EXPANDED TABLE OF CONTENTS

EARLIER PUBLICATIONS IN THIS SERIES
Edited by Oscar Krisen Buros

TESTS IN PRINT II

TESTS
IN PRINT II

AN INDEX TO TESTS
TEST REVIEWS, AND THE LITERATURE
ON SPECIFIC TESTS

Edited by

OSCAR KRISEN BUROS
Director, The Institute of Mental Measurements

THE GRYPHON PRESS
HIGHLAND PARK · NEW JERSEY
1974

DESIGNED BY LUELLA BUROS

COPYRIGHT 1974 BY OSCAR KRISEN BUROS, PUBLISHED BY THE GRYPHON PRESS,
220 MONTGOMERY STREET, HIGHLAND PARK, NEW JERSEY 08904. No part of this publication may
be reproduced in any form, nor may any of the contents be used in an informational storage,
retrieval, or transmission system without the prior written permission of the publisher.

ISBN 910674-14-0

MANUFACTURED BY QUINN & BODEN COMPANY, INC., RAHWAY, NEW JERSEY
PRINTED IN THE UNITED STATES OF AMERICA

To

Anne Anastasi

Howard R. Anderson

Walter V. Kaulfers

Victor H. Noll

Arthur E. Traxler

TABLE OF CONTENTS

MMY TEST REVIEWERS

IRA E. AARON, 6–7 [1]
HAROLD H. ABELSON, 3
MURRAY ABORN, 4
CLIFFORD R. ADAMS, 6
ELIZABETH C. ADAMS, 4
GEORGIA S. ADAMS, 7
C. J. ADCOCK, 5–7
DOROTHY C. ADKINS, 3–7
DAN L. ADLER, 5
JANET G. AFFLERBACH, 5
LOIS G. AFFLERBACH, 5
FREDERICK B. AGARD, 3
J. STANLEY AHMANN, 6–7
MARY D. AINSWORTH, 5
LEWIS E. ALBRIGHT, 6–7
NORMA A. ALBRIGHT, 2
HENRY A. ALKER, 7
JOHN C. ALMACK, 1–2
WILLIAM D. ALTUS, 4
JEAN D. AMBERSON, 4
VERA M. AMERSON, 3
ANNE ANASTASI, 1–7
NICHOLAS ANASTASIOW, 7
OLIVER F. ANDERHALTER, 4, 6–7
HOWARD R. ANDERSON, 1–7
IRVING H. ANDERSON, 1, 3
JAMES M. ANDERSON, 3–4, 6
KENNETH E. ANDERSON, 4, 6
LAWRENCE ANDRUS, 2
HARVEY A. ANDRUSS, 3
EDGAR ANSTEY, 6
CHRISTIAN O. ARNDT, 2
DWIGHT L. ARNOLD, 4–5
GWEN F. ARNOLD, 4
THEODORE A. ASHFORD, 3, 5
ALEXANDER W. ASTIN, 6–7
SAMUEL D. ATKINS, 1–2
MARY C. AUSTIN, 6
FREDERIC L. AYER, 3–4
J. DOUGLAS AYERS, 6–7
JAMES C. BABCOCK, 2
ANDREW R. BAGGALEY, 5–6
LEONARD L. BAIRD, 7

THOMAS S. BALDWIN, 7
BENJAMIN BALINSKY, 4–5
RACHEL S. BALL, 2
WARREN R. BALLER, 4–5
IROL W. BALSLEY, 6
CHARLOTTE E. K. BANKS, 4–5
ALLAN G. BARCLAY, 7
WALTER BARNES, 1
A. S. BARR, 3
REBECCA C. BARR, 7
RICHARD S. BARRETT, 6
THOMAS C. BARRETT, 6
FRANK BARRON, 5
W. L. BASHAW, 7
ROBERT H. BAUERNFEIND, 5–7
BRENT BAXTER, 3–5
ERNEST EDWARD BAYLES, 1
NANCY BAYLEY, 2–3, 5
KENNETH L. BEAN, 5–6
ROBERT M. BEAR, 3–4
HAROLD P. BECHTOLDT, 4–7
ROLAND L. BECK, 2–3
SAMUEL J. BECK, 2, 5
WESLEY C. BECKER, 6
RALPH C. BEDELL, 3, 5
H. R. BEECH, 6
FRED S. BEERS, 1
EDWARD G. BEGLE, 7
JOHN E. BELL, 4–6
ALBERT A. BENNETT, 2–3
GEORGE K. BENNETT, 3–7
PETER M. BENTLER, 6–7
ARTHUR L. BENTON, 3–4, 7
H. E. BENZ, 2
RALPH F. BERDIE, 3–7
HARRY D. BERG, 3–7
PAUL CONRAD BERG, 7
ALLEN BERGER, 7
ROBERT G. BERNREUTER, 1–4
EMMETT A. BETTS, 6
WILLIAM BETZ, 1, 3
CHARLES L. BICKEL, 2
MARION A. BILLS, 3

WALTER V. BINGHAM, 1
WILLIAM C. BINGHAM, 6
L. B. BIRCH, 6–7
REIGN H. BITTNER, 3–4
HAROLD H. BIXLER, 3–4
ÅKE BJERSTEDT, 5–6
DONALD B. BLACK, 6–7
HILLEL BLACK, 6
JOHN D. BLACK, 5–6
J. M. BLACKBURN, 2
JAMES H. BLACKHURST, 1
E. G. BLACKSTONE, 3
C. B. BLAKEMORE, 6
EMERY P. BLIESMER, 6
PAUL J. BLOMMERS, 3–6
BENJAMIN S. BLOOM, 3–5, 7
BRUCE BLOXOM, 7
MILTON L. BLUM, 3–4
JACK L. BODDEN, 7
JOAN BOLLENBACHER, 5
GUY L. BOND, 2
IVAN A. BOOKER, 1–4
DANIEL R. BOONE, 7
EDWARD S. BORDIN, 3–5
FRED H. BORGEN, 7
HAROLD BORKO, 6–7
JOHN R. BORMUTH, 7
MORTON BORTNER, 6
THOMAS J. BOUCHARD, JR., 7
JOHN E. BOWERS, 6
E. J. G. BRADFORD, 3–4
FRANCIS F. BRADSHAW, 1
JAMES BRASWELL, 7
JOHN R. BRAUN, 7
ARTHUR H. BRAYFIELD, 4–6
W. C. BRENKE, 3
ANN BREWINGTON, 3
ANN BRICKNER, 7
ROBERT G. BRIDGHAM, 7
M. ALAN BRIMER, 5–7
HUBERT E. BROGDEN, 3–4
NELSON BROOKS, 1–6

1 *Mental Measurements Yearbooks* in which reviews appear.

M. EUSTACE BROOM, 2
R. A. BROTEMARKLE, 3
ALFRED S. BROWN, 3
ANDREW W. BROWN, 2
CHARLES M. BROWN, 6
CLARA M. BROWN, 1–2
FREDERICK G. BROWN, 7
WILLIAM A. BROWNELL, 1–5
LEO J. BRUECKNER, 1–4
JAMES E. BRYAN, 5–7
MIRIAM M. BRYAN, 4, 6–7
N. DALE BRYANT, 5–7
ROBERT L. BURCH, 4
THOMAS C. BURGESS, 6
CAROLYN L. BURKE, 7
R. WILL BURNETT, 4
PAUL S. BURNHAM, 3
DONALD G. BURNS, 4
EMILY T. BURR, 3
ALVIN G. BURSTEIN, 6–7
CYRIL BURT, 3, 5
NANCY W. BURTON, 7
GUY T. BUSWELL, 2
H. J. BUTCHER, 7
KATHARINE G. BUTLER, 7
MARGARET C. BYRNE, 7
LEONARD S. CAHEN, 7
G. P. CAHOON, 3–4
JAMES R. CALDWELL, 7
DAVID P. CAMPBELL, 6–7
DONALD T. CAMPBELL, 4–6
DUGAL CAMPBELL, 6
J. A. CAMPBELL, 6
JOEL T. CAMPBELL, 6–7
VINCENT N. CAMPBELL, 7
THORSTEN R. CARLSON, 7
W. L. CARR, 2
JOHN B. CARROLL, 4–7
L. RAY CARRY, 7
HAROLD D. CARTER, 1–4
LAUNOR F. CARTER, 4
W. H. CARTWRIGHT, 3
FRANK P. CASSARETTO, 5
BURTON M. CASTNER, 2
ROBERT S. CATHCART, 5
PSYCHE CATTELL, 1, 3
RAYMOND B. CATTELL, 2
COURTNEY B. CAZDEN, 7
STELLA CENTER, 1
HESTER CHADDERDON, 1–2, 4
ROBERT C. CHALLMAN, 4, 6–7
E. G. CHAMBERS, 3–5
CLINTON I. CHASE, 7
HENRY CHAUNCEY, 3, 6
MAURICE CHAZAN, 7
BRAD S. CHISSOM, 7
EDMUND P. CHURCHILL, 3
RUTH D. CHURCHILL, 3, 5
CHERRY ANN CLARK, 5
D. F. CLARK, 7
GALE W. CLARK, 5
J. F. CLARK, 5
JOHN L. D. CLARK, 7
JOHN R. CLARK, 2
KENNETH E. CLARK, 4
STANLEY CLARK, 4–6
WILLIS W. CLARK, 6

H. HARRISON CLARKE, 4
GLEN U. CLEETON, 3
W. V. CLEMANS, 6
DOROTHY M. CLENDENEN, 5–7
VICTOR B. CLINE, 7
RICHARD W. COAN, 6–7
CHARLES N. COFER, 3–5
WILLIAM E. COFFMAN, 3, 5–7
BERTRAM D. COHEN, 6
JACOB COHEN, 6–7
JOHN COHEN, 3
S. ALAN COHEN, 7
NANCY S. COLE, 7
ROBERTA R. COLLARD, 7
RICHARD COLWELL, 7
W. D. COMMINS, 1–4
ANDREW L. COMREY, 5, 7
CLINTON C. CONRAD, 2
HERBERT S. CONRAD, 1–4
JOHN COOK, 7
WALTER W. COOK, 2–3, 5
WILLIAM W. COOLEY, 6
CLYDE H. COOMBS, 3
STEPHEN M. COREY, 1–2
ETHEL L. CORNELL, 1
WILLIAM C. COTTLE, 5
STUART A. COURTIS, 1, 4
DOUGLAS COURTNEY, 3–4
JOHN A. COX, JR., 5
MARION MONROE COX, 1, 3
ALBERT B. CRAWFORD, 2
WILLIAM R. CRAWFORD, 6–7
WILLIAM J. E. CRISSY, 4
R. LENOX CRISWELL, 2
JOHN O. CRITES, 6–7
LYSLE W. CROFT, 3–4
LEE J. CRONBACH, 3–7
DOUGLAS P. CROWNE, 6
WILLIAM M. CRUICKSHANK, 4
THOMAS E. CULLITON, JR., 6
EDWARD E. CURETON, 1–2, 4
LOUISE W. CURETON, 4
THOMAS K. CURETON, 3
WILLIAM CURR, 5
FRANCIS D. CURTIS, 1–2
W. GRANT DAHLSTROM, 4–6
JOHN T. DAILEY, 4–5
EDGAR DALE, 3
REGINALD R. DALE, 5
RICHARD H. DANA, 5–7
JOHN C. DANIELS, 5
JOHN G. DARLEY, 1–2
JOHN H. DAUGHERTY, 3
CHARLOTTE CROON DAVIS, 3–6
D. RUSSELL DAVIS, 4–5
EDWIN W. DAVIS, 3
FREDERICK B. DAVIS, 1–5, 7
PARKER DAVIS, JR., 3
PAUL C. DAVIS, 6
ROBERT A. DAVIS, 3
STANLEY E. DAVIS, 6
HELEN C. DAWE, 3
LESTER W. DEARBORN, 6
JAMES DEESE, 5
FRANK P. DELAY, 2
GABRIEL M. DELLA-PIANA, 6
DENNIS J. DELORIA, 7

HAROLD A. DELP, 4
ROBERT G. DEMAREE, 4, 7
GEORGE D. DEMOS, 6
EVELYN DENO, 7
SUSAN K. DERI, 3
CLARENCE DERRICK, 4–7
MAYHEW DERRYBERRY, 3
LAWRENCE G. DERTHICK, 5
HARRY R. DESILVA, 2
M. VERE DEVAULT, 7
JOSEPH C. DEWEY, 1–2
LOUIS M. DICARLO, 6
CHARLES F. DICKEN, 6
GWENDOLEN S. DICKSON, 1, 3
PAUL B. DIEDERICH, 1–2, 7
JOHN S. DIEKHOFF, 3–5
RICHARD F. DOCTER, 7
ROBERT H. DOLLIVER, 7
GEORGE DOMINO, 7
JEROME E. DOPPELT, 4–7
HARL R. DOUGLASS, 2–3
N. M. DOWNIE, 6
VINCENT R. D'OYLEY, 7
RALEIGH M. DRAKE, 2–5
RICHARD M. DRAKE, 2–3
ARNOLD DRESDEN, 1
PAUL L. DRESSEL, 3–7
JAMES DREVER, 2
ROBERT C. DROEGE, 7
PHILIP H. DUBOIS, 3, 6–7
GERALD G. DUFFY, 7
LYDIA A. DUGGINS, 5
STANLEY G. DULSKY, 2–3
HAROLD B. DUNKEL, 2–6
JACK W. DUNLAP, 1–3
JAMES A. DUNN, 7
S. S. DUNN, 5–6
MARVIN D. DUNNETTE, 6
WALTER N. DUROST, 4–7
RALPH D. DUTCH, 6–7
AUGUST DVORAK, 2
BEATRICE J. DVORAK, 3
HENRY S. DYER, 5–6
ROBERT DYKSTRA, 7
NORMAN EAGLE, 5, 7
HOWARD EASLEY, 2
ROBERT L. EBEL, 4–7
ALLEN L. EDWARDS, 6
BATEMAN EDWARDS, 2
REGINALD EDWARDS, 5
WILLIAM J. EICHMAN, 6–7
DOROTHY H. EICHORN, 5–7
PHILIP EISENBERG, 3
WILLIAM ELLER, 6
M. H. ELLIOTT, 3
ALBERT ELLIS, 3–7
W. G. EMMETT, 3–4
MAX D. ENGELHART, 1–2, 4–6
BERTRAM EPSTEIN, 4
GERALD L. ERICKSEN, 6–7
LAWRENCE W. ERICKSON, 6–7
EMANUEL E. ERICSON, 2
LEONARD D. ERON, 5–7
ANNA S. ESPENSCHADE, 4–5
BARBARA F. ESSER, 6–7
ALVIN C. EURICH, 1–2
ALEXANDER EVEN, 7

Hans J. Eysenck, 3–7
Paul R. Farnsworth, 1–3, 5–6
Roger Farr, 7
Ray N. Faulkner, 1–2
Harold P. Fawcett, 2–5
Jay W. Fay, 1
Ethel M. Feagley, 3
Howard F. Fehr, 4
Elizabeth Fehrer, 3
Henry Feinberg, 1
Leonard S. Feldt, 5–7
George A. Ferguson, 3–6
Leonard W. Ferguson, 6
Robert H. Ferrell, 5
C. E. Ficken, 2
James A. Field, Jr., 5
Gordon Fifer, 5
Warren G. Findley, 2–7
Seymour Fisher, 6
Wayne D. Fisher, 6
Joshua A. Fishman, 5
Donald W. Fiske, 5
James A. Fitzgerald, 5
Robert Fitzpatrick, 7
John C. Flanagan, 1, 3–4, 6
C. M. Fleming, 4
W. G. Fleming, 6
Charles D. Flory, 1, 3
John P. Foley, Jr., 5–7
Mary O. Folsom, 7
Thomas G. Foran, 1
Bertram R. Forer, 6
Frank J. Fornoff, 6
Elaine Forsyth, 3
Robert A. Forsyth, 7
Tomlinson Fort, 2
Judson W. Foust, 2
Hanford M. Fowler, 4–5
Raymond D. Fowler, Jr., 7
Charles Fox, 2
Thomas T. Frantz, 7
Elizabeth D. Fraser, 5–6
Wayne A. Frederick, 5
Norman Frederiksen, 3–7
Frank S. Freeman, 4–5
David Freides, 7
John W. French, 3–7
Joseph L. French, 7
Robert L. French, 6
Sidney J. French, 3
Benno G. Fricke, 5–6
Clifford P. Froehlich, 4–5
Gustav J. Froehlich, 3–6
Benjamin Fruchter, 5
F. P. Frutchey, 1
Edward B. Fry, 6–7
Douglas H. Fryer, 3
Verne C. Fryklund, 2
Paul H. Furfey, 1
Edward J. Furst, 6–7
N. L. Gage, 4–5
Eugene L. Gaier, 5
Rosslyn Gaines, 7
Bessie Lee Gambrill, 2
Eric F. Gardner, 4–7
Sol L. Garfield, 7
Edgar R. Garrett, 7

Henry E. Garrett, 1–5
Ann L. Gebhardt, 2
Karl W. Gehrkens, 2
Kenneth E. Gell, 2
J. Raymond Gerberich, 2–6
John J. Geyer, 7
Edwin E. Ghiselli, 3
Cecil A. Gibb, 5–7
H. H. Giles, 1–2
John W. Gittinger, 5
Gene V Glass, 7
James R. Glennon, 6
Goldine C. Gleser, 6–7
Marvin D. Glock, 5–7
Lewis R. Goldberg, 7
Bert A. Goldman, 6–7
Leo Goldman, 6
Marcel L. Goldschmid, 7
Keith Goltry, 2
Elizabeth J. Goodacre, 7
Florence L. Goodenough, 2–3
Clarence J. Goodnight, 7
Leonard D. Goodstein, 6–7
Edwin Gordon, 7
Hans C. Gordon, 2–3
Leonard V. Gordon, 6–7
Harrison G. Gough, 4–7
Neil Gourlay, 5
Grace Graham, 2
William S. Gray, 1, 3–4
Russel F. Green, 6–7
Edward B. Greene, 3–5
Harry A. Greene, 2–3
Konrad Gries, 4–5
Arnold B. Grobman, 7
Hulda Grobman, 7
Richard E. Gross, 5–7
Foster E. Grossnickle, 1–4
William R. Grove, 3–4
Wilson H. Guertin, 5–6
Walter S. Guiler, 4
J. P. Guilford, 1–5
Arlen R. Gullickson, 7
R. Gulliford, 7
Harold Gulliksen, 1–2, 4
John Flagg Gummere, 2
John W. Gustad, 5
John T. Guthrie, 7
Malcolm D. Gynther, 7
Laura B. Hadley, 2
John H. Haefner, 5–6
Elizabeth Hagen, 5–7
Michio P. Hagiwara, 7
Milton E. Hahn, 3–4, 6
A. Ralph Hakstian, 7
W. E. Hall, 3
Wallace B. Hall, 6
Raphael M. Haller, 7
E. W. Hamilton, 6
Nelson G. Hanawalt, 3–5
C. H. Handschin, 2
Lavone A. Hanna, 2–3
Paul R. Hanna, 4
Gary R. Hanson, 7
Robert A. Harper, 6–7
Thomas W. Harrell, 3
Philip L. Harriman, 4–6

Albert J. Harris, 3, 6–7
Chester W. Harris, 3–4
Dale B. Harris, 4–7
David P. Harris, 7
Jesse G. Harris, Jr., 6
Larry A. Harris, 7
Robert C. Harris, 7
Theodore L. Harris, 6
Mary T. Harrison, 7
Charles M. Harsh, 3–4
George W. Hartmann, 1, 4
Louis D. Hartson, 1
Maurice L. Hartung, 1, 3
Glen Hass, 3
J. O. Hassler, 1–2
J. Thomas Hastings, 4–6
Richard S. Hatch, 6
Starke R. Hathaway, 3
G. E. Hawkins, 2
David G. Hawkridge, 7
Mary R. Haworth, 5–6
Edward N. Hay, 3–5
James R. Hayden, 5–6
Leslie M. Haynes, 4
Kenneth L. Heaton, 4
Earle R. Hedrick, 2
David K. Heenan, 5–6
Lloyd H. Heidgerd, 6
Louis M. Heil, 2
Alfred B. Heilbrun, Jr., 5–7
Alice W. Heim, 4–7
Harry Heller, 2
William H. Helme, 6
G. C. Helmstadter, 7
John K. Hemphill, 6–7
V. A. C. Henmon, 1
Edwin R. Henry, 4
William E. Henry, 4–5
William Hered, 6
David O. Herman, 6–7
Virgil E. Herrick, 4–5
A. N. Hieronymus, 5–7
E. H. C. Hildebrandt, 3
Walker H. Hill, 5
John R. Hills, 6–7
Philip Himelstein, 7
Elmer D. Hinckley, 4
C. B. Hindley, 6
Marshall S. Hiskey, 6–7
Jean Hoard, 2
James R. Hobson, 2–5
Elton Hocking, 3–4
Robert Hogan, 7
Dorothy E. Holberg, 3
Raymond H. Holden, 7
Warren S. Holmes, 2
Robert R. Holt, 4
Wayne H. Holtzman, 5, 7
Charles Holzwarth, 2
Charles H. Honzik, 4
Marjorie P. Honzik, 6–7
Florence E. Hooper, 3
Kenneth D. Hopkins, 6–7
John L. Horn, 7
Thomas D. Horn, 7
John E. Horrocks, 5–6
Clark W. Horton, 2–5

CARL I. HOVLAND, 3–5
ROBERT W. HOWARD, 2
DUNCAN HOWIE, 5
MONICA M. HOYE, 3
CYRIL J. HOYT, 4–7
KENNETH B. HOYT, 6
CARL J. HUBERTY, 7
EDITH M. HUDDLESTON, 4
MILDRED H. HUEBNER, 7
VIOLET HUGHES, 2
DONCASTER G. HUMM, 2
LLOYD G. HUMPHREYS, 3–6
JOHN D. HUNDLEBY, 6
STEPHEN HUNKA, 6
ALBERT L. HUNSICKER, 4
E. PATRICIA HUNT, 2
JANE V. HUNT, 7
THELMA HUNT, 3
WILLIAM A. HUNT, 3
GEORGE W. HUNTER, 1–2
ARCHER W. HURD, 1
LUDWIG IMMERGLUCK, 3
HENRY A. IMUS, 3
MARGARET IVES, 3
DOUGLAS N. JACKSON, 7
JOSEPH F. JACKSON, 2–3
ROBERT W. B. JACKSON, 5
ALICE N. JAMESON, 3
COLLEEN B. JAMISON, 7
FRANK C. JEAN, 1
JOHN R. JENNINGS, 5
ARTHUR R. JENSEN, 5–7
CARL F. JESNESS, 7
RICHARD JESSOR, 5
FRANK B. JEX, 6
A. PEMBERTON JOHNSON, 5
CECIL D. JOHNSON, 5
LAURA B. JOHNSON, 2
LELAND P. JOHNSON, 4
PALMER O. JOHNSON, 1–5
RICHARD T. JOHNSON, 6–7
JOSEPH A. JOHNSTON, 7
CARLETON C. JONES, 1–2
CLIVE JONES, 7
DAVID JONES, 7
DOROTHY L. JONES, 7
EDWARD S. JONES, 1–2
F. NOWELL JONES, 3
H. GWYNNE JONES, 6
HAROLD E. JONES, 1–4
KENNETH J. JONES, 6
ROBERT A. JONES, 5
WORTH R. JONES, 5–6
A. M. JORDAN, 2
RICHARD H. JORDAN, 3
CLIFFORD E. JURGENSEN, 3–6
JOSEPH JUSTMAN, 5
PAUL E. KAMBLY, 4
HARRY W. KARN, 4
M. RAY KARNES, 4
LAWRENCE M. KASDON, 7
WALTER KASS, 5
WALTER KATKOVSKY, 6
MARTIN R. KATZ, 5–7
RAYMOND A. KATZELL, 3–7
WALTER V. KAULFERS, 1–7
T. J. KEATING, 2

J. A. KEATS, 5–6
GERTRUDE KEIR, 4
TRUMAN L. KELLEY, 2
THEODORE E. KELLOGG, 4–5
E. LOWELL KELLY, 3–7
WILLIAM E. KENDALL, 6
KATHERINE G. KENEALLY, 4
JAMES E. KENNEDY, 6–7
DOUGLAS T. KENNY, 5
GRACE H. KENT, 2–3
ROBERT E. KEOHANE, 2
NEWELL C. KEPHART, 7
WILLARD A. KERR, 3–4, 6–7
GILBERT C. KETTELKAMP, 6
JEREMY KILPATRICK, 7
ELAINE F. KINDER, 1
JOSEPH E. KING, 3
FORREST A. KINGSBURY, 2
ALBERT J. KINGSTON, 6–7
LUCIEN B. KINNEY, 2, 4
JOHN R. KINZER, 3
WAYNE K. KIRCHNER, 6
BARBARA A. KIRK, 7
PHILIP M. KITAY, 6–7
PAUL M. KJELDERGAARD, 6
SEYMOUR G. KLEBANOFF, 4
BENJAMIN KLEINMUNTZ, 6–7
MILTON V. KLINE, 6
PAUL KLINE, 7
WILLIAM E. KLINE, 7
MARTIN KLING, 7
ROBERT R. KNAPP, 7
JOHN F. KNUTSON, 7
KATE L. KOGAN, 3–4
WILLIAM S. KOGAN, 4
DAVID KOPEL, 1–2
DAVID R. KRATHWOHL, 5
CHARLES J. KRAUSKOPF, 7
ROY A. KRESS, 7
A. C. KREY, 1
PHILIP H. KRIEDT, 6
RUSSELL P. KROPP, 5
MORRIS KRUGMAN, 3–5
JOHN D. KRUMBOLTZ, 6
FREDERIC KUDER, 2–3
F. KUHLMANN, 2
DANA G. KURFMAN, 7
ALBERT K. KURTZ, 4–6
W. C. KVARACEUS, 3–4
LOU LaBRANT, 2
ROBERT LADO, 7
TOM A. LAMKE, 5
W. ELMER LANCASTER, 2
DANIEL LANDIS, 7
HERBERT A. LANDRY, 2
EDWARD LANDY, 5
THEOS A. LANGLIE, 1
CHARLES R. LANGMUIR, 3–6
GERALD V. LANNHOLM, 3–5
RICHARD I. LANYON, 7
PETER A. LAPPAN, JR., 6–7
WILLIAM S. LARSON, 2–6
JULIAN J. LASKY, 7
ROBERT L. LATHROP, 7
J. S. LAWES, 6–7
C. H. LAWSHE, JR., 3
MARTHA E. LAYMAN, 4

WILBUR L. LAYTON, 4–7
RICHARD LEDGERWOOD, 1
J. MURRAY LEE, 1, 5
S. G. LEE, 6–7
D. WELTY LEFEVER, 1–6
PAUL R. LEHMAN, 7
IRVIN J. LEHMANN, 6–7
ROGER T. LENNON, 4–5
THEODORE F. LENTZ, 3
J. PAUL LEONARD, 2–3
DONALD A. LETON, 7
EUGENE E. LEVITT, 6–7
PHILIP M. LEVY, 6
SEYMOUR LEVY, 6
ROY D. LEWIS, 5
LESTER M. LIBO, 7
JOHN LIGGETT, 5–6
PAUL M. LIMBERT, 1
E. F. LINDQUIST, 5
C. M. LINDVALL, 7
W. LINE, 2
JAMES C. LINGOES, 6
WILLIAM M. LITTELL, 7
ORREL E. LITTLE, 3
ALICE K. LIVERIGHT, 2
AILEENE S. LOCKHART, 7
JANE LOEVINGER, 4
PAUL R. LOHNES, 6–7
WALTER F. W. LOHNES, 7
PAUL S. LOMAX, 3
JOHN W. LOMBARD, 7
JOHN A. LONG, 3
LOUIS LONG, 3
ANDREW LONGACRE, 2
FRANK M. LOOS, 4
PETER G. LORET, 6
IRVING LORGE, 2–3, 5
MARGARET F. LORIMER, 6
MAURICE LORR, 5–7
C. M. LOUTTIT, 1–4
KENNETH LOVELL, 6–7
RUTH LOWES, 3
ARDIE LUBIN, 4
WILLIAM H. LUCIO, 6
WILLIAM H. LUCOW, 5
JAMES LUMSDEN, 5
ROBERT W. LUNDIN, 5–7
CLIFFORD E. LUNNEBORG, 7
DAVID T. LYKKEN, 6–7
HOWARD B. LYMAN, 6–7
HENRY S. MAAS, 3
CHARLES C. McARTHUR, 7
JOHN N. McCALL, 7
RAYMOND J. McCALL, 5
W. C. McCALL, 2
WILLIAM A. McCALL, 2
JAMES M. McCALLISTER, 3
BOYD R. McCANDLESS, 4, 6–7
JAMES J. McCARTHY, 7
ROBERT L. McCAUL, 2–3
CLARA J. McCAULEY, 2
R. W. McCULLOCH, 5
CONSTANCE M. McCULLOUGH, 2–3,
    5, 7
S. P. McCUTCHEN, 1–2
ARTHUR S. McDONALD, 6
D. W. McELWAIN, 4–5

CHRISTINE H. McGUIRE, 5–7
MICHAEL G. McKEE, 7
GORDON N. MACKENZIE, 3–4
MARGARET G. McKIM, 3–4
ARTHUR C. MacKINNEY, 6–7
SAUNDERS MAC LANE, 6
KENNETH F. McLAUGHLIN, 6
JOHN McLEISH, 4, 7
JONATHON C. McLENDON, 6
DOUGLAS M. McNAIR, 7
JEANETTE McPHERRIN, 2
JOHN V. McQUITTY, 3–4
LOUIS L. McQUITTY, 4
PAUL McREYNOLDS, 7
FAITH MADDEN, 4
THOMAS W. MAHAN, JR., 6
JAMES MAINWARING, 5
JULIUS B. MALLER, 1–2
GEORGE G. MALLINSON, 6–7
JACQUELINE V. MALLINSON, 6–7
BERENICE MALLORY, 2
MILTON M. MANDELL, 4
LESTER MANN, 7
M. JACINTA MANN, 5
JOHN MANNING, 5, 7
WINTON H. MANNING, 6
HERSCHEL T. MANUEL, 2–5
MELVIN R. MARKS, 6
STANLEY S. MARZOLF, 3
BERTRAM B. MASIA, 6
ROSS W. MATTESON, 4
FRANCIS N. MAXFIELD, 1–2
JAMES MAXWELL, 3–5
SAMUEL T. MAYO, 6–7
ARTHUR B. MAYS, 2
RICHARD A. MEADE, 5
ARTHUR W. MEADOWS, 5
I. G. MEDDLETON, 5
ALBERT E. MEDER, JR., 5
PAUL E. MEEHL, 3
EDWIN I. MEGARGEE, 7
HOWARD D. MEHLINGER, 7
WILLIAM A. MEHRENS, 7
MANFRED J. MEIER, 7
NORMAN C. MEIER, 2
WILLIAM B. MELDRUM, 1, 3
P. L. MELLENBRUCH, 5
RICHARD S. MELTON, 6
H. MELTZER, 3
GERALD A. MENDELSOHN, 6
IVAN N. MENSH, 4
GERALD M. MEREDITH, 7
PHILIP R. MERRIFIELD, 6
JACK C. MERWIN, 6–7
BERNADINE MEYER, 5
DONALD L. MEYER, 6
JOHN H. MEYER, 3
JOAN J. MICHAEL, 7
WILLIAM B. MICHAEL, 4–7
WILLIAM J. MICHEELS, 4–5
T. R. MILES, 5–6
JOHN E. MILHOLLAND, 5–7
LOVICK C. MILLER, 7
JASON MILLMAN, 6–7
J. B. MINER, 2
J. H. MINNICK, 2
LORENZ MISBACH, 3

JAMES V. MITCHELL, JR., 7
RONALD W. MITCHELL, 7
ARTHUR MITTMAN, 6–7
WILLIAM G. MOLLENKOPF, 3–4
FLOYD V. MONAGHAN, 7
EASON MONROE, 3
MARION MONROE, 1, 3
JOSEPH E. MOORE, 2–4, 6
TERENCE MOORE, 6
WALTER J. MOORE, 7
G. A. V. MORGAN, 5–7
ALICE E. MORIARTY, 7
JOHN B. MORRIS, 5
COLEMAN MORRISON, 6
FRANCES CROOK MORRISON, 5–6
HARRIET B. MORRISON, 1–2
NATHAN MORRISON, 3
THOMAS F. MORRISON, 2
H. T. MORSE, 3
N. W. MORTON, 1–2, 4
R. L. MORTON, 2
HAROLD E. MOSER, 5
DONALD L. MOSHER, 7
CHARLES I. MOSIER, 2–3
C. SCOTT MOSS, 6
KATE HEVNER MUELLER, 5
LEO A. MUNDAY, 7
ALLYN M. MUNGER, 6
JOSEPH A. MURPHY, 7
WILBUR F. MURRA, 1–2
ELSIE MURRAY, 4
JAMES L. MURSELL, 1–3
BERNARD I. MURSTEIN, 6–7
CHARLES T. MYERS, 5
SHELDON S. MYERS, 6–7
THEODOR F. NAUMANN, 6–7
LOUIS C. NANASSY, 5
LEO NEDELSKY, 5–6
CHARLES O. NEIDT, 5–6
CLARENCE H. NELSON, 3–7
THEODORE NEWCOMB, 2
T. ERNEST NEWLAND, 6–7
BERNARD H. NEWMAN, 7
JOSEPH NEWMAN, 4
KENNETH R. NEWTON, 5
ROBERT C. NICHOLS, 6
JOHN NISBET, 5–7
STANLEY D. NISBET, 4–7
VICTOR H. NOLL, 1–7
CLAUDE E. NORCROSS, 4
WARREN T. NORMAN, 5–7
RAYMOND C. NORRIS, 5
ROBERT D. NORTH, 5–7
PAUL A. NORTHROP, 1–2
EDWARD S. NOYES, 2–3
JUM C. NUNNALLY, 7
C. A. OAKLEY, 2–3
C. O. OAKLEY, 3
THOMAS C. O'BRIEN, 7
CHARLES W. ODELL, 1–3
DONALD W. OLIVER, 6
MARY E. OLIVERIO, 5, 7
CARL J. OLSON, 7
PEDRO T. ORATA, 2
JACOB S. ORLEANS, 2–6
DAVID B. ORR, 6–7
AGNES E. OSBORNE, 3

ALAN R. OSBORNE, 7
R. T. OSBORNE, 7
WORTH J. OSBURN, 1–2, 4
STUART OSKAMP, 7
ALTON O'STEEN, 2
JAY L. OTIS, 3–4
WILLIAM A. OWENS, 6
C. ROBERT PACE, 3–7
ALBERT G. PACKARD, 3
ELLIS B. PAGE, 6–7
ORVILLE PALMER, 5
OSMOND E. PALMER, 5–7
JEAN M. PALORMO, 6
JOSEPHINE B. PANE, 7
GINO PARISI, 7
ANNA PARSEK, 2
A. HARRY PASSOW, 4
DONALD G. PATERSON, 2–4
GERALD R. PATTERSON, 5
WILLARD W. PATTY, 4
WALTER PAUK, 7
JEROME D. PAUKER, 6–7
DAVID A. PAYNE, 6–7
R. W. PAYNE, 6–7
WILLIAM G. PEACHER, 4
JOHN GRAY PEATMAN, 2
E. A. PEEL, 4–5
L. S. PENROSE, 3
WILLIAM H. PERKINS, 7
KATHLEEN N. PERRET, 5
CHARLES C. PETERS, 1
DONALD R. PETERSON, 6
HAROLD A. PETERSON, 7
SHAILER PETERSON, 3
ROGER P. PHELPS, 7
THEODORE G. PHILLIPS, 5–7
HALE C. PICKETT, 3
DOUGLAS A. PIDGEON, 5–7
JOHN PIERCE-JONES, 5–6
ELLEN V. PIERS, 6
MYRTLE L. PIGNATELLI, 2
LEN PIKAART, 7
A. E. G. PILLINER, 5–7
PAUL PIMSLEUR, 6
RUDOLF PINTNER, 1
GUS P. PLESSAS, 6–7
LYNNETTE B. PLUMLEE, 3, 5–7
ROBERT C. POOLEY, 2–7
JAMES M. PORTER, JR., 3
LYMAN W. PORTER, 6
STANLEY D. PORTEUS, 2
WINIFRED L. POST, 4–5
NORMAN T. PRATT, JR., 1–2
DANIEL A. PRESCOTT, 1
JOAN PRESTON, 7
RALPH C. PRESTON, 3–4
H. VERNON PRICE, 5
JACK PRICE, 7
RAY G. PRICE, 3, 6–7
ROY A. PRICE, 2–3
HUGH F. PRIEST, 7
M. L. KELLMER PRINGLE, 4–7
GLEN W. PROBST, 7
EARL V. PULLIAS, 2
ALAN C. PURVES, 7
M. Y. QUERESHI, 7
ALBERT I. RABIN, 4–5, 7

W. L. Sumner, 4
Norman D. Sundberg, 5–7
Donald E. Super, 3–6
J. P. Sutcliffe, 5
John Sutherland, 5–6
Marilyn N. Suydam, 7
Edward O. Swanson, 6
Richard A. Swanson, 7
Clifford H. Swensen, Jr., 5
Percival M. Symonds, 2–5
Hilda Taba, 1–2, 4
Abraham J. Tannenbaum, 6
Calvin W. Taylor, 5
Erwin K. Taylor, 3–7
Howard R. Taylor, 3–4
Hugh Taylor, 7
Wallace W. Taylor, 2–3
Florence M. Teagarden, 2–5
Lorene Teegarden, 2
Mildred C. Templin, 4
Edward A. Tenney, 2
W. Wesley Tennyson, 5
James B. Tharp, 2, 4
Paul W. Thayer, 6
Herbert A. Thelen, 3
William N. Thetford, 6
C. L. Thiele, 2–3
Charles S. Thomas, 1–2
Cleveland A. Thomas, 5
Albert S. Thompson, 1–2, 4–6
Anton Thompson, 4
John H. Thompson, 1
Edith I. M. Thomson, 3
Godfrey H. Thomson, 2
Robert L. Thorndike, 2–7
Louis P. Thorpe, 3
Robert H. Thouless, 3
David V. Tiedeman, 4–7
Ernest W. Tiegs, 1–3
Joseph Tiffin, 1
Miles A. Tinker, 1–4
Carol K. Tittle, 7
Hazel M. Toliver, 3
Herbert A. Tonne, 1, 3, 5
Herbert A. Toops, 3
T. L. Torgerson, 3
Agatha Townsend, 3, 5–6
Marion R. Trabue, 1–2
Kenneth J. Travers, 7
Robert M. W. Travers, 3–5
Arthur E. Traxler, 1–7
Frances O. Triggs, 3
Harold C. Trimble, 6–7
Marie E. Trost, 2
Maurice E. Troyer, 3
R. M. Tryon, 1–2
Robert C. Tryon, 2
Simon H. Tulchin, 2–3
Mary E. Turnbull, 4–6
William W. Turnbull, 3–6
Clarence E. Turner, 2–6
Mervyn L. Turner, 5

Austin H. Turney, 1–2
Lawrence J. Turton, 7
F. T. Tyler, 3
Leona E. Tyler, 4–7
Ralph W. Tyler, 2–3, 5
C. C. Upshall, 3
Marguerite Uttley, 3
Curtis C. Vail, 1
Paolo Valesio, 7
Robert E. Valett, 7
Forrest L. Vance, 6–7
Henry Van Engen, 4
Byron H. Van Roekel, 5–7
Neil J. Van Steenberg, 4–5
Donald J. Veldman, 6–7
Magdalen D. Vernon, 5–6
Philip E. Vernon, 2, 4–7
Verna L. Vickery, 5
Roland Vinette, 3
Morris S. Viteles, 2–3
J. R. Jefferson Wadkins, 7
Guy W. Wagner, 1
John Wagner, 7
William W. Waite, 3–4
J. V. Waits, 3
David A. Walker, 7
Helen M. Walker, 1
W. D. Wall, 4
S. Rains Wallace, 4–5
Wimburn L. Wallace, 5–7
Norman E. Wallen, 6
James A. Walsh, 7
W. Bruce Walsh, 7
Edwin Wandt, 4, 7
Morey J. Wantman, 4–6
F. W. Warburton, 4–5
Charles F. Ward, 7
William C. Ward, 7
David M. Wark, 7
Charles F. Warnath, 6
Neil D. Warren, 3, 5
Willard G. Warrington, 5–7
Ruth W. Washburn, 3
Alan T. Waterman, 2
Eugene A. Waters, 2
John G. Watkins, 6
Ralph K. Watkins, 2
Richard W. Watkins, 7
Goodwin Watson, 1–3
Robert I. Watson, 3
J. Fred Weaver, 5
Harold Webster, 5–6
William J. Webster, 7
David Wechsler, 2–3
Charles C. Weidemann, 1–2
David P. Weikart, 7
Sheldon A. Weintraub, 7
David J. Weiss, 7
Henry Weitz, 3–7
Carolyn M. Welch, 3
A. T. Welford, 4
Beth L. Wellman, 3

F. L. Wells, 1–3
Joseph M. Wepman, 7
Emmy E. Werner, 6–7
Edgar B. Wesley, 1–4
Alexander G. Wesman, 4–7
Leonard J. West, 7
Bert W. Westbrook, 7
George Westby, 4–6
Frederick L. Westover, 4
Harry G. Wheat, 2
D. K. Wheeler, 5
Howard R. White, 4
Dean K. Whitla, 6
Carroll A. Whitmer, 2–3
Jerry S. Wiggins, 6–7
Katherine W. Wilcox, 3
S. S. Wilks, 1–2
Haydn S. Williams, 5
J. Robert Williams, 6
Edmund G. Williamson, 1–2
Warren W. Willingham, 6
Carl G. Willis, 7
Margaret Willis, 2
John M. Willits, 3, 5
J. Richard Wilmeth, 6
Guy M. Wilson, 1–3
James W. Wilson, 7
Herbert D. Wing, 4–6
William L. Winnett, 7
George P. Winship, Jr., 6–7
R. Winterbourn, 5
Robert D. Wirt, 6–7
Emory E. Wiseman, 7
Stephen Wiseman, 3, 5
Ernest C. Witham, 2
J. Richard Wittenborn, 3–4
Paul A. Witty, 3
Dael L. Wolfle, 1–2, 4
Leroy Wolins, 6
Frank B. Womer, 6–7
E. F. Wonderlic, 3
Hugh B. Wood, 2
Ray G. Wood, 3
Clifford Woody, 1, 3
D. A. Worcester, 2–4
Blaine R. Worthen, 7
F. Lynwood Wren, 3
C. Gilbert Wrenn, 1–2, 5
Robert L. Wright, 7
J. Wayne Wrightstone, 1–3, 5
Jack Wrigley, 5
Ll. Wynn Jones, 2
Alfred Yates, 5
Aubrey J. Yates, 7
Albert H. Yee, 7
Dale Yoder, 4
Louis C. Zahner, 2–3, 5
O. L. Zangwill, 3
Edwin Ziegfeld, 2–4
Wayne S. Zimmerman, 6–7
Donald G. Zytowski, 7

TESTS IN PRINT II

PREFACE

THE FIRST edition of *Tests in Print* (TIP I) was finally published in November 1961 after several unsuccessful attempts to launch a series of similar publications to complement the *Mental Measurements Yearbooks*. Earlier bibliographies [1] had been compiled largely from secondary sources. They made no distinction between in print and out of print tests, or between tests commercially available and those available only in articles, books, and theses, and they were badly out of date. Although the first five *Mental Measurements Yearbooks* covered all new and revised tests published between 1933 and 1958, there was a pressing need for a comprehensive and up-to-date bibliography of all tests in print. Furthermore, TIP I was needed to serve as a guide and index to the contents of the first five MMY's.

Originally we had planned to prepare a new *Tests in Print* after each new *Mental Measurements Yearbook* was published. We had thought that TIP would outsell the MMY's since we reasoned that testing specialists and frequent users of tests would want to have their own copies of TIP even if they were unable or unwilling to purchase a set of the five *Mental Measurements Yearbooks*. We couldn't have been more mistaken.

Although TIP I was enthusiastically acclaimed by reviewers, the book sold extremely poorly. Very few copies were purchased by individuals. We were so concerned about our stock of unsold books that arrangements were made with a national testing organization to sell copies of TIP I to its members at the manufacturing cost—which did not include the greater cost of preparing the manuscript! Because of poor sales, we were forced to abandon plans for a new edition of *Tests in Print* following publication of *The Sixth Mental Measurements Yearbook* in 1965. Much to our surprise, however, sales of *Tests in Print* began to pick up the following year—five years after its publication in 1961. In 1973, twelve years after its publication, TIP I outsold more recent books such as the 1965 *Sixth Mental Measurements Yearbook,* the 1968 *Reading Tests and Reviews* (RTR), and the 1970 *Personality Tests and Reviews* (PTR). Encouraged by the upturn in sales, we began concentrated work on *Tests in Print II* late in 1971.

This volume has a much broader scope than the 1961 TIP. Like the first volume, TIP II presents: (*a*) a comprehensive bibliography of all known tests published as separates for use with English-speaking subjects; (*b*) a classified index to the contents of all *Mental Measurements Yearbooks* published to date; and (*c*) a reprinting of the 1974 APA-AERA-NCME *Standards for Educational and Psychological Tests*. In addition, TIP II presents several new features: (*d*) comprehensive bibliographies through 1971 on the construction, use, and validity of specific tests—some of the bibliographies are complete in this volume; others supplement bibliographies in earlier publica-

---

[1] Hildreth, Gertrude H. *A Bibliography of Mental Tests and Rating Scales, Second Edition.* New York: Psychological Corporation, 1939. Pp. xxiv, 295. (*1945 Supplement,* 1946. Pp. ix, 86.) For reviews, see 2:B937, 1:B384, and 36:B136.
Wang, Charles K. A. *An Annotated Bibliography of Mental Tests and Scales, Volumes 1 and 2.* Peiping, China: Catholic University Press, 1939. Pp. vi, 725; vii, 698. For reviews, see 3:1221–3.

tions; (*e*) a classified list of tests which have gone out of print since TIP I; (*f*) a cumulative name index for each test with references; (*g*) title and name indexes covering all in print and out of print tests and all authors of tests, reviews, excerpts, and references in the seven MMY's and PTR; (*h*) a publishers directory with a complete listing of each publisher's test titles; and (*i*) a classified scanning index with a description of the population for which each test is intended.

Although this volume is useful in and of itself, its maximum usefulness requires the availability and use of the seven *Mental Measurements Yearbooks* and, in the case of references for personality tests, *Personality Tests and Reviews*. Although up-to-date information on available tests and specific test bibliographies is valuable, the greatest service which *Tests in Print* can perform is to encourage test users to choose tests more wisely by consulting the test reviews in the *Mental Measurements Yearbooks*. We do not consider it of great importance merely to present readers with a comprehensive list of tests—most of which are of unknown or questionable validity. Our major objective is to direct readers to the MMY test reviews, the excerpted test reviews from journals, and to the professional literature on the construction, use, and validity of the tests being considered. Test users should be extremely cautious about choosing tests which have not been favorably reviewed by competent specialists. Relatively few test users will have the experience and time to make such appraisals for themselves.

The cost of preparing and manufacturing this volume has been tremendous. TIP II contains a huge amount of material. In order to reduce costs, references and cumulative name indexes were set in an extremely small type size, while the test entries and the extensive end-of-the-book indexes were set in a larger but still relatively small type size. Had we chosen commonly used larger type sizes, the book would have been two to three times bigger. Although we do not have exact figures, we are confident that the editorial cost alone of preparing this volume has been at least a quarter of a million dollars. This does not include salaries for my wife and myself or the extremely high costs of paper, typesetting, presswork, and binding. It may be that spiraling costs will price us out of the market. We hope,

however, that our clientele will consider the volume an especially good value because of the wealth of useful information. With the hope that there will be general agreement about the worth of TIP II, we have begun working on TIP III.

Since TIP III will not have cumulative indexing and will have only about three-fifths as many references, it will be a smaller work. Although the test coverage will be as of mid-1975, the specific test bibliographies will include only references published through 1973. Our plans are to publish TIP III in mid-1976, with a new edition every two years thereafter.

Tests in Print III will supplement but not supplant this volume. TIP II will continue to be useful for many years to come because of its 16,574 references, its cumulative name indexes for specific tests, its cumulative title index covering both in print and out of print tests, and its overall cumulative name index listing authors of all tests, reviews, excerpts, and references. These cumulative indexes, covering not only this volume but our thirteen earlier publications produced over the past thirty-nine years, will never be superseded.

Unlike TIP II, which will continue to have considerable value even after the publication of later editions, the 1961 *Tests in Print* will have only marginal value after the publication of this volume. Although TIP I does not present specific test bibliographies, it does have three features of historical value: (*a*) a classified bibliography of tests out of print as of mid-1961; (*b*) information about tests in print as of mid-1961 but now out of print; and (*c*) a reprinting of two important monographs which were pioneer attempts to set standards for test manuals: the 1954 *Technical Recommendations for Psychological Tests and Diagnostic Techniques* and the 1955 *Technical Recommendations for Achievement Tests*. These historical values seemed important enough to warrant the 1974 reprinting of *Tests in Print I*.

References on the construction, use, and validity of specific tests will no longer be included in the *Mental Measurements Yearbooks*. Hereafter, references will be presented only in *Tests in Print* and, possibly, in our special monographs. By shifting these specific test bibliographies to TIP, the preparation and manufacture of the MMY's will become more manageable and will, therefore, permit us to publish the *Mental Measurements Yearbooks* more frequently, perhaps every three years.

The cumulative indexing and the MMY-like format of *Tests in Print II* will enable us to publish separate monographs in each of the following specific areas: English, foreign languages, intelligence, mathematics, personality, reading, science, social studies, and vocations. These monographs will consist of the relevant sections in the seven MMY's and TIP II, ranging in size from 250 to 1500 pages. The monographs will make it possible for persons especially interested in one of these nine areas to purchase a single volume (two volumes for personality or reading) containing a 1974 bibliography of in print tests, a reprinting of all the relevant materials in the seven MMY's, and cumulative indexes.

The first two of the nine monographs, *Personality Tests and Reviews II* (PTR II) and *Reading Tests and Reviews II* (RTR II), are scheduled for publication early in 1975. These monographs will supplement the 1968 RTR and the 1970 PTR by reprinting the relevant sections from *The Seventh Mental Measurements Yearbook* and *Tests in Print II*. The cumulative indexes, however, will include all of the material published in the earlier monographs.

Although we may find it impossible to finance all of these monographs because of runaway inflation and its effect on sales, we feel reasonably confident that we shall be able to publish at least four or five monographs before the end of 1975.

We are, of course, glad to have our publications used as widely as possible. No requests to reprint our materials have been refused. We are disturbed, however, by the use of our material without permission and, what is worse, without giving us credit. We are most concerned about the use of our specific test bibliographies. More than 60,000 references have been presented in this and earlier volumes at a tremendous cost in time and money. All references (except unpublished theses) have been personally examined by me to make sure that they meet our criteria for relevancy with regard to specific tests. We never rely on secondary sources in listing articles, books, chapters, or monographs. In light of this, we feel that we have succeeded in producing bibliographies unequaled in their accuracy, comprehensiveness, and relevancy. Yet, we regret to report

that, to our knowledge, not one of these uniquely prepared bibliographies has even been cited in a test manual, article, or book dealing with a specific test. (Had we published any of these bibliographies—say, the 4,578 references for Rorschach—in a separate monograph, it very likely would have been cited in the literature.) What disturbs us even more, however, is that some authors unabashedly present parts of our material as their own. We feel strongly that proper credit should be given for the use of our costly and laboriously prepared bibliographies. We have a suggestion which some authors and publishers of tests generating a substantial number of references may like to consider. In your test manuals, refer your readers to our bibliographies and then present your own supplementary bibliography of references not found in the specific test bibliographies published by us.

With very few exceptions, test publishers have been most cooperative in providing specimen sets of their tests to facilitate our preparation of accurate test entries. Their contribution, however, did not end when they sent us the specimen sets. We frequently found it necessary to request from them additional information and materials needed in order to prepare test entries. Lastly, the final drafts of the entries had to be submitted to the publishers for checking. Test publishers, I am sure, can attest to the care with which our entries are prepared. We would urge new test publishers who may not be known to us, and authors publishing their own tests or having their tests published by a new or obscure publisher to send us specimen sets of their tests soon after publication for inclusion in our biennial TIP's. Unless we actually see the test materials, we will not list them in an MMY or TIP.

Numerous libraries in this country and abroad have been used in preparing the specific test bibliographies in this volume. The greatest use has been made of the excellent periodical collections in the Rutgers University libraries. I am pleased to express my appreciation for the assistance given us by staff members of the Rutgers libraries.

We are especially pleased that the American Psychological Association is permitting us to reprint its 1974 *Standards for Educational and Psychological Tests* prepared by a joint committee of the American Psychological Association, American Educational Research Association, and National Council on Measurements in Education. This important monograph should receive the widest possible readership. We hope that the accessibility of the APA-AERA-NCME *Standards* will result in their being read and applied by many who might otherwise have given the *Standards* little or no attention.

The preparation and production of this work has required a larger staff and more of my time than any of our previous publications. Fortunately, five of our staff members are veterans of at least three earlier publications. To these five—Ethel Kersting, Doris G. McCan, Mary T. Mooney, Joan S. Paszamant, and Natalie J. Turton—I am especially indebted; their dedication, experience, and high standards have been a great satisfaction to me and have, I am sure, inspired newer members of the staff, namely, Mary Anne Becker and Susan Vogel. Because of the important contributions made by these seven staff members, their names have been listed on the page opposite the title page. My editorial colleagues—Ethel Kersting, Joan S. Paszamant, and Susan Vogel—have been responsible for preparing test entries, corresponding with test publishers, editing manuscript copy, as well as sharing with other staff members the tremendous task of proofreading. Without their dedicated and competent assistance, I wonder whether I would continue with these publications.

Since the responsibilities of our secretarial staff go far beyond the usual clerical and secretarial assignments, their duties are more appropriately described as "secretarial and production." They have copyread, proofread, sightread, compiled statistics, and made indexes as well as performed the usual clerical tasks. These staff members—Mary Anne Becker, Doris G. McCan, Mary T. Mooney, and Natalie J. Turton—have efficiently and conscientiously carried out these numerous and varied assignments.

In addition to expressing my appreciation and thanks to the above seven staff members, I also wish to acknowledge and thank two new staff members, Sandra Boxer Discenza and Barbara Ruis Martko, who have been on our staff approximately six months. They quickly demonstrated a flair for the exacting work demanded by our publications. I hopefully look forward to their continued assistance in preparing future publications.

Having such a large and experienced staff is not without its drawbacks. For the first six yearbooks, relatively small staffs were required and were hired only for a particular book. As soon as the last page proof was approved, the staff would be reduced to one person, sometimes only part time, which gave me a respite to work on other things or to go off to teach or travel in Africa. Because I highly value our present staff and since I am very reluctant to have to train a new staff to handle each upcoming publication, I hope to continue our experienced staff members working indefinitely. This means, however, that I must keep them continuously involved in new projects. Since I do not foresee discontinuing our service to test users, we must always be working on new publications, even while a current volume is being prepared or in press. Two months before a book is off the press, the entire staff is working on other new books in the series.

I also wish to mention the continuing efforts which my wife has devoted to these publications as book designer, co-publisher, and counselor. As grateful as I am for her constant support and active assistance, I am even more appreciative that she has reluctantly concluded that we should not retire.

One of the satisfactions in editing the *Mental Measurements Yearbooks* has been my working relationships with the contributing reviewers. I am deeply indebted to the hundreds of persons, representing a wide range of disciplines, who have helped us in providing critical test reviews to all who use tests. As a token of my appreciation, this book is being dedicated in particular to the five persons who have reviewed for all seven *Mental Measurements Yearbooks*: Anne Anastasi, Howard R. Anderson, Walter V. Kaulfers, Victor H. Noll, and Arthur E. Traxler; and, in general, to all MMY reviewers over the years. My warmest thanks to all of you.

OSCAR KRISEN BUROS

Highland Park, New Jersey
September 10, 1974

INTRODUCTION

THIS volume is the fourteenth in a series of publications [1] initiated in 1935 to assist educators, personnel workers, and psychologists in the selection and use of tests. Although the earliest three publications are noncritical bibliographies, the original intent had been to prepare an annual critical review of new tests for journal publication. It soon became apparent, however, that this was far beyond the capacity of a single individual. A more modest goal was substituted, the publication of an annual bibliography of tests, as described in the Introduction to the first of our fourteen publications:

To locate the standard tests recently published in specific areas is a laborious task. The usual biblio-

[1] The thirteen earlier publications, all edited by Oscar K. Buros and now published by The Gryphon Press, are listed from the most recent to the oldest:
   a) The Seventh Mental Measurements Yearbook, Vols. I and II, 1974. Pp. xl, 935; vi, 937–1986. $70 per set.
   b) Personality Tests and Reviews: Including an Index to The Mental Measurements Yearbooks, 1972. Pp. xxxi, 1659. $45.00. For reviews, see 7:B120.
   c) Reading Tests and Reviews: Including a Classified Index to The Mental Measurements Yearbook, 1968. Pp. xxii, 520. $20.00. For reviews, see 7:B121.
   d) The Sixth Mental Measurements Yearbook, 1965. Pp. xxxvii, 1714. $45.00. (Reprinted 1971) For reviews, see 7:B122.
   e) Tests in Print: A Comprehensive Bibliography of Tests for Use in Education, Psychology, and Industry, 1961. Pp. xxix, 479. $15.00. (Reprinted 1974) For reviews, see 6:B105.
   f) The Fifth Mental Measurements Yearbook, 1959. Pp. xxix, 1292. $35.00. (Reprinted 1961) For reviews, see 6:B104.
   g) The Fourth Mental Measurements Yearbook, 1953. Pp. xxv, 1163. $30.00. (Reprinted 1974) For reviews, see 5:B84.
   h) The Third Mental Measurements Yearbook, 1949. Pp. xv, 1047. $25.00. (Reprinted 1974) For reviews, see 4:B71.
   i) The Nineteen Forty Mental Measurements Yearbook, 1941. Pp. xxv, 674. $22.50. (Reissued 1972) For reviews, see 3:788 and 4:B70.
   j) The Nineteen Thirty Eight Mental Measurements Yearbook, 1938. Pp. xv, 415. $20.00. (Reissued 1972) For reviews, see 2:B858.
   k) Educational, Psychological, and Personality Tests of 1936: Including a Bibliography and Book Review Digest of Measurement Books and Monographs of 1933-36, 1937. Pp. 141. For reviews, see 1:B326.
   l) Educational, Psychological, and Personality Tests of 1933, 1934, and 1935, 1936. Pp. 83. For reviews, see 36:B46.
   m) Educational, Psychological, and Personality Tests of 1933 and 1934, 1935. Pp. 44. For a review, see 36:B45.

graphic aids for locating periodical, monograph, and book publications are of little value in locating standard tests. New tests are being published so rapidly that the test technicians themselves find it difficult to locate the test titles of the past year without an inordinate amount of searching. For these reasons, the writer has undertaken the task of preparing a bibliography of psychological, achievement, character, and personality tests published in 1933 and 1934. This bibliography will be the first of a series to be published annually by the School of Education, Rutgers University.[2]

This 44-page bibliography lists 257 tests that were new, revised, or supplemented in 1933 and 1934. Many of these tests, usually revised editions, are still in print today.

Similar test bibliographies [3] were published in 1936 and 1937. During this time, attempts were being made to obtain a grant to initiate a research organization which would serve as a bureau of standards for the evaluation of educational and psychological tests. It was only after we despaired of raising such funds that we decided to set up a test reviewing service.

THE SEVEN MMY'S

Since tests, unlike books, were rarely reviewed in professional journals, it was a revolutionary step forward when we published *The 1938 Mental Measurements Yearbook* 36 years ago. In his Foreword, Clarence E. Partch's comments reflect our excitement and mood in those early days:

The publication of *The 1938 Mental Measurements Yearbook* of the School of Education, Rutgers Uni-

[2] *Educational, Psychological, and Personality Tests of 1933 and 1934*, p. 5.
[3] *Educational, Psychological, and Personality Tests of 1933, 1934, and 1935.*
Educational, Psychological, and Personality Tests of 1936.

versity is likely to prove a landmark of considerable importance in the history of tests and measurements. Heretofore, despite the obvious need of test users for frank evaluations of tests by competent reviewers, few standardized tests have been critically appraised in the professional journals and textbooks for students of education and psychology. Now, for the first time, a large number of frankly evaluative reviews by able test technicians, subject-matter specialists, and psychologists are available to assist test users in making more discriminating selections from among the hundreds of tests on the market.[4]

Except for a few test authors and publishers who objected to unfavorable reviews, *The 1938 Yearbook* (also referred to as *The First Yearbook*) was enthusiastically acclaimed in this country and abroad. It took some time, however, before most of the protesting publishers were able to accept unfavorable test reviews with equanimity.

Before *The 1938 Yearbook* was off the press, we began sending out invitations to review tests for a 1939 yearbook. Unfortunately, because of financing and production problems, we were unable to maintain our annual production schedule. It took us over two years to publish the next volume, *The 1940 Mental Measurements Yearbook.*

Much enlarged and greatly improved over its predecessor, *The 1940 Yearbook* (also referred to as *The Second Yearbook*) has been the prototype for all later yearbooks. In addition to the increased number of tests, reviews, and references, there were many qualitative changes: (*a*) The objectives which have characterized all MMY's were presented in detail for the first time. (*b*) The format was standardized. (*c*) The classification of tests was changed from 40 specific categories to 12 broad categories. (*d*) The practice of including very short reviews of 100 words or less was discontinued. (*e*) The review coverage was extended to old tests and to tests previously reviewed as well as new tests. (*f*) The instructions given to reviewers concerning the preparation of their test reviews were presented. (*g*) The reactions of test authors and publishers—most of them objecting strenuously to unfavorable reviews—were reprinted for the first and last time.

In the Preface of *The 1940 Yearbook* we announced that the yearbooks would be published every two years. Because of World War II, however, *The Third Mental Measurements Yearbook* was not published until 1949. Except

4 *The 1938 Mental Measurements Yearbook,* p. xi.

for its larger size and more thorough preparation, *The Third Yearbook*—like all later yearbooks—is very similar in its coverage, format, indexing, and organization to *The 1940 Yearbook.* There were, however, several improvements: (*a*) The "Classified Index of Tests," an expanded table of contents, was introduced. (*b*) Stars and asterisks were used preceding test titles to indicate, respectively, tests listed in a yearbook for the first time and tests revised or supplemented since last listed. (*c*) Asterisks were used at the end of a reference to indicate that the reference had been examined personally for accuracy and relevance. (*d*) Whenever possible, the abstract in *Psychological Abstracts* was cited for each reference. (*e*) Two improvements were made in the name index. Previously authors of references for specific tests had been indexed merely by citing the test for which the reference appears. After locating the test, one then had to search through the references to find those by that author. The new index eliminated this searching by citing each reference both to the test number and the reference number. Secondly, the index was converted into an "analytic index" in which *"test," "rev," "exc," "bk,"* and *"ref"* were used to indicate whether a citation referred to authorship of a test, review, excerpted review, book, or reference. These five features have been included in all later yearbooks.

In *The Fourth Mental Measurements Yearbook,* published in 1953, our review coverage was extended for the first time to many tests restricted to testing programs administered by organizations such as the College Entrance Examination Board. Six years later, in 1959, *The Fifth Yearbook* was published. Upon the completion of that volume, we were concerned that some cutbacks would be necessary to stem the phenomenal growth of production costs, as well as the ever increasing length of each MMY. As a result, we decided to discontinue specific test bibliographies and almost all reviews of foreign tests. The appreciative reviews *The Fifth Yearbook* received, however, especially those mentioning the value of the specific bibliographies to students of testing, caused us to reconsider. Consequently, despite the expanding literature on specific tests, we decided to continue all features of the earlier volumes. As a result, it took us six years to publish in 1965 *The Sixth Mental Measurements Yearbook,* a

1751-page volume, approximately one-third larger than the previous yearbook. In addition to its more extensive coverage, *The Sixth Yearbook* presents a comprehensive listing of all tests in print as of mid-1964. The latest yearbook to date, *The Seventh Yearbook,* was published in 1972. This massive two-volume work of 2032 pages may well be considered the zenith of the MMY's.

Like all other volumes published since 1938, *The Seventh Yearbook* supplements rather than supplants earlier yearbooks. For complete coverage, therefore, a reader must have access to all seven MMY's. A person using only the latest, *The Seventh Yearbook,* will miss a tremendous amount of valuable information in the six earlier volumes. Although the more recent yearbooks—especially the last three—are of greatest value, the third and fourth yearbooks also contain much useful information on many in print tests. Even though the first two yearbooks are mainly of historical interest, they also include some critical information on currently used tests. Our faith in the value of the first four MMY's, published between 1938 and 1953, is attested to by our reissuing of the first and second yearbooks in 1972 and reprinting of the third and fourth in 1974. Consequently, all seven yearbooks are now in print.

MMY MONOGRAPHS

It is with amusement and wonder that we look back at some of the dreams of our youth. *The 1940 Mental Measurements Yearbook* was the first yearbook published by my wife and myself. In those depression days, money was scarce but printing was cheap and penny postcards could be used for advertising. Borrowed capital of $3500 was sufficient to launch us into book publishing. Even before our first book was off the press we were planning to publish not only a new MMY every two years, but also a series of derivative monographs. Our plans were confidently announced in the Preface of *The 1940 Yearbook* thus:

In order to make the material in the yearbooks more easily accessible to individuals who are interested in only a small part of each volume, a new series of monographs is being planned. If the first two or three monographs prove successful, others will eventually be prepared to cover tests in each of the following fields: business education, English and reading, fine arts, foreign languages, health and physical education, home economics, industrial arts, intelligence, mathematics, sciences, social studies, and vocational apti-

tudes. The first publication in each field will include: a comprehensive bibliography of all standard tests in print in that area; a reprinting, in part or in full, of all reviews of these tests which have appeared in previous yearbooks or in the journal literature; new reviews written especially for the monograph (to be, in turn, reprinted, in part or in full, in the following yearbook); and an extensive list of references on the construction, validation, use, and limitations of the tests. Separates in each field will be issued every four, six, or eight years depending upon the frequency of test publication. These monographs will range in size from fifty to two hundred pages. This new series will make it possible for an individual to purchase, at a nominal cost, every four, six, or eight years a monograph devoted solely to the tests and reviews of most interest to him.[5]

However, the publishing of the MMY's alone, even at intervals of 4 to 8 years, proved to be so time consuming and difficult that initiating the monograph series had to be continually postponed. But the dreams were never abandoned.

In 1968, 27 years after the monograph series was initially announced, the first monograph, *Reading Tests and Reviews* (RTR), was published. This 542-page volume consists of: the reading sections of the first six MMY's; a comprehensive bibliography of reading tests as of May, 1968, including 52 new tests and 36 revised tests not previously listed in an MMY; a classified listing of all tests listed in one or more MMY's; and cross references to reviews, excerpts, and references of all tests appearing in the yearbooks to date. The second monograph, *Personality Tests and Reviews* (PTR), was published in 1970. This 1695-page work, which reprints the personality sections of all previous MMY's, also includes much new material: a comprehensive bibliography of tests through mid-1969, over 7000 new references, separate author indexes to tests with over 25 references, and a scanning index of 513 personality tests listed in the volume. Unlike RTR, PTR features: (*a*) a reprinting of the 1966 APA-AERA-NCME *Standards for Educational and Psychological Tests and Manuals,* and (*b*) an index to all reviews of measurement books excerpted in the first six MMY's. Because of the large number of specific test bibliographies, PTR must be used along with the MMY's.

Early in 1975, we plan to publish two new monographs to supplement the personality and reading volumes. We are also hoping to publish later in 1975 monographs in seven additional areas: English, foreign languages, intelligence,

[5] *The 1940 Mental Measurements Yearbook,* p. xx.

mathematics, science, social studies, and vocations.

TESTS IN PRINT I

In 1961, we published the eighth volume in the MMY series: *Tests in Print: A Comprehensive Bibliography of Tests for Use in Education, Psychology, and Industry.* The objectives and nature of *Tests in Print* (hereafter called *Tests in Print I* or TIP I) are described in its Introduction as follows:

> The objectives of *Tests in Print* are threefold: first, to present a comprehensive bibliography of tests—achievement, aptitude, intelligence, personality, and certain sensory-motor skills—published as separates and currently available in English-speaking countries; second, to serve as a classified index and supplement to the volumes of the *Mental Measurements Yearbook* series published to date; third, to give a wider distribution to the excellent recommendations for improving test manuals made by committees of the American Psychological Association, the American Educational Research Association, and the National Council on Measurements Used in Education.[6]

TIP I lists 2967 tests—2126 in print and 841 out of print as of early 1961, and also serves as a master index to the contents of the first five MMY's. Originally, we had planned to publish a new edition of TIP shortly after the publication of each new MMY, but poor sales of TIP I caused these plans to be abandoned. *The Sixth Yearbook,* in effect, served as a new edition of *Tests in Print* by referring to the tests in TIP I which were still in print as of mid-1964. Surprisingly, however, sales of the 1961 *Tests in Print* began to pick up after publication of *The Sixth Yearbook* in 1965. This unexpected upturn encouraged us to begin devoting all of our time to the preparation of a new edition of TIP immediately after approving the last proofs for *The Seventh Yearbook.*

TESTS IN PRINT II

Users of TIP I may well marvel at the expansion in the scope and size of this volume. TIP II has easily been the most expensive volume to prepare and manufacture to date. Spiraling inflation is, of course, an important factor. Of even greater importance, however, is the sheer magnitude of the task undertaken. Had we estimated more accurately the work involved, we might never have undertaken it.

[6] *Tests in Print,* p. xv.

Like the 1961 volume, *Tests in Print II* presents: (*a*) a comprehensive bibliography of all known tests published as separates for use with English-speaking subjects; (*b*) a classified index to the contents of the test sections of all *Mental Measurements Yearbooks* published to date; and (*c*) a reprinting of the 1974 APA-AERA-NCME *Standards for Educational and Psychological Tests.*

In addition, TIP II introduces the following new features: (*d*) comprehensive bibliographies through 1971 on the construction, use, and validity of specific tests; (*e*) a classified list of tests which have gone out of print since TIP I; (*f*) a cumulative name index for each test with references; (*g*) a title index covering in print and out of print tests, as well as inverted, series, and superseded titles in the MMY's and monographs; (*h*) an analytic name index covering all authors of tests, reviews, excerpts, and references in the MMY's and monographs; (*i*) a publishers directory with a complete listing of each publisher's test titles; (*j*) a classified scanning index which describes the population for which each test is intended; (*k*) identification of foreign tests and journals by presenting the country of origin in brackets immediately after a test entry or journal title; (*l*) inclusions of factual statements implying criticism such as "1971 tests identical with tests copyrighted 1961 except for format," and "no manual"; (*m*) listing of test titles at the foot of each page to permit immediate identification of pages consisting only of references or names; and (*n*) directions on how to use the book and an expanded table of contents printed on the endpages to greatly facilitate its use.

TESTS

This volume contains 2467 test entries, 16.0 percent more than TIP I. Over a 13-year period this increase averages slightly more than 1.1 percent per year. Table 1 indicates that the number of personality tests—the area in which we know least about testing— is, as it was in 1961, greater than any other classification. In 1961, one out of seven tests was a personality test; by 1974, this ratio had increased to one out of six. Multi-aptitude, reading, sensory-motor, speech and hearing, and vocations are other areas with proportionately more tests in 1974. In all achievement areas, the proportion

TABLE 1

Tests by Major Classification
TIP II (1974) and TIP I (1961)

Classification	Tests		Percentage	
	1974	1961	1974	1961
Achievement Batteries	50	45	2.0	2.1
English	131	183 †	5.3	8.6
Fine Arts	35	29	1.4	1.4
Foreign Languages	105	92	4.3	4.3
Intelligence	274	238	11.1	11.2
Mathematics	168	198	6.8	9.3
Miscellaneous	291	278 †	11.8	13.1
Multi-Aptitude	26	20	1.1	0.9
Personality	441	306	17.9	14.4
Reading	248	159	10.1	7.5
Science	97	106	3.9	5.0
Sensory-Motor	62	42 †	2.5	2.0
Social Studies	85	113 †	3.4	5.3
Speech and Hearing	79	22	3.2	1.0
Vocations	375	295 †	15.2	13.9
Total	2467	2126	100.0	100.0

† An adjusted count to make 1961 classifications comparable to 1974 classifications.

of tests in 1974 is lower than in 1961. Four categories—intelligence, personality, reading, and vocations—make up 54.3 percent of the tests in this volume, compared to 47.0 percent in 1961. It is interesting to compare the overall 16.0 percent increase in the number of tests with the 138.0 percent increase in the number of specific test references over approximately the same period, 1960–62 to 1969–71.

NEW AND REVISED TESTS

Table 2 presents information on the percentages of tests new or revised (or supplemented in some way) since last listed in an MMY. Of the 2467 tests listed in this volume,

TABLE 2

New and Revised (or Supplemented) Tests
by Major Classifications

Classification	Tests	Percentage		
		New	Revised	Total
Achievement Batteries	50	10.0	48.0	58.0
English	131	9.2	27.5	36.6
Fine Arts	35	17.1	22.9	40.0
Foreign Languages	105	12.4	43.8	56.2
Intelligence	274	14.2	17.2	31.4
Mathematics	168	14.3	30.4	44.6
Miscellaneous	291	22.3	29.9	52.2
Multi-Aptitude	26	19.2	23.1	42.3
Personality	441	15.9	11.3	27.2
Reading	248	20.6	11.3	31.9
Science	97	4.1	52.6	56.7
Sensory-Motor	62	30.6	9.7	40.3
Social Studies	85	11.8	44.7	56.5
Speech and Hearing	79	29.1	22.8	51.9
Vocations	375	10.9	22.1	33.1
Total	2467	15.7	23.5	39.2

TABLE 3

Tests by Countries
TIP II (1974) and TIP I (1961)

Country	Number		Percentage	
	1974	1961	1974	1961
United States	2204	1875	85.3	87.7
Great Britain	181	149	7.0	7.0
South Africa	64	23	2.5	1.1
Australia	53	38	2.1	1.8
Canada	50	39	1.9	1.8
India	9		0.3	
Switzerland	8	6	0.3	.3
New Zealand	6	3	0.2	.1
Sweden	3	2	0.1	.1
Japan	2		0.1	
Netherlands	2	3	0.1	.1
Belgium	1		0.0	
France	1		0.0	
Papua New Guinea	1		0.0	
Total	2585 †	2138	99.9	100.0

† This total is larger than the total given in Table 1 since some of the 2467 entries are either for two or more tests or for tests published in two or more countries giving the above total of 2585.

15.7 percent are new and 23.5 percent have been revised or supplemented over a three year period. These statistics represent annual increases of 4.9 and 7.3 percent, respectively.

Because of the numerous secure achievement tests (e.g., College Entrance Examination Board tests) which annually have new forms, it is understandable that achievement tests generally have the lowest percentages of new tests and the highest percentages of revised tests. The categories with the most tests —personality, vocations, intelligence, and reading—have the smallest percentages of new and revised tests, an overall percentage of 16.6.

As in all our earlier publications, *Tests in Print II* attempts to cover the English-speaking world. In addition, if a test published in a non-English-speaking country is written in English, or intended for use with English-speaking subjects, we endeavor to list it too. In the entries, these foreign tests are identified by the name of the country in brackets immediately after the publisher's name. Test titles in the Scanning Index are also identified in the same way. Table 3 does not reflect the entire number of tests distributed abroad.

REVIEWS AND EXCERPTS

This volume is a master index to the 2682 original test reviews and the 381 excerpted test reviews in the first seven MMY's. As shown in Table 4, personality, intelligence, vocations, and reading account for 61.5 percent of the original

TABLE 4

REVIEWS, EXCERPTS, AND REFERENCES FOR TESTS IN TIP II

Classification	Number			
	Tests	Rev's	Exc's	Ref's
Achievement Batteries	50	113	14	984
English	131	136	6	569
Fine Arts	35	54	4	549
Foreign Languages	105	68	9	266
Intelligence	274	393	85	11,798
Mathematics	168	173	4	335
Miscellaneous	291	189	14	2,279
Multi-Aptitude	26	73	11	1,297
Personality	441	631	132	29,464
Reading	248	300	32	1,812
Science	97	98	11	277
Sensory-Motor	62	38	14	937
Social Studies	85	53	1	78
Speech & Hearing	79	38	11	394
Vocations	375	325	33	4,906
Total	2,467	2,682	381	55,945

TABLE 5

TESTS WITH 100 OR MORE REFERENCES THROUGH 1971

Test (Rank)	Total	TIP II
Rorschach (1)	4578	376
Minnesota Multiphasic Personality Inventory (2)	3855	549
Thematic Apperception Test (3)	1765	231
Stanford-Binet Intelligence Scale (4)	1408	438
Edwards Personal Preference Schedule (5)	1314	226
Strong Vocational Interest Blank for Men (6)	1231	133
Wechsler Intelligence Scale for Children (7)	1035	229
Wechsler-Bellevue Intelligence Scale (8)	990	243
Wechsler Adult Intelligence Scale (9)	938	178
California Psychological Inventory (10)	934	166
Sixteen Personality Factor Questionnaire (11)	898	244
Kuder Preference Record—Vocational (12)	867	302
Study of Values (13)	836	149
Bender-Gestalt Test (14)	765	144
College Board Scholastic Aptitude Test (15)	567	148
Maudsley Personality Inventory (16)	542	273
Progressive Matrices (17)	509	122
Guilford-Zimmerman Temperament Survey (18)	494	189
Personality Inventory (19)	465	124
General Aptitude Test Battery (20)	447	45
Minnesota Teacher Attitude Inventory (21)	442	287
California Test of Personality (22)	438	196
Rosenzweig Picture-Frustration Study (23)	416	106
Goodenough-Harris Drawing Test (24)	388	93
ACT Assessment (25)	376	97
Illinois Test of Psycholinguistic Abilities (26)	374	113
SRA Primary Mental Abilities (27)	368	57
Human Figure Drawing Techniques (29)	331	150
Torrance Tests of Creative Thinking (29)	331	88
Differential Aptitude Tests (29)	331	64
Cooperative School and College Ability Tests (31)	319	62
Adjective Check List (32)	318	85
Eysenck Personality Inventory (33)	314	140
Machover Draw-A-Person Test (34)	304	83
Cooperative English Tests (35)	300	107
Peabody Picture Vocabulary Test (36)	299	77
California Test of Mental Maturity (37)	277	72
Otis Self-Administering Tests of Mental Ability (38)	262	139
Holtzman Inkblot Technique (39)	260	42
Adjustment Inventory (40)	249	77
Seashore Measures of Musical Talent (41.5)	241	97
Porteus Maze Test (41.5)	241	52
Embedded Figures Test (43)	229	149
Mooney Problem Check List (44)	228	92
Interpersonal Check List (45)	224	115
Stanford Achievement Test (46)	216	87
Omnibus Personality Inventory (47)	215	62
Szondi Test (48)	210	24
College and University Environment Scales	208	69
Personal Orientation Inventory (50)	203	80
Otis Quick-Scoring Mental Ability Tests (51)	202	136
Strong Vocational Interest Blank for Women (52)	201	30
Tennessee Self-Concept Scale (53)	198	80
H-T-P (54.5)	197	61
Metropolitan Readiness Tests (54.5)	197	55
Revised Minnesota Paper Form Board Test (56)	196	37
IPAT Anxiety Scale Questionnaire (57)	188	120
Myers-Briggs Type Indicator (58)	186	120
Vineland Social Maturity Scale (59)	185	50
Stern Environment Indexes (60)	181	38
FIRO Scales (61)	174	59
Ohio State University Psychological Test (62)	169	89
Marianne Frostig Developmental Test of Visual Perception (63)	167	43
Blacky Pictures (64)	165	47
Inpatient Multidimensional Psychiatric Scale (65)	161	47
Kent-Rosanoff Free Association Test (66)	160	44

reviews and 74.0 percent of the excerpted reviews. Authors of reviews and excerpts are named following the test entries in cross references to the appropriate MMY. Although TIP II will serve a useful function by providing a comprehensive bibliography of tests in print, the cross references to the critical reviews are of even greater importance if tests are to be used wisely. It is necessary to consult TIP I to learn which tests were out of print in 1961 and to learn whether they had been reviewed and by whom. This volume indicates which tests have gone out of print since TIP I, whether there were any reviews or excerpts for the tests, and the latest yearbooks listing these tests. TIP II does not, however, mention names of reviewers of these out of print tests.

A total of 1317 persons have contributed reviews to one or more MMY's. Because of their important contributions to the *Mental Measurements Yearbooks,* a complete listing of MMY test reviewers is presented beginning on page xi. These reviewers were selected to represent a wide variety of viewpoints and disciplines. The number of reviewers per yearbook increased from 133 in 1938 to 439 in 1972. One-third of the 1317 contributors reviewed for *The Seventh Yearbook.* Approximately one-fifth reviewed for two or more yearbooks.

REFERENCES

This volume presents specific test bibliographies for all in print tests for which we have located references (written in English) on their construction, use, and validity. The 16,574

Test (Rank)	Total	TIP II
Shipley-Institute of Living Scale (67)	155	34
Stern Activities Index (68)	152	23
Cornell Medical Index (69)	151	42
Lorge-Thorndike Intelligence Tests (70)	150	38
AAHPER Youth Fitness Test (71)	148	23
Medical College Admission Test (72)	145	30
Multiple Affect Adjective Check List (73.5)	144	56
Watson-Glaser Critical Thinking Appraisal (73.5)	144	35
Leader Behavior Description Questionnaire (75)	143	35
Miller Analogies Test (76)	142	15
Jr.-Sr. High School Personality Questionnaire (77)	140	37
Bennett Mechanical Comprehension Test (78)	139	9
Survey of Interpersonal Values (79)	138	78
Vocational Preference Inventory (80.5)	131	48
Ortho-Rater (80.5)	131	31
Kuhlmann-Anderson Intelligence Test (82.5)	129	53
Remote Associates Test (82.5)	129	29
Survey of Study Habits and Attitudes (84)	128	33
Goldstein-Scheerer Tests of Abstract and Concrete Thinking (85)	127	36
Inventory of Factors STDCR (86)	125	43
Rotter Incomplete Sentence Blank (87)	124	48
Wonderlic Personnel Test (88)	123	10
Reading Comprehension: Cooperative English Tests (89)	121	51
Iowa Tests of Educational Development (90.5)	120	85
Gordon Personal Profile (90.5)	120	56
Minnesota Clerical Test (92)	119	23
Guilford-Martin Inventory of Factors GAMIN (93)	112	29
Iowa Silent Reading Tests (94.5)	109	42
Tests of General Educational Development (94.5)	109	11
Gesell Developmental Schedules (96)	108	48
Iowa Tests of Basic Skills (97)	104	87
Henmon-Nelson Tests of Basic Skills (98.5)	102	52
California Achievement Test (98.5)	102	28
Alternate Uses (101)	101	94
Benton Visual Retention Test (101)	101	71
A-S Reaction Study (101)	101	36
Test for Colour Blindness (103)	100	29
Total for the 103 tests	40,944	10,055
Total for the remaining 2,364 tests	15,001	6,519
Grand Total	55,945	16,574

references reported for the first time in this volume supplement through 1971 the 39,371 references previously listed for these same tests in an MMY or PTR. The 55,945 references represent a tremendous number of journals, greater than the journal coverage in any of the educational or psychological indexing and abstracting services.

These bibliographies are unique in several respects: (*a*) All references, except unpublished theses, have been examined for relevancy. (*b*) References are made to abstracts, if any, in *Dissertation Abstracts International* (DAI) and *Psychological Abstracts* (PA). (*c*) Beginning with PTR, all citations to unpublished theses not listed in DAI have been checked for accuracy by the graduate office of the degree granting institution. (*d*) The bibliographies are arranged chronologically to make it easier to check the most recent references first.

(*e*) A cumulative name index covering all yearbooks and PTR has been provided for each test with references.

As shown in Table 4, personality tests account for 29,464 references, 52.7 percent of all references. The only other categories generating a large number of references are intelligence and vocations, with 11,798 (21.0 percent) and 4,906 (8.8 percent), respectively.

For the first time, we have some trustworthy statistics comparing the literature output generated by specific tests across all fields. Table 5 ranks the 103 tests with 100 or more references. These 103 tests together have 40,944 references, 73.2 percent of the references for all 2467 tests in TIP II. Stated differently, 4.2 percent of the tests generated 73.2 percent of the references. Seven tests have 1000 or more references and 17 have 500 or more references.

Since Table 5 reports total reference counts, recent tests which are generating a great deal of writing do not stand out. A fairly accurate picture of the current literature output for specific tests is shown in Table 6. Although the Rorschach has a total reference count 18.7 percent larger than the MMPI, the MMPI generated 139.8 percent more references than the Rorschach in the triennium 1969–71. Estimates of trends may be made by comparing the reference counts for 1966–68 with those for 1969–71. Of the five tests averaging 100 or more references per year in 1969–71, the MMPI and EPPS remained approximately the same; 16PF and WISC increased 41.8 and 31.4 percent, respectively; and Rorschach decreased 26.6 percent. The total number of references for all tests in 1969–71 is 21.2 percent larger than for 1966–68. If this trend continues, we may expect approximately 15,000 references in 1972–74, an average of 5000 new references per year.

It is always a source of wonder to us that this voluminous literature has produced so little knowledge. Some of our reflections on this point were expressed in the Introduction of *Personality Tests and Reviews:*

In this era of remarkable progress in science and technology, it is sobering to think that our most widely used instruments for personality assessment were published 20, 30, 40, and even more years ago. Despite the tremendous amount of research devoted to these old, widely used tests, they have not been replaced by instruments more acceptable to the profession. Nor has the research resulted in a consensus among psychologists concerning the validities of a

TABLE 6

TESTS WITH 23 OR MORE REFERENCES
IN THE TRIENNIUM 1969–71

Test (Rank)	1969–71	1966–68
Minnesota Multiphasic Personality Inventory (1)	772	786
Sixteen Personality Factor Questionnaire (2)	370	261
Edwards Personal Preference Schedule (3)	334	320
Rorschach (4)	329	448
Wechsler Intelligence Scale for Children (5)	322	245
California Psychological Inventory (6)	281	247
Wechsler Adult Intelligence Scale (7)	262	265
Strong Vocational Interest Blank for Men (8)	222	203
Bender Gestalt Test (9)	220	140
Eysenck Personality Inventory (10)	217	81
Thematic Apperception Test (11)	188	255
Illinois Test of Psycholinguistic Abilities (12)	182	115
College Board Scholastic Aptitude Test (13)	176	139
ACT Assessment (14)	167	135
Study of Values (15)	162	194
Maudsley Personality Inventory (16)	153	134
Torrance Tests of Creative Thinking (17)	148	115
Stanford-Binet Intelligence Scale (18)	147	117
Peabody Picture Vocabulary Test (19)	135	108
Personal Orientation Inventory (20)	134	63
College and University Environment Scales (21)	133	69
Adjective Check List (22)	132	93
Tennessee Self Concept Scale (23)	131	50
Minnesota Teacher Attitude Inventory (24)	111	88
Omnibus Personality Inventory (25)	109	67
Progressive Matrices (26)	105	104
FIRO Scales (27)	94	38
Cooperative School and College Ability Tests (28)	89	76
Holtzman Inkblot Technique (29)	86	85
Embedded Figures Test (30.5)	83	62
Guilford-Zimmerman Temperament Survey (30.5)	83	105
Goodenough Harris Drawing Test (32)	82	84
Metropolitan Readiness Tests (33.5)	80	52
Marianne Frostig Developmental Test of Visual Perception (33.5)	80	68
General Aptitude Test Battery (35)	78	59
California Test of Personality (36)	77	70
Vocational Preference Inventory (37)	74	30
IPAT Anxiety Scale Questionnaire (38.5)	73	50
Myers-Briggs Type Indicator (38.5)	73	65
College Student Questionnaire (40)	72	14
Human Figure Drawing Technique (41)	70	51
Multiple Affect Adjective Check List (42)	69	50
Wechsler Preschool and Primary Scale of Intelligence (43)	67	19
Stern Environment Indexes (44)	62	61
State-Trait Anxiety Inventory (45)	61	4
Kuder Preference Record—Vocational (46)	57	86
California Test of Mental Maturity (47)	56	48
Strong Vocational Interest Blank for Women (48)	55	40
Leader Behavior Description Questionnaire (49)	54	34
Jr.-Sr. High School Personality Questionnaire (51)	53	40
Remote Associates Test (51)	53	48
Interpersonal Check List (51)	53	63
Lorge-Thorndike Intelligence Tests (53.5)	51	39
Watson-Glaser Critical Thinking Appraisal (53.5)	51	32
Differential Aptitude Tests (55.5)	50	61
Wide Range Achievement Test (55.5)	50	19
Survey of Interpersonal Values (57)	49	54
Personality Research Form (58)	46	16
AAHPER Youth Fitness Test (59.5)	43	38
Survey of Study Habits and Attitudes (59.5)	43	26
SRA Primary Mental Abilities (61)	42	45
H-T-P (62)	39	15
Barron-Welsh Art Scale (63)	38	28
Cornell Medical Index (65)	37	44
Mooney Problem Check List (65)	37	34

Test (Rank)	1969–71	1966–68
Auditory Discrimination Test (65)	37	33
Opinion, Attitude, and Interest Survey (68)	36	25
Rokeach Value Survey (68)	36	3
Children's Personality Questionnaire (68)	36	26
Hidden Figures Test (71.5)	35	13
Stern Activities Index (71.5)	35	54
Rosenzweig Picture-Frustration Study (71.5)	35	41
Hostility and Direction of Hostility Questionnaire (71.5)	35	11
Machover Draw-A-Person Test (75.5)	34	46
Otis Quick-Scoring Mental Ability Tests (75.5)	34	40
Wechsler-Bellevue Intelligence Scale (75.5)	34	37
Alternate Uses (75.5)	34	37
Gordon Personal Profile (78.5)	32	25
Vineland Social Maturity Scale (78.5)	32	14
Iowa Tests of Basic Skills (80.5)	31	28
Junior Eysenck Personality Inventory (80.5)	31	7
Slosson Intelligence Test (82)	30	13
Consequences (84)	29	22
Graduate Record Examinations Aptitude Test (84)	29	17
Stanford Achievement Test (84)	29	25
Benton Visual Retention Test (88.5)	28	23
Iowa Tests of Educational Development (88.5)	28	27
Leader Behavior Description Questionnaire, Form 12 (88.5)	28	19
Memory-for-Designs Test (88.5)	28	16
Self-Rating Depression Scale (88.5)	28	11
Shipley-Institute of Living Scale (88.5)	28	30
Children's Embedded Figures Test (92.5)	27	6
Purdue Teacher Opinionaire (92.5)	27	11
Leadership Opinion Questionnaire (94)	26	14
Fear Survey Schedule (97)	25	2
Medical College Admission Test (97)	25	31
Metropolitan Achievement Tests (97)	25	6
Miller Analogies Test (97)	25	25
Minnesota Counseling Inventory (97)	25	29
Inpatient Multidimensional Psychiatric Scale (101)	24	50
Porteus Maze Test (101)	24	31
Scale to Measure Attitudes Toward Disabled Persons (101)	24	15
Motivation Analysis Test (103.5)	23	10
Security-Insecurity Inventory (103.5)	23	11
Total for the 104 tests	9,207	7,579
Total for the remaining 2,363 tests	3,227	2,681
Grand Total	12,434	10,260

particular test. The vast literature on personality testing has failed to produce a body of knowledge generally acceptable to psychologists. In fact, all personality instruments may be described as controversial, each with its own following of devotees. * It seems incredible, for example, that the MMPI—now being researched at the rate of 200 articles, books, and theses per year—is still the same instrument published 27 years ago. The 2474 references (over 400 are doctoral dissertations) reported in this monograph apparently have not generated enough new knowledge to bring about a revision or replacement of the test. Nor has this concentrated research on the MMPI resulted in a consensus among psychologists as to what it can and cannot do. The search for correlates to MMPI responses, scores, and patterns continues to be a favorite research project for hundreds of psychologists and others; despite this intensive study of the MMPI, the inventory is probably just as controversial, if not more so, than it was ten or twenty years ago. * This monograph reports 3747 references (over 530 are doctoral dissertations) for the Rorschach, with a current output of about 120 references per year. This vast amount of writing and research has produced astonishingly little, if any, agreement among psychologists regarding the specific validities of the Rorschach. It is amazing to think that this voluminous research and experimental writing over a period of nearly a half a century has not produced a body of knowledge generally accepted by competent psychologists. Even among the Rorschach disciples, there are various schools of thought, each with its own following. * The sterility of the research and experiential writing on the Rorschach and the MMPI is also applicable to other personality tests which have generated fewer publications. In no case, however, has the accumulated research produced an enduring body of generally accepted knowledge concerning the validities of the test under study. We are still at the stage where every test, regardless of its merits and deficiencies, is considered useful by some and useless by others.[7]

APA-AERA-NCME STANDARDS

An important development in testing was the publication in 1954 of a 40-page monograph *Technical Recommendations for Psychological Tests and Diagnostic Techniques*[8] and the 1955 publication of the derivative 36-page booklet *Technical Recommendations for Achievement Tests.*[9] These two small monographs, commonly referred to as the *Technical Recommendations,* were jointly prepared by three professional organizations in education and psychology: American Psychological Association, American Educational Research Association, and National Council on Measurements Used in Education. A major objective in publishing these monographs was to persuade test authors and publishers to supply more information in their manuals concerning the construction, use, and validity of their tests. Both of these monographs were reprinted in *Tests in Print I* with the permission of the American Psychological Association and the American Educational Research Association.

In 1966, the two monographs were replaced by a single monograph, the revised *Standards for Educational and Psychological Tests and Manuals.*[10] This revision, the product of a joint

committee representing the same three organizations, was reprinted in *Personality Tests and Reviews* with the permission of the American Psychological Association.

The third edition, *Standards for Educational and Psychological Tests,*[11] was published early in 1974. We are pleased that the American Psychological Association has given us permission to reprint the 1974 *Standards* in TIP II. Their action will, we hope, greatly extend the readership of this important monograph.

PUBLISHERS DIRECTORY AND INDEX

The Publishers Directory and Index lists 493 test publishers in 13 countries: United States, 427; England, 28; Canada, 16; India, 5; Union of South Africa, 4; Australia, 3; Japan, 2; Sweden, 2; Switzerland, 2; France, 1; Netherlands, 1; New Zealand, 1; and Papua New Guinea, 1.

Instead of listing only the entry numbers for the tests of a given publisher, as in our earlier volumes, the test titles themselves are presented alphabetically with test entry numbers. Stars denote publishers with test catalogs listing 10 or more tests. Tests not originating in the country of publication are identified by listing in brackets the country in which the test was originally prepared and published.

Table 7 ranks the 45 publishers with 10 or more tests. These 45 publishers, 9.1 percent of the total number, publish 64.9 percent of the tests in print. Most test publishers are very small; 57.6 percent publish only one test and 67.0 percent publish only one or two tests. It is this extraordinary scatter of tests which makes our task of presenting a comprehensive bibliography so difficult.

Although the number of test entries does not necessarily reflect the size and importance of a publisher, the statistics reported in Table 7 are of some interest. Two nonprofit organizations, the Educational Testing Service and the College Entrance Examination Board, lead with 130 and 111 tests, respectively. ETS has

[7] *Personality Tests and Reviews,* pp. xxv–xxvi.
[8] *Technical Recommendations for Psychological Tests and Diagnostic Techniques.* Prepared by a Joint Committee of the American Psychological Association, American Educational Research Association, and National Council on Measurements Used in Education. Lee J. Cronbach, Chairman. Supplement to the *Psychological Bulletin,* Vol. 51, No. 2, March 1954. Washington, D.C.: American Psychological Association, Inc., March 1954. Pp. ii, 38.
[9] *Technical Recommendations for Achievement Tests.* Prepared by the Committees on Test Standards of the American Educational Research Association and the National Council on Measurements Used in Education. Jacob S. Orleans, Chairman. Washington, D.C.: American Educational Research Association, 1955. Pp. 36.
[10] *Standards for Educational and Psychological Tests and Manuals.* Prepared by a Joint Committee of the American Psychological Association, American Educational Research Association, and National Council on Measurement in Education. John W. French and William B. Michael, Cochairmen. Wash-

ington, D.C.: American Psychological Association, Inc., 1966. Pp. iii, 40.
[11] *Standards for Educational and Psychological Tests.* Prepared by a Joint Committee of the American Psychological Association, American Educational Research Association, and National Council on Measurement in Education. Frederick B. Davis, Chair. Washington, D.C.: American Psychological Association, Inc., 1974. Pp. iv, 76.

TABLE 7

PUBLISHERS WITH 10 OR MORE TESTS
TIP II (1974) AND TIP I (1961)

Publisher (Rank)	1974	1961
Educational Testing Service (1)	130	65
College Entrance Examination Board (2)	111	36
Psychometric Affiliates (3)	101	37
Western Psychological Services (4)	98	26
Psychological Corporation (5)	94	77
Science Research Associates, Inc. (6)	75	73
Bobbs-Merrill Co., Inc. (7)	69	88
Cooperative Tests & Services (8.5)	64	50
Harcourt Brace Jovanovich, Inc. (8.5)	64	107
Consulting Psychologists Press, Inc. (10)	51	21
NFER Publishing Co. Ltd. [England] (11)	49	33
Australian Council for Educational Research [Australia] (12)	47	40
Houghton Mifflin Co. (13)	46	28
American Guidance Service, Inc. (15)	39	71
Bureau of Educational Measurements (15)	39	125
CTB/McGraw-Hill (15)	39	63
Sheridan Psychological Services, Inc. (17)	36	20
University of London Press Ltd. [England] (18)	33	38
National Institute for Personnel Research [South Africa] (19)	31	15
Human Sciences Research Council [South Africa] (20)	30	8
Ginn & Co. Ltd. [England] (21)	28	
Stoelting Co. (22)	24	39
Bureau of Educational Research & Service (24)	23	32
Psychologists & Educators, Inc. (24)	23	
Richardson, Bellows, Henry & Co., Inc. (24)	23	
Martin M. Bruce, Ph.D., Publishers (27.5)	21	13
Educational & Industrial Testing Service (27.5)	21	
Guidance Centre [Canada] (27.5)	21	29
University Book Store (27.5)	21	21
American Printing House for the Blind, Inc. (30.5)	19	
George G. Harrap & Co. Ltd. [England] (30.5)	19	20
Examinations Committee, American Chemical Society (32.5)	19	9
Industrial Relations Center (32.5)	18	15
Family Life Publications, Inc. (34.5)	16	6
Grune & Stratton, Inc. (34.5)	16	7
Institute for Personality & Ability Testing (36)	15	15
Robert Gibson & Sons, Glasgow, Ltd. [Scotland] (38)	14	14
Instructional Materials Laboratory (38)	14	
Perfection Form Co. (38)	14	10
Educators'-Employers' Tests & Services Associates (41)	11	
McCann Associates (41)	11	
Psychological Test Specialists (41)	11	11
Educational Records Bureau (44)	10	9
Monitor (44)	10	
Scholastic Testing Service, Inc. (44)	10	9
Total for the 45 publishers	1678	1280
Total for the remaining 448 publishers	907	
Grand Total	2585	

doubled the number of its tests since 1961 and CEEB has more than tripled its list. Psychometric Affiliates' accession to the tests of the Acorn Publishing Company is largely responsible for its large increase in titles. Four California publishers have expanded their lists considerably: Consulting Psychologists Press, Educational and Industrial Testing Service, Sheridan Psychological Services, and Western

Psychological Services. Nine foreign publishers are among the 45 with 10 or more tests.

Test publishing is even more concentrated among a few publishers than Table 7 indicates. There are two huge conglomerates of jointly owned or interlocking publishing organizations. Although listed separately, Educational Testing Service includes the Cooperative Tests and Services and Educational Records Bureau. Since ETS also constructs all CEEB tests, the ETS conglomerate is represented by 315 tests, 14.3 percent of the tests published in the United States. The other publishing giant, Harcourt Brace Jovanovich with its subsidiaries, Grune and Stratton and the Psychological Corporation, has a total of 174 tests, 7.9 percent of the same total. Together these two publishing groups account for 22.2 percent of the domestic tests in TIP II. Their dominating positions are even greater than these statistics reflect—their tests are among the most widely used in the country.

INDEX OF TITLES

The 62-page Index of Titles lists not only the tests in TIP II but also all out of print tests once listed in an MMY, PTR, RTR, or TIP I. Out of print tests are immediately recognizable since their cited numbers always include colons. For example, 4:507 refers to test 507 in the 4th MMY and R:177 refers to test 177 in RTR. These citations refer to the last listing of the out of print test in our publications. Out of print tests listed in both a yearbook and either the personality or reading monograph have citations to both volumes. Test titles consisting of two parts separated by a colon have been entered twice so that each part will be listed first; e.g., there are listings for both *Cooperative Mathematics Test: Algebra* and the inverted title *Algebra: Cooperative Mathematics Test.* Superseded and nonpreferred titles are also listed followed by the correct or preferred title and its entry number. Series titles also list all tests in the series, such as Evaluation and Adjustment Series, General Education Series, and Every Pupil Scholarship Tests. These series listings have been broken up into groupings such as English, foreign languages, and intelligence, which quickly reveal the areas covered by a given series of tests. Also included are some non-title listings providing information of historical value; e.g.,

Evaluation in the Eight Year Study Tests and USAFI Subject Examinations. Acronyms for tests having ten or more references follow the alphabetical listing of test titles.

INDEX OF NAMES

The 190-page Index of Names lists approximately 30,000 names—authors of practically all tests, reviews, excerpts, and references listed in our fourteen publications. It is an analytical index indicating authorship of a test, test review, excerpted review, or reference dealing with a specific test. Furthermore, the index indicates whether the relevant test is in print or out of print. Numbers with colons refer to out of print tests not listed in this volume; readers interested in these tests are referred to the last volume listing the test in question.

Forenames have been reduced to initials to lower the cost of indexing. Since authors are not always consistent in how they list their names, two or more listings may refer to the same person. On the other hand, the use of initials increases the probability of one name representing two or more persons. References to the cited material in the text will resolve these difficulties in almost all cases, since it is our practice to list authors' names exactly as reported in an article, book, or test.

Except for test authors listed in this volume, the use of the Index of Names is a two-step process. For example, if the name index reports *"rev, 163"* for John Doe, the reader must look at the cross reference for test 163 to learn where John Doe's review may be found in the yearbooks. Similarly, if the name index reports *"ref, 1189"* for John Doe, the reader must look at the Cumulative Name Index for test 1189 to learn where John Doe's reference or references on that test may be found in TIP II, PTR, and the MMY's. For example, in the Index of Names, the only reference listed for S. J. Beck is *"ref, 1499"*; however, the Cumulative Name Index for test 1499, the Rorschach, cites sixty-six references by S. J. Beck. This two-step indexing has made it possible for us to provide both a specific name index for each test and an all-inclusive name index covering all tests. Had we tried to make the complete name index independent of the specific name indexes, the preparation and printing costs would have overwhelmed us. Each of

these two sets of indexes covers all authors of approximately 70,000 items—tests, reviews, excerpts, and references.

SCANNING INDEX

The Scanning Index is an expanded table of contents designed to facilitate searches for titles of possible interest. Stars indicate tests listed for the first time in TIP II; asterisks indicate tests revised or supplemented since last listed in an MMY or monograph. Foreign tests are identified by listing the country of origin in brackets following the title. The Scanning Index will probably be most useful in helping readers locate all tests in a particular area which are suitable for a given population, since descriptions of these populations are reported immediately after the test titles, or, with foreign tests, immediately after the country of origin.

HOW TO USE THIS BOOK

The reader who wishes to get the maximum information in as brief a time as possible from *Tests in Print II* should read the following suggestions and explanations. Hopefully, if this is done, the reader will find the book well organized and easy to use. If the reader attempts to use the volume without understanding its organization, he may well have feelings of frustration or, at best, use the volume ineffectively.

1) *Page and Entry Numbers.* Page numbers appear in the running heads next to the inside margins. Entry numbers (i.e., the numbers assigned to specific tests) appear in the running heads next to the outside margins. Except for the inclusion of both page and entry numbers in the Table of Contents, all citations are to entry numbers; that is why they are placed next to the outside margins where they can be seen quickly. Probably the most common error in using an MMY or TIP is to confuse entry numbers with page numbers.

2) *Table of Contents.* The Table of Contents should be consulted to get an overall view of the book's contents and the classification plan used in the main section, *Tests in Print*. With the exception of two classifications—Achievement Batteries and Multi-Aptitude Batteries— each of the fifteen categories is further subdivided. For the complete classification plan,

consult either the Expanded Table of Contents printed on the endpapers or the Scanning Index —the last index in the book.

3) *Scanning Index*. This index presents a classified listing of all tests along with a description of the population for which the test is suitable. This index permits the reader to quickly locate tests suitable for a given population.

4) *Index of Titles*. If the title of a test is known, the title index is, of course, the quickest way of locating a particular test. It is important that the instructions on its use, appearing on page 823 (the first page of the index), are read before attempting to use the index.

5) *Index of Names*. If the title of a test is not known but the name of an author is, consult the name index. Because of the extensive information provided in this analytical name index, it is imperative that the instructions on page 884 (the first page of the index) are read before using the index.

6) *Publishers Directory and Index*. Following the publisher's address, all the tests of a publisher are listed in alphabetical sequence. If the title or author cannot be recalled but the name of the publisher is known, the test may be located by scanning the publisher's test list. These lists may also be useful in identifying the publishers having tests in areas of one's interests.

7) *Catchwords*. In the main section, containing test entries, the running heads on the right-hand pages list the first display heading appearing on the facing pages and, if none appears, the last heading used on preceding pages. For example, if the heading "Diagnostic" appears first on one of two facing pages in the section "Reading," the catchword in the right-hand running head would be "Reading—Diagnostic." The entry numbers on the outside margins and the corresponding test titles in the running feet correspond to the first and last lines of type on facing pages. This system of catchwords makes it possible to open to any page in the test section and immediately know the relevant tests for all material on the facing pages. Since there are many runs of solid pages of references or cumulative name indexes, readers will find the listing of test titles in the running feet quite helpful.

8) *Test Entries*. Test entries in TIP II are similar to those in the yearbooks and PTR, but shorter. Only the MMY and PTR entries include such information as: listings of all test materials with the copyright date and number of pages for each item, price information, scoring services, administration time, and a lack of reliability, validity, and normative data. Cross references to additional information are always made from the shorter TIP entries to the longer MMY and PTR entries.

An attempt has been made to present the following information, in the order given, for each test:

a) TITLE. Test titles are printed in boldface type. Secondary or series titles are set off from main titles by a colon. Titles are always presented exactly as reported in the test materials. Stars precede titles of tests listed for the first time in TIP II; asterisks precede titles of tests which have been revised or supplemented since last listed.

b) TEST POPULATION. The grade, chronological age, or semester range, or the employment category is usually given. Commas are used to indicate separate grade levels. "Grades 1.5–2.5, 2–3, 4–12, 13–17" means that there are four test booklets: a booklet for the middle of the first grade through the middle of the second grade, a booklet for the beginning of the second grade through the end of the third grade, a booklet for grades 4 through 12 inclusive, and a booklet for undergraduate and graduate students in colleges and universities. "First, second semester" means that there are two test booklets: one covering the work of the first semester, the other covering the work of the second semester. "1, 2 semesters" indicates that the second booklet covers the work of the two semesters. "Ages 10-2 to 11-11" means ages 10 years 2 months to 11 years 11 months and "Grades 4-6 to 5-9" means the sixth month in the fourth grade through the ninth month in the fifth grade. "High school and college" denotes a single test booklet for both levels; "High school, college" denotes two test booklets, one for high school and one for college.

c) COPYRIGHT DATE. The range of copyright dates (or publication dates if not copyrighted) includes the various forms, accessories, and editions of a test. When the publication date differs from the copyright date, both dates are given; e.g., "1971, c1965–68" means that the test materials were copyrighted between 1965 and 1968 but were not published until 1971. Publication or copyright dates enclosed in brackets do not appear on the test materials but were obtained from other sources.

d) ACRONYM. An acronym is given for many tests. Following the alphabetical sequence of test titles in the Index of Titles, there is an alphabetical listing of acronyms for tests with 10 or more references.

e) SPECIAL COMMENTS. Some entries contain special notations, such as: "for research use only"; "revision of the *ABC Test*"; "tests administered monthly at centers throughout the United States"; "subtests available as separates"; and "verbal creativity." "For research use only" should be interpreted to mean that the *only* use of the test should be in research designed to assess its usefulness; contrary to what the implications seem to be, "for research use only" does not mean that a test has any use, whatsoever, as a research instrument. Tests used in research studies should have demonstrated validity before being selected as research tools.

A statement such as "verbal creativity" is intended to further describe what the test claims to measure.

f) PART SCORES. The number and description of part scores is presented.

g) FACTUAL STATEMENTS IMPLYING CRITICISM. Some of the test entries include factual statements which imply criticism of the test, such as "1970 test identical with test copyrighted 1960" and "no manual."

h) AUTHOR. For most tests, all authors are reported. In the case of tests which appear in a new form each year, only authors of the most recent forms are listed. Names are reported exactly as printed on test materials. Names of editors are generally not reported.

i) PUBLISHER. The name of the publisher or distributor is reported for each test. Foreign publishers are identified by listing the country in brackets immediately following the name of the publisher. The Publishers Directory and Index must be consulted for a publisher's address.

j) FOREIGN ADAPTATIONS. Revisions and adaptations of tests for foreign use are listed in parentheses following the description of the original edition.

k) CLOSING ASTERISK. An asterisk following the publisher's name indicates that the entry was prepared from a first-hand examination of the test materials.

l) CROSS REFERENCES WITHIN TIP II. Some tests are listed twice; first, as a part of a battery, program, or series entry and, second, as a separate test entry. Cross references are presented from the separate listings to the battery or program listings.

m) SUBLISTINGS. Levels, editions, subtests, or parts of a test which are available in separate booklets are sometimes presented as sublistings with titles set in small capitals. Sub-sublistings are indented with titles set in italic type.

n) CROSS REFERENCES TO OTHER VOLUMES. Except for new tests not previously listed in an MMY or PTR, a test entry includes a second paragraph with a cross reference to relevant material in those volumes. These cross references may be only "for additional information" presented in the longer entries or for reviews, excerpts, and references, when they are available for a specific test.

EDITORIAL REITERATIONS

Throughout the history of the MMY's, *Tests in Print,* and the monographs, our objectives have remained constant. The Introduction of *The Seventh Yearbook* restates them succinctly:

(*a*) to provide information about tests published as separates throughout the English-speaking world; (*b*) to present frankly critical test reviews written by testing and subject specialists representing various viewpoints; (*c*) to provide extensive bibliographies of verified references on the construction, use, and validity of specific tests; (*d*) to make readily available the critical portions of test reviews appearing in professional journals; and (*e*) to present fairly exhaustive listings of new and revised books on testing, along with evaluative excerpts from representative reviews which these books receive in professional journals. * Concomitantly, we attach considerable importance to other objectives of a crusading nature: (*f*) to impel test authors and publishers to publish better tests and to provide test users with detailed information on the validity and limitations of their tests; (*g*) to inculcate test users with a keener awareness of the values and limitations of standardized tests; (*h*) to stimulate contributing reviewers to think through more carefully their own beliefs and values relevant to testing; (*i*) to suggest to test users better methods of appraising tests in light of their own particular needs; and (*j*) to impress test users with the need to suspect all tests unaccompanied by detailed data on their construction, validity, uses, and limitations—even when products of distinguished authors and reputable publishers.[12]

To better understand our objectives, it is of interest to consider the following basic assumptions and principles which have guided us in the preparation of the MMY's:

(*a*) Because of the technical nature of standardized tests, most test users cannot, on their own, make an intelligent assessment of a test's validity in a given situation for a given purpose. (*b*) Just as an ill person wants to believe in the efficacy of a drug, the typical test user wants to believe in the validity of a test. If the claims for a test are accepted as true, decisions can be made in a "scientific" manner. If such claims are questioned, the would-be test user is forced to rely upon his unaided judgment. (*c*) Most commercially marketed tests are poorly constructed, inadequately validated, and of unknown value. Even the best of the tests tend to make some claims not supported by research data. (*d*) The test reviews in the MMY's should reflect a great variety of views and disciplines. (*e*) Each test should receive multiple reviews in order to get a better representation of different viewpoints. (*f*) Reviewers should use their own criteria in evaluating tests. (*g*) Test publishers should present whatever information they want test reviewers to consider in the manuals and technical reports which are routinely sold with their tests. (*h*) Reviewers should not be asked to review tests by their former teachers or by past or present colleagues.[13]

Dating back to the publication of *The Fifth Yearbook* in 1959, we expressed concern as to whether our objectives were being achieved—at least, not as rapidly as we had expected when we began to publish critical test reviews in 1938:

It is easy to look back over the period since the first publication in this series and to note that a great number of high quality tests have been published, that more publishers are including more detailed information about their tests in manuals, that tests are being more widely used (with, it is hoped, more recognition of the need for discriminating use) by more sophisticated users, and that the quality of test and book reviews has steadily increased. It would, of course, be presumptuous to conclude that *The Mental Measurements Yearbooks* are responsible for these changes. Yet it does not seem too much to say that the series, particularly since the introduction of critical test reviews 21 years ago, has made some contribution to these trends. * Whatever the influence of the yearbook series, it is a fact that the testing industry has grown tremendously both in quality and quantity of production in the past quarter century. It seems to us that this growth

12 *The Seventh Mental Measurements Yearbook,* p. xxvii.
13 *The Sixth Mental Measurements Yearbook,* p. xxix.

alone has made some assistance in sorting through the many test titles available more and more vital. To the extent that *The Mental Measurements Yearbook* has helped busy teachers, personnel workers, psychologists, and others to be acquainted with and form some opinions concerning tests existing in their areas, to the extent that it has caused authors and publishers to be more aware of the needs and expectations of the test-purchasing public, to the extent that it has furnished some organized information on existing tests and books where less was available before— to this extent it has achieved its goal of being of service to test users.[14]

In the Preface of *The Sixth Yearbook,* we expressed discouragement that more progress was not being made in improving tests, or in influencing test publishers to produce or test users to select tests based on the research and critical information presented in the MMY's. The following conviction, presented thirteen years ago in *Tests in Print I,* is still held today:

At present, no matter how poor a test may be, if it is nicely packaged and if it promises to do all sorts of things which no test can do, the test will find many gullible buyers. When we initiated critical test reviewing in *The 1938 Yearbook,* we had no idea how difficult it would be to discourage the use of poorly constructed tests of unknown validity. Even the better informed test users who finally become convinced that a widely used test has no validity after all are likely to rush to use a new instrument which promises far more than any good test can possibly deliver. Counselors, personnel directors, psychologists, and school administrators seem to have an unshakable will to believe the exaggerated claims of test authors and publishers. If these test users were better informed regarding the merits and limitations of their testing instruments, they would probably be less happy and less successful in their work. The test user who has faith—however unjustified— can speak with confidence in interpreting test results and in making recommendations. The well informed test user cannot do this; he knows that the best of our tests are still highly fallible instruments which are extremely difficult to interpret with assurance in individual cases. Consequently, he must interpret test results cautiously and with so many reservations that others wonder whether he really knows what he is talking about.[15]

Although the number and use of poor tests —as well as the unproductive research, especially in personality assessment—are discouraging, there are some encouraging developments in testing. Progress is being made in eliminating some of the most flagrant discriminatory abuses in the use of tests. Disturbing questions are being raised with increasing frequency regarding the fair use of tests in the selection of students and employees. Lay persons, courts, and legislatures are raising legitimate concerns which are forcing us to reconsider our traditional views in testing. Tests are

under attack from many sides; frequently unjustly—but often the criticisms are deserved. We believe that the misuse of tests is still more common than good usage; but we also believe that progress is being made toward eliminating these abuses. Nevertheless, much work remains to be done to diminish testing practices which are biased, discriminatory, and invasive of privacy. We are confident that we shall move steadily ahead.

TESTS NOT PUBLISHED AS SEPARATES

For every test published as a separate, there are several tests which are not and are found only in books, journals, and unpublished theses. For more than thirty years, we have been compiling bibliographies on thousands of these unpublished tests for two reasons: (*a*) we wanted to have a bibliography ready if the test were later published as a separate; and (*b*) we thought that we might some day be able to complement the MMY's with a guide to tests not available as separates. We are still compiling these bibliographies, but it is unlikely that we shall ever have the resources to publish them.

In recent years, however, there have been others who have prepared somewhat similar works in specific areas. For those of our readers who may be interested in these unpublished tests, we are presenting a bibliography of publications listing tests not available as separates. Since all of the following publications list some published tests as well, there is some overlap with the MMY's and TIP:

1. *Test Collection ·Bulletin.* Published quarterly by Educational Testing Service, Princeton, N.J. (Lists new and old tests, including tests not published commercially as separates, added to the Test Collection of the Educational Testing Service. This bulletin is a good source of continuously updated information on new tests.)

2. BONJEAN, CHARLES M.; HILL, RICHARD J.; AND McLEMORE, S. DALE. *Sociological Measurement: An Inventory of Scales and Indices.* San Francisco, Calif.: Chandler Publishing Co., 1967. Pp. xv, 580. For a review, see 7:B93.

3. COMREY, ANDREW L.; BACKER, THOMAS E.; AND GLASER, EDWARD M. *A Sourcebook for Mental Health Measures: Incorporating the Final Report on "A Taxonomy of Data-Collecting Devices," NIMH Grant No. MH 19611.* Los Angeles, Calif.: Human Interaction Research Institute, 1973. Pp. vii, 462.

4. GOLDMAN, BERT A., AND SAUNDERS, JOHN L. *Directory of Unpublished Experimental Measures,*

14 *The Fifth Mental Measurements Yearbook,* pp. xxi–xxiii.
15 *Tests in Print,* pp. xxii–xxiii.

Volume 1. New York: Behavioral Publications, 1974. Pp. xiv, 223.

5. JOHNSON, ORVAL G., AND BOMMARITO, JAMES W. *Tests and Measurements in Child Development: A Handbook.* San Francisco, Calif.: Jossey-Bass Inc., Publishers,. 1971. Pp. xv, 518.

6. LAKE, DALE G.; MILES, MATTHEW B.; AND EARLE, RALPH B., JR. *Measuring Human Behavior: Tools for the Assessment of Social Functioning.* New York: Teachers College Press, 1973. Pp. xviii, 422.

7. LYERLY, SAMUEL B. *Handbook of Psychiatric Rating Scales, Second Edition.* DHEW Publication No. (HSM) 42–69–77. Washington, D.C.: United States Government Printing Office, 1973. Pp. viii, 71.

8. ROBINSON, JOHN P., AND SHAVER, PHILLIP R. *Measures of Social Psychological Attitudes, Revised Edition.* Ann Arbor, Mich.: Institute for Social Research, University of Michigan, 1973. Pp. viii, 750.

9. ROBINSON, JOHN P.; ATHANASIOU, ROBERT; AND HEAD, KENDRA B. *Measures of Occupational Attitudes and Characteristics (Appendix A to Measures of Political Attitudes).* Ann Arbor, Mich.: Institute for Social Research, University of Michigan, 1969. Pp. xiv, 460. For a review, see 7:B503.

10. ROBINSON, JOHN P.; RUSK, JERROLD G.; AND HEAD, KENDRA B. *Measures of Political Attitudes.* Ann Arbor, Mich.: Institute for Social Research, University of Michigan, 1968. Pp. viii, 702. For a review, see 7:B504.

11. SHAW, MARVIN E., AND WRIGHT, JACK M. *Scales for the Measurement of Attitudes.* New York: McGraw-Hill Book Co., 1967. Pp. xxi, 604. For reviews, see 7:B574.

12. SIMON, ANITA, AND BOYER, E. GIL., EDITORS. *Mirrors for Behavior III: An Anthology of Observation Instruments.* Philadelphia, Pa.: Research for Better Schools, Inc., 1974. Pp. xxi, 758.

13. STRAUS, MURRAY A. *Family Measurement Techniques: Abstracts of Published Instruments.* Minneapolis, Minn.: University of Minnesota Press, 1969. Pp. viii, 316. For reviews, see 7:B601.

TESTS IN PRINT

ACHIEVEMENT BATTERIES

---

[1]

Academic Proficiency Battery. College entrants; 1969; APB; 5 scores: social sciences, commercial sciences, natural sciences, mathematical sciences, languages (either English or Afrikaans); F. A. Fouché, N. F. Alberts, and C. L. J. Minnaar (test); Human Sciences Research Council [South Africa]. *
For additional information, see 7:1.

[2]

Adult Basic Education Student Survey. Poorly educated adults in basic education classes; 1966–67; ABESS; 4 parts in 2 booklets; Elvin Rasof and Monroe C. Neff; Educational Opportunities Division, Follett Publishing Co. *
a) PARTS 1 AND 2. 2 scores: reading comprehension, word recognition.
b) PARTS 3 AND 4. 2 scores: arithmetic computation, arithmetic problems.
For additional information and reviews by Dorothy C. Adkins and A. N. Hieronymus, see 7:2.

[3]

Adult Basic Learning Examination. Adults with achievement levels grades 1–4, 5–8, 9–12; 1967–71; ABLE; 6 scores: vocabulary, reading, spelling, arithmetic (computation, problem solving, total); Bjorn Karlsen, Richard Madden, and Eric F. Gardner; Harcourt Brace Jovanovich, Inc. *
For additional information, a review by A. N. Hieronymus, and excerpted reviews by Edward B. Fry and James W. Hall, see 7:3.

REFERENCES THROUGH 1971

1. KNIGHT, DAVID, AND ALCORN, JOHN D. "Comparisons of the Performance of Educationally Disadvantaged Adults and Elementary Children on Selected Measures of Reading Performance." *South J Ed Res* 4(4):262–72 O '70. *
2. GRIFFIN, JOYCE ZEFFRE. *The Relationship Between Behavioral Objectives and Measurement Instruments Used to Evaluate Student Progress in an Urban Adult Basic Education Program.* Doctor's thesis, Catholic University of America (Washington, D.C.), 1971. (*DAI* 32:1335A)

3. KNIGHT, DAVID, AND ALCORN, JOHN D. "Comparisons of the Performance of Educationally Disadvantaged Adults and Elementary Children on Selected Measures of Reading Performance." *Yearb Nat Read Conf* 19(2):113–7 '71. *

CUMULATIVE NAME INDEX

[4]

American School Achievement Tests. Grades 1, 2–3, 4–6, 7–9; 1941–63; ASAT; subtests in reading, arithmetic, language and spelling, and social studies and science available as separates; partial batteries are available without social studies and science; 4 levels; parts 1–3 of Forms D, E, F are essentially the same as Forms A, B, C copyrighted 1941–43; Willis E. Pratt, Robert V. Young (parts 1–3), Miriam E. Wilt (*a*), and Clara Cockerille (part 4); Bobbs-Merrill Co., Inc. *
a) PRIMARY BATTERY 1. Grade 1; 1941–56; 5 scores: reading (word recognition, word meaning, total), numbers, total; numbers subtest available as a separate entitled *American School Achievement Tests: Arithmetic Readiness* for grades kgn–1.
b) PRIMARY BATTERY 2. Grades 2–3; 1941–58; 9 scores: reading (sentences and words, paragraphs, total), arithmetic (computation, problems, total), language, spelling, total.
c) INTERMEDIATE BATTERY. Grades 4–6; 1942–61; 11 scores: reading (sentences and words, paragraphs, total), arithmetic (computation, problems, total), language, spelling, social studies, science, total.
d) ADVANCED BATTERY. Grades 7–9; 1947–63; 11 scores: same as for Intermediate Battery.
For additional information and reviews by Robert H. Bauernfeind and Frank B. Womer, see 6:2; for reviews by J. Raymond Gerberich and Virgil E. Herrick, see 5:1; for a review by Ralph C. Preston of an earlier edition, see 4:1 (1 reference); for reviews by Walter W. Cook and Gordon N. Mackenzie (with Glen Hass), see 3:1. For reviews of the language and spelling sub-

test, see 5:174 (2 reviews); the arithmetic readiness subtest, see 5:455 (1 review); the arithmetic subtest, see 5:456 (2 reviews); and the reading subtest, see 5:620 (2 reviews).

REFERENCES THROUGH 1971

1. See 4:1.
2. BENSBERG, GERARD J., JR. "The Relation of Academic Achievement of Mental Defectives to Mental Age, Sex, Institutionalization and Etiology." *Am J Mental Def* 58:327-30 O '53. * (*PA* 28:4530)

CUMULATIVE NAME INDEX

Bauernfeind, R. H.: *rev*, 6:2　　Herrick, V. E.: *rev*, 5:1
Bensberg, G. J.: 2　　　　　　　Mackenzie, G. N.: *rev*, 3:1
Cook, W. W.: *rev*, 3:1　　　　Preston, R. C.: *rev*, 4:1
Gerberich, J. R.: *rev*, 5:1　　Stone, C. R.: 1
Hass, G.: *rev*, 3:1　　　　　　Womer, F. B.: *rev*, 6:2

[5]

Bristol Achievement Tests. Ages 8-0 to 9-11, 9-0 to 10-11, 10-0 to 11-11, 11-0 to 12-11, 12-0 to 13-11; 1969; BAT; 3 tests available as separates; Thomas Nelson & Sons Ltd. [England]. *
a) ENGLISH LANGUAGE. 6 scores: word meaning, paragraph meaning, sentence organisation, organisation of ideas, spelling and punctuation, total; Alan Brimer and Herbert Gross.
b) MATHEMATICS. 6 scores: number, reasoning, space, measurement, arithmetic laws and processes, total; Alan Brimer.
c) STUDY SKILLS. 6 scores: properties, structures, processes, explanations, interpretations, total; Alan Brimer, Margaret Fidler, Wynne Harlen, and John Taylor.
For additional information and reviews by G. A. V. Morgan and A. E. G. Pilliner, see 7:4. For a review of the English language subtest, see 7:185; the mathematics subtest, see 7:453; and the study skills subtest, see 7:776.

[6]

*CLEP General Examinations: Humanities. 1–2 years of college or equivalent; 1964–73; for college accreditation of nontraditional study, advanced placement, or assessment of educational attainment; a retired subtest of the *College-Level Examination Program General Examinations* published as a separate for local administration through the *Testing Academic Achievement* program (see 1061); 3 scores: fine arts, literature, total; program administered for the College Entrance Examination Board by Educational Testing Service. * For the testing program entry, see 1050.
For additional information concerning earlier forms, see 7:8b. For reviews of the testing program, see 7:664 (3 reviews).

[7]

*California Achievement Tests. 1934–72; CAT; earlier editions called *Progressive Achievement Tests*; subtests available as separates; 2 editions; Ernest W. Tiegs and Willis W. Clark; CTB/McGraw-Hill. *
a) 1957 EDITION WITH 1963 NORMS. Grades 1–2, 2.5–4.5, 4–6, 7–9, 9–14; 1934–63; 11 scores: reading (vocabulary, comprehension, total), arithmetic (reasoning, fundamentals, total), language (mechanics of English, spelling, total), total, handwriting; 1963 tests identical with tests copyrighted 1957 except for profile and reading subtest (grades 7–9, Form X).
b) 1970 EDITION. Grades 1.5–2.5, 2.5–4.5, 4–6, 6–9, 9–12; 1934–72; 11 or 12 scores: reading (vocabulary, comprehension, total), mathematics (computation, concepts and problems, total), language (auding [grades 1.5–2.5 only], mechanics, usage and structure, total, spelling), total.
For additional information concerning the 1970 edi-

tion, see 7:5 (32 references); for reviews by Jack C. Merwin and Robert D. North of the 1957 edition, see 6:3 (20 references); for a review by Charles O. Neidt, see 5:2 (10 references); for reviews by Warren G. Findley, Alvin W. Schindler, and J. Harlan Shores of an earlier edition, see 4:2 (8 references); for a review by Paul A. Witty, see 3:15 (3 references); for reviews by C. W. Odell and Hugh B. Wood, see 2:1193 (1 reference); for a review by D. Welty Lefever and an excerpted review by E. L. Abell, see 1:876. For reviews of the 1957 edition of the language subtest, see 6:251 (1 review) and 5:177 (2 reviews); earlier editions of the language subtest, see 4:151 (2 reviews) and 2:1292 (2 reviews); the 1957 edition of the arithmetic subtest, see 5:468 (1 review); earlier editions of the arithmetic subtest, see 4:411 (1 review), 2:1459 (2 reviews), and 1:893 (1 review); and earlier editions of the reading subtest, see 4:530 (2 reviews, 1 excerpt), 2:1563 (1 review), and 1:1110 (2 reviews).

REFERENCES THROUGH 1971

1. See 2:1193.
2–4. See 3:15.
5–12. See 4:2.
13–22. See 5:2.
23–41. See 6:3.
42–73. See 7:5.
74. HOLMES, JACK A., AND FINLEY, CARMEN J. "Relative Importance of Curricular Areas for Grade Placement Deviations in Grade V." *Calif J Ed Res* 6:213-8 N '55. * (*PA* 30:6268)
75. DURFLINGER, GLENN W. "The Fundamentals Forgotten by College Students." *J Ed Res* 49:571-9 Ap '56. * (*PA* 31:5143)
76. CARROW, MARY ARTHUR. "Linguistic Functioning of Bilingual and Monolingual Children." *J Speech & Hearing Disorders* 22:371-80 S '57. * (*PA* 33:4258)
77. HOLMES, JACK A., AND FINLEY, CARMEN J. "Under- and Over-Age Grade Placements and School Achievement." *J Ed Psychol* 48:447-56 N '57. * (*PA* 33:2063)
78. GARRISON, MORTIMER, JR. "A Comparison of Psychological Measures in Mentally Retarded Boys Over a Three-Year Period as a Function of Etiology." *Training Sch B* 55:54-60 N '58. * (*PA* 34:1664)
79. MORRISON, IDA E., AND PERRY, IDA F. "Spelling and Reading Relationships With Incidence of Retardation and Acceleration." *J Ed Res* 52:222-7 F '59. * (*PA* 34:2012)
80. LLOYD, DAVID O. "Comparison of Standardized Test Results of Indian and Non-Indian in an Integrated School System." *J Am Indian Ed* 1:8-16 Ja '61. *
81. CURRY, ROBERT L. "The Effect of Socio-Economic Status on the Scholastic Achievement of Sixth-Grade Children: Part I." *Brit J Ed Psychol* 32:46-9 F '62. * (*PA* 37:2007)
82. ANDERSON, HARRY E., JR., AND SLIVINSKE, ALEC J. "A Study of Intelligence and Achievement at the Fourth-, Fifth-, and Sixth-Grade Levels." *J Exp Ed* 31:425-32 su '63. * (*PA* 38:5756)
83. TOBIAS, MILTON, AND MICHAEL, WILLIAM B. "Dimensions of Biological and Psychological Function in Two Samples of Children in the Third Grade." *Psychol Rep* 12:759-62 Je '63. * (*PA* 38:5756)
84. YOUNG, J. A., AND JENKINSON, M. D. "An Objective Comparison of Achievement in the Basic Subjects for Matched Groups of Children in Manchester, England and Edmonton, Alberta." *Alberta J Ed Res* (Canada) 10:59-66 Je '64. * (*PA* 39:12096)
85. DIZNEY, HENRY F., AND YAMAMOTO, KAORU. "Note on Effects of Practice and Fatigue in Group Testing of Intelligence and Achievement." *Psychol Rep* 16:537-8 Ap '65. * (*PA* 39:10193)
86. SPAIGHTS, ERNEST. "Accuracy of Self-Estimation of Junior High School Students." *J Ed Res* 58:416-9 My-Je '65. * (*PA* 39:16327)
87. CENTER, CLARE CALL. *A Correlational Study of the Relationship Between Eighth Grade Test Scores and First Semester Grades at Del Oro High School.* Master's thesis, Sacramento State College (Sacramento, Calif.), 1966.
88. FINLEY, CARMEN J. "How Well Can Teachers Judge Pupil Achievement? The Case of the Illusive Criterion." *Calif J Ed Res* 17:126-32 My '66. * (*PA* 40:10449)
89. GRAY, JAMES A. *A Study to Determine the Effectiveness of Certain Lehi Junior High School Variables in Predicting Senior High School Success.* Master's thesis, Brigham Young University (Provo, Utah), 1966.
90. MACARTHUR, R. S., AND MOSYCHUK, H. "Lower and Upper Socioeconomic Group Contrasts in Long-Term Predictability of Grade Nine Achievement." *J Ed Meas* 3:167-8 su '66. *
91. CICIRELLI, VICTOR G. "Sibling Constellation, Creativity,

IQ, and Academic Achievement." *Child Develop* 38:481–90 Je '67. * (*PA* 41:10210)

92. MOULIN, EUGENE K. "The Effects of Client-Centered Group Counseling Using Play Media on the Intelligence, Achievement, and Psycholinguistic Abilities of Underachieving Primary School Children." *El Sch Guid & Counsel* 5(2):85–98 D '70. *

93. WONZER, ANN CUSHMAN. *A Study of the Relationships Among Creativity, Intelligence, and Achievement Measures Based on Longitudinal Data.* Doctor's thesis, University of Michigan (Ann Arbor, Mich.), 1970. (*DAI* 32:1205A)

94. FLEISCHMAN, HOWARD L.; ORR, DAVID B.; AND STRASEL, H. C. "Relationships Between the Subtests of Six Achievement Test Batteries." Abstract. *Proc 79th Ann Conv Am Psychol Assn* 6(1):109–10 '71. * (*PA* 46:3727)

95. GLAVIN, JOHN P., AND ANNESLEY, FREDERICK R. "Reading and Arithmetic Correlates of Conduct-Problem and Withdrawn Children." *J Spec Ed* 5(3):213–9 f '71. * (*PA* 48:12263)

96. HOLLY, KEITH ALLEN. *Structure-of-Intellect Factor Abilities and a Self-Concept Measure in Mathematics Relative to Performance in High School Modern Algebra.* Doctor's thesis, University of Southern California (Los Angeles, Calif.), 1971. (*DAI* 32:2484A)

97. KEEN, CHARLES FLOYD. *A Study of Relationships Between Growth and Developmental Variables, Creativity, and Musicality.* Doctor's thesis, University of Michigan (Ann Arbor, Mich.), 1971. (*DAI* 32:3791A)

98. RUBIN, HOWARD STANLEY. *The Prevention of Student Attrition in Nursing Education: A Community Psychology Approach.* Doctor's thesis, Illinois Institute of Technology (Chicago, Ill.), 1971. (*DAI* 33:1296B)

99. STACY, BOBBY FANT. *A Comparison of Academic Achievement and Mental Maturity Test Scores of Negro High School Seniors in Predominantly White Schools With Academic Achievement and Mental Maturity Test Scores of Negro Seniors in Predominantly Negro Schools.* Doctor's thesis, Mississippi State University (State College, Miss.), 1971. (*DAI* 32:1815A)

100. TURES, ROBERT STEPHEN. *The Analysis of Sex Differences in Intelligence, Achievement, Behavior, and Personality of the Same Student Sample at the Third and Tenth Grade Levels: A Longitudinal Study.* Doctor's thesis, West Virginia University (Morgantown, W.Va.), 1971. (*DAI* 32:4363A)

101. VON DRACH, ROBERT BORKORT. *An Investigation of the Correlation Between Reading Achievement and the Performance on Physical Tests of the Second Grade Students of the Centennial Schools.* Doctor's thesis, Temple University (Philadelphia, Pa.), 1971. (*DAI* 32:1820A)

CUMULATIVE NAME INDEX

[8]

Canadian Tests of Basic Skills. Grades 3–8; 1955–70; CTBS; Canadian adaptation of *Iowa Tests of Basic Skills*; 15 scores: vocabulary, reading comprehension, language (spelling, capitalization, punctuation, usage, total), work-study skills (maps, graphs and tables, reference materials, total), mathematics skills (concepts, problem solving, total), total; original test by E. F. Lindquist and A. N. Hieronymus; adaptation by Ethel M. King; Thomas Nelson & Sons (Canada) Ltd. [Canada]. *

For additional information and a review by L. B. Birch, see 7:6.

[9]

Classification and Placement Examination. Grade 8 and high school entrants; 1967–68; CAPE; 8 scores: aptitude (verbal, quantitative, total), achievement (reading, mathematics, English, total), total; Richard Madden and Eric F. Gardner; Harcourt Brace Jovanovich, Inc. *

For additional information and a review by Leonard S. Cahen, see 7:7.

[10]

*College-Level Examination Program General Examinations. 1–2 years of college or equivalent; 1964–73; for college accreditation of nontraditional study, advanced placement, or assessment of educational attainment; program administered for the College Entrance Examination Board by Educational Testing Service. * For the testing program entry, see 1050.

a) COMPLETE BATTERY. Tests administered monthly at centers throughout the United States; 5 tests, 13 scores as listed below.

1) *Book 1.* 3 tests, 7 scores: English composition, natural sciences (biological, physical, total), mathematics (basic skills, advanced topics, total).

2) *Book 2.* 2 tests, 6 scores: humanities (fine arts, literature, total), social sciences—history (social sciences, history, total).

b) SEPARATE TEST BOOKLETS. 5 tests; available only through *Testing Academic Achievement* (see 1061).

1) *English Composition.*

2) *Humanities.* 3 scores: fine arts, literature, total.

3) *Mathematics.* 3 scores: basic skills, advanced topics, total.

4) *Natural Sciences.* 3 scores: biological, physical, total.

5) *Social Sciences and History.* 3 scores: social sciences, history, total.

For additional information concerning earlier forms,

see 7:8. For reviews of the testing program, see 7:664 (3 reviews).

REFERENCES THROUGH 1971

1. BURKETT, EVA. "Composition Tests for Screening Prospective Teachers." *Col Comp & Commun* 22(5):355–62 D '71. *
2. FAGIN, MARGARET C. "Analysis of Performance of Adult Women in Missouri on Three General Examinations of the College Level Examination Program." *Adult Ed* 21(3):148–65 sp '71. * (*PA* 46:11498)
3. FAGIN, MARGARET C. "CLEP Credit Encourages Adults to Seek Degrees." *Col Board R* 81:18–22 f '71. *
4. SHARON, AMIEL T. "Adult Academic Achievement in Relation to Formal Education and Age." *Adult Ed* 21(4):231–7 su '71. *
5. SHARON, AMIEL T. "Measurement of College Achievement by the College-Level Examination Program." *Ed & Psychol Meas* 31(2):477–84 su '71. *
6. STETSON, ROBERT F. "Getting a Head Start on College." *Col Board R* 81:23–5 f '71. *
7. WERMERS, DONALD JOSEPH. *A Study of Achievement by Junior College Tranfer, Four-Year College Transfer, and Native Juniors as Measured by the CLEP General Examinations.* Doctor's thesis, University of Illinois (Urbana, Ill.), 1971. (*DAI* 32:4387A)

CUMULATIVE NAME INDEX

Burkett, E.: 1
Fagin, M. C.: 2–3
Sharon, A. T.: 4–5
Stetson, R. F.: 6
Wermers, D. J.: 7

[11]

*Comprehensive Tests of Basic Skills. 1968–73; CTBS; 2 editions; CTB/McGraw-Hill. *

a) FORMS Q AND R. Grades 2.5–4, 4–6, 6–8, 8–12; 1968–71; 13–15 scores: reading (vocabulary, comprehension, total), language (mechanics, expression, spelling, total), arithmetic (computation, concepts, applications, total), total, study skills (reference materials [except grades 2.5–4], graphic materials [except grades 2.5–4], total); subtests available as separates.

b) EXPANDED EDITION, FORM S. Grades kgn–1.5, kgn.5–1.9, 1.5–2.9, 2.5–4.9, 4.5–6.9, 6.5–8.9. 8.5–12.9; 1968–73; except for the substitution of subtests in science and social studies for the graphic skills subtest in grades 4–12, Levels 1–4 are "moderate revisions" of Forms Q and R; subtest in reading (grades 4.5–8.9) available as separate; 7 levels.

1) *Level A.* Grades kgn–1.5; 11 scores: alphabet skills (letter forms, letter names, total), listening for information, letter sounds, visual and auditory discrimination (visual discrimination, sound matching, total), language, total, mathematics.

2) *Level B.* Grades kgn.5–1.9; 12 scores: reading (letter sounds, word recognition [2 scores], reading comprehension, total), language (oral comprehension, grammar, total), mathematics (concepts and applications, computation, total), total.

3) *Level C.* Grades 1.5–2.9; 14 scores: reading (vocabulary, sentences, passages, total), language (expression, spelling, mechanics, total), mathematics (computation, concepts and applications, total), total, science, social studies.

4) *Level 1.* Grades 2.5–4.9; 15 scores: reading (vocabulary, comprehension, total), language (spelling, mechanics, expression, total), mathematics (computation, concepts, applications, total), total, reference skills, science, social studies.

5) *Level 2.* Grades 4.5–6.9; 15 scores: same as for level 1.

6) *Level 3.* Grades 6.5–8.9; 15 scores: same as for level 1.

7) *Level 4.* Grades 8.5–12.9; 15 scores: same as for level 1.

For additional information, reviews by J. Stanley Ahmann and Frederick G. Brown, and excerpted reviews by Brooke B. Collison and Peter A. Taylor (rejoinder by Verna White) of a, see 7:9. For reviews

of the arithmetic subtest, see 7:514 (2 reviews); the reading subtest, see 7:685 (1 review); and the study skills subtest, see 7:778 (1 review).

REFERENCES THROUGH 1971

1. BROWN, FREDERICK G. "Comprehensive Tests of Basic Skills: A Review." *Meas & Eval Guid* 4(1):59–62 Ap '71. *

CUMULATIVE NAME INDEX

Ahmann, J. S.: *rev*, 7:9
Brown, F. G.: 1; *rev*, 7:9
Collison, B. B., *exc*, 7:9
Taylor, P. A.: *exc*, 7:9
White, V.: *exc*, 7:9

[12]

Cooperative Primary Tests. Grades 1.5–2.5, 2.5–3; 1965–67; CPT; subtests available as separates; 2 levels; Cooperative Tests and Services. *

a) FORMS 12A AND 12B. Grades 1.5–2.5; 4 scores: listening, word analysis, mathematics, reading.

b) FORMS 23A AND 23B. Grades 2.5–3; 7 scores: listening, word analysis, mathematics, reading, writing skills (spelling, capitalization-punctuation-usage, total).

For additional information and excerpted reviews by Gerald S. Hanna and Esin Kaya, see 7:10 (1 reference).

REFERENCES THROUGH 1971

1. See 7:10.

CUMULATIVE NAME INDEX

Hanna, G. S.: *exc*, 7:10
Kaya, E.: *exc*, 7:10
Pickering, C. T.: 1

[13]

★Educational Skills Tests: College Edition. Open-door college entrants; 1971; EST; 11 scores: English (phonetic, syntactic, semantic, organizational, editing, total), mathematics (basic information, computation, problem analysis, total), total; CTB/McGraw-Hill. *

[14]

General Tests of Language and Arithmetic. Standards 5–7; 1964–67; GTLA; 3 scores: first language (English or Afrikaans), arithmetic, second language (English or Afrikaans); Human Sciences Research Council [South Africa]. *

For additional information, see 7:12.

[15]

The Gray-Votaw-Rogers General Achievement Tests. Grades 1–3, 4–6, 7–9; 1934–63; 3 levels; Hob Gray, David F. Votaw, Sr., and J. Lloyd Rogers; Steck-Vaughn Co. *

a) PRIMARY. Grades 1–3; 1934–63; 6 scores: reading comprehension, reading vocabulary, spelling, arithmetic reasoning, arithmetic computation, total.

b) INTERMEDIATE. Grades 4–6; 1934–62; 10 or 11 scores: same as for primary level plus elementary science, language, literature (optional), social studies, health and safety.

c) ADVANCED. Grades 7–9; 1934–62; 10 or 11 scores: same as for intermediate level.

For additional information and reviews by Kenneth D. Hopkins, Victor H. Noll, and Ellis Batten Page, see 6:10; for reviews by Warren G. Findley and Douglas E. Scates of an earlier edition, see 5:11 (1 reference); for a review by Oliver F. Anderhalter, see 4:12; for a review by Roland L. Beck, see 3:9 (3 references); for reviews by Joseph E. Moore and C. C. Ross, see 2:1187 (1 reference).

REFERENCES THROUGH 1971

1. See 2:1187.
2–4. See 3:9.
5. See 5:11.

CUMULATIVE NAME INDEX

Anderhalter, O. F.: *rev,* 4:12
Barber, D.: 2
Beck, R. L.: *rev,* 3:9
Drake, T.: 3
Findley, W. G.: *rev,* 5:11
Fruchter, B.: 5
Hopkins, K. D.: *rev,* 6:10

Moore, J. E.: *rev,* 2:1187
Noll, V. H.: *rev,* 6:10
Oehler, C. A.: 4
Page, E. B.: *rev,* 6:10
Ross, C. C.: *rev,* 2:1187
Scates, D. E.: *rev,* 5:11
Votaw, D. F.: 1

[16]

★**Guidance Test for Junior Secondary Bantu Pupils in Form III.** 1969–71; GJB; 7 scores: English vocabulary, English sentences, series completion, arithmetic, Afrikaans vocabulary, Afrikaans sentences, verbal reasoning; all test materials (except language subtests) in both English and Afrikaans; J. D. van Staden, G. J. Ligthelm, J. P. du Toit, A. P. J. Pottas, and G. Engelbrecht (revision); Human Sciences Research Council [South Africa]. *

[17]

High School Fundamentals Evaluation Test. Grades 9–12; 1955–59; catalog uses the title *Fundamentals Evaluation Test;* 6 scores: reading vocabulary, reading comprehension, history and social studies, science, mathematics, total; David F. Votaw, Sr.; Steck-Vaughn Co. *

For additional information and reviews by George D. Demos and Jason Millman, see 6:12 (1 reference); for reviews by Victor H. Noll and Verner M. Sims, see 5:14.

REFERENCES THROUGH 1971

1. See 6:12.

CUMULATIVE NAME INDEX

Demos, G. D.: *rev,* 6:12
Millman, J.: *rev,* 6:12
Noll, V. H.: *rev,* 5:14

Sims, V. M.: *rev,* 5:14
Votaw, D. F.: 1

[18]

Iowa High School Content Examination. Grades 11–13; 1924–43; 5 scores: English and literature, mathematics, science, history and social studies, total; D. B. Stuit, H. A. Greene, and G. M. Ruch; Bureau of Educational Research and Service. *

For additional information and a review by David V. Tiedeman, see 4:16 (4 references); for a review by Maurice E. Troyer, see 3:11 (7 references).

REFERENCES THROUGH 1971

1–7. See 3:11.
8–11. See 4:16.
12. Ruch, G. M. "A Mental-Educational Survey of 1550 High School Seniors." *Univ Iowa Studies Ed* 2(5):1–29 '23. *
13. Kornhauser, Arthur W. "Test and High-School Records as Indicators of Success in an Undergraduate School of Business." *J Ed Res* 16:342–56 D '27. * (*PA* 2:1072)
14. Ruch, G. M., and Stoddard, George D. *Tests and Measurements in High School Instruction,* pp. 202–4. Yonkers, N.Y.: World Book Co., 1927. Pp. xxi, 381. * (*PA* 1:1454)
15. Hall, Robert T. "How Athletes and Non-Athletes Compare in Mental Ability and in Educational Achievement." *Am Phys Ed R* 33:388–9 Je '28. * (*PA* 2:3710)
16. Eells, Walter Crosby. "The California Junior College Mental-Educational Survey." *Ed Rec* 11:281–91 O '30. *
17. Nelson, M. J. "Some Data From Freshman Tests." *Sch & Soc* 31:772–4 Je 7 '30. * (*PA* 4:3694)
18. Segel, David. "The Automatic Prediction of Scholastic Success by Using the Multiple Regression Technique With Electric Tabulating and Accounting Machines." *J Ed Psychol* 22:139–44 F '31. * (*PA* 5:2573)
19. Eells, Walter Crosby, and Fox, Clement S. "Sex Differences in Mathematical Achievement of Junior College Students." *J Ed Psychol* 23:381–6 My '32. * (*PA* 6:4166)
20. Segel, David. "Differential Prediction of Scholastic Success." *Sch & Soc* 39:91–6 Ja 20 '34. *
21. Wagner, Mazie Earle, and Strabel, Eunice. "Predicting Success and Failure in College Ancient and Modern Foreign Languages." *Mod Lang J* 19:285–93 Ja '35. * (*PA* 9:2995)
22. Read, Cecil B. "The Prediction of Scholastic Success in a Municipal University." *Sch & Soc* 48:187–8 Ag 6 '38. * (*PA* 12:6645)

23. Butsch, R. L. C. "Improving the Prediction of Academic Success Through Differential Weighting." *J Ed Psychol* 30:401–2 S '39. * (*PA* 14:1058)
24. Bullock, Henry Allen. "A Comparison of the Academic Achievement of White and Negro High School Graduates." *J Ed Res* 44:179–92 N '50. * (*PA* 25:6457)
25. Driscoll, Justin A. *Factors in Intelligence and Achievement: A Study of the Factor Pattern Resulting From Analysis of the Scores of Boys in Junior Year of High School on Intelligence and Achievement Tests.* Catholic University of America, Educational Research Monographs, Vol. 16, No. 7. Washington, D.C.: Catholic University of America Press, Inc., June 15, 1952. Pp. viii, 56. * (*PA* 27:3330)
26. Fruchter, Benjamin. "Orthogonal and Oblique Solutions of a Battery of Aptitude, Achievement and Background Variables." *Ed & Psychol Meas* 12:20–38 sp '52. * (*PA* 27:6180)
27. Stewart, Roy A. *An Analysis of the Performance on the Iowa High School Content Examination of High School Seniors by Sex and Place of Residence.* Master's thesis, Fisk University (Nashville, Tenn.), 1952.
28. Toumey, Sylvester L. *An Analytical Study of Certain Correlates of Responses to the Illinois Inventory of Parent Opinion.* Master's thesis, University of Georgia (Athens, Ga.), 1952.
29. Hardaway, Charles. "Orientation Tests and Freshmen Scholarship." *Teach Col J* 25:10–1 O '53. *
30. Ridley, Walter Nathaniel. *Prognostic Values of Freshman Tests Used at Virginia State College.* Doctor's thesis, University of Virginia (Charlottesville, Va.), 1953. (*DA* 14:1042)
31. Stoner, William Gerald. *Factors Related to the Underachievement of High School Students.* Doctor's thesis, Stanford University (Stanford, Calif.), 1956. (*DA* 17:96)
32. Lowry, Carmen Ercell. *The Prediction of Academic Success in a Private Liberal Arts College for Negroes.* Doctor's thesis, University of Texas (Austin, Tex.), 1957. (*DA* 17:2500)

CUMULATIVE NAME INDEX

Adams, M.: 6
Adams, W. M.: 7
Bullock, H. A.: 24
Bushong, G. E.: 9
Butsch, R. L. C.: 23
Cleeton, G. U.: 1
Donnelly, M. C.: 5
Driscoll, J. A.: 25
Eells, W. C.: 16, 19
Fox, C. S.: 19
Fruchter, B.: 26
Gerberich, J. R.: 2
Giesecke, G. E.: 8
Hall, R. T.: 15
Hardaway, C.: 29
Kornhauser, A. W.: 13
Larsen, R. P.: 8
Leaf, C. T.: 4

Lowry, C. E.: 32
Nelson, M. J.: 17
Portenier, L. G.: 10
Read, C. B.: 22
Ridley, W. N.: 30
Ruch, G. M.: 12, 14
Segel, D.: 18, 20
Stewart, R. A.: 27
Stoddard, G. D.: 14
Stoner, W. G.: 31
Strabel, E.: 3, 21
Stuit, D. B.: 5
Tiedeman, D. V.: *rev,* 4:16
Toumey, S. L.: 28
Troyer, M. E.: *rev,* 3:11
Uhrbrock, R. S.: 11
Wagner, M. E.: 3, 21
Wittenborn, J. R.: 8

[19]

Iowa Tests of Basic Skills. Grades 1.7–3.5, 3–9; 1955–73; ITBS; E. F. Lindquist and A. N. Hieronymus; Houghton Mifflin Co. *

a) PRIMARY BATTERY: LEVELS 7–8. Grades 1.7–3.5; 1972; 16 scores: listening, vocabulary, word analysis, reading comprehension, language skills (spelling, capitalization, punctuation, usage, total), work-study skills (maps/graphs and tables, references, total), mathematics skills (mathematics concepts, mathematics problems, total), composite.

b) LEVELS EDITION: LEVELS 9–14. Grades 3–9; 1955–72; 15 scores: vocabulary, reading comprehension, language (spelling, capitalization, punctuation, usage, total), work-study skills (map reading, reading graphs and tables, knowledge and use of reference materials, total), mathematics skills (mathematics concepts, mathematics problem solving, total), total; 2 editions.

1) *Forms 1–4.* 1955–66; 6 levels in a single booklet; a Braille edition (omitting map reading) is available from American Printing House for the Blind, Inc.
2) *Forms 5–6.* 1955–73.
(*a*) Multilevel Edition.
(*b*) Separate Booklet Edition.

For additional information concerning Forms 1–2, see 6:13 (17 references); for reviews by Virgil E.

Herrick, G. A. V. Morgan, and H. H. Remmers and an excerpted review by Laurence Siegel, see 5:16.

REFERENCES THROUGH 1971

1–17. See 6:13.
18. LUMSDEN, FLORENCE M. "Growth and Achievement in Basic English Skills." *J Exp Ed* 13:9–14 S '44. * (*PA* 19:1577)
19. ZINTZ, MILES V. "Academic Achievement and Social and Emotional Adjustment of Handicapped Children." *El Sch J* 51:502–7 My '51. * (*PA* 25:7670)
20. GAFFNEY, PHILIP DANIAL. *A Ten-Year Follow-Up Study of Students Identified as Talented on the Basis of Sixth-Grade Achievement Test Scores.* Doctor's thesis, State University of Iowa (Iowa City, Iowa), 1957. (*DA* 17:2918)
21. KRANTZ, L. L. "The Relationship of Reading Abilities and Basic Skills of the Elementary School to Success in the Interpretation of the Content Materials in the High School." *J Exp Ed* 26:97–114 D '57. * (*PA* 33:4579)
22. LARSON, ROBERT E., AND SELLAND, CYNTHIA T. "A Comparison of Reading Ages With Mental Ages." *J Ed Res* 52:55–9 O '58. * (*PA* 34:2105)
23. KOEHN, EDNA BERTHA. *The Relationship of the Basic Skill Development of Sixth Grade Gifted Children to Ninth Grade Achievement in the Content Fields.* Doctor's thesis, University of Minnesota (Minneapolis, Minn.), 1960. (*DA* 21:133)
24. KRAMER, KLAAS. "Work-Study Skills in Iowa and the Netherlands." *El Sch J* 61:81–5 N '60. *
25. FISCHER, ROBERT FREDERICK. *Relationships Between School Achievement and the Verbal and Nonverbal Abilities of Children.* Doctor's thesis, University of Wisconsin (Madison, Wis.), 1961. (*DA* 21:3357)
26. FAUST, CLAIRE EDWARD. *A Study of the Relationship Between Attitude and Achievement in Selected Elementary School Subjects.* Doctor's thesis, State University of Iowa (Iowa City, Iowa), 1962. (*DA* 23:2752)
27. BROWN, SANDRA ROSE. *A Comparison of Five Widely Used Standardized Reading Tests and an Informal Reading Inventory for a Selected Group of Elementary School Children.* Doctor's thesis, University of Georgia (Athens, Ga.), 1963. (*DA* 25:996)
28. GOOLSBY, THOMAS MORRIS, JR. *Interrelationships Among Seven Measures of Competency in Elementary School Social Studies.* Doctor's thesis, State University of Iowa (Iowa City, Iowa), 1963. (*DA* 24:4540)
29. KAMII, CONSTANCE K., AND WEIKART, DAVID P. "Marks, Achievement, and Intelligence of Seventh Graders Who Were Retained (Nonpromoted) Once in Elementary School." *J Ed Res* 56:452–9 My–Je '63. *
30. SONNEMAN, LAWRENCE J. *A Study of the Relationships Between Four Tests of Intelligence and One Test of Scholastic Achievement.* Doctor's thesis, State University of South Dakota (Vermillion, S.D.), 1963. (*DA* 24:4555)
31. CAUBLE, BEN LEROY. *Anxiety in Intermediate Grade Children and Its Relationship With Their Scores on Measures of Intelligence, Academic Achievement, and Several Personality Factors.* Doctor's thesis, Southern Illinois University (Carbondale, Ill.), 1964. (*DA* 25:5150)
32. DE BOER, DOROTHY LOUISE. *A Study of the Relationship of Creativity to Intelligence and Achievement.* Doctor's thesis, Northwestern University (Evanston, Ill.), 1964. (*DA* 25:3968)
33. HOPKINS, KENNETH D. "Extrinsic Reliability: Estimating and Attenuating Variance From Response Styles, Chance, and Other Irrelevant Sources." *Ed & Psychol Meas* 24:271–81 su '64. * (*PA* 39:3152)
34. MILLMAN, JASON, AND LINDLOF, JOHN. "The Comparability of Fifth-Grade Norms of the California, Iowa, and Metropolitan Achievement Tests." *J Ed Meas* 1:135–7 D '64. * (*PA* 39:10143)
35. COHEN, S. ALAN. *A Study of the Relationships Among Measurements of Reading, Intelligence and Vision Development, Using a Dynamic Theory of Vision, in Socially Disadvantaged Junior High School Children.* Doctor's thesis, Boston University (Boston, Mass.), 1965. (*DA* 26:5222)
36. DAVIS, O. L., JR., AND YAMAMOTO, KAORU. "Creative Thinking and Achievement Item Responses of Elementary School Pupils: A Preliminary Investigation." *J Peabody Ed* 42:349–55 My '65. *
37. DIZNEY, HENRY F., AND BEGGS, DONALD L. "A Comparison of Grade Equivalent Scores Between Grade Levels on Two Subtests of the Iowa Tests of Basic Skills." *J Ed Meas* 2:187–91 D '65. *
38. GUILFORD, J. P.; HOEPFNER, RALPH; AND PETERSEN, HUGH. "Predicting Achievement in Ninth-Grade Mathematics From Measures of Intellectual-Aptitude Factors." *Ed & Psychol Meas* 25:659–82 au '65. * (*PA* 40:3376)
39. HANNA, GERALD STANLEY. *An Investigation of Selected Ability, Aptitude, Interest, and Personality Characteristics Relevant to Success in High School Geometry.* Doctor's thesis, University of Southern California (Los Angeles, Calif.), 1965. (*DA* 26:3152)
40. HARRISON, BARBARA. *The Development of Local Norms for the Otis Mental Ability Test and the Iowa Tests of Basic Skills With Selected Relationships to Teacher Marks in Orange,*

Connecticut. Master's thesis, Southern Connecticut State College (New Haven, Conn.), 1965.
41. JOHNSON, HALVIN SHERWOOD. *The Relationship of Scores on Aptitude and Achievement Tests Taken at Late Elementary and Junior High School Levels to Scholarship in Ninth Grade.* Doctor's thesis, University of South Dakota (Vermillion, S.D.), 1965. (*DA* 26:4449)
42. KANGAS, RONALD D. "Factors Related to Success in 7th Grade Foreign Language Study." *Mod Lang J* 49:97–8 F '65. *
43. LONG, BARBARA H., AND HENDERSON, EDMUND H. "Originality, Reading, and Arithmetic." *Percept & Motor Skills* 21:553–4 O '65. * (*PA* 40:2871)
44. MCCAULEY, JOHN HOWARD, JR. *Rorschach, WISC, and ITBS Patterns of Nine-Year-Old School Boys With Labile and Stabile IQ Scores.* Doctor's thesis, University of Maryland (College Park, Md.), 1965. (*DA* 27:1663A)
45. RAINEY, ROBERT G. "A Study of Four School-Ability Tests." *J Exp Ed* 33:305–19 su '65. * (*PA* 39:12306)
46. CRAWSHAW, TED CATHCART. *Comparative Validities of Eleven Predictors of Student Success in Ninth Grade Spanish and French: Aurora-West Public Schools, 1961–63.* Master's thesis, Northern Illinois University (DeKalb, Ill.), 1966.
47. CUNNINGHAM, WILLIAM. *A Thirteen-Year Retrospective Study of Standardized Test Data.* Doctor's thesis, Western Reserve University (Cleveland, Ohio), 1966. (*DA* 27:3305A)
48. FINLEY, CARMEN J. "How Well Can Teachers Judge Pupil Achievement? The Case of the Illusive Criterion." *Calif J Ed Res* 17:126–32 My '66. * (*PA* 40:10449)
49. FUQUA, NORMAN VINCE. *An Analysis of the Relationships and Differences Among Measures of Creative Thinking and Selected Other Factors in Educable and Less Educable Groups of Negro Children.* Doctor's thesis, Wayne State University (Detroit, Mich.), 1966. (*DA* 27:2314A)
50. GOOLSBY, THOMAS M., JR. "Differentiating Between Measures of Different Outcomes in the Social Studies." *J Ed Meas* 3:219–22 f '66. *
51. DUNN, JAMES A. "Validity Coefficients for the New Harris-Goodenough Draw-A-Man Test." *Percept & Motor Skills* 24:299–301 F '67. * (*PA* 41:8149)
52. GALLIAN, RICHARD DONALD. *A Content Validation Study of the Arithmetic Test Items of Four Arithmetic Achievement Tests Compared With the Content of Six Arithmetic Series at the Intermediate Level.* Doctor's thesis, University of Missouri (Columbia, Mo.), 1967. (*DA* 28:3361A)
53. HOOVER, HIRAM D. *A Factor Analytic Study of the Iowa Tests of Basic Skills.* Master's thesis, University of Iowa (Iowa City, Iowa), 1967.
54. LANIER, PERRY EUGENE. *A Study of Creativity, Intelligence and Discovery Teaching as Related to Performance in Elementary School Mathematics.* Doctor's thesis, University of Oklahoma (Norman, Okla.), 1967. (*DA* 28:1004A)
55. POEHLEIN, PAUL O. *The Correlation Between Iowa Tests of Basic Skills Scores and Achievement in Related Subject Areas at Merrill Junior High School, Des Moines, Iowa.* Master's thesis, Drake University (Des Moines, Iowa), 1967.
56. PRINE, DONALD L. *Prediction of Academic Achievement in 9th Grade Algebra by the Use of Selected Scores on the Iowa Tests of Basic Skills.* Master's thesis, Drake University (Des Moines, Iowa), 1967.
57. RICE, VICTOR. *An Appraisal of the Predictive Value of Patterns of Subtest Scores in Achievement Test Batteries.* Doctor's thesis, American University (Washington, D.C.), 1967. (*DA* 28:1267A)
58. RUDNICK, MARK; STERRITT, GRAHAM M.; AND FLAX, MORTON. "Auditory and Visual Rhythm Perception and Reading Ability." *Child Develop* 38:581–7 Je '67. * (*PA* 41:10263)
59. STROWBRIDGE, EDWIN DAVID, JR. *Relationships Between Twelve Characteristics of Ability in Mathematics and Successful Achievement in an Eighth Grade SMSG Algebra Program.* Doctor's thesis, University of Oregon (Eugene, Ore.), 1967. (*DA* 28:1014A)
60. WILLIAMSON, MALCOM L., AND HOPKINS, KENNETH D. "The Use of 'None-of-These' Versus Homogeneous Alternatives on Multiple-Choice Tests: Experimental Reliability and Validity Comparisons." *J Ed Meas* 4:53–8 su '67. *
61. WOOD, SUSAN. *An Evaluation of Published English Tests,* pp. 35–40. Madison, Wis.: Wisconsin Department of Public Instruction, 1967. Pp. 91. *
62. BEGGS, DONALD L., AND HIERONYMUS, ALBERT N. "Uniformity of Growth in the Basic Skills Throughout the School Year and During the Summer." *J Ed Meas* 5:91–7 su '68. *
63. COOKE, BRYAN EDWARD MARSHALL. *The Relationship Between Balance and Cognitive Abilities of Children Aged Eight to Thirteen Years.* Doctor's thesis, University of Illinois (Urbana, Ill.), 1968. (*DAI* 30:154A)
64. FREVERT, RITA K. *The Ability of Elementary School Students to Estimate High and Low Sub-Test Scores on the Iowa Tests of Basic Skills.* Master's thesis, Iowa State University (Ames, Iowa), 1968.
65. GORDON, EDWIN. "A Study of the Efficacy of General Intelligence and Musical Aptitude Tests in Predicting Achievement in Music." *Council Res Music Ed B* 13:40–5 sp '68. * (*PA* 42:15436)

Iowa Tests of Basic Skills

66. MANN, LESTER; HAUGHEY, CHARLES; TREFSGAR, THEODORE F.; AND KEFFER, CHARLES E. "Achievement and Personality Measurements Associated With Progress in a Programmed Course in Decimals and Fractions at a Fifth Grade Level." *Scientia Paedagogica Experimentalis* (Belgium) 5(1):76–83 '68. * (*PA* 45:3108)

67. MERENDA, PETER F., AND JACKSON, ROBERT M. "Relationship Between Fourth Grade and Seventh Grade Performance on the Iowa Tests of Basic Skills." *J Ed Meas* 5:163–5 su '68. * Erratum: 6(1):31 sp '69. *

68. PLACK, JERALYN J. "Relationship Between Achievement in Reading and Achievement in Selected Motor Skills in Elementary School Children." *Res Q* 39:1063–8 D '68. *

69. PUGH, RICHARD C. "Tests for Creative Thinking—Potential for School Testing Programs." *B Sch Ed Ind Univ* 44(6):1–30 N '68. * (*PA* 46:5483)

70. SABERS, DARRELL L., AND FELDT, LEONARD S. "The Predictive Validity of the Iowa Algebra Aptitude Test for Achievement in Modern Mathematics and Algebra." *Ed & Psychol Meas* 28:901–7 au '68. * (*PA* 43:4435)

71. SATTABANASUK, THIRAPAN. *Junior High Student Performance and Related Student and Parent Characteristics.* Doctor's thesis, Colorado State College (Greeley, Colo.), 1968. (*DA* 29:1052A)

72. SCHREINER, ROBERT LEE. *A Study of Interrelationships Among Different Approaches to Measuring Reading Comprehension.* Doctor's thesis, University of Iowa (Iowa City, Iowa), 1968. (*DA* 29:3882A)

73. WOODFIN, MARY JO. "Correlations Among Certain Factors and the Written Expression of Third Grade Children." *Ed & Psychol Meas* 28:1237–42 w '68. * (*PA* 44:6509)

74. AMES, WILBUR S. "Reading Programs: Use of Test Data as a Vital Factor." *Clearing House* 43(9):515–8 My '69. *

75. ANTTONEN, RALPH G. "A Longitudinal Study in Mathematics Attitude." *J Ed Res* 62(10):467–71 Jl–Ag '69. *

76. BARROW, LLOYD HARLEY. *Development of a Prediction Equation for the Placement of Students in Seventh Grade Life Science.* Master's thesis, University of Northern Iowa (Cedar Falls, Iowa), 1969.

77. BARZ, ANITA I. *Prediction of Secondary School Achievement From Primary Grade Aptitude and Achievement Measures.* Doctor's thesis, St. John's University (Jamaica, N.Y.), 1969. (*DAI* 30:3271A)

78. BOTEL, MORTON. "A Comparative Study of the Validity of the Botel Reading Inventory and Selected Standardized Tests." *Proc Ann Conv Int Read Assn* 13(1):721–7 '69. *

79. DYER, HENRY S.; LINN, ROBERT L.; AND PATTON, MICHAEL J. "A Comparison of Four Methods of Obtaining Discrepancy Measures Based on Observed and Predicted School System Means on Achievement Tests." *Am Ed Res J* 6(4):591–605 N '69. * (*PA* 45:6966)

80. EAGLE, NORMAN, AND HARRIS, ANNA S. "Interaction of Race and Test on Reading Performance Scores." *J Ed Meas* 6(3):131–5 f '69. * (*PA* 44:15298)

81. FITZSIMMONS, MARGARET ELAINE. *An Analytic Study of the Retention of Selected Skills by Intermediate Grade Pupils After the Summer Recess.* Doctor's thesis, Fordham University (New York, N.Y.), 1969. (*DAI* 30:5163A)

82. FOXWORTHY, ESTHER G. *The Effects of Listening Training on Selected Scores of the Iowa Tests of Basic Skills.* Master's thesis, Drake University (Des Moines, Iowa), 1969.

83. HITTI, FRED JOSEPH. *The Reliability and Concurrent Validity of Objective Spelling Tests With and Without Optional Items.* Doctor's thesis, University of Rochester (Rochester, N.Y.), 1969. (*DAI* 30:3321A)

84. LINN, ROBERT L. "A Note on the Stability of the Iowa Tests of Basic Skills." *J Ed Meas* 6(1):29–30 sp '69. * (*PA* 44:15305)

85. MILLER, WILLIAM G. "Ability Grouping by Multiple Discriminant Analysis." *Fla J Ed Res* 11(1):25–37 Ja '69. *

86. SCHREINER, ROBERT L.; HIERONYMUS, A. N.; AND FORSYTH, ROBERT. "Differential Measurement of Reading Abilities at the Elementary School Level." *Read Res Q* 5(1):84–99 f '69. *

87. SHADEED, CHARLES T. *A Study of Available Criteria for Predicting Success in Algebra.* Master's thesis, Western Connecticut State College (Danbury, Conn.), 1969.

88. WESTPHAL, M. ELIZABETH; LEUTENEGGER, RALPH R.; AND WAGNER, DOROTHEA L. "Some Psycho-Acoustic and Intellectual Correlates of Achievement in German Language Learning of Junior High School Students." *Mod Lang J* 53(4):258–66 Ap '69. * (*PA* 44:21623)

89. YOUNG, WILLIAM THOMAS. *An Investigation of the Relative and Combined Power of Musical Aptitude, General Intelligence, and Academic Achievement Tests to Predict Musical Attainment.* Doctor's thesis, University of Iowa (Iowa City, Iowa), 1969. (*DAI* 30:758A)

90. COTLER, SHELDON, AND PALMER, RICHARD J. "The Relationships Among Sex, Sociometric, Self, and Test Anxiety Factors and the Academic Achievement of Elementary School Children." *Psychol Sch* 7(3):211–6 Jl '70. * (*PA* 45:5019)

91. EDWARDS, RONNIE PHILIP. *A Comparison Between Standardized and Listening-Reading Administrations of the Iowa Tests of Basic Skills.* Doctor's thesis, University of Iowa (Iowa City, Iowa), 1970. (*DAI* 31:4542A)

92. GREEN, TIMOTHY MACK. *Self-Conceptions, Physical Fitness Factors, School Achievement and Their Interrelations With Sixth-Grade Students.* Doctor's thesis, University of Oklahoma (Norman, Okla.), 1970. (*DAI* 31:2613A)

93. GUSTAFSON, RICHARD A. "Factor Analyzing the Iowa Tests of Basic Skills." *Psychol Sch* 7(3):226–7 Jl '70. * (*PA* 45:4919)

94. THOMPSON, LOWELL H. *The Critical Thinking Ability of New School Sixth Grade Students.* Doctor's thesis, University of North Dakota (Grand Forks, N.D.), 1970. (*DAI* 31:4609A)

95. TUMANGDAY, MARIA G. *The Performance of Filipino Fifth-Grade Children on the Test of Work-Study Skills of the Iowa Tests of Basic Skills.* Doctor's thesis, University of Iowa (Iowa City, Iowa), 1970. (*DAI* 31:4395A)

96. CHANG, SUNNYUH SHIN, AND RATHS, JAMES. "The Schools' Contribution to the Cumulating Deficit." *J Ed Res* 64(6):272–6 F '71. *

97. DOUGHTY, EARL. "Test Rankings and Selection Procedures for Identifying Gifted Intermediate Elementary Students." *Ill Sch Res* 8(1):29–32 f '71. *

98. FLEISCHMAN, HOWARD L.; ORR, DAVID B.; AND STRASEL, H. C. "Relationships Between the Subtests of Six Achievement Test Batteries." Abstract. *Proc 79th Ann Conv Am Psychol Assn* 6(1):109–10 '71. * (*PA* 46:3727)

99. HOPKINS, KENNETH D., AND BRACHT, GLENN H. "A Longitudinal Study of Constancy of Reading Performance," pp. 103–12. In *Diagnostic Viewpoints in Reading*. Edited by Robert E. Leibert. Newark, Del.: International Reading Association, 1971. Pp. viii, 133. *

100. JONES, DOROTHY M. "Language Skills as an Indication of Success in Junior High School Typewriting." *Ball State J Bus Educators* 42(3):2–7 My '71. *

101. NIEDERKORN, ROBERT HENRY. *Assessing Relative Effectiveness of Standardized and Experimental Tests in Measuring Mathematics Achievement in Selected Fifth Grades.* Doctor's thesis, University of Montana (Missoula, Mont.), 1971. (*DAI* 32:2314A)

102. STOCKWELL, KEITH WILLIAM. *The Identification and Analysis of Selected Factors Contributing to High Achievement in Elementary School Science.* Doctor's thesis, Wayne State University (Detroit, Mich.), 1971. (*DAI* 32:3012A)

103. WILLIAMS, JOHN D.; HARLOW, STEVEN D.; AND BORGEN, JEROME S. "Creativity, Dogmatism, and Arithmetic Achievement." *J Psychol* 78(2):217–22 Jl '71. * (*PA* 46:9760)

104. YOUNG, WILLIAM T. "The Role of Musical Aptitude, Intelligence, and Academic Achievement in Predicting the Musical Attainment of Elementary Instrumental Music Students." *J Res Music Ed* 19(4):385–98 w '71. * (*PA* 48:7918)

CUMULATIVE NAME INDEX

[20]

*The Iowa Tests of Educational Development.
Grades 9–12; 1942–72; ITED; 2 editions; prepared
under the direction of E. F. Lindquist and Leonard S.
Feldt with the assistance of Robert A. Forsyth (*b*)
and Esther D. Neckere (*b*) ; Science Research Associates, Inc. *

a) FORMS X-4 AND Y-4. 1942–67; 11 scores: understanding of basic social concepts, general background
in the natural sciences, correctness and appropriateness
of expression, ability to do quantitative thinking, ability to interpret reading materials (social studies, natural sciences, literary, total), general vocabulary, total,
use of sources of information ; 2 editions.

1) *Single Booklet Edition.*

2) *Separate Booklet Edition.* 9 tests (titles are the
same as scores listed above) available as separates.

b) FORMS X5 AND Y5. 1942–72; *SRA Assessment Survey* is title used by publisher for combination of these
forms and Forms E and F of *SRA Achievement Series*,
which together cover the grade range 1–12; 8–11
scores: reading (comprehension, vocabulary, total),
language arts (usage, spelling, total), mathematics,
composite, social studies background (optional), science background (optional), use of sources (optional)
plus 44 optional skill scores.

For additional information and reviews by Ellis Batten Page and Alexander G. Wesman of Forms X-4
and Y-4, see 6:14 (23 references) ; for reviews by
J. Murray Lee and Stephen Wiseman of earlier forms,
see 5:17 (9 references) ; for a review by Eric F.
Gardner, see 4:17 (3 references) ; for reviews by
Henry Chauncey, Gustav J. Froehlich, and Lavone A.
Hanna, see 3:12. For reviews of earlier forms of the
quantitative thinking subtest, see 6:579 (1 review) ;
the background in natural sciences subtest, see 6:876
(2 reviews) ; and the basic social concepts subtest, see
6:969 (1 review).

REFERENCES THROUGH 1971

1–3. See 4:17.
4–12. See 5:17.
13–35. See 6:14.
36. HIERONYMUS, A. N. "A Study of Social Class Motivation:
Relationships Between Anxiety for Education and Certain Socio-Economic and Intellectual Variables." *J Ed Psychol* 42:193–205
Ap '51. * (*PA* 26:2400)
37. KRANTZ, L. L. "The Relationship of Reading Abilities
and Basic Skills of the Elementary School to Success in the
Interpretation of the Content Materials in the High School."
J Exp Ed 26:97–114 D '57. * (*PA* 33:4579)
38. GREEN, DONALD A. *A Study of the Relationships Between
School Persistence and Grades, Ability and Achievement of
Secondary School Pupils.* Doctor's thesis, State University of
Iowa (Iowa City, Iowa), 1958. (*DA* 19:1616)
39. STOKER, HOWARD W., AND KROPP, RUSSELL P. "The
Predictive Validities and Factorial Content of the Florida

State-Wide Ninth-Grade Testing Program Battery." *Fla J Ed
Res* 2:105–14 Ja '60. *
40. DEISSLER, KENNETH L. "A Study of South Dakota
Indian Achievement Problems." *J Am Indian Ed* 1:19–21 My
'62. *
41. QUILLER, GORDON FREDERICK. *A Study of College Predictors for First Year Students at Colorado State University.*
Doctor's research study No. 1, Colorado State College (Greeley,
Colo.), 1962. (*DA* 23:1253)
42. BRUNO, ANN T. *An Analysis of the Iowa Tests of
Educational Development Using the Taxonomy of Educational
Objectives as Criterion.* Master's thesis, Boston University
(Boston, Mass.), 1963.
43. CRAWFORD, W. R., AND MOYEL, I. S. "Predicting Academic
Achievement From Intelligence and Personality Data." *Fla J
Ed Res* 5:19–28 Ja '63. *
44. OSTROW, JEANNE. *A Comparative Study of Certain Aspects
of Intellectual Functioning in Achieving and Low-Achieving
High School Students.* Doctor's thesis, University of Michigan
(Ann Arbor, Mich.), 1963. (*DA* 25:617)
45. BROWN, MARY MARGARET. *A Study of the Relationships
of Selected Tests and Grade Point Averages for a Land Grant
Institution.* Doctor's thesis, University of South Dakota (Vermillion, S.D.), 1964. (*DA* 27:664A)
46. CAPLAN, STANLEY W., AND RUBLE, RONALD A. "A Study
of Culturally Imposed Factors on School Achievement in a
Metropolitan Area." *J Ed Res* 58:16–21 S '64. *
47. FORD, THOMAS G. *A Study of the Predictive Value of
the ITED at Guilford High School, Rockford, Illinois.* Master's
thesis, Northern Illinois University (DeKalb, Ill.), 1964.
48. HAHN, CHARLES WALTER. *A Study of Scores Obtained
From Iowa Tests of Educational Development in Selected
Schools in Iowa Prior to and Subsequent to School District
Reorganization.* Doctor's thesis, State University of Iowa (Iowa
City, Iowa), 1964. (*DA* 25:5016)
49. JORDAN, BILLY HARRISON, JR. *Analysis of the Interrelationship of Intelligence, Achievement, and Socio-Economic
Status in a Selected Population of High-School Seniors.* Doctor's
thesis, North Texas State University (Denton, Tex.), 1964.
(*DA* 25:1006)
50. MOORE, EARL JAMES. *A Study of the Relationship Between
High School and College Scholarship and Selected Test Results
for Grades K–12.* Doctor's thesis, University of South Dakota
(Vermillion, S.D.), 1964. (*DA* 27:679A)
51. SHEA, MARIE. *Results of Test 4 of the ITED for Predicting Success in Algebra I.* Master's thesis, Marywood College
(Scranton, Pa.), 1964.
52. SPACE, MARGARET NIVEN. *A Study of Individual Predictability Based on Intra-Individual Variability on Certain
Achievement Measures.* Doctor's thesis, University of Minnesota (Minneapolis, Minn.), 1964. (*DA* 26:879)
53. TYLER, LEONA E. "The Antecedents of Two Varieties of
Vocational Interests." *Genetic Psychol Monogr* 70:177–227 N
'64. * (*PA* 39:10878)
54. YAMAMOTO, KAORU. "Role of Creative Thinking and
Intelligence in High School Achievement." *Psychol Rep* 14:783–
9 Je '64. * (*PA* 39:5140)
55. ZIMMER, JOSEPH H. *Predicting High School Success From
the Differential Aptitude Tests and the Iowa Tests of Educational Development.* Master's thesis, Catholic University of
America (Washington, D.C.), 1964.
56. CHRISTOFANELLI, DONALD J. *A Statistical Study for
Predicting the Probable Success in First Year Algebra at
Auburn Senior High School, Rockford, Illinois.* Master's thesis,
Northern Illinois University (DeKalb, Ill.), 1965.
57. HUTCHERSON, DONALD. "Junior High School Social
Studies Teacher-Pupil Compatibility—Its Relation to Pupil Sex,
Social Level, and Indexes of Achievement." *J Ed Res* 59:39–44
S '65. *
58. JOSELYN, EDWIN GARY. "'Educational Growth' and the
Iowa Tests of Educational Development." *Personnel & Guid J*
44:35–9 S '65. *
59. KOSAI, JOSEPH HIDEO. *A Proposed Basis for Predicting
the Grades in Elementary Algebra of Tenth Grade Students at
Stadium High School.* Master's thesis, University of Puget
Sound (Tacoma, Wash.), 1965.
60. PABST, ROBERT LEROY. *A Validation Study of the Relationship of Size of High School and Certain Intellective Factors
to Academic Achievement in College.* Doctor's thesis, Indiana
University (Bloomington, Ind.), 1965. (*DA* 27:331A)
61. PETERSON, DONALD FREDERICK. *A Predictive Study of
Success in First Year Bookkeeping.* Master's thesis, San Diego
State College (San Diego, Calif.), 1965.
62. POPE, BILLY NEWTON. *Factorial Study of Teacher Marks
and Standardized Tests.* Doctor's thesis, University of Houston
(Houston, Tex.), 1965. (*DA* 26:6452)
63. SASSENRATH, JULIUS M. "The Factorial Composition of
the Iowa Tests of Educational Development." *Calif J Ed Res*
16:80–4 Mr '65. * (*PA* 39:10822)
64. SLAGLE, LLOYD T. *A Study of the Validity of Iowa Tests
of Educational Development Scores When Correlated With
Teachers' Needs.* Doctor's thesis, University of Tulsa (Tulsa,
Okla.), 1965.

65. THORDERSON, PARLEY E. *An Item Analysis Study of Selected Phases of the Language Responses of Eleventh Grade Students on the ITED.* Master's thesis, Utah State University (Logan, Utah), 1965.

66. ALLEN, JOYCE CARMEN YANDELL. *A Study of the Relationships Between Achievement and Intelligence Test Scores for Charleston High School Juniors and Seniors.* Master's thesis, Eastern Illinois University (Charleston, Ill.), 1966.

67. AYERS, LONNIE DOUGLAS. *An Evaluation of the Iowa Tests of Educational Development and the General Aptitude Test Battery for Predicting Academic Success at Cedar City High School.* Master's thesis, University of Utah (Salt Lake City, Utah), 1966.

68. BELK, FLOYD EDMOND. *The Construction of a Simple Instrument to Predict Junior College Freshmen Attrition.* Doctor's thesis, Oklahoma State University (Stillwater, Okla.), 1966. (*DA* 27:4061A)

69. CERWINSKE, JOE G. *Academic Growth of Students in an Iowa High School as Measured by the Iowa Test of Educational Development in 10th and 12th Grades.* Master's thesis, Drake University (Des Moines, Iowa), 1966.

70. COPPEDGE, FLOYD LEVON. *The Relationship of Selected Factors to Occupational and College Success.* Doctor's thesis, University of Oklahoma (Norman, Okla.), 1966 (*DA* 26:6441)

71. GADZELLA, BERNADETTE M., AND BENTALL, GRACE. "Differences in Mental Ability and Academic Achievement of Two Groups of High School Graduates." *J Ed Res* 60:104–6 N '66. *

72. LITHERLAND, RONALD LEE. *The Iowa Tests of Educational Development as a Predictor of Academic Success in Iowa Schools of Professional Nursing.* Doctor's thesis, University of Iowa (Iowa City, Iowa), 1966. (*DA* 27:1240A)

73. MAYHON, WOODROW G. *The Relationship of Creativity to Achievement and Other Student Variables.* Doctor's thesis, University of New Mexico (Albuquerque, N.M.), 1966. (*DA* 27:1713A)

74. WOMACK, RALPH HENRY. *An Exploration for Evidence of Construct Validity Within Selected Subtests of a Standardized Achievement Test Battery.* Doctor's thesis, University of Houston (Houston, Tex.), 1966. (*DA* 28:68A)

75. ABBOTT, GEORGE WILLIAM. *An Investigation of the Use of Results of the Iowa Test of Educational Development.* Master's thesis, Kearney State College (Kearney, Neb.), 1967.

76. CRITES, JOHN O., AND SEMLER, IRA J. "Adjustment, Educational Achievement, and Vocational Maturity as Dimensions of Development in Adolescence." *J Counsel Psychol* 14:489–96 N '67. * (*PA* 42:3783)

77. DONELSON, KENNETH L. "Variables Distinguishing Between Effective and Ineffective Writers in the Tenth Grade." *J Exp Ed* 35:37–41 su '67. *

78. EVANS, G. T. "Growth Factor Analysis of the Iowa Tests of Educational Development." *J Ed Meas* 4:179–90 f '67. * (*PA* 42:3194)

79. GARLAND, KENNETH EDWARD. *An Investigation of the Academic Achievement of Ninth Graders, With Varying Elementary School Backgrounds, From Selected Minnesota School Districts.* Doctor's thesis, University of Minnesota (Minneapolis, Minn.), 1967. (*DA* 28:2894A)

80. HENDRICKS, JAMES V. *The Iowa Tests of Educational Development as Predictors of Academic Success at Utah State University.* Master's thesis, Utah State University (Logan, Utah), 1967.

81. HILL, JAMES T. *A Longitudinal Study of the Iowa Tests of Educational Development Scores at the Ninth and Eleventh Grade Levels in the Franklin Pierce School.* Master's thesis, Pacific Lutheran University (Tacoma, Wash.), 1967.

82. MINETTI, GARY L. *The Composite Score on the Iowa Tests of Educational Development as a Predictor of Initial College Success.* Master's thesis, Pacific Lutheran University (Tacoma, Wash.), 1967.

83. SCHWALB, JOSEPH E. *An Analysis of Achievement Test Scores for Three Groups of Lakeview High School Students.* Master's thesis, Eastern Illinois University (Charleston, Ill.), 1967.

84. WOOD, SUSAN. *An Evaluation of Published English Tests,* pp. 41–5. Madison, Wis.: Wisconsin Department of Public Instruction, 1967. Pp. 91. *

85. YAMAMOTO, KAORU. "Creativity and Unpredictability in School Achievement." *J Ed Res* 60:321–5 Mr '67. *

86. BEERS, MORRIS I. *A Study of the Use of Correlations Between Computational Ability, Reading Comprehension, and Achievement in Algebra as a Method of Grouping Students in Algebra One.* Master's thesis, Western Connecticut State College (Danbury, Conn.), 1968.

87. CHANCELLOR, GEORGE A., JR. *Standardized Tests as Predictors of Academic Success in Either One or Two Forms of High School Biology.* Master's thesis, Stetson University (DeLand, Fla.), 1968.

88. COLGAN, RICHARD THOMAS. *A Longitudinal Study of the Relationship of Teacher Judgment Versus Objective Test Data With Respect to College Success.* Doctor's thesis, Southern Illinois University (Carbondale, Ill.), 1968. (*DA* 29:3413B)

89. FRANDSEN, ARDEN, AND SORENSON, MAURICE. "Interests as Motives in Academic Achievement." *J Sch Psychol* 7(1): 52–6 '68–69. * (*PA* 43:10415)

90. SABERS, DARRELL L., AND FELDT, LEONARD S. "The Predictive Validity of the Iowa Algebra Aptitude Test for Achievement in Modern Mathematics and Algebra." *Ed & Psychol Meas* 28:901–7 au '68. * (*PA* 43:4435)

91. TOCK, WILLIAM ANDREW. *The Relationship of Selected Educational Factors to Pupil Test Scores in English.* Doctor's thesis, University of Nebraska (Lincoln, Neb.), 1968. (*DA* 29:4258A)

92. WESSON, JANET C. *Predicting Success at Snyder High School in Geometry and Chemistry From the Iowa Tests of Educational Development.* Master's thesis, University of Alabama (University, Ala.), 1968.

93. COPPEDGE, FLOYD L. "Relation of Selected Variables from High School Records to Occupational and College Success." *J Ed Res* 63(2):71–3 O '69. *

94. DUNN, CHARLETA J. "A Statistical Analysis of Data Used in Critical Decision Making by Secondary School Personnel." *H Sch J* 52(4):199–205 Ja '69. *

95. HAMILTON, DOROTHY DEE HOWE. *A Comparison of School Achievement, Teachers' Ratings, Self-Ratings, and a Personality Score as Predictors of Creative Thinking Potential.* Doctor's thesis, University of Nebraska (Lincoln, Neb.), 1969. (*DAI* 30:2905A)

96. HARMAN, ROBERT LEE. *Predicting Persistence in College From Information in High School Cumulative Records.* Doctor's thesis, University of Nebraska (Lincoln, Neb.), 1969. (*DAI* 30:1397A)

97. HUSEMOLLER, KENNETH E. *The Prediction of Freshmen Academic Success at Eastern New Mexico University, Roswell, by Means of Selected Demographic and Standardized Tests Data.* Doctor's thesis, Colorado State College (Greeley, Colo.), 1969. (*DAI* 30:1467A)

98. LONNING, PHILIP EUGENE. *Characteristics of Full-Time Students Enrolled in Area II and Area V Community Colleges.* Doctor's thesis, Iowa State University (Ames, Iowa), 1969. (*DAI* 30:4779A)

99. MACCHIONE, RUDOLPH J. *The Relationship of Age, IQ, and Certain Scores on the Iowa Tests of Educational Development to Achievement Scores on the Tests for Programmed Business Mathematics.* Master's thesis, Northern Illinois University (DeKalb, Ill.), 1969.

100. MILLER, WILLIAM G. "Ability Grouping by Multiple Discriminant Analysis." *Fla J Ed Res* 11(1):25–37 Ja '69. *

101. PATRICK, WILLIAM H. *A Comparison of the Iowa Tests of Educational Development With Student Achievement as Predictors of Future Student Success in Mathematics.* Master's thesis, Central Washington State College (Ellensburg, Wash.), 1969.

102. RAJPAL, PURAN L. "Relationship Between Expenditures and Quality Characteristics of Education in Public Schools." *J Ed Res* 63(2):57–9 O '69. *

103. RICHTSMEIER, HERMAN L. *An Evaluation Using Behavioral Objectives of Test 4, "Ability to Do Quantitative Thinking" From Iowa Test of Educational Development.* Master's thesis, Drake University (Des Moines, Iowa), 1969.

104. STONE, THOMAS CARL. *A Case Study: Predictors of Success in Post-High School Vocational Trade, Industrial, and Technical Programs.* Doctor's thesis, Colorado State University (Ft. Collins, Colo.), 1969. (*DAI* 30:4348A)

105. TRONSUE, MARY ELIZABETH. *A Study of Relationships of Selected Variables With Shorthand Transcription Speed.* Doctor's thesis, University of Maryland (College Park, Md.), 1969. (*DAI* 30:1760A)

106. AUCKER, JOHN ROBERT. *The Prediction of Success in Vocational Education From Student Characteristics.* Doctor's thesis, University of Northern Colorado (Greeley, Colo.), 1970. (*DAI* 31:3864A)

107. CALDWELL, JAMES R.; MICHAEL, WILLIAM B.; SCHRADER, DONALD R.; AND MEYERS, C. E. "Comparative Validities and Working Times for Composites of Structure-of-Intellect Tests and Algebra Grades and Composites of Traditional Test Measures and Algebra Grades in the Prediction of Success in Tenth-Grade Geometry." *Ed & Psychol Meas* 30(4):955–9 w '70. *

108. CASSEL, RUSSELL N., AND KNOX, PATRICIA. "Improving High School Learning Predictions With Multiple Junior High Test Scores." *Calif J Ed Res* 21(1):14–20 Ja '70. *

109. HILPERT, FREDERICK MARTIN. *School District Norms for ITED Growth and Difference Scores and the Relationship of Student Achievement to Selected Environmental Characteristics.* Doctor's thesis, University of Iowa (Iowa City, Iowa), 1970. (*DAI* 31:4546A)

110. JERDONEK, AGNES CLARE. *Correlates of School-Average Science Achievement in the Secondary Schools of the Catholic Diocese of Cleveland.* Doctor's thesis, Case Western Reserve University (Cleveland, Ohio), 1970. (*DAI* 32:268A)

111. ARMSTRONG, KENNETH EUGENE. *A Comparative Validity Study of the General Aptitude Test Battery, Differential Aptitude Tests, and the Iowa Tests of Educational Development in Idaho Area Vocational Schools.* Doctor's thesis, University of Idaho (Moscow, Idaho), 1971. (*DAI* 32:3613B)

112. BRUE, ELDON J.; ENGEN, HAROLD B.; AND MAXEY, E. JAMES. "How Do Community College Transfer and Occupa-

tional Students Differ?" *ACT Res Rep* 41:1–33 F '71. * (*PA* 47:1775)

113. CARDWELL, JESSE FRANKLIN. *A Comparative Study of Intellectually Able Students Who Completed and Who Did Not Complete an Honors and Advanced Placement Program.* Doctor's thesis, George Peabody College for Teachers (Nashville, Tenn.), 1971. (*DAI* 32:1939A)

114. CORDES, JOHN HENRY. *An Analysis of Test Resistance in the ITED Testing Program.* Doctor's thesis, University of Iowa (Iowa City, Iowa), 1971. (*DAI* 32:1214A)

115. HOPKINS, KENNETH D., AND BRACHT, GLENN H. "A Longitudinal Study of Constancy of Reading Performance," pp. 103–12. In *Diagnostic Viewpoints in Reading.* Edited by Robert E. Leibert. Newark, Del.: International Reading Association, 1971. Pp. viii, 133. *

116. KENNEDY, MARY THERESA. *The Relationship of Achievement to Different Socio-Economic Status Levels for Selected Groups of Tenth Grade Students in a Public and a Private High School.* Doctor's thesis, Fordham University (New York, N.Y.), 1971. (*DAI* 32:1918A)

117. OMVIG, CLAYTON P. "Effects of Guidance on the Results of Standardized Achievement Testing." *Meas & Eval Guid* 4(1):47–52 Ap '71. *

118. PINKHAM, THOMAS C. *A Correlation of Academic Achievement as Measured by the Iowa Tests of Educational Development With Success of Varsity Players in Football in Iowa High Schools.* Master's thesis, University of North Dakota (Grand Forks, N.D.), 1971.

119. TURES, ROBERT STEPHEN. *The Analysis of Sex Differences in Intelligence, Achievement, Behavior, and Personality of the Same Student Sample at the Third and Tenth Grade Levels: A Longitudinal Study.* Doctor's thesis, West Virginia University (Morgantown, W.Va.), 1971. (*DAI* 32:4363A)

120. WHITNEY, DOUGLAS R., AND BOYD, NORLIN W. "Limiting Effect of Predictive Validity on the Expected Accuracy of Admissions Decisions." *Col & Univ* 46(3):180–90 sp '71. *

CUMULATIVE NAME INDEX

[21]

Ligondé Equivalence Test. Adults who left elementary or secondary school 15–20 years ago; 1967; LET; also called *School Equivalence Test;* Paultre Ligondé; Institute of Psychological Research, Inc. [Canada]. *

For additional information, see 7:13.

[22]

*Metropolitan Achievement Tests.** 1931–72; MAT; 2 editions; Walter N. Durost, Harold H. Bixler, J. Wayne Wrightstone, Gertrude H. Hildreth (*a*), Kenneth W. Lund (*a*), George A. Prescott (*b*), and Irving H. Balow (*b*); Harcourt Brace Jovanovich, Inc. *

a) 1958 EDITION. Grades 1.5–1.9, 2, 3–4, 5–6, 7–9; 1931–64; 5 levels; subtests in reading (grades 2–9) and arithmetic (grades 3–9) available as separates; partial batteries are available without science and social studies information (grades 5–9).

1) *Primary 1.* Grades 1.5–1.9; 4 scores: word knowledge, word discrimination, reading, arithmetic concepts and skills.

2) *Primary 2.* Grade 2; 7 scores: word knowledge, word discrimination, reading, spelling, arithmetic (concepts and problem solving, computation, total).

3) *Elementary.* Grades 3–4; 9 scores: word knowledge, word discrimination, reading, spelling, language (usage, punctuation and capitalization, total), arithmetic (computation, problem solving and concepts).

4) *Intermediate.* Grades 5–6; 13 scores: word knowledge, reading, spelling, language (usage, parts of speech, punctuation and capitalization, total), language study skills, arithmetic (computation, problem solving and concepts), social studies (study skills, information), science.

5) *Advanced.* Grades 7–9; 14 scores: same as for intermediate level plus kinds of sentences under language.

b) 1970 EDITION. Grades kgn–1.4, 1.5–2.4, 2.5–3.4, 3.5–4.9, 5.0–6.9, 7.0–9.5; 1931–72; 6 levels; subtests in reading (grades 2.5–9.5) and mathematics (grades 3.5–9.5) available as separates.

1) *Primer.* Grades kgn–1.4; 1971–72; 3 scores: listening for sounds, reading, numbers.

2) *Primary 1.* Grades 1.5–2.4; 1931–72; 5 scores: reading (word knowledge, reading, total), word analysis, mathematics.

3) *Primary 2.* Grades 2.5–3.4; 1932–72; 9 scores: reading (word knowledge, reading, total), word analysis, spelling, mathematics (computation, concepts, problem solving, total).

4) *Elementary.* Grades 3.5–4.9; 1932–72; 9 scores: reading (word knowledge, reading, total), language, spelling, mathematics (computation, concepts, problem solving, total).

5) *Intermediate.* Grades 5.0–6.9; 1932–71; 11 scores: reading (word knowledge, reading, total), language, spelling, mathematics (computation, concepts, problem solving, total), science, social studies.

6) *Advanced.* Grades 7.0–9.5; 1932–71; 11 scores: same as for intermediate level.

For additional information concerning the 1970 edition, see 7:14 (25 references); for reviews by Henry S. Dyer and Warren G. Findley of an earlier edition, see 6:15 (16 references); for a review by Warren G. Findley, see 4:18 (10 references); see also 3:13 (7 references); for reviews by E. V. Pullias and Hugh B. Wood, see 2:1189 (3 references); for reviews by Jack W. Dunlap, Charles W. Odell, and Richard Ledgerwood, see 1:874. For reviews of earlier editions of the arithmetic subtest, see 6:627 (2 reviews), 4:416 (1 review), 2:1458.1 (2 reviews), and 1:892 (2 reviews); the reading subtest, see 6:797 (1 review), 4:543 (2 reviews), 2:1551 (1 review), and 1:1105 (2 reviews); the science subtest, see 6:877 (2 reviews); and the social studies subtest, see 6:970 (2 reviews).

REFERENCES THROUGH 1971

1-3. See 2:1189.
4-10. See 3:13.
11-20. See 4:18.
21-36. See 6:15.
37-61. See 7:14.
62. NOTTINGHAM, RUTH D. "A Psychlogical Study of Forty Unmarried Mothers." *Genetic Psychol Monogr* 19:157-228 My '37. * (*PA* 11:4670)
63. HAYES, SAMUEL P. "A New Series of Achievement Tests for Use in Schools for the Blind." *Outl Blind* 43:1-6 Jan '49. * (*PA* 23:3432)
64. THORNDIKE, ROBERT L. "Community Variables as Predictors of Intelligence and Academic Achievement." *J Ed Psychol* 42:321-38 O '51. * (*PA* 26:5397)
65. BURKE, NORRIS F., AND ANDERSON, KENNETH E. "A Comparative Study of 1939 and 1950 Achievement Test Results in the Hawthorne Elementary School in Ottawa, Kansas." *J Ed Res* 47:19-33 S '53. * (*PA* 28:4930)
66. LOHNES, PAUL R., AND MARSHALL, THOMAS O. "Redundancy in Student Records." *Am Ed Res J* 2:19-23 Ja '65. *
67. FINLEY, CARMEN J. "How Well Can Teachers Judge Pupil Achievement? The Case of the Illusive Criterion." *Calif J Ed Res* 17:126-32 My '66. * (*PA* 40:10449)
68. PERSONKE, CARL. "Spelling Achievement of Scottish and American Children." *El Sch J* 66:337-43 Mr '66. * (*PA* 40:7010)
69. WOOD, SUSAN. *An Evaluation of Published English Tests*, pp. 47-53. Madison, Wis.: Wisconsin Department of Public Instruction, 1967. Pp. 91. *
70. PUGH, RICHARD C. "Tests for Creative Thinking—Potential for School Testing Programs." *B Sch Ed Ind Univ* 44(6): 1-30 N '68. * (*PA* 46:5483)
71. MACDONALD, H. A., AND NETHERTON, A. H. "Contribution of a Non-Verbal General Ability Test to the Educational Assessment of Pupils in the Cross-Cultural Setting of the Canadian North." *J Ed Res* 62(7):315-9 Mr '69. *
72. ANASTASIOW, NICHOLAS J.; STEDMAN, DONALD J.; AND SPAULDING, ROBERT L. "Language and Reading Achievement Among Disadvantaged Nursery and Primary Grade Children." *Slow Learning Child* (Australia) 17(1):39-51 Mr '70. * (*PA* 44:18316)
73. KAPEL, MARILYN B., AND KAPEL, DAVID E. "Hebrew English Reading Achievement in a Jewish Day School: A Comparison Among Reading Achievements and Attitudes Towards the Two Languages." *Jewish Ed* 40(3):23-32 w '70. *
74. DUROST, WALTER N. "Interpreting and Using Standardized Tests in the 70's: A View From One Man's Mountaintop." *Fla J Ed Res* 13:123-53 '71. *
75. GOOLSBY, THOMAS M., JR. "Appropriateness of Subtests in Achievement Tests Selection." *Ed & Psychol Meas* 31(4): 969-72 w '71. * (*PA* 48:1640)
76. HAMMILL, DONALD, AND WIEDERHOLT, J. LEE. "Appropriateness of the Metropolitan Tests in an Economically Deprived, Urban Neighborhood." *Psychol Sch* 8(1):49-50 Ja '71. * (*PA* 46:7446)
77. HANSEN, ROGER L. *The Effects of Social, Symbolic and Material Reinforcers on the Metropolitan Test Performance of Normal Primary II Pupils*. Doctor's thesis, University of Northern Colorado (Greeley, Colo.), 1971 (*DAI* 32:3787A)
78. JOHNSON, GERALDINE F. "Metropolitan Tests: Inappropriate for ESEA Pupils." *Integrated Ed* 9(6):22-6 N-D '71. *
79. MASON, GEORGE E., AND BLANTON, WILLIAM E. "Semantic Constructs and Beginning Reading." *Yearb Nat Read Conf* 19(1):39-45 '71. *
80. MYKLEBUST, HELMER R.; BANNOCHIE, MARGARET N.; AND KILLEN, JAMES R. Chap. 9, "Learning Disabilities and Cognitive Processes," pp. 213-51. In *Progress in Learning Disabilities, Vol. 2*. Edited by Helmer R. Myklebust. New York: Grune & Stratton, Inc., 1971. Pp. ix, 404. *
81. SWIZE, MYRON THEODORE. *Prediction of Piagetian Conservation for Second Grade Mexican-American and Anglo-American Children*. Doctor's thesis, University of Northern Colorado (Greeley, Colo.), 1971. (*DAI* 32:5624A)

[23]

National Achievement Tests. Grades 4-6, 7-9; 1954-62; 4 scores: language, mathematics, social studies-science-health, total; 2 levels; Lester D. Crow, Alice Crow, and William H. Bristow (b); Psychometric Affiliates. *

a) INTERMEDIATE BATTERY. Grades 4-6; 1957-62; 1960 test identical with test copyrighted 1957 except for revision in 1 item, item sequence, and response procedure.
b) ADVANCED BATTERY. Grades 7-9; 1954-57; 1957 manual identical with manual copyrighted 1955.

For additional information, see 6:16; for a review by William E. Coffman, see 5:19.

[24]

***National Educational Development Tests.** Grades 7-8, 9-10; 1959-73, c1959-72; NEDT; tests administered annually in February and October by individual schools; 7 scores: English usage, mathematics usage, social studies reading, natural sciences reading, word usage, total, learning ability; 2 levels; Test of Learning Ability by Thelma Gwinn Thurstone; Science Research Associates, Inc. *

a) LEVEL 1. Grades 7-8; 1963-73, c1963-72.
b) LEVEL 2. Grades 9-10; 1959-73, c1959-72; test booklet includes the optional *Educational Planning Ques-*

tionnaire (also called *Counselor's Program Questionnaire*) by Samuel A. Stouffer.

For additional information concerning earlier forms, see 7:16 (2 references); for reviews by Willis W. Clark, Arthur E. Traxler, and Alexander G. Wesman of Level 2, see 6:17.

REFERENCES THROUGH 1971

1-2. See 7:16.
3. SUMMERS, BARBARA L. *A Study of Predictive Devices for Placement in Ninth-Grade English and Algebra Classes for Wheaton Community High School-Central.* Master's thesis, Northern Illinois University (DeKalb, Ill.), 1964.

CUMULATIVE NAME INDEX

Clark, W. W.: *rev,* 6:17   Tolor, A.: 2
Kushinka, M.: 1   Traxler, A. E.: *rev,* 6:17
Summers, B. L.: 3   Wesman, A. G.: *rev,* 6:17

[25]

*National Teacher Examinations: Common Examinations.** College seniors and teachers; 1940–73; 7 scores: professional education, subtotal, general education (English expression, social studies-literature-the fine arts, science and mathematics, subtotal), total; a modification of an inactive form (1966), entitled *Teacher Education Examination Program: General Professional Examinations,* is available to colleges for local administration; another inactive form (1970) is available to school systems for local use as part of the program entitled *School Personnel Research and Evaluation Services;* Educational Testing Service. * For the testing program entry, see 869.

For additional information concerning earlier forms, see 7:582a. For reviews of the testing program, see 7:582 (2 reviews), 6:700 (1 review), 5:538 (3 reviews), and 4:802 (1 review).

[26]

Peabody Individual Achievement Test. Grades kgn–12; 1970; PIAT; 6 scores: mathematics, reading recognition, reading comprehension, spelling, general information, total; Lloyd M. Dunn and Frederick C. Markwardt, Jr.; American Guidance Service, Inc. *

For additional information, a review by Joseph L. French, and an excerpted review by Howard B. Lyman, see 7:17.

REFERENCES THROUGH 1971

1. PROGER, BARTON B. "Peabody Individual Achievement Test: A Review." *J Spec Ed* 4(4):461–7 f-w '70. * (*PA* 47: 5624)
2. SITLINGTON, PATRICIA L. *Validity of the Peabody Individual Achievement Test for Educable Mentally Retarded Adolescents.* Master's thesis, University of Hawaii (Honolulu, Hawaii), 1970.

CUMULATIVE NAME INDEX

French, J. L.: *rev,* 7:17   Proger, B. B.: 1
Lyman, H. B.: *exc,* 7:17   Sitlington, P. L.: 2

[27]

★[**Primary Survey Tests.**] Grades 2, 3; 1973; 4 scores: reading, spelling, language, mathematics; subtests in reading and mathematics available as separates; 2 levels; E. Glenadine Gibb, Kenneth S. Goodman, John C. Manning, Marion Monroe, Andrew Schiller, and Joseph M. Wepman; Scott, Foresman & Co. *
a) EARLY PRIMARY SURVEY TEST. Grade 2.
b) LATE PRIMARY SURVEY TEST. Grade 3.

[28]

Public School Achievement Tests. Grades 3–8; 1928–61; subtests in reading, arithmetic computation, and arithmetic reasoning available as separates; 7 scores: reading, arithmetic computation, arithmetic reasoning, language usage, spelling, grammar (grades 6–8

only), total; 1959 and 1961 tests identical with tests copyrighted 1928 except for addition of the grammar subtest in both forms; 1959 manual essentially the same —including norms—as 1928 manual; Jacob S. Orleans; Bobbs-Merrill Co., Inc. *

For additional information, see 6:19 (2 references); for reviews by Herbert S. Conrad and E. V. Pullias, see 2:1194.

REFERENCES THROUGH 1971

1-2. See 6:19.
3. COERS, WALTER CLARENCE. *Comparative Achievement of White and Mexican Junior High School Pupils.* Master's thesis, George Peabody College for Teachers (Nashville, Tenn.), 1933.
4. COERS, WALTER C. "Comparative Achievement of White and Mexican Junior High School Pupils." *Peabody J Ed* 12: 157–62 Ja '35. * (*PA* 9:2957)

CUMULATIVE NAME INDEX

Coers, W. C.: 3–4   Pullias, E. V.: 2; *rev,* 2:1194
Conrad, H. S.: *rev,* 2:1194   Wilson, G. M.: 1
Parsons, A. R.: 1

[29]

*SRA Achievement Series.** Grades 1–9; 1954–73; 2 editions; Robert A. Naslund, Louis P. Thorpe, and D. Welty Lefever; Science Research Associates, Inc. *
a) FORMS C AND D. Grades 4–9; 1954–69; tests for grades 1–4 are out of print; 14 or 17 scores: social studies, science, language arts (capitalization and punctuation, grammatical usage, spelling, total), arithmetic (reasoning, concepts, computation, total), reading (comprehension, vocabulary, total), total, plus optional work-study skills (references, charts, total); *SRA Modern Math Understanding Test* (see 7:485) may be used as a substitute for the arithmetic subtest; 3 levels: blue (grades 4.5–6.5), green (grades 6.5–8.5), and red (grades 8.5–9) in a single booklet (except work-study skills); subtests available as separates.
b) FORMS E AND F. Grades 1–3, 2–4, 4–5, 6–7, 8–9; 1954–73; *SRA Assessment Survey* is title used by publisher for combination of these forms and Forms X5 and Y5 of *The Iowa Tests of Educational Development,* which together cover the grade range 1–12.
 1) *Primary Edition.* Grades 1–3, 2–4; 1955–73; 4 scores (reading, language arts, mathematics, composite) plus 28 or 30 optional skill scores; 2 levels.
   (*a*) Primary 1. Grades 1–3; 1958–73.
   (*b*) Primary 2. Grades 2–4; 1955–73.
 2) *Multilevel Edition.* Grades 4–5, 6–7, 8–9; 1955–73; 10–13 scores [reading (comprehension, vocabulary, total), language arts (usage, spelling, total), mathematics (concepts, computation, total), composite, social studies (optional), science (optional), use of sources (optional)] plus 40 optional skill scores; 3 overlapping levels in a single booklet.
   (*a*) Blue Level. Grades 4–5.
   (*b*) Green Level. Grades 6–7.
   (*c*) Red Level. Grades 8–9.

For additional information and reviews by Miriam M. Bryan and Fred M. Smith of Forms C and D, see 7:18 (9 references); for a review by Jacob S. Orleans of earlier forms, see 6:21 (3 references); for reviews by Warren G. Findley and Worth R. Jones, see 5:21. For reviews of earlier forms of the arithmetic subtest, see 6:632 (1 review) and 5:483 (2 reviews); the reading subtest, see 6:808 (1 review) and 5:649 (2 reviews); the language arts subtest, see 5:200 (2 reviews); and the work-study skills subtest, see 5:696 (2 reviews).

REFERENCES THROUGH 1971

1-3. See 6:21.
4-12. See 7:18.

National Educational Development Tests

13. THOMPSON, LOWELL H. *The Critical Thinking Ability of New School Sixth Grade Students.* Doctor's thesis, University of North Dakota (Grand Forks, N.D.), 1970. (*DAI* 31:4609A)

14. BARNES, JEROME MEDWICK. *An Analysis of the Education of the Children of Migrant Agricultural Workers in Arkansas Public Schools.* Doctor's thesis, North Texas State University (Denton, Tex.), 1971. (*DAI* 32:1738A)

15. TAYLOR, ALTON L. "Regression Analysis of Antecedent Measures of Slow Sections in High School Biology." *Sci Ed* 55(3):395–402 Jl–S '71. *

CUMULATIVE NAME INDEX

Barnes, J. M.: 14	Hopkins, K. D.: 4–5
Barz, A. I.: 10	Jones, W. R.: *rev,* 5:21
Bryan, M. M.: *rev,* 7:18	Lemke, E. A.: 8
Cawley, J. F.: 9	Meinke, D. L.: 8
Crandall, J. H.: 3	Neale, D. C.: 12
Findley, W. G.: 2; *rev,* 5:21	Orleans, J. S.: *rev,* 6:21
Garlock, J. C.: 1	Smith, F. M.: *rev,* 7:18
Gill, N.: 12	Tagatz, G. E.: 8
Goodman, J. O.: 9	Taylor, A. L.: 6, 15
Harsh, J. R.: 1	Taylor, E. A.: 3
Hayes, E. M.: 11	Thompson, L. H.: 13
Hickey, D. E.: 7	Tismer, W.: 12

[30]

*SRA Assessment Survey. Grades 1–3, 2–4, 4–5, 6–7, 8–9, 9–12; 1973, c1942–73; a title used by the publisher for the combination of the current revisions of *SRA Achievement Series* and *The Iowa Tests of Educational Development;* Science Research Associates, Inc. *

a) SRA ACHIEVEMENT SERIES. Grades 1–3, 2–4, 4–5, 6–7, 8–9; 1954–73; Forms E and F. See 29.

b) IOWA TESTS OF EDUCATIONAL DEVELOPMENT. Grades 9–12; 1942–72; Forms X5 and Y5. See 20.

[31]

*SRA High School Placement Test. Entering ninth grade students; 1957–73; 7 or 8 scores: educational ability, reading, language arts, arithmetic or modern mathematics, total, social studies, science methodology, Catholic religion (optional); new form published annually; Science Research Associates, Inc. *

For additional information concerning the 1970 form, see 7:19 (8 references); for reviews by Walter N. Durost and Charles O. Neidt of earlier forms, see 6:22 (3 references); for reviews by Cyril J. Hoyt (with W. Wesley Tennyson) and William W. Turnbull, see 5:22.

REFERENCES THROUGH 1971

1–3. See 6:22.
4–11. See 7:19.

12. KIZIOR, EUGENIA A. *A Study of Factors That Aid in the Prediction of Secondary School Foreign Language Achievement.* Master's thesis, Northwestern University (Evanston, Ill.), 1965.

13. BUIKEMA, ROGER J. *The Development of a Multiple Regression Equation for Predicting Ninth Grade English Grades at Morrison Community High School.* Master's thesis, Northern Illinois University (DeKalb, Ill.), 1967.

CUMULATIVE NAME INDEX

Bauernfeind, R. H.: 2–3	Marini, J. L.: 10
Blumenfeld, W. S.: 2–4	Neidt, C. O.: *rev,* 6:22
Buikema, R. J.: 13	Simmer, L.: 7
Durost, M. N.: *rev,* 6:22	Tennyson, W. W.: *rev,* 5:22
Giles, G. C.: 5	Turnbull, W. W.: *rev,* 5:22
Gruber, E. C.: 1	Waldron, C.: 8
Hoyt, C. J.: *rev,* 5:22	Wickiser, R.: 7
Impellitteri, J. T.: 6, 11	Wittmer, R. E.: 9
Kizior, E. A.: 12	

[32]

*STS Closed High School Placement Test. Grade 9 entrants; 1955–72; 7 scores: ability (verbal, quantitative, total), skills (reading, modern mathematics or traditional arithmetic, language), composite; new series issued annually; Scholastic Testing Service, Inc. *

For additional information concerning an earlier series, see 7:21 (2 references); for reviews by Marion F. Shaycoft and James R. Hayden, see 6:6; for reviews

by William C. Cottle and Robert A. Jones of the 1955 "open" test, see 5:15.

REFERENCES THROUGH 1971

1–2. See 7:21.

CUMULATIVE NAME INDEX

Cottle, W. C.: *rev,* 5:15	Jones, R. A.: *rev,* 5:15
Dodson, R. G.: 1	Shaycoft, M. F.: *rev,* 6:6
Hayden, J. R.: *rev,* 6:6	Westphal, J. H.: 2

[33]

*STS Educational Development Series: Scholastic Tests. Grades 2–3, 3–4, 4–6, 6–9, 9–12; 1963–73; EDS; a battery of ability and achievement tests and questions on interests and plans; 14 reports and scores for grades 4–12: 3 interest areas (school plans, career plans, school interests), 3 ability scores (verbal, nonverbal, total), 7 achievement scores (reading, English, mathematics, basic skills total, science, social studies, everyday problems), composite of ability and achievement scores; 9 reports and scores for grades 2–4: omitting school plans, career plans, science, social studies, and everyday problems; a basic skills battery (reading, English, and mathematics), a core achievement battery (reading, English, mathematics, science, and social studies), and an ability/skills battery (verbal, nonverbal, reading, English, and mathematics) are also available as separates (except for primary levels for which only the basic skills battery is available separately); Scholastic Testing Service, Inc. *

For additional information and a review by Robert D. North, see 7:22.

REFERENCES THROUGH 1971

1. MAGRUDER, ALAN WILLETT. *A Study of the Stability of Career Choices, School Plans and Interests of Students During the Secondary School Years, With Special Emphasis on the Factors Related With Instability.* Doctor's thesis, St. Louis University (St. Louis, Mo.), 1970. (*DAI* 32:849A)

CUMULATIVE NAME INDEX

Magruder, A. W.: 1	North, R. D.: *rev,* 7:22

[34]

*Scholastic Proficiency Battery. Standards 8–10; 1969–71; SPB; 5 scores: social sciences, commercial sciences, natural sciences, arithmetic, languages (either English or Afrikaans); F. A. Fouché, N. F. Alberts, and V. H. Paul (test); Human Sciences Research Council [South Africa]. *

For additional information, see 7:23.

[35]

*Sequential Tests of Educational Progress. Grades 4–6, 7–9, 10–12, 13–14; 1956–72; STEP; subtests available as separates; 2 editions; Cooperative Tests and Services. *

a) ORIGINAL SERIES [70 MINUTE TESTS]. 1956–63; 7 tests: reading, writing, mathematics, science, social studies, listening, essay (out of print); Braille and large type editions (grades 4–12) are available from American Printing House for the Blind, Inc.

b) SERIES 2 [40–60 MINUTE TESTS]. 1956–72, c1956–71; 7 tests, 9 scores: English expression, reading, mechanics of writing (spelling, capitalization and punctuation, total), mathematics computation, mathematics basic concepts, science, social studies.

For additional information and reviews by Harold Seashore and John E. Stecklein of *a,* see 6:25 (6 references); for reviews by Robert W. B. Jackson and Wilbur L. Layton and an excerpted review by Laurence Siegel, see 5:24. For reviews of the original edition of the writing test, see 6:292 (2 reviews, 1 excerpt) and 5:207 (3 reviews); the mathematics test, see 6:590 (2 reviews) and 5:438 (3 reviews); the reading test, see

6:810 (2 reviews) and 5:653 (3 reviews) ; the science test, see 6:882 (2 reviews) and 5:716 (3 reviews) ; the social studies test, see 6:971 (2 reviews) and 5:792 (3 reviews) ; the essay test, see 5:206 (3 reviews) ; and the listening test, see 5:578 (2 reviews).

REFERENCES THROUGH 1971

1-6. See 6:25.

7. BATES, CHARLES O. *A Study of Creative Potential as Found in Elementary Student Teachers.* Doctor's thesis, Ball State Teachers College (Muncie, Ind.), 1963. (*DA* 24:4561)

8. SMITH, FREDERICK R. "The Academic Achievement of Academically Talented Students." *J Ed Res* 56:255–9 Ja '63. *

9. BONEY, JEW DON. *A Study of the Use of Intelligence Aptitude, and Mental Ability Measures in Predicting the Academic Achievement of Negro Students in Secondary School.* Doctor's thesis, University of Texas (Austin, Tex.), 1964. (*DA* 25:5726)

10. ENDLER, NORMAN S. "Factors Related to the Prediction of Academic Success." *Ont J Ed Res* (Canada) 7:147–54 w '64–65. *

11. EVANS, RICHARD WILLIAM. *The School Counselor and Objective Measures as Predictors of High School Achievement and Relationship of Load to Achievement.* Doctor's thesis, Rutgers—The State University (New Brunswick, N.J.), 1964. (*DA* 25:2848)

12. HAUGEN, EARL STUART. *A Study of the Validity of the WAIS, SCAT, and STEP as Predictors of Success in College Mathematics.* Doctor's research study No. 1, Colorado State College (Greeley, Colo.), 1964. (*DA* 28:124A)

13. HOPKINS, KENNETH D. "Extrinsic Reliability: Estimating and Attenuating Variance From Response Styles, Chance, and Other Irrelevant Sources." *Ed & Psychol Meas* 24:271–81 su '64. * (*PA* 39:3152)

14. QUINLAN, CLAIRE A. *The Prediction of Freshman Academic Success at Colorado State College by Means of Selected Standardized Tests and Admission Data.* Doctor's research study No. 1, Colorado State College (Greeley, Colo.), 1964. (*DA* 25:5124)

15. FELDHUSEN, JOHN F.; DENNY, TERRY; AND CONDON, CHARLES F. "Anxiety, Divergent Thinking, and Achievement." *J Ed Psychol* 56:40–5 F '65. * (*PA* 39:10771)

16. HOLTBY, VANITA J. *A Set of Expectancy Tables for Use With SCAT-STEP Tests at Lewis and Clark Junior High School, Omaha, Nebraska.* Master's thesis, University of Kansas (Lawrence, Kan.), 1965.

17. LEEP, ALBERT GENE. *Selected Pre-Service Measures as Predictors of First Year Teaching Performance of Elementary Teachers.* Doctor's thesis, Ball State Teachers College (Muncie, Ind.), 1965. (*DA* 26:3163)

18. MORRIS, ROBERT O. *A Study of the Effects of Test Sequence on the Results of the SCAT-STEP Test Battery.* Master's thesis, University of Washington (Seattle, Wash.), 1965.

19. WALLACH, MICHAEL A., AND KOGAN, NATHAN. *Modes of Thinking in Young Children: A Study of the Creativity-Intelligence Distinction,* pp. 25–65. New York: Henry Holt & Winston, Inc., 1965. Pp. ix, 357. * (*PA* 40:429, title only)

20. BYLER, JESSE THOMAS. *The Relative Influence of Selected Variables in Determining Level of Vocational Preference.* Doctor's thesis, University of Virginia (Charlottesville, Va.), 1966. (*DA* 27:2385A) (Abstract: *Ed R* 4:56–8)

21. IRVINE, DONALD W. "Relationships Between the STEP Tests and Overachievement/Underachievement." *J Ed Res* 59:294–6 Mr '66. * (*PA* 40:10452)

22. MEANS, HESTER RICE. *An Analysis of the First Freshman Class of the DeKalb Junior College.* Doctor's thesis, University of Georgia (Athens, Ga.), 1966. (*DA* 27:1552A)

23. COYLE, PAUL J. "A Study of the Predictive Validity of the Sequential Tests of Educational Progress." Abstract. *J Sch Psychol* 5:317–8 su '67. *

24. GRECO, GERALDINE F. *A Study of STEP and SCAT as Predictors of School Achievement.* Master's thesis, Central Connecticut State College (New Britain, Conn.), 1967.

25. HILTON, THOMAS L., AND MYERS, ALBERT E. "Personal Background, Experience and School Achievement: An Investigation of the Contribution of Questionnaire Data to Academic Prediction." *J Ed Meas* 4:69–80 su '67. * (*PA* 42:4570)

26. TENOPYR, MARY L. "Symbolic Tests as Predictors of High-School Grades." *Ed & Psychol Meas* 27:385–91 su '67. * (*PA* 41:14227)

27. TRISMEN, DONALD A. "Equating Braille Forms of the Sequential Tests of Educational Progress." *Excep Children* 33:419–24 F '67. *

28. TUCKER, WILLIAM FRANCIS. *The Prediction of Achievement in Selected High School Subjects From Junior High School Data.* Doctor's thesis, New York University (New York, N.Y.), 1967. (*DA* 28:1317A)

29. WARD, JAMES. "An Oblique Factorization of Wallach and Kogan's 'Creativity' Correlations." *Brit J Ed Psychol* 37:380–2 N '67. * (*PA* 42:4784)

30. BLAI, BORIS, JR. "Measuring Educational Progress Through 'Before' and 'After' Testing." *Psychol* 5:39–41 My '68. * (*PA* 42:14567)

31. FEE, FRANCIS. "An Alternative to Ward's Factor Analysis

of Wallach and Kogan's 'Creativity' Correlations." Comment by James Ward. *Brit J Ed Psychol* 38:319–21 N '68. * (*PA* 43:6128)

32. FISHER, RHEUA DALE SPICKELMIER. *A Study of Grades and Test Scores in a Selective Admissions Program for Teacher Education.* Doctor's thesis, Oklahoma State University (Stillwater, Okla.), 1968. (*DAI* 30:986A)

33. MEDLER, BYRON WAYNE. *A Comparative Study of Selected Variables Between Students Completing the Elementary Education Curriculum and Those Students Who Left the Elementary Education Curriculum Due to Academic Disqualification or Change of Major.* Doctor's thesis, Ball State University (Muncie, Ind.), 1968. (*DA* 29:3503A)

34. CUNNINGHAM, ROOSEVELT. *A Study to Determine Whether There Were Any Relationships Between High School Grade Point Averages and SCAT and STEP Tests.* Master's thesis, Virginia State College (Petersburg, Va.), 1969.

35. HALL, LUCIEN TALMAGE, JR. *The Prediction of Success in Each of Six Four-Year Selections of Secondary Mathematics Courses.* Doctor's thesis, University of Virginia (Charlottesville, Va.), 1969. (*DAI* 30:4141A)

36. SUTHERLAND, KELLEY. *The Predictive Value of School and College Ability Test, Sequential Test of Educational Progress, Differential Aptitude Test, Iowa Silent Reading Test, and California Test of Mental Maturity Scores at Clintwood High School, Clintwood, Virginia.* Master's thesis, East Tennessee State University (Johnson City, Tenn.), 1969.

37. FELDHUSEN, JOHN F.; TREFFINGER, DONALD J.; AND ELIAS, ROBERT M. "Prediction of Academic Achievement With Divergent and Convergent Thinking and Personality Variables." *Psychol Sch* 7(1):46–52 Ja '70. * (*PA* 44:11410)

38. LIBBY, WILLIAM L., JR. "Reaction Time and Remote Association in Talented Male Adolescents." *Develop Psychol* 3(3):285–97 N '70. * (*PA* 45:4001)

39. HALL, LUCIEN T., JR. "The Prediction of Success in Each of Six Four-Year Selections of Secondary Mathematics Courses." *Sch Sci & Math* 71(8):693–6 N '71. *

40. ROSENFELD, MICHAEL, AND HILTON, THOMAS L. "Negro-White Differences in Adolescent Educational Growth." *Am Ed Res J* 8(2):267–83 Mr '71. *

41. TAYLOR, ALTON L. "Regression Analysis of Antecedent Measures of Slow Sections in High School Biology." *Sci Ed* 55(3):395–402 Jl–S '71. *

42. TISDALE, JOSEPH CHRISTOPHER, III. *Prediction of Success in First-Year Community College Mathematics.* Doctor's thesis, University of Virginia (Charlottesville, Va.), 1971. (*DAI* 32:4485A)

43. WEBB, HAROLD QUENTIN. *The Prognostic Potential of Selected Factors for Predicting Achievement in the Study of High School Bookkeeping and Accounting.* Doctor's thesis, Ohio State University (Columbus, Ohio), 1971. (*DAI* 32:3645A)

CUMULATIVE NAME INDEX

[36]

*Stanford Achievement Test. 1923–74; SAT; 2 editions; Richard Madden, Eric F. Gardner, Herbert C. Rudman, Truman L. Kelley (*a*), Bjorn Karlsen (*b*), and Jack C. Merwin (*b*) ; Harcourt Brace Jovanovich, Inc. *

a) 1964 EDITION. Grades 1.5–2.4, 2.5–3.9, 4.0–5.4, 5.5–6.9, 7.0–9.9; 1923–68; subtests in spelling and language, arithmetic, reading, science, and social studies available as separates; partial batteries are available without science and social studies (grades 4.0–9.9); 5 levels; Braille and large type editions (grades 2.5–9.9) are available from American Printing House for the Blind, Inc.

1) *Primary 1 Battery*. Grades 1.5–2.4; 6 scores: word reading, paragraph meaning, vocabulary, spelling, word study skills, arithmetic.

2) *Primary 2 Battery*. Grades 2.5–3.9; 8 scores: word meaning, paragraph meaning, science and social studies concepts, spelling, word study skills, language, arithmetic computation, arithmetic concepts.

3) *Intermediate 1 Battery*. Grades 4.0–5.4; 10 scores: word meaning, paragraph meaning, spelling, word study skills, language, arithmetic computation, arithmetic concepts, arithmetic applications, social studies, science.

4) *Intermediate 2 Battery*. Grades 5.5–6.9; 9 scores: same as for Intermediate 1 Battery except for omission of word study skills.

5) *Advanced Battery*. Grades 7.0–9.9; 8 scores: same as for Intermediate 1 Battery except for omission of word meaning and word study skills.

b) 1973 EDITION. Grades 1.5–2.4, 2.5–3.4, 3.5–4.4, 4.5–5.4, 5.5–6.9, 7.0–9.5; 1923–74; subtests in mathematics and reading available as separates; partial batteries are available without science, social science, and listening comprehension (grades 2.5–6.9), without science and social science (grades 7.0–9.5); 6 levels.

1) *Primary Level 1*. Grades 1.5–2.4; 12 or 13 scores: reading (word, comprehension, word plus comprehension), word study skills, total, mathematics (concepts, computation and applications, total), auditory (vocabulary, listening comprehension, total), total, spelling (optional).

2) *Primary Level 2*. Grades 2.5–3.4; 16 scores: reading (word, comprehension, word plus comprehension), word study skills, total, mathematics (concepts, computation, applications, total), spelling, social science, science, auditory (vocabulary, listening comprehension, total), total.

3) *Primary Level 3*. Grades 3.5–4.4; 15 scores: reading comprehension, word study skills, total, mathematics (concepts, computation, applications, total), spelling, language, social science, science, auditory (vocabulary, listening comprehension, total), total.

4) *Intermediate Level 1*. Grades 4.5–5.4; 15 scores: same as for Primary Level 3.

5) *Intermediate Level 2*. Grades 5.5–6.9; 15 scores: same as for Primary Level 3.

6) *Advanced*. Grades 7.0–9.5; 12 scores: vocabulary, reading comprehension, total, mathematics (concepts, computation, applications, total), spelling, language, social science, science, total.

For additional information and an excerpted review by Peter F. Merenda of the 1964 edition, see 7:25 (44 references); for a review by Miriam M. Bryan and an excerpted review by Robert E. Stake (with J. Thomas Hastings), see 6:26 (13 references); for a review by N. L. Gage of an earlier edition, see 5:25 (19 references); for reviews by Paul R. Hanna (with Claude E. Norcross) and Virgil E. Herrick, see 4:25 (20 references); for reviews by Walter W. Cook and Ralph C. Preston, see 3:18 (33 references). For reviews of the spelling and language subtest, see 7:209 (2 reviews); the 1964 edition of the arithmetic subtest, see 7:527 (1 review); earlier editions of the arithmetic subtest, see 6:637 (1 review) and 4:419 (1 review); the 1964 edition of the reading subtest, see 7:708 (1 review); earlier editions of the reading subtest, see 5:656 (2 reviews), 4:555 (1 review), and 3:503 (1 review);

the science subtest, see 7:802 (1 review); an earlier edition of the science subtest, see 4:593 (2 reviews); the social studies subtest, see 7:895 (1 review); earlier editions of the social studies subtest, see 5:799 (1 review) and 3:595 (1 review); and an earlier edition of the study skills subtest, see 5:698 (2 reviews).

REFERENCES THROUGH 1971

1–34. See 3:18.
35–54. See 4:25.
55–73. See 5:25.
74–86. See 6:26.
87–130. See 7:25.
131. KELLEY, TRUMAN L. "Distinctive Ability." *Sch & Soc* 18:424–8 O 13 '23. *
132. GATES, ARTHUR I.; ASSISTED BY GRACE A. TAYLOR, ELOISE BOEKER, AND DOROTHY VAN ALSTYNE. "The Nature and Educational Significance of Physical Status and of Mental, Physiological, Social and Emotional Maturity." *J Ed Psychol* 15:329–58 S '24. *
133. MERRILL, MAUD A. "On the Relation of Intelligence to Achievement in the Case of Mentally Retarded Children." *Comp Psychol Monogr* 2(10):1–100 S '24. *
134. DeVoss, JAMES C. Chap. 12, "Specialization of the Abilities of Gifted Children," pp. 307–62. In *Genetic Studies of Genius: Vol. 1, Mental and Physical Traits of a Thousand Gifted Children*. By Lewis M. Terman. Palo Alto, Calif.: Stanford University Press, 1925. Pp. xv, 648. *
135. FRANZEN, CARL G. F., AND YOUNG, HERMAN H. "An Experiment in Interference and Learning in Giving the Stanford Achievement Tests." *Ann Conf Ed Meas* 11:3–9 '25. *
136. HILDRETH, GERTRUDE HOWELL. "The Resemblance of Siblings in Intelligence and Achievement." *Teach Col Contrib Ed* 186:1–65 '25. *
137. TERMAN, LEWIS M. *Genetic Studies of Genius: Vol. 1, Mental and Physical Traits of a Thousand Gifted Children*, pp. 289–306. Palo Alto, Calif.: Stanford University Press, 1925. Pp. xv, 648. *
138. WILSON, G. M. "Standard Deviations of Age Scores and Quotients in Typical Groups." *J Ed Psychol* 16:193–207 Mr '25. *
139. COURTIS, S. A. "The Influence of Certain Social Factors Upon Scores in the Stanford Achievement Tests." *J Ed Res* 13:311–24 My; 14:33–42 Je '26. * (*PA* 1:691)
140. DARSIE, MARVIN L. "The Mental Capacity of American-Born Japanese Children." *Comp Psychol Monogr* 3(15):1–89 Ja '26. * (*PA* 1:133)
141. WILSON, F. T. "Some Achievements of Pupils of the Same Mental Ages but Different Intelligence Quotients." *J Ed Res* 14:43–53 Je '26. *
142. WRIGHT, WENDELL W. "A Cooperative Project." *Ann Conf Ed Meas* 13:80–9 '26. *
143. WALTERS, FRED C. "A Statistical Study of Certain Aspects of the Time Factor in Intelligence." *Teach Col Contrib Ed* 248:1–82 '27. *
144. WILLOUGHBY, RAYMOND ROYCE. "Family Similarities in Mental-Test Abilities (With a Note on the Growth and Decline of These Abilties)." *Genetic Psychol Monogr* 2:237–77 Jl '27. * (*PA* 2:112)
145. WITTY, PAUL A., AND DECKER, A. I. "A Comparative Study of the Educational Attainment of Negro and White Children." *J Ed Psychol* 18:497–500 O '27. * (*PA* 2:482)
146. BALDWIN, BIRD T. "The Educational Growth of Elementary School Children." *J Ed Psychol* 19:521–35 N '28. * (*PA* 3:903)
147. BRUENE, E. "Effect of the Summer Vacation on the Achievement of Pupils in the Fourth, Fifth and Sixth Grades." *J Ed Res* 18:309–14 N '28. * (*PA* 3:911)
148. COMMINS, W. D. "More About Sex Differences." *Sch & Soc* 28:599–600 N 10 '28. * (*PA* 3:968)
149. DENWORTH, KATHARINE M. "The Effect of Length of School Attendance Upon Mental and Educational Ages." *Yearb Nat Soc Study Ed* 27(2):67–91 '28. * (*PA* 2:2608)
150. ECKERT, DANA Z. "Report on the Stanford Achievement Test." *Pittsburgh Sch* 3:40–122 N–D '28. *
151. HOEFER, CAROLYN, AND HARDY, MATTIE CRUMPTON. "The Influence of Improvement in Physical Condition on Intelligence and Educational Achievement." *Yearb Nat Soc Study Ed* 27(1):371–87 '28. * (*PA* 2:2342)
152. McDOWELL, ELIZABETH DICKINSON. "Educational and Emotional Adjustments of Stuttering Children." *Teach Col Contrib Ed* 314:1–59 '28. * (*PA* 3:299)
153. WILLOUGHBY, RAYMOND R. "Family Similarities in Mental-Test Abilities." *Yearb Nat Soc Study Ed* 27(1):55–9 '28. * (*PA* 2:1513)
154. CHAUNCEY, MARLIN R. "The Relation of the Home Factor to Achievement and Intelligence Test Scores." *J Ed Res* 20:88–90 S '29. * (*PA* 3:4672)
155. LENTZ, THEO. F., JR. "Sex Differences in School Marks With Achievement Test Scores Constant." *Sch & Soc* 29:65–8 Ja 12 '29. * (*PA* 3:1703)
156. PRATT, HELEN G. "Some Conclusions From a Comparison

of School Achievement of Certain Racial Groups." *J Ed Psychol* 20:661–8 D '29. * (*PA* 4:1371)

157. SCOTT, ADELIN WHITE. "A Comparative Study of Responses of Children of Different Nationalities and Environments on Intelligence and Achievement Tests." *Teach Col Contrib Ed* 367:1–30 '29. *

158. DAVIS, THOMAS ROYAL. *The Prognostic Value of Certain Tests for Predicting the Success of High School Freshmen.* Master's thesis, University of Chicago (Chicago, Ill.), 1930.

159. DEARBORN, WALTER F., AND CATTELL, PSYCHE. "The Intelligence and Achievement of Private School Pupils." *J Ed Psychol* 21:197–211 Mr '30. * (*PA* 4:2864)

160. HILDRETH, GERTRUDE. "Results of Repeated Measurement of Pupil Achievement." *J Ed Psychol* 21:286–96 Ap '30. * (*PA* 4:3275)

161. MORLEY, CLYDE A. "The Reliability of the Achievement Quotient." *J Ed Psychol* 21:351–60 My '30. * (*PA* 4:4052)

162. BROWN, ANDREW W., AND LIND, CHRISTINE. "School Achievement in Relation to Mental Age—A Comparative Study." *J Ed Psychol* 22:561–76 N '31. * (*PA* 6:856)

163. DUNLAP, JACK W. "Race Differences in the Organization of Numerical and Verbal Abilities." *Arch Psychol* 124:1–72 My '31. * (*PA* 5:4187)

164. BROOM, M. E. "Measuring Mental Ability in the Intermediate Grades of the Elementary School." *Sch & Soc* 35:323–4 Mr 5 '32. * (*PA* 6:2575)

165. CHASE, VERA A. "Educational Achievement of Delinquent Boys." *J Juvenile Res* 16:189–92 Jl '32. * (*PA* 7:312)

166. McCRORY, JOHN R. "The Reliability of the Accomplishment Quotient." *J Ed Res* 25:27–39 Ja '32. * (*PA* 6:2016)

167. SANCHEZ, GEORGE I. "Scores of Spanish-Speaking Children on Repeated Tests." *J Genetic Psychol* 40:223–31 Mr '32. * (*PA* 6:3795)

168. HEILMAN, J. D. "Sex Differences in Intellectual Abilities." *J Ed Psychol* 24:47–62 Ja '33. * (*PA* 7:2121)

169. CARROLL, NANCY LEE. *The Relative Values of Certain Factors in Predicting Success in First-Year Latin.* Master's thesis, University of North Carolina (Chapel Hill, N.C.), 1934.

170. CRAMER, JOHN FRANCIS. "Australian Pupils Take an American Test." *Sch R* 42:362–7 My '34. *

171. FRITZ, RALPH A., AND RANKIN, NELLIE R. "The English Handicap of Junior High-School Pupils From Foreign Speaking Homes, and Remedial Suggestions." *J Ed Res* 27:412–21 F '34. * (*PA* 8:2766)

172. LANE, HOWARD A., AND WITTY, PAUL A. "The Educational Attainment of Delinquent Boys." *J Ed Psychol* 25:695–702 D '34. * (*PA* 9:1984)

173. WELLER, LOUISE, AND BROOM, M. E. "A Study of the Validity of Six Types of Spelling Tests." *Sch & Soc* 40:103–4 Jl 21 '34. * (*PA* 8:5670)

174. WITTY, PAUL A., AND JENKINS, MARTIN D. "The Educational Achievement of a Group of Gifted Negro Children." *J Ed Psychol* 25:585–97 N '34. * (*PA* 9:1358)

175. ANDERSON, H. DEWEY, AND EELLS, WALTER CROSBY. *Alaska Natives: A Survey of Their Sociological and Educational Status,* pp. 298–370. Stanford, Calif.: Stanford University Press, 1935. Pp. xvi, 472. * (*PA* 9:2346)

176. HILL, GEORGE E. "Educational Attainments of Young Male Offenders." *El Sch J* 36:53–8 S '35. * (*PA* 10:507)

177. WEISENBURG, THEODORE; ROE, ANNE; AND McBRIDE, KATHARINE E. *Adult Intelligence: A Psychological Study of Test Performances.* New York: Commonwealth Fund, 1936. Pp. xiii, 155. * (*PA* 10:3771)

178. FORNEY, ROY S. *Sex Differences and Educational Achievement of Public School Children.* Master's thesis, Temple University (Philadelphia, Pa.), 1938.

179. DENNIS, FLAVIUS ELIAS. *An Investigation of the Mental Ability, Educational Achievement, and Neurotic Tendencies of a Group of Partially Seeing Pupils.* Master's thesis, University of Colorado (Boulder, Colo.), 1939. (Abstract: *Univ Colo Studies* 26:48)

180. RIES, ARTHUR J. *A Survey of the Intelligence and Achievement Scores of White and Negro Children Entering the Junior High Schools of Louisville in September, 1938.* Master's thesis, University of Louisville (Louisville, Ky.), 1940.

181. PATTERSON, R. MELCHER, AND PHILLEO, CHARLOTTE. "Academic Achievement of Differentiated Groups at the Moron Level [Part 1]." *Am J Mental Def* 47:406–13 Ap '43. * (*PA* 18:3635)

182. PATTERSON, R. MELCHER, AND PHILLEO, CHARLOTTE. "Academic Achievement of Differentiated Groups at the Moron Level [Part 2]." *Am J Mental Def* 48:261–8 Ja '44. * (*PA* 18:3635)

183. SCHREIBER, PAUL R. "Measurements of Growth and Adjustment After Four Years in High School." *J Ed Res* 39:210–9 N '45. * (*PA* 20:2095)

184. FOX, WILLIAM H., AND EATON, MERRILL T. *Analysis of the Spelling Proficiency of 82,833 Pupils in Grades 2 to 8 in 3,547 Teaching Units of the City Schools in Indiana.* Bulletin of the School of Education, Indiana University, Vol. 22, No. 2. Bloomington, Ind.: Bureau of Cooperative Research and Field Service, the University, 1946. Pp. 45. *

185. FERRELL, GUY V. "Comparative Study of Sex Differences in School Achievement of White and Negro Children." *J Ed Res* 43:116–21 O '49. * (*PA* 24:2783)

186. BARBER, HERBERT O. *The Relationships Between Stanford Achievement Test Scores and Teachers' Marks for Flowing Wells School Eighth Grade Students.* Master's thesis, University of Arizona (Tucson, Ariz.), 1952.

187. DUNHAM, RALPH E. "Factors Related to Recidivism in Adults." *J Social Psychol* 39:77–91 F '54. * (*PA* 28:8866)

188. SCHOONOVER, SARAH M. "A Longitudinal Study of Sibling Resemblances in Intelligence and Achievement." *J Ed Psychol* 47:436–42 N '56. * (*PA* 32:4617)

189. FEINBERG, HENRY, AND MOSCOVITCH, EDWARD. "Achievement on the Stanford Achievement Test of Children in Difficult Own Home Situations Compared With Children Placed Out of the Home." *J Exp Ed* 26:67–80 S '57. * (*PA* 33:6908)

190. SALZINGER, KURT. "Academic Achievement in a Group of Mentally Disturbed Adolescents in a Residential Treatment Setting." *J Genetic Psychol* 90:239–53 Je '57. * (*PA* 35:1033)

191. PHILLIPS, BEEMAN N., AND WEATHERS, GARRETT. "Analysis of Errors Made in Scoring Standardized Tests." *Ed & Psychol Meas* 18:563–7 au '58. * (*PA* 33:9336)

192. WARREN, SUE ALLEN. "Academic Achievement of Trainable Pupils With Five or More Years of Schooling." *Training Sch B* 60:75–88 Ag '63. * (*PA* 38:4573)

193. MEYER, PEGGY ELLEN. *Analysis of Stanford Achievement Test Scores of Sixth Grade Students From Broadmor, Guadalupe, and Salt River Day Schools.* Master's thesis, Arizona State University (Tempe, Ariz.), 1965.

194. ASHFORD, ZELODIOUS WILLIAMS. *Personality: Reading and Spelling Achievement of Mentally Retarded Pupils.* Master's thesis, Illinois State University (Normal, Ill.), 1966.

195. LEVY, RUSSELL H. "The Gauging of Academic Achievement Among 'Court-Labelled' Delinquent Boys (Second of a Series)." *J Correct Ed* 18:14–7 O '66. *

196. LEVY, RUSSELL H., AND HENNING, JOHN A. "The Gauging of Achievement Among 'Court-Labelled' Delinquent Boys." *J Correct Ed* 18:16–8+ Ap '66. *

197. OHNMACHT, FRED W. "Correlates of Change in Academic Achievement." *J Ed Meas* 5:41–4 sp '68. *

198. GENTILE, AUGUSTINE, AND DIFRANCESCA, SAL. *Academic Achievement Test Performance of Hearing Impaired Students, United States, Spring 1969.* Office of Demographic Studies, Gallaudet College, Series D, No. 1. Washington, D.C.: Gallaudet College Book Store, September 1969. Pp. iv, 45. *

199. BROWN, ROSCOE C., JR. "The Relationship Between Physical Performance and Personality in Elementary School Children," pp. 439–45. In *Contemporary Psychology of Sport.* Proceedings of the Second International Congress of Sport Psychology, Washington, D.C., 1968. Chicago, Ill.: Athletic Institute, 1970. Pp. xix, 878. *

200. CYTANOVICH, KATHRYN. *A Study of the Validity of the Publisher's Interpolated May Norms of the First Grade Stanford Achievement Tests as Used in the State of California.* Master's thesis, Fresno State College (Fresno, Calif.), 1970.

201. DESKINS, L. R. "Need/Drive Plus a System Equals General Educational Development." *Training & Develop J* 24(3):30–2 Mr '70. * (*PA* 45:3078)

202. GENTILE, AUGUSTINE, AND DIFRANCESCA, SAL. *Item Analysis of Academic Achievement Tests Hearing Impaired Students, United States, Spring 1969.* Office of Demographic Studies, Gallaudet College, Series D, No. 2. Washington, D.C.: Gallaudet College Book Store, April 1970. Pp. iv, 41. *

203. ISMAIL, A. H., AND KIRKENDALL, D. R. "Relationship Among Three Domains of Development," pp. 451–60. In *Contemporary Psychology of Sport.* Proceedings of the Second International Congress of Sport Psychology, Washington, D.C., 1968. Chicago, Ill.: Athletic Institute, 1970. Pp. xix, 878. *

204. OLIPHANT, GENEVIEVE G. "A Study of Factors Involved in Early Identification of Specific Language Disability." *B Orton Soc* 20:81–92 '70. *

205. COOPER, STIRLING M. "The Decline of American Education: A Five-Year Report on the Denver Public Schools." *J Nat Assn Col Adm Counsel* 15(4):8–11+ F '71. *

206. FAIR, DENNIS T., AND BIRCH, JACK W. "Effect of Rest on Test Scores of Physically Handicapped and Nonhandicapped Children." *Excep Children* 38(4):335–6 D '71. * (*PA* 49:11893)

207. FULK, BARBARA F. *Correlations Between Scores of the Metropolitan Readiness Tests of Matching and Copying and the Stanford Achievement Tests Primary I Battery of Word Reading, Paragraph Meaning, Vocabulary, and Word Study Skills.* Master's thesis, Texas Woman's University (Denton, Tex.), 1971.

208. GOOLSBY, THOMAS M., JR. "Appropriateness of Subtests in Achievement Tests Selection." *Ed & Psychol Meas* 31(4): 969–72 w '71. * (*PA* 48:1640)

209. HAMMERMEISTER, FRIEDA K. "Reading Achievement in Deaf Adults." *Am Ann Deaf* 116(1):25–8 F '71. *

210. JENSEN, ARTHUR R. "Do Schools Cheat Minority Children?" *Ed Res* (England) 14(1):3–28 N '71. * (*PA* 49:11953)

211. JOHNSON, GARY L., AND HUMMEL, THOMAS J. "The Effect of Three Modes of Test Administration on the Reading Achievement Scores of Fifth Graders." *El Sch Guid & Counsel* 6(1):21–6 O '71. * (*PA* 49:7853)

212. JONES, W. PAUL, AND DeBLASSIE, RICHARD R. "Social Class Contrasts in Short Term Predictability of Grade 7 Achievement." *J Ed Res* 65(1):11–4 S '71. *

Stanford Achievement Test

213. LANDRY, RICHARD G. "The Factorial Orthogonality of the Torrance Tests of Creative Thinking and the Culture-Fair Intelligence Test." *Col Ed Rec Univ N Dak* 57(2):20–6 N '71. *

214. LEVONIAN, EDWARD. "Student Personality and Academic Achievement." *Personality* 1(1):25–39 sp '71. * (*PA* 47:9804)

215. MILLER, MAX. "Use of the Stanford Achievement Test as a Predictor of Success on the High School Equivalency Test." *J Employ Counsel* 8(2):65–71 Je '71. * (*PA* 47:11783)

216. OTTO, WAYNE; CANMAN, MARY JANE; AND JENSEN, DELORES. "Factors Related to Poor Readers' Achievement Test Performance." *J Read Behav* 3(4):1–5 f '71. *

217. PROGER, BARTON B.; MCGOWAN, JOHN R.; BAYUK, ROBERT J., JR.; MANN, LESTER; TREVORROW, RUTH L.; AND MASSA, EDWARD. "The Relative Predictive and Construct Validities of the Otis-Lennon Mental Ability Test, the Lorge-Thorndike Intelligence Test, and the Metropolitan Readiness Test in Grades Two and Four: A Series of Multivariate Analyses." *Ed & Psychol Meas* 31(2):529–38 su '71. *

CUMULATIVE NAME INDEX

[37]

Stanford Achievement Test: High School Basic Battery. Grades 9–12; 1965–66; 9 scores: English, numerical competence, mathematics (Part A, total), reading, science (Part A, total), social studies, spelling; was referred to as the High School Battery when 3 supplementary tests (arts and humanities, business and economics, and technical comprehension—now out of print) were included; subtests (English and spelling combined) available as separates; Eric F. Gardner, Jack C. Merwin, Robert Callis, and Richard Madden; Harcourt Brace Jovanovich, Inc. *

For additional information and reviews by Georgia S. Adams and G. C. Helmstadter, see 7:27. For reviews of the high school arts and humanities subtest, see 7:26 (1 review); the high school English and spelling subtest, see 7:208 (2 reviews); the high school mathematics subtest, see 7:488 (2 reviews); the high school numerical competence subtest, see 7:489 (2 reviews); the high school technical comprehension subtest, see 7:633 (1 review); the high school reading subtest, see 7:707 (2 reviews); and the high school science subtest, see 7:801 (2 reviews).

[38]

*Stanford Early School Achievement Test. Grades kgn-1.1, 1.1–1.5; 1969–71; SESAT; 2 levels; Richard Madden and Eric F. Gardner; Harcourt Brace Jovanovich, Inc. *

a) LEVEL 1. Grades kgn-1.1; 1969; 5 scores: environment, mathematics, letters and sounds, aural comprehension, total.

b) LEVEL 2. Grades 1.1–1.5; 1970–71; 7 scores: environment, mathematics, letters and sounds, aural comprehension, word reading, sentence reading, total.

For additional information and reviews by Elizabeth Hagen and William A. Mehrens of Level 1, see 7:28.

REFERENCES THROUGH 1971

1. BLAKSLEE, ROBERT WAYNE. *The Relationship Between the Bender Gestalt Test and Reading Achievement in First Grade Children.* Doctor's thesis, University of New Mexico (Albuquerque, N.M.), 1971. (*DAI* 32:4934A)

CUMULATIVE NAME INDEX

Blakslee, R. W.: 1   Mehrens, W. A.: *rev,* 7:28
Hagen, E.: *rev,* 7:28

[39]

★**Stanford Test of Academic Skills.** Grades 8–10, 11–12 and grade 13 in junior/community college; 1972–74; TASK; also called *Stanford TASK;* 3 scores: reading, English, mathematics; Eric F. Gardner, Robert Callis, Jack C. Merwin, and Richard Madden; Harcourt Brace Jovanovich, Inc. *

[40]

Survey of College Achievement. Grades 13–14; 1966–69; SCA; for institutional research use only; 5 scores: English composition, mathematics, social sciences and history, humanities, natural sciences; Educational Testing Service. *

For additional information and reviews by Paul L. Dressel and H. Bradley Sagen, see 7:29.

[41]

*****Teacher Education Examination Program: General Professional Examinations.** College seniors preparing to teach; 1957–72; modification of inactive 1966 form of *National Teacher Examinations: Common Examinations;* test available to colleges for local administration; 5 scores: social-philosophical-historical bases of education, learning and instruction, written English expression, cultural background—social sciences-literature-fine arts, science and mathematics—basic concepts and principles; Educational Testing Service. * For the testing program entry, see 898.

For additional information concerning an earlier form, see 6:709a. For a review of the testing program, see 5:543.

[42]

*****Test for High School Entrants.** High school entrants; 1945–69; THSE; 5 scores: English, reading comprehension, arithmetic, general information, total; 1969 test identical with test copyrighted 1947 except for 2 items; 1953 manual identical with manual copyrighted 1947; Lester D. Crow and Alice Crow; Psychometric Affiliates. *

For additional information and a review by Jacob S. Orleans, see 5:26; for a review by Benjamin S. Bloom, see 3:19.

[43]

Test of Reading and Number: Inter-American Series. Grade 4 entrants; 1969; TRN; experimental form; 3 scores: reading, number, total; parallel editions in English and Spanish; Herschel T. Manuel; Guidance Testing Associates. *

For additional information, see 7:30.

[44]

*****Tests of Academic Progress.** Grades 9–12; 1964–72; TAP; 7 scores: social studies, composition, science, reading, mathematics, literature, total; 2 nonequivalent editions; Dale P. Scannell, Oscar M. Haugh (composition and literature), William B. Reiner (science),

Alvin H. Schild (social studies), Henry P. Smith (reading), and Gilbert Ulmer (mathematics); Houghton Mifflin Co. *

a) FORMS 1 AND 2. 1964–66; subtests available as separates.

b) FORM S. 1971–72, c1964–72; ("Form S was developed from specifications that reflect current goals and content of secondary education. Form S differs from Forms 1 and 2 to the extent that the goals have changed; the similarities reflect the constancy of secondary school goals."—Dale P. Scannell).

For additional information and a review by C. M. Lindvall of Forms 1 and 2, see 7:31. For reviews of the composition subtest, see 7:210 (2 reviews); the literature subtest, see 7:225 (3 reviews); the mathematics subtest, see 7:491 (2 reviews); the reading subtest, see 7:710 (1 review); the science subtest, see 7:805 (1 review); and the social studies subtest, see 7:896 (1 review).

[45]

Tests of Adult Basic Education. Adults at reading levels of children in grades 2–4, 4–6, 7–9; 1967, c1957–67; TABE; 3 levels; CTB/McGraw-Hill. *

a) LEVEL E. Adults at reading levels of children in grades 2–4; except for very minor changes, the tests are identical with the 1957 *California Achievement Tests* for grades 2–4; 6 scores: reading (vocabulary, comprehension, total), arithmetic (reasoning, fundamentals, total).

b) LEVEL M. Adults at reading levels of children in grades 4–6; except for very minor changes, the tests are identical with the 1957 *California Achievement Tests* for grades 4–6; 10 scores: same as for Level E plus language (mechanics, spelling, total), total.

c) LEVEL D. Adults at reading levels of children in grades 7–9; except for very minor changes, the tests are identical with the 1957 *California Achievement Tests* for grades 7–9; 10 scores: same as for Level M.

d) PRACTICE EXERCISES AND LOCATOR TEST. For determining level of test to be administered.

For additional information, a review by A. N. Hieronymus, and an excerpted review by S. Alan Cohen, see 7:32. For reference to reviews of the *California Achievement Tests,* see 7.

[46]

★**Tests of Arithmetic and Language for Indian South Africans.** Standards 6–8; 1968; TALISA; adaptation for Indian pupils of the *General Tests of Language and Arithmetic;* 2 scores: arithmetic, English language; Human Sciences Research Council [South Africa].*

[47]

*****Tests of Basic Experiences.** Prekgn-kgn, kgn-grade 1; 1970–72; TOBE; test of experiences and concepts involving no reading; battery of 4 tests (language, mathematics, science, social studies) and a composite test (*General Concepts Test*) used for screening or as a post-test; subtests available as separates; Margaret H. Moss; CTB/McGraw-Hill. *

For additional information and a review by Courtney B. Cazden, see 7:33.

[48]

*****Tests of General Educational Development.** Candidates for high school equivalency certificates; 1944–72; TGED, also GED; 6 scores: correctness and effectiveness of expression, interpretation of reading materials in the social studies, interpretation of reading materials in the natural sciences, interpretation of literary materials, general mathematical ability, average; Educational Testing Service; General Educational Development Testing Service of the American Council on Education.

a) CIVILIAN RESTRICTED FORMS. Civilian adults including veterans; tests administered throughout the year only at Official GED Centers; new form issued each September; special editions available for blind and partially sighted.

b) MILITARY RESTRICTED FORMS. Military personnel on active duty; tests administered only at USAFI Testing Sections.

For additional information, see 7:34 (21 references); for a review by Robert J. Solomon of earlier forms, see 5:27 (39 references); for a review by Gustav J. Froehlich, see 4:26 (27 references); for reviews by Herbert S. Conrad and Warren G. Findley, see 3:20 (11 references). For a review by Charlotte W. Croon of an earlier form of the expression subtest, see 3:122; for reviews by W. E. Hall and C. Robert Pace of an earlier form of the social studies reading subtest, see 3:528.

REFERENCES THROUGH 1971

1–11. See 3:20.
12–38. See 4:26.
39–77. See 5:27.
78–98. See 7:34.
99. JAMES, RICHARD WARREN. *Selection of Graduate Students: (1) The Adequacy of Certain Measures for Differentiating Between Two Groups of Master Candidates; (2) The Value of These Measures in Prognosing Graduate Academic Achievement.* Doctor's thesis, New York University (New York, N.Y.), 1950.
100. TRAVERS, ROBERT M. W., AND WALLACE, WIMBURN L. "Inconsistency in the Predictive Value of a Battery of Tests." *J Appl Psychol* 34:237–9 Ag '50. * *(PA* 25:6480)
101. GLASER, ROBERT. "The Validity of Some Tests for Predicting Achievement in Medical School." Abstract. *Am Psychologist* 6:298 Jl '51. *
102. WEISS, IRVING. "Prediction of Academic Success in Dental School." *J Appl Psychol* 36:11–4 F '52. * *(PA* 26:7296)
103. LAYTON, WILBUR L. "Predicting Success in Dental School." *J Appl Psychol* 37:251–5 Ag '53. * *(PA* 28:6712)
104. MARTIN, RICHARD RALPH. *An Investigation of the Effectiveness of an Entrance Test Battery for Predicting Success in Law School.* Doctor's thesis, Temple University (Philadelphia, Pa.), 1954. *(DA* 16:575)
105. BAIR, JOHN T.; LOCKMAN, ROBERT F.; AND MARTOCCIA, CHARLES T. "Validity and Factor Analyses of Naval Air Training Predictor and Criterion Measures." *J Appl Psychol* 40:213–9 Ag '56. * *(PA* 31:6701)
106. WEBB, SAM C. "The Prediction of Achievement for First Year Dental Students." *Ed & Psychol Meas* 16:543–8 w '56. * *(PA* 32:962)
107. MONTGOMERY, TRAVIS. "Use of the GATB in Predicting Success on the High School Equivalency Tests." *J Employ Counsel* 4:117–21 D '67. *
108. DESKINS, L. R. "Need/Drive Plus a System Equals General Educational Development." *Training & Develop J* 24(3):30–2 Mr '70. * *(PA* 45:3078)
109. MILLER, MAX. "Use of the Stanford Achievement Test as a Predictor of Success on the High School Equivalency Tests." *J Employ Counsel* 8(2):65–71 Je '71. * *(PA* 47:11783)

CUMULATIVE NAME INDEX

American Council on Education, Commission on Accreditation of Service Experiences: 72, 76
American Council on Education, Committee on the Evaluation of the Tyler Fact-Finding Study of the American Council on Education: 66
Anderson, G. V.: 19
Andregg, N. B.: 29
Andrew, D. C.: 45, 47, 56
Aslin, N. C.: 79
Bair, J. T.: 105
Baird, T. B.: 85
Batmale, L. F.: 20, 65
Berdie, R. F.: 44
Bernard, J.: 57
Berns, S. A.: 52
Bledsoe, J. C.: 48, 53, 80
Bloom, B. S.: 67, 73
Bradley, M. E.: 4
Brenna, D. W.: 90
Burnham, P. S.: 2

Callis, R.: 7
Carbuhn, W. M.: 91, 95
Cauffman, P. F.: 81
Chausow, H. M.: 49
Conrad, H. S.: *rev,* 3:20
Crabtree, A. P.: 88
Crawford, A. B.: 2
Croon, C. W.: *rev,* 3:122
D'Amico, L. A.: 54, 74–5
DeNoyelles, L. C.: 86
Deskins, L. R.: 108
Dittrick, A. R.: 68
Dixon, P. T.: 21
Dixon, W. R.: 22
Donahue, W. T.: 5
Dressel, P. L.: 8, 38
Dyer, H. S.: 3
Eckelberry, R. H.: 12
Edberg, G.: 23
Enochs, J. B.: 24
Farley, E. J.: 88
Findley, W. G.: 29, 43; *rev,* 3:20
Frandsen, A.: 14
Froehlich, G. J.: *rev,* 4:26

Glaser, R.: 46, 58, 101
Graham, W. R.: 59
Hall, W. E.: *rev,* 3:528
Hartung, A. W.: 25
Heston, J. C.: 34
Humphreys, J. A.: 9
Irwin, I. A.: 35
Jacobs, O.: 58
James, R. W.: 99
Johnston, W. C.: 40
Jones, R. S.: 60
Keller, L. J.: 83
Klein, F.: 92, 96
Klein, M. A.: 97
Koehler, L. E.: 10
Kovnar, M. R.: 55, 61
LaPine, H. J.: 77, 84
Layton, W. L.: 103
Leton, D. A.: 82
Lins, L. J.: 26
Little, K.: 26
Lockman, R. F.: 105
Love, L. L.: 10, 15
McConagha, G. L.: 30
McCracken, N. M.: 41
Martin, R. R.: 104
Martoccia, C. T.: 105
Miller, M.: 109
Milligan, E. E.: 26
Monahan, F. X.: 50
Montgomery, T.: 107
Mosel, J. N.: 62
Moser, W. E.: 31–2
Muirhead, J. V.: 31–2
Mumma, R. A.: 36

Olson, E. H.: 63
Pace, C. R.: *rev,* 3:528
Peters, F. R.: 69
Pipho, C. C.: 87
Putnam, P. H.: 39
Roeber, E. C.: 37
Rohrer, J. H.: 42
Rosenlof, G. W.: 13
Russo, J. F.: 93
Schmid, J.: 38
Schmidt, L. G.: 75
Schultz, F. G.: 16
Segel, D.: 6
Shoemaker, H. A.: 42
Soderberg, P. B.: 98
Solomon, R. J.: *rev,* 5:27
Statler, C. R.: 73
Super, D. E.: 33
Sutter, N. A.: 44
Travers, R. M. W.: 100
Trione, V.: 96
Turner, C. P.: 68, 78
Tyler, H. E.: 70
Tyler, R. W.: 64
Van Winkle, H. G.: 71
Wallace, W. L.: 100
Wardlaw, H. P.: 51
Webb, S. C.: 106
Weinhold, C. E.: 88
Weiss, I.: 102
Westover, H. T.: 27
Wiegel, D. F.: 17
Wilcox, G. M.: 28
Wrenn, C. G.: 7

[49]

*The Undergraduate Program Area Tests. College; 1954–73; formerly called *The Undergraduate Record Examinations: Area Tests;* still earlier called *The Graduate Record Examinations: The Area Tests;* tests available to colleges for local administration; 3 tests: social sciences, humanities, natural science; Educational Testing Service. * For the testing program entry, see 1062.

For additional information, see 7:35 (4 references); for reviews by Paul L. Dressel and Everett B. Sackett of earlier forms, see 6:9 (10 references); for reviews by Benjamin S. Bloom and Frederick B. Davis, see 5:10. For reviews of the testing program, see 7:671 (2 reviews) and 5:601 (1 review).

REFERENCES THROUGH 1971

1–9. See 6:9.
10–13. See 7:35.
14. HOUSTON, SAMUEL R. "Generating a Projected Criterion of Graduate School Success via Normative Judgment Analysis." *J Exp Ed* 37:53–8 w '68. *
15. CENTRA, JOHN A., AND ROCK, DONALD. "College Environments and Student Academic Achievement." *Am Ed Res J* 8(4):623–34 N '71. * *(PA* 47:11755)
16. CREAGER, JOHN A. "Academic Achievement and Institutional Environments: Two Research Strategies." *J Exp Ed* 40(2):9–23 w '71. * *(PA* 47:11757)

CUMULATIVE NAME INDEX

Astin, A. W.: 11–2
Bloom, B. S.: *rev,* 5:10
Centra, J. A.: 15
Creager, J. A.: 16
Davis, F. B.: *rev,* 5:10
Dressel, P. L.: *rev,* 6:9
Elton, C. F.: 10
Gibbons, B. D.: 3
Houston, S. R.: 13–4
Johnson, J. W.: 5
Johnston, R. A.: 9
Jones, R. A.: 3
Lannholm, G. V.: 1

Maberly, N. C.: 6, 8
Michael, W. B.: 3
Panos, R. J.: 12
Pemberton, W. A.: 8a
Rock, D.: 15
Roscoe, J. T.: 13
Sackett, E. B.: *rev,* 6:9
Scarborough, B. B.: 2
Thomsen, S. J.: 4
Tully, G. E.: 7
Williams, J. E.: 9
Wright, J. C.: 2

[50]

Wide Range Achievement Test, Revised Edition. Ages 5–11, 12 and over; 1940–65; WRAT; 3 scores: spelling, arithmetic, reading; J. F. Jastak, S. R. Jastak, and S. W. Bijou (test); Guidance Associates of Delaware, Inc. *

For additional information and reviews by Jack C. Merwin and Robert L. Thorndike, see 7:36 (49 refer-

ences) ; see also 6:27 (15 references) ; for reviews by
Paul Douglas Courtney, Verner M. Sims, and Louis P.
Thorpe of the 1946 edition, see 3:21.

REFERENCES THROUGH 1971

1–15. See 6:27.
16–64. See 7:36.
65. JENSEN, MILTON B., AND SCHMID, JOHN. "An Analysis
of Some Clinical Judgments on Male Basic Airmen Who Failed
the Group Psychological Tests." *J Clin Psychol* 10:325–32 O
'54. * (*PA* 29:4753)
66. BURCHINAL, LEE G. "Social Status, Measured Intelligence, Achievement, and Personality Adjustment of Rural
Iowa Girls." *Sociometry* 22:75–80 Mr '59. * (*PA* 34:1254)
67. PANTON, JAMES H. "The Relationship Between Education and Measures of Intelligence and Educational Achievement
Within a State Prison Population." *J Correct Ed* 12:18–20
Ja '60. *
68. DOWIS, JAMES L., AND BUCHANAN, CHARLES E. "Some
Relationships Between Intellectual Efficiency and the Severity
of Psychiatric Illness." *J Psychol* 51:371–81 Ap '61. * (*PA*
35:6905)
69. WITHERSPOON, Y. T. "The Measurement of Indian
Children's Achievement in the Academic Tool Subjects." *J Am
Indian Ed* 1:5–9 My '62. *
70. WARREN, SUE ALLEN. "Academic Achievement of Trainable Pupils With Five or More Years of Schooling." *Training
Sch B* 60:75–88 Ag '63. * (*PA* 38:4573)
71. TAYLOR, JAMES BENTLEY. "The Structure of Ability in
the Lower Intellectual Range." *Am J Mental Def* 68:766–74
My '64. * (*PA* 39:1793)
72. CAPOBIANCO, R. J. "Ocular-Manual Laterality and Reading in Adolescent Mental Retardates." *Am J Mental Def*
70:781–5 Mr '66. * (*PA* 40:6970)
73. WAMPLER, JOE F. "Prediction of Achievement in College
Mathematics." *Math Teach* 59:364–9 Ap '66. *
74. CANTER, FRANCIS M. "Motivation for Self-Confrontation
in Alcoholic Patients." *Psychother Theory Res & Prac* 6(1):21–3
w '69. * (*PA* 43:11581)
75. KIDD, LOR RHEBA R. *A Comparison of the Wide Range
Achievement Test With the Stanford Achievement Test and
Comprehensive Tests of Basic Skills as a Measurement of
Reading Achievement.* Master's thesis, California State College
(Hayward, Calif.), 1970.
76. MCDONALD, NORMA LEE HALE. *A Study of Creativity in
Educable Mentally Retarded Children.* Doctor's thesis, University of Denver (Denver, Colo.), 1970. (*DAI* 31:4587A)
77. SCHAIE, K. WARNER, AND ROBERTS, JEAN. "School
Achievement of Children 6–11 Years as Measured by the Reading
and Arithmetic Subtests of the Wide Range Achievement Test:
United States." *Vital & Health Stat* Series 11(103):1–47 Je
'70. * (*PA* 45:7066)
78. BALDWIN, THOMAS S. "Relationships Among Student
Achievement and 'Pure Factors' of Intellect." *J Indus Teach
Ed* 9(1):15–25 f '71. *
79. BRAFF, REBA GERTRUDE. *Signal-to-Noise Speech Discrimi-
nation of Black and White Children With Varying Socio-
Economic Backgrounds.* Doctor's thesis, University of Southern
California (Los Angeles, Calif.), 1971. (*DAI* 32:3686B)
80. COWDEN, JAMES E.; PETERSON, WILLIAM M.; AND PACHT,
ASHER R. "The Validation of a Brief Screening Test for Verbal
Intelligence at Several Correctional Institutions in Wisconsin."
J Clin Psychol 27(2):216–8 Ap '71. * (*PA* 46:7125)
81. DEICH, RUTH F. "Reading Time and Error Rates for
Normal and Retarded Readers." *Percept & Motor Skills* 32(3):
689–90 Je '71. * (*PA* 47:3751)
82. FINNERTY, RICHARD J.; SOLTYS, JOHN J.; AND COLE,
JONATHAN O. "The Use of D-Amphetamine With Hyperkinetic
Children." *Psychopharmacologia* (West Germany) 21(3):302–8
'71. * (*PA* 47:9150)
83. FRIEDMAN, GERALDINE H. PROBE. *A Comparative Study
of Psychoeducational Test Scores of Emotionally Disturbed
Children and Children With Learning Disabilities.* Doctor's
thesis, St. Louis University (St. Louis, Mo.), 1971. (*DAI* 33:
1043A)
84. GREEN, JOSEPH B., AND HARTLAGE, LAWRENCE C. "Comparative Performance of Epileptic and Nonepileptic Children
and Adolescents." *Dis Nerv System* 32(6):418–21 Je '71. *
(*PA* 48:3530)
85. HARDY, MIRIAM P.; MELLITS, DAVID; AND WILLIG, SHA-
RON N. "Reading: A Function of Language Usage." *Johns
Hopkins Med J* 129(1):43–53 Jl '71. *
86. HARTLAGE, LAWRENCE C., AND GREEN, JOSEPH B. "EEG
Differences in Children's Reading, Spelling, and Arithmetic
Abilities." *Percept & Motor Skills* 32(1):133–4 F '71. * (*PA*
46:3571)
87. HINTON, GEORGE G., AND KNIGHTS, ROBERT M. "Children With Learning Problems: Academic History, Academic
Prediction, and Adjustment Three Years After Assessment."
Excep Children (7(7):513–9 Mr '71. * (*PA* 47:3663)
88. KARADENES, MARK. *A Comparison of Differences in
Achievement and Learning Abilities Between Anglo and Mexican-American Children When the Two Groups Are Equated by

Intelligence. Doctor's thesis, University of Virginia (Charlottesville, Va.), 1971. (*DAI* 32:4422A)
89. MASON, GEORGE E., AND BLANTON, WILLIAM E. "Semantic Constructs and Beginning Reading." *Yearb Nat Read
Conf* 19(1):39–45 '71. *
90. MOORE, MARY, AND WELCHER, DORIS W. "A Descriptive
Analysis of the Seven-Year Psychological Data." *Johns Hopkins
Med J* 128(6):332–46 Je '71. *
91. MYKLEBUST, HELMER R.; BANNOCHIE, MARGARET N.;
AND KILLEN, JAMES R. Chap. 9, "Learning Disabilities and Cognitive Processes," pp. 213–51. In *Progress in Learning Disabilities, Vol. 2.* Edited by Helmer R. Myklebust. New York: Grune
& Stratton, Inc., 1971. Pp. ix, 404. *
92. NELSON, JOHN CLEMENT. *Relating Student and Teacher
Personality and Cognitive Characteristics With School Achieve-
ment of Educable Mentally Retarded Children.* Doctor's thesis,
George Peabody College for Teachers (Nashville, Tenn.), 1971.
(*DAI* 32:1948A)
93. OWEN, FREYA WEAVER; ADAMS, PAULINE AUSTIN; FOR-
REST, THOMAS; STOLZ, LOIS MEEK; AND FISHER, SARA. "Learn-
ing Disorders in Children: Sibling Studies." *Monogr Soc Res
Child Develop* 36(4):1–77 N '71. * (*PA* 48: 12196)
94. ROURKE, B. P.; YOUNG, G. C.; AND FLEWELLING, R. W.
"The Relationships Between WISC Verbal-Performance Dis-
crepancies and Selected Verbal, Auditory-Perceptual, Visual-
Perceptual, and Problem-Solving Abilities in Children With
Learning Disabilities." *J Clin Psychol* 27(4):475–9 O '71. *
(*PA* 47:9738)
95. SCHAIE, K. WARNER, AND ROBERTS, JEAN. "School
Achievement of Children by Demographic and Socioeconomic
Factors: United States." *Vital & Health Stat* Series 11(109):
1–88 N '71. * (*PA* 48:7868)
96. SINGHAL, SUSHILA, AND CRAGO, PRISCILLA H. "Sex Differences in the School Gains of Migrant Children." *J Ed Res*
64(9):417–9 My–Je '71. *
97. SUNDEAN, DAVID A., AND SALOPEK, THOMAS F. "Achievement and Intelligence in Primary and Elementary Classes for
the Educable Mentally Retarded." *J Sch Psychol* 9(2):150–6
'71. * (*PA* 47:7610)
98. WAGONSELLER, BILL R. *A Comparison of Intellectual
Ability, Achievement Level, Self-Concept, and Behavior Problems Exhibited by Children Labeled as Learning Disabilities
and Emotionally Disturbed.* Doctor's thesis, University of Kansas (Lawrence, Kan.), 1971. (*DAI* 32:5644A)
99. WELCHER, DORIS W.; MELLITS, E. DAVID; AND HARDY,
JANET B. "A Multivariate Analysis of Factors Affecting Psychological Performance." *Johns Hopkins Med J* 129(1):19–35
Jl '71. *

CUMULATIVE NAME INDEX

Wide Range Achievement Test

Merwin, J. C.: *rev*, 7:36
Moore, M.: 90
Myklebust, H. R.: 91
Nelson, J. C.: 92
Oldridge, O. A.: 11, 19
Oppel, W. C.: 40
Owen, F. W.: 93
Owens, R. T.: 47
Pacht, A. R.: 80
Panton, J. H.: 67
Pedrini, D. T.: 20, 43
Peterson, W. M.: 80
Pinney, E. L.: 35
Rabin, A.: 3
Rankin, R. J.: 36
Reed, J. C.: 48
Reger, R.: 16, 26
Reitan, R. M.: 14, 25, 48
Rice, J. A.: 49
Rider, W. V.: 40
Roberts, J.: 77, 95
Rourke, B. P.: 94
Rowley, V. N.: 21
Sabatino, D. A.: 37–8, 50, 60–2
Salopek, T. F.: 97
Saxton, G.: 15
Schaie, K. W.: 30, 77, 95
Scherer, I. W.: 7
Schmid, J.: 65
Schuell, H.: 17

Schwarz, R. H.: 51
Sells, S. B.: 27
Seybold, F. R.: 20
Shepherd, C. W.: 52
Simpson, R. L.: 63
Sims, V. M.: *rev*, 3:21
Singhal, S.: 96
Smith, B. S.: 8
Soltys, J. J.: 82
Stolz, L. M.: 93
Stone, F. B.: 21
Sundean, D. A.: 97
Taylor, J. B.: 71
Teska, J. A.: 64
Thompson, W. H.: 34
Thorndike, R. L.: *rev*, 7:36
Thorpe, L. P.: *rev*, 3:21
Topetzes, N. J.: 6
Tretakoff, M. I.: 15
Vacc, N. A.: 39
Wagonseller, B. R.: 98
Wampler, J. F.: 73
Warren, S. A.: 70
Washington, E. D.: 64
Welcher, D. W.: 90, 99
Wickham, W.: 38
Wiener, G.: 40
Willig, S. N.: 85
Witherspoon, Y. T.: 69
Young, G. C.: 94

[Out of Print Since TIP I]

Burt Scholastic Tests, T :3
California Basic Skills Tests, 6:4 (1 review)
California Tests in Social and Related Sciences, 5:4 (3 reviews)
Canadian Test of General Information, 6:5 (2 reviews, 2 references)
Cooperative General Achievement Tests [General Proficiency Series], 6:7 (4 reviews, 25 references)
Cooperative General Culture Test, 5:7 (8 reviews, 35 references)

Coordinated Scales of Attainment, 4:8 (5 reviews)
DIGEST: Diagnostic Inventory Group Evaluation Survey Tests, 7:11 (2 reviews, 1 reference)
Eighth Grade Test, 6:8 (1 reference)
Essential High School Content Battery, 4:9 (3 reviews)
Every Pupil Primary Achievement Test, 3:7 (1 review)
General Scholarship Test for High School Seniors, 6:8a (1 review, 2 references)
Group Achievement Test: Dominion Tests, 1934 Edition, 5:12
Group Achievement Tests: Niagara Edition: Dominion Tests, 5:13
Harlow Achievement Tests for Texas, 4:13
Harlow Battery Achievement Test, 4:14
High School Classification Examination, 6:11 (2 reviews, 1 reference)
Iowa Every-Pupil Tests of Basic Skills, 4:15 (9 reviews, 12 references)
Metropolitan Achievement Tests: High School Battery, 7:15 (5 reviews)
Modern School Achievement Tests, 4:19 (4 reviews, 3 references)
Municipal Battery: National Achievement Tests, 5:18 (4 reviews)
Public School Attainment Tests for High School Entrance, 3:17 (3 reviews, 1 reference)
Pupil Record of Educational Progress, 6:20 (2 reviews)
Scholastic Achievement Series, 6:23 (4 reviews)
Seven Plus Assessment: The Northumberland Series, 4:24 (1 review)
Standard Graduation Examination for Elementary Schools, T :41, 35:18
Stanford Achievement Test: High School Arts and Humanities Test, 7:26 (1 review)

ENGLISH

[51]

*Advanced Placement Examination in English. High school students desiring credit for college level courses or admission to advanced courses; 1954–73; replaces separate tests in English composition and literature; available to secondary schools for annual administration on specified days in May; inactive forms are available to colleges for local administration in the *Testing Academic Achievement* program; program administered for the College Entrance Examination Board by Educational Testing Service. * For the testing program entry, see 1045.

For additional information concerning earlier forms, see 7:184 (1 reference); for a review by Robert C. Pooley of an earlier form of the English composition test, see 5:205; for a review by John S. Diekhoff of an earlier form of the literature test, see 5:211. For reviews of the testing program, see 7:662 (2 reviews).

REFERENCES THROUGH 1971
1. See 7:184.
2. THOMAS, CLEVELAND A. "English Composition for Advanced Placement Students." *Col Board R* 38:33–6 sp '59. *
3. NEILSON, JOAN BUTLER. *Predicting Success in the English*

Advanced Placement Program in Utah Public Schools. Master's thesis, University of Utah (Salt Lake City, Utah), 1965.

CUMULATIVE NAME INDEX
Diekhoff, J. S.: *rev*, 5:211 Smith, E. H.: 1
Neilson, J. B.: 3 Thomas, C. A.: 2
Pooley, R. C.: *rev*, 5:205

[52]

American School Achievement Tests: Part 3, Language and Spelling. Grades 4–6, 7–9; 1941–63; 2 scores: language, spelling; forms copyrighted 1955–57 are identical with forms copyrighted 1941–43 except for format; Willis E. Pratt, Robert V. Young, and Clara E. Cockerille (manuals); Bobbs-Merrill Co., Inc. * For the complete battery, see 4.

For additional information, see 6:248 (1 reference); for reviews by M. A. Brimer and Clarence Derrick, see 5:174. For reviews of the complete battery, see 6:2 (2 reviews), 5:1 (2 reviews), 4:1 (1 review), and 3:1 (2 reviews).

REFERENCES THROUGH 1971
1. See 6:248.
CUMULATIVE NAME INDEX
Brimer, M. A.: *rev*, 5:174 Groff, P. J.: 1
Derrick, C.: *rev*, 5:174

[53]
Analytical Survey Test in English Fundamentals.
Grades 9–13; 1932–57; formerly called *Diagnostic Survey Test in English Fundamentals;* 8 scores: spelling, capitalization, punctuation, sentence organization, sentence structure, grammatical usage, grammatical terminology, total; J. Helen Campbell and Walter Scribner Guiler; Bobbs-Merrill Co., Inc. *

For additional information and reviews by Leonard S. Feldt and Roger A. Richards, see 6:249 (2 references).

REFERENCES THROUGH 1971
1–2. See 6:249.
3. GUILER, W. S., AND CAMPBELL, J. HELEN. "Remedial English at the College Level." *J Am Assn Col Reg* 18:246–55 Ap '43. *
4. GUILER, WALTER SCRIBNER. "Disabilities of College Freshmen in Sentence Structure." *Sch R* 54:480–7 O '46. * (*PA* 21:601)
5. KOSTYSHAK, THEODORE. *An Analytical Study of the Guiler-Campbell English Test.* Master's thesis, Miami University (Oxford, Ohio), 1953.

CUMULATIVE NAME INDEX
Campbell, J. H.: 3
Feldt, L. S.: *rev,* 6:249
Guiler, W. S.: 1–4
Kostyshak, T.: 5
Richards, R. A.: *rev,* 6:249

[54]
Barrett-Ryan English Test. Grades 7–13; 1926–61; E. R. Barrett, Teresa M. Ryan, M. W. Sanders (Forms 1, 2, 3), H. E. Schrammel (Forms 1948, 1954, manual), and E. R. Wood (manual); Bureau of Educational Measurements. *

For additional information and a review by Clarence Derrick, see 6:250 (2 references); for a review by J. Raymond Gerberich, see 5:175.

REFERENCES THROUGH 1971
1–2. See 6:250.
3. WOOD, SUSAN. *An Evaluation of Published English Tests,* pp. 9–12. Madison, Wis.: Wisconsin Department of Public Instruction, 1967. Pp. 91. *

CUMULATIVE NAME INDEX
Anderson, M. R.: 1
Derrick, C.: *rev,* 6:250
Gerberich, J. R.: *rev,* 5:175
Groff, P. J.: 2
Stegman, E. J.: 1
Wood, S.: 3

[55]
★**Berry-Talbott Language Test: Comprehension of Grammar.** Ages 5–8; 1966; BTLT; experimental; "to *explore* the child's ability to make up and to use rules of grammar and syntax" using nonsense words; 8 scores: plural noun, past tense, third person singular, possessive singular-plural, derived adjective, adjective: comparative-superlative, diminutive-derived word, progressive-derived word; Mildred F. Berry and Ruth Talbott; Berry Language Tests. *

[56]
Bristol Achievement Tests: English Language.
Ages 8-0 to 9-11, 9-0 to 10-11, 10-0 to 11-11, 11-0 to 12-11, 12-0 to 13-11; 1969; 6 scores: word meaning, paragraph meaning, sentence organisation, organisation of ideas, spelling and punctuation, total; Alan Brimer and Herbert Gross; Thomas Nelson & Sons Ltd. [England]. * For the complete battery entry, see 5.

For additional information and a review by Ralph D. Dutch, see 7:185. For reviews of the complete battery, see 7:4 (2 reviews).

[57]
Business English Test: The Dailey Vocational Tests. Grades 8–12 and adults; 1964–65; BET; John T. Dailey and Kenneth B. Hoyt (manual); Houghton Mifflin Co. * For the complete battery entry, see 2105.

For additional information, see 7:976c. For reviews

of the complete battery, see 7:976 (2 reviews, 2 excerpts).

[58]
*****CLEP General Examinations: English Composition.** 1–2 years of college or equivalent; 1964–73; for college accreditation of nontraditional study, advanced placement, or assessment of educational attainment; a retired subtest of the *College-Level Examination Program General Examinations* published as a separate for local administration through the *Testing Academic Achievement* program (see 1061); program administered for the College Entrance Examination Board by Educational Testing Service. * For the testing program entry, see 1050.

For additional information concerning earlier forms, see 7:8b. For reviews of the testing program, see 7:664 (3 reviews).

REFERENCES THROUGH 1971
1. BURKETT, EVA. "Composition Tests for Screening Prospective Teachers." *Col Comp & Commun* 22(5):355–62 D '71. *

CUMULATIVE NAME INDEX
Burkett, E.: 1

[59]
*****CLEP Subject Examination in English Composition.** 1 year or equivalent; 1965–73; for college accreditation of nontraditional study, advanced placement, or assessment of educational achievement; tests administered monthly at centers throughout the United States; program administered for the College Entrance Examination Board by Educational Testing Service. * For the testing program entry, see 1050.

For additional information and a review by David P. Harris, see 7:186. For reviews of the testing program, see 7:664 (3 reviews).

[60]
★**CLEP Subject Examination in Freshman English.** 1 year or equivalent; 1973; for college accreditation of nontraditional study, advanced placement, or assessment of educational achievement; tests administered monthly at centers throughout the United States; program administered for the College Entrance Examination Board by Educational Testing Service. * For the testing program entry, see 1050.

For reviews of the testing program, see 7:664 (3 reviews).

[61]
*****California Achievement Tests: Language.** 1933–72; earlier editions called *Progressive Language Tests;* 2 editions; Ernest W. Tiegs and Willis W. Clark; CTB/McGraw-Hill. * For the complete battery entry, see 7.

a) 1957 EDITION WITH 1963 NORMS. Grades 1–2, 2.5–4.5, 4–6, 7–9, 9–14; 1933–63; test booklet title is *California Language Test;* 4 scores: mechanics of English, spelling, total, handwriting; 1963 tests identical with tests copyrighted 1957 except for profile.

b) 1970 EDITION. Grades 1.5–2.5, 2.5–4.5, 4–6, 6–9, 9–12; 1933–72; 4 or 5 scores: auding (grades 1.5–2.5 only), mechanics, usage and structure, total, spelling.

For additional information concerning the 1970 edition, see 7:187 (2 references); for a review by Richard E. Schutz of the 1957 edition, see 6:251 (1 reference); for reviews by Constance M. McCullough and Winifred L. Post, see 5:177 (3 references); for reviews by Gerald V. Lannholm and Robert C. Pooley of an earlier edition, see 4:151; for reviews by Harry A. Greene and J. Paul Leonard, see 2:1292. For reviews of the complete battery, see 6:3 (2 reviews), 5:2 (1 review), 4:2 (3 reviews), 3:15 (1 review), 2:1193 (2 reviews), and 1:876 (1 review, 1 excerpt).

REFERENCES THROUGH 1971

1-3. See 5:177.
4. See 6:251.
5-6. See 7:187.
7. McGuire, Carson. "Sex Role and Community Variability in Test Performances." *J Ed Psychol* 52:61–73 Ap '61. * (*PA* 38:3207)
8. Katz, Stanley S. "Selection and Evaluation of Students in Medical Technology Degree Programs." *Am J Med Technol* 30:51–63 Ja '64. *
9. Winston, Wilma Essex. *A Correlation Between Language Achievement and Musical Aptitude of Thirty Sixth Grade Pupils at Booker T. Washington School, East Gadsden, Alabama.* Master's thesis, Alabama A & M College (Normal, Ala.), 1967.
10. Wood, Susan. *An Evaluation of Published English Tests,* pp. 13–7. Madison, Wis.: Wisconsin Department of Public Instruction, 1967. Pp. 91. *

CUMULATIVE NAME INDEX

Conquest, G. R.: 1
Greene, H. A.: *rev,* 2:1292
Groff, P. J.: 4
Katz, S. S.: 8
Lannholm, G. V.: *rev,* 4:151
Leonard, J. P.: *rev,* 2:1292
McCullough, C. M.: *rev,* 5:177
McGuire, C.: 7
Palate, E. L.: 6
Pooley, R. C.: *rev,* 4:151
Post, W. L.: *rev,* 5:177
Reid, T. J.: 1
Sangster, C. H.: 2
Schutz, R. E.: *rev,* 6:251
Sopchak, A. L.: 3
Turner, D.: 5
Winston, W. E.: 9
Wood, S.: 10

[62]

*Canadian Achievement Test in English. Grade 10; 1961–68; CATE; a test in the *Canadian Test Battery, Grade 10;* Ontario Institute for Studies in Education; distributed by Guidance Centre [Canada]. * For the complete battery entry, see 1046.

For additional information and a review by Bernard Spolsky, see 6:252 (2 references).

REFERENCES THROUGH 1971

1-2. See 6:252.

CUMULATIVE NAME INDEX

D'Oyley, V. R.: 1–2   Spolsky, B.: *rev,* 6:252

[63]

*Canadian English Achievement Test. Grades 8.5–9.0; 1959–68; CEAT; a test in the *Canadian Test Battery, Grades 8–9;* 3 or 4 scores; the reading subtest is also listed separately; Ontario Institute for Studies in Education; distributed by Guidance Centre [Canada]. * For the complete battery entry, see 1047.
a) PART 1, READING COMPREHENSION.
b) PART 2, MECHANICS OF EXPRESSION. 2 scores in grade 8 (separate scores are obtained for the first 60 and the last 60 items).
c) PART 3, EFFECTIVENESS OF EXPRESSION. Items selected from early forms of the *Cooperative English Tests.*

For additional information and reviews by J. Douglas Ayers and Bernard Spolsky, see 6:253 (2 references).

REFERENCES THROUGH 1971

1-2. See 6:253.

CUMULATIVE NAME INDEX

Ayers, J. D.: *rev,* 6:253   Spolsky, B.: *rev,* 6:253
D'Oyley, V. R.: 1–2

[63A]

★**Canadian English Language Achievement Test.** Candidates for college entrance; 1968–73; CELAT; test administered annually in April and December at centers established by the publisher; parallel edition for French language available; Service for Admission to College and University [Canada]. * For the testing program entry, see 1060.

REFERENCES THROUGH 1971

1. D'Oyley, Vincent R., and Scott, Douglas M. "Objective Testing and the Evaluation of English: Some Comments." *Engl Q* (Canada) 3(1):87–93 sp '70. *
2. D'Oyley, Vincent R. "Development of the SACU Tests." *Sch Guid Worker* (Canada) 26(4):12–6 Mr–Ap '71. *
3. Elley, W. B. "SACU English Language Achievement and Verbal Aptitude Tests." *Interchange* (Canada) 2(3):83–6 '71. * (*PA* 48:5618)
4. Elliott, H. A. "SACU and the SACU Tests: Past, Present, and Future." *Sch Guid Worker* (Canada) 26(4):6–11 Mr–Ap '71. *
5. Holmes, Mark. "The Relationship Between SACU Test Scores and Other Criteria of High School Academic Performance." *Sch Guid Worker* (Canada) 26(4):25–30 Mr–Ap '71. *

CUMULATIVE NAME INDEX

D'Oyley, V. R.: 1–2
Elley, W. B.: 3
Elliott, H. A.: 4
Holmes, M.: 5
Scott, D. M.: 1

[64]

College Board Achievement Test in English Composition. Candidates for college entrance; 1943–73; test administered on specified dates at centers established by the publisher; inactive forms, entitled *College Placement Tests in English Composition,* are available to colleges for local administration; program administered for the College Entrance Examination Board by Educational Testing Service. * For the testing program entry, see 1048.

For additional information, see 7:188 (10 references); for reviews by Charlotte Croon Davis, Robert C. Pooley, and Holland Roberts of earlier forms, see 6:287 (6 references); see also 5:204 (14 references); for a review by Charlotte Croon Davis (with Frederick B. Davis), see 4:178 (6 references). For reviews of the testing program, see 6:760 (2 reviews).

REFERENCES THROUGH 1971

1-6. See 4:178.
7-20. See 5:204.
21-26. See 6:287.
27-36. See 7:188.
37. Muhlenkamp, Ann F. "Prediction of State Board Scores in a Baccalaureate Program." *Nursing Outl* 19(1):57 Ja '71. *

CUMULATIVE NAME INDEX

Barth, C. A.: 32
Black, D. B.: 21
Bobbitt, J. M.: 7
Clark, E. W.: 27
College Entrance Examination Board: 11, 17, 28
Davis, C. C.: *rev,* 4:178, 6:287
Davis, F. B.: *rev,* 4:178
Davis, S. E.: 3
Dyer, H. S.: 8, 13
Eley, E. G.: 14
Elledge, S.: 35
Evenson, A. B.: 19
Farmer, P.: 23
Fels, W. C.: 6
Fishman, J. A.: 18
French, J. W.: 7, 20, 24, 29
Halladay, R. E.: 33
Huddleston, E. M.: 5
Ivanoff, J. M.: 30
King, R. G.: 13
Ludlow, H. G.: 36
McCall, J. N.: 10
Malloy, J. P.: 30
Marshall, J. J.: 34
Miller, P. M.: 12
Morgan, J. M.: 36
Muhlenkamp, A. F.: 37
Newman, S. H.: 7
Noyes, E. S.: 1, 26
Olsen, M. A.: 9
Palmer, O.: 22
Pearson, R.: 15
Peixotto, H. E.: 4
Pooley, R. C.: *rev,* 6:287
Pugh, R. C.: 36
Roberts, H.: *rev,* 6:287
Rose, J. R.: 30
Shostak, J.: 31
Smith, D. E.: 19
Stoke, S. M.: 2
Swineford, F.: 16
Weaver, L. J.: 2
Webb, S. C.: 10

[65]

College English Placement Test. College entrants; 1969; CEPT; Oscar M. Haugh and James I. Brown; Houghton Mifflin Co. *

For additional information and reviews by Clarence Derrick and Osmond E. Palmer, see 7:189.

REFERENCES THROUGH 1971

1. Novak, Mary Lou Bayer. *The English Language Proficiency of Secondary Student Teachers in Selected Nebraska Colleges and Universities.* Doctor's thesis, University of Nebraska (Lincoln, Neb.), 1970. (*DAI* 31:4016A)
2. Neal, L. Ramon, and Ellis, W. Geiger. "College English Placement Test: A Review." *J Ed Meas* 8(3):228–30 f '71. *

[66]

College English Test: National Achievement Tests. Grades 12–13; 1937–43; 7 scores: punctuation, capitalization, language usage, sentence structure, modifiers, miscellaneous principles, total; 1942 form identical with test copyrighted 1937 except for minor changes; A. C. Jordan; Psychometric Affiliates. *

For additional information and a review by Osmond E. Palmer, see 5:178; for reviews by Constance M. McCullough and Robert W. Howard, see 2:1269.1.

[67]

*College Placement Tests in English Composition. Entering college freshmen; 1962–72, c1958–72; reprintings of inactive 1966 and 1967 forms of *College Board Achievement Test in English Composition;* tests available to colleges for local administration; 2 tests: 1-hour version, shortened version entitled *College Placement Test in English Composition (Forty Minute Version)*; program administered for the College Entrance Examination Board by Educational Testing Service. * For the testing program entry, see 1051.

For additional information and a review by John C. Sherwood, see 7:190 (3 references). For a review of the testing program, see 7:665. For reference to reviews of the *College Board Achievement Test in English Composition,* see 64.

REFERENCES THROUGH 1971
1–3. See 7:190.

[68]

*Comprehensive Tests of Basic Skills: Language. Grades 2.5–4, 4–6, 6–8, 8–12; 1968–71; 4 scores: mechanics, expression, spelling, total; CTB/McGraw-Hill. * For the complete battery entry, see 11.

For additional information, see 7:191. For reviews of the complete battery, see 7:9 (2 reviews, 3 excerpts).

[69]

Cooperative English Tests. Grades 9–12, 13–14; 1940–60; CET; 6 scores: reading comprehension (vocabulary, level, speed, total), English expression, total; subtests available as separates; revision by Clarence Derrick, David P. Harris, and Biron Walker; Cooperative Tests and Services. *

For additional information, reviews by Leonard S. Feldt and Margaret F. Lorimer, and an excerpted review by Laurence Siegel, see 6:256 (52 references); see also 5:179 (58 references) and 4:155 (53 references); for reviews by J. Paul Leonard, Edward S. Noyes, and Robert C. Pooley of an earlier edition, see 3:120 (29 references); see also 2:1276 (1 reference). For reviews of the expression subtest, see 6:258 (2 reviews); the reading subtest, see 6:806 (2 reviews); and an earlier edition of the reading subtest, see 3:497 (2 reviews).

REFERENCES THROUGH 1971
1–2. See 2:1276.
3–31. See 3:120.
32–84. See 4:155.
85–142. See 5:179.
143–194. See 6:256.

195. GLADFELTER, M. E. "The Value of the Cooperative English Test in Prediction in College." *Sch & Soc* 44:383–4 S 10 '36. * (*PA* 11:460)

196. DRAKE, LEWIS E., AND HENMON, V. A. C. "The Prediction of Scholarship in the College of Letters and Science at the University of Wisconsin." *Sch & Soc* 45:191–4 F 6 '37. * (*PA* 11:2441)

197. MANNING, FRANK LEROY. "How Accurately Can We Predict Success in College?" *J Am Assn Col Reg* 14:35–8 O '38. * (*PA* 13:4365)

198. DOUGLASS, LOWELL N. "A Study of Certain Factors Influencing Academic Achievement With Special Reference to the Health Factor." *J Exp Ed* 7:235–44 Mr '39. * (*PA* 13:5911)

199. ARSENIAN, SETH. "Own Estimate and Objective Measurement." *J Ed Psychol* 33:291–302 Ap '42. * (*PA* 17:934)

200. MCCLANAHAN, WALTER R., AND MORGAN, DAVID H. "Use of Standard Tests in Counseling Engineering Students in College." *J Ed Psychol* 39:491–501 D '48. * (*PA* 23:3448)

201. RAUSCH, OSCAR P. "The Effects of Individual Variability on Achievement." *J Ed Psychol* 39:469–78 D '48. * (*PA* 23:3450)

202. BERGERON, WILBUR LEE. *An Analysis of the Relationship Between Selected Characteristics and Academic Success of Freshmen at the University of Arkansas.* Doctor's thesis, University of Arkansas (Fayetteville, Ark.), 1953. (*DA* 13:505)

203. JARVIS, JOHN ASA. *Student Survival Factors in the Stout Institute: A Statistical Study of High School Records, Entrance Test Scores, College Course Grades and Other Measures With Relation to Survival in and Graduation by a College of Teacher Training Type-Male Students, Industrial Arts Division, Four Years, 1947–51.* Doctor's thesis, University of Minnesota (Minneapolis, Minn.), 1953. (*DA* 13:700)

204. SMITH, ALLAN B. *The Prediction of Scholastic Success for Freshman Entrants to the University of Connecticut 1933–1951.* Doctor's thesis, University of Connecticut (Storrs, Conn.), 1953. (*DA* 13:1121)

205. HENDRICKS, RICHARD. *Relationships Among Tests of Intelligibility, Word-Reception, and Other Measures of Symbolic Formulation.* Doctor's thesis, Ohio State University (Columbus, Ohio), 1956. (*DA* 16:2239)

206. JONES, TOM M. *Comparisons of Test Scores of High School Graduates of 1954 Who Go to College With Those Who Do Not Go, and a Study of Certain Factors Associated With Going to College.* Doctor's thesis, University of Arkansas (Fayetteville, Ark.), 1956. (*DA* 16:1373)

207. PEPPARD, PAULA LAFORGE, AND VOTAW, DAVID F., SR. "Objective Methods of Detecting Needs for Remedial Work in Writing." *J Ed Res* 49:537–41 Mr '56. * (*PA* 31:5148)

208. SHEA, ELLEN MARIE. *The Prognostic Value of Admissions Procedures in a State Teachers College.* Doctor's thesis, University of Connecticut (Storrs, Conn.), 1957. (*DA* 17:2503)

209. ENGELBRECHT, GLADYS M. *Scholastic Success of Students Changing School or College Within the University of Connecticut.* Doctor's thesis, University of Connecticut (Storrs, Conn.), 1958. (*DA* 19:986)

210. KING, EDWARD S., AND KING, DONALD B. "English Usage and Spelling in Law School: An Experiment and Possible Solution." *J Legal Ed* 11(2):253–6 '58. *

211. KRATTIGER, JOHN TRUBERT. *An Evaluation of the Freshman Testing Program of Southeastern State College of Oklahoma.* Doctor's thesis, University of Oklahoma (Norman, Okla.), 1958. (*DA* 19:718)

212. FLETCHER, JUNIOR EUGENE. *A Study of the Relationships Between Ability to Use Context as an Aid in Reading and Other Verbal Abilities.* Doctor's thesis, University of Washington (Seattle, Wash.), 1959. (*DA* 20:2674)

213. FRADENBURG, LEO GLENN. *An Investigation of the Correlation Between Pre-Course Test Results and Academic Success in the Air Force Squadron Officer School for Prediction Purposes.* Doctor's thesis, Purdue University (Lafayette, Ind.), 1959. (*DA* 20:3193)

214. KITTELL, JACK E. "Relationship of Language Scores to Residence Classifications of College Freshmen." *J Ed Res* 52:190–3 Ja '59. * (*PA* 34:12104)

215. KUNHART, WILLIAM E., AND OLSEN, LIONEL R. "An Analysis of Test Scores and Grades for Predicting Success of College Students in English Composition." *J Ed Res* 53:79 O '59. *

216. PAERATAKUL, CHAWAL. "Differences in Performance on the Doctoral Admission Examinations at Indiana University by Thai Students, Foreign Non-Thai Students, and American Students." *B Sch Ed Ind Univ* 35(3):41–64 My '59. * (*PA* 34:6571)

217. GOWAN, J. C., AND DIBLE, ISABEL. "Age Effects on the Test Scores of Women Teaching Candidates." *Calif J Ed Res* 11:37–8 Ja '60. * (*PA* 34:8417)

218. HILL, EDWIN S. *An Analysis of the Results of Special Training in Listening Compared to Special Training in Reading Skills.* Doctor's thesis, Indiana University (Bloomington, Ind.), 1961. (*DA* 22:3093)

219. BALLANTYNE, ROBERT HUBBARD. *An Analysis of Criteria for Selecting Freshmen Students for an Honors Program at Washington State University.* Doctor's thesis, Washington State University (Pullman, Wash.), 1962. (*DA* 23:2439)

220. BASHAW, W. L. "The Prediction of Grades of First-Time Florida Freshmen at the Florida State University." *Fla J Ed Res* 4:27–36 Ja '62. *

221. DeHart, Arla Lando, Jr. *Possible Selective Admissions Criteria for the California Public Junior College.* Doctor's thesis, Stanford University (Stanford, Calif.), 1962. (*DA* 22:4233)

222. Medlin, Yancey Leonard. *An Analysis of Some Aspects of the English Proficiency of White Secondary School Teacher Candidates in North Carolina, 1959–1961.* Doctor's thesis, University of North Carolina (Chapel Hill, N.C.), 1962. (*DA* 24:1495)

223. Babbott, Edward French. *The Differential Effectiveness of Eight 9th Grade Variables in Predicting Success in Three 10th Grade Academic Subjects at Summit High School: A Study in Differential Prediction.* Doctor's thesis, New York University (New York, N.Y.), 1963. (*DA* 25:993)

224. Cieutat, Victor J. "Individual Differences in Verbal Learning." *Percept & Motor Skills* 17:275–8 Ag '63. * (*PA* 38:7320)

225. Hermsen, Leon Paul. *A Comparative Study of the Background Data, Academic Achievement and the Persistence of Students Electing Business Teacher Education With Those in Other Subject Fields at Wisconsin State College, Whitewater.* Doctor's thesis, University of Wisconsin (Madison, Wis.), 1963. (*DA* 24:1492)

226. Lehmkuhl, Carlton Burdell. *Test Performance Relationships Among Occupational Patterns of Educational Administration Program Graduates.* Doctor's thesis, University of Minnesota (Minneapolis, Minn.), 1963. (*DA* 24:4510)

227. Taulbee, George C., Sr. *Construction and Validation of a Scale for Predicting Graduation From a College of Optometry.* Doctor's thesis, University of Houston (Houston, Tex.), 1963. (*DA* 24:387)

228. Torres, Leonard. *A Study of the Relationship Between Selected Variables and the Achievement of Industrial Arts Students at Long Beach State College.* Doctor's research study No. 1, Colorado State College (Greeley, Colo.), 1963. (*DA* 25:316)

229. Williams, Robert A. *An Assessment of the Success of C Average High School Graduates in Grand Rapids Junior College.* Doctor's thesis, Michigan State University (East Lansing, Mich.), 1963. (*DA* 25:317)

230. Zimmerman, William George, Jr. *An Analysis of Selected Aspects of the Master of Education Program at the University of Miami.* Doctor's thesis, University of Miami (Coral Gables, Fla.), 1963. (*DA* 28:95A)

231. Anderson, A. W. "Reading and English Scores of a Group of Foreign Students Entering the University of Western Australia in 1964." *Austral J Higher Ed* 2:84–90 N '64. *

232. Boe, Erling E. "The Prediction of Academic Performance of Engineering Students." *Ed & Psychol Meas* 24:377–83 su '64. * (*PA* 39:5975)

233. Brown, Frederick G., and Dubois, Thomas E. "Correlates of Academic Success for High-Ability Freshman Men." *Personnel & Guid J* 42:603–7 F '64. * (*PA* 39:5820)

234. Chase, Clinton I.; Ludlow, H. Glenn; and Pugh, Richard C. *Predicting Success for Master's Degree Students in Education.* Indiana Studies in Prediction No. 5. Bloomington, Ind.: Bureau of Educational Studies and Testing, Indiana University, 1964. Pp. v, 25. *

235. Chase, Clinton I.; Ludlow, H. Glenn; Pugh, Richard C.; and Pomeroy, Martha C. *Predicting Success for Advanced Graduate Students in Education.* Indiana Studies in Prediction No. 4. Bloomington, Ind.: Bureau of Educational Studies and Testing, Indiana University, 1964. Pp. v, 18. *

236. Cooper, Carl J. "Some Relationships Between Paired-Associates Learning and Foreign-Language Aptitude." *J Ed Psychol* 55:132–8 Je '64. * (*PA* 39:5823)

237. Engen, Harold Bernard, Jr. *Differential Prediction of Academic Success and Attrition-Survival of Entering Freshmen at the University of South Dakota.* Doctor's thesis, State University of South Dakota (Vermillion, S.D.), 1964. (*DA* 25:2847)

238. Hughes, Donald L. *A Study to Predict the Academic Success of Low Achieving High School Students at Brigham Young University With Selected Tests.* Master's thesis, Brigham Young University (Provo, Utah), 1964.

239. Schreck, Thomas C. "Selected Factors Related to Academic Success in College." *Ed & Psychol R* (India) 4:71–6 Ap '64. *

240. Space, Margaret Niven. *A Study of Individual Predictability Based on Intra-Individual Variability on Certain Achievement Measures.* Doctor's thesis, University of Minnesota (Minneapolis, Minn.), 1964. (*DA* 26:879)

241. Webb, Sam C. "The Psychological Components of Scores for Two Tests of Report Writing Ability." *Ed & Psychol Meas* 24:31–46 sp '64. * (*PA* 39:1770)

242. Chaudhry, Ghulam Mohammed, and Kayani, Mohammed Rashid. "A Comparative Study of the DAT Verbal Reasoning, ACE Psychological Examination and Cooperative English Comprehension Tests as Predictors of Academic Success in the Institute of Education and Research, University of the Panjab." *B Ed & Res* (Pakistan) 4(2):1–21 '65. *

243. Davis, Luther Edward, Jr. *A Study of Selected Traits of St. Petersburg Junior College Students and Their Value in Predicting Academic Success in Certain Courses of Study at the Senior College Level.* Doctor's thesis, Auburn University (Auburn, Ala.), 1965. (*DA* 26:791)

244. Jungeblut, Ann. "A Note on the 1960 Revision of the Cooperative English Test." *Ed Rec B* 88:64–6 Jl '65. *

245. Kimball, Webster H. *Persistence and Success Prediction in Accounting.* Master's thesis, California State College (Long Beach, Calif.), 1965.

246. Leutenegger, Ralph R.; Mueller, Theodore H.; and Wershow, Irving R. "Auditory Factors in Foreign Language Acquisition." *Mod Lang J* 49:22–31 Ja '65. *

247. Stone, Donald Bradford. *Predicting Student Retention and Withdrawal in a Selected State University College of New York.* Doctor's thesis, Cornell University (Ithaca, N.Y.), 1965. (*DA* 26:5184)

248. Taylor, Jean. *An Examination of the Relationships Between Test Scores and Grades in Eleventh Grade English Groups at Hillcrest High School.* Master's thesis, University of Utah (Salt Lake City, Utah), 1965.

249. Troy, Elizabeth McGoldrick. *A Study of the Predictive Value of Eleven Variables Used at King's College to Determine General Scholastic Achievement of Two Hundred Forty-Three Entering Students.* Master's thesis, Marywood College (Scranton, Pa.), 1965.

250. Wenberg, Burness G., and Ingersoll, Ralph W. "Medical Dietetics: Part 2, The Development of Evaluative Techniques." *J Am Dietetic Assn* 47:298–300 O '65. *

251. Wyeth, Ezra R. "Evaluation of the Effectiveness of the Leadership Training Program in the Area of the Deaf at San Fernando Valley State College." *Am Ann Deaf* 110:479–82 S '65. * (*PA* 40:5848)

252. Bretnall, Doris, and Davis, Frederick B. "The Effect of the Conventional Correction for Chance on Distributions of Scores From Form B of the 1960 Edition of the Cooperative English Tests." *Ed Rec B* 90:55–7 Jl '66. *

253. Campbell, John P. "Comparison of Criterion Clusters Obtained by Analyzing the Homogeneity of a Set of Regression Equations and the Matrix of Intercorrelations." *Ed & Psychol Meas* 26:405–17 su '66. * (*PA* 40:12757)

254. Cunningham, William. *A Thirteen-Year Retrospective Study of Standardized Test Data.* Doctor's thesis, Western Reserve University (Cleveland, Ohio), 1966. (*DA* 27:3305A)

255. Gross, Nathan. *English Grades as a Function of Intellectual Ability, Performance, and the Congruency of Teacher-Pupil Perceptions of Interpersonal Values.* Doctor's thesis, Harvard University (Cambridge, Mass.), 1966. (*DA* 28:123A)

256. Jex, Frank B. *Predicting Academic Success Beyond High School.* Salt Lake City, Utah: University of Utah Bookstore, 1966. Pp. vi, 41. *

257. Schofield, William, and Merwin, Jack C. "The Use of Scholastic Aptitude, Personality, and Interest Test Data in the Selection of Medical Students." *J Med Ed* 41:502–9 Je '66. *

258. Schroeder, Pearl. "Relative Spelling Ability as a Predictor of the Academic Performance of Superior Ability College Freshmen." *J Ed Res* 59:427–8 My–Je '66. * (*PA* 40:11463)

259. Smith, William Charles. *A Factor Analytic Study of the "Test of Sound Reasoning."* Doctor's thesis, University of Missouri (Kansas City, Mo.), 1966. (*DA* 28:408A)

260. Stallings, William Marion. *A Study of Non-Intellective Factors in the Prediction of Academic Success for Master's Degree Level Students in the School of Education, Indiana University.* Doctor's thesis, Indiana University (Bloomington, Ind.), 1966. (*DA* 27:3324A)

261. Tucker, Harmon. *A Statistical Study to Determine the Relationship Between Scores of the Cooperative English Test and the Aptitude Sections of the Graduate Record Examinations.* Master's thesis, Stetson University (DeLand, Fla.), 1966.

262. Barnett, Thomas Marvin. *The Predictive Validities, as Measured by Multiple Correlation, of Two Batteries Using Academic Achievement as Criterion.* Doctor's thesis, North Texas State University (Denton, Tex.), 1967. (*DA* 28:2006A)

263. Ingram, John Allen. *Factors Affecting the Success of Transfer Students at Drake University.* Doctor's thesis, Iowa State University (Ames, Iowa), 1967. (*DA* 28:1341A)

264. Lohnes, Paul R., and McIntire, Paul H. "Classification Validities of a Statewide 10th Grade Test Program." *Personnel & Guid J* 45:561–7 F '67. *

265. Pickle, John H. *Analysis of the Relation of Entrance Examination Scores and Marks Earned in Eight Semesters by Graduates of the College of Education.* Doctor's thesis, University of Arkansas (Fayetteville, Ark.), 1967. (*DA* 28:405A)

266. Walters, Nancy Rockhill. *Predictive Characteristics of Depauw University Freshman Dropouts Over a Three Year Period.* Doctor's thesis, Indiana University (Bloomington, Ind.), 1967. (*DA* 28:3471A)

267. Wood, Susan. *An Evaluation of Published English Tests,* pp. 19–21. Madison, Wis.: Wisconsin Department of Public Instruction, 1967. Pp. 91. *

268. Brown, Thomas O. *The Urban University Student. Selected Factors Related to Continuation and Withdrawal.* Doctor's thesis, Kent State University (Kent, Ohio), 1968. (*DA* 29:4318A)

269. Colgan, Richard Thomas. *A Longitudinal Study of the Relationship of Teacher Judgment Versus Objective Test Data With Respect to College Success.* Doctor's thesis, Southern Illinois University (Carbondale, Ill.), 1968. (*DA* 29:3413B)

270. Conklin, R. C., and Ogston, D. G. "Prediction of

Academic Success for Freshmen at the University of Calgary."
Alberta J Ed Res (Canada) 14:185–92 S '68. * (*PA* 44:4244)

271. COY, MICHAEL. *Factorial Study of Variables Related to College Grade Point Average.* Master's thesis, Humboldt State College (Arcata, Calif.), 1968.

272. DALY, JOSEPH L., AND STAHMANN, ROBERT F. "The Effect of Time Limits on a University Placement Test." *J Ed Res* 62:103–4 N '68. *

273. HEDLEY, CAROLYN NEAL. "Learning Relationship Differences and Curriculum Choice." *Improving Col & Univ Teach* 16:268–72 au '68. *

274. JOHNSON, RICHARD W.; KEOCHAKIAN, SIMON V.; MORNINGSTAR, MONA; AND SOUTHWORTH, J. ALFRED. "Validation of Freshman Orientation Test Battery." *Ed & Psychol Meas* 28:437–40 su '68. * (*PA* 42:1927J)

275. MCGEE, JIM ED. *Selected Factors Associated With Success or Failure on the Junior English Examination at the University of Arkansas.* Doctor's thesis, University of Arkansas (Fayetteville, Ark.), 1968. (*DA* 29:99A)

276. MILLER, RICHARD HADDEN. *A Descriptive Study of the Relationship Between Potential and Performance of Freshman Students at the University of South Dakota.* Doctor's thesis, University of South Dakota (Vermillion, S.D.), 1968. (*DA* 29:2612A)

277. MUNDAY, LEO. "Correlations Between ACT and Other Predictors of Academic Success in College." *Col & Univ* 44:67–76 f '68. *

278. VAN DERSLICE, JOHN FREDERICK. *The Educational, Social, and Economic Background of Engineering and Technical Students Analyzed for the Purpose of Establishing Profiles for Use in Counseling.* Doctor's thesis, Utah State University (Logan, Utah), 1968. (*DA* 29:1431A)

279. WILSON, ANAISE VICTORIANNE. *A Study of the Relationship of Selected Factors to the Academic Achievement of College Freshmen in the School of Education of Tuskegee Institute.* Doctor's thesis, New York University (New York, N.Y.), 1968. (*DAI* 30:144A)

280. DAVIS, J. MICHAEL. *The Relationship of Selection Factors in the Cuban Teacher Retraining Program to the Effective Classroom Performance of Cuban Teachers.* Doctor's thesis, University of Miami (Coral Gables, Fla.), 1969. (*DAI* 30:3222A)

281. ELTING, ROBERT A., AND BUTTERFIELD, MARY. "Academic Performance of Cuban-Teacher Students at the University of Miami." *Col & Univ* 44(3):263–7 sp '69. *

282. EVANS, JAMES D. "The Relationships of Three Personality Scales to Grade Point Average and Verbal Ability in College Freshmen." *J Ed Res* 63(3):121–5 N '69. * (*PA* 46:5658)

283. FOLLMAN, JOHN. "Factor Analysis of Three Critical Thinking Tests, One Logical Reasoning Test, and One English Test." *Yearb Nat Read Conf* 18:154–60 '69. *

284. FOLLMAN, JOHN COSGROVE. *A Factor Analytic Study of Three Critical Thinking Tests, One English Test, and One Logical Reasoning Test.* Doctor's thesis, Indiana University (Bloomington, Ind.), 1969. (*DAI* 30:1015A)

285. GEORGE, WARREN EDWIN. *Significant Predictors for College Achievement in Specified Areas of Music Education and Identification of Potential Graduates.* Doctor's thesis, University of Kansas (Lawrence, Kan.), 1969. (*DAI* 30:3040A)

286. HUCKABEE, MALCOM W. "Personality and Academic Aptitude Correlates of Cognitive Control Principles." *South J Ed Res* 3(1):1–9 Ja '69. *

287. HUSEMOLLER, KENNETH E. *The Prediction of Freshmen Academic Success at Eastern New Mexico University, Roswell, by Means of Selected Demographic and Standardized Tests Data.* Doctor's thesis, Colorado State College (Greeley, Colo.), 1969. (*DAI* 30:1467A)

288. MILLER, RICHARD H. "Students Show a Preparation Increase but No Increase in Grades Was Shown." *Col & Univ* 45(1):28–30 f '69. *

289. POSTON, WILLIAM KENNETH, JR. *Educational Administrator Job Performance and Training Program Admission Criteria.* Doctor's thesis, Arizona State University (Tempe, Ariz.), 1969. (*DAI* 30:532A)

290. PREAS, NANCY BUSH. *A Study of the Relationship Between Selected Variables and Academic Achievement in a Community College.* Doctor's thesis, North Carolina State University (Raleigh, N.C.), 1969. (*DAI* 30:5245A)

291. WENBERG, BURNESS G.; INGERSOLL, RALPH W.; AND DOHNER, CHARLES W. "Evaluation of Dietetic Interns." *J Am Dietetic Assn* 54(4):297–301 Ap '69. *

292. WILLIAMS, VERNON. *A Multi-Predictive Measure to Predict Success at Two Levels in Freshman College Mathematics.* Doctor's thesis, Oklahoma State University (Stillwater, Okla.), 1969. (*DAI* 31:4026A)

293. ELTING, ROBERT ARTHUR. *The Prediction of Freshman Year Academic Performance of Foreign Students From Pre-Admission Data.* Doctor's thesis, New York University (New York, N.Y.), 1970. (*DAI* 31:5697A)

294. FOLLMAN, JOHN. "Correlational and Factor Analysis of Critical Thinking, Logical Reasoning, and English Total Test Scores." *Fla J Ed Res* 12(1):91–4 Ja '70. *

295. FOLLMAN, JOHN; BROWN, LAURENCE; AND BURG, ELDON. "Factor Analysis of Critical Thinking, Logical Reasoning, and English Subtests." *J Exp Ed* 38(4):11–6 su '70. *

296. JANSEN, DAVID G.; ROBB, GEORGE P.; AND BONK, EDWARD C. "Characteristics of High-Rated and Low-Rated Master's Degree Candidates in Counseling and Guidance." *Counselor Ed & Sup* 9(3):162–70 sp '70. * (*PA* 46:5559)

297. LAUTZ, ROBERT; MACLEAN, G. DONALD; VAUGHAN, ANDREW T.; AND OLIVER, THOMAS C. "Characteristics of Successful Students Following Academic Suspension." *Col & Univ* 45(2):192–202 w '70. *

298. LIBBY, WILLIAM L., JR. "Reaction Time and Remote Association in Talented Male Adolescents." *Develop Psychol* 3(3):285–97 N '70. * (*PA* 45:4001)

299. RUSSELL, WENDELL PHILLIPS. *Intellectual and Non-Intellectual Factors Affecting the Attrition Rate of Students Entering Virginia Union University in 1965.* Doctor's thesis, University of Virginia (Charlottesville, Va.), 1970. (*DAI* 31:4474A)

300. MAZUR, JAMES MATTHEW. *A Study of Predictive Validity of Standardized Tests Used for Placement of Vocational Students at Rockingham Community College.* Master's thesis, North Carolina State University (Raleigh, N.C.), 1971.

301. SMITH, RICHARD LEE. *A Factor-Analytic Study of Critical Reading/Thinking, Influenceability, and Related Factors.* Doctor's thesis, University of Maine (Orono, Me.), 1971. (*DAI* 32:6229A)

CUMULATIVE NAME INDEX

[70]

Cooperative Primary Tests: Writing Skills.
Grades 2.5–3; 1965–67; 3 scores: spelling, capitalization-punctuation-usage, total; Cooperative Tests and Services. * For the complete battery entry, see 12.

For reviews of the complete battery, see 7:10 (2 excerpts).

[71]

*Cotswold Junior English Ability Test. Ages 8.5–9.5, 9.5–10.5; 1949–70; 2 levels; tests A, B, and E are out of print; C. M. Fleming; Robert Gibson & Sons, Glasgow, Ltd. [Scotland]. *
a) JUNIOR ENGLISH C AND D. Ages 8.5–9.5; 1967–70, c1954–57.
b) JUNIOR ENGLISH F. Ages 9.5–10.5; 1968–70, c1961.

For additional information and reviews by M. A. Brimer and John C. Daniels of earlier forms, see 5:182.

[72]

*Cotswold Measurement of Ability: English. Ages 10–12; 1947–69; C. M. Fleming; Robert Gibson & Sons, Glasgow, Ltd. [Scotland]. *

For additional information and reviews by M. A. Brimer and S. C. Richardson of earlier forms, see 5:183.

[73]

English Expression: Cooperative English Tests. Grades 9–12, 13–14; 1940–60; this subtest of the *Cooperative English Tests* is a revision of the subtests *Effectiveness of Expression* and *Mechanics of Expression* in earlier editions of the battery; revision by Clarence Derrick, David P. Harris, and Biron Walker; Cooperative Tests and Services. * For the complete battery entry, see 69.

For additional information and reviews by John C. Sherwood and John M. Stalnaker, see 6:258; for a review by Chester W. Harris of an earlier edition, see 4:155. For reviews of the complete battery, see 6:256 (2 reviews, 1 excerpt) and 3:120 (3 reviews).

[74]

English IX–XII: Achievement Examinations for Secondary Schools. Grades 9, 10, 11, 12; 1951–54; Form 4 ('54) of a series of tests, currently (1973) entitled *Language Arts: Minnesota High School Achievement Examinations* (see 90), issued annually for May testing; 4 levels; Bobbs-Merrill Co., Inc. *
a) ENGLISH IX. Grade 9; Carl Towley.
b) ENGLISH X. Grade 10; Ina Engburg.
c) ENGLISH XI. Grade 11; Winifred Murray.
d) ENGLISH XII. Grade 12; Ina Engburg.

For additional information concerning later and earlier forms, see 90, 7:197, 6:268 (1 review), 5:185, and 5:186 (1 review).

REFERENCES THROUGH 1971
1. GROFF, PATRICK J. "Parts of Speech in Standardized English Tests." *Sch R* 69:457–60 w '61. *

CUMULATIVE NAME INDEX
Groff, P. J.: 1

[75]

*English Progress Tests. Various ages 7-3 to 15-6; 1952–72; 13 tests; tests B, C, D, and F are out of print; published for the National Foundation for Educational Research in England and Wales; Ginn & Co. Ltd. [England]. *
a) ENGLISH PROGRESS TEST A. Ages 8-0 to 9-0; 1952–60; A. F. Watts.
b) ENGLISH PROGRESS TEST E. Ages 12-0 to 13-0; 1956; M. A. Brimer and A. F. Watts.

c) ENGLISH PROGRESS TEST G. Ages 13-0 to 15-6; 1962; test by S. M. Unwin.

d) ENGLISH PROGRESS TEST A2. Ages 7-3 to 8-11; 1962–66; test by Betsy Barnard.

e) ENGLISH PROGRESS TEST B2. Ages 8-6 to 10-0; 1959–60; manual by Valerie C. Land.

f) ENGLISH PROGRESS TEST C2. Ages 9-6 to 11-0; 1961; Valerie Land.

g) ENGLISH PROGRESS TEST D2. Ages 10-6 to 12-0; 1963–64; Jennifer Henchman.

h) ENGLISH PROGRESS TEST E2. Ages 11-0 to 13-0; 1962–72; test by S. M. Unwin.

i) ENGLISH PROGRESS TEST F2. Ages 12-0 to 13-6; 1963–72; test by Jennifer Henchman and Elsa Hendry.

j) ENGLISH PROGRESS TEST B3. Ages 8-0 to 9-6; 1970–72.

k) ENGLISH PROGRESS TEST C3. Ages 9-0 to 10-9; 1970–72.

l) ENGLISH PROGRESS TEST D3. Ages 10-0 to 11-8; 1970–72.

m) ENGLISH PROGRESS TEST F3. Ages 12-0 to 13-6; 1969.

For additional information, see 7:192; for reviews by Neil Gourlay and Stanley Nisbet of Tests A–F, see 5:187.

[76]

English Test FG. Ages 12–13; 1952; formerly called *English Test 2;* G. A. V. Morgan; published for the National Foundation for Educational Research in England and Wales; Ginn & Co. Ltd. [England]. *

For additional information and reviews by Reginald Edwards, S. C. Richardson, and Cleveland A. Thomas, see 5:192.

[77]

English Test: Municipal Tests: National Achievement Tests. Grades 3–6, 6–8; 1938–56; subtest of *Municipal Battery;* 5 scores: language usage-words, language usage-sentences, punctuation and capitalization, expressing ideas, total; 1952–56 tests identical with tests copyrighted 1938–39; Robert K. Speer and Samuel Smith; Psychometric Affiliates. *

For additional information, see 5:190. For reviews of the complete battery, see 5:18 (1 review), 4:20 (1 review), and 2:1191 (2 reviews).

REFERENCES THROUGH 1971
1. GROFF, PATRICK J. "Parts of Speech in Standardized English Tests." *Sch R* 69:457–60 w '61. *

CUMULATIVE NAME INDEX
Groff, P. J.: 1

[78]

English Test: National Achievement Tests. Grades 3–8, 7–12; 1936–57; 2 levels; Robert K. Speer and Samuel Smith; Psychometric Affiliates. *

a) GRADES 3–8. 1936–38; 7 scores: capitalization, punctuation, language usage (sentences), language usage (words), expressing ideas, letter writing, total.

b) GRADES 7–12. 1936–57; 7 scores: word usage, punctuation, vocabulary, language usage (sentences), expressing ideas, expressing feeling, total; 1952 test identical with test copyrighted 1938.

For additional information, see 5:191; for a review by Winifred L. Post, see 4:162; for a review by Harry A. Greene, see 3:126.

REFERENCES THROUGH 1971
1. GROFF, PATRICK J. "Parts of Speech in Standardized English Tests." *Sch R* 69:457–60 w '61. *

CUMULATIVE NAME INDEX
Greene, H. A.: *rev,* 3:126   Post, W. L.: *rev,* 4:162
Groff, P. J.: 1

[79]

English Tests (Adv.). Ages 12–13; 1954–67; 5 tests; distribution restricted to directors of education; published for the National Foundation for Educational Research in England and Wales; Ginn & Co. Ltd. [England]. *

a) ENGLISH TEST (ADV.) 1. 1954–55; G. A. V. Morgan.

b) ENGLISH TEST (ADV.) 2. 1957. *Out of print.*

c) ENGLISH TEST (ADV.) 3. 1958.

d) ENGLISH TEST (ADV.) 4. 1960.

e) ENGLISH TEST (ADV.) 5. 1962–67.

For additional information and a review by Stanley Nisbet, see 7:193; for a review by A. E. G. Pilliner of Tests 1–4, see 6:262.

[80]

*****English Tests 14–20 and 22.** Ages 10–11; 1951–71; new test published annually except for 1970; tests 1 and 3–13 are out of print; distribution restricted to directors of education; published for the National Foundation for Educational Research in England and Wales; Ginn & Co. Ltd. [England]. *

a) ENGLISH TEST 14. 1963–64.

b) ENGLISH TEST 15. 1964–65.

c) ENGLISH TEST 16. 1965–66.

d) ENGLISH TEST 17. 1966–67.

e) ENGLISH TEST 18. 1967–68.

f) ENGLISH TEST 19. 1968–69.

g) ENGLISH TEST 20. 1969–70.

h) ENGLISH TEST 22. 1971.

For additional information and a review by R. Gulliford of tests 13–20, see 7:194; for reviews by Stanley Nisbet and H. J. Sants of earlier tests, see 6:264 (1 reference).

REFERENCES THROUGH 1971
1. See 6:264.

CUMULATIVE NAME INDEX
Butcher, H. J.: 1   Nisbet, S.: *rev,* 6:264
Gulliford, R.: *rev,* 7:194   Sants, H. J.: *rev,* 6:264
Moreton, C. A.: 1

[81]

Essentials of English Tests, Revised Edition. Grades 7–13; 1939–61; 6 scores: spelling, grammatical usage, word usage, sentence structure, punctuation and capitalization, total; 1961 forms identical with forms copyrighted 1939 and 1940 except for revisions in 12 items; 1961 manual essentially the same as 1944 manual except for wording changes; original edition by Dora V. Smith and Constance M. McCullough, revision by Carolyne Green; American Guidance Service, Inc. *

For additional information and a review by J. Raymond Gerberich, see 6:266; for reviews by Charlotte W. Croon and Gerald V. Lannholm and an excerpted review by William J. Jones, see 3:128.

REFERENCES THROUGH 1971
1. WOOD, SUSAN. *An Evaluation of Published English Tests,* pp. 27–9. Madison, Wis.: Wisconsin Department of Public Instruction, 1967. Pp. 91. *

CUMULATIVE NAME INDEX
Croon, C. W.: *rev,* 3:128   Lannholm, G. V.: *rev,* 3:128
Gerberich, J. R.: *rev,* 6:266 Wood, S.: 1
Jones, W. J.: *exc,* 3:128

[82]

★**Functional Grammar Test.** High school and college; 1970; FGT; Joyce E. Lackey; Psychometric Affiliates. *

[83]

*****Grammar and Usage Test Series.** Grades 7–9, 10–12; 1950–70; 2 levels; no manual; Perfection Form Co. *

a) JUNIOR HIGH SCHOOL SERIES. Grades 7–9; formerly called *Objective Tests in English;* 6 tests.

1) *Plurals and Possessives.*
2) *Punctuation.*
3) *Parts of Speech.*
4) *Pronoun Usage.*
5) *Word Usage.*
6) *Final Examination.*

b) SENIOR HIGH SCHOOL SERIES. Grades 10–12; formerly called *Objective Test in Grammar;* 7 tests.

1) *Plurals and Possessives.*
2) *Punctuation.*
3) *Parts of Speech.*
4) *Pronoun Usage.*
5) *Verbals.*
6) *Word Usage.*
7) *Final Examination.*

For additional information concerning the earlier tests, see 4:171 and 4:172.

[84]

Grammar, Usage, and Structure Test and Vocabulary Test. College entrants; 1963–68; William A. McCartney; the Author. *

For additional information, see 7:195.

[85]

Hoyum-Sanders English Tests. 1, 2 semesters in grades 2–4, 5–6, 7–8; 1962–64; first published 1962–63 in the Every Pupil Scholarship Test series; 3 tests; Vera Davis Hoyum and M. W. Sanders; Bureau of Educational Measurements. *

a) HOYUM-SANDERS ELEMENTARY ENGLISH TEST. 1, 2 semesters in grades 2–4.

b) HOYUM-SANDERS INTERMEDIATE ENGLISH TEST. 1, 2 semesters in grades 5–6.

c) HOYUM-SANDERS JUNIOR HIGH SCHOOL ENGLISH TEST. 1, 2 semesters in grades 7–8.

For additional information and a review by Paul B. Diederich, see 7:196.

[86]

Iowa Placement Examinations: English Aptitude. Grades 12–13; 1925–26; test by M. F. Carpenter and G. D. Stoddard; Bureau of Educational Research and Service. *

For additional information and reviews by Clarence Derrick and W. C. Kvaraceus, see 4:166 (5 references); for a review by Robert C. Pooley, see 3:115 (9 references).

REFERENCES THROUGH 1971

1–9. See 3:115.
10–14. See 4:166.
15. HAMMOND, H. P., AND STODDARD, GEORGE DINSMORE. "A Study of Placement Examinations." *Univ Iowa Studies Ed* 4(7):1–59 '28. * (*PA* 3:2069)

CUMULATIVE NAME INDEX

Derrick, C.: *rev*, 4:166
Edmonson, L. D.: 12
Gerberich, J. R.: 7
Hammond, H. P.: 15
Hansen, G. W.: 10
Kvaraceus, W. C.: *rev*, 4:166
Langlie, T. A.: 2–3, 5
Larsen, H. P.: 11
Leaf, C. T.: 9
Miller, L. W.: 8
O'Brien, C. C.: 14
Pooley, R. C.: *rev*, 3:115
Stalnaker, J. M.: 6
Stoddard, G. D.: 1, 4, 15
Topetzes, N. J.: 14
Uhrbrock, R. S.: 13
Wittenborn, J. R.: 11

[87]

Iowa Placement Examinations: English Training. Grades 12–13; 1925–44; 2 editions; test by M. F. Carpenter, G. D. Stoddard, L. W. Miller (*b*), and D. B. Stuit (*b*); Bureau of Educational Research and Service. *

a) SERIES ET-1, REVISED. 1925–26.

b) NEW SERIES ET-2, REVISED. 1925–44.

For additional information and reviews by Clarence Derrick and W. C. Kvaraceus, see 4:167 (5 references); for a review by Robert C. Pooley, see 3:131 (15 references).

REFERENCES THROUGH 1971

1–15. See 3:131.
16–20. See 4:167.
21. HAMMOND, H. P., AND STODDARD, GEORGE DINSMORE. "A Study of Placement Examinations." *Univ Iowa Studies Ed* 4(7):1–59 '28. * (*PA* 3:2069)
22. NELSON, M. J. "Some Data From Freshman Tests." *Sch & Soc* 31:772–4 Je 7 '30. * (*PA* 4:3694)
23. GARNETT, WILLIAM LESLIE. "A Study of Status and Improvement of College Freshmen in Certain Skills of English Composition." *J Exp Ed* 6:29–34 S '37. * (*PA* 12:2108)
24. LONG, JOHN MARSHALL. *The Prediction of College Success From a Battery of Tests and From High School Achievement.* Doctor's thesis, University of Virginia (Charlottesville, Va.), 1960. (*DA* 21:1100)
25. CRANE, WILLIAM J. "Screening Devices for Occupational Therapy Majors." *Am J Occup Ther* 16:131–2 My–Je '62. * (*PA* 37:4078)
26. LONG, JOHN M. "Sex Differences in Academic Prediction Based on Scholastic, Personality and Interest Factors." *J Exp Ed* 32:239–48 sp '64. * (*PA* 39:6058)

CUMULATIVE NAME INDEX

Adams, M.: 14
Adams, W. M.: 15
Barnette, W. L.: 11
Crane, W. J.: 25
Derrick, C.: *rev*, 4:167
Donnelly, M. C.: 12
Freeman, K. H.: 19
Garnett, W. L.: 23
Gerberich, J. R.: 7
Giesecke, G. E.: 17
Hammond, H. P.: 21
Hansen, G. W.: 16
Kvaraceus, W. C.: *rev*, 4:167
Langlie, T. A.: 2–3, 5
Larsen, R. P.: 17–8
Long, J. M.: 24, 26
Merrill, R. A.: 10
Miller, L. W.: 8
Nelson, M. J.: 22
Pankaskie, M.: 13
Pooley, R. C.: *rev*, 3:131
Root, A. R.: 9
Stalnaker, J. M.: 6
Stoddard, G. D.: 1, 4, 21
Stuit, D. B.: 12
Uhrbrock, R. S.: 20
Wittenborn, J. R.: 17–8

[88]

*****The Iowa Tests of Educational Development: Test 3, Correctness and Appropriateness of Expression.** Grades 9–12; 1942–67; Forms X-4 and Y-4; more recent Forms X5 and Y5 are not available as separates; prepared under the direction of E. F. Lindquist and Leonard S. Feldt; Science Research Associates, Inc. * For the complete battery entry, see 20.

For additional information concerning earlier forms, see 6:267 (1 reference). For reviews of the complete battery, see 6:14 (2 reviews), 5:17 (2 reviews), 4:17 (1 review), and 3:12 (3 reviews).

REFERENCES THROUGH 1971

1. See 6:267.

CUMULATIVE NAME INDEX

Groff, P. J.: 1

[89]

★**Language Arts Diagnostic Probes.** Grades 3–9; 1970; also called SALI (Systems Approach to Language Instruction); **2** tests; Stella B. Warner; American Testing Co. *

a) LANGUAGE ARTS DIAGNOSTIC PROBE I: PROBES INTO CAPITALIZATION. SALI I; 3 scores: Probe 40 (8 skills), 41 (9 skills), 42 (9 skills).

b) LANGUAGE ARTS DIAGNOSTIC PROBE II: PROBES INTO PUNCTUATION. SALI II; 2 scores: Probes 43 (17 skills), 44 (8 skills).

[90]

Language Arts: Minnesota High School Achievement Examinations. Grades 7, 8, 9, 10, 11, 12; 1951–70; a new, revised, or previously inactive form issued each May; Achievement Examinations for Secondary Schools, High School Achievement Examinations, and

Midwest High School Achievement Examinations have also been used as series titles; Form GJ Rev ('70, some tests for grade 10 have 1973 copyright) used in 1970 and 1973 testings; Form 4 ('54), entitled *English IX-XII: Achievement Examinations for Secondary Schools,* is available from another publisher (see 74); 6 levels; edited by V. L. Lohmann; American Guidance Service, Inc. *

a) LANGUAGE ARTS GRADE 7. 1962–70.
b) LANGUAGE ARTS GRADE 8. 1962–70.
c) LANGUAGE ARTS GRADE 9. 1951–70.
d) LANGUAGE ARTS GRADE 10. 1951–70.
e) LANGUAGE ARTS GRADE 11. 1951–70.
f) LANGUAGE ARTS GRADE 12. 1951–70.

For additional information, see 7:197; for a review by Marvin D. Glock of Forms E (1962) and F (1963), see 6:268; see also 5:185; for a review by Roger A. Richards of Form A (1955) and Form B (1957), see 5:186.

[91]

Language Arts Tests: Content Evaluation Series. Grades 7–9; 1969; 3 tests in 1 booklet; Elsa Graser (*a*), Leonard Freyman (*b*), and Ruth Reeves (*c*); Houghton Mifflin Co. *

a) LANGUAGE ABILITY TEST: CONTENT EVALUATION SERIES.
b) COMPOSITION TEST: CONTENT EVALUATION SERIES.
c) LITERATURE TEST: CONTENT EVALUATION SERIES.

For additional information and reviews by Joan J. Michael and Blaine R. Worthen, see 7:198.

[92]

Language Perception Test. Business and industry; 1959–63; Richardson, Bellows, Henry & Co., Inc. *
For additional information, see 6:269.

[93-4]

*Language Usage: Differential Aptitude Tests. Grades 8–12 and adults; 1947–73; 2 editions; George K. Bennett, Harold G. Seashore, and Alexander G. Wesman; Psychological Corporation. * For the complete battery entry, see 1069.

a) FORM A. 1947–59; 2 scores: spelling, sentences. *Out of print.*
b) FORM T. 1947–73; revision of Form M ('62).

For reviews of the complete battery, see 7:673 (1 review, 1 excerpt), 6:767 (2 reviews), 5:605 (2 reviews), 4:711 (3 reviews), and 3:620 (1 excerpt).

REFERENCES THROUGH 1971
1. BOURNE, ROBERT K., AND ROTHNEY, JOHN W. M. "Assessments of Counselees Writing Skills by Tests and Essays." *Voc Guid Q* 9:21–4 au '60. *
2. WOOD, SUSAN. *An Evaluation of Published English Tests,* pp. 23–5. Madison, Wis.: Wisconsin Department of Public Instruction, 1967. Pp. 91. *

CUMULATIVE NAME INDEX
Bourne, R. K.: 1   Wood, S.: 2
Rothney, J. W. M.: 1

[95]

Moray House English Tests. Ages 8.5–10.5, 10–12, 12–14; 1935–70; 3 levels; Godfrey Thomson Unit, University of Edinburgh; University of London Press Ltd. [England]. *

a) MORAY HOUSE JUNIOR ENGLISH TEST. Ages 8.5–10.5; 1952–70.
b) MORAY HOUSE ENGLISH TEST. Ages 10–12; 1935–69.
c) MORAY HOUSE ENGLISH TEST (ADV.). Ages 12–14; 1947–58.

For additional information, see 7:202 (1 reference); for a review by M. Alan Brimer, see 6:271 (7 references).

REFERENCES THROUGH 1971
1–7. See 6:271.
8. See 7:202.
9. DOCKRELL, W. B. "The Relationship Between Socio-Economic Status, Intelligence and Attainment in Some Scottish Primary Schools." *Indian Psychol B* 4:1–6 Ja '59. * (*PA* 37:4715)
10. LEWIS, D. G. "Differences in Attainment Between Primary-Schools in Mixed-Language Areas: Their Dependence on Intelligence and Linguistic Background." *Brit J Ed Psychol* 30:63–70 F '60. *
11. MANLEY, D. R. "Mental Ability in Jamaica: (An Examination of the Performance of Children in the Jamaican Common Entrance Examination, 1959)." *Social & Econ Studies* (Jamaica) 12:51–71 Mr '63. * (*PA* 38:767)
12. HALLWORTH, H. J. "Personality Ratings of Adolescents: A Study in a Comprehensive School." *Brit J Ed Psychol* 34:171–7 Je '64. * (*PA* 39:3180)
13. HOROBIN, GORDON; OLDMAN, DAVID; AND BYTHEWAY, BILL. "The Social Differentiation of Ability." *Sociology* 1:113–29 My '67. *
14. NISBET, J. D., AND ENTWISTLE, N. J. "Intelligence and Family Size, 1949–1965." *Brit J Ed Psychol* 37:188–93 Je '67. * (*PA* 41:15274)

CUMULATIVE NAME INDEX
Armstrong, H. G.: 5   Lewis, D. G.: 10
Brimer, M. A.: *rev,* 6:271 MacNamara, J.: 8
Buchan, J.: 7   Manley, D. R.: 11
Bytheway, B.: 13   Mukherjee, L.: 6
Dockrell, W. B.: 9   Nisbet, J.: 7
Emmett, W. G.: 3, 4   Nisbet, J. D.: 14
Entwistle, N. J.: 14   Oldman, D.: 13
Hallworth, H. J.: 12   Peel, E. A.: 5
Horobin, G.: 13   Pilliner, A. E. G.: 2
Lambert, C. M.: 1   Wilmut, F. S.: 3

[96]

*National Teacher Examinations: English Language and Literature. College seniors and teachers; 1940–73; an inactive form (1966) entitled *Teacher Education Examination Program: English Language and Literature* is available to colleges for local administration; another inactive form (1968) entitled *Specialty Examinations: English Language and Literature* is available to school systems for local use as part of the program entitled *School Personnel Research and Evaluation Services;* Educational Testing Service. * For the testing program entry, see 869.

For additional information concerning earlier forms, see 7:203 (1 reference); for a review by Holland Roberts, see 6:259. For reviews of the testing program, see 7:582 (2 reviews), 6:700 (1 review), 5:538 (3 reviews), and 4:802 (1 review).

REFERENCES THROUGH 1971
1. See 7:203.

CUMULATIVE NAME INDEX
Medlin, Y. L.: 1   Roberts, H.: *rev,* 6:259

[97]

Nationwide English Composition Examination. Grades 4–12; 1959–63; no manual; [Donald R. Honz]; Educational Stimuli. *
For additional information, see 6:290.

[98]

Nationwide English Grammar Examination. Grades 4–12; 1957–63; no manual; [Donald R. Honz]; Educational Stimuli. *
For additional information, see 6:272.

[99]

The New Purdue Placement Test in English. Grades 11–16; 1931–55; revision of *The Purdue Placement Test in English;* 8 scores: punctuation, grammar, sentence structure, reading (study), reading (pleasure), vocabulary, spelling, total; G. S. Wykoff, J. H. McKee, and H. H. Remmers; Houghton Mifflin Co. *
For additional information and reviews by Gerald V.

Lannholm and M. J. Wantman, see 5:199 (5 references) ; see also 4:173 (9 references).

REFERENCES THROUGH 1971
1-9. See 4:173.
10-14. See 5:199.
15. PERRY, ROBERT D. *Prediction Equations for Success in College Mathematics.* Contribution to Education No. 122. Nashville, Tenn.: George Peabody College for Teachers, 1934. Pp. xiii, 58. * (*PA* 8:3277)
16. READ, CECIL B. "The Prediction of Scholastic Success in a Municipal University." *Sch & Soc* 48:187-8 Ag 6 '38. * (*PA* 12:6645)
17. DOUGLASS, LOWELL N. "A Study of Certain Factors Influencing Academic Achievement With Special Reference to the Health Factor." *J Exp Ed* 7:235-44 Mr '39. * (*PA* 13:5911)
18. SPOERL, DOROTHY TILDEN. "The Academic and Verbal Adjustment of College Age Bilingual Students." *J Genetic Psychol* 64:139-57 Mr '44. * (*PA* 18:2275)
19. ADAMS, SAM, AND GARRETT, H. L. "Scholastic Background as Related to Success in College Physics." *J Ed Res* 47:545-9 Mr '54. * (*PA* 28:7951)
20. LEBOLD, WILLIAM KERNS. *A Longitudinal Study of Purdue Engineering Students.* Doctor's thesis, Purdue University (Lafayette, Ind.), 1957. (*DA* 17:2057)
21. SPAHR, BETTE JEANNE WEINTZ. *A Study of the Correlation Between Scores on the Purdue Placement Test in English and Success in Graduate Education Programs at Purdue University.* Master's thesis, Purdue University (Lafayette, Ind.), 1960.

CUMULATIVE NAME INDEX

Adams, S.: 19	Lawrence, W. A.: 2
Baker, P. C.: 12	LeBold, W. K.: 20
Belman, H. S.: 7, 9	Lott, H. V.: 3
Bonner, L. W.: 14	Perry, R. D.: 15
Brown, J. I.: 5	Pred, G. D.: 8
Douglass, L. N.: 17	Quaid, T. D. D.: 1
Dungan, E. W.: 13	Read, C. B.: 16
Elliott, D. N.: 6	Remmers, H. H.: 6
Evans, R. N.: 7, 9	Severance, K. M.: 11
Gage, N. L.: 6	Spahr, B. J. W.: 21
Garrett, H. L.: 19	Spoerl, D. T.: 18
Johnson, A. P.: 10	Varnado, G. R.: 4
Lannholm, G. V.: *rev*, 5:199	Wantman, M. J.: *rev*, 5:199

[100]

*Objective Tests in Constructive English.** Grades 7, 8, 9, 10-12; 1955-64; 1964 tests identical with tests copyrighted 1955 except for format and directions ; no manual ; Gunnar Horn ; Perfection Form Co. *

[101]

*Objective Tests in Punctuation.** Grades 7, 8, 9, 10-12; 1955-64; 1964 tests identical with tests copyrighted 1955 except for format and directions ; no manual ; Gunnar Horn ; Perfection Form Co. *

[102]

Pacific Tests of English Attainment and Skills: Pacific Test Series. Job applicants in Papua and New Guinea; 1933-68; PTEAS; 3 tests; I. G. Ord; Australian Council for Educational Research [Australia]. *
a) PACIFIC READING COMPREHENSION TEST. 1933-68; PRCT; adaptation of Part 3 of *A.C.E.R. Silent Reading Test,* Forms A and B.
b) PACIFIC WORD KNOWLEDGE TEST. 1933-68; PWKT.
c) PACIFIC WORD FORMATION TEST. 1968; PWFT.
For additional information, see 7:204.

[103]

Picture Story Language Test. Ages 7-17; 1965; PSLT; developmental scale for written language; 5 scores: productivity (total words, total sentences, words per sentence), syntax, abstract-concrete; Helmer R. Myklebust; Grune & Stratton, Inc. *
For additional information, reviews by Nicholas Anastasiow and William H. Perkins, and excerpted reviews by C. H. Ammons and Joseph M. Wepman, see 7:205 (5 references).

REFERENCES THROUGH 1971
1-5. See 7:205.
6. MYKLEBUST, HELMER R.; BANNOCHIE, MARGARET N.; AND KILLEN, JAMES R. Chap. 9, "Learning Disabilities and Cognitive Processes," pp. 213-51. In *Progress in Learning Disabilities, Vol. 2.* Edited by Helmer R. Myklebust. New York: Grune & Stratton, Inc., 1971. Pp. ix, 404. *

CUMULATIVE NAME INDEX

Ammons, C. H.: *exc*, 7:205	Mason, C. W.: 2
Anastasiow, N.: *rev*, 7:205	Moore, A. B.: 3
Anderson, R. P.: 5	Myklebust, H. R.: 1, 6
Bannochie, M. N.: 6	O'Toole, T. J.: 4
Bell, D. B.: 5	Perkins, W. H.: *rev*, 7:205
Killen, J. R.: 6	Wepman, J. M.: *exc*, 7:205
Lewis, F. D.: 5	

[104]

Pressey Diagnostic Tests in English Composition. Grades 7-12; 1923-24; 4 tests; Bobbs-Merrill Co., Inc. *
a) CAPITALIZATION. S. L. Pressey, E. V. Bowers, and Blythe Pearce.
b) PUNCTUATION. S. L. Pressey, Helen Ruhlen, and Blythe Pearce.
c) GRAMMAR. F. R. Conkling, S. L. Pressey, and L. C. Pressey.
d) SENTENCE STRUCTURE. F. R. Conkling, S. L. Pressey, and L. C. Pressey.
For additional information and reviews by Harry A. Greene and Jean Hoard, see 2:1274.

REFERENCES THROUGH 1971
1. PRESSEY, SIDNEY L. "Measurement of Progress in English in the Upper Grades." *Ann Conf Ed Meas* 8:35-45 '21. *
2. CAVINS, L. V. "An Experiment With Standardized Tests in a State Teachers' Examination." *J Ed Res* 14:206-12 O '26. * (*PA* 1:489)
3. DEAN, CECIL H. "Report of Diagnostic Tests in English Composition Given in Schenley High School." *Pittsburgh Sch* 1:8-14 N-D '26. *
4. WILLING, MATTHEW H. "Valid Diagnosis in High School Composition." *Teach Col Contrib Ed* 230:1-64 '26. *
5. BELL, J. CARLETON. Chap. 15, "Attainments of High School Pupils in the Pressey Diagnostic Tests in English Composition," pp. 87-96. In *Contributions to Education, Vol. 2.* Edited by J. Carleton Bell and Ambrose L. Suhrie. Yonkers, N.Y.: World Book Co., 1928. Pp. xi, 425. * (*PA* 2:2313)
6. LYONS, ELVA ANNE. "Objective Measurements in English." *Ed Res B* (Los Angeles City Schools) 9:481-9 N 19 '30. *
7. WERNER, OSCAR H. Chap. 2, "The Influence of the Study of Modern Foreign Languages on the Development of Desirable Abilities in English," pp. 97-145. (*PA* 4:2847) In *Studies in Modern Language Teaching.* By E. W. Bagster-Collins and Others. New York: Macmillan Co., 1930. Pp. xxxi, 491. *

CUMULATIVE NAME INDEX

Bell, J. C.: 5	Lyons, E. A.: 6
Cavins, L. V.: 2	Pressey, S. L.: 1
Dean, C. H.: 3	Werner, O. H.: 7
Greene, H. A.: *rev*, 2:1274	Willing, M. H.: 4
Hoard, J.: *rev*, 2:1274	

[105]

The Purdue High School English Test. Grades 9-12; 1931-62; abbreviated modification of *New Purdue Placement Test in English* which is also available; all items selected from the earlier test; 6 scores: grammar, punctuation, effective expression, vocabulary, spelling, total; H. H. Remmers, R. D. Franklin, G. S. Wykoff, and J. H. McKee; Houghton Mifflin Co. *
For additional information and reviews by Charlotte Croon Davis and Benjamin Rosner, see 6:276.

REFERENCES THROUGH 1971
1. BONNER, LEON WILLIAM. *Factors Associated With the Academic Achievement of Freshmen Students at a Southern Agricultural College.* Doctor's thesis, Pennsylvania State University (University Park, Pa.), 1956. (*DA* 17:266)
2. PALACIOS, JOHN RAYMOND. *A Validation Study of Selected Tests for Possible Use in Admission to Professional Education Sequences at Purdue University.* Doctor's thesis, Purdue University (Lafayette, Ind.), 1959. (*DA* 20:2679)
3. BATES, CHARLES O. *A Study of Creative Potential as Found in Elementary Student Teachers.* Doctor's thesis, Ball State Teachers College (Muncie, Ind.), 1963. (*DA* 24:4561)

4. FOURNET, FRANCIS GARY, JR. *A Study of Various Factors Related to Success in College General Mathematics.* Doctor's thesis, Louisiana State University (Baton Rouge, La.), 1963. (*DA* 24:5239)

5. BLACK, HUBERT PERRY. *The Predictive Value of Selected Factors for Achievement of Lee College Freshmen.* Doctor's thesis, University of Tennessee (Knoxville, Tenn.), 1965. (*DA* 27:618A)

6. LEEP, ALBERT GENE. *Selected Pre-Service Measures as Predictors of First Year Teaching Performance of Elementary Teachers.* Doctor's thesis, Ball State Teachers College (Muncie, Ind.), 1965. (*DA* 26:3163)

7. WOOD, SUSAN. *An Evaluation of Published English Tests,* pp. 57-9. Madison, Wis.: Wisconsin Department of Public Instruction, 1967. Pp. 91. *

8. MEDLER, BYRON WAYNE. *A Comparative Study of Selected Variables Between Students Completing the Elementary Education Curriculum and Those Students Who Left the Elementary Education Curriculum Due to Academic Disqualification or Change of Major.* Doctor's thesis, Ball State University (Muncie, Ind.), 1968. (*DA* 29:3503A)

9. MUNDAY, LEO. "Correlations Between ACT and Other Predictors of Academic Success in College." *Col & Univ* 44:67-76 f '68. *

10. SHALLCROSS, MARCIA KEEL. *Predicting Success in Written Communications in Business by Using the New Purdue Placement Test in English.* Master's thesis, San Diego State College (San Diego, Calif.), 1968.

11. CHERRY, ADA LOU. *A Comparison of Selected Characteristics of Graduated Students and Academically Disqualified Students Who Were Admitted With Warning to Ball State University Autumns, 1963 and 1964.* Doctor's thesis, Ball State University (Muncie, Ind.), 1969. (*DAI* 30:4217A)

12. CHIMONIDES, STELIOS GEORGIOU. *Some Relationships Associated With Academic Success in Graduate Work at a Midwestern University.* Master's thesis, Western Michigan University (Kalamazoo, Mich.), 1969. (*Masters Abstracts* 7:200)

CUMULATIVE NAME INDEX

Bates, C. O.: 3	Leep, A. G.: 6
Black, H. P.: 5	Medler, B. W.: 8
Bonner, L. W.: 1	Munday, L.: 9
Cherry, A. L.: 11	Palacios, J. R.: 2
Chimonides, S. G.: 12	Rosner, B.: *rev*, 6:276
Davis, C. C.: *rev*, 6:276	Shallcross, M. K.: 10
Fournet, F. G.: 4	Wood, S.: 7

[106]

RBH Spelling Test and Word Meaning Test. Business and industry; 1957-63; Richardson, Bellows, Henry & Co., Inc. *

For additional information, see 6:324.

[107]

RBH Test of Language Skills. Business and industry; 1949-63; Richardson, Bellows, Henry & Co., Inc. *
For additional information, see 6:285.

[108-9]

SRA Achievement Series: Language Arts. Grades 2-4, 4-9; 1954-69; Forms C and D; more recent Forms E and F are not available as separates; 4 scores: capitalization and punctuation, grammatical usage, spelling, total; Louis P. Thorpe, D. Welty Lefever, and Robert A. Naslund; Science Research Associates, Inc. * For the complete battery entry, see 29.
a) HAND SCORED EDITION. Grades 2-4; 1955-68; test booklet title is *How Should We Say This? Out of print.*
b) MULTILEVEL EDITION. Grades 4-9; 1963-69.

For additional information, see 7:206; for a review by Miriam M. Bryan of earlier forms, see 6:277 (1 reference) ; for reviews by Constance M. McCullough and Winifred L. Post, see 5:200. For reviews of the complete battery, see 7:18 (2 reviews), 6:21 (1 review), and 5:21 (2 reviews).

REFERENCES THROUGH 1971
1. See 6:277.
2. WOOD, SUSAN. *An Evaluation of Published English Tests,* pp. 65-8. Madison, Wis.: Wisconsin Department of Public Instruction, 1967. Pp. 91. *

Purdue High School English Test

CUMULATIVE NAME INDEX

Bryan, M. M.: *rev*, 6:277	Post, W. L.: *rev*, 5:200
Groff, P. J.: 1	Wood, S.: 2
McCullough, C. M.: *rev*, 5:200	

[110]

The Schonell Diagnostic English Tests. Ages 9.5-16; 1940; 5 scores: English usage, capital letters and punctuation, vocabulary, sentence structure, composition; F. Eleanor Schonell; Oliver & Boyd [Scotland]. *

For additional information and reviews by John Cohen and Robert H. Thouless, see 3:135.

REFERENCES THROUGH 1971
1. SCHONELL, FLORENCE ELEANOR. *An Experimental Study of Diagnostic Tests in English.* Master's thesis, University of London (London, England), 1941.

CUMULATIVE NAME INDEX

Cohen, J.: *rev*, 3:135	Thouless, R. H.: *rev*, 3:135
Schonell, F. E.: 1	

[111]

*Senior English Test. Technical college entrants; 1963-71; 1971 manual essentially the same as 1964 manual except for deletion of 3 paragraphs and inclusion of 1963 norms formerly published separately; distribution restricted to colleges of further education; published for the National Foundation for Educational Research in England and Wales; Ginn & Co. Ltd. [England]. *

For additional information and reviews by M. A. Brimer and David A. Walker, see 7:207.

[112]

★Sequential Tests of Educational Progress, Series 2: English Expression. Grades 4-6, 7-9, 10-12, 13-14; 1969-72; Cooperative Tests and Services. * For the complete battery entry, see 35.

For reviews of the original edition of the complete battery, see 6:25 (2 reviews) and 5:24 (2 reviews, 1 excerpt).

[113]

*Sequential Tests of Educational Progress: Writing. Grades 4-6, 7-9, 10-12, 13-14 (except *b*); 1956-72; 2 editions; Cooperative Tests and Services. * For the complete battery entry, see 35.
a) ORIGINAL SERIES: WRITING [70 MINUTE TESTS]. Grades 4-6, 7-9, 10-12, 13-14; 1956-63; Braille and large type editions (grades 4-12) are available from American Printing House for the Blind, Inc.
b) SERIES 2: MECHANICS OF WRITING [40 MINUTE TESTS]. Grades 4-6, 7-9, 10-12; 1956-72; 3 scores: spelling, capitalization and punctuation, total.

For additional information, reviews by Hillel Black and Albert N. Hieronymus, and an excerpted review by Dean A. Allen of *a,* see 6:292 (3 references) ; for reviews by Charlotte Croon Davis, John M. Stalnaker, and Louis C. Zahner, see 5:207. For reviews of the original edition of the complete battery, see 6:25 (2 reviews) and 5:24 (2 reviews, 1 excerpt).

REFERENCES THROUGH 1971
1-3. See 6:292.
4. MICHAEL, WILLIAM B.; CATHCART, ROBERT; AND ZIMMERMAN, WAYNE S. "Linguistic Factors in Various Measures of Communication Skills for College Students With Implications for Predictive Validity." *Ed & Psychol Meas* 24:363-7 su '64. * (*PA* 39:3192)
5. CHASE, CLINTON I. *The University Freshman Dropout.* Indiana University, Monograph of the Bureau of Educational Studies and Testing, Indiana Studies in Prediction, No. 6. Bloomington, Ind.: the Bureau, 1965. Pp. 36. *
6. ELLIOTT, MERLE H., AND BADAL, ALDEN W. "Achievement and Racial Composition of Schools." *Calif J Ed Res* 16:158-66 S '65. * (*PA* 40:1478)
7. WHEELER, FRED. "An Experimental Study of Means to Improve Writing." *J Sec Ed* 40:331-5 N '65. *

8. MADAUS, GEORGE F., AND RIPPEY, ROBERT M. "Zeroing in on the STEP Writing Test: What Does It Tell a Teacher?" *J Ed Meas* 3:19–25 sp '66. *

9. PHELPS, ARTHUR M. *Predicting First Semester Grades in the Junior College Two-Year Terminal Vocational-Technical Programs.* Master's thesis, Stetson University (DeLand, Fla.), 1966.

10. PIERSON, HOWARD. *Peer and Teacher Correction: A Comparison of the Effects of Two Methods of Teaching Composition in Grade Nine English Classes.* Doctor's thesis, New York University (New York, N.Y.), 1967. (*DA* 28:1350A)

11. TENOPYR, MARY L. "Social Intelligence and Academic Success." *Ed & Psychol Meas* 27:961–5 w '67. * (*PA* 42:9509)

12. WOOD, SUSAN. *An Evaluation of Published English Tests,* pp. 73–8. Madison. Wis.: Wisconsin Department of Public Instruction, 1967. Pp. 91. *

13. WILSON, ANAISE VICTORIANNE. *A Study of the Relationship of Selected Factors to the Academic Achievement of College Freshmen in the School of Education of Tuskegee Institute.* Doctor's thesis, New York University (New York, N.Y.), 1968. (*DAI* 30:144A)

14. RIPPEY, ROBERT M. "A Comparison of Five Different Scoring Functions for Confidence Tests." *J Ed Meas* 7(3):165–70 f '70. *

15. HALL, LUCIEN T., JR. "The Prediction of Success in Each of Six Four-Year Selections of Secondary Mathematics Courses." *Sch Sci & Math* 71(8):693–6 N '71. *

16. SHAVER, JAMES P., AND NUHN, DEE. "The Effectiveness of Tutoring Underachievers in Reading and Writing." *J Ed Res* 65(3):107–12 N '71. * (*PA* 48:1878)

CUMULATIVE NAME INDEX

Allen, D. A.: *exc,* 6:292	Milfs, M.: 3
Badal, A. W.: 6	Nuhn, D.: 16
Black, H.: *rev,* 6:292	Phelps, A. M.: 9
Cathcart, R.: 3–4	Pierson, H.: 10
Chase, C. I.: 5	Rippey, R. M.: 8, 14
Davis, C. C.: *rev,* 5:207	Shaver, J. P.: 16
Elliott, M. H.: 6	Stalnaker, J. M.: *rev,* 5:207
Endler, N. S.: 2	Steinberg, D.: 2
Groff, P. J.: 1	Tenopyr, M. L.: 11
Hall, L. T.: 15	Wheeler, F.: 7
Hieronymus, A. N.: *rev,* 6: 292	Wilson, A. V.: 13
	Wood, S.: 12
Madaus, G. F.: 8	Zahner, L. C.: *rev,* 5:207
Michael, W. B.: 3–4	Zimmerman, W. S.: 3–4

[114]

Stanford Achievement Test: High School English and Spelling Tests. Grades 9–12; 1965–66; catalog uses the title *Stanford High School English and Spelling Tests;* subtest of *Stanford Achievement Test: High School Basic Battery;* Eric F. Gardner, Jack Merwin, Robert Callis, and Richard Madden; Harcourt Brace Jovanovich, Inc. * For the complete battery entry, see 37.

For additional information and reviews by Vincent R. D'Oyley and Leonard S. Feldt, see 7:208. For reviews of the complete battery, see 7:27 (2 reviews).

[115]

Stanford Achievement Test, 1964 Edition: Spelling and Language Tests. Grades 4.0–5.4, 5.5–6.9, 7.0–9.9; 1940–68; catalog uses the title *Stanford Language Tests;* same as spelling and language subtests of *Stanford Achievement Test;* not available as a separate in the 1973 edition of the battery; 2 scores: spelling, language; Braille editions are available from American Printing House for the Blind, Inc.; Truman L. Kelley, Richard Madden, Eric F. Gardner, and Herbert C. Rudman; Harcourt Brace Jovanovich, Inc. * For the complete battery entry, see 36.

For additional information and reviews by William E. Coffman and Carleton B. Shay, see 7:209. For reviews of the complete battery, see 7:25 (1 excerpt), 6:26 (1 review, 1 excerpt), 5:25 (1 review), 4:25 (2 reviews), and 3:18 (2 reviews).

REFERENCES THROUGH 1971

1. WILLING, MATTHEW H. "Valid Diagnosis in High School Composition." *Teach Col Contrib Ed* 230:1–64 '26. *

CUMULATIVE NAME INDEX

Coffman, W. E.: *rev,* 7:209	Willing, M. H.: 1
Shay, C. B.: *rev,* 7:209	

[116]

Survey Tests of English Usage. Grades 9–13; 1947–49; title on some forms is *Achievement Test of English Usage;* L. J. O'Rourke; O'Rourke Publications. *

For additional information and a review by Holland Roberts, see 6:281 (1 reference).

REFERENCES THROUGH 1971

1. See 6:281.

CUMULATIVE NAME INDEX

Groff, P. J.: 1	Roberts, H.: *rev,* 6:281

[117]

*Teacher Education Examination Program: English Language and Literature. College seniors preparing to teach secondary school; 1957–72; reprinting of inactive 1966 form of *National Teacher Examinations: English Language and Literature;* test available to colleges for local administration; Educational Testing Service. * For the testing program entry, see 898.

For additional information concerning an earlier form, see 6:260. For a review of the testing program, see 5:543. For reference to a review of the *National Teacher Examinations: English Language and Literature,* see 96.

[118]

A Test of English Usage. English-speaking high school and college students and adults; 1963–64; A. Edwin Harper, Jr., and Rhea S. Das; Manasayan [India]. *

For additional information, see 6:284.

[119]

Tests of Academic Progress: Composition. Grades 9–12; 1964–66; Dale P. Scannell and Oscar H. Haugh; Houghton Mifflin Co. * For the complete battery entry, see 44.

For additional information and reviews by Ellis Batten Page and Osmond E. Palmer, see 7:210 (1 reference). For a review of the complete battery, see 7:31.

REFERENCES THROUGH 1971

1. See 7:210.

CUMULATIVE NAME INDEX

Goolsby, T. M.: 1	Palmer, O. E.: *rev,* 7:210
Page, E. B.: *rev,* 7:210	

[120]

*Tests of Basic Experiences: Language. Prekgn-kgn, grade 1; 1970–72; Margaret H. Moss; CTB/McGraw-Hill. * For the complete battery entry, see 47.

For additional information, see 7:211 (1 reference). For a review of the complete battery, see 7:33.

REFERENCES THROUGH 1971

1. See 7:211.

2. COMPTON, MARY ELIZABETH. *A Study of the Relationship Between Oral Language Facility and Reading Achievement of Selected First-Grade Children.* Doctor's thesis, University of North Carolina (Chapel Hill, N.C.), 1971. (*DAI* 32:6848A)

CUMULATIVE NAME INDEX

Compton, M. E.: 2	Moss, M. H.: 1

[121]

Tressler English Minimum Essentials Test, Revised Edition. Grades 8–12; 1932–56; 8 scores: grammatical correctness, vocabulary, punctuation and capitalization, the sentence and its parts, sentence sense, inflection and accent, spelling, total; 1954 test identical with test copyrighted 1941 except for changes in 4 items; 1955 manual identical with sheet copyrighted 1941 except for minor changes; J. C. Tressler; Bobbs-Merrill Co., Inc. *

For additional information and reviews by Osmond E. Palmer and Roger A. Richards, see 6:286 (1 reference).

REFERENCES THROUGH 1971
1. See 6:286.

CUMULATIVE NAME INDEX
Groff, P. J.: 1   Richards, R. A.: rev, 6:286
Palmer, O. E.: rev, 6:286

[122]
Walton-Sanders English Test. 1, 2 semesters in grades 9–13; 1962–64; first published 1962–63 in the Every Pupil Scholarship Test series; Charles E. Walton and M. W. Sanders; Bureau of Educational Measurements. *
For additional information, see 7:212.

[123]
Watson English Usage and Appreciation Test, Fourth Edition. Grades 4–8; 1966; G. Milton Watson; Book Society of Canada Ltd. [Canada]. *
For additional information and a review by Vincent R. D'Oyley, see 7:213.

[124]
Writing Skills Test. Grades 9–12; 1961, c1960–61; Macklin Thomas; Science Research Associates, Inc. *
For additional information and reviews by William E. Coffman and Osmond E. Palmer, see 6:293.

[125]
Writing Test: McGraw-Hill Basic Skills System. Grades 11–14; 1970; also called *MHBSS Writing Test*; although designed for use with the MHBSS instructional program, the test may be used independently; 4 scores: language mechanics, sentence patterns, paragraph patterns, total; Alton L. Raygor; McGraw-Hill Book Co., Inc. *
For additional information and a review by Leonard S. Feldt, see 7:214.

[Out of Print Since TIP I]
A.C.E.R. English Usage Tests, 5:173 (1 review)
Ability for English (Language): Fife Tests of Ability, Test 1, 3:114 (1 reference)
Barrett-Ryan-Schrammel English Test, 5:176 (5 reviews, 1 reference)
Basic Language Skills: Iowa Every-Pupil Tests of Basic Skills, Test C, 4:150
Clapp-Young English Test, 3:117 (1 review)
College Entrance Examination Board Writing Sample, 6:289 (1 review, 2 references)
College Placement Test in English, 4:153 (1 review)
College Preparatory Test in English, 4:154 (1 review)
Columbia Research Bureau English Test, 2:1270 (2 reviews)
Cooperative English Test: Usage, Spelling, and Vocabulary, 6:255 (10 reviews, 16 references)
Coordinated Scales of Attainment: English, 5:180
Correct English Usage Test, 4:156
Correctness and Effectiveness of Expression, 5:181 (1 review); now available only as a subtest of *Tests of General Educational Development,* 48
Cross English Test, 2:1272 (2 reviews, 3 references)
Eaton Diagnostic-Accomplishment Tests in English, T:421
Eleventh Year English Fundamentals: Manchester Semester-End Achievement Tests, T:422, 36:639
English: Every Pupil Scholarship Test, 6:257 (1 reference)
English: Northumberland Standardised Tests (1925 Series), T:428
English Survey Test: Ohio Scholarship Tests: Ohio Senior Survey Tests, 5:188 (2 reviews, 1 reference)

English Test (Four-Year Course): Affiliation Testing Program for Catholic Secondary Schools, 6:263 (1 review)
English: Thanet Mental Tests, 2:1279 (1 review)
English Usage: Every Pupil Test, 6:265 (1 review, 2 references)
Greene-Stapp Language Abilities Test, 5:195 (2 reviews, 1 reference)
Hoyum-Schrammel English Essentials Tests, 5:196 (2 reviews)
Iowa Grammar Information Test, 4:164 (1 review)
Iowa Language Abilities Test, 4:165 (1 review)
Iowa Primary Language Test, T:446, 36:642
Kentucky English Test, 3:132 (1 review, 1 reference); revised edition was available only as a part of *Kentucky Classification Battery,* 4:301 (1 review, 4 references)
Kirby Grammar Test, T:448
Language Battery: National Institute for Personnel Research High Level Battery, T:450; revised edition now available only as a subtest of *High Level Battery: Test A/75,* 1075
Language Battery: National Institute for Personnel Research Normal Battery, T:451; now available only as a subtest of *National Institute for Personnel Research Normal Battery,* 1085
Language Essentials Tests, 3:133 (1 review)
Linguistic Awareness Test, 2:1287
Mechanics of Written English, 7:199
Metropolitan Achievement Tests: High School Language Tests, 7:200 (2 reviews)
Missouri College English Test, 7:201 (2 reviews, 1 reference)
Nelson's High School English Test, 2:1290 (2 reviews)
Ninth Year English Fundamentals: Manchester Semester-End Achievement Tests, T:459, 36:644
Novelty Grammar Tests (status unknown), 6:273
Pribble-Dallmann Diagnostic Tests in Elementary Language Skills, 6:274 (2 reviews)
Pribble-McCrory Diagnostic Tests in Practical English Grammar, 6:275 (1 review)
Public School Achievement Tests: Grammar, T:439; *Language Usage,* T:453
Rinsland-Beck Natural Test of English Usage, 2:1293 (2 reviews, 1 excerpt, 3 references)
Scholastic Achievement Series: English-Spelling, 6:278 (2 reviews, 1 reference)
Sequential Tests of Educational Progress: Essay Test, 6:291 (3 reviews, 3 references)
Survey of Language Achievement: California Survey Series, 6:280 (1 review)
T.C. English Test, 6:282
Tenth Year English Fundamentals: Manchester Semester-End Achievement Tests, T:475, 36:646
Test of Creative Writing Aptitude and Ability, T:484
Test of English Usage, 6:283 (2 reviews)
Tests of Language Usage: Cooperative Inter-American Tests, 4:176 (1 review, 3 references)
Twelfth Year English Fundamentals: Manchester Semester-End Achievement Tests, 36:647; for revision, see *Senior English Fundamentals: Manchester Semester-End Achievement Tests,* T:472
20th Century Test for English—9th Grade, 4:159; *10th Grade,* 4:160

LITERATURE

[126]
*****American Literature Anthology Tests.** High school; 1959–70; revisions of the *Objective Tests in*

Tressler English Minimum Essentials Test

American Anthology by Carl H. Larson and the *Alternate Objective Tests in American Anthology* by Dorothy A. Mason; 7 tests; no manual; Perfection Form Co. *
a) COLONIAL TIMES AND MAKING OF A NATION.
b) FLOWERING OF THE EAST.
c) THE GENIUS OF NEW ENGLAND.
d) CIVIL WAR AND THE WESTWARD MOVEMENT.
e) GROWTH OF REALISM.
f) MODERN AMERICAN LITERATURE.
g) FINAL TEST.

For additional information concerning the earlier tests, see 7:223.

[127]

★**CLEP Subject Examination in American Literature.** 1 year or equivalent; 1971–73, c1970–73; for college accreditation of nontraditional study, advanced placement, or assessment of educational achievement; tests administered monthly at centers throughout the United States; program administered for the College Entrance Examination Board by Educational Testing Service. * For the testing program entry, see 1050.

[128]

*CLEP Subject Examination in Analysis and Interpretation of Literature.** 1 year or equivalent; 1964–73; for college accreditation of nontraditional study, advanced placement, or assessment of educational achievement; tests administered monthly at centers throughout the United States; program administered for the College Entrance Examination Board by Educational Testing Service. * For the testing program entry, see 1050.

For additional information concerning an earlier form, see 7:215. For reviews of the testing program, see 7:664 (3 reviews).

[129]

*CLEP Subject Examination in English Literature.** 1 year or equivalent; 1970–73; for college accreditation of nontraditional study, advanced placement, or assessment of educational achievement; tests administered monthly at centers throughout the United States; program administered for the College Entrance Examination Board by Educational Testing Service. * For the testing program entry, see 1050.

For additional information, see 7:216. For reviews of the testing program, see 7:664 (3 reviews).

[130]

*College Board Achievement Test in Literature.** Candidates for college entrance; 1968–73; test administered on specified dates at centers established by the publisher; inactive forms, entitled *College Placement Test in Literature,* are available to colleges for local administration; program administered for the College Entrance Examination Board by Educational Testing Service. * For the testing program entry, see 1048.

For additional information, see 7:217 (2 references). For reviews of the testing program, see 6:760 (2 reviews).

REFERENCES THROUGH 1971
1–2. See 7:217.

CUMULATIVE NAME INDEX
Elledge, S.: 2   Purves, A. C.: 1

[131]

*College Placement Test in Literature.** Entering college freshmen; 1968–72; reprinting of inactive 1968 form of *College Board Achievement Test in Literature;* test available to colleges for local administration; program administered for the College Entrance Examination Board by Educational Testing Service. * For the testing program entry, see 1051.

For additional information, see 7:218. For a review of the testing program, see 7:665.

[132]

★**Cooperative Literature Tests.** Grades 9–12; 1972–73; CLT; 19 tests: The Bridge of San Luis Rey, Great Expectations, Hamlet, Huckleberry Finn, Julius Caesar, Macbeth, The Merchant of Venice, Moby Dick, The Odyssey, Oedipus the King, The Old Man and the Sea, Our Town, Pride and Prejudice, Pygmalion, The Red Badge of Courage, The Return of the Native, The Scarlet Letter, Silas Marner, A Tale of Two Cities; Cooperative Tests and Services. *

[133]

*English Literature Anthology Tests.** High school; 1959–70; slight revisions of the *Objective Tests in English Anthology* by Carl H. Larson and the *Alternate Objective Tests in English Anthology* by Dorothy A. Mason; 9 tests; no manual; Perfection Form Co. *
a) BEGINNINGS OF ENGLISH LITERATURE. 1959–70.
b) THE EIGHTEENTH CENTURY. 1959–70.
c) THE ELIZABETHAN PERIOD. 1959–70.
d) THE ENGLISH NOVEL. 1964–70.
e) THE PURITAN PERIOD. 1959–70.
f) THE ROMANTIC PERIOD. 1959–70.
g) THE TWENTIETH CENTURY. 1959–70.
h) THE VICTORIAN PERIOD. 1959–70.
i) FINAL EXAMINATION. 1959–70.

For additional information concerning the earlier tests, see 7:224.

[134]

English Tests for Outside Reading. Grades 9–10, 11–12; 1939; 100 tests on specific literary works; Henrietta Silliman; the Author. *

For additional information, see 2:1301.

[135]

*The Graduate Record Examinations Advanced Literature in English Test.** Graduate school candidates; 1939–73; Educational Testing Service. * For the testing program entry, see 1053.

For additional information concerning earlier forms, see 7:219 (1 reference); for a review by Robert C. Pooley, see 5:215. For reviews of the testing program, see 7:667 (1 review) and 5:601 (1 review).

REFERENCES THROUGH 1971
1. See 7:219.

CUMULATIVE NAME INDEX
Lannholm, G. V.: 1   Pooley, R. C.: *rev,* 5:215
Marco, G. L.: 1   Schrader, W. B.: 1

[136]

Hollingsworth-Sanders Junior High School Literature Test. 1, 2 semesters in grades 7–8; 1962–64; first published 1962–63 in the Every Pupil Scholarship Test series; Leon Hollingsworth and M. W. Sanders; Bureau of Educational Measurements. *

For additional information and a review by Paul B. Diederich, see 7:220.

[137]

Hoskins-Sanders Literature Test. 1, 2 semesters grades 9–13; 1962–64; first published 1962–63 in the Every Pupil Scholarship Test series; Thomas Hoskins and M. W. Sanders; Bureau of Educational Measurements. *

For additional information and a review by Alan C. Purves, see 7:221.

[138]

*The Iowa Tests of Educational Development: Test 7, Ability to Interpret Literary Materials. Grades 9–12; 1942–67; Forms X-4 and Y-4; more recent Forms X5 and Y5 are not available as separates; prepared under the direction of E. F. Lindquist and Leonard S. Feldt; Science Research Associates, Inc. * For the complete battery entry, see 20.

For additional information concerning earlier forms, see 6:300 (1 reference). For reviews of the complete battery, see 6:14 (2 reviews), 5:17 (2 reviews), 4:17 (1 review), and 3:12 (3 reviews).

REFERENCES THROUGH 1971
1. See 6:300.
2. WEISGERBER, CHARLES A. "Accuracy in Judging Emotional Expressions as Related to Understanding of Literature." *J Social Psychol* 46:253–8 N '57. * (*PA* 34:2619)
3. TRELA, THADDEUS M. "Comparing Achievement on Tests of General and Critical Reading." *J Read Specialist* 6:140–2 My '67. * (*PA* 41:14190)

CUMULATIVE NAME INDEX
Trela, T. M.: 1, 3　　Weisgerber, C. A.: 2

[139]

Literature Test: National Achievement Tests. Grades 7–12; 1937–57; 5 scores: recognizing effects, recognizing qualities, analyzing moods, miscellaneous facts, total; 1944 and 1954 tests identical with tests copyrighted 1937 and 1939, respectively; Robert K. Speer and Samuel Smith; Psychometric Affiliates. *

For additional information, see 5:219; for reviews by H. H. Giles and Robert C. Pooley, see 2:1304.

[140]

*Literature Tests/Objective. High school; 1929–71; 2 series; no manual; Perfection Form Co. *
a) 50-QUESTION SERIES. 1950–71; 284 tests on specific literary works; formerly called *Book Review Tests.*
b) 100-QUESTION SERIES. 1929–70; 174 tests on specific literary works; formerly called *Objective Tests in English.*
For additional information concerning earlier editions, see 6:295 and 6:304.

[141]

A Look at Literature: The NCTE Cooperative Test of Critical Reading and Appreciation. Grades 4–6; 1968–69; 3 scores: Parts 1 (selections read aloud by examiner while read silently by examinee), 2 (selections read silently by examinee), total; developed and sponsored jointly by Research Foundation of the National Council of Teachers of English and Educational Testing Service; Cooperative Tests and Services. *

For additional information and reviews by Nancy W. Burton and Walter J. Moore, see 7:222.

[142]

★Poetry Test/Objective. Grades 7–9, 10–12; 1968; no manual; Perfection Form Co. *

[143]

Tests of Academic Progress: Literature. Grades 9–12; 1964–66; Dale P. Scannell and Oscar H. Haugh; Houghton Mifflin Co. * For the complete battery entry, see 44.

For additional information and reviews by Robert C. Pooley, Alan C. Purves, and John C. Sherwood, see

7:225 (1 reference). For a review of the complete battery, see 7:31.

REFERENCES THROUGH 1971
1. See 7:225.

CUMULATIVE NAME INDEX
Goolsby, T. M.: 1　　　Purves, A. C.: *rev*, 7:225
Pooley, R. C.: *rev*, 7:225　Sherwood, J. C.: *rev*, 7:225

[144]

*The Undergraduate Program Field Tests: Literature Tests. College; 1969–73; formerly called *The Undergraduate Record Examinations: Literature Tests;* tests available to colleges for local administration; 2 tests: field, modular; Educational Testing Service. * For the testing program entry, see 1062.
a) LITERATURE TEST.
b) EUROPEAN AND AMERICAN LITERATURE TEST: A MODULAR TEST DESIGNED TO COMPLEMENT THE TWO-HOUR LITERATURE TEST.

For additional information, see 7:226. For reviews of the testing program, see 7:671 (2 reviews).

REFERENCES THROUGH 1971
1. SCHNITZEN, JOSEPH P., AND COX, JOHN A. "Concurrent Validity of a Literature Test in Relation to Selection of Persons for Graduate Study in English." *Ed & Psychol Meas* 31(2):485–9 su '71. *

CUMULATIVE NAME INDEX
Cox, J. A.: 1　　　　Schnitzen, J. P.: 1

[145]

★World Literature Anthology Tests. High school; 1964–70; revision of *Objective Tests in World Anthology* by Dorothy A. Mason; 5 tests; no manual; Perfection Form Co. *
a) CLASSICAL LITERATURE.
b) EUROPEAN LITERATURE.
c) ORIENTAL LITERATURE.
d) RUSSIAN LITERATURE.
e) FINAL TEST.

[Out of Print Since TIP I]

Objective Tests in English [Turner E. Smith & Co.], 4:194

Objective Tests in English Literature, T:513

Outside Reading Tests for Freshmen and Sophomores (status unknown), 6:305

Outside Reading Tests for Junior High Schools, 6:307

Outside Reading Tests for Juniors and Seniors (status unknown), 6:306

Rigg Poetry Judgment Test, 3:146 (2 reviews, 2 references)

Survey Test in American Literature, 3:147

Survey Test in English Literature, 4:196 (1 review)

Test of Literary Essentials, 4:217

Ullman-Clark Test on Classical References and Allusions, 4:197

SPELLING

[146]

Buckingham Extension of the Ayres Spelling Scale. Grades 2–9; [1918?]; B. R. Buckingham; Bobbs-Merrill Co., Inc. *

REFERENCES THROUGH 1971

1. OTIS, ARTHUR S. "The Reliability of Spelling Scales, Involving a 'Deviation Formula' for Correlation." *Sch & Soc* 4:676–83, 716–22, 750–6, 793–6 O 28, N 4, 11, 18 '16. *
2. FRANZEN, RAYMOND. "The Geography of Intelligence." *J Ed Psychol* 15:499–512 N '24. *
3. GARRISON, S. C., AND RYAN, FLORENCE. "Age-Grade-Sex Percentile Norms for Some Educational Tests." *Peabody J Ed* 1:191–200 Ja '24. *
4. GATES, ARTHUR I., AND LaSALLE, JESSIE. "A Study of Writing Ability and Its Relation to Other Abilities Based on Repeated Tests During a Period of 20 Months." *J Ed Psychol* 15:205–16 Ap '24. *
5. SYMONDS, PERCIVAL M. "The Accuracy of Certain Standard Tests for School Classification." *J Ed Res* 9:315–29 Ap '24. *
6. TRABUE, MARION REX. *Measuring Results in Education*, pp. 128–43. New York: American Book Co., 1924. Pp. 492. *
7. OMWAKE, KATHARINE T. "The Relation of Abstract Intelligence to Ability to Spell." *Pub Personnel Studies* 3:197–201 Jl '25. *
8. SIFFERD, CALVIN S. "A Survey of Spelling Ability." *El Sch J* 47:340–6 F '47. *
9. DOYLE, ANDREW M. "A Study of Spelling Achievement." *Cath Ed R* 48:171–4 Mr '50. *

CUMULATIVE NAME INDEX

Doyle, A. M.: 9	Otis, A. S.: 1
Franzen, R.: 2	Ryan, F.: 3
Garrison, S. C.: 3	Sifferd, C. S.: 8
Gates, A. I.: 4	Symonds, P. M.: 5
LaSalle, J.: 4	Trabue, M. R.: 6
Omwake, K. T.: 7	

[147]

★**Correct Spelling.** Grades 10–13; 1967; "cognition of symbolic units" and "clerical aptitude"; Ralph Hoepfner and J. P. Guilford; Sheridan Psychological Services, Inc. *

[148]

Group Diagnostic Spelling Test. Grades 9–13; 1958; Thomas G. Kemp; Reading Laboratory and Clinic. *

For additional information, see 6:319.

[149]

The Iowa Spelling Scales. Grades 2, 3, 5, 6, 7, 8; 1921–45; no manual; Ernest J. Ashbaugh; Bureau of Educational Research and Service. *

REFERENCES THROUGH 1971

1. ASHBAUGH, ERNEST J. *The Iowa Spelling Scales: Their Derivation, Uses, and Limitations.* Bloomington, Ill.: Public School Publishing Co., 1922. Pp. 144. *
2. TIDYMAN, W. F. "The Iowa Spelling Scales: A Review." *J Ed Res* 7:163–4 F '23. *

CUMULATIVE NAME INDEX

Ashbaugh, E. J.: 1   Tidyman, W. F.: 2

[150]

Kansas Spelling Tests. 1, 2 semesters in grades 3, 4–6, 7–8; 1962–64; first published 1962–63 in the Every Pupil Scholarship Test series; 3 tests; Connie Moritz, Alice Robinson, Mary T. Williams, and M. W. Sanders; Bureau of Educational Measurements. *

a) KANSAS ELEMENTARY SPELLING TEST. 1, 2 semesters in grade 3.

b) KANSAS INTERMEDIATE SPELLING TEST. 1, 2 semesters in grades 4–6.

c) KANSAS JUNIOR HIGH SCHOOL SPELLING TEST. 1, 2 semesters in grades 7–8.

For additional information, see 7:227.

[151]

Kelvin Measurement of Spelling Ability. Ages 7–12; 1933; C. M. Fleming; Robert Gibson & Sons, Glasgow, Ltd. [Scotland]. *

For additional information, see 1:1160.

[152]

Lincoln Diagnostic Spelling Tests. Grades 2–4 or 2–5, 4–8, 8–12 or 9–12; 1941–62; 2 editions; A. L. Lincoln.

a) EDUCATIONAL RECORDS BUREAU EDITION. Grades 2–4 or 2–5, 4–8, 8–12; 1941–62; 3 levels; Educational Records Bureau. *

1) *Lincoln Primary Spelling Test.* Grades 2–4 in independent schools or 2–5 in public schools; 1960–62.

2) *Lincoln Intermediate Spelling Test.* Grades 4–8; 1941–62; three of the 1949 forms identical with tests published 1947–48.

3) *Lincoln Diagnostic Spelling Test.* Grades 8–12; 1941–62; 1949 test identical with test copyrighted 1941.

b) BOBBS-MERRILL COMPANY EDITION. Grades 9–12; 1949–56; 1956 tests same as Forms 1, 2 of *Lincoln Diagnostic Spelling Test* published 1941 and 1942; Bobbs-Merrill Co., Inc. *

For additional information and a review by Gus P. Plessas, see 6:320 (6 references); for reviews by Walter Scribner Guiler and George Spache of the tests for grades 4–12, see 4:202–3.

REFERENCES THROUGH 1971

1–6. See 6:320.
7. TOWNSEND, AGATHA. "An Investigation of Certain Relationships of Spelling With Reading and Academic Aptitude." *J Ed Res* 40:465–71 F '47. * (*PA* 21:3763)
8. NEWTON, BERTHA M. "A Study of Certain Factors Related to Achievement in Spelling." *Alberta J Ed Res* (Canada) 7:202–8 D '61. * (*PA* 36:5KLo2N)
9. BABBOTT, EDWARD FRENCH. *The Differential Effectiveness of Eight 9th Grade Variables in Predicting Success in Three 10th Grade Academic Subjects at Summit High School: A Study in Differential Prediction.* Doctor's thesis, New York University (New York, N.Y.), 1963. (*DA* 25:993)

CUMULATIVE NAME INDEX

Babbott, E. F.: 9	Townsend, A.: 1–2, 7
Guiler, W. S.: *rev*, 4:202–3	Traxler, A. E.: 5
Luntz, L.: 3	Triggs, F. O.: 4
Newton, B. M.: 8	Vecchione, N.: 6
Plessas, G. P.: *rev*, 6:320	Waldman, J.: 4
Spache, G.: *rev*, 4:202–3	

[153]

N.B. Spelling Tests. Standards 1–3, 3–5, 6–8, 8–10 for English pupils and 3–5, 6–8, 9–10 for Afrikaans pupils; [1962–64]; Human Sciences Research Council [South Africa]. *

For additional information, see 7:228.

[154]

Nationwide Spelling Examination. Grades 4–12; 1959–63; no manual; [Donald R. Honz]; Educational Stimuli. *

For additional information, see 6:321.

[155]

The New Iowa Spelling Scale. Grades 2–8; 1954; master word list with difficulty values by grades from which teacher may compile tests; Harry A. Greene; Bureau of Educational Research and Service. *

For additional information, see 6:322 (1 reference).

REFERENCES THROUGH 1971

1. See 6:322.

CUMULATIVE NAME INDEX

Groff, P. J.: 1

[156]

Sanders-Fletcher Spelling Test. 1, 2 semesters in grades 9–13; 1962–64; first published 1962–63 in the Every Pupil Scholarship Test series; Gwen Fletcher and M. W. Sanders; Bureau of Educational Measurements. *

For additional information and a review by Thomas D. Horn, see 7:229.

[157]

***Spelling: Differential Aptitude Tests.** Grades 8–12 and adults; 1947–73; revision of the spelling subtest of Form B of the DAT *Language Usage* (1947), later called Form M of the DAT *Language Usage—Spelling* (1962); George K. Bennett, Harold G. Seashore, and Alexander G. Wesman; Psychological Corporation. * For the complete battery entry, see 1069.

For reviews of the complete battery, see 7:673 (1 review, 1 excerpt), 6:767 (2 reviews), 5:605 (2 reviews), 4:711 (3 reviews), and 3:620 (1 excerpt).

REFERENCES THROUGH 1971

1. VINEYARD, EDWIN E., AND MASSEY, HAROLD W. "The Interrelationship of Certain Linguistic Skills and Their Relationship With Scholastic Achievement When Intelligence Is Ruled Constant." *J Ed Psychol* 48:279–86 My '57. * (*PA* 33: 2200)

2. RICHMAN, JAY T. *A Comparison of the Phonetic Structure of a Basal Vocabulary List and the Spelling Section of the Differential Aptitude Test.* Master's thesis, Utah State University (Logan, Utah), 1965.

CUMULATIVE NAME INDEX

Massey, H. W.: 1   Vineyard, E. E.: 1
Richman, J. T.: 2

[158]

Spelling Errors Test. Grades 2–4, 5–6, 7–8; 1948–55; George Spache; Reading Laboratory and Clinic. *

For additional information, see 5:228 (1 reference).

REFERENCES THROUGH 1971

1. See 5:228.

CUMULATIVE NAME INDEX

Lampard, D. M.: 1

[159]

Spelling Test for Clerical Workers: [Personnel Research Institute Clerical Battery]. Stenographic applicants and high school; 1947; Jay L. Otis, David J. Chesler, and Irene Salmi; Personnel Research Institute. * For the complete battery entry, see 2140.

For additional information and a review by Harold H. Bixler, see 4:211. For reviews of the complete battery, see 4:729 (2 reviews).

REFERENCES THROUGH 1971

1. STAPLES, JOHN DIXON. *An Experimental Study to Identify the Basic Abilities Needed to Detect Typescript Errors With*

Implications for the Improvement of Instruction in Typewriting. Doctor's thesis, University of North Dakota (Grand Forks, N.D.), 1965. (*DA* 27:1693A)

CUMULATIVE NAME INDEX

Bixler, H. H.: *rev*, 4:211   Staples, J. D.: 1

[160]

Spelling Test: McGraw-Hill Basic Skills System. Grades 11–14; 1970; also called *MHBSS Spelling Test;* although designed for use with the MHBSS instructional program, the test may be used independently; Alton L. Raygor; McGraw-Hill Book Co., Inc. *

For additional information and reviews by Thomas D. Horn and Albert H. Yee, see 7:230.

[161]

Spelling Test: National Achievement Tests. Grades 3–4, 5–8, 7–9, 10–12; 1936–57; 1956–57 tests identical with tests copyrighted 1939; Robert K. Speer and Samuel Smith; Psychometric Affiliates. *

For additional information and a review by James A. Fitzgerald, see 5:230; for a review by W. J. Osburn, see 1:1161.

[162]

Traxler High School Spelling Test. Grades 9–12; 1937–55; 1955 tests same as tests published 1937–40; Arthur E. Traxler; Bobbs-Merrill Co., Inc. *

For additional information and a review by Gus P. Plessas, see 6:326; for a review by Henry D. Rinsland, see 4:212.

[Out of Print Since TIP I]

A.C.E.R. Spelling Test, 2:1309 (1 review)
A.C.E.R. Spelling Test (Form C), 5:222 (2 reviews);
Ayer Standardized Spelling Test, 6:317 (2 reviews); see also 4:198 (1 reference)
Coordinated Scales of Attainment: Spelling, 5:223
Davis-Schrammel Spelling Test, 4:199 (3 reviews)
Gates-Russell Spelling Diagnostic Tests, 6:318 (3 reviews); see also 4:200 (1 reference)
Graded Word Spelling Test, 5:224 (1 review)
Iowa Dictation Exercise and Spelling Test, T:539
Kansas Spelling Test, 3:153 (2 reviews)
Morrison-McCall Spelling Scale, 4:205 (1 review, 2 references)
New Standard High School Spelling Scale, 4:206
Rich-Engelson Spelling Test, 4:207 (1 review)
Spelling and Vocabulary: Every Pupil Test, 6:323
Spelling: Every Pupil Scholarship Test, 6:325
Spelling: Public School Achievement Tests, T:554
Spelling: Seven Plus Assessment: Northumberland Series, 4:210
Wellesley Spelling Scale, 5:232 (3 reviews, 1 reference)

VOCABULARY

[163]

A.C.E.R. Word Knowledge Test—Adult Form B. Ages 18 and over; 1933–60; identical with part 1 of *A.C.E.R. Silent Reading Tests,* Form B for grades 3–8 except for directions; manual by T. M. Whitford; Australian Council for Educational Research [Australia]. *

For additional information, see 6:327 (1 reference).

REFERENCES THROUGH 1971

1. See 6:327.

CUMULATIVE NAME INDEX

Bucklow, M.: 1   Doughty, P.: 1

[164]

American Literacy Test. Adults; 1962; vocabulary; John J. McCarty; Psychometric Affiliates. *
For additional information and a review by Victor H. Noll, see 6:328.

[165]

Bruce Vocabulary Inventory. Business and industry; 1959–67; Martin M. Bruce; Martin M. Bruce, Ph.D., Publishers. *
For additional information and reviews by Fred H. Borgen and Robert Fitzpatrick, see 7:231.

[166]

*The Iowa Tests of Educational Development: Test 8, General Vocabulary. Grades 9–12; 1942–67; Forms X-4 and Y-4; more recent Forms X5 and Y5 are not available as separates; prepared under the direction of E. F. Lindquist and Leonard S. Feldt; Science Research Associates, Inc. * For the complete battery entry, see 20.
For additional information concerning earlier forms, see 6:332. For reviews of the complete battery, see 6:14 (2 reviews), 5:17 (2 reviews), 4:17 (1 review), and 3:12 (3 reviews).

[167]

Johnson O'Connor English Vocabulary Worksamples. Ages 9–14, 15 and over, "high vocabulary students and adults"; 1934–62; 3 levels; Johnson O'Connor and others; Human Engineering Laboratory Inc. *
a) INTERMEDIATE FORM WORKSAMPLE 176. Ages 9–14.
b) WORKSAMPLE 95. Ages 15 and over; all but 3–7 items of Forms AD, BC, and CC are revisions of items from *The Inglis Tests of English Vocabulary.*
c) ADVANCED FORM WORKSAMPLE 180. "High vocabulary students and adults."
For additional information, see 6:333 (5 references).

REFERENCES THROUGH 1971
1–5. See 6:333.
6. DODGE, ARTHUR F. "Occupational Ability Patterns." *Teach Col Contrib Ed* 658:1–97 '35. * (*PA* 9:5877)
7. GUTHRIE, GEORGE M., AND ZEKTICK, IDA N. "Predicting Performance in the Peace Corps." *J Social Psychol* 71:11–21 F '67. * (*PA* 41:6319)

CUMULATIVE NAME INDEX
Achard, F. H.: 2	Gelman, B.: 3
Clarke, F. H.: 2	Guthrie, G. M.: 7
Dodge, A. F.: 6	O'Connor, J.: 1
Filley, M. E.: 1	Uhrbrock, R. S.: 5
Fisher, F.: 4	Zektick, I. N.: 7

[168]

Johnson O'Connor Vocabulary Tests. Professionals; 1937–58; 6 tests; no manual; [Johnson O'Connor and staff]; Human Engineering Laboratory Inc. *
a) JOHNSON O'CONNOR VOCABULARY OF MATHEMATICS. 1945–56.
b) JOHNSON O'CONNOR VOCABULARY OF ARCHITECTURE. 1946–56.
c) JOHNSON O'CONNOR VOCABULARY OF MUSIC. 1945–56.
d) JOHNSON O'CONNOR VOCABULARY OF PHYSICS. 1937–58.
e) JOHNSON O'CONNOR VOCABULARY OF RADIO AND PHYSICS. 1952–56.
f) JOHNSON O'CONNOR VOCABULARY OF SPORTS. 1953–56.
For additional information, see 6:334.

[169]

Nationwide English Vocabulary Examination. Grades 4–12; 1959–63; [Donald R. Honz]; Educational Stimuli. *
For additional information, see 6:335.

[170]

Purdue Industrial Supervisors Word-Meaning Test. Supervisors; 1952; Joseph Tiffin and Donald A. Long; University Book Store. *
For additional information and reviews by Jerome E. Doppelt and Bernadine Meyer, see 5:237 (2 references).

REFERENCES THROUGH 1971
1–2. See 5:237.
3. GRUENFELD, LEOPOLD WILHELM. *Selection of Executives for a Training Program.* Doctor's thesis, Purdue University (Lafayette, Ind.), 1960. (*DA* 21:1247)
4. KIRCHNER, WAYNE; HANSON, RICHARD; AND BENSON, DALE. "Selecting Foremen With Psychological Tests." *Personnel Adm* 23:27–30 N–D '60. *
5. GRUENFELD, LEOPOLD W. "Selection of Executives for a Training Program." *Personnel Psychol* 14:421–31 w '61. * (*PA* 37:3922)

CUMULATIVE NAME INDEX
Benson, D.: 4	Kirchner, W.: 4
Doppelt, J. E.: *rev*, 5:237	Long, D. A.: 1
Gruenfeld, L. W.: 3, 5	Meyer, B.: *rev*, 5:237
Hanson, R.: 4	Sawyer, J.: 2

[171]

RBH Vocabulary Test. Applicants for clerical and stenographic positions; 1948–63; Richardson, Bellows, Henry & Co., Inc. *
For additional information and a review by Fred H. Borgen, see 7:232.

[172]

Sanders-Fletcher Vocabulary Test. 1, 2 semesters in grades 9–13; 1938–64; first published 1938 in the Every Pupil Scholarship Test series; Gwen Fletcher and M. W. Sanders; Bureau of Educational Measurements. *
For additional information, see 7:233.

[173]

Survey Test of Vocabulary. Grades 3–12; 1931–65; 1940 test identical with test copyrighted 1931; no manual; L. J. O'Rourke; O'Rourke Publications. *
For additional information, see 7:234; see also 5:239 (3 references); for reviews by Verner M. Sims and Clifford Woody, see 3:167 (1 reference).

REFERENCES THROUGH 1971
1. See 3:167.
2–4. See 5:239.
5. POND, FREDERICK L. "Influence of Reading Abilities on School Success in Grade IX." *Sch R* 48:437–44 Je '40. *
6. BURTON, MARY. "The Hearing and Reading Comprehension of Vocabulary Among High-School Seniors." *Sch R* 52:47–50 Ja '44. * (*PA* 18:1862)

CUMULATIVE NAME INDEX
Burton, M.: 6	Stead, W. H.: 2
Janus, S.: 3	War Manpower Commission,
Littleton, I. T.: 4	Division of Occupational
Pond, F. L.: 5	Analysis, Staff: 1
Sims, V. M.: *rev*, 3:167	Woody, C.: *rev*, 3:167

[174]

A Test of Active Vocabulary. Grades 9–12; 1961; Paul W. Lehmann; Educational Publications. *
For additional information, see 6:338.

[175]

★Vocabulary Survey Test. Grades kgn–1; 1971; oral vocabulary; 3 scores: part 1 (nouns, mathematical terms), part 2 (place relationship terms, verbs, adjectives, pronouns, mathematical concepts), total; Marion Monroe, John C. Manning, and Joseph M. Wepman; Scott, Foresman & Co. *

[176]

Vocabulary Test for High School Students and College Freshmen. Grades 9–13; 1964; Arthur E. Traxler; Bobbs-Merrill Co., Inc. *

For additional information, a review by George P. Winship, Jr., and an excerpted review by Joan Bollenbacher, see 7:235 (1 reference).

REFERENCES THROUGH 1971

1. See 7:235.

CUMULATIVE NAME INDEX

Bollenbacher, J.: exc, 7:235   Winship, G. P.: rev, 7:235
Traxler, A. E.: 1

[177]

Vocabulary Test: McGraw-Hill Basic Skills System. Grades 11-14; 1970; also called *MHBSS Vocabulary Test;* although designed for use with the MHBSS instructional program, the test may be used independently; Alton L. Raygor; McGraw-Hill Book Co., Inc. *

For additional information and a review by George P. Winship, Jr., see 7:236.

[178]

Vocabulary Test: National Achievement Tests. Grades 3-8, 7-12; 1939-57; 1951-57 tests identical with tests copyrighted 1939; Robert K. Speer and Samuel Smith; Psychometric Affiliates. *

For additional information, see 5:241; for a review by Clifford Woody, see 3:168.

[179]

Wide Range Vocabulary Test. Ages 8 and over; 1937-45; C. R. Atwell and F. L. Wells; Psychological Corporation. *

For additional information and a review by Paul S. Burnham, see 3:169 (1 reference).

REFERENCES THROUGH 1971

1. See 3:169.
2. KNEHR, CHARLES A. "Psychological Assessment of Differential Impairment in Cerebral Organic Conditions and Schizophrenics." *J Psychol* 54:165-89 Jl '62. * (*PA* 37:3695)
3. REGER, ROGER. "Brief Tests of Intelligence and Academic Achievement." *Psychol Rep* 11:82 Ag '62. * (*PA* 37:5654)
4. JOHNSTON, JAMES ORRIN. *Relationships Between Intelligence and Personality Variables.* Doctor's thesis, Oklahoma State University (Stillwater, Okla.), 1965. (*DA* 27:315B)
5. RICHARDS, JAMES M., JR. "Can Computers Write College Admissions Tests?" *ACT Res Rep* 15:1-11 O '66. * (*PA* 41:2242)

CUMULATIVE NAME INDEX

Atwell, C. R.: 1   Reger, R.: 3
Burnham, P. S.: rev, 3:169   Richards, J. M.: 5
Johnston, J. O.: 4   Wells, F. L.: 1
Knehr, C. A.: 2

[180]

Word Clue Tests. Grades 7-13 and adults; 1962-65; designed primarily for use with instructional booklets in the Word Clues series; 2 tests; Stanford E. Taylor, Helen Frackenpohl, and Arthur S. McDonald; Educational Developmental Laboratories, Inc. *

a) WORD CLUE TEST.
b) WORD CLUE APPRAISAL.

For additional information, see 7:237.

[181]

Word Dexterity Test. Grades 7-16; 1942-50; Shailer Peterson; the Author. *

For additional information, see 4:218; see also 3:170 (2 references).

REFERENCES THROUGH 1971

1-2. See 3:170.

CUMULATIVE NAME INDEX

Peterson, S.: 2   Peterson, S. A.: 1

[182]

Word Understanding. Grades 6-12; 1969; R. Hoepfner, M. Hendricks, and R. H. Silverman; Monitor. *

For additional information, see 7:238.

[Out of Print Since TIP I]

College Vocabulary Test (status unknown), T:562
Cooperative Vocabulary Test, 4:213 (2 reviews, 4 references)
Durost-Center Word Mastery Test, 6:330 (2 reviews)
English Vocabulary Tests for High School and College Students, T:565
Gulick Vocabulary Survey, 6:331 (1 review, 1 reference)
Holborn Vocabulary Test for Young Children, 4:215 (1 review, 1 reference)
Inglis Tests of English Vocabulary, 5:234 (1 review, 10 references)
Kansas Vocabulary Test, 3:164 (1 review)
Lower Extension of the Inglis Tests of English Vocabulary, T:571, 35:225 (1 reference)
Michigan Vocabulary Profile Test, 4:216 (7 reviews, 1 excerpt, 15 references)
New Standard Vocabulary Test, 6:336 (2 reviews)
Quick-Scoring Vocabulary Test: Dominion Tests, 6:337 (1 review)
Schrammel-Wharton Vocabulary Test, 2:1321 (1 review)
Sentence Vocabulary Scale, T:577
Vocabulary: Every Pupil Scholarship Test, 6:339
Vocabulary Test [Management Service Co.] (status unknown), 6:340
Vocabulary Test—GT, 6:342 (1 review, 6 references)

FINE ARTS

[Out of Print Since TIP I]
Oberlin Test of Music and Art, 6:344

ART

[183]

★**Advanced Placement Examination in Art.** High school students desiring credit for college level courses or admission to advanced courses; 1972–73; available to secondary schools for annual administration on specified days in May; inactive forms are available to colleges for local administration in the *Testing Academic Achievement* program; 2 tests; program administered for the College Entrance Examination Board by Educational Testing Service. * For the testing program entry, see 1045.
a) HISTORY OF ART. Test consists of essays and an individual study.
b) STUDIO ART. Candidate submits materials for evaluation of quality, concentration, and breadth.

For reviews of the testing program, see 7:662 (2 reviews).

[184]

Art Vocabulary. Grades 6–12; 1969; R. H. Silverman, R. Hoepfner, and M. Hendricks; Monitor. *
For additional information, see 7:239.

[185]

Graves Design Judgment Test. Grades 7–16 and adults; 1948; Maitland Graves; Psychological Corporation. *
For additional information, reviews by William B. Michael and Edwin Ziegfeld, and an excerpted review by Laurance F. Shaffer, see 4:220 (2 references).

REFERENCES THROUGH 1971

1–2. See 4:220.
3. CRANNELL, C. W. "The Validity of Certain Measures of Art Appreciation in Relation to a Drawing Task." *J Psychol* 35:131–42 Ja '53. * (*PA* 27:6436)
4. BOLTON, EURI BELLE. "Brief Evaluation of Two Tests of Aesthetic Judgment." *Peabody J Ed* 32:211–23 Ja '55. * (*PA* 29:6947)
5. GRANGER, G. W. "An Experimental Study of Colour Preferences." *J General Psychol* 52:3–20 Ja '55. * (*PA* 30:2493)
6. GUTEKUNST, JOSEF GRANT. *The Prediction of Art Achievement of Art Education Students by Means of Standardized Tests.* Doctor's thesis, Temple University (Philadelphia, Pa.), 1959. (*DA* 20:3202)
7. WOLD, STANLEY GORDON. *A Comparison of College Students' Performance on Selected Art Tasks and on the Graves Design Judgment Test.* Doctor's thesis, University of Minnesota (Minneapolis, Minn.), 1960. (*DA* 21:2997)
8. BROWN, ROBERT LEWIS. *A Study of the Relationship Between Ability Ratings of Art and Architecture Students, Intelligence, and Scores on Two Art Aptitude Tests.* Doctor's thesis, University of Arkansas (Fayetteville, Ark.), 1962. (*DA* 23:528)
9. LANSDELL, H. "A Sex Difference in Effect of Temporal-Lobe Neurosurgery on Design Preference." *Nature* (England) 194:852–4 Je 2 '62. * (*PA* 38:5375)
10. SILVERMAN, RONALD H. *Comparing the Effects of Two Versus Three-Dimensional Art Activity Upon Spatial Visualization, Aesthetic Judgment, and Art Interest.* Doctor's thesis, Stanford University (Stanford, Calif.), 1962. (*DA* 23:2017)
11. ALFORD, MARY LEE. *Teacher Judgments as Related to Certain Predictors of Artistic Creativity in Senior High-School*

Students. Doctor's thesis, North Texas State University (Denton, Tex.), 1964. (*DA* 25:1039)
12. GERARD, HAROLD B.; BLEVANS, STEPHEN A.; AND MALCOLM, THOMAS. "Self-Evaluation and the Evaluation of Choice Alternatives." *J Personality* 32:395–410 S '64. * (*PA* 39:7633)
13. BOAZ, MARY EVELYN. *Identification and Evaluation of Creative Abilities of Students in the Area of Textiles and Clothing.* Doctor's thesis, Oklahoma State University (Stillwater, Okla.), 1965. (*DA* 27:219B)
14. GUION, ROBERT M. "Synthetic Validity in a Small Company: A Demonstration." *Personnel Psychol* 18:49–63 sp '65. * (*PA* 39:16490)
15. LANSDELL, H., AND URBACH, NELLY. "Sex Differences in Personality Measures Related to Size and Side of Temporal Lobe Ablations." Abstract. *Proc Ann Conv Am Psychol Assn* 73:113–4 '65. * (*PA* 39:14113)
16. SEIFERT, GEORGE GUSTAV. *The Development of Aesthetic Awareness and Creativity in Fifth Graders Utilizing a Design Procedure.* Doctor's thesis, Western Reserve University (Cleveland, Ohio), 1965. (*DA* 27:422A)
17. MILLMAN, MARCIA, AND CHANG, TERESA. "Inter-Correlations Among Three Widely Used Art Tests." *Percept & Motor Skills* 23:1002 D '66. * (*PA* 41:6434, title only)
18. EYSENCK, H. J. "Factor-Analytic Study of the Maitland Graves Design Judgment Test." *Percept & Motor Skills* 24:73–4 F '67. * (*PA* 41:8900)
19. KEESEE, CURTIS GORDON, JR. *The Relationship of Performance on the Scholastic Aptitude Test, the Meier Art Judgment Test, and the Graves Design Judgment Test to Successful Completion of Freshmen Commercial Art Courses.* Doctor's thesis, University of Virginia (Charlottesville, Va.), 1967. (*DA* 28:2516A) (Abstract: *Ed R* 5:58–60)
20. JASNOSZ, THOMAS ADAM. *A Comparison of Student Achievement in Visual Communication and in the Traditional Graphic Arts Approach.* Doctor's thesis, Arizona State University (Tempe, Ariz.), 1969. (*DAI* 30:1416A)
21. EYSENCK, H. J. "An Application of the Maitland Graves Design Judgment Test to Professional Artists." *Percept & Motor Skills* 30(2):589–90 Ap '70. * (*PA* 46:7444)
22. SLOANE, PATRICIA. "Art and Art Token in Tests Involving Art Evaluation." *Psychol Rec* 20(2):191–6 sp '70. * (*PA* 45:2366)
23. EYSENCK, H. J., AND CASTLE, M. "Comparative Study of Artists and Nonartists on the Maitland Graves Design Judgment Test." *J Appl Psychol* 55(4):389–92 Ag '71. * (*PA* 47:2908)
24. JENSEN, OLIVE MARIE JACOBSON. *Differences in Perception Through Teaching Drawing in Contrasting Groups of Fifth Grade Students.* Doctor's thesis, University of Minnesota (Minneapolis, Minn.), 1971. (*DAI* 32:3156A)

CUMULATIVE NAME INDEX

Alford, M. L.: 11
Blevans, S. A.: 12
Boaz, M. E.: 13
Bolton, E. B.: 4
Brown, R. L.: 8
Castle, M.: 23
Chang, T.: 17
Crannell, C. W.: 3
Eysenck, H. J.: 18, 21, 23
Gerard, H. B.: 12
Granger, G. W.: 5
Graves, M.: 1–2
Guion, R. M.: 14
Gutekunst, J. G.: 6

Jasnosz, T. A.: 20
Jensen, O. M. J.: 24
Keesee, C. G.: 19
Lansdell, H.: 9, 15
Malcolm, T.: 12
Michael, W. B.: *rev*, 4:220
Millman, M.: 17
Seifert, G. G.: 16
Shaffer, L. F.: *exc*, 4:220
Silverman, R. H.: 10
Sloane, P.: 22
Urbach, N.: 15
Wold, S. G.: 17
Ziegfeld, E.: *rev*, 4:220

[186]

Horn Art Aptitude Inventory. Grades 12–16 and adults; 1939–53; 2 scores: scribbling and doodling, imagery; Charles C. Horn; Stoelting Co. *
For additional information and a review by Orville Palmer, see 5:242; for a review by Edwin Ziegfeld, see 3:171 (1 reference).

REFERENCES THROUGH 1971

1. See 3:171.

[187]

Knauber Art Ability Test. Grades 7–16; 1932–35; Alma Jordan Knauber; the Author. *

For additional information and a review by Edwin Ziegfeld, see 4:222; for a review by Norman C. Meier, see 2:1323 (4 references).

REFERENCES THROUGH 1971

1–4. See 2:1323.
5. Gunn, Chester E. "Art Ability of Junior High School Pupils in a Cosmopolitan Community." *Sch R* 45:769–75 D '37. *
6. Gutekunst, Josef Grant. *The Prediction of Art Achievement of Art Education Students by Means of Standardized Tests.* Doctor's thesis, Temple University (Philadelphia, Pa.), 1959. (*DA* 20:3202)

[188]

Knauber Art Vocabulary Test. Grades 7–16; 1932–35; Alma Jordan Knauber; the Author. *

For additional information and a review by Edwin Ziegfeld, see 4:223 (2 references); for reviews by Ray Faulkner and Joseph E. Moore, see 2:1324 (4 references).

REFERENCES THROUGH 1971

1–4. See 2:1324.
5–6. See 4:223.

[189]

The Meier Art Tests. Grades 7–16 and adults, 9–16 and adults; 1929–63; 2 tests; Norman Charles Meier; Bureau of Educational Research and Service. *

a) THE MEIER ART TESTS: 1, ART JUDGMENT. Grades 7–16 and adults; 1929–42; revision of *Meier-Seashore Art Judgment Test.*

b) THE MEIER ART TESTS: 2, AESTHETIC PERCEPTION. Grades 9–16 and adults; 1963.

For additional information and an excerpted review by Laurence Siegel of test 2, see 7:240 (7 references); for a review by Harold A. Schultz, see 6:346 (8 references); for a review by Harold A. Schultz of test 1, see 4:224 (9 references); for a review by Edwin Ziegfeld, see 3:172 (4 references); for reviews by Paul R. Farnsworth and Aulus Ward Saunders of the original edition of test 1, see 2:1326 (15 references).

REFERENCES THROUGH 1971

1–15. See 2:1326.
16–19. See 3:172.
20–28. See 4:224.
29–36. See 6:346.
37–43. See 7:240.
44. Meier, Norman C. "A Measure of Art Talent." *Psychol Monogr* 39(2):184–99 '28. * (*PA* 3:2311)
45. Carroll, Herbert A. "A Preliminary Report on a Study of the Interrelationships of Certain Appreciations." *J Ed Psychol* 23:505–10 O '32. * (*PA* 7:1452)
46. Carroll, Herbert A. "A Preliminary Report on a Study of the Relationship Between Ability in Art and Certain Personality Traits." *Sch & Soc* 36:285–8 Ag 27 '32. * (*PA* 7:230)
47. Hevner, Kate. "A Method of Correcting for Guessing in True-False Tests and Empirical Evidence in Support of It." *J Social Psychol* 3:359–62 Ag '32. * (*PA* 7:1177)
48. Mausner, Bernard. "Studies in Social Interaction: 3, Effect of Variation in One Partner's Prestige on the Interaction

Horn Art Aptitude Inventory

---

of Observer Pairs." *J Appl Psychol* 37:391–3 O '53. * (*PA* 29:689)

[190]

*National Teacher Examinations: Art Education. College seniors and teachers; 1961–73; an inactive form (1966) entitled *Teacher Education Examination Program: Art Education* is available to colleges for local administration; another inactive form (1968) entitled *Specialty Examinations: Art Education* is available to school systems for local use as part of the program entitled *School Personnel Research and Evaluation Services;* Educational Testing Service. * For the testing program entry, see 869.

For additional information concerning earlier forms, see 7:241; for a review by Harold A. Schultz, see 6:345. For reviews of the testing program, see 7:582 (2 reviews), 6:700 (1 review), 5:538 (3 reviews), and 4:802 (1 review).

[191]

★Teacher Education Examination Program: Art Education. College seniors preparing to teach secondary school; 1971–72; reprinting of inactive 1966 form of *National Teacher Examinations: Art Education;* test available to colleges for local administration; Educational Testing Service. * For the testing program entry, see 898.

For a review of the testing program, see 5:543. For reference to a review of the *National Teacher Examinations: Art Education,* see 190.

[192]

*The Undergraduate Program Field Test: Art History Test. College; 1970–73; formerly called *The Undergraduate Record Examinations: Art History Test;* test available to colleges for local administration; Educational Testing Service. * For the testing program entry, see 1062.

For additional information, see 7:242. For reviews of the testing program, see 7:671 (2 reviews).

[Out of Print Since TIP I]

Cooper Union Art School Imagination Test, T:587
Measuring Scale for Freehand Drawing, 1:896
Tests in Fundamental Abilities of Visual Arts, 2:1329
(2 reviews, 6 references)

MUSIC

[193]

★Advanced Placement Examination in Music.
High school students desiring credit for college level courses or admission to advanced courses; 1971–73; available to secondary schools for annual administration on specified days in May; inactive forms are available to colleges for local administration in the *Testing Academic Achievement* program; program administered for the College Entrance Examination Board by Educational Testing Service. * For the testing program entry, see 1045.
For reviews of the testing program, see 7:662 (2 reviews).

REFERENCES THROUGH 1971
1. LANDIS, BETH. "Advanced Placement Comes to Music." *Music Ed J* 58(1):65–6 S '71. *

CUMULATIVE NAME INDEX
Landis, B.: 1

[194]

[Aliferis-Stecklein Music Achievement Tests.]
Music students; 1954–62, c1947–62; 2 levels; James Aliferis and John E. Stecklein (b); University of Minnesota Press. *
a) ALIFERIS MUSIC ACHIEVEMENT TEST: COLLEGE ENTRANCE LEVEL. Entering freshman music students; 1954, c1947–54; 4 scores: melody, harmony, rhythm, total.
b) ALIFERIS-STECKLEIN MUSIC ACHIEVEMENT TEST: COLLEGE MIDPOINT LEVEL. Music students at end of grade 14 or beginning of grade 15; 1962, c1952–62; subtitle is *A Measure of Auditory-Visual Discrimination;* 4 scores: melodic interval, chord, rhythm, total.
For additional information and reviews by Paul R. Farnsworth and Herbert D. Wing of *b,* see 6:347 (5 references); for a review by Herbert D. Wing of *a,* see 5:243 (5 references).

REFERENCES THROUGH 1971
1–5. See 5:243.
6–10. See 6:347.
11. JUNG, JOSEPH WEILAND. *A Study of the Factors Associated With Music Participation by Secondary School Pupils in the Suburban Areas of Minneapolis and St. Paul.* Doctor's thesis, University of Minnesota (Minneapolis, Minn.), 1954. (*DA* 14:2007)
12. NEICE, THOMAS ELBERT. *An Investigation of the Relationships of Selected Factors in the Preparation of Music Education Majors to Musical Achievement.* Doctor's thesis, University of Illinois (Urbana, Ill.), 1964. (*DA* 25:4743)
13. DOUGLAS, CHARLES HERBERT. *Measuring and Equalizing Music Theory Competence of Freshmen College Music Majors.* Doctor's thesis, Florida State University (Tallahassee, Fla.), 1965. (*DA* 26:4712)
14. FOLSTROM, ROGER JAMES. *A Comparative Study of the Musical Achievement of Students in Three Illinois High Schools.* Doctor's thesis, Northwestern University (Evanston, Ill.), 1967. (*DA* 28:3697A)
15. BUTLER, JOHN HARRISON. *Personality Factors as Correlates of Receptivity to Electronic Music.* Doctor's thesis, University of Georgia (Athens, Ga.), 1968. (*DA* 29:4514A)

CUMULATIVE NAME INDEX
Aliferis, J.: 1–2, 4 Neice, T. E.: 12
Butler, J. H.: 15   Roby, A. R.: 9
Colwell, R.: 6, 10   Stecklein, J. E.: 1–4
Douglas, C. H.: 13   White, A.: 8
Duda, W. B.: 7   Williams, R. E.: 5
Farnsworth, P. R.: *rev,* 6:347 Wing, H. D.: *rev,* 5:243,
Folstrom, R. J.: 14   6:347
Jung, J. W.: 11

[195]

★The Belwin-Mills Singing Achievement Test.
Grades 5–16; 1971; sight singing; Richard W. Bowles with validations by Charles Corbin; Belwin-Mills Publishing Corporation. *

[196]

★Elementary Rhythm and Pitch Test: For Selecting Band and Orchestra Members in Grades Four to Eight. Grades 4–8; 1937–70; C. L. McCreery; National School Music Service, Inc. *

[197]

*The Graduate Record Examinations Advanced Music Test. Graduate school candidates; 1951–73; 3 scores: music theory, music history, total; Educational Testing Service. * For the testing program entry, see 1053.
For additional information concerning earlier forms, see 7:243; for a review by William S. Larson, see 5:247. For reviews of the testing program, see 7:667 (1 review) and 5:601 (1 review).

[198]

The Gretsch-Tilson Musical Aptitude Test.
Grades 4–12; 1938; Lowell Mason Tilson; Fred Gretsch Co., Inc. *
For additional information, see 7:244 (2 references).

REFERENCES THROUGH 1971
1–2. See 7:244.

CUMULATIVE NAME INDEX
Jung, J. W.: 2   Tilson, L. M.: 1

[199]

*Iowa Tests of Music Literacy. Grades 4–12, 7–12; 1970–71; ITML; 9 scores: tonal concepts (aural perception, reading recognition, notational understanding, total), rhythmic concepts (aural perception, reading recognition, notational understanding, total), total; Edwin Gordon; Bureau of Educational Research and Service. *
For additional information, see 7:245 (2 references).

REFERENCES THROUGH 1971
1–2. See 7:245.
3. GORDON, EDWIN. "The Second-Year Results of a Five-Year Longitudinal Study of the Musical Achievement of Culturally-Disadvantaged Students," pp. 131–43. (*PA* 50:7719) In his *Experimental Research in the Psychology of Music:* 7. Studies in the Psychology of Music, Vol. 7. Iowa City, Iowa: University of Iowa Press, 1971. Pp. vii, 179. *
4. MOHATT, JAMES L. "An Investigation of the Criterion-Related Validity of the Iowa Tests of Music Literacy," pp. 144–67. (*PA* 50:7801) In *Experimental Research in the Psychology of Music:* 7. Edited by Edwin Gordon. Studies in the Psychology of Music, Vol. 7. Iowa City, Iowa: University of Iowa Press, 1971. Pp. vii, 179. *
5. MOHATT, JAMES LEO. *A Study of the Validity of the Iowa Tests of Music Literacy.* Doctor's thesis, University of Iowa (Iowa City, Iowa). 1971. (*DAI* 32:1553A)
6. SCHLEUTER, STANLEY LEROY. *An Investigation of the Interrelation of Personality Traits, Musical Aptitude and Musical Achievement.* Doctor's thesis, University of Iowa (Iowa City, Iowa), 1971. (*DAI* 32:1556A)
7. THAYER, ROBERT WILCOX. *An Investigation of the Interrelation of Personality Traits, Musical Achievement, and Different Measures of Musical Aptitude.* Doctor's thesis, University of Iowa (Iowa City, Iowa), 1971. (*DAI* 32:2734A)

CUMULATIVE NAME INDEX
Gordon, E.: 3   Schleuter, S. L.: 6
Huyser, B. H.: 1   Swindell, W. C.: 2
Mohatt, J. L.: 4–5   Thayer, R. W.: 7

[200]

Jones Music Recognition Test. Grades 4–8, 9–16; 1949; Archie N. Jones; Carl Fischer, Inc. *
For additional information and a review by Herbert D. Wing, see 6:349.

[201]

Knuth Achievement Tests in Music: Recognition of Rhythm and Melody. Grades 3–4, 5–6, 7–12; 1936–68; KATM; manual title is *Achievement Tests in*

Music; reissue of the 1936 edition using filmstrips and prerecorded tapes; William E. Knuth; Creative Arts Research Associates, Inc. *

For additional information, see 7:246 (1 reference); for a review by Carl E. Seashore, see 2:1332 (1 reference); for reviews by Jay W. Fay and James L. Mursell, see 1:1085.

REFERENCES THROUGH 1971

1. See 2:1332.
2. See 7:246.
3. SEASHORE, CARL E. "The Psychology of Music: Measures of Musical Achievement, XXIV." *Music Ed J* 26:24+ F '40. * (*PA* 14:3096)
4. WHEELER, LESTER R., AND WHEELER, VIOLA D. "The Relationship Between Music Reading and Language Reading Abilities." *J Ed Res* 45:439-50 F '52. * (*PA* 27:2208)
5. COLWELL, RICHARD. *An Investigation of Achievement in Music in the Public Schools of Sioux Falls, South Dakota.* Doctor's thesis, University of Illinois (Urbana, Ill.), 1961. (*DA* 22:1653)
6. COLWELL, RICHARD. "An Investigation of Musical Achievement Among Vocal Students, Vocal-Instrumental Students, and Instrumental Students." *J Res Music Ed* 11:123-30 f '63. * (*PA* 38:6655)
7. COLWELL, RICHARD. "An Investigation of Musical Achievement Among Public School Students." *J Ed Res* 57:355-9 Mr '64. *

CUMULATIVE NAME INDEX

Colwell, R.: 5-7
Fay, J. W.: *rev,* 1:1085
Knuth, W. E.: 1
Mursell, J. L.: *rev,* 1:1085
Seashore, C. E.: 3; *rev,* 2:1332
Slagle, H. C.: 2
Wheeler, L. R.: 4
Wheeler, V. D.: 4

[202]

Kwalwasser-Dykema Music Tests. Grades 4-16 and adults; 1930; 11 scores: tonal memory, quality discrimination, intensity discrimination, tonal movement, time discrimination, rhythm discrimination, pitch discrimination, melodic taste, pitch imagery, rhythm imagery, total; Jacob Kwalwasser and Peter W. Dykema; Carl Fischer, Inc. *

For additional information and a review by William S. Larson, see 3:176 (29 references).

REFERENCES THROUGH 1971

1-29. See 3:176.
30. SWARD, KEITH. "Jewish Musicality in America." *J Appl Psychol* 17:675-712 D '33. * (*PA* 8:3725)
31. FARNSWORTH, PAUL R. "Studies in the Psychology of Tone and Music." *Genetic Psychol Monogr* 15:1-94 Ja '34. * (*PA* 8:3682)
32. DRAKE, RALEIGH M. "Factor Analysis of Music Tests." Abstract. *Psychol B* 36:608-9 O '39. * (*PA* 14:414, title only)
33. ODE, SIGURD J. *A Survey to Show What Percentage of Musically Talented Pupils Are Overlooked by School Music Educators.* Master's thesis, University of North Dakota (Grand Forks, N.D.), 1939.
34. SHEPARD, EUGENE L. *Measurements of Certain Nonverbal Abilities of Urban and Rural Children.* Doctor's thesis, New York University (New York, N.Y.), 1940.
35. GROSS, BETHUEL, AND SEASHORE, ROBERT H. "Psychological Characteristics of Student and Professional Musical Composers." *J Appl Psychol* 25:159-70 Ap '41. * (*PA* 15:4297)
36. HOLT, VEE JANE. *An Evaluation of the Seashore and the Kwalwasser-Dykema Music Tests at the College Level.* Master's thesis, University of Minnesota (Minneapolis, Minn.), 1941.
37. HARRIS, JACK H. *The Reliability and Validity of the McCreery Tests of Pitch and Rhythm.* Master's thesis, University of North Dakota (Grand Forks, N.D.), 1945.
38. RAMM, KATHERINE M. "Personality Maladjustment Among Monotones." *Smith Col Studies Social Work* 17:264-84 Je '47. * (*PA* 21:3590)
39. LEHMAN, CHARLES F., JR. *A Comparative Study of Instrumental Musicians on the Basis of the Kwalwasser Dykema Music Tests, the Otis I.Q. Intelligence Test and the Minnesota Multiphasic Personality Inventory.* Doctor's thesis, Syracuse University (Syracuse, N.Y.), 1949.
40. O'BRIEN, CYRIL C. "Music Aptitude Tests by Radio." *J AER* 8:52-3 Ja '49. *
41. LEHMAN, CHARLES F. "A Comparative Study of Instrumental Musicians on the Basis of the Otis Intelligence Test, the Kwalwasser-Dykema Music Test, and the Minnesota Multiphasic Personality Inventory." *J Ed Res* 44:57-61 S '50. * (*PA* 25:2927)
42. HOLMES, J. A. "Increased Reliabilities Resulting From Certain Modifications of the Kwalwasser-Dykema Tests of Musical Aptitudes." Abstract. *Calif J Ed Res* 3:181 S '52. *

43. LEHMAN, CHARLES F. "An Investigation of Musical Achievement and Relationship to Intelligence and Musical Talent." *J Ed Res* 45:623-9 Ap '52. * (*PA* 27:2962)
44. LEHMAN, CHARLES F. "A Study of Musically Superior and Inferior Subjects as Selected by the Kwalwasser-Dykema Music Tests." *J Ed Res* 45:517-22 Mr '52. * (*PA* 27:2199)
45. LUNDIN, ROBERT W. *An Objective Psychology of Music,* pp. 209-15. New York: Ronald Press Co., 1953. Pp. ix, 303. * (*PA* 28:590)
46. HOLMES, JACK A. "Increased Reliabilities, New Keys, and Norms for a Modified Kwalwasser-Dykema Test of Musical Aptitudes." *J Genetic Psychol* 85:65-73 S '54. * (*PA* 29:5709)
47. SIMPSON, SHIRLEY EVELYN. *To Develop and Validate an Objective Measure of Locomotor Response to Auditory Rhythmic Stimuli.* Doctor's thesis, Boston University (Boston, Mass.), 1957. (*DA* 18:141)
48. LUNDIN, ROBERT W. "What Next in the Psychology of Musical Measurement?" *Psychol Rec* 8:1-6 Ja '58. * (*PA* 33:7960)
49. COLWELL, RICHARD. *An Investigation of Achievement in Music in the Public Schools of Sioux Falls, South Dakota.* Doctor's thesis, University of Illinois (Urbana, Ill.), 1961. (*DA* 22:1653)
50. COLWELL, RICHARD. "An Investigation of Musical Achievement Among Vocal Students, Vocal-Instrumental Students, and Instrumental Students." *J Res Music Ed* 11:123-30 f '63. * (*PA* 38:6655)
51. ANASTASIOW, NICHOLAS J., AND SHAMBAUGH, ROBERT F. "Experimental Use of Pre-Instrumental Music Melody Instruments." *J Res Music Ed* 13:246-8 w '65. * (*PA* 40:4558)
52. HOLMES, JACK A., AND SINGER, HARRY. *Speed and Power of Reading in High School.* Cooperative Research Monograph No. 14. Washington, D.C.: United States Government Printing Office, 1966. Pp. xii, 183. *
53. LUNDIN, ROBERT W. *An Objective Psychology of Music, Second Edition,* pp. 244-51. New York: Ronald Press Co., 1967. Pp. vii, 345. *
54. TUCKER, DAVID WALTER. *Factors Related to Musical Reading Ability of Senior High School Students Participating in Choral Groups.* Doctor's thesis, University of California (Berkeley, Calif.), 1969. (*DAI* 31:2427A)

CUMULATIVE NAME INDEX

Anastasiow, N. J.: 51
Barnard, B.: 4
Beckham, A. S.: 16
Bienstock, S. F.: 24-5
Bower, L. B.: 28
Colwell, R.: 49-50
Drake, R. M.: 8, 32
Farnsworth, P. R.: 2, 5, 31
Gilbert, G. M.: 17, 21, 26
Gross, B.: 35
Harris, J. H.: 37
Holmes, J. A.: 42, 46, 52
Holt, V. J.: 36
Larson, W. S.: *rev,* 3:176
Lehman, C. F.: 39, 41, 43-4
Lundin, R. W.: 45, 48, 53
Mangan, M. R.: 12
Manzer, C. W.: 10
Marowitz, S.: 10
Martin, L. R.: 27
Monk, L. P.: 18
More, G. V. D.: 6
O'Brien, C. C.: 29, 40
Ode, S. J.: 33
Pechstein, L. A.: 18
Pike, H.: 11
Ramm, K. M.: 38
Rhoades, F. L.: 15
Sanderson, H. E.: 9
Schoen, M.: 19
Seashore, R. H.: 35
Shambaugh, R. F.: 51
Shepard, E. L.: 34
Simpson, S. E.: 47
Singer, H.: 52
Sward, K.: 30
Swift, F. F.: 20
Taylor, E. M.: 22-3
Tilson, L. M.: 3
Tucker, D. W.: 54
Webster, B. S.: 13
Whitley, M. T.: 7
Wiener, M.: 14
Williams, C. O.: 1
Woods, R. C.: 27

[203]

Kwalwasser Music Talent Test. Grades 4-6, 7-16 and adults; 1953; Jacob Kwalwasser; Belwin-Mills Publishing Corporation. *

For additional information and reviews by Paul R. Farnsworth and Kate Hevner Mueller, see 5:248.

REFERENCES THROUGH 1971

1. BENTLEY, RICHARD RAYMOND. *A Critical Comparison of Certain Music Aptitude Tests.* Doctor's thesis, University of Southern California (Los Angeles, Calif.), 1955.
2. BENTLEY, RICHARD R. "A Critical Comparison of Certain Music Aptitude Tests." Abstract. *Calif J Ed Res* 7:139 My '56. *
3. ANDERSON, JOHN MARTIN. *The Use of Musical Talent, Personality and Vocational Interest Factors in Predicting Success for Student Music Teachers.* Doctor's thesis, University of Southern California (Los Angeles, Calif.), 1965. (*DA* 26:6523)
4. PRESCOTT, PEGGY-LYNN. *A Study of the Relationship Between Musical Aptitude and Intelligence in Elementary School Children.* Master's thesis, East Tennessee State University (Johnson City, Tenn.), 1967.

[204]

Kwalwasser-Ruch Test of Musical Accomplishment. Grades 4–12; 1924–27; Jacob Kwalwasser and G. M. Ruch; Bureau of Educational Research and Service. *

For additional information and reviews by William S. Larson and James L. Mursell, see 2:1333 (1 reference).

REFERENCES THROUGH 1971

1. See 2:1333.
2. KWALWASSER, JACOB. "The Status of Music Education as Revealed by an Objective Test." *Music Sup J* 13:65–70 Mr '27. *
3. ANDERSON, H. DEWEY, AND EELLS, WALTER CROSBY. *Alaska Natives: A Survey of Their Sociological and Educational Status,* pp. 298–370. Stanford, Calif.: Stanford University Press, 1935. Pp. xvi, 472. * (*PA* 9:2346)
4. SCHMITZ, SYLVESTER M. *An Investigation of the Prognostic Value of the Revised Seashore Tests and the Kwalwasser-Ruch Test of Musical Accomplishment for Academic Success in a Music Education Program.* Doctor's thesis, Northwestern University (Evanston, Ill.), 1956. (*DA* 17:3042)
5. LEASE, GUS C. *A Study of the Musicality, Intelligence, and Music Achievement of Vocalists and Instrumentalists in Selected High Schools.* Doctor's thesis, State University of South Dakota (Vermillion, S.D.), 1959. (*DA* 19:3631)
6. ANASTASIOW, NICHOLAS J., AND SHAMBAUGH, ROBERT F. "Experimental Use of Pre-Instrumental Music Melody Instruments." *J Res Music Ed* 13:246–8 w '65. * (*PA* 40:4558)
7. BOLDEN, JOYCE INEZ. *The Influence of Selected Factors on Growth in Sight Singing and Rhythmic Reading.* Doctor's thesis, Michigan State University (East Lansing, Mich.), 1967. (*DA* 28:2278A)

[205]

Kwalwasser Test of Music Information and Appreciation. High school and college; 1927; Jacob Kwalwasser; Bureau of Educational Research and Service. *

For additional information and reviews by Raleigh M. Drake and Karl W. Gehrkens, see 2:1334 (1 reference).

REFERENCES THROUGH 1971

1. See 2:1334.
2. DYKEMA, PETER W. "Recent Developments in Music Testing Material." *Music Sup J* 13:59–64 F '27. *
3. KAPPEA, MARION. "Measures of Musical Talent." *Teach Forum* 4:2–7 S '31. * (*PA* 5:5059)

[206]

Measures of Musical Abilities. Ages 7–14; 1966; MMA; Arnold Bentley; George G. Harrap & Co. Ltd. [England]. * (United States distributor: October House, Inc.)

For additional information, reviews by Richard Colwell and John McLeish, and excerpted reviews by Richard R. Bentley and Paul R. Farnsworth, see 7:247 (13 references).

REFERENCES THROUGH 1971

1–13. See 7:247.
14. PARKER, D. H. H. "Musical Perception and Backwardness in Reading." *Ed Res* (England) 12(3):244–6 Je '70. * (*PA* 47:1754)
15. MCLEISH, JOHN, AND THOMAS, CYRIL. "Nationality and Musicality Used to Test the Lamarckian Hypothesis." *Nature* (England) 230(5292):337–8 Ap 2 '71. *
16. VAUGHAN, MARGERY, AND MYERS, R. E. "Examination of

Musical Process as Related to Creative Thinking." *J Res Music Ed* 19(3):337–41 f '71. * (*PA* 48:5879)

[207]

Music Achievement Tests. Grades 3–12; 1967–70; MAT; first edition called *Elementary Music Achievement Tests;* 4 tests; Richard Colwell; Follett Publishing Co. *

a) TEST 1. Grades 3–12; 1967–69; 4 scores: pitch discrimination, interval discrimination, meter discrimination, total.

b) TEST 2. Grades 4–12; 1967–69; 6 scores: major-minor mode discrimination, feeling for tonal center, auditory-visual discrimination (pitch, rhythm, total), total.

c) TEST 3. Grades 4–12; 1970; 5 scores: tonal memory, melody recognition, pitch recognition, instrument recognition, total.

d) TEST 4. Grades 5–12; 1970; 7 scores: musical style (composers, texture, total), auditory-visual discrimination, chord recognition, cadence recognition, total.

For additional information and a review by Paul R. Lehman, see 7:248 (5 references).

REFERENCES THROUGH 1971

1–5. See 7:248.
6. CIRCLE, DAVID EDISON. *An Investigation of the Relationship Between the Musical Achievement of Sixth Grade Students and Teachers in Kansas.* Doctor's thesis, George Peabody College for Teachers (Nashville, Tenn.), 1971. (*DAI* 33:1762A)
7. CROSS, J. DIANE. *An Investigation of the Relative Correlation Between the Music Aptitude Profile and the Elementary Music Achievement Tests at the Elementary Level.* Master's thesis, East Tennessee State University (Johnson City, Tenn.), 1971.
8. GALLAGHER, FULTON DENT. *A Study of the Relationships Between the Gordon Musical Aptitude Profile, the Colwell Music Achievement Tests, and the Drake-Oregon Music Discrimination Test.* Doctor's thesis, Indiana University (Bloomington, Ind.), 1971. (*DAI* 32:2728A)
9. SWICKARD, JOHN HARPER. *A Comparative Study of Music Achievement of Students in Grades Four, Five and Six.* Doctor's thesis, University of Illinois (Urbana, Ill.), 1971. (*DAI* 32:4653A)
10. ZAHRT, HILDA ELIZABETH. *A Study of the Relationships Between Musical Background, Aptitude, College Grades, and Music Achievement of Selected Elementary Education Majors.* Doctor's thesis, University of Southern Mississippi (Hattiesburg, Miss.), 1971. (*DAI* 32:2540A)

[208]

★**Music Aptitude Test.** Grades 4–8; 1948–55; C. G. Conn Ltd. *

REFERENCES THROUGH 1971

1. ETERNO, JOHN A. "Foreign Language Pronunciation and Musical Aptitude." *Mod Lang J* 45:168–70 Ap '61. *
2. PELLETIER, HAROLD WALDO. *An Investigation of the Relation Between Training in Instrumental Music and Selected Aspects of Language Growth in Third Grade Children.* Doctor's thesis, Arizona State University (Tempe, Ariz.), 1963. (*DA* 25:6440)

[209]

Musical Aptitude Profile. Grades 4–12; 1965; MAP; 11 scores: tonal imagery (melody, harmony, total), rhythm imagery (tempo, meter, total), musical sensitivity (phrasing, balance, style, total), total; Edwin Gordon; Houghton Mifflin Co. *

For additional information and reviews by Robert W. Lundin and John McLeish, see 7:249 (33 references). For an excerpt from a related book review, see 7:B246.

REFERENCES THROUGH 1971

1-33. See 7:249.

34. LUMMIS, RUTH MARGARET. *A Study of the Musical Aptitudes of the Educable Mentally Retarded.* Master's thesis, Sacramento State College (Sacramento, Calif.), 1967.

35. BEINKE, JAMES L. *A Study to Determine the Correlation of a System of Teacher Evaluation to Otis IQ Scores and the Gordon Musical Aptitude Profile Test.* Master's thesis, Wisconsin State University (Whitewater, Wis.), 1970.

36. CROSS, J. DIANE. *An Investigation of the Relative Correlation Between the Musical Aptitude Profile and the Elementary Music Achievement Tests at the Elementary Level.* Master's thesis, East Tennessee State University (Johnson City, Tenn.), 1971.

37. FROSETH, JAMES O. "Using MAP Scores in the Instruction of Beginning Students in Instrumental Music." *J Res Music Ed* 19(1):98–105 sp '71. * (*PA* 46:11748)

38. GALLAGHER, FULTON DENT. *A Study of the Relationships Between the Gordon Musical Aptitude Profile, the Colwell Music Achievement Tests, and the Indiana-Oregon Music Discrimination Test.* Doctor's thesis, Indiana University (Bloomington, Ind.), 1971. (*DAI* 32:2728A)

39. GORDON, EDWIN. "The Second-Year Results of a Five-Year Longitudinal Study of the Musical Achievement of Culturally-Disadvantaged Students," pp. 131–43. (*PA* 50:7719) In his *Experimental Research in the Psychology of Music: 7.* Studies in the Psychology of Music, Vol. 7. Iowa City, Iowa: University of Iowa Press, 1971. Pp. vii, 179. *

40. KEEN, CHARLES FLOYD. *A Study of Relationships Between Growth and Developmental Variables, Creativity, and Musicality.* Doctor's thesis, University of Michigan (Ann Arbor, Mich.), 1971. (*DAI* 32:3791A)

41. SCHLEUTER, STANLEY LEROY. *An Investigation of the Interrelation of Personality Traits, Musical Aptitude and Musical Achievement.* Doctor's thesis, University of Iowa (Iowa City, Iowa), 1971. (*DAI* 32:1556A)

42. THAYER, ROBERT WILCOX. *An Investigation of the Interrelation of Personality Traits, Musical Achievement, and Different Measures of Musical Aptitude.* Doctor's thesis, University of Iowa (Iowa City, Iowa), 1971. (*DAI* 32:2734A)

43. VOKAS, CONSTANCE S. *The Musical Aptitude Profile as a Predictor of Success in the Tenth Grade General Music Class.* Master's thesis, John Carroll University (Cleveland, Ohio), 1971.

44. YOUNG, WILLIAM T. "The Role of Musical Aptitude, Intelligence, and Academic Achievement in Predicting the Musical Attainment of Elementary Instrumental Music Students." *J Res Music Ed* 19(4):385–98 w '71. * (*PA* 48:7918)

CUMULATIVE NAME INDEX

Beinke, J. L.: 35	Keen, C. F.: 40
Bixler, J.: 16	Lee, R. E.: 7, 15
Brown, R.: 25	Lummis, R. M.: 34
Brown, M. E.: 8	Lundin, R. W.: rev, 7:249
Colwell, R.: exc, 7:B246	McCarthy, K. J.: 28
Cross, J. D.: 36	McGlothlin, D. E.: 32
Culver, F. R.: 3	McLeish, J.: rev, 7:249
Dittemore, E. E.: 17	Raim, R. L.: 5
Fosha, R. L.: 1	Rice, J. A.: 33
Froseth, J. O.: 18, 37	Schleuter, S. L.: 41
Gallagher, F. D.: 38	Standifer, J. A.: 24
Gordon, E.: 4, 9–12, 19–21, 26, 30–1, 39	Tarrell, V. V.: 2, 6
Harrington, C. J.: 13, 27	Thayer, R. W.: 42
Hatfield, W. G.: 14	Vokas, C. S.: 43
Hill, J. D.: 22–3	Young, W. T.: 29, 44

[210]

*National Teacher Examinations: Music Education. College seniors and teachers; 1957–73; an inactive form (1966) entitled *Teacher Education Examination: Music Education* is available to colleges for local administration; another inactive form (1968) entitled *Specialty Examinations: Music Education* is available to school systems for local use as part of the program entitled *School Personnel Research and Evaluation Services;* Educational Testing Service. * For the testing program entry, see 869.

For additional information and reviews by Paul R. Lehman and Roger P. Phelps of earlier forms, see 7:250; for a review by William S. Larson, see 6:350.

For reviews of the testing program, see 7:582. (2 reviews), 6:700 (1 review), 5:538 (3 reviews), and 4:802 (1 review).

[211]

Seashore Measures of Musical Talents. Grades 4–16 and adults; 1919–60; 6 scores: pitch, loudness, rhythm, time, timbre, tonal memory; 1957 test essentially the same as 1939 revision except for record size and modifications in directions; Carl E. Seashore, Don Lewis, and Joseph G. Saetveit; Psychological Corporation. *

For additional information and reviews by Kenneth L. Bean and Robert W. Lundin, see 6:353 (13 references); see also 5:251 (9 references); for reviews by John McLeish and Herbert D. Wing of the 1939 revision, see 4:229 (16 references); for reviews by Paul R. Farnsworth, William S. Larson, and James L. Mursell, see 3:177 (46 references); see also 2:1338 (60 references).

REFERENCES THROUGH 1971

1–55. See 2:1338.
56–101. See 3:177.
102–117. See 4:229.
118–126. See 5:251.
127–139. See 6:353.

140. SEASHORE, C. E. "The Discovery and Encouragement of Musical Talent in the Public Schools by Means of Measurement: Some Suggestions on Organization." *Ann Conf Ed Meas* 7:28–30 '20. *

141. GAW, ESTHER ALLEN. "Some Individual Difficulties in the Study of Music." *J Ed Res* 5:381–8 My '22. *

142. WEAVER, ANDREW THOMAS. "Experimental Studies in Vocal Expression: 2, The Prediction of Talent for Vocal Expression in Reading." *J Appl Psychol* 8:159–86 Je '24. *

143. NORRIS, HERBERT T. "A Critical Review of Tests and Measurements in Music Education." *Music Sup J* 13:57–60 D '26. *

144. TRAVIS, LEE EDWARD, AND DAVIS, MILDRED G. "The Relation Between Faulty Speech and Lack of Certain Musical Talents." *Psychol Monogr* 36(2):71–81 '26. * (*PA* 1:1135)

145. WORTHINGTON, MYRTLE RAYMAKER. "Performance Test Scores of Behavior and Non-Behavior Children." *Welfare Mag* 17:97–103 O '26. * (*PA* 1:439)

146. LANIER, LYLE H. "Prediction of the Reliability of Mental Tests and Tests of Special Abilities." *J Exp Psychol* 10:69–113 Ap '27. * (*PA* 2:1692)

147. RUCH, G. M., AND STODDARD, GEORGE D. *Tests and Measurements in High School Instruction,* pp. 192–5. Yonkers, N.Y.: World Book Co., 1927. Pp. xxi, 381. * (*PA* 1:1454)

148. STINCHFIELD, SARA M. "Some Relationships Between Speech Defects, Musical Disability, Scholastic Attainment and Maladjustment." *Q J Speech Ed* 13:268–75 Je '27. *

149. DAVIDS, INA. "An Experiment With Seashore Tests in Manual Arts High School." *Ed Res B* (Los Angeles City Schools) 7:11–3 My '28. *

150. FARNSWORTH, PAUL R. "The Effects of Nature and Nurture on Musicality." *Yearb Nat Soc Study Ed* 27(2):233–45 '28. * (*PA* 2:2467)

151. FRACKER, GEORGE CUTLER, AND HOWARD, VIRGIE M. "Correlation Between Intelligence and Musical Talent Among University Students." *Psychol Monogr* 39(2):157–61 '28. * (*PA* 3:2298)

152. GAW, ESTHER ALLEN. "Five Studies of Musical Tests." *Psychol Monogr* 39(2):145–56 '28. * (*PA* 3:2300)

153. NATHANSON, YALE S. "The Musical Ability of the Negro." *Ann Am Acad Pol & Social Sci* 140:186–90 N '28. *

154. STANTON, HAZEL M. "Seashore's Measures of Musical Talent." *Psychol Monogr* 39(2):135–44 '28. * (*PA* 3:2323)

155. PETERSON, JOSEPH, AND LANIER, LYLE H. Part 2, "Comparisons of Certain Mental Abilities in White and Negro Adults," pp. 103–56. In their *Studies in the Comparative Abilities of Whites and Negroes.* Mental Measurements Monographs, Serial No. 5. Baltimore, Md.: Williams & Wilkins Co., 1929. Pp. vi, 156. * (*PA* 3:2316)

156. CHURCH, NORVAL LUTHER. *A Statistical Study of the Seashore "Measures of Musical Talent" and the Kwalwasser "Test of Melodic and Harmonic Sensitivity."* Master's thesis, Stanford University (Stanford, Calif.), 1930.

157. LARSON, RUTH CREWDSON. *Studies on Seashore's Measures of Musical Talent.* Doctor's thesis, University of Iowa (Iowa City, Iowa), 1930.

158. EELLS, WALTER CROSBY. "Mechanical, Physical, and Musical Ability of the Native Races of Alaska." *J Appl Psychol* 17:493–506 O '33. * (*PA* 8:2669)

159. SWARD, KEITH. "Jewish Musicality in America." *J Appl Psychol* 17:675–712 D '33. * (*PA* 8:3725)

160. Wheeler, Lester R., and Wheeler, Viola D. "The Musical Ability of Mountain Children as Measured by the Seashore Test of Musical Talent." *J Genetic Psychol* 43:352–76 D '33. * (*PA* 8:3733)

161. Capurso, Alexander A. "The Effect of an Associative Technique in Teaching Pitch and Interval Discrimination." *J Appl Psychol* 18:811–8 D '34. * (*PA* 9:4259)

162. Farnsworth, Paul R. "Studies in the Psychology of Tone and Music." *Genetic Psychol Monogr* 15:1–94 Ja '34. * (*PA* 8:3682)

163. Loudon, Mary V. "The Required Music Course in the Light of Pupil Ability." *El Sch J* 35:103–6 O '34. * (*PA* 9:399)

164. Stanton, Hazel M. "Predicting Musical Progress—A Technique for Guidance." *Psychol Clinic* 22(4):270–6 '34. * (*PA* 9:1352)

165. Anderson, H. Dewey, and Eells, Walter Crosby. *Alaska Natives: A Survey of Their Sociological and Educational Status*, pp. 298–370. Stanford, Calif.: Stanford University Press, 1935. Pp. xvi, 472. * (*PA* 9:2346)

166. Lamp, Charles J., and Keys, Noel. "Can Aptitude for Specific Musical Instruments Be Predicted?" *J Ed Psychol* 26:587–96 N '35. * (*PA* 10:1624)

167. Hunt, Thelma. *Measurement in Psychology*, pp. 143–53. New York: Prentice-Hall, Inc., 1936. Pp. xx, 471. * (*PA* 11:19)

168. Paterson, Donald G.; Schneidler, Gwendolen, G.; and Williamson, Edmund G. *Student Guidance Techniques*, pp. 216–21. New York: McGraw-Hill Book Co., Inc., 1938. Pp. xviii, 316. * (*PA* 12:2131)

169. Woodrow, H. "The Common Factors in Fifty-Two Mental Tests." *Psychometrika* 4:99–107 Je '39. * (*PA* 13:5390)

170. Fay, Paul J., and Middleton, Warren C. "Relationship Between Musical Talent and Preferences for Different Types of Music." *J Ed Psychol* 32:573–83 N '41. * (*PA* 16:2760)

171. Gross, Bethuel, and Seashore, Robert H. "Psychological Characteristics of Student and Professional Musical Composers." *J Appl Psychol* 25:159–70 Ap '41. * (*PA* 15:4297)

172. Hansen, Burrell F. "The Application of Sound Discrimination Tests to Functional Articulatory Defectives With Normal Hearing." *J Speech Disorders* 9:347–55 D '44. * (*PA* 19:616)

173. Harris, Jack H. *The Reliability and Validity of the McCreery Tests of Pitch and Rhythm*. Master's thesis, University of North Dakota (Grand Forks, N.D.), 1945.

174. Graves, Winifred Sibley. "Factors Associated With Children's Taking Music Lessons, Including Some Parent-Child Relationships: 1, History and Procedures; 2, Results and Conclusions." *J Genetic Psychol* 70:65–89, 91–125 Mr '47. * (*PA* 21:3495–6)

175. Cooley, John Christopher. *A Study of the Relation Between Certain Mental and Personality Traits and Ratings of Musical Abilities*. Doctor's thesis, Michigan State College (East Lansing, Mich.), 1952. (*DA* 13:240)

176. Reynolds, Maynard Clinton. "A Study of the Relationships Between Auditory Characteristics and Specific Silent Reading Abilities." *J Ed Res* 46:439–49 F '53. * (*PA* 28:1492)

177. Wheeler, Lester R., and Wheeler, Viola D. "A Study of the Relationship of Auditory Discrimination to Silent Reading Abilities." *J Ed Res* 48:103–13 O '54. * (*PA* 29:6186)

178. Damgaard, Thelma Louise Johnson. *Auditory Acuity and Discrimination Differences as Factors in Spelling Competence*. Doctor's thesis, Stanford University (Stanford, Calif.), 1956. (*DA* 16:1856)

179. Ottman, Robert William. *A Statistical Investigation of the Influence of Selected Factors on the Skill of Sight-Singing*. Doctor's thesis, North Texas State College (Denton, Tex.), 1956. (*DA* 16:763)

180. Schmitz, Sylvester M. *An Investigation of the Prognostic Value of the Revised Seashore Tests and the Kwalwasser-Ruch Test of Musical Accomplishment for Academic Success in a Music Education Program*. Doctor's thesis, Northwestern University (Evanston, Ill.), 1956. (*DA* 17:3042)

181. Shook, Andrew Woodson. *Auditory Sensitivity and Speech Defects—A Comparative Study of the Incidence of Selected Factors of Auditory Sensitivity and Defects of Voice and Articulation*. Doctor's thesis, New York University (New York, N.Y.), 1956. (*DA* 17:918)

182. Rosenstein, Joseph. "Tactile Perception of Rhythmic Patterns by Normal, Blind, Deaf, and Aphasic Children." *Am Ann Deaf* 102:399–403 N '57. * (*PA* 33:6788)

183. Cramer, William F. *The Relation of Maturation and Other Factors to Achievement in Beginning Instrumental Music Performance at the Fourth Through Eighth Grade Levels*. Doctor's thesis, Florida State University (Tallahassee, Fla.), 1958. (*DA* 19:540)

184. Eisenson, Jon; Kastein, Shulamith; and Schneiderman, Norma. "An Investigation Into the Ability of Voice Defectives to Discriminate Among Differences in Pitch and Loudness." *J Speech & Hearing Disorders* 23:577–82 N '58. * (*PA* 34:6290)

185. Gesler, Harriet Lillian. *An Analysis of the Relation Between Pitch Discrimination and Phonic Sensitivity in First Grade Children*. Doctor's thesis, University of Connecticut (Storrs, Conn.), 1958. (*DA* 19:988)

186. Bond, Marjorie Helen. "Rhythmic Perception and Gross Motor Performance." *Res Q* 30:259–65 O '59. * (*PA* 35:4869)

187. Simmons, Audrey Ann. "Factors Related to Lipreading." *J Speech & Hearing Res* 2:340–52 D '59. * (*PA* 34:6510)

188. Longwell, Jerrold W. *The Relationship Between Auditory Acuity and Scores on Selected Items of the Seashore Measures of Musical Talents*. Master's thesis, Texas Christian University (Ft. Worth, Tex.), 1961.

189. Stitt, Clyde LeRoy. *Relationships Between Certain Measures of Auditory Abilities and Judgments of Articulation Proficiency*. Doctor's thesis, Stanford University (Stanford, Calif.), 1961. (*DA* 22:677)

190. Peterson, Floyd Henry, Jr. *A Study of the Relationships Between Music Aptitude and Academic Achievement of Graduate Music Students*. Doctor's thesis, Indiana University (Bloomington, Ind.), 1963. (*DA* 26:408)

191. Pimsleur, Paul. "A Study of Foreign Language Learning Ability: Parts 1 and 2," pp. 57–72. In *Report of the Twelfth Annual Round Table Meeting on Linguistics and Language Studies*. Edited by Michael Zarechnak. Washington, D.C.: Georgetown University Press, 1963. Pp. 132. *

192. Leutenegger, Ralph R., and Mueller, Theodore H. "Auditory Factors and the Acquisition of French Language Mastery." *Mod Lang J* 48:141–6 Mr '64. *

193. Sheldon, John Maurice. *Prediction of Success in Pitch Reproduction for the Nonmusic Major in College*. Doctor's thesis, University of Southern California (Los Angeles, Calif.), 1964. (*DA* 25:5326)

194. Diggs, Ruth Winstead. *A Study of the Levels of Musical Aptitude and Musical Achievement Among Institutionalized and Noninstitutionalized Educable Mentally Retarded Children*. Doctor's thesis, University of Virginia (Charlottesville, Va.), 1965. (*DA* 26:6087)

195. Leutenegger, Ralph R.; Mueller, Theodore H.; and Wershow, Irving R. "Auditory Factors in Foreign Language Acquisition." *Mod Lang J* 49:22–31 Ja '65. *

196. Radus, Libby. *Dysphasia: Musical Perception as a Stimulus in Communication*. Doctor's thesis, University of Florida (Gainesville, Fla.), 1965. (*DA* 26:6230)

197. Rainbow, Edward L. "A Pilot Study to Investigate the Constructs of Musical Aptitude." *J Res Music Ed* 13:3–14 sp '65. * (*PA* 39:13031)

198. Reed, Homer B. C., Jr.; Reitan, Ralph M.; and Klove, Hallgrim. "Influence of Cerebral Lesions on Psychological Test Performances of Older Children." *J Consult Psychol* 29:247–51 Je '65. * (*PA* 39:12702)

199. Blickley, J. Ford. *Musical Discrimination as a Predictor of Success in Foreign Language Learning*. Master's thesis, Northern Illinois University (DeKalb, Ill.), 1966.

200. Coy, Richard Vining. *An Experimental Investigation of Factors in Children's Selection of and Adaptation to Four Orchestral Instruments*. Doctor's thesis, University of California (Los Angeles, Calif.), 1966. (*DA* 26:5471)

201. Greenberg, Marvin, and MacGregor, Beatrix. "Correlation of Musical Talents and Behavioral Traits." *Council Res Music Ed B* 7:24–33 sp '66. * (*PA* 40:11155)

202. Arendt, Jermaine Delos. *Predicting Success in Foreign Language Study: A Study Made in Selected Minneapolis Schools From 1963 to 1964*. Doctor's thesis, University of Minnesota (Minneapolis, Minn.), 1967. (*DA* 28:4869A)

203. Davis, Demaris S., and Boone, Daniel R. "Pitch Discrimination and Tonal Memory Abilities in Adult Voice Patients." *J Speech & Hearing Res* 10:811–5 D '67. * (*PA* 42:5943)

204. Huff, Joan. *An Investigation of Auditory and Visual Perception of Rhythm and Its Relation to Skill in Selected Motor Activities*. Doctor's thesis, University of Utah (Salt Lake City, Utah), 1967. (*DA* 28:1281A)

205. Lundin, Robert W. *An Objective Psychology of Music, Second Edition*, pp. 236–44. New York: Ronald Press Co., 1967. Pp. vii, 345. *

206. McLeish, John, and Higgs, Geoffrey. *An Inquiry Into the Musical Capacities of Educationally Sub-Normal Children*. Occasional Research Papers No 1. Cambridge, England: Cambridge Institute of Education, [1967]. Pp. ii, 12. *

207. Prescott, Peggy-Lynn. *A Study of the Relationship Between Musical Aptitude and Intelligence in Elementary School Children*. Master's thesis, East Tennessee State University (Johnson City, Tenn.), 1967.

208. Tanner, Jane, and Loess, Henry. "Intercorrelations Among Rhythm Subtests of Three Tests of Musical Aptitude." *Percept & Motor Skills* 25:721–6 D '67. * (*PA* 42:8738)

209. Winston, Wilma Essex. *A Correlation Between Language Achievement and Musical Aptitude of Thirty Sixth Grade Pupils at Booker T. Washington School, East Gadsden, Alabama*. Master's thesis, Alabama A & M College (Normal, Ala.), 1967.

210. Butler, John Harrison. *Personality Factors as Cor-*

relates of Receptivity to Electronic Music. Doctor's thesis, University of Georgia (Athens, Ga.), 1968. (*DA* 29:4514A)

211. DAVIS, SAMUEL EUGENE. *Predicting Probable Failure in College-Level Music Theory Courses.* Doctor's thesis, University of Montana (Missoula, Mont.), 1968. (*DAI* 30:354A)

212. MCLEISH, JOHN. *The Factor of Musical Cognition in Wing's and Seashore's Tests.* Music Education Research Papers No. 2. London: Novello & Co. Ltd., 1968. Pp. 10. *

213. PEAK, DANIEL T. "Changes in Short-Term Memory in a Group of Aging Adults." *J Gerontol* 23:9–16 Ja '68. *

214. READ, JOHN WILLIAM. *An Investigation of the Relationship of Selected Variables to Sight-Singing Ability.* Doctor's thesis, North Texas State University (Denton, Tex.), 1968. (*DAI* 30:358A)

215. STOCK, WILLIAM H., JR. *Some Psychological and Physiological Factors Affecting Excellence in Acting.* Doctor's thesis, Michigan State University (East Lansing, Mich.), 1968. (*DA* 29:3716A)

216. TURBEVILLE, WINSTON CHARLES. *An Experimental Study of Audio and Visual Perception of Rhythm Patterns Used in Seashore Measures of Musical Talents.* Master's thesis, Texas Christian University (Ft. Worth, Tex.), 1968.

217. BRAUN, JOHN R. "Search for Correlates of Self-Actualization." *Percept & Motor Skills* 28(2):557–8 Ap '69. * (*PA* 43:15764)

218. BRUTON-SIMMONDS, I. V. "A Critical Note on the Value of the Seashore Measures of Musical Talents." *Psychologia Africana* (South Africa) 13(1):50–4 O '69. * (*PA* 44:18639)

219. CARPENTER, ROBERT LEWIS. *A Study of Acoustic Cue Discrimination Abilities of Aphasic, Brain-Damaged Nonaphasic, and Normal Adults.* Doctor's thesis, Northwestern University (Evanston, Ill.), 1969. (*DAI* 30:3422B)

220. GEORGE, WARREN EDWIN. *Significant Predictors for College Achievement in Specified Areas of Music Education and Identification of Potential Graduates.* Doctor's thesis, University of Kansas (Lawrence, Kan.), 1969. (*DAI* 30:3040A)

221. GOEWEY, GORDON IRA. *An Experimental Study of the Effectiveness of the Melodic Line Score Approach to Music Listening in Developing Musical Literacy in General College Students.* Doctor's thesis, Boston University (Boston, Mass.), 1969. (*DAI* 31:2421A)

222. GORDON, EDWIN. "Intercorrelations Among Musical Aptitude Profile and Seashore Measures of Musical Talent Subtests." *J Res Music Ed* 17(3):263–71 f '69. * (*PA* 44:7263)

223. HIGGINS, JANIS. *A Correlational Study of Language Development and Musical Ability.* Master's thesis, Texas Tech University (Lubbock, Tex.), 1969.

224. NICHOLS, ALAN C. "Correlations Between Timbre Discrimination and Articulation Scoring." *Speech Monogr* 36(2): 148–51 Je '69. * (*PA* 44:12330)

225. SPREEN, O., AND GADDES, W. H.; in collaboration with S. MEIKLE AND F. J. SPELLACY. "Developmental Norms for 15 Neuropsychological Tests Age 6 to 15." *Cortex* (Italy) 5(2): 170–91 Je '69. * (*PA* 44:8165)

226. WESTPHAL, M. ELIZABETH; LEUTENEGGER, RALPH R.; AND WAGNER, DOROTHEA L. "Some Psycho-Acoustic and Intellectual Correlates of Achievement in German Language Learning of Junior High School Students." *Mod Lang J* 53(4):258–66 Ap '69. * (*PA* 44:21623)

227. WILCOX, ROGER. "Music Ability Among Negro Grade School Pupils: Or, I Got Ryhthm?" *Percept & Motor Skills* 29(1):167–8 Ag '69. * (*PA* 44:2191)

228. DEBRODER, GORDON WAYNE. *The Relationship of Improvement in Training of Musical Perception to Dimensions of the Personality.* Doctor's thesis, University of Denver (Denver, Colo.), 1970. (*DAI* 31:4197A)

229. FLYNN, PAULINE T., AND BYRNE, MARGARET C. "Relationship Between Reading and Selected Auditory Abilities of Third-Grade Children." *J Speech & Hearing Res* 13(4):731–40 D '70. *

230. LACKS, PATRICIA BRILLIANT; COLBERT, JOHN; HARROW, MARTIN; AND LEVINE, JACOB. "Further Evidence Concerning the Diagnostic Accuracy of the Halstead Organic Test Battery." *J Clin Psychol* 26(4):480–1 O '70. * (*PA* 45:4541)

231. GOLDSTEIN, GERALD, AND SHELLY, CAROLYN H. "Field Dependence and Cognitive, Perceptual and Motor Skills in Alcoholics." *Q J Studies Alcohol* 32(1A):29–40 Mr '71. * (*PA* 46:7095)

232. NABORS, MARTHA G. *A Study of the Effect of Temporal Redundancy on Aphasic Subjects' Performance on the Seashore Measures of Musical Talents.* Master's thesis, University of Tennessee (Knoxville, Tenn.), 1971.

233. ROURKE, B. P.; YOUNG, G. C.; AND FLEWELLING, R. W. "The Relationships Between WISC Verbal-Performance Discrepancies and Selected Verbal, Auditory-Perceptual, Visual-Perceptual, and Problem-Solving Abilities in Children With Learning Disabilities." *J Clin Psychol* 27(4):475–9 O '71. * (*PA* 47:9738)

234. THAYER, ROBERT WILCOX. *An Investigation of the Interrelation of Personality Traits, Musical Achievement, and Different Measures of Musical Aptitude.* Doctor's thesis, University of Iowa (Iowa City, Iowa), 1971. (*DAI* 32:2734A)

235. WERNER, LAWRENCE KURT. *The Relationships Among the Psycho-Motor, Motor Coordination, Personality, and Intellectual Domains of Development in Preadolescent Children.* Doctor's thesis, Purdue University (Lafayette, Ind.), 1971. (*DAI* 32:4435A)

236. WILCOX, ROGER. "Further Ado About Negro Music Ability." *J Negro Ed* 40(4):361–4 f '71. * (*PA* 48:6949)

CUMULATIVE NAME INDEX

Ruch, G. M.: 147
Saetveit, J. G.: 81, 86
Salisbury, F. S.: 16
Sanderson, H. E.: 63
Schmitz, S. M.: 180
Schneiderman, N.: 184
Schneidler, G. G.: 168
Schoen, M.: 7, 87
Seagoe, M.: 126
Seashore, C. E.: 1–2, 24, 43, 45, 50, 54, 74, 82, 86, 101, 140
Seashore, R. H.: 171
Sheldon, J. M.: 193
Shelly, C. H.: 231
Shook, A. W.: 181
Simmons, A. A.: 187
Smith, H. B.: 16
Smith, O. W.: 130
Sorensen, M. B.: 116
Spellacy, F. J.: 225
Spreen, O.: 225
Stanton, H. M.: 8, 17–8, 39–40, 44, 73, 154, 164
Stinchfield, S. M.: 148
Stitt, C. L.: 189
Stock, W. H.: 215
Stoddard, G. D.: 147
Streep, R.: 60
Super, D. E.: 112, 139
Sward, K.: 159

Takamune, T. H.: 96
Tanner, J.: 208
Taylor, E. M.: 92–3
Thayer, R. W.: 234
Tilson, L. M.: 30–1, 35, 69
Trafton, H. R.: 62
Travis, L. E.: 144
Turbeville, W. C.: 216
Viteles, M. S.: 9
Wagner, D. L.: 226
Weaver, A. T.: 142
Werner, L. K.: 235
Wershow, I. R.: 195
Westphal, M. E.: 226
Wheeler, L. R.: 160, 177
Wheeler, V. D.: 160, 177
Whitley, M. T.: 36
Wilcox, R.: 227, 236
Williams, C. O.: 19
Williamson, E. G.: 168
Wilson, M. E.: 25
Wilson, W. E.: 120
Wing, H. D.: rev, 4:229
Winston, W. E.: 209
Wood, W. F.: 108
Woodrow, H.: 169
Worthington, M. R.: 145
Wright, F. A.: 10
Wyatt, R.: 55
Wyatt, R. F.: 99
Young, G. C.: 233

[212]

Snyder Knuth Music Achievement Test. Elementary education and music majors; 1968; Alice Snyder Knuth; Creative Arts Research Associates, Inc. *

For additional information and reviews by Richard Colwell and Edwin Gordon, see 7:251 (3 references).

REFERENCES THROUGH 1971

1–3. See 7:251.

CUMULATIVE NAME INDEX

Colwell, R.: rev, 7:251
Garder, B. W.: 3
Gordon, E.: rev, 7:251
Slagle, H. C.: 2
Snyder, A. M.: 1

[213]

*Teacher Education Examination Program: Music Education. College seniors preparing to teach secondary school; 1958–72; reprinting of inactive 1966 form of *National Teacher Examinations: Music Education;* test available to colleges for local administration; Educational Testing Service. * For the testing program entry, see 898.

For additional information concerning an earlier form, see 6:351. For a review of the testing program, see 5:543. For reference to reviews of the *National Teacher Examinations: Music Education,* see 210.

[214]

Test of Musicality, Fourth Edition. Grades 4–12; 1942–58; E. Thayer Gaston; Test of Musicality. *

For additional information and reviews by Paul R. Farnsworth and Kate Hevner Mueller, see 5:252 (1 reference).

REFERENCES THROUGH 1971

1. See 5:252.
2. GRAVES, WINIFRED SIBLEY. "Factors Associated With Children's Taking Music Lessons, Including Some Parent-Child Relationships." 1, History and Procedures; 2, Results and Conclusions." *J Genetic Psychol* 70:65–89, 91–125 Mr '47. * (PA 21:3495–6)
3. BENTLEY, RICHARD R. "A Critical Comparison of Certain Music Aptitude Tests." Abstract. *Calif J Ed Res* 7:139 My '56. *
4. OKEY, JUDITH N. *Intelligence and Musicality: The Relationship Between Scores on the Otis Intelligence Test and the Gaston Test of Musicality.* Master's thesis, University of Tennessee (Knoxville, Tenn.), 1958.
5. CAIN, MARTHA LEE. *A Comparison of the Wing Standardized Tests of Musical Intelligence With a Test of Musicality by Gaston and the Drake Musical Aptitude Tests.* Master's thesis, University of Kansas (Lawrence, Kan.), 1960.

6. FRENCH, ELIZABETH I. *A Study of the Relationship of Scores Obtained on the Gaston Test of Musicality and the Seashore Measures of Musical Talents to Responses to Four Thematic Apperception Test Pictures.* Master's thesis, University of Tennessee (Knoxville, Tenn.), 1962.
7. DEIHL, NED CHARLES. *Certain Relationships Among Concept Development, Listening Achievement, Musicality, and the Quantification of Musical Performance Experience.* Doctor's thesis, Pennsylvania State University (University Park, Pa.), 1963. (DA 24:5449)
8. GILLETT, ROBERT. *An Analysis of the Gaston Test of Musicality When Administered at the Junior High School Level.* Master's thesis, Northern Illinois University (DeKalb, Ill.), 1963.
9. EBY, JANE M. *The Relationship Between Selected Factors Concerning Elementary Education Majors and Their Achievements in Specified Music Fundamentals Classes.* Doctor's thesis, Indiana University (Bloomington, Ind.), 1969. (DAI 30: 750A)
10. GEORGE, WARREN EDWIN. *Significant Predictors for College Achievement in Specified Areas of Music Education and Identification of Potential Graduates.* Doctor's thesis, University of Kansas (Lawrence, Kan.), 1969. (DAI 30:3049A)
11. MICHALSKI, STANLEY F., JR. "Development and Evaluation of a Visual-Aural Program in Conceptual Understanding of the Basic Elements of Music." *J Res Music Ed* 19(1):92–7 sp '71. * (PA 47:1824)
12. WERMUTH, ROBERT FRED. *Relationship of Musical Aptitude to Family and Student Activity in Music, Student Interest in Music, Socioeconomic Status, and Intelligence Among Caucasian and Negro Middle School Students.* Doctor's thesis, Ohio State University (Columbus, Ohio), 1971. (DAI 32: 4054A)

CUMULATIVE NAME INDEX

Bentley, R. R.: 1, 3
Cain, M. L.: 5
Deihl, N. C.: 7
Eby, J. M.: 9
Farnsworth, P. R.: rev, 5:252
French, E. I.: 6
George, W. E.: 10
Gillett, R.: 8
Graves, W. S.: 2
Michalski, S. F.: 11
Mueller, K. H.: rev, 5:252
Okey, J. N.: 4
Wermuth, R. F.: 12

[215]

*The Undergraduate Program Field Tests: Music Tests. College; 1969–73; formerly called *The Undergraduate Record Examinations: Music Tests;* tests available to colleges for local administration; 2 tests: field, modular; Educational Testing Service. * For the testing program entry, see 1062.
a) MUSIC TEST.
b) AURAL MUSIC: A MODULAR TEST DESIGNED TO COMPLEMENT THE TWO–HOUR MUSIC TEST.

For additional information and a review by Roger P. Phelps, see 7:252. For reviews of the testing program, see 7:671 (2 reviews).

[216]

*The Watkins-Farnum Performance Scale: A Standardized Achievement Test for All Band Instruments. Music students; 1942–62; John G. Watkins and Stephen E. Farnum; Hal Leonard Music, Inc. *

For additional information and a review by Herbert D. Wing, see 5:253 (2 references); for related reviews, see 3:1228 (4 excerpts).

REFERENCES THROUGH 1971

1–2. See 5:253.
3. CHILDS, CARROLL ARTHUR. *A Comparison of Two Distributed Instructional Periods in the Teaching of Beginning Instrumental Music Students.* Doctor's research study No. 1, Colorado State College (Greeley, Colo.), 1963. (DA 25:517)
4. STRACHAN, EDWIN DUANE. *The Designation of the Appropriate Grade Level for Beginning Instrumental Study.* Doctor's research study No. 1, Colorado State College (Greeley, Colo.), 1964. (DA 28:161A)
5. McGARRY, ROBERT J. *A Teaching Experiment to Measure the Extent to Which Vocalization Contributes to the Development of Selected Instrumental Music Performance Skills. A Comparison of the Effectiveness of Two Teaching Techniques on Instrumental Music Performance Utilizing the Watkins-Farnum Performance Scale.* Doctor's thesis, New York University (New York, N.Y.), 1967. (DA 28:4385A)
6. MEWES, GORDEN EUGENE. *An Attempt to Determine the Association, if Any, Between Crossed Dominance and Achievement Levels in Instrumental Music Reading.* Doctor's thesis, University of Oklahoma (Norman, Okla.), 1969. (DAI 31:416A)

CUMULATIVE NAME INDEX

Ahrens, A. W.: *exc*, 3:1228   Pepinsky, A.: *exc*, 3:1228
Cheslock, L.: *exc*, 3:1228   Strachan, E. D.: 4
Childs, C. A.: 3   Watkins, J. G.: 1
Farnum, S. E.: 2   Wilson, M. E.: *exc*, 3:1228
McGarry, R. J.: 5   Wing, H. D.: *rev*, 5:253
Mewes, G. E.: 6

[217]

Wing Standardised Tests of Musical Intelligence.
Ages 8 and over; 1939–61; 8 scores: chord analysis,
pitch change, memory, rhythmic accent, harmony, intensity, phrasing, total; H. D. Wing; distributed by
NFER Publishing Co. Ltd. [England]. *
    For additional information and reviews by William S.
Larson and Robert W. Lundin, see 6:354 (6 references) ; see also 5:254 (4 references) ; for a review by
John McLeish of an earlier edition, see 4:230 (6 references). For excerpts from related book reviews, see
7:B647 (2 excerpts) and 4:231 (5 excerpts).

REFERENCES THROUGH 1971

1–6. See 4:230.
7–10. See 5:254.
11–15. See 6:354.
16. BEARD, R. M. "The Structure of Perception: A Factorial
Study." *Brit J Ed Psychol* 35:210–22 Je '65. * (*PA* 39:13425)
    17. McCLUNE, D. J. C.; FAIRBROTHER, C. J.; AND FAULDS,
B. D. "Musical Intelligence and Scale Preference." *Percept &
Motor Skills* 20:938–40 Je '65. * (*PA* 40:12304)
    18. PITMAN, DEREK J. "The Musical Ability of Blind Chil-
dren." *Am Found Blind Res B* 11:63–79 O '65. * (*PA* 40:4520)
    19. SHUTER, ROSAMUND. "Hereditary and Environmental
Factors in Musical Ability." *Eug R* (England) 58:149–56 S
'66. *
    20. McLEISH, JOHN, AND HIGGS, GEOFFREY. *An Inquiry Into
the Musical Capacities of Educationally Sub-Normal Children.*
Occasional Research Papers No. 1. Cambridge, England: Cam-
bridge Institute of Education, [1967]. Pp. ii, 12. *
    21. TANNER, JANE, AND LOESS, HENRY. "Intercorrelations
Among Rhythm Subtests of Three Tests of Musical Aptitude."
Percept & Motor Skills 25:721–6 D '67. * (*PA* 42:8738)
    22. CRICKMORE, LEON. "An Approach to the Measurement of
Music Appreciation (II)." *J Res Music Ed* 16:291–301 w '68.
* (*PA* 43:8756)
    23. McLEISH, JOHN. *The Factor of Musical Cognition in
Wing's and Seashore's Tests.* Music Education Research Papers
No. 2. London: Novello & Co. Ltd., 1968. Pp. 10. *
    24. WING, HERBERT. *Tests of Musical Ability and Appreci-
ation: An Investigation Into the Measurement, Distribution, and*

Development of Musical Capacity, Second Edition. London:
Cambridge University Press, 1968. Pp. vii, 98. *
    25. EGGER, G. J., AND IVINSKIS, A. "An Investigation Into
the Development of Melodic Interval Discrimination." *Austral
J Psychol* 21(2):187–91 Ag '69. * (*PA* 45:5388) *
    26. MITCHUM, JOHN PIOS. *The Wing "Standardised Tests
of Musical Intelligence": An Investigation of Predictability
With Selected Seventh-Grade Beginning-Band Students.* Doc-
tor's thesis, Florida State University (Tallahassee, Fla.), 1969.
(*DAI* 30:5017A)
    27. SHUTER, ROSAMUND. "Measurement and Development of
Musical Abilities: Some Problems in Psychology of Musical
Ability." *J Res Music Ed* 17(1):90–3 sp '69. *
    28. TUCKER, DAVID WALTER. *Factors Related to Musical
Reading Ability of Senior High School Students Participating
in Choral Groups.* Doctor's thesis, University of California
(Berkeley, Calif.), 1969. (*DAI* 31:2427A)
    29. WHELLAMS, FREDERICK S. "The Relative Efficiency of
Aural-Musical and Non-Musical Tests as Predictors of Achieve-
ment in Instrumental Music." *Council Res Music Ed B* 21:15–21
su '70. *

CUMULATIVE NAME INDEX

Beard, R. M.: 16   Loess, H.: 21
Bentley, R. R.: 8   Lundin, R. W.: *rev*, 6:354
Burt, C.: *exc*, 4:231   McClune, D. J. C.: 17
Cain, M. L.: 11   McLeish, J.: 5, 20, 23; *rev*,
Crickmore, L.: 22   4:230
Egger, G. J.: 25   Mitchum, J. P.: 26
Fairbrother, C. J.: 17   Pitman, D. J.: 18
Farnsworth, P. R.: *exc*, 7: Shuter, R.: 19, 27
   B647   Tanner, J.: 21
Faulds, B. D.: 17   Tucker, D. W.: 28
Franklin, E.: 9   Vernon, P. E.: *exc*, 4:231
Heim, K. E.: 14   Wertz, C. B.: 15
Heller, J. J.: 12   Whellams, F. S.: 29
Higgs, G.: 20   Whittington, R. W. T.: 10
Ivinskis, A.: 25   Wing, H.: 4, 7, 24
Larson, W. S.: *rev*, 6:354 Wing, H. D.: 1–3, 6, 11a, 13
Lehman, P. R.: *exc*, 7:B647

[Out of Print Since TIP I]

Beach Music Test, 3:174 (1 review)
Diagnostic Tests of Achievement in Music, 4:226 (2
reviews)
Drake Musical Aptitude Tests, 5:245 (2 reviews, 1
reference)
Farnum Music Notation Test, 5:246 (2 reviews, 1 ref-
erence)
Musical Aptitude Test: Series A, 6:352 (3 reviews,
2 references)
Strouse Music Test, 2:1339 (3 reviews, 1 reference)

FOREIGN LANGUAGES

[218]

Foreign Language Prognosis Test. Grades 8–9;
1930–59; 2 tests labeled Forms A, B; 1958–59 tests
identical with tests copyrighted 1930 except for cover
page; Percival M. Symonds; Teachers College Press. *
a) FORM A. 5 scores: English inflection, word transla-
tion-English to Esperanto, sentence translation-Esperanto to English, related words, total.
b) FORM B. 5 scores: word translation-Esperanto to
English, artificial language, sentence translation-Eng-
lish to Esperanto, formation of parts of speech in English, total.
    For additional information and a review by Wayne D.
Fisher (with Bertram B. Masia), see 6:355 (1 reference) ; for a review by William B. Michael, see 4:232;

for a review by Walter V. Kaulfers, see 2:1340 (6
references).

REFERENCES THROUGH 1971

1–6. See 2:1340.
7. See 6:355.

CUMULATIVE NAME INDEX

Fisher, W. D.: *rev*, 6:355   Michael, W. B.: *rev*, 4:232
Kaulfers, W. V.: *rev*, 2:1340 Richardson, H. D.: 4
Lau, L. M.: 3   Symonds, P. M.: 1–2
Maronpot, R. P.: 6   Veon, D. H.: 7
Masia, B. B.: *rev*, 6:355   Virgil, *Sister*: 5

[219]

***The Graduate School Foreign Language Testing
Program.** Graduate level degree candidates required
to demonstrate foreign language reading proficiency;

Watkins-Farnum Performance Scale

1963–73; GSFLT; French, German, and Spanish administered 4 times annually (January, April, June, October) at centers established by the publisher; Russian administered on a special basis; Educational Testing Service. *

For additional information, see 7:668 (3 references). For a review of the Spanish test, see 7:320; an earlier edition of the French test, see 6:377; and the German test, see 6:391.

REFERENCES THROUGH 1971
1–3. See 7:668.

CUMULATIVE NAME INDEX

[220]

Iowa Placement Examinations: Foreign Language Aptitude. Grades 12–13; 1925–44; 2 editions; Bureau of Educational Research and Service. *
a) SERIES FAI, REVISED. 1925–26; test by G. D. Stoddard and G. E. Vander Beke (Form A).
b) NEW SERIES FA-2, REVISED. 1925–44; original test by G. D. Stoddard; revision by Grace Cochran, J. R. Nielson, and D. B. Stuit.

For additional information and a review by H. E. Brogden, see 3:178 (7 references).

REFERENCES THROUGH 1971
1–7. See 3:178.
8. HAMMOND, H. P., AND STODDARD, GEORGE DINSMORE. "A Study of Placement Examinations." *Univ Iowa Studies Ed* 4(7): 1–59 '28. * (*PA* 3:2069)
9. THARP, JAMES BURTON. Chap. 10, "Sectioning in Romance Language Classes at the University of Illinois." pp. 365–432. In *Studies in Modern Language Teaching.* By E. W. Bagster-Collins and Others. New York: Macmillan Co., 1930. Pp. xxxi, 491. *
10. FEDER, DANIEL D. "An Evaluation of Some Problems in the Prediction of Achievement at the College Level." *J Ed Psychol* 26:597–603 N '35. * (*PA* 10:1681)
11. VEON, DOROTHY HELENE. *The Relationship of Learning Factors Found in Certain Modern Foreign-Language Aptitude Tests to the Prediction of Shorthand Achievement in College.* Foreword by M. Herbert Freeman. Stillwater, Okla.: Division of Commerce, Oklahoma Agricultural and Mechanical College, 1950. Pp. 74. *
12. MORGAN, WILLIAM J. "A Validity Study of the Iowa Language Aptitude Examination." Abstract. *Am Psychologist* 7:287 Jl '52. *
13. HASCALL, EDWARD ORSON, JR. *Predicting Success in High School Foreign Language Study.* Doctor's thesis, University of Michigan (Ann Arbor, Mich.), 1959. (*DA* 19:3245)
14. LANG, MARY JANE. *The Relationship Between Certain Psychological Tests and Shorthand Achievement at Three Instructional Levels.* Doctor's thesis, University of Missouri (Columbia, Mo.), 1960. (*DA* 21:2632)
15. HASCALL, EDWARD O. "Predicting Success in High School Foreign Language Study." *Personnel & Guid J* 40:361–7 D '61. * (*PA* 36:4KL61H)
16. LANG, MARY JANE. "Predicting Elementary Shorthand Achievement." *Balance Sheet* 45:300–2 Mr '64. *

CUMULATIVE NAME INDEX

[221]

Modern Language Aptitude Test. Grades 9 and over; 1959, c1955–58; MLAT; earlier experimental form called *Psi-Lambda Foreign Language Aptitude Battery;* 6 scores: number learning, phonetic script, spelling clues, words in sentences, paired associates, total; John B. Carroll and Stanley M. Sapon; Psychological Corporation. *

For additional information, reviews by Wayne D. Fisher (with Bertram B. Masia) and Marion F. Shay-

coft, and excerpted reviews by Edward S. Bordin, Harold B. Dunkel, Herschel T. Manuel, and Laurence Siegel, see 6:357 (10 references).

REFERENCES THROUGH 1971
1–10. See 6:357.
11. HARDING, FRANCIS D. "Tests as Selectors of Language Students." *Mod Lang J* 42:120–2 Mr '58. * (*PA* 34:2153)
12. CARROLL, JOHN B. Chap. 4, "The Prediction of Success in Intensive Foreign Language Training," pp. 87–136. In *Training Research and Education.* Edited by Robert Glaser. Pittsburgh, Pa.: University of Pittsburgh Press, 1962. Pp. xi, 596. * (*PA* 38:1380)
13. CARROLL, JOHN B. "Programed Instruction and Student Ability." *J Programed Instr* 2:7–11 w '63. * (*PA* 40:7018)
14. PIMSLEUR, PAUL. "A Study of Foreign Language Learning Ability: Parts 1 and 2," pp. 57–72. In *Report of the Twelfth Annual Round Table Meeting on Linguistics and Language Studies.* Edited by Michael Zarechnak. Monograph Series on Language and Linguistics, No. 14. Washington, D.C.: Georgetown University Press, 1963. Pp. 132. *
15. CLOOS, ROBERT IRA. *A Comparative Study of Fourteen Predictors of Success in the Audio-Lingual Approach to First-Year German at the High School Level.* Doctor's thesis, Rutgers University (New Brunswick, N.J.), 1964. (*DA* 25:7106)
16. COOPER, CARL J. "Some Relationships Between Paired-Associates Learning and Foreign-Language Aptitude." *J Ed Psychol* 55:132–8 Je '64. * (*PA* 39:5823)
17. GALLAGHER, JOSEPH W., AND SPENCER, RICHARD E. "Prediction of Success in Basic German at the College Level." *Ed & Psychol Meas* 24:955–60 w '64. * (*PA* 39:8701)
18. SCHERER, GEORGE A. C., AND WERTHEIMER, MICHAEL. *A Psycholinguistic Experiment in Foreign-Language Teaching.* New York: McGraw-Hill Book Co., 1964. Pp. xiii, 256. *
19. ACKERMAN, THOMAS J. *Language Laboratory Instruction and the Achievement of First-Year Students of Spanish in Florida.* Doctor's thesis, Florida State University (Tallahassee, Fla.), 1965. (*DA* 27:134A)
20. CLARK, MARGARET G. *The Modern Language Aptitude Test as a Predictor at the University of Rochester.* Master's thesis, University of Rochester (Rochester, N.Y.), 1965.
21. GARDNER, R. C. "A Language Aptitude Test for Blind Students." *J Appl Psychol* 49:135–41 Ap '65. * (*PA* 39:10107)
22. GARDNER, R. C., AND LAMBERT, W. E. "Language Aptitude, Intelligence, and Second-Language Achievement." *J Ed Psychol* 56:191–9 Ag '65. * (*PA* 39:15290)
23. KIZIOR, EUGENIA A. *A Study of Factors That Aid in the Prediction of Secondary School Foreign Language Achievement.* Master's thesis, Northwestern University (Evanston, Ill.), 1965.
24. CRAWSHAW, TED CATHCART. *Comparative Validities of Eleven Predictors of Student Success in Ninth Grade Spanish and French: Aurora-West Public Schools, 1961–63.* Master's thesis, Northern Illinois University (DeKalb, Ill.), 1966.
25. HORTON, DAVID L.; WILEY, RONALD E.; AND DIXON, THEODORE R. "Predicting Paired-Associate Learning Speed: An Alternate MLAT." *Psychol Rep* 18:93–4 F '66. * (*PA* 40:6249)
26. RENFER, MARY EMMA FEWELL. *Predicting Success in the Study of Descriptive Linguistics.* Doctor's thesis, University of Southern California (Los Angeles, Calif.), 1966. (*DA* 27: 1268A)
27. ARENDT, JERMAINE DELOS. *Predicting Success in Foreign Language Study: A Study Made in Selected Minneapolis Schools From 1963 to 1964.* Doctor's thesis, University of Minnesota (Minneapolis, Minn.), 1967. (*DA* 28:4869A)
28. MASSAD, CAROLYN EMRICK. *A Comparative Study of Creativity, Language Aptitude, and Intelligence in Sixth-Grade Children From Low-Socioeconomic and Middle-Socioeconomic Levels.* Doctor's thesis, Kent State University (Kent, Ohio), 1967. (*DA* 29:4331A)
29. PAYNE, DAVID A., AND VAUGHN, HAROLD A. "Forecasting Italian Language Proficiency of Culturally Immersed Students." *Mod Lang J* 51:3–6 Ja '67. *
30. STURGIS, THEODORE GILBERT. *A Study of the Statistical Relationships Between Certain Variables and Success in Learning Certain African Languages.* Doctor's thesis, Syracuse University (Syracuse, N.Y.), 1967. (*DA* 28:4393A)
31. ZAHN, JANE C. "Some Characteristics of Successful and Less Successful Overseas Community Development Advisers." *Adult Ed* 18:15–23 f '67. *
32. MUELLER, THEODORE H. "Programmed Language Instruction—Help for the Linguistically 'Underprivileged.'" *Mod Lang J* 52:79–84 F '68. * (*PA* 44:20888)
33. BARTLEY, DIANA E. "A Pilot Study of Aptitude and Attitude Factors in Language Dropout." *Calif J Ed Res* 20(2):48–55 Mr '69. *
34. CARROLL, JOHN B. "What Does the Pennsylvania Foreign Language Project Tell Us?" *Foreign Lang Ann* 3(2):214–36 D '69. *
35. CHASTAIN, KENNETH. "Prediction of Success in Audio-Lingual and Cognitive Classes." *Lang Learning* 19(1–2):27–39 Je '69. *
36. DICKEN, CHARLES. "Predicting the Success of Peace Corps Community Development Workers." *J Consult & Clin Psychol* 33(5):597–606 O '69. * (*PA* 44:2919)

37. HALSALL, ELIZABETH. "Linguistic Aptitude." *Mod Lang* (England) 50(1):18–23 Mr '69. *
38. JAKOBOVITS, LEON A. "Research Findings and Foreign Language Requirements in Colleges and Universities." *Foreign Lang Ann* 2(4):436–56 My '69. *
39. NEUFELD, GERALD G. *How Personality, Foreign Language Aptitude, and Anomie Relate to Foreign Language Acquisition.* Doctor's thesis, University of California (Berkeley, Calif.), 1969. (*DAI* 31:1651A)
40. SMITH, PHILIP D., JR. "The Pennsylvania Foreign Language Research Project: Teacher Proficiency and Class Achievement in Two Modern Languages." *Foreign Lang Ann* 3(2):194–207 D '69. *
41. WEAVER, WENDELL W.; KINGSTON, ALBERT J.; BICKLEY, A. C.; AND WHITE, WILLIAM F. "Information-Flow Difficulty in Relation to Reading Comprehension." *J Read Behav* 1(3):41–9 su '69. * (*PA* 45:2355)
42. POLITZER, ROBERT L. "On the Use of Aptitude Variables in Research in Foreign Language Teaching." *IRAL* (West Germany) 8(4): 333–40 N '70. *
43. SMITH, PHILIP D., JR. *A Comparison of the Cognitive and Audiolingual Approaches to Foreign Language Instruction: The Pennsylvania Foreign Language Project.* Philadelphia, Pa.: Center for Curriculum Development, Inc., 1970. Pp. xxv, 380. *
44. CLOOS, ROBERT I. "A Four-Year Study of Foreign Language Aptitude at the High School Level." *Foreign Lang Ann* 4(4):411–9 My '71. *

CUMULATIVE NAME INDEX

Ackerman, T. J.: 19
Arendt, J. D.: 27
Bartley, D. E.: 33
Bickley, A. C.: 41
Bordin, E. S.: *exc,* 6:357
Carroll, J. B.: 1–3, 12–3, 34
Chastain, K.: 35
Cieutat, V. J.: 7
Clark, M. G.: 20
Cloos, R. I.: 15, 44
Comrey, A. L.: 6
Cooper, C. J.: 16
Crawshaw, T. C.: 24
Dicken, C.: 36
Dixon, T. R.: 25
Dunkel, H. B.: *exc,* 6:357
Fisher, W. D.: *rev,* 6:357
Gallagher, J. W.: 17
Gardner, R. C.: 21–2
Halsall, E.: 37
Harding, F. D.: 11
Horton, D. L.: 25
Jakobovits, L. A.: 38
Kingston, A. J.: 10, 41
Kizior, E. A.: 23
Kjeldergaard, P. M.: 5
Kurlander, E. D.: 8

Lambert, W. E.: 22
Manuel, H. T.: *exc,* 6:357
Marquardt, W. F.: 4
Masia, B. B.: *rev,* 6:357
Massad, C. E.: 28
Mueller, K. A.: 9
Mueller, T. H.: 32
Neufeld, G. G.: 39
Payne, D. A.: 29
Pimsleur, P.: 6, 14
Politzer, R. L.: 42
Renfer, M. E. F.: 26
Scherer, G. A. C.: 18
Shaycoft, M. F.: *rev,* 6:357
Siegel, L.: *exc,* 6:357
Smith, P. D.: 40, 43
Spencer, R. E.: 17
Stockwell, R. P.: 6
Sturgis, T. G.: 30
Vaughn, H. A.: 29
Weaver, W. W.: 10, 41
Wertheimer, M.: 18
White, W. F.: 41
Wiersma, W.: 9
Wiley, R. E.: 25
Zahn, J. C.: 31

[222]
Modern Language Aptitude Test—Elementary. Grades 3–6; 1960–67; EMLAT; downward extension of the *Modern Language Aptitude Test*; 5 scores: hidden words, matching words, finding rhymes, number learning, total; John B. Carroll and Stanley M. Sapon; Psychological Corporation. *
For additional information and a review by A. Ralph Hakstian, see 7:255.

REFERENCES THROUGH 1971
1. MILLER, BERNEICE BEADLES. *The Effects of Continuing or Changing Foreign Languages on Listening Comprehension and Selected Tests as Predictors of Success in Spanish or French at the Seventh-Grade Level.* Doctor's thesis, University of Oklahoma (Norman, Okla.), 1970. (*DAI* 31:2618A)

CUMULATIVE NAME INDEX
Hakstian, A. R.: *rev,* 7:255   Miller, B. B.: 1

[223]
Pimsleur Language Aptitude Battery. Grades 6–12; 1966–67; 5 scores: grade-point average, interest, verbal, auditory, total; Paul Pimsleur; Harcourt Brace Jovanovich, Inc. *
For additional information, a review by A. Ralph Hakstian, and an excerpted review by Donald C. Ryberg, see 7:256 (5 references).

REFERENCES THROUGH 1971
1–5. See 7:256.
6. CLOOS, ROBERT I. "A Four-Year Study of Foreign Lan-

guage Aptitude at the High School Level." *Foreign Lang Ann* 4(4):411–9 My '71. *
7. LAFAYETTE, ROBERT CLAUDE. *An Investigation of Causes Leading to Early Attrition in Foreign Language Study.* Doctor's thesis, Ohio State University (Columbus, Ohio), 1971. (*DAI* 32:1752A)
8. LEAL, AUREA M. *A Study of the Factors Involved in the Correlation Between Pimsleur's Aptitude Test Scores and Academic Achievement in Beginning Spanish.* Master's thesis, John Carroll University (Cleveland, Ohio), 1971.
9. LESTER, KENNETH ALLEN. *Factors Related to Dropouts Between Levels Two and Three of Modern Foreign Language Study in the Public Secondary Schools of Connecticut.* Doctor's thesis, Boston University (Boston, Mass.), 1971. (*DAI* 32:1839A)
10. VON WITTICH, BARBARA. *The Impact of Method of Evaluation Upon Achievement in Elementary Foreign Language Courses.* Doctor's thesis, Iowa State University (Ames, Iowa), 1971. (*DAI* 32:5576A)

CUMULATIVE NAME INDEX

Cloos, R. I.: 6
Comrey, A. L.: 1
Fay, B. L.: 3
Hakstian, A. R.: *rev,* 7:256
Lafayette, R. C.: 7
Leal, A. M.: 8
Lester, K. A.: 9

Pimsleur, P.: 1–2, 4
Ryberg, D. C.: *exc,* 7:256
Stockwell, R. P.: 1
Struth, J. F.: 4
Thomas, J. C.: 5
Von Wittich, B.: 10

[Out of Print Since TIP I]
Common Concepts Foreign Language Test, 7:253 (1 review)
Luria-Orleans Modern Language Prognosis Test, 2:1341 (1 review, 3 references)

ARABIC

[224]
*First Year Arabic Final Examination, 1972 Edition. 1 year college; 1964–72; 1964 edition called *First-Year Arabic Qualifying Examination;* no manual; Sami A. Hanna; Middle East Center, University of Utah. *
For additional information concerning the 1964 edition, see 7:258.

CHINESE

[225]
Harvard-MLA Tests of Chinese Language Proficiency. College and adults; 1959–65; 2 tests; Modern Language Association of America and Educational Testing Service; program administered by Educational Testing Service (Atlanta Office). *
a) PICTORIAL AUDITORY COMPREHENSION TEST. 2 semesters; 1959–65; John B. Carroll and Wai-Ching Ho.
b) INTERMEDIATE READING COMPREHENSION TEST IN MODERN CHINESE. 4 semesters; 1964–65; 4 scores: vocabulary, structure, reading comprehension, total; K. P. Chou, John de Francis, Y. K. Kao, H. C. Mills, R. C. Pian, and J. Wrenn.
For additional information, see 7:259.

ENGLISH

[226]
A Comprehensive English Language Test for Speakers of English as a Second Language. Nonnative speakers of English; 1970; CELT; 3 tests; David P. Harris and Leslie A. Palmer; McGraw-Hill Book Co., Inc. *

a) LISTENING.
b) STRUCTURE.
c) VOCABULARY.

For additional information and a review by John B. Carroll, see 7:260.

[227]

Diagnostic Test for Students of English as a Second Language. Applicants from non-English language countries for admission to American colleges; 1953; A. L. Davis; McGraw-Hill Book Co., Inc. *

For additional information and reviews by Nelson Brooks and Herschel T. Manuel, see 5:255.

REFERENCES THROUGH 1971
1. BLATCHFORD, CHARLES H. "A Theoretical Contribution to ESL Diagnostic Test Construction." *TESOL Q* 5(3):209–15 S '71. *

CUMULATIVE NAME INDEX
Blatchford, C. H.: 1   Manuel, H. T.: *rev,* 5:255
Brooks, N.: *rev,* 5:255

[228]

English Knowledge and Comprehension Test. High school; 1965; S. Chatterji and M. Mukerjee; S. Chatterji [India]. *

For additional information, see 7:261.

[229]

★**English Placement Test.** College entrants from non-English language countries; 1972; test by Mary Spaan and Laura Strowe; published by the English Language Institute, University of Michigan and distributed by Follett's Michigan Book Store, Inc. *

[230]

*English Usage Test for Non-Native Speakers of English.** Non-native speakers of English; 1955–72; distribution restricted to the Agency for International Development and the Bureau of Educational and Cultural Affairs of the U.S. Department of State; David P. Harris and Leslie A. Palmer assisted by B. Jean Longmire (Forms L and U-B); American Language Institute. *

For additional information, see 7:262.

[231]

Examination in Structure (English as a Foreign Language). College entrants from non-English language countries; 1947; published by the English Language Institute, University of Michigan and distributed by Follett's Michigan Book Store, Inc. *

For additional information, see 5:260.

REFERENCES THROUGH 1971
1. LADO, ROBERT. *Measurement in English as a Foreign Language With Special Reference to Spanish-Speaking Adults.* Doctor's thesis, University of Michigan (Ann Arbor, Mich.), 1950.

CUMULATIVE NAME INDEX
Lado, R.: 1

[232]

★**Michigan Test of Aural Comprehension.** College applicants from non-English language countries; 1969–72; MTAC; John Upshur, Mary Spaan, and Rudolph Thrasher; published by the English Language Institute, University of Michigan and distributed by Follett's Michigan Book Store, Inc. *

[233]

*Michigan Test of English Language Proficiency.** College applicants from non-English language countries; 1961–66; MTELP; test by John Upshur, Leslie

Palmer (Form A), John Harris (Forms A and E), Geraldine May (Forms A and B), Miho Tanaka (Form B), Rudolph Thrasher (Forms B and D), A. Palmer (Form D), M. Spaan (Forms D and E), and E. Loundon (Form E); manual by Division of Testing and Certification, English Language Institute, University of Michigan; distributed for the Institute by Follett's Michigan Book Store, Inc. *

For additional information, see 7:264 (2 references); for a review by John B. Carroll, see 6:360.

REFERENCES THROUGH 1971
1–2. See 7:264.
3. BEBEAU, DONALD E. "Administration of a TOEFL Test to Sioux Indian High School Students." *J Am Indian Ed* 9(1):7–16 O '69. *

CUMULATIVE NAME INDEX
Bebeau, D. E.: 3   Dizney, H.: 1
Carroll, J. B.: *rev,* 6:360   Ursua, A. R.: 2

[234]

Oral Rating Form for Rating Language Proficiency in Speaking and Understanding English. Non-native speakers of English; 1959–67; also called *AULC Interview Rating Form;* 6 ratings by interviewers: comprehension, pronunciation, grammar and word-order, vocabulary, general speed of speech and sentence length, total; 1962 form identical with form published 1959 except for title; [David P. Harris]; American Language Institute. *

For additional information, see 7:265.

[235]

★**Test A/65.** Matriculants and higher; [1956?]; also called *English Language Achievement Test;* 3 scores: spelling, comprehension, vocabulary; no manual; National Institute for Personnel Research [South Africa]. *

[236]

Test of Aural Perception in English for Japanese Students. Japanese students in American colleges; 1950; for research use only; Robert Lado and R. D. Andrade; published by the English Language Institute, University of Michigan and distributed by Follett's Michigan Book Store, Inc. *

For additional information, see 6:362.

REFERENCES THROUGH 1971
1. STRAIN, JERIS E. "Difficulties in Measuring Pronunciation Improvement." *Lang Learning* 13(3–4):217–24 '63. *

CUMULATIVE NAME INDEX
Strain, J. E.: 1

[237]

Test of Aural Perception in English for Latin-American Students. Latin-American students of English; 1947–57; Robert Lado; published by the English Language Institute, University of Michigan and distributed by Follett's Michigan Book Store, Inc. *

For additional information, see 5:262.

REFERENCES THROUGH 1971
1. LADO, ROBERT. *Measurement in English as a Foreign Language With Special Reference to Spanish-Speaking Adults.* Doctor's thesis, University of Michigan (Ann Arbor, Mich.), 1950.
2. SISSON, CYRUS R. "The Effect of Delayed Comparison in the Language Laboratory on Phoneme Discrimination and Pronunciation Accuracy." *Lang Learning* 20(1):69–88 Je '70. *

CUMULATIVE NAME INDEX
Lado, R.: 1   Sisson, C. R.: 2

[238]

*Test of English as a Foreign Language.** College applicants from non-English language countries; 1964–

73; TOEFL; test administered 4 times annually (January, March, June, October) in approximately 100 countries; 6 scores: listening comprehension, English structure, vocabulary, reading comprehension, writing ability, total; program sponsored jointly by the College Entrance Examination Board and Educational Testing Service; Educational Testing Service. * For additional information and reviews by Clinton I. Chase and George Domino of earlier forms, see 7:266 (10 references).

REFERENCES THROUGH 1971

1–10. See 7:266.
11. ERICKSON, DOUGLAS EUGENE. *Differential Personality, Academic, and Biographical Characteristics of International Graduate Students at the University of North Dakota.* Doctor's thesis, University of North Dakota (Grand Forks, N.D.), 1970. (*DAI* 32:6756A)
12. ANGOFF, WILLIAM H., AND SHARON, AMIEL T. "A Comparison of Scores Earned on the Test of English as a Foreign Language by Native American College Students and Foreign Applicants to U.S. Colleges." *TESOL Q* 5(2):129–36 Je '71. *
13. MARTIN, GALE MACLANE. *A Model for the Cultural and Statistical Analysis of Academic Achievement of Foreign Graduate Students at the University of North Carolina at Chapel Hill.* Doctor's thesis, University of North Carolina (Chapel Hill, N.C.), 1971. (*DAI* 32:2311A)
14. REILLY, RICHARD R. "A Note on 'Clozentrophy: A Procedure' for Testing English Language Proficiency of Foreign Students.'" *Speech Monogr* 38(4):350–3 N '71. *

CUMULATIVE NAME INDEX

Angoff, W. H.: 12
Chase, C. I.: 5; *rev*, 7:266
Darnell, D. K.: 8
Dizney, H.: 3
Dizney, H. F.: 9
Domino, G.: *rev*, 7:266
Erickson, D. E.: 11
Harris, D.: 1
Hwang, K. Y.: 7, 9
Lado, R.: 2
Martin, G. M.: 13
Maxwell, A.: 6
Palmer, L. A.: 4
Reilly, R. R.: 14
Sharon, A. T.: 12
Stallings, W. M.: 5
Vroman, C.: 10
Wilcox, L.: 10

[239]

*A Vocabulary and Reading Test for Students of English as a Second Language. Non-native speakers of English; 1960–72; distribution restricted to the Agency for International Development and the Bureau of Educational and Cultural Affairs of the U.S. Department of State; David P. Harris and Leslie A. Palmer; American Language Institute. *
For additional information, see 7:267.

[Out of Print Since TIP I]

English Examinations for Foreign Students, 5:256 (3 reviews)
English Language Test for Foreign Students, 5:257 (2 reviews, 3 references)
English Reading Test for Students of English as a Foreign Language (status unknown), 5:258 (2 reviews)
Listening Test for Students of English as a Second Language, 7:263
Rating Language Proficiency in Speaking and Understanding English (status unknown), T:625
Test of Aural Comprehension, 5:261 (2 reviews)

FRENCH

[240]

*Advanced Placement Examination in French. High school students desiring credit for college level courses or admission to advanced courses; 1954–73; 2 tests (candidate elects one or both); available to secondary schools for annual administration on specified days in May; inactive forms are available to colleges for local administration in the *Testing Academic Achievement* program; program administered for the College Entrance Examination Board by Educational

Test of English as a Foreign Language

Testing Service. * For the testing program entry, see 1045.
a) FRENCH LANGUAGE.
b) FRENCH LITERATURE.
For additional information concerning earlier forms, see 7:268 (1 reference); see also 6:368 (3 references). For reviews of the testing program, see 7:662 (2 reviews).

REFERENCES THROUGH 1971

1–3. See 6:368.
4. See 7:268.

CUMULATIVE NAME INDEX

Nelson, R. J.: 3
Niess, R. J.: 2
Valley, J. R.: 1

[241]

Baltimore County French Test. 1 year high school; 1962; 2 scores: parts A, B; Baltimore County French Language Committee; Bobbs-Merrill Co., Inc. *
For additional information and reviews by Nelson Brooks and Mary E. Turnbull, see 6:364 (1 reference).

REFERENCES THROUGH 1971

1. See 6:364.

CUMULATIVE NAME INDEX

Brooks, N.: *rev*, 6:364
Jungeblut, A.: 1
Turnbull, M. E.: *rev*, 6:364

[242]

*Canadian Achievement Test in French. Grade 10; 1961–68; CATF; a test in the *Canadian Test Battery, Grade 10;* Ontario Institute for Studies in Education; distributed by Guidance Centre [Canada]. * For the complete battery entry, see 1046.
For additional information and a review by Mary E. Turnbull, see 6:365 (2 references).

REFERENCES THROUGH 1971

1–2. See 6:365.

CUMULATIVE NAME INDEX

D'Oyley, V. R.: 1–2
Turnbull, M. E.: *rev*, 6:365

[243]

★College Board Achievement Test in French Listening-Reading. Candidates for college entrance with 2–4 years high school French; 1971–73; test administered each spring at centers established by the publisher; inactive forms, entitled *College Placement Test in French Listening-Reading,* are available to colleges for local administration; program administered for the College Entrance Examination Board by Educational Testing Service. * For the testing program entry, see 1048.
For reviews of the testing program, see 6:760 (2 reviews).

[244]

*College Board Achievement Test in French Reading. Candidates for college entrance with 2–4 years high school French; 1901–73; test administered on specified dates at centers established by the publisher; inactive forms, entitled *College Placement Test in French Reading,* are available to colleges for local administration; program administered for the College Entrance Examination Board by Educational Testing Service. * For the testing program entry, see 1048.
For additional information, see 7:269; see also 6:366 (4 references) and 5:263 (2 references); for a review by Walter V. Kaulfers of earlier forms, see 4:237 (7 references). For reviews of the testing program, see 6:760 (2 reviews).

REFERENCES THROUGH 1971

1–7. See 4:237.
8–9. See 5:263.
10–13. See 6:366.

[245]

*College Placement Test in French Listening Comprehension. Entering college freshmen; 1962–72, c1955–72; reprintings of inactive 1963 and 1967 forms of *College Board Achievement Test in French Listening Comprehension;* test available to colleges for local administration; program administered for the College Entrance Examination Board by Educational Testing Service. * For the testing program entry, see 1051.

For additional information, see 7:270 (1 reference). For a review of the testing program, see 7:665.

REFERENCES THROUGH 1971
1. See 7:270.

[246]

*College Placement Test in French Listening-Reading. Entering college freshmen; 1971–72; reprinting of inactive 1971 form of *College Board Achievement Test in French Listening-Reading;* test available to colleges for local administration; program administered for the College Entrance Examination Board by Educational Testing Service. * For the testing program entry, see 1051.

For a review of the testing program, see 7:665.

[247]

*College Placement Test in French Reading. Entering college freshmen; 1962–72, c1955–72; reprinting of inactive 1964 forms of *College Board Achievement Test in French Reading;* test available to colleges for local administration; program administered for the College Entrance Examination Board by Educational Testing Service. * For the testing program entry, see 1051.

For additional information, see 7:271 (1 reference). For a review of the testing program, see 7:665. For reference to a review of the *College Board Achievement Test in French Reading,* see 244.

REFERENCES THROUGH 1971
1. See 7:271.

[248]

Cooperative French Listening Comprehension Test. 2–5 semesters high school or college; 1955; Nelson Brooks; Cooperative Tests and Services. *

For additional information and reviews by Walter V. Kaulfers and Kathleen N. Perret, see 5:265 (1 reference).

REFERENCES THROUGH 1971
1. See 5:265.
2. VECCHIONE, NICHOLAS. "A Further Study of the Cooperative French Listening Comprehension Test." *Ed Rec B* 77:75–82 Jl '60. *
3. TRAXLER, ARTHUR E. "Some Further Information on the Cooperative French Listening Comprehension Test Among Independent School Pupils." *Ed Rec B* 82:61–2 Jl '62. *
4. SIMON-HERMANN, *Sister.* "A Report on an Applied Linguistics Method Used to Improve the Spoken French of French-Speaking Students at the Grade Seven Level." *Alberta J Ed Res* (Canada) 9:111–9 Je '63. *

5. GARDNER, R. C., AND LAMBERT, W. E. "Language Aptitude, Intelligence, and Second-Language Achievement." *J Ed Psychol* 56:191–9 Ag '65. * (*PA* 39:15290)

[249]

First Year French Test. High school and college; 1956–68; Jean Leblon and Minnie M. Miller; Bureau of Educational Measurements. *

For additional information, see 7:273; for reviews by Nelson Brooks and Mary E. Turnbull of an earlier edition, see 5:266.

[250]

Ford-Hicks French Grammar Completion Tests. High school; 1944; test booklet title is *Dents' Modern Language Tests: French Grammar;* H. E. Ford and R. K. Hicks; J. M. Dent & Sons (Canada) Ltd. [Canada]. *

For additional information, see 6:372.

[251]

French I and II: Achievement Examinations for Secondary Schools. 1–2 years high school; 1951–60; Form 4 ('55) is the only form in print; Midwest High School Achievement Examinations and Minnesota High School Achievement Examinations were also used as series titles; Lee Stark; Bobbs-Merrill Co., Inc. *

For additional information concerning later and earlier forms, see 6:373 and 5:268; for a review by Mary E. Turnbull of Form A [1955, same as A-E (1962)], see 5:267; for a review by Elton Hocking of Form 1 (1951), see 4:239.

[252]

*The Graduate Record Examinations Advanced French Test. Graduate school candidates; 1939–73; 3 scores: interpretive reading skills, literature and civilization, total; Educational Testing Service. * For the testing program entry, see 1053.

For additional information concerning earlier forms, see 7:274; for a review by Nelson Brooks, see 6:376; for a review by Walter V. Kaulfers, see 5:270. For reviews of the testing program, see 7:667 (1 review) and 5:601 (1 review).

[253]

*Graduate School Foreign Language Test: French. Graduate level degree candidates required to demonstrate reading proficiency in French; 1963–73; test administered 4 times annually (January, April, June, October) at centers established by the publisher; Educational Testing Service. * For the testing program entry, see 219.

For additional information, see 7:275 (3 references); for a review by Clarence E. Turner of an earlier edition, see 6:377.

REFERENCES THROUGH 1971
1–3. See 7:275.

[254]

Iowa Placement Examinations: French Training. Grades 12–13; 1925–26; test by G. E. Vander Beke, G. D. Stoddard, and C. E. Young (Form B); Bureau of Educational Research and Service. *

For additional information and a review by Geraldine Spaulding, see 3:189 (4 references).

REFERENCES THROUGH 1971

1-4. See 3:189.
5. HAMMOND, H. P., AND STODDARD, GEORGE DINSMORE. "A Study of Placement Examinations." *Univ Iowa Studies Ed* 4(7):1-59 '28. * (*PA* 3:2069)
6. RICE, GEORGE A. Chap. 11, "A Study of Achievement in French and Spanish in Junior and Senior High School, With Consideration of Some of the Factors That Condition Achievement," pp. 433-71. In *Studies in Modern Language Teaching.* By E. W. Bagster-Collins and Others. New York: Macmillan Co., 1930. Pp. xxxi, 491. *
7. THARP, JAMES BURTON. Chap. 10, "Sectioning in Romance Language Classes at the University of Illinois," pp. 365-432. In *Studies in Modern Language Teaching.* By E. W. Bagster-Collins and Others. New York: Macmillan Co., 1930. Pp. xxxi, 491. *

CUMULATIVE NAME INDEX

Hammond, H. P.: 5   Spaulding, G.: *rev,* 3:189
Miller, L. W.: 4   Stoddard, G. D.: 1-2, 5
Rice, G. A.: 6   Tharp, J. B.: 3, 7

[255]

MLA Cooperative Foreign Language Proficiency Tests: French. French majors and advanced students in college; 1960-68; formerly called *MLA Foreign Language Proficiency Tests for Teachers and Advanced Students: French;* 7 tests in 3 booklets; 1966 test identical with tests copyrighted 1961 except for format and directions; Modern Language Association of America and Educational Testing Service; Cooperative Tests and Services. *
a) BOOK 1: READING, LISTENING COMPREHENSION, SPEAKING.
b) BOOK 2: WRITING.
c) BOOK 3: APPLIED LINGUISTICS, CIVILIZATION AND CULTURE, PROFESSIONAL PREPARATION.

For additional information and reviews by Joseph A. Murphy and Jean-Guy Savard, see 7:276 (9 references); for reviews by Paul Pimsleur and James H. Ricks, Jr., see 6:379 (3 references).

REFERENCES THROUGH 1971

1-3. See 6:379.
4-12. See 7:276.
13. SMITH, PHILIP D., JR. "An Assessment of Three Foreign Language Teaching Strategies and Three Language Laboratory Systems." *French R* 43(2):289-304 D '69. *
14. VILLARREAL, JOSE A. *The MLA-Cooperative Foreign Language Proficiency Test as an Evaluating Instrument of the Competency of Prospective Student Teachers of Spanish, French, and German.* Master's thesis, University of Texas (Austin, Tex.), 1970.

CUMULATIVE NAME INDEX

Bashour, D. S.: 5   Perkins, J. A.: 9
Beaujour, M.: 5   Pimsleur, P.: *rev,* 6:379
Carroll, J. B.: 6, 10   Ricks, J. H.: *rev,* 6:379
Churchill, F. J.: 4   Savard, J. G.: *rev,* 7:276
Dizney, H. F.: 7   Sheppard, D. C.: 5
Ehrmann, J.: 5   Smith, P. D.: 12-3
Gromen, L.: 7   Spencer, R. E.: 4
Hull, A.: 5   Starr, W. H.: 1-3
Ladu, T. T.: 5   Tollinger, S.: 5
McKinney, J. C.: 5   Valette, R. M.: 5
Murphy, J. A.: *rev,* 7:276   Villarreal, J. A.: 14
Otto, F.: 11   Wallmark, M.: 4, 8
Paquette, F. A.: 4-5, 8

[256]

MLA-Cooperative Foreign Language Tests: French. 1-2 years high school or 2 semesters college, 3-4 years high school or 4 semesters college; 1963-65; 4 tests in a single booklet: listening, speaking, reading, writing; writing test available as separate; prepared in cooperation with the Modern Language Association of America; Cooperative Tests and Services. *

For additional information and a review by Michio Peter Hagiwara, see 7:277 (5 references). For an excerpted review by John L. D. Clark of the series, see 7:254.

REFERENCES THROUGH 1971

1-5. See 7:277.
6. SMITH, PHILIP D., JR. *A Comparison of the Cognitive and Audiolingual Approaches to Foreign Language Instruction: The Pennsylvania Foreign Language Project.* Philadelphia, Pa.: Center for Curriculum Development, Inc., 1970. Pp. xxv, 380. *

CUMULATIVE NAME INDEX

Aleamoni, L. M.: 5   Paquette, F. A.: 1
Churchill, F. J.: 1   Smith, P. D.: 6
Clark, J. L. D.: *exc,* 7:254   Spencer, R. E.: 1-2, 5
Hagiwara, M. P.: *rev,* 7:277   Vocolo, J. M.: 3
Mueller, T. H.: 4   Wallmark, M.: 1

[257]

*National Teacher Examinations: French. College seniors and teachers; 1970-73; derived from *MLA Foreign Language Proficiency Tests for Teachers and Advanced Students: French;* an inactive form (1967) entitled *Teacher Education Examination Program: French* is available to colleges for local administration; the same inactive form entitled *French* is available to school systems for local use as part of the program entitled *School Personnel Research and Evaluation Services;* Educational Testing Service. * For the testing program entry, see 869.

For additional information, see 7:278. For reviews of the testing program, see 7:582 (2 reviews), 6:700 (1 review), 5:538 (3 reviews), and 4:802 (1 review).

[258]

Pimsleur French Proficiency Tests. "First-level,... second-level" courses in grades 7-16; 1967; 4 tests; Paul Pimsleur; Harcourt Brace Jovanovich, Inc. *
a) TEST 1, LISTENING COMPREHENSION.
b) TEST 2, SPEAKING PROFICIENCY.
c) TEST 3, READING COMPREHENSION.
d) TEST 4, WRITING PROFICIENCY.

For additional information, reviews by John L. D. Clark and Michio Peter Hagiwara, and an excerpted review by C. Richards Pusey, see 7:279 (1 reference). For an excerpted review by A. Ralph Hakstian of this and other tests (German, Spanish) in the series, see 7:257.

REFERENCES THROUGH 1971

1. See 7:279.

CUMULATIVE NAME INDEX

Clark, J. L. D.: *rev,* 7:279   Pimsleur, P.: 1
Hagiwara, M. P.: *rev,* 7:279   Pusey, C. R.: *exc,* 7:279
Hakstian, A. R.: *exc,* 7:257

[259]

Second Year French Test. High school and college; 1956-68; Jean Leblon and Minnie M. Miller; Bureau of Educational Measurements. *

For additional information and a review by John L. D. Clark, see 7:280; for reviews by Geraldine Spaulding and Clarence E. Turner of an earlier edition, see 5:271.

[260]

*Teacher Education Examination Program: French. College seniors preparing to teach secondary school; 1957-72; reprinting of inactive 1967 form of *National Teacher Examinations: French;* test available to colleges for local administration; Educational Testing Service. * For the testing program entry, see 898.

For additional information concerning an earlier form, see 6:374. For a review of the testing program, see 5:543.

[261]

*The Undergraduate Program Field Tests: French Test. College; 1969-73; formerly called *The Undergraduate Record Examinations: French Test;*

test available to colleges for local administration; Educational Testing Service. * For the testing program entry, see 1062.

For additional information and a review by Joseph A. Murphy of an earlier form, see 7:281. For reviews of the testing program, see 7:671 (2 reviews).

[Out of Print Since TIP I]

American Council Beta French Test, 2:1344 (1 review, 2 references)

Cohen French Test, 4:236 (1 review)

College Entrance Examination Board Achievement Test: French Listening Comprehension, 6:367

Common Concepts Foreign Language Test: French, 7:272

Cooperative French Test: Elementary and Advanced Forms, 3:181 (7 reviews, 7 references)

French Recognition Vocabulary Test: State High School Tests for Indiana, 4:240 (1 review, 1 reference); for a revision, see *French, First Year—Second Semester: State High School Tests for Indiana*, T:639

French Test (Two-Year Course): Affiliation Testing Program for Catholic Secondary Schools, 6:375 (1 review)

Lundeberg-Tharp Audition Test in French, 2:1354 (1 review, 3 references)

Standard French Test: Vocabulary, Grammar, and Comprehension, 2:1356 (1 review, 2 references)

Standardised French Grammar Test, 6:380 (2 reviews, 1 reference)

Standardised French Vocabulary Test, 6:381 (2 reviews, 1 reference)

GERMAN

[262]

*Advanced Placement Examination in German. High school students desiring credit for college level courses or admission to advanced courses; 1954–73; available to secondary schools for annual administration on specified days in May; inactive forms are available to colleges for local administration in the *Testing Academic Achievement* program; program administered for the College Entrance Examination Board by Educational Testing Service. * For the testing program entry, see 1045.

For additional information concerning earlier forms, see 7:282 (4 references); see also 6:385 (5 references); for a review by Herbert Schueler, see 5:273. For reviews of the testing program, see 7:662 (2 reviews).

REFERENCES THROUGH 1971
1–5. See 6:385.
6–9. See 7:282.

CUMULATIVE NAME INDEX

Lederer, H.: 7	Scheider, R. M.: 9
Newmark, M.: 5	Scherer, P.: 5
Presel, R.: 1	Schueler, H.: *rev*, 5:273
Reichard, J. R.: 2, 4, 8	Valley, J. R.: 3

[263]

★College Board Achievement Test in German Listening-Reading. Candidates for college entrance with 2–4 years high school German; 1971–73; test administered each spring at centers established by the publisher; inactive forms, entitled *College Placement Test in German Listening-Reading*, are available to colleges for local administration; program administered for the College Entrance Examination Board by Educational

Testing Service. * For the testing program entry, see 1048.

For reviews of the testing program, see 6:760 (2 reviews).

[264]

*College Board Achievement Test in German Reading. Candidates for college entrance with 2–4 years high school German; 1901–73; test administered on specified dates at centers established by the publisher; inactive forms, entitled *College Placement Test in German Reading,* are available to colleges for local administration; program administered for the College Entrance Examination Board by Educational Testing Service. * For the testing program entry, see 1048.

For additional information, see 7:283; for a review by Gilbert C. Kettelkamp of earlier forms, see 6:383; for a review by Harold B. Dunkel, see 5:272 (3 references); for a review by Herbert Schueler, see 4:244 (3 references). For reviews of the testing program, see 6:760 (2 reviews).

REFERENCES THROUGH 1971
1–3. See 4:244.
4–6. See 5:272.

CUMULATIVE NAME INDEX

College Entrance Examination Board: 4	Kettelkamp, G. C.: *rev*, 6:383
	King, R. G.: 5
Dunkel, H. B.: *rev*, 5:272	Schueler, H.: *rev*, 4:244
Dyer, H. S.: 1–2	Tucker, L. R.: 3
Hollmann, W.: 6	

[265]

*College Placement Test in German Listening Comprehension. Entering college freshmen; 1962–72, c1955–72; reprintings of inactive 1966 and 1967 forms of *College Board Achievement Test in German Listening Comprehension;* test available to colleges for local administration; program administered for the College Entrance Examination Board by Educational Testing Service. * For the testing program entry, see 1051.

For additional information, see 7:284 (2 references). For a review of the testing program, see 7:665; for reviews of the *College Board Achievement Test in German Listening Comprehension,* see 6:384 (2 reviews).

REFERENCES THROUGH 1971
1–2. See 7:284.

CUMULATIVE NAME INDEX

Aleamoni, L. M.: 2	Seguin, E. L.: 1
Matsunaga, A.: 2	Spencer, R. E.: 1

[266]

★College Placement Test in German Listening-Reading. Entering college freshmen; 1971–72; reprinting of inactive 1971 form of *College Board Achievement Test in German Listening-Reading;* test available to colleges for local administration; program administered for the College Entrance Examination Board by Educational Testing Service. * For the testing program entry, see 1051.

For a review of the testing program, see 7:665.

[267]

*College Placement Test in German Reading. Entering college freshmen; 1962–72, c1957–72; reprintings of inactive 1965 and 1966 forms of *College Board Achievement Test in German Reading;* test available to colleges for local administration; program administered for the College Entrance Examination Board by Educational Testing Service. * For the testing program entry, see 1051.

For additional information, see 7:285 (2 references). For a review of the testing program, see 7:665. For reference to reviews of the *College Board Achievement Test in German Reading,* see 264.

REFERENCES THROUGH 1971

1–2. See 7:285.

CUMULATIVE NAME INDEX

Aleamoni, L. M.: 2   Seguin, E. L.: 1
Matsunaga, A.: 2   Spencer, R. E.: 1

[268]

German I and II: Achievement Examinations for Secondary Schools. 1–2 years high school; 1951–60; Form 4 ['54] is the only form in print; Midwest High School Achievement Examinations and Minnesota High School Achievement Examinations were also used as series titles; Emma Marie Birkmaier; Bobbs-Merrill Co., Inc. *

For additional information concerning earlier forms, see 6:390 and 5:275; for a review by Harold B. Dunkel of Form A (1955) and Form B (1953, same as Form 2), see 5:276.

[269]

*The Graduate Record Examinations Advanced German Test. Graduate school candidates; 1939–73; Educational Testing Service. * For the testing program entry, see 1053.

For additional information concerning earlier forms, see 7:287. For reviews of the testing program, see 7:667 (1 review) and 5:601 (1 review).

REFERENCES THROUGH 1971

1. Schultz, Margaret K., and Angoff, William H. "The Development of New Scales for the Aptitude and Advanced Tests of the Graduate Record Examinations." *J Ed Psychol* 47: 285–94 My '56. * (*PA* 32:2127)

CUMULATIVE NAME INDEX

Angoff, W. H.: 1   Schultz, M. K.: 1

[270]

*Graduate School Foreign Language Test: German. Graduate level degree candidates required to demonstrate reading proficiency in German; 1963–73; test administered 4 times annually (January, April, June, October) at centers established by the publisher; Educational Testing Service. * For the testing program entry, see 219.

For additional information, see 7:288 (3 references); for a review by Jack M. Stein of an earlier edition, see 6:391.

REFERENCES THROUGH 1971

1–3. See 7:288.

CUMULATIVE NAME INDEX

Bartlett, A. A.: 1   Harvey, P. R.: 3
Clark, J. L. D.: 2   Stein, J. M.: *rev,* 6:391

[271]

MLA Cooperative Foreign Language Proficiency Tests: German. German majors and advanced students in college; 1960–68; formerly called *MLA Foreign Language Proficiency Tests for Teachers and Advanced Students: German;* 7 tests in 3 booklets; 1966 test identical with tests copyrighted 1961 except for format and directions; Modern Language Association of America and Educational Testing Service; Cooperative Tests and Services. *

a) BOOK 1: READING, LISTENING COMPREHENSION, SPEAKING.
b) BOOK 2: WRITING.
c) BOOK 3: APPLIED LINGUISTICS, CIVILIZATION AND CULTURE, PROFESSIONAL PREPARATION.

For additional information, see 7:289 (8 references);

for reviews by Harold B. Dunkel and Herbert Schueler, see 6:393 (3 references).

REFERENCES THROUGH 1971

1–3. See 6:393.
4–11. See 7:289.
12. Villarreal, Jose A. *The MLA-Cooperative Foreign Language Proficiency Test as an Evaluating Instrument of the Competency of Prospective Student Teachers of Spanish, French, and German.* Master's thesis, University of Texas (Austin, Tex.), 1970.

CUMULATIVE NAME INDEX

Carroll, J. B.: 6, 10   Rehder, H.: 5
Churchill, F. J.: 4–5   Ryder, F. G.: 5
Dizney, H. F.: 7   Schueler, H.: *rev,* 6:393
Dunkel, H. B.: *rev,* 6:393   Sheppard, D. C.: 5
Gromen, L.: 7   Smith, P. D.: 11
Ladu, T. T.: 5   Spencer, R. E.: 4
McKinney, J. C.: 5   Starr, W. H.: 1–3
Marchand, J. W.: 5   Tollinger, S.: 5
Mueller, K. A.: 5   Villarreal, J. A.: 12
Paquette, F. A.: 4–5, 8   Wallmark, M.: 4, 8
Perkins, J. A.: 9

[272]

MLA-Cooperative Foreign Language Tests: German. 1–2 years high school or 2 semesters college, 3–4 years high school or 4 semesters college; 1963–65; 4 tests in a single booklet: listening, speaking, reading, writing; writing test available as separate; prepared in cooperation with the Modern Language Association of America; Cooperative Tests and Services. *

For additional information and a review by T. F. Naumann, see 7:290 (2 references). For an excerpted review by John L. D. Clark of the series, see 7:254.

REFERENCES THROUGH 1971

1–2. See 7:290.
3. Smith, Philip D., Jr. *A Comparison of the Cognitive and Audiolingual Approaches to Foreign Language Instruction: The Pennsylvania Foreign Language Project.* Philadelphia, Pa.: Center for Curriculum Development, Inc., 1970. Pp. xxv, 380. *

CUMULATIVE NAME INDEX

Aleamoni, L. M.: 2   Paquette, F. A.: 1
Churchill, F. J.: 1   Smith, P. D.: 3
Clark, J. L. D.: *exc,* 7:254   Spencer, R. E.: 1–2
Naumann, T. F.: *rev,* 7:290   Wallmark, M.: 1

[273]

*National German Examination for High School Students. 2, 3, or 4 years high school; 1960–73; formerly called *AATG German Test* and *National German Contest for High School Students;* tests administered annually in February/March under auspices of high school guidance departments or centers established by the publisher; American Association of Teachers of German with the technical assistance of Educational Testing Service; program administered by American Association of Teachers of German, Inc. *

For additional information and reviews by Gilbert C. Kettelkamp and Theodor F. Naumann of an earlier edition, see 6:382.

[274]

*National Teacher Examinations: German. College seniors and teachers; 1970–73; derived from *MLA Foreign Language Proficiency Tests for Teachers and Advanced Students: German;* Educational Testing Service. * For the testing program entry, see 869.

For additional information, see 7:291. For reviews of the testing program, see 7:582 (2 reviews), 6:700 (1 review), 5:538 (3 reviews), and 4:802 (1 review).

[275]

Pimsleur German Proficiency Tests. "First-level, . . . second-level" courses in grades 7–16; 1967; 4 tests; Paul Pimsleur; Harcourt Brace Jovanovich, Inc. *

a) TEST 1, LISTENING COMPREHENSION.
b) TEST 2, SPEAKING PROFICIENCY.
c) TEST 3, READING COMPREHENSION.
d) TEST 4, WRITING PROFICIENCY.
For additional information, reviews by Walter F. W. Lohnes and Jack M. Stein, and an excerpted review by Garold N. Davis, see 7:292. For an excerpted review by A. Ralph Hakstian of this and other tests (French, Spanish) in the series, see 7:257.

[276]
*The Undergraduate Program Field Tests: German Test.** College; 1969–73; formerly called *The Undergraduate Record Examinations: German Test;* test available to colleges for local administration; Educational Testing Service. * For the testing program entry, see 1062.
For additional information, see 7:293. For reviews of the testing program, see 7:671 (2 reviews).

[Out of Print Since TIP I]
College Entrance Examination Board Achievement Test: German Listening Comprehension, 6:384 (2 reviews, 1 reference)
Common Concepts Foreign Language Test: German, 7:286 (1 review)
First Year German Test, 5:274 (1 review)
German: Every Pupil Test, 6:389
Lundeberg-Tharp Audition Test in German, 3:194 (1 review)

GREEK

[277]
*College Placement Test in Greek Reading.** Entering college freshmen; 1962–72, c1957–72; formerly called *College Placement Test in Greek;* reprinting of inactive 1957 form of *College Board Achievement Test in Greek;* test available to colleges for local administration; program administered for the College Entrance Examination Board by Educational Testing Service. * For the testing program entry, see 1051.
For additional information, see 7:295. For a review of the testing program, see 7:665. For a review of the *College Board Achievement Test in Greek,* see 5:277.

[Out of Print Since TIP I]
College Board Achievement Test in Greek, 7:294 (1 review)

HEBREW

[278]
★Achievement Test—Hebrew Language. Grades 5–7; 1973; Testing Bureau of the National Curriculum Research Institute; American Association for Jewish Education. *

[279]
*College Board Achievement Test in Hebrew.** Candidates for college entrance with 2–4 years high school Hebrew; 1961–73; test administered on a specified date at centers established by the publisher; inactive forms, entitled *College Placement Test in Hebrew Reading,* are available to colleges for local administration; program administered for the College Entrance Examination Board by Educational Testing Service. * For the testing program entry, see 1048.

For additional information, see 7:296. For reviews of the testing program, see 6:760 (2 reviews).

[280]
*College Placement Test in Hebrew Reading.** Entering college freshmen; 1962–72, c1961–72; reprinting of inactive 1964 form of *College Board Achievement Test in Hebrew;* test available to colleges for local administration; program administered for the College Entrance Examination Board by Educational Testing Service. * For the testing program entry, see 1051.
For additional information, see 7:297. For a review of the testing program, see 7:665.

[281]
[NCRI Achievement Tests in Hebrew.] Grades 5–7, 7–9; 1965–67; Simon Bugatch and Judah Pilch (test); National Curriculum Research Institute, American Association for Jewish Education. *
For additional information, see 7:298.

REFERENCES THROUGH 1971
1. KAPEL, MARILYN B., AND KAPEL, DAVID E. "Hebrew English Reading Achievement in a Jewish Day School: A Comparison Among Reading Achievements and Attitudes Towards the Two Languages." *Jewish Ed* 40(3):23–32 w '70. *

CUMULATIVE NAME INDEX
Kapel, D. E.: 1   Kapel, M. B.: 1

[282]
Test on the Fundamentals of Hebrew. Grades 2–5, 3–6, 4–7; 1955–59; 4 or 5 scores: sentences (grades 3–7 only), vocabulary, stories, grammar, total; Committee on Tests of the American Association for Jewish Education; the Association. *
For additional information, see 6:397.

ITALIAN

[283]
*College Placement Test in Italian Listening Comprehension.** Entering college freshmen; 1962–72; reprinting of inactive 1966 form of *College Board Achievement Test in Italian Listening Comprehension;* test available to colleges for local administration; program administered for the College Entrance Examination Board by Educational Testing Service. * For the testing program entry, see 1051.
For additional information and a review by Paolo Valesio, see 7:299. For a review of the testing program, see 7:665.

[284]
★College Placement Test in Italian Listening-Reading. Entering college freshmen; 1971–72; reprinting of inactive 1971 form of *College Board Achievement Test in Italian Listening-Reading;* program administered for the College Entrance Examination Board by Educational Testing Service. * For the testing program entry, see 1051.
For a review of the testing program, see 7:665.

[285]
*College Placement Test in Italian Reading.** Entering college freshmen; 1962–72, c1957–72; reprinting of inactive 1966 form of *College Board Achievement Test in Italian Reading;* test available to colleges for local administration; program administered for the College Entrance Examination Board by Educational Testing Service. * For the testing program entry, see 1051.

For additional information and a review by Paolo Valesio, see 7:300. For a review of the testing program, see 7:665.

[286]

MLA Cooperative Foreign Language Proficiency Tests: Italian. Italian majors and advanced students in colleges; 1961-68; formerly called *MLA Foreign Language Proficiency Tests for Teachers and Advanced Students: Italian;* 7 tests in 3 booklets; Modern Language Association of America and Educational Testing Service; Cooperative Tests and Services. *

a) BOOK 1: READING, LISTENING COMPREHENSION, SPEAKING.

b) BOOK 2: WRITING.

c) BOOK 3: APPLIED LINGUISTICS, CIVILIZATION AND CULTURE, PROFESSIONAL PREPARATION.

For additional information and a review by Josephine Bruno Pane, see 7:301 (2 references); see also 6:403 (3 references).

REFERENCES THROUGH 1971

1-3. See 6:403.
4-5. See 7:301.

CUMULATIVE NAME INDEX

Castiglione, P. B.: 4	Pane, J. B.: *rev,* 7:301
Di Pietro, R. J.: 4	Paquette, F. A.: 4-5
Ladu, T. T.: 4	Sheppard, D. C.: 4
Lazzarino, G.: 4	Starr, W. H.: 1-3
MacAllister, A. T.: 4	Tollinger, S.: 4
McKinney, J. C.: 4	Wallmark, M.: 5
Olson, P. R.: 4	

[287]

MLA-Cooperative Foreign Language Tests: Italian. 1-2 years high school or 2 semesters college, 3-4 years high school or 4 semesters college; 1963-65; 4 tests in a single booklet: listening, speaking, reading, writing; writing test available as separate; prepared in cooperation with the Modern Language Association of America; Cooperative Tests and Services. *

For additional information and a review by Josephine Bruno Pane, see 7:302. For an excerpted review by John L. D. Clark of the series, see 7:254.

[Out of Print Since TIP I]

College Entrance Examination Board Achievement Test: Italian Listening Comprehension, 6:398
College Entrance Examination Board Achievement Test: Italian Reading and Essay, 6:399; formerly called *College Entrance Examination Board Achievement Test in Italian,* 5:279

LATIN

[288]

*Advanced Placement Examination in Classics. High school students desiring credit for college level courses or admission to advanced courses; 1954-73; formerly called *Advanced Placement Examination in Latin;* 3 tests (candidate elects 1 or 2): Vergil, Lyric, Prose; available to secondary schools for annual administration on specified days in May; inactive forms are available to colleges for local administration in the *Testing Academic Achievement* program; program administered for the College Entrance Examination Board by Educational Testing Service. * For the testing program entry, see 1045.

For additional information concerning earlier forms, see 7:303. For reviews of the testing program, see 7: 662 (2 reviews).

College Placement Test in Italian Reading

[289]

*College Board Achievement Test in Latin. Candidates for college entrance with 2-4 years high school Latin; 1901-73; test administered on specified dates at centers established by the publisher; inactive forms, entitled *College Placement Test in Latin Reading,* are available to colleges for local administration; program administered for the College Entrance Examination Board by Educational Testing Service. * For the testing program entry, see 1048.

For additional information, see 7:304; for a review by Konrad Gries of an earlier form, see 5:280 (1 reference); for a review by Harold B. Dunkel, see 4:250 (2 references). For reviews of the testing program, see 6:760 (2 reviews).

REFERENCES THROUGH 1971

1-2. See 4:250.
3. See 5:280.

CUMULATIVE NAME INDEX

Colby, J. K.: 2	Harwood, F. C.: 2
College Entrance Examination Board: 3	Murphy, C. T.: 2
	Shero, L. R.: 2
Dunkel, H. B.: *rev,* 4:250	Spaeth, J. W.: 2
Gries, K.: *rev,* 5:280	Tucker, L. R.: 1

[290]

*College Placement Test in Latin Reading. Entering college freshmen; 1962-72, c1955-72; reprintings of inactive 1963 and 1964 forms of *College Board Achievement Test in Latin;* test available to colleges for local administration; program administered for the College Entrance Examination Board by Educational Testing Service. * For the testing program entry, see 1051.

For additional information, see 7:305. For a review of the testing program, see 7:665. For reference to reviews of the *College Board Achievement Test in Latin,* see 289.

[291]

Cooperative Latin Test: Elementary and Advanced Levels. 1-4 semesters high school or 1-2 semesters college, more than 4 semesters high school or more than 2 semesters college; 1932-41; 4 scores: reading, vocabulary, grammar, total; George A. Land; Cooperative Tests and Services. *

For additional information, see 3:204 (1 reference); for reviews by Harold B. Dunkel and John Flagg Gummere of an earlier form of the elementary level, see 2:1365; for a review by S. D. Atkins, see 1:1065; for a review by Norman T. Pratt, Jr. of an earlier form of the advanced level, see 1:1064.

REFERENCES THROUGH 1971

1. See 3:204.
2. TRAXLER, ARTHUR E. "The Correlation Between Achievement Scores and School Marks in an Independent School for Boys." *J Appl Psychol* 24:58-63 F '40. * (*PA* 14:3766)
3. TRAXLER, ARTHUR E. "Reliability of Cooperative Achievement Tests for Independent Secondary School Pupils." *Ed Rec B* 68:64-8 Jl '56. * (*PA* 31:8853)

CUMULATIVE NAME INDEX

Atkins, S. D.: *rev,* 1:1065	Pratt, N. T.: *rev,* 1:1064
Dunkel, H. B.: *rev,* 2:1365	Traxler, A. E.: 1-3
Gummere, J. F.: *rev,* 2:1365	

[292]

Emporia First Year Latin Test. 1 year high school; 1962-64; first published 1962-63 in the Every Pupil Scholarship Test series; Bernadine Sitts, Minnie M. Miller, Lillian A. Wall, and M. W. Sanders; Bureau of Educational Measurements. *

For additional information, see 7:306.

[293]

Emporia Second Year Latin Test. 2 years high school; 1962–64; first published 1962–63 in the Every Pupil Scholarship Test series; Bernadine Sitts, Minnie M. Miller, Lillian A. Wall, and M. W. Sanders; Bureau of Educational Measurements. *
For additional information, see 7:307.

[294]

Latin I and II: Achievement Examinations for Secondary Schools. 1–2 years high school; 1951–59; Form 4 ('55) is the only form in print; High School Achievement Examinations, Midwest High School Achievement Examinations, and Minnesota High School Achievement Examinations were also used as series titles; Margaret M. Forbes; Bobbs-Merrill Co., Inc. *
For additional information concerning later and earlier forms, see 6:409, 5:284, and 5:286.

[Out of Print Since TIP I]

Cicero Test, 2:1363 (1 review)
First- and Second-Year Latin: Every Pupil Test, 6:407
First Year Latin: Every Pupil Scholarship Test, 6:408
First Year Latin: Manchester Semester-End Achievement Tests, T:670, 36:765
First Year Latin Test: State High School Tests for Indiana, 4:252
Holtz Vergil Test, 2:1366 (2 reviews)
Kansas First Year Latin Test, 5:283 (2 reviews)
Kansas Second Year Latin Test, 4:254 (2 reviews)
Latin Test (Two-Year Course): Affiliation Testing Program for Catholic Secondary Schools, 6:410 (1 review)
Orleans-Solomon Latin Prognosis Test, 3:207 (1 review)
Powers Diagnostic Latin Test, 2:1370 (2 reviews)
Second Year Latin: Every Pupil Scholarship Test, 6:411
Second Year Latin: Manchester Semester-End Achievement Tests, T:683, 36:771
Second Year Latin Test: State High School Tests for Indiana, 4:257
Ullman-Kirby Latin Comprehension Test, T:684

RUSSIAN

[295]

★College Board Achievement Test in Russian Listening-Reading. Candidates for college entrance with 2–4 years high school Russian; 1971–73; test administered each spring at centers established by the publisher; inactive forms, entitled *College Placement Test in Russian Listening-Reading,* are available to colleges for local administration; program administered for the College Entrance Examination Board by Educational Testing Service. * For the testing program entry, see 1048.
For reviews of the testing program, see 6:760 (2 reviews).

[296]

*College Placement Test in Russian Listening Comprehension. Entering college freshmen; 1962–72; reprinting of inactive 1968 form of *College Board Achievement Test in Russian Listening Comprehension;* test available to colleges for local administration; program administered for the College Entrance Examination Board by Educational Testing Service. * For the testing program entry, see 1051.

For additional information, see 7:308 (1 reference). For a review of the testing program, see 7:665.

REFERENCES THROUGH 1971
1. See 7:308.

CUMULATIVE NAME INDEX
Aleamoni, L. M.: 1   Matsunaga, A.: 1

[297]

★College Placement Test in Russian Listening-Reading. Entering college freshmen; 1971–72; reprinting of inactive 1971 form of *College Board Achievement Test in Russian Listening-Reading;* test available to colleges for local administration; program administered for the College Entrance Examination Board by Educational Testing Service. * For the testing program entry, see 1051.
For a review of the testing program, see 7:665.

[298]

*College Placement Test in Russian Reading. Entering college freshmen; 1962–72; reprintings of inactive 1964 and 1965 forms of *College Board Achievement Test in Russian;* test available to colleges for local administration; program administered for the College Entrance Examination Board by Educational Testing Service. * For the testing program entry, see 1051.
For additional information, see 7:309. For a review of the testing program, see 7:665.

[299]

*Graduate School Foreign Language Test: Russian. Graduate level degree candidates required to demonstrate reading proficiency in Russian; 1963–73; test administered on a special basis; Educational Testing Service. * For the testing program entry, see 219.
For additional information, see 7:310 (4 references).

REFERENCES THROUGH 1971
1–4. See 7:310.

CUMULATIVE NAME INDEX
Aleamoni, L. M.: 4   Harvey, P. R.: 3
Bartlett, A. A.: 1   Matsunaga, A.: 4
Clark, J. L. D.: 2

[300]

MLA Cooperative Foreign Language Proficiency Tests: Russian. Russian majors and advanced students in college; 1960–68; formerly called *MLA Foreign Language Proficiency Tests for Teachers and Advanced Students: Russian;* 7 tests in 3 booklets; 1966 test identical with tests copyrighted 1961 except for format and directions; Modern Language Association of America and Educational Testing Service; Cooperative Tests and Services. *
a) BOOK 1: READING, LISTENING COMPREHENSION, SPEAKING.
b) BOOK 2: WRITING.
c) BOOK 3: APPLIED LINGUISTICS, CIVILIZATION AND CULTURE, PROFESSIONAL PREPARATION.
For additional information, see 7:311 (3 references); for a review by Wayne D. Fisher, see 6:417 (3 references).

REFERENCES THROUGH 1971
1–3. See 6:417.
4–6. See 7:311.

CUMULATIVE NAME INDEX
Baker, R. L.: 4   Moser, C. A.: 4
Carroll, J. B.: 5   Paquette, F. A.: 4
Chandler, D.: 4   Perkins, J. A.: 6
Fisher, W. D.: *rev,* 6:417   Sheppard, D. C.: 4
Ignatieff, E.: 4   Starr, W. H.: 1–3
Ladu, T. T.: 4   Tollinger, S.: 4
McKinney, J. C.: 4   Twarog, L. I.: 4

[301]

MLA-Cooperative Foreign Language Tests: Russian. 1–2 years high school or 2 semesters college, 3–4 years high school or 4 semesters college; 1963–65; 4 tests in a single booklet: listening, speaking, reading, writing; writing test available as separate; prepared in cooperation with the Modern Language Association of America; Cooperative Tests and Services. *

For additional information and an excerpted review by Raymond L. Bair, see 7:312 (2 references). For an excerpted review by John L. D. Clark of the series, see 7:254.

REFERENCES THROUGH 1971

1–2. See 7:312.
3. SHANE, ALEX M. "An Evaluation of the Existing College Norms for the MLA-Cooperative Russian Test and Its Efficacy as a Placement Examination." *Mod Lang J* 55(2):93–9 F '71.*

CUMULATIVE NAME INDEX

Aleamoni, L. M.: 2   Shane, A. M.: 3
Bair, R. L.: 1; *exc*, 7:312   Spencer, R. E.: 2
Clark, J. L. D.: *exc*, 7:254

[Out of Print Since TIP I]

College Entrance Examination Board Achievement Test: Russian, 6:412
College Entrance Examination Board Achievement Test: Russian Listening Comprehension, 6:413

SPANISH

[302]

*Advanced Placement Examination in Spanish. High school students desiring credit for college level courses or admission to advanced courses; 1954–73; available to secondary schools for annual administration on specified days in May; inactive forms are available to colleges for local administration in the *Testing Academic Achievement* program; program administered for the College Entrance Examination Board by Educational Testing Service. * For the testing program entry, see 1045.

For additional information concerning earlier forms, see 7:313 (2 references); see also 6:421 (1 reference). For reviews of the testing program, see 7:662 (2 reviews).

REFERENCES THROUGH 1971

1. See 6:421.
2–3. See 7:313.

CUMULATIVE NAME INDEX

Englekirk, J. E.: 2   Valley, J. R.: 1
Turner, A. R.: 3

[303]

Baltimore County Spanish Test. 1 year high school; 1962; 2 scores: parts A, B; Baltimore County Spanish Language Committee; Bobbs-Merrill Co., Inc. *

For additional information and a review by Mariette Schwarz, see 6:418.

[304]

★College Board Achievement Test in Spanish Listening-Reading. Candidates for college entrance with 2–4 years high school Spanish; 1971–73; test administered each spring at centers established by the publisher; inactive forms, entitled *College Placement Test in Spanish Listening-Reading,* are available to colleges for local administration; program administered for the College Entrance Examination Board by Educational Testing Service. * For the testing program entry, see 1048.

For reviews of the testing program, see 6:760 (2 reviews).

[305]

*College Board Achievement Test in Spanish Reading. Candidates for college entrance with 2–4 years high school Spanish; 1902–73; test administered on specified dates at centers established by the publisher; inactive forms, entitled *College Placement Test in Spanish Reading,* are available to colleges for local administration; program administered for the College Entrance Examination Board by Educational Testing Service. * For the testing program entry, see 1048.

For additional information, see 7:314; see also 6:419 (1 reference), 5:287 (1 reference), and 4:259 (3 references). For reviews of the testing program, see 6:760 (2 reviews).

REFERENCES THROUGH 1971

1–3. See 4:259.
4. See 5:287.
5. See 6:419.

CUMULATIVE NAME INDEX

Cabat, L.: 5   Godin, J. D.: 5
College Entrance Examination   Tucker, L. R.: 2
   Board: 4   Walsh, D. D.: 3
Dyer, H. S.: 1

[306]

*College Placement Test in Spanish Listening Comprehension. Entering college freshmen; 1962–72, c1955–72; reprintings of inactive 1969 and 1970 forms of *College Board Achievement Test in Spanish Listening Comprehension;* test available to colleges for local administration; program administered for the College Entrance Examination Board by Educational Testing Service. * For the testing program entry, see 1051.

For additional information concerning earlier forms, see 7:315 (1 reference); see also 6:422 (1 reference). For a review of the testing program, see 7:665.

REFERENCES THROUGH 1971

1. See 6:422.
2. See 7:315.

CUMULATIVE NAME INDEX

Aleamoni, L. M.: 2   Scheider, R. M.: 1
Matsunaga, A.: 2

[307]

★College Placement Test in Spanish Listening-Reading. Entering college freshmen; 1971–72; reprinting of inactive 1971 form of *College Board Achievement Test in Spanish Listening-Reading;* test available to colleges for local administration; program administered for the College Entrance Examination Board by Educational Testing Service. * For the testing program entry, see 1051.

For a review of the testing program, see 7:665.

[308]

*College Placement Test in Spanish Reading. Entering college freshmen; 1962–72, c1955–72; reprintings of inactive 1963 forms of *College Board Achievement Test in Spanish Reading;* test available to colleges for local administration; program administered for the College Entrance Examination Board by Educational Testing Service. * For the testing program entry, see 1051.

For additional information, see 7:316 (1 reference). For a review of the testing program, see 7:665.

REFERENCES THROUGH 1971

1. See 7:316.

CUMULATIVE NAME INDEX

Aleamoni, L. M.: 1   Matsunaga, A.: 1

[309]

First Year Spanish Test. High school and college; 1947–68; revision of *Kansas First Year Spanish Test;* Oscar F. Hernández and Minnie M. Miller; Bureau of Educational Measurements. *

For additional information, see 7:318.

[310]

Furness Test of Aural Comprehension in Spanish. 1–3 years high school or 1–2 years college; 1945–51; 2 editions; Edna Lue Furness; National Textbook Co. *

a) ORIGINAL EDITION. 1945–46; 4 scores: vocabulary, completion, identification, total; 1946 tests identical with tests copyrighted 1945.

b) RECORDED EDITION. 1951; 5 scores: vocabulary, completion, identification, question-answer, total.

For additional information, see 4:262; for reviews by Frederick B. Agard and Walter V. Kaulfers of *a*, see 3:213.

REFERENCES THROUGH 1971

1. FURNESS, EDNA L. *An Experiment in Objective Measurement of Aural Comprehension of Spanish.* Doctor's thesis, University of Colorado (Boulder, Colo.), 1952.

CUMULATIVE NAME INDEX

Agard, F. B.: *rev, 3*:213   Kaulfers, W. V.: *rev, 3*:213
Furness, E. L.: 1

[311]

*The Graduate Record Examinations Advanced Spanish Test. Graduate school candidates; 1946–72; 4 scores: language knowledge, peninsular topics, Hispano-American topics, total; Educational Testing Service. * For the testing program entry, see 1053.

For additional information and a review by Gino Parisi of an earlier form, see 7:319. For reviews of the testing program, see 7:667 (1 review) and 5:601 (1 review).

[312]

*Graduate School Foreign Language Test: Spanish. Graduate level degree candidates required to demonstrate reading proficiency in Spanish; 1963–73; test administered 4 times annually (January, April, June, October) at centers established by the publisher; Educational Testing Service. * For the testing program entry, see 219.

For additional information and a review by Robert Lado, see 7:320 (3 references).

REFERENCES THROUGH 1971

1–3. See 7:320.

CUMULATIVE NAME INDEX

Bartlett, A. A.: 1   Harvey, P. R.: 3
Clark, J. L. D.: 2   Lado, R.: *rev, 7*:320

[313]

Iowa Placement Examinations: Spanish Training. Grades 12–13; 1925–26; test by G. E. Vander Beke and G. D. Stoddard; Bureau of Educational Research and Service. *

For additional information and a review by Harry J. Russell, see 3:212 (2 references).

REFERENCES THROUGH 1971

1–2. See 3:212.
3. HAMMOND, H. P., AND STODDARD, GEORGE DINSMORE. "A Study of Placement Examinations." *Univ Iowa Studies Ed* 4(7):1–59 '28. * (*PA* 3:2069)
4. RICE, GEORGE A. Chap. 11, "A Study of Achievement in French and Spanish in Junior and Senior High School, With Consideration of Some of the Factors That Condition Achievement," pp. 433–71. In *Studies in Modern Language Teaching.* By E. W. Bagster-Collins and Others. New York: Macmillan Co., 1930. Pp. xxxi, 491. *

5. THARP, JAMES BURTON. Chap. 10, "Sectioning in Romance Language Classes at the University of Illinois," pp. 365–432. In *Studies in Modern Language Teaching.* By E. W. Bagster-Collins and Others. New York: Macmillan Co., 1930. Pp. xxxi, 491. *

CUMULATIVE NAME INDEX

Hammond, H. P.: 3   Russell, H. J.: *rev, 3*:212
Miller, L. W.: 2   Stoddard, G. D.: 1, 3
Rice, G. A.: 4   Tharp, J. B.: 5

[314]

MLA Cooperative Foreign Language Proficiency Tests: Spanish. Spanish majors and advanced students in college; 1960–68; formerly called *MLA Foreign Language Proficiency Tests for Teachers and Advanced Students: Spanish;* 7 tests in 3 booklets; 1966 test identical with tests copyrighted 1961 except for format and directions; Modern Language Association of America and Educational Testing Service; Cooperative Tests and Services. *

a) BOOK 1: READING, LISTENING COMPREHENSION, SPEAKING.

b) BOOK 2: WRITING.

c) BOOK 3: APPLIED LINGUISTICS, CIVILIZATION AND CULTURE, PROFESSIONAL PREPARATION.

For additional information and a review by Glen W. Probst, see 7:321 (6 references); for a review by Walter V. Kaulfers, see 6:427 (3 references).

REFERENCES THROUGH 1971

1–3. See 6:427.
4–9. See 7:321.
10. VILLARREAL, JOSE A. *The MLA-Cooperative Foreign Language Proficiency Test as an Evaluating Instrument of the Competency of Prospective Student Teachers of Spanish, French, and German.* Master's thesis, University of Texas (Austin, Tex.), 1970.

CUMULATIVE NAME INDEX

Carroll, J. B.: 6   Perkins, J. A.: 9
Churchill, F. J.: 4   Probst, G. W.: *rev, 7*:321
Ciruti, J. E.: 5   Ruisanchez-Lopez, L.: 5
Dizney, H. F.: 7   Sheppard, D. C.: 5
Griffin, D.: 5   Spencer, R. E.: 4
Gromen, L.: 7   Starr, W. H.: 1–3
Kaulfers, W. V.: *rev, 6*:427   Tollinger, S.: 5
Ladu, T. T.: 5   Villarreal, J. A.: 10
McKinney, J. C.: 5   Wallmark, M.: 4, 8
Meade, R. G.: 5   Wilkins, G. W.: 5
Paquette, F. A.: 4–5, 8

[315]

MLA-Cooperative Foreign Language Tests: Spanish. 1–2 years high school or 2 semesters college, 3–4 years high school or 4 semesters college; 1963–65; 4 tests in a single booklet: listening, speaking, reading, writing; writing test available as separate; prepared in cooperation with the Modern Language Association of America; Cooperative Tests and Services. *

For additional information and a review by Robert Lado, see 7:322 (2 references). For an excerpted review by John L. D. Clark of the series, see 7:254.

REFERENCES THROUGH 1971

1–2. See 7:322.

CUMULATIVE NAME INDEX

Aleamoni, L. M.: 2   Paquette, F. A.: 1
Churchill, F. J.: 1   Spencer, R. E.: 1–2
Clark, J. L. D.: *exc, 7*:254   Wallmark, M.: 1
Lado, R.: *rev, 7*:322

[316]

*National Spanish Examination. 1, 2, 3, 4, 5 years junior high school and high school; 1957–73; NSE; new form issued annually for administration in April at local secondary schools or centers established by local chapters of the AATSP; 4 scores: aural, usage, reading comprehension, total; [Test Development Committee, American Association of Teachers of Spanish and Portuguese]; the Association (distributed by local chapter treasurers and the national chairman). *

For additional information and a review by Walter V. Kaulfers of earlier forms, see 7:323 (1 reference); see also 6:428 (8 references).

REFERENCES THROUGH 1971
1–8. See 6:428.
9. See 7:323.

CUMULATIVE NAME INDEX
Boyer, M. V.: 8   Kaulfers, W. V.: rev, 7:323
Charly, H. T.: 1, 3–9   Powell, J. D.: 2–4
Hartsook, J. H.: 4–6   Saporta, S.: 1

[317]
*National Teacher Examinations: Spanish. College seniors and teachers; 1970–73; derived from MLA Foreign Language Proficiency Tests for Teachers and Advanced Students: Spanish; an inactive form (1967) entitled Teacher Education Examination Program: Spanish is available to colleges for local administration; the same inactive form entitled Spanish is available to school systems for local use as part of the program entitled School Personnel Research and Evaluation Services; Educational Testing Service. * For the testing program entry, see 869.

For additional information, see 7:324. For reviews of the testing program, see 7:582 (2 reviews), 6:700 (1 review), 5:538 (3 reviews), and 4:802 (1 review).

[318]
Pimsleur Spanish Proficiency Tests. "First-level, ...second-level" courses in grades 7–16; 1967; 4 tests; Paul Pimsleur; Harcourt Brace Jovanovich, Inc. *
a) TEST 1, LISTENING COMPREHENSION.
b) TEST 2, SPEAKING PROFICIENCY.
c) TEST 3, READING COMPREHENSION.
d) TEST 4, WRITING PROFICIENCY.

For additional information, a review by Gino Parisi, and an excerpted review by E. E. Bilyeu, see 7:325. For an excerpted review by A. Ralph Hakstian of this and other tests (French, German) in the series, see 7:257.

[319]
Second Year Spanish Test. High school and college; 1953–68; revision of Kansas Second Year Spanish Test; Oscar F. Hernández and Minnie M. Miller; Bureau of Educational Measurements. *
For additional information, see 7:326.

[320]
Spanish I and II: Achievement Examinations for Secondary Schools. 1–2 years high school; 1951–55;

Form 4 ('55) is the only form in print; Midwest High School Achievement Examinations and Minnesota High School Achievement Examinations were also used as series titles; Emma Marie Birkmaier and Walter Pederson; Bobbs-Merrill Co., Inc. *
For additional information concerning earlier forms, see 6:429 and 5:292–3.

[321]
*Teacher Education Examination Program: Spanish. College seniors preparing to teach secondary school; 1957–72; reprinting of inactive 1967 form of National Teacher Examinations: Spanish; test available to colleges for local administration; Educational Testing Service. * For the testing program entry, see 898.

For additional information concerning an earlier form, see 6:430. For a review of the testing program, see 5:543.

[322]
*The Undergraduate Program Field Tests: Spanish Test. College; 1969–73; formerly called The Undergraduate Record Examinations: Spanish Test; test available to colleges for local administration; Educational Testing Service. * For the testing program entry, see 1062.

For additional information concerning an earlier form, see 7:327. For reviews of the testing program, see 7:671 (2 reviews).

[Out of Print Since TIP I]
College Entrance Examination Board Achievement Test: Spanish Listening Comprehension, 6:420
Common Concepts Foreign Language Test: Spanish, 7:317
Cooperative Spanish Test: Elementary and Advanced Forms, 2:1373–4 (4 reviews, 1 reference)
First Year Spanish Test: State High School Tests for Indiana, 4:261
Lundeberg-Tharp Audition Test in Spanish, 3:211 (2 reviews, 1 excerpt)
Silent Reading Test in Spanish, T:704b
Spanish and Latin American Life and Culture, 5:291 (1 review)
Spanish Test (Two-Year Course): Affiliation Testing Program for Catholic Secondary Schools, 6:431 (1 review)
Test of Spanish Vocabulary, T:704a

INTELLIGENCE

GROUP

[323]
A.C.E.R. Advanced Test B40. Ages 13 and over; 1940–66; formerly called Adult Test (B40); 1965 test identical with test copyrighted 1940 except for 2 revised items; 1966 manual identical with manual published

1964 except for key to 2 items; Australian Council for Educational Research [Australia]. *
For additional information, see 7:328 (4 references); for a review by C. Sanders, see 5:296 (3 references).

REFERENCES THROUGH 1971
1–3. See 5:296.
4–7. See 7:328.
8. ANDERSON, A. W. "School of Entry and First-Year Aca-

demic Performance in the University of Western Australia."
Austral J Higher Ed 1:20–3 N '61. *

9. HOGBEN, D. "The Academic Progress of Science Students in the University of Western Australia." *Austral J Higher Ed* 1:24–8 N '61. *

10. SMALL, J. J. "A Case Study Approach to Success and Failure Among First Year Students in New Zealand." *Austral J Higher Ed* 1:80–90 N '63.*

11. POND, L. "A Study of High-Achieving and Low-Achieving University Freshmen." *Austral J Higher Ed* 2:73–8 N '64. *

12. START, K. B. "Intelligence and the Improvement in a Gross Motor Skill After Mental Practice." *Brit J Ed Psychol* 34:85–90 F '64. * (*PA* 38:7246)

13. ADCOCK, C. J., AND WEBBERLEY, M. "Primary Mental Abilities." *J General Psychol* 84(2):229–43 Ap '71. * (*PA* 46:4979)

CUMULATIVE NAME INDEX

Adcock, C. J.: 13
Anderson, A. W.: 4, 6, 8
Cook, P. H.: 1
Hogben, D.: 5, 7, 9
Hohne, H. H.: 2–3
Pond, L.: 11
Sanders, C.: *rev,* 5:296
Small, J. J.: 10
Start, K. B.: 12
Webberley, M.: 13

[324]

*A.C.E.R. Advanced Tests AL and AQ. College and superior adults; 1953–73; 2 tests; D. Spearritt (manual); Australian Council for Educational Research [Australia]. *

a) TEST AL. 1953–55; linguistic.

b) TEST AQ. 1953–73; quantitative; 1973 metric edition identical with test published 1954 except for 2 new and 4 revised items.

For additional information and a review by Duncan Howie, see 5:295.

REFERENCES THROUGH 1971

1. POND, L. "A Study of High-Achieving and Low-Achieving University Freshmen." *Austral J Higher Ed* 2:73–8 N '64. *

2. CHEONG, GEORGE S. C. "Relations Among Age, Schooling, Differential Aptitude Test, and the ACER Test." *Ed & Psychol Meas* 30(2):479–82 su '70. *

3. GAUDRY, ERIC, AND SPIELBERGER, CHARLES D. "Anxiety and Intelligence in Paired-Associate Learning." *J Ed Psychol* 61(5):386–91 O '70. * (*PA* 45:1705)

CUMULATIVE NAME INDEX

Cheong, G. S. C.: 2
Gaudry, E.: 3
Howie, D.: *rev,* 5:295
Pond, L.: 1
Spielberger, C. D.: 3

[325]

*A.C.E.R. Higher Tests. Ages 13 and over; 1944–73; formerly called *A.C.E.R. General Ability Test: Advanced M;* 3 scores: linguistic, quantitative, total; 2 parts; D. Spearritt (original manual), M. L. Clark (revised manual), and B. Christeson (form W); Australian Council for Educational Research [Australia]. *

a) FORMS ML AND WL [LINGUISTIC]. 1973 metric edition of form WL identical with form published 1959 except for 2 revised items.

b) FORMS MQ AND WQ [QUANTITATIVE]. 1973 metric edition identical with forms published 1948 (MQ) and 1959 (WQ) except for 6 new and 5 revised items for MQ and 4 new and 2 revised items for WQ.

For additional information, see 6:432 (1 reference); for a review by C. Sanders, see 5:297.

REFERENCES THROUGH 1971

1. See 6:432.

2. PHILLIPS, G. R. "A Study of Psychological Tests for the Selection of Trainee Nurses: 1, General Approach." *Personnel Prac B* 20:28–32 D '64. * (*PA* 39:10886)

CUMULATIVE NAME INDEX

Casey, D. L.: 1
Mason, P. L.: 1
Phillips, G. R.: 2
Sanders, C.: *rev,* 5:297

[326]

A.C.E.R. Intermediate Test A. Ages 10-0 to 14-0; 1938–61; 1961 test essentially the same as *A.C.E.R. General Test A* ['38]; Australian Council for Educational Research [Australia]. *

For additional information, see 6:433. For excerpts from related book reviews, see 3:1110 (1 excerpt) and 2:B1005 (1 excerpt).

[327]

*A.C.E.R. Intermediate Tests C and D. Ages 10-0 to 14-0; 1939–72; 2 tests; Australian Council for Educational Research [Australia]. *

a) TEST C. 1939–53; formerly called *A.C.E.R. General Test C. Out of print.*

b) TEST D. 1947–72; 1972 metric edition of test identical with test published 1947 except for 3 new and 5 revised items; not available to government schools; D. Spearritt (original manual) and M. L. Clark (revised manual).

For additional information and a review by James Lumsden, see 5:298 (2 references).

REFERENCES THROUGH 1971

1–2. See 5:298.

3. DEWING, K. "Some Correlates of Creativity Test Performance in Seventh Grade Children." *Austral J Psychol* 22(3):269–76 D '70. * (*PA* 46:889)

CUMULATIVE NAME INDEX

Brownless, V. T.: 2
Dewing, K.: 3
Dunn, S.: 1
Dunn, S. S.: 2
Lumsden, J.: *rev,* 5:298
Spearritt, D.: 1

[328]

A.C.E.R. Junior Non-Verbal Test. Ages 8.5–12.0; 1949–53; manual by D. Spearritt; Australian Council for Educational Research [Australia]. *

For additional information and a review by D. A. Pidgeon, see 5:301 (1 reference).

REFERENCES THROUGH 1971

1. See 5:301.

2. HOWIE, DUNCAN. "Scholastic Aptitude, Reasoning, Fluency and Concentration." *Austral J Psychol* 2:100–13 D '50. * (*PA* 26:737)

3. COCHRANE, R. G.; ELKINS, J.; AND RICHMOND, DAWN M. "Analysis of Fourth Grade Testing." *Slow Learning Child* (Australia) 16(3):131–42 N '69. * (*PA* 44:18351)

4. ELKINS, J. "Some Recent Queensland Norms for Widely Used Standardized Tests." *Slow Learning Child* (Australia) 18(3):142–7 N '71. *

CUMULATIVE NAME INDEX

Cochrane, R. G.: 3
Dunn, S.: 1
Elkins, J.: 3–4
Howie, D.: 2
Pidgeon, D. A.: *rev,* 5:301
Richmond, D. M.: 3
Spearritt, D.: 1

[329]

A.C.E.R. Junior Test A. Ages 8.5–12.0; 1946–58; formerly called *General Test T;* Australian Council for Educational Research [Australia]. *

For additional information, see 6:434; for a review by R. Winterbourn, see 5:299.

[330]

A.C.E.R. Lower Grades General Ability Scale, Second Edition. Ages 6-6 to 9-1; 1962–66; 5 scores: picture vocabulary, picture arrangement, picture analogies, picture series, total; 1964 test identical with test copyrighted 1962 except for minor revisions in format; manual by M. L. Clark; Australian Council for Educational Research [Australia]. *

For additional information, see 7:329.

REFERENCES THROUGH 1971

1. ELKINS, J. "Some Recent Queensland Norms for Widely Used Standardized Tests." *Slow Learning Child* (Australia) 18(3):142–7 N '71. *

CUMULATIVE NAME INDEX

Elkins, J.: 1

[331]

*AH4, AH5, and AH6 Tests. Ages 10 and over, 13 and over, 16 and over; 1955–73; 4 tests; A. W. Heim,

K. P. Watts (*c*), and V. Simmonds (*c*); NFER Publishing Co. Ltd. [England]. *

a) AH4: GROUP TEST OF GENERAL INTELLIGENCE (1968 REVISION). Ages 10 and over; 1955–73; 2 editions.

  1) *Hand Scored Edition.* 1955–70.

  2) *Machine Scorable Edition.* 1973; manual by Peter Saville and Janice Hare.

b) AH5: GROUP TEST OF HIGH-GRADE INTELLIGENCE. Ages 13 and over; 1956–68.

c) AH6: GROUP TESTS OF HIGH-LEVEL INTELLIGENCE. Ages 16 and over; 1970; 2 tests: SEM for Scientists, Engineers and Mathematicians (potential or qualified), AG for Arts and General.

For additional information and a review by John Nisbet, see 7:331 (12 references); for a review by John Liggett of AH5 and the original edition of AH4, see 6:506; for reviews by George A. Ferguson of AH4 and J. A. Keats of AH5, see 5:390 (11 references).

REFERENCES THROUGH 1971

1–11. See 5:390.
12–23. See 7:331.
24. HEIM, ALICE W., AND WALLACE, JEAN G. "The Effects of Repeatedly Retesting the Same Group on the Same Intelligence Test: Part 1, Normal Adults." *Q J Exp Psychol* (England) 1:151–9 O '49. * (*PA* 25:6022)
25. DAVIDSON, M. A.; LEE, D.; PARNELL, R. W.; AND SPENCER, S. J. G. "The Detection of Psychological Vulnerability in Students." *J Mental Sci* (England) 101:810–25 O '55. * (*PA* 30:7161)
26. HUDSON, L. "A Differential Test of Art/Science Aptitude." *Nature* (England) 186:413–4 Ap 30 '60. *
27. EVANS, E. G. S. "Reasoning Ability and Personality Differences Among Student-Teachers." *Brit J Ed Psychol* 34:305–14 N '64. * (*PA* 39:8718)
28. GIBBONS, K. C., AND SAVAGE, R. D. "Intelligence Study Habits and Personality Factors in Academic Success—A Preliminary Report." *Durham Res R* (England) 5:8–12 S '65. *
29. OJHA, A. B.; KELVIN, R. P.; AND LUCAS, C. J. "A Note on Season of Birth and Intelligence." *Brit J Ed Psychol* 36:94–5 F '66. * (*PA* 40:6630)
30. POPPLETON, PAMELA K. "Puberty, Family Size and the Educational Progress of Girls." *Brit J Ed Psychol* 38:286–92 N '68. * (*PA* 43:6777)
31. STRINGER, PETER, AND TYSON, MOYA. "University Selection Interviewers' Ratings Related to Interviewee Self-Image." *Occup Psychol* (England) 42:49–60 Ja '68. * (*PA* 43:4563)
32. LI, ANITA KING-FUN. "Student Attitudes and Teacher Training Performance." *Ed Res* (England) 12(1):60–3 N '69. *
33. BRIERLEY, HARRY. "A Fully Automated Intellectual Test." *Brit J Social & Clin Psychol* 10(3):286–8 S '71. * (*PA* 48:3255)
34. BYRNE, P. S., AND FREEMAN, JAMES. "Postgraduate Training for General Practice: An Assessment of Aptitudes and Abilities of Trainee Entrants." *Brit J Med Ed* 5(4):293–304 D '71. *
35. CHILD, DENNIS, AND SMITHERS, ALAN. "Some Cognitive and Affective Factors in Subjective Choice." *Res Ed* (England) 5:1–9 My '71. *
36. CRAWSHAW, JOYCE E. "Investigation Into Correlation Between Scores on Tests of Creativity and Ability in Modern Educational Dance." *Brit J Phys Ed* 2(6):xliii–xlv N '71. *
37. DACEY, JOHN S., AND MADAUS, GEORGE F. "An Analysis of Two Hypotheses Concerning the Relationship Between Creativity and Intelligence." *J Ed Res* 64(5):213–6 Ja '71. * (*PA* 46:4712)
38. FRANSELLA, FAY. "A Personal Construct Theory and Treatment of Stuttering." *J Psychosom Res* (England) 15(4):433–8 D '71. *
39. HAMILTON, V., AND FREEMAN, P. "Academic Achievement and Student Personality Characteristics: Multivariate Study." *Brit J Sociol* 22(1):31–52 Mr '71. * (*PA* 47:3755)
40. HARTLEY, JAMES, AND HOLT, JANET. "The Validity of a Simplified Version of Baddeley's Three-Minute Reasoning Test." *Ed Res* (England) 14(1):70–3 N '71. * (*PA* 49:10254)
41. MEHRYAR, A. H., AND SHAPURIAN, R. "The Reliability and Validity of the Persian Form of AH5." *Brit J Ed Psychol* 41(2):209–13 Je '71. * (*PA* 47:9657)
42. SINGH, AMARJIT. "Norms for First-Year Student Nurses: General Intelligence and Personality." *Nursing Times* (England) 67(30, sup):117–9 Jl 29 '71. *
43. WATERS, W. E. "Migraine: Intelligence, Social Class, and Familial Prevalence." *Brit Med J* 2(5753):77–81 Ap 10 '71. * (*PA* 47:3566)

CUMULATIVE NAME INDEX

[332]

APT Performance Test. Adults; 1954–57; 2 tests: verbal, quantitative; distribution restricted to clients; Bentley Barnabas; Associated Personnel Technicians, Inc. *

For additional information, see 5:302.

REFERENCES THROUGH 1971

1. SANCHEZ, JOHN TRIJILLO. *A Statistical Appraisal of the APT Form of the Wonderlic Personnel Test.* Master's thesis, Kansas State College (Manhattan, Kan.), 1954.

CUMULATIVE NAME INDEX

[333]

*Abstract Reasoning: Differential Aptitude Tests. Grades 8–12 and adults; 1947–73; 2 editions; George K. Bennett, Harold G. Seashore, and Alexander G. Wesman; Psychological Corporation. * For the complete battery entry, see 1069.

a) FORM A. 1947–59. *Out of print.*

b) FORM T. 1947–73; 1972 test identical with tests copyrighted 1947 and 1961 except for item sequence.

For reviews of the complete battery, see 7:673 (1 review, 1 excerpt), 6:767 (2 reviews), 5:605 (2 reviews), 4:711 (3 reviews), and 3:620 (1 excerpt).

REFERENCES THROUGH 1971

1. WILLIAMS, NANCY. "A Study of the Validity of the Verbal Reasoning Subtests and the Abstract Reasoning Subtest of the Differential Aptitude Tests." *Ed & Psychol Meas* 12:129–31 sp '52. * (*PA* 27:5914)
2. PASRICHA, P. "A Try-out of Abstract Reasoning Test With Children of Baroda." *J Voc & Ed Guid* (India) 9:118–21 Ag '63. * (*PA* 38:6571)
3. GILES, GEORGE C., JR. "Predictive Validity of Progressive Matrices and Two Other Nonlanguage Tests of Mental Ability." *J Ed Meas* 1:65–7 Je '64. * (*PA* 39:7757)
4. SCHRECK, THOMAS C. "Selected Factors Related to Academic Success in College." *Ed & Psychol R* (India) 4:71–6 Ap '64. *
5. MARTIN, WILLIAM T. "Analysis of the Abstracting Function in Reasoning Using an Experimental Test." *Psychol Rep* 21:593–8 O '67. * (*PA* 42:4815)
6. KIRKPATRICK, JAMES J.; EWEN, ROBERT B.; BARRETT, RICHARD S.; AND KATZELL, RAYMOND A. *Testing and Fair Employment: Fairness and Validity of Personnel Tests for Different Ethnic Groups,* pp. 17–9, 25–7, 51–69. New York: New York University Press, 1968. Pp. x, 145. *
7. GRANT, DONALD L., AND BRAY, DOUGLAS W. "Validation of Employment Tests for Telephone Company Installation and Repair Occupations." *J Appl Psychol* 54(1):7–14 F '70. * (*PA* 44:5738)

CUMULATIVE NAME INDEX

[334]

Academic Alertness "AA": Individual Placement Series. Adults; 1957–66; 7 scores: general knowledge, arithmetic, vocabulary, reasoning ability, logical sequence, accuracy, total; J. H. Norman; Personnel Research Associates, Inc. *

For additional information and a review by Joel T. Campbell, see 7:332.

[335]

Academic Aptitude Test: Non-Verbal Intelligence: Acorn National Aptitude Tests. Grades 7–16 and adults; 1943–57; 4 scores: spatial relations, physical relations, graphic relations, total; 1957 test identical with test copyrighted 1944; Andrew Kobal, J. Wayne Wrightstone, and Karl R. Kunze; Psychometric Affiliates. *

For additional information, see 5:303; for a review by William B. Schrader, see 4:274.

[336]

Academic Aptitude Test: Verbal Intelligence: Acorn National Aptitude Tests. Grades 7–16 and adults; 1943–52; 4 scores: general information, mental alertness, comprehension of relations, total; 1952 test identical with test copyrighted 1943 except for minor changes; Andrew Kobal, J. Wayne Wrightstone, and Karl R. Kunze; Psychometric Affiliates. *

For additional information, see 5:304; for a review by William B. Schrader, see 4:275; for a review by Marion A. Bills, see 3:215.

[337]

Adaptability Test. Job applicants; 1942–67; Joseph Tiffin and C. H. Lawshe; Science Research Associates, Inc. *

For additional information, see 7:333 (6 references); for a review by John M. Willits, see 5:305 (13 references); for reviews by Anne Anastasi and Marion A. Bills, see 3:216 (3 references).

REFERENCES THROUGH 1971

1–3. See 3:216.
4–16. See 5:305.
17–22. See 7:333.
23. LAWSHE, C. H., AND PATINKA, PAUL J. "An Empirical Comparison of Two Methods of Test Selection and Weighting." *J Appl Psychol* 42:210–2 Je '58. * (*PA* 33:9093)
24. WRIGHTSMAN, LAWRENCE S., JR. "The Effects of the Purported Validity of a Test Upon Level of Motivation and Performance." *J Ed Res* 54:153–6 D '60. *
25. GRUENFELD, LEOPOLD W. "Selection of Executives for a Training Program." *Personnel Psychol* 14:421–31 w '61. * (*PA* 37:3922)

CUMULATIVE NAME INDEX

Albright, L. E.: 15–6   Page, H. E.: 17
Anastasi, A.: *rev*, 3:216   Patinka, P. J.: 23
Baehner, V. M.: 21   Patton, W. M.: 14
Berg, I. A.: 12   Poe, W. A.: 12
Bills, M. A.: *rev*, 3:216   Pred, G. D.: 5
Buel, W. D.: 21   Rosensteel, R. K.: 13
Chandler, R. E.: 18   Sartain, A. Q.: 3
Giese, W. J.: 7   Stromberg, E. L.: 6
Gruenfeld, L. W.: 20, 25   Thornton, G. R.: 1
Guion, R. M.: 22   Tiffin, J.: 2
Hadley, J. M.: 8–9   Wallace, S. R.: 11
Kahn, D. F.: 4, 8–9   Willits, J. M.: *rev*, 5:305
Kazmier, L. J.: 19   Wrightsman, L. S.: 24
Lawshe, C. H.: 1–2, 10, 23

[338]

Advanced Test N. Ages 15 and over; 1951–52; not available to government schools; Australian Council for Educational Research [Australia]. *

For additional information and reviews by A. E. G. Pilliner and C. Sanders, see 5:307.

[339]

American School Intelligence Test. Grades kgn–3, 4–6, 7–9, 10–12; 1961–63; ASIT; tests for grades 4–12 "developed from the *Illinois General Intelligence Scale*" ('20–26) for grades 3–8; Willis E. Pratt, M. R. Trabue, Rutherford B. Porter, and George A. W. Stouffer, Jr.; Bobbs-Merrill Co., Inc. *

For additional information and reviews by David A. Payne and Frank B. Womer, see 6:439 (1 reference).

REFERENCES THROUGH 1971

1. See 6:439.

CUMULATIVE NAME INDEX

Hofforth, R. A.: 1   Womer, F. B.: *rev*, 6:439
Payne, D. A.: *rev*, 6:439

[340]

*****Analysis of Learning Potential.** Grades 1, 2–3, 4–6, 7–9, 10–12; 1970–71; ALP; *complete test option:* 2 scores derived from the same total raw score: learning potential ("estimate of the pupil's general learning ability" compared to the same age group), general composite ("estimate of the pupil's general learning ability" compared to the same grade group); in grades 4–12 a reading-mathematics difference score (called "reading-mathematics composite prognostic differential") is also reported; *reading prognostic subtests option:* reading composite prognostic score ("an estimate of the pupil's capacity for school learning" in reading compared to the same grade group); *mathematics prognostic subtests option:* mathematics composite prognostic score ("an estimate of the pupil's capacity for school learning" in mathematics compared to the same grade group); Walter N. Durost, Eric F. Gardner, Richard Madden, and George A. Prescott; Harcourt Brace Jovanovich, Inc. *

For additional information and reviews by Lee J. Cronbach and Arthur R. Jensen, see 7:334.

REFERENCES THROUGH 1971

1. GIRARD, JUDITH ANDERSON FUNK. *A Study of the Correlations Between the Gates-MacGinitie Reading Comprehension Test and Various Subtests From the Analysis of Learning Potential.* Doctor's thesis, University of Northern Colorado (Greeley, Colo.), 1971. (*DAI* 32:5468A)
2. HEYDENBERK, WARREN ROBERT. *A Comparison of Four Methods of Estimating Reading Potential.* Doctor's thesis, University of Northern Colorado (Greeley, Colo.), 1971. (*DAI* 32:3558A)

CUMULATIVE NAME INDEX

Cronbach, L. J.: *rev*, 7:334   Heydenberk, W. R.: 2
Girard, J. A. F.: 1   Jensen, A. R.: *rev*, 7:334

[341]

Analysis of Relationships. Grades 12–16 and industry; 1960; manual subtitle is *A Test of Mental Ability;* Edwin E. Ghiselli; Consulting Psychologists Press, Inc. *

For additional information and reviews by Gustav J. Froehlich and Wimburn L. Wallace, see 6:440 (2 references).

REFERENCES THROUGH 1971

1–2. See 6:440.
3. ROSS, PAUL F., AND DUNFIELD, NEIL M. "Selecting Salesmen for an Oil Company." *Personnel Psychol* 17:75–84 sp '64. *

CUMULATIVE NAME INDEX

Dunfield, N. M.: 3   Ross, P. F.: 3
Froehlich, G. J.: *rev*, 6:440 Wallace, W. L.: *rev*, 6:440
Ghiselli, E. E.: 1–2

[341A]

The Army Alpha Examination: First Nebraska Revision. Grades 6–16 and adults; 1937–40; a revision of *Army Group Examination Alpha;* 4 scores: verbal, numerical computation, relationships, total; 1940 test identical with test copyrighted 1937; J. P. Guilford; Sheridan Psychological Services, Inc. *

For additional information and a review by Robert G. Demaree (with Louis L. McQuitty), see 4:279 (5 references); for a review by W. D. Commins, see 1:1039; see also 3:220 (77 references for *Army Group Examination Alpha* and revisions).

REFERENCES THROUGH 1971

1–4. See 3:220 (61, 66, 69, 73).
5. See 4:279.

CUMULATIVE NAME INDEX

Blakemore, A. M.: 2
Commins, W. D.: *rev*, 1:1039
Demaree, R. G.: *rev*, 4:279
Guilford, J. P.: 1, 5
Hay, E. N.: 2–3
McQuitty, L. L.: *rev*, 4:279
Rabin, A. I.: 4
Weinik, H. M.: 4

[342]

Army General Classification Test, First Civilian Edition. Grades 9–16 and adults; 1940–60; AGCT; 1947 test identical with the 1940 form 1a of the Army edition; test by Personnel Research Section, the Adjutant General's Office, War Department; Science Research Associates, Inc. *

For additional information and reviews by Bert A. Goldman and Howard B. Lyman, see 6:441 (5 references); see also 5:310 (17 references); for a review by John T. Dailey, see 4:280 (15 references); for an excerpted review, see 3:219 (14 references).

REFERENCES THROUGH 1971

1–14. See 3:219.
15–29. See 4:280.
30–46. See 5:310.
47–51. See 6:441.
52. LAYMAN, JAMES W., AND BOGUSLAVSKY, GEORGE W. "The Relationship Between Ability and Achievement in the Army Specialized Training Program." *J Psychol* 18:45–54 Jl '44. * (*PA* 19:254)
53. BINGHAM, WALTER V. "Inequalities in Adult Capacity — From Military Data." *Sci* 104:147–52 Ag 16 '46. * (*PA* 20:3967)
54. FOX, VERNON. "A Study of the Promotion of Enlisted Men in the Army." *J Appl Psychol* 31:298–305 Je '47. * (*PA* 21:4101)
55. WILLIAMS, S. B., AND LEAVITT, H. J. "Prediction of Success in Learning Japanese." *J Appl Psychol* 31:164–8 Ap '47. * (*PA* 21:2796)
56. ALTUS, W. D. "Some Correlates of Enlisted Grades in a Specialized Type of Army Installation." *J Social Psychol* 31:303–4 My '50. * (*PA* 25:3446)
57. FUCHS, EDMUND F., AND CHYATTE, CONRAD. "On the Intelligence of Soldier Criminals." *J Crim Law Criminol & Police Sci* 40:753–5 Mr–Ap '50. * (*PA* 25:1927)
58. CANTER, AARON HERMAN. "Direct and Indirect Measures of Psychological Deficit in Multiple Sclerosis: Part 1." *J General Psychol* 44:3–25 Ja '51. * (*PA* 25:7027)
59. CANTER, AARON HERMAN. "Direct and Indirect Measures of Psychological Deficit in Multiple Sclerosis: Part 2." *J General Psychol* 44:27–50 Ja '51. * (*PA* 25:7028)
60. MASON, CHARLES F. "Pre-Illness Intelligence of Mental Hospital Patients." *J Consult Psychol* 20:297–300 Ag '56. * (*PA* 31:7418)
61. FIRESTONE, RICHARD W. "Education, Intelligence, and Military Recruit Performance." *J Clin Psychol* 13:93–5 Ja '57. * (*PA* 32:6039)
62. WEINSTEIN, SIDNEY, AND TEUBER, HANS-LUKAS. "Effects of Penetrating Brain Injury on Intelligence Test Scores." *Sci* 125:1036–7 My 24 '57. * (*PA* 32:5817)
63. WEINSTEIN, SIDNEY, AND TEUBER, HANS-LUKAS. "The Role of Preinjury Education and Intelligence Level in Intellectual Loss After Brain Injury." *J Comp & Physiol Psychol* 50:535–9 O '57. * (*PA* 33:4493)
64. BRADLEY, ARTHUR DICKINSON. *Estimating Success in Technical and Skilled Trade Courses Using a Multivariate Statistical Analysis.* Doctor's thesis, University of Minnesota (Minneapolis, Minn.), 1958. (*DA* 21:313)
65. ROSS, ALAN O. "Brain Injury and Intellectual Performance." *J Consult Phychol* 22:151–2 Ap '58. * (*PA* 35:3415)
66. CROUCH, HENRIETTA H. "An Inquiry Into the Relationship of Achievement Scores and Certain Variables in an Adult High School." *J Ed Res* 55:323–6 Ap '62. * (*PA* 38:6558)
67. CURRIE, JOHN S.; ANDERSON, RICHARD J.; AND PRICE, A. COOPER. "Timed Block Counting as a Test for Organic Brain Impairment." *J Gerontol* 20:372–3 Jl '65. *
68. SILVER, MIRIAM ROST. *Characteristics and Functions of Teacher-Aides in Classes for Trainable Mentally Retarded Chil-*

dren. Doctor's thesis, University of Pittsburgh (Pittsburgh, Pa.), 1965. (*DA* 27:988A)
69. WOLINS, LEROY, AND PERLOFF, ROBERT. "The Factorial Composition of AGCT 'Subtests' Along With College Aptitude Items and High School Grades." *Ed & Psychol Meas* 25:73–8 sp '65. * (*PA* 39:13028)
70. BINGHAM, WILLIAM C.; BURKE, HENRY R.; AND MURRAY, STEWART. "Raven's Progressive Matrices: Construct Validity." *J Psychol* 62:205–9 Mr '66. * (*PA* 40:7203)
71. KINGSLEY, LEONARD, AND STRUENING, ELMER L. "Changes in Intellectual Performance of Acute and Chronic Schizophrenics." *Psychol Rep* 18:791–800 Je '66. * (*PA* 40:10283)
72. BLUMENKRANTZ, JACK; WILKIN, WENDELL R.; AND TUDDENHAM, READ D. "Relationships Between the Progressive Matrices and AGOT-3a Among Older Military Personnel." *Ed & Psychol Meas* 28:931–5 au '68. * (*PA* 43:3317)
73. PERLMAN, LEONARD G. *A Predictive Model for the Identification of Potential Dropouts From Vocational Training in a Comprehensive Rehabilitation Center.* Doctor's thesis, Pennsylvania State University (University Park, Pa.), 1968. (*DA* 29:3424A)
74. TUDDENHAM, R. D.; BLUMENKRANTZ, J.; AND WILKIN, W. R. "Age Changes on AGCT: A Longitudinal Study of Average Adults." *J Consult & Clin Psychol* 32:659–63 D '68. * (*PA* 43:4017)
75. WATSON, CHARLES G., AND KLETT, WILLIAM G. "Prediction of WAIS IQ's From the Shipley-Hartford, the Army General Classification Test and the Revised Beta Examination." *J Clin Psychol* 24:338–41 Jl '68. * (*PA* 42:16437)
76. BURKE, HENRY R., AND BINGHAM, WILLIAM C. "Raven's Progressive Matrices: More on Construct Validity." *J Psychol* 72(2):247–51 Jl '69. * (*PA* 44:71)
77. HOLLENDER, JOHN W., AND BROMAN, HARVEY J. "Intellectual Assessment in a Disadvantaged Population." *Meas & Eval Guid* 2(1):19–24 sp '69. *
78. PERLMAN, LEONARD G., AND HYLBERT, KENNETH W. "Identifying Potential Dropouts at a Rehabilitation Center." *Rehabil Counsel B* 13(2):217–25 D '69. *

CUMULATIVE NAME INDEX

Adjutant General's Office, Classification and Replacement Branch, Personnel Research Section: 5
Altus, W. D.: 19, 21, 56
Anderson, R. J.: 51, 67
Aylesworth, H. C.: 22
Bailey, H. W.: 16
Barnette, W. L.: 39
Barrett, R. S.: 46
Bernard, J.: 35
Billeter, P. E.: 4
Bingham, W. C.: 70, 76
Bingham, W. V.: 53
Bittner, R. H.: 18
Blumenkrantz, J.: 72, 74
Boguslavsky, G. W.: 52
Bond, G. L.: 30
Bradley, A. D.: 64
Bradley, G. H.: 23
Broman, H. J.: 77
Burke, H. R.: 70, 76
Callis, R.: 36
Canter, A. H.: 58–9
Chappell, T. L.: 36, 40
Christensen, T. E.: 8
Chyatte, C.: 57
Conover, D. M.: 6
Crites, J. O.: 50
Crouch, H. H.: 66
Cureton, E. E.: 24
Currie, J. S.: 67
Dailey, J. T.: *rev*, 4:280
Dallenbach, K. M.: 16
Darley, J. G.: 48
DuBois, P. H.: 26, 37
Duncan, A. J.: 10
Estes, B. W.: 49
Ferson, R. F.: 32
Firestone, R. W.: 61
Fox, V.: 54
Fruchter, B.: 33
Fuchs, E. F.: 57
Fulk, B. E.: 34
Glaser, R.: 27–8, 38
Goldman, B. A.: *rev*, 6:441
Griffith, R. M.: 9
Harrell, M. S.: 7

Harrell, T. W.: 7, 9, 17, 34
Hollender, J. W.: 77
Hylbert, K. W.: 78
Jacobs, O.: 38
Jensen, M. B.: 11
Johnson, R. H.: 30, 43
Kent, E. G.: 51
Kingsley, L.: 71
Kirkpatrick, J. J.: 24
Klett, W. G.: 75
Layman, J. W.: 52
Leavitt, H. J.: 55
LeShan, L.: 47
Lyerly, O.: 47
Lyman, H. B.: *rev*, 6:441
Marvin, S.: 47
Mason, C. F.: 31, 60
Mullineaux, J. E.: 41
Murray, S.: 70
Otterness, W. B.: 43
Patterson, C. H.: 42–4
Perlman, L. G.: 73, 78
Perloff, R.: 45, 69
Peterson, L. R.: 43
Price, A. C.: 51, 67
Renzaglia, G. A.: 36
Ross, A. O.: 65
Rotter, J. B.: 11
Silver, M. R.: 68
Spohrer, M. A.: 36
Stewart, N.: 12–3
Struening, E. L.: 71
Super, D. E.: 25, 50
Tamminen, A. W.: 29
Teuber, H. L.: 62–3
Thompson, R. B.: 15
Tuddenham, R. D.: 20, 72, 74
War Department, Adjutant General's Office, Personnel Research Section: 14
Watson, C. G.: 75
Watson, R. I.: 26, 37
Weinstein, S.: 62–3
Wilkin, W. R.: 72, 74
Williams, S. B.: 55
Wolins, L.: 45, 69
Zerof, S. A.: 49

[343]

★The BITCH Test (Black Intelligence Test of Cultural Homogeneity). Adolescents and adults; 1972; BITCH; a vocabulary test of Afro-American expressions used as an intelligence test for blacks and as "a measure of sensitivity and responsivity" to black experience when administered to whites; manual also uses the other titles: *The Bitch-100: A Culture-Specific Test* and *Black Intelligence Test of Cultural Homogeneity;* Robert L. Williams; Williams and Associates. *

[344]

*Boehm Test of Basic Concepts. Grades kgn–2; 1969–71, c1967–71; BTBC; Ann E. Boehm; Psychological Corporation. *

For additional information, reviews by Boyd R. McCandless and Charles D. Smock, and excerpted reviews by Frank S. Freeman, George Lawlor, Victor H. Noll, and Barton B. Proger, see 7:335 (1 reference).

REFERENCES THROUGH 1971
1. See 7:335.
2. VANE, JULIA R. "Importance of Considering Background Factors When Evaluating the Effects of Compensatory Education Programs Designed for Young Children." *J Sch Psychol* 9(4):393–8 w '71. * *(PA 47:11817)*

CUMULATIVE NAME INDEX

Boehm, A. E.: 1	Noll, V. H.: *exc,* 7:335
Freeman, F. S.: *exc,* 7:335	Proger, B. B.: *exc,* 7:335
Lawlor, G.: *exc,* 7:335	Smock, C. D.: *rev,* 7:335
McCandless, B. R.: *rev,* 7:335	Vane, J. R.: 2

[345]

*Business Test. Clerical workers; 1952–71; intelligence; 1971 test identical with test copyrighted in 1952; Edward N. Hay; Aptitude Test Service, Inc. *

For additional information and reviews by Louis C. Nanassy and James H. Ricks, Jr., see 5:311.

[346]

CGA Mental Ability Tests. Grades 6–9, 9–12; 1957–68; items identical with *The Henmon-Nelson Tests of Mental Ability;* for use in Canada only; Canadian Guidance Associates; distributed by Guidance Centre [Canada]. *

For additional information, see 7:336.

[347]

★C.P.66 Test. Ages 13 and over; 1966; CP66 is acronym for Comparability Project 1966; title on test booklet is *Aptitude Test C.P. 66;* 3 scores: verbal, quantitative, total; Ian M. Connaughton; NFER Publishing Co. Ltd. [England]. *

REFERENCES THROUGH 1971
1. CONNAUGHTON, I. M., AND SKURNIK, L. S. "The Comparative Effectiveness of Several Short-Cut Item Analysis Procedures." *Brit J Ed Psychol* 39(3):225–32 N '69. * *(PA 44:9257)*

CUMULATIVE NAME INDEX

Connaughton, I. M.: 1	Skurnik, L. S.: 1

[348]

California Short-Form Test of Mental Maturity, 1963 Revision. Grades kgn–1.5, 1.5–3.5, 3–4, 4–6, 6–7, 7–8, 9–12, 12–16 and adults; 1938–65; CTMM-SF; all items drawn from the long form, *California Test of Mental Maturity;* 7 scores: logical reasoning, numerical reasoning, verbal concepts, memory, language total, nonlanguage total, total; Elizabeth T. Sullivan, Willis W. Clark, and Ernest W. Tiegs; CTB/McGraw-Hill. *

For the regular edition entry, see 349.

For additional information, see 7:337 (41 references); for a review by Julian C. Stanley, see 6:443 (11 references); for a review by Cyril Burt of an earlier edition, see 5:313 (15 references); for an excerpted review by Laurance F. Shaffer, see 4:282. For reference to reviews of the regular edition, see 349.

REFERENCES THROUGH 1971
1–15. See 5:313.
16–26. See 6:443.
27–67. See 7:337.
68. WOODY, CLIFFORD. *Aptitudes, Achievements and Interests of High School Pupils.* University of Michigan, Bureau of Educational Reference and Research Bulletin No. 157. Ann Arbor, Mich.: School of Education, the University, 1945. Pp. vi, 159. *
69. EELLS, KENNETH; DAVIS, ALLISON; HAVIGHURST, ROBERT J.; HERRICK, VERGIL E.; AND TYLER, RALPH W. *Intelligence and Cultural Differences: A Study of Cultural Learning and Problem-Solving.* Chicago, Ill.: University of Chicago Press, 1951. Pp. xii, 388. * *(PA 27:5738)*
70. KITTELL, JACK E. "Bilingualism and Language: Non-Language Intelligence Scores of Third-Grade Children." *J Ed Res* 52:263–8 Mr '59. * *(PA 34:4038)*
71. MORRISON, IDA E., AND PERRY, IDA F. "Spelling and Reading Relationships With Incidence of Retardation and Acceleration." *J Ed Res* 52:222–7 F '59. * *(PA 34:2012)*
72. LLOYD, DAVID O. "Comparison of Standardized Test Results of Indian and Non-Indian in an Integrated School System." *J Am Indian Ed* 1:8–16 Je '61. *
73. KITTELL, JACK E. "Intelligence-Test Performance of Children From Bilingual Environments." *El Sch J* 64:76–83 N '63. *
74. POLLARD, ALICE G. *A Comparison of the Performance of a Group of Intellectually Retarded Children on Three Group Tests of Intelligence.* Master's thesis, Catholic University of America (Washington, D.C.), 1963.
75. BACKE, EDWARD B. *Predicting the Outcome in Second Year Algebra.* Master's thesis, Northern Illinois University (DeKalb, Ill.), 1964.
76. DIZNEY, HENRY F., AND YAMAMOTO, KAORU. "Note on Effects of Practice and Fatigue in Group Testing of Intelligence and Achievement." *Psychol Rep* 16:537–8 Ap '65. * *(PA 39:10193)*
77. FOSTER, MARION E. "A Comparison of Reading Achievement of Christchurch, New Zealand and Edmonton Alberta Public School Students of the Same Age and Number of Years of Schooling." *Alberta J Ed Res* (Canada) 11:21–31 Mr '65. * *(PA 39:16455)*
78. SINKS, NAOMI B., AND POWELL, MARVIN. "Sex and Intelligence as Factors in Achievement in Reading in Grades 4 Through 8." *J Genetic Psychol* 106:67–79 Mr '65. * *(PA 39:12952)*
79. GRAY, JAMES A. *A Study to Determine the Effectiveness of Certain Lehi Junior High School Variables in Predicting Senior High School Success.* Master's thesis, Brigham Young University (Provo, Utah), 1966.
80. WHITTEMORE, ROBERT G.; ECHEVERRIA, BEN P.; AND GRIFFIN, JOHN V. "Can We Use Existing Tests for Adult Basic Education?" *Adult Ed* 17:19–29 au '66. *
81. CICIRELLI, VICTOR G. "Sibling Constellation, Creativity, IQ, and Academic Achievement." *Child Develop* 38:481–90 Je '67. * *(PA 41:10210)*
82. SCHORR, MORTIMER. *A Study to Determine the Relationships Between Non-Language Mental Maturity and Achievement in the California Physical Performance Test.* Master's thesis, Humboldt State College (Arcata, Calif.), 1967.
83. DATTA, LOIS-ELLIN, AND SCHAEFER, EARL. "Sex and Scholastic Aptitude as Variables in Teachers' Ratings of the Adjustment and Classroom Behavior of Negro and Other Seventh-Grade Students." *J Ed Psychol* 59:94–101 Ap '68. * *(PA 42:9407)*
84. KELSEY, ANN E. *A Study of the Relationship Between Ability and Achievement.* Master's thesis, Texas Tech College (Lubbock, Tex.), 1968.
85. PAGE, BEN H. *Predicting Performance in Seventh Grade Advanced Mathematics at Kearns Junior High School.* Master's thesis, University of Utah (Salt Lake City, Utah), 1969.
86. ELEFAÑO, INOCENCIA PATIÑO. *Predicting the Educability of Children From Low Socioeconomic Status Homes.* Doctor's thesis, Rutgers—The State University (New Brunswick, N.J.), 1970. *(DAI 32:667A)*
87. MOULIN, EUGENE K. "The Effects of Client-Centered Group Counseling Using Play Media on the Intelligence, Achievement, and Psycholinguistic Abilities of Underachieving Primary School Children." *El Sch Guid & Counsel* 5(2):85–98 D '70. *
88. SMALL, JAMES FRANKLIN, II. *Auditory-Vocal and Visual-Motor Language Orientations in Elementary School Children.* Doctor's thesis, Duke University (Durham, N.C.), 1970. *(DAI 31:6268B)*
89. SMITH, PHILIP D., JR. *A Comparison of the Cognitive and Audiolingual Approaches to Foreign Language Instruction: The Pennsylvania Foreign Language Project.* Philadelphia, Pa.: Center for Curriculum Development, Inc., 1970. Pp. xxv, 380. *
90. DOUGHTY, EARL. "Test Rankings and Selection Procedures for Identifying Gifted Intermediate Elementary Students." *Ill Sch Res* 8(1):29–32 f '71. *
91. FRIEDRICHS, THOMAS DONNELLY. *Prediction of First Grade Teachers' Ratings and Objective Achievement From*

Ability and Biographical Data. Doctor's thesis, University of North Carolina (Chapel Hill, N.C.), 1971. (*DAI* 32:1211B)

92. HALL, LUCIEN T., JR. "The Prediction of Success in Each of Six Four-Year Selections of Secondary Mathematics Courses." *Sch Sci & Math* 71(8):693–6 N '71. *

93. LIEDTKE, WERNER. "Mathematics Learning and Pupil Characteristics." *Alberta J Ed Res* (Canada) 17(3):143–53 S '71. * (*PA* 48:1864)

94. O'PIELA, JOAN MARIE. *Identification of Predictor Variables of Success in First Grade Reading in Culturally Disadvantaged Inner-City Children Who Have Had a Preschool Experience.* Doctor's thesis, Wayne State University (Detroit, Mich.), 1971. (*DAI* 32:6109A)

95. STACY, BOBBY FANT. *A Comparison of Academic Achievement and Mental Maturity Test Scores of Negro High School Seniors in Predominantly White Schools With Academic Achievement and Mental Maturity Test Scores of Negro Seniors in Predominantly Negro Schools.* Doctor's thesis, Mississippi State University (State College, Miss.), 1971. (*DAI* 32:1815A)

CUMULATIVE NAME INDEX

[349]

California Test of Mental Maturity, 1963 Revision. Grades kgn–1.5, 1.5–3.5, 4–6, 7–9, 9–12, 12–16 and adults; 1936–65; CTMM; 8 scores: logical reasoning, spatial relationships, numerical reasoning, verbal concepts, memory, language total, nonlanguage total, total; Elizabeth T. Sullivan, Willis W. Clark, and Ernest W. Tiegs; CTB/McGraw-Hill. * For the short form entry, see 348.

For additional information and reviews by Bert A. Goldman and John H. Rosenbach, see 7:338 (102 ref-

erences) ; see also 6:444 (30 references) ; for reviews by Frank S. Freeman and John E. Milholland of an earlier edition, see 5:314 (34 references) ; see also 4:282 (24 references) ; for a review by Henry E. Garrett and excerpted reviews by W. Line and one other, see 3:223 (10 references) ; for reviews by Raymond B. Cattell and F. Kuhlmann and an excerpted review by David Kopel, see 2:1384 (5 references) ; for reviews by W. D. Commins, Rudolf Pintner, and Arthur E. Traxler, and an excerpted review of the short form, see 1:1042. For reference to reviews of the short form, see 348.

REFERENCES THROUGH 1971

1–5. See 2:1384.
6–15. See 3:223.
16–39. See 4:282.
40–73. See 5:314.
74–103. See 6:444.
104–205. See 7:338.

206. BONNEY, MERL E. "The Relative Stability of Social, Intellectual, and Academic Status in Grades II to IV, and the Inter-Relationships Between These Various Forms of Growth." *J Ed Psychol* 34:88–102 F '43. * (*PA* 17:3943)

207. HANSEN, CARL W. "Factors Associated With Successful Achievement in Problem Solving in Sixth Grade Arithmetic." *J Ed Res* 38:111–8 O '44. * (*PA* 19:1039)

208. WAGGONER, R. W., AND ZEIGLER, THORNTON WOODWARD. "Psychiatric Factors in Medical School Students Who Fail." *Am J Psychiatry* 103:369–76 N '46. * (*PA* 21:1671)

209. SMITH, HERBERT A. "The Relationship Between Intelligence and the Learning Which Results From the Use of Educational Sound Motion Pictures." *J Ed Res* 43:241–9 D '49. * (*PA* 24:3879)

210. STRAUS, MURRAY A. "Mental Ability and Cultural Needs: A Psychocultural Interpretation of the Intelligence Performance of Ceylon University Entrants." *Indian J Psychol* 25:21–32 pts 1–4 '50. * (*PA* 27:7158)

211. CURTIN, JAMES T. *A Factor Analysis of Verbal and Non-Verbal Tests of Intelligence.* Washington, D.C.: Catholic University of America, 1951. Pp. vii, 63. * (*PA* 27:981)

212. HOPKA, ERICH. "Correlation of College Freshmen Chemistry Marks With Some California Mental Maturity Test Scores." *Trans Kans Acad Sci* 55:465–7 D '52. * (*PA* 27:7409)

213. STRAUS, MURRAY A. "Subcultural Variation in Ceylonese Mental Ability: A Study in National Character." *J Social Psychol* 39:129–41 F '54. * (*PA* 28:8662)

214. KRANTZ, L. L. "The Relationship of Reading Abilities and Basic Skills of the Elementary School to Success in the Interpretation of the Content Materials in the High School." *J Exp Ed* 26:97–114 D '57. * (*PA* 33:4579)

215. COLEMAN, J. M.; ISCOE, IRA; AND BRODSKY, MARVIN. "The 'Draw-A-Man' Test as a Predictor of School Readiness and as an Index of Emotional and Physical Maturity." *Pediatrics* 24:275–81 Ag '59. *

216. HIRSCH, MONROE J. "The Relationship Between Refractive State of the Eye and Intelligence Test Scores." *Am J Optom* 36:12–21 Ja '59. * (*PA* 34:1099)

217. McBEE, GEORGE, AND DUKE, RALPH L. "Relationship Between Intelligence, Scholastic Motivation, and Academic Achievement." *Psychol Rep* 6:3–8 F '60. * (*PA* 34:8404)

218. SNIDER, JAMES G., AND COLADARCI, ARTHUR P. "Intelligence Test Performance of Acculturated Indian Children." *Calif J Ed Res* 11:34–6+ Ja '60. * (*PA* 34:7662)

219. McGUIRE, CARSON. "Sex Role and Community Variability in Test Performances." *J Ed Psychol* 52:61–73 Ap '61. * (*PA* 38:3207)

220. TOBIAS, MILTON, AND MICHAEL, WILLIAM B. "An Exploration Into Child Ecology: Physiological and Maturational Indices as Predictors of Measures of Achievement, Aptitude, and Adjustment." *Ed & Psychol Meas* 21:967–74 w '61. *

221. CURRY, ROBERT L. "The Effect of Socio-Economic Status on the Scholastic Achievement of Sixth-Grade Children: Part I," *Brit J Ed Psychol* 32:46–9 F '62. * (*PA* 37:2007)

222. WILLIAMS, J. R., AND KNECHT, WALTER W. "Teachers' Ratings of High-School Students on 'Likability' and Their Relation to Measures of Ability and Achievement." *J Ed Res* 56:152–5 N '62. *

223. ANDERSON, HARRY E., JR., AND SLIVINSKE, ALEC J. "A Study of Intelligence and Achievement at the Fourth-, Fifth-, and Sixth-Grade Levels." *J Exp Ed* 31:425–32 su '63. *

224. BAYLOR, CONSTANCE C. *The Predictive Efficiency of the California Test of Mental Maturity.* Master's thesis, Glassboro State College (Glassboro, N.J.), 1963.

225. BLACK, DONALD B., AND FOSTER, MARION E. "A Comparative Study of the Performance in Arithmetic of Edmonton, Alberta, and Christchurch, New Zealand, Public School Pupils of Comparable Age and Grade Level." *Alberta J Ed Res* (Canada) 9:49–59 Mr '63. *

226. KAMII, CONSTANCE K., AND WEIKART, DAVID P. "Marks, Achievement, and Intelligence of Seventh Graders Who Were

Retained (Nonpromoted) Once in Elementary School." *J Ed Res* 56:452–9 My–Je '63. *

227. PETERS, HERBERT D. "Performance of Hopi Children on Four Intelligence Tests." *J Am Indian Ed* 2:27–31 Ja '63. *

228. RUSH, ALLEN C. "Better Police Personnel Selection." *Police Chief* 30:18+ S '63. *

229. TOBIAS, MILTON, AND MICHAEL, WILLIAM B. "Dimensions of Biological and Psychological Function in Two Samples of Children in the Third Grade." *Psychol Rep* 12:759–62 Je '63. * (*PA* 38:5756)

230. YOUNG, FRANCIS A. "Reading, Measures of Intelligence and Refractive Errors." *Am J Optom* 40:257–64 My '63. *

231. BARBEE, EUNICE W. *A Comparison of the Validity of Individual and Group Administration of Intelligence Tests With First Grade Pupils.* Master's thesis, Furman University (Greenville, S.C.), 1964.

232. NADEAU, CORINNE. *A Comparison of the Performance of a Group of Intellectually Normal Children on Three Group Tests of Intelligence.* Master's thesis, Catholic University of America (Washington, D.C.), 1964.

233. ROBERTS, HERBERT CLIVE. *Predicting Performance in Shorthand at Skyline High School.* Master's thesis, University of Utah (Salt Lake City, Utah), 1964.

234. TRITES, DAVID K., AND COBB, BART B. "Problems in Air Traffic Management: 4, Comparison of Pre-Employment, Job Related Experience With Aptitude Tests as Predictors of Training and Job Performance of Air Traffic Control Specialists." *Aerospace Med* 35:428–36 My '64. *

235. PETERSON, DONALD FREDERICK. *A Predictive Study of Success in First Year Bookkeeping.* Master's thesis, San Diego State College (San Diego, Calif.), 1965.

236. ROZYNKO, VITALLI, AND WENK, ERNEST. "Intellectual Performance of Three Delinquent Groups of Different Ethnic Origin." Abstract. *J Consult Psychol* 29:282 Je '65. * (*PA* 39:12810, title only)

237. CENTER, CLARE CALL. *A Correlational Study of the Relationship Between Eighth Grade Test Scores and First Semester Grades at Del Oro High School.* Master's thesis, Sacramento State College (Sacramento, Calif.), 1966.

238. GOOD, RONALD K. *Factors Used to Predict Achievement in Algebra I.* Master's thesis, Millersville State College (Millersville, Pa.), 1966.

239. LANE, BETTY RUBINO. *A Study of the Predictive Values of the Tests Being Used to Determine Success in Algebra I in the Lockport Township High Schools.* Master's thesis, Northern Illinois University (DeKalb, Ill.), 1966.

240. TAGG, HOWARD R. *Correlation Between Intelligence Test Scores and Modern Mathematics Test Scores of Fifty Seventh-Grade Hillcrest Junior High School Students.* Master's thesis, Brigham Young University (Provo, Utah), 1966.

241. WILSON, GERALD E. *An Investigation of the Relationship of Mental Ability to Manual Dexterity and Coordination in Adolescents.* Master's thesis, California State College (Long Beach, Calif.), 1966.

242. AMUNRUD, KATHERINE D. *A Study of Intelligence and Personality Factors Influencing Teacher Effectiveness.* Master's thesis, Northwestern University (Evanston, Ill.), 1967.

243. HUFF, BETTY. *The Predictive Value of Standardized Testing in Relation to Mathematical Achievement at Virginia High School.* Master's thesis, East Tennessee State University (Johnson City, Tenn.), 1967.

244. HURLEY, JOHN R. "Parental Malevolence and Children's Intelligence." *J Consult Psychol* 31:199–204 Ap '67. * (*PA* 41:7151)

245. PARK, GAIL RODNEY. *The Predictive Efficiency of Selected Data for Eighth Grade Algebra Students at Bonneville Junior High.* Master's thesis, University of Utah (Salt Lake City, Utah), 1967.

246. CHANCELLOR, GEORGE A., JR. *Standardized Tests as Predictors of Academic Success in Either One or Two Forms of High School Biology.* Master's thesis, Stetson University (DeLand, Fla.), 1968.

247. CRUMLEY, FRANCES S. *The Relationship of Personal-Social Adjustment and Intellectual Capacity to the Academic Achievement of Ninety-Three Junior High School Students.* Master's thesis, East Tennessee State University (Johnson City, Tenn.), 1968.

248. DE LUCA, JOSEPH N. "Motivation and Performance in Chronic Schizophrenia." *Psychol Rep* 22:1261–9 Je '68. * (*PA* 42:19082)

249. OBERSTEIN, RITA M. *Reading Achievement: Its Relationship to Visual Motor Perception and Mental Age in First and Third Grade Students.* Master's thesis, Adelphi University (Garden City, N.Y.), 1968.

250. COFFEY, FRANK HOLMES. *The Relationship of Intelligence to Creativity.* Master's thesis, Wisconsin State University (Oshkosh, Wis.), 1969.

251. KING, F. J.; ROBERTS, DENNIS; AND KROPP, RUSSELL P. "Relationship Between Ability Measures and Achievement Under Four Methods of Teaching Elementary Set Concepts." *J Ed Psychol* 60(3):244–7 Je '69. * (*PA* 43:13392)

252. LOWE, WALTER EDWARD, SR. *A Study of the Relationship Between the Socioeconomic Status and the Reading Performance of Negro Students Enrolled in the Public Schools of Caroline County, Virginia.* Doctor's thesis, George Washington University (Washington, D.C.), 1969. (*DAI* 31:1141A)

253. MORE, ARTHUR. "The Relation of High School Grades, Achievement and Intelligence Test Scores to Success in Dental School." *Can Counsellor* 3(1):56–8 Ja '69. *

254. SHIELDS, RUTH VIRGINIA. *Relationship of Schematic Concept Formation to Mental Ability in Adolescents.* Master's thesis, Southern Methodist University (Dallas, Tex.), 1969.

255. ELLISON, ROBERT L.; JAMES, LAWRENCE R.; FOX, DAVID G.; AND TAYLOR, CALVIN W. *The Identification of Talent Among Negro and White Students From Biographical Data.* An unpublished report to the U.S. Office of Education, Research Project No. 9-H-033, Institute for Behavioral Research in Creativity, 1970. Pp. iv, 71. *

256. HOOPES, JANET L.; SHERMAN, EDMUND A.; LAWDER, ELIZABETH; ANDREWS, ROBERTA G.; AND LOWER, KATHERINE D. *A Follow-Up Study of Adoptions (Vol. II): Post-Placement Functioning of Adopted Children.* New York: Child Welfare League of America, Inc., 1970. Pp. v, 126. *

257. PLUMLEIGH, GEORGE ELWOOD, JR. *The Relationship of Selected Variables to the Ability of First-Grade Children to Read and Interpret Maps.* Doctor's thesis, University of Southern California (Los Angeles, Calif.), 1970. (*DAI* 31:5946A)

258. POMERANTZ, NORMAN ELIOT. *An Investigation of the Relationship Between Intelligence and Reading Achievement for Various Samples of Bilingual Spanish-Speaking Children.* Doctor's thesis, New Mexico State University (University Park, N.M.), 1970. (*DAI* 31:4558A)

259. WONZER, ANN CUSHMAN. *A Study of the Relationships Among Creativity, Intelligence, and Achievement Measures Based on Longitudinal Data.* Doctor's thesis, University of Michigan (Ann Arbor, Mich.), 1970. (*DAI* 32:1205A)

260. BROUSSEAU, PAULA JOAN. *A Study of the Interrelationships of Reading Ability, Listening Ability and Intelligence of Ninth and Tenth Grade Students.* Doctor's thesis, Southern Illinois University (Carbondale, Ill.), 1971. (*DAI* 32:4828A)

261. CHOATE, HUBERT HUGH. *Selected Factors Contributing to Learning Potential of Children of Spanish Heritage.* Doctor's thesis, University of Southern California (Los Angeles, Calif.), 1971. (*DAI* 32:3778A)

262. DEBERARDINIS, ACHILLE. *The Relationship Between Group IQ Sub-Scale Discrepancy and Specific Reading Comprehension Abilities.* Doctor's thesis, University of Rochester (Rochester, N.Y.), 1971. (*DAI* 32:1393A)

263. ENDE, RUSSELL S. "Reading for Understanding in Grades 7, 8, and 9." *Ill Sch Res* 7(2):32–7 w '71. *

264. HAFNER, LAWRENCE E.; GWALTNEY, WAYNE; AND ROBINSON, RICHARD. "Reading in Bookkeeping: Predictions and Performance." *J Read* 14(8):537–46 My '71. *

265. HAYNES, ELIZABETH FINGER. *An Analysis of the Relationships Between Pupil Performance in the Learning of Transformational Grammar and Intelligence Test Scores.* Doctor's thesis, University of Virginia (Charlottesville, Va.), 1971. (*DAI* 32:4591A)

266. HOLLY, KEITH ALLEN. *Structure-of-Intellect Factor Abilities and a Self-Concept Measure in Mathematics Relative to Performance in High School Modern Algebra.* Doctor's thesis, University of Southern California (Los Angeles, Calif.), 1971. (*DAI* 32:2484A)

267. HOPKINS, KENNETH D., AND BIBELHEIMER, MILO. "Five-Year Stability of Intelligence Quotients From Language and Nonlanguage Group Tests." *Child Develop* 42(2):645–9 Je '71. * (*PA* 47:652)

268. RAMSEYER, GARY C., AND CASHEN, VALJEAN M. "The Effect of Practice Sessions on the Use of Separate Answer Sheets by First and Second Graders." *J Ed Meas* 8(3):177–81 f '71. *

269. ROTTER, DORIS M.; LANGLAND, LOIS; AND BERGER, DALE. "The Validity of Tests of Creative Thinking in Seven-Year-Old Children." *Gifted Child Q* 15(4):273–8 w '71. * (*PA* 48:5633)

270. SEITHER, FRANCES GARDNER. *An Investigation of the Predictive Validity of Selected Admission Screening Measures Relative to Success in Practical Nursing.* Doctor's thesis. University of Maryland (College Park, Md.), 1971. (*DAI* 32:5890B)

271. SHAVER, JAMES P., AND NUHN, DEE. "The Effectiveness of Tutoring Underachievers in Reading and Writing." *J Ed Res* 65(3):107–12 N '71. * (*PA* 48:1878)

272. STEVENS, FRANCES ANN BENNETT. *Predicting Third Grade Reading Achievement for Mexican-American Students From Lower Socioeconomic Levels.* Doctor's thesis, New Mexico State University (University Park, N.M.), 1971. (*DAI* 32:5480A)

273. TAYLOR, ALTON L. "Regression Analysis of Antecedent Measures of Slow Sections in High School Biology." *Sci Ed* 55(3):395–402 Jl–S '71. *

274. WETHERELL, RICHARD H. *A Study of the Relationship Between Visual Perception and School Achievement.* Doctor's thesis, University of Southern Mississippi (Hattiesburg, Miss.), 1971. (*DAI* 32:2324A)

275. WICKWIRE, PATRICIA JOANNE NELLOR. *The Academic Achievement and Language Development of American Children of Latin Heritage: Factors of Intellect, Home Educational*

Environment, and Personality. Doctor's thesis, University of Texas (Austin, Tex.), 1971. (*DAI* 32:6232A)

276. WILLIAMS, J. R.; DEWITT, WILLARD R.; AND HURT, ROBERT W. "Ability, Likability, and Motivation of Students as They Relate to Prediction of Achievement." *J Ed Res* 65(4):155–8 D '71. * (*PA* 48:1873)

277. WILLIAMS, PATSY RUTH. *Comparison of the Cattell Culture Fair Test With the California Mental Maturity Test.* Master's thesis, Southern Methodist University (Dallas, Tex.), 1971.

CUMULATIVE NAME INDEX

Altus, G. T.: 53, 59
American Gas Association, Personnel Committee: 43
Amunrud, K. D.: 242
Anderson, H. E.: 86–7, 123, 178, 223
Anderson, M.: 204
Andrews, R. G.: 256
Arena, T.: 192
Arnold, E. R.: 40
Arth, A. A.: 167
Bailey, A. E.: 8
Bailey, H. K.: 26
Baldauf, R. J.: 99
Baldwin, J. W.: 94
Barbee, E. W.: 231
Barnowe, T. J.: 18
Barry, C. A.: 75
Barz, A. I.: 179
Baylor, C. C.: 224
Benoit, E. P.: 62
Berger, D.: 269
Bessemer, D. W.: 98
Bibelheimer, M.: 267
Bibelheimer, M. H.: 119
Bish, G. G.: 124
Black, D. B.: 225
Bliesmer, E. P.: 60
Bobbe, C.: 100
Boger, J. H.: 44
Bolton, F. B.: 14
Boney, J. D.: 125, 143
Bonney, M. E.: 206
Bosworth, D. L.: 158
Boyce, R. W.: 136
Boyd, H. F.: 62
Bradshaw, D. H.: 126
Brady, W. J.: 137
Breen, J. M.: 138
Brendemuehl, F. L.: 80, 157
Brodsky, M.: 215
Brousseau, P. J.: 260
Buck, J. R.: 127
Burnette, R.: 92
Caffrey, J.: 58
Caldwell, J. R.: 193
California Test Bureau, Division of Professional Services: 61
Callaway, W. R.: 180
Campbell, W.: 100
Canabal, J. V.: 194
Carl, P. M.: 41
Carlson, H. B.: 31
Carney, R. E.: 95
Carroll, I. V.: 195
Cashen, V. M.: 268
Cassel, R. N.: 79, 88
Cattell, R. B.: *rev,* 2:1384
Center, C. C.: 237
Centi, P.: 89
Chambers, J. A.: 76
Chancellor, G. A.: 246
Choate, H. H.: 261
Church, A. M.: 19
Clark, B. P.: 98
Clark, J. H.: 27, 104
Clark, W. W.: 28–9, 45, 48, 96
Cleveland, G. A.: 158
Cline, V. B.: 101
Clymer, T.: 80, 90, 102
Cobb, B. B.: 97, 128, 164, 234
Coffey, F. H.: 250
Coffey, H. S.: 16
Coladarci, A. P.: 218
Coleman, J. C.: 61
Coleman, J. M.: 215
Colgan, R. T.: 168
Commins, W. D.: *rev,* 1:1042
Comrey, A. L.: 54
Cooke, B. E. M.: 169
Cooper, J. G.: 72

Coppedge, F. L.: 144, 181
Coppedge, L. L.: 145
Corrigan, F. V.: 196
Cox, O.: 182
Crumley, F. S.: 247
Cunningham, W.: 146
Curry, R. L.: 109, 221
Curtin, J. T.: 211
Damm, V. J.: 197
Davis, W. A.: 20
DeBerardinis, A.: 262
De Boer, D. L.: 129
Deich, R. F.: 170
Dejmek, F. W.: 21
De Luca, J. N.: 248
DeWitt, W. R.: 276
Dirr, P. M.: 147
Dizney, H.: 130–1
Driscoll, J. A.: 46
Duke, R. L.: 217
Elias, J. Z.: 36
Elley, W. B.: 103
Ellison, K. L.: 255
Ende, R.: 159
Ende, R. S.: 263
Erlandson, F. L.: 77
Evans, M. C.: 22
Failor, L. M.: 7
Fleming, E.: 131
Foster, M. E.: 225
Fox, D. G.: 255
Freeman, F. S.: *rev,* 5:314
French, J. L.: 91
Fuller, G. B.: 159
Fuqua, N. V.: 148
Gallagher, J. J.: 62
Gardner, S. F.: 118
Garrett, H. E.: *rev,* 3:223
Gates, J. A.: 198
Gilman, R. H.: 160
Goldman, B. A.: *rev,* 7:338
Good, R. K.: 238
Gordon, M. A.: 188
Griess, J. A.: 149
Guilford, J. P.: 139, 150
Gundersen, R. O.: 107
Gwaltney, W.: 264
Hackman, R. B.: 23
Hafner, L. E.: 264
Hammer, E. F.: 49
Hansen, C. W.: 207
Harootunian, B.: 151–2
Harootunian, B. A.: 108
Hatfield, R. C.: 171
Havighurst, R. J.: 20
Haynes, E. F.: 265
Henderson, N.: 31
Herrmann, M.: 23
Hieronymus, A. N.: 183
High, W. S.: 54
Hindsman, E.: 113
Hirsch, M. J.: 216
Hoepfner, R.: 139, 150
Hoffman, C. B.: 110
Holly, K. A.: 266
Hoopes, J. L.: 256
Hopka, E.: 212
Hopkins, K. D.: 119, 184, 267
Huff, B.: 243
Hurley, J. R.: 244
Hurt, R. W.: 276
Iscoe, I.: 215
Jackson, B. J.: 42
Jacobs, R. E.: 81
James, L. R.: 255
Jennings, E.: 113
Johnson, J. K.: 199
Johnson, W. E.: 111
Jones, A. L.: 75
Jones, K. J.: 200
Jones, P. P.: 200
Jogeward, P. A.: 132
Kamii, C. K.: 226

Kandel, A.: 153
Keach, C. C.: 154
King, F. J.: 113, 251
King, P.: 77
Knecht, W. W.: 222
Knezevich, S. J.: 12
Kopel, D.: *exc,* 2:1384
Kortmeyer, H. A.: 78
Krantz, L. L.: 214
Krebs, S. O.: 74
Krop, H.: 185
Kropp, R. P.: 251
Kuhlmann, F.: *rev,* 2:1384
Kurek, A.: 164
Lamberti, E.: 100
Lane, B. R.: 239
Langland, L.: 269
Lauten, D. A. H.: 172
Lawder, E.: 256
Leton, D. A.: 123
Line, W.: *exc,* 3:223
Lloyd, B. A.: 161
Lloyd, R.: 161
Lovett, C. J.: 186
Lowe, W. E.: 252
Lower, K. D.: 256
Lucier, O.: 92
MacArthur, R. S.: 103, 115, 175
McBee, G.: 217
McCall, J. R.: 55
McCall, R. A.: 140
McCall, R. B.: 140
McCauley, J. H.: 141
McCracken, R. A.: 201
McDonald, D.: 6
McGuire, C.: 93, 113, 219
McHugh, A. F.: 68
McLeod, J. D.: 173
Mandel, R.: 162
Manolakes, G.: 51, 56
Manson, M. P.: 32
Maples, V. S.: 187
Marshall, J. J.: 174
Marshall, T. A.: 57
Maxfield, F. N.: 2
Mehrens, W. A.: 84
Meyers, C. E.: 193
Michael, W. B.: 193, 220, 229
Milholland, J. E.: *rev,* 5:314
Moe, I. L.: 106
More, A.: 253
Moulin, E. K.: 202
Mullen, N. D.: 201
Mumaw, M. J.: 120
Nadeau, C.: 232
Nair, R. K.: 33
Needham, W. E.: 101
Nelson, A. G.: 9
Nicholson, A.: 69, 73
Nolan, E. G.: 17
Norman, R. D.: 98
Norrell, G.: 77
Nuhn, D.: 271
Oberstein, R. M.: 249
Olson, D. R.: 115
Onarheim, J.: 15
Ordahl, V. E.: 13
Osborne, R. T.: 82
Owen, J. C.: 70
Parish, R. L.: 155
Park, G. R.: 245
Parker, A. D.: 156
Paxson, R. C.: 136
Peters, H. D.: 227
Petersen, H.: 139
Peterson, D. F.: 235
Pintner, R.: *rev,* 1:1042
Plessas, G. P.: 121
Plumb, G. R.: 37
Plumbleigh, G. E.: 257
Pomerantz, N. E.: 258
Ramsey, W.: 83
Ramseyer, G. C.: 268

Rattan, M. S.: 175
Rawlings, T. D.: 105
Ray, M. R.: 176
Richards, J. M.: 101
Ringness, T. A.: 203
Rinsland, H. D.: 30
Roberts, D.: 251
Roberts, H. C.: 233
Robinson, R.: 264
Rosenbach, J. H.: *rev,* 7:338
Rosilda, M.: 38
Rotter, D. M.: 269
Rozynko, V.: 236
Rubin, S. S.: 116
Rush, A. C.: 228
Schell, R. E.: 163
Schellenberg, E. D.: 24
Schrader, D. R.: 193
Schwellenbach, J. A.: 50
Seither, F. G.: 270
Shanner, W. M.: 64
Shaver, J. P.: 271
Sheldon, W. D.: 51, 56
Sheppard, C.: 100
Sherman, E. A.: 256
Shields, R. V.: 188, 254
Sitkei, E. G.: 184
Skubic, V.: 204
Slivinske, A. J.: 223
Smith, H. A.: 209
Smith, P. D.: 189
Smith, R. H.: 133
Smith, T. W.: 58, 65–6
Snider, J. G.: 218
Spiers, D. E.: 142
Stake, R. E.: 84
Stancik, E. J.: 79, 88
Stein, H. L.: 25
Stevens, F. A. B.: 272
Stevens, J. C.: 178
Strang, R.: 10
Straus, M. A.: 39, 210, 213
Stroud, J. B.: 183
Sutherland, K.: 190
Sweeney, F. J.: 52
Tagg, H. R.: 240
Tate, M. W.: 67
Taylor, A. L.: 273
Taylor, C. W.: 255
Thomas, H.: 177
Tiegs, E. W.: 1
Tilker, H. A.: 163
Tobias, M.: 220, 229
Topetzes, N. J.: 71
Traxler, A. E.: 3–5; *rev,* 1: 1042
Trites, D. K.: 134, 164, 234
Trowbridge, N.: 95
Tully, G. E.: 165
Vertein, L. D.: 112
Voss, C. E.: 67
Waggoner, R. W.: 208
Wagner, H. E.: 166
Waldron, C.: 135
Walsh, N. E.: 122
Weikart, D. P.: 226
Welch, W. B.: 47
Welna, C. T.: 85
Welter, M. B.: 114
Wenk, E.: 236
Wetherell, R. H.: 274
White, W. F.: 178
Wickwire, P. J. N.: 275
Wiley, L. N.: 34
Williams, J. R.: 222, 276
Williams, P. R.: 277
Willmarth, J. G.: 191
Wilson, G. E.: 241
Winans, J. M.: 35
Wonzer, A. C.: 259
Woody, C.: 11
Young, F. A.: 230
Younge, J. W.: 205
Zeigler, T. W.: 208

[350]

Canadian Academic Aptitude Test. Grades 8.5–9.0; 1959–68; CAAT; a test in the *Canadian Test Battery, Grades 8–9;* 3 parts; Ontario Institute for Studies in Education; distributed by Guidance Centre [Canada]. * For the complete battery entry, see 1047.

a) PART I, VERBAL REASONING.

b) PART 2, MATHEMATICAL REASONING.
c) PART 3, NON-VERBAL REASONING. 1962 test identical with test copyrighted 1959.

For additional information, see 7 :339 (1 reference) ; for reviews by Donald B. Black and George A. Ferguson, see 6 :445 (2 references).

REFERENCES THROUGH 1971

1–2. See 6:445.
3. See 7:339.

CUMULATIVE NAME INDEX

Black, D. B.: *rev*, 6:445   Khan, S. B.: 3
D'Oyley, V. R.: 1–2   Roberts, D. M.: 3
Ferguson, G. A.: *rev*, 6:445

[351]

Canadian Cognitive Abilities Test. Grades kgn–1, 2–3 ; 1954–70 ; CCAT ; adaptation of *Cognitive Abilities Test;* original test by Robert L. Thorndike, Elizabeth Hagen, and Irving Lorge ; adaptation by Edgar N. Wright ; Thomas Nelson & Sons (Canada) Ltd. [Canada]. *

For additional information, see 7 :340.

[352]

Canadian Lorge-Thorndike Intelligence Tests, Multi-Level Edition. Grades 3–9 ; 1954–67 ; CLTIT ; adaptation of *Lorge-Thorndike Intelligence Tests,* Multi-Level Edition ; 3 scores : verbal, non-verbal, composite ; original test by Irving Lorge, Robert L. Thorndike, and Elizabeth Hagen ; adaptation by Edgar N. Wright ; Thomas Nelson & Sons (Canada) Ltd. [Canada]. *

For additional information, see 7 :341.

[353]

★**Canadian Scholastic Aptitude Test.** Candidates for college entrance ; 1968–73 ; CSAT ; test administered annually in April and December at centers established by the publisher ; 2 scores : verbal, mathematical ; French edition available ; Service for Admission to College and University [Canada]. * For the testing program entry, see 1060.

REFERENCES THROUGH 1971

1. D'OYLEY, VINCENT R. "Development of the SACU Tests." *Sch Guid Worker* (Canada) 26(4):12–6 Mr–Ap '71. *
2. ELLEY, W. B. "SACU English Language Achievement and Verbal Aptitude Tests." *Interchange* (Canada) 2(3):83–6 '71. * (*PA* 48:5618)
3. ELLIOTT, H. A. "SACU and the SACU Tests: Past, Present, and Future." *Sch Guid Worker* (Canada) 26(4):6–11 Mr–Ap '71. *
4. EVANS, G. T. "The Canadian Scholastic Aptitude Test: Mathematical Sections." *Interchange* (Canada) 2(3):86–90 '71. * (*PA* 48:5620)
5. HOLMES, MARK. "The Relationship Between SACU Test Scores and Other Criteria of High School Academic Performance." *Sch Guid Worker* (Canada) 26(4):25–30 Mr–Ap '71. *
6. ROSEVEAR, DAVID. "Reflections on the Mathematics Section of CSAT." *Sch Guid Worker* (Canada) 26(4):31–3 Mr–Ap '71. *

CUMULATIVE NAME INDEX

D'Oyley, V. R.: 1   Evans, G. T.: 4
Elley, W. B.: 2   Holmes, M.: 5
Elliott, H. A.: 3   Rosevear, D.: 6

[354]

Cattell Intelligence Tests. Mental ages 4–8, 8–11, 11–15, 15 and over ; 1930–52 ; 4 levels ; R. B. Cattell ; George G. Harrap & Co. Ltd. [England]. *
a) SCALE 0 (DARTINGTON SCALE). Mental ages 4–8 ; 1933. *Out of print.* Identical with Scale 1 of *IPAT Culture Fair Intelligence Test* (see 364a1).
b) SCALE 1 (NON-VERBAL), NEW EDITION, REVISED. Mental ages 8–11 ; 1930–52.

c) SCALE 2, NEW EDITION, REVISED. Mental ages 11–15 ; 1930–52.
d) SCALE 3, NEW EDITION, REVISED. Mental ages 15 and over ; 1930–52.

For additional information and a review by I. Macfarlane Smith, see 5 :315 (9 references) ; for a review by Godfrey H. Thomson, see 2 :1386 (3 references).

REFERENCES THROUGH 1971

1–3. See 2:1386 (There is no reference 4.)
5–13. See 5:315.
14. CATTELL, RAYMOND B. "Intelligence Levels in Schools of the South-West." *Forum Ed* (England) 8:201–5 N '30. * (*PA* 5:2058)
15. PEEL, E. A., AND GRAHAM, D. "Differentiation of Ability in Primary School Children." *Durham Res R* (England) 1(2):40–8 S '51. *
16. PEEL, E. A., AND GRAHAM, D. "Differentiation of Ability in Primary School Children—II." *Durham Res R* (England) 1(3):31–4 S '52. * (*PA* 27:5157)

CUMULATIVE NAME INDEX

Bristol, H.: 1   Peel, E. A.: 13, 15–6
Cattell, R. B.: 1–3, 10, 14   Rogers, C. A.: 11
Chase, V. E.: 6   Rohan, J. C.: 5
Crawford, J. M.: 12   Slater, P.: 7
Fitt, A. B.: 11   Smith, C. A.: 8
Graham, D.: 15–6   Smith, I. M.: *rev*, 5:315
Halstead, H.: 6   Thomson, G. H.: *rev*, 2:1386
Moore, B. G. R.: 13   Tizard, J.: 12
O'Connor, N.: 12   Uhrbrock, R. S.: 9

[355]

Chicago Non-Verbal Examination. Ages 6 and over ; 1936–54 ; Andrew W. Brown, Seymour P. Stein, and Perry L. Rohrer ; Psychological Corporation. *

For additional information and a review by Raleigh M. Drake, see 5 :316 (10 references) ; for reviews by Robert G. Bernreuter, Myrtle Luneau Pignatelli, and S. D. Porteus, see 2 :1387.

REFERENCES THROUGH 1971

1–10. See 5:316.
11. CARY, LEE ALLAN. *A Comparative Analysis of the Sub-Test Scores of Two Groups of Deaf Children for the Chicago Non-Verbal Examination and the Reading and Arithmetic Reasoning Sections of the Stanford Achievement Test.* Doctor's thesis, University of Denver (Denver, Colo.), 1964. (*DA* 25:7023)
12. FARRANT, ROLAND H. "The Intellective Abilities of Deaf and Hearing Children Compared by Factor Analyses." *Am Ann Deaf* 109:306–25 My '64. * (*PA* 39:2442)
13. GOETZINGER, CORNELIUS P.; WILLS, ROBERT C.; AND DEKKER, LYNN CROUTER. "Non-Language IQ Tests Used With Deaf Pupils." *Volta R* 69:500–6 O '67. *
14. LARSON, STANFORD S. *A Comparison of Two Non-Verbal Intelligence Tests as Predictors of Academic Success of Navajo Students.* Master's thesis, Utah State University (Logan, Utah), 1967.
15. SEIDEL, H. E., JR.; BARKLEY, MARY JO; AND STITH, DORIS. "Evaluation of a Program for Project Head Start." *J Genetic Psychol* 110:185–97 Je '67. * (*PA* 41:11718)
16. McLELLAND, PAUL EUGENE. *A Comparative Study of the Reasoning Ability of Two Groups of Hearing Impaired Children in a Residential School.* Doctor's thesis, University of Virginia (Charlottesville, Va.), 1968. (*DA* 29:3005A)

CUMULATIVE NAME INDEX

Allen, R. M.: 4   Johnson, E. H.: 3
Barkley, M. J.: 15   Larson, S. S.: 14
Bernreuter, R. G.: *rev*, 2:   Lavos, G.: 6, 9
   1387   Lawrence, W. C.: 8
Bessell, T.: 4   Levine, B.: 10
Brown, A. W.: 1–2   McLelland, P. E.: 16
Cary, L. A.: 11   Newland, T. E.: 8
Cotton, C. B.: 2   Pignatelli, M. L.: *rev*, 2:1387
Dekker, L. C.: 13   Porteus, S. D.: *rev*, 2:1387
Drake, R. M.: *rev*, 5:316   Roper, G. E.: 7
Ewing, R. M.: 5   Seidel, H. E.: 15
Farrant, R. H.: 12   Stith, D.: 15
Goetzinger, C. P.: 13   Wills, R. C.: 13
Iscoe, I.: 10

[356]

★**Cognitive Abilities Test.** Grades kgn–1, 2–3, 3–12 ; 1954–72 ; CAT ; Robert L. Thorndike, Elizabeth Hagen, and Irving Lorge (*a*) ; Houghton Mifflin Co. *

a) PRIMARY BATTERIES. Grades kgn–1, 2–3; 1954–68; revision of Levels 1 and 2 of still-in-print *Lorge-Thorndike Intelligence Tests;* 2 levels.

  1) *Primary 1.* Grades kgn–1.
  2) *Primary 2.* Grades 2–3.

b) MULTI-LEVEL EDITION. Grades 3–12; 1971–72; 3 scores: verbal, quantitative, nonverbal.

For additional information, reviews by Marcel L. Goldschmid and Carol K. Tittle, and an excerpted review by Richard C. Cox, see 7:343.

[357]

*College Board Scholastic Aptitude Test. Candidates for college entrance; 1926–73; SAT; test administered on specified dates at centers established by the publisher; 2 scores: verbal, mathematical; special editions available for the visually handicapped; program administered for the College Entrance Examination Board by Educational Testing Service. * For the testing program entry, see 1048.

For additional information and reviews by Philip H. DuBois and Wimburn L. Wallace of an earlier form, see 7:344 (298 references); for reviews by John E. Bowers and Wayne S. Zimmerman, see 6:449 (79 references); for a review by John T. Dailey, see 5:318 (20 references); for a review by Frederick B. Davis, see 4:285 (22 references). For reviews of the testing program, see 6:760 (2 reviews).

REFERENCES THROUGH 1971

1–22. See 4:285.
23–42. See 5:318.
43–121. See 6:449.
122–419. See 7:344.
420. BRIGHAM, CARL C.; ANGIER, ROSWELL P.; MacPHAIL, ANDREW H.; ROGERS, DAVID C.; AND STONE, CHARLES L. "General Report [First] on the Scholastic Aptitude Test." *Col Entr Exam Board Ann Rep* 26:159–98 S '26. * (PA 1:1627)
421. BRIGHAM, CARL C.; ANGIER, ROSWELL P.; MacPHAIL, ANDREW H.; ROGERS, DAVID C.; AND STONE, CHARLES L. "General Report [Second] on the Scholastic Aptitude Test, June 25, 1927." *Col Entr Exam Board Ann Rep* 27:173–211 S '27. * (PA 2:1390)
422. BRIGHAM, CARL C. "General Report [Third] on the Scholastic Aptitude Test, June 23, 1928." *Col Entr Exam Board Ann Rep* 28:147–99 S '28. * (PA 3:965)
423. BRIGHAM, CARL C. "General Report [Fourth] on the Scholastic Aptitude Test, June 19, 1929." *Col Entr Exam Board Ann Rep* 29:161–200 S '29. * (PA 4:913)
424. BROLYER, CECIL R. "General Report [Fifth] on the Scholastic Aptitude Test, June 21, 1930." *Col Entr Exam Board Ann Rep* 30:202–32 S '30. * (PA 5:1681)
425. CRAWFORD, ALBERT BEECHER. "Forecasting Freshman Achievement." *Sch & Soc* 31:125–32 Ja 25 '30. *
426. BROLYER, CECIL R. "General Report [Sixth] on the Scholastic Aptitude Test, June 20, 1931." *Col Entr Exam Board Ann Rep* 31:173–205 S '31. * (PA 6:1652)
427. BRIGHAM, CARL C. *A Study of Error: A Study and Evaluation of Methods Used in Six Years of Study of the Scholastic Aptitude Test of the College Entrance Examination Board.* New York: College Entrance Examination Board, 1932. Pp. xiii, 384. * (PA 6:4597)
428. BROLYER, CECIL R. "General Report [Seventh] on the Scholastic Aptitude Test, June 25, 1932." *Col Entr Exam Board Ann Rep* 32:173–95 S '32. * (PA 7:1170)
429. CRAWFORD, ALBERT B., AND BURNHAM, PAUL S. "Entrance Examinations and College Achievement." *Sch & Soc* 36:344–52, 378–84 S 10, 17 '32. * (PA 7:349)
430. BROLYER, CECIL R. "General Report [Eighth] on the Scholastic Aptitude Test, June 24, 1933." *Col Entr Exam Board Ann Rep* 33:171–96 S '33. * (PA 8:1362)
431. BROLYER, CECIL R. "General Report [Ninth] on the Scholastic Aptitude Test, June 23, 1934." *Col Entr Exam Board Ann Rep* 34:157–82 S '34. * (PA 9:924)
432. BRIGHAM, CARL C. *Examining Fellowship Applicants: A Report Made to the Social Science Research Council on the Method of Selecting Fellows for First-Year Graduate Study.* Social Science Research Council Bulletin No. 23. Princeton, N.J.: Princeton University Press, 1935. Pp. vii, 58. * (PA 10:1724)
433. BROLYER, CECIL R. "General Report [Tenth] on the Scholastic Aptitude Test, June 22, 1935." *Col Entr Exam Board Ann Rep* 35:151–74 S '35. * (PA 10:1725)
434. BROLYER, CECIL R. "General Report [Eleventh] on

the Scholastic Aptitude Test, June 13, 1936." *Col Entr Exam Board Ann Rep* 36:145–53 S '36. *
435. BROLYER, CECIL R. "General Report [Twelfth] on the Scholastic Aptitude Test." *Col Entr Exam Board Ann Rep* 37:135–43 S '37. *
436. LANDRY, HERBERT A. "The Relative Predictive Value of Certain College Entrance Criteria." *J Exp Ed* 5:256–60 Mr '37. * (PA 11:3887)
437. STALNAKER, JOHN M. "Thirteenth Annual Report on the Scholastic Aptitude Test." *Col Entr Exam Board Ann Rep* 38:79–95 S '38. * (PA 13:2733)
438. STALNAKER, JOHN M., AND STALNAKER, RUTH C. "Fourteenth Annual Report on the Scholastic Aptitude Test." *Col Entr Exam Board Ann Rep* 39:97–114 S '39. *
439. WOLF, RALPH ROBINSON, JR. "Differential Forecasts of Achievement and Their Use in Educational Counseling." *Psychol Monogr* 51(1):1–53 '39. * (PA 13:6506)
440. CHILD, IRVIN L., AND SHELDON, WILLIAM H. "The Correlation Between Components of Physique and Scores on Certain Psychological Tests." *Char & Pers* 10:23–34 S '41. * (PA 16:1040)
441. STALNAKER, JOHN M. "Identification of the Best Southern Negro High-School Seniors." *Sci Mo* 67:237–9 S '48. * (PA 23:1269)
442. DAVIS, JUNIUS A., AND FREDERIKSEN, NORMAN. "Public and Private School Graduates in College." *J Teach Ed* 6:18–22 Mr '55. * (PA 30:3359)
443. SARASON, IRWIN G. "Test Anxiety, General Anxiety, and Intellectual Performance." *J Consult Psychol* 21:485–90 D '57. * (PA 33:3867)
444. SEVIER, FRANCIS A. C. "Testing the Assumptions Underlying Multiple Regression." *J Exp Ed* 25:323–30 Je '57. * (PA 33:5133)
445. BIERI, JAMES; BRADBURN, WENDY M.; AND GALINSKY, M. DAVID. "Sex Differences in Perceptual Behavior." *J Personality* 26:1–12 Mr '58. * (PA 33:5426)
446. FRENCH, JOHN W. "The Relationship of Home and School Experiences to Scores on Achievement Tests." *J Ed Psychol* 50:75–82 Ap '59. * (PA 35:2795)
447. WORELL, LEONARD. "Level of Aspiration and Academic Success." *J Ed Psychol* 50:47–54 Ap '59. * (PA 35:2783)
448. FREDERIKSEN, NORMAN, AND GILBERT, ARTHUR C. F. "Replication of a Study of Differential Predictability." *Ed & Psychol Meas* 20:759–67 w '60. * (PA 35:7953)
449. ALTUS, WILLIAM D. "Questionnaire Items and Types of Intelligence." *J Genetic Psychol* 98:265–71 Je '61. * (PA 36:2KK65A)
450. GETTYS, RICHARD H. *An Analysis of Variables at Spartanburg High School in Predicting College Success.* Master's thesis, Furman University (Greenville, S.C.), 1963.
451. HEARD, WILLIAM G.; FINLEY, JUDSON R.; AND STAATS, ARTHUR W. "The Relationship of Intelligence-Test Scores to the Ease of Language Conditioning." *J Genetic Psychol* 103:227–31 D '63. * (PA 38:7786)
452. SCHNEYER, J. WESLEY. "Factors Associated With the Progress of Students Enrolled in a College Reading Program." *J Ed Res* 56:340–5 Mr '63. *
453. WESTCOTT, MALCOLM R., AND RANZONI, JANE H. "Correlates of Intuitive Thinking." *Psychol Rep* 12:595–613 Ap '63. * (PA 38:4257)
454. AIKEN, LEWIS R., JR. "Rank in High School Graduating Classes of Various Sizes as a Predictor of College Grades." *J Ed Res* 58:56–60 O '64. *
455. AIKEN, LEWIS R., JR. "Some Nomographs for Academic Prediction Work." *Ed & Psychol Meas* 24:913–20 w '64. * (PA 39:8678)
456. BEHRING, DANIEL W. *The Prediction of Academic Success From an Inventory of Student Preferences for Activities.* Master's thesis, Ohio University (Athens, Ohio), 1964.
457. BROD, DIANE; KERNOFF, PHYLLIS; AND TERWILLIGER, ROBERT F. "Anxiety and Semantic Differential Responses." *J Abn & Social Psychol* 68:570–4 My '64. * (PA 39:4647)
458. FOREE, SHERRELL S. *Selection of Factors for Prediction of Scholastic Success in Introductory Food and Nutrition Courses.* Master's thesis, Texas Technological College (Lubbock, Tex.), 1964.
459. SPIELBERGER, CHARLES D., AND WEITZ, HENRY. "Improving the Academic Performance of Anxious College Freshmen: A Group-Counseling Approach to the Prevention of Underachievement." *Psychol Monogr* 78(13):1–20 '64. * (PA 39:5919)
460. BOVINETTE, ROBERT L. *Establishing a Prediction Equation for Determining Academic Success at MacMurray College.* Master's thesis, Northern Illinois University (DeKalb, Ill.), 1965.
461. BURKE, RONALD J., AND MAIER, NORMAN R. F. "Attempts to Predict Success on an Insight Problem." *Psychol Rep* 17:303–10 Ag '65. * (PA 40:1115)
462. CAUTELA, JOSEPH R., AND BARLOW, DAVID H. "The Relation Between Intelligence and Critical Flicker Fusion." *Psychon Sci* 3:559–60 D 15 '65. * (PA 40:2219)
463. HOWELL, WALLACE J. "Influence of Curriculum Enrichment in a High School Honors Group on College Board

Examination Scores." *J Ed Res* 59:113–4 N '65. * (*PA* 40:3332)

464. LARIMORE, DAVID LEE. *A Study of the Relationship Between the Scholastic Aptitude Test Scores and Converted High School Rank Scores and Success in a School of Education.* Master's thesis, North Carolina State University (Raleigh, N.C.), 1965.

465. MATHIS, CLAUDE, AND PARK, YOUNG HORN. "Some Factors Relating to Success in Student Teaching." *J Ed Res* 58:420–2 My–Je '65. * (*PA* 39:16472)

466. BURKE, RONALD J. "The Relationship of Some Interest, Intellectual Ability, and Nonintellectual Ability Tests to Problem-Solving Success and Effective Use of Hints in Individual Problem-Solving." *Mich Acad Sci Arts & Letters* 51:353–60 '66. * (*PA* 41:14722)

467. DENNY, J. PETER. "Effects of Anxiety and Intelligence on Concept Formation." *J Exp Psychol* 72:596–602 O '66. *

468. HILLS, JOHN R. "Diversity and the Effect of Selective Admissions." *J Ed Meas* 3:235–42 f '66. *

469. HILLS, JOHN R.; BUSH, MARILYN L.; AND KLOCK, JOSEPH A. "Keeping College Prediction Equations Current." *J Ed Meas* 3:33–4 sp '66. *

470. PHILLIPS, LYNDA N. *A Statistical Analysis of Selected Factors Influencing Performance of Students Enrolled in Physics 218 at Texas A & M University.* Master's thesis, Texas A & M University (College Station, Tex.), 1966.

471. BAGGALEY, ANDREW R., AND CAMPBELL, JAMES P. "Multiple-Discriminant Analysis of Academic Curricula by Interest and Aptitude Variables." *J Ed Meas* 4:143–9 f '67. * (*PA* 42:4434)

472. CROW, JOHNNY LEE. *Factors Associated With Improvement in Ability to Visualize Shapes Described by Orthographic Projection Drawings.* Master's thesis, North Carolina State University (Raleigh, N.C.), 1967.

473. MARKS, EDMOND. "Student Perceptions of College Persistence, and Their Intellective, Personality and Performance Correlates." *J Ed Psychol* 58:210–21 Ag '67. * (*PA* 41:15798)

474. NEIDT, CHARLES O., AND HEDLUND, DALVA E. "The Relationship Between Changes in Attitudes Toward a Course and Final Achievement." *J Ed Res* 61:56–8 O '67. *

475. NICHOLI, ARMAND M., JR. "Harvard Dropouts: Some Psychiatric Findings." *Am J Psychiatry* 124:651–8 N '67. * (*PA* 42:5637)

476. WALKER, C. EUGENE, AND TAHMISIAN, JAMES. "Birth Order and Student Characteristics: A Replication." Abstract. *J Consult Psychol* 31:219 Ap '67. * (*PA* 41:7349, title only)

477. CARRUTH, BETTY RUTH ROBERTS. *Development of Criteria for Student Placement in an Introductory Food and Nutrition Course.* Master's thesis, Texas Tech University (Lubbock, Tex.), 1968.

478. COY, MICHAEL. *Factorial Study of Variables Related to College Grade Point Average.* Master's thesis, Humboldt State College (Arcata, Calif.), 1968.

479. DIMALTA, VINCENT F. *Statistical Differences Between Science and Non-Science Freshmen Entering Indiana University of Pennsylvania During the Fall Term, 1967.* Master's thesis, Indiana University of Pennsylvania (Indiana, Pa.), 1968.

480. GENTRY, JOANNE. "Abstract of a Study of the Relationship Between High School Grades and Test Scores and the Achievement of Students Enrolled in BEOA 326 (Shorthand) at Ball State University in the Autumn Quarter of 1966." *Ball State J Bus Educators* 40:12–6 N '68. *

481. OPPENHEIM, DON B. "The Relation Between Intelligence and Different Patterns of Feedback in a Linear Teaching Program." *J Exp Ed* 36:82–5 sp '68. *

482. PETERSON, RICHARD E. "Predictive Validity of a Brief Test of Academic Aptitude." *Ed & Psychol Meas* 28:441–4 su '68. * (*PA* 42:19279)

483. TILLINGHAST, B. S., AND NORRIS, BETTY N. "The Relation of Selected Admission Variables to Student Achievement." *Nursing Outl* 16:58 Jl '68. *

484. BROUSSEAU, MARY ALINE. *Comparison of Disciplined and Non-Disciplined Women Residents Marquette University 1967–68.* Doctor's thesis, Marquette University (Milwaukee, Wis.), 1969. (*DAI* 31:4451A)

485. KLEIN, STEPHEN P.; FREDERIKSEN, NORMAN; AND EVANS, FRANKLIN R. "Anxiety and Learning to Formulate Hypotheses." *J Ed Psychol* 60(6):465–75 D '69. * (*PA* 44:3087)

486. LAPP, C. J. "Evaluation and Selection of Graduate Students." *Eng Ed* 60(2):112–6 O '69. *

487. LINDEMAN, RICHARD H.; GORDON, RICHARD E.; AND GORDON, KATHERINE K. "Further Relationships Between Blood Chemical Values and College Student Performance and Attitudes." *J Am Col Health Assn* 18(2):156–61 D '69. *

488. ROGGENKAMP, RONALD R. *A Study to Determine the Validity of Using College Entrance Exams and I.Q. as Predictors of College Performance for Falls City Senior High Graduates.* Master's thesis, Kearney State College (Kearney, Neb.), 1969.

489. WILLIAMS, HELEN B. *Interests and Prediction of Academic Performance of Associate Degree Nursing Students.* Master's thesis, Alfred University (Alfred, N.Y.), 1969.

490. *Normative Data for the 1969–70 Freshman Class, University System of Georgia.* Atlanta, Ga.: Regents of the University System of Georgia, November 1970. Pp. xi, 94. *

491. ASTIN, ALEXANDER W. "How Colleges Are Rated." *Change H* 2(6):11+ N–D '70. *

492. BARRETT, S BARRE. *A Study of the Interrelationship and Influences of Scholastic Aptitude and Perception Upon Aesthetic Sensitivity in College Students.* Doctor's thesis, University of Kansas (Lawrence, Kan.), 1970. (*DAI* 31:5835A)

493. BEAN, ANDREW GEORGE. *Personality Measures as Multiple Moderators in the Prediction of College Student Attrition.* Doctor's thesis, University of Pennsylvania (Philadelphia, Pa.), 1970. (*DAI* 32:229A)

494. BELLICO, RUSSELL PAUL. *The Relationship of Selected Factors to Academic Achievement in Economics.* Doctor's thesis, University of Massachusetts (Amherst, Mass.), 1970. (*DAI* 31:5022A)

495. BROWN, JOAN LOBIS. *A Descriptive Analysis of Some Common Predictors of Academic Achievement Applied in a Predominantly Black State University in North Carolina.* Master's thesis, Wake Forest University (Winston-Salem, N.C.), 1970.

496. CHERDACK, ARTHUR NORMAN. *The Predictive Validity of the Scholastic Aptitude Test for Disadvantaged College Students Enrolled in a Special Education Program.* Doctor's thesis, University of California (Los Angeles, Calif.), 1970. (*DAI* 31:5193A)

497. CHRISTOFF, PATRICK LEO. *The Relationship Between Attendance at a Summer Orientation Program, Expectation-Press Congruence, and Selected Behavioral Correlates.* Doctor's thesis, University of Maryland (College Park, Md.), 1970. (*DAI* 31:4454A)

498. D'ANGELO, ROCCO DOMENICK. *Variations in Instructional and General Expenditures Associated With Seven Administrative Factors in Private Liberal Arts Colleges for the Academic Year, 1966–67.* Doctor's thesis, Ohio University (Athens, Ohio), 1970. (*DAI* 31:4484A)

499. DANIERE, ANDRE, AND MECHLING, JERRY. "Direct Marginal Productivity of College Education in Relation to College Aptitude of Students and Production Costs of Institutions." *J Hum Resources* 5(1):51–70 w '70. *

500. ELLISON, ROBERT L.; JAMES, LAWRENCE R.; FOX, DAVID G.; AND TAYLOR, CALVIN W. *The Identification of Talent Among Negro and White Students From Biographical Data.* An unpublished report to the U.S. Office of Education, Research Project No. 9-H-033, Institute for Behavioral Research in Creativity, 1970. Pp. iv, 71. *

501. GARMS, JOE D. "A Nonintellectual Scale for Predicting Achievement in Introductory Psychology." *Psychol* 7(1):40–3 F '70. * (*PA* 44:13377)

502. GRUNEBERG, MICHAEL M. "Scholastic Aptitude and Attainment Related to Employment Choice: A Study of Senior Secondary School Leavers in Scotland." *Voc Aspect Ed* (England) 22(53):159–68 N '70. *

503. HARTNETT, RODNEY T. "Differences in Selected Attitudes and College Orientations Between Black Students Attending Traditionally Negro and Traditionally White Institutions." *Sociol Ed* 43(4):419–36 f '70. * (*PA* 47:9611)

504. KALOGER, JAMES HERACLES. *Characteristics of Grosse Pointe High School Students in Advanced Placement Programs.* Doctor's thesis, University of Michigan (Ann Arbor, Mich.), 1970. (*DAI* 31:6440A)

505. KIRKENDALL, DON R., AND GRUBER, JOSEPH J. "Canonical Relationships Between the Motor and Intellectual Achievement Domains in Culturally Deprived High School Pupils." *Res Q* 41(4):496–502 D '70. * (*PA* 46:5712)

506. MOORE, LELAND B. *Predicting Levels of Success in Baccalaureate Technology Curriculums.* Doctor's thesis, Southern Illinois University (Carbondale, Ill.), 1970. (*DAI* 31:5151A)

507. MORRISON, JOHN W. "The Vocational Response of High School Students to Science Courses." *Sch Sci & Math* 70(8):720–34 N '70. *

508. NOWKA, HARRY EDWARD. *The Relationship Between Student Characteristics and Collegiate Termination of Vocational Business Certificate Holders.* Doctor's thesis, Oklahoma State University (Stillwater, Okla.), 1970. (*DAI* 31:5151A)

509. OATES, WALLACE E., AND QUANDT, RICHARD E. "The Effectiveness of Graduate Students as Teachers of the Principles of Economics." *J Econ Ed* 1(2):131–8 sp '70. *

510. PINTEL, GERALD. *The Effectiveness of Admissions Criteria in Relation to the Timely Completion of a Business Administration Curriculum by Students Enrolled in a Community College.* Doctor's thesis, New York University (New York, N.Y.), 1970. (*DAI* 32:1303A)

511. ROBERTS, JOSEPH PORTER. *Intellectually Gifted Adolescents: A Multivariate Analysis of Certain Educationally Relevant Attributes.* Doctor's thesis, University of Virginia (Charlottesville, Va.), 1970. (*DAI* 31:4588A)

512. SHINN, STEVEN MARKHAM. *A Comparative Investigation of Three Predictors of Academic Success at Springfield College.* Master's thesis, Springfield College (Springfield, Mass.), 1970.

513. WALL, K. WAYNE. "The Continuing Problem of Predicting Success in the Basic College Speech Course." *Speech Teach* 19(4):310–2 N '70. *

514. WILSON, KENNETH M. "Increasing Selectivity and Institutional Grading Standards." *Col & Univ* 46(1):46–53 f '70. *

515. YOUNG, RICHARD O. "A Study of Sophomores Who Used Career Counseling Services." *J Col Stud Personnel* 11(6):457 N '70. * (*PA* 45:8960)

516. *Normative Data for the 1970–71 Freshman Class, University System of Georgia.* Atlanta, Ga.: Regents of the University System of Georgia, November 1971. Pp. xi, 95. *

517. ALKER, HENRY A., AND CLOSSON, MICHAEL B. "Admission Standards, Institutional Racism, and Black Student Political Participation." Abstract. *Proc 79th Ann Conv Am Psychol Assn* 6(1):397–8 '71. * (*PA* 46:3703)

518. ASTIN, ALEXANDER W. *Predicting Academic Performance in College: Selectivity Data for 2300 American Colleges.* New York: Free Press, 1971. Pp. ix, 299. * (*PA* 48:3832, title only)

519. BACKMAN, MARGARET E., AND STEINDLER, FRANCES M. "Cognitive Abilities Related to Attrition in a Collegiate Nursing Program." *Nursing Outl* 19(12):807–8 D '71. *

520. BACKMAN, MARGARET E., AND STEINDLER, FRANCES M. "Prediction of Achievement in a Collegiate Nursing Program and Performance on State Board Examinations." *Nursing Outl* 19(7):487 Jl '71. *

521. BADGETT, JOHN L.; HOPE, LANNES H.; AND KERLEY, S. AUSTON. "The Relationship Between Self-Concept and Academic Aptitude of Entering Male College Freshmen." *Psychol* 8(2):43–7 My '71. * (*PA* 47:5736)

522. BELZ, HELENE FULTON. *The Relation of Convergent and Divergent Thinking Processes to Complex Problem-Solving.* Doctor's thesis, Stanford University (Stanford, Calif.), 1971. (*DAI* 32:5604A)

523. BLANCHFIELD, W. C. "College Dropout Identification: A Case Study." *J Exp Ed* 40(2):1–4 w '71. * (*PA* 48:1856)

524. BOHRNSTEDT, GEORGE W.; LAMBERT, PHILIP; AND BORGATTA, EDGAR F. "The Reliability and Validity of Quick Tests With High School Seniors." *J Exp Ed* 39(4):22–3 su '71. * (*PA* 47:1573)

525. BRADY, WILLIAM JOHN. *A Comparison of the Academic Performances of Native Students and Junior College Transfer Students in the Colleges of Agriculture, Business, and Education at the University of Georgia.* Doctor's thesis, University of Georgia (Athens, Ga.), 1971. (*DAI* 32:5561A)

526. BRANDENBURG, JUDITH BERMAN. *The Relationship Between Future Time Perspective and Academic Achievement: The Relationship of Three Dimensions of Future Time Perspective to Academic Achievement With Respect to Scholastic Aptitude, Sex and Socioeconomic Status Among College Freshmen.* Doctor's thesis, New York University (New York, N.Y.), 1971. (*DAI* 32:2982B)

527. BURKE, RONALD J. "Correlates of the Ability to Fragment and Reorganize Stored Information." *J General Psychol* 84(2):183–9 Ap '71. * (*PA* 46:4255)

528. BURNHAM, PAUL S., AND HEWITT, BENJAMIN A. "Advanced Placement Scores: Their Predictive Validity." *Ed & Psychol Meas* 31(4):939–45 w '71. * (*PA* 48:1631)

529. CARRUTH, BETTY RUTH, AND LAMB, MINA W. "Prediction of Student Performance Through Pretesting in Food and Nutrition: Home Economics Majors and Nonmajors." *J Home Econ* 63(1):41–4 Ja '71. *

530. CHAMBERS, JEAN FORBES. *Predicting the Academic Achievement Level of Deaf Students.* Doctor's thesis, University of Arizona (Tucson, Ariz.), 1971. (*DAI* 31:6396A)

531. CHAUNCEY, HENRY. "Educational Testing and Human Diversity." *Ed Rec* 52(2):117–24 sp '71. *

532. CLARK, KENNETH, AND PLOTKIN, LAWRENCE. "Aptitude Test Bias." Letter. *Sci* 174(4016):1278–9 D 12 '71. *

533. CREIGHTON, SAMUEL LESLEY. *The Quest for New Methods for Predicting the Academic Achievement of Economically Disadvantaged College Students.* Doctor's thesis, University of Toledo (Toledo, Ohio), 1971. (*DAI* 32:3717A)

534. DAVIS, JUNIUS A., AND TEMP, GEORGE. "Is the SAT Biased Against Black Students?" *Col Board R* 81:4–9 f '71. *

535. DENNEHY, ROBERT F. *The Relationship Between "Satisfaction" and "Satisfactoriness" in a Sample of College Freshmen: An Exploration of the Applicability of the Minnesota Theory of Work Adjustment to Scholastic Performance.* Doctor's thesis, New York University (New York, N.Y.), 1971. (*DAI* 32:5543A)

536. DINNAN, JAMES A.; BICKLEY, RACHEL T.; AND WILLIAMS, JOHN C. "Syntagmatic Oral Responses and SAT Scores of College Freshmen." *Yearb Nat Read Conf* 20:17–9 '71. *

537. DI SCIPIO, WILLIAM J. "Divergent Thinking: A Complex Function of Interacting Dimensions of Extraversion-Introversion and Neuroticism-Stability." *Brit J Psychol* 62(4):545–50 N '71. * (*PA* 47:8899)

538. FEDELL, JOHN C. *A Study of the Relationship Between the Need for Academic Achievement Motive and Student Grade Point Average at the Community College Level.* Doctor's

thesis, American University (Washington, D.C.), 1971. (*DAI* 32:1332A)

539. GOOLSBY, THOMAS M., JR., AND WILLIAMSON, DONALD A. "Use of the ROTC Qualifying Examination for Selection of Students to Enroll in Advanced Courses in ROTC as Juniors." *Ed & Psychol Meas* 31(2):513–6 su '71. *

540. HENDRICKSON, GERRY F. "The Effect of Differential Option Weighting on Multiple-Choice Objective Tests." *J Ed Meas* 8(4):291–6 w '71. * (*PA* 47:9651)

541. IRVINE, DONALD W. "Predicting the Persistence of Summer Trial Freshmen." *Cont Ed* 42(4):184–6 F '71. *

542. JAMES, REUBEN J. *Traits Associated With the Initial and Persistent Interest in the Study of College Science.* Doctor's thesis, State University of New York (Buffalo, N.Y.), 1971. (*DAI* 32:1296A)

543. KEPKA, EDWARD J., AND BRICKMAN, PHILIP. "Consistency Versus Discrepancy as Clues in the Attribution of Intelligence and Motivation." *J Pers & Social Psychol* 20(2):223–9 N '71. * (*PA* 47:6717)

544. KINCANNON, SUE GUNTER. *The Relationship of Selected Variables and Length of College Attendance at the University of Arkansas.* Doctor's thesis, University of Arkansas (Fayetteville, Ark.), 1971. (*DAI* 32:740A)

545. KIPNIS, DAVID, AND RESNICK, JEROME H. "Experimental Prevention of Underachievement Among Intelligent Impulsive College Students." *J Consult & Clin Psychol* 36(1):53–60 F '71. * (*PA* 45:10969)

546. LINN, MOTT ROBERTSON. *Achievement, Aptitude, Interest, and Personality Variables as Predictors of Curriculum, Graduation, and Placement.* Doctor's thesis, University of Pennsylvania (Philadelphia, Pa.), 1971. (*DAI* 32:1857A)

547. MACCHIA, WALTER. *Prediction of Senior Year SAT Scores From Freshman Year SCAT Scores and Final Grade Averages in English and Algebra.* Master's thesis, Jersey City State College (Jersey City, N.J.), 1971.

548. McCONNELL, DARLENE S. "A Study to Determine the Difference Between Selected Factors and Success in Shorthand I (BEOA 321) at Ball State University." *Ball State J Bus Educators* 43(1):9–14 N '71. *

549. MICHALSKI, STANLEY F., JR. "Development and Evaluation of a Visual-Aural Program in Conceptual Understanding of the Basic Elements of Music." *J Res Music Ed* 19(1):92–7 sp '71. * (*PA* 47:1824)

550. MOLNAR, GEORGE E.; DELAURETIS, ROBERT J.; AND LEBOLD, WILLIAM K. "Discriminant and Regression Models of College Persistence and Vocational Decisions." Abstract. *Proc 79th Ann Conv Am Psychol Assn* 6(2):519–20 '71. * (*PA* 46:5707)

551. MORGAN, ROBERT EARLE. *A Study of the Choices of Majors of Gardner-Webb College's Senior Class 1970–1971.* Doctor's thesis, University of North Carolina (Chapel Hill, N.C.), 1971. (*DAI* 32:4991A)

552. MUHLENKAMP, ANN F. "Prediction of State Board Scores in a Baccalaureate Prgoram." *Nursing Outl* 19(1):57 Ja '71. *

553. PFEIFER, C. MICHAEL, JR., AND SEDLACEK, WILLIAM E. "The Validity of Academic Predictors for Black and White Students at a Predominantly White University." *J Ed Meas* 8(4):253–61 w '71. * (*PA* 47:11785)

554. POWERS, RICHARD J. *Selected Noncognitive Variables as Predictors of Academic Achievement.* Doctor's thesis, St. John's University (Jamaica, N.Y.), 1971. (*DAI* 32:4194B)

555. SCHELLHAMMER, JAMES ROBERT. *A Longitudinal Analysis of the Academic Performance of Probationary Matriculants at Indiana University.* Doctor's thesis, Indiana University (Bloomington, Ind.), 1971. (*DAI* 32:1885A)

556. SHERRILL, DAVID, AND DRUGER, MARVIN. "Relationships Among Student Variables in an Audio-Tutorial Biology Course." *J Res Sci Teach* 8(2):191–4 '71. *

557. SIEGELMAN, MARVIN. "SAT and High School Average Predictions of Four Year College Achievement." *Ed & Psychol Meas* 31(4):947–50 w '71. * (*PA* 48:1871)

558. SMITH, JOHN STEPHEN. *A Multivariate Combination of Academic and Non-Academic Factors Related to Student Attrition.* Doctor's thesis, University of Pittsburgh (Pittsburgh, Pa.), 1971. (*DAI* 32:6786A)

559. SNYDER, C. R., AND RAY, WILLIAM J. "Observed Body Movement in the College Test-Taking Situation and Scores on the Scholastic Aptitude Test." *Percept & Motor Skills* 32(1):265–8 F '71. * (*PA* 46:3733)

560. STANLEY, JULIAN C. "Predicting College Success of the Educationally Disadvantaged: Admission to Selective Colleges Should Be Based Substantially on Test Scores and High School Grades." *Sci* 171(3972):640–7 F 19 '71. * (*PA* 46:9771)

561. SZABO, MICHAEL, AND FELDHUSEN, JOHN F. "Success in an Independent Study Science Course at the College Level as Related to Intellective, Personality, and Biographical Variables." *J Res Sci Teach* 8(3):225–9 '71. *

562. TEMP, GEORGE. "Validity of the SAT for Blacks and Whites in Thirteen Integrated Institutions." *J Ed Meas* 8(4):245–51 w '71. * (*PA* 47:11635)

563. THOMAS, CHARLES LEO. *The Relative Effectiveness of High School Grades and Standardized Test Scores for Predicting College Grades of Black Students.* Doctor's thesis, Johns

Hopkins University (Baltimore, Md.), 1971. (*DAI* 32:2495A)

564. ULIN, RICHARD O., AND BELSKY, THEODORE B. "Screening Prospective English Teachers: Criteria for Admission to Teacher Education Programs." *Res Teach Engl* 5(2):165–78 f '71. *

565. WHEELER, ROBERT G. "Computer Predicts Student Success as They Register." *Col Mgmt* 6(4):36–8 Ap '71. *

566. WILHELM, HOWARD McDONALD. *Predicting Academic Achievement at a Multipurpose College.* Doctor's thesis, University of Virginia (Charlottesville, Va.), 1971. (*DAI* 32: 4261A)

567. WING, CLIFF W., AND WALLACH, MICHAEL A. *College Admissions and the Psychology of Talent.* New York: Holt, Rinehart & Winston, Inc., 1971. Pp. ix, 165. * (*PA* 46:3701)

CUMULATIVE NAME INDEX

[358]

College Qualification Tests. Candidates for college entrance; 1955–61; CQT; 2 editions; distribution of Forms B and C restricted to colleges and universities; George K. Bennett, Marjorie G. Bennett, Wimburn L. Wallace, and Alexander G. Wesman; Psychological Corporation. *

a) COMBINED BOOKLET EDITION. 6 scores: verbal, numerical, information (science, social studies, total), total.

b) SEPARATE BOOKLET EDITION.

1) *Test V [Verbal].*

2) *Test N [Numerical].*

3) *Test I [Information].* 3 scores: science, social studies, total.

For additional information, see 7:345 (24 references); for reviews by Ralph F. Berdie and Warren G. Findley, see 6:450 (11 references); for reviews by Gustav J. Froehlich, A. E. G. Pilliner, and David V. Tiedeman, see 5:320.

REFERENCES THROUGH 1971

1–11. See 6:450.

12–35. See 7:345.

36. ROBERTSON, MALCOLM H. "Test Scores and Self-Estimates of Two Curricula Groups." *Personnel & Guid J* 38:746–50 My '60. * (*PA* 35:2767)

37. CUMMINGS, ROGER W., AND KIRK, BARBARA A. ["Norms of the College Qualification Test."] Letter. *J Counsel Psychol* 9:282 f '62. *

38. SEASHORE, HAROLD G. "Women Are More Predictable Than Men." *J Counsel Psychol* 9:261–70 f '62. * (*PA* 38:3194)

39. OBST, FRANCES. "A Study of Abilities of Women Students Entering the Colleges of Letters and Science and Applied Arts at the University of California, Los Angeles." *J Ed Res* 57:84–6 O '63. *

40. TROY, ELIZABETH McGOLDRICK. *A Study of the Predictive Value of Eleven Variables Used at King's College to Determine General Scholastic Achievement of Two Hundred Forty-Three Entering Students.* Master's thesis, Marywood College (Scranton, Pa.), 1965.

41. CUMMINS, EMERY J. "A Study of Differences Among Four Types of Disciplinary Offenders on Selected Cognitive and Affective Measures." *J Ed Res* 60:444–7 Jl–Ag '67. *

42. DeLONG, JOAN J. *The College Qualification Tests and Predictability of First Semester Grade Point Average at Chadron State College.* Master's thesis, Chadron State College (Chadron, Neb.), 1969.

43. ARNDT, JOHN RICHARD. *A Study of Selected Factors Characterizing Freshmen Who Entered Michigan State University in Fall 1968 Identified as Under-, Over- or Normal Achievers After One Term of College.* Doctor's thesis, Michigan State University (East Lansing, Mich.), 1970. (*DAI* 32:191A)

44. DUTHLER, BERNARD THOMAS. *A Study of the Prediction of Transfer Students' Academic Success in a College of Educa-*

tion. Doctor's thesis, University of Toledo (Toledo, Ohio), 1970. (*DAI* 31:4457A)

45. JOHNS, DANIEL JAY. *Correlates of Academic Success in a Predominantly Black, Open-Door, Public, Urban Community College.* Doctor's thesis, University of Virginia (Charlottesville, Va.), 1970. (*DAI* 31:4464A)

46. KALLINGAL, ANTHONY K. *Differential Validities of Selected Variables in the Prediction of College Success for Blacks and Whites.* Doctor's thesis, Michigan State University (East Lansing, Mich.), 1970. (*DAI* 31:5848A)

47. KALLINGAL, ANTHONY. "The Prediction of Grades for Black and White Students at Michigan State University." *J Ed Meas* 8(4):263–5 w '71. *

48. SMITH, DONALD MICHAEL. *The Validity of Factor Score Estimates of Speed and Accuracy as Predictors of First Term Grade Point Average.* Doctor's thesis, Florida State University (Tallahassee, Fla.), 1971. (*DAI* 32:6228A)

49. SMITH, LELAND. "A 5-Year Follow-Up Study of High Ability Achieving and Nonachieving College Freshmen." *J Ed Res* 64(5):220–2 Ja '71. * (*PA* 46:5716)

50. WILLETT, ELIZABETH A.; RIFFEL, P. A.; BREEN, LAWRENCE J.; AND DICKSON, ELINOR J. "Selection and Success of Students in a Hospital School of Nursing." *Can Nurse* 67(1):41–5 Ja '71. *

CUMULATIVE NAME INDEX

[359]

Concept Mastery Test. Grades 15–16 and graduate students and applicants for executive and research positions; 1956, c1950; CMT; Lewis M. Terman; Psychological Corporation. *

For additional information, see 6:451 (8 references); for reviews by J. A. Keats and Calvin W. Taylor, see 5:321 (4 references).

REFERENCES THROUGH 1971

1–4. See 5:321.

5–12. See 6:451.

13. CAMPBELL, MARY LOU. *Verbal Analogies Tests: A Comparison of Vocabulary and Reasoning Components Using the Miller Analogies Test and the Concept Mastery Test.* Master's thesis, University of Utah (Salt Lake City, Utah), 1964.

14. CHASE, CLINTON I.; LUDLOW, H. GLENN; AND PUGH, RICHARD C. *Predicting Success for Master's Degree Students in Education.* Indiana Studies in Prediction No. 5. Bloomington, Ind.: Bureau of Educational Studies and Testing, Indiana University, 1964. Pp. v, 25. *

15. CHASE, CLINTON I.; LUDLOW, H. GLENN; PUGH, RICHARD C.; AND POMEROY, MARTHA C. *Predicting Success for Advanced Graduate Students in Education.* Indiana Studies in Prediction No. 4. Bloomington, Ind.: Bureau of Educational Studies and Testing, Indiana University, 1964. Pp. v, 18. *

16. KNAPP, ROBERT H. "An Experimental Study of a Triadic Hypothesis Concerning the Sources of Aesthetic Imagery." *J Proj Tech & Pers Assess* 28:49–54 Mr '64. * (*PA* 39:1641)

17. FLEISCHER, GERALD, AND COHEN, IRA S. "The Relationship Between Test Anxiety and Tests of Creativity." Abstract. *Proc Ann Conv Am Psychol Assn* 73:311–2 '65. * (*PA* 39:15458)

18. GLAD, JOAN ROGERS BOURNE. *Evaluation of the Remedial Reading Program in Utah Public Schools.* Doctor's thesis, University of Utah (Salt Lake City, Utah), 1965. (*DA* 26:5864)

19. MCDERMID, CHARLES D. "Some Correlates of Creativity in Engineering Personnel." *J Appl Psychol* 49:14–9 F '65. * (*PA* 39:7782)

20. ALEXAKOS, C. E. "Predictive Efficiency of Two Multivariate Statistical Techniques in Comparison With Clinical Predictions." *J Ed Psychol* 57:297–306 O '66. * (*PA* 40:12756)

21. BYERS, JOE L. "A Set of Norms for the Concept Mastery Test Based Upon a Sample of Students in Teacher Education." *Calif J Ed Res* 17:133–43 My '66. * (*PA* 40:9429)

22. WELSH, GEORGE S. "Comparison of D-48, Terman CMT, and Art Scale Scores of Gifted Adolescents." Abstract. *J Consult Psychol* 30:88 F '66. * (*PA* 40:4105)

23. GAMEWELL, JOYCE. *An Investigation of the Use of Two Instruments for Assessing Intellective and Nonintellective Aspects of Intelligence as Predictors of Post Degree Success of Psychology Graduate Students.* Doctor's thesis, Colorado State College (Greeley, Colo.), 1967. (*DA* 28:3022A)

24. LAUGHLIN, PATRICK R. "Incidental Concept Formation as a Function of Creativity and Intelligence." *J Pers & Social Psychol* 5:115–9 Ja '67. * (*PA* 41:3958)

25. NEIDT, CHARLES O., AND HEDLUND, DALVA E. "The Relationship Between Changes in Attitudes Toward a Course and Final Achievement." *J Ed Res* 61:56–8 O '67. *

26. SLAKTER, MALCOLM J. "Risk Taking On Objective Examinations." *Am Ed Res J* 4:31–43 Ja '67. * (*PA* 41:7850)

27. WALLEN, NORMAN E., AND CAMPBELL, MARY LOU A. "Vocabulary and Non-verbal Reasoning Components of Verbal Analogies Tests (Miller Analogies Test and Concept Mastery Test)." *J Ed Res* 61:87–9 O '67. *

28. WELSH, GEORGE S. "Verbal Interests and Intelligence: Comparison of Strong VIB, Terman CMT, and D-48 Scores of Gifted Adolescents." *Ed & Psychol Meas* 27:349–52 su '67. * (*PA* 41:13633)

29. ZAHN, JANE C. "Some Characteristics of Successful and Less Successful Overseas Community Development Advisers." *Adult Ed* 18:15–23 f '67. *

30. GRIMSRUD, RICHARD ARLO. *A Method for Predicting Success in a Counselor Education Training Program.* Doctor's thesis, University of Minnesota (Minneapolis, Minn.), 1968. (*DA* 29:2115A)

31. MCCLOUD, THOMAS E. "Persistency as a Motivational Factor of Vocational Interest in the Prediction of Academic Success of Twelfth-Grade Superior Students." *Psychol* 5:34–46 N '68. * (*PA* 43:5984)

32. ROHLF, RICHARD JOHN. *A Higher-Order Alpha Factor Analysis of Interest, Personality, and Ability Variables, Including an Evaluation of the Effect of Scale Interdependency.* Doctor's thesis, University of Kansas (Lawrence, Kan.), 1968. (*DA* 29:1758A)

33. SLAKTER, MALCOLM J. "The Penalty for Not Guessing." *J Ed Meas* 5:141–4 su '68. *

34. SLAKTER, MALCOLM J., AND RODEN, AUBREY H. "Comparison of a Disguised and Reported Measure of Risk Taking on Objective Examinations." *Alberta J Ed Res* (Canada) 14:123–8 Je '68. * (*PA* 44:4173)

35. HINRICHS, J. R. "Comparison of 'Real Life' Assessments of Management Potential With Situational Exercises, Paper-and-Pencil Ability Tests, and Personality Inventories." *J Appl Psychol* 53(5):425–32 O '69. * (*PA* 44:1442)

36. KRAUT, ALLEN I. "Intellectual Ability and Promotional Success Among High Level Managers." *Personnel Psychol* 22(3):281–90 au '69. * (*PA* 44:9440)

37. LAUGHLIN, PATRICK R.; BRANCH, LAURENCE G.; AND JOHNSON, HOMER H. "Individual Versus Triadic Performance on a Unidimensional Complementary Task as a Function of Initial Ability Level." *J Pers & Social Psychol* 12(2):144–50 Je '69. * (*PA* 43:12897)

38. WELSH, GEORGE S. *Gifted Adolescents: A Handbook of Test Results.* Greensboro, N.C.: Prediction Press, June 1969. Pp. viii, 89. *

39. ROHLF, RICHARD J. "A Higher-Order Alpha Factor Analysis of Interest, Personality, and Ability Variables. Including an Evaluation of the Effect of Scale Interdependency." *Ed & Psychol Meas* 31(2):381–96 su '71. * (*PA* 46:11516)

40. WELSH, GEORGE S. "Vocational Interests and Intelligence in Gifted Adolescents." *Ed & Psychol Meas* 31(1):155–64 sp '71. * (*PA* 46:10645)

CUMULATIVE NAME INDEX

[360]

Cooperative Academic Ability Test. Superior grade
12 students; 1963–64; AAT; also published in 1966 as
Level 1 of *Cooperative School and College Ability
Tests: Series 2,* Forms A and B; 3 scores: verbal,
mathematical, total; Cooperative Tests and Services. *
For additional information, reviews by Eric F. Gardner and William B. Michael, and an excerpted review
by Kenneth D. Hopkins (with Darrell L. Sander), see
7:346 (3 references).

REFERENCES THROUGH 1971

1–3. See 7:346.

CUMULATIVE NAME INDEX

[361]

*Cooperative School and College Ability Tests.
1955–73; SCAT; 3 scores: verbal, quantitative, total;
2 editions; Cooperative Tests and Services. *
a) ORIGINAL SERIES [70 MINUTE TESTS]. Grades 4–6, 6–
8, 8–10, 10–12, 12–14, 15–16; 1955–63; 6 levels.
  1) *School Ability Test.* Grades 4–6, 6–8, 8–10, 10–12;
  Braille and large type editions are available from
  American Printing House for the Blind, Inc.
  2) *College Ability Test.* Grades 12–14, 15–16.
b) SERIES 2 [40 MINUTE TESTS]. Grades 4–6, 7–9, 10–12,
12–14; 1955–73.
For additional information, a review by H. J. Butcher,
and excerpted reviews by S. David Farr, Esin Kaya,
and Douglas McKie (with Peggy Rae Koopman) of
Series 2, see 7:347 (186 references); for a review by
Russel F. Green of the original series, see 6:452 (64
references); for reviews by Frederick B. Davis, Hanford M. Fowler, and Julian C. Stanley, see 5:322 (7 references).

REFERENCES THROUGH 1971

1–7. See 5:322.
8–71. See 6:452.
72–257. See 7:347.
258. CLIFF, ROSEMARY. "The Predictive Value of Chance-
Level Scores." *Ed & Psychol Meas* 18:607–16 au '58. * (PA
33:9269)
259. FOREHAND, G. A., JR., AND McQUITTY, LOUIS L.
"Configurations of Factor Standings as Predictors of Educational
Achievement." *Ed & Psychol Meas* 19:31–43 sp '59. * (PA
34:119)
260. DAHLKE, ARNOLD E., AND DANA, RICHARD H. "Intra-
individual Verbal-Numerical Discrepancies and Personality."
Abstract. *J Consult Psychol* 27:182 Ap '63. *
261. CHABASSOL, DAVID J., AND MANSON, GORDON G. "An
Investigation to Identify Creativity in Teaching." *Alberta J
Ed Res* (Canada) 10:201–8 D '64. *
262. EDMONDS, WILLIAM S. "Sex Differences in the Verbal
Ability of Socio-Economically Depressed Groups." *J Ed Res*
58:61–4 O '64. *
263. GAZDA, GEORGE M., AND FOLDS, JANELL H. "The Effects
of Three Methods of Test Interpretation on the Recall of Test
Scores and Change in Self Concept." *J Stud Pers Assn Teach
Ed* 4:10–21 D '64. *
264. HUGHES, DONALD L. *A Study to Predict the Academic
Success of Low Achieving High School Students at Brigham
Young University With Selected Tests.* Master's thesis, Brigham
Young University (Provo, Utah), 1964.
265. KATZ, STANLEY S. "Selection and Evaluation of Students
in Medical Technology Degree Programs." *Am J Med Technol*
30:51–63 Ja '64. *
266. ALTUS, WILLIAM D. "Birth Order and Mean Score on

a Ten-Item Aptitude Test." *Psychol Rep* 16:956 Je '65. * (PA
39:14628)
267. BARGER, BEN, AND HALL, EVERETTE. "The Interaction
of Ability Levels and Socioeconomic Variables in the Prediction
of College Dropouts and Grade Achievement." *Ed & Psychol
Meas* 25:501–8 su '65. * (PA 39:14896)
268. ELLIOTT, MERLE H., AND BADAL, ALDEN W. "Achievement and Racial Composition of Schools." *Calif J Ed Res*
16:158–66 S '65. * (PA 40:1478)
269. KIMBALL, WEBSTER H. *Persistence and Success Prediction in Accounting.* Master's thesis, California State College
(Long Beach, Calif.), 1965.
270. LUNDQUIST, RUSSELL M. *Prognosis of Success in Ninth
Grade Algebra.* Master's thesis, Mankato State College (Mankato, Minn.), 1965.
271. PEDERSEN, DARHL M. "The Measurement of Individual
Differences in Perceived Personality-Trait Relationships and
Their Relation to Certain Determinants." *J Social Psychol*
65:233–58 Ap '65. * (PA 39:14976)
272. AMAREL, MARIANNE; CHEEK, FRANCES E.; AND STIER-
HEM, ROBERT J. "Studies in the Sources of Variation in Cloze
Scores: 1, The Raters." *J Abn Psychol* 71:444–8 D '66. *
(PA 41:1574)
273. HARDING, WILLIAM THOMAS. *Differential Verbal and
Quantitative Scores and Interests.* Master's thesis, Illinois State
University (Normal, Ill.), 1966.
274. PHELPS, ARTHUR M. *Predicting First Semester Grades
in the Junior College Two-Year Terminal Vocational-Technical
Programs.* Master's thesis, Stetson University (DeLand, Fla.),
1966.
275. BIDINIAN, ROSE JOHNSON. *Predicting Probability of
Success in Selected First Semester Curriculum Areas of Sac-
ramento State College.* Master's thesis, Sacramento State College
(Sacramento, Calif.), 1967.
276. HUFF, BETTY. *The Predictive Value of Standardized
Testing in Relation to Mathematical Achievement at Virginia
High School.* Master's thesis, East Tennessee State University
(Johnson City, Tenn.), 1967.
277. STEWART, LAWRENCE H.; DOLE, ARTHUR A.; AND
HARRIS, YEUELL Y. "Cultural Differences in Abilities During
High School." *Am Ed Res J* 4:19–29 Ja '67. * (PA 41:7189)
278. WILLIAMSON, MALCOLM L., AND HOPKINS, KENNETH D.
"The Use of 'None-of-These' Versus Homogeneous Alternatives
on Multiple-Choice Tests: Experimental Reliability and Validity
Comparisons." *J Ed Meas* 4:53–8 su '67. *
279. ZOOK, HOWARD A. *A Comparative Study of the Validity
of Three Variables as Predictors of GPI at Kearney State
College.* Master's thesis, Kearney State College (Kearney, Neb.),
1967.
280. BLAI, BORIS, JR. "Measuring Educational Progress
Through 'Before' and 'After' Testing." *Psychol* 5:39–41 My
'68. * (PA 42:14567)
281. GENTRY, JOANNE. "Abstract of a Study of the Relationship Between High School Grades and Test Scores and the
Achievement of Students Enrolled in BEOA 326 (Shorthand)
at Ball State University in the Autumn Quarter of 1966." *Ball
State J Bus Educators* 40:12–6 N '68. *
282. GOEDICKE, RITA. *The Relation Between Academic Success
and Personality Variables.* Master's thesis, University of Alberta
(Edmonton, Alta., Canada), 1968.
283. MILLER, RICHARD H. "Students Show a Preparation
Increase but No Increase in Grades Was Shown." *Col & Univ*
45(1):28–30 f '69. *
284. MORE, ARTHUR. "The Relation of High School Grades,
Achievement and Intelligence Test Scores to Success in Dental
School." *Can Counsellor* 3(1):56–8 Ja '69. *
285. BACHMAN, ALFRED MORRY. "The Relationship Between a
Seventh-Grade Pupil's Academic Self-Concept and Achievement
in Mathematics." *J Res Math Ed* 1(3):173–9 My '70. *
286. CARPENTER, CORINNE TAYLOR. *Study of the Relationship
of Selected Factors to the Performance of Business Education
Graduates at Grambling College on the Commons Section of the
National Teacher Examinations.* Doctor's thesis, Indiana University (Bloomington, Ind.), 1970. (DAI 31:5900A)
287. DURHAM, JAMES ALFRED, JR. *An Analysis of Academic
Success Predictors for Selected Students at a Florida Junior
College.* Doctor's thesis, University of Southern Mississippi
(Hattiesburg, Miss.), 1970. (DAI 31:5790A)
288. EDDY, BERDYNE BUTCHER. *A Study of the Relationship
of Selected Student Characteristics to Persistence and With-
drawal of a Sample of Full-Time Freshmen at a Community
College.* Doctor's thesis, American University (Washington,
D.C.), 1970. (DAI 32:89A)
289. ELBERFELD, STEPHAN, AND LOVE, BETHOLENE. "Identifica-
tion of Aptitude Criteria for Medical Technology." *Am J Med
Technol* 36(8):388–99 Ag '70. *
290. FOXWORTH, CHARLES LEONARD. *Factors Related to
Academic Performance of Students Admitted to the Roswell
Community College 1958–1967.* Doctor's thesis, Louisiana State
University (Baton Rouge, La.), 1970. (DAI 31:4487A)
291. HALCROW, JOHN HAROLD. *The Relationship of Selected
Variables to the Academic Performance of Transfer Students
at the University of North Dakota.* Doctor's thesis, University
of North Dakota (Grand Forks, N.D.), 1970. (DAI 32:6759A)
292. KALOGER, JAMES HERACLES. *Characteristics of Grosse

Pointe High School Students in Advanced Placement Programs. Doctor's thesis, University of Michigan (Ann Arbor, Mich.), 1970. (*DAI* 31:6440A)

293. KIMBLES, SAMUEL LEWIS. *A Measure of Cultural Deprivation.* Doctor's thesis, University of Southern California (Los Angeles, Calif.), 1970. (*DAI* 31:4552A)

294. PARSLEY, JAMES FRANCIS, JR. *A Comparison of the Ability of Ninth Grade Students to Apply Several Critical Thinking Skills to Problematic Content Presented Through Two Different Media.* Doctor's thesis, Ohio University (Athens, Ohio), 1970. (*DAI* 31:4629A)

295. POINDEXTER, CHARLES CRAWFORD, JR. *Degrees and Dropouts: A Profile of Student Characteristics in North Carolina Community Colleges.* Doctor's thesis, University of North Carolina (Chapel Hill, N.C.), 1970. (*DAI* 31:5776A)

296. ROBERTS, JOSEPH PORTER. *Intellectually Gifted Adolescents: A Multivariate Analysis of Certain Educationally Relevant Attributes.* Doctor's thesis, University of Virginia (Charlottesville, Va.), 1970. (*DAI* 31:4588A)

297. RUSSELL, WENDELL PHILLIPS. *Intellectual and Non-Intellectual Factors Affecting the Attrition Rate of Students Entering Virginia Union University in 1965.* Doctor's thesis, University of Virginia (Charlottesville, Va.), 1970. (*DAI* 31:4474A)

298. SCHRECK, JOHN FREDERICK. *An Experimental Study of the Influence of Human Color Sensitivity Upon the Reliability of Student Responses on the School and College Ability Test Series II, Forms 1A and 1B.* Doctor's thesis, American University (Washington, D.C.), 1970. (*DAI* 32:1347A)

299. SODHI, SURINDER. "Personality Factors in Second Language Acquisition." *Ed & Psychol R* (India) 10(2):70–6 Ap '70. *

300. AUSTIN, GILBERT R., AND RYAN, BRUCE. "Computer Assisted Guidance in Predicting Probable Admission to Institutions of Higher Education." *J Ed Data Processing* 8(2–3):18–23 '71. *

301. BAUER, DAVID H. "The Effect of Test Instructions, Test Anxiety, Defensiveness, and Confidence in Judgment on Guessing Behavior in Multiple-Choice Test Situations." *Psychol Sch* 8(3):208–15 Jl '71. * (*PA* 47:9634)

302. BRADLEY, RICHARD W., AND SANBORN, MARSHALL P. "Using Tests to Predict Four-Year Patterns of College Grade Point." *J Col Stud Personnel* 12(2):138–42 Mr '71. * (*PA* 46:5699)

303. CLARK, NEWTON CECIL, JR. *Test Anxiety, Locus of Control, and Feedback in Self-Instruction.* Doctor's thesis, George Peabody College for Teachers (Nashville, Tenn.), 1971. (*DAI* 32:1912A)

304. DAMPEL, DAVID D., AND SEYMOUR, WARREN R. "The Academic Success of Black Students: A Dilemma." *J Col Stud Personnel* 12(4):243–7 Jl '71. *

305. DIXON, PAUL W.; FUKUDA, NOBUKO K.; AND BERENS, ANNE E. "A Factor Analysis of EPPS Scales, Ability, and Achievement Measures." *J Exp Ed* 39(4):31–41 su '71. * (*PA* 47:1723)

306. FRANK, AUSTIN C. "Men's Strong Vocational Interest Blank Academic Achievement Scale: An Attempted Validation." *J Counsel Psychol* 18(4):324–31 Jl '71. * (*PA* 46:11572)

307. HALL, LUCIEN T., JR. "The Prediction of Success in Each of Six Four-Year Selections of Secondary Mathematics Courses." *Sch Sci & Math* 71(8):693–6 N '71. *

308. HEATON, JEAN MOSSMAN. *Adolescent Orientation, Achievement and Family Interaction.* Doctor's thesis, Florida State University (Tallahassee, Fla.), 1971. (*DAI* 32:6486B)

309. KIRBY, BARBARA JANE. *An Analysis of the Relationships Between Academic Performance and Scores on Licensure Examinations of Mortuary Science Students at Miami-Dade Junior College 1966–1969.* Doctor's thesis, University of Miami (Coral Gables, Fla.), 1971. (*DAI* 32:3122A)

310. LESCARBEAU, WILFRED J. *A Study of the Relationship Between Selected Fine Manipulative Motor Abilities and Achievement in the Introductory Physical Science Course.* Doctor's thesis, University of Houston (Houston, Tex.), 1971. (*DAI* 33:900A)

311. MACCHIA, WALTER. *Prediction of Senior Year SAT Scores From Freshman Year SCAT Scores and Final Grade Averages in English and Algebra.* Master's thesis, Jersey City State College (Jersey City, N.J.), 1971.

312. PANDEY, R. E. "The SCAT and Race." *Psychol Rep* 28(2):459–62 Ap '71. * (*PA* 46:7456)

313. ROSENFELD, MICHAEL, AND HILTON, THOMAS L. "Negro-White Differences in Adolescent Educational Growth." *Am Ed Res J* 8(2):267–83 Mr '71. *

314. SISSON, ELEANOR RUTH. *A Longitudinal Study of Recent Counselor Information as a Broader Base for Academic Prediction.* Doctor's thesis, Purdue University (Lafayette, Ind.), 1971. (*DAI* 32:3045A)

315. STEPHENSON, ROBERT S., AND BEARD, JACOB G. "Common Dimensions of the School, Social, and Economic Environment in Florida: An Empirical Study." *Fla J Ed Res* 13:49–57 '71. *

316. TAYLOR, ALTON L. "Regression Analysis of Antecedent Measures of Slow Sections in High School Biology." *Sci Ed* 55(3):395–402 Jl–S '71. *

317. TISDALE, JOSEPH CHRISTOPHER, III. *Prediction of Success in First-Year Community College Mathematics.* Doctor's thesis, University of Virginia (Charlottesville, Va.), 1971. (*DAI* 32:4385A)

318. WAGMAN, MORTON. "Clinical and Research Use of the Strong Vocational Interest Blank Academic Achievement Scale." *J Counsel Psychol* 18(4):337–430 Jl '71. * (*PA* 46:11599)

319. WEBB, HAROLD QUENTIN. *The Prognostic Potential of Selected Factors for Predicting Achievement in the Study of High School Bookkeeping and Accounting.* Doctor's thesis, Ohio State University (Columbus, Ohio), 1971. (*DAI* 32:3645A)

CUMULATIVE NAME INDEX

[362]

*Cotswold Junior Ability Tests. Ages 8.5–9.5, 9.5–10.5; 1949–69; 2 levels; tests A, B, C, and E are out of print; C. M. Fleming; Robert Gibson & Sons, Glasgow, Ltd. [Scotland]. *

a) JUNIOR MENTAL ABILITY D. Ages 8.5–9.5; 1967–69, c1957.

b) JUNIOR MENTAL ABILITY F. Ages 9.5–10.5; 1967–69, c1961.

For additional information concerning earlier forms, see 5:323.

[363]

*Cotswold Measurement of Ability. Ages 10–12; 1947–70; earlier forms entitled *Cotswold Measurement of Mental Ability* and *Cotswold Mental Ability Test;* C. M. Fleming; Robert Gibson & Sons, Glasgow, Ltd. [Scotland]. *

For additional information and a review by A. W. Heim of earlier forms, see 5:324.

REFERENCES THROUGH 1971

1. JONES, W. R., AND STEWART, W. A. C. "Bilingualism and Verbal Intelligence." *Brit J Psychol* (Stat Sect) 4:3–8 Mr '51. * (*PA* 25:7930)

CUMULATIVE NAME INDEX

Heim, A. W.: *rev,* 5:324   Stewart, W. A. C.: 1
Jones, W. R.: 1

[364]

*Culture Fair Intelligence Test. Ages 4–8 and mentally retarded adults, 8–14 and average adults, 13–16 and superior adults or grades 9–16 and superior adults; 1933–73; CFIT; formerly called *Culture Free Intelligence Test;* 2 editions; Raymond B. Cattell and A. K. S. Cattell (Scales 2 and 3).

a) IPAT CULTURE FAIR INTELLIGENCE TEST. 1933–73; formerly called *IPAT Culture Free Intelligence Test;* test booklet titles are *Test of g: Culture Fair* or *Test of g: Culture Free;* 3 levels; Institute for Personality and Ability Testing. *

1) *Scale 1.* Ages 4–8 and mentally retarded adults; 1933–69; test copyrighted 1950 identical with *Cattell Intelligence Tests, Scale 0: Dartington Scale* (see 354a) copyrighted 1933.

2) *Scale 2.* Ages 8–14 and average adults; 1949–73.

3) *Scale 3.* Ages 13–16 and superior adults; 1950–73; Form A copyrighted 1963 identical with Form A copyrighted 1959 except for slight change in scale of some drawings.

b) CATTELL CULTURE FAIR INTELLIGENCE TEST. 1960–61; 2 levels; Bobbs-Merrill Co., Inc. *

1) *Scale 2.* Ages 8–14 and average adults; 1960; test copyrighted 1960 identical with Forms A (1957) and B (1960) of Scale 2 of *IPAT Culture Fair Intelligence Test* presented in a single test booklet.

2) *Scale 3.* Grades 9–16 and superior adults; 1961; test copyrighted 1961 identical with Forms A (1959) and B (1961) of Scale 3 of *IPAT Culture Fair Intelligence Test* presented in a single test booklet.

For additional information and reviews by John E. Milholland and Abraham J. Tannenbaum, see 6:453 (15 references); for a review by I. Macfarlane Smith of *a*, see 5:343 (11 references); for reviews by Raleigh M. Drake and Gladys C. Schwesinger, see 4:300 (2 references).

REFERENCES THROUGH 1971

1–2. See 4:300.
3–13. See 5:343.

14–28. See 6:453.

29. ELLIS, EARNEST. *A Comparison of the Wechsler Intelligence Scale for Children and the I.P.A.T. Culture Free Intelligence Test.* Master's thesis, San Francisco State College (San Francisco, Calif.), 1953.

30. ROGERS, LORENE L., AND PELTON, RICHARD B. "Effect of Glutamine on IQ Scores of Mentally Deficient Children." *Tex Rep Biol & Med* 15:84–90 sp '57. * (*PA* 31:8272)

31. RODD, WILLIAM G. "The Role of a 'Culture Free' Intelligence Test." *J Ed* (Hong Kong) 20:10–7 '62. *

32. MOORE, RICHARD V. *Comparative Influences of Material Incentives on Cattell Culture-Free Intelligence Scores for Children From Different Socio-economic Groups.* Master's thesis, Kent State University (Kent, Ohio), 1963.

33. POLLARD, ALICE G. *A Comparison of the Performance of a Group of Intellectually Retarded Children on Three Group Tests of Intelligence.* Master's thesis, Catholic University of America (Washington, D.C.), 1963.

34. DOMINO, GEORGE. "Comparison of the D48, Cattell Culture Fair, and Army Beta Tests in a Sample of College Males." *J Consult Psychol* 28:468–9 O '64. * (*PA* 39:5052)

35. FARRANT, ROLAND H. "The Intellective Abilities of Deaf and Hearing Children Compared by Factor Analyses." *Am Ann Deaf* 109:306–25 My '64. * (*PA* 39:2442)

36. KEARNEY, GEORGE E. "Comment on 'The Use of a Non-Verbal Test of Intelligence in the Trust Territory of the Pacific' by Jordheim and Olsen." *Am Anthrop* 66:1395–6 D '64. *

37. KING, A. RICHARD. "Comments on Jordheim and Olsen's Use of a Non-Verbal Test of Intelligence in the Pacific Islands Trust Territory." Letter. *Am Anthrop* 66:640–4 Je '64. *

38. NADEAU, CORINNE. *A Comparison of the Performance of a Group of Intellectually Normal Children on Three Group Tests of Intelligence.* Master's thesis, Catholic University of America (Washington, D.C.), 1964.

39. GERSTEIN, ALVIN I. "Development of a Selection Program for Nursing Candidates." *Nursing Res* 14:254–7 su '65. *

40. KIDD, ALINE H., AND RIVOIRE, JEANNE L. "The Culture-Fair Aspects of the Development of Spatial Perception." *J Genetic Psychol* 106:101–11 Mr '65. * (*PA* 39:12291)

41. RAO, SHARADAMBA. "Use of Culture Free Intelligence Tests in India." *Indian J Psychol* 40:61–5 Je '65. * (*PA* 40:9359)

42. RAO, SHARADAMBA. "A Useful Intelligence Test for Senior High School and College Students in India." *Indian J Psychol* 40:19–26 Mr '65. * (*PA* 40:5453)

43. STEWART, HORACE F., JR., AND KEELER, CLYDE E. "A Comparison of the Intelligence and Personality of Moon-Child Albino and Control Cuna Indians." *J Genetic Psychol* 106:319–24 Je '65. * (*PA* 39:14888)

44. CATTELL, R. B.; SEALY, A. P.; AND SWENEY, A. B. "What Can Personality and Motivation Source Trait Measurements Add to the Prediction of School Achievement?" *Brit J Ed Psychol* 36:280–95 N '66. * (*PA* 41:804)

45. HORN, JOHN L., AND CATTELL, RAYMOND B. "Age Differences in Primary Mental Ability Factors." *J Gerontol* 21:210–20 Ap '66. *

46. MACARTHUR, R. S., AND MOSYCHUK, H. "Lower and Upper Socio-economic Group Contrasts in Long-Term Predictability of Grade Nine Achievement." *J Ed Meas* 3:167–8 su '66. *

47. TATHAM, CLIFFORD B., AND DOLE, ARTHUR A. "Academic Success of Foreign Undergraduates." *J Col Stud Personnel* 7:167–71 My '66. *

48. AINSWORTH, MARJORIE E. "The Relationship Between Motivation, Personality, Intelligence and School Attainment in a Secondary Modern School." *Brit J Ed Psychol* 37:135–7 F '67. * Abstract of master's thesis, University of Manchester (Manchester, England), 1966.

49. CATE, CLARENCE C. "Test Behavior of ESL Students." *Calif J Ed Res* 18:184–7 S '67. * (*PA* 42:4480)

50. HORN, JOHN L., AND CATTELL, RAYMOND B. "Age Differences in Fluid and Crystallized Intelligence." *Acta Psychologica* (Netherlands) 26(2):107–29 '67. * (*PA* 41:10446)

51. HUMPHREYS, LLOYD G. "Critique of Cattell's 'Theory of Fluid and Crystallized Intelligence: A Critical Experiment.'" *J Ed Psychol* 58:129–36 Je '67. * (*PA* 41:10447)

52. LARSON, STANFORD S. *A Comparison of Two Non-Verbal Intelligence Tests as Predictors of Academic Success of Navajo Students.* Master's thesis, Utah State University (Logan, Utah), 1967.

52a. MOGOR, ALBERT GARY. *The Concurrent Validity of Scale 2, Cattell Culture Fair Test of Intelligence for Three Levels of Socioeconomic Status.* Master's thesis, New Mexico State University (University Park, N.M.), 1967.

53. ALZOBAIE, ABDUL JALIL; METFESSEL, NEWTON S.; AND MICHAEL, WILLIAM B. "Alternative Approaches to Assessing the Intellectual Abilities of Youth From a Culture of Poverty." *Ed & Psychol Meas* 28:449–55 su '68. * (*PA* 42:19264)

54. ARNOLD, RICHARD D. "Reliability Coefficients of Certain Tests Used in the San Antonio Language Research Project." Abstract. *AERA Paper Abstr* 1968:92 '68. *

55. AX, ALBERT F., AND BAMFORD, JACQUELINE L. "Validation of a Psychophysiological Test of Aptitude for Learning Social Motives." *Psychophysiol* 5:316–32 S '68. * (*PA* 43:3943)

56. BECICA, BOZA. *A Comparison of Selected Characteristics of Students With Higher Grades in Their Foreign Language*

Courses Than in Their Nonlanguage Courses. Doctor's thesis, University of Texas (Austin, Tex.), 1968. (*DA* 29:4315A)

57. CATTELL, RAYMOND B., AND BUTCHER, H. J. *The Prediction of Achievement and Creativity*, pp. 161–79, passim. Indianapolis, Ind.: Bobbs-Merrill Co., Inc., 1968. Pp. xiv, 386. *

58. CATTELL, RAYMOND BERNARD. "Are I.Q. Tests Intelligent?" *Psychol Today* 1:56–62 Mr '68. *

59. DOMINO, GEORGE. "Culture-Free Tests and the Academic Achievement of Foreign Students." Abstract. *J Consult & Clin Psychol* 32:102 F '68. * (*PA* 42:7843)

60. GADDES, W. H.; MCKENZIE, AUDREY; AND BARNSLEY, ROGER. "Psychometric Intelligence and Spatial Imagery in Two Northwest Indian and Two White Groups of Children." *J Social Psychol* 75:35–42 Je '68. * (*PA* 42:13575)

61. HARRIS, A. J., AND LOVINGER, R. J. "Longitudinal Measures of the Intelligence of Disadvantaged Negro Adolescents." *Sch R* 76:60–6 Mr '68. * (*PA* 43:3138)

62. MACARTHUR, R. S. "Assessing Intellectual Potential of Native Canadian Pupils: A Summary." *Alberta J Ed Res* (Canada) 14:115–22 Je '68. * (*PA* 44:4170)

63. MACARTHUR, RUSSELL. "Some Differential Abilities of Northern Canadian Native Youth." *Int J Psychol* (France) 3(1):43–50 '68. * (*PA* 42:15325)

64. PELOSI, JOHN WILLIAM. *A Study of the Effects of Examiner Race, Sex, and Style on Test Responses of Negro Examinees.* Doctor's thesis, Syracuse University (Syracuse, N.Y.), 1968. (*DA* 29:4105A)

65. SCHLICHT, WILLIAM J., JR.; ANDERSON, DERWYN L.; HELIN, WILLIAM C.; HIPPE, DOUGLAS L.; LISTIAK, RICHARD L.; MOSER, RICHARD J.; AND WALKER, JAMES L. "Creativity and Intelligence: Further Findings." *J Clin Psychol* 24:458 O '68. * (*PA* 43:4025)

66. WILLARD, LOUISA A. "A Comparison of Culture Fair Test Scores With Group and Individual Intelligence Test Scores of Disadvantaged Negro Children." *J Learn Dis* 1:584–9 O '68. * (*PA* 45:3968)

67. ARNOLD, RICHARD D. "Reliability of Test Scores for the Young 'Bilingual' Disadvantaged." *Read Teach* 22(4):341–5 Ja '69. *

68. KANDERIAN, SUAD SIROP. *Study of the Relationship Between School Achievement and Measures of Intelligence and Creativity for Students in Iraq.* Doctor's thesis, University of Southern California (Los Angeles, Calif.), 1969. (*DAI* 31:644A)

69. MACARTHUR, RUSSELL S. "Some Cognitive Abilities of Eskimo, White, and Indian-Métis Pupils Aged 9 to 12 Years." *Can J Behav Sci* 1(1):50–9 Ja '69. * (*PA* 44:12319)

70. WIGGINS, NANCY; HOFFMAN, PAUL J.; AND TABER, THOMAS. "Types of Judges and Cue Utilization in Judgments of Intelligence." *J Pers & Social Psychol* 12(1):52–9 My '69. * (*PA* 43:11266)

71. ISMAIL, A. H., AND KIRKENDALL, D. R. "Relationship Among Three Domains of Development," pp. 451–60. In *Contemporary Psychology of Sport.* Proceedings of the Second International Congress of Sport Psychology, Washington, D.C., 1968. Chicago, Ill.: Athletic Institute, 1970. Pp. xix, 878. *

72. KAKKAR, S. B. "Popularity, Intelligence, Economic Status and Academic Achievement." *Indian J Psychol* 45(3):233–7 S '70. *

73. KALEHOFF, DOROTHY W. *Selected Personal Characteristics of the Adult Basic Education Student in Mississippi.* Doctor's thesis, Mississippi State University (State College, Miss.), 1970. (*DAI* 31:5109A)

74. KNIGHT, DAVID, AND ALCORN, JOHN D. "Comparisons of the Performance of Educationally Disadvantaged Adults and Elementary Children on Selected Measures of Reading Performance." *South J Ed Res* 4(4):262–72 O '70. *

75. SINGH, R. N. "A Study of the Scores on Cattell's Culture Fair Test of Intelligence (Scale 2) in an Indian Background: A Special Reference to Socio-Economic Variable." Doctor's thesis abstract. *Indian Psychol R* 7(1):74–6 Jl '70. *

76. VROMAN, CLYDE, AND WILCOX, LEE. "Research on A.I.D. Sponsored Foreign Students." *Col & Univ* 45(4):717–23 su '70. *

77. ADCOCK, C. J., AND WEBBERLEY, M. "Primary Mental Abilities." *J General Psychol* 84(2):229–43 Ap '71. * (*PA* 46:4979)

78. BARTON, K.; DIELMAN, T. E.; AND CATTELL, R. B. "The Prediction of School Grades From Personality and IQ Measures." *Personality* 2(4):325–33 w '71. * (*PA* 48:7878)

79. COWDEN, JAMES E.; PETERSON, WILLIAM M.; AND PACHT, ASHER R. "The Validation of a Brief Screening Test for Verbal Intelligence at Several Correctional Institutions in Wisconsin." *J Clin Psychol* 27(2):216–8 Ap '71. * (*PA* 46:7125)

80. DIELMAN, T. E.; BARTON, K.; AND CATTELL, R. B. "The Prediction of Junior High School Achievement From Objective Motivation Tests." *Personality* 2(4):279–87 w '71. * (*PA* 48:7881)

81. GOODWIN, NANCY-LEE. *The Prediction of Artistic Performance From Cognitive and Non-Cognitive Measures.* Doctor's thesis, University of Illinois (Urbana, Ill.), 1971. (*DAI* 32:4419A)

82. GREENBERG, BERNARD L., AND GREENBERG, SALLY H. "The Measurement of College Potential in the Hearing Handicapped." *Am Ann Deaf* 116(3):372-81 Je '71. * (*PA* 47:1410)

83. KNIGHT, DAVID, AND ALCORN, JOHN D. "Comparisons of the Performance of Educationally Disadvantaged Adults and Elementary Children on Selected Measures of Reading Performance." *Yearb Nat Read Conf* 19(2):113-7 '71. *

84. LANDRY, RICHARD G. "The Factorial Orthogonality of the Torrance Tests of Creative Thinking and the Culture-Fair Intelligence Tests." *Col Ed Rec Univ N Dak* 57(2):20-6 N '71. *

85. POWELL, RICHARD R., AND POHNDORF, RICHARD H. "Comparison of Adult Exercisers and Nonexercisers on Fluid Intelligence and Selected Physiological Variables." *Res Q* 42(1):70-7 Mr '71. * (*PA* 46:6635)

86. SINGH, AMIR, AND HUNDAL, P. S. "Age Differences in Fluid and Crystallized Intelligence." *Indian J Psychol* 46(1):85-94 Mr '71. *

87. WILLIAMS, PATSY RUTH. *Comparison of the Cattell Culture Fair Test With the California Mental Maturity Test.* Master's thesis, Southern Methodist University (Dallas, Tex.), 1971.

88. ZEDECK, SHELDON. "Identification of Moderator Variables by Discriminant Analysis in a Multipredictable Group Validation Model." *J Appl Psychol* 55(4):364-71 Ag '71. * (*PA* 47:1947)

CUMULATIVE NAME INDEX

[365-6]

The D48 Test. Grades 5 and over; 1963, c1961; intelligence; translation of the French edition published in 1948; for research use only; translation and American

manual by John D. Black; Consulting Psychologists Press, Inc. *

For additional information and reviews by Paul C. Davis and S. S. Dunn, see 6:454 (3 references).

REFERENCES THROUGH 1971

1-3. See 6:454.

4. DOMINO, GEORGE. "Comparison of the D48, Cattell Culture Fair, and Army Beta Tests in a Sample of College Males." *J Consult Psychol* 28:468-9 O '64. * (*PA* 39:5052)

5. BOYD, MAYNARD E. *Characteristics of the D48 Test When Used at the College Level.* Master's thesis, Marshall University (Huntington, W.Va.), 1966.

6. CANTWELL, ZITA M. "Relationships Between Scores on the Standard Progressive Matrices (1938) and on the D.48 Test of Non-Verbal Intelligence and 3 Measures of Academic Achievement." *J Exp Ed* 34:28-31 su '66. * (*PA* 40:11152)

7. WELSH, GEORGE S. "Comparison of D-48, Terman CMT, and Art Scale Scores of Gifted Adolescents." Abstract. *J Consult Psychol* 30:88 F '66. * (*PA* 40:4105)

8. BOYD, MAYNARD E., AND WARD, GEORGE, II. "Validities of the D-48 Test for Use With College Students." *Ed & Psychol Meas* 27:1137-8 w '67. * (*PA* 8:8933)

9. RAFI, A. ABI. "The Progressive Matrices (1938) and the Dominoes (D48) Tests: A Cross-Cultural Study." *Brit J Ed Psychol* 37:117-9 F '67. *

10. WELSH, GEORGE S. "Verbal Interests and Intelligence: Comparison of Strong VIB, Terman CMT, and D-48 Scores of Gifted Adolescents." *Ed & Psychol Meas* 27:349-52 su '67. * (*PA* 41:13633)

11. DOMINO, GEORGE. "Culture-Free Tests and the Academic Achievement of Foreign Students." Abstract. *J Consult & Clin Psychol* 32:102 F '68. * (*PA* 42:7843)

12. DOMINO, GEORGE. "A Non-Verbal Measure of Intelligence for Totally Blind Adults." *New Outl Blind* 62:247-52 O '68. *

13. KARNES, LUCIA ROONEY. *The Comparison of Scores of Eighth-Grade Reading and Nonreading Boys on the Lorge-Thorndike Tests, Wechsler Intelligence Scale for Children, the D48 Test, and the Welsh Figure Preference Test, GW Scale.* Doctor's thesis, University of North Carolina (Chapel Hill, N.C.), 1968. (*DAI* 30:585A)

14. WELSH, GEORGE S. *Gifted Adolescents: A Handbook of Test Results.* Greensboro, N.C.: Prediction Press, June 1969. Pp. viii, 89. *

15. CHISSOM, BRAD S., AND LIGHTSEY, RALPH. "A Comparison of the D-48 Test and the Otis Quick Score for High School Dropouts." *Ed & Psychol Meas* 31(2):525-7 su '71. *

16. WELSH, GEORGE S. "Vocational Interests and Intelligence in Gifted Adolescents." *Ed & Psychol Meas* 31(1):155-64 sp '71. * (*PA* 46:10645)

CUMULATIVE NAME INDEX

[367]

Deeside Non-Verbal Reasoning Test: English-Welsh Bilingual Version. Ages 10-12; 1961-63; distribution restricted to directors of education; W. G. Emmett; George G. Harrap & Co. Ltd. [England]. *

For additional information, see 6:455.

[368]

Deeside Picture Puzzles. Ages 6.5-8.5; 1956-58; W. G. Emmett; George G. Harrap & Co. Ltd. [England]. *

For additional information and reviews by Charlotte E. K. Banks and M. L. Kellmer Pringle, see 5:327.

[369]

Dennis Test of Scholastic Aptitude. Grades 4-8, 5-8; DTSA; 1961-63; William H. Dennis; the Author. *

For additional information, see 7:348.

[370]

Detroit General Intelligence Examination. Grades 7-12; 1938-54; consists of 8 of the 10 subtests used to get an intelligence score in the *Detroit General Apti-*

tudes Examination; 1954 test identical with subtests copyrighted 1938; Harry J. Baker and Paul H. Voelker; Bobbs-Merrill Co., Inc. *
For additional information, see 5:328.

[371]

Doppelt Mathematical Reasoning Test. Grades 16–17 and employees; 1954–68; DMRT; distribution restricted and test administered at specified licensed university centers; Jerome E. Doppelt; Psychological Corporation. *
For additional information, see 7:349 (2 references); for a review by W. V. Clemans, see 6:456 (2 references).

REFERENCES THROUGH 1971

1–2. See 6:456.
3–4. See 7:349.

CUMULATIVE NAME INDEX

Carleton, F. O.: 4   Jones, W. S.: 3
Clark, F. E.: 1   Roemmich, H.: 2
Clemans, W. V.: *rev,* 6:456   Schwartz, M. M.: 1
Hardesty, D. L.: 3

[372]

Draw-A-Man Test for Indian Children. Ages 6–10; 1956–66; adaptation of *Goodenough Intelligence Test;* Pramila Phatak; distributed by Anand Agencies [India]. *
For additional information and an excerpted review by M. A. Faroqi, see 7:350 (4 references).

REFERENCES THROUGH 1971

1–4. See 7:350.
5. MAJUMDAR, S. K. "Relationship Between Old (1956) and New (1966) Norms for Goodenough's Draw-a-Man Test (Pramila Phatak's Indian Adaptation) on Normal and Retarded Children." *Indian Ed R* 4(2):97–102 Jl '69. *

CUMULATIVE NAME INDEX

Faroqi, M. A.: *exc,* 7:350   Misra, A. N.: 4
Majumdar, S. K.: 5   Phatak, P.: 1–3

[373]

The Essential Intelligence Test. Ages 8–12; 1940–52; manual title is *Essential Junior Intelligence Test;* Fred J. Schonell and R. H. Adams; Oliver & Boyd [Scotland]. *
For additional information and a review by R. Winterbourn, see 5:333; for a review by F. W. Warburton, see 4:290.

REFERENCES THROUGH 1971

1. PEEL, E. A., AND GRAHAM, D. "Differentiation of Ability in Primary School Children." *Durham Res R* (England) 1(2): 40–8 S '51. *
2. PEEL, E. A., AND GRAHAM, D. "Differentiation of Ability in Primary School Children—II." *Durham Res R* (England) 1(3):31–4 S '52. * (*PA* 27:5157)
3. MADDOX, H. "Mental Age Scales." *Brit J Ed Psychol* 29:72–3 F '59. * (*PA* 34:2731)
4. NISBET, J. D., AND ILLESLEY, R. "The Influence of Early Puberty on Test Performance at Age Eleven." *Brit J Ed Psychol* 33:169–76 Je '63. * (*PA* 38:4096)
5. RILEY, CONAL STUART. "The Relationship Between Reading Ability and Verbal Intelligence Test Performance." Abstract. *Brit J Ed Psychol* 36:117 F '66. * (*PA* 40:7056; title only)
6. HOROBIN, GORDON; OLDMAN, DAVID; AND BYTHEWAY, BILL. "The Social Differentiation of Ability." *Sociology* 1:113–29 My '67. *
7. NISBET, J. D., AND ENTWISTLE, N. J. "Intelligence and Family Size, 1949–1965." *Brit J Ed Psychol* 37:188–93 Je '67. * (*PA* 41:15274)

CUMULATIVE NAME INDEX

Bytheway, B.: 6   Nisbet, J. D.: 4, 7
Entwistle, N. J.: 7   Oldman, D.: 6
Graham, D.: 1–2   Peel, E. A.: 1–2
Horobin, G.: 6   Riley, C. S.: 5
Illesley, R.: 4   Warburton, F. W.: *rev,* 4:290
Maddox, H.: 3   Winterbourn, R.: *rev,* 5:333

[374]

Executive Employment Review. Applicants for executive level positions; 1964–70; revision of *General Interest Review;* formerly called *General Employment Review;* 4 scores: vocabulary, mathematics, perception-general knowledge, total; no manual; L & L Associates. *
For additional information, see 7:992c.

[375]

Figure Reasoning Test: A Non-Verbal Intelligence Test, Second Edition. Ages 10 and over; 1949–62; 1962 test identical with test copyrighted 1949 except for format; John C. Daniels; Crosby Lockwood Staples [England]. *
For additional information and a review by A. W. Heim, see 6:457; for reviews by E. J. G. Bradford and James Maxwell and an excerpted review, see 4:291 (1 reference).

REFERENCES THROUGH 1971

1. See 4:291.
2. MESSER, MICHAEL E., AND ALLEN, ROBERT M. "Verbal Recognition and Non-Verbal Reasoning of Retardates." *Percept & Motor Skills* 28(1):334 F '69. * (*PA* 43:11764)

CUMULATIVE NAME INDEX

Allen, R. M.: 2   Heim, A. W.: *rev,* 6:457
Bradford, E. J. G.:. *rev,* 4:291   Maxwell, J.: *rev,* 4:291
Daniels, J. C.: 1   Messer, M. E.: 2

[376-7]

*Fundamental Achievement Series. Semiliterate job applicants and employees; 1968–70, c1965–70; FAS; 3 scores: numerical, verbal, total; 2 tests; distribution of Form A restricted to personnel departments; George K. Bennett and Jerome E. Doppelt; Psychological Corporation. *
a) NUMERICAL.
b) VERBAL.
For additional information, a review by Norman Frederiksen, and an excerpted review by Lewis R. Aiken, Jr., see 7:978.

[378]

*General Mental Ability Test: ETSA Test 1A. Job applicants; 1960–72, c1957–66; manual and technical handbook by S. Trevor Hadley and George A. W. Stouffer, Jr.; test by Psychological Services Bureau; Educators'-Employers' Tests & Services Associates. *
For the complete battery entry, see 2106.
For reviews of the complete battery, see 6:1025 (2 reviews).

[379]

General Verbal Practice Tests G1–G3. Ages 10–11; 1954–61; to be given at least 3 weeks before administering a verbal intelligence test in order to equalize coaching effects; distribution restricted to directors of education; published for the National Foundation for Educational Research in England and Wales; Ginn & Co. Ltd. [England]. *
For additional information, see 6:458.

[380]

*Gilliland Learning Potential Examination. Ages 6 and over; 1966–71; GLPE; an intelligence test "for use with remedial readers and the culturally disadvantaged"; 1 to 4 scores: total score for all subjects, non-reading-noncultural, predicted comprehension, and visual memory for subjects with reading problems; some subtests may be omitted in grades 3 and over to obtain a quick score and in grades 3 and under to obtain a primary score; Hap Gilliland; Montana Reading Publications. *

For additional information and reviews by Albert J. Harris and Howard B. Lyman, see 7:351.

[381]
Goodenough-Harris Drawing Test. Ages 3–15; 1926–63; revision and extension of the *Goodenough Intelligence Test;* Florence L. Goodenough and Dale B. Harris; Harcourt Brace Jovanovich, Inc. *

For additional information, reviews by Anne Anastasi and James A. Dunn, and excerpted reviews by M. L. Kellmer Pringle, Marjorie P. Honzik, Carol Hunter, Adolph G. Woltmann, Marvin S. Kaplan, and Mary J. Rouse, see 7:352 (158 references) ; see also 6:460 (43 references) and 5:335 (34 references) ; for a review by Naomi Stewart of the original edition, see 4:292 (60 references).

REFERENCES THROUGH 1971

1–60. See 4:292.
61–94. See 5:335.
95–137. See 6:460.
138–295. See 7:352.
296. HECKMAN, SAMUEL B. Chap. 3, "A Comparative Study of Group Intelligence Tests Applicable to Children of Kindergarten Age," pp. 17–44. In *Contributions to Education, Vol 1.* Edited by J. Carleton Bell. Yonkers, N.Y.: World Book Co., 1924. Pp. ix, 364. *
297. CUNNINGHAM, BESS V. "Measurement of Intelligence by Drawings: A Review." *J Ed Psychol* 18:66–7 Ja '27. *
298. WAGONER, LOVISA C., AND ARMSTONG, EDNA M. "The Motor Control of Children as Involved in the Dressing Process." *J Genetic Psychol* 35:84–97 Mr '28. * (*PA* 2:3692)
299. PORTEUS, STANLEY D. Chap. 23, "Aboriginal Children's Intelligence," pp. 408–20. In his *The Psychology of a Primitive People: A Study of the Australian Aborigine.* New York: Longmans, Green & Co., 1931. Pp. xvi, 438. * (*PA* 6:1168, title only)
300. DAVENPORT, E. LEE. "The Intelligence Quotients of Mexican and Non-Mexican Siblings." *Sch & Soc* 36:304–6 S 3 '32. * (*PA* 7:232)
301. EELLS, WALTER CROSBY. "Mental Ability of the Native Races of Alaska." *J Appl Psychol* 17:417–38 Ag '33. * (*PA* 8:478)
302. SCHILLER, BELLE. "Verbal, Numerical and Spatial Abilities of Young Children." *Arch Psychol* 161:1–69 Mr '34. * (*PA* 8:3874)
303. ANDERSON, H. DEWEY, AND EELLS, WALTER CROSBY. *Alaska Natives: A Survey of Their Sociological and Educational Status,* pp. 298–370. Stanford, Calif.: Stanford University Press, 1935. Pp. xvi, 472. * (*PA* 9:2346)
304. TIEBOUT, CAROLYN. "The Measurement of Quality in Children's Painting by the Scale Method." *Psychol Monogr* 48(1):85–94 '36. * (*PA* 11:391)
305. TIEBOUT, CAROLYN, AND MEIER, NORMAN C. "Artistic Ability and General Intelligence." *Psychol Monogr* 48(1):95–125 '36. * (*PA* 11:392)
306. WEISENBURG, THEODORE; ROE, ANNE; AND McBRIDE, KATHARINE E. *Adult Intelligence: A Psychological Study of Test Performances.* New York: Commonwealth Fund, 1936. Pp. xiii, 155. * (*PA* 10:3771)
307. SPRINGER, N. NORTON. "A Comparative Study of the Intelligence of a Group of Deaf and Hearing Children." *Am Ann Deaf* 83:138–52 Mr '38. * (*PA* 13:750)
308. SPRINGER, N. NORTON. "The Influence of General Social Status on the Emotional Stability of Children." *J Genetic Psychol* 53:321–8 D '38. * (*PA* 13:3348)
309. ABEL, THEODORA M. "Subnormal Girls With Discrepant Test Patterns." *J Appl Psychol* 23:398–404 Je '39. * (*PA* 13:5668)
310. MOTT, SINA M. "The Growth of an Abstract Concept." *Child Develop* 10:21–5 Mr '39. * (*PA* 13:4408)
311. ROHRER, JOHN H. "The Test Intelligence of Osage Indians." *J Social Psychol* 16:99–105 Ag '42. * (*PA* 16:4724)
312. SEASHORE, HAROLD G., AND BAVELAS, ALEX. "A Study of Frustration in Children." *J Genetic Psychol* 61:279–314 D '42. * (*PA* 17:1002)
313. GREENE, CHARLOTTE L. "A Study of Personal Adjustment in Mentally Retarded Girls." *Am J Mental Def* 49:472–6 Ap '45. * (*PA* 20:145)
314. NOTCUTT, B. "The Measurement of Zulu Intelligence." *J Social Res* (South Africa) 1:195–206 D '50. * (*PA* 27:4186)
315. BENNETT, EDWARD M., AND JOHANNSEN, DOROTHEA E. "Psychodynamics of the Diabetic Child." *Psychol Monogr* 68(11):1–23 '54. * (*PA* 29:6072)
316. GUREVITZ, SAUL, AND HELME, WILLIAM H. "Effects of Electroconvulsive Therapy on Personality and Intellectual Functioning of the Schizophrenic Child." *J Nerv & Mental Dis* 120:213–26 S-O '54. * (*PA* 29:7650)
317. KARLSEN, BJÖRN. *A Comparison of Some Educational and Psychological Characteristics of Successful and Unsuccessful Readers at the Elementary School Level.* Doctor's thesis, University of Minnesota (Minneapolis, Minn.), 1954. (*DA* 15:456)
318. GÜNZBURG, H. C. "Projection in Drawings: A Case Study." *Brit J Med Psychol* 28:72–81 pt 1 '55. * (*PA* 30:1028)
319. WHEELER, JOHN I., JR., AND CALDWELL, BETTYE McDONALD. "Psychological Evaluation of Women With Cancer of the Breast and of the Cervix." *Psychosom Med* 17:256–68 Jl–Ag '55. * (*PA* 30:5074)
320. DENNIS, WAYNE, AND NAJARIAN, PERGROUHI. "Infant Development Under Environmental Handicap." *Psychol Monogr* 71(7):1–13 '57. * (*PA* 33:5830)
321. HELLER, ARTHUR D. "The Draw-a-Person Test in Mental Defectives." *Mental Health* (England) 16:90–5 S '57. * (*PA* 33:1636)
322. MELIKIAN, LEVON. "Preference for Delayed Reinforcement: An Experimental Study Among Palestinian Arab Refugee Children." *J Social Psychol* 50:81–6 Ag '59. * (*PA* 35:3240)
323. SAMPSON, OLIVE C. "The Speech and Language Development of 5-Year-Old Children." *Brit J Ed Psychol* 29:217–22 N '59. *
324. CURTI, MARGARET WOOSTER. "Intelligence Tests of White and Colored Children in Grand Cayman." *J Psychol* 49:13–27 Ja '60. * (*PA* 34:7628)
325. CARKHUFF, ROBERT R. "The Face Supplement: A Quick Index of Intelligence for Adult Subnormals." *J Clin Psychol* 18:346–7 Jl '62. * (*PA* 39:1721)
326. CARKHUFF, ROBERT R. "Perseveration of Habit in Drawing Tasks as a Characteristic Distinguishing Mental Defectives From Normals." *J Clin Psychol* 18:413–5 O '62. * (*PA* 39:5658)
327. MACKAY, G. W. S., AND VERNON, P. E. "The Measurement of Learning Ability." *Brit J Ed Psychol* 33:177–86 Je '63. * (*PA* 38:4067)
328. PETERS, HERBERT D. "Performance of Hopi Children on Four Intelligence Tests." *J Am Indian Ed* 2:27–31 Ja '63. *
329. TAYLOR, JAMES BENTLEY. "The Structure of Ability in the Lower Intellectual Range." *Am J Mental Def* 68:766–74 My '64. * (*PA* 39:1793)
330. KING, AUDREY J., AND WAKE, F. R. "The Effect of Motivation on 'Draw-a-Man' Scores." *Ont Psychol Assn Q* (Canada) 19(4):97–101 '66. *
331. McPHERSON, MARION WHITE; POPPLESTONE, JOHN A.; AND EVANS, KATHERINE A. "Perceptual Carelessness, Drawing Precision, and Oral Activity Among Six-Year-Olds." *Percept & Motor Skills* 22:327–30 F '66. * (*PA* 40:5241)
332. SPOCK, ALEXANDER, AND STEDMAN, DONALD J. "Psychologic Characteristics of Children With Cystic Fibrosis." *N C Med J* 27:426–8 S '66. *
333. MOLEMA, SEODI Y. *A Comparison of Associative and Conceptual Thinking as Indicated by Two Non-Language Tests Among Lower and Higher Socioeconomic Negro Children in Elementary School.* Master's thesis, Catholic University of America (Washington, D.C.), 1967.
334. VERNON, PHILIP E. "A Cross-Cultural Study of 'Creativity Tests' With 11-Year Boys." *New Res Ed* (England) 1:135–46 Je '67. *
335. BELLER, E. KUNO. "Intellectual Development in Educationally Disadvantaged Pre-School Children." *Proc 1966 Ann Read Inst Temple Univ* 5:73–83 '68. *
336. DE-NOUR, ATARA K.; SHALTIEL, JUDITH; AND CZACZKES, J. W. "Emotional Reactions of Patients on Chronic Hemodialysis." *Psychosom Med* 30:521–33 S-O '68. * (*PA* 43:8624)
337. DOMRATH, RICHARD P. "Constructional Praxis and Visual Perception in School Children." *J Consult & Clin Psychol* 32:186–92 Ap '68. * (*PA* 42:8174)
338. GLUCKSMAN, MYRON L.; HIRSCH, JULES; McCULLY, ROBERT S.; BARRON, BRUCE A.; AND KNITTLE, JEROME L. "The Response of Obese Patients to Weight Reduction: 2, A Quantitative Evaluation of Behavior." *Psychosom Med* 30:359–73 Jl–Ag '68. * (*PA* 43:2314)
339. MONEY, JOHN; COHEN, STEPHEN M.; LEWIS, VIOLA; AND DRASH, PHILIP W. Chap. 40, "Human Figure Drawings as Index of Body Image in Dwarfism," pp. 582–91. In *Human Growth, Body Composition, Cell Growth, Energy, and Intelligence.* Edited by Donald B. Cheek. Philadelphia, Pa.: Lea & Febiger, 1968. Pp. xxx, 781. *
340. PRENTICE, NORMAN M., AND BIERI, JAMES. "Intellectual Development of Culturally Deprived Children in a Day Care Program." Abstract. *Proc 76th Ann Conv Am Psychol Assn* 3:599–600 '68. * (*PA* 43:1328, title only)
341. GRANDOVIC, MARGARET CLARK. *A Study of the Usefulness of the Bender Gestalt Test With Young Educable Retarded Children Using the Koppitz Procedures.* Doctor's thesis, Temple University (Philadelphia, Pa.), 1969. (*DAI* 32:1335A)
342. HARRIS, DALE B. *Comparison of Timed and Untimed Presentation of the Goodenough-Harris Test of Intellectual Maturity.* Public Health Service Publication No. 1000, Series 2, No. 35. Washington, D.C.: United States Government Printing Office, June 1969. Pp. vi, 16. *
343. MAJUMDAR, S. K. "Relationship Between Old (1956) and New (1966) Norms for Goodenough's Draw-a-Man Test (Pramila Phatak's Indian Adaptation) on Normal and Retarded Children." *Indian Ed R* 4(2):97–102 Jl '69. *

344. SINHA, MAYA. *A Study of the Harris Revision of the Goodenough Draw-A-Man Test.* Doctor's thesis, University of London (London, England), 1969.

345. CICERO, JANE. *An Analysis of the Effectiveness of the Goodenough Draw-A-Person Test in Predicting Achievement Among Selected Third Graders.* Master's thesis, John Carroll University (Cleveland, Ohio), 1970.

346. EAVES, LINDA C.; NUTTALL, J. C.; KLONOFF, H.; AND DUNN, H. G. "Developmental and Psychological Test Scores in Children of Low Birth Weight." *Pediatrics* 45(1):9–20 Ja '70. * Correction: 45(5):886–7 My '70. *

347. HARRIS, DALE B.; ROBERTS, JEAN; AND PINDNER, GLENN D. "Intellectual Maturity of Children as Measured by the Goodenough-Harris Drawing Test." *Vital & Health Stat* Series 11(105):1–40 D '70. * (*PA* 50:2691)

348. HARTMAN, ROBERT KINTZ. *An Investigation of the Incremental Validity of Human Figure Drawings in the Diagnosis of Learning Disabilities.* Doctor's thesis, University of Connecticut (Storrs, Conn.), 1970. (*DAI* 31:6403A)

349. KEOGH, BARBARA K., AND VORMELAND, ODDVAR. "Performance of Norwegian Children on the Bender Gestalt and Draw-A-Person Tests." *Scand J Ed Res* (Norway) 14(3):105–11 '70. * (*PA* 47:10628)

350. LECRONE, EDDIE M. *A Comparison of the Goodenough-Harris "Self" and "Adult" Drawings of Children Having Corrected Cleft-Palates With Similar Drawings of Children Having No Speech Impediments.* Master's thesis, Northern Illinois University (DeKalb, Ill.), 1970.

351. MUSGROVE, WALTER J. "Comparisons of Low Socioeconomic Black and White Kindergarten Children." *Acad Ther* 6(2):163–7 w '70. *

352. NATHAN, SUSAN, AND PISULA, DOROTHY. "Psychological Observations of Obese Adolescents During Starvation Treatment." *J Am Acad Child Psychiatry* 9(4):722–40 O '70. * (*PA* 45:8849)

353. NORDÉN, K. "The Structure of Abilities in a Group of Deaf Adolescents." *Ed & Psychol Interactions* (Sweden) 32:1–22 '70. * (*PA* 44:15094)

354. WHITE, GENEVIEVE. *Procedures for Predicting Children's Success in First Grade Achievement.* Master's thesis, Arkansas State University (State University, Ark.), 1970.

355. ABLES, BILLIE S. "The Use of the Draw-A-Man Test With Borderline Retarded Children Without Pronounced Pathology." *J Clin Psychol* 27(2):262–3 Ap '71. * (*PA* 46:7068)

356. ACUFF, NANCY HAMBLEN. *Paternal Effectiveness in a Selected Cognitive Task.* Doctor's thesis, Ohio State University (Columbus, Ohio), 1971. (*DAI* 32:3771A)

357. ARMENTROUT, JAMES A. "Effects of Perceptual Training on Children's Human Figure Drawings." *J Genetic Psychol* 119(2):281–7 D '71. * (*PA* 47:11789)

358. BRAUN, JEAN S., AND BRANE, MARIA. "Comparison of the Performance of Children With Dysrhythmia Grade 1 and Normal EEG on Psychological Tests." Abstract. *Proc 79th Ann Conv Am Psychol Assn* 6(1):457–8 '71. * (*PA* 46:5135)

359. CONNERS, C. KEITH. "The Effect of Stimulant Drugs on Human Figure Drawings in Children With Minimal Brain Dysfunction." *Psychopharmacologia* (West Germany) 19(4):329–33 '71. * (*PA* 46:3568)

360. GAYTON, WILLIAM F.; EVANS, H. EUGENE; AND WILSON, WINSTON S. "Comparative Validity of Harris Point and Quality Scales." *Percept & Motor Skills* 33(3):1111–3 D '71. * (*PA* 48:687)

361. GOLDSTEIN, HARRIS S., AND PECK, ROSALIND. "Cognitive Functions in Negro and White Children in a Child Guidance Clinic." *Psychol Rep* 28(2):379–84 Ap '71. * (*PA* 46:7556)

362. HALL, JOSEPH C., AND CHANSKY, NORMAN M. "Relationships Between Selected Ability and Achievement Tests in an Economically Disadvantaged Negro Sample." *Psychol Rep* 28(3):741–2 Je '71. * (*PA* 46:11501)

363. IRETON, HAROLD; QUAST, WENTWORTH; AND GANTCHER, PHYLLIS. "The Draw-A-Man Test as an Index of Developmental Disorders in a Pediatric Outpatient Population." *Child Psychiatry & Hum Develop* 2(1):42–9 f '71. * (*PA* 49:4143)

364. JENSEN, DIANA E.; PRANDONI, JOGUES R.; AND ABUDABBEH, NUHA N. "Figure Drawings by Sex Offenders and a Random Sample of Offenders." *Percept & Motor Skills* 32(1):295–300 F '71. * (*PA* 46:3356)

365. JENSEN, OLIVE MARIE JACOBSON. *Differences in Perception Through Teaching Drawing in Contrasting Groups of Fifth Grade Students.* Doctor's thesis, University of Minnesota (Minneapolis, Minn.), 1971. (*DAI* 32:3156A)

366. JOHNSON, DALE L., AND JOHNSON, CARMEN A. "Comparison of Four Intelligence Tests Used With Culturally Disadvantaged Children." *Psychol Rep* 28(1):209–10 F '71. * (*PA* 46:5736)

367. L'ABATE, LUCIANO. "Receptive-Expressive Functions in Kindergarten Children and Adolescents." *Psychol Sch* 8(3):253–9 Jl '71. * (*PA* 47:9699)

368. LAOSA, LUIS M.; SWARTZ, JON D.; AND HOLTZMAN, WAYNE H. "Human Figure Drawings by Normal Children Over Four Years of Repeated Testing." Abstract. *Proc 79th Ann Conv Am Psychol Assn* 6(1):167–8 '71. * (*PA* 46:2607)

369. LEHMAN, ELYSE BRAUCH, AND LEVY, BERNARD I. "Discrepancies in Estimates of Children's Intelligence: WISC

and Human Figure Drawings." *J Clin Psychol* 27(1):74–6 Ja '71. * (*PA* 46:1427)

370. LEVI, HELENE S., AND WELCHER, DORIS W. "Social Class and Race as Determinants of the Sex of Human Figures Drawn by Seven-Year-Olds." *Johns Hopkins Med J* 129(1):10–8 Jl '71. *

371. LEVY, IRWIN S. "The Harris-Goodenough Drawing Test and Educable Mentally Retarded Adolescents." *Am J Mental Def* 75(6):760–1 My '71. *

372. McCORMICK, CLARENCE C., AND SCHNOBRICH, JANICE N. "Perceptual-Motor Training and Improvement in Concentration in a Montessori Preschool." *Percept & Motor Skills* 32(1):71–7 F '71. * (*PA* 46:3865)

373. McGILLIGAN, ROBERT P.; YATER, ALLAN C.; AND HUESING, RALPH. "Goodenough-Harris Drawing Test Reliabilities." *Psychol Sch* 8(4):359–62 O '71. * (*PA* 47:11621)

374. MOORE, MARY, AND WELCHER, DORIS W. "A Descriptive Analysis of the Seven-Year Psychological Data." *Johns Hopkins Med J* 128(6):332–46 Je '71. *

375. MUSGROVE, WALTER J., AND LAWSON, JOHN R. "A Comparison of Lower Class Negro and White Children on Three Standardized Tests." *J Negro Ed* 40(1):53–5 w '71. *

376. MYKLEBUST, HELMER R.; BANNOCHIE, MARGARET N.; AND KILLEN, JAMES R. Chap. 9, "Learning Disabilities and Cognitive Processes," pp. 213–51. In *Progress in Learning Disabilities, Vol. 2.* Edited by Helmer R. Myklebust. New York: Grune & Stratton, Inc., 1971. Pp. ix, 404. *

377. O'KEEFE, RIP; LESKOSKY, RICHARD J.; O'BRIEN, THOMAS G.; YATER, ALLAN C.; AND BARCLAY, ALLAN. "Influences of Age, Sex, and Ethnic Origin on Goodenough-Harris Drawing Test Performances by Disadvantaged Preschool Children." *Percept & Motor Skills* 33(3):708–10 D '71. * (*PA* 48:691)

378. OWEN, FREYA WEAVER; ADAMS, PAULINE AUSTIN; FORREST, THOMAS; STOLZ, LOIS MEEK; AND FISHER, SARA. "Learning Disorders in Children: Sibling Studies." *Monogr Soc Res Child Develop* 36(4):1–77 N '71. * (*PA* 48:12196)

379. PARKER, HARRY J.; STERNLOF, RICHARD E.; AND McCOY, JOHN F. "Objective Versus Individual Mental Ability Tests With Former Head Start Children in the First Grade." *Percept & Motor Skills* 32(1):287–92 F '71. * (*PA* 46:3868)

380. PELC, ROBERT E. "Advancement Along a Complexity Gradient in Perceptual Level and Brain Damage." *Percept & Motor Skills* 32(1):251–4 F '71. * (*PA* 46:3322)

381. SAPIR, SELMA G. "Learning Disability and Deficit Centered Classroom Training." *Cognitive Studies* 2:324–38 '71. * (*PA* 49:1359, title only)

382. SCHAEFER, CHARLES E., AND STERNFIELD, MELVIN. "Comparative Validity of the Harris Quality and Point Scales." *Percept & Motor Skills* 33(3):997–8 D '71. * (*PA* 48:1325)

383. SINHA, MAYA. "Draw-A-Man Test Scores of British and Non-British Children." *Indian Ed R* 6(2):79–87 Jl '71. *

384. STRUEMPFER, D. J. W. "Validation of Two Quality Scales for Children's Figure Drawings." *Percept & Motor Skills* 32(3):887–93 Je '71. * (*PA* 47:2675)

385. WELCHER, DORIS W.; MELLITS, E. DAVID; AND HARDY, JANET B. "A Multivariate Analysis of Factors Affecting Psychological Performance." *Johns Hopkins Med J* 129(1):19–35 Jl '71. *

386. WELLS, DONALD G., AND PEDRINI, DUILIO T. "Relationships Among Wechsler Adult Intelligence Scale, Goodenough-Harris, and Peabody Picture Vocabulary Tests With Institutionalized Retarded Adults." *Percept & Motor Skills* 33(1):227–32 Ag '71. * (*PA* 47:3549)

387. WICKWIRE, PATRICIA JOANNE NELLOR. *The Academic Achievement and Language Development of American Children of Latin Heritage: Factors of Intellect, Home Educational Environment, and Personality.* Doctor's thesis, University of Texas (Austin, Tex.), 1971. (*DAI* 32:6232A)

388. YATER, ALLAN C.; BARCLAY, ALLAN; AND LESKOSKY, RICHARD. "Goodenough-Harris Drawing Test and WPPSI Performance of Disadvantaged Preschool Children." *Percept & Motor Skills* 33(3):967–70 D '71. * (*PA* 48:698)

CUMULATIVE NAME INDEX

Singh, B.: 123
Sinha, M.: 292, 344, 383
Sinnett, E. R.: 71
Sjah, A.: 124
Smith, A. A.: 225
Smith, F. O.: 25
Spadafore, G. J.: 293
Spock, A.: 332
Spoerl, D. T.: 30
Spotts, J. V.: 107
Spotts, W. S.: 167
Springer, N. N.: 32, 307-8
Springfield, L.: 264
Stedman, D. J.: 332
Steer, M. D.: 112
Steinman, W. M.: 226
Sternfield, M.: 382
Sternlof, R. E.: 257, 379
Stewart, N.: rev, 4:292
Stolz, L. M.: 378
Stone, P. A.: 186
Stonesifer, F. A.: 55
Struempfer, D. J. W.: 384
Strümpfer, D. J. W.: 258-9
Sturgis, L. H.: 253
Sundberg, N.: 260
Swartz, J. D.: 368
Sweeney, N. R.: 172
Tauber, R.: 206
Taylor, J. B.: 207, 329
Telford, C. W.: 12, 61
Teska, P. T.: 291
Thomas, R. M.: 124
Thompson, C. W.: 261
Thompson, J. M.: 137
Thorpe, J. S.: 187
Throne, F. M.: 185, 188
Tiebout, C.: 304-5
Tobias, J.: 113
Tracy, D. B.: 238
Trowbridge, N.: 126
Tsao, D. F.: 62

Tuska, S. A.: 78
Tyson, M. C.: 189
Utsugi, E.: 96
Vahar, M.: 179
Vane, J. R.: 131, 173, 227
Varva, F. I.: 145
Vernon, P. E.: 327, 334
Vogel, F. X.: 228
Vormeland, O.: 349
Vroegh, K.: 275
Wagoner, L. C.: 298
Wake, F. R.: 330
Wang, C.: 221
Warren, S. A.: 114
Watkins, D. G.: 208
Watson, B. L.: 276
Weir, M. W.: 117
Weisenburg, T.: 306
Welcher, D. W.: 370, 374, 385
Wells, D. G.: 229-30, 386
Werner, E. E.: 294
West, J. H.: 115
West, P. C.: 174
Wheeler, J. I.: 319
White, G.: 354
White, M. F. R.: 44
Whitten, C. F.: 133
Wickwire, P. J. N.: 387
Williams, B. K.: 295
Williams, J. H.: 21
Williams, M. L.: 5
Wilson, J. L.: 146
Wilson, W. S.: 360
Winter, W. D.: 71
Woltmann, A. G.: exc, 7:352
Yater, A. C.: 277, 373, 377, 388
Yen, S. M. Y.: 278
Yepsen, L. N.: 3-4
Yule, W.: 231
Zangwill, O. L.: 209

[382]

*The Graduate Record Examinations Aptitude Test. Graduate school candidates; 1949-73; GREAT; 2 scores: verbal, quantitative; Educational Testing Service. * For the testing program entry, see 1053.

For additional information concerning earlier forms, see 7:353 (43 references); for reviews by Robert L. French and Warren W. Willingham, see 6:461 (17 references); for a review by John T. Dailey, see 5:336 (7 references); for reviews by J. P. Guilford and Carl I. Hovland, see 4:293 (2 references). For an excerpt from a related book review, see 7:B113. For reviews of the testing program, see 7:667 (1 review) and 5:601 (1 review).

REFERENCES THROUGH 1971

1-2. See 4:293.
3-9. See 5:336.
10-26. See 6:461.
27-69. See 7:353.
70. WYETH, EZRA R. "Evaluation of the Effectiveness of the Leadership Training Program in the Area of the Deaf at San Fernando Valley State College." *Am Ann Deaf* 110:479-82 S '65. * (*PA* 40:5848)
71. HOUSTON, SAMUEL R. "Generating a Projected Criterion of Graduate School Success via Normative Judgment Analysis." *J Exp Ed* 37:53-8 w '68. *
72. JARDIN, ROBERT PATRICK. *An Analysis of Peer Ratings and Subordinate Ratings as a Potential Feedback and Self-Selection Device for School Counselor Candidates.* Doctor's thesis, American University (Washington, D.C.), 1970. (*DAI* 32:178A)
73. ROBERTS, PAMELA T. *An Analysis of the Relationship Between Graduate Record Examination Scores and Success in the Graduate School of Wake Forest University.* Master's thesis, Wake Forest University (Winston-Salem, N.C.), 1970.
74. CRAWFORD, FRANCES W. *An Investigation of the Graduate Record Examination and Other Variables Used as Predictors of Success in the Graduate Program of the Department of Psychology of East Tennessee State University.* Master's thesis, East Tennessee State University (Johnson City, Tenn.), 1971.
75. ELSTER, RICHARD S.; GITHENS, WILLIAM H.; AND WISKOFF, MARTIN. "Predicting the Graduate School Performance of Military Officers," pp. 91-8. In *Second Annual Symposium: Psychology in the Air Force, 20-22 April 1971.* Edited by Hal W. Hendrick. Colorado Springs, Colo.: United States Air Force Academy, [1971]. Pp. x, 409. *

76. HANSEN, W. LEE. "Prediction of Graduate Performance in Economics." *J Econ Ed* 3(1):49-53 f '71. *
77. HARRIS, JOHN A. *A Study of Selected Graduate Students' Performances on Graduate Record Examination, Iowa Silent Reading Test, and Grade-Point Average.* Master's thesis, Fort Valley State College (Ft. Valley, Ga.), 1971.
78. LEDFORD, KENNETH B. *An Analysis of the Predictive Value of the Graduate Record Examination in Relation to Success in Four Disciplines at East Tennessee State University.* Master's thesis, East Tennessee State University (Johnson City, Tenn.), 1971.
79. MARSTON, ALBERT R. "It Is Time to Reconsider the Graduate Record Examination." *Am Psychologist* 26(7):653-5 Jl '71. * (*PA* 47:11620)
80. MERENDA, PETER F., AND REILLY, RAYMOND. "Validity of Selection Criteria in Determining Success of Graduate Students in Psychology." *Psychol Rep* 28(1):259-66 F '71. * (*PA* 46:5705)
81. MICHAEL, WILLIAM B.; JONES, ROBERT A.; AL-AMIR, HUDHAIL; PULLIAS, CALVIN M.; JACKSON, MICHEL; AND GOO, VALERIE. "Correlates of a Pass-Fail Decision for Admission to Candidacy in a Doctoral Program in Education." *Ed & Psychol Meas* 31(4):965-7 w '71. * (*PA* 48:1832)
82. PAYNE, DAVID A.; WELLS, ROBERT A.; AND CLARKE, ROBERT R. "Another Contribution to Estimating Success in Graduate School: A Search for Sex Differences and Comparison Between Three Degree Types." *Ed & Psychol Meas* 31(2):497-503 su '71. *
83. WITTMER, JOE, AND LISTER, JAMES L. "The Graduate Record Examination, 16 PF Questionnaire, and Counseling Effectiveness." *Counselor Ed & Sup* 10(3):293 sp '71. *
84. WRIGHT, MATTHEW THOMAS. *An Analysis of Selected Factors of Education Doctoral Programs at Washington State University.* Doctor's thesis, Washington State University (Pullman, Wash.), 1971. (*DAI* 32:4388A)

CUMULATIVE NAME INDEX

Al-Amir, H.: 81
Alexakos, C. E.: 47
Angoff, W. H.: 5, 7
Baillie, G. S.: 27
Bass, A. R.: 66
Besco, R. O.: 13-4
Blackburn, M.: 53, 63
Borg, W. R.: 24
Breimeier, K. H.: 42
Burdick, L. A.: 31
Capps, M. P.: 8
Carbonari, J. P.: 48
Chimonides, S. G.: 54
Cieboter, F. J.: 55
Clarke, R. R.: 82
Colvin, G. F.: 49
Conway, M. T.: 10
Crawford, F. W.: 74
Creager, J. A.: 35
Crosby, D. W.: 4
Cureton, E. E.: 43
Dailey, J. T.: rev, 5:336
DeCosta, F. A.: 8
Donaghy, R. T.: 46
Duperre, M. R.: exc, 7:B113
Elster, R. S.: 75
Elton, C. F.: 36
Ewen, R. B.: 56
Frank, A. C.: 57
French, R. L.: rev, 6:461
Gab, D.: 58, 64, 69
Gibbons, B. D.: 16
Githens, W. H.: 75
Goo, V.: 81
Green, E. J.: 68
Guilford, J. P.: rev, 4:293
Hackman, J. R.: 53, 63, 66
Hall, E.: 34
Hansen, W. L.: 76
Harlow, S. D.: 69
Harris, J. A.: 77
Harrison, C. W.: 60
Horton, C. P.: 61
Houston, S. R.: 62, 71
Hovland, C. I.: rev, 4:293
Howard, J. S.: 20
Huber, J. T.: 44
Jackson, M.: 81
Jardin, R. P.: 72
Johnson, B. G.: 28
Johnson, J. W.: 21
Jones, R. A.: 16, 81
King, D. C.: 14
King, F. J.: 29
Kirk, B. A.: 57
Law, A.: 15
Ledford, K. B.: 78

Lister, J. L.: 83
Maberly, N. C.: 22, 25
Madaus, G. F.: 37
Manuel, H. T.: 6
Marston, A. R.: 79
Mehrabian, A.: 59, 67
Merenda, P. F.: 80
Michael, W. B.: 16, 81
Moghrabi, K. M.: 38
Mosher, R. L.: 46
Newman, R. I.: 50
Nichols, R. C.: 32
Nielsen, W.: 17
Palmer, R. H.: 39
Payne, D. A.: 82
Poniatowski, R. A.: 33
Pullias, C. M.: 81
Rawls, D. J.: 60
Rawls, J. R.: 60
Reilly, R.: 80
Richter, W. R.: 51
Rindone, R.: 40
Roberts, B. T.: 61
Roberts, P. T.: 73
Roberts, S. O.: 61
Robertson, M.: 17, 34
Robinson, D. W.: 9
Roscoe, J. T.: 62
Rudman, J.: 26
Rupiper, O. J.: 11
Saum, J. A.: 1, 3
Schultz, M. K.: 5, 7
Scott, T. B.: 43
Sleeper, M. L.: 18
Sprinthall, N. A.: 46
Stafford, J. W.: 2
Stein, R. F.: 68
Stricker, G.: 44
Thomsen, S. J.: 19
Tookey, M. D.: 52
Tucker, H.: 41
Tully, G. E.: 23, 29
Walsh, J. J.: 37
Wells, R. A.: 82
White, G. W.: 45
Whiteley, J. M.: 46
Wiggins, N.: 53, 63, 66
Williams, D. J.: 64, 69
Williams, O. H.: 12
Willingham, W. W.: rev, 6:461
Wiskoff, M.: 75
Wittmer, J.: 83
Woodard, D. B.: 65
Wright, M. T.: 84
Wyeth, E. R.: 70
Zimmerman, W. G.: 30

[383]

★**Group Test for Indian South Africans.** Standards 4–6, 7–8, 9–10; 1967–71; GTISA; adaptation for Indian pupils of the *New South African Group Test;* 3 scores: verbal, nonverbal, total; 3 levels; Human Sciences Research Council [South Africa]. *
a) JUNIOR. Standards 4–6; 1968–71; Indian standardization by F. W. O. Heinichen, R. J. Prinsloo, and S. Oosthuizen.
b) INTERMEDIATE. Standards 7–8; 1967–69.
c) SENIOR. Standards 9–10; 1968–69.

[384]

Group Test 36. Ages 10–14; 1937–45; verbal intelligence; National Institute of Industrial Psychology; NFER Publishing Co. Ltd. [England]. *
For additional information, see 4:296.

REFERENCES THROUGH 1971
1. HOLLIDAY, FRANK. "An Investigation Into the Selection of Apprentices for the Engineering Industry." *Occup Psychol* (England) 14:69–81 Ap '40. * (*PA* 14:3710)
2. SHUTTLEWORTH, CLIFFORD W. "Tests of Technical Aptitude." *Occup Psychol* (England) 16:175–82 O '42. *
3. FRISBY, C. B.; VINCENT, D. F.; AND LANCASHIRE, RUTH. *Tests for Engineering Apprentices: A Validation Study.* National Institute of Industrial Psychology, Report 14. London: the Institute, 1959. Pp. iii, 24. *
4. JAMIESON, G. H. "Psychological Aspects of Craftsmanship in Pottery-Making at a Secondary School." *Brit J Ed Psychol* 35:179–82 Je '65. * (*PA* 39:16457)

CUMULATIVE NAME INDEX
Frisby, C. B.: 3   Lancashire, R.: 3
Holliday, F.: 1   Shuttleworth, C. W.: 2
Jamieson, G. H.: 4   Vincent, D. F.: 3

[385]

Group Test 75. Ages 12–13; 1957; nonverbal intelligence; National Institute of Industrial Psychology; NFER Publishing Co. Ltd. [England]. *
For additional information, see 5:338.

REFERENCES THROUGH 1971
1. JAMIESON, G. H. "Psychological Aspects of Craftsmanship in Pottery-Making at a Secondary School." *Brit J Ed Psychol* 35:179–82 Je '65. * (*PA* 39:16457)

CUMULATIVE NAME INDEX
Jamieson, G. H.: 1

[386]

Group Test 91. Industrial applicants; 1949–68; verbal intelligence; National Institute of Industrial Psychology; NFER Publishing Co. Ltd. [England]. *
For additional information, see 7:354.

REFERENCES THROUGH 1971
1. CASTLE, P. F. C., AND GARFORTH, F. I. DE LA P. "Selection, Training and Status of Supervisors: 1, Selection." *Occup Psychol* (England) 25:109–23 Ap '51. * (*PA* 26:5858)

CUMULATIVE NAME INDEX
Castle, P. F. C.: 1   Garforth, F. I. de la P.: 1

[386A]

★**Group Test 95.** Ages 14 and over; [1972]; verbal intelligence; no manual; National Institute of Industrial Psychology; NFER Publishing Co. Ltd. [England]. *

[387]

*****Group Test of Learning Capacity: Dominion Tests.** Grades kgn–1, 4–6, 7–9, 10–12 and adults; 1934–70; formerly called *Group Test of Intelligence;* various titles used by publisher: *Dominion Group Test of Learning Capacity, Dominion Tests of Learning Capacity;* 4 levels; Ontario Institute for Studies in Education; distributed by Guidance Centre [Canada]. *

a) PRIMARY. Grades kgn–1; 1934–56. *Out of print.* (Replaced by *OISE Picture Reasoning Test: Primary.*)
b) JUNIOR. Grades 4–6; 1940–56.
c) MACHINE-SCORING GROUP TEST OF LEARNING CAPACITY, MACHINE- AND HAND-SCORING EDITION. Grades 7–9, 10–12 and adults; 1934–70; revision of *Quick-Scoring Group Test of Learning Capacity: Dominion Tests* (test items identical except for deletion of 5 items); 2 levels; technical report by Mohindra P. Gill, Ross E. Traub, and R. Schweiker.
    1) *Intermediate.* Grades 7–9; 1934–70.
    2) *Advanced.* Grades 10–12 and adults; 1939–70.
For additional information and reviews by Donald B. Black and George A. Ferguson of the intermediate and advanced levels, see 6:493; for additional information concerning the primary and junior levels, see 5:341; for a review by W. G. Emmett, see 4:294 (3 references); for a review by F. T. Tyler, see 3:231.

REFERENCES THROUGH 1971
1–3. See 4:294.
4. PIPHER, J. A. "An Appraisal of the Use of the Dominion Group Test of Learning Capacity (Advanced) in the Atkinson Study of Utilization of Student Resources." *Ont J Ed Res* (Canada) 3:17–23 O '60. *
5. RUSSELL, H. H., AND DILLING, H. J. "Comparison of General Intelligence Test Results and Student Achievement in Grade 8 and Grade 9 of Scarborough Schools." *Ont J Ed Res* (Canada) 8:267–77 sp '66. *
6. GORDON, JAMES ROSCOE. *Listening, Attitude, and Intelligence Tests to Predict Academic Achievement.* Doctor's thesis, Colorado State College (Greeley, Colo.), 1968. (*DA* 29:2522A)

CUMULATIVE NAME INDEX
Black, D. B.: *rev*, 6:493   Gordon, J. R.: 6
Department of Educational   Ontario Commercial Teachers'
  Research, Ontario College   Association: 2
  of Education, University of   Phillips, A. J.: 1
  Toronto: 2   Pipher, J. A.: 4
Dilling, H. J.: 5   Russell, H. H.: 5
Emmett, W. G.: *rev*, 4:294   Tyler, F. T.: *rev*, 3:231
Ferguson, G. A.: *rev*, 6:493   Yule, D. L. G.: 3

[388]

Group Tests 70 and 70B. Ages 15 and over; 1939–70; subtest of *N.I.I.P. Engineering Apprentice Selection Test Battery;* nonverbal intelligence; National Institute of Industrial Psychology; NFER Publishing Co. Ltd. [England]. * For the complete battery entry, see 2345.
For additional information, see 7:355 (5 references); for a review by George Westby of form 70, see 4:297 (5 references).

REFERENCES THROUGH 1971
1–5. See 4:297.
6–10. See 7:355.
11. SLATER, PATRICK, AND BENNETT, ELIZABETH. "The Development of Spatial Judgment and Its Relation to Some Educational Problems." *Occup Psychol* (England) 17:139–55 Jl '43. *
12. ADCOCK, CYRIL. "A Re-Analysis of Slater's Spatial Judgment Research." *Occup Psychol* (England) 22:213–6 O '48. * (*PA* 23:1691)
13. HIMMELWEIT, HILDE T., AND SUMMERFIELD, ARTHUR. "Student Selection—An Experimental Investigation: II." *Brit J Sociol* 2:59–75 Mr '51. * (*PA* 26:542)
14. GASKILL, P. Chap. 9, "Tests of Ability and Attainments: Pilot Experiments in Selection and Guidance," pp. 188–212. In *Educational Guidance and the Deaf Child.* Edited by A. W. G. Ewing. Manchester, England: Manchester University Press, 1957. Pp. xiii, 345. *
15. MURPHY, K. P. Chap. 11, "Tests of Abilities and Attainments: Pupils in Schools for the Deaf Aged Twelve," pp. 252–77. In *Educational Guidance and the Deaf Child.* Edited by A. W. G. Ewing. Manchester, England: Manchester University Press, 1957. Pp. xiii, 345. *
16. CATTELL, RAYMOND B., AND SCHEIER, IVAN H. "The Objective Test Measurement of Neuroticism, U.I. 23 (—)." *Indian J Psychol* 33:217–36 pt 4 '58. * (*PA* 35:3427, title only)
17. MEHROTRA, S. N. "An Educational-Vocational Guidance Project for Intermediate Students: A Follow-Up Study." *Indian J Psychol* 34:148–62 pt 3 '59. * (*PA* 36:4KJ48M)
18. MOSHIN, S. M. "Plea for a Scientific Aptitude Test and

a Preliminary Report of the Development of Such Test." *Indian J Psychol* 34:36–42 pt 1 '59. *

19. DAS, RHEA S. "Validity Information Exchange, No. 14-05: D.O.T. Code 2-66.01, Police Lieutenant." *Personnel Psychol* 14:459–61 w '61. *

CUMULATIVE NAME INDEX

Adcock, C.: 12
Aga, H.: 10
Bennett, E.: 11
Cattell, R. B.: 16
Das, R. S.: 19
Dhar, C.: 7
Frisby, C. B.: 8
Gaskill, P.: 14
Himmelweit, H. T.: 13
Jog, R. N.: 9–10
Lancashire, R.: 8
Marr, E.: 7

Mehrotra, S. N.: 6, 17
Mills, L. F.: 2
Moshin, S. M.: 18
Murphy, K. P.: 15
Parry, J. B.: 4
Scheier, I. H.: 16
Slater, P.: 1, 11
Summerfield, A.: 13
Vernon, P. E.: 3–4
Vincent, D. F.: 8
Westby, G.: *rev*, 4:297

[389]

Group Tests 72 and 73. Industrial applicants; 1949–68; nonverbal intelligence; National Institute of Industrial Psychology; NFER Publishing Co. Ltd. [England]. *

For additional information, see 7:356 (1 reference).

REFERENCES THROUGH 1971

1. See 7:356.

CUMULATIVE NAME INDEX

Castle, P. F. C.: 1   Garforth, F. I. de la P.: 1

[390]

Group Tests 90A and 90B. Ages 15 and over; 1950–70; subtest of *N.I.I.P. Engineering Apprentice Selection Test Battery;* verbal intelligence; National Institute of Industrial Psychology; NFER Publishing Co. Ltd. [England]. * For the complete battery entry, see 2345.

For additional information, see 7:357 (1 reference); for a review by John Liggett of form 90A, see 5:340.

REFERENCES THROUGH 1971

1. See 7:357.
2. VINCENT, D. F. "The Linear Relationship Between Age and Score of Adults in Intelligence Tests." *Occup Psychol* (England) 26:243–9 O '52. * (*PA* 27:7044)
3. GARSIDE, R. F. "The Prediction of Examination Marks of Mechanical Engineering Students at King's College, Newcastle." *Brit J Psychol* 48:219–20 Ag '57. * (*PA* 33:2157)

CUMULATIVE NAME INDEX

Garside, R. F.: 3
Liggett, J.: *rev*, 5:340

Vincent, D. F.: 2
Williams, A. P.: 1

[391]

*The Henmon-Nelson Tests of Mental Ability. Grades kgn–2, 3–6, 6–9, 9–12, 13–17; 1931–73; 2 editions; Tom A. Lamke (except *b1*) and Martin J. Nelson; Houghton Mifflin Co. *

a) REVISED EDITION. Grades 3–6, 6–9, 9–12, 13–17; 1931–61; 4 levels.

1) *Grades 3–6.* 1931–58.
2) *Grades 6–9.* 1931–57.
3) *Grades 9–12.* 1931–58.
4) *Grades 13–17.* 1931–61; 3 scores: quantitative, verbal, total; Paul C. Kelso.

b) 1973 REVISION. Grades kgn–2, 3–6, 6–9, 9–12; 1931–73; 4 levels; no manual; Joseph L. French.

1) *Primary Battery.* Grades kgn–2; 1973.
2) *Grades 3–6.* 1931–73.
3) *Grades 6–9.* 1931–73.
4) *Grades 9–12.* 1931–73.

For additional information, a review by Norman E. Wallen, and an excerpted review by John O. Crites of the college level, see 6:462 (11 references); for reviews by D. Welty Lefever and Leona E. Tyler and an excerpted review by Laurance F. Shaffer of the other levels in the Revised Edition, see 5:342 (14 references); for a review by H. M. Fowler of an earlier edition, see

4:299 (25 references); for reviews by Anne Anastasi, August Dvorak, Howard Easley, and J. P. Guilford and an excerpted review by Francis N. Maxfield, see 2:1398.

REFERENCES THROUGH 1971

1–25. See 4:299.
26–39. See 5:342.
40–50. See 6:462.
51. BYRNS, RUTH. "The Mental Ability of Twins." *Sch & Soc* 40:671–2 N 17 '34. * (*PA* 9:1187)
52. LYON, VERGIL E. "The Variation of High School Senior and College Freshman Classes." *J Exp Ed* 3:25–35 S '34. * (*PA* 9:1418)
53. OMWAKE, KATHARINE T.; DEXTER, EMILY S.; AND LEWIS, L. WAYVE. "The Inter-Relations of Certain Physiological Measurements and Aspects of Personality." *Char & Pers* 3:64–71 S '34. * (*PA* 9:291)
54. BYRNS, RUTH. "Intelligence and Nationality of Wisconsin School Children." *J Social Psychol* 7:455–70 N '36. * (*PA* 11:4220)
55. OLANDER, HERBERT T., AND WALKER, BERT S. "Can Teachers Estimate I.Q.'s?" *Sch & Soc* 44:744–6 D 5 '36. * (*PA* 11:1490)
56. DENNIS, FLAVIUS ELIAS. *An Investigation of the Mental Ability, Educational Achievement, and Neurotic Tendencies of a Group of Partially Seeing Pupils.* Master's thesis, University of Colorado (Boulder, Colo.), 1939. (Abstract: *Univ Colo Studies* 26:48)
57. MACKENZIE, D. M. "Placement Tests and Freshman Week." *Sch & Soc* 50:351–2 S 9 '39. * (*PA* 14:547)
58. MORRIS, CHARLES M. "A Critical Analysis of Certain Performance Tests." *J Genetic Psychol* 54:85–105 Mr '39. * (*PA* 13:5387)
59. FROEHLICH, GUSTAV J. *The Prediction of Academic Success at the University of Wisconsin, 1909–1941.* Bulletin of the University of Wisconsin, Serial No. 2574, General Series No. 2358. Madison, Wis.: Bureau of Guidance and Records, the University, 1941. Pp. 44. * (*PA* 16:3775)
60. JOHNSON, DONALD M., AND REYNOLDS, FLOYD. "A Factor Analysis of Verbal Ability." *Psychol Rec* 4:183–95 Ja '41. * (*PA* 15:3315)
61. DEXTER, EMILY S. "Relation of Imagination to Certain Other Factors." *J General Psychol* 28:139–41 Ja '43. * (*PA* 17:1106)
62. SPOERL, DOROTHY TILDEN. "The Academic and Verbal Adjustment of College Age Bilingual Students." *J Genetic Psychol* 64:139–57 Mr '44. * (*PA* 18:2275)
63. BERRY, GEORGE S. "An Experiment in Self-Analysis." *J Ed Psychol* 37:111–24 F '46. * (*PA* 20:2061)
64. MOSER, W. E. "Vocational Preference as Related to Mental Ability." *Occupations* 27:460–1 Ap '49. * (*PA* 23:4870)
65. BARRETT, HARRY O. "Differences in Intelligence Between Two- and Four-Year Course Pupils in a Commercial High School." *J Ed Res* 44:143–7 O '50. * (*PA* 25:5681)
66. EELLS, KENNETH; DAVIS, ALLISON; HAVIGHURST, ROBERT J.; HERRICK, VERGIL E.; AND TYLER, RALPH W. *Intelligence and Cultural Differences: A Study of Cultural Learning and Problem-Solving.* Chicago, Ill.: University of Chicago Press, 1951. Pp. xii, 388. * (*PA* 27:5738)
67. WILLIAMS, HENRIETTA V., AND McQUARY, JOHN P. "The High-School Performance of College Freshmen." *Ed Adm & Sup* 39:303–8 My '53. * (*PA* 28:4955)
68. PROTHRO, E. TERRY. "An Alternative Approach in Cross-Cultural Intelligence Testing." *J Psychol* 39:247–51 Ap '55. * (*PA* 29:8553)
69. HOFSTAETTER, PETER R.; O'CONNOR, JAMES P.; AND SUZIEDELIS, ANTANAS. "Sequences of Restricted Associative Responses and Their Personality Correlates." *J General Psychol* 57:219–27 O '57. * (*PA* 33:9818)
70. LITTLE, J. KENNETH. "The Persistence of Academically Talented Youth in University Studies." *Ed Rec* 40:237–41 Jl '59. * (*PA* 34:4815)
71. PIPPERT, RALPH REINHARD. *The Prediction of the Correctness of Post-High School Written Language Performance.* Doctor's thesis, University of Wisconsin (Madison, Wis.), 1959. (*DA* 20:2104)
72. MARTIN, JACK R. "The Correlation Between Preadmission Tests and Graduation From Nursing School." *J Nursing Ed* 1:3–4+ D '62. *
73. KIENLEN, JOSEPH S. *A Study to Predict the Success of Students in Plane Geometry in Worland High School, Worland, Wyoming.* Master's thesis, Fort Hays Kansas State College (Hays, Kan.), 1963.
74. MUMAW, MYRON JAY. *Test Predictability for Culturally Deprived Students.* Master's thesis, Ohio State University (Columbus, Ohio), 1963.
75. GLIDDEN, GEORGE WAYNE. *Factors That Influence Achievement in Senior High School American History.* Doctor's thesis, University of Nebraska (Lincoln, Neb.), 1964. (*DA* 25:3429)
76. ZAHN, JANE. "Dropout and Academic Ability in University Extension Courses." *Adult Ed* 15:35–46 au '64. *
77. RIGHTHAND, HERBERT. "Identifying Technical Institute Dropouts." *Personnel & Guid J* 44:68–72 S '65. *

78. Swan, Robert J., and Hopkins, Kenneth D. "An Investigation of Theoretical and Empirical Chance Scores on Selected Standardized Group Tests." *Calif J Ed Res* 16:34–41 Ja '65. * (*PA* 39:10156)

79. Pearson, Richard E., and Ohlsen, Merle M. "Factors Associated With Teacher Over- Or Under-Estimation of Student Intellectual Ability." *J Stud Pers Assn Teach Ed* 5:1–13 Ap '66. *

80. Renfer, Mary Emma Fewell. *Predicting Success in the Study of Descriptive Linguistics.* Doctor's thesis, University of Southern California (Los Angeles, Calif.), 1966. (*DA* 27:1268A)

81. Conklin, Bernice B. *The Correlation of High School Students' Intelligence and Aptitude in Relation to the Understanding of Automated Data Processes.* Master's thesis, San Diego State College (San Diego, Calif.), 1967.

82. Schurdak, John J. "An Approach to the Use of Computers in the Instructional Process and an Evaluation." *Am Ed Res J* 4:59–73 Ja '67. * (*PA* 41:7947)

83. Westbrook, Bert W., and Sellers, James R. "Critical Thinking, Intelligence, and Vocabulary." *Ed & Psychol Meas* 27:443–6 su '67. * (*PA* 41:13634)

84. Gordon, Edwin. "A Study of the Efficacy of General Intelligence and Musical Aptitude Tests in Predicting Achievement in Music." *Council Res Music Ed B* 13:40–5 sp '68. * (*PA* 42:15436)

85. Hansen, Eda A. *The Relationship Between Grade Point Averages of the Henmon-Nelson Test of Mental Ability and the American College Test.* Master's thesis, Utah State University (Logan, Utah), 1968.

86. Mann, Lester; Haughey, Charles; Trefsgar, Theodore F.; and Keffer, Charles E. "Achievement and Personality Measurements Associated With Progress in a Programmed Course in Decimals and Fractions at a Fifth Grade Level." *Scientia Paedagogica Experimentalis* (Belgium) 5(1):76–83 '68. * (*PA* 45:3108)

87. Munday, Leo. "Correlations Between ACT and Other Predictors of Academic Success in College." *Col & Univ* 44:67–76 f '68. *

88. Sewell, William H., and Shah, Vimal P. "Social Class, Parental Encouragement, and Educational Aspirations." *Am J Sociol* 73:559–72 Mr '68. * (*PA* 42:11147)

89. Welch, Wayne W., and Rothman, Arthur I. "The Success of Recruited Students in a New Physics Course." *Sci Ed* 52:270–3 Ap '68. *

90. Berger, Vincent F.; Munz, David C.; Smouse, Albert D.; and Angelino, Henry. "The Effects of Item Difficulty Sequencing and Anxiety Reaction Type on Aptitude Test Performance." *J Psychol* 71(2):253–8 Mr '69. * (*PA* 43:8674)

91. Hamilton, Dorothy Dee Howe. *A Comparison of School Achievement, Teachers' Ratings, Self-Ratings, and a Personality Score as Predictors of Creative Thinking Potential.* Doctor's thesis, University of Nebraska (Lincoln, Neb.), 1969. (*DAI* 30:2905A)

92. Hieronymus, A. N., and Stroud, James B. "Comparability of IQ Scores on Five Widely Used Intelligence Tests." *Meas & Eval Guid* 2(3):135–40 f '69. * (*PA* 44:13285)

93. Walberg, Herbert J. "Predicting Class Learning: An Approach to the Class as a Social System." *Am Ed Res J* 6(4):529–42 N '69. * (*PA* 45:7078)

94. Westphal, M. Elizabeth; Leutenegger, Ralph R.; and Wagner, Dorothea L. "Some Psycho-Acoustic and Intellectual Correlates of Achievement in German Language Learning of Junior High School Students." *Mod Lang J* 53(4):258–66 Ap '69. * (*PA* 44:21623)

95. Cassel, Russell N., and Knox, Patricia. "Improving High School Learning Predictions With Multiple Junior High Test Scores." *Calif J Ed Res* 21(1):14–20 Ja '70. *

96. Johnson, Marie Louise. *Black Adolescents' Nonstandard English and Its Relation to Intellectual Skills.* Doctor's thesis, Illinois Institute of Technology (Chicago, Ill.), 1970. (*DAI* 31:7573B)

97. Walberg, Herbert J., and Ahlgren, Andrew. "Predictors of the Social Environment of Learning." *Am Ed Res J* 7(2):153–67 Mr '70. * (*PA* 46:11680)

98. Walker, Larry Dale. *The Effect of Reactive Inhibition and Extroversion on the Standardized Test Scores of Selected Groups of Students.* Doctor's thesis, Mississippi State University (State College, Miss.), 1970. (*DAI* 31:6249B)

99. Berman, Graham, and Eisenberg, Mildred. "Psycho-Social Aspects of Academic Achievement." *Am J Orthopsychiatry* 41(3):406–15 Ap '71. * (*PA* 46:7673)

100. Butler, Ralph Backstrom. *Aptitude Test Performance of Negro College Students as Affected by Item Difficulty Sequence, Anxiety Reaction Type, and Sex Differences.* Doctor's thesis, University of Oklahoma (Norman, Okla.), 1971. (*DAI* 32:3776A)

101. Davis, Gary A., and Belcher, Terence L. "How Shall Creativity Be Measured? Torrance Tests, RAT, Alpha Biographical, and IQ." *J Creative Behav* 5(3):153–61 '71. *

102. Vaughan, Margery, and Myers, R. E. "Examination of Musical Process as Related to Creative Thinking." *J Res Music Ed* 19(3):337–41 f '71. * (*PA* 48:5879)

CUMULATIVE NAME INDEX

[392]

Illinois Index of Scholastic Aptitude. Grades 9–12; 1966; IISA; B. Everard Blanchard; Western Psychological Services. *

For additional information and reviews by J. Stanley Ahmann and David A. Payne, see 7:358.

[393]

Inventory No. 2. Ages 16 and over; 1956; "a mental ability test"; Stevens, Thurow and Associates, Inc. *

For additional information, see 6:463.

[394]

Junior Scholastic Aptitude Test, Revised Edition. Grades 7–9; 1935–60; for independent schools; 2 scores:

verbal, numerical; 1959–60 tests identical with tests copyrighted 1957 except for cover page directions; Secondary Education Board (original edition); Geraldine Spaulding (revised edition); distributed for the National Association of Independent Schools by Educational Records Bureau. *

For additional information and a review by Jerome E. Doppelt, see 6:464 (5 references); see also 5:345 (7 references) and 3:233 (3 references).

REFERENCES THROUGH 1971

1–3. See 3:233.
4–10. See 5:345.
11–15. See 6:464.
16. TRAXLER, ARTHUR E. "A Note on the Correlation of the Secondary Education Board Junior Scholastic Aptitude Test With the College Entrance Examination Board Scholastic Aptitude Test." *Ed Rec B* 51:63–5 Ja '49. * (*PA* 23:3453)
17. TRAXLER, ARTHUR E. "A Further Study of Relationship Between the SEB Junior Scholastic Aptitude Test and the CEEB Scholastic Aptitude Test." *Ed Rec B* 53:48–51 Ja '50. * (*PA* 24:3898)
18. TOWNSEND, AGATHA. "The Junior Scholastic Aptitude Test in the Independent-School Program." *Ed Rec B* 57:58–65 Jl '51. * (*PA* 26:1107)
19. CLAWAR, HARRY J. "Some Examples of Best-Weighted Combinations of Junior Scholastic Aptitude Test Verbal and Numerical Scores When Predicting Standardized Achievement Test Performance." *Ed Rec B* 93:34–40 F '68. *

CUMULATIVE NAME INDEX

Clawar, H. J.: 19   Townsend, A.: 3, 5, 18
Doppelt, J. E.: *rev*, 6:464   Traxler, A. E.: 1–2, 4–7, 16–7
Jungeblut, A.: 14   Vecchione, N.: 13
Spaulding, G.: 8–12, 15

[395]

Kelvin Measurement of Ability in Infant Classes.
Ages 5–8; 1935; C. M. Fleming; Robert Gibson & Sons, Glasgow, Ltd. [Scotland]. *
For additional information, see 5:346.

REFERENCES THROUGH 1971

1. THACKRAY, D. V. *The Relationship Between Reading Readiness and Reading Progress.* Master's thesis, University of London (London, England), 1964. (Abstract: *Brit J Ed Psychol* 35:252–4)

CUMULATIVE NAME INDEX

Thackray, D. V.: 1

[396]

Kelvin Measurement of Mental Ability. Ages 8–12; 1933; C. M. Fleming; Robert Gibson & Sons, Glasgow, Ltd. [Scotland]. *
For additional information, see 1:1047.

[397]

The Kingston Test of Intelligence. Ages 10–12; 1953–63; M. E. Hebron; George G. Harrap & Co. Ltd. [England]. *
For additional information and a review by H. J. Sants, see 6:465; for a review by A. W. Heim, see 5:347.

[398]

*Kuhlmann-Anderson Test, Seventh Edition.
Grades kgn, 1, 2, 3–4, 4–5, 5–7, 7–9, 9–12; 1927–67; KAT, also MAP; publisher uses title *Kuhlmann-Anderson Measure of Academic Potential* in promotional literature; 8 levels; F. Kuhlmann (fourth and earlier editions) and Rose G. Anderson; Personnel Press. *
a) BOOKLETS K, A, B, AND CD. Grades kgn, 1, 2, 3–4; 1927–65.
b) SEPARATE ANSWER SHEET EDITION. Grades 4–5, 5–7, 7–9, 9–12; 1927–67.
  1) *Booklets D and EF.* Grades 4–5, 5–7; 1927–67.
  2) *Booklets G and H.* Grades 7–9, 9–12; 1927–65; 3 scores: verbal, quantitative, total.
For additional information, reviews by William B. Michael and Douglas A. Pidgeon, and an excerpted re-

view by Frederick B. Davis, see 6:466 (11 references); see also 5:348 (15 references); for reviews by Henry E. Garrett and David Segel of an earlier edition, see 4:302 (10 references); for reviews by W. G. Emmett and Stanley S. Marzolf, see 3:236 (25 references); for a review by Henry E. Garrett, see 2:1404 (15 references); for reviews by Psyche Cattell, S. A. Courtis, and Austin H. Turney, see 1:1049.

REFERENCES THROUGH 1971

1–15. See 2:1404.
16–40. See 3:236.
41–50. See 4:302.
51–65. See 5:348.
66–76. See 6:466.
77. HENRY, MARY BESS. "The Kuhlmann-Anderson Test of Intelligence—IX to Maturity." *Ed Res B* (Los Angeles City Schools) 8:15 D '28. *
78. McALPIN, ALICE S. "Changes in the Intelligence Quotients of Negro Children." *J Negro Ed* 1:44–8 Ap '32. * (*PA* 8:3826)
79. COERS, WALTER CLARENCE. *Comparative Achievement of White and Mexican Junior High School Pupils.* Master's thesis, George Peabody College for Teachers (Nashville, Tenn.), 1933.
80. NILSON, KENNETH. "Certain Intelligence Aspects of a Group of Physically Disabled Pupils in Minnesota Public Schools." *J Ed Res* 26:513–6 Mr '33. * (*PA* 7:3061)
81. PRICE, ORVILLE K. *Comparative Validity and Reliability of Four Intelligence Tests in the Ninth Grade.* Master's thesis, University of Kentucky (Lexington, Ky.), 1933.
82. JAGGERS, CRADDOCK H. "The Relation of Intelligence to Behavior in School Children." *Peabody J Ed* 11:254–9 My '34. * (*PA* 9:997)
83. LEE, J. MURRAY, AND HUGHES, W. HARDIN. "Predicting Success in Algebra and Geometry." *Sch R* 42:188–96 Mr '34. *
84. LONG, HOWARD H. "The Intelligence of Colored Elementary Pupils in Washington, D.C." *J Negro Ed* 3:205–22 Ap '34. * (*PA* 8:3699)
85. LONG, HOWARD HALE. "Test Results of Third-Grade Negro Children Selected on the Basis of Socio-Economic Status." *J Negro Ed* 4:192–212, 523–52 Ap, O '35. * (*PA* 10:1089)
86. CHARLES, C. M. "A Comparison of the Intelligence Quotients of Incarcerated Delinquent White and American Negro Boys and of Groups of St. Louis Public School Boys." *J Appl Psychol* 20:499–510 Ag '36. * (*PA* 11:400)
87. OLANDER, HERBERT T., AND WALKER, BERT S. "Can Teachers Estimate I.Q.'s?" *Sch & Soc* 44:744–6 D 5 '36. * (*PA* 11:1490)
88. RYANS, DAVID G. "An Experimental Study of the Transfer of Training With Special Attention to the Relation of Intelligence Test Performance." *J Ed Psychol* 27:492–500 O '36. * (*PA* 11:1523)
89. TIEBOUT, CAROLYN. "The Measurement of Quality in Children's Painting by the Scale Method." *Psychol Monogr* 48(1):85–94 '36. * (*PA* 11:391)
90. TIEBOUT, CAROLYN, AND MEIER, NORMAN C. "Artistic Ability and General Intelligence." *Psychol Monogr* 48(1):95–125 '36. * (*PA* 11:392)
91. CRISSEY, ORLO L. *Mental Development as Related to Institutional Residence and Educational Achievement.* University of Iowa Studies in Child Welfare Vol. 13, No. 1. Iowa City, Iowa: the University, 1937. Pp. 81. * (*PA* 11:3477)
92. DESING, MINERVA F. *The Relation of Pupil Achievement Gain to Certain Personal and Environmental Elements.* Philadelphia, Pa.: University of Pennsylvania, 1940. Pp. xii, 169. *
93. BOYNTON, PAUL L. "The Relationship Between Children's Tested Intelligence and Their Hobby Participations." *J Genetic Psychol* 58:353–62 Je '41. * (*PA* 16:374)
94. BONNEY, MERL E. "The Relative Stability of Social, Intellectual, and Academic Status in Grades II to IV, and the Inter-Relationships Between These Various Forms of Growth." *J Ed Psychol* 34:88–102 F '43. * (*PA* 17:3943)
95. KOBLER, FRANK J. "Cultural Differences in Intelligence." *J Social Psychol* 18:279–303 S '43. * (*PA* 18:1145)
96. GILL, LESTER N., AND GILL, MYRTLE PAINE. "The Correlation of Reading Rate With Intelligence Scores of Grade School Children After Training in Phonics." *Proc Iowa Acad Sci* 51:377–81 '44. * (*PA* 20:3306)
97. LEWIS, W. DRAYTON. "Sex Distribution of Intelligence Among Inferior and Superior Children." *J Genetic Psychol* 67:67–75 S '45. * (*PA* 20:592)
98. ROBINSON, MARY LOUISE, AND MEENES, MAX. "The Relationship Between Test Intelligence of Third Grade Negro Children and the Occupations of Their Parents." *J Negro Ed* 16:136–41 W '47. * (*PA* 21:2933)
99. TOWNSEND, AGATHA. "An Investigation of Certain Relationships of Spelling With Reading and Academic Aptitude." *J Ed Res* 40:465–71 F '47. * (*PA* 21:3763)
100. JOHNSON, J. T. "On the Nature of Problem-Solving in Arithmetic." *J Ed Res* 43:110–5 O '49. * (*PA* 24:2791)
101. EELLS, KENNETH; DAVIS, ALLISON; HAVIGHURST, ROBERT J.; HERRICK, VERGIL E.; AND TYLER, RALPH W. *Intelligence and Cultural Differences: A Study of Cultural Learning*

and Problem-Solving. Chicago, Ill.: University of Chicago Press, 1951. Pp. xii, 388. * *(PA 27:5738)*

102. WALLIHAN, ROBERT SYLVANUS. *A Comparative Study of Retardation in the Primary Grades of the San Diego, California, City Schools.* Doctor's thesis, University of Colorado (Boulder, Colo.), 1955. *(DA 16:1418)*

103. HEBER, RICK F. "The Relation of Intelligence and Physical Maturity to Social Status of Children." *J Ed Psychol* 47: 158–62 Mr '56. * *(PA 31:7514)*

104. EDWARDS, ROBERTA MILLER. *Factorial Comparison of Arithmetic Performance of Girls and Boys in the Sixth Grade.* Washington: D.C.: Catholic University of America, 1957. Pp. viii, 45. * *(PA 32:842)*

105. LARSON, ROBERT E., AND SELLAND, CYNTHIA T. "A Comparison of Reading Ages With Mental Ages." *J Ed Res* 52:55–9 O '58. * *(PA 34:2105)*

106. SMITH, GARY RICHARD. *An Examination of Selected Measures of Achievement and Aptitude for Use in Normative Grade Placement of Science Concepts on Light.* Doctor's thesis, Northwestern University (Evanston, Ill.), 1960. *(DA 21:2952)*

107. WOZENCRAFT, MARIAN. "Sex Comparisons of Certain Abilities." *J Ed Res* 57:21–7 S '63. *

108. BRYAN, QUENTIN R. "Relative Importance of Intelligence and Visual Perception in Predicting Reading Achievement." *Calif J Ed Res* 15:44–8 Ja '64. * *(PA 38:9228)*

109. MOORE, EARL JAMES. *A Study of the Relationship Between High School and College Scholarship and Selected Test Results for Grades K-12.* Doctor's thesis, University of South Dakota (Vermillion, S.D.), 1964. *(DA 27:679A)*

110. NORTH, ROBERT D. "An Appraisal of the Kuhlmann-Anderson Seventh Edition Test for Grades K-3 in Independent Schools." *Ed Rec B* 85:48–54 Ja '64. "

111. SHAFFER, RAYMOND GEORGE. *A Study of Four Group Intelligence Tests to Identify Ambiguous Pictures as a Factor Which Causes Some Children to Select Incorrect Answers.* Doctor's research study No. 1, Colorado State College (Greeley, Colo.), 1964. *(DA 25:1014)*

112. JOHNSON, MARILYN C. *Relationship Between Kuhlmann-Anderson Intelligence Tests and Reading Ability in Grade 3.* Master's thesis, University of Tulsa (Tulsa, Okla.), 1965.

113. NORTH, ROBERT D. "Kuhlmann-Anderson and Stanford Achievement Test Results of Sixth-Grade Students in Suburban Public Schools." *Ed Rec B* 88:67–70 Jl '65. *

114. NORTH, ROBERT D. "Kuhlmann-Anderson Seventh Edition IQs of Pupils in Independent Elementary Schools." *Ed Rec B* 87:50–6 F '65. *

115. RAINEY, ROBERT G. "A Study of Four School-Ability Tests." *J Exp Ed* 33:305–19 su '65. * *(PA 39:12306)*

116. WIMBY, EUGENE B. *A Comparative Study of the Kuhlmann-Anderson and the Otis Quick Scoring Intelligence Tests as Predictors of High School Performance.* Master's thesis, Atlanta University (Atlanta, Ga.), 1965.

117. YAMAMOTO, KAORU, AND DIZNEY, HENRY F. "Effects of Three Sets of Test Instructions on Scores on an Intelligence Scale." *Ed & Psychol Meas* 25:87–94 sp '65. * *(PA 39:13029)*

118. CUNNINGHAM, WILLIAM. *A Thirteen-Year Retrospective Study of Standardized Test Data.* Doctor's thesis, Western Reserve University (Cleveland, Ohio), 1966. *(DA 27:3305A)*

119. DAVIS, BARBARA H. *Comparison of the Row Peterson First Year Readiness Test Scores and the Kuhlmann-Anderson IQ as Predictors of Reading Achievement in Second Grade Boys.* Master's thesis, Kent State University (Kent, Ohio), 1966.

120. ZWIER, MARCIA D. "Interrelations Among Measured and Perceived Psychosocial Variables." *Percept & Motor Skills* 22:910 Je '66. * *(PA 40:10998)*

121. PATTERSON, BARBARA. *Comparison of Students From High and Low Socio-Economic Backgrounds Using Kuhlmann-Anderson and SCAT Total Test Scores.* Master's thesis, California State College (Hayward, Calif.), 1967.

122. GORDON, JAMES ROSCOE. *Listening, Attitude, and Intelligence Tests to Predict Academic Achievement.* Doctor's thesis, Colorado State College (Greeley, Colo.), 1968. *(DA 29:2522A)*

123. MAZUR, JOSEPH LAWRENCE. *Validity of Scholastic Aptitude Scores as Predictors of Achievement.* Doctor's thesis, Case Western Reserve University (Cleveland, Ohio), 1968. *(DAI 30:171A)*

124. GOFF, CHARLES EDWARD. *A Study of the Relationship Between Noncognitive Factors and General Intelligence to Academic Achievement at the Junior High School Level.* Doctor's thesis, Boston University (Boston, Mass.), 1969. *(DAI 31:220A)*

125. HIERONYMUS, A. N., AND STROUD, JAMES B. *Comparability of IQ Scores on Five Widely Used Intelligence Tests.* *Meas & Eval Guid* 2(3):135–40 f '69. * *(PA 44:13285)*

126. ANNESLEY, FRED; ODHNER, FRED; MADOFF, ELLEN; AND CHANSKY, NORMAN. "Identifying the First Grade Underachiever." *J Ed Res* 63(10):459–62 Jl-Ag '70. *

127. JOSE, TERESITA A. "Convergent-Divergent Thinking Abilities and Risk-Taking in Children." *Philippine J Psychol* 3(1): 22–35 Je '70. * *(PA 49:11231)*

128. BRESKIN, STEPHEN, AND RICH, KENNETH D. "Correlation of Non-Verbal Rigidity and Intelligence in Elementary School Children." *Percept & Motor Skills* 32(1):194 F '71. * *(PA 46:2729)*

129. GWALTNEY, WAYNE KEITH. *Reading in Upward Bound: An Evaluation of a Reading Improvement Course and an Analysis of Some Correlates of Reading Achievement.* Doctor's thesis, University of Georgia (Athens, Ga.), 1971. *(DAI 32:3557A)*

CUMULATIVE NAME INDEX

[399]

Kuhlmann-Finch Tests. Grades 1, 2, 3, 4, 5, 6, 7–9, 10–12; 1951–60; catalog uses the title *Kuhlmann-Finch Scholastic Aptitude Tests;* 1957 test identical with tests copyrighted 1951–52; Frank H. Finch; American Guidance Service, Inc. *

For additional information and reviews by Walter N. Durost, Henry E. Garrett, and Charles O. Neidt, see 5:349 (3 references).

REFERENCES THROUGH 1971

1–3. See 5:349.

4. SCHMUCK, RICHARD A., AND SCHMUCK, ROBERT W. "Upward Mobility and I.Q. Performance." *J Ed Res* 55:123–7 N '61. * *(PA 36:5GC23S)*

5. CLYMER, THEODORE. "A Study of the Influence of Reading

Ability on the Validity of Group Intelligence Tests." *Slow Learning Child* (England) 10:76–84 N '63. *

6. SNIFFEN, ALLAN MEAD. *A Correlation Study of Group Intelligence Tests With Achievement in Reading and Arithmetic in Grade Four: An Investigation of the Effectiveness of Using Group Intelligence Test Scores for Evaluating Academic Achievement in the Tool Subject Areas of Reading and Arithmetic in Public Elementary Schools.* Doctor's thesis, New York University (New York, N.Y.), 1963. (*DA* 24:826)

7. LARSON, ANNE A. *A Study to Determine the Correlation Between a Set of Scores Received on the SRA Primary Mental Abilities Test Given in Kindergarten and a Set of Scores Received on the Kuhlmann-Finch Group Intelligence Test in Third Grade.* Master's thesis, Moorehead State College (Moorehead, Minn.), 1966.

8. DOMRATH, RICHARD P. "Constructional Praxis and Visual Perception in School Children." *J Consult & Clin Psychol* 32:186–92 Ap '68. * (*PA* 42:8174)

9. MENDENHALL, DIANA R. *The Influences of Various Methods of Test Interpretation of the Kuhlmann-Finch Tests.* Master's thesis, Wisconsin State University (Platteville, Wis.), 1970.

CUMULATIVE NAME INDEX

[400]

Lorge-Thorndike Intelligence Tests. Grades kgn–13; 1954–66; LTIT; 2 editions; Irving Lorge, Robert L. Thorndike, and Elizabeth Hagen (*b*); Houghton Mifflin Co. *

a) SEPARATE LEVEL EDITION. Grades kgn–1, 2–3, 4–6, 7–9, 10–12; 1954–62; 5 levels; 2 tests (verbal, nonverbal) for levels 3–5.

1) *Level 1, Nonverbal Battery.* Grades kgn–1.
2) *Level 2, Nonverbal Battery.* Grades 2–3.
3) *Level 3.* Grades 4–6.
4) *Level 4.* Grades 7–9.
5) *Level 5.* Grades 10–12.

b) MULTI-LEVEL EDITION. Grades 3–13; 1954–66; revision of levels 3–5 of the separate level edition; 3 scores: verbal, nonverbal, composite; 8 levels (grades 3, 4, 5, 6, 7, 8–9, 10–11, 12–13) in a single booklet; test for grades 12–13 also available as a separate (see 401).

For additional information and a review by Carol K. Tittle of the multi-level edition, see 7:360 (95 references); see also 6:467 (11 references); for reviews by Frank S. Freeman, John E. Milholland, and D. A. Pidgeon of the separate level edition, see 5:350 (6 references).

REFERENCES THROUGH 1971

1–6. See 5:350.
7–17. See 6:467.
18–112. See 7:360.

113. NEWTON, BERTHA M. "A Study of Certain Factors Related to Achievement in Spelling." *Alberta J Ed Res* (Canada) 7:202–8 D '61. * (*PA* 36:5KL02N)

114. CONVERSE, HAROLD D., AND COURTNEY, JOHN MICHAEL. "A Comparative Study of the Lorge-Thorndike Group Intelligence Tests With an Individual Intelligence Test." *J Res Services* 1:1–5 My '62. *

115. POLLARD, ALICE G. *A Comparison of the Performance of a Group of Intellectually Retarded Children on Three Group Tests of Intelligence.* Master's thesis, Catholic University of America (Washington, D.C.), 1963.

116. NADEAU, CORINNE. *A Comparison of the Performance of a Group of Intellectually Normal Children on Three Group Tests of Intelligence.* Master's thesis, Catholic University of America (Washington, D.C.), 1964.

117. RAPHAEL, SHARON. *The Relationship of Intelligence and Personality on the Reading Achievement of Culturally Deprived Second-Grade Students.* Master's thesis, Central Connecticut State College (New Britain, Conn.), 1965.

118. ROFF, MERRILL, AND SELLS, S. B. "Relations Between Intelligence and Sociometric Status in Groups Differing in Sex and Socio-Economic Background." *Psychol Rep* 16:511–6 Ap '65. * (*PA* 39:9929)

119. TRAD, MICHAEL, JR. *Intelligence: Relationship With Achievement of Junior High School Students.* Master's thesis, Illinois State University (Normal, Ill.), 1965.

120. MACARTHUR, R. S., AND MOSYCHUK, H. "Lower and Upper Socioeconomic Group Contrasts in Long-Term Predictability of Grade Nine Achievement." *J Ed Meas* 3:167–8 su '66. *

121. BATH, JOHN A. "Mental Ability of Residents in a State School for Dependent and Neglected Youth." *Psychol Rep* 20:469–70 Ap '67. * (*PA* 41:8716)

122. GUSTAFSON, RAYMOND G. *Predicting Student Success in Ninth Grade Algebra in the Public Schools of Watertown, Minnesota.* Master's thesis, St. Cloud State College (St. Cloud, Minn.), 1967.

123. HOHENSHIL, THOMAS H. *The Effects of Discouragement on the Verbal Section of a Group Intelligence Test.* Master's thesis, Kent State University (Kent, Ohio), 1967.

124. RUDNICK, MARK; STERRITT, GRAHAM M.; AND FLAX, MORTON. "Auditory and Visual Rhythm Perception and Reading Ability." *Child Develop* 38:581–7 Je '67. * (*PA* 41:10263)

125. YAMAMOTO, KAORU. "Creativity and Unpredictability in School Achievement." *J Ed Res* 60:321–5 Mr '67. *

126. OHNMACHT, FRED W. "Correlates of Change in Academic Achievement." *J Ed Meas* 5:41–4 sp '68. *

127. AMES, WILBUR S. "Reading Programs: Use of Test Data as a Vital Factor." *Clearing House* 43(9):515–8 My '69. *

128. HAMMOND, LONNIE L. *A Non-Linear Relationship Study of Personality and Intelligence.* Master's thesis, East Tennessee State University (Johnson City, Tenn.), 1969.

129. EHRHART, PATRICIA MAULDIN. *A Study of Selected Mental Ability Tests as Predictors of Achievement for Chamorro Pupils.* Master's thesis, University of Guam (Agana, Guam), 1970.

130. MANCOTT, ANATOL. "Prediction of Performance in Chemistry II." *Nursing Outl* 18(11):57 N '70. *

131. MIRON, MORDECHAI. *Principles for Equivalent Cross-Cultural Utilization of Group Intelligence Tests.* Doctor's thesis, University of Pittsburgh (Pittsburgh, Pa.), 1970. (*DAI* 31:6474A)

132. MITCHELL, KATHARINE E. *An Early Predictive Test and Its Relationship to Junior High School Achievement.* Doctor's thesis, Syracuse University (Syracuse, N.Y.), 1970. (*DAI* 32:97A)

133. BUSCH, JOHN CHRISTIAN, AND DE RIDDER, LAWRENCE M. "Note on Control for Intelligence in Studies of Field Dependence With Young Children." *Percept & Motor Skills* 32(1):337–8 F '71. * (*PA* 46:2634)

134. COUNTS, PERRY DALMOND. *A Study of the Relationship Between Academic Achievement and Creativity.* Doctor's thesis, University of Tennessee (Knoxville, Tenn.), 1971. (*DAI* 32:4342A)

135. DACEY, JOHN S., AND MADAUS, GEORGE F. "An Analysis of Two Hypotheses Concerning the Relationship Between Creativity and Intelligence." *J Ed Res* 64(5):213–6 Ja '71. * (*PA* 46:4712)

136. FOLLMAN, JOHN; LOWE, A. J.; AND WILEY, RUSSELL. "Correlational and Factor Analysis of Critical Reading and Thinking Test Scores—Twelfth Grade." *Yearb Nat Read Conf* 20:128–36 '71. *

137. GREEN, RICHARD B., AND ROHWER, WILLIAM D., JR. "SES Differences on Learning and Ability Tests in Black Children." *Am Ed Res J* 8(4):601–9 N '71. * (*PA* 47:11611)

138. JENSEN, ARTHUR R. "Do Schools Cheat Minority Children?" *Ed Res* (England) 14(1):3–28 N '71. * (*PA* 49:11953)

139. JOHNSON, ROGER; FOLLMAN, JOHN; WILEY, RUSSELL; LOWE, A. J.; AND MILLER, WILLIAM. "Canonical and Partial Correlation of Critical Reading and Critical Thinking Test Scores—Twelfth Grade." *Yearb Nat Read Conf* 20:137–41 '71. *

140. KAUFFMAN, JAMES M.; WEAVER, S. JOSEPH; AND WEAVER, ANN. "Age and Intelligence as Correlates of Perceived Family Relationships of Underachievers." *Psychol Rep* 28(2):522 Ap '71. * (*PA* 46:7758)

141. KAUFMAN, ALAN S. "Piaget and Gesell: A Psychometric Analysis of Tests Built From Their Tasks." *Child Develop* 42(5):1341–60 N '71. * (*PA* 48:4592)

142. LOWE, A. J.; FOLLMAN, JOHN; BURLEY, WADE; AND FOLLMAN, JOHNNY. "Psychometric Analysis of Critical Reading and Critical Thinking Test Scores—Twelfth Grade." *Yearb Nat Read Conf* 20:142–7 '71. *

143. PROGER, BARTON B.; MCGOWAN, JOHN R.; BAYUK, ROBERT J., JR.; MANN, LESTER; TREVORROW, RUTH L.; AND MASSA, EDWARD. "The Relative Predictive and Construct Validities of the Otis-Lennon Mental Ability Test, the Lorge-Thorndike Intelligence Test, and the Metropolitan Readiness Test in Grades Two and Four: A Series of Multivariate Analyses." *Ed & Psychol Meas* 31(2):529–38 su '71. *

144. RICHMOND, BERT O. "Creative and Cognitive Abilities of White and Negro Children." *J Negro Ed* 40(2):111–6 sp '71. * (*PA* 47:7566)

145. ROSENAU, CHARLES B., AND WILLIAMS, JOHN D. "A Comparison of the Lorge-Thorndike Intelligence Test Total IQ and the General Aptitude Test Battery Aptitude G." *Col Ed Rec Univ N Dak* 56(9):167–70 Je '71. *

146. SMITH, I. LEON. "IQ, Creativity, and Achievement: Interaction and Threshold." *Multiv Behav Res* 6(1):51–62 Ja '71. * (*PA* 46:9753)

147. TAYLOR, ALTON L. "Regression Analysis of Antecedent

Measures of Slow Sections in High School Biology." *Sci Ed* 55(3):395–402 Jl–S '71. *

148. WILLIAMSON, HELEN THORWORTH. *Tolerance of Ambiguity and Creativity Thinking in Elementary School Children: A Study of the Relationships Among Tolerance of Ambiguity, Intelligence, Training in Creative Thinking, and Flexibility of Concept Formation.* Doctor's thesis, New York University (New York, N.Y.), 1971. (*DAI* 32:6821A)

149. YOLOYE, EMMANUEL AYOTUNDE. "The Effect of Schooling on the Performance of Bilingual Students in Tests of Intelligence." *Res Ed* (England) 5:25–34 My '71. * (*PA* 47:3646)

150. YOUNG, WILLIAM T. "The Role of Musical Aptitude, Intelligence, and Academic Achievement in Predicting the Musical Attainment of Elementary Instrumental Music Students." *J Res Music Ed* 19(4):385–98 w '71. * (*PA* 48:7918)

CUMULATIVE NAME INDEX

[401]

Lorge-Thorndike Intelligence Tests, College Edition. Grades 12–13; 1954–66; LTIT-H; Level H of the Multi-Level Edition (see 400); 3 scores: verbal, nonverbal, composite; Irving Lorge, Robert L. Thorndike, and Elizabeth Hagen; Houghton Mifflin Co. *

For additional information and reviews by Eric F. Gardner, William B. Michael, and John H. Rosenbach, see 7:359.

[402]

***Mental Alertness: Tests A/1 and A/2.** Job applicants with 9–11, 12 or more years of education; 1945–68; 2 levels; no manual; National Institute for Personnel Research [South Africa]. *

a) TEST A/2. Job applicants with 9–11 years of education; 1945–68; revision of Test A(G) of the South African Air Force.

b) TEST A/1. Job applicants with 12 or more years of education; 1945–62; revision of Test A(F) of the South African Air Force.

For additional information, see 7:362.

[403]

Mill Hill Vocabulary Scale. Ages 4 and over, 11–14, 14 and over; 1943–58; intelligence; 2 editions; John C. Raven; H. K. Lewis & Co. Ltd. [England]. *

a) ORAL DEFINITIONS FORM. Ages 4 and over; consists of all words from both forms of the junior and senior levels below.

b) WRITTEN TEST. Ages 11–14, 14 and over. (Australian edition of senior level: Australian Council for Educational Research [Australia].)

For additional information and a review by Morton Bortner, see 6:471 (16 references); see also 4:303 (7 references); for a review by David Wechsler, see 3:239 (3 references).

REFERENCES THROUGH 1971

1–3. See 3:239.
4–10. See 4:303.
11–26. See 6:471.

27. CROWN, SIDNEY. "An Experimental Study of Psychological Changes Following Prefrontal Lobotomy." *J General Psychol* 47:3–41 Jl '52. * (*PA* 27:6024)

28. DAVIES-EYSENCK, MARGARET. "Cognitive Factors in Epilepsy." *J Neurol Neurosurg & Psychiatry* (England) 15:39–44 F '52. * (*PA* 27:2918)

29. FOULDS, G. A. "The Reliability of Psychiatric, and the Validity of Psychological, Diagnoses." *J Mental Sci* (England) 101:851–62 O '55. * (*PA* 30:7165)

30. HOPKINS, BARBARA, AND POST, FELIX. "The Significance of Abstract and Concrete Behaviour in Elderly Psychiatric Patients and Control Subjects." *J Mental Sci* (England) 101: 841–50 O '55. * (*PA* 30:7000)

31. MEYER, VICTOR, AND YATES, AUBREY J. "Intellectual Changes Following Temporal Lobectomy for Psychomotor Epilepsy: Preliminary Communication." *J Neurol Neurosurg & Psychiatry* (England) 18:44–52 F '55. * (*PA* 29:7775)

32. MONTGOMERY, G. W. G. "Predicting Success in Engineering." *Occup Psychol* (England) 36:59–68 Ja–Ap '62. *

33. ROSS, JEAN. "Predicting Practical Skill in Engineering Apprentices." *Occup Psychol* (England) 36:69–74 Ja–Ap '62. *

34. SAMPSON, OLIVE C. "Reading Skill at Eight Years in

Relation to Speech and Other Factors." *Brit J Ed Psychol* 32:12–7 F '62. *

35. FOULDS, G. A., AND OWEN, ANNA. "Speed and Accuracy on Mazes in Relation to Diagnosis and Personality." *Brit J Social & Clin Psychol* 3:34–5 F '64. * (*PA* 38:8870)

36. GIBSON, H. B. "A Slang Vocabulary Test as an Indicator of Delinquent Association." *Brit J Social & Clin Psychol* 3:50–5 F '64. * (*PA* 38:8999)

37. KENDRICK, D. C. "Assessment of Pre-Morbid Intelligence of Elderly Patients With Diffuse Brain Pathology." *Psychol Rep* 15:188 Ag '64. * (*PA* 39:1389)

38. VINODA, K. S. "A Comparative Study of the Personality Characteristics of Attempted Suicides, Psychiatric Patients and Normals." *Trans All-India Inst Mental Health* 5:67–74 D '65. * (*PA* 40:7860)

39. GIBSON, H. B. "The Validation of a Technique for Measuring Delinquent Association by Means of Vocabulary." *Brit J Social & Clin Psychol* 5:190–5 S '66. * (*PA* 40:13338)

40. LEY, P.; SPELMAN, M. S.; DAVIES, ANN D. M.; AND RILEY, S. "The Relationships Between Intelligence, Anxiety, Neuroticism and Extraversion." *Brit J Ed Psychol* 36:185–91 Je '66. * (*PA* 40:10100)

41. HERON, ALASTAIR, AND CHOWN, SHEILA. *Age and Function.* London: J. & A. Churchill Ltd., 1967. Pp. x, 182. *

42. PAYNE, R. W.; NETLEY, C. T.; AND SLOANE, R. B. "Rigidity, Drive and Conditioning in Neurotics." *Brit J Psychol* 58:111–26 My '67. * (*PA* 42:10857)

43. MONTGOMERY, G. W. G. "A Factorial Study of Communication and Ability in Deaf School Leavers." *Brit J Ed Psychol* 38:27–37 F '68. * (*PA* 42:12755)

44. MUNRO, HELLE. "Verbal Fluency in Test and Group Situations." *Brit J Proj Psychol & Pers Study* 13:25–9 Je '68. * (*PA* 45:946)

45. FARLEY, FRANK H. "Further Data on Multiple-Choice Versus Open-Ended Estimates of Vocabulary." *Brit J Social & Clin Psychol* 8(1):67–8 F '69. * (*PA* 43:7551)

46. JAMIESON, G. HARRY. "Prior Learning and Response Flexibility in Two Age Groups." *J Gerontol* 24(2):179–83 Ap '69. *

47. ROMNEY, DAVID. "The Validity of Certain Tests of Overinclusion." *Brit J Psychiatry* 115(522):591–2 My '69. * (*PA* 44:3689)

48. FOULDS, G. A. "Progressive Matrices and the Mill Hill Vocabulary Scale as a Diagnostic Aid Among Psychiatric Patients." *Brit J Social & Clin Psychol* 9(1):80–2 F '70. *

49. GIBSON, H. B., AND WEST, D. J. "Social and Intellectual Handicaps as Precursors of Early Delinquency." *Brit J Criminol* 10(1):21–32 Ja '70. * (*PA* 44:16949)

50. IRVING, G.; ROBINSON, R. A.; AND McADAM, W. "The Validity of Some Cognitive Tests in the Diagnosis of Dementia." *Brit J Psychiatry* 117(537):149–56 Ag '70. * (*PA* 45:4539)

51. KEAR-COLWELL, J. J. "The B Factor Scale of the 16 PF as a Measure of Intelligence in Psychiatric Patients." *J Clin Psychol* 26(4):477–9 O '70. * (*PA* 45:4540)

52. McKERRACHER, D. W.; ZWIRNER, W.; AND HARSHMAN, R. C. "Personality and Attainment: A Pilot Study." *West Psychologist* (Canada) 1(2):62–70 Ja '70. *

53. ORME, J. E. "A Practical Guide to Estimating Intelligence, Attainments and Intellectual Deficit." *Acta Psychologica* (Netherlands) 32(2):145–61 Ap '70. * (*PA* 44:16684)

54. PECK, DAVID F. "The Conversion of Progressive Matrices and Mill Hill Vocabulary Raw Scores Into Deviation IQ's." *J Clin Psychol* 26(1):67–70 Ja '70. * (*PA* 44:10420)

55. WARDER, JOHN; PRESLY, ALLAN S.; AND KIRK, JOAN. "Intelligence and Literacy in Prison and Hospital Populations." *Brit J Criminol* 10(3):286–7 Jl '70. * (*PA* 46:1469)

56. EYSENCK, HANS J. "Relation Between Intelligence and Personality." *Percept & Motor Skills* 32(2):637–8 Ap '71. * (*PA* 46:10929)

57. LOVIUS, B. B. J. "Speech and Intelligence in Adult Cleft-Palate Patients." *Dental Prac & Dental Rec* 21(8):290–3 Ap '71. *

58. SPELMAN, MICHAEL S.; HARRISON, ARTHUR W.; AND MELLSOP, GRAHAM W. "Grid Test for Schizophrenic Thought Disorder in Acute and Chronic Schizophrenia." *Psychol Med* (England) 1(3):234–8 My '71. * (*PA* 47:11296)

CUMULATIVE NAME INDEX

[404]

Miller Analogies Test. Candidates for graduate school; 1926–70; MAT; Forms J and R also published under the title *Advanced Personnel Test* for use in business; distribution restricted and test administered at specified licensed university centers; W. S. Miller (test); Psychological Corporation. *

For additional information, see 7:363 (57 references); for reviews by Lloyd G. Humphreys, William B. Schrader, and Warren W. Willingham, see 6:472 (26 references); for a review by John T. Dailey, see 5:352 (28 references); for reviews by J. P. Guilford and Carl I. Hovland, see 4:304 (16 references).

REFERENCES THROUGH 1971

1–16. See 4:304.
17–44. See 5:352.
45–70. See 6:472.
71–127. See 7:363.

128. SORENSON, HERBERT. "Adult Ages as a Factor in Learning." *J Ed Psychol* 21:451–9 S '30. * (*PA* 5:108)

129. BLAKE, ROBERT R. "The Relation Between Childhood Environment and the Scholastic Aptitude and Intelligence of Adults." *J Social Psychol* 29:37–41 F '49. * (*PA* 23:4132)

130. DUMLER, MARVIN J. "A Study of Factors Related to Gains in the Reading Rate of College Students Trained With the Tachistoscope and Accelerator." *J Ed Res* 52:27–30 S '58. * (*PA* 33:10956)

131. WIDENER, SUE ELLEN. *A Statistical Analysis for Predicting Success in Graduate School.* Master's thesis, East Tennessee State University (Johnson City, Tenn.), 1964.

132. "Science and Nursing Knowledge of Graduate Students." *Nursing Outl* 15:53 D '67. *

133. HARTSOCK, WOODROW WILSON. *The Prediction of Academic Performance in a Seminary.* Master's thesis, Southern Methodist University (Dallas, Tex.), 1967.

134. FELKER, SALLY ANNA. *The Relationship Between Communication and Discrimination Skills and Selected Factors of Personality, Intellect, and Experience in Counselor Trainees.* Doctor's thesis, Kent State University (Kent, Ohio), 1970. (*DAI* 31:5122A)

135. JARDIN, ROBERT PATRICK. *An Analysis of Peer Ratings and Subordinate Ratings as a Potential Feedback and Self-Selection Device for School Counselor Candidates.* Doctor's thesis, American University (Washington, D.C.), 1970. (*DAI* 32:178A)

136. POROZNY, GEORGE HAROLD JOHN. *Relationship of Selected Intellectual and Personal Factors to Completion of the Business Education Doctoral Program at Selected American Universities.* Doctor's thesis, University of North Dakota (Grand Forks, N.D.), 1970. (*DAI* 31:6488A)

137. AYERS, JERRY B. "Predicting Quality Point Averages in Master's Degree Programs in Education." *Ed & Psychol Meas* 31(2):491–5 su '71. *

138. BURRELL, LEON FREDERICK. *Non-Academic Variables as They Relate to Academic Achievement of Male Black Doctoral Candidates.* Doctor's thesis, Michigan State University (East Lansing, Mich.), 1971. (*DAI* 32:4863A)

139. DOPPELT, JEROME E. "Differences Between the Miller Analogies Test Scores of People Tested Twice." *Ed & Psychol Meas* 31(3):735–44 au '71. * (*PA* 47:7556)

140. KOOKER, EARL W. "The Relationship Between Performance in a Graduate Course in Statistics and the Miller Analogies Test and the Watson-Glaser Critical Thinking Appraisal." *J Psychol* 77(2):165–9 Mr '71. * (*PA* 46:1772)

141. PAYNE, DAVID A.; WELLS, ROBERT A.; AND CLARKE, ROBERT R. "Another Contribution to Estimating Success in Graduate School: A Search for Sex Differences and Comparison

Between Three Degree Types." *Ed & Psychol Meas* 31(2):497–503 su '71. *

142. WRIGHT, MATTHEW THOMAS. *An Analysis of Selected Factors of Education Doctoral Programs at Washington State University.* Doctor's thesis, Washington State University (Pullman, Wash.), 1971. (*DAI* 32:4388A)

CUMULATIVE NAME INDEX

[405]

★**Minnesota Scholastic Aptitude Test.** High school and college; 1969–70, c1940–70; MSAT; short form of *Ohio State University Psychological Test*, Form 23; originally prepared for use in Minnesota secondary schools; Wilbur L. Layton; original test by Herbert A. Toops; Wilbur L. Layton. *

REFERENCES THROUGH 1971

1. LAYTON, WILBUR L. "Construction of a Short Form of the Ohio State University Psychological Examination." *Yearb Nat Council Meas Used Ed* 12(pt 1):81–5 '55. *

2. SWANSON, EDWARD O., AND BERDIE, RALPH F. "Predictive Validities in an Institute of Technology." *Ed & Psychol Meas* 21:1001–8 w '61. * Errata: 22:258 su '62.

3. BERDIE, RALPH F.; LAYTON, WILBUR L.; HAGENAH, THEDA; AND SWANSON, EDWARD O. *Who Goes to College? Comparison of Minnesota College Freshmen, 1930–1960.* Minneapolis, Minn.: University of Minnesota Press, 1962. Pp. vii, 56. *

4. RAY, PHILIP BOND. *A Descriptive Study of Certain Characteristics of "High Creative" Freshman Arts College Students as Compared With "High Academic Potential" Students.* Doctor's thesis, University of Minnesota (Minneapolis, Minn.), 1962. (*DA* 24:1924)

5. LESTER, ROBERT ANDREW. *The Relationship of SVIB and ACT Scores to Differential Academic Achievement.* Doctor's thesis, University of Minnesota (Minneapolis, Minn.), 1963. (*DA* 24:1076)

6. HAAK, LOUIS ANDREW. *An Investigation of the Validation Characteristics of Four Statistical Techniques in the Prediction of Certain Educational Achievement Variables.* Doctor's thesis, University of Minnesota (Minneapolis, Minn.), 1964. (*DA* 26:867)

7. HOOD, ALBERT B., AND BERDIE, RALPH F. "The Relationship of Ability to College Attendance." *Col & Univ* 39:309–18 sp '64. *

8. SPACE, MARGARET NIVEN. *A Study of Individual Predictability Based on Intra-Individual Variability on Certain Achievement Measures.* Doctor's thesis, University of Minnesota (Minneapolis, Minn.), 1964. (*DA* 26:879)

9. WATLEY, DONIVAN J. "Type, Location, and Size of High School and Prediction of Achievement in an Institute of Technology." *Ed & Psychol Meas* 24:331–8 su '64. * (*PA* 39:5987)

10. CAMPBELL, DAVID P. "A Cross-Sectional and Longitudinal Study of Scholastic Abilities Over Twenty-Five Years." *J Counsel Psychol* 12:55–61 sp '65. * (*PA* 39:10814)

11. HEWER, VIVIAN H. "Are Tests Fair to College Students From Homes With Low Socio-Economic Status?" *Personnel & Guid J* 43:764–9 Ap '65. * (*PA* 39:16441)

12. BERDIE, RALPH F., AND HOOD, ALBERT B. "How Effectively Do We Predict Plans for College Attendance?" *Personnel & Guid J* 44:487–93 Ja '66. * (*PA* 40:5899)

13. BERDIE, RALPH F., AND STEIN, JUNE. "A Comparison of New University Students Who Do and Do Not Seek Counseling." *J Counsel Psychol* 13:310–7 f '66. * (*PA* 40:12631)

14. CAMPBELL, JOHN P. "Comparison of Criterion Clusters Obtained by Analyzing the Homogeneity of a Set of Regression Equations and the Matrix of Intercorrelations." *Ed & Psychol Meas* 26:405–17 su '66. * (*PA* 40:12757)

15. HAKEL, MILTON D. "Prediction of College Achievement From the Edwards Personal Preference Schedule Using Intellectual Ability as a Moderator." *J Appl Psychol* 50:336–40 Ag '66. * (*PA* 40:11489)

16. BROWN, F. G., AND SCOTT, D. A. "Differential Predictability in College Admissions Testing." *J Ed Meas* 4:163–6 f '67. *

17. HOOD, ALBERT B. "A Method of Comparing Student Achievement Levels at Different Colleges." *Personnel & Guid J* 45:799–803 Ap '67. *

18. HOOD, ALBERT B. "Predicting College Achievement of Students From Farm Backgrounds." *Personnel & Guid J* 45:996–1000 Je '67. *

19. PETRIK, NORMAN D. "Socio-Economic Status, Vocational Interests, and Persistence in Selected College Curricula." *Voc Guid Q* 16:39–44 S '67. *

20. WATLEY, DONIVAN J., AND MERWIN, JACK C. "An Attempt to Improve Prediction of College Success by Adjusting for High School Characteristics." *Am Ed Res J* 4:229–40 My '67. * (*PA* 41:14173)

21. LUNDGREN, ELIZABETH J. "Predicting Student Success in Medical Technology and Clinical Laboratory Assistant Programs." *Am J Med Technol* 34:349–61 Je '68. *

22. MUNDAY, LEO. "Correlations Between ACT and Other Predictors of Academic Success in College." *Col & Univ* 44:67–76 f '68. *

23. BERDIE, RALPH F. "Intra-Individual Temporal Variability

and Predictability." *Ed & Psychol Meas* 29(2):235–57 su '69. * (*PA* 44:17502)

24. TAYLOR, RONALD G., AND HANSON, GARY R. "Pre-College Math-Workshop and Freshman Achievement." *J Ed Res* 63(4): 157–60 D '69. *

25. BIGGS, DONALD A.; ROTH, JOHN D.; AND STRONG, STANLEY R. "Self-Made Academic Predictions and Academic Performance." *Meas & Eval Guid* 3(2):81–5 su '70. * (*PA* 45:1357)

26. BYERLY, RICHARD LEE. *The Use of Multiple Regression and Path Analysis in Analyzing Success in Journalism at Iowa State University.* Doctor's thesis, Iowa State University (Ames, Iowa), 1970. (*DAI* 31:4617A)

27. ERNEST, DAVID J. "The Predication of Academic Success of College Music Majors." *J Res Music Ed* 18(3):273–6 f '70. * (*PA* 45:8994)

28. HANSON, GARY R., AND TAYLOR, RONALD G. "Interaction of Ability and Personality: Another Look at the Drop-Out Problem in an Institute of Technology." *J Counsel Psychol* 17(6): 540–5 N '70. * (*PA* 45:3036)

29. IM, IN JAE. *A Multivariate Analysis of the Relationship of Academic, Personality, and Family Background Variables to the Different Patterns of Collegiate Attendance.* Doctor's thesis, University of Minnesota (Minneapolis, Minn.), 1970. (*DAI* 32:240A)

30. SHERMAN, RICHARD C., AND POE, CHARLES A. "Factor-Analytic Scales of a Normative Form of the EPPS." *Meas & Eval Guid* 2(4):243–8 w '70. *

31. FRYETT, HOWARD LESLIE. *An Interpretation of Student Self Concept and Analysis of Relationships Between the Self and Selected Characteristics of Business Education Students Enrolled in Minnesota Area Vocational-Technical Schools.* Doctor's thesis, University of North Dakota (Grand Forks, N.D.), 1971. (*DAI* 33:76A)

CUMULATIVE NAME INDEX

Berdie, R. F.: 2–3, 7, 12–3, 23
Biggs, D. A.: 25
Brown, F. G.: 16
Byerly, R. L.: 26
Campbell, D. P.: 10
Campbell, J. P.: 14
Ernest, D. J.: 27
Fryett, H. L.: 31
Haak, L. A.: 6
Hagenah, T.: 3
Hakel, M. D.: 15
Hanson, G. R.: 24, 28
Hewer, V. H.: 11
Hood, A. B.: 7, 12, 17–8
Im, I. J.: 29
Layton, W. L.: 1, 3

Lester, R. A.: 5
Lundgren, E. J.: 21
Merwin, J. C.: 20
Munday, L.: 22
Petrik, N. D.: 19
Poe, C. A.: 30
Ray, P. B.: 4
Roth, J. D.: 25
Scott, D. A.: 16
Sherman, R. C.: 30
Space, M. N.: 8
Stein, J.: 13
Strong, S. R.: 25
Swanson, E. O.: 2–3
Taylor, R. G.: 24, 28
Watley, D. J.: 9, 20

[406]
Mitchell Vocabulary Test. Adults; 1958; intelligence; [A. Mitchell]; distributed by NFER Publishing Co. Ltd. [England]. *

For additional information, see 6:473 (1 reference).

REFERENCES THROUGH 1971
1. See 6:473.

CUMULATIVE NAME INDEX

Semeonoff, B.: 1   Trist, E.: 1

[407]
Modified Alpha Examination Form 9. Grades 7–12 and adults; 1941–51; a revision of *Army Group Examination Alpha;* 3 scores: numerical, verbal, total; F. L. Wells; Psychological Corporation. *

For additional information and a review by Dael Wolfle, see 4:305 (8 references); see also 3:220 (77 references for *Army Group Examination Alpha* and revisions).

REFERENCES THROUGH 1971
1–3. See 3:220(68, 70, 72).
4–8. See 4:305.
9. RUBIN, EDMUND JOSEPH. *Performance of Totally-Blind and Sighted Subjects on Tests of Abstraction.* Doctor's thesis, Fordham University (New York, N.Y.), 1963. (*DA* 24:2989)
10. MATHAE, DAVID E. "Norms and Correlations of Scores From the Modified Alpha Examination Form 9 and the Shipley Institute of Living Scale for Hospitalized Female Neuropsychiatric Patients." *Newsl Res Psychol* 10:22–6 My '68. *

CUMULATIVE NAME INDEX

Allen, R. M.: 7
Bennett, G. K.: 1
Bessell, H.: 7

Demand, J. W.: 3
Eimicke, V. W.: 4, 8
Fish, H. L.: 4

Mathae, D. E.: 10
Murray, J. E.: 6
Rubin, E. J.: 9
Savage, B. M.: 2

Seltzer, C. C.: 5
Wells, F. L.: 2
Wolfle, D.: *rev,* 4:305

[408]
Moray House Picture Tests. Ages 6.5–8.5; 1944–61; 2 tests; Department of Education, University of Edinburgh; University of London Press Ltd. [England]. *
a) MORAY HOUSE PICTURE INTELLIGENCE TEST 1. Ages 6.5–8.5; 1944–48; test booklet title is *Picture Intelligence Test 1;* Margaret A. Mellone.
b) MORAY HOUSE PICTURE TEST 2. Ages 6.5–8.0; 1961.

For additional information concerning *b*, see 6:475; for reviews by Gertrude Keir and M. L. Kellmer Pringle of *a*, see 4:306 (5 references).

REFERENCES THROUGH 1971
1–5. See 4:306.
6. PEEL, E. A., AND GRAHAM, D. "Differentiation of Ability in Primary School Children." *Durham Res R* (England) 1(2): 40–8 S '51. *
7. PEEL, E. A., AND GRAHAM, D. "Differentiation of Ability in Primary School Children—II." *Durham Res R* (England) 1(3):31–4 S '52. * (*PA* 27:5157)
8. POTTS, ERIC. "A Factorial Study of the Relationship Between the Child's Vocabulary and His Reading Progress at the Infants' Stage." Abstract. *Brit J Ed Psychol* 30:84–6 F '60. *
9. NISBET, J. D., AND ILLESLEY, R. "The Influence of Early Puberty on Test Performance at Age Eleven." *Brit J Ed Psychol* 33:169–76 Je '63. * (*PA* 38:4096)
10. HOROBIN, GORDON; OLDMAN, DAVID; AND BYTHEWAY, BILL. "The Social Differentiation of Ability." *Sociology* 1:113–29 My '67. *
11. NISBET, J. D., AND ENTWISTLE, N. J. "Intelligence and Family Size, 1949–1965." *Brit J Ed Psychol* 37:188–93 Je '67. * (*PA* 41:15274)
12. PUMFREY, P. D. "Effect of Selection Procedure on the Placement of Children in Special Schools." *Res Ed* (England) 5:10–24 My '71. *

CUMULATIVE NAME INDEX

Bytheway, B.: 10
Emmett, W. C.: 4
Entwistle, N. J.: 11
Graham, D.: 6–7
Horobin, G.: 10
Hughes, H. O.: 5
Illesley, R.: 9
Keir, G.: *rev,* 4:306

Mellone, M. A.: 1–3
Nisbet, J. D.: 9, 11
Oldman, D.: 10
Peel, E. A.: 6–7
Potts, E.: 8
Pringle, M. L. K.: *rev,* 4:306
Pumfrey, P. D.: 12

[409]
Moray House Verbal Reasoning Tests. Ages 8.5–10.5, 10–12, 12–14.5, 13.5 and over; 1930–72; formerly listed as *Moray House Intelligence Tests;* 5 levels; Godfrey Thomson Unit, University of Edinburgh; University of London Press Ltd. [England]. *
a) MORAY HOUSE JUNIOR REASONING TEST FOR NINE YEAR OLDS. Ages 8.5–10.5; 1947–70; formerly called *Moray House Junior Intelligence Test.*
b) MORAY HOUSE VERBAL REASONING TEST. Ages 10–12; 1930–72; formerly called *Moray House Intelligence Tests;* 1–3 new forms issued annually; distribution of forms 75–89 restricted to education authorities.
c) MORAY HOUSE VERBAL REASONING TEST: VERNIER TEST 2. Ages 10–12 of above average ability; 1954–57. *Out of print.*
d) MORAY HOUSE VERBAL REASONING TEST (ADV.). Ages 12–14.5; 1940–68.
e) MORAY HOUSE VERBAL REASONING TEST (ADULT) 1. Ages 13.5 and over; 1952–70; formerly called *Moray House Adult Intelligence Test 1.*

For additional information, see 7:364 (3 references); see also 6:474 (13 references) and 5:353 (2 references); for a review by Patrick Slater of earlier forms, see 3:241 (2 references); for a review by C. Ebblewhite Smith, see 2:1409.

REFERENCES THROUGH 1971
1–2. See 3:241.
3–4. See 5:353.
5–17. See 6:474.

18–20. See 7:364.

21. SUTHERLAND, H. E. G. "The Relationship Between IQ and Size of Family." *J Ed Psychol* 20:81–90 F '29. * (*PA* 3:2242)

22. McRAE, HUGH. "The Inconstancy of Group Test IQ's." *Brit J Ed Psychol* 12:59–70 F '42. * (*PA* 16:2905)

23. RUTTER, D. "An Inquiry Into the Predictive Value of the Grammar School Entrance Examination." *Durham Res R* (England) 1(1):3–11 Jl '50. *

24. JONES, W. R. "The Influence of Reading Ability in English on the Intelligence Test Scores of Welsh-Speaking Children." *Brit J Ed Psychol* 23:114–20 F '53. * (*PA* 28:4835)

25. PEEL, E. A. "Footnote on 'Practice Effects Between Three Consecutive Tests of Intelligence.'" *Brit J Ed Psychol* 23:126 F '53. * (*PA* 28:4382)

26. SMITH, I. MACFARLANE. "The Development of a Spatial Test." *Durham Ed R* (England) 1(5):19–33 S '54. * (*PA* 29:7298)

27. DOCKRELL, W. B. "The Relationship Between Socio-Economic Status, Intelligence and Attainment in Some Scottish Primary Schools." *Indian Psychol B* 4:1–6 Ja '59. * (*PA* 37:4715)

28. KING, NORMAN W. "Sources of Fluctuation in Scores From Successive Group Intelligence Tests." Abstract of bachelor's thesis. *Brit J Ed Psychol* 30:83 F '60. *

29. PILLINER, A. E. G.; SUTHERLAND, J.; AND TAYLOR, E. G. "Zero Error in Moray House Verbal Reasoning Tests." *Brit J Ed Psychol* 30:53–62 F '60. *

30. MANLEY, D. R. "Mental Ability in Jamaica: (An Examination of the Performance of Children in the Jamaican Common Entrance Examination, 1959)." *Social & Econ Studies* (Jamaica) 12:51–71 Mr '63. * (*PA* 38:767)

31. NISBET, J. D., AND ILLESLEY, R. "The Influence of Early Puberty on Test Performance at Age Eleven." *Brit J Ed Psychol* 33:169–76 Je '63. * (*PA* 38:4096)

32. HALLWORTH, H. J. "Personality Ratings of Adolescents: A Study in a Comprehensive School." *Brit J Ed Psychol* 34:171–7 Je '64. * (*PA* 39:3180)

33. HOROBIN, GORDON; OLDMAN, DAVID; AND BYTHEWAY, BILL. "The Social Differentiation of Ability." *Sociology* 1:113–29 My '67. *

34. NISBET, J. D., AND ENTWISTLE, N. J. "Intelligence and Family Size, 1949–1965." *Brit J Ed Psychol* 37:188–93 Je '67. * (*PA* 41:15274)

35. HADDON, F. A., AND LYTTON, HUGH. "Teaching Approach and the Development of Divergent Thinking Abilities in Primary Schools." *Brit J Ed Psychol* 38:171–80 Je '68. * (*PA* 42:17790)

36. HOCKEY, S. W. "Intelligence, Common Entrance and the General Certificate of Education." *Brit J Ed Psychol* 38:140–7 Je '68. * (*PA* 43:17796)

37. RICHARDS, P. N., AND BOLTON, N. "Type of Mathematics Teaching, Mathematical Ability and Divergent Thinking in Junior School Children." *Brit J Ed Psychol* 41(1):32–7 F '71. * (*PA* 46:9822)

38. WILSON, J. D. "Predicting Levels of First Year University Performance." *Brit J Ed Psychol* 41(2):163–70 Je '71. * (*PA* 47:9821)

CUMULATIVE NAME INDEX

Armstrong, H. G.: 15
Bolton, N.: 37
Boyne, A. W.: 18
Buchan, J.: 16
Bytheway, B.: 33
Clark, J. R.: 18
Dempster, J. J. B.: 4
Dockrell, W. B.: 27
Emmett, W. G.: 10, 14
Entwistle, N. J.: 19, 34
Haddon, F. A.: 35
Hallworth, H. J.: 32
Herbert, N.: 17
Hockey, S. W.: 36
Horobin, G.: 33
Illesley, R.: 31
Jones, W. R.: 11, 24
King, N. W.: 28
Lambert, C. M.: 7
Lytton, H.: 35
McIntosh, D. M.: 20
McRae, H.: 22
Manley, D. R.: 30

Nisbet, J.: 16
Nisbet, J. D.: 31, 34
Oldman, D.: 33
Peel, E. A.: 8–9, 12, 15, 25
Pilliner, A. E. G.: 29
Richards, P. N.: 37
Rodger, A. G.: 1
Rutter, D.: 23
Slater, P.: *rev*, 3:241
Smith, C. E.: *rev*, 2:1409
Smith, I. M.: 26
Sutherland, H. E. G.: 21
Sutherland, J.: 29
Taylor, E. G.: 29
Thomson, G. H.: 2–3, 5–6
Turnbull, G. H.: 17
Walker, D. A.: 20
Welsh, J.: 19
Wilmut, F. S.: 10
Wilson, J. D.: 38
Wiseman, S.: 13
Wrigley, J.: 13

[410]

[N.B. Group Tests.] Ages 5–6, 7–8; 1958; 2 levels; Human Sciences Research Council [South Africa]. *

a) N.B. GROUP TEST FOR FIVE AND SIX YEAR OLDS.

b) N.B. GROUP TEST FOR SEVEN AND EIGHT YEAR OLDS.

For additional information, see 6:477.

Moray House Verbal Reasoning Tests

[411]

New South African Group Test. Ages 8–11, 10–14, 13–17; 1931–65; NSAGT; 3 scores: verbal, nonverbal, total; 3 levels; Human Sciences Research Council [South Africa]. *

a) JUNIOR. Ages 8–11; 1931–65.

b) INTERMEDIATE. Ages 10–14; 1931–63.

c) SENIOR. Ages 13–17; 1931–65.

For additional information, see 7:365 (3 references).

REFERENCES THROUGH 1971

1–3. See 7:365.

4. STRÜMPFER, D. J. W. "The Relation of Draw-A-Person Test Variables to Psychometric and Inventory Measures." *J Social Res* (South Africa) 15(1):1–9 '66. * (*PA* 42:2613)

CUMULATIVE NAME INDEX

Elder, C. M.: 1
Mienie, C. J. P.: 3
Strümpfer, D. J. W.: 3–4
Sugarman, L.: 2

[412]

★**Non-Language Test of Verbal Intelligence—Form 768.** Class 8 (ages 11–13); 1968; 4 scores: analogy, classification, opposites, picture arrangement; S. Chatterji and Manjula Mukerjee; Statistical Publishing Society [India]. *

REFERENCES THROUGH 1971

1. CHATTERJI, S., AND MUKERJEE, MANJULA. "The Development of Non-Language Test of Verbal Intelligence." *J Psychol Res* (India) 11:58–68 My '67. * (*PA* 42:6379)

2. CHATTERJI, S., AND MUKERJEE, M. "Verbal Intelligence as Measured by the NLTVI and Its Relation With Different Subjects Taught in School." *Psychol Studies* (India) 15(2):71–83 Jl '70. *

CUMULATIVE NAME INDEX

Chatterji, S.: 1–2   Mukerjee, M.: 1–2

[413]

Non-Readers Intelligence Test. Ages 6–9 to 8–11; 1964; D. Young; University of London Press Ltd. [England]. *

For additional information, see 7:366.

[414]

Non-Verbal Reasoning Test. Job applicants and industrial employees; 1961; Raymond J. Corsini (test) and Measurement Research Division, Industrial Relations Center, University of Chicago (manual); the Center. * [The publisher has not replied to our four requests to check the accuracy of this entry.]

For additional information and reviews by James E. Kennedy and David G. Ryans, see 6:478.

REFERENCES THROUGH 1971

1. LAURENT, HARRY. Chap. 1, "Research on the Identification of Management Potential," pp. 1–34. In *Predicting Managerial Success*. Edited by John A. Myers, Jr. Ann Arbor, Mich.: Foundation for Research on Human Behavior, April 1968. Pp. v, 173. *

2. BAEHR, MELANY E.; FURCON, JOHN E.; AND FROEMEL, ERNEST C. *Psychological Assessment of Patrolman Qualifications in Relation to Field Performance*. Washington, D.C.: United States Government Printing Office, 1969. Pp. vii, 246. *

CUMULATIVE NAME INDEX

Baehr, M. E.: 2
Froemel, E. C.: 2
Furcon, J. E.: 2
Kennedy, J. E.: *rev*, 6:478
Laurent, H.: 1
Ryans, D. G.: *rev*, 6:478

[415]

Non-Verbal Tests. Ages 8 to 11–0, 10 to 12, 10 to 15; 1947–65; 3 levels; published for the National Foundation for Educational Research in England and Wales; Ginn & Co. Ltd. [England]. *

a) NON-VERBAL TESTS 1–2. Ages 10 to 12; 1947–59; 2 forms.

1) *Non-Verbal Test 1*. 1947–59; test booklet title is *A Scale of Non-Verbal Mental Ability*; J. W. Jenkins. (An Australian adaptation, *Jenkins Non-Verbal*

Test, is available from Australian Council for Educational Research [Australia].)

2) *Non-Verbal Test 2.* 1948–51; D. M. Lee and J. W. Jenkins.

b) NON-VERBAL TEST DH. Ages 10 to 15; 1953–58; formerly called *Non-Verbal Test 3;* B. Calvert (test) and I. Macfarlane Smith (original manual).

c) NON-VERBAL TEST BD. Ages 8 to 11–0; 1953–65; formerly called *Non-Verbal Test 5;* D. A. Pidgeon.

For additional information, see 7:367 (1 reference); for reviews by T. R. Miles and John Nisbet, see 6:479 (1 reference); for a review by Cyril A. Rogers, see 5:356 (1 reference); for a review by E. A. Peel of the original edition, see 4:307 (3 references).

REFERENCES THROUGH 1971

1–3. See 4:307.
4. See 5:356.
5. See 6:479.
6. See 7:367.
7. JONES, W. R., AND STEWART, W. A. C. "Bilingualism and Verbal Intelligence." *Brit J Psychol* (Stat Sect) 4:3–8 Mr '51. * (*PA* 25:7930)
8. JONES, W. R. "The Influence of Reading Ability in English on the Intelligence Test Scores of Welsh-Speaking Children." *Brit J Ed Psychol* 23:114–20 F '53. * (*PA* 28:4835)
9. McINTYRE, W. "Difficulty of Understanding Instructions as a Factor in Coaching and Practice Effects in Intelligence Testing." Abstract. *Brit J Ed Psychol* 24:122–3 Je '54. * (*PA* 29:2456)
10. SMITH, I. MACFARLANE. "The Development of a Spatial Test." *Durham Ed R* (England) 1(5):19–33 S '54. * (*PA* 29:7298)
11. DUNN, S., AND SPEARRITT, D. "A Comparative Study of the Reliability of Some Verbal and Non-Verbal Intelligence Tests." *Austral J Psychol* 7:169–74 D '55. * (*PA* 31:1030)
12. DUNN, S. S., AND BROWNLESS, V. T. "Differences in Test and Retest Responses of a Group of Children to a Verbal and a Non-Verbal Test." *Austral J Psychol* 8:84–7 Je '56. * (*PA* 31:7910)
13. MORGAN, G. A. V. "Verbal Abilities of Primary School Children." *Durham Ed R* (England) 2(7):97–107 S '56. *
14. LEWIS, D. G. "Differences in Attainment Between Primary-Schools in Mixed-Language Areas: Their Dependence on Intelligence and Linguistic Background." *Brit J Ed Psychol* 30:63–70 F '60. *
15. LLOYD, F., AND PIDGEON, D. A. "An Investigation Into the Effects of Coaching on Non-Verbal Test Material With European, Indian and African Children." *Brit J Ed Psychol* 31:145–51 Je '61. * (*PA* 36:3KJ45L)
16. LOVELL, K.; SHAPTON, D.; AND WARREN, N. S. "A Study of Some Cognitive and Other Disabilities in Backward Readers of Average Intelligence as Assessed by a Non-Verbal Test." *Brit J Ed Psychol* 34:58–64 F '64. * (*PA* 38:9233)
17. NISBET, J. D., AND ENTWISTLE, N. J. "Intelligence and Family Size, 1949–1965." *Brit J Ed Psychol* 37:188–93 Je '67. * (*PA* 41:15274)
18. PARKER, D. H. H. "Musical Perception and Backwardness in Reading." *Ed Res* (England) 12(3):244–6 Je '70. * (*PA* 47:1754)

CUMULATIVE NAME INDEX

Brownless, V. T.: 12
Dunn, S.: 11
Dunn, S. S.: 12
Entwistle, N. J.: 6, 17
Jones, W. R.: 4, 7–8
Lewis, D. G.: 5, 14
Lloyd, F.: 15
Lovell, K.: 16
McIntyre, W.: 9
Miles, T. R.: *rev,* 6:479
Mills, L. F.: 1
Morgan, G. A. V.: 13
Nisbet, J.: *rev,* 6:479

Nisbet, J. D.: 17
Parker, D. H. H.: 18
Peel, E. A.: 2; *rev,* 4:307
Pidgeon, D. A.: 15
Rogers, C. A.: *rev,* 5:356
Scott, G. C.: 3
Shapton, D.: 16
Smith, I. M.: 10
Spearritt, D.: 11
Stewart, W. A. C.: 7
Warren, N. S.: 16
Welsh, J.: 6

[416]

The Northumberland Mental Tests. Ages 10–12.5; 1922; manual and higher level test (for ages 11–16) are out of print; Godfrey H. Thomson; George G. Harrap & Co. Ltd. [England]. *

REFERENCES THROUGH 1971

1. THOMSON, GODFREY H. "The Northumberland Mental Tests." *Brit J Psychol* 12:201–22 D '21. *
2. BALLARD, PHILIP BOSWOOD. Chap. 11, "The Northumberland Mental Tests," pp. 76–89. In his *Group Tests of Intelligence.* London: University of London Press, Ltd., 1922. Pp. x, 252. *

3. WILSON, J. H. "Comparison of Certain Intelligence Scales." *Brit J Psychol* 15:44–63 Jl '24. *
4. BOWIE, S., AND LAWS, A. R. "A School Intelligence Test." *Forum Ed* (England) 3:134–40 Je '25. *
5. STAINER, W. J. "Intelligence Tests in Scholarship Examinations." *Forum Ed* (England) 3:32–9 F '25. *
6. RUSSELL, J. B. "The Measurement of Intelligence in a Rural Area." *Brit J Psychol* 20:274–95 Ja '30. * (*PA* 4:2940)
7. GHOSH, S. "Investigation Into the Validity of an Intelligence-Test-Element Such as the Hindustani Test (A6, B6) in the Northumberland Mental Test (No. 1)." *Indian J Psychol* 6:61–70 Ja '31. * (*PA* 6:909)
8. WILSON, J. H. "The Exactness of '*g*' as Determined by Certain Intelligence Tests." *Brit J Psychol* 26:93–8 Jl '35. *
9. NIJHAWAN, HARBANS KAUR. *The Reliability and Validity of the Northumberland Intelligence Test.* Doctor's thesis, University College, University of London (London, England), 1956. *
10. NIJHAWAN, H. K. "The Reliability and Validity of the Northumberland Test of Intelligence." *Psychol Studies* (India) 10:115–20 Jl '65. * (*PA* 39:15255)

CUMULATIVE NAME INDEX

Ballard, P. B.: 2
Bowie, S.: 4
Ghosh, S.: 7
Laws, A. R.: 4
Nijhawan, H. K.: 9–10

Russell, J. B.: 6
Stainer, W. J.: 5
Thomson, G. H.: 1
Wilson, J. H.: 3, 8

[417]

OISE Picture Reasoning Test: Primary. Grades 1–2; 1969–70; replaces *Group Test of Learning Capacity: Dominion Tests: Primary;* Ontario Institute for Studies in Education; distributed by Guidance Centre [Canada]. *

For additional information, see 7:368.

[418]

The Ohio Penal Classification Test. Penal institutions; 1952–54; also available for industrial use under the title *Ohio Classification Test* ('57); 5 scores: block counting, digit-symbol, number series, memory span, total; DeWitt E. Sell; manual for industrial edition by the author and Robert W. Scollay and Leroy N. Vernon; Psychometric Affiliates. *

For additional information and a review by Norman Eagle, see 5:358.

REFERENCES THROUGH 1971

1. KERR, WILLARD A., AND McGEHEE, EDWARD M. "Creative Temperament as Related to Aspects of Strategy and Intelligence." *J Social Psychol* 62:211–6 Ap '64. * (*PA* 39:5126)
2. KELLEHER, EDWARD J.; KERR, WILLARD A.; AND MELVILLE, NORBERT T. "The Prediction of Subprofessional Nursing Success." *Personnel Psychol* 21:379–88 au '68. * (*PA* 47:4063)

CUMULATIVE NAME INDEX

Eagle, N.: *rev,* 5:358
Kelleher, E. J.: 2
Kerr, W. A.: 1–2

McGehee, E. M.: 1
Melville, N. T.: 2

[419]

Ohio State University Psychological Test. Grades 9–16 and adults; 1919–68; OSUPT; 4 scores: same-opposites, analogies, reading comprehension, total; Herbert A. Toops; originally published by the Ohio College Association; now distributed by Wilbur L. Layton. *

For additional information and a review by Cyril J. Hoyt (with W. Wesley Tennyson), see 5:359 (29 references); for a review by George A. Ferguson, see 4:308 (23 references); for a review by J. P. Guilford, see 3:244 (28 references); for reviews by Louis D. Hartson, Theos A. Langlie, and Rudolf Pintner, see 1:1051.

REFERENCES THROUGH 1971

1–28. See 3:244.
29–51. See 4:308.
52–80. See 5:359.
81. ERFFMEYER, C. E. "Intelligence Tests as an Aid in the Diagnosis of Academic Maladies." *Sch & Soc* 20:317–20 S 6 '24. *
82. WHINERY, S. M. "Psychological Test Ratings and College Entrance Age." *Sch & Soc* 24:370–2 S 18 '26. * (*PA* 1:506)

83. FARNSWORTH, P. R.; SEASHORE, R. H.; AND TINKER, M. A. "Speed in Simple and Serial Action as Related to Performance in Certain 'Intelligence' Tests." *J Genetic Psychol* 34:537–51 D '27. * (*PA* 2:1700)

84. EDGERTON, HAROLD A., AND TOOPS, HERBERT A. *Academic Progress: A Follow-Up Study of the Freshmen Entering the University in 1923.* Ohio State University Studies, Contributions in Administration, No. 1. Columbus, Ohio: Ohio State University Press, 1929. Pp. x, 150. *

85. NEEL, MARY O., AND MEAD, A. R. "Correlations Between Certain Group Factors in Preparation of Secondary School Teachers." *Ed Adm & Sup* 17:675–6 D '31. *

86. FREEMAN, FRANK S. "The Factor of Speed." *J General Psychol* 6:462–8 Ap '32. * (*PA* 7:773)

87. HARTSON, L. D. "The Validation of the Rating Scales Used With Candidates for Admission to Oberlin College." *Sch & Soc* 36:413–6 S 24 '32. * (*PA* 7:354)

88. PATRICK, JAMES R., AND ROWLES, EMMETT. "Intercorrelations Among Metabolic Rate, Vital Capacity, Blood Pressure, Intelligence, Scholarship, Personality and Other Measures on University Women." *J Appl Psychol* 17:507–21 O '33. * (*PA* 8:2498)

89. LYON, VERGIL E. "The Variation of High School Senior and College Freshman Classes." *J Exp Ed* 3:25–35 S '34. * (*PA* 9:1418)

90. CLARK, GENEVIEVE Y., AND SOUTH, EARL B. "Some Suggestions for Measuring Nursing Aptitude." *Am J Nursing* 35:865–71 S '35. * (*PA* 10:550)

91. LORENZ, ALICE B., AND MCCLURE, WILLIAM E. "The Influence of Color Blindness on Intelligence and Achievement of College Men." *J Appl Psychol* 19:320–30 Je '35. * (*PA* 10:85)

92. SMITH, HARRY P. "Psychological Examinations Administered by Syracuse University." *Sch & Soc* 41:134–6 Ja 26 '35. * (*PA* 9:2986)

93. STRABEL, EUNICE. "How Academically Apt Are Collegiate College Students?" *Sch & Soc* 41:814–6 Je 15 '35. * (*PA* 9:4822)

94. WELLER, DALE C. *Predictive Value of the Ohio State University Psychological Test Toward College Success.* Master's thesis, University of Wyoming (Laramie, Wyo.), 1936.

95. HARTSON, L. D. "Intellectual Output of Sixty-One Secondary Schools." *J Higher Ed* 9:42–4 Ja '38. * (*PA* 12:2632)

96. READ, CECIL B. "The Prediction of Scholastic Success in a Municipal University." *Sch & Soc* 48:187–8 Ag 6 '38. * (*PA* 12:6645)

97. STUIT, DEWEY B. "A Follow-Up Study of Freshmen in the Teachers College of the University of Nebraska." *Sch & Soc* 48:282–4 Ag 27 '38. * (*PA* 13:558)

98. HARTSON, L. D. "Relative Value of School Marks and Intelligence Tests as Bases for Rating Secondary Schools." *Sch & Soc* 49:354–6 Mr 18 '39. * (*PA* 13:3849)

99. ODGERS, JOHN GARNET, JR. *An Attempt to Broaden the Bases of Prognosis for Marginal Students in the College of Education.* Master's thesis, Ohio State University (Columbus, Ohio), 1939.

100. SHEDDAN, BOYD R., AND WITMER, LOUISE R. "Employment Tests for Relief Visitors." *J Appl Psychol* 23:270–9 Ap '39. * (*PA* 13:4837)

101. OSBORN, RICHARDS C. "How Is Intellectual Performance Related to Social and Economic Background." *J Ed Psychol* 34:215–28 Ap '43. * (*PA* 17:'4276)

102. LANE, G. GORHAM. "Studies in Pilot Selection: 1, The Prediction of Success in Learning to Fly Light Aircraft." *Psychol Monogr* 61(5):1–17 '47. * (*PA* 22:5166)

103. PORTENIER, LILLIAN G. "Abilities and Interests of Japanese-American High School Seniors." *J Social Psychol* 25:53–61 F '47. * (*PA* 21:3177)

104. ROACH, JAMES H. L. "Autosuggestion in Extroverts and Introverts." *J Personality* 15:215–21 Mr '47. * (*PA* 22:2536)

105. BUMGARNER, FAYNE. "Social Factors and OSPE Scores for 46 Women Enrolled in the University of Oklahoma Fall Semester 1951." *Proc Okla Acad Sci* 32:110–3 '52. * (*PA* 27:3781)

106. SMITH, ALLAN B. *The Prediction of Scholastic Success for Freshman Entrants to the University of Connecticut 1933–1951.* Doctor's thesis, University of Connecticut (Storrs, Conn.), 1953. (*DA* 13:1121)

107. MALLINSON, GEORGE GREISEN, AND SAMS, CONWAY C. "The Relationship Among Scientific Knowledge, Intelligence, and Achievement in General Psychology." *J Ed Res* 48:29–36 S '54. * (*PA* 29:3341)

108. MERRILL, REED M. "An Evaluative Study of Probation Students' Academic Performance in a University." *J Ed Res* 48:37–45 S '54. * (*PA* 29:4639)

109. MARTIN, JUDSON PHILLIPS. *Prediction of Scholastic Success as One Phase of Counseling Service for Entering Freshmen in a State Teachers College.* Doctor's thesis, University of Wisconsin (Madison, Wis.), 1955. (*DA* 16:267)

110. CHAHBAZI, PARVIZ. "Use of Projective Tests in Predicting College Achievement." *Ed & Psychol Meas* 16:538–42 w '56. * (*PA* 32:939)

111. MUNGER, PAUL. "Student Persistence in College." *Personnel & Guid J* 35:241–3 D '56. * (*PA* 31:8836)

112. PIHLBLAD, C. T., AND GREGORY, C. L. "The Role of Test

Intelligence and Occupational Background as Factors in Occupational Choice." *Sociometry* 19:192–9 S '56. * (*PA* 31:8191)

113. HILL, SUZANNE D. "The Relationship Between Grades and a Predictive Test Battery in the School of Pharmacy of the George Washington University." *J Appl Psychol* 41:61–2 F '57. * (*PA* 32:946)

114. SHERWOOD, EMILY J. *An Investigation of the Relationship Between the Academic Achievement and Goal-Orientations of College Students.* Doctor's thesis, Temple University (Philadelphia, Pa.), 1957. (*DA* 17:2924)

115. CHAMPION, JOHN MILLS. *A Method For Predicting Success of Commerce Students.* Doctor's thesis, Purdue University (Lafayette, Ind.), 1958. (*DA* 19:2134)

116. NEBERGALL, ROGER E. "An Experimental Investigation of Rhetorical Clarity." *Speech Monogr* 25:243–54 N '58. *

117. PIERSON, LEROY R. "High School Teacher Prediction of College Success." *Personnel & Guid J* 37:142–5 O '58. * (*PA* 36:2KJ42P)

118. WEBB, SAM C., AND GOODLING, RICHARD A. "Test Validity in a Methodist Theology School." *Ed & Psychol Meas* 18:859–66 w '58. * (*PA* 34:2123)

119. PAERATAKUL, CHAWAL. "Differences in Performance on the Doctoral Admission Examinations at Indiana University by Thai Students, Foreign Non-Thai Students, and American Students." *B Sch Ed Ind Univ* 35(3):41–64 My '59. * (*PA* 34:6571)

120. SPAULDING, HELEN. "The Prediction of First-Year Grade Averages in a Private Junior College." *Ed & Psychol Meas* 19:627–8 w '59. * (*PA* 34:6574)

121. BARTLETT, CLAUDE J.; RONNING, ROYCE R.; AND HURST, JOHN G. "A Study of Classroom Evaluation Techniques With Special Reference to Application of Knowledge." *J Ed Psychol* 51:152–8 Je '60. * (*PA* 35:3871)

122. BROWN, DONALD JAMES. *An Investigation of the Relationships Between Certain Personal Characteristics of Guidance Counselors and Performance in Supervised Counseling Interviews.* Doctor's thesis, Ohio State University (Columbus, Ohio). 1960. (*DA* 21:810)

123. GARRETT, WILEY S. "Prediction of Academic Success in a School of Nursing." *Personnel & Guid J* 38:500–3 F '60. * (*PA* 35:3954)

124. JUOLA, ARVO E. "Predictive Validity of Five College-Level Academic Aptitude Tests at One Institution." *Personnel & Guid J* 38:637–41 Ap '60. * (*PA* 35:2791)

125. KETCHAM, HERBERT E., (MRS.) "Reading Tests and College Performance," pp. 63–6. In *Research and Evaluation in College Reading.* Ninth Yearbook of the National Reading Conference for College and Adults. Ft. Worth, Tex.: Texas Christian University Press, 1960. Pp. 137. *

126. MCFARLAND, JOHN ANTHONY. *A Study to Determine the Correlation Between the Ohio State University Psychological Test Scores and Academic Success Among Students at North Idaho Junior College.* Master's thesis, Gonzaga University (Spokane, Wash.), 1960.

127. PEDERSEN, FRANK, AND MARLOWE, DAVID. "Capacity and Motivational Differences in Verbal Recall." *J Clin Psychol* 16:219–22 Ap '60. * (*PA* 36:2HJ19P)

128. TOOPS, HERBERT A. "A Comparison, by Work-Limit and Time-Limit, of Item Analysis Indices for Practical Test Construction." *Ed & Psychol Meas* 20:251–66 su '60. * (*PA* 35:6395)

129. ISARD, ELEANORE S., AND LASKY, DAVID I. "A Discrepancy Score Method in Predicting Scholastic Achievement of College Freshmen Counseled During Probation." *Personnel & Guid J* 39:725–8 My '61. * (*PA* 36:1KL25I)

130. LUNN, MERVEL SAMUEL, JR. *The Prediction of Success of Students Enrolled in Professional Education Courses at the University of Oklahoma.* Doctor's thesis, University of Oklahoma (Norman, Okla.), 1961. (*DA* 22:1490)

131. PETERS, FRANK R., AND PLOG, EUGENIA L. "The Effectiveness of the ACT for Selection and Placement at the Ohio State University." *Ed Res B* 40:232–41+ D '61. *

132. RISHEL, DARRELL FRED. *The Development and Validation of Instruments and Techniques for the Selective Admission of Applicants for Graduate Studies in Counselor Education.* Doctor's thesis, Pennsylvania State University (University Park, Pa.), 1961. (*DA* 22:2271)

133. CASH, W. L., JR. "Relationship of Personality Traits and Scholastic Aptitude to Academic Achievement in Theological Studies." *J Psychol Studies* 13:105–10 Je '62 [issued F '64]. * (*PA* 39:1718)

134. DARLEY, JOHN G. "The Basis for Equivalent Scores on the Annual Editions of the American Council on Education Psychological Examination (ACE), 1941 to 1954," pp. 170–83. In his *Promise and Performance: A Study of Ability and Achievement in Higher Education.* Berkeley, Calif.: Center for Study of Higher Education, University of California, 1962. Pp. vii, 191. *

135. TURRENTINE, EDGAR MAYER. *Predicting Success in Practice Teaching in Music.* Doctor's thesis, State University of Iowa (Iowa City, Iowa), 1962. (*DA* 23:2814)

136. BROWN, ELIZABETH A., AND CRITES, JOHN O. "The Ohio State Psychological Test Today: A Current Evaluation for Counseling." *Personnel & Guid J* 41:677–9 Ap '63. * (*PA* 39:1718)

Ohio State University Psychological Test

137. Hughes, Billie Edward. *Predicting Achievement in a Graduate School of Education.* Doctor's thesis, North Texas State University (Denton, Tex.), 1963. (*DA* 24:1448)

138. Jarmin, Martin Valencia. *Prediction of Success in the Student Teaching Program for Prospective Teachers of Vocational Agriculture at the New York State College of Agriculture at Cornell University.* Doctor's thesis, Cornell University (Ithaca, N.Y.), 1963. (*DA* 24:3219)

139. Land, Melvin. "Psychological Tests as Predictors for Scholastic Achievement of Dental Students." *J Dental Ed* 27:25–30 Mr '63. *

140. Porter, Albert. "Intelligence-Test Score as a Predictor of Executive Success." *J Bus* 36:65–8 Ja '63. * [The *Ohio State University Psychological Examination*—not the "Otis intelligence test"—was used in this study according to the author.]

141. Vorreyer, Warren J. "Relationship of Selected Adjustment Factors, College Ability, and Achievement to Drop-Outs and Nondrop-Outs of College Freshmen." *J Ed Res* 56:362–5 Mr '63. *

142. Weaver, Wendell W., and Kingston, Albert J. "A Factor Analysis of the Cloze Procedure and Other Measures of Reading and Language Ability." *J Commun* 13:252–61 D '63. * (*PA* 39:188)

143. Zimmerman, William George, Jr. *An Analysis of Selected Aspects of the Master of Education Program at the University of Miami.* Doctor's thesis, University of Miami (Coral Gables, Fla.), 1963. (*DA* 28:95A)

144. Brown, Frederick G., and Dubois, Thomas E. "Correlates of Academic Success for High-Ability Freshman Men." *Personnel & Guid J* 42:603–7 F '64. * (*PA* 39:5820)

145. Callis, Robert, and Prediger, Dale J. "Predictors of Achievement in Counseling and Guidance Graduate Study." *Counselor Ed & Sup* 3:63–9 w '64. *

146. De Sante, David A. *The Effectiveness of the Ohio State University Psychological Examination in Predicting First Year Scholastic Averages of the Class of 1966 College of Liberal Arts, and Local Application at Niagara University.* Master's thesis, Niagara University (Niagara University, N.Y.), 1964.

147. Feinberg, Abraham. *The Relative Efficiency of Several Variables Used in the Selection Process for Candidates in a Graduate Certification Program.* Doctor's thesis, Rutgers—The State University (New Brunswick, N.J.), 1964. (*DA* 25:2871)

148. Chaika, John J. *Norms and Validity of the Total Scores of the Ohio State Psychological Examination, Form 26, in Predicting First Year Averages in the College of Business Administration of Niagara University.* Master's thesis, Niagara University (Niagara University, N.Y.), 1965.

149. Hewer, Vivian H. "Are Tests Fair to College Students From Homes With Low Socio-Economic Status?" *Personnel & Guid J* 43:764–9 Ap '65. * (*PA* 39:16441)

150. Lynch, Peter L. *A Study of the Effectiveness of the Ohio State University Psychological Examination in Predicting First Year Averages in the College of Liberal Arts in the Class of 1967 at Niagara University.* Master's thesis, Niagara University (Niagara University, N.Y.), 1965.

151. Sciortino, Rio. "Relationships Among Originality, Intelligence, Scholastic Achievement, and Scholastic Ability Measures." *Psychol Rep* 17:943–54 D '65. * (*PA* 40:4218)

152. Tollefson, Bruce E. *The Conditioning and Extinction of Verbal Responses as a Function of Scores on the Ohio State Psychological Examination.* Master's thesis, University of Wyoming (Laramie, Wyo.), 1965.

153. Belk, Floyd Edmond. *The Construction of a Simple Instrument to Predict Junior College Freshmen Attrition.* Doctor's thesis, Oklahoma State University (Stillwater, Okla.), 1966. (*DA* 27:4061A)

154. Havens, Robert Innis. *An Exploratory Search for Characteristic Patterns of High Performance Rated and Low Performance Rated Counselor-Candidates in a Counselling Practicum.* Doctor's thesis, University of Michigan (Ann Arbor, Mich.), 1966. (*DA* 28:104A)

155. Owens, Thomas R., and Roaden, Arliss L. "Predicting Academic Success in Master's Degree Programs in Education." *J Ed Res* 60:124–6 N '66. *

156. Prien, Erich P., and Botwin, David E. "The Reliability and Correlates of an Achievement Index." *Ed & Psychol Meas* 26:1047–52 w '66. * (*PA* 41:4998)

157. Breimeier, Kenneth H. *Relationship Between Various Psychological Measures in Use at Theological Seminaries.* Comments by James E. Dittes. Occasional Papers No. 1. Washington, D.C.: Ministry Studies Board, 1967. Pp. iii, 59. *

158. Lane, James Albert. *Assessment of Physically Handicapped Adult Students in College.* Doctor's thesis, Ohio State University (Columbus, Ohio), 1967. (*DA* 28:3511A)

159. Nelson, Arvid Kaye. *Differential Predictability of Academic Success.* Doctor's thesis, University of Missouri (Columbia, Mo.), 1967. (*DA* 28:3975A)

160. Denney, Loren L. *The Relationships Between Teaching Method, Critical Thinking and Other Selected Teacher Traits.* Doctor's thesis, University of Missouri (Columbia, Mo.), 1968. (*DA* 29:2586A)

161. Grimsrud, Richard Arlo. *A Method for Predicting Success in a Counselor Education Training Program.* Doctor's

thesis, University of Minnesota (Minneapolis, Minn.), 1968. (*DA* 29:2115A)

162. Keough, Mary Joan. *The Validity of the Ohio State Psychological Examination in Predicting First Year Averages of the College of Nursing at Niagara University.* Master's thesis, Niagara University (Niagara University, N.Y.), 1968.

163. Levine, Louis Gerald. *The Relationship of Selected Intellective Factors in the High School Record to First Semester Community College Grade Point Average.* Doctor's thesis, Case Western Reserve University (Cleveland, Ohio), 1968. (*DA* 29:4286A)

164. Munday, Leo. "Correlations Between ACT and Other Predictors of Academic Success in College." *Col & Univ* 44:67–76 f '68. *

165. Pendergast, Mary Carita. *Assessment of a Psychological Screening Program for Candidates to a Religious Congregation of Women.* Doctor's thesis, Fordham University (New York, N.Y.), 1968. (*DA* 29:2572A)

166. DiGiorgio, Anthony Joseph. *Discriminant Function Analysis of Measured Characteristics Among Committed Career Groups With Requisite Graduate Training.* Doctor's thesis, Purdue University (Lafayette, Ind.), 1969. (*DAI* 30:4769A)

167. Dielman, T. E., and Wilson, Warner R. "Convergent and Discriminant Validity of Three Measures of Ability, Aspiration-Level, Achievement, Adjustment and Dominance." *J Ed Meas* 7(3):185–90 f '70. * (*PA* 45:4915)

168. Dielman, Lois June. *Selected Factors as Related to Success in Student Teaching of Home Economics.* Doctor's thesis, University of Missouri (Columbia, Mo.), 1970. (*DAI* 31:5249A)

169. Jansen, David G.; Robb, George P.; and Bonk, Edward C. "Characteristics of High-Rated and Low-Rated Master's Degree Candidates in Counseling and Guidance." *Counselor Ed & Sup* 9(3):162–70 sp '70. * (*PA* 46:5559)

CUMULATIVE NAME INDEX

Merrill, R. M.: 108
Munday, L.: 164
Munger, P.: 111
Munger, P. F.: 72
Nebergall, R. E.: 116
Neel, M. O.: 85
Nelson, A. K.: 159
Newman, S. E.: 58
Norman, W. T.: 66
Odgers, J. G.: 99
Osborn, R. C.: 101
Owens, T. R.: 155
Paeratakul, C.: 119
Patrick, J. R.: 88
Paulsen, G. B.: 36
Pedersen, F.: 127
Pendergast, M. C.: 165
Peters, F. R.: 131
Pierson, L. R.: 117
Pihlblad, C. T.: 112
Pintner, R.: rev, 1:1051
Plog, E. L.: 131
Portenier, L. G.: 40–1, 48, 103
Porter, A.: 140
Porter, J. P.: 8
Prediger, D. J.: 145
Prien, E. P.: 156
Quaid, T. D. D.: 7, 11
Read, C. B.: 96
Reusser, W. C.: 4
Richards, J. M.: 79
Rinsland, H. D.: 44
Rishel, D. F.: 132
Roach, J. H. L.: 104
Roaden, A. L.: 155
Robb, G. P.: 169
Ronning, R. R.: 121
Rowles, E.: 88
Ryan, S. E.: 49

Sabeh, R.: 50
Samenfeld, H. W.: 62
Sams, C. C.: 107
Saum, A. L.: 12
Schmitz, R. M.: 68
Sciortino, R.: 151
Seashore, R. H.: 83
Selover, R. B.: 8
Sharp, H. C.: 35
Sheddan, B. R.: 100
Sherwood, E. J.: 114
Smith, A. B.: 106
Smith, H. P.: 92
South, E. B.: 2, 90
Spaulding, H.: 120
Sprow, A. J.: 21
Stackhouse, H. A.: 80
Staton, T. F.: 14
Stopher, E. C.: 22
Strabel, C.: 93
Stuit, D. B.: 9, 13, 97
Tennyson, W. W.: rev, 5:359
Thompson, R. B.: 33
Tinker, M. A.: 83
Tollefson, B. E.: 152
Toops, H. A.: 15, 84, 128
Turrentine, E. M.: 135
Uhrbrock, R. S.: 45
Vorreyer, W. J.: 141
Weaver, W. W.: 142
Webb, S. C.: 118
Weller, D. C.: 94
Welsh, M. L.: 56
Whinery, S. M.: 82
Wilson, W. R.: 167
Witmer, L. R.: 100
Woodruff, A. D.: 42
Wrenn, C. G.: 46
Zimmerman, W. G.: 143

[419A]

★Oral Verbal Intelligence Test. Ages 7.5–14; 1973; OVIT; D. Young; University of London Press Ltd. [England]. *

[420]

The Oregon Academic Ranking Test. Gifted children grades 3–7; 1965; OART; for rapid identification of the top 3 percent; 9 scores: making sentences, making comparisons, numbers, secret words, working problems, reasoning, completing sentences, sayings, total; Charles H. Derthick; Western Psychological Services. *
For additional information and a review by Robert H. Bauernfeind, see 7:369.

[421]

O'Rourke General Classification Test, Senior Grade. Grades 12–13 and adults; 1927–42; L. J. O'Rourke; O'Rourke Publications. *
For additional information and a review by Marion A. Bills, see 3:246 (3 references).

REFERENCES THROUGH 1971

1–3. See 3:246.
4. CUMMINGS, D. E. "Iron Men for Iron Ships." Personnel J 6:87–92 Ag '27. * (PA 2:736)
5. "Validity Information Exchange, No. 7-095: D.O.T. Code 7-94.112 and 7-94.100, Tool and Die and Machinist Apprentice." Personnel Psychol 7:573 w '54. *

CUMULATIVE NAME INDEX

Bills, M. A.: rev, 3:246
Cummings, D. E.: 4
Davidson, C. M.: 1–2
Lawshe, C. H.: 3
Thornton, G. R.: 3

[422]

The "Orton" Intelligence Test, No. 4. Ages 10–14; 1931; Robert Gibson & Sons, Glasgow, Ltd. [Scotland]. *
For additional information, see 1:1052.

[423]

Otis Employment Tests. Applicants for employment; 1943, c1922; tests identical with Forms A and B

of Otis Self-Administering Tests of Mental Ability; Arthur S. Otis; Harcourt Brace Jovanovich, Inc. *
For additional information, see 4:310. For reference to a review of the Otis Self-Administering Tests of Mental Ability, see 426.

REFERENCES THROUGH 1971

1. HILL, G. H.; STOUTENBOROUGH, ANN; AND SAUNDERS, WILLIAM J., JR. "Normative Data Information Exchange, No. 29." Personnel Psychol 9:539–40 w '56. *
2. COOK, JOHN M., AND FARBRO, PATRICK C. "Normative Data Information Exchange, No. 10-3." Personnel Psychol 10:97 sp '57. *
3. SHORE, RICHARD P. "Normative Data Information Exchange, Nos. 11-27, 11-28." Personnel Psychol 11:593–4 w '58. *
4. SHORE, RICHARD P. "Validity Information Exchange, No. 11-22: D.O.T. Code 1-02.01, Bookkeeping-Machine Operator (Banking)." Personnel Psychol 11:435–6 au '58. *
5. SHORE, RICHARD P. "Validity Information Exchange, No. 11-23: D.O.T. Code 1-06.02, Teller." Personnel Psychol 11:437 au '58. *
6. SHORE, RICHARD P. "Validity Information Exchange, No. 11-24: D.O.T. Code 1-25.68, Proof-Machine Operator." Personnel Psychol 11:438–9 au '58. *
7. ARON, JOEL E., AND HECHT, ROBERT M. "Normative Data Information Exchange, No. 12-26." Personnel Psychol 12:645 w '59. *
8. KAZMIER, LEONARD J. "Normative Data Information Exchange, No. 12-20." Personnel Psychol 12:502 au '59. *
9. HARRELL, THOMAS W. "The Relation of Test Scores to Sales Criteria." Personnel Psychol 13:65–9 sp '60. * (PA 35:7192)
10. MACKINNEY, ARTHUR C., AND WOLINS, LEROY. "Validity Information Exchange, No. 13-01, Foreman II, Home Appliance Manufacturing." Personnel Psychol 13:443–7 w '60. *
11. RHODE, JACK FERDINAND. A Pilot Study of the Prediction of Salesmen's Success in an Electronics Organization. Doctor's thesis, University of Minnesota (Minneapolis, Minn.), 1963. (DA 25:2283)

CUMULATIVE NAME INDEX

Aron, J. E.: 7
Cook, J. M.: 2
Farbro, P. C.: 2
Harrell, T. W.: 9
Hecht, R. M.: 7
Hill, G. H.: 1
Kazmier, L. J.: 8
MacKinney, A. C.: 10
Rhode, J. F.: 11
Saunders, W. J.: 1
Shore, R. P.: 3–6
Stoutenborough, A.: 1
Wolins, L.: 10

[424]

Otis-Lennon Mental Ability Test. Grades kgn, 1.0–1.5, 1.6–3, 4–6, 7–9, 10–12; 1936–70; revision of still-in-print Otis Quick-Scoring Mental Ability Tests; Arthur S. Otis and Roger T. Lennon; Harcourt Brace Jovanovich, Inc. *
For additional information, a review by John E. Milholland, and excerpted reviews by Arden Grotelueschen and Arthur E. Smith, see 7:370 (6 references). For reference to reviews of the Otis Quick-Scoring Mental Ability Tests, see 425.

REFERENCES THROUGH 1971

1–6. See 7:370.
7. ADKISSON, JACK. A Study of the Value of Selected Curiosity Tests for Predicting Academic Achievement in First and Second-Grades. Doctor's thesis, North Texas State University (Denton, Tex.), 1970. (DAI 31:5833A)
8. BUDDE, ELAINE HELEN. The Relationship Between Performance of Kindergarten Children on Selected Motor Tests and the Metropolitan Readiness Tests—Otis-Lennon Mental Ability Test, Doctor's thesis, University of Wisconsin (Madison, Wis.), 1970. (DAI 31:5820A)
9. EHRHART, PATRICIA MAULDIN. A Study of Selected Mental Ability Tests as Predictors of Achievement for Chamorro Pupils. Master's thesis, University of Guam (Agana, Guam), 1970.
10. EICHELBERGER, R. TONY. Practice Effects of Repeated IQ Testing and the Relationship Between IQ Change Scores and Selected Individual Characteristics. Doctor's thesis, Southern Illinois University (Carbondale, Ill.), 1970. (DAI 31:5196A)
11. CHISSOM, BRAD S., AND THOMAS, JERRY R. "Multivariate Validity of the Otis-Lennon Mental Ability Tests Primary I Level." Ed & Psychol Meas 31(4):991–3 w '71. * (PA 48:1635)
12. GRUEN, RONALD STEVEN. Prediction of End-of-Year Reading Achievement for First and Third Grade Pupils. Doctor's thesis, Pennsylvania State University (University Park, Pa.), 1971. (DAI 32:6198A)
13. HASSON, DAVID JOSEPH. An Evaluation of Two Methods

of Test Item Selection. Doctor's thesis, University of Maine (Orono, Me.), 1971. (*DAI* 32:6200A)

14. PROGER, BARTON B.; McGOWAN, JOHN R.; BAYUK, ROBERT J., JR.; MANN, LESTER; TREVORROW, RUTH L.; AND MASSA, EDWARD. "The Relative Predictive and Construct Validities of the Otis-Lennon Mental Ability Test, the Lorge-Thorndike Intelligence Test, and the Metropolitan Readiness Test in Grades Two and Four: A Series of Multivariate Analyses." *Ed & Psychol Meas* 31(2):529–38 su '71. *

15. RICE, JAMES A. "Head Start Screening: Effectiveness of a Teacher-Administered Battery." *Percept & Motor Skills* 32(2): 675–8 Ap '71. * (*PA* 46:11733)

16. TRIDER, MARY S. "The Right to Read and Standardized Testing: A Necessary Dimension." *Read Teach* 24(4):320–30 Ja '71. * (*PA* 46:11521)

CUMULATIVE NAME INDEX

[425]

Otis Quick-Scoring Mental Ability Tests. Grades 1–4, 4–9, 9–16; 1936–54; 3 levels; Beta and Gamma levels are revisions of still-in-print *Otis Self-Administering Tests of Mental Ability;* for revised edition, see 424; Arthur S. Otis; Harcourt Brace Jovanovich, Inc. *
a) ALPHA TEST. Grades 1–4; 1936–54; 2 editions.
1) *Alpha Test [Long Form].* 3 scores: nonverbal, verbal, total. *Out of print.*
2) *Alpha Short Form.*
b) BETA TEST. Grades 4–9; 1937–54.
c) GAMMA TEST. Grades 9–16; 1937–54.

For additional information, see 6:481 (24 references) ; for reviews by D. Welty Lefever and Alfred Yates, see 5:362 (33 references) ; for a review by Frederic Kuder, see 3:249 (9 references) ; for a review by F. Kuhlmann, see 2:1413 ; for a review by C. Spearman of this and the *SRA Primary Mental Abilities,* see 2:1427 ; for reviews by Psyche Cattell and R. Pintner and excerpted reviews by J. A. Long and one other, see 1:1053. For reference to reviews of the earlier edition, see 426.

REFERENCES THROUGH 1971

1–9. See 3:249.
10–42. See 5:362.
43–66. See 6:481.

67. WILLMOTT, JOHN N. "High School Boys Electing Industrial Arts: A Study of Certain Factors Differentiating the Industrial Arts Group From the Group Not Electing Industrial Arts." *Teach Col Contrib Ed* 836:1–71 '41. * (*PA* 16:2490)

68. SHEPARD, EUGENE L. "Measurements of Certain Nonverbal Abilities of Urban and Rural Children." *J Ed Psychol* 33:458–62 S '42. * (*PA* 17:809)

69. THOMPSON, GEORGE G., AND WITRYOL, SAM L. "The Relationship Between Intelligence and Motor Learning Ability, as Measured by a High Relief Finger Maze." *J Psychol* 22:237–46 O '46. * (*PA* 21:713)

70. SUPER, DONALD E.; BRAASCH, WILLIAM F., JR.; AND SHAY, JOSEPH B. "The Effect of Distractions on Test Results." *J Ed Psychol* 38:373–7 O '47. * (*PA* 22:2159)

71. POTTER, MURIEL CATHERINE. "Perception of Symbol Orientation and Early Reading Success." *Teach Col Contrib Ed* 939:1–69 '49. * (*PA* 24:6511)

72. BARRETT, HARRY O. "Differences in Intelligence Between Two- and Four-Year Course Pupils in a Commercial High School." *J Ed Res* 44:143–7 O '50. * (*PA* 25:5681)

73. EELLS, KENNETH; DAVIS, ALLISON; HAVIGHURST, ROBERT J.; HERRICK, VERGIL E.; AND TYLER, RALPH W. *Intelligence and Cultural Differences: A Study of Cultural Learning and Problem-Solving.* Chicago, Ill.: University of Chicago Press, 1951. Pp. xii, 388. * (*PA* 27:5738)

74. PEEL, E. A., AND GRAHAM, D. "Differentiation of Ability in Primary School Children." *Durham Res R* (England) 1(2): 40–8 S '51. *

75. PEEL, E. A., AND GRAHAM, D. "Differentiation of Ability in Primary School Children—II." *Durham Res R* (England) 1(3):31–4 S '52. * (*PA* 27:5157)

76. CARTER, ROBERT SCRIVEN. "Non-Intellectual Variables Involved in Teachers' Marks." *J Ed Res* 47:81–95 O '53. * (*PA* 28:6587)

77. COLEMAN, JAMES C. "Perceptual Retardation in Reading Disability Cases." *J Ed Psychol* 44:497–503 D '53. * (*PA* 28:7966)

78. GRAHAM, D. "The Differentiation of Ability in Primary School-Children: A Comment." *Durham Res R* (England) 1(4):27–30 S '53. * (*PA* 28:8077)

79. GREEN, CLINTON WALLACE. "The Relationship Between Intelligence as Determined by Intelligence Tests and the Ability to Learn as Determined by Performance on Learning Tests." *J Ed Res* 47:191–200 N '53. * (*PA* 28:6494)

80. GARDINER, CHARLES S.; HALL, HENRY E.; AND PARKER, LEE L., JR. "Identification and Measurement of Case Worker Characteristics: Part II." *Pub Personnel R* 16:153–9 Jl '55. * (*PA* 30:3654)

81. HARRINGTON, MARY JAMES, AND DURRELL, DONALD D. "Mental Maturity Versus Perception Abilities in Primary Reading." *J Ed Psychol* 46:375–80 O '55. * (*PA* 30:7676)

82. WEBB, WILSE B. "Self-Evaluations, Group Evaluations, and Objective Measures." *J Consult Psychol* 19:210–2 Je '55. * (*PA* 30:2935)

83. BRICE, MARSHALL MOORE. *A Comparison of Subjective Predictions With Objective Predictions of College Achievement.* Doctor's thesis, University of Virginia (Charlottesville, Va.), 1956. (*DA* 16:1622)

84. BEAMER, GEORGE C., AND BONK, EDWARD C. "Reliability of Mental Ability Tests." *J Counsel Psychol* 4:322 w '57. * (*PA* 33:5720)

85. CURRIE, CAROLINE. *The Relationship of Certain Selected Factors to Achievement in Freshman Composition.* Doctor's thesis, Northwestern University (Evanston, Ill.), 1957. (*DA* 18:884)

86. HUTSON, BILLY T., AND VINCENT, NICHOLAS M. "Motivation and Prognosis in Shorthand." *J Bus Ed* 33:29–31 O '57. *

87. OLSON, GARETH RAYMOND. *A Study of Predictive Efficiency of Selected Mental and Motor Measures and Success in Athletics.* Doctor's thesis, University of Minnesota (Minneapolis, Minn.), 1958. (*DA* 19:2530)

88. PEGNATO, CARL V. *An Evaluation of Various Initial Methods of Selecting Intellectually Gifted Children at the Junior High School Level.* Doctor's thesis, Pennsylvania State University (University Park, Pa.), 1958. (*DA* 19:1254)

89. BURCHINAL, LEE G. "Social Status, Measured Intelligence, Achievement, and Personality Adjustment of Rural Iowa Girls." *Sociometry* 22:75–80 Mr '59. * (*PA* 34:1254)

90. HAROOTUNIAN, BERJ AVEDIS. *The Relationships Among Tests of Intelligence, Learning, and Reasoning.* Doctor's thesis, University of Pennsylvania (Philadelphia, Pa.), 1959. (*DA* 20:203)

91. KELLY, JOHN PATRICK. *The Influence of Reading Ability on Group Intelligence Test Scores.* Doctor's thesis, State University of Iowa (Iowa City, Iowa), 1959. (*DA* 20:3629)

92. LIGHTHALL, FREDERICK; RUEBUSH, BRITTON; SARASON, SEYMOUR; AND ZWEIBELSON, IRVING. "Change in Mental Ability as a Function of Test Anxiety and Type of Mental Test." *J Consult Psychol* 23:34–8 F '59. * (*PA* 34:981)

93. OLANDER, HERBERT T., AND KLEYLE, HELEN M. "Differences in Personal and Professional Characteristics of a Selected Group of Elementary Teachers With Contrasting Success Records." *Ed Adm & Sup* 45:191–8 Jl '59. * (*PA* 34:6582)

94. FITZGERALD, LOUIS ALLEN. *Some Effects of Reading Ability on Group Intelligence Test Scores in the Intermediate Grades.* Doctor's thesis, State University of Iowa (Iowa City, Iowa), 1960. (*DA* 21:1844)

95. HOLOWINSKY, IVAN ZENOVI. *The Relationship Between Intelligence (80–110 I.Q.) and Achievement in Basic Educational Skills for a Selected Sample in Camden, New Jersey.* Doctor's thesis, Temple University (Philadelphia, Pa.), 1961. (*DA* 22:1509)

96. MORRISON, HUGH E., AND COLLISTER, E. GORDON. "The Use of Difference Scores in the Interpretation of Test Results in Elementary Schools." *Univ Kan B Ed* 16:19–25 N '61. *

97. TURRENTINE, EDGAR MAYER. *Predicting Success in Practice Teaching in Music.* Doctor's thesis, State University of Iowa (Iowa City, Iowa), 1962. (*DA* 23:2814)

98. BABBOTT, EDWARD FRENCH. *The Differential Effectiveness of Eight 9th Grade Variables in Predicting Success in Three 10th Grade Academic Subjects at Summit High School: A Study in Differential Prediction.* Doctor's thesis, New York University (New York, N.Y.), 1963. (*DA* 25:993)

99. BOND, CONSTANCE McCURRY. *A Study of the Predictive Value of Two Measures of Scholastic Aptitude in the Middle Elementary Grades.* Master's thesis, Northern Illinois University (DeKalb, Ill.), 1963.

100. GUSTAFSON, EDWIN A. *A Study of the Relationship of IQ Scores to the Grades and Curriculum Choices Among the Students of Little Falls High School.* Master's thesis, St. Cloud State College (St. Cloud, Minn.), 1963.

101. HAAS, MARY GERALDINE. *A Comparative Study of Critical*

Thinking, Flexibility of Thinking, and Reading Ability Involving Religious and Lay College Seniors. Doctor's thesis, Fordham University (New York, N.Y.), 1963. (*DA* 24:622)

102. PETERS, HERBERT D. "Performance of Hopi Children on Four Intelligence Tests." *J Am Indian Ed* 2:27–31 Ja '63. *

103. SILVAROLI, NICHOLAS JOSEPH. *Intellectual and Emotional Factors as Predictors of Children's Success in First Grade Reading.* Doctor's thesis, Syracuse University (Syracuse, N.Y.), 1963. (*DA* 24:5098)

104. URAY, RICHARD MARTIN. *An Analysis of Scores Made by a Group of Radio Announcers in Texas on Selected Psychological Tests.* Doctor's thesis, University of Houston (Houston, Tex.), 1963. (*DA* 25:950)

105. WEBER, LYLE E. *An Experimental Study on the Effect of Age, Reading Score, I.Q., and Sex on High School Students' Ability to Learn to Typewrite.* Master's thesis, Northwestern University (Evanston, Ill.), 1963.

106. CHARLES, C. M. "Bicultural Children and Science Achievement." *Sci Ed* 48:93–6 F '64. *

107. JOHNSON, EDWARD E. "Time Concepts as Related to Sex, Intelligence and Academic Performance." *J Ed Res* 57:377–9 Mr '64. *

108. LYSAUGHT, JEROME P. "Further Analysis of Success Among Auto-Instructional Programmers." *Teaching Aid News* 4:6–11 O 15 '64. *

109. LYSAUGHT, JEROME P. "Selecting Instructional Programmers: New Research Into Characteristics of Successful Programmers." *Training Directors J* 18:8–14 Je '64. *

110. LYSAUGHT, JEROME P., AND PIERLEONI, ROBERT G. "A Comparison of Predicted and Actual Success in Auto-Instructional Programing." *J Programed Instr* 3(4):14–23 '64. * (*PA* 40:13506)

111. McCORMICK, JAMES H., AND ASHER, WILLIAM. "Aspects of the High School Record Related to the First Semester College Grade Point Average." *Personnel & Guid J* 42:699–703 Mr '64. *

112. SHAFFER, RAYMOND GEORGE. *A Study of Four Group Intelligence Tests to Identify Ambiguous Pictures as a Factor Which Causes Some Children to Select Incorrect Answers.* Doctor's research study No. 1, Colorado State College (Greeley, Colo.), 1964. (*DA* 25:1014)

113. SLATER, RICHARD D. "The Equivalency of IBM Mark-Sense Answer Cards and IBM Answer Sheets When Used as Answer Formats for a Precisely-Timed Test of Mental Ability." *J Ed Res* 57:545–7 Jl–Ag '64. *

114. BRADY, WILLIAM JOSEPH. *Twenty Quantitative Predictors of Academic Success in College as Measured by Grade Point Averages.* Doctor's thesis, University of Connecticut (Storrs, Conn.), 1965. (*DA* 26:5121)

115. CASTIGLIONE, LAWRENCE VIRGIL. *The Relation of Intelligence to Selected Measures of Creativity.* Doctor's thesis, New York University (New York, N.Y.), 1965. (*DA* 27:1278B)

116. CAUTELA, JOSEPH R., AND BARLOW, DAVID H. "The Relation Between Intelligence and Critical Flicker Fusion." *Psychon Sci* 3:559–60 D 15 '65. * (*PA* 40:2219)

117. DICKEN, CHARLES F., AND BLACK, JOHN D. "Predictive Validity of Psychometric Evaluations of Supervisors." *J Appl Psychol* 49:34–47 F '65. * (*PA* 39:8793)

118. ESTES, BETSY WORTH. "Relationships Between the Otis, 1960 Stanford-Binet and WISC." *J Clin Psychol* 21:296–7 Jl '65. * (*PA* 39:15230)

119. FOSTER, MARION E. "A Comparison of Reading Achievement of Christchurch, New Zealand and Edmonton Alberta Public School Students of the Same Age and Number of Years of Schooling." *Alberta J Ed Res* (Canada) 11:21–31 Mr '65. * (*PA* 39:16455)

120. GOSHAL, AVTAR H. SINGH. "Indian Adaptation of Otis Mental Ability Test Gamma C—A Normative Study." *J Indian Acad Appl Psychol* 2:24–9 Ja '65. * (*PA* 39:12284)

121. JAMAL, SHABNAM. "The Validity of Raven's Coloured Progressive Matrices and Otis Quick Scoring Mental Ability Test for Pakistani Children." *B Ed & Res* (Pakistan) 4(1): 25–41 '65. *

122. JUSTMAN, JOSEPH. "Academic Aptitude and Reading Test Scores of Disadvantaged Children Showing Varying Degrees of Mobility." *J Ed Meas* 2:151–5 D '65. * (*PA* 40:5943)

123. PETIT, JEAN L. *Selecting Variables Found in the Cumulative Folder of Belvidere High School Students Predicting Academic Success.* Master's thesis, Northern Illinois University (DeKalb, Ill.), 1965.

124. PLAPP, JON M.; PSATHAS, GEORGE; AND CAPUTO, DANIEL V. "Intellective Predictors and Success in Nursing School." Abstract. *Proc Ann Conv Am Psychol Assn* 73:307–8 '65. * (*PA* 39:16458)

125. PLAPP, JON M.; PSATHAS, GEORGE; AND CAPUTO, DANIEL V. "Intellective Predictors of Success in Nursing School." *Ed & Psychol Meas* 25:565–77 su '65. * (*PA* 39:15259)

126. SCOTT, RUSSELL H.; PHIPPS, GRANT T.; AND MORGART, HELEN S. "Prediction of Success in a Dental Assisting Course." *J Dental Ed* 29:348–57 D '65. *

127. STAPLES, JOHN DIXON. *An Experimental Study to Identify the Basic Abilities Needed to Detect Typescript Errors With Implications for the Improvement of Instruction in Typewriting.*

Doctor's thesis, University of North Dakota (Grand Forks, N.D.), 1965. (*DA* 27:1693A)

128. WIMBY, EUGENE B. *A Comparative Study of the Kuhlmann-Anderson and the Otis Quick Scoring Intelligence Tests as Predictors of High School Performance.* Master's thesis, Atlanta University (Atlanta, Ga.), 1965.

129. BRENNAN, JOSEPH T., JR. *Estimating Expected Reading Achievement in the Junior High School.* Doctor's thesis, University of Pittsburgh (Pittsburgh, Pa.), 1966. (*DA* 27:4033A)

130. CASHMAN, JEROME PATRICK. *A Study of the Relationship Between Organic Factors, Certain Selected Variables and Progress in a Reading Improvement Program.* Doctor's thesis, Fordham University (New York, N.Y.), 1966. (*DA* 27:1648A)

131. CONAWAY, BARON DARVIS. *A Modification of Group Intelligence Test Administration and Its Relation to the Reading Abilities of Sixth-Grade Pupils.* Doctor's thesis, Auburn University (Auburn, Ala.), 1966. (*DA* 27:945A)

132. DARBES, ALEX. "Some Test Characteristics of Female Student Beauticians." *Proc W Va Acad Sci* 37:286–8 F '66. * (*PA* 40:8250)

133. DIRR, PIERRE MARIE. *Intellectual Variables in Achievement in Modern Algebra.* Doctor's thesis, Catholic University of America (Washington, D.C.), 1966. (*DA* 27:2873A)

134. FOX, A. M., AND AINSWORTH, L. L. "Otis Prediction of Graduate Education Course Grades." *Ed & Psychol Meas* 26: 1055–6 w '66. * (*PA* 41:4990)

135. GAY, CLEVELAND JOHNSON. *Academic Achievement and Intelligence Among Negro Eighth Grade Students as a Function of the Self Concept.* Doctor's thesis, North Texas State University (Denton, Tex.), 1966. (*DA* 27:112A)

136. HAROOTUNIAN, BERJ. "Intelligence and the Ability to Learn." *J Ed Res* 59:211–4 Ja '66. * (*PA* 40:6627)

137. JEX, FRANK B. *Predicting Academic Success Beyond High School.* Salt Lake City, Utah: University of Utah Bookstore, 1966. Pp. vi, 41. *

138. KANDEL, ARTHUR. *Discrepancies Between the Stanford-Binet and Three Group Tests of Intelligence in the Identification of Low I.Q. Children.* Doctor's thesis, Catholic University of America (Washington, D.C.), 1966. (*DA* 27:1659A)

139. KEACH, CHARLES CAMPBELL. *Discrepancies Between the Stanford-Binet and Three Group Tests of Intelligence in the Identification of High I.Q. Children.* Doctor's thesis, Catholic University of America (Washington, D.C.), 1966. (*DA* 27: 1660A)

140. McCORMICK, ALBERT GRANT. *An Investigation of Reading Skills, General Mental Ability and Personality Variables Used in the Selection of Practical Nursing Students.* Doctor's thesis, Oklahoma State University (Stillwater, Okla.), 1966. (*DA* 27:4136A)

141. McCRORY, MARGARET ANNE. *An Analysis of Mental Emotional and Social Factors Related to Success in Student Teaching.* Doctor's thesis, Boston University (Boston, Mass.), 1966. (*DA* 27:3318A)

142. RUSSELL, H. H., AND DILLING, H. J. "Comparison of General Intelligence Test Results and Student Achievement in Grade 8 and Grade 9 of Scarborough Schools." *Ont J Ed Res* (Canada) 8:267–77 sp '66. *

143. SAVAGE, R. D., AND O'CONNOR, D. J. "The Assessment of Reading and Arithmetic Retardation in the School." *Brit J Ed Psychol* 36:317–8 N '66. *

144. SCHUSLER, MARIAN M. "Prediction of Grades by Computer for High School Students: A Cross-Validation and Experimental Placement Study." *J Ed Data Processing* 3:97–110 su '66. *

145. STAFFORD, RICHARD LINDSAY. *The Effects of Creativity and Intelligence on Information Seeking Strategies Used in a Problem Solving Task by Sixth Grade Boys.* Doctor's thesis, University of Houston (Houston, Tex.), 1966. (*DA* 27:973B)

146. WEBER, DORIS S. *The Relationship Between Verbal and Non-Verbal Ability and Achievement in Elementary Mathematics.* Master's thesis, Adelphi University (Garden City, N.Y.), 1966.

147. WHITTEMORE, ROBERT G.; ECHEVERRIA, BEN P.; AND GRIFFIN, JOHN V. "Can We Use Existing Tests for Adult Basic Education?" *Adult Ed* 17:19–29 au '66. *

148. AINSWORTH, L. L., AND FOX, A. M. "Otis IQ: Forecasting Efficiency for Undergraduate Education Courses." *Ed & Psychol Meas* 27:431 su '67. *

149. BHUSHAN, VIDYA. "The Translation of the Otis Quick-Scoring Mental Ability Tests Into Hindi Language." *J Ed & Psychol* (India) 24:192–5 Ja '67. *

150. HUSTON, BEATRICE MOORE. *A Normative Survey of the Personal and Academic Characteristics of the Freshmen Women Students Enrolled in Mary Hardin-Baylor College, 1966–1967.* Doctor's thesis, Baylor University (Waco, Tex.), 1967. (*DA* 28:1209A)

151. SANTORO, ROSEANN MARIE. *The Relationship of Reading Achievement to Specific Measures of Visual Perception, Visual-Motor Perception and Intelligence.* Doctor's thesis, Fordham University (New York, N.Y.), 1967. (*DA* 28:4010A)

152. SERVIS, MARGERY, AND FROST, REUBEN B. "Qualities Related to Success in Women's Physical Education Professional Preparation Program." *Res Q* 38:283–90 My '67. *

153. TUCKER, WILLIAM FRANCIS. *The Prediction of Achievement in Selected High School Subjects From Junior High School*

Data. Doctor's thesis, New York University (New York, N.Y.), 1967. (*DA* 28:1317A)

154. WILLIAMS, JACK, AND FOX, A. M. "Prediction of Performance in Student Teaching." *Ed & Psychol Meas* 27:1169–70 w '67. * (*PA* 42:9491)

155. WINSTON, WILMA ESSEX. *A Correlation Between Language Achievement and Musical Aptitude of Thirty Sixth Grade Pupils at Booker T. Washington School, East Gadsden, Alabama.* Master's thesis, Alabama A & M College (Normal, Ala.), 1967.

156. AHMAD, FARRUKH Z. "Is the Otis Quick Scoring Mental Ability Test a Good Predictor of Academic Success in West Pakistan?" *Ed & Psychol Meas* 28:947–9 au '68. * (*PA* 43:4513)

157. ARTH, ALFRED ARTHUR. *A Study of the Relationship Between Non-Completion and Intelligence Exhibited by Sixth Grade Elementary School Students.* Doctor's thesis, University of Oklahoma (Norman, Okla.), 1968. (*DA* 29:1666A)

158. BAILEY, LARRY J. "Factors Related to Success in Practical Nursing Programs." *Nursing Outl* 16:59 N '68. *

159. BUSZEK, BEATRICE R. "Differential Treatment of Test Scores." *Col & Univ* 43:294–307 sp '68. *

160. GREEN, JOHNNIE HENDERSON. *An Analysis of Academic Proficiency of the 1965–66 Beginning Freshman Class, School of Business, Texas Southern University, Houston, Texas.* Doctor's thesis, University of Houston (Houston, Tex.), 1968. (*DA* 29:3323A)

161. HARRIS, A. J., AND LOVINGER, R. J. "Longitudinal Measures of the Intelligence of Disadvantaged Negro Adolescents." *Sch R* 76:60–6 Mr '68. * (*PA* 43:3138)

162. HAYDEN, DAVID LEE. *Factors of Intelligence of College Students in the Philippines as Determined by the Otis Quick-Scoring Mental Ability Test, Gamma, FM, and the Measure of Intellectual Maturation.* Doctor's thesis, Catholic University of America (Washington, D.C.), 1968. (*DA* 29:3874A)

163. MACARTHUR, R. S. "Assessing Intellectual Potential of Native Canadian Pupils: A Summary." *Alberta J Ed Res* (Canada) 14:115–22 Je '68. * (*PA* 44:4170)

164. MACARTHUR, RUSSELL. "Some Differential Abilities of Northern Canadian Native Youth." *Int J Psychol* (France) 3(1):43–50 '68. * (*PA* 42:15325)

165. PUGH, RICHARD C. "Tests for Creative Thinking—Potential for School Testing Programs." *B Sch Ed Ind Univ* 44(6):1–30 N '68. * (*PA* 46:5483)

166. RUTHERFORD, BRENT M., AND KOPLYAY, JANOS B. "Program COGITO: Computerized General IQ Testing—Otis, in the FORTRAN IV Language." *Ed & Psychol Meas* 28:177–9 sp '68. * (*PA* 42:11395)

167. SOLKOFF, NORMAN. "The Use of Personality and Attitude Tests in Predicting the Academic Success of Medical and Law Students." *J Med Ed* 43:1250–3 D '68. * (*PA* 44:7336)

168. STOCK, WILLIAM H., JR. *Some Psychological and Physiological Factors Affecting Excellence in Acting.* Doctor's thesis, Michigan State University (East Lansing, Mich.), 1968. (*DA* 29:3716A)

169. ARMBRUST, ROBERT. *An Investigation of the Role of Selected Non-Verbal Intelligence Factors in Beginning Drafting Success.* Doctor's thesis, Southern Illinois University (Carbondale, Ill.), 1969. (*DAI* 30:2895A)

170. BOWERS, JOHN. "Interactive Effects of Creativity and IQ on Ninth-Grade Achievement." *J Ed Meas* 6(3):173–7 f '69. * (*PA* 44:15469)

171. DE BOTTARI, LINDA. "Primary School Correlates of Secondary School Achievement." *Personnel & Guid J* 47(7):675–8 Mr '69. * (*PA* 43:13362)

172. ERTL, JOHN P., AND SCHAFER, EDWARD W. P. "Brain Response Correlates of Psychometric Intelligence." *Nature* 223(5204):421–2 Jl 26 '69. *

173. FAIRCHILD, PATRICIA CARLETTE. *Grade Point Average and Variance as Criteria of College Academic Performance.* Doctor's thesis, University of Oklahoma (Norman, Okla.), 1969. (*DAI* 30:3318A)

174. GROPPER, ROBERT L. *Comprehension of Narrative Passages by Fourth-Grade Children as a Function of Listening Rate and Eleven Predictor Variables.* Doctor's thesis, George Peabody College for Teachers (Nashville, Tenn.), 1969. (*DAI* 30:4827A)

175. HIERONYMUS, A. N., AND STROUD, JAMES B. "Comparability of IQ Scores on Five Widely Used Intelligence Tests." *Meas & Eval Guid* 2(3):135–40 f '69. * (*PA* 44:13285)

176. MEEHAN, KATHRYN S. *Predicting Future Achievement From the Detroit Beginning First Grade Intelligence Test and the Otis Quick Scoring Test of Mental Ability.* Master's thesis, Jersey City State College (Jersey City, N.J.), 1969.

177. MORE, ARTHUR. "The Relation of High School Grades, Achievement and Intelligence Test Scores to Success in Dental School." *Can Counsellor* 3(1):56–8 Ja '69. *

178. NELSON, C. MICHAEL, AND HUDSON, FLOYD G. "Predicting the Reading Achievement of Junior High School EMR Children." *Am J Mental Def* 74(3):415–20 N '69. * (*PA* 44:5559)

179. ROGGENKAMP, RONALD R. *A Study to Determine the Validity of Using College Entrance Exams and I.Q. as Predictors of College Performance for Falls City Senior High Graduates.* Master's thesis, Kearney State College (Kearney, Neb.), 1969.

180. TOLOR, ALEXANDER. "Incidence of Underachievement at the High School Level." *J Ed Res* 63(2):63–5 O '69. *

181. URLOCKER, WILFRID THOMAS. *A Pilot Study to Determine the Validity of the Otis Quick-Scoring Mental Ability Beta Test and the Dominion Achievement Test in Silent Reading Type II: Diagnostic Test in Paragraph Reading in Predicting Grade VII Averages at St. Anthony Senior Elementary School.* Master's thesis, Niagara University (Niagara University, N.Y.), 1969.

182. BEINKE, JAMES L. *A Study to Determine the Correlation of a System of Teacher Evaluation to Otis IQ Scores and the Gordon Musical Aptitude Profile Test.* Master's thesis, Wisconsin State University (Whitewater, Wis.), 1970.

183. BICKLEY, A. C.; DINNAN, JAMES A.; AND BICKLEY, RACHEL. "Language Responses as a Predictor of Performance on Intelligence Tests." *J Read Behav* 2(4):291–4 f '70. * (*PA* 46:4980)

184. CHASE, CLINTON I. "Comparable Intelligence Test Performance by Extreme Social Classes." Abstract. *Proc 78th Ann Conv Am Psychol Assn* 5(2):645–6 '70. * (*PA* 44:18350)

185. ISMAIL, A. H., AND KIRKENDALL, D. R. "Relationship Among Three Domains of Development," pp. 451–60. In *Contemporary Psychology of Sport.* Proceedings of the Second International Congress of Sport Psychology, Washington, D.C., 1968. Chicago, Ill.: Athletic Institute, 1970. Pp. xix, 878. *

186. KENNETT, K. F., AND CROPLEY, A. J. "Intelligence, Family Size and Socio-Economic Status." *J Biosocial Sci* (England) 2(3):227–36 Jl '70. * (*PA* 46:4670)

187. LEUNES, ARNOLD, AND CHRISTENSEN, LARRY. "Reliability and Inmate Test Results." *Correct Psychologist* 4(3):85–93 N–D '70. * (*PA* 49:2670)

188. LYSAUGHT, JEROME P., AND PIERLEONI, ROBERT G. "Predicting Individual Success in Programing Self-Instructional Materials." *AV Commun R* 18(1):5–24 sp '70. * (*PA* 44:13334)

189. PARTIN, RONALD L. *The Value of Four Selected Test Scores in Predicting Advanced Placement American History Test Scores.* Master's thesis, Bowling Green State University (Bowling Green, Ohio), 1970.

190. PIERLEONI, ROBERT G., AND LYSAUGHT, JEROME P. "A Decision Ladder for Predicting Programmer Success." *NSPI J* 9(5):6–7 + Je '70. *

191. SMITH, I. MACFARLANE. "The Use of Diagnostic Tests for Assessing the Abilities of Overseas Students Attending Institutions of Further Education, Part I." *Voc Aspect Ed* (England) 22(51):1–8 Mr '70. *

192. BAILEY, KENT G., AND GIBBY, ROBERT G., SR. "Developmental Differences in Self-Ratings on Intelligence." *J Clin Psychol* 27(1):51–4 Ja '71. * (*PA* 46:791)

193. CHASE, CLINTON I., AND PUGH, RICHARD C. "Social Class and Performance on an Intelligence Test." *J Ed Meas* 8(3):197–202 f '71. * (*PA* 47:11604)

194. CHISSOM, BRAD S., AND LIGHTSEY, RALPH. "A Comparison of the D-48 Test and the Otis Quick Score for High School Dropouts." *Ed & Psychol Meas* 31(2):525–7 su '71. *

195. FARR, JAMES L.; O'LEARY, BRIAN S.; AND BARTLETT, C. J. "Ethnic Group Membership as a Moderator of the Prediction of Job Performance." *Personnel Psychol* 24(4):609–36 w '71. *

196. LANGEVIN, R. "Is Curiosity a Unitary Construct?" *Can J Psychol* 25(4):360–74 au '71. * (*PA* 47:5607)

197. LEMKE, ELMER A., AND KIRCHNER, JOHN H. "A Multivariate Study of Handwriting, Intelligence, and Personality Correlates." *J Pers Assess* 35(6):584–92 D '71. * (*PA* 47:10876)

198. SHANLEY, LUKE A.; WALKER, RONALD E.; AND FOLEY, JEANNE M. "Social Intelligence: A Concept in Search of Data." *Psychol Rep* 29(3):1123–32 D '71. * (*PA* 48:1661)

199. SMITH, I. MACFARLANE. "The Use of Diagnostic Tests for Assessing the Abilities of Overseas Students Attending Institutions of Further Education, Part II." *Voc Aspect Ed* (England) 23(54):39–48 Ap '71. *

200. SMITH, RICHARD LEE. *A Factor-Analytic Study of Critical Reading/Thinking, Influenceability, and Related Factors.* Doctor's thesis, University of Maine (Orono, Me.), 1971. (*DAI* 32:6229A)

201. VARNER, DONALD GILES. *The Relationship of Selected Cumulative Grade Point Averages to Intelligence Quotient.* Master's thesis, Eastern Illinois University (Charleston, Ill.), 1971.

202. WILSON, GLENN D.; TUNSTALL, OLIVE A.; AND EYSENCK, H. J. "Individual Differences in Tapping Performance as a Function of Time on the Task." *Percept & Motor Skills* 33(2):375–8 O '71. * (*PA* 47:6073)

CUMULATIVE NAME INDEX

[426]
Otis Self-Administering Tests of Mental Ability.
Grades 4-9, 9-16; 1922-29; Arthur S. Otis and Thomas N. Barrows (Forms D, intermediate C); Harcourt Brace Jovanovich, Inc. (Australian adaptation: Ages 9-14, 12.5 and over; 1936-73; 1972-73 metric editions identical with tests published 1936-51 except for 2-9 revised items; manuals by D. Spearritt; Australian Council for Educational Research [Australia]. New Zealand adaptation: Ages 9-14, 12-17; 1937-69; New Zealand Council for Educational Research [New Zealand].) * For later edition entries, see 424 and 425.

For additional information, see 5:363 (52 references); for a review by Frederic Kuder, see 3:250 (71 references). For additional information concerning the original Australian edition, see 2:1412.

REFERENCES THROUGH 1971

1-71. See 3:250.
72-123. See 5:363.
124. BINNEWIES, W. G. "Freshmen Grades and Mental Tests: A Correlation Made at South Dakota State College, Brookings." *Ed Adm & Sup* 9:161-2 Mr '23. *
125. HUGHES, J. M. "The Use of Tests in the Evaluation of Factors Which Condition the Achievement of Pupils in High School Physics." *J Ed Psychol* 16:217-31 Ap '25. *
126. KEENER, E. E. "Mental Ability of Freshman High-School Pupils." *J Ed Res* 11:113-22 F '25. *
127. ODELL, C. W. "Some Data as to the Effect of Previous Testing Upon Intelligence Test Scores." *J Ed Psychol* 16:482-6 O '25. *
128. SCHREIBER, EDWIN W. "A Study of the Factors of Success in First-Year Algebra." *Math Teach* 18:65-78, 141-63 F, Mr '25. *
129. BEAR, ROBT. B. "Factors in the Achievement of College Freshmen." *Sch & Soc* 24:802-4 D 25 '26. * (*PA* 1:689)
130. BRIGHAM, CARL C.; ANGIER, ROSWELL P.; MACPHAIL, ANDREW H.; ROGERS, DAVID C.; AND STONE, CHARLES L. "The Otis Self-Administering Test." *Col Entr Exam Board Ann Rep* 26:185-7 S '26. *
131. ELDER, HARRY E. "Percentile Rank in Intelligence as a Prognosis in Algebra." *Sch R* 34:542-6 S '26. *
132. GROVES, J. W. "Some Correlations in a Teacher-Training Class." *J Ed Res* 13:305-6 Ap '26. *
133. HURD, A. W. "The Intelligence Quotient as a Prognosis of Success in Physics." *Sch R* 34:123-8 F '26. *
134. LACY, L. D. "Relative Intelligence of White and Colored Children." *El Sch J* 26:542-6 Mr '26. *
135. PEAK, HELEN, AND BORING, EDWIN G. "The Factor of Speed in Intelligence." *J Exp Psychol* 9:71-94 Ap '26. * (*PA* 1:64)
136. JANUS, MORRIS. *I.Q. as Indicative of Achievement in Townsend Harris Hall High School.* Master's thesis, College of the City of New York (New York, N.Y.), 1927.
137. KORNHAUSER, ARTHUR W. "Test and High-School Records as Indicators of Success in an Undergraduate School of Business." *J Ed Res* 16:342-56 D '27. * (*PA* 2:1072)
138. LANIER, LYLE H. "Prediction of the Reliability of Mental Tests and Tests of Special Abilities." *J Exp Psychol* 10:69-113 Ap '27. * (*PA* 2:1692)
139. ANDERSON, ERNEST MITCHELL. *Individual Differences in the Reading Ability of College Students.* The University of Missouri Bulletin, Vol. 29, No. 39: Education Series, No. 25. Columbia, Mo.: the University, 1928. Pp. 79. *
140. BEAR, ROBERT M. "Factors Affecting the Success of College Freshmen." *J Appl Psychol* 12:517-23 O '28. * (*PA* 3:460)

141. Brown, William M. *Validity of Certain Group Intelligence Tests.* Master's thesis, State College of Washington (Pullman, Wash.), 1928.

142. Burger, Bertrand. *Correlations of Standardized English Tests, School Marks in English and Intelligence Tests.* Master's thesis, College of the City of New York (New York, N.Y.), 1928.

143. Fowler, O. F. "The Civic Attitudes of High School Sophomores." *Sch R* 36:25–37 Ja '28. *

144. Garrison, K. C. "Correlation Between Intelligence Test Scores and Success in Certain Rational Organization Problems." *J Appl Psychol* 12:621–30 D '28. * (*PA* 3:1747)

145. Garrison, K. C. "Intelligence Test Scores and Choice of Major Field." *Sch & Soc* 28:630–2 N 17 '28. * (*PA* 3:923)

146. Garrison, Karl C. *An Analytic Study of Rational Learning.* George Peabody College for Teachers Contributions to Education, No. 44. Nashville, Tenn.: the College, 1928. Pp. 52. * (*PA* 2:2701)

147. Main, H. V. "A Simplified Table for Otis I.Q." *Sch Sci & Math* 28:730 O '28. *

148. Spence, Ralph B. "Factors Related to College Achievement." *Teach Col Rec* 29:504–14 Mr '28. * (*PA* 2:2326)

149. Travis, Lee Edward, and Hunter, Theodore A. "The Relation Between 'Intelligence' and Reflex Conduction Rate." *J Exp Psychol* 11:342–54 O '28. * (*PA* 3:987)

150. Balyeat, Ray M. "The General Health and Mental Activity of Allergic Children." *Am J Dis Children* 37:1193–7 Je '29. * (*PA* 4:3885)

151. Garrison, Karl C. "An Investigation of Some Simple Speed Activities." *J Appl Psychol* 13:167–72 Ap '29. * (*PA* 3:3428)

152. Kefauver, Grayson N. "Need of Equating Intelligence Quotients Obtained From Group Tests." *J Ed Res* 19:92–101 F '29. * (*PA* 3:2105)

153. Peterson, Joseph, and Lanier, Lyle H. Part 2, "Comparisons of Certain Mental Abilities in White and Negro Adults," pp. 103–56. In their *Studies in the Comparative Abilities of Whites and Negroes.* Mental Measurements Monographs, Serial No. 5. Baltimore, Md.: Williams & Wilkins Co., 1929. Pp. vi, 156. * (*PA* 3:2316)

154. Price, J. St. Clair. "The Intelligence of Negro College Freshmen." *Sch & Soc* 30:749–54 N 30 '29. * (*PA* 4:739)

155. Schutte, T. H. "Students' Estimates of Their Ability and Achievement." *J Ed Res* 20:394–6 D '29. * (*PA* 4:883)

156. Wood, Margaret M. "Mental Test Findings With Armenian, Turkish, Greek and Bulgarian Subjects." *J Appl Psychol* 13:266–73 Je '29. * (*PA* 3:3737)

157. Commins, W. D. "A Factor in Language Ability." *J Ed Res* 21:77–8 Ja '30. *

158. Davis, Thomas Royal. *The Prognostic Value of Certain Tests for Predicting the Success of High School Freshmen.* Master's thesis, University of Chicago (Chicago, Ill.), 1930.

159. Graham, James L. "A Quantitative Comparison of Certain Mental Traits of Negro and White College Students." *J Social Psychol* 1:97–121, 267–85 F, My '30. * (*PA* 5:503)

160. Morley, Clyde A. "The Reliability of the Achievement Quotient." *J Ed Psychol* 21:351–60 My '30. * (*PA* 4:4052)

161. Odell, Charles W. *Predicting the Scholastic Success of College Students.* University of Illinois Bulletin, Vol. 28, No. 5; Bureau of Educational Research Bulletin No. 37. Urbana, Ill.: the Bureau, 1930. Pp. 43. *

162. Bray, Willis Joseph. "Achievement in General Chemistry as It Is Related to Certain Learning Abilities." *Sci J* 16:149–60 D '31. *

163. Brooks, Fowler D. "Predicting Scholarship in the Junior High School." *Ann Conf Ed Meas* 18:73–80 '31. *

164. Sims, Verner Martin. "The Influence of Blood Relationship and Common Environment on Measured Intelligence." *J Ed Psychol* 22:56–65 Ja '31. * (*PA* 5:2290)

165. Symonds, P. M. "Shall the I.Q. Be Used for Sectioning in the High School?" *J Ed Res* 24:138–40 S '31. * (*PA* 6:505)

166. Bousfield, Maudelle B. "The Intelligence and School Achievement of Negro Children." *J Negro Ed* 1:388–95 O '32. * (*PA* 8:3671)

167. Bowman, Herbert Lloyd. "Reported Preference and Performance in Problem Solving According to Intelligence Groups." *J Ed Res* 25:295–9 Ap–My '32. * (*PA* 6:3381)

168. Engelhart, Max D. "The Relative Contribution of Certain Factors to Individual Differences in Arithmetical Problem Solving Ability." *J Exp Ed* 1:19–27 S 15 '32. * (*PA* 7:1126)

169. Grace, Alonzo G. "The Relationship of Mental Ability to Occupational Choices of Adults." *Voc Guid Mag* 10:354–8 My '32. * (*PA* 7:2543)

170. Hendrickson, Gordon, and Huskey, John F. "Extroversion as a Factor Conditioning Achievement in the Fifth and Sixth Grades of an Elementary School." *J Ed Res* 25:6–13 Ja '32. * (*PA* 6:2005)

171. McMurry, Robert N. "Efficiency, Work-Satisfaction and Neurotic Tendency: A Study of Bank Employees." *Personnel J* 11:201–10 D '32. * (*PA* 7:1086)

172. Maller, J. B. "Age Versus Intelligence as Basis for Prediction of Success in High School." *Teach Col Rec* 33:402–15 F '32. * (*PA* 6:2015)

173. Miller, Andrew J., and Manwiller, C. E. "A Study of Trade School Pupils." *Pittsburgh Sch* 6:219–69 My–Je '32. *

174. Durrell, Donald D. "The Influence of Reading Ability on Intelligence Measures." *J Ed Psychol* 24:412–6 S '33. * (*PA* 8:654)

175. Boynton, Paul L., and Lowe, Paul E. "The Developmental Age of Industrial School Boys." *Child Develop* 5:59–62 Mr '34. * (*PA* 8:4803)

176. Brown, Andrew W.; Lyon, Verne W.; and Stein, Seymour. "The Influence of Distraction Upon Mental-Test Performance." *Psychol Clinic* 22(4):213–9 '34. * (*PA* 9:1086)

177. Jaggers, Craddock H. "The Relation of Intelligence to Behavior in School Children." *Peabody J Ed* 11:254–9 My '34. * (*PA* 9:997)

178. Laslett, H. R., and Manning, Juanita. "A Delinquency Survey of a Medium-Size High School." *J Juvenile Res* 18:71–8 Ap '34. * (*PA* 8:5147)

179. Patterson, Herbert. "The Chronological Age of Highly Intelligent Freshmen." *Peabody J Ed* 12:19–20 Jl '34. * (*PA* 9:953)

180. Triplett, Richard J. "Intelligence of Commercial College Students." *Personnel J* 13:92–3 Ag '34. * (*PA* 8:5668)

181. Finch, F. H., and Nemzek, C. L. "Attendance and Achievement in the High School." *Sch & Soc* 41:207–8 F 9 '35. * (*PA* 9:2967)

182. Leahy, A. M. "Nature-Nurture and Intelligence." *Genetic Psychol Monogr* 17:236–308 Ag '35. * (*PA* 9:5664)

183. Mitchell, Claude. "Prognostic Value of Intelligence Tests." *J Ed Res* 28:577–81 Ap '35. * (*PA* 9:3904)

184. Odoroff, M. E. "A Correlational Method Applicable to the Study of the Time Factor in Intelligence Tests." *J Ed Psychol* 26:307–11 Ap '35. * (*PA* 9:4843)

185. Quayle, Margaret Sidney. "A Study of Some Aspects of Satisfaction in the Vocation of Stenography." *Teach Col Contrib Ed* 659:1–121 '35. * (*PA* 10:2644)

186. Wells, F. L., and Hylan, N. W. "Psychometric Practice in Adults of Superior Intelligence." *Am J Orthopsychiatry* 5:286–301 Jl '35. * (*PA* 10:1224)

187. Benton, Arthur L. "Influence of Incentives Upon Intelligence Test Scores of School Children." *J Genetic Psychol* 49:494–7 D '36. * (*PA* 11:2971)

188. Fendrick, Paul, and Bond, Guy. "Delinquency and Reading." *J Genetic Psychol* 48:236–43 Mr '36. * (*PA* 10:3619)

189. Hill, Harry Segner. "Correlation Between I.Q.'s of Bilinguals at Different Ages on Different Intelligence Tests." *Sch & Soc* 44:89–90 Jl 18 '36. * (*PA* 10:5164)

190. Lorge, Irving. "The Influence of the Test Upon the Nature of Mental Decline as a Function of Age." *J Ed Psychol* 27:100–10 F '36. * (*PA* 10:3760)

191. Moore, Joseph E. "A Comparative Study of the Educational Achievement of Delinquent and Dependent Boys." *Peabody J Ed* 14:1–6 Jl '36. * (*PA* 11:969)

192. Olander, Herbert T., and Walker, Bert S. "Can Teachers Estimate I.Q.'s?" *Sch & Soc* 44:744–6 D 5 '36. * (*PA* 11:1490)

193. Steer, Max D. "The General Intelligence of College Stutterers." *Sch & Soc* 44:862–4 D 26 '36. * (*PA* 11:1427)

194. Tiebout, Carolyn, and Meier, Norman C. "Artistic Ability and General Intelligence." *Psychol Monogr* 48(1):95–125 '36. * (*PA* 11:392)

195. Ferguson, Henry H. "Incentives and an Intelligence Test." *Austral J Psychol & Philos* 15:39–53 Mr '37. * (*PA* 11:3924)

196. Moore, Joseph E. "A Comparative Study of the Intelligence of Delinquent and Dependent Boys." *J Ed Psychol* 28:355–66 My '37. * (*PA* 12:478)

197. Schmitz, Sylvester B. "Predicting Success in College: A Study of Various Criteria." *J Ed Psychol* 28:465–73 S '37. * (*PA* 12:538)

198. Seashore, R. H.; Stockford, L. B. O.; and Swartz, B. K. "A Correlational Analysis of Factors in Speed of Reading Tests." *Sch & Soc* 46:187–92 Ag 7 '37. * (*PA* 11:5346)

199. Stone, C. P., and Barker, R. G. "Aspects of Personality and Intelligence in Post Menarcheal and Premenarcheal Girls of the Same Chronological Age." *J Comp Psychol* 23:439–45 Je '37. * (*PA* 11:4871)

200. Goldberg, Woolf. *The Carnegie Examinations at Temple University: A Study of the Examinations of the Carnegie Foundation in the Teachers College of Temple University.* Philadelphia, Pa.: Temple University, 1938. Pp. 105. *

201. Manning, Frank Leroy. "How Accurately Can We Predict Success in College?" *J Am Assn Col Reg* 14:35–8 O '38. * (*PA* 13:4365)

202. Otis, Jay L. "The Prediction of Success in Power Sewing Machine Operating." *J Appl Psychol* 22:350–66 Ag '38. * (*PA* 13:1688)

203. Krueger, Raymond Leslie. "Grades and Intelligence Quotients. (A Study of the Figures for Three Years in One Private School.)" *Sch & Soc* 50:6–4 Jl 8 '39. * (*PA* 13:5920)

204. Pond, Frederick L. "Influence of Reading Abilities on School Success in Grade IX." *Sch R* 48:437–44 Je '40. *

205. Ries, Arthur J. *A Survey of the Intelligence and Achievement Scores of White and Negro Children Entering the*

Junior High Schools of Louisville in September, 1938. Master's thesis, University of Louisville (Louisville, Ky.), 1940.

206. BEAN, KENNETH L. "Negro Responses to Verbal and Non-Verbal Test Materials." *J Psychol* 13:343–53 Ap '42. * (*PA* 16:3487)

207. ROHRER, JOHN H. "The Test Intelligence of Osage Indians." *J Social Psychol* 16:99–105 Ag '42. * (*PA* 16:4724)

208. WILSON, M. T. "Detection of Reading Difficulties in a Rural Public School." *Training Sch B* 39:41–6 My '42. * (*PA* 16:3818)

209. EBERT, ELIZABETH, AND SIMMONS, KATHERINE. *The Brush Foundation Study of Child Growth and Development: 1, Psychometric Tests.* Monographs of the Society for Research in Child Development, Vol. 8, No. 2, Serial No. 35. Washington, D.C.: the Society, National Research Council, 1943. Pp. xiv, 113. * (*PA* 18:3322)

210. OSBORNE, AGNES ELIZABETH. "The Relationship Between Certain Psychological Tests and Shorthand Achievement." *Teach Col Contrib Ed* 873:1–58 '43. *

211. LORGE, IRVING. "Schooling Makes a Difference." *Teach Col Rec* 46:483–92 My '45. * (*PA* 19:2773)

212. CLARK, WALTER H. "Perseverance and Repetition as Factors in Gain in IQ." *J Ed Psychol* 37:557–62 D '46. * (*PA* 21:1420)

213. BROWER, DANIEL. "The Experimental Study of Imagery: 1, The Relation of Imagery to Intelligence." *J General Psychol* 36:229–31 Ja '47. * (*PA* 22:2927)

214. LANE, G. GORHAM. "Studies in Pilot Selection: 1, The Prediction of Success in Learning to Fly Light Aircraft." *Psychol Monogr* 61(5):1–17 '47. * (*PA* 22:5166)

215. STAUDT, VIRGINIA M. "The Relationship of Testing Conditions and Intellectual Level to Errors and Correct Responses in Several Types of Tasks Among College Women." *J Psychol* 26:125–40 Jl '48. * (*PA* 23:1163)

216. KNEHR, CHARLES A., AND SOBOL, ALBERT. "Mental Ability of Prematurely Born Children at Early School Age." *J Psychol* 27:355–61 Ap '49. * (*PA* 23:4160)

217. BRUCE, MARTIN MARC. *The Importance of Certain Personality Characteristics, Skills and Abilities in Effectiveness as a Factory Foreman.* Doctor's thesis, New York University (New York, N.Y.), 1952. (*DA* 13:116)

218. HANES, BERNARD. *A Factor Analysis of the MMPI, Aptitude Test Data and Personal Information Using a Population of Criminals.* Doctor's thesis, Ohio State University (Columbus, Ohio), 1952. (*DA* 18:1483)

219. LAWRENCE, P. J. "Some Characteristics of Incorrect Responses to Intelligence Test Items." *Austral J Psychol* 9:1–11 Je '57. *

220. KRATTIGER, JOHN TRUBERT. *An Evaluation of the Freshman Testing Program of Southeastern State College of Oklahoma.* Doctor's thesis, University of Oklahoma (Norman, Okla.), 1958. (*DA* 19:718)

221. LAVER, A. B. "Testing in Canada: Report No. 1." *Can Psychologist* 8:102–3 O '59. *

222. BROWN, THELMA E. "Factors Relating to Turnover Among Veterans Administration Nursing Assistants." *J Clin & Exp Psychopathol* 22:226–34 D '61. *

223. HASCALL, EDWARD O. "Predicting Success in High School Foreign Language Study." *Personnel & Guid J* 40:361–7 D '61. * (*PA* 36:4KL61H)

224. ROTH, ROBERT M., AND GILBERT, JEAN. "AF: A New Approach to the Concept of Achievement." *J Ed Res* 55:90–2 O '61. *

225. BLAZSANYIK, J. "Clinical Diagnostic Use of P.M. 38 and Verbal Tests." *Austral J Psychol Res* 3:5–8 au '62. *

226. CRANE, WILLIAM J. "Screening Devices for Occupational Therapy Majors." *Am J Occup Ther* 16:131–2 My–Je '62. * (*PA* 37:4078)

227. DARLEY, JOHN G. "The Basis for Equivalent Scores on the Annual Editions of the American Council on Education Psychological Examination (ACE), 1941 to 1954," pp. 170–83. In his *Promise and Performance: A Study of Ability and Achievement in Higher Education.* Berkeley, Calif.: Center for Study of Higher Education, University of California, 1962. Pp. vii, 194. *

228. ROOS, PHILIP, AND LEWIS, JERRY M. "Differential Abstraction Deficits in a Normal Population." *J Nerv & Mental Dis* 134:535–8 Je '62. * (*PA* 37:3708)

229. SUPER, DONALD E., AND CRITES, JOHN O. *Appraising Vocational Fitness by Means of Psychological Tests, Revised Edition,* pp. 102–9. New York: Harper & Brothers, 1962. Pp. xv, 688. * (*PA* 37:2038)

230. ADKINS, ARLIE ANDREW. *Prediction of College Success at Middle Tennessee State College.* Doctor's thesis, University of Florida (Gainesville, Fla.), 1963. (*DA* 25:211)

231. BECKER, JAMES A. "An Exploratory Factor Analytic Study of Interests, Intelligence, and Personality." *Psychol Rep* 13:847–51 D '63. * (*PA* 38:8399)

232. BLAKENEY, ADOLPH L. *An Analysis of the Relationships Between Certain Ability and Personality Variables and Clinical Performance During Psychiatric-Mental Health Nursing Education.* Doctor's thesis, University of Alabama (University, Ala.), 1963. (*DA* 25:1732)

233. HACKETT, JOHN R., AND FARNUM, HOLLIS B. "A New

Look at the Evening College Student." *Adult Ed* 13:148–52 sp '63. *

234. JONES, KENNETH J. "Predicting Achievement in Chemistry: A Model." *J Res Sci Teach* 1:226–31 S '63. *

235. TWAIN, DAVID C., AND BROOKS, EDWARD M. "A Comparison of Wechsler, Revised Beta and Otis Scores of Delinquents." *Brit J Criminol* 3:288–90 Ja '63. *

236. WOEHLKE, ARNOLD B., AND WILDER, DAVID H. "Differences in Difficulty of Forms A and B of the Otis Self-Administering Test of Mental Ability." *Personnel Psychol* 16:395–8 w '63. * (*PA* 38:8440)

237. CREELMAN, ARTHUR G. *The Prediction of Physics Grades at the University Level From Previously Recorded Data.* Master's thesis, University of British Columbia (Vancouver, B.C., Canada), 1964.

238. SPITZER, MORTON EDWARD, AND MCNAMARA, WALTER J. "A Managerial Selection Study." *Personnel Psychol* 17:19–40 sp '64. * (*PA* 39:2045)

239. DOUGLAS, MARCELINE J. *A Study of Test-Retest Scores of the Otis Test of Mental Ability for Seabreeze High School Students.* Master's thesis, Stetson University (DeLand, Fla.), 1965.

240. HARRISON, BARBARA. *The Development of Local Norms for the Otis Mental Ability Test and the Iowa Tests of Basic Skills With Selected Relationships to Teacher Marks in Orange, Connecticut.* Master's thesis, Southern Connecticut State College (New Haven, Conn.), 1965.

241. JOG, R. N., AND AGA, H. "A Comparative Study of the Prediction of Academic Achievement of Engineering." *J Voc & Ed Guid* (India) 12:45–50 My '66. *

242. LEVY, RUSSELL H. "The Gauging of Academic Achievement Among 'Court-Labelled' Delinquent Boys (Second of a Series)." *J Correct Ed* 18:14–7 O '66. *

243. LEVY, RUSSELL H., AND HENNING, JOHN A. "The Gauging of Achievement Among 'Court-Labelled' Delinquent Boys." *J Correct Ed* 18:16–8+ Ap '66. *

244. LEVY, RUSSELL H., AND MOORE, WINSTON E. "Cross-Sectional Psychometric Evaluation of Court-Labelled Delinquent Boys." *J Correct Ed* 18:7–9 Jl '66. *

245. MCCREARY, J. R. "Reading Tests With Maori Children." *N Zeal J Ed Studies* 1(1–2):40–50 '66. *

246. DONELSON, KENNETH L. "Variables Distinguishing Between Effective and Ineffective Writers in the Tenth Grade." *J Exp Ed* 35:37–41 su '67. *

247. HAWKES, NORMA JEANNE. *Analysis of Channel Selection by Junior Secondary School Students on the Reorganized Curriculum in British Columbia Schools.* Doctor's thesis, University of Oregon (Eugene, Ore.), 1967. (*DA* 28:3463A)

248. HINMAN, SUSAN LEE. *A Predictive Validity Study of Creative Managerial Performance.* Greensboro, N.C.: Creativity Research Institute of the Richardson Foundation, Inc., November 1967. Pp. vi, 124. *

249. MOFFIE, D. J., AND GOODNER, SUSAN. *A Predictive Validity Study of Creative and Effective Managerial Performance.* Greensboro, N.C.: Creativity Research Institute of the Richardson Foundation, Inc., December 1967. Pp. 80. *

250. WELSCH, LAWRENCE A. *The Supervisor's Employee Appraisal Heuristic: The Contribution of Selected Measures of Employee Aptitude, Intelligence and Personality.* Doctor's thesis, University of Pittsburgh (Pittsburgh, Pa.), 1967. (*DA* 28: 4321A)

251. BILES, DAVID. "Test Performance and Imprisonment." *Austral & N Zeal J Criminol* (Australia) 1:46–58 Mr '68. *

252. LEVY, RUSSELL H. "Group Administered Intelligence Tests Which Appropriately Reflect the Magnitude of Mental Retardation Among Wards of the Illinois Youth Commission." *J Correct Ed* 20:7–10 su '68. *

253. SOLKOFF, NORMAN. "The Use of Personality and Attitude Tests in Predicting the Academic Success of Medical and Law Students." *J Med Ed* 43:1250–3 D '68. * (*PA* 44:7336)

254. THUMIN, FRED J. "Ability Scores as Related to Age Among Male Job Applicants." *J Gerontol* 23:390–2 Jl '68. *

255. ELLEY, W. B. "Changes in Mental Ability in New Zealand School Children." *N Zeal J Ed Studies* 4(2):140–55 N '69. * (*PA* 47:4547)

256. WITT, NORMAN ERNEST. *A Study of Significant Factors Which Tend to Predict Selection as a Candidate for the Position of Commercial Airline Pilot.* Doctor's thesis, University of California (Los Angeles, Calif.), 1969. (*DAI* 30:3291A)

257. BRADLEY, M. "Statistical Comparison of the Otis Self-Administering Tests of Mental Ability and PSC Examinations 302A and 5A (GIT Series)." *Studies Pers Psychol* (Canada) 2(1):74–80 Ap '70. * (*PA* 46:4042)

258. DODD, W. E.; WOLLOWICK, H. B.; AND MCNAMARA, W. J. "Task Difficulty as a Moderator of Long-Range Prediction." *J Appl Psychol* 54(3):265–70 Je '70. * (*PA* 44:13452)

259. GROSVENOR, THEODORE. "Refractive State, Intelligence Test Scores, and Academic Ability." *Am J Optom* 47(5):355–61 My '70. * (*PA* 46:4624)

260. THUMIN, FRED J. "Comparative Study of Three Mental Ability Tests." *J Indus Psychol* 5(1):1–7 Mr '70. * (*PA* 45:7117)

261. COWDEN, JAMES E.; PETERSON, WILLIAM M.; AND PACHT, ASHER R. "The Validation of a Brief Screening Test

for Verbal Intelligence at Several Correctional Institutions in Wisconsin." *J Clin Psychol* 27(2):216–8 Ap '71. * (*PA* 46:7125)
262. ELKINS, J. "Some Recent Queensland Norms for Widely Used Standardized Tests." *Slow Learning Child* (Australia) 18(3):142–7 N '71. *

[427]

Pacific Reasoning Series Tests: Pacific Test Series. Job applicants in Papua New Guinea; 1962–68; PRST; I. G. Ord; Australian Council for Educational Research [Australia]. *

For additional information, see 7:371 (1 reference).

REFERENCES THROUGH 1971
1. See 7:371.

CUMULATIVE NAME INDEX

[428]

Pattern Perception Test. Ages 6 and over; 1943; no manual; L. S. Penrose; Kennedy-Galton Centre [England]. *

For additional information and a review by Alice W. Heim, see 4:312 (3 references).

REFERENCES THROUGH 1971
1–3. See 4:312.
4. LEE, TERENCE. "The Selection of Student Nurses: A Revised Procedure." *Occup Psychol* (England) 33:209–16 O '59. *

CUMULATIVE NAME INDEX

[429]

Performance Alertness "PA" (With Pictures): Individual Placement Series. Adults; 1961–66; J. H. Norman; Personnel Research Associates, Inc. *

For additional information and a review by Joel T. Campbell, see 7:372.

[430]

Personal Classification Test. Business and industry; 1953–59; no manual for Form H; W. E. Brown, W. H. E. Geiger, R. W. Henderson, and L. C. Steckle; William, Lynde & Williams. *
For additional information, see 6:483.

[431]

Personnel Research Institute Classification Test. Adults; 1943–54; formerly called *Classification Test for Industrial and Office Personnel;* Jay L. Otis, Evelyn Katz (Form A), Robert W. Henderson (A), Mary Aiken (A), David J. Chesler (Form B), and Gardner E. Lindzey (B) ; Personnel Research Institute. *
For additional information and reviews by James R. Glennon and Melvin R. Marks, see 6:484 (2 references). For reviews by Louise Witmer Cureton and Albert K. Kurtz of this and other tests in the *Personnel Research Institute Clerical Battery,* see 4:729.

REFERENCES THROUGH 1971
1–2. See 6:484.
3. HILTON, ANDREW C.; BOLIN, STANLEY F.; PARKER, JAMES W., JR.; TAYLOR, ERWIN K.; AND WALKER, WILLIAM B. "The Validity of Personnel Assessments by Professional Psychologists." *J Appl Psychol* 39:287–93 Ag '55. * (*PA* 30:5294)

CUMULATIVE NAME INDEX
Bolin, S. F.: 3   Marks, M. R.: *rev,* 6:484
Campbell, J. T.: 2   Otis, J. L.: 1
Chesler, D. J.: 1   Parker, J. W.: 3
Glennon, J. R.: *rev,* 6:484   Taylor, E. K.: 3
Hilton, A. C.: 3   Walker, W. B.: 3

[432]

Personnel Research Institute Factory Series Test. Applicants for routine industrial positions; 1950–56; Jay L. Otis and Alfred H. Exton; Personnel Research Institute. *
For additional information and a review by N. M. Downie, see 6:485.

[433]

Personnel Tests for Industry. Trade school and adults; 1945–69; PTI; 3 tests; Psychological Corporation. *
a) PTI-VERBAL TEST. 1952–69; PTI-V; Alexander G. Wesman.
b) PTI-NUMERICAL TEST. 1952–69; PTI-N; Jerome E. Doppelt.
c) PTI-ORAL DIRECTIONS TEST. 1945–54; ODT; Charles R. Langmuir.
For additional information, see 7:373 (3 references) ; for a review by Erwin K. Taylor, see 5:366; see also 4:309 (1 reference) ; for reviews by Charles D. Flory, Irving Lorge, and William W. Turnbull of the *Oral Directions Test,* see 3:245.

REFERENCES THROUGH 1971
1. See 4:309.
2–4. See 7:373.
5. VACCARO, JOSEPH JOHN. *A Study of Psychological Factors That Contrast the Most and Least Efficient Psychiatric Aides in Mental Hospitals.* Doctor's thesis, Fordham University (New York, N.Y.), 1951.
6. SANUA, VICTOR D. "A Note on the Spanish Language Form of the Oral Directions Test of Intelligence." *J Appl Psychol* 40:350–2 O '56. * (*PA* 31:7968)
7. DOPPELT, JEROME E., AND SEASHORE, HAROLD G. "Psychological Testing in Correctional Institutions." *J Counsel Psychol* 6:81–92 sp '59. * (*PA* 34:6012)
8. STERN, FERDINAND, AND GORDON, LEONARD V. "Ability to Follow Instructions as a Predictor of Success in Recruit Training." *J Appl Psychol* 45:22–4 F '61. * (*PA* 36:2LD22S)
9. RAFFEL, SHERMAN C.; SWINK, RICHARD; AND LAMPTON, T. D. "The Influence of Chlorphenesin Carbamate and Carisoprodol on Psychological Test Scores." *Curr Ther Res* 11(9): 553–60 S '69. *

CUMULATIVE NAME INDEX
Campbell, S. C.: 2   Sanua, V. D.: 6
Davis, J. A.: 4   Seashore, H. G.: 1, 7
Doppelt, J. E.: 7   Stern, F.: 8
Flory, C. D.: *rev,* 3:245   Swink, R.: 9
Gordon, L. V.: 8   Taylor, E. K.: *rev,* 5:366
Haber, W.: 3   Turnbull, W. W.: *rev,* 3:245
Lampton, T. D.: 9   Vaccaro, J. J.: 5
Lorge, I.: *rev,* 3:245   Wolfe, R. N.: 4
Raffel, S. C.: 9

[434]

Picture Test A. Ages 7-0 to 8-1; 1955–70; formerly called *Picture Test 1* and, earlier, *Picture Intelligence Test 1;* 1970 test identical with test published 1955 except for title; 1961 manual identical with 1955 manual; Joan E. Stuart; published for the National Foundation for Educational Research in England and Wales; Ginn & Co. Ltd. [England]. *
For additional information, see 7:374; for reviews by Charlotte E. K. Banks and M. L. Kellmer Pringle, see 5:367.

[435]

Pintner–Cunningham Primary Test. Grades kgn–2; 1923–66; revision of *Pintner-Cunningham Primary Mental Test;* a test in the *Pintner General Ability Tests: Verbal Series;* tests for grades 2–12 are out of print; Rudolf Pintner, Bess V. Cunningham, and Walter N. Durost; Harcourt Brace Jovanovich, Inc. *
For additional information, see 5:368a; for an excerpted review by J. Wayne Wrightstone, see 2:1416. For reviews of the *Pintner General Ability Tests: Verbal Series,* see 3:255 (2 reviews) and 2:1416 (2 excerpts).

REFERENCES THROUGH 1971
1. PINTNER, R., AND CUNNINGHAM, BESS V. "The Problem of Group Intelligence Tests for Very Young Children." *J Ed Psychol* 13:465–72 N '22. *
2. CUNNINGHAM, BESS V. "The Prognostic Value of a Primary Group Test: A Study of Intelligence and Relative Achievement in the First Grade." *Teach Col Contrib Ed* 139: 1–54 '23. *
3. FORAN, THOMAS GEORGE. "A Study of Some Group Intelligence Tests in the First Grade." *Cath Ed R* 22:81–9 F '24. *
4. HECKMAN, SAMUEL B. Chap. 3, "A Comparative Study of Group Intelligence Tests Applicable to Children of Kindergarten Age," pp. 17–44. In *Contributions to Education, Vol. 1.* Edited by J. Carleton Bell. Yonkers, N.Y.: World Book Co., 1924. Pp. ix, 364. *
5. PRESSEY, LUELLA C. "The Prognostic Value of a Primary Group Test: A Review." *J Ed Res* 11:223–4 Mr '25. *
6. RAYBOLD, EMMA. "An Experiment With Primary Intelligence Tests." *Ed Res B* (Los Angeles City Schools) 4:8 Je 15 '25. *
7. VIELE, ADA B. "A Study of Four Primary Mental Tests." *El Sch J* 25:675–81 My '25. *
8. HIRSCH, NATHANIEL D. MTTRON. "A Study of Natio-Racial Mental Differences." *Genetic Psychol Monogr* 1:231–406 My–Jl '26. * (*PA* 2:179)
9. KOCH, HELEN LOIS, AND SIMMONS, RIETTA. "A Study of the Test-Performance of American, Mexican, and Negro Children." *Psychol Monogr* 35(5):1–116 '26. *
10. BERG, B. C., AND PARKS, ETTA. "Comparison of the Scores on Pintner-Cunningham Test at the Beginning of the Kindergarten Course in the Second Grade." *J Ed Res* 15:293–4 Ap '27. *
11. FOX, EDNA J. "The Diagnostic Value of Group Tests as Determined by the Qualitative Differences Between Normal and Feeble-Minded Children." *J Appl Psychol* 11:127–34 Ap '27. * (*PA* 2:2945)
12. PINTNER, RUDOLF. "The Pintner-Cunningham Primary Test." *J Ed Psychol* 18:52–8 Ja '27. * (*PA* 1:977)
13. JAMIESON, ELMER, AND SANDIFORD, PETER. "The Mental Capacity of Southern Ontario Indians." *J Ed Psychol* 19:313–28, 536–51 My, N '28. * (*PA* 2:2841, 3:817)
14. KUHLMANN, F. "The Kuhlmann-Anderson Intelligence Tests Compared With Seven Others." *J Appl Psychol* 12:545–94 D '28. * (*PA* 3:1751)
15. McGRAW, MARY LOUISE, AND MANGOLD, MARIE CECILIA. "Group Intelligence Tests in the Primary Grades." *Cath Univ Am Ed Res B* 4(2):1–41 F '29. * (*PA* 3:3902)
16. SANGREN, PAUL V. "Comparative Validity of Primary Intelligence Tests." *J Appl Psychol* 13:394–412 Ag '29. * (*PA* 3:4324)

17. DEPUTY, ERBY CHESTER. "Predicting First-Grade Reading Achievement: A Study in Reading Readiness." *Teach Col Contrib Ed* 426:1–61 '30. * (*PA* 7:2114)

18. JONES, CHARLES H. *Reliability of Group Intelligence Tests Administered to Children From Foreign Language Homes.* Master's thesis, New York State College for Teachers (Albany, N.Y.), 1930.

19. PORTER, M. POWELL, AND LAUDERBACH, J. CALVIN. "On the Constancy of the IQ." *Sch & Soc* 33:675–6 My 16 '31. * (*PA* 5:3570)

20. SEAGOE, M. V. "An Evaluation of Certain Intelligence Tests." *J Appl Psychol* 18:432–6 Je '34. * (*PA* 8:6140)

21. WALKER, ELLIS WOODS. *The Predictive Value of the Pintner-Cunningham Primary Mental Test: A Follow-up Study.* Master's thesis, Birmingham-Southern College (Birmingham, Ala.), 1935.

22. GRANT, ALBERT. "A Comparison of the Metropolitan Readiness Tests and the Pintner-Cunningham Primary Mental Test." *El Sch J* 38:118–26 O '37. * (*PA* 15:3195)

23. GRANT, ALBERT. "The Comparative Validity of the Metropolitan Readiness Tests and the Pintner-Cunningham Primary Mental Tests." *El Sch J* 38:599–605 Ap '38. * (*PA* 12:4990)

24. GATES, ARTHUR I. "A Further Evaluation of Reading Readiness Tests." *El Sch J* 40:577–91 Ap '40. * (*PA* 15:3581)

25. BAILEY, ALBERT ERNEST. *The Relative Validity of Ten Different Intelligence Tests.* Doctor's thesis, University of Washington (Seattle, Wash.), 1942.

26. HERR, SELMA E. "The Effect of Pre-First-Grade Training Upon Reading Readiness and Reading Achievement Among Spanish-American Children." *J Ed Psychol* 37:87–102 F '46. * (*PA* 20:2076)

27. MOREAU, MARGARET. "Long Term Prediction of Reading Success." *Calif J Ed Res* 1:173–6 S '50. *

28. SAWREY, JAMES M. "The Predictive Effectiveness of Two Non-Verbal Tests of Intelligence Used in the First Grade in the Santa Clara County Schools." Abstract. *Calif J Ed Res* 6:133 My '55. *

29. WALLIHAN, ROBERT SYLVANUS. *A Comparative Study of Retardation in the Primary Grades of the San Diego, California, City Schools.* Doctor's thesis, University of Colorado (Boulder, Colo.), 1955. (*DA* 16:1418)

30. BRENNER, ANTON, AND MORSE, NANCY C. "The Measurement of Children's Readiness for School." *Papers Mich Acad Sci Arts & Letters* 41:333–40 '56. * (*PA* 37:6453)

31. MORGAN, ELMER F., JR. "Efficacy of Two Tests in Differentiating Potentially Low From Average and High First Grade Achievers." *J Ed Res* 53:300–4 Ap '60. *

32. AVAKIAN, SONIA ASTRID. "An Investigation of Trait Relationships Among Six-Year-Old Children." *Genetic Psychol Monogr* 63:339–94 My '61. * (*PA* 36:1FF39A)

33. GNAUCK, JOHANNA, AND KACZKOWSKI, HENRY. "Prediction of Junior High School Performance." *Ed & Psychol Meas* 21:485–8 su '61. * (*PA* 36:2KL85G)

34. GASKILL, A. R., AND FOX, W. C. "How Useful Are Psychological Tests for Screening Underage School Beginners?" *J Ed Res* 57:333–6 F '64. * (*PA* 39:5832)

35. WIDEEN, MARVIN FRANK. *The Predictive Validity of the Pintner-Cunningham Primary Test, Form A.* Master's thesis, University of Saskatchewan (Saskatoon, Sask., Canada), 1964.

36. LOHNES, PAUL R., AND MARSHALL, THOMAS O. "Redundancy in Student Records." *Am Ed Res J* 2:19–23 Ja '65. *

37. BEAUCHAMP, JOAN M. *The Relationship Between Selected Factors Associated With Reading Readiness and the First Grade Reading Achievement of Students Instructed in the Initial Teaching Alphabet.* Doctor's thesis, Syracuse University (Syracuse, N.Y.), 1967. (*DA* 28:1200A)

38. BOND, GUY L., AND DYKSTRA, ROBERT. "The Cooperative Research Program in First-Grade Reading Instruction." *Read Res Q* 2:5–142 su '67. * (*PA* 42:4557)

39. WILSON, ROBERT M., AND ANDERSON, CATHIE A. "Prediction of Success in Reading." *Acad Ther* 4(3):199–200 sp '69. * (*PA* 43:17992)

40. BILKA, LOISANNE PFEIFER. *An Evaluation of the Predictive Value of Certain Reading Readiness Measures as Related to Method of Instruction, Sex, and Mental Age.* Doctor's thesis, University of Pittsburgh (Pittsburgh, Pa.), 1970. (*DAI* 31:5922A)

41. SANDY, CLAUDE ASHBURN. *The Effects of Material Reward, Sex, Race, and Socioeconomic Strata on the Pintner-Cunningham Primary Test Scores of Kindergarten Students.* Doctor's thesis, University of Virginia (Charlottesville, Va.), 1970. (*DAI* 31:5213A)

CUMULATIVE NAME INDEX

[436]

*Preliminary Scholastic Aptitude Test/National Merit Scholarship Qualifying Test.

Grades 10–12; 1959–73; PSAT/NMSQT; formerly called *Preliminary Scholastic Aptitude Test;* "a two-hour version of the [College Board] *Scholastic Aptitude Test"*; for guidance in grades 10–12 and scholarship testing in grade 11; administered in October at participating secondary schools; 3 scores: verbal, mathematical, selection index (for scholarship consideration by NMSC); program administered for College Entrance Examination Board and National Merit Scholarship Corporation by Educational Testing Service. *

For additional information concerning earlier forms, see 7:375 (10 references); for a review by Wayne S. Zimmerman, see 6:487 (2 references).

REFERENCES THROUGH 1971

1–2. See 6:487.

3–12. See 7:375.

13. SKAGER, RODNEY W.; BUSSIS, ANNE M.; AND SCHULTZ, CHARLES B. "Comparison of Information Scales and Like-Indifferent-Dislike Scales as Measures of Interest." *Psychol Rep* 16:251–61 F '65. * (*PA* 39:8691)

14. PARTIN, RONALD L. *The Value of Four Selected Test Scores in Predicting Advanced Placement American History Test Scores.* Master's thesis, Bowling Green State University (Bowling Green, Ohio), 1970.

15. DISPENZIERI, ANGELO; GINIGER, SEYMOUR; REICHMAN, WALTER; AND LEVY, MARGUERITE. "College Performance of Disadvantaged Students as a Function of Ability and Personality." *J Counsel Psychol* 18(4):298–305 Jl '71. * (*PA* 46:11687)

16. RUTLAND, EUGENE. *A Study to Determine the Influence of the Preliminary Scholastic Aptitude Test on the Results on the Scholastic Aptitude Test Scores of a Group of Students Enrolled in the Senior Class at the Wilcox County High School, Rochelle, Georgia.* Master's thesis, Fort Valley State College (Ft. Valley, Ga.), 1971.

CUMULATIVE NAME INDEX

[437]

★Preschool and Early Primary Skill Survey, Preliminary Edition.

Ages 3-3 to 7-2; 1971; PEPSS; 4 or 5 scores: picture recognition, picture relationship, picture sequence, total, form completion (optional); John A. Long, Jr., Morton Morris, and George A. W. Stouffer, Jr.; distributed by Mafex Associates, Inc. *

[438]

[Pressey Classification and Verifying Tests.]

Grades 1-2, 3-6, 7-12 and adults; 1922–58; 3 levels; S. L. Pressey (except *a*) and L. C. Pressey; Bobbs-Merrill Co., Inc. *

a) PRIMARY CLASSIFICATION TEST. Grades 1–2; 1922.
b) PRESSEY INTERMEDIATE CLASSIFICATION-VERIFYING TESTS. Grades 3–6; 1922–58; 1958 test identical with tests copyrighted 1922 and 1923 except for format, directions, and minor changes in a few items; 2 tests.
  1) *Pressey Intermediate Classification Test.*
  2) *Pressey Intermediate Verifying Test.*
c) PRESSEY SENIOR CLASSIFICATION-VERIFYING TESTS. Grades 7–12 and adults; 1922–58; 2 tests.
  1) *Pressey Senior Classification Test.*
  2) *Pressey Senior Verifying Test.* 1958 test identical with test copyrighted 1922 except for format, directions, and minor changes in a few items.
For additional information and a review by Walter N. Durost, see 6:488 (11 references).

REFERENCES THROUGH 1971

1–11. See 6:488.
12. FORAN, THOMAS GEORGE. "A Study of Some Group Intelligence Tests in the First Grade." *Cath Ed R* 22:81–9 F '24. *
13. HECKMAN, SAMUEL B. Chap. 3, "A Comparative Study of Group Intelligence Tests Applicable to Children of Kindergarten Age," pp. 17–44. In *Contributions to Education, Vol. 1.* Edited by J. Carleton Bell. Yonkers, N.Y.: World Book Co., 1924. Pp. ix, 364. *
14. MILLER, W. S. "The Variation and Significance of Intelligence Quotients Obtained From Group Tests." *J Ed Psychol* 15:359–66 S '24. *
15. PRESSEY, L. W. "The Primary Classification Test." *J Ed Res* 9:305–14 Ap '24. *
16. PRESSEY, S. L., AND LONG, GLENN S. "A New Idea in Intelligence Testing." *Ed Res B* 3:365–8 D 10 '24. *
17. STROUD, J. B. "A Study of the Relation of Intelligence Test Scores on Public School Children to the Economic Status of Their Parents." *J Genetic Psychol* 35:105–10 Mr '28. * (*PA* 2:3758)
18. McGRAW, MARY LOUISE, AND MANGOLD, MARIE CECILIA. "Group Intelligence Tests in the Primary Grades." *Cath Univ Am Ed Res B* 4(2):1–41 F '29. * (*PA* 3:3902)
19. SOUTH, EARL B., AND CLARK, GENEVIEVE Y. "Some Uses of Psychological Tests in Schools of Nursing." *Am J Nursing* 29:1495–501 D '29. * (*PA* 4:1740)
20. NEMZEK, CLAUDE L.; CRONIN, MARION; AND BRANNOM, EDNA. "Motor Ability of High-School Girls." *J Ed Res* 26:593–4 Ap '33. * (*PA* 7:4070)
21. DODGE, ARTHUR F. "Occupational Ability Patterns." *Teach Col Contrib Ed* 658:1–97 '35. * (*PA* 9:5877)
22. BRENTLINGER, W. H. "The Abilities and Occupational History of Transients: A Preliminary Study." *J Appl Psychol* 20:105–13 F '36. * (*PA* 10:3673)
23. FIALKIN, H. N., AND BECKMAN, R. O. "The Influence of Month of Birth on the Intelligence Test Scores of Adults." *J Genetic Psychol* 52:203–9 Mr '38. * (*PA* 13:172)
24. PATERSON, DONALD G.; SCHNEIDLER, GWENDOLEN G.; AND WILLIAMSON, EDMUND G. *Student Guidance Techniques,* pp. 63–6. New York: McGraw-Hill Book Co., Inc., 1938. Pp. xviii, 316. * (*PA* 12:2131)
25. NEMZEK, CLAUDE L. "A Note Concerning Direct and Differential Prediction of Academic Success." *J Social Psychol* 15:325–30 My '42. * (*PA* 16:4543)
26. SHULTZ, IRVIN T., AND RUSH, HARVEY. "Comparison of the Occupational Ranking and Interests, Education and Intelligence of Patients at Sunnyside Sanatorium." *J Appl Psychol* 26:218–26 Ap '42. * (*PA* 16:4184)

CUMULATIVE NAME INDEX

Beckman, R. O.: 23
Bender, W. R. G.: 11
Berman, I. R.: 7
Brannom, E.: 20
Brentlinger, W. H.: 22
Clark, G. Y.: 19
Cronin, M.: 20
Dodge, A. F.: 21
Durost, W. N.: *rev,* 6:488
Fialkin, H. N.: 23
Finch, F. H.: 6
Foran, T. G.: 12
Ghiselli, E. E.: 10
Green, H. J.: 7
Hackman, R. C.: 9
Heckman, S. B.: 13
Henmon, V. A. C.: 1
Long, G. S.: 16
Lorge, I.: 8

Loveless, H. E.: 11
McGraw, M. L.: 18
Mangold, M. C.: 18
Miller, W. S.: 3, 5, 14
Nemzek, C. L.: 20, 25
Paterson, D. G.: 7, 24
Pressey, L. C.: 2
Pressey, L. W.: 15
Pressey, S. L.: 2, 16
Rush, H.: 26
Sangren, P. V.: 4
Schneidler, G. G.: 24
Shultz, I. T.: 26
South, E. B.: 19
Streitz, R.: 1
Stroud, J. B.: 17
Trabue, M. R.: 7
Williamson, E. G.: 24

[439]

Progressive Matrices. Ages 5 and over; 1938–65; PM; 3 levels; J. C. Raven; H. K. Lewis & Co. Ltd.

Pressey Classification and Verifying Tests

[England]. * (United States distributor: Psychological Corporation.)
a) STANDARD PROGRESSIVE MATRICES. Ages 6 and over; 1938–60; manual also uses the title *Progressive Matrices (1938), 1956 Revision;* 1956 test identical with test copyrighted 1938 except for 1 revised item and item sequence; 1960 manual identical with 1956 manual except for bibliography.
b) COLOURED PROGRESSIVE MATRICES. Ages 5–11 and mental patients and senescents; 1947–63.
c) ADVANCED PROGRESSIVE MATRICES. Ages 11 and over; 1943–65; 2 editions.
  1) *Progressive Matrices (1947): Set 1.* For use either as a practice test for Set 2 or as a rough screening test.
  2) *Advanced Progressive Matrices, Set 2: 1962 Revision.*
For additional information, see 7:376 (194 references); for a review by Morton Bortner, see 6:490 (78 references); see also 5:370 (62 references); for reviews by Charlotte Banks, W. D. Wall, and George Westby, see 4:314 (32 references); for reviews by Walter C. Shipley and David Wechsler of the 1938 edition, see 3:258 (13 references); for a review by T. J. Keating, see 2:1417 (8 references).

REFERENCES THROUGH 1971

1–8. See 2:1417.
9–21. See 3:258.
22–53. See 4:314.
54–115. See 5:370.
116–193. See 6:490.
194–387. See 7:376.
388. ADCOCK, CYRIL. "A Re-Analysis of Slater's Spatial Judgment Research." *Occup Psychol* (England) 22:213–6 O '48. * (*PA* 23:1691)
389. BIESHEUVEL, S. Chap. 4, "Psychological Tests and Their Applications to Non-European Peoples," pp. 87–126. In *The Yearbook of Education, 1949.* London: Evans Brothers Ltd., 1949. Pp. xv, 660. *
390. WICKHAM, MARY. "Follow-Up of Personnel Selection in the A.T.S." *Occup Psychol* (England) 23:153–69 Jl '49. * (*PA* 24:1504)
391. NOTCUTT, B. "The Measurement of Zulu Intelligence." *J Social Res* (South Africa) 1:195–206 D '50. * (*PA* 27:4186)
392. SUTTON, R. V., AND MITCHELL, L. "Preliminary Report on the Validation of Aptitude Tests for the Selection of Articled Clerks." *B Nat Inst Pers Res* (South Africa) 3:4–13 F '51. * (*PA* 27:1488)
393. DAVIES-EYSENCK, MARGARET. "Cognitive Factors in Epilepsy." *J Neurol Neurosurg & Psychiatry* (England) 15:39–44 F '52. * (*PA* 27:2918)
394. KALDEGG, A. "Migraine Patients: A Discussion of Some Test Results." *J Mental Sci* (England) 98:672–82 O '52. * (*PA* 27:6067)
395. PINKERTON, PHILIP, AND KELLEY, JOSEPH. "An Attempted Correlation Between Clinical and Psychometric Findings in Senile-Arteriosclerotic Dementia." *J Mental Sci* (England) 98:244–55 Ap '52. * (*PA* 27:585)
396. STRUCKETT, PAULINE B. A. "Effect of Prefrontal Lobotomy on Intellectual Functioning in Chronic Schizophrenia." *Arch Neurol & Psychiatry* 69:293–304 Mr '53. * (*PA* 28:1346)
397. PITTS, R., AND SIMON, A. "A Psychological and Educational Study of a Group of Male Prisoners." *Brit J Ed Psychol* 24:106–21 Je '54. * (*PA* 29:2748)
398. SMITH, I. MACFARLANE. "The Development of a Spatial Test." *Durham Ed R* (England) 1(5):19–33 S '54. * (*PA* 29:7298)
399. FOULDS, G. A. "The Reliability of Psychiatric, and the Validity of Psychological, Diagnoses." *J Mental Sci* (England) 101:851–62 O '55. * (*PA* 30:7165)
400. HOPKINS, BARBARA, AND POST, FELIX. "The Significance of Abstract and Concrete Behaviour in Elderly Psychiatric Patients and Control Subjects." *J Mental Sci* (England) 101:841–50 O '55. * (*PA* 30:7000)
401. MARCUS, B. "Intelligence, Criminality and the Expectation of Recidivism." *Brit J Deling* 6:147–51 S '55. * (*PA* 30:4914)
402. MEYER, VICTOR, AND YATES, AUBREY J. "Intellectual Changes Following Temporal Lobectomy for Psychomotor Epilepsy: Preliminary Communication." *J Neurol Neurosurg & Psychiatry* (England) 18:44–52 F '55. * (*PA* 29:7775)
403. PICHOT, PIERRE. "Language Disturbances in Cerebral Disease; Concept of Latent Aphasia." *Arch Neurol & Psychiatry* 74:92–6 Jl '55. * (*PA* 30:3225)
404. JAHODA, GUSTAV. "Assessment of Abstract Behavior in a

Non-Western Culture." *J Abn & Social Psychol* 53:237–43 S '56. * *(PA 32:2798)*

405. JORDAN, THOMAS E. "Psychological Findings in a Case of Von Recklinghausen's Disease and Hyperpituitarism." *J Clin Psychol* 12:389–91 O '56. * *(PA 32:4470)*

406. WARBURTON, F. W., AND VENABLES, E. C. "Relationship Between the Intelligence of Technical College Students and Size of Family." *Eug R* (England) 47:245 Ja '56. * *(PA 31:2530)*

407. BAUER, ROBERT W., AND JOHNSON, DERWOOD E. "The Question of Deterioration in Alcoholism." Abstract. *J Consult Psychol* 21:296 Ag '57. * *(PA 33:1669)*

408. HANDEL, AMOS. "The Suitability of Certain Non-Verbal Tests for Testing Immigrants in Israel." *J Ed Res* 51:55–8 S '57. * *(PA 33:2164)*

409. MUNDY, LYDIA. "Environmental Influence on Intellectual Function as Measured by Intelligence Tests." *Brit J Med Psychol* 30:194–201 pt 3 '57. * *(PA 33:791)*

410. YOUNG, CECIL, AND McCONNELL, FREEMAN. "Retardation of Vocabulary Development in Hard of Hearing Children." *Excep Children* 23:368–70 My '57. * *(PA 33:4509)*

411. CALLAWAY, ENOCH, III, AND BAND, RAYMOND I. "Some Psychopharmacological Effects of Atropine: Preliminary Investigation of Broadened Attention." *Arch Neurol & Psychiatry* 79:91–102 Ja '58. * *(PA 33:5502)*

412. HILDEBRAND, H. P. "A Factorial Study of Introversion-Extraversion." *Brit J Psychol* 49:1–11 F '58. * *(PA 33:8632)*

413. VIEL, BENJAMIN, AND REQUENA, MARIANO. "Analysis of the Results Obtained With the Entrance Examination in the School of Medicine of the University of Chile." *J Med Ed* 33:352–62 Ap '58. * *(PA 34:2291)*

414. JAHODA, GUSTAV. "Development of the Perception of Social Differences in Children From 6 to 10." *Brit J Psychol* 50:159–75 My '59. * *(PA 34:2826)*

415. JARVIE, HUGH. "Problem-Solving Deficits Following Wounds of the Brain." *J Mental Sci* (England) 106:1377–82 O '60. * *(PA 35:5145)*

416. MORAN, R. E. "Levels of Attainment of Educable Subnormal Adolescents." *Brit J Ed Psychol* 30:201–10 N '60. * *(PA 37:3584)*

417. RAO, C. K. VASUDEVA. "Intelligence in a Group of Convicts: An Analysis of 35 Cases." *Trans All-India Inst Mental Health* 1:44–53 D '60. * *(PA 37:3649)*

418. WILLIAMS, MOYRA. "The Effect of Past Experience on Mental Test Performance in the Elderly." *Brit J Med Psychol* 33:215–9 pt 2 '60. * *(PA 36:4FI15W)*

419. DOWIS, JAMES L., AND BUCHANAN, CHARLES E. "Some Relationships Between Intellectual Efficiency and the Severity of Psychiatric Illness." *J Psychol* 51:371–81 Ap '61. * *(PA 35:6905)*

420. BIGGS, J. B. "The Relation of Neuroticism and Extraversion to Intelligence and Educational Attainment." *Brit J Ed Psychol* 32:188–99 Je '62. * *(PA 37:3123)*

421. BRENGELMANN, JOHANNES C., AND LINDAHL, LESLIE E. H. "Personality, Task Difficulty, and Level of Memory Performance." *Archiv für die Gesamte Psychologie* (West Germany) 114:242–59 D '62. * *(PA 38:1179)*

422. DAS, J. P., AND MITRA, A. K. "Relative Effectiveness of Electric Shock and Praise and Reproof in Verbal Conditioning." *J General Psychol* 67:141–6 Jl '62. * *(PA 37:2442)*

423. KNEHR, CHARLES A. "Psychological Assessment of Differential Impairment in Cerebral Organic Conditions and Schizophrenics." *J Psychol* 54:165–89 Jl '62. * *(PA 37:3695)*

424. ORME, J. E. "Intelligence and Season of Birth." *Brit J Med Psychol* 35:233–4 pt 3 '62. * *(PA 37:4963)*

425. PIERCY, MALCOLM M., AND SMYTH, V. O. G. "Right Hemisphere Dominance for Certain Non-Verbal Intellectual Skills." *Brain* (England) 85:775–90 D '62. *

426. SAMPSON, OLIVE C. "Reading Skill at Eight Years in Relation to Speech and Other Factors." *Brit J Ed Psychol* 32: 12–7 F '62. *

427. SHAFFER, JOHN W.; FREINEK, WILFRIED R.; WOLF, SIDNEY; FOXWELL, NANCY H.; AND KURLAND, ALBERT A. "A Controlled Evaluation of Chlordiazepoxide (Librium) in the Treatment of Convalescing Alcoholics." *J Nerv & Mental Dis* 137:494–507 N '63. * *(PA 39:5332)*

428. HALLWORTH, H. J. "Personality Ratings of Adolescents: A Study in a Comprehensive School." *Brit J Ed Psychol* 34: 171–7 Je '64. * *(PA 39:3180)*

429. JUEL-NIELSEN, NIELS. "Individual and Environment: A Psychiatric-Psychological Investigation of Monozygotic Twins Reared Apart." *Acta Psychiatrica Scandinavica Supplementum* (Denmark) 183:1–292 '64. *

430. LEVITA, ERIC; RIKLAN, MANUEL; AND COOPER, IRVING S. "Cognitive and Perceptual Performance in Parkinsonism as a Function of Age and Neurological Impairment." *J Nerv & Mental Dis* 139:516–20 D '64. * *(PA 39:10554)*

431. DAS, RHEA S. "An Application of Factor and Canonical Analysis to Multivariate Data." *Brit J Math & Stat Psychol* 18:57–67 My '65. * *(PA 39:13270)*

432. DIXON, JAMES C. "Cognitive Structure in Senile Conditions With Some Suggestions for Developing a Brief Screening Test of Mental Status." *J Gerontol* 20:41–9 Ja '65. *

433. JAMAL, SHABNAM. "The Validity of Raven's Coloured Progressive Matrices and Otis Quick Scoring Mental Ability Test for Pakistani Children." *B Ed & Res* (Pakistan) 4(1):25–41 '65. *

434. KNEHR, CHARLES A. "Revised Approach to Detection of Cerebral Damage: Progressive Matrices Revisited." *Psychol Rep* 17:71–7 Ag '65. * *(PA 40:1891)*

435. BARRY, ALAN J.; STEINMETZ, JOHN R.; PAGE, HENRY F.; AND RODAHL, KAARE. "The Effects of Physical Conditioning on Older Individuals: 2, Motor Performance and Cognitive Function." *J Gerontol* 21:192–9 Ap '66. *

436. BEVANS, H. G. "Confidence (Probability) Scoring for the Standard Progressive Matrices (1956) and the Advanced Matrices." Abstract. *B Brit Psychol Soc* 19:A15 Ap '66. *

437. EVANS, LIONEL. "A Comparative Study of the Wechsler Intelligence Scale for Children (Performance) and Raven's Progressive Matrices With Deaf Children." *Teach Deaf* (England) 64:76–82 Mr '66. *

438. MACARTHUR, R. S., AND MOSYCHUK, H. "Lower and Upper Socioeconomic Group Contrasts in Long-Term Predictability of Grade Nine Achievement." *J Ed Meas* 3:167–8 su '66. *

439. ARNOLD, ELIZABETH M. "Is Temporal Integration a Distinct Mental Ability?" *Austral J Psychol* 19:41–7 Ap '67. * *(PA 41:11914)*

440. KINSBOURNE, MARCEL. "Effect of Focal Cerebral Lesions on Perspective and Movement Reversals." *J Nerv & Mental Dis* 144:139–44 F '67. * *(PA 41:12356)*

441. LEVITA, ERIC, AND RIKLAN, MANUEL. "Patterns of Psychological Function Before, After Unilateral, and After Bilateral Thalamic Surgery." *Percept & Motor Skills* 24:619–26 Ap '67. * *(PA 41:9973)*

442. MOLEMA, SEODI Y. *A Comparison of Associative and Conceptual Thinking as Indicated by Two Non-Language Tests Among Lower and Higher Socioeconomic Negro Children in Elementary School.* Master's thesis, Catholic University of America (Washington, D.C.), 1967.

443. CHOPRA, SUKHENDRA L. "Measured Intelligence and Academic Achievement as Related to Urban-Rural Residence." Letter. *Rural Sociol* 33:214–7 Je '68. * *(PA 43:730)*

444. DAVIES, ANN D. M. "Measurement of Mental Deterioration in Aging and Brain Damage." Discussion by Walter W. Surwillo. *Interdiscipl Topics Gerontol* 1:78–92 '68. *

445. DE-NOUR, ATARA K.; SHALTIEL, JUDITH; AND CZACZKES, J. W. "Emotional Reactions of Patients on Chronic Hemodialysis." *Psychosom Med* 30:521–33 S–O '68. * *(PA 43:8624)*

446. FREYBERG, P. S. "Fluctuations in Children's Cognitive Test Scores Over a Two-Year Period." *Brit J Ed Psychol* 38: 82–6 F '68. * *(PA 42:12731)*

447. HALSTEAD, HERBERT, AND NEAL, C. DAVID. "Intelligence and Personality in Drug Addicts: A Pilot Study." *Brit J Addict* 63:237–40 D '68. *

448. HICHENS, JOHN H. "Speed, Level, Power and Progressive Matrices." Abstract. *Papers Psychol* (Northern Ireland) 2:72–3 O '68. *

449. JACOBS, PAUL I. "The Development, Use and Evaluation of Self-Instructional Programs in Israel." *J Exp Ed* 36:59–69 sp '68. *

450. JENSEN, ARTHUR R. "Patterns of Mental Ability and Socioeconomic Status." *Proc Nat Acad Sci* 60:1330–7 Ag 15 '68. *

451. MONTGOMERY, G. W. G. "A Factorial Study of Communication and Ability in Deaf School Leavers." *Brit J Ed Psychol* 38:27–37 F '68. * *(PA 42:12755)*

452. BROADHURST, ANNE. "Time Estimation Related to Personality, Cognitive Speed and Schizophrenia." *Life Sci* (England) 8(pt 2, 2):69–78 Ja 15 '69. * *(PA 45:2722)*

453. FREEMAN, JAMES; M'COMISKY, JAMES G.; AND BUTTLE, DEREK. "Student Selection: A Comparative Study of Student Entrants to Architecture and Economics." *Ed Sci* (England) 3(3):189–97 D '69. *

454. HASETH, KJELL; SHAGASS, CHARLES; AND STRAUMANIS, JOHN J. "Perceptual and Personality Correlates of EEG and Evoked Response Measures." *Biol Psychiatry* 1(1):49–60 Ja '69. * *(PA 46:4440)*

455. IRVINE, S. H. "How Fair Is Culture? Factorial Studies of Raven's Progressive Matrices Across Cultures in Africa," pp. 372–87. In *Developments in Educational Testing: The Proceedings of an International Conference Held Under the Aegis of the Pädagogisches Zentrum, Berlin, Vols. 1 and 2.* Edited by Karlheinz Ingenkamp. London: University of London Press Ltd., 1969. Pp. 446, 502. *

456. JAMIESON, G. HARRY. "Prior Learning and Response Flexibility in Two Age Groups." *J Gerontol* 24(2):179–83 Ap '69. *

457. WETHERICK, N. E.; FITZSIMMONS, ELIZABETH K.; AND HILLS, D. A. "Inductive Thinking in Subnormals." *J Mental Subnorm* (England) 15(2):79–84 D '69. * *(PA 44:16917)*

458. BEACH, JOE EDWARD. *A Study of the Relationship of Intelligence and Academic Achievement of a Selected Group of Deaf Pupils.* Master's thesis, Mississippi State University (State College, Miss.), 1970.

459. BLANTON, WILLIAM ELGIT. *The Interactive Effects of Perceptual Centration and Decentration on Reading Readiness and Reading Achievement at the First Grade Level.* Doctor's thesis, University of Georgia (Athens, Ga.), 1970. *(DAI 31: 5837A)*

460. BOLLINGER, RICK LEONARD. *Communication Abilities of*

"Chronic Brain Syndrome" Patients. Doctor's thesis, University of Washington (Seattle, Wash.), 1970. (*DAI* 32:610B)

461. COMSTOCK, JOHN ALLAN. *The Relationship Between Clinically Derived Scores of Employability and Employability Scores Predicted by an Employability Model for Mentally Retarded Adolescents.* Doctor's thesis, University of Minnesota (Minneapolis, Minn.), 1970. (*DAI* 32:271A)

462. DAS, J. P.; JACHUCK, KASTURI; AND PANDA, T. P. Chap. 23, "Cultural Deprivation and Cognitive Growth," pp. 587–604. In *Social-Cultural Aspects of Mental Retardation: Proceedings of the Peabody-NIMH Conference.* Edited by H. Carl Haywood. New York: Appleton-Century-Crofts, 1970. Pp. xvii, 798. *

463. DAVAGE, P. P. E., AND WILKINSON, V. J. "The Intelligence of Voluntary Mental Hospital Admissions: A Pilot Study." *N Zeal Med J* 72(459):96–8 Ag '70. *

464. DICKER, LEO. *Retardation of 9–14 Year Old Deaf Students on the 1938 Raven's Progressive Matrices.* Doctor's thesis, University of Kansas (Lawrence, Kan.), 1970. (*DAI* 31:5884A)

465. DURR, LEWIS. "Personality Profile of the Successful Pilot." *Airline Mgmt & Marketing* 2(10):79–80+ O '70. *

466. ELEFAÑO, INOCENCIA PATIÑO. *Predicting the Educability of Children From Low Socioeconomic Status Homes.* Doctor's thesis, Rutgers—The State University (New Brunswick, N.J.), 1970. (*DAI* 32:667A)

467. FAROQI, M. A. "A Study of Errors Made by Children on Progressive Matrices Test." *J Ed Res & Exten* (India) 7(2): 65–73 O '70. *

468. FEIN, SOPHIA RICHMAN. *Conceptual Tempo and Abstract Reasoning in College Students: A Study of the Effects of Individual Differences in Speed and Confidence of Judgment on Abstract Reasoning Performance of College Females.* Doctor's thesis, New York University (New York, N.Y.), 1970. (*DAI* 31:5840A)

469. NORDÉN, K. "The Structure of Abilities in a Group of Deaf Adolescents." *Ed & Psychol Interactions* (Sweden) 32: 1–22 '70. * (*PA* 44:15094)

470. PAITICH, DANIEL. "The Clarke Automated Psychological Examination and Report (CAPER)." *Ont Psychologist* (Canada) 2(5):304–14 '70. *

471. SHANAN, JOEL; KEDAR, HANNAH; ELIAKIM, MARCEL; OSTER, ZVI H.; AND PRYWES, MOSHE. "Evolution of Selection Methods for Admission to Medical School: 3, Psychological Tests in the Selection of Medical Students." *Israel J Med Sci* 6(1): 132–44 Ja–F '70. *

472. WOOSTER, ARTHUR D. "Social and Ethnic Differences in Understanding the Spoken Word." *Brit J Dis Commun* 5(2): 118–25 O '70. *

473. BART, LEONARD EUGENE. *A Comparison of the Effectiveness of Televised and Conventional Administrations of Objective Scales.* Doctor's thesis, St. John's University (Jamaica, N.Y.), 1971. (*DAI* 32:2980B)

474. BERRY, J. W. "Ecological and Cultural Factors in Spatial Perceptual Development." *Can J Behav Sci* 3(4):324–36 O '71. * (*PA* 47:8577)

475. BEYEL, VIRGINIA; FRACCHIA, JOHN; SHEPPARD, CHARLES; AND MERLIS, SIDNEY. "Relationships Among Raven Progressive Matrices Avoidable and Atypical Errors and Bender Gestalt Errors." *Percept & Motor Skills* 33(3):1269–70 D '71. * (*PA* 48:3366)

476. BIGGS, J. B.; FITZGERALD, D.; AND ATKINSON, SONIA M. "Convergent and Divergent Abilities in Children and Teachers' Ratings of Competence and Certain Classroom Behaviours." *Brit J Ed Psychol* 41(3):277–86 N '71. * (*PA* 47:11600)

477. BOLTON, BRIAN. "A Factor Analytic Study of Communication Skills and Nonverbal Abilities of Deaf Rehabilitation Clients." *Multiv Behav Res* 6(4):485–501 O '71. * (*PA* 47: 11373)

478. CANTWELL, ZITA M. "Teachers' Perceptions of Levels of Performances of Students From an Economically Disadvantaged Urban Area." *Percept & Motor Skills* 32(2):593–4 Ap '71. * (*PA* 46:11646)

479. CARLSON, J. S. "Some Relationships Between Class Inclusion, Perceptual Capabilities, Verbal Capabilities and Race." *Hum Develop* (Switzerland) 14(1):30–8 '71. * (*PA* 47:2617)

480. CARLSON, JERRY S. "Some Relationships Between Verbal and Perceptual Capabilities and the Development of Relative Thinking." *J Genetic Psychol* 118(1):115–9 Mr '71. * (*PA* 46:8724)

481. CHEYNE, WILLIAM M., AND JAHODA, GUSTAV. "Emotional Sensitivity and Intelligence in Children From Orphanages and Normal Homes." *J Child Psychol & Psychiatry* (England) 12(2):77–90 Je '71. * (*PA* 47:4505)

482. DESHPANDE, M. V. "Sex Differences on Raven's Matrices Test—(Coloured Form)." *J Psychol Res* (India) 15(3):101–3 S '71. *

483. EISENTHAL, SHERMAN, AND HARFORD, THOMAS. "Correlation Between the Raven Progressive Matrices Scale and the Shipley Institute of Living Scale." *J Clin Psychol* 27(2):213–5 Ap '71. * (*PA* 46:7158)

484. EYSENCK, HANS J. "Relation Between Intelligence and Personality." *Percept & Motor Skills* 32(2):637–8 Ap '71. * (*PA* 46:10929)

485. FITZ-GIBBON, CAROL T. *An Investigation of Advanced Progressive Matrices (1962) as a Selection Instrument for*

Mentally Gifted Students in Inner-City Schools. Master's thesis, University of California (Los Angeles, Calif.), 1971.

486. FURR, KARL D., AND LANDRUS, GARY. "Raven Progressive Matrices Norms for Toronto, Canada." *Ont Psychologist* (Canada) 3(3):160–2 '71. *

487. GRANICK, SAMUEL. "Brief Tests and Their Interrelations as Intelligence Measures of Aged Subjects." Abstract. *Proc 79th Ann Conv Am Psychol Assn* 6(2):599–600 '71. * (*PA* 46:4727)

488. GREEN, RICHARD B., AND ROHWER, WILLIAM D., JR. "SES Differences on Learning and Ability Tests in Black Children." *Am Ed Res J* 8(4):601–9 N '71. * (*PA* 47:11611)

489. GUINAGH, BARRY J. "An Experimental Study of Basic Learning Ability and Intelligence in Low-Socioeconomic-Status Children." *Child Develop* 42(1):27–36 Mr '71. * (*PA* 46:4669)

490. HUNDAL, P. S., AND SINGH, MOHINDER. "A Factor Analytical Study of Intellectual and Non-Intellectual Characteristics." *Multiv Behav Res* 6(4):503–14 O '71. * (*PA* 47:11735)

491. JACOBS, PAUL I., AND VANDEVENTER, MARY. "The Learning and Transfer of Double-Classification Skills by First Graders." *Child Develop* 42(1):149–59 Mr '71. * (*PA* 46:4642)

492. JENSEN, ARTHUR R. "Do Schools Cheat Minority Children?" *Ed Res* (England) 14(1):3–28 N '71. * (*PA* 49:11953)

493. JONES, BEN MORGAN. "Verbal and Spatial Intelligence in Short and Long Term Alcoholics." *J Nerv & Mental Dis* 153(4):292–7 O '71. * (*PA* 47:11157)

494. KLINGELHOFER, E. L. "A Note on Language, School, and Examiner Effects on the Performance of Tanzanian Schoolchildren on Raven's Standard Progressive Matrices Test." *J Social Psychol* 83(1):145–6 F '71. * (*PA* 45:8230)

495. LANGEVIN, R. "Is Curiosity a Unitary Construct?" *Can J Psychol* 25(4):360–74 au '71. * (*PA* 45:5607)

496. LEMKE, ELMER A., AND KIRCHNER, JOHN H. "A Multivariate Study of Handwriting, Intelligence, and Personality Correlates." *J Pers Assess* 35(6):584–92 D '71. * (*PA* 47: 10876)

497. LOVIUS, B. B. J. "Speech and Intelligence in Adult Cleft-Palate Patients." *Dental Prac & Dental Rec* 21(8):290–3 Ap '71. *

498. MATHER, LEONARD JOSEPH. *A Causal Comparative Study of Intellectual Functioning in Good and Poor Readers.* Doctor's thesis, Catholic University of America (Washington, D.C.), 1971. (*DAI* 32:1920A)

499. MOHAN, VIDHU, AND MOHAN, JITENDRA. "Scores on Two Intelligence Tests and Seasons of Birth." *Psychologia* (Japan) 14(3–4):170–4 D '71. * (*PA* 49:863)

500. MOYLES, E. WILLIAM, AND WOLINS, MARTIN. "Group Care and Intellectual Development." *Develop Psychol* 4(3):370–80 My '71. * (*PA* 46:6543)

501. PRICE, JAMES DAVID. *Analysis of Changes in Intelligence Test Scores of Mexican-American Youth Assigned to Special Classes in Relation to Jensen's Two-Level Theory of Mental Abilities.* Doctor's thesis, University of Arizona (Tucson, Ariz.), 1971. (*DAI* 32:3125A)

502. PRINGLE, ROGER K., AND HAANSTAD, MARTIN. "Estimating WAIS IQs From Progressive Matrices and Shipley-Hartford Scores." *J Clin Psychol* 27(4):479–81 O '71. * (*PA* 47:8929)

503. RAMIREZ, JUDITH VALLA. "Effects of Tutorial Experiences on the Problem-Solving Behavior of Sixth-Graders." *Calif J Ed Res* 22(2):80–90 Mr '71. *

504. RAO, S. NARAYANA. "A Prognostic Study of Achievement in Relation to Academic Adjustment." *Indian Ed R* 6(2):196–213 Jl '71. *

505. ROHWER, WILLIAM D., JR.; AMMON, MARY SUE; SUZUKI, NANCY; AND LEVIN, JOEL R. "Population Differences and Learning Proficiency." *J Ed Psychol* 62(1):1–14 F '71. * (*PA* 46:3844)

506. ROHWER, WILLIAM D., JR., AND LEVIN, JOEL R. "Elaboration Preferences and Differences in Learning Proficiency." *Cognitive Studies* 2:127–48 '71. * (*PA* 49:1354, title only)

507. THORSEN, ERIC EDWARD. *The Heritability of "G" and Figural Divergent Thinking.* Doctor's thesis, Boston College (Chestnut Hill, Mass.), 1971. (*DAI* 32:1351A)

508. WEINER, PAUL S. "The Cognitive Functioning of Language Deficient Children." *Cognitive Studies* 2:338–63 '71. *

509. WILSON, GLENN D.; TUNSTALL, OLIVE A.; AND EYSENCK, H. J. "Individual Differences in Tapping Performance as a Function of Time on the Task." *Percept & Motor Skills* 33(2):375–8 O '71. * (*PA* 47:6073)

CUMULATIVE NAME INDEX

Beach, J. E.: 458
Beck, E. J.: 218
Bennett, C. M.: 106
Bennett, E.: 56
Berry, J. W.: 474
Besijn, J. W.: 384
Bevan, W. E.: 343
Bevans, H. G.: 436
Beyel, V.: 475
Biesheuvel, S.: 116, 389
Biggs, J. B.: 420, 476
Bingham, W. C.: 254, 345
Birkemeyer, F.: 219, 236
Birren, J. E.: 213
Blanton, W. E.: 459
Blazsanyik, J.: 167
Blue, A. W.: 344
Blumenkrantz, J.: 310
Boeke, P. E.: 384
Bolin, B. J.: 83
Bollinger, R. L.: 460
Bolton, B.: 477
Bolton, F. B.: 84
Bortner, M.: rev, 6:490
Botwinick, J.: 213
Bradford, E. J. G.: 11
Bradley, B. H.: 220
Brengelmann, J. C.: 421
Brimble, A. R.: 230
Broadhurst, A.: 452
Bromley, D. B.: 69
Brown, R.: 149
Buchanan, C. E.: 419
Bucklow, M.: 103
Budoff, M.: 282
Burke, H. R.: 112, 254, 345
Burnett, A.: 182
Buttle, D.: 453
Caine, T. A.: 121
Callaway, E.: 411
Canabal, J. V.: 368
Cankardas, A.: 119
Cantwell, Z. M.: 255, 283, 478
Carleton, F. O.: 93
Carlson, J. S.: 369, 479–80
Casey, D. L.: 150
Cashdan, A.: 237
Cassel, R. H.: 34
Castetter, J. S.: 98
Cate, C. C.: 284
Cattell, R. B.: 120
Cheyne, W. M.: 481
Chopra, S. L.: 443
Chown, S.: 289
Chun, R. W. M.: 323
Clark, P. J.: 154
Collins, L.: 334–5, 366
Collins, M. G.: 118
Colonna, A.: 256
Comstock, J. A.: 461
Cook, C.: 278, 308
Cooper, I. S.: 430
Costa, L. D.: 346
Costello, C. G.: 126
Cowley, J. J.: 116
Crawford, A.: 85
Crawford, J. M.: 48
Crickmore, L.: 311
Crookes, T. G.: 155
Curr, W.: 99
Curtin, M. E.: 156
Czaczkes, J. W.: 445
Das, J. P.: 312, 422, 462
Das, R. S.: 431
Dasgupta, J.: 297
Dash, S. C.: 127
Davage, P. P. E.: 463
Davidson, M.: 3
Davies, A. D. M.: 265, 444
Davies-Eysenck, M.: 393
Davis, L.: 115
Davis, W. E.: 370
Davison, L.: 115
DeBurger, R. A.: 156
DeCharms, R.: 132
Dekker, L. C.: 287
Denny, C.: 156
De-Nour, A. K.: 445
De Renzi, E.: 238
Desai, M.: 19, 62
Desai, M. M.: 86, 142
Deshpande, M. V.: 482
DeWolfe, A. S.: 370
Dhar, C.: 198

Dicker, L.: 464
Dils, C. W.: 143
Dingman, H. F.: 177
Dirks, D. D.: 204
Dixon, J. C.: 432
Dixon, P.: 169–71
Dizzonne, M. F.: 370
Domino, G.: 313
Doughty, P.: 103
Dowis, J. L.: 419
Durr, L.: 465
Dutta, D.: 297
Dutta, T.: 312
Dwarshuis, L.: 303
Edelstein, G.: 189
Edholm, O. G.: 15
Edwards, A. E.: 183
Eisenthal, S.: 347, 351, 483
Elefaño, I. P.: 466
Eliakim, M.: 471
Elkin, L.: 314
Elley, W. B.: 168, 188
Elonen, A. S.: 71
Esbenshade, A. A.: 203
Esher, F. J. S.: 54
Estes, B. W.: 156
Evans, L.: 437
Evans, R. B.: 184, 221
Ewert, J. C.: 87
Eysenck, H. J.: 12, 16, 19, 484, 509
Eysenck, M. D.: 17
Faglioni, P.: 238, 256
Faroqi, M. A.: 467
Fein, S. R.: 468
Feinberg, I.: 157
Fiedler, E. R.: 349
Finney, B. J.: 315
Finnie, F. R.: 316
Fiorentino, D.: 334–5, 348, 366, 372
Fitch, M. J.: 257
Fitzgerald, D.: 476
Fitz-Gibbon, C. T.: 485
Fitzsimmons, E. K.: 457
Fleming, J. M.: 285
Forbes, A. R.: 222
Foulds, G. A.: 26–7, 35, 42–3, 121, 128, 169–71, 223, 371, 399
Foxwell, N. H.: 427
Fracchia, J.: 372–3, 475
Fracchia, J. F.: 348
Frank, H.: 349
Freeman, S.: 113
Freinek, W. R.: 427
French, J. G.: 155
Freyberg, P. S.: 258, 446
Frisby, C. B.: 208
Fuller, C. W.: 199
Furneaux, W. D.: 19
Furr, K. D.: 486
Gabriel, K. R.: 78
Ganguly, A.: 286
Garman, E. M.: 157
Gaskill, P.: 104
Gibbens, T. C. N.: 214
Gibson, H. B.: 374
Gibson, Q. H.: 15, 57
Giles, G. C.: 224
Gill, M. R.: 94
Goetzinger, C. P.: 204, 287
Goetzinger, M. R.: 350
Gordon, I. E.: 160
Gourlay, N.: 99
Gowan, J. C.: 226, 294
Grabow, J. D.: 323
Granick, S.: 487
Gray, J. E.: 343
Green, M. W.: 87
Green, R. B.: 488
Grosvenor, T.: 375
Guinagh, B. J.: 489
Gupta, G. C.: 259
Gupta, K. P.: 239
Gupta, S.: 259
Gwynne Jones, H.: 100
Haanstad, M.: 502
Hake, D.: 149
Hall, J. C.: 105
Hallworth, H. J.: 428
Halstead, H.: 13, 18–9, 44, 447
Hamilton, V.: 185
Handel, A.: 408

Harding, D. W.: 14
Harford, T.: 288, 317, 347, 351, 483
Harris, D. B.: 129
Häseth, K.: 454
Hazari, A.: 144, 376
Hegge, T. G.: 71
Heim, A. W.: 45, 59
Heron, A.: 289
Hichens, J. H.: 448
Higashimachi, W. H.: 186
Higdon, B. P.: 158
Higgins, C.: 122
Hildebrand, H. P.: 412
Hills, D. A.: 457
Himmelweit, H. T.: 19
Holden, R. H.: 51
Hopkins, B.: 70, 75, 400
Horwitz, M.: 346
Houchins, R. R.: 350
Hundal, P. S.: 490
Hutchins, B. E.: 318
Hwang, C. H.: 352
Irvine, S. H.: 230, 260, 353–4, 455
Irving, G.: 377
Iscoe, I.: 79, 90, 269
Jachuck, K.: 462
Jacobs, G. F.: 116
Jacobs, P. I.: 261, 319, 378, 449, 491
Jahoda, G.: 404, 414, 481
Jain, K. S. P.: 225
Jamal, S.: 433
Jamieson, G. H.: 456
Jamuar, K. K.: 159
Jarvie, H.: 415
Jastak, J.: 36
Jensen, A. R.: 130, 450, 492
Johnson, C. A.: 290
Johnson, D. E.: 407
Johnson, D. L.: 290
Johnson, E. Z.: 63–4, 71–3
Johnson, J. E.: 379
Johnson, S. A. H.: 262
Jones, B. M.: 493
Jones, L. V.: 279–80
Jordan, T. E.: 88, 106, 131–2, 172, 405
Juel-Nielsen, N.: 429
Jurjevich, R. M.: 291–2
Kakkar, A.: 240
Kaldegg, A.: 394
Kanungo, R.: 127
Kasper, S.: 113
Kear-Colwell, J. J.: 380
Keating, T. J.: rev, 2:1417
Kebbon, L.: 241
Kedar, H.: 471
Keehn, J. D.: 89
Keir, G.: 37
Kelley, J.: 395
Kenchaveeraiah, B.: 320
Kern, F. E.: 278, 308
Khatena, J.: 226, 242–3, 293–4
Kiang, C. G.: 226
Kilburn, K. L.: 263–4
King, W. H.: 187
Kingsley, L.: 355
Kinsbourne, M.: 440
Kirchner, J. H.: 496
Kirk, J.: 386
Klein, J.: 244
Klingelhofer, E. L.: 295, 494
Klonoff, H.: 60
Knehr, C. A.: 101, 173, 423, 434
Knief, L. M.: 133
Kobler, F. J.: 81
Kothari, S.: 362, 381
Kullberg, G.: 342
Kumar, P.: 296
Kundu, R.: 227
Kurland, A. A.: 427
Kuroda, J.: 134
Landrus, G.: 486
Lange, U. A.: 356
Langevin, R.: 495
Larson, K. H.: 228
Lemke, E. A.: 496
Levin, J. R.: 505–6
Levine, B.: 79, 90
Levine, B. D.: 74

Levinson, B. M.: 135–6, 174, 205
Levita, E.: 430, 441
Ley, P.: 265
Li, A. K.: 229
Lindahl, L. E. H.: 421
Lingwood, J.: 65
Loranger, A. W.: 137, 145
Lovius, B. B. J.: 497
Lunzer, E. A.: 146
Lynn, R.: 160
McAdam, W.: 377
MacArthur, R.: 322
MacArthur, R. S.: 147, 168, 188, 210, 230, 234, 321, 333, 357, 438
McClelland, M.: 171
McClelland, W. J.: 171
M'Comisky, J. G.: 453
McConnell, F.: 410
Macdonald, H. A.: 358
McDonald, R. P.: 245
McDonnell, M. W.: 175
McGee, E.: 82
McKinlay, M.: 19
McLeod, H. N.: 161, 176
McNamara, J. R.: 359
Maher, B. A.: 148
Maitra, A. K.: 246
Majumdar, P. K.: 297
Malpass, L. F.: 149
Mandel, R.: 298
Marcus, B.: 401
Marmorston, J.: 184, 221
Marr, E.: 198
Marriage, A.: 214
Martin, A. W.: 80
Martin, D. R.: 58
Martin, F.: 202
Marum, O.: 19
Marzolf, S. S.: 96
Mason, P. L.: 150
Mather, L. J.: 498
Matthews, C. G.: 323
Maxwell, A. E.: 123
Mears, F. G.: 299
Mehrotra, K. K.: 324–5
Mehrotra, S. N.: 138, 197
Meier, J. H.: 247
Melton, K.: 264
Menon, A. S.: 320
Merlis, M.: 373
Merlis, S.: 334–5, 348, 366, 372–3, 475
Meyer, V.: 402
Meyers, E.: 177
Michael, W. B.: 271
Midkiff, K. L.: 91
Miller, F. M.: 4
Miller, L. E.: 359
Mills, L. F.: 25
Misiak, H.: 137, 145
Mitchell, L.: 392
Mitra, A. K.: 422
Mogensen, A.: 231
Mohan, J.: 499
Mohan, V.: 499
Molema, S. Y.: 442
Montemagni, G.: 181
Montgomery, G. W. G.: 209, 266, 451
Moore, B. G. R.: 52
Morán, R. E.: 416
Morris, A. B.: 152
Morrison, M.: 215
Moshin, S. M.: 139
Mosychuk, H.: 438
Moyles, E. W.: 500
Mueller, M. W.: 248–9, 326
Mundy, L.: 123, 409
Munro, H.: 327
Murray, S.: 254
Neal, C. D.: 447
Nelson, M. O.: 189
Netherton, A. H.: 358
Newbrough, J. R.: 338
Newcomb, W. B.: 300
Nicholson, C. L.: 360, 382
Nickols, J.: 301
Nickols, J. E.: 178
Nordén, K.: 469
Norman, R. D.: 91
Notcutt, B.: 38, 391
Nyman, G. E.: 151
O'Connor, N.: 48, 53, 66

[440]

Proverbs Test. Grades 5–16 and adults; 1954–56; 2 scores: abstract, concrete; Donald R. Gorham; Psychological Test Specialists. *

For additional information and reviews by Eugene L. Gaier and Alfred B. Heilbrun, Jr., see 5:371 (4 references).

REFERENCES THROUGH 1971

1–4. See 5:371.
5. O'REILLY, P. O., AND HARRISON, K. "Experimentation With an Objective Test Battery." *Can Psychiatric Assn J* 5:108–23 Ap '60. *
6. O'REILLY, P. O., AND HARRISON, K. "The Gorham Proverbs Test." *Dis Nerv System* 21:382–5 Je '60. *
7. GORHAM, DONALD R. "Verbal Abstraction in Psychiatric Illness: Assay of Impairment Utilizing Proverbs." *J Mental Sci* 107:52–9 Ja '61. * (*PA* 36:1JP52G)
8. HERRON, WILLIAM G. "Abstract Ability in the Process-Reactive Classification of Schizophrenia." *J General Psychol* 67:147–54 Jl '62. * (*PA* 37:3691)
9. SATZ, PAUL, AND CARROLL, L. T. "Utilization of the Proverbs Test as a Projective Instrument: An Objective Approach Through Language Behavior." *J General Psychol* 67:205–13 O '62. * (*PA* 37:8020)
10. GORHAM, DONALD R. "Additional Norms and Scoring Suggestions for the Proverbs Test." *Psychol Rep* 13:487–92 O '63. * (*PA* 38:8415)
11. HARKEY, SHARON M., AND HOWELL, ROBERT J. "The Effect of Anxiety as Measured by the Taylor MAS Scale on Performance on the Gorham Proverb Tests." *J Clin Psychol* 19:106–8 Ja '63. * (*PA* 39:1667)
12. RUBIN, EDMUND JOSEPH. *Performance of Totally-Blind and Sighted Subjects on Tests of Abstraction.* Doctor's thesis, Fordham University (New York, N.Y.), 1963. (*DA* 24:2989)
13. HOLTZMAN, WAYNE H.; GORHAM, DONALD R.; AND MORAN, LOUIS J. "A Factor-Analytic Study of Schizophrenic Thought Processes." *J Abn & Social Psychol* 69:355–64 O '64. * (*PA* 39:8491)
14. LEWINSOHN, PETER M., AND NICHOLS, ROBERT C. "The Evaluation of Changes in Psychiatric Patients During and After Hospitalization." *J Clin Psychol* 20:272–9 Ap '64. * (*PA* 39:8200)
15. PETTINATO, GAETANO CARL. *The Effect of Stress and the Sex of the Examiner on the Conceptual Performance of Male Schizophrenics.* Doctor's thesis, Temple University (Philadelphia, Pa.), 1964. (*DA* 25:1343)
16. SUEHS, JAMES ERNEST. *A Comparative Study of Brain-Damaged and Schizophrenic Subjects on Several Psychological Tests.* Doctor's thesis, University of Houston (Houston, Tex.), 1964. (*DA* 25:1347)
17. FOGEL, MAX L. "The Proverbs Test in the Appraisal of Cerebral Disease." *J General Psychol* 72:269–75 Ap '65. * (*PA* 39:12281)
18. GOLDSTEIN, ROBERT H., AND SALZMAN, LEONARD F. "Proverb Word Counts as a Measure of Overinclusiveness in Delusional Schizophrenics." *J Abn Psychol* 70:244–5 Ag '65. * (*PA* 39:16197)
19. SMITH, LAURENCE C., JR. "The Effects of Heat Stroke on Cognitive Functioning." *Proc Ann Conf Air Force Behav Sci* 11:130–42 Jl '65. *
20. WEISSMAN, HERBERT, AND KOSTLAN, ALBERT. "Use of the Proverbs Test in Differential Diagnosis in the Intensive Treatment Setting." *Newsl Res Psychol* 7:33–4 My '65. *
21. MAY, A. E. "Anxiety and Overinclusion." *Brit J Psychiatry* 112:41–2 Ja '66. * (*PA* 40:5745)
22. SALZMAN, LEONARD F.; GOLDSTEIN, ROBERT H.; ATKINS, ROBERT; AND BABIGIAN, HAROUTUN. "Conceptual Thinking in Psychiatric Patients." *Arch Gen Psychiatry* 14:55–9 Ja '66. * (*PA* 40:4443)
23. SHIMKUNAS, ALGIMANTAS M.; GYNTHER, MALCOLM D.; AND SMITH, KATHLEEN. "Abstracting Ability of Schizophrenics Before and During Phenothiazine Therapy." *Arch Gen Psychiatry* 14:79–83 Ja '66. * (*PA* 40:4468)
24. GOLDSTEIN, ROBERT H., AND SALZMAN, LEONARD F. "Cognitive Functioning in Acute and Remitted Psychiatric Patients." *Psychol Rep* 21:24–6 Ag '67. * (*PA* 42:2738)
25. JURJEVICH, R. M. "Intellectual Assessment With Gorham's Proverbs Test, Raven's Progressive Matrices, and WAIS." *Psychol Rep* 20:1285–6 Je '67. * (*PA* 41:15271)
26. LASKY, LAWRENCE. "Alternate Forms of the Multiple Choice Version of the Proverbs Test." *J Psychol* 65:59–60 Ja '67. * (*PA* 41:4746)
27. LEWINSOHN, PETER M., AND NICHOLS, ROBERT C. "Dimensions of Change in Mental Hospital Patients." *J Clin Psychol* 23:498–503 O '67. * (*PA* 42:2624)

28. MARTIN, WILLIAM T. "Analysis of the Abstracting Function in Reasoning Using an Experimental Test." *Psychol Rep* 21:593–8 O '67. * (*PA* 42:4815)

29. SHIMKUNAS, ALGIMANTAS M.; GYNTHER, MALCOLM D.; AND SMITH, KATHLEEN. "Schizophrenic Responses to the Proverbs Test: Abstract, Concrete, or Autistic?" *J Abn Psychol* 72:128–33 Ap '67. * (*PA* 41:7605)

30. TURNER, WILLIAM J. "The Usefulness of Diphenylhydantoin in Treatment of Nonepileptic Emotional Disorders." *Int J Neuropsychiatry* 3(sup 2):S8–20 D '67. * (*PA* 42:14005)

31. POWELL, J. C. "The Interpretation of Wrong Answers From a Multiple Choice Test." *Ed & Psychol Meas* 28:403–12 su '68. * (*PA* 42:18104)

32. AFTANAS, M. S., AND ROYCE, J. R. "A Factor Analysis of Brain Damage Tests Administered to Normal Subjects With Factor Score Comparisons Across Ages." *Multiv Behav Res* 4(4):459–81 O '69. * (*PA* 44:11030)

33. KINGSLEY, LEONARD. "Functioning of Acute and Chronic Schizophrenics on Measures of Abstract Reasoning." *J Clin Psychol* 25(2):144–7 Ap '69. * (*PA* 43:14470)

34. L'ABATE, LUCIANO, AND GALE, ELLIOT N. "Neurological Status and Psychological Functioning." *Percept & Motor Skills* 29(3):999–1007 D '69. * (*PA* 46:5330)

35. SHIMKUNAS, ALGIMANTAS M. "Reciprocal Shifts in Schizophrenic Thought Processes." *J Abn Psychol* 76(3):423–6 D '70. * (*PA* 45:6724)

36. REED, J. L. "The Relationship Between Results on Some Psychological Tests and Outcome in Schizophrenia." *Acta Psychiatrica Scandinavica* (Denmark) 47(3):223–9 '71. *

37. SMITH, ROGER C. "Use of the Proverbs Test for the Identification of Psychotic Disorder." *J Clin Psychol* 27(2):227 Ap '71. * (*PA* 46:7083)

CUMULATIVE NAME INDEX

Aftanas, M. S.: 32	Lasky, L.: 26
Atkins, R.: 22	Lewinsohn, P. M.: 14, 27
Babigian, H.: 22	Martin, W. T.: 28
Carroll, L. T.: 9	May, A. E.: 21
Elmore, C. M.: 4	Moran, L. J.: 13
Fogel, M. L.: 17	Nichols, R. C.: 14, 27
Gaier, E. L.: *rev,* 5:371	O'Reilly, P. O.: 5–6
Gale, E. N.: 34	Pettinato, G. C.: 15
Goldstein, R. H.: 18, 22, 24	Pounders, D. J.: 3
Gorham, D. R.: 1–2, 4, 7, 10, 13	Powell, J. C.: 31
	Reed, J. L.: 36
Gynther, M. D.: 23, 29	Royce, J. R.: 32
Harkey, S. M.: 11	Rubin, E. J.: 12
Harrison, K.: 5–6	Salzman, L. F.: 18, 22, 24
Heilbrun, A. B.: *rev,* 5:371	Satz, P.: 9
Herron, W. G.: 8	Shimkunas, A. M.: 23, 29, 35
Holtzman, W. H.: 13	Smith, K.: 23, 29
Howell, R. J.: 11	Smith, L. C.: 19
Jurjevich, R. M.: 25	Smith, R. C.: 37
Kingsley, L.: 33	Suehs, J. E.: 16
Kostlan, A.: 20	Turner, W. J.: 30
L'Abate, L.: 34	Weissman, H.: 20

[441]

Public School Primary Intelligence Test. Grades 2–4; 1924–56; revision of *Detroit Primary Intelligence Test;* 1954 test identical with test copyrighted 1924 except for minor changes; Harry J. Baker; Bobbs-Merrill Co., Inc. *

For additional information, see 5:329*a;* for a review by W. Line of this and two other Detroit intelligence tests, see 2:1393.

REFERENCES THROUGH 1971

1. KUHLMANN, F. "The Kuhlmann-Anderson Intelligence Tests Compared With Seven Others." *J Appl Psychol* 12:545–94 D '28. * (*PA* 3:1751)

2. KUHLMANN, F. "Effect of Degree of Difficulty on Operation of Intelligence Tests." *J Juvenile Res* 14:8–21 Ja '30. * (*PA* 4:2866)

3. SEAGOE, M. V. "An Evaluation of Certain Intelligence Tests." *J Appl Psychol* 18:432–6 Je '34. * (*PA* 8:6140)

4. TILTON, J. W. "The Relation Between IQ and Trait Difference as Measured by Group Intelligence Tests." *J Ed Psychol* 38:343–52 O '47. * (*PA* 22:2066)

CUMULATIVE NAME INDEX

Kuhlmann, F.: 1–2	Tilton, J. W.: 4
Seagoe, M. V.: 3	

[442]

Purdue Non-Language Personnel Test. Business and industry; 1957–69; abbreviated revision of *Purdue Non-Language Test;* Joseph Tiffin; University Book Store. *

For additional information, see 7:377; for reviews by John D. Hundleby and Benjamin Rosner of the earlier test, see 6:491.

REFERENCES THROUGH 1971

1. GRUENFELD, LEOPOLD W. "Selection of Executives for a Training Program." *Personnel Psychol* 14:421–31 w '61. * (*PA* 37:3922)

CUMULATIVE NAME INDEX

Gruenfeld, L. W.: 1	Rosner, B.: *rev,* 6:491
Hundleby, J. D.: *rev,* 6:491	

[443]

Quantitative Evaluative Device. Entering graduate students; 1959–62; also called QED; tests administered at college centers established by the author; "potential for quantitative sophistication"; R. E. Stake; Lincoln Test Service. *

For additional information, see 6:492 (1 reference).

REFERENCES THROUGH 1971

1. See 6:492.

2. STAKE, ROBERT EARL. *Predicting Success in Quantification at the Graduate Level.* Master's thesis, University of Nebraska (Lincoln, Neb.), 1955.

CUMULATIVE NAME INDEX

Stake, R. E.: 1–2

[444]

RBH Test of Learning Ability. Business and industry; 1947–63; TLA; 3 editions; Richardson, Bellows, Henry & Co., Inc. *

a) FORMS S AND T.

b) FORMS DS-12 AND DT-12. Identical with Forms S and T except for removal of directions from testing time; formerly titled *Test for Office Personnel;* 1961 test identical with tests copyrighted 1947.

c) FORM ST. Consists of Forms S and T combined.

For additional information and a review by Erwin K. Taylor, see 7:379 (2 references); see also 6:504 (2 references).

REFERENCES THROUGH 1971

1–2. See 6:504.

3–4. See 7:379.

5. SPARKS, CHARLES P. "Validity of Psychological Tests." *Personnel Psychol* 23(1):39–46 sp '70. * (*PA* 44:17556)

CUMULATIVE NAME INDEX

Dunfield, N. M.: 3	Ross, P. F.: 3
MacNaughton, J. F.: 4	Sparks, C. P.: 2, 5
Moore, C. L.: 4	Taylor, E. K.: *rev,* 7:379
Osborn, H. G.: 4	Waite, W. D.: 2
Perrine, M. W.: 1	

[445]

RBH Test of Non-Verbal Reasoning. Business and industry; 1948–63; catalog uses title *The RBH Non-Verbal Reasoning Test;* Richardson, Bellows, Henry & Co., Inc. *

For additional information and a review by Erwin K. Taylor, see 7:380 (1 reference); see also 6:505 (3 references).

REFERENCES THROUGH 1971

1–3. See 6:505.

4. See 7:380.

CUMULATIVE NAME INDEX

Benson, D.: 3	Meyer, H. H.: 2
Cuomo, S.: 1–2	Moore, C. L.: 4
Hanson, R.: 3	Osburn, H. G.: 4
Kirchner, W.: 3	Taylor, E. K.: *rev,* 7:380
MacNaughton, J. F.: 4	

[446]

Reasoning Tests for Higher Levels of Intelligence. College entrants; 1954; C. W. Valentine; Oliver & Boyd [Scotland]. *

For additional information and a review by Reginald R. Dale, see 5:374.

REFERENCES THROUGH 1971

1. VALENTINE, C. W. "The Use of a New Reasoning Test for Selection of University and Training College Students." *Brit J Ed Psychol* 31:227–31 N '61. * (*PA* 36:5KK27V)
2. HALLWORTH, H. J. "An Analysis of C. W. Valentine's Reasoning Test for Higher Levels of Intelligence." *Brit J Ed Psychol* 33:41–6 F '63. * (*PA* 38:954)
3. EVANS, E. G. S. "Reasoning Ability and Personality Differences Among Student-Teachers." *Brit J Ed Psychol* 34:305–14 N '64. * (*PA* 39:8718)
4. ELTON, CHARLES F. "The Effect of Logic Instruction on the Valentine Reasoning Test." *Brit J Ed Psychol* 35:339–41 N '65. * (*PA* 40:3374)
5. BACKHOUSE, J. K. "The Use of Valentine's Reasoning Tests in an Investigation Into Transfer From Mathematics to Reasoning." *Brit J Ed Psychol* 37:121–3 F '67. *
6. PILKINGTON, G. W., AND HARRISON, G. J. "The Relative Value of Two High Level Intelligence Tests, Advanced Level, and First Year University Examination Marks for Predicting Degree Classification." *Brit J Ed Psychol* 37:382–9 N '67. * (*PA* 42:6148)
7. BANKS, C.; KARDAK, V. S.; JONES, E. M.; AND LUCAS, C. J. "The Relation Between Mental Health, Academic Performance and Cognitive Test Scores Among Chemistry Students." *Brit J Ed Psychol* 40(1):74–9 F '70. * (*PA* 44:11366)

CUMULATIVE NAME INDEX

[447]

Revised Beta Examination. Ages 16–59; 1931–57; revision of *Army Group Examination Beta* ('20); non-language; 1946 revision by Robert M. Lindner and Milton Gurvitz; basic revision by C. E. Kellogg and N. W. Morton; Psychological Corporation. *

For additional information and a review by Bert A. Goldman, see 6:494 (13 references); see also 5:375 (14 references); for reviews by Raleigh M. Drake and Walter C. Shipley, see 3:259 (5 references); for reviews by S. D. Porteus and David Wechsler, see 2:1419 (4 references).

REFERENCES THROUGH 1971

1–4. See 2:1419.
5–9. See 3:259.
10–23. See 5:375.
24–36. See 6:494.
37. BERAN, MARIANNE; PERKINS, JOHN C.; AND SCOLLON, ROBERT W. "Psychological Studies on Patients Undergoing Nonconvulsive Electric-Stimulation Treatment." *Am J Psychiatry* 109:367–74 N '52. * (*PA* 27:5168)
38. HANES, BERNARD. *A Factor Analysis of the MMPI, Aptitude Test Data and Personal Information Using a Population of Criminals.* Doctor's thesis, Ohio State University (Columbus, Ohio), 1952. (*DA* 18:1483)
39. DUNHAM, RALPH E. "Factors Related to Recidivism in Adults." *J Social Psychol* 39:77–91 F '54. * (*PA* 28:8866)
40. MARTIN, RICHARD PANTALL. *The Adjustment of Latin-American Male Students in Selected Private Secondary Schools in the United States.* Doctor's thesis, Northwestern University (Evanston, Ill.), 1954. (*DA* 14:1605)
41. PANTON, JAMES H. "The Relationship Between Education and Measures of Intelligence and Educational Achievement Within a State Prison Population." *J Correct Ed* 12:18–20 Ja '60. *
42. WOODS, JAMES E., AND MYERS, ROGER A. "A Comparison of IQ Scores on the Revised Beta Examination and the Wechsler Adult Intelligence Scale." *Rehabil Counsel B* 7:54–8 S '63. *
43. DOMINO, GEORGE. "Comparison of the D48, Cattell Culture Fair, and Army Beta Tests in a Sample of College Males." *J Consult Psychol* 28:468–9 O '64. * (*PA* 39:5052)
44. LEVINE, BERNARD L. *A Sub-Test Comparison of Negro and White Delinquents on the Revised Beta Examination.* Master's thesis, De Paul University (Chicago, Ill.), 1964.
45. WATSON, CHARLES G., AND CAHOON, D. D. "A Note on the Relationship Between the Revised Beta Examination and the Wechsler Adult Intelligence Scale." *Rehabil Counsel B* 8:47–9 D '64. *
46. BORTNER, RAYMAN W. "The IES Test and a Performance Measure of Intelligence." *Percept & Motor Skills* 22:171–5 F '66. * (*PA* 40:5449)
47. LEVY, RUSSELL H., AND MOORE, WINSTON E. "Cross-Sectional Psychometric Evaluation of Court-Labelled Delinquent Boys." *J Correct Ed* 18:7–9 Jl '66. *

48. WATSON, CHARLES G., AND BAUGH, VERNER S. "Patterns of Psychiatric Patients on the Revised Beta Examination." *J Clin Psychol* 22:188–90 Ap '66. * (*PA* 40:7861)
49. WHITTEMORE, ROBERT G.; ECHEVERRIA, BEN P.; AND GRIFFIN, JOHN V. "Can We Use Existing Tests for Adult Basic Education?" *Adult Ed* 17:19–29 au '66. *
50. BARTZ, WAYNE R. "Relationship of WAIS, BETA and Shipley-Hartford Scores." *Psychol Rep* 22:676 Ap '68. * (*PA* 42:12089)
51. DOMINO, GEORGE. "Culture-Free Tests and the Academic Achievement of Foreign Students." Abstract. *J Consult & Clin Psychol* 32:102 F '68. * (*PA* 42:7843)
52. FUNKHOUSER, THOMAS R. "Correlational Study of the 'Revised Beta Examination' in a Female Retarded Population." *Am J Mental Def* 72:875–8 My '68. * (*PA* 42:13754)
53. LEVY, RUSSELL H. "Group Administered Intelligence Tests Which Appropriately Reflect the Magnitude of Mental Retardation Among Wards of the Illinois Youth Commission." *J Correct Ed* 20:7–10 su '68. *
54. PATRICK, JERRY H., AND OVERALL, JOHN E. "Validity of Beta IQ's for White Female Patients in a State Psychiatric Hospital." *J Clin Psychol* 24:343–5 Jl '68. * (*PA* 42:16422)
55. WATSON, CHARLES G., AND KLETT, WILLIAM G. "Prediction of WAIS IQ's From the Shipley-Hartford, the Army General Classification Test and the Revised Beta Examination." *J Clin Psychol* 24:338–41 Jl '68. * (*PA* 42:16437)
56. FOSTER, ASHLEY. "The Use of Psychological Testing in Rehabilitation Planning for Alaskan Native People." *Austral Psychologist* 4(2–3):146–52 N '69. * (*PA* 46:5260)
57. OSBORNE, R. T. "Psychometric Correlates of the Visual Evoked Potential." *Acta Psychologica* (Netherlands) 29(3):303 My '69. * (*PA* 44:1912)
58. PHILLIPS, RICHARD MARTIN. *A Multiple Regression Study of Academic Prediction at Gallaudet College.* Doctor's thesis, University of Maryland (College Park, Md.), 1969. (*DAI* 30:5257A)
59. RAFFEL, SHERMAN C.; SWINK, RICHARD; AND LAMPTON, T. D. "The Influence of Chlorphenesin Carbamate and Carisoprodol on Psychological Test Scores." *Curr Ther Res* 11(9):553–60 S '69. *
60. ROCHESTER, DEAN E., AND BODWELL, AARON. "Beta-WAIS Comparisons for Illiterate and Indigent Male and Female Negroes." *Meas & Eval Guid* 3(3):164–8 f '70. * (*PA* 45:9974)
61. SMITH, HARRY ELMER. *The Beta-WAIS Relationship and the Intercorrelations Among Beta Subtests for a Youthful Offender Population.* Master's thesis, Millersville State College (Millersville, Pa.), 1970.
62. BOLTON, BRIAN. "A Factor Analytic Study of Communication Skills and Nonverbal Abilities of Deaf Rehabilitation Clients." *Multiv Behav Res* 6(4):485–501 O '71. * (*PA* 47: 11373)
63. DUDLEY, HAROLD K., JR.; WILLIAMS, JACK D.; AND OVERALL, JOHN E. "Relationships of Beta IQ Scores to Socio-Cultural Factors in a Psychiatric Population." *J Clin Psychol* 27(1):68–74 Ja '71. * (*PA* 46:1421)
64. LIBB, J. WESLEY, AND COLEMAN, JOHN M. "Correlation Between the WAIS and Revised Beta, Wechsler Memory Scale and Quick Test in a Vocational Rehabilitation Center." *Psychol Rep* 29(3):863–5 D '71. * (*PA* 47:2910)
65. MILLER, BRIAN P. "IQ Tests and Minority Groups." *Training & Develop J* 25(10):26–7 O '71. * (*PA* 48:2801)

CUMULATIVE NAME INDEX

Overall, J. E.: 54, 63
Panton, J. H.: 33, 41
Pastore, N.: 28
Patrick, J. H.: 54
Perkins, J. C.: 37
Phillips, R. M.: 58
Porteus, S. D.: rev, 2:1419
Raffel, S. C.: 59
Rochester, D. E.: 60
Ross, L. W.: 12, 19
Saucer, R. T.: 35
Scollon, R. W.: 37
Seashore, H. G.: 32
Shipley, W. C.: rev, 3:259
Smith, H. E.: 61
Stotsky, B. A.: 22

Swink, R.: 59
Toal, R.: 23
Twain, D. C.: 36
Watson, C. G.: 45, 48, 55
Wechsler, D.: rev, 2:1419
Wegman, M.: 13
Wesman, A. G.: 9
Whittemore, R. G.: 49
Williams, H. M.: 13
Williams, J. D.: 63
Woods, J. E.: 42
Woods, W. A.: 23
Yerbury, E. C.: 16
Yerkes, R. M.: 1–2
Yoakum, C. S.: 1
Zakolski, F. C.: 14

[448]

The Ryburn Group Intelligence Tests. Ages 6.5–12.5, 9.5–15.5; [1936–40]; H. V. Clark; Robert Gibson & Sons, Glasgow, Ltd. [Scotland]. *

For additional information, see 2:1421.

[449]

SRA Nonverbal Form. Ages 12 and over; 1946–73; formerly called *SRA Non-Verbal Classification Form;* Robert N. McMurry and Joseph E. King; Science Research Associates, Inc. *

For additional information and a review by W. D. Commins, see 4:318; for an excerpted review, see 3:261 (incorrectly listed under 3:260 in the first printing of *The Third Mental Measurements Yearbook*).

REFERENCES THROUGH 1971

1. Buswell, G. T. "The Relationship Between Rate of Thinking and Rate of Reading." *Sch R* 59:339–46 S '51. *
2. Eber, Herbert W.; Cochrane, Carl M.; and Branca, Albert A. "Brief Intellectual Assessment of Patients With Behavior Disorders." Abstract. *J Consult Psychol* 18:396 D '54. * (*PA* 29:7271, title only)
3. Foote, Richard Paul. *The Prediction of Success in Automotive Mechanics in a Vocational-Industrial Curriculum on the Secondary School Level.* Doctor's thesis, New York University (New York, N.Y.), 1960. (*DA* 21:3014)
4. Holden, Raymond H.; Mendelson, Martin A.; and DeVault, Spencer. "Relationship of the WAIS to the SRA Non-Verbal Test Scores." *Psychol Rep* 19:987–90 D '66. * (*PA* 41:3721)
5. Levy, Russell H. "The Gauging of Academic Achievement Among 'Court-Labelled' Delinquent Boys (Second of a Series)." *J Correct Ed* 18:14–7 O '66. *
6. Levy, Russell H., and Moore, Winston E. "Cross-Sectional Psychometric Evaluation of Court-Labelled Delinquent Boys." *J Correct Ed* 18:7–9 Jl '66. *
7. Phillips, Robert, and Berg, Thomas. "Use of the SRA Verbal and Non-Verbal Forms at Gallaudet College." *J Rehabil Deaf* 1:59–62 O '67. *
8. Kirkpatrick, James J.; Ewen, Robert B.; Barrett, Richard S.; and Katzell, Raymond A. *Testing and Fair Employment: Fairness and Validity of Personnel Tests for Different Ethnic Groups,* pp. 17–9, 25–7, 51–69. New York: New York University Press, 1968. Pp. x, 145. *
9. Levy, Russell H. "Group Administered Intelligence Tests Which Appropriately Reflect the Magnitude of Mental Retardation Among Wards of the Illinois Youth Commission." *J Correct Ed* 20:7–10 su '68. *
10. Stratton, Albert J. "Validity of the SRA Non-Verbal Form for Adults." *Psychol Rep* 22:163–7 F '68. * (*PA* 42:10577)
11. Phillips, Richard Martin. *A Multiple Regression Study of Academic Prediction at Gallaudet College.* Doctor's thesis, University of Maryland (College Park, Md.), 1969. (*DAI* 30:5257A)
12. Odell, Louise M. "Maternal Intellectual Functioning." *Johns Hopkins Med J* 128(6):362–8 Je '71. *

CUMULATIVE NAME INDEX

Barrett, R. S.: 8
Berg, T.: 7
Branca, A. A.: 2
Buswell, G. T.: 1
Cochrane, C. M.: 2
Commins, W. D.: rev, 4:318
DeVault, S.: 4
Eber, H. W.: 2
Ewen, R. B.: 8
Foote, R. P.: 3

Holden, R. H.: 4
Katzell, R. A.: 8
Kirkpatrick, J. J.: 8
Levy, R. H.: 5–6, 9
Mendelson, M. A.: 4
Moore, W. E.: 6
Odell, L. M.: 12
Phillips, R.: 7
Phillips, R. M.: 11
Stratton, A. J.: 10

[450]

SRA Pictorial Reasoning Test. Ages 14 and over; 1966–73; PRT; "to measure the learning potential of individuals from diverse backgrounds with reading difficulties"; test by Robert N. McMurry and Phyllis D. Arnold; manual by Bruce A. Campbell with the editorial assistance of Marita Schofield; Science Research Associates, Inc. *

For additional information, reviews by Raymond A. Katzell and John E. Milholland, and an excerpted review by John L. Horn, see 7:381.

[451]

SRA Short Test of Educational Ability. Grades kgn–1, 2–3, 3–6, 6–9, 9–12; 1966–72; STEA; approximately 80 percent of the items were taken from *SRA Primary Mental Abilities* and *SRA Tests of Educational Ability;* Science Research Associates, Inc. *

For additional information, reviews by Russel F. Green and Henry Weitz, and an excerpted review by Raynard J. Dooley (rejoinder by W. Paul Jones), see 7:382 (2 references).

REFERENCES THROUGH 1971

1–2. See 7:382.
3. Jones, W. Paul, and DeBlassie, Richard R. "Social Class Contrasts in Short Term Predictability of Grade 7 Achievement." *J Ed Res* 65(1):11–4 S '71. *

CUMULATIVE NAME INDEX

DeBlassie, R. R.: 3
Dooley, R. J.: exc, 7:382
Green, R. F.: rev, 7:382

Jones, W. P.: 1–3; exc, 7:382
Weitz, H.: rev, 7:382

[452]

SRA Verbal Form. Grades 7–16 and adults; 1946–73; formerly called *SRA Verbal Classification Form;* abbreviated adaptation of *Thurstone Test of Mental Alertness* which is an abbreviated adaptation of *American Council on Education Psychological Examination for High School Students,* 1940 Edition; 3 scores: quantitative, linguistic, total; test by Thelma Gwinn Thurstone and L. L. Thurstone; manual by Bruce A. Campbell with the editorial assistance of LaVonne Macaitis and Marita Schofield; Science Research Associates, Inc. *

For additional information, see 7:383 (2 references); for reviews by W. D. Commins and Willis C. Schaefer, see 4:319.

REFERENCES THROUGH 1971

1–2. See 7:383.
3. Phillips, Robert, and Berg, Thomas. "Use of the SRA Verbal and Non-Verbal Forms at Gallaudet College." *J Rehabil Deaf* 1:59–62 O '67. *

CUMULATIVE NAME INDEX

Berg, T.: 3
Commins, W. D.: rev, 4:319
Filer, R. J.: 1
Grigg, A. E.: 1

Phillips, R.: 3
Phillips, R. M.: 2
Schaefer, W. C.: rev, 4:319

[453]

Safran Culture Reduced Intelligence Test. Grades 1–6, 4 and over; 1960–69; SCRIT; C. Safran; the Author [Canada]. *

For additional information and a review by Lee J. Cronbach, see 7:384 (6 references); see also 6:497 (1 reference).

REFERENCES THROUGH 1971

1. See 6:497.
2–7. See 7:384.
8. Neville, Mary H., and Frost, Barry P. "Differential Achievement in Reading and Arithmetic." *Alberta J Ed Res* (Canada) 10:192–200 D '64. *

CUMULATIVE NAME INDEX

Cronbach, L. J.: rev, 7:384
Frost, B. P.: 3, 8

MacArthur, R.: 5
MacArthur, R. S.: 2, 4, 6

Neville, M. H.: 8   Solis, M. M.: 7
Rattan, M. S.: 6   West, L. W.: 2
Safran, C.: 1

[454]

Scholastic Mental Ability Tests. Grades kgn–1, 2–3, 4–5, 6–8; 1953–67; SMAT; various titles used by publisher; Oliver F. Anderhalter; Scholastic Testing Service, Inc. *

For additional information, see 7:385; for reviews by Walter N. Durost and Alexander G. Wesman of earlier editions, see 5:380.

[455]

Schubert General Ability Battery. Grades 12–16 and adults; 1946–65; 5 scores: vocabulary, analogies, arithmetic problems, syllogisms, total; 1965 test identical with test copyrighted 1946 except for 4 revised items and 3 omitted items; 1965 manual identical with manual published 1953 except for revised analogies norms for grade 12 boys; Herman J. P. Schubert and Daniel S. P. Schubert (test); Herman J. P. Schubert. *

For additional information, see 7:386 (1 reference); for a review by William B. Schrader, see 5:382.

REFERENCES THROUGH 1971

1. See 7:386.

CUMULATIVE NAME INDEX

Drebus, R. W.: 1   Schrader, W. B.: rev, 5:382
Neidt, C. O.: 1

[456]

Scott Company Mental Alertness Test. Applicants for office positions; 1923; Scott Co.; Stoelting Co. *

REFERENCES THROUGH 1971

1. FRYER, DOUGLAS, AND SPARLING, E. J. "Intelligence and Occupational Adjustment." *Occupations* 12:55–63 Je '34. *

CUMULATIVE NAME INDEX

Fryer, D.: 1   Sparling, E. J.: 1

[457]

Ship Destination Test. Grades 9 and over; 1955–56; general reasoning; Paul R. Christensen and J. P. Guilford; Sheridan Psychological Services, Inc. *

For additional information and a review by William B. Schrader, see 6:500 (8 references); for a review by C. J. Adcock, see 5:383.

REFERENCES THROUGH 1971

1–8. See 6:500.
9. MARKS, ALVIN; MICHAEL, WILLIAM B.; AND KAISER, HENRY F. "Comparison of Manual and Analytic Techniques of Rotation in a Factor Analysis of Aptitude Test Variables." *Psychol Rep* 7:519–22 D '60. * (PA 35:2792)
10. MERRIFIELD, P. R.; GUILFORD, J. P.; CHRISTENSEN, P. R.; AND FRICK, J. W. "Interrelationships Between Certain Abilities and Certain Traits of Motivation and Temperament." *J General Psychol* 65:57–74 Jl '61. * (PA 36:2HD57M)
11. DE MILLE, RICHARD. "Intellect After Lobotomy in Schizophrenia: A Factor Analytic Study." *Psychol Monogr* 76(16):1–18 '62. * (PA 38:2784)
12. LOCKE, EDWIN A. "Some Correlates of Classroom and Out-of-Class Achievement in Gifted Science Students." *J Ed Psychol* 54:238–48 O '63. * (PA 38:4649)
13. PIMSLEUR, PAUL. "A Study of Foreign Language Learning Ability: Parts 1 and 2," pp. 57–72. In *Report of the Twelfth Annual Round Table Meeting on Linguistics and Language Studies.* Edited by Michael Zarechnak. Washington, D.C.: Georgetown University Press, 1963. Pp. 132. *
14. LEMKE, ELMER A.; KLAUSMEIER, HERBERT J.; AND HARRIS, CHESTER W. "Relationship of Selected Cognitive Abilities to Concept Attainment and Information Processing." *J Ed Psychol* 58:27–35 F '67. * (PA 41:3959)
15. VERY, PHILIP S. "Differential Factor Structures in Mathematical Ability." *Genetic Psychol Monogr* 75:169–207 My '67. * (PA 41:10451)
16. BERGER, RAYMOND M. "Selection of Systems Analysts and Programmer Trainees." *Proc Ann Computer Personnel Res Conf* 6:44–63 '68. *
17. BROWN, STEPHEN W.; GUILFORD, J. P.; AND HOEPFNER, RALPH. "Six Semantic-Memory Abilities." *Ed & Psychol Meas* 28:691–717 au '68. * (PA 43:4427)

18. GUILFORD, J. P., AND HOEPFNER, RALPH. "Comparisons of Varimax Rotations With Rotations to Theoretical Targets." *Ed & Psychol Meas* 29(1):3–22 sp '69. * (PA 44:15668)
19. KRAUT, ALLEN I. "Intellectual Ability and Promotional Success Among High Level Managers." *Personnel Psychol* 22(3):281–90 au '69. * (PA 44:9440)
20. VANDENBERG, STEVEN G. "A Twin Study of Spatial Ability." *Multiv Behav Res* 4(3):273–94 Jl '69. * (PA 44:356)
21. BALDWIN, THOMAS S. "Relationships Among Student Achievement and 'Pure Factors' of Intellect." *J Indus Teach Ed* 9(1):15–25 f '71. *

CUMULATIVE NAME INDEX

Adcock, C. J.: rev, 5:383   Kaiser, H. F.: 6–7, 9
Baldwin, T. S.: 21   Kettner, N. W.: 4
Berger, R. M.: 1, 16   Klausmeier, H. J.: 14
Brown, S. W.: 17   Kraut, A. I.: 19
Christensen, P. R.: 1, 4, 8, 10   Lemke, E. A.: 14
de Mille, R.: 11   Locke, E. A.: 12
Frick, J. W.: 8, 10   Marks, A.: 6–7, 9
Guilford, J. P.: 1, 4, 8, 10,   Merrifield, P. R.: 8, 10
   17–8   Michael, W. B.: 3, 5–7, 9
Haney, R.: 3, 5   Pimsleur, P.: 13
Harris, C. W.: 14   Schrader, W. B.: rev, 6:500
Hills, J. R.: 2   Vandenberg, S. G.: 20
Hoepfner, R.: 17–8   Very, P. S.: 15
Jones, R. A.: 3, 5

[458]

Short Form Test of Academic Aptitude. Grades 1.5–3.4, 3.5–4, 5–6, 7–9, 9–12; 1936–70; SFTAA; revision of still-in-print *California Test of Mental Maturity;* 3 scores: language, nonlanguage, total; Elizabeth T. Sullivan, Willis W. Clark, and Ernest W. Tiegs; CTB/McGraw-Hill. *

For additional information, see 7:387.

[459]

The Simplex GNV Intelligence Tests. Ages 11–13.0; 1952–57; titles on tests are, for example for form 1, *The Simplex Intelligence Test GNV 1;* C. A. Richardson; George G. Harrap & Co. Ltd. [England]. *

For additional information and a review by Philip M. Levy, see 6:501 (2 references).

REFERENCES THROUGH 1971

1–2. See 6:501.

CUMULATIVE NAME INDEX

Levy, P. M.: rev, 6:501   Shuttleworth, C. W.: 1
Nisbet, J. D.: 2

[460]

The Simplex Group Intelligence Scale. Ages 10 and over; 1922–39; C. A. Richardson; George G. Harrap & Co. Ltd. [England]. *

For additional information and a review by James Mainwaring, see 5:385.

REFERENCES THROUGH 1971

1. WILSON, J. H. "Comparison of Certain Intelligence Scales." *Brit J Psychol* 15:44–63 Jl '24. *
2. JONES, D. CARADOG, AND CARR-SAUNDERS, A. M. "The Relation Between Intelligence and Social Status Among Orphan Children." *Brit J Psychol* 17:343–64 Ap '27. * (PA 1:2271)
3. DALE, A. BARBARA. "The Use of Mental Tests With University Women Students." *Brit J Ed Psychol* 5:59–75 F '35. * (PA 9:3448)

CUMULATIVE NAME INDEX

Carr-Saunders, A. M.: 2   Mainwaring, J.: rev, 5:385
Dale, A. B.: 3   Wilson, J. H.: 1
Jones, D. C.: 2

[461]

[The Simplex Junior Intelligence Tests.] Ages 7–14; 1932–51; 2 forms; C. A. Richardson; George G. Harrap & Co. Ltd. [England]. *

a) THE SIMPLEX JUNIOR INTELLIGENCE SCALE. 1932.
b) THE SIMPLEX JUNIOR 'A' INTELLIGENCE TEST. 1950–51; test booklet title is *The Simplex Junior 'A' Test.*

For additional information and a review by Arthur B. Royse, see 5:386 (1 reference); see also 4:322 (2 references).

Safran Culture Reduced Intelligence Test

REFERENCES THROUGH 1971

1–2. See 4:322.
3. See 5:386.
4. LAWRENCE, EVELYN M. "An Investigation Into the Relation Between Intelligence and Inheritance." *Brit J Psychol Monogr Sup* 16:1–80 '31. *
5. RICHARDSON, C. A., AND STOKES, C. W. "The Growth and Variability of Intelligence." *Brit J Psychol Monogr Sup* 18:1–83 '33. * (*PA* 9:4390)
6. McRAE, HUGH. "The Inconstancy of Group Test IQ's." *Brit J Ed Psychol* 12:59–70 F '42. * (*PA* 16:2905)
7. MADDOX, H. "Mental Age Scales." *Brit J Ed Psychol* 29:72–3 F '59. * (*PA* 34:2731)
8. KING, W. H. "The Development of Scientific Concepts in Children." *Brit J Ed Psychol* 33:240–52 N '63. * (*PA* 38:8062)

CUMULATIVE NAME INDEX

Curr, W.: 3   Maddox, H.: 7
Gourlay, N.: 3   Richardson, C. A.: 5
Keir, G.: 1   Royse, A. B.: *rev,* 5:386
King, W. H.: 8   Stokes, C. W.: 5
Lawrence, E. M.: 4   Wilson, J. T.: 2
McRae, H.: 6

[462]
Sleight Non-Verbal Intelligence Test. Ages 8–9, 6–10; 1931–63; 2 tests; George F. Sleight and Preston Education Committee (revision of *a*); George G. Harrap & Co. Ltd. [England]. *
a) SLEIGHT NON-VERBAL INTELLIGENCE TEST: PRESTON REVISION. Ages 8–9; 1931–63; distribution restricted to directors of education.
b) SLEIGHT NON-VERBAL INTELLIGENCE TEST. Ages 6–10; 1931.
For additional information, see 6:502 (1 reference); for reviews by John C. Daniels and M. L. Kellmer Pringle of *b*, see 5:387.

REFERENCES THROUGH 1971

1. See 6:502.
2. PEEL, E. A., AND GRAHAM, D. "Differentiation of Ability in Primary School Children." *Durham Res R* (England) 1(2): 40–8 S '51. *
3. PEEL, E. A., AND GRAHAM, D. "Differentiation of Ability in Primary School Children—II." *Durham Res R* (England) 1(3): 31–4 S '52. * (*PA* 27:5157)
4. GRAHAM, D. "The Differentiation of Ability in Primary School-Children: A Comment." *Durham Res R* (England) 1(4):27–30 S '53. * (*PA* 28:8077)

CUMULATIVE NAME INDEX

Daniels, J. C.: *rev,* 5:387   Peel, E. A.: 2–3
Graham, D.: 2–4   Pringle, M. L. K.: *rev,* 5:387
Lytton, H.: 1

[463]
The Southend Test of Intelligence. Ages 10–12; 1939–53; revision of *Southend Group Test of Intelligence;* M. E. Hebron and W. Stephenson; George G. Harrap & Co. Ltd. [England]. *
For additional information and a review by James Mainwaring, see 5:388; for a review by Gertrude Keir of the original edition, see 4:323 (1 reference); for an excerpted review, see 2:1423.

REFERENCES THROUGH 1971

1. See 4:323.

CUMULATIVE NAME INDEX

Keir, G.: *rev,* 4:323   Peel, E. A.: 1
Mainwaring, J.: *rev,* 5:388

[464]
Spiral Nines, Sixth Edition. Job applicants with 7–8 years of education; 1960–65; also called *Nines;* intelligence; no manual; National Institute for Personnel Research [South Africa]. *
For additional information, see 7:388 (2 references).

REFERENCES THROUGH 1971

1–2. See 7:388.

CUMULATIVE NAME INDEX

Brimble, A. R.: 1   MacArthur, R. S.: 1
Irvine, S. H.: 1–2

[465]
Test of Adult College Aptitude. Evening college entrants; 1966; TACA; King M. Wientge and Philip H. DuBois; TACA Development Fund. *
For additional information and a review by Kenneth D. Hopkins, see 7:389.

[466]
*Test of Perceptual Organization. Ages 12 and over; 1967–70; formerly called *Test of Abstract Reasoning;* William T. Martin; Psychologists and Educators, Inc. *
For additional information, see 7:390 (1 reference).

REFERENCES THROUGH 1971

1. See 7:390.

CUMULATIVE NAME INDEX

Martin, W. T.: 1

[467]
Tests of General Ability. Grades kgn–2, 2–4, 4–6, 6–9, 9–12; 1959–60, c1957–60; TOGA; test booklets for grades 4–12 have the title *SRA Tests of General Ability;* 3 scores: verbal (cultural), reasoning (noncultural), total; John C. Flanagan; Science Research Associates, Inc. *
For additional information, reviews by John E. Horrocks and Richard E. Schutz, and an excerpted review by Laurence Siegel, see 6:496.

REFERENCES THROUGH 1971

1. BERNARDONI, LOUIS C. "Results of the TOGA With First Grade Children." *J Am Indian Ed* 1:24–8 Je '61. *
2. CATE, CLARENCE C. "Test Behavior of ESL Students." *Calif J Ed Res* 18:184–7 S '67. * (*PA* 42:4480)
3. CONN, LANE K.; EDWARDS, CARL N.; ROSENTHAL, ROBERT; AND CROWNE, DOUGLAS. "Perception of Emotion and Response to Teachers' Expectancy by Elementary School Children." *Psychol Rep* 22:27–34 F '68. * (*PA* 42:11118)
4. STOUGH, KENNETH FRANCIS. *An Analysis of Selected Factors as Predictors of Success in Vocational Industrial Certification Courses.* Doctor's thesis, University of Maryland (College Park, Md.), 1968. (*DA* 29:2595A)
5. BRAGG, JANE K. *Six Predictive Reading Capacity Formulas With Actual Reading Achievement for Children in Grades 3–6.* Master's thesis, Rutgers—The State University (New Brunswick, N.J.), 1971.
6. DAVISON, DONALD G., AND KILGORE, JOHN H. "A Model for Evaluating the Effectiveness of Economic Education in Primary Grades." *J Econ Ed* 3(1):17–25 f '71. *
7. FIELDER, WILLIAM R.; COHEN, RONALD D.; AND FEENEY, STEPHANIE. "An Attempt to Replicate the Teacher Expectancy Effect." *Psychol Rep* 29(3):1223–8 D '71. * (*PA* 48:1638)
8. LOWELL, ROBERT E. "Reading Readiness Factors as Predictors of Success in First Grade Reading." *J Learn Dis* 4(10):563–7 D '71. * (*PA* 47:11782)

CUMULATIVE NAME INDEX

Bernardoni, L. C.: 1   Fielder, W. R.: 7
Bragg, J. K.: 5   Horrocks, J. E.: *rev,* 6:496
Cate, C. C.: 2   Kilgore, J. H.: 6
Cohen, R. D.: 7   Lowell, R. E.: 8
Conn, L. K.: 3   Rosenthal, R.: 3
Crowne, D.: 3   Schutz, R. E.: *rev,* 6:496
Davison, D. G.: 6   Siegel, L.: *exc,* 6:496
Edwards, C. N.: 3   Stough, K. F.: 4
Feeney, S.: 7

[468]
*Tests of General Ability: Inter-American Series. Preschool, grades kgn–1.5, 2–3, 4–6, 7–9, 10–13.5; 1961–73; TGA; revision of *Tests of General Ability: Co-operative Inter-American Tests;* 6 levels; parallel editions in English and Spanish; Herschel T. Manuel; Guidance Testing Associates. *
a) PRESCHOOL LEVEL. Ages 4–5; 1966–73; 3 scores: verbal-numerical, nonverbal, total.
b) LEVEL 1—PRIMARY. Grades kgn–1.5; 1962–73; 3 scores: same as in *a*.
c) LEVEL 2—PRIMARY. Grades 2–3; 1964–73; 3 scores: same as in *a*.

d) LEVEL 3—ELEMENTARY. Grades 4–6; 1961–73; 4 scores: verbal, nonverbal, numerical, total.

e) LEVEL 4—INTERMEDIATE. Grades 7–9; 1962–73; 4 scores: same as in *d.*

f) LEVEL 5—ADVANCED. Grades 10–13.5; 1962–67; 4 scores: same as in *d.*

For additional information and reviews by Russel F. Green and Richard E. Schutz, see 7:391 (2 references); for reviews by Raleigh M. Drake and Walter N. Durost of the earlier edition, see 4:325 (8 references).

REFERENCES THROUGH 1971

1–8. See 4:325.
9–10. See 7:391.
11. CHENAULT, VIVIAN MARGARET. *A Study of the Cooperative Inter-American Tests of General Ability and Reading at the Primary Level.* Master's thesis, University of Texas (Austin, Tex.), 1951.

CUMULATIVE NAME INDEX

Chenault, V. M.: 11	McCranie, J.: 2
Drake, R. M.: *rev,* 4:325	Manuel, H. T.: 8–10
Dunham, C. V.: 6	Schutz, R. E.: *rev,* 7:391
Durost, W. N.: *rev,* 4:325	Stovall, F. L.: 1, 7
Fife, R. H.: 8	Willhauk, R. C.: 4
Green, R. F.: *rev,* 7:391	Zaccaria, M. A.: 5
Kelley, F.: 3	

[469]

Thurstone Test of Mental Alertness. Grades 9–12 and adults; 1943–68; TTMA; abbreviated adaptation of *American Council on Education Psychological Examination for High School Students,* 1940 Edition; for a shorter adaptation of this test, see *SRA Verbal Form;* 3 scores: quantitative, linguistic, total; Thelma Gwinn Thurstone and L. L. Thurstone; Science Research Associates, Inc. *

For additional information and a review by Robert D. North, see 7:392 (4 references); for a review by Joshua A. Fishman, see 5:391; see also 4:326 (3 references); for reviews by Anne Anastasi and Emily T. Burr of an earlier edition, see 3:265.

REFERENCES THROUGH 1971

1–3. See 4:326.
4–7. See 7:392.
8. BASS, BERNARD M. "Further Evidence on the Dynamic Character of Criteria." *Personnel Psychol* 15:93–7 sp '62. * (*PA* 37:3906)
9. MAHER, HOWARD. "Validity Information Exchange, No. 16-01: D.O.T. Code 0-06.71, Feature Writer; 0-06.73, Columnist; 0-06.92, Copyreader (Rewrite Man)." *Personnel Psychol* 16:71–3 sp '63. *
10. MAHER, HOWARD. "Validity Information Exchange, No. 16-02: D.O.T. Code 1-87.26, Advertising Space Salesman." *Personnel Psychol* 16:74–7 sp '63. *
11. BENTZ, V. JON. Chap. 7, "The Sears Experience in the Investigation, Description, and Prediction of Executive Behavior," pp. 147–205; critique by Ross Stagner, pp. 206–27. In *Measuring Executive Effectiveness.* Edited by Frederic R. Wickert and Dalton E. McFarland. New York: Appleton-Century-Crofts, 1967. Pp. viii, 242. *
12. FARR, JAMES L.; O'LEARY, BRIAN S.; AND BARTLETT, C. J. "Ethnic Group Membership as a Moderator of the Prediction of Job Performance." *Personnel Psychol* 24(4):609–36 w '71. *

CUMULATIVE NAME INDEX

Anastasi, A.: *rev,* 3:265	Hackney, K. U.: 1
Bartlett, C. J.: 12	Maher, H.: 2, 9–10
Bass, B. M.: 8	North, R. D.: *rev,* 7:392
Bentz, V. J.: 6, 11	O'Leary, B. S.: 12
Borg, W. R.: 3	Peterson, F. E.: 4
Burr, E. T.: *rev,* 3:265	Stagner, R.: 11
Farr, J. L.: 12	Vivers, R. B. B.: 5
Fife, I. E.: 2	Wheeler, R. W.: 7
Fishman, J. A.: *rev,* 5:391	

[470]

*The Undergraduate Program Aptitude Test. Grades 15–16; 1969–73; formerly called *The Undergraduate Record Examinations: Aptitude Test;* test available to colleges for local administration; 2 scores: verbal, quantitative; Educational Testing Service. * For the testing program entry, see 1062.

Tests of General Ability

For additional information, see 7:393. For reviews of the testing program, see 7:671 (2 reviews).

[471]

The Verbal Power Test of Concept Equivalence. Ages 14 and over; 1959–63; VPT; E. Francesco; Western Psychological Services. *

For additional information and a review by Erwin K. Taylor, see 7:394; see also 6:508 (3 references).

REFERENCES THROUGH 1971

1–3. See 6:508.
4. FRANCESCO, E. "Performance of the VPT With Low-Variance Samples." *J Social Psychol* 62:343–9 Ap '64. * (*PA* 39:5057)
5. BORGATTA, EDGAR F. "Intelligent Word Associations." *Multiv Behav Res* 6(3):301–11 Jl '71. * (*PA* 47:4828)
6. LAMBERT, PHILIP; HANSEN, LEE H.; AND BORGATTA, EDGAR F. "Intelligent Word Associations in High School Students." *J Ed Res* 64(6):269–70 F '71. * (*PA* 46:11510)

CUMULATIVE NAME INDEX

Borgatta, E. F.: 5–6	Lambert, P.: 6
Francesco, E.: 1–4	Taylor, E. K.: *rev,* 7:394
Hansen, L. H.: 6	

[472]

Verbal Reasoning. Job applicants and industrial employees; 1958–61; Raymond J. Corsini, Richard Renck, and Measurement Research Division, Industrial Relations Center, University of Chicago (manual); the Center. *

For additional information and reviews by James E. Kennedy and David G. Ryans, see 6:509.

[473]

*Verbal Reasoning: Differential Aptitude Tests. Grades 8–12 and adults; 1947–73; 2 editions; George K. Bennett, Harold G. Seashore, and Alexander G. Wesman; Psychological Corporation. * For the complete battery entry, see 1069.

a) FORM A. 1947–59. *Out of print.*

b) FORM T. 1947–73; revision of Forms L and M ('61).

For reviews of the complete battery, see 7:673 (1 review, 1 excerpt), 6:767 (2 reviews), 5:605 (2 reviews), 4:711 (3 reviews), and 3:620 (1 excerpt).

REFERENCES THROUGH 1971

1. WILLIAMS, NANCY. "A Study of the Validity of the Verbal Reasoning Subtest and the Abstract Reasoning Subtest of the Differential Aptitude Tests." *Ed & Psychol Meas* 12:129–31 sp '52. * (*PA* 27:5914)
2. CATTELL, RAYMOND B., AND SCHEIER, IVAN H. "The Objective Test Measurement of Neuroticism, U.I. 23 (—)." *Indian J Psychol* 33:217–36 pt 4 '58. * (*PA* 35:3427, title only)
3. MOSHIN, S. M. "Plea for a Scientific Aptitude Test and a Preliminary Report of the Development of Such Test." *Indian J Psychol* 34:36–42 pt 1 '59. *
4. MILTON, OHMER. "Primitive Thinking and Reasoning Among College Students." *J Higher Ed* 31:218–20 Ap '60. *
5. AIJAZ, SAIYID MOHAMMAD. *Predictive Validity of the Three Versions of the "Verbal Reasoning" and the "Numerical Ability" Subtests of the Differential Aptitude Tests for East Pakistan.* Doctor's research study No. 1, Colorado State College (Greeley, Colo.), 1963. (*DA* 24:1068)
6. DAYAL, P. "Study of the Relationship Between a Verbal Intelligence Test (B.P.T. 15) and Verbal Reasoning Plus Numerical Ability Test Scores of the D.A.T." *J Voc & Ed Guid* (India) 10:83–9 Ag '64. * (*PA* 39:5114)
7. BUSBY, WALTER ALVIN. *A Multivariate Analysis of the Relationship of Academic Motivation, Aptitude, Socio-Economic Status, and Age to Persistence in Adult Evening School.* Doctor's thesis, Michigan State University (East Lansing, Mich.), 1965. (*DA* 26:4414)
8. CHAUDHRY, GHULAM MOHAMMED, AND KAYANI, MOHAMMED RASHID. "A Comparative Study of the DAT Verbal Reasoning, ACE Psychological Examination and Cooperative English Comprehension Tests as Predictors of Academic Success in the Institute of Education and Research, University of the Panjab." *B Ed & Res* (Pakistan) 4(2):1–21 '65. *
9. BAROYA, GEORGE MANORANJAN. *Reliability, Validity, and Comparability of Forms L and M of the "Verbal Reasoning" and the "Numerical Ability" Subtests of the Differential Aptitude Tests for Use in East Pakistan.* Doctor's research study No. 1, Colorado State College (Greeley, Colo.), 1966. (*DA* 27:2865A)

10. CAIN, RALPH W. "Relationships of Verbal Reasoning and Numerical Ability to Achievement in First-Year Algebra." *Sch Sci & Math* 66:131–4 F '66. *

11. HASHMI, SHAMIM AHMAD. *Effect of Previous Academic Achievement on the Performance of First-Year College Students of East Pakistan on the "Verbal Reasoning" and the "Numerical Ability" Subtests of the Differential Aptitude Tests.* Doctor's research study No. 1, Colorado State College (Greeley, Colo.), 1966. (*DA* 27:2391A)

12. NELSON, LEONARD THEODORE, JR. *The Relationship Between Verbal, Visual-Spatial, and Numerical Abilities and the Learning of the Mathematical Concept of Function.* Doctor's thesis, University of Michigan (Ann Arbor, Mich.), 1968. (*DAI* 30:218A)

CUMULATIVE NAME INDEX

Aijaz, S. M.: 5	Hashmi, S. A.: 11
Baroya, G. M.: 9	Kayani, M. R.: 8
Busby, W. A.: 7	Milton, O.: 4
Cain, R. W.: 10	Moshin, S. M.: 3
Cattell, R. B.: 2	Nelson, L. T.: 12
Chaudhry, G. M.: 8	Scheier, I. H.: 2
Dayal, P.: 6	Williams, N.: 1

[474]

Verbal Tests (Adv.). Ages 12–13; 1954–67; 5 tests; distribution restricted to directors of education; published for National Foundation for Educational Research in England and Wales; Ginn & Co. Ltd. [England]. *

a) VERBAL TEST (ADV.) 1. 1954–55; D. A. Pidgeon.
b) VERBAL TEST (ADV.) 2. 1957. *Out of print.*
c) VERBAL TEST (ADV.) 3. 1958.
d) VERBAL TEST (ADV.) 4. 1960.
e) VERBAL TEST (ADV.) 5. 1962–67.

For additional information, see 7:395; for reviews by J. S. Lawes and John Nisbet of Tests 1–4, see 6:510.

[475]

Verbal Tests BC, CD, C, and D. Ages 8-0 to 10-6, 9-0 to 11-6, 9-6 to 12-0; 1953–66; 3 levels; published for the National Foundation for Educational Research in England and Wales; Ginn & Co. Ltd. [England]. *

a) VERBAL TEST BC. Ages 8-0 to 10-6; 1953–62; formerly called *Primary Verbal Test 1;* adaptation of *A.C.E.R. Junior A Test* and *A.C.E.R. Junior B Test;* D. A. Pidgeon.

b) VERBAL TESTS CD AND C. Ages 9-0 to 11-6; 1959–66; 2 tests.

1) *Verbal Test CD.* Ages 9-0 to 11-6; formerly called *Primary Verbal Test 2;* Valerie Land.

2) *Verbal Test C.* Ages 9-4 to 11-0; formerly called *Primary Verbal Test 2G.*

c) VERBAL TEST D. Ages 9-6 to 12-0; 1962; formerly called *Primary Verbal Test 3;* T. Neville Postlethwaite.

For additional information, see 7:396; for reviews by John Nisbet and F. W. Warburton of *a*, see 5:369.

[476]

Verbal Tests EF and GH. Ages 11.0–13.5, 13.5–15.0; 1960–66; 2 levels; Valerie Land and Olive Wood (*a*); published for the National Foundation for Educational Research in England and Wales; Ginn & Co. Ltd. [England]. *

a) VERBAL TEST EF. Ages 11.0–13.5; 1960; formerly called *Secondary Verbal Test 1.*

b) VERBAL TEST GH. Ages 13.5–15.0; 1962–66; formerly called *Secondary Verbal Test 2.*

For additional information, see 7:397; for a review by Stanley Nisbet of *a*, see 6:499.

[477]

***Verbal Tests 15–23 and 69.** Ages 10–12; 1951–72; 10 tests; new test published annually; tests 1–2 and 4–14 are out of print; distribution restricted to directors of education; published for the National Foundation

for Educational Research in England and Wales; Ginn & Co. Ltd. [England]. *

a) VERBAL TEST 15. 1964–65.
b) VERBAL TEST 16. 1965–66.
c) VERBAL TEST 17. 1966–67.
d) VERBAL TEST 18. 1967–68.
e) VERBAL TEST 19. 1968–69.
f) VERBAL TESTS 20 AND 69. 1969–70; 2 editions.

1) *Verbal Test 20.* 1969–70.
2) *Verbal Test 69.* 1969; multiple choice version of form 20A.

g) VERBAL TEST 21. 1970–71.
h) VERBAL TEST 22. 1971.
i) VERBAL TEST 23. 1972.

For additional information and a review by David A. Walker of tests 13–20, see 7:398; for a review by Arthur B. Royse of earlier tests, see 6:511 (1 reference).

REFERENCES THROUGH 1971
1. See 6:511.

CUMULATIVE NAME INDEX

Butcher, H. J.: 1	Royse, A. B.: *rev,* 6:511
Moreton, C. A.: 1	Walker, D. A.: *rev,* 7:398

[478]

★**WLW Employment Inventory III.** Job applicants; 1954–72; approximately 65 percent of the items are from *WLW Culture Fair Inventory, WLW Mental Alertness Inventory,* and *WLW Employment Inventory, Short Form;* 4 scores: verbal, numerical, nonverbal, total; L. D. Edmonson, W. E. Brown, T. L. Chappell, W. H. E. Geiger, R. W. Henderson, T. E. Sutherland, W. S. Jones, and L. C. Steckle; William, Lynde & Williams. *

[479]

★**WLW Mental Alertness Inventory.** Job applicants; 1955; 3 scores: verbal, nonverbal, total; R. W. Henderson, W. E. Brown, T. L. Chappell, L. D. Edmonson, W. H. E. Geiger, R. L. Kaiser, L. E. Saddler, and L. C. Steckle; William, Lynde & Williams. *

[480]

Wesman Personnel Classification Test. Grades 8–16 and adults; 1946–65; WPCT; title on Forms A and B is *Personnel Classification Test;* 3 scores: verbal, numerical, total; Alexander G. Wesman; Psychological Corporation. *

For additional information, a review by Arthur C. MacKinney, and an excerpted review by Jack C. Merwin, see 7:400 (7 references); see also 5:399 (8 references); for reviews by John C. Flanagan and Erwin K. Taylor, see 4:331 (3 references); for an excerpted review, see 3:253.

REFERENCES THROUGH 1971
1–3. See 4:331.
4–11. See 5:399.
12–18. See 7:400.

19. GARBER, W. F. "Evaluation of Psychometric Tests for Optometry." *Optom Weekly* 40:1927–32+, 1953–7 D 22, 29 '49. * (*PA* 24:3477)

20. FRANKLE, A. H. "Indirect Measurement of Personal Adjustment by Use of a Conventional Industrial Aptitude Test." *Proc Inter Congr Appl Psychol* 16:284–90 '68. *

CUMULATIVE NAME INDEX

Abrahams, N.: 16	Gerken, C. d'A.: 5
Abt, L. E.: 1	Gilbert, H. B.: 3–4
Ash, P.: 12–3	Haner, C. F.: 6
Baier, D. E.: 9–10	Holt, W. G.: 7, 11
Cottle, W. C.: 11	Kirchner, W. K.: 14
Dugan, R. D.: 9–10, 15	MacKinney, A. C.: *rev,* 7:400
Dunnette, M. D.: 14, 16	Merwin, J. C.: *exc,* 7:400
Flanagan, J. C.: *rev,* 4:331	Ottman, D. K.: 11
Frankle, A. H.: 20	Parry, M. E.: 18
Garber, W. F.: 19	Perrine, M. W.: 8

Poruben, A.: 2
Taylor, E. K.: *rev*, 4:331
Vincent, N. L.: 15

Welsch, L. A.: 17
Wernimont, P.: 16
Williams, J. E.: 5

[481]
The Western Personnel Tests. College and adults; 1962; WPT; Robert L. Gunn and Morse P. Manson; Western Psychological Services. *

For additional information and reviews by Lewis E. Albright and Erwin K. Taylor, see 6:512.

REFERENCES THROUGH 1971

1. MONROE, KENTON L. "Note on the Estimation of the WAIS Full Scale IQ." *J Clin Psychol* 22:79–81 Ja '66. * (*PA* 40:4217)

CUMULATIVE NAME INDEX

Albright, L. E.: *rev*, 6:512   Taylor, E. K.: *rev*, 6:512
Monroe, K. L.: 1

[482]
Wonderlic Personnel Test. Adults; 1938–72; WPT; Forms D and F are adaptations of *Otis Self-Administering Tests of Mental Ability*, Higher Form; E. F. Wonderlic; E. F. Wonderlic & Associates, Inc.*

For additional information and reviews by Robert C. Droege and John P. Foley, Jr., see 7:401 (28 references) ; for reviews by N. M. Downie and Marvin D. Dunnette, see 6:513 (17 references) ; see also 5:400 (59 references) ; for reviews by H. E. Brogden, Charles D. Flory, and Irving Lorge, see 3:269 (7 references) ; see also 2:1415 (2 references).

REFERENCES THROUGH 1971

1–2. See 2:1415.
3–9. See 3:269.
10–68. See 5:400.
69–85. See 6:513.
86–113. See 7:401.

114. GUEST, LESTER, AND NUCKOLS, ROBERT. "A Laboratory Experiment in Recording in Public Opinion Interviewing." *Int J Opin & Attitude Res* (Mexico) 4:336–52 f '50. * (*PA* 25:7387)
115. WEIDER, ARTHUR. "Some Aspects of an Industrial Mental Hygiene Program." *J Appl Psychol* 35:383–5 D '51. * (*PA* 26:6560)
116. BASS, BERNARD M. "Validity Information Exchange, No. 10-25: D.O.T. Code 1-85.22, Salesman, Foodstuffs." *Personnel Psychol* 10:343–4 au '57. *
117. BIAMONTE, A. J. "A Study of the Effect of Attitudes on the Learning of Computer Programming." *Proc Ann Computer Personnel Res Conf* 3:68–74 '65. *
118. GETZELS, J. W., AND CSIKSZENTMIHALYI, M. Chap. 15, "The Study of Creativity in Future Artists: The Criterion Problem," pp. 349–68. In *Experience, Structure and Adaptability*. Edited by O. J. Harvey. New York: Springer Publishing Co., Inc., 1966. Pp. ix, 406. *
119. GORDON, BRUCE F., AND DENNIS, RICHARD A. "Characteristics and Performance Predictors of 7094 Computer Service Operators." *Proc Ann Computer Personnel Res Conf* 4:96–106 '66. *
120. BLANK, STANLEY S. "An Examination of the Usefulness of Various Psychological Instruments for Predicting Department Managers' Ratings of Clerical Sales Personnel." *Can Counsellor* 2:46–50 Ja '68. *
121. BOTTEGAL, J. DAVID, AND DECKER, ROBERT L. "An Industrial Test-Validation to Meet the Requirements of Title VII of the Civil Rights Act of 1964." *Proc W Va Acad Sci* 41(1969): 204–9 '70. *
122. COX, WRAY KENT. *Personality, Intelligence, and Work Performance of Disadvantaged Adolescents*. Doctor's thesis, University of Missouri (Columbia, Mo.), 1971. (*DAI* 32:4939A)
123. GLUSKINOS, URY, AND BRENNAN, THOMAS F. "Selection and Evaluation Procedure for Operating Room Personnel." *J Appl Psychol* 55(2):165–9 Ap '71. * (*PA* 46:3909)

CUMULATIVE NAME INDEX

Albright, L. E.: 64, 67, 72, 85, 100, 102
American Gas Association, Personnel Committee: 30
Aursand, I. M.: 43
Barnabas, B.: 48–9
Barrett, R. S.: 65
Barton, G.: 69
Bass, B. M.: 35, 116
Benson, D.: 80
Biamonte, A. J.: 117
Blakemore, A.: 26

Blank, S. S.: 120
Bolanovich, D. J.: 5
Boneau, C. A.: 54, 59
Bottegal, J. D.: 121
Braaten, L. J.: 43
Brailey, L. G.: 78
Brennan, T. F.: 123
Bridgman, C. S.: 66
Brogden, H. E.: *rev*, 3:269
Browne, C. G.: 76
Busch, A. C.: 73–4
Butler, P. C.: 104

Campbell, J. T.: 78
Canfield, A. A.: 56
Capwell, D. F.: 15
Carlson, W. A.: 3
Chesler, D. J.: 14
Coats, J. E.: 82
Cox, W. K.: 122
Csikszentmihalyi, M.: 118
Cuomo, S.: 50
Decker, R. L.: 121
Dennis, R. A.: 119
Dignan, F.: 66
Doub, B. A.: 19
Downie, N. M.: *rev*, 6:513
Droege, R. C.: *rev*, 7:401
Dulsky, S. G.: 20
Dunn, R. E.: 81
Dunnette, M. D.: *rev*, 6:513
Fiske, D. W.: 13
Fitzpatrick, E. D.: 41, 44–6, 51, 57
Flory, C. D.: *rev*, 3:269
Foley, J. P.: *rev*, 7:401
Garner, R. G.: 82
Getzels, J. W.: 118
Glaser, R.: 16
Glennon, J. R.: 64, 67, 72, 85
Gluskinos, U.: 123
Goldhor, H.: 55
Goldman, S.: 103
Gordon, B. F.: 119
Grohsmeyer, F. A.: 36
Guest, L.: 114
Haner, C. F.: 37
Hanson, R.: 80
Harding, F. D.: 52
Harrison, R.: 53
Hawkins, W. A.: 79
Hay, E. N.: 21, 27, 31, 38
Hodgson, R. W.: 89
Holmes, F. J.: 22–3
Hoskins, J. E.: 90
Hovland, C. I.: 1–2
Hunt, W.: 53
Huttner, L.: 70
Irish, T. E.: 99
Jackson, T. A.: 53
Jacobson, C. F.: 10
Jennings, E. E.: 32
Jensen, M. B.: 8
Jerdee, T. H.: 87
Jex, F. B.: 92
Johnson, D. L.: 7
Kaplan, M.: 105
Karlins, M.: 105
Karstendiek, B.: 35
Kazmier, L. J.: 75–6
Keillor, J. S.: 109
Keim, L.: 93
King, D. C.: 83
Kirchner, W.: 80
Knauft, E. B.: 17, 39
Kopff, R. G.: 94

Krout, M. H.: 20
Kushmar, H. S.: 56
Laing, D. M.: 4
Laney, A. R.: 28
Lindzey, G.: 18
Lindzey, G. E.: 11
Lord, R. M.: 106
Lorge, I.: *rev*, 3:269
McCarty, J. J.: 40–1, 44–6, 51, 57, 60–3
McCullough, G.: 35
MacKinney, A. C.: 77
McMurry, F. D.: 100
McMurry, R. N.: 7
McNamara, W. J.: 84
Mahoney, T. A.: 87
Martin, F.: 42
Meyer, H. H.: 29, 50
Miller, R. B.: 24
Mitchell, M. D.: 100
Morrison, W. E.: 88
Nash, A. N.: 87
Neel, R. G.: 81
Nuckols, R.: 114
Parry, M. E.: 101
Penfield, R. V.: 95
Phillips, J. C.: 68
Prien, E. P.: 78, 110
Pruitt, R. C.: 35
Richardson, B. K.: 107
Robbins, J. E.: 83
Roberts, W. H.: 12
Ronan, W. W.: 111
Rotter, J. B.: 8
Rowe, F. B.: 86
Ruda, E.: 102
Rusmore, J.: 42
Rusmore, J. T.: 104
Schuerhoff, C.: 105
Schuh, A. J.: 98
Seashore, H. G.: 33
Shott, G. L.: 85
Skard, Ø.: 43
Skolnicki, J.: 71
Smith, W. J.: 64, 67, 72
Spaethe, M.: 66
Stene, D. M.: 70
Thompson, C. E.: 9
Thumin, F.: 103
Thumin, F. J.: 91, 112
Walker, F. C.: 58
Weaver, H. B.: 54, 59
Wechsler, I. R.: 25
Weider, A.: 115
Westberg, W. C.: 41, 44–6
Wevrick, L.: 113
Wille, G. R.: 108
Wittenberg, A.: 91
Wolins, L.: 77
Wonderlic, E. F.: 1–2, 6, 96–7
Woodward, R. H.: 73–4
Wright, J. H.: 4
Young, M. B.: 47

[Out of Print Since TIP I]

Carlton Picture Intelligence Test, 6:447 (2 reviews)

Classification Test 40-A, 6:448 (2 reviews)

Cole-Vincent Group Intelligence Test for School Entrants, 3:226 (1 review)

College Placement Test, 5:319 (2 reviews)

Comprehension Tests: Supplementary Mentality Tests for Superior Adults, T:741

Daneshill Intelligence Test, 5:325 (2 reviews)

Davis-Eells Test of General Intelligence or Problem-Solving Ability, 5:326 (3 reviews, 36 references)

Dawson Mental Test, 2:1389 (2 reviews, 2 excerpts)

Detroit Advanced First-Grade Intelligence Test, 2:1392 (1 review)

Detroit Advanced Intelligence Test, 5:329c (1 review, 6 references—3, 4, 6, 7, 8, 9)

Detroit Alpha Intelligence Test, 5:329b (1 review, 7 references—1, 3, 5, 6, 8, 10, 11)

Detroit Beginning First-Grade Intelligence Test, 1:1044 (1 review, 1 excerpt)

Dominion Group Test of Intelligence, 5:330

Duplex Series of Ability Tests, 4:289 (2 reviews, 1 excerpt, 2 references)

Easel Age Scale, 5:332 (2 reviews)

FR-CR Test, 4:339 (1 review, 1 reference); now available only as a subtest of Leiter Adult Intelligence Scale, 504

General Intelligence: Northumberland Standardised Tests (1925 Series), T:760

Gestalt Continuation Test (status unknown), 6:459 (3 references)

Group Tests 33 and 33B, 5:339 (11 references)

Group Test 90A, 5:340 (1 review)

Inductive Reasoning Test, 3:232 (1 review)

Job Alertness Tests, T:776

Junior School Grading Test, 2:1400 (1 review)

Kentucky General Ability Test, 3:234 (1 review, 3 references); revised edition was available only as a part of Kentucky Classification Battery, 4:301 (1 review, 4 references)

Kingsway Intelligence Tests, 3:235 (2 excerpts)

Laycock Mental Ability Test, 3:237 (2 reviews)

Leiter Adaptation of Arthur's Stencil Design Test, 4:347 (1 excerpt, 1 reference); now available only as a subtest of Leiter Adult Intelligence Scale, 504

Leiter Adaptation of the Painted Cube Test, 4:348 (1 excerpt, 1 reference); now available only as a subtest of Leiter Adult Intelligence Scale, 504

Lowry-Lucier Reasoning Test Combination, 7:361 (2 reviews, 7 references)

Maddox Verbal Reasoning Test, 6:469 (2 reviews, 1 excerpt)

Manchester General Ability Test (Senior), 6:470 (3 reviews, 1 reference)

Multi-Racial Picture Intelligence Tests Suitable for Use in African and Asian Schools, 6:476

New Rhode Island Intelligence Test, 5:354 (1 review, 6 references)

Non-Language Multi-Mental Test, 3:243 (1 review, 1 reference)

"Northern" Test of Educability, T:805

Orally Presented Group Test of Intelligence for Juniors, 5:360 (1 review, 2 references)

Otis Classification Test, 3:247 (1 excerpt, 3 references)

Otis General Intelligence Examination, 3:248 (1 review)

Otis Group Intelligence Scale, 6:480 (1 review, 44 references)

Partington's Pathways Test, 4:355 (1 review, 1 excerpt, 1 reference); now available only as a subtest of Leiter Adult Intelligence Scale, 504

Pintner General Ability Tests: Non-Language Series, 3:254 (1 review)

Pintner General Ability Tests: Verbal Series, 5:368 (2 reviews, 2 excerpts, 23 references); the lowest level, Pintner-Cunningham Primary Test, 435, is still in print

Purdue Non-Language Test, 6:491 (2 reviews)

Quick Word Test, 7:378 (1 review, 2 excerpts, 8 references)

Roback Mentality Tests for Superior Adults, T:837

SRA College Classification Tests, 5:376

SRA Tests of Educational Ability, 6:495 (5 reviews, 1 excerpt, 1 reference)

School Aptitude Test: Thanet Mental Tests, 2:1422 (1 review)

Schrammel General Ability Test, 6:498 (1 review)

Scientific Ingenuity and Juristic Aptitude Test, T:848

Selective Service System College Qualification Test, T:851

Survey of Mental Maturity: California Survey Series, 6:503 (1 review)

Terman-McNemar Test of Mental Ability, 4:324 (4 reviews, 62 references)

Test of General Knowledge, 2:1425 (1 reference)

Test of Word-Number Ability, 5:389 (3 reviews, 1 reference)

Tomlinson Junior School Test, 5:392 (1 review)

Verbal and Non-Verbal Test 1, 5:393 (1 review)

Verbal Capacity Sampler, 5:394

Vocabulary Tests, 5:398 (1 review)

WLW Culture Fair Inventory, 7:399 (2 reviews)

"West Riding" Tests of Mental Ability, 2:1430 (1 review)

"West Yorkshire" Group Test of Intelligence, 4:332

INDIVIDUAL

[483]

Arthur Point Scale of Performance Tests. Ages 4.5 or 5.5 to superior adults; 1925–47; 2 editions; Grace Arthur. *

a) FORM I. Ages 5.5 to superior adults; 1925–43; 10 tests: *Knox Cube Test (Arthur Revision), Seguin Form Board (Arthur Revision), Two-Figure Form Board, Casuist Form Board, Manikin Test, Feature Profile Test, Mare and Foal Formboard, Healy Pictorial Completion Test I, Porteus Maze Test (1924 Series), The Block-Design Test (Arthur Modification)*; Stoelting Co.

b) REVISED FORM II. Ages 4.5 to superior adults; 1933–47; 5 tests: *Knox Cube Test (Arthur Revision), Seguin Form Board (Arthur Revision), Arthur Stencil Design Test I, Porteus Maze Test (Arthur Revision), Healy Pictorial Completion Test II*; Psychological Corporation.

For additional information and a review by William R. Grove, see 4:335 (12 references); for an excerpted review, see 3:271 (20 references); for reviews by Andrew W. Brown and Carroll A. Whitmer and an excerpted review by Donald Snedden, see 2:1379 (17 references). For excerpts from related book reviews, see 2:B830 (1 excerpt), 1:B304 (7 excerpts), and 36:B19 (1 excerpt).

REFERENCES THROUGH 1971

1–16. See 2:1379.

17–35. See 3:271.

36–47. See 4:335.

48. BALKEN, EVA RUTH; MAURER, SIEGFRIED; AND FALSTEIN, EUGENE K. "Variations in Psychological Measurements Associated With Increased Feeding of Vitamins A, D, B₁, and B₂ and

Iron in Dementia Praecox." *J Comp Psychol* 21:387–403 Je '36. * (*PA* 10:5019)

49. HINTON, RALPH T., JR. "The Role of the Basal Metabolic Rate in the Intelligence of Ninety Grade-School Students." *J Ed Psychol* 27:546–50 O '36. * (*PA* 11:1247)

50. NAROSNY, ELEANOR HELEN. *A Comparative Study of the Performanie of Juvenile Delinquents and Educational Problem Children on the Stanford-Binet and Grace Arthur Scales.* Master's thesis, Ohio State University (Columbus, Ohio), 1937.

51. HASLAM, PHYLLIS. *The Prediction of Ability on the Arthur Point Performance Scale From the Merrill-Palmer Scale.* Master's thesis, State University of Iowa (Iowa City, Iowa), 1938.

52. HINTON, RALPH T., JR. "A Further Study of the Role of the Basal Metabolic Rate in the Intelligence of Children." *J Ed Psychol* 30:309–14 Ap '39. * (*PA* 13:5462)

53. BIJOU, S. W., AND MCCANDLESS, B. R. "An Approach to a More Comprehensive Analysis of Mentally Retarded Pre-Delinquent Boys." *J Genetic Psychol* 65:147–60 S '44. * (*PA* 19:440)

54. ZIMMERMAN, FREDERIC T.; BURGEMEISTER, BESSIE B.; AND PUTNAM, TRACY J. "A Group Study of the Effect of Glutamic Acid Upon Mental Functioning in Children and Adolescents." *Psychosom Med* 9:175–83 My–Je '47. * (*PA* 21:3474)

55. JOSEPH, ALICE, AND MURRAY, VERONICA F. *Chamorros and Carolinians of Saipan: Personality Studies,* pp. 119–35, 329–36, passim. Cambridge, Mass.: Harvard University Press, 1951. Pp. xviii, 381. * (*PA* 26:3359)

56. COHEN, BERTRAM D., AND COLLIER, MARY J. "A Note on the WISC and Other Tests of Children Six to Eight Years Old." *J Consult Psychol* 16:226–7 Je '52. * (*PA* 27:5145)

57. GELLERMAN, SAUL W. "Forms I and II of the Arthur Performance Scales With Mental Defectives." *J Consult Psychol* 16:127–31 Ap '52. * (*PA* 27:2719)

58. JOHNSON, ELIZABETH Z. "Sex Differences and Variability in the Performance of Retarded Children on Raven, Binet and Arthur Tests." *J Clin Psychol* 8:298–301 Jl '52. * (*PA* 27:5981)

59. MANOLAKES, GEORGE, AND SHELDON, WILLIAM D. "A Comparison of the Grace Arthur, Revised Form II, and the Stanford-Binet, Revised Form L." *Ed & Psychol Meas* 12:105–8 sp '52. * (*PA* 27:5886)

60. GLOWATSKY, EDWARD. "The Verbal Element in the Intelligence Scores of Congenitally Deaf and Hard of Hearing Children." *Am Ann Deaf* 98:328–35 My '53. * (*PA* 28:7921)

61. VARVA, FRANK IRVIN. *An Investigation of the Effect of Auditory Deficiency Upon Performance With Special Reference to Concrete and Abstract Tasks.* Doctor's thesis, University of Pittsburgh (Pittsburgh, Pa.), 1956. (*DA* 16:2532)

62. SHONTZ, FRANKLIN C. "Evaluation of Intellectual Potential in Hemiplegic Individuals." *J Clin Psychol* 13:267–9 Jl '57. * (*PA* 32:5816)

63. LEVINSON, BORIS M. "A Research Note on the Knox Cubes as an Intelligence Test for Aged Males." *J Gerontol* 15: 85–6 Ja '60. * (*PA* 35:6234)

64. SHECHTMAN, AUDREY M. *The Relationship of Variability in Children's Verbal and Non-Language Test Performance to Current and Later Behavioral Functions.* Doctor's thesis, University of Minnesota (Minneapolis, Minn.), 1961. (*DA* 22:2065)

65. BERGÈS, JEAN, AND LÉZINE, IRÈNE. *The Imitation of Gestures: A Technique for Studying the Body Schema and Praxis of Children Three to Six Years of Age,* pp. 83–7. Clinics in Developmental Medicine No. 18. Translated from the 1963 French edition by Arthur H. Parmelee, Jr. Published for the Spastics Society Medical Education and Information Unit, 1965. Pp. x, 116. *

66. KOWITZ, GERALD T., AND LEVY, LOIS E. "Underachievement in Deaf Children." *Am Ann Deaf* 110:414–9 My '65. * (*PA* 39:15990)

67. SANTORO, ROSEANN MARIE. *The Relationship of Reading Achievement to Specific Measures of Visual Perception, Visual-Motor Perception and Intelligence.* Doctor's thesis, Fordham University (New York, N.Y.), 1967. (*DA* 28:4010A)

68. SILBERBERG, NORMAN E., AND BOURESTOM, NORMAN C. "The Knox Cubes as a Screening Measure of Intelligence for Hemiparetic Patients." *J Clin Psychol* 24:348–9 Jl '68. * (*PA* 42:16431)

CUMULATIVE NAME INDEX

[484]

Bayley Scales of Infant Development. Ages 2–30 months; 1969; BSID; 2 scores: mental, motor, plus 30 behavior ratings; Nancy Bayley; Psychological Corporation. *

For additional information and reviews by Roberta R. Collard and Raymond H. Holden, see 7:402 (20 references).

REFERENCES THROUGH 1971

1–20. See 7:402.

21. ROSENBLITH, JUDY F. "Prognostic Value of Behavioral Assessments of Neonates." *Biologia Neonatorum* (Switzerland) 6(1–2):76–103 '64. *

22. VANDENBERG, STEVEN G.; STAFFORD, RICHARD E.; AND BROWN, ANNE E. Chap. 10, "The Louisville Twin Study," pp. 153–204. In *Progress in Human Behavior Genetics.* Edited by Steven G. Vandenberg. Baltimore, Md.: Johns Hopkins Press, 1968. Pp. xi, 356. *

23. HERMAN, SUSAN JANE. *The Relationship Between Maternal Variable Scores and Infant Performance in a Negro Experimental Stimulation Training Population.* Doctor's thesis, University of Florida (Gainesville, Fla.), 1970. (*DAI* 32:239A)

24. KILBRIDE, JANET E.; ROBBINS, MICHAEL C.; AND KILBRIDE, PHILIP L. "The Comparative Motor Development of Baganda, American White, and American Black Infants." *Am Anthrop* 72(6):1422–8 D '70. * (*PA* 46:8847)

25. BAYLEY, NANCY, AND HUNT, JANE V. "Explorations Into Patterns of Mental Development and Prediction From Bayley Scales of Infant Development," pp. 52–71. In *Minnesota Symposia on Child Psychology, Vol. 5.* Edited by John P. Hill. Minneapolis, Minn.: University of Minnesota Press, 1971. Pp. xiii, 216. *

26. BLAINE, HENRY MYRATE, II. *The Relationship of Attention Span in a Selected Group of Infants to Performance on a Test of Mental Abilities.* Doctor's thesis, University of Alabama (University, Ala.), 1971. (*DAI* 32:2511A)

27. GOFFENEY, BARBARA; HENDERSON, NORMAN B.; AND BUTLER, BRUCE V. "Negro-White, Male-Female Eight-Month Developmental Scores Compared With Seven-Year WISC and Bender Test Scores." *Child Develop* 42(2):595–604 Je '71. * (*PA* 47:651)

28. HIGUCHI, JUDITH L. *Applications of the Bayley Scales of Infant Development to Multiply Handicapped Children.* Master's thesis, George Peabody College (Nashville, Tenn.), 1971.

29. HUNT, JANE V., AND BAYLEY, NANCY. "Explorations Into Patterns of Mental Development From the Bayley Scales of Infant Development." *Minn Symposia Child Psychol* 5:52–71 '71. *

30. ROBINSON, HALBERT B., AND ROBINSON, NANCY M. "Longitudinal Development of Very Young Children in a Comprehensive Day Care Program: The First Two Years." *Child Develop* 42(6):1673–83 D '71. * (*PA* 48:8827)

31. WELCHER, DORIS W.; MELLITS, E. DAVID; AND HARDY, JANET B. "A Multivariate Analysis of Factors Affecting Psychological Performance." *Johns Hopkins Med J* 129(1):19–35 Jl '71. *

CUMULATIVE NAME INDEX

Goffeney, B.: 27
Gravem, H.: 18
Hardy, J. B.: 31
Henderson, N. B.: 27
Herman, S. J.: 23
Higuchi, J. L.: 28
Holden, R. H.: rev, 7:402
Hunt, J. V.: 25, 29
Ireton, H.: 18
Johnson, N. M.: 17
Jones, W. S.: 19
Kilbride, J. E.: 24
Kilbride, P. L.: 24
Klatskin, E. H.: 5
Kohen-Raz, R.: 6, 9, 14
Lord, R. M.: 19
McGarry, M. E.: 5
Man, E. B.: 19
Mellits, E. D.: 31

Mendelson, M. A.: 10
Patel, A.: 2
Phatak, P.: 2
Poffenberger, T.: 2
Robbins, M. C.: 24
Robinson, H. B.: 30
Robinson, J. S.: 11
Robinson, N. M.: 30
Rosenblith, J. F.: 21
Schaefer, E. S.: 1
Stafford, R. E.: 22
Steward, M. S.: 5
Thwing, E.: 18
Vanderberg, S. G.: 22
Welcher, D. W.: 31
Werner, E. E.: 7
Willerman, L.: 20
Yule, W.: 8

[485]

★**Bingham Button Test.** Disadvantaged children ages 3–6; 1967; BBT; "knowledge and understanding of simple terms and relationships"; William J. Bingham; Bingham Button Test. *

[486]

Canadian Intelligence Test, 1966 Revision. Ages 3–16; 1940–66; formerly called *Canadian Intelligence Examination;* modification of the 1916 *Stanford Revision of the Binet-Simon Intelligence Scale;* Carman E. Stothers, Beverly R. Collier, James W. Covert, and James C. Williams; McGraw-Hill Ryerson Ltd. [Canada]. *

For additional information and a review by Hugh Taylor, see 7:403; for a review by Gwen F. Arnold of the 1947 edition, see 4:336; for excerpted reviews by Clara Blacklock and one other, see 3:272 (1 reference).

REFERENCES THROUGH 1971

1. See 3:272.

CUMULATIVE NAME INDEX

Arnold, G. F.: rev, 4:336
Blacklock, C.: exc, 3:272

Stothers, C. E.: 1
Taylor, H.: rev, 7:403

[487]

Cattell Infant Intelligence Scale. Ages 3–30 months; 1940–60; downward extension of *Stanford-Binet Intelligence Scale, Second Revision;* Psyche Cattell; Psychological Corporation. *

For additional information, see 6:515 (22 references); for reviews by Florence M. Teagarden and Beth L. Wellman and excerpted reviews by Rachel Stutsman Ball, C. M. Louttit, T. L. McCulloch, Norma V. Scheidemann, and Helen Speyer, see 3:281–2.

REFERENCES THROUGH 1971

1–22. See 6:515.
23. SIMON, ABRAHAM J., AND BASS, LIBBY G. "Toward a Validation of Infant Testing." *Am J Orthopsychiatry* 26:340–50 Ap '56. * (PA 31:4713)
24. DENNIS, WAYNE, AND NAJARIAN, PERGROUHI. "Infant Development Under Environmental Handicap." *Psychol Monogr* 71(7):1–13 '57. * (PA 33:5830)
25. HOHMAN, LESLIE B., AND FREEDHEIM, DONALD K. "A Study of IQ Retest Evaluations on 370 Cerebral Palsied Children." *Am J Phys Med* 38:180–7 O '59. *
26. WIEMERS, IRENE HOLLINGSWORTH. *Evaluating Adequacy of Adjustment in Normal Infants.* Doctor's thesis, University of Utah (Salt Lake City, Utah), 1960. (DA 21:2791)
27. DUNPHY, DONAL, AND PESSIN, VIVIAN. "Correlation Between Cord Blood Oxygen Values and Psychological Test Scores." *J Iowa Med Soc* 52:212–6 Ap '62. *
28. BIERMAN, JESSIE M.; CONNOR, ANGIE; VAAGE, MARILYN; AND HONZIK, MARJORIE P. "Pediatricians' Assessments of the Intelligence of Two-Year-Olds and Their Mental Test Scores." *Pediatrics* 34:680–90 N '64. *
29. KARELITZ, SAMUEL; FISICHELLI, VINCENT R.; COSTA, JOAN; KARELITZ, RUTH; AND ROSENFIELD, LAURA. "Relation of Crying Activity in Early Infancy to Speech and Intellectual Development at Age Three Years." *Child Develop* 35:769–77 S '64. * (PA 39:4513)
30. GERSON, ELAINE F., AND SCOTT, ROLAND B. "Growth and Development of Negro Infants: 7, The Relationship of Parental

Attitudes and Socioeconomic Pressures to Intelligence and Gross Motor Quotients During the Second Year of Life." *Med Ann DC* 35:5–8 Ja '66. *
31. LUSZKI, WALTER A. "Intellectual Functioning of Spastic Cerebral Palsied." *Cereb Palsy J* 27:7–9 Mr–Ap '66. * (PA 40:8010)
32. MATHENY, ADAM P., JR. "Improving Diagnostic Forecasts Made on a Developmental Scale." *Am J Mental Def* 71:371–5 N '66. * (PA 41:1706)
33. SIDERITS, MARY ANNE TERESA. *Indices of Change in the Cattell-Binet Ratings of Intellectually Sub-Average Children.* Doctor's thesis, University of Michigan (Ann Arbor, Mich.), 1966. (DA 27:2519B)
34. STOTT, LELAND H., AND BALL, RACHEL STUTSMAN. *Infant and Preschool Mental Tests: Review and Evaluation.* Monographs of the Society for Research in Child Development, Vol. 30, No. 3, Serial No. 101. Chicago, Ill.: University of Chicago Press, 1966. Pp. iv, 151. * (PA 40:7220)
35. ALPERN, GERALD D. "Measurement of 'Untestable' Autistic Children." *J Abn Psychol* 72:478–86 D '67. * (PA 42:4183)
36. LINDE, LEONARD M.; RASOF, BEATRICE; AND DUNN, OLIVE JEAN. "Mental Development in Congenital Heart Disease." *J Pediatrics* 71:198–203 Ag '67. *
37. RASOF, BEATRICE; LINDE, LEONARD M.; AND DUNN, OLIVE JEAN. "Intellectual Development in Children With Congenital Heart Disease." *Child Develop* 38:1043–53 D '67. * (PA 42:7687)
38. WERNER, EMMY; SIMONIAN, KENNETH; BIERMAN, JESSIE M.; AND FRENCH, FERN E. "Cumulative Effect of Perinatal Complications and Deprived Environment on Physical, Intellectual, and Social Development of Preschool Children." *Pediatrics* 39:490–505 Ap '67. *
39. BONACCORSI, MARIE-THÉRÈSE; GAGNON, JACQUES; DESTROOPER, JOHAN; AND TOUSIGNANT, FRANCINE. "The Relationship Between Mongoloid Phenotype and Genotype: A Comparative Study of the Psychological and Social Developments of Diplo 21/Triplo 21 Mosaic and Standard Trisomy 21." *Proc 4th World Congr Psychiatry* 1966(pt 3):1584–6 '68. *
40. ERICKSON, MARILYN T. "The Predictive Validity of the Cattell Infant Intelligence Scale for Young Mentally Retarded Children." *Am J Mental Def* 72:728–33 Mr '68. * (PA 42:11047)
41. GOLDEN, MARK, AND BIRNS, BEVERLY. "Social Class and Cognitive Development in Infancy." *Merrill-Palmer Q* 14:139–49 Ap '68. * (PA 43:2423)
42. WERNER, EMMY E.; HONZIK, MARJORIE P.; AND SMITH, RUTH S. "Prediction of Intelligence and Achievement at Ten Years From Twenty Months Pediatric and Psychologic Examinations." *Child Develop* 39:1063–75 D '68. * (PA 43:8145)
43. WERNER, EMMY E.; SIMONIAN, KENNETH; AND SMITH, RUTH S. "Ethnic and Socioeconomic Status Differences in Abilities and Achievement Among Preschool and School-Age Children in Hawaii." *J Social Psychol* 75:43–59 Je '68. * (PA 42:13553)
44. ALPERN, GERALD D., AND KIMBERLIN, CAROLYN C. "Short Intelligence Test Ranging From Infancy Levels Through Childhood Levels for Use With the Retarded." *Am J Mental Def* 75(1):65–71 Jl '70. * (PA 45:1185)
45. BAYLEY, NANCY. Chap. 16, "Development of Mental Abilities," pp. 1163–209. In *Carmichael's Manual of Child Psychology, Third Edition, Vol. 1.* Edited by Paul H. Mussen. New York: John Wiley & Sons, Inc., 1970. Pp. xiii, 1519. *
46. ERICKSON, MARILYN T.; JOHNSON, NANCY M.; AND CAMPBELL, FRANCES A. "Relationships Among Scores on Infant Tests for Children With Developmental Problems." *Am J Mental Def* 75(1):102–4 Jl '70. * (PA 45:926)
47. BECKWITH, LEILA. "Relationships Between Attributes of Mothers and Their Infants' IQ Scores." *Child Develop* 42(4):1083–97 O '71. * (PA 48:2692)
48. GOLDEN, MARK; BIRNS, BEVERLY; BRIDGER, WAGNER; AND MOSS, ABIGAIL. "Social-Class Differentiation in Cognitive Development Among Black Preschool Children." *Child Develop* 42(1):37–45 Mr '71. * (PA 46:4621)
49. HUSTED, J.; WALLIN, K.; AND WOODEN, H. "The Psychological Evaluation of Profoundly Retarded Children With the Use of Concrete Reinforcers." *J Psychol* 77(2):173–9 Mr '71. * (PA 46:1701)

CUMULATIVE NAME INDEX

Allen, R. M.: 15
Alpern, G. D.: 35, 44
Ball, R. S.: 34; exc, 3:282
Bass, L. G.: 23
Bayley, N.: 45
Beckwith, L.: 47
Bierman, J. M.: 28, 38
Birns, B.: 41, 48
Bonaccorsi, M. T.: 39
Bridger, W.: 48
Brodie, F. H.: 14
Campbell, F. A.: 46
Cattell, P.: 1–2, 10, 18
Cavanaugh, M. C.: 12
Cohen, I.: 12
Connor, A.: 28

Costa, J.: 29
Dennis, W.: 24
Destrooper, J.: 39
Dunn, O. J.: 36–7
Dunphy, D.: 12, 27
Erickson, M. T.: 40, 46
Escalona, S.: 4–5, 20
Fisichelli, V. R.: 29
Freedheim, D. K.: 25
French, F. E.: 38
Fromm, E.: 13
Gagnon, J.: 39
Gallagher, J. J.: 11
Gerson, E. F.: 30
Gerstein, R. A.: 3
Goldberg, I. D.: 12

Golden, M.: 41, 48
Harms, I. E.: 6, 16
Hartman, L. D.: 13
Hohman, L. B.: 25
Honzik, M. P.: 28, 42
Husted, J.: 49
Johnson, N. M.: 46
Karelitz, R.: 29
Karelitz, S.: 29
Kimberlin, C. C.: 44
Klatskin, E. H.: 8
Kralovich, A. M.: 17
Linde, L. M.: 36–7
London, S. K.: 22
Louttit, C. M.: *exc*, 3:282
Luszki, W. A.: 31
McCulloch, T. L.: *exc*, 3:282
Marschak, M.: 13
Matheny, A. P.: 32
Miller, E.: 9
Moriarty, A.: 20
Moss, A.: 48
Najarian, P.: 24
Norris, M.: 14
Pease, D.: 21
Pessin, V.: 27
Rasof, B.: 36–7

Ringwall, E. A.: 12
Rosauer, J. K.: 21
Rosenfeld, G. B.: 9
Rosenfeld, L.: 29
Scheidemann, N. V.: *exc*, 3:281
Scott, R. B.: 30
Siderits, M. A. T.: 33
Simon, A. J.: 23
Simonian, K.: 38, 43
Smith, R. S.: 42–3
Spaulding, P. J.: 14
Speyer, H.: *exc*, 3:282
Spiker, C. C.: 16
Stott, L. H.: 34
Teagarden, F. M.: *rev*, 3:281
Tousignant, F.: 39
Vaage, M.: 28
Wallin, K.: 49
Watson, R. I.: 7
Wellman, B. L.: *rev*, 3:281
Werner, E.: 38
Werner, E. E.: 42–3
Wiemers, I. H.: 26
Wiggin, M. K.: 19
Wolins, L.: 21
Wooden, H.: 49

[488]

★Classification Tasks, Experimental Edition. Ages 5–9; 1971; for research use only; 2 scores (response, response plus explanation) for each of 2 tasks (cross-classification, equivalence); Mary Nixon; Australian Council for Educational Research [Australia]. *

REFERENCES THROUGH 1971

1. NIXON, MARY. *Children's Classification Skills.* Hawthorn, Vic., Australia: Australian Council for Educational Research, 1971. Pp. 107. *

CUMULATIVE NAME INDEX

Nixon, M.: 1

[489]

*Columbia Mental Maturity Scale, Third Edition. Ages 3.5–9; 1954–72; CMMS; Bessie B. Burgemeister, Lucille Hollander Blum, and Irving Lorge; Harcourt Brace Jovanovich, Inc. *

For additional information and reviews by Marshall S. Hiskey and T. Ernest Newland of an earlier edition, see 6:517 (22 references); see also 5:402 (12 references).

REFERENCES THROUGH 1971

1–13. See 5:402.
14–35. See 6:517.
36. STEPHENSON, GEORGE ROTHWELL. *Form Perception, Abstract Thinking and Intelligence Test Validity in Cerebral Palsy.* Doctor's thesis, Columbia University (New York, N.Y.), 1957. (*DA* 17:1600)
37. BOONE, DANIEL R. "Communication Skills and Intelligence in Right and Left Hemiplegics." *J Speech & Hearing Disorders* 24:241–8 Ag '59. * (*PA* 34:8233)
38. LEREA, LOUIS, AND KOHUT, SUZANNE. "A Comparative Study of Monolinguals and Bilinguals in a Verbal Task Performance." *J Clin Psychol* 17:49–52 Ja '61. * (*PA* 37:2480)
39. BRENGELMANN, JOHANNES C., AND STANDEN, JOHN L. "Task Difficulty and Response Time in the Retardate." *Training Sch B* 60:89–93 Ag '63. * (*PA* 38:4557)
40. SONNEMAN, LAWRENCE J. *A Study of the Relationships Between Four Tests of Intelligence and One Test of Scholastic Achievement.* Doctor's thesis, State University of South Dakota (Vermillion, S.D.), 1963. (*DA* 24:4555)
41. BIBB, JOHN JAMES, JR. *A Study of the Quick Test as a Screening Instrument for Educable Mentally Retarded Children.* Doctor's thesis, University of Virginia (Charlottesville, Va.), 1963. (*DA* 25:3386) (Abstract: *Ed R* 2:69–71)
42. MARLEY, ALBERT D. *A Validity Study of the Columbia Mental Maturity Scale and the Peabody Picture Vocabulary Test, Using the Wechsler Intelligence Scale for Children as the Validating Criterion, With a Selected Sample of Educable Mentally Retarded Children.* Doctor's research study No. 1, Colorado State College (Greeley, Colo.), 1964. (*DA* 25:5386)
43. TUTTLE, LESTER EUGENE, JR. *The Comparative Effect on Intelligence Test Scores of Negro and White Children When Certain Verbal and Time Factors Are Varied.* Doctor's thesis, University of Florida (Gainesville, Fla.), 1964. (*DA* 25:7093)
44. BRENGELMANN, JOHANNES C., AND HILLMAN, WILLIAM

A., JR. "Determinants of Learning in the Retardate: A Pilot Study." *Training Sch B* 61:156–62 F '65. * (*PA* 39:10570)
45. BRENGELMANN, JOHANNES C., AND HILLMAN, WILLIAM A., JR. "Perceptual and Conceptual Response Time Effects in the Retardate." *Training Sch B* 62:57–65 Ag '65. * (*PA* 40:713)
46. CORWIN, BETTY JANE. "The Influence of Culture and Language on Performance of Individual Ability Tests." *J Sch Psychol* 3:41–7 sp '65. * (*PA* 39:15217)
47. BRENGELMANN, JOHANNES C., AND HILLMAN, WILLIAM A., JR. "Response Time to Passed and Failed Problems in the Retardate." *Training Sch B* 62:128–35 N '66. * (*PA* 41:3230)
48. BRUNJE, JOHN. *Suitability of the Revised Columbia Mental Maturity Scale for Use With Educable Mentally Retarded Children.* Master's thesis, Fresno State College (Fresno, Calif.), 1966.
49. HIRSCHENFANG, SAMUEL; JARAMILLO, SELENE; AND BENTON, JOSEPH G. "Comparison of Scores on the Revised Stanford-Binet (L), Columbia Mental Maturity Scale (CMMS) and Goodenough Draw-A-Man Test of Children With Neurological Disorders." *Psychol Rep* 19:15–6 Ag '66. * (*PA* 40:12564)
50. ROBINSON, H. ALAN. "Reliability of Measures Related to Reading Success of Average, Disadvantaged, and Advantaged Kindergarten Children." Comments by Samuel Weintraub. *Read Teach* 20:203–9 D '66. * (*PA* 41:3344).
51. ROSENBERG, LEON A., AND STROUD, MICHAEL. "Limitations of Brief Intelligence Testing With Young Children." *Psychol Rep* 19:721–2 D '66. * (*PA* 41:4999)
52. TUTTLE, LESTER EUGENE, JR. "The Comparative Effect on Intelligence Test Scores of Negro and Caucasian Children When Certain Verbal and Time Factors Are Varied by Use of the WISC, PPVT, and CMMS." *Fla J Ed Res* 8:49–61 Ja '66. *
53. BUFFMIRE, JUDY A. *A Comparative Study of the Performance of Retarded Children on the Columbia Mental Maturity Scale.* Master's thesis, University of Utah (Salt Lake City, Utah), 1967.
54. MILLER, BILLY. *A Comparison of the Columbia Mental Maturity Scale, the Leiter International Performance Scale, and the Wright Short Form of the Stanford Binet, Form L-M, With the Full Scale Stanford Binet, Form L-M, on a Group of Trainable Retardates.* Master's thesis, Central Missouri State College (Warrensburg, Mo.), 1967.
55. BERMAN, ALLAN. *An Investigation of the Relationship Between Cerebral Dominance and Intelligence.* Doctor's thesis, Louisiana State University (Baton Rouge, La.), 1968. (*DA* 29:3476B)
56. HYMAN, JOANNE R. *A Study of Concept Identification in Elementary School Children Using the Columbia Mental Maturity Scale.* Master's thesis, Kent State University (Kent, Ohio), 1968.
57. LEREA, LOUIS, AND SINCLAIR, JANET K. "A Preliminary Study of Verbal Style Among Normal and Speech Defective Children." *Psychol Rec* 18:75–80 Ja '68. * (*PA* 42:9318)
58. SEKYRA, FRANCIS, III, AND ARNOULT, JOSEPH FRANCIS, III. "Negro Intellectual Assessment With Three Instruments Contrasting Caucasian and Negro Norms." *J Learn Dis* 1:564–9 O '68. * (*PA* 45:2174)
59. STERNLOF, R. E.; PARKER, H. J.; AND McCOY, J. F. "Relationships Between the Goodenough DAM Test and the Columbia Mental Maturity Test for Negro and White Headstart Children." *Percept & Motor Skills* 27:424–6 O '68. * (*PA* 43:5328)
60. DUNDORE, JAMES M., JR. *A Study of the Relationship Between Scores Earned on the Columbia Mental Maturity Scale and Peabody Picture Vocabulary Test and School Achievement of Culturally Disadvantaged Negro Children.* Master's thesis, Mississippi State University (State College, Miss.), 1969.
61. FREY, JOAN H. *A Study of the Feasibility of Using the Columbia Mental Maturity Scale to Predict School Achievement of Young Deaf Children.* Master's thesis, University of Tennessee (Knoxville, Tenn.), 1969.
62. GIOIOSO, JOSEPH V., AND ADERMAN, MORRIS. "The Combination Test as a Quick Screening Device to Differentiate Levels of Retardation." *Psychol Rep* 25(3):843–8 D '69. * (*PA* 44:18906)
63. GROSS, MORRIS. "Learning Readiness in Two Groups: A Study in 'Cultural Deprivation.'" *Jewish Ed* 39(1):36–48 Ja '69. *
64. NICHOLSON, CHARLES L. "The Use of Four Screening Instruments." *Ann Inter Conf Assn Children Learn Dis* 6:101–7 '69. *
65. VINGOE, FRANK J.; BIRNEY, S. DARYL; AND KORDINAK, S. THOMAS. "Note on Psychological Screening of Preschool Children." *Percept & Motor Skills* 29(2):661–2 O '69. * (*PA* 44:4182)
66. GOLDSTEIN, LEO S.; COLLER, ALAN R.; DILL, JOHN; AND TILIS, HOWARD S. "The Effect of a Special Curriculum for Disadvantaged Children on Test-Retest Reliabilities of Three Standardized Instruments." *J Ed Meas* 7(3):171–4 f '70. * (*PA* 45:4917)
67. NICHOLSON, CHARLES L. "Correlations Among CMMS, PPVT, and RCPM for Cerebral Palsied Children." *Percept & Motor Skills* 30(3):715–8 Je '70. * (*PA* 44:17151)
68. REUTER, JEANETTE, AND MINTZ, JOANNE. "Columbia

Cattell Infant Intelligence Scale

Mental Maturity Scale as a Test of Concept Formation." *J Consult & Clin Psychol* 34(3):387–93 Je '70. * (*PA* 44:13635)

69. BART, LEONARD EUGENE. *A Comparison of the Effectiveness of Televised and Conventional Administrations of Objective Scales.* Doctor's thesis, St. John's University (Jamaica, N.Y.), 1971. (*DAI* 32:2980B)

70. BERMAN, ALLAN. "The Problem of Assessing Cerebral Dominance and Its Relationship to Intelligence." *Cortex* (Italy) 7(4):372–86 D '71. * (*PA* 49:11336)

71. HOLLINGSWORTH, JACK DAREL. *A Comparison of Motor Ability of Mentally Retarded Children of Specific Mental and Chronological Ages and Normal Children.* Doctor's thesis, University of Georgia (Athens, Ga.), 1971. (*DAI* 32:3760A)

72. JEFFREE, D. M., AND CASHDAN, A. "Severely Subnormal Children and Their Parents: An Experiment in Language Improvement." *Brit J Ed Psychol* 41(2):184–94 Je '71. * (*PA* 47:9728)

73. KANFER, FREDERICK H.; DUERFELDT, PRYSE H.; MARTIN, BARBARA; AND DORSEY, THOMAS E. "Effects of Model Reinforcement, Expectation to Perform, and Task Performance on Model Observation." *J Pers & Social Psychol* 20(2):214–7 N '71. * (*PA* 47:6449)

74. L'ABATE, LUCIANO. "Receptive-Expressive Functions in Kindergarten Children and Adolescents." *Psychol Sch* 8(3):253–9 Jl '71. * (*PA* 47:9699)

75. PARKER, HARRY J.; STERNLOF, RICHARD E.; AND McCOY, JOHN F. "Objective Versus Individual Mental Ability Tests With Former Head Start Children in the First Grade." *Percept & Motor Skills* 32(1):287–92 F '71. * (*PA* 46:3868)

76. SWIZE, LYDIA MARIE. *The Relationship Between Performance on Piagetian Conservation Tasks and Intelligence and Achievement in Educable Mentally Retarded Children.* Doctor's thesis, University of Northern Colorado (Greeley, Colo.), 1971. (*DAI* 32:3806A)

77. SWIZE, MYRON THEODORE. *Prediction of Piagetian Conservation for Second Grade Mexican-American and Anglo-American Children.* Doctor's thesis, University of Northern Colorado (Greeley, Colo.), 1971. (*DAI* 32:5624A)

78. VANCE, SANDRA B. *A Comparison of the Wechsler Intelligence Scale for Children and the Columbia Mental Maturity Scale With Mental Retardates.* Master's thesis, East Tennessee State University (Johnson City, Tenn.), 1971.

CUMULATIVE NAME INDEX

[490]

Cooperative Preschool Inventory, Revised Edition. Ages 3–6; 1965–70; CPI; achievement in areas necessary for success in school; test booklet title is *Preschool Inventory;* standardized on disadvantaged children; Bettye M. Caldwell; Cooperative Tests and Services. *

For additional information, a review by Joseph L. French, and an excerpted review by Dale Carlson, see 7:404 (5 references).

REFERENCES THROUGH 1971

1–5. See 7:404.

6. SONTAG, MARVIN; SELLA, ADINA P.; AND THORNDIKE, ROBERT L. "The Effect of Head Start Training on the Cognitive Growth of Disadvantaged Children." *J Ed Res* 62(9):387–9 My–Je '69. * (*PA* 46:1899)

7. SLAUGHTER, DIANA T. "Parental Potency and the Achievements of Inner-City Black Children." *Am J Orthopsychiatry* 40(3):433–40 Ap '70. * (*PA* 45:8989)

8. FORMANEK, RUTH, AND WOOG, PIERRE. "Attitudes of Preschool and Elementary School Children to Authority Figures." *Child Study J* 1(2):100–10 w '71. * (*PA* 47:7523)

9. ROBINSON, HALBERT B., AND ROBINSON, NANCY M. "Longitudinal Development of Very Young Children in a Comprehensive Day Care Program: The First Two Years." *Child Develop* 42(6):1673–83 D '71. * (*PA* 48:8827)

CUMULATIVE NAME INDEX

[491]

Crichton Vocabulary Scale. Ages 4–11; 1950; John C. Raven; H. K. Lewis & Co. Ltd. [England]. *

For additional information and a review by Morton Bortner, see 6:518 (1 reference); for reviews by Charlotte Banks and W. D. Wall, see 4:337.

REFERENCES THROUGH 1971

1. See 6:518.

2. JAHODA, GUSTAV. "Development of the Perception of Social Differences in Children From 6 to 10." *Brit J Psychol* 50:159–75 My '59. * (*PA* 34:2826)

3. PAYNE, J. F. "A Comparative Study of the Mental Ability of Seven- and Eight-Year-Old British and West Indian Children in a West Midland Town." *Brit J Ed Psychol* 39(3):326–7 N '69. *

4. WOOSTER, ARTHUR D. "Social and Ethnic Differences in Understanding the Spoken Word." *Brit J Dis Commun* 5(2):118–25 O '70. *

CUMULATIVE NAME INDEX

[492]

Denver Developmental Screening Test. Ages 2 weeks to 6 years; 1968–70; DDST; 4 scores: gross motor, fine motor-adaptive, language, personal-social; William K. Frankenburg, Josiah B. Dodds, and Alma W. Fandal (manual); Ladoca Project and Publishing Foundation, Inc. *

For additional information and reviews by Alice E. Moriarty and Emmy E. Werner, see 7:405 (6 references).

REFERENCES THROUGH 1971

1–6. See 7:405.

7. "Development Screening Test." *Nursing Mirror & Midwives J* (England) 130(5):27–9 Ja 30 '70. *

8. HILL, BEVERLY E. *Developmental Screening of the Pre-School Child.* Master's thesis, Dominican College (San Rafael, Calif.), 1970.
9. BLACK, ROBERT BEN. *An Investigation of Early Childhood Development as Related to Age and Social Class.* Doctor's thesis, Ohio University (Athens, Ohio), 1971. (*DAI* 32:4934A)
10. FRANKENBURG, WILLIAM K.; CAMP, BONNIE W.; AND VAN NATTA, PEARL A. "Validity of the Denver Developmental Screening Test." *Child Develop* 42(2):475-85 Je '71. * (*PA* 47:596)
11. FRANKENBURG, WILLIAM K.; CAMP, BONNIE W.; VAN NATTA, PEARL A.; DEMERSSEMAN, JOHN A.; AND VOORHEES, SUSAN F. "Reliability and Stability of the Denver Developmental Screening Test." *Child Develop* 42(5):1315-25 N '71. * (*PA* 48:4065)
12. FRANKENBURG, WILLIAM K.; GOLDSTEIN, ARNOLD D.; AND CAMP, BONNIE W. "The Revised Denver Developmental Screening Test: Its Accuracy as a Screening Instrument." *J Pediatrics* 79(6):988-95 D '71. *

CUMULATIVE NAME INDEX

Black, R. B.: 9
Camp, B. W.: 10–2
Desmersseman, J. A.: 11
Dodds, J. B.: 1
Frankenburg, W. K.: 1, 3, 10–2
Goldstein, A. D.: 12
Hill, B. E.: 8
Koupernik, C.: 2
Moriarty, A. E.: *rev, 7:*405
Ratner, G.: 5
Robischon, P.: 4
Sandler, L.: 5
Smith, J. H.: 6
Stafford, C.: 5
VanCampen, J.: 5
Van Natta, P. A.: 10–1
Voorhees, S. F.: 11
Weismar, R.: 5
Werner, E. E.: *rev, 7:*405

[493]

Detroit Tests of Learning Aptitude. Ages 3 and over; 1935-68; DTLA; 20 scores: pictorial absurdities, verbal absurdities, pictorial opposites, verbal opposites, motor speed and precision, auditory attention span (for unrelated words, for related syllables), oral commissions, social adjustment A, visual attention span (for objects, for letters), orientation, free association, memory for designs, number ability, social adjustment B, broken pictures, oral directions, likenesses and differences, total; Harry J. Baker and Bernice Leland; Bobbs-Merrill Co., Inc. *

For additional information, see 7:406 (10 references) ; for a review by F. L. Wells, see 3:275 (1 reference) ; for reviews by Anne Anastasi and Henry Feinberg and an excerpted review by D. A. Worcester (with S. M. Corey) of an earlier edition, see 1:1058.

REFERENCES THROUGH 1971

1. See 3:275.
2–11. See 7:406.
12. ENGELHARDT, GEORGE MICHAEL. *Predicting Rehabilitation of Socially Maladjusted Boys From the Detroit Tests of Learning Aptitude.* Doctor's thesis, Wayne State University (Detroit, Mich.), 1969. (*DAI* 32:6191A)
13. FALK, LIBBY JANET. *A Profile of Learning Abilities and Behavioral Characteristics of Elementary School-Age Children With Phenylketonuria.* Doctor's thesis, Temple University (Philadelphia, Pa.), 1971. (*DAI* 32:1913A)
14. MYKLEBUST, HELMER R.; BANNOCHIE, MARGARET N.; AND KILLEN, JAMES R. Chap. 9, "Learning Disabilities and Cognitive Processes," pp. 213–51. In *Progress in Learning Disabilities, Vol. 2.* Edited by Helmer R. Myklebust. New York: Grune & Stratton, Inc., 1971. Pp. ix, 404. *

CUMULATIVE NAME INDEX

Anastasi, A.: *rev,* 1:1058
Ashlock, P.: 4
Ashlock, P. R.: 2
Banas, N.: 8
Bannochie, M. N.: 14
Bruininks, R. H.: 9
Charry, L. B.: 5
Chiappone, A. D.: 7
Corey, S. M.: 1; *exc,* 1:1058
Engelhardt, G. M.: 11–2
Falk, L. J.: 13
Feinberg, H.: *rev,* 1:1058
Hudson, F. G.: 10
Killen, J. R.: 14
Myklebust, H. R.: 14
Nelson, C. M.: 10
Sandstedt, B.: 3
Wartenberg, H.: 6
Wells, F. L.: *rev,* 3:275
Wills, I. H.: 8
Worcester, D. A.: 1; *exc,* 1:1058

[494]

A Developmental Screening Inventory. Ages 1–18 months; 1966; DSI; test consists of selected items from *Gesell Developmental Schedules;* abnormal development; history and observation ratings in 5 areas: adaptive, gross motor, fine motor, language, personal-social; Hilda Knobloch, Benjamin Pasamanick, and Earl S. Sherard, Jr.; Hilda Knobloch. *

For additional information, see 7:407 (1 reference).

REFERENCES THROUGH 1971

1. See 7:407.
2. KNOBLOCH, HILDA, AND PASAMANICK, BENJAMIN. "A Developmental Questionnaire for Infants Forty Weeks of Age: An Evaluation." *Monogr Soc Res Child Develop* 20(2):1–112 '55. * (*PA* 31:673)
3. KNOBLOCH, HILDA; RIDER, ROWLAND; PASAMANICK, BENJAMIN; AND HARPER, PAUL. "An Evaluation of a Questionnaire on Infant Development." *Am J Pub Health* 45:1309-20 O '55. * (*PA* 30:8137)

CUMULATIVE NAME INDEX

Harper, P.: 3
Knobloch, H.: 1–3
Pasamanick, B.: 1–3
Rider, R.: 3
Sherard, E. S.: 1

[495]

***English Picture Vocabulary Test.** Ages 5–8, 7–11, 11 and over; 1962–68; EPVT; derived from *Peabody Picture Vocabulary Test;* 3 levels; M. A. Brimer and Lloyd M. Dunn; Educational Evaluation Enterprises [England]. *

a) TEST 1. Ages 5–8; 1962–66.
b) TEST 2. Ages 7–11; 1962–66.
c) TEST 3. Ages 11 and over; 1968.

For additional information and a review by Kenneth Lovell of Tests 1–2, see 7:408 (5 references) ; for reviews by L. B. Birch and Philip M. Levy, see 6:520.

REFERENCES THROUGH 1971

1–5. See 7:408.
6. WOOSTER, ARTHUR D. "Social and Ethnic Differences in Understanding the Spoken Word." *Brit J Dis Commun* 5(2): 118–25 O '70. *
7. CHEYNE, WILLIAM M., AND JAHODA, GUSTAV. "Emotional Sensitivity and Intelligence in Children From Orphanages and Normal Homes." *J Child Psychol & Psychiatry* (England) 12(2):77–90 Je '71. * (*PA* 47:4505)
8. CONRAD, R. "The Chronology of the Development of Covert Speech in Children." *Develop Psychol* 5(3):398-405 N '71. * (*PA* 47:4506)
9. CREED, C. D., AND ROBINSON, W. P. "Intelligence Test Scores in the Evaluation of a 'Use of Language' Programme for Infant School Children." *Res Ed* (England) 6:1–11 N '71. * (*PA* 48:12239)

CUMULATIVE NAME INDEX

Bannon, W. J.: 2
Birch, L. B.: *rev,* 6:520
Brimer, M. A.: 3
Cheyne, W. M.: 7
Conrad, R.: 8
Creed, C. D.: 9
Horne, I. E.: 4
Jahoda, G.: 7
Levy, P. M.: *rev,* 6:520
Lovell, K.: *rev,* 7:408
Marshall, A.: 1
O'Kelly, E.: 5
Phillips, C. J.: 2
Robinson, W. P.: 9
Wedell, K.: 4
Wooster, A. D.: 6

[496]

Full-Range Picture Vocabulary Test. Ages 2 and over; 1948; Robert B. Ammons and Helen S. Ammons; Psychological Test Specialists. *

For additional information, see 6:521 (30 references) ; for reviews by William D. Altus and William M. Cruickshank, see 4:340 (10 references).

REFERENCES THROUGH 1971

1–10. See 4:340.
11–40. See 6:521.
41. JENSEN, MILTON B., AND SCHMID, JOHN. "An Analysis of Some Clinical Judgments on Male Basic Airmen Who Failed the Group Psychological Tests." *J Clin Psychol* 10:325-32 O '54. * (*PA* 29:4753)
42. STEPHENSON, GEORGE ROTHWELL. *Form Perception, Abstract Thinking and Intelligence Test Validity in Cerebral Palsy.* Doctor's thesis, Columbia University (New York, N.Y.), 1957. (*DA* 17:1600)
43. TIKOFSKY, RONALD SHERWOOD. *An Investigation of Some Possible Relationships Between Neurologic and Psychologic Techniques in the Study of Aphasia.* Doctor's thesis, University of Utah (Salt Lake City, Utah), 1957. (*DA* 18:1903)
44. WINTHROP, HENRY. "Scoring, Validation, and Construction Problems in the Picture Recognition Type of Vocabulary Test." *J General Psychol* 56:269-79 Ap '57. * (*PA* 33:11039)
45. YOUNG, CECIL, AND MCCONNELL, FREEMAN. "Retardation

of Vocabulary Development in Hard of Hearing Children."
Excep Children 23:368–70 My '57. * (*PA* 33:4509)

46. INGLIS, JAMES. "Learning, Retention, and Conceptual Usage in Elderly Patients With Memory Disorder." *J Abn & Social Psychol* 59:210–5 S '59. * (*PA* 34:3317)

47. WINITZ, HARRIS. "Language Skills of Male and Female Kindergarten Children." *J Speech & Hearing Res* 2:377–86 D '59. * (*PA* 34:5895)

48. WINTHROP, HENRY. "Relative Variability With Visually Mediated Vocabulary Among the Retarded." *Psychol Rep* 5:318 Je '59. * (*PA* 34:3186)

49. DOEHRING, DONALD G., AND ROSENSTEIN, JOSEPH. "Visual Word Recognition by Deaf and Hearing Children." *J Speech & Hearing Res* 3:320–6 D '60. * (*PA* 35:2488)

50. SCHUELL, HILDRED; JENKINS, JAMES; AND LANDIS, LYDIA. "Relationship Between Auditory Comprehension and Word Frequency in Aphasia." *J Speech & Hearing Res* 4:30–6 Mr '61. * (*PA* 35:6801)

51. SPRAGUE, ANN LEE. *The Relationship Between Selected Measures of Expressive Language and Motor Skill in Eight-Year-Old Boys.* Doctor's thesis, State University of Iowa (Iowa City, Iowa), 1961. (*DA* 21:3696)

52. OHLSEN, ROBERT L., JR. *The Effects of Concretion and Abstraction on Vocabulary Performance of Mentally Retarded, Average and Bright Children.* Doctor's thesis, University of Kansas (Lawrence, Kan.), 1963. (*DA* 25:1664)

53. GROSSBERG, JOHN M. "A Comparison of the Full-Range Picture Vocabulary Test and WISC in Clinical Use." Abstract. *J Consult Psychol* 28:188 Ap '64. * (*PA* 39:1732, title only)

54. JACKSON, CECIL LEE. *Factor Structure of the Wechsler Intelligence Scale for Children and Selected Reference Tests at Pre-School Level and After First Grade: A Longitudinal Study.* Doctor's thesis, University of Georgia (Athens, Ga.), 1964. (*DA* 25:6052)

55. RUGG, ROGER H. *A Comparison of the Relative Effectiveness of the Peabody Picture Vocabulary Test and the Ammons Full Range Picture Vocabulary Test With Educable Mentally Retarded Children.* Master's thesis, Sacramento State College (Sacramento, Calif.), 1964.

56. STERNE, DAVID M. "Use of a Picture Vocabulary in Evaluating Comprehension in Residual Aphasia After CVA." *J Clin Psychol* 20:357–9 Jl '64. * (*PA* 39:10543)

57. HEDGER, MABLE F. Chap. 3, "An Analysis of Three Picture Vocabulary Tests for Use With the Deaf," pp. 12–9. In *Research Studies on the Psycholinguistic Behavior of Deaf Children.* Edited by Joseph Rosenstein and Walter H. MacGinitie. CEC Research Monograph, Series B, No. B-2. Washington, D.C.: Council for Exceptional Children, 1965. Pp. v, 40. *

58. KIMBRELL, DON L. "Comparison of PPVT, FRPVT, RS-B, and Academic Achievement Scores Among Institutionalized Educable Mental Retardates." *Percept & Motor Skills* 23:1178 D '66. * (*PA* 41:6185)

59. LINDSEY, JAMES MORRISON. *The Factorial Organization of Intelligence in Children as Related to the Variables of Age, Sex and Subculture.* Doctor's thesis, University of Georgia (Athens, Ga.), 1966. (*DA* 27:3664B)

60. VELLUTINO, FRANK R., AND HOGAN, TERRENCE P. "The Relationship Between the Ammons and WAIS Test Performances of Unselected Psychiatric Subjects." *J Clin Psychol* 22:69–71 Ja '66. * (*PA* 40:4221)

61. COOPER, G. DAVID; YORK, MICHAEL W.; DASTON, PAUL G.; AND ADAMS, HENRY B. "The Porteus Test and Various Measures of Intelligence With Southern Negro Adolescents." *Am J Mental Def* 71:787–92 Mr '67. * (*PA* 41:8879)

62. OSBORNE, R. T.; ANDERSON, HARRY E., JR.; AND BASHAW, W. L. "The Stability of the WISC Factor Structure at Three Age Levels." *Multiv Behav Res* 2:443–51 O '67. * (*PA* 42:6388)

63. SILVERSTEIN, A. B., AND HILL, THOMAS VERNON. "Comparability of Three Picture Vocabulary Tests With Retarded School Children." *Training Sch B* 64:58–61 Ag '67. * (*PA* 42:1057)

64. SYDIAHA, DANIEL. "Prediction of WAIS IQ for Psychiatric Patients Using the Ammons' FRPV and Raven's Progressive Matrices." *Psychol Rep* 20:823–6 Je '67. * (*PA* 41:13602)

65. DICKINSON, THOMAS C.; NEUBERT, JOAN; AND McDERMOTT, DOROTHY. "Relationship of Scores on the Full-Range Picture Vocabulary Test and the Wechsler Adult Intelligence Scale in a Vocational Rehabilitation Setting." *Psychol Rep* 23:1263–6 D '68. * (*PA* 43:8448)

66. FINE, MARVIN J., AND TRACY, D. B. "Performance of Normal and EMR Boys on the FRPV and GHDT." *Am J Mental Def* 72:648–52 Mr '68. * (*PA* 42:11049)

67. CARDONE, SAMUEL S., AND OLSON, RONALD E. "Chlorpromazine and Body Image: Effects on Chronic Schizophrenics." *Arch Gen Psychiatry* 20(5):576–82 My '69. * (*PA* 43:16118)

68. FRANK, HARRY, AND FIEDLER, EDNA R. "A Multifactor Behavioral Approach to the Genetic-Etiological Diagnosis of Mental Retardation." *Multiv Behav Res* 4(2):131–45 Ap '69. * (*PA* 43:16258)

69. GIOIOSO, JOSEPH V., AND ADERMAN, MORRIS. "The Combination Test as a Quick Screening Device to Differentiate Levels of Retardation." *Psychol Rep* 25(3):843–8 D '69. * (*PA* 44:18906)

70. HOGAN, TERRENCE P. "Relationship Between the Ammons

IQ Norms and WAIS Test Performances of Psychiatric Subjects." *J Clin Psychol* 25(3):275–6 Jl '69. * (*PA* 44:3679)

71. MARKIDES, M. "The Speech of Deaf and Partially-Hearing Children With Special Reference to Factors Affecting Intelligibility." *Brit J Dis Commun* 5(2):126–40 O '70. * (*PA* 46:7484)

72. GRANICK, SAMUEL. "Brief Tests and Their Interrelations as Intelligence Measures of Aged Subjects." Abstract. *Proc 79th Ann Conv Am Psychol Assn* 6(2):599–600 '71. * (*PA* 46:4727)

73. MOORE, N. I. "Cognitive Styles and the Schizophrenias and Character Disorders." *Percept & Motor Skills* 33(2):475–82 O '71. * (*PA* 47:7200)

CUMULATIVE NAME INDEX

[497]

Gesell Developmental Schedules, 1940 Series.
Ages 4 weeks to 6 years; 1925–49; GDS; Arnold Gesell and others; Psychological Corporation. *

For additional information and a review by Emmy E. Werner, see 6:522 (27 references); see also 4:341 (5 references); for reviews by Nancy Bayley and Florence M. Teagarden, see 3:276 (28 references). For excerpts from related book reviews, see 3:277 (11 excerpts), 3:278 (4 excerpts), 3:279 (8 excerpts), 3:280 (1 excerpt), 2:B912 (3 excerpts), 2:B913 (13 excerpts), 2:B914 (6 excerpts), 2:B915 (8 excerpts), and 2:B916 (15 excerpts).

REFERENCES THROUGH 1971

1–28. See 3:276.
29–33. See 4:341.
34–60. See 6:522.
61. GESELL, ARNOLD, AND LORD, ELIZABETH EVANS. "A Psychological Comparison of Nursery School Children From Homes

of Low and High Economic Status." *J Genetic Psychol* 34:339–56 S '27. * (*PA* 2:751)

62. GESELL, ARNOLD L. "Developmental Diagnosis of Infant and Child: Its Role in Clinical Medicine." *Post Grad Med J* (England) 1:29–35 Ja '47. * (*PA* 21:4408)

63. BERKO, MARTIN J. "Measurement of Behavioral Development in Cerebral Palsy." *Cereb Palsy R* 15:16–7 Je–Jl '54. * (*PA* 29:6088)

64. APGAR, VIRGINIA; GIRDANY, B. R.; McINTOSH, R.; AND TAYLOR, H. C., JR. "Neonatal Anoxia: 1, A Study of the Relation of Oxygenation at Birth to Intellectual Development." *Pediatrics* 15:653–62 Je '55. *

65. DU PAN, R. MARTIN, AND ROTH, S. "The Psychologic Development of a Group of Children Brought Up in a Hospital Type Residential Nursery." *J Pediatrics* 47:124–9 Jl '55. * (*PA* 30:4251)

66. KNOBLOCH, HILDA, AND PASAMANICK, BENJAMIN. "A Developmental Questionnaire for Infants Forty Weeks of Age: An Evaluation." *Monogr Soc Res Child Develop* 20(2):1–112 '55. * (*PA* 31:673)

67. KNOBLOCH, HILDA; RIDER, ROWLAND; PASAMANICK, BENJAMIN; AND HARPER, PAUL. "An Evaluation of a Questionnaire on Infant Development." *Am J Pub Health* 45:1309–20 O '55. * (*PA* 30:8137)

68. FISH, BARBARA. "The Detection of Schizophrenia in Infancy: A Preliminary Report." *J Nerv & Mental Dis* 125:1–24 Ja–Mr '57. * (*PA* 33:4353)

69. GEBER, MARCELLE, AND DEAN, R. F. A. "Gesell Tests on African Children." *Pediatrics* 20:1055–65 D '57. *

70. KNOBLOCH, HILDA, AND PASAMANICK, BENJAMIN. "The Relationship of Race and Socioeconomic Status to the Development of Motor Behavior Patterns in Infants." *Psychiatric Res Rep* 10:123–33 D '58. * (*PA* 35:1971)

71. KNOBLOCH, HILDA, AND PASAMANICK, BENJAMIN. "Environmental Factors Affecting Human Development, Before and After Birth." *Pediatrics* 26:210–8 Ag '60. *

72. WIEMERS, IRENE HOLLINGSWORTH. *Evaluating Adequacy of Adjustment in Normal Infants.* Doctor's thesis, University of Utah (Salt Lake City, Utah), 1960. (*DA* 21:2791)

73. PELZ, KURT; PIKE, FRANCES; AND AMES, LOUISE B. "A Proposed Battery of Childhood Tests for Discriminating Between Different Levels of Intactness of Function in Elderly Subjects." *J Genetic Psychol* 100:23–40 Mr '62. * (*PA* 37:975)

74. WOODWARD, MARY, AND STERN, DIANA J. "Developmental Patterns of Severely Subnormal Children." *Brit J Ed Psychol* 33:10–21 F '63. * (*PA* 38:673)

75. AMES, LOUISE B., AND ILG, FRANCES L. "Sex Differences in Test Performance of Matched Girl-Boy Pairs in the Five-to-Nine-Year-Old Age Range." *J Genetic Psychol* 104:25–34 Mr '64. * (*PA* 39:4582)

76. FISHLER, KAROL; SHARE, JACK; AND KOCH, RICHARD. "Adaptation of the Gesell Developmental Scales for Evaluation of Development in Children With Down's Syndrome (Mongolism)." *Am J Mental Def* 68:642–6 Mr '64. *

77. SHARE, JACK; KOCH, RICHARD; WEBB, ALLEN; AND GRALIKER, BETTY. "The Longitudinal Development of Infants and Young Children With Down's Syndrome (Mongolism)." *Am J Mental Def* 68:689–92 My '64. * (*PA* 39:2533)

78. STECHLER, GERALD. "A Longitudinal Follow-Up of Neonatal Apnea." *Child Develop* 35:333–48 Je '64. * (*PA* 39:4520)

79. DONOFRIO, A. F. "Clinical Value of Infant Testing." *Percept & Motor Skills* 21:571–4 O '65. * (*PA* 40:1029)

80. FISHLER, KAROL; GRALIKER, BETTY V.; AND KOCH, RICHARD. "The Predictability of Intelligence With Gesell Developmental Scales in Mentally Retarded Infants and Young Children." *Am J Mental Def* 69:515–25 Ja '65. * (*PA* 39:9821)

81. WALTERS, C. ETTA. "Prediction of Postnatal Development From Fetal Activity." *Child Develop* 36:801–8 Je '65. * (*PA* 39:14616)

82. DICKS-MIREAUX, MARIE-JOSÉ. "Development of Intelligence of Children With Down's Syndrome: Preliminary Report." *J Mental Def Res* (England) 10:89–93 Je '66. * (*PA* 41:1827)

83. FISHLER, KAROL; KOCH, RICHARD; DONNELL, GEORGE; AND GRALIKER, BETTY V. "Psychological Correlates in Galactosemia." *Am J Mental Def* 71:116–25 Jl '66. * (*PA* 40:11430)

84. GERSON, ELAINE F., AND SCOTT, ROLAND B. "Growth and Development of Negro Infants: 7, The Relationship of Parental Attitudes and Socioeconomic Pressures to Intelligence and Gross Motor Quotients During the Second Year of Life." *Med Ann DC* 35:5–8 Ja '66. *

85. KNOBLOCH, HILDA; PASAMANICK, BENJAMIN; AND SHERARD, EARL S., JR. "A Developmental Screening Inventory for Infants." *Pediatrics* 38(sup):1095–108 D '66. *

86. STOTT, LELAND H., AND BALL, RACHEL STUTSMAN. *Infant and Preschool Mental Tests: Review and Evaluation.* Monographs of the Society for Research in Child Development, Vol. 30, No. 3, Serial No. 101. Chicago, Ill.: University of Chicago Press, 1966. Pp. iv, 151. * (*PA* 40:7220)

87. AMES, LOUISE B. "Predictive Value of Infant Behavior Examinations," pp. 207–39. In *Exceptional Infant: The Normal Infant, Vol. 1.* Edited by Jerome Hellmuth. Seattle, Wash.: Special Child Publications, 1967. Pp. 568. *

88. FULLER, RENEE. "Psychological Results in Treated Phenyl-

ketonuria: 1, Gesell Findings." *Proc Am Psychopath Assn* 56:153–80, 190–2 '67. *

89. KNOBLOCH, HILDA, AND PASAMANICK, BENJAMIN. "Prediction From the Assessment of Neuromotor and Intellectual Status in Infancy." *Proc Am Psychopath Assn* 56:387–400 '67. *

90. LINDE, LEONARD M.; RASOF, BEATRICE; AND DUNN, OLIVE JEAN. "Mental Development in Congenital Heart Disease." *J Pediatrics* 71:198–203 Ag '67. *

91. RASOF, BEATRICE; LINDE, LEONARD M.; AND DUNN, OLIVE JEAN. "Intellectual Development in Children With Congenital Heart Disease." *Child Develop* 38:1043–53 D '67. * (*PA* 42:7687)

92. WALTERS, C. ETTA. "Comparative Development of Negro and White Infants." *J Genetic Psychol* 110:243–51 Je '67. * (*PA* 41:11696)

93. ROE, KIKI VLACHOULI. *A Longitudinal Study of Infant Vocalizations.* Doctor's thesis, University of California (Los Angeles, Calif.), 1968. (*DA* 29:3472B)

94. AYRES, A. JEAN. "Relation Between Gesell Developmental Quotients and Later Perceptual-Motor Performance." *Am J Occup Ther* 23(1):11–7 Ja–F '69. * (*PA* 44:439)

95. DALES, RUTH J. "Motor and Language Development of Twins During the First Three Years." *J Genetic Psychol* 114(2):263–71 Je '69. * (*PA* 43:17029)

96. LEVESQUE, CLAIRE E. *The Correlation Between the Gesell Developmental Examination and Four Common Ability Tests.* Master's thesis, Southern Connecticut State College (New Haven, Conn.), 1969.

97. MURALIDHARAN, RAJALAKSHMI. "Developmental Norms of Children Aged 2½–5 Years: A Pilot Study." *Indian Ed R* 4(1):67–91 Ja '69. * (*PA* 46:840)

98. BAYLEY, NANCY. Chap. 16, "Development of Mental Abilities," pp. 1163–209. In *Carmichael's Manual of Child Psychology, Third Edition, Vol. 1.* Edited by Paul H. Mussen. New York: John Wiley & Sons, Inc., 1970. Pp. xiii, 1519. *

99. CRANDALL, VIRGINIA C., AND BATTLE, ESTHER S. "The Antecedents and Adult Correlates of Academic and Intellectual Achievement." *Minn Symposia Child Psychol* 4:36–93 '70. *

100. DEMPSEY, MARIA PETRA. *A Comparative Study of the Developmental Quotients of the 30–36-Months-Old Negro and Indian Child as Measured by the Gesell Schedules.* Doctor's thesis, Florida State University (Tallahassee, Fla.), 1970. (*DAI* 31:5660A)

101. HELSETH, BETTY J. *A Comparative Study of Intelligence and Maturity as Measured by the Gesell Developmental Placement Test and Other Selected Tests.* Master's thesis, Pacific Lutheran University (Tacoma, Wash.), 1970.

102. PARMELEE, ARTHUR H., JR., AND SCHULTE, FRANZ J. "Developmental Testing of Pre-Term and Small-for-Date Infants." *Pediatrics* 45(1):21–8 Ja '70. *

103. BARBER, LUCIE W. "Effect of an Infancy Curriculum on Motor and Personal-Social Behaviors." *Char Potential* 5(3):128–47 F '71. * (*PA* 45:7837)

104. BARBER, LUCIE W. "Language Development in Infants Enrolled in the Infancy Design." *Char Potential* 5(3):118–28 F '71. * (*PA* 45:7838)

105. BECKWITH, LEILA. "Relationships Between Attributes of Mothers and Their Infants' IQ Scores." *Child Develop* 42(4):1083–97 O '71. * (*PA* 48:2692)

106. COLLARD, ROBERTA R. "Exploratory and Play Behaviors of Infants Reared Apart in an Institution and in Lower- and Middle-Class Homes." *Child Develop* 42(4):1003–15 O '71. * (*PA* 48:2709)

107. GRANTHAM-McGREGOR, SALLY M., AND HAWKE, W. A. "Development Assessment of Jamaican Infants." *Develop Med & Child Neurol* (England) 13(5):582–9 O '71. *

108. POPOVICS, ALEXANDER J. *A Comparison of the Effectiveness of Actuarial and Clinical Scoring of the Gesell Incomplete Man Test as a Predictor of School Success.* Master's thesis, Southern Connecticut State College (New Haven, Conn.), 1971.

CUMULATIVE NAME INDEX

Fish. B.: 68
Fishler, K.: 76, 80, 83
Foxe, A. N.: *exc*, 3:277
Fuller, R.: 88
Gardener, D. B.: 43
Gardner, W. H.: *exc*, 3:277
Geber, M.: 69
Gerson, E. F.: 84
Gerstein, R. A.: 30
Gesell, A.: 1–5, 10–1, 13, 17, 20, 22, 26–7, 31, 34, 36, 61
Gesell, A. L.: 62
Girdany, B. R.: 64
Good, C. V.: *exc*, 3:277
Goodenough, F. L.: *exc*, 2:B915
Graliker, B.: 77
Graliker, B. V.: 58, 80, 83
Grant, W. W.: 40
Grantham-McGregor, S. M.: 107
Halverson, H. M.: 20
Harper, P.: 67
Hawke, W. A.: 107
Helseth, B. I.: 101
Henderson, E. M.: 12
Hendrick, I.: *exc*, 3:B279
Hildreth, G.: *exc*, 2:B916
Howard, W. H. R.: 44
Hrdlicka, A.: *exc*, 3:B279
Ilg, F. L.: 20, 24, 34, 57, 75
Illingworth, R. S.: 48, 52
Irwin, O. C.: *exc*, 2:B914
Janoff, I. Z.: 40
Jenkins, J. W.: *exc*, 3:B279
Jensen, K.: *exc*, 2:B916
Kasambi, K.: 29
Knobloch, H.: 44, 49, 56, 66–7, 70–1, 85, 89
Koch, H. L.: *exc*, 3:277
Koch, R.: 55, 58, 76–7, 80, 83
Koshuk, R. P.: *exc*, 2:B916
Koza, C.: 59
Kugel, R. B.: 40, 46
Lamm, S. S.: *exc*, 2:B916
Learned, J.: 34
Leiter, R. G.: *exc*, 2:B916
Levesque, C. W.: 96
Liddicoat, R.: 59
Linde, L. M.: 90–1
Line. W.: *exc*, 3:278
Lis, E. F.: 47
Lord, E. E.: 61; *exc*, 3:278
McIntosh, R.: 64
MacRae, J. M.: 38
Malcove, L.: *exc*, 2:B916
Marshall, F. B.: 12
Mead, M.: 28
Moriarty. A.: 51
Munn, N. L.: *exc*, 2:B915
Muralidharan, R.: 97
Myers, B. J.: 40
Nelson, A. K.: *exc*, 2:B916

Nelson, V.: 21
Nelson, V. L.: 14–5, 18–9
Norman, R. D.: 37
Parmelee, A. H.: 102
Pasamanick, B.: 49, 56, 66–7, 70–1, 85, 89
Pease, D.: 53
Peatman, J. G.: *exc*, 2:B916
Pelz, K.: 73
Pelz, K. S.: 54
Pike, F.: 54, 73
Popovics, A. J.: 108
Rasof, B.: 90–1
Ribble, M. A.: *exc*, 2:B916
Rich, G. J.: *exc*, 2:B916
Richards, T. W.: 14–5, 18–9, 21
Rider, R.: 67
Riess, A.: 40
Roe, K. V.: 93
Rosauer, J. K.: 53
Roth, S.: 65
Ruess, A. L.: 47
Russell, E. C.: 40
Ryan, M. S.: *exc*, 2:B913
Ryans, D. G.: *exc*, 2:B914
Sayers, M. P.: 44
Schmidt, A. G.: *exc*, 2:B914
Schulte, F. J.: 102
Scott, R. B.: 84
Share, J.: 55, 58, 76–7
Sherard, E. S.: 85
Shirley, M.: *exc*, 2:B913
Sievers, D. J.: 37
Silver, A. A.: 35
Simon, A. J.: 39
Stechler, G.: 78
Steckel, M. L.: 7
Steggerda, M.: 12
Stern, D. J.: 74
Stoddard, G. D.: *exc*, 2:B915
Stott, L. H.: 86
Swiger, M. K.: 43
Symmes, E. F.: 9
Taylor, H. C.: 64
Teagarden, F. M.: *rev*, 3:276
Thompson, H.: 11, 13, 17, 20
Valentine, C. W.: *exc*, 2: B913, 2:B915, 3:B279
Veeder, B. S.: *exc*, 2:B912
Walters, C. E.: 81, 92
Washburn, A. A.: *exc*, 3:277
Webb, A.: 55, 58, 77
Welch, L.: *exc*, 3:278
Werner, E. E.: *rev*, 6:522
Wiemers, I. H.: 72
Wile, I. S.: *exc*, 2:B914
Wilson, M. G.: 60
Wilson, M. T.: *exc*, 3:277
Wittenborn, J. R.: 40
Wolins, L.: 53
Wolk, S. M.: 41
Woodward, M.: 74

[498]

Haptic Intelligence Scale for Adult Blind. Blind and partially sighted adults; 1964; HIS; 7 scores: digit symbol, block design, object assembly, object completion, pattern board, bead arithmetic, total; Harriett C. Shurrager and Phil S. Shurrager; Harriett C. Shurrager. *

For additional information and a review by Marshall S. Hiskey, see 7:409 (9 references).

REFERENCES THROUGH 1971

1–9. See 7:409.
10. MILLER, LAURENCE RICHARD. *A Factor Analytic Study of Cognitive Variables in Congenitally Blind Individuals.* Doctor's thesis, Case Western Reserve University (Cleveland, Ohio), 1970. (*DAI* 32:248A)

CUMULATIVE NAME INDEX

Alston, P. P.: 9
Avery, C. D.: 7–8
Curtis, W. S.: 6
Dauterman, W. L.: 3
Eber, H. W.: 4
Gallagher, P.: 5
Hiskey, M. S.: *rev*, 7:409
Kamin, H. S.: 2

Miller, L. R.: 10
Naddeo, C. L.: 6
Porter, T. L.: 9
Saxon, J. P.: 9
Shapiro, B.: 3
Streitfeld, J. W.: 7–8
Suinn, R. M.: 3
Watson, S. B.: 1

[499]

Hiskey-Nebraska Test of Learning Aptitude. Ages 3–17 (deaf and hearing); 1941–66; HNTLA; revision of *Nebraska Test of Learning Aptitude;* Marshall S. Hiskey; the Author. *

For additional information and a review by T. Ernest Newland, see 7:410 (14 references); for a review by William Sloan of an earlier edition, see 5:409 (8 references); for a review by Mildred C. Templin, see 4:353 (1 reference); see also 3:289 (3 references).

REFERENCES THROUGH 1971

1–3. See 3:289.
4. See 4:353.
5–12. See 5:409.
13–26. See 7:410.
27. VASA, STANLEY FRANK. *A Comparison of Selected Intelligence Scales With Bilingual Children.* Doctor's thesis, University of Nebraska (Lincoln, Neb.), 1971. (*DAI* 32:802A)

CUMULATIVE NAME INDEX

Bach, L. C.: 21
Casjens, C. C.: 17
Davis, K. A.: 8
Gentile, J. R.: 19
Giangreco, C. J.: 18, 20
Hiskey, M. S.: 1–3, 11–2
Howard, J. O.: 25
Kirk, S. A.: 13
Lane, H. S.: 14
Lewis, J. F.: 26
Ludlow, M.: 5
MacPherson, J. G.: 6, 14
Mira, M. P.: 16

Morris, B. E. J. VanC.: 22
Morris, G. L.: 23
Newland, T. E.: *rev*, 7:410
Paul, G. T.: 24
Perry, I.: 13
Perry, J. A.: 7
Ross, G.: 9
Sloan, W.: *rev*, 5:409
Templin, M. C.: *rev*, 4:353
Thomure, E.: 4
Varva, F. I.: 15
Vasa, S. F.: 27
Walsh, R.: 10

[500]

The Immediate Test: A Quick Verbal Intelligence Test. Adults; 1951; Raymond J. Corsini; Sheridan Psychological Services, Inc. *

For additional information and reviews by Jerome E. Doppelt and Ivan Norman Mensh, see 4:342 (1 reference).

REFERENCES THROUGH 1971

1. See 4:342.
2. NEWTON, G. MACKIE. "A Comparison of the Immediate Test and WAIS Verbal Scale in Vocational Rehabilitation Use." *J Clin Psychol* 21:300 Jl '65. * (*PA* 39:15368)
3. CULL, JOHN G., AND HARDY, RICHARD E. "Correlation Between the Immediate Test and the Wechsler Adult Intelligence Scale Verbal Scale in the Rehabilitation Setting." *J Psychol* 77(2):203–5 Mr '71. * (*PA* 46:1627)

CUMULATIVE NAME INDEX

Corsini, R.: 1
Cull, J. G.: 3
Doppelt, J. E.: *rev*, 4:342

Hardy, R. E.: 3
Mensh, I. N.: *rev*, 4:342
Newton, G. M.: 2

[501]

★**Individual Scale for Indian South Africans.** Ages 8–17; 1971; ISISA; adaptation for Indian pupils of the *New South African Individual Scale;* 13 scores: verbal (vocabulary, comprehension, similarities, problems, memory, total), nonverbal (pattern completion, blocks, absurdities, form board, mazes, total), total; R. J. Prinsloo and F. W. O. Heinichen in collaboration with D. J. Swart; Human Sciences Research Council [South Africa]. *

[502]

Kahn Intelligence Tests: Experimental Form. Ages 1 month and over (particularly the verbally or culturally handicapped); 1960; KIT; uses same test objects as *Kahn Test of Symbol Arrangement;* main scale plus 6 optional scales: brief scale, concept formation, recall, motor coordination, scale for use with the deaf, scale for use with the blind; Theodore C. Kahn; Psychological Test Specialists. *

For additional information and a review by Marjorie P. Honzik, see 7:411 (6 references); see also 6:524 (2 references).

REFERENCES THROUGH 1971

1–2. See 6:524.
3–8. See 7:411.
9. CHAWLA, TILAK R. "Cultural Factors and Kahn Intelligence Test." *Indian Psychol R* 6(2):77–9 Ja '70. * (*PA* 46: 9569)

CUMULATIVE NAME INDEX

[503]

Kent Series of Emergency Scales. Ages 5–7, 6–8, 6.5–10, 9–14; 1932–46; 4 scales; Grace H. Kent; Psychological Corporation. *

a) SCALE A. Ages 5–7; 1944–46; formerly called *Andover School-Entrance Test.*
b) SCALES B AND C. Ages 6–8, 6.5–10; 1946.
c) SCALE D. Ages 9–14; 1932–46; revision of *Emergency Test* (also called *Kent E-G-Y Test*).

For additional information and a review by Ivan Norman Mensh, see 4:346 (8 references); for a review by Charles N. Cofer, see 3:284 (26 references).

REFERENCES THROUGH 1971

1–26. See 3:284.
27–34. See 4:346.
35. TROWBRIDGE, LOWELL; MOORE, MERRILL; AND GRAY, M. GENEVA. "An Estimate of the Intelligence of Alcoholic Patients at the Haymarket Square Relief Station as Related to Chronological Age, Marital Status, and Occupation." *New Engl J Med* 221:59–62 Jl 13 '39. * (*PA* 14:1437)
36. WILSON, M. T. "Detection of Reading Difficulties in a Rural Public School." *Training Sch B* 39:41–6 My '42. * (*PA* 16:3818)
37. ORR, DAVID HAMILTON. *A Field Study of a Psychiatric Aide Applicant Group at a State Mental Hospital.* Doctor's thesis, University of Kentucky (Lexington, Ky.), 1950. (*DA* 18:666)
38. CROWLEY, MIRIAM E. "The Use of the Kent EGY for the Detection of Malingering." *J Clin Psychol* 8:332–7 O '52. * (*PA* 27:5864)
39. DELP, HAROLD A. "Correlations Between the Kent EGY and the Wechsler Batteries." *J Clin Psychol* 9:73–5 Ja '53. * (*PA* 27:7764)
40. MASON, EVELYN P. "Some Correlates of Self-Judgments of the Aged." *J Gerontol* 9:324–37 Jl '54. * (*PA* 29:5429)
41. ROBINOWITZ, RALPH. "Performances of Hospitalized Psychiatric Patients on the Kent Emergency Test and the Wechsler-Bellevue Intelligence Scale." *J Clin Psychol* 12:199–200 Ap '56. * (*PA* 31:4711)
42. GOERTZEN, STAN M. "A Study of Some Aspects of the Kent E.G.Y. Scales." *Calif J Ed Res* 8:140 My '57. *
43. WEST, DORAL N. "Reducing Chance in Test Selection." *Personnel & Guid J* 36:420–1 F '58. * (*PA* 33:6935)
44. GYNTHER, MALCOLM D., AND MAYER, ANNE D. "The Prediction of Mental Deficiency by Means of the Kent-EGY." *Am J Mental Def* 64:988–90 My '60. * (*PA* 35:6834)
45. GUERRANT, JOHN; ANDERSON, WILLIAM W.; FISCHER, AMES; WEINSTEIN, MORTON R.; JAROS, R. MARY; AND DESKINS, ANDREW. Chap. 5, "Psychological Considerations," pp. 66–92. In their *Personality in Epilepsy.* Springfield, Ill.: Charles C Thomas, Publisher, 1962. Pp. xii, 112. *
46. KATZ, LAWRENCE, AND CROOK, HAMILTON. "Use of the Kent E-G-Y With an Aged Population." *J Gerontol* 17:186–9 Ap '62. * (*PA* 37:2953)
47. CLORE, GERALD L., JR. "Kent E-G-Y: Differential Scoring and Correlation With the WAIS." Abstract. *J Consult Psychol* 27:372 Ag '63. * (*PA* 38:2665)
48. CLORE, GERALD L., JR. "The Kent E-G-Y: Differential Scoring and Correlation With the WAIS." *Newsl Res Psychol* 5:9 F '63. *
49. McDONALD, ROBERT L.; GYNTHER, MALCOLM D.; AND CHRISTAKOS, ARTHUR C. "Relations Between Maternal Anxiety and Obstetric Complications." *Psychosom Med* 25:357–63 Jl–Ag '63. * (*PA* 38:9104)
50. NELSON, DON A. "Group vs. Individual Administration of the Kent E-G-Y." *Newsl Res Psychol* 5:12–3 F '63. *
51. GENDEL, HOWARD, AND RICE, WARREN. "Correlation of the Kent EGY With WAIS IQ's and Scaled Scores." *Newsl Res Psychol* 6:43–4 Ag '64. *
52. MEER, BERNARD, AND BAKER, JANET A. "Reliability of Measurements of Intellectual Functioning of Geriatric Patients." *J Gerontol* 20:410–4 Jl '65. *
53. SCHWARTZ, MARK S. "Relationships Between the Kent EGY and WAIS Scores, Functioning Levels and Subtests in a

Veterans Neuropsychiatric Population." *Newsl Res Psychol* 7: 8–9 My '65. *
54. PIERCE, ROBERT C. Chap. 4, "Intellectual Functioning and Mental Health," pp. 82–100. In *Aging and Mental Disorder in San Francisco: A Social Psychiatric Study.* By Marjorie Fiske Lowenthal, Paul L. Berkman, and Associates. San Francisco, Calif.: Jossey-Bass Inc., Publishers, 1967. Pp. xix, 341. *
55. PIERCE, ROBERT C. Chap. 6, "Intellectual Status Compared," pp. 112–9. In *Aging and Mental Disorder in San Francisco: A Social Psychiatric Study.* By Marjorie Fiske Lowenthal, Paul L. Berkman, and Associates. San Francisco, Calif.: Jossey-Bass Inc., Publishers, 1967. Pp. xix, 341. *
56. PIERCE, ROBERT C., AND BERKMAN, PAUL L. Chap. 11, "Change in Intellectual Functioning," pp. 176–89. In *Aging and Mental Disorder in San Francisco: A Social Psychiatric Study.* By Marjorie Fiske Lowenthal, Paul L. Berkman, and Associates. San Francisco, Calif.: Jossey-Bass Inc., Publishers, 1967. Pp. xix, 341. *
57. DE CASTRO, FERNANDO J.; VAUGHN, KENNETH L.; AND GIBSON, RALPH M. "A Rapid Screening Psychometric Test: Evaluation of the Kent Emergency Scale." *Clin Pediatrics* 8(5): 258–62 My '69. *
58. O'CONNOR, PATRICIA A.; SCHWARTZ, EDWARD M.; AND ROKICKI, ROBERT R. "Use of the Kent Scales to Evaluate Development in Children." *Univ Mich Med Center J* 35(4):217–9 O–D '69. *
59. TEMPLER, DONALD I., AND HARTLAGE, LAWRENCE C. "Physicians' I.Q. Estimates and Kent I.Q. Compared With WAIS I.Q." *J Clin Psychol* 25(1):74–5 Ja '69. * (*PA* 43:10025)
60. DE CASTRO, F. J., AND GIBSON, R. M. "Psychometric Screening by Allied Medical Personnel." *Clin Pediatrics* 9(4): 192 Ap '70. *
61. MYKLEBUST, HELMER R.; BANNOCHIE, MARGARET N.; AND KILLEN, JAMES R. Chap. 9, "Learning Disabilities and Cognitive Processes," pp. 213–51. In *Progress in Learning Disabilities,* Vol. 2. Edited by Helmer R. Myklebust. New York: Grune & Stratton, Inc., 1971. Pp. ix, 404. *

CUMULATIVE NAME INDEX

[504]

*The Leiter Adult Intelligence Scale. Adults; 1949–72; LAIS; revision of *Leiter-Partington Adult Performance Scale;* includes *The FR-CR Test, Partington's Pathways Test, The Leiter Adaptation of Arthur's Stencil Design Test,* and *The Leiter Adapta-*

tion of the Painted Cube Test; 3 scores: verbal, performance, total; Russell Graydon Leiter; Stoelting Co. *

For additional information, reviews by Paul C. Davis and Frank B. Jex, and an excerpted review by Laurance F. Shaffer, see 6:525 (15 references); for reviews by Harold A. Delp and Herschel Manuel and an excerpted review by Laurance F. Shaffer of the original edition, see 4:350 (4 references). For a review of *The FR-CR Test,* see 4:339; for an excerpted review of *The Leiter Adaptation of Arthur's Stencil Design Test,* see 4:347; for an excerpted review of *The Leiter Adaptation of the Painted Cube Test,* see 4:348; and for reviews of *Partington's Pathways Test,* see 4:355 (1 review, 1 excerpt).

REFERENCES THROUGH 1971

1–4. See 4:350.
5–19. See 6:525.
20. PAYNE, R. W. "Some Aspects of Perception and Thought Disorder in Schizophrenic Subjects." *Schweizerische Zeitschrift für Psychologie und Ihre Anwendungen* (Switzerland) 17(4): 300–8 '58. * (*PA* 34:1791)
21. CRAWFORD, PAUL L. "The Relative Sensitivity of the LAIS, WAIS, and PM in Differentiating Between Psychopathic and Psychotic Patients in a Mental Hospital." *Psychol Service Center J* 11(2):93–7 '59. * (*PA* 34:4374)
22. CRAWFORD, PAUL L. "The Statistical Significance of Difference in Performance on the Leiter Adult Intelligence Scale, the Wechsler Adult Intelligence Scale, and the Porteus Maze by a Heterogeneous Mental Hospital Population." *Psychol Service Center J* 11(2):89–92 '59. * (*PA* 34:4510)
23. SCHERER, ISIDORE W., AND WINNE, JOHN F. "A Five Year Follow-Up Study of the Pathways Test With Lobotomized Patients." *Psychol Service Center J* 11(2):98–101 '59. * (*PA* 34:4408)
24. DOERRING, PAUL LUTHER. *Psychological Deficits in Children as Sequelae of Western and St. Louis Encephalitis.* Doctor's thesis, Stanford University (Stanford, Calif.), 1962. (*DA* 23: 2006)
25. WASSENAAR, G. M. C. "The Effect of General Anxiety as an Index of Lability on the Performance of Various Psychomotor Tasks." *J General Psychol* 71:351–7 O '64. * (*PA* 39:3667)
26. CRAWFORD, PAUL L., AND SNYDER, WILLIAM U. "Differentiating the Psychopath and Psychoneurotic With the LAIS." Abstract. *J Consult Psychol* 30:178 Ap '66. * (*PA* 40:6637, title only)
27. BERKE, NORMAN DANIEL. *An Investigation of Adult Negro Illiteracy: Prediction of Reading Achievement and Description of Educational Characteristics of a Sample of City Core Adult Negro Illiterates.* Doctor's thesis, State University of New York (Buffalo, N.Y.), 1967. (*DA* 28:931A)
28. BLUNDELL, ELIZABETH. "A Psychological Study of the Effects of Surgery on Eighty-Six Elderly Patients." *Brit J Social & Clin Psychol* 6:297–303 D '67. * (*PA* 42:7707)
29. GOLDSAMT, MILTON R. "An Evaluation of the Leiter Adult Intelligence Scale (LAIS)." *Percept & Motor Skills* 28(3): 959–71 Je '69. * (*PA* 43:16633)
30. LUBER, SHULA A., AND WALKER, RONALD E. "Sex Difference on the Free Recall-Controlled Recall Test of the Leiter Adult Intelligence Scale." *J Clin Psychol* 25(4):412–3 O '69. * (*PA* 44:10417)
31. CLARK, JACK MANNING. *The Prediction of Gain in Reading Among Adult Illiterates From an Analysis of Items on the Wechsler, Leiter and Davis-Eells Scales.* Doctor's thesis, State University of New York (Buffalo, N.Y.), 1971. (*DAI* 32:2512A)

CUMULATIVE NAME INDEX

Adjutant General's Office, Classification and Replacement Branch, Personnel Research Section: 1
Armitage, S. G.: 2
Berke, N. D.: 27
Blundell, E.: 28
Brown, R. C.: 4
Clark, J. M.: 31
Cozan, L. W.: 12, 15
Crawford, P. L.: 21–2, 26
Davis, P. C.: *rev,* 6:525
Delp, H. A.: *rev,* 4:350
Doerman, L. H.: 4
Doerring, P. L.: 24
Gaitz, C. M.: 19
George, E. I.: 16
Goldsamt, M. R.: 29
Hewlett, J. H. G.: 17

International Psychological Service Center: 5
Jex, F. B.: *rev,* 6:525
Leiter, R. G.: 3, 6–7, 9, 13
Luber, S. A.: 30
Manuel, H.: *rev,* 4:350
Mattussek, P.: 16
Partington, J. E.: 3, 8–9
Payne, R. W.: 16–7, 20
Scherer, I. W.: 23
Shaffer, L. F.: *exc,* 4:350, 6:525
Snyder, W. U.: 26
Sydow, D. W.: 14
Vinson, D. B.: 18–9
Walker, R. E.: 30
Wassenaar, G. M. C.: 25
Watson, N.: 10–1
Weaver, H. B.: 4
Winne, J. F.: 23

[505]
Leiter International Performance Scale. Ages 2–18, 3–8; 1936–55; 2 editions; Russell Graydon Leiter and Grace Arthur (*b*); Stoelting Co. *
a) 1948 REVISION. Ages 2–18; 1936–52.
b) ARTHUR ADAPTATION. Ages 3–8; 1952–55; author recommends use with *Arthur Point Scale of Performance Tests.*

For additional information and a review by Emmy E. Werner, see 6:526 (10 references); see also 5:408 (17 references); for a review by Gwen F. Arnold and an excerpted review by Laurance F. Shaffer of *a*, see 4:349 (25 references). For an excerpt from a related book review, see 2:B989.

REFERENCES THROUGH 1971

1–25. See 4:349.
26–42. See 5:408.
43–52. See 6:526.
53. VARVA, FRANK IRVIN. *An Investigation of the Effect of Auditory Deficiency Upon Performance With Special Reference to Concrete and Abstract Tasks.* Doctor's thesis, University of Pittsburgh (Pittsburgh, Pa.), 1956. (*DA* 16:2532)
54. BRENGELMANN, JOHANNES C., AND HILLMAN, WILLIAM A., JR. "Determinants of Learning in the Retardate: A Pilot Study." *Training Sch B* 61:156–62 F '65. * (*PA* 39:10570)
55. KORST, JOSEPH W. *A Comparison of the Results Obtained for the Peabody Picture Vocabulary Test and the Leiter International Performance Scale With Children Having Functional Articulatory Disorders.* Master's thesis, Wichita State University (Wichita, Kan.), 1965.
56. STEWART, HORACE F., JR., AND KEELER, CLYDE E. "A Comparison of the Intelligence and Personality of Moon-Child Albino and Control Cuna Indians." *J Genetic Psychol* 106:319–24 Je '65. * (*PA* 39:14888)
57. CLEGG, STANLEY J., AND WHITE, WILLIAM F. "Assessment of General Intelligence of Negro Deaf Children in a Public Residential School for the Deaf." *J Clin Psychol* 22:93–4 Ja '66. * (*PA* 40:4523)
58. GENTILE, J. RONALD. "In Search of Research: Four Children's Tests." *J Sch Psychol* 5:1–13 au '66. * (*PA* 41:3335)
59. KORST, JOSEPH W. "A Comparison of Results From the Peabody Vocabulary Test and Leiter International Performance Scale With Children Having Functional Articulatory Disorders." *Cereb Palsy J* 27:3–5 Ja–F '66. * (*PA* 40:5851)
60. MCBRIDE, DON W. "Longitudinal Study of Performance of Childhood Aphasics on Mental Ability Tests," pp. 118–25. In *Special Education: Strategies for Educational Progress.* Selected Convention Papers, 44th Annual CEC Convention, 1966. Washington, D.C.: Council for Exceptional Children, [1966]. Pp. viii, 259. *
61. BEANS, DAVID T. *The Leiter International Performance Scale as a Measure of Intelligence in Navahos.* Master's thesis, Utah State University (Logan, Utah), 1967.
62. MIEZITIS, SOLVEIGA AUSMA. *An Exploratory Study of Divergent Production in Preschoolers.* Doctor's thesis, University of Toronto (Toronto, Ont., Canada), 1968. (*DAI* 30:589A)
63. COSTELLO, JOAN, AND DICKIE, JOYCE. "Leiter and Stanford-Binet IQ's of Preschool Disadvantaged Children." Abstract. *Develop Psychol* 2(2):314 Mr '70. * (*PA* 44:6523)
64. KING, SUSAN HOFMAN. *The Relationships Between Mental Age, Level of Language Functioning and Social Acceptability in the Trainable Mentally Retarded.* Doctor's thesis, Louisiana State University (Baton Rouge, La.), 1970. (*DAI* 31:5691B)
65. MATHER, LEONARD JOSEPH. *A Causal Comparative Study of Intellectual Functioning in Good and Poor Readers.* Doctor's thesis, Catholic University of America (Washington, D.C.), 1971. (*DAI* 32:1920A)
66. MYKLEBUST, HELMER R.; BANNOCHIE, MARGARET N.; AND KILLEN, JAMES R. Chap. 9, "Learning Disabilities and Cognitive Processes," pp. 213–51. In *Progress in Learning Disabilities,* Vol. 2. Edited by Helmer R. Myklebust. New York: Grune & Stratton, Inc., 1971. Pp. ix, 404. *
67. NEDLER, SHARI, AND SEBERA, PEGGY. "Intervention Strategies for Spanish-Speaking Preschool Children." *Child Develop* 42(1):259–67 Mr '71. * (*PA* 46:5743)
68. ROBINSON, HALBERT B., AND ROBINSON, NANCY M. "Longitudinal Development of Very Young Children in a Comprehensive Day Care Program: The First Two Years." *Child Develop* 42(6):1673–83 D '71. * (*PA* 48:8827)
69. RUBINO, C. A.; KROCCO, D.; AND SHEA, M. "An Analysis of Right Hemispheric Deficits in the Moderately Retarded Child as Measured by the WISC and Leiter." *Ont Psychologist* (Canada) 3(2):85–95 '71. * (*PA* 47:9488)
70. WEINER, PAUL S. "Stability and Validity of Two Measures of Intelligence Used With Children Whose Language Development Is Delayed." *J Speech & Hearing Res* 14(2):254–61 Je '71. * (*PA* 48:5419)

CUMULATIVE NAME INDEX

[506]

★**McCarthy Scales of Children's Abilities.** Ages 2.5–8.5; 1972, c1970–72; MSCA; 6 scores: verbal, perceptual-performance, quantitative, composite (general cognitive), memory, motor; Dorothea McCarthy; Psychological Corporation. *

[507]

Merrill-Palmer Scale of Mental Tests. Ages 24–63 months; 1926–31; Rachel Stutsman; Stoelting Co. *

For additional information and a review by Marjorie P. Honzik, see 6:527 (16 references); for reviews by Nancy Bayley, B. M. Castner, Florence L. Goodenough, and Florence M. Teagarden, see 2:1406 (13 references). For excerpts from related book reviews, see 2:B1123 (5 excerpts).

REFERENCES THROUGH 1971

1–13. See 2:1406.
14–29. See 6:527.
30. WOOLEY, HELEN T. "The Validity of Standards of Mental Measurement in Young Childhood." *Sch & Soc* 21:476–82 Ap 18 '25. *
31. GOODENOUGH, FLORENCE L. "The Reliability and Validity of the Wallin Peg Boards." *Psychol Clinic* 16:199–215 O '27. * (*PA* 2:1395)
32. BALDWIN, BIRD T., AND WELLMAN, BETH L. "The Peg Board as a Means of Analyzing Form Perception and Motor Control in Young Children." *J Genetic Psychol* 35:389–414 S '28. * (*PA* 3:1358)
33. WAGONER, LOVISA C., AND ARMSTRONG, EDNA M. "The Motor Control of Children as Involved in the Dressing Process." *J Genetic Psychol* 35:84–97 Mr '28. * (*PA* 2:3692)
34. HERTZBERG, OSCAR E. "The Relationship of Motor Ability to the Intelligence of Kindergarten Children." *J Ed Psychol* 20:507–19 O '29. * (*PA* 4:373)
35. GOODENOUGH, FLORENCE L. "Inter-Relationships in the Behavior of Young Children." *Child Develop* 1:29–48 Mr '30. * (*PA* 4:3637)
36. VANCE, THOMAS F. "The Effect of Size of Peg and Form Boards Upon the Performance Scores of Young Children." *Proc Iowa Acad Sci* 40:181–4 '33. * (*PA* 9:3048)
37. WELLMAN, BETH L. "Mental Measurement of Preschool Children: A Review." *J Ed Res* 26:536–7 Mr '33. *
38. HASLAM, PHYLLIS. *The Prediction of Ability on the Arthur

Point Performance Scale From the Merrill-Palmer Scale. Master's thesis, State University of Iowa (Iowa City, Iowa), 1938.
39. SKEELS, HAROLD M.; UPDEGRAFF, RUTH; WELLMAN, BETH L.; AND WILLIAMS, HAROLD M. *A Study of Environmental Stimulation: An Orphanage Preschool Project*, pp. 60–73. University of Iowa Studies in Child Welfare, Vol. 15, No. 4. Iowa City, Iowa: the University, 1938. Pp. 191. * (*PA* 13:1758)
40. GROVER, V. M. "The Coloured Nursery School Child and the Merrill Palmer Test." Abstract. *Proc South African Psychol Assn* 3:26–7 '52. * (*PA* 30:2881, title only)
41. MORIARTY, ALICE. "Coping Patterns of Preschool Children in Response to Intelligence Test Demands." *Genetic Psychol Monogr* 64:3–127 Ag '61. * (*PA* 36:2FF03M)
42. KLATSKIN, ETHELYN HENRY. "Relationships of Deficits in Intelligence Test Performance of Preschool Children to Perinatal Experience." *J Consult Psychol* 28:228–33 Je '64. * (*PA* 39: 4590)
43. KEIR, GERTRUDE. "The Merrill-Palmer Test With the Children From the Island of Tristan da Cunha." *J Child Psychol & Psychiatry* (England) 7:133–42 O '66. * (*PA* 41:4399, title only)
44. STOTT, LELAND H., AND BALL, RACHEL STUTSMAN. *Infant and Preschool Mental Tests: Review and Evaluation.* Monographs of the Society for Research in Child Development, Vol. 30, No. 3, Serial No. 101. Chicago, Ill.: University of Chicago Press, 1966. Pp. iv, 151. * (*PA* 40:7220)
45. DUROJAIYE, M. O. A., AND SUCH, M. "Predicting Educational Suitability of Children in an Assessment Unit." *J Exp Ed* 40(2):27–36 w '71. * (*PA* 47:11608)
46. TAKACS, CAROL PAULA. *Comparison of Mental Abilities Between Lower Socioeconomic Status Five-Year-Old Negro and White Children on Individual Intelligence Measures.* Doctor's thesis, Kent State University (Kent, Ohio), 1971. (*DAI* 32: 3806A)

CUMULATIVE NAME INDEX

[508]

★**Minnesota Child Development Inventory.** Ages 1–6; 1968–72; MCDI; observations by mother; 8 scores: gross motor, fine motor, expressive language, comprehension-conceptual, situation comprehension, self help, personal-social, general development; Harold R. Ireton and Edward J. Thwing; NCS Interpretive Scoring Systems. *

[509]

Minnesota Preschool Scale. Ages 1.5–6.0; 1932–40; MPS; 3 scores: verbal, nonverbal, total; Florence L. Goodenough, Katherine M. Maurer, and M. J. Van Wagenen; American Guidance Service, Inc. *

For additional information and a review by Marjorie P. Honzik, see 6:528 (3 references); see also 4:351 (2 references); for a review by Beth L. Wellman, see 3:286 (2 references); for reviews by Rachel Stutsman Ball, Nancy Bayley, and Florence M. Teagarden of the original edition, see 2:1407 (3 references). For excerpts from related book reviews, see 4:352 (5 excerpts), 3:287 (5 excerpts), and 3:288 (2 excerpts).

REFERENCES THROUGH 1971

1-3. See 2:1407.
4-5. See 3:286.
6-7. See 4:351.
8-10. See 6:528.
11. GOODENOUGH, FLORENCE L. "Inter-Relationships in the Behavior of Young Children." *Child Develop* 1:29-48 Mr '30. * (*PA* 4:3637)
12. WELLMAN, BETH L. *The Intelligence of Preschool Children as Measured by the Merrill-Palmer Scale of Performance Tests.* University of Iowa Studies in Child Welfare, Vol. 15, No. 3. Iowa City, Iowa: the University, 1938. Pp. 150. * (*PA* 13:1730)

CUMULATIVE NAME INDEX

Ball, R. S.: *rev,* 2:1407
Bayley, N.: *rev,* 2:1407; *exc,* 3:287, 4:352
Coffey, H. S.: 6
Cronbach, L. J.: *exc,* 4:352
Curti, M. W.: 2
DeForrest, R.: 3, 7
Eysenck, H. J.: *exc,* 4:352
Fleming, C. M.: *exc,* 4:352
Froehlich, G. J.: *exc,* 3:287
Goodenough, F. L.: 4, 11
Honzik, M. P.: *rev,* 6:528
Lyle, J. G.: 8-10
McNemar, Q.: *exc,* 4:352
Maurer, K. M.: 4-5
Mowrer, W. M. C.: 1
Olson, W. C.: *exc,* 3:287
Steggerda, M.: 2
Teagarden, F. M.: *rev,* 2:1407
Valentine, C. W.: *exc,* 3:287
Wellman, B. L.: 12; *rev,* 3:286

[510]

New Guinea Performance Scales. Pre-literates ages 17 and over; 1961-71; NGPS; based (except *f*) on the unpublished *PIR Test* used for screening for the Pacific Island Regiment; test (except *e*) is essentially the same as the *Queensland Test* except for minor differences in some of the testing materials and differences in administration, scoring, and norms population; 6 tests; 7 scores: 6 scores listed below plus total; I. G. Ord; Society for New Guinea Psychological Research and Publications [Papua New Guinea]. *
a) CUBE IMITATION TEST. An adaptation of *Knox Cube Test: Pintner Modification.*
b) BEAD THREADING TEST.
c) PASSALONG TEST. Modification of a subtest of *Alexander Performance Scale;* test booklet title is *Passalong Test (New Guinea Version).*
d) FORM ASSEMBLY TEST.
e) OBSERVATION TEST.
f) DESIGN CONSTRUCTION TEST. Published separately as *Pacific Design Construction Test.*
For additional information, see 7:412 (4 references).

REFERENCES THROUGH 1971

1-4. See 7:412.

CUMULATIVE NAME INDEX

Ord, I. G.: 1-4

[511]

New South African Individual Scale. Ages 6-17; 1964; NSAIS; 12 scores: verbal (vocabulary, comprehension, reasoning, problems, memory, total), nonverbal (pattern completion, blocks, absurdities, form board, total), total; both power and power-time scores are obtained for 4 subtests (problems, pattern completion, blocks, absurdities), verbal total, nonverbal total, and overall total; Human Sciences Research Council [South Africa]. *
For additional information, see 7:413 (1 reference).

REFERENCES THROUGH 1971

1. See 7:413.

CUMULATIVE NAME INDEX

Mienie, C. J. P.: 1   Strümpfer, D. J. W.: 1

[512]

Non-Verbal Intelligence Tests for Deaf and Hearing Subjects. Ages 3-16; 1939-59; NVIT, also

SON; record booklet title is *S.O.N. Snijders-Oomen Non-Verbal Intelligence Scale;* 9 scores: mosaic, picture memory, arrangement, analogies, completion, Knox cubes, drawing, sorting, IQ; J. Th. Snijders and N. Snijders-Oomen; distributed by Swets and Zeitlinger B.V. [The Netherlands]. (South African standardization entitled *Snijders-Oomen Non-Verbal Intelligence Scale.* 1964; W. Backer; Human Sciences Research Council [South Africa].) *
For additional information and a review by J. S. Lawes, see 6:529 (2 references).

REFERENCES THROUGH 1971

1-2. See 6:529.
3. HART, N. W. M. "The Use of the S.O.N. Test With Deaf Children in Queensland as a Measure of Their Academic Potential." *Spec Sch B* 5:11-23 N '63. *
4. MONTGOMERY, G. W. G. "A Factorial Study of Communication and Ability in Deaf School Leavers." *Brit J Ed Psychol* 38:27-37 F '68. * (*PA* 42:12755)
5. KEARNEY, JACQUELINE E. "A New Performance Scale of Cognitive Capacity for Use With Deaf Subjects." *Am Ann Deaf* 114(1):2-14 Ja '69. * (*PA* 43:7197)
6. CANABAL, JUANA VILLANUEVA. *Comparison of Deaf and Normally Hearing Children on Analogy Items Under Different Methods of Instruction at Different Age Levels.* Doctor's thesis, St. John's University (Jamaica, N.Y.), 1970. (*DAI* 31:3700B)
7. GASKILL, P.; LONGWORTH, A.; AND NEILSON, J. R. "The Administration of Snijders-Oomen Non-Verbal Intelligence Tests to Deaf Children." *Teach Deaf* (England) 68(400):137-42 Mr '70. *

CUMULATIVE NAME INDEX

Canabal, J. V.: 6
Gaskill, P.: 7
Hart, N. W. M.: 3
Kearney, J. E.: 5
Lawes, J. S.: *rev,* 6:529
Longworth, A.: 7
Montgomery, G. W. G.: 4
Neilson, J. R.: 7
Neuhaus, M.: 2
Snijders, J. T.: 1
Snijders-Oomen, N.: 1

[513]

The Ohwaki-Kohs Tactile Block Design Intelligence Test for the Blind. Blind ages 6 and over; 1965; OKTBD; record booklet title is *The Ohwaki-Kohs Tactile Block-Design Intelligence Test;* adaptation of *Kohs' Block Design Test;* for American revision, see 527; Yoshikazu Ohwaki; Western Psychological Services. *
For additional information and an excerpted review by Richard J. Rankin, see 7:414 (4 references).

REFERENCES THROUGH 1971

1-4. See 7:414.
5. SUINN, RICHARD M. "The Theory of Cognitive Style: A Partial Replication." *J General Psychol* 77:11-5 Jl '67. * (*PA* 41:14063)

CUMULATIVE NAME INDEX

Bozzo, M. T.: 2
Dauterman, W.: 4
Hariu, T.: 1
Hayasaka, K.: 1
Miyake, K.: 1
Ohwaki, M.: 1
Ohwaki, Y.: 1
Rankin, R. J.: *exc,* 7:414
Shapiro, B.: 4
Suinn, R. M.: 3-5
Tanno, Y.: 1
Zecca, G.: 2

[514]

Pacific Design Construction Test. Illiterates and semiliterates in Papua New Guinea; 1962-68; PDCT; based upon *Kohs' Block-Design Test* and block design subtest of *Wechsler Adult Intelligence Scale;* subtest of *New Guinea Performance Scales;* subtest (with minor modifications) of *Queensland Test* in which it is called *Pattern Matching Test;* I. G. Ord; Australian Council for Educational Research [Australia]. *
For additional information, see 7:415 (3 references).

REFERENCES THROUGH 1971

1-3. See 7:415.
4. ORD, I. G. "The P.I.R. Test and Derivatives." *Austral Psychologist* 2:137-46 Mr '68. * (*PA* 42:18798)

CUMULATIVE NAME INDEX

Kearney, G. E.: 2   Ord, I. G.: 1, 3-4

[515]

The Passalong Test: A Performance Test of Intelligence. Ages 8 and over; 1932–37; W. P. Alexander; Stoelting Co. *

For additional information and reviews by James Drever, T. J. Keating, and Grace H. Kent, see 2:1414 (5 references).

REFERENCES THROUGH 1971

1–5. See 2:1414.
6. PRICE, E. J. J. "The Nature of the Practical Factor (F)." *Brit J Psychol* 30:341–51 Ap '40. * (*PA* 14:3783)
7. BRADFORD, E. J. G. "Performance Tests in the Diagnosis of Mental Deficiency." *Brit J Med Psychol* 19:394–414 pts 3–4 '43. * (*PA* 17:3783)
8. AMIN, D. L. "Differences Among the Deaf and Hearing Children." *Indian J Psychol* 21:91–2 pts 1–4 '46. * (*PA* 22:4571)
9. BRADFORD, E. J. G. "Selection for Technical Education: Parts I and II." *Brit J Ed Psychol* 16:20–31, 69–81 F, Je '46. * (*PA* 20:2887, 4881)
10. KAPAT, G., AND BHATTACHARYYA, C. C. "Some Critical Observations on Pass-along Test." *Indian J Psychol* 23:51–4 pts 1–4 '48. * (*PA* 28:6032, title only)
11. BIESHEUVEL, S. Chap. 4, "Psychological Tests and Their Applications to Non-European Peoples," pp. 87–126. In *The Yearbook of Education, 1949.* London: Evans Brothers Ltd., 1949. Pp. xv, 660. *
12. YELA, MARIANO. "Application of the Concept of Simple Structure to Alexander's Data." *Psychometrika* 14:121–35 Je '49. * (*PA* 24:1066)
13. WOODWARD, JOHN C. *Relationship of the Passalong Intelligence Test and Eighth Grade Achievement.* Master's thesis, University of Nebraska (Lincoln, Neb.), 1953.
14. RAY-CHOWDHURY, K. "Imagery and Performance Tests of Intelligence." *Indian Psychol B* 2:25–30 S '57. * (*PA* 37:4964)
15. JAYALAKSHMI, G. "Correlation of Tests of Psychomotor Ability With Intelligence and Non-motor Tests." *J Psychol Res* (India) 3:78–84 S '59. *
16. RAO, C. K. VASUDEVA. "Intelligence in a Group of Convicts: An Analysis of 35 Cases." *Trans All-India Inst Mental Health* 1:44–53 D '60. * (*PA* 37:3649)
17. KUNDU, RAMANATH. "An Investigation Into the Relationship Between Intelligence and Memory." *J Psychol Res* (India) 7:32–6 Ja '63. * (*PA* 38:2685)
18. FAHMY, MOSTAFA. "Initial Exploring of the Intelligence of Shilluk Children: Studies in the Southern Sudan." *Vita Hum* (Switzerland) 7(3–4):164–77 '64. * (*PA* 39:7815)
19. CHATTERJEE, NEERA. "A Comparison of Performance of Tribal and Non-Tribal Boys of Tripura (India) on Five Performance Tests." *J Psychol Res* (India) 9:151–8 S '65. * (*PA* 40:6561)
20. DEB, SUBIMAL, AND RAY, TAPATI. "Nature of Consistency Between Scores of Two Different Performance Tests in Normal and Subnormals." *Psychol Studies* (India) 13:16–20 Ja '68. *

CUMULATIVE NAME INDEX

[516]

Peabody Picture Vocabulary Test. Ages 2.5–18; 1959–70; PPVT; Lloyd M. Dunn; American Guidance Service, Inc. *

For additional information, see 7:417 (201 references); for reviews by Howard B. Lyman and Ellen V. Piers, see 6:530 (21 references).

REFERENCES THROUGH 1971

1–21. See 6:530.
22–223. See 7:417.
224. BRENGELMANN, JOHANNES C., AND HILLMAN, WILLIAM A., JR. "Determinants of Learning in the Retardate: A Pilot Study." *Training Sch B* 61:156–62 F '65. * (*PA* 39:10570)
225. LIEBERMAN, J. NINA. "Playfulness and Divergent Thinking: An Investigation of Their Relationship at the Kindergarten Level." *J Genetic Psychol* 107:219–24 D '65. * (*PA* 40:5252)
226. BENGER, KATHLYN. *A Study of the Relationships Be-*

tween *Perception, Personality, Intelligence and Grade One Reading Achievement.* Master's thesis, University of Alberta (Edmonton, Alta., Canada), 1966.
227. CORAH, NORMAN L.; JONES, SALLY ANN; AND MILLER, BARBARA B. "The Relation of Verbal Intelligence and Color-Form Discriminative Ability to Children's Color-Matching and Form-Matching Behavior." *J Psychol* 62:221–8 Mr '66. * (*PA* 40:7569)
228. SPOCK, ALEXANDER, AND STEDMAN, DONALD J. "Psychologic Characteristics of Children With Cystic Fibrosis." *N C Med J* 27:426–8 S '66. *
229. TILLMANS, SUSAN JEAN. *A Pilot Program on Language Development for Cerebral Palsied Children.* Master's thesis, St. Cloud State College (St. Cloud, Minn.), 1967.
230. BELLER, E. KUNO. "Intellectual Development in Educationally Disadvantaged Pre-School Children." *Proc 1966 Ann Read Inst Temple Univ* 5:73–83 '68. *
231. BURNS, GARY W. *A Comparison of the Peabody Picture Vocabulary Test With the Stanford-Binet Intelligence Scale and With the Wechsler Intelligence Scale for Children.* Master's thesis, Sacramento State College (Sacramento, Calif.), 1968.
232. GIEBINK, JOHN W., AND MARDEN, MARY L. "Verbal Expression, Verbal Fluency, and Grammar Related to Cultural Experience." *Psychol Sch* 5:365–8 O '68. * (*PA* 43:5912)
233. IRVINE, JAMES. *Correlates of Grade One Achievement.* Master's thesis, University of Alberta (Edmonton, Alta., Canada), 1968.
234. PAULUS, DIETER H., AND RENZULLI, JOSEPH S. "Improving the Validity of the Peabody Picture Vocabulary Test Through Item Analysis." *Univ Va Ed R* 6:67–71 '68. *
235. SMITH, MARSHALL P. "Intellectual Differences in Five-Year-Old Underprivileged Girls and Boys With and Without Pre-Kindergarten School Experience." *J Ed Res* 61:348–50 Ap '68. *
236. TEASDALE, G. R., AND KATZ, F. M. "Psycholinguistic Abilities of Children From Different Ethnic and Socio-Economic Backgrounds." *Austral J Psychol* 20:155–9 D '68. * (*PA* 45:3957)
237. FEDIO, PAUL, AND MIRSKY, ALLAN F. "Selective Intellectual Deficits in Children With Temporal Lobe or Centrencephalic Epilepsy." *Neuropsychologia* (England) 7(4):287–300 S '69. * (*PA* 44:4022)
238. GROSS, MORRIS. "Learning Readiness in Two Groups: A Study in 'Cultural Deprivation.' " *Jewish Ed* 39(1):36–48 Ja '69. *
239. BENNINGER, CLEO A. *A Study of the Interrelations Among Articulation, Chronological Age, Memory for Digits and Sentences, and Measures of the Peabody Picture Vocabulary Test for Kindergarten Children.* Master's thesis, Sacramento State College (Sacramento, Calif.), 1970.
240. COMSTOCK, JOHN ALLAN. *The Relationship Between Clinically Derived Scores of Employability and Employability Scores Predicted by an Employability Model for Mentally Retarded Adolescents.* Doctor's thesis, University of Minnesota (Minneapolis, Minn.), 1970. (*DAI* 32:271A)
241. KARNES, MEREL B.; TESKA, JAMES A.; AND HODGINS, AUDREY S. "The Effects of Four Programs of Classroom Intervention on the Intellectual and Language Development of 4-Year-Old Disadvantaged Children." *Am J Orthopsychiatry* 40(1):58–76 Ja '70. * (*PA* 45:1373)
242. KING, SUSAN HOFMAN. *The Relationships Between Mental Age, Level of Language Functioning and Social Acceptability in the Trainable Mentally Retarded.* Doctor's thesis, Louisiana State University (Baton Rouge, La.), 1970. (*DAI* 31:5691B)
243. LANEY, BILLIE JOHNSON. *A Comparative Study of Expressive and Comprehensive Vocabulary Development in Male and Female Kindergarten Children.* Doctor's thesis, East Texas State University (Commerce, Tex.), 1970. (*DAI* 31:4386A)
244. WHITMAN, MYRON A. "Discrimination Learning as a Function of MA, IQ and Institutionalization." *Training Sch B* 67(2):123–30 Ag '70. * (*PA* 44:21460)
245. ALI, FAIZUNISA, AND COSTELLO, JOAN. "Modification of the Peabody Picture Vocabulary Test." *Develop Psychol* 5(1):86–91 Jl '71. * (*PA* 46:8740)
246. AMDUR, JEANETTE LORRAINE READ. *Oral Language Abilities in a Low Socio-Economic Status Kindergarten Spanish-Surnamed Population Varying in Reading Achievement.* Doctor's thesis, University of Denver (Denver, Colo.), 1971. (*DAI* 32:779A)
247. BART, LEONARD EUGENE. *A Comparison of the Effectiveness of Televised and Conventional Administrations of Objective Scales.* Doctor's thesis, St. John's University (Jamaica, N.Y.), 1971. (*DAI* 32:2980B)
248. BERG, NORMAN L., AND BERG, SANDRA D. "Comparison of Verbal Intelligence of Young Children From Low and Middle Socioeconomic Status." *Psychol Rep* 28(2):559–62 Ap '71. * (*PA* 46:6531)
249. BIGELOW, GORDON S. "Field Dependence-Field Independence in 5- to 10-Year-Old Children." *J Ed Res* 64(9):397–400 My–Je '71. * (*PA* 47:6507)
250. BURLAND, R., AND CARROLL, V. M. "The Misuse of a Test of a Specific Ability as an Estimate of General Ability." *B Brit Psychol Soc* 24(85):317–8 O '71. * (*PA* 48:3515)
251. CARLSON, J. S. "Some Relationships Between Class Inclu-

sion, Perceptual Capabilities, Verbal Capabilities and Race." *Hum Develop* (Switzerland) 14(1):30–8 '71. * (*PA* 47:2617)

252. CARLSON, JERRY S. "Some Relationships Between Verbal and Perceptual Capabilities and the Development of Relative Thinking." *J Genetic Psychol* 118(1):115–9 Mr '71. * (*PA* 46:8724)

253. COSTELLO, JOAN, AND ALI, FAIZUNISA. "Reliability and Validity of Peabody Picture Vocabulary Test Scores of Disadvantaged Preschool Children." *Psychol Rep* 28(3):755–60 Je '71. * (*PA* 46:11495)

254. DE LACEY, P. R. "Classificatory Ability and Verbal Intelligence Among High-Content Aboriginal and Low Socioeconomic White Australian Children." *J Cross-Cultural Psychol* 2(4):393–6 D '71. * (*PA* 48:655)

255. DE LACEY, P. R. "Verbal Intelligence, Operational Thinking and Environment in Part-Aboriginal Children." *Austral J Psychol* 23(2):145–9 Ag '71. * (*PA* 47:10681)

256. DICK, ROBERT MARCUS, II. *Screening Identification of First Grade Problems in an American Indian Population.* Doctor's thesis, University of North Carolina (Chapel Hill, N.C.), 1971. (*DAI* 32:1209B)

257. DOLL, PADDY A.; FAGOT, HACKER J.; AND HIMBERT, JOANNA D. "Experimenter Effect on Sex-Role Preference Among Black and White Lower-Class Male Children." *Psychol Rep* 29(3):1295–301 D '71. * (*PA* 48:709)

258. ELLIOTT, R., AND MACKAY, D. N. "Social Competence of Subnormal and Normal Children Living Under Different Types of Residential Care." *Brit J Mental Subnormal* 17(32):48–53 Je '71. * (*PA* 47:11471)

259. FALK, LIBBY JANET. *A Profile of Learning Abilities and Behavioral Characteristics of Elementary School-Age Children With Phenylketonuria.* Doctor's thesis, Temple University (Philadelphia, Pa.), 1971. (*DAI* 32:1913A)

260. FAY, WARREN H., AND BUTLER, BRUCE V. "Echo-Reaction as an Approach to Semantic Resolution." *J Speech & Hearing Res* 14(3):645–51 S '71. * (*PA* 48:2699)

261. HALL, JOSEPH C., AND CHANSKY, NORMAN M. "Relationships Between Selected Ability and Achievement Tests in an Economically Disadvantaged Negro Sample." *Psychol Rep* 28(3):741–2 Je '71. * (*PA* 46:11501)

262. HARDY, MIRIAM P.; MELLITS, DAVID; AND WILLIG, SHARON N. "Reading: A Function of Language Usage." *Johns Hopkins Med J* 129(1):43–53 Jl '71. *

263. HEYDENBERK, WARREN ROBERT. *A Comparison of Four Methods of Estimating Reading Potential.* Doctor's thesis, University of Northern Colorado (Greeley, Colo.), 1971. (*DAI* 32:3558A)

264. HINTON, GEORGE G., AND KNIGHTS, ROBERT M. "Children With Learning Problems: Academic History, Academic Prediction, and Adjustment Three Years After Assessment." *Excep Children* 37(7):513–9 Mr '71. * (*PA* 47:3663)

265. JEFFREE, D. M., AND CASHDAN, A. "Severely Subnormal Children and Their Parents: An Experiment in Language Improvement." *Brit J Ed Psychol* 41(2):184–94 Je '71. * (*PA* 47:9728)

266. JERROLDS, BOB W.; CALLAWAY, BYRON; AND GWALTNEY, WAYNE. "A Comparative Study of Three Tests of Intellectual Potential, Three Tests of Reading Achievement, and the Discrepancy Scores Between Potential and Achievement." *J Ed Res* 65(4):168–72 D '71. * (*PA* 48:1647)

267. JERUCHIMOWICZ, RITA; COSTELLO, JOAN; AND BAGUR, J. SUSANA. "Knowledge of Action and Object Words: A Comparison of Lower- and Middle-Class Negro Preschoolers." *Child Develop* 42(2):455–64 Je '71. * (*PA* 47:637)

268. JOESTING, JOAN, AND JOESTING, ROBERT. "Correlation of Scores on the Picture Interpretation Test and Stanford-Binet Form L-M IQs." *Psychol Rep* 28(3):906 Je '71. * (*PA* 46:10576)

269. JOHNSON, DALE L., AND JOHNSON, CARMEN A. "Comparison of Four Intelligence Tests Used With Culturally Disadvantaged Children." *Psychol Rep* 28(1):209–10 F '71. * (*PA* 46:5736)

270. KASPAR, JOSEPH C.; MILLICHAP, J. GORDON; BACKUS, RENO; CHILD, DAVID; AND SCHULMAN, JEROME L. "A Study of the Relationship Between Neurological Evidence of Brain Damage in Children and Activity and Distractibility." *J Consult & Clin Psychol* 36(3):329–37 Je '71. * (*PA* 46:9475)

271. KOOLS, JOSEPH A.; WILLIAMS, AMANDA F.; VICKERS, MARJORIE JO; AND COELL, ANN. "Oral and Limb Apraxia in Mentally Retarded Children With Deviant Articulation." *Cortex* (Italy) 7(4):387–400 D '71. * (*PA* 49:11425)

272. L'ABATE, LUCIANO. "Receptive-Expressive Functions in Kindergarten Children and Adolescents." *Psychol Sch* 8(3):253–9 Jl '71. * (*PA* 47:9699)

273. MCCALL, CAROL IRENE. *An Investigation of Language Deficiency in a Female Prison Population.* Doctor's thesis, University of Florida (Gainesville, Fla.), 1971. (*DAI* 32:6101B)

274. MCCOOK, WILLIAM. *A Statistical Analysis of the Item Validity of the Peabody Picture Vocabulary Test.* Master's thesis, University of Connecticut (Storrs, Conn.), 1971.

275. MCCORMICK, CLARENCE C., AND SCHNOBRICH, JANICE N. "Perceptual-Motor Training and Improvement in Concentration in a Montessori Preschool." *Percept & Motor Skills* 32(1):71–7 F '71. * (*PA* 46:3865)

276. MALONEY, MICHAEL P.; WARD, MICHAEL P.; SCHENCK, HERBERT U.; AND BRAUCHT, GEORGE N. "Re-Evaluation of the Use of the Quick Test With a Sample of Institutionalized Mentally Retarded Subjects." *Psychol Rep* 29(3):1155–9 D '71. * (*PA* 48:1517)

277. MARSHALL, M. S., AND BENTLER, P. M. "IQ Increases of Disadvantaged Minority-Group Children Following Innovative Enrichment Program." *Psychol Rep* 29(3):805–6 D '71. * (*PA* 47:9836)

278. MATHENY, ADAM P., JR. "Comparability of WISC and PPVT Scores Among Young Children." *Excep Children* 38(2):147–50 O '71. * (*PA* 48:3673)

279. MILGRAM, NORMAN A. "IQ Constancy in Disadvantaged Negro Children." *Psychol Rep* 29(1):319–26 Ag '71. * (*PA* 47:2652)

280. NEDLER, SHARI, AND SEBERA, PEGGY. "Intervention Strategies for Spanish-Speaking Preschool Children." *Child Develop* 42(1):259–67 Mr '71. * (*PA* 46:5743)

281. ODELL, LOUISE M. "Maternal Intellectual Functioning." *Johns Hopkins Med J* 128(6):362–8 Je '71. *

282. O'PIELA, JOAN MARIE. *Identification of Predictor Variables of Success in First Grade Reading in Culturally Disadvantaged Inner-City Children Who Have Had a Preschool Experience.* Doctor's thesis, Wayne State University (Detroit, Mich.), 1971. (*DAI* 32:6109A)

283. PASEWARK, RICHARD A.; FITZGERALD, BERNARD J.; AND GLOECKLER, TED. "Relationship of Peabody Picture Vocabulary Test and Wechsler Intelligence Scale for Children in an Educable Retarded Group: A Cautionary Note." *Psychol Rep* 28(2):405–6 Ap '71. * (*PA* 46:7516)

284. RADIN, NORMA. "Maternal Warmth, Achievement Motivation, and Cognitive Functioning in Lower-Class Preschool Children." *Child Develop* 42(5):1560–5 N '71. * (*PA* 48:4724)

285. RASKIN, LARRY M.; OFFENBACH, STUART I.; AND SCOONOVER, DELMER L. "A Developmental Study of PPVT Temporal Stability Over Two 6-Mo. Intervals." *Psychol Rep* 28(2):501–2 Ap '71. * (*PA* 46:7458)

286. ROBINSON, HALBERT B., AND ROBINSON, NANCY M. "Longitudinal Development of Very Young Children in a Comprehensive Day Care Program: The First Two Years." *Child Develop* 42(6):1673–83 D '71. * (*PA* 48:8827)

287. ROHWER, WILLIAM D., JR.; AMMON, MARY SUE; SUZUKI, NANCY; AND LEVIN, JOEL R. "Population Differences and Learning Proficiency." *J Ed Psychol* 62(1):1–14 F '71. * (*PA* 46:3844)

288. ROHWER, WILLIAM D., JR., AND LEVIN, JOEL R. "Elaboration Preferences and Differences in Learning Proficiency." *Cognitive Studies* 2:127–48 '71. * (*PA* 49:1354, title only)

289. ROSENBERG, JOHN BENJAMIN. *The Relationship of Minor Congenital Anomalies to Behavioral and Intellectual Variables in Early School Age Children.* Doctor's thesis, Temple University (Philadelphia, Pa.), 1971. (*DAI* 32:2384B)

290. ROURKE, B. P.; YOUNG, G. C.; AND FLEWELLING, R. W. "The Relationships Between WISC Verbal-Performance Discrepancies and Selected Verbal, Auditory-Perceptual, Visual-Perceptual, and Problem-Solving Abilities in Children With Learning Disabilities." *J Clin Psychol* 27(4):475–9 O '71. * (*PA* 47:9738)

291. SEDA, MARIA S. A., AND MICHAEL, JOAN J. "The Concurrent Validity of the Sprigle School Screening Readiness Test for a Sample of Preschool and Kindergarten Children." *Ed & Psychol Meas* 31(4):995–7 w '71. * (*PA* 48:1660)

292. SELMAN, ROBERT L. "The Relation of Role Taking to the Development of Moral Judgment in Children." *Child Develop* 42(1):79–91 Mr '71. * (*PA* 46:4699)

293. SILOAC, KENNETH THOMAS. *An Investigation of Selected Perceptual Abilities in Educable Retarded and Normal Children.* Doctor's thesis, Wayne State University (Detroit, Mich.), 1971. (*DAI* 32:6719B)

294. STAFFIERI, J. ROBERT. "Performance of Preschool Children on the Quick Test (QT)." *Psychol Rep* 29(2):472 O '71. * (*PA* 47:9667)

295. SWIZE, LYDIA MARIE. *The Relationship Between Performance on Piagetian Conservation Tasks and Intelligence and Achievement in Educable Mentally Retarded Children.* Doctor's thesis, University of Northern Colorado (Greeley, Colo.), 1971. (*DAI* 32:3806A)

296. THOMAS, CLIFTON D.; ALCORN, JOHN D.; AND HOLMES, WILLIAM R. "Intellectual Performance of Headstart Children." *South J Ed Res* 5(1):51–6 Ja '71. *

297. TOLIVER, GLORIA DEAN. *The Measurement of Language Abilities of Black Children From Low Socioeconomic Environments.* Doctor's thesis, Ohio State University (Columbus, Ohio), 1971. (*DAI* 32:1903B)

298. WEINER, PAUL S. "Stability and Validity of Two Measures of Intelligence Used With Children Whose Language Development Is Delayed." *J Speech & Hearing Res* 14(2):254–61 Je '71. * (*PA* 48:5419)

299. WELLS, DONALD G., AND PEDRINI, DUILIO T. "Relationships Among Wechsler Adult Intelligence Scale, Goodenough-Harris, and Peabody Picture Vocabulary Tests With Institutionalized Retarded Adults." *Percept & Motor Skills* 33(1):227–32 Ag '71. * (*PA* 47:3549)

300. WILLIAMS, JOHN E., AND ROUSSEAU, CYNTHIA A. "Evaluation and Identification Responses of Negro Preschoolers to the Colors Black and White." *Percept & Motor Skills* 33(2):587–99 O '71. * (*PA* 47:6522)

301. WOLF, GERALD PHILLIP. *The Reliability and Validity of the Peabody Picture Vocabulary Test With Institutionalized Educable Retarded Children and Adolescents and Its Use as a Group Test With This Population.* Doctor's thesis, Catholic University of America (Washington, D.C.), 1971. (*DAI* 32:1871A)

CUMULATIVE NAME INDEX

Taylor, J. R.: 20
Teasdale, G. R.: 186, 236
Tempero, H. E.: 47
Tenhoff, M. L.: 23
Teska, J. A.: 241
Thomas, C. D.: 296
Throne, F. M.: 54
Tilis, H. S.: 206
Tillinghast, B. S.: 77, 151
Tillmans, S. J.: 229
Tobias, J.: 9
Toliver, G. D.: 297
Tolley, J.: 152
Tuttle, L. E.: 37, 78
Uhl, N. P.: 221
Vickers, M. J.: 271
Wakefield, H. E.: 137
Walker, A. J. M.: 187
Wallach, E. S.: 156
Ward, M. P.: 276
Ward, W. C.: 79

Ware, W. B.: 205
Weaver, A. S.: 115
Weeks, R. W.: 21
Weiner, P. S.: 298
Wells, D. G.: 116, 299
Whipple, C. I.: 80
Whitman, M. A.: 244
Wight, B. W.: 19
Williams, A. F.: 271
Williams, J. E.: 300
Williams, T. M.: 188
Willig, S. N.: 262
Winschel, J. F.: 27
Wolf, G. P.: 301
Wolfensberger, W.: 16
Womack, M.: 148
Woody, R. H.: 222
Yen, S. M. Y.: 189
Young, G. C.: 290
Zaeske, A.: 223
Zunich, M.: 152

[517]

Pictorial Test of Intelligence. Ages 3–8; 1964; PTI; prepublication titles were *North Central Individual Test of Mental Ability* and *Pictorial Intelligence Test;* 7 scores: picture vocabulary, form discrimination, information and comprehension, similarities, size and number, immediate recall, total; Joseph L. French; Houghton Mifflin Co. *

For additional information and reviews by Philip Himelstein and T. Ernest Newland, see 7:418 (17 references); see also 6:531 (2 references).

REFERENCES THROUGH 1971

1–2. See 6:531.
3–19. See 7:418.
20. MANDELBAUM, DAVID. *The Feasibility of an Audio-Taped Administration of the Pictorial Test of Intelligence.* Master's thesis, Pennsylvania State University (University Park, Pa.), 1971.

CUMULATIVE NAME INDEX

Bonfield, J. R.: 11
Brito, H.: 10
Dell, D.: 10
Elliott, R. N.: 18
French, J. L.: 1–3
Gentile, J. R.: 7
Greer, D.: 3
Himelstein, P.: *rev*, 7:418
Honstead, C. A.: 8
Howard, J. L.: 9
Jenson, G.: 4
Lee, R.: 10

Mandelbaum, D.: 20
Mueller, M. W.: 5–6, 12, 18
Newland, T. E.: *rev*, 7:418
Ortiz, K. K.: 13
Pasewark, R. A.: 10
Patterson, H. J.: 14
Plant, W. T.: 9, 15
Sawyer, R. N.: 10, 16
Smith, E.: 10
Southern, M. L.: 15
Vogler, J. D.: 17
Wasserberger, M.: 10

[518]

The Porteus Maze Test. Ages 3 and over; 1914–65; PMT; 2 scores: quantitative, qualitative; 3 editions and 2 supplements; Stanley D. Porteus. *

a) VINELAND REVISION. Ages 3 and over; 1914–24; Stoelting Co.

b) VINELAND REVISION: NEW SERIES. Ages 3 and over; 1914–65; Psychological Corporation.

c) PORTEUS MAZE EXTENSION. Ages 7 and over; 1953–65; for use only as a supplement to the *Vineland Revision: New Series;* Psychological Corporation.

d) PORTEUS MAZE SUPPLEMENT. Ages 7 and over; 1959–65; a retesting series; Psychological Corporation.

e) BRITISH EDITION. Ages 3 and over; 1914–65; George G. Harrap & Co. Ltd. [England].

For additional information, reviews by Richard F. Docter and John L. Horn, and excerpted reviews by William D. Altus, H. B. Gibson, D. C. Kendrick, and Laurance F. Shaffer, see 7:419 (67 references); see also 6:532 (38 references) and 5:412 (28 references); for reviews by C. M. Louttit and Gladys C. Schwesinger, see 4:356 (56 references). For excerpts from related book reviews, see 6:B400 (3 excerpts), 4:357 (4 excerpts), 1:B453 (2 excerpts), and 36:B210 (3 excerpts).

REFERENCES THROUGH 1971

1–56. See 4:356.
57–84. See 5:412.
85–122. See 6:532.
123–189. See 7:419.
190. BASSETT, DOROTHY M., AND PORTEUS, STANLEY D. "Sex Differences in Porteus Maze Test Performance." *Training Sch B* 17:1–16 N '20. *
191. PORTEUS, S. D. Chap. 4, "Porteus Maze Tests," pp. 75–115. In his *Studies in Mental Deviations.* Publications of the Training School at Vineland, N.J., Department of Research, No. 24, October 1922. Vineland, N.J.: the School, 1923. Pp. xi, 276. *
192. FOX, J. TYLOR. "The Response of Epileptic Children to Mental and Educational Tests." *Brit J Med Psychol* 4:235–48 N '24. *
193. HERRING, JOHN P. "Diagnosis of Feeble-Mindedness by Subjective Means." *J Ed Psychol* 17:270–4 Ap '26. *
194. BABCOCK, MARJORIE E. *Applications of Clinical Psychology in Hawaii.* University of Hawaii Research Publications No. 1. Honolulu, Hawaii: Mercantile Press, 1927. Pp. 88. *
195. PETERSON, JOSEPH. "A Review of *Temperament and Race.*" *Am J Psychol* 40:640–1 O '28 *; PORTEUS, S. D. "A Protest." *Am J Psychol* 41:336–8 Ap '29 *; PETERSON, JOSEPH. "A Reply to Porteus' 'Protest.'" *Am J Psychol* 41:338–41 Ap '29. *
196. BROOM, EUSTACE. "The Validity of Four Individual Tests of Mental Ability." *Ed Res B* (Los Angeles City Schools) 8:9–10 Mr '29. *
197. TREAT, KATHARINE. "Tests for Garment Machine Operators." *Personnel J* 8:19–28 Je '29. * *(PA 3:3767)*
198. PORTEUS, STANLEY D. Chap. 21, "Tests of Temperament and Intelligence," pp. 351–77. In his *The Psychology of a Primitive People: A Study of the Australian Aborigine.* New York: Longmans, Green & Co., 1931. Pp. xvi, 438. * *(PA 6:1168, title only)*
199. PORTEUS, STANLEY D. Chap. 23, "Aboriginal Children's Intelligence," pp. 408–20. In his *The Psychology of a Primitive People: A Study of the Australian Aborigine.* New York: Longmans, Green & Co., 1931. Pp. xvi, 438. * *(PA 6:1168, title only)*
200. PORTEUS, STANLEY D. "Mentality of Australian Aborigines." *Oceania* (Australia) 4:30–6 S '33. *
201. REICHARD, J. D. "The Intelligence of the Prospective Immigrant: 1, A Study of the Mental Ability, Measured by Language and Non-Language Tests, of Applicants for Immigrant Visas at Warsaw, Poland." *Pub Health B* 206:1–35 Jl '33. * *(PA 8:1774)*
202. SHAKOW, DAVID, AND MILLARD, MARY S. "A Psychometric Study of One Hundred and Fifty Adult Delinquents." *J Social Psychol* 6:437–57 N '35. * *(PA 10:3652)*
203. WEISENBURG, THEODORE; ROE, ANNE; AND McBRIDE, KATHARINE E. *Adult Intelligence: A Psychological Study of Test Performances.* New York: Commonwealth Fund, 1936. Pp. xiii, 155. * *(PA 10:3771)*
204. COWLES, KATHARINE. *The Correlation of Non-Language Mental Tests and Scholastic Achievement of Deaf Children.* Master's thesis, Temple University (Philadelphia, Pa.), 1937.
205. MARSH, CHARLES JUDD. *Performance Test Abilities of Adults.* Doctor's thesis, Stanford University (Stanford, Calif.), 1938.
206. MORRIS, CHARLES M. "A Critical Analysis of Certain Performance Tests." *J Genetic Psychol* 54:85–105 Mr '39. * *(PA 13:5387)*
207. PENROSE, L. S. "Intelligence Test Scores of Mentally Defective Patients and Their Relatives." *Brit J Psychol* 30:1–18 Jl '39. * *(PA 13:5734)*
208. PETERS, MARY FRIDIANA. *A Comparative Study of Some Measures of Emotional Instability in School Children.* Lafayette, Ind.: St. Francis Community Press, 1939. Pp. x, 71. *
209. MUENCH, GEORGE A. "A Follow-Up of Mental Defectives After Eighteen Years." *J Abn & Social Psychol* 39:407–18 O '44. * *(PA 19:420)*
210. BIESHEUVEL, S. Chap. 4, "Psychological Tests and Their Applications to Non-European Peoples," pp. 87–126. In *The Yearbook of Education, 1949.* London: Evans Brothers Ltd., 1949. Pp. xv, 660. *
211. PETRIE, ASENATH. "Personality Changes After Pre-Frontal Leucotomy." *Brit J Med Psychol* 22:200–1 pts 3–4 '49. * *(PA 25:2002)*
212. PETRIE, ASENATH. "Preliminary Report of Changes After Prefrontal Leucotomy." *J Mental Sci* (England) 95:449–55 Ap '49. * *(PA 24:278)*
213. JENSEN, MILTON B., AND SCHMID, JOHN. "An Analysis of Some Clinical Judgments on Male Basic Airmen Who Failed the Group Psychological Tests." *J Clin Psychol* 10:325–32 O '54. * *(PA 29:4753)*
214. FOULDS, G. A. "The Reliability of Psychiatric, and the Validity of Psychological, Diagnoses." *J Mental Sci* (England) 101:851–62 O '55. * *(PA 30:7165)*
215. GARDNER, M. J.; HAWKINS, H. M.; JUDAH, L. N.; AND MURPHREE, O. D. "Objective Measurement of Psychiatric Changes Produced by Chlorpromazine and Reserpine in Chronic Schizophrenia." *Psychiatric Res Rep* 1:77–83 Jl '55. * *(PA 30: 8411)*
216. PORTEUS, STANLEY D. "Some Commonsense Implications

of Psychosurgery." *Brit J Med Psychol* 28:167–76 pts 2–3 '55. * (*PA* 30:2982)

217. TOW, P. MACDONALD. Chap. 22, "Porteus Mazes," pp. 171–80. In his *Personality Changes Following Frontal Leucotomy.* London: Oxford University Press, 1955. Pp. xv, 262. * (*PA* 30:8319)

218. DURLING, DOROTHY, AND ESEN, FATMA MUNIRE. "Irregular Test Profiles Correlated With Personality Traits." *Am J Mental Def* 61:409–12 O '56. * (*PA* 32:1772)

219. DENNIS, WAYNE, AND NAJARIAN, PERGROUHI. "Infant Development Under Environmental Handicap." *Psychol Monogr* 71(7):1–13 '57. * (*PA* 33:5830)

220. GARRISON, MORTIMER, JR. "A Comparison of Psychological Measures in Mentally Retarded Boys Over a Three-Year Period as a Function of Etiology." *Training Sch B* 55:54–60 N '58. * (*PA* 34:1664)

221. SMITH, AARON, AND KINDER, ELAINE F. "Changes in Psychological Test Performances of Brain-Operated Schizophrenics After 8 Years." *Sci* 129:149–50 Ja 16 '59. * (*PA* 34:4700)

222. RAO, C. K. VASUDEVA. "Intelligence in a Group of Convicts: An Analysis of 35 Cases." *Trans All-India Inst Mental Health* 1:44–53 D '60. * (*PA* 37:3649)

223. SHAPIRO, M. B.; KESSELL, R.; AND MAXWELL, A. E. "Speed and Quality of Psychomotor Performance in Psychiatric Patients." *J Clin Psychol* 16:266–71 Jl '60. * (*PA* 36:2HI66S)

224. PORTEUS, STANLEY D., AND DIAMOND, A. L. "Measurement of Psychomotor Perseverative Tendencies." Letter. *Nature* (England) 189(4765):691–2 F 25 '61. *

225. JENKINS, C. DAVID. "The Relation of EEG Slowing to Selected Indices of Intellective Impairment." *J Nerv & Mental Dis* 135:162–70 Ag '62. *

226. AGNEW, NEIL, AND AGNEW, MARY. "Drive Level Effects on Tasks of Narrow and Broad Attention." *Q J Exp Psychol* 15:58–62 F '63. * (*PA* 37:7549)

227. CONNERS, C. KEITH, AND EISENBERG, LEON. "The Effects of Methylphenidate on Symptomatology and Learning in Disturbed Children." *Am J Psychiatry* 120:458–63 N '63. * (*PA* 38:6177)

228. HELPER, MALCOLM M.; WILCOTT, R. C.; AND GARFIELD, SOL L. "Effects of Chlorpromazine on Learning and Related Processes in Emotionally Disturbed Children." *J Consult Psychol* 27:1–9 F '63. * (*PA* 37:7710)

229. SMITH, AARON. "Mental Deterioration in Chronic Schizophrenia." *J Nerv & Mental Dis* 139:479–87 N '64. *

230. BROMLEY, D. B. "Age Differences in the Porteus Maze Test." *Proc Int Congr Gerontol* 6:225–8 '65. *

231. MUSSEN, PAUL H., AND PARKER, ANN L. "Mother Nurturance and Girls' Incidental Imitative Learning." *J Pers & Social Psychol* 2:94–7 Jl '65. * (*PA* 39:12022)

232. MEIER, MANFRED J., AND FRENCH, LYLE A. "Longitudinal Assessment of Intellectual Functioning Following Unilateral Temporal Lobectomy." *J Clin Psychol* 22:22–7 Ja '66. * (*PA* 40:4283)

233. PORTEUS, STANLEY D., AND DAVID, KENNETH. "Australid Mental Development and Geriatric Decline." *Percept & Motor Skills* 23:75–87 Ag '66. *

234. PORTEUS, STANLEY D. *A Psychologist of Sorts: The Autobiography and Publications of the Inventor of the Porteus Maze Tests.* Palo Alto, Calif.: Pacific Books, Publishers, 1969. Pp. x, 325. *

235. MEIER, MANFRED J. "Effects of Focal Cerebral Lesions on Contralateral Visuomotor Adaptation to Reversal and Inversion of Visual Feedback." *Neuropsychologia* (England) 8(3): 269–79 Jl '70. * (*PA* 44:21410)

236. ERIKSON, ROBERT V., AND ROBERTS, ALAN H. "Some Ego Functions Associated With Delay of Gratification in Male Delinquents." *J Consult & Clin Psychol* 36(3):378–82 Je '71. * (*PA* 46:9318)

237. FALCONER, A. D. "Measurement of Cognitive Function in Two Groups of Alcoholics." *J Alcoholism* (England) 6(4): 118–23 W '71. *

238. FRESTON, CYRUS WHEELOCK, II. *Verbal and Porteus Maze Performance of Learning Disabled Children: Effects of Methylphenidate and Input Organization.* Doctor's thesis, University of Texas (Austin, Tex.), 1971. (*DAI* 32:6246A)

239. LOGOTHETIS, JOHN; HARITOS-FATOUROS, MARY; CONSTANTOULAKIS, MATHIOS; ECONOMIDOU, JOANNA; AUGOUSTAKI, OLGA; AND LOEWENSON, RUTH B. "Intelligence and Behavioral Patterns in Patients With Cooley's Anemia (Homozygous Beta-thalassemia); A Study Based on 138 Consecutive Cases." *Pediatrics* 48(5):740–4 N '71. *

240. MEICHENBAUM, DONALD H., AND GOODMAN, JOSEPH. "Training Impulsive Children to Talk to Themselves." *J Abn Psychol* 77(2):115–26 Ap '71. * (*PA* 46:3785)

241. SHIPE, DOROTHY. "Impulsivity and Locus of Control as Predictors of Achievement and Adjustment in Mildly Retarded and Borderline Youth." *Am J Mental Def* 76(1):12–22 Jl '71. * (*PA* 47:5484)

CUMULATIVE NAME INDEX

O'Keefe, E. J.: 185
Owen, A.: 134
Palkes, H.: 170
Palmer, R. J.: 182
Parker, A. L.: 231
Penrose, L. S.: 207
Peretz, D.: 109
Peters, H. N.: 42–3, 53; *exc*, 6:B400
Peters, M. F.: 208
Peterson, J.: 14, 195
Petrie, A.: 211–2
Phillips, E. L.: 45
Piddington, M.: 85
Piddington, R.: 85
Pierce, R. A.: 142
Pintner, R.: *exc*, 1:B453
Porteus, S. D.: 1–2, 4–5, 8, 15, 22, 26, 28, 31, 33, 35–6, 39–40, 42–3, 49–50, 54, 65–6, 70, 74, 77, 82–3, 89, 94–5, 102–3, 108, 112–3, 121, 143, 162, 171, 178, 190–1, 195, 198–200, 216, 224, 233–4
Poull, L. E.: 13
Prange, A. J.: 181
Pulleine, R. H.: 16
Purcell, K.: 78, 114
Query, W. T.: 186
Ralph, D. W.: 17
Rankin, R.: 152
Rankin, R.: 151
Rao, C. K. V.: 222
Reichard, J. D.: 201
Resch, J. A.: 150, 161
Riley, J. E.: 144
Roberts, A. H.: 147, 172, 236
Roe, A.: 203
Rosén, A. S.: 173
Rosen, M.: 187
Royce, J. R.: 174
Ruebush, B. K.: 104, 122
Russell, J.: 162
Sacks, J. M.: 79
Salzinger, K.: 109
Salzinger, S.: 109
Sanderson, M. H.: 41
Sarason, S. B.: 104
Satter, G.: 71, 75
Schalling, D.: 173
Schell, R. E.: 148, 163
Schmid, J.: 213
Schmidt, A. G.: *exc*, 36:B210
Schwesinger, G. C.: *rev*, 4:356

Shaffer, L. F.: *exc*, 4:357, 7:419
Shakow, D.: 202
Shapiro, M. B.: 223
Sharp, E. Y.: 188
Shimota, H. E.: 87
Shipe, D.: 241
Simmons, K.: 123
Small, K.: 72
Smith, A.: 105, 221, 229
Spano, R. M.: 159
Sparling, M. E.: 32
Stackman, H.: 23
Stephenson, G.: 110
Sterne, D. M.: 153, 179
Stewart, M.: 170
Stone, C. L.: *exc*, 36:B210
Story, J. L.: 160
Stotsky, B. A.: 79
Sunukjian, H.: 47
Sutton, S.: 109
Sydow, D. W.: 67
Telford, C. W.: 14, 20
Thomas, R. R.: 81
Thompson, K.: 151–2
Thompson, W. H.: 169
Tilker, H. A.: 163
Tilton, J. W.: *exc*, 1:B453
Tizard, J.: 51, 55
Tobias, J.: 115
Tow, P. M.: 217
Trail, B. M.: 180
Treadway, C. R.: 181
Treat, K.: 197
Turnbull, J. W.: 114
Van de Castle, R. L.: 176
van der Kolk, J. J.: 29
Vernon, P. E.: 27
Verrill, B. V.: 90
Waite, R. R.: 104
Walker, A.: 131
Wassenaar, G. M. C.: 135
Watson, R. I.: 56
Weisenburg, T.: 203
Werner, E. E.: 189
Whybrow, P. C.: 181
Wilcott, R. C.: 228
Winder, C. L.: 68
Worcester, D. A.: *exc*, 4:357
Worthington, M. R.: 11
Wright, C.: 37
York, M. W.: 155
Zeckel, A.: 29
Zubin, J.: 109

[519]
Preschool Attainment Record, Research Edition.

Ages 6 months to 7 years; 1966–67; PAR; 9 scores: ambulation, manipulation, rapport, communication, responsibility, information, ideation, creativity, total; Edgar A. Doll; American Guidance Service, Inc. *

For additional information, a review by Roberta R. Collard, and an excerpted review by C. H. Ammons, see 7:420 (5 references).

REFERENCES THROUGH 1971

1–5. See 7:420.
6. JORDAN, THOMAS E. "Early Developmental Adversity and the First Two Years of Life." *Multiv Behav Res Monogr* 6(1): 1–80 '71. * (*PA* 49:2132)
7. PHILLIPS, DORIS CAMPBELL. *An Exploratory Study of the Relationship Between Mothers' Individualization of Their Children and the Children's Developmental Progress.* Doctor's thesis, Washington University (St. Louis, Mo.), 1971. (*DAI* 32:2201A)

CUMULATIVE NAME INDEX

Ammons, C. H.: *exc*, 7:420
Blair, J. R.: 4
Bowling, D. H.: 5
Clifford, M.: 3
Collard, R. R.: *rev*, 7:420
Doll, E. A.: 1–2
Jordan, T. E.: 6
McKnight, E. L.: 1
Owens, E. P.: 5
Phillips, D. C.: 7
Spitznagel, A.: 3
Stedman, D. J.: 3

[520]
Queensland Test.

Ages 7 and over; 1968–70; QT; based (except for pattern matching subtest) on the unpublished *PIR Test* used for screening for the Pacific Island Regiment; essentially the same as 5 of the 6 subtests in *New Guinea Performance Scales* except

for minor differences in some testing materials and differences in administration, scoring, and norms population; for the selection of subjects "likely to be able to learn rapidly the complex skills of westernized urbanized cultures from among groups who had had little contact with that culture"· 6 scores: *Knox Cube Test*, beads, modified *Passalong Test*, form assembly, pattern matching, total; D. W. McElwain, G. E. Kearney, and I. G. Ord (test and record form); Australian Council for Educational Research [Australia]. * (United States distributor: Educational and Industrial Testing Service.)

For additional information, see 7:421 (7 references).

REFERENCES THROUGH 1971

1–7. See 7:421.
8. BIANCHI, G. N.; McELWAIN, D. W.; AND CAWTE, J. E. "The Dispensary Syndrome in Australian Aborigines: Origins of Their Bodily Preoccupation and Sick Role Behavior." *Brit J Med Psychol* 43(4):375–82 D '70. *

CUMULATIVE NAME INDEX

Bianchi, G. N.: 8
Cawte, J. E.: 8
Kearney, G. E.: 2, 4
Kearney, J. E.: 3, 6–7
McElwain, D. W.: 8
Ord, I. G.: 1, 5

[521]
Quick Screening Scale of Mental Development.

Ages 6 months to 10 years; 1963; 6 mental age ratings: body coordination, manual performance, speech and language, listening attention and number, play interests, general mental level (mean of preceding 5 ratings); Katharine M. Banham; Psychometric Affiliates. *

For additional information and a review by Boyd R. McCandless, see 6:533.

[522]
The Quick Test.

Ages 2 and over; 1958–62; QT; picture vocabulary; R. B. Ammons and C. H. Ammons; Psychological Test Specialists. *

For additional information and excerpted reviews by Peter F. Merenda and B. Semeonoff, see 7:422 (30 references); for reviews by Boyd R. McCandless and Ellen V. Piers, see 6:534 (3 references).

REFERENCES THROUGH 1971

1–3. See 6:534.
4–33. See 7:422.
34. DIXON, JAMES C. "Cognitive Structure in Senile Conditions With Some Suggestions for Developing a Brief Screening Test of Mental Status." *J Gerontol* 20:41–9 Ja '65. *
35. MERENDA, PETER F. "The Provisional Manual for the Quick Test: A Review." *Ed & Psychol Meas* 25:268–71 sp '65. *
36. FLOWER, RICHARD M.; VIEHWEG, RICHARD; AND RUZICKA, WILLIAM R. "The Communicative Disorders of Children With Kernicteric Athetosis: 2, Problems in Language Comprehension and Use." *J Speech & Hearing Disorders* 31:60–8 F '66. * (*PA* 40:9108)
37. PATON, RICHARD. "Use of the Quick Test With Retarded Children." *Ont Psychol Assn Q* (Canada) 19:60–3 su '66. *
38. BOHRNSTEDT, GEORGE W.; LAMBERT, PHILIP; AND BORGATTA, EDGAR F. "The Reliability and Validity of Quick Tests With High School Seniors." *J Exp Ed* 39(4):22–3 su '71. * (*PA* 47:1573)
39. ERNHART, CLAIRE B.; JORDAN, THOMAS E.; AND SPANER, STEVEN D. "Maternal Quick Test (QT) Scores in Child Development Research." *Psychol Rep* 28(2):669–70 Ap '71. * (*PA* 46:6594)
40. JERROLDS, BOB W.; CALLAWAY, BYRON; AND GWALTNEY, WAYNE. "A Comparative Study of Three Tests of Intellectual Potential, Three Tests of Reading Achievement, and the Discrepancy Scores Between Potential and Achievement." *J Ed Res* 65(4):168–72 D '71. * (*PA* 48:1647)
41. JOESTING, JOAN, AND JOESTING, ROBERT. "Comparison of Scores on Quick Test and Stanford-Binet, Form L-M." *Psychol Rep* 29(3):1178 D '71. * (*PA* 48:1648)
42. JOESTING, JOAN, AND JOESTING, ROBERT. "The Quick Test as a Screening Device in a Welfare Setting." *Psychol Rep* 29(3):1289–90 D '71. * (*PA* 48:992)
43. LAMBERT, PHILIP; HANSEN, LEE H.; AND BORGATTA, EDGAR F. "Intelligent Word Associations in High School Students." *J Ed Res* 64(6):269–70 F '71. * (*PA* 46:11510)
44. LEVINE, NIRA R. "Validation of the Quick Test for Intel-

ligence Screening of the Elderly." *Psychol Rep* 29(1):167–72 Ag '71. * (*PA* 47:2717)

45. LIBB, J. WESLEY, AND COLEMAN, JOHN M. "Correlation Between the WAIS and Revised Beta, Wechsler Memory Scale and Quick Test in a Vocational Rehabilitation Center." *Psychol Rep* 29(3):863–5 D '71. * (*PA* 47:9410)

46. MALONEY, MICHAEL P.; WARD, MICHAEL P.; SCHENCK, HERBERT U.; AND BRAUCHT, GEORGE N. "Re-Evaluation of the Use of the Quick Test With a Sample of Institutionalized Mentally Retarded Subjects." *Psychol Rep* 29(3):1155–9 D '71. * (*PA* 48:1517)

47. SEITZ, FRANK C., AND BRAUCHT, GEORGE N. "Ammons' Quick Test as a Measure of Adult Intelligence in a Psychiatric Sample." *Psychol Rep* 29(2):356–8 O '71. * (*PA* 47:9302)

48. STAFFIERI, J. ROBERT. "Performance of Preschool Children on the Quick Test (QT)." *Psychol Rep* 29(2):472 O '71. * (*PA* 47:9667)

CUMULATIVE NAME INDEX

Abidin, R. R.: 13
Ammons, C. H.: 2
Ammons, R. B.: 2
Anderson, J.: 12
Andrews, R. J.: 12
Barclay, A.: 16, 26
Bibb, J. J.: 4
Bohrnstedt, G. W.: 38
Bonfield, J. R.: 20
Borgatta, E. F.: 38, 43
Braucht, G. N.: 46–7
Burgess, T. C.: 1, 3
Byrne, A. V.: 13
Callaway, B.: 40
Carlisle, A. L.: 6
Cole, S.: 14, 18
Coleman, J. M.: 45
Colvin, C. R.: 32
Connolly, J. K.: 21
Coyle, F. A.: 22
Cull, J. G.: 32
Davis, W. E.: 33
Dixon, J. C.: 34
Dizzone, M. F.: 33
Doyle, E. D.: 7
Eaton, A. E.: 10
Erdberg, P.: 22
Ernhart, C. B.: 39
Feldman, S. E.: 23
Flower, R. M.: 36
Griffith, J.: 31
Gwaltney, W.: 40
Hansen, L. H.: 43
Houston, C.: 24–5
Jerrolds, B. W.: 40
Joesting, J.: 41–2
Joesting, R.: 41–2
Jordan, T. E.: 39

Kearsley, R. B.: 10
King, F. W.: 15
Lambert, P.: 38, 43
Lamp, R. E.: 16, 26
Levine, N. R.: 27, 44
Libb, J. W.: 45
McCandless, B. R.: *rev*, 6:534
McMenemy, R. A.: 9
Maloney, M. P.: 46
Mednick, M. T.: 17, 28
Merenda, P. F.: 35; *exc*, 7:422
Methvin, M.: 5
Metzger, R.: 11
Miner, L.: 31
Ogilvie, R. D.: 8
Otto, W.: 9, 24–5
Paton, R.: 37
Piers, E. V.: *rev*, 6:534
Pless, I. B.: 10
Plotkin, R.: 19
Quattlebaum, L. F.: 29–30
Ruzicka, W. R.: 36
Schenck, H. U.: 46
Seitz, F. C.: 47
Semeonoff, B.: *exc*, 7:422
Snider, M.: 10
Spaner, S. D.: 39
Staffieri, J. R.: 48
Stewart, H.: 18
Strandberg, T. E.: 31
Viehweg, R.: 36
Ward, M. P.: 46
White, W. F.: 29–30
Whitney, V.: 11
Williams, R.: 14, 18
Wirls, C. J.: 19
Wright, D. D.: 3

[523]

Ring and Peg Tests of Behavior Development.

Birth to age 6; 1958–64; experimental; 6 scores: ambulative, manipulative, communicative, social adaptive, emotive, total; Katharine M. Banham; Psychometric Affiliates. *

For additional information and reviews by Jane V. Hunt and Emmy E. Werner, see 7:423.

[524]

Slosson Intelligence Test.

Ages 2 weeks and over; 1961–63; SIT; based in part upon *Stanford-Binet Intelligence Scale, Third Revision* and *Gesell Developmental Schedules;* Richard L. Slosson; Slosson Educational Publications, Inc. *

For additional information and reviews by Philip Himelstein and Jane V. Hunt, see 7:424 (31 references).

REFERENCES THROUGH 1971

1–31. See 7:424.

32. MESINGER, JOHN F. "An Intelligence Test to Assess Compensatory Education Programs for Disadvantaged Youth?" *Univ Va Ed R* 7:52–8 '69. *

33. MILLER, CHARLES K. "Conservation in Blind Children." *Ed Visually Handicapped* 1(4):101–5 D '69. * (*PA* 44:9017)

34. CHARLTON, NORMAN WOOD, II. *An Investigation of Selected Visual-Perceptual and Motor Parameters of Young Trainable Mentally Retarded Children.* Doctor's thesis, University of Houston (Houston, Tex.), 1970. (*DAI* 32:271A)

35. KAPEL, MARILYN B., AND KAPEL, DAVID E. "Hebrew English Reading Achievement in a Jewish Day School: A Comparison Among Reading Achievements and Attitudes Towards the Two Languages." *Jewish Ed* 40(3):23–32 w '70. *

36. MAXWELL, MICHAEL T. *The Relationship Between the Wechsler Intelligence Scale for Children and the Slosson Intelligence Test.* Master's thesis, Eastern Montana College (Billings, Mont.), 1970.

37. RUDOLPH, LINDA. *Correlates of the Slosson Intelligence Test, Wechsler Adult Intelligence Scale, ACT Scores and Grade Point Averages.* Master's thesis, Austin Peay State University (Clarksville, Tenn.), 1970.

38. ARMSTRONG, ROBERT J., AND MOONEY, ROBERT F. "The Slosson Intelligence Test: Implications for Reading Specialists." *Read Teach* 24(4):336–40+ Ja '71. * (*PA* 46:11492)

39. ARMSTRONG, ROBERT J.; MOONEY, ROBERT F.; AND JENSEN, JOHN A. "A Short, Reliable, Easy to Administer Individual Intelligence Test for Special Class Placement." *Child Study J* 1(3):156–63 sp '71. * (*PA* 48:1701)

40. GARRISON, MORTIMER, JR., AND HAMMILL, DONALD D. "Who Are the Retarded?" *Excep Children* 38(1):13–20 S '71. * (*PA* 47:7598)

41. HEDL, JOHN J., JR.; O'NEIL, HAROLD F., JR.; AND HANSEN, DUNCAN N. "Affective Nature of Computer-Based Testing Procedures." Abstract. *Proc 79th Ann Conv Am Psychol Assn* 6(2):535–6 '71. * (*PA* 46:5468)

42. LESSLER, KEN, AND GALINSKY, M. DAVID. "Relationship Between Slosson Intelligence Test and WISC Scores in Special Education Candidates." *Psychol Sch* 8(4):341–4 O '71. * (*PA* 47:9677)

43. MAXWELL, MICHAEL T. "The Relationship Between the Wechsler Intelligence Scale for Children and the Slosson Intelligence Test." *Child Study J* 1(3):164–71 sp '71. * (*PA* 48:1709)

CUMULATIVE NAME INDEX

Ames, L. B.: 3
Armstrong, R. J.: 38–9
Bonfield, J. R.: 4
Burns, L. M.: 5
Carlisle, A. L.: 24
Charlton, N. W.: 34
Colarusso, R.: 26
Crandell, J. M.: 26
DeLapa, G.: 1, 6
Duggan, M. D.: 7
Fagert, C. M.: 8
Galinsky, M. D.: 42
Garrison, M.: 40
Gillespie, P. H.: 25
Hammill, D.: 14
Hammill, D. D.: 26, 40
Hansen, D. N.: 41
Hedl, J. J.: 41
Himelstein, P.: *rev*, 7:424
Houston, C.: 9–10
Hunt, J. V.: *rev*, 7:424
Hutton, J. B.: 15, 27
Ivanoff, J.: 18
Jacobson, A.: 31
Jensen, J. A.: 39
Jongeward, P. A.: 16–7

Kapel, D. E.: 35
Kapel, M. B.: 35
Kaufman, H.: 18
Keany, M.: 11
Kilduff, C. T.: 19
Lessler, K.: 42
McRae, J.: 12
Maxwell, M. T.: 36, 43
Meissler, G. R.: 28
Mesinger, J. F.: 32
Miller, C. K.: 33
Mooney, R. F.: 38–9
Nash, M. S.: 20
Nicholson, C. L.: 21, 29
O'Keefe, S. L.: 2
O'Neil, H. F.: 41
O'Neill, H. D.: 22
Otto, W.: 9–10
Rudolph, L.: 37
Shepherd, C. W.: 23
Shinedling, M. M.: 24
Stuhler, M. A.: 30
Swanson, M. S.: 31
Weaver, R.: 24
Whitacre, R. L.: 13

[525]

*Stanford-Binet Intelligence Scale.

Ages 2 and over; 1916–73; S-B; 2 editions; Lewis M. Terman and Maud A. Merrill; Houghton Mifflin Co. * (British edition: George G. Harrap & Co. Ltd. [England].)

a) SECOND REVISION. 1916–37; title on test material is *Revised Stanford-Binet Scales;* only printed materials available.

b) THIRD REVISION. 1916–73; a single form combination of items selected from Forms L and M ('37) of the second revision; test materials and directions in 1972 standardization identical with 1960 edition except for minor changes in two items; Samuel R. Pinneau (1960 norms) and Robert L. Thorndike (1972 norms).

For additional information and a review by David Freides of the third revision, see 7:425 (258 references); for a review by Elizabeth D. Fraser and excerpted reviews by Benjamin Balinsky, L. B. Birch, James Maxwell, Marie D. Neale, and Julian C. Stanley, see 6:536 (110 references); for reviews by Mary R. Haworth and Norman D. Sundberg of the second revision, see 5:413 (121 references); for a review by Boyd R. McCandless, see 4:358 (142 references); see also 3:292 (217 references); for excerpted reviews by Cyril Burt, Grace H. Kent, and M. Krugman, see 2:1420 (132 references); for reviews by Francis N. Maxfield, J. W. M. Rothney, and F. L. Wells, see 1:1062. For excerpts from related book reviews, see 6:B396 (2 excerpts), 3:293 (6 excerpts), 3:294 (2 excerpts), 2:B1093 (3 excerpts), and 1:B497 (23 excerpts).

REFERENCES THROUGH 1971

1-134. See 2:1420.
135-351. See 3:292.
352-493. See 4:358.
494-620. See 5:413.
621-728. See 6:536.
729-986. See 7:425.

987. PYLE, W. H. "A Suggestion for the Improvement and Extension of Mental Tests." *J Ed Psychol* 3:95-6 F '12. *

988. HICKS, VINNIE CRANDALL. "The Value of the Binet Mental Age Tests for First-Grade Entrants." *J Ed Psychol* 6:157-66 Mr '15. *

989. HOUSER, J. DAVID. "The Relation of Spelling Ability to General Intelligence and to Meaning Vocabulary." *El Sch J* 16:190-9 D '15. *

990. TERMAN, LEWIS M., AND KNOLLIN, H. E. "Some Problems Relating to the Detection of Borderline Cases of Mental Deficiency." *J Psycho-Asthenics* 20:1-15 S-D '15. *

991. WILLIAMS, J. HAROLD. "The Problem of the Delinquent Boy." *Child* 6:29-32 O '15. *

992. BRIGGER, GRETCHEN. "A Study of Twenty-Five Repeaters at the Associated Charities, Portland, Oregon." *J Delinq* 1:187-94 S '16. *

993. TERMAN, LEWIS M. "Mentality Tests: A Symposium." *J Ed Psychol* 7:348-51 Je '16. *

994. WELLS, F. L. "The Measurement of Intelligence: A Review." *Sch & Soc* 4:296-8 Ag 19 '16. *

995. DOLL, E. A. "The Measurement of Intelligence: A Review." *J Ed Psychol* 8:111-6 F '17. *

996. DOWNEY, J. E. "University Instructors Tested by the Stanford Scale." Abstract. *Psychol B* 14:70-1 F '17. *

997. DOWNEY, JUNE E. "The Stanford Adult Intelligence Tests." *J Delinq* 2:144-55 My '17. *

998. KOHS, SAMUEL C. "The Stanford (1915) and the Vineland (1911) Revisions of the Binet Scale." *Psychol R* 24:174-9 Mr '17. *

999. PRATT, CARROL C. "The Measurement of Intelligence: A Review." *J Appl Psychol* 1:191-2 Je '17. *

1000. WELLS, F. L. "Aphasic Performance in the Terman Vocabulary Test." *J Ed Psychol* 8:343-7 O '17. *

1001. COLE, LAWRENCE W. "Mental Age and School Entrance." *Sch & Soc* 8:418-9 O 5 '18. *

1002. DOWNEY, JUNE E. "The Constancy of the I.Q." *J Delinq* 3:122-31 My '18. *

1003. LACY, WILLIAM I. "A Study of 100 Retarded Fourth Grade Pupils Tested by the Binet Scale." *Psychol Clinic* 12:16-23 Mr 15 '18. *

1004. MATEER, FLORENCE. "The Diagnostic Fallability of Intelligence Ratios." *Pedagog Sem* 25:369-92 D '18. *

1005. MAXFIELD, FRANCIS N. "Some Mathematical Aspects of the Binet-Simon Tests." *J Ed Psychol* 9:1-12 Ja '18. *

1006. CALDWELL, HELEN HUBBERT. "Adult Tests of the Stanford Revision Applied to College Students." *J Ed Psychol* 10:477-88 D '19. *

1007. CHASE, H. W., AND CARPENTER, C. C. "The Response of a Composite Group to the Stanford Revision of the Binet-Simon Tests." *J Ed Psychol* 10:179-88 Ap '19. *

1008. GORDON, KATE. "Report of Psychological Tests of Orphan Children." *J Delinq* 4:46-55 Ja '19. *

1009. SAAM, THEODORE. "Intelligence Tests as an Aid in Supervision." *El Sch J* 20:26-32 S '19. *

1010. SUNNE, DAGNY. "The Relation of Scholarships to the Yerkes and Terman Adult Tests." *J Ed Psychol* 10:520-4 D '19. *

1011. TERMAN, LEWIS M. "Some Data on the Binet Test of Naming Words." *J Ed Psychol* 10:29-35 Ja '19. *

1012. WALLIN, J. E. WALLACE. "The Value of the Intelligence Quotient for Individual Diagnosis." *J Delinq* 4:109-24 My '19. *

1013. WASHBURN, M. F. "A Note on the Terman Superior Adult Tests, as Applied to Vassar Freshmen." *Am J Psychol* 30:310 Jl '19. *

1014. WASHBURNE, CARLETON W. "A Classified Scale for Measuring Intelligence." *J Ed Psychol* 10:309-22 S '19. *

1015. BUCKINGHAM, B. R. "The Intelligence of School Children: A Review." *J Ed Res* 1:144-7 F '20. *

1016. CLARK, WILLIS W. "Success Record of Delinquent Boys in Relation to Intelligence." *J Delinq* 5:174-82 S '20. *

1017. DERRICK, S. M. "A Comparative Study of the Intelligence of Seventy-Five White and Fifty-Five Colored College Students by the Stanford Revision of the Binet-Simon Scale." *J Appl Psychol* 4:316-29 D '20. *

1018. DICKSON, VIRGIL E. "What First-Grade Children Can Do in School as Related to What Is Shown by Mental Tests." *J Ed Res* 2:475-80 Je '20. *

1019. EDMONDSON, MARGARET B. "A Mental Survey of First-Grade School Children." *Pedagog Sem* 27:354-70 D '20. *

1020. FRASIER, GEORGE W. "The Measurement of Intelligence as an Aid to Administration." *Ed Adm & Sup* 6:361-6 O '20. *

1021. NORTON, JOHN K. "The Mental Ages of a Group of 127 Prostitutes." *J Delinq* 5:63-6 My '20. *

1022. PINTNER, RUDOLF, AND NOBLE, HELEN. "The Classification of School Children According to Mental Age." *J Ed Res* 2:713-28 N '20. *

1023. PROCTOR, W. M. "Psychological Tests as a Means of Measuring the Probable School Success of High School Pupils." *J Ed Res* 1:258-70 Ap '20. *

1024. PROCTOR, W. M. "The Use of Psychological Tests in the Educational Guidance of High School Pupils." *J Ed Res* 1:369-81 My '20. *

1025. ROSENOW, CURT. "The Stability of the Intelligence Quotient." *J Delinq* 5:160-73 S '20. *

1026. RUCH, G. M., AND STRACHAN, LEXIE. "Intelligence Ratings by Group Scales and by the Stanford Revision of the Binet Tests." *J Ed Psychol* 11:421-9 N '20. *

1027. SCHWEGLER, R. A., AND WINN, EDITH. "A Comparative Study of the Intelligence of White and Colored Children." *J Ed Res* 2:838-48 D '20. *

1028. TERMAN, LEWIS M. "The Use of Intelligence Tests in the Grading of School Children." *J Ed Res* 1:20-32 Ja '20. *

1029. WALCOTT, GREGORY D. "The Intelligence of Chinese Students." *Sch & Soc* 11:474-80 Ap 17 '20. *

1030. CHASSELL, CLARA F., AND CHASSELL, LAURA M. "A Survey of the Three First Grades of the Horace Mann School by Means of Psychological Tests and Teachers' Estimates, and a Statistical Evaluation of the Measures Employed." *J Ed Psychol* 12:72-81, 243-52 F, My '21. *

1031. DECAMP, J. E. "Studies in Mental Tests: Army Alpha, Thurstone IV, and Binet-Simon (SR)." *Sch & Soc* 14:353-8 O 1 '21. *

1032. GARRISON, S. C. "Fluctuation of Intelligence Quotient." *Sch & Soc* 13:647-9 Je 4 '21. *

1033. GATES, ARTHUR I. "An Experimental and Statistical Study of Reading and Reading Tests." *J Ed Psychol* 12:303-14, 378-91, 445-64 S, O, N '21. *

1034. MATHEWS, JULIA. "Irregularity in Intelligence Tests of Delinquents." *J Delinq* 6:355-61 Mr '21. *

1035. ODELL, C. W. "Correlation of Certain Intelligence Tests for the Lower Grades." *J Ed Res* 3:308-10 Ap '21. *

1036. OTIS, ARTHUR S., AND KNOLLIN, HERBERT E. "The Reliability of the Binet Scale and of Pedagogical Scales." *J Ed Res* 4:121-42 S '21. *

1037. POULL, LOUISE E. "Constancy of I.Q. in Mental Defectives, According to the Stanford-Revision of Binet Tests." *J Ed Psychol* 12:323-4 S '21. *

1038. PROCTOR, WILLIAM MARTIN. *The Use of Psychological Tests in the Educational and Vocational Guidance of High School Pupils, Revised Edition.* Journal of Educational Research Monographs No. 1. Bloomington, Ill.: Public School Publishing Co., 1921. Pp. 125. *

1039. ROOT, W. T. "Two Cases Showing Marked Change in I.Q." *J Appl Psychol* 5:156-8 Je '21. *

1040. TERMAN, L. M. "Mental Growth and the I.Q." *J Ed Psychol* 12:325-41, 401-7 S, O '21. *

1041. WALLIN, J. E. WALLACE. "A Comparison of Three Methods for Making the Initial Selection of Presumptive Mental Defectives." Abstract. *Psychol B* 18:85-6 F '21. *

1042. WALLIN, J. E. WALLACE. "A Comparison of Three Methods for Making the Initial Selection of Presumptive Mental Defectives." *Sch & Soc* 13:31-45 Ja 8 '21. *

1043. WALLIN, J. E. WALLACE. "The Results of Retests by Means of the Binet Scale." *J Ed Psychol* 12:392-400 O '21. *

1044. WEEKS, ANGELINA L. "Terman Vocabulary as a Group Test." *J Ed Psychol* 12:532-6 D '21. *

1045. WEISMAN, FRANCES. "The Use of Mental Tests in the Whitman School." *J Ed Res* 4:155-8 S '21. *

1046. BAKER, HARRY J. "Mental Tests as an Aid in the Analysis of Mental Constitution." *J Appl Psychol* 6:349-77 D '22. *

1047. BALDWIN, BIRD T. "The Relation Between Mental and Physical Growth." *J Ed Psychol* 13:193-203 Ap '22. *

1048. BROWN, GILBERT L. "Intelligence as Related to Nationality." *J Ed Res* 5:324-7 Ap '22. *

1049. CALDWELL, HELEN HUBBERT. "Adult Tests of the Stanford Revision Applied to University Faculty Members." *J Exp Psychol* 5:247-62 Ag '22. *

1050. CLARK, WILLIS W. "Home Conditions and Native Intelligence." *J Delinq* 7:17-23 Ja '22. *

1051. COBB, MARGARET V. "One Element in the Probable Error of a Mental Age Measurement." *J Ed Psychol* 13:236-40 Ap '22. *

1052. COBB, MARGARET V. "Tentative Order of Difficulty of the Terman Vocabulary With Very Young Children." *J Ed Psychol* 13:357-62 S '22. *

1053. COWDERY, KARL M. "Measures of General Intelligence as Indices of Success in Trade Learning." *J Appl Psychol* 6:311-30 D '22. *

1054. DAWSON, CHARLES D. "Classification of Kindergarten

Children for First Grade by Means of the Binet Scale." *J Ed Res* 6:412–22 D '22. *

1055. FREEMAN, FRANK N. "The Mental Age of Adults." Editorial. *J Ed Res* 6:441–4 D '22. *

1056. GATES, ARTHUR I. "The Correlations of Achievement in School Subjects With Intelligence Tests and Other Variables." *J Ed Psychol* 13:129–39, 223–35, 277–85 Mr, Ap, My '22. *

1057. GLENN, IRENE. "A Report on the Correlation of Psychological Tests With Academic and Manual Subjects." *J Ed Psychol* 13:496–500 N '22. *

1058. GUILER, WALTER S. "How Different Mental Tests Agree in Rating Children." *El Sch J* 22:734–44 Je '22. *

1059. JOHNSON, BUFORD, AND SCHRIEFER, LOUISE. "A Comparison of Mental Age Scores Obtained by Performance Tests and the Stanford Revision of the Binet-Simon Scale." *J Ed Psychol* 13:408–17 O '22. *

1060. LINCOLN, EDWARD A. "The Constancy of Intelligence Quotients (A Case Study)." *J Ed Psychol* 13:484–95 N '22. *

1061. LINCOLN, EDWARD A. "Time-Saving in the Stanford-Binet Test." *J Ed Psychol* 13:94–7 F '22. *

1062. MITCHELL, DAVID. "Psychological Examination and Pre-School Age Children." *Sch & Soc* 15:561–8 My 20 '22. *

1063. ROOT, W. T. "The Intelligence Quotient From Two Viewpoints." *J Appl Psychol* 6:267–75 S '22. *

1064. TEAGARDEN, FLORENCE M. " 'The Constancy of the IQ' Again." *J Ed Psychol* 13:366–72 S '22. *

1065. WALLIN, J. E. W. "Intelligence Irregularity as Measured by Scattering in the Binet Scale." *J Ed Psychol* 13:140–51 Mr '22. *

1066. AVERY, GEORGE T. "A Study of the Binet and Terman Intelligence Tests With Eleven-Year-Old Children." *J Ed Res* 7:429–33 My '23. *

1067. BALDWIN, B. T. "Additional Data From Consecutive Stanford-Binet Tests." *J Ed Res* 8:375 N '23. *

1068. COLVIN, STEPHEN S., AND ALLEN, RICHARD D. "Mental Tests and Linguistic Ability." *J Ed Psychol* 14:1–20 Ja '23. *

1069. DEBUSK, B. W. "The Economic Status and the Intelligence of Children." *J Ed Res* 8:370–2 N '23. *

1070. EATON, H. T. "The Intelligence of Pupils Who Repeat." *Sch & Soc* 17:139–40 F 3 '23. *

1071. GATES, ARTHUR I., AND LASALLE, JESSIE. "The Relative Predictive Values of Certain Intelligence and Educational Tests Together With a Study of the Effect of Educational Achievement Upon Intelligence Test Scores." *J Ed Psychol* 14:517–39 D '23. *

1072. GORDON, KATE. "Some Notes on the Mental Status of the Left-Handed." *J Delinq* 8:154–7 My–Jl '23. *

1073. GRAY, P. L., AND MARSDEN, R. E. "The Constancy of the Intelligence Quotient." *Brit J Psychol* 13:315–24 Ja '23. *

1074. GRAY, P. L., AND MARSDEN, R. E. "The Stanford-Binet Tests in Some English Schools." *J Ed Res* 8:150–5 S '23. *

1075. JORDAN, A. M. "The Validation of Intelligence Tests." *J Ed Psychol* 14:348–66, 414–28 S, O '23. *

1076. ORDAHL, GEORGE. "Diagnosis of the Unstable Moron." *J Delinq* 8:99–112 Mr '23. *

1077. PORTEUS, S. D. Chap. 7, "Binet-Simon Scale," pp. 187–208. In his *Studies in Mental Deviations*. Publications of the Training School at Vineland, N.J., Department of Research, No. 24, October 1922. Vineland, N.J.: the School, 1923. Pp. xi, 276. *

1078. ROOT, W. T. "Transmutation of Scores Between Binet Tests and Group Tests." *J Ed Res* 7:338–43 Ap '23. *

1079. SCRIPTURE, MAY KIRK, AND KITTREDGE, WINIFRED BOYD. "An Attempt to Determine Another Etiological Factor of Stuttering Through Objective Measurement." *J Ed Psychol* 14:162–73 Mr '23. *

1080. WALLIN, J. E. W. "The Diagnostic Findings From Seven Years of Experience in the Same School Clinic." *J Delinq* 8:169–95 My–Jl '23. *

1081. WILNER, CHARLES F. "Mental Age Equivalents for a Group of Non-Reading Tests of the Herring Revision of the Binet-Simon Tests." *J Ed Psychol* 14:296–9 My '23. *

1082. GATES, ARTHUR I., AND LASALLE, JESSIE. "A Study of Writing Ability and Its Relation to Other Abilities Based on Repeated Tests During a Period of 20 Months." *J Ed Psychol* 15:205–16 Ap '24. *

1083. GATES, ARTHUR I.; ASSISTED BY GRACE A. TAYLOR, ELOISE BOEKER, AND DOROTHY VAN ALSTYNE. "The Nature and Educational Significance of Physical Status and of Mental, Physiological, Social and Emotional Maturity." *J Ed Psychol* 15:329–58 S '24. *

1084. GRAVES, KATHARINE B. "The Influence of Specialized Training on Tests of General Intelligence." *Teach Col Contrib Ed* 143:1–78 '24. *

1085. GRAY, P. L., AND MARSDEN, R. E. "The Constancy of the Intelligence Quotient—Further Results." *Brit J Psychol* 15:169–73 O '24. *

1086. HART, HORNELL. "Correlations Between Intelligence Quotients of Siblings." *Sch & Soc* 20:382 S 20 '24. *

1087. HECKMAN, SAMUEL B. Chap. 3, "A Comparative Study of Group Intelligence Tests Applicable to Children of Kindergarten Age," pp. 17–44. In *Contributions to Education, Vol. 1*. Edited by J. Carleton Bell. Yonkers, N.Y.: World Book Co., 1924. Pp. ix, 364. *

1088. HERRING, JOHN P. "Herring Revision of the Binet-Simon Tests." *J Ed Psychol* 15:172–9 Mr '24. *

1089. HEWES, AMY; HOLT, MILDRED; MERANSKI, SOPHIE; AND SNELL, JULIA. "Mental Age and School Attainment of 1007 Retarded Children in Massachusetts." *J Ed Psychol* 15:297–301 My '24. *

1090. MERRILL, MAUD A. "On the Relation of Intelligence to Achievement in the Case of Mentally Retarded Children." *Comp Psychol Monogr* 2(10):1–100 S '24. *

1091. MERRIMAN, CURTIS. "The Intellectual Resemblance of Twins." *Psychol Monogr* 33(5):1–58 '24. *

1092. MITCHELL, DAVID. "Psychological Examination of Pre-School Age Children: A Demonstration of the Classification of Children According to Ability." *Pedagog Sem* 31:108–46 Je '24. *

1093. SHELDON, WILLIAM H. "The Intelligence of Mexican Children." *Sch & Soc* 19:139–42 F 2 '24. *

1094. ABERNETHY, ETHEL M. "Correlations in Physical and Mental Growth." *J Ed Psychol* 16:458–66, 539–46 O, N '25. *

1095. CARMICHAEL, LEONARD. "Eidetic Imagery and the Binet Test." *J Ed Psychol* 16:251–2 Ap '25. *

1096. DASHIELL, J. F., AND GLENN, W. D. "A Re-examination of a Socially Composite Group With Binet and With Performance Tests." *J Ed Psychol* 16:335–40 My '25. *

1097. DAVIDSON, HELEN PYE. *Some Effects of Training on the Stanford Binet Scale.* Master's thesis, Stanford University (Stanford, Calif.), 1925.

1098. DEVOSS, JAMES C. Chap. 12, "Specialization of the Abilities of Gifted Children," pp. 307–62. In *Genetic Studies of Genius: Vol. 1, Mental and Physical Traits of a Thousand Gifted Children.* By Lewis M. Terman. Palo Alto, Calif.: Stanford University Press, 1925. Pp. xv, 648. *

1099. FERNALD, MABLE R., AND ARLITT, ADA H. "A Psychological Study of a Group of Crippled Children of Various Types." *Sch & Soc* 21:449–52 Ap 11 '25. *

1100. FUKUDA, TONAN. "A Survey of the Intelligence and Environment of School Children." *Am J Psychol* 36:124–39 Ja '25. *

1101. GARRISON, S. C., AND ROBINSON, M. S. "A Study of Re-Tests." *J Ed Res* 11:190–6 Mr '25. *

1102. GATES, ARTHUR I., AND TAYLOR, GRACE A. "An Experimental Study of the Nature of Improvement Resulting From Practice in a Mental Function." *J Ed Psychol* 16:583–92 D '25. *

1103. GOODENOUGH, F. L. "The Reading Tests of the Stanford Achievement Scale and Other Variables." *J Ed Psychol* 16:523–31 N '25. *

1104. HARTER, DORIS IRENE. *Some Results of Coaching Some of the Tests of the Stanford Revision of the Binet-Simon Scale.* Master's thesis, Stanford University (Stanford, Calif.), 1925.

1105. HILDRETH, GERTRUDE HOWELL. "The Resemblance of Siblings in Intelligence and Achievement." *Teach Col Contrib Ed* 186:1–65 '25. *

1106. JOHNSON, BUFORD J. Chap. 4, "Mental Development as Measured by Graded Series of Tests," pp. 79–107. In his *Mental Growth of Children in Relation to the Rate of Growth in Bodily Development: A Report of the Bureau of Educational Experiments, New York City*. New York: E. P. Dutton & Co., 1925. Pp. 160. *

1107. JONES, A. M. "An Analytical Study of One Hundred Twenty Superior Children." *Psychol Clinic* 16:19–76 Ja–F '25. * (*PA* 3:1656)

1108. JONES, VERNON A. "A Study of Children's Ability to Note Similarities and Differences." *J Ed Psychol* 16:253–60 Ap '25. *

1109. KOLB, LAURENCE. "The Relation of Intelligence to the Etiology of Drug Addiction." *Am J Psychiatry* 82:163–7 Jl '25. * (*PA* 1:618)

1110. RAND, GERTRUDE. "A Discussion of the Quotient Method of Specifying Test Results." *J Ed Psychol* 16:599–618 D '25. *

1111. RAYBOLD, EMMA. "An Experiment With Primary Intelligence Tests." *Ed Res B* (Los Angeles City Schools) 4:8 Je 15 '25. *

1112. RUGG, L. S. "Retests and the Constancy of the IQ." *J Ed Psychol* 16:341–3 My '25. *

1113. SUNNE, DAGNY. "Comparison of White and Negro Children by the Terman and Yerkes-Bridges Revisions of the Binet Tests." *J Comp Psychol* 5:209–20 Je '25. * (*PA* 1:1409)

1114. WILSON, G. M. "Standard Deviations of Age Scores and Quotients in Typical Groups." *J Ed Psychol* 16:193–207 Mr '25. *

1115. WOODS, ELIZABETH L. "Intellectual and Emotional Improvement in Nutrition Classes." *Ed Res B* (Los Angeles City Schools) 5:6–11 O '25. *

1116. WOOLEY, HELEN T. "The Validity of Standards of Mental Measurement in Young Childhood." *Sch & Soc* 21:476–82 Ap 18 '25. *

1117. BROOKS, FOWLER D. "The Accuracy of Group Test Mental Ages and Intelligence Quotients of Junior High School Pupils." *Sch R* 34:333–42 My '26. *

1118. CASEY, MARY LOUISE. *Some Results of Training in Material Similar to the Stanford Revision of the Binet-Simon Scale.* Master's thesis, Stanford University (Stanford, Calif.), 1926.

1119. DARSIE, MARVIN L. "The Mental Capacity of American-Born Japanese Children." *Comp Psychol Monogr* 3(15):1–89 Ja '26. * (*PA* 1:133)

1120. GATES, ARTHUR I. "A Study of the Role of Visual Per-

Stanford-Binet Intelligence Scale

ception, Intelligence, and Certain Associative Processes in Reading and Spelling." *J Ed Psychol* 17:433–45 O '26. * (*PA* 1:175)

1121. GRAHAM, VIRGINIA TAYLOR. "The Intelligence of Chinese Children in San Francisco." *J Comp Psychol* 6:43–71 F '26. * (*PA* 1:663)

1122. GRAY, P. L., AND MARSDEN, R. E. "The Constancy of the Intelligence Quotient—Final Results." *Brit J Psychol* 17: 20–6 Jl '26. *

1123. HOLLINGWORTH, LETA S. "Musical Sensitivity of Children Who Test Above 135 IQ (Stanford-Binet)." *J Ed Psychol* 17:95–109 F '26. *

1124. HOLLINGWORTH, LETA S., AND MONAHAN, JANE E. "Tapping-Rate of Children Who Test Above 135 IQ (Stanford-Binet)." *J Ed Psychol* 17:505–18 N '26. * (*PA* 1:285)

1125. LACY, L. D. "Relative Intelligence of White and Colored Children." *El Sch J* 26:542–6 Mr '26. *

1126. MERRILL, MAUD A. "Mental Differences Among Juvenile Delinquents." *J Delinq* 10:312–23 Mr '26. *

1127. MINOGUE, BLANCHE M. "The Constancy of the I.Q. of Mental Defectives." *Mental Hyg* 10:751–8 O '26. * (*PA* 1:870)

1128. STRACHAN, LEXIE. "Distribution of Intelligence Quotients of Twenty-Two Thousand Primary-School Children." *J Ed Res* 14:169–77 O '26. * (*PA* 1:209)

1129. SULLIVAN, ELIZABETH T. "The Use of a Psychographic Representation of Results of the Stanford Revision of the Binet-Simon Tests." *J Delinq* 10:284–5 plus 2 inserts Ja '26. *

1130. WECHSLER, DAVID. "On the Influence of Education on Intelligence as Measured by the Binet-Simon Tests." *J Ed Psychol* 17:248–57 Ap '26. *

1131. WORTHINGTON, MYRTLE RAYMAKER. "Performance Test Scores of Behavior and Non-Behavior Children." *Welfare Mag* 17:97–103 O '26. * (*PA* 1:439)

1132. WORTHINGTON, MYRTLE RAYMAKER. "A Study of Some Commonly Used Performance Tests." *J Appl Psychol* 10:216–27 Je '26. *

1133. ASHER, E. J. "Training Needs of Reform School Boys Experimentally Determined." *J Delinq* 11:151–8 S '27. * (*PA* 2:746)

1134. BROOM, M. EUSTACE. "A Study of the Constancy of the I.Q." *Ed Res B* (Los Angeles City Schools) 7:2–3 O–N '27. *

1135. MONAHAN, JANE E., AND HOLLINGWORTH, LETA S. "Neuro-Muscular Capacity of Children Who Test Above 135 IQ (Stanford-Binet)." *J Ed Psychol* 18:88–96 F '27. * (*PA* 1:1170)

1136. SEROTA, KATHRYN EWART. "A Comparative Study of One Hundred Italian Children at the Six-Year Level." *Psychol Clinic* 16:216–31 O '27. * (*PA* 2:1347)

1137. SLOCOMBE, C. S. "Why the IQ Is Not, and Cannot Be Constant." *J Ed Psychol* 18:421–3 S '27. * (*PA* 2:277)

1138. STALNAKER, ELIZABETH M., AND ROLLER, R. D., JR. "A Study of One Hundred Nonpromoted Children." *J Ed Res* 16: 265–70 N '27. * (*PA* 2:781)

1139. WALTERS, FRED C. "A Statistical Study of Certain Aspects of the Time Factor in Intelligence." *Teach Col Contrib Ed* 248:1–82 '27. *

1140. ABELSON, HAROLD H. Chap. 12, "What Hope for the Low I.Q.?" pp. 64–70. In *Contributions to Education, Vol. 2.* Edited by J. Carleton Bell and Ambrose L. Suhrie. Yonkers, N.Y.: World Book Co., 1928. Pp. xi, 425. * (*PA* 2:2313)

1141. BIDDLE, A. E. "An Analytical Study of One Class in High School." *Psychol Clinic* 17:97–118 S–O '28. * (*PA* 3: 1676)

1142. BURKS, BARBARA STODDARD. "The Relative Influence of Nature and Nurture Upon Mental Development: A Comparative Study of Foster Parent-Foster Child Resemblance and True Parent-True Child Resemblance." *Yearb Nat Soc Study Ed* 27(1):219–316 '28. * (*PA* 2:2464)

1143. CASEY, MARY L.; DAVIDSON, HELEN P.; AND HARTER, DORIS I. "Three Studies on the Effect of Training in Similar and Identical Material Upon Stanford-Binet Test Scores." *Yearb Nat Soc Study Ed* 27(1):431–9 '28. * (*PA* 2:2338)

1144. DENWORTH, KATHARINE M. "The Effect of Length of School Attendance Upon Mental and Educational Ages." *Yearb Nat Soc Study Ed* 27(2):67–91 '28. * (*PA* 2:2608)

1145. DIETSCH, MILDRED KATHRYN. *A Correlation of the Intelligence Quotients of the Drawing Test With the Stanford Binet.* Master's thesis, Ohio State University (Columbus, Ohio), 1928.

1146. ESTABROOKS, G. H. "The Relation Between Cranial Capacity, Relative Cranial Capacity and Intelligence in School Children." *J Appl Psychol* 12:524–9 O '28. * (*PA* 3:499)

1147. FREEMAN, FRANK N.; HOLZINGER, KARL J.; AND MITCHELL, BLYTHE CLAYTON. "The Influence of Environment on the Intelligence, School Achievement, and Conduct of Foster Children." *Yearb Nat Soc Study Ed* 27(1):102–217 '28. * (*PA* 2:2469)

1148. FREEMAN, FRANK S. "Influence of Educational Attainment Upon Tests of Intelligence." *J Ed Psychol* 19:230–42 Ap '28. * (*PA* 2:2651)

1149. GREENE, KATHARINE B. "The Influence of Specialized Training on Tests of General Intelligence." *Yearb Nat Soc Study Ed* 27(1):421–8 '28. * (*PA* 2:2063)

1150. HALLOWELL, D. K. "Mental Tests for Pre-School Children." *Psychol Clinic* 16:235–76 N–D '28. * (*PA* 2:2948)

1151. HILDRETH, GERTRUDE. "The Effect of School Environ-

ment Upon Stanford Binet Tests of Young Children." *Yearb Nat Soc Study Ed* 27(1):355–9 '28. * (*PA* 2:1649)

1152. HOEFER, CAROLYN, AND HARDY, MATTIE CRUMPTON. "The Influence of Improvement in Physical Condition on Intelligence and Educational Achievement." *Yearb Nat Soc Study Ed* 27(1):371–87 '28. * (*PA* 2:2342)

1153. JONES, ALICE M. "A Vocabulary Study of Children in a Foreign Industrial Community." *Psychol Clinic* 17:13–21 Mr '28. * (*PA* 2:2950)

1154. LINCOLN, EDWARD A. "Studies of the Validity of the Dearborn General Intelligence Examinations." *J Ed Psychol* 19:346–9 My '28. * (*PA* 2:2952)

1155. McANULTY, ELLEN ALICE. "A Comparison of the Terman, the National and the Stanford Binet Tests." *Ed Res B* (Los Angeles City Schools) 8:5–7 O '28. *

1156. MATTHEW, JANET, AND LUCKEY, BERTHA. "Notes on Factors That May Alter the Intelligence Quotient in Successive Examinations." *Yearb Nat Soc Study Ed* 27(1):411–9 '28. * (*PA* 2:2345)

1157. MURPHY, MILES. "The Ten Year Level of Competency." *Psychol Clinic* 17:33–60 My–Je '28. *

1158. ROGERS, AGNES L.; DURLING, DOROTHY; AND McBRIDE, KATHARINE. "The Constancy of the IQ and the Training of Examiners." *J Ed Psychol* 19:257–62 Ap '28. * (*PA* 2:2657)

1159. ROGERS, AGNES L.; DURLING, DOROTHY; AND McBRIDE, KATHARINE. "The Effect on the Intelligence Quotient of Change From a Poor to a Good Environment." *Yearb Nat Soc Study Ed* 27(1):323–31 '28. * (*PA* 2:1708)

1160. THORNDIKE, ROBERT L.; FLEMMING, CECILE WHITE; HILDRETH, GERTRUDE; AND STANGER, MARGARET. "Retest Changes in the IQ in Certain Superior Schools." *Yearb Nat Soc Study Ed* 27(2):351–61 '28. *

1161. WAGONER, LOVISA C., AND ARMSTRONG, EDNA M. "The Motor Control of Children as Involved in the Dressing Process." *J Genetic Psychol* 35:84–97 Mr '28. * (*PA* 2:3692)

1162. WITTY, PAUL A. "Some Results of a Pre-School Clinic." *J Genetic Psychol* 35:139–41 Mr '28. * (*PA* 2:3694)

1163. WOODWORTH, R. S. "Computing the Standard Deviation and Probable Error of a Binet Mental Age." Abstract. *Psychol B* 25:167 Mr '28. *

1164. ABT, ISAAC A.; ADLER, HERMAN M.; AND BARTELME, PHYLLIS. "The Relationship Between the Onset of Speech and Intelligence." *J Am Med Assn* 93:1351–5 N 2 '29. * (*PA* 4: 1285)

1165. BROOM, EUSTACE. "The Validity of Four Individual Tests of Mental Ability." *Ed Res B* (Los Angeles City Schools) 8:9–10 Mr '29. *

1166. CHIPMAN, CATHERINE E. "The Constancy of the Intelligence Quotient of Mental Defectives." *Psychol Clinic* 18:103–11 My–Je '29. * (*PA* 4:1110)

1167. FORD, CHARLES A. "The Variability of I.Q.'s for Psychopaths Retested Within Fifteen Days." *Psychol Clinic* 18:199–204 N–D '29. * (*PA* 4:4082)

1168. HERTZBERG, OSCAR E. "The Relationship of Motor Ability to the Intelligence of Kindergarten Children." *J Ed Psychol* 20:507–19 O '29. * (*PA* 4:373)

1169. McCLURE, W. E., AND GOLDBERG, BRONETT. "Intelligence of Unmarried Mothers." *Psychol Clinic* 18:119–27 My–Je '29. * (*PA* 4:1202)

1170. MARSDEN, R. E. "The Intelligence of Children in Some Remote Country Schools." *Forum Ed* (England) 7:83–90 Je '29. * (*PA* 3:4320)

1171. RUCH, FLOYD L. "Defensibility of Certain Abridgments of the Stanford Achievement Examination." *J Ed Res* 20:66–9 Je '29. *

1172. THURSTONE, L. L., AND JENKINS, RICHARD L. "Birth Order and Intelligence." *J Ed Psychol* 20:641–51 D '29. * (*PA* 4:1057)

1173. CARROLL, HERBERT A., AND HOLLINGWORTH, LETA S. "The Systematic Error of Herring-Binet in Rating Gifted Children." *J Ed Psychol* 21:1–11 Ja '30. * (*PA* 4:1840)

1174. CATTELL, PSYCHE. "Comparability of I.Q.'s Obtained From Different Tests at Different I.Q. Levels." *Sch & Soc* 31: 437–42 Mr 29 '30. * (*PA* 4:2561)

1175. CATTELL, PSYCHE. "IQ's and the Otis' Measure of Brightness." *J Ed Res* 22:31–5 Je '30. * (*PA* 4:3726)

1176. COX, JOHN FREMONT. *Differences Between Negro and Native White Convicts Tested With the Stanford-Binet Scale and Retested With a Reorganized Form of This Scale.* Master's thesis, University of Pittsburgh (Pittsburgh, Pa.), 1930.

1177. DAVENPORT, CHARLES B., AND MINOGUE, BLANCHE M. "The Intelligence Quotient and the Physical Quotient: Their Fluctuation and Intercorrelation." *Hum Biol* 2:473–507 D '30. * (*PA* 6:440)

1178. DEARBORN, WALTER F., AND CATTELL, PSYCHE. "The Intelligence and Achievement of Private School Pupils." *J Ed Psychol* 21:197–211 Mr '30. * (*PA* 4:2864)

1179. KEEN, ANGELINE M. "Growth Curves and IQ's as Determined by Testing Large Families." *Sch & Soc* 32:737–42 N 29 '30. * (*PA* 5:1740)

1180. ALTMAIER, CARL L. "The Performance Level of Children in the Sixth Grade in Two Philadelphia Public Schools." *Psychol Clinic* 19:233–57 Ja '31. * (*PA* 5:3986)

1181. BROOKS, FOWLER D. "Predicting Scholarship in the Junior High School." *Ann Conf Ed Meas* 18:73–80 '31. *

1182. CATTELL, PSYCHE. "Why Otis' 'IQ' Cannot Be Equivalent to the Stanford-Binet IQ." *J Ed Psychol* 22:599–603 N '31. * (*PA* 6:906)

1183. HSIAO, HSIAO HUNG. "The Status of the First-Born With Special Reference to Intelligence." *Genetic Psychol Monogr* 9:1–118 Ja–F '31. * (*PA* 5:2689)

1184. LAWRENCE, EVELYN M. "An Investigation Into the Relation Between Intelligence and Inheritance." *Brit J Psychol Monogr Sup* 16:1–80 '31. *

1185. LEE, MARY V. "The Children's Orthopedic Hospital: A Survey of the Intelligence of Crippled Children." *J Ed Res* 23:164–6 F '31. * (*PA* 5:2503)

1186. DAWSON, SHEPHERD. "Intelligence and Fertility." *Brit J Psychol* 23:42–51 Jl '32. * (*PA* 7:2829)

1187. McELWEE, EDNA WILLIS. "An Analysis of the Binet Test of Naming Words." *Psychol Clinic* 21:59–61 Mr–My '32. * (*PA* 7:379)

1188. OBELKEVICH, HENRY. *A Comparison of Detroit Boy Truants With Boy Non-Truants on Stanford-Binet Test Failures and on Certain Tangible Home Factors.* Master's thesis, University of Alabama (University, Ala.), 1932.

1189. RICHARDS, T. W. "Psychological Tests in the First Grade." *Psychol Clinic* 21:235–42 D–F '32–33. * (*PA* 8:665)

1190. RICHARDS, T. W. "The Relationship of Psychological Tests in the First Grade to School Progress: A Follow-Up Study." *Psychol Clinic* 21:137–71 S–N '32. *

1191. STEINER, MELVIN ARTHUR. "Yearly Variation in the Average Intelligence of Pupils Entering the First Grade." *J Ed Psychol* 23:161–72 Mr '32. * (*PA* 6:3003)

1192. UPDEGRAFF, RUTH. "The Determination of a Reliable Intelligence Quotient for the Young Child." *J Genetic Psychol* 41:152–66 S '32. * (*PA* 7:2164)

1193. WELLMAN, BETH L. "The Effect of Pre-School Attendance Upon IQ." *J Exp Ed* 1:48–69 D '32. * (*PA* 7:3106)

1194. BECKHAM, ALBERT SIDNEY. "A Study of the Intelligence of Colored Adolescents of Different Social-Economic Status in Typical Metropolitan Areas." *J Social Psychol* 4:70–91 F '33. * (*PA* 7:2459)

1195. CATTELL, PSYCHE. "The Heinis Personal Constant as a Substitute for the IQ." *J Ed Psychol* 24:221–8 Mr '33. * (*PA* 7:4176)

1196. DURRELL, DONALD D. "The Influence of Reading Ability on Intelligence Measures." *J Ed Psychol* 24:412–6 S '33. * (*PA* 8:654)

1197. EELLS, WALTER CROSBY. "Mental Ability of the Native Races of Alaska." *J Appl Psychol* 17:417–38 Ag '33. * (*PA* 8:478)

1198. FARSON, MABEL R. "A Comparison of Orthogenic Backward Children and Regular Grade Children at the Six Year Performance Level." *Psychol Clinic* 22:149–80 S–N '33. * (*PA* 8:5685)

1199. HARRIMAN, PHILIP L. "Ethical Discrimination as a Function of Intelligence." *Sch & Soc* 38:812 D 16 '33. * (*PA* 8:3175)

1200. HEILMAN, J. D. "Sex Differences in Intellectual Abilities." *J Ed Psychol* 24:47–62 Ja '33. * (*PA* 7:2121)

1201. LINE, W., AND KAPLAN, E. "Variation in I.Q. at the Preschool Level." *J Exp Ed* 2:95–100 D '33. * (*PA* 8:2316)

1202. McCLURE, W. E. "Intelligence of Six Hundred Juvenile Delinquents." *J Juvenile Res* 17:35–43 Ja '33. * (*PA* 7:2509)

1203. MURPHY, MILES. "The Relation Between Intelligence and Age of Walking in Normal and Feeble-Minded Children." *Psychol Clinic* 22:187–97 S–N '33. * (*PA* 8:5712)

1204. OUTHIT, MARION CURRIE. "A Study of the Resemblance of Parents and Children in General Intelligence." *Arch Psychol* 149:1–60 Ap '33. * (*PA* 8:310)

1205. REICHARD, J. D. "The Intelligence of the Prospective Immigrant: 1, A Study of the Mental Ability, Measured by Language and Non-Language Tests, of Applicants for Immigrant Visas at Warsaw, Poland." *Pub Health B* 206:1–35 Jl '33. * (*PA* 8:1774)

1206. SCHELL, M. "Infection by Intestinal Protozoa in Relation to the Intelligence of Siblings." *Child Develop* 4:253–8 S '33. * (*PA* 8:721)

1207. SIMMONS, PERSIS WHITE. "Statistical Results of an Eight Year Testing Program of a Psychological Clinic in a Charity Hospital." *Psychol Clinic* 22:128–37 Je–Ag '33. * (*PA* 8:4681)

1208. BRYAN, ALICE I. "Organization of Memory in Young Children." *Arch Psychol* 162:1–56 Mr '34. * (*PA* 8:3836)

1209. CUNNINGHAM, BESS V. "Infant IQ Ratings Evaluated After an Interval of Seven Years." *J Exp Ed* 3:84–7 D '34. * (*PA* 9:2493)

1210. RAPPAPORT, MITCHELL E. "The Selection of the Intelligence Quotient Divisor for Clinical Cases Between Fourteen and Nineteen Years of Age." *J Ed Psychol* 25:101–14 F '34. * (*PA* 8:2812)

1211. STEINBACH, ALEXANDER ALAN. "Intelligence and Juvenile Delinquency." *El Sch J* 34:691–7 My '34. * (*PA* 8:4682)

1212. ANDERSON, H. DEWEY, AND EELLS, WALTER CROSBY. *Alaska Natives: A Survey of Their Sociological and Educational Status,* pp. 298–370. Stanford, Calif.: Stanford University Press, 1935. Pp. xvi, 472. * (*PA* 9:2346)

1213. ASHER, E. J. "The Inadequacy of Current Intelligence Tests for Testing Kentucky Mountain Children." *J Genetic Psychol* 46:480–6 Je '35. * (*PA* 9:6005)

1214. AXELBAUM, ETHEL M. *Differences Between the Kohs and Stanford-Binet in a Group of Artistically Gifted Children.* Master's thesis, Columbia University (New York, N.Y.), 1935.

1215. BRADWAY, KATHERINE PRESTON. "Paternal Occupational Intelligence and Mental Deficiency." *J Appl Psychol* 19:527–41 O '35. * (*PA* 10:2019)

1216. LANE, HOWARD A., AND WITTY, PAUL A. "The Mental Ability of Delinquent Boys." *J Juvenile Res* 19:1–12 Ja '35. * (*PA* 9:4718)

1217. LEAHY, A. M. "Nature-Nurture and Intelligence." *Genetic Psychol Monogr* 17:236–308 Ag '35. * (*PA* 9:5664)

1218. LINCOLN, EDWARD A. "A Study of Changes in the Intelligence Quotients of Superior Children." *J Ed Res* 29:272–5 D '35. * (*PA* 10:2764)

1219. LONG, HOWARD HALE. "Test Results of Third-Grade Negro Children Selected on the Basis of Socio-Economic Status." *J Negro Ed* 4:192–212, 523–52 Ap, O '35. * (*PA* 10:1089)

1220. McELWEE, EDNA WILLIS. "Differences in Reading Attainment of Italian and Jewish Children." *J Appl Psychol* 19:730–2 D '35. * (*PA* 10:3637)

1221. ROTHBART, H. B., AND HAW, ARTHUR B. "Basal Metabolism in Children of Normal and Subnormal Intelligence With Blood Cholesterol and Creatinine Values." *Am J Dis Children* 49:672–88 Mr '35. *

1222. SHAKOW, DAVID, AND MILLARD, MARY S. "A Psychometric Study of One Hundred and Fifty Adult Delinquents." *J Social Psychol* 6:437–57 N '35. * (*PA* 10:3652)

1223. CANADY, HERMAN G. "The Effect of 'Rapport' on the I.Q.: A New Approach to the Problem of Racial Psychology." *J Negro Ed* 5:209–19 Ap '36. * (*PA* 10:4136)

1224. FENDRICK, PAUL, AND BOND, GUY. "Delinquency and Reading." *J Genetic Psychol* 48:236–43 Mr '36. * (*PA* 10:3619)

1225. HILL, HARRY SEGNER. "Correlation Between I.Q.'s of Bilinguals at Different Ages on Different Intelligence Tests." *Sch & Soc* 44:89–90 Jl 18 '36. * (*PA* 10:5164)

1226. HINTON, RALPH T., JR. "The Role of the Basal Metabolic Rate in the Intelligence of Ninety Grade-School Students." *J Ed Psychol* 27:546–50 O '36. * (*PA* 11:1247)

1227. JENKINS, MARTIN D. "A Socio-Psychological Study of Negro Children of Superior Intelligence." *J Negro Ed* 5:175–90 Ap '36. * (*PA* 10:4157)

1228. LORGE, IRVING, AND HOLLINGWORTH, LETA S. "Adult Status of Highly Intelligent Children." *J Genetic Psychol* 49:215–26 S '36. * (*PA* 11:3007)

1229. SKEELS, HAROLD M. "The Relation of the Foster Home Environment to the Mental Development of Children Placed in Infancy." *Child Develop* 7:1–5 Mr '36. * (*PA* 10:4443)

1230. SMITTER, FAITH WINTERS. *The Serviceability of the Merrill-Palmer and the Stanford-Binet Scales for Ages Three to Six.* Master's thesis, University of Southern California (Los Angeles, Calif.), 1936.

1231. WEISENBURG, THEODORE; ROE, ANNE; AND McBRIDE, KATHARINE E. *Adult Intelligence: A Psychological Study of Test Performances.* New York: Commonwealth Fund, 1936. Pp. xiii, 155. * (*PA* 10:3771)

1232. BAYLEY, NANCY, AND JONES, HAROLD E. "Environmental Correlates of Mental and Motor Development: A Cumulative Study From Infancy to Six Years." *Child Develop* 8:329–41 D '37. * (*PA* 12:3201)

1233. CRISSEY, ORLO L. *Mental Development as Related to Institutional Residence and Educational Achievement.* University of Iowa Studies in Child Welfare Vol. 13, No. 1. Iowa City, Iowa: the University, 1937. Pp. 81. * (*PA* 11:3477)

1234. GLANVILLE, A. DOUGLAS. "Psychometric Patterns in Industrial School Boys." *Delaware State Med J* 11:91–4 Ap '37. * (*PA* 11:4270)

1235. HONZIK, MARJORIE P., AND JONES, HAROLD E. "Mental-Physical Relationships During the Preschool Period." *J Exp Ed* 6:139–46 D '37. * (*PA* 12:3216)

1236. JASTAK, JOSEPH. "Psychometric Patterns of State Hospital Patients." *Delaware State Med J* 11:87–91 Ap '37. * (*PA* 11:4152)

1237. KYTE, GEORGE C. "Causes of First-Grade Non-Promotion in the Light of Measured Intelligence." *El Sch J* 37:415–28 F '37. * (*PA* 11:3886)

1238. NAROSNY, ELEANOR HELEN. *A Comparative Study of the Performance of Juvenile Delinquents and Educational Problem Children on the Stanford-Binet and Grace Arthur Scales.* Master's thesis, Ohio State University (Columbus, Ohio), 1937.

1239. NOTTINGHAM, RUTH D. "A Psychological Study of Forty Unmarried Mothers." *Genetic Psychol Monogr* 19:157–228 My '37. * (*PA* 11:4670)

1240. PINESS, GEORGE; MILLER, HYMAN; AND SULLIVAN, ELLEN G. "The Intelligence Rating of the Allergic Child." *J Allergy* 8:168–74 Ja '37. * (*PA* 12:994)

1241. WELLMAN, BETH L. "Mental Growth From Preschool to College." *J Exp Ed* 6:127–38 D '37. * (*PA* 12:3244)

1242. WOLF, S. J. "A Comparative Study of Two Groups of Girls of Relatively Equal Intelligence but Differing Markedly in Achievement." *J Appl Psychol* 21:304–10 Je '37. * (*PA* 11:4815)

1243. LAMSON, EDNA E. "To What Extent Are Intelligence

Stanford-Binet Intelligence Scale

Quotients Increased by Children Who Participate in a Rich, Vital School Curriculum?" *J Ed Psychol* 29:67–70 Ja '38. * (PA 12:3950)

1244. ROBERTS, CHARLES STEPHEN. "Ordinal Position and Its Relationship to Some Aspects of Personality." *J Genetic Psychol* 53:173–213 Je '38. * (PA 13:2034)

1245. SKEELS, HAROLD M.; UPDEGRAFF, RUTH; WELLMAN, BETH L.; AND WILLIAMS, HAROLD M. *A Study of Environmental Stimulation: An Orphanage Preschool Project*, pp. 37–60. University of Iowa Studies in Child Welfare, Vol. 15, No. 4. Iowa City, Iowa: the University, 1938. Pp. 191. * (PA 13:1758)

1246. WELLMAN, BETH L. *The Intelligence of Preschool Children as Measured by the Merrill-Palmer Scale of Performance Tests*. University of Iowa Studies in Child Welfare, Vol. 15, No. 3. Iowa City, Iowa: the University, 1938. Pp. 150. * (PA 13:1730)

1247. WILE, IRA S., AND DAVIS, ROSE M. "A Study of the Behavior of 250 Children With Mental Age Ten Years." *Am J Orthopsychiatry* 8:689–709 O '38. * (PA 13:1345)

1248. ABEL, THEODORA M. "Subnormal Girls With Discrepant Test Patterns." *J Appl Psychol* 23:398–404 Je '39. * (PA 13:5668)

1249. BIJOU, S. W. "Psychometric Similarities Between Habitual Criminals and Psychotics." *Delaware State Med J* 11:126–9 My '39. * (PA 14:3687)

1250. BRODY, LEON. "Adult Intelligence and Pre-Adult Schooling." *Sch & Soc* 49:746–8 Je 10 '39. * (PA 13:5063)

1251. HINTON, RALPH T., JR. "A Further Study of the Role of the Basal Metabolic Rate in the Intelligence of Children." *J Ed Psychol* 30:309–14 Ap '39. * (PA 13:5602)

1252. JASTAK, JOSEPH. "Psychometric Changes Following Insulin Therapy." *Delaware State Med J* 11:114–9 My '39. * (PA 14:3410)

1253. PENROSE, L. S. "Intelligence Test Scores of Mentally Defective Patients and Their Relatives." *Brit J Psychol* 30:1–18 Jl '39. * (PA 13:5734)

1254. TEAGARDEN, FLORENCE M. "The Intelligence of Diabetic Children With Some Case Reports." *J Appl Psychol* 23:337–46 Je '39. * (PA 13:5613)

1255. WELLS, F. L. "The Plan of Search at Various Levels of Abstraction." *J General Psychol* 21:163–85 Jl '39. * (PA 14:242)

1256. BAYLEY, NANCY. "Mental Growth in Young Children." *Yearb Nat Soc Study Ed* 39(2):11–47 '40. * (PA 14:3260)

1257. BRADLEY, CHARLES, AND GREEN, EMILY. "Psychometric Performance of Children Receiving Amphetamine (Benzedrine) Sulfate." *Am J Psychiatry* 97:388–94 S '40. * (PA 15:1997)

1258. CONRAD, HERBERT S., AND JONES, HAROLD E. "A Second Study of Familial Resemblance in Intelligence: Environmental and Genetic Implications of Parent-Child and Sibling Correlations in the Total Sample." *Yearb Nat Soc Study Ed* 39(2):97–141 '40. * (PA 14:2870)

1259. FRANDSEN, ARDEN, AND BARLOW, FRANCES P. "Influence of the Nursery School on Mental Growth." *Yearb Nat Soc Study Ed* 39(2):143–8 '40. * (PA 14:3202)

1260. GRAHAM, VIRGINIA TAYLOR. "Psychological Studies of Hypoglycemia Therapy." *J Psychol* 10:327–58 O '40. * (PA 15:1337)

1261. HONZIK, MARJORIE PYLES. "Age Changes in the Relationship Between Certain Environmental Variables and Children's Intelligence." *Yearb Nat Soc Study Ed* 39(2):185–205 '40. * (PA 14:2888)

1262. JENKINS, RICHARD L.; BROWN, ANDREW W.; AND CISLER, LILLIAN E. "Influence of Syphilis on Intelligence of Children." *Am J Dis Children* 60:341–51 Ag '40. * (PA 15:3627)

1263. KATZ, EVELYN. "The Relationship of IQ to Height and Weight From Three to Five Years." *J Genetic Psychol* 57:65–82 S '40. * (PA 15:1109)

1264. KVARACEUS, W. C. "Intelligence Quotients of Retarded Children in the Same Families." *El Sch J* 40:527–8 Mr '40. * (PA 15:4066)

1265. LAYMAN, JAMES W. "A Quantitative Study of Certain Changes in Schizophrenic Patients Under the Influence of Sodium Amytal." *J General Psychol* 22:67–86 Ja '40. * (PA 14:2439)

1266. SPEER, GEORGE S. "The Intelligence of Foster Children." *J Genetic Psychol* 57:49–55 S '40. * (PA 15:1128)

1267. PAGE, JAMES D. "Twin, Sibling and Chance IQ Differences." *J Ed Psychol* 32:73–6 Ja '41. * (PA 15:2947)

1268. ROFF, MERRILL. "A Statistical Study of the Development of Intelligence Test Performance." *J Psychol* 11:371–86 Ap '41. * (PA 15:3738)

1269. DULSKY, STANLEY G. "Affect and Intellect: An Experimental Study." *J General Psychol* 27:199–220 O '42. * (PA 17:77)

1270. MCRAE, HUGH. "The Inconstancy of Group Test IQ's." *Brit J Ed Psychol* 12:59–70 F '42. * (PA 16:2905)

1271. WILSON, M. T. "Detection of Reading Difficulties in a Rural Public School." *Training Sch B* 39:41–6 My '42. * (PA 16:3818)

1272. JENKINS, MARTIN D. "Case Studies of Negro Children of Binet IQ of 160 and Above." *J Negro Ed* 12:159–66 sp '43. * (PA 17:2410)

1273. BIJOU, S. W., AND MCCANDLESS, B. R. "An Approach to a More Comprehensive Analysis of Mentally Retarded Pre-Delinquent Boys." *J Genetic Psychol* 65:147–60 S '44. * (PA 19:440)

1274. BROWN, FRED. "A Comparative Study of the Intelligence of Jewish and Scandinavian Kindergarten Children." *J Genetic Psychol* 64:67–92 Mr '44. * (PA 18:2003)

1275. MUENCH, GEORGE A. "A Follow-Up of Mental Defectives After Eighteen Years." *J Abn & Social Psychol* 39:407–18 O '44. * (PA 19:420)

1276. SPOERL, DOROTHY TILDEN. "The Academic and Verbal Adjustment of College Age Bilingual Students." *J Genetic Psychol* 64:139–57 Mr '44. * (PA 18:2275)

1277. FALK, R.; PENROSE, L. S.; AND CLARK, E. A. "The Search for Intellectual Deterioration Among Epileptic Patients." *Am J Mental Def* 49:469–71 Ap '45. * (PA 20:139)

1278. KEIR, GERTRUDE. "An Experiment in Mental Testing Under Hypnosis." *J Mental Sci* (England) 91:346–52 Jl '45. * (PA 20:425)

1279. SPIEGEL, HERBERT; SHOR, JOEL; AND FISHMAN, SIDNEY. "An Hypnotic Ablation Technique for the Study of Personality Development: A Preliminary Report." *Psychosom Med* 7:273–8 S '45. * (PA 20:209)

1280. WAGGONER, R. W., AND ZEIGLER, THORNTON WOODWARD. "Psychiatric Factors in Medical School Students Who Fail." *Am J Psychiatry* 103:369–76 N '46. * (PA 21:1671)

1281. MARTIN, FLORENCE. "Comparative Study of Intelligence of Children From Private Homes and Those From an Institutional Home." *Peabody J Ed* 24:198–202 Ja '47. * (PA 21:3950)

1282. SLOAN, WILLIAM, AND HARMAN, HARRY H. "Constancy of IQ in Mental Defectives." *J Genetic Psychol* 71:177–85 D '47. * (PA 22:3525)

1283. ZIMMERMAN, FREDERIC T.; BURGEMEISTER, BESSIE B.; AND PUTNAM, TRACY J. "A Group Study of the Effect of Glutamic Acid Upon Mental Functioning in Children and Adolescents." *Psychosom Med* 9:175–83 My–Je '47. * (PA 21:3474)

1284. COLLINS, JEANNE. "The Correlation Between Perseveration Test Scores and the Intelligence Quotient: An Experimental Study." *J Genetic Psychol* 72:47–55 Mr '48. * (PA 22:4834)

1285. ZIMMERMAN, FREDERIC T.; BURGEMEISTER, BESSIE B.; AND PUTNAM, TRACY J. "The Ceiling Effect of Glutamic Acid Upon Intelligence in Children and in Adolescents." *Am J Psychiatry* 104:593–9 Mr '48. * (PA 23:634)

1286. SKODAK, MARIE, AND SKEELS, HAROLD M. "A Final Follow-Up Study of One Hundred Adopted Children." *J Genetic Psychol* 75:85–125 S '49. * (PA 24:3651)

1287. ASHER, PATRIA, AND SCHONELL, F. ELEANOR. "A Survey of 400 Cases of Cerebral Palsy in Childhood." *Arch Dis Childh* (England) 25:360–79 D '50. *

1288. GERVER, JOHN M., AND DAY, RICHARD. "Intelligence Quotient of Children Who Have Recovered From Erythroblastosis Fetalis." *J Pediatrics* 36:342–8 Mr '50. * (PA 24:4490)

1289. KREEZER, GEORGE L., AND SMITH, FRANKLIN W. "The Relation of the Alpha Rhythm of the Electroencephalogram, and Intelligence Level in the Non-Differentiated Familial Type of Mental Deficiency." *J Psychol* 29:47–51 Ja '50. * (PA 24:4170)

1290. ALBERT, K.; HOCH, P.; AND WAELSCH, H. "Glutamic Acid and Mental Deficiency." *J Nerv & Mental Dis* 114:471–91 D '51. * (PA 26:4871)

1291. REED, HOMER R. "The Intelligence of Epileptics." *J Genetic Psychol* 78:145–52 Je '51. * (PA 26:2942)

1292. BENSBERG, GERARD J., JR. "The Relation of Academic Achievement of Mental Defectives to Mental Age, Sex, Institutionalization and Etiology." *Am J Mental Def* 58:327–30 O '53. * (PA 28:4530)

1293. GHOSH, S. P., AND SEN, ROMA. "An Attempt to Standardise the Bengali Adaptation of Terman 'M' Form." *Indian J Psychol* 28:111–5 pts 1–4 '53. * (PA 29:2446)

1294. REYNOLDS, MAYNARD CLINTON. "A Study of the Relationships Between Auditory Characteristics and Specific Silent Reading Abilities." *J Ed Res* 46:439–49 F '53. * (PA 28:1492)

1295. BAYLEY, NANCY. "Some Increasing Parent-Child Similarities During the Growth of Children." *J Ed Psychol* 45:1–21 Ja '54. * (PA 28:7257)

1296. GUREVITZ, SAUL, AND HELME, WILLIAM H. "Effects of Electroconvulsive Therapy on Personality and Intellectual Functioning of the Schizophrenic Child." *J Nerv & Mental Dis* 120:213–26 S–O '54. * (PA 29:7650)

1297. PAZEIAN, BESSIE. "Classification and Treatment Problems in a Case of Encephalopathy." *J Clin Psychol* 10:149–55 Ap '54. * (PA 29:1376)

1298. UECKER, ALBERT E.; FRENCH, LYLE A.; AND JOHNSON, DAVID R. "Psychological Studies of Seven Epileptic Hemiparetics Before and After Hemispherectomy." *Arch Neurol & Psychiatry* 72:555–64 N '54. * (PA 29:6114)

1299. BAYLEY, NANCY. "On the Growth of Intelligence." *Am Psychologist* 10:805–18 D '55. * (PA 30:6898)

1300. GRANICK, SAMUEL. "Intellectual Performance as Related to Emotional Instability in Children." *J Abn & Social Psychol* 51:653–6 N '55. * (PA 31:2632)

1301. SONTAG, L. W.; BAKER, CHARLES T.; AND NELSON, VIRGINIA. "Personality as a Determinant of Performance." *Am J Orthopsychiatry* 25:555–62 Jl '55. * (PA 30:4173)

1302. MONEY, JOHN. "Psychologic Studies in Hypothyroidism: Recommendations for Case Management." *Arch Neurol & Psychiatry* 76:296–309 S '56. * (PA 31:4827)

Stanford-Binet Intelligence Scale

1303. PEARSON, JOHN S., AND AMACHER, PHYLLIS L. "Intelligence Test Results and Observations of Personality Disorder Among 3594 Unwed Mothers in Minnesota." *J Clin Psychol* 12:16–21 Ja '56. * *(PA* 30:4476)

1304. REBHUN, ALBERT M. "The Level-Sharpening Dimension as Manifested in Other Perceptual or Non-Perceptual Tasks." *Psychol Newsl* 7:43–6 Ja–F '56. * *(PA* 31:1767)

1305. SCHOONOVER, SARAH M. "A Longitudinal Study of Sibling Resemblances in Intelligence and Achievement." *J Ed Psychol* 47:436–42 N '56. * *(PA* 32:4617)

1306. ELLIS, N. R., AND SLOAN, W. "Relationship Between Intelligence and Simple Reaction Time in Mental Defectives." *Percept & Motor Skills* 7:65–7 Je '57. * *(PA* 32:3041)

1307. LEVINSON, BORIS M. "A Comparative Study of the Intelligence of Jewish Preschool Boys and Girls of Orthodox Parentage." *J Genetic Psychol* 90:17–22 Mr '57. * *(PA* 35:2198)

1308. LEVINSON, BORIS M. "The Intelligence of Applicants for Admission to Jewish Day Schools." *Jewish Social Studies* 19:129–40 Jl–O '57. * *(PA* 34:2728, 35:781)

1309. LEWIS, D. G. "The Normal Distribution of Intelligence: A Critique." *Brit J Psychol* 48:98–104 My '57. * *(PA* 32:5220)

1310. MUNDY, LYDIA. "Environmental Influence on Intellectual Function as Measured by Intelligence Tests." *Brit J Med Psychol* 30:194–201 pt 3 '57. * *(PA* 33:791)

1311. BAKER, CHARLES T.; SONTAG, LESTER W.; AND NELSON, VIRGINIA L. "Individual and Group Differences in the Longitudinal Measurement of Change in Mental Ability." *Monogr Soc Res Child Develop* 23(2):11–85 '58. * *(PA* 33:5719)

1312. GARRISON, MORTIMER, JR. "A Comparison of Psychological Measures in Mentally Retarded Boys Over a Three-Year Period as a Function of Etiology." *Training Sch B* 55:54–60 N '58. * *(PA* 34:1664)

1313. SONTAG, LESTER W., AND BAKER, CHARLES T. "Personality, Familial, and Physical Correlates of Change in Mental Ability." *Monogr Soc Res Child Develop* 23(2):87–143 '58. * *(PA* 33:5729)

1314. BRAEN, BERNARD B., AND MASLING, JOSEPH M. "Intelligence Tests Used With Special Groups of Children." *Excep Children* 26:42–5 S '59. * *(PA* 35:2194)

1315. HIRSCH, MONROE J. "The Relationship Between Refractive State of the Eye and Intelligence Test Scores." *Am J Optom* 36:12–21 Ja '59. * *(PA* 34:1099)

1316. HOHMAN, LESLIE B., AND FREEDHEIM, DONALD K. "A Study of IQ Retest Evaluations on 370 Cerebral Palsied Children." *Am J Phys Med* 38:180–7 O '59. * *(PA* 34:1669)

1317. HUNT, BETTY M. "Performance of Mentally Deficient Brain-Injured Children and Mentally Deficient Familial Children on Construction From Patterns." *Am J Mental Def* 63:679–87 Jl '59. * *(PA* 34:1669)

1318. SAMPSON, OLIVE C. "The Speech and Language Development of 5-Year-Old Children." *Brit J Ed Psychol* 29:217–22 N '59. *

1319. MORAN, R. E. "Levels of Attainment of Educable Subnormal Adolescents." *Brit J Ed Psychol* 30:201–10 N '60. * *(PA* 37:3584)

1320. DUNPHY, DONAL, AND PESSIN, VIVIAN. "Correlation Between Cord Blood Oxygen Values and Psychological Test Scores." *J Iowa Med Soc* 52:212–6 Ap '62. *

1321. JENKINS, C. DAVID. "The Relation of EEG Slowing to Selected Indices of Intellective Impairment." *J Nerv & Mental Dis* 135:162–70 Ag '62. *

1322. WORDEN, DON K., AND VIGNOS, PAUL J., JR. "Intellectual Function in Childhood Progressive Muscular Dystrophy." *Pediatrics* 29:968–77 Je '62. *

1323. CHODORKOFF, JOAN, AND WHITTEN, CHARLES F. "Intellectual Status of Children With Sickle Cell Anemia." *J Pediatrics* 63:29–35 Jl '63. *

1324. FRANCIS, GARY MILLS. *Mental Age as a Criterion of School Entrance.* Master's thesis, University of Utah (Salt Lake City, Utah), 1963.

1325. HAAN, NORMA. "Proposed Model of Ego Functioning: Coping and Defense Mechanisms in Relationship to IQ Change." *Psychol Monogr* 77(8):1–23 '63. * *(PA* 38:4234)

1326. YOUNG, FRANCIS A. "Reading Measures of Intelligence and Refractive Errors." *Am J Optom* 40:257–64 My '63. *

1327. KARELITZ, SAMUEL; FISICHELLI, VINCENT R.; COSTA, JOAN; KARELITZ, RUTH; AND ROSENFIELD, LAURA. "Relation of Crying Activity in Early Infancy to Speech and Intellectual Development at Age Three Years." *Child Develop* 35:769–77 S '64. * *(PA* 39:4513)

1328. KLATSKIN, ETHELYN HENRY. "Relationships of Deficits in Intelligence Test Performance of Preschool Children to Perinatal Experience." *J Consult Psychol* 28:228–33 Je '64. * *(PA* 39:4590)

1329. POLLITT, ERNESTO, AND MONEY, JOHN. "Studies in the Psychology of Dwarfism: 1, Intelligence Quotient and School Achievement." *J Pediatrics* 64:415–21 Mr '64. *

1330. QUERESHI, MOHAMMED Y. "Performance on Individual Ability Tests as a Function of Various Scoring Cutoffs." *Ed & Psychol Meas* 24:481–512 f '64. * *(PA* 39:3173)

1331. REINHART, RICHARD A. "Some Relationships Between Early Rheumatic Fever, Intelligence and Anxiety Scores." *J Child Psychol & Psychiatry* (England) 6:243–50 D '65. * *(PA* 40:8694)

1332. SILVERSTEIN, A. B. "'Validity' of Short-Form Intelligence Tests." *J Consult Psychol* 29:392–3 Ag '65. * *(PA* 39:15267)

1333. SPREEN, OTFRIED, AND BENTON, ARTHUR L. "Comparative Studies of Some Psychological Tests for Cerebral Damage." *J Nerv & Mental Dis* 140:323–33 My '65. * *(PA* 40:700)

1334. MONEY, JOHN, AND LEWIS, VIOLA. "IQ, Genetics and Accelerated Growth: Adrenogenital Syndrome." *Johns Hopkins Med J* 118:365–73 My '66. *

1335. PATON, RICHARD. "Use of the Quick Test With Retarded Children." *Ont Psychol Assn Q* (Canada) 19:60–3 su '66. *

1336. BALL, T. S., AND WILSONCROFT, W. E. "Perceptual-Motor Deficits and the Phi Phenomenon." *Am J Mental Def* 71:797–800 Mr '67. * *(PA* 41:9259)

1337. GITTELMAN, MARTIN, AND BIRCH, HERBERT G. "Childhood Schizophrenia: Intellect, Neurologic Status, Perinatal Risk, Prognosis, and Family Pathology." *Arch Gen Psychiatry* 17:16–25 Jl '67. * *(PA* 41:15552)

1338. HARTER, SUSAN. "Mental Age, IQ, and Motivational Factors in the Discrimination Learning Set Performance of Normal and Retarded Children." *J Exp Child Psychol* 5:123–41 Je '67. * *(PA* 41:12393)

1339. LINDE, LEONARD M.; RASOF, BEATRICE; AND DUNN, OLIVE JEAN. "Mental Development in Congenital Heart Disease." *J Pediatrics* 71:198–203 Ag '67. *

1340. MONEY, JOHN; DRASH, PHILIP W.; AND LEWIS, VIOLA. "Dwarfism and Hypopituitarism: Statural Retardation Without Mental Retardation." *Am J Mental Def* 72:122–6 Jl '67. * *(PA* 41:15732)

1341. QUERESHI, MOHAMMED Y. "The Invariance of Certain Ability Factors." *Ed & Psychol Meas* 27:803–10 w '67. * *(PA* 42:8734)

1342. BELLER, E. KUNO. "Intellectual Development in Educationally Disadvantaged Pre-School Children." *Proc 1966 Ann Read Inst Temple Univ* 5:73–83 '68. *

1343. DRASH, PHILIP W.; GREENBERG, NANCY E.; AND MONEY, JOHN. Chap. 39, "Intelligence and Personality in Four Syndromes of Dwarfism," pp. 568–81. In *Human Growth, Body Composition, Cell Growth, Energy, and Intelligence.* Edited by Donald B. Cheek. Philadelphia, Pa.: Lea & Febiger, 1968. Pp. xxx, 781. *

1344. PRENTICE, NORMAN M., AND BIERI, JAMES. "Intellectual Development of Culturally Deprived Children in a Day Care Program." Abstract. *Proc 76th Ann Conv Am Psychol Assn* 3:599–600 '68. * *(PA* 43:1328, title only)

1345. PRINGLE, M. L. KELLMER, AND COX, T. "The Association Between Sarason's Test Anxiety and Intelligence Test Performance." *Ed Sci* (England) 2:227–36 S '68. *

1346. SMITH, MARSHALL P. "Intellectual Differences in Five-Year-Old Underprivileged Girls and Boys With and Without Pre-Kindergarten School Experience." *J Ed Res* 61:348–50 Ap '68. *

1347. BABSON, S. GORHAM; HENDERSON, NORMAN; AND CLARK, WILLIAM M., JR. "The Preschool Intelligence of Oversized Newborns." *Pediatrics* 44(4):536–8 O '69. *

1348. BARCLAY, A. "Longitudinal Changes in Intellectual and Social Development of Non-Institutionalized Retardates." *Am J Mental Def* 73(5):831–7 Mr '69. * *(PA* 43:10216)

1349. BOZARTH, DOROTHY CRAIG. *The Relationship of Intelligence Test Scatter and Self-Concept.* Master's thesis, Millersville State College (Millersville, Pa.), 1969.

1350. BRUCH, CATHERINE. "A Creative Score From the Stanford-Binet and Its Application." *CEC Selected Conv Papers* 1969:1–3 '69. *

1351. FRASER, DON. "Mental Abilities of British Columbia Indian Children." *Can Counsellor* 3(3):42–8 Je '69. *

1352. FRASER, WILLIAM D. *Mental Abilities of British Columbia Indian Children.* Master's thesis, University of British Columbia (Vancouver, B.C., Canada), 1969.

1353. GROSS, MORRIS. "Learning Readiness in Two Groups: A Study in 'Cultural Deprivation.'" *Jewish Ed* 39(1):36–48 Ja '69. *

1354. HONZIK, MARJORIE P.; COLLART, DONNA S.; ROBINSON, SAUL J.; AND FINLEY, KNOX H. "Sex Differences in Verbal and Performance IQ's of Children Undergoing Open-heart Surgery." *Sci* 164(3878):445–7 Ap 25 '69. * *(PA* 45:6906)

1355. SONTAG, MARVIN; SELLA, ADINA P.; AND THORNDIKE, ROBERT L. "The Effect of Head Start Training on the Cognitive Growth of Disadvantaged Children." *J Ed Res* 62(9):387–9 My–Je '69. * *(PA* 46:1899)

1356. BROWN, JOE, AND ZEMANEK, DON. "Variables Affecting the Gross Motor Performance of Trainable Retardates," pp. 489–98. In *Contemporary Psychology of Sport.* Proceedings of the Second International Congress of Sport Psychology, Washington, D.C., 1968. Chicago, Ill.: Athletic Institute, 1970. Pp. xix, 878. *

1357. EAVES, LINDA C.; NUTTALL, J. C.; KLONOFF, H.; AND DUNN, H. G. "Developmental and Psychological Test Scores in Children of Low Birth Weight." *Pediatrics* 45(1):9–20 Ja '70. * Correction: 45(5):886–7 My '70. *

1358. GROSS, MORRIS B. "Pre-School Prediction of Academic Achievement." Abstract. *Psychol Rep* 26(1):278 F '70. * *(PA* 45:5056)

1359. KARNES, MEREL B.; TESKA, JAMES A.; AND HODGINS, AUDREY S. "The Effects of Four Programs of Classroom Intervention on the Intellectual and Language Development of 4-Year-Old Disadvantaged Children." *Am J Orthopsychiatry* 40(1):58–76 Ja '70. * (*PA* 45:1373)

1360. O'KELLY, E. "A Method for Detecting Slow Learning Juniors." *Ed Res* (England) 12(2):135–9 F '70. *

1361. SHATUS, ERWIN L. "Validation of the Wechsler Preschool and Primary Scale of Intelligence With the Stanford-Binet, Form L-M, on Culturally Deprived Children." *South J Ed Res* 4(1):18–36 Ja '70 [My '71]. *

1362. SIMMERS, CATHERINE POWELL. *Cognitive Correlates of Attitudinal Rigidity.* Doctor's thesis, Case Western Reserve University (Cleveland, Ohio), 1970. (*DAI* 32:1348A)

1363. SLAUGHTER, DIANA T. "Parental Potency and the Achievements of Inner-City Black Children." *Am J Orthopsychiatry* 40(3):433–40 Ap '70. * (*PA* 45:8989)

1364. WHITE, GENEVIEVE. *Procedures for Predicting Children's Success in First Grade Achievement.* Master's thesis, Arkansas State University (State University, Ark.), 1970.

1365. WRIGHT, ELSIE LOUISE. *A Correlational Study of Selected Sociological Variables and Two Ranges of Stanford-Binet Intelligence Quotients Among Culturally Disadvantaged Preschool Children.* Doctor's thesis, University of Alabama (University, Ala.), 1970. (*DAI* 31:5219A)

1366. ABLES, BILLIE S. "The Use of the Draw-A-Man Test With Borderline Retarded Children Without Pronounced Pathology." *J Clin Psychol* 27(2):262–3 Ap '71. * (*PA* 46:7068)

1367. ACHENBACH, THOMAS M. "Stanford-Binet Short-Form Performance of Retarded and Nonretarded Persons Matched for MA." *Am J Mental Def* 76(1):30–2 Jl '71. * (*PA* 47:7069)

1368. ARMSTRONG, ROBERT J., AND MOONEY, ROBERT F. "The Slosson Intelligence Test: Implications for Reading Specialists." *Read Teach* 24(4):336–40+ Ja '71. * (*PA* 46:11492)

1369. ARMSTRONG, ROBERT J.; MOONEY, ROBERT F.; AND JENSEN, JOHN A. "A Short, Reliable, Easy to Administer Individual Intelligence Test for Special Class Placement." *Child Study J* 1(3):156–63 sp '71. * (*PA* 48:1701)

1370. BERSOFF, DONALD N. "Short Forms of Individual Intelligence Tests for Children: Review and Critique." *J Sch Psychol* 9(3):310–20 '71. * (*PA* 47:8924)

1371. BROWN, DARRELL LEE. *Variations in Test Response of Preschool Children by Sex and Socioeconomic Level Related to Guilford's Structure-of-Intellect.* Doctor's thesis, University of Pittsburgh (Pittsburgh, Pa.), 1971. (*DAI* 32:4412A)

1372. BRUCH, CATHERINE B. "Modification of Procedures for Identification of the Disadvantaged Gifted." *Gifted Child Q* 15(4):267–72 w '71. * (*PA* 48:5647)

1373. BUCK, CAROL; GREGG, ROSE; HARPER, MARY; AND SNIDER, SANDRA. "The Effect of Kindergarten Experiences Upon IQ Test Performance." *Psychol Sch* 8(1):62–4 Ja '71. * (*PA* 46:7677)

1374. BUDOFF, M.; MESKIN, J.; AND HARRISON, R. H. "Educational Test of the Learning-Potential Hypothesis." *Am J Mental Def* 76(2):159–69 S '71. * (*PA* 47:9717)

1375. DUROJAIYE, M. O. A., AND SUCH, M. "Predicting Educational Suitability of Children in an Assessment Unit." *J Exp Ed* 40(2):27–36 w '71. * (*PA* 47:11608)

1376. ELLIOTT, R., AND MACKAY, D. N. "Social Competence of Subnormal and Normal Children Living Under Different Types of Residential Care." *Brit J Mental Subnormal* 17(32):48–53 Je '71. * (*PA* 47:11471)

1377. FIELDS, DONALD L., AND GIBSON, DAVID. "Forecasting Mental Growth for At-Home Mongols (Down's Syndrome)." *J Mental Def Res* (England) 15(3):163–8 S '71. * (*PA* 49:11377)

1378. FOREHAND, REX, AND GORDON, DONALD A. "Application of Two Short Forms of the Stanford-Binet With Retardates." *Am J Mental Def* 75(6):763–4 My '71. *

1379. GAYTON, WILLIAM F. "An Evaluation of Two Short Forms of the Stanford-Binet, Form L-M, for Use With a Child Guidance Population." *Psychol Rep* 28(2):355–7 Ap '71. * (*PA* 46:7553)

1380. GOLDEN, MARK; BIRNS, BEVERLY; BRIDGER, WAGNER; AND MOSS, ABIGAIL. "Social-Class Differentiation in Cognitive Development Among Black Preschool Children." *Child Develop* 42(1):37–45 Mr '71. * (*PA* 46:4621)

1381. HERSH, JEFFREY B. "Effects of Referral Information on Testers." *J Consult & Clin Psychol* 37(1):116–22 Ag '71. * (*PA* 47:1578)

1382. HERTZIG, MARGARET E., AND BIRCH, HERBERT G. "Longitudinal Course of Measured Intelligence in Preschool Children of Different Social and Ethnic Backgrounds." *Am J Orthopsychiatry* 41(3):416–26 Ap '71. * (*PA* 46:6537)

1383. HUIZINGA, RALEIGH JAMES. *The Relationship of the Illinois Test of Psycholinguistic Abilities to the Stanford-Binet Form L-M and the Wechsler Intelligence Scale for Children.* Doctor's thesis, University of Arizona (Tucson, Ariz.), 1971. (*DAI* 32:3823A)

1384. JACOBSON, LEONARD I.; BERGER, STEPHEN E.; BERGMAN, RONALD L.; MILLHAM, JIM; AND GREESON, LARRY E. "Effects of Age, Sex, Systematic Conceptual Learning, Acquisition of Learning Sets, and Programmed Social Interaction on the Intellectual and Conceptual Development of Preschool Children From Poverty Backgrounds." *Child Develop* 42(5):1399–415 N '71. * (*PA* 48:5847)

1385. JOESTING, JOAN, AND JOESTING, ROBERT. "Comparison of Scores on Quick Test and Stanford-Binet, Form L-M." *Psychol Rep* 29(3):1178 D '71. * (*PA* 48:1648)

1386. JOHNSON, DALE L., AND JOHNSON, CARMEN A. "Comparison of Four Intelligence Tests Used With Culturally Disadvantaged Children." *Psychol Rep* 28(1):209–10 F '71. * (*PA* 46:5736)

1387. JORDAN, THOMAS E. "Early Developmental Adversity and the First Two Years of Life." *Multiv Behav Res Monogr* 6(1):1–80 '71. * (*PA* 49:2132)

1388. KANGAS, JON, AND BRADWAY, KATHERINE. "Intelligence at Middle Age: A Thirty-Eight-Year Follow-Up." *Develop Psychol* 5(2):333–7 S '71. * (*PA* 47:2985)

1389. KARADENES, MARK. *A Comparison of Differences in Achievement and Learning Abilities Between Anglo and Mexican-American Children When the Two Groups Are Equated by Intelligence.* Doctor's thesis, University of Virginia (Charlottesville, Va.), 1971. (*DAI* 32:4422A)

1390. KOLLER, JAMES RAYMOND. *Mental Age: A Test of Certain Underlying Assumptions.* Doctor's thesis, University of Missouri (Columbia, Mo.), 1971. (*DAI* 32:2485A)

1391. LEITHWOOD, KENNETH A. "Motor, Cognitive, and Affective Relationships Among Advantaged Preschool Children." *Res Q* 42(1):47–53 Mr '71. * (*PA* 46:6539)

1392. LEVINSON, ELIZABETH J. "The Modification of Intelligence by Training in the Verbalization of Word Definitions and Simple Concepts." *Child Develop* 42(5):1361–80 N '71. * (*PA* 48:4673)

1393. LEWIS, RUTH. "Survey of the Intelligence of Cleft-Lip and Cleft-Palate Children in Ontario." *Brit J Dis Commun* 6(1):17–25 Ap '71. * (*PA* 49:9395)

1394. LOBL, MICHELE; WELCHER, DORIS W.; AND MELLITS, E. DAVID. "Maternal Age and Intellectual Functioning of Offspring." *Johns Hopkins Med J* 128(6):347–61 Je '71. *

1395. MCKINNEY, JAMES D., AND CORTER, HAROLD M. "Flexibility Training With Educable Retarded Children." *J Sch Psychol* 9(4):455–61 w '71. * (*PA* 48:1711)

1396. MAXWELL, MICHAEL T. "The Relationship Between the Wechsler Intelligence Scale for Children and the Slosson Intelligence Test." *Child Study J* 1(3):164–71 sp '71. * (*PA* 48:1709)

1397. MILGRAM, NORMAN A. "IQ Constancy in Disadvantaged Negro Children." *Psychol Rep* 29(1):319–26 Ag '71. * (*PA* 47:2652)

1398. OAKLAND, THOMAS D.; KING, JOHN D.; WHITE, LINDA ANN; AND ECKMAN, ROBERT. "A Comparison of Performance on the WPPSI, WISC, and SB With Preschool Children: Companion Studies." *J Sch Psychol* 9(2):144–9 '71. * (*PA* 47:7563)

1399. O'GRADY, DONALD J.; BERRY, HELEN K.; AND SUTHERLAND, BETTY S. "Cognitive Development in Early Treated Phenylketonuria." *Am J Dis Children* 121(1):20–3 Ja '71. *

1400. PASEWARK, RICHARD A.; RARDIN, MAX W.; AND GRICE, JOHN E., JR. "Relationship of the Wechsler Pre-School and Primary Scale of Intelligence and the Stanford-Binet (L-M) in Lower Class Children." *J Sch Psychol* 9(1):43–50 '71. * (*PA* 47:5609)

1401. PHILLIPS, DORIS CAMPBELL. *An Exploratory Study of the Relationship Between Mothers' Individualization of Their Children and the Children's Developmental Progress.* Doctor's thesis, Washington University (St. Louis, Mo.), 1971. (*DAI* 32:2201A)

1402. PRASAD, R.; MUKHERJEE, A.; AND VARMA, S. K. "The Role of Intelligence Testing in the Assessment of Cerebral Palsy Children." *J Assn Physicians India* 19(10):715–7 O '71. *

1403. PROSSER, NANETTE S., AND CRAWFORD, VEDA B. "Relationship of Scores on the Wechsler Preschool and Primary Scale of Intelligence and the Stanford-Binet Intelligence Scale Form LM." *J Sch Psychol* 9(3):278–83 '71. * (*PA* 47:8634)

1404. QUAY, LORENE C. "Language Dialect, Reinforcement, and the Intelligence-Test Performance of Negro Children." *Child Develop* 42(1):5–15 Mr '71. * (*PA* 46:4660)

1405. RADIN, NORMA. "Maternal Warmth, Achievement Motivation, and Cognitive Functioning in Lower-Class Preschool Children." *Child Develop* 42(5):1560–5 N '71. * (*PA* 48:4724)

1406. SANDSTEAD, HAROLD H.; CARTER, JAMES P.; HOUSE, FAYE R.; MCCONNELL, FREEMAN; HORTON, KATHRYN B.; AND VANDER ZWAAG, ROGER. "Nutritional Deficiencies in Disadvantaged Preschool Children: Their Relationship to Mental Development." *Am J Dis Children* 121(6):455–63 Je '71. *

1407. SCHWARZ, ROBERT H., AND COOK, JOHN J. "Mental Age as a Predictor of Academic Achievement." *Ed & Train Mental Retard* 6(1):12–5 F '71. *

1408. SCHWARZ, ROBERT H., AND FLANIGAN, PATRICK J. "Evaluation of Examiner Bias in Intelligence Testing." *Am J Mental Def* 76(2):262–5 S '71. * (*PA* 47:9664)

1409. SILVERSTEIN, A. B. "Reliability and Constancy of a New Measure of Intelligence for Institutionalized Retardates." *Am J Mental Def* 76(2):257–8 S '71. * (*PA* 47:9514)

1410. SPENCE, ALLYN G.; MISHRA, SHITALA P.; AND GHOZEIL, SUSAN. "Home Language and Performance on Standardized Tests." *El Sch J* 71(6):309–13 Mr '71. * (*PA* 47:2655)

1411. SUNDEAN, DAVID A., AND SALOPEK, THOMAS F. "Achievement and Intelligence in Primary and Elementary

Classes for the Educable Mentally Retarded." *J Sch Psychol* 9(2):150–6 '71. * (*PA* 47:7610)

1412. TAYLOR, JOHN F. "A Table for Predicting Retardate Mental Age Growth." *Am J Mental Def* 75(4):499–503 Ja '71. * (*PA* 46:3623)

1413. WELCHER, DORIS W.; MELLITS, E. DAVID; AND HARDY, JANET B. "A Multivariate Analysis of Factors Affecting Psychological Performance." *Johns Hopkins Med J* 129(1):19–35 Jl '71. *

1414. WIKOFF, RICHARD L. "Subscale Classification Schemata for the Stanford-Binet, Form L-M." *J Sch Psychol* 9(3):329–37 '71. * (*PA* 47:8931)

CUMULATIVE NAME INDEX

Kato, J. G.: 805
Katz, E.: 217, 571, 592, 617, 633–5, 1263
Kaunitz, R. M.: 377
Kavruck, S.: 257
Kawin, E.: *exc*, 1:B497
Keach, C. C.: 812
Kebbon, L.: 788
Keen, A. M.: 365, 1179
Keim, R. P.: 927
Keir, G.: 1278
Kendig, I.: 131
Kennedy, V.: 422
Kennedy, W.: 715a
Kennedy, W. A.: 674, 716, 776, 928
Kennedy-Fraser, D.: 322, 454
Kenny, J. T.: 663
Kent, G. H.: 21, 158; *exc*, 2:1420
Kent, N.: 608
Kepner, R. D.: 407
Keston, M. J.: 555
Kicklighter, R. M.: 813
Kidd, A. H.: 651, 699
Kidder, J. W.: 919
Kilburn, K. L.: 814
Killian, C. D.: 389
Kilman, B. A.: 668
Kimberlin, C. C.: 943
Kimbrell, D. L.: 815
Kinder, E. F.: 381–2
King, J. D.: 1398
Kirkpatrick, F. H.: *exc*, 3:293
Kittredge, W. B.: 1079
Klapper, Z. S.: 842
Klatskin, E. H.: 1328
Klebanoff, S. G.: 434
Klonoff, H.: 1357
Klugman, S. F.: 306
Knight, D.: 951
Knight, M. W.: 72
Knollin, H. E.: 4, 990, 1036
Knox, S.: 763
Kobler, F. J.: 560
Kodman, F.: 970
Kogan, K. L.: 456
Koh, T. H.: 843
Kohs, S. C.: 998
Kolb, C.: 1109
Koller, J. R.: 1390
Kolstoe, O. P.: 731
Konstans, D. J.: 652
Koppitz, E. M.: 844
Korner, A. F.: 429
Kovalinsky, T.: 960
Kreezer, G. L.: 172, 1289
Kroske, W. H.: 789
Krugman, J. I.: 485
Krugman, M.: 122, 485; *exc*, 2:1420
Kuhlmann, F.: 258
Kundu, R.: 845
Kureth, G.: 521, 539
Kurko, V. K.: 487
Kushner, R.: 308
Kutash, S. B.: 323
Kvaraceus, W. C.: 186, 218, 1264
Kyte, G. C.: 1237
Lacy, L. D.: 1125
Lacy, W. I.: 1003
Lair, C. V.: 940
Lambert, R. A.: 728
Lamp, R. E.: 886
Lamson, E. E.: 1243
Lane, H. A.: 1216
Lantz, B.: 593
Lantz, C. M. B.: 395
Larsen, M. J.: 971
Larsen, M. R. J.: 887
LaSalle, J.: 1071, 1082
Lawrence, E. M.: 1184
Laycock, S. R.: 259, 324
Layman, J. W.: 260, 383, 396, 1265
Leahy, A. M.: 1217
Leberfeld, D. T.: 734
Lebovitz, L.: 828
Lee, M. V.: 1185
Lehmann, I. J.: 643, 738
Lehmann, M. M.: 556
Leitch, M.: 440
Leithwood, K. A.: 1391

Lennox, W. G.: 730
Lessing, E. E.: 675
Levi, J.: 296
Levin, J.: 475, 491
Levine, D.: 768
Levinson, B. M.: 594, 609, 618, 644, 653–4, 743, 1307–8
Levinson, E. J.: 756, 1392
Levy, P.: 888
Lewis, D. G.: 1309
Lewis, J. F.: 929
Lewis, R.: 1393
Lewis, V.: 1334, 1340
Lidz, T.: 626
Lincoln, E. A.: 32, 62, 79, 85, 1060–1, 1154, 1218
Linde, L. M.: 854, 1339
Lindholm, B. W.: 769, 790
Lindner, R.: 674
Line, W.: 1201
Lively, M. L.: 329–30
Livingston, J. S.: 610, 619
Lobl, M.: 1394
Lodge, T.: 108
Long, H. H.: 140, 1219
Lore, J.: 870
Lorge, I.: 468, 1228
Lorr, M.: 219, 261
Louden, M. V.: 63–4
Lourie, D. K.: 384
Louttit, C. M.: 86
Lowden, G. L.: 20
Lowell, F. E.: 220
Lucker, W. G.: 949
Luckey, B.: 1156
Ludlow, M. E.: 494
Luh, C. W.: 366
Lumsden, J.: 595
Luong, C. K. M.: 889
Luszki, W. A.: 816
Lyman, G.: 4
Lytton, H.: 676
McAnulty, E. A.: 1155
McArthur, C. R.: 890
McBride, K.: 1158–9
McBride, K. E.: 1231
McCandless, B. R.: 345, 1273; *rev*, 4:358
McCloskey, E. P.: 223
McClure, W. E.: 1169, 1202
McConnell, F.: 1406
McCulloch, T. L.: 311, 572
McCullough, B. R.: 436, 469
McElwee, E. W.: 1187, 1220
McFadden, J. H.: 51, 367
Macfarlane, J. W.: 433
McFie, J.: 629, 677
McGee, E.: 561
McGrath, R. F.: 390
McHugh, G.: 290
McIntosh, R.: 736
McKay, B. E.: 402
MacKay, D. N.: 1376
McKerracher, D. W.: 817
McKinney, J. D.: 1395
McKinstry, E.: 241
Macmeeken, A. M.: 123
MacMurray, D.: 94
McNemar, Q.: 164, 264, 540, 627–8
Macomber, L.: 319
McRae, H.: 1270
MacRae, J. M.: 573
Madden, R.: 56
Madow, A. A.: 843
Madsen, I. N.: 26, 73
Magaret, A.: 351, 419, 472
Mahan, H. C.: 87
Maity, H.: 31
Maizlish, I. L.: 221, 262
Malamud, W.: 163
Mann, A.: 486
Mann, C. W.: 124
Mann, H. P.: 124
Manolakes, G.: 522, 562
Manuel, H. T.: 187, 379
Marine, E. L.: 41, 361
Marks, E. S.: 421
Marquart, D. I.: 574
Marschak, M.: 605
Marsden, R. E.: 1073–4, 1085, 1122, 1170
Marshall, A.: 846
Marshall, H.: 263, 628

Martin, A. H.: *exc*, 1:B497
Martin, F.: 1281
Martinson, B.: 222
Marx, B.: 360
Masling, J. M.: 1314
Mason, A. W.: 847, 967
Massari, D.: 930
Mateer, F.: 173, 621, 1004
Matheny, A. P.: 818
Mathews, J.: 1034
Matthew, J.: 1156
Matthews, C. G.: 891
Matyas, R. P.: 557, 589
Maurer, K. M.: 416
Maxfield, F. N.: 152, 1005; *rev*, 1:1062; *exc*, 1:B497, 3:293–4
Maxwell, A. E.: 640
Maxwell, J.: 655, 931; *exc*, 6:536
Maxwell, M. T.: 1396
May, W. T.: 611, 828, 862
Mayer, B. A.: 80–1, 153
Mayman, M.: 325, 339
Meeker, M.: 791
Meeker, M. M.: 718
Meeker, M. N.: 932
Meier, J. H.: 792
Mein, R.: 700
Meissler, G. R.: 972
Meister, R. K.: 191, 219, 230, 261, 422, 487
Mellits, E. D.: 1394, 1413
Mellone, M. A.: 526
Melton, K.: 814
Mensh, I. N.: 434
Meranski, S.: 1089
Mercer, M.: 870
Merrill, M. A.: 98–9, 109, 545, 657a, 1090, 1126
Merriman, C.: 1091
Meskin, J.: 1374
Meyer, W. J.: 930
Meyers, C. E.: 803
Michael, W. B.: 826
Michaels, J. J.: 155–6
Miezitis, S. A.: 892
Milgram, N. A.: 1397
Millard, M. S.: 1222
Miller, B.: 848
Miller, E.: 630
Miller, H.: 1240
Miller, I.: 660
Miller, J. O.: 973
Miller, L. R.: 291
Miller, V. J.: 558
Millham, J.: 1384
Minogue, B. M.: 1127, 1177
Miscevich, M. B.: 849
Mishra, S. P.: 1410
Mitchell, B. C.: 1147
Mitchell, D.: 1062, 1092
Mitchell, M. B.: 188, 224–5, 265, 292
Mitchell, R. J.: 793
Mittler, P.: 709
Mittler, P. J.: 779
Mohan, P. J.: 861
Monahan, J. E.: 1124, 1135
Money, J.: 1302, 1329, 1334, 1340, 1343
Moon, H.: 674
Mooney, R. F.: 1368–9
Moore, T.: 850
Morán, R. E.: 1319
Morgenthau, D. R.: 17
Moriarty, A.: 746
Morris, H. L.: 959
Moss, A.: 1380
Motter, M. E.: 241
Mowrer, W. M. C.: 65
Mueller, M. W.: 794–5, 893, 933
Muench, G. A.: 1275
Muhr, J. P.: 521
Mukherjee, A.: 1402
Mullen, F. A.: 266
Mumbauer, C. C.: 973
Mundy, L.: 640, 1310
Munson, C.: 174, 226
Murphy, M.: 1157, 1203
Mussen, P.: 523
Muzekari, L. H.: 851
Myers, C. R.: 293, 399

Nagler, E.: 881
Nakamura, H.: 747, 796
Nale, S.: 488
Nale, S. L.: 645
Narosny, E. H.: 1238
Nash, P. N.: 717
Neale, M. D.: *exc*, 6:536
Needham, N. R.: 307
Needham, W. E.: 934
Neely, J. H.: 591
Nelson, K. B.: 974
Nelson, T. M.: 701
Nelson, V.: 1301
Nelson, V. L.: 547, 564, 579, 1311
Nelson, W.: 674
Nemzek, C. L.: 66–7
Nevill, E. M.: *exc*, 1:B497
Nevins, F. A.: 267
New York Public Schools, Division of Tests and Measurements: 227
Newland, T. E.: 718
Newlyn, D.: 615
Nicholson, C. L.: 975
Noble, H.: 1022
Noller, P. A.: 493
Norman, R. D.: 543
Norman, R. M.: 110, 625
Norton, J. K.: 135, 1021
Nottingham, R. D.: 1239
Nunnally, J. C.: 770
Nurss, J. R.: 976
Nuttall, J. C.: 1357
Oakland, T. D.: 1398
Obelkevich, H.: 1188
Oblinger, B.: 350
O'Connor, G.: 937
O'Connor, N.: 476, 596
Odell, C. W.: 10, 1035
Oden, M. H.: 81, 628
Odoroff, M. E.: 258
Oexle, H. M.: 228
O'Grady, D. J.: 1399
O'Kelly, E.: 1360
Olivier, K.: 852
Oppel, W.: 727
Ordahl, G.: 4, 1076
Ordahl, L. E.: 4
Ordahl, V. E.: 417
Orgel, A. R.: 575
Otis, A. S.: 135, 1036
Outhit, M. C.: 1204
Page, H. A.: 982
Page, J. D.: 189, 1267
Pal, S.: 29
Palmer, A. B.: 771
Palmer, E. M.: 157, 163
Palmer, F. H.: 977, 980
Papania, N.: 559
Papurt, M. J.: 380
Parker, H. T.: 74
Parkyn, G. W.: 326
Parsley, K. M.: 678
Pasewark, R. A.: 1400
Pastovic, J. J.: 506
Paton, R.: 1335
Patterson, H. J.: 894
Payne, R. W.: 679
Pazeian, B.: 1297
Pearson, J. S.: 1303
Peatman, J. G.: 88
Peatman, L. B.: 88
Pedrini, D. T.: 864–6, 913, 978
Pedrini, L. N.: 978
Pegram, E. L.: 316
Penrose, L. S.: 1253, 1277
Perce, F. C.: 391
Perkins, R. E.: 57
Perry, H. W.: 611
Pessin, V.: 1320
Phillips, A.: 58
Phillips, C. J.: 772, 895
Phillips, D. C.: 1401
Phillips, E. L.: 437
Pickles, D. G.: 853
Pickup, K. T.: 719
Pierce, H. O.: 338, 438
Piercy, M. F.: 629
Pignatelli, M. L.: 268, 294
Pilliner, A. E. G.: 655
Piness, G.: 1240
Pinneau, S. R.: 657a, 680

Wells, D. G.: 864–6
Wells, F. L.: 35, 994, 1000, 1255; *rev*, 1:1062
Welsh, G. B.: 735
Wentworth, M. M.: 356–7
Werner, H.: 134, 197
Wesman, A. G.: 457
Wexberg, E.: 237
Whitacre, R. L.: 903
Whitcomb, M. A.: 334
White, D. T.: 714
White, G.: 1364
White, J. C.: 705, 715a, 716
White, L. A.: 904, 1398
White, M. L.: 276
White, R. R.: 772
Whitten, C. F.: 1323
Wiener, G.: 727
Wikoff, R. L.: 1414
Wilcock, J. C.: 833
Wile, I. S.: 238, 386, 1247
Wilk, W. S.: 706
Willerman, L.: 985
Williams, H. M.: 458, 1245
Williams, J. H.: 4, 991
Williams, J. R.: 833, 867
Williams, M.: 434
Williams, R. D. B.: 900
Wilner, C. F.: 28, 1081
Wilson, B. A.: 642
Wilson, C. A.: 47
Wilson, G. M.: 1114
Wilson, J. A. R.: 773
Wilson, M. T.: 392, 1271
Wilsoncroft, W. E.: 1336
Winn, E.: 1027
Winslow, C. N.: 982
Winter, W. N.: 502
Wise, J. H.: 905
Wiser, W. C.: 934
Wisler, M. L.: 374

Witkin, H. A.: 752
Witmer, L.: 87
Witty, P. A.: 1162, 1216
Wladkowsky, E.: 165
Wolf, R.: 593
Wolf, S. J.: 1242
Wolf, W. C.: 601
Woodall, C. S.: 145
Woods, E. L.: 1115
Woodward, W. M.: 709
Woodworth, R. S.: 1163
Wooley, H. T.: 1116
Woo-Sam, J.: 986
Worbois, G. M.: 277
Worcester, D. A.: 239
Worden, D. K.: 1322
Worthington, M. R.: 1131–2
Wrenn, C. G.: 459
Wright, C.: 278, 419
Wright, E. L.: 1365
Wright, R. E.: 126
Wrightstone, J. W.: 485, 544
Wu, T. M.: 366
Yater, A. C.: 910
Yates, L. G.: 868
Yen, S. M. Y.: 941
Yerkes, R. M.: 12, 136
Young, F. A.: 1326
Young, F. M.: 280
Zabin, D. H.: 370
Zeaman, D.: 707, 961
Zeidler, R.: 4
Zeigler, T. W.: 1280
Zemanek, D.: 1356
Zigler, E.: 906, 950
Zimmerman, F. T.: 1283, 1285
Zimmerman, I. L.: 986
Zingle, H. W.: 728
Zuk, G. H.: 659
Zunich, M.: 907

[526]

[Re Stanford-Binet Intelligence Scale] A Clinical Profile for the Stanford Binet Intelligence Scale (L-M). Ages 5 and over; 1965; title on profile is *A Profile for the Stanford Binet (L-M)*; an item classification system for use by school psychologists in analyzing and reporting performance in 6 categories: general comprehension, visual-motor ability, arithmetic reasoning, memory and concentration, vocabulary and verbal fluency, judgment and reasoning; Robert E. Valett; Consulting Psychologists Press, Inc. *

For additional information, see 7:426.

[527]

Stanford-Ohwaki-Kohs Block Design Intelligence Test for the Blind: American Revision of the Ohwaki-Kohs Test. Blind and partially sighted ages 16 and over; 1965–66; uses same testing materials as *The Ohwaki-Kohs Tactile Block Design Intelligence Test for the Blind*; Richard M. Suinn and William L. Dauterman; Western Psychological Services. *

For additional information, see 7:427.

[528]

Vane Kindergarten Test. Ages 4–6; 1968; VKT; 4 scores: perceptual motor, vocabulary, drawing a man, total; Julia R. Vane; Clinical Psychology Publishing Co., Inc. *

For additional information and reviews by Dorothy H. Eichorn and Marcel L. Goldschmid, see 7:428 (3 references).

REFERENCES THROUGH 1971

1–3. See 7:428.
4. POWERS, SANDRA MATTHEWS. *Long-Term Reliability and Predictive Validity of the Vane Kindergarten Test*. Doctor's thesis, University of Connecticut (Storrs, Conn.), 1970. (*DAI* 31:6411A)
5. D'ANGELO, R.; WALSH, J.; AND LOMANGINO, L. "IQs of Negro Head Start Children on the Vane Kindergarten Test." *J Clin Psychol* 27(1):82–3 Ja '71. * (*PA* 46:821)
6. JOHNSON, ROBERT E. L., JR. *Psycho-Social Correlates of*

Black Pre-School Children's Educational Progress. Doctor's thesis, University of Oklahoma (Norman, Okla.), 1971. (*DAI* 32:4137A)
7. VANE, JULIA R. "Importance of Considering Background Factors When Evaluating the Effects of Compensatory Education Programs Designed for Young Children." *J Sch Psychol* 9(4): 393–8 w '71. * (*PA* 47:11817)
8. VANE, JULIA R., AND DAVIS, WILLIAM M. "Factors Related to the Effectiveness of Preschool Programs With Disadvantaged Children." *J Ed Res* 64(7):297–9 Mr '71. *
9. WALSH, JOHN F., AND D'ANGELO, RITA. "IQs of Puerto Rican Head Start Children on the Vane Kindergarten Test." *J Sch Psychol* 9(2):173–6 '71. * (*PA* 47:7806)
10. WALSH, JOHN F.; D'ANGELO, RITA; AND LOMANGINO, LOUIS. "Performance of Negro and Puerto Rican Head Start Children on the Vane Kindergarten Test." *Psychol Sch* 8(4): 357–8 O '71. * (*PA* 47:11641)

CUMULATIVE NAME INDEX

D'Angelo, R.: 5, 9–10
Davis, W. M.: 8
Eichorn, D. H.: *rev*, 7:428
Ellerman, R. A.: 2
Goldschmid, M. L.: *rev*, 7:428
Johnson, R. E. L.: 6
Lomangino, L.: 5, 10
Powers, S. M.: 4
Vane, J. R.: 1, 7–8
Wadley, J. A.: 2
Walsh, J.: 5
Walsh, J. F.: 9–10
Willis, D. J.: 3

[529]

Wechsler Adult Intelligence Scale. Ages 16 and over; 1939–55; WAIS; revision of Form 1 of *Wechsler-Bellevue Intelligence Scale*; 14 scores: verbal (information, comprehension, arithmetic, similarities, digit span, vocabulary, total), performance (digit symbol, picture completion, block design, picture arrangement, object assembly, total), total; David Wechsler; Psychological Corporation. (South African edition: Ages 18–59; 1969; National Institute for Personnel Research [South Africa]. British manual supplement: 1971; Peter Saville; NFER Publishing Co. Ltd. [England].) *

For additional information and reviews by Alvin G. Burstein and Howard B. Lyman, see 7:429 (538 references); see also 6:538 (180 references); for reviews by Nancy Bayley and Wilson H. Guertin, see 5:414 (42 references). For reference to reviews of an earlier edition, see 532. For excerpts from related book reviews, see 6:B503 (3 excerpts).

REFERENCES THROUGH 1971

1–42. See 5:414.
43–222. See 6:538.
223–762. See 7:429.
763. KALDEGG, A. "Migraine Patients: A Discussion of Some Test Results." *J Mental Sci* (England) 98:672–82 O '52. * (*PA* 27:6067)
764. WEST, ALICE A., III. *A Comparison of Subtest Scatter on the Wechsler-Bellevue Form I and the WAIS*. Master's thesis, University of Arizona (Tucson, Ariz.), 1956.
765. BAUER, ROBERT W., AND JOHNSON, DERWOOD E. "The Question of Deterioration in Alcoholism." Abstract. *J Consult Psychol* 21:296 Ag '57. * (*PA* 33:1669)
766. BEHRENS, BARBARA, AND MILES, GUY H. "A Test of 'Tendency to Analyze' for Use With College Men." *Proc Iowa Acad Sci* 64:508–13 '57. * (*PA* 33:3814)
767. THROP, JAMES L. *Scatter on the Wechsler Adult Intelligence Scale as a Measure of Personality Adjustment*. Master's thesis, University of Arizona (Tucson, Ariz.), 1957.
768. INGLIS, JAMES. "Learning, Retention, and Conceptual Usage in Elderly Patients With Memory Disorder." *J Abn & Social Psychol* 59:210–5 S '59. * (*PA* 34:3317)
769. JONES, NELSON F., JR. "The Validity of Clinical Judgments of Schizophrenic Pathology Based on Verbal Responses to Intelligence Test Items." *J Clin Psychol* 15:396–400 O '59. * (*PA* 36:1HI96J)
770. KENNEDY, WALLACE A.; SMITH, MARION; VAN DE RIET, HANNAH; VAN DE RIET, VERNON; SMITH, HERBERT; RAPP, DON; AND PAINE, R. W. "A Multidimensional Study of Mathematically Gifted Adolescents." *Child Develop* 31:655–66 D '60. * (*PA* 36:2FH55K)
771. MIRSKY, ALLAN F.; PRIMAC, DANIEL W.; MARSAN, COSIMO AJMONE; ROSVOLD, H. ENGER; AND STEVENS, JANICE R. "A Comparison of the Psychological Test Performance of Patients With Focal and Nonfocal Epilepsy." *Exp Neurol* 2:75–89 F '60. *
772. SHAPIRO, M. B.; KESSELL, R.; AND MAXWELL, A. E. "Speed and Quality of Psychomotor Performance in Psychiatric Patients." *J Clin Psychol* 16:266–71 Jl '60. * (*PA* 36:2HI66S)

773. WENDLAND, LEONARD V.; URMER, ALBERT H.; AND SAFFORD, H. WILLIAM. "The Intellectual Functioning of Post-poliomyelitic Patients." *J Clin Psychol* 16:179–81 Ap '60. * (*PA* 36:2HD79W)

774. SHNEIDMAN, EDWIN S. "The Case of El: Psychological Test Data." *J Proj Tech* 25:131–54 Je '61. * (*PA* 36:21K31S)

775. SPERBER, ZANWIL, AND ADLERSTEIN, ARTHUR M. "The Accuracy of Clinical Psychologists' Estimates of Interviewees' Intelligence." *J Consult Psychol* 25:521–4 D '61. * (*PA* 37:4969)

776. VASSILIOU, VASSO, AND HIMWICH, H. E. "Psychological Effects of Isocarboxazid and Nialamide on a Group of Depressed Patients." *J Clin Psychol* 17:319–20 Jl '61. * (*PA* 38:7581)

777. CARKHUFF, ROBERT R. "The Face Supplement: A Quick Index of Intelligence for Adult Subnormals." *J Clin Psychol* 18:346–7 Jl '62. * (*PA* 39:1721)

778. GRUEN, ARNO. "Psychologic Aging as a Pre-existing Factor in Strokes." *J Nerv & Mental Dis* 134:109–16 F '62. * (*PA* 37:965)

779. HERRON, WILLIAM G. "Abstract Ability in the Process-Reactive Classification of Schizophrenia." *J General Psychol* 67:147–54 Jl '62. * (*PA* 37:3691)

780. JENKINS, C. DAVID. "The Relation of EEG Slowing to Selected Indices of Intellective Impairment." *J Nerv & Mental Dis* 135:162–70 Ag '62. *

781. PEARL, DAVID. "Phenothiazine Effects in Chronic Schizophrenia." *J Clin Psychol* 18:86–9 Ja '62. * (*PA* 38:7573)

782. PIERCY, MALCOLM M., AND SMYTH, V. O. G. "Right Hemisphere Dominance for Certain Non-Verbal Intellectual Skills." *Brain* (England) 85:775–90 D '62. *

783. SCHULBERG, HERBERT C. "Insight, Authoritarianism and Tendency to Agree." *J Nerv & Mental Dis* 135:481–8 D '62. *

784. WYKE, MARIA. "An Experimental Study of Verbal Association in Dysphasic Subjects." *Brain* (England) 85:679–82 D '62. *

785. CLARK, MERVIN L.; RAY, THOMAS S.; AND RAGLAND, ROBERT E. "Chlorpromazine in Chronic Schizophrenic Women: Rate of Onset and Rate of Dissipation of Drug Effects." *Psychosom Med* 25:212–7 My–Je '63. * (*PA* 38:4397)

786. MULERO, RICARDO; IN COLLABORATION WITH J. WHITNEY KELLEY AND DONALD L. FAUTH. "The Effects of Valium on Psychological Testing." *Neb Med J* 48:499–505 S '63. *

787. SHAFFER, JOHN W.; FREINEK, WILFRIED R.; WOLF, SIDNEY; FOXWELL, NANCY H.; AND KURLAND, ALBERT A. "A Controlled Evaluation of Chlordiazepoxide (Librium) in the Treatment of Convalescing Alcoholics." *J Nerv & Mental Dis* 137:494–507 N '63. * (*PA* 39:5332)

788. WHEELER, LAWRENCE, AND REITAN, RALPH M. "Discriminant Functions Applied to the Problem of Predicting Cerebral Damage From Behavioral Tests: A Cross-Validation Study." *Percept & Motor Skills* 16:681–701 Je '63. * (*PA* 38:6415)

789. WHEELER, LAWRENCE; BURKE, CLETUS J.; AND REITAN, RALPH M. "An Application of Discriminant Functions to the Problem of Predicting Brain Damage Using Behavioral Variables." *Percept & Motor Skills* 16:417–40 Ap '63. * (*PA* 38:2991)

790. WOODS, JAMES E., AND MYERS, ROGER A. "A Comparison of IQ Scores on the Revised Beta Examination and the Wechsler Adult Intelligence Scale." *Rehabil Counsel B* 7:54–8 S '63. *

791. CARR, ARTHUR C. "Psychological Defect and Psychological Testing." *Int Psychiatry Clinics* 1:773–98 O '64. *

792. LEVITA, ERIC; RIKLAN, MANUEL; AND COOPER, IRVING S. "Cognitive and Perceptual Performance in Parkinsonism as a Function of Age and Neurological Impairment." *J Nerv & Mental Dis* 139:516–20 D '64. * (*PA* 39:10554)

793. MCLEOD, H. N. "The Use of Information and Block Design Subtests of the W.A.I.S. as a Measure of Intelligence in Psychiatric Hospital Patients." *Ont Psychol Assn Q* (Canada) 17:60–1 su '64. *

794. OBERLEDER, MURIEL. "Effects of Psycho-Social Factors on Test Results of the Aging." *Psychol Rep* 14:383–7 Ap '64. * (*PA* 39:1390)

795. SPIETH, WALTER. "Cardiovascular Health Status, Age, and Psychological Performance." *J Gerontol* 19:277–84 Jl '64. *

796. TAYLOR, JAMES BENTLEY. "The Structure of Ability in the Lower Intellectual Range." *Am J Mental Def* 68:766–74 My '64. * (*PA* 39:1793)

797. WATSON, CHARLES G., AND CAHOON, D. D. "A Note on the Relationship Between the Revised Beta Examination and the Wechsler Adult Intelligence Scale." *Rehabil Counsel B* 8:47–9 D '64. *

798. BEARD, BELLE BOON. "Survival Traits: Adaptive Intelligence of Centenarians." *Proc Int Congr Gerontol* 6:233–6 '65. *

799. BLATT, SIDNEY J. Chap. 23, "The Wechsler Scales and Acting Out," pp. 242–51. In *Acting Out: Theoretical and Clinical Aspects*. By Lawrence Edwin Abt and Stuart L. Weissman. New York: Grune & Stratton, Inc., 1965. Pp. xiii, 336. *

800. BRENGELMANN, JOHANNES C., AND HILLMAN, WILLIAM A., JR. "Determinants of Learning in the Retardate: A Pilot Study." *Training Sch B* 61:156–62 F '65. * (*PA* 39:10570)

801. DIXON, JAMES C. "Cognitive Structure in Senile Conditions With Some Suggestions for Developing a Brief Screening Test of Mental Status." *J Gerontol* 20:41–9 Ja '65. *

802. GRAD, B.; KRAL, V. A.; AND CRAMER-AZIMA, F. "Correlations Between Salivary Sodium and Potassium Concentration and Memory Function in Elderly Persons, Normal and Psychotic." *Recent Adv Biol Psychiatry* 7:97–106 '65. *

803. KASWAN, JAQUES; HARALSON, SALLY; AND CLINE, RUTH. "Variables in Perceptual and Cognitive Organization and Differentiation." *J Personality* 33:164–77 Je '65. * (*PA* 40:2418)

804. LAWRENCE, RONALD M., AND LEICHMAN, NATHAN S. "Comparison of the Effects of Heparin Sodium, Xanthinol Niacinate (Complamin) and 2-Dimethyl-Aminoethanol (Deaner) in Institutionalized Geriatric Groups." *J Am Geriatrics Soc* 13:325–42 Ap '65. *

805. MACKIE, JAMES B., AND BECK, EDWARD C. "Relations Among Age, Intelligence, and Critical Flicker Fusion." *Percept & Motor Skills* 21:875–8 D '65. * (*PA* 40:4535)

806. SPREEN, OTFRIED, AND BENTON, ARTHUR L. "Comparative Studies of Some Psychological Tests for Cerebral Damage." *J Nerv & Mental Dis* 140:323–33 My '65. * (*PA* 40:700)

807. STEWART, HORACE F., JR., AND KEELER, CLYDE E. "A Comparison of the Intelligence and Personality of Moon-Child Albino and Control Cuna Indians." *J Genetic Psychol* 106:319–24 Je '65. * (*PA* 39:14888)

808. CORRELL, ROBERT E.; ROKOSZ, SAUNDRA; AND BLANCHARD, BRADFORD M. "Some Correlates of WAIS Performance in the Elderly." *J Gerontol* 21:544–9 O '66. *

809. FELIX, R., AND ARIELI, S. "The Pattern of the Human Hand." *Israel Ann Psychiatry* 4:30–42 sp '66. * (*PA* 41:656)

810. GRISWOLD, BARBARA B.; WILTSE, KERMIT T.; AND ROBERTS, ROBERT W. "Some Personality and Intellectual Correlates of Repeated Out-of-Wedlock Childbirth Among Welfare Recipients." *J Clin Psychol* 22:348–53 Jl '66. * (*PA* 40:11141)

811. LEVY, RUSSELL H., AND MOORE, WINSTON E. "Cross-Sectional Psychometric Evaluation of Court-Labelled Delinquent Boys." *J Correct Ed* 18:7–9 Jl '66. *

812. MACKIE, JAMES B., AND BECK, EDWARD C. "Relations Among Rigidity, Intelligence and Perception in Brain-Damaged and Normal Individuals." *J Nerv & Mental Dis* 142:310–7 Ap '66. * (*PA* 40:13429)

813. MAUPIN, EDWARD W., AND HUNTER, DIANE. "Digit Span as Measure of Attention: Attempted Validation Studies." *Psychol Rep* 18:457–8 Ap '66. * (*PA* 40:8398)

814. MEIER, MANFRED J., AND FRENCH, LYLE A. "Longitudinal Assessment of Intellectual Functioning Following Unilateral Temporal Lobectomy." *J Clin Psychol* 22:22–7 Ja '66. * (*PA* 40:4283)

815. NORDVIK, HILMAR. "Factor Analytical Research on Aging by the Wechsler Adult Intelligence Scale." *Proc Int Congr Gerontol* 6(sup):525–8 '66. *

816. PAREDES, ALFONSO; BAUMGOLD, JOHN; PUGH, LAWRENCE A.; AND RAGLAND, ROBERT. "Clinical Judgment in the Assessment of Psychopharmacological Effects." *J Nerv & Mental Dis* 142:153–60 F '66. * (*PA* 40:11294)

817. SATZ, PAUL. "Specific and Non-Specific Effects of Brain Lesions in Man." *J Abn Psychol* 71:65–70 F '66. * (*PA* 40:4292)

818. SIM, MYRE; TURNER, ERIC; AND SMITH, W. THOMAS. "Cerebral Biopsy in the Investigation of Presenile Dementia: 1, Clinical Aspects." *Brit J Psychiatry* 112:119–25 F '66. *

819. BLUNDELL, ELIZABETH. "A Psychological Study of the Effects of Surgery on Eighty-Six Elderly Patients." *Brit J Social & Clin Psychol* 6:297–303 D '67. * (*PA* 42:7707)

820. FALBERG, ROGER M. "The Psychological Evaluation of Prelingually Deaf Adults." *J Rehabil Deaf* 1:31–46 Jl '67. *

821. FISHER, JEROME, AND PIERCE, ROBERT C. "Dimensions of Intellectual Functioning in the Aged." *J Gerontol* 22:166–73 Ap '67. *

822. GRANICK, SAMUEL, AND FRIEDMAN, ALFRED S. "The Effect of Education on the Decline of Psychometric Test Performance With Age." *J Gerontol* 22:191–5 Ap '67. *

823. LEVITA, ERIC, AND RIKLAN, MANUEL. "Patterns of Psychological Function Before, After Unilateral, and After Bilateral Thalamic Surgery." *Percept & Motor Skills* 24:619–26 Ap '67. * (*PA* 41:9973)

824. LEVY, PHILIP. "The Correction for Spurious Correlation in the Evaluation of Short-Form Tests." *J Clin Psychol* 23:84–6 Ja '67. * (*PA* 41:5253)

825. LEVY, RUSSELL H. "Dimensions of Mental Retardation Among Wards of the Illinois Youth Commission." *J Correct Ed* 19:12–6 O '67. *

826. MONEY, JOHN, AND EPSTEIN, RALPH. "Verbal Aptitude in Eonism and Prepubertal Effeminacy—A Feminine Trait." *Trans N Y Acad Sci* 29:448–54 F '67. * (*PA* 41:16833)

827. RAMALINGASWAMI, P. "A Comparative Study on the Use of Block Design Test." *Indian J Psychol* 42(1–4):29–33 '67. *

828. SHIMKUNAS, ALGIMANTAS M.; GYNTHER, MALCOLM D.; AND SMITH, KATHLEEN. "Schizophrenic Responses to the Proverbs Test: Abstract, Concrete, or Autistic?" *J Abn Psychol* 72:128–33 Ap '67. * (*PA* 41:7605)

829. SUINN, RICHARD M. "The Theory of Cognitive Style: A Partial Replication." *J General Psychol* 77:11–5 Jl '67. * (*PA* 41:14063)

830. BARRINGTON, BYRON L. "Special Education Students—

How Many Are Misplaced?" *J Learn Dis* 1:726-9 D '68. *
(*PA* 45:6998)
831. BLOCK, J. BRADFORD. Chap. 13, "Hereditary Components
in the Performance of Twins on the WAIS," pp. 221-8. In
Progress in Human Behavior Genetics. Edited by Steven G.
Vandenberg. Baltimore, Md.: Johns Hopkins Press, 1968. Pp. xi,
356. *
832. DE LUCA, JOSEPH N. "Motivation and Performance in
Chronic Schizophrenia." *Psychol Rep* 22:1261-9 Je '68. * (*PA*
42:19082)
833. GOLDSTEIN, NORMAN P.; EWERT, JOSEPHINE C.; RAN-
DALL, RAYMOND V.; AND GROSS, JOHN B. "Psychiatric Aspects
of Wilson's Disease (Hepatolenticular Degeneration): Results
of Psychometric Tests During Long-Term Therapy." *Am J
Psychiatry* 124:1555-61 My '68. * (*PA* 42:12656)
834. LEWIS, VIOLA G.; MONEY, JOHN; AND EPSTEIN, RALPH.
"Concordance of Verbal and Nonverbal Ability in the Adrenogenital Syndrome." *Johns Hopkins Med J* 122:192-5 Ap '68. *
835. LOEWER, H. D. "The Dependence of the Factorial
Structure of Intelligence From the Level of Intelligence and
From the Brain State." *Proc Inter Congr Appl Psychol* 16:707-
12 '68. *
836. FREEMAN, JAMES; M'COMISKY, JAMES G.; AND BUTTLE,
DEREK. "Student Selection: A Comparative Study of Student
Entrants to Architecture and Economics." *Ed Sci* (England)
3(3):189-97 D '69. *
837. GIANNITRAPANI, DUILIO. "EEG Average Frequency and
Intelligence." *Electroenceph & Clin Neurophysiol* (Netherlands)
27(5):480-6 N '69. * (*PA* 45:2021)
838. HALPERN, ANDREW S., AND EQUINOZZI, ARTHUR M.
"Verbal Expressivity as an Index of Adaptive Behavior."
Am J Mental Def 74(2):180-6 S '69. * (*PA* 44:5551)
839. HOLMES, DOUGLAS S. "Comment on Levy's Reply."
Psychol Rep 24(3):936 Je '69. * (*PA* 44:707)
840. KEEVIL-ROGERS, PATRICIA, AND SCHNORE, MORRIS M.
"Short-Term Memory as a Function of Age in Persons of Above
Average Intelligence." *J Gerontol* 24(2):184-8 Ap '69. *
841. MANN, EDWARD T. "Use of the KTSA as a Technique
for Assessing Intelligence and Psychodynamics in Drug Addicts."
Int J Symbol 1(2):57-66 D '69. * (*PA* 45:10218)
842. MASICA, DANIEL N.; EHRHARDT, ANKE A.; AND LEWIS,
VIOLA G. "IQ, Fetal Sex Hormones and Cognitive Patterns:
Studies in the Testicular Feminizing Syndrome of Androgen
Insensitivity." *Johns Hopkins Med J* 124(1):34-43 Ja '69. *
843. MONEY, JOHN, AND BRENNAN, JOHN G. "Achievement
Versus Failure: Intelligence, Education and Career in Seven
Female Transsexuals." *J Learn Dis* 2(2):76-81 F '69. * (*PA*
45:6641)
844. MYERS, SUSAN SLOAT. *Investigation of Creativity of
Female Electronics Assemblers.* Master's thesis, Southern Methodist University (Dallas, Tex.), 1969.
845. RAFFEL, SHERMAN C.; SWINK, RICHARD; AND LAMPTON,
T. D. "The Influence of Chlorphenesin Carbamate and Carisoprodol on Psychological Test Scores." *Curr Ther Res* 11(9):
553-60 S '69. *
846. THETFORD, WILLIAM N., AND SCHUCMAN, HELEN. "Self-
Choices, Preferences, and Personality Traits." *Psychol Rep*
25(2):659-67 O '69. * (*PA* 44:5171)
847. WEINBERG, H. "Correlation of Frequency Spectra of
Averaged Visual Evoked Potentials With Verbal Intelligence."
Nature (England) 224(5221):813-5 N 22 '69. *
848. ALEXANDER, SHIRLEY MAE. *A Study of Perceptual and
Verbal Differentiation Among Male College Students.* Doctor's
thesis, George Washington University (Washington, D.C.),
1970. (*DAI* 31:6887B)
849. BEACH, JOE EDWARD. *A Study of the Relationship of
Intelligence and Academic Achievement of a Selected Group of
Deaf Pupils.* Master's thesis, Mississippi State University (State
College, Miss.), 1970.
850. BERRINGER, DALTON EARL. *An Examination of Geometric
Errors in the WAIS Block Design Test and the Effects Upon
Performance as a Function of Spatial Relations Ability.* Doctor's
thesis, University of Northern Colorado (Greeley, Colo.), 1970.
(*DAI* 31:6393A)
851. BOCK, R. DARRELL; VANDENBERG, STEVEN G.; BRAMBLE,
WILLIAM; AND PEARSON, WRIGHT. "A Behavioral Correlate of
Blood-Group Discordance in Dizygotic Twins." *Behav Genetics*
1(2):89-98 My '70. * (*PA* 47:10428)
852. GIANNITRAPANI, D. "WAIS I.Q. as Related to EEG
Frequency Scores." Abstract. *Electroenceph & Clin Neurophysiol*
(Netherlands) 28(1):102 Ja '70. *
853. GREEN, RUSSEL F., AND REIMANIS, GUNARS. "The Age-
Intelligence Relationship—Longitudinal Studies Can Mislead."
Indus Gerontol 6:1-16 su '70. * (*PA* 45:7981)
854. KIMBALL, CHASE P. "The Experience of Open Heart
Surgery: 2, Determinants of Post-Operative Behavior." *Psychother & Psychosom* (Switzerland) 18(1-6):259-74 '70. * (*PA*
47:5515)
855. LABERTEAUX, THOMAS E. *A Comparison of Single and
Multiple Stimuli Overinclusion Measures.* Doctor's thesis, St.
Louis University (St. Louis, Mo.), 1970. (*DAI* 32:1216B)
856. LYNCH, WILLIAM JOHN. *The Performance of LSD Users
on Certain Neuropsychological Tests.* Doctor's thesis, University
of Tennessee (Knoxville, Tenn.), 1970. (*DAI* 31:5630B)

857. MEIER, MANFRED J. "Effects of Focal Cerebral Lesions
on Contralateral Visuomotor Adaptation to Reversal and Inversion of Visual Feedback." *Neuropsychologia* (England) 8(3):
269-79 Jl '70. * (*PA* 44:21410)
858. MILLER, LAURENCE RICHARD. *A Factor Analytic Study
of Cognitive Variables in Congenitally Blind Individuals.* Doctor's thesis, Case Western Reserve University (Cleveland, Ohio),
1970. (*DAI* 32:248A)
859. PAGE, STEWART. "Examiner Effect, Expertise, and Intelligence Testing." *Ont Psychologist* (Canada) 2(3):181-4 '70. *
860. ROSS, DONALD R. "A Technique of Verbal Ability Assessment of Deaf Adults." *J Rehabil Deaf* 3(3):7-15 Ja '70. *
861. RUDOLPH, LINDA. *Correlates of the Slosson Intelligence
Test, Wechsler Adult Intelligence Scale, ACT Scores and Grade
Point Averages.* Master's thesis, Austin Peay State University
(Clarksville, Tenn.), 1970.
862. TARNOPOL, LESTER. "Delinquency and Minimal Brain
Dysfunction." *J Learn Dis* 3(4):200-7 Ap '70. * (*PA* 47:3517)
863. WAGNER, NATHANIEL N. "Malaysian Medical Students:
Intellectual Performance and Ethnic Background." *Brit J Med
Ed* 4(2):109-13 Je '70. *
864. WHITMAN, JAMES R. "Learning Impairment in Schizophrenic and Brain-Damaged Patients." *Percept & Motor Skills*
30(1):311-6 F '70. * (*PA* 46:9296)
865. BACKMAN, MARGARET E., AND STEINDLER, FRANCES M.
"Cognitive Abilities Related to Attrition in a Collegiate Nursing Program." *Nursing Outl* 19(12):807-8 D '71. *
866. BACKMAN, MARGARET E., AND STEINDLER, FRANCES M.
"Prediction of Achievement in a Collegiate Nursing Program
and Performance on State Board Examinations." *Nursing Outl*
19(7):487 Jl '71. *
867. BEARDSLEY, JAMES V., AND PULETTI, FLAVIO. "Personality (MMPI) and Cognitive (WAIS) Changes After Levodopa
Treatment: Occurrence in Patients With Parkinson's Disease."
Arch Neurol 25(2):145-50 Ag '71. * (*PA* 48:1446)
868. BEN-YISHAY, YEHUDA; DILLER, LEONARD; MANDLEBERG,
IAN; GORDON, WAYNE; AND GERSTMAN, LOUIS J. "Similarities
and Differences in Block Design Performance Between Older
Normal and Brain-Injured Persons: A Task Analysis." *J Abn
Psychol* 78(1):17-25 Ag '71. * (*PA* 47:3261)
869. BETZ, ROGER CHARLES. *Predicting Rehabilitation Outcomes Through Selected Personal, Psychological and Program
Variables.* Doctor's thesis, University of Northern Colorado
(Greeley, Colo.), 1971. (*DAI* 32:3681A)
870. BOWERS, KENNETH S. "Sex and Susceptibility as Moderator Variables in the Relationship of Creativity and Hypnotic
Susceptibility." *J Abn Psychol* 78(1):93-100 Ag '71. * (*PA*
47:2042)
871. BREWER, COLIN, AND PERRETT, LANCE. "Brain Damage
Due to Alcoholic Consumption: An Air-encephalographic, Psychometric and Electroencephalographic Study." *Brit J Addict*
66(3):170-82 N '71. * (*PA* 48:5229)
872. BROWN, DON A. "Intelligence of Adult Illiterates."
Yearb Nat Read Conf 19(1):94-8 '71. *
873. BUCKLEY, FELICITY. "Preliminary Report on Intelligence
Quotient Scores of Patients With Turner's Syndrome: A Replication Study." *Brit J Psychiatry* 119(552):513-4 N '71. * (*PA*
48:3046)
874. CHAMBERS, JEAN FORBES. *Predicting the Academic
Achievement Level of Deaf Students.* Doctor's thesis, University
of Arizona (Tucson, Ariz.), 1971. (*DAI* 31:6396A)
875. CLARK, JACK MANNING. *The Prediction of Gain in Reading Among Adult Illiterates From an Analysis of Items on the
Wechsler, Leiter and Davis-Eells Scales.* Doctor's thesis, State
University of New York (Buffalo, N.Y.), 1971. (*DAI* 32:
2512A)
876. COWDEN, JAMES E.; PETERSON, WILLIAM M.; AND PACHT,
ASHER R. "The Validation of a Brief Screening Test for Verbal
Intelligence at Several Correctional Institutions in Wisconsin."
J Clin Psychol 27(2):216-8 Ap '71. * (*PA* 46:7125)
877. CULL, JOHN G., AND HARDY, RICHARD E. "Correlation
Between the Immediate Test and the Wechsler Adult Intelli-
gence Scale Verbal Scale in the Rehabilitation Setting." *J Psy-
chol* 77(2):203-5 Mr '71. * (*PA* 46:1627)
878. DAVIS, WILLIAM E.; BECKER, BRUCE C.; AND DEWOLFE,
ALAN S. "Categorization of Patients With Personality Disorders
and Acute Brain Trauma Through WAIS Subtest Variations."
J Clin Psychol 27(3):358-60 Jl '71. * (*PA* 47:5077)
879. DAVIS, WILLIAM E.; DIZZONNE, MICHAEL F.; AND DE-
WOLFE, ALAN S. "Relationships Among WAIS Subtest Scores,
Patient's Premorbid History, and Institutionalization." *J Consult
& Clin Psychol* 36(3):400-3 Je '71. * (*PA* 46:9377)
880. DEMERS, ROBERT G., AND HENINGER, GEORGE R. "Visual-
Motor Performance During Lithium Treatment—A Preliminary
Report." *J Clin Pharmacol* 11(4):274-9 Jl '71. * (*PA* 47:3169)
881. DEWOLFE, ALAN S. "Differentiation of Schizophrenia and
Brain Damage With the WAIS." *J Clin Psychol* 27(2):209-11
Ap '71. * (*PA* 46:7073)
882. DEWOLFE, ALAN S.; BARRELL, ROBERT P.; BECKER,
BRUCE C.; AND SPANER, FRED E. "Intellectual Deficit in Chronic
Schizophrenia and Brain Damage." *J Consult & Clin Psychol*
36(2):197-204 Ap '71. * (*PA* 46:3117)
883. DICKSTEIN, LOUIS S., AND MACEVITT, MARJORIE. "Com-

prehension Subtest of the WAIS and Need for Approval." *Psychol Rep* 28(2):482 Ap '71. * (*PA* 46:6845)

884. DISPENZIERI, ANGELO; GINIGER, SEYMOUR; REICHMAN, WALTER; AND LEVY, MARGUERITE. "College Performance of Disadvantaged Students as a Function of Ability and Personality." *J Counsel Psychol* 18(4):298–305 Jl '71. * (*PA* 46:11687)

885. DONAHUE, DANIEL, AND SATTLER, JEROME M. "Personality Variables Affecting WAIS Scores." Abstract. *J Consult & Clin Psychol* 36(3):441 Je '71. * (*PA* 46:9041)

886. DUJOVNE, BEATRIZ E., AND LEVY, BERNARD I. "The Psychometric Structure of the Wechsler Memory Scale." *J Clin Psychol* 27(3):351–4 Jl '71. * (*PA* 47:5081)

887. FIELDS, FRANCIS R. J. "Relative Effects of Brain Damage on the Wechsler Memory and Intelligence Quotients." *Dis Nerv System* 32(10):673–5 O '71. * (*PA* 48:12023)

888. FIELDS, FRANCIS R. J. "Relative Effects of Brain Damage on the Wechsler Memory and Intelligence Quotients." *Newsl Res Psychol* 13(2):5–6 My '71. *

889. FIRETTO, ANTHONY C., AND DAVEY, HEATHER. "Subjectively Reported Anxiety as a Discriminator of Digit Span Performance." *Psychol Rep* 28(1):98 F '71. * (*PA* 46:5001)

890. FLICK, GRAD L., AND EDWARDS, KENNETH R. "Prediction of Lateralized Organic Brain Dysfunction With a Neuropsychological Test Battery: A Discriminant Function Analysis." *Newsl Res Psychol* 13(2):16–7 My '71. *

891. FREYMARK, BARRY A. *WAIS Block Design Performance as a Function of Amount of Exposure to Embedded Figures Tasks.* Master's thesis, Illinois State University (Normal, Ill.), 1971.

892. GEORGAS, JAMES G.; VASSILIOU, VASSO; AND KATAKIS, HARRIS. "The Verbal Intelligence of Athenians." *J Social Psychol* 83(2):165–73 Ap '71. * (*PA* 46:3084)

893. GOLDSTEIN, GERALD, AND SHELLY, CAROLYN H. "Field Dependence and Cognitive, Perceptual and Motor Skills in Alcoholics." *Q J Studies Alcohol* 32(1A):29–40 Mr '71. * (*PA* 46:7095)

894. GRANICK, SAMUEL. "Brief Tests and Their Interrelations as Intelligence Measures of Aged Subjects." Abstract. *Proc 79th Ann Conv Am Psychol Assn* 6(2):599–600 '71. * (*PA* 46:4727)

895. GRIFFITHS, A. W. "Prisoners of XYY Constitution: Psychological Aspects." *Brit J Psychiatry* 119(549):193–4 Ag '71. * (*PA* 47:7155)

896. GUERTIN, WILSON H.; LADD, CLAYTON E.; FRANK, GEORGE H.; RABIN, ALBERT I.; AND HIESTER, DOUGLAS S. "Research With the Wechsler Intelligence Scales for Adults: 1965–1970." *Psychol Rec* 21(3):289–339 su '71. * (*PA* 47:8926)

897. HANNINEN, HELENA. "Psychological Picture of Manifest and Latent Carbon Disulphide Poisoning." *Brit J Indus Med* 28(4):374–81 O '71. *

898. HARWOOD, ELSIE, AND NAYLOR, G. F. K. "Changes in the Constitution of the WAIS Intelligence Pattern With Advancing Age." *Austral J Psychol* 23(3):297–303 D '71. * (*PA* 48:2746)

899. HEDL, JOHN J., JR.; O'NEIL, HAROLD F., JR.; AND HANSEN, DUNCAN N. "Affective Nature of Computer-Based Testing Procedures." Abstract. *Proc 79th Ann Conv Am Psychol Assn* 6(2):535–6 '71. * (*PA* 46:5468)

900. HUNT, WILLIAM A., AND WALKER, RONALD E. "Cue Utilization in Diagnostic Judgment." *J Clin Psychol* 27(1):62–4 Ja '71. * (*PA* 46:1425)

901. IVINSKIS, ALGIS; ALLEN, STEPHEN; AND SHAW, ELVA. "An Extension of Wechsler Memory Scale Norms to Lower Age Groups." *J Clin Psychol* 27(3):354–7 Jl '71. * (*PA* 47:5087)

902. KAHN, MARVIN W. "Murderers Who Plead Insanity: A Descriptive Factor-Analytic Study of Personality, Social, and History Variables." *Genetic Psychol Monogr* 84(2):275–360 N '71. * (*PA* 49:990)

903. KANGAS, JON, AND BRADWAY, KATHERINE. "Intelligence at Middle Age: A Thirty-Eight-Year Follow-Up." *Develop Psychol* 5(2):333–7 S '71. * (*PA* 47:2985)

904. LEVENSON, MARVIN, AND NEURINGER, CHARLES. "Problem-Solving Behavior in Suicidal Adolescents." *J Consult & Clin Psychol* 37(3):433–6 D '71. * (*PA* 47:9261)

905. LEVINE, NIRA R. "Validation of the Quick Test for Intelligence Screening of the Elderly." *Psychol Rep* 29(1):167–72 Ag '71. * (*PA* 47:2717)

906. LIBB, J. WESLEY, AND COLEMAN, JOHN M. "Correlation Between the WAIS and Revised Beta, Wechsler Memory Scale and Quick Test in a Vocational Rehabilitation Center." *Psychol Rep* 29(3):863–5 D '71. * (*PA* 47:9410)

907. LOGOTHETIS, JOHN; HARITOS-FATOUROS, MARY; CONSTANTOULAKIS, MATHIOS; ECONOMIDOU, JOANNA; AUGOUSTAKI, OLGA; AND LOEWENSON, RUTH B. "Intelligence and Behavioral Patterns in Patients With Cooley's Anemia (Homozygous Betathalassemia); A Study Based on 138 Consecutive Cases." *Pediatrics* 48(5):740–4 N '71. *

908. LOGUE, PATRICK E., AND ALLEN, KATHE. "WAIS-Predicted Category Test Scores With the Halstead Neuropsychological Battery." *Percept & Motor Skills* 33(3):1095–6 D '71. * (*PA* 48:1463)

909. LORANGER, ARMAND W.; GOODELL, HELEN; McDOWELL, FLETCHER; LEE, JOHN; AND SWEET, RICHARD D. "Cognitive

Impairment in Parkinson's Syndrome." Abstract. *Proc 79th Ann Conv Am Psychol Assn* 6(1):463–4 '71. * (*PA* 46:5322)

910. McCORMICK, CLARENCE C.; KLAPPAUF, JEANNIE; SCHNOBRICH, JANICE N.; AND HARVEY, JOHN. "Relationships Among Arrow-Dot IES Scores and Wechsler IQs and MMPI Scales for Hospitalized, Disturbed Adolescents." *Percept & Motor Skills* 33(3):1227–34 D '71. * (*PA* 48:3263)

911. McKERRACHER, D. W. "Psychological Aspects of a Sex Chromatin Abnormality." *Can Psychologist* 12(2):270–81 Ap '71. * (*PA* 46:9096)

912. MILLHAM, JIM; JACOBSON, LEONARD I.; AND BERGER, STEPHEN E. "Effects of Intelligence, Information Processing, and Mediation Conditions on Conceptual Learning." *J Ed Psychol* 62(4):293–9 Ag '71. * (*PA* 47:220)

913. MISHRA, SHITALA P. "Wechsler Adult Intelligence Scale: Examiner vs Machine Administration?" *Psychol Rep* 29(3):759–62 D '71. * (*PA* 47:8928)

914. MOLISH, H. BARRY; KRAFT, IRVIN A.; AND WIGGINS, P. Y. "Psychodiagnostic Evaluation of the Heart Transplant Patient." *Seminars Psychiatry* 3(1):46–57 F '71. * (*PA* 49:7577)

915. MOSHER, LOREN R.; POLLIN, WILLIAM; AND STABENAU, JAMES R. "Identical Twins Discordant for Schizophrenia: Neurologic Findings." *Arch Gen Psychiatry* 24(5):422–30 My '71. * (*PA* 47:9365)

916. PAGE, STEWART. "On Wessler's 'Estimating IQ: Expertise or Examiner Effect?': Research and Discussion." *Percept & Motor Skills* 33(2):435–8 O '71. * (*PA* 47:7094)

917. PETERSEN, PAUL W. *Predicting Work Evaluation Results From the Wechsler Adult Intelligence Scale.* Doctor's thesis, Brigham Young University (Provo, Utah), 1971. (*DAI* 32:4454A)

918. PRINGLE, ROGER K., AND HAANSTAD, MARTIN. "Estimating WAIS IQs From Progressive Matrices and Shipley-Hartford Scores." *J Clin Psychol* 27(4):479–81 O '71. * (*PA* 47:8929)

919. ROYER, FRED L. "Information Processing of Visual Figures in the Digit Symbol Substitution Task." *J Exp Psychol* 87(3):335–42 Mr '71. * (*PA* 46:109)

920. ROYER, FRED L. "Information Processing of Visual Figures in the Digit-Symbol Substitution Task." *Newsl Res Psychol* 13(1):15–9 F '71. *

921. RUSSELL, ELBERT W. "Reexamination of Halstead's Biological Intelligence Factors." Abstract. *Proc 79th Ann Conv Am Psychol Assn* 6(1):461–2 '71. * (*PA* 46:5335)

922. SCHOFIELD, LARRY F., AND KUNCE, JOSEPH T. "The WAIS Adaptability Scale and Vocational Behavior." *J Voc Behav* 1(4):355–60 O '71. * (*PA* 48:5351)

923. SCHOOLER, CARMI, AND SILVERMAN, JULIAN. "Differences Between Correlates of Perceptual Style and Petrie Task Performance in Chronic and Acute Schizophrenics." *Percept & Motor Skills* 32(2):595–601 Ap '71. * (*PA* 46:11261)

924. SEITZ, FRANK C., AND BRAUCHT, GEORGE N. "Ammons' Quick Test as a Measure of Adult Intelligence in a Psychiatric Sample." *Psychol Rep* 29(2):356–8 O '71. * (*PA* 47:9302)

925. SHIMKUNAS, ALGIMANTAS M.; GROHMANN, MARY; AND ZWIBELMAN, BARRY. "Sources of Intellectual Inefficiency." *Psychol Rep* 29(3):747–54 D '71. * (*PA* 47:9374)

926. SHORE, CELIA; SHORE, HOWARD; AND PIHL, R. O. "Correlations Between Performance on the Category Test and the Wechsler Adult Intelligence Scale." *Percept & Motor Skills* 32(1):70 F '71. * (*PA* 46:3068)

927. SILVERSTEIN, A. B. "A Corrected Formula for Assessing the Validity of WAIS, WISC, and WPPSI Short Forms." *J Clin Psychol* 27(2):212–3 Ap '71. * (*PA* 46:6881)

928. SIMPSON, C. DENE, AND VEGA, ARTHUR. "Unilateral Brain Damage and Patterns of Age-Corrected WAIS Subtest Scores." *J Clin Psychol* 27(2):204–8 Ap '71. * (*PA* 46:7308)

929. SMITH, W. LYNN, AND LOWREY, J. B. "Differential Effects of Cyclandelate on Psychological Test Performance in Patients With Cerebral Vascular Insufficiency," pp. 69–73. In *Assessment in Cerebrovascular Insufficiency.* Edited by G. Stöcker and Others. Stuttgart, Germany: Georg Thieme Verlag, 1971. Pp. viii, 152. *

930. TOOMEY, TIMOTHY CHARLES. *The Effect of a Televised Model in Altering a Behavioral Correlate of Field Dependence and Field Independence.* Doctor's thesis, University of Georgia (Athens, Ga.), 1971. (*DAI* 32:4231B)

931. TOPPEN, J. T. "Underemployment: Economic or Psychological." *Psychol Rep* 28(1):111–22 F '71. * (*PA* 46:4762)

932. TRIESCHMANN, ROBERTA B., AND SAND, PATRICIA L. "WAIS and MMPI Correlates of Increasing Renal Failure in Adult Medical Patients." *Psychol Rep* 29(3):1251–62 D '71. * (*PA* 48:1559)

933. TSAI, LOH SENG, AND HAINES, RICHARD B. "Tsai Number-Joining Test Scores Correlated With College Students' Performance on WAIS and DAT." *Percept & Motor Skills* 33(1):35–44 Ag '71. * (*PA* 47:3643)

934. VEGA, ARTHUR, AND PARSONS, OSCAR A. "Lateralized Brain Damage and Differential Psychological Effects: Reply to Dr. Woo-Sam." *Percept & Motor Skills* 33(1):269–70 Ag '71. * (*PA* 47:3518)

935. WARRINGTON, ELIZABETH K.; LOGUE, VALENTINE; AND PRATT, R. T. C. "The Anatomical Localisation of Selective

Impairment of Auditory Verbal Short-Term Memory." *Neuropsychologia* (England) 9(4):377–87 D '71. * (*PA* 48:5435)

936. WEINSTOCK, CAMILDA, AND BENNETT, RUTH. "From 'Waiting on the List' to Becoming a 'Newcomer' and an 'Old-timer' in a Home for the Aged: Two Studies of Socialization and Its Impact Upon Cognitive Functioning." *Aging & Hum Develop* 2(1):46–58 F '71. * (*PA* 48:8893)

937. WELLS, DONALD G., AND PEDRINI, DUILIO T. "Relationships Among Wechsler Adult Intelligence Scale, Goodenough-Harris, and Peabody Picture Vocabulary Tests With Institutionalized Retarded Adults." *Percept & Motor Skills* 33(1):227–32 Ag '71. * (*PA* 47:3549)

938. WILKIE, FRANCES, AND EISDORFER, CARL. "Intelligence and Blood Pressure in the Aged." *Sci* 172(3986):959–62 My 28 '71. * (*PA* 46:8804)

939. WILLNER, ALLEN E. "Abstraction, Associative Focusing, and Similarities Tests: Towards More Clinically Sensitive and Better Understood Tests." *Psychol Rep* 29(3):683–731 D '71. * (*PA* 47:8001)

940. WOO-SAM, JAMES. "Lateralized Brain Damage and Differential Psychological Effects: Parsons, *et al.*, Re-Examined." *Percept & Motor Skills* 33(1):259–62 Ag '71. * (*PA* 47:3519)

CUMULATIVE NAME INDEX

[530]

[Re Wechsler Adult Intelligence Scale] Rhodes WAIS Scatter Profile. Ages 16 and over; 1971; a form for profiling WAIS scores; Fen Rhodes; Educational and Industrial Testing Service. *

For additional information, see 7:430.

[531]

★[Re Wechsler Adult Intelligence Scale] WAIS Test Profile. Ages 16 and over; 1968–69; Consulting Psychologists Press, Inc. *

[532]

Wechsler-Bellevue Intelligence Scale. Ages 10 and over; 1939–47; W-B; 2 forms; David Wechsler; Psychological Corporation. (South African adaptation: National Institute for Personnel Research [South Africa].) *

a) FORM I. 1939–47; out of print except for record form.

b) FORM 2. 1946–47; catalog states that "Form 2 is the retest instrument for the WAIS as well as for Form 1"; 14 scores: verbal (general information, general comprehension, digit span, arithmetic, similarities, voca-

bulary, total), performance (picture arrangement, picture completion, block design, object assembly, digit symbol, total), total; for a downward extension, see 533.

For additional information, see 6:539 (123 references); see also 5:415 (253 references); for reviews by Murray Aborn and William D. Altus, see 4:361 (250 references); for a review by Robert I. Watson, see 3:298 (119 references); for a review by F. L. Wells and excerpted reviews by Grace H. Kent and one other, see 2:1429 (2 references). For excerpts from related book reviews, see 6:B503 (3 excerpts), 5:B332 (2 excerpts), 4:362 (1 excerpt), 3:299 (7 excerpts), 3:300 (7 excerpts), 3:301 (5 excerpts), and 2:B1121 (10 excerpts).

REFERENCES THROUGH 1971

1–2. See 2:1429.
3–121. See 3:298.
122–371. See 4:361.
372–625. See 5:415.
626–748. See 6:539.
749. PETERSON, RACHEL. *The Use of the Wechsler-Bellevue Intelligence Scale With the Visually Handicapped.* Master's thesis, MacMurray College (Jacksonville, Ill.), 1944.
750. ALTUS, WILLIAM D. "Racial and Bi-Lingual Group Differences in Predictability and in Mean Aptitude Test Scores in an Army Special Training Center." *Psychol B* 42:310–20 My '45. * (*PA* 19:3049)
751. ALTUS, WILLIAM D., AND MAHLER, CLARENCE A. "The Significance of Verbal Aptitude in the Type of Occupation Pursued by Illiterates." *J Appl Psychol* 30:155–60 Ap '46. * (*PA* 20:3265)
752. WAGGONER, R. W., AND ZEIGLER, THORNTON WOODWARD. "Psychiatric Factors in Medical School Students Who Fail." *Am J Psychiatry* 103:369–76 N '46. * (*PA* 21:1671)
753. COLLINS, A. LOUISE, AND LENNOX, WILLIAM G. "The Intelligence of 300 Private Epileptic Patients." *Res Publ Assn Res Nerv & Mental Dis* 26:586–603 '47. *
754. SANDS, HARRY, AND PRICE, JERRY C. "A Pattern Analysis of the Wechsler-Bellevue Adult Intelligence Scale in Epilepsy." *Res Publ Assn Res Nerv & Mental Dis* 26:604–15 '47. *
755. ZIMMERMAN, FREDERIC T.; BURGEMEISTER, BESSIE B.; AND PUTNAM, TRACY J. "A Group Study of the Effect of Glutamic Acid Upon Mental Functioning in Children and Adolescents." *Psychosom Med* 9:175–83 My–Je '47. * (*PA* 21:3474)
756. BOWIE, CAROL C. "The Meaning of the Marriage Contract to 674 Negro Male Veterans." *Int J Sexol* 2:42–3 Ag '48. * (*PA* 24:6297)
757. ALTUS, WILLIAM D. "The Relationship of Intelligence and Years of Schooling When Literacy Is Held Constant." *J Consult Psychol* 13:375–6 O '49. * (*PA* 24:2757)
758. PETRIE, ASENATH. "Personality Changes After Pre-Frontol Leucotomy." *Brit J Med Psychol* 22:200–1 pts 3–4 '49. * (*PA* 25:2002)
759. PETRIE, ASENATH. "Preliminary Report of Changes After Prefrontal Leucotomy." *J Mental Sci* (England) 95:449–55 Ap '49. * (*PA* 24:278)
760. WHITEMAN, MORDECAI, AND WHITEMAN, DORIT B. "The Application of Cluster Analysis to the Wechsler-Bellevue Scale." *Delaware State Med J* 21:174–6 Ag '49. * (*PA* 25:483)
761. DIERS, WALLACE C., AND BROWN, CLINTON C. "Psychometric Patterns Associated With Multiple Sclerosis: 1, Wechsler-Bellevue Patterns." *Arch Neurol & Psychiatry* 63:760–5 My '50. * (*PA* 25:4779)
762. GOLDSTEIN, M. J. "A Preliminary Evaluation of the Use of the Wechsler-Bellevue Adult Intelligence Scale in South Africa." *J Social Res* (South Africa) 1:220–6 D '50. * (*PA* 27:4256)
763. GURVITZ, MILTON S. *An Experimental Application of Wechsler-Bellevue Type Tests in an Attempt to Discriminate and Diagnose Psychopathic Personality Types Resident in a Penal Institution.* Doctor's thesis, New York University (New York, N.Y.), 1950. (*DA* 10:234)
764. KOGAN, WILLIAM SANFORD. "An Investigation Into the Relationship Between Psychometric Patterns and Psychiatric Diagnosis." *J General Psychol* 43:17–46 Jl '50. * (*PA* 25:6215)
765. RAPAPORT, DAVID. "Diagnostic Testing in Psychiatric Practice." *B N Y Acad Med* 26:115–25 F '50. * (*PA* 24:5250)
766. WEBER, GEORGE H. "Some Qualitative Aspects of an Exploratory Personality Study of 15 Juvenile Automobile Thieves." *Trans Kans Acad Sci* 53:548–56 '50. * (*PA* 25:7574)
767. CANTER, AARON HERMAN. "Direct and Indirect Measures of Psychological Deficit in Multiple Sclerosis: Part 1." *J General Psychol* 44:3–25 Ja '51. * (*PA* 25:7027)
768. CANTER, AARON HERMAN. "Direct and Indirect Measures of Psychological Deficit in Multiple Sclerosis: Part 2." *J General Psychol* 44:27–50 Ja '51. * (*PA* 25:7028)
769. CARSCALLEN, H. B.; BUCK, C. W.; AND HOBBS, G. E.

"Clinical and Psychological Investigation of Prefrontal Lobotomy in Chronic Schizophrenia." *Arch Neurol & Psychiatry* 65:206–20 F '51. * (*PA* 25:6996)

770. KANTOR, ROBERT E., AND BOYES, FREDERICK E. "Effects of a Supranormal Diet of Glutamic Acid on the Test Performance of Paretics." *Sci* 113:681–2 Je 15 '51. * (*PA* 26:1646)

771. KLINE, MILTON V. "Hypnosis and Age Progression: A Case Report." *J Genetic Psychol* 78:195–205 Je '51. * (*PA* 26:2613)

772. KRAL, V. A., AND DÖRKEN, HERBERT, JR. "Comparative Psychological Study of Hyperkinetic and Akinetic Extrapyramidal Disorders." *Arch Neurol & Psychiatry* 66:431–42 O '51. * (*PA* 26:2937)

773. LUCHINS, ABRAHAM S. "The Einstellung Test of Rigidity: Its Relation to Concreteness of Thinking." *J Consult Psychol* 15:303–10 Ag '51. * (*PA* 26:6071)

774. MERCER, MARGARET, AND HECKER, ARTHUR O. "The Use of Tolserol (Myanesin) in Psychological Testing." *J Clin Psychol* 7:263–6 Jl '51. * (*PA* 26:926)

775. REED, HOMER R. "The Intelligence of Epileptics." *J Genetic Psychol* 78:145–52 Je '51. * (*PA* 26:2942)

776. STEISEL, IRA M. "The Relation Between Test and Retest Scores on the Wechsler–Bellevue Scale (Form I) for Selected College Students." *J Genetic Psychol* 79:155–62 D '51. * (*PA* 26:5633)

777. STEISEL, IRA M. "Retest Changes in Wechsler-Bellevue Scores as a Function of the Time Interval Between Examinations." *J Genetic Psychol* 79:199–203 D '51. * (*PA* 26:5634)

778. THOMPSON, CLARE WRIGHT. "Decline in Limit of Performance Among Adult Morons." *Am J Psychol* 64:203–15 Ap '51. * (*PA* 26:3489)

779. WILLENSON, DAVID. *Relation of Subtest Performance on the Wechsler-Bellevue Intelligence Scale to the Effects of Psychosurgery.* Master's thesis, Columbia University (New York, N.Y.), 1951.

780. BERGER, DAVID G. *The Emotional Reaction on Admission to a Tuberculosis Hospital.* Doctor's thesis, Michigan State College (East Lansing, Mich.), 1952. (*DA* 14:550)

781. CALDWELL, BETTYE McDONALD, AND WATSON, ROBERT I. "An Evaluation of Psychologic Effects of Sex Hormone Administration in Aged Women: 1, Results of Therapy After Six Months." *J Gerontol* 7:228–44 Ap '52. * (*PA* 27:1874)

782. DILLER, LEONARD. "A Comparison of the Test Performances of Delinquent and Non-Delinquent Girls." *J Genetic Psychol* 81:167–83 D '52. * (*PA* 27:6658)

783. MENSH, IVAN N.; SCHWARTZ, HENRY G.; MATARAZZO, RUTH G.; AND MATARAZZO, JOSEPH D. "Psychological Functioning Following Cerebral Hemispherectomy in Man." *Arch Neurol & Psychiatry* 67:787–96 Je '52. * (*PA* 27:2167)

784. RAUB, EDWIN S.; MERCER, MARGARET; AND HECKER, ARTHUR O. "A Study of Psychotic Patients Assumed To Be Mentally Deficient on the Basis of School Progress and Social Adjustment." *Am J Mental Def* 57:82–8 O '52. * (*PA* 27:3704)

785. SUMMERSKILL, JOHN; SEEMAN, WILLIAM; AND MEALS, DONALD W. "An Evaluation of Postelectroshock Confusion With the Reiter Apparatus." *Am J Psychiatry* 108:835–8 My '52. * (*PA* 27:515)

786. DOUST, JOHN W. LOVETT; SCHNEIDER, ROBERT A.; TALLAND, GEORGE A.; WALSH, MICHAEL A.; AND BARKER, G. B. "Studies on the Physiology of Awareness: The Correlation Between Intelligence and Anoxemia in Senile Dementia." *J Nerv & Mental Dis* 117:383–98 My '53. * (*PA* 29:1258)

787. DOZIER, JUSTIN P., AND GETZ, S. B. "Problems Involved in the Placement of a Deaf Puerto Rican Child in an Educational Environment in the United States." *Am Ann Deaf* 98:260–7 Mr '53. * (*PA* 28:3253)

788. FLANARY, WOODROW. *A Study of the Possible Use of the Wechsler-Bellevue Scale in Diagnosis of Reading Difficulties of Adolescent Youth.* Doctor's thesis, University of Virginia (Charlottesville, Va.), 1953. (*DA* 14:1045)

789. MURPHY, MARY MARTHA. "Social Class Differences in Intellectual Characteristics of Alcoholics." *Q J Studies Alcohol* 14:192–6 Je '53. * (*PA* 28:2923)

790. STEVENSON, WILLIAM D. *Form II of the Wechsler-Bellevue Scale as a Predictor of Academic Success.* Master's thesis, University of Arizona (Tucson, Ariz.), 1953.

791. STRUCKETT, PAULINE B. A. "Effect of Prefrontal Lobotomy on Intellectual Functioning in Chronic Schizophrenia." *Arch Neurol & Psychiatry* 69:293–304 Mr '53. * (*PA* 28:1346)

792. VAN LENNEP, J. E. "Some Considerations Regarding the Clinical-Psychological Examination of Paranoid States." *Folia Psychiatrica Neurologica et Neurochirurgica Neerlandica* (Netherlands) 56:769–78 '53. *

793. WEXLER, MURRAY. *The Relationship Between Personality Organization and Electroshock: A Comparative Study of the Personality Characteristics of Psychotic Patients Who Improve or Do Not Improve From Electroshock Therapy.* Doctor's thesis, New York University (New York, N.Y.), 1953. (*DA* 14:2281)

794. CADMAN, WILLIAM H., MISBACH, LORENZ; AND BROWN, DONALD V. "An Assessment of Round-Table Psychotherapy." *Psychol Monogr* 68(13):1–48 '54. * (*PA* 29:7345)

795. CALDWELL, BETTYE McDONALD, AND WATSON, ROBERT I. "An Evaluation of Sex Hormone Replacement in Aged Women." *J Genetic Psychol* 85:181–200 D '54. * (*PA* 29:7046)

796. CHANCE, JUNE; LOTSOF, ERWIN J.; PINE, IRVING; PATTERSON, RALPH M.; AND CRAIG, JAMES. "Effects of Cortisone on Psychiatric Patients." *Psychosom Med* 16:516–25 N–D '54. * (*PA* 29:6020)

797. CLARKE, A. D. B., AND CLARKE, A. M. "Cognitive Changes in the Feebleminded." *Brit J Psychol* 45:173–9 Ag '54. * (*PA* 29:4256)

798. COLGAN, CARROLL M. "Critical Flicker Frequence, Age, and Intelligence." *Am J Psychol* 67:711–3 D '54. * (*PA* 30:2126)

799. DUNHAM, RALPH E. "Factors Related to Recidivism in Adults." *J Social Psychol* 39:77–91 F '54. * (*PA* 28:8866)

800. GALLAHER, PHILLIP J. *The Influence of Sex Differences and Handedness on the Digit Symbol Subtest of the Wechsler-Bellevue.* Master's thesis, San Diego State College (San Diego, Calif.), 1954.

801. HEILBRUN, ALFRED B., JR. *The Localization of Cerebral Lesions by the Use of Psychological Tests.* Doctor's thesis, State University of Iowa (Iowa City, Iowa), 1954. (*DA* 14:1804)

802. HERNDON, C. NASH. "Intelligence in Family Groups in the Blue Ridge Mountains." *Eug Q* (England) 1:53–7 Mr '54. * (*PA* 28:8556)

803. HILER, EDWARD WESLEY. *An Investigation of Psychological Factors Associated With Premature Termination of Psychotherapy.* Doctor's thesis, University of Michigan (Ann Arbor, Mich.), 1954. (*DA* 14:712)

804. HOLZBERG, JULES D.; ALESSI, SALVATORE L.; AND TALKOFF, ALVIN. "Judgments of Premorbid Intellectual Functioning in Severely Impaired Psychiatric Patients." *J Clin Psychol* 10:219–24 Jl '54. * (*PA* 29:2793)

805. LEWINSKI, ROBERT J. "Variations in Mental Ability According to Month, Season, and Period of Birth." *J Genetic Psychol* 85:281–8 D '54. * (*PA* 29:6914)

806. MAILER, AUDREY B. "Effects on Mephenesin and Prenderol on Intellectual Functions of Mental Patients." *J Clin Psychol* 10:283–5 Jl '54. * (*PA* 29:2643)

807. REITAN, RALPH M. "Intelligence and Language Functions in Dysphasic Patients." *Dis Nerv System* 15:131–7 My '54. * (*PA* 29:6114)

808. ROGERS, LAWRENCE S., AND TAYLOR, JAMES W. "Case Report on a Mental Hygiene Clinic Patient Tested Before and After Frontal Lobe Injury." *J Clin Psychol* 10:75–9 Ja '54. * (*PA* 28:7908)

809. RUBIN-RABSON, GRACE. "Correlates of the Non-Committal Test-Item Response." *J Clin Psychol* 10:93–5 Ja '54. * (*PA* 28:7546)

810. RUBIN-RABSON, GRACE. "Intelligence and Conservative-Liberal Attitudes." *J Psychol* 37:151–4 Ja '54. * (*PA* 28:7408)

811. UECKER, ALBERT E.; FRENCH, LYLE A.; AND JOHNSON, DAVID R. "Psychological Studies of Seven Epileptic Hemiparetics Before and After Hemispherectomy." *Arch Neurol & Psychiatry* 72:555–64 N '54. * (*PA* 29:6114)

812. BAYLEY, NANCY. "On the Growth of Intelligence.". *Am Psychologist* 10:805–18 D '55. * (*PA* 30:6898)

813. GARDNER, M. J.; HAWKINS, H. M.; JUDAH, L. N.; AND MURPHREE, O. D. "Objective Measurement of Psychiatric Changes Produced by Chlorpromazine and Reserpine in Chronic Schizophrenia." *Psychiatric Res Rep* 1:77–83 Jl '55. * (*PA* 30:8411)

814. HOVEY, H. B., AND KOOL, KENNETH A. "Transient Disturbances of Thought Processes and Epilepsy." *Arch Neurol & Psychiatry* 74:287–91 S '55. * (*PA* 30:5102)

815. LEVINSON, BORIS M. "The Intelligence of Middle-Aged White Homeless Men in Receipt of Public Assistance." *Psychol Rep* 1:35–6 Mr '55. * (*PA* 30:2602)

816. LEVIT, HERBERT I. *A Study of the Effects of Electroconvulsive Therapy on Certain Psychological and Physiological Functions in Paranoid Schizophrenia.* Doctor's thesis, Temple University (Philadelphia, Pa.), 1955. (*DA* 15:1440)

817. MEYER, VICTOR, AND YATES, AUBREY J. "Intellectual Changes Following Temporal Lobectomy for Psychomotor Epilepsy: Preliminary Communication." *J Neurol Neurosurg & Psychiatry* (England) 18:44–52 F '55. * (*PA* 29:7775)

818. MORROW, ROBERT S., AND MARK, JOSEPH C. "The Correlation of Intelligence and Neurological Findings on Twenty-Two Patients Autopsied for Brain Damage." *J Consult Psychol* 19:283–9 Ag '55. * (*PA* 30:1512)

819. QUADFASEL, ANGELA FOLSOM, AND PRUYSER, PAUL W. "Cognitive Deficit in Patients With Psychomotor Epilepsy." *Epilepsia* (United States) 4:80–90 N '55. * (*PA* 30:8437)

820. TATERKA, JOHN H., AND KATZ, JOSEPH. "Study of Correlations Between Electroencephalographic and Psychological Patterns in Emotionally Disturbed Children." *Psychosom Med* 17:62–72 Ja–F '55. * (*PA* 29:7565)

821. BLANK, LEONARD, AND RAWN, MOSS L. "An Experimental Method to Measure Intellectual Functioning With Verbal and Motor Factors Minimal (1)." *J Psychol* 41:119–26 Ja '56. * (*PA* 30:8106)

822. HUNT, WILLIAM A., AND ARNHOFF, FRANKLYN N. "The Repeat Reliability of Clinical Judgments of Test Responses." *J Clin Psychol* 12:289–90 Jl '56. * (*PA* 31:6088)

823. PEYMAN, D. A. R. "An Investigation of the Effects of Group Psychotherapy on Chronic Schizophrenic Patients." *Group Psychother* 9:35–9 Ap '56. * (*PA* 33:4391)

Wechsler-Bellevue Intelligence Scale

824. REITAN, RALPH M. "Investigation of Relationships Between 'Psychometric' and 'Biological' Intelligence." *J Nerv & Mental Dis* 123:536–41 Je '56. * (*PA* 32:1345)

825. SEYMOUR, JOHN H. *Some Changes in Psychometric, Perceptual and Motor Performance as a Function of Sleep Deprivation.* Doctor's thesis, New York University (New York, N.Y.), 1956. (*DA* 16:2216)

826. TALLENT, NORMAN. "Behavioral Control and Intellectual Achievement of Secondary School Boys." *J Ed Psychol* 47: 490–503 D '56. * (*PA* 32:4624)

827. WEST, ALICE A., III. *A Comparison of Subtest Scatter on the Wechsler-Bellevue Form I and the WAIS.* Master's thesis, University of Arizona (Tucson, Ariz.), 1956.

828. YATES, AUBREY J. "The Rotation of Drawings by Brain-Damaged Patients." *J Abn & Social Psychol* 53:178–81 S '56. * (*PA* 32:3248)

829. ABRAMS, JULIAN. *Chlorpromazine in the Treatment of Chronic Schizophrenia: A Comparative Investigation of the Therapeutic Value of Chlorpromazine in Effecting Certain Psychological and Behavioral Changes in Chronic Schizophrenic Patients.* Doctor's thesis, New York University (New York, N.Y.), 1957. (*DA* 17:1589)

830. OLSON, RAY WILLARD. *A Comparison of Mental Deterioration and Intellectual Functioning in Senescent and Brain-Damaged Subjects.* Doctor's thesis, University of Utah (Salt Lake City, Utah), 1957. (*DA* 17:1813)

831. ALTROCCHI, JOHN, AND ROSENBERG, B. G. "A New Sorting Technique for Diagnosing Brain Damage." *J Clin Psychol* 14:36–40 Ja '58. * (*PA* 33:6202)

832. BLANK, LEONARD. "The Intellectual Functioning of Delinquents." *J Social Psychol* 47:9–14 F '58. * (*PA* 34:3237)

833. BROMLEY, DENNIS B. "Some Effects of Age on Short Term Learning and Remembering." *J Gerontol* 13:398–406 O '58. * (*PA* 33:9786)

834. EPPLEY, MARY VINEITA (BOOTS). *The Relationship of Personal Factors and Reading Performance to Academic Achievement of Selected Oregon State College Students.* Doctor's thesis, Oregon State University (Corvallis, Ore.), 1958. (*DA* 19:730)

835. HEILBRUN, ALFRED B., JR. "Vocabulary Response as Related to Lateralization of Cerebral Lesion: An Investigation of 'Latent Aphasia.'" *J Abn & Social Psychol* 57:237–9 S '58. * (*PA* 33:10876)

836. REITAN, RALPH M. "Qualitative Versus Quantitative Mental Changes Following Brain Damage." *J Psychol* 46: 339–46 O '58. * (*PA* 34:3350)

837. TANCK, ROLAND H. "Psychologic Changes Induced by Reserpine Therapy on a Group of Severely Disturbed Psychotics." *J Nerv & Mental Dis* 126:353–9 Ap '58. * (*PA* 33:8581)

838. FAULS, JOHN THOMAS. *Superior Readers Versus Mediocre Readers: A Comparison of Ego Organizations.* Doctor's thesis, Florida State University (Tallahassee, Fla.), 1959. (*DA* 20:3376)

839. FOSTER, ARTHUR L. "A Note Concerning the Intelligence of Delinquents." *J Clin Psychol* 15:78–9 Ja '59. * (*PA* 34:3200)

840. HABER, WILFRED. *The Contribution of Selected Variables to Success or Failure in a Vocational Rehabilitation Evaluation.* Doctor's thesis, New York University (New York, N.Y.), 1959. (*DA* 20:4171)

841. HEILBRUN, ALFRED B., JR. "Lateralization of Cerebral Lesion and Performance on Spatial-Temporal Tasks." *Arch Neurol* 1:282–7 S '59. * (*PA* 34:6461)

842. LEVINE, MURRAY; SPIVACK, GEORGE; FUSCHILLO, JEAN; AND TAVERNIER, ANN. "Intelligence, and Measures of Inhibition and Time Sense." *J Clin Psychol* 15:224–6 Ap '59. * (*PA* 35:4859)

843. PAOLINO, ALBERT F., AND FRIEDMAN, IRA. "Intellectual Changes Following Frontal Lobe Procainization." *J Clin Psychol* 15:437–9 O '59. * (*PA* 36:1DC37P)

844. RIKLAN, MANUEL; WEINER, HERMAN; AND DILLER, LEONARD. "Somato-Psychologic Studies in Parkinson's Disease." *J Nerv & Mental Dis* 129:263–72 S '59. * (*PA* 34:6482)

845. ROYO, D., AND MARTIN, F. "Standardized Psychometrical Tests Applied to the Analysis of the Effects of Anti-Convulsive Medication on the Intellectual Proficiency of Young Epileptics." *Epilepsia* (Netherlands) 1:189–207 D '59. *

846. SIMMONS, AUDREY ANN. "Factors Related to Lipreading." *J Speech & Hearing Res* 2:340–52 D '59. * (*PA* 34:6510)

847. SMITH, AARON, AND KINDER, ELAINE F. "Changes in Psychological Test Performances of Brain-Operated Schizophrenics After 8 Years." *Sci* 129:149–50 Ja 16 '59. * (*PA* 34:4700)

848. VICTOR, MAURICE; TALLAND, GEORGE A.; AND ADAMS, RAYMOND D. "Psychological Studies of Korsakoff's Psychosis: 1, General Intellectual Functions." *J Nerv & Mental Dis* 128:528–37 Je '59. * (*PA* 34:4702)

849. BORTNER, MORTON, AND BIRCH, HERBERT G. "Perceptual and Perceptual-Motor Dissociation in Brain-Damaged Patients." *J Nerv & Mental Dis* 130:49–53 Ja '60. * (*PA* 35:6742)

850. CROKES, T. G., AND KELLER, ANNA J. "Rorschach Card Rejection and IQ." *J Clin Psychol* 16:424–6 O '60. * (*PA* 37:3140)

851. FITZHUGH, LOREN C.; FITZHUGH, KATHLEEN B.; AND REITAN, RALPH M. "Adaptive Abilities and Intellectual Functioning in Hospitalized Alcoholics." *Q J Studies Alcohol* 21: 414–23 S '60. * (*PA* 35:6863)

852. ORCHINIK, C. W. "Some Psychological Aspects of Circumscribed Lesions of the Diencephalon." *Confinia Neurologica* (Switzerland) 20:292–310 '60. * (*PA* 35:2522)

853. O'REILLY, P. O., AND HARRISON, K. "The Gorham Proverbs Test." *Dis Nerv System* 21:382–5 Je '60. *

854. PHELPS, HENRY BEVERIDGE. *Conceptual Ability and the Perception of Interaction in Movement by Elderly Persons.* Doctor's thesis, Columbia University (New York, N.Y.), 1960. (*DA* 21:2007)

855. WILLIAMS, MOYRA. "The Effect of Past Experience on Mental Test Performance in the Elderly." *Brit J Med Psychol* 33:215–9 pt 2 '60. * (*PA* 36:4FI15W)

856. BRIERLEY, HARRY. "A Comparison of the Test Responses of Criminals and Mental Defectives." *Brit J Ed Psychol* 31: 212–4 Je '61. *

857. O'BRIEN, CYRIL C. "Exceptional Tonal Memory and Intelligence." *Percept & Motor Skills* 12:282 Je '61. * (*PA* 36:2HD82O)

858. TUCK, JAMES A. "Wechsler Verbal Scale Propensity in Psychopathic Patients." *Ont Psychol Assn Q* (Canada) 14:12–3 Mr '61. *

859. DE MILLE, RICHARD. "Intellect After Lobotomy in Schizophrenia: A Factor Analytic Study." *Psychol Monogr* 76(16):1–18 '62. * (*PA* 38:2784)

860. DE MILLE, RICHARD. "Intellectual Effects of Transorbital Versus Prefrontal Lobotomy in Schizophrenia: A Follow-Up Study." *J Clin Psychol* 18:61–2 Ja '62. * (*PA* 38:9042)

861. DOEHRING, DONALD G., AND REITAN, RALPH M. "Concept Attainment of Human Adults With Lateralized Cerebral Lesions." *Percept & Motor Skills* 14:27–33 F '62. * (*PA* 37:3531)

862. FITZHUGH, LOREN C.; FITZHUGH, KATHLEEN B.; AND REITAN, RALPH M. "Sensorimotor Deficits of Brain-Damaged SS in Relation to Intellectual Level." *Percept & Motor Skills* 15:603–8 D '62. * (*PA* 38:2983)

863. LASKOWITZ, DAVID. "A Comparison of the Intellectual Performance of the Juvenile Addict With Standardization Norms." *J Correct Ed* 14:31–2 Ap '62. *

864. PETERSON, PAUL G. Chap. 4, "Intellectual Abilities and Social Attitudes," pp. 55–70, 219–25. In *Aging and Personality: A Study of Eighty-Seven Older Men.* By Suzanne Reichard and Others. New York: John Wiley & Sons, Inc., 1962. Pp. xv, 237. * (*PA* 37:2962)

865. PIERCY, MALCOLM M., AND SMYTH, V. O. G. "Right Hemisphere Dominance for Certain Non-Verbal Intellectual Skills." *Brain* (England) 85:775–90 D '62. *

866. SCHEIN, EDGAR H., AND SINGER, MARGARET T. "Follow-Up Intelligence Test Data on Prisoners Repatriated From North Korea." *Psychol Rep* 11:193–4 Ag '62. * (*PA* 37:4877)

867. SKLAR, MAURICE. "Psychological Test Scores, Language Disturbances, and Autopsy Findings in Aphasia Patients." *Newsl Res Psychol* 4:65–79 Ag '62. *

868. SMITH, AARON. "Psychodiagnosis of Patients With Brain Tumors: The Validity of Hewson's Ratios in Neurological and Mental Hospital Populations." *J Nerv & Mental Dis* 135:513–33 D '62. *

869. BERGER, LESLIE; BERNSTEIN, ALVIN; KLEIN, EDWARD; COHEN, JACOB; AND LUCAS, GERALD. "Effects of Aging and Pathology on the Factorial Structure of Intelligence." *Newsl Res Psychol* 5:35–6 Ag '63. * (*PA* 38:8442)

870. BERKOWITZ, BERNARD, AND GREEN, RUSSEL F. "Changes in Intellect With Age: 1, Longitudinal Study of Wechsler-Bellevue Scores." *Newsl Res Psychol* 5:2–4 My '63. *

871. BURKE, JOAN L.; ISAAC, DONALD M.; AND LAFAVE, HUGH G. "Reappraisal of the Diagnosis of Mental Deficiency in Mental Hospitals." *J Clin Psychol* 19:359–61 Jl '63. * (*PA* 39:8369)

872. GREEN, RUSSEL F., AND BERKOWITZ, BERNARD. "Changes in Intellect With Age: 2, Factorial Analysis of Wechsler-Bellevue Scores." *Newsl Res Psychol* 5:17–8 Ag '63. * (*PA* 38:8455)

873. KRAMISH, ARTHUR A. "Examining for Mental Deficiency at an Induction Center (W.W. II)." *Mental Retard* 1:95–6+ Ap '63. * (*PA* 38:8692)

874. OSTROW, JEANNE. *A Comparative Study of Certain Aspects of Intellectual Functioning in Achieving and Low-Achieving High School Students.* Doctor's thesis, University of Michigan (Ann Arbor, Mich.), 1963. (*DA* 25:617)

875. SKLAR, MAURICE. "Relation of Psychological and Language Test Scores and Autopsy Findings in Aphasia." *J Speech & Hearing Res* 6:84–90 Mr '63. * (*PA* 38:1201)

876. BERKOWITZ, BERNARD. "Changes in Intellect With Age: 4, Changes in Achievement and Survival." *Newsl Res Psychol* 6:18–20 Ag '64. * (*PA* 39:4632)

877. BERKOWITZ, BERNARD, AND GREEN, RUSSEL. "Changes in Intellect With Age: 3, The Relationship of Heterogeneous Brain Damage to Achievement in Older People." *Newsl Res Psychol* 6:36–7 F '64. * Also repeated 6:20–1 My '64. *

878. BROVERMAN, DONALD M. "Generality and Behavioral Correlates of Cognitive Styles." *J Consult Psychol* 28:487–500 D '64. * (*PA* 39:7680)

879. FITZHUGH, KATHLEEN B., AND FITZHUGH, LOREN C. "Patterns of Abilities in Relation to Abstraction Ability and

Wechsler-Bellevue Intelligence Scale

Age in Subjects With Longstanding Cerebral Dysfunction."
J Gerontol 19:479–84 O '64. *

880. FITZHUGH, KATHLEEN B.; FITZHUGH, LOREN C.; AND REITAN, RALPH M. "Influence of Age Upon Measures of Problem Solving and Experiential Background in Subjects With Longstanding Cerebral Dysfunction." *J Gerontol* 19:132–4 Ap '64. * (*PA* 39:5632)

881. FITZHUGH, LOREN C., AND FITZHUGH, KATHLEEN B. "Relationships Between Wechsler-Bellevue Form I and WAIS Performances of Subjects With Longstanding Cerebral Dysfunction." *Percept & Motor Skills* 19:539–43 O '64. * (*PA* 39:8348)

882. GINETT, LYNDON E., AND MORAN, LOUIS J. "Stability of Vocabulary Performance by Schizophrenics." *J Consult Psychol* 28:178–9 Ap '64. * (*PA* 39:2675)

883. GREEN, RUSSEL F., AND BERKOWITZ, BERNARD. "Changes in Intellect With Age: 2, Factorial Analysis of Wechsler-Bellevue Scores." *J Genetic Psychol* 104:3–18 Mr '64. * (*PA* 39:5120)

884. HARROWER, MOLLY. *Appraising Personality: An Introduction to Projective Techniques, Revised Edition*, pp. 101–23. New York: Franklin Watts, Inc., 1964. Pp. xiv, 302. * (*PA* 39:7895)

885. JENKIN, NOEL; SPIVACK, GEORGE; LEVINE, MURRAY; AND SAVAGE, WILLIAM. "Wechsler Profiles and Academic Achievement in Emotionally Disturbed Boys." Abstract. *J Consult Psychol* 28:290 Je '64. * (*PA* 39:5926, title only)

886. JUEL-NIELSEN, NIELS. "Individual and Environment: A Psychiatric-Psychological Investigation of Monozygotic Twins Reared Apart." *Acta Psychiatrica Scandinavica Supplementum* (Denmark) 183:1–292 '64. *

887. KIRSCHNER, DAVID. "Differences in Gradients of Stimulus Generalization as a Function of 'Abstract' and 'Concrete' Attitude." *J Consult Psychol* 28:160–4 Ap '64. * (*PA* 39:2389)

888. KRAL, V. A.; GRAD, B.; CRAMER-AZIMA, F.; AND RUSSELL, L. "Biologic, Psychologic, and Sociologic Studies in Normal Aged Persons and Patients With Senile Psychosis." *J Am Geriatrics Soc* 12:21–37 Ja '64. *

889. LANSDELL, HERBERT, AND MIRSKY, ALLAN F. "Attention in Focal and Centrencephalic Epilepsy." *Exp Neurol* 9:463–9 Je '64. * (*PA* 39:5620)

890. LEVINSON, BORIS M. "The 'Beat' Phenomenon in Wechsler Tests." *J Clin Psychol* 20:118–20 Ja '64. * (*PA* 39:10133)

891. MATTHEWS, CHARLES G., AND FOLK, EARL D. "Finger Localization, Intelligence, and Arithmetic in Mentally Retarded Subjects." *Am J Mental Def* 69:107–13 Jl '64. * (*PA* 39:2525)

892. MATTHEWS, CHARLES G., AND MANNING, GEORGE C., JR. "Psychological Test Performances in Three Electroencephalographic Classifications of Mentally Retarded Subjects." *Am J Mental Def* 68:485–92 Ja '64. * (*PA* 39:2526)

893. MATTHEWS, CHARLES G., AND REITAN, RALPH M. "Correlations of Wechsler-Bellevue Rank Orders of Subtest Means in Lateralized and Non-lateralized Brain-damaged Groups." *Percept & Motor Skills* 19:391–9 O '64. * (*PA* 39:8354)

894. PRESTON, CAROLINE E. "Psychological Testing With Northwest Coast Alaskan Eskimos." *Genetic Psychol Monogr* 69:323–419 My '64. * (*PA* 39:4713)

895. REITAN, RALPH M. Chap. 14, "Psychological Deficits Resulting From Cerebral Lesions in Man," pp. 295–312. In *The Frontal Granular Cortex and Behavior: A Symposium*. Edited by J. M. Warren and K. Akert. New York: McGraw-Hill Co., 1964. Pp. x, 492. *

896. RIKLAN, MANUEL, AND LEVITA, ERIC. "Psychological Effects of Lateralized Basal Ganglia Lesions: A Factorial Study." *J Nerv & Mental Dis* 138:233–40 Mr '64. * (*PA* 39:4087)

897. SCHON, MARTHA. "Hypothyroidism: A Psychoendocrinological Evaluation." *Psychosomatics* 5:203–12 Jl–Ag '64. *

898. SEYBOLD, FRED R., AND PEDRINI, DUILIO T. "The Relation Between Wechsler-Bellevue Subtests and Academic Achievement Using Institutionalized Retardates." *Psychiatirc Q* 38:635–49 O '64. * (*PA* 39:12755)

899. SHIMOTA, HELEN E. "Reading Skills in Emotionally Disturbed, Institutionalized Adolescents." *J Ed Res* 58:106–11 N '64. *

900. SMITH, AARON. "Mental Deterioration in Chronic Schizophrenia." *J Nerv & Mental Dis* 139:479–87 N '64. *

901. SWENSON, EDWIN WAYNE. *A Comparison of the Wechsler-Bellevue, Form I, and the Wechsler Adult Intelligence Scale for a Population of Average Intelligence*. Master's thesis, University of Utah (Salt Lake City, Utah), 1964.

902. TAVRIS, EDWARD. "An Attempt to Distinguish Between 'Successful' and 'Unsuccessful' Separation Groups in a Hospital for Mentally Retarded Patients." *Training Sch B* 60:184–91 F '64. * (*PA* 39:5488)

903. BERKOWITZ, BERNARD. "Changes in Intellect With Age: 4, Changes in Achievement and Survival in Older People." *J Genetic Psychol* 107:3–14 S '65. *

904. BERKOWITZ, BERNARD, AND GREEN, RUSSEL F. "Changes in Intellect With Age: 5, Differential Changes as Functions of Time Interval and Original Score." *J Genetic Psychol* 107:179–92 D '65. * (*PA* 40:5284)

905. BURNETT, ALASTAIR. "Comparison of the PPVT, Wechsler-Bellevue, and Stanford-Binet on Educable Retardates." *Am J Mental Def* 69:712–5 Mr '65. * (*PA* 39:12715)

906. COHEN, EDWIN. "Examiner Differences With Individual Intelligence Tests." *Percept & Motor Skills* 20:1324 Je '65. * (*PA* 39:15316)

907. DE MILAN, JEAN. "Bilingualism and the Wechsler Vocabulary Scales." *J Clin Psychol* 21:298 Jl '65. * (*PA* 39:15346)

908. FITZHUGH, KATHLEEN B., AND FITZHUGH, LOREN C. "Effects of Early and Later Onset of Cerebral Dysfunction Upon Psychological Test Performance." *Percept & Motor Skills* 20:1099–100 Je '65. * (*PA* 39:15321)

909. FITZHUGH, LOREN C.; FITZHUGH, KATHLEEN B.; AND REITAN, RALPH M. "Adaptive Abilities and Intellectual Functioning of Hospitalized Alcoholics: Further Considerations." *Q J Studies Alcohol* 26:402–11 Je '65. * (*PA* 40:2900)

910. GREEN, RUSSEL F., AND BERKOWITZ, BERNARD. "Changes in Intellect With Age: 3, The Relationship of Heterogeneous Brain Damage to Achievement in Older People." *J Genetic Psychol* 106:349–59 Je '65. * (*PA* 39:14787)

911. HAMILTON, J., AND McKENNA, B. "Sex Differences in the Wechsler Intelligence Tests." *Can Psychologist* 6a:353–7 O '65. *

912. HUNT, WILLIAM A.; SCHWARTZ, MELVIN L.; AND WALKER, RONALD E. "Judgmental Bias in the Differentiation of Process and Reactive Schizophrenia." *J Clin Psychol* 21:172 Ap '65. * (*PA* 39:12847)

913. KRAUS, J. "Discriminatory Power of the Wechsler-Bellevue Intelligence Scale Subtests Within the Range of Mental Defective Functioning." *Am J Mental Def* 69:571–4 Ja '65. * (*PA* 39:10129)

914. LANSDELL, H., AND URBACH, NELLY. "Sex Differences in Personality Measures Related to Size and Side of Temporal Lobe Ablations." Abstract. *Proc Ann Conv Am Psychol Assn* 73:113–4 '65. * (*PA* 39:14113)

915. POLLACK, MAX; KLEIN, DONALD F.; WILLNER, ARTHUR; BLUMBERG, ARNOLD; AND FINK, MAX. "Imipramine-Induced Behavioral Disorganization in Schizophrenic Patients: Physiological and Psychological Correlates." *Recent Adv Biol Psychiatry* 7:53–61 '65. *

916. PRADO, WILLIAM M., AND CANNON, ROBERT C. "Shipley-Hartford and Wechsler-Bellevue Intellectual Functioning: A Selection Screening Approach." *Psychol Rep* 16:853–6 Je '65. * (*PA* 39:15260)

917. PRADO, WILLIAM M., AND SCHNADT, FREDERICK. "Differences in WAIS—WB Functioning of Three Psychiatric Groups." *J Clin Psychol* 21:184–6 Ap '65. * (*PA* 39:12305)

918. REED, HOMER B. C., JR.; REITAN, RALPH M.; AND KLØVE, HALLGRIM. "Influence of Cerebral Lesions on Psychological Test Performances of Older Children." *J Consult Psychol* 29:247–51 Je '65. * (*PA* 39:12702)

919. RIKLAN, MANUEL; LEVITA, ERIC; AND COOPER, IRVING S. "Psychological Effects of Bilateral Subcortical Surgery for Parkinson's Disease." *J Nerv & Mental Dis* 141:403–9 O '65. * (*PA* 40:5052)

920. SPREEN, OTFRIED, AND BENTON, ARTHUR L. "Comparative Studies of Some Psychological Tests for Cerebral Damage." *J Nerv & Mental Dis* 140:323–33 My '65. * (*PA* 40:700)

921. BAILEY, MATTOX A. "Normalized Vocabulary Scores Equivalent to Wechsler-Bellevue Intelligence Quotient." *Newsl Res Psychol* 8:23–5 F '66. *

922. BATMAN, ROBERT H.; ALBEE, GEORGE W.; AND LANE, ELLEN A. "Intelligence Test Performance of Chronic and Recovered Schizophrenics." Abstract. *Proc 74th Ann Conv Am Psychol Assn* 1:173–4 '66. * (*PA* 41:6108)

923. BLACK, ALAN H., AND DAVIS, LEO J., JR. "The Relationship Between Intelligence and Sensorimotor Proficiency in Retardates." *Am J Mental Def* 71:55–9 Jl '66. * (*PA* 40:11420)

924. BLUNDELL, ELIZABETH. "Parietal Lobe Dysfunction in Subnormal Patients." *J Mental Def Res* (England) 10:141–52 Je '66. * (*PA* 41:1814)

925. BURNETT, ALASTAIR. "Borderline Intelligence: Some Problems and Implications." *Mental Retard* 4:3–8 Je '66. *

926. DAVIS, LEO J., JR., AND REITAN, RALPH M. "Methodological Note on the Relationship Between Ability to Copy a Simple Configuration and Wechsler Verbal and Performance IQs." *Percept & Motor Skills* 22:381–2 Ap '66. * (*PA* 40:8850)

927. DAVIS, LEO J., JR.; HAMLETT, IONA C.; AND REITAN, RALPH M. "Relationship of Conceptual Ability and Academic Achievement to Problem-Solving and Experiential Backgrounds of Retardates." *Percept & Motor Skills* 22:499–505 Ap '66. * (*PA* 40:9152)

928. GOLDBERG, LEWIS R., AND WERTS, CHARLES E. "The Reliability of Clinicians' Judgments: A Multitrait-Multimethod Approach." *J Consult Psychol* 30:199–206 Je '66. * (*PA* 40:8999)

929. GUERTIN, WILSON H.; LADD, CLAYTON E.; FRANK, GEORGE H.; RABIN, ALBERT I.; AND HIESTER, DOUGLAS S. "Research With the Wechsler Intelligence Scales for Adults: 1960–1965." *Psychol B* 66:385–409 N '66. * (*PA* 41:40)

930. HILER, E. WESLEY. "Prognostic Indicators for Children in a Psychiatric Hospital." *J Consult Psychol* 30:169–71 Ap '66. * (*PA* 40:6773)

Wechsler-Bellevue Intelligence Scale

931. HOROWITZ, FRANCES DEGEN. "The Relationship Between Wechsler Intelligence Quotients and Parsons Language-Sample Scores of Mentally Retarded Children." *J Genetic Psychol* 108:59–63 Mr '66. * *(PA* 40:10400)

932. HUNT, WILLIAM A.; QUAY, HERBERT C.; AND WALKER, RONALD E. "The Validity of Clinical Judgments of Asocial Tendency." *J Clin Psychol* 22:116–8 Ja '66. * *(PA* 40:4410)

933. MATTHEWS, CHARLES G.; FOLK, EARL D.; AND ZERFAS, PHILIP G. "Lateralized Finger Localization Deficits and Differential Wechsler-Bellevue Results in Retardates." *Am J Mental Def* 70:695–702 Mr '66. * *(PA* 40:6983)

934. PURDY, RUTH SANDERS. *The Developmental Process, the Inhibition Process, and the Production of Human Movement on the Kinget Drawing Completion Test.* Doctor's thesis, University of Oklahoma (Norman, Okla.), 1966. *(DA* 27:1680A)

935. REED, HOMER B. C., JR., AND FITZHUGH, KATHLEEN B. "Patterns of Deficits in Relation to Severity of Cerebral Dysfunction in Children and Adults." *J Consult Psychol* 30:98–102 Ap '66. * *(PA* 40:6963)

936. REITAN, RALPH M. "Diagnostic Inferences of Brain Lesions Based on Psychological Test Results." *Can Psychologist* 7a(4):368–83 '66. * *(PA* 41:2477)

937. RUBINO, CARL A. "Chronic Brain Damage and the Wechsler-Bellevue." *Ont Psychol Assn Q* (Canada) 19:64–9 su '66. *

938. SHANAN, JOEL; COHEN, MARGALITH; AND ADLER, EMIL. "Intellectual Functioning in Hemiplegic Patients After Cerebrovascular Accidents." *J Nerv & Mental Dis* 143:181–9 Ag '66. * *(PA* 41:4893)

939. SHARON (SINGER), SHLOMO. "Family Interaction With Schizophrenics and Their Siblings." *J Abn Psychol* 71:345–53 O '66. * *(PA* 40:13385)

940. SMITH, AARON. "Intellectual Functions in Patients With Lateralized Frontal Tumours." *J Neurol Neurosurg & Psychiatry* (England) 29:52–9 F '66. *

941. SMITH, AARON. "Verbal and Nonverbal Test Performances of Patients With 'Acute' Lateralized Brain Lesions (Tumors)." *J Nerv & Mental Dis* 141:517–23 N '66. * *(PA* 40:6964)

942. SPREEN, OTFRIED, AND ANDERSON, CHARLES W. G. "Sibling Relationship and Mental Deficiency Diagnosis as Reflected in Wechsler Test Patterns." *Am J Mental Def* 71:406–10 N '66. * *(PA* 41:1850)

943. DAVIS, LEO J., JR., AND REITAN, RALPH M. "Dysphasia and Constructional Dyspraxia Items, and Wechsler Verbal and Performance IQs in Retardates." *Am J Mental Def* 71:604–8 Ja '67. * *(PA* 41:6179)

944. HONZIK, MARJORIE P. "Prediction of Differential Abilities at Age 18 From the Early Family Environment." Abstract. *Proc 75th Ann Conv Am Psychol Assn* 2:151–2 '67. * *(PA* 41:13595)

945. KUNDU, RAMANATH. "A Comparison of Stanford-Binet and Wechsler-Bellevue Scales." *Indian Psychol R* 3:114–8 Ja '67. * *(PA* 41:8901)

946. REED, JAMES C., AND FITZHUGH, KATHLEEN B. "Factor Analysis of WB-1 and WAIS Scores of Patients With Chronic Cerebral Dysfunction." *Percept & Motor Skills* 25:517–21 O '67. * *(PA* 42:5964)

947. REED, JAMES C., AND REED, HOMER C., JR. "Concept Formation Ability and Non-Verbal Abstract Thinking Among Older Children With Chronic Cerebral Dysfunction." *J Spec Ed* 1:157–61 w '67. * *(PA* 41:12362)

948. ASKAR, A. M.; RAKHAWY, Y. T.; AND SHAALAN, M. "Conceptual Measurement as a Means of Assessing Therapeutic Changes in Schizophrenia." *J Egypt Med Assn* 51(1):1–17 '68. *

949. ASKAR, A. M.; SHAALAN, M.; AND RAKHAWY, Y. T. "The Stability of Vocabulary in Schizophrenics." *J Egypt Med Assn* 51(4):227–33 '68. *

950. BAYLEY, NANCY. "Behavioral Correlates of Mental Growth: Birth to Thirty-Six Years." *Am Psychologist* 23:1–17 Ja '68. * *(PA* 42:8705)

951. DRASH, PHILIP W.; GREENBERG, NANCY E.; AND MONEY, JOHN. Chap. 39, "Intelligence and Personality in Four Syndromes of Dwarfism," pp. 568–81. In *Human Growth, Body Composition, Cell Growth, Energy, and Intelligence.* Edited by Donald B. Cheek. Philadelphia, Pa.: Lea & Febiger, 1968. Pp. xxx, 781. *

952. KISSIN, BENJAMIN; ROSENBLATT, SIDNEY M.; AND MACHOVER, SOLOMON. "Prognostic Factors in Alcoholism." *Psychiatric Res Rep Am Psychiatric Assn* 24:22–43 Mr '68. * *(PA* 43:1099)

953. LANSDELL, HERBERT. "The Use of Factor Scores From the Wechsler-Bellevue Scale of Intelligence in Assessing Patients With Temporal Lobe Removals." *Cortex* (Italy) 4:257–68 S '68. * *(PA* 43:4325)

954. PEAK, DANIEL T. "Changes in Short-Term Memory in a Group of Aging Adults." *J Gerontol* 23:9–16 Ja '68. *

955. RAPAPORT, DAVID; GILL, MERTON M.; AND SCHAFER, ROY; EDITED BY ROBERT R. HOLT. Chap. 3, "The Wechsler-Bellevue Scale," pp. 71–160. In their *Diagnostic Psychological Testing, Revised Edition.* New York: International Universities Press, Inc., 1968. Pp. xi, 562. *

956. SCHUCMAN, HELEN, AND THETFORD, WILLIAM N. "Expressed Symptoms and Personality Traits in Conversion Hysteria." *Psychol Rep* 23:231–43 Ag '68. * *(PA* 43:7148)

957. WILLARD, LOUISA A. "A Comparison of Culture Fair Test Scores With Group and Individual Intelligence Test Scores of Disadvantaged Negro Children." *J Learn Dis* 1:584–9 O '68. * *(PA* 45:3968)

958. APPELBAUM, STEPHEN A.; COYNE, LOLAFAYE; AND SIEGAL, RICHARD S. "Change in IQ During and After Long-Term Psychotherapy." *J Proj Tech & Pers Assess* 33(3):290–7 Je '69. * *(PA* 43:14310)

959. ASKAR, A. M.; EL-GUNDY, T.; AND SHAHEEN, O. "Effect of Thioproperazine (Majeptil) on Some Wechsler Bellevue Subtests." *J Egypt Med Assn* 52(10):807–12 '69. *

960. BLUM, JUNE E. *Psychological Changes Between the 7th and 9th Decades of Life.* St. John's University (Jamaica, N.Y.), 1969. *(DAI* 30:3854B)

961. BLUM, JUNE E., AND JARVIK, LISSY F. "Variations in Intellectual Decline as Indicators of Pathology: A Longitudinal Twin Study." Abstract. *Proc 77th Ann Conv Am Psychol Assn* 4(2):743–4 '69. * *(PA* 44:499)

962. HAMLIN, ROY M. "The Stability of Intellectual Function in Chronic Schizophrenia." *J Nerv & Mental Dis* 149(6):496–503 D '69. * *(PA* 44:8863)

963. JANSSEN, R. H. C.; WELMAN, A. J.; AND COLLA, P. "Wechsler-Bellevue Test and Brain-Damaged Patients." *Nederlands Tijdschrift voor de Psychologie en haar Grensgebieden* (Netherlands) 24(5):257–66 My–Je '69. * *(PA* 44:5517)

964. LANSDELL, H. "Verbal and Nonverbal Factors in Right-Hemisphere Speech: Relation to Early Neurological History." *J Comp & Physiol Psychol* 69(4):734–8 D '69. * *(PA* 44:2694)

965. SATTLER, JEROME M. "Effects of Cues and Examiner Influence on Two Wechsler Subtests." *J Consult & Clin Psychol* 33(6):716–21 D '69. * *(PA* 44:4171)

966. SERAFETINIDES, E. A. "Psychological Effects of Sudden Complete Hemianopia." *Percept & Motor Skills* 28(1):206 F '69. * *(PA* 43:11749)

967. WYSOCKI, BOLESLAW A., AND WYSOCKI, AYDIN C. "Cultural Differences as Reflected in Wechsler-Bellevue Intelligence (WBII) Test." *Psychol Rep* 25(1):95–101 Ag '69. * *(PA* 44:3623)

968. APPELBAUM, STEPHEN A.; COYNE, LOLAFAYE; AND SIEGAL, RICHARD S. "Routes to Change in IQ During and After Long Term Psychotherapy." *J Nerv & Mental Dis* 151(5): 310–5 N '70. * *(PA* 45:10050)

969. BLUM, JUNE E.; JARVIK, LISSY F.; AND CLARK, EDWARD T. "Rate of Change on Selective Tests of Intelligence: A Twenty-Year Longitudinal Study." *J Gerontol* 25(3):171–6 Jl '70. *

970. BOLL, THOMAS J., AND REITAN, RALPH M. "Deficits in Adaptive Abilities in Parkinson's Disease." Abstract. *Proc 78th Ann Conv Am Psychol Assn* 5(2):549–50 '70. * *(PA* 44:19137)

971. CRANDALL, VIRGINIA C., AND BATTLE, ESTHER S. "The Antecedents and Adult Correlates of Academic and Intellectual Achievement." *Minn Symposia Child Psychol* 4:36–93 '70. *

972. DHAPOLA, T. S. "Some Observations on the Use of the W-B Intelligence Scale in India." *Indian Psychol R* 7(1):55–9 Jl '70. *

973. FRANK, GEORGE H. "The Measurement of Personality From the Wechsler Tests." *Prog Exp Pers Res* 5:169–94 '70. *

974. GREEN, RUSSEL F., AND REIMANIS, GUNARS. "The Age-Intelligence Relationship—Longitudinal Studies Can Mislead." *Indus Gerontol* 6:1–16 su '70. * *(PA* 45:7981)

975. HAMLIN, ROY M. "Intellectual Function 14 Years After Frontal Lobe Surgery." *Cortex* (Italy) 6(3):299–307 S '70. * *(PA* 46:1513)

976. HIRSCH, ERNEST A. *The Troubled Adolescent: As He Emerges From Psychological Tests.* New York: International Universities Press, Inc., 1970. Pp. xv, 645. *

977. LANSDELL, H. "Relation of Extent of Temporal Removals to Closure and Visuomotor Factors." *Percept & Motor Skills* 31(2):491–8 O '70. * *(PA* 45:6846)

978. MIGNONE, R. J.; DONNELLY, E. F.; AND SADOWSKY, DORIS. "Psychological and Neurological Comparisons of Psychomotor and Non-Psychomotor Epileptic Patients." *Epilepsia* (Netherlands) 11(4):345–59 D '70. *

979. OBUCHOWSKI, K.; ZIENKIEWICZ, H.; AND GRACZYKOWSKA-KOCZOROWSKA, A. "Psychological Studies in Pituitary Dwarfism." *Polish Med J* 9(5):1229–35 '70. * *(PA* 48:1554)

980. QUERESHI, M. Y., AND MILLER, JEFFREY M. "The Comparability of the WAIS, WISC, and WBII." *J Ed Meas* 7(2):105–11 su '70. * *(PA* 44:18711)

981. QUERESHI, M. Y., AND WIDLAK, FREDERIC W. "Perceptual Diversity as a Function of Intelligence." Abstract. *Proc 78th Ann Conv Am Psychol Assn* 5(1):379–80 '70. * *(PA* 44:18613)

982. REITAN, RALPH M. "Sensorimotor Functions, Intelligence and Cognition, and Emotional Status in Subjects With Cerebral Lesions." *Percept & Motor Skills* 31(1):275–84 Ag '70. * *(PA* 45:4773)

983. RUBINO, CARL A. "Psychometric Procedures and the Detection and Exploration of Behavioral Deficits Due to Cerebral Dysfunction in Man." *Can Psychologist* 11(3):239–60 Jl '70. * *(PA* 44:21180)

984. SCHUT, DIEN; BESIJN, J. W.; BOEKE, P. E.; AND ULEMAN, A. L. "Psychological Examination Before and After Stereotactic Operations in Parkinson Patients." *Psychiatria*

Neurologia Neurochirurgia (Netherlands) 73(5):375–86 S–O '70. * (*PA* 47:11421)

985. WOO-SAM, JAMES. "Note on Wechsler Comprehension and Picture Arrangement Scores of Head-Injured Epileptics." *Percept & Motor Skills* 31(3):818 D '70. * (*PA* 45:10513)

986. LANSDELL, H. "A General Intellectual Factor Affected by Temporal Lobe Dysfunction." *J Clin Psychol* 27(2):182–4 Ap '71. * (*PA* 46:7303)

987. REDDY, MICHAEL JOSEPH. *Interaction Testing in the Measurement Marital Disturbance.* Doctor's thesis, Ohio State University (Columbus, Ohio), 1971. (*DAI* 32:6659B)

988. REITAN, RALPH M., AND BOLL, THOMAS J. "Intellectual and Cognitive Functions in Parkinson's Disease." *J Consult & Clin Psychol* 37(3):364–9 D '71. * (*PA* 47:9471)

989. REITAN, RALPH M., AND FITZHUGH, KATHLEEN B. "Behavioral Deficits in Groups With Cerebral Vascular Lesions." *J Consult & Clin Psychol* 37(2):215–23 O '71. * (*PA* 47:9486)

990. REITAN, RALPH M.; REED, JAMES C.; AND DYKEN, MARK L. "Cognitive, Psychomotor, and Motor Correlates of Multiple Sclerosis." *J Nerv & Mental Dis* 153(3):218–24 S '71. * (*PA* 47:11420)

991. WOO-SAM, JAMES; ZIMMERMAN, IRLA LEE; AND ROGAL, RICHARD. "Location of Injury and Wechsler Indices of Mental Deterioration." *Percept & Motor Skills* 32(2):407–11 Ap '71. * (*PA* 46:11364)

CUMULATIVE NAME INDEX

Aborn, M.: 269–70; *rev,* 4:361
Abrams, J.: 829
Abramson, H. A.: 548
Adams, N. A.: 408
Adams, R. D.: 848
Adcock, C. J.: 501
Adler, E.: 938
Aita, J. A.: 107
Albee, G. W.: 922
Alderdice, E. T.: 406
Alessi, S. L.: 804
Alexander, F. S.: 108
Alimena, B.: 333
Allen, L.: 166
Allen, R. M.: 109, 146–7, 189–91, 502, 504
Altrocchi, J.: 831
Altus, W. D.: 59, 80, 148, 192–4, 391, 750–1, 757; *rev,* 4:361; *exc,* 6:B503
Anastasi, A.: *exc,* 3:300
Andersen, A. L.: 258, 334
Anderson, C. W. G.: 942
Anderson, E. E.: 20
Anderson, S. F.: 20
Angers, W. P.: 528, 613, 731
Appelbaum, S. A.: 958, 968
Arenberg, D.: 633
Armitage, S. G.: 81, 107, 614
Armstrong, C. P.: 32
Armstrong, D. M.: 646
Armstrong, R. G.: 458
Arnhoff, F. N.: 822
Arnold, G. F.: 124
Askar, A. M.: 948–9, 959
Atkey, R. R.: 195
Atwell, C. R.: *exc,* 2:B1121
Azima, F. C.: 667
Bacon, C. S.: 503
Baggett, M. P.: 111
Bailey, M. A.: 921
Baldwin, A. L.: *exc,* 3:299
Balinsky, B.: 1, 3, 6, 18
Balthazar, E. E.: 687–8, 732–3
Barker, G. B.: 786
Barnett, I.: 259
Barrett, A. M.: 697
Barry, J. R.: 565
Batman, R. H.: 922
Battle, E. S.: 971
Bay, M. S.: 149
Bayley, N.: 196, 593, 812, 950
Beach, H. D.: 735
Becker, G. J.: 150
Beech, H. R.: 730
Bell, A.: 668
Bell, J. E.: 197
Belmont, L.: 434
Bensberg, G. J.: 260, 496
Benson, S.: 529
Benton, A. L.: 7–8, 920
Berger, D. G.: 780
Berger, L.: 869
Berk, R. L.: 407
Berkowitz, B.: 459, 734, 870, 872, 876–7, 883, 903–4, 910
Berks, M. D.: 149

Berman, I. R.: 181
Bernstein, A.: 869
Bernstein, L.: 620
Bernstein, R.: 460
Besijn, J. W.: 984
Biesheuvel, S.: 461, 647
Bilodeau, I. M.: 349
Binks, V. M.: 408
Birch, H. G.: 849
Birren, J. E.: 277–80, 335–6, 379, 392, 409
Black, A. H.: 923
Blackburn, A. R.: 303
Blake, R. R.: 151, 443–4
Blank, L.: 821, 832
Blatt, S. J.: 648
Blauvelt, J.: 8
Blum, J. E.: 960–1, 969
Blumberg, A.: 915
Blumberg, E.: 348
Blundell, E.: 924
Boehm, A. E.: 110
Boeke, P. E.: 984
Boll, T. J.: 970, 988
Bonier, R. J.: 689
Bortner, M.: 849
Bortner, R. W.: 737
Botwinick, J.: 336, 392, 462
Bowie, C. C.: 756
Bowman, K. M.: 163
Boyes, F. E.: 770
Brackbill, G. A.: 592
Bradway, K.: 529
Brecher, S.: 82
Breiger, B.: 566
Bressler, M. B.: 530
Bridges, C.: 649
Brierley, H.: 856
Brierley, J.: 730
Brody, A. B.: 261
Bromley, D. B.: 833
Brooks, L. E.: 126
Broverman, D. M.: 878
Brower, D.: 152
Brown, C. C.: 761
Brown, D. V.: 794
Brown, F.: 669
Brown, J. F.: 9
Brown, M. H.: 531–2, 594–5, 631
Brown, M. N.: 198
Brown, R. R.: 21
Bryan, G. E.: 531–3, 594–5, 631
Buck, C. W.: 769
Burgemeister, B. B.: 755
Burik, T. E.: 199, 262
Burke, J. L.: 871
Burnett, A.: 735, 905, 925
Burnham, C. A.: 200
Burns, W. H.: 708
Burton, A.: 201
Butler, A.: 504
Butler, A. J.: 406
Cadman, W. H.: 794
Calden, G.: 525
Caldwell, B. M.: 781, 795

Caldwell, M. B.: 567
Campbell, E. F.: 410
Campbell, J. C.: 650
Cannicott, R. G.: 349
Cannon, R. C.: 916
Canter, A. H.: 202, 270, 767–8
Caputo, D. V.: 736
Carment, D. W.: 505
Carp, A.: 153, 263
Carscallen, H. B.: 769
Carse, D.: 382
Cassel, R. H.: 708
Catterall, C. D.: 203
Chambers, W. R.: 618
Chance, J.: 796
Charles, D. C.: 557
Chesrow, E. J.: 204
Clark, E. T.: 969
Clark, J. H.: 154, 193–4, 205–6, 264–5
Clarke, A. D. B.: 797
Clarke, A. M.: 797
Clarke, F. R.: 383
Clarke, H. J.: 83
Clarke, W. V.: *exc,* 2:B1121
Cleveland, S. E.: 47
Cofer, C. N.: 132
Cohen, B.: 60, 127, 133
Cohen, D.: 134
Cohen, E.: 384, 906
Cohen, J.: 266, 337, 411–2, 534, 869
Cohen, M.: 938
Cole, D.: 418
Cole, E. M.: 111
Colgan, C. M.: 798
Colla, P.: 963
Collins, A. L.: 338, 753
Collins, J. J.: 527
Cook, M.: 506
Cook, R. A.: 690
Coon, G. P.: 86–8
Cooper, I. S.: 684, 919
Coppinger, N. W.: 737
Copple, G. E.: 155
Corotto, L. V.: 691
Corrie, C. C.: 507, 538
Corsini, R. J.: 413–4, 460, 463
Corter, H. M.: 415
Cortes, C. F.: 416
Cotzin, M.: 207, 267
Cowley, J. J.: 461
Coyne, L.: 958, 968
Coyne, W. J.: 709
Craddick, R. A.: 692
Craig, J.: 796
Cramer-Azima, F.: 888
Crandall, V. C.: 971
Crokes, T. G.: 850
Cronbach, L. J.: 208
Cronholm, B.: 738
Crookes, T. G.: 693
Crutchlow, E.: 108
Cummings, S. B.: 84, 117, 257
Cummins, J. F.: 695
Cureton, E. E.: *exc,* 3:299
Cutts, R. A.: 61, 77, 112
Daley, M. F.: 659
Dana, R. H.: 596
Darbes, A.: 694
Davidson, J. L.: 582
Davidson, K. S.: 268
Davis, J. C.: 96, 567, 597
Davis, L. J.: 923, 926–7, 943
Davis, P. C.: 417, 568
Deane, M. A.: 297
De Haan, H.: 368
DeLange, W. H.: 700
Delattre, L.: 418
Della Piana, G. M.: 540
Delli Colli, P.: 598
Demarest, R.: 128
DeMartino, H. A.: 464, 508
De Milan, J.: 907
de Mille, R.: 859–60
Denny, J. P. 744
Denton, L. R.: 627
Derner, G. F.: 269–70
Desai, M. M.: 535
DeStephens, W. P.: 465
Devonshire, M. E.: 419
Dhapola, T. S.: 972
Diamond, S.: 113
Dibner, A. S.: 695

Diers, W. C.: 761
Diller, J. C.: 536
Diller, L.: 684, 782, 844
Doehring, D. G.: 696, 861
Donnelly, E. F.: 978
Doppelt, J.: 209
Dorcus, R. M.: 399
Dore, J. J.: 466
Dörken, H.: 467, 772
Doust, J. W. L.: 786
Dozier, J. P.: 787
Drash, P. W.: 951
Dubin, S. S.: 9, 156
DuBois, P. H.: 433
Duncan, D. R.: 697
Duncan, J. O.: 468
Dunham, R. E.: 799
Durea, M. A.: 157
Dyken, M. L.: 990
Dysinger, D. W.: 47
Edmonston, W. E.: 736
Edrington, T. C.: 271
Eglash, A.: 272
Ehrmann, J. C.: 559
Eisen, V. W.: 526
El-Gundy, T.: 959
Ellis, A.: 158
Engen, T.: 420
Eppley, M. V. (B.): 834
Erwin, E. F.: 273
Escalona, S. K.: 640
Estes, S. G.: 22, 85
Everett, E. G.: 569
Everson, R. R.: 393
Falek, A.: 715, 717
Farber, I. E.: 602
Fassett, K. K.: 413–4, 463
Fauls, J. T.: 838
Fellers, G. L.: 469
Ferguson, C.: 20
Fey, W. F.: 162
Ficca, S. C.: 274
Field, J. G.: 670
Fink, M.: 915
Finkelstein, M.: 421
Fishbein, S.: 372
Fisher, G. C.: 210, 615
Fisher, G. M.: 671, 698, 710, 748
Fisher, K. A.: 211
Fisher, S.: 275
Fitzhugh, K. B.: 699, 711–2, 719, 739, 851, 862, 879–81, 908–9, 935, 946, 989
Fitzhugh, L. C.: 699, 711–2, 739, 851, 862, 8-9–81, 908–9
Flanary, W.: 788
Flynn, J. J.: 509
Fogel, J.: 507, 538
Folk, E. D.: 891, 933
Forster, C. R.: 537
Fortson, C. B.: 570
Foster, A.: 135, 510
Foster, A. L.: 839
Foster, C.: 394
Foster, C. G.: 136
Foster, D. V.: 408
Fox, C.: 137, 277–80, 379
Frandsen, A. N.: 276
Frank, G. H.: 507, 538, 571, 575, 713, 929, 973
Franklin, J. C.: 62
Freeburne, C. M.: 740
Freeman, A. V.: 159–60
Freeman, F. S.: 281
French, E. G.: 167, 225
French, L. A.: 811
Friedman, I.: 843
Fry, L. M.: 572
Frye, C. S.: 573
Fulkerson, S. C.: 565
Fuschillo, J.: 842
Gainer, W. L.: 422
Gallagher, J. J.: 207, 267
Gallaher, P. J.: 800
Gardner, M. J.: 813
Garfield, S. L.: 114, 138, 161–2, 212, 672
Gaskill, P.: 599
Gaston, C. O.: 637, 700
Geertsma, R.: 555
Geil, A.: 63
Gerboth, R.: 282, 421
Germain, G. L.: 423

[533]
Wechsler Intelligence Scale for Children.

Ages 5–15; 1949; WISC; downward extension of Form 2 of *Wechsler-Bellevue Intelligence Scale;* 13–15 scores: verbal (information, comprehension, arithmetic, similarities, vocabulary, digit span [optional], total), performance (picture completion, picture arrangement, block design, object assembly, mazes [optional], coding, total), total; David Wechsler; Psychological Corporation. (Australian edition: 1968; manual by J. A. Radcliffe and F. E. Trainer; Australian Council for Educational Research [Australia]. British edition: 1971; manual supplement by Peter Saville; NFER Publishing Co. Ltd. [England].) *

For additional information and reviews by David Freides and R. T. Osborne, see 7:431 (518 references); for a review by Alvin G. Burstein, see 6:540 (155 references); for reviews by Elizabeth D. Fraser, Gerald R. Patterson, and Albert I. Rabin, see 5:416 (111 references); for reviews by James M. Anderson, Harold A. Delp, and Boyd R. McCandless, and an excerpted review by Laurance F. Shaffer, see 4:363 (22 references). For excerpts from related book reviews, see 7:B234 (2 excerpts).

REFERENCES THROUGH 1971
1–22. See 4:363.
23–133. See 5:416.
134–288. See 6:540.
289–807. See 7:431.
808. KARLSEN, BJÖRN. *A Comparison of Some Educational and Psychological Characteristics of Successful and Unsuccessful Readers at the Elementary School Level.* Doctor's thesis, University of Minnesota (Minneapolis, Minn.), 1954. (*DA* 15:456)
809. JORDAN, THOMAS E. "Psychological Findings in a Case of Von Recklinghausen's Disease and Hyperpituitarism." *J Clin Psychol* 12:389–91 O '56. * (*PA* 32:4470)
810. MONEY, JOHN. "Psychologic Studies in Hypothyroidism: Recommendations for Case Management." *Arch Neurol & Psychiatry* 76:296–309 S '56. * (*PA* 31:4827)
811. REBHUN, ALBERT M. "The Level-Sharpening Dimension as Manifested in Other Perceptual or Non-Perceptual Tasks." *Psychol Newsl* 7:43–6 Ja-F '56. * (*PA* 31:1767)
812. RICHARDS, T. W., AND HOOPER, SARA. "Brain-Injury at Birth (Cerebral Palsy) and Perceptual Responses During Childhood and Adolescence." *J Nerv & Mental Dis* 123:117–24 F '56. * (*PA* 31:8608)
813. SPACHE, GEORGE D. "Intellectual and Personality Characteristics of Retarded Readers." *Psychol Newsl* 9:9–12 S-O '57. * (*PA* 32:4526)
814. MURSTEIN, BERNARD I. "Personality and Intellectual Changes in Leukemia: A Case Study." *J Proj Tech* 22:421–6 D '58. * (*PA* 34:1401)
815. BECK, HARRY S. "A Comparison of Convulsive Organic, Non-Convulsive Organic, and Non-Organic Public School Children." *Am J Mental Def* 63:866–75 Mr '59. * (*PA* 34:1656)
816. BRAEN, BERNARD B., AND MASLING, JOSEPH M. "Intelligence Tests Used With Special Groups of Children." *Excep Children* 26:42–5 S '59. * (*PA* 35:2194)
817. HOHMAN, LESLIE B., AND FREEDHEIM, DONALD K. "A Study of IQ Retest Evaluations on 370 Cerebral Palsied Children." *Am J Phys Med* 38:180–7 O '59. *
818. SCHACTER, FRANCES F., AND APGAR, VIRGINIA. "Perinatal Asphyxia and Psychologic Signs of Brain Damage in Childhood." *Pediatrics* 24:1016–25 D '59. *
819. WINITZ, HARRIS. "Language Skills of Male and Female Kindergarten Children." *J Speech & Hearing Res* 2:377–86 D '59. * (*PA* 34:5895)
820. HAND, JACK, AND MARTIN, J. D. "An Abbreviated Form of the Wechsler Intelligence Scale for Children." *J Crim Law Criminol & Police Sci* 51:81 My-Je '60. *
821. JACKSON, PHILIP W.; GETZELS, JACOB W.; AND XYDIS, GEORGE A. "Psychological Health and Cognitive Functioning in Adolescence: A Multivariate Analysis." *Child Develop* 31:285–98 Je '60. * (*PA* 36:3FH85J)
822. KENNEDY, WALLACE A.; SMITH, MARION; VAN DE RIET, HANNAH; VAN DE RIET, VERNON; SMITH, HERBERT; RAPP, DON; AND PAINE, R. W. "A Multidimensional Study of Mathematically Gifted Adolescents." *Child Develop* 31:655–66 D '60. * (*PA* 36:2FH55K)
823. ELKIND, DAVID. "The Development of Quantitative Thinking: A Systematic Replication of Piaget's Studies." *J Genetic Psychol* 98:37–46 Mr '61. * (*PA* 35:6143)
824. GOODSTEIN, LEONARD D. "Intellectual Impairment in Children With Cleft Palates." *J Speech & Hearing Res* 4:287–94 S '61. * (*PA* 36:2JB87G)

825. CONVERSE, HAROLD D., AND COURTNEY, JOHN MICHAEL. "A Comparative Study of the Lorge-Thorndike Group Intelligence Tests With an Individual Intelligence Test." *J Res Services* 1:1–5 My '62. *
826. MORAN, ROBERTA E. "Observations and Recommendations on the Puerto Rican Version of the Wechsler Intelligence Scale for Children." *Pedagogía* (Puerto Rico) 10:89–98 Ja-Je '62. * (*PA* 37:1205)
827. SACKS, LENORA; FEINSTEIN, ALVAN R.; AND TARANTA, ANGELO. "A Controlled Psychologic Study of Sydenham's Chorea." *J Pediatrics* 61:714–22 N '62. *
828. WITHERSPOON, Y. T. "The Measurement of Indian Children's Achievement in the Academic Tool Subjects." *J Am Indian Ed* 1:5–9 My '62. *
829. CROOKES, T. G., AND GREENE, MARGARET C. L. "Some Characteristics of Children With Two Types of Speech Disorder." *Brit J Ed Psychol* 33:31–40 F '63. * (*PA* 38:1221)
830. HARITOS-FATOUROS, MARY. *A Study of the Wechsler Intelligence Scale for Children Applied to Greek School Children.* Master's thesis, University of London (London, England), 1963.
831. KRIPPNER, STANLEY. "Sociopathic Tendencies and Reading Retardation in Children." *Excep Children* 29:258–66 F '63. *
832. ORTAR, GINA. "Is a Verbal Test Cross-Cultural?" pp. 219–35. (*PA* 39:1753) In *Scripta Hierosolymitana: Studies in Education, Vol. 13.* Jerusalem, Israel: Magnes Press, 1963. Pp. viii, 264. *
833. ROBEY, MILDRED C. "Readers Who Lacked Word Analysis Skills: A Group Diagnosis." *J Ed Res* 56:432–4 Ap '63. *
834. SEMLER, IRA J., AND ISCOE, IRA. "Comparative and Developmental Study of the Learning Abilities of Negro and White Children Under Four Conditions." *J Ed Psychol* 54:38–44 F '63. * (*PA* 37:7996)
835. BARBEE, EUNICE W. *A Comparison of the Validity of Individual and Group Administration of Intelligence Tests With First Grade Pupils.* Master's thesis, Furman University (Greenville, S.C.), 1964.
836. LOVELL, K.; SHAPTON, D.; AND WARREN, N. S. "A Study of Some Cognitive and Other Disabilities in Backward Readers of Average Intelligence as Assessed By a Non-Verbal Test." *Brit J Ed Psychol* 34:58–64 F '64. * (*PA* 38:9233)
837. POLLITT, ERNESTO, AND MONEY, JOHN. "Studies in the Psychology of Dwarfism: 1, Intelligence Quotient and School Achievement." *J Pediatrics* 64:415–21 Mr '64. *
838. WRIGHT, HELEN C. *The Analysis of WISC Profiles and Bender-Gestalt Protocols of a Sample of Elementary School Children With Reading Disability.* Master's thesis, University of Arizona (Tucson, Ariz.), 1964.
839. BELL, D. A.; TAYLOR, W. C.; AND DOCKRELL, W. B. "A Ten Year Follow-Up of Low Birth Weight Infants: Intellectual Functioning." *Alberta J Ed Res* (Canada) 11:220–5 D '65. * (*PA* 40:7538)
840. CLEVELAND, SIDNEY E.; REITMAN, E. EDWARD; AND BREWER, EARL J., JR. "Psychological Factors in Juvenile Rheumatoid Arthritis." *Arthr & Rheum* 8:1152–8 D '65. *
841. CORAH, NORMAN L.; ANTHONY, E. JAMES; PAINTER, PAUL; STERN, JOHN A.; AND THURSTON, DONALD. "Effects of Perinatal Anoxia After Seven Years." *Psychol Monogr* 79(3): 1–34 '65. * (*PA* 39:9776)
842. DREW, ARTHUR L., AND NORTON, JAMES A. "A Study of the Inheritance of Measured Intelligence." *Recent Adv Biol Psychiatry* 7:171–82 '65. *
843. MCBEATH, MARCIA. "The Effect of Pretest Interaction on a Perceptual Task." *Calif J Ed Res* 16:203–9 N '65. * (*PA* 40:4609)
844. RAJALAKSHMI, R., AND JEEVES, M. A. "Comparative Performance of Normals and Retardates of the Same Mental Age on Certain Psychological Tasks." *J Genetic Psychol* 106:39–43 Mr '65. * (*PA* 39:12748)
845. RUESS, AUBREY L. "A Comparative Study of Cleft Palate Children and Their Siblings." *J Clin Psychol* 21:354–60 O '65. * (*PA* 40:1880)
846. CAPOBIANCO, R. J. "Ocular-Manual Laterality and Reading in Adolescent Mental Retardates." *Am J Mental Def* 70:781–5 Mr '66. * (*PA* 40:6970)
847. EVANS, LIONEL. "A Comparative Study of the Wechsler Intelligence Scale for Children (Performance) and Raven's Progressive Matrices With Deaf Children." *Teach Deaf* (England) 64:76–82 Mr '66. *
848. FLOWER, RICHARD M.; VIEHWEG, RICHARD; AND RUZICKA, WILLIAM R. "The Communicative Disorders of Children With Kernicteric Athetosis: 2, Problems in Language Comprehension and Use." *J Speech & Hearing Disorders* 31:60–8 F '66. * (*PA* 40:9108)
849. GRIFFIN, DONALD CASSATT. *Admission Tests as Predictors of Gain in Reading in a Remedial School.* Master's thesis, University of California (Los Angeles, Calif.), 1966.
850. LEVY, RUSSELL H., AND MOORE, WINSTON E. "Cross-Sectional Psychometric Evaluation of Court-Labelled Delinquent Boys." *J Correct Ed* 18:7–9 Jl '66. *
851. MONEY, JOHN, AND LEWIS, VIOLA. "IQ, Genetics and Accelerated Growth: Adrenogenital Syndrome." *Johns Hopkins Med J* 118:365–73 My '66. *

852. MONEY, JOHN; WEINBERG, ROBERT S.; AND LEWIS, VIOLA. "Intelligence Quotient and School Performance in Twenty-Two Children With a History of Thyrotoxicosis." *B Johns Hopkins Hosp* 118:275–81 Mr '66. *

853. MONTGOMERY, G. W. G. "Differences in the Interrelationships of Non-Verbal Intelligence Test Scores, Educational Attainments and Residual Hearing in Selected and Unselected Populations." *Teach Deaf* (England) 64:29–33 Ja '66. *

854. ORPET, R. E., AND MEYERS, C. E. "Six Structure-of-Intellect Hypotheses in Six-Year-Old Children." *J Ed Psychol* 57:341–6 D '66. * (*PA* 41:1416)

855. PICKLES, DENNIS G. "The Wechsler Performance Scale and Its Relationship to Speech and Educational Response in Deaf Slow-Learning Children." *Teach Deaf* (England) 64:382–92 N '66. *

856. WILHELM, ROWENA. "Diagnostic Value of Test Score Differentials Found Between Measures of Visual and Auditory Memory in Severely Disabled Readers." *Acad Ther Q* 2:42–4 f '66. * (*PA* 40:13545)

857. EVERETT, GARY D. *An Analysis of the Performance of Children With Severe Articulation Problems and Children With Minimal Brain Dysfunction as Manifested on a Selected Battery of Tests.* Master's thesis, Texas Technological College (Lubbock, Tex.), 1967.

858. GITTELMAN, MARTIN, AND BIRCH, HERBERT G. "Childhood Schizophrenia: Intellect, Neurologic Status, Perinatal Risk, Prognosis, and Family Pathology." *Arch Gen Psychiatry* 17:16–25 Jl '67. * (*PA* 41:15552)

859. LEVY, RUSSELL H. "Dimensions of Mental Retardation Among Wards of the Illinois Youth Commission." *J Correct Ed* 19:12–6 O '67. *

860. MONEY, JOHN; DRASH, PHILIP W.; AND LEWIS, VIOLA. "Dwarfism and Hypopituitarism: Statural Retardation Without Mental Retardation." *Am J Mental Def* 72:122–6 Jl '67. * (*PA* 41:15732)

861. VANDENBERG, STEVEN G. "Hereditary Factors in Psychological Variables in Man, With a Special Emphasis on Cognition," pp. 99–133. In *Genetic Diversity and Human Behavior.* Viking Fund Publications in Anthropology No. 45. Edited by J. N. Spuhler. Chicago, Ill.: Aldine Publishing Co., 1967. Pp. xi, 291. *

862. BURNS, GARY W. *A Comparison of the Peabody Picture Vocabulary Test With the Stanford-Binet Intelligence Scale and With the Wechsler Intelligence Scale for Children.* Master's thesis, Sacramento State College (Sacramento, Calif.), 1968.

863. COHEN, S. ALAN. "Socially Disadvantaged Americans: Slow Learners." *Slow Learning Child* (Australia) 14:153–60 Mr '68. * (*PA* 42:19298)

864. DOMRATH, RICHARD P. "Constructional Praxis and Visual Perception in School Children." *J Consult & Clin Psychol* 32:186–92 Ap '68. * (*PA* 42:8174)

865. IRVINE, JAMES. *Correlates of Grade One Achievement.* Master's thesis, University of Alberta (Edmonton, Alta., Canada), 1968.

866. LEWIS, VIOLA G.; MONEY, JOHN; AND EPSTEIN, RALPH. "Concordance of Verbal and Nonverbal Ability in the Adrenogenital Syndrome." *Johns Hopkins Med J* 122:192–5 Ap '68. *

867. MALIN, A. J. "Adaptation of the Wechsler Intelligence Scale for Children." *J Rehabil Asia* (India) 9:19–20 O '68. *

868. MANN, LESTER; HAUGHEY, CHARLES; TREFSGAR, THEODORE F.; AND KEFFER, CHARLES E. "Achievement and Personality Measurements Associated With Progress in a Programmed Course in Decimals and Fractions at a Fifth Grade Level." *Scientia Paedagogica Experimentalis* (Belgium) 5(1):76–83 '68. * (*PA* 45:3108)

869. GRANDOVIC, MARGARET CLARK. *A Study of the Usefulness of the Bender Gestalt Test With Young Educable Retarded Children Using the Koppitz Procedures.* Doctor's thesis, Temple University (Philadelphia, Pa.), 1969. (*DAI* 32:1335A)

870. HONZIK, MARJORIE P.; COLLART, DONNA S.; ROBINSON, SAUL J.; AND FINLEY, KNOX H. "Sex Differences in Verbal and Performance IQ's of Children Undergoing Open-heart Surgery." *Sci* 164(3878):445–7 Ap 25 '69. * (*PA* 45:6906)

871. JOINER, LEE M.; ERICKSON, EDSEL L.; CRITTENDEN, JERRY B.; AND STEVENSON, VIVIAN M. "Predicting the Academic Achievement of the Acoustically-Impaired Using Intelligence and Self-Concept of Academic Ability." *J Spec Ed* 3(4):425–31 f '69. * (*PA* 44:15092)

872. MASICA, DANIEL N.; EHRHARDT, ANKE A.; AND LEWIS, VIOLA G. "IQ, Fetal Sex Hormones and Cognitive Patterns: Studies in the Testicular Feminizing Syndrome of Androgen Insensitivity." *Johns Hopkins Med J* 124(1):34–43 Ja '69. *

873. PARKER, JAMES. "Adapting School Psychological Evaluation to the Blind Child." *New Outl Blind* 63(10):305–11 D '69. * (*PA* 47:3654)

874. ROSENQUIST, CARL M., AND MEGARGEE, EDWIN I. *Delinquency in Three Cultures,* pp. 208–24. Austin, Tex.: University of Texas Press, 1969. Pp. xvi, 554. *

875. RUSCHIVAL, MARY LENA. *The Effectiveness of the Wechsler Preschool and Primary Scale of Intelligence in the Identification of Gifted Preschool Children.* Master's thesis, East Carolina University (Greenville, N.C.), 1969.

876. CARING, LILLIAN COTT. *The Relation of Cognitive Style, Sex and Intelligence to Moral Judgment in Children.* Doctor's

thesis, New York University (New York, N.Y.), 1970. (*DAI* 31:7568B)

877. COHEN, LEO. "The Effects of Material and Non-Material Reinforcement Upon Performance of the WISC Block Design Subtest by Children of Different Social Classes: A Follow-up Study." *Psychol* 7(4):41–7 N '70. * (*PA* 46:2794)

878. CRONIN, ROBERT. "I Give I.Q. Tests Without Looking." *New Outl Blind* 64(5):142–7 My '70. * (*PA* 46:9446)

879. CROWN, PHYLLIS JO. *The Effects of Race of Examiner and Standard vs. Dialect Administration of the Wechsler Preschool and Primary Scale of Intelligence on the Performance of Negro and White Children.* Doctor's thesis, Florida State University (Tallahassee, Fla.), 1970. (*DAI* 32:232A)

880. DANGEL, HARRY LEWIS. *The Biasing Effect of Pretest Information on the WISC Scores of Mentally Retarded Children.* Doctor's thesis, Pennsylvania State University (University Park, Pa.), 1970. (*DAI* 32:233A)

881. EARLY, GEORGE H., AND SHARPE, THEODORE M. "Developing Perceptual-Motor Skills: Perceptual-Motor Training and Basic Abilities." *Acad Ther* 5(3):235–40+ sp '70. * (*PA* 44:19036)

882. EAVES, LINDA C.; NUTTALL, J. C.; KLONOFF, H.; AND DUNN, H. G. "Developmental and Psychological Test Scores in Children of Low Birth Weight." *Pediatrics* 45(1):9–20 Ja '70. * Correction: 45(5):886–7 My '70. *

883. FRETZ, BRUCE R.; JOHNSON, WARREN R.; AND JOHNSON, JULIA A. "Intellectual and Perceptual Motor Development as a Function of Therapeutic Play," pp. 475–80. In *Contemporary Psychology of Sport.* Proceedings of the Second International Congress of Sport Psychology, Washington, D.C., 1968. Chicago, Ill.: Athletic Institute, 1970. Pp. xix, 878. *

884. GARMS, JOE D. "Factor Analysis of the WISC and ITPA." *Psychol* 7(4):30–1 N '70. * (*PA* 46:3067)

885. HAFNER, LAWRENCE E., AND WEAVER, WENDELL W. "Correlates of Error Rate in the Pronunciation of WISC Vocabulary Items." *J Read Behav* 3(2):27–31 sp '70–71 ['71]. *

886. HARTMAN, ROBERT KINTZ. *An Investigation of the Incremental Validity of Human Figure Drawings in the Diagnosis of Learning Disabilities.* Doctor's thesis, University of Connecticut (Storrs, Conn.), 1970. (*DAI* 31:6403A)

887. JAYAGOPAL, RAJABATHER. *Problem Solving Abilities and Psychomotor Skills of Navajo Indians, Spanish Americans and Anglos in Junior High School.* Doctor's thesis, University of New Mexico (Albuquerque, N.M.), 1970. (*DAI* 31:5035A)

888. KAUFMAN, MARTIN JOEL. *Level, Shape and Dispersion as Relevant Variables in WISC Profiles of Minimally Brain-Injured Children.* Doctor's thesis, University of Texas (Austin, Tex.), 1970. (*DAI* 31:5888A)

889. LANEY, BILLIE JOHNSON. *A Comparative Study of Expressive and Comprehensive Vocabulary Development in Male and Female Kindergarten Children.* Doctor's thesis, East Texas State University (Commerce, Tex.), 1970. (*DAI* 31:4386A)

890. LEVINE, MAUREEN. *Psychological, Neuropsychological, and Educational Correlates of Reading Deficit: Etiological and Normative Comparison.* Master's thesis, Central Michigan University (Mt. Pleasant, Mich.), 1970.

891. McCONOCHIE, WILLIAM A. "Juvenile Delinquents: Relationship Between WISC Scores, Offenses, Race, Chronological Age and Residence." *Correct Psychologist* 4(3):103–10 N–D '70. * (*PA* 49:2685)

892. McNINCH, GEORGE HAAS WILEY. *The Relationships Between Selected Perceptual Factors and Measured First Grade Reading Achievement.* Doctor's thesis, University of Georgia (Athens, Ga.), 1970. (*DAI* 31:3965A)

893. MARCHI, JACK UGO. *Comparison of Selected Piagetian Tasks With the Wechsler Intelligence Scale for Children as Measures of Mental Retardation.* Doctor's thesis, University of California (Berkeley, Calif.), 1970. (*DAI* 31:6442A)

894. MAXWELL, MICHAEL T. *The Relationship Between the Wechsler Intelligence Scale for Children and the Slosson Intelligence Test.* Master's thesis, Eastern Montana College (Billings, Mont.), 1970.

895. MOENY, WILLIAM COWIN. *An Investigation of the Relationships Between Ocular-Motor Skill and Intelligence in Mentally Retarded and Normal Children.* Doctor's thesis, University of New Mexico (Albuquerque, N.M.), 1970. (*DAI* 31:5889A)

896. NEAVES, ALISON I. "To Establish a Basis for Prognosis in Stammering." *Brit J Dis Commun* 5(1):46–58 Ap '70. * (*PA* 46:5319)

897. OWEN, DAVID R., AND SINES, JACOB O. "Heritability of Personality in Children." *Behav Genetics* 1(3–4):235–48 Ag–N '70. * (*PA* 47:10446)

898. PAGE, STEWART. "Examiner Effect, Expertise, and Intelligence Testing." *Ont Psychologist* (Canada) 2(3):181–4 '70. *

899. RAJATASILPIN, ANUSITH; SUEPSAMAN, BANCHONG; AND YAMARAT, VALAITIP. "Intellectual Development and Its Relationship to the Nutritional Status Among School Children." *J Med Assn Thailand* 53(11):788–93 N '70. *

900. REBISH, DELLA. *Learning Ability as a Function of Verbal and Nonverbal Intelligence.* Doctor's thesis, Claremont Graduate School (Claremont, Calif.), 1970. (*DAI* 31:7609B)

901. REED, JAMES C. "The Deficits of Retarded Readers—Fact or Artifact?" *Read Teach* 23(4):347–52+ Ja '70. * (*PA* 45:2972)

902. RICHARDS, HYRUM E., AND STONE, DAVID R. "The Learning and Transference of the Piagetian Concept of Conservation." *Mental Retard* 8(4):34–7 Ag '70. * (*PA* 48:1714)

903. ROSENBERGER, PETER B. "Visual Matching and Clinical Findings Among Good and Poor Readers." *Am J Dis Children* 119(2):103–10 F '70. * (*PA* 44:16376)

904. RYCHLAK, JOSEPH F. "Personality Factors in Self- and Peer-Evaluations of WISC Performance Among Middle-Class Children." *J Spec Ed* 4(3):269–77 su–f '70. * (*PA* 46:6585)

905. SCHNEIDER, JUDY H. *A Correlation Study Between Performance Scores of the Wechsler Intelligence Scale for Children and Experimental Preschool and School Age Scale of Intellectual Function With Deaf Children.* Master's thesis, Bowling Green State University (Bowling Green, Ohio), 1970.

906. SILBERBERG, NORMAN, AND FELDT, LEONARD S. "Intellectual and Perceptual Correlates of Reading Disabilities." *Skolepsykologi* (Denmark) 7(2):67–81 '70. * (*PA* 46:5502)

907. SIMMERS, CATHERINE POWELL. *Cognitive Correlates of Attitudinal Rigidity.* Doctor's thesis, Case Western Reserve University (Cleveland, Ohio), 1970. (*DAI* 32:1348A)

908. SMITH, MAXINE McGOWAN. *Patterns of Intellectual Abilities in Educationally Handicapped Children.* Doctor's thesis, Claremont Graduate School (Claremont, Calif.), 1970. (*DAI* 31:6415A)

909. WELLS, CLINTON GEORGE. *A Comparative Study of Children Grouped by Three Basic Score Patterns on the Wechsler Intelligence Scale for Children.* Doctor's thesis, University of Northern Colorado (Greeley, Colo.), 1970. (*DAI* 31:6444A)

910. WIENER, GERALD. "The Relationship of Birth Weight and Length of Gestation to Intellectual Development at Ages 8 to 10 Years." *J Pediatrics* 76(5):694–9 My '70. *

911. WYNE, MARVIN D.; COOP, RICHARD H.; AND BROOKHOUSE, DIANE B. "Information Processing in Young Mildly Retarded Children." *Am J Mental Def* 75(3):371–5 N '70. *

912. ABLES, BILLIE S. "The Use of the Draw-A-Man Test With Borderline Retarded Children Without Pronounced Pathology." *J Clin Psychol* 27(2):262–3 Ap '71. * (*PA* 46:7068)

913. ACKERMAN, PEGGY T.; PETERS, JOHN E.; AND DYKMAN, ROSCOE A. "Children With Specific Learning Disabilities: Bender Gestalt Test Findings and Other Signs." *J Learn Dis* 4(8):437–46 O '71. * (*PA* 47:9714)

914. ACKERMAN, PEGGY T.; PETERS, JOHN E.; AND DYKMAN, ROSCOE A. "Children With Specific Learning Disabilities: WISC Profiles." *J Learn Dis* 4(3):150–66 Mr '71. * (*PA* 47:9713)

915. BAGWELL, FRANCES IMOGENE. *The Effects of a Selected Language Training Program on the Measured Verbal and Intellectual Ability of Educable Mentally Retarded Pupils.* Doctor's thesis, Texas Tech University (Lubbock, Tex.), 1971. (*DAI* 32:5064A)

916. BARRON, ROBERT CHARLTON. *A Comparison of Patterns of Intellectual and Psycho-Linguistic Abilities Among First Graders With Average and Very Low Reading Ability.* Doctor's thesis, University of Minnesota (Minneapolis, Minn.), 1971. (*DAI* 32:1817B)

917. BARTIN, NORMA GLADYS. *The Intellectual and Psycholinguistic Characteristics of Three Groups of Differentiated Third Grade Readers.* Doctor's thesis, State University of New York (Buffalo, N.Y.), 1971. (*DAI* 32:228A)

918. BELLAMY, EDWARD ELLSWORTH. *A Study of Productive Thinking in Mentally Retarded Children.* Doctor's thesis, University of Illinois (Urbana, Ill.), 1971. (*DAI* 32:4411A)

919. BERGAN, ALENE; McMANIS, DONALD L.; AND MELCHERT, PAUL A. "Effects of Social and Token Reinforcement on WISC Block Design Performance." *Percept & Motor Skills* 32(3):871–80 Je '71. * (*PA* 47:3622)

920. BERSOFF, DONALD N. "Short Forms of Individual Intelligence Tests for Children: Review and Critique." *J Sch Psychol* 9(3):310–20 '71. * (*PA* 47:8924)

921. BLACK, BOB GENE. *Determining the Predictive Value of Selected Measures for First Grade Reading Success.* Doctor's thesis, North Texas State University (Denton, Tex.), 1971. (*DAI* 32:3548A)

922. BLACK, F. WILLIAM. "An Investigation of Intelligence as a Causal Factor in Reading Problems." *J Learn Dis* 4(3):139–42 Mr '71. * (*PA* 47:9695)

923. BOLL, THOMAS J. "Correlation of WISC With Motor Speed and Strength for Brain-Damaged and Normal Children." *J Psychol* 77(2):169–72 Mr '71. * (*PA* 46:1674)

924. BORREANO, PAUL M. *A Replication and Extension of Studies of the Relations Between Distractibility and the WISC Digit Span Test.* Master's thesis, University of Wisconsin (LaCrosse, Wis.), 1971.

925. BRAFF, REBA GERTRUDE. *Signal-to-Noise Speech Discrimination of Black and White Children With Varying Socio-Economic Backgrounds.* Doctor's thesis, University of Southern California (Los Angeles, Calif.), 1971. (*DAI* 32:3686B)

926. BURNES, KAY. "Clinical Assumptions About WISC Subtest Score and Test Behavior Relationships." Abstract. *J Consult & Clin Psychol* 36(2):299 Ap '71. * (*PA* 46:2633)

927. BUSH, WILMA JO. *A Comparative Study of the WISC Test Patterns of the Bright and Gifted Underachievers With the Test Patterns of Underachievers With Normal Intelligence.* Doctor's thesis, Texas Tech University (Lubbock, Tex.), 1971. (*DAI* 32:5066A)

928. BUTLER, GARY D. *The Performance of Sixth Grade Over and Underachievers on the Information, Arithmetic, Digit Span, and Coding Subtests of the Wechsler Intelligence Scale for Children.* Master's thesis, East Tennessee State University (Johnson City, Tenn.), 1971.

929. CERBUS, GEORGE, AND OZIEL, L. JEROME. "Correlation of the Bender-Gestalt and WISC for Negro Children." *Percept & Motor Skills* 32(1):276 F '71. * (*PA* 46:2703)

930. CLARKE, BRYAN R., AND LESLIE, PERRY T. "Visual-Motor Skills and Reading Ability of Deaf Children." *Percept & Motor Skills* 33(1):263–8 Ag '71. * (*PA* 47:3463)

931. COLE, SPURGEON, AND HUNTER, MILDRED. "Pattern Analysis of WISC Scores Achieved by Culturally Disadvantaged Children." *Psychol Rep* 29(1):191–4 Ag '71. * (*PA* 47:2647)

932. CREED, C. D., AND ROBINSON, W. P. "Intelligence Test Scores in the Evaluation of a 'Use of Language' Programme for Infant School Children." *Res Ed* (England) 6:1–11 N '71. * (*PA* 48:12239)

933. DAHLKE, ANITA B. "Predicting True Reading Gains After Remedial Tutoring," pp. 81–102. In *Diagnostic Viewpoints in Reading.* Edited by Robert E. Leibert. Newark, Del.: International Reading Association, 1971. Pp. viii, 133. *

934. DERSHOWITZ, ZACHARY. "Jewish Subcultural Patterns and Psychological Differentiation." *Int J Psychol* (France) 6(3):223–31 '71. * (*PA* 49:672)

935. DREYER, ALBERT S.; DREYER, CECILY A.; AND NEBELKOPF, EDWIN B. "Portable Rod-and-Frame Test as a Measure of Cognitive Style in Kindergarten Children." *Percept & Motor Skills* 33(3):775–81 D '71. * (*PA* 48:710)

936. DUFFY, ROBERT J., AND MOORE, MARCIA CZYZEWSKI. "The Relationship Between Intelligence and Gestural Behavior in a Mentally Retarded Population." *J Genetic Psychol* 119(2):195–202 D '71. * (*PA* 48:1508)

937. DUROJAIYE, M. O. A., AND SUCH, M. "Predicting Educational Suitability of Children in an Assessment Unit." *J Exp Ed* 40(2):27–36 w '71. * (*PA* 47:11608)

938. FALK, LIBBY JANET. *A Profile of Learning Abilities and Behavioral Characteristics of Elementary School-Age Children With Phenylketonuria.* Doctor's thesis, Temple University (Philadelphia, Pa.), 1971. (*DAI* 32:1913A)

939. FELDMAN, SOLOMON E., AND SULLIVAN, DAVID S. "Factors Mediating the Effects of Enhanced Rapport on Children's Performance." Abstract. *J Consult & Clin Psychol* 36(2):302 Ap '71. * (*PA* 46:3726)

940. FINNERTY, RICHARD J.; SOLTYS, JOHN J.; AND COLE, JONATHAN O. "The Use of D-Amphetamine With Hyperkinetic Children." *Psychopharmacologia* (West Germany) 21(3):302–8 '71. * (*PA* 47:9150)

941. FREER, FRANK J. *Visual and Auditory Perceptual Modality Differences as Related to Success in First Grade Reading Word Recognition.* Doctor's thesis, Rutgers—The State University (New Brunswick, N.J.), 1971. (*DAI* 32:6193A)

942. FRIEDMAN, GERALDINE H. PROBE. *A Comparative Study of Psychoeducational Test Scores of Emotionally Disturbed Children and Children With Learning Disabilities.* Doctor's thesis, St. Louis University (St. Louis, Mo.), 1971. (*DAI* 33:1043A)

943. GALDIERI, ANTHONY AUGUST. *The Effect of Verbal Approval Upon the Performance of Middle- and Lower-Class Third-Grade Children on the Wechsler Intelligence Scale for Children.* Doctor's thesis, Ohio University (Athens, Ohio), 1971. (*DAI* 32:1270A)

944. GARNER, JOHN; PERCY, LYNDA M.; AND LAWSON, TOM. "Sex Differences in Behavioral Impulsivity, Intellectual Impulsivity, and Attainment in Young Children: OSCAR and WISC." *J Child Psychol & Psychiatry* (England) 12(4):261–71 D '71. *

945. GOFFENEY, BARBARA; HENDERSON, NORMAN B.; AND BUTLER, BRUCE V. "Negro-White, Male-Female Eight-Month Developmental Scores Compared With Seven-Year WISC and Bender Test Scores." *Child Develop* 42(2):595–604 Je '71. * (*PA* 47:651)

946. GOLDSTEIN, HARRIS S., AND PECK, ROSALIND. "Cognitive Functions in Negro and White Children in a Child Guidance Clinic." *Psychol Rep* 28(2):379–84 Ap '71. * (*PA* 46:7556)

947. GRIEF, ELLEN G. *An Analysis of the Performance of Children With Learning Disabilities on the Illinois Test of Psycholinguistic Abilities and the Wechsler Intelligence Scale for Children.* Doctor's thesis, University of Kansas (Lawrence, Kan.), 1971. (*DAI* 32:5638A)

948. HANNAFORD, ALONZO E. "Factors Affecting Motor and Cognitive Performance of the Educable Mentally Retarded." *Am Correct Ther* 25(4):105–10 Jl–Ag '71. *

949. HARDY, MIRIAM P.; MELLITS, DAVID; AND WILLIG, SHARON N. "Reading: A Function of Language Usage." *Johns Hopkins Med J* 129(1):43–53 Jl '71. *

950. HEISS, WARREN ESLER. *Intersensory Integration and Intelligence in Learning Disabled Children.* Doctor's thesis, Yeshiva University (New York, N.Y.), 1971. (*DAI* 32:5639A)

951. HENDERSON, N. B.; BUTLER, B. V.; AND CLARK, W. M., JR. "Relationships Between Selected Perinatal Variables and Seven-Year Intelligence." Abstract. *Proc 79th Ann Conv Am Psychol Assn* 6(1):139–40 '71. * (*PA* 46:2707)

952. HILDMAN, LEE K., AND LOWE, JAMES D., JR. "The Usefulness of Parental Occupation as a Criterion for Standardization of the WISC." *South J Ed Res* 5(3):120–9 Jl '71. * (*PA* 49:9933)

953. HINTON, GEORGE G., AND KNIGHTS, ROBERT M. "Children With Learning Problems: Academic History, Academic Prediction, and Adjustment Three Years After Assessment." *Excep Children* 37(7):513–9 Mr '71. * (*PA* 47:3663)

954. HOWELL, ROBERT WAYNE. *Evaluation of Cognitive Abilities of Emotionally Disturbed Children: An Application of Piaget's Theories.* Doctor's thesis, Southern Illinois University (Carbondale, Ill.), 1971. (*DAI* 32:5037A)

955. HUIZINGA, RALEIGH JAMES. *The Relationship of the Illinois Test of Psycholinguistic Abilities to the Stanford-Binet Form L-M and the Wechsler Intelligence Scale for Children.* Doctor's thesis, University of Arizona (Tucson, Ariz.), 1971. (*DAI* 32:3823A)

956. HUNTER, EDNA J., AND JOHNSON, LAVERNE C. "Developmental and Psychological Differences Between Readers and Nonreaders." *J Learn Dis* 4(10):572–7 D '71. * (*PA* 47:11671)

957. JERROLDS, BOB W.; CALLAWAY, BYRON; AND GWALTNEY, WAYNE. "A Comparative Study of Three Tests of Intellectual Potential, Three Tests of Reading Achievement, and the Discrepancy Scores Between Potential and Achievement." *J Ed Res* 65(4):168–72 D '71. * (*PA* 48:1647)

958. JOESTING, JOAN, AND JOESTING, ROBERT. "The Quick Test as a Screening Device in a Welfare Setting." *Psychol Rep* 29(3):1289–90 D '71. * (*PA* 48:992)

959. KAPPELMAN, MURRAY M.; LUCK, ELIZABETH; AND GANTER, ROBERT L. "Profile of the Disadvantaged Child With Learning Disorders." *Am J Dis Children* 121(5):371–9 My '71. *

960. KILLIAN, L. R. "WISC, Illinois Test of Psycholinguistic Abilities, and Bender Visual-Motor Gestalt Test ·Performance of Spanish-American Kindergarten and First-Grade School Children." *J Consult & Clin Psychol* 37(1):38–43 Ag '71. * (*PA* 47:1738)

961. KLONOFF, HARRY. "Factor Analysis of a Neuropsychological Battery for Children Aged 9 to 15." *Percept & Motor Skills* 32(2):603–16 Ap '71. * (*PA* 46:11508)

962. KLUEVER, RAYMOND. Chap. 8, "Mental Abilities and Disorders of Learning," pp. 196–212. In *Progress in Learning Disabilities, Vol. 2.* Edited by Helmer R. Myklebust. New York: Grune & Stratton, Inc., 1971. Pp. ix, 404. *

963. KOPPITZ, ELIZABETH MUNSTERBERG. *Children With Learning Disabilities: A Five Year Follow-Up Study.* New York: Grune & Stratton, Inc., 1971. Pp. xv, 218. *

964. LEHMAN, ELYSE BRAUCH, AND LEVY, BERNARD I. "Discrepancies in Estimates of Children's Intelligence: WISC and Human Figure Drawings." *J Clin Psychol* 27(1):74–6 Ja '71. * (*PA* 46:1427)

965. LEICHTMAN, SANDRA ROSE. *Correlates of Role-Taking and Communication Skill in Children.* Doctor's thesis, University of North Carolina (Chapel Hill, N.C.), 1971. (*DAI* 32:7314B)

966. LESSLER, KEN, AND GALINSKY, M. DAVID. "Relationship Between Slosson Intelligence Test and WISC Scores in Special Education Candidates." *Psychol Sch* 8(4):341–4 O '71. * (*PA* 47:9677)

967. LEVI, HELENE S., AND WELCHER, DORIS W. "Social Class and Race as Determinants of the Sex of Human Figures Drawn by Seven-Year-Olds." *Johns Hopkins Med J* 129(1):10–8 Jl '71. *

968. LEVINSON, ELIZABETH J. "The Modification of Intelligence by Training in the Verbalization of Word Definitions and Simple Concepts." *Child Develop* 42(5):1361–80 N '71. * (*PA* 48:4673)

969. LOGOTHETIS, JOHN; HARITOS-FATOUROS, MARY; CONSTANTOULAKIS, MATHIOS; ECONOMIDOU, JOANNA; AUGOUSTAKI, OLGA; AND LOEWENSON, RUTH B. "Intelligence and Behavioral Patterns in Patients With Cooley's Anemia (Homozygous Betathalassemia); A Study Based on 138 Consecutive Cases." *Pediatrics* 48(5):740–4 N '71. *

970. McKINNEY, JAMES D., AND CORTER, HAROLD M. "Flexibility Training With Educable Retarded Children." *J Sch Psychol* 9(4):455–61 w '71. * (*PA* 48:1711)

971. McNINCH, GEORGE. "Auditory Perceptual Factors and Measured First-Grade Reading Achievement." *Read Res Q* 6(4):472–92 su '71. * (*PA* 47:11769)

972. McPROUTY, VIVIAN HELEN. *Piaget's Theory as the Basis for the Assessment of Reading Disability and Suggested Remediation Through an Adapted Science Curriculum.* Doctor's thesis, University of the Pacific (Stockton, Calif.), 1971. (*DAI* 32:2488A)

973. MATHENY, ADAM P., JR. "Comparability of WISC and PPVT Scores Among Young Children." *Excep Children* 38(2):147–50 O '71. * (*PA* 48:3673)

974. MATHER, LEONARD JOSEPH. *A Causal Comparative Study of Intellectual Functioning in Good and Poor Readers.* Doctor's thesis, Catholic University of America (Washington, D.C.), 1971. (*DAI* 32:1920A)

975. MEICHENBAUM, DONALD H., AND GOODMAN, JOSEPH. "Training Impulsive Children to Talk to Themselves." *J Abn Psychol* 77(2):115–26 Ap '71. * (*PA* 46:3785)

976. MIKLICH, DONALD R. "A Device to Facilitate Administering the Object Assembly Test." *Meas & Eval Guid* 4(2):115–6 Jl '71. *

977. MOORE, MARY, AND WELCHER, DORIS W. "A Descriptive Analysis of the Seven-Year Psychological Data." *Johns Hopkins Med J* 128(6):332–46 Je '71. *

978. MOORE, TELFORD IRA. *The Relationship Among Differentiated Cognitive Abilities, Field Dependency, Achievement, and Rated Classroom Behavior of Ninth Grade Junior High School Students.* Doctor's thesis, University of Southern California (Los Angeles, Calif.), 1971. (*DAI* 32:249A)

979. MYKLEBUST, HELMER R.; BANNOCHIE, MARGARET N.; AND KILLEN, JAMES R. Chap. 9, "Learning Disabilities and Cognitive Processes," pp. 213–51. In *Progress in Learning Disabilities, Vol. 2.* Edited by Helmer R. Myklebust. New York: Grune & Stratton, Inc., 1971. Pp. ix, 404. *

980. NEWMAN, ANABEL POWELL. *Longitudinal Study of Pupils Who Were Underachieving in Reading in First Grade.* Doctor's thesis, State University of New York (Buffalo, N.Y.), 1971. (*DAI* 32:2313A)

981. OAKLAND, THOMAS D.; KING, JOHN D.; WHITE, LINDA ANN; AND ECKMAN, ROBERT. "A Comparison of Performance on the WPPSI, WISC, and SB With Preschool Children: Companion Studies." *J Sch Psychol* 9(2):144–9 '71. * (*PA* 47:7563)

982. OLSHIN, DAVID. *The Relationship of Race and Social Class to Intelligence and Reading Achievement at Grades One and Five.* Doctor's thesis, Temple University (Philadelphia, Pa.), 1971. (*DAI* 32:1923A)

983. OROS, JAMES ALLAN. *Effects of Induced Anxiety on the Wechsler Intelligence Scale for Children.* Master's thesis, Illinois State University (Normal, Ill.), 1971.

984. OWEN, FREYA WEAVER; ADAMS, PAULINE AUSTIN; FORREST, THOMAS; STOLZ, LOIS MEEK; AND FISHER, SARA. "Learning Disorders in Children: Sibling Studies." *Monogr Soc Res Child Develop* 36(4):1–77 N '71. * (*PA* 48:12196)

985. PASEWARK, RICHARD A.; FITZGERALD, BERNARD J.; AND GLOECKLER, TED. "Relationship of Peabody Picture Vocabulary Test and Wechsler Intelligence Scale for Children in an Educable Retarded Group: A Cautionary Note." *Psychol Rep* 28(2):405–6 Ap '71. * (*PA* 46:7516)

986. PAUL, LEONARD MARC. *WISC and Bender as Predictors of Reading Performance in Children With Learning Disabilities.* Doctor's thesis, University of Pennsylvania (Philadelphia, Pa.), 1971. (*DAI* 32:1923A)

987. POLLEY, DALE. *The Relationship of the Channels of Communication of the Illinois Test of Psycholinguistic Abilities to the Wechsler Intelligence Scale for Children.* Doctor's thesis, University of Northern Colorado (Greeley, Colo.), 1971. (*DAI* 32:4194B)

988. PRICE, JAMES DAVID. *Analysis of Changes in Intelligence Test Scores of Mexican-American Youth Assigned to Special Classes in Relation to Jensen's Two-Level Theory of Mental Abilities.* Doctor's thesis, University of Arizona (Tucson, Ariz.), 1971. (*DAI* 32:3125A)

989. PROSSER, NANETTE S., AND CRAWFORD, VEDA B. "Relationship of Scores on the Wechsler Preschool and Primary Scale of Intelligence and the Stanford-Binet Intelligence Scale Form LM." *J Sch Psychol* 9(3):278–83 '71. * (*PA* 47:8634)

990. PYLE, ROBERT FORREST. *Shortening the Information, Arithmetic, and Picture Completion Subtests of the Wechsler Intelligence Scale for Children.* Doctor's thesis, University of Northern Colorado (Greeley, Colo.), 1971. (*DAI* 32:2408B)

991. REBISH, DELLA. "Mask of Competence." *Claremont Read Conf Yearb* 35:109–19 '71. *

992. REDMOND, NEIL JOSEPH. *Rorschach Correlates of Underachievement and Cognitive Deficits of Underachievers.* Doctor's thesis, St. John's University (Jamaica, N.Y.), 1971. (*DAI* 32:3015B)

993. RESNICK, ROBERT J., AND ENTIN, ALAN D. "Is an Abbreviated Form of the WISC Valid for Afro-American Children?" *J Consult & Clin Psychol* 36(1):97–9 F '71. * (*PA* 45:9973)

994. RITZINGER, FRANCES CONNOR. *Psychological and Physiological Differentiation in Children Six to Eleven Years of Age.* Doctor's thesis, Washington University (St. Louis, Mo.), 1971. (*DAI* 32:2409B)

995. ROBERTS, JEAN. *Intellectual Development of Children as Measured by the Wechsler Intelligence Scale for Children: United States.* U.S. Department of Health, Education, and Welfare Publication No. (HSM) 72-1004; Vital Health Statistics, Series 11, No. 107. Washington, D.C.: Government Printing Office, August 1971. Pp. iv, 41. * (*PA* 48:2696)

996. ROBERTS, JEAN. "Intellectual Development of Children as Measured by the Wechsler Intelligence Scale for Children: United States." *Vital & Health Stat* Series 11(107):1–41 Ag '71. * (*PA* 48:2696)

997. ROBERTS, JEAN. "Intellectual Development of Children by Demographic and Socioeconomic Factors: United States." *Vital & Health Stat* Series 11(110):1–71 D '71. * (*PA* 48:7748)

998. ROURKE, B. P.; YOUNG, G. C.; AND FLEWELLING, R. W. "The Relationships Between WISC Verbal-Performance Discrepancies and Selected Verbal, Auditory-Perceptual, Visual-Perceptual, and Problem-Solving Abilities in Children With Learning Disabilities." *J Clin Psychol* 27(4):475–9 O '71. * (*PA* 47:9738)

Wechsler Intelligence Scale for Children

999. ROURKE, BYRON P., AND TELEGDY, GABOR A. "Lateralizing Significance of WISC Verbal-Performance Discrepancies for Older Children With Learning Disabilities." *Percept & Motor Skills* 33(3):875-83 D '71. * (PA 48:1715)

1000. RUBINO, C. A.; KROCCO, D.; AND SHEA, M. "An Analysis of Right Hemispheric Deficits in the Moderately Retarded Child as Measured by the WISC and Leiter." *Ont Psychologist* (Canada) 3(2):85-95 '71. * (PA 47:9488)

1001. RUDEL, RITA G., AND TEUBER, H.-L. "Spatial Orientation in Normal Children and in Children With Early Brain Injury." *Neuropsychologia* (England) 9(4):401-7 D '71. * (PA 48:5446)

1002. RUSCHIVAL, M. LENA, AND WAY, JOHN GILBERT. "The WPPSI and the Stanford-Binet: A Validity and Reliability Study Using Gifted Preschool Children." Abstract. *J Consult & Clin Psychol* 37(1):163 Ag '71. * (PA 47:1586)

1003. SABATINO, DAVID A., AND BECKER, JOHN T. "Relationship Between Lateral Preference and Selected Behavioral Variables for Children Failing Academically." *Child Develop* 42(6):2055-60 D '71. * (PA 48:9861)

1004. SACHS, DAVID A. "WISC Changes as an Evaluative Procedure Within a Token Economy." *Am J Mental Def* 76(2):230-4 S '71. * (PA 47:9683)

1005. SAPIR, SELMA G. "Learning Disability and Deficit Centered Classroom Training." *Cognitive Studies* 2:324-38 '71. * (PA 49:1359, title only)

1006. SATTLER, JEROME M., AND MARTIN, SANDER. "Anxious and Nonanxious Examiner Roles on Two WISC Subtests." *Psychol Sch* 8(4):347-9 O '71. * (PA 47:11628)

1007. SCHWARZ, ROBERT H., AND COOK, JOHN J. "Mental Age as a Predictor of Academic Achievement." *Ed & Train Mental Retard* 6(1):12-5 F '71. *

1008. SCHWARZ, ROBERT H., AND FLANIGAN, PATRICK J. "Evaluation of Examiner Bias in Intelligence Testing." *Am J Mental Def* 76(2):262-5 S '71. * (PA 47:9664)

1009. SCOTT, RALPH, AND SATTEL, LUDWIG. "School and Home: Not Either-Or." *Merrill-Palmer Q* 17(4):335-45 O '71. * (PA 47:9666)

1010. SEARLS, EVELYN FITCH. *WISC and WPPSI IQ's and Subtest Patterns Related to First Grade Reading Achievement.* Doctor's thesis, University of Miami (Coral Gables, Fla.), 1971. (DAI 32:6225A)

1011. SHELDON, HARRY JAY. *An Investigation of Syntactical Ability and Vocabulary Knowledge of First Graders as Related to Reading and Vocabulary Achievement as Measured by the Stanford Achievement Test.* Doctor's thesis, University of Iowa (Iowa City, Iowa), 1971. (DAI 32:1201A)

1012. SILVERSTEIN, A. B. "A Corrected Formula for Assessing the Validity of WAIS, WISC, and WPPSI Short Forms." *J Clin Psychol* 27(2):212-3 Ap '71. * (PA 46:6881)

1013. SMITH, NATHANIEL C., JR. "A Comparison of Short-Form Estimation Methods in the WISC in Juvenile Public Offenders." *J Clin Psychol* 27(1):77-9 Ja '71. * (PA 46:1476)

1014. SMITH, PHILIP A., AND MARX, RONALD W. "The Factor Structure of the Revised Edition of the Illinois Test of Psycholinguistic Abilities." *Psychol Sch* 8(4):349-56 O '71. * (PA 47:9666)

1015. SOUTHERN, MARA L., AND PLANT, WALTER T. "Differential Cognitive Development Within and Between Racial and Ethnic Groups of Disadvantaged Preschool and Kindergarten Children." *J Genetic Psychol* 119(2):259-66 D '71. * (PA 48:637)

1016. SPENCE, ALLYN G.; MISHRA, SHITALA P.; AND GHOZEIL, SUSAN. "Home Language and Performance on Standardized Tests." *El Sch J* 71(6):309-13 Mr '71. * (PA 47:2655)

1017. STEWART, JOE GLENN. *The Relationship of Selected Abilities to Gross Motor Performance of Educable Mentally Retarded Students.* Doctor's thesis, North Texas State University (Denton, Tex.), 1971. (DAI 32:6799A)

1018. SUNDEAN, DAVID A., AND SALOPEK, THOMAS F. "Achievement and Intelligence in Primary and Elementary Classes for the Educable Mentally Retarded." *J Sch Psychol* 9(2):150-6 '71. * (PA 47:7610)

1019. SURWILLO, W. W. "Digit Span and EEG Frequency in Normal Children." *Electroenceph & Clin Neurophysiol* (Netherlands) 31(1):93-5 Jl '71. * (PA 47:10315)

1020. SWADE, ROBERTA EDYTHE. *Relationship of the Block Design Subtest of the WISC to Reading Achievement.* Doctor's thesis, Temple University (Philadelphia, Pa.), 1971. (DAI 32:1927A)

1021. SWANSON, ELINOR, AND DEBLASSIE, RICHARD. "Interpreter Effects on the WISC Performance of First Grade Mexican-American Children." *Meas & Eval Guid* 4(3):172-5 O '71. * (PA 49:12095)

1022. SWEET, ROGER C., AND RINGNESS, THOMAS A. "Variations in the Intelligence Test Performance of Referred Boys of Differing Racial and Socioeconomic Backgrounds as a Function of Feedback or Monetary Reinforcement." *J Sch Psychol* 9(4):399-409 w '71. * (PA 48:1664)

1023. SWIZE, LYDIA MARIE. *The Relationship Between Performance on Piagetian Conservation Tasks and Intelligence and Achievement in Educable Mentally Retarded Children.* Doctor's thesis, University of Northern Colorado (Greeley, Colo.), 1971. (DAI 32:3806A)

1024. THOMAS, ALEXANDER; HERTZIG, MARGARET E.; DRYMAN, IRVING; AND FERNANDEZ, PAULINA. "Examiner Effect in IQ Testing of Puerto Rican Working-Class Children." *Am J Orthopsychiatry* 41(5):809-21 O '71. * (PA 47:11636)

1025. TIGAY, BARRY, AND KEMPLER, HYMAN L. "Stability of WISC Scores of Children Hospitalized for Emotional Disturbance." *Percept & Motor Skills* 32(2):487-90 Ap '71. * (PA 46:11229)

1026. VANCE, SANDRA B. *A Comparison of the Wechsler Intelligence Scale for Children and the Columbia Mental Maturity Scale With Mental Retardates.* Master's thesis, East Tennessee State University (Johnson City, Tenn.), 1971.

1027. VASA, STANLEY FRANK. *A Comparison of Selected Intelligence Scales With Bilingual Children.* Doctor's thesis, University of Nebraska (Lincoln, Neb.), 1971. (DAI 32:802A)

1028. WAGONSELLER, BILL R. *A Comparison of Intellectual Ability, Achievement Level, Self-Concept, and Behavior Problems Exhibited by Children Labeled as Learning Disabilities and Emotionally Disturbed.* Doctor's thesis, University of Kansas (Lawrence, Kan.), 1971. (DAI 32:5644A)

1029. WALLBROWN, FRED HAROLD. *A Validity Study of the Wallach-Kogan Creativity Test: The Prediction of Six Concurrent Criteria in Visual Art.* Doctor's thesis, Ohio State University (Columbus, Ohio), 1971. (DAI 32:6630B)

1030. WEINER, PAUL S. "The Cognitive Functioning of Language Deficient Children." *Cognitive Studies* 2:338-63 '71. *

1031. WEINER, PAUL S. "Stability and Validity of Two Measures of Intelligence Used With Children Whose Language Development Is Delayed." *J Speech & Hearing Res* 14(2):254-61 Je '71. * (PA 48:5419)

1032. WELCHER, DORIS W.; MELLITS, E. DAVID; AND HARDY, JANET B. "A Multivariate Analysis of Factors Affecting Psychological Performance." *Johns Hopkins Med J* 129(1):19-35 Jl '71. *

1033. WHITEHOUSE, DENNIS. "Psychological and Neurological Correlates of Seizure Disorders." *Johns Hopkins Med J* 129(1):36-42 Jl '71. *

1034. WILLS, I. H., AND BANAS, NORMA. "The Vulnerable Child: Prescriptive Teaching From WISC Patterns." *Acad Ther* 7(1):79-83 f '71. *

1035. WILSON, GERALDINE O. *The Difference in Approach to the Block Subtest of the Wechsler Intelligence Scale for Children and the Bender Visual-Motor Gestalt Test by Subjects With Organic Brain Dysfunction and Normal Subjects.* Master's thesis, Southern Connecticut State College (New Haven, Conn.), 1971.

1036. WITMER, J. MELVIN; BORNSTEIN, ALAN V.; AND DUNHAM, RICHARD M. "The Effects of Verbal Approval and Disapproval Upon the Performance of Third and Fourth Grade Children on Four Subtests of the Wechsler Intelligence Scale for Children." *J Sch Psychol* 9(3):347-56 '71. * (PA 47:9668)

1037. WRIGHT, LOGAN, AND JIMMERSON, STEVE. "Intellectual Sequelae of Hemophilus Influenzae Meningitis." *J Abn Psychol* 77(2):181-3 Ap '71. * (PA 46:3584)

CUMULATIVE NAME INDEX

Harris, H.: 750
Harris, R.: 137
Harte, M. L.: 449
Hartlage, L. C.: 751
Hartman, R. K.: 886
Haskell, S. H.: 398
Haughey, C.: 868
Haupt, T. D.: 376
Hawkins, W. F.: 255, 433, 674
Haworth, M. R.: 241
Hayden, B. S.: 721
Hayden, D. L.: 778–80
Hecht, P. J.: 399
Heiss, W. E.: 950
Hemberger, L. W.: 678
Henderson, N. B.: 679, 945, 951
Hendrix, R.: 71
Henning, J. J.: 511
Herndon, J. D.: 231
Herrell, J. M.: 680
Herron, W. G.: 711
Hershenson, D. B.: 512
Hertel, R. K.: 782
Hertzig, M. E.: 1024
Hewitt, P. S.: 681
Higginson, J. B.: 10
Hildman, L. K.: 952
Hillix, W. A.: 781
Himelstein, P.: 231
Hine, W. D.: 752–3
Hinton, G. G.: 953
Hirsch, E. A.: 754
Hirst, L. S.: 172
Hite, L.: 54
Hofmann, L. J.: 698
Hohman, L. B.: 817
Holland, G. A.: 55
Holland, W. R.: 173
Hollingsworth, B. H.: 72
Holloway, H. D.: 56, 73
Holroyd, J.: 400, 597
Holroyd, J. C.: 341
Holtzman, W. H.: 450
Hommel, R. W.: 598
Honzik, M. P.: 870
Hooper, S.: 812
Hopkins, K. D.: 203, 342, 451, 513
Horowitz, F. D.: 452
Houston, C.: 599–600
Howell, R. W.: 954
Hudson, F. G.: 700
Hueftle, M. K.: 514
Huelsman, C. B.: 755
Hughes, D. H.: 299
Hughes, R. B.: 401
Hughes, V. A.: 398
Huizinga, R. J.: 955
Hunt, D.: 204
Hunter, E. J.: 956
Hunter, M.: 931
Huntress, D. W.: 136
Hutton, J. B.: 343
Indow, T.: 139
Ingham, J. G.: 601
Irvine, J.: 865
Irwin, D. O.: 344, 453
Irwin, O. C.: 515
Iscoe, I.: 345, 469, 834
Ison, M. G.: 116
Iverson, I. A.: 712
Jackson, C. L.: 346
Jackson, E. M.: 602
Jackson, M. A.: 174
Jackson, P. W.: 821
Jacobson, A.: 796
Jacobson, F. N.: 516
Jacobson, S.: 672
James, P.: 269
Jaros, E.: 430
Jastak, J. F.: 347
Jastak, S. R.: 347
Jayagopal, R.: 887
Jeeves, M. A.: 418, 844
Jenkin, N.: 348
Jerrolds, B. W.: 957
Jillson, R. P.: 150
Jimmerson, S.: 1037
Joesting, J.: 958
Joesting, R.: 958
Johnson, C. I.: 682
Johnson, D. D.: 683
Johnson, D. L.: 618

Johnson, J. A.: 883
Johnson, L. C.: 956
Johnson, O. L.: 232
Johnson, W. R.: 883
Joiner, L. M.: 871
Jonckheere, J.: 328
Jones, G. T.: 517
Jones, R. L.: 630
Jones, R. W.: 376
Jones, S.: 151, 233
Jongeward, P. A.: 684–5
Jordan, T. E.: 809
Jurjevich, R.: 263–4
Justman, J.: 12
Kaback, G. R.: 402
Kahn, J. H.: 238
Kaiser, M. D.: 349
Kallos, G. L.: 205
Kalter, N.: 693
Kappelman, M. M.: 959
Kardos, M. S.: 74
Karlsen, B.: 808
Karp, S. A.: 202, 313, 686
Kaspar, J. C.: 249, 421, 425, 603
Kass, C. E.: 687
Kaufman, M. J.: 888
Kearney, J. E.: 688
Kearsley, R. B.: 417
Keffer, C. E.: 868
Kell, E. R.: 785
Keller, J. E.: 117
Kelly, F. J.: 273
Kempler, H. L.: 1025
Kennedy, W. A.: 822
Kent, N.: 118
Kern, K. C.: 692
Kicklighter, R.: 749
Killen, J. R.: 979
Killian, L. R.: 960
Kilman, B. A.: 175
Kimbrell, D. L.: 176
King, J. D.: 981
Kissel, S.: 454–5
Klahn, J. E.: 208
Klausmeier, H. J.: 308
Klonoff, H.: 664, 737, 882, 961
Kløve, H.: 470
Kluever, R.: 962
Knights, R. M.: 953
Knopf, I. J.: 57, 75
Knott, J. R.: 412
Kogan, N.: 428
Kolstoe, O. P.: 76, 289
Koos, E. M.: 350
Koppitz, E. M.: 130, 518, 963
Korst, J. W.: 515
Koutstaal, C. W.: 318
Kovalinsky, T.: 672
Kraft, I. A.: 571
Kralovich, A. M.: 77
Kranzler, G. D.: 474
Kriegman, G.: 403
Kriegman, L. S.: 403
Krippner, S.: 319, 351–2, 756, 831
Krocco, D.: 1000
Krugman, J. I.: 12
Krugman, M.: 12
Kureth, G.: 37, 58
L'Abate, L.: 257
LaDriere, L.: 677
La Driere, M. L.: 748
Lair, C. V.: 766
Laird, D. S.: 119
Lam, R. L.: 92
Lamp, R. E.: 519
Landrum, J. P.: 265
Laney, B. J.: 889
Larr, A. L.: 152
Larson, K. H.: 353
Lauber, M.: 123
Lauer, B. A.: 456
Lavitt, J. A.: 520
Lavos, G.: 234
Lawson, T.: 944
Lee, R.: 536
Lehman, E. B.: 964
Lehmann, M. M.: 78
Leichtman, S. R.: 965
Lerand, L. W.: 457
Leslie, P. T.: 930
Lessing, E. E.: 266, 757
Lessing, J. C.: 266

Lessler, K.: 401, 966
Lester, E. P.: 586, 667–8, 758
Lester, L. P.: 498
Levi, H. S.: 967
Levin, J.: 19
Levine, M.: 348, 890
Levinson, B. M.: 153–4, 177, 206, 301
Levinson, E. J.: 968
Levitt, E. E.: 186
Levy, B. I.: 964
Levy, P.: 604
Levy, R. H.: 511, 605, 850, 859
Lewis, F. D.: 759
Lewis, L. L.: 138
Lewis, V.: 851–2, 860
Lewis, V. G.: 866, 872
Lindsey, J. M.: 458, 534
Litaker, R. G.: 493
Littell, W. M.: 178
Livermore, G.: 734
Lockyer, L.: 689, 760
Loewenson, R. B.: 969
Logothetis, J.: 969
Loos, F. M.: 100
Loper, D. J.: 404
Lotsof, E. J.: 131
Lovell, K.: 354, 521, 836
Lovinger, R. J.: 596
Lovinger, S. L.: 761
Lowe, J. D.: 952
Lucito, L. J.: 179
Lucito, L. J.: 201
Luck, E.: 959
Luong, C. K. M.: 606
Lusienski, D. R.: 355
Luszki, W. A.: 356, 405
Lyle, J. G.: 607, 690–1
Lytton, H.: 608
McArthur, C. R.: 609
McBeath, M.: 843
McBrearty, J. F.: 13
McBride, J. W.: 337
McCandless, B. R.: rev, 4:363
McCauley, J. H.: 406
McConochie, W. A.: 891
McCulloch, T. L.: 99
McElhaney, M. L.: 459
McFie, J.: 762
McGraw, J. J.: 460
McGuire, L.: 451, 513
Machi, V. S.: 126
McHugh, A. F.: 267
McKenzie, A.: 593
McKerracher, D. W.: 610
McKinney, J. D.: 970
McLean, T. K.: 320
McLeod, J.: 407, 461, 522
McManis, D. L.: 919
McMenemy, R. A.: 415
McMullen, C. P.: 408
McNinch, G. H. W.: 892, 971
McPherson, M. W.: 254
McProuty, V. H.: 972
Mac Vicar, D. B.: 357
Mahan, T. W.: 268
Malin, A. J.: 409, 867
Mann, L.: 868
Marchi, J. U.: 893
Margach, C.: 692
Marks, J. B.: 208
Marley, A. D.: 358
Marsden, G.: 693, 763
Martin, A. W.: 79
Martin, J. D.: 820
Martin, S.: 1006
Marx, R. W.: 1014
Mascarenhas, J.: 666
Masica, D. N.: 872
Masling, J.: 816
Massey, J. O.: 410, 681
Matheny, A. P.: 973
Mather, A. J.: 974
Mathews, A.: 559
Matthews, C. G.: 132, 470, 611
Matyas, R. P.: 80, 109
Maxwell, A. E.: 155–6, 180, 209–10
Maxwell, M. T.: 894
Maycock, G. A.: 764
Mayer, R. W.: 140
Meeker, M. N.: 694

Megargee, E. I.: 874
Mehrotra, K. K.: 612–3
Meichenbaum, D. H.: 975
Meier, J. H.: 411
Melchert, P. A.: 919
Mellits, D.: 949
Mellits, E. D.: 1032
Meyers, C. E.: 854
Michael, W. B.: 203
Miele, J. A.: 141
Miezitis, S. A.: 614
Miklich, D. R.: 976
Milgram, N. A.: 390, 523
Miller, C. K.: 765
Miller, H. R.: 695
Miller, J. M.: 771
Milstein, V.: 57, 75
Mirsky, A. F.: 671
Mishra, S. P.: 1016
Moed, G.: 269
Moeny, W. C.: 895
Mogel, S.: 544
Mohan, P. J.: 281
Moller, H.: 181
Money, J.: 359, 462, 524, 810, 837, 851–2, 860, 866
Montgomery, G. W. G.: 853
Moon, W. H.: 766
Moore, D.: 627
Moore, M.: 977
Moore, M. C.: 936
Moore, T. I.: 978
Moore, W. E.: 850
Morán, R. E.: 826
Mordock, J. B.: 615
Morgan, C. E.: 294
Moriarty, A.: 594–5
Morledge, J.: 540
Morper, J.: 463
Morris, H. L.: 739
Morrison, D. H.: 193
Morrison, E. B.: 295
Morrison, M.: 321
Muehl, S.: 412
Muhr, J. P.: 37–8
Muir, R.: 758
Mukherjee, B. N.: 182
Mumpower, D. L.: 360
Munger, P. F.: 474
Munz, A.: 767
Murfett, B. J.: 57, 75
Murphy, L. J.: 120
Murstein, B. I.: 814
Mussen, P.: 39
Myers, C. E.: 769
Myklebust, H. R.: 979
Naar, R.: 413
Nale, S.: 14
Nalven, F. B.: 525, 616, 696–8
Namy, E.: 526
Naumann, T. F.: 391
Neaves, A. I.: 896
Nebelkopf, E. B.: 935
Needham, W. E.: 699
Neher, L. A.: 781
Nelson, C. C.: 142
Nelson, C. M.: 700
Nelson, D.: 757
Neuhaus, M.: 527
Neville, D.: 211
Newland, T. E.: 399, 528
Newman, A. P.: 980
Newman, J. R.: 100
Nickols, J.: 270, 464, 529
Nickols, M.: 270, 464
Nix, A. P.: 493
Noller, P. A.: 21
Norton, J. A.: 842
Nowakiwska, M.: 628
Nunnally, J. C.: 361
Nurss, J. R.: 768
Nuttall, J. C.: 882
Oakland, J. A.: 701
Oakland, T. D.: 981
O'Connell, A. W.: 322
Ogdon, D. P.: 183, 530
Oki, T.: 531
Oliver, D. E.: 354
Olshin, D.: 982
O'Neil, W. M.: 235
O'Neill, H. D.: 702
Oppel, W. C.: 649
Oros, J. A.: 983
Orpet, R. E.: 769, 854

[534]
**[Re Wechsler Intelligence Scale for Children]
California Abbreviated WISC.** Educable mentally retarded ages 8–13.5, intellectually gifted elementary school children; 1966; consists of 5 subtests of *Wechsler Intelligence Scale for Children;* 2 levels; Carmen J. Finley and Jack M. Thompson; Western Psychological Services. *
a) FORM 1. Educable mentally retarded ages 8–13.5; CAW-MR; 6 scores: information, picture arrangement, picture completion, block design, coding, total.
b) FORM 2. Intellectually gifted elementary school children; CAW-IG; 6 scores: information, picture arrangement, picture completion, block design, similarities, total.
For additional information and a review by A. B. Silverstein, see 7:432 (1 reference).

REFERENCES THROUGH 1971
1. See 7:432.

CUMULATIVE NAME INDEX

[535]
**[Re Wechsler Intelligence Scale for Children]
Rhodes WISC Scatter Profile.** Ages 5–15; 1969; a form for profiling WISC scores; Fen Rhodes; Educational and Industrial Testing Service. *
For additional information, see 7:433.

[536]
★**[Re Wechsler Intelligence Scale for Children]
WISC Mental Description Sheet.** Ages 5–15; 1970–71; a form for profiling WISC scores; 1971 form identical with form copyrighted 1970; no manual; John A. Blazer; Psychologists and Educators, Inc. *

[537]
★**[Re Wechsler Intelligence Scale for Children]
WISC Test Profile.** Ages 5–15; 1968–69; Consulting Psychologists Press, Inc. *

[538]
Wechsler Preschool and Primary Scale of Intelligence. Ages 4–6.5; 1967, c1949–67; WPPSI; 8 of the 11 tests provide the same measures as the *Wechsler Intelligence Scale for Children* and approximately ⅓ of the total number of items are essentially the same; 13 or 14 scores: verbal (information, vocabulary, arithmetic, similarities, comprehension, sentences [optional], total), performance (animal house, picture completion, mazes, geometric design, block design, total), total; David Wechsler; Psychological Corporation. (British edition: 1971; manual supplement by Peter Saville; NFER Publishing Co. Ltd. [England].) *
For additional information, reviews by Dorothy H. Eichorn and A. B. Silverstein, and excerpted reviews by C. H. Ammons and O. A. Oldridge (with E. E. Allison), see 7:434 (56 references).

REFERENCES THROUGH 1971
1–56. See 7:434.
57. HARTMAN, ROBERT K. "The Wechsler Preschool and Primary Scale of Intelligence." *Dig Mental Retard* 5(2):107–9 w '68–69 ['69]. *
58. RUSCHIVAL, MARY LENA. *The Effectiveness of the Wechsler Preschool and Primary Scale of Intelligence in the Identification of Gifted Preschool Children.* Master's thesis, East Carolina University (Greenville, N.C.), 1969.
59. BOYD, MILLER WILLIAMS, JR. *A Factor Analysis of the Wechsler Preschool and Primary Scale of Intelligence.* Doctor's thesis, St. Louis University (St. Louis, Mo.), 1970. (*DAI* 32:1186B)
60. GUEST, KRISTIN ELIZABETH. *Relationships Among the Illinois Test of Psycholinguistic Abilities, Receptive and Expressive Language Tasks, Intelligence, and Achievement.* Doctor's thesis, University of Wisconsin (Madison, Wis.), 1970. (*DAI* 31:5845A)
61. KINNIE, ERNEST J. *The Influence of Nonintellective Factors on the IQ Scores of Middle- and Lower-Class Children.* Doctor's thesis, Purdue University (Lafayette, Ind.), 1970. (*DAI* 31:6260B)
62. LIVO, NORMA J. "Reading Readiness Factors and Beginning Reading Success." *Read Teach* 24(2):124–9+ N '70. * (*PA* 45:10960)
63. MUSGROVE, WALTER J. "Comparisons of Low Socioeconomic Black and White Kindergarten Children." *Acad Ther* 6(2):163–7 w '70. *
64. SHATUS, ERWIN L. "Validation of the Wechsler Preschool and Primary Scale of Intelligence With the Stanford-Binet, Form L-M, on Culturally Deprived Children." *South J Ed Res* 4(1):18–36 Ja '70 [My '71]. *
65. BERSOFF, DONALD N. "Short Forms of Individual Intelligence Tests for Children: Review and Critique." *J Sch Psychol* 9(3):310–20 '71. * (*PA* 47:8924)
66. FREER, FRANK J. *Visual and Auditory Perceptual Modality Differences as Related to Success in First Grade Reading Word Recognition.* Doctor's thesis, Rutgers—The State University (New Brunswick, N.J.), 1971. (*DAI* 32: 6193A)
67. GORDON, GEORGE, AND HYMAN, IRWIN. "The Measurement of Perceptual-Motor Abilities of Head Start Children." *Psychol Sch* 8(1):41–8 Ja '71. * (*PA* 46:7777)
68. HAGIN, ROSA A.; SILVER, ARCHIE A.; AND CORWIN, CAROL G. "Clinical-Diagnostic Use of the WPPSI in Predicting Learning Difficulties in Grade 1." *J Spec Ed* 5(3):221–32 f '71. * (*PA* 48:12188)
69. HAYWOOD, NANCY ROBERTS. *The Wechsler Preschool and Primary Scale of Intelligence and Picture Motivation Scale as Predictors of Academic Achievement in First-Grade Children.* Master's thesis, George Peabody College (Nashville, Tenn.), 1971.
70. KINNIE, ERNEST J., AND STERNLOF, RICHARD E. "The Influence of Nonintellective Factors on the IQ Scores of Middle- and Lower-Class Children." *Child Develop* 42(6):1989–95 D '71. * (*PA* 48:8823)
71. KRUSEN, MARGARET MARY MORROW. *The Relationship of Physical Condition at Birth to Intellectual Functioning at Early School Age.* Doctor's thesis, University of Nebraska (Lincoln, Neb.), 1971. (*DAI* 32:2485A)
72. MATHENY, ADAM P., JR., AND BROWN, ANNE M. "Activity, Motor Coordination and Attention: Individual Differences in Twins." *Percept & Motor Skills* 32(1):151–8 F '71. * (*PA* 46:2639)
73. MOFFITT, P.; NURCOMBE, B.; PASSMORE, M.; AND MCNEILLY, A. "Intervention in Cultural Deprivation: The Comparative Success of Preschool Techniques for Rural Aborigines and Europeans." *Austral Psychologist* 6(1):51–61 Mr '71. * (*PA* 47:3795)
74. MUSGROVE, WALTER J., AND LAWSON, JOHN R. "A Comparison of Lower Class Negro and White Children on Three Standardized Tests." *J Negro Ed* 40(1):53–5 w '71. *
75. OAKLAND, THOMAS D.; KING, JOHN D.; WHITE, LINDA ANN; AND ECKMAN, ROBERT. "A Comparison of Performance on the WPPSI, WISC, and SB With Preschool Children:

Companion Studies." *J Sch Psychol* 9(2):144–9 '71. * (*PA* 47:7563)

76. OLSHIN, DAVID. *The Relationship of Race and Social Class to Intelligence and Reading Achievement at Grades One and Five.* Doctor's thesis, Temple University (Philadelphia, Pa.), 1971. (*DAI* 32:1923A)

77. PASEWARK, RICHARD A.; RARDIN, MAX W.; AND GRICE, JOHN E., JR. "Relationship of the Wechsler Pre-School and Primary Scale of Intelligence and the Stanford-Binet (L-M) in Lower Class Children." *J Sch Psychol* 9(1):43–50 '71. * (*PA* 47:5609)

78. PROSSER, NANETTE S., AND CRAWFORD, VEDA B. "Relationship of Scores on the Wechsler Preschool and Primary Scale of Intelligence and the Stanford-Binet Intelligence Scale Form LM." *J Sch Psychol* 9(3):278–83 '71. * (*PA* 47:8634)

79. ROBINSON, HALBERT B., AND ROBINSON, NANCY M. "Longitudinal Development of Very Young Children in a Comprehensive Day Care Program: The First Two Years." *Child Develop* 42(6):1673–83 D '71. * (*PA* 48:8827)

80. RUSCHIVAL, M. LENA, AND WAY, JOHN GILBERT. "The WPPSI and the Stanford-Binet: A Validity and Reliability Study Using Gifted Preschool Children." Abstract. *J Consult & Clin Psychol* 37(1):163 Ag '71. * (*PA* 47:1586)

81. SCHWARZ, ROBERT H., AND FLANIGAN, PATRICK J. "Evaluation of Examiner Bias in Intelligence Testing." *Am J Mental Def* 76(2):262–5 S '71. * (*PA* 47:9664)

82. SEARLS, EVELYN FITCH. *WISC and WPPSI IQ's and Subtest Patterns Related to First Grade Reading Achievement.* Doctor's thesis, University of Miami (Coral Gables, Fla.), 1971. (*DAI* 32:6225A)

83. SEITZ, ELAINE KELLER. *The Relationship Between Cognitive Abilities and Impulse Control in Project Headstart Children.* Doctor's thesis, New York University (New York, N.Y.), 1971. (*DAI* 32:6061B)

84. SILVERSTEIN, A. B. "A Corrected Formula for Assessing the Validity of WAIS, WISC, and WPPSI Short Forms." *J Clin Psychol* 27(2):212–3 Ap '71. * (*PA* 46:6881)

85. TAKACS, CAROL PAULA. *Comparison of Mental Abilities Between Lower Socioeconomic Status Five-Year-Old Negro and White Children on Individual Intelligence Measures.* Doctor's thesis, Kent State University (Kent, Ohio), 1971. (*DAI* 32:3806A)

86. YATER, ALLAN C.; BARCLAY, ALLAN; AND LESKOSKY, RICHARD. "Goodenough-Harris Drawing Test and WPPSI Performance of Disadvantaged Preschool Children." *Percept & Motor Skills* 33(3):967–70 D '71. * (*PA* 48:698)

CUMULATIVE NAME INDEX

Allen, M.: 25
Allison, E. E.: *exc*, 7:434
Ammons, C. H.: *exc*, 7:434
Bach, L. C.: 2
Barclay, A.: 19, 86
Berger, M.: 41
Bersoff, D. N.: 65
Birney, S. D.: 40
Bonfield, J. R.: 3
Boyd, M. W.: 59
Brittain, M.: 20
Broughton, E.: 25
Brown, A. M.: 72
Brudenell, G. A.: 21
Butler, S.: 41
Campanella, S.: 4
Clark, B.: 25
Corwin, C. G.: 68
Crawford, V. B.: 78
Cundick, B. P.: 42
Curry, D. R.: 22
Delaney, R. J.: 43
Dienstag, R.: 23
Dokecki, P. R.: 24
Eckman, R.: 75
Eichorn, D. H.: *rev*, 7:434
Emerson, P.: 25
Fagan, J.: 25
Flanigan, P. J.: 81
Frede, M. C.: 24
Freer, F. J.: 66
Fuller, B. L.: 5
Futterer, J. W.: 44
Garver, S. A.: 26
Gautney, D. B.: 24
Goens, B. D.: 27
Gordon, C.: 67
Graham, G. A.: 45
Green, R. M.: 28
Grice, J. E.: 77
Guest, K. E.: 60
Hagin, R. A.: 68
Handley, W. B.: 46
Hartman, R. K.: 57
Haywood, N. R.: 69
Herman, D. O.: 6

Hyman, I.: 67
Jones, E. L. H.: 47
Kavajecz, L. G.: 29
King, J. D.: 75
Kinnie, E. J.: 61, 70
Knoll, D. B.: 7
Kordinak, S. T.: 40
Krebs, E. G.: 30
Krusen, M. M. M.: 71
Lawson, J. R.: 74
Leskosky, R.: 86
Lichtman, M. V.: 31
Livo, N. J.: 32, 62
McNamara, J. R.: 33
McNeilly, A.: 73
McRae, J.: 8
Matheny, A. P.: 72
Meeker, M. N.: 34
Miezitis, S.: 38
Miller, L. E.: 33
Milliren, A. P.: 35
Moffitt, P.: 48, 73
Musgrove, W. J.: 63, 74
Nase, R. R.: 36
Newham, V.: 41
Newland, T. E.: 35
Nurcombe, B.: 48, 73
Oakland, T. D.: 75
O'Keefe, G. S.: 49
Olshin, D.: 76
Pasewark, R. A.: 77
Passmore, M.: 73
Paul, G. T.: 9
Plant, W. T.: 10
Porterfield, C. L.: 33
Prosser, N. S.: 78
Rardin, M. W.: 77
Rellas, A. J.: 37
Richards, J. T.: 11, 50
Robinson, H. B.: 79
Robinson, N. M.: 79
Ruschival, M. L.: 58, 80
Schwarz, R. H.: 81
Searls, E. F.: 82
Seitz, E. K.: 83

Shatus, E. L.: 64
Shipe, D.: 38
Silver, A. A.: 68
Silverstein, A. B.: 1, 12–6, 39, 51–2, 84; *rev*, 7:434
Smith, R. A.: 17
Southern, M. L.: 10
Sternlof, R. E.: 70
Takacs, C. P.: 85
Taylor, V. C.: 53
Tizard, J.: 41

Vingoe, F. J.: 40
Wasik, B. H.: 54
Wasik, J. L.: 54
Way, J. G.: 80
White, L. A.: 18, 75
Woo-Sam, J.: 56
Works, M. N.: 55
Yater, A. C.: 19, 86
Yule, W.: 41
Zimmerman, I. L.: 56

[539]

★[Re Wechsler Preschool and Primary Scale of Intelligence] **WPPSI Test Profile.** Ages 4–6.5; 1968–69; Consulting Psychologists Press, Inc. *

[540]

Williams Intelligence Test for Children With Defective Vision. Blind and partially sighted ages 5–15; 1956; M. Williams; distributed by NFER Publishing Co. Ltd. [England]. *

For additional information and a review by T. Ernest Newland, see 6:541 (2 references).

REFERENCES THROUGH 1971

1–2. See 6:541.
3. WILLIAMS, M. "Superior Intelligence of Children Blinded From Retinoblastoma." *Arch Dis Childh* (England) 43:204–10 Ap '68. * (*PA* 42:17499)

CUMULATIVE NAME INDEX

Newland, T. E.: *rev*, 6:541   Williams, M.: 1–3

[Out of Print Since TIP I]

Alexander Performance Scale, 6:514 (1 review, 11 references); see also 4:334 (3 reviews, 2 excerpts)

Carl Hollow Square Scale, 3:273 (2 reviews, 5 references)

Children's Picture Information Test, 6:516 (2 reviews, 2 references)

Detroit Kindergarten Test, 3:274 (2 reviews, 1 reference)

Diagnostic Performance Tests, 6:519 (1 review, 1 reference)

Griffiths Mental Development Scale for Testing Babies From Birth to Two Years, 6:523 (2 reviews, 7 references)

Intelligence Tests for Children, 5:405 (2 reviews, 8 excerpts, 5 references)

Northwestern Intelligence Tests, 5:411 (2 reviews, 1 excerpt, 9 references)

Ontario School Ability Examination, 2:1411 (1 review, 2 references)

Pacific Infants Performance Scale, 7:416 (1 reference)

Performance Tests of Intelligence: A Series of Non-Linguistic Tests for Deaf and Normal Children, 3:290 (3 excerpts, 2 references)

Preliminary Test of Intelligence, 3:291

Randall's Island Performance Series, T:908

Tests of Mental Development, 2:1426 (4 reviews, 2 excerpts, 1 reference)

Van Alstyne Picture Vocabulary Test, 6:537 (3 reviews, 6 references)

SPECIFIC

[541]

★**Abstract Spatial Relations Test, Second Edition.** Bantu industrial workers with 0–12 years of education; ?–1969; ASRT; J. Kelmovitz (test); National Institute for Personnel Research [South Africa]. *

REFERENCES THROUGH 1971

1. GRANT, G. V. "Spatial Thinking: A Dimension in African Intellect." *Psychologia Africana* (South Africa) 13(2–3):222–39 O '70. *

CUMULATIVE NAME INDEX

[542]

Alternate Uses. Grades 6–16 and adults; 1960; revision of *Unusual Uses*; experimental form; spontaneous flexibility; for a downward extension, see 554i; Paul R. Christensen, J. P. Guilford, Philip R. Merrifield, and Robert C. Wilson; Sheridan Psychological Services, Inc. *

For additional information, see 6:542 (7 references).

REFERENCES THROUGH 1971

1–7. See 6:542.

8. MEADOW, ARNOLD, AND PARNES, SIDNEY J. "Evaluation of Training in Creative Problem-Solving." *J Appl Psychol* 43:189–94 Je '59. * (*PA* 34:5568)

9. MARKS, ALVIN; MICHAEL, WILLIAM B.; AND KAISER, HENRY F. "Comparison of Manual and Analytic Techniques of Rotation in a Factor Analysis of Aptitude Test Variables." *Psychol Rep* 7:519–22 D '60. * (*PA* 35:2792)

10. GARWOOD, DOROTHY SEMENOW. *Some Personality Factors Related to Creativity in Young Scientists.* Doctor's thesis, Claremont Graduate School (Claremont, Calif.), 1961. (*DA* 22:3273)

11. MCGUIRE, CARSON; HINDSMAN, EDWIN; KING, F. J.; AND JENNINGS, EARL. "Dimensions of Talented Behavior." *Ed & Psychol Meas* 21:3–38 sp '61. * (*PA* 36:1KH03M)

12. MALTZMAN, IRVING; SEYMORE, SIMON; AND LICHT, LEONARD. "Verbal Conditioning of Common and Uncommon Word Associations." *Psychol Rep* 10:363–9 Ap '62. * (*PA* 37:2450)

13. PENNY, R. K., AND MCCANN, B. "Application of Originality Training to the Mentally Retarded." *Psychol Rep* 11:347–51 O '62. * (*PA* 37:8161)

14. BARRON, FRANK. *Creativity and Psychological Health: Origins of Personal Vitality and Creative Freedom.* Princeton, N.J.: D. Van Nostrand Co., Inc., 1963. Pp. xi, 292. *

15. HAAS, MARY GERALDINE. *A Comparative Study of Critical Thinking, Flexibility of Thinking, and Reading Ability Involving Religious and Lay College Seniors.* Doctor's thesis, Fordham University (New York, N.Y.), 1963. (*DA* 24:622)

16. IRVINE, DAVID JAMES. *An Empirical Study of the Relationship Between Certain Pupil Characteristics and Selected Measures of Creativity.* Doctor's thesis, University of North Carolina (Chapel Hill, N.C.), 1963. (*DA* 25:4543)

17. CASTELLI, CHARLES DOMINIC. *An Exploration of the Relationship Between Teacher Creative Ability and Teacher-Pupil Classroom Behavior.* Doctor's thesis, State University of New York (Buffalo, N.Y.), 1964. (*DA* 25:3320)

18. FLEISCHER, GERALD. *The Effects of Anxiety Upon Tests of Creativity.* Doctor's thesis, State University of New York (Buffalo, N.Y.), 1964. (*DA* 25:5372)

19. GARWOOD, DOROTHY SEMENOW. "Personality Factors Related to Creativity in Young Scientists." *J Abn & Social Psychol* 68:413–9 Ap '64. * (*PA* 39:1729)

20. GRIFFIN, WILLIAM MAXWELL. *A Study of the Relationship of Certain Characteristics of High School Seniors to Effectiveness in Independent Study.* Doctor's thesis, Syracuse University (Syracuse, N.Y.), 1964. (*DA* 25:5787)

21. ISCOE, IRA, AND PIERCE-JONES, JOHN. "Divergent Thinking, Age, and Intelligence in White and Negro Children." *Child Develop* 35:785–97 S '64. * (*PA* 39:4589)

22. MCGLOTHLIN, WILLIAM H.; COHEN, SIDNEY; AND MCGLOTHLIN, MARCELLA S. "Short-Term Effects of LSD on Anxiety, Attitudes and Performance." *J Nerv & Mental Dis* 139:266–73 S '64. * (*PA* 39:7046)

23. RAINWATER, JANETTE MUNKITTRICK. *Effects of Set on Problem Solving in Subjects of Varying Levels of Assessed Creativity.* Doctor's thesis, University of California (Berkeley, Calif.), 1964. (*DA* 25:6753)

24. SEITZ, THEODORE LEE. *The Relationship Between Creativity and Intelligence, Personality, and Value Patterns in Adolescence.* Doctor's thesis, University of Denver (Denver, Colo.), 1964. (*DA* 25:3679)

25. WHITE, LOUISE ELIZABETH. *Creativity as a Function of Feelings of Self Worth.* Doctor's thesis, Vanderbilt University (Nashville, Tenn.), 1964. (*DA* 25:2619)

26. ABOU-GHORRA, I. M. "Dynamic Predictors of Production of Creative Novel Solutions in Counseling Among College Students." Abstract. *Proc Ann Conv Am Psychol Assn* 73:353–4 '65. * (*PA* 39:15850)

27. BACHELIS, LEONARD A. *Body-Field Perceptual Differentiation as a Variable in Creative Thinking.* Doctor's thesis, Yeshiva University (New York, N.Y.), 1965. (*DA* 26:3475)

28. DIXON, JAMES C. "Cognitive Structure in Senile Conditions With Some Suggestions for Developing a Brief Screening Test of Mental Status." *J Gerontol* 20:41–9 Ja '65. *

29. FELDHUSEN, JOHN F.; DENNY, TERRY; AND CONDON, CHARLES F. "Anxiety, Divergent Thinking, and Achievement." *J Ed Psychol* 56:40–5 F '65. * (*PA* 39:10771)

30. FLEISCHER, GERALD, AND COHEN, IRA S. "The Relationship Between Test Anxiety and Tests of Creativity." Abstract. *Proc Ann Conv Am Psychol Assn* 73:311–2 '65. * (*PA* 39:15458)

31. CORDER, BILLIE FARMER. *A Study of Shift in Set in Relation to Intelligence, Rigidity Measured as a Cognitive and Personality Variable, and Educational Set.* Doctor's thesis, University of Kentucky (Lexington, Ky.), 1966. (*DAI* 30:1861A)

32. EISENSTADT, J. MARVIN. "Problem-Solving Ability of Creative and Non-Creative College Students." *J Consult Psychol* 30:81–3 F '66. * (*PA* 40:4223)

33. FLAX, MORTON LEWIS. *The Stability of Relationships Between Creativity and Personality Variables.* Doctor's research study No. 1, Colorado State College (Greeley, Colo.), 1966. (*DA* 27:2857B)

34. GETZELS, J. W., AND CSIKSZENTMIHALYI, M. Chap. 15, "The Study of Creativity in Future Artists: The Criterion Problem," pp. 349–68. In *Experience, Structure and Adaptability.* Edited by O. J. Harvey. New York: Springer Publishing Co., Inc., 1966. Pp. ix, 406. *

35. HAYNES, CAROLYN R. *The Relationships of Performances of Seventh Grade Students on Measures of Creativity, Study Habits and Attitudes, Expressed Need for Counseling and Achievement.* Master's thesis, Texas A & M University (College Station, Tex.), 1966.

36. HELSON, RAVENNA. "Personality of Women With Imaginative and Artistic Interests: The Role of Masculinity, Originality, and Other Characteristics in Their Creativity." *J Personality* 34:1–25 Mr '66. * (*PA* 40:8830)

37. JANSSEN, CALVIN WAYNE. *Comparative Creativity Scores of Lower Socio-Economic Dropouts and Non-Dropouts.* Doctor's thesis, University of Tennessee (Knoxville, Tenn.), 1966. (*DA* 27:1659A)

38. MAHAL, BARBARA KRUEGER. *Achievement and Rigidity.* Doctor's thesis, Rutgers—The State University (New Brunswick, N.J.), 1966. (*DA* 27:1661A)

39. NICOLAY, GLEN C. *Relationship Between a Risk-Taking Questionnaire and Selected Personality Characteristics.* Doctor's thesis, Fordham University (New York, N.Y.), 1966. (*DA* 27:2142B)

40. RAY, WILBERT S. "Absence of Transfer in Unusual Uses Tests." *Psychol Rep* 18:237–8 F '66. * (*PA* 40:6644)

41. SMITH, ROBERT M., AND NEISWORTH, JOHN T. "Creative Thinking Abilities of Intellectually Superior Children in the Regular Grades." *Psychol Rep* 18:335–41 Ap '66. * (*PA* 40:8832)

42. BRUCH, CATHERINE BELL. *Cognitive Characteristics of Effectively Creative Teachers.* Doctor's thesis, University of California (Los Angeles, Calif.), 1967. (*DA* 28:3524A)

43. COMPTON, MARY FRANCES. *An Attempt to Foster Creative Thinking in Teachers.* Doctor's thesis, University of Florida (Gainesville, Fla.), 1967. (*DA* 29:164A)

44. GIVENS, PAUL R.; PINKARD, CAROLYN A.; AND RICH, THOMAS A. "Relationship of Personality Factors, Creativity and Academic Achievement Among High School Seniors." *Fla J Ed Res* 9:45–56 Ja '67. *

45. JACKSON, ROBERT LEON. *An Investigation of the Creative Growth Curves of University Students.* Doctor's thesis, East Texas State University (Commerce, Tex.), 1967. (*DA* 28:3508A)

46. JENKINS, JOHN MERVIN. *A Study of the Characteristics Associated With Innovative Behavior in Teachers.* Doctor's thesis, University of Miami (Coral Gables, Fla.), 1967. (*DA* 28:903A)

47. MANGAN, GORDON L. "Studies of the Relationship Between Neo-Pavlovian Properties of Higher Nervous Activity and Western Personality Dimensions: 3, The Relations of Transformation Mobility to Thinking Flexibility." *J Exp Res Personality* 2:117–23 My '67. * (*PA* 41:11907)

48. PANKOVE, ETHEL WASSERMAN. *The Relationship Between Creativity and Risk Taking in Fifth-Grade Children.* Doctor's thesis, Rutgers—The State University (New Brunswick, N.J.), 1967. (*DA* 28:1308A)

49. RIDLEY, DENNIS R., AND BIRNEY, ROBERT C. "Effects of Training Procedures on Creativity Test Scores." *J Ed Psychol* 58:158–64 Je '67. * (*PA* 41:10457)

50. SIDLE, ALLAN CHARLES. *Creativity and Delusional Thinking in Schizophrenics.* Doctor's thesis, Stanford University (Stanford, Calif.), 1967. (*DA* 28:353B)

51. SKAGER, R. W.; KLEIN, S. P.; AND SCHULTZ, C. B. "The Prediction of Academic and Artistic Achievement at a School of Design." *J Ed Meas* 4:105–17 su '67. *

52. SMITH, ROBERT M. "Creative Thinking Abilities of Educable Mentally Handicapped Children in the Regular Grades." *Am J Mental Def* 71:571–5 Ja '67. * (*PA* 41:6197)

53. WINDHOLZ, GEORGE, AND MCINTOSH, WILLIAM A. "Concurrent Validation of Guilford's Six Convergent Tests." *Ed & Psychol Meas* 27:393–400 su '67. * (*PA* 41:12843)

54. ADAMS, JOHN C., JR. "The Relative Effects of Various Testing Atmospheres on Spontaneous Flexibility, a Factor of Divergent Thinking." *J Creative Behav* 2:187–94 su '68. * (*PA* 43:5882)

55. ARMSTRONG, CARMEN LAPP GERBERDING. *Changes Evidenced in the Art Products of Elementary Education Majors Exhibiting the Characteristic of Flexibility.* Doctor's thesis, Indiana University (Bloomington, Ind.), 1968. (*DA* 29:1799A)

56. BROWN, STEPHEN W.; GUILFORD, J. P.; AND HOEFFNER, RALPH. "Six Semantic-Memory Abilities." *Ed & Psychol Meas* 28:691–717 au '68. * (*PA* 43:4427)

57. CRAVER, ANN APRIL. *Convergent and Divergent Creative Thinking as a Function of Stimulation.* Doctor's thesis, University of Georgia (Athens, Ga.), 1968. (*DA* 29:4842B)

58. EDWARDS, ARTHUR B. *An Analysis of the Creative Ability Levels of the Potential Dropout in the Average Mental Ability Range.* Doctor's thesis, University of Tennessee (Knoxville, Tenn.), 1968. (*DA* 29:3828A)

59. GETZELS, J. W., AND CSIKSZENTMIHALYI, M. "The Value-Orientations of Art Students as Determinants of Artistic Specialization and Creative Performance." *Studies Art Ed* 10:5–16 f '68. *

60. GIBSON, JAMES W.; KIBLER, ROBERT J.; AND BARKER, LARRY L. "Some Relationships Between Selected Creativity and Critical Thinking Measures." *Psychol Rep* 23:707–14 D '68. * (*PA* 43:9748)

61. HINTON, BERNARD L. "Environmental Frustration and Creative Problem Solving." *J Appl Psychol* 52:211–7 Je '68. * (*PA* 42:11701)

62. JANSSEN, CALVIN. "Comparative Creativity Scores of Lower Socio-Economic Dropouts and Non-Dropouts." *Psychol Sch* 5:183–4 Ap '68. * (*PA* 43:17498)

63. LETT, WARREN ROBERT. *Some Postulated Correlates of Creativity and Need Achievement.* Doctor's thesis, University of California (Berkeley, Calif.), 1968. (*DA* 29:1106A)

64. MANSKE, MARY E., AND DAVIS, GARY A. "Effects of Simple Instructional Biases Upon Performance in the Unusual Uses Test." *J General Psychol* 79:25–33 Jl '68. * (*PA* 42:16417)

65. STIMSON, ROGER C., JR. "Factor Analytic Approach to the Structural Differentiation of Description." *J Counsel Psychol* 15:301–7 Jl '68. * (*PA* 42:15457)

66. WHITE, KINNARD. "Anxiety, Extraversion-Intraversion, and Divergent Thinking Ability." *J Creative Behav* 2:119–27 sp '68. * (*PA* 42:17233)

67. WINDHOLZ, GEORGE. "The Relation of Creativity and Intelligence Constellations to Traits of Temperament, Interest, and Value in College Students." *J General Psychol* 79:291–9 O '68. * (*PA* 43:3998)

68. ALKER, HENRY A.; CARLSON, JULIA A.; AND HERMANN, MARGARET G. "Multiple-Choice Questions and Student Characteristics." *J Ed Psychol* 60(3):231–43 Je '69. * (*PA* 43:13299)

69. BLACKHURST, A. EDWARD; MARKS, CLAUDE H.; AND TISDALL, WILLIAM J. "Relationship Between Mobility and Divergent Thinking in Blind Children." *Ed Visually Handicapped* 1(2):33–6 My '69. * (*PA* 43:14813)

70. GRIMSLEY, WILLIAM GERALD. *The Relationship Between Creativity and Leader Behavior of School Superintendents.* Doctor's thesis, University of Missouri (Columbia, Mo.), 1969. (*DAI* 30:5193A)

71. GUILFORD, J. P., AND HOEFFNER, RALPH. "Comparisons of Varimax Rotations With Rotations to Theoretical Targets." *Ed & Pyschol Meas* 29(1):3–22 sp '69. * (*PA* 44:15668)

72. HAAG, RICHARD A., AND DAVID, KENNETH H. "The Latent Dimensionality of Several Measures of Creativity." *J General Psychol* 80(2):279–85 Ap '69. * (*PA* 43:11328)

73. LEHRER, ARNOLD CURTIS. *The Personality Correlates of Creativity in Undergraduates.* Doctor's thesis, Colorado State College (Greeley, Colo.), 1969. (*DAI* 31:397B)

74. OLIVE, HELEN. *Sibling Resemblances in Divergent Thinking.* Doctor's thesis, Columbia University (New York, N.Y.), 1969. (*DAI* 33:3289B)

75. ROELKE, PATRICIA LYNN. *Reading Comprehension as a Function of Three Dimensions of Word Meaning.* Doctor's thesis, Indiana University (Bloomington, Ind.), 1969. (*DAI* 30:5300A)

76. SIMPSON, DONALD JAMES. *The Effect of Selected Musical Studies on Growth in General Creative Potential.* Doctor's thesis, University of Southern California (Los Angeles, Calif.), 1969. (*DAI* 30:502A)

77. BARRON, FRANK. "Heredability of Factors in Creative Thinking and Judgment." *Acta Geneticae Medicae et Gemellologiae* (Italy) 19(1–2):294–8 Ja–Ap '70. *

78. DELLAS, MARIE. *Effects of Creativity Training, Defensiveness, and Intelligence on Divergent Thinking.* Doctor's thesis, State University of New York (Buffalo, N.Y.), 1970. (*DAI* 31:4540A)

79. FELDHUSEN, JOHN F.; TREFFINGER, DONALD J.; AND ELIAS, ROBERT M. "Prediction of Academic Achievement With Divergent and Convergent Thinking and Personality Variables." *Psychol Sch* 7(1):46–52 Ja '70. * (*PA* 44:11410)

80. HEUSSENSTAMM, FRANCES K. "Creativity and Alienation: An Exploration of Their Relationship in Adolescence." *Calif J Ed Res* 21(3):140–6 My '70. *

81. HINTON, BERNARD L. "Personality Variables and Creative Potential." *J Creative Behav* 4(3):210–7 su '70. *

82. LAKE, A. E., III, AND TEDFORD, W. H., JR. "Influence of Creativity on Formation of Subjective Units." *J General Psychol* 83(2):227–37 O '70. * (*PA* 45:2406)

83. LAMONTAGNE, CHARLES WARREN. *An Exploration of the Relationship of Creativity and Educational Administration.* Doctor's thesis, Boston University (Boston, Mass.), 1970. (*DAI* 31:2064A)

84. OLESON, D. S., AND ZUBEK, JOHN P. "Effect of One Day of Sensory Deprivation on a Battery of Open-Ended Cognitive Tests." *Percept & Motor Skills* 31(3):919–23 D '70. * (*PA* 46:358)

85. OWEN, STEVEN V.; FELDHUSEN, JOHN F.; AND THURSTON, JOHN R. "Achievement Prediction in Nursing Education With Cognitive, Attitudinal, and Divergent Thinking Variables." *Psychol Rep* 26(3):867–70 Je '70. * (*PA* 45:1361)

86. REESE, HAYNE W., AND PARNES, SIDNEY J. "Programming Creative Behavior." *Child Develop* 41(2):413–23 Je '70. * (*PA* 44:15509)

87. RICHMOND, BERT O. "Creativity: Its Relationship to the Counselor's Approach." *J Stud Pers Assn Teach Ed* 8(2):56–63 w '70. * (*PA* 44:19438)

88. SIMMS, JEANNE THOMAS. *An Investigation of the Differences Between Creative High Socio-Economic College Freshmen and Creative Low-Socio-Economic College Freshmen on Measures of Vocational Interests and Certain Motivational Factors.* Doctor's thesis, Catholic University of America (Washington, D.C.), 1970. (*DAI* 31:2693A)

89. ABRAHAM, CAROL. *The Relationship of Authoritarianism to Independence and Creativity Among College Students.* Doctor's thesis, New York University (New York, N.Y.), 1971. (*DAI* 32:6023B)

90. ANASTASI, ANNE, AND SCHAEFER, CHARLES E. "Note on the Concepts of Creativity and Intelligence." *J Creative Behav* 5(2):113–6 '71. * (*PA* 48:7724)

91. BYRNE, MARY ANN; FELDHUSEN, JOHN F.; AND KANE, ROBERT B. "The Relationships Among Two Cloze Measurement Procedures and Divergent Thinking Abilities." *Read Res Q* 6(3):378–93 sp '71. * (*PA* 47:3624)

92. MARINO, CHARLES. "Cross-National Comparisons of Catholic-Protestant Creativity Differences." *Brit J Social & Clin Psychol* 10(2):132–7 Je '71. *

93. RENNER, VIVIAN, AND RENNER, JOHN C. "Effects of a Creativity Training Program on Stimulus Preferences." *Percept & Motor Skills* 33(3):872–4 D '71. * (*PA* 48:1002)

94. SCHOEL, DORIS R., AND BUSSE, THOMAS V. "Humor and Creative Abilities." *Psychol Rep* 29(1):34 Ag '71. * (*PA* 47:2958)

95. SHAW, FILIZ. "Verbal Time Stress and Divergent Thinking." *J Ed & Psychol* (India) 29(1):41–4 Ap '71. *

96. SHEEHAN, PETER W. "Task Structure as a Limiting Condition of the Occurrence of the Treatment Effects of Simulation Instruction in Application of the Real-Simulating Model of Hypnosis." *Int J Clin & Exp Hyp* 19(4):260–76 O '71. * (*PA* 47:4066)

97. TAFT, RONALD. "Creativity: Hot and Cold." *J Personality* 39(3):345–61 S '71. * (*PA* 47:6804)

98. TISDALL, WILLIAM J.; BLACKHURST, A. EDWARD; AND MARKS, CLAUDE H. "Divergent Thinking in Blind Children." *J Ed Psychol* 62(6):468–73 D '71. * (*PA* 47:9708)

99. TUELLER, REX LAMAR. *The Use of Personality Traits in Predicting Doctoral Student Success at Utah State University.* Doctor's thesis, Utah State University (Logan, Utah), 1971. (*DAI* 32:3732A)

100. WADE, SERENA E. "Adolescents, Creativity, and Media: An Exploratory Study." *Am Behav Sci* 14(3):341–51 Ja '71. * (*PA* 46:8797)

101. WILLIAMSON, HELEN THORWORTH. *Tolerance of Ambiguity and Creativity Thinking in Elementary School Children: A Study of the Relationships Among Tolerance of Ambiguity, Intelligence, Training in Creative Thinking, and Flexibility of Concept Formation.* Doctor's thesis, New York University (New York, N.Y.), 1971. (*DAI* 32:6821A)

CUMULATIVE NAME INDEX

Grimsley, W. G.: 70
Guilford, J. P.: 2, 56, 71
Haag, R. A.: 72
Haas, M. G.: 15
Haynes, C. R.: 35
Helson, R.: 36
Hermann, M. G.: 68
Heussenstamm, F. K.: 80
Hindsman, E.: 11
Hinton, B. L.: 61, 81
Hoepfner, R.: 56, 71
Irvine, D. J.: 16
Iscoe, I.: 21
Jackson, R. L.: 45
Janssen, C.: 62
Janssen, C. W.: 37
Jenkins, J. M.: 46
Jennings, E.: 11
Kaiser, H. F.: 4–5, 9
Kane, R. B.: 91
Kibler, R. J.: 60
King, F. J.: 11
Klein, S. P.: 51
Lake, A. E.: 82
Lamontagne, C. W.: 83
Lehrer, A. C.: 73
Lett, W. R.: 63
Licht, L.: 12
McCann, B.: 13
McGlothlin, M. S.: 22
McGlothlin, W. H.: 22
McGuire, C.: 11
McIntosh, W. A.: 53
Mahal, B. K.: 38
Maltzman, I.: 12
Mangan, G. L.: 47
Manske, M. E.: 64
Marino, C.: 92
Marks, A.: 4–5, 9
Marks, C. H.: 69, 98
Meadow, A.: 8
Michael, W. B.: 4–5, 9
Neisworth, J. T.: 41

Nicolay, G. C.: 39
Oleson, D. S.: 84
Olive, H.: 74
Owen, S. V.: 85
Pankove, E. W.: 48
Parnes, S. J.: 8, 86
Penney, R. K.: 13
Pierce-Jones, J.: 21
Pinkard, C. A.: 44
Rainwater, J. M.: 23
Ray, W. S.: 40
Reese, H. W.: 86
Renner, J. C.: 93
Renner, V.: 93
Rich, T. A.: 44
Richmond, B. O.: 87
Ridley, D. R.: 49
Roelke, P. L.: 75
Schaefer, C. E.: 90
Schoel, D. R.: 94
Schultz, C. B.: 51
Seitz, T. L.: 24
Seymore, S.: 12
Shaw, F.: 95
Sheehan, P. W.: 96
Sidle, A. C.: 50
Simms, J. T.: 88
Simpson, D. J.: 76
Skager, R. W.: 51
Smith, R. M.: 41, 52
Stimson, R. C.: 65
Taft, R.: 97
Tedford, W. H.: 82
Thurston, J. R.: 85
Tisdall, W. J.: 69, 98
Treffinger, D. J.: 79
Tueller, R. L.: 99
Wade, S. E.: 100
White, K.: 66
White, L. E.: 25
Williamson, H. T.: 101
Windholz, G.: 53, 67
Zubek, J. P.: 84

[543]

Benton Visual Retention Test, Revised Edition.
Ages 8 and over; 1946–55; BVRT; title on manual
is *Revised Visual Retention Test;* Arthur L. Benton;
distributed by Psychological Corporation. *

For additional information, see 6:543 (22 references) ; for a review by Nelson G. Hanawalt, see 5:401
(5 references) ; for reviews by Ivan Norman Mensh,
Joseph Newman, and William Schofield of the original
edition, see 4:360 (3 references) ; for an excerpted review, see 3:297.

REFERENCES THROUGH 1971

1–3. See 4:360.
4–8. See 5:401.
9–30. See 6:543.
31. KOLSTOE, OLIVER PAUL. *A Comparison of Mental Abilities of Bright and Dull Children Having the Same Mental Ages.* Doctor's thesis, State University of Iowa (Iowa City, Iowa), 1952. (*DA* 12:707)
32. STRUCKETT, PAULINE B. A. "Effect of Prefrontal Lobotomy on Intellectual Functioning in Chronic Schizophrenia." *Arch Neurol & Psychiatry* 69:293–304 Mr '53. * (*PA* 28:1346)
33. HEILBRUN, ALFRED B., JR. *The Localization of Cerebral Lesions by the Use of Psychological Tests.* Doctor's thesis, State University of Iowa (Iowa City, Iowa), 1954. (*DA* 14:1804)
34. WAHLER, HARRY JOE. *Analysis of the Performance of Brain-Damaged Patients on a Memory-For-Designs Test.* Doctor's thesis, State University of Iowa (Iowa City, Iowa), 1954. (*DA* 14:2406)
35. KAPLAN, HENRY KAY. *A Study of Relationships Between Handwriting Legibility and Perception Adjustment and Personality Factors.* Doctor's thesis, University of Wisconsin (Madison, Wis.), 1957. (*DA* 17:1950)
36. HEILBRUN, ALFRED, JR. "Lateralization of Cerebral Lesion and Performance on Spatial-Temporal Tasks." *Arch Neurol* 1:282–7 S '59. * (*PA* 34:6461)
37. BENTON, A. L. "The Visual Retention Test as a Constructional Praxis Task." *Confinia Neurologica* (Switzerland) 22(2):141–55 '62. *
38. JENKINS, C. DAVID. "The Relation of EEG Slowing to Selected Indices of Intellectual Impairment." *J Nerv & Mental Dis* 135:162–70 Ag '62. *
39. PEARL, DAVID. "Phenothiazine Effects in Chronic Schizophrenia." *J Clin Psychol* 18:86–9 Ja '62. * (*PA* 38:7573)
40. SEVERSON, ROGER ALFRED. *Some Nonreading Correlates*

of *Reading Retardation.* Doctor's thesis, State University of Iowa (Iowa City, Iowa), 1962. (*DA* 23:2798)
41. BARNES, CHARLES MANLY. *Prediction of Brain Damage Using the Holtzman Inkblot Technique and Other Selected Variables.* Doctor's thesis, State University of Iowa (Iowa City, Iowa), 1963. (*DA* 24:4789)
42. HUBER, THEODORE G. *A Comparative Study of Visual Retention Between Deaf and Hearing Adolescents Using the Benton Visual Retention Test.* Master's thesis, University of Kansas (Lawrence, Kan.), 1963.
43. NICKOLS, JOHN. "Mental Deficit, Schizophrenia and the Benton Test." *J Nerv & Mental Dis* 136:279–82 Mr '63. * (PA 38:4615)
44. BENTON, ARTHUR L., AND SPREEN, OTFRIED. "Visual Memory Test Performance in Mentally Deficient and Brain-Deficient Patients." *Am J Mental Def* 68:630–3 Mr '64. * (*PA* 39:2494)
45. GOETZINGER, C. P., AND HUBER, T. G. "A Study of Immediate and Delayed Visual Retention With Deaf and Hearing Adolescents." *Am Ann Deaf* 109:297–305 My '64. * (*PA* 39:2443)
46. GRANT, THOMAS NICHOLAS. *The Effect of Narcotic Addiction on CFF, Digit Symbol and the Benton Visual Retention Test.* Master's thesis, Fordham University (New York, N.Y.), 1965.
47. KLONOFF, HARRY, AND KENNEDY, MARGARET. "Memory and Perceptual Functioning in Octogenarians and Nonagenarians in the Community." *J Gerontol* 20:328–33 Jl '65. *
48. SIMMS, LORRAINE G. *A Validation Study of Benton's Visual Retention Test as a Measure of Intelligence.* Master's thesis, North Carolina State University (Raleigh, N.C.), 1965.
49. SMITH, LAURENCE C., JR. "The Effects of Heat Stroke on Cognitive Functioning." *Proc Ann Conf Air Force Behav Sci* 11:130–42 Jl '65. *
50. SPREEN, OTFRIED, AND BENTON, ARTHUR L. "Comparative Studies of Some Psychological Tests for Cerebral Damage." *J Nerv & Mental Dis* 140:323–33 My '65. * (*PA* 40:700)
51. ALEXANDER, DUANE; EHRHARDT, ANKE A.; and MONEY, JOHN. "Defective Figure Drawings, Geometric and Human, in Turner's Syndrome." *J Nerv & Mental Dis* 142:161–7 F '66. * (*PA* 40:11185)
52. BRENNER, MAY WOOLF, AND GILLMAN, SELMA. "Visuomotor Ability in Schoolchildren: A Survey." *Develop Med & Child Neurol* (England) 8:686–703 D '66. * (*PA* 41:4397)
53. CHANSKY, NORMAN M. "Measuring the Intelligence and Achievement of School Dropouts With the Benton Visual Retention Test." *Am J Mental Def* 71:191–5 S '66. * (*PA* 40:13186)
54. FJELD, STANTON P.; SMALL, IVER F.; SMALL, JOYCE G.; AND HAYDEN, MARY P. "Clinical, Electrical and Psychological Tests and the Diagnosis of Organic Brain Disorder." *J Nerv & Mental Dis* 142:172–9 F '66. * (*PA* 40:11285)
55. KLONOFF, HARRY, AND KENNEDY, MARGARET. "A Comparative Study of Cognitive Functioning in Old Age." *J Gerontol* 21:239–43 Ap '66. *
56. MONEY, JOHN; ALEXANDER, DUANE; AND EHRHARDT, ANKE. "Visual-Constructional Deficit in Turner's Syndrome." *J Pediatrics* 69:126–7 Jl '66. *
57. NICKOLS, JOHN. "Schizophrenic Deficit as a Function of the Test Materials." *J Clin Psychol* 22:77–9 Ja '66. * (*PA* 40:4465)
58. SHANAN, JOEL; COHEN, MARGALITH; AND ADLER, EMIL. "Intellectual Functioning in Hemiplegic Patients After Cerebrovascular Accidents." *J Nerv & Mental Dis* 143:181–9 Ag '66. * (*PA* 41:4893)
59. BENTON, A. L.; SPREEN, O.; FANGMAN, M. W.; AND CARR, D. L. "Visual Retention Test, Administration C: Norms for Children." *J Spec Ed* 1:151–6 w '67. * (*PA* 41:11175)
60. CHANSKY, NORMAN M. "Validity of the Benton Visual Retention Test." *Percept & Motor Skills* 24:1126 Je '67. * (*PA* 41:14437, title only)
61. EGELAND, BYRON; RICE, JAMES; AND PENNY, SUSAN. "Inter-Scorer Reliability on the Bender Gestalt Test and the Revised Visual Retention Test." *Am J Mental Def* 72:96–9 Jl '67. * (*PA* 41:15715)
62. OLIVER, J. E., AND RESTELL, MARY. "Serial Testing in Assessing the Effect of Meclofenoxate on Patients With Memory Defects." *Brit J Psychiatry* 113:219–22 F '67. * (*PA* 41:7456)
63. PETTIFOR, R. E. "The Effects of Unilateral Brain Damage on Performance on the Benton Visual Retention Test." *Alberta Psychologist* (Canada) 8(1):5–11 Ja '67. * (*PA* 41:10840)
64. SIMPSON, SEYMOUR AARON. *Perceptual Functions in Cerebral-Palsied Children.* Doctor's thesis, Yeshiva University (New York, N.Y.), 1967. (*DA* 28:508A)
65. TEMPLER, DONALD I. "Relation Between Immediate and Short-Term Memory and Clinical Implications." *Percept & Motor Skills* 24:1011–2 Je '67. * (*PA* 41:13086)
66. ALLEY, GORDON R. "Visual Retention Test, Administration C: Norms for Mentally Retarded Children." *Percept & Motor Skills* 27:438 O '68. * (*PA* 43:5776)
67. CRONHOLM, BÖRJE, AND SCHALLING, DAISY. "Cognitive Test Performances in Cerebrally Palsied Adults Without Men-

tal Retardation." *Acta Psychiatrica Scandinavica* (Denmark) 44(1):37–50 '68. * (*PA* 43:2937)

68. DOMRATH, RICHARD P. "Constructional Praxis and Visual Perception in School Children." *J Consult & Clin Psychol* 32:186–92 Ap '68. * (*PA* 42:8174)

69. LOEWER, H. D. "The Dependence of the Factorial Structure of Intelligence From the Level of Intelligence and From the Brain State." *Proc Inter Congr Appl Psychol* 16:707–12 '68. *

70. LOISELLE, ROBERT H.; YOUNG, KATHLEEN M.; AND MC-DONALD, MARGARET A. "Four Common Tests of Brain Damage Compared." *Psychiatric Commun* 10(2):41–4 '68. *

71. RICE, JAMES A. "Form Equivalence of the Revised Visual Retention Test in Mental Retardates: An Extension." *J Psychol* 68:159–63 Ja '68. * (*PA* 42:7666)

72. TEMPLER, DONALD I. "Memory and Grade Point Average of College Students." *Psychol Rep* 22:944 Je '68. * (*PA* 42:14591)

73. WATSON, CHARLES G. "The Separation of NP Hospital Organics From Schizophrenics With Three Visual Motor Screening Tests." *J Clin Psychol* 24:412–4 O '68. * (*PA* 43:4168)

74. ALLEY, GORDON R. "Comparative Constructional Praxis Performance of Organically Impaired and Cultural-Familial Mental Retardates." *Am J Mental Def* 74(2):279–82 S '69. * (*PA* 44:5526)

75. DEE, HENRY LEE. *Visuoconstructive and Visuoperceptive Deficit in Patients With Unilateral Cerebral Lesions.* Doctor's thesis, University of Iowa (Iowa City, Iowa), 1969. (*DAI* 30:3383B)

76. HALL, JOSEPH CLARENCE. *A Comparative Study of Selected Measures of Intelligence as Predictors of First-Grade Reading Achievement in a Culturally Disadvantaged Population.* Doctor's thesis, Temple University (Philadelphia, Pa.), 1969. (*DAI* 31:1074A)

77. L'ABATE, LUCIANO, AND GALE, ELLIOT N. "Neurological Status and Psychological Functioning." *Percept & Motor Skills* 29(3):999–1007 D '69. * (*PA* 46:5330)

78. LANGE, UNA ANN. *Differential Performances of Minimally Brain-Damaged Boys and of Non-Brain-Damaged Boys on Selected Tests.* Doctor's thesis, University of Nebraska (Lincoln, Neb.), 1969. (*DAI* 30:2852A)

79. ORGASS, B., AND POECK, K. "Assessment of Aphasia by Psychometric Methods." *Cortex* (Italy) 5(4):317–30 D '69. * (*PA* 44:17125)

80. OWENS, RICHARD THOMAS. *A Study of the Performance of Minimally Brain-Damaged and Emotionally Disturbed Boys on Six Selected Psychological Tests.* Doctor's thesis, University of Nebraska (Lincoln, Neb.), 1969. (*DAI* 31:383B)

81. STERNE, DAVID M. "The Benton, Porteus and WAIS Digit Span Tests With Normal and Brain-Injured Subjects." *J Clin Psychol* 25(2):173–5 Ap '69. * (*PA* 43:14481)

82. VITALE, JOHN H.; STEINHELBER, JOHN C.; DRAKE, WILLIAM E., JR.; AND DAHLGREN, HELEN. "Psychological Dimensions of Cerebrovascular Insufficiency." *Percept & Motor Skills* 29(2):555–63 O '69. * (*PA* 44:3996)

83. BIDDER, T. G.; STRAIN, J. J.; AND BRUNSCHWIG, L. "Bilateral and Unilateral ECT: Follow-Up Study and Critique." *Am J Psychiatry* 127(6):737–45 D '70. * (*PA* 47:5329)

84. BURGESS, MICHAEL M.; KODANAZ, ALTAN; AND ZIEGLER, DEWEY K. "Prediction of Brain Damage in a Neurological Population With Cerebrovascular Accidents." *Percept & Motor Skills* 31(2):595–601 O '70. * (*PA* 45:6841)

85. BURGESS, MICHAEL M.; KODANAZ, ALTAN; ZIEGLER, DEWEY; AND GREENBURG, HOWARD. "Prediction of Brain Damage in Two Clinical Populations." *Percept & Motor Skills* 30(2):523–32 Ap '70. * (*PA* 46:7299)

86. DEE, H. L. "Visuoconstructive and Visuoperceptive Deficit in Patients With Unilateral Cerebral Lesions." *Neuropsychologia* (England) 8(3):305–14 Jl '70. * (*PA* 44:21403)

87. DEE, H. L., AND BENTON, A. L. "A Cross-Modal Investigation of Spatial Performances in Patients With Unilateral Cerebral Disease." *Cortex* (Italy) 6(3):261–72 S '70. * (*PA* 46:1677)

88. ADAMS, JERRY, AND RUSHTON, SUSAN Y. "Immediate and Delayed Responses From Memory in Brain-Damaged Patients." Abstract. *J Consult & Clin Psychol* 37(2):305 O '71. * (*PA* 47:9479)

89. BLAKE, MARION ELIZABETH. *A Hierarchical Presentation of Tasks in Visual Perception and Their Relationship to Reading Performance.* Doctor's thesis, State University of New York (Buffalo, N.Y.), 1971. (*DAI* 32:779A)

90. BRAFF, RHODA A. *Imagery, Activity Level, and Learning Modality Preference as Indications of Sensory-Motor Stage Behavior in Low-Income Kindergarten Children.* Doctor's thesis, New York University (New York, N.Y.), 1971. (*DAI* 32:5605A)

91. BREWER, COLIN, AND PERRETT, LANCE. "Brain Damage Due to Alcoholic Consumption: An Air-encephalographic, Psychometric and Electroencephalographic Study." *Brit J Addict* 66(3):170–82 N '71. * (*PA* 48:5229)

92. CRARY, HELEN L., AND RIDGWAY, ROBERT W. "Relationships Between Visual Form Perception Abilities and Reading Achievement in the Intermediate Grades." *J Exp Ed* 40(1):17–22 f '71. * (*PA* 47:9796)

93. FALCONER, A. D. "Measurement of Cognitive Function in Two Groups of Alcoholics." *J Alcoholism* (England) 6(4):118–23 w '71. *

94. FREER, FRANK J. *Visual and Auditory Perceptual Modality Differences as Related to Success in First Grade Reading Word Recognition.* Doctor's thesis, Rutgers—The State University (New Brunswick, N.J.), 1971. (*DAI* 32:6193A)

95. GLAISTER, BRIAN R. "An Ordinate Comparison Method of Calculating Brain Damage Probability." *Brit J Social & Clin Psychol* 10(4):367–74 D '71. * (*PA* 48:1489)

96. GOLDSMITH, R. W., AND BRENGELMANN, J. C. "Rotation of Brain-Damaged and Schizophrenic Subjects." *Archiv für die Gesamte Psychologie* (West Germany) 123:164–70 '71. *

97. HALL, JOSEPH C., AND CHANSKY, NORMAN M. "Relationships Between Selected Ability and Achievement Tests in an Economically Disadvantaged Negro Sample." *Psychol Rep* 28(3):741–2 Je '71. * (*PA* 46:11501)

98. HANNINEN, HELENA. "Psychological Picture of Manifest and Latent Carbon Disulphide Poisoning." *Brit J Indus Med* 28(4):374–81 O '71. * (*PA* 46:11508)

99. KLONOFF, HARRY. "Factor Analysis of a Neuropsychological Battery for Children Aged 9 to 15." *Percept & Motor Skills* 32(2):603–16 Ap '71. * (*PA* 46:11508)

100. LACKS, PATRICIA BRILLIANT. "Revised Interpretation of Benton Visual Retention Test Scores." *J Clin Psychol* 27(4):481–2 O '71. * (*PA* 47:9205)

101. SHUKLA, T. R.; JHA, J.; AND MISRA, M. N. "The Diagnostic Usefulness of the Benton Revised Visual Retention Test of Brain Damage." *Psychol Studies* (India) 16(1):35–41 Ja '71. *

CUMULATIVE NAME INDEX

Benton Visual Retention Test

Wahler, H. J.: 8, 34
Watson, C. G.: 73
Wharton, L. H.: 4

Young, K. M.: 70
Ziegler, D. K.: 84–5

[544]

★**Biographical Inventory—Creativity.** "Adolescents and young adults"; 1970; BIC; 2 scores for boys: art-writing, mathematics-science; 2 scores for girls: art, writing; Charles E. Schaefer; Educational and Industrial Testing Service. *

REFERENCES THROUGH 1971

1. ANASTASI, ANNE, AND SCHAEFER, CHARLES E. "Biographical Correlates of Artistic and Literary Creativity in Adolescent Girls." *J Appl Psychol* 53(4):267–73 Ag '69. * (*PA* 43:15812)
2. SCHAEFER, CHARLES E. " 'Onomatopoeia and Images': Further Evidence of Validity." *Percept & Motor Skills* 31(3): 786 D '70. * (*PA* 45:9979)

CUMULATIVE NAME INDEX

Anastasi, A.: 1   Schaefer, C. E.: 1–2

[545]

The Block-Design Test. Mental ages 5–20; [1919]; also called *Kohs' Block-Design Test;* modifications appear in *Arthur Point Scale of Performance Tests, New Guinea Performance Scales, Ohwaki-Kohs Tactile Block Design Intelligence Test for the Blind,* and *Pacific Design Construction Test;* S. C. Kohs; Stoelting Co. *

REFERENCES THROUGH 1971

1. DOLL, EDGAR A. "Intelligence Measurement: A Review." *J Ed Res* 11:218–9 Mr '25. *
2. RAYBOLD, EMMA. "An Experiment With Primary Intelligence Tests." *Ed Res B* (Los Angeles City Schools) 4:8 Je 15 '25. *
3. GRAHAM, VIRGINIA TAYLOR. "The Intelligence of Chinese Children in San Francisco." *J Comp Psychol* 6:43–71 F '26. * (*PA* 1:663)
4. STEIN, MARTIN L. "A Trial With Criteria of the MacQuarrie Test of Mechanical Ability." *J Appl Psychol* 11:391–3 O '27. * (*PA* 2:2964)
5. BROOM, EUSTACE. "The Validity of Four Individual Tests of Mental Ability." *Ed Res B* (Los Angeles City Schools) 8:9–10 Mr '29. *
6. LESTER, OLIVE P. "Performance Tests and Foreign Children." *J Ed Psychol* 20:303–9 Ap '29. * (*PA* 3:2889)
7. BROWN, A. JEAN. "An Enquiry Into the Standardization of the Kohs' Block-Design Test." *J Appl Psychol* 14:178–81 Ap '30. * (*PA* 4:3309)
8. EIGLER, PAULINE. "The Kohs Block Design Test." *Child Develop* 1:341–2 D '30. * (*PA* 5:2582)
9. HUTT, MAX L. "A Simplified Scoring Method for the Kohs Block-Design Tests." *Am J Psychol* 42:450–2 Jl '30. * (*PA* 4:4578)
10. PORTEUS, S. D.; WITH THE ASSISTANCE OF DORIS M. DEWEY AND ROBERT G. BERNREUTER. "Race and Social Differences in Performance Tests." *Genetic Psychol Monogr* 8:93–208 Ag '30. * (*PA* 4:4947)
11. WILE, IRA S., AND DAVIS, ROSE. "A Comparative Study of the Kohs Block Design Test." *Am J Orthopsychiatry* 1:89–103 O '30. * (*PA* 5:2593)
12. McDONALD, JANE REGINA. *A Comparative Study of Deaf Children by Means of the Kohs Block Design Tests and Porteus Maze.* Master's thesis, Ohio State University (Columbus, Ohio), 1931.
13. KENT, GRACE H. "Modification of the Kohs Block Design Test." *J Appl Psychol* 18:578–98 Ag '34. * (*PA* 9:982)
14. AXELBAUM, ETHEL M. *Differences Between the Kohs and Stanford-Binet in a Group of Artistically Gifted Children.* Master's thesis, Columbia University (New York, N.Y.), 1935.
15. WILE, IRA S., AND DAVIS, ROSE. "The Use of the Kohs Test as an Indicator of Mental Confusion." Discussion by Rose Anderson. *Am J Orthopsychiatry* 6:1–17 Ja '36. * (*PA* 10:3586)
16. EARL, C. J. C. "The Performance Test Behavior of Adult Morons." *Brit J Med Psychol* 17:78–92 pt 1 '37. * (*PA* 12:1400)
17. GREENE, EDWARD B. "Practice Effects on Various Types of Standard Tests." *Am J Psychol* 49:67–75 Ja '37. * (*PA* 11:2482)
18. BENTON, ARTHUR L. "The Performance of Pre-School Children on the Kohs Block Design Test." *J Genetic Psychol* 53:231–3 Je '38. * (*PA* 13:2217)
19. NADEL, AARON B. *A Qualitative Analysis of Behavior Following Cerebral Lesions Diagnosed as Primarily Affecting the Frontal Lobes.* Archives of Psychology, No. 224. Washington, D.C.: American Psychological Association, April 1938. Pp. 60. * (*PA* 13:83)
20. BENTON, ARTHUR L. "The Performance of Young Adults

on the Kohs Block Designs Test." Abstract. *Psychol B* 37:513 Jl '40. * (*PA* 14:5728, title only)
21. EARL, C. J. C. "A Psychograph for Morons." *J Abn & Social Psychol* 35:428–48 Jl '40. * (*PA* 14:5403)
22. PRICE, E. J. J. "The Nature of the Practical Factor (F)." *Brit J Psychol* 30:341–51 Ap '40. * (*PA* 14:3783)
23. BENTON, ARTHUR L. "Application of Hutt's Revised Scoring of the Kohs Block Designs Test to the Performances of Adult Subjects." *Am J Psychol* 54:131–2 Ja '41. * (*PA* 15:1991)
24. BENTON, ARTHUR L. "A Study of the Performances of Young Adults on the Kohs Block Designs Test." *J Appl Psychol* 25:420–7 Ag '41. * (*PA* 15:5400)
25. BENTON, ARTHUR L., AND HOWELL, IRA L. "The Use of Psychological Tests in the Evaluation of Intellectual Function Following Head Injury: Report of a Case of Post-Traumatic Personality Disorder." *Psychosom Med* 3:138–51 Ap '41. * (*PA* 15:4206)
26. THOMSON, GODFREY H. "The Speed Factor in Performance Tests." *Brit J Psychol* 32:131–5 O '41. * (*PA* 16:368)
27. WECHSLER, DAVID. *The Measurement of Adult Intelligence, Second Edition,* pp. 93–6, 177–9. Baltimore, Md.: Williams & Wilkins Co., 1941. Pp. xi, 248. *
28. BENTON, ARTHUR L., AND PERRY, JAMES D. "Short Method of Administering the Kohs Block Designs Test." *Am J Orthopsychiatry* 12:231–3 Ap '42. * (*PA* 16:3322)
29. LIDZ, THEODORE; GAY, JAMES R.; AND TIETZE, CHRISTOPHER. "Intelligence in Cerebral Deficit States and Schizophrenia Measured by the Kohs Block Design Test." *Arch Neurol & Psychiatry* 48:568–82 O '42. * (*PA* 17:862)
30. YACORZYNSKI, G. K. "Degree of Effort: 2, Quality of Work and Time of Completion of Performance Tests." *J Exp Psychol* 30:342–4 Ap '42. * (*PA* 16:2635)
31. BRADFORD, E. J. G. "Performance Tests in the Diagnosis of Mental Deficiency." *Brit J Med Psychol* 19:394–414 pts 3–4 '43. * (*PA* 17:3783)
32. EBERT, ELIZABETH, AND SIMMONS, KATHERINE. *The Brush Foundation Study of Child Growth and Development: 1, Psychometric Tests.* Monographs of the Society for Research in Child Development, Vol. 8, No. 2, Serial No. 35. Washington, D.C.: the Society, National Research Council, 1943. Pp. xiv, 113. * (*PA* 18:3322)
33. GOLDFARB, WILLIAM. "Note on a Revised Block Design Test as a Measure of Abstract Performance." *J Ed Psychol* 36:247–51 Ap '45. * (*PA* 19:2392)
34. BRADFORD, E. J. G. "Selection for Technical Education: Parts I and II." *Brit J Ed Psychol* 16:20–31, 69–81 F, Je '46. * (*PA* 20:2887, 4881)
35. SARASON, SEYMOUR B., AND SARASON, ESTHER KROOP. "The Discriminatory Value of a Test Pattern With Cerebral Palsied, Defective Children." Abstract. *Am Psychologist* 1:288 Jl '46. * (*PA* 20:3668, title only)
36. LANDISBERG, SELMA. "A Personality Study of Institutionalized Epileptics." *Am J Mental Def* 52:16–22 Jl '47. * (*PA* 22:2267)
37. POTTER, ELMER H., AND SARASON, SEYMOUR B. "Color in the Rorschach and Kohs Block Designs." Abstract. *Am Psychologist* 2:269–70 Ag 47. * (*PA* 22:4391, title only)
38. SARASON, SEYMOUR B., AND POTTER, ELMER H. "Color in the Rorschach and Kohs Block Designs." *J Consult Psychol* 11:202–6 Jl–Ag '47. * (*PA* 22:205)
39. TOOTH, GEOFFREY. "On the Use of Mental Tests for the Measurement of Disability After Head Injury: With a Comparison Between the Results of These Tests in Patients After Head Injury and Psychoneurotics." *J Neurol Neurosurg & Psychiatry* (England) 10:1–11 F '47. *
40. BIESHEUVEL, S. Chap. 4, "Psychological Tests and Their Applications to Non-European Peoples," pp. 87–126. In *The Yearbook of Education, 1949.* London: Evans Brothers Ltd., 1949. Pp. xv, 660. *
41. FREUDENBERG, R. K., AND ROBERTSON, J. P. S. "Investigation Into Intellectual Changes Following Prefrontal Leucotomy." *J Mental Sci* (England) 95:826–41 O '49. * (*PA* 24:3833)
42. YELA, MARIANO. "Application of the Concept of Simple Structure to Alexander's Data." *Psychometrika* 14:121–35 Je '49. * (*PA* 24:1066)
43. ROGERS, BARBARA ELLEN. *An Investigation to Examine the Results of Kohs' Block Design Test When Used With Young Deaf Children.* Master's thesis, MacMurray College for Women (Jacksonville, Ill.), 1950.
44. TIZARD, J.; IN COLLABORATION WITH N. O'CONNOR AND J. M. CRAWFORD. "The Abilities of Adolescent and Adult High-Grade Male Defectives." *J Mental Sci* 96:888–907 O '50. * (*PA* 25:5421)
45. MANDLER, GEORGE, AND SARASON, SEYMOUR B. "Anxiety as a Factor in Test Performance." Abstract. *Am Psychologist* 6:341 Jl '51. *
46. SHAPIRO, M. B. "Experimental Studies of a Perceptual Anomaly: 1, Initial Experiments." *J Mental Sci* 97:90–110 Ja '51. * (*PA* 25:6220)
47. LIDZ, THEODORE; CARTER, JAMES D.; LEWIS, BERNARD I.; AND SURRATT, CAROLYN. "Effect of ACTH and Cortisone on

Mood and Mentation." *Psychosom Med* 14:363–77 S–O '52. * (*PA* 27:4457)

48. McFie, J., and Piercy, M. F. "Intellectual Impairment With Localized Cerebral Lesions." *Brain* (England) 75:292–311 S '52. * (*PA* 27:7649)

49. Mandler, George, and Sarason, Seymour B. "A Study of Anxiety and Learning." *J Abn & Social Psychol* 47:166–73 Ap '52. * (*PA* 27:2743)

50. Shapiro, M. B. "Experimental Studies of a Perceptual Anomaly: 2, Confirmatory and Explanatory Experiments." *J Mental Sci* (England) 98:605–17 O '52. * (*PA* 27:6085)

51. Shapiro, M. B. "An Experimental Investigation of the Block Design Rotation Effect: An Analysis of a Psychological Effect of Brain Damage." *Brit J Med Psychol* 27:84–8 pts 1 and 2 '54. * (*PA* 28:8947)

52. Yates, Aubrey J. "The Validity of Some Psychological Tests of Brain Damage." *Psychol B* 51:359–79 Jl '54. *

53. Lachmann, Frank Michael. *Perceptual-Motor Development in Children Retarded in Reading Ability*. Doctor's thesis, Northwestern University (Evanston, Ill.), 1955. (*DA* 15:1900)

54. Ray-Chowdhury, K. "Imagery and Performance Tests of Intelligence." *Indian Psychol B* 2:25–30 S '57. * (*PA* 37:4964)

55. Bilger, Robert C. "Limitations on the Use of Intelligence Scales to Estimate the Mental Ages of Children." *Volta R* 60:321–5 S '58. *

56. Gutekunst, Josef Grant. *The Prediction of Art Achievement of Art Education Students by Means of Standardized Tests*. Doctor's thesis, Temple University (Philadelphia, Pa.), 1959. (*DA* 20:3202)

57. Jayalakshmi, G. "Correlation of Tests of Psychomotor Ability With Intelligence and Non-motor Tests." *J Psychol Res* (India) 3:78–84 S '59. *

58. Taylor, A. J. W. "Social Isolation and Imprisonment." *Psychiatry* 24:373–6 N '61. * (*PA* 37:5462)

59. Warhapdande, N. R., and Khullar, B. M. P. "Factorial Analysis of Intelligence Tests." *Manas* (India) 10(2):89–100 '63. * (*PA* 38:10180)

60. Budoff, Milton, and Friedman, Martin. " 'Learning Potential' as an Assessment Approach to the Adolescent Mentally Retarded." *J Consult Psychol* 28:434–9 O '64. * (*PA* 39:5651)

61. Coates, Gerald E. *Basic Components of Performance on the Block Design Test: A Validation Study*. Master's thesis, University of Chicago (Chicago, Ill.), 1964.

62. Larson, Richard K. *The Kohs Block Design Test as a Diagnostic Tool in the Area of Remedial Reading*. Master's thesis, Moorhead State College (Moorhead, Minn.), 1964.

63. Chatterjee, Neera. "A Comparison of Performance of Tribal and Non-Tribal Boys of Tripura (India) on Five Performance Tests." *J Psychol Res* (India) 9:151–8 S '65. * (*PA* 40:6561)

64. Kosc, Ladislav. "Kohs Test and Its Qualitative Analysis in Psychological Clinical Practice." *Studia Psychologica* (Czechoslovakia) 8(3):241–4 '66. *

65. Thune, Jeanne; Tine, Sebastian; and Cherry, Nancy. "Personality Characteristics of Successful Older Leaders." *J Gerontol* 21:463–70 Jl '66. *

66. Budoff, Milton. "Learning Potential Among Institutionalized Young Adult Retardates." *Am J Mental Def* 72:404–11 N '67. * (*PA* 42:7631)

67. Dawson, John L. M. "Cultural and Physiological Influences Upon Spatial-Perceptual Processes in West Africa, Part I." *Int J Psychol* (France) 2(2):115–28 '67. * (*PA* 41:15125)

68. Dawson, John L. M. "Cultural and Physiological Influences Upon Spatial-Perceptual Processes in West Africa, Part II." *Int J Psychol* (France) 2(3):171–85 '67. * (*PA* 43:5194)

69. Kessler, Michael R., and Kronenberger, Earl J. "Dogmatism and Perceptual Synthesis." *Percept & Motor Skills* 24:179–82 F '67. * (*PA* 41:8210)

70. Shrivastava, Radhika Pd. "Kohs Block Design Test Norms for Children." *Indian Psychol R* 4:68–70 Jl '67. *

71. De-Nour, Atara K.; Shaltiel, Judith; and Czaczkes, J. W. "Emotional Reactions of Patients on Chronic Hemodialysis." *Psychosom Med* 30:521–33 S–O '68. * (*PA* 43:8624)

72. Elkin, Lorne. "Predicting Performance of the Mentally Retarded on Sheltered Workshop and Non-Institutional Jobs." *Am J Mental Def* 72:533–9 Ja '68. * (*PA* 42:7638)

73. Kimball, Chase P. "The Experience of Open Heart Surgery: 2, Determinants of Post-operative Behavior." *Psychother & Psychosom* (Switzerland) 18(1–6):259–74 '70. * (*PA* 47:5515)

74. Berry, J. W. "Ecological and Cultural Factors in Spatial Perceptual Development." *Can J Behav Sci* 3(4):324–36 O '71. * (*PA* 47:8577)

CUMULATIVE NAME INDEX

[546]

*Christensen-Guilford Fluency Tests. Grades 7–16 and adults; 1957–73; 4 tests; Paul R. Christensen and J. P. Guilford; Sheridan Psychological Services, Inc. *
a) WORD FLUENCY.
b) IDEATIONAL FLUENCY I.
c) ASSOCIATIONAL FLUENCY I.
d) EXPRESSIONAL FLUENCY.

For additional information and reviews by J. A. Keats and Albert S. Thompson, see 6:544 (4 references).

REFERENCES THROUGH 1971

1–4. See 6:544.

5. Bereiter, Carl Edward. *Verbal and Ideational Fluency in Superior Tenth-Grade Students*. Doctor's thesis, University of Wisconsin (Madison, Wis.), 1959. (*DA* 20:2139)

6. Merrifield, P. R.; Guilford, J. P.; Christensen, P. R.; and Frick, J. W. "Interrelationships Between Certain Abilities and Certain Traits of Motivation and Temperament." *J General Psychol* 65:57–74 Jl '61. * (*PA* 36:2HD57M)

7. de Mille, Richard. "Intellect After Lobotomy in Schizophrenia: A Factor Analytic Study." *Psychol Monogr* 76(16):1–18 '62. * (*PA* 38:2784)

8. Irvine, David James. *An Empirical Study of the Relationship Between Certain Pupil Characteristics and Selected Measures of Creativity*. Doctor's thesis, University of North Carolina (Chapel Hill, N.C.), 1963. (*DA* 25:4543)

9. Locke, Edwin A. "Some Correlates of Classroom and Out-of-Class Achievement in Gifted Science Students." *J Ed Psychol* 54:238–48 O '63. * (*PA* 38:4649)

10. May, Lomax Louis. *A Study of the Relationships Between Achievement on a Complex Visual-Auditory Learning Task and Certain Selected Variables*. Doctor's thesis, University of Alabama (University, Ala.), 1963. (*DA* 25:1750)

11. Atkinson, Bea Henrietta. *The Relationship Between Problem-Solving Strategies and Measures of Convergent and Divergent Thinking in a Selelcted Group of Secondary School Pupils*. Doctor's thesis, University of Florida (Gainesville, Fla.), 1964. (*DA* 25:7070)

12. McGlothlin, William H.; Cohen, Sidney; and McGlothlin, Marcella S. "Short-Term Effects of LSD on Anxiety, Attitudes and Performance." *J Nerv & Mental Dis* 139:266–73 S '64. * (*PA* 39:7046)

13. Seitz, Theodore Lee. *The Relationship Between Creativity and Intelligence, Personality, and Value Patterns in Adolescence*. Doctor's thesis, University of Denver (Denver, Colo.), 1964. (*DA* 25:3679)

14. Bachelis, Leonard A. *Body-Field Perceptual Differentiation as a Variable in Creative Thinking*. Doctor's thesis, Yeshiva University (New York, N.Y.), 1965. (*DA* 26:3475)

15. BUTLER, MARJORIE JOHNSON. *Criteria for Creativity in Counseling.* Doctor's thesis, University of Pittsburgh (Pittsburgh, Pa.), 1965. (*DA* 27:977B)

16. CASTIGLIONE, LAWRENCE VIRGIL. *The Relation of Intelligence to Selected Measures of Creativity.* Doctor's thesis, New York University (New York, N.Y.), 1965. (*DA* 27:1278B)

17. FLAX, MORTON LEWIS. *The Stability of Relationships Between Creativity and Personality Variables.* Doctor's research study No. 1, Colorado State College (Greeley, Colo.), 1966. (*DA* 27:2857B)

18. HAYNES, CAROLYN R. *The Relationships of Performances of Seventh Grade Students on Measures of Creativity, Study Habits and Attitudes, Expressed Need for Counseling and Achievement.* Master's thesis, Texas A & M University (College Station, Tex.), 1966.

19. JANSSEN, CALVIN WAYNE. *Comparative Creativity Scores of Lower Socio-Economic Dropouts and Non-Dropouts.* Doctor's thesis, University of Tennessee (Knoxville, Tenn.), 1966. (*DA* 27:1659A)

20. JOHN, MARTHA ADELINE TYLER. *The Relationship of Symbolic Peer-Modeling to Ideational Fluency in Homogeneous and Heterogeneous Groups.* Doctor's thesis, Stanford University (Stanford, Calif.), 1966. (*DA* 27:2070A)

21. SMITH, ROBERT M., AND NEISWORTH, JOHN T. "Creative Thinking Abilities of Intellectually Superior Children in the Regular Grades." *Psychol Rep* 18:335-41 Ap '66. * (*PA* 40:8832)

22. GIVENS, PAUL R.; PINKARD, CAROLYN A.; AND RICH, THOMAS A. "Relationship of Personality Factors, Creativity and Academic Achievement Among High School Seniors." *Fla J Ed Res* 9:45-56 Ja '67. *

23. GRAY, JAMES JOSEPH. *An Investigation of the Relationship Between Primary Process Thinking and Creativity.* Doctor's thesis, Fordham University (New York, N.Y.), 1967. (*DA* 28:5206B)

24. JACKSON, ROBERT LEON. *An Investigation of the Creative Growth Curves of University Students.* Doctor's thesis, East Texas State University (Commerce, Tex.), 1967. (*DA* 28:3508A)

25. JENKINS, JOHN MERVIN. *A Study of the Characteristics Associated With Innovative Behavior in Teachers.* Doctor's thesis, University of Miami (Coral Gables, Fla.), 1967. (*DA* 28:903A)

26. MANGAN, GORDON L. "Studies of the Relationship Between Neo-Pavlovian Properties of Higher Nervous Activity and Western Personality Dimensions: 4, A Factor Analytic Study of Extraversion and Flexibility, and the Sensitivity and Mobility of the Nervous System." *J Exp Res Personality* 2:124-7 My '67. * (*PA* 41:11908)

27. SMITH, ROBERT M. "Creative Thinking Abilities of Educable Mentally Handicapped Children in the Regular Grades." *Am J Mental Def* 71:571-5 Ja '67. * (*PA* 41:6197)

28. WINDHOLZ, GEORGE, AND MCINTOSH, WILLIAM A. "Concurrent Validation of Guilford's Six Convergent Tests." *Ed & Psychol Meas* 27:393-400 su '67. * (*PA* 41:12843)

29. ANDERSON, RONALD JUDE. *Divergent Thinking Within Superior, Average, and Retarded Subjects.* Doctor's thesis, University of Nebraska (Lincoln, Neb.), 1968. (*DA* 29:1126A)

30. BROWN, STEPHEN W.; GUILFORD, J. P.; AND HOEPFNER, RALPH. "Six Semantic-Memory Abilities." *Ed & Psychol Meas* 28:691-717 au '68. * (*PA* 43:4427)

31. EDWARDS, ARTHUR B. *An Analysis of the Creative Ability Levels of the Potential Dropout in the Average Mental Ability Range.* Doctor's thesis, University of Tennessee (Knoxville, Tenn.), 1968. (*DA* 29:3828A)

32. GETZELS, J. W., AND CSIKSZENTMIHALYI, M. "The Value-Orientations of Art Students as Determinants of Artistic Specialization and Creative Performance." *Studies Art Ed* 10:5-16 f '68. *

33. JANSSEN, CALVIN. "Comparative Creativity Scores of Lower Socio-Economic Dropouts and Non-Dropouts." *Psychol Sch* 5:183-4 Ap '68. * (*PA* 43:17498)

34. LETT, WARREN ROBERT. *Some Postulated Correlates of Creativity and Need Achievement.* Doctor's thesis, University of California (Berkeley, Calif.), 1968. (*DA* 29:1106A)

35. STIMSON, ROGER C., JR. "Factor Analytic Approach to the Structural Differentiation of Description." *J Counsel Psychol* 15:301-7 Jl '68. * (*PA* 42:15457)

36. WINDHOLZ, GEORGE. "The Relation of Creativity and Intelligence Constellations to Traits of Temperament, Interest, and Value in College Students." *J General Psychol* 79:291-9 O '68. * (*PA* 43:3998)

37. BLACKHURST, A. EDWARD; MARKS, CLAUDE H.; AND TISDALL, WILLIAM J. "Relationship Between Mobility and Divergent Thinking in Blind Children." *Ed Visually Handicapped* 1(2):33-6 My '69. * (*PA* 43:14813)

38. GRAY, JAMES J. "The Effect of Productivity on Primary Process and Creativity." *J Proj Tech & Pers Assess* 33(3):213-8 Je '69. * (*PA* 43:14302)

39. GRIMSLEY, WILLIAM GERALD. *The Relationship Between Creativity and Leader Behavior of School Superintendents.* Doctor's thesis, University of Missouri (Columbia, Mo.), 1969. (*DAI* 30:5193A)

40. GUILFORD, J. P., AND HOEPFNER, RALPH. "Comparisons of Varimax Rotations With Rotations to Theoretical Targets." *Ed & Psychol Meas* 29(1):3-22 sp '69. * (*PA* 44:15668)

41. HAAKONSEN, HARRY OLAV. *An Investigation of the Relationships Between Selected Psychological Characteristics of Students and Performance in an Audio-Tutorial Genetics Program.* Doctor's thesis, Syracuse University (Syracuse, N.Y.), 1969. (*DAI* 31:63A)

42. LEHRER, ARNOLD CURTIS. *The Personality Correlates of Creativity in Undergraduates.* Doctor's thesis, Colorado State College (Greeley, Colo.), 1969. (*DAI* 31:397B)

43. OLIVE, HELEN. *Sibling Resemblances in Divergent Thinking.* Doctor's thesis, Columbia University (New York, N.Y.), 1969. (*DAI* 33:3289B)

44. SIMPSON, DONALD JAMES. *The Effect of Selected Musical Studies on Growth in General Creative Potential.* Doctor's thesis, University of Southern California (Los Angeles, Calif.), 1969. (*DAI* 30:502A)

45. BARRON, FRANK. "Heredability of Factors in Creative Thinking and Judgment." *Acta Geneticae Medicae et Gemellologiae* (Italy) 19(1-2):294-8 Ja-Ap '70. *

46. OLESON, D. S., AND ZUBEK, JOHN P. "Effect of One Day of Sensory Deprivation on a Battery of Open-Ended Cognitive Tests." *Percept & Motor Skills* 31(3):919-23 D '70. * (*PA* 46:358)

47. REESE, HAYNE W., AND PARNES, SIDNEY J. "Programming Creative Behavior." *Child Develop* 41(2):413-23 Je '70. * (*PA* 44:15509)

48. SIMMS, JEANNE THOMAS. *An Investigation of the Differences Between Creative High Socio-Economic College Freshmen and Creative Low-Socio-Economic College Freshmen on Measures of Vocational Interests and Certain Motivational Factors.* Doctor's thesis, Catholic University of America (Washington, D.C.), 1970. (*DAI* 31:2693A)

49. ABRAHAM, CAROL. *The Relationship of Authoritarianism to Independence and Creativity Among College Students.* Doctor's thesis, New York University (New York, N.Y.), 1971. (*DAI* 32:6023B)

50. BYRNE, MARY ANN; FELDHUSEN, JOHN F.; AND KANE, ROBERT B. "The Relationships Among Two Cloze Replacement Procedures and Divergent Thinking Abilities." *Read Res Q* 6(3):378-93 sp '71. * (*PA* 47:3624)

51. TISDALL, WILLIAM J.; BLACKHURST, A. EDWARD; AND MARKS, CLAUDE H. "Divergent Thinking in Blind Children." *J Ed Psychol* 62(6):468-73 D '71. * (*PA* 47:9708)

52. WADE, SERENA E. "Adolescents, Creativity, and Media: An Exploratory Study." *Am Behav Sci* 14(3):341-51 Ja '71. * (*PA* 46:8797)

CUMULATIVE NAME INDEX

[547]

Closure Flexibility (Concealed Figures). Industrial employees; 1956–65; revision of *Gottschaldt Figures*; L. L. Thurstone (test), T. E. Jeffrey (test), and Manpower Research and Development Division, Industrial Relations Center, University of Chicago (manual); the Center. * [The publisher has not replied to our four requests to check the accuracy of this entry.]

For additional information, see 7:435 (9 references); for a review by Leona E. Tyler, see 6:545 (4 references).

REFERENCES THROUGH 1971

1–4. See 6:545.
5–13. See 7:435.
14. LONG, ROBERT I. "Field-Articulation as a Factor in Verbal Learning and Recall." *Percept & Motor Skills* 15:151–8 Ag '62. * (*PA* 37:4375)
15. KARP, STEPHEN A. "Field Dependence and Occupational Activity in the Aged." *Percept & Motor Skills* 24:603–9 Ap '67. * (*PA* 41:10284)
16. DICKSTEIN, LOUIS S. "Field Independence in Concept Attainment." *Percept & Motor Skills* 27:635–42 O '68. * (*PA* 43:4803)
17. DAUGHERTY, ROBERT A., AND WATERS, THOMAS J. "Closure Flexibility, Field Dependence and Student Leadership." *Percept & Motor Skills* 29(1):256–8 Ag '69. * (*PA* 44:2341)
18. HASETH, KJELL; SHAGASS, CHARLES; AND STRAUMANIS, JOHN J. "Perceptual and Personality Correlates of EEG and Evoked Response Measures." *Biol Psychiatry* 1(1):49–60 Ja '69. * (*PA* 46:4440)
19. KEISER, THOMAS WILLARD. *Some Correlates of Perceptual Differentiation.* Doctor's thesis, Wayne State University (Detroit, Mich.), 1969. (*DAI* 32:3007B)
20. TARNOPOL, LESTER. "Delinquency and Minimal Brain Dysfunction." *J Learn Dis* 3(4):200–7 Ap '70. * (*PA* 47:3517)
21. LANGLEY, C. W. "Differentiation and Integration of Systems of Personal Constructs." *J Personality* 39(1):10–25 Mr '71. * (*PA* 46:4956)
22. RESNICK, HARVEY. *The Relationship of Client Cognitive Style to Counselor Verbal Style in a Counseling Analogue.* Doctor's thesis, Ohio State University (Columbus, Ohio), 1971. (*DAI* 32:3015B)

CUMULATIVE NAME INDEX

Baehr, M. E.: 11
Blewett, D. B.: 2
Brayer, R.: 4
Corter, H. M.: 1
Daugherty, R. A.: 6, 17
Dickstein, L. S.: 16
Froemel, E. C.: 11
Furcon, J. E.: 11
Gardner, R. W.: 12
Gordon, O.: 4
Gordon, O. J.: 3
Häseth, K.: 18
Karp, S. A.: 15
Keiser, T. W.: 19
Langley, C. W.: 21
Lewin, P. B.: 7
Lohrenz, L. J.: 12
Long, R. I.: 14
Mangan, G. L.: 8
Ohnmacht, F. W.: 9
Resnick, H.: 22
Scheibner, R. M.: 13
Shagass, C.: 18
Steinmetz, A.: 10
Straumanis, J. J.: 18
Tarnopol, L.: 20
Tikofsky, R.: 4
Tikofsky, R. S.: 3
Tyler, L. E.: *rev*, 6:545
Uhlmann, F. W.: 5
Waters, T. J.: 17
Weckowicz, T. E.: 2

[548]

Closure Speed (Gestalt Completion). Industrial employees; 1956–66; formerly called *Gestalt Completion: A Test of Speed of Closure*; L. L. Thurstone (test), T. E. Jeffrey (test), and Norman J. Kantor (manual); Industrial Relations Center, University of Chicago. * [The publisher has not replied to our four requests to check the accuracy of this entry.]

For additional information, see 7:436 (2 references); for a review by Leona E. Tyler, see 6:546 (3 references).

REFERENCES THROUGH 1971

1–3. See 6:546.
4–5. See 7:436.
6. HASETH, KJELL; SHAGASS, CHARLES; AND STRAUMANIS, JOHN J. "Perceptual and Personality Correlates of EEG and Evoked Response Measures." *Biol Psychiatry* 1(1):49–60 Ja '69. * (*PA* 46:4440)

CUMULATIVE NAME INDEX

Baehr, M. E.: 4
Bass, B. M.: 1–2
Coates, C. H.: 1
Coscarelli, J. E.: 5
Froemel, E. C.: 4
Furcon, J. E.: 4
Häseth, K.: 6
Karstendiek, B.: 2
McCarty, J. J.: 3
McCullough, G.: 2
Pruitt, R. C.: 2
Sanders, J. W.: 5
Shagass, C.: 6
Straumanis, J. J.: 6
Tyler, L. E.: *rev*, 6:546

[549]

Concept Assessment Kit—Conservation. Ages 4–7; 1968; CAKC; 2 editions; Marcel L. Goldschmid

and Peter M. Bentler; Educational and Industrial Testing Service. *

a) FORMS A AND B. 13 scores: 2 scores (behavior, explanation) in each of 6 areas (2-dimensional space, number, substance, continuous quantity, weight, discontinuous quantity), total.

b) FORM C. 13 scores: 2 scores (behavior, explanation) in area (3 scores) and length (3 scores), total.

For additional information, a review by J. Douglas Ayers, and excerpted reviews by Rheta DeVries (with Lawrence Kohlberg), Vernon C. Hall (with Michael Mery), and Charles D. Smock, see 7:437 (5 references).

REFERENCES THROUGH 1971

1–5. See 7:437.
6. GOLDSCHMID, MARCEL L. "Role of Experience in the Acquisition of Conservation." Abstract. *Proc 76th Ann Conv Am Psychol Assn* 3:361–2 '68. * (*PA* 43:665, title only)
7. RARDIN, DONALD R., AND MOAN, CHARLES E. "Peer Interaction and Cognitive Development." *Child Develop* 42(6):1685–99 D '71. * (*PA* 48:8760)
8. SWIZE, LYDIA MARIE. *The Relationship Between Performance on Piagetian Conservation Tasks and Intelligence and Achievement in Educable Mentally Retarded Children.* Doctor's thesis, University of Northern Colorado (Greeley, Colo.), 1971. (*DAI* 32:3806A)
9. SWIZE, MYRON THEODORE. *Prediction of Piagetian Conservation for Second Grade Mexican-American and Anglo-American Children.* Doctor's thesis, University of Northern Colorado (Greeley, Colo.), 1971. (*DAI* 32:5624A)
10. WASIK, BARBARA H., AND WASIK, JOHN L. "Performance of Culturally Deprived Children on the Concept Assessment Kit—Conservation." *Child Develop* 42(5):1586–90 N '71. * (*PA* 48:4660)

CUMULATIVE NAME INDEX

Ayers, J. D.: *rev*, 7:437
Baker, E. A.: 4
Bentler, P. M.: 3, 5
DeVries, R.: *exc*, 7:437
Goldschmid, M. L.: 1–3, 6
Hall, V. C.: *exc*, 7:437
Kohlberg, L.: *exc*, 7:437
Mery, M.: *exc*, 7:437
Moan, C. E.: 7
Rardin, D. R.: 7
Smock, C. D.: *exc*, 7:437
Swize, L. M.: 8
Swize, M. T.: 9
Wasik, B. H.: 10
Wasik, J. L.: 10

[550]

★**Concept Attainment Test.** College and adults; 1959; CAT; J. M. Schepers; National Institute for Personnel Research [South Africa]. *

[551]

Consequences. Grades 9–16 and adults; 1958–62; 2 scores: originality, ideational fluency; the original 1958 single-form, 10-item test has been divided into two 5-item tests, Forms A-1 (first 5 items) and A-2 (last 5 items); no manual for the 5-item tests; P. R. Christensen, P. R. Merrifield, and J. P. Guilford; Sheridan Psychological Services, Inc. *

For additional information and a review by Goldine C. Gleser of the 10-item test, see 6:547 (13 references).

REFERENCES THROUGH 1971

1–13. See 6:547.
14. MARKS, ALVIN; MICHAEL, WILLIAM B.; AND KAISER, HENRY F. "Comparison of Manual and Analytic Techniques of Rotation in a Factor Analysis of Aptitude Test Variables." *Psychol Rep* 7:519–22 D '60. * (*PA* 35:2792)
15. GARWOOD, DOROTHY SEMENOW. *Some Personality Factors Related to Creativity in Young Scientists.* Doctor's thesis, Claremont Graduate School (Claremont, Calif.), 1961. (*DA* 22:3273)
16. MCGUIRE, CARSON; HINDSMAN, EDWIN; KING, F. J.; AND JENNINGS, EARL. "Dimensions of Talented Behavior." *Ed & Psychol Meas* 21:3–38 sp '61. * (*PA* 36:1KH03M)
17. MERRIFIELD, P. R.; GUILFORD, J. P.; CHRISTENSEN, P. R.; AND FRICK, J. W. "Interrelationships Between Certain Abilities and Certain Traits of Motivation and Temperament." *J General Psychol* 65:57–74 Jl '61. * (*PA* 36:2HD57M)
18. BARRON, FRANK. *Creativity and Psychological Health: Origins of Personal Vitality and Creative Freedom.* Princeton, N.J.: D. Van Nostrand Co., Inc., 1963. Pp. xi, 292. *
19. IRVINE, DAVID JAMES. *An Empirical Study of the Relationship Between Certain Pupil Characteristics and Selected Measures of Creativity.* Doctor's thesis, University of North Carolina (Chapel Hill, N.C.), 1963. (*DA* 25:4543)

20. LOCKE, EDWIN A. "Some Correlates of Classroom and Out-of-Class Achievement in Gifted Science Students." *J Ed Psychol* 54:238–48 O '63. * (*PA* 38:4649)

21. WHITTEMORE, ROBERT GEORGE, JR. *Modification of Originality Responses in Academically Talented, Male University Freshmen.* Doctor's thesis, Arizona State University (Tempe, Ariz.), 1963. (*DA* 25:6403)

22. CASTELLI, CHARLES DOMINIC. *An Exploration of the Relationship Between Teacher Creative Ability and Teacher-Pupil Classroom Behavior.* Doctor's thesis, State University of New York (Buffalo, N.Y.), 1964. (*DA* 25:3320)

23. FLEISCHER, GERALD. *The Effects of Anxiety Upon Tests of Creativity.* Doctor's thesis, State University of New York (Buffalo, N.Y.), 1964. (*DA* 25:5372)

24. GARWOOD, DOROTHY SEMENOW. "Personality Factors Related to Creativity in Young Scientists." *J Abn & Social Psychol* 68:413–9 Ap '64. * (*PA* 39:1729)

25. GRIFFIN, WILLIAM MAXWELL. *A Study of the Relationship of Certain Characteristics of High School Seniors to Effectiveness in Independent Study.* Doctor's thesis, Syracuse University (Syracuse, N.Y.), 1964. (*DA* 25:5787)

26. MCGLOTHLIN, WILLIAM H.; COHEN, SIDNEY; AND MCGLOTHLIN, MARCELLA S. "Short-Term Effects of LSD on Anxiety, Attitudes and Performance." *J Nerv & Mental Dis* 139:266–73 S '64. * (*PA* 39:7046)

27. RAINWATER, JANETTE MUNKITTRICK. *Effects of Set on Problem Solving in Subjects of Varying Levels of Assessed Creativity.* Doctor's thesis, University of California (Berkeley, Calif.), 1964. (*DA* 25:6753)

28. RICHARDS, JAMES M., JR.; CLINE, VICTOR B.; AND NEEDHAM, WALTER E. "Creativity Tests and Teacher and Self Judgments of Originality." *J Exp Ed* 32:281–5 sp '64. * (*PA* 39:5135)

29. SEITZ, THEODORE LEE. *The Relationship Between Creativity and Intelligence, Personality, and Value Patterns in Adolescence.* Doctor's thesis, University of Denver (Denver, Colo.), 1964. (*DA* 25:3679)

30. BACHELIS, LEONARD A. *Body-Field Perceptual Differentiation as a Variable in Creative Thinking.* Doctor's thesis, Yeshiva University (New York, N.Y.), 1965. (*DA* 26:3475)

31. BUTLER, MARJORIE JOHNSON. *Criteria for Creativity in Counseling.* Doctor's thesis, University of Pittsburgh (Pittsburgh, Pa.), 1965. (*DA* 27:977B)

32. FELDHUSEN, JOHN F.; DENNY, TERRY; AND CONDON, CHARLES F. "Anxiety, Divergent Thinking, and Achievement." *J Ed Psychol* 56:40–5 F '65. * (*PA* 39:10771)

33. FLEISCHER, GERALD, AND COHEN, IRA S. "The Relationship Between Test Anxiety and Tests of Creativity." Abstract. *Proc Ann Conv Am Psychol Assn* 73:311–2 '65. * (*PA* 39:15458)

34. CROPLEY, A. J. "Creativity and Intelligence." *Brit J Ed Psychol* 36:259–66 N '66. * (*PA* 41:573)

35. EISENSTADT, J. MARVIN. "Problem-Solving Ability of Creative and Non-Creative College Students." *J Consult Psychol* 30:81–3 F '66. * (*PA* 40:4223)

36. FLAX, MORTON LEWIS. *The Stability of Relationships Between Creativity and Personality Variables.* Doctor's research study No. 1, Colorado State College (Greeley, Colo.), 1966. (*DA* 27:2857B)

37. HARDYCK, CURTIS D. "Personality Characteristics and Motor Activity: Some Empirical Evidence." *J Pers & Social Psychol* 4:181–8 Ag '66. * (*PA* 40:11183)

38. NICOLAY, GLEN C. *Relationship Between a Risk-Taking Questionnaire and Selected Personality Characteristics.* Doctor's thesis, Fordham University (New York, N.Y.), 1966. (*DA* 27:2142B)

39. SMITH, ROBERT M., AND NEISWORTH, JOHN T. "Creative Thinking Abilities of Intellectually Superior Children in the Regular Grades." *Psychol Rep* 18:335–41 Ap '66. * (*PA* 40:8832)

40. COMPTON, MARY FRANCES. *An Attempt to Foster Creative Thinking in Teachers.* Doctor's thesis, University of Florida (Gainesville, Fla.), 1967. (*DA* 29:164A)

41. CROPLEY, A. J. "Creativity, Intelligence, and Achievement." *Alberta J Ed Res* (Canada) 13:51–8 Mr '67. * (*PA* 41:15253)

42. GIVENS, PAUL R.; PINKARD, CAROLYN A.; AND RICH, THOMAS A. "Relationship of Personality Factors, Creativity and Academic Achievement Among High School Seniors." *Fla J Ed Res* 9:45–56 Ja '67. *

43. JACKSON, ROBERT LEON. *An Investigation of the Creative Growth Curves of University Students.* Doctor's thesis, East Texas State University (Commerce, Tex.), 1967. (*DA* 28:3508A)

44. MANGAN, GORDON L. "Studies of the Relationship Between Neo-Pavlovian Properties of Higher Nervous Activity and Western Personality Dimensions: 3, The Relations of Transformation Mobility to Thinking Flexibility." *J Exp Res Personality* 2:117–23 My '67. * (*PA* 41:11907)

45. SIDLE, ALLAN CHARLES. *Creativity and Delusional Thinking in Schizophrenics.* Doctor's thesis, Stanford University (Stanford, Calif.), 1967. (*DA* 28:353B)

46. SMITH, ROBERT M. "Creative Thinking Abilities of Educable Mentally Handicapped Children in the Regular Grades." *Am J Mental Def* 71:571–5 Ja '67. * (*PA* 41:6197)

47. ADAMS, JOHN C., JR. "The Relative Effects of Various Testing Atmospheres on Spontaneous Flexibility, a Factor of Divergent Thinking." *J Creative Behav* 2:187–94 su '68. * (*PA* 43:5882)

48. ANDERSON, RONALD JUDE. *Divergent Thinking Within Superior, Average, and Retarded Subjects.* Doctor's thesis, University of Nebraska (Lincoln, Neb.), 1968. (*DA* 29:1126A)

49. BOWERS, KENNETH. "Hypnosis and Creativity: A Preliminary Investigation." *Int J Clin & Exp Hyp* 16:38–52 Ja '68. * (*PA* 42:11537)

50. BROWN, STEPHEN W.; GUILFORD, J. P.; AND HOEFFNER, RALPH. "Six Semantic-Memory Abilities." *Ed & Psychol Meas* 28:691–717 au '68. * (*PA* 43:4427)

51. HINTON, BERNARD L. "Environmental Frustration and Creative Problem Solving." *J Appl Psychol* 52:211–7 Je '68. * (*PA* 42:11701)

52. LETT, WARREN ROBERT. *Some Postulated Correlates of Creativity and Need Achievement.* Doctor's thesis, University of California (Berkeley, Calif.), 1968. (*DA* 29:1106A)

53. ROGERS, MARTIN IRVING. *Self-Actualization as Process.* Doctor's thesis, Case Western Reserve University (Cleveland, Ohio), 1968. (*DAI* 30:4380B)

54. SHAPIRO, R. J. *Creative Research Scientists.* Psychologica Africana Monograph Supplement No. 4. Johannesburg, South Africa: National Institute for Personnel Research, 1968. Pp. 180. * (*PA* 43:923)

55. WHITE, KINNARD. "Anxiety, Extraversion-Intraversion, and Divergent Thinking Ability." *J Creative Behav* 2:119–27 sp '68. * (*PA* 42:17233)

56. BLACKHURST, A. EDWARD; MARKS, CLAUDE H.; AND TISDALL, WILLIAM J. "Relationship Between Mobility and Divergent Thinking in Blind Children." *Ed Visually Handicapped* 1(2):33–6 My '69. * (*PA* 43:14813)

57. GRIMSLEY, WILLIAM GERALD. *The Relationship Between Creativity and Leader Behavior of School Superintendents.* Doctor's thesis, University of Missouri (Columbia, Mo.), 1969. (*DAI* 30:5193A)

58. GUILFORD, J. P., AND HOEFFNER, RALPH. "Comparisons of Varimax Rotations With Rotations to Theoretical Targets." *Ed & Psychol Meas* 29(1):3–22 sp '69. * (*PA* 44:15668)

59. KLEIN, STEPHEN P.; FREDERIKSEN, NORMAN; AND EVANS, FRANKLIN R. "Anxiety and Learning to Formulate Hypotheses." *J Ed Psychol* 60(6):465–75 D '69. * (*PA* 44:3087)

60. KROP, HARRY. "Effects of Extrinsic Motivation, Intrinsic Motivation, and Intelligence on Creativity: A Factorial Approach." *J General Psychol* 80(2):259–66 Ap '69. * (*PA* 43:11332)

61. KROP, HARRY D.; ALEGRE, CECILIA E.; AND WILLIAMS, CARL D. "Effect of Induced Stress on Convergent and Divergent Thinking." *Psychol Rep* 24(3):895–8 Je '69. * (*PA* 44:218)

62. OLIVE, HELEN. *Sibling Resemblances in Divergent Thinking.* Doctor's thesis, Columbia University (New York, N.Y.), 1969. (*DAI* 33:289B)

63. SCHNITZER, LEAH PALTIEL, AND STEWART, ROBERT A. C. "Originality and Personality Variables in High School Art Students." *Psychol* 6(1):36–9 F '69. * (*PA* 43:11334)

64. BARRON, FRANK. "Heredability of Factors in Creative Thinking and Judgment." *Acta Geneticae Medicae et Gemellologiae* (Italy) 19(1–2):294–8 Ja–Ap '70. *

65. BOWERS, KENNETH S., AND VAN DER MEULEN, SANDRA J. "Effect of Hypnotic Susceptibility on Creativity Test Performance." *J Pers & Social Psychol* 14(3):247–56 Mr '70. * (*PA* 44:8441)

66. DELLAS, MARIE. *Effects of Creativity Training, Defensiveness, and Intelligence on Divergent Thinking.* Doctor's thesis, State University of New York (Buffalo, N.Y.), 1970. (*DAI* 31:4540A)

67. FELDHUSEN, JOHN F.; TREFFINGER, DONALD J.; AND ELIAS, ROBERT M. "Prediction of Academic Achievement With Divergent and Convergent Thinking and Personality Variables." *Psychol Sch* 7(1):46–52 Ja '70. * (*PA* 44:11410)

68. FRUIN, DAVID JOHN. *Response Styles and Creativity.* Doctor's thesis, Johns Hopkins University (Baltimore, Md.), 1970. (*DAI* 31:436IB)

69. HINTON, BERNARD L. "Personality Variables and Creative Potential." *J Creative Behav* 4(3):210–7 su '70. *

70. LAMONTAGNE, CHARLES WARREN. *An Exploration of the Relationship of Creativity and Educational Administration.* Doctor's thesis, Boston University (Boston, Mass.), 1970. (*DAI* 31:2064A)

71. OLESON, D. S., AND ZUBEK, JOHN P. "Effect of One Day of Sensory Deprivation on a Battery of Open-Ended Cognitive Tests." *Percept & Motor Skills* 31(3):919–23 D '70. * (*PA* 46:358)

72. OWEN, STEVEN V.; FELDHUSEN, JOHN F.; AND THURSTON, JOHN R. "Achievement Prediction in Nursing Education With Cognitive, Attitudinal, and Divergent Thinking Variables." *Psychol Rep* 26(3):867–70 Je '70. * (*PA* 45:1361)

73. REESE, HAYNE W., AND PARNES, SIDNEY J. "Programming Creative Behavior." *Child Develop* 41(2):413–23 Je '70. * (*PA* 44:15509)

74. RENNER, VIVIAN. "Effects of Modification of Cognitive Style on Creative Behavior." *J Pers & Social Psychol* 14(3):257–62 Mr '70. * (*PA* 44:8435)

Consequences

75. RICHMOND, BERT O. "Creativity: Its Relationship to the Counselor's Approach." *J Stud Pers Assn Teach Ed* 8(2):56–63 w '70. * (*PA* 44:19438)

76. SMITH, I. LEON. "IQ, Creativity, and the Taxonomy of Educational Objectives: Cognitive Domain." *J Exp Ed* 38(4):58–60 su '70. * (*PA* 46:5688)

77. ABRAHAM, CAROL. *The Relationship of Authoritarianism to Independence and Creativity Among College Students.* Doctor's thesis, New York University (New York, N.Y.), 1971. (*DAI* 32:6023B)

78. ANASTASI, ANNE, AND SCHAEFER, CHARLES E. "Note on the Concepts of Creativity and Intelligence." *J Creative Behav* 5(2):113–6 '71. * (*PA* 48:7724)

79. BOWERS, KENNETH S. "Sex and Susceptibility as Moderator Variables in the Relationship of Creativity and Hypnotic Susceptibility." *J Abn Psychol* 78(1):93–100 Ag '71. * (*PA* 47:2042)

80. CROPLEY, A. J., AND CLAPSON, L. "Long Term Test-Retest Reliability of Creativity Tests." *Brit J Ed Psychol* 41(2):206–8 Je '71. * (*PA* 47:9640)

81. SMITH, I. LEON. "IQ, Creativity, and Achievement: Interaction and Threshold." *Multiv Behav Res* 6(1):51–62 Ja '71. * (*PA* 46:9753)

82. TISDALL, WILLIAM J.; BLACKHURST, A. EDWARD; AND MARKS, CLAUDE H. "Divergent Thinking in Blind Children." *J Ed Psychol* 62(6):468–73 D '71. * (*PA* 47:9708)

83. WADE, SERENA E. "Adolescents, Creativity, and Media: An Exploratory Study." *Am Behav Sci* 14(3):341–51 Ja '71. * (*PA* 46:8797)

84. WILLIAMS, JOHN D.; HARLOW, STEVEN D.; AND BORGEN, JEROME S. "Creativity, Dogmatism, and Arithmetic Achievement." *J Psychol* 78(2):217–22 Jl '71. * (*PA* 46:9760)

CUMULATIVE NAME INDEX

Abdel-Razik, T. M.: 10
Abe, C.: 9
Abraham, C.: 77
Adams, J. C.: 47
Alegre, C. E.: 61
Anastasi, A.: 78
Anderson, R. J.: 48
Asher, J. J.: 13
Bachelis, L. A.: 30
Barron, F.: 1, 11, 18, 64
Beittel, K. R.: 5
Berger, R. M.: 2
Blackhurst, A. E.: 56, 82
Borgen, J. S.: 84
Bowers, K.: 49
Bowers, K. S.: 65, 79
Brittain, W. L.: 5
Brown, S. W.: 50
Butler, M. J.: 31
Castelli, C. D.: 22
Christensen, P. R.: 2, 4, 17
Clapson, L.: 80
Cline, V. B.: 9, 12, 28
Cohen, I. S.: 33
Cohen, S.: 26
Compton, M. F.: 40
Condon, C. F.: 32
Cropley, A. J.: 34, 41, 80
Dellas, M.: 66
Denny, T.: 32
Eisenstadt, J. M.: 35
Elias, R. M.: 67
Evans, F. R.: 59
Feldhusen, J. F.: 32, 67, 72
Flax, M. L.: 36
Fleischer, G.: 23, 33
Frederiksen, N.: 59
Frick, J. W.: 17
Fruin, D. J.: 68
Garwood, D. S.: 15, 24
Givens, P. R.: 42
Gleser, G. C.: rev, 6:547
Griffin, W. M.: 25
Grimsley, W. G.: 57
Guilford, J. P.: 2–4, 17, 50, 58
Hardyck, C. D.: 37
Harlow, S. D.: 84
Hindsman, E.: 16
Hinton, B. L.: 51, 69
Hoepfner, R.: 50, 58
Irvine, D. J.: 19
Jackson, R. L.: 43

Jacobsen, T. L.: 13
Jennings, E.: 16
Kaiser, H. F.: 7–8, 14
Kettner, N. W.: 4
King, F. J.: 16
Klein, S. P.: 59
Krop, H.: 60
Krop, H. D.: 61
Lamontagne, C. W.: 70
Lett, W. R.: 52
Locke, E. A.: 20
McGlothlin, M. S.: 26
McGlothlin, W. H.: 26
McGuire, C.: 6, 16
Mangan, G. L.: 44
Marks, A.: 7–8, 14
Marks, C. H.: 56, 82
Merrifield, P. R.: 17
Michael, W. B.: 7–8, 14
Needham, W. E.: 12, 28
Neisworth, J. T.: 39
Nicolay, G. C.: 38
Oleson, D. S.: 71
Olive, H.: 62
Owen, S. V.: 72
Parnes, S. J.: 73
Pinkard, C. A.: 42
Rainwater, J. M.: 27
Reese, H. W.: 73
Renner, V.: 74
Rich, T. A.: 42
Richards, J. M.: 9, 12, 28
Richmond, B. O.: 75
Rogers, M. I.: 53
Schaefer, C. E.: 78
Schnitzer, L. P.: 63
Seitz, T. L.: 29
Shapiro, R. J.: 54
Sidle, A. C.: 45
Smith, I. L.: 76, 81
Smith, R. M.: 39, 46
Stewart, R. A. C.: 63
Thurston, J. R.: 72
Tisdall, W. J.: 56, 82
Treffinger, D. J.: 67
van der Meulen, S. J.: 65
Wade, S. E.: 83
White, K.: 55
Whittemore, R. G.: 21
Williams, C. D.: 61
Williams, J. D.: 84
Zubek, J. P.: 71

[552]

★**Consequences [NIPR].** Ages 15 and over; 1972; verbal creativity; H. E. Schmidt (manual); National Institute for Personnel Research [South Africa]. *

Consequences

[553]

★**Creativity Attitude Survey.** Grades 4–6; 1971; CAS; Charles E. Schaefer; Psychologists and Educators, Inc. *

REFERENCES THROUGH 1971

1. SCHAEFER, CHARLES E., AND BRIDGES, CAROLYN I. "Development of a Creativity Attitude Survey for Children." *Percept & Motor Skills* 31(3):861–2 D '70. * (*PA* 45:9980)

CUMULATIVE NAME INDEX

Bridges, C. I.: 1   Schaefer, C. E.: 1

[554]

★**Creativity Tests for Children.** Grades 4–6; 1971; CTC; "divergent production abilities"; 10 tests; J. P. Guilford and others listed below; Sheridan Psychological Services, Inc. *

a) ADDING DECORATIONS. Identical with first half of *Decorations* (see 555); Arthur Gershon, Sheldon Gardner, and Philip R. Merrifield.

b) DIFFERENT LETTER GROUPS. Arthur Gershon.

c) HIDDEN LETTERS.

d) KINDS OF PEOPLE. Adaptation of *Possible Jobs* (see 573); Arthur Gershon.

e) MAKE SOMETHING OUT OF IT.

f) MAKING OBJECTS. Adaptation of adult test with the same title (see 562); Sheldon Gardner, Arthur Gershon, and Philip R. Merrifield.

g) NAMES FOR STORIES. Adaptation of *Plot Titles* (see 572).

h) SIMILAR MEANINGS. Adaptation of *Associational Fluency 1* (see 546c); Philip R. Merrifield.

i) WHAT TO DO WITH IT. Adaptation of *Alternate Uses* (see 542); Philip R. Merrifield.

j) WRITING SENTENCES.

[555]

Decorations. Grades 9–16 and adults; 1963; "divergent production of figural implications" or "ability to add meaningful details"; Arthur Gershon, Sheldon Gardner, Philip R. Merrifield, and J. P. Guilford; Sheridan Psychological Services, Inc. *

For additional information, see 6:548 (1 reference).

REFERENCES THROUGH 1971

1. See 6:548.

2. MACKLER, BERNARD, AND SHONTZ, FRANKLIN C. "Life Style and Creativity: An Empirical Investigation." *Percept & Motor Skills* 20:873–96 Je '65. * (*PA* 39:15302)

3. MACKLER, BERNARD, AND SPOTTS, JAMES V. "Characteristics of Responses to Tests of Creativity: A Second Look." *Percept & Motor Skills* 21:595–9 O '65. * (*PA* 40:2880)

4. HEUSSENSTAMM, FRANCES K. "Creativity and Alienation: An Exploration of Their Relationship in Adolescence." *Calif J Ed Res* 21(3):140–6 My '70. *

5. OLESON, D. S., AND ZUBEK, JOHN P. "Effect of One Day of Sensory Deprivation on a Battery of Open-Ended Cognitive Tests." *Percept & Motor Skills* 31(3):919–23 D '70. * (*PA* 46:358)

6. RAIA, JAMES R., AND OSIPOW, SAMUEL H. "Creative Thinking Ability and Susceptibility to Persuasion." *J Social Psychol* 82(2):181–6 D '70. * (*PA* 45:6341)

CUMULATIVE NAME INDEX

Guilford, J. P.: 1   Raia, J. R.: 6
Heussenstamm, F. K.: 4   Shontz, F. C.: 2
Mackler, B.: 2–3   Spotts, J. V.: 3
Oleson, D. S.: 5   Zubek, J. P.: 5
Osipow, S. H.: 6

[556]

Feature Profile Test: Pintner-Paterson Modification. Ages 4 and over; [1917–23]; modification of *Knox-Kempf Feature Profile Test* ['14]; subtest of *Arthur Point Scale of Performance Tests* and *Performance Tests of Intelligence*; R. Pintner and D. G. Paterson; Stoelting Co.

REFERENCES THROUGH 1971

1. WECHSLER, DAVID. *The Measurement of Adult Intelligence, Second Edition*, pp. 98–100, 175–7. Baltimore, Md.: Williams & Wilkins Co., 1941. Pp. xi, 248. *

CUMULATIVE NAME INDEX

Wechsler, D.: 1

[557]

★**Gottschaldt Figures [NIPR].** Job applicants with at least 10 years of education; 1943–56; adaptation of U.S. Army Air Forces Test AC121; test in English and Afrikaans; no manual; National Institute for Personnel Research [South Africa]. *

[558]

Healy Pictorial Completion Tests. Ages 5 and over; [1914–21]; 2 tests; William Healy; Stoelting Co. *

a) TEST I. 1914; modification appears in *Arthur Point Scale of Performance Tests*.

b) TEST II. [1917–21]; subtest of *Arthur Point Scale of Performance Tests*.

REFERENCES THROUGH 1971

1. HEALY, WILLIAM. "A Pictorial Completion Test." *Psychol R* 21:189–203 My '14. *
2. PINTNER, RUDOLF, AND PATERSON, DONALD G. *A Scale of Performance Tests*, pp. 44–53, 122–6. New York: D. Appleton & Co., 1917. Pp. xi, 218. *
3. WALKER, MIRIAM A., AND WASHBURN, M. F. "The Healy-Fernald Picture Completion Test as a Test of the Perception of the Comic." *Am J Psychol* 30:304–7 Jl '19. *
4. GAULT, ROBERT H. "Picture Completion." *J Appl Psychol* 4:310–5 D '20. *
5. SKAGGS, E. B. "A Comparison of Results Obtained by the Terman Binet Tests and the Healy Picture Completion Test." *J Ed Psychol* 11:418–420a O '20. *
6. HEALY, WILLIAM. "Pictorial Completion Test II." *J Appl Psychol* 5:225–39 S '21. *
7. JOHNSON, BUFORD, AND SCHRIEFER, LOUISE. "A Comparison of Mental Age Scores Obtained by Performance Tests and the Stanford Revision of the Binet-Simon Scale." *J Ed Psychol* 13:408–17 O '22. *
8. MORGENTHAU, DOROTHY RUTH. "Some Well-Known Mental Tests Evaluated and Compared." *Arch Psychol* 52:1–54 My '22. *
9. PERRY, DORIS E. "Interpretations of the Reactions of the Feeble-Minded on the Healy Pictorial Completion Test II—Social Implications." *J Deling* 7:75–85 Mr '22. *
10. GAW, FRANCES. "A Study of Performance Tests." *Brit J Psychol* 15:374–92 Ap '25. *
11. JOHNSON, BUFORD J. *Mental Growth of Children in Relation to the Rate of Growth in Bodily Development: A Report of the Bureau of Educational Experiments, New York City*, pp. 123–5. New York: E. P. Dutton & Co., 1925. Pp. 160. *
12. McCAULLEY, SELINA. "One Hundred Non-Conformed Boys." *Psychol Clinic* 16:141–66 My–Je '25. * (*PA* 3:1607)
13. PASCHAL, FRANKLIN C., AND SULLIVAN, LOUIS R. "Racial Influences in the Mental and Physical Development of Mexican Children." *Comp Psychol Monogr* 3(14):1–76 O '25. * (*PA* 1:393)
14. JONES, GRACE L. *A Study of the Healy Completion Test II.* Master's thesis, Ohio Wesleyan University (Delaware, Ohio), 1926.
15. WORTHINGTON, MYRTLE RAYMAKER. "A Study of Some Commonly Used Performance Tests." *J Appl Psychol* 10:216–27 Je '26. *
16. DORCUS, MILDRED DAY. "Analysis of Specific Responses of Children in the Healy Pictorial Completion Test II." *J Genetic Psychol* 35:574–86 D '28. * (*PA* 3:2436)
17. SCHIEFFELIN, BARBARA, AND SCHWESINGER, GLADYS C. *Mental Tests and Heredity: Including a Survey of Non-Verbal Tests*, pp. 148–50. New York: Galton Publishing Co., Inc., 1930. Pp. ix, 298. *
18. ECCLES, AUGUST M. "The Performance of Delinquent Boys on the Healy Completion Test II." *Training Sch B* 28:61–70 Je '31. * (*PA* 7:1981, title only)
19. LOUTTIT, C. M. "Test Performance of a Selected Group of Part-Hawaiians." *J Appl Psychol* 15:43–52 F '31. * (*PA* 5:4204)
20. SCOVILL, MARY SOPHIA. *A Comparative Study of the Performance of Normal and Feebleminded Subjects on the Healy Pictorial Completion Test II.* Master's thesis, Ohio State University (Columbus, Ohio), 1931.
21. NOTTINGHAM, RUTH D. "A Psychological Study of Forty Unmarried Mothers." *Genetic Psychol Monogr* 19:157–228 My '37. * (*PA* 11:4670)

22. VERNON, P. E. "A Study of the Norms and the Validity of Certain Mental Tests at a Child Guidance Clinic: Part II." *Brit J Ed Psychol* 7:115–37 Je '37. * (*PA* 11:4827)
23. WILSON, FRANK T., AND FLEMING, CECILE WHITE. "Correlations of Performance Tests With Other Abilities and Traits in Grade I." *Child Develop* 8:80–8 Mr '37. * (*PA* 11:4814)
24. CARPENTER, RACHEL STANLEY. *What Value Has Healy's Picture Completion Test II as a Prognostic Test for Success in Geometry?* Master's thesis, Trinity College (Hartford, Conn.), 1938.
25. HAMLIN, ROY, AND ABEL, THEODORA M. "Test Pattern of Mental Defectives Skilled in Weaving." *J Appl Psychol* 22:385–9 Ag '38. * (*PA* 13:1642)
26. MARSH, CHARLES JUDD. *Performance Test Abilities of Adults.* Doctor's thesis, Stanford University (Stanford, Calif.), 1938.
27. HANFMANN, EUGENIA. "A Qualitative Analysis of the Healy Pictorial Completion Test II." *Am J Orthopsychiatry* 9:325–30 Ap '39. * (*PA* 13:5385)
28. WERNER, HENRY. "A Comparative Study of a Small Group of Clinical Tests." *J Appl Psychol* 24:231–6 Ap '40. * (*PA* 14:4775)
29. WOOD, LOUISE. "A New Picture Completion Test." *J Genetic Psychol* 56:383–409 Je '40. * (*PA* 15:576)
30. SCHWERIN, ERNA. *A Study of Comparative Reliability and Validity of the Healy Completion Test II and a Revised Form.* Master's thesis, Bowling Green State University (Bowling Green, Ohio), 1953.
31. SCHWERIN, ERNA, AND FITZWATER, MYLEN E. "Comparative Reliability and Validity of the Healy Completion Test II and a Revised Form." Abstract. *Am Psychologist* 9:468 Ag '54. *
32. SCHWERIN, ERNA, AND FITZWATER, MYLEN E. "Comparative Reliability and Validity of the Healy Completion Test II and a Revised Form." *J Clin Psychol* 10:248–51 Jl '54. * (*PA* 29:2475)
33. CLARK, KENNETH C. *The Healy Picture Completion Test II as an Indicator of Emotional Disorder in Elementary School Children.* Master's thesis, Fresno State College (Fresno, Calif.), 1956.
34. FITZPATRICK, CONSTANCE H. *A Study of the Performance of a Group of Mentally Retarded Children on the Healy Pictorial Completion Test II.* Master's thesis, Boston University (Boston, Mass.), 1957.
35. BILGER, ROBERT C. "Limitations on the Use of Intelligence Scales to Estimate the Mental Ages of Children." *Volta R* 60:321–5 S '58. *
36. JUDGE, CAROLE HESSE. *Thought Disorder in Parents of Schizophrenics.* Doctor's thesis, University of Minnesota (Minneapolis, Minn.), 1967. (*DA* 28:3473B)
37. MYKLEBUST, HELMER R.; BANNOCHIE, MARGARET N.; AND KILLEN, JAMES R. Chap. 9, "Learning Disabilities and Cognitive Processes," pp. 213–51. In *Progress in Learning Disabilities, Vol. 2*. Edited by Helmer R. Myklebust. New York: Grune & Stratton, Inc., 1971. Pp. ix, 404. *

CUMULATIVE NAME INDEX

Abel, T. M.: 25
Bannochie, M. N.: 37
Bilger, R. C.: 35
Carpenter, R. S.: 24
Clark, K. C.: 33
Dorcus, M. D.: 16
Eccles, A. M.: 18
Fitzpatrick, C. H.: 34
Fitzwater, M. E.: 31–2
Fleming, C. W.: 23
Gault, R. H.: 4
Gaw, F.: 10
Hamlin, R.: 25
Hanfmann, E.: 27
Healy, W.: 1, 6
Johnson, B.: 7
Johnson, B. J.: 11
Jones, G. L.: 14
Judge, C. H.: 36
Killen, J. R.: 37
Louttit, C. M.: 19
McCaulley, S.: 12

Marsh, C. J.: 26
Morgenthau, D. R.: 8
Myklebust, H. R.: 37
Nottingham, R. D.: 21
Paschal, F. C.: 13
Paterson, D. G.: 2
Perry, D. E.: 9
Pintner, R.: 2
Schieffelin, B.: 17
Schriefer, L.: 7
Schwerin, E.: 30–2
Schwesinger, G. C.: 17
Scovill, M. S.: 20
Skaggs, E. B.: 5
Sullivan, L. R.: 13
Vernon, P. E.: 22
Walker, M. A.: 3
Washburn, M. F.: 3
Werner, H.: 28
Wilson, F. T.: 23
Wood, L.: 29
Worthington, M. R.: 15

[559]

Hidden Figures Test. Grades 6–16; 1962–63; HFT; for research use only; flexibility of closure; 2 tests; Educational Testing Service (Atlanta Office). *

a) FORM CF-1. 1962–63; manual by John W. French, Ruth B. Ekstrom, and Leighton B. Price.

b) FORM 5. 1962.

For additional information, see 7:440 (31 references).

REFERENCES THROUGH 1971

1–31. See 7:440.
32. BOERSMA, FREDERIC J.; MUIR, WALTER; WILTON, KERI;

AND BARHAM, RICHARD. "Eye Movements During Embedded Figure Tasks." *Percept & Motor Skills* 28(1):271-4 F '69. * (*PA* 43:11294)

33. EVANS, FREDERICK J. "Effects of Practice on the Validity of a Group-Administered Embedded Figures Test." *Acta Psychologica* (Netherlands) 29(2):172-80 Mr '69. * (*PA* 44:1634)

34. STRAUSS, MILTON E. "Cognitive Style and the Use of Incidental Cues in Problem Solving." *J Psychol* 73(1):69-74 S '69. * (*PA* 44:4548)

35. GREENFIELD, ADELAIDE. *Perceptual Style, Attitudes Toward Problem Solving, and Problem-Solving Performance.* Doctor's thesis, New York University (New York, N.Y.), 1970. (*DAI* 31:7571B)

36. McDONAGH, JOHN MICHAEL. *The Relationship Between Familial Characteristics and Two Measures of Dependency.* Doctor's thesis, University of Oklahoma (Norman, Okla.), 1970. (*DAI* 32:542B)

37. ADCOCK, C. J., AND WEBBERLEY, M. "Primary Mental Abilities." *J General Psychol* 84(2):229-43 Ap '71. * (*PA* 46:4979)

38. BRILHART, BARBARA LIEB, AND BRILHART, JOHN K. "Field Independence and Academic Achievement of Engineering Students." *Percept & Motor Skills* 32(2):443-6 Ap '71. * (*PA* 46:11645)

39. COOPER, WALTER, AND ARMSTRONG, WAYNE. "Beginning Tennis Skill and Field Independence." *South J Ed Res* 5(2):114-9 Ap '71. *

40. DARGEL, RUSSELL, AND KIRK, ROGER E. "Manifest Anxiety, Field Dependency, and Task Performance." *Percept & Motor Skills* 32(2):383-93 Ap '71. * (*PA* 46:10865)

41. DINGMAN, ROBERT LEWIS. *A Study of Cognitive Style Differences as a Factor of Communications in School Counseling.* Doctor's thesis, Wayne State University (Detroit, Mich.), 1971. (*DAI* 32:6756A)

42. GRIEVE, TARRANCE DON, AND DAVIS, J. KENT. "The Relationship of Cognitive Style and Method of Instruction to Performance in Ninth Grade Geography." *J Ed Res* 65(3):137-41 N '71. * (*PA* 48:1927)

43. HOCHMAN, SIDNEY H. "Field Independence and Stroop Color-Word Performance." *Percept & Motor Skills* 33(3):782 D '71. * (*PA* 48:953)

44. HUCKABEE, MALCOM W., AND MC GOWN, W. P. "Differences Between Field Independent and Field Dependent Persons on the Stroop Color-Word Test: A Failure to Replicate." *J Clin Psychol* 27(2):226 Ap '71. * (*PA* 46:6888)

45. KAZELSKIS, RICHARD. "Field Independence and Serial Verbal Learning." *South J Ed Res* 5(1):31-8 Ja '71. *

46. PARLETT, T. A. A., AND AYERS, J. D. "The Modification of Criminal Personality Through Massed Learning by Programmed Instruction." *Can J Criminol & Correct* 13(2):155-65 Ap '71. *

47. RICHARDS, TERRY D. *The Effects of Cognitive Style Sets of Flexibility Upon Counselor Perception: Field Dependence and Repression-Sensitization in Relation to Empathic Accuracy.* Doctor's thesis, New York University (New York, N.Y.), 1971. (*DAI* 32:1865A)

48. FLEISHMAN, JOSEPH J., AND FINE, BERNARD J. "Note on Cognitive Factors Related to Factor B of the 16 PF Test." *Psychol Rep* 29(3):1075-7 D '71. * (*PA* 48:988)

49. FLEISHMAN, JOSEPH J., AND DUSEK, E. RALPH. "Reliability and Learning Factors Associated With Cognitive Tests." *Psychol Rep* 29(2):523-30 O '71. * (*PA* 47:7996)

CUMULATIVE NAME INDEX

Acker, M. B.: 5	Fine, B. J.: 48
Adcock, C. J.: 37	Fleishman, J. J.: 48-9
Anderson, C. C.: 2	Frederick, W. C.: 9
Armstrong, W.: 39	Graham, J.: 29
Ayers, J. D.: 46	Greenfield, A.: 35
Barham, R.: 32	Grieve, T. D.: 42
Barrett, G. V.: 10, 15, 23	Gruenfeld, L. W.: 26
Bartelt, C. A.: 16	Hochman, S. H.: 43
Beckerle, G. P.: 3	Huckabee, M. W.: 21, 44
Boersma, F. J.: 11, 32	Kazelskis, R.: 27, 45
Brigham, B. W.: 6	Kirk, R. E.: 40
Brilhart, B. L.: 38	Klausmeier, H. J.: 25
Brilhart, J. K.: 38	Kohler, E. T.: 30
Brinton, G.: 17	McDonagh, J. M.: 36
Bryan, V.: 12	Mc Gown, W. P.: 44
Cabe, P. A.: 10, 15, 23	McWhinnie, H. J.: 28
Cline, V. B.: 1	Mausner, B.: 29
Conklin, R. C.: 18	Muir, W.: 32
Cooper, W.: 39	Needham, W. E.: 1
Crego, C. A.: 24	Ohnmacht, F. W.: 30
Cropley, A. J.: 2, 4, 7	Parlett, T. A. A.: 46
Dargel, R.: 40	Richards, J. M.: 1
Davis, J. K.: 8, 25, 42	Richards, T. D.: 47
Dingman, R. L.: 41	Rouleau, R. A.: 17
Dusek, E. R.: 49	Sharp, E. Y.: 31
Duvall, N. S.: 19	Strauss, M. E.: 34
Erginel, A.: 20	Thornton, C. L.: 10, 15, 23
Evans, F. J.: 33	Titus, H. E.: 22
Farr, R. S.: 13	Weaver, W. W.: 30

Hidden Figures Test

Webberley, M.: 37	Wilton, K.: 32
Weissenberg, P.: 26	Zingle, H. W.: 18
Werbel, S. A.: 14	

[560]

Higgins-Wertman Test: Threshold of Visual Closure. Ages 5-15; 1968; manual title is *Visual Closure Assessment;* 6 scores: initial closure, final closure, number of responses prior to final closure (whole and detail), perseveration, impotence; Conwell Higgins and Howard Wertman; Higgins-Wertman Associates. *

For additional information, see 7:441 (1 reference).

REFERENCES THROUGH 1971

1. See 7:441.
2. RUSCH, REUBEN R. "Note on the Validity of the Claim That Final Closure Is Related to Reading Achievement." *Percept & Motor Skills* 32(2):394 Ap '71. * (*PA* 46:11669)

CUMULATIVE NAME INDEX

Rusch, R. R.: 1-2

[560A]

Jensen Alternation Board. Ages 5 and over; 1959-60; JAB; learning age; Milton B. Jensen; Lafayette Instrument Co. *

For additional information, see 6:550 (2 references).

REFERENCES THROUGH 1971

1-2. See 6:550.
3. FLICK, GRAD L., AND WATKINS, ERNEST O. "Alternation Learning and Its Relationship to Intellectual Functioning in Primary Retardates." *Psychol Rep* 16:931-2 Je '65. * (*PA* 39:16045)
4. CHAPA, DOLORES G. *An Investigation of the Jensen Alternation Board, Social Maturity and Intelligence as Predictive Factors of Achievement in Retardates.* Master's thesis, Texas Woman's University (Denton, Tex.), 1966.
5. GATES, DONALD O. *The Relationship Between the Jensen Alternation Board and Objective Measures of Ability and Emotional Adjustment.* Doctor's thesis, University of Southern Mississippi (Hattiesburg, Miss.), 1966. (*DA* 28:339B)

CUMULATIVE NAME INDEX

Chapa, D. G.: 4	Jensen, M. B.: 1-2
Flick, G. L.: 3	Watkins, E. O.: 3
Gates, D. O.: 5	

[561]

Kit of Reference Tests for Cognitive Factors, 1963 Revision. Various grades 6-16; 1954-63; previously called *Kit of Selected Tests for Reference Aptitude and Achievement Factors;* for research use only; groups of 2-5 tests measuring 24 (16 in the 1954 Kit) "of the better established factors in the cognitive area"; 4 of the 16 factors presented in the 1954 Kit have been dropped and 12 new factors added; "whereas the tests in the first Kit [1954] were usually exact copies of those used in earlier factor studies, most of the tests in the present edition have been newly adapted"; although most tests have been "adapted" or revised, the same titles are used in both the 1954 and 1963 Kits; unless otherwise indicated, all tests were prepared by the Educational Testing Service; tests compiled and manual written by John W. French, Ruth B. Ekstrom, and Leighton A. Price; Educational Testing Service (Atlanta Office) unless otherwise indicated. *

a) FACTOR CF: FLEXIBILITY OF CLOSURE. Grades 6-16; 1962; 3 tests.

    1) *Hidden Figures Test, Cf-1.*
    2) *Hidden Patterns Test, Cf-2.*
    3) *Copying Test, Cf-3.* Out of print.

b) FACTOR CS: SPEED OF CLOSURE. Grades 6-16; 1962; 2 tests.

    1) *Gestalt Completion Test, Cs-1.*
    2) *Concealed Words Test, Cs-2.*

c) FACTOR FA: ASSOCIATIONAL FLUENCY. Grades 6-16; 1957-62; 3 tests.

1) *Controlled Associations Test, Fa-1.* 1962. *Out of print.*

2) *Associational Fluency 1, Form A, [Fa-2].* See 546c; 1957; Paul R. Christensen and J. P. Guilford; Sheridan Psychological Services, Inc.

3) *Associations 4, Fa-3.* 1962; J. P. Guilford. *Out of print.*

d) FACTOR FE: EXPRESSIONAL FLUENCY. Grades 8–16; 1958–62; 3 tests.

1) *Expressional Fluency, [Fe-1].* See 546d; 1958; Paul R. Christensen and J. P. Guilford; Sheridan Psychological Services, Inc.

2) *Simile Interpretations, Fe-2.* 1962; J. P. Guilford. *Out of print.* For a revision consisting of the 4 items of this test plus 4 new items, see 579.

3) *Word Arrangement, Fe-3.* 1962; J. P. Guilford. *Out of print.*

e) FACTOR FI: IDEATIONAL FLUENCY. Grades 8–16; 1962; 3 tests. *Out of print.*

1) *Topics Test, Fi-1.*

2) *Theme Test, Fi-2.*

3) *Thing Categories Test, Fi-3.*

f) FACTOR FW: WORD FLUENCY. Grades 6–16; 1962; 3 tests. *Out of print.*

1) *Word Endings Test, Fw-1.*

2) *Word Beginnings Test, Fw-2.*

3) *Word Beginnings and Endings Test, Fw-3.*

g) FACTOR I: INDUCTION. Grades 8–16; 1962; 3 tests.

1) *Letter Sets Test, I-1.*

2) *Locations Test, I-2.*

3) *Figure Classification, I-3.*

h) FACTOR LE: LENGTH ESTIMATION. Grades 6–16; 1962; 3 tests.

1) *Estimation of Length Test, Le-1.*

2) *Shortest Road Test, Le-2. Out of print.*

3) *Nearer Point Test, Le-3.*

i) FACTOR MA: ASSOCIATIVE (ROTE) MEMORY. Grades 6–16; 1962; 3 tests. *Out of print.*

1) *Picture-Number Test, Ma-1.*

2) *Object-Number Test, Ma-2.*

3) *First and Last Names Test, Ma-3.*

j) FACTOR MK: MECHANICAL KNOWLEDGE. 1962; 3 tests. *Out of print.*

1) *Tool Knowledge Test, Mk-1.* Grades 6–16.

2) *Mechanical Information Test, Mk-2.* Grades 8–16.

3) *Electrical Information Test, Mk-3.* Grades 8–16.

k) FACTOR MS: MEMORY SPAN. Grades 6–16; 1962; 3 tests.

1) *Auditory Number Span Test, Ms-1. Out of print.*

2) *Visual Number Span Test, Ms-2. Out of print.*

3) *Auditory Letter Span Test, Ms-3.*

l) FACTOR N: NUMBER FACILITY. Grades 6–16; 1953–62; 3 tests; 1962 tests essentially the same as tests copyrighted 1953 except for an increase in items.

1) *Addition Test, N-1.*

2) *Division Test, N-2.*

3) *Subtraction and Multiplication Test, N-3.*

m) FACTOR O: ORIGINALITY. Grades 10–16; 1958–62; 3 tests. *Out of print.*

1) *Plot Titles, O-1.* 1962. For a 1969 reissued edition of this test with revised administration instructions, see 572.

2) *Symbol Production, O-2.* 1962.

3) *Consequences, O-3 [10-Item Edition].* 1958; P. R. Christensen, P. R. Merrifield, and J. P. Guilford. For a revision of this 10-item test into two 5-item tests, Forms A-1 (first 5 items) and A-2 (last 5 items), see 551.

n) FACTOR P: PERCEPTUAL SPEED. Grades 6–16; 1962; 3 tests.

1) *Finding A's Test, P-1.*

2) *Number Comparison Test, P-2. Out of print.*

3) *Identical Pictures Test, P-3.*

o) FACTOR R: GENERAL REASONING. 1955–62; 4 tests.

1) *Mathematics Aptitude Test, R-1.* Grades 6–12; 1962. *Out of print.*

2) *Mathematics Aptitude Test, R-2.* Grades 11–16; 1962.

3) *Ship Destination Test, [R-3].* See 457; 1955; Paul R. Christensen and J. P. Guilford; Sheridan Psychological Services, Inc.

4) *Necessary Arithmetic Operations Test, R-4.* Grades 6–16; 1962.

p) FACTOR RE: SEMANTIC REDEFINITION. Grades 10–16; 1962; 3 tests. *Out of print.*

1) *Gestalt Transformation, Re-1.*

2) *Object Synthesis, Re-2.* J. P. Guilford.

3) *Picture Gestalt, Re-3.* J. P. Guilford. For a revision, see *New Uses* (568).

q) FACTOR RS: SYLLOGISTIC REASONING. Grades 11–16; 1955–62; 3 tests.

1) *Nonsense Syllogisms Test, Rs-1.* 1962.

2) *Logical Reasoning, [Rs-2].* See 1761; 1955; Alfred F. Hertzka and J. P. Guilford; Sheridan Psychological Services, Inc.

3) *Inference Test, Rs-3.* 1962.

r) FACTOR S: SPATIAL ORIENTATION. 1947–62; 3 tests.

1) *Card Rotations Test, S-1.* Grades 8–16; 1962.

2) *Cube Comparisons Test, S-2.* Grades 8–16; 1962.

3) *Guilford-Zimmerman Aptitude Survey: Part 5, Spatial Orientation, [S-3].* See 1074; 1947; J. P. Guilford and Wayne S. Zimmerman; Sheridan Psychological Services, Inc.

s) FACTOR SEP: SENSITIVITY TO PROBLEMS. Grades 8–16; 1962; 3 tests. *Out of print.*

1) *Apparatus Test, Sep-1.* J. P. Guilford.

2) *Seeing Problems, Sep-2.* For a test published in 1969 consisting of the first 2 of the 4 problems in this test, see 577.

3) *Seeing Deficiencies, Sep-3.* J. P. Guilford.

t) FACTOR SS: SPATIAL SCANNING. Grades 6–16; 1962; 3 tests.

1) *Maze Tracing Speed Test, Ss-1.*

2) *Choosing a Path, Ss-2.*

3) *Map Planning Test, Ss-3.*

u) FACTOR V: VERBAL COMPREHENSION. 1962; 5 tests.

1) *Vocabulary Test, V-1.* Grades 7–12. *Out of print.*

2) *Vocabulary Test, V-2.* Grades 7–12.

3) *Wide Range Vocabulary Test, V-3.* Grades 7–16.

4) *Advanced Vocabulary Test, V-4.* Grades 11–16.

5) *Vocabulary Test, V-5.* Grades 11–16. *Out of print.*

v) FACTOR VZ: VISUALIZATION. Grades 9–16; 1962; 3 tests.

1) *Form Board Test, Vz-1.*

2) *Paper Folding Test, Vz-2.*

3) *Surface Development Test, Vz-3.*

w) FACTOR XA: FIGURAL ADAPTIVE FLEXIBILITY. Grades 11–16; 1962; 3 tests. *Out of print.*

1) *Match Problems 2, Xa-1.* For a 1963 test identical with this 1962 test except for change of title to *Match Problems,* see 564.

2) *Match Problems 5, Xa-2.* For a 1969 test identical with this 1962 test except for one new item, one revised item, and administration instructions, see 565.

3) *Planning Air Maneuvers, Xa-3.*

x) FACTOR XS: SEMANTIC SPONTANEOUS FLEXIBILITY. Grades 6–16; 1960–62; 3 tests.

1) *Utility Test, Xs-1.* 1962. *Out of print.* For a 1969 test identical with this 1962 test except for administration instructions, see 591.

2) *Alternate Uses, [Xs-2].* See 542; 1960; Paul R. Christensen, J. P. Guilford, Philip R. Merrifield, and

Robert C. Wilson; Sheridan Psychological Services, Inc.

3) *Object Naming, Xs-3.* 1962; J. P. Guilford. *Out of print.*

For additional information, see 6:551.

REFERENCES THROUGH 1971

1. BARRON, FRANK. "The Disposition Toward Originality." *J Abn & Social Psychol* 51:478–85 N '55. * *(PA* 31:2533)

2. MEADOW, ARNOLD, AND PARNES, SIDNEY J. "Evaluation of Training in Creative Problem-Solving." *J Appl Psychol* 43:189–94 Je '59. * *(PA* 34:5568)

3. GARDNER, RILEY W.; JACKSON, DOUGLAS N.; AND MESSICK, SAMUEL J. "Personality Organization in Cognitive Controls and Intellectual Abilities." *Psychol Issues* 2(4):i–x, 1–148 '60. * *(PA* 36:2HA49G)

4. MARKS, ALVIN; MICHAEL, WILLIAM B.; AND KAISER, HENRY F. "Comparison of Manual and Analytic Techniques of Rotation in a Factor Analysis of Aptitude Test Variables." *Psychol Rep* 7:519–22 D '60. * *(PA* 35:2792)

5. GARWOOD, DOROTHY SEMENOW. *Some Personality Factors Related to Creativity in Young Scientists.* Doctor's thesis, Claremont Graduate School (Claremont, Calif.), 1961. *(DA* 22:3273)

6. MERRIFIELD, P. R.; GUILFORD, J. P.; CHRISTENSEN, P. R.; AND FRICK, J. W. "Interrelationships Between Certain Abilities and Certain Traits of Motivation and Temperament." *J General Psychol* 65:57–74 Jl '61. * *(PA* 36:2HD57M)

7. DE MILLE, RICHARD. "Intellect After Lobotomy in Schizophrenia: A Factor Analytic Study." *Psychol Monogr* 76(16):1–18 '62. * *(PA* 38:2784)

8. OWEN, CRAMER. "An Investigation of Creative Potential at the Junior High Level." *Studies Art Ed* 3:16–33 sp '62. *

9. BARRON, FRANK. *Creativity and Psychological Health: Origins of Personal Vitality and Creative Freedom.* Princeton, N.J.: D. Van Nostrand Co., Inc., 1963. Pp. xi, 292. *

10. ATKINSON, BEA HENRIETTA. *The Relationship Between Problem-Solving Strategies and Measures of Convergent and Divergent Thinking in a Selected Group of Secondary School Pupils.* Doctor's thesis, University of Florida (Gainesville, Fla.), 1964. *(DA* 25:7070)

11. EDWARDS, ALLEN JACK, AND PARKS, PAULA. "Note on Normative Data of Tests Measuring Flexibility in Cognitive Processes." *Psychol Rep* 14:741–2 Je '64. * *(PA* 39:5116)

12. MOLOMO, RAYMOND R-S. *Two Spatial Factors in Two-Dimensional and Three-Dimensional Spatial Aptitude.* Master's thesis, University of Ottawa (Ottawa, Ont., Canada), 1964.

13. MORAN, LOUIS J.; KIMBLE, JAMES P., JR.; AND MEFFERD, ROY B., JR. "Repetitive Psychometric Measures: Equating Alternate Forms." *Psychol Rep* 14:335–8 Ap '64. * *(PA* 39:302)

14. RAINWATER, JANETTE MUNKITTRICK. *Effects of Set on Problem Solving in Subjects of Varying Levels of Assessed Creativity.* Doctor's thesis, University of California (Berkeley, Calif.), 1964. *(DA* 25:6253)

15. KELLY, FRANCIS J.; HUNKA, STEPHEN; AND CONKLIN, RODNEY. "Further Normative Data on Tests Measuring Flexibility in Cognitive Processes." *Psychol Rep* 17:683–6 D '65. * *(PA* 40:3575)

16. VINT, VIRGINIA HOLLISTER. *The Effect of Prior Convergent or Divergent Art Training on Subsequent Art Activity.* Doctor's thesis, Stanford University (Stanford, Calif.), 1965. *(DA* 26:914)

17. ANDERSON, C. C., AND CROPLEY, A. J. "Some Correlates of Originality." *Austral J Psychol* 18:218–27 D '66. * *(PA* 41:4572)

18. CROPLEY, A. J. "Creativity and Intelligence." *Brit J Ed Psychol* 36:259–66 N '66. * *(PA* 41:573)

19. EDWARDS, ALLEN JACK. "Reliability of Selected Tests of Flexibility in Cognitive Processes." *Psychol Rep* 19:1267–70 D '66. * *(PA* 41:3710)

20. JANSSEN, CALVIN WAYNE. *Comparative Creativity Scores of Lower Socio-Economic Dropouts and Non-Dropouts.* Doctor's thesis, University of Tennessee (Knoxville, Tenn.), 1966. *(DA* 27:1659A)

21. NEEDHAM, WALTER EVANS. *Intellectual, Personality and Biographical Characteristics of Southern Negro and White College Students.* Doctor's thesis, University of Utah (Salt Lake City, Utah), 1966. *(DA* 27:1609B)

22. SMITH, ROBERT M., AND NEISWORTH, JOHN T. "Creative Thinking Abilities of Intellectually Superior Children in the Regular Grades." *Psychol Rep* 18:335–41 Ap '66. * *(PA* 40:8832)

23. WAMPLER, JOE F. "Prediction of Achievement in College Mathematics." *Math Teach* 59:364–9 Ap '66. *

24. WEISS, DAVID J.; DAWIS, RENE V.; LOFQUIST, LLOYD H.; AND ENGLAND, GEORGE W. *Instrumentation for the Theory of Work Adjustment.* University of Minnesota, Industrial Relations Center Bulletin 44; Minnesota Studies in Vocational Rehabilitation 21. Minneapolis, Minn.: the Center, December 1966. Pp. viii, 85. *

25. BRAUND, ROBERT A. "Pilot Study of a Cognitive Restructuring Paradigm." *Psychol Rep* 20:275–9 F '67. * *(PA* 41:7919)

26. COMPTON, MARY FRANCES. *An Attempt to Foster Creative Thinking in Teachers.* Doctor's thesis, University of Florida (Gainesville, Fla.), 1967. *(DA* 29:164A)

27. CROPLEY, A. J. "Creativity, Intelligence, and Achievement." *Alberta J Ed Res* (Canada) 13:51–8 Mr '67. * *(PA* 41:15253)

28. EKSTROM, RUTH BURT. *A Comparison of Two Groups of Reference Tests Measuring Selected Perception and Closure Factors.* Doctor's thesis, Rutgers—The State University (New Brunswick, N.J.), 1967. *(DA* 28:1703A)

29. GRAY, JAMES JOSEPH. *An Investigation of the Relationship Between Primary Process Thinking and Creativity.* Doctor's thesis, Fordham University (New York, N.Y.), 1967. *(DA* 28:5206B)

30. JENKINS, JOHN MERVIN. *A Study of the Characteristics Associated With Innovative Behavior in Teachers.* Doctor's thesis, University of Miami (Coral Gables, Fla.), 1967. *(DA* 28:903A)

31. KARSTEN, MARY O'KEEFFE. *The Relationship of Tested Creative Abilities and Selected Factors of Academic Achievement, Intelligence, Sex, Socioeconomic Status, and Pupil Attitudes.* Doctor's thesis, University of Southern California (Los Angeles, Calif.), 1967. *(DA* 28:2557A)

32. LEMKE, ELMER A.; KLAUSMEIER, HERBERT J.; AND HARRIS, CHESTER W. "Relationship of Selected Cognitive Abilities to Concept Attainment and Information Processing." *J Ed Psychol* 58:27–35 F '67. * *(PA* 41:3959)

33. MANGAN, GORDON L. "Studies of the Relationship Between Neo-Pavlovian Properties of Higher Nervous Activity and Western Personality Dimensions: 3, The Relations of Transformation Mobility to Thinking Flexibility." *J Exp Res Personality* 2:117–23 My '67. * *(PA* 41:11907)

34. MILES, DAVID T. *An Experimental Investigation of Programed Creativity.* Doctor's thesis, Southern Illinois University (Carbondale, Ill.), 1967. *(DA* 28:2099A)

35. PLOGMAN, BERNARD EDWARD. *The Creative Relationship Between Art Teachers and Their Ninth Grade Art Students in Art Room Practices, Personality and Pencil Drawing in Catholic Schools.* Doctor's thesis, University of Cincinnati (Cincinnati, Ohio), 1967. *(DA* 28:3534A)

36. RICHARDS, JAMES M., JR. "Can Computers Write College Admissions Tests?" *J Appl Psychol* 51:211–5 Je '67. * *(PA* 41:10942)

37. RIDLEY, DENNIS R., AND BIRNEY, ROBERT C. "Effects of Training Procedures on Creativity Test Scores." *J Ed Psychol* 58:158–64 Je '67. * *(PA* 41:10457)

38. SIDLE, ALLAN CHARLES. *Creativity and Delusional Thinking in Schizophrenics.* Doctor's thesis, Stanford University (Stanford, Calif.), 1967. *(DA* 28:353B)

39. SKAGER, R. W.; KLEIN, S. P.; AND SCHULTZ, C. B. "The Prediction of Academic and Artistic Achievement at a School of Design." *J Ed Meas* 4:105–17 su '67. *

40. SMITH, ROBERT M. "Creative Thinking Abilities of Educable Mentally Handicapped Children in the Regular Grades." *Am J Mental Def* 71:571–5 Ja '67. * *(PA* 41:6197)

41. STOKER, H. W., AND KROPP, R. P. "Note on the Kit of Reference Tests." *Ed & Psychol Meas* 27:1171–2 w '67. * *(PA* 42:8944)

42. VERY, PHILIP S. "Differential Factor Structures in Mathematical Ability." *Genetic Psychol Monogr* 75:169–207 My '67. * *(PA* 41:10451)

43. WINDHOLZ, GEORGE, AND MCINTOSH, WILLIAM A. "Concurrent Validation of Guilford's Six Convergent Tests." *Ed & Psychol Meas* 27:393–400 su '67. * *(PA* 41:12843)

44. ADAMS, JOHN C., JR. "The Relative Effects of Various Testing Atmospheres on Spontaneous Flexibility, a Factor of Divergent Thinking." *J Creative Behav* 2:187–94 su '68. * *(PA* 43:5882)

45. ALZOBAIE, ABDUL JALIL; METFESSEL, NEWTON S.; AND MICHAEL, WILLIAM B. "Alternative Approaches to Assessing the Intellectual Abilities of Youth From a Culture of Poverty." *Ed & Psychol Meas* 28:449–55 su '68. * *(PA* 42:19264)

46. ANDERSON, RONALD JUDE. *Divergent Thinking Within Superior Average, and Retarded Subjects.* Doctor's thesis, University of Nebraska (Lincoln, Neb.), 1968. *(DA* 29:1126A)

47. BROWN, STEPHEN W.; GUILFORD, J. P.; AND HOEPFNER, RALPH. "Six Semantic-Memory Abilities." *Ed & Psychol Meas* 28:691–717 au '68. * *(PA* 43:4427)

48. BRYAN, VINCENT. *The Experimental Induction of Stress in Relation to Field Articulation.* Doctor's thesis, Yeshiva University (New York, N.Y.), 1968. *(DAI* 30:1354B)

49. EDWARDS, ARTHUR B. *An Analysis of the Creative Ability Levels of the Potential Dropout in the Average Mental Ability Range.* Doctor's thesis, University of Tennessee (Knoxville, Tenn.), 1968. *(DA* 29:3828A)

50. GIBSON, JAMES W.; KIBLER, ROBERT J.; AND BARKER, LARRY L. "Some Relationships Between Selected Creativity and Critical Thinking Measures." *Psychol Rep* 23:707–14 D '68. * *(PA* 43:9748)

51. HETRICK, SUZANNE H.; LILLY, ROY S.; AND MERRIFIELD, PHILIP R. "Figural Creativity, Intelligence, and Personality in Children." *Multiv Behav Res* 3:173–87 Ap '68. * *(PA* 42:15273)

52. JANSSEN, CALVIN. "Comparative Creativity Scores of Lower Socio-Economic Dropouts and Non-Dropouts." *Psychol Sch* 5:183–4 Ap '68. * *(PA* 43:17498)

53. WINDHOLZ, GEORGE. "The Relation of Creativity and Intelligence Constellations to Traits of Temperament, Interest, and Value in College Students." *J General Psychol* 79:291–9 O '68. * (*PA* 43:3998)

54. ANDERSON, HARRY E., JR.; WHITE, WILLIAM F.; AND STEVENS, JOHN C. "Student Creativity, Intelligence, Achievement, and Teacher Classroom Behavior." *J Social Psychol* 78(1):99–107 Je '69. * (*PA* 43:16427)

55. BLACKHURST, A. EDWARD; MARKS, CLAUDE H.; AND TISDALL, WILLIAM J. "Relationship Between Mobility and Divergent Thinking in Blind Children." *Ed Visually Handicapped* 1(2):33–6 My '69. * (*PA* 43:14813)

56. DICKSTEIN, LOUIS S. "Prospective Span as a Cognitive Ability." *J Consult & Clin Psychol* 33(6):757–60 D '69. * (*PA* 44:3616)

57. EDWARDS, ALLEN JACK. "Order Effects on Scores and Reliability Estimates Obtained With a Divergent-Thinking Task." *Psychol Rep* 24(2):610 Ap '69. * (*PA* 43:14999)

58. GARDNER, RILEY W., AND LOHRENZ, LEANDER J. "Some Old and New Group Tests for the Study of Cognitive Controls and Intellectual Abilities." *Percept & Motor Skills* 29(3):935–50 D '69. * (*PA* 46:4981)

59. GOODMAN, P.; FURCON, J.; AND ROSE, J. "Examination of Some Measures of Creative Ability by the Multitrait-Multimethod Matrix." *J Appl Psychol* 53(3):240–3 Je '69. * (*PA* 43:11327)

60. GRAY, JAMES J. "The Effect of Productivity on Primary Process and Creativity." *J Proj Tech & Pers Assess* 33(3):213–8 Je '69. * (*PA* 43:14302)

61. GRIMSLEY, WILLIAM GERALD. *The Relationship Between Creativity and Leader Behavior of School Superintendents.* Doctor's thesis, University of Missouri (Columbia, Mo.), 1969. (*DAI* 30:5193A)

62. GUILFORD, J. P., AND HOEPFNER, RALPH. "Comparisons of Varimax Rotations With Rotations to Theoretical Targets." *Ed & Psychol Meas* 29(1):3–22 sp '69. * (*PA* 44:15668)

63. KANDERIAN, SUAD SIROP. *Study of the Relationship Between School Achievement and Measures of Intelligence and Creativity for Students in Iraq.* Doctor's thesis, University of Southern California (Los Angeles, Calif.), 1969. (*DAI* 31:644A)

64. KARLINS, MARVIN; SCHUERHOFF, CHARLES; AND KAPLAN, MARTIN. "Some Factors Related to Architectural Creativity in Graduating Architecture Students." *J General Psychol* 81(2):203–15 O '69. * (*PA* 44:6775)

65. KLEIN, STEPHEN P.; FREDERIKSEN, NORMAN; AND EVANS, FRANKLIN R. "Anxiety and Learning to Formulate Hypotheses." *J Ed Psychol* 60(6):465–75 D '69. * (*PA* 44:3087)

66. SCHNITZER, LEAH PALTIEL, AND STEWART, ROBERT A. C. "Originality and Personality Variables in High School Art Students." *Psychol* 6(1):36–9 F '69. * (*PA* 43:11334)

67. STRAUSS, MILTON E. "Cognitive Style and the Use of Incidental Cues in Problem Solving." *J Psychol* 73(1):69–74 S '69. * (*PA* 44:4548)

68. VANDENBERG, STEVEN G. "A Twin Study of Spatial Ability." *Multiv Behav Res* 4(3):273–94 Jl '69. * (*PA* 44:356)

69. ALEXANDER, SHIRLEY MAE. *A Study of Perceptual and Verbal Differentiation Among Male College Students.* Doctor's thesis, George Washington University (Washington, D.C.), 1970. (*DAI* 31:6887B)

70. EL-ABD, HAMED A. "The Intellect of East African Students." *Multiv Behav Res* 5(4):423–33 O '70. * (*PA* 45:8037)

71. FRUIN, DAVID JOHN. *Response Styles and Creativity.* Doctor's thesis, Johns Hopkins University (Baltimore, Md.), 1970. (*DAI* 31:4361B)

72. GREENFIELD, ADELAIDE. *Perceptual Style, Attitudes Toward Problem Solving, and Problem-Solving Performance.* Doctor's thesis, New York University (New York, N.Y.), 1970. (*DAI* 31:7571B)

73. JOHNSON, MARIE LOUISE. *Black Adolescents' Nonstandard English and Its Relation to Intellectual Skills.* Doctor's thesis, Illinois Institute of Technology (Chicago, Ill.), 1970. (*DAI* 31:7573B)

74. KHAN, S. B. "Development of Mental Abilities: An Investigation of the 'Differentiation Hypothesis.'" *Can J Psychol* 24(3):199–205 Je '70. * (*PA* 46:5667)

75. MCDONAGH, JOHN MICHAEL. *The Relationship Between Familial Characteristics and Two Measures of Dependency.* Doctor's thesis, University of Oklahoma (Norman, Okla.), 1970. (*DAI* 32:542B)

76. OHNMACHT, FRED W.; WEAVER, WENDELL W.; AND KOHLER, EMMETT T. "Cloze and Closure: A Factorial Study." *J Psychol* 74(2):205–17 Mr '70. * (*PA* 44:12542)

77. PARLETT, T. A. A. *The Modification of Criminal Personality Through Massed Learning by Programmed Instruction.* Master's thesis, University of Victoria (Victoria, B.C., Canada), 1970.

78. REESE, HAYNE W., AND PARNES, SIDNEY J. "Programming Creative Behavior." *Child Develop* 41(2):413–23 Je '70. * (*PA* 44:15509)

79. SHARP, ELIZABETH YERXA. *The Relationship of Visual Closure to Speechreading Among Deaf Children.* Doctor's thesis, University of Arizona (Tucson, Ariz.), 1970. (*DAI* 31:2198A)

80. ADCOCK, C. J., AND WEBBERLEY, M. "Primary Mental Abilities." *J General Psychol* 84(2):229–43 Ap '71. * (*PA* 46:4979)

81. BALDWIN, THOMAS S. "Relationships Among Student Achievement and 'Pure Factors' of Intellect." *J Indus Teach Ed* 9(1):15–25 f '71. *

82. BRILHART, BARBARA LIEB, AND BRILHART, JOHN K. "Field Independence and Academic Achievement of Engineering Students." *Percept & Motor Skills* 32(2):443–6 Ap '71. * (*PA* 46:11645)

83. BYRNE, MARY ANN; FELDHUSEN, JOHN F.; AND KANE, ROBERT B. "The Relationships Among Two Cloze Measurement Procedures and Divergent Thinking Abilities." *Read Res Q* 6(3):378–93 sp '71. * (*PA* 47:3624)

84. COOPER, WALTER, AND ARMSTRONG, WAYNE. "Beginning Tennis Skill and Field Independence." *South J Ed Res* 5(2):114–9 Ap '71. *

85. DARGEL, RUSSELL, AND KIRK, ROGER E. "Manifest Anxiety, Field Dependency, and Task Performance." *Percept & Motor Skills* 32(2):383–93 Ap '71. * (*PA* 46:10865)

86. DINGMAN, ROBERT LEWIS. *A Study of Cognitive Style Differences as a Factor of Communications in School Counseling.* Doctor's thesis, Wayne State University (Detroit, Mich.), 1971. (*DAI* 32:6756A)

87. FLEISHMAN, JOSEPH J., AND DUSEK, E. RALPH. "Reliability and Learning Factors Associated With Cognitive Tests." *Psychol Rep* 29(2):523–30 O '71. * (*PA* 47:7996)

88. FLEISHMAN, JOSEPH J., AND FINE, BERNARD J. "Note on Cognitive Factors Related to Factor B of the 16 PF Test." *Psychol Rep* 29(3):1075–7 D '71. * (*PA* 48:988)

89. GRIEVE, TARRANCE DON, AND DAVIS, J. KENT. "The Relationship of Cognitive Style and Method of Instruction to Performance in Ninth Grade Geography." *J Ed Res* 65(3):137–41 N '71. * (*PA* 48:1927)

90. GUTHRIE, GEORGE M.; SINAIKO, H. WALLACE; AND BRISLIN, RICHARD. "Nonverbal Abilities of Americans and Vietnamese." *J Social Psychol* 84(2):183–90 Ag '71. *

91. HOCHMAN, SIDNEY H. "Field Independence and Stroop Color-Word Performance." *Percept & Motor Skills* 33(3):782 D '71. * (*PA* 48:953)

92. HUCKABEE, MALCOM W., AND MC GOWN, W. P. "Differences Between Field Independent and Field Dependent Persons on the Stroop Color-Word Test: A Failure to Replicate." *J Clin Psychol* 27(2):226 Ap '71. * (*PA* 46:6888)

93. KAZELSKIS, RICHARD. "Field Independence and Serial Verbal Learning." *South J Ed Res* 5(1):31–8 Ja '71. *

94. KORAN, MARY LOU. "Differential Response to Inductive and Deductive Instructional Procedures." *J Ed Psychol* 62(4):300–7 Ag '71. * (*PA* 47:1820)

95. KORAN, MARY LOU; SNOW, RICHARD E.; AND MCDONALD, FREDERICK J. "Teacher Aptitude and Observational Learning of a Teaching Skill." *J Ed Psychol* 62(3):219–28 Je '71. * (*PA* 46:9703)

96. LINKER, JERRY MAC. *The Interaction of Cognitive Factors, Visual Fidelity, and Learning Tasks in Learning From Pictures.* Doctor's thesis, University of Texas (Austin, Tex.), 1971. (*DAI* 33:144A)

97. MILLER, JEFFREY O. "Personality Factors and Perceptual Factors in Motor Performance." *ICHPER* 13:46–61 '71. *

98. OHNMACHT, FRED W., AND MCMORRIS, ROBERT F. "Creativity as a Function of Field Independence and Dogmatism." *J Psychol* 79(2):165–8 N '71. * (*PA* 47:6800)

99. PARLETT, T. A. A., AND AYERS, J. D. "The Modification of Criminal Personality Through Massed Learning by Programmed Instruction." *Can J Criminol & Correct* 13(2):155–65 Ap '71. *

100. RICHARDS, TERRY D. *The Effects of Cognitive Style Sets of Flexibility Upon Counselor Perception: Field Dependence and Repression-Sensitization in Relation to Empathic Accuracy.* Doctor's thesis, New York University (New York, N.Y.), 1971. (*DAI* 32:1865A)

101. RYBACK, RALPH S.; LEWIS, OLIVER F.; AND LESSARD, CHARLES S. "Psychobiologic Effects of Prolonged Bed Rest (Weightless) in Young Healthy Volunteers (Study II)." *Aerospace Med* 42(5):529–35 My '71. *

102. TISDALL, WILLIAM J.; BLACKHURST, A. EDWARD; AND MARKS, CLAUDE H. "Divergent Thinking in Blind Children." *J Ed Psychol* 62(6):468–73 D '71. * (*PA* 47:9708)

103. WILLIAMS, JOHN D.; HARLOW, STEVEN D.; AND BORGEN, JEROME S. "Creativity, Dogmatism, and Arithmetic Achievement." *J Psychol* 78(2):217–22 Jl '71. * (*PA* 46:9760)

CUMULATIVE NAME INDEX

Cooper, W.: 84
Cropley, A. J.: 17–8, 27
Dargel, R.: 85
Davis, J. K.: 89
Dawis, R. V.: 24
de Mille, R.: 7
Dickstein, L. S.: 56
Dingman, R. L.: 86
Dusek, E. R.: 87
Edwards, A. B.: 49
Edwards, A. J.: 11, 19, 57
Ekstrom, R. B.: 28
El-Abd, H. A.: 70
England, G. W.: 24
Evans, F. R.: 65
Feldhusen, J. F.: 83
Fine, B. J.: 88
Fleishman, J. J.: 87–8
Frederiksen, N.: 65
Frick, J. W.: 6
Fruin, D. J.: 71
Furcon, J.: 59
Gardner, R. W.: 3, 58
Garwood, D. S.: 5
Gibson, J. W.: 50
Goodman, P.: 59
Gray, J. J.: 29, 60
Greenfield, A.: 72
Grieve, T. D.: 89
Grimsley, W. G.: 61
Guilford, J. P.: 6, 47, 62
Guthrie, G. M.: 90
Harlow, S. D.: 103
Harris, C. W.: 32
Hetrick, S. H.: 51
Hochman, S. H.: 91
Hoepfner, R.: 47, 62
Huckabee, M. W.: 92
Hunka, S.: 15
Jackson, D. N.: 3
Janssen, C.: 52
Janssen, C. W.: 20
Jenkins, J. M.: 30
Johnson, M. L.: 73
Kaiser, H. F.: 4
Kanderian, S. S.: 63
Kane, R. B.: 83
Kaplan, M.: 64
Karlins, M.: 64
Karsten, M. O.: 31
Kazelskis, R.: 93
Kelly, F. J.: 15
Khan, S. B.: 74
Kibler, R. J.: 50
Kimble, J. P.: 13
Kirk, R. E.: 85
Klausmeier, H. J.: 32
Klein, S. P.: 39, 65
Kohler, E. T.: 76
Koran, M. L.: 94–5
Kropp, R. P.: 41
Lemke, E. A.: 32
Lessard, C. S.: 101

Lewis, O. F.: 101
Lilly, R. S.: 51
Linker, J. M.: 96
Lofquist, L. H.: 24
Lohrenz, L. J.: 58
McDonagh, J. M.: 75
McDonald, F. J.: 95
Mc Gown, W. P.: 92
McIntosh, W. A.: 43
McMorris, R. F.: 98
Mangan, G. L.: 33
Marks, A.: 4
Marks, C. H.: 55, 102
Meadow, A.: 2
Mefferd, R. B.: 13
Merrifield, P. R.: 6, 51
Messick, S. J.: 3
Metfessel, N. S.: 45
Michael, W. B.: 4, 45
Miles, D. T.: 34
Miller, J. O.: 97
Molomo, R. R-S.: 12
Moran, L. J.: 13
Needham, W. E.: 21
Neisworth, J. T.: 22
Ohnmacht, F. W.: 76, 98
Owen, C.: 8
Parks, P.: 11
Parlett, T. A. A.: 77, 99
Parnes, S. J.: 2, 78
Plogman, B. E.: 35
Rainwater, J. M.: 14
Reese, H. W.: 78
Richards, J. M.: 36
Richards, T. D.: 100
Ridley, D. R.: 37
Rose, J.: 59
Ryback, R. S.: 101
Schnitzer, L. P.: 66
Schuerhoff, C.: 64
Schultz, C. B.: 39
Sharp, E. Y.: 79
Sidle, A. C.: 38
Sinaiko, H. W.: 90
Skager, R. W.: 39
Smith, R. M.: 22, 40
Snow, R. E.: 95
Stevens, J. C.: 54
Stewart, R. A. C.: 66
Stoker, H. W.: 41
Strauss, M. E.: 67
Tisdall, W. J.: 55, 102
Vandenberg, S. G.: 68
Very, P. S.: 42
Vint, V. H.: 16
Wampler, J. F.: 23
Weaver, W. W.: 76
Webberley, M.: 80
Weiss, D. J.: 24
White, W. F.: 54
Williams, J. D.: 103
Windholz, G.: 43, 53

[562]

Making Objects. Grades 9–16 and adults; 1963; "divergent production of figural systems" or "figural expressional fluency"; for a downward extension, see 554f; Sheldon Gardner, Arthur Gershon, Philip R. Merrifield, and J. P. Guilford; Sheridan Psychological Services, Inc. *

For additional information, see 6:552 (1 reference).

REFERENCES THROUGH 1971

1. See 6:552.
2. SMITH, ROBERT M., AND NEISWORTH, JOHN T. "Creative Thinking Abilities of Intellectually Superior Children in the Regular Grades." *Psychol Rep* 18:335–41 Ap '66. * (*PA* 40: 8832)
3. FORD, ELEANOR DIANE. *The Relationship of Certain Socio-Cultural Factors Among Junior High School Students to Creativity in Art.* Doctor's thesis, North Texas State University (Denton, Tex.), 1967. (*DA* 28:3502A)
4. KARSTEN, MARY O'KEEFFE. *The Relationship of Tested Creative Abilities and Selected Factors of Academic Achievement, Intelligence, Sex, Socioeconomic Status, and Pupil Attitudes.* Doctor's thesis, University of Southern California (Los Angeles, Calif.), 1967. (*DA* 28:2557A)
5. SMITH, ROBERT M. "Creative Thinking Abilities of Educable Mentally Handicapped Children in the Regular Grades." *Am J Mental Def* 71:571–5 Ja '67. * (*PA* 41:6197)

6. ALZOBAIE, ABDUL JALIL; METFESSEL, NEWTON S.; AND MICHAEL, WILLIAM B. "Alternative Approaches to Assessing the Intellectual Abilities of Youth From a Culture of Poverty." *Ed & Psychol Meas* 28:449–55 su '68. * (*PA* 42:19264)
7. KANDERIAN, SUAD SIROP. *Study of the Relationship Between School Achievement and Measures of Intelligence and Creativity for Students in Iraq.* Doctor's thesis, University of Southern California (Los Angeles, Calif.), 1969. (*DAI* 31:644A)
8. SIMPSON, DONALD JAMES. *The Effect of Selected Musical Studies on Growth in General Creative Potential.* Doctor's thesis, University of Southern California (Los Angeles, Calif.), 1969. (*DAI* 30:502A)
9. OLESON, D. S., AND ZUBEK, JOHN P. "Effect of One Day of Sensory Deprivation on a Battery of Open-Ended Cognitive Tests." *Percept & Motor Skills* 31(3):919–23 D '70. * (*PA* 46:358)

CUMULATIVE NAME INDEX

Alzobaie, A. J.: 6   Michael, W. B.: 6
Ford, E. D.: 3   Neisworth, J .T.: 2
Guilford, J. P.: 1   Oleson, D. S.: 9
Kanderian, S. S.: 7   Simpson, D. J.: 8
Karsten, M. O.: 4   Smith, R. M.: 2, 5
Metfessel, N. S.: 6   Zubek, J. P.: 9

[563]

Manikin Test. Ages 2 and over; [1917]; subtest of *Merrill-Palmer Scale of Mental Tests* and *Arthur Point Scale of Performance Tests, Form 1;* R. Pintner; Stoelting Co.

REFERENCES THROUGH 1971

1. WECHSLER, DAVID. *The Measurement of Adult Intelligence, Second Edition,* pp. 98–100, 175–7. Baltimore, Md.: Williams & Wilkins Co., 1941. Pp. xi, 248. *

CUMULATIVE NAME INDEX

Wechsler, D.: 1

[564]

Match Problems. Grades 9–16 and adults; 1963; formerly called *Match Problems 2;* "divergent production of figural transformations" or "originality in dealing with concrete visual material"; identical with the 1962 *Match Problems 2* (see 561w1); Raymond M. Berger and J. P. Guilford; Sheridan Psychological Services, Inc. *

For additional information, see 6:554 (7 references).

REFERENCES THROUGH 1971

1–7. See 6:554.
8. GARWOOD, DOROTHY SEMENOW. *Some Personality Factors Related to Creativity in Young Scientists.* Doctor's thesis, Claremont Graduate School (Claremont, Calif.), 1961. (*DA* 22:3273)
9. OWEN, CRAMER. "An Investigation of Creative Potential at the Junior High Level." *Studies Art Ed* 3:16–33 sp '62. *
10. GARWOOD, DOROTHY SEMENOW. "Personality Factors Related to Creativity in Young Scientists." *J Abn & Social Psychol* 68:413–9 Ap '64. * (*PA* 39:1729)
11. RAINWATER, JANETTE MUNKITTRICK. *Effects of Set on Problem Solving in Subjects of Varying Levels of Assessed Creativity.* Doctor's thesis, University of California (Berkeley, Calif.), 1964. (*DA* 25:6753)
12. RICHARDS, JAMES M., JR.; CLINE, VICTOR B.; AND NEEDHAM, WALTER E. "Creativity Tests and Teacher and Self Judgments of Originality." *J Exp Ed* 32:281–5 sp '64. * (*PA* 39:5135)
13. FORD, ELEANOR DIANE. *The Relationship of Certain Socio-Cultural Factors Among Junior High School Students to Creativity in Art.* Doctor's thesis, North Texas State University (Denton, Tex.), 1967. (*DA* 28:3502A)
14. ARMSTRONG, CARMEN LAPP GERBERDING. *Changes Evidenced in the Art Products of Elementary Education Majors Exhibiting the Characteristic of Flexibility.* Doctor's thesis, Indiana University (Bloomington, Ind.), 1968. (*DA* 29:1799A)
15. BUSSE, THOMAS V. "Establishment of the Flexible Thinking Factor in Fifth-Grade Boys." *J Psychol* 69:93–100 My '68. * (*PA* 42:11690)
16. HINTON, BERNARD L. "Environmental Frustration and Creative Problem Solving." *J Appl Psychol* 52:211–7 Je '68. * (*PA* 42:11701)
17. LEHRER, ARNOLD CURTIS. *The Personality Correlates of Creativity in Undergraduates.* Doctor's thesis, Colorado State College (Greeley, Colo.), 1969. (*DAI* 31:397B)
18. HEUSSENSTAMM, FRANCES K. "Creativity and Alienation: An Exploration of Their Relationship in Adolescence." *Calif J Ed Res* 21(3):140–6 My '70. *
19. HINTON, BERNARD L. "Personality Variables and Creative Potential." *J Creative Behav* 4(3):210–7 su '70. *

20. OLESON, D. S., AND ZUBEK, JOHN P. "Effect of One Day of Sensory Deprivation on a Battery of Open-Ended Cognitive Tests." *Percept & Motor Skills* 31(3):919–23 D '70. * (*PA* 46:358)

21. ADCOCK, C. J., AND WEBBERLEY, M. "Primary Mental Abilities." *J General Psychol* 84(2):229–43 Ap '71. * (*PA* 46:4979)

22. ARBUTHNOT, JACK BRAEDEN. *Field Independence and Maturity of Moral Judgment, Critical Distinctive Feature Analysis, and Perceived Locus of Control.* Doctor's thesis, Cornell University (Ithaca, N.Y.), 1971. (*DAI* 32:2190A)

CUMULATIVE NAME INDEX

[565]

*Match Problems 5, [Revised Edition]. Grades 9–16; 1962–69; "divergent production of figural transformations"; 1969 test identical with test copyrighted 1962 (see 561w2) except for one new and one revised item; no manual; Philip R. Merrifield and J. P. Guilford; Sheridan Psychological Services, Inc. *

For additional information, see 6:551w2.

[566]

★Memory for Events. Grades 9–13; 1969; "memory for semantic systems"; J. P. Guilford; Sheridan Psychological Services, Inc. *

[567]

★Memory for Meanings. Grades 7–16; 1969; "memory for semantic units"; Ralph Hoepfner and J. P. Guilford; Sheridan Psychological Services, Inc. *

[568]

*New Uses. Grades 10–16; 1962–69; "convergent production of semantic transformations"; revision of *Picture Gestalt* (see 561p3); Ralph Hoepfner and J. P. Guilford; Sheridan Psychological Services, Inc. *

[569]

★Pattern Relations Test. College graduates; 1968–69; PRT; abstract reasoning; test in English and Afrikaans; D. Daneel (test) and Delene Barker (manual); National Institute for Personnel Research [South Africa]. *

[570]

Perceptual Speed (Identical Forms). Grades 9–16 and industrial employees; 1956–66; L. L. Thurstone (test), T. E. Jeffrey (test), and Norman J. Kantor (manual); Industrial Relations Center, University of Chicago. * [The publisher has not replied to our four requests to check the accuracy of this entry.]

For additional information, see 7:444 (2 references); for a review by Leroy Wolins, see 6:556.

REFERENCES THROUGH 1971

1–2. See 7:444.
3. BILKA, LOISANNE PFEIFER. *An Evaluation of the Predictive Value of Certain Reading Readiness Measures as Related to Method of Instruction, Sex, and Mental Age.* Doctor's thesis, University of Pittsburgh (Pittsburgh, Pa.), 1970. (*DAI* 31:5922A)
4. BORDEAUX, ELIZABETH ANN. *Auditory and Visual Readiness Factors Related to Reading Achievement in First Grade Based on Three Methods of Instruction.* Doctor's thesis, University of North Carolina (Chapel Hill, N.C.), 1970. (*DAI* 31:5924A)

CUMULATIVE NAME INDEX

[571]

Pertinent Questions. Grades 9–16 and adults; 1960; experimental form; conceptual foresight; Raymond M. Berger, J. P. Guilford, and P. R. Merrifield (manual); Sheridan Psychological Services, Inc. *

For additional information, see 6:557 (3 references).

REFERENCES THROUGH 1971

1–3. See 6:557.
4. LOCKE, EDWIN A. "Some Correlates of Classroom and Out-of-Class Achievement in Gifted Science Students." *J Ed Psychol* 54:238–48 O '63. * (*PA* 38:4649)

CUMULATIVE NAME INDEX

[572]

*Plot Titles. Grades 9–16; 1962–69; PT; 2 scores: ideational fluency, originality; 1969 test identical with test copyrighted 1962 (see 561m1) except for administration instructions; for a downward extension, see 554g; Raymond M. Berger and J. P. Guilford; Sheridan Psychological Services, Inc. *

For additional information, see 6:551m1.

REFERENCES THROUGH 1971

1. BARRON, FRANK. "The Disposition Toward Originality." *J Abn & Social Psychol* 51:478–85 N '55. * (*PA* 31:2533)
2. MEADOW, ARNOLD, AND PARNES, SIDNEY J. "Evaluation of Training in Creative Problem-Solving." *J Appl Psychol* 43:189–94 Je '59. * (*PA* 34:5568)
3. MARKS, ALVIN; MICHAEL, WILLIAM B.; AND KAISER, HENRY F. "Comparison of Manual and Analytic Techniques of Rotation in a Factor Analysis of Aptitude Test Variables." *Psychol Rep* 7:519–22 D '60. * (*PA* 35:2792)
4. BARRON, FRANK. *Creativity and Psychological Health: Origins of Personal Vitality and Creative Freedom.* Princeton, N.J.: D. Van Nostrand Co., Inc., 1963. Pp. xi, 292. *
5. VINT, VIRGINIA HOLLISTER. *The Effect of Prior Convergent or Divergent Art Training on Subsequent Art Activity.* Doctor's thesis, Stanford University (Stanford, Calif.), 1965. (*DA* 26:914)
6. GUILFORD, J. P., AND HOEPFNER, RALPH. "Sixteen Divergent-Production Abilities at the Ninth-Grade Level." *Multiv Behav Res* 1:43–66 Ja '66. * (*PA* 41:1602)
7. HILL, ARTHUR H. "A Longitudinal Study of Attrition Among High Aptitude College Students." *J Ed Res* 60:166–73 D '66. *
8. JANSSEN, CALVIN WAYNE. *Comparative Creativity Scores of Lower Socio-Economic Dropouts and Non-Dropouts.* Doctor's thesis, University of Tennessee (Knoxville, Tenn.), 1966. (*DA* 27:1659A)
9. GRAY, JAMES JOSEPH. *An Investigation of the Relationship Between Primary Process Thinking and Creativity.* Doctor's thesis, Fordham University (New York, N.Y.), 1967. (*DA* 28:5206B)
10. JENKINS, JOHN MERVIN. *A Study of the Characteristics Associated With Innovative Behavior in Teachers.* Doctor's thesis, University of Miami (Coral Gables, Fla.), 1967. (*DA* 28:903A)
11. MANGAN, GORDON L. "Studies of the Relationship Between Neo-Pavlovian Properties of Higher Nervous Activity and Western Personality Dimensions: 3, The Relations of Transformation Mobility to Thinking Flexibility." *J Exp Res Personality* 2:117–23 My '67. * (*PA* 41:11907)
12. MILES, DAVID T. *An Experimental Investigation of Programed Creativity.* Doctor's thesis, Southern Illinois University (Carbondale, Ill.), 1967. (*DA* 28:2099A)
13. RIDLEY, DENNIS R., AND BIRNEY, ROBERT C. "Effects of Training Procedures on Creativity Test Scores." *J Ed Psychol* 58:158–64 Je '67. * (*PA* 41:10457)
14. WINDHOLZ, GEORGE, AND MCINTOSH, WILLIAM A. "Concurrent Validation of Guilford's Six Convergent Tests." *Ed & Psychol Meas* 27:393–400 su '67. * (*PA* 41:12843)
15. BROWN, STEPHEN W.; GUILFORD, J. P.; AND HOEPFNER, RALPH. "Six Semantic-Memory Abilities." *Ed & Psychol Meas* 28:691–717 au '68. * (*PA* 43:4427)
16. EDWARDS, ARTHUR B. *An Analysis of the Creative Ability Levels of the Potential Dropout in the Average Mental Ability*

Range. Doctor's thesis, University of Tennessee (Knoxville, Tenn.), 1968. (*DA* 29:3828A)

17. JANSSEN, CALVIN. "Comparative Creativity Scores of Lower Socio-Economic Dropouts and Non-Dropouts." *Psychol Sch* 5:183–4 Ap '68. * (*PA* 43:17498)

18. WINDHOLZ, GEORGE. "The Relation of Creativity and Intelligence Constellations to Traits of Temperament, Interest, and Value in College Students." *J General Psychol* 79:291–9 O '68. * (*PA* 43:3998)

19. ANDERSON, HARRY E., JR.; WHITE, WILLIAM F.; AND STEVENS, JOHN C. "Student Creativity, Intelligence, Achievement, and Teacher Classroom Behavior." *J Social Psychol* 78(1):99–107 Je '69. * (*PA* 43:16427)

20. GRAY, JAMES J. "The Effect of Productivity on Primary Process and Creativity." *J Proj Tech & Pers Assess* 33(3):213–8 Je '69. * (*PA* 43:14302)

21. GUILFORD, J. P., AND HOEPFNER, RALPH. "Comparisons of Varimax Rotations With Rotations to Theoretical Targets." *Ed & Psychol Meas* 29(1):3–22 sp '69. * (*PA* 44:15668)

22. SCHNITZER, LEAH PALTIEL, AND STEWART, ROBERT A. C. "Originality and Personality Variables in High School Art Students." *Psychol* 6(1):36–9 F '69. * (*PA* 43:11334)

23. FRUIN, DAVID JOHN. *Response Styles and Creativity.* Doctor's thesis, Johns Hopkins University (Baltimore, Md.), 1970. (*DAI* 31:4361B)

CUMULATIVE NAME INDEX

Anderson, H. E.: 19	McIntosh, W. A.: 14
Barron, F.: 1, 4	Mangan, G. L.: 11
Birney, R. C.: 13	Marks, A.: 3
Brown, S. W.: 15	Meadow, A.: 2
Edwards, A. B.: 16	Michael, W. B.: 3
Fruin, D. J.: 23	Miles, D. T.: 12
Gray, J. J.: 9, 20	Parnes, S. J.: 2
Guilford, J. P.: 6, 15, 21	Ridley, D. R.: 13
Hill, A. H.: 7	Schnitzer, L. P.: 22
Hoepfner, R.: 6, 15, 21	Stevens, J. C.: 19
Janssen, C.: 17	Stewart, R. A. C.: 22
Janssen, C. W.: 8	Vint, V. H.: 5
Jenkins, J. M.: 10	White, W. F.: 19
Kaiser, H. F.: 3	Windholz, G.: 14, 18

[573]

Possible Jobs. Grades 6–16 and adults; 1963; "divergent production of semantic implications" or "ability to suggest alternative deductions"; for a downward extension, see 554d; Arthur Gershon and J. P. Guilford; Sheridan Psychological Services, Inc. *

For additional information, see 6:558 (1 reference).

REFERENCES THROUGH 1971

1. See 6:558.

2. HAYNES, CAROLYN R. *The Relationships of Performances of Seventh Grade Students on Measures of Creativity, Study Habits and Attitudes, Expressed Need for Counseling and Achievement.* Master's thesis, Texas A & M University (College Station, Tex.), 1966.

3. GRAY, JAMES JOSEPH. *An Investigation of the Relationship Between Primary Process Thinking and Creativity.* Doctor's thesis, Fordham University (New York, N.Y.), 1967. (*DA* 28:5206B)

4. WINDHOLZ, GEORGE. "The Relation of Creativity and Intelligence Constellations to Traits of Temperament, Interest, and Value in College Students." *J General Psychol* 79:291–9 '68. * (*PA* 43:3998)

5. GRAY, JAMES J. "The Effect of Productivity on Primary Process and Creativity." *J Proj Tech & Pers Assess* 33(3):213–8 Je '69. * (*PA* 43:14302)

6. SIMPSON, DONALD JAMES. *The Effect of Selected Musical Studies on Growth in General Creative Potential.* Doctor's thesis, University of Southern California (Los Angeles, Calif.), 1969. (*DAI* 30:502A)

7. HEUSSENSTAMM, FRANCES K. "Creativity and Alienation: An Exploration of Their Relationship in Adolescence." *Calif J Ed Res* 21(3):140–6 My '70. *

8. OLESON, D. S., AND ZUBEK, JOHN P. "Effect of One Day of Sensory Deprivation on a Battery of Open-Ended Cognitive Tests." *Percept & Motor Skills* 31(3):919–23 D '70. * (*PA* 46:358)

9. SMITH, I. LEON. "IQ, Creativity, and the Taxonomy of Educational Objectives: Cognitive Domain." *J Exp Ed* 38(4):58–60 su '70. * (*PA* 46:5688)

10. SMITH, I. LEON. "IQ, Creativity, and Achievement: Interaction and Threshold." *Multiv Behav Res* 6(1):51–62 Ja '71. * (*PA* 46:9753)

CUMULATIVE NAME INDEX

Gray, J. J.: 3, 5	Simpson, D. J.: 6
Guilford, J. P.: 1	Smith, I. L.: 9–10
Haynes, C. R.: 2	Windholz, G.: 4
Heussenstamm, F. K.: 7	Zubek, J. P.: 8
Oleson, D. S.: 8	

Plot Titles

[574]

*****Remote Associates Test.** High school, college and adults; 1967–71, c1959–71; RAT; "ability to think creatively"; 2 levels; Sarnoff A. Mednick and Martha T. Mednick; Houghton Mifflin Co. *

a) HIGH SCHOOL LEVEL. 1971.

b) COLLEGE AND ADULT LEVEL. 1967, c1959–67.

For additional information and reviews by Leonard L. Baird, George K. Bennett, and Philip E. Vernon of *b*, see 7:445 (100 references).

REFERENCES THROUGH 1971

1–100. See 7:445.

101. HOUSTON, JOHN P., AND MEDNICK, SARNOFF A. "Creativity and the Need for Novelty." *J Abn & Social Psychol* 66:137–41 F '63. * (*PA* 37:6699)

102. McGLOTHLIN, WILLIAM H.; COHEN, SIDNEY; AND McGLOTHLIN, MARCELLA S. "Short-Term Effects of LSD on Anxiety, Attitudes and Performance." *J Nerv & Mental Dis* 139:266–73 S '64. * (*PA* 39:7046)

103. MENDELSOHN, GERALD A., AND GRISWOLD, BARBARA B. "Differential Use of Incidental Stimuli in Probem Solving as a Function of Creativity." *J Abn & Social Psychol* 68:431–6 Mr '64. * (*PA* 39:740)

104. MENDELSOHN, GERALD A.; GRISWOLD, BARBARA B.; AND ANDERSON, MILTON L. "Individual Differences in Anagram-Solving Ability." *Psychol Rep* 19:799–809 D '66. * (*PA* 41:3943)

105. WHITTEMORE, ROBERT G., JR., AND HEIMANN, ROBERT A. "Modification of Originality Responses." *J Counsel Psychol* 13:213–8 su '66. * (*PA* 40:8833)

106. GALL, MEREDITH, AND MENDELSOHN, GERALD A. "Effects of Facilitating Techniques and Subject-Experimenter Interaction on Creative Problem Solving." *J Pers & Social Psychol* 5:211–6 F '67. * (*PA* 41:3953)

107. KLEIN, PETER, AND KELLNER, HAROLD. "Creativity in a Two-Choice Probability Situation." *J General Psychol* 76:193–200 Ap '67. * (*PA* 41:8394)

108. LAUGHLIN, PATRICK R. "Incidental Concept Formation as a Function of Creativity and Intelligence." *J Pers & Social Psychol* 5:115–9 Ja '67. * (*PA* 41:3958)

109. McDONALD, DONALD C., JR., AND MARTIN, RANDALL B. "Word Association Training and Creativity." *Psychol Rep* 20:319–22 F '67. * (*PA* 41:6681)

110. DESIDERATO, OTELLO, AND SIGAL, SUSAN. "Associative Productivity as a Function of Creativity Level and Type of Verbal Stimulus." *Psychon Sci* 18(6):357–8 Mr 25 '70. * (*PA* 44:12581)

111. KORIAT, ASHER. *Creativity and the Structure of Memory.* Doctor's thesis, University of California (Berkeley, Calif.), 1970. (*DAI* 31:6242B)

112. WARREN, THOMAS FRANKLIN. *Creative Thinking Techniques: Four Methods of Stimulating Original Ideas in Sixth Grade Students.* Doctor's thesis, University of Wisconsin (Madison, Wis.), 1970. (*DAI* 31:5863A)

113. BOWERS, KENNETH S., AND KEELING, KENNETH R. "Heart-Rate Variability in Creative Functioning." *Psychol Rep* 29(1):160–2 Ag '71. * (*PA* 47:2468)

114. BURKE, RONALD J. "Correlates of the Ability to Fragment and Reorganize Stored Information." *J General Psychol* 84(2):183–9 Ap '71. * (*PA* 46:4255)

115. DACEY, JOHN S., AND MADAUS, GEORGE F. "An Analysis of Two Hypotheses Concerning the Relationship Between Creativity and Intelligence." *J Ed Res* 64(5):213–6 Ja '71. * (*PA* 46:4712)

116. DAVIS, GARY A., AND BELCHER, TERENCE L. "How Shall Creativity Be Measured? Torrance Tests, RAT, Alpha Biographical, and IQ." *J Creative Behav* 5(3):153–61 '71. *

117. DEL GAUDIO, ANDREW CHARLES. *Psychological Differentiation and Mobility as Related to Creativity.* Doctor's thesis, Fordham University (New York, N.Y.), 1971. (*DAI* 32:2393B)

118. ENRIQUEZ, VIRGILIO GASPAR. *Language and Originality: Recall of Postnominal Adjectives and Semantically Ill-Formed Sentences as a Function of the Structural Locus and Anomaly.* Doctor's thesis, Northwestern University (Evanston, Ill.), 1971. (*DAI* 32:5336A)

119. LEFCOURT, HERBERT M., AND TELEGDI, MELANIE SMITH. "Perceived Locus of Control and Field Dependence as Predictors of Cognitive Activity." *J Consult & Clin Psychol* 37(1):53–6 Ag '71. * (*PA* 47:903)

120. OHNMACHT, FRED W., AND McMORRIS, ROBERT F. "Creativity as a Function of Field Independence and Dogmatism." *J Psychol* 79(2):165–8 N '71. * (*PA* 47:6800)

121. PERRONE, JAMES V. *An Investigation of Two Approaches to the Measurement of Creative Potential in College Students.* Doctor's thesis, St. John's University (Jamaica, N.Y.), 1971. (*DAI* 32:2989B)

122. PHILLIPS, VICTOR K., AND TORRANCE, E. PAUL. "Divergent Thinking, Remote Associations, and Concept Attainment Strategies." *J Psychol* 77(2):223–8 Mr '71. * (*PA* 46:361)

123. PIERS, ELLEN V., AND KIRCHNER, ELIZABETH P. "Pro-

ductivity and Uniqueness in Continued Word Association as a Function of Subject Creativity and Stimulus Properties." *J Personality* 39(2):264–76 Je '71. * (*PA* 47:210)

124. PIZAM, ABRAHAM. *Some Socio-Psychological Correlates of Innovation Within Industrial Suggestion Systems.* Doctor's thesis, Cornell University (Ithaca, N.Y.), 1971. (*DAI* 32:606B)

125. SCHOEL, DORIS R., AND BUSSE, THOMAS V. "Humor and Creative Abilities." *Psychol Rep* 29(1):34 Ag '71. * (*PA* 47:2958)

126. SUTER, BARBARA ANN. *Masculinity-Femininity in Creative Women.* Doctor's thesis, Fordham University (New York, N.Y.), 1971. (*DAI* 32:2411B)

127. TURNEY, JOHN R.; ROSEN, NED A.; AND CONKLYN, ELIZABETH D. "Early Identification of Managerial Potential in a Technical-Professional Organization." Abstract. *Proc 79th Ann Conv Am Psychol Assn* 6(2):481–2 '71. * (*PA* 46:5909)

128. WIRWICK-VAN DUSEN, MAXINE, AND HALL, ALFRED E. "Need for Associative Novelty: An Unreliable Effect." *J Exp Res Personality* 5(2):119–23 Je '71. * (*PA* 48:1004)

129. WORTHEN, BLAINE R., AND CLARK, PHILIP M. "Toward an Improved Measure of Remote Associational Ability." *J Ed Meas* 8(2):113–23 su '71. * (*PA* 46:10884)

CUMULATIVE NAME INDEX

[575]

The Rutgers Drawing Test. Ages 4–6, 6–9; 1952–69; RDT; Anna Spiesman Starr; the Author. *

For additional information and a review by Melvyn I. Semmel, see 7:446 (6 references); see also 6:559 (2 references).

REFERENCES THROUGH 1971

1–2. See 6:559.
3–8. See 7:446.

CUMULATIVE NAME INDEX

[576]

★**Seeing Faults.** Ages 15 and over; 1971; verbal creativity; H. E. Schmidt (manual); National Institute for Personnel Research [South Africa]. *

[577]

Seeing Problems. Grades 9–16; 1962–69; 1969 test identical with half of test copyrighted 1962 (see 56182) except for administration instructions; Philip R. Merrifield and J. P. Guilford; Sheridan Psychological Services, Inc. *

For additional information, see 6:55182.

REFERENCES THROUGH 1971

1. DE MILLE, RICHARD. "Intellect After Lobotomy in Schizophrenia: A Factor Analytic Study." *Psychol Monogr* 76(16):1–18 '62. * (*PA* 38:2784)

2. ATKINSON, BEA HENRIETTA. *The Relationship Between Problem-Solving Strategies and Measures of Convergent and Divergent Thinking in a Selected Group of Secondary School Pupils.* Doctor's thesis, University of Florida (Gainesville, Fla.), 1964. (*DA* 25:7070)

3. ANDERSON, C. C., AND CROPLEY, A. J. "Some Correlates of Originality." *Austral J Psychol* 18:218–27 D '66. * (*PA* 41:4572)

4. CROPLEY, A. J. "Creativity and Intelligence." *Brit J Ed Psychol* 36:259–66 N '66. * (*PA* 41:573)

5. GUILFORD, J. P., AND HOEFFNER, RALPH. "Sixteen Divergent-Production Abilities at the Ninth-Grade Level." *Multiv Behav Res* 1:43–66 Ja '66. * (*PA* 41:1602)

6. HILL, ARTHUR H. "A Longitudinal Study of Attrition Among High Aptitude College Students." *J Ed Res* 60:166–73 D '66. *

7. NEEDHAM, WALTER EVANS. *Intellectual, Personality and Biographical Characteristics of Southern Negro and White College Students.* Doctor's thesis, University of Utah (Salt Lake City, Utah), 1966. (*DA* 27:1609B)

8. SMITH, ROBERT M., AND NEISWORTH, JOHN T. "Creative Thinking Abilities of Intellectually Superior Children in the Regular Grades." *Psychol Rep* 18:335–41 Ap '66. * (*PA* 40:8832)

9. CROPLEY, A. J. "Creativity, Intelligence, and Achievement." *Alberta J Ed Res* 13:51–8 Mr '67. * (*PA* 41:15253)

10. KARSTEN, MARY O'KEEFFE. *The Relationship of Tested Creative Abilities and Selected Factors of Academic Achievement, Intelligence, Sex, Socioeconomic Status, and Pupil Attitudes.* Doctor's thesis, University of Southern California (Los Angeles, Calif.), 1967. (*DA* 28:2557A)

11. SMITH, ROBERT M. "Creative Thinking Abilities of Educable Mentally Handicapped Children in the Regular Grades." *Am J Mental Def* 71:571–5 Ja '67. * (*PA* 41:6197)

12. BLACKHURST, A. EDWARD; MARKS, CLAUDE H.; AND TISDALL, WILLIAM J. "Relationship Between Mobility and Divergent Thinking in Blind Children." *Ed Visually Handicapped* 1(2):33–6 My '69. * (*PA* 43:14813)

13. GOODMAN, P.; FURCON, J.; AND ROSE, J. "Examination of Some Measures of Creative Ability by the Multitrait-Multi-

method Matrix." *J Appl Psychol* 53(3):240–3 Je '69. * (*PA* 43:11327)

14. GRIMSLEY, WILLIAM GERALD. *The Relationship Between Creativity and Leader Behavior of School Superintendents.* Doctor's thesis, University of Missouri (Columbia, Mo.), 1969. (*DAI* 30:5193A)

15. TISDALL, WILLIAM J.; BLACKHURST, A. EDWARD; AND MARKS, CLAUDE H. "Divergent Thinking in Blind Children." *J Ed Psychol* 62(6):468–73 D '71. * (*PA* 47:9708)

CUMULATIVE NAME INDEX

Anderson, C. C.: 3
Atkinson, B. H.: 2
Blackhurst, A. E.: 12, 15
Cropley, A. J.: 3–4, 9
de Mille, R.: 1
Furcon, J.: 13
Goodman, P.: 13
Grimsley, W. G.: 14
Guilford, J. P.: 5

Hill, A. H.: 6
Hoepfner, R.: 5
Karsten, M. O.: 10
Marks, C. H.: 12, 15
Needham, W. E.: 7
Neisworth, J. T.: 8
Rose, J.: 13
Smith, R. M.: 8, 11
Tisdall, W. J.: 12, 15

[578]

Seguin-Goddard Formboard. Ages 5–14; [1911]; modifications appear in *Arthur Point Scale of Performance Tests* and *Merrill-Palmer Scale of Mental Tests;* E. Seguin, H. H. Goddard, and N. Norsworthy; Stoelting Co.

REFERENCES THROUGH 1971

1. GAW, FRANCES. "A Study of Performance Tests." *Brit J Psychol* 15:374–92 Ap '25. *

2. WORTHINGTON, MYRTLE RAYMAKER. "A Study of Some Commonly Used Performance Tests." *J Appl Psychol* 10:216–27 Je '26. *

3. PORTEUS, S. D.; WITH THE ASSISTANCE OF DORIS M. DEWEY AND ROBERT G. BERNREUTER. "Race and Social Differences in Performance Tests." *Genetic Psychol Monogr* 8:93–208 Ag '30. * (*PA* 4:4947)

4. PORTEUS, STANLEY D. Chap. 21, "Tests of Temperament and Intelligence," pp. 351–77. In his *The Psychology of a Primitive People: A Study of the Australian Aborigine.* New York: Longmans, Green & Co., 1931. Pp. xvi, 438. * (*PA* 6:1168, title only)

5. PORTEUS, STANLEY D. Chap. 23, "Aboriginal Children's Intelligence," pp. 408–20. In his *The Psychology of a Primitive People: A Study of the Australian Aborigine.* New York: Longmans, Green & Co., 1931. Pp. xvi, 438. * (*PA* 6:1168, title only)

6. VANCE, THOMAS F. "The Effect of Size of Peg and Form Boards Upon the Performance Scores of Young Children." *Proc Iowa Acad Sci* 40:181–4 '33. * (*PA* 9:3048)

7. NOTTINGHAM, RUTH D. "A Psychological Study of Forty Unmarried Mothers." *Genetic Psychol Monogr* 19:157–228 My '37. * (*PA* 11:4670)

8. VERNON, P. E. "A Study of the Norms and the Validity of Certain Mental Tests at a Child Guidance Clinic: Part II." *Brit J Ed Psychol* 7:115–37 Je '37. * (*PA* 11:4827)

9. HAMLIN, ROY, AND ABEL, THEODORA M. "Test Pattern of Mental Defectives Skilled in Weaving." *J Appl Psychol* 22:385–9 Ag '38. * (*PA* 13:1642)

10. BERKO, MARTIN J. "Some Factors in the Perceptual Deviations of Cerebral Palsied Children." *Cerebral Palsy R* 15:3–4+ F '54. * (*PA* 28:7892)

11. TEUBER, HANS-LUKAS, AND WEINSTEIN, SIDNEY. "Performance on a Formboard-Task After Penetrating Brain Injury." *J Psychol* 38:177–90 Jl '54. * (*PA* 29:4573)

12. BILGER, ROBERT C. "Limitations on the Use of Intelligence Scales to Estimate the Mental Ages of Children." *Volta R* 60:321–5 S '58. *

13. REITAN, RALPH M. "Effects of Brain Damage on a Psychomotor Problem-Solving Task." *Percept & Motor Skills* 9:211–5 S '59. * (*PA* 34:6479)

14. MATTHEWS, CHARLES G., AND REITAN, RALPH M. "Psychomotor Abilities of Retardates and Patients With Cerebral Lesions." *Am J Mental Def* 66:607–12 Ja '62. * (*PA* 36:4JI07M)

15. REED, HOMER B. C., JR., AND REITAN, RALPH M. "The Significance of Age in the Performance of a Complex Psychomotor Task by Brain-Damaged and Non-Brain-Damaged Subjects." *J Gerontol* 17:193–6 Ap '62. * (*PA* 37:2961)

16. FAHMY, MOSTAFA. "Initial Exploring of the Intelligence of Shilluk Children: Studies in the Southern Sudan." *Vita Hum* (Switzerland) 7(3–4):164–77 '64. * (*PA* 39:7815)

17. KLATSKIN, ETHELYN HENRY. "Relationships of Deficits in Intelligence Test Performance of Preschool Children to Perinatal Experience." *J Consult Psychol* 28:228–33 Je '64. * (*PA* 39:4590)

18. MARSHALL, ANNE. *The Abilities and Attainments of Children Leaving Junior Training Centres.* London: National Association for Mental Health, 1967. Pp. i, 62. *

19. MEIER, MANFRED J., AND RESCH, JOSEPH A. "Behavioral Prediction of Short-Term Neurologic Change Following Acute Onset of Cerebrovascular Symptoms." *Mayo Clin Proc* 42:641–7 O '67. *

20. SANTORO, ROSEANN MARIE. *The Relationship of Reading Achievement to Specific Measures of Visual Perception, Visual-Motor Perception and Intelligence.* Doctor's thesis, Fordham University (New York, N.Y.), 1967. (*DA* 28:4010A)

21. BOURESTOM, NORMAN C., AND HOWARD, MARY T. "Behavioral Correlates of Recovery of Self-Care in Hemiplegic Patients." *Arch Phys Med & Rehabil* 49:449–54 Ag '68. *

22. COLE, SPURGEON; BURKHEIMER, G. J.; AND STEINBERG, JAY. "Validity of Seguin Formboard With Retarded Children." *Psychol Rep* 22:1143–4 Je '68. * (*PA* 42:19179)

23. MEIER, MANFRED J., AND OKAYAMA, MASAHIRO. "Behavior Assessment." *Geriatrics* 24(11):95–110 N '69. *

24. MEIER, MANFRED J. "Effects of Focal Cerebral Lesions on Contralateral Visuomotor Adaptation to Reversal and Inversion of Visual Feedback." *Neuropsychologia* (England) 8(3): 269–79 Jl '70. * (*PA* 44:21410)

25. GORDON, GEORGE, AND HYMAN, IRWIN. "The Measurement of Perceptual-Motor Abilities of Head Start Children." *Psychol Sch* 8(1):41–8 Ja '71. * (*PA* 46:7777)

CUMULATIVE NAME INDEX

Abel, T. M.: 9
Berko, M. J.: 10
Bernreuter, R. G.: 3
Bilger, R. C.: 12
Bourestom, N. C.: 21
Burkheimer, G. J.: 22
Cole, S.: 22
Dewey, D. M.: 3
Fahmy, M.: 16
Gaw, F.: 1
Gordon, G.: 25
Hamlin, R.: 9
Howard, M. T.: 21
Hyman, I.: 25
Klatskin, E. H.: 17
Marshall, A.: 18

Matthews, C. G.: 14
Meier, M. J.: 19, 23–4
Nottingham, R. D.: 7
Okayama, M.: 23
Porteus, S. D.: 3–5
Reed, H. B. C.: 15
Reitan, R. M.: 13–5
Resch, J. A.: 19
Santoro, R. M.: 20
Steinberg, J.: 22
Teuber, H. L.: 11
Vance, T. F.: 6
Vernon, P. E.: 8
Weinstein, S.: 11
Worthington, M. R.: 2

[579]

*Simile Interpretations [Sheridan Edition]. Grades 10–16; 1962–69; "divergent production of semantic systems"; consists of the 4 items in the 1962 test of the same title (see 561d2) plus 4 new items; Paul R. Christensen, J. P. Guilford, and Ralph Hoepfner; Sheridan Psychological Services, Inc. *
For additional information, see 6:551d2.

REFERENCES THROUGH 1971

1. GUILFORD, J. P., AND HOEPFNER, RALPH. "Sixteen Divergent-Production Abilities at the Ninth-Grade Level." *Multiv Behav Res* 1:43–66 Ja '66. * (*PA* 41:1602)

CUMULATIVE NAME INDEX

Guilford, J. P.: 1   Hoepfner, R.: 1

[580]

★Similes Test. Grades 4–16 and adults; 1971; ST; creativity; Charles E. Schaefer; Research Psychologists Press, Inc. *

REFERENCES THROUGH 1971

1. SCHAEFER, CHARLES E. "The Similes Test: A New Measure of Metaphorical Thinking." Abstract. *Proc 78th Ann Conv Am Psychol Assn* 5(1):169–70 '70. * (*PA* 44:18718)

CUMULATIVE NAME INDEX

Schaefer, C. E.: 1

[581]

★Sketches. Grades 9 and over; 1967; "divergent production of figural units" or "visual-figural fluency"; S. Gardner, A. Gershon, P. R. Merrifield, and J. P. Guilford; Sheridan Psychological Services, Inc. *

REFERENCES THROUGH 1971

1. GUILFORD, J. P., AND HOEPFNER, RALPH. "Sixteen Divergent-Production Abilities at the Ninth-Grade Level." *Multiv Behav Res* 1:43–66 Ja '66. * (*PA* 41:1602)

CUMULATIVE NAME INDEX

Guilford, J. P.: 1   Hoepfner, R.: 1

[582]

Subsumed Abilities Test. Ages 9 and over; 1957–63; 5 scores: recognition, abstraction, conceptualiza-

Seeing Problems

tion, total (demonstrated abilities), potential abilities; Joseph R. Sanders; Martin M. Bruce, Ph.D., Publishers. *

For additional information and a review by Naomi Stewart, see 6:560.

REFERENCES THROUGH 1971

1. BRUCE, MARTIN M. "Normative Data Information Exchange, No. 11–14." *Personnel Psychol* 11:280 su '58. *
2. BRUCE, MARTIN M. "Normative Data Information Exchange, No. 11–15." *Personnel Psychol* 11:281 su '58. *

CUMULATIVE NAME INDEX

Bruce, M. M.: 1–2   Stewart, N.: *rev,* 6:560

[583]

★**Symbol Identities.** Grades 10 and over; 1967; "evaluation of symbolic units"; Ralph Hoepfner and J. P. Guilford; Sheridan Psychological Services, Inc. *

[584]

Symbol Series Test: I.B.P. Edition, 1968. Illiterate and semi-literate adults; 1969; abstract reasoning; G. V. Grant; National Institute for Personnel Research [South Africa]. *
For additional information, see 7:447.

[585]

★**Test of Concept Utilization.** Ages 4.5–18.5; 1972; TCU; 24 scores: 6 equivalence scores (color, shape, homogeneous function, abstract, stimulus bound, object bound), 2 relational scores (relational function, minor relational), 3 structure scores (total equivalence, total relational, total unilateral), 6 reality match scores (color, shape, homogeneous function, abstract, relational function, total), 2 concept articulation scores (acceptable mains, inferior mains), 4 qualitative scores (action, object qualities, infusions, creations), negations; Richard L. Crager and Ann J. Spriggs; Western Psychological Services. *

REFERENCES THROUGH 1971

1. CRAGER, RICHARD L., AND SPRIGGS, ANN J. "Development of Concept Utilization." *Develop Psychol* 1(4):415–24 Jl '69. * (*PA* 43:14117)

CUMULATIVE NAME INDEX

Crager, R. L.: 1   Spriggs, A. J.: 1

[586]

★**Test of Creative Potential.** Grades 2–12 and adults; 1973; TCP; Ralph Hoepfner and Judith Hemenway; Monitor. *

[587]

★**Thinking Creatively With Sounds and Words, Research Edition.** Grades 3–12, adults; 1973; TCSW; 2 tests; technical manual by Joe Khatena and E. Paul Torrance; Personnel Press. *
a) SOUNDS AND IMAGES. SI; Bert F. Cunnington and E. Paul Torrance.
b) ONOMATOPEIA AND IMAGES. OI; Joe Khatena.

REFERENCES THROUGH 1971

1. WHITTEMORE, ROBERT GEORGE, JR. *Modification of Originality Responses in Academically Talented, Male University Freshmen.* Doctor's thesis, Arizona State University (Tempe, Ariz.), 1963. (*DA* 25:6403)
2. WHITTEMORE, ROBERT G., JR., AND HEIMANN, ROBERT A. "Modification of Originality Responses." *J Counsel Psychol* 13:213–8 su '66. * (*PA* 40:8833)
3. KHATENA, JOE. "'Onomatopoeia and Images': Preliminary Validity Study of a Test of Originality." *Percept & Motor Skills* 28(1):335–8 F '69. * (*PA* 43:11331)
4. KHATENA, JOE. *The Training of Creative Thinking Strategies and Its Effects on Originality.* Doctor's thesis, University of Georgia (Athens, Ga.), 1969. (*DAI* 30:3324A)
5. TORRANCE, E. P. "Originality of Imagery in Identifying Creative Talent in Music." *Gifted Child Q* 13(1):3–8 sp '69. * (*PA* 43:14320)

6. KHATENA, JOE. "Note on Reliability and Validity of Onomatopoeia and Images." *Percept & Motor Skills* 31(1):86 Ag '70. * (*PA* 45:4282)
7. KHATENA, JOE. "Repeated Presentation of Stimuli and Production of Original Responses." *Percept & Motor Skills* 30(1):91–4 F '70. * (*PA* 46:9071)
8. KHATENA, JOE. "Training College Adults to Think Creatively With Words." *Psychol Rep* 27(1):279–81 Ag '70. * (*PA* 45:6340)
9. SCHAEFER, CHARLES E. "'Onomatopoeia and Images': Further Evidence of Validity." *Percept & Motor Skills* 31(3):786 D '70. * (*PA* 45:9979)
10. KHATENA, JOE. "Adolescents and the Meeting of Time Deadlines in the Production of Original Verbal Images." *Gifted Child Q* 15(3):201–4 f '71. * (*PA* 47:11651)
11. KHATENA, JOE. "Breaking Away From Perceptual Set and Statistical Infrequency in Production of Original Verbal Images." *Percept & Motor Skills* 32(3):958 Je '71. * (*PA* 47:2991)
12. KHATENA, JOE. "Children's Version of 'Onomatopoeia and Images': A Preliminary Validity Study of Verbal Originality." *Percept & Motor Skills* 33(1):26 Ag '71. * (*PA* 47:2992)
13. KHATENA, JOE. "Evaluation and the Creative Potential in Music." *Gifted Child Q* 15(1):19–22 sp '71. * (*PA* 47:11802)
14. KHATENA, JOE. "Production of Original Verbal Images by Children Between Ages 8 and 19 as Measured by the Alternate Forms of Onomatopoeia and Images." Abstract. *Proc 79th Ann Conv Am Psychol Assn* 6(1):187–8 '71. * (*PA* 46:2605)
15. KHATENA, JOE. "A Second Study Training College Adults to Think Creatively With Words." *Psychol Rep* 28(2):385–6 Ap '71. * (*PA* 46:6162)
16. KHATENA, JOE. "'Sounds and Images': Further Evidence of Validity of a Test of Originality." *Percept & Motor Skills* 32(3):850 Je '71. * (*PA* 47:2993)
17. KHATENA, JOE, AND TORRANCE, E. PAUL. "Attitude Patterns and the Production of Original Verbal Images: A Study in Construct Validity." *Gifted Child Q* 15(2):117–22 su '71. * (*PA* 47:9614)

CUMULATIVE NAME INDEX

Heimann, R. A.: 2   Torrance, E. P.: 5, 17
Khatena, J.: 3–4, 6–8, 10–7   Whittemore, R. G.: 1–2
Schaefer, C. E.: 9

[588]

The Time Appreciation Test. Ages 10 and over; 1943–46; test sheet title is *JNB Time Test;* John N. Buck; Western Psychological Services. *

For additional information and reviews by E. J. G. Bradford and Charles N. Cofer, see 3:266 (2 references).

REFERENCES THROUGH 1971

1–2. See 3:266.
3. COFER, CHARLES N., AND BIEGEL, MARK M. "A Study of the Kent and Buck Screen Tests of Mental Ability in Relation to Otis and Stanford Achievement Test Scores." *J Consult Psychol* 12:187–9 My–Je '48. * (*PA* 22:4943)
4. ENGLE, T. L., AND HAMLETT, IONA C. "The Use of the Time Appreciation Test as a Screening or Supplementary Test for Mentally Deficient Patients." *Am J Mental Def* 54:521–5 Ap '50. * (*PA* 25:410)
5. ENGLE, T. L., AND HAMLETT, IONA C. "Constancy of the I.Q. With Mentally Deficient Patients as Measured by the Time Appreciation Test." *Am J Mental Def* 56:775–6 Ap '52. * (*PA* 26:7081)
6. HAMMER, EMANUEL F. "Comparison of the Performances of Negro Children and Adolescents on Two Tests of Intelligence, One an Emergency Scale." *J Genetic Psychol* 84:85–93 Mr '54. * (*PA* 28:8659)
7. JOHNSON, EDWARD E. "Time Concepts as Related to Sex, Intelligence and Academic Performance." *J Ed Res* 57:377–9 Mr '64. *

CUMULATIVE NAME INDEX

Biegel, M. M.: 3   Hamlett, I. C.: 4–5
Bradford, E. J. G.: *rev,* 3:266   Hammer, E. F.: 6
Buck, J.: 1   Johnson, E. E.: 7
Cofer, C. N.: 3; *rev,* 3:266   Landisberg, S.: 2
Engle, T. L.: 4–5

[589]

Torrance Tests of Creative Thinking, Research Edition. Kgn through graduate school; 1966; TTCT; revision of *Minnesota Tests of Creative Thinking;* 2 tests; E. Paul Torrance; Personnel Press. *
a) VERBAL TEST. Test booklet title is *Thinking Creatively With Words;* 3 scores: fluency, flexibility, originality.

b) FIGURAL TEST. Test booklet title is *Thinking Creatively With Pictures;* 4 scores: fluency, flexibility, originality, elaboration.

For additional information, reviews by Leonard L. Baird and Robert L. Thorndike, and excerpted reviews by Ralph Hoepfner, John L. Holland, and Michael A. Wallach, see 7:448 (243 references).

REFERENCES THROUGH 1971

1–243. See 7:448.

244. FLEMING, ELYSE S., AND WEINTRAUB, SAMUEL. "Attitudinal Rigidity as a Measure of Creativity in Gifted Children." *J Ed Psychol* 53:81–5 Ap '62. * (*PA* 37:1918)

245. TORRANCE, E. PAUL. "Cultural Discontinuities and the Development of Originality of Thinking." *Excep Children* 29:2–13 S '62. * (*PA* 37:6707)

246. YAMAMOTO, KAORU. "Creativity and Sociometric Choice Among Adolescents." *J Social Psychol* 64:249–61 D '64. * (*PA* 39:7828)

247. CREEKMORE, FLORINE. *A Study of the Creative Thinking Abilities of Teachers and the Tested Creativity of Their Pupils.* Master's thesis, Central Washington College of Education (Ellensburg, Wash.), 1965.

248. HAVEN, GEORGE A., JR. "Creative Thought, Productivity, and the Self-Concept." *Psychol Rep* 16:750–2 Je '65. * (*PA* 39:15291)

249. LONG, BARBARA H., AND HENDERSON, EDMUND H. "Originality, Reading, and Arithmetic." *Percept & Motor Skills* 21:553–4 O '65. * (*PA* 40:2871)

250. MACKLER, BERNARD, AND SHONTZ, FRANKLIN C. "Life Style and Creativity: An Empirical Investigation." *Percept & Motor Skills* 20:873–96 Je '65. * (*PA* 39:15302)

251. TORRANCE, E. PAUL. *Rewarding Creative Behavior: Experiments in Classroom Activity.* Englewood Cliffs, N.J.: Prentice-Hall, Inc., 1965. Pp. xiii, 353. *

252. WODTKE, KENNETH H., AND WALLEN, NORMAN E. "The Effects of Teacher Control in the Classroom on Pupils' Creativity-Test Gains." *Am Ed Res J* 2:75–82 Mr '65. *

253. YAMAMOTO, KAORU. "A Note on Fifth-Grade Children's Vocational World and Creative Thinking." *Gifted Child Q* 9:187–91 w '65. * (*PA* 40:5254)

254. SMITH, ROBERT M., AND NEISWORTH, JOHN T. "Creative Thinking Abilities of Intellectually Superior Children in the Regular Grades." *Psychol Rep* 18:335–41 Ap '66. * (*PA* 40:8832)

255. CICIRELLI, VICTOR G. "Sibling Constellation, Creativity, IQ, and Academic Achievement." *Child Develop* 38:481–90 Je '67. * (*PA* 41:10210)

256. MCWHINNIE, HAROLD J. "Some Relationships Between Creativity and Perception in Sixth-Grade Children." *Percept & Motor Skills* 25:979–80 D '67. * (*PA* 42:8733)

257. PANEY, HENRY, AND HORROCKS, CAROL. "Creativity in a Troop of Low Average Intelligent Boy Scouts." *Adolescence* 2:231–41 su '67. * (*PA* 42:3962)

258. YAMAMOTO, KAORU. "Creativity and Unpredictability in School Achievement." *J Ed Res* 60:321–5 Mr '67. *

259. BUDOFF, MILTON; MESKIN, JOAN D.; AND KEMLER, DEBORAH. "Training Productive Thinking of EMRs: A Failure to Replicate." *Am J Mental Def* 73:195–9 S '68. * (*PA* 43:4371)

260. BURNHAM, RUTH ELIZABETH. *The Relationship Between the Intelligence Quotient and the Creative Ability of Second Grade Children in the Villa Park School System.* Master's thesis, Northern Illinois University (DeKalb, Ill.), 1968.

261. HADDON, F. A., AND LYTTON, HUGH. "Teaching Approach and the Development of Divergent Thinking Abilities in Primary Schools." *Brit J Ed Psychol* 38:171–80 Je '68. * (*PA* 42:17790)

262. PUGH, RICHARD C. "Tests for Creative Thinking—Potential for School Testing Programs." *B Sch Ed Ind Univ* 44(6):1–30 N '68. * (*PA* 46:5483)

263. COFFEY, FRANK HOLMES. *The Relationship of Intelligence to Creativity.* Master's thesis, Wisconsin State University (Oshkosh, Wis.), 1969.

264. KOONS, NANCY. *The Relationship Between E. Paul Torrance's Tests for Creativity in Art and Performance in Art Class.* Master's thesis, Millersville State College (Millersville, Pa.), 1969.

265. SHACKEL, D. S. J., AND LAWRENCE, P. J. "Improving Creativity Through Programmed Instruction." *N Zeal J Ed Studies* 4(1):41–56 My '69. *

266. TORRANCE, E. PAUL. "New Types of Items for Measuring the Creative Thinking Abilities," pp. 293–309. In *Developments in Educational Testing, Vol. I.* Edited by Karlheinz Ingenkamp. London: University of London Press Ltd., 1969. Pp. 446. *

267. ARCHAMBAULT, FRANCIS XAVIER, JR. *A Computerized Approach to Scoring Verbal Responses to the Torrance Tests of Creative Thinking.* Doctor's thesis, University of Connecticut (Storrs, Conn.), 1970. (*DAI* 31:6464A)

268. BATES, BRIAN C.; SUNDBERG, NORMAN D.; AND TYLER, LEONA E. "Divergent Problem Solving: A Comparison of

Adolescents in India and America." *Int J Psychol* (France) 5(4):231–44 '70. * (*PA* 47:10696)

269. BURGESS, WILLIAM VANDER. *The Analysis of Teacher Creativity, Pupil Age, and Pupil Sex as Sources of Variation Among Elementary Pupils' Performances on Pre- and Post-Tests of Creative Thinking.* Doctor's thesis, University of California (Berkeley, Calif.), 1970. (*DAI* 32:747A)

270. JOSE, TERESITA A. "Convergent-Divergent Thinking Abilities and Risk-Taking in Children." *Philippine J Psychol* 3(1):22–35 Je '70. * (*PA* 49:11231)

271. MCDONALD, NORMA LEE HALE. *A Study of Creativity in Educable Mentally Retarded Children.* Doctor's thesis, University of Denver (Denver, Colo.), 1970. (*DAI* 31:4587A)

272. MARBURG, GALEN SANFORD. *The Relationship Between Classroom Climate and Creative Performance Among Fifth Grade Elementary School Children.* Doctor's thesis, University of Maryland (College Park, Md.), 1970. (*DAI* 31:6407A)

273. MAUL, TERRY LEE. *An Investigation of the Relationships Between Self-Actualization and Creative Thinking Processes.* Doctor's thesis, University of California (Berkeley, Calif.), 1970. (*DAI* 32:793A)

274. OVERSTREET, GEORGE CLARK. *A Study of Teacher Characteristics in Changing and Stable Schools.* Doctor's thesis, University of Kentucky (Lexington, Ky.), 1970. (*DAI* 32:796A)

275. RANZAU, MARIE-LOUISE. *Correlates of Creativity in Nursing Education.* Doctor's thesis, University of Texas (Austin, Tex.), 1970. (*DAI* 31:6715B)

276. SHIVELY, JOE E. *Evaluation of the Effects of Creativity Training Programs in the Elementary School.* Doctor's thesis, Purdue University (Lafayette, Ind.), 1970. (*DAI* 31:5215A)

277. SILVERBERG, ROBERT ALLAN. *The Relationship of Children's Perceptions of Parental Behavior to the Creativity of Their Children.* Doctor's thesis, New York University (New York, N.Y.), 1970. (*DAI* 31:6413A)

278. STEVENS, HOWARD LAMAR. *A Study of Creative and Causal Thinking Skills and Student-Faculty Perceptions in a Mexican Institution.* Doctor's thesis, University of Georgia (Athens, Ga.), 1970. (*DAI* 31:6416A)

279. WALTON, JOSEPH MOSES. *Predicting the Success of Prospective Teachers in an Urban Teacher Education Project.* Doctor's thesis, Ohio State University (Columbus, Ohio), 1970. (*DAI* 32:190A)

280. WARREN, THOMAS FRANKLIN. *Creative Thinking Techniques: Four Methods of Stimulating Original Ideas in Sixth Grade Students.* Doctor's thesis, University of Wisconsin (Madison, Wis.), 1970. (*DAI* 31:5863A)

281. WEISER, JOHN C. "Personality Variables Associated With Creativity in Prospective Female Teachers." *J Stud Pers Assn Teach Ed* 8(3):77–84 sp '70. * (*PA* 44:18682)

282. WONZER, ANN CUSHMAN. *A Study of the Relationships Among Creativity, Intelligence, and Achievement Measures Based on Longitudinal Data.* Doctor's thesis, University of Michigan (Ann Arbor, Mich.), 1970. (*DAI* 32:1205A)

283. ALSTON, DOROTHY JEAN. *A Comparison of Motor Creativity With Verbal Creativity and Figural Creativity of Black Culturally Deprived Children.* Doctor's thesis, University of North Carolina (Greensboro, N.C.), 1971. (*DAI* 32:2458A)

284. BELLAMY, EDWARD ELLSWORTH. *A Study of Productive Thinking in Mentally Retarded Children.* Doctor's thesis, University of Illinois (Urbana, Ill.), 1971. (*DAI* 32:2411A)

285. BERRETTA, SHIRLEY. *Comparative Effects of Play on Creative Thinking: The Immediate Influence of Art, Drama, and Playground Experiences on Children.* Doctor's thesis, University of Southern Mississippi (Hattiesburg, Miss.), 1971. (*DAI* 32:2981B)

286. BLOCKER, LARRY PAUL. *Effect of In-Service Training for Teachers on the Creative Production of Students.* Doctor's thesis, United States International University (San Diego, Calif.), 1971. (*DAI* 32:1952A)

287. CACHA, FRANCES BLACKHALL. *A Study of the Relation of Creative Thinking Abilities to Personality Factors and Peer Nominations of Fifth Grade Children.* Doctor's thesis, New York University (New York, N.Y.), 1971. (*DAI* 32:1329A)

288. CULLINA, JAMES JOSEPH. *The Effects of Ambiguous Visual Stimuli in Art Instruction on Divergent Thinking Abilities.* Doctor's thesis, Ball State University (Muncie, Ind.), 1971. (*DAI* 32:3085A)

289. DACEY, JOHN S., AND MADAUS, GEORGE F. "An Analysis of Two Hypotheses Concerning the Relationship Between Creativity and Intelligence." *J Ed Res* 64(5):213–6 Ja '71. * (*PA* 46:4712)

290. DAFFRON, MARTHA RUTH. *The Influence of Selective Factors on the Divergent Thinking Abilities of Fourth Grade School Children.* Doctor's thesis, Mississippi State University (State College, Miss.), 1971. (*DAI* 32:3780A)

291. DAVIS, GARY A., AND BELCHER, TERENCE L. "How Shall Creativity Be Measured? Torrance Tests, RAT, Alpha Biographical, and I.Q." *J Creative Behav* 5(3):153–61 '71. *

292. DILCHER, RONALD CLARENCE. *Relationships Among Independent Study, Divergent Thinking, Convergent Thinking, Attitudes and Achievement in General College Biology.* Doctor's thesis, State University of New York (Buffalo, N.Y.), 1971. (*DAI* 32:1743A)

293. DILL, JOHN RICHARD. *A Study of the Influence of Race of the Experimenter and Verbal Reinforcement on Creativity*

Test Performance of Lower Socioeconomic Status Black Children. Doctor's thesis, New York University (New York, N.Y.), 1971. (*DAI* 32:6071B)

294. EMRICK, CAROL SHAW. *Language Performance of Stuttering and Nonstuttering Children.* Doctor's thesis, University of Iowa (Iowa City, Iowa), 1971. (*DAI* 32:5509B)

295. FELDHUSEN, JOHN F.; TREFFINGER, DONALD J.; VAN MONDFRANS, ADRIAN P.; AND FERRIS, DONALD R. "The Relationship Between Academic Grades and Divergent Thinking Scores Derived From Four Different Methods of Testing." *J Exp Ed* 40(1):35–40 f '71. * (*PA* 47:9798)

296. FERENCE, CAMILLE. *Prediction of Creativity by Means of Interest Measures.* Doctor's thesis, Ohio State University (Columbus, Ohio), 1971. (*DAI* 32:3685A)

297. GREENE, JOHN FRANCIS. *Scoring Creativity Tests by Computer Simulation.* Doctor's thesis, University of Connecticut (Storrs, Conn.), 1971. (*DAI* 32:237A)

298. JOESTING, JOAN, AND JOESTING, ROBERT. "The Picture Interpretation Test and Its Relationship to the Stanford-Binet." *Psychol Rep* 29(3):1146 D '71. * (*PA* 48:1649)

299. KALTSOUNIS, BILL. "Differences in Creative Thinking of Black and White Deaf Children." *Percept & Motor Skills* 32(1):243–8 F '71. * (*PA* 46:3745)

300. KALTSOUNIS, BILL, AND STEPHENS, HOWARD G. "Learning Mathematics by Discovery: Implications for a Creative Child." *Percept & Motor Skills* 33(3):884–6 D '71. * (*PA* 48:1929)

301. KANITZ, HUGO EDWARD. *Predicting Effectiveness in Potential Teachers.* Doctor's thesis, Ohio State University (Columbus, Ohio), 1971. (*DAI* 32:1855A)

302. KEEN, CHARLES FLOYD. *A Study of Relationships Between Growth and Developmental Variables, Creativity, and Musicality.* Doctor's thesis, University of Michigan (Ann Arbor, Mich.), 1971. (*DAI* 32:3791A)

303. KELLENBERGER, LONNIE ROBERT. *Student Question-Asking Behavior in Grade Six Social Studies.* Doctor's thesis, University of Oregon (Eugene, Ore.), 1971. (*DAI* 32:4881A)

304. KHATENA, JOE. "Teaching Disadvantaged Preschool Children to Think Creatively With Pictures." *J Ed Psychol* 62(5):384–6 O '71. * (*PA* 47:5851)

305. LADNER, JUDITH LEE. *Enhancement of Productive Thinking in Institutionalized Mental Retardates.* Doctor's thesis, Fordham University (New York, N.Y.), 1971. (*DAI* 32:2401B)

306. LANDRY, RICHARD G. "The Factorial Orthogonality of the Torrance Tests of Creative Thinking and the Culture-Fair Intelligence Test." *Col Ed Rec Univ N Dak* 57(2):20–6 N '71. *

307. LANGGULUNG, HASAN. *A Cross-Cultural Study of the Child's Conception of Situational Causality in India, Western Samoa, Mexico, and the United States.* Doctor's thesis, University of Georgia (Athens, Ga.), 1971. (*DAI* 32:5040A)

308. LOW, HELEN E. *Identification of Gifted Mexican-American Children by Using the Torrance Tests of Creative Thinking.* Master's thesis, California State College (Long Beach, Calif.), 1971.

309. MAR'I, SAMI KHALIL. *Creativity of American and Arab Rural Youth: A Cross-Cultural Study.* Doctor's thesis, University of Wisconsin (Madison, Wis.), 1971. (*DAI* 31:6407A)

310. MEERBACH, JOHN CALVIN. *A Study of the Relationship of Creativity, Vocational Maturity and Vocational Choice Among Eighth Grade Students.* Doctor's thesis, University of Toledo (Toledo, Ohio), 1971. (*DAI* 32:3695A)

311. MITCHELL, BRUCE. "The Classroom Pursuit of Creativity: One Strategy That Worked." *J Res & Develop Ed* 4(3):57–61 sp '71. *

312. MOSIER, JACK ARTHUR. *A Study of Parent Occupational Expectations for Gifted and Average Children Compared With the Child's Occupational Goals and Creativity.* Doctor's thesis, Brigham Young University (Provo, Utah), 1971. (*DAI* 32:4297A)

313. OGLETREE, EARL. "A Cross-Cultural Examination of the Creative Thinking Ability of Public and Private School Pupils in England, Scotland, and Germany." *J Social Psychol* 83(2):301–2 Ap '71. * (*PA* 47:2836)

314. OGLETREE, EARL J. "Are Creativity Tests Valid in Cultures Outside the United States?" *J Res & Develop Ed* 4(3):129–30 sp '71. *

315. PHILLIPS, VICTOR K., AND TORRANCE, E. PAUL. "Divergent Thinking, Remote Associations, and Concept Attainment Strategies." *J Psychol* 77(2):223–8 Mr '71. * (*PA* 46:361)

316. RAMIREZ, JUDITH VALLA. "Effects of Tutorial Experiences on the Problem-Solving Behavior of Sixth-Graders." *Calif J Ed Res* 22(2):80–90 Mr '71. *

317. RENZULLI, JOSEPH S.; HARTMAN, ROBERT K.; AND CALLAHAN, CAROLYN M. "Teacher Identification of Superior Students." *Excep Children* 38(3):211–4+ N '71. * (*PA* 49:7941)

318. RICHARDS, P. N., AND BOLTON, N. "Type of Mathematics Teaching, Mathematical Ability and Divergent Thinking in Junior School Children." *Brit J Ed Psychol* 41(1):32–7 F 71. * (*PA* 46:9822)

319. RICHMOND, BERT O. "Creative and Cognitive Abilities of White and Negro Children." *J Negro Ed* 40(2):111–6 sp '71. * (*PA* 47:7566)

320. SPEEDIE, STUART M.; ASHER, J. WILLIAM; AND TREFFINGER, DONALD J. "Comment on 'Fluency as a Pervasive Element in the Measurement of Creativity.'" *J Ed Meas* 8(2):125–6 su '71. * (*PA* 46:10883)

321. STRUM, IRENE S. *The Relationship of Creativity and Academic Risk-Taking Among Fifth Graders.* Doctor's thesis, Fordham University (New York, N.Y.), 1971. (*DAI* 32:801A)

322. STUDER, MARILYN RITA. *The Relationship of Discovery Methods in Mathematics to Creative Thinking and Attitudes Toward Mathematics.* Doctor's thesis, Ohio State University (Columbus, Ohio), 1971. (*DAI* 32:3816A)

323. THORSEN, ERIC EDWARD. *The Heritability of "G" and Figural Divergent Thinking.* Doctor's thesis, Boston College (Chestnut Hill, Mass.), 1971. (*DAI* 32:1351A)

324. TORRANCE, E. PAUL. "Are the Torrance Tests of Creative Thinking Biased Against, or in Favor of 'Disadvantaged' Groups?" *Gifted Child Q* 15(2):75–80 su '71. * (*PA* 47:8656)

325. TORRANCE, E. PAUL. "Is Bias Against Job Changing Bias Against Giftedness?" *Gifted Child Q* 15(4):244–8 w '71. * (*PA* 48:5010)

326. TORRANCE, E. PAUL. "Stimulation, Enjoyment, and Originality in Dyadic Creativity." *J Ed Psychol* 62(1):45–8 F '71. * (*PA* 46:3079)

327. TURKNETT, ROBERT LAVALE. *A Study of the Differential Effects of Individual Versus Group Reward Conditions on the Creative Productions of Elementary School Children.* Doctor's thesis, University of Georgia (Athens, Ga.), 1971. (*DAI* 32:5625A)

328. TURNER, THOMAS NOEL. *A Correlational Study of Creative Verbal Behavior and Perception in the Elementary School.* Doctor's thesis, Pennsylvania State University (University Park, Pa.), 1971. (*DAI* 33:89A)

329. VAN MONDFRANS, ADRIAN P.; FELDHUSEN, JOHN F.; TREFFINGER, DONALD J.; AND FERRIS, DONALD R. "The Effects of Instructions and Response Time on Divergent Thinking Test Scores." *Psychol Sch* 8(1):64–71 Ja '71. * (*PA* 46:7464)

330. VAUGHAN, MARGERY, AND MYERS, R. E. "Examination of Musical Process as Related to Creative Thinking." *J Res Music Ed* 19(3):337–41 f '71. * (*PA* 48:5879)

331. WILLIAMS, ROBERT L. "Relationship of Class Participation to Personality, Ability, and Achievement Variables." *J Social Psychol* 83(2):193–8 Ap '71. * (*PA* 46:3721)

CUMULATIVE NAME INDEX

[590]

Two-Figure Formboard. Ages 4 and over; [1917];
modification appears in *Arthur Point Scale of Performance Tests;* R. Pintner; Stoelting Co.

[591]

*****Utility Test.** Grades 9–12; 1962–69; for research
use only; 2 scores: divergent production of semantic
units, divergent production of semantic classes; 1969
test identical with test copyrighted 1962 (see 561x1)
except for administration instructions; Robert C. Wilson, Philip R. Merrifield, and J. P. Guilford; Sheridan
Psychological Services, Inc. *

For additional information, see 6:551x1.

REFERENCES THROUGH 1971

1. GUILFORD, J. P., AND HOEPFNER, RALPH. "Sixteen Divergent-Production Abilities at the Ninth-Grade Level." *Multiv
Behav Res* 1:43–66 Ja '66. * (*PA* 41:1602)
2. BRAUND, ROBERT A. "Pilot Study of a Cognitive Restructuring Paradigm." *Psychol Rep* 20:275–9 F '67. * (*PA* 41:7919)
3. GRAY, JAMES JOSEPH. *An Investigation of the Relationship
Between Primary Process Thinking and Creativity.* Doctor's
thesis, Fordham University (New York, N.Y.), 1967. (*DA*
28:5206B)
4. KARSTEN, MARY O'KEEFFE. *The Relationship of Tested
Creative Abilities and Selected Factors of Academic Achievement, Intelligence, Sex, Socioeconomic Status, and Pupil Attitudes.* Doctor's thesis, University of Southern California (Los
Angeles, Calif.), 1967. (*DA* 28:2557A)
5. MANGAN, GORDON L. "Studies of the Relationship Between
Neo-Pavlovian Properties of Higher Nervous Activity and
Western Personality Dimensions: 3, The Relations of Transformation Mobility to Thinking Flexibility." *J Exp Res Person-
ality* 2:117–23 My '67. * (*PA* 41:11907)
6. PLOGMAN, BERNARD EDWARD. *The Creative Relationship
Between Art Teachers and Their Ninth Grade Art Students in
Art Room Practices, Personality and Pencil Drawing in Catholic
Schools.* Doctor's thesis, University of Cincinnati (Cincinnati,
Ohio), 1967. (*DA* 28:3534A)
7. ALZOBAIE, ABDUL JALIL; METFESSEL, NEWTON S.; AND
MICHAEL, WILLIAM B. "Alternative Approaches to Assessing
the Intellectual Ability of Youth From a Culture of Poverty."
Ed & Psychol Meas 28:449–55 su '68. * (*PA* 42:19264)
8. ANDERSON, RONALD JUDE. *Divergent Thinking Within
Superior, Average, and Retarded Subjects.* Doctor's thesis,
University of Nebraska (Lincoln, Neb.), 1968. (*DA* 29:1126A)
9. BROWN, STEPHEN W.; GUILFORD, J. P.; AND HOEPFNER,
RALPH. "Six Semantic-Memory Abilities." *Ed & Psychol Meas*
28:691–717 au '68. * (*PA* 43:4427)
10. ANDERSON, HARRY E., JR.; WHITE, WILLIAM F.; AND
STEVENS, JOHN C. "Student Creativity, Intelligence, Achievement, and Teacher Classroom Behavior." *J Social Psychol*
78(1):99–107 Je '69. * (*PA* 43:16427)
11. GRAY, JAMES J. "The Effect of Productivity on Primary
Process and Creativity." *J Proj Tech & Pers Assess* 33(3):
213–8 Je '69. * (*PA* 43:14302)
12. KANDERIAN, SUAD SIROP. *Study of the Relationship
Between School Achievement and Measures of Intelligence and
Creativity for Students in Iraq.* Doctor's thesis, University of
Southern California (Los Angeles, Calif.), 1969. (*DAI* 31:644A)
13. RYBACK, RALPH S.; LEWIS, OLIVER F.; AND LESSARD,
CHARLES S. "Psychobiologic Effects of Prolonged Bed Rest
(Weightless) in Young Healthy Volunteers (Study II)." *Aerospace Med* 42(5):529–35 My '71. *
14. WILLIAMS, JOHN D.; HARLOW, STEVEN D.; AND BORGEN,
JEROME S. "Creativity, Dogmatism, and Arithmetic Achieve-
ment." *J Psychol* 78(2):217–22 Jl '71. * (*PA* 46:9760)

CUMULATIVE NAME INDEX

[592]

Wechsler Memory Scale. Adults; 1945–63; 1962–63 tests are slight revisions of tests copyrighted 1945 and 1948; David Wechsler and Calvin P. Stone (Form 2); Psychological Corporation. *

For additional information, see 6:561 (9 references); for reviews by Ivan Norman Mensh and Joseph Newman, see 4:364 (6 references); for a review by Kate Levine Kogan, see 3:302 (3 references).

REFERENCES THROUGH 1971

1–3. See 3:302.
4–9. See 4:364.
10–18. See 6:561.
19. BERAN, MARIANNE; PERKINS, JOHN C.; AND SCOLLON, ROBERT W. "Psychological Studies on Patients Undergoing Nonconvulsive Electric-Stimulation Treatment." *Am J Psychiatry* 109:367–74 N '52. * (*PA* 27:5168)
20. CALDWELL, BETTYE McDONALD, AND WATSON, ROBERT I. "An Evaluation of Psychologic Effects of Sex Hormone Administration in Aged Women: 1, Results of Therapy After Six Months." *J Gerontol* 7:228–44 Ap '52. * (*PA* 27:1874)
21. MENSH, IVAN N.; SCHWARTZ, HENRY G.; MATARAZZO, RUTH G.; AND MATARAZZO, JOSEPH D. "Psychological Functioning Following Cerebral Hemispherectomy in Man." *Arch Neurol & Psychiatry* 67:787–96 Je '52. * (*PA* 27:2167)
22. STRUCKETT, PAULINE B. A. "Effect of Prefrontal Lobotomy on Intellectual Functioning in Chronic Schizophrenia." *Arch Neurol & Psychiatry* 69:293–304 Mr '53. * (*PA* 28:1346)
23. CALDWELL, BETTYE McDONALD, AND WATSON, ROBERT I. "An Evaluation of Sex Hormone Replacement in Aged Women." *J Genetic Psychol* 85:181–200 D '54. * (*PA* 29:7046)
24. STANDLEE, LLOYD S. "Validity of Archimedes Spiral in Discriminating Memory Ability of Psychotics and of Normals." *Arch Neurol & Psychiatry* 71:648–50 My '54. * (*PA* 29:2839)
25. UECKER, ALBERT E.; FRENCH, LYLE A.; AND JOHNSON, DAVID R. "Psychological Studies of Seven Epileptic Heminaretics Before and After Hemispherectomy." *Arch Neurol & Psychiatry* 72:555–64 N '54. * (*PA* 29:6114)
26. MEYER, VICTOR, AND YATES, AUBREY J. "Intellectual Changes Following Temporal Lobectomy for Psychomotor Epilepsy: Preliminary Communication." *J Neurol Neurosurg & Psychiatry* (England) 18:44–52 F '55. * (*PA* 29:7775)
27. QUADFASEL, ANGELA FOLSOM, AND PRUYSER, PAUL W. "Cognitive Deficit in Patients With Psychomotor Epilepsy." *Epilepsia* (United States) 4:80–90 N '55. * (*PA* 30:8437)
28. SEYMOUR, JOHN H. *Some Changes in Psychometric, Perceptual and Motor Performance as a Function of Sleep Deprivation.* Doctor's thesis, New York University (New York, N.Y.), 1956. (*DA* 16:2216)
29. STONESIFER, FRED A. *Intellectual and Perceptual Performance of Defective Idiopathic Epileptics and Familial Mental Defectives.* Doctor's thesis, Pennsylvania State University (University Park, Pa.), 1956. (*DA* 17:400)
30. STENBACK, ASSER; VIITAMKI, R. OLAVI; AND KUKKONEN, SIMO. "Personality Changes in Electroconvulsive Treatment. A Study of the Effect of Three Successive Electroconvulsive Treatments With Special Reference to Spacing of Treatments." *Acta Psychiatrica et Neurologica Scandinavica* (Denmark) 32(3):345–59 '57. * (*PA* 33:1500)
31. DASTON, PAUL G. "Effects of Two Phenothiazine Drugs on Concentrative Attention Span of Chronic Schizophrenics." *J Clin Psychol* 15:106–9 Ja '59. * (*PA* 34:3050)
32. KRAL, V. A., AND WIGDOR, B. T. "Androgen Effect on Senescent Memory Function." *Geriatrics* 14:450–6 Jl '59. * (*PA* 34:5687)
33. SANTOS, BERTHA. *A Comparison of Memory and Learning Ability With Social Competence and Social Participation in Aged Senile Dements in a Mental Institution.* Doctor's thesis, New York University (New York, N.Y.), 1959. (*DA* 20:1441)
34. VICTOR, MAURICE; TALLAND, GEORGE A.; AND ADAMS, RAYMOND D. "Psychological Studies of Korsakoff's Psychosis: 1, General Intellectual Functions." *J Nerv & Mental Dis* 128:528–37 Je '59. * (*PA* 34:4702)
35. HUMPHRIES, CHARLES C. *Temporal Variability and Pre-Morbid Adjustment in Schizophrenia.* Doctor's thesis, University of Florida (Gainesville, Fla.), 1960. (*DA* 21:2003)

36. MIRSKY, ALLAN F.; PRIMAC, DANIEL W.; MARSAN, COSIMO AJMONE; ROSVOLD, H. ENGER; AND STEVENS, JANICE R. "A Comparison of the Psychological Test Performance of Patients With Focal and Nonfocal Epilepsy." *Exp Neurol* 2:75–89 F '60. *
37. NELSON, LOIS AUDREY. *A Study of Certain Cognitive Aspects of the Speech of Multiple Sclerotic Patients.* Doctor's thesis, University of Wisconsin (Madison, Wis.), 1960. (*DA* 21:1666)
38. ORCHINIK, C. W. "Some Psychological Aspects of Circumscribed Lesions of the Diencephalon." *Confinia Neurologica* (Switzerland) 20:292–310 '60. * (*PA* 35:2522)
39. WILLIAMS, MOYRA. "The Effect of Past Experience on Mental Test Performance in the Elderly." *Brit J Med Psychol* 33:215–9 pt 2 '60. * (*PA* 36:4FI15W)
40. BERKOWITZ, PEARL H. "Some Psychophysical Aspects of Mental Illness in Children." *Genetic Psychol Monogr* 63:103–48 F '61. * (*PA* 35:6452)
41. GUERRANT, JOHN; ANDERSON, WILLIAM W.; FISCHER, AMES; WEINSTEIN, MORTON R.; JAROS, R. MARY; AND DESKINS, ANDREW. Chap. 5, "Psychological Considerations," pp. 66–92. In their *Personality in Epilepsy.* Springfield, Ill.: Charles C Thomas, Publisher, 1962. Pp. xii, 112. *
42. PEARL, DAVID. "Phenothiazine Effects in Chronic Schizophrenia." *J Clin Psychol* 18:86–9 Ja '62. * (*PA* 38:7573)
43. ZUCKERMAN, MARVIN; ALBRIGHT, RICHARD J.; MARKS, CLIFFORD S.; AND MILLER, GERALD L. "Stress and Hallucinatory Effects of Perceptual Isolation and Confinement." *Psychol Monogr* 76(30):1–15 '62. * (*PA* 38:7226)
44. CAMERON, D. EWEN; SVED, S.; SOLYOM, L.; WAINRIB, B.; AND BARIK, H. "Effects of Ribonucleic Acid on Memory Defect in the Aged." *Am J Psychiatry* 120:320–5 O '63. * (*PA* 38:5511)
45. CARROLL, WAYNE R. "The Differentiation of Organic and Non-Organic Hospital Patients by Use of the Wechsler Memory Scale." *Newsl Res Psychol* 5:11 F '63. *
46. KRAL, V. A., AND WIGDOR, B. T. "Clinical and Psychological Observations in a Group of Well-Preserved Aged People." *Med Services J Can* 19:1–11 Ja '63. *
47. KRAL, V. A.; GRAD, B.; CRAMER-AZIMA, F.; AND RUSSELL, L. "Biologic, Psychologic, and Sociologic Studies in Normal Aged Persons and Patients With Senile Psychosis." *J Am Geriatrics Soc* 12:21–37 Ja '64. *
48. LEVITA, ERIC; RIKLAN, MANUEL; AND COOPER, IRVING S. "Cognitive and Perceptual Performance in Parkinsonism as a Function of Age and Neurological Impairment." *J Nerv & Mental Dis* 139:516–20 D '64. * (*PA* 39:10554)
49. SUEHS, JAMES ERNEST. *A Comparative Study of Brain-Damaged and Schizophrenic Subjects on Several Psychological Tests.* Doctor's thesis, University of Houston (Houston, Tex.), 1964. (*DA* 25:1347)
50. DIXON, JAMES C. "Cognitive Structure in Senile Conditions With Some Suggestions for Developing a Brief Screening Test of Mental Status." *J Gerontol* 20:41–9 Ja '65. *
51. GRAD, B.; KRAL, V. A.; AND CRAMER-AZIMA, F. "Correlations Between Salivary Sodium and Potassium Concentration and Memory Function in Elderly Persons, Normal and Psychotic." *Recent Adv Biol Psychiatry* 7:97–106 '65. *
52. KLONOFF, HARRY, AND KENNEDY, MARGARET. "Memory and Perceptual Functioning in Octogenarians and Nonagenarians in the Community." *J Gerontol* 20:328–33 Jl '65. *
53. MEER, BERNARD, AND BAKER, JANET A. "Reliability of Measurements of Intellectual Functioning of Geriatric Patients." *J Gerontol* 20:410–4 Jl '65. *
54. ZAMORA, EMIL L., AND KAELBLING, RUDOLF. "Memory and Electroconvulsive Therapy." *Am J Psychiatry* 122:546–54 N '65. * (*PA* 40:3046)
55. HOWARD, ALVIN R. "A Fifteen-Year Follow-Up With the Wechsler Memory Scale." *J Consult Psychol* 30:175–6 Ap '66. * (*PA* 40:6958)
56. HULICKA, IRENE M. "Age Differences in Wechsler Memory Scale Scores." *J Genetic Psychol* 109:135–45 S '66. * (*PA* 40:13204)
57. KLONOFF, HARRY, AND KENNEDY, MARGARET. "A Comparative Study of Cognitive Functioning in Old Age." *J Gerontol* 21:239–43 Ap '66. *
58. BAER, P.; MERRYMAN, P.; AND GAITZ, C. "Performance Deficit Related to Chronic Brain Syndrome, Schizophrenia and Age." *Gerontologist* 7(3, pt 2):37 S '67. * (*PA* 41:16721)
59. BOURESTOM, NORMAN C., AND HOWARD, MARY T. "Behavioral Correlates of Recovery of Self-Care in Hemiplegic Patients." *Arch Phys Med & Rehabil* 49:449–54 Ag '68. *
60. GILBERSTADT, HAROLD. "Relationships Among Scores of Tests Suitable for the Assessment of Adjustment and Intellectual Functioning." *J Gerontol* 23:483–7 O '68. *
61. GOLDSTEIN, NORMAN P.; EWERT, JOSEPHINE C.; RANDALL, RAYMOND V.; AND GROSS, JOHN B. "Psychiatric Aspects of Wilson's Disease (Hepatolenticular Degeneration): Results of Psychometric Tests During Long-Term Therapy." *Am J Psychiatry* 124:1555–61 My '68. * (*PA* 42:12656)
62. KAHN, EDWIN, AND FISHER, CHARLES. "Individual Differences and Amount of Rapid Eye Movement Sleep in Aged Adulthood." Abstract. *Psychophysiol* 4:393–4 Ja '68. * (*PA* 42:15311)

63. KAHN, EDWIN, AND FISHER, CHARLES. "The Relationship of REM Sleep to Various Measures in the Aged." Abstract. *Psychophysiol* 5:228–9 S '68. * (*PA* 43:14153)

64. KASTL, ALBERT J.; DAROFF, ROBERT B.; AND BLOCKER, W. WEBSTER. "Psychological Testing of Cerebral Malaria Patients." *J Nerv & Mental Dis* 147:553–61 D '68. * (*PA* 43:14654)

65. LEVY, RAYMOND. "The Clinical Evaluation of Unilateral Electroconvulsive Therapy." *Brit J Psychiatry* 114:459–63 Ap '68. * (*PA* 42:12248)

66. SCHAIE, K. W., AND STROTHER, C. R. "Limits of Optimal Functioning in Superior Old Adults." Discussion by Joseph H. Britton. *Interdiscipl Topics Gerontol* 1:132–53 '68. *

67. SCHAIE, K. WARNER, AND STROTHER, CHARLES R. "Cognitive and Personality Variables in College Graduates of Advanced Age," pp. 281–308. (*PA* 43:15628, title only) In *Human Aging and Behavior: Recent Advances in Research and Theory.* Edited by George A. Talland. New York: Academic Press Inc., 1968. Pp. xiii, 322. *

68. FOWLER, ROY S., JR. "A Simple Non-Language Test of New Learning." *Percept & Motor Skills* 29(3):895–901 D '69. * (*PA* 46:7301)

69. JACOBS, ELEANOR A.; WINTER, PETER M.; ALVIS, HARRY J.; AND SMALL, S. MOUCHLY. "Hyperoxygenation Effect on Cognitive Functioning in the Aged." Abstract. *Proc 77th Ann Conv Am Psychol Assn* 4(2):721–2 '69. * (*PA* 44:505)

70. JACOBS, ELEANOR A.; WINTER, PETER M.; ALVIS, HARRY J.; AND SMALL, S. MOUCHLY. "Hyperoxygenation Effect on Cognitive Functioning in the Aged." *New Engl J Med* 281(14):753–7 O 2 '69. * (*PA* 44:7205)

71. KAHN, EDWIN, AND FISHER, CHARLES. "Some Correlates of Rapid Eye Movement Sleep in the Normal Aged Male." *J Nerv & Mental Dis* 148(5):495–505 My '69. * (*PA* 44:507)

72. RAFFEL, SHERMAN C.; SWINK, RICHARD; AND LAMPTON, T. D. "The Influence of Chlorphenesin Carbamate and Carisoprodol on Psychological Test Scores." *Curr Ther Res* 11(9):553–60 S '69. *

73. VITALE, JOHN H.; STEINHELBER, JOHN C.; DRAKE, WILLIAM E., JR.; AND DAHLGREN, HELEN. "Psychological Dimensions of Cerebrovascular Insufficiency." *Percept & Motor Skills* 29(2):555–63 O '69. * (*PA* 44:3996)

74. BIDDER, T. G.; STRAIN, J. J.; AND BRUNSCHWIG, L. "Bilateral and Unilateral ECT: Follow-Up Study and Critique." *Am J Psychiatry* 127(6):737–45 D '70. * (*PA* 47:5329)

75. CRONON, D.; BODLEY, P.; POTTS, L.; MATHER, MARCIA D.; GARDNER, R. K.; AND TOBIN, JEAN C. "Unilateral and Bilateral ECT: A Study of Memory Disturbance and Relief From Depression." *J Neurol Neurosurg & Psychiatry* (England) 33(5):705–13 O '70. * (*PA* 47:9139)

76. DAVIS, LEO J., JR., AND SWENSON, WENDELL M. "Factor Analysis of the Wechsler Memory Scale." Abstract. *J Consult & Clin Psychol* 35(3):430 D '70. * (*PA* 45:6577)

77. FLEMINGER, J. J.; DE L. HORNE, D. J.; AND NOTT, P. N. "Unilateral Electroconvulsive Therapy and Cerebral Dominance: Effect of Right- and Left-Sided Electrode Placement on Verbal Memory." *J Neurol Neurosurg & Psychiatry* (England) 33(3):408–11 Je '70. * (*PA* 47:9140)

78. CRARY, HELEN L., AND RIDGWAY, ROBERT W. "Relationships Between Visual Form Perception Abilities and Reading Achievement in the Intermediate Grades." *J Exp Ed* 40(1):17–22 f '71. * (*PA* 47:9796)

79. DUJOVNE, BEATRIZ E., AND LEVY, BERNARD I. "The Psychometric Structure of the Wechsler Memory Scale." *J Clin Psychol* 27(3):351–4 Jl '71. * (*PA* 47:5081)

80. FALCONER, A. D. "Measurement of Cognitive Function in Two Groups of Alcoholics." *J Alcoholism* (England) 6(4):118–23 w '71. *

81. FIELDS, FRANCIS R. J. "Relative Effects of Brain Damage on the Wechser Memory and Intelligence Quotients." *Dis Nerv System* 32(10):673–5 O '71. * (*PA* 48:12023)

82. FIELDS, FRANCIS R. J. "Relative Effetcs of Brain Damage on the Wechsler Memory and Intelligence Quotients." *Newsl Res Psychol* 13(2):5–6 My '71. *

83. FLICK, GRAD L., AND EDWARDS, KENNETH R. "Prediction of Lateralized Organic Brain Dysfunction With a Neuropsychological Test Battery: A Discriminant Function Analysis." *Newsl Res Psychol* 13(2):16–7 My '71. *

84. IVINSKIS, ALGIS; ALLEN, STEPHEN; AND SHAW, ELVA. "An Extension of Wechsler Memory Scale Norms to Lower Age Groups." *J Clin Psychol* 27(3):354–7 Jl '71. * (*PA* 47:5087)

85. LIBB, J. WESLEY AND COLEMAN, JOHN M. "Correlation Between the WAIS and Revised Beta, Wechsler Memory Scale and Quick Test in a Vocational Rehabilitation Center." *Psychol Rep* 29(3):863–5 D '71. * (*PA* 47:9410)

86. MOLISH, H. BARRY; KRAFT, IRVIN A.; AND WIGGINS, P. Y. "Psychodiagnostic Evaluation of the Heart Transplant Patient." *Seminars Psychiatry* 3(1):46–57 F '71. * (*PA* 49:7557)

87. SMALL, IVER F., AND SMALL, JOYCE G. "Electroencephalographic (EEG), Evoked Potential, and Direct Current (DC) Responses With Unilateral Electroconvulsive Treatment (ECT)." *J Nerv & Mental Dis* 152(6):396–404 Je '71. * (*PA* 47:11054)

88. SOMASUNDARAM, C. P.; KALIAPPAN, K. V.; AND POLNAYA, MEERA. "A Psychometric Study of Patients Disabled by Cerebrovascular Disease (A Preliminary Study of 54 Cases)." *Neurol India* 19(1):34–7 Mr '71. *

CUMULATIVE NAME INDEX

Adams, R. D.: 34
Albrecht, R.: 2
Albright, R. J.: 43
Allen, S.: 84
Alvis, H. J.: 69–70
Anderson, W. W.: 41
Baer, P.: 58
Baker, J. A.: 53
Barik, H.: 44
Beran, M.: 19
Berkowitz, P. H.: 40
Bidder, T. G.: 74
Blocker, W. W.: 64
Bloom, B. L.: 16
Bodley, P.: 75
Bourestom, N. C.: 59
Britton, J. H.: 66
Brunschwig, L.: 74
Caldwell, B. M.: 20, 23
Cameron, D. E.: 44
Carroll, W. R.: 45
Cohen, J.: 7
Coleman, J. M.: 85
Cooper, I. S.: 48
Cramer-Azima, F.: 47, 51
Crary, H. L.: 78
Cronon, D.: 75
Dahlgren, H.: 73
Daroff, R. B.: 64
Daston, P. G.: 31
Davis, L. J.: 76
de L. Horne, D. J.: 77
Deskins, A.: 41
Dixon, J. C.: 50
Drake, W. E.: 73
Dujovne, B. E.: 79
Edwards, K. R.: 83
Ewert, J. C.: 61
Falconer, A. D.: 80
Fanelli, G. C.: 5
Fields, F. R. J.: 81–2
Fischer, A.: 41
Fisher, C.: 62–3, 71
Fleminger, J. J.: 77
Flick, G. L.: 83
Fowler, R. S.: 68
French, L. A.: 25
Gaitz, C.: 58
Gardner, R. K.: 75
Gilberstadt, H.: 60
Girdner, J.: 2
Goldstein, N. P.: 61
Grad, B.: 47, 51
Gross, J. B.: 61
Guerrant, J.: 41
Herman, K.: 17
Horst, P.: 14
Howard, A. R.: 8, 11, 55
Howard, M. T.: 59
Hulicka, I. M.: 56
Humphries, C. C.: 35
Ivinskis, A.: 84
Jacobs, E. A.: 69–70
Jaros, R. M.: 41
Johnson, D. R.: 25
Kaelbling, R.: 54
Kahn, E.: 62–3, 71
Kaliappan, K. V.: 88
Kastl, A. J.: 64
Kennedy, M.: 52, 57
Klonoff, H.: 52, 57
Kogan, K. L.: *rev*, 3:302
Kraft, I. A.: 86
Kral, V. A.: 32, 46–7, 51
Kukkonen, S.: 30
Lampton, T. D.: 72
Levita, E.: 48
Levy, B. I.: 79
Levy, R.: 65

Libb, J. W.: 85
Marks, C. S.: 43
Marsan, C. A.: 36
Matarazzo, J. D.: 21
Matarazzo, R. G.: 21
Mather, M. D.: 75
Meer, B.: 53
Mensh, I. N.: 21; *rev*, 4:364
Merryman, P.: 58
Meyer, V.: 26
Miller, G. L.: 43
Mirsky, A. F.: 36
Molish, H. B.: 86
Nelson, L. A.: 37
Newman, J.: *rev*, 4:364
Nott, P. N.: 77
Orchinik, C. W.: 38
Parker, J. W.: 12
Pearl, D.: 42
Perkins, J. C.: 19
Polnaya, M.: 88
Potts, L.: 75
Primac, D. W.: 36
Pruyser, P. W.: 27
Quadfasel, A. F.: 27
Raffel, S. C.: 72
Randall, R. V.: 61
Ridgway, R. W.: 78
Riklan, M.: 48
Rosvold, H. E.: 36
Russell, L.: 47
Santos, B.: 33
Schaie, W. K.: 14, 66–7
Schwartz, H. G.: 21
Scollon, R. W.: 19
Seymour, J. H.: 28
Shaw, E.: 84
Shaw, J. H.: 18
Shontz, F. C.: 13
Silva, J. J.: 6
Small, I. F.: 87
Small, J. G.: 87
Small, S. M.: 69–70
Solyon, L.: 44
Somasundaram, C. P.: 88
Standlee, L.: 24
Steinhelber, J. C.: 73
Stenbäck, A.: 30
Stevens, J. R.: 36
Stone, C. P.: 2–4
Stonesifer, F. A.: 29
Strain, J. J.: 74
Strother, C. R.: 14, 66–7
Struckett, P. B. A.: 22
Suehs, J. E.: 49
Sved, S.: 44
Swenson, W. M.: 76
Swink, R.: 72
Talland, G. A.: 34
Tobin, J. C.: 75
Uecker, A. E.: 25
Victor, M.: 17, 34
Viitamäki, R. O.: 30
Vitale, J. H.: 73
Wainrib, B.: 44
Walton, D.: 15
Watson, R. I.: 9, 20, 23
Wechsler, D.: 1
Weider, A.: 10
Weinstein, M. R.: 41
White, E. E.: 17
Wigdor, B. T.: 32, 46
Wiggins, P. Y.: 86
Williams, M.: 39
Winter, P. M.: 69–70
Yates, A. J.: 26
Zamora, E. L.: 54
Zuckerman, M.: 43

[593]

★**Willner Instance Similarities Test.** Adults; 1971; WIST; no manual; Allen E. Willner; Cognitive Test Center. *

REFERENCES THROUGH 1971

1. WILLNER, ALLEN E. "Crucial Flaw in Similarities Tests and a Remedy." Abstract. *Proc 76th Ann Conv Am Psychol Assn* 3:457–8 '68. * (*PA* 43:932, title only)

2. WILLNER, ALLEN E. "Abstraction, Associative Focusing, and Similarities Tests: Towards More Clinically Sensitive and Better Understood Tests." *Psychol Rep* 29(3):683–731 D '71. * (*PA* 47:8001)

CUMULATIVE NAME INDEX

Willner, A. E.: 1–2

[594]

Word Fluency. Industrial employees; 1959–61; Raymond J. Corsini and Measurement Research Division, Industrial Relations Center, University of Chicago; the Center. * [The publisher has not replied to our four requests to check the accuracy of this entry.]

For additional information and a review by James E. Kennedy, see 6:562.

REFERENCES THROUGH 1971

1. BLACKHURST, A. EDWARD; MARKS, CLAUDE H.; AND TISDALL, WILLIAM J. "Relationship Between Mobility and Divergent Thinking in Blind Children." *Ed Visually Handicapped* 1(2):33–6 My '69. * (*PA* 43:14813)

2. HEUSSENSTAMM, FRANCES K. "Creativity and Alienation: An Exploration of Their Relationship in Adolescence." *Calif J Ed Res* 21(3):140–6 My '70. *

CUMULATIVE NAME INDEX

Blackhurst, A. E.: 1   Marks, C. H.: 1
Heussenstamm, F. K.: 2   Tisdall, W. J.: 1
Kennedy, J. E.: *rev*, 6:562

[Out of Print Since TIP I]

Creative Ability Inventory, T :1138
Cube Construction Test, T :921
Fret Continuation Test, 7 :438
Fret Repetition Test, 7 :439
Mare and Foal Formboard, T :929
Meyer Finger Mazes, T :930
Nufferno Tests of Speed and Level, 6:555 (2 reviews, 7 references)
Stencil Design Tests I and II, 4:359 (2 reviews, 4 references)

MATHEMATICS

[595]

★**ACER Mathematics Tests: AM Series Topic Tests.** Grades 4–6; 1971–72, c1969–72; 6 tests; tests prepared under the direction of J. Izard; handbook prepared by D. Arney in collaboration with B. Rechter and M. L. Clark; Australian Council for Educational Research [Australia]. *

a) TEST AM1, NUMERATION, COUNTING AND NUMBER PATTERNS.
b) TEST AM2, PLACE VALUE.
c) TEST AM4, WHOLE NUMBERS. 4 parts: mathematical ideas, mathematical terms, applications, computation.
d) TEST AM5, MONEY.
e) TEST AM12, CAPACITY AND VOLUME.
f) TEST AM13, TIME.

[596]

ACT Mathematics Placement Examination. College entrants; 1968, c1965–68; MPE; 6 scores: algebra (intermediate, college, total), trigonometry, total, special topics; manuals by Linda R. Shevel and Douglas R. Whitney; American College Testing Program. *

For additional information and a review by William E. Kline, see 7:449 (1 reference).

REFERENCES THROUGH 1971

1. See 7:449.
2. REINER, JOHN R. "Differential Effects of Initial Course Placement as a Function of ACT Mathematics Scores and High-School Rank-in-Class in Predicting General Performance in Chemistry." *Ed & Psychol Meas* 31(4):977–81 w '71. * (*PA* 48:1870)

CUMULATIVE NAME INDEX

Kline, W. E.: *rev,* 7:449   Shevel, L. R.: 1
Reiner, J. R.: 2   Whitney, D. R.: 1

[597]

*****Advanced Mathematics (Including Trigonometry): Minnesota High School Achievement Examinations.** High school; 1951–70; a new, revised, or previously inactive form issued each May; title was *Advanced Algebra* through 1968; Achievement Examinations for Secondary Schools, High School Achievement Examinations, and Midwest High School Achievement Examinations have also been used as series titles; Form GJ Rev ('70) used in 1970 and 1973 testings; Form 4 ('54), entitled *Advanced Algebra: Achievement Examinations for Secondary Schools* (see 664), is available from another publisher; edited by V. L. Lohmann; American Guidance Service, Inc. *

For additional information concerning out of print and inactive forms, see 7:450 and 5:441; for reviews by Lynnette B. Plumlee and James P. Rizzo of Forms E (1962) and F (1963), see 6:593; for a review by Emma Spaney of Form A (1955), see 5:442.

[598]

★**Annual High School Mathematics Examination.** High school students competing for individual and school awards; 1950–73; AHSME; title on 1973 test booklet is *Twenty Fourth Annual Mathematics Examination;* test administered annually in March at participating secondary schools; special editions available for the visually handicapped; sponsored jointly by the Mathematical Association of America, Society of Actuaries, Mu Alpha Theta, National Council of Teachers of Mathematics, and Casualty Actuarial Society; M.A.A. Committee on High School Contests. *

REFERENCES THROUGH 1971

1. TURNER, NURA D. "Whither Mathematics Contest Winners?" *Sci Ed* 47:452–4 D '63. *
2. SALKIND, C. T. "Annual High School Mathematics Contest." *Math Teach* 57:75–8 F '64. *
3. TURNER, NURA D., AND DALY, SALOME S. "Attitudes of Upstate New York Section Students Toward the MAA-SA Contest." *Sci Ed* 49:491–3 D '65. *

CUMULATIVE NAME INDEX

Daly, S. S.: 3   Turner, N. D.: 1, 3
Salkind, C. T.: 2

[599]

*****Basic Mathematics Tests.** Ages 7-0 to 8-0, 8-0 to 9-0, 9-7 to 10-10, 10-0 to 12-6, 12-0 to 14-6; 1969–72; 5 levels; published for the National Foundation for Educational Research in England and Wales; Ginn & Co. Ltd. [England]. *

a) BASIC MATHEMATICS TEST A [ORAL]. Ages 7-0 to 8-0; 1971.
b) BASIC MATHEMATICS TEST B [ORAL]. Ages 8-0 to 9-0; 1971.
c) BASIC MATHEMATICS TEST C. Ages 9-7 to 10-10; 1970-72.
d) BASIC MATHEMATICS TEST DE. Ages 10-0 to 12-6; 1969-72.
e) BASIC MATHEMATICS TEST FG. Ages 12-0 to 14-6; 1969.
For additional information concerning *c–e*, see 7:452.

[600]

Bristol Achievement Tests: Mathematics. Ages 8-9, 9-10, 10-11, 11-12, 12-13; 1969; 6 scores: number, reasoning, space, measurement, arithmetic laws and processes, total; Alan Brimer; Thomas Nelson & Sons Ltd. [England]. * For the complete battery entry, see 5.
For additional information and a review by Kenneth Lovell, see 7:453. For a review of the complete battery, see 7:4.

[601]

*CLEP General Examinations: Mathematics. 1–2 years of college or equivalent; 1964-73; for college accreditation of nontraditional study, advanced placement, or assessment of educational attainment; a retired subtest of the *College-Level Examination Program General Examinations* published as a separate for local administration through the *Testing Academic Achievement* program (see 1061); 3 scores: basic skills, advanced topics, total; program administered for the College Entrance Examination Board by Educational Testing Service. * For the testing program entry, see 1050.
For additional information concerning earlier forms, see 7:8*b*. For reviews of the testing program, see 7:664 (3 reviews).

[602]

*CLEP Subject Examination in College Algebra and Trigonometry. 1 semester or equivalent; 1968-73; for college accreditation of nontraditional study, advanced placement, or assessment of educational achievement; tests administered monthly at centers throughout the United States; program administered for the College Entrance Examination Board by Educational Testing Service. * For the testing program entry, see 1050.
For additional information and a review by Carl G. Willis, see 7:454. For reviews of the testing program, see 7:664 (3 reviews).

[603]

*California Achievement Tests: Mathematics. 1933-72; earlier editions called *Progressive Arithmetic Tests;* 2 editions; Ernest W. Tiegs and Willis W. Clark; CTB/McGraw-Hill. * For the complete battery entry, see 7.
a) 1957 EDITION WITH 1963 NORMS. Grades 1-2, 2.5-4.5, 4-6, 7-9, 9-14; 1933-63; test booklet titles are *California Arithmetic Test* (grades 1-9) and *California Mathematics Test* (grades 9-14); 3 scores: reasoning, fundamentals, total; 1963 tests identical with tests copyrighted 1957 except for profile.
b) 1970 EDITION. Grades 1.5-2.5, 2.5-4.5, 4-6, 6-9, 9-12; 1933-72; 3 scores: computation, concepts and problems, total.
For additional information concerning the 1970 edition, see 7:455 (25 references); for a review by Robert D. North of the 1957 edition, see 5:468; for a review by Robert L. Burch of an earlier edition of the tests for

grades 1-9, see 4:411; for reviews by C. L. Thiele and Harry Grove Wheat, see 2:1459; for a review by William A. Brownell, see 1:893. For reviews of the complete battery, see 6:3 (2 reviews), 5:2 (1 review), 4:2 (3 reviews), 3:15 (1 review), 2:1193 (2 reviews), and 1:876 (1 review, 1 excerpt).

REFERENCES THROUGH 1971
1-25. See 7:455.
26. McBee, George, and Duke, Ralph L. "Relationship Between Intelligence, Scholastic Motivation, and Academic Achievement." *Psychol Rep* 6:3-8 F '60. * (*PA* 34:8404)
27. McGuire, Carson. "Sex Role and Community Variability in Test Performances." *J Ed Psychol* 52:61-73 Ap '61. * (*PA* 38:3207)
28. Tobias, Milton, and Michael, William B. "An Exploration Into Child Ecology: Physiological and Maturational Indices as Predictors of Measures of Achievement, Aptitude, and Adjustment." *Ed & Psychol Meas* 21:967-74 w '61. *
29. Black, Donald B., and Foster, Marion E. "A Comparative Study of the Performance in Arithmetic of Edmonton, Alberta, and Christchurch, New Zealand, Public School Pupils of Comparable Age and Grade Level." *Alberta J Ed Res* (Canada) 9:49-59 Mr '63. *
30. Parsley, Kenneth M., Jr.; Powell, Marvin; O'Connor, Henry A.; and Deutsch, Murray. "Are There Really Sex Differences in Achievement?" *J Ed Res* 57:210-2 D '63. *
31. Katz, Stanley S. "Selection and Evaluation of Students in Medical Technology Degree Programs." *Am J Med Technol* 30:51-63 Ja '64. *
32. Neville, Mary H., and Frost, Barry P. "Differential Achievement in Reading and Arithmetic." *Alberta J Ed Res* (Canada) 10:192-200 D '64. *
33. McRae, James A. *The Relationship of Mathematical Ability and Physical Coordination.* Master's thesis, North Carolina State University (Raleigh, N.C.), 1966.
34. Williamson, Malcom L., and Hopkins, Kenneth D. "The Use of 'None-of-These' Versus Homogeneous Alternatives on Multiple-Choice Tests: Experimental Reliability and Validity Comparisons." *J Ed Meas* 4:53-8 su '67. *
35. Greenberg, Bernard L., and Greenberg, Sally H. "The Measurement of College Potential in the Hearing Handicapped." *Am Ann Deaf* 116(3):372-81 Je '71. * (*PA* 47:1410)
36. Johnson, Theola Gae. *Influence of Selected Factors on the Ability of Fourth, Fifth, and Sixth Graders to Read Graphs.* Doctor's thesis, University of Southern California (Los Angeles, Calif.), 1971. (*DAI* 32:726A)
37. Michael, William B.; Haney, Russell; Lee, Young B.; and Michael, Joan J. "The Criterion-Related Validities of Cognitive and Noncognitive Predictors in a Training Program for Nursing Candidates." *Ed & Psychol Meas* 31(4):983-7 w '71. * (*PA* 48:1866)

CUMULATIVE NAME INDEX

[604]

*Canadian Achievement Test in Mathematics. Grade 10; 1961-68; CATM; a test in the *Canadian Test Battery, Grade 10;* Ontario Institute for Studies in Education; distributed by Guidance Centre [Canada]. * For the complete battery entry, see 1046.

For additional information and a review by Frances Crook Morrison, see 6 :565 (2 references).

REFERENCES THROUGH 1971
1–2. See 6:565.

CUMULATIVE NAME INDEX

D'Oyley, V. R.: 1–2   Morrison, F. C.: *rev,* 6:565

[605]

*Canadian Achievement Test in Technical and Commercial Mathematics.** Grade 10; 1961–68; CATTCM; a test in the *Canadian Test Battery, Grade 10;* Ontario Institute for Studies in Education; distributed by Guidance Centre [Canada]. * For the complete battery entry, see 1046.

For additional information and a review by Stanley Clark, see 6:566 (2 references).

REFERENCES THROUGH 1971
1–2. See 6:566.

CUMULATIVE NAME INDEX

Clark, S.: *rev,* 6:566   D'Oyley, V. R.: 1–2

[606]

*Canadian Mathematics Achievement Test.** Grades 8.5–9.0; 1959–68; CMAT; a test in the *Canadian Test Battery, Grades 8–9;* 3 parts; Ontario Institute for Studies in Education; distributed by Guidance Centre [Canada]. * For the complete battery entry, see 1047.
a) PART 1, ARITHMETIC COMPUTATION.
b) PART 2, FACTS, TERMS AND CONCEPTS.
c) PART 3, MEASUREMENT.

For additional information and reviews by Stanley Clark and Frances Crook Morrison, see 6:567 (2 references).

REFERENCES THROUGH 1971
1–2. See 6:567.

CUMULATIVE NAME INDEX

Clark, S.: *rev,* 6:567   Morrison, F. C.: *rev,* 6:567
D'Oyley, V. R.: 1–2

[607]

*College Board Achievement Test in Mathematics, Level 1.** Candidates for college entrance; 1901–73; test administered on specified dates at centers established by the publisher; inactive forms, entitled *College Placement Test in Mathematics, Level 1,* are available to colleges for local administration; program administered for the College Entrance Examination Board by Educational Testing Service. * For the testing program entry, see 1048.

For additional information, see 7 :456 (4 references). For reviews of the testing program, see 6 :760 (2 reviews).

REFERENCES THROUGH 1971
1–4. See 7:456.

CUMULATIVE NAME INDEX

Burgess, T. C.: 1   Nelson, B. E.: 2
Hutchcraft, G.: 3   Pugh, R. C.: 3
Ludlow, H. G.: 3   Stover, D. W.: 4

[608]

*College Board Achievement Test in Mathematics, Level 2.** Candidates for college entrance; 1901–73; test administered on specified dates at centers established by the publisher; inactive forms, entitled *College Placement Test in Mathematics, Level 2,* are available to colleges for local administration; program administered for the College Entrance Examination Board by Educational Testing Service. * For the testing program entry, see 1048.

For additional information, see 7 :457 (1 reference).

For reviews of the testing program, see 6 :760 (2 reviews).

REFERENCES THROUGH 1971
1. See 7:457.

CUMULATIVE NAME INDEX

Stover, D. W.: 1

[609]

*College Placement Test in Advanced Mathematics.** Entering college freshmen; 1962–72, c1957–72; reprintings of inactive 1957 and 1958 forms of *College Board Achievement Test in Advanced Mathematics;* test available to colleges for local administration; program administered for the College Entrance Examination Board by Educational Testing Service. * For the testing program entry, see 1051.

For additional information, see 7 :458. For a review of the testing program, see 7 :665. For reviews of the *College Board Achievement Test in Advanced Mathematics,* see 6 :568 (1 review) and 4 :367 (1 review).

[610]

*College Placement Test in Intermediate Mathematics.** Entering college freshmen; 1962–72, c1956–72; reprintings of inactive 1956 and 1957 forms of *College Board Achievement Test in Intermediate Mathematics;* test available to colleges for local administration; program administered for the College Entrance Examination Board by Educational Testing Service. * For the testing program entry, see 1051.

For additional information, see 7 :459. For a review of the testing program, see 7 :665. For reviews of the *College Board Achievement Test in Intermediate Mathematics,* see 6 :569 (1 review) and 4 :368 (1 review).

[611]

*College Placement Test in Mathematics, Level 1.** Entering college freshmen; 1964–72; reprintings of inactive 1965 forms of *College Board Achievement Test in Mathematics, Level 1;* test available to colleges for local administration; program administered for the College Entrance Examination Board by Educational Testing Service. * For the testing program entry, see 1051.

For additional information, see 7 :460. For a review of the testing program, see 7 :665.

[612]

*College Placement Test in Mathematics, Level 2.** Entering college freshmen; 1965–72; reprinting of inactive 1965 form of *College Board Achievement Test in Mathematics, Level 2;* test available to colleges for local administration; program administered for the College Entrance Examination Board by Educational Testing Service. * For the testing program entry, see 1051.

For additional information, see 7 :461. For a review of the testing program, see 7 :665.

[613]

Cooperative Mathematics Tests: Structure of the Number System. Grades 7–8; 1963–65; Cooperative Tests and Services. *

For additional information and reviews by M. Vere DeVault and Leslie P. Steffe, see 7 :466. For excerpted reviews by John R. Hills and Jack C. Merwin of the series, see 7 :465.

REFERENCES THROUGH 1971
1. TAGG, HOWARD R. *Correlation Between Intelligence Test Scores and Modern Mathematics Test Scores of Fifty Seventh-*

Grade Hillcrest Junior High School Students. Master's thesis, Brigham Young University (Provo, Utah), 1966.

CUMULATIVE NAME INDEX

DeVault, M. V.: *rev*, 7:466   Steffe, L. P.: *rev*, 7:466
Hills, J. R.: *exc*, 7:465   Tagg, H. R.: 1
Merwin, J. C.: *exc*, 7:465

[614]

Cooperative Primary Tests: Mathematics. Grades 1.5–2.5, 2.5–3; 1965–67; Cooperative Tests and Services. * For the complete battery entry, see 12.

For reviews of the complete battery, see 7:10 (2 excerpts).

[615]

★Diagnostic Test in Mathematics—Level 1. Grades 8–9; 1970; DTM; 8 scores: operations with whole numbers, operations with positive fractions, problems with fractions and percents, properties of numbers, set notation, operations with integers, number sentences, geometry; Ontario Institute for Studies in Education (test) and Frances Crook Morrison (manual); distributed by Guidance Centre [Canada]. *

[616]

*ERB Modern Mathematics Test. Grades 7–8; 1965–71; 1971 test identical with test copyrighted 1965 except for directions; no manual; Educational Records Bureau. *

For additional information, see 7:468 (1 reference).

REFERENCES THROUGH 1971

1. See 7:468.

CUMULATIVE NAME INDEX

Litterick, W. S.: 1

[617]

General Mathematics III: Achievement Examinations for Secondary Schools. Grade 9; 1951–54; Form 4 of a series of tests, currently (1973) entitled *Mathematics Grade 9: Minnesota High School Achievement Examinations* (see 631c), issued annually for May testing; Wallace M. Bernards; Bobbs-Merrill Co., Inc. *

For additional information concerning later and earlier forms, see 631, 7:473, 6:577, and 5:424–5.

[618]

*Graded Arithmetic-Mathematics Test: Decimal Currency Edition. Ages 7–21; 1949–71; 1970 test identical with test published 1949 except for 8 items; P. E. Vernon; University of London Press Ltd. [England]. *

For additional information and a review by Stanley Nisbet of the original edition, see 5:476.

REFERENCES THROUGH 1971

1. McKenzie, Helen M. *The Standardisation of an Arithmetic-Mathematics Test in a Midland Area.* Bachelor's thesis, Glasgow University (Glasgow, Scotland), 1951. (Abstract: *Brit J Ed Psychol* 22:73)
2. Venables, Ethel C. "Placement Problems Among Engineering Apprentices in Part-Time Technical College Courses: Part II, Level of Ability Needed for Success in National Certificate Courses." *Brit J Ed Psychol* 31:56–8 F '61. * (*PA* 36:1KJ56V)
3. Montgomery, G. W. G. "Predicting Success in Engineering." *Occup Psychol* (England) 36:59–68 Ja–Ap '62. *
4. Ross, Jean. "Predicting Practical Skill in Engineering Apprentices." *Occup Psychol* (England) 36:69–74 Ja–Ap '62. *
5. Chappel, Susan. "Pre-Selection of Apprentice Motor Mechanics—A Preliminary Validation Study." *Personnel Prac B* (Australia) 23:204–13 S '67. *
6. Gooch, Stan; Levy, Philip; and Pringle, M. L. Kellmer. "The Interaction of Four Status Variables and Measured Intelligence and Their Effect on Attainment in Two Junior Schools." *Ed Sci* (England) 2:37–46 O '67. *
7. Smith, I. Macfarlane. "The Use of Diagnostic Tests for Assessing the Abilities of Overseas Students Attending Institu-

tions of Further Education, Part I." *Voc Aspect Ed* (England) 22(51):1–8 Mr '70. *
8. Smith, I. Macfarlane. "The Use of Diagnostic Tests for Assessing the Abilities of Overseas Students Attending Institutions of Further Education, Part II." *Voc Aspect Ed* (England) 23(54):39–48 Ap '71. *

CUMULATIVE NAME INDEX

Chappel, S.: 5   Nisbet, S.: *rev*, 5:476
Gooch, S.: 6   Pringle, M. L. K.: 6
Levy, P.: 6   Ross, J.: 4
McKenzie, H. M.: 1   Smith, I. M.: 7–8
Montgomery, G. W. G.: 3 Venables, E. C.: 2

[619]

*The Graduate Record Examinations Advanced Mathematics Test. Graduate school candidates; 1939–73; Educational Testing Service. * For the testing program entry, see 1053.

For additional information concerning earlier forms, see 7:469; for a review by Paul C. Rosenbloom, see 6:578; for a review by Eric F. Gardner, see 5:427 (1 reference). For reviews of the testing program, see 7:667 (1 review) and 5:601 (1 review).

REFERENCES THROUGH 1971

1. See 5:427.

CUMULATIVE NAME INDEX

Angoff, W. H.: 1   Rosenbloom, P. C.: *rev*, 6:578
Gardner, E. F.: *rev*, 5:427 Schultz, M. K.: 1

[620]

★Group Mathematics Test. Ages 6.5–8.5; 1970; GMT; 3 scores: oral, computation, total; D. Young; University of London Press Ltd. [England]. *

[621]

Iowa Placement Examinations: Mathematics Aptitude. Grades 12–13; 1925–44; 2 editions; test by G. D. Stoddard, E. W. Chittenden, L. W. Miller (*b*), and D. B. Stuit (*b*); Bureau of Educational Research and Service. *

a) SERIES MA-1, REVISED. 1925–26.
b) NEW SERIES MA-2, REVISED. 1925–44.

For additional information and reviews by Edmund P. Churchill and Paul L. Dressel, see 3:308 (18 references).

REFERENCES THROUGH 1971

1–18. See 3:308.
19. Hammond, H. P., and Stoddard, George Dinsmore. "A Study of Placement Examinations." *Univ Iowa Studies Ed* 4(7):1–59 '28. * (*PA* 3:2069)
20. Stalnaker, John M. *A Statistical Study of Some Aspects of the Purdue Orientation Testing Program.* Bulletin of Purdue University, Vol. 28, No. 6; Studies in Higher Education VIII. Lafayette, Ind.: Division of Educational Reference, the University, February 1928. Pp. 68. * (*PA* 5:831)
21. Feder, Daniel D. "The Effect of Directions and Arrangement of Items on Student Performance in a Test." *J Ed Res* 30:28–35 S '36. * (*PA* 10:5979)
22. Herrmann, William Charles. *A Follow-Up Study and Evaluation of a Pre-college Program of Educational Guidance at an Engineering College.* Master's thesis, Clark University (Worcester, Mass.), 1940.
23. Jones, Vernon. "An Annual Ten-Day Guidance Program—Methods and Results." *J Ed Psychol* 34:129–41 Mr '43. * (*PA* 17:4271)
24. Barnette, Warren Leslie, Jr. *Occupational Aptitude Patterns of Counseled Veterans.* Doctor's thesis, New York University (New York, N.Y.), 1949.
25. Edmonson, Lawrence Davis. *Comparative Analyses of a Test Battery Used for the Prediction of Scholastic Success at the University of Missouri.* Doctor's thesis, University of Missouri (Columbia, Mo.), 1949.
26. Jenson, Ralph E. *Predicting Scholastic Achievement of First-Year Graduate Students.* Doctor's thesis, University of Pittsburgh (Pittsburgh, Pa.), 1949.
27. Krathwohl, William C. "Effects of Industrious and Indolent Work Habits on Grade Prediction in College Mathematics." *J Ed Res* 43:32–40 S '49. * (*PA* 24:2063)
28. Krathwohl, William C. "The Persistence in College of Industrious and Indolent Work Habits." *J Ed Res* 42:365–70 Ja '49. * (*PA* 23:3900)

29. RINSLAND, HENRY D. "The Prediction of Veterans' Success From Test Scores at the University of Oklahoma," Part 1, pp. 59–72. In *The Sixth Yearbook of the National Council on Measurements Used in Education, 1948–1949.* Fairmont, W.Va.: the Council, Fairmont State College, 1949. Pp. v, 140. *
30. UHRBROCK, RICHARD STEPHEN. "Construction of a Selection Test for College Graduates." *J General Psychol* 41:153–93 O '49. * (*PA* 24:4874)
31. BARNETTE, W. LESLIE, JR. "Occupational Aptitude Pattern Research." *Occupations* 29:5–12 O '50. * (*PA* 25:3239)
32. BARNETTE, W. LESLIE, JR. "Occupational Aptitude Patterns of Selected Groups of Counseled Veterans." *Psychol Monogr* 65(5):1–49 '51. * (*PA* 26:2794)
33. JENSON, RALPH E. "Predicting Scholastic Achievement of First-Year Graduate Students." *Ed & Psychol Meas* 13:322–9 su '53. * (*PA* 28:4833)
34. KRATHWOHL, WILLIAM C. "Relative Contributions of Aptitude and Work Habits to Achievement in College Mathematics." *J Ed Psychol* 44:140–8 Mr '53. * (*PA* 28:3210)
35. CHATTERJI, S. "Standardisation of Iowa Math Aptitude Test Under Indian Conditions." *Indian J Psychol* 32:217–22 pts 3–4 '57. * (*PA* 33:2507)

CUMULATIVE NAME INDEX

Adams, M.: 13	Jones, V.: 23
Adams, W. M.: 16	Krathwohl, W. C.: 18, 27–8,
Barnette, W. L.: 24, 31–2	34
Chatterji, S.: 35	Langlie, T. A.: 2–3, 5
Churchill, E. P.: *rev*, 3:308	Lapp, C. J.: 12
Crane, J. M.: 14	McGehee, W.: 15
Crose, J. M.: 11	Miller, L. W.: 7
Donnelly, M. C.: 10	Moffie, D. J.: 15
Dressel, P. L.: *rev*, 3:308	Nutting, M. L.: 8
Edmonson, L. D.: 25	Pankaskie, M.: 17
Feder, D. D.: 21	Rinsland, H. D.: 29
Gerberich, J. R.: 6	Stalnaker, J. M.: 20
Hammond, H. P.: 19	Stoddard, G. D.: 1, 4, 19
Herrmann, W. C.: 22	Stuit, D. B.: 9–10, 12
Jenson, R. E.: 26, 33	Uhrbrock, R. S.: 30

[622]

Iowa Placement Examinations: Mathematics Training: Series MT1, Revised. Grades 12–13; 1925–26; test by G. D. Stoddard and E. W. Chittenden; Bureau of Educational Research and Service. *
For additional information and reviews by Edmund P. Churchill and Paul L. Dressel, see 3:309 (8 references).

REFERENCES THROUGH 1971

1–8. See 3:309.
9. HAMMOND, H. P., AND STODDARD, GEORGE DINSMORE. "A Study of Placement Examinations." *Univ Iowa Studies Ed* 4(7):1–59 '28. * (*PA* 3:2069)
10. PERRY, ROBERT D. *Prediction Equations for Success in College Mathematics.* Contribution to Education No. 122. Nashville, Tenn.: George Peabody College for Teachers, 1934. Pp. xiii, 58. * (*PA* 8:3277)
11. REMMERS, H. H., AND GEIGER, H. E. "Predicting Success and Failure of Engineering Students in the Schools of Engineering in Purdue University," pp. 10–9. In *Studies in Engineering Education.* Purdue University, Division of Educational Reference, Studies in Higher Education, [No.] 38. Lafayette, Ind.: the Division, May 1940. Pp. 33. *
12. UHRBROCK, RICHARD STEPHEN. "Construction of a Selection Test for College Graduates." *J General Psychol* 41:153–93 O '49. * (*PA* 24:4874)
13. WEAVER, HERBERT B. "The Mathematical Proficiency of Students of Psychology." *J Ed Res* 51:261–70 D '57. *
14. WHIPKEY, KENNETH LEE. *A Study of the Interrelationship Between Mathematical Attitude and Mathematical Achievement.* Doctor's thesis, Case Western Reserve University (Cleveland, Ohio), 1969. (*DAI* 30:3808A)

CUMULATIVE NAME INDEX

Churchill, E. P.: *rev*, 3:309	Perry, R. D.: 10
Dressel, P. L.: *rev*, 3:309	Remmers, H. H.: 11
Geiger, H. E.: 11	Stoddard, G. D.: 1, 4, 9
Hammond, H. P.: 9	Uhrbrock, R. S.: 12
Johnson, A. P.: 7–8	Weaver, H. B.: 13
Langlie, T. A.: 2–3, 5	Whipkey, K. L.: 14
Miller, L. W.: 6	

[623]

*The Iowa Tests of Educational Development: Test 4, Ability to Do Quantitative Thinking. Grades 9–12; 1942–67; Forms X-4 and Y-4; more recent Forms X5 and Y5 are not available as separates; prepared under the direction of E. F. Lindquist and Leonard S. Feldt; Science Research Associates, Inc. * For the complete battery entry, see 20.

For additional information and a review by Peter A. Lappan, Jr. of earlier forms, see 6:579. For reviews of the complete battery, see 6:14 (2 reviews), 5:17 (2 reviews), 4:17 (1 review), and 3:12 (3 reviews).

REFERENCES THROUGH 1971

1. ANTTONEN, RALPH G. "A Longitudinal Study in Mathematics Attitude." *J Ed Res* 62(10):467–71 Jl–Ag '69. *

CUMULATIVE NAME INDEX

Anttonen, R. G.: 1　　　　Lappan, P. A.: *rev*, 6:579

[624]

Junior High School Mathematics Test: Acorn Achievement Tests. Grades 7–9; 1942–52; 4 scores: concepts, problem analysis, problems, total; 1952 test identical with test copyrighted 1942 except for minor changes; Harry Eisner; Psychometric Affiliates. *
For additional information and a review by Myron F. Rosskopf, see 5:429; for a review by William Betz, see 3:310.

[625]

★Leicester Number Test. Ages 7-1 to 8-1; 1970; LNT; Charles Gillham and K. A. Hesse; University of London Press Ltd. [England]. *

[626]

★Mathematics Attainment Test EF. Ages 11-0 to 13-0; 1972; published for the National Foundation for Educational Research in England and Wales; Ginn & Co. Ltd. [England]. *

[627]

Mathematics Attainment Tests C1 and C3. Ages 9-3 to 10-8; 1965–69; 2 tests; published for the National Foundation for Educational Research in England and Wales; Ginn & Co. Ltd. [England]. *
a) MATHEMATICS ATTAINMENT TEST C1. 1965–69; formerly called *Junior Mathematics Test C1.*
b) MATHEMATICS ATTAINMENT TEST C3. 1966–69; formerly called *Junior Mathematics Test C3.*
For additional information and a review by John Cook, see 7:470.

[628]

Mathematics Attainment Tests DE1 and DE2. Ages 10-0 to 12-0; 1966–70; 2 tests; published for the National Foundation for Educational Research in England and Wales; Ginn & Co. Ltd. [England]. *
a) MATHEMATICS ATTAINMENT TEST DE1. 1966–70; modification of *Mathematics Test 17;* 1970 test essentially the same as test published 1966 except for 12 items revised for metrication and decimalization.
b) MATHEMATICS ATTAINMENT TEST DE2. 1967–70; formerly called *Intermediate Mathematics Test 1;* 1970 test identical with test published 1969 except for title.
For additional information, see 7:471.

[629]

*Mathematics Attainment Tests (Oral). Ages 7-0 to 8-6, 8-6 to 9-8; 1965–72; 2 levels; published for the National Foundation for Educational Research in England and Wales; Ginn & Co. Ltd. [England]. *
a) MATHEMATICS ATTAINMENT TEST A (ORAL). Ages 7-0 to 8-6; 1969–72; formerly called *Junior Mathematics Test A1.*
b) MATHEMATICS ATTAINMENT TEST B (ORAL). Ages 8-6 to 9-8; 1965–69; formerly called *Junior Mathematics Test B1.*
For additional information and a review by John Cook, see 7:472.

[630]

★**Mathematics Inventory Tests.** Grades 4–12; 1970; MIT; 3 tests; American Testing Co. *
a) MATHEMATICS INVENTORY TEST 1: GENERAL MATHE-MATICS.
b) MATHEMATICS INVENTORY TEST 2: CONTEMPORARY MATHEMATICS.
c) MATHEMATICS INVENTORY TEST 3: PROBLEM SOLVING.

[631]

*Mathematics: Minnesota High School Achievement Examinations.** Grades 7, 8, 9; 1951–70; a new, revised, or previously inactive form issued each May; Achievement Examinations for Secondary Schools, High School Achievement Examinations, and Midwest High School Achievement Examinations have also been used as series titles; Form GJ Rev ('70) used in 1970 and 1973 testings; 3 levels; edited by V. L. Lohmann; American Guidance Service, Inc. *
a) MATHEMATICS GRADE 7. 1962–70; Form E ('62) called *Arithmetic: Midwest High School Achievement Examinations.*
b) MATHEMATICS GRADE 8. 1962–70; Form E ('62) called *Arithmetic: Midwest High School Achievement Examinations.*
c) MATHEMATICS GRADE 9. 1951–70; Form 4 ('54), entitled *General Mathematics III: Achievement Examinations for Secondary Schools* (see 617), is available from another publisher.
For additional information concerning out of print and inactive forms, see 7:473, 6:582, and 5:424–5; for a review by Gerald L. Ericksen of Form F ('63) of the test for grade 9, see 6:577.

[632]

*Mathematics Test (Adv.) 6.** Ages 12–13; 1954–72; earlier tests, *Arithmetic Test (Adv.) 1* and *Mathematics Tests (Adv.) 2–5,* are out of print; distribution restricted to directors of education; published for the National Foundation for Educational Research in England and Wales; Ginn & Co. Ltd. [England]. *
For additional information concerning earlier tests, see 7:474; for a review by Kenneth Lovell, see 6:585.

[633]

Mathematics Test: Content Evaluation Series. Grades 7–9; 1969; Gilbert Ulmer; Houghton Mifflin Co. *
For additional information and a review by Robert A. Forsyth, see 7:475.

[634]

A Mathematics Test for Grades Four, Five and Six. Grades 4–6; 1969; 13 scores: numeration systems, set terminology, mathematical structure, addition and subtraction, multiplication, division, common fractions, decimal fractions and per cent, measurements, geometry, problems, graphs and scales, total; Stanley J. LeJeune; Psychometric Affiliates. *
For additional information and a review by Arthur Mittman, see 7:476.

[635]

Mathematics Test: McGraw-Hill Basic Skills System. Grades 11–14; 1970; also called *MHBSS Mathematics Test;* although designed for use with the MHBSS instructional program, the test may be used independently; 4 scores: arithmetic, elementary algebra, intermediate algebra, total; McGraw-Hill Book Co., Inc. *
For additional information and reviews by James Braswell and Carl J. Huberty, see 7:477.

[636]

*Mathematics Tests 20–22.** Ages 10-0 to 12-0; 1951–71; 3 tests; new test published annually; earlier tests, *Arithmetic Tests 1–2* and *4–16* and *Mathematics Tests 17–19,* are out of print; distribution restricted to directors of education; published for the National Foundation for Educational Research in England and Wales; Ginn & Co. Ltd. [England]. *
a) MATHEMATICS TEST 20. 1969–70.
b) MATHEMATICS TEST 21. 1970–71.
c) MATHEMATICS TEST 22. 1971.
For additional information, see 7:478; see also 6:614 (1 reference).

REFERENCES THROUGH 1971
1. See 6:614.

CUMULATIVE NAME INDEX
Butcher, H. J.: 1   Moreton, C. A.: 1

[637]

*Metropolitan Achievement Tests: Mathematics Tests.** 1932–71; 2 editions; Walter N. Durost, Harold H. Bixler, J. Wayne Wrightstone, Gertrude H. Hildreth (a), Kenneth W. Lund (a), George A. Prescott (b), and Irving H. Balow (b); Harcourt Brace Jovanovich, Inc. * For the complete battery entry, see 22.
a) 1958 EDITION. Grades 3–4, 5–6, 7–9; 1932–62; catalog uses the title 1958 *Metropolitan Arithmetic Tests;* 2 scores: computation, problem solving and concepts.
b) 1970 EDITION. Grades 3.5–4.9, 5.0–6.9, 7.0–9.5; 1932–71; catalog uses the title 1970 *Metropolitan Mathematics Tests;* 4 scores: computation, concepts, problem solving, total.
For additional information concerning the 1970 edition, see 7:480 (4 references); for reviews by O. F. Anderhalter and E. W. Hamilton of the 1958 edition, see 6:627 (1 reference); for a review by Robert L. Burch of an earlier edition, see 4:416; for reviews by Peter L. Spencer and Harry Grove Wheat, see 2:1458.1; for reviews by Foster E. Grossnickle and Guy M. Wilson, see 1:892. For reviews of the complete battery, see 6:15 (2 reviews), 4:18 (1 review), 2:1189 (2 reviews), and 1:874 (3 reviews).

REFERENCES THROUGH 1971
1. See 6:627.
2–5. See 7:480.
6. LANE, BETTY RUBINO. *A Study of the Predictive Values of the Tests Being Used to Determine Success in Algebra I in the Lockport Township High Schools.* Master's thesis, Northern Illinois University (DeKalb, Ill.), 1966.
7. FLEISCHMAN, HOWARD L.; ORR, DAVID B.; AND STRASEL, H. C. "Relationships Between the Subtests of Six Achievement Test Batteries." Abstract. *Proc 79th Ann Conv Am Psychol Assn* 6(1):109–10 '71. * (*PA* 46:3727)
8. GRIDLEY, JOHN DAVID, JR. *An Empirical Investigation of the Construct of Mathematics Achievement in the Elementary Grades Based on the Method of Homogeneous Keying.* Doctor's thesis, Fordham University (New York, N.Y.), 1971. (*DAI* 32:1914A)
9. NORLAND, CHARLES R. *Mathematics Achievement: Changes in Achievement Scores for Grades Six and Eight After Instruction in Modern Mathematics Programs for Four Years or More, 1969.* Doctor's thesis, Northern Illinois University (DeKalb, Ill.), 1971. (*DAI* 32:2363A)

CUMULATIVE NAME INDEX
Anderhalter, O. F.: *rev*, 6:627   Lane, B. R.: 6
Brennan, J. T.: 2   Norland, C. R.: 9
Burch, R. L.: *rev*, 4:416   Orr, D. B.: 7
Fleischman, H. L.: 7   Spencer, P. L.: *rev*, 2:1458.1
Gallian, R. D.: 3   Stilgebauer, L. K.: 4
Gridley, J. D.: 8   Strasel, H. C.: 7
Grossnickle, F. E.: *rev*, 1:892   Walker, C. E.: 5
Hamilton, E. W.: *rev*, 6:627   Wheat, H. G.: *rev*, 2:1458.1
Jacobs, J. N.: 1   Wilson, G. M.: *rev*, 1:892

[638]

*Minimum Essentials for Modern Mathematics.** Grades 6–8; 1963–71; Ernest Hayes; Hayes Educational Test Laboratory. *

For additional information and a review by Gerald L. Ericksen, see 6:587.

[639]

Modern Mathematics Supplement to the Iowa Tests of Basic Skills. Grades 3–9; 1968; E. F. Lindquist, A. N. Hieronymus, and H. D. Hoover; Houghton Mifflin Co. *

For additional information and reviews by E. G. Begle and Thomas C. O'Brien, see 7:481.

[640]

Moray House Mathematics Tests. Ages 8.5–10.5, 10–12; 1964–70; 2 levels; distribution restricted to education authorities; Godfrey Thomson Unit, University of Edinburgh; University of London Press Ltd. [England]. *
a) MORAY HOUSE JUNIOR MATHEMATICS TEST. Ages 8.5–10.5; 1964–70.
b) MORAY HOUSE MATHEMATICS TEST. Ages 10–12; 1964–69.

For additional information, see 7:482.

[641]

★**The Moreton Mathematics Tests—Level 2.** Grades 3–5; 1970; MMT; 2 tests; R. J. Andrews, R. G. Cochrane, and J. Elkins; Teaching and Testing Resources [Australia]. *
a) FORM N [NUMERICAL OPERATIONS].
b) FORM P [MATHEMATICAL APPLICATIONS].

REFERENCES THROUGH 1971
1. ELKINS, J. "Some Recent Queensland Norms for Widely Used Standardized Tests." *Slow Learning Child* (Australia) 18(3):142–7 N '71. *

CUMULATIVE NAME INDEX
Elkins, J.: 1

[642]

N.B. Mathematics Tests. Standards 7–8 (ages 14–15); 1967; NBMT; 7 tests; Human Sciences Research Council [South Africa]. *
a) ALGEBRA.
b) ALGEBRA: FUNDAMENTAL CONCEPTS.
c) ALGEBRA: BASIC COMPUTATIONS.
d) ALGEBRA: EQUATIONS.
e) ALGEBRA: PROBLEMS.
f) ALGEBRA: FACTORS.
g) GEOMETRY AND GRAPHS.

For additional information, see 7:483.

[643]

*National Teacher Examinations: Mathematics.** College seniors and teachers; 1940–73; an inactive form (1966) entitled *Teacher Education Examination Program: Mathematics* is available to colleges for local administration; another inactive form (1968) entitled *Specialty Examinations: Mathematics* is available to school systems for local use as part of the program entitled *School Personnel Research and Evaluation Services;* Educational Testing Service. * For the testing program entry, see 869.

For additional information concerning earlier forms, see 7:484; for a review by Paul Blommers, see 6:583. For reviews of the testing program, see 7:582 (2 reviews), 6:700 (1 review), 5:538 (3 reviews), and 4:802 (1 review).

[644]

*Numerical Ability: Differential Aptitude Tests.** Grades 8–12 and adults; 1947–73; 2 editions; George K. Bennett, Harold G. Seashore, and Alexander G.

Wesman; Psychological Corporation. * For the complete battery entry, see 1069.
a) FORM A. 1947–59. *Out of print.*
b) FORM T. 1947–73; revision of Form M ('61).

For reviews of the complete battery, see 7:673 (1 review, 1 excerpt), 6:767 (2 reviews), 5:605 (2 reviews), 4:711 (3 reviews), and 3:620 (1 excerpt).

REFERENCES THROUGH 1971
1. PIPPERT, RALPH REINHARD. *The Prediction of the Correctness of Post-High School Written Language Performance.* Doctor's thesis, University of Wisconsin (Madison, Wis.), 1959. (*DA* 20:2104)
2. JENKINS, THOMAS VINNEDGE. *A Study of the Relationship Between Music Aptitudes and Mental Ability, Science Aptitudes, and Mathematics Aptitudes Among Secondary School Pupils in Texas.* Doctor's thesis, University of Texas (Austin, Tex.), 1960. (*DA* 21:2592)
3. AIJAZ, SAIYID MOHAMMAD. *Predictive Validity of the Three Versions of the "Verbal Reasoning" and the "Numerical Ability" Subtests of the Differential Aptitude Tests for East Pakistan.* Doctor's research study No. 1, Colorado State College (Greeley, Colo.), 1963. (*DA* 24:1068)
4. CHASE, CLINTON I.; LUDLOW, H. GLENN; AND PUGH, RICHARD C. *Predicting Success for Master's Degree Students in Education.* Indiana Studies in Prediction No. 5. Bloomington, Ind.: Bureau of Educational Studies and Testing, Indiana University, 1964. Pp. v, 25. *
5. CHASE, CLINTON I.; LUDLOW, H. GLENN; PUGH, RICHARD C.; AND POMEROY, MARTHA C. *Predicting Success for Advanced Graduate Students in Education.* Indiana Studies in Prediction No. 4. Lafayette, Ind.: Bureau of Educational Studies and Testing, Indiana University, 1964. Pp. v, 18. *
6. DAYAL, P. "Study of the Relationship Between a Verbal Intelligence Test (B.P.T. 15) and Verbal Reasoning Plus Numerical Ability Test Scores of the D.A.T." *J Voc & Ed Guid* (India) 10:83–9 Ag '64. * (*PA* 39:5114)
7. BAROYA, GEORGE MANORANJAN. *Reliability, Validity, and Comparability of Forms L and M of the "Verbal Reasoning" and the "Numerical Ability" Subtests of the Differential Aptitude Tests for Use in East Pakistan.* Doctor's research study No. 1, Colorado State College (Greeley, Colo.), 1966. (*DA* 27:2865A)
8. CAIN, RALPH W. "Relationships of Verbal Reasoning and Numerical Ability to Achievement in First-Year Algebra." *Sch Sci & Math* 66:131–4 F '66. *
9. HASHMI, SHAMIM AHMAD. *Effect of Previous Academic Achievement on the Performance of First-Year College Students of East Pakistan on the "Verbal Reasoning" and the "Numerical Ability" Subtests of the Differential Aptitude Tests.* Doctor's research study No. 1, Colorado State College (Greeley, Colo.), 1966. (*DA* 27:2391A)
10. NELSON, LEONARD THEODORE, JR. *The Relationship Between Verbal, Visual-Spatial, and Numerical Abilities and the Learning of the Mathematical Concept of Function.* Doctor's thesis, University of Michigan (Ann Arbor, Mich.), 1968. (*DAI* 30:218A)
11. PETERSON, JOANNE E. *A Comparative Investigation of Student Scores on the Numerical Ability Section of the Differential Aptitude Test and the Same Students' First Semester Grades in Algebra at Keithley Junior High School.* Master's thesis, Pacific Lutheran University (Tacoma, Wash.), 1971.

CUMULATIVE NAME INDEX
Aijaz, S. M.: 3
Baroya, G. M.: 7
Cain, R. W.: 8
Chase, C. I.: 4–5
Dayal, P.: 6
Hashmi, S. A.: 9
Jenkins, T. V.: 2
Ludlow, H. G.: 4–5
Nelson, L. T.: 10
Peterson, J. E.: 11
Pippert, R. R.: 1
Pomeroy, M. C.: 5
Pugh, R. C.: 4–5

[645]

★**Objective Tests in Mathematics: Arithmetic and Trigonometry.** Ages 15 and over; 1970; no manual; B. C. Erricker; University of London Press Ltd. [England]. *

[646]

*Portland Prognostic Test for Mathematics.** Grades 6.9–8.0, 8.5–9.0; 1960–71; Ernest Hayes; Hayes Educational Test Laboratory. *

For additional information and a review by Cyril J. Hoyt, see 6:588 (1 reference).

REFERENCES THROUGH 1971
1. See 6:588.
2. STROWBRIDGE, EDWIN DAVID, JR. *Relationships Between Twelve Characteristics of Ability in Mathematics and Success-*

ful Achievement in an Eighth Grade SMSG Algebra Program.
Doctor's thesis, University of Oregon (Eugene, Ore.), 1967.
(*DA* 28:1014A)

CUMULATIVE NAME INDEX

Hoyt, C. J.: *rev*, 6:588   Strowbridge, E. D.: 2
Kearney, C. P.: 1

[647]

★**Prescriptive Mathematics Inventory.** Grades 4–5,
5–6, 6–7, 7–8; 1971–72; PMI; no scores other than an
item score for each of "351 instructional objectives in
traditional and contemporary mathematics" and the
identification in each category of "students who did not
show mastery of at least 60% of the related objectives
[i.e., items] in a category"; for a series of longer tests
(4–6 items, rather than 1 item, per objective) which
may be used immediately after studying a topic prescribed by this test (3 lowest levels only) see *Prescriptive Mathematics Inventory Interim Evaluation Tests;*
4 levels; John Gessel; CTB/McGraw-Hill. *
a) ORANGE BOOK. Grades 4–5; 102 items in 14 categories:
whole numbers (addition, subtraction, multiplication,
division), fractions, decimal numbers (addition, subtraction), properties, rounded numbers, inequalities and
number theory, measurement, non-metric geometry,
place value, problem solving.
b) AQUA BOOK. Grades 5–6; 136 items in 16 categories:
whole numbers (addition and subtraction, multiplication, division), positive fractions (addition, subtraction,
multiplication), decimal numbers (addition, subtraction,
multiplication and division), properties, rounded numbers, inequalities and number theory, measurement,
non-metric geometry, place value, problem solving.
c) PURPLE BOOK. Grades 6–7; 169 items in 20 categories:
whole numbers, fractions (addition, subtraction, multiplication, division), decimal numbers (addition, subtraction, multiplication, division), negative integers,
properties, rounded numbers, missing addends and factors, inequalities and number theory, measurement, non-
metric geometry, numeration systems, percent, sets,
problem solving.
d) LEVEL C. Grades 7–8; 193 items in 24 categories:
positive integers (operations, addition and subtraction,
multiplication and division), decimal numbers, negative
integers (operations, addition and subtraction, multiplication and division), rounded numbers, transform,
properties, number sequences, number theory, mathematical sentences, sets, numeration systems, geometry
(metric, non-metric), percent, functions and graphs,
measurement, statistics, probability, trigonometry, problem solving.

[648]

★**Prescriptive Mathematics Inventory Interim
Evaluation Tests.** Grades 4–5, 5–6, 6–7; 1973; developmental edition; primarily for use immediately after
studying a topic prescribed by the *Prescriptive Mathematics Inventory;* a series of 4–6 item tests (2–6 tests
per sheet or booklet); each test is designed to measure
mastery of 1 of "208 specific instructional objectives
.... taught in both traditional and contemporary
mathematics curricula"; number of correct items indicating mastery of an objective to be determined
locally; 3 levels; John Gessel; CTB/McGraw-Hill. *
a) ORANGE LEVEL. Grades 4–5; 94 "mastery" scores.
b) AQUA LEVEL. Grades 5–6; 127 "mastery" scores.
c) PURPLE LEVEL. Grades 6–7; 143 "mastery" scores.

[649]

★**[Primary Mathematics Survey Tests.]** Grades 2,
3; 1973; subtest of *Primary Survey Tests;* 2 levels;
E. Glenadine Gibb and Marion Monroe; handbooks by

Kenneth S. Goodman, John C. Manning, Andrew
Schiller, and Joseph M. Wepman; Scott, Foresman &
Co. * For the complete battery entry, see 27.
a) EARLY PRIMARY MATHEMATICS SURVEY TEST. Grade 2.
b) LATE PRIMARY MATHEMATICS SURVEY TEST. Grade 3.

[650]

Purdue Industrial Mathematics Test. Adults;
1946; C. H. Lawshe, Jr. and Dennis H. Price; University Book Store. *
For additional information and reviews by Clyde H.
Coombs and C. C. Upshall, see 3:314.

REFERENCES THROUGH 1971

1. BROADHURST, JOHN C. *A Differential Prediction of Success in Vocational-Technical and Vocational-Industrial Courses
in a Vocational High School.* Doctor's thesis, New York University (New York, N.Y.), 1948.
2. PAGE, HOWARD E. "A Note on Norms for the Purdue
Industrial Mathematics Test and the Adaptability Test." *J Appl
Psychol* 34:306–8 O '50. * (*PA* 26:559)
3. CHANDLER, ROBERT E. *Validation of Apprentice Screening
Tests in an Oil Refinery.* Doctor's thesis, Purdue University
(Lafayette, Ind.), 1956. (*DA* 27:325B)
4. GRUENFELD, LEOPOLD WILHELM. *Selection of Executives
for a Training Program.* Doctor's thesis, Purdue University
(Lafayette, Ind.), 1960. (*DA* 21:1247)
5. GRUENFELD, LEOPOLD W. "Selection of Executives for a
Training Program." *Personnel Psychol* 14:421–31 w '61. *
(*PA* 37:3922)
6. FINCH, CURTIS R. "Predicting Mathematics Achievement
in Technical Training." *Voc Guid Q* 16:193–7 Mr '68. *

CUMULATIVE NAME INDEX

Broadhurst, J. C.: 1   Gruenfeld, L. W.: 4–5
Chandler, R. E.: 3   Page, H. E.: 2
Coombs, C. H.: *rev*, 3:314   Upshall, C. C.: *rev*, 3:314
Finch, C. R.: 6

[651]

*****Senior Mathematics Test.** Technical college en-
trants; 1963–71; 1971 test identical with test copyrighted 1963 except for decimalization change in 2
items; distribution restricted to colleges of further education; published for the National Foundation for Educational Research in England and Wales; Ginn & Co.
Ltd. [England]. *
For additional information, see 7:487.

[652]

*****Sequential Tests of Educational Progress:
Mathematics.** Grades 4–6, 7–9, 10–12, 13–14 (except
*b*2); 1956–72; 2 editions; Cooperative Tests and Services. * For the complete battery entry, see 35.
a) ORIGINAL SERIES [70 MINUTE TESTS]. Grades 4–6,
7–9, 10–12, 13–14; 1956–63; Braille and large type
editions (grades 4–12) are available from American
Printing House for the Blind, Inc.
b) SERIES 2 [40 MINUTE TESTS]. Grades 4–6, 7–9, 10–12,
13–14; 1956–72; 2 tests.
  1) *Mathematics Basic Concepts.* Grades 4–6, 7–9,
10–12, 13–14; 1956–72.
  2) *Mathematics Computation.* Grades 4–6, 7–9, 10–12;
1969–72.
For additional information and reviews by Arthur
Mittman and Douglas A. Pidgeon of *a,* see 6:590 (5
references); for reviews by Paul L. Dressel, Gordon
Fifer, and Tom A. Lamke, see 5:438. For reviews of
the original edition of the complete battery, see 6:25
(2 reviews) and 5:24 (2 reviews, 1 excerpt).

REFERENCES THROUGH 1971

1–5. See 6:590.
6. RUSSELL, JAMES WILLIAM. *An Analysis of the Academic
Performance of Transfer and Native Students and Their Major
Fields in the College of Arts and Sciences at the University of
Georgia.* Doctor's thesis, University of Georgia (Athens, Ga.),
1963. (*DA* 25:1668)
7. ANDERSON, ROBERT ARNOLD. *Mathematical Student Achievement of Third Form (Ninth Grade) Students in London and*

St. Paul-Minneapolis Metropolitan Areas. Doctor's thesis, University of Minnesota (Minneapolis, Minn.), 1964. (*DA* 25:5008)

8. ELLIOTT, MERLE H., AND BADAL, ALDEN W. "Achievement and Racial Composition of Schools." *Calif J Ed Res* 16:158–66 S '65. * (*PA* 40:1478)

9. FORREST, DON R. *The Development of Prediction Tables To Be Used in Predicting Students' Performance in High School Trigonometry.* Master's thesis, University of Utah (Salt Lake City, Utah), 1966.

10. JONES, FRANKLIN McGEHEE. *A Controlled Comparison of the Academic Performance of Native and Transfer Students at the University of Georgia.* Doctor's thesis, University of Georgia (Athens, Ga.), 1966. (*DA* 27:3227A)

11. MARTIN, BERNARD LOYAL. *Spatial Visualization Abilities of Central Washington State College Prospective Elementary and Secondary Teachers of Mathematics.* Doctor's thesis, Oregon State University (Corvallis, Ore.), 1966. (*DA* 27:2427A)

12. FERRIS, MANFORD J. "Validity as a Function of Empirical Scaling of Test Items by a Logistic Model." *Ed & Psychol Meas* 27:829–35 w '67. * (*PA* 42:8091)

13. HUFF, BETTY. *The Predictive Value of Standardized Testing in Relation to Mathematical Achievement at Virginia High School.* Master's thesis, East Tennessee State University (Johnson City, Tenn.), 1967.

14. PARK, GAIL RODNEY. *The Predictive Efficiency of Selected Data for Eighth Grade Algebra Students at Bonneville Junior High.* Master's thesis, University of Utah (Salt Lake City, Utah), 1967.

15. TENOPYR, MARY L. "Social Intelligence and Academic Success." *Ed & Psychol Meas* 27:961–5 w '67. * (*PA* 42:9509)

16. GUPTA, RAM K. "Certain Techniques of Multivariate Analysis Applied to Different Measures of Inter-Item Relationships for Developing Unifactor Tests." *J Ed Meas* 5:223–30 f '68. * (*PA* 44:11217)

17. WILSON, ANAISE VICTORIANNE. *A Study of the Relationship of Selected Factors to the Academic Achievement of College Freshmen in the School of Education of Tuskegee Institute.* Doctor's thesis, New York University (New York, N.Y.), 1968. (*DAI* 30:144A)

18. ANASTASIOW, NICHOLAS J. "Fourth Through Sixth Grade Student Performance Differences on STEP and SRA Achievement Tests." *Meas & Eval Guid* 2(3):149–52 f '69. * (*PA* 44:13276)

19. FUJITA, GEORGE Y., AND O'REILLY, JOSEPH P. "A Two-Stage Sequential Strategy in the Placement of Students in an Undergraduate Curriculum." *J Res Math Ed* 1(4):241–50 N '70. *

20. FLEISCHMAN, HOWARD L.; ORR, DAVID B.; AND STRASEL, H. C. "Relationships Between the Subtests of Six Achievement Test Batteries." Abstract. *Proc 79th Ann Conv Am Psychol Assn* 6(1):109–10 '71. * (*PA* 46:3727)

For additional references, see the bibliography for the series, 35.

CUMULATIVE NAME INDEX

[653]

Stanford Achievement Test: High School Mathematics Test. Grades 9–12; 1965–66; catalog uses the title *Stanford High School Mathematics Test;* subtest of *Stanford Achievement Test: High School Basic Battery;* 2 scores: Part A (basic), total (basic and advanced); Part A is for all students in grades 9–12, Part B is only for students enrolled in 3rd and 4th year advanced mathematics courses; Eric F. Gardner, Jack C. Merwin, Robert Callis, and Richard Madden; Harcourt Brace Jovanovich, Inc. * For the complete battery entry, see 37.

For additional information and reviews by James Braswell and James W. Wilson, see 7:488. For reviews of the complete battery, see 7:27 (2 reviews).

[654]

Stanford Achievement Test: High School Numerical Competence Test. Grades 9–12; 1965–66; catalog uses the title *Stanford High School Numerical Competence Test;* subtest of *Stanford Achievement Test: High School Basic Battery;* Eric F. Gardner, Jack C. Merwin, Robert Callis, and Richard Madden; Harcourt Brace Jovanovich, Inc. * For the complete battery entry, see 37.

For additional information and reviews by Sheldon S. Myers and Len Pikaart, see 7:489. For reviews of the complete battery, see 7:27 (2 reviews).

[655]

*Stanford Achievement Test: Mathematics Tests. 1923–74; 2 editions; Richard Madden, Eric F. Gardner, Herbert C. Rudman, Truman L. Kelley (*a*), Bjorn Karlsen (*b*), and Jack C. Merwin (*b*); Harcourt Brace Jovanovich, Inc. * For the complete battery entry, see 36.

a) 1964 EDITION. Grades 4.0–5.4, 5.5–6.9, 7.0–9.9; 1923–68; catalog uses the title *Stanford Arithmetic Tests;* 3 scores: computation, concepts, applications; Braille and large type editions available from American Printing House for the Blind, Inc.

b) 1973 EDITION. Grades 1.5–2.4, 2.5–3.4, 3.5–4.4, 4.5–5.4, 5.5–6.9, 7.0–9.5; 1923–74; 4 scores (concepts, computation, applications, total) except for grades 1.5–2.4 (concepts, computation and applications, total).

For additional information and a review by Harold C. Trimble of the 1964 edition, see 7:527 (6 references); for a review by C. Alan Riedesel of an earlier edition, see 6:637 (7 references); for a review by Robert L. Burch, see 4:419. For reviews of the complete battery, see 7:25 (1 excerpt), 6:26 (1 review, 1 excerpt), 5:25 (1 review), 4:25 (2 reviews), and 3:18 (2 reviews).

REFERENCES THROUGH 1971

1–7. See 6:637.
8–13. See 7:527.

14. LEONHARDY, ALMA. "Arithmetic Accomplishment of Pupils in Los Angeles Junior High Schools." *Ed Res B* (Los Angeles City Schools) 4:10–1 Ja 15 '25. *

15. GARRISON, S. C., AND HODGSON, JULIA. "The Reliability and Validity of Certain Arithmetic Tests." *Peabody J Ed* 5:339–41 My '28. *

16. BOUSFIELD, MAUDELLE B. "The Intelligence and School Achievement of Negro Children." *J Negro Ed* 1:388–95 O '32. * (*PA* 8:3671)

17. ENGELHART, MAX D. "The Relative Contribution of Certain Factors to Individual Differences in Arithmetical Problem Solving Ability." *J Exp Ed* 1:19–27 S 15 '32. * (*PA* 7:1126)

18. MILLER, ANDREW J., AND MANWILLER, C. E. "A Study of Trade School Pupils." *Pittsburgh Sch* 6:219–69 My–Je '32. *

19. THORNDIKE, EDWARD L.; BREGMAN, ELSIE O.; LORGE, IRVING; METCALFE, ZAIDA F.; ROBINSON, ELEANOR E.; AND WOODYARD, ELLA. *Prediction of Vocational Success.* New York: Commonwealth Fund, 1934. Pp. xxiv, 284. * (*PA* 8:2796)

20. CANADY, HERMAN G. "Individual Differences Among Freshmen at West Virginia State College." *J Negro Ed* 4:246–58 Ap '35. *

21. LONG, HOWARD HALE. "Test Results of Third-Grade Negro Children Selected on the Basis of Socio-Economic Status." *J Negro Ed* 4:192–212, 523–52 Ap, O '35. * (*PA* 10:1089)

22. MANUEL, H. T. "A Comparison of Spanish-Speaking and English-Speaking Children in Reading and Arithmetic." *J Appl Psychol* 19:189–202 Ap '35. * (*PA* 9:5346)

23. WEISENBURG, THEODORE; ROE, ANNE; AND McBRIDE, KATHARINE E. *Adult Intelligence: A Psychological Study of Test Performances.* New York: Commonwealth Fund, 1936. Pp. xiii, 155. * (*PA* 10:3771)

24. JOHNSON, J. T. "On the Nature of Problem-Solving in Arithmetic." *J Ed Res* 43:110–5 O '49. * (*PA* 24:2791)

25. EDWARDS, ROBERTA MILLER. *Factorial Comparison of Arithmetic Performance of Girls and Boys in the Sixth Grade.* Washington, D.C.: Catholic University of America, 1957. Pp. viii, 45. * (*PA* 32:842)

26. GOWAN, J. C., AND DIBLE, ISABEL. "Age Effects on the Test Scores of Women Teaching Candidates." *Calif J Ed Res* 11:37–8 Ja '60. * (*PA* 34:8417)

27. PAGE, BEN H. *Predicting Performance in Seventh Grade Advanced Mathematics at Kearns Junior High School.* Master's thesis, University of Utah (Salt Lake City, Utah), 1969.

28. FLEISCHMAN, HOWARD L.; ORR, DAVID B.; AND STRASEL, H. C. "Relationships Between the Subtests of Six Achievement Test Batteries." Abstract. *Proc 79th Ann Conv Am Psychol Assn* 6(1):109–10 '71. * (*PA* 46:3727)

29. Kapes, Jerome T., and Long, Thomas E. "An Assessment of the Criterion-Related Validity of the Ohio Trade and Industrial Education Achievement Test Battery." *J Indus Teach Ed* 9(1):6–14 f '71. *

30. Kay, Patricia M.; Tittle, Carol J.; and Weiner, Max. "Selecting Tests to Predict the Need for Remediation in a University Open Admissions Population." *Meas & Eval Guid* 4(3):154–9 O '71. * (*PA* 49:11964)

CUMULATIVE NAME INDEX

Ashcroft, S. C.: 6	Lorge, I.: 19
Bousfield, M. B.: 16	McBride, K. E.: 23
Bregman, E. O.: 19	McTaggart, H. P.: 4
Burch, R. L.: *rev,* 4:419	Manuel. H. T.: 22
Canady, H. G.: 20	Manwiller, C. E.: 18
Cohen, J. M.: 12	Metcalfe, Z. F.: 19
Dible, I.: 26	Miller, A. J.: 18
Edwards, R. M.: 25	Namkin, S.: 10
Emm, M. E.: 3	Nolan, C. Y.: 5–6
Engelhart, M. D.: 17	Orr, D. B.: 28
Fleischman, H. L.: 28	Page, B. H.: 27
Gallian, R. D.: 11	Riedesel, C. A.: *rev,* 6:637
Garrison, S. C.: 15	Riley, M. F.: 9
Gowan, J. C.: 2, 26	Robinson, E. E.: 19
Hodgson, J.: 15	Roe, A.: 23
Johnson, J. T.: 24	Rudd, J. P.: 7
Kapes, J. T.: 29	Slocum, T. J.: 13
Kay, P. M.: 30	Strasel, H. C.: 28
Laney, A. R.: 1	Thorndike, E. L.: 19
Leonhardy, A.: 14	Tittle, C. J.: 30
Lieberman, M.: 13	Trimble, H. C.: *rev,* 7:527
Long, H. H.: 21	Weiner, M.: 30
Long, J. A.: 8	Weisenburg, T.: 23
Long, T. E.: 29	Woodyard, E.: 19

[656]

Stanford Modern Mathematics Concepts Test. Grades 5.5–6.9, 7.0–9.5; 1965; test booklet title is *Stanford Achievement Test: Modern Mathematics Concepts Test;* Truman L. Kelley, Richard Madden, Eric F. Gardner, and Herbert C. Rudman; Harcourt Brace Jovanovich, Inc. *

For additional information, a review by James R. Caldwell, and an excerpted review by B. R. Hopkins, see 7:490 (3 references).

REFERENCES THROUGH 1971
1–3. See 7:490.

CUMULATIVE NAME INDEX

Caldwell, J. R.: *rev,* 7:490	Qualls, L. J.: 2
Erickson, B. L.: 3	Woodward, J. W.: 1
Hopkins, B. R.: *exc,* 7:490	

[657]

*Teacher Education Examination Program: Mathematics. College seniors preparing to teach secondary school; 1957–72; reprinting of inactive 1966 form of *National Teacher Examinations: Mathematics;* test available to colleges for local administration; Educational Testing Service. * For the testing program entry, see 898.

For additional information concerning an earlier form, see 6:584. For a review of the testing program, see 5:543. For reference to a review of the *National Teacher Examinations: Mathematics,* see 643.

[658]

★Test A/16 [Mathematical Achievement Test]. Job applicants with at least 10 years of education; 1957–63; no manual; National Institute for Personnel Research [South Africa]. *

[659]

Tests of Academic Progress: Mathematics. Grades 9–12; 1964–66; Dale P. Scannell and Gilbert Ulmer; Houghton Mifflin Co. * For the complete battery entry, see 44.

For additional information and reviews by Carl J. Huberty and J. R. Jefferson Wadkins, see 7:491 (1 reference). For a review of the complete battery, see 7:31.

REFERENCES THROUGH 1971
1. See 7:491.

CUMULATIVE NAME INDEX

Goolsby, T. M.: 1	Wadkins, J. R. J.: *rev,* 7:491
Huberty, C. J.: *rev,* 7:491	

[660]

*Tests of Achievement in Basic Skills: Mathematics. Grades 4–6, 7–9, 10–12; 1970–73; TABS-M; 3 levels; tests consist of 69 (Level B), 64 (Level C), and 44 (Level D) items each of which is designed to measure a particular objective; James C. Young and Robert R. Knapp (manual for Level C); Educational and Industrial Testing Service. *

a) LEVEL B. Grades 4–6; 1972–73; 4 scores: arithmetic skills, geometry-measurement-application, modern mathematics concepts, total.

b) LEVEL C. Grades 7–9; 1970–71; 4 scores: same as for *a*.

c) LEVEL D. Grades 10–12; 1972; 3 scores: arithmetic skills, arithmetic application, total.

For additional information concerning Level C, see 7:492 (1 reference).

REFERENCES THROUGH 1971
1. See 7:492.

CUMULATIVE NAME INDEX

Knapp, R. R.: 1	Young, J. C.: 1
Michael, W. B.: 1	

[661]

*Tests of Basic Experiences: Mathematics. Pre-kgn–kgn, kgn–grade 1; 1970–72; Margaret H. Moss; CTB/McGraw-Hill. * For the complete battery entry, see 47.

For additional information, see 7:493. For a review of the complete battery, see 7:33.

[662]

*The Undergraduate Program Field Tests: Mathematics Tests. College; 1969–73; formerly called *The Undergraduate Record Examinations: Mathematics Tests;* tests available to colleges for local administration; 5 tests: 1 field test, 4 modular tests; Educational Testing Service. * For the testing program entry, see 1062.

a) MATHEMATICS TEST.

b) MODULAR TESTS DESIGNED TO COMPLEMENT THE TWO-HOUR MATHEMATICS TEST.

1) *Abstract Algebra.*
2) *Linear Algebra.*
3) *Real Analysis 1.*
4) *Real Analysis 2.*

For additional information and a review by L. Ray Carry, see 7:494. For reviews of the testing program, see 7:671 (2 reviews).

[663]

★Watson Diagnostic Mathematics Test: Computation, Fourth Edition. Grades 1–3, 4–6, 7–10; 1973; WDMT; 3 levels; G. Milton Watson; Book Society of Canada Ltd. [Canada]. *

a) PRIMARY. Grades 1–3; 22 scores: grade 1 level (basic concepts, counting, addition, subtraction, fractions, time, total), grade 2 level (counting, addition, subtraction, multiplication, fractions, time, total), grade 3 level (basic concepts, counting, addition, subtraction, multiplication, fractions, total), total.

b) JUNIOR. Grades 4–6; 14 scores: addition (whole numbers, fractions), subtraction (whole numbers, fractions), total, multiplication (whole numbers, fractions), division (whole numbers, fractions), total (unsorted review, decimals-percent-fractions, total), total.

c) INTERMEDIATE. Grades 7–10; 16 scores: addition (whole numbers and decimals, fractions), subtraction (whole numbers and decimals, fractions), total, multiplication (whole numbers and decimals, fractions), division (whole numbers and decimals, fractions), total (rules of signs review, fractions and decimals, percent, stretchers, total), total.

[Out of Print Since TIP I]

Business Mathematics: Every Pupil Scholarship Test, 6:563
College Entrance Examination Board Achievement Test: Advanced Mathematics, 6:568 (2 reviews, 10 references) ; *Intermediate Mathematics,* 6:569 (2 reviews, 6 references)
Contemporary Mathematics Tests, 7:464 (2 excerpts) ; *Advanced (Senior High),* 7:462 (2 reviews) ; *Elementary and Junior High,* 7:463 (2 reviews, 1 reference)
Cooperative General Achievement Tests [General Proficiency Series] :Test 3, Mathematics, 6:573 (1 review, 4 references)
Cooperative General Mathematics Test for High School Classes, 2:1432 (2 reviews, 1 reference)
Cooperative Mathematics Pre-Test for College Students, 4:369 (3 reviews)
Cooperative Mathematics Tests for Grades 7, 8, and 9, 5:421 (5 reviews, 6 references)
Davis Test of Functional Competence in Mathematics, 5:422 (2 reviews, 2 references)
ERB Mathematics Tests, 7:467 (2 references)
Functional Evaluation in Mathematics, 4:372 (1 review)
General Mathematical Ability, 5:426; now available only as a subtest of *Tests of General Educational Development,* 48
General Mathematics: Every Pupil Scholarship Test, 6:575
General Mathematics: Every Pupil Test, 6:576
Junior Math Reasoning Test (status unknown), 6:580
Kansas Mathematics Test, 5:430 (1 review)
Kentucky Mathematics Test, 3:311; revised edition was available only as a part of *Kentucky Classification Battery,* 4:301 (1 review, 4 references)
Mathematical Ability Test, 1:1075
Mathematical Literacy for High School Seniors, 5:431
Mathematics: Every Pupil Test, 6:581
Mathematics Test I, 5:436 (1 review)
Metropolitan Achievement Tests: High School Mathematics Tests, 7:479 (2 reviews)
Morgan Achievement Test in Mathematics for Employee Selection (status unknown), 5:437 (1 review)
Purdue Mathematics Training Test: Arithmetic and Algebra, 6:589 (1 review, 8 references)
Rasmussen General Mathematics Test, 3:315 (1 review, 1 reference)
SRA Modern Math Understanding Test, 7:485 (2 reviews) ; now available only as an optional substitute for the arithmetic subtest of *SRA Achievement Series, Forms C and D,* 29
Sanders-Schrader General Mathematics Test, 7:486
Snader General Mathematics Test, 5:439 (2 reviews)
Survey of Mathematics Achievement: California Survey Series, 6:591 (2 reviews)
T.C. Mathematics Test, 6:592
Test of Mathematical Fundamentals for Grades 7 to 12, 5:440 (1 review)
Wisconsin Contemporary Test of Elementary Mathematics, 7:495 (1 review, 1 excerpt)

ALGEBRA

[664]

Advanced Algebra: Achievement Examinations for Secondary Schools. High school; 1951–54; Form 4 ('54) of a series of tests, currently (1973) entitled *Advanced Mathematics (Including Trigonometry)* : *Minnesota High School Achievement Examinations* (see 597), issued annually for May testing; Harvey O. Jackson; Bobbs-Merrill Co., Inc. *
For additional information concerning later and earlier forms, see 597, 7:450, 6:593 (2 reviews), 5:441, and 5:442 (1 review).

[665]

Algebra Readiness Test. Grades 8–9; 1947; 6 scores: fundamental operations, fractions, decimals, problem solving, general numbers, total; William R. Lueck; Bobbs-Merrill Co., Inc. *
For additional information and a review by Harold Gulliksen, see 4:384.

[666–7]

Algebra Test for Engineering and Science: National Achievement Tests. College entrants; 1958–61 ; 2 scores: part 1, total; 1961 test identical with test copyrighted 1958 except for option order for some items and use of letters to designate options; A. B. Lonski; Psychometric Affiliates. *
For additional information and a review by Peter A. Lappan, Jr., see 6:595.

[668]

Blyth Second-Year Algebra Test, Revised Edition. Grades 9–12; 1953–66; M. Isobel Blyth; Harcourt Brace Jovanovich, Inc. *
For additional information and reviews by Peter A. Lappan, Jr. and G. Edith Robinson, see 7:497; for reviews by Paul Blommers and Myron F. Rosskopf of the original edition, see 5:443.

[669]

Breslich Algebra Survey Test. 1, 2 semesters high school; 1930–31; 7 scores: algebraic concepts, simplifying expressions, solving equations, deriving equations, formulas and graphs, factoring, total; E. R. Breslich; Bobbs-Merrill Co., Inc. *
For additional information and a review by John R. Clark, see 2:1435.

[670]

*****CLEP Subject Examination in College Algebra.** 1 semester or equivalent; 1968–73; for college accreditation of nontraditional study, advanced placement, or assessment of educational achievement; tests administered monthly at centers throughout the United States; program administered for the College Entrance Examination Board by Educational Testing Service. * For the testing program entry, see 1050.
For additional information, see 7:498. For reviews of the testing program, see 7:664 (3 reviews).

[671]

California Algebra Aptitude Test. High school; 1940–58; 1958 test identical with test copyrighted 1940: 1958 manual essentially the same as manual copyrighted 1950; Noel Keys and Muriel McCrum; American Guidance Service, Inc. *
For additional information, see 5:444; for a review by William G. Mollenkopf, see 4:385; for a review by David Segel, see 3:320.

REFERENCES THROUGH 1971
1. BALDAUF, ROBERT J. "Predicting Success in Eighth Grade Algebra." *Psychol Rep* 12:810 Je '63. * (*PA* 38:6580)
2. GUSTAFSON, RAYMOND G. *Predicting Student Success in Ninth Grade Algebra in the Public Schools of Watertown, Minnesota.* Master's thesis, St. Cloud State College (St. Cloud, Minn.), 1967.
3. VANDEWALL, CLIFFORD E. *The California Algebra Aptitude Test: Its Predictive Validity.* Master's thesis, Drake University (Des Moines, Iowa), 1968.

CUMULATIVE NAME INDEX
Baldauf, R. J.: 1   Segel, D.: *rev,* 3:320
Gustafson, R. G.: 2   Vandewall, C. E.: 3
Mollenkopf, W. G.: *rev,* 4:385

[672]
Cooperative Mathematics Tests: Algebra I and II.
Grades 8–9, 10–12; 1962–65; 2 levels; Cooperative Tests and Services. *
a) ALGEBRA I. 1 semester grades 8–9.
b) ALGEBRA II. Grades 10–12.
For additional information and a review by Kenneth J. Travers, see 7:500 (4 references); for a review by Paul Blommers, see 6:594. For excerpted reviews by John R. Hills and Jack C. Merwin of the series, see 7:465.

REFERENCES THROUGH 1971
1–4. See 7:500.

CUMULATIVE NAME INDEX
Ali, M. B.: 1   Meyers, C. E.: 3
Blommers, P.: *rev,* 6:594   Michael, W. B.: 3
Caldwell, J. R.: 3   Morgan, W. P.: 4
Hills, J. R.: *exc,* 7:465   Schrader, D. R.: 3
Lovett, C. J.: 2   Travers, K. J.: *rev,* 7:500
Merwin, J. C.: *exc,* 7:465

[673]
Cooperative Mathematics Tests: Algebra III.
High school and college; 1963–65; Cooperative Tests and Services. *
For additional information and reviews by James R. Caldwell and Willard G. Warrington, see 7:501. For excerpted reviews by John R. Hills and Jack C. Merwin of the series, see 7:465.

REFERENCES THROUGH 1971
1. TATHAM, CLIFFORD B., AND TATHAM, ELAINE J. "A Note on the Predictive Validity of the Cooperative Algebra III." *Ed & Psychol Meas* 31(2):517–8 su '71. *

CUMULATIVE NAME INDEX
Caldwell, J. R.: *rev,* 7:501   Tatham, E. J.: 1
Hills, J. R.: *exc,* 7:465   Warrington, W. G.: *rev,* 7:
Merwin, J. C.: *exc,* 7:465   501
Tatham, C. B.: 1

[674]
Diagnostic Test in Basic Algebra. 2, 3 semesters high school; 1956; John H. Henshaw; Australian Council for Educational Research [Australia]. *
For additional information and a review by Stanley Clark, see 5:445.

[675]
***ERB Modern Elementary Algebra Test.** Grades 8–9; 1965–71; 1971 test identical with test copyrighted 1965 except for directions; no manual; Educational Records Bureau. *
For additional information, see 7:502 (1 reference).

REFERENCES THROUGH 1971
1. See 7:502.

CUMULATIVE NAME INDEX
Litterick, W. S.: 1

[676]
ERB Modern Second Year Algebra Test. High school; 1968–69; no manual; Frederic P. Bonan, Philip

Avirett, Karl S. Kalman (Form X), Stephen S. Ober, Foye Perry, Randolph Stone, Reinhoud H. van der Linde (Form X), Frederick Watson, and Arthur Weeks (Form Y); Educational Records Bureau. *
For additional information, see 7:503.

[677]
Elementary Algebra: Achievement Examinations for Secondary Schools. High school; 1951–54; Form 4 ('54) of a series of tests, currently (1973) entitled *Elementary Algebra: Minnesota High School Achievement Examinations* (see 678), issued annually for May testing; Lyle M. Eakins; Bobbs-Merrill Co., Inc. *
For additional information concerning later and earlier forms, see 678, 7:504, 6:597, 5:446, and 5:448 (1 review).

[678]
***Elementary Algebra: Minnesota High School Achievement Examinations.** High school; 1951–70; a new, revised, or previously inactive form issued each May; Achievement Examinations for Secondary Schools, High School Achievement Examinations, and Midwest High School Achievement Examinations have also been used as series titles; Form GJ Rev ('70) used in 1970 and 1973 testings; Form 4 ('54), entitled *Elementary Algebra: Achievement Examinations for Secondary Schools* (see 677), is available from another publisher; edited by V. L. Lohmann; American Guidance Service, Inc. *
For additional information concerning out of print and inactive forms, see 7:504, 6:597, and 5:446; for a review by Lynnette B. Plumlee of Form A (1955), see 5:448.

[679]
First Year Algebra Test: National Achievement Tests. 1 year high school; 1958–62; 1962 test identical with test copyrighted 1958; Ray Webb and Julius H. Hlavaty; Psychometric Affiliates. *
For additional information and a review by Donald L. Meyer, see 6:600.

[680]
Illinois Algebra Test. 1, 1.5, 2 semesters high school; 1956–58; formerly called *Chicago Algebra Test;* 1958 test identical with test copyrighted 1956 except for title and 1 revised item; Charles H. Schutter; Bobbs-Merrill Co., Inc. *
For additional information and reviews by Stanley Clark and Theodore E. Kellogg, see 5:450.

[681]
Iowa Algebra Aptitude Test, Third Edition. Grade 8; 1931–69; IAAT; H. A. Greene and Darrell Sabers; Bureau of Educational Research and Service. *
For additional information, reviews by W. L. Bashaw and Cyril J. Hoyt, and an excerpted review by Russell A. Chadbourn, see 7:505 (8 references); for reviews by Harold Gulliksen and Emma Spaney of an earlier edition, see 4:393; for a review by David Segel, see 3:327 (2 references); for reviews by Richard M. Drake and M. W. Richardson, see 2:1441 (1 reference).

REFERENCES THROUGH 1971
1. See 2:1441.
2–3. See 3:327.
4–11. See 7:505.
12. SCHWELLENBACH, JOHN A. "An Experiment in Predicting the Ability of Eighth Grade Students to Work Simple Algebra Problems." *Calif J Ed Res* 5:36–41 Ja '54. * (*PA* 28:7998)
13. KENNEDY, WILLIAM D. *The Predictive Value of the Iowa Algebra Aptitude Test in the Des Moines Schools.* Master's thesis, Drake University (Des Moines, Iowa), 1956.

14. SHAW, GERALDINE SAX. "Prediction of Success in Elementary Algebra." *Math Teach* 49:173–8 Mr '56. *
15. NORTON, DANIEL P. "The Relationship of Study Habits and Other Measures to Achievement in Ninth-Grade General Science." *J Exp Ed* 27:211–7 Mr '59. * (*PA* 35:1283)
16. OSBURN, H. G., AND MELTON, R. S. "Prediction of Proficiency in a Modern and Traditional Course in Beginning Algebra." *Ed & Psychol Meas* 23:277–87 su '63. * (*PA* 38:1386)
17. LAVENAU, BRUCE A. *A Study of Five Factors and Their Simple and Multiple Correlation With Advanced Algebra Grades.* Master's thesis, Northern Illinois University (DeKalb, Ill.), 1965.
18. SABERS, DARRELL L., AND WHITE, GORDON W. "The Effect of Differential Weighting of Individual Item Responses on the Predictive Validity and Reliability of an Aptitude Test." *J Ed Meas* 6(2):93–6 su '69. * (*PA* 44:13299)

CUMULATIVE NAME INDEX

Bashaw, W. L.: *rev,* 7:505	McCabe, M. S.: 5
Chadbourn, R. A.: *exc,* 7:505	Melton, R. S.: 16
Coffie, F. L.: 6	Norton, D. P.: 15
Drake, R. M.: *rev,* 2:1441	Osburn, H. G.: 16
Feldt, L. S.: 9–10	Piper, A. H.: 1
Grime, H. E.: 3	Richardson, M. W.: *rev,* 2:
Guiler, W. S.: 2	1441
Gulliksen, H.: *rev,* 4:393	Sabers, D. L.: 8–10, 18
Hoyt, C. J.: *rev,* 7:505	Schwellenbach, J. A.: 12
Hulling, R. H.: 7	Segel, D.: *rev,* 3:327
Kearney, C. P.: 4	Shaw, G. S.: 14
Kennedy, W. D.: 13	Spaney, E.: *rev,* 4:393
Lavenau, B. A.: 17	White, G. W.: 18
Lippincott, W. R.: 11	

[682]

Kepner Mid-Year Algebra Achievement Tests. 1 semester high school; 1969; KMAAT; Henry S. Kepner, Jr. and Darrell Sabers; Bureau of Educational Research and Service. *

For additional information, a review by Gerald L. Ericksen, and an excerpted review by Arthur Mittman, see 7:506.

[683]

Lankton First-Year Algebra Test, Revised Edition. Grades 8–12; 1950–65; Robert S. Lankton; Harcourt Brace Jovanovich, Inc. *

For additional information and reviews by Lynnette B. Plumlee and Kenneth J. Travers, see 7:507 (3 references); for a review by Emma Spaney of the original edition, see 5:451; for a review by Stanley Clark, see 4:394 (1 reference).

REFERENCES THROUGH 1971

1. See 4:394.
2–4. See 7:507.
5. STEPHENS, JAMES ALBERT. *A Study of the Correlation Between Critical Thinking Abilities and Achievement in Algebra Involving Advanced Placement.* Master's thesis, North Carolina State University (Raleigh, N.C.), 1966.

CUMULATIVE NAME INDEX

Caldwell, J. R.: 4	Schrader, D. R.: 4
Clark, S.: *rev,* 4:394	Sommerfeld, R. E.: 2
Dirr, P. M.: 3	Spaney, E.: *rev,* 5:451
Lankton, R. S.: 1	Stephens, J. A.: 5
Meyers, C. E.: 4	Tracy, N. H.: 2
Michael, W. B.: 4	Travers, K. J.: *rev,* 7:507
Plumlee, L. B.: *rev,* 7:507	

[684]

Lee Test of Algebraic Ability, Revised. Grades 7–8; 1930–64; TAA; identical with the 1930 edition except for adaptation to machine scoring; J. Murray Lee; Bobbs-Merrill Co., Inc. *

For additional information, reviews by W. L. Bashaw and Cyril J. Hoyt, and an excerpted review by William Mehrens, see 7:508 (2 references); for a review by S. S. Wilks, see 2:1443 (1 reference).

REFERENCES THROUGH 1971

1. See 2:1443.
2–3. See 7:508.
4. LEE, DORRIS MAY, AND LEE, J. MURRAY. "Some Relationships Between Algebra and Geometry." *J Ed Psychol* 22:551–60 O '31. * (*PA* 6:873)

5. LEE, J. MURRAY, AND HUGHES, W. HARDIN. "Predicting Success in Algebra and Geometry." *Sch R* 42:188–96 Mr '34. *
6. LAYTON, R. B. "A Study of Prognosis in High School Algebra." *J Ed Res* 34:601–5 Ap '41. * (*PA* 15:3157)

CUMULATIVE NAME INDEX

Aamodt, G. P.: 1	Lee, D. M.: 4
Bashaw, W. L.: *rev,* 7:508	Lee, J. M.: 4–5
Grothus, J. R.: 2	Mehrens, W.: *exc,* 7:508
Hoyt, C. J.: *rev,* 7:508	Stilgebauer, L. K.: 3
Hughes, W. H.: 5	Torgerson, T. L.: 1
Layton, R. B.: 6	Wilks, S. S.: *rev,* 2:1443

[685]

Mid-Year Algebra Test. High school; 1968; Harcourt Brace Jovanovich, Inc. *

For additional information and a review by Gerald L. Ericksen, see 7:509.

[686]

★**Modern Algebra Test: Content Evaluation Series.** 1 year high school; 1972; Gerald S. Hanna; Houghton Mifflin Co. *

[687]

★**Objective Tests in Mathematics: Algebra.** Ages 15 and over; 1970; no manual; B. C. Erricker; University of London Press Ltd. [England]. *

[688]

Orleans-Hanna Algebra Prognosis Test. Grades 7–11; 1928–69; revision of *Orleans Algebra Prognosis Test;* Joseph B. Orleans and Gerald S. Hanna; Harcourt Brace Jovanovich, Inc. *

For additional information and reviews by W. L. Bashaw and Cyril J. Hoyt, see 7:510 (3 references); for reviews by Harold Gulliksen and Emma Spaney of an earlier edition, see 4:396 (1 reference); for a review by S. S. Wilks, see 2:1444 (4 references).

REFERENCES THROUGH 1971

1–4. See 2:1444.
5. See 4:396.
6–8. See 7:510.
9. JOHNSON, ELLIS. *An Investigation of Prognosis in First Year High School Algebra.* Doctor's thesis, Fordham University (New York, N.Y.), 1934.
10. DUNN, WILLIAM HUDSON. "The Influence of the Teacher Factor in Predicting Success in Ninth Grade Algebra." *J Ed Res* 30:577–82 Ap '37. * (*PA* 11:3405)
11. JOHNSON, LOAZ W. "Do the Benefits Derived From the Orleans Algebra Prognosis Test Justify Time and Expense to Administer It?" Abstract. *Calif J Ed Res* 5:185 S '54. *
12. McQUEEN, ROBERT, AND WILLIAMS, KENNETH C. "Predicting Success in Beginning High School Algebra." *Psychol Rep* 4:603–6 D '58. * (*PA* 34:2009)
13. ANDERSON, ETHEL P. *An Investigation of the Validity of the Orleans Algebra Prognosis Test in Predicting Success in Algebra in Williamsville Junior-Senior High School.* Master's thesis, Niagara University (Niagara University, N.Y.), 1959.
14. DUNCAN, ROGER LEE. *The Prediction of Success in Eighth Grade Algebra.* Doctor's thesis, University of Oklahoma (Norman, Okla.), 1969. (*DA* 21:1869)
15. BARNES, WARD EWING, AND ASHER, JOHN WILLIAM. "Predicting Students' Success in First-Year Algebra." *Math Teach* 55:651–4 D '62. *
16. OSBURN, H. G., AND MELTON, R. S. "Prediction of Proficiency in a Modern and Traditional Course in Beginning Algebra." *Ed & Psychol Meas* 23:277–87 su '63. * (*PA* 38:1386)
17. LUNDQUIST, RUSSELL M. *Prognosis of Success in Ninth Grade Algebra.* Master's thesis, Mankato State College (Mankato, Minn.), 1965.
18. ARMSTRONG, RONALD V. *Predicting Students' Success in Elementary Algebra.* Master's thesis, Bowling Green State University (Bowling Green, Ohio), 1966.
19. LENKE, JOANNE M.; BLIGH, HAROLD F.; AND KANE, BERNARD H. "Cross-Validation of the Orleans-Hanna Algebra Prognosis Test and the Orleans-Hanna Geometry Prognosis Test." *Ed & Psychol Meas* 31(2):521–3 su '71. *

CUMULATIVE NAME INDEX

Aamodt, G. P.: 2	Bligh, H. F.: 8, 19
Anderson, E. P.: 13	Duncan, R. L.: 14
Armstrong, R. V.: 18	Dunn, W. H.: 10
Asher, J. W.: 15	Grover, C. C.: 1
Barnes, W. E.: 15	Gulliksen, H.: *rev,* 4:396
Bashaw, W. L.: *rev,* 7:510	Hanna, G. S.: 8

Hines, A. C.: 6
Hoyt, C. J.: *rev*, 7:510
Johnson, E.: 9
Johnson, L. W.: 11
Kane, B. H.: 19
Katz, E. M.: 7
Lenke, J. M.: 8, 19
Lundquist, R. M.: 17
McQueen, R.: 12

Melton, R. S.: 16
Orleans, J. B.: 3, 8
Osburn, H. G.: 16
Seagoe, M. V.: 4–5
Spaney, E.: *rev*, 4:396
Torgerson, T. L.: 2
Wilks, S. S.: *rev*, 2:1444
Williams, K. C.: 12

[689]

Survey Test of Algebraic Aptitude: California Survey Series. Grade 8; 1959; Robert E. Dinkel; CTB/McGraw-Hill. *

For additional information and reviews by Cyril J. Hoyt and Donald L. Meyer, see 6:602.

REFERENCES THROUGH 1971

1. LANE, BETTY RUBINO. *A Study of the Predictive Values of the Tests Being Used to Determine Success in Algebra I in the Lockport Township High Schools.* Master's thesis, Northern Illinois University (DeKalb, Ill.), 1966.
2. SLADE, SHERRY L. *A Comparison of Methods Used to Predict Success in Ninth Grade Elementary Algebra.* Master's thesis, Utah State University (Logan, Utah), 1969.

CUMULATIVE NAME INDEX

Hoyt, C. J.: *rev*, 6:602
Lane, B. R.: 1

Meyer, D. L.: *rev*, 6:602
Slade, S. L.: 2

[Out of Print Since TIP I]

Ability for Algebra: Fife Tests of Ability, Test 3, 4:380 (1 review, 3 references)
Algebra Tests, 7:496
Colvin-Schrammel Algebra Test, 2:1437 (2 reviews)
Contemporary Mathematics Test: Algebra, 7:499 (2 reviews)
Cooperative Algebra Test: Elementary Algebra Through Quadratics, 4:387 (7 reviews, 4 references)
Cooperative Intermediate Algebra Test: Quadratics and Beyond, 4:388 (7 reviews, 3 references)
Elementary Algebra: Every Pupil Test, 6:596
Elementary Algebra Test: Affiliation Testing Program for Catholic Secondary Schools, 6:598 (1 review, 2 references)
First Year Algebra: Every Pupil Scholarship Test, 6:599
First Year Algebra: 20th Century Test, 4:392
Garman-Schrammel Algebra Test, 3:326 (2 reviews)
Larson-Greene Unit Tests in First-Year Algebra, 4:395
Seattle Algebra Test, 6:601 (3 reviews, 1 reference)
Second Year Algebra: Manchester Semester-End Achievement Tests, T:1010, 36:516
Tucker-Sanders First Year Algebra Test, 7:511
Votaw Algebra Test, 6:603 (3 reviews)

ARITHMETIC

[690]

A.C.E.R. Arithmetic Tests: Standardized for Use in New Zealand. Ages 9–12; 1957; identical with corresponding parts of *A.C.E.R. Arithmetic Tests* (see 4:398); 4 tests: addition, multiplication, subtraction, division; manual by A. E. Fieldhouse; New Zealand Council for Educational Research [New Zealand]. *

For additional information, see 5:453 (the 2 references listed for this test are incorrectly placed and are for 5:454).

REFERENCES THROUGH 1971

1. McCREARY, J. R. "Reading Tests With Maori Children." *N Zeal J Ed Studies* 1(1–2):40–50 '66. *

CUMULATIVE NAME INDEX

McCreary, J. R.: 1

Orleans-Hanna Algebra Prognosis Test

[691]

A.C.E.R. Number Test. Ages 13.5 and over; 1942–55; 1964 test identical with test copyrighted 1952; 1962 manual identical with manual published 1955; manual by D. Spearritt; Australian Council for Educational Research [Australia]. *

For additional information, see 5:454; for a review by Leslie M. Haynes of the original edition, see 4:399.

REFERENCES THROUGH 1971

1. HOHNE, H. H. *Success and Failure in Scientific Faculties of the University of Melbourne.* Melbourne, Australia: Australian Council for Educational Research, 1955. Pp. vii, 129. * (*PA* 31:3787)
2. BUCKLOW, MAXINE, AND DOUGHTY, PATRICIA. "The Use of Aptitude Tests in Clerical Employment: The Selection of Accounting Machinists." *Personnel Prac B* (Australia) 13: 35–44 S '57. * (*PA* 33:2256)

CUMULATIVE NAME INDEX

Bucklow, M.: 2
Doughty, P.: 2

Haynes, L. M.: *rev*, 4:399
Hohne, H. H.: 1

[692]

★**Adston Diagnostic Instruments in Elementary School Mathematics: Whole Numbers.** Grades 4–8; 1971; 9 tests: survey test plus 2 tests (facts, operations) for addition, subtraction, multiplication, division; Sam Adams and Leslie Ellis; Adston Educational Enterprises, Inc. *

[693]

American Numerical Test. Adults in "that great middle and upper middle block of vocations which emphasize shop and white collar skills involving number competence"; 1962; John J. McCarty; Psychometric Affiliates. *

For additional information and reviews by Marvin D. Glock and Richard T. Johnson, see 6:604.

[694]

American School Achievement Tests: Arithmetic Readiness. Grades kgn–1; 1941–55; identical with the numbers subtest of the Primary Battery I of *American School Achievement Tests;* Robert V. Young, Willis E. Pratt, and Frank Gatto; Bobbs-Merrill Co., Inc. *
For the complete battery entry, see 4.

For additional information and a review by Harold E. Moser, see 5:455. For reviews of the complete battery, see 6:2 (2 reviews), 5:1 (2 reviews), 4:1 (1 review), and 3:1 (2 reviews).

[695]

American School Achievement Tests: Part 2, Arithmetic. Grades 2–3, 4–6, 7–9; 1941–63; 3 scores: computation, problems, total; 1955–57 tests identical with tests copyrighted 14 years earlier except for format; Willis E. Pratt, Robert V. Young, and Clara E. Cockerille (manuals); Bobbs-Merrill Co., Inc. * For the complete battery entry, see 4.

For additional information, see 6:605 (1 reference); for reviews by Joseph Justman and J. Fred Weaver, see 5:456. For reviews of the complete battery, see 6:2 (2 reviews), 5:1 (2 reviews), 4:1 (1 review), and 3:1 (2 reviews).

REFERENCES THROUGH 1971

1. See 6:605.

CUMULATIVE NAME INDEX

Cleland, D. L.: 1
Justman, J.: *rev*, 5:456

Toussaint, I. H.: 1
Weaver, J. F.: *rev*, 5:456

[696]

Analytical Survey Test in Computational Arithmetic. Grades 7–12; 1930–57; H. C. Christofferson and W. S. Guiler; Bobbs-Merrill Co., Inc. *

For additional information and a review by Emma Spaney, see 5:457.

REFERENCES THROUGH 1971

1. GUILER, W. S. "Forecasting Achievement in Elementary Algebra." *J Ed Res* 38:25–53 S '44. * (*PA* 19:799)
2. GUILER, WALTER SCRIBNER. "Difficulties Encountered by College Freshmen in Fractions." *J Ed Res* 39:102–15 O '45. *
3. GUILER, WALTER SCRIBNER. "Difficulties Encountered by College Freshmen in Decimals." *J Ed Res* 40:1–13 S '46. * (*PA* 21:280)

CUMULATIVE NAME INDEX

Guiler, W. S.: 1–3   Spaney, E.: *rev,* 5:457

[697]

Arithmetic Computation: Public School Achievement Tests. Grades 3–8; 1928–59; Jacob S. Orleans; Bobbs-Merrill Co., Inc. * For the complete battery entry, see 28.

For additional information, see 6:606. For reviews of the complete battery, see 2:1194 (2 reviews).

[698]

Arithmetic Reasoning: Public School Achievement Tests. Grades 3–8; 1928–59; Jacob S. Orleans; Bobbs-Merrill Co., Inc. * For the complete battery entry, see 28.

For additional information, see 6:612. For reviews of the complete battery, see 2:1194 (2 reviews).

REFERENCES THROUGH 1971

1. TREACY, JOHN P. "The Relationship of Reading Skills to the Ability to Solve Arithmetic Problems." *J Ed Res* 38:86–96 O '44. * (*PA* 19:809)

CUMULATIVE NAME INDEX

Treacy, J. P.: 1

[699]

Arithmetic Reasoning Test: [Personnel Research Institute Clerical Battery]. Clerical applicants and high school; 1948; Jay L. Otis and David J. Chesler; Personnel Research Institute. * For the complete battery entry, see 2140.

For additional information, see 4:403. For reviews of the complete battery, see 4:729 (2 reviews).

[700]

Arithmetic Test (Fundamentals and Reasoning): Municipal Tests: National Achievement Tests. Grades 3–6, 6–8; 1938–56; subtest of *Municipal Battery;* Robert K. Speer and Samuel Smith; Psychometric Affiliates. *

For additional information, see 5:463; for reviews by Foster E. Grossnickle and Charles S. Ross, see 4:406. For reviews of the complete battery, see 5:18 (1 review), 4:20 (1 review), and 2:1191 (2 reviews).

[701]

Arithmetic Test: National Achievement Tests. Grades 3–8; 1936–61; 2 tests; no manual; Robert K. Speer and Samuel Smith; Psychometric Affiliates. *
a) FUNDAMENTALS. 1938–61; 4 scores: fundamentals-speed, number comparisons, fundamentals-skills, total; 1958–60 tests identical with tests copyrighted 1938.
b) REASONING. 1936–60; 5 scores: comparisons, problem analysis, finding problem key, problems, total; 1950 and 1954 tests identical with tests copyrighted 1938 except for 1 item.

For additional information, see 6:613; for reviews by R. L. Morton and Leroy H. Schnell, see 2:1449; for reviews by William A. Brownell and W. J. Osburn, see 1:889.

[702]

*****Arithmetic Tests EA2A and EA4.** Ages 14.5 and over; 1947–72; subtest of *N.I.I.P. Engineering Appren-*

tice Selection Test Battery; arithmetic attainment; 2 tests; National Institute of Industrial Psychology; NFER Publishing Co. Ltd. [England]. * For the complete battery entry, see 2345.
a) TEST EA2A. 1947–71; decimalized version of *Test EA2;* also referred to as *Engineering Arithmetic Test 2;* 1971 test identical with test copyrighted 1947 except for 1 revised item.
b) TEST EA4. 1972; metricated version of *a*; no manual.

For additional information concerning Test EA2, see 7:1096d.

[703]

*****Arithmetical Problems: Test A/68.** Job applicants with at least 10 years of education; 1955–62; 1962 test identical with 1955 edition except for revision of 9 items involving sterling notation; test in English and Afrikaans; no manual; National Institute for Personnel Research [South Africa]. *

[704]

Basic Skills in Arithmetic Test. Grades 6–12; 1945; William L. Wrinkle, Juanita Sanders, and Elizabeth H. Kendel; Science Research Associates, Inc. *

For additional information and reviews by Jacob S. Orleans and F. Lynwood Wren, see 3:335.

REFERENCES THROUGH 1971

1. PETRO, PETER K. *Student Aptitudes and Abilities Correlated With Achievement in First Semester High School Bookkeeping.* Master's thesis, Iowa State Teachers College (Cedar Falls, Iowa), 1957.

CUMULATIVE NAME INDEX

Orleans, J. S.: *rev,* 3:335   Wren, F. L.: *rev,* 3:335
Petro, P. K.: 1

[705]

Bobbs-Merrill Arithmetic Achievement Tests. Grades 1, 2, 3, 4, 5, 6, 7, 8–9; 1963; 3 scores: concepts and problems, computation, total; William E. Kline and Harry J. Baker; Bobbs-Merrill Co., Inc. *

For additional information and a review by C. Alan Riedesel, see 7:513.

[706]

A Brief Survey of Arithmetic Skills, Revised Edition. Grades 7–12; 1947–53; 3 scores: computation, reasoning, total; Arthur E. Traxler; Bobbs-Merrill Co., Inc. *

For additional information and a review by H. Vernon Price, see 5:467 (1 reference); for reviews by William A. Brownell and Henry Van Engen of the original edition, see 4:409.

REFERENCES THROUGH 1971

1. See 5:467.
2. TRAXLER, ARTHUR E. "An Analysis of the Results of a Brief Survey of Arithmetic Skills Among Independent-School Pupils." *Ed Rec B* 49:59–67 F '48. * (*PA* 22:3281)

CUMULATIVE NAME INDEX

Brownell, W. A.: *rev,* 4:409   Traxler, A. E.: 1–2
Price, H. V.: *rev,* 5:467   Van Engen, H.: *rev,* 4:409

[707]

*****Comprehensive Tests of Basic Skills: Arithmetic.** Grades 2.5–4, 4–6, 6–8, 8–12; 1968–71; 4 scores: computation, concepts, applications, total; CTB/McGraw-Hill. * For the complete battery entry, see 11.

For additional information and reviews by Jack Price and C. Alan Riedesel, see 7:514. For reviews of the complete battery, see 7:9 (2 reviews, 3 excerpts).

REFERENCES THROUGH 1971

1. AL-NASSER, BHANI VISISSOBHA. *The Relationship Between the Cultural Background of Disadvantaged Children and Their*

Performance on an Arithmetic Test. Doctor's thesis, Ohio State University (Columbus, Ohio), 1971. (*DAI* 32:6281A)

CUMULATIVE NAME INDEX

Al-Nasser, B. V.: 1   Riedesel, C. A.: *rev*, 7:514
Price, J.: *rev*, 7:514

[708]

Computation Test A/67. Job applicants with at least 6 years of education; 1956–63; multiplication; National Institute for Personnel Research [South Africa]. *
For additional information, see 6:618.

[709]

Cooperative Mathematics Tests: Arithmetic. Grades 7–9; 1962–65; Cooperative Tests and Services. *
For additional information and a review by Alan R. Osborne, see 7:515 (2 references); for a review by O. F. Anderhalter, see 6:607. For excerpted reviews by John R. Hills and Jack C. Merwin of the series, see 7:465.

REFERENCES THROUGH 1971

1–2. See 7:515.
3. DIELMAN, T. E.; BARTON, K.; AND CATTELL, R. B. "The Prediction of Junior High School Achievement From Objective Motivation Tests." *Personality* 2(4):279–87 w '71. * (*PA* 48:7881)
4. MAZUR, JAMES MATTHEW. *A Study of Predictive Validity of Standardized Tests Used for Placement of Vocational Students at Rockingham Community College.* Master's thesis, North Carolina State University (Raleigh, N.C.), 1971.

CUMULATIVE NAME INDEX

Ali, M. B.: 1   Hills, J. R.: *exc*, 7:465
Anderhalter, O. F.: *rev*, 6:607   Mazur, J. M.: 4
Barton, K.: 3   Merwin, J. C.: *exc*, 7:465
Cahen, L. S.: 2   Osborne, A. R.: *rev*, 7:515
Cattell, R. B.: 3   Romberg, T. A.: 2
Dielman, T. E.: 3   Zwirner, W.: 2

[710]

*Cotswold Junior Arithmetic Ability Test. Ages 8.5–9.5, 9.5–10.5; 1949–70; 2 levels; C. M. Fleming; Robert Gibson & Sons, Glasgow, Ltd. [Scotland]. *
a) JUNIOR ARITHMETIC A AND B. *Out of print.*
b) JUNIOR ARITHMETIC C AND D. Ages 8.5–9.5; 1964–70, c1954–58.
c) JUNIOR ARITHMETIC E AND F. Ages 9.5–10.5; 1965–67, c1958–61.
For additional information and reviews by William Curr and George W. Sturrock of *a*, see 5:470.

[711]

*Cotswold Measurement of Ability: Arithmetic. Ages 10–12; 1947–68; C. M. Fleming; Robert Gibson & Sons, Glasgow, Ltd. [Scotland]. *
For additional information concerning earlier forms, see 5:471; for a review by W. L. Sumner, see 4:412.

[712]

*Diagnostic Arithmetic Tests. Standards 2–5 (ages 9–12); 1951–66; 9 tests in separate booklets: addition, subtraction, multiplication, division, money, weights and measures, fractions, decimals, percentages; Human Sciences Research Council [South Africa]. *
For additional information, see 6:619.

[713]

Diagnostic Chart for Fundamental Processes in Arithmetic. Grades 2–8; 1925; G. T. Buswell and Lenore John; Bobbs-Merrill Co., Inc. *
For additional information and a review by Leo J. Brueckner, see 4:413; for reviews by H. E. Benz and Foster E. Grossnickle, see 2:1456.

REFERENCES THROUGH 1971

1. See 2:1456.
2. SCHILLER, BELLE. "Verbal, Numerical and Spatial Abilities of Young Children." *Arch Psychol* 161:1–69 Mr '34. * (*PA* 8:3874)

3. CRUICKSHANK, WILLIAM M. "Arithmetic Work Habits of Mentally Retarded Boys." *Am J Mental Def* 52:318–30 Ap '48. * (*PA* 22:5123)

CUMULATIVE NAME INDEX

Benz, H. E.: *rev*, 2:1456   Grossnickle, F. E.: *rev*, 2:1456
Brueckner, L. J.: *rev*, 4:413   John, L.: 1
Buswell, G. T.: 1   Schiller, B.: 2
Cruickshank, W. M.: 3

[714]

★Diagnostic Decimal Tests. Ages 9–12, 10–12, 10–13; 1966; 3 tests; E. W. Seville; Australian Council for Educational Research [Australia]. *
a) DIAGNOSTIC DECIMAL TESTS 1. Ages 9–12; addition and subtraction.
b) DIAGNOSTIC DECIMAL TESTS 2. Ages 10–12; simple multiplication and simple division.
c) DIAGNOSTIC DECIMAL TESTS 3. Ages 10–13; long multiplication and long division.

[715]

Diagnostic Fractions Test 3. Ages 7–11; 1957–66; E. W. Seville; Australian Council for Educational Research [Australia]. *
For additional information, see 7:516.

[716]

Diagnostic Number Tests 1–2. Ages 8–11, 9–12; 1951–66; formerly called *Diagnostic Arithmetic Tests 1–2*; 2 tests; 1966 tests identical with tests published 1951; E. W. Seville; Australian Council for Educational Research [Australia]. *
a) TEST 1. Ages 8–11.
b) TEST 2. Ages 9–12.
For additional information, see 7:517.

[717]

Diagnostic Tests and Self-Helps in Arithmetic. Grades 3–12; 1955; Leo J. Brueckner; CTB/McGraw-Hill. *
a) SCREENING TESTS. Grades 4–6, 5–6, 6, 7 and over.
b) DIAGNOSTIC TESTS. Grades 3, 4, 5, 6, 7.
For additional information and a review by Harold E. Moser, see 5:472.

[718]

*ERB Modern Arithmetic Test. Grades 5–6; 1969–71; no manual; Educational Records Bureau. *
For additional information, see 7:518.

[719]

Emporia Arithmetic Tests. Grades 1, 2–3, 4–6, 7–8; 1962–64; first published 1962–63 in the Every Pupil Scholarship Test series; 4 tests; M. W. Sanders, Ieleen Engelson (manual, *d*), Ruth Otterstrom (manual, *c*), and Patricia M. Pease (manual, *a, b*); Bureau of Educational Measurements. *
a) EMPORIA PRIMARY ARITHMETIC TEST. I, 2 semesters in grade 1.
b) EMPORIA ELEMENTARY ARITHMETIC TEST. I, 2 semesters in grades 2–3.
c) EMPORIA INTERMEDIATE ARITHMETIC TEST. I, 2 semesters in grades 4–6.
d) EMPORIA JUNIOR HIGH SCHOOL ARITHMETIC TEST. I, 2 semesters in grades 7–8.
For additional information and reviews by Marilyn N. Suydam and Blaine R. Worthen, see 7:519.

[720]

Kelvin Measurement of Ability in Arithmetic. Ages 7–12; 1933; C. M. Fleming; Robert Gibson & Sons, Glasgow, Ltd. [Scotland]. *
For additional information, see 1:891.

Comprehensive Tests of Basic Skills: Arithmetic

[721]

★**KeyMath Diagnostic Arithmetic Test.** Grades kgn–7; 1972, c1971; 15 scores: content (numeration, fractions, geometry and symbols), operations (addition, subtraction, multiplication, division, mental computation, numerical reasoning), applications (word problems, missing elements, money, measurement, time), total; Austin J. Connolly, William Nachtman, and E. Milo Pritchett; American Guidance Service, Inc. *

[722]

Moray House Arithmetic Test. Ages 10–12; 1935–69; form 43; earlier forms (1–42) are out of print; distribution restricted to education authorities; Godfrey Thomson Unit for Educational Research, University of Edinburgh; University of London Press Ltd. [England]. *

For additional information, see 7:521; see also 6:628 (9 references); for a review by John Cohen of earlier forms, see 3:346.

REFERENCES THROUGH 1971

1–9. See 6:628.
10. DOCKRELL, W. B. "The Relationship Between Socio-Economic Status, Intelligence and Attainment in Some Scottish Primary Schools." *Indian Psychol B* 4:1–6 Ja '59. * (*PA* 37:4715)
11. MANLEY, D. R. "Mental Ability in Jamaica: (An Examination of the Performance of Children in the Jamaican Common Entrance Examination. 1959)." *Social & Econ Studies* (Jamaica) 12:51–71 Mr '63. * (*PA* 38:767)
12. HALLWORTH, H. J. "Personality Ratings of Adolescents: A Study in a Comprehensive School." *Brit J Ed Psychol* 34:171–7 Je '64. * (*PA* 39:3180)
13. HOROBIN, GORDON; OLDMAN, DAVID; AND BYTHEWAY, BILL. "The Social Differentiation of Ability." *Sociology* 1:113–29 My '67. *
14. NISBET, J. D., AND ENTWISTLE, N. J. "Intelligence and Family Size, 1949–1965." *Brit J Ed Psychol* 37:188–93 Je '67. * (*PA* 41:15274)

CUMULATIVE NAME INDEX

Buchan, J.: 9
Bytheway, B.: 13
Cohen, J.: *rev*, 3:346
Dockrell, W. B.: 10
Emmett, W. G.: 6, 8
Entwistle, N. J.: 14
Hallworth, H. J.: 12
Horobin, G.: 13
Lambert, C. M.: 3
Manley, D. R.: 11
Nisbet, J.: 9
Nisbet, J. D.: 14
Oldman, D.: 13
Pilliner, A. E. G.: 4
Sutherland, J.: 5, 7
Thomson, G. H.: 1–2
Wilmut, F. S.: 6

[723]

★**The Moreton Arithmetic Tests.** Grades 6–7; 1967; MAT; 2 tests; R. G. Cochrane and R. J. Andrews; Teaching and Testing Resources [Australia]. *
a) FORM M [MECHANICAL ARITHMETIC].
b) FORM P [PROBLEM ARITHMETIC].

REFERENCES THROUGH 1971

1. COCHRANE, R. G.; ELKINS, J.; AND RICHMOND, DAWN M. "Analysis of Fourth Grade Testing." *Slow Learning Child* (Australia) 16(3):131–42 N '69. * (*PA* 44:18351)

CUMULATIVE NAME INDEX

Cochrane, R. G.: 1
Elkins, J.: 1
Richmond, D. M.: 1

[724]

N.B. Arithmetic Tests. Standards 2–3 (ages 9–11), 4–5 (ages 11–13), 6–8 (ages 13–15); 1961–63; 4 scores: ready knowledge, fundamentals, mechanical computations and problems, total; Human Sciences Research Council [South Africa]. *

For additional information, see 6:629.

[725]

Number Test DE. Ages 10.5–12.5; 1965; formerly called *Number Test 1;* E. L. Barnard; published for the National Foundation for Educational Research in England and Wales; Ginn & Co. Ltd. [England]. *

For additional information, see 7:522.

[726]

*****Office Arithmetic Test: ETSA Test 2A.** Job applicants; 1960–72, c1957–59; manual and technical handbook by S. Trevor Hadley and George A. W. Stouffer, Jr.; test by Psychological Services Bureau; Educators'-Employers' Tests & Services Associates. * For the complete battery entry, see 2106.

For reviews of the complete battery, see 6:1025 (2 reviews).

[727]

RBH Arithmetic Fundamentals Test. Business and industry; 1951–63; Richardson, Bellows, Henry & Co., Inc. *

For additional information and a review by John W. Lombard, see 7:523.

[728]

The RBH Arithmetic Reasoning Test. Business and industry; 1948–63; Richardson, Bellows, Henry & Co., Inc. *

For additional information and a review by John W. Lombard, see 7:524.

[729]

RBH Shop Arithmetic Test. Industry; 1948–63; Richardson, Bellows, Henry & Co., Inc. *

For additional information and a review by John W. Lombard, see 7:525; see also 6:636 (2 references).

REFERENCES THROUGH 1971

1–2. See 6:636.
3. SPARKS, CHARLES P. "Validity of Psychological Tests." *Personnel Psychol* 23(1):39–46 sp '70. * (*PA* 44:17556)

CUMULATIVE NAME INDEX

Cuomo, S.: 1–2
Lombard, J. W.: *rev*, 7:525
Meyer, H. H.: 2
Sparks, C. P.: 3

[730]

Revised Southend Attainment Test in Mechanical Arithmetic. Ages 7–15; 1939–50; manual discontinued; M. E. Hebron; George G. Harrap & Co. Ltd. [England]. * For the earlier edition entry, see 736.

For additional information, see 6:631.

[731]

SRA Achievement Series: Arithmetic. Grades 1–2, 2–4, 4–9; 1954–69; Forms C and D; more recent Forms E and F are not available as separates; 4 scores: concepts, reasoning, computation, total; Louis P. Thorpe, D. Welty Lefever, and Robert A. Naslund; Science Research Associates, Inc. * For the complete battery entry, see 29.
a) HAND SCORED EDITION. Grades 1–2, 2–4; 1955–68. *Out of print.*
b) MULTILEVEL EDITION. Grades 4–9; 1963–69.

For additional information and a review by Mary O. Folsom, see 7:526 (3 references); for a review by E. W. Hamilton of earlier forms, see 6:632 (1 reference); for reviews by Robert D. North and J. Fred Weaver, see 5:483. For reviews of the complete battery, see 7:18 (2 reviews), 6:21 (1 review), and 5:21 (2 reviews).

REFERENCES THROUGH 1971

1. See 6:632.
2–4. See 7:526.
5. WILLIAMSON, MALCOM L., AND HOPKINS, KENNETH D. "The Use of 'None-of-These' Versus Homogeneous Alternatives on Multiple-Choice Tests: Experimental Reliability and Validity Comparisons." *J Ed Meas* 4:53–8 su '67. *
6. FLEISCHMAN, HOWARD L.; ORR, DAVID B.; AND STRASEL, H. C. "Relationships Between the Subtests of Six Achievement Test Batteries." Abstract. *Proc 79th Ann Conv Am Psychol Assn* 6(1):109–10 '71. * (*PA* 46:3727)

[732-3]

SRA Arithmetic Index. Job applicants with poor educational backgrounds; 1968; Science Research Associates, Inc. *

For additional information and a review by Dorothy C. Adkins of this test and the *SRA Reading Index,* see 7:20.

[734]

Schonell Diagnostic Arithmetic Tests. Ages 7–13; 1936–57; 12 scores: combinations (addition, subtraction, multiplication, division, miscellaneous), graded addition, graded subtraction, graded multiplication, graded simple division, graded long division (2 tests), graded mental arithmetic; Fred J. Schonell; Oliver & Boyd [Scotland]. *

For additional information and a review by John Sutherland, see 5:485 (1 reference); see also 3:350 (1 reference); for a review by C. Ebblewhite Smith of an earlier edition, see 2:1461 (2 references).

REFERENCES THROUGH 1971
1-2. See 2:1461.
3. See 3:350.
4. See 5:485.

[735]

***Seeing Through Arithmetic Tests.** Grades 1, 2, 3, 4, 5, 6; 1960–69; STAT; intended for use with the text of the same title; Maurice L. Hartung, Henry Van Engen, E. Glenadine Gibb, James E. Stochl, Lois Knowles, and Ray Walch; Scott, Foresman & Co. *
a) GRADES 1–2. 1966; 3 scores: concepts and applications, basic facts, total.
b) GRADES 3–6. 1960–69; 7 scores: selecting answers, computation, selecting sentences, finding solutions, information, concepts, total.

For additional information and a review by William H. Lucio of an earlier edition of *b*, see 6:635.

[736]

Southend Attainment Test in Mechanical Arithmetic. Ages 6–7, 7–8, 8–9, 9–10, 10–11, 11–12, 12–13, 13–14; 1939; M. E. Hebron; George G. Harrap & Co. Ltd. [England]. * For the revised edition entry, see 730.

For additional information and a review by Stephen Wiseman, see 3:352.

REFERENCES THROUGH 1971
1. HILL, M. E. *The Education of Backward Children.* London: George G. Harrap & Co. Ltd., 1939. Pp. 174. * (*PA* 14:3735)

[737]

The Staffordshire Arithmetic Test. Ages 7–15; 1938–58; identical in part with *Revised Southend Attainment Test in Mechanical Arithmetic;* M. E. Hebron; George G. Harrap & Co. Ltd. [England]. *
For additional information, see 5:486.

[738]

Stanford Diagnostic Arithmetic Test. Grades 2.5–4.5, 4.5–8.5; 1966–68; SDAT; 2 levels; Leslie S. Beatty,

Richard Madden, and Eric F. Gardner; Harcourt Brace Jovanovich, Inc. *
a) LEVEL 1. Grades 2.5–4.5; 13 scores grouped in 3 categories: concepts (number system and counting, operations, decimal place value, total), computation (A—addition, B—subtraction, C—multiplication, D—division, A + B for grade 3 or A + B + C + D for grade 4), number facts (addition, subtraction, multiplication, division).
b) LEVEL 2. Grades 4.5–8.5; 16 scores grouped in 5 categories: concepts (number system and operations, decimal place value, total), computation (addition and subtraction, multiplication, division, total), common fractions (understanding, computation, total), decimal fractions and percent, number facts (addition, subtraction, multiplication, division, carrying).

For additional information and a review by W. Todd Rogers, see 7:528.

[739]

Survey Tests of Arithmetic Fundamentals: Dominion Tests. Grades 3–5, 5–8; 1957–58; 2 levels; Department of Educational Research, Ontario College of Education, University of Toronto; distributed by Guidance Centre [Canada]. *
a) GRADES 3–5. 7 scores: addition, subtraction, multiplication, division, measurement, fractions, total.
b) GRADES 5–8. 5 scores: whole numbers, fractions, decimals and percentage, measurement, total.

For additional information and a review by Frances E. Crook, see 5:488.

[740]

Test A/8: Arithmetic. Technical college students and applicants for clerical and trade positions with 8–12 years of education; 1943–57; National Institute for Personnel Research [South Africa]. *
For additional information, see 6:639.

REFERENCES THROUGH 1971
1. BEEZHOLD, F. W. "The Use of the Second Language as a Medium for a Mathematical Achievement and a Scientific Information Test." *B Nat Inst Pers Res* (South Africa) 3:9–18 D '51. * (*PA* 27:1456)
2. SUTTON, R. V., AND MITCHELL, L. "Preliminary Report on the Validation of Aptitude Tests for the Selection of Articled Clerks." *B Nat Inst Pers Res* (South Africa) 3:4–13 F '51. * (*PA* 27:1488)

[741]

Watson Number-Readiness Test, Fifth Edition. Grades kgn–1; 1963; 6 scores: subjective test (teacher's ratings of social, emotional, and psychological readiness, total), objective test, total; G. Milton Watson; Book Society of Canada Ltd. [Canada]. *
For additional information, see 7:529.

[Out of Print Since TIP I]

A.C.E.R. Arithmetic Tests, 4:398
Analytical Scales of Attainment: Arithmetic, 2:1447 (3 reviews)
Arithmetic Essentials Test, 5:458 (3 reviews)
Arithmetic: Every Pupil Scholarship Test, 6:608
Arithmetic: Every Pupil Test, 6:609
Arithmetic Fundamentals Test, 7:512
Arithmetic: Northumberland Standardised Tests, T: 1026
Arithmetic Progress Test, 6:610 (2 reviews)
Arithmetic Reasoning, 3:331 (1 review)
Arithmetic: Seven Plus Assessment, 4:404 (1 review)

Arithmetic Test: Fundamental Operations: Dominion Tests, 5:462 (2 reviews)
Arithmetic: Thanet Mental Tests, 2:1450 (2 reviews)
Basic Arithmetic Skills: Iowa Every-Pupil Tests of Basic Skills, 4:408 (2 reviews)
Basic Number Skills Test for Employee Selection (status unknown), 5:466 (2 reviews)
Brueckner Diagnostic Arithmetic Test in Decimals; in Fractions; in Whole Numbers, 4:410 (1 review)
Cardall Arithmetic Reasoning Test (status unknown), 6:617 (1 review)
Clapp-Young Arithmetic Test, 3:339 (1 review)
Commercial Arithmetic: Manchester Semester-End Achievement Tests, T:1046, 36:532
Commercial Arithmetic Test: State High School Tests for Indiana, 4:448
Coordinated Scales of Attainment: Arithmetic, 5:469
Diagnostic Tests in Arithmetic Fundamentals: Dominion Tests, 5:473 (2 reviews)
Diagnostic Tests in Money, 6:620 (2 reviews)
Diagnostic Tests in Vulgar Fractions, Decimal Fractions and Percentages, 5:474 (1 review)
Essential Mechanical Arithmetic Test, 3:342a (2 reviews)
Essential Problem Arithmetic Test, 3:342b (2 reviews)
Gilbert Business Arithmetic, 4:450 (1 review)
Group Test of Speed and Accuracy in Arithmetic Computation: Dominion Tests, 5:477 (2 reviews)
Hundred Problem Arithmetic Test, 3:344 (1 review, 1 excerpt, 2 references) ; see also 2:1462 (1 review)
Intermediate Diagnostic Arithmetic Test, 6:621 (1 review)
Kansas Arithmetic Test, 2:1457 (2 reviews)
Kansas Primary Arithmetic Test, 2:1458 (2 reviews)
Lee-Clark Arithmetic Fundamentals Survey Test, 3:345 (2 reviews)
Los Angeles Diagnostic Tests: Fundamentals of Arithmetic, 6:622 ; *Reasoning in Arithmetic*, 6:623
Madden-Peak Arithmetic Computation Test, 6:624 (2 reviews)
Manchester Mechanical Arithmetic Test (Sen.) 1, 7:520 (1 review)
Mechanical Arithmetic Tests, 6:626 (2 reviews)
Milne Arithmetic Test, 5:479
Moray House Arithmetic Test (Adv.), 6:628c
Moray House Junior Arithmetic Test, 6:628a
New York Test of Arithmetical Meanings, 5:480 (1 review)
Number Fact Check Sheet, 4:417 (1 review)
Oral Diagnostic Test in Addition: Dominion Tests, 3:348 (1 review)
Otis Arithmetic Reasoning Test, T:1078
Primary Arithmetic: Every Pupil Scholarship Test, 6:630
Readiness and Achievement Tests in Arithmetic, T:1080
Scholastic Achievement Series: Arithmetic, 6:633 (2 reviews)
Schrammel-Otterstrom Arithmetic Test, 6:634 (1 review)
Speed and Diagnostic Tests of Arithmetic (status unknown), T:1088
Survey of Arithmetic Achievement: California Survey Series, 6:638 (2 reviews)
Tiedeman Arithmetical Knowledge and Information Test, 5:490 (1 review)
Understanding the Meanings in Arithmetic: A Diagnostic Test, 6:641 (2 reviews, 2 references)
Wilson General Survey Tests in Arithmetic, T:1098
Wilson Inventory and Diagnostic Tests in Arithmetic, T:1099
Wirral Mechanical Arithmetic Tests (status unknown), 6:642 (1 review)

CALCULUS

[742]

*Advanced Placement Examination in Mathematics. High school students desiring credit for college level courses or admission to advanced courses; 1954–73; available to secondary schools for annual administration on specified days in May; inactive forms are available to colleges for local administration in the *Testing Academic Achievement* program; 2 levels; program administered for the College Entrance Examination Board by Educational Testing Service. * For the testing program entry, see 1045.

a) CALCULUS AB. Equivalent of 1 semester college calculus.

b) CALCULUS BC. Equivalent of 1 year college calculus.

For additional information concerning earlier forms, see 7:451 (2 references) ; see also 6:570 (4 references) ; for a review by Paul L. Dressel, see 5:419. For reviews of the testing program, see 7:662 (2 reviews).

REFERENCES THROUGH 1971

1–4. See 6:570.
5–6. See 7:451.
7. FINKBEINER, DANIEL T.; NEFF, JOHN D.; AND WILLIAMS, S. IRENE. "The Advanced Placement Examinations in Mathematics—Complete and Unexpurgated." *Math Teach* 64(6): 499–516 O '71. *

CUMULATIVE NAME INDEX

Douglas, E. C.: 1	Grossman, G.: 4
Dressel, P. L.: *rev*, 5:419	Neff, J. D.: 7
Finkbeiner, D. T.: 7	Ralston, N. C.: 5
Francis, R. L.: 6	Valley, J. R.: 2
Gilbert, A. C. F.: 3	Williams, S. I.: 7

[743]

*CLEP Subject Examination in Introductory Calculus. 1 year or equivalent; 1964–73; for college accreditation of nontraditional study, advanced placement, or assessment of educational achievement; tests administered monthly at centers throughout the United States; program administered for the College Entrance Examination Board by Educational Testing Service. * For the testing program entry, see 1050.

For additional information, see 7:530. For reviews of the testing program, see 7:664 (3 reviews).

[744]

Cooperative Mathematics Tests: Calculus. High school and college; 1963–65; Cooperative Tests and Services. *

For additional information and reviews by William E. Kline and G. Edith Robinson, see 7:531. For excerpted reviews by John R. Hills and Jack C. Merwin of the series, see 7:465.

GEOMETRY

[745]

Cooperative Mathematics Tests: Analytic Geometry. High school and college; 1963–65; Cooperative Tests and Services. *

For additional information and a review by L. Ray Carry, see 7:532. For excerpted reviews by John R. Hills and Jack C. Merwin of the series, see 7:465.

[746]

Cooperative Mathematics Tests: Geometry. Grades 10–12; 1962–65; 2 scores: Part 1 (Euclidean geometry), total; Cooperative Tests and Services. *

For additional information and a review by Evan D. Shull, see 7:533 (2 references) ; see also 6:645 (1 reference). For excerpted reviews by John R. Hills and Jack C. Merwin of the series, see 7:465.

REFERENCES THROUGH 1971
1. See 6:645.
2–3. See 7:533.

CUMULATIVE NAME INDEX

Ali, M. B.: 2   North, R. D.: 3
Hills, J. R.: *exc*, 7:465   Shull, E. D.: *rev*, 7:533
Merwin, J. C.: *exc*, 7:465   Traxler, A. E.: 1

[747]

Diagnostic Test in Basic Geometry. 1, 2 years high school; 1962; John H. Henshaw; Australian Council for Educational Research [Australia]. *
For additional information, see 6:644.

[748-9]

Geometry (Including Plane and Solid Geometry): Minnesota High School Achievement Examinations. High school; 1969–71; a new, revised, or previously inactive form issued each May; in 1969 this test replaced the plane geometry (see 756) and solid geometry (see 758) test in the same series; Form GJ Rev ('70, some tests have 1973 copyright) used in 1970 and 1973 testings; edited by V. L. Lohmann; American Guidance Service, Inc. *
For additional information, see 7:534.

[750]

Howell Geometry Test. Grades 9–12; 1969; Edgar N. Howell; Harcourt Brace Jovanovich, Inc. *
For additional information and reviews by Dorothy L. Jones and John Wagner, see 7:536.

[751]

Iowa Geometry Aptitude Test, Third Edition. High school; 1935–69; IGAT; revision of *Iowa Plane Geometry Aptitude Test;* James Maxey and Darrell Sabers; Bureau of Educational Research and Service. *
For additional information and a review by Lynnette B. Plumlee, see 7:537 (2 references); for a review by Philip H. DuBois of an earlier edition, see 3:360; for reviews by Edward E. Cureton and Charles C. Weidemann, see 2:1469.

REFERENCES THROUGH 1971
1–2. See 7:537.
3. HOHMAN, MARIE. *The Comparative Value of Three Geometry Prognosis Tests and an Arithmetic Achievement Test in Predicting Success in Plane Geometry.* Master's thesis, Catholic University of America (Washington, D.C.), 1959. (Abstract: *Cath Ed R* 59:621)
4. BRISTOL, JOHN L. *A Study of the Predictive Validity of the Iowa Plane Geometry Aptitude Test, as Used in Elgin, Illinois.* Master's thesis, Northern Illinois University (DeKalb, Ill.), 1961.

CUMULATIVE NAME INDEX

Bristol, J. L.: 4   Hohman, M.: 3
Cureton, E. E.: *rev*, 2:1469 Plumlee, L. B.: *rev*, 7:537
DuBois, P. H.: *rev*, 3:360   Weidemann, C. C.: *rev*, 2:
Hanna, G. S.: 1–2   1469

[752]

Mid-Year Geometry Test. High school; 1968; Harcourt Brace Jovanovich, Inc. *
For additional information and a review by Evan D. Shull, see 7:538.

[753]

★**Modern Geometry Test: Content Evaluation Series.** Grades 10–12; 1971; Gerald S. Hanna; Houghton Mifflin Co. *

[754]

★**Objective Tests in Mathematics: Geometry.** Ages 15 and over; 1970; no manual; B. C. Erricker; University of London Press Ltd. [England]. *

[755]

Orleans-Hanna Geometry Prognosis Test. Grades 8–11; 1929–68; revision of *Orleans Geometry Prognosis Test;* Joseph B. Orleans and Gerald S. Hanna; Harcourt Brace Jovanovich, Inc. *
For additional information and a review by Lynnette B. Plumlee, see 7:539 (4 references); for reviews by Edward E. Cureton and Charles C. Weidemann of the original edition, see 2:1471 (3 references).

REFERENCES THROUGH 1971
1–3. See 2:1471.
4–5. See 4:427.
6–9. See 7:539.
10. HOHMAN, MARIE. *The Comparative Value of Three Geometry Prognosis Tests and an Arithmetic Achievement Test in Predicting Success in Plane Geometry.* Master's thesis, Catholic University of America (Washington, D.C.), 1959. (Abstract: *Cath Ed R* 59:621)
11. DAVIS, WENDELL R. *A Critical Evaluation of the Use of the Orleans Geometry Prognosis Test in the Lodi Union High School.* Master's thesis, College of the Pacific (Stockton, Calif.), 1960.
12. KIENLEN, JOSEPH S. *A Study to Predict the Success of Students in Plane Geometry in Worland High School, Worland, Wyoming.* Master's thesis, Fort Hays Kansas State College (Hays, Kan.), 1963.
13. HANNA, GERALD STANLEY. *An Investigation of Selected Ability, Aptitude, Interest, and Personality Characteristics Relevant to Success in High School Geometry.* Doctor's thesis, University of Southern California (Los Angeles, Calif.), 1965. (*DA* 26:3152)
14. LENKE, JOANNE M.; BLIGH, HAROLD F.; AND KANE, BERNARD H. "Cross-Validation of the Orleans-Hanna Algebra Prognosis Test and the Orleans-Hanna Geometry Prognosis Test." *Ed & Psychol Meas* 31(2):521–3 su '71. *

CUMULATIVE NAME INDEX

Bligh, H. F.: 14   Meyers, C. E.: 8
Caldwell, J. R.: 8   Michael, W. B.: 8
Cooke, D. H.: 2   Orleans, J. B.: 3
Crane, M. P.: 4   Pearson, M.: 2
Cureton, E. E.: *rev*, 2:1471   Perry, W. M.: 1
Davis, W. R.: 11   Plumlee, L. B.: *rev*, 7:539
Hanna, G. S.: 6–7, 9, 13   Roscoe, J. T.: 7
Hohman, M.: 10   Schrader, D. R.: 8
Kane, B. H.: 14   Uhrbrock, R. S.: 5
Kienlen, J. S.: 12   Weidemann, C. C.: *rev*, 2:
Lenke, J. M.: 9, 14   1471

[756]

Plane Geometry: Achievement Examinations for Secondary Schools. High school; 1951–68; a new, revised, or previously inactive form was issued each May from 1951 through 1968; Form 4 ('54) is the only form in print; this and the solid geometry test (see 758) in the same series were replaced in 1969 by *Geometry (Including Plane and Solid Geometry): Minnesota High School Achievement Examinations* (see 748); High School Achievement Examinations, Midwest High School Achievement Examinations, and Minnesota High School Achievement Examinations have also been used as series titles; Emil J. Berger; Bobbs-Merrill Co., Inc. *
For additional information concerning later and earlier forms, see 6:649 and 5:493; for a review by Harold P. Fawcett of Form A (1955), see 5:495.

[757]

Plane Geometry: National Achievement Tests. High school; 1958–70; 1970 test identical with test copyrighted 1958 except for cover page and format; Ray Webb and Julius H. Hlavaty; Psychometric Affiliates. *
For additional information and a review by Dorothy L. Jones, see 7:540.

[758]

*****Solid Geometry: Achievement Examinations for Secondary Schools.** High school; 1951–68; a new, revised, or previously inactive form was issued each

May from 1951 through 1968; Form 4 ('54) is the only form in print; this and the plane geometry test (see 756) were replaced in 1969 by *Geometry (Including Plane and Solid Geometry): Minnesota High School Achievement Examinations* (see 748); High School Achievement Examinations, Midwest High School Achievement Examinations, and Minnesota High School Achievement Examinations have also been used as series titles; Emil J. Berger; Bobbs-Merrill Co., Inc. *

For additional information concerning later and earlier forms, see 6:652 and 5:499–500.

[759]
Solid Geometry: National Achievement Tests. High school; 1958–60; 1960 test identical with test copyrighted 1958; Ray Webb and Julius H. Hlavaty (manual); Psychometric Affiliates. *

For additional information and a review by Sheldon S. Myers, see 6:653.

[Out of Print Since TIP I]
Ability for Geometry: Fife Tests of Ability, 3:356 (2 references)
American Council Solid Geometry Test, T:1101
Becker-Schrammel Plane Geometry, 2:1465 (2 reviews, 1 reference)
Cooperative Plane Geometry Test, 4:423 (6 reviews, 1 reference)
Cooperative Solid Geometry Test, 2:1468 (2 reviews)
Geometry Attainment Test, 4:424 (2 reviews)
Geometry: Every Pupil Test, 6:646
Geometry Survey Test, T:1107
Geometry Test, 7:535
Illinois Plane Geometry Test, 5:491 (1 review)
Lane-Greene Unit Tests in Plane Geometry, 4:426
Lee Test of Geometric Aptitude, 6:647 (4 reviews, 5 references)
Plane Geometry: Every Pupil Scholarship Test, 6:648
Plane Geometry: Manchester Semester-End Achievement Tests, T:1116, 36:686
Plane Geometry Test: Affiliation Testing Program for Catholic Secondary Schools, 6:651 (1 review)
Plane Geometry: 20th Century Test, 4:430
Schrammel-Reed Solid Geometry Test, 5:496 (1 review)
Seattle Plane Geometry Test, 5:497 (1 review)
Seattle Solid Geometry Test Series, T:1123
Shaycoft Plane Geometry Test, 5:498 (2 reviews)
Solid Geometry: Manchester Semester-End Achievement Tests, T:1126, 36:689
Solid Geometry Test: State High School Tests for Indiana, 4:435
Tucker-Sanders Plane Geometry Test, 7:541

SPECIAL FIELDS

[760]
★**Decimal Currency Test.** Primary and secondary school; 1969; published for the National Foundation for Educational Research in England and Wales; Ginn & Co. Ltd. [England]. *

[761]
★**NM Consumer Mathematics Test.** Grades 9–12; 1973; NMCMT; Monitor. *

TRIGONOMETRY

[762]
*****CLEP Subject Examination in Trigonometry.** 1 semester or equivalent; 1968–73; for college accreditation of nontraditional study, advanced placement, or assessment of educational achievement; tests administered monthly at centers throughout the United States; program administered for the College Entrance Examination Board by Educational Testing Service. * For the testing program entry, see 1050.

For additional information, see 7:542. For reviews of the testing program, see 7:664 (3 reviews).

[763]
Cooperative Mathematics Tests: Trigonometry. High school and college; 1962–65; Cooperative Tests and Services. *

For additional information and a review by Thomas A. Romberg, see 7:543. For excerpted reviews by John R. Hills and Jack C. Merwin of the series, see 7:465.

[764]
Plane Trigonometry: National Achievement Tests. Grades 10–16; 1958–60; 1960 test identical with test copyrighted 1959; Ray Webb and Julius H. Hlavaty; Psychometric Affiliates. *

For additional information, see 6:656.

[765]
*****Trigonometry: Minnesota High School Achievement Examinations.** High school; 1961–70; a new, revised, or previously inactive form issued each May; Midwest High School Achievement Examinations used as series title in 1961; Form GJ Rev ['70, same as Forms GJ ('67) and G ('64)] used in 1970 and 1973 testings; edited by V. L. Lohmann; American Guidance Service, Inc. *

For additional information concerning earlier forms, see 7:544 and 6:658.

[Out of Print Since TIP I]
American Council Trigonometry Test, 2:1473 (2 reviews)
Cooperative Plane Trigonometry Test, 4:438 (3 reviews, 1 reference)
Rasmussen Trigonometry Test, 5:501 (1 review)
Trigonometry: Manchester Semester-End Achievement Tests, T:1135
Trigonometry Test: State High School Tests for Indiana, 4:440

MISCELLANEOUS

[766]

Modern Photography Comprehension Test. Photography students; 1953–69; MPCT; revision of *What Do You Know About Photography?*; 1969 test essentially the same as test copyrighted 1953 except for format and 6 new items; Martin M. Bruce; Martin M. Bruce, Ph.D., Publishers. *

For additional information and a review by David P. Campbell, see 7:547.

[767]

★**NM Consumer Rights and Responsibilities Test.** Grades 9–12; 1973; NMCRRT; Monitor. *

AGRICULTURE

[768]

★**Agribusiness Achievement Test: Content Evaluation Series.** Grades 9–12; 1973; 4 scores: animal science, plant and soil science, mechanics, management; Roland L. Peterson, Leo M. Harvill, and James T. Horner; Houghton Mifflin Co. *

[Out of Print Since TIP I]

Agriculture: Every Pupil Scholarship Test, 6:659
Animal Husbandry Test: State High School Tests for Indiana, 3:365
Farm Shop Tools: State High School Tests for Indiana, 4:441 (1 review, 1 reference)

BLIND

[769]

Colorado Braille Battery: Literary Code Tests. Grades 1–2.5, 2–3.5, 3.5 and over; 1963–66; grade 2 braille; 3 levels; Richard W. Woodcock and Stanley E. Bourgeault; American Printing House for the Blind, Inc. *
a) LITERARY PRETEST. For selection of appropriate level of testing.
b) LITERARY BEGINNING TEST. Grades 1–2.5; 4 scores: letters, punctuation, word form, total.
c) LITERARY INTERMEDIATE TEST. Grades 2–3.5; 3 scores: punctuation, word form, total.
d) LITERARY ADVANCED TEST. Grades 3.5 and over; 3 scores: same as for *c.*

For additional information, see 7:549 (2 references).
REFERENCES THROUGH 1971
1–2. See 7:549.
CUMULATIVE NAME INDEX
Bourgeault, S. E.: 1–2   Woodcock, R. W.: 1–2

[770]

Colorado Braille Battery: Nemeth Code Tests. Grades 4–8, 9 and over; 1963–66; braille mathematics code; 2 levels; Richard W. Woodcock and Stanley E.

Bourgeault; American Printing House for the Blind, Inc. *
a) NEMETH BEGINNING TEST. Grades 4–8.
b) NEMETH INTERMEDIATE TEST. Grades 9 and over.
For additional information, see 7:550 (2 references).
REFERENCES THROUGH 1971
1–2. See 7:550.
CUMULATIVE NAME INDEX
Bourgeault, S. E.: 1–2   Woodcock, R. W.: 1–2

[771]

Lorimer Braille Recognition Test: A Test of Ability in Reading Braille Contractions. Students (ages 7–13) in grade 2 braille; 1962; John Lorimer; College of Teachers of the Blind [England]. *
For additional information, see 6:854 (1 reference).
REFERENCES THROUGH 1971
1. See 6:854.

[772]

Roughness Discrimination Test. Blind children in grades kgn–1; 1965; RDT; test of tactual ability for predicting Braille reading readiness; Carson Y. Nolan and June E. Morris; American Printing House for the Blind, Inc. *
For additional information, see 7:551 (4 references).
REFERENCES THROUGH 1971
1–4. See 7:551.
CUMULATIVE NAME INDEX
Morris, J. E.: 3–4   Roach, E. G.: 1
Nolan, C. Y.: 2–4

[773]

★**Stanford Multi-Modality Imagery Test.** Blind and partially sighted ages 16 and over; 1972, c1969; SMIT; "functional imagery ability of blind persons"; William L. Dauterman; American Foundation for the Blind, Inc. *

REFERENCES THROUGH 1971
1. SUINN, RICHARD M.; DAUTERMAN, W. L.; AND SHAPIRO, BERNICE. "The Stanford Multi-Modality Imagery Test for the Blind." *Rehabil Counsel B* 10:23–7 S '66. *
CUMULATIVE NAME INDEX
Dauterman, W. L.: 1   Suinn, R. M.: 1
Shapiro, B.: 1

[774]

Tooze Braille Speed Test: A Test of Basic Ability in Reading Braille. Students (ages 7–13) in grades 1 or 2 braille; 1962; F. H. G. Tooze; College of Teachers of the Blind [England]. *
For additional information, see 6:855.

BUSINESS EDUCATION

[775]

Bookkeeping: Achievement Examinations for Secondary Schools. High school; 1951–54; Form 4 ('54) of a series of tests, currently (1973) entitled

Bookkeeping: Minnesota High School Achievement Examinations (see 776), issued annually for May testing; Helen Haberman; Bobbs-Merrill Co., Inc. *

For additional information concerning later and earlier forms, see 776, 7:553, 6:35 (1 review), 5:502, and 5:504 (1 review).

[776]

*Bookkeeping: Minnesota High School Achievement Examinations. High school; 1951–70; a new, revised, or previously inactive form issued each May; Achievement Examinations for Secondary Schools, High School Achievement Examinations, and Midwest High School Achievement Examinations have also been used as series titles; Form GJ Rev ('70) used in 1970 and 1973 testings; Form 4 ('54), entitled *Bookkeeping: Achievement Examinations for Secondary Schools* (see 775), is available from another publisher; edited by V. L. Lohmann; American Guidance Service, Inc. *

For additional information concerning out of print and inactive forms, see 7:553 and 5:502; for a review by Harold L. Royer of Form F (1963), see 6:35; for a review by I. David Satlow of Form A (1955) and Form B (1952), see 5:504.

[777]

*Bookkeeping Test: National Business Entrance Tests. Grades 11–16 and adults; 1938–72; National Business Education Association. * For the complete battery entry, see 786.

For additional information, see 6:36; for reviews by Harvey A. Andruss and Ray G. Price of an earlier form, see 3:368. For reviews of the complete battery, see 6:33 (1 review), 5:515 (3 reviews), and 3:396 (1 review).

[778]

*Business Fundamentals and General Information Test: National Business Entrance Tests. Grades 11–16 and adults; 1938–72; National Business Education Association. * For the complete battery entry, see 786.

For additional information, see 6:30; for reviews by Vera M. Amerson and C. C. Upshall of an earlier form, see 3:369. For reviews of the complete battery, see 6:33 (1 review), 5:515 (3 reviews), and 3:396 (1 review).

[779]

*Business Relations and Occupations: Achievement Examinations for Secondary Schools. High school; 1951–61; a new, revised, or previously inactive form was issued each May from 1951 through 1961; Form 4 ('54) is the only form in print; High School Achievement Examinations and Midwest High School Achievement Examinations have also been used as series titles; A. Donald Beattie; Bobbs-Merrill Co., Inc. *

For additional information concerning later and earlier forms, see 5:509–10.

[780]

Clerical Aptitude Test: Acorn National Aptitude Tests. Grades 7–16 and adults; 1943–50; 4 scores: business practice, number checking, date-name-address checking, total; 1950 test materials identical with those copyrighted 1943; Andrew Kobal, J. Wayne Wrightstone, and Karl R. Kunze; Psychometric Affiliates. *

For additional information, see 5:847 (1 reference); for reviews by Marion A. Bills, Donald G. Paterson, Henry Weitz, and E. F. Wonderlic, see 3:623.

REFERENCES THROUGH 1971

1. See 5:847.

CUMULATIVE NAME INDEX

Bair, J. T.: 1   Weitz, H.: *rev,* 3:623
Bills, M. A.: *rev,* 3:623   Wonderlic, E. F.: *rev,* 3:623
Paterson, D. G.: *rev,* 3:623

[781]

*Clerical Speed and Accuracy: Differential Aptitude Tests. Grades 8–12 and adults; 1947–73; 2 editions; George K. Bennett, Harold G. Seashore, and Alexander G. Wesman; Psychological Corporation. * For the complete battery entry, see 1069.
a) FORM A. 1947–59. *Out of print.*
b) FORM T. 1947–73; 1972 test (Part I) identical with tests copyrighted 1947 and 1961 (i.e., Forms A, B, L, and M).

For reviews of the complete battery, see 7:673 (1 review, 1 excerpt), 6:767 (2 reviews), 5:605 (2 reviews), 4:711 (3 reviews), and 3:620 (1 excerpt).

REFERENCES THROUGH 1971

1. "Results of the Space Relations, Mechanical Reasoning, and Clerical Speed and Accuracy Tests of the Differential Aptitude Test Battery in Six Public Schools." *Ed Rec B* 58:79–84 F '52. * (*PA* 26:7240)
2. GARNER, GLENN LAMAR. *High School Freshmen DAT Clerical Speed and Accuracy Scores and English Grades as Predictors of Success in Business Courses.* Master's thesis, Millersville State College (Millersville, Pa.), 1969.

CUMULATIVE NAME INDEX

Garner, G. L.: 2

[781A]

Clerical Tests FG and 2. Ages 12-0 to 13-11; 1952–54; 2 tests; published for the National Foundation for Educational Research in England and Wales; Ginn & Co. Ltd. [England]. *
a) CLERICAL TEST FG. Ages 12-0 to 13-11; 1952–53; formerly called *Clerical Test 1;* M. K. B. Richards.
b) CLERICAL TEST 2. Ages 12-3 to 13-1; 1953–54; distribution restricted to directors of education; G. A. V. Morgan.

For additional information, see 5:848.

[782]

Detroit Clerical Aptitudes Examination. Grades 9–12; 1937–44; 12 scores: motor (circles, classification, total), visual imagery (likenesses and differences, disarranged pictures, total), trade information, educational (handwriting, arithmetic, alphabetizing, total), total; includes *Ayres Measuring Scale for Handwriting;* Harry J. Baker and Paul H. Voelker; Bobbs-Merrill Co., Inc. *

For additional information and a review by E. F. Wonderlic, see 3:626 (1 reference); for reviews by Irving Lorge and M. W. Richardson of an earlier edition, see 2:1655.

REFERENCES THROUGH 1971

1. See 3:626.
2. GUINN, MARY PAULINE. *Aids for the Prognosis of Success in Typewriting.* Master's thesis, Kansas State Teachers College (Pittsburg, Kan.), 1948.
3. BAIR, JOHN T. "Factor Analysis of Clerical Aptitude Tests." *J Appl Psychol* 35:245–9 Ag '51. * (*PA* 26:3067)
4. COOK, FRED SOLOMON. *A Study to Determine the Predictive Value of the Detroit Clerical Aptitudes Examination.* Doctor's thesis, University of Michigan (Ann Arbor, Mich.), 1953. (*DA* 13:333)

CUMULATIVE NAME INDEX

Anderson, R. N.: 1   Lorge, I.: *rev,* 2:1655
Bair, J. T.: 3   Richardson, M. W.: *rev,* 2:
Cook, F. S.: 4   1655
Guinn, M. P.: 2   Wonderlic, E. F.: *rev,* 3:626

[783]

*General Office Clerical Test: National Business Entrance Tests. Grades 11–16 and adults; 1948–72; National Business Education Association. * For the complete battery entry, see 786.

For additional information, see 6:32 (1 reference). For reviews of the complete battery, see 6:33 (1 review), 5:515 (3 reviews), and 3:396 (1 review).

REFERENCES THROUGH 1971

1. See 6:32.

CUMULATIVE NAME INDEX

Hamilton, H. A.: 1

[784]

Hiett Simplified Shorthand Test (Gregg). 1, 2 semesters high school; 1951–63; an identical edition, entitled *Hiett Diamond Jubilee Shorthand Test* ('63), is available without a manual; Victor C. Hiett and H. E. Schrammel (manual); Bureau of Educational Measurements. *

For additional information, see 7:555; for a review by Gale W. Clark, see 5:512.

[785]

*Machine Calculation Test: National Business Entrance Tests. Grades 11–16 and adults; 1941–72; earlier tests called *Key-Driven Calculating Machine Ability Test;* National Business Education Association. * For the complete battery entry, see 786.

For additional information, see 6:39; for a review by Dorothy C. Adkins of earlier forms, see 5:514; for a review by Elizabeth Fehrer, see 3:384. For reviews of the complete battery, see 6:33 (1 review), 5:515 (3 reviews), and 3:396 (1 review).

[786]

*National Business Entrance Tests. Grades 11–16 and adults; 1938–72; formerly called *National Clerical Ability Tests* and *United-NOMA Business Entrance Tests;* subtests available as separates; 3 series; National Business Education Association. *

a) [GENERAL TESTING SERIES (SERIES 2500).] 1938–72; 6 tests.

 1) *Business Fundamentals and General Information Test.* 1938–72.
 2) *Bookkeeping Test.* 1938–72.
 3) *General Office Clerical Test.* 1948–72.
 4) *Machine Calculation Test.* 1941–72.
 5) *Stenographic Test.* 1938–72.
 6) *Typewriting Test.* 1941–72.

b) [SHORT FORM SERIES.] 1938–55; 2 tests. *Out of print.*

 1) *Stenographic Test.* 1938–55.
 2) *Typewriting Test.* 1941–55.

c) [OFFICIAL TESTING SERIES (SERIES 2000 AND 2100).] 1938–65; administered only at NBET Centers which may be established in any community; 1965 tests identical with tests copyrighted 1959 (2000 series) and 1960 (2100 series) except for deletion of authorship; 6 tests.

 1) *Business Fundamentals and General Information Test.* 1938–65.
 2) *Bookkeeping Test.* 1938–65.
 3) *General Office Clerical Test.* 1948–65.
 4) *Machine Calculation Test.* 1941–65.
 5) *Stenographic Test.* 1938–65.
 6) *Typewriting Test.* 1941–65.

For additional information and a review by Melvin R. Marks, see 6:33 (5 references); for reviews by Edward N. Hay, Jacob S. Orleans, and Wimburn L. Wallace of earlier forms, see 5:515; see also 4:453 (1 reference); for a review by Paul S. Lomax, see 3:396; see also 2:1476 (9 references). For a review of the typewriting test, see 6:55; earlier editions of the machine calculation test, see 5:514 (1 review) and 3:384 (1 review); the stenographic test, see 5:522 (1 review) and 3:391 (2 reviews); the typewriting test, see 5:526

General Office Clerical Test

(1 review) and 3:394 (2 reviews); the bookkeeping test, see 3:368 (2 reviews); the business fundamentals test, see 3:369 (2 reviews); and the clerical test, see 3:379 (2 reviews).

REFERENCES THROUGH 1971

1–9. See 2:1476.
10. See 4:453.
11–16. See 6:33.

CUMULATIVE NAME INDEX

Baird, M. W.: 15	Joint Committee on Tests: 4
Brigham, L. H.: 2	Liles, P.: 13
Cowan, H. E.: 3	Lomax, P. S.: *rev,* 3:396
Crissy, W. J.: 11	Marks, M. R.: *rev,* 6:33
Eastern Commercial Teachers'	Nelson, J. H.: 10, 12
Association: 1	Orleans, J. S.: *rev,* 5:515
Ford, G. C.: 7	Slaughter, R. E.: 14
Hay, E. N.: *rev,* 5:515	Wallace, W. L.: *rev,* 5:515
Hittler, G. M.: 8	Wantman, M. J.: 11

[787]

*National Teacher Examinations: Business Education. College seniors and teachers; 1956–73; an inactive form (1966) entitled *Teacher Education Examination Program: Business Education* is available to colleges for local administration; another inactive form (1968) entitled *Specialty Examinations: Business Education* is available to school systems for local use as part of the program entitled *School Personnel Research and Evaluation Services;* Educational Testing Service. * For the testing program entry, see 869.

For additional information and a review by Ray G. Price of an earlier form, see 7:556. For reviews of the testing program, see 7:582 (2 reviews), 6:700 (1 review), 5:538 (3 reviews), and 4:802 (1 review).

[788]

★Office Information and Skills Test: Content Evaluation Series. High school; 1971–72; 4 scores: office information, error location and correction, typewriting, transcription; G. Elizabeth Ripka; Houghton Mifflin Co. *

[789]

Reicherter-Sanders Typewriting I and II. 1, 2 semesters high school; 1962–64; first published 1962–63 in the Every Pupil Scholarship Test series; Richard F. Reicherter and M. W. Sanders; Bureau of Educational Measurements. *

For additional information and a review by Lawrence W. Erickson, see 7:557.

[790]

Russell-Sanders Bookkeeping Test. 1, 2 semesters high school; 1962–64; first published 1962–63 in the Every Pupil Scholarship Test series; Raymond B. Russell and M. W. Sanders; Bureau of Educational Measurements. *

For additional information and a review by Bernard H. Newman, see 7:558.

[791]

SRA Clerical Aptitudes. Grades 9–12 and adults; 1947–50; 4 scores: office vocabulary, office arithmetic, office checking, total; Richardson, Bellows, Henry & Co., Inc.; Science Research Associates, Inc. *

For additional information and reviews by Edward N. Hay and G. A. Satter, see 4:732.

REFERENCES THROUGH 1971

1. SEASHORE, HAROLD G. "Validation of Clerical Testing in Banks." *Personnel Psychol* 6:45–56 sp '53. * (*PA* 28:1670)
2. HAY, EDWARD N. "Comparative Validities in Clerical Testing." *J Appl Psychol* 38:299–301 O '54. * (*PA* 29:6351)

CUMULATIVE NAME INDEX

Hay, E. N.: 2; *rev,* 4:732	Seashore, H. G.: 1
Satter, G. A.: *rev,* 4:732	

[792]

SRA Typing Skills. Grades 9-12 and adults; 1947; 2 scores: speed, accuracy; Marion W. Richardson and Ruth A. Pedersen; Science Research Associates, Inc. *

For additional information and reviews by Lawrence W. Erickson and Jacob S. Orleans, see 6:51 (2 references).

REFERENCES THROUGH 1971

1-2. See 6:51.
3. THUMIN, FRED J., AND BOERNKE, CAROL. "Ability Scores as Related to Age Among Female Job Applicants." *J Gerontol* 21:369-71 Jl '66. *

CUMULATIVE NAME INDEX

Ash, P.: 2	Skula, M.: 1
Boernke, C.: 3	Spillane, R. F.: 1
Erickson, L. W.: *rev,* 6:51	Thumin, F. J.: 3
Orleans, J. S.: *rev,* 6:51	

[793]

Shorthand Aptitude Test. High school; 1953-54; V. Brownless, S. Dunn, and the Queensland Department of Public Instruction; Australian Council for Educational Research [Australia]. *

For additional information and a review by James Lumsden, see 5:520.

[794]

Stenographic Aptitude Test. Grades 9-16; 1939-46; 3 scores: transcription, spelling, total; George K. Bennett; Psychological Corporation. *

For additional information and reviews by Philip H. DuBois and Edward A. Rundquist, see 3:390 (1 reference) ; see also 2:1677 (1 reference).

REFERENCES THROUGH 1971

1. See 2:1677.
2. See 3:390.
3. SEASHORE, HAROLD G. "Psychological Testing With Phonograph Recordings." Abstract. *Am Psychologist* 1:248 Jl '46. * (*PA* 20:3932, title only)
4. WIGHTWICK, BEATRICE. *The Effect of Retesting on the Predictive Power of Aptitude Tests.* Doctor's thesis, New York University (New York, N.Y.), 1949.

CUMULATIVE NAME INDEX

Barrett, D. M.: 2	Rundquist, E. A.: *rev,* 3:390
Bennett, G. K.: 1	Seashore, H. G.: 3
DuBois, P. H.: *rev,* 3:390	Wightwick, B.: 4

[795]

*Stenographic Test: National Business Entrance Tests. Grades 11-16 and adults; 1938-72; earlier tests called *Stenographic Ability Tests;* National Business Education Association. * For the complete battery entry, see 786.

For additional information, see 6:47 (1 reference) ; for a review by Edward B. Greene of earlier forms, see 5:522; for reviews by Ann Brewington and Elizabeth Fehrer, see 3:391. For reviews of the complete battery, see 6:33 (1 review), 5:515 (3 reviews), and 3:396 (1 review).

REFERENCES THROUGH 1971

1. See 6:47.
2. NATALE, GLORIA MARIE. *Measurement Aspects of the Stenographic and Typewriting Tests of the National Business Entrance Tests.* Doctor's thesis, Columbia University (New York, N.Y.), 1963. (*DA* 24:1887)
3. ROTHWELL, WADE BROWNELL. *The Relationship of Certain Predictive Factors Including Personality Traits to Job Success of Graduates of Stenographic and Secretarial Programs of Public Supported Technical Institutes and Junior Colleges in the State of Alabama.* Doctor's thesis, Auburn University (Auburn, Ala.), 1970. (*DAI* 31:4055A)
4. REID JAYNE. *The Relationship of Selected Aspects of Attitude, Personality, and Achievement to the Post-High School Employment of Senior Stenographic Students.* Doctor's thesis, University of Cincinnati (Cincinnati, Ohio), 1971. (*DAI* 32: 3570A)

CUMULATIVE NAME INDEX

Brewington, A.: *rev,* 3:391	Nelson, J. H.: 1
Fehrer, E.: *rev,* 3:391	Reid, J.: 4
Greene, E. B.: *rev,* 5:522	Rothwell, W. B.: 3
Natale, G. M.: 2	

[796]

*The Tapping Test: A Predictor of Typing and Other Tapping Operations. High school; 1959-70; John C. Flanagan, Grace Fivars (manual), Shirley A. Tuska (manual), and Carol F. Hershey (manual) ; Psychometric Techniques Associates. *

For additional information and reviews by Ray G. Price and Henry Weitz, see 6:52 (2 references).

REFERENCES THROUGH 1971

1-2. See 6:52.
3. FLANAGAN, JOHN C., AND FIVARS, GRACE. "Predicting Success in Typewriting." *Balance Sheet* 46:7-9 S '64. *
4. FLANAGAN, JOHN C., AND FIVARS, GRACE. "The Tapping Test—A New Tool to Predict Aptitude for Typing." *Delta Pi Epsilon J* 6:33-9 F '64. *
5. WILEY, EDITH S. *An Evaluation of the Effectiveness of the Flanagan Tapping Test as a Predictor of Typing Achievement in Adult Classes.* Master's thesis, California State College (Hayward, Calif.), 1969.

CUMULATIVE NAME INDEX

Banas, P.: 2	Price, R. G.: *rev,* 6:52
Fivars, G.: 1, 3-4	Tuska, S. A.: 1
Flanagan, J. C.: 1, 3-4	Weitz, H.: *rev,* 6:52
Kirchner, W. K.: 2	Wiley, E, S.: 5

[797]

*Teacher Education Examination Program: Business Education. College seniors preparing to teach secondary school; 1957-72; reprinting of inactive 1966 form of *National Teacher Examinations: Business Education;* test available to colleges for local administration; Educational Testing Service. * For the testing program entry, see 898.

For additional information concerning an earlier form, see 6:29. For a review of the testing program, see 5:543. For reference to a review of the *National Teacher Examinations: Business Education,* see 787.

[798]

Turse Shorthand Aptitude Test. Grades 8 and over; 1937-40; 8 scores: stroking, spelling, phonetic association, symbol transcription, word discrimination, dictation, word sense, total; Paul L. Turse; Harcourt Brace Jovanovich, Inc. *

For additional information and a review by Leslie M. Haynes, see 4:460 (5 references) ; for a review by Philip H. DuBois, see 3:393.

REFERENCES THROUGH 1971

1-5. See 4:460.
6. HOLMES, JACK A. "Factors Underlying Major Reading Disabilities at the College Level." *Genetic Psychol Monogr* 49:3-95 F '54. * (*PA* 28:8982)
7. STRICKLAND, ESTHER HEDGES. *Criteria for Predicting Success in Shorthand at East High School, Columbus, Ohio.* Master's thesis, Ohio State University (Columbus, Ohio), 1957.
8. BENDER, W. R. G., AND LOVELESS, H. E. "Validation Studies Involving Successive Classes of Trainee Stenographers." *Personnel Psychol* 11:491-508 w '58. * (*PA* 34:2143)
9. DI BONA, LUCILLE J. "Predicting Success in Shorthand.' *J Bus Ed* 35:213-4 F '60. *
10. PAUK, WALTER. "Comparison of the Validities of Selected Test Procedures to Predict Shorthand Success." *Ed & Psychol Meas* 23:831-5 w '63. *
11. PAUK, WALTER. "What's the Best Way to Predict Success in Shorthand?" *Bus Ed World* 43:7-8+ Ap '63. *
12. DAVIS, ROSE ANNE. "Will Half a Turse Do Just as Well?" *Bus Ed World* 46:11-2 Ja '66. *
13. HANSON, ROBERT NELTON. *Visual Stimulus Versus Combined Audio-Visual Stimuli for Out-of-Class Practice in First-Semester College Gregg Shorthand.* Doctor's thesis, University of North Dakota (Grand Forks, N.D.), 1966. (*DA* 27:3224A)
14. HEEMSTRA, JOYCE J. "Shorthand Prognosis: Can We Be Sure?" *Bus Ed Forum* 20:21+ F '66. *
15. O'CONNELL, MARY MARGARET, AND HOSLER, RUSSEL J. "Predictors of Success in Shorthand." *J Bus Ed* 44:96-8 D '68. *

16. PEHRSON, PATRICIA J. *A Comparison of Student Achievement in Shorthand and Performance on the Turse Test and the ACT Test at Mankato State College.* Master's thesis, Mankato State College (Mankato, Minn.), 1970.

CUMULATIVE NAME INDEX

[799]

Typewriting Test: National Business Entrance Tests. Grades 11–16 and adults; 1941–72; earlier tests called *Typing Ability Test;* National Business Education Association. * For the complete battery entry, see 786.

For additional information and a review by Lawrence W. Erickson, see 6:55 (1 reference); for a review by Clifford E. Jurgensen of earlier forms, see 5:526; for reviews by E. G. Blackstone and Beatrice J. Dvorak, see 3:394. For reviews of the complete battery, see 6:33 (1 review), 5:515 (3 reviews), and 3:396 (1 review).

REFERENCES THROUGH 1971

1. See 6:55.
2. NATALE, GLORIA MARIE. *Measurement Aspects of the Stenographic and Typewriting Tests of the National Business Entrance Tests.* Doctor's thesis, Columbia University (New York, N.Y.), 1963. (*DA* 24:1887)

CUMULATIVE NAME INDEX

[800]

The Undergraduate Program Field Tests: Business Test. College; 1969–73; formerly called *The Undergraduate Record Examinations: Business Test;* test available to colleges for local administration; Educational Testing Service. * For the testing program entry, see 1062.

For additional information concerning an earlier form, see 7:1086. For reviews of the testing program, see 7:671 (2 reviews).

[801]

United Students Typewriting Tests, Volume 14. 1, 2, 3, 4 semesters; 1932–58; Committee on Tests, UBEA Research Foundation; National Business Education Association. *

For additional information, see 5:527.

[Out of Print Since TIP I]

Bookkeeping Achievement Test: Business Education Achievement Test Series, 7:552 (2 reviews)
Bookkeeping: Every Pupil Scholarship Test, 6:34
Byers' First-Year Shorthand Aptitude Tests, 6:41 (1 review, 1 reference)
Commercial Law: Every Pupil Scholarship Test, 6:38
First-Year Bookkeeping: Every Pupil Test, 6:37
First-Year Shorthand: Every Pupil Test, 6:42
First-Year Typewriting: Every Pupil Test, 6:49
General Business Achievement Test: Business Education Achievement Test Series, 7:554 (2 reviews)
General Business: Every Pupil Scholarship Test, 6:31 (1 review)
Revised Standard Graded Tests for Stenographers, 6:44
SRA Typing Adaptability Test, 5:518 (2 reviews)

Stanford Achievement Test: High School Business and Economics Test, 7:559 (1 review)
Typewriting Achievement Test: Business Education Achievement Test Series, 7:559A (2 reviews)
Typewriting I and II: Every Pupil Scholarship Test, 6:54

COMPUTATIONAL AND TESTING DEVICES

[802]

★The Bowman Chronological Age Calculator. 1964; perpetual age scale; Howard A. Bowman; Personnel Press. *

[803]

The Bowman M.A. and I.Q. Kalculator. 1957; for calculating IQ's from MA's and CA's between 4 and 22; formerly called *The Bowman I.Q. Kalculator;* Howard A. Bowman; Personnel Press. *

For additional information, see 5:528.

[804]

*Chronological Age Computer. Ages 3-7 to 19-5; 1961–73; for determining CA's at month of testing from birthdate; new set of computing slides issued each September; B. A. Linsday; American Guidance Service, Inc. *

For additional information, see 6:660.

[805]

Dominion Table for Converting Mental Age to I.Q. 1948; for determining IQ's from MA's and CA's between 5 and 17; Department of Educational Research, Ontario College of Education, University of Toronto; distributed by Guidance Centre [Canada]. *

For additional information, see 6:662.

[806]

[Grade Averaging Charts.] 1956–61; E. P. Harvey; Teaching Aids Co. *
a) SCORE-QUICK GRADER. 1961; for determining per cent correct from number wrong.
b) QUICK PER CENT GRADE AVERAGING CHART. 1960; for averaging per cent grades.
c) TIME-SAVER GRADE AVERAGING CHART. 1956; for averaging letter grades.

For additional information, see 6:664.

[807]

I.Q. Calculator. 1952; for determining IQ's from MA's and CA's between 3.5 and 20; identical (except for directions) with *Mental Age Calculator,* see 808; Milo M. Bolstad; American Guidance Service, Inc. *

[808]

★Mental Age Calculator. [1952]; for determining MA's from IQ's and CA's between 3.5 and 20; identical (except for directions) with *I.Q. Calculator,* see 807; M. M. Bolstad; American Guidance Service, Inc. *

[809]

*The Multiple Purpose Self Trainer. High school and adults; 1951–67; a teaching-testing pull-tab device for use with any set of objective questions keyed to the given answer pattern; Charles W. Nelson; Management Research Associates. *
a) SCALE OF VALUES FORM.
b) TRUE-FALSE FORM.

[810]

Psychometric Research and Service Chart Showing the Davis Difficulty and Discrimination Indices for Item Analysis. 1962; A. Edwin Harper, Jr., S. P. Sangal, and B. Das Gupta; Manasayan [India]. *

For additional information and an excerpted review, see 6:672.

[811]

The Rapid-Rater. 1961–68; special answer sheets and hand punch device for use with classroom tests and for self-testing; Research Media, Inc. *

For additional information, see 7:658.

[812]

★**Ratio I.Q. Computer.** 1966; for calculating IQ from MA and CA (3.0–17.5) or for calculating MA from IQ and CA (3.0–17.5); B. A. Linsday; American Guidance Service, Inc. *

[Out of Print Since TIP I]

Baltimore Age Calculator, T :1147
EB Punch-Key Scoring and Answer Sheet System, 6:663
Grade Master, 6:665
Grade-O-Mat, 6:666
Hammond Matrix Sorter, T :1151
Inglis Intelligence Quotient Values, T :1155
Jensen I. Q. Dial, T :1156
Normal Percentile Chart, T :1159
STAR Score Teach Answer Record, 6:674
Scorule Response Aid (status unknown), 7:659 (1 excerpt, 1 reference)
Tweeddale I.Q. Conversion Tables, 4:469
V.G.C. Answer Strips and Scoring Sleeves, 4:470

COURTSHIP AND MARRIAGE

[813]

★**The Albert Mate Selection Check List.** Premarital counselees; 1971; for self-rating or rating of prospective mate; Gerald Albert; Personal Growth Press, Inc. *

[814]

California Marriage Readiness Evaluation. Premarital counselees; 1965; CMRE; 12 scores: personality (character, emotional maturity, marriage readiness, total), preparation for marriage (family experiences, dealing with money, planning ability, total), interpersonal compatibility (marriage motivation, compatibility, total), total; Morse P. Manson; Western Psychological Services. *

For additional information and a review by Robert A. Harper, see 7:560.

[815]

Caring Relationship Inventory. Marital counselees; 1966; CRI; research edition; 7 scores: affection, friendship, eros, empathy, self-love, being love, deficiency love; Everett L. Shostrom; Educational and Industrial Testing Service. *

For additional information and a review by Albert Ellis, see 7:561; see also P:31 (1 reference).

REFERENCES THROUGH 1971
1. See P:31.

CUMULATIVE NAME INDEX
Ellis, A.: *rev*, 7:561   Pang, H.: 1
Frost, L. J.: 1

[816]

A Courtship Analysis, [Revised]. Adults; 1961–66; unscored counseling and teaching aid for analysis of the attitudes and behavior traits of each partner as seen by the other; Gelolo McHugh; Family Life Publications, Inc. *

For additional information, see P:52; for a review by William R. Reevy of the original edition, see 6:675.

[817]

A Dating Problems Checklist. High school and college; 1961; DPC; unscored counseling and teaching aid; experimental form; Family Life Publications, Inc. *

For additional information, see P:55; for reviews by Clifford R. Adams and Robert A. Harper, see 6:676.

[818]

The El Senoussi Multiphasic Marital Inventory. Premarital and marital counselees; 1963–68; SMMI; 10 scores: frustration and chronic projection, cumulative ego strain, adolescent hangover or immaturity, revolt against femininity, flight into rejection, early conditioning against marriage, will-o'-the-wisp, sex dissatisfaction, sex dissatisfaction and projection, total; Ahmed El Senoussi; Western Psychological Services. *

For additional information and a review by Donald L. Mosher, see 7:562.

[819]

★**The I-Am Sentence Completion Test.** Marital counselees; 1971; no scores; Gerald Albert; Personal Growth Press, Inc. *

[820]

Individual and Family Developmental Review. Counselees and therapy patients; 1969; IFDR; Israel W. Charny; Western Psychological Services. *

For additional information and an excerpted review by Hirsch Lazaar Silverman, see 7:563.

[821]

★**A Love Attitudes Inventory.** Grades 12–16; 1971; LAI; David Knox; Family Life Publications, Inc. *

REFERENCES THROUGH 1971
1. KNOX, DAVID H., JR., AND SPORAKOWSKI, MICHAEL J. "Attitudes of College Students Toward Love." *J Marriage & Family* 30:638–42 N '68. * (*PA* 44:19341)

CUMULATIVE NAME INDEX
Knox, D. H.: 1   Sporakowski, M. J.: 1

[822]

The Male Impotence Test. Adult males; 1964; MIT; 5 scores: reaction to female rejection, flight from male role, reaction to male inadequacy, organic factor, total; Ahmed El Senoussi; Western Psychological Services. *

For additional information and a review by Albert Ellis, see 7:564.

[823]

A Marital Communication Inventory. Adults; 1968–69; MCI; Millard J. Bienvenu, Sr.; Family Life Publications, Inc. *

For additional information, see 7:565 (1 reference).

REFERENCES THROUGH 1971
1. See 7:565.
2. MURPHY, DONALD CLARENCE. *Verbal and Nonverbal Communication in High and Low Marital Adjustment.* Doctor's thesis, Florida State University (Tallahassee, Fla.), 1970. (*DAI* 31:4919A)

CUMULATIVE NAME INDEX

Bienvenu, M. J.: 1   Murphy, D. C.: 2

[824]

★**Marital Diagnostic Inventory.** Marital counselees; 1973; MDI; checklist in 3 areas (reasons for marrying, problems, motivation for counseling) for use at initial contact with counselor; Leslie Navran; Western Psychological Services. *

[825]

Marital Roles Inventory. Marital counselees; 1961; MRI; 4 derived scores: index of marital strain, index of deviation of role performances, index of deviation of role expectations, corrected index of marital strain; Nathan Hurvitz; Western Psychological Services. *

For additional information, see P:153 (3 references); for a review by Robert A. Harper, see 6:680.

REFERENCES THROUGH 1971

1-3. See 6:680 or P:153.
4. HURVITZ, NATHAN. "Control Roles, Marital Strain, Role Deviation, and Marital Adjustment." *J Marriage & Family* 27:29–31 F '65. * (*PA* 39:8236)
5. HURVITZ, NATHAN. "The Marital Roles Inventory as a Counseling Inventory." *J Marriage & Family* 27:492–501 N '65. *

CUMULATIVE NAME INDEX

Harper, R. A.: *rev*, 6:680   Hurvitz, N.: 1–5

[826]

A Marriage Adjustment Form. Adults; 1939–61; MAF; problems checklist; Ernest W. Burgess; distributed by Family Life Publications, Inc. *

For additional information, see P:154 (1 reference); for a review by Lester W. Dearborn, see 6:681.

REFERENCES THROUGH 1971

1. See 6:681 or P:154.
2. BURGESS, ERNEST W., AND COTTRELL, LEONARD S., JR. "The Prediction of Adjustment in Marriage." *Am Sociol R* 1:737–51 O '36. * (*PA* 11:1393)
3. BURGESS, ERNEST W., AND WALLIN, PAUL. "Predicting Adjustment in Marriage From Adjustment in Engagement." *Am J Sociol* 49:324–30 Ja '44. * (*PA* 18:3197)
4. CHRISTENSEN, HAROLD T., AND PHILBRICK, ROBERT E. "Family Size as a Factor in the Marital Adjustments of College Couples." *Am Sociol R* 17:306–12 Je '52. * (*PA* 27:4190)

CUMULATIVE NAME INDEX

Burgess, E. W.: 1–3   Dearborn, L. W.: *rev*, 6:681
Christensen, H. T.: 4   Philbrick, R. E.: 4
Cottrell, L. S.: 1–2   Wallin, P.: 3

[827]

The Marriage Adjustment Inventory. Marital counselees; 1962; MAI; problems checklist; 52 scores: 4 scores (self-evaluation, spouse-evaluation, husband-wife evaluation, total) in each of 12 areas (family relationships, dominance, immaturity, neurotic traits, sociopathic traits, money-management, children, interests, physical, abilities, sexual, incompatibility) and total scores for self-evaluation, spouse-evaluation, husband-wife evaluation, total; Morse P. Manson and Arthur Lerner; Western Psychological Services. *

For additional information, see P:155; for reviews by Clifford R. Adams and Albert Ellis, see 6:682.

[828]

The Marriage Adjustment Sentence Completion Survey. Marital counselees; 1962–65; MASCS; 5 scores: needs, problems, maturity level, goals, values; 1965 test materials identical with materials copyrighted 1962 except for format of manual; Morse P. Manson and Arthur Lerner; Western Psychological Services. *

For additional information, see P:453; for a review by Albert Ellis, see 6:683.

[829]

A Marriage Analysis, Experimental Edition. Married couples in counseling; 1966; 8 scores: role concepts, self image, feelings toward spouse, emotional openness, knowledge of spouse, sexual adjustment and security, common traits, meaning of marriage; Daniel C. Blazier and Edgar T. Goosman; Family Life Publications, Inc. *

For additional information and reviews by Robert C. Challman and Robert A. Harper, see 7:566.

[830]

★**The Marriage Expectation Inventories.** Engaged and married couples; 1972; 2 inventories; Patrick J. McDonald; Family Life Publications, Inc. *
a) FORM 1: FOR ENGAGED COUPLES.
b) FORM 2: FOR MARRIED COUPLES.

[831]

Marriage-Personality Inventory, Educational Research Edition. Individuals and couples; 1963–69; MP1; 24 profiled scores: items completed, satisfaction, growing up years (3 scores), life style preferences (2 scores), personality traits (2 scores), growth inviting (3 scores), life engaging (6 scores), flexibility (3 scores), dependability (3 scores); 4 booklets; 1967 tests essentially the same as Clinical Research Edition copyrighted 1966; Karl V. Schultz; Psychological Services Press. *
a) FORM 1, INDIVIDUAL PERSONALITY. 1963–67; responses in terms of self-image, desired self-image, and satisfaction with differences.
b) FORM 2, MATCH-MATE. 1963–69; responses in terms of self-image, desired mate image, importance of desired mate image.
c) FORM 3, COURTSHIP PRE-MARRIAGE. 1963–67; responses in terms of self-image, prospective mate image, effect of combination on marriage if married.
d) FORM 4, MARRIAGE. 1963–67; responses in terms of self-image, mate image, effect of combination on marriage.

For additional information and reviews by Robert C. Challman and Bernard I. Murstein, see 7:567.

[832]

A Marriage Prediction Schedule. Adults; 1939–61; MPS; Ernest W. Burgess; Family Life Publications, Inc. *

For additional information, see P:158; for a review by Lester W. Dearborn, see 6:684; see also 5:84 (8 references).

REFERENCES THROUGH 1971

1-8. See 5:84.

CUMULATIVE NAME INDEX

Burgess, E. W.: 1   King, C. E.: 4, 6
Cottrell, L. S.: 1   McPhee, W. M.: 5
Dearborn, L. W.: *rev*, 6:684   Skidmore, R. A.: 5
Frumkin, R. M.: 3, 7–8   Stroup, A. L.: 2

[833]

Marriage Role Expectation Inventory. Adolescents and adults; 1960–63; MREI; role expectations in 7 areas (authority, homemaking, care of children, personal characteristics, social participation, education, employment and support) yielding an equalitarian-traditional rating; Marie S. Dunn; Family Life Publications, Inc. *

For additional information, see P:159 (6 references); for a review by Robert C. Challman, see 6:685.

REFERENCES THROUGH 1971

1-6. See 6:685 or P:159.

[834]

***Marriage Scale (For Measuring Compatibility of Interests).** Premarital or married counselees; 1970–73; self-rating scale; J. Gustav White; Psychologists and Educators, Inc. *

For additional information, see 7:568.

[835]

★Marriage Skills Analysis. Marital counselees; 1970; MSA; experimental; 80 scores: 16 scale scores (physical, sex, loving, togetherness, talking, listening, adapting and conforming, money management, learning, family goal setting, reconciliation, creating, helping, sense of humor, aggression, total) in each of 5 areas (feeling, thinking, acting, relationship with people, total); Robert W. Henderson and Jack G. Wiggins; Personal Growth Press, Inc. *

[836]

Otto Pre-Marital Counseling Schedules. Adult couples; 1961, c1951–61; checklist for use as a discussion stimulator; 3 parts; Herbert A. Otto; Consulting Psychologists Press, Inc. *
a) PRE-MARITAL SURVEY SECTION.
b) FAMILY FINANCE SECTION.
c) SEXUAL ADJUSTMENT SECTION.

For additional information, see P:189 (2 references); for reviews by Robert C. Challman and William R. Reevy, see 6:686.

REFERENCES THROUGH 1971
1–2. See 6:686 or P:189.

[837]

★Pair Attraction Inventory, Preliminary Edition. College and adults; 1970–71; PAI; for research use only; 7 scale scores: mother–son, daddy–doll, bitch–nice guy, master–servant, hawks, doves, person-person; Everett L. Shostrom; Educational and Industrial Testing Service. *

[838]

Sex Knowledge Inventory. Sex education classes in high school and college and adults; 1950–68; SKI; 2 tests; Gelolo McHugh; Family Life Publications, Inc. *
a) SEX KNOWLEDGE INVENTORY: VOCABULARY AND ANATOMY, SECOND REVISION (EXPERIMENTAL EDITION). High school and college and adults; 1950–55; 1955 test identical with first revision ('50) except for format.
b) SEX KNOWLEDGE INVENTORY, REVISED. College and adults; 1950–68.

For additional information, see 7:570 (6 references); for a review by Clifford R. Adams, see 6:687 (3 references); for a review by Albert Ellis and an excerpted review by Donald F. Schroeder, see 4:488.

REFERENCES THROUGH 1971
1–3. See 6:687.
4–9. See 7:570.
10. PRICE, QUENTIN L. E. *Influence of Sex and Family Life Education on Student Attitude Toward Traditional Family Ideology and Sex Knowledge.* Doctor's thesis, United States International University (San Diego, Calif.), 1969. (*DAI* 31:6161A)
11. BENDER, STEPHEN J. "Human Reproductive Knowledge of Prospective Elementary Teachers." *J Sch Health* 41(5):273–4 My '71. *

[839]

Sexual Development Scale for Females. Adult females; 1968–69; SDSF; frigidity; 38 scores: 7 factor scores (lack of feminine identity, free floating identity, unpleasant sexual encounter, passive sex aversion, flight into sex, sexual insufficiency, early negative conditioning toward sex), 5 to 9 cluster scores and a total score for each of 4 time periods (childhood to age 10, ages 10–15, 16–21, 21 and over), and a total frigidity score; Ahmed El Senoussi; Western Psychological Services. *

For additional information and a review by Albert Ellis, see 7:571.

[840]

***Taylor-Johnson Temperament Analysis.** Grades 7–12, 9–16 and adults; 1941–73; TJTA; revision of *Johnson Temperament Analysis;* individual, premarital, and marital counseling; 9 trait scores (nervous-composed, depressive-lighthearted, active/social-quiet, expressive/responsive-inhibited, sympathetic-indifferent, subjective-objective, dominant-submissive, hostile-tolerant, self disciplined-impulsive) plus test-taking attitude scale; 2 editions; original edition by Roswell H. Johnson; revision by Robert M. Taylor; Psychological Publications, Inc. *
a) SECONDARY EDITION. Grades 7–12; no manual; W. Lee Morrison (test).
b) [REGULAR EDITION.] Grades 9–16 and adults; Lucile P. Morrison (manual).

For additional information and a review by Donald L. Mosher of *b,* see 7:572 (1 reference); see also P:264 (3 references and 6:130 (10 references); for a review by Albert Ellis of the original edition, see 4:62 (6 references); for a review by H. Meltzer, see 3:57.

REFERENCES THROUGH 1971
1–6. See 4:62.
7–16. See 6:130.
17–19. See P:264.
20. See 7:572.
21. BERBIGLIA, JAMES C. *The AWOL Syndrome: A Study of the Early Identification of Potential AWOLS by the Use of the Taylor-Johnson Temperament Analysis Leading to the Development of a Preventive Program.* Los Angeles, Calif.: Psychological Publications, Inc., 1971. Pp. 20. *
22. HUANG, DAVID DARMING. *An Investigation of Probationary and Non-Probationary Engineering Students' Self Perceived Versus Measured Temperaments, Values and Vocational Preferences.* Doctor's thesis, Purdue University (Lafayette, Ind.), 1971. (*DAI* 32:3030A)
23. LEVI, MARIO, AND TRACY, FRED. "Prediction of Success of Drug Addicts in Outpatient Release Status Based Upon a Personality Inventory." *Int J Addic* 6(3):533–41 S '71. * (*PA* 48:1227)

[841]

The Thorman Family Relations Conference Situation Questionnaire. Families receiving therapy; 1965; also called *Thorman Family Relations Evaluation;* George Thorman; Western Psychological Services. *

For additional information, see P:275.

Psychotherapy Inventory, 7:569, P:123
Sex Knowledge Test (status unknown), 6:688

DRIVING AND SAFETY EDUCATION

[842]

*[American Automobile Association Driver Test-
ing Apparatus.] Drivers; 1939–72; 13 tests; Traffic
Engineering and Safety Department, American Automobile Association; the Association. *
a) AUTOMATIC REACTION TIME. 1958–60; braking reaction to electrically operated signals.
b) COLOR VISION. 1947–60.
c) COMPLEX REACTION TIME. 1940–72; braking and
turning reactions to electrically operated signals.
d) DETONATORS. 1939–60; braking reaction and distance.
e) DISTANCE JUDGMENT. 1939–60.
f) DISTANCE JUDGMENT AND VISION. 1940; incorporates
essential features of *e* and *m*.
g) DRIVER EVALUATOR. 1950–60; incorporates essential
features of *b, e, h,* and *m*.
h) FIELD OF VISION. 1939–72.
i) JERK RECORDER. 1950.
j) NIGHT SIGHT METER. 1952–70; 3 scores: glare vision,
night vision, recovery.
k) [SIMPLE] REACTION TIME. 1943–60; braking reaction to manually operated signals.
l) STEADINESS. 1939–60.
m) VISUAL ACUITY. 1943–60.
For additional information, see 4:521.

REFERENCES THROUGH 1971
1. LAUER, A. R.; SUHR, VIRTUS W.; AND ALLGAIER, E.
"Development of a Criterion for Driving Performance." *Traffic
Safety Res R* 2:24–7 Mr '58. *

CUMULATIVE NAME INDEX
Allgaier, E.: 1   Suhr, V. W.: 1
Lauer, A. R.: 1

[843]

*Bicycle Safety—Performance and Skill Tests,
[1962 Revision]. Ages 10–16; 1940–62, c1940–58;
tests 1, 2, 4, and 6 are modifications of the *National
Bicycle Tests* by Alfred L. Lorenz; 12 tests, 13 scores:
balance test (straight lane), pedaling and braking,
straight line test, signaling-mounting-dismounting,
single obstacle test, double obstacle test, double zig-zag
obstacle test, figure-eight steering, figure-eight balance
test, turning around, emergency turn and stop, cruising
test, total; no manual; Ben W. Miller; National Safety
Council. *

[844]

Driver Attitude Survey. Drivers; 1962–70; DAS; 6
scores: violations, accidents, alcohol, faking, deviance,
misses; Donald H. Schuster and J. P. Guilford; Sheridan Psychological Services, Inc. *
For additional information, see 7:574 (3 references).

REFERENCES THROUGH 1971
1–3. See 7:574.
4. SCHUSTER, D. H., AND GUILFORD, J. P. "The Psychometric Prediction of Problem Drivers." *Hum Factors* 6:393–421
Ag '64. *
5. SCHUSTER, D. H. "Prediction of Current Accident Record
for Youthful Drivers." *Traffic Safety Res R* 10:22–5 Mr '66. *
6. PERRINE, M. W. "Identification of Personality, Attitudinal,
and Biographical Characteristics of Drinking Drivers." *Behav
Res Highway Safety* 1(4):207–26 w '70. *
7. SCHUSTER, D. H. "Attitudes Toward Driving Safety and

Their Modification." *Hum Factors* 12(1):89–94 F '70. * (*PA*
44:9481)

CUMULATIVE NAME INDEX
Guilford, J. P.: 1, 4   Schuster, D. H.: 1–5, 7
Perrine, M. W.: 6

[845]

★Driving Skill Exercises. Automobile drivers; 1961;
7 scores: driving in a straight line, steering in close
limits, stopping smoothly from 20 mph, determining
front and rear limits, parallel parking, measuring reaction and braking distance, total; Amos E. Neyhart;
published jointly by American Automobile Association
and Institute of Public Safety. *

[846]

General Test on Traffic and Driving Knowledge.
Drivers; 1949–50; Traffic Engineering and Safety Department, American Automobile Association; the Association. *
For additional information, see 5:922.

[847]

Hannaford Industrial Safety Attitude Scales. In-
dustry; 1959; attitude toward safety; 2 editions;
Earle S. Hannaford; Center for Safety. *
a) INDUSTRIAL SAFETY ATTITUDE SCALE FOR MALE EM-
PLOYEES.
b) INDUSTRIAL SAFETY ATTITUDE SCALE FOR MALE SUPER-
VISORS.
For additional information and a review by David O.
Herman, see 6:690.

[848]

The McGlade Road Test for Use in Driver Licensing, Education and Employment. Prospective
drivers; 1961–62; manual title is *A New Road Test for
Use in Driver Licensing, Education & Employment
(out of print);* Francis S. McGlade; Center for
Safety. *
For additional information, see 6:691 (1 reference).

REFERENCES THROUGH 1971
1. See 6:691.

CUMULATIVE NAME INDEX
McGlade, F. S.: 1

[849]

Road Test Check List for Passenger Car Drivers.
Passenger car drivers; 1947–55; formerly called *Road
Test in Traffic for Passenger Car Drivers;* 3 scores:
specific driving errors, general attitude and driving
practices, total; Amos E. Neyhart; published jointly
by American Automobile Association and Institute of
Public Safety. *
For additional information, see 5:594.

[850]

Siebrecht Attitude Scale. Grades 9–16 and adults;
1941–58; attitude toward safe driving practices; Elmer
B. Siebrecht; Center for Safety. *
For additional information, see 6:693 (3 references).

REFERENCES THROUGH 1971
1–3. See 6:693.
4. BEAMISH, JEROME J., AND MALFETTI, JAMES L. "A Psychological Comparison of Violator and Non-Violator Automobile
Drivers in the 16 to 19 Year Age Group." *Traffic Safety Res R*
6:12–5 Mr '62. *
5. CRAWFORD, PAUL L. "Reliability and Validity of the
Siebrecht Attitude Scale." *Ed & Psychol Meas* 28:609–13 su
'68. * (*PA* 42:18086)

CUMULATIVE NAME INDEX
Beamish, J. J.: 4   Malfetti, J. L.: 4
Crawford, P. L.: 5   Siebrecht, E. B.: 1–2
Forlano, G.: 3   Wrightstone, J. W.: 3

[851]

★**Simplified Road Test.** Drivers; 1969; Traffic Engineering and Safety Department, American Automobile Association; the Association. *

[Out of Print Since TIP I]

Columbia Driver Judgment Test, 7:573 (1 review)
Driver Education Teacher Performance Inventory, 7:575 (1 review)
Driver Scalogram, T:1163
Examination for Driving Instructors, 4:522
Lauer Driver Reaction Inventory, 5:593 (2 references)
National Test in Driver Education, 6:692
Rating Scale for Automobile-Driver Skills: The Abercrombie Driver Test, 4:524
Revere Safety Test, 4:525 (2 reviews)
Rogers-Lauer Driver Rating Inventory, 5:595
Safety Education: Manchester Semester-End Achievement Tests, T:1173
Student Record in Driver Education, 6:694
Test of Safety Mindedness, T:1176

EDUCATION

[852]

Academic Freedom Survey. College students and faculty; 1954; 3 scores: student, faculty, total; Paul Slivnick and Academic Freedom Committee, Illinois Division, American Civil Liberties Union; Psychometric Affiliates. *

For additional information, see 5:531.

[853]

*****CLEP Subject Examination in History of American Education.** 1 semester or equivalent; 1967–73; for college accreditation of nontraditional study, advanced placement, or assessment of educational achievement; tests administered monthly at centers throughout the United States; program administered for the College Entrance Examination Board by Educational Testing Service. * For the testing program entry, see 1050.

For additional information, see 7:576. For reviews of the testing program, see 7:664 (3 reviews).

[854]

*****CLEP Subject Examination in Tests and Measurements.** 1 semester or equivalent; 1964–73; for college accreditation of nontraditional study, advanced placement, or assessment of educational achievement; tests administered monthly at centers throughout the United States; program administered for the College Entrance Examination Board by Educational Testing Service. * For the testing program entry, see 1050.

For additional information, see 7:577. For reviews of the testing program, see 7:664 (3 reviews).

[855]

★**Classroom Atmosphere Questionnaire.** Grades 4–9; 1971; CAQ; ratings of teacher by students; 2 scores: acceptance-understanding, problem solving skills; James K. Hoffmeister; Test Analysis and Development Corporation. *

[856]

★**Comprehensive Teaching and Training Evaluation.** College and training programs; 1969; CTTE; ratings by students; 4 scores: how we learn, what the instructor was like, our class (or course) was, total; no manual; John M. Gullo; Psychologists and Educators, Inc. *

[857]

★**Counseling Services Assessment Blank.** College and adult counseling clients; 1968; CSAB; for evaluating services provided by counseling agencies; no manual; James C. Hurst and Richard G. Weigel; Rocky Mountain Behavioral Science Institute, Inc. *

REFERENCES THROUGH 1971

1. HURST, JAMES C.; WEIGEL, RICHARD G.; THATCHER, RITA; AND NYMAN, ARIE J. "Counselor-Client Diagnostic Agreement and Perceived Outcomes of Counseling." *J Counsel Psychol* 16(5):421–6 S '69. * (PA 43:17583)
2. HARMAN, ROBERT L. "Client Assessment of a University Counseling Service." Abstract. *J Counsel Psychol* 18(5):496–7 S '71. * (PA 47:3692)
3. HURST, JAMES C., AND MORRILL, WESTON H. "Personal Versus General Requests for Client Feedback in Evaluating Counseling Services." *J Col Stud Personnel* 12(1):32–5 Ja '71. * (PA 46:1821)

CUMULATIVE NAME INDEX

Harman, R. L.: 2   Nyman, A. J.: 1
Hurst, J. C.: 1, 3   Thatcher, R.: 1
Morrill, W. H.: 3   Weigel, R. G.: 1

[858]

★**Course Evaluation Questionnaire.** High school and college; 1971; CEQ; ratings by students; 5 scores: openness to students and ideas, contextual approach to learning, dynamism-enthusiasm, organization-clarity, quality-meaningfulness; James K. Hoffmeister; Test Analysis and Development Corporation. *

[859]

Diagnostic Teacher-Rating Scale. Grades 4–12; 1938–52; ratings by pupils; originally published in 1938 for use in grades 4–8; 8 ratings: liking for teacher, ability to explain, kindness-friendliness-understanding, fairness in grading, discipline, work required, liking for lessons, total; 1952 tests identical with tests published 1938 except for format and revision in directions; Mary Amatora; Educators'-Employers' Tests & Services Associates. *

For additional information, see 6:696; for a review by Dorothy M. Clendenen, see 5:534 (5 references); see also 4:795 (2 references).

REFERENCES THROUGH 1971

1–2. See 4:795.
3–7. See 5:534.

CUMULATIVE NAME INDEX

Amatora, M.: 3–7   Hipskind, M. J. F.: 1
Amatora, S. M.: 2   Remmers, H. H.: 1
Clendenen, D. M.: *rev*, 5:534   Tschechtelin, M. A.: 1

[860]

★**Educational Values Assessment Questionnaire.** Adults; 1973; EVAQ; for research use only; rating scale "on the beliefs people have about what is important educationally for the child of elementary or junior high school age"; 8 scores: community involvement, strictness/standards, professional specialists, innovation, health-recreation-practical training, economic considerations, parent education, special handling of difficult children; Harry Gottesfeld; Behavioral Publications, Inc. *

[861]

Faculty Morale Scale for Institutional Improvement. College faculty; 1954–63; A Local Chapter Committee, American Association of University Professors; Psychometric Affiliates. *

For additional information, see 6:697.

[862]

★**General Tests of Language and Arithmetic for Students.** First and second year Bantu candidates for primary teacher's certificate; 1972–73; GTLAS; 13

scores: arithmetic (ready knowledge, computations, problems, total), English (language usage, vocabulary, reading comprehension, total), Afrikaans (language usage, vocabulary, reading comprehension, total), total; arithmetic subtest and manual in both English and Afrikaans; J. C. Chamberlain, B. S. Claasen (test), J. Fourie (test), and F. W. Gericke (test); Human Sciences Research Council [South Africa]. *

[863]

*The Graduate Record Examinations Advanced Education Test. Graduate school candidates; 1946–73; Educational Testing Service. * For the testing program entry, see 1053.

For additional information concerning earlier forms, see 7:578 (9 references); for a review by D. Welty Lefever, see 6:698 (7 references); for a review by Harry N. Rivlin, see 5:537. For reviews of the testing program, see 7:667 (1 review) and 5:601 (1 review).

REFERENCES THROUGH 1971

1–7. See 6:698.
8–16. See 7:578.
17. HOUSTON, SAMUEL R. "Generating a Projected Criterion of Graduate School Success via Normative Judgment Analysis." *J Exp Ed* 37:53–8 w '68. *

CUMULATIVE NAME INDEX

Angoff, W. H.: 6
Capps, M. P.: 7
Colvin, G. F.: 12
DeCosta, F. A.: 7
Feinberg, A.: 10
Gab, D.: 16
Gab, D. D.: 13
Hall, J. G.: 11
Harlow, S. D.: 16
Houston, S. R.: 14, 17
Johnson, B. G.: 8
Lannholm, G. V.: 5
Lefever, D. W.: *rev,* 6:698
Manuel, H. T.: 4
Rivlin, H. N.: *rev,* 5:537
Roscoe, J. T.: 14
Saum, J. A.: 1–2
Schultz, M. K.: 6
Treacy, J. P.: 3
Williams, J. D.: 16
Woodard, D. B.: 15
Zimmerman, W. G.: 9

[864]

*Illinois Course Evaluation Questionnaire. College; 1965–72; ICEQ; ratings by students; 7 scores: general course attitude, method of instruction, course content, interest-attention, instructor, specific items, total; Richard E. Spencer and Lawrence M. Aleamoni (manual); Measurement and Research Division, University of Illinois. *

For additional information, see 7:579 (2 references).

REFERENCES THROUGH 1971

1–2. See 7:579.
3. STALLINGS, WILLIAM M., AND SINGHAL, SUSHILA. "Some Observations on the Relationships Between Research Productivity and Student Evaluations of Courses and Teaching." *Am Sociologist* 5(2):141–3 My '70. *

CUMULATIVE NAME INDEX

Aleamoni, L. M.: 2
Meredith, G. M.: 1
Singhal, S.: 3
Spencer, R. E.: 2
Stallings, W. M.: 3

[865]

Illinois Ratings of Teacher Effectiveness. Grades 9–12; 1967; IRTE; ratings by students; 11 scores: appearance, explaining lessons, friendliness, grading, discipline, work assignments, teaching, voice, mannerisms, knowledge of subject, total; B. Everard Blanchard; Western Psychological Services. *

For additional information and a review by Gerald M. Meredith, see 7:580.

[866]

Illinois Teacher Evaluation Questionnaire. Grades 7–12; 1968–70; ITEQ; ratings by students; 5 scores: general impressions, competence, interest in class, attitude, total; Richard E. Spencer and J. Maurice Mahan (manual); Measurement and Research Division, University of Illinois. *

For additional information, see 7:581.

[867]

*Junior Index of Motivation. Grades 7–12; 1965–70; JIM; test booklet title is *JIM Scale Student Questionnaire;* motivation toward school; Jack R. Frymier; University Publications Sales, Ohio State University. *

For additional information, see P:132.

REFERENCES THROUGH 1971

1. AGER, MERLIN FRED. *A Study of the Relationships Between Selected Personality Variables and Verbal Behavior, Supervisory Ratings and Grades of Student Teachers.* Doctor's thesis, Ohio State University (Columbus, Ohio), 1967. (*DA* 28:4926A)
2. MOSS, ALLEN MILLER. *Differences in Academic Achievement, Motivation, and Personality Traits Between High School Dropouts and Persisters.* Doctor's thesis, University of Alabama (University, Ala.), 1968. (*DA* 29:4832B)
3. SHAPPELL, DEAN LEROY. *The Relationship of Socio-Economic Status to School Motivation and Occupational Orientation.* Doctor's thesis, Ohio State University (Columbus, Ohio), 1969. (*DAI* 30:2345A)
4. FRYMIER, JACK R. "Development and Validation of a Motivation Index." *Theory Into Prac* 9(1):56–88 F '70. *
5. FRYMIER, JACK R. "Motivation: The Mainspring and Gyroscope of Learning." *Theory Into Prac* 9(1):23–32 F '70. *
6. SHAPPELL, DEAN L.; HALL, LACY G.; AND TARRIER, RANDOLPH B. "School Motivation and Occupational Orientation." *Voc Guid Q* 19(2):97–103 D '70. *
7. SCHOCK, NORVILLE H. *An Analysis of the Relationship Which Exists Between Cognitive and Affective Educational Objectives in Selected Biology Classrooms of Wayne County, Michigan.* Doctor's thesis, Wayne State University (Detroit, Mich.), 1971. (*DAI* 32:6016A)

CUMULATIVE NAME INDEX

Ager, M. F.: 1
Frymier, J. R.: 4–5
Hall, L. G.: 6
Moss, A. M. 2
Schock, N. H.: 7
Shappell, D. L.: 3, 6
Tarrier, R. B.: 6

[868]

Minnesota Teacher Attitude Inventory. Elementary and secondary school teachers and students in grades 12–17; 1951; MTAI; Walter W. Cook, Carroll H. Leeds, and Robert Callis; Psychological Corporation. *

For additional information, see 6:699 (146 references); for reviews by Dwight L. Arnold and Lee J. Cronbach, see 4:801 (9 references).

REFERENCES THROUGH 1971

1–9. See 4:801.
10–155. See 6:699.
156. SHAW, JACK. "The Function of the Interview in Determining Fitness for Teacher-Training." *J Ed Res* 45:667–81 My '52. * (*PA* 27:3007)
157. ANDERSON, PHILIP STANLEY. *The Effects of Teacher Attitudes Toward Learning Theories and Toward Children on Pupil Achievement in Fourth Grade Arithmetic and Reading.* Doctor's thesis, University of Minnesota (Minneapolis, Minn.), 1955. (*DA* 16:296)
158. PEARSON, ARVID NEIL. *A Study of the Relationships Between Attitudes, Intelligence, and Achievement of University of Minnesota Majors in Education Grouped by Major Area of Specialization.* Doctor's thesis, University of Minnesota (Minneapolis, Minn.), 1955. (*DA* 15:1562)
159. TAYLOR, MARVIN. *The Effects of Three Cue Conditions, Interpersonal Relations Attitudes and Ideology of Judges on the Formation and Modification of First Impressions.* Doctor's thesis, Syracuse University (Syracuse, N.Y.), 1955. (*DA* 15:2476)
160. KRUMBOLTZ, HELEN BRANDHORST. *The Relationship of Birth Rank and Number of Siblings to Certain Personality Characteristics of Teacher Education Candidates.* Doctor's thesis, University of Minnesota (Minneapolis, Minn.), 1956. (*DA* 16:1841)
161. CLINKER, BERNARD KEITH. *An Experimental Study of Selected Factors Important in Successful Teaching.* Doctor's thesis, Indiana University (Bloomington, Ind.), 1957. (*DA* 18:508)
162. CORCORAN, MARY ELIZABETH. *The Role of Personal Attitudes in Student Evaluation of an Introductory Education Course.* Doctor's thesis, University of Minnesota (Minneapolis, Minn.), 1957. (*DA* 18:144)
163. GLOTZBACH, CHARLES JEROME. *Intellectual and Non-intellectual Characteristics Associated With Persistence of Women in an Elementary and Nursery School Teacher-Education Program.* Doctor's thesis, University of Minnesota (Minneapolis, Minn.), 1957. (*DA* 18:146)

164. ISENBERGER, WILMA E. *Self-Attitudes of Women Physical Education Majors as Related to Measures of Interest and Success.* Doctor's thesis, State University of Iowa (Iowa City, Iowa), 1957. (*DA* 17:2911)

165. RUZICKA, WILLIAM JOSEPH. *Personality Variables and Student-Centered Learning Experiences in Educational Psychology Classes.* Doctor's thesis, Ohio State University (Columbus, Ohio), 1957. (*DA* 19:175)

166. TIMSON, IRIS MARIE. *The Relationship of Personal Characteristics to Performance in the Initial Teaching Experience.* Doctor's thesis, Stanford University (Stanford, Calif.), 1957. (*DA* 17:818)

167. HARDER, DONALD F. "A Suggestion Pertaining to a More Sensitive Indication of Change of Attitude as Measured by the MTAI." *Psychol Rep* 4:553–4 D '58. * (*PA* 34:1371)

168. POPHAM, W. JAMES. *Relationships Between Out-of-School Activities of Teachers and Their Attitudes Toward Pupil-Teacher Relations.* Doctor's thesis, Indiana University (Bloomington, Ind.), 1958. (*DA* 19:992)

169. BERRYESSA, MAX JOSEPH. *Factors Contributing to the Competency of Elementary Teachers in Teaching Science.* Doctor's thesis, Stanford University (Stanford, Calif.), 1959. (*DA* 20:558)

170. FOSTER, LUCILLE ESTELLE CASTER. *Perceived Competencies of School Supervisors.* Doctor's thesis, Stanford University (Stanford, Calif.), 1959. (*DA* 20:568)

171. LaBUE, ANTHONY C. "Teachers' Classroom Attitudes." *J Teach Ed* 10:433–4 D '59. * (*PA* 34:8420)

172. McCARDLE, HUGH JOSEPH. *An Investigation of the Relationships Between Pupil Achievement in First-Year Algebra and Some Teacher Characteristics.* Doctor's thesis, University of Minnesota (Minneapolis, Minn.), 1959. (*DA* 20:165)

173. OLANDER, HERBERT T., AND KLEYLE, HELEN M. "Differences in Personal and Professional Characteristics of a Selected Group of Elementary Teachers With Contrasting Success Records." *Ed Adm & Sup* 45:191–8 Jl '59. * (*PA* 34:6582)

174. SANFORD, ALPHEUS. *The Practice Teaching Experience and Its Effect on Cadet Teacher Attitudes Toward Pupils.* Doctor's thesis, Boston University (Boston, Mass.), 1959. (*DA* 20:3212)

175. SCHOR, THEODORE. *Some Variables Among Elementary School Teachers That Affect the Utilization of Audio-Visual Materials.* Doctor's thesis, Rutgers University (New Brunswick, N.J.), 1959. (*DA* 20:2662)

176. TROISI, NICHOLAS FRANCIS. *The Effect of Student-Teaching Upon Student Teachers' Objectives and Their Relation to Achievement and Attitudes Toward Children.* Doctor's thesis, Pennsylvania State University (University Park, Pa.), 1959. (*DA* 20:609)

177. DEL POPOLO, JOSEPH A. "Authoritarian Trends in Personality as Related to Attitudinal and Behavioral Traits of Student Teachers." *J Ed Res* 53:252–7 Mr '60. *

178. FIELDER, WILLIAM RODNEY. *A Study of Certain Antecedent Factors Associated With Perseverance in Training and Entry Into Classroom Teaching.* Doctor's thesis, Stanford University (Stanford, Calif.), 1960. (*DA* 21:97)

179. GABERMAN, FLORENCE KILGORE. *A Scale for Measuring Teacher Class Control and Its Relation to Personality.* Doctor's thesis, Pennsylvania State University (University Park, Pa.), 1960. (*DA* 21:1845)

180. MYERS, BETTYE BLANCHE. *Evaluation of the Effectiveness of the University of Michigan's Summer Counselor Education Program at the National Music Camp.* Doctor's thesis, University of Michigan (Ann Arbor, Mich.), 1960. (*DA* 21:2196)

181. RIBBECK, JAMES C. *High School Counselor and Teacher Prediction of College Success as Related to Objective Predictor Measures and to Counselor and Teacher Characteristics.* Doctor's thesis, State University of Iowa (Iowa City, Iowa), 1960. (*DA* 21:1852)

182. STANDLEE, LLOYD S., AND POPHAM, W. JAMES. "Teacher Variables Related to Job Performance." *Psychol Rep* 6:458 Je '60. * (*PA* 35:7139)

183. VERTEIN, LESTER DALE. *A Study of the Personal-Social and Intellectual Characteristics of a Group of State College Students Preparing to Teach.* Doctor's thesis, University of Wisconsin (Madison, Wis.), 1960. (*DA* 21:1473)

184. CLARKE, GERALD EUGENE. *Some Aspects of Attitudinal Perception in School Supervision.* Doctor's thesis, Cornell University (Ithaca, N.Y.), 1961. (*DA* 22:2649)

185. LETON, DONALD A. "An Evaluation of Course Methods in Teaching Child Development." *J Ed Res* 55:118–22 N '61. *

186. LUNN, MERVEL SAMUEL, JR. *The Prediction of Success of Students Enrolled in Professional Education Courses at the University of Oklahoma.* Doctor's thesis, University of Oklahoma (Norman, Okla.), 1961. (*DA* 22:1490)

187. NEWMAN, WILLIAM HENRY. *Factors Affecting Leadership.* Doctor's thesis, Stanford University (Stanford, Calif.), 1961. (*DA* 21:3329)

188. RISHEL, DARRELL FRED. *The Development and Validation of Instruments and Techniques for the Selective Admission of Applicants for Graduate Studies in Counselor Education.* Doctor's thesis, Pennsylvania State University (University Park, Pa.), 1961. (*DA* 22:2271)

189. STAHLY, HAROLD LeROY. *A Theoretical and Empirical Study of Decisional Behavior of Teachers.* Doctor's thesis, Indiana University (Bloomington, Ind.), 1961. (*DA* 22:1090)

190. STORLIE, THEODORE RUDOLPH. *Selected Characteristics of Teachers Whose Verbal Behavior Is Influenced by an In-Service Course in Interaction Analysis.* Doctor's thesis, University of Minnesota (Minneapolis, Minn.), 1961. (*DA* 22:3941)

191. BERNARDO, ROSE ANN. *Cultural Backgrounds of Students and Cooperating Teachers as Related to Attitudes Toward Children, Problems of Student Teaching, and Achievement of Student Teachers.* Doctor's thesis, Pennsylvania State University (University Park, Pa.), 1962. (*DA* 23:3791)

192. FOWLER, BEVERLY DAVIS. *Relation of Teacher Personality Characteristics and Attitudes to Teacher-Pupil Rapport and Emotional Climate in the Elementary Classroom.* Doctor's thesis, University of South Carolina (Columbia, S.C.), 1962. (*DA* 23:1614)

193. FRINSKO, WILLIAM. *Experimental Post-Degree Program at Wayne State University—An Analysis of the Selective and Predictive Factors in Student Teaching.* Doctor's thesis, Wayne State University (Detroit, Mich.), 1962. (*DA* 24:1901)

194. HINELY, REGINALD TERRY. *Prediction of Readiness for Teaching as Measured by Performance in Internship.* Doctor's thesis, University of Florida (Gainesville, Fla.), 1962. (*DA* 23:2806)

195. MEISGEIER, CHARLES HENRY. *Variables Which May Identify Successful Student Teachers of Mentally or Physically Handicapped Children.* Doctor's thesis, Pennsylvania State University (University Park, Pa.), 1962. (*DA* 23:3583)

196. PERRY, JAMES OLDEN. *A Study of a Selective Set of Criteria for Determining Success in Secondary Student Teaching at Texas Southern University.* Doctor's thesis, University of Texas (Austin, Tex.), 1962. (*DA* 23:1617)

197. WEBB, HARRY CHARLES. *An Investigation of Teacher Characteristics and Educational Film Utilization in Three Minnesota Urban Public School Systems.* Doctor's thesis, University of Minnesota (Minneapolis, Minn.), 1962. (*DA* 28:554A)

198. WEISER, JOHN CONRAD. *A Study of College of Education Students Divided According to Creative Ability.* Doctor's thesis, University of Missouri (Columbia, Mo.), 1962. (*DA* 23:4611)

199. BATES, CHARLES O. *A Study of Creative Potential as Found in Elementary Student Teachers.* Doctor's thesis, Ball State Teachers College (Muncie, Ind.), 1963. (*DA* 24:4561)

200. LACONICO, NORMA VALMONTE. *A Validation Study of the Minnesota Teacher Attitude Inventory in the Philippines.* Doctor's thesis, University of Colorado (Boulder, Colo.), 1963. (*DA* 28:2582A)

201. RICHARDSON, JOHN FRANCIS, III. *A Comparison of Certain Characteristics of a Group of Negro Education and Non-Education College Students: An Investigation to Determine the Nature and Significance of the Differences in Various Characteristics Between Negro College Students Who Select Teaching and Those Who Choose Other Vocational Goals.* Doctor's thesis, New York University (New York, N.Y.), 1963. (*DA* 24:2789)

202. SOLOMON, ADRIAN. "Authoritarian Attitude Changes and Group Homogeneity." *J Social Psychol* 59:129–35 F '63. * (*PA* 38:855)

203. BRODE, ELVIN LELAND. *Imitation of Supervisors by Teachers in Experimental Situations.* Doctor's thesis, University of Michigan (Ann Arbor, Mich.), 1964. (*DA* 25:7037)

204. BUTTON, HENRY WARREN, AND IANNACCONE, LAURANCE. "Correlates of the MTAI Validation Instrument." *J Ed Res* 58:184–5 D '64. *

205. CROWELL, THOMAS ROLLA, JR. *A Comparative Study of Teacher Personalities, Attitudes, and Values in Relation to Student Nonpromotion in the Elementary Schools of Rockford, Illinois.* Doctor's research study No. 1, Colorado State College (Greeley, Colo.), 1964. (*DA* 25:2823)

206. DANIELSON, ELAINE LOUISE. *A Study of Minnesota Teacher Attitude Inventory Scores and Grade Variables in Predicting Inter-Personal Relationships Between Elementary Student Teachers and Co-Operating Teachers.* Master's thesis, University of Kansas (Lawrence, Kan.), 1964.

207. DOLE, ARTHUR A. "The Prediction of Effectiveness in School Counseling." Comment by Edward Landy. *J Counsel Psychol* 11:112–22 su '64. * (*PA* 39:5956)

208. EASTERBROOK, CAROLYN M. *Pursuit of a Quest: Mortalities Along the Way. A Study of a Selected Group of Variables Relative to the Holding Power of the Art Teaching Profession.* Doctor's thesis, Wayne State University (Detroit, Mich.), 1964. (*DA* 26:4478)

209. FISCHER, WYMAN EDWIN. *A Study in the Prediction of Academic and Teaching Success—Concordia Teachers College, River Forest, Illinois.* Doctor's thesis, Southern Illinois University (Carbondale, Ill.), 1964. (*DA* 25:5137)

210. GORALSKI, PATRICIA SCHWARZ. *Creativity: Student Teachers' Perceptions of Approaches to Classroom Teaching.* Doctor's thesis, University of Minnesota (Minneapolis, Minn.), 1964. (*DA* 25:2851)

211. HERMAN, WILLIAM LANE. *Relationship Between Selected Characteristics and Teaching Attitude of Male Senior Physical Education Majors and Minors at Colorado State College.* Doctor's research study No. 1, Colorado State College (Greeley, Colo.), 1964. (*DA* 25:272)

Minnesota Teacher Attitude Inventory

212. JOHNSON, ROBERT KEECH. *Personal Characteristics of Effective Teachers of Slow Learning but Educable Students.* Doctor's thesis, Indiana University (Bloomington, Ind.), 1964. (*DA* 25:5681)

213. JOSHI, MOHAN C., AND SRIVASTAVA, R. P. "Intelligence and Teaching Attitude." *Guid R* (India) 2:95–103 Jl '64. * (*PA* 40:7069)

214. McDANIEL, ERNEST. "A Disguised Minnesota Teacher Attitude Test." *J Ed Res* 58:91 O '64. *

215. MUNRO, BARRY C. "The Minnesota Teacher Attitude Inventory as a Predictor of Teaching Success." *J Ed Res* 58:138–9 N '64. *

216. NELSON, ROBERT EUGENE. *A Study of the Intra-Faculty Sociometric Position of the Teacher of the Educable Mentally Retarded.* Doctor's thesis, Syracuse University (Syracuse, N.Y.), 1964. (*DA* 25:5746)

217. ORB, VERGIL K. "A Study of Some Techniques Used for Predicting the Success of Teachers." *J Teach Ed* 15:67–71 Mr '64. *

218. PALMER, WILLIAM FISHER. *Relationships of Certain Personality, Attitude, and Classroom Behavior Factors of Classroom Supervisors and Student Teachers.* Doctor's thesis, University of North Carolina (Chapel Hill, N.C.), 1964. (*DA* 25:6411)

219. POLESZAK, LEONARD J. *A Study of Student Teachers' Expected and Actual Outcomes and the Student Teaching Program of the Industrial Arts Education Division at the State University of New York, College at Buffalo.* Doctor's thesis, Michigan State University (East Lansing, Mich.), 1964. (*DA* 25:6413)

220. RANDLES, HARRY EDWARD. *The Effects of Organizational Climate on Beginning Elementary Teachers.* Doctor's thesis, Ohio State University (Columbus, Ohio), 1964. (*DA* 25:7049)

221. VEAL, LELAND RAMON. *A Comparison of the Professional Growth of Student Teachers Under Two Different Time-Arrangements for Student Teaching at the Secondary Level.* Doctor's thesis, University of South Carolina (Columbia, S.C.), 1964. (*DA* 25:7104)

222. WOLAVER, KATHRYN EVANS. *A Longitudinal Study of the Stability of Teachers' Attitudes and Personality as Related to Teacher Education and Teaching Experience.* Doctor's thesis, Purdue University (Lafayette, Ind.), 1964. (*DA* 25:2866)

223. ZIMILES, HERBERT; BIBER, BARBARA; RABINOWITZ, WILLIAM; AND HAY, LOUIS. "Personality Aspects of Teaching: A Predictive Study." *Genetic Psychol Monogr* 69:101–49 F '64. * (*PA* 39:2902)

224. BURKARD, M. INNOCENTIA. "Effectiveness of the MTAI in a Parochial School Setting." *J Exp Ed* 33:225–9 sp '65. * (*PA* 39:10843)

225. CHANCE, WILLIAM GEORGE. *A Study of Selected Factors as They Relate to the Establishment of Interpersonal Relations by Student Teachers.* Doctor's thesis, Oklahoma State University (Stillwater, Okla.), 1965. (*DA* 27:47A)

226. CONDELL, JAMES F., AND TONN, MARTIN H. "A Comparison of MTAI Scores." *Mental Retard* 3:23–4 F '65. * (*PA* 39:10846)

227. CONLEY, NAOMI LEE. *Factors Related to Teacher Effectiveness of High School Distributive Education Teacher-Coordinators.* Doctor's thesis, University of Tennessee (Knoxville, Tenn.), 1965. (*DA* 26:6440)

228. HORN, JOHN L., AND MORRISON, W. LEE. "Dimensions of Teacher Attitudes." *J Ed Psychol* 56:118–25 Je '65. * (*PA* 39:13048)

229. KEYTON, FREDERICK R. *Some Relationships Between a Measure of Self-Actualization and Various Aspects of Intermediate Grade Teacher Effectiveness.* Doctor's thesis, Catholic University of America (Washington, D.C.), 1965. (*DA* 26:4450)

230. LANTZ, DONALD L. "The Relationship of Minnesota Teacher Attitude Inventory Scores to Certain Biographical Information." *J Ed Res* 59:160–5 D '65. * (*PA* 40:5956)

231. LEEP, ALBERT GENE. *Selected Pre-Service Measures as Predictors of First Year Teaching Performance of Elementary Teachers.* Doctor's thesis, Ball State Teachers College (Muncie, Ind.), 1965. (*DA* 26:3163)

232. McCRACKEN, OLIVER, JR. *Changes in the Personality, Attitudes, and Classroom Behavior of Beginning Elementary Teachers in Niles Township, Niles, Illinois.* Doctor's thesis, University of Missouri (Columbia, Mo.), 1965. (*DA* 27:1663A)

233. McFADDEN, JACK DONALD. *The Relationship of Values, Attitude and Personality Characteristics of Student Teachers to Ratings by Their Supervisors.* Doctor's thesis, Northwestern University (Evanston, Ill.), 1965. (*DA* 26:7169)

234. MEISGEIER, CHARLES. "The Identification of Successful Teachers of Mentally or Physically Handicapped Children." *Excep Children* 32:229–35 D '65. * (*PA* 40:3409)

235. MOSER, JAMES MICHAEL. *A Case Study of the Effect of Information Feedback on the Performance of Student Teachers in Mathematics.* Doctor's thesis, University of Colorado (Boulder, Colo.), 1965. (*DA* 26:5895)

236. NULL, ELDON JAMES. *The Relationships Between the Organizational Climate of a School and Personal Variables of Members of the Teaching Staff.* Doctor's thesis, University of Minnesota (Minneapolis, Minn.), 1965. (*DA* 26:4392)

237. NYMAN, ERNEST LESLIE. *A Study of Drop-Outs Among Beginning Teachers.* Doctor's thesis, University of California (Los Angeles, Calif.), 1965. (*DA* 26:3770)

238. OANA, ROBERT GEORGE. *An Analysis of the Use of the Minnesota Teacher Attitude Inventory in a Preservice Program in Childhood Education.* Doctor's thesis, Columbia University (New York, N.Y.), 1965. (*DA* 27:129A)

239. RAICHE, ALOISE. *Selected Teacher Characteristics and Verbal Behavior in the Classroom.* Doctor's thesis, University of Minnesota (Minneapolis, Minn.), 1965. (*DA* 26:6508)

240. RENFRO, VIRGIL RALPH. *A Study of the Relationship Between Selected Influences and Changes of Attitude Toward Pupils That Occur During an Eighteen-Week Student-Teaching Experience.* Doctor's thesis, Oklahoma State University (Stillwater, Okla.), 1965. (*DA* 27:407A)

241. SCHMITT, PATRICIA ANN. *Descriptive Characteristics of Successful Girls' Camp Cabin Counselors and Their Attitudes Toward Children.* Master's thesis, Texas Woman's University (Denton, Tex.), 1965.

242. TARPEY, M. SIMEON. "Personality Factors in Teacher Trainee Selection." *Brit J Ed Psychol* 35:140–9 Je '65. * (*PA* 39:16480)

243. YEE, ALBERT HOY. *Causality in the Relationships Between Teachers' and Pupils' Interpersonal Attitudes.* Doctor's thesis, Stanford University (Stanford, Calif.), 1965. (*DA* 26:6572)

244. AMERSHEK, KATHLEEN GRACE. *The Structure of Verbal Behavior of Student Teachers and Children During the First Student Teaching Quarter.* Doctor's thesis, University of Minnesota (Minneapolis, Minn.), 1966. (*DA* 27:4148A)

245. BARTLETT, C. J. "A Forced-Choice Teacher Attitude Inventory." *J Ed Meas* 3:296 w '66. *

246. BLAIR, MARGARET SNYDER MORRIS. *Climate and Attitude: A Study of the Organizational Climate of Schools and Teachers' Attitudes Toward Students.* Doctor's thesis, Rutgers —The State University (New Brunswick, N.J.), 1966. (*DA* 27:1573A)

247. BRIM, BURL J. "Attitude Changes in Teacher Education Students." *J Ed Res* 59:441–5 Jl–Ag '66. * (*PA* 40:11510)

248. BUSCHER, ROBERT E. *An Analysis of Student Teaching and Organizational Climate.* Master's thesis, Eastern Illinois University (Charleston, Ill.), 1966.

249. CLOS, MARJORIE. "Evaluation of Mental Health Workshops in Kentucky." *J Ed Res* 59:278–81 F '66. * (*PA* 40:6916)

250. DIENER, RUSSELL EDWARD. *A Comparative Study of Selected Needs, Values, and Attitudes of Negro and White Elementary Education Students.* Doctor's thesis, University of Michigan (Ann Arbor, Mich.), 1966. (*DA* 27:2825A)

251. EVANS, K. M. "The Minnesota Teacher Attitude Inventory." *Ed Res* (England) 8:134–41 F '66. * (*PA* 40:9222)

252. HAMPTON, CAROL DEAN. *An Analysis of Pupil Progress as Related to Selected Teacher Behaviors: A Study of the Senior High School Associate Teachers Enrolled in the Fifth-Year Program in Teacher Education at the University of North Carolina, 1964–1965.* Doctor's thesis, University of North Carolina (Chapel Hill, N.C.), 1966. (*DA* 27:3755A)

253. ROSSI, PHILIP; YENGO, CARMINE; AND BOYD, WILLIAM. "A Comparison of Methodology on the Fakability of the Minnesota Teacher Attitude Inventory." *J Ed Res* 59:475–8 Jl–Ag '66. * (*PA* 40:10638)

254. SORENSON, GARTH; SCHAEFER, SHIRLEY; AND NYMAN, ERNEST L. "A Teacher Drop-Out for the MTAI?" *Calif J Ed Res* 17:91–5 Mr '66. * (*PA* 40:7074)

255. TEIGLAND, JOHN J. "The Relationship Between Measured Teacher Attitude Change and Certain Personality Characteristics." *J Ed Res* 60:84–5 O '66. *

256. VACCHIANO, RALPH B.; SCHIFFMAN, DAVID C.; AND CROWELL, ARETA V. "Attitude Change as a Function of Intensive Training, Dogmatism and Authoritarianism." *Psychol Rep* 19:359–62 O '66. * (*PA* 41:525)

257. WALKER, URSIN STUART. *The Relationship of Achievement and Attitudes to Selected Secondary School Factors of Teacher Education Candidates.* Doctor's thesis, Mississippi State University (State College, Miss.), 1966. (*DA* 27:3281A)

258. WARD, PAUL, AND BAILEY, JOHN A. "Community Participation and Attitudinal Changes Among Teacher Education Students." *Personnel & Guid J* 44:628–30 F '66. * (*PA* 40:7075)

259. WILLIAMS, JACK. *An Investigation of the Relationships Between Selected Factors Concerning Student Teachers and Their Success in Student Teaching.* Doctor's thesis, University of Houston (Houston, Tex.), 1966. (*DA* 27:2820A)

260. WILLMAN, CAROL ELSIE. *A Comparison of Prospective Special Education and Elementary Teachers on Selected Personality Characteristics.* Doctor's thesis, University of Michigan (Ann Arbor, Mich.), 1966. (*DA* 28:100A)

261. AGER, MERLIN FRED. *A Study of the Relationships Between Selected Personality Variables and Verbal Behavior, Supervisory Ratings and Grades of Student Teachers.* Doctor's thesis, Ohio State University (Columbus, Ohio), 1967. (*DA* 28:4926A)

262. ANDERSON, ROBERT E. "Seminar Experiences for Changing Attitudes of Graduating Seniors in Education." *J Exp Ed* 36:87–92 f '67. *

263. BRIDGMAN, JOHN NORTHAN, JR. *Selected Teacher Characteristics and Their Relationships With Certain Behavior Patterns and Teaching Effectiveness.* Doctor's thesis, University of North Carolina (Chapel Hill, N.C.), 1967. (*DA* 28:3524A)

Minnesota Teacher Attitude Inventory

264. BROADBENT, FRANK WILLIAM. *An Application of the Social Judgment-Involvement Approach to Predicting Changes in the Attitudes of Student Teachers.* Doctor's thesis, University of Rochester (Rochester, N.Y.), 1967. *(DA 28:138A)*

265. CAMPBELL, DONALD E. "Dimensional Attitude Changes of Student Teachers." *J Ed Res* 61:160–2 D '67. *

266. DAVIS, KATHLEEN L. *The Sensitivity of Selected Instruments to Personality Changes Produced by Group Counseling.* Doctor's thesis, University of Georgia (Athens, Ga.), 1967. *(DA 28:3968A)*

267. EVANS, K. M. "Teacher Training Courses and Students' Personal Qualities." *Ed Res* (England) 10:72–7 N '67. * *(PA 42:9394)*

268. FISCHLE, MILDRED JULIA. *A Study of Attitude and Behavior Change of Teachers Attending an NDEA Institute for Teachers of Disadvantaged Children.* Doctor's thesis, Ball State University (Muncie, Ind.), 1967. *(DA 28:4023A)*

269. FOX, A. M. "Temperament and Attitude Correlates of Leadership Behavior." *Ed & Psychol Meas* 27:1167–8 w '67. * *(PA 42:8953)*

270. FRANK, JAMES BERNELL. *Attitude Change of Secondary School Student Teachers During Student Teaching.* Doctor's thesis, University of Texas (Austin, Tex.), 1967. *(DA 28: 1717A)*

271. GEWINNER, MARCUS N. *A Study of the Results of the Interaction of Student Teachers With Their Supervising Teachers During the Student Teaching Period.* Doctor's thesis, Mississippi State University (State College, Miss.), 1967. *(DA 29: 165A)*

272. GIEBINK, JOHN W. "A Failure of the Minnesota Teacher Attitude Inventory to Relate to Teacher Behavior." *J Teach Ed* 18:233–9 su '67. * *(PA 41:12830)*

273. GREENE, GEORGE GORDON. *A Comparison on Selected Factors of a Group of College Undergraduate Volunteers in a Tutoring Program for Culturally Disadvantaged Children.* Doctor's thesis, Ball State University (Muncie, Ind.), 1967. *(DA 28:3052A)*

274. HAGADONE, THEODORE EDWARD. *A Study of Teacher Personal and Professional Attitudes as They Relate to Student Self-Concepts and Attitudes Toward School in the Six Highest Achieving Schools in Flint, Michigan.* Doctor's thesis, Michigan State University (East Lansing, Mich.), 1967. *(DA 28:3932A)*

275. HERMAN, WILLIAM L. "Teaching Attitude as Related to Academic Grades and Athletic Ability of Prospective Physical Education Teachers." *J Ed Res* 61:40–2 S '67. *

276. HICKOX, WILLIAM ANDERSON. *A Measurement of Professional Compatibility Between a Teacher and His Principal.* Doctor's thesis, University of Mississippi (University, Miss.), 1967. *(DA 28:429A)*

277. KRACHT, CONRAD RALPH. *The Relationship of Scores on the Minnesota Teacher Attitude Inventory and the IPAT Anxiety Scale Questionnaire to Evaluation of Student Teachers' Classroom Performance.* Doctor's thesis, Southern Illinois University (Carbondale, Ill.), 1967. *(DA 28:3529A)*

278. McCAW, W. RALPH. "Cognitive Dissonance and Teachers-in-Training." *J Exp Ed* 35:50–2 su '67. *

279. MAXWELL, ROBERT EARL. *Leader Behavior of Principals: A Study in Ten Inner-City Elementary Schools of Flint, Michigan.* Doctor's thesis, Wayne State University (Detroit, Mich.), 1967. *(DA 28:2950A)*

280. MORRISON, W. LEE, AND ROMOSER, R. C. "Personality Structure and Dimensions of Teacher Attitudes." *J Exp Ed* 36:55–8 w '67. *

281. MORRISON, W. LEE, AND ROMOSER, R. C. " 'Traditional' Classroom Attitudes, the A.C.T. and the 16 P.F." *J Ed Res* 60:326–9 Mr '67. *

282. MORRISON, WAYLAND LEE. *Dimensions of Personality and Teacher Related Attitudes in Prospective Teachers.* Doctor's thesis, University of Denver (Denver, Colo.), 1967. *(DA 28: 502A)*

283. MUTO, NICK FRANCIS. *A Study of Changes in Teaching Style During the Student Teaching Experience.* Doctor's thesis, Syracuse University (Syracuse, N.Y.), 1967. *(DA 28:4387A)*

284. REBSTOCK, CHARLES WESLEY. *Changes in the Personality, Values, Attitudes, and Verbal Behavior of Student Teachers Through the Use of Certain Objective Observational Techniques.* Doctor's thesis, University of Minnesota (Minneapolis, Minn.), 1967. *(DA 28:4939A)*

285. SEIBEL, DEAN W. "Predicting the Classroom Behavior of Teachers." *J Exp Ed* 36:26–32 f '67. *

286. SPAIGHTS, ERNEST, AND BLUM, LAWRENCE P. "Social Reinforcement Counseling as an Adjunct to a Course in Education." *J Ed Res* 60:256–9 F '67. *

287. TAN, CONCHITA ABELLA. *Creativity in Teaching.* Doctor's thesis, University of Minnesota (Minneapolis, Minn.), 1967. *(DA 28:4917A)*

288. THOMPSON, JAMES NEWTON. *Stability and Change in Measured Attitudes and Vocational Interests of Women in a Teacher Education Program.* Doctor's thesis, University of Missouri (Columbia, Mo.), 1967. *(DA 28:4035A)*

289. WALBERG, HERBERT J. "The Development of Teacher Personality: Multivariate Theory and Analysis." *Sch R* 75: 187–96 su '67. *

290. WALBERG, HERBERT J., AND WELCH, WAYNE W. "Per-

sonality Characteristics of Innovative Physics Teachers." *J Creative Behav* 1:163–71 sp '67. * *(PA 41:15285)*

291. WILLIAMS, JACK, AND FOX, A. M. "Prediction of Performance in Student Teaching." *Ed & Psychol Meas* 27:1169–70 w '67. * *(PA 42:9491)*

292. YEE, ALBERT H. "Is the Minnesota Teacher Attitude Inventory Valid and Homogeneous?" *J Ed Meas* 4:151–61 f '67. * *(PA 43:11887)*

293. BLACKWELL, ROBERT BRENNAN. *A Study of Effective and Ineffective Teachers of the Trainable Mentally Retarded.* Doctor's thesis, Colorado State College (Greeley, Colo.), 1968. *(DA 29:1147A)*

294. BRADBERRY, RONALD DAVID. *Relationships Among Critical Thinking Ability, Personality Attributes, and Attitudes of Students in a Teacher Education Program.* Doctor's thesis, North Texas State University (Denton, Tex.), 1968. *(DA 29:163A)*

295. BRODY, ERNESS EDWYNA BRIGHT. *The Relationships Between Student Teacher Effectiveness and Student Characteristics: A Moderator Variable Analysis.* Doctor's thesis, University of Michigan (Ann Arbor, Mich.), 1968. *(DA 29:757A)*

296. CAMPBELL, GENE VIRGINIA. *A Descriptive Study of the Effects of Student Teaching Upon Attitudes, Anxieties, and Perceived Problems of Student Teachers.* Doctor's thesis, University of Houston (Houston, Tex.), 1968. *(DA 29:3890A)*

297. CLARK, WINIFRED BRADLEY. *An Empirical Study of Attitudes Toward Teaching Selected Values, and Demographic Information of Freshmen and Seniors.* Doctor's thesis, Auburn University (Auburn, Ala.), 1968. *(DA 28:3992A)*

298. COMBS, CLYDE MAURICE, JR. *An Experiment With Independent Study in Science Education.* Doctor's thesis, University of Mississippi (University, Miss.), 1968. *(DA 29:3489A)*

299. CONLEY, JAMES LEROY. *A Study of Selected Biographical Data, Personality Characteristics and Attitudes of Elementary Intern Program Students at Michigan State University.* Doctor's thesis, Michigan State University (East Lansing, Mich.), 1968. *(DA 29:3490A)*

300. CZAJKOWSKI, THEODORE JOSEPH, JR. *The Relationship of Confidence for Teaching to Selected Personal Characteristics and Performance of Student Teachers.* Doctor's thesis, Michigan State University (East Lansing, Mich.), 1968. *(DAI 30:185A)*

301. DAVIS, O. L., JR., AND YAMAMOTO, KAORU. "Teachers in Preparation: 2, Professional Attitudes and Motivations." *J Teach Ed* 19:365–9 f '68. * *(PA 43:3094, title only)*

302. EVANS, K. M. "Teachers and Some Others: A Comparative Study." *Ed Res* (England) 11:153–6 F '68. *

303. FRANK, RUTH E. "Can Changes in Professional Attitudes Be Catalyzed by Coursework in Social Foundations of Education?" *Int J Exp Res Ed* (Belgium) 5(1):68–75 '68. * *(PA 45:3019)*

304. FURR, ONETA ROBERTS. *Effects of Observational Feedback on Verbal and Nonverbal Classroom Behavior of Student Teachers.* Doctor's thesis, North Texas State University (Denton, Tex.), 1968. *(DA 29:3495A)*

305. GATES, CARL JAY. *A Study of Attitude, Need, and Personality Trait Correlates of Effective Teaching in Three Selected School Systems.* Doctor's thesis, University of Southern Mississippi (Hattiesburg, Miss.), 1968. *(DA 29:3021A)*

306. GILL, NEWELL T.; KING, ROY; AND WILBURN, RON G. "A Helping Relationship Experience in Teacher Education." *J Exp Ed* 37:24–33 w '68. *

307. GNAGEY, WILLIAM J. "Parental Acceptance and the Professional Attitudes of Students in Teacher Education." *J Ed Res* 61:234–7 Ja '68. *

308. GNAGEY, WILLIAM J. "Student Attitude Learning as a Function of Parental Acceptance and Sex of Teacher." *J Teach Ed* 19:313–6 f '68. * *(PA 43:3095)*

309. GOOD, RONALD GLENN. *An Analysis of the Self-Perceptions and Other Selected Characteristics of Effective and Ineffective Teachers: A Study Based on the Educational Philosophy of the Fifth-Year Program in Teacher Education at the University of North Carolina.* Doctor's thesis, University of North Carolina (Chapel Hill, N.C.), 1968. *(DA 29:4373A)*

310. JUSTIZ, THOMAS BENSON. *A Method for Identifying the Effective Teacher.* Doctor's thesis, University of California (Los Angeles, Calif.), 1968. *(DA 29:3022A)*

311. LLOYD, THOMAS C. *The Relationship of Selected Characteristics of Teacher Education Students and Selected Measures of Achievement in Teacher Education.* Doctor's thesis, Texas Technological College (Lubbock, Tex.), 1968. *(DA 29:3332A)*

312. McEWIN, TOM. *Attitudinal Change of Students During Methods Courses and Student Teaching.* Doctor's thesis, East Texas State University (Commerce, Tex.), 1968. *(DA 29:169A)*

313. McFADDEN, JACK D. "The Discrimination of Student Teaching Performance on the Basis of Psychological Attributes." *J Ed Res* 61:215–7 Ja '68. *

314. MAKOVIC, MARY VERNICE. *The Relationships Between Nun-Teachers' Manifest Psychogenic Needs and Attitudes Toward Students and Student Behavior.* Doctor's thesis, Case Western Reserve University (Cleveland, Ohio), 1968. *(DAI 30: 170A)*

315. MEDLER, BYRON WAYNE. *A Comparative Study of Selected Variables Between Students Completing the Elementary Education Curriculum and Those Students Who Left the Elementary Education Curriculum Due to Academic Disqualifi-

cation or Change of Major. Doctor's thesis, Ball State University (Muncie, Ind.), 1968. (*DA* 29:3503A)

316. NORWALK-POLSKY, ZITA. *A Preliminary Study of the Belief Systems and Selected Values and Attitudes of Faculty and Students in a State College for Teachers.* Doctor's thesis, New York University (New York, N.Y.), 1968. (*DA* 29:1466A)

317. PITKIN, TONY RAY. *A Comparison of the Attitudes Toward Mathematics and Toward Pupils of Selected Groups of Elementary School Teachers Who Had Different Types and Amounts of College Education in Modern Mathematics.* Doctor's thesis, University of South Dakota (Vermillion, S.D.), 1968. (*DA* 29:3025A)

318. ROSEN, JULIUS. "School Counselor Dogmatism and Vocational Identity." *Psychol Rep* 23:24-6 Ag '68. * (*PA* 43:7350)

319. ROTHROCK, JULIA E. *An Assessment of the Validity of the Minnesota Teacher Attitude Inventory in a Field Situation.* Master's thesis, Chico State College (Chico, Calif.), 1968.

320. SENOFF, GEORGE. *The Influence of Flamidon Interaction Analysis Instruction on Student Teachers' Prediction and Performance of Select Objectives.* Doctor's thesis, University of North Dakota (Grand Forks, N.D.), 1968. (*DA* 29:2592A)

321. SHUSTER, ARNOLD ALLAN. *The Relationship Between Varying Scores on the Minnesota Teacher Attitude Inventory and Patterns of Behavior Both Perceived and Enacted in a Recreation Setting.* Doctor's thesis, University of Illinois (Urbana, Ill.), 1968. (*DA* 29:2581A)

322. THOMPSON, RICHARD ARLEN. *An Evaluation of a Two-Week Workshop in Education (Exploring Creativity).* Doctor's thesis, Ball State University (Muncie, Ind.), 1968. (*DA* 29:1470A)

323. THORUP, ROINE FIFE HUNT. *A Study of the Relationship of Certain Attitudes and Characteristics of Home Economics Student Teacher Candidates and Their Subsequent Effectiveness as Secondary School Teachers.* Doctor's thesis, University of Minnesota (Minneapolis, Minn.), 1968. (*DA* 29:2513B)

324. VERGIELS, JOHN MAURICE. *A Cross-National Study of Relationships Between Professional Variables of Secondary Teacher Education Students.* Doctor's thesis, University of Toledo (Toledo, Ohio), 1968. (*DA* 29:2595A)

325. WALBERG, HERBERT J. "Personality Correlates of Factored Teaching Attitudes." *Psychol Sch* 5:67-74 Ja '68. *

326. WALBERG, HERBERT J. "Teacher Personality and Classroom Climate." *Psychol Sch* 5:163-9 Ap '68. *

327. WALBERG, HERBERT J., AND WELCH, WAYNE W. "Dimensions of Personality in Selected Physics Teachers." *J Res Sci Teach* 5(4):357-61 '67-68 ['68]. *

328. WALBERG, HERBERT J.; METZNER, SEYMOUR; TODD, ROBERT M.; AND HENRY, PHYLLIS M. "Effects of Tutoring and Practice Teaching on Self-Concept and Attitudes in Education Students." *J Teach Ed* 19:283-91 f '68. * (*PA* 43:3104)

329. WHITE, JOSEPH MARTIN, JR. *Effects on Teacher Attitude and Behavior When Teachers Plan the Student Teaching Program for Students Assigned to a Participating School in a Teaching Center.* Doctor's thesis, Michigan State University (East Lansing, Mich.), 1968. (*DA* 29:1470A)

330. WHITE, THOMAS ROBERT. *A Study of the Values and Attitudes of Distributive Education Teacher-Coordinators as Compared to Two Groups of Potential Teacher-Coordinators.* Doctor's thesis, Ohio State University (Columbus, Ohio), 1968. (*DAI* 30:610A)

331. YEE, ALBERT H. "Source and Direction of Causal Influence in Teacher-Pupil Relationships." *J Ed Psychol* 59:275-82 Ag '68. * (*PA* 42:16008)

332. BEHLING, MARY ALICE. *The Development of a Screening Program for the Selection and Retention of Women Physical Education Major Students.* Doctor's thesis, Florida State University (Tallahassee, Fla.), 1969. (*DAI* 30:4258A)

333. BELT, GORDON ANTHONY. *A Study of the Changes in Personality Variables and Attitudes of Students in an Education Class.* Doctor's thesis, Wayne State University (Detroit, Mich.), 1969. (*DAI* 31:1654A)

334. BRASHEARS, ELIZABETH FITZGERALD. *Attitudes of Student Teachers in Team Teaching and Self-Contained Classrooms.* Doctor's thesis, University of Tennessee (Knoxville, Tenn.), 1969. (*DAI* 31:1657A)

335. BRUCE, LARRY RHEA. *A Determination of the Relationships Among SCIS Teachers' Personality Traits, Attitude Toward Teacher-Pupil Relationship, Understanding of Science Process Skills and Question Types.* Doctor's thesis, Michigan State University (East Lansing, Mich.), 1969. (*DAI* 30:4850A)

336. COLLINS, ERIK. *The Relationship of Perceptiveness and Attitude of Elementary Teachers to Certain Dimensions of Classroom Mental Health.* Doctor's thesis, University of Michigan (Ann Arbor, Mich.), 1969. (*DAI* 30:3775A)

337. FINCH, CURTIS R. "The Trade and Industrial Education Teacher's Background, Values, and Attitude Toward Teaching." *J Indus Teach Ed* 6(2):55-64 w '69. *

338. GEISS, DORIS THERESA. *Faculty and Administrator Perceptions of the Decision-Making Authority in Collegiate Nursing Programs.* Doctor's thesis, Columbia University (New York, N.Y.), 1969. (*DAI* 30:1359A)

339. GILBERT, CHARLES DAVID. *Interrelationships Among Interstaff Rankings of Elementary School Teachers in Respect to Classroom Management, Social Living Effectiveness, and Other*

Selected Factors. Doctor's thesis, Ball State University (Muncie, Ind.), 1969. (*DAI* 30:489A)

340. GOLDMAN, BERT A. "Effect of Classroom Experience and Video Tape Self-Observation Upon Undergraduate Attitudes Toward Self and Toward Teaching." Abstract. *Proc 77th Ann Conv Am Psychol Assn* 4(2):647-8 '69. * (*PA* 44:1317)

341. GORMLEY, JOSEPH DONLAN. *Dogmatism and Change in Teachers.* Doctor's thesis, University of Kentucky (Lexington, Ky.), 1969. (*DAI* 31:63A)

342. HAYNES, ROBERT CLAYTON. *The Role of In-Service Education in Attitudinal Change for Teachers of Slow Learners in Mathematics and Science.* Doctor's thesis, George Peabody College for Teachers (Nashville, Tenn.), 1969. (*DAI* 30:4307A)

343. HOGAN, ROBERT A. "Academic Excellence and Its Philosophical Motivation." *Ill State Univ J* 31(4):25-30 My '69. *

344. INGLIS, JOAN DIETHELM. *The Effect of a Professional Laboratory Experience on the Attitudes of Student Teachers Toward Children and Teaching.* Doctor's thesis, University of Toledo (Toledo, Ohio), 1969. (*DAI* 31:1666A)

345. JABS, MAX LEWIS. *An Experimental Study of the Comparative Effects of Initiating Structure and Consideration Leadership on the Educational Growth of College Students.* Doctor's thesis, University of Connecticut (Storrs, Conn.), 1969. (*DAI* 30:2762A)

346. JOHNSTON, DONALD P. "The Relationships of Self-Supervision to Change in Selected Attitudes and Behaviors of Secondary Student Teachers." *Ed Leadership* 27(1):57-63 O '69. *

347. JUSTIZ, THOMAS B. "A Reliable Measure of Teacher Effectiveness." *Ed Leadership* 27(1):49-55 O '69. *

348. LAGANA, JOSEPH FRANCIS. *Attitude Changes Among Beginning Teachers Toward Students and Teaching.* Doctor's thesis, University of Pittsburgh (Pittsburgh, Pa.), 1969. (*DAI* 30:4189A)

349. LANTZ, ALBERT WESLEY. *Relationship of Sensitivity Training to Change in Attitudes Held by Student Teachers.* Doctor's thesis, United States International University (San Diego, Calif.), 1969. (*DAI* 30:2402A)

350. LEEDS, C. H. "Predictive Validity of the *Minnesota Teacher Attitude Inventory.*" *J Teach Ed* 20(1):51-6 sp '69. * (*PA* 43:16418)

351. LI, ANITA KING-FUN. "Student Attitudes and Teacher Training Performance." *Ed Res* (England) 12(1):60-3 N '69. *

352. LINDEN, KATHRYN W., AND LINDEN, JAMES D. "A Longitudinal Study of Teachers' Attitudes and Personality Characteristics." *J Teach Ed* 20(3):351-60 f '69. * (*PA* 44:11336)

353. MINTER, JOSEPH ROBERT. *The Effects of Sensitivity Training on Self Concept and Attitudes of Student Teachers.* Doctor's thesis, East Texas State University (Commerce, Tex.), 1969. (*DAI* 30:5323A)

354. MORITZ, FLOYD C. *A Human Relations Laboratory as an Inservice Education Program.* Doctor's thesis, Arizona State University (Tempe, Ariz.), 1969. (*DAI* 30:3694A)

355. MUUSS, ROLF E. "Differential Effects of Studying Versus Teaching on Teachers' Attitudes." *J Ed Res* 63(4):185-9 D '69. *

356. PADOVER, ANN FEINGOLD. *Impact on Attitudes, Personality Factors, and Behavior of an N.D.E.A. Summer Institute for Teachers and Other Professional School Personnel of Disadvantaged Youth.* Doctor's thesis, University of Michigan (Ann Arbor, Mich.), 1969. (*DAI* 30:4780B)

357. PORTER, JAMES HURT, JR. *Correlation of Teacher Attitudes With Learning Among Selected Disadvantaged Elementary Students.* Doctor's thesis, Texas A & M University (College Station, Tex.), 1969. (*DAI* 31:79A)

358. POWELL, JUDITH ANN JOURDAN, AND BENSON, GERALD B. "Relationship Between Students' Personalities and Their Attitudes Toward Young Children." *J Home Econ* 61(9):687-92 N '69. *

359. RANDALL, WILLIAM THEODORE. *The Relationship of Teacher Attitudes and Verbal Behavior to Participation in a Workshop Utilizing the Instrument for the Observation of Teaching Activities.* Doctor's thesis, Arizona State University (Tempe, Ariz.), 1969. (*DAI* 30:2305A)

360. ROTHMAN, ARTHUR I.; WELCH, WAYNE W.; AND WALBERG, HERBERT J. "Physics Teacher Characteristics and Student Learnings." *J Res Sci Teach* 6(1):59-63 '69. *

361. SAWIN, MARGARET MAY. *A Study of Sunday Church School Teachers' Personality Characteristics and Attitudes Toward Children.* Doctor's thesis, University of Maryland (College Park, Md.), 1969. (*DAI* 31:245A)

362. SMITH, CHARLES FRANK, JR. *A Study of the Attitudes of Teachers in Title I and Non-Title I Depressed Area Elementary Schools Toward Pupil-Teacher Relations as Measured by the Minnesota Teacher Attitude Inventory.* Doctor's thesis, Michigan State University (East Lansing, Mich.), 1969. (*DAI* 31:85A)

363. STEDTFELD, RICHARD WARREN. *Performance Level Effectiveness of Training Prospective Teachers in Interpersonal Skills.* Doctor's thesis, University of Minnesota (Minneapolis, Minn.), 1969. (*DAI* 30:5329A)

364. STOCKTON, REX ARTHUR. *An Investigation of the Effect of Sensitivity Training on the Attitudes of Teacher Education*

Students. Doctor's thesis, Ball State University (Muncie, Ind.), 1969. (*DAI* 30:2156A)

365. SUMMERS, GENE F.; SHUSTER, ARNOLD A.; AND SHUSTER, SUSAN K. "The Minnesota Teacher Attitude Inventory and Counselor-Camper Interaction: A Note on Predictive Validity." *Ed & Psychol Meas* 29(4):999–1004 w '69. * (*PA* 44:21006)

366. TAYLOR, JUDSON HARRY. *Some Changes in and Correlates of Attitudinal Profile Similarity Between Student and Supervising Teachers.* Doctor's thesis, Arizona State University (Tempe, Ariz.), 1969. (*DAI* 30:3804A)

367. THOMAS, RANDALL L. *A Study of the Relationship Between Scores on the Minnesota Teacher Attitude Inventory and the Academic Classification and Sex of Secondary Education Majors at the Time They Entered the College of Education at Mississippi State University.* Master's thesis, Mississippi State University (State College, Miss.), 1969.

368. WEINSTOCK, HENRY R.; PECCOLO, CHARLES M.; COPPEDGE, FLOYD L.; AND COPPEDGE, LLOYD L. "Logical Consistency of Student Teachers in Different Educational Environments." *J Exp Ed* 37(3):78–84 sp '69. *

369. YEE, ALBERT H. "Do Cooperating Teachers Influence the Attitudes of Student Teachers?" *J Ed Psychol* 60(4):327–32 Ag '69. * (*PA* 43:16422)

370. YEE, ALBERT H. "Social Interaction in Classrooms: Implications for the Education of Disadvantaged Pupils." *Urban Ed* 4(3):203–19 O '69. * (*PA* 44:7275)

371. YEE, ALBERT H., AND KRIEWALL, THOMAS. "A New Logical Scoring Key for the Minnesota Teacher Attitude Inventory." *J Ed Meas* 6(1):11–4 sp '69. * (*PA* 44:15313)

372. ZIMMERMAN, DONALD DREW. *The Effects of Differentiated Community Placement Upon Attitudes and Personality Characteristics of College Juniors in a Laboratory Setting.* Doctor's thesis, Temple University (Philadelphia, Pa.), 1969. (*DAI* 32:1390A)

373. ASBURY, FRANK R.; BALL, ROBERT L.; AND CONSTANTINO, NICHOLAS V. "Some General Effects of a Foundations of Education Course on Selected Personality Variables of Teacher Candidates." *J Stud Pers Assn Teach Ed* 9(1):23–32 f '70. * (*PA* 46:5604)

374. BRADEN, JAMES NEIL. *A Study of the Relationship Between Teacher, Principal and Student Attitudes and Organizational Climate.* Doctor's thesis, University of Missouri (Columbia, Mo.), 1970. (*DAI* 31:3801A)

375. BRICKNER, SALLY ANN MARY. *Observed Classroom Behaviors and Personality Types of 178 Beginning Teachers.* Doctor's thesis, Michigan State University (East Lansing, Mich.), 1970. (*DAI* 31:5898A)

376. BRODY, ERNESS B. "A Note on the Validity of the Minnesota Teacher Attitude Inventory (MTAI)." *J Ed Res* 64(2):67 O '70. * (*PA* 46:7617)

377. CICIRELLI, VICTOR G., AND CICIRELLI, JEAN S. "Counselors' Creative Ability and Attitude in Relation to Counseling Behavior With Disadvantaged Counselees." *J Counsel Psychol* 17(2):177–83 Mr '70. * (*PA* 44:8550)

378. CLAYCOMB, CLYDE MORGAN. *An Exploratory Study of Attitudes Toward Children Expressed by Undergraduate Teacher Candidates.* Doctor's thesis, Michigan State University (East Lansing, Mich.), 1970. (*DAI* 31:5657A)

379. COCKRIEL, IRVIN WAYNE. *Stability of Responses to the Minnesota Teacher Attitude Inventory of College Freshmen in Education.* Doctor's thesis, University of Missouri (Columbia, Mo.), 1970. (*DAI* 31:5118A)

380. DEWALD, ANNA LUCILLE KENT. *A Study to Determine Factors Influencing Attitude Change of Student Teachers in the Elementary School.* Doctor's thesis, University of Houston (Houston, Tex.), 1970. (*DAI* 31:2769A)

381. FREEBERG, HOWARD GLYNN. *A Comparative Study of Secondary Student Teacher Attitudinal Change and Satisfaction With Student Teaching.* Doctor's thesis, University of North Dakota (Grand Forks, N.D.), 1970. (*DAI* 31:6451A)

382. GEORGE, PAUL STEINER. *A Study of the Effects of Mutually Perceived Facilitative Relationships Upon the Attitudes and Satisfactions of Student Teachers.* Doctor's thesis, George Peabody College for Teachers (Nashville, Tenn.), 1970. (*DAI* 31:2771A)

383. HENSRUD, NEIL BARRY. *The Relation of Scores on the MTAI to Selected Non-Intellective and Demographic Variables.* Doctor's thesis, University of North Dakota (Grand Forks, N.D.), 1970. (*DAI* 31:2229A)

384. HOLCOMB, J. DAVID. "Improving Attitudes and Verbal Behavior Through Kinescope Observation." *Ed Leadership* 27(8):809–14 My '70. *

385. HUGHES, LOIS JUNE. *Selected Factors as Related to Success in Student Teaching of Home Economics.* Doctor's thesis, University of Missouri (Columbia, Mo.), 1970. (*DAI* 31:5249A)

386. HUGHES, THOMAS HENRY. *A Study of Selected Characteristics and Behaviors of Effective Cooperating Teachers.* Doctor's thesis, Northern Illinois University (DeKalb, Ill.), 1970. (*DAI* 31:5905A)

387. INMAN, GERALD DUANE. *A Study of Expectations Held by Intern Teachers With Selected Personal Characteristics for Intern Consultant Role.* Doctor's thesis, Michigan State University (East Lansing, Mich.), 1970. (*DAI* 31:4007A)

388. JANSEN, DAVID G.; ROBB, GEORGE P.; AND BONK, EDWARD C. "Characteristics of High-Rated and Low-Rated Master's Degree Candidates in Counseling and Guidance." *Counselor Ed & Sup* 9(3):162–70 sp '70. * (*PA* 46:5559)

389. KAKKAR, S. B. "Teacher Attitude Change and Value Structure." *Manas* (India) 17(2):103–9 N '70. * (*PA* 47:9784)

390. KIMBROUGH, BROWNIE MITCHELL. *A Study of Attitude Changes of Student Teachers Toward Discipline of Elementary Pupils as Measured by the Minnesota Teacher Attitude Inventory.* Doctor's thesis, Oklahoma State University (Stillwater, Okla.), 1970. (*DAI* 31:5251A)

391. KNAPP, WILLIAM MARTIN. *A Study of Teacher Personality Characteristics and Rated Effectiveness.* Doctor's thesis, University of Southern Mississippi (Hattiesburg, Miss.), 1970. (*DAI* 31:5712A)

392. LAMB, RONALD WRIGHT. *Factors Affecting Cooperating Teacher Influence Upon Student Teacher Attitude and Role Perception.* Doctor's thesis, University of Arizona (Tucson, Ariz.), 1970. (*DAI* 31:4600A)

393. LEE, WALTER S. "Human Relations Training for Teachers: The Effectiveness of Sensitivity Training." *Calif J Ed Res* 21(1):28–34 Ja '70. * (*PA* 45:8966)

394. MORTENSON, ROBERT ALBERT. *Student Teacher Attitudinal Changes.* Doctor's thesis, University of Missouri (Columbia, Mo.), 1970. (*DAI* 31:5912A)

395. QUINN, PETER JOHN, JR. *The Effects of Field Teaching Assignments, Made on the Basis of the Teaching Behavior of the Student Teachers and the Cooperating Teachers, on the Attitudes and Dogmatism of Student Teachers.* Doctor's thesis, University of Massachusetts (Amherst, Mass.), 1970. (*DAI* 31:4605A)

396. RAINES, BOB GENE. *Personal, Situational, and Behavioral Predisposition Factors Related to the Elementary Teacher's Attitude Toward Teaching Mathematics.* Doctor's thesis, University of Virginia (Charlottesville, Va.), 1970. (*DAI* 31:4631A)

397. RAWLINS, GEORGE MIMMS, III. *A Study of Prospective Teachers' Problem Perceptions Compared With Problems Encountered and Attitude Changes Occurring During Student Teaching.* Doctor's thesis, University of Tennessee (Knoxville, Tenn.), 1970. (*DAI* 31:3397A)

398. ROBERTS, LAUNEY FRANKLIN, JR. *Selected Perceptions of Parents and Elementary School Staff Attitudes Related to Organizational Climate and Income.* Doctor's thesis, University of Missouri (Columbia, Mo.), 1970. (*DAI* 31:5096A)

399. RONDEAU, JAMES HENRY. *A Study of Selected Group and Individual Characteristics of Fifty-Two Teacher Candidates Enrolled in a Secondary Social Studies Methods Course at the University of Idaho.* Doctor's thesis, University of Idaho (Moscow, Idaho), 1970. (*DAI* 31:3399A)

400. ROTHWELL, ELIZABETH ANN. *The Relationship of Personality Traits, Teacher Attitude, Anxiety Level, and Academic Achievement to Ratings of Teacher Interns.* Doctor's thesis, Auburn University (Auburn, Ala.), 1970. (*DAI* 31:4021A)

401. SMITH, DAVID LARRY. *An Analysis of Attitudes of Teacher Education Majors at Florida Atlantic University Toward School Age Students.* Doctor's thesis, University of Nebraska (Lincoln, Neb.), 1970. (*DAI* 31:5258A)

402. STEVENSON, WARREN ALLEN. *Authoritarian and Equalitarian Attitudes of Classroom Teachers.* Doctor's thesis, University of California (Los Angeles, Calif.), 1970. (*DAI* 31:1556A)

403. TALLANT, WELDON J. *Changes in Pre-Service Teachers Involved in a Multi-Cultural Training Program Utilizing Formal Presentations, Sensitivity Training, Planned Social Activities, and a Cooperative Living Arrangement.* Doctor's thesis, East Texas State University (Commerce, Tex.), 1970. (*DAI* 31:4608A)

404. YEE, ALBERT H. "Do Principals' Interpersonal Attitudes Agree With Those of Teachers and Pupils?" *Ed Adm Q* 6(2):1–13 sp '70. * (*PA* 44:19329)

405. ZURHELLEN, HENRY SCOTT. *A Study of Teacher Attitudes During an In-Service Education Program in Selected East Tennessee Schools.* Doctor's thesis, University of Tennessee (Knoxville, Tenn.), 1970. (*DAI* 31:4613A)

406. ZURHELLEN, JOAN HARRIS. *An Evaluation of Attitude Changes Among Science Teachers During an ESCP In-Service Institute.* Doctor's thesis, University of Tennessee (Knoxville, Tenn.), 1970. (*DAI* 31:4613A)

407. BELL, RAYMOND. *A Comparison of Attitudes of Teachers in Selected Urban Comprehensive Secondary Schools of England and Pennsylvania.* Doctor's thesis, Lehigh University (Bethlehem, Pa.), 1971. (*DAI* 32:4826A)

408. BRADFIELD, PHYLLIS G. KAPLAN. *Interrelationships Between Teacher Attitudes, Student Achievement and Student Behavior Ratings in the Public School Classrooms for the Emotionally Disturbed.* Doctor's thesis, Wayne State University (Detroit, Mich.), 1971. (*DAI* 32:2511A)

409. BROWN, JAMES C.; STARNES, THOMAS A.; AND WATSON, J. ALLEN. "Southern Negro and White Educators: A Comparison of Pertinent Characteristics." *J Negro Ed* 40(2):159–62 sp '71. *

410. COX, JOHN ALFRED. *The Effectiveness of Teacher Verbal Feedback as Measured by the Withall Climate Index.* Doctor's thesis, Pennsylvania State University (University Park, Pa.), 1971. (*DAI* 33:72A)

411. DAVIDSON, CHARLES WINFREY. *Relationships Between Remuneration and Attitudes and Qualifications and Attitudes of*

Cooperating Teachers in Public Secondary Schools. Doctor's thesis, University of Arkansas (Fayetteville, Ark.), 1971. (*DAI* 32:2522A)

412. EL-ABD, HAMED A. "Application of the Minnesota Teacher Attitude Inventory (MTAI) to British and East African Diploma Students." *J Cross-Cultural Psychol* 2(2):203–4 Je '71. * (*PA* 47:4649)

413. GABRIELLI, RALPH B. *A Study of the Characteristics of Pre-Service Teachers Identified on an Experimental Instrument as High or Low in Problem Solving Ability.* Doctor's thesis, Syracuse University (Syracuse, N.Y.), 1971. (*DAI* 32:5650A)

414. GIESE, RONALD NORMAN. *An Analysis of Selected Aspects of the ISCS Model of Science Teaching: Part 1, Relationships of Selected Characteristics and Behaviors of Teachers Using the Intermediate Science Curriculum Study.* Doctor's thesis, Temple University (Philadelphia, Pa.), 1971. (*DAI* 32:4466A)

415. GOLDENBURG, IRENE. "Social Class Differences in Teacher Attitudes Toward Children." *Child Develop* 42(5):1637–40 N '71. * (*PA* 48:5756)

416. GREEN, POWELL A. *Factor Structure of the Minnesota Teacher Attitude Inventory and Correlations With Selected Personality Measures.* Master's thesis, University of California (Los Angeles, Calif.), 1971.

417. HOUSER, RONALD L. *Development of Affective Scales to Predict Career Commitment to Education.* Doctor's thesis, Purdue University (Lafayette, Ind.), 1971. (*DAI* 32:788A)

418. JACOBSON, PHYLLIS COLLEEN. *The Importance of Certain Factors in Teacher Preparation for Teacher-Pupil Relations.* Doctor's thesis, University of Utah (Salt Lake City, Utah), 1971. (*DAI* 32:3076A)

419. JOHN, ALEYAMMA KOSHY. *Investigation of Personality and Teacher-Pupil Rapport as Related to Sex, Religion, Education, Subjects Taught, Training, Age and Experience of Selected Secondary Teachers of Bangalore, India.* Doctor's thesis, Catholic University of America (Washington, D.C.), 1971. (*DAI* 32:1338A)

420. KAKKAR, S. B., AND JAWANDA, J. S. "Fakability of a Test of Honesty." *Indian J Psychol* 46(2):179–84 Je '71. *

421. KEARNS, HOMER H., JR. *An Analysis of Attitudes Toward Children and the Teaching Role of Students Who Have Participated in Education 482, the Urban Tutorial Program.* Doctor's thesis, Michigan State University (East Lansing, Mich.), 1971. (*DAI* 32:5654A)

422. KILANSKI, DORIS MARIE. *A Study to Measure the Attitudes of Sixth Grade Teachers Toward Their Students and the Relationship of These Attitudes Toward the Achievement of Sixth Grade Students in Acquiring Reading Skills.* Doctor's thesis, University of Michigan (Ann Arbor, Mich.), 1971. (*DAI* 32:1259A)

423. LANTZ, DONALD L., AND BOTT, WILLIAM K. "Effects of F Scale Scores on Changes of MTAI Scores." *J Stud Pers Assn Teach Ed* 10(1):20–4 f '71. *

424. MENTLEY, MARC CHARLES. *Some Relationships Between Personality, Class Selection Characteristics and Teacher Attitude Change of Secondary Teaching Methods Students, Michigan State University, Winter Term, 1971.* Doctor's thesis, Michigan State University (East Lansing, Mich.), 1971. (*DAI* 32:5093A)

425. MOORE, SHELDON L. *The Effect of Group Counseling on Attitudes of Student Teachers Toward Interpersonal Relationships With Children.* Doctor's thesis, Lehigh University (Bethlehem, Pa.), 1971. (*DAI* 32:184A)

426. NULL, ELDON J. "Relationships Between Personal Variables of Teachers and Their Perception of the Behavior of School Personnel." *J Ed Res* 64(8):351–4 Ap '71. * (*PA* 46:11627)

427. O'TUEL, FRANCES SETTLE. *A Study of Attitude and Personality Changes in Teachers and Teacher Aides in Williamsburg County, South Carolina as Related to Formal Training and Experience.* Doctor's thesis, University of South Carolina (Columbia, S.C.), 1971. (*DAI* 32:2489A)

428. PARKER, JAMES ARTHUR. *A Comparative Study of the Michigan State University Cluster Program and the Conventional Program of Student Teaching in the Saginaw Area With Reference to Stereotypic Beliefs and Attitude Formation.* Doctor's thesis, Michigan State University (East Lansing, Mich.), 1971. (*DAI* 32:5657A)

429. POWER, D. J. "Characteristics of Successful Student Teachers of the Deaf." *Volta R* 73(9):529–37 D '71. * (*PA* 47:11741)

430. PRICE, WILLIAM J. *A Study of the Effects of the Student Teaching Experience and the Student Teaching Assignment Upon the Educational Attitudes of Secondary Student Teachers at Michigan State University.* Doctor's thesis, Michigan State University (East Lansing, Mich.), 1971. (*DAI* 32:3142A)

431. PSENCIK, LEROY FLOYD. *Some Relationships Between Attitude, Verbal Behavior, and Cognitive Level of Classroom Questions of Secondary American History Teachers.* Doctor's thesis, Texas A & M University (College Station, Tex.), 1971. (*DAI* 32:4250A)

432. PUM, ROBERT JOSEPH. *Differential Characteristics of Art-Teaching Majors and Elementary-Education Majors in College; as Measured by Selected Attitude, Value, and Personality*

Factors. Doctor's thesis, Ball State University (Muncie, Ind.), 1971. (*DAI* 32:5659A)

433. RAINA, T. N. "Effect of Internship on Attitude Change." *J Ed & Psychol* (India) 29(1):51–6 Ap '71. *

434. RALPH, LEONARD DONALD. *A Study of the Effects of In-Service Involvement on Selected Characteristics of Teachers.* Doctor's thesis, University of Kentucky (Lexington, Ky.), 1971. (*DAI* 32:1964A)

435. ROTH, ROBERT AUGUST. *The Relationship of Verbal Interaction Patterns and Teacher-Student Rapport of Selected ESCP Teachers.* Doctor's thesis, Kent State University (Kent, Ohio), 1971. (*DAI* 33:2622A)

436. SCHALL, ROBERT PHILIP. *A Study of the Effect of the Allegheny College Off-Campus Student Teaching Program Upon Student Teacher Self Concept and Attitude Toward Teacher-Pupil Relations.* Doctor's thesis, George Peabody College for Teachers (Nashville, Tenn.), 1971. (*DAI* 32:1966A)

437. SHOEMAKER, EVELYN JEAN. *Satisfaction of Student Needs Through Humanistic Attributes of Personality in Teachers.* Doctor's thesis, University of Wisconsin (Madison, Wis.), 1971. (*DAI* 32:3636A)

438. SHUSTER, ARNOLD A. "The Minnesota Teacher Attitude Inventory as a Prediction of Leadership Styles in a Recreation Setting." *J Leisure Res* 3(2):168–77 su '71. *

439. SORGE, DENNIS HAROLD. *Effectiveness of Interaction Analysis Feedback on Verbal Behavior of College Teachers and Attendant Effect Upon Pupil Attitude and Achievement.* Doctor's thesis, Purdue University (Lafayette, Ind.), 1971. (*DAI* 32:2984A)

440. VERMA, I. B. "Sex Differences in the Impact of Training on the Values and Attitudes of Student Teachers." *J Ed Res & Exten* (India) 7(4):233–7 Ap '71. *

441. WILBORN, BOBBIE LARUE. *The Relaltionship Between Teacher Attitudes and Teacher Ratings of Pupil Behavior.* Doctor's thesis, University of Missouri (Columbia, Mo.), 1971. (*DAI* 32:4974A)

442. YEE, ALBERT H., AND FRUCHTER, BENJAMIN. "Factor Content of the Minnesota Teacher Attitude Inventory." *Am Ed Res J* 8(1):119–33 Ja '71. * (*PA* 46:7670)

CUMULATIVE NAME INDEX

[869]

National Teacher Examinations. College seniors and teachers; 1940–73; NTE; tests administered 4 times a year (January or February, April, July, November) at centers established by the publisher (French, German, Spanish, and Guidance Counselor offered in April and November only); a composite NTE score is available for examinees taking both *a* and *b;* inactive forms of *a* and 15 tests in *b* are available to colleges for local administration in the *Teacher Education Examination Program;* other inactive forms of *a* and 16 tests in *b* are available to school systems for local use in the program entitled

School Personnel Research and Evaluation Service; Educational Testing Service. *

a) COMMON EXAMINATIONS. See 25; 7 scores: professional education, subtotal, general education (written English expression, social studies-literature-the fine arts, science and mathematics, subtotal), total.

b) TEACHING AREA EXAMINATIONS. 27 tests listed separately: Art Education, Audiology, Biology and General Science, Business Education, Chemistry-Physics-General Science, Early Childhood Education, Education in an Urban Setting, Education in the Elementary School, Education of Mentally Retarded, Educational Administration and Supervision, English Language and Literature, French, German, Guidance Counselor, Home Economics Education, Industrial Arts Education, Mathematics, Media Specialist—Library and Audio-Visual Services, Men's Physical Education, Music Education, Reading Specialist, Social Studies, Spanish, Speech-Communication and Theatre, Speech Pathology, Texas Government, Women's Physical Education.

For additional information and reviews by Wayne H. Holtzman and Edwin Wandt of earlier forms, see 7:582 (25 references); for a review by Harold Seashore, see 6:700 (5 references); for reviews by William A. Brownell, Walter W. Cook, and Lawrence G. Derthick, see 5:538 (6 references); for a review by Harry N. Rivlin, see 4:802 (43 references). For reviews of earlier forms of the music education test, see 7:250 (2 reviews) and 6:350 (1 review); the business education test, see 7:556 (1 review); the English language and literature test, see 6:259 (1 review); the art education test, see 6:345 (1 review); the mathematics test, see 6:583 (1 review); and the social studies test, see 6:974 (1 review).

REFERENCES THROUGH 1971

1–43. See 4:802.
44–49. See 5:538.
50–54. See 6:700.
55–79. See 7:582.
80. OLANDER, HERBERT T., AND KLEYLE, HELEN M. "Differences in Personal and Professional Characteristics of a Selected Group of Elementary Teachers With Contrasting Success Records." *Ed Adm & Sup* 45:191–8 Jl '59. * (*PA* 34:6582)
81. GREENE, JAMES E., SR. "A Comparison of Certain Characteristics of White and Negro Teachers in a Large Southeastern School System." *J Social Psychol* 58:383–91 D '62. * (*PA* 37:7210)
82. LEWIS, JAMES N. "Tests for Teachers: Survey Report." *Tex Outl* 52:20–1 Jl '68. *
83. CARPENTER, CORINNE TAYLOR. *Study of the Relationship of Selected Factors to the Performance of Business Education Graduates at Grambling College on the Commons Section of the National Teacher Examinations.* Doctor's thesis, Indiana University (Bloomington, Ind.), 1970. (*DAI* 31:5900A)
84. McGEE, THURMAN ELZIE, JR. *A Study of Certain Factors and Their Interrelationships in Teacher Education at the University of Tennessee, Knoxville.* Doctor's thesis, University of Tennessee (Knoxville, Tenn.), 1970. (*DAI* 31:4602A)
85. AYERS, JERRY B. "Predicting Quality Point Averages in Master's Degree Programs in Education." *Ed & Psychol Meas* 31(2):491–5 su '71. *
86. DUNCAN, JOE P. *A Statistical Analysis of Student Grades in Teacher Education Curricula and Certain Scores on the National Teacher Examination.* Master's thesis, East Tennessee State University (Johnson City, Tenn.), 1971.
87. PAYNE, DAVID A.; WELLS, ROBERT A.; AND CLARKE, ROBERT R. "Another Contribution to Estimating Success in Graduate School: A Search for Sex Differences and Comparison Between Three Degree Types." *Ed & Psychol Meas* 31(2):497–503 su '71. *

CUMULATIVE NAME INDEX

Anderson, J. H.: 73
Anderson, W. A.: 7
Antley, E. M.: 56
Ayers, J. B.: 85
Benson, A. L.: 46
Boozer, H. R.: 61
Bowles, E.: 65
Brownell, W. A.: *rev,* 5:538
Capps, M. P.: 49
Carpenter, C. T.: 83
Carson, E. M.: 75
Clarke, R. R.: 87

Collins, E. R.: 2
Cook, W. W.: *rev,* 5:538
Crissy, W. J. E.: 8, 22–3
Croon, C. W.: 9
Crow, E. R.: 30
Davis, F. B.: 10
DeCosta, F. A.: 49, 55
Delaney, E. C.: 47
Derthick, L. G.: *rev,* 5:538
Douglass, H. R.: 11
Dukes, A. C.: 76
Duncan, J. P.: 86

Eckelberry, R. H.: 37
Eissey, E. M.: 66
Emens, J. R.: 31
Engelhardt, G.: 67
Fenstermacher, G. M.: 50
Flanagan, J. C.: 12–3, 23
Greene, J. E.: 81
Gruber, E. C.: 53
Harvey, E. D.: 77
Hauff, A. C.: 68
Hebert, D. J.: 69
Holtzman, W. H.: *rev,* 7:582
Howard, W. T.: 78
Hunter, E. C.: 74
Jenkins, J. M.: 70
Johnson, B. G.: 57
Jones, L. H.: 62
Kandel, I. L.: 44
King, F. J.: 58
King, H. V.: 14
Kleyle, H. M.: 80
Leavitt, W. C.: 79
Lewis, J. N.: 82
Lins, L. J.: 28
McCamey, J. E.: 51
McGee, T. E.: 84
Nichols, A. S.: 24
Olander, H. T.: 80
Payne, D. A.: 87

Pearson, C. A.: 25
Perry, H. T.: 59, 64
Pilley, J. G.: 15
Reed, C. R.: 16
Rivlin, H. N.: *rev,* 4:802
Rooks, J. E.: 63
Rowland, A. L.: 3
Ryans, D. G.: 4, 17, 25, 27, 29, 32–6, 38–41, 43
Seagoe, M. V.: 42
Seashore, H.: *rev,* 6:700
Shea, J. A.: 48
Simpson, H. D.: 54
Spaney, E.: 18
Spaulding, G.: 19
Starcher, G.: 52
Stoddard, A. J.: 5
Swineford, F.: 50
Thacker, J. A.: 60
Townsend, M. E.: 1
Tullos, S. J.: 71
Tully, A. G.: 45
Tully, G. E.: 58
Walberg, H. J.: 72
Wandt, E.: *rev,* 7:582
Wells, R. A.: 87
Winetrout, K.: 20
Wood, B. D.: 6, 21, 26

[870]

*National Teacher Examinations: Early Childhood Education. College seniors and teachers; 1953–73; an inactive form (1966) entitled *Teacher Education Examination Program: Early Childhood Education* is available to colleges for local administration; another inactive form (1968) entitled *Specialty Examinations: Early Childhood Education* is available to school systems for local use as part of the program entitled *School Personnel Research and Evaluation Services;* Educational Testing Service. * For the testing program entry, see 869.

For additional information concerning earlier forms, see 7:583. For reviews of the testing program, see 7:582 (2 reviews), 6:700 (1 review), 5:538 (3 reviews), and 4:802 (1 review).

[871]

*National Teacher Examinations: Education in an Urban Setting. College seniors and teachers; 1970–73; Educational Testing Service. * For the testing program entry, see 869.

For additional information, see 7:584. For reviews of the testing program, see 7:582 (2 reviews), 6:700 (1 review), 5:538 (3 reviews), and 4:802 (1 review).

[872]

*National Teacher Examinations: Education in the Elementary School. College seniors and teachers; 1940–73; an inactive form (1966) entitled *Teacher Education Examination Program: Elementary School Education* is available to colleges for local administration; another inactive form (1969) entitled *Specialty Examinations: Education in the Elementary School* is available to school systems for local use as part of the program entitled *School Personnel Research and Evaluation Services;* Educational Testing Service. * For the testing program entry, see 869.

For additional information concerning earlier forms, see 7:585. For reviews of the testing program, see 7:582 (2 reviews), 6:700 (1 review), 5:538 (3 reviews), and 4:802 (1 review).

[873]

*National Teacher Examinations: Education of Mentally Retarded. College seniors and teachers; 1970–73; Educational Testing Service. * For the testing program entry, see 869.

For additional information concerning an earlier form,

see 7:586. For reviews of the testing program, see 7:582 (2 reviews), 6:700 (1 review), 5:538 (3 reviews), and 4:802 (1 review).

[874]

★**National Teacher Examinations: Educational Administration and Supervision.** Prospective principals; 1971–73; Educational Testing Service. * For the testing program entry, see 869.

For reviews of the testing program, see 7:582 (2 reviews), 6:700 (1 review), 5:538 (3 reviews), and 4:802 (1 review).

[875]

★**National Teacher Examinations: Guidance Counselor.** Prospective guidance counselors; 1972–73; Educational Testing Service. * For the testing program entry, see 869.

For reviews of the testing program, see 7:582 (2 reviews), 6:700 (1 review), 5:538 (3 reviews), and 4:802 (1 review).

[876]

*****National Teacher Examinations: Media Specialist—Library and Audio-Visual Services.** College seniors and teachers; 1970–73; Educational Testing Service. * For the testing program entry, see 869.

For additional information concerning earlier forms, see 7:587. For reviews of the testing program, see 7:582 (2 reviews), 6:700 (1 review), 5:538 (3 reviews), and 4:802 (1 review).

[877]

Ohio Teaching Record: Anecdotal Observation Form, Second Revised Edition. Teachers; 1940–45; ratings by supervisors; University Publications Sales, Ohio State University. *

For additional information and an excerpted review by Thomas O. Marshall, see 3:402 (1 reference).

REFERENCES THROUGH 1971
1. See 3:402.

CUMULATIVE NAME INDEX
Marshall, T. O.: *exc*, 3:402   Raths, L.: 1

[878]

★**Oral School Attitude Test.** Grades kgn–3; 1973; downward extension of *School Attitude Test* (see 888); test booklet title is *School Attitude Test: Oral Version;* students' "perception of the school environment"; 4 scores: interpersonal relations, student-instruction interaction, general school factor, total; directions in English and Spanish; Juan Rivera; Learning Concepts. *

[879]

Pictographic Self Rating Scale. High school and college; 1955–57; attitude toward classroom and study activities; Einar R. Ryden; Psychometric Affiliates. *

For additional information and reviews by Stanley E. Davis and John D. Krumboltz, see 6:701 (2 references).

REFERENCES THROUGH 1971
1–2. See 6:701.

CUMULATIVE NAME INDEX
Davis, S. E.: *rev*, 6:701   Romanowski, W. V.: 1
Krumboltz, J. D.: *rev*, 6:701   Sales, R. C.: 2

[880]

The Purdue Instructor Performance Indicator. College teachers; 1960; ratings by students; John H. Snedeker and H. H. Remmers; University Book Store. *

For additional information and a review by C. Robert Pace, see 6:704 (3 references).

REFERENCES THROUGH 1971
1–3. See 6:704.
4. KRAUSS, MARTIN LUTHER. *A Comparison Between Student Evaluations of Full-Time and Part-Time Faculty in University College, University of Louisville.* Doctor's thesis, Indiana University (Bloomington, Ind.), 1962. (*DA* 24:589)

CUMULATIVE NAME INDEX
Krauss, M. L.: 4   Remmers, H. H.: 2
Leftwich, W. H.: 2–3   Snedeker, J. H.: 1
Pace, C. R.: *rev*, 6:704

[881]

The Purdue Rating Scale for Instruction. College teachers; 1927–65; PRSI; revision of *The Purdue Rating Scale for Instructors;* student ratings on 26 characteristics of the instructor and teaching situation; H. H. Remmers, D. N. Elliott (scale), and J. A. Weisbrodt (manual and response card); University Book Store. *

For additional information, see 7:588 (9 references); for a review by C. Robert Pace, see 6:705 (5 references); for a review by Kenneth L. Heaton, see 4:803 (26 references).

REFERENCES THROUGH 1971
1–26. See 4:803.
27–31. See 6:705.
32–40. See 7:588.
41. PATERSON, DONALD G., AND TINKER, MILES A. "Studies of Typographical Factors Influencing Speed of Reading: 2, Size of Type." *J Appl Psychol* 13:120–30 Ap '29. * (*PA* 3:3392)
42. BOWMAN, EARL C. "Pupil Ratings of Student Teachers." *Ann Conf Ed Meas* 21:28–37 '34. *
43. WARD, WILLIAM DUNHAM. *A Study of the Purdue Rating Scale for Instructors as a Training Device for Prospective Teachers.* Master's thesis, Purdue University (Lafayette, Ind.), 1935.
44. HEILMAN, J. D., AND ARMENTROUT, W. D. "The Rating of College Teachers on Ten Traits by Their Students." *J Ed Psychol* 27:197–216 Mr '36. * (*PA* 10:3710)
45. VENEMANN, MINNIE ADELLE. *A Diagnostic Study of Student Attitudes Towards Their Teachers.* Master's thesis, Purdue University (Lafayette, Ind.), 1939.
46. BENDIG, A. W. "The Relation of Level of Course Achievement to Students' Instructor and Course Ratings in Introductory Psychology." *Ed & Psychol Meas* 13:437–48 au '53. * (*PA* 28:3655)
47. BENDIG, A. W. "Student Achievement in Introductory Psychology and Student Ratings of the Competence and Empathy of Their Instructors." *J Psychol* 36:427–33 O '53. * (*PA* 28:4956)
48. LAIRD, CLAUD ALTON. *A Study of the College-Level Educational Program of the Texas Department of Corrections.* Doctor's thesis, University of Houston (Houston, Tex.), 1971. (*DAI* 32:4376A)
49. WALTER, JAMES EDGAR. *Relationships Between Selected Values of Students and Their Perception of a University Instructor.* Doctor's thesis, Purdue University (Lafayette, Ind.), 1971. (*DAI* 32:4387A)

CUMULATIVE NAME INDEX
Armentrout, W. D.: 44   Miklich, D. R.: 35
Baker, P. C.: 24   Morris, M. J.: 36
Bendig, A. W.: 27–8, 46–7   Pace, C. R.: *rev*, 6:705
Bowman, E. C.: 42   Paterson, D. G.: 41
Brandenburg, G. C.: 1–2   Potter, A. A.: 15–6
Carter, G. C.: 25   Remmers, H. H.: 1–11, 13–6,
Creager, J. A.: 20–1 | 18–9, 22, 24, 26, 30
Davenport, K. S.: 15–6   Scarbrough, J. P.: 33
Drinkwater, B. L.: 32   Schmalzried, N. T.: 13–4
Drucker, A. J.: 22, 26   Shock, N. W.: 3
Elkin, A.: 29   Stalnaker, J. M.: 5
Elliott, D. N.: 17–9, 23   Starks, D. D.: 37
Feldhusen, J. F.: 37, 39   Tinker, M. A.: 41
Heaton, K. L.: *rev*, 4:803   Treffinger, D. J.: 39
Heilman, J. D.: 44   Venemann, M. A.: 45
Hoshaw, L. D.: 12   Walker, B. D.: 34
Kelly, E. L.: 3   Walter, J. E.: 49
Laird, C. A.: 48   Ward, W. D.: 13, 43
Leftwich, W. H.: 30–1   Willingham, D. C.: 40
McCarbery, R. J.: 38   Wykoff, G. S.: 7
Martin, F. D.: 19

[882]

The Purdue Student-Teacher Opinionaire. Student teachers; 1969–70; PSTO; for group measurement only; 100 median item scores grouped by 12 factors (rapport with supervising teacher, rapport with principal, teaching as a profession, rapport with university supervisor, community support of education, student teacher load, rapport with students, rapport with other teachers, satisfaction with housing, professional preparation, school facilities, curriculum issues), 12 median factor scores, total; Ralph R. Bentley and Jo-Ann Price; University Book Store. *

For additional information, see 7:589 (1 reference).

REFERENCES THROUGH 1971

1. See 7:589.
2. Ross, Colvin, and Swick, Kevin. "An Explanatory Study in the Development of Positive Changes in Student-Teacher Attitudes Toward Inner-City Teaching." *Ed & Urban Soc* 2(1):112-7 N '69. *
3. Turner, Ruth Donham. *Assessment of Supervising and Student Teacher Morale in Relationship to Supervisory Practices.* Doctor's thesis, Purdue University (Lafayette, Ind.), 1971. (*DAI* 32:1968A)

CUMULATIVE NAME INDEX

Price, J. A.: 1	Swick, K.: 2
Ross, C.: 2	Turner, R. D.: 3

[883]

The Purdue Teacher Evaluation Scale. Grades 7-12; 1969-70; PTES; student ratings of teachers; 60 median item scores grouped in 6 scales: ability to motivate students, ability to control students, subject matter orientation, student-teacher communication, teaching methods and procedures, fairness; Ralph R. Bentley and Allan R. Starry; University Book Store. *

For additional information, see 7:590 (1 reference).

REFERENCES THROUGH 1971

1. See 7:590.

CUMULATIVE NAME INDEX

Woolfolk, T. V.: 1

[884]

The Purdue Teacher Opinionaire. Teachers; 1961-70; PTO; revision of *The Purdue Teacher Morale Inventory;* for group measurement only; 100 median item scores grouped by 10 factors (teacher rapport with principal, satisfaction with teaching, rapport among teachers, teacher salary, teacher load, curriculum issues, teacher status, community support of education, school facilities and services, community pressures), 10 median factor scores, total; Ralph R. Bentley and Averno M. Rempel; University Book Store. *

For additional information and reviews by Bert A. Goldman and Benjamin Rosner, see 7:591 (26 references).

REFERENCES THROUGH 1971

1-26. See 7:591.
27. Ross, Colvin, and Swick, Kevin. "An Explanatory Study in the Development of Positive Changes in Student-Teacher Attitudes Toward Inner-City Teaching." *Ed & Urban Soc* 2(1):112-7 N '69. *
28. Cook, Richard Paul. *The Relationship of Principal Leader Behavior and Teacher Morale to Certain Other Variables in Selected Urban Elementary Schools.* Doctor's thesis, Purdue University (Lafayette, Ind.), 1970. (*DAI* 31:5063A)
29. Halliday, Malcolm Frank. *An Investigation of Parent Attitudes and Teacher Morale in Relationship to Community Unrest.* Doctor's thesis, Michigan State University (East Lansing, Mich.), 1970. (*DAI* 32:125A)
30. Johnson, Paul O'Neal. *Relationships Between the Morale of Georgia Extension Agents and the Leader Behavior of Georgia County Agent Chairman.* Doctor's thesis, University of Georgia (Athens, Ga.), 1970. (*DAI* 31:5748A)
31. Rempel, Averno M., and Bentley, Ralph R. "Teacher Morale: Relationship With Selected Factors." *J Teach Ed* 21(4):534-9 w '70. *
32. Schott, James Lawrence. *The Leader Behavior of Non-White Principals in Inner-City Elementary Schools With Integrated Teaching Staffs Under Conditions of High and Low Morale.* Doctor's thesis, Purdue University (Lafayette, Ind.), 1970. (*DAI* 31:5097A)
33. Zimmerman, Robert Edgar. *Teacher Perceptions and Personality Characteristics Associated With Innovation.* Doctor's thesis, University of North Dakota (Grand Forks, N.D.), 1970. (*DAI* 31:6462A)

34. Collins, Harold W. "A Comparative Study of Public School Teacher Opinion and State Laboratory Teacher Opinion." *Ill Sch Res* 7(2):38-42 w '71. *
35. Foley, Gerald Francis. *A Study of the Relationships Between Team Leaders' Leadership Behavior and the Morale and Effectiveness of Their Team Members.* Doctor's thesis, State University of New York (Buffalo, N.Y.), 1971. (*DAI* 32:2944A)
36. Herrmann, William M. *Relationship of Faculty Morale to Faculty Involvement in School Policy Determination in Selected Communities of Mercer and Mahoning Counties.* Doctor's thesis, University of Akron (Akron, Ohio), 1971. (*DAI* 32:2950A)
37. Morris, James Riley, Jr. *A Study of Teacher Morale as Affected by Teacher Assignment to Achieve Faculty Desegregation.* Doctor's thesis, University of Southern Mississippi (Hattiesburg, Miss.), 1971. (*DAI* 32:4893A)
38. Olatunji, Stella Adeninhun. *The Relationship Between Selected Teacher Variables and Teacher Job Satisfaction in Western Nigerian Secondary Schools.* Doctor's thesis, New York University (New York, N.Y.), 1971. (*DAI* 32:6059A)
39. Snyder, William Carroll. *Morale as an Effect of Teachers' Perceptions of Their Role in Educational Decision Making.* Doctor's thesis, University of Pittsburgh (Pittsburgh, Pa.), 1971. (*DAI* 32:6071A)
40. Turner, Ruth Donham. *Assessment of Supervising and Student Teacher Morale in Relationship to Supervisory Practices.* Doctor's thesis, Purdue University (Lafayette, Ind.), 1971. (*DAI* 32:1968A)
41. Wallace, Charles William. *An Investigation of the Relationships Among Selected Attitudinal-Personality Characteristics and Success of Teachers in Installing an Innovative Elementary Science Curriculum.* Doctor's thesis, Syracuse University (Syracuse, N.Y.), 1971. (*DAI* 32:5064A)
42. Wolf, Robert Charles. *A Study of Relationships Among Faculty Morale, Philosophies of Human Nature of High School Principals, and Teachers' Perceived Participation in Educational Decision-Making.* Doctor's thesis, George Peabody College for Teachers (Nashville, Tenn.), 1971. (*DAI* 32:1823A)

CUMULATIVE NAME INDEX

Andrews, R. L.: 7	Kokovich, S.: 19
Bahnsen, J. F.: 22	Lambert, D. B.: 14
Beharka, C. H.: 16	Morris, J. R.: 37
Bentley, R. R.: 1-3, 31	Nelson, N. J.: 9
Berger, E. H.: 8	Olatunji, S. A.: 38
Brinkman, M. J.: 5	Pennebaker, W. K.: 20
Collins, H. W.: 4, 9, 34	Price, J. A.: 21
Cook, R. P.: 28	Reahard, R. R.: 25
Diemert, N. E.: 23	Rempel, A. M.: 1-3, 31
Edgecombe, W. D.: 10	Robinson, C. D.: 26
Foley, G. F.: 35	Rosner, B.: *rev*, 7:591
Forrest, L. C.: 24	Ross, C.: 27
Frisbie, K. G.: 17	Schott, J. L.: 32
Goldman, B. A.: *rev*, 7:591	Snyder, W. C.: 39
Gubser, M. M.: 11, 18	Strouse, J. P.: 15
Halliday, M. F.: 29	Swick, K.: 27
Herrmann, W. M.: 36	Turner, R. D.: 40
Hoagland, R. M.: 12	Wallace, C. W.: 41
Holdaway, E. A.: 23	Westfall, H. R.: 6
Houston, D. E.: 13	Wolf, R. C.: 42
Johnson, P. O.: 30	Zimmerman, R. E.: 33

[885]

Remmlein's School Law Test. Teacher education classes in school law; 1957; 3 or 4 scores: acquaintance with legal terms, knowledge of principles and cases, use of law books (optional), total; [Madaline Kinter Remmlein]; Interstate Printers & Publishers, Inc. *

For additional information, see 6:707.

[886]

★**School Administration and Supervision.** Prospective elementary school administrators and supervisors; 1968-71; available to school systems for local use as part of the *School Personnel Research and Evaluation Services;* originally available as part of the discontinued *School Administrative and Supervisory Examination Services;* Educational Testing Service. *
For the testing program entry, see 889.

[887]

★**School Atmosphere Questionnaire.** Grades 7-12; 1971; SAQ; ratings by students; 3 scores: enthusiasm for school, school acceptance-understanding, school dynamism-enthusiasm; James K. Hoffmeister; Test Analysis and Development Corporation. *

Purdue Student-Teacher Opinionaire

[888]

★School Attitude Test. Grades 4–6; 1973; students' "perception of the school environment"; for a lower level test, see 878; 4 scores: interpersonal relations, student-instruction interaction, general school factor, total; test booklets and directions in English and Spanish; Earl McCallon; Learning Concepts. *

[889]

★School Personnel Research and Evaluation Services. Teachers and prospective administrators and supervisors; 1971, c1967–71; SPRES; derived from discontinued School Administrative and Supervisory Examination Services; tests available to school systems for local use; 20 tests; Educational Testing Service. *
a) COMMON EXAMINATIONS. 1971, c1970–71; reprinting of inactive 1970 form of National Teacher Examinations: Common Examinations; 5 scores: professional education, written English expression, social studies-literature-the fine arts, science and mathematics, total.
b) SPECIALTY EXAMINATIONS. 1971, c1967–71; all tests are reprints of inactive forms (1967–69) of National Teacher Examinations except School Administration and Supervision, Secondary School Administration, and Secondary School Supervision, which were originally published as part of the School Administrative and Supervisory Examination Services; 19 tests, 3 of which are listed separately: Art Education, Biology and General Science, Business Education, Chemistry-Physics-General Science, Early Childhood Education, Education in the Elementary School, English Language and Literature, French, Home Economics Education, Industrial Arts Education, Mathematics, Music Education, Physical Education, Reading Specialist—Elementary School, School Administration and Supervision (see 886), Secondary School Administration (see 891), Secondary School Supervision (see 892), Social Studies, Spanish.
For reference to reviews of the National Teacher Examinations, see 869.

[890]

★The School Survey of Interpersonal Relationships. Teachers; 1971; SSIR; a measure of a "school's interpersonal learning climate"; 3 main scores: affective (teachers' feelings toward students and other staff members), cognitive (teachers' knowledge regarding students and other staff members), total, and 7 subscores (teachers' feelings toward or perception of principal, fellow teachers, counselors, non-teaching staff, self, students in general, different types of students); Joe Wittmer; Remediation Associates, Inc. *

REFERENCES THROUGH 1971
1. AYERS, HERBERT BOYD, JR. The School Interpersonal Climate as Perceived by Teachers, Counselors, and Administrators. Doctor's thesis, University of Florida (Gainesville, Fla.), 1969.
2. TAYLOR, STEPHEN ST. CLAIR. A Study of the Effects of Teacher Sex and Contract Status as Variables Influencing Teacher Interpersonal Relations With Principals and Students. Master's thesis, Stetson University (DeLand, Fla.), 1969.

CUMULATIVE NAME INDEX
Ayers, H. B.: 1   Taylor, S. St. C.: 2

[891]

★Secondary School Administration. Prospective secondary school administrators; 1968–71; available to school systems for local use as part of the School Personnel Research and Evaluation Services; originally available as part of the discontinued School Administrative and Supervisory Examination Services; Educational Testing Service. * For the testing program entry, see 889.

[892]

★Secondary School Supervision. Prospective secondary school supervisors; 1968–71; available to school systems for local use as part of the School Personnel Research and Evaluation Services; originally available as part of the discontinued School Administrative and Supervisory Examination Services; Educational Testing Service. * For the testing program entry, see 889.

[893]

A Self Appraisal Scale for Teachers. Teachers; 1957; 1965 scale identical with scale copyrighted 1957; Howard Wilson; Administrative Research Associates, Inc. *
For additional information, see 5:541.

[894]

★Student Instructional Report. College teachers; 1971–73; SIR; ratings and background data by students on 39 items concerning the instructor, course, and student; Institutional Research Program for Higher Education; Educational Testing Service. *

REFERENCES THROUGH 1971
1. BLANK, LOGAN FINK. Relationship Between Student Instructional Ratings and Student-Faculty Psychological Types. Doctor's thesis, Michigan State University (East Lansing, Mich.), 1970. (DAI 31:2123A)

CUMULATIVE NAME INDEX
Blank, L. F.: 1

[895]

★Student Reactions to College. Two-year college; 1974, c1971–73; SRC; for group measurement only; 171 percentage item response distributions for all students tested and for each of 5 locally identified subgroups in 6 areas: instruction and classroom experiences, studying, student goals and planning, administrative regulations—registration and class scheduling, student activities and out-of-class faculty contact, living; Jonathan Warren and Pamela Roelfs; Educational Testing Service. *

[896]

*A Student's Rating Scale of an Instructor. High school and college; 1952–69; no manual; Russell M. Eidsmoe; the Author. *
For additional information and a review by James R. Hayden of an earlier form, see 6:702.

REFERENCES THROUGH 1971
1. MEREDITH, GERALD M. "Dimensions of Faculty-Course Evaluation." J Psychol 73(1):27–32 S '69. * (PA 44:5656)

CUMULATIVE NAME INDEX
Hayden, J. R.: rev, 6:702   Meredith, G. M.: 1

[897]

★Survey of Educational Leadership Practices. Teachers and school administrators; 1955–67; SELP; an adaptation of Leadership Practices Inventory; 2 scores (desirable practices marked as ideal, desirable practices marked as in actual practice) for total, each of 4 leadership styles (using style answer form), and each of 5 management areas (using area answer form); J. J. Valenti and Charles W. Nelson; Management Research Associates. *

REFERENCES THROUGH 1971
1. RIPPY, MARK LEO, JR. Certain Relationships Between Classroom Behavior and Attitude and Personality Characteristics of Selected Elementary Teachers. Doctor's thesis, George Peabody College for Teachers (Nashville, Tenn.), 1960. (DA 21:814)

CUMULATIVE NAME INDEX
Rippy, M. L.: 1

[898]

*Teacher Education Examination Program. College seniors preparing to teach; 1957–72; TEEP; all tests are reprints (except *a*, which is a modification) of inactive forms of *National Teacher Examinations;* tests available to colleges for local administration; 16 tests; Educational Testing Service. *

a) GENERAL PROFESSIONAL EXAMINATIONS. See 41; 5 scores: social-philosophical-historical bases of education, learning and instruction, written English expression, cultural background—social sciences-literature-fine arts, science and mathematics—basic concepts and principles.

b) TEACHING FIELD TESTS. 15 tests listed separately: Art Education, Biology and General Science, Business Education, Chemistry-Physics-General Science, Early Childhood Education, Elementary School Education, English Language and Literature, French, Home Economics Education, Industrial Arts, Mathematics, Music Education, Physical Education, Social Studies, Spanish.

For additional information concerning earlier forms, see 6:709; for a review by Walter W. Cook, see 5:543. For reference to reviews of the *National Teacher Examinations,* see 869.

REFERENCES THROUGH 1971

1. MEADORS, PONNIE R. *An Evaluation on the Performance of Tennessee A & I State University Students on the Teacher Education Examination, Nashville, Tennessee.* Master's thesis, Tennessee A & I State University (Nashville, Tenn.), 1965.
2. VERGIELS, JOHN MAURICE. *A Cross-National Study of Relationships Between Professional Variables of Secondary Teacher Education Students.* Doctor's thesis, University of Toledo (Toledo, Ohio), 1968. (*DA* 29:2595A)

CUMULATIVE NAME INDEX

Cook, W. W.: *rev,* 5:543   Vergiels, J. M.: 2
Meadors, P. R.: 1

[899]

*Teacher Education Examination Program: Early Childhood Education. College seniors preparing to teach kgn–grade 3; 1957–72; reprinting of inactive 1966 form of *National Teacher Examinations: Early Childhood Education;* test available to colleges for local administration; Educational Testing Service. * For the testing program entry, see 898.

For additional information concerning an earlier form, see 6:709b. For a review of the testing program, see 5:543.

[900]

*Teacher Education Examination Program: Elementary School Education. College seniors preparing to teach grades 1–8; 1957–72; reprinting of inactive 1966 form of *National Teacher Examinations: Elementary School Education;* test available to colleges for local administration; Educational Testing Service. * For the testing program entry, see 898.

For additional information concerning an earlier form, see 6:709b. For a review of the testing program, see 5:543.

[901]

Teacher Opinionaire on Democracy. Teachers; 1949; democratic aspects of teacher philosophy; Enola Ledbetter and Theodore F. Lentz; Character Research Association. *

For additional information and reviews by George W. Hartmann and C. Robert Pace, see 4:805.

REFERENCES THROUGH 1971

1. WELLMAN, FRANK EDWIN. *Factors Related to Attitudes of Iowa Educators Toward Democracy in Education.* Doctor's thesis, University of Nebraska (Lincoln, Neb.), 1952.
2. WOLFSON, BEATRICE NATALIE. *A Study of Personality Variables, as Measured by Certain Instruments, That May*

Differentiate School Guidance Counselors From Classroom Teachers. Doctor's thesis, University of Connecticut (Storrs, Conn.), 1958. (*DA* 19:2816)

CUMULATIVE NAME INDEX

Hartmann, G. W.: *rev,* 4:805   Wellman, F. E.: 1
Pace, C. R.: *rev,* 4:805   Wolfson, B. N.: 2

[902]

Teacher Preference Schedule. Elementary school teachers and prospective teachers; [1960]; TPS; experimental form; unconscious motivations for teaching; 2 parts, 10 scores for each part (practical, status-striving, nurturant, non-directive, rebellious, preadult fixated, orderliness, dependency, exhibition, dominance), plus 5 combination scores (task oriented, affection-seeking, dependent, vicarious youth leader, professional spokesman); George G. Stern and Joseph M. Masling; distributed by Psychological Research Center. *

a) FORM A [ATTITUDES].

b) FORM G [GRATIFICATIONS].

REFERENCES THROUGH 1971

1. STERN, GEORGE G.; MASLING, JOSEPH; DENTON, BARNETT; HENDERSON, JOHN; AND LEVIN, RACHEL. "Two Scales for the Assessment of Unconscious Motivations for Teaching." *Ed & Psychol Meas* 20:9–29 sp '60. * (*PA* 34:7181)
2. WODTKE, KENNETH H.; REID, IAN E.; WALLEN, NORMAN E.; AND TRAVERS, ROBERT M. W. "Patterns of Needs as Predictors of Classroom Behavior of Teachers." *Ed & Psychol Meas* 23:569–77 au '63. * (*PA* 38:6671)
3. JONES, REGINALD L., AND GOTTFRIED, NATHAN W. "Psychological Needs and Preferences for Teaching Exceptional Children." *Excep Children* 32:313–21 Ja '66. * (*PA* 40:4615)
4. JONES, REGINALD L.; GOTTFRIED, NATHAN W.; AND BERKOWITZ, HOWARD. "Partial Construct Validation of a Scale Developed to Reflect Unconscious Motives Fulfilled by Teaching." *Ed & Psychol Meas* 27:97–112 sp '67. * (*PA* 41:8157)

CUMULATIVE NAME INDEX

Berkowitz, H.: 4   Masling, J.: 1
Denton, B.: 1   Reid, I. E.: 2
Gottfried, N. W.: 3–4   Stern, G. G.: 1
Henderson, J.: 1   Travers, R. M. W.: 2
Jones, R. L.: 3–4   Wallen, N. E.: 2
Levin, R.: 1   Wodtke, K. H.: 2

[903]

★Teacher Self-Rating Inventory. Teachers; 1971; TSRI; no manual; Harold F. Burks; Arden Press. *

[904]

Teaching Aptitude Test: George Washington University Series. Grades 12–16; 1927; F. A. Moss, T. Hunt, and F. C. Wallace; Center for Psychological Service. *

For additional information and a review by May V. Seagoe, see 4:806; for a review by A. S. Barr, see 3:405 (8 references).

REFERENCES THROUGH 1971

1–8. See 3:405.
9. GIPSON, THEODORE H. "Relationship of Teaching Aptitude to Age, Sex, and Classification of Students at Southern University." *Ed Adm & Sup* 45:283–9 S '59. *
10. GIPSON, THEODORE H. "Relationship of Teaching Aptitude to Age, Sex, and Classification of Students at Southern University." *J Negro Ed* 29:96–9 w '60. *

CUMULATIVE NAME INDEX

Barr, A. S.: *rev,* 3:405   Markt, A. R.: 2
Gilliland, A. R.: 2   Moss, F. A.: 3
Gipson, T. H.: 9–10   Seagoe, M. V.: 7–8; *rev,*
Greene, J. E.: 6   4:806
Hunt, T.: 1, 3   Staton, T. F.: 6
Jorgensen, C.: 4   Stump, F. N.: 5
Loman, W.: 3

[905]

The Teaching Evaluation Record. Teachers; 1953–56; ratings by supervisors; Dwight E. Beecher; Educators Publishing Co. *

For additional information, see 5:542.

REFERENCES THROUGH 1971

1. HOOKER, WILLIAM DOUGLAS. *A Study of Certain Personal Characteristics and Attitudes of Full-Time and Part-Time Student Teachers and Certified Beginning Teachers.* Doctor's thesis, University of Texas (Austin, Tex.), 1959. (*DA* 20:2677)
2. KLEYLE, HELEN MURRAY. *Differences in Personal and Professional Characteristics of a Selected Group of Elementary Teachers With Contrasting Success Records.* Doctor's thesis, University of Pittsburgh (Pittsburgh, Pa.), 1959. (*DA* 20:185)
3. MAGRATH, GEORGE. *An Evaluation of Teachers Trained Under the Intensive Program for College Graduates.* Doctor's thesis, University of Connecticut (Storrs, Conn.), 1960. (*DA* 21:1864)
4. PRICE, EDWIN FRANK. *A Study of the Relationships of Characteristics of Senior High School Teachers to an Evaluation of Teaching Effectiveness by Supervising Principals.* Doctor's thesis, Washington State University (Pullman, Wash.), 1966. (*DA* 27:1603A)
5. SIEGEL, WAYNE GERALD. *A Study of the Relationship Between Selected Undergraduate Academic Achievement Variables and Teaching Success.* Doctor's thesis, Washington State University (Pullman, Wash.), 1969. (*DAI* 30:4320A)

CUMULATIVE NAME INDEX

[906]

*The Undergraduate Program Field Tests: Education Test. College; 1969–73; formerly called *The Undergraduate Record Examinations: Education Test;* test available to colleges for local administration; Educational Testing Service. * For the testing program entry, see 1062.

For additional information concerning an earlier form, see 7:592. For reviews of the testing program, see 7:671 (2 reviews).

[907]

The Wilson Teacher-Appraisal Scale. Ratings by students in grades 7–16; 1948–57; also available as part of *A Self Appraisal Scale for Teachers* (see 893); Howard Wilson; Administrative Research Associates, Inc. *

For additional information and a review by James R. Hayden, see 6:711.

[Out of Print Since TIP I]

ETIQUETTE

[Out of Print Since TIP I]

HANDWRITING

[908]

Ayres Measuring Scale for Handwriting: Gettysburg Edition. Grades 5–8; 1912–17; revision of *Ayres Measuring Scale for Handwriting: Three Slant Edition;* 2 scores: quality, speed; Leonard P. Ayres; distributed by Bureau of Educational Research and Service. *

For additional information, see 5:550; for a review by Worth J. Osburn, see 4:475 (9 references).

REFERENCES THROUGH 1971

1–9. See 4:475.
10. LEWIS, E. E. "The Present Standard of Handwriting in Iowa Normal Training High Schools." *Ed Adm & Sup* 1:663–71 N '15. *
11. JUDD, CHARLES HUBBARD. *Measuring the Work of the Public Schools,* pp. 61–93, 234–6. Cleveland, Ohio: The Survey Committee of the Cleveland Foundation, 1916. Pp. 290. *
12. MONROE, WALTER SCOTT. *Measuring the Results of Teaching,* pp. 207–12, *passim.* Boston, Mass.: Houghton Mifflin Co., 1918. Pp. xviii, 297. *
13. STARCH, DANIEL. "A Scale for Measuring Handwriting." *Sch & Soc* 9:154–8, 184–8 F 1, 8 '19. *
14. BIRD, GRACE E. "A Test of Some Standard Tests." *J Ed Psychol* 11:275–83 My '20. *
15. KOOS, FRANK H. "Educational Measurements in a Small School System." *J Ed Res* 2:493–501 Je '20. *
16. WILSON, G. M., AND HOKE, KREMER J. *How to Measure,* pp. 24–42. New York: Macmillan Co., 1920. Pp. vii, 285. *
17. MORTON, R. L. "The Value of a Handwriting Scale to an Untrained Teacher." *J Ed Res* 3:133–7 F '21. *
18. BEATTY, WILLARD W. "Judging Handwriting: A Critical Weakness of the Thorndike Scale Revealed by a Comparative Study." *J Ed Psychol* 13:170–2 Mr '22. *
19. BROOKS, FOWLER D. "The Accuracy and Comparative Variability of Ratings According to Three Handwriting Scales." *Ed Res B* 2:148–51+ My 16 '23. *
20. BLACK, W. W., AND RUSSELL, JOHN DALE. "A Study of Handwriting in Forty Indiana Cities: A Preliminary Report." *Ann Conf Ed Meas* 12:43–57 '25. *
21. KIRK, JOHN G. "Handwriting Survey to Determine Grade Standards." *J Ed Res* 13:259–72 Ap '26. * (*PA* 1:181, 467)
22. WEST, PAUL V. "Improving Handwriting Through Diagnosis and Remedial Treatment." *J Ed Res* 14:187–98 O '26. * (*PA* 1:479)
23. JAMIESON, ELMER, AND SANDIFORD, PETER. "The Mental Capacity of Southern Ontario Indians." *J Ed Psychol* 19:313–28, 536–51 My, N '28. * (*PA* 2:2841, 3:817)
24. ANDERSON, H. DEWEY, AND EELLS, WALTER CROSBY. *Alaska Natives: A Survey of Their Sociological and Educational Status,* pp. 298–370. Stanford, Calif.: Stanford University Press, 1935. Pp. xvi, 472. * (*PA* 9:2346)
25. ERLEBACHER, ADRIENNE, AND HERRICK, VIRGIL E. "Quality of Handwriting Today and Yesterday." *El Sch J* 62:89–93 N '61. *
26. RONDINELLA, ORESTE RENATO. *An Evaluation of Subjectivity of Elementary-School Teachers in Grading Handwriting.* Doctor's thesis, Fordham University (New York, N.Y.), 1962. (*DA* 23:2820)
27. LANDWEHR, BERNARD JOHN. *An Analysis of Selected Factors Related to Success in the Study of College Accounting in an Attempt to Establish Minimum Requirements for Accounting Students at West Liberty State College.* Doctor's thesis, University of Pittsburgh (Pittsburgh, Pa.), 1963. (*DA* 25:2280)
28. RONDINELLA, ORESTE R. "An Evaluation of Subjectivity of Elementary-School Teachers in Grading Handwriting." *El Engl* 40:531–2 My '63. *
29. LOVE, HAROLD D. "Comparison of Quality, Speed and Use of Handwriting Among Special and Regular Classroom Children." *J Ed Res* 58:475–7 Jl–Ag '65. * (*PA* 40:731)

CUMULATIVE NAME INDEX

Lewis, E. E.: 10
Love, H. D.: 29
Manuel, H. T.: 6
Monroe, W. S.: 12
Morton, R. L.: 17
Osburn, W. J.: *rev*, 4:475
Pintner, R.: 3

Rondinella, O. R.: 26, 28
Russell, J. D.: 20
Sandiford, P.: 23
Starch, D.: 13
Traxler, A. E.: 9
West, P. V.: 22
Wilson, G. M.: 16

[909]

*Expressional Growth Through Handwriting Evaluation Scale. Grades 1, 2, 3, 4, 5, 6, 7, 8–9, high school; 1958–68; formerly called *Evaluation Scales for Guiding Growth in Handwriting;* 1968 scales identical with 1958 scales except for grading instructions; no manual; original edition by Frank N. Freeman; Zaner-Bloser Co. *

For additional information and a review by Theodore L. Harris, see 6:713 (2 references).

REFERENCES THROUGH 1971
1–2. See 6:713.

CUMULATIVE NAME INDEX
Feldt, L. S.: 2
Freeman, F. N.: 1
Harris, T. L.: *rev*, 6:713

[Out of Print Since TIP I]

American Handwriting Scale, 6:712 (1 review)
Metropolitan Primary Cursive Handwriting Scale and Metropolitan Primary Manuscript Handwriting Scale, T:1220
Normal Handwriting Scale, 6:714 (1 review)

HEALTH AND PHYSICAL EDUCATION

[910]

★AAHPER Cooperative Health Education Test. Grades 5–6, 7–9; 1971–72; Cooperative Tests and Services. *

[911]

AAHPER Cooperative Physical Education Tests. Grades 4–6, 7–9, 10–12; 1970; Cooperative Tests and Services. *

For additional information, see 7:593.

REFERENCES THROUGH 1971
1. KIYOGUCHI, JULIA. *Assessment of Knowledge and Understanding of Physical Education Concepts in Selected Sub-Populations in Arizona.* Doctor's thesis, Arizona State University (Tempe, Ariz.), 1971. (*DAI* 32:3077A)

CUMULATIVE NAME INDEX
Kiyoguchi, J.: 1

[912]

AAHPER-Kennedy Foundation Special Fitness Test for the Mentally Retarded. Ages 8–18; 1968; adaptation of *AAHPER Youth Fitness Test;* 7 scores: flexed arm hang, sit-up, shuttle run, standing broad jump, 50-yard dash, softball throw, 300-yard run-walk; adaptation by G. Lawrence Rarick; American Association for Health, Physical Education, and Recreation. *

For additional information, see 7:594 (2 references).

REFERENCES THROUGH 1971
1–2. See 7:594.

CUMULATIVE NAME INDEX
Brown, B. J.: 1
Davis, R. M.: 2

[913]

AAHPER Sport Skills Tests. Ages 10–18; 1965–69; 5 tests; Donald K. Brace (*a–d*) and Frank D. Sills (*e*); American Association for Health, Physical Education, and Recreation. *

a) ARCHERY SKILLS TEST. 1967; 4 scores for boys, 3 scores for girls.
b) BASKETBALL SKILLS TEST. 1966; 9 scores.
c) FOOTBALL SKILLS TEST. Boys; 1965; 10 scores.
d) SOFTBALL SKILLS TEST. 1966; 8 scores.
e) VOLLEYBALL SKILLS TEST. 1969; 4 scores.

For additional information, see 7:595 (3 references).

REFERENCES THROUGH 1971
1–3. See 7:595.

CUMULATIVE NAME INDEX
Bettencourt, R. M.: 2
Stockton, G. E.: 3
Walter, R. J.: 1

[914]

AAHPER Youth Fitness Test. Ages 10-30 (grades 5–16); 1958–65; 7 scores: pull-up, sit-up, shuttle run, standing broad jump, 50-yard dash, softball throw, 600-yard run-walk; AAHPER Youth Fitness Project; American Association for Health, Physical Education, and Recreation. *

For additional information and a review by Aileene S. Lockhart, see 7:596 (104 references); see also 6:715 (21 references).

REFERENCES THROUGH 1971
1–21. See 6:715.
22–126. See 7:596.
127. SENGSTOCK, WAYNE L. "Physical Fitness of Mentally Retarded Boys." *Alberta J Ed Res* (Canada) 9:264–73 D '63. * (*PA* 40:6988)
128. GROOMS, RICHARD A. *A Comparative Statistical Analysis of the Physical Fitness Scores of Seventh Grade Boys at Washington Junior High School, Nashville, Tennessee, During the School Year 1963–64.* Master's thesis, Tennessee A & I State University (Nashville, Tenn.), 1964.
129. HONEYCUTT, JULIA M. *Physical Fitness and Academic Success of Northwestern State College Freshmen Women.* Master's thesis, Northwestern State College (Natchitoches, La.), 1964.
130. KEOGH, JACK, AND BENSON, DAVID. "Motor Characteristics of Underachieving Boys." *J Ed Res* 57:339–44 Mr '64. * (*PA* 39:5839)
131. BROWN, S. R., AND KITAMURA, F. "Difference Between Rubber and Leather Balls in Distance Achieved in the AAHPER Softball Throw." *J Can Assn Health Phys Ed & Rec* 32:12–3+ Je–Jl '66. *
132. HUNSICKER, PAUL A., AND REIFF, GUY G. "A Survey and Comparison of Youth Fitness 1958–1965." *J Health Phys Ed & Rec* 37:23–5 Ja '66. *
133. BROWN, S. R., AND FIELD, A. "Reliability and Errors of Measurement of the AAHPER Youth Fitness Test." *J Can Assn Health Phys Ed & Rec* 33:15–9 Ag–S '67. *
134. BROWN, STANLEY R. "AAHPER Youth Fitness Test Results of University of British Columbia Students." *J Can Assn Health Phys Ed & Rec* 33:19–21 F–Mr '67. *
135. FLETCHER, ORVILLE. *A Correlated Study of the Physical Fitness Level and Academic Achievement of the Freshmen at Sul Ross State College, 1966.* Master's thesis, Sul Ross State College (Alpine, Tex.), 1967.
136. DRAKE, V.; JONES, G.; BROWN, J. R.; AND SHEPHARD, R. J. "Fitness Performance Tests and Their Relationship to Maximal Oxygen Uptake of Adults." *Can Med Assn J* 99:844–8 N 2 '68. *
137. BUZAHORA, RONALD G. *Modified AAHPER Youth Fitness Test Norms for Freshmen College Males at the University of North Dakota.* Master's thesis, University of North Dakota (Grand Forks, N.D.), 1970.
138. KESTNER, RICHARD A. *A Study of Peer Social Acceptance as Related to the Modified AAHPER Youth Fitness Test.* Master's thesis, Kansas State Teachers College (Emporia, Kan.), 1970.
139. SHYIAK, DAVID P. *A Study of the Reliability of the AAHPER Youth Fitness Test as Applied to Male Visually Handicapped Students at the North Dakota State School for the Blind.* Master's thesis, University of North Dakota (Grand Forks, N.D.), 1970.
140. SODERBERG, PAUL O. *The Reliability and Validity of the Modified AAHPER Fitness Test as Applied to Freshmen College Males at the University of North Dakota.* Master's thesis, University of North Dakota (Grand Forks, N.D.), 1970.
141. WIDDOP, JAMES H. "A Comparative Study of the Motor Performance of Educable Retarded and Normal Children," pp. 523–39. In *Contemporary Psychology of Sport.* Proceedings of the Second International Congress of Sport Psychology, Washington, D.C., 1968. Chicago, Ill.: Athletic Institute, 1970. Pp. xix, 878. *

142. CAMPBELL, JOHN WILLIAM. *Evaluation of a Contingency Managed Physical Fitness Program for Mentally Retarded Boys.* Doctor's thesis, Pennsylvania State University (University Park, Pa.), 1971. (*DAI* 33:1042A)

143. LASHLEY, KENT ADRIAN. *A Comparative Study of Negro and Caucasian Junior High School Boys on Selected Factors of Personality, Socioeconomic Status, and Physical Fitness.* Doctor's thesis, East Texas State University (Commerce, Tex.), 1971. (*DAI* 32:5022A)

144. MILES, HELEN M. *A Study of Comparisons of Test Results From the AAHPER Youth Fitness Test, the 600-Yard Run-Walk Test, and the 12 Minute Run-Walk Test for Selected High School Girls.* Master's thesis, Fort Hays Kansas State College (Hays, Kan.), 1971.

145. MILLER, JEFFREY O. "Personality Factors and Perceptual Factors in Motor Performance." *ICHPER* 13:46–61 '71. *

146. MONTGOMERY, JOHN RAY. *Comparative Effects of Two Physical Conditioning Programs and Evaluation of Instruments for Measuring Physical Fitness.* Doctor's thesis, North Texas State University (Denton, Tex.), 1971. (*DAI* 32:3763A)

147. MURPHY, THOMAS MICHAEL. *The Relationship Between the AAHPER Youth Fitness Test Scores and Athletic Ability in Football, Basketball, and Paddleball.* Master's thesis, Florida State University (Tallahassee, Fla.), 1971.

148. REED, PAMELA R. *A Study of the Relationship of Age, Height, and Weight to Performance on the AAHPER Youth Fitness Test.* Master's thesis, Texas Tech University (Lubbock, Tex.), 1971.

149. STASKEY, PAUL J. "Physical Fitness and the Computer." *J Ed Data Processing* 8(5):14–6 '71. *

CUMULATIVE NAME INDEX

[915]

Action-Choice Tests for Competitive Sports Situations. High school and college; 1960; sportsmanship; Mary Jane Haskins and Betty Grant Hartman; Mary Jane Haskins. *

For additional information, see 6:716 (2 references).

REFERENCES THROUGH 1971

1–2. See 6:716.

CUMULATIVE NAME INDEX

[916]

Attitude Inventory. College women; [1959]; attitudes about values of physical education; 5 scores: spiritual, sociological, psychological, general, total; June P. Galloway; the Author. *

[917]

Basic Fitness Tests. Ages 12–18; 1964; BFT; 11 scores: extent flexibility, dynamic flexibility, shuttle run (explosive strength), softball throw (explosive strength), hand grip (static strength), pull-ups (dynamic strength), leg lifts (trunk strength), cable jump (coordination), balance A (equilibrium), 600-yard run-walk (stamina), fitness index; Edwin A. Fleishman; Prentice-Hall, Inc. *

For additional information, a review by Aileene S. Lockhart, and an excerpted review by C. H. Ammons, see 7:597 (7 references); see also 6:716a (1 reference). For excerpts from related book reviews, see 7:B214 (2 excerpts).

REFERENCES THROUGH 1971

1. See 6:716a.

2–8. See 7:597.

9. FLEISHMAN, EDWIN A., AND HEMPEL, WALTER E., JR. "Factorial Analysis of Complex Psychomotor Performance and Related Skills." *J Appl Psychol* 40:96–104 Ap '56. * (*PA* 31:6757)

10. FLEISHMAN, EDWIN A. "The Measurement of Physical Proficiency: A Problem in Skill Classification," pp. 328–40. In *Manpower Research in a Defense Context: The Proceedings of a Conference Under the Aegis of the NATO Scientific Affairs Committee.* New York: American Elsevier Publishing Co., Inc., 1969. Pp. x, 463. *

11. JOHNSON, JOSEPH BENJAMIN. *A Comparison of Physical Fitness and Self-Concept Between Junior High Negro and White Male Students.* Doctor's thesis, University of Alabama (University, Ala.), 1970. (*DAI* 31:5180A)

12. KANE, JOHN E. "Personality and Physical Abilities," pp. 131–41. In *Contemporary Psychology of Sport.* Proceedings of the Second International Congress of Sport Psychology, Washington, D.C., 1968. Chicago, Ill.: Athletic Institute, 1970. Pp. xix, 878. *

13. SCHILTZ, JACK HERBERT. *Level of Aspiration of High and Low Motor Ability Children in a Failure Task Preceded by Successful and Unsuccessful Pretask Conditions.* Doctor's thesis, Columbia University (New York, N.Y.), 1970. (*DAI* 31:3351A)

14. JACKSON, ANDREW S. "Factor Analysis of Selected Muscular Strength and Motor Performance Tests." *Res Q* 42(2):164–72 My '71. * (*PA* 47:2082)

CUMULATIVE NAME INDEX

[918]

The Belmont Measures of Athletic Performance.
Females grades 9–16; 1963–64; ratings by 6 or more
classmates; 4 scales; Logan Wright and Patsy K.
Wright; Psychometric Affiliates. *
a) BASKETBALL SCALE FOR WOMEN. 1964.
b) FIELD HOCKEY SCALE. 1963.
c) SOFTBALL SCALE FOR WOMEN. 1964.
d) VOLLEYBALL SCALE FOR WOMEN. 1964.
For additional information, see 7:598 (2 references).

REFERENCES THROUGH 1971
1–2. See 7:598.

CUMULATIVE NAME INDEX

[919]

*The CAHPER Fitness-Performance Test. Ages
7–17, 18–44; 1966–71; 2 levels; Canadian Association
for Health, Physical Education and Recreation [Can-
ada]. *
a) CHILDREN. Ages 7–17; 1966; 6 scores: speed sit up,
standing broad jump, shuttle run, flexed arm hang, 50
yard run, 300 yard run.
b) ADULTS. Ages 18–44; 1971; 5 scores: speed sit up,
standing broad jump, adipose tissue mensuration, grip
strength, flexibility.
For additional information, see 7:599 (1 reference).

REFERENCES THROUGH 1971
1. See 7:599.
2. CUMMING, GORDON R., AND KEYNES, RHODA. "A Fitness
Performance Test for School Children and Its Correlation With
Physical Working Capacity and Maximal Oxygen Uptake."
Can Med Assn J 96:1262–9 My 6 '67. *
3. CRAWFORD, GERALD LYN. *A Reliability Study of the
CAHPER Fitness-Performance Test.* Master's thesis, University
of Victoria (Victoria, B.C., Canada), 1971.

CUMULATIVE NAME INDEX

[920]

***CLEP Subject Examination in Human Growth
and Development.** 1 semester or equivalent; 1969–73;
for college accreditation of nontraditional study, advanced placement, or assessment of educational achievement; tests administered monthly at centers throughout
the United States; program administered for the College Entrance Examination Board by Educational Testing Service. * For the testing program entry, see 1050.
For additional information, see 7:600. For reviews of
the testing program, see 7:664 (3 reviews).

[921]

College Health Knowledge Test, Personal Health.
College; 1950–59; 12 scores: social and biological background, nutrition and diet, excretion and cleanliness,
exercise and body mechanics, fatigue and rest, mental
hygiene, reproduction and heredity, prevention and control of disease, eye-ear-teeth hygiene, hygiene of environment, use of medical care, total; Terry H. Dearborn; Stanford University Press. *
For additional information and reviews by James E.
Bryan and Peter G. Loret, see 6:718 (4 references);
for a review by H. Harrison Clarke, see 4:478.

REFERENCES THROUGH 1971
1–4. See 6:718.
5. BAKER, BARBARA; FRANK, JIM; AND PANGLE, ROY. "A New
Approach in Determining Health Misconceptions." *J Sch Health*
34:300–2 Je '64. *
6. FARRIS, JEFFERSON DAVIS, JR. *The Relationship of Selected
Factors to the Health Knowledge of Entering College Freshmen.*
Doctor's thesis, University of Arkansas (Fayetteville, Ark.),
1964. (*DA* 25:1720)
7. HEFLIN, BAILEY, AND PANGLE, ROY. "Health Misconceptions of College Students." *J Am Col Health Assn* 14:154–7 F
'66. *
8. TOMPKINS, ROBERT NEILL. *A Comparative Study of Divergent Levels of Physical Fitness With Reference to Selected
Health Factors.* Doctor's thesis, University of Utah (Salt Lake
City, Utah), 1968. (*DA* 29:1123A)

CUMULATIVE NAME INDEX

[922]

★Drug Abuse Knowledge Test. Grades 10–12; 1973,
c1969; DAKT; test booklet title is *Drug Abuse Test;*
Madge Louise Attwood; the Author. *

[923]

**A Drug Knowledge Inventory, Experimental Edi-
tion.** Grades 7–16 and adults; 1969–70; DKI; Gelolo
McHugh and Jay C. Williams; Family Life Publica-
tions, Inc. *
For additional information and a review by James E.
Bryan, see 7:601.

[924]

Emporia Elementary Health Test. 1, 2 semesters in
grades 6–8; 1962–64; first published 1962–63 in the
Every Pupil Scholarship Test series; Gary Adamson
and M. W. Sanders; Bureau of Educational Measurements. *
For additional information and a review by James E.
Bryan, see 7:602.

[925]

Emporia High School Health Test. High school
and college; 1962–64; first published 1962–63 in the
Every Pupil Scholarship Test series; Ron Blaylock and
M. W. Sanders; Bureau of Educational Measure-
ments. *
For additional information, see 7:603.

[926]

**Health and Safety Education Test: National
Achievement Tests.** Grades 3–6; 1947–60; 5 scores:
good habits, cause and effect, facts, application of rules,
total; 1960 test identical with test copyrighted 1947; no
manual; Lester D. Crow and Loretta C. Ryan; Psychometric Affiliates. *
For additional information, see 6:724; for a review
by Clarence H. Nelson, see 5:555.

[927]

Health Behavior Inventory. Grades 3–6, 7–9, 10–12,
college; 1962–66; HBI; 4 levels; CTB/McGraw-Hill. *
a) ELEMENTARY LEVEL. Grades 3–6; 1962–64; 9 scores:
personal health, personal cleanliness, nutrition, safety,
community health, infection and disease, mental health,
dental health, total; Sylvia Yellen.
b) JUNIOR HIGH LEVEL. Grades 7–9; 1962–64; 15 scores:
nutrition, personal cleanliness and skin care, mental
health, personal health, community health, smoking and
drinking, infection and disease, safety, care of eyes,
dental health, rest and recreation, practices total, attitudes total, knowledge total, total; Albert D. Colebank.

c) SENIOR HIGH LEVEL. Grades 10–12; 1962–64; 11 scores: personal health, safety and first aid, family health, infection and disease, mental health, nutrition, community health, exercise-rest-recreation, drinking-smoking-narcotics, dental health, total; E. Harold Le-Maistre and Marion B. Pollock.

d) COLLEGE LEVEL. 1965–66; Carmen Patricia Reid.

For additional information, see 7:604 (4 references); for reviews by James E. Bryan and Peter G. Loret of the first three levels, see 6:723.

REFERENCES THROUGH 1971

1–4. See 7:604.
5. SLOBOF, HAROLD. *Health Knowledge of Senior Students and Health Education Programs of the Secondary Schools in Toledo and Lucas County, Ohio.* Doctor's thesis, University of Toledo (Toledo, Ohio), 1970. (*DAI* 31:3942A)
6. BUCK, JOHN WILLIAM. *Relationship of Health Behavior to the Adjustment of Selected High School Seniors.* Doctor's thesis, University of Utah (Salt Lake City, Utah), 1971. (*DAI* 32:3073A)

CUMULATIVE NAME INDEX

Bryan, J. E.: *rev,* 6:723   Dennison, D.: 3
Buck, J. W.: 6   Loret, P. G.: *rev,* 6:723
Colebank, A.: 1   Slobof, H.: 5
Cremer, A. G.: 4   Yellen, S.: 2

[928]

Health Education Test: Knowledge and Application: Acorn National Achievement Tests, Revised Edition. Grades 7–13; 1946–56; 3 scores: knowledge, application, total; 1956 test materials identical with materials copyrighted 1946 except for minor changes in test; John H. Shaw and Maurice E. Troyer; Psychometric Affiliates. *

For additional information, see 5:557 (1 reference); for reviews by H. H. Remmers and Mabel E. Rugen, see 3:421.

REFERENCES THROUGH 1971

1. See 5:557.
2. FISHER, MILLARD JAY. *The Relationship of Health Knowledges to Health Practices of College Freshmen at North Texas State University.* Doctor's thesis, North Texas State University (Denton, Tex.), 1969. (*DAI* 30:2766B)

CUMULATIVE NAME INDEX

Fisher, M. J.: 2   Shaw, J. H.: 1
Remmers, H. H.: *rev,* 3:421   Troyer, M. E.: 1
Rugen, M. E.: *rev,* 3:421

[929]

Health Knowledge Test for College Freshmen: National Achievement Tests. Grade 13; 1956; A. Frank Bridges; Psychometric Affiliates. *

For additional information and a review by James E. Bryan, see 5:558 (3 references).

REFERENCES THROUGH 1971

1–3. See 5:558.

CUMULATIVE NAME INDEX

Boydston, D. N.: 3   Kilander, H. F.: 1
Bridges, F.: 2   Sells, J. A.: 3
Bryan, J. E.: *rev,* 5:558   Whelan, R. F.: 3

[930]

Health Test: National Achievement Tests. Grades 3–8; 1937–57; 5 scores: recognizing best habits, health comparisons, causes and effects, health facts, total; 1949 and 1957 tests identical with tests copyrighted 1938 except for 1 item in each; Robert K. Speer and Samuel Smith; Psychometric Affiliates. *

For additional information and a review by Benno G. Fricke, see 5:560; for a review by Jacob S. Orleans, see 4:485.

[931]

Illinois Ratings of Character in Physical Education. High school; 1969; IRC; ratings by 2 classmates of same sex; 10 scores: leadership, positive physical qualities, positive mental qualities, self-control, cooperation, social action standards, ethical social qualities, efficiency, sociability, total; B. Everard Blanchard; Western Psychological Services. *

For additional information, see 7:605.

[932]

Indiana Physical Fitness Test. Grades 4–12; 1964; modification of *Indiana University Motor Fitness Index* (see 3:424); 4 scores: straddle chins, squat thrusts, push ups, vertical jump; Karl W. Bookwalter and Harold J. Walter (norms); Indiana Public Health Foundation, Inc. *

For additional information, see 7:606.

[933]

***Information Test on Drugs and Drug Abuse.** Grades 9–16 and adults; 1957–68; 1968 test essentially the same as 1966 *Information Test on Stimulants and Depressants* and 1957 *Stimulants and Depressants* except for deletion of 8 items and minor changes in format and 6 options; for research use only; no manual; H. Frederick Kilander; Glenn C. Leach, Publisher. *

[934]

***Information Test on Human Reproduction.** Grades 9–16 and adults; 1950–67; for research use only; no manual; H. Frederick Kilander; Glenn C. Leach, Publisher. *

REFERENCES THROUGH 1971

1. KILANDER, H. FREDERICK. "A Survey of the Public's Knowledge of Certain Aspects of Human Reproduction." *J Sch Health* 29:211–5 Je '59. *

CUMULATIVE NAME INDEX

Kilander, H. F.: 1

[935]

Kilander-Leach Health Knowledge Test. Grades 12–16; 1936–72; KLHKT; formerly called *Kilander Health Knowledge Test;* 1972 test identical with test copyrighted 1969 except for title; original test by H. Frederick Kilander, revision by Glenn C. Leach; Glenn C. Leach, Publisher. *

For additional information and a review by James E. Bryan, see 7:609 (2 references); see also 5:562 (3 references); for excerpted reviews by Lois M. Shoemaker and one other of an earlier form, see 2:1503.

REFERENCES THROUGH 1971

1–3. See 5:562.
4–5. See 7:609.
6. KILANDER, H. F. "The Public's Knowledge of Nutrition." *J Home Econ* 36:78–9 F '44. *
7. WICKERSHAM, BILL. *The Health Knowledge of Rural and Urban Youths in Missouri.* Doctor's thesis, University of Missouri (Columbia, Mo.), 1963. (*DA* 24:3301)
8. DUNGEE, GRANT ALAN, III. *A Comparison of the Health Knowledge Level of Students in Selected Secondary Negro Schools With the Ratings of Their Schools' Health Service and Health Instruction Programs.* Doctor's thesis, Indiana University (Bloomington, Ind.), 1964. (*DA* 26:1597)
9. DEES, MYRON HENRY. *Status of Health Education in Selected Texas Secondary Schools in 1966.* Doctor's thesis, University of Texas (Austin, Tex.), 1968. (*DA* 29:2103A)
10. KRUEGER, ESTHER SIEGEL. *A Study of the Health Knowledge of Graduating Elementary Teachers at Newark State College.* Doctor's thesis, Columbia University (New York, N.Y.), 1970. (*DAI* 31:2072B)

CUMULATIVE NAME INDEX

Bryan, J. E.: *rev,* 7:609   Lee, M. C.: 4
Campbell, D. E.: 5   Masley, J. W.: 3
Dees, M. H.: 9   Shoemaker, L. M.: *exc,* 2:1503
Dungee, G. A.: 8
Early, R. G.: 5   Trice, E. W.: 2
Kilander, H. F.: 1, 6   Wickersham, B.: 7
Krueger, E. S.: 10

[936]

*The Modified Sjöstrand Physical Work Capacity Test. Ages 7–17, 18–44; 1968–71; measures physical work capacity concurrent with a steady state heart rate of 170 beats per minute (PWC_{170}) by means of the Quinton-Monark Bicycle Ergometer; 2 scores: PWC_{170}, PWC_{170}/body weight (kg.) ; Canadian Association for Health, Physical Education and Recreation [Canada]. *
For additional information, see 7 :610 (6 references).

REFERENCES THROUGH 1971
1–6. See 7:610.
7. HOWELL, MAXWELL L., AND McNAB, ROSS B. J. "Interests and Attitudes Toward Physical Activity, Strength, Fitness-Performance, and Work Capacity of Canadian Children." *ICHPER* 10:36–45 '68. *

CUMULATIVE NAME INDEX

Adams, F. H.: 1–2	Linde, L. M.: 2
Bengtsson, E.: 1	Lovsin, J. L.: 3
Berven, H.: 1	McNab, R. B. J.: 7
Ellis, W. T.: 5	Miyaka, H.: 2
Fedoruk, D. E.: 6	Taylor, P. S.: 4
Howell, M. L.: 7	Wegelius, C.: 1

[937]

*National Teacher Examinations: Men's Physical Education. College seniors and teachers; 1954–73; this and *Women's Physical Education* replace the former single *Physical Education* test; an inactive form (1966) of the single test, entitled *Teacher Education Examination Program: Physical Education,* is available to colleges for local administration; another inactive form (1967) of the single test, entitled *Specialty Examinations: Physical Education,* is available to school systems for local use as part of the program entitled *School Personnel Research and Evaluation Services;* Educational Testing Service. * For the testing program entry, see 869.
For additional information concerning earlier forms, see 7 :611. For reviews of the testing program, see 7 :582 (2 reviews), 6 :700 (1 review), 5 :538 (3 reviews), and 4 :802 (1 review).

[938]

*National Teacher Examinations: Women's Physical Education. College seniors and teachers; 1954–73; this and *Men's Physical Education* replace the former single *Physical Education* test; an inactive form (1966) of the single test, entitled *Teacher Education Examination Program: Physical Education,* is available to colleges for local administration; another inactive form (1967) of the single test, entitled *Specialty Examinations: Physical Education,* is available to school systems for local use as part of the program entitled *School Personnel Research and Evaluation Services;* Educational Testing Service. * For the testing program entry, see 869.
For additional information concerning earlier forms, see 7 :612. For reviews of the testing program, see 7 :582 (2 reviews), 6 :700 (1 review), 5 :538 (3 reviews), and 4 :802 (1 review).

[939]

Patient's Self-History Form, Second Edition. Patients; 1948–58; Oliver E. Byrd; Stanford University Press. *
For additional information, see 4 :486.

[940]

★A Self Administered Health Questionnaire for Secondary School Students. High school; 1968; no manual; N. G. Alexiou and G. Weiner; N. G. Alexiou. *

REFERENCES THROUGH 1971
1. ALEXIOU, NICHOLAS G., AND WIENER, GERALD. "Reliability of a Self-Administered Health Questionnaire for Secondary

School Students (Adolescents)." *Am J Pub Health* 58:1439–46 Ag '68. *
2. ALEXIOU, NICHOLAS G.; WIENER, GERALD; SILVERMAN, MARY; AND MILTON, TOBY. "Validity Studies of a Self-Administered Health Questionnaire for Secondary School Students." *Am J Pub Health* 59(8):1400–13 Ag '69. *

CUMULATIVE NAME INDEX

Alexiou, N. G.: 1–2	Silverman, M.: 2
Milton, T.: 2	Wiener, G.: 1–2

[941]

Swimming Ability Scales for Boys in Secondary Schools: National Swimming Norms. Boys ages 11–18; 1964; 5 scores: breaststroke, crawlstroke, backstroke, butterfly, 5 minute distance swim; J. Atha; Physical Education and Industrial Fitness Unit, Loughborough University of Technology [England]. *
For additional information, see 7 :613.

[942]

*Teacher Education Examination Program: Physical Education. College seniors preparing to teach secondary school; 1957–72; reprinting of inactive 1966 form of *National Teacher Examinations: Physical Education;* test available to colleges for local administration; Educational Testing Service. * For the testing program entry, see 898.
For additional information concerning an earlier form, see 6 :728. For a review of the testing program, see 5 :543.

[943]

★[Tests for Venereal Disease Education.] Junior high school, high school and college; 1965–67; 3 tests; Family Life Publications, Inc. *
a) TEACHING TEST ON SYPHILIS AND GONORRHEA. Junior high school; 1965–66; TTSG; also called *A Standard Test on Syphilis and Gonorrhea;* William F. Schwartz.
b) A VENEREAL DISEASE KNOWLEDGE INVENTORY, EXPERIMENTAL EDITION. High school and college; 1966–67; VDKI; teaching test; Gelolo McHugh.
c) ACHIEVEMENT TEST ON SYPHILIS AND GONORRHEA. Junior high school through college; 1965–66; ATSG; to follow teaching with *a* or *b;* William F. Schwartz.

REFERENCES THROUGH 1971
1. SCHWARTZ, WILLIAM F. *Teacher's Handbook on Venereal Disease Education: Includes Complete Student's Manual.* Washington, D.C.: American Association for Health, Physical Education, and Recreation, 1965. Pp. 216. *
2. WALLACE, ROBERT CLAYTON. *Sex Education Knowledge, Verbal Interaction, and Attitudes: An Exploratory Study in High School Human Biology Classes.* Doctor's thesis, University of Illinois (Urbana, Ill.), 1970. (*DAI* 31:6434A)

CUMULATIVE NAME INDEX

Schwartz, W. F.: 1	Wallace, R. C.: 2

[944]

★Thompson Smoking and Tobacco Knowledge Test. Grades 7–16; 1964–67; no manual; Clem W. Thompson; the Author. *

REFERENCES THROUGH 1971
1. THOMPSON, CLEM W. "Thompson Smoking and Tobacco Knowledge Test." *Res Q* 35:60–8 Mr '64. *
2. ATHA, DANIEL RAY. *A Study of Smoking Habits and Tobacco Knowledges of Ninth Grade Students in Washington County, Arkansas.* Doctor's thesis, University of Arkansas (Fayetteville, Ark.), 1968. (*DA* 29:133A)

CUMULATIVE NAME INDEX

Atha, D. R.: 2	Thompson, C. W.: 1

[945]

*The Undergraduate Program Field Tests: Physical Education Test. College; 1969–73; formerly called *The Undergraduate Record Examinations: Physical Education Test;* test available to colleges for local administration; Educational Testing Service. * For the testing program entry, see 1062.

For additional information concerning an earlier form, see 7:614. For reviews of the testing program, see 7:671 (2 reviews).

[946]

★VD Knowledge Test. Grades 6 and over; 1973; primarily for use with the instructional booklet *A Shortcut to Venereal Disease Education;* "self-administered remedial test"; Joseph Chiappa and Gelolo McHugh; Family Life Publications, Inc. *

[947]

[Wetzel Grid Charts.] Ages birth–3, 2–18; 1940–48; chart for evaluating physical growth and development; 2 levels; Norman C. Wetzel; NEA Service, Inc. *
a) THE BABY GRID: A GUIDE TO INDIVIDUAL PROGRESS DURING INFANCY. Ages birth–3; 1946–48.
b) GRID FOR EVALUATING PHYSICAL FITNESS IN TERMS OF PHYSIQUE (BODY BUILD), DEVELOPMENT LEVEL AND BASAL METABOLISM—A GUIDE TO INDIVIDUAL PROGRESS FROM INFANCY TO MATURITY. Ages 2–18; 1940–48.

For additional information and a review by Dorothy Eichorn, see 6:731 (26 references); see also 4:489 (9 references).

REFERENCES THROUGH 1971

1–9. See 4:489.
10–35. See 6:731.
36. WETZEL, NORMAN C. "The Grid Technique of Evaluating Growth and Development in Infants and Children." Abstract. *Am J Phys Anthropol* 4:255–6 '46. * (*PA* 21:331, title only)
37. MANN, ARVIN W.; DREIZEN, SAMUEL; SPIES, TOM D.; WITH THE TECHNICAL ASSISTANCE OF S. IDELL PYLE. "The Determination of Status and Progress in Children With Nutritive Failure." *J Pediatrics* 31:161–71 Ag '47. * (*PA* 22:239)
38. BOOKWALTER, KARL W., AND OTHERS. "The Relationship of Body Size and Shape to Physical Performance." *Res Q* 23:271–9 O '52. * (*PA* 27:4870)
39. BRENNER, ANTON, AND MORSE, NANCY C. "The Measurement of Children's Readiness for School." *Papers Mich Acad Sci Arts & Letters* 41:333–40 '56. * (*PA* 37:6453)
40. FISH, BARBARA. "The Detection of Schizophrenia in Infancy: A Preliminary Report." *J Nerv & Mental Dis* 125:1–24 Ja–Mr '57. * (*PA* 33:4353)
41. SOLLEY, WILLIAM H. "Ratio of Physical Development as a Factor in Motor Coordination of Boys Ages 10–14." *Res Q* 28:295–304 O '57. * (*PA* 33:5485)
42. CARLSON, HOWARD ERIC. *Wetzel Grid Classification Techniques as Bases for Evaluating Individual Performances in Selected Physical Ability Tests.* Master's thesis, University of Washington (Seattle, Wash.), 1961.
43. SERL, JOHN W. *Relationships Between Physical Performance and Growth Characteristics of Fifth and Sixth Grade Children as Characterized by the Wetzel Grid Technique.* Master's thesis, University of Washington (Seattle, Wash.), 1962.
44. GEARHART, EVERETT E. *An Evaluation of Performances in Selected Physical Ability Tests by Elementary School Boys Classified on the Basis of Wetzel Grid Developmental Levels.* Master's thesis, University of Washington (Seattle, Wash.), 1963.
45. ELLIS, RICHARD ROMAINE. *A Longitudinal Study to Determine the Relationship Between Physical Development as Measured by the Wetzel Grid, and Academic Achievement of Elementary School Children, Grades 1–6, as Measured by the Metropolitan Achievement Tests.* Doctor's thesis, Columbia University (New York, N.Y.), 1965. (*DA* 26:4328)
46. MILLS, FRED M. *The Relationship of the Speed of Growth as Assessed by the Wetzel Grid to Physical Fitness and Academic Achievement of Seventh-Grade Students.* Master's thesis, University of Washington (Seattle, Wash.), 1965.
47. VAN IDEN, STARR STANLEY. *Scholastic Progress of Boys Classified by the Wetzel Grid Technique: A Ten-Year Longitudinal Study.* Doctor's thesis, Western Reserve University (Cleveland, Ohio), 1965. (*DA* 27:614A)
48. SCHWARTZ, SAMUEL. *The Validity of the Human Dentition as an Indicator of Physical Maturity of Boys Ranging From Seven Years to Twelve Years and Six Months of Age.* Doctor's thesis, Temple University (Philadelphia, Pa.), 1966. (*DA* 28:954A)
49. HURSTER, MADELINE, AND ARCHER, MORTON. "Selected Parameters of School Achievement Among Urban Adolescents: A Study in Four New York City Junior High Schools." *J Sch Health* 37:511–8 D '67. * (*PA* 42:9497)

50. RIVERA, EMILIO, JR. *The Contribution of Non-Intellectual Variables to the Prediction of Academic Performance of Junior High School Pupils.* Doctor's thesis, New York University (New York, N.Y.), 1967. (*DA* 28:4058A)
51. BUCKELLEW, WILLIAM FRANKLIN. *A Cross Sectional and Longitudinal Study of Various Factors of Growth and Development of Fifth, Sixth, Seventh, and Eighth Grade Boys.* Doctor's thesis, University of Arkansas (Fayetteville, Ark.), 1968. (*DA* 29:1445A)
52. KURLE, HAROLD B. *A Comparison of the AAHPER and Renton Physical Fitness Tests to Determine the Effect of a Wetzel Grid Equated Classification System on the Fitness Scores of Renton Junior High School Physical Education Students.* Master's thesis, University of Washington (Seattle, Wash.), 1968.
53. WEAR, CARL L. "An Analysis of Height-Weight Relationships of Midwestern Boys." *Res Q* 40(3):607–12 O '69. *
54. BROWN, ROSCOE C., JR. "The Relationship Between Physical Performance and Personality in Elementary School Children," pp. 439–45. In *Contemporary Psychology of Sport.* Proceedings of the Second International Congress of Sport Psychology, Washington, D.C., 1968. Chicago, Ill.: Athletic Institute, 1970. Pp. xix, 878. *

CUMULATIVE NAME INDEX

[Out of Print Since TIP I]

Smoking Habits Questionnaire (status unknown), 6:729
Trusler-Arnett Health Knowledge Test, 3:426 (1 review)
Veenker Health Knowledge Test, 6:730 (1 reference)
Width-Weight Tables, 4:490 (1 reference)
Winsberg Tests: Examinations for Physical Education Major Students, 5:567

HOME ECONOMICS

[948]

Compton Fabric Preference Test. Females in grades 7 and over; 1965; CFPT; Norma H. Compton; the Author. *
For additional information and a review by Dorothy M. Clendenen, see 7:619 (9 references).

REFERENCES THROUGH 1971
1–9. See 7:619.
10. SEARS, NANCY JANE. *Fabric Preferences as Related to Selected Personality Characteristics of Delinquent and Nondelinquent Adolescent Girls.* Master's thesis, University of North Carolina (Greensboro, N.C.), 1966.
11. COMPTON, NORMA H. "Body Perception in Relation to Anxiety Among Women." *Percept & Motor Skills* 28(1):215–8 F '69. * (PA 43:11299)

CUMULATIVE NAME INDEX
Clendenen, D. M.: *rev,* 7:619   Sears, N. J.: 10
Compton, N. H.: 1–7, 11   Taylor, L. C.: 7
Matthews, L. B.: 8   Torreta, D. M.: 9

[949]

Emporia Clothing Test. High school; 1962–64; first published 1962–63 in the Every Pupil Scholarship Test series; Margaret C. Parkman, Patricia Duncan, and M. W. Sanders; Bureau of Educational Measurements. *
For additional information, see 7:620.

[950]

Emporia Foods Test. High school; 1962–64; first published 1962–63 in the Every Pupil Scholarship Test series; Margaret C. Parkman, Patricia Duncan, and M. W. Sanders; Bureau of Educational Measurements. *
For additional information, see 7:621.

[951]

Minnesota Check List for Food Preparation and Serving, Third Edition. Grades 7–16 and adults; 1938–51; Clara Brown Arny; University of Minnesota Press. *
For additional information, see 5:571; for an excerpted review, see 2:1509 (1 reference).

REFERENCES THROUGH 1971
1. See 2:1509.
CUMULATIVE NAME INDEX
Amidon, E. P.: 1

[952]

*National Teacher Examinations: Home Economics Education. College seniors and teachers; 1960–73; an inactive form (1966) entitled *Teacher Education Examination Program: Home Economics Education* is available to colleges for local administration; another inactive form (1968) entitled *Specialty Examinations: Home Economics Education* is available to school systems for local use as part of the program entitled *School Personnel Research and Evaluation Services;* Educational Testing Service. * For the testing program entry, see 869.

For additional information concerning earlier forms, see 7:626. For reviews of the testing program, see 7:582 (2 reviews), 6:700 (1 review), 5:538 (3 reviews), and 4:802 (1 review).

[953]

*Nutrition Information Test. Grades 9–16 and adults; 1942–68; for research use only; no manual; H. Frederick Kilander; Glenn C. Leach, Publisher. *
For additional information, see 3:425 (1 reference).

REFERENCES THROUGH 1971
1. See 3:425.
2. KILANDER, H. F. "The Public's Knowledge of Nutrition." *J Home Econ* 36:78–9 F '44. *
3. KILANDER, H. FREDERICK. "The Public's Beliefs in Nutrition Facts and Fallacies." *J Sch Health* 34:218–21 My '64. *
CUMULATIVE NAME INDEX
Kilander, H. F.: 1–3

[954]

Scales for Appraising High School Homemaking Programs. Pupils, teachers, community members, and administrators; 1953; 3 scales; Clara Brown Arny and Sara Blackwell; University of Minnesota Press. *
a) SCALE 1, THE CURRICULUM.
b) SCALE 2, REFERENCE AND ILLUSTRATIVE MATERIALS.
c) SCALE 3, SPACE AND EQUIPMENT.
For additional information, see 5:572.

[955]

★Teacher Education Examination Program: Home Economics Education. College seniors preparing to teach secondary school; 1971–72; reprinting of inactive 1966 form of *National Teacher Examinations: Home Economics Education;* test available to colleges for local administration; Educational Testing Service. * For the testing program entry, see 898.
For a review of the testing program, see 5:543.

[956-66]

★Test of Family Life Knowledge and Attitudes: Betty Crocker Search for Leadership in Family Living. Grade 12 boys and girls seeking Betty Crocker college scholarships and awards; 1955–73; formerly called *Knowledge and Attitude Test: Betty Crocker Search for American Homemakers of Tomorrow;* test administered annually in December at participating secondary schools; test prepared and administered for General Mills, Inc. by Science Research Associates, Inc. *

[Out of Print Since TIP I]

Assisting With Care and Play of Children: State High School Tests for Indiana, 3:427 (1 review)
Chart for Diagnosing Defects in Buttonholes, T:1256
Child Development, 7:615 (1 review)
Clothing I and II, 7:616–7
Clothing: Every Pupil Scholarship Test, 6:732
Clothing Problems, 7:618
Family Life, 7:622
Food in the Home, 7:623 (1 review)
Foods I, 7:624 (1 review); *Foods II*, 7:625
Foods: Every Pupil Scholarship Test, 6:733
Helping With the Housekeeping: State High School Tests for Indiana, 4:499 (1 review)
Home Art Placement Test, T:1266
Home Care of the Sick Test: State High School Tests for Indiana, 4:500
Homemaking I and II: Every Pupil Scholarship Test, 6:735
Housing the Family: State High School Tests for Indiana, 4:501 (1 review)

Johnson Home Economics Interest Inventory, 5:570
(2 reviews, 6 references)
*Ninth Year Home Economics: Manchester Semester-
End Achievement Tests,* T:1273, 36:626
*Unit Scales of Attainment in Foods and Household
Management,* 2:1511 (2 reviews)

INDUSTRIAL ARTS

[967]

Drawing: Cooperative Industrial Arts Tests. 1 se-
mester grades 7–9; 1969–70; Cooperative Tests and
Services. *
For additional information and a review by Robert
C. Harris, see 7:627.

REFERENCES THROUGH 1971

1. TUCKMAN, BRUCE W., AND CORMAN, MYRON N. "Cooperative Industrial Arts Tests: A Review." *J Ed Meas* 8(4):
341–2 w '71. *

CUMULATIVE NAME INDEX

Corman, M. N.: 1   Tuckman, B. W.: 1
Harris, R. C.: *rev,* 7:627

[968]

**Electricity/Electronics: Cooperative Industrial
Arts Tests.** 1 semester grades 7–9; 1969–70; Coopera-
tive Tests and Services. *
For additional information and a review by Alan R.
Suess, see 7:628.

REFERENCES THROUGH 1971

1. TUCKMAN, BRUCE W., AND CORMAN, MYRON N. "Cooperative Industrial Arts Tests: A Review." *J Ed Meas* 8(4):341–2
w '71. *

CUMULATIVE NAME INDEX

Corman, M. N.: 1   Tuckman, B. W.: 1
Suess, A. R.: *rev,* 7:628

[969]

Emporia Industrial Arts Test. High school; 1962–
64; first published 1962–63 in the Every Pupil Scholarship Test series; David E. Hill, Elton Amburn, and
M. W. Sanders; Bureau of Educational Measurements. *
For additional information, see 7:629.

[970]

**General Industrial Arts: Cooperative Industrial
Arts Tests.** 1 year grades 7–9; 1969–70; Cooperative
Tests and Services. *
For additional information and a review by Thomas
S. Baldwin, see 7:630.

REFERENCES THROUGH 1971

1. TUCKMAN, BRUCE W., AND CORMAN, MYRON N. "Cooperative Industrial Arts Tests: A Review." *J Ed Meas* 8(4):341–2
w '71. *

CUMULATIVE NAME INDEX

Baldwin, T. S.: *rev,* 7:630   Tuckman, B. W.: 1
Corman, M. N.: 1

[971]

Metals: Cooperative Industrial Arts Tests. 1
semester grades 7–9; 1969–70; Cooperative Tests and
Services. *
For additional information, see 7:631.

REFERENCES THROUGH 1971

1. TUCKMAN, BRUCE W., AND CORMAN, MYRON N. "Cooperative Industrial Arts Tests: A Review." *J Ed Meas* 8(4):341–2
w '71. *

CUMULATIVE NAME INDEX

Corman, M. N.: 1   Tuckman, B. W.: 1

[972]

*****National Teacher Examinations: Industrial
Arts Education.** College seniors and teachers; 1947–

73; an inactive form (1966) entitled *Teacher Education Examination Program: Industrial Arts* is available to colleges for local administration; another inactive form (1968) entitled *Specialty Examinations:
Industrial Arts Education* is available to school systems for local use as part of the program entitled
School Personnel Research and Evaluation Services;
Educational Testing Service. * For the testing program entry, see 869.
For additional information, see 7:632. For reviews
of the testing program, see 7:582 (2 reviews), 6:700
(1 review), 5:538 (3 reviews), and 4:802 (1 review).

[973]

*****Teacher Education Examination Program: In-
dustrial Arts.** College seniors preparing to teach
secondary school; 1957–72; reprinting of inactive 1966
form of *National Teacher Examinations: Industrial
Arts Education;* test available to colleges for local
administration; Educational Testing Service. * For
the testing program entry, see 898.
For additional information concerning an earlier
form, see 6:738. For a review of the testing program,
see 5:543.

[974]

**Technical and Scholastic Test: The Dailey Voca-
tional Tests.** Grades 8–12 and adults; 1964–65; TST;
3 scores for males in grades 8–10 and females: technical, scholastic, total; 11 scores for others: technical
(electricity, electronics, mechanics, science, total),
scholastic (arithmetic, algebra, vocabulary, total),
total, mechanical (mechanics and arithmetic); John T.
Dailey and Kenneth B. Hoyt (manual); Houghton
Mifflin Co. * For the complete battery entry, see 2105.
For reviews of the complete battery, see 7:976 (2
reviews, 2 excerpts).

[975]

Woods: Cooperative Industrial Arts Tests. 1
semester grades 7–9; 1969–70; Cooperative Tests and
Services. *
For additional information and a review by Richard
A. Swanson, see 7:634.

REFERENCES THROUGH 1971

1. TUCKMAN, BRUCE W., AND CORMAN, MYRON N. "Cooperative Industrial Arts Tests: A Review." *J Ed Meas* 8(4):341–2
w '71. *

CUMULATIVE NAME INDEX

Corman, M. N.: 1   Tuckman, B. W.: 1
Swanson, R. A.: *rev,* 7:634

[Out of Print Since TIP I]

Industrial Arts: Every Pupil Scholarship Test, 6:737
Mechanical Drawing, 2:1513 (1 review)
*Mechanical Drawing Test: State High School Tests
for Indiana,* 4:503 (1 review)
Middleton Industrial Arts Test, 4:504 (1 review)
*Stanford Achievement Test: High School Technical
Comprehension Test,* 7:633 (1 review)

LEARNING DISABILITIES

[976]

★**Automated Graphogestalt Technique.** Grades
1–4; 1970–72; AGT; test booklet title is *Intermediate
A.G.T.;* identification of "children with incipient learning problems"; computer scored copying of 10 geometric forms; Theodore I. Friedman and Robert G.
Gatza; Computer Psychometric Affiliates, Inc. *

[977]

★**A Basic Screening and Referral Form for Children With Suspected Learning and Behavioral Disabilities.** Grades 1–12; 1972; teacher ratings in 8 areas: social-personal, conceptual-cognitive, language, perceptual-motor (visual-motor, visual, auditory), sensory-motor, gross-motor plus a pupil work sample; no manual; Robert E. Valett; Lear Seigler, Inc./Fearon Publishers. *

[978]

★**Cutrona Child Study Profile of Psycho-Educational Abilities.** Grades kgn–3; 1970; ratings in 10 areas: general behavior, gross-motor development, fine-motor development, body image and awareness, tactile-kinesthetic development, visual-motor perception, auditory perception, time orientation, non-verbal conceptualization, numerical conceptualization; Michael P. Cutrona; Cutronics Educational Institute. *

[979]

First Grade Screening Test. First grade entrants; 1966–69; FGST; intellectual deficiency, central nervous system dysfunction, and emotional disturbance; John E. Pate and Warren W. Webb; American Guidance Service, Inc. *

For additional information and an excerpted review by Grayce A. Ransom, see 7:748.

REFERENCES THROUGH 1971

1. PATE, JOHN E., AND WEBB, WARREN W. "Screening Beginning First Graders for Potential Problems." *Excep Children* 32:111 O '65. * (PA 40:762)
2. WEBB, WARREN W., AND PATE, JOHN E. "Predicting Failure in the Primary Grades." *Ed & Psychol Meas* 30(2): 459–62 su '70. * (PA 45:3071)
3. PAULUS, DIETER H., AND RENZULLI, JOSEPH S. "A Factor-Analytic Study of the First Grade Screening Test." *Psychol Sch* 8(1):57–9 Ja '71. * (PA 46:7457)

CUMULATIVE NAME INDEX

Pate, J. E.: 1–2   Renzulli, J. S.: 3
Paulus, D. H.: 3   Webb, W. W.: 1–2
Ransom, G. A.: *exc*, 7:748

[980]

★**Grassi Basic Cognitive Evaluation.** Ages 3–9; 1973; GBCE; "identification of developmental deficits"; 29 scores: discriminations (5 scores), conceptualization (5 scores), identifications (3 scores), orientation (3 scores), visualization, number concepts (3 scores), kinesthesia (2 scores), auditory perception, sequencing (2 scores), recall (2 scores), total, basic learning quotient (ratio of a GBCE score to mental age on the *Stanford-Binet Intelligence Scale*); Joseph R. Grassi; Scoptec Labs, Inc. *

[981]

Illinois Test of Psycholinguistic Abilities, Revised Edition. Ages 2–10; 1961–68; ITPA; 11–13 scores: auditory reception, visual reception, visual sequential memory, auditory association, auditory sequential memory, visual association, visual closure, verbal expression, grammatic closure, manual expression, auditory closure (optional), sound blending (optional), total; Samuel A. Kirk, James J. McCarthy, and Winifred D. Kirk; University of Illinois Press. *

For additional information and reviews by John B. Carroll and Clinton I. Chase, see 7:442 (239 references); see also 6:549 (22 references).

REFERENCES THROUGH 1971

1–22. See 6:549.
23–261. See 7:442.
262. SMITH, JAMES OTTO. "Group Language Development for Educable Mental Retardates." *Excep Children* 29:95–101 O '62. *

263. QUERESHI, MOHAMMED Y. "Performance on Individual Ability Tests as a Function of Various Scoring Cutoffs." *Ed & Psychol Meas* 24:481–512 f '64. * (PA 39:3173)
264. FROSTIG, MARIANNE. "The Relationship of Diagnosis to Remediation in Learning Problems." *Selected Papers Learn Disabilities* 3:45–66 '66. *
265. EVERETT, GARY D. *An Analysis of the Performance of Children With Severe Articulation Problems and Children With Minimal Brain Dysfunction as Manifested on a Selected Battery of Tests.* Master's thesis, Texas Technological College (Lubbock, Tex.), 1967.
266. KIRK, SAMUEL A. Chap. 13, "Amelioration of Mental Disabilities Through Psychodiagnostic and Remedial Procedures," pp. 186–219. In *Mental Retardation: A Symposium.* Edited by George A. Jervis. Springfield, Ill.: Charles C Thomas, Publisher, 1967. Pp. viii, 248. *
267. LITTLEDIKE, LILA JACLYN. *A Comparison of Certain Psycholinguistic Skills in Normal and Articulately Impaired Children.* Master's thesis, Utah State University (Logan, Utah), 1967.
268. QUERESHI, MOHAMMED Y. "The Invariance of Certain Ability Factors." *Ed & Psychol Meas* 27:803–10 w '67. * (PA 42:8734)
269. SEMMEL, MELVYN I. "Language Behavior of Mentally Retarded and Culturally Disadvantaged Children," pp. 31–47. (PA 42:7301) In *Fifth Annual Distinguished Lectures in Special Education, Summer Session 1966.* Edited by James F. Magary and Robert B. McIntyre. Los Angeles, Calif.: School of Education, University of Southern California Press, 1967. Pp. vii, 91. *
270. TILLMANS, SUSAN JEAN. *A Pilot Program on Language Development for Cerebral Palsied Children.* Master's thesis, St. Cloud State College (St. Cloud, Minn.), 1967.
271. ELLIS, JANET KOCH. *An Approach to Language Development Based on a Perceptual-motor Training Program.* Master's thesis, Southern Methodist University (Dallas, Tex.), 1968.
272. GIEBINK, JOHN W., AND MARDEN, MARY L. "Verbal Expression, Verbal Fluency, and Grammar Related to Cultural Experience." *Psychol Sch* 5:365–8 O '68. * (PA 43:5912)
273. LOVELL, K., AND GORTON, A. "A Study of Some Differences Between Backward and Normal Readers of Average Intelligence." *Brit J Ed Psychol* 38:240–8 N '68. * (PA 43:7398)
274. SLOBODZIAN, EVELYN B. "Use of the Illinois Test of Psycholinguistic Abilities as a Readiness Measure." *Proc Ann Conv Int Read Assn* 13(4):43–8 '68. *
275. SOWADA, LENORE. *An Experimental Investigation of the Illinois Test of Psycholinguistic Abilities With Non-Verbal Children.* Master's thesis, St. Cloud State College (St. Cloud, Minn.), 1968.
276. TEASDALE, G. R., AND KATZ, F. M. "Psycholinguistic Abilities of Children From Different Ethnic and Socio-Economic Backgrounds." *Austral J Psychol* 20:155–9 D '68. * (PA 45:3957)
277. CLASEN, ROBERT E.; SPEAR, JO ELLEN; AND TOMARO, MICHAEL P. "A Comparison of the Relative Effectiveness of Two Types of Preschool Compensatory Programming." *J Ed Res* 62(9):401–5 My–Je '69. *
278. HIGGINS, JANIS. *A Correlational Study of Language Development and Musical Ability.* Master's thesis, Texas Tech University (Lubbock, Tex.), 1969.
279. LAMB, STANFORD H. Chap. 13, "The Illinois Test of Psycholinguistic Abilities: Implications for Diagnosis and Remediation," pp. 256–88. In *Learning Disabilities: Introduction to Educational and Medical Management.* Edited by Lester Tarnopol. Springfield, Ill.: Charles C Thomas, Publisher, 1969. Pp. xix, 389. * (PA 44:3681)
280. MITTLER, PETER JOSEPH. *Psycholinguistic Skills in Four Year Old Twins and Singletons.* Doctor's thesis, University of London (London, England), 1969.
281. RUPERT, HAROLD A. "Application of the ITPA for Mentally Retarded Children." Abstract. *CEC Selected Conv Papers* 1969:136–7 '69. *
282. WEINTHALER, JUDITH. "Application of the ITPA for Children With Learning Disabilities." *CEC Selected Conv Papers* 1969:241–5 '69. *
283. ANASTASIOW, NICHOLAS J.; STEDMAN, DONALD J.; AND SPAULDING, ROBERT L. "Language and Reading Achievement Among Disadvantaged Nursery and Primary Grade Children." *Slow Learning Child* (Australia) 17(1):39–51 Mr '70. * (PA 44:18316)
284. BUTTS, TED MERRILL. *A Study of Race and Social Class Variables and Psycholinguistic, Cognitive, and Perceptual Measures of Selected First Grade Children.* Doctor's thesis, University of Alabama (University, Ala.), 1970. (DAI 31:5193A)
285. CAWLEY, JOHN F.; BURROW, WILL H.; AND GOODSTEIN, HENRY A. "Performance of Head Start and Non-Head Start Participants at First Grade." *J Negro Ed* 39(2):124–31 sp '70. * (PA 46:7770)
286. EARLY, GEORGE H., AND SHARPE, THEODORE M. "Developing Perceptual-Motor Skills: Perceptual-Motor Training and Basic Abilities." *Acad Ther* 5(3):235–40+ sp '70. * (PA 44:19036)
287. FAIRCHILD, MILES RICHARD. *Case Studies Concerning the Effects of Intensive, Short-Term Remediation of Psycho-*

linguistic Abilities. Doctor's thesis, University of South Dakota (Vermillion, S.D.), 1970. (*DAI* 31:5885A)

288. GARMS, JOE D. "Factor Analysis of the WISC and ITPA." *Psychol* 7(4):30–1 N '70. * (*PA* 46:3067)

289. GLOVSKY, LEON. "A Comparison of Two Groups of Mentally Retarded Children on the Illinois Test of Psycholinguistic Abilities." *Training Sch B* 67(1):4–14 My '70. * (*PA* 44:17214)

290. GUEST, KRISTIN ELIZABETH. *Relationships Among the Illinois Test of Psycholinguistic Abilities, Receptive and Expressive Language Tasks, Intelligence, and Achievement.* Doctor's thesis, University of Wisconsin (Madison, Wis.), 1970. (*DAI* 31:5845A)

291. HUTTON, WILBUR ORAN, JR. *The Performance of Educable Mentally Retarded Children on a Three-Trial Paired-Associate Learning Task as a Function of Conceptual Instructions and Chronological Age.* Doctor's thesis, University of Oregon (Eugene, Ore.), 1970. (*DAI* 31:5233A)

292. IKEDA, MIYOSHI. *The Relationships Between the Illinois Test of Psycholinguistic Abilities, Reading Performance, and IQ of Third-Grade Children.* Doctor's thesis, University of New Mexico (Albuquerque, N.M.), 1970. (*DAI* 31:5270A)

293. JOHNSON, K. E. "Increasing the Capacity to Learn." *Slow Learning Child* (Australia) 17(3):163–9 N '70. * (*PA* 46:9630)

294. KARNES, MEREL B.; TESKA, JAMES A.; AND HODGINS, AUDREY S. "The Effects of Four Programs of Classroom Intervention on the Intellectual and Language Development of 4-Year-Old Disadvantaged Children." *Am J Orthopsychiatry* 40(1):58–76 Ja '70. * (*PA* 45:1373)

295. KING, SUSAN HOFMAN. *The Relationships Between Mental Age, Level of Language Functioning and Social Acceptability in the Trainable Mentally Retarded.* Doctor's thesis, Louisiana State University (Baton Rouge, La.), 1970. (*DAI* 31:5691B)

296. LAGERMAN, AUDREY PHYLLIS. *Psycholinguistic Characteristics of Children With Reading Disabilities and the Effects of Remediation on Psycholinguistic Development and Reading Achievement.* Doctor's thesis, Marquette University (Milwaukee, Wis.), 1970. (*DAI* 32:791A)

297. LUCAS, MARILYN S. "Assessment of Coding Behavior of Trainable Retardates." *Am J Mental Def* 75(3):309–15 N '70. * (*PA* 46:3612)

298. MITTLER, PETER. "The Use of Morphological Rules by Four Year Old Children: An Item Analysis of the Auditory-Vocal Automatic Subtest of the Illinois Test of Psycholinguistic Abilities." *Brit J Dis Commun* 5(2):99–109 O '70. * (*PA* 46:6542)

299. PAGE, EDWIN RICHARD. *Comparisons of the Illinois Test of Psycholinguistic Abilities and the Adaptive Behavior Checklist With Institutionalized Mentally Retarded Children.* Doctor's thesis, Ohio University (Athens, Ohio), 1970. (*DAI* 32:613B)

300. ROSENFIELD, ABBY GREENBERG. *Psycholinguistic Abilities as Predictors of Reading Abilities and Disabilities in First Grade Children.* Doctor's thesis, St. Louis University (St. Louis, Mo.), 1970. (*DAI* 32:798A)

301. SAUDARGAS, RICHARD A.; MADSEN, CHARLES H., JR.; AND THOMPSON, FAITH. "Prescriptive Teaching in Language Arts Remediation for Black Rural Elementary School Children." *J Learn Dis* 3(7):364–70 Jl '70. *

302. SILVER, MERYL. "A Comparison Between Visual Association and Auditory Association in Disadvantaged and Middle Class Children: Subtests of the ITPA." *Grad Res Ed & Related Discip* 6(1):2–29 f '70. * (*PA* 48:8829)

303. SMALL, JAMES FRANKLIN, II. *Auditory-Vocal and Visual-Motor Language Orientations in Elementary School Children.* Doctor's thesis, Duke University (Durham, N.C.), 1970. (*DAI* 31:6268B)

304. STALLINGS, JANE AINEL. *Reading Methods and Sequencing Abilities: An Interaction Study in Beginning Reading.* Doctor's thesis, Stanford University (Stanford, Calif.), 1970. (*DAI* 31:6415A)

305. WELLS, CLINTON GEORGE. *A Comparative Study of Children Grouped by Three Basic Score Patterns on the Wechsler Intelligence Scale for Children.* Doctor's thesis, University of Northern Colorado (Greeley, Colo.), 1970. (*DAI* 31:6444A)

306. AMDUR, JEANETTE LORRAINE READ. *Oral Language Abilities in a Low Socio-Economic Status Kindergarten Spanish-Surnamed Population Varying in Reading Achievement.* Doctor's thesis, University of Denver (Denver, Colo.), 1971. (*DAI* 32:779A)

307. ATKINSON, SANDRA L. *The Preschool Inventory and the Illinois Test of Psycholinguistic Abilities.* Master's thesis, California State College (Fullerton, Calif.), 1971.

308. BAGWELL, FRANCES IMOGENE. *The Effects of a Selected Language Training Program on the Measured Verbal and Intellectual Ability of Educable Mentally Retarded Pupils.* Doctor's thesis, Texas Tech University (Lubbock, Tex.), 1971. (*DAI* 32:5064A)

309. BARRON, ROBERT CHARLTON. *A Comparison of Patterns of Intellectual and Psycho-Linguistic Abilities Among First Graders With Average and Very Low Reading Ability.* Doctor's thesis, University of Minnesota (Minneapolis, Minn.), 1971. (*DAI* 32:1817B)

310. BARTIN, NORMA GLADYS. *The Intellectual and Psycholinguistic Characteristics of Three Groups of Differentiated Third Grade Readers.* Doctor's thesis, State University of New York (Buffalo, N.Y.), 1971. (*DAI* 32:228A)

311. BRAFF, REBA GERTRUDE. *Signal-to-Noise Speech Discrimination of Black and White Children With Varying Socio-Economic Backgrounds.* Doctor's thesis, University of Southern California (Los Angeles, Calif.), 1971. (*DAI* 32:3686B)

312. BRAFF, RHODA A. *Imagery, Activity Level, and Learning Modality Preference as Indications of Sensory-Motor Stage Behavior in Low-Income Kindergarten Children.* Doctor's thesis, New York University (New York, N.Y.), 1971. (*DAI* 32:5605A)

313. CACCAMO, JAMES MICHAEL. *An Investigation of Psycholinguistic Abilities of Negro Children With Down's Syndrome.* Doctor's thesis, St. Louis University (St. Louis, Mo.), 1971. (*DAI* 33:1041A)

314. CARTER, JOHN L. "An Analysis of the Effects of a Language Development Program With First Grade Children of the New Orleans Education Improvement Department." *J Negro Ed* 40(4):352–5 f '71. * (*PA* 48:7897)

315. CELEBRE, GERALD. *Psycholinguistic Abilities and Oral Word Recognition Associated With Relative Level of Personality Adjustment in Primary School-Age Children With "Minimal Brain Dysfunction."* Doctor's thesis, Temple University (Philadelphia, Pa.), 1971. (*DAI* 32:781A)

316. CHOATE, HUBERT HUGH. *Selected Factors Contributing to Learning Potential of Children of Spanish Heritage.* Doctor's thesis, University of Southern California (Los Angeles, Calif.), 1971. (*DAI* 32:3778A)

317. CICIRELLI, VICTOR G.; GRANGER, ROBERT; SCHEMMEL, DENNY; COOPER, WILLIAM; AND HOLTHOUSE, NORMAN. "Performance of Disadvantaged Primary-Grade Children on the Revised Illinois Test of Psycholinguistic Abilities." *Psychol Sch* 8(3):240–6 Jl '71. * (*PA* 47:9639)

318. DEESE, JEANETTE CLEVELAND. *A Study of the Discrimination by the Subtests of the Revised Illinois Test of Psycholinguistic Abilities Between Successful and Unsuccessful Readers of Normal Intelligence.* Doctor's thesis, Memphis State University (Memphis, Tenn.), 1971. (*DAI* 32:4483A)

319. DUFFY, ROBERT J., AND MOORE, MARCIA CZYZEWSKI. "The Relationship Between Intelligence and Gestural Behavior in a Mentally Retarded Population." *J Genetic Psychol* 119(2):195–202 D '71. * (*PA* 48:1508)

320. ELLNER, SUSAN R. *The Relationship of the Illinois Test of Psycholinguistic Abilities to Selected Perceptual Tests With Retarded Children.* Master's thesis, Pennsylvania State University (University Park, Pa.), 1971.

321. ESHBAUGH, ROHE H. "Illinois Test of Psycholinguistic Abilities, Revised Edition: A Review." *Prof Psychol* 2(2):206–8 sp '71. *

322. FINKENBINDER, RONALD LEON. *The Concurrent and Predictive Validity of Selected Auditory Perceptual Tests With Children.* Doctor's thesis, Pennsylvania State University (University Park, Pa.), 1971. (*DAI* 32:6192A)

323. FRIEDMAN, GERALDINE H. PROBE. *A Comparative Study of Psychoeducational Test Scores of Emotionally Disturbed Children and Children With Learning Disabilities.* Doctor's thesis, St. Louis University (St. Louis, Mo.), 1971. (*DAI* 33:1043A)

324. GARRISON, MORTIMER, JR., AND HAMMILL, DONALD D. "Who Are the Retarded?" *Excep Children* 38(1):13–20 S '71. * (*PA* 47:7598)

325. GOEBEL, ALICE KATHRINE. *A Comparison of Visual Perceptual Abilities Between Learning Disabled Kindergarten Children and Non-Learning Disabled Kindergarten Children.* Doctor's thesis, University of Oklahoma (Norman, Okla.), 1971. (*DAI* 32:6618B)

326. GREIF, SUSAN ANN. *A Study of the Relationship Between Auditory, Visual, and Haptic Perception and Selected Parameters of Language and Articulation in Children With Central Processing Dysfunction.* Doctor's thesis, Wayne State University (Detroit, Mich.), 1971. (*DAI* 32:6717B)

327. GRIEF, ELLEN G. *An Analysis of the Performance of Children With Learning Disabilities on the Illinois Test of Psycholinguistic Abilities and the Wechsler Intelligence Scale for Children.* Doctor's thesis, University of Kansas (Lawrence, Kan.), 1971. (*DAI* 32:5638A)

328. GUTKNECHT, BRUCE ARTHUR. *A Psycholinguistic Analysis of the Oral Reading Behavior of Selected Children Identified as Perceptually Handicapped.* Doctor's thesis, Wayne State University (Detroit, Mich.), 1971. (*DAI* 32:6101A)

329. HANNAH, BETTY RUPARD. *Visual Behavior of Children With Nystagmus While Reading Orally.* Doctor's thesis, University of Arizona (Tucson, Ariz.), 1971. (*DAI* 32:3821A)

330. HARDY, MIRIAM P.; MELLITS, DAVID; AND WILLIG, SHARON N. "Reading: A Function of Language Usage." *Johns Hopkins Med J* 129(1):43–53 Jl '71. *

331. HATCH, ERIC, AND FRENCH, JOSEPH L. "The Revised ITPA: Its Reliability and Validity for Use With EMRs." *J Sch Psychol* 9(1):16–23 '71. * (*PA* 47:5651)

332. HAYES, MABEL E., AND DEMBO, MYRON H. "A Diagnostic-Prescriptive Approach to Preschool Education." *Psychol Sch* 8(1):37–40 Ja '71. * (*PA* 46:7780)

333. HORN, WILLIAM ANTHONY. *An Investigation of Language and Reading Abilities of Educable Mentally Retarded and Normal Students in Rural and Urban Areas.* Doctor's thesis,

West Virginia University (Morgantown, W.Va.), 1971. (*DAI* 32:6249A)

334. HUIZINGA, RALEIGH JAMES. *The Relationship of the Illinois Test of Psycholinguistic Abilities to the Stanford-Binet Form L-M and the Wechsler Intelligence Scale for Children.* Doctor's thesis, University of Arizona (Tucson, Ariz.), 1971. (*DAI* 32:3823A)

335. JENKINS, CHARLES F. *A Study of the Illinois Test of Psycholinguistic Abilities, 1968 Revision.* Master's thesis, Central Missouri State University (Warrensburg, Mo.), 1971.

336. JORSTAD, DOROTHY. "Psycholinguistic Learning Disabilities in 20 Mexican-American Students." *J Learn Dis* 4(3):143–9 Mr '71. * (*PA* 47:9698)

337. KILLIAN, L. R. "WISC, Illinois Test of Psycholinguistic Abilities, and Bender Visual-Motor Gestalt Test Performance of Spanish-American Kindergarten and First-Grade School Children." *J Consult & Clin Psychol* 37(1):38–43 Ag '71. * (*PA* 47:1738)

338. KIRK, SAMUEL A., AND KIRK, WINIFRED D. *Psycholinguistic Learning Disabilities: Diagnosis and Remediation.* Urbana, Ill.: University of Illinois Press, 1971. Pp. x, 198. *

339. LARSEN, STEPHEN. "Performance of Achieving and Underachieving Second, Third, and Fourth Grade Children on Tests of Auditory Ability and Oral Form Discrimination." *Kan Studies Ed* 21(1–2):53–9 sp–su '71. *

340. LAVIN, CLAIRE MARIE. *The Effect of a Structured Sensory-Motor Training Program on Selected Cognitive and Psycholinguistic Abilities of Preschool Disadvantaged Children.* Doctor's thesis, Fordham University (New York, N.Y.), 1971. (*DAI* 32:1984A)

341. LYONS, ELLEN RAE. *Evaluation of the Illinois Test of Psycholinguistic Abilities.* Master's thesis, University of Utah (Salt Lake City, Utah), 1971.

342. McCALL, CAROL IRENE. *An Investigation of Language Deficiency in a Female Prison Population.* Doctor's thesis, University of Florida (Gainesville, Fla.), 1971. (*DAI* 32:6101B)

343. McCORMICK, CLARENCE C., AND SCHNOBRICH, JANICE N. "Perceptual-Motor Training and Improvement in Concentration in a Montessori Preschool." *Percept & Motor Skills* 32(1):71–7 F '71. * (*PA* 46:3865)

344. McPROUTY, VIVIAN HELEN. *Piaget's Theory as the Basis for the Assessment of Reading Disability and Suggested Remediation Through an Adapted Science Curriculum.* Doctor's thesis, University of the Pacific (Stockton, Calif.), 1971. (*DAI* 32:2488A)

345. MANN, LESTER. "Psychometric Phrenology and the New Faculty Psychology: The Case Against Ability Assessment and Training." *J Spec Ed* 5(1):3–14 w–sp '71. * (*PA* 48:3684)

346. MERLIN, SHIRLEY B. *The Psycholinguistic and Reading Abilities of Educable Mentally Retarded Readers.* Doctor's thesis, West Virginia University (Morgantown, W.Va.), 1971. (*DAI* 32:1921A)

347. MESSINEO, LOUIS V. *Comparison Between Poor and Good Readers in Relation to Skill Development at the Automatic Level of Organization.* Doctor's thesis, Syracuse University (Syracuse, N.Y.), 1971. (*DAI* 32:4452A)

348. MITTLER, PETER. "The Influence of Social Class on Psycholinguistic Abilities: Some Implications for Special Education." *Forward Trends* 15(1):6–11 Mr '71. *

349. MOFFITT, P.; NURCOMBE, B.; PASSMORE, M.; AND McNEILLY, A. "Intervention in Cultural Deprivation: The Comparative Success of Preschool Techniques for Rural Aborigines and Europeans." *Austral Psychologist* 6(1):51–61 Mr '71. * (*PA* 47:3795)

350. MOORE, MARY, AND WELCHER, DORIS W. "A Descriptive Analysis of the Seven-Year Psychological Data." *Johns Hopkins Med J* 128(6):332–46 Je '71. *

351. MORGAN, ARTHUR T., JR. *An Analysis of Auditory Abilities as Predictors of First-Grade Reading Achievement.* Doctor's thesis, University of Houston (Houston, Tex.), 1971. (*DAI* 32:3125A)

352. O'GRADY, DONALD J.; BERRY, HELEN K.; AND SUTHERLAND, BETTY S. "Cognitive Development in Early Treated Phenylketonuria." *Am J Dis Children* 121(1):20–3 Ja '71. *

353. PEROZZI, JOSEPH A., AND KUNZE, LuVERN H. "Relationship Between Speech Sound Discrimination Skills and Language Abilities of Kindergarten Children." *J Speech & Hearing Res* 14(2):382–90 Je '71. *

354. PHILLIPS, DORIS CAMPBELL. *An Exploratory Study of the Relationship Between Mothers' Individualization of Their Children and the Children's Developmental Progress.* Doctor's thesis, Washington University (St. Louis, Mo.), 1971. (*DAI* 32:2201A)

355. POLLEY, DALE. *The Relationship of the Channels of Communication of the Illinois Test of Psycholinguistic Abilities to the Wechsler Intelligence Scale for Children.* Doctor's thesis, University of Northern Colorado (Greeley, Colo.), 1971. (*DAI* 32:4194B)

356. RICE, JAMES A. "Head Start Screening: Effectiveness of a Teacher-Administered Battery." *Percept & Motor Skills* 32(2):675–8 Ap '71. * (*PA* 46:11733)

357. SABATINO, DAVID A., AND BECKER, JOHN T. "Relationship Between Lateral Preference and Selected Behavioral Variables for Children Failing Academically." *Child Develop* 42(6):2055–60 D '71. * (*PA* 48:9861)

358. SAPIR, SELMA G. "Learning Disability and Deficit Centered Classroom Training." *Cognitive Studies* 2:324–38 '71. * (*PA* 49:1359, title only)

359. SCHIFANI, JOHN WILLIAM. *The Relationship Between the Illinois Test of Psycholinguistic Abilities and the Peabody Language Development Kit With a Select Group of Intermediate Educable Mentally Retarded Children.* Doctor's thesis, University of Alabama (University, Ala.), 1971. (*DAI* 32:5076A)

360. SCRUGGS, ALLIE W. *The Effect of the Fall River and Lowell Head Start Programs on Behavioral Characteristics Associated With Lower Socio-Economic Class Preschool Children.* Doctor's thesis, Boston University (Boston, Mass.), 1971. (*DAI* 32:1949A)

361. SMITH, CAROLYN M. "The Relationship of Reading Method and Reading Achievement to ITPA Sensory Modalities." *J Spec Ed* 5(2):143–9 su '71. * (*PA* 48:9854)

362. SMITH, PHILIP A., AND MARX, RONALD W. "The Factor Structure of the Revised Edition of the Illinois Test of Psycholinguistic Abilities." *Psychol Sch* 8(4):349–56 O '71. * (*PA* 47:9666)

363. SOUTHERN, MARA L., AND PLANT, WALTER T. "Differential Cognitive Development Within and Between Racial and Ethnic Groups of Disadvantaged Preschool and Kindergarten Children." *J Genetic Psychol* 119(2):259–66 D '71. * (*PA* 48:637)

364. SWALLOW, ROSE-MARIE. *Automatic Processing of Perceptual-Linguistic Stimuli in Second Grade Achieving and Non-Achieving Readers.* Doctor's thesis University of Southern California (Los Angeles, Calif.), 1971. (*DAI* 32:3827A)

365. SWISHER, LINDA PECK, AND PINSKER, ESTHER JILL. "The Language Characteristics of Hyperverbal Hydrocephalic Children." *Develop Med & Child Neurol* (England) 13(6):746–55 D '71. * (*PA* 48:7620)

366. TIEL, EILEEN M. *The Aphasoid Child: Psycholinguistic Abilities as Assessed by the Illinois Test of Psycholinguistic Abilities.* Master's thesis, California State College (Fullerton, Calif.), 1971.

367. UNOH, SOLOMON O. "Psycholinguistic Perspectives on the Education of Exceptional Children." *Papers Psychol* (Northern Ireland) 5(2):36–43 D '71. * (*PA* 48:9691)

368. WAGNER, RUDOLPH F. "Symbolization Deficits in Dyslexic Conditions." *Acad Ther* 6(4):359–65 su '71. *

369. WAUGH, RUTH PETERSON. *The Relationship Between Individual Modality Preference and Performance Under Four Instructional Procedures.* Doctor's thesis, University of Oregon, (Eugene, Ore.), 1971. (*DAI* 32:5077A)

370. WEINER, PAUL S. "The Cognitive Functioning of Language Deficient Children." *Cognitive Studies* 2:338–63 '71. *

371. WELCHER, DORIS W.; MELLITS, E. DAVID; AND HARDY, JANET B. "A Multivariate Analysis of Factors Affecting Psychological Performance." *Johns Hopkins Med J* 129(1):19–35 Jl '71. *

372. WHITCRAFT, CAROL JONES. *Levels of Generative Syntax and Linguistic Performance of Young Children From Standard and Non-Standard English Language Environments.* Doctor's thesis, University of Texas (Austin, Tex.), 1971. (*DAI* 32:5644A)

373. WHITE, JOHN A. *An Investigation of the Reliability of the Illinois Test of Psycholinguistic Abilities With Fourth Grade Children.* Master's thesis, Glassboro State College (Glassboro, N.J.), 1971.

374. WICKWIRE, PATRICIA JOANNE NELLOR. *The Academic Achievement and Language Development of American Children of Latin Heritage: Factors of Intellect, Home Educational Environment, and Personality.* Doctor's thesis, University of Texas (Austin, Tex.), 1971. (*DAI* 32:6232A)

CUMULATIVE NAME INDEX

Illinois Test of Psycholinguistic Abilities

[982]

[Re Illinois Test of Psycholinguistic Abilities] A Filmed Demonstration of the ITPA. 1969; University of Illinois Press.

For additional information and an excerpted review by Don Mahler, see 7:443.

[983]

★Individual Learning Disabilities Classroom Screening Instrument. Grades 1-3; 1970-72; 8 scoring categories: high risk disability, auditory perceptual disability, neurological involvement, visual acuity disability, visual perception disability, spatial orientation disability, sequential memory disability, social-emotional involvement; John H. Meier, Verl O. Cazier, and Marian T. Giles; Learning Pathways, Inc. *

REFERENCES THROUGH 1971

1. Meier, John H. "Prevalence and Characteristics of Learning Disabilities Found in Second Grade Children." *J Learn Dis* 4(1):6-21 Ja '71. *

CUMULATIVE NAME INDEX

Meier, J. H.: 1

[984]

The Meeting Street School Screening Test. Grades kgn-1; 1969; MSSST; 4 scores: motor patterning, visual-perceptual-motor, language, total; Peter K. Hainsworth and Marian L. Siqueland; Crippled Children and Adults of Rhode Island, Inc. *

For additional information and an excerpted review by William Yule, see 7:756 (4 references).

REFERENCES THROUGH 1971

1-4. See 7:756.
5. Denhoff, Eric; Hainsworth, Peter; and Hainsworth, Marian. Chap. 5, "Learning Disabilities and Early Childhood Education: An Information-Processing Approach," pp. 111-50. In *Progress in Learning Disabilities, Vol. 2.* Edited by Helmer R. Myklebust. New York: Grune & Stratton, Inc., 1971. Pp. ix, 404. *

CUMULATIVE NAME INDEX

Denhoff, E.: 1-2, 4-5	Hainsworth, P. K.: 1-2
Gavino, P. G.: 3	Komich, M. P.: 2
Hainsworth, M.: 5	Siqueland, M. L.: 1-2
Hainsworth, P.: 5	Yule, W.: *exc*, 7:756

[985]

★**A Psychoeducational Inventory of Basic Learning Abilities.** Ages 5-12 with suspected learning disabilities; 1968; rating scale of 53 basic learning abilities in 6 areas: gross motor development, sensory-motor integration, perceptual-motor skills, language development, conceptual skills, social skills; no manual; Robert E. Valett; Lear Siegler, Inc./Fearon Publishers. *

[986]

Psychoeducational Profile of Basic Learning Abilities. Ages 2-14 with learning disabilities; 1966; booklet for recording clinical and standardized test data in 5 areas: motor integration and physical development, perceptual abilities, language, social-personal adaptivity, general intellectual functioning; Robert E. Valett; Consulting Psychologists Press, Inc. *

For additional information, see 7:548.

[987]

★**The Pupil Rating Scale: Screening for Learning Disabilities.** Grades 3-4; 1971; PRS; 8 scores: verbal (auditory comprehension, spoken language, total), nonverbal (orientation, motor coordination, personal-social behavior, total), total; Helmer R. Myklebust; Grune & Stratton, Inc. *

[988]

Screening Test for the Assignment of Remedial Treatments. Ages 4-6 to 6-5; 1968; START; 5 scores: visual memory, auditory memory, visual copying, visual discrimination, total; A. Edward Ahr; Priority Innovations, Inc. *

For additional information and a review by Evelyn Deno, see 7:764.

REFERENCES THROUGH 1971

1. Proger, Barton B. "Screening Test for the Assignment of Remedial Treatments: A Review." *J Spec Ed* 5(2):191-4 su '71. *

CUMULATIVE NAME INDEX

Deno, E.: *rev,* 7:764	Proger, B. B.: 1

[989]

Screening Tests for Identifying Children With Specific Language Disability, Revised Edition. Grades 1-2.5, 2.5-3.5, 3.5-4; 1964-70, c1962-70; 8 tests

(visual copying far point, visual copying near point, visual perception-memory, visual discrimination, visual perception-memory in association with kinesthetic memory, auditory recall, auditory perception of beginning and ending sounds, auditory associations) with 21 scores for each (right, wrong, total, recall, substitution, insertion, reversal, inversion, transposition, number reversal, letter formation, number formation, geometric figure, mixed cursive and manuscript, mixed capitals and lowercase, omission, incompletion, spelling error, spatial organization, circling, kinesthetic) plus 2 optional individual tests (echolalia and story telling); Beth H. Slingerland; Educators Publishing Service, Inc. *

For additional information and reviews by Evelyn Deno and Joseph M. Wepman, see 7:969 (3 references).

REFERENCES THROUGH 1971

1-3. See 7:969.
4. Irvine, James. *Correlates of Grade One Achievement.* Master's thesis, University of Alberta (Edmonton, Alta., Canada), 1968.
5. Oliphant, Genevieve G. "A Study of Factors Involved in Early Identification of Specific Language Disability." *B Orton Soc* 20:81-92 '70. *
6. Early, George H.; Early, Frances G.; and Heath, Earl J. "Classroom Evaluation of Learning Disabilities." *Ed Technol* 11(9):40-3 S '71. * (*PA* 47:9644)
7. Proger, Barton B. "Screening Tests for Identifying Children With Specific Language Disability: A Review." *J Spec Ed* 5(3):293-9 f '71. * (*PA* 48:12168)

CUMULATIVE NAME INDEX

Baker, G. A. P.: 1	Irvine, J.: 4
Deno, E.: *rev,* 7:969	Oliphant, G. G.: 2, 5
Early, F. G.: 6	Proger, B. B.: 7
Early, G. H.: 6	Wepman, J. M.: *rev,* 7:969
Heath, E. J.: 6	Wharry, R. E.: 3

[990]

Specific Language Disability Test. "Average to high IQ" children in grades 6-8; 1967-68; SLDT; upward extension of *Screening Tests for Identifying Children With Specific Language Disability;* 10 tests (visual copying far point, visual copying near point, visual discrimination, visual perception memory for words, visual perception memory in association with kinesthetic memory, auditory discrimination, auditory perception and recall, auditory-visual discrimination, comprehension, spelling) with 4 scores (omissions, errors, self-corrections, reversals) for each; Neva Malcomesius; Educators Publishing Service, Inc. *

For additional information and reviews by S. Alan Cohen and Robert E. Valett, see 7:971.

[991]

Valett Developmental Survey of Basic Learning Abilities. Ages 2-7; 1966; largely a selection and adaptation of items from many scales, particularly the *Gesell Developmental Schedules;* 7 areas of development: motor integration and physical development, tactile discrimination, auditory discrimination, visual-motor coordination, visual discrimination, language development and verbal fluency, conceptual development; Robert E. Valett; Consulting Psychologists Press, Inc. *

For additional information and reviews by Lester Mann and Roger A. Ruth, see 7:767 (2 references).

REFERENCES THROUGH 1971

1-2. See 7:767.
3. Compton, Mary Elizabeth. *A Study of the Relationship Between Oral Language Facility and Reading Achievement of Selected First-Grade Children.* Doctor's thesis, University of North Carolina (Chapel Hill, N.C.), 1971. (*DAI* 32:6848A)

CUMULATIVE NAME INDEX

Compton, M. E.: 3	Ruth, R. A.: *rev,* 7:767
Mann, L.: *rev,* 7:767	Valett, R.: 1-2

Individual Learning Disabilities Classroom Screening Instrument

Evanston Early Identification Scale, 7:747 (2 reviews, 1 reference)

LISTENING COMPREHENSION

[992]

*Assessment of Children's Language Comprehension. Ages 2–6; 1969–73; ACLC; 4 scores: vocabulary, 2-word phrases, 3-word phrases, 4-word phrases; Rochana Foster, Jane J. Giddan, and Joel Stark; Consulting Psychologists Press, Inc. *

For additional information, see 7:635.

[993]

Brown-Carlsen Listening Comprehension Test. Grades 9–16 and adults; 1953–55; James I. Brown and G. Robert Carlsen; Harcourt Brace Jovanovich, Inc. *

For additional information, see 6:739 (9 references); for reviews by E. F. Lindquist and Irving Lorge, see 5:577 (13 references).

REFERENCES THROUGH 1971

1–13. See 5:577.
14–22. See 6:739.
23. SHAPIRO, GEORGE L. *An Inductive Investigation Into the Correlates of Ability to Predict Opinion.* Doctor's thesis, University of Minnesota (Minneapolis, Minn.), 1960. (*DA* 21:3196)
24. KELLY, CHARLES MILBURN. *"Actual Listening Behavior" of Industrial Supervisors, as Related to "Listening Ability," General Mental Ability, Selected Personality Factors and Supervisory Effectiveness.* Doctor's thesis, Purdue University (Lafayette, Ind.), 1962. (*DA* 23:4019)
25. FRIESEN, WALTER S. *A Descriptive Study of Freshman Performance in English Composition I at Kansas State University, 1961, in Relation to Fifty-Two Variables.* Doctor's research study No. 1, Colorado State College (Greeley, Colo.), 1963. (*DA* 25:290)
26. BATEMAN, DAVID; FRANDSEN, KENNETH; AND DEDMON, DONALD. *"Dimensions of 'Lecture Comprehension': A Factor Analysis of Listening Test Items." J Commun* 14:183–9 S '64. * (*PA* 39:6603)
27. CLOOS, ROBERT IRA. *A Comparative Study of Fourteen Predictors of Success in the Audio-Lingual Approach to First-Year German at the High School Level.* Doctor's thesis, Rutgers University (New Brunswick, N.J.), 1964. (*DA* 25:7106)
28. HIGGINS, IVAN DUKE. *An Empirical Study of Listening Related to Anxiety and to Certain Other Measures of Ability and Achievement.* Doctor's thesis, University of Southern California (Los Angeles, Calif.), 1964. (*DA* 25:1745)
29. JONES, ROBERT A.; KAPLAN, ROBERT; AND MICHAEL, WILLIAM B. *"The Predictive Validity of a Modified Battery of Tests in Language Skills for Foreign Students at an American University." Ed & Psychol Meas* 24:961–5 w '64. * (*PA* 39:8687)
30. KAPLAN, ROBERT B., AND JONES, ROBERT A. *"Evaluation of Relative Foreign Student Success." Lang Learning* 14(3–4):161–6 '64. *
31. SCHERER, GEORGE A. C., AND WERTHEIMER, MICHAEL. *A Psycholinguistic Experiment in Foreign-Language Teaching.* New York: McGraw-Hill Book Co., Inc., 1964. Pp. xiii, 256. *
32. WAKELAND, WILLIAM FLOYD. *A Study of the Teaching of Sightsinging of Melodic Configurations to a Group of Secondary-School Students by Means of a Teaching Machine.* Doctor's thesis, Southern Illinois University (Carbondale, Ill.), 1964. (*DA* 25:5165)
33. CONDON, EDWYNA FORSYTH. *An Analysis of the Differences Between Good and Poor Listeners in Grades Nine, Eleven, and Thirteen.* Doctor's thesis, University of Kansas (Lawrence, Kan.), 1965. (*DA* 26:3106)
34. KELLY, CHARLES M. *"Investigation of the Construct Validity of Two Commercially Published Listening Tests." Speech Monogr* 32:139–43 Je '65. *
35. LANGHOLZ, ARMIN PAUL. *A Study of the Relationship of Listening Test Scores to Test Item Difficulty.* Doctor's thesis, Ohio State University (Columbus, Ohio), 1965. (*DA* 26:6912)
36. BURKE, JACK DALE. *The Predictive Validity of English Language Screening Instruments for Foreign Students Entering the University of Southern California.* Doctor's thesis, University of Southern California (Los Angeles, Calif.), 1968. (*DA* 29:3118A)
37. GORDON, JAMES ROSCOE. *Listening, Attitude, and Intelligence Tests to Predict Academic Achievement.* Doctor's thesis, Colorado State College (Greeley, Colo.), 1968. (*DA* 29:2522A)
38. JOHNSON, MARTHA, AND RICHARDSON, DON. *"Listening

Training in the Fundamentals of Speech Class." Speech Teach* 17:292–6 N '68. *
39. BROILES, MACK ROBINSON. *A Study of the Effectiveness of Teaching Listening.* Doctor's thesis, East Texas State University (Commerce, Tex.), 1969. (*DAI* 30:2613A)
40. GOODYEAR, FINIS HERBERT. *An Experimental Study of the Motivational Effect of Punishment and Reward Anticipation on the Listening Comprehension of College Students.* Doctor's thesis, University of Texas (Austin, Tex.), 1969. (*DAI* 30:5551A)
41. HARRISON, CARROL F., JR. *The Development of a Descriptive Listening Paradigm.* Doctor's thesis, Southern Illinois University (Carbondale, Ill.), 1969. (*DAI* 30:3125A)
42. SAYRE, MARY LOUISE. *An Investigation of the Relationship of Listening Comprehension to Academic Achievement.* Master's thesis, Glassboro State College (Glassboro, N.J.), 1970. *
43. GWALTNEY, WAYNE KEITH. *Reading in Upward Bound: An Evaluation of a Reading Improvement Course and an Analysis of Some Correlates of Reading Achievement.* Doctor's thesis, University of Georgia (Athens, Ga.), 1971. (*DAI* 32:3557A)

CUMULATIVE NAME INDEX

Bateman, D.: 26	Kaplan, R.: 29
Broiles, M. R.: 39	Kaplan, R. B.: 30
Brown, J. I.: 1–5, 7	Kelly, C. M.: 22, 24, 34
Burke, J. D.: 36	Kramar, E. J. J.: 8
Cloos, R. I.: 27	Langholz, A. P.: 35
Condon, E. F.: 33	Lindquist, E. F.: *rev*, 5:577
Dedmon, D.: 26	Lorge, I.: *rev*, 5:577
Duncan, C. H.: 15	Michael, W. B.: 17–8, 29
Frandsen, K.: 21, 26	Murphy, W. C.: 19
Friesen, W. S.: 25	Publicover, P. R.: 6
Goodyear, F. H.: 40	Richardson, D.: 38
Gordon, J. R.: 37	Rose, E.: 14
Gwaltney, W. K.: 43	Sayre, M. L.: 42
Haberland, J. A.: 10–1, 13, 16	Scherer, G. A. C.: 31
Harrison, C. F.: 41	Shapiro, G. L.: 23
Higgins, I. D.: 28	Stark, J.: 12
Johnson, F. C.: 21	Still, D. S.: 9
Johnson, M.: 38	Wakeland, W. F.: 32
Jones, R. A.: 17–8, 29–30	Wertheimer, M.: 31

[994]

Cooperative Primary Tests: Listening. Grades 1.5–2.5, 2.5–3; 1965–67; Cooperative Tests and Services. *
For the complete battery entry, see 12.

For reviews of the complete battery, see 7:10 (2 excerpts).

[995]

Orr-Graham Listening Test. Junior high school boys; 1968; OGLT; designed to be "especially appropriate for disadvantaged eighth grade boys"; David B. Orr (test), Warren R. Graham (test), and Ronald P. Carver; American Institutes for Research. *

For additional information and reviews by Jum C. Nunnally and Roger A. Richards, see 7:636 (5 references).

REFERENCES THROUGH 1971

1–5. See 7:636.

CUMULATIVE NAME INDEX

Carver, R. P.: 2–3, 5	Orr, D. B.: 1, 4
Graham, W. R.: 1, 4	Richards, R. A.: *rev*, 7:636
Nunnally, J. C.: *rev*, 7:636	

[996]

★Progressive Achievement Tests of Listening Comprehension. Standards 1–4 and Forms I–IV (ages 7–14); 1971–72; PATLC; manual by Warwick B. Elley and Neil A. Reid; New Zealand Council for Educational Research [New Zealand]. *

[997]

Sequential Tests of Educational Progress [Original Series]: Listening. Grades 4–6, 7–9, 10–12, 13–14; 1956–63; Braille and large type editions (grades 4–12) are available from American Printing House for the Blind, Inc.; Cooperative Tests and Services. * For the complete battery entry, see 35.

For additional information, see 6:740 (11 references); for reviews by E. F. Lindquist and Irving Lorge, see

5:578. For reviews of the complete battery, see 6:25 (2 reviews) and 5:24 (2 reviews, 1 excerpt).

REFERENCES THROUGH 1971

1–11. See 6:740.
12. WELCH, ISOM LIN. *An Investigation of the Listening Proficiency of Stutterers.* Doctor's thesis, University of Missouri (Columbia, Mo.), 1960. (*DA* 21:270)
13. MCGUIRE, CARSON; HINDSMAN, EDWIN; KING, F. J.; AND JENNINGS, EARL. "Dimensions of Talented Behavior." *Ed & Psychol Meas* 21:3–38 sp '61. * (*PA* 36:1KH03M)
14. TOUSSAINT, ISABELLA HASTIE. *Interrelationships of Reading, Listening, Arithmetic, and Intelligence and Their Implications.* Doctor's thesis, University of Pittsburgh (Pittsburgh, Pa.), 1961. (*DA* 22:819)
15. KELLY, CHARLES MILBURN. *"Actual Listening Behavior" of Industrial Supervisors, as Related to "Listening Ability," General Mental Ability, Selected Personality Factors and Supervisory Effectiveness.* Doctor's thesis, Purdue University (Lafayette, Ind.), 1962. (*DA* 23:4019)
16. FAWCETT, ANNABEL ELIZABETH. *The Effect of Training in Listening Upon the Listening Skills of Intermediate Grade Children.* Doctor's thesis, University of Pittsburgh (Pittsburgh, Pa.), 1963. (*DA* 25:7108)
17. DOLCINI, MARY ELLEN. *Children's Listening Comprehension of Fictional and Factual Materials at Two Levels of Difficulty.* Doctor's thesis, University of California (Berkeley, Calif.), 1964. (*DA* 25:6428)
18. HIGGINS, IVAN DUKE. *An Empirical Study of Listening Related to Anxiety and to Certain Other Measures of Ability and Achievement.* Doctor's thesis, University of Southern California (Los Angeles, Calif.), 1964. (*DA* 25:1745)
19. KELLY, FRANCIS J.; VELDMAN, DONALD J.; AND MCGUIRE, CARSON. "Multiple Discriminant Prediction of Delinquency and School Dropouts." *Ed & Psychol Meas* 24:535–44 f '64. * (*PA* 39:5713)
20. MICHAEL, WILLIAM B.; CATHCART, ROBERT; AND ZIMMERMAN, WAYNE S. "Linguistic Factors in Various Measures of Communication Skills for College Students With Implications for Predictive Validity." *Ed & Psychol Meas* 24:363–7 su '64. * (*PA* 39:3192)
21. STARR, FAY HAVEN. *Antecedents and Concomitants of Change in Teacher Evaluation of Pupil Performance.* Doctor's thesis, University of Texas (Austin, Tex.), 1964. (*DA* 25:2862)
22. KELLY, CHARLES M. "Investigation of the Construct Validity of Two Commercially Published Listening Tests." *Speech Monogr* 32:139–43 Je '65. *
23. MILLER, DORIS KOTEEN. *A Study of Differences Between Auditory and Visual Learners in Respect to Extraversion-Introversion.* Doctor's thesis, New York University (New York, N.Y.), 1965. (*DA* 26:4078)
24. WINTER, CLOTILDA. "Listening and Learning." *El Engl* 43:569–72 O '66. *
25. WENGER, THELMA WOOD. *A Study of the Effect on Listening Test Scores of Change in Methods of Presentation.* Doctor's thesis, University of Virginia (Charlottesville, Va.), 1967. (*DA* 28:2466A)
26. ORR, DAVID B., AND GRAHAM, WARREN R. "Development of a Listening Comprehension Test to Identify Educational Potential Among Disadvantaged Junior High School Students." *Am Ed Res J* 5:167–80 Mr '68. *
27. REDDIN, ESTOY. "Characteristics of Good Listeners and Poor Listeners." *J Read Specialist* 7:109–13 Mr '68. *
28. REEVES, RACHAEL JOANNE. *A Study of the Relation Between Listening Performance and Reading Performance of Sixth-Grade Pupils as Measured by Certain Standardized Tests.* Doctor's thesis, University of Alabama (University, Ala.), 1968. (*DA* 29:4196A)
29. BROOKS, WILLIAM D., AND HANNAH, LARRY K. "Pretest Effects of the STEP Listening Test." *Speech Monogr* 36(1): 66–7 Mr '69. *
30. CARVER, RONALD P. "Use of a Recently Developed Listening Comprehension Test to Investigate the Effect of Disadvantagement Upon Verbal Proficiency." *Am Ed Res J* 6(2):263–70 Mr '69. *
31. DREYER, DOROTHY E. *Listening Performance Related to Selected Academic and Psychological Measures.* Doctor's thesis, Michigan State University (East Lansing, Mich.), 1969. (*DAI* 30:5735B)
32. GRASTY, WILLIAM KENDRICK. *The Effectiveness of Direct and Indirect Instruction in Listening on College Freshmen.* Doctor's thesis, University of Texas (Austin, Tex.), 1969. (*DAI* 30:5342A)
33. MATHEWS, MARILYN. *The Relationships Between Listening and Writing Abilities of Selected Sixth Grade Children.* Doctor's thesis, University of Georgia (Athens, Ga.), 1969. (*DAI* 30: 5347A)
34. MONTGOMERY, MARY ANN. *An Investigation of Students Who Succeed Academically and Those Who Do Not Succeed Academically in a Community College.* Doctor's thesis, University of Pittsburgh (Pittsburgh, Pa.), 1969. (*DAI* 31:1578A)
35. BUTLER, JOSEPH. *Comparisons of Listening Abilities, Categorized as Good and Poor, of Inner-City Children in the Sixth*

Grade. Doctor's thesis, Indiana University (Bloomington, Ind.), 1970. (*DAI* 31:5655A)
36. CHILDERS, PERRY R. "Black Pupils Can Be Taught to Listen." *J Exp Ed* 39(4):24–5 su '71. *
For additional references, see the bibliography for the series, 35.

CUMULATIVE NAME INDEX

Anderson, H. M.: 8
Bailey, R. B.: 4
Baldauf, R. J.: 2, 8
Bonner, M. C. S.: 3
Brooks, W. D.: 29
Butler, J.: 35
Carver, R. P.: 30
Cathcart, R.: 10, 20
Cleland, D. L.: 6
Dolcini, M. E.: 17
Dreyer, D. E.: 31
Fawcett, A. E.: 16
Graham, W. R.: 26
Grasty, W. K.: 32
Hannah, L. K.: 29
Higgins, I. D.: 18
Hindsman, E.: 13
Jennings, E.: 13
Kelly, C. M.: 9, 15, 22
Kelly, F. J.: 19
King, F. J.: 13
Kingston, A. J.: 11
Lindquist, E. F.: *rev*, 5:578
Lorge, I.: *rev*, 5:578
McGuire, C.: 5, 13, 19
Mathews, M.: 33
Michael, W. B.: 10, 20
Milfs, M.: 10
Miller, D. K.: 23
Montgomery, M. A.: 34
North, R. D.: 1
Orr, D. B.: 26
Reddin, E.: 27
Reeves, R. J.: 28
Spearritt, D.: 7
Starr, F. H.: 21
Toussaint, I.: 6, 14
Veldman, D. J.: 19
Vineyard, E. E.: 4
Weaver, W. W.: 11
Welch, I. L.: 12
Wenger, T. W.: 25
Winter, C.: 24
Zimmerman, W. S.: 10, 20

[997A]

★**Tests for Auditory Comprehension of Language.** Ages 3–7; 1973; 2 tests which may be administered in English or Spanish; Elizabeth Carrow; Learning Concepts. *

a) SCREENING TEST FOR AUDITORY COMPREHENSION OF LANGUAGE. STACL; short form for identifying children who need further testing with long form.
b) TEST FOR AUDITORY COMPREHENSION OF LANGUAGE. TACL; long form.

REFERENCES THROUGH 1971

1. CARROW, MARY ARTHUR. "The Development of Auditory Comprehension of Language Structure in Children." *J Speech & Hearing Disorders* 33:99–111 My '68. * (*PA* 42:15279)
2. CARROW, ELIZABETH. "Comprehension of English and Spanish by Preschool Mexican-American Children." *Mod Lang J* 55(5):299–306 My '71. *

CUMULATIVE NAME INDEX

Carrow, E.: 2   Carrow, M. A.: 1

PHILOSOPHY

[998]

*****The Graduate Record Examinations Advanced Philosophy Test.** Graduate school candidates; 1939–73; Educational Testing Service. * For the testing program entry, see 1053.
For additional information concerning earlier forms, see 7:637 (1 reference). For reviews of the testing program, see 7:667 (1 review) and 5:601 (1 review).

REFERENCES THROUGH 1971

1. See 7:637.

CUMULATIVE NAME INDEX

Lannholm, G. V.: 1   Schrader, W. B.: 1
Marco, G. L.: 1

[999]

*****The Undergraduate Program Field Tests: Philosophy Test.** College; 1969–73; formerly called *The Undergraduate Record Examinations: Philosophy Test;* test available to colleges for local administration; Educational Testing Service. * For the testing program entry, see 1062.
For additional information concerning an earlier form, see 7:638. For reviews of the testing program, see 7:671 (2 reviews).

[1000]

*The Undergraduate Program Field Tests: Scholastic Philosophy Test. College; 1969–73; formerly called *The Undergraduate Record Examinations: Scholastic Philosophy Test;* test available to Roman Catholic colleges for local administration; Educational Testing Service. * For the testing program entry, see 1062.

For additional information, see 7:639. For reviews of the testing program, see 7:671 (2 reviews).

[Out of Print Since TIP I]

Graduate Record Examinations Advanced Tests: Scholastic Philosophy, 6:742 (2 references)

PSYCHOLOGY

[1001]

Aden-Crosthwait Adolescent Psychology Achievement Test. College; 1963–70; Robert C. Aden and Charles Crosthwait; Psychometric Affiliates. *

For additional information, see 7:640 (1 reference).

REFERENCES THROUGH 1971

1. See 7:640.

CUMULATIVE NAME INDEX

Aden, R. C.: 1

[1002]

*CLEP Subject Examination in Educational Psychology. 1 semester or equivalent; 1967–73; for college accreditation of nontraditional study, advanced placement, or assessment of educational achievement; tests administered monthly at centers throughout the United States; program administered for the College Entrance Examination Board by Educational Testing Service. * For the testing program entry, see 1050.

For additional information, see 7:641. For reviews of the testing program, see 7:664 (3 reviews).

[1003]

*CLEP Subject Examination in General Psychology. 1 semester or equivalent; 1967–73; for college accreditation of nontraditional study, advanced placement, or assessment of educational achievement; tests administered monthly at centers throughout the United States; program administered for the College Entrance Examination Board by Educational Testing Service. * For the testing program entry, see 1050.

For additional information, see 7:642. For reviews of the testing program, see 7:664 (3 reviews).

[1004]

Cass-Sanders Psychology Test. High school and college; 1964; Dal H. Cass and M. W. Sanders; Bureau of Educational Measurements. *

For additional information, see 7:643.

[1005]

*The Graduate Record Examinations Advanced Psychology Test. Graduate school candidates; 1939–73; 3 scores: experimental, social, total; Educational Testing Service. * For the testing program entry, see 1053.

For additional information concerning earlier forms, see 7:644 (9 references); for a review by Harold Seashore, see 5:583. For reviews of the testing program, see 7:667 (1 review) and 5:601 (1 review).

REFERENCES THROUGH 1971

1–9. See 7:644.
10. CRAWFORD, FRANCES W. *An Investigation of the Graduate Record Examination and Other Variables Used as Predictors of Success in the Graduate Program of the Department of Psychology of East Tennessee State University.* Master's thesis, East Tennessee State University (Johnson City, Tenn.), 1971.
11. MERENDA, PETER F., AND REILLY, RAYMOND. "Validity of Selection Criteria in Determining Success of Graduate Students in Psychology." *Psychol Rep* 28(1):259–66 F '71. * (*PA* 46:5705)

CUMULATIVE NAME INDEX

Bass, A. R.: 8
Blackburn, M.: 4, 6
Crawford, F. W.: 10
Ewen, R. B.: 5
Hackman, J. R.: 4, 6, 8
Huber, J. T.: 1
Lannholm, G. V.: 2
Marco, G. L.: 2
Merenda, P. F.: 11
Newman, R. I.: 3
Reilly, R.: 11
Schrader, W. B.: 2
Seashore, H.: *rev*, 5:583
Shand, J.: 9
Stricker, G.: 1
Wiggins, N.: 4, 6, 8
Woodard, D. B.: 7

[1006]

*The Undergraduate Program Field Tests: Psychology Test. College; 1969–73; formerly called *The Undergraduate Record Examinations: Psychology Test;* test available to colleges for local administration; Educational Testing Service. * For the testing program entry, see 1062.

For additional information, see 7:646. For reviews of the testing program, see 7:671 (2 reviews).

[Out of Print Since TIP I]

Engle Psychology Test, 5:582 (1 review)
Hogan Psychology Test, 5:584 (1 review)
Psychological Publications Press Achievement Test in General Psychology, 7:645
Psychology Test: Every Pupil Scholarship Test, 6:744
Tests of Human Growth and Development, 3:406 (2 reviews, 3 references)

RECORD AND REPORT FORMS

[1007]

*A/9 Cumulative Record Folder. Grades kgn–12; 1951–72; 1972 folder essentially the same as folder published 1951 except for omission of reference to race and economic status, and minor wording changes; American Guidance Service, Inc. *

For additional information, see 6:745.

[1008]

American Council on Education Cumulative Record Folders. Grades 1–3, 4–6, 7–12, 13–16; 1928–47; Committee on Cumulative Records of the American Council on Education; the Council. *

For additional information and reviews by Warren R. Baller and Arthur H. Brayfield of the folders for grades 1–3 and 4–6, see 4:510; for reviews by Herbert A. Toops of the folders for grades 7–12 and 13–16, see 3:444–5.

[1009]

[California Cumulative Record and Health Insert.] Grades 1–12; 1944–58; Carlisle Graphics. *
a) CALIFORNIA CUMULATIVE RECORD. Grades 1–8, 9–12; 1944–55.
b) HEALTH INSERT. Grades 1–12; 1957–58; c1943–58; Noelle Anderson, Patricia Hill, Margaret Leonard, and David Van der Slice.

For additional information and a review by Warren R. Baller of the original edition, see 4:511.

California Cumulative Record and Health Insert

[1010]

*The Cassel Developmental Record. Birth to death;
1955–71, c1954–70; profile of 6 areas of development
(physiological, emotional, psycho-sexual, intellectual,
social, educational) and average development; Russell
N. Cassel; Psychologists and Educators, Inc. *
For additional information and a review by William
E. Henry, see 5:586.

[1011]

Florida Cumulative Guidance Record, Revised.
Grades 1–12; 1950–59; Edward Drew Co. *

[1012]

G.C. Anecdotal Record Form. Teachers' recordings
of student actions; 1943; formerly called V.G.C. Anecdotal Record Form; Guidance Centre [Canada]. *

[1013]

*[Guidance Cumulative Folder and Record
Forms.] Grades kgn–12; 1941–70; folder and 5 insert
sheets; Chronicle Guidance Publications, Inc. *
a) INTERVIEW RECORD SHEET. 1958.
b) OBSERVATION RECORD SHEET. 1958; reports by teachers.
c) PERSONALITY REPORT SHEET. 1958; ratings by teachers.
d) FOUR YEAR EDUCATIONAL PLAN. Grades 9–12; 1961.
e) DIVISION OF VOCATIONAL EDUCATION—COOPERATIVE
TRAINING. Grades 11–12; 1970; vocational education
report.
For additional information, see 6:746.

[1014]

*[Height Weight Interpretation Folders.] Ages
4.0–18.0; 1947–64; 2 editions; Howard V. Meredith and
Virginia B. Knott; Joint Committee on Health Problems in Education of the National Education Association and the American Medical Association; distributed by American Association for Health, Physical
Education, and Recreation. *
a) HEIGHT WEIGHT INTERPRETATION FOLDER FOR GIRLS.
Formerly called Physical Growth Record for Girls.
b) HEIGHT WEIGHT INTERPRETATION FOLDER FOR BOYS.
Formerly called Physical Growth Record for Boys.
For additional information concerning earlier forms,
see 6:748 (1 reference).
REFERENCES THROUGH 1971
1. See 6:748.
2. WEAR, CARL L. "An Analysis of Height-Weight Relationships of Midwestern Boys." Res Q 40(3):607–12 O '69. *
CUMULATIVE NAME INDEX
Meredith, H. V.: 1   Wear, C. L.: 2

[1015]

Junior High School Record. Grades 7–10; 1955;
also available in combination with the Personality Record (Revised); National Association of Secondary-
School Principals. *

[1016]

*Ontario School Record System, 1972 Edition.
Grades kgn–13; 1950–72; OSRS; 3 parts: Ontario Stu-
dent Record Folder, Ontario School Office Index Card,
Student Achievement Form; Ministry of Education,
Ontario; Guidance Centre [Canada]. *
For additional information concerning an earlier edi-
tion, see 6:747.

[1017]

★Permanent Record Folder. Exceptional children;
1966; Educational Performance Associates, Inc. *

[1018]

★Psychodiagnostic Test Report Blank. Psychologists' test data on clients; 1965; Leopold Bellak; C.P.S.,
Inc. *

[1019]

*Secondary-School Record. Grades 9–12; 1941–64;
SSR; National Association of Secondary-School Principals. *
a) TRANSCRIPT.
b) STUDENT DESCRIPTION SUMMARY. For summarizing
ratings by several teachers of 8 characteristics on Student Description Form.
For additional information concerning an earlier edition, see 4:516 (1 reference).
REFERENCES THROUGH 1971
1. See 4:516.
CUMULATIVE NAME INDEX
Elicker, P. E.: 1

[Out of Print Since TIP I]

Ayer's Cumulative Records, T:1302
Blum-Fieldsteel Development Charts, 5:585 (1 refer-
ence)
Cumulative Personnel Record, 4:513
Merrill-Palmer Logarithmic Developmental Graph,
T:1312
Permanent Record Card, 4:515 (1 reference)
Pre-School Record Form, 5:587
Ready Record Forms, T:1316
School Records (status unknown), T:1317
Standard Profile Chart, 3:448 (1 review)
Steck Cumulative Record Folder, T:1320
Universal Cumulative Record (status unknown),
T:1321
V.G.C. Cumulative Record Folder, 4:517; for a re-
vision, see G.C. Cumulative Record Folder, T:1307
V.G.C. Interview Record Form, 3:451; for a revision,
see G.C. Interview Record Form, T:1308
V.G.C. Student Information Form, 3:452; for a re-
vision, see G.C. Student Information Form, T:1309

RELIGIOUS EDUCATION

[1020]

Achievement Test in Jewish History. Junior high
school; 1962; 4 scores: informational background,
terms and concepts, personalities, total; original forms
by Leon H. Spotts; revision, manual, and technical report by Gerhard Lang; National Curriculum Research
Institute, American Association for Jewish Education. *
For additional information, see 6:749.

[1021]

★Achievement Test—Jewish Life and Observances. Grades 5–7; 1973; Testing Bureau of the National Curriculum Research Institute; American Association for Jewish Education. *

[1022]

★Achievement Test—The State of Israel. "Pupils
who have completed an organized course of study on
the State of Israel"; 1973; Testing Bureau of the National Curriculum Research Institute; American Association for Jewish Education. *

[1023]

★The Bible and You (A Test of Factual Knowledge About the Bible). Ages 13 and over; 1961–64;
Sunday School Board of the Southern Baptist Conven-

tion; Broadman Press; distributed by Baptist Book Store. *

[1024]

★**Biblical Survey Test.** College; 1961; 2 scores: New Testament, Old Testament; Edna SoRelle and Joseph V. West; distributed by Baylor University Press. *

[1025]

*Concordia Bible Information Inventory. Grades 4–8; 1954–71; formerly called *Test on Biblical Information;* Martin J. Maehr; Concordia Publishing House. *

For additional information concerning earlier forms, see 6:754.

REFERENCES THROUGH 1971

1. MAEHR, MARTIN J. "Biblical Information Test," pp. 67–71. In *Tests and Measurements in Lutheran Education.* Edited by Arthur L. Miller. Lutheran Education Association, Fourteenth Yearbook. 1957. River Forest, Ill.: the Association, 1959. Pp. xi, 115. *

CUMULATIVE NAME INDEX

Maehr, M. J.: 1

[1025A]

*An Inventory of Religious Activities and Interests. High school and college students considering church-related occupations and theological school students; 1967–70; IRAI; for research use only; 11 scales: counselor, administrator, teacher, scholar, evangelist, spiritual guide, preacher, reformer, priest, musician, check scale; Sam C. Webb; Educational Testing Service (Atlanta Office). *

For additional information and a review by Donald G. Zytowski, see 7:1023.

REFERENCES THROUGH 1971

1. HEINTZEN, ERICH HUGO, III. *The Religious Attitudes and Interests of Seminary Students and Clergymen of the Lutheran Church-Missouri Synod.* Doctor's thesis, University of North Dakota (Grand Forks, N.D.), 1971. (*DAI* 32:7078A)
2. HULTGREN, DAYTON DELANO. *Interests and Job Activities of Ministers in a Variety of Preferred Roles.* Doctor's thesis, University of Minnesota (Minneapolis, Minn.), 1971. (*DAI* 32:5038A)

CUMULATIVE NAME INDEX

Heintzen, E. H.: 1　　　　Zytowski, D. G.: *rev,* 7:1023
Hultgren, D. D.: 2

[1026]

A Religious Attitudes Inventory. Religious counselees; 1964; W. E. Crane and J. Henry Coffer, Jr.; Family Life Publications, Inc. *

For additional information, see 7:650.

[1027]

*Standardized Bible Content Tests. Bible college; 1956–73; Standardized Bible Content Test Committee of the Accrediting Association of Bible Colleges; the Association. *

For additional information, see 7:651 (1 reference).

REFERENCES THROUGH 1971

1. See 7:651.

CUMULATIVE NAME INDEX

Hakes, J. E.: 1

[1028]

*Theological School Inventory. Incoming seminary students; 1962–72; TSI; motivation for entering the ministry; 12 scores (definiteness, natural leading, special leading, concept of the call, flexibility, acceptance by others, intellectual concern, self-fulfillment, leadership success, evangelistic witness, social reform, service

to persons) plus unscored sections on biographical information and reactions to demands of the ministry; Educational Testing Service (test), James E. Dittes (manual and supplements), Frederick Kling (test and 1 supplement), Ellery Pierson (1 supplement), and Harry DeWire (1 supplement); Ministry Studies Board; distributed by Theological Schools Scoring Service. *

For additional information concerning an earlier edition, see P:273 (5 references).

REFERENCES THROUGH 1971

1–5. See P:273.
6. TAGGART, MORRIS. *A Study of Attitude Change in a Group of Theological Students.* Doctor's thesis, Northwestern University (Evanston, Ill.), 1962. (*DA* 23:2236)
7. BREIMEIER, KENNETH H. *Relationship Between Various Psychological Measures in Use at Theological Seminaries.* Comments by James E. Dittes. Occasional Papers No. 1. Washington, D.C.: Ministry Studies Board, 1967. Pp. iii, 59. *
8. GILBERT, ALBIN R. "The Superiority of Latency-Weighted Scores Over Unweighted Scores in the Assessment of Professional Suitability." *Proc W Va Acad Sci* 40:192–5 '68. *
9. STEERE, JAMES LINDLEY. *The Relationship of a Measure of Personality Factors to a Measure of Motivation for Ministerial Work and Success in a Selected B. D. Program.* Doctor's thesis, Ball State University (Muncie, Ind.), 1969. (*DAI* 30:4235A)
10. HOUTS, DONALD CHARLES. *The Use of Ego Identity Measures in Evaluating a Seminary Curriculum.* Doctor's thesis, Northwestern University (Evanston, Ill.), 1970. (*DAI* 31: 3362A)
11. HOUTS, DONALD C. "Ego Identity and Professional Preparation for the Ministry." *J Pastoral Care* 25(1):12–23 Mr '71. * (*PA* 46:8839)
12. WEISGERBER, CHARLES. "The Theological School Inventory and Some Roman Catholic and Protestant Differences." *Counsel & Values* 16(1):54–65 f '71. * (*PA* 49:2308)

CUMULATIVE NAME INDEX

Breimeier, K. H.: 7　　　　Otte, H. W.: 4
Dittes, J. E.: 3, 7　　　　Spiers, D. E.: 5
Embree, R. A.: 1　　　　Steere, J. L.: 9
Gilbert, A. R.: 8　　　　Taggart, M.: 6
Houts, D. C.: 10–1　　　Weisgerber, C.: 12
Knott, T. G.: 2

[1029]

*Youth Research Survey. Ages 13–19; 1958–71; YRS; revision of *CYR Youth Survey* (CYR is acronym for Church Youth Research) which was a revision of *LYR Youth Inventory* (LYR is acronym for Lutheran Youth Research); for group and individual measurement in religious congregations and high schools; yields 25 profiled scores: concerns (family unity, parental understanding, family pressures, life partner, lack of self-confidence, academic problems, personal faults, classroom relationships, national issues, God relationship), beliefs-values (interest in help, maturity of values, orientation for change, moral responsibility, meaningful life, religious participation, social action, self regard, human relations, God awareness, biblical concepts), perception (youth group vitality, adult caring, family social concerns), frankness plus a computer group report of about 120 pages of narrative statements and percentage responses in 36 areas: general description of your youth (tally, frankness, family, school, leisure), life perspective (world view, self regard), concerns about family (family unity, parental understanding, family pressures), concerns about oneself (lack of self-confidence, academic problems, personal faults, classroom relationships), personal battles (dating and emotions, moral issues, maturity of values, moral responsibility, drug use), feeling for people (national issues, orientation for change, human relations), perception of church (youth group vitality, adult caring, family social concern), religious commitment (God awareness, God relationship, participation in religious activities, biblical concepts, meaningful life, social action, needs of others), interest in help (marriage concerns—life partner, interest in the worship service, focal points for a ministry, interest in help items) ; Merton P. Strommen and Ram K. Gupta ; Youth Research Center. *

For additional information on the CYR edition, see P :22 (2 references).

REFERENCES THROUGH 1971

1–2. See P:22.
3. ROA, CLAYTON DURWARD. *An Investigation of Factors Leading to the Withdrawal of Waldorf Junior College Freshmen.* Doctor's thesis, Michigan State University (East Lansing, Mich.), 1965. (*DA* 27:681A)

CUMULATIVE NAME INDEX

Roa, C. D.: 3   Strommen, M. P.: 1–2

[Out of Print Since TIP I]

Achievement Test for Weekday Afternoon Congregational Schools, 6:750
Bible History Tests, 5:589
Comprehensive Test on Luther's Small Catechism, 7:647 (1 reference)
Concordia PBK Inventory, 7:648 (2 references)
How I Think and Feel, 7:649 (1 reference)
Northwestern University Religious Education Tests, T:1326
Peters Biblical Knowledge Test, 5:590 (1 review)
Religion Test for Grades Two and Three, 5:591
Religion Test for High Schools, 5:592
Religion Test (Four-Year Course): Affiliation Testing Program for Catholic Secondary Schools, 6:751 (1 review)
Scholastic Achievement Series: Religion, 6:752
Southern Baptist Theological Seminary Bible Tests, T:1330
Test in Religious Instruction for High School Students, 2:1520
Unit Tests on Luther's Catechism, 6:756; for a short adaptation, see *Comprehensive Test on Luther's Small Catechism,* 7:647
Wilson Tests of Religious Aptitude, 3:456 (1 review, 1 reference)

SCORING MACHINES AND SERVICES

[1030]

*Automata EDT 1200 Educational Data Terminal. 1967–72; replaces *Automata 450 Test Scorer;* an optical scanner for scoring special answer cards (Data Dot Cards) ; Automata Corporation. *

For additional information on the earlier model, see 7:652.

[1031]

**Hankes Scoring Service. 1946–62; special answer sheets, scoring services, and profiles available for *Minnesota Multiphasic Personality Inventory, The Personality Inventory,* and *Strong Vocational Interest Blank;* E. J. Hankes ; Testscor. *

For additional information, see 6:667; see also 5:529 (1 reference) and 4:466 (5 references).

REFERENCES THROUGH 1971

1–5. See 4:466.
6. See 5:529.
7. BURACK, BENJAMIN. "Have You Checked Machine-Scoring Error Lately?" *Voc Guid Q* 9:191–3 sp '61. * (*PA* 36:1KI91B)
8. ADAMS, JAMES F. "The Reliability and Accuracy of Commercial Machine Scoring of the Strong Vocational Interest Blank." *J Ed Meas* 2:85–90 Je '65. *
9. CAMPBELL, DAVID P. "Note: A Comparison of the Performance of Four SVIB Scoring Services." *J Ed Meas* 2:218–9 D '65. *
10. MERWIN, JACK C.; BRADLEY, ARTHUR D.; JOHNSON, RALPH H.; AND JOHN, ELMER R. "S.V.I.B. Machine Scoring

Provided by a Test Scoring Agency." *Personnel & Guid J* 43:665–8 Mr '65. *
11. WEIGEL, RICHARD; ROEHLKE, ART; AND POE, CHARLES. "Re-evaluating Machine Scoring Consistency." *Voc Guid Q* 13:209–11 sp '65. *
12. WEIGEL, RICHARD G., AND PHILLIPS, MARYANN. "An Evaluation of MMPI Scoring Accuracy by Two National Scoring Agencies." *J Clin Psychol* 23:102–3 Ja '67. * (*PA* 41:5977)
13. FOWLER, RAYMOND D., JR., AND COYLE, F. A., JR. "Scoring Error on the MMPI." *J Clin Psychol* 24:68–9 Ja '68. * (*PA* 42:9159)
14. WEIGEL, RICHARD G.; PHILLIPS, MARYANN; AND LEWIS, RAYMOND. "Machine-Scoring Consistency of the Strong Vocational Interest Blank." *J Ed Res* 62(5):200+ Ja '69. *

CUMULATIVE NAME INDEX

Adams, J. F.: 8	Layton, W. L.: 4
Bradley, A. D.: 10	Lewis, R.: 14
Burack, B.: 7	Merwin, J. C.: 10
Campbell, D. P.: 9	Phillips, M.: 12, 14
Coyle, F. A.: 13	Poe, C.: 11
Cuadra, C. A.: 6	Roehlke, A.: 11
Fowler, R. D.: 13	Stone, C. H.: 5
Hankes, E. J.: 1	Strong, E. K.: 1
John, E. R.: 10	Weigel, R.: 11
Johnson, R. H.: 10	Weigel, R. G.: 12, 14
Kriedt, P. H.: 2–3, 5	

[1032]

**IBM 1230 Optical Mark Scoring Reader. 1962–63; for scoring IBM 1230 answer sheets (maximum of 1,000 response positions) marked with ordinary lead pencils ; scores up to 1,200 sheets per hour and prints out part and total scores on the answer sheets; when used with the IBM 534 card punch, data may be transferred to punched cards ; machine printed reports (score distributions, item analyses, correlations, and other statistics) are obtainable from the 1230/534 combination ; International Business Machines Corporation. *

For additional information, see 6:668.

REFERENCES THROUGH 1971

1. JONES, ROBERT A.; PULLIAS, CALVIN; AND MICHAEL, WILLIAM B. "An IBM 1401 Computer Program for Item and Test Analysis." *Ed & Psychol Meas* 25:217–9 sp '65. * (*PA* 39:13017)
2. DIZNEY, HENRY F.; MERRIFIELD, PHILIP R.; AND DAVIS, O. L., JR. "Effects of Answer-Sheet Format on Arithmetic Test Scores." *Ed & Psychol Meas* 26:491–3 su '66. * (*PA* 40:13532)
3. FINGER, JOHN A., JR. "A Machine Scoring Answer Sheet Form for the IBM 1231 Optical Scanner." *Ed & Psychol Meas* 26:725–7 au '66. * (*PA* 41:981)
4. GUGEL, JOHN F. "Designing and Printing IBM 1230 Optical Mark Scoring Reader Answer Sheets by Photo-Offset." *Ed & Psychol Meas* 26:729–31 au '66. * (*PA* 41:1020)
5. GUGEL, JOHN F. "An IBM 1620 SPS Computer Program for Unpacking the IBM 1230 Special Code." *Ed &Psychol Meas* 26:733–7 au '66. *
6. GUGEL, JOHN F. "Punching Multiresponse Questions With the IBM 1230 Optical Mark Scoring Reader: A Procedure and an IBM 1620 SPS Computer Program." *Ed & Psychol Meas* 26:739–42 au '66. *
7. GUGEL, JOHN F. "Scoring Multiresponse Questions With the IBM 1230 Optical Mark Scoring Reader." *Ed & Psychol Meas* 26:743–5 au '66. *
8. SWANSON, JAMES R., AND TULLY, G. EMERSON. "Answer Sheet Format as a Variable in the Test Performance." *J Col Stud Personnel* 7:33–6 Ja '66. *
9. ENGLISH, HOWARD H., AND KUBINIEC, CATHLEEN M. "An Objective Test Analysis Program Utilizing the IBM 1230 Optical Mark Scoring Reader." *Ed & Psychol Meas* 27:165–70 sp '67. *
10. JONES, ROBERT A.; PULLIAS, CALVIN M.; AND MICHAEL, WILLIAM B. "An IBM Scoring Routine for Three-Choice Inventories." *Ed & Psychol Meas* 27:197–9 sp '67. * (*PA* 41:8132)
11. MILLER, C. DEAN; DOIG, MARILYN; AND MILLIKEN, GEORGE. "Scoring, Analyzing, and Reporting Classroom Tests Using an Optical Reader and 1401 Computer." *Ed & Psychol Meas* 27:159–64 sp '67. * (*PA* 41:8133)
12. MOORE, JAMES C., AND SCHUTZ, RICHARD E. "An Item and Test Analysis Program Used in Conjunction With the IBM 1230 Optical Mark Scoring Reader and IBM 534 Card Punch Attachment." *Ed & Psychol Meas* 27:171–4 sp '67. * (*PA* 41:8134)
13. WUEBBEN, PAUL LANE; TIMMERMANS, GRETCHEN B.; AND TIMMERMANS, PERRY R. "Data Processing of Machine Scored Questionnaires." *Ed & Psychol Meas* 27:195–6 sp '67. * (*PA* 41:8139)
14. EVANS, ROBERT C., JR., AND WESTBROOK, BERT W. "A Fortran Program for Generalized Item Analysis Using IBM

1230 Punched Output." *Ed & Psychol Meas* 28:849–50 au '68. * (*PA* 43:3311)

15. SMITH, VIRGIL B. "Adapting a Machine-Read Response Sheet for Combined Use as a Semantic Differential Scale Questionnaire." *Ed & Psychol Meas* 28:181–3 sp '68. * (*PA* 42:11396)

16. JOHNSON, RICHARD T. "Test Processing and Reporting Programs for the IBM S360/20." *Ed & Psychol Meas* 29(3): 693–6 au '69. * (*PA* 44:17749)

17. KIMBALL, JACK E. "Scoring Local College Entrance Tests by Use of the IBM 1130 Computer and the IBM 1230 Optical Reader." *J Ed Data Processing* 6(3):192–3 su '69. *

18. GAFFNEY, RICHARD F., AND MAGUIRE, THOMAS O. "Use of Optically Scored Test Answer Sheets With Young Children." *J Ed Meas* 8(2):103–6 su '71. * (*PA* 46:11500)

19. GEISLER, ROBERT, AND PAPERT, ANTONY. "Computerized Test Analysis." *J Med Ed* 46(8):666–9 Ag '71. *

CUMULATIVE NAME INDEX

Davis, O. L.: 2	Michael, W. B.: 1, 10
Dizney, H. F.: 2	Miller, C. D.: 11
Doig, M.: 11	Milliken, G.: 11
English, H. H.: 9	Moore, J. C.: 12
Evans, R. C.: 14	Papert, A.: 19
Finger, J. A.: 3	Pullias, C.: 1
Gaffney, R. F.: 18	Pullias, C. M.: 10
Geisler, R.: 19	Schutz, R. E.: 12
Gugel, J. F.: 4–7	Smith, V. B.: 15
Johnson, R. T.: 16	Swanson, J. R.: 8
Jones, R. A.: 1, 10	Timmermans, G. B.: 13
Kimball, J. E.: 17	Timmermans, P. R.: 13
Kubiniec, C. M.: 9	Tully, G. E.: 8
Maguire, T. O.: 18	Westbrook, B. W.: 14
Merrifield, P. R.: 2	Wuebben, P. L.: 13

[1033]

★**IBM 3881 Optical Mark Reader.** 1972; for reading IBM 3881 answer sheets (maximum of 2,480 response positions) marked with ordinary lead pencils; 2 models: Model 1 reads up to 4,000 sheets per hour and transmits data directly to a computer (System/3, System/370 Model 135 or 145), Model 2 reads up to 3,700 sheets per hour and uses IBM 3410 magnetic tape subsystem to record data on magnetic tape for use with various computers; International Business Machines Corporation. *

[1034]

*****MRC Scoring and Reporting Services.** 1956–71; special answer sheets and cards, scoring and reporting services, and profiles for 48 tests: *ACT Assessment, ACT Mathematics Placement Examination, Academic Promise Tests, Adult Basic Learning Examination, Analysis of Learning Potential, Canadian Lorge-Thorndike Intelligence Tests, Canadian Tests of Basic Skills, Classification and Placement Examination, Cognitive Abilities Test, College English Placement Test, Content Evaluation Series, Dailey Vocational Tests, Differential Aptitude Tests, Durrell Listening-Reading Series, Gates-MacGinitie Reading Tests, Henmon-Nelson Tests of Mental Ability, Iowa Silent Reading Tests, Iowa Tests of Basic Skills, Iowa Tests of Educational Development, Iowa Tests of Music Literacy, Lorge-Thorndike Intelligence Tests, Metropolitan Achievement Tests, Minnesota Vocational Interest Inventory, Modern Mathematics Supplement to the Iowa Tests of Basic Skills, Musical Aptitude Profile, Nelson-Denny Reading Test, Nelson Reading Test, Ohio Vocational Interest Survey, Omnibus Personality Inventory, Opinion, Attitude, and Interest Survey, Orleans-Hanna Algebra Prognosis Test, Orleans-Hanna Geometry Prognosis Test, Otis-Lennon Mental Ability Test, Otis Quick Scoring Mental Ability Tests, Primary Reading Profiles, Primary Social Studies Test, Purdue High School English Test, SRA Achievement Series, School Interest Inventory, Stanford Achievement Test, Stanford Achievement Test: High School Basic Battery, Stanford Diagnostic Reading Test, Strong Vocational Interest Blank for Men, Strong Vocational Interest Blank for Women, Study of Values, Tests of Academic*

Progress, Vocational Planning Inventory, and *Work Values Inventory;* Measurement Research Center, Inc. *

For additional information, see 7:653 (2 references).

REFERENCES THROUGH 1971

1–2. See 7:653.

CUMULATIVE NAME INDEX

Bell, F. O.: 1	Hoff, A. L.: 1
Campbell, D. P.: 2	Hoyt, K. B.: 1

[1035]

NCS Scoring and Reporting Services. 1962–68; special answer sheets, scoring and reporting services, and profiles for 38 tests: *Adjective Check List, California Achievement Tests, California Psychological Inventory, California Short-Form Test of Mental Maturity, Cognitive Abilities Test, Comprehensive Tests of Basic Skills, Cooperative English Tests, Cooperative School and College Ability Tests, Differential Aptitude Tests, Edwards Personal Preference Schedule, Gates-MacGinitie Reading Tests, General Aptitude Test Battery, Inventory of College Activities, Iowa Tests of Basic Skills, Iowa Tests of Educational Development, Lorge-Thorndike Intelligence Tests, Metropolitan Achievement Tests, Minnesota Child Development Inventory, Minnesota Multiphasic Personality Inventory, Minnesota Vocational Interest Inventory, Nonreading Aptitude Test Battery, Ohio Vocational Interest Survey, Omnibus Personality Inventory, Otis-Lennon Mental Ability Test, SRA Achievement Series, SRA Short Test of Educational Ability, Sequential Tests of Educational Progress, Short Form Test of Academic Aptitude, Sixteen Personality Factor Questionnaire, Stanford Achievement Test, Stanford Achievement Test: High School Basic Battery, Stanford Test of Academic Skills, Stern Activities Index, Stern Environment Indexes, Strong Vocational Interest Blank for Men, Strong Vocational Interest Blank for Women, Tests of Academic Progress,* and *USES Clerical Skills Tests;* NCS Interpretive Scoring Systems. *

For additional information, see 7:654 (6 references).

REFERENCES THROUGH 1971

1–6. See 7:654.

CUMULATIVE NAME INDEX

Adams, J. F.: 1	Phillips, M.: 4, 6
Campbell, D. P.: 2	Poe, C.: 3
Coyle, F. A.: 5	Roehlke, A.: 3
Fowler, R. D.: 5	Weigel, R.: 3
Lewis, R.: 6	Weigel, R. G.: 4, 6

[1036]

NCS Sentry 70. 1962–70; an optical mark reader (Model 7015) for scoring answer sheets and processing documents at speeds up to 6,000 per hour, both sides of sheet in one pass; processes any answer sheet format up to 11 by 17 inches, including stapled multiple-sheet booklets; an 8½ by 11 inch sheet will take about 240 5-position responses or about 280 4-position responses; the Stored Program Controller, a 2.4 micro-second computer with 8,192 words of 12-bit memory, takes the responses from the mark reading element, validates, scores, and writes a record on the magnetic tape unit; peripheral devices such as line printers, card readers, and magnetic tape units are available to make an independent computer system; general purpose answer sheets available; for answer sheets available for specific tests, see 1035; NCS Interpretive Scoring Systems. *

For additional information and reviews by O. F. Anderhalter and Walter N. Durost, see 7:655.

[1037]

*OpScan Test Scoring and Document Scanning System. 1963–70; formerly called *Digitek Optical Test Scoring and Document Scanning System;* the answer sheets continue to be called Digitek answer sheets; for optical scanning scoring of Digitek answer sheets marked with ordinary lead pencils; reads alphabetic as well as numeric grids on answer sheets and other data sheets and will also score IBM 805 answer sheets; 3 systems; Optical Scanning Corporation. *

a) MODEL 100 [DB]. 1964–67.

b) MODEL 100 DC. 1964–70.

c) MODEL 100 DM. 1964–69.

For additional information and reviews by O. F. Anderhalter and Walter N. Durost, see 7:656 (3 references).

REFERENCES THROUGH 1971

1–3. See 7:656.

CUMULATIVE NAME INDEX

Anderhalter, O. F.: *rev,* 7:656   Finger, J. A.: 2
Dick, W.: 1   Spencer, R. E.: 1, 3
Durost, W. N.: *rev,* 7:656

[1038]

Psychological Resources. 1970; PR; formerly called *Psychological Resources Support Systems;* computer scoring and interpreting service for data from combinations of several tests: 16PF, MMPI, MAT, SVIB, and CAQ; Herbert W. Eber, Robert S. Stein, and Marvin Kliman; Psychological Resources, Inc. *

For additional information, see 7:657.

[Out of Print Since TIP I]

Datronics Optical Test Scoring Machine (status unknown), 7:652A

IBM Test Scoring Machine, 6:669 (3 reviews, 54 references)

SOCIOECONOMIC STATUS

[1039]

The American Home Scale. Grades 8–16; 1942; socioeconomic status; 5 scores: cultural, aesthetic, economic, miscellaneous, total; W. A. Kerr and H. H. Remmers; Psychometric Affiliates. *

For additional information, see 5:596 (2 references); for reviews by Henry S. Maas and Verner M. Sims, see 3:417 (7 references).

REFERENCES THROUGH 1971

1–7. See 3:417.

8–9. See 5:596.

10. KARAS, SHAWKY FALTAOUS. *A Study of Personality and Socioeconomic Factors and Mathematics Achievement.* Doctor's thesis, Columbia University (New York, N.Y.), 1964. (*DA* 28:5191B)

11. BAILEY, RUBELLIA JOHNSON. *The Relationship of Educational Background, Socio-Economic Status, Level of Aspiration, and Intelligence to Success in Business Education.* Doctor's thesis, Temple University (Philadelphia, Pa.), 1965. (*DA* 26:1396)

12. ROWLAND, GEORGE WILLIAM. *A Study of the Relationship Between Socio-Economic Status and Elementary School Science Achievement.* Doctor's thesis, University of Missouri (Columbia, Mo.), 1965. (*DA* 26:5306)

13. STEINBERG, MARVIN; SEGEL, RUEBEN H.; AND LEVINE, HARRY D. "Psychological Determinants of Academic Success: A Pilot Study." *Ed & Psychol Meas* 27:413–22 su '67. * (*PA* 41:14226)

14. LASHLEY, KENT ADRIAN. *A Comparative Study of Negro and Caucasian Junior High School Boys on Selected Factors of Personality, Socioeconomic Status, and Physical Fitness.* Doctor's thesis, East Texas State University (Commerce, Tex.), 1971. (*DAI* 32:5022A)

CUMULATIVE NAME INDEX

Bailey, R. J.: 11   Gough, H. G.: 7–8
Finch, F. H.: 9   Hoehn, A. J.: 9

Karas, S. F.: 10   Remmers, H. H.: 1–3, 6
Kerr, W. A.: 1–6   Rowland, G. W.: 12
Lashley, K. A.: 14   Segel, R. H.: 13
Levine, H. D.: 13   Sims, V. M.: *rev,* 3:417
Maas, H. S.: *rev,* 3:417   Steinberg, M.: 13

[1040]

Environmental Participation Index. Culturally disadvantaged ages 12 and over; 1966–67; EPI; cultural deprivation; 3 scores: possessions, activities, total; Harold Mathis; the Author. *

For additional information and a review by Carl F. Jesness, see 7:660 (2 references).

REFERENCES THROUGH 1971

1–2. See 7:660.

CUMULATIVE NAME INDEX

Jesness, C. F.: *rev,* 7:660   Rosenberg, E.: 2
Kassinove, H.: 2   Trudeau, P.: 2
Mathis, H. I.: 1

[1040A]

*The Home Index. Grades 4–12; 1949–70; for research use only; 1970 index identical with index copyrighted 1953 except for deletion of 2 items; no manual; Harrison G. Gough; the Author. *

REFERENCES THROUGH 1971

1. GOUGH, HARRISON G. "A Short Social Status Inventory." *J Ed Psychol* 40:52–6 Ja '49. * (*PA* 23:4499)

2. O'HARA, ROBERT P., AND TIEDEMAN, DAVID V. "The Vocational Self-Concept in Adolescence." *J Counsel Psychol* 6:292–301 w '59. * (*PA* 35:3279)

3. PARKER, AILEEN WEBBER. *A Comparative Study of Selected Factors in the Vocational Development of College Women.* Doctor's thesis, Indiana University (Bloomington, Ind.), 1961. (*DA* 22:1087)

4. WILSON, JACK FRANCIS. *The Factor Structure and Some Correlates of Parental Identification.* Doctor's thesis, Pennsylvania State University (University Park, Pa.), 1963. (*DA* 24:3418)

5. CROPLEY, A. J. "Differentiation of Abilities, Socioeconomic Status, and the WISC." *J Consult Psychol* 28:512–7 D '64. * (*PA* 39:7749)

6. GOUGH, HARRISON G. "A Cluster Analysis of Home Index Status Items." *Psychol Rep* 28(3):923–9 Je '71. * (*PA* 46:10670)

7. GOUGH, HARRISON G. "Socioeconomic Status as Related to High School Graduation and College Attendance." *Psychol Sch* 8(3):226–31 Jl '71. * (*PA* 47:9815)

8. JENSEN, ARTHUR R. "Do Schools Cheat Minority Children?" *Ed Res* (England) 14(1):3–28 N '71. * (*PA* 49:11953)

CUMULATIVE NAME INDEX

Cropley, A. J.: 5   Parker, A. W.: 3
Gough, H. G.: 1, 6–7   Tiedeman, D. V.: 2
Jensen, A. R.: 8   Wilson, J. F.: 4
O'Hara, R. P.: 2

[1041]

Socio-Economic Status Scales. Urban students, adults, rural families; 1962–64; 2 editions; Manasayan [India]. *

a) SOCIO-ECONOMIC STATUS SCALE (URBAN). Urban students, adults; 1962; 3 ratings (education, occupation, income) yielding a total status score; B. Kuppuswamy.

b) SOCIO-ECONOMIC STATUS SCALE (RURAL). Rural families; 1964; 9 ratings (caste, occupation, education, social participation, land, house, farm powers, material possessions, family type and size) yielding a total status score; Udai Pareek and G. Trivedi.

For additional information and excerpted reviews by Anwar Ansari, E. G. Parameswaran, and one other, see 7:661 (1 reference); for an excerpted review by D. Gopal Rao, see 6:757.

REFERENCES THROUGH 1971

1. See 7:661.

2. PANDEY, R. N. "Construct Validity of a Social Class Evaluation Scale (SCES)." *Indian Psychol R* 6(2):123–4 Ja '70. * (*PA* 46:7992)

CUMULATIVE NAME INDEX

Ansari, A.: *exc,* 7:661   Pareek, U.: 1
Pandey, R. N.: 2   Rao, D. G.: *exc,* 6:757
Parameswaran, E. G.: *exc,* 7:661   Trivedi, G.: 1

[Out of Print Since TIP I]

Minnesota Home Status Index, 1 :983 (1 review, 4 excerpts, 1 reference)
Sims SCI Occupational Rating Scale, 5 :597 (1 review, 10 references)
Social Status Scale, 5 :598 (7 references)

STATISTICS

[1042]

*CLEP Subject Examination in Statistics. 1 semester or equivalent; 1967–73; for college accreditation of nontraditional study, advanced placement, or assessment of educational achievement; tests administered monthly at centers throughout the United States; program administered for the College Entrance Examination Board by Educational Testing Service. * For the testing program entry, see 1050.

For additional information, see 7 :545. For reviews of the testing program, see 7 :664 (3 reviews).

[1043]

★Objective Tests in Mathematics: Statistics. Ages 15 and over; 1970; no manual; B. C. Erricker; University of London Press Ltd. [England]. *

TEST PROGRAMS

[1044]

*ACT Assessment. Candidates for college entrance; 1959–73; ACT; formerly called *ACT Test Battery;* tests administered 5 times a year (February, April, June or July, October, December) at centers established by the publisher; 3 parts in 1 booklet; special editions available for the visually handicapped; American College Testing Program. *

a) ACADEMIC TESTS. 5 scores: English usage, mathematics usage, social studies reading, natural sciences reading, composite.

b) STUDENT PROFILE SECTION. Survey inventory of admissions/enrollment data, out-of-class accomplishments, educational/vocational plans, special educational needs and interests, extracurricular activities, high school coursework information, and self-reported high school grades in 4 general areas (English, mathematics, social studies, natural sciences).

c) ACT INTEREST INVENTORY. 6 scores: social service, business contact, business detail, technical, science, creative arts.

For additional information and a review by Wimburn L. Wallace of an earlier program, see 7 :330 (265 references); for reviews by Max D. Engelhart and Warren G. Findley and an excerpted review by David V. Tiedeman, see 6 :1 (14 references).

REFERENCES THROUGH 1971

1–14. See 6:1.
15–279. See 7:330.
280. SHEPHERD, LINDA MAE. *Some Relationships Between Measured Ability, Achievement, Social Class, and Anxiety.* Master's thesis, Illinois State University (Normal, Ill.), 1963.
281. WILLIAMS, HILDA LEE. *A Comparative Study of the Differences Existent Between the Academic Ability, Motor Ability and Personality Adjustment of Physical Education Majors and Non-majors at Sam Houston State Teachers College, Huntsville, Texas.* Master's thesis, Sam Houston State Teachers College (Huntsville, Tex.), 1964.
282. WILSON, JOHN NORTON. *Prediction of Success in a Basic College Mathematics Course.* Master's thesis, Illinois State University (Normal, Ill.), 1964.
283. RICHARDS, JAMES M., JR., AND HOLLAND, JOHN L. "A

Factor Analysis of Student 'Explanations' of Their Choice of a College." *ACT Res Rep* 8:1–22 O '65. * (*PA* 40:8059)
284. SICURO, NATALE A. "A Comparison of Academic Aptitudes, Certain Values, and Personal and Background Characteristics of Students in Off-Campus Centers and on Central Campus of the Same University." *J Ed Res* 58:220–32 Ja '65. *
285. STONE, LEROY A. "A Discriminate Analysis and Prediction of Dropouts for Freshman Year With Agricultural Students." *J Ed Res* 59:37–8 S '65. *
286. BERDIE, RALPH F., AND STEIN, JUNE. "A Comparison of New University Students Who Do and Do Not Seek Counseling." *J Counsel Psychol* 13:310–7 f '66. * (*PA* 40:12631)
287. PHILLIPS, JAMES STEPHEN. *A Study of the Relationships of Selected Variables to Attrition of the Entering Freshmen at Tennessee Technological University in the Fall Quarter 1964.* Master's thesis, Tennessee Technological University (Cookeville, Tenn.), 1966.
288. RICHARDS, JAMES M., JR., AND HOLLAND, JOHN L. "A Factor Analysis of Student 'Explanations' of Their Choice of a College." *Ed Sci* (England) 1:103–12 O '66. *
289. HOLLAND, JOHN L., AND LUTZ, SANDRA W. "Predicting a Student's Vocational Choice." *ACT Res Rep* 18:1–21 Mr '67. * (*PA* 41:9342)
290. MILLER, AARON J., AND TWYMAN, J. PASCHAL. "Persistence in Engineering and Technical Institute Programs: A Study of Some Nonintellective Concomitants." *J Hum Resources* 2:254–62 sp '67. *
291. THALBERG, STANTON P. "Reading Rate and Immediate Versus Delayed Retention." *J Ed Psychol* 58:373–8 D '67. * (*PA* 42:3379)
292. ZOOK, HOWARD A. *A Comparative Study of the Validity of Three Variables as Predictors of GPI at Kearney State College.* Master's thesis, Kearney State College (Kearney, Neb.), 1967.
293. GROOM, HARRY DEE. *Predicting Achievement Behavior of Academic Probation Students at Brigham Young University.* Master's thesis, Brigham Young University (Provo, Utah), 1968.
294. HONN, MAX MICHAEL. *Relationship Between Inter-Test Variability on the ACT and Personality Characteristics.* Master's thesis, Illinois State University (Normal, Ill.), 1968.
295. LANDMAN, STEPHEN H. *Prediction of College Grades From Measures of Manifest Anxiety, Achievement Motivation, Test Anxiety, Study Habits, and Scholastic Aptitude.* Master's thesis, Kent State University (Kent, Ohio), 1968.
296. LUNDGREN, ELIZABETH J. "Predicting Student Success in Medical Technology and Clinical Laboratory Assistant Programs." *Am J Med Technol* 34:349–61 Je '68. *
297. MEYER, GENEVIEVE L. *Prediction Equations for the Placement of Entering Freshmen in Advanced Mathematics Courses at Wisconsin State University—Platteville.* Master's thesis, Wisconsin State University (Platteville, Wis.), 1968.
298. MOYER, M. E., AND PADEN, D. W. "On the Efficiency of the High School Economics Course." *Am Econ R* 58:870–7 S '68. *
299. ANDERSON, EDITH E. *Syntactic Differences in the Writing of Two Groups of College Freshmen With Different ACT Test Scores.* Master's thesis, St. Cloud State College (St. Cloud, Minn.), 1969.
300. ASTIN, ALEXANDER W. "Recent Findings From the ACE Research Program: Implications for College Choice and Admissions." *Col & Univ* 44(4):341–56 su '69. *
301. BAIRD, LEONARD L. "Patterns of Educational Aspiration." *ACT Res Rep* 32:1–22 D '69. * (*PA* 45:3030)
302. HAMMES, RICHARD R. "Characteristics Related to the Success of the Transfer Program of the University of Wisconsin Center System." *J Ed Res* 62(9):417–21 My–Je '69. *
303. LAWLER, JOYCE ELAM. *An Investigation of the Relationship Between Selected Achievement and Aptitude Variables and Freshman Academic Performance at Tennessee Technological University.* Master's thesis, Tennessee Technological University (Cookeville, Tenn.), 1969.
304. MILLER, RICHARD H. "Students Show a Preparation Increase but No Increase in Grades Was Shown." *Col & Univ* 45(1):28–30 f '69. *
305. REESE, JAMES LLOYD. *Determining the Probability of Success in Business Data Processing at Northeastern Oklahoma A & M College.* Master's thesis, Kansas State College (Pittsburgh, Kan.), 1969.
306. ROGGENKAMP, RONALD R. *A Study to Determine the Validity of Using College Entrance Exams and I.Q. as Predictors of College Performance for Falls City Senior High Graduates.* Master's thesis, Kearney State College (Kearney, Neb.), 1969.
307. AUVENSHINE, C. D.; SMITH, DAVID F.; AND HENAGHAN, MARGARET B. "Need for Achievement: Relation to Academic Achievement and Inventoried Needs." *J Stud Pers Assn Teach Ed* 8(4):105–14 su '70. * (*PA* 45:2386)
308. BATEMAN, JOHN KEITH. *A Multivariate and Univariate Validity Study of the OAIS.* Doctor's thesis, University of Kansas (Lawrence, Kan.), 1970. (*DAI* 31:5753A)
309. COBB, ROBERT L. *The Establishment and Comparison of Prediction Equations for Determining Minimum GPA's in Applied Arts Programs at Dixie College.* Master's thesis, Utah State University (Logan, Utah), 1970.

310. CURL, GERALD ALLEN. *A Comparison of Freshman Achievers and Non-Achievers From Economically Deprived Families.* Doctor's thesis, University of Illinois (Urbana, Ill.), 1970. (*DAI* 31:4455A)

311. DEFRAIN, DAVID MURRAY. *The Effects of Self-Concept and Selected Personal and Educational Variables Upon Attrition in a Non-Credit College Reading Improvement Program.* Doctor's thesis, Oklahoma State University (Stillwater, Okla.), 1970. (*DAI* 31:5195A)

312. FARMER, LOYAL. *The Predictive Validities, as Measured by Multiple Correlation, of Certain Mathematics Grades and a Test Battery Using Academic Achievement as Criteria.* Doctor's thesis, North Texas State University (Denton, Tex.), 1970. (*DAI* 32:1850A)

313. FERRARA, SYLVIA L. *A Comparison of the Predictive Validities of an Achievement Test Battery and an Ability Test Battery in the Prediction of Course Category GPA's for First Quarter Kent State University Freshmen.* Master's thesis, Kent State University (Kent, Ohio), 1970.

314. GERY, FRANK W. "Mathematics and the Understanding of Economic Concepts." Letter. *J Econ Ed* 2(1):100–4 f '70. *

315. HENDERSON, ARNOLD RICHARD. *Factors Relating to Success of Students in Physical Geology in Higher Education.* Doctor's thesis, Mississippi State University (State College, Miss.), 1970. (*DAI* 31:5148A)

316. IM, IN JAE. *A Multivariate Analysis of the Relationship of Academic, Personality, and Family Background Variables to the Different Patterns of Collegiate Attendance.* Doctor's thesis, University of Minnesota (Minneapolis, Minn.), 1970. (*DAI* 32:240A)

317. LAMB, GLEN W. *Correlation Study of Entrance Examination Scores in Mathematics and Performance in Mathematics 12.* Master's thesis, University of Arizona (Tucson, Ariz.), 1970.

318. LARSON, ALLAN D. *The Relationship of Student Academic Success in Selected California Junior College Business Data Processing Programs to Special Aptitudes and Secondary School Academic Achievement.* Doctor's thesis, University of North Dakota (Grand Forks, N.D.), 1970. (*DAI* 31:6454A)

319. LEE, DAVID LAWRENCE. *Selected Interest Factors Related to Academic Achievement at the University of North Dakota.* Doctor's thesis, University of North Dakota (Grand Forks, N.D.), 1970. (*DAI* 32:6762A)

320. MOYER, M. EUGENE, AND PADEN, DONALD W. "Economics Achievement and Mathematics Training." Letter. *J Econ Ed* 2(1):104–6 f '70. *

321. MUHICH, DOLORES. *Multivariable Prediction of Selected Measures of College Success.* Doctor's thesis, Southern Illinois University (Carbondale, Ill.), 1970. (*DAI* 31:5209A)

322. OKHOWAT, VALIOLLAH. *Multiple Discriminant Analysis Applied to American College Test Scores for Three Groups of College Majors in Four Oklahoma State Colleges.* Doctor's thesis, University of Oklahoma (Norman, Okla.), 1970. (*DAI* 31:6879B)

323. ROMINE, PHILIP GORDON. *The Combined Moderating Influences of Personality Variables on the Accuracy of Prediction of Academic Success.* Doctor's thesis, University of Alabama (University, Ala.), 1970. (*DAI* 31:5213A)

324. ROOT, EDWARD LAKIN. *A Regression Analysis of Selected Variables Predicting Academic Success of Full- and Part-Time Students at Allegany Community College, 1963–1970.* Doctor's thesis, University of Maryland (College Park, Md.), 1970. (*DAI* 31:5730A)

325. RUDOLPH, LINDA. *Correlates of the Slosson Intelligence Test, Wechsler Adult Intelligence Scale, ACT Scores and Grade Point Averages.* Master's thesis, Austin Peay State University (Clarksville, Tenn.), 1970.

326. STARKS, WALTER LIVINGSTON. *The Relationship of Residence and Economic Factors to the First Semester Academic Achievement of College of Business Administration and College of Agriculture 1969 Freshmen, Male Students.* Doctor's thesis, Oklahoma State University (Stillwater, Okla.), 1970. (*DAI* 31:5805A)

327. TAYLOR, GLORIA BRUEMMER. *Factors Related to the Academic Performance of Students Transferring From Mississippi Public Junior Colleges to the Department of Business Education, University of Southern Mississippi.* Doctor's thesis, University of Southern Mississippi (Hattiesburg, Miss.), 1970. (*DAI* 31:5805A)

328. VANDER WELL, ALLEN R. "Influence of Financial Need on the Vocational Development of College Students." *ACT Res Rep* 36:1–29 S '70. * (*PA* 47:1845)

329. WILLIAMS, BERTHA M. *A Study of the Relationship Between the American College Test Scores and the Grade-Point Average of Selected Freshman Students of Alabama Agricultural and Mechanical University for 1966–67.* Master's thesis, Alabama A. & M. University (Normal, Ala.), 1970.

330. ASTIN, ALEXANDER W. *Predicting Academic Performance in College: Selectivity Data for 2300 American Colleges.* New York: Free Press, 1971. Pp. ix, 299. * (*PA* 48:3832, title only)

331. BAIRD, LEONARD L. "Cooling Out and Warming Up in the Junior College." *Meas & Eval Guid* 4(3):160–71 O '71. * (*PA* 49:11825)

332. BEASLEY, STEWART RUSSELL, JR. *The Use of Biographical Data as a Predictor of Academic Success for Minority Stu-*

dents at the University of Colorado. Doctor's thesis, University of Colorado (Boulder, Colo.), 1971. (*DAI* 32:6753A)

333. BEYER, DARRELL ERICK. *An Analysis of Selected Intellectual and Nonintellectual Characteristics of Dropouts and Survivors in a Private College.* Doctor's thesis, Baylor University (Waco, Tex.), 1971. (*DAI* 32:3773A)

334. BOHRNSTEDT, GEORGE W.; LAMBERT, PHILIP; AND BORGATTA, EDGAR F. "The Reliability and Validity of Quick Tests With High School Seniors." *J Exp Ed* 39(4):22–3 su '71. * (*PA* 47:1573)

335. BORUP, JERRY H. "The Validity of American College Test for Discerning Potential Academic Achievement Levels—Ethnic and Sex Groups." *J Ed Res* 65(1):3–6 S '71. * (*PA* 47:9813)

336. BOY, JERRY LEONARD. *Grade Prediction of Educational Opportunity Grant Recipients at the University of Arizona, 1967–1969.* Doctor's thesis, University of Arizona (Tucson, Ariz.), 1971. (*DAI* 32:1845A)

337. BRIMM, JACK LESLIE. *Selected Factors Associated With the Academic Performance of Students Who Transfer From the University of Tennessee, Knoxville, to Community Colleges.* Doctor's thesis, University of Tennessee (Knoxville, Tenn.), 1971. (*DAI* 32:4368A)

338. BROOKS, JO NELL BLOOD. *An Identification of Factors Which Appear to Exert a Holding Power on Eastern New Mexico University Students.* Doctor's thesis, New Mexico State University (University Park, N.M.), 1971. (*DAI* 32:1266A)

339. DUTT, LOUISE ELIZABETH GETTYS. *Student Persistence in College: An Analysis.* Doctor's thesis, University of Kentucky (Lexington, Ky.), 1971. (*DAI* 32:4943A)

340. FARLEY, FRANK H., AND TRUOG, ANTHONY L. "Academic Achievement and Resultant and Academic Achievement Motivation." *Psychol Rep* 28(3):843–8 Je '71. * (*PA* 46:11647)

341. FENSKE, ROBERT H., AND CARMODY, JAMES F. "Correlates of Student Interest in Social Issues." *ACT Res Rep* 46:1–7 O '71. *

342. GARBER, JOHN RODNEY. *Characteristics of Students Enrolled in the Guided Studies Program at Rockingham Community College and Their Implications for Curriculum Development.* Doctor's thesis, North Carolina State University (Raleigh, N.C.), 1971. (*DAI* 32:3555A)

343. GARY, BRYN EDWIN. *Prediction of Achievement in Analytic Geometry at East Texas State University.* Doctor's thesis, East Texas State University (Commerce, Tex.), 1971. (*DAI* 32:5059A)

344. HAUSELMAN, ALBERT J. *Personality and the Choice of Undergraduate Major: A Test of Holland's Theory.* Doctor's thesis, University of Kentucky (Lexington, Ky.), 1971. (*DAI* 32:4948A)

345. HEIDY, NICHOLAS J. *A Comparison of Accelerated and Nonaccelerated Fort Lewis College Baccalaureate Graduates.* Doctor's thesis, University of Northern Colorado (Greeley, Colo.), 1971. (*DAI* 32:5567A)

346. HOWELL, JAMES OLIVER. *A Comparison of Academic Characteristics and Predictability of Academic Success of Mexican American Students With That of Non-Mexican American Students at New Mexico State University.* Doctor's thesis, New Mexico State University (University Park, N.M.), 1971. (*DAI* 32:1227A)

347. JOHNSON, ROBERT GORDON, AND WILSON, KAY MACLELLAN. "Performance Variables in a Freely Structured Educational Psychology Course." *Proc W Va Acad Sci* 42(1970):223–32 '71. *

348. KEEFER, KARL E. "Characteristics of Students Who Make Accurate and Inaccurate Self-Predictions of College Achievement." *J Ed Res* 64(9):401–4 My–Je '71. * (*PA* 47:7751)

349. LANGTON, RUSSELL GEORGE. *Iowa Two-Year College Transfer Students at the University of Iowa: Academic Success and Satisfaction.* Doctor's thesis, University of Iowa (Iowa City, Iowa), 1971. (*DAI* 32:4955A)

350. LEBLANC, JOHN READER, JR. *The ACT Test Battery as a Predictor of Completion of a Baccalaureate Degree in Music or Music Education.* Doctor's thesis, University of Southern Mississippi (Hattiesburg, Miss.), 1971. (*DAI* 32:4956A)

351. LEONARD, REX LEE. *An Educational Index for the Prediction of Freshmen Success.* Doctor's thesis, University of Northern Colorado (Greeley, Colo.), 1971. (*DAI* 32:1937A)

352. McKENZIE, CHARLES RAY. *A Comparison of Success in Academic Foundation College Courses Between Students Presenting High School Credits in Practical Arts Courses and Those With Credits in Academic Courses.* Doctor's thesis, North Texas State University (Denton, Tex.), 1971. (*DAI* 32:1839A)

353. MAXEY, E. JAMES, AND ORMSBY, VICTOR J. "The Accuracy of Self-Report Information Collected on the ACT Test Battery: High School Grades and Items of Nonacademic Achievement." *ACT Res Rep* 45:1–25 Jl '71. * (*PA* 47:7561)

354. MENACKER, JULIUS; PARASKEVOPOULOS, JOHN; AND ROBINSON, L. F. "A Problem in Selective College Admission Policy: Performance of Students With Discrepant Admission Scores." *Col & Univ* 46(3):259–64 sp '71. *

355. NELSON, DAVID ALEXANDER. *Trait Anxiety as an Individual Factor in Prediction and as It Correlates With Other Variables in Predicting Academic Achievement.* Doctor's thesis, University of Northern Colorado (Greeley, Colo.), 1971. (*DAI* 32:3699A)

356. NOVICK, MELVIN R.; JACKSON, PAUL H.; THAYER, DOROTHY T.; AND COLE, NANCY S. "Applications of Bayesian Methods to the Prediction of Educational Performance." *ACT Res Rep* 42:1–23 Ap '71. * (*PA* 47:3773)

357. O'CONNELL, TIMOTHY J. *A Comparison of ACT Scores Between Matched Students in Traditional and Experimental School Systems.* Master's thesis, Mankato State College (Mankato, Minn.), 1971.

358. OSBORN, MICHAEL ERNEST. *Factors Associated With the Classification of Clients in a University Counseling Service.* Doctor's thesis, University of Iowa (Iowa City, Iowa), 1971. (*DAI* 32:2423A)

359. SCHOBEL, JAMES ALLAN. *The Use of the OAIS Psychological Test, the ACT Achievement Test and High School Rank in a Discriminant Analysis to Predict Freshmen Attrition at a Midwestern State College.* Doctor's thesis, Ohio University (Athens, Ohio), 1971. (*DAI* 32:4995A)

360. SHELLY, MICHAEL BERT. *Prediction of Undergraduate Journalism Grade Point Average at Southern Illinois University.* Doctor's thesis, Southern Illinois University (Carbondale, Ill.), 1971. (*DAI* 33:1135A)

361. SISSON, ELEANOR RUTH. *A Longitudinal Study of Recent Counselor Information as a Broader Base for Academic Prediction.* Doctor's thesis, Purdue University (Lafayette, Ind.), 1971. (*DAI* 32:3045A)

362. SPEARS, BILLY GENE. *Factors Identified as Affecting the Choice of a College by Senior Students in Public High Schools in Mississippi.* Doctor's thesis, University of Mississippi (University, Miss.), 1971. (*DAI* 32:1868A)

363. STEFANICH, GREGORY PAUL. *University of Montana Freshman Dropout Study, 1968–1970.* Doctor's thesis, University of Montana (Missoula, Mont.), 1971. (*DAI* 32:2425A)

364. THOMAS, CHARLES LEO. *The Relative Effectiveness of High School Grades and Standardized Test Scores for Predicting College Grades of Black Students.* Doctor's thesis, Johns Hopkins University (Baltimore, Md.), 1971. (*DAI* 32:2495A)

365. VON WITTICH, BARBARA. *The Impact of Method of Evaluation Upon Achievement in Elementary Foreign Language Courses.* Doctor's thesis, Iowa State University (Ames, Iowa), 1971. (*DAI* 32:5576A)

366. VRAA, CALVIN W. "Predicting Academic Achievement of Canadian College Freshmen." *J Col Stud Personnel* 12(4):303–8 Jl '71. *

367. WANGER, RUTH SCHWARTZ. *The Relationship of Selected Variables to the Performance and Persistence of Career-Oriented Community College Students.* Doctor's thesis, George Washington University (Washington, D.C.), 1971. (*DAI* 32:3044A)

368. WEAVER, CHARLES N. "A Comparison of the Achievement of Graduates of Catholic High Schools and Non Catholic High Schools Measured by ACT Scores and by Grade Point Averages." *J Mex Am Studies* 1(2):97–105 w '71. *

369. WHITE, JAMES HOWARD. *Individual and Environmental Factors Associated With Freshman Attrition at a Multi-Campus Community College.* Doctor's thesis, George Washington University (Washington, D.C.), 1971. (*DAI* 32:3709A)

370. WHITNEY, DOUGLAS R., AND BOYD, NORLIN W. "Limiting Effect of Predictive Validity on the Expected Accuracy of Admissions Decisions." *Col & Univ* 46(3):180–90 sp '71. *

371. WITTMEYER, ALMA L.; CAMISCIONI, JOHN S.; AND PURDY, PATRICIA A. "A Longitudinal Study of Attrition and Academic Performance in a Collegiate Nursing Program." *Nursing Res* 20(4):339–47 Jl–Ag '71. *

372. WORTHINGTON, LOIS H., AND GRANT, CLAUDE W. "Factors of Academic Success: A Multivariate Analysis." *J Ed Res* 65(1):7–10 S '71. *

373. WRAY, FREDERICK EARL, AND LEISCHUCK, GERALD S. "Predicting Academic Success of Junior College Transfers." *Col & Univ* 47(1):10–6 f '71. *

374. ZACCARIA, LUCY, AND CREASER, JAMES. "Factors Related to Persistence in an Urban Commuter University." *J Col Stud Personnel* 12(4):286–91 Jl '71. * (*PA* 47:7550)

375. ZEDECK, SHELDON. "Identification of Moderator Variables by Discriminant Analysis in a Multipredictable Group Validation Model." *J Appl Psychol* 55(4):364–71 Ag '71. * (*PA* 47:1947)

376. ZEDECK, SHELDON; CRANNY, C. J.; VALE, CAROL A.; AND SMITH, PATRICIA CAIN. "Comparison of 'Joint Moderators' in Three Prediction Techniques." *J Appl Psychol* 55(3):234–40 Je '71. * (*PA* 46:9774)

CUMULATIVE NAME INDEX

[1045]

*Advanced Placement Examinations. High school students desiring credit for college level courses or admission to advanced courses; 1954–73; APE; available to secondary schools for annual administration on specified days in May; inactive forms are available to colleges for local administration in the *Testing Academic Achievement* program; 13 tests listed separately: American History, Art, Biology, Chemistry, Classics, English, European History, French, German, Mathematics, Music, Physics, Spanish; program administered for the College Entrance Examination Board by Educational Testing Service. *

For additional information and reviews by Warren G. Findley and Alexander G. Wesman of earlier forms, see 7:662 (3 references); see also 6:761 (5 references). For reviews of earlier forms of the biology test, see 6:893 (1 review) and 5:724 (1 review); the American history test, see 6:1000 (1 review) and 5:812 (2 reviews); the English composition test, see 5:205 (1 review); the literature test, see 5:211 (1 review); the German test, see 5:273 (1 review); the mathematics test, see 5:419 (1 review); the chemistry test, see 5:743 (1 review); and the physics test, see 5:750 (1 review).

REFERENCES THROUGH 1971

1–5. See 6:761.
6–8. See 7:662.
9. KELLER, CHARLES R. "Piercing the 'Sheepskin Curtain': A Report on the Advanced Placement Program in Its First Year of Sponsorship by the College Board." *Col Board R* 30:19–23 f '56. *
10. CASSERLY, PATRICIA L. "What's Really Happening in Advanced Placement?-II." *Col Board R* 59:16–22 sp '66. *
11. FRIEDRICH, GERHARD. "Advanced Placement: Some Concerns and Principles." *Col Board R* 78:20–1 w '70–71 ['71]. *
12. BURNHAM, PAUL S., AND HEWITT, BENJAMIN A. "Advanced Placement Scores: Their Predictive Validity." *Ed & Psychol Meas* 31(4):939–45 w '71. * (*PA* 48:1631)

CUMULATIVE NAME INDEX

[1046]

*Canadian Test Battery, Grade 10. 1961–68; 5 tests; subtests available as separates; Ontario Institute for Studies in Education; distributed by Guidance Centre [Canada]. *
a) CANADIAN ACHIEVEMENT TEST IN ENGLISH.
b) CANADIAN ACHIEVEMENT TEST IN FRENCH.
c) CANADIAN ACHIEVEMENT TEST IN MATHEMATICS.
d) CANADIAN ACHIEVEMENT TEST IN TECHNICAL AND COMMERCIAL MATHEMATICS. 2 tests in a single booklet.
1) *Canadian Achievement Test in Commercial Mathematics.*
2) *Canadian Achievement Test in Technical Mathematics.*
For reference to reviews of the *Canadian Achievement Test in English,* see 62; the *Canadian Achievement Test in French,* see 242; the *Canadian Achievement Test in Mathematics,* see 604; and the *Canadian Achievement Test in Technical and Commercial Mathematics,* see 605.

[1047]

*Canadian Test Battery, Grades 8–9. Grades 8.5–9.0; 1959–68; subtests available as separates; 9 or 10 scores; Ontario Institute for Studies in Education; distributed by Guidance Centre [Canada]. *

a) CANADIAN ACADEMIC APTITUDE TEST.
   1) *Part 1, Verbal Reasoning.*
   2) *Part 2, Mathematical Reasoning.*
   3) *Part 3, Non-Verbal Reasoning.*
b) CANADIAN ENGLISH ACHIEVEMENT TEST.
   1) *Part 1, Reading Comprehension.*
   2) *Part 2, Mechanics of Expression.* 2 scores in grade 8 (separate scores are obtained for the first 60 and the last 60 items).
   3) *Part 3, Effectiveness of Expression.*
c) CANADIAN MATHEMATICS ACHIEVEMENT TEST.
   1) *Part 1, Arithmetic Computation.*
   2) *Part 2, Facts, Terms, and Concepts.*
   3) *Part 3, Measurement.*

For reference to reviews of the *Canadian English Achievement Test,* see 63; the *Canadian Academic Aptitude Test,* see 350; and the *Canadian Mathematics Achievement Test,* see 606.

[1048]

*College Board Admissions Testing Program. Candidates for college entrance; 1901–73; ATP; special administration arrangements available for the physically handicapped; an optional questionnaire, *Student Descriptive Questionnaire,* provides background information to colleges; program administered for the College Entrance Examination Board by Educational Testing Service. *

a) COLLEGE BOARD SCHOLASTIC APTITUDE TEST. See 357; 2 scores: verbal, mathematical.

b) COLLEGE BOARD ACHIEVEMENT TESTS. 18 tests listed separately (candidates elect 1–3 tests as specified by individual college or scholarship program requirements) : American History and Social Studies, Biology, Chemistry, English Composition, European History and World Cultures, French Listening-Reading, French Reading, German Listening-Reading, German Reading, Hebrew, Latin, Literature, Mathematics Level 1, Mathematics Level 2, Physics, Russian Listening-Reading, Spanish Listening-Reading, Spanish Reading; inactive forms, entitled *College Placement Tests,* are available to colleges for local administration.

c) SUPPLEMENTARY ACHIEVEMENT TESTS. *Out of print.*

For additional information, see 7:663 (16 references); for reviews by Benno G. Fricke and Dean K. Whitla of an earlier program, see 6:760 (12 references); see also 5:599 (3 references) and 4:526 (9 references). For reviews of the Scholastic Aptitude Test, see 7:344 (2 reviews); earlier forms of the English composition test, see 6:287 (3 reviews) and 4:178 (1 review); the German test, see 6:383 (1 review), 5:272 (1 review), and 4:244 (1 review); the Scholastic Aptitude Test, see 6:449 (2 reviews), 5:318 (1 review), and 4:285 (1 review); the chemistry test, see 6:914 (1 review), 5:742 (1 review), and 4:617 (1 review); the American history and social studies test, see 6:966 (1 review), 5:786 (1 review), and 4:662 (1 review); the European history and world cultures test, see 6:967 (1 review); the Latin test, see 5:280 (1 review) and 4:250 (1 review); the biology test, see 5:723 (1 review) and 4:600 (1 review); the physics test, see 5:749 (1 review) and 4:633 (1 review); and the French test, see 4:237 (1 review). For reviews of discontinued tests, see 6:289 (1 review), 6:384 (2 reviews), 6:568 (1 review), 6:569 (1 review), 5:277 (1 review), 4:367 (1 review), and 4:368 (1 review).

REFERENCES THROUGH 1971

1–9. See 4:526.
10–12. See 5:599.
13–24. See 6:760.
25–40. See 7:663.
41. LINCOLN, E. A. "Relative Standing of Pupils in High School, in Early College, and on College Entrance Examinations." *Sch & Soc* 5:417–20 Ap 7 '17. *
42. GERRY, HENRY LESTER. "College Entrance Examination Board Questions in Chemistry." *Sch Sci & Math* 20:845–50 D '20. *
43. WHITMAN, A. D. "The Selective Value of the Examinations of the College Entrance Examination Board." *Sch & Soc* 25:522–5 Ap 30 '27. * (*PA* 1:1858)
44. CRAWFORD, ALBERT B., AND BURNHAM, PAUL S. "Entrance Examinations and College Achievement." *Sch & Soc* 36:344–52, 378–84 S 10, 17 '32. * (*PA* 7:349)
45. WHITCRAFT, LESLIE HARPER. "Some Influences of the Requirements and Examinations of the College Entrance Examination Board on Mathematics in Secondary Schools in the United States." *Teach Col Contrib Ed* 557:1–115 '33. *
46. WEBER, CHRISTIAN O. "Comparative Values of College Entrance Examinations." *Sch & Soc* 55:247–51 F 28 '42. * (*PA* 16:2488)
47. FELS, WILLIAM C. "Who Should Know the Score?" *Col Board R* 30:16–8 f '56. * (*PA* 32:943)
48. BAIRD, LEONARD L. "The Student Descriptive Questionnaire: How Valid Is Its Information? How Can It Be Used?" *Col Board R* 81:10–6 f '71. *
49. SIMS, ALBERT G. "The Case of the Student Descriptive Questionnaire." *Col Board R* 80:13–20 su '71. *

CUMULATIVE NAME INDEX

Angoff, W. H.: 31, 35–6
Ashburn, F. D.: 4
Baird, L. L.: 48
Benson, L.: 30
Black, D. B.: 14
Brownstein, S. C.: 17
Burnham, P. S.: 44
Chandler, M. O.: 38
Chauncey, H.: 5
Coffman, W. E.: 13, 37
College Entrance Examination Board: 16, 18, 21–7, 32–3
Crawford, A. B.: 44
Dyer, H. S.: 10–1, 19, 28, 36
Fels, W. C.: 47
Fishman, J. A.: 12
Foose, R. L.: 30
Fremer, J.: 38
Fricke, B. G.: *rev,* 6:760
Fuess, C. M.: 6
Gagnon, J. B.: 29
Gerry, H. L.: 42
Groesbeck, B. L.: 30
Kellogg, T. E.: 30
Kendrick, S. A.: 15
Kille, F. R.: 9
King, R. G.: 11
Landis, J.: 7
Lincoln, E. A.: 41
Nicholson, E.: 34
Pearson, R.: 30
Schrader, W. B.: 39–40
Sims, A. G.: 49
Stewart, E. E.: 40
Stoke, S. M.: 1
Swineford, F.: 7
Trump, P. L.: 30
Turnbull, M. E.: 8
Turnbull, W. W.: 2–3
Weaver, L. J.: 1
Weber, C. O.: 46
Weiner, M.: 17
Whitcraft, L. H.: 45
Whitla, D. K.: *rev,* 6:760
Whitman, A. D.: 43

[1049]

★College Guidance Program. Grade 11; 1972–73; CGP; an academic ability test, interest survey (optional), and guidance material for students considering college; tests administered annually in spring or fall by participating high schools; 2 tests; Esther E. Diamond and George Heigho; Science Research Associates, Inc. *

a) THE COLLEGE PLANNING TEST. CPT; 8 scores: reading, verbal, mathematics, composite, 4 derived predicted senior-year scores (ACT composite, SAT verbal, SAT mathematics, SAT total).

b) KUDER INTEREST SURVEY, COLLEGE LEVEL. Optional; differs from the *Kuder Occupational Interest Survey* only "in the format of the score report and the number of occupational scores reported"; 38 or 40 scores: 27 (women) or 29 (men) college major scales and 11 professional scales.

[1050]

*College-Level Examination Program. 1–2 years of college or equivalent; 1964–73; CLEP; for college accreditation of nontraditional study, advanced placement, or assessment of eductional achievement; tests administered monthly at centers throughout the United States; 2 series of examinations; program administered for the College Entrance Examination Board by Educational Testing Service. *

a) GENERAL EXAMINATIONS. See 10; retired forms (separate booklet edition) are available for local administration in the *Testing Academic Achievement* program; 13 scores: English composition, natural sciences (biological, physical, total), mathematics (basic skills, advanced topics, total), humanities (fine arts, literature, total), social sciences—history (social sciences, history, total).

b) SUBJECT EXAMINATIONS. 35 tests listed separately: Afro-American History, American Government, American History, American Literature, Analysis and Interpretation of Literature, Biology, Clinical Chemistry, College Algebra, College Algebra and Trigonometry, Computers and Data Processing, Educational Psychology, Elementary Computer Programming—Fortran IV, English Composition, English Literature, Freshman English, General Chemistry, General Psychology, Geology, Hematology, History of American Education, Human Growth and Development, Immunohematology, Introduction to Business Management, Introductory Accounting, Introductory Business Law, Introductory Calculus, Introductory Economics, Introductory Marketing, Introductory Sociology, Microbiology, Money and Banking, Statistics, Tests and Measurements, Trigonometry, Western Civilization.

c) BRIEF TESTS. *Out of print.*

For additional information and reviews by Alexander W. Astin, Benjamin S. Bloom, and Warren G. Findley, see 7:664 (7 references). For reviews of the English composition test, see 7:186 (1 review); and the college algebra and trigonometry test, see 7:454 (1 review).

REFERENCES THROUGH 1971

1–7. See 7:664.
8. BURNETTE, RICHARD R. "Here's How: Developing and Implementing Credit by Examination." *Col Board R* 81:26–8 f '71. *
9. FAGIN, MARGARET C. "CLEP Credit Encourages Adults to Seek Degrees." *Col Board R* 81:18–22 f '71. *
10. STETSON, ROBERT F. "Getting a Head Start on College." *Col Board R* 81:23–5 f '71. *
11. WISNER, ROSCOE W. "Broadening Management Opportunities: The Port Authority's Use of the College Level Examination." *Pub Personnel R* 32(1):8–11 Ja '71. *

CUMULATIVE NAME INDEX

Allyn, N. C.: 6	Findley, W. G.: *rev,* 7:664
Arbolino, J. N.: 5	Gibel, I. L.: 2
Astin, A. W.: *rev,* 7:664	Goolsby, T. M.: 1, 7
Bloom, B. S.: *rev,* 7:664	Stetson, R. F.: 10
Burnette, R. R.: 8	Stuit, D. B.: 3
Fagin, M. C.: 9	Wisner, R. W.: 11

[1051]

*College Placement Tests. Entering college freshmen; 1962–72; CPT; all tests are reprints of inactive forms of *College Board Achievement Tests;* tests available to colleges for local administration; 31 tests listed separately: American History and Social Studies, Biology, Chemistry, English Composition, English Composition (Forty-Minute Version), European History and World Cultures, French Listening Comprehension, French Listening-Reading, French Reading, German Listening Comprehension, German Listening-Reading, German Reading, Greek Reading, Hebrew Reading, Italian Listening Comprehension, Italian Listening-Reading, Italian Reading, Latin Reading, Literature, Advanced Mathematics, Intermediate Mathematics, Mathematics-Level 1, Mathematics-Level 2, Physics, Russian Listening Comprehension, Russian Listening-Reading, Russian Reading, Spanish Listening Comprehension, Spanish Listening-Reading, Spanish Reading, Spatial Relations; program administered for the College Entrance Examination Board by Educational Testing Service. *

For additional information and a review by John R. Hills, see 7:665.

[1052]

*Comparative Guidance and Placement Program. Entrants to two-year colleges and vocational-technical institutes; 1969–73, c1954–73; CGP; a battery of background, abilities, and interest measures which may be administered at any time by participating institutions; program administered for the College Entrance Examination Board by Educational Testing Service. *

a) INTEREST AND BACKGROUND MEASURES.
1) *Biographical Inventory.* Modification of the *College Student Questionnaires;* yields an academic motivation score.
2) *Comparative Interest Index.* Revision of *Academic Interest Measures;* 11 scores: mathematics, physical sciences, engineering technology, biology, health, home economics, secretarial, business, social sciences, fine arts, music.

b) PLACEMENT MEASURES. 3 scores: reading, sentences, mathematics (students take either computation and applied arithmetic, computation and elementary algebra, or algebra).

c) SPECIAL ABILITIES. 3 scores: year 2000 (ability to follow directions), letter groups (inductive reasoning), mosaic comparisons (perceptual speed and accuracy).

For additional information and reviews by C. Robert Pace and H. Bradley Sagen of earlier forms, see 7:666 (2 references).

REFERENCES THROUGH 1971

1–2. See 7:666.
3. CURRAN, EUGENE EDWARD. *An Evaluation of the Significance of Selected Personal Characteristics of Community College Students as Determiners of Achievement in College.* Doctor's thesis, University of Connecticut (Storrs, Conn.), 1971. (*DAI* 32:2431A)
4. DAY, RICHARD THOMAS. *An Analysis of Prison Inmate Versus Community College Student Performance of the CGP.* Doctor's thesis, University of Connecticut (Storrs, Conn.), 1971. (*DAI* 32:2479A)
5. DEVECCHIO, RICHARD CHARLES. *Scholastic Aptitudes, Academic Motivation, Personality and Biographical Characteristics of Non-Returning and Returning Community College Freshmen.* Doctor's thesis, University of Virginia (Charlottesville, Va.), 1971. (*DAI* 32:4371A)
6. EDWARDS, RONALD ROBERT. *Predicting Success in Remediation Programs in Mathematics for the Public Community Junior College.* Doctor's thesis, University of Connecticut (Storrs, Conn.), 1971. (*DAI* 32:2432A)
7. GRIMALDI, JOSEPH; LOVELESS, EUGENE; HENNESSY, JAMES; AND PRIOR, JOHN. "Factor Analysis of 1970–71 Version of the Comparative Guidance and Placement Battery." *Ed & Psychol Meas* 31(4):959–63 w '71. * (*PA* 48:1641)
8. MEYERS, HERMAN WILSON. *The Significance of Certain Academic and Socioeconomic Characteristics to the Stability of Program Choice Among Community College Students.* Doctor's thesis, University of Connecticut (Storrs, Conn.), 1971. (*DAI* 32:2440A)
9. TISDALE, JOSEPH CHRISTOPHER, III. *Prediction of Success in First-Year Community College Mathematics.* Doctor's thesis, University of Virginia (Charlottesville, Va.), 1971. (*DAI* 32:4385A)
10. TROUT, ROBERT W., SR. "CGP—After One Year." *Am Voc J* 46(7):25–7 O '71. *

CUMULATIVE NAME INDEX

Curran, E. E.: 3	Lunneborg, C. E.: 1–2
Day, R. T.: 4	Lunneborg, P. W.: 1–2
DeVecchio, R. C.: 5	Meyers, H. W.: 8
Edwards, R. R.: 6	Pace, C. R.: *rev,* 7:666
Greenmun, R.: 1–2	Prior, J.: 7
Grimaldi, J.: 7	Sagen, H. B.: *rev,* 7:666
Hennessy, J.: 7	Tisdale, J. C.: 9
Loveless, E.: 7	Trout, R. W.: 10

[1053]

*Graduate Record Examinations: National Program for Graduate School Selection. Graduate school candidates; 1939–73; GRE; tests administered 6 times annually (January, February, April, June, October, December) at centers established by the publisher; Educational Testing Service. *

a) APTITUDE TEST. See 382.
b) ADVANCED TESTS. Candidate elects 1 test as specified by individual college requirements; 19 tests listed separately: Biology, Chemistry, Economics, Education, Engineering, French, Geography, Geology, German,

History, Literature in English, Mathematics, Music, Philosophy, Physics, Political Science, Psychology, Sociology, Spanish.

For additional information and a review by Leona E. Tyler of an earlier program, see 7:667 (10 references); see also 6:762 (1 reference); for a review by Harold Seashore, see 5:601 (12 references); see also 4:527 (24 references). For reviews of earlier forms of the advanced Spanish test, see 7:319 (1 review); the area tests, see 6:9 (2 reviews) and 5:10 (2 reviews); the advanced French test, see 6:376 (1 review) and 5:270 (1 review); the aptitude test, see 6:461 (2 reviews), 5:336 (1 review), and 4:293 (2 reviews); the mathematics test, see 6:578 (1 review) and 5:427 (1 review); the education test, see 6:698 (1 review) and 5:537 (1 review); the chemistry test, see 6:919 (1 review); the physics test, see 6:931 (1 review) and 5:754 (1 review); the sociology test, see 6:1021 (1 review); the literature in English test, see 5:215 (1 review); the music test, see 5:247 (1 review); the psychology test, see 5:583 (1 review); the biology test, see 5:727 (1 review); the history test, see 5:818 (1 review); and the political science test, see 5:835 (1 review).

REFERENCES THROUGH 1971

1-24. See 4:527.
25-36. See 5:601.
37. See 6:762.
38-47. See 7:667.

CUMULATIVE NAME INDEX

Abernethy, J.: 26
Angoff, W. H.: 32, 36
Burns, R. L.: 47
Campbell, J. T.: 39
Clark, H.: 40
Conway, M. T.: 35
Crawford, A. B.: 3
Creager, J. A.: 38
Eckelberry, R. H.: 7
Findley, W. G.: 27
Gruber, E. C.: 37
Harvey, P. R.: 41
Herke, M. L.: 30
Heston, J. C.: 13, 21
Hilton, T. L.: 39
Jones, E. S.: 28
King, D. W.: 31
Lannholm, G. V.: 23, 42-4
Learned, W. S.: 5, 8

Marco, G. L.: 44
Osborne, R. T.: 33
Peterson, S. C.: 4, 24
Pitcher, B.: 39
Reed, H. B.: 6
Sanders, W. B.: 33
Schrader, W. B.: 23, 44
Schultz, M. K.: 32, 36
Seashore, H.: rev, 5:601
Speer, G. S.: 10
Springer, G. P.: 41
Stuit, D. B.: 24
Tyler, L. E.: rev, 7:667
Vaughn, K. W.: 9, 12, 14-8, 25
Wallace, A. D.: 29
Wallmark, M. M.: 45
Washington, M.: 46
White, E. L.: 34

[1054]
Junior College Placement Program. Junior college entrants; 1967-69; JCPP; level of instruction appropriate for a student; 4 scores: intelligence, English, mathematics, reading; the intelligence section is Level 5 of *Short Test of Educational Ability;* Science Research Associates, Inc. *

For additional information and reviews by Norman Eagle, Jack C. Merwin, and Richard W. Watkins, see 7:669 (1 reference).

REFERENCES THROUGH 1971
1. See 7:669.

CUMULATIVE NAME INDEX

Eagle, N.: rev, 7:669
Kee, B. E.: 1

Merwin, J. C.: rev, 7:669
Watkins, R. W.: rev, 7:669

[1055]
*National Guidance Testing Program: Series 2. Grades 1.5-14; 1958-71; NGTP; school selects one or more of the *Cooperative Primary Tests, Cooperative School and College Ability Tests,* and *Sequential Tests of Educational Progress;* Cooperative Tests and Services. *

For additional information, see 6:763. For reference to reviews of the CPT, STEP, and SCAT, see 12, 35, and 361.

[1056]
*[National Science Foundation Graduate Fellowship Testing Program.] Applicants for N.S.F. fellowships for graduate study in the sciences; 1951-72; applicant takes 2 tests from the *Graduate Record Examinations:* the Aptitude Test and 1 Advanced Test (Biology, Chemistry, Economics, Engineering, Geography, Geology, Mathematics, Physics, Political Science, Psychology, or Sociology); program administered for the National Science Foundation by Educational Testing Service. *

[1057]
★Ohio Survey Tests. Grades 4, 6, 8, 10; 1965-73; OST; an aptitude and achievement testing program for April-May and September testing in Ohio schools but also available for use elsewhere; 6 scores: academic ability (verbal, mathematical, total), achievement (reading, English expression, mathematics); Roger Trent (manual); Ohio Testing Services. *

[1058]
Project Talent Test Battery: A National Inventory of Aptitudes and Abilities. Grades 9-12; 1960-61; for research use and normative studies only; 8 booklets containing 22 tests and 3 questionnaires; Project Talent Office. *

a) TEST BOOKLET A. 3 tests, 26 scores.
1) *Information Test—Part 1.* 16 scores: screening, vocabulary, literature, music, social studies, mathematics, physical science, biological science, scientific attitude, aeronautics and space, electricity and electronics, mechanics, farming, home economics, sports, total.
2) *Student Activities Inventory.* 10 scores: sociability, social sensitivity, impulsiveness, vigor, calmness, tidiness, culture, leadership, self-confidence, mature personality.
3) *[Preferences Test.]* Characteristics preferred in friends and associates.

b) TEST BOOKLET B. 3 tests, 30 scores.
1) *Interest Inventory.* 17 scores: physical science-engineering, biological science-medicine, computation, mechanical-technical, skilled trades, literary-linguistic, social service, public service, musical, artistic, business management, sales, office work, labor, farming, outdoor recreation, sports.
2) *Information Test—Part 2.* 13 scores: art, law, medicine, engineering, architecture, military, accounting-business-sales, Bible, hunting and fishing, other outdoor activities, theater and ballet, miscellaneous, total.
3) *Student Information Blank.* Personal and family background data, activities, experiences, and plans.

c) TEST BOOKLET CI-X. 1 test (arithmetic computation) plus study materials for memory for words and memory for sentences below.

d) TEST BOOKLET CI. 4 tests, 12 scores: memory for words, memory for sentences, mathematics (arithmetic reasoning, introductory, advanced, total), English (usage, effective expression, punctuation, spelling, capitalization, total).

e) TEST BOOKLET C2. 11 tests, 11 scores: abstract reasoning, mechanical reasoning, disguised words, creativity, clerical checking, visualization in 2 dimensions, reading comprehension, visualization in 3 dimensions, word functions in sentences, table reading, object inspection.

f) SCHOOL QUESTIONNAIRE: GENERAL SCHOOL CHARACTERISTICS. Principals.

g) SCHOOL QUESTIONNAIRE: GUIDANCE PROGRAM. Guidance counselors.

h) SCHOOL QUESTIONNAIRE: COUNSELOR'S QUESTION-
NAIRE. Guidance counselors.

For additional information, see 6:764 (5 references).
For excerpts from related book reviews, see 6:B178 (2
excerpts).

REFERENCES THROUGH 1971

1–5. See 6:764.
6. FLANAGAN, JOHN C.; DAILEY, JOHN T.; SHAYCOFT, MAR-
ION F.; ORR, DAVID B.; AND GOLDBERG, ISADORE. *Studies of
the American High School.* Cooperative Research Project No.
226. Pittsburgh, Pa.: Project Talent, University of Pittsburgh,
1964. Pp. [375]. *
7. FLANAGAN, JOHN C.; DAVIS, FREDERICK B.; DAILEY,
JOHN T.; SHAYCOFT, MARION F.; ORR, DAVID B.; GOLDBERG,
ISADORE; AND NEYMAN, CLINTON A., JR. *The American High
School Student.* Technical Report to the United States Office
of Education, Cooperative Research Project No. 635, Project
Talent: The Identification, Development, and Utilization of
Human Talents. Pittsburgh, Pa.: Project Talent Office, University of Pittsburgh, 1964. Pp. xxiii, [700]. *
8. SHAYCOFT, MARION F.; DAILEY, JOHN T.; ORR, DAVID B.;
NEYMAN, CLINTON A., JR.; AND SHERMAN, STUART E. *Studies
of a Complete Age Group, Age 15.* Cooperative Research Project
No. 566, The Identification, Development, and Utilization of
Human Talents. Pittsburgh, Pa.: Project Talent Office, University of Pittsburgh, 1964. Pp. [270]. *
9. COOLEY, WILLIAM W. "Further Relationships With the
TALENT Battery." *Personnel & Guid J* 44:295–303 N '65. *
10. COOLEY, WILLIAM W., AND MILLER, JUDY D. "The Project
TALENT Tests as a National Standard." *Personnel & Guid J*
43:1038–44 Je '65. *
11. HOROWITZ, HERBERT. "Prediction of Adolescent Popularity
and Rejection From Achievement and Interest Tests." *J Ed
Psychol* 58:170–4 Je '67. * (*PA* 41:10279)
12. CARP, ABRAHAM, AND SCHOENFELDT, LYLE F. "Project
TALENT: A Computer Based Study." *J Sch Psychol* 6:186–92
sp '68. * (*PA* 42:17642)
13. COMBS, JANET, AND COOLEY, WILLIAM W. "Dropouts:
In High School and After School." *Am Ed Res J* 5:343–63 My
'68. *
14. SCHOENFELDT, LYLE F. "The Hereditary Components of
the Project TALENT Two-Day Test Battery." *Meas & Eval
Guid* 1:130–40 su '68. * (*PA* 44:9268)
15. LIPE, DEWEY. "Trait Validity of Airline Stewardess
Performance Ratings." *J Appl Psychol* 54(4):347–52 Ag '70. *
(*PA* 44:21690)
16. SCHOENFELDT, LYLE F.; BAYER, ALAN E.; AND BROWN,
MARSHA D. "Delayed and Normal Progress College Students:
A Comparison of Psycho-Social Characteristics and Career
Plans." *Am Ed Res J* 7(2):235–50 Mr '70. * (*PA* 46:11671)

CUMULATIVE NAME INDEX

Bayer, A. E.: 16	Horowitz, H.: 11
Brown, M. D.: 16	Lipe, D.: 15
Carp, A.: 12	Miller, J. D.: 10
Combs, J.: 13	Neyman, C. A.: 5, 7–8
Cooley, W. W.: 9–10, 13	Orr, D. B.: 3–8
Dailey, J. T.: 3–8	Schoenfeldt, L. F.: 12, 14, 16
Davis, F. B.: 7	Sherman, S. E.: 5, 8
Flanagan, J. C.: 1–4, 6–7	Stanley, J. C.: *exc*, 6:B178
Goldberg, I.: 3–4, 6–7	Tiedeman, D. V.: *exc*, 6:B178
Gorham, W. A.: 3	

[1059]

*Secondary School Admission Test.** Grades 5–7, 8–
10; 1957–73; SSAT; tests administered 4 times annually (January, March, May, December) at centers established by the publisher; also called National Program; 4 scores: reading comprehension, ability (verbal,
quantitative, total); a single score test, the *Secondary
School Admission Test Short Form,* is available for
local administration and scoring between June 1 and
September 15 to schools participating in the national
program; program administered for the Secondary
School Admission Test Board, Inc. by Educational
Testing Service. *

For additional information concerning an earlier
form, see 7:24 (1 reference); for reviews by Charles O.
Neidt and David V. Tiedeman, see 6:24 (1 reference).

REFERENCES THROUGH 1971

1. See 6:24.
2. See 7:24.

CUMULATIVE NAME INDEX

Dizney, H. F.: 2	Spaulding, G.: 1
Neidt, C. O.: *rev*, 6:24	Tiedeman, D. V.: *rev*, 6:24
Schuerger, J. M.: 2	

Project Talent Test Battery

[1060]

★**Service for Admission to College and University Testing Program.** Candidates for college entrance; 1968–73; SACU; tests administered annually in
April and December at centers established by the publisher; 4 tests: 2 tests for students whose native language is English (listed below) and 2 parallel tests in
French; Service for Admission to College and University [Canada]. *

a) CANADIAN SCHOLASTIC APTITUDE TEST. See 353.

b) CANADIAN ENGLISH LANGUAGE ACHIEVEMENT TEST.
See 63A.

REFERENCES THROUGH 1971

1. D'OYLEY, VINCENT R. "Development of the SACU Tests."
Sch Guid Worker (Canada) 26(4):12–6 Mr–Ap '71. *
2. ELLIOTT, H. A. "SACU and the SACU Tests: Past,
Present, and Future." *Sch Guid Worker* (Canada) 26(4):6–11
Mr–Ap '71. *
3. HOLMES, MARK. "The Relationship Between SACU Test
Scores and Other Criteria of High School Academic Perform-
ance." *Sch Guid Worker* (Canada) 26(4):25–30 Mr–Ap '71. *

CUMULATIVE NAME INDEX

D'Oyley, V. R.: 1	Holmes, M.: 3
Elliott, H. A.: 2	

[1061]

★**Testing Academic Achievement.** High school students desiring credit for college level courses or advanced placement, entering college freshmen, and 1–2
years of college or equivalent; 1973; TAA; college
rents retired forms of one or more of the *Advanced
Placement Examinations* (see 1045), *College-Level Examination Program General Examinations* (see 10),
and *College Placement Tests* (see 1051); for local administration and scoring; program administered for the
College Entrance Examination Board by Educational
Testing Service. *

For reference to reviews of the APE and CPT programs, see 1045 and 1051.

[1062]

*The Undergraduate Program for Counseling and
Evaluation.** College; 1954–73; UP; replaced The
Graduate Record Examinations Institutional Testing
Program in 1969; tests formerly called The Undergrad-
uate Record Examinations; tests available to colleges
for local administration; 4 parts; Educational Testing
Service. *

a) APTITUDE TEST. Grades 15–16; see 470; 1969–73; 2
scores: verbal, quantitative.

b) AREA TESTS. See 49; 1954–73; 3 tests: social science,
humanities, natural science.

c) FIELD TESTS. 1969–73; successor to Advanced Tests
in the Graduate Record Examinations Institutional
Testing Program; 25 tests listed separately: Art History, Biology, Business, Chemistry, Drama and Theatre,
Economics, Education, Engineering, French, Geography, Geology, German, History, Literature, Mathematics, Music, Philosophy, Physical Education, Physics,
Political Science, Psychology, Scholastic Philosophy,
Sociology, Spanish, Speech Pathology and Audiology.

d) MODULAR TESTS. Specialized concentration within a
major field; may be taken alone or to complement the
Field Test; 6 tests in 3 fields: literature (European and
American Literature, see 144), mathematics (Abstract
Algebra, Linear Algebra, Real Analysis 1, Real Analy-
sis 2, see 662), music (Aural Music, see 215).

For additional information and reviews by Robert L.
Lathrop and Lyman J. Smith, see 7:671. For reviews of
the music tests, see 7:252 (1 review); the French test,
see 7:281 (1 review); and the mathematics tests, see
7:494 (1 review).

MULTI-APTITUDE BATTERIES

[1063]

Academic Promise Tests. Grades 6–9; 1959–69; APT; 7 scores: abstract reasoning, numerical, nonverbal total, language usage, verbal, verbal total, total; George K. Bennett, Marjorie G. Bennett, Dorothy M. Clendenen, Jerome E. Doppelt, James H. Ricks, Jr., Harold G. Seashore, and Alexander G. Wesman; Psychological Corporation. *

For additional information, see 7:672 (6 references); for reviews by Julian C. Stanley and William W. Turnbull, see 6:766.

REFERENCES THROUGH 1971
1–6. See 7:672.
7. MORSE, JOHN L. "The Adaptation of a Non-Verbal Abstract Reasoning Test for Use With the Blind." *Ed Visually Handicapped* 2(3):79–80 O '70. * (PA 46:1795)

CUMULATIVE NAME INDEX

Beymer, C. L.: 1	Proger, B. B.: 5
Church, J. J.: 4	Stanley, J. C.: *rev,* 6:766
Dungan, R. H.: 5	Taylor, R. G.: 5
Johnson, H. S.: 2	Tidey, W. J.: 5
Mann, L.: 5	Turnbull, W. W.: *rev,* 6:766
Morse, J. L.: 6–7	Willard, L. A.: 3

[1064]

★Academic-Technical Aptitude Tests. "Coloured pupils" in standards 6–8; 1970; ATA; the coordination and writing speed tests are taken from the *N.B. Aptitude Tests (Junior);* 10 scores: verbal reasoning, nonverbal reasoning, computations, spatial perception (2-D), mechanical reasoning, language comprehension, spatial perception (3-D), comparison, coordination, writing speed; all test materials are in both English and Afrikaans except the Technical Report which is in Afrikaans; K. Owen (7 tests and manual) and C. P. Celliers (language comprehension test); Human Sciences Research Council [South Africa]. *

[1065]

★Aptitude Test for Junior Secondary Pupils. Bantus in Form I; 1970–72; AJB; formerly called *Aptitude Test for Junior Secondary Bantu Pupils in Form I;* 6–11 scores: core battery (English, spatial perception, nonverbal reasoning, mathematics, Afrikaans, verbal reasoning), supplementary battery (comparison, numerical, mechanical insight, eye-hand coordination, writing speed); some subtests in both English and Afrikaans; test by J. D. van Staden, J. P. du Toit, F. W. Gericke, R. R. C. Horne, and D. P. Lombard; manual by G. J. Ligthelm; Human Sciences Research Council [South Africa]. *

[1066]

Aptitude Tests for Occupations. Grades 9–13 and adults; 1951; 6 tests; Wesley S. Roeder and Herbert B. Graham; CTB/McGraw-Hill. *

a) PERSONAL-SOCIAL APTITUDE.
b) MECHANICAL APTITUDE.
c) GENERAL SALES APTITUDE.
d) CLERICAL ROUTINE APTITUDE.
e) COMPUTATIONAL APTITUDE.
f) SCIENTIFIC APTITUDE.

For additional information and a review by Lloyd G. Humphreys, see 5:891; for a review by Clifford P. Froehlich and an excerpted review by Laurance F. Shaffer, see 4:710.

REFERENCES THROUGH 1971
1. CURETON, EDWARD E. "Service Tests of Multiple Aptitudes." *Proc Inv Conf Testing Probl* 1955:22–39 '56. * (PA 31:3017)
2. DURFLINGER, GLENN W. "Personality Correlates of Success in Student-Teaching." *Ed & Psychol Meas* 23:383–90 su '63. * (PA 38:1427)
3. PRICE, THOMAS HUGH. *Psychological Case Studies of Successful Workers in the Field of Retailing.* Doctor's thesis, University of North Carolina (Chapel Hill, N.C.), 1967. (DA 28:4790B)

CUMULATIVE NAME INDEX

Cureton, E. E.: 1	Humphreys, L. G.: *rev,* 5:891
Durflinger, G. W.: 2	Price, T. H.: 3
Froehlich, C. P.: *rev,* 4:710	Shaffer, L. F.: *exc,* 4:710

[1067]

★Armed Services Vocational Aptitude Battery. High school (some seniors must be included); 1967–73; ASVAB; administered free of charge at participating high schools by Department of Defense personnel; for use in counseling and to stimulate "student interest in service job and training opportunities"; a battery of 9 tests "selected to represent 'common' content among the military service classification batteries"; 9 scores: coding speed, word knowledge, arithmetic reasoning, tool knowledge, space perception, mechanical comprehension, shop information, automotive information, electronics information plus 5 aptitude composites: general-technical, clerical, electronics, general mechanics, motor mechanics; Armed Forces Vocational Testing Group. *

REFERENCES THROUGH 1971
1. BAYROFF, A. G., AND FUCHS, EDMUND F. "The Armed Services Vocational Aptitude Battery." Abstract. *Proc 76th Ann Conv Am Psychol Assn* 3:635–6 '68. * (PA 43:125, title only)

CUMULATIVE NAME INDEX
Bayroff, A. G.: 1   Fuchs, E. F.: 1

[1068]

Detroit General Aptitudes Examination. Grades 6–12; 1938–54; assembled from *Detroit Mechanical Aptitudes Examination, Detroit Clerical Aptitudes Examination, Detroit General Intelligence Examination,* and *Detroit Advanced Intelligence Test;* 20 scores: intelligence, mechanical, clerical, total, and 16 subtest scores; 1954 manual identical with manual copyrighted

1941 except for minor changes; Harry J. Baker, Alex C. Crockett, and Paul H. Voelker; Bobbs-Merrill Co., Inc. *

For additional information, see 5:603; for reviews by G. Frederic Kuder, Irving Lorge, and John Gray Peatman, see 2:1654.

REFERENCES THROUGH 1971

1. WOODY, CLIFFORD. *Aptitudes, Achievements and Interests of High School Pupils.* University of Michigan, Bureau of Educational Reference and Research Bulletin No. 157. Ann Arbor, Mich.: School of Education, the University, 1945. Pp. vi, 159. *
2. ROSENZWEIG, SAUL; WITH THE COLLABORATION OF KATE LEVINE KOGAN. *Psychodiagnosis: An Introduction to Tests in the Clinical Practice of Psychodynamics,* pp. 76–80. New York: Grune & Stratton, Inc., 1949. Pp. xii, 380. * (*PA* 23:3761)
3. CHRISTEL, ROBERT I. *A Correlation Study of General Mental Ability, Mechanical Aptitude and Clerical Aptitude as Measured by the Detroit General Aptitudes Examination, Form A, With Teachers' Marks in Sophomore Exploratory and Junior-Senior Industrial Arts Subjects in the Springfield, Ohio, Senior High School.* Master's thesis, Miami University (Oxford, Ohio), 1958.

CUMULATIVE NAME INDEX

Christel, R. I.: 3
Kogan, K. L.: 2
Kuder, G. F.: *rev, 2:1654*
Lorge, I.: *rev, 2:1654*
Peatman, J. G.: *rev, 2:1654*
Rosenzweig, S.: 2
Woody, C.: 1

[1069]

*Differential Aptitude Tests. Grades 8–12 and adults; 1947–73; DAT; 3 editions; George K. Bennett, Harold G. Seashore, and Alexander G. Wesman; Psychological Corporation. *

a) FORMS A AND B. 1947–59; 9 scores: verbal reasoning, numerical ability, total (scholastic aptitude), abstract reasoning, clerical speed and accuracy, mechanical reasoning, space relations, language usage (spelling, sentences). *Out of print.*

b) FORMS L AND M. 1947–67; 2 booklets.

1) *Booklet 1.* 5 scores: verbal reasoning, numerical ability, total, abstract reasoning, clerical speed and accuracy; verbal reasoning and numerical ability also available in a single booklet; 1961 tests identical with Forms A and B copyrighted 1947 except for number of response options in verbal reasoning test.

2) *Booklet 2.* 4 scores: mechanical reasoning, space relations, spelling, grammar; 1962 mechanical reasoning and spelling tests identical with Forms A and B copyrighted 1947.

c) FORMS S AND T. 1947–73; 1972 tests in abstract reasoning identical with tests copyrighted 1947 and 1961 except for sequence of items; 1972 test in space relations identical with earlier forms copyrighted 1962 except for sequence of items; part 1 of the clerical speed and accuracy test identical in all forms (A, B, L, M, S, and T), part 2 identical in all forms except Form T and a different item sequence in Forms B and M; 9 scores: verbal reasoning, numerical ability, total, abstract reasoning, clerical speed and accuracy, mechanical reasoning, space relations, spelling, language usage; subtests available as separates.

For additional information, a review by M. Y. Qureshi, and an excerpted review by Jack C. Merwin of *b,* see 7:673 (139 references); for reviews by J. A. Keats and Richard E. Schutz, see 6:767 (52 references); for reviews by John B. Carroll and Norman Frederiksen of *a,* see 5:605 (49 references); for reviews by Harold Bechtoldt, Ralph F. Berdie, and Lloyd G. Humphreys, see 4:711 (27 references); for an excerpted review see 3:620.

REFERENCES THROUGH 1971

1–28. See 4:711.
29–77. See 5:605.
78–129. See 6:767.
130–268. See 7:673.
269. BARRATT, ERNEST S. "The Space-Visualization Factors

Related to Temperament Traits." *J Psychol* 39:279–87 Ap '55. * (*PA* 29:8424)
270. MENDICINO, LORENZO. *The Effect of Certain Educational Experiences Upon Achievement in Mechanical Reasoning and Space Perception.* Doctor's thesis, University of Pittsburgh (Pittsburgh, Pa.), 1955. (*DA* 16:65)
271. BAIR, JOHN T.; LOCKMAN, ROBERT F.; AND MARTOCCIA, CHARLES T. "Validity and Factor Analyses of Naval Air Training Predictor and Criterion Measures." *J Appl Psychol* 40: 213–9 Ag '56. * (*PA* 31:6701)
272. DRESSEL, PAUL L. "Working With Youth of Below Average Ability." *Personnel & Guid J* 34:348–50 F '56. * (*PA* 31:3745)
273. FROEHLICH, CLIFFORD P. "Must Counseling Be Individual?" *Ed & Psychol Meas* 18:681–9 w '58. * (*PA* 34:2079)
274. WALCH, SHELBY LEWIS. *Self-Estimates of Aptitudes and Preferences and Test-Score Defensiveness.* Doctor's thesis, University of Texas (Austin, Tex.), 1959. (*DA* 20:210)
275. FRANKEL, EDWARD. "A Comparative Study of Achieving and Underachieving High School Boys of High Intellectual Ability." *J Ed Res* 53:172–80 Ja '60. * (*PA* 35:7115)
276. PAUK, WALTER J. "Are Present Reading Tests Valid for Both Girls and Boys?" *J Ed Res* 53:279–80 Mr '60. *
277. ROBERTSON, MALCOLM H. "Test Scores and Self-Estimates of Two Curricula Groups." *Personnel & Guid J* 38:746–50 My '60. * (*PA* 35:2767)
278. WESMAN, ALEXANDER G. "Some Effects of Speed in Test Use." *Ed & Psychol Meas* 20:267–74 su '60. * (*PA* 35:6396)
279. AIKEN, LEWIS R., JR., AND DREGER, RALPH MASON. "The Effect of Attitudes on Performance in Mathematics." *J Ed Psychol* 52:19–24 F '61. * (*PA* 36:2KD19A)
280. McGUIRE, CARSON. "Sex Role and Community Variability in Test Performances." *J Ed Psychol* 52:61–73 Ap '61. * (*PA* 38:3207)
281. SEASHORE, HAROLD G. "Women Are More Predictable Than Men." *J Counsel Psychol* 9:261–70 f '62. * (*PA* 38:3194)
282. D'AOUST, THÉRÈSE. *Predictive Validity of Four Psychometric Tests in a Selected School of Nursing.* Master's thesis, Catholic University of America (Washington, D.C.), 1963.
283. HUGHES, HERBERT H., AND NELSON, WILLARD H. "The Effect of Reward on Expectancy and Test Performance of Low and High Achievers With High Ability Scores." *J Res Services* 3:22–9 D '63. *
284. RUTT, ROBERT JAMES. *A Study in Predicting Student Success in Plane Geometry Classes of a Minneapolis Senior High School.* Master's thesis, St. Cloud State College (St. Cloud, Minn.), 1963.
285. MOLOMO, RAYMOND R-S. *Two Spatial Factors in Two-Dimensional and Three-Dimensional Spatial Aptitude.* Master's thesis, University of Ottawa (Ottawa, Ont., Canada), 1964.
286. PETERSON, AUDREY J. *A Statistical Analysis of Selected Factors for Predicting Academic Success at Wheaton Community High School, Central.* Master's thesis, Northern Illinois University (DeKalb, Ill.), 1964.
287. SUMMERS, BARBARA L. *A Study of Predictive Devices for Placement in Ninth-Grade English and Algebra Classes for Wheaton Community High School-Central.* Master's thesis, Northern Illinois University (DeKalb, Ill.), 1964.
288. TRITES, DAVID K., AND COBB, BART B. "Problems in Air Traffic Management: 4, Comparison of Pre-Employment, Job Related Experience With Aptitude Tests as Predictors of Training and Job Performance of Air Traffic Control Specialists." *Aerospace Med* 35:428–36 My '64. *
289. CHAUDHRY, GHULAM MOHAMMED, AND KAYANI, MOHAMMED RASHID. "A Comparative Study of the DAT Verbal Reasoning, ACE Psychological Examination and Cooperative English Comprehension Tests as Predictors of Academic Success in the Institute of Education and Research, University of the Panjab." *B Ed & Res* (Pakistan) 4(2):1–21 '65. *
290. KOSAI, JOSEPH HIDEO. *A Proposed Basis for Predicting the Grades in Elementary Algebra of Tenth Grade Students at Stadium High School.* Master's thesis, University of Puget Sound (Tacoma, Wash.), 1965.
291. PETERSON, DONALD FREDERICK. *A Predictive Study of Success in First Year Bookkeeping.* Master's thesis, San Diego State College (San Diego, Calif.), 1965.
292. PETIT, JEAN L. *Selecting Variables Found in the Cumulative Folder of Belvidere High School Students Predicting Academic Success.* Master's thesis, Northern Illinois University (DeKalb, Ill.), 1965.
293. STILLWELL, DOUGLAS JAMES. *A Study of Some Relationships Between the Differential Aptitude Test Scores and Course Marks of Students in the Elk River Public Schools.* Master's thesis, St. Cloud State College (St. Cloud, Minn.), 1965.
294. TAYLOR, JEAN. *An Examination of the Relationships Between Test Scores and Grades in Eleventh Grade English Groups at Hillcrest High School.* Master's thesis, University of Utah (Salt Lake City, Utah), 1965.
295. WHITTEMORE, ROBERT G.; ECHEVERRIA, BEN P.; AND GRIFFIN, JOHN V. "Can We Use Existing Tests for Adult Basic Education?" *Adult Ed* 17:19–29 au '66. *
296. BUIKEMA, ROGER J. *The Development of a Multiple Regression Equation for Predicting Ninth Grade English Grades*

at Morrison Community High School. Master's thesis, Northern Illinois University (DeKalb, Ill.), 1967.

297. COXFORD, LOLA MAE. *A Predictive Study of Success in Shorthand at Mayfair High School.* Master's thesis, California State College (Long Beach, Calif.), 1967.

298. HUDSON, DONALD K. *Relationship of Student Aptitude and Extra-Class Participation to Student Success.* Master's thesis, Illinois State University (Normal, Ill.), 1967.

299. HUFF, BETTY. *The Predictive Value of Standardized Testing in Relation to Mathematical Achievement at Virginia High School.* Master's thesis, East Tennessee State University (Johnson City, Tenn.), 1967.

300. KARPOFF, JOHN T. *Aptitudes for Achievement in the Vocational Programs of One Composite High School in Alberta.* Master's thesis, University of Alberta (Edmonton, Alta., Canada), 1967.

301. MARTIN, BERNARD L. "Spatial Visualization Abilities of Prospective Mathematics Teachers." *J Res Sci Teach* 5(1):11–9 '67. *

302. WOOD, SUSAN. *An Evaluation of Published English Tests,* pp. 23–5. Madison, Wis.: Wisconsin Department of Public Instruction, 1967. Pp. 91. *

303. BOCK, R. DARRELL, AND VANDENBERG, STEVEN G. Chap. 14, "Components of Heritable Variation in Mental Test Scores," pp. 233–60. In *Progress in Human Behavior Genetics.* Edited by Steven G. Vandenberg. Baltimore, Md.: Johns Hopkins Press, 1968. Pp. xi, 356. *

304. CHANCELLOR, GEORGE A., JR. *Standardized Tests as Predictors of Academic Success in Either One or Two Forms of High School Biology.* Master's thesis, Stetson University (DeLand, Fla.), 1968.

305. BEVERIDGE, MARTIN DOYLE. *The Correlation of Selected Characteristics to Achievement in Orthographic Projection.* Master's thesis, California State College (California, Pa.), 1969.

306. LUCAS, ROBERT J., AND SHROCK, JOHN G. "Identifying Socially Sensitive Applicants for Dental Schools." *J Pub Health Dent* 29(2):92–5 sp '69. *

307. SHADEED, CHARLES T. *A Study of Available Criteria for Predicting Success in Algebra.* Master's thesis, Western Connecticut State College (Danbury, Conn.), 1969.

308. DE MARTINO, ALICE J. *The Relations Among Adaptive Regression, Independence, and Creativity in Adolescents.* Doctor's thesis, New York University (New York, N.Y.), 1970. (*DAI* 32:539B)

309. FLYE, LINDA M. *Knowledge of Aptitude as a Source of Change in Inventoried Interests.* Master's thesis, East Tennessee State University (Johnson City, Tenn.), 1970.

310. KALOGER, JAMES HERACLES. *Characteristics of Grosse Pointe High School Students in Advanced Placement Programs.* Doctor's thesis, University of Michigan (Ann Arbor, Mich.), 1970. (*DAI* 31:6440A)

311. SIMPSON, D. "The Aptitudes of Computer Programmers." *Computer B* (England) 14(2):37–40 F '70. *

312. STEVENS, NORMA YOUNG. *A Longitudinal Study of Biographical, Intelligence, and Personality Variables in Predicting Achievement of Mexican Theological Students.* Doctor's thesis, University of Georgia (Athens, Ga.), 1970. (*DAI* 31:4564A)

313. ZUPKA, ANSELM J. *The Development of Expectancy Tables to Estimate the Probable Success of Freshmen Students at Benedictine High School Utilizing Selected Parts of the Differential Aptitude Tests and Grades in Specified Subject Areas.* Master's thesis, John Carroll University (Cleveland, Ohio), 1970.

314. ADCOCK, C. J., AND WEBBERLEY, M. "Primary Mental Abilities." *J General Psychol* 84(2):229–43 Ap '71. * (*PA* 46:4979)

315. ANDERSON, RUTH. *A Study of the Predictability of High School Grades and the Differential Aptitude Tests for Success in Vocational Programs in Health Careers.* Master's thesis, University of Wisconsin (LaCrosse, Wis.), 1971.

316. ARMBRUST, KENNETH EUGENE. *A Comparative Validity Study of the General Aptitude Test Battery, Differential Aptitude Tests, and the Iowa Tests of Educational Development in Idaho Area Vocational Schools.* Doctor's thesis, University of Idaho (Moscow, Idaho), 1971. (*DAI* 32:3613B)

317. BRADLEY, RICHARD W., AND SANBORN, MARSHALL P. "Using Tests to Predict Four-Year Patterns of College Grade Point." *J Col Stud Personnel* 12(2):138–42 Mr '71. * (*PA* 46:5699)

318. FRYETT, HOWARD LESLIE. *An Interpretation of Student Self Concept and Analysis of Relationships Between the Self and Selected Characteristics of Business Education Students Enrolled in Minnesota Area Vocational-Technical Schools.* Doctor's thesis, University of North Dakota (Grand Forks, N.D.), 1971. (*DAI* 33:76A)

319. HALL, LUCIEN T., JR. "The Prediction of Success in Each of Six Four-Year Selections of Secondary Mathematics Courses." *Sch Sci & Math* 71(8):693–6 N '71. *

320. HELWIG, CARL, AND PENDERGRAPH, ANITA. "Data Processing—Success or Failure?" *J Bus Ed* 47(3):99–100 D '71. *

321. HOOD, DUANE. *A Study of Selected Factors Related to Achievement in Applied and Abstract Mathematics for College*

Juniors and Seniors. Doctor's thesis, East Texas State University (Commerce, Tex.), 1971. (*DAI* 32:4985A)

322. KING, MICHAEL, AND KING, JOHANNA. "Some Correlates of University Performance in a Developing Country: The Case of Ethiopia." *J Cross-Cultural Psychol* 2(3):293–300 S '71. * (*PA* 47:7735)

323. LANSDELL, H. "A General Intellectual Factor Affected by Temporal Lobe Dysfunction." *J Clin Psychol* 27(2):182–4 Ap '71. * (*PA* 46:7303)

324. MEEKER, MARY, AND MEYERS, C. E. "Memory Factors and School Success of Average and Special Groups of Ninth-Grade Boys." *Genetic Psychol Monogr* 83(2):275–308 My '71. * (*PA* 46:5673)

325. MOORE, TELFORD IRA. *The Relationship Among Differentiated Cognitive Abilities, Field Dependency, Achievement, and Rated Classroom Behavior of Ninth Grade Junior High School Students.* Doctor's thesis, University of Southern California (Los Angeles, Calif.), 1971. (*DAI* 32:249A)

326. PETERSON, JOANNE E. *A Comparative Investigation of Student Scores on the Numerical Ability Section of the Differential Aptitude Test and the Same Students' First Semester Grades in Algebra at Keithley Junior High School.* Master's thesis, Pacific Lutheran University (Tacoma, Wash.), 1971.

327. SIMPSON, D. "An Analysis of the Aptitudes of HND Business Studies Students." *Voc Aspect Ed* (England) 23(56):127–36 N '71. *

328. SMITH, RICHARD LEE. *A Factor-Analytic Study of Critical Reading/Thinking, Influenceability, and Related Factors.* Doctor's thesis, University of Maine (Orono, Me.), 1971. (*DAI* 32:6229A)

329. SOUTHALL, BARBARA J. *A Comparative Investigation of the Relationship Between Algebra Grades and Differential Aptitude Test Subtests to Geometry Grades.* Master's thesis, University of Richmond (Richmond, Va.), 1971.

330. SUMMERS, GENE F.; BURKE, MARIANNE; SALTIEL, SUZANNE; AND CLARK, JOHN P. "Stability of the Structure of Work Orientations Among High School Students." *Multiv Behav Res* 6(1):35–50 Ja '71. * (*PA* 46:9686)

331. TAYLOR, ALTON L. "Regression Analysis of Antecedent Measures of Slow Sections in High School Biology." *Sci Ed* 55(3):395–402 Jl–S '71. *

332. TSAI, LOH SENG, AND HAINES, RICHARD B. "Tsai Number-Joining Test Scores Correlated With College Students' Performance on WAIS and DAT." *Percept & Motor Skills* 33(1):35–44 Ag '71. * (*PA* 47:3643)

CUMULATIVE NAME INDEX

[1070]

Differential Test Battery. Ages 11 to "top university level" (range for Test 1 extends downward to age 7); 1955–59; 12 tests in 7 booklets; J. R. Morrisby; distributed by Educational and Industrial Test Services [England]. *

a) TEST I, COMPOUND SERIES TEST. Ages 7 and over; "mental work power"; 1955.

b) GENERAL ABILITY TESTS. Ages 11 and over; 1955; 3 tests.

   1) *Test 2, General Ability Tests: Verbal.*

   2) *Test 3, General Ability Tests: Numerical.*

   3) *Test 4, General Ability Tests: Perceptual.*

c) TEST 5, SHAPES TEST. Ages 11 and over; 1955; spatial ability.

d) TEST 6, MECHANICAL ABILITY TEST. Ages 11 and over; 1955.

e) SPEED TESTS. Ages 11 and over; 1955–59; 6 tests in a single booklet.

   1) *Test 7 (Speed Test 1), Routine Number and Name Checking.*

   2) *Test 8 (Speed Test 2), Perseveration.*

   3) *Test 9 (Speed Test 3), Word Fluency.*

   4) *Test 10 (Speed Test 4), Ideational Fluency.*

   5) *Test 11 (Speed Test 5), Motor Speed.*

   6) *Test 12 (Speed Test 6), Motor Skill.*

For additional information, see 6:768; for reviews by E. A. Peel, Donald E. Super, and Philip E. Vernon, see 5:606.

REFERENCES THROUGH 1971

1. MORRISBY, J. R. "The Differential Test Battery: A Preliminary Notice." *B Nat Found Ed Res Engl & Wales* (England) (6):27–31 N '55. *
2. BEARD, RUTH M.; LEVY, P. M.; AND MADDOX, H. "Academic Performance at University: Test Performance, Motivation and Course of Training." *Ed R* (England) 16:163–74 Je '64. *
3. EL-SHARKAWY, M. K. L., AND LEE, D. M. "A Study of Some Contributions of the Morrisby Differential Test Battery to Vocational Selection." *Brit J Ed Psychol* 35:223–41 Je '65. * (*PA* 39:15227)
4. LEWIS, D. G. "Ability in Science at Ordinary Level of the General Certificate of Education." *Brit J Ed Psychol* 37:361–70 N '67. * (*PA* 42:6146)
5. SMITH, I. MACFARLANE. "The Use of Diagnostic Tests for Assessing the Abilities of Overseas Students Attending Insti-

tutions of Further Education, Part I." *Voc Aspect Ed* (England) 22(51):1–8 Mr '70. *

6. SMITH, I. MACFARLANE. "The Use of Diagnostic Tests for Assessing the Abilities of Overseas Students Attending Institutions of Further Education, Part II." *Voc Aspect Ed* (England) 23(54):39–48 Ap '71. *

[1071]

Employee Aptitude Survey. Ages 16 and over; 1952–63; EAS; 10 tests; G. Grimsley (*a–h*), F. L. Ruch (*a–g, i, j*), N. D. Warren (*a–g*), and J. S. Ford (*a, c, e–g, j*); Psychological Services, Inc. *

a) TEST 1, VERBAL COMPREHENSION. 1952–63.
b) TEST 2, NUMERICAL ABILITY. 1952–63.
c) TEST 3, VISUAL PURSUIT. 1956–63.
d) TEST 4, VISUAL SPEED AND ACCURACY. 1952–63.
e) TEST 5, SPACE VISUALIZATION. 1952–63.
f) TEST 6, NUMERICAL REASONING. 1952–63.
g) TEST 7, VERBAL REASONING. 1952–63.
h) TEST 8, WORD FLUENCY. 1953–63.
i) TEST 9, MANUAL SPEED AND ACCURACY. 1953–63.
j) TEST 10, SYMBOLIC REASONING. 1956–63.

For additional information, reviews by Paul F. Ross and Erwin K. Taylor, and an excerpted review by John O. Crites, see 6:769 (4 references); for reviews by Dorothy C. Adkins and S. Rains Wallace, see 5:607.

REFERENCES THROUGH 1971

1–4. See 6:769.
5. BARRATT, ERNEST S. "The Space-Visualization Factors Related to Temperament Traits." *J Psychol* 39:279–87 Ap '55. * (*PA* 29:8424)
6. FOY, GLENN ARTHUR. *A Study of the Relationship Between Certain Factor-Analyzed Ability Measures and Success in College Engineering.* Doctor's thesis, University of Southern California (Los Angeles, Calif.), 1959. (*DA* 20:368)
7. BROE, JOHN RICHARD. *Prediction of Success in Training Among Electronics Technicians.* Doctor's thesis, University of Southern California (Los Angeles, Calif.), 1962. (*DA* 23:2417)
8. GUION, ROBERT M. "Synthetic Validity in a Small Company: A Demonstration." *Personnel Psychol* 18:49–63 sp '65. * (*PA* 39:16490)
9. RUDE, H. NEIL, AND KING, DONALD C. "Aptitude Levels in a Depressed Area." *Personnel & Guid J* 43:785–9 Ap '65. * (*PA* 39:14918)
10. LUNNEBORG, CLIFFORD E., AND LUNNEBORG, PATRICIA W. "Uniqueness of Selected Employment Aptitude Tests to a General Academic Guidance Battery." *Ed & Psychol Meas* 27:953–60 w '67. * (*PA* 42:9425)
11. THUMIN, FRED J. "Ability Scores as Related to Age Among Male Job Applicants." *J Gerontol* 23:390–2 Jl '68. * (*PA* 43:7254)
12. CARLSON, ROBERT E.; DAWIS, RENE V.; AND WEISS, DAVID J. "The Effect of Satisfaction on the Relationship Between Abilities and Satisfactoriness." *Occup Psychol* (England) 43(1):39–46 '69. * (*PA* 44:17573)
13. DUBIN, JERRY A.; OSBURN, HOBART; AND WINICK, DARVIN M. "Speed and Practice: Effects on Negro and White Test Performances." *J Appl Psychol* 53:19–23 F '69. * (*PA* 43:7254)
14. DUBIN, JERRY ALAN. *Effects of Practice and Speed on Negro and White Mental Ability Test Performances.* Doctor's thesis, University of Houston (Houston, Tex.), 1969. (*DAI* 30:367B)
15. TENOPYR, MARY L. "The Comparative Validity of Selected Leadership Scales Relative to Success in Production Management." *Personnel Psychol* 22(1):77–85 sp '69. * (*PA* 43:14924)
16. WIGGINS, NANCY; HOFFMAN, PAUL J.; AND TABER, THOMAS. "Types of Judges and Cue Utilization in Judgments of Intelligence." *J Pers & Social Psychol* 12(1):52–9 My '69. * (*PA* 43:11266)
17. POUNDERS, CEDRIC J. "The Admissions Test for Graduate Study in Business: A Factor Analytic Study." *Ed & Psychol Meas* 30(2):469–73 su '70. * (*PA* 45:2955)
18. BETZ, ELLEN L. "An Investigation of Job Satisfaction as a Moderator Variable in Predicting Job Success." *J Voc Behav* 1(2):123–8 Ap '71. * (*PA* 47:11882)

[1072]

Flanagan Aptitude Classification Tests. Grades 9–12, 10–12 and adults; 1951–60; FACT; 2 editions; John C. Flanagan; Science Research Associates, Inc. *

a) SEPARATE BOOKLET 16-TEST EDITION. Grades 10–12 and adults; 1951–60; 16 tests.
1) *FACT 1A, Inspection.* 1953–56.
2) *FACT 2A and 2B, Coding.* 1953–56.
3) *FACT 3A and 3B, Memory.* 1953–56.
4) *FACT 4A, Precision.* 1953–56.
5) *FACT 5A, Assembly.* 1953–56.
6) *FACT 6A, Scales.* 1953–56.
7) *FACT 7A, Coordination.* 1953–56.
8) *FACT 8A, Judgment and Comprehension.* 1953–56.
9) *FACT 9A, Arithmetic.* 1953–56.
10) *FACT 10A, Patterns.* 1953–56.
11) *FACT 11A, Components.* 1953–56.
12) *FACT 12A, Tables.* 1953–56.
13) *FACT 13A and 13B, Mechanics.* 1953–56.
14) *FACT 14A. Expression.* 1953–56.
15) *FACT 15A, Reasoning.* 1957–60.
16) *FACT 16A, Ingenuity.* 1957–60.

b) 19-TEST EDITION. Grades 9–12; 1957–60; 19 tests (same as for *a* plus vocabulary, planning, alertness) in 2 booklets.

For additional information and an excerpted review by Harold D. Murphy (with John P. McQuary), see 7:675 (10 references); for reviews by Norman Frederiksen and William B. Michael, see 6:770 (7 references); for reviews by Harold P. Bechtoldt, Ralph F. Berdie, and John B. Carroll, see 5:608.

REFERENCES THROUGH 1971

1–7. See 6:770.
8–17. See 7:675.
18. LATHAM, ELLEN DIXON. *An Investigation of the Influence of Instructional Sets Upon the Test Performance, Expectancy Levels, and Post-Performance Estimates of Selected Students at Western Carolina University.* Doctor's thesis, University of North Carolina (Chapel Hill, N.C.), 1971. (*DAI* 32:2486A)

[1073]

General Aptitude Test Battery. Grades 9–12 and adults; 1946–73; GATB; for a nonreading adaptation, *Nonreading Aptitude Test Battery,* see 1086; developed by the United States Employment Service for use in its occupational counseling program and released for use by State Employment Services; orders for test materials must be cleared through a State Employment Service office; test booklets and manuals distributed by United States Government Printing Office. *

a) SCREENING DEVICE AND PRETESTING EXERCISES. 1966–73.

　　1) *GATB-NATB Screening Device*. 1966–73; test sheet title is *Wide-Range Scale;* to identify examinees who are deficient in reading and arithmetic skills and should be tested with *Nonreading Aptitude Test Battery.*

　　2) *USES Pretesting Orientation Exercises*. 1968; test-taking practice for disadvantaged persons.

b) GATB, B-I001, [EXPENDABLE BOOKLET EDITION]. *Out of print.*

c) GATB, B-1002, [SEPARATE ANSWER SHEET EDITION]. 1952–70; 9 scores: intelligence, verbal, numerical, spatial, form perception, clerical perception, motor coordination, finger dexterity, manual dexterity; 12 tests: 8 paper and pencil tests plus 4 performance tests.

　　1) *Book 1*. 1965 test identical with test published 1952; 4 tests: name comparison, computation, three-dimensional space, vocabulary.

　　2) *Book 2*. 3 tests: tool matching, arithmetic reasoning, form matching.

　　3) *Part 8* [*Mark Making*]. 1965.

　　4) *Pegboard*. 2 tests: place, turn; K & W Products Co., Inc., Specialty Case Manufacturing Co., and Warwick Products Co.

　　5) *Finger Dexterity Board*. 2 tests: assemble, disassemble; K & W Products Co., Inc., Specialty Case Manufacturing Co., and Warwick Products Co.

For additional information and a review by David J. Weiss, see 7:676 (138 references); for reviews by Harold P. Bechtoldt and John B. Carroll of earlier forms, see 6:771 (55 references); for reviews by Andrew L. Comrey, Clifford P. Froehlich, and Lloyd G. Humphreys, see 5:609 (176 references); for reviews by Milton L. Blum, Edward B. Greene, and Howard R. Taylor, see 4:714 (33 references).

REFERENCES THROUGH 1971

1–33. See 4:714.
34–209. See 5:609.
210–264. See 6:771.
265–402. See 7:676.
403. HERON, ALASTAIR. "The Objective Assessment of Personality Among Factory Workers." *J Social Psychol* 39:161–85 My '54. * (*PA* 29:4728)
404. TRATTNER, MARVIN H.; FINE, SIDNEY A.; AND KUBIS, JOSEPH F. "A Comparison of Worker Requirement Ratings Made by Reading Job Descriptions and by Direct Job Observation." *Personnel Psychol* 8:183–94 su '55. * (*PA* 30:5309)
405. AYRES, A. JEAN. "A Study of the Manual Dexterity and Workshop Wages of Thirty-Nine Cerebral Palsied Trainees." *Am J Phys Med* 36:6–10 F '57. * (*PA* 32:4463)
406. CAIRD, W. K.; SLOANE, BRUCE; AND INGLIS, JAMES. "The Effects of Nialamide and Ethyl Alcohol on Some Personality, Cognitive and Psychomotor Variables in Normal Volunteers." *J Neuropsychiatry* 2:31–4 S–O '61. *
407. INGLIS, J.; CAIRD, W. K.; AND SLOANE, R. B. "An Objective Assessment of the Effects of Nialamide on Depressed Patients." *Can Med Assn J* 84:1059–63 My 13 '61. *
408. WILLIAMS, RUTH. "A Preliminary Report on the Validity of Aptitude Tests as a Predictor of Success in Medical Technology." *Am J Med Technol* 29:157–62 My–Je '63. *
409. DVORAK, BEATRICE J. "Changing Emphasis in Occupational Test Development." *Employ Service R* 2:45–7 Ag '65. *
410. DVORAK, BEATRICE J. "Program Research on Effectiveness of USES Tests." *Employ Service R* 2:62–4 O '65. *
411. PASKEWITZ, DORIS L. *A Prediction Study of Senior High Course Grades and Test Scores*. Master's thesis, Stetson University (DeLand, Fla.), 1965.
412. ROZYNKO, VITALI, AND WENK, ERNEST. "Intellectual Performance of Three Delinquent Groups of Different Ethnic Origin." Abstract. *J Consult Psychol* 29:282 Je '65. * (*PA* 39:12810)
413. SEILER, JOSEPH. "Abilities for ADP Occupations: Assessment of High and Low Education Job Applicants." *Proc Ann Computer Personnel Res Conf* 3:52–9 '65. *
414. WILLIAMS, RUTH. "Aptitude Tests for Med. Tech. Recruits?" *Hosp Progr* 46:30+ O '65. *
415. WHITTEMORE, ROBERT G.; ECHEVERRIA, BEN P.; AND GRIFFIN, JOHN V. "Can We Use Existing Tests for Adult Basic Education?" *Adult Ed* 17:19–29 au '66. *
416. BENDER, LLOYD D.; HOBBS, DARYL J.; AND GOLDEN, JAMES F. "Congruence Between Aspirations and Capabilities of Youth in a Low-Income Rural Area." *Rural Sociol* 32:278–89 S '67. * (*PA* 41:16572)
417. MONTGOMERY, TRAVIS. "Use of the GATB in Predicting Success on the High School Equivalency Tests." *J Employ Counsel* 4:117–21 D '67. *
418. SOUTHWICK, RICHARD NEPHI. *Relationship of Intelligence to Vocational Adjustment*. Master's thesis, University of Utah (Salt Lake City, Utah), 1967.
419. WILLIAMS, RUTH; KONECNY, PATRICIA WARNER; AND CHAMPION, JOAN. "Validity and Predictive Studies on the General Aptitude Test Battery." *Am J Med Technol* 33:142–7 Mr–Ap '67. *
420. BAIRD, ROBERT G. *A Comparison of Success Predictions With Performance of Disadvantaged Apprenticeship Candidates*. Master's thesis, Seattle University (Seattle, Wash.), 1969.
421. BOYD, HELEN L. *Freedom to Vary: Environment and Perceptual Aptitude; the General Aptitude Test Battery*. Master's thesis, East Texas State University (Commerce, Tex.), 1970.
422. KASL, STANISLAV V.; BROOKS, GEORGE W.; AND RODGERS, WILLARD L. "Serum Uric Acid and Cholesterol in Achievement Behavior and Motivation: 1, The Relationship to Ability, Grades, Test Performance, and Motivation." *J Am Med Assn* 213(7):1158–64 Ag 17 '70. * (*PA* 45:9556)
423. MYERS, RICHARD WAYNE. *Effects of Motivational Incentives on GATB "F" and "M" Subtest Performance With Hospitalized Neuropsychiatric Patients*. Doctor's thesis, Iowa State University (Ames, Iowa), 1970. (*DAI* 31:4470A)
424. NOLEN, DONOVAN R. *Validation of the GATB Tests for Predicting LPN State Board Examination Success*. Master's thesis, University of Tennessee (Knoxville, Tenn.), 1970.
425. SUBBERT, DWIGHT C. *Predicting School Success Through the Use of GATB Scores and Core Area Grades*. Master's thesis, Drake University (Des Moines, Iowa), 1970.
426. TURNER, JEANINE F. *A Comparison of the General Aptitude Test Battery Scores of Disadvantaged and Non-Disadvantaged Individuals*. Master's thesis, Gonzaga University (Spokane, Wash.), 1970.
427. ARMSTRONG, KENNETH EUGENE. *A Comparative Validity Study of the General Aptitude Test Battery, Differential Aptitude Tests, and the Iowa Tests of Educational Development in Idaho Area Vocational Schools*. Doctor's thesis, University of Idaho (Moscow, Idaho), 1971. (*DAI* 32:3613B)
428. BEARD, R. B., AND BLACKBURN, H. L. "Factors Affecting General Aptitude Test Battery Scores Among Schizophrenic Patients." *Newsl Res Psychol* 13(3):3–4 Ag '71. *
429. BEMIS, STEPHEN E. "Use of Aptitude Scores as Predictors of Success in Occupational Training Under the MDTA." *J Employ Counsel* 8(1):11–8 Mr '71. * (*PA* 47:11868)
430. CASSEL, RUSSELL N., AND REIER, GEROLD W. "Comparative Analysis of Concurrent and Predictive Validity for the GATB Clerical Aptitude Test Battery." *J Psychol* 79(1):135–40 S '71. * (*PA* 47:5603)
431. FOZARD, JAMES L., AND NUTTALL, RONALD L. "General Aptitude Test Battery Scores for Men Differing in Age and Socioeconomic Status." *J Appl Psychol* 55(4):372–9 Ag '71. * (*PA* 47:3835)
432. GOLDMAN, ROBERT CHARLIE. *The General Aptitude Test Battery as a Predictor of Student Success in Seven Area Vocational-Technical Schools in Arkansas*. Doctor's thesis, University of Mississippi (University, Miss.), 1971. (*DAI* 32:3686A)
433. GRINA, ALONDA A. *Effectiveness of the GATB in Predicting Training Success of Practical Nurse Students When the Confidence Band Principle Is Employed*. Master's thesis, Duquesne University (Pittsburgh, Pa.), 1971.
434. HENDEL, DARWIN D. "Test Format and Administration Variables as Related to the Performance of Mentally Retarded Adults on Multifactor Tests of Vocational Abilities." Abstract. *Proc 79th Ann Conv Am Psychol Assn* 6(2):615–6 '71. * (*PA* 46:5374)
435. KAPES, JEROME THEODORE. *The Relationship Between Selected Characteristics of Ninth Grade Boys and Curriculum Selection and Success in Tenth Grade*. Doctor's thesis, Pennsylvania State University (University Park, Pa.), 1971. (*DAI* 32:6131A)
436. MARTIN, GEORGE E. *The General Aptitude Test Battery in Enrolling Vocational Students at Haskell Institute*. Master's thesis, Kansas State Teachers College (Emporia, Kan.), 1971.
437. MAZUR, JAMES MATTHEW. *A Study of Predictive Validity of Standardized Tests Used for Placement of Vocational Students at Rockingham Community College*. Master's thesis, North Carolina State University (Raleigh, N.C.), 1971.
438. MILLER, DELBERT G. *A Comparative Study of the Rorschach F+ Per Cent to the General Aptitude Test Battery Subtests S, Spatial Aptitude and P, Form Perception*. Master's thesis, University of Idaho (Moscow, Idaho), 1971.
439. NUTTALL, RONALD L., AND FOZARD, JAMES L. "A Reexamination of the Structure of the General Aptitude Test Battery Aptitudes." *Indus Gerontol* 8:1–18 w '71. * (*PA* 46:11781)
440. NUTTALL, RONALD L.; FOZARD, JAMES L.; ROSE, CHARLES L.; AND BURNEY, SPENCER W. "Ages of Man: Ability Age,

Personality Age, and Biochemical Age." Abstract. *Proc 79th Ann Conv Am Psychol Assn* 6(2):605–6 '71. * (*PA* 46:4729)

441. PRIMMER, RICHARD D., AND TIPTON, ROBERT M. "Effects on Test Performance of Test Apparatus Boards Made of Different Material." *Percept & Motor Skills* 32(3):916–8 Je '71. * (*PA* 47:39)

442. ROSENAU, CHARLES B., AND WILLIAMS, JOHN D. "A Comparison of the Lorge-Thorndike Intelligence Test Total IQ and the General Aptitude Test Battery Aptitude G." *Col Ed Rec Univ N Dak* 56(9):167–70 Je '71. *

443. WANGER, RUTH SCHWARTZ. *The Relationship of Selected Variables to the Performance and Persistence of Career-Oriented Community College Students.* Doctor's thesis, George Washington University (Washington, D.C.), 1971. (*DAI* 32:3044A)

444. WEBER, THOMAS R. "An Evaluation of the Effectiveness of SATB Norms in MDTA Selection." *J Employ Counsel* 8(1):2–10 Mr '71. * (*PA* 47:11878)

445. WENK, ERNEST A.; ROZYNKO, VITALI V.; SARBIN, THEODORE R.; AND ROBISON, JAMES O. "The Effect of Incentives Upon Aptitude Scores of White and Negro Inmates." *J Res Crime & Del* 8(1):53–64 Ja '71. *

446. WILHIDE, EARLE R. *An Investigation of the Usefulness of the GATB for Beginning Tenth Grade Vocational Students.* Master's thesis, Western Maryland College (Westminster, Md.), 971.

447. ZIEGLER, ELWOOD. "An Evaluation of the Effect of Pre-Testing Orientation on GATB Scores." *J Employ Counsel* 8(1):31–6 Mr '71. * (*PA* 47:11867)

CUMULATIVE NAME INDEX

The Guilford-Zimmerman Aptitude Survey. Grades 9–16 and adults; 1947–56; GZAS; 7 parts; J. P.

Guilford-Zimmerman Aptitude Survey

Guilford and Wayne S. Zimmerman; Sheridan Psychological Services, Inc. *

a) PART 1, VERBAL COMPREHENSION.
b) PART 2, GENERAL REASONING.
c) PART 3, NUMERICAL OPERATIONS.
d) PART 4, PERCEPTUAL SPEED.
e) PART 5, SPATIAL ORIENTATION.
f) PART 6, SPATIAL VISUALIZATION.
g) PART 7, MECHANICAL KNOWLEDGE.

For additional information, see 6:772 (17 references); for reviews by Anne Anastasi, Harold Bechtoldt, John B. Carroll, and P. E. Vernon, see 4:715 (15 references).

REFERENCES THROUGH 1971

1–15. See 4:715.
16–32. See 6:772.
33. BARRATT, ERNEST S. "The Space-Visualization Factors Related to Temperament Traits." *J Psychol* 39:279–87 Ap '55. * (*PA* 29:8424)
34. BAIR, JOHN T.; LOCKMAN, ROBERT F.; AND MARTOCCIA, CHARLES T. "Validity and Factor Analyses of Naval Air Training Predictor and Criterion Measures." *J Appl Psychol* 40:213–9 Ag '56. * (*PA* 31:6701)
35. DREWES, HENRY WALTER. *An Experimental Study of the Relationship Between Electroencephalographic Imagery Variables and Perceptual-Cognitive Processes.* Doctor's thesis, Cornell University (Ithaca, N.Y.), 1958. (*DA* 19:87)
36. FRANCESCO, E. "The General Orientations Profile (GOP)." *Psychol Rep* 5:561–9 S '59. * (*PA* 38:4264)
37. BALLANTYNE, ROBERT HUBBARD. *An Analysis of Criteria for Selecting Freshmen Students for an Honors Program at Washington State University.* Doctor's thesis, Washington State University (Pullman, Wash.), 1962. (*DA* 23:2439)
38. DE MILLE, RICHARD. "Intellect After Lobotomy in Schizophrenia: A Factor Analytic Study." *Psychol Monogr* 76(16):1–18 '62. * (*PA* 38:2784)
39. LOCKE, EDWIN A. "Some Correlates of Classroom and Out-of-Class Achievement in Gifted Science Students." *J Ed Psychol* 54:238–48 O '63. * (*PA* 38:4649)
40. PIMSLEUR, PAUL. "A Study of Foreign Language Learning Ability: Parts 1 and 2," pp. 57–72. In *Report of the Twelfth Annual Round Table Meeting on Linguistics and Language Studies.* Edited by Michael Zarechnak. Washington, D.C.: Georgetown University Press, 1963. Pp. 132. *
41. RONAN, W. W. "Evaluation of Skilled Trades Performance Predictors." *Ed & Psychol Meas* 24:601–8 f '64. * (*PA* 39:6074)
42. COLLIER, BOY N., AND NUGENT, FRANK A. "Characteristics of Self-referred, Staff-referred, and Non-Counseled College Students." *J Counsel Psychol* 12:208–12 su '65. * (*PA* 39:12609, title only)
43. SCOTT, RUSSELL H.; PHIPPS, GRANT T.; AND MORGART, HELEN E. "Prediction of Success in a Dental Assisting Course." *J Dental Ed* 29:348–57 D '65. *
44. GETZELS, J. W., AND CSIKSZENTMIHALYI, M. Chap. 15, "The Study of Creativity in Future Artists: The Criterion Problem," pp. 349–68. In *Experience, Structure and Adaptability.* Edited by O. J. Harvey. New York: Springer Publishing Co., Inc., 1966. Pp. ix, 406. *
45. NEEDHAM, WALTER EVANS. *Intellectual, Personality and Biographical Characteristics of Southern Negro and White College Students.* Doctor's thesis, University of Utah (Salt Lake City, Utah), 1966. (*DA* 27:1609B)
46. SINAY, RUTH DORIS. *Creative Aptitude Patterns of College Honors Students.* Doctor's thesis, University of Southern California (Los Angeles, Calif.), 1967. (*DA* 28:5212B)
47. VERY, PHILIP S. "Differential Factor Structures in Mathematical Ability." *Genetic Psychol Monogr* 75:169–207 My '67. * (*PA* 41:10451)
48. LUNNEBORG, CLIFFORD E., AND LUNNEBORG, PATRICIA W. "Architecture School Performance Predicted From ASAT, Intellective, and Nonintellective Measures." *J Appl Psychol* 53(3):209–13 Je '69. * (*PA* 43:11928)
49. HAYNES, JACK R. "Factor-Analytic Study of Performance on the Bender-Gestalt." *J Consult & Clin Psychol* 34(3):345–7 Je '70. * (*PA* 44:13618)
50. HAYNES, JACK R., AND CARLEY, JOHN W. "Relation of Spatial Abilities and Selected Personality Traits." *Psychol Rep* 26(1):214 F '70. * (*PA* 45:4238)
51. VINCENT, WILLIAM J., AND ALLMANDINGER, MICHAEL F. "Relationships Among Selected Tests of Spatial Orientation Ability." *J Motor Behav* 3(3):259–64 S '71. * (*PA* 48:8830)

CUMULATIVE NAME INDEX

Allmandinger, M. F.: 51
Anastasi, A.: *rev*, 4:715
Bair, J. T.: 34
Ball, J. M.: 16, 24
Ballantyne, R. H.: 37
Barratt, E. S.: 33
Bechtoldt, H.: *rev*, 4:715
Berger, R. M.: 21
Blakemore, A.: 14
Borko, H.: 5

Buchanan, P. C.: 10
Carley, J. W.: 50
Carroll, J. B.: *rev*, 4:715
Christensen, P. R.: 21, 31
Collier, B. N.: 42
Cottle, W. C.: 23
Csikszentmihalyi, M.: 44
Cureton, E. E.: 19
de Mille, R.: 38
Drewes, H. W.: 35
Francesco, E.: 36
Frick, J. W.: 31
Getzels, J. W.: 44
Guilford, J. P.: 1–4, 11, 15, 20–1, 26, 31
Haney, R.: 27–8
Haynes, J. R.: 49–50
Hills, J. R.: 22
Jones, R. A.: 27–8
Locke, E. A.: 39
Lockman, R. F.: 34
Long, J. M.: 30
Lunneborg, C. E.: 48
Lunneborg, P. W.: 48
Martin, G. C.: 17

Martoccia, C. T.: 34
Merrifield, P. R.: 31
Michael, W. B.: 3, 6, 11, 15, 27–8
Miller, R. S.: 23
Morgart, H. S.: 43
Needham, W. E.: 45
Nugent, F. A.: 42
Phipps, G. T.: 43
Pimsleur, P.: 40
Razor, B. A. L.: 12
Ronan, W. W.: 41
Scott, R. H.: 43
Sinay, R. D.: 46
Stinson, P. J.: 25
Thompson, P. O.: 13
Tomkins, S. S.: 18
Vernon, P. E.: *rev*, 4:715
Very, P. S.: 47
Vincent, W. J.: 51
Wilson, J. E.: 29
Zimmerman, W. S.: 2, 4, 7, 11, 15
Zubin, J.: 18

[1075]

*High Level Battery: Test A/75. Adults with at least 12 years of education; 1960–72; formerly listed as *National Institute for Personnel Research High Level Battery;* 6 tests in a single booklet: mental alertness, arithmetical problems, reading comprehension (English, Afrikaans), vocabulary (English, Afrikaans); manual by D. P. M. Beukes; National Institute for Personnel Research [South Africa]. *

For additional information, see 6:778 (1 reference).

REFERENCES THROUGH 1971

1. See 6:778.

CUMULATIVE NAME INDEX

Schepers, J. M.: 1

[1076]

★International Primary Factors Test Battery. Grades 5 and over; 1973; also called IPF; 17 scores: vocabulary (subtest 1), word fluency (2), memory [words (3), numbers (4), designs (5)], mazes (6), reasoning [designs (7), letters and numbers (8)], hidden designs (9), space (10), mutilated pictures (11), mutilated words (12), spelling (13), addition (14), comparison [words (15), numbers (16)], total, plus 6 "potential" scores based upon overlapping combinations of subtests in 6 areas: mathematics (subtests 1, 7, 8, 13, 14), English (1, 2, 8, 12, 13), clerical (12–16), technological (1, 7–10), practical (6, 7, 9–11), fluid intelligence (3–7); W. O. Horn; International Tests, Inc. *

[1077]

*The Jastak Test of Potential Ability and Behavior Stability. Ages 11.5–14.5; 1958–67; the publisher's catalog lists this test under a new title, *Wide Range Intelligence and Personality Test* (for ages 9.5–54), but all currently available test materials bear the original title; test booklet title is *The Jastak Test;* 1967 test identical with test copyrighted 1959 except for the title page; 16 scores: 10 direct scores (vocabulary, number series, coding, picture reasoning, space series, verbal reasoning, social concept, arithmetic, space completion, spelling) and 6 derived scores (language, reality, motivation, psychomotor, intelligence, capacity); J. F. Jastak; Guidance Associates of Delaware, Inc. *

For additional information, reviews by Anne Anastasi and Benjamin Kleinmuntz, and excerpted reviews by Edward S. Bordin and Earl C. Butterfield, see 6:773 (3 references).

REFERENCES THROUGH 1971

1–3. See 6:773.

[1078]

Job-Tests Program. Adults; 1947–60; battery of aptitude tests, personality tests, and biographical forms used in various combinations in different jobs in business and industry; 3 series; Industrial Psychology, Inc. *

a) FACTORED APTITUDE SERIES. 1947–60; also called *Aptitude-Intelligence Tests*; 15 tests; Joseph E. King (1–2, 4–15) and H. B. Osborn, Jr. (3).

1) *Office Terms.* 1947–60.
2) *Sales Terms.* 1948–60.
3) *Factory Terms.* 1957–60.
4) *Tools.* 1948–60.
5) *Numbers.* 1947–60.
6) *Perception.* 1948–60.
7) *Judgment.* 1947–60.
8) *Precision.* 1947–60.
9) *Fluency.* 1947–60; 2 scores: words ending in tion and jobs, or words beginning with pre and equipment.
10) *Memory.* 1948–60.
11) *Parts.* 1949–60.
12) *Blocks.* 1948–60; adapted from *Army General Classification Test.*
13) *Dimension.* 1947–60.
14) *Dexterity.* 1949–60; 3 scores: maze, checks, dots.
15) *Motor.* 1948–60.

b) EMPLOYEE ATTITUDE SERIES. 1954–60; 3 tests; R. B. Cattell, J. E. King (1–2), and A. K. Schuettler (1–2).

1) *CPF.* 1954; also published by Institute for Personality and Ability Testing as Form A of *IPAT Contact Personality Factor Test.*
2) *NPF.* 1954; also published by Institute for Personality and Ability Testing as *IPAT Neurotic Personality Factor Test* with 1955 copyright.
3) *16 PF.* 1956–60; special printing with new item format, labeled Industrial Edition A, of *Sixteen Personality Factor Questionnaire,* 1956 edition of Form C.

c) APPLICATION-INTERVIEW SERIES. 1948–60; questions in 8 areas: job stability, job experience, education, financial maturity, health-physical condition, family, domestic, outside activities; 5 biography booklets; Joseph E. King.

1) *Biography-Clerical.*
2) *Biography-Mechanical.*
3) *Biography-Sales.*
4) *Biography-Technical.*
5) *Biography-Supervisor.*

For additional information and reviews by William H. Helme and Stanley I. Rubin, see 6:774; for a review by Harold P. Bechtoldt of the *Factored Aptitude Series,* see 5:602; for a review by D. Welty Lefever and an excerpted review by Laurance F. Shaffer of an earlier edition of this series, see 4:712 (1 reference). For reviews of the personality tests, see 6:174 (1 review), 5:71 (2 reviews), 5:74 (2 reviews), 5:112 (1 review), and 4:87 (3 reviews).

REFERENCES THROUGH 1971

1. See 4:712.
2. KNIEVEL, WILLIAM R. "A Vocational Aptitude Test Battery for the Deaf." *Am Ann Deaf* 99:314–9 My '54. * (*PA* 29:4595)
3. ASH, PHILIP. "Claimed and Reported Use of an Industrial Aptitude Test Battery." Abstract. *Am Psychologist* 10:473 Ag '55. *
4. CURETON, EDWARD E. "Service Tests of Multiple Aptitudes." *Proc Inv Conf Testing Probl* 1955:22–39 '56. * (*PA* 31:3017)
5. KIRCHNER, WAYNE K.; LAW, MARY L.; AND DUNNETTE, MARVIN D. "Validity Information Exchange, No. 9-46; D.O.T.

Code 1-86.10, Salesman (Machinery, Equipment, & Supplies)." *Personnel Psychol* 9:525 w '56. *
6. KING, JOSEPH E. "Factored Aptitude Series of Business and Industrial Tests." Comments by Donald E. Super. *Personnel & Guid J* 35:351–60 F '57. * (*PA* 32:998)
7. SHORE, RICHARD P. "Validity Information Exchange, No. 11-22: D.O.T. Code 1-02.01, Bookkeeping-Machine Operator (Banking)." *Personnel Psychol* 11:435–6 au '58. *
8. SHORE, RICHARD P. "Validity Information Exchange, No. 11-23: D.O.T. Code 1-06.02, Teller." *Personnel Psychol* 11:437 au '58. *
9. SHORE, RICHARD P. "Validity Information Exchange, No. 11-24: D.O.T. Code 1-25.68, Proof-Machine Operator." *Personnel Psychol* 11:438–9 au '58. *
10. MACKINNEY, ARTHUR C., AND WOLINS, LEROY. "Validity Information Exchange, No. 12-19: D.O.T. Code 1-36.05, Coding Clerk; 1-17.02, File Clerk II, Circulation Clerk." *Personnel Psychol* 12:482–3 au '59. *
11. BILASKI, I., AND ZUBEK, JOHN P. "The Effects of Age on Factorially 'Pure' Mental Abilities." *J Gerontol* 15:175–82 Ap '60. * (*PA* 35:6223)
12. RONAN, W. W. "Evaluation of Skilled Trades Performance Predictors." *Ed & Psychol Meas* 24:601–8 f '64. * (*PA* 39:6074)
13. CARRON, THEODORE J. "Validity of Tests for Chemical Plant Personnel." *Personnel Psychol* 22(3):307–12 au '69. * (*PA* 44:9414)

[1079]

★**Junior Aptitude Tests for Indian South Africans.** Standards 6–8; 1971; JATISA; 10 scores: verbal reasoning, series completion, social insight, language usage, numerical reasoning, spatial perception (2 dimensional, 3 dimensional), visual arts, clerical speed and accuracy, mechanical insight; S. Oosthuizen; Human Sciences Research Council [South Africa]. *

[1080]

Measurement of Skill: A Battery of Placement Tests for Business, Industrial and Educational Use. Adults; 1956–67; MOS; 8 tests; Walter V. Clarke Associates, Inc.; AVA Publications, Inc. *

a) SKILL WITH VOCABULARY.
b) SKILL WITH NUMBERS.
c) SKILL WITH SHAPE.
d) SPEED AND ACCURACY.
e) SKILL IN ORIENTATION.
f) SKILL IN THINKING.
g) SKILL WITH MEMORY. 1966 test identical with test copyrighted 1960 except for format.
h) SKILL WITH FINGERS.

For additional information, see 7:677 (4 references); for reviews by Dorothy C. Adkins, Lloyd G. Humphreys, and Joseph E. Moore, see 6:775 (2 references).

REFERENCES THROUGH 1971

1–2. See 6:775.
3–6. See 7:677.

[1081]

The Multi-Aptitude Test. College courses in testing; 1955; miniature battery of 10 tests for instructional use; Edward E. Cureton, Louise Witmer Cureton, and students; Psychological Corporation. *

For additional information and a review by H. H. Remmers, see 5:612 (1 reference).

REFERENCES THROUGH 1971
1. See 5:612.

CUMULATIVE NAME INDEX
Remmers, H. H.: *rev*, 5:612   Wesman, A. G.: 1

[1082]

Multiple Aptitude Tests, 1959 Edition. Grades 7–13; 1955–60; tests identical with those of 1955 edition except for booklet organization; 14 scores: scholastic potential plus 13 scores listed below; 9 tests in 4 booklets; David Segel and Evelyn Raskin; CTB/McGraw-Hill. *

a) FACTOR 1, VERBAL COMPREHENSION. 3 scores: word meaning, paragraph meaning, total.

b) FACTOR 2, PERCEPTUAL SPEED. 3 scores: language usage, routine clerical facility, total.

c) FACTOR 3, NUMERICAL REASONING. 3 scores: arithmetic reasoning, arithmetic computation, total.

d) FACTOR 4, SPATIAL VISUALIZATION. 4 scores: applied science and mechanics, 2-dimensional spatial relations, 3-dimensional spatial relations, total.

For additional information, reviews by S. S. Dunn and Leroy Wolins, and an excerpted review by Laurence Siegel, see 6:776 (8 references) ; for reviews by Ralph F. Berdie and Benjamin Fruchter of the original edition, see 5:613.

REFERENCES THROUGH 1971
1–8. See 6:776.
9. SILVERMAN, RONALD H. *Comparing the Effects of Two Versus Three-Dimensional Art Activity Upon Spatial Visualization, Aesthetic Judgment, and Art Interest.* Doctor's thesis, Stanford University (Stanford, Calif.), 1962. (*DA* 23:2017)
10. BOWERS, ORVON REX. *The Effects of Varied Amounts of Pre-Test Orientation and Types of Post-Test Interpretation on the Accuracy of Students' Vocational Self-Perception.* Doctor's thesis, University of Missouri (Columbia, Mo.), 1963. (*DA* 24:4535)
11. CAPLAN, STANLEY W., AND RUBLE, RONALD A. "A Study of Culturally Imposed Factors on School Achievement in a Metropolitan Area." *J Ed Res* 58:16–21 S '64. *
12. CHANSKY, NORMAN M. "Race, Aptitude and Vocational Interests." *Personnel & Guid J* 43:780–4 Ap '65. * (*PA* 39:16499)
13. CHASE, CLINTON I. *The University Freshman Dropout.* Indiana University, Monoraph of the Bureau of Educational Studies and Testing, Indiana Studies in Prediction, No. 6. Bloomington, Ind.: the Bureau, 1965. Pp. 36. *
14. GARBER, JOHN RODNEY. *Characteristics of Students Enrolled in the Guided Studies Program at Rockingham Community College and Their Implications for Curriculum Development.* Doctor's thesis, North Carolina State University (Raleigh, N.C.), 1971. (*DAI* 32:3555A)

CUMULATIVE NAME INDEX
Berdie, R. F.: *rev*, 5:613   Garber, J. R.: 14
Bowers, O. R.: 10   Khan, L.: 5, 7
Bryant, J. H.: 4   Mendenhall, G. V.: 1
Caplan, S. W.: 8, 11   Miner, J. B.: 6
Chansky, N. M.: 12   Prahl, M. R.: 4
Chase, C. I.: 13   Ruble, R. A.: 8, 11
Cureton, E. E.: 2   Segel, D.: 3, 8
D'Amico, L. A.: 4   Siegel, L.: *exc*, 6:776
Dunn, S. S.: *rev*, 6:776   Silverman, R. H.: 9
Fruchter, B.: *rev*, 5:613   Wolins, L.: *rev*, 6:776

[1083]

N.B. Aptitude Tests (Junior). Standards 4–8; 1961–62; 12 scores: reasoning, classification, computations, spare parts, synonyms, squares, name comparison, figure perception, memory for names and faces, word fluency, coordination, writing speed; Human Sciences Research Council [South Africa]. *

For additional information, see 6:777.

[1084]

National Institute for Personnel Research Intermediate Battery. Standards 7–10 and job applicants with 9–12 years of education; 1964–69; 7 tests in a single booklet: mental alertness, arithmetical problems, computation, spot-the-error (speed, accuracy), reading comprehension, vocabulary, spelling; manual by Anne-Marie Wilcocks; National Institute for Personnel Research [South Africa]. *

For additional information, see 7:678.

REFERENCES THROUGH 1971
1. GIESEKE, MARTHA. "Predicting the Ability to Learn a Foreign Language." *Psychologia Africana* (South Africa) 13(2–3):218–21 O '70. * (*PA* 46:6812)

CUMULATIVE NAME INDEX
Gieseke, M.: 1

[1085]

***National Institute for Personnel Research Normal Battery.** Standards 6–10 and job applicants with 8–11 years of education; 1960–73; 1973 metricated battery identical with battery copyrighted 1960 except for 8 revised items; 5 tests in a single booklet: mental alertness, reading comprehension, vocabulary, spelling, computation; manual by S. M. A. Waterhouse; National Institute for Personnel Research [South Africa]. *

For additional information concerning an earlier edition, see 6:779.

REFERENCES THROUGH 1971
1. MACARTHUR, R. S.; IRVINE, S. H.; AND BRIMBLE, A. R. *The Northern Rhodesia Mental Ability Survey 1963.* Rhodes-Livingstone Communication No. 27. Lusaka, Zambia: Rhodes-Livingstone Institute, 1964. Pp. ix, 100. *
2. IRVINE, S. H. "Factor Analysis of African Abilities and Attainments: Constructs Across Cultures." *Psychol B* 71(1): 20–32 Ja '69. * (*PA* 43:7553)

CUMULATIVE NAME INDEX
Brimble, A. R.: 1   MacArthur, R. S.: 1
Irvine, S. H.: 1–2

[1086]

***Nonreading Aptitude Test Battery, 1969 Edition.** Disadvantaged grades 9–12 and adults; 1965–73; NATB; nonreading adaptation of the *General Aptitude Test Battery;* 9 scores: intelligence, verbal, numerical, spatial, form perception, clerical perception, motor coordination, finger dexterity, manual dexterity; 14 tests: 10 paper and pencil tests plus 4 performance tests; United States Employment Service; orders for test materials must be cleared through a State Employment Service office; manuals, accessóries and GATB Part 8 distributed by United States Government Printing Office; Books 1–8 and scoring keys distributed by NCS Interpretive Scoring Systems. *

a) GATB-NATB SCREENING DEVICE. 1972–73; test sheet title is *Wide-Range Scale;* to identify examinees who are sufficiently skilled in reading and arithmetic to be tested with the *General Aptitude Test Battery.*

b) BOOK 1, PICTURE WORD MATCHING.

c) BOOK 2, COIN MATCHING.

d) BOOK 3, MATRICES.

e) BOOK 4, TOOL MATCHING.

f) BOOK 5, THREE-DIMENSIONAL SPACE.

g) BOOK 6, FORM MATCHING.

h) BOOK 7, COIN SERIES.

i) BOOK 8, NAME COMPARISON.

j) GATB PART 8 [MARK MAKING].

k) PEGBOARD. 2 tests: place, turn; K & W Products Co., Inc., Specialty Case Manufacturing Co., and Warwick Products Co.

l) FINGER DEXTERITY BOARD. 2 tests: assemble, disassemble; K & W Products Co., Inc., Specialty Case Manufacturing Co., and Warwick Products Co.

For additional information, see 7:679 (3 references).

REFERENCES THROUGH 1971
1–3. See 7:679.

Multi-Aptitude Test

[1087]
SRA Primary Mental Abilities, 1962 Edition.
Grades kgn–1, 2–4, 4–6, 6–9, 9–12, adults; 1946–69;
PMA; earlier editions entitled *Tests of Primary Mental
Abilities* and *Chicago Tests of Primary Mental Abilities;* 6 levels; L. L. Thurstone (earlier editions) and
Thelma Gwinn Thurstone; Science Research Associates, Inc. *
a) GRADES KGN–1. 1946–65; 5 scores: verbal meaning,
perceptual speed, number facility, spatial relations, total.
b) GRADES 2–4. 1946–65; 5 scores: same as for grades
kgn–1.
c) GRADES 4–6. 1946–69; 6 scores: same as for grades
kgn–1 plus reasoning.
d) GRADES 6–9. 1946–69; 5 scores: verbal meaning,
number facility, reasoning, spatial relations, total.
e) GRADES 9–12. 1946–69; 5 scores: same as for grades
6–9.
f) ADULT. 1946–69; 5 scores: same as for grades 6–9;
1965 test identical with test copyrighted 1962 for grades
9–12 except for title.

For additional information and reviews by M. Y.
Quereshi and Richard E. Schutz, see 7:680 (98 references); for a review by John E. Milholland of *a–e*, see
6:780 (50 references); for reviews by Norman Frederiksen and Albert K. Kurtz of an earlier edition, see
5:614 (58 references); for reviews by Anne Anastasi,
Ralph F. Berdie, John B. Carroll, Stuart A. Courtis,
and P. E. Vernon, see 4:716 (42 references); for reviews by Cyril Burt, James R. Hobson, and F. L. Wells,
see 3:225 (52 references); for a review by Florence L.
Goodenough of *a*, see 3:264; for reviews by Henry E.
Garrett, Truman L. Kelley, C. Spearman, Godfrey H.
Thomson, and Robert C. Tryon and excerpted reviews
by A. B. Crawford and John M. Stalnaker, see 2:1427
(11 references). For excerpts from related book reviews, see 2:B1099 (9 excerpts) and 1:B503 (4 excerpts).

REFERENCES THROUGH 1971

1–10. See 2:1427.
11–60. See 3:225.
61–102. See 4:716.
103–161. See 5:614.
162–211. See 6:780.
212–309. See 7:680.
310. JOHNSON, J. T. "On the Nature of Problem-Solving in
Arithmetic." *J Ed Res* 43:110–5 O '49. * (*PA* 24:2791)
311. EELLS, KENNETH; DAVIS, ALLISON; HAVIGHURST, ROB-
ERT J.; HERRICK, VERGIL E.; AND TYLER, RALPH W. *Intelligence and Cultural Differences: A Study of Cultural Learning
and Problem Solving.* Chicago, Ill.: University of Chicago Press,
1951. Pp. xii, 388. * (*PA* 27:5738)
312. HIMMELWEIT, HILDE T., AND SUMMERFIELD, ARTHUR.
"Student Selection—An Experimental Investigation: II." *Brit J
Sociol* 2:59–75 Mr '51. * (*PA* 26:542)
313. LEE, EVERETT S. "Negro Intelligence and Selective
Migration: A Philadelphia Test of the Klineberg Hypothesis."
Am Sociol R 16:227–33 Ap '51. * (*PA* 27:1093)
314. O'BRIEN, MARY C. *A Computation of Norms for Science
Research Associates Primary Mental Abilities Test for the
State of West Virginia.* Master's thesis, West Virginia University (Morgantown, W.Va.), 1953.
315. DUNHAM, RALPH E. "Factors Related to Recidivism in
Adults." *J Social Psychol* 39:77–91 F '54. * (*PA* 28:8866)
316. RUSSELL, DAVID H. "A Second Study of Characteristics
of Good and Poor Spellers." *J Ed Psychol* 46:129–41 Mr '55. *
(*PA* 30:1531)
317. BINDER, ARNOLD. "Schizophrenic Intellectual Impairment: Uniform or Differential?" *J Abn & Social Psychol*
52:11–8 Ja '56. * (*PA* 31:3444)
318. DREVDAHL, JOHN E. "Factors of Importance for Creativity." *J Clin Psychol* 12:21–6 Ja '56. * (*PA* 30:4160)
319. DURLING, DOROTHY, AND ESEN, FATMA MUNIRE. "Irregular Test Profiles Correlated With Personality Traits." *Am J
Mental Def* 61:409–12 O '56. * (*PA* 32:1772)
320. TALLENT, NORMAN. "Behavioral Control and Intellectual

Achievement of Secondary School Boys." *J Ed Psychol* 47:
490–503 D '56. * (*PA* 32:4624)
321. HOFSTAETTER, PETER R.; O'CONNOR, JAMES P.; AND
SUZIEDELIS, ANTANAS. "Sequences of Restricted Associative
Responses and Their Personality Correlates." *J General Psychol*
57:219–27 O '57. * (*PA* 33:9818)
322. OVERTON, ELEAZER C. "Factors That Influence Personality Behavior of High School Students." *Optom Weekly* 48:
583–6 Mr 28 '57. * (*PA* 32:2464)
323. GARRISON, MORTIMER, JR. "A Comparison of Psychological Measures in Mentally Retarded Boys Over a Three-Year
Period as a Function of Etiology." *Training Sch B* 55:54–60
N '58. * (*PA* 34:1664)
324. WRIGLEY, CHARLES; SAUNDERS, DAVID R.; AND NEUHAUS,
JACK O. "Application of the Quartimax Method of Rotation to
Thurstone's Primary Mental Abilities Study." *Psychometrika*
23:151–70 Je '58. * (*PA* 33:7329)
325. CLARK, JAMES W. "The Aging Dimension: A Factorial
Analysis of Individual Differences With Age on Psychological
and Physiological Measurements." *J Gerontol* 15:183–7 Ap '60. *
(*PA* 35:6227)
326. GROVER, V. M. "The Basis of Reading Disability in the
Elementary School Years." *J Social Res* (South Africa) 13:
29–38 D '62. * (*PA* 38:9229)
327. PETERS, HERBERT D. "Performance of Hopi Children on
Four Intelligence Tests." *J Am Indian Ed* 2:27–31 Ja '63. *
328. RANDECKER, HELEN. *A Study to Determine if Chronological Age, Mental Age Scores, and Reading Readiness Tests
Predict the Probable Achievement in Reading of First Grade
Pupils.* Master's thesis, Wisconsin State University (Whitewater, Wis.), 1963.
329. ANASTASIOW, NICHOLAS J. "Maximizing Identification
of the Gifted." *J Ed Res* 57:538–41 Jl–Ag '64. *
330. PETERSON, DONALD FREDERICK. *A Predictive Study of
Success in First Year Bookkeeping.* Master's thesis, San Diego
State College (San Diego, Calif.), 1965.
331. VANDENBERG, STEVEN G. "Multivariate Analysis of Twin
Differences," pp. 29–43. In his *Methods and Goals in Human
Behavior Genetics.* New York: Academic Press Inc., 1965.
Pp. xiii, 351. *
332. FREYBERG, P. S. "Concept Development in Piagetian
Terms in Relation to School Attainment." *J Ed Psychol* 57:
164–8 Je '66. * (*PA* 40:9223)
333. HOLMES, JACK A., AND SINGER, HARRY. *Speed and
Power of Reading in High School.* Cooperative Research Mon-
ograph No. 14. Washington, D.C.: United States Government
Printing Office, 1966. Pp. xii, 183. *
334. ORPET, R. E., AND MEYERS, C. E. "Six Structure-of-
Intellect Hypotheses in Six-Year-Old Children." *J Ed Psychol*
57:341–6 D '66. * (*PA* 41:1416)
335. OWENS, CHARLES D. *Development of a Regression
Equation for Predicting Academic Achievement in the Lake
City, Arkansas, High School.* Master's thesis, Arkansas State
College (State University, Ark.), 1966.
336. VANDENBERG, STEVEN G. "Hereditary Factors in Psy-
chological Variables in Man, With a Special Emphasis on
Cognition," pp. 99–133. In *Genetic Diversity and Human
Behavior.* Viking Fund Publications in Anthropology No. 45.
Edited by J. N. Spuhler. Chicago, Ill.: Aldine Publishing Co.,
1967. Pp. xi, 291. *
337. BURNHAM, RUTH ELIZABETH. *The Relationship Between
the Intelligence Quotient and the Creative Ability of Second
Grade Children in the Villa Park School System.* Master's thesis,
Northern Illinois University (DeKalb, Ill.), 1968.
338. FREYBERG, P. S. "Fluctuations in Children's Cognitive
Test Scores Over a Two-Year Period." *Brit J Ed Psychol* 38:
82–6 F '68. * (*PA* 42:12731)
339. LOEHLIN, JOHN C., AND VANDENBERG, STEVEN G. Chap.
15, "Genetic and Environmental Components in the Covariation
of Cognitive Abilities: An Additive Model," pp. 261–78. In
Progress in Human Behavior Genetics. Edited by Steven G.
Vandenberg. Baltimore, Md.: Johns Hopkins Press, 1968. Pp.
xi, 356. *
340. ROUDABUSH, GLENN E. Chap. 17, "Analyzing Dyadic
Relationships," pp. 303–33. In *Progress in Human Behavior
Genetics.* Edited by Steven G. Vandenberg. Baltimore, Md.:
Johns Hopkins Press, 1968. Pp. xi, 356. *
341. SCHAIE, K. W., AND STROTHER, C. R. "Limits of
Optimal Functioning in Superior Old Adults." Discussion by
Joseph H. Britton. *Interdiscipl Topics Gerontol* 1:132–53 '68. *
342. SCHAIE, K. WARNER, AND STROTHER, CHARLES R. "Cog-
nitive and Personality Variables in College Graduates of
Advanced Age," pp. 281–308. (*PA* 43:15628, title only) In
*Human Aging and Behavior: Recent Advances in Research
and Theory.* Edited by George A. Talland. New York: Academic
Press Inc., 1968. Pp. xiii, 322. *
343. KING, F. J.; ROBERTS, DENNIS; AND KROPP, RUSSELL P.
"Relationship Between Ability Measures and Achievement
Under Four Methods of Teaching Elementary Set Concepts."
J Ed Psychol 60(3):244–7 Je '69. * (*PA* 43:13392)
344. DIELMAN, T. E., AND FURUNO, SETSU. "Interrelationships
Among Selected Environmental, Cognitive, and Achievement
Variables: A Further Analysis of the Ten-Year Follow-Up of

the Children of the Kauai Pregnancy Study." *Personality* 1(3):185–99 au '70. * (*PA* 47:9797)

345. MARJORIBANKS, KEVIN McLEOD. *Ethnic and Environmental Influences on Levels and Profiles of Mental Abilities.* Doctor's thesis, University of Toronto (Toronto, Ont., Canada), 1970. (*DAI* 32:6052A)

346. RENNELS, MAX RAYMOND. "The Effects of Instructional Methodology in Art Education Upon Achievement on Spatial Tasks by Disadvantaged Negro Youths." *J Negro Ed* 39(2): 116–23 sp '70. * (*PA* 46:7841)

347. RIVERS, LARRY WENDELL. *The Stability of Differential Patterns of Mental Abilities in Children From Different Ethnic Groups.* Doctor's thesis, St. Louis University (St. Louis, Mo.), 1970. (*DAI* 32:1194B)

348. VAN CAMP, SARAH STREET. *An Auditory and Visual Discrimination Test for Kindergarten and First Grade Children: A New Approach.* Doctor's thesis, University of Massachusetts (Amherst, Mass.), 1970. (*DAI* 31:5680A)

349. WOOD, MILDRED HOPE. *A Longitudinal Study of the Effectiveness of Certain Kindergarten Tests in Predicting Reading Achievement, School Failure, and the Need for Special Services.* Doctor's thesis, Indiana University (Bloomington, Ind.), 1970. (*DAI* 31:5683A)

350. BALTES, PAUL B.; SCHAIE, K. WARNER; AND NARDI, ANNE H. "Age and Experimental Mortality in a Seven-Year Longitudinal Study of Cognitive Behavior." *Develop Psychol* 5(1):18–26 Jl '71. * (*PA* 46:8800)

351. CRARY, HELEN L., AND RIDGWAY, ROBERT W. "Relationships Between Visual Form Perception Abilities and Reading Achievement in the Intermediate Grades." *J Exp Ed* 40(1): 17–22 f '71. * (*PA* 47:9796)

352. JOHNSON, THEOLA GAE. *Influence of Selected Factors on the Ability of Fourth, Fifth, and Sixth Graders to Read Graphs.* Doctor's thesis, University of Southern California (Los Angeles, Calif.), 1971. (*DAI* 32:726A)

353. LAVELY, ROBERT HENRY. *An Investigation Comparing Primary Mental Abilities of Trainable Mentally Retarded Children, Educable Mentally Retarded Children, and Normal Children With Comparable Mental Ages.* Doctor's thesis, Ohio State University (Columbus, Ohio), 1971. (*DAI* 32:3823A)

354. LOO, CHALSA, AND WENAR, CHARLES. "Activity Level and Motor Inhibition: Their Relationship to Intelligence-Test Performance in Normal Children." *Child Develop* 42(3):967–71 S '71. * (*PA* 47:6495)

355. McGILLIGAN, ROBERT PATRICK. *Psychological Differentiation, Abilities and Personality.* Doctor's thesis, St. Louis University (St. Louis, Mo.), 1971. (*DAI* 33:1291B)

356. MARJORIBANKS, KEVIN. "Environmental Correlates of Diverse Mental Abilities." *J Exp Ed* 39(4):64–8 su '71. * (*PA* 47:655)

357. MARJORIBANKS, KEVIN. "The Learning Environment of the Home—An Instrument." *Austral & N Zeal J Sociol* (Australia) 7(2):69–77 O '71. *

358. MARTIN, WILLIAM A. "Word Fluency—Intellect or Personality?" *J Genetic Psychol* 118(1):17–24 Mr '71. * (*PA* 46:8848)

359. MUSSIO, JERRY J., AND WAHLSTROM, MERLIN W. "Predicting Performance of Programmer Trainees in a Post-High School Setting." Discussion by Charles D. Lothridge. *Proc Ann Computer Personnel Res Conf* 9:26–53 '71. *

360. MYKLEBUST, HELMER R.; BANNOCHIE, MARGARET N.; AND KILLEN, JAMES R. Chap. 9, "Learning Disabilities and Cognitive Processes," pp. 213–51. In *Progress in Learning Disabilities, Vol. 2.* Edited by Helmer R. Myklebust. New York: Grune & Stratton, Inc., 1971. Pp. ix, 404. *

361. NELSON, JOHN CLEMENT. *Relating Student and Teacher Personality and Cognitive Characteristics With School Achievement of Educable Mentally Retarded Children.* Doctor's thesis, George Peabody College for Teachers (Nashville, Tenn.), 1971. (*DAI* 32:1948A)

362. PARKER, HARRY J.; STERNLOF, RICHARD E.; AND McCOY, JOHN F. "Objective Versus Individual Mental Ability Tests With Former Head Start Children in the First Grade." *Percept & Motor Skills* 32(1):287–92 F '71. * (*PA* 46:3868)

363. RAJU, VIJAYA, AND RAMAMURTHI, P. V. "Verbal Ability and Educational Achievement." *Indian J Appl Psychol* 8(2):59–60 Jl '71. *

364. SCOTT, RALPH, AND SATTEL, LUDWIG. "School and Home: Not Either-Or." *Merrill-Palmer Q* 17(4):335–45 O '71. *

365. UPCHURCH, WINIFRED BROOK. *The Relationship Between Perceptual-Motor Skills and Word Recognition Achievement at the Kindergarten Level.* Doctor's thesis, Syracuse University (Syracuse, N.Y.), 1971. (*DAI* 32:4497A)

366. VARNER, DONALD GILES. *The Relationship of Selected Cumulative Grade Point Averages to Intelligence Quotient.* Master's thesis, Eastern Illinois University (Charleston, Ill.), 1971.

CUMULATIVE NAME INDEX

Larson, A. A.: 263
Lavely, R. H.: 353
Lee, E. S.: 313
Lepkin, M.: 136
Levine, S.: 98
Lewis, D. G.: 242
Lewis, L. H.: 285
Lighthall, F. K.: 191
Lloyd, C. J.: 168
Loehlin, J. C.: 339
Long, J. R.: 157
Loo, C.: 354
Loranger, A. W.: 179, 189
Lothridge, C. D.: 359
Lundberg, G. A.: exc, 1:B503
Maccoby, E. E.: 260
McCormick, J. H.: 234
McCoy, J. F.: 362
McElwee, A. R.: 43
McFarland, R. L.: 201
McGilligan, R. P.: 355
McKee, J. P.: 112
McNemar, Q.: exc, 2:B1099
McTaggart, H. P.: 180
Mangan, G. L.: 221
Marjoribanks, K.: 356–7
Marjoribanks, K. M.: 345
Marquis, F. N.: 113
Martin, W. A.: 303, 358
Maslany, G. W.: 296
Mearig, J. S.: 243
Melton, R. S.: 209
Meredith, P.: 144
Meyer, H. H.: 99
Meyer, W. J.: 190, 195, 206
Meyers, C. E.: 257, 286, 334
Meyers, E.: 202
Michael, W. B.: 76, 100
Micheli, G. S.: 114
Milholland, J. E.: rev, 6:780
Mill, C. R.: 145
Misiak, H.: 179, 189
Mitchell, J. V.: 153
Moffie, D. J.: 21–2, 44
Money, J.: 264
Moody, C. B.: 115
Mueller, M. W.: 252–3, 287, 304
Mukherjee, B. N.: 254
Murray, J. E.: 77
Mussio, J. J.: 359
Myklebust, H. R.: 360
Nardi, A. H.: 350
Nelson, C. L.: 201
Nelson, J. C.: 361
Neuhaus, J. O.: 324
Nicholls, J. G.: 269
Nixon, M.: 72
Novack, H. S.: 222
O'Brien, M. C.: 314
O'Connor, J. P.: 321
Olson, D. J.: 105
Orpet, R. E.: 202, 286, 334
Osburn, H. G.: 209
Overton, E. C.: 322
Owens, C. D.: 335
Pankaskie, M.: 31
Parker, H. J.: 362
Perlman, R. M.: 124

Perry, J. O.: 229
Peters, H. D.: 327
Peterson, D. F.: 330
Plant, W. T.: 248
Pont, H. B.: 295
Pooler, M. H.: 146
Poteet, J. A.: 309
Pouncey, A. T.: 215
Proctor, C. H.: 194
Quereshi, M. Y.: rev, 7:680
Racky, D. J.: 181
Rainey, R. G.: 255
Raju, V.: 363
Ramamurthi, P. V.: 363
Ramaseshan, R. S.: 92
Randecker, H.: 328
Rawlings, T. D.: 218
Reddig, G. L.: 256
Reining, H.: 45
Rennels, M. R.: 346
Ridgway, R. W.: 351
Rivers, L. W.: 347
Roberts, D.: 343
Roberts, S. O.: 116
Robinson, F. P.: 61
Robinson, J. B.: 32
Robinson, J. M.: 116
Rochlin, I.: 117
Rogers, C. A.: 154
Ronan, W. W.: 244
Rosenthal, F.: 124
Rossi, A. M.: 201
Rothney, J. W. M.: 140
Roudabush, G. E.: 340
Rowan, T. C.: 164
Ruebush, B. K.: 191
Russell, D. H.: 316
Sanders, J. R.: 93
Sanders, R. M.: 210
Sarason, S. B.: 191
Sattel, L.: 364
Satter, G.: 147
Saunders, D. R.: 324
Schaefer, W. C.: 23
Schafer, E. W. P.: 297
Schaffer, M. C.: 305
Schaie, K. W.: 124, 148, 165, 169–70, 182, 288–9, 341–2, 350
Schalling, D.: 281
Schmidt, L. G.: 78, 125, 140
Schutz, R. E.: rev, 7:680
Scott, R.: 364
Seashore, H. G.: 85
Shalloe, M. P.: 141
Shanner, W. M.: 6, 33, 52
Shaw, D. C.: 69, 79
Shinn, E. O.: 155
Shofstall, W. P.: exc, 2: B1099
Silverstein, A. B.: 196
Simonian, K.: 272, 290
Singer, H.: 333
Smith, A. E.: 80
Smith, C. E.: exc, 1:B503
Smith, D. D.: 160, 171
Smith, G. R.: 225
Smith, H. C.: 8
Smith, R. S.: 272, 290

Spaulding, G.: 118
Spearman, C.: rev, 2:1427
Spivey, G. M.: 94
Stalnaker, J. M.: 7, 9; exc, 2:1427
Staveley, B.: 270
Stempel, E. F.: 126
Stene, D. M.: 166
Sternlof, R. E.: 362
Stier, L. D.: 205
Stonesifer, F. A.: 219
Stonesifer, J. N.: exc, 2: B1099
Stromsen, K. E.: 45
Strother, C. R.: 148, 165, 288–9, 341–2
Stuit, D. B.: 34, 46
Summerfield, A.: 312
Super, D. E.: 82, 203
Sutherland, T. E.: 216
Suziedelis, A.: 321
Tallent, N.: 320
Taylor, P. L.: 163
Thomson, G. H.: rev, 2:1427
Thurstone, L. L.: 1–5, 24, 35, 53–4, 57, 70, 83
Thurstone, T. G.: 25, 35–6, 62, 71, 84, 95, 101, 159
Toussaint, I. H.: 198, 227
Townsend, A.: 59, 118
Traxler, A. E.: 37
Tredick, V. D.: 16
Trumbull, R.: 127
Tryon, R. C.: rev, 2:1427
Tuel, J. K.: 257
Turner, C. J.: 145
Tutt, M. L.: 245
Tyler, L. E.: 102, 128, 172

Tyler, R. W.: 311
Upchurch, W. B.: 365
Van Camp, S. S.: 348
Vandenberg, S. G.: 183, 194, 217, 230, 271, 331, 336, 339
Van Voorhis, W. R.: 38
Varner, D. G.: 366
Vernon, P. E.: rev, 4:716
Wagner, R. M.: 204
Wahlstrom, M. W.: 359
Waite, R. R.: 191
Walters, R. H.: 161
Weise, P.: 257
Wellington, J. A.: 149
Wellman, F. E.: 158
Wells, F. L.: rev, 3:225
Wenar, C.: 354
Werner, E. E.: 272, 290
Wesman, A. G.: 85
Weston, L. D.: 291
Wheatley, M. M.: 103
White, H. G.: 211
White, I. W.: 47
Wilkins, M. F.: 184
Willis, W. K.: 262
Wilson, J. A. R.: 173, 205
Wilson, R. C.: 223, 228
Wolking, W. D.: 150
Wood, M. H.: 349
Wright, R. E.: 7.1
Wrigley, C.: 324
Yates, L. G.: 273
Young, E. F.: exc, 1:B503
Yum, K. S.: 39
Zaidi, S. W. H.: 235
Zimmerman, W. S.: 100, 129
Zubin, J.: exc, 2:B1099

[1088]

*Senior Aptitude Tests. Standards 8–10 and college and adults; 1969–71; SAT; 12 scores: verbal comprehension, numerical fluency, word fluency, visual perception speed, reasoning (deductive, inductive), spatial visualization (2 dimensional, 3 dimensional), memory (paragraphs, symbols), psychomotor coordination, writing speed; F. A. Fouche and N. F. Alberts; Human Sciences Research Council [South Africa]. *

For additional information, see 7:681.

[Out of Print Since TIP I]

Differential Ability Tests, 5:604
Experimental Comparative Prediction Batteries, 7:674 (3 references)
Fife Tests of Ability, 4:713 (2 reviews, 3 references)
Holzinger-Crowder Uni-Factor Tests, 5:610 (3 reviews, 3 references)
United States Employment Service Special Aptitude Tests, 4:717
Vocational Guidance Program, 6:781 (1 review)
Yale Educational Aptitude Test Battery, 5:615 (2 reviews, 11 references)

PERSONALITY

NONPROJECTIVE

[1089]

★Ai3Q: A Measure of the Obsessional Personality or Anal Character. Sixth form and intelligent adults; 1971; test sheet title is *Ai3Q Questionnaire;* ex-

perimental; Paul Kline; NFER Publishing Co. Ltd. [England]. *

REFERENCES THROUGH 1971

1. KLINE, PAUL. *An Investigation Into the Freudian Concept of the Anal Character.* Doctor's thesis, University of Manchester (Manchester, England), 1968.
2. KLINE, PAUL. "Obsessional Traits, Obsessional Symptoms

and Anal Erotism." *Brit J Med Psychol* 41:299–305 S '68. * (*PA* 43:1061)

3. KLINE, PAUL. "The Anal Character: A Cross-Cultural Study in Ghana." *Brit J Social & Clin Psychol* 8(3):201–10 S '69. * (*PA* 44:3517)

4. KLINE, PAUL. "The Validity of the Brook Reaction Test." *Brit J Social & Clin Psychol* 9(1):42–5 F '70. * (*PA* 44:12609)

5. KLINE, PAUL. "Obsessional Traits and Academic Performance in the Sixth Form." *Ed Res* (England) 13(3):230–2 Je '71. * (*PA* 49:11969)

CUMULATIVE NAME INDEX

Kline, P.: 1–5

[1090]

A-S Reaction Study: A Scale for Measuring Ascendance-Submission in Personality. College and adults; 1928–39; ASRS; Gordon W. Allport and Floyd H. Allport; Houghton Mifflin Co. *

For additional information, see P:1 (9 references); for a review by Warren T. Norman, see 6:57 (11 references); see also 5:28 (15 references); for a review by William U. Snyder, see 3:23 (11 references); for a review by Doncaster G. Humm of the 1928 edition, see 2:1198 (19 references).

REFERENCES THROUGH 1971

1–19. See 2:1198.
20–30. See 3:23.
31–45. See 5:28.
46–56. See 6:57.
57–65. See P:1.

66. COOPER, PETER. "Notes on Psychological Race Differences." *Social Forces* 8:425–6 Mr '30. * (*PA* 5:470)

67. OLIVER, R. A. C. "The Traits of Extroverts and Introverts." *J Social Psychol* 1:345–66 Ag '30. * (*PA* 5:308)

68. VETTER, GEORGE B. "The Measurement of Social and Political Attitudes and the Related Personality Factors." *J Abn & Social Psychol* 25:149–89 Jl–S '30. * (*PA* 5:1899)

69. MCLAUGHLIN, MARY AQUINAS. "The Genesis and Constancy of Ascendance and Submission as Personality Traits." *Univ Iowa Studies* Ed 6(5):1–95 '31. * (*PA* 6:1404)

70. STAGNER, ROSS. "Differential Factors in the Testing of Personality: 1, Sex Differences; 2, Differences in Maturity." *J Social Psychol* 3:477–87 N '32. * (*PA* 7:182)

71. BOWDEN, A. O. "Change—The Test of Teaching." *Sch & Soc* 40:133–6 Jl 28 '34. * (*PA* 8:5652)

72. HARVEY, O. L. "The Measurement of Handwriting Considered as a Form of Expressive Movement." *Char & Pers* 2:310–21 Je '34. * (*PA* 8:5136)

73. MOORE, LAWRENCE H. "Leadership Traits of College Women." *Sociol & Social Res* 20:136–9 N–D '35. * (*PA* 10:3640)

74. QUAYLE, MARGARET SIDNEY. "A Study of Some Aspects of Satisfaction in the Vocation of Stenography." *Teach Col Contrib Ed* 659:1–121 '35. * (*PA* 10:2644)

75. GARTH, THOMAS R., AND GARTH, THOMAS R., JR. "The Personality of Indians." *J Appl Psychol* 21:464–7 Ag '37. * (*PA* 12:886)

76. CABOT, P. S. DE Q. "The Relationship Between Characteristics of Personality and Physique in Adolescents." *Genetic Psychol Monogr* 20:3–120 F '38. * (*PA* 12:3592)

77. WEBER, C. O. "Function-Fluctuation and Personality Trends of Normal Subjects." *Am J Psychol* 51:702–8 O '38. * (*PA* 13:1536)

78. WEBER, C. O. "The Relation of Personality Trends to Degrees of Visual Constancy Correction for Size and Form." *J Appl Psychol* 23:703–8 D '39. * (*PA* 14:2482)

79. SPERLING, ABRAHAM P. "A Comparison Between Jews and Non-Jews With Respect to Several Traits of Personality." *J Appl Psychol* 26:828–40 D '42. * (*PA* 17:2819)

80. SPERLING, ABRAHAM P. "The Relationship Between Personality Adjustment and Achievement in Physical Education Activities." *Res Q* 13:351–63 O '42. * (*PA* 17:600)

81. HOOD, PHILIP N.; SHANK, KENNON H.; AND WILLIAMSON, DORIS B. "Environmental Factors in Relation to the Speech of Cerebral Palsied Children." *J Speech & Hearing Disorders* 13:325–31 D '48. * (*PA* 23:3301)

82. GARBER, W. F. "Evaluation of Psychometric Tests for Optometry." *Optom Weekly* 40:1927–32+, 1953–7 D 22, 29 '49. * (*PA* 24:3477)

83. BARNETTE, W. LESLIE. "Occupational Aptitude Pattern Research." *Occupations* 29:5–12 O '50. * (*PA* 25:3239)

84. TRESSELT, M. E., AND BECKER, MAXWELL. "Scales of Judgment and Personality Correlates." *J General Psychol* 43:221–30 O '50. * (*PA* 25:6005)

85. MCCARTHY, MARY VITERBO. "An Empirical Study of the Personality Profiles Characterizing Differential Quantitative and Linguistic Ability." *Studies Psychol & Psychiatry* 8(4):1–45 Je '53. * (*PA* 28:4043)

86. MISIAK, HENRYK, AND FRANGHIADI, GEORGE J. "The Thumb and Personality." *J General Psychol* 48:241–4 Ap '53. * (*PA* 28:564)

87. FABIAN, WALTER ALBERT, JR. *An Investigation of the Relationship Between Measures of Insight and Measures of Projection and Distortion in Ratings.* Doctor's thesis, University of Buffalo (Buffalo, N.Y.), 1954. (*DA* 14:711)

88. DOUGLASS, ROBERT RAYMOND. *Personality of the Librarian.* Doctor's thesis, University of Chicago (Chicago, Ill.), 1957.

89. KEMP, CLARENCE GRATTON. *Changes in Patterns of Personal Values in Relation to Open-Closed Belief Systems.* Doctor's thesis, Michigan State University (East Lansing, Mich.), 1957. (*DA* 19:271)

90. RODEN, AUBREY HENRY. *The Effects of Residual, Background, and Stimulus on Contributing Behavior.* Doctor's thesis, University of Texas (Austin, Tex.), 1957. (*DA* 18:503)

91. SARGENT, S. STANSFELD, AND BEARDSLEY, KATHERINE PEASE. "Social Roles and Personality Traits." *Int J Social Psychiatry* (England) 6:66–70 su '60. * (*PA* 37:4993)

92. MATTHEWS, LILLIAN BEATRICE. *College Students' Attitudes Toward Clothing and Their Relation to Certain Personality Traits.* Doctor's thesis, Ohio State University (Columbus, Ohio), 1963. (*DA* 24:2887)

93. HAFEEZ, A., AND DHARANENDRIAH, K. S. "Distribution of Ascendance-Submission Scores Among College Students." *Manas* (India) 13(1):29–32 '66. * (*PA* 40:13192)

94. MCAULIFFE, MARY EILEEN. *Manifest Anxiety, Ascendance, and Values in Students Planning to Teach.* Doctor's thesis, Northwestern University (Evanston, Ill.), 1966. (*DA* 27:2403A)

95. NUCHO, AINA OZOLINS. *The Problem of Psychological Similarity and the Process of Codification in Therapeutic Interaction.* Doctor's thesis, Bryn Mawr College (Bryn Mawr, Pa.), 1966. (*DA* 27:3678B)

96. SHOUKSMITH, GEORGE. "Personality Attributes Associated With Two Measures of Cognitive Style." *Acta Psychologica* (Netherlands) 31(4):353–64 D '69. * (*PA* 44:14589)

97. BHUSHAN, L. I. "An Investigation Into Certain Personality Correlates of Leadership Preference." *Psychol Studies* (India) 15(1):40–5 Ja '70. *

98. BHUSHAN, L. I. "Personality Factors and Leadership Preference." Thesis abstract. *Indian Psychol R* 6(2):125–6 Ja '70. * (*PA* 46:9028)

99. DUTT, N. K. "A Study of Anxiety and Some Correlates." *J Psychol Res* (India) 14(2):50–2 My '70. *

100. PRAKASH, JAI. "A Study of Group Convergence in Relation to Ascendance and Submission." *Manas* (India) 17(2):125–33 N '70. * (*PA* 47:10795)

101. HAFEEZ, A. "A Study of Ascendance-Submission Among Engineering, Humanities and Science Students, Employed Engineers and Supervisors." *Indian J Social Work* 32(1):95–8 Ap '71. * (*PA* 48:2998)

CUMULATIVE NAME INDEX

Achilles, P. S.: 24	Herr, V. V.: 50
Allport, F. H.: 1	Holcomb, G. W.: 10
Allport, G. W.: 1–2, 4, 18	Holmes, F. J.: 39
Barnette, W. L.: 34, 40, 83	Holzberg, J. D.: 41
Beardsley, K. P.: 91	Hood, P. N.: 81
Beaver, A. P.: 44	Horrall, B. M.: 36
Becker, M.: 84	Humm, D. G.: *rev*, 2:1198
Beckman, R. O.: 5	Hundal, P. S.: 49, 62
Bender, I. E.: 3, 38	Jersild, A.: 7
Bhushan, L. I.: 97–8	Kemp, C. G.: 89
Bowden, A. O.: 71	Koltuv, M.: 52–3
Bronzaft, A.: 52–3	Laslett, H. R.: 10
Broom, M. E.: 6	Levine, M.: 5
Brower, D.: 32	Link, H. C.: 30
Brower, J. L.: 55	McAuliffe, M. E.: 94
Cabot, P. S. de Q.: 76	McCarthy, M. V.: 85
Carter, L.: 35	McGeoch, J. A.: 22
Chamberlain, F.: 17	McKenna, F. S.: 42
Child, I. L.: 28	McLaughlin, M. A.: 69
Cooper, P.: 66	Mann, R. D.: 51
Decker, C. E.: 20	Manzer, C. W.: 11
Dharanendriah, K. S.: 93	Matthews, L. B.: 92
Dhillon, P. K.: 64	Misiak, H.: 86
Douglass, R. R.: 88	Moore, H.: 13
Dow, C. W.: 29	Moore, L. H.: 73
Dutt, N. K.: 99	Nixon, M.: 35
English, H. B.: 46	Norman, W. T.: *rev*, 6:57
Fabian, W. A.: 87	Nucho, A. O.: 95
Farram, F.: 16	Oliver, A. G.: 54
Flanagan, J. J.: 50	Oliver, R. A. C.: 67
Franghiadi, G. J.: 86	Parameswaran, E. G.: 54, 56, 60
Gandhi, J. S.: 48	
Garber, W. F.: 82	Perry, R. C.: 14
Garth, T. R.: 75	Posner, R.: 41
Hafeez, A.: 93, 101	Prakash, J.: 100
Hanna, J. V.: 8	Quayle, M. S.: 74
Hardy, V. T.: 33	Ray-Chowdhury, K.: 48–9, 57–9
Harvey, O. L.: 72	
Hastorf, A. H.: 38	Reader, N.: 46
Hayes, R.: 52–3	Reindl, M. O.: 45

Roden, A. H.: 90
Ruggles, R.: 18
Santhanam, M. L.: 60
Sargent, S. S.: 91
Schultz, R. S.: 24, 26
Shank, K. H.: 81
Sheldon, W. H.: 28
Shouksmith, G.: 96
Sinha, J. N.: 65
Skiff, S. C.: 47
Snyder, W. U.: *rev*, 3:23
Sperling, A. P.: 79–80
Stagner, R.: 12, 23, 70
Starer, E.: 43
Steele, I.: 13
Stevens, S. N.: 15

Sundaram, K.: 56
Thompson, C. E.: 31
Tillman, K.: 63
Tillman, K. G.: 61
Tresselt, M. E.: 84
Uhrbrock, R. S.: 37
Vetter, G. B.: 68
Wang, C. K. A.: 9, 21
Wasson, M. M.: 19, 27
Weber, C. O.: 77–8
Weiss, L.: 25
Welch, L.: 52–3
Whitely, L.: 22
Williams, G. W.: 17
Williamson, D. B.: 81
Wonderlic, E. F.: 15

Schulz, H.: 48, 51, 54
Shapurian, R.: 55, 57–8
Strehse, W.: 48, 51, 54
Wallace, S. R.: 7

Whisler, L. D.: 9
Whiteley, D. P.: 38
Winneke, G.: 48, 51, 54

[1091]

*Activity Vector Analysis. Ages 16 and over; 1945–72; AVA; test booklet title is *Placement Analysis;* personality characteristics related to job success; 6 scores: aggressiveness, sociability, emotional stability, social adaptability, social adjustment, activity ratio; Walter V. Clarke Associates, Inc.; AVA Publications, Inc. *

For additional information, see P:2 (16 references) ; for reviews by Lewis E. Albright, Alexander W. Astin, and Winton H. Manning, see 6:58 (21 references) ; for reviews by Brent Baxter and George K. Bennett, see 5:29 (11 references).

REFERENCES THROUGH 1971

1–11. See 5:29.
12–32. See 6:58.
33–48. See P:2.
49. MERENDA, PETER F., AND CLARKE, WALTER V. "Differences in Results of Inferential Self Measurement in Self-Concept Analysis." *Percept & Motor Skills* 25:317–22 Ag '67. * (*PA* 42:2588)
50. HASLER, KERMIT R., AND CLARKE, WALTER V. "Reexamination of Test-Retest Reliability of AVA Placement Analysis Scores." *Psychol Rep* 23:1035–8 D '68. * (*PA* 43:8808)
51. MERENDA, PETER F.; CLARKE, WALTER V.; SCHULZ, HARTMUT; STREHSE, WOLFGANG; AND WINNEKE, GERHARD. "Cross-Cultural Perceptions of the Ideal Self-Concept." *Int R Appl Psychol* 18(2):129–34 O '69. * (*PA* 44:8214)
52. MUSIKER, HAROLD R., AND LUNDIN, WILLIAM H. "Activity Vector Analysis vs. Clinical Appraisal in Personality Description." *J Clin Psychol* 25(1):26–9 Ja '69. * (*PA* 43:8943)
53. MERENDA, PETER F., AND MOHAN, JITENDRA. "Indian Students' Pre- and Post-Election Perceptions of Nixon and Humphrey." *Percept & Motor Skills* 30(2):677–8 Ap '70. * (*PA* 46:6799)
54. MERENDA, PETER F.; CLARKE, WALTER V.; SCHULZ, HARTMUT; STREHSE, WOLFGANG; AND WINNEKE, GERHARD. "Differences in Perception of Concept of Ideal-Self and Ideal-Person Between American and German Samples." *Percept & Motor Skills* 30(3):783–6 Je '70. * (*PA* 44:16465)
55. MERENDA, PETER F.; BASSIRI, TORAB; SHAPURIAN, REZA; AND CLARKE, WALTER V. "Iranian Perceptions of the Reza Shah, Presidents Nixon and Johnson, and the Ideal Self." *Percept & Motor Skills* 33(2):428–30 O '71. * (*PA* 47:6784)
56. MERENDA, PETER F.; MOHAN, JITENDRA; AND CLARKE, WALTER V. "Indian Students' Perceptions of Eight Internationally Known Personalities." *Percept & Motor Skills* 33(2): 611–4 O '71. * (*PA* 47:6723)
57. MERENDA, PETER F.; SHAPURIAN, REZA; AND CLARKE, WALTER V. "Iranian Students' Perception of the Reza Shah and the Ideal Self." *Percept & Motor Skills* 33(2):431–4 O '71. * (*PA* 47:6785)
58. MERENDA, PETER F.; SHAPURIAN, REZA; BASSIRI, TORAB; AND CLARKE, WALTER V. "Iranian Perceptions of the Reza Shah and President Johnson." *Percept & Motor Skills* 32(1):239–41 F '71. * (*PA* 46:2970)

CUMULATIVE NAME INDEX

Albright, L. E.: *rev*, 6:58
Astin, A. W.: *rev*, 6:58
Bassiri, T.: 55, 58
Baxter, B.: *rev*, 5:29
Bennett, G. K.: *rev*, 5:29
Clarke, W. V.: 2–5, 7, 10–1, 14–27, 30–2, 36, 39–42, 44–5, 48–51, 54–8
Dry, R. J.: 7
Dunnette, M. D.: 28
Farrington, A. D.: 12, 21
Fitzpatrick, E. D.: 6
Hall, C. E.: 26
Hammer, C. H.: 13

Harker, J. B.: 8
Hasler, K. R.: 39–42, 50
Hulin, C. L.: 29
Kessler, S.: 23, 27
Kirchner, W. K.: 28
Locke, E. A.: 29
Lundin, W. H.: 52
McCarty, J. J.: 6
Manning, W. H.: *rev*, 6:58
Merenda, P. F.: 10, 14–27, 30–2, 33–7, 43–9, 51, 53–8
Mohan, J.: 37, 43, 46–8, 53, 56
Mosel, J. N.: 1
Musiker, H. R.: 11, 24, 27, 52

[1092]

*Adaptive Behavior Scales. Mentally retarded and emotionally maladjusted ages 3–12, 13 and over; 1969–70, c1969; ABS; ratings in 24 areas: Part 1 (independent functioning, physical development, economic activity, language development, number and time concept, occupation—domestic, occupation—general, self-direction, responsibilities, socialization), Part 2 (violent and destructive behavior, antisocial, rebellious behavior, untrustworthy behavior, withdrawal, stereotyped behavior and odd mannerisms, inappropriate interpersonal manners, inappropriate vocal habits, unacceptable or eccentric habits, self-abusive behavior, hyperactive tendencies, sexually aberrant behavior, psychological disturbances, use of medications) ; Kazuo Nihira, Ray Foster, Max Shellhaas, and Henry Leland; American Association on Mental Deficiency. *

For additional information and reviews by Lovick C. Miller and Melvyn I. Semmel, see 7:37 (9 references).

REFERENCES THROUGH 1971

1–9. See 7:37.
10. LELAND, HENRY; NIHIRA, KAZUO; FOSTER, RAY; SHELLHAAS, MAX D.; AND KAGIN, EDWIN F. *Conference on Measurement of Adaptive Behavior: III.* Unpublished report to the National Institute of Mental Health, Project MH 14901, Parsons State Hospital and Training Center, 1968. Pp. 159. *
11. PAGE, EDWIN RICHARD. *Comparisons of the Illinois Test of Psycholinguistic Abilities and the Adaptive Behavior Checklist With Institutionalized Mentally Retarded Children.* Doctor's thesis, Ohio University (Athens, Ohio), 1970. (*DAI* 32:613B)
12. NIHIRA, KAZUO. "Environmental Expectations and Adaptive Behavior." Abstract. *Proc 79th Ann Conv Am Psychol Assn* 6(2):619–20 '71. * (*PA* 46:5353)

CUMULATIVE NAME INDEX

Fiedler, E. R.: 4
Foster, R.: 1–3, 10
Frank, H.: 4
Kagin, E. F.: 10
Leland, H.: 1, 10
Miller, L. C.: *rev*, 7:37

Nihira, K.: 1–3, 5–10, 12
Page, E. R.: 11
Semmel, M. I.: *rev*, 7:37
Shellhaas, M.: 1, 9
Shellhaas, M. D.: 10
Spencer, L.: 2

[1093]

Addiction Research Center Inventory. Drug addicts; 1961–67; ARCI; test booklet title is *The ARC Inventory;* subjective effects of drugs and various dimensions of psychiatric disorders; 29 scales: carelessness, general drug, psychopathic deviate, alcohol withdrawal, opiate withdrawal, 7 empirical drug scales (alcohol, amphetamine, chlorpromazine, LSD, morphine, pentobarbital, pyrahexyl), 7 group pattern scales (alcohol, amphetamine, chlorpromazine, LSD, morphine, morphine-amphetamine, pentobarbital-chlorpromazine-alcohol), 10 factor scales (reactivity, efficiency, patience-impatience, sentimental, uncritical, immaturity, masculinity-femininity, inadequacy, impulsivity, neurotic sensitivity versus psychopathic toughness) ; Harris E. Hill, Charles A. Haertzen, and Richard E. Belleville; Addiction Research Center (Att. Charles A. Haertzen), National Institute of Mental Health. *

For additional information, see P:3 (15 references).

REFERENCES THROUGH 1971

1–15. See P:3.
16. HAERTZEN, C. A., AND HOOKS, N. T., JR. "Effects of Adaptation Level, Context and Face Validity on Responses to Self-Report Psychological Inventories." *Psychol Rec* 18:339–49 Jl '68. * (*PA* 42:16412)
17. HAERTZEN, C. A. "Contrast Effect on Subjective Experience in Drug Experiments." *Psychol Rep* 24(1):69–70 F '69. * (*PA* 43:13881)
18. HAERTZEN, CHARLES A., AND HOOKS, NALL T., JR. "Changes in Personality and Subjective Experience Associated

With the Chronic Administration and Withdrawal of Opiates."
J Nerv & Mental Dis 148(6):606–14 Je '69. * (*PA* 44:875)
19. HAERTZEN, C. A.; MEKETON, M. J.; AND HOOKS, N. T., JR. "Subjective Experiences Produced by the Withdrawal of Opiates." *Brit J Addict* 65(3):245–55 N '70. *
20. HAERTZEN, CHARLES A. "Subjective Effects of Narcotic Antagonists Cyclazocine and Nalorphine on the Addiction Research Center Inventory (ARCI)." *Psychopharmacologia* (West Germany) 18(4):366–77 '70. * (*PA* 46:7030)
21. JAFFE, JEROME H.; SCHUSTER, CHARLES R.; SMITH, BETH B.; AND BLACHLEY, PAUL H. "Comparison of Acetylmethadol and Methadone in the Treatment of Long-Term Heroin Users." *J Am Med Assn* 211(11):1834–6 Mr 16 '70. * (*PA* 45:6605)
22. HAERTZEN, C. A., AND HOOKS, N. T., JR. "Contrast Effects From Simulation of Subjective Experiences: A Possible Standard for Behavioral Modification." *Brit J Addict* 66(3):225–7 N '71. * (*PA* 48:5223)
23. KIPLINGER, GLENN F.; MANNO, JOSEPH E.; RODDA, BRUCE E.; AND FORNEY, ROBERT B.; WITH THE TECHNICAL ASSISTANCE OF SUSAN E. HAINE, RITA EAST, AND ALICE B. RICHARDS. "Dose-Response Analysis of the Effects of Tetrahydrocannabinol in Man." *Clin Pharmacol & Therapeu* 12(4):650–7 Jl–Ag '71. *

CUMULATIVE NAME INDEX

Belleville, R. E.: 3
Blachley, P. H.: 21
East, R.: 23
Forney, R. B.: 23
Fuller, G.: 12
Fuller, G. B.: 15
Haertzen, C. A.: 1–20, 22
Haine, S. E.: 23
Hill, H. E.: 2–5
Hooks, N. T.: 15–6, 18–9, 22
Jaffe, J. H.: 21
Kiplinger, G. F.: 23

Manno, J. E.: 23
Meketon, M. J.: 14, 19
Miner, E. J.: 4–5, 9, 15
Monroe, J. J.: 15
Panton, J. H.: 13
Richards, A. B.: 23
Rodda, B. E.: 23
Schuster, C. R.: 21
Sharp, H.: 15
Smith, B. B.: 21
Wolbach, A. B.: 4–5

[1094]

The Adjective Check List. Grades 9–16 and adults; 1952–65; ACL; 24 scores: number of adjectives checked, defensiveness, favorable adjectives checked, unfavorable adjectives checked, self-confidence, self-control, lability, personal adjustment, achievement, dominance, endurance, order, intraception, nurturance, affiliation, heterosexuality, exhibition, autonomy, aggression, change, succorance, abasement, deference, counseling readiness; Harrison G. Gough and Alfred B. Heilbrun, Jr. (manual); Consulting Psychologists Press, Inc. *

For additional information and reviews by Leonard G. Rorer and Forrest L. Vance, see 7:38 (131 references); see also P:4 (102 references).

REFERENCES THROUGH 1971

1–102. See P:4.
103–233. See 7:38.
234. ALLEN, MARK KNIGHT. *Personality and Cultural Factors Related to Religious Authoritarianism.* Doctor's thesis, Stanford University (Stanford, Calif.), 1955. (*DA* 15:2324)
235. SHELSKY, IRVING. *The Effect of Disability on Self-Concept.* Doctor's thesis, Columbia University (New York, N.Y.), 1957. (*DA* 17:1598)
236. GRIGG, AUSTIN E. "Experience of Clinicians, and Speech Characteristics and Statements of Clients as Variables in Clinical Judgment." *J Consult Psychol* 22:315–9 Ag '58. * (*PA* 34:1367)
237. LEVITT, EUGENE E.; DEN BREEIJEN, ARDIE; AND PERSKY, HAROLD. "The Induction of Clinical Anxiety by Means of a Standardized Hypnotic Technique." *Am J Clin Hyp* 2:206–14 Ap '60. * (*PA* 35:3623)
238. HEILBRUN, A. B. "Psychological Factors Related to Counseling Readiness and Implications for Counselor Behavior." *J Counsel Psychol* 9:353–8 w '62. * (*PA* 39:2298)
239. HEILBRUN, ALFRED B., JR. "Further Validation of the Need Scales: The Order Scale." Abstract. *J Consult Psychol* 26:478 O '62. * (*PA* 39:1734)
240. HEILBRUN, ALFRED B., JR. "Social Desirability and the Relative Validities of Achievement Scales." *J Consult Psychol* 26:383–6 Ag '62. * (*PA* 38:4310)
241. MACKINNON, DONALD W. Chap. 11, "Creativity and Images of the Self," pp. 250–78. In *The Study of Lives: Essays in Honor of Henry A. Murray.* Edited by Robert W. White and Katherine F. Bruner. New York: Atherton Press, 1963. Pp. xxi, 442. * (*PA* 38:6039)
242. POLDER, GORDON JAMES. *An Experimental Evaluation of Male Sensitivity to Deviance From Sex-Typical Behavior and Its Relationship to Counseling Readiness.* Doctor's thesis, State University of Iowa (Iowa City, Iowa), 1963. (*DA* 24:4805)
243. HEILBRUN, ALFRED B., JR. "Conformity to Masculinity-Femininity Stereotypes and Ego Identity in Adolescents." *Psychol Rep* 14:351–7 Ap '64. * (*PA* 39:1417)

244. HEILBRUN, ALFRED B., JR. "Further Validation of a Counseling Readiness Scale." *J Counsel Psychol* 11:290–2 f '64. *
245. MCGURK, ETHEL LA NOUE. *Determinants of Differential Susceptibility to Visual Illusions.* Doctor's thesis, University of California (Berkeley, Calif.), 1964. (*DA* 25:7382)
246. PEYTON, PATRICIA. *A Comparison of Values, Self Concept, and Success in College of Negro and White College Students.* Master's thesis, Ohio University (Athens, Ohio), 1964.
247. RASMUSSEN, JOHN E. "Relationship of Ego Identity to Psychosocial Effectiveness." *Psychol Rep* 15:815–25 D '64. * (*PA* 39:7951)
248. HEATH, DOUGLAS H.; WITH THE ASSISTANCE OF HARRIET E. HEATH. *Explorations of Maturity: Studies of Mature and Immature College Men.* New York: Appleton-Century-Crofts, 1965. Pp. xv, 423. * (*PA* 39:12057)
249. HEILBRUN, ALFRED B., JR. "On Predicting Defection From Psychotherapy." *Psychol Rep* 19:61–2 Ag '65. * (*PA* 40:12382)
250. SPITZER, STEPHEN P.; STRATTON, JOHN R.; FITZGERALD, JACK D.; AND MACH, BRIGITTE K. "The Self Concept: Test Equivalence and Perceived Validity." *Sociol Q* 7:265–80 su '66. *
251. BARRON, FRANK, AND ROSENBERG, MARVIN. "King Lear and His Fool: A Study of the Conception and Enactment of Dramatic Role in Relation to Self-Conception." Abstract. *Proc 76th Ann Conv Am Psychol Assn* 3:369–70 '68. * (*PA* 43:883, title only)
252. EKMAN, PAUL, AND FRIESEN, WALLACE V. "Nonverbal Behavior in Psychotherapy Research," pp. 186–92. *Res Psychother* 3:179–216 '68. *
253. GOLDMEIER, JOHN. "A Study of Selected Personality Attributes and Treatment Preferences of Caseworkers and Casework Students." *Social Service R* 42:231–40 Je '68. *
254. LAPLACE, ROSABELLE; STEIN, DAVID D.; AND WEISSMAN, HERBERT N. "Clinical Experience and the Perception of the Schizophrenic Patient." *J Consult & Clin Psychol* 32:134–9 Ap '68. * (*PA* 42:9147)
255. REHM, LYNN P., AND MARSTON, ALBERT R. "Reduction of Social Anxiety Through Modification of Self-Reinforcement: An Instigation Therapy Technique." *J Consult & Clin Psychol* 32:565–74 O '68. * (*PA* 43:1018)
256. SANDERS, ERIC P. "Evolutionary Performance, Managerial Abilities, and Change: An Exploratory Investigation of Organizations." *J Appl Psychol* 52:362–5 O '68. * (*PA* 42:19536)
257. TARLETON, M. ROSS BERNARD. *The Relation of Perceived Attitudes of Reference Group Members to Personal Attitudes Toward and Decisions to Enter Roman Catholic Sisterhoods.* Doctor's thesis, Catholic University of America (Washington, D.C.), 1968. (*DAI* 30:838A)
258. BERRY, GORDON LA VERN. *A Comparative Study of Selected Personality Characteristics of Educationally Disadvantaged Adolescents Enrolled in a Continuation School and Adolescents Enrolled in a Public High School.* Doctor's thesis, Marquette University (Milwaukee, Wis.), 1969. (*DAI* 31:140A)
259. BROUSSEAU, MARY ALINE. *Comparison of Disciplined and Non-Disciplined Women Residents Marquette University 1967–68.* Doctor's thesis, Marquette University (Milwaukee, Wis.), 1969. (*DAI* 31:4451A)
260. NOLAND, SARAH JANE, AND CATRON, DAVID W. "Cooperative Behavior Among High School Students on the Prisoner's Dilemma Game." *Psychol Rep* 24(3):711–8 Je '69. * (*PA* 44:234)
261. CARTWRIGHT, LILLIAN KAUFMAN. *Women in Medical School.* Doctor's thesis, University of California (Berkeley, Calif.), 1970. (*DAI* 31:6237B)
262. GIER, DOROTHY LAURETTA. *An Investigation of Dogmatism and Stress of Elementary Student Teachers.* Doctor's thesis, University of Michigan (Ann Arbor, Mich.), 1970. (*DAI* 31:4004A)
263. GOLDMAN, ROY DAVID. *Parameters in the Choice of Cognitive Strategies.* Doctor's thesis, University of California (Berkeley, Calif.), 1970. (*DAI* 31:7571B)
264. HULAC, GEORGIA MAY. *Measurement of Activation, Competitiveness, and Sociability Through an Activity Selection Questionnaire.* Doctor's thesis, University of New Mexico (Albuquerque, N.M.), 1970. (*DAI* 31:5179A)
265. KITCHIN, WILLIAM WILLIS. *Relationships of Autonomy and Succorance to Adult Students' References, Satisfactions, and Performance in University Evening College Classes.* Doctor's thesis, University of North Carolina (Chapel Hill, N.C.), 1970. (*DAI* 31:3858A)
266. NAOR, NEHAMA KLIBAN. *Configurational Analysis of the Strong Vocational Interest Blank (SVIB) and Concomitant Personality Correlates.* Doctor's thesis, University of North Carolina (Chapel Hill, N.C.), 1970. (*DAI* 31:6908B)
267. OAKES, MERILEE R. *Pills, Periods, and Personality.* Doctor's thesis, University of Michigan (Ann Arbor, Mich.), 1970. (*DAI* 31:7577B)
268. POINDEXTER, CHARLES CRAWFORD, JR. *Degrees and Dropouts: A Profile of Student Characteristics in North Carolina Community Colleges.* Doctor's thesis, University of North Carolina (Chapel Hill, N.C.), 1970. (*DAI* 31:5776A)
269. RUBIN, GERALD. *Reduction of Egocentrism in Chronic-*

Schizophrenic Patients as a Function of a Conservation Learning Task. Doctor's thesis, University of Maryland (College Park, Md.), 1970. (*DAI* 31:5007B)

270. RUTSTEIN, ELEANOR H. *The Effects of Aggressive Stimulation on Suicidal Patients: An Experimental Study of the Psychoanalytic Theory of Suicide.* Doctor's thesis, New York University (New York, N.Y.), 1970. (*DAI* 31:7611B)

271. SEEVERS, CHARLES J. *Problems and Psychological Needs of Lutheran Confirmands.* Doctor's thesis, University of Notre Dame (Notre Dame, Ind.), 1970. (*DAI* 31:4572A)

272. TOM, VICTOR R. *The Role of Personality and Organizational Images in the Recruiting Process.* Doctor's thesis, University of California (Berkeley, Calif.), 1970. (*DAI* 31:7662B)

273. TRAILL, RONALD DAVID. *The Effects of Supervisory Feedback of Interaction Analysis on the Verbal Behavior of Elementary Student Teachers.* Doctor's thesis, University of California (Berkeley, Calif.), 1970. (*DAI* 31:6460A)

274. TUCKER, BERNICE ZIPIN. *Feminine Sex-Role and Occupational Choice: A Study of Self and Intergroup Perceptions of Three Groups of Women.* Doctor's thesis, Temple University (Philadelphia, Pa.), 1970. (*DAI* 31:5783A)

275. WEISER, JOHN C. "Personality Variables Associated With Creativity in Prospective Female Teachers." *J Stud Pers Assn Teach Ed* 8(3):77–84 sp '70. * (*PA* 44:18682)

276. APFELDORF, MAX, AND HUNLEY, PHYLLIS J. "The Adjective Check List Applied to Older Institutionalized Men." *J Pers Assess* 35(5):457–62 O '71. * (*PA* 47:9583)

277. ASTIN, HELEN S. "Self-Perceptions of Student Activists." *J Col Stud Personnel* 12(4):263–70 Jl '71. * (*PA* 47:7512)

278. BARNETT, ROSALIND. "Personality Correlates of Vocational Planning." *Genetic Psychol Monogr* 83(2):309–56 My '71. * (*PA* 46:5539)

279. BATES, HENRY D. "Toward the Development of a Screening Scale for Assertive Training." *Psychol Rep* 28(1):99–107 F '71. *

280. BERG, NORMAN L. "Effect of Alcoholic Intoxication on Self-Concept: Studies of Alcoholics and Controls in Laboratory Conditions." *Q J Studies Alcohol* 32(2):442–53 Je '71. *

281. BOHN, MARTIN J. JR. "Psychological Needs of Engineering, Pre-Law, Pre-Medical, and Undecided College Freshmen." *J Col Stud Personnel* 12(5):359–61 S '71. * (*PA* 47:11569)

282. BRAUN, ROBERT W. *Curricular Choice, Achievement, and Self-Concept in Engineering and Engineering Technology Programs at a College of Engineering.* Doctor's thesis, Marquette University (Milwaukee, Wis.), 1971. (*DAI* 32:4411A)

283. BROWN, BARRY S.; DUPONT, ROBERT L.; KOZEL, NICHOLAS J.; AND SPEVACEK, JOHN D. "Staff Conceptions of Inmate Characteristics: A Comparison of Treatment and Custodial Staffs at Two Differing Institutions." *Criminol* 9(2–3):316–29 Ag–N '71. *

284. BRUHN, JOHN G.; HAMPTON, JAMES W.; AND CHANDLER, BETTY C. "Clinical Marginality and Psychological Adjustment in Hemophilia." *J Psychosom Res* (England) 15(2):207–13 Je '71. * (*PA* 49:7094)

285. BRUHN, JOHN G.; HAMPTON, JAMES W.; AND PHILIPS, BILLY U. "A Psycho-Social Study of Married Hemophiliacs and Their Wives and Hemophiliac Adolescents and Their Parents." *J Psychosom Res* (England) 15(2):293–303 Je '71. *

286. CASTELLOW, WILBUR ALLEN. *Relationships Between the Spiral After-Effect and Extraversion, Neuroticism, Sex, and Induced Arousal.* Doctor's thesis, University of North Carolina (Chapel Hill, N.C.), 1971. (*DAI* 32:7287B)

287. CHEIFETZ, DAVID I.; GARRON, DAVID C.; LEAVITT, FRANK; KLAWANS, HAROLD L.; AND GARVIN, JOHN S. "Emotional Disturbance Accompanying the Treatment of Parkinsonism With L-Dopa." *Clin Pharmacol & Therapeu* 12(1):56–61 Ja–F '71. *

288. EVANS, RAY B. "Adjective Check List Scores of Homosexual Men." *J Pers Assess* 35(4):344–9 Ag '71. * (*PA* 47:5206)

289. GANTZ, BENJAMIN S., JR.; ERICKSON, CLARA; AND STEPHENSON, ROBERT W. "Measuring the Motivation to Manage in a Research and Development Population." Abstract. *Proc 79th Ann Conv Am Psychol Assn* 6(1):129–30 '71. * (*PA* 46:3949)

290. GOUGH, HARRISON G. "The Assessment of Wayward Impulse by Means of the Personnel Reaction Blank." *Personnel Psychol* 24(4):669–77 w '71. *

291. GRAVES, WILLIAM H., AND SHEARER, ROBERT A. "Use of the Adjective Check List to Elicit Description of Self-Ideal Discrepancy." *Percept & Motor Skills* 32(3):781–2 Je '71. * (*PA* 47:900)

292. HEILBRUN, ALFRED B., JR. "Female Preference for Therapist Initial Interview Style as a Function of 'Client' and Therapist Social Role Variables." *J Counsel Psychol* 18(4):285–91 Jl '71. * (*PA* 46:10954)

293. HEILBRUN, ALFRED B., JR. "Maternal Child Rearing and Creativity in Sons." *J Genetic Psychol* 119(2):175–9 D '71. * (*PA* 48:999)

294. HOOKE, JAMES F., AND KRAUSS, HERBERT H. "Personality Characteristics of Successful Police Sergeant Candidates." *J Crim Law Criminol & Police Sci* 62(1):104–6 Mr '71. * (*PA* 46:11787)

295. JOHNSON, DAVID JAN. *Job Complexity, Job Attitude, and Self Concept Among Probation Officers.* Doctor's thesis, University of Minnesota (Minneapolis, Minn.), 1971. (*DAI* 32:6544A)

296. KAPLAN, MARTIN F. "The Effect of Judgmental Dispositions on Forming Impressions of Personality." *Can J Behav Sci* 3(3):259–67 Jl '71. * (*PA* 47:2874)

297. KNIGHT, BRENT MALCOLM. *A Study of Selected Variables Associated With Idiosyncrasy Credit.* Doctor's thesis, Western Michigan University (Kalamazoo, Mich.), 1971. (*DAI* 32:2957A)

298. LEWIS, EVELYN GARY. *The Difference Among Normal, Social Disability and Physically Disabled Groups in Body Image and Self Concept.* Doctor's thesis, University of Connecticut (Storrs, Conn.), 1971. (*DAI* 32:3096A)

299. LOHMAN, KEITH DOUGLASS. *The Ideal Colleague: An Analysis of University Faculty Perceptions.* Doctor's thesis, University of Northern Colorado (Greeley, Colo.), 1971. (*DAI* 32:4188B)

300. McLAUGHLIN, FRANK E. "Personality Changes Through Alternate Group Leadership." *Nursing Res* 20(2):123–30 Mr–Ap '71. * (*PA* 47:3073) *

301. MARTIN, ROGER D. "Personality Correlates of Life Insurance Underwriters." *Studies Pers Psychol* (Canada) 3(1):63–7 Ap '71. * (*PA* 46:11769)

302. PARKER, GEORGE V. C. "Prediction of Individual Stability." *Ed & Psychol Meas* 31(4):875–86 w '71. * (*PA* 48:1009)

303. RODGERS, ROBERT FLOYD. *The Relationship Between Personality and Style of Interpersonal Relationships and Effectiveness and Satisfaction as a Residence Hall Counselor.* Doctor's thesis, Ohio State University (Columbus, Ohio), 1971. (*DAI* 32:1282A)

304. SIMPSON, ALAN ROGER. *A Comparison of Selected Characteristics of Counselors Leaving the State Rehabilitation Agency With Counselors Who Stay.* Doctor's thesis, University of Iowa (Iowa City, Iowa), 1971. (*DAI* 32:4362A)

305. SUTER, BARBARA ANN. *Masculinity-Femininity in Creative Women.* Doctor's thesis, Fordham University (New York, N.Y.), 1971. (*DAI* 32:2411B)

306. TAKACS, GEORGE GABRIEL. *A Comparison of Selected Self-Concept Variables of Tenth Grade Male Students and Their Course of Study.* Doctor's thesis, University of Connecticut (Storrs, Conn.), 1971. (*DAI* 33:3410A)

307. THOMPSON, NORMAN L., JR.; McCANDLESS, BOYD R.; AND STRICKLAND, BONNIE R. "Personal Adjustment of Male and Female Homosexuals and Heterosexuals." *J Abn Psychol* 78(2):237–40 O '71. * (*PA* 47:9286)

308. THOMPSON, NORMAN LEE, JR. *Family Background and Sexual Identity in Male and Female Homosexuals.* Doctor's thesis, Emory University (Atlanta, Ga.), 1971. (*DAI* 32:1863B)

309. TOM, VICTOR R. "The Role of Personality and Organizational Images in the Recruiting Process." *Organiz Behav & Hum Perfor* 6(5):573–92 S '71. * (*PA* 47:9882)

310. UCHIYAMA, ANDY, AND LINDGREN, HENRY CLAY. "Ideal Teacher Concepts: Attitude Shift After Practice Teaching." *Psychol Rep* 28(2):470 Ap '71. * (*PA* 46:7667)

311. VAN HEERDEN, LEONORA ENGELA. *Job Satisfaction and Personality of the Hospital Dietitian.* Doctor's thesis, Cornell University (Ithaca, N.Y.), 1971. (*DAI* 32:5269B)

312. WHITTAKER, DAVID. "The Psychological Adjustment of Intellectual, Nonconformist, Collegiate Dropouts." *Adolescence* 6(24):415–24 w '71. * (*PA* 48:7723)

313. WHITTAKER, DAVID, AND WATTS, WILLIAM A. "Personality Characteristics Associated With Activism and Disaffiliation in Today's College-Age Youth." *J Counsel Psychol* 18(3):200–6 My '71. * (*PA* 46:5451)

314. WIGGINS, JERRY S.; GOLDBERG, LEWIS R.; AND APPELBAUM, MARK. "MMPI Content Scales: Interpretative Norms and Correlations With Other Scales." *J Consult & Clin Psychol* 37(3):403–10 D '71. * (*PA* 47:8950)

315. WILLIAMS, CLARK EUGENE. *Role-Taking Aptitude and Instructor Effectiveness Among Appointed Seminar Leaders.* Doctor's thesis, American University (Washington, D.C.), 1971. (*DAI* 32:1930A)

316. YARNELL, THOMAS. "Percentile Norms for the Adjective Check List (ACL) Creativity Scale." *Psychol Rep* 29(2):675–8 O '71. * (*PA* 47:8933)

317. YARNELL, THOMAS D. "A Common Item Creativity Scale for the Adjective Check List." *Psychol Rep* 29(2):466 O '71. * (*PA* 47:8934)

318. ZACKER, JOSEPH; RUTTER, ELLIOT; AND BARD, MORTON. "Evaluation of Attitudinal Changes in a Program of Community Consultation." *Commun Mental Health J* 7(3):236–41 S '71. * (*PA* 47:5545)

CUMULATIVE NAME INDEX

[1095]

The Adjustment Inventory. Grades 9–16, adults;
1934–63; AI; 2 levels; Hugh M. Bell; Consulting Psychologists Press, Inc. *

a) REVISED (1962) STUDENT FORM. Grades 9–16; 1934–
63; 6 scores: home, health, submissiveness, emotionality, hostility, masculinity.

b) ADULT FORM. Adults; 1938–39; 6 scores: home, occupational, health, social, emotional, total.

For additional information, see P:5 (16 references);
for a review by Forrest L. Vance and an excerpted review by Laurence Siegel, see 6:59 (11 references); see
also 5:30 (26 references); for reviews by Nelson G.
Hanawalt and Theodore R. Sarbin, see 4:28 (104 references); for reviews by Raymond B. Cattell, John G.
Darley, C. M. Louttit, and Percival M. Symonds of the
original Student Form, reviews by S. J. Beck, J. P.
Guilford, and Doncaster G. Humm of the Adult Form,
and an excerpted review by Ruth A. Pedersen, see 2:
1200 (15 references); for a review by Austin H. Turney
of the Student Form, see 1:912.

REFERENCES THROUGH 1971

1–15. See 2:1200.
16–119. See 4:28.

120–145. See 5:30.
146–156. See 6:59.
157–172. See P:5.
173. LUNGER, RUTH, AND PAGE, JAMES D. "Worries of College Freshmen." *J Genetic Psychol* 54:457–60 Je '39. * (*PA* 14:614)
174. ABERNETHY, ETHEL MARY. "Further Data on Personality and Family Position." *J Psychol* 10:303–7 O '40. * (*PA* 15:917)
175. BILLIG, ALBERT LEROY. "Finger Nail-Biting: Its Incipience, Incidence, and Amelioration." *Genetic Psychol Monogr* 24:123–218 Ag '41. * (*PA* 16:795)
176. ARSENIAN, SETH. "Own Estimate and Objective Measurement." *J Ed Psychol* 33:291–302 Ap '42. * (*PA* 17:934)
177. TRAVERS, R. M. W. "Who Are the Best Judges of the Public?" *Pub Opin Q* 6:628–33 w '42. * (*PA* 17:1274)
178. CRIDER, BLAKE. "A Study of a Character Analyst." *J Social Psychol* 20:315–8 N '44. * (*PA* 19:713)
179. LONG, HERMAN H. "Tested Personality Adjustment in Jewish and Non-Jewish Groups." *J Negro Ed* 13:64–9 w '44. * (*PA* 18:1757)
180. ROSE, ANNELIES ARGELANDER. "Insecurity Feelings in Adolescent Girls." *Nerv Child* 4:46–59 O '44. * (*PA* 19:1834)
181. TODD, J. E. "Measurement in the Continuous Selection and Counseling of Students in a College of Physical Education and Social Work." *Ed & Psychol Meas* 4:233–43 au '44. * (*PA* 19:1810)
182. BOLLINGER, RUSSELL V. "The Social Impact of the Teacher on the Pupil." *J Exp Ed* 13:153–73 Je '45. * (*PA* 19:3483)
183. PREVEY, ESTHER ELIZABETH. "A Quantitative Study of Family Practices in Training Children in the Use of Money." *J Ed Psychol* 36:411–28 O '45. * (*PA* 20:1596)
184. SEAGOE, MAY V. "Permanence of Interest in Teaching." *J Ed Res* 38:678–84 My '45. * (*PA* 19:3183)
185. SMITH, HENRY P. "A Study in the Selective Character of American Secondary Education: Participation in School Activities as Conditioned by Socio-Economic Status and Other Factors." *J Ed Psychol* 36:229–46 Ap '45. * (*PA* 19:2378)
186. BERRY, GEORGE S. "An Experiment in Self-Analysis." *J Ed Psychol* 37:111–24 F '46. * (*PA* 20:2061)
187. ALTUS, WILLIAM D., AND BELL, HUGH M. "An Analysis of Four Orally Administered Measures of Adjustment." *Ed & Psychol Meas* 7:101–15 sp '47. * (*PA* 22:623)
188. BARNES, T. C., AND AMOROSO, MARIE D. "Electroencephalograms Correlated With Scores of the Bell Adjustment Inventory for Personality." Abstract. *Federation Proc* 6:75 Mr '47. * (*PA* 21:3954, title only)
189. DUNCAN, MELBA HURD. "Personality Adjustment Techniques in Voice Therapy." *J Speech Disorders* 12:161–7 Je '47. * (*PA* 22:1768)
190. POWELL, MARGARET. "An Analysis of Relationships Existent Between Health Practice, Adjustment, and Physical Performance of Freshmen Women." *Res Q* 18:176–86 O '47. * (*PA* 22:2309)
191. ROSE, ANNELIES ARGELANDER. "A Study of Homesickness in College Freshmen." *J Social Psychol* 26:185–202 N '47. * (*PA* 22:4613)
192. PORTENIER, LILLIAN G. "Personality Tests in a University Guidance Program." *J Ed Psychol* 39:479–87 D '48. * (*PA* 23:3218)
193. ROSE, ANNELIES ARGELANDER. "The Homes of Homesick Girls." *J Child Psychiatry* 1(2):181–9 '48. * (*PA* 23:2312)
194. THERON, P. A. "Peripheral Vasometer Reactions as Indices of Basic Emotional Tension and Lability." *Psychosom Med* 10:335–46 N–D '48. *
195. ALTUS, WILLIAM D., AND CLARK, JERRY H. "The Effect of Adjustment Patterns Upon the Intercorrelation of Intelligence Subtest Variables." *J Social Psychol* 30:39–48 Ag '49. * (*PA* 24:2362)
196. DAMRIN, DORA E. "Family Size and Sibling Age, Sex, and Position as Related to Certain Aspects of Adjustment." *J Social Psychol* 29:93–102 F '49. * (*PA* 23:4224)
197. LANDIS, PAUL H. "Personality Differences of Girls From Farm, Town, and City." *Rural Sociol* 14:10–20 Mr '49. *
198. STONE, CAROL LARSON. "Sorority Status and Personality Adjustment." *Am Sociol R* 16:538–41 Ag '51. * (*PA* 27:1442)
199. DARLING, C. D., AND SUMMERSKILL, JOHN. "Emotional Factors in Obesity and Weight Reduction." *J Am Dietetic Assn* 29:1204–7 D '53. *
200. MARTINSON, FLOYD M. *Some Personality Adjustment Differences of Rural Nonmigrants and Migrants.* Doctor's thesis, University of Minnesota (Minneapolis, Minn.), 1953. (*DA* 13:1291)
201. CAREY, JOAN. *An Analysis of Certain Traits as Exhibited by a Group of Women Selected for Elementary Education at Syracuse University.* Doctor's thesis, Syracuse University (Syracuse, N.Y.), 1954. (*DA* 15:1356)
202. LaBUE, ANTHONY CHARLES. *An Analysis of Some Factors Associated With Persistence of Interest in Teaching as a Vocational Choice.* Doctor's thesis, Syracuse University (Syracuse, N.Y.), 1954. (*DA* 14:2001)
203. McGLOTHLIN, WILLIAM H. "A Psychometric Study of Gambling." *J Consult Psychol* 18:145–9 Ap '54. * (*PA* 29:2232)

204. MARTIN, RICHARD PANTALL. *The Adjustment of Latin-American Male Students in Selected Private Secondary Schools in the United States.* Doctor's thesis, Northwestern University (Evanston, Ill.), 1954. (*DA* 14:1605)
205. SMITH, GEORGE HORSLEY. "Personality Scores and the Personal Distance Effect." *J Social Psychol* 39:57–62 F '54. * (*PA* 28:8632)
206. CANTONI, LOUIS J. "Men, Emotions and Jobs." *Sch & Soc* 81:40–1 F 5 '55. * (*PA* 30:5345)
207. MARTINSON, FLOYD M. "Ego Deficiency as a Factor in Marriage." *Am Sociol R* 20:161–4 Ap '55. * (*PA* 31:912)
208. SANDERS, WILLIAM B.; OSBORNE, R. TRAVIS; AND GREENE, J. E. "Intelligence and Academic Performance of College Students of Urban, Rural, and Mixed Backgrounds." *J Ed Res* 49:185–93 N '55. * (*PA* 30:7774)
209. SUMMERSKILL, JOHN, AND DARLING, C. DOUGLAS. "Emotional Adjustment and Dieting Performance." *J Consult Psychol* 19:151–3 Ap '55. * (*PA* 30:1272)
210. WITTICH, JOHN J. "The Generality of the Prediction of Self Reports." *J Consult Psychol* 19:445–8 D '55. * (*PA* 30:7237)
211. GREEN, LEAH ANN. *A Study of Creativity and the Self-Attitudes and Sociability of High School Students.* Doctor's thesis, Columbia University (New York, N.Y.), 1957. (*DA* 17:1807)
212. YOUNG, CHARLOTTE M.; BERRESFORD, KATHLEEN; AND MOORE, NORMAN S. "Psychologic Factors in Weight Control." *Am J Clin Nutr* 5:186–91 Mr–Ap '57. * (*PA* 32:4456)
213. IRWIN, JACK MENZENWERTH. *A Study of Certain Personal and Social Factors Differentiating the Nonevidently Handicapped From the Physically Normal Adolescent.* Doctor's thesis, Cornell University (Ithaca, N.Y.), 1960. (*DA* 21:3852)
214. GREENE, JAMES E., SR. "Factors Associated With Absenteeism Among Students in Two Metropolitan High Schools." *J Exp Ed* 31:389–94 su '63. *
215. SMITH, PAUL M. "Some Implications for Freshman Orientation Activities With Negro College Students." *J Col Stud Personnel* 5:176–9+ Mr '64. *
216. HOFFMAN, MARY FRANCINE JOHNSON. *An Investigation of the Comparative Scholastic Success and Personality Adjustment of Texas Public Junior College Transfers and Native Students Who Graduated From East Texas State University in May, 1965.* Doctor's thesis, East Texas State University (Commerce, Tex.), 1965. (*DA* 27:1545A)
217. McKINNEY, DORLIS JOHNSON. *A Comparison Between Women Physical Education Majors and Non-Majors in Selected Personal and Social Characteristics.* Master's thesis, Arkansas State College (State College, Ark.), 1965.
218. MEANS, HESTER RICE. *An Analysis of the First Freshman Class of the DeKalb Junior College.* Doctor's thesis, University of Georgia (Athens, Ga.), 1966. (*DA* 27:1552A)
219. STRÜMPFER, D. J. W. "The Relation of Draw-A-Person Test Variables to Psychometric and Inventory Measures." *J Social Res* (South Africa) 15(1):1–9 '66. * (*PA* 42:2613)
220. GEORGE, E. I.; PILLAY, P. GOPALA; AND DHARMANGADAN, B. "Effect of Physical Disability on Personality Adjustment and Achievement of Secondary School Pupils." *J Ed & Psychol* (India) 24:180–7 Ja '67. *
221. HARTNETT, RODNEY T., AND SELIGSOHN, HARRIET C. "The Effects of Varying Degrees of Anonymity on Responses to Different Types of Psychological Questionnaires." *J Ed Meas* 4:95–103 su '67. * (*PA* 42:3199)
222. KAKKAR, S. B. "Adjustment and Self-Acceptance." *Manas* (India) 14(1):31–5 '67. * (*PA* 42:7135)
223. FROILAND, DONALD JOSEPH. *Parental Attitudes: A Predictor of Academic Achievement.* Doctor's thesis, Marquette University (Milwaukee, Wis.), 1968. (*DAI* 31:1618A)
224. HEILMAN, HENRIETTA. *A Study of the Relationships Between Certain Factors Associated With Employability and the Rehabilitation Status of Selected Psychiatric Clients in a Vocational Rehabilitation Program.* Doctor's thesis, New York University (New York, N.Y.), 1968. (*DA* 29:2564A)
225. MAZUREK, FREDERICK H. *The Occupational Interests of Superior Ninth-Grade Boys as Related to Their Aspects of Adjustment.* Master's thesis, Catholic University of America (Washington, D.C.), 1968.
226. PANDEY, J., AND SINHA, J. B. P. "Dependence Proneness and Perceived Problems of Adjustment." *J Psychol Res* (India) 12:104–10 S '68. *
227. TURNER, MARY MALISSA. *Personality Factors for Major Students in Health, Physical Education, and Recreation.* Doctor's thesis, University of Alabama (University, Ala.), 1968. (*DA* 29:3861A)
228. BANGS, ARTHUR J. *The Parental Perception of Certain Inventoried Traits of a Selected Group of Male Adolescent Offspring.* Doctor's thesis, Catholic University of America (Washington, D.C.), 1969. (*DAI* 30:1810A)
229. BAZIK, ANNA MARIE. *Characteristics of Junior College Male Students Who Seek Counseling Services.* Doctor's thesis, Northwestern University (Evanston, Ill.), 1969. (*DAI* 30:2793A)
230. BOTTRILL, JOHN H. "Personality Change in LSD Users." *J General Psychol* 80(2):157–61 Ap '69. * (*PA* 43:11280)
231. CHANG, CHUN-HSING. "EEG Alpha Frequency Correlate

of Emotional Stability in Normal Adult Subjects." *Psychol & Ed* (Taiwan) 3:49–56 D '69. *

232. GRANLUND, ELNORE, AND KNOWLES, LOIS. "Child-Parent Identification and Academic Underachievement." *J Consult & Clin Psychol* 33(4):495–6 Ag '69. * (*PA* 43:16456)

233. HAZARI, ANANDI, AND SINGH, RAMADHAR. "Social Maladaptation as a Factor in the Recall of Completed and Interrupted Tasks." *Indian Psychol R* 5(2):122–5 Ja '69. *

234. JAMUAR, K. K. "Study Habits and Some Personality Variables." *Psychol Studies* (India) 14(2):100–3 Jl '69. *

235. KUMAR, K. "Effects of Puberty on the Adjustments of Girls." *J Ed & Psychol* (India) 26(4):232–7 Ja '69. *

236. KUNDU, RAMANATH, AND MITRA, IRA. "Personality Adjustment Pattern of Post-Graduate Male Students." *Psychol Studies* (India) 14(2):94–9 Jl '69. *

237. RAMIREZ, MANUEL, III. "Identification With Mexican-American Values and Psychological Adjustment in Mexican-American Adolescents." *Int J Social Psychiatry* (England) 15(2):151–6 sp '69. * (*PA* 44:6537)

238. WEIR, CAROL E. *Personal and Social Adjustment of Male Students in Selected Secondary Schools in Western North Carolina.* Master's thesis, University of Tennessee (Knoxville, Tenn.), 1969.

239. WOTRUBA, RICHARD T. "Can Residence Hall Staff Be Selected Scientifically?" *NASPA* 7(2):107–11 O '69. *

240. BROWN, DUANE, AND JONES, ELLA. "Using the Bell Adjustment Inventory With the Mentally Retarded." *Rehabil Counsel B* 13(3):288–94 Mr '70. *

241. DE, BIMALESWAR, AND SINGH, RAMADHAR. "Home Adjustment as a Determinant of Academic Motivation." *Indian Ed R* 5(2):52–8 Jl '70. * (*PA* 46:5654)

242. DIELMAN, T. E., AND WILSON, WARNER R. "Convergent and Discriminant Validity of Three Measures of Ability, Aspiration-Level, Achievement, Adjustment and Dominance." *J Ed Meas* 7(3):185–90 f '70. * (*PA* 45:4915)

243. ELBERFELD, STEPHAN, AND LOVE, BETHOLENE. "Identification of Aptitude Criteria for Medical Technology." *Am J Med Technol* 36(8):388–99 Ag '70. *

244. RUSSELL, WENDELL PHILLIPS. *Intellectual and Non-Intellectual Factors Affecting the Attrition Rate of Students Entering Virginia Union University in 1965.* Doctor's thesis, University of Virginia (Charlottesville, Va.), 1970. (*DAI* 31:4474A)

245. THIMMAPPA, M. S. "Intelligence and Personality Adjustment in Epileptic Patients: A Preliminary Study." *Trans All-India Inst Mental Health* 10:81–8 D '70. * (*PA* 47:11455)

246. BAILEY, ROGER C., AND SHAW, WILLIAM R. "Direction of Self-Estimate of Ability and College-Related Criteria." *Psychol Rep* 29(3):959–64 D '71. * (*PA* 47:9602)

247. MURPHY, SOLBRITT; NICKOLS, JACKSON; EDDY, ROGER; AND UMPHRESS, AGNES. "Behavioral Characteristics of Adolescent Enuretics." *Adolescence* 6(21):1–18 sp '71. * (*PA* 46:11223)

248. OSBORN, WILLIAM P. "Adjustment Differences of Selected Foreign-Born Pupils." *Calif J Ed Res* 22(3):131–9 My '71. * (*PA* 46:11481)

249. ROSS, LOUIS. "Forecasting the Academic Achievement of Engineering Freshmen." *J Ed Res* 64(7):307–10 Mr '71. *

CUMULATIVE NAME INDEX

Adjustment Inventory

Watson, R. I.: 57
Weir, C. E.: 238
Weiss, A. J.: 170
Williams, H. M.: 17, 21
Williams, J. L.: 144
Williamson, E. G.: 11, 30
Wilson, C. E.: 106
Wilson, W. R.: 242
Winthrop, H.: 151

Wittich, J. J.: 210
Wittman, M. P.: 62, 71
Wood, A. L.: 89
Woodruff, L.: 64
Woolf, M. D.: 63
Wotruba, R. T.: 239
Young, C. M.: 212
Zakolski, F. C.: 107

[1096]

★**Adolescent Alienation Index.** Ages 12–19; 1971; AAI; F. K. Heussenstamm; Monitor. *

REFERENCES THROUGH 1971

1. HEUSSENSTAMM, FRANCES KOVACS. *Creativity and Alienation: An Exploration of Their Relationship in Adolescence.* Doctor's thesis, University of Southern California (Los Angeles, Calif.), 1968. (*DA* 29:2888A)

CUMULATIVE NAME INDEX

Heussenstamm, F. K.: 1

[1097]

★**Affect Scale.** College; 1960–71; AS; 4 scores: myself, others, myself plus others, myself minus others; no manual; Ricardo Girona; the Author. *

[1098]

The Alcadd Test. Adults; 1949; identification of alcoholic addicts and individuals with alcoholic problems; 6 scores: regularity of drinking, preference for drinking over other activities, lack of controlled drinking, rationalization of drinking, excessive emotionality, total; Morse P. Manson; Western Psychological Services. *
For additional information, see P :7 (3 references); for a review by Dugal Campbell, see 6 :60 (6 references); for reviews by Charles H. Honzik and Albert L. Hunsicker, see 4 :30.

REFERENCES THROUGH 1971

1–6. See 6:60.
7–9. See P:7.
10. PARKER, FREDERICK B. "Self-Role Strain and Drinking Disposition at a Prealcoholic Age Level." *J Social Psychol* 78(1):55–61 Je '69. * (*PA* 43:15761)

CUMULATIVE NAME INDEX

Barillas, M. G.: 2
Clark, J. W.: 5
Honzik, C. H.: *rev,* 4:30
Hunsicker, A. L.: *rev,* 4:30

Manson, M. P.: 1
Murphy, D. G.: 3–4
Parker, F. B.: 10
Smart, R. G.: 6

Campbell, D.: *rev,* 6:60

[1099]

★**Animal Crackers: A Test of Motivation to Achieve, Research Edition.** Grades kgn–1; 1973; 6 scores: school enjoyment, self-confidence, purposiveness, instrumental activity, self-evaluation, total; Dorothy C. Adkins and Bonnie L. Ballif; CTB/McGraw-Hill. *

[1100]

The Anxiety Scale for the Blind. Blind and partially sighted ages 13 and over; 1966–68; ASB; experimental form; Richard E. Hardy; American Foundation for the Blind, Inc. *
For additional information, see P :8 (3 references).

REFERENCES THROUGH 1971

1–3. See P:8.
4. MILLER, WILLIAM H. "Manifest Anxiety in Visually Impaired Adolescents." *Ed Visually Handicapped* 2(3):91–5 O '70. * (*PA* 46:1794)

CUMULATIVE NAME INDEX

Hardy, R. E.: 1–3   Miller, W. H.: 4

[1101]

Attitude-Interest Analysis Test. Early adolescents and adults; 1936–38; AIAT; also called *M-F Test;* masculinity-femininity; manual out of print; Lewis M.

Terman and Catherine Cox Miles; McGraw-Hill Book Co., Inc. *
For additional information, see P :9 (5 references); see also 6 :61 (16 references); for a review by Starke R. Hathaway, see 3 :24 (20 references). For excerpts from related book reviews, see 2 :B1094 (3 excerpts) and 1 :B498 (14 excerpts).

REFERENCES THROUGH 1971

1–20. See 3:24.
21–36. See 6:61.
37–41. See P:9.
42. BECK, MAURICE P. *An Analysis of Popularity: A Study of the Social Aspects of Personality.* Master's thesis, Western Reserve University (Cleveland, Ohio), 1940.
43. KLINE, MILTON V. "A Measure of Mental Masculinity and Femininity in Relation to Hypnotic Age Progression." *J Genetic Psychol* 78:207–15 Je '51. * (*PA* 26:2614)
44. GERTLER, MENARD M., AND WHITE, PAUL D. Chap. 6, "Findings on Masculinity," pp. 67–79. In their *Coronary Heart Disease in Young Adults: A Multidisciplinary Study.* Cambridge, Mass.: Harvard University Press, 1954. Pp. xix, 218. *
45. WEITZENHOFFER, ANDRÉ MULLER. *Hypnotic Susceptibility as Related to Masculinity-Femininity.* Doctor's thesis, University of Michigan (Ann Arbor, Mich.), 1956. (*DA* 1⁷:1397)
46. BERENBERG, ALBERT N. *A Study of the Relationship Between Skills in Certain Cognitive Areas and Certain Patterns Involving Attitudes, Interests and Identifications in Eighth Grade Students.* Doctor's thesis, New York University (New York, N.Y.), 1957. (*DA* 18:651)
47. DOUGLASS, ROBERT RAYMOND. *Personality of the Librarian.* Doctor's thesis, University of Chicago (Chicago, Ill.), 1957.
48. WARMAN, ROY ELTON, JR. *Differential Perceptions of the Counseling Role of a University Counseling Center.* Doctor's thesis, Ohio State University (Columbus, Ohio), 1958. (*DA* 19:874)
49. YAMAMOTO, JOE, AND SEEMAN, WILLIAM. "Psychological Study of Castrated Males." *Psychiatric Res Rep Am Psychiatric Assn* 12:97–103 Ja '60. * (*PA* 35:6527)
50. MILGRAM, NORMAN A. "Role-Taking in Female Schizophrenic Patients." *J Clin Psychol* 17:409–11 O '61. * (*PA* 38:9060)
51. LESSLER, KENNETH JAY. *The Anatomical and Cultural Dimensions of Sexual Symbols.* Doctor's thesis, Michigan State University (East Lansing, Mich.), 1962. (*DA* 23:3976)
52. WEISS, PETER. *Some Aspects of Femininity.* Doctor's thesis, University of Colorado (Boulder, Colo.), 1962. (*DA* 23:1083)
53. LAMKIN, FLOYD DUANE. *Masculinity-Femininity of Preadolescent Youth in Relation to Behavior Acceptability, Tested and Graded Achievement, Inventoried Interests and General Intelligence.* Doctor's thesis, University of Virginia (Charlottesville, Va.), 1967. (*DA* 28:2558A)
54. FARR, ROBERTA SIEGEL. *Personality Variables and Problem Solving Performance: An Investigation of the Relationships Between Field-Dependence-Independence, Sex-Role Identification, Problem Difficulty and Problem Solving Performance.* Doctor's thesis, New York University (New York, N.Y.), 1968. (*DA* 29:2561A)
55. MEREDITH, GERALD M. "Sex Temperament Among Japanese-American College Students in Hawaii." *J Social Psychol* 77(2):149–56 Ap '69. * (*PA* 43:9606)
56. PARKER, FREDERICK B. "Self-Role Strain and Drinking Disposition at a Prealcoholic Age Level." *J Social Psychol* 78(1):55–61 Je '69. * (*PA* 43:15761)
57. FISHER, A. CRAIG. *The Relationship Between Participation in Selected Sport Activities and Sex Role Orientation of Institutionalized Males.* Doctor's thesis, Ohio State University (Columbus, Ohio), 1970. (*DAI* 31:5175A)
58. FLEMING, PATRICIA ANN DINNEEN. *Masculinity-Femininity and the Generation Gap as Reflected in University Graduates Twenty Years Ago and Today.* Doctor's thesis, University of Northern Colorado (Greeley, Colo.), 1971. (*DAI* 32:6028B)
59. LEFLEY, HARRIET P. "Masculinity-Femininity in Obese Women." *J Consult & Clin Psychol* 37(2):180–6 O '71. * (*PA* 47:9542)

CUMULATIVE NAME INDEX

Aronson, M. L.: 27
Balogh, B.: 40
Barnette, W. L.: 14
Beck, M. P.: 9, 42
Berenberg, A. N.: 46
Bilsky, H. B.: 17
Bosselman, B.: 10
Botwinick, J.: 28
Bryson, G.: *exc,* 1:B498
Burger, F. E.: 15
Capwell, D. F.: 19
Carter, L.: 23
Cerf, A. Z.: 21

Child, I. L.: 11
de Cillis, O. E.: 24
Disher, D. R.: 7, 16
Douglass, R. R.: 47
Dunlap, J. W.: 3
Durea, M. A.: 17
Edgerton, H. A.: 3
Engel, I. M.: 36, 39
Farr, R. S.: 54
Fisher, A. C.: 57
Fisher, S.: 29
Fleming, P. A. D.: 58
Flügel, J. C.: *exc,* 2:B1094

Ford, C. F.: 32
Forlano, G.: 18
Franz, J. G.: 38
Gertler, M. M.: 44
Gilkinson, H.: 4, 8, 12
Hardy, V. T.: 22
Hartmann, G. W.: *exc,* 1:B498
Hathaway, S. R.: *rev,* 3:24
Hinds, E.: 29
Kelly, E. L.: 2–3
Kline, M. V.: 43
Knower, F. H.: 8, 12
Kurtz, A. K.: 3
Lamkin, F. D.: 53
Lee, M. C.: 25, 33
Lefley, H. P.: 59
Lessler, K. J.: 51
McAnulty, E. A.: 3
McCarthy, D.: 41
McCurdy, H.: *exc,* 1:B498
Machover, S.: 28
McNemar, Q.: 3
Meredith, G. M.: 55
Merrill, M. A.: 3
Miles, C. C.: 1–3
Milgram, N. A.: 50
Nemzek, C. L.: 15
Nixon, M.: 23
Orbison, W. D.: 24
Page, J.: 5
Parker, F. B.: 34, 56
Pintner, R.: 18

Rosenzweig, S.: 6
Ross, R. T.: 26
Ruch, F. L.: 3
Sappenfield, B. R.: 40
Schiro, F. M.: 41
Schwesinger, G. C.: *exc,* 1:B498
Seeman, W.: 49
Sheldon, W. H.: 11
Shepler, B. F.: 30
Silverberg, W. V.: *exc,* 2:B1094
Skorodin, B.: 10
Smith, J. H.: 20
Stanek, R. J.: 35
Stephenson, W.: *exc,* 1:B498
Sudimack, J. P.: 41
Terman, L. M.: 1–3
Tyler, L. E.: 32
Uhrbrock, R. S.: *exc,* 2:B1094
Vaccaro, J. J.: 31
Vaughn, C. L.: 15
Walker, E. L.: 13
Warkentin, J.: 5
Warman, R. E.: 48
Weiss, P.: 52
Weitzenhoffer, A. M.: 45
White, P. D.: 44
Wyatt, H. G.: 3
Yamamoto, J.: 49
Young, K.: *exc,* 1:B498
Zuckman, L.: 37

[1102]

Attitudes Toward Industrialization. Adults; 1959; Donald E. Kaldenberg; Psychometric Affiliates. *

For additional information, see P:10; for a review by Marvin D. Dunnette, see 6:62.

[1103]

Attitudes Toward Parental Control of Children. Adults; 1936; Ralph M. Stogdill and Henry H. Goddard; Ralph M. Stogdill. *

For additional information, see P:11; see also 2:1205 (2 references).

REFERENCES THROUGH 1971

1–2. See 2:1205.

CUMULATIVE NAME INDEX

Stogdill, R. M.: 1–2

[1104]

The Ayres Space Test. Ages 3 and over; 1962; AST; also available as a subtest of *Southern California Sensory Integration Tests;* brain damage; 3 scores: accuracy, time, accuracy less adjustment for time; A. Jean Ayres; Western Psychological Services. *

For additional information, see P:12 (3 references); for reviews by Alvin G. Burstein and Alfred B. Heilbrun, Jr., see 6:63 (2 references).

REFERENCES THROUGH 1971

1–2. See 6:63.
3–5. See P:12.
6. AYRES, A. JEAN. "Interrelationships Among Perceptual-Motor Functions in Children." *Am J Occup Ther* 20:68–71 Mr–Ap '66. * (*PA* 40:8678)
7. FOX, FRANK HEWITT. *A Description of Language and Perceptual Function of Culturally Deprived Children.* Doctor's thesis, University of Wisconsin (Madison, Wis.), 1968. (*DA* 29:4323A)
8. AYRES, A. JEAN. "Deficits in Sensory Integration in Educationally Handicapped Children." *J Learn Dis* 2(3):160–8 Mr '69. * (*PA* 45:6978)
9. PUNWAR, ALICE. "Spatial Visualization, Reading, Spelling, and Mathematical Abilities in Second- and Third-Grade Children." *Am J Occup Ther* 24(7):495–9 O '70. *

CUMULATIVE NAME INDEX

Ayres, A. J.: 1, 3–6, 8
Burstein, A. G.: *rev,* 6:63
Fox, F. H.: 7
Heilbrun, A. B.: *rev,* 6:63
Punwar, A.: 9
Reid, W.: 5
Sleeper, M. L.: 2

[1105]

The Babcock Test of Mental Efficiency. Ages 7 and over; 1930–65; BTME; formerly called *Babcock Test of Mental Deterioration;* 14 scores: easy tests, repetition, initial learning, recall and recognition, motor A, motor B, perception time, easy continuous work, total mental efficiency (based on 8 previous scores), efficiency deviation, verbal (untimed, timed), motor control, recognition; Harriet Babcock and Lydia Levy (test); Western Psychological Services. *

For additional information and a review by Aubrey J. Yates, see 7:39 (1 reference); see also P:13 (6 references) and 6:64 (6 references); for reviews by D. Russell Davis and Seymour G. Klebanoff, see 4:31 (10 references); see also 3:71 (21 references) and 2:1248 (16 references). For excerpts from related book reviews, see 3:72 (4 excerpts).

REFERENCES THROUGH 1971

1–14. See 2:1248.
15–35. See 3:71.
36–45. See 4:31.
46–51. See 6:64.
52–57. See P:13.
58. See 7:39.
59. CANTER, AARON HERMAN. "Direct and Indirect Measures of Psychological Deficit in Multiple Sclerosis: Part 1." *J General Psychol* 44:325 Ja '51. * (*PA* 25:7027)
60. CANTER, AARON HERMAN. "Direct and Indirect Measures of Psychological Deficit in Multiple Sclerosis: Part 2." *J General Psychol* 44:27–50 Ja '51. * (*PA* 25:7028)
61. SCHERER, ISIDOR W. "Prognoses and Psychological Scores in Electroconvulsive Therapy, Psychosurgery, and Spontaneous Remission." *Am J Psychiatry* 107:926–31 Je '51. * (*PA* 27:477)
62. FRYER, DAVID G., AND RICH, MARGARET P. "Denial of Illness in Relation to Intellectual Function." *J Nerv & Mental Dis* 131:523–7 D '60. * (*PA* 35:4955)
63. SHAPIRO, M. B.; KESSELL, R.; AND MAXWELL, A. E. "Speed and Quality of Psychomotor Performance in Psychiatric Patients." *J Clin Psychol* 16:266–71 Jl '60. * (*PA* 36:2HI66S)
64. PETERSON, PAUL G. Chap. 4, "Intellectual Abilities and Social Attitudes," pp. 55–70, 219–25. In *Aging and Personality: A Study of Eighty-Seven Older Men.* By Suzanne Reichard and Others. New York: John Wiley & Sons, Inc., 1962. Pp. xv, 237. * (*PA* 37:2962)
65. DIXON, JAMES C. "Cognitive Structure in Senile Conditions With Some Suggestions for Developing a Brief Screening Test of Mental Status." *J Gerontol* 20:41–9 Ja '65. *
66. HAWKS, D. V., AND MARSHALL, W. L. "A Parsimonious Theory of Overinclusive Thinking and Retardation in Schizophrenia." *Brit J Med Psychol* 44(1):75–83 Mr '71. * (*PA* 46:11244)

CUMULATIVE NAME INDEX

Allen, F. H.: 9.1
Altman, C. H.: 9
Babcock, H.: 1–2, 4, 14, 17–8, 46
Barnes, M. R.: 11
Benton, A. L.: *exc,* 3:72
Birren, J. E.: 42–3, 45
Bookhammer, R. S.: 9.1
Botwinick, J.: 45
Brody, M. B.: 22–3
Burr, E.: 38
Caird, W. K.: 54
Canter, A. H.: 59–60
Capps, H. M.: 12.1
Davis, D. R.: *rev,* 4:31
Dixon, J. C.: 65
Fetterman, J. L.: 11
Finch, F. H.: 29
Foulds, G. A.: 55
Fox, C.: 42–3
Fryer, D. G.: 62
George, E. I.: 49
Gilbert, J. G.: 6, 19, 26
Gill, M.: 25, 27, 32
Gill, M. M.: 57
Gonen, Y.: 56
Hall, M. E.: 12
Harbinson, M. R.: 8
Hawks, D. V.: 66
Hayman, M.: 24
Hewlett, J. H. G.: 50
Holt, R. R.: 57
Hook, M. E.: 47
Hope, K.: 55

Hunt, H. F.: 30
Jambor, K. L.: 58
Jastak, J.: 10, 40
Kendig, I.: 13
Kessell, R.: 63
Klebanoff, S. G.: *rev,* 4:31
Knight, R. P.: 25
Landisberg, S.: 34
Laverty, S. G.: 54
Lorge, I.: *exc,* 3:72
Lozoff, M.: 25
McFie, J.: 52
McPherson, F. M.: 55
Marshall, W. L.: 66
Mattussek, P.: 49
Maxwell, A. E.: 63
Mayman, M.: 31
Mayo, P. R.: 55
Nelson, E. H.: 48
Newton, R. L.: 44
Noyes, A. P.: 9.1
Partington, J. E.: 36
Payne, R. W.: 49–51, 54
Peterson, P. G.: 64
Piercy, M. F.: 52
Rabin, A. I.: 35
Rapaport, D.: 25, 27, 32, 57
Rautman, A. L.: 20
Rich, M. P.: 62
Richmond, W. V.: 13
Rubin, B.: 9.1
Schafer, R.: 27–8, 32, 39, 57
Scherer, I. W.: 41, 61
Schwarz, R.: 3

Seidenfeld, M. A.: 29
Shakow, D.: 9, 26
Shapiro, M. B.: 48, 63
Sharp, A. A.: 15
Shoore, A. B.: 33
Simmons, C.: 7
Warburton, J. W.: 53

Wesley, S. M.: 37
Wittman, P.: 5
Yacorzynski, G. K.: 16, 21; *exc,* 3:72
Yaskin, J. C.: 9.1
Yates, A. J.: *rev,* 7:39

[1106]

Baker-Schulberg Community Mental Health Ideology Scale. Mental health professionals; 1967; CMHI; primarily intended for measuring groups; Frank Baker and Herbert C. Schulberg; Behavioral Publications, Inc. *

For additional information and reviews by Robert Fitzpatrick and Lester M. Libo, see 7:40 (2 references) ; see also P:14 (1 reference).

REFERENCES THROUGH 1971

1. See P:14.
2-3. See 7:40.
4. LANGSTON, ROBERT D. "Community Mental Health Centers and Community Mental Health Ideology." *Commun Mental Health J* 6(5):387-92 O '70. * (*PA* 45:6924)
5. HOWARD, LUCY ANN. "Ideology and Role Function of the Nurse in Community Mental Health." *Nursing Res* 20(5):450-4 S-O '71. *
6. PANTLEO, PAUL MORRIS. *Community Mental Health Ideology: An Analysis of Community Oriented and Traditional Mental Health Facilities.* Doctor's thesis, University of Colorado (Boulder, Colo.), 1971. (*DAI* 33:447B)

CUMULATIVE NAME INDEX

Baker, F.: 1-2
Fitzpatrick, R.: *rev,* 7:40
Howard, L. A.: 5
Langston, R. D.: 4

Libo, L. M.: *rev,* 7:40
Pantleo, P. M.: 6
Schulberg, H. C.: 1-2
Walker, L. J.: 3

[1107]

★Balthazar Scales of Adaptive Behavior. "Profoundly and severely mentally retarded adults and the younger less retarded"; 1971-73; BSAB; formerly called Central Wisconsin Colony Scales of Adaptive Behavior; 2 sections; Earl E. Balthazar; Consulting Psychologists Press, Inc. *

a) SECTION 1: THE SCALES OF FUNCTIONAL INDEPENDENCE. 1971; 8 ratings: eating (dependent feeding, finger foods, spoon usage, fork usage, drinking, total), dressing, toileting.

b) SECTION 2: SCALES OF SOCIAL ADAPTATION. 1973; 19 ratings grouped in 7 categories: unadaptive self-directed behaviors (5 ratings), unadaptive interpersonal behaviors (2 ratings), adaptive self-directed behaviors (1 rating), adaptive interpersonal behaviors (3 ratings), verbal communication (2 ratings), play activities (3 ratings), response to instructions (3 ratings), plus 9 checklist items of personal care and other behaviors.

REFERENCES THROUGH 1971

1. BALTHAZAR, EARL E., AND ENGLISH, GEORGE E. "A Factorial Study of Unstructured Ward Behaviors." *Am J Mental Def* 74(3):353-60 N '69. * (*PA* 44:5528)
2. BALTHAZAR, EARL E., AND ENGLISH, GEORGE E. "A System for the Social Classification of the More Severely Mentally Retarded." *Am J Mental Def* 74(3):361-8 N '69. * (*PA* 44:5529)

CUMULATIVE NAME INDEX

Balthazar, E. E.: 1-2   English, G. E.: 1-2

[1108]

★Barclay Classroom Climate Inventory. Grades 3-6; 1971-74, c1967-74; BCCI; "social interaction and expectation variables" of children and "the classroom climate"; teacher, peer, and self-ratings in classes of 25-35; 1-page individual computer printout yields narrative statements on self-competency scores, vocational awareness, peer group judgments, teacher ratings, and summary statements plus diagnostic code and 42 scores: 5 self-competency scores (artistic-intellectual, realistic-outdoor, social-conventional, enterprising, total), 7

group nomination skill scores (artistic-intellectual, realistic-outdoor, social-conventional, enterprising, total, reticence, disruptiveness), 10 vocational preference scales (realistic-outdoor, intellectual-scientific, social, conventional, enterprising, artistic, control, masculinity-femininity, status, total), 12 teacher-rating scores (2 personal adjustment scores, 2 social adjustment scores, 2 effort and motivation scores, 4 temperament scores, total positive, total negative), 8 self-rated behavioral interest scores (self-stimulating, esthetic, intellectual task-oriented, familial, conventional, peer male, peer female, classroom climate index) ; group printouts (separate for boys, girls) include narrative report of statements in 4 areas (self-competency ratings, group nominations, teacher judgments, vocational interests), grids, analysis of teacher ratings, summary of problems; reports based on 5 diagnostic temperament clusters (extroverted-divergent, extroverted-convergent, introverted-divergent, introverted-convergent, blend) and 15 factor scores: self-esteem, sociability, dominance, aggression, seclusion, physical skills, vocational awareness, affiliation-succorance, intellectuality, instability, conventional-peer, intellectual-task-order, familial, peer female (males), esthetic-self-stimulating (females), classroom climate; James R. Barclay with the assistance of Lisa K. Barclay, William E. Stillwell, Calvin D. Catterall (user's manual), David A. Santoro (user's manual), and George Tapp (user's manual) ; Educational Skills Development, Inc. *

[1109]

Barron-Welsh Art Scale: A Portion of the Welsh Figure Preference Test. Ages 6 and over; 1959-63, c1949-63; BWAS; a separate booklet printing of the art scale and revised art scale items from *Welsh Figure Preference Test, Research Edition;* George S. Welsh and Frank Barron (test) ; Consulting Psychologists Press, Inc. *

For additional information and reviews by Leonard L. Baird and G. C. Helmstadter, see 7:41 (40 references) ; see also P:15 (20 references). For reference to reviews of the *Welsh Figure Preference Test,* see 1437.

REFERENCES THROUGH 1971

1-20. See P:15.
21-60. See 7:41.
61. ALLEN, MARK KNIGHT. *Personality and Cultural Factors Related to Religious Authoritarianism.* Doctor's thesis, Stanford University (Stanford, Calif.), 1955. (*DA* 15:2324)
62. BIERI, JAMES; BRADBURN, WENDY M.; AND GALINSKY, M. DAVID. "Sex Differences in Perceptual Behavior." *J Personality* 26:1-12 Mr '58. * (*PA* 33:5426)
63. DAY, HY. "Looking Time as a Function of Stimulus Variables and Individual Differences." *Percept & Motor Skills* 22:423-8 Ap '66. * (*PA* 40:8320)
64. BIASE, D. VINCENT, AND ZUCKERMAN, MARVIN. "Sex Differences in Stress Responses to Total and Partial Sensory Deprivation." *Psychosom Med* 29:380-90 Jl-Ag '67. * (*PA* 42:1602)
65. PANEY, HENRY, AND HORROCKS, CAROL. "Creativity in a Troop of Low Average Intelligent Boy Scouts." *Adolescence* 2:231-41 su '67. * (*PA* 42:3962)
66. PANG, HENRY, AND FROST, LINDA. "Relatedness of Creativity, Values, and ESP." *Percept & Motor Skills* 24:650 Ap '67. * (*PA* 41:9549)
67. DAY, HY. "Role of Specific Curiosity in School Achievement." *J Ed Psychol* 59:37-43 F '68. * (*PA* 42:7841)
68. HETRICK, SUZANNE H.; LILLY, ROY S.; AND MERRIFIELD, PHILIP R. "Figural Creativity, Intelligence, and Personality in Children." *Multiv Behav Res* 3:173-87 Ap '68. * (*PA* 42:15273)
69. BARRON, FRANK. "Hereditability of Factors in Creative Thinking and Judgment." *Acta Geneticae Medicae et Gemellologiae* (Italy) 19(1-2):294-8 Ja-Ap '70. *
70. BAKKE, LARRY H. *A Study of the Relationship of Aesthetic Judgment to Self-Esteem and Security in University Women.* Doctor's thesis, Syracuse University (Syracuse, N.Y.), 1971. (*DAI* 32:4410A)
71. BLOOMBERG, MORTON. "Creativity as Related to Field

Independence and Mobility." *J Genetic Psychol* 118(1):3–12 Mr '71. * (*PA* 46:9065)

72. BOROD, JOAN; GROSSMAN, JAN CARL; AND EISENMAN, RUSSELL. "Extraversion, Anxiety, Creativity and Grades." *Percept & Motor Skills* 33(3):1106 D '71. * (*PA* 48:966)

73. BOWERS, KENNETH S. "Sex and Susceptibility as Moderator Variables in the Relationship of Creativity and Hypnotic Susceptibility." *J Abn Psychol* 78(1):93–100 Ag '71. * (*PA* 47:2042)

74. BOWERS, KENNETH S., AND KEELING, KENNETH R. "Heart-Rate Variability in Creative Functioning." *Psychol Rep* 29(1):160–2 Ag '71. * (*PA* 47:2468)

75. GARFIELD, S. JEFFREY; COHEN, HELEN A.; ROTH, ROBERT M.; AND BERENBAUM, HARRIS L. "Effects of Group Counseling on Creativity." *J Ed Res* 64(5):235–7 Ja '71. * (*PA* 46:5553)

76. LEWIS, NEIL PHILLIP. *Cognitive Style, Cognitive Complexity, and Behavior Prediction in Process and Reactive Schizophrenia.* Doctor's thesis, Fordham University (New York, N.Y.), 1971. (*DAI* 32:1217B)

77. MITCHELL, MARLYS M. "Personality Assessment of Retarded Children." *Training Sch B* 68(3):186–91 N '71. * (*PA* 48:1712)

78. MITCHELL, MARLYS MARIE. "Analysis of Welsh Figure Preference Test Scores of Educable Mentally Handicapped Children." *Training Sch B* 67(4):214–9 F '71. * (*PA* 46:7513)

79. MONTGOMERY, JOY T. *A Comparison of Creativity of Ninth Grade Students as Determined by Peer Ratings, Teacher Ratings, and the Welsh Revised Art Scale.* Master's thesis, Wake Forest University (Winston-Salem, N.C.), 1971.

80. PIERS, ELLEN V., AND KIRCHNER, ELIZABETH P. "Productivity and Uniqueness in Continued Word Association as a Function of Subject Creativity and Stimulus Properties." *J Personality* 39(2):264–76 Je '71. * (*PA* 47:210)

81. RAYCHAUDHURI, MANAS. "Associative Reactions and Aesthetic Choice." *J Psychol Res* (India) 15(3):104–7 S '71. *

82. RENNER, VIVIAN, AND RENNER, JOHN C. "Effects of a Creativity Training Program on Stimulus Preferences." *Percept & Motor Skills* 33(3):872–4 D '71. * (*PA* 48:1002)

83. WEISSMAN, HERBERT N.; SELDMAN, MARTIN; AND RITTER, KENNETH. "Changes in Awareness of Impact Upon Others as a Function of Encounter and Marathon Group Experiences." *Psychol Rep* 28(2):651–61 Ap '71. * (*PA* 46:6770)

CUMULATIVE NAME INDEX

Barron-Welsh Art Scale

[1110]

Behavior Cards: A Test-Interview for Delinquent Children. Delinquents having a reading grade score 4.5 or higher; 1941–50; Ralph M. Stogdill; distributed by Stoelting Co. *

For additional information, see P:16; see also 6:65 (1 reference); for reviews by W. C. Kvaraceus and Simon H. Tulchin, see 3:25 (3 references).

REFERENCES THROUGH 1971

1–3. See 3:25.
4. See 6:65.

CUMULATIVE NAME INDEX

[1111]

Behavior Status Inventory. Psychiatric inpatients; 1969; BSI; ratings in 7 areas (personal appearance, manifest behavior, attitude, verbal behavior, social behavior, work or school behavior, cognitive behavior) and total patient asset score; William T. Martin; Psychologists and Educators, Inc. *

For additional information, see 7:42.

[1112]

Bristol Social Adjustment Guides. Ages 5–15; 1956–66; BSAG; ratings by teachers and others; adjustment score and an optional delinquency prediction score for boys; 3 editions; D. H. Stott and E. G. Sykes (*a*, *b*); University of London Press Ltd. [England]. *
a) THE CHILD IN SCHOOL. 1956–66. (American edition: Ages 5–16; 1956–67; 1967 test identical in 1956 British edition except for minor changes in wording; Educational and Industrial Testing Service. *)
b) THE CHILD IN RESIDENTIAL CARE. 1956–66.
c) THE CHILD IN THE FAMILY. 1956–66.
d) DELINQUENCY PREDICTION INSTRUMENT. Boys ages 5–15; 1961–66; consists of a delinquency prediction key to be used with the diagnostic form for *The Child in School* scale and a teacher's questionnaire for preliminary identification of pupils to be rated on the scale.

For additional information, see P:20 (6 references); for reviews by G. A. V. Morgan and M. L. Kellmer Pringle and excerpted reviews by R. G. Andry, Mary Engel, A. W. Heim, Read D. Tuddenham, and P. E. Vernon, see 6:68 (13 references).

REFERENCES THROUGH 1971

1–13. See 6:68.
14–19. See P:20.

20. BRENNAN, W. K. "The Relation of Social Adaptation, Emotional Adjustment and Moral Judgment to Intelligence in Primary School Children." Abstract. *Brit J Ed Psychol* 32:200–4 Je '62. *

21. STOTT, D. H. "Delinquency and Cultural Stress." *Brit J Social & Clin Psychol* 1:182–91 O '62. * (*PA* 37:5461)

22. WINDER, W. E. P. "Forgetting in Emotionally Disturbed Secondary School Children." Abstract. *Brit J Ed Psychol* 32:82–3 F '62. *

23. BELFIELD, D. J. "The Social Adjustment of Most Accepted and Least Accepted Children in Junior Schools." *Brit J Ed Psychol* 34:324–7 N '64. *

24. SAMPSON, OLIVE C. "Written Composition at 10 Years as an Aspect of Linguistic Development." *Brit J Ed Psychol* 34:143–50 Je '64. * (*PA* 39:4958)

25. CHAZAN, MAURICE. "Factors Associated With Maladjustment in Educationally Subnormal Children." *Brit J Ed Psychol* 35:277–85 N '65. * (*PA* 40:3328)

26. FISHER, BRIAN. "The Social and Emotional Adjustment of Children With Impaired Hearing Attending Ordinary Classes." *Brit J Ed Psychol* 36:319–21 N '66. *

27. MARSHALL, ANNE. *The Abilities and Attainments of Children Leaving Junior Training Centres.* London: National Association for Mental Health, 1967. Pp. i, 62. *

28. BURTON, LINDY. *Vulnerable Children: Three Studies of Children in Conflict: Accident Involved Children, Sexually Assaulted Children, and Children With Asthma.* New York: Schocken Books Inc., 1968. Pp. x, 277. *

29. CHAZAN, MAURICE. "Inconsequential Behaviour in School Children." *Brit J Ed Psychol* 38:5–9 F '68. * *(PA 42:12706)*
30. STOTT, D. H., AND WILSON, D. M. "The Prediction of Early-Adult Criminality From School-Age Behaviour." *Int J Social Psychiatry* (England) 14:5–8 w '67–68 ['68]. * *(PA 42:14125)*
31. McKENZIE, D. J., AND WILSON, P. E. "A Pilot Study of the Bristol Social Adjustment Guides Used With Pre-school Children." *Austral Psychologist* 3(3):177–80 Mr '69. * *(PA 45:6590)*
32. MARSH, R. W. "The Validity of the Bristol Social Adjustment Guides in Delinquency Prediction." *Brit J Ed Psychol* 39(3):278–83 N '69. * *(PA 44:8824)*
33. MARSTON, N., AND STOTT, D. H. "Inconsequence as a Primary Type of Behaviour Disturbance in Children." *Brit J Ed Psychol* 40(1):15–20 F '70. * *(PA 44:10749)*
34. DUROJAIYE, M. O. A., AND SUCH, M. "Predicting Educational Suitability of Children in an Assessment Unit." *J Exp Ed* 40(2):27–36 w '71. * *(PA 47:11613)*
35. HINE, W. D. "The Social Adjustment of Partially Hearing Children." *Teach Deaf* (England) 69(405):5–13 Ja '71. * *(PA 47:11608)*
36. STOTT, D. H. "Classification of Behavior Disturbance Among School-Age Students: Principles, Epidemiology and Syndromes." *Psychol Sch* 8(3):232–9 Jl '71. * *(PA 47:9624)*

CUMULATIVE NAME INDEX

[1113]

Brook Reaction Test. Ages 13 and over; 1969; BRT; experimental form; may be administered by examiner but tape recording is recommended; 27 scores: 22 interest scores (aesthetic, business, clothing, dances-social functions, entertainment, food and drink, agricultural, humanitarian, intellectual interests, practical, literary, law, military, outdoor activities, people, political, religion, biological sciences, physical sciences, secretarial, sport, travel) and 5 temperament indices (omissions, unclassifiable, questionable responses, sexual responses, multiple themes); A. W. Heim, K. P. Watts, and V. Simmonds; NFER Publishing Co. Ltd. [England]. *

For additional information, see 7:44 (7 references).

REFERENCES THROUGH 1971

1–7. See 7:44.
8. HEIM, ALICE. Chap. 11, "The Brook Reaction Test," pp. 97–110. In her *Intelligence and Personality: Their Assessment and Relationship.* Harmondsworth, Middlesex, England: Penguin Books Ltd., 1970. Pp. 206. * *(PA 48:936, title only)*
9. HOCKEY, S. W., AND HILL, G. C. "The Predictive Validity of the Brook Reaction Test." *Brit J Ed Psychol* 41(3):322–4 N '71. * *(PA 47:11613)*
10. KLINE, P., AND THOMAS, M. "The Brook Reaction Test as a Measure of Temperament With Children of 13 and 14 Years." *Brit J Ed Psychol* 41(3):317–21 N '71. * *(PA 47:11580)*
11. UNDERWOOD, K. "The Brook Reaction Test—Some Australian Data." *Austral Psychologist* 6(2):113–7 Jl '71. * *(PA 47:9875)*

CUMULATIVE NAME INDEX

[1114]

Burks' Behavior Rating Scale for Organic Brain Dysfunction. Grades kgn–6; 1968; BBRS; ratings by teachers; 4 scores: vegetative-autonomic, perceptual-discriminative, social-emotional, total; Harold F. Burks; Arden Press. *

For additional information, see 7:45.

[1115]

Burks' Behavior Rating Scales. Preschool and kgn, grades 1–8; 1968–69; BBRS; experimental; ratings of problem children by teachers or parents in 18 or 20 areas: self blame, anxiety, withdrawal, dependency, ego strength, physical strength, coordination, intellectuality, academics (upper level), attention, impulse control, reality contact, sense of identity, suffering, anger control, sense of persecution, sexuality (upper level), aggressiveness, resistance, social conformity; Harold F. Burks; Arden Press. *

For additional information, see 7:46 (2 references).

REFERENCES THROUGH 1971

1–2. See 7:46.
3. BURKS, HAROLD F. "A Behavior Rating Scale for Screening Brain Impaired Children," pp. 89–98. In *Proceedings Regional Institute on Neurological Handicapping Conditions in Children.* Edited by Eleanor H. Boydston. Berkeley, Calif.: University of California, 1961. Pp. iv, 151. *

CUMULATIVE NAME INDEX

[1116]

C-R Opinionaire. Grades 11–16 and adults; 1935–46, c1935; CRO; conservatism-radicalism; 1946 tests identical with tests copyrighted 1935 except for 8 revised items; Theodore F. Lentz; Character Research Association. *

For additional information, see P:21 (3 references); for a review by George W. Hartmann, see 4:39 (5 references); for a review by Goodwin Watson, see 2:1212 (5 references); for a review by H. H. Remmers, see 1:899.

REFERENCES THROUGH 1971

1–5. See 2:1212.
6–10. See 4:39.
11–13. See P:21.
14. NELSON, ERLAND. "Radicalism-Conservatism in Student Attitudes." *Psychol Monogr* 50(4):1–32 '38. * *(PA 13:970)*
15. NELSON, E. "Student Attitudes Toward Religion." *Genetic Psychol Monogr* 22:325–423 Ag '40. * *(PA 15:399)*
16. SAPPENFIELD, BERT R. "The Attitudes and Attitude Estimates of Catholic, Protestant, and Jewish Students." *J Social Psychol* 16:173–97 N '42. * *(PA 17:908)*
17. SKAGGS, E. B. "Sex Differences in Feeling and Emotional Disposition in a University Population." *J Social Psychol* 16:21–7 Ag '42. * *(PA 16:4763)*
18. HOOD, PHILIP N.; SHANK, KENNON H.; AND WILLIAMSON, DORIS B. "Environmental Factors in Relation to the Speech of Cerebral Palsied Children." *J Speech & Hearing Disorders* 13:325–31 D '48. * *(PA 23:3301)*
19. NELSON, ERLAND N. P. "Persistence of Attitudes of College Students Fourteen Years Later." *Psychol Monogr* 68(2):1–13 '54. * *(PA 29:3002)*
20. KLINE, MILTON V., AND CUMINGS, RUTH. "A Study of the Learning Characteristics of Public Health Nurses in Relation to Mental Health Education and Consultation: 3. Comparative Study of Some Aspects of Personality and Learning Skill in Relation to In-Service Educational Performance." *J Social Psychol* 42:43–60 Ag '55. * *(PA 30:7149)*

CUMULATIVE NAME INDEX

[1117]

Cain-Levine Social Competency Scale. Mentally retarded children ages 5–13; 1963; CLSCS; rating scale based upon information obtained from parents; 5 scores: self-help, initiative, social skills, communication, total; Leo F. Cain, Samuel Levine, and Freeman F. Elzey; Consulting Psychologists Press, Inc. *

For additional information, see P :23 (3 references) ; for a review by Marshall S. Hiskey, see 6 :69.

REFERENCES THROUGH 1971

1–3. See P :23.

4. KATZ, ELIAS. "Rating the 'Vocational Potential' of Seriously Mentally Handicapped Young Adults." *Calif J Ed Res* 16:116–22 My '65. * (*PA* 39:15923)

5. CONGDON, DAVID M. "The Vineland and Cain-Levine: A Correlational Study and Program Evaluation." *Am J Mental Def* 74(2):231–4 S '69. * (*PA* 44:5594)

6. TAYLOR, GEORGE ROBERT. *The Relationship Between Varying Amounts of Physical Education Upon the Development of Certain Motor Skills in Trainable Mentally Retarded Children.* Doctor's thesis, Catholic University of America (Washington, D.C.), 1969. (*DAI* 30:2364A)

7. GARDNER, JAMES M., AND GIAMPA, FRANKLYN L. "Utility of Three Behavioral Indices for Studying Severely and Profoundly Retarded Children." *Am J Mental Def* 76(3):352–6 N '71. * (*PA* 48:1509)

8. LAWRENCE, WAYNE, AND KARTYE, JOSEPH. "Extinction of Social Competency Skills in Severely and Profoundly Retarded Females." *Am J Mental Def* 75(5):630–4 Mr '71. *

CUMULATIVE NAME INDEX

Anderson, D. F.: 3	Kartye, J.: 8
Congdon, D. M.: 5	Katz, E.: 4
Domino, G.: 1	Lawrence, W.: 8
Elzey, F. F.: 2	Levine, S.: 2
Gardner, J. M.: 7	Paulson, F. L.: 2
Giampa, F. L.: 7	Rosenthal, R.: 3
Goldschmid, M. L.: 1	Taylor, G. R.: 6
Hiskey, M. S.: *rev*, 6:69	

[1118]

The California Life Goals Evaluation Schedules. Ages 15 and over ; 1966–69; CLGES ; 10 scores : esteem, profit, fame, power, leadership, security, social service, interesting experiences, self-expression, independence ; Milton E. Hahn; Western Psychological Services. *

For additional information and a review by Robert W. Lundin, see 7 :47 (3 references).

REFERENCES THROUGH 1971

1–3. See 7 :47.

4. PATRICK, MAXINE LAMBRECHT. *A Study of Middle-Aged Women and Menopause.* Doctor's thesis, University of California (Los Angeles, Calif.), 1970. (*DAI* 32:408B)

5. BACKER, THOMAS E.; COMREY, ANDREW L.; AND HAHN, MILTON E. "Comparison of the Comrey Personality Scales and the California Life Goals Evaluation Schedules." *Psychol Rep* 29(2):513–4 O '71. * (*PA* 47:8935)

CUMULATIVE NAME INDEX

Backer, T. E.: 5	Lundin, R. W.: *rev*, 7:47
Comrey, A. L.: 5	Patrick, A. L.: 4
Hahn, M. E.: 5	Sinha, S. N.: 1
Keith-Spiegel, P.: 3	Spiegel, D.: 3
Kohler, A. T.: 2	

[1119]

The California Medical Survey. Medical patients ages 10–18, adults; 1962; CMS ; checklist of medical and psychological information; 18 or 23 scores : chronicity of illness, emotional conditions, familial background, basic medical information, psychiatric symptoms, specific disorder, medical background, genitourinary, neuro-mus-skeletal, cardio-vas-blood, sensory, digestive, respiratory, 5 gynecologic scores (women only), anxiety-stress, psychiatric, habits-traits, sexual-social, energy level; 2 levels; Harold L. Snow and Morse P. Manson; Western Psychological Services. *

a) CHILDREN'S FORM. Ages 10–18.

b) ADULT FORMS.

For additional information, see P :26.

[1120]

California Preschool Social Competency Scale. Ages 2.5–5.5; 1969; CPSCS; ratings by teachers;

Samuel Levine, Freeman F. Elzey, and Mary Lewis; Consulting Psychologists Press, Inc. *

For additional information, see 7 :48.

[1121]

California Psychological Inventory. Ages 13 and over; 1956–69; CPI; 18 scores : dominance (Do), capacity for status (Cs), sociability (Sy), social presence (Sp), self-acceptance (Sa), sense of well-being (Wb), responsibility (Re), socialization (So), self-control (Sc), tolerance (To), good impression (Gi), communality (Cm), achievement via conformance (Ac), achievement via independence (Ai), intellectual efficiency (Ie), psychological-mindedness (Py), flexibility (Fx), femininity (Fe) ; Harrison G. Gough ; Consulting Psychologists Press, Inc. *

For additional information, reviews by Lewis R. Goldberg and James A. Walsh, and an excerpted review by John O. Crites, see 7 :49 (370 references) ; see also P :27 (249 references) ; for a review by E. Lowell Kelly, see 6 :71 (116 references) ; for reviews by Lee J. Cronbach and Robert L. Thorndike and an excerpted review by Laurance F. Shaffer, see 5 :37 (33 references).

REFERENCES THROUGH 1971

1–33. See 5 :37.

34–144. See 6 :71.

145–393. See P :27.

394–764. See 7 :49.

765. WEBSTER, HAROLD. "Some Quantitative Results." *J Social Issues* 12(4):29–41 '56. * (*PA* 32:4546)

766. RECKLESS, WALTER C.; DINITZ, SIMON; AND MURRAY, ELLEN. "The 'Good' Boy in a High Delinquency Area." *J Crim Law Criminol & Police Sci* 48:18–25 My–Je '57. * (*PA* 33:1783)

767. JACKSON, DOUGLAS N., AND MESSICK, SAMUEL. "Content and Style in Personality Assessment." *Psychol B* 55:243–52 Jl '58. * (*PA* 33:7926)

768. RAMEY, J. W. "The Relationship of Peer Group Rating to Certain Individual Perceptions of Personality." *J Exp Ed* 27:143–9 D '58. * (*PA* 34:2783)

769. REHFISCH, JOHN M. "Some Scale and Test Correlates of a Personality Rigidity Scale." *J Consult Psychol* 22:372–4 O '58. * (*PA* 34:1050)

770. HEINBERG, PAUL. "Factors Related to an Individual's Ability to Perceive Implications of Dialogues." *Speech Monogr* 28:274–81 N '61. * (*PA* 36:4GH74H)

771. KRASNER, LEONARD; ULLMANN, LEONARD P.; WEISS, ROBERT L.; AND COLLINS, BEVERLY J. "Responsivity to Verbal Conditioning as a Function of Three Different Examiners." *J Clin Psychol* 17:411–5 O '61. * (*PA* 38:7295)

772. ROBERTS, HELEN ERSKINE. "Factors Affecting the Academic Underachievement of Bright High-School Students." *J Ed Res* 56:175–83 D '62. *

773. WINBORN, BOB, AND SCHMIDT, LOUIS G. "The Effectiveness of Short-Term Group Counseling Upon the Academic Achievement of Potentially Superior but Underachieving College Freshmen." *J Ed Res* 55:169–73 D–Ja '62. * (*PA* 37:1985)

774. COOK, JOHN J. "Acquiescence on the Parental Attitude Research Instrument (PARI), the California Personality Inventory (CPI), and the Interpersonal Interview." *Ont Psychol Assn Q* (Canada) 16:8–18 sp '63. *

775. DONOVAN, GEORGE LENWOOD. *Personality Characteristics of Freshman Women Applying for Positions in the Activities Program at Washington State University.* Master's thesis, Washington State University (Pullman, Wash.), 1963.

776. HAAN, NORMA. "Proposed Model of Ego Functioning: Coping and Defense Mechanisms in Relationship to IQ Change." *Psychol Monogr* 77(8):1–23 '63. * (*PA* 38:4234)

777. ROUNDY, CHARLES OWEN. *A Study of Personality Characteristics of Students and Student Leaders at the College of Southern Utah 1963.* Master's thesis, University of Utah (Salt Lake City, Utah), 1963.

778. CAPLAN, STANLEY W., AND RUBLE, RONALD A. "A Study of Culturally Imposed Factors on School Achievement in a Metropolitan Area." *J Ed Res* 58:16–21 S '64. *

779. DIERMAN, FREDERICK G. *The Relationship Between Personality Traits and Aptitude for the Service in Naval ROTC Students.* Master's thesis, University of Utah (Salt Lake City, Utah), 1964.

780. KAHN, ROBERT L.; WOLFE, DONALD M.; QUINN, ROBERT P.; AND SNOEK, J. DIEDRICK; IN COLLABORATION WITH ROBERT A. ROSENTHAL. Part 5, "Personality Processes in Role Stress," pp. 223–333. In their *Organizational Stress: Studies in Role Conflict and Ambiguity.* New York: John Wiley & Sons, Inc., 1964. Pp. xiii, 470. * (*PA* 39:8866)

781. MOORE, ROSEMARIE K. "Susceptibility to Hypnosis and

Susceptibility to Social Influence." *J Abn & Social Psychol* 68:282–94 Mr '64. * *(PA* 38:8193)

782. WILLIAMS, HILDA LEE. *A Comparative Study of the Differences Existent Between the Academic Ability, Motor Ability and Personality Adjustment of Physical Education Majors and Non-majors at Sam Houston State Teachers College, Huntsville, Texas.* Master's thesis, Sam Houston State Teachers College (Huntsville, Tex.), 1964.

783. CONONELOS, BERTHA PAPANIKOLAS. *Measuring the Personality Patterns of Sixth Grade Children.* Master's thesis, University of Utah (Salt Lake City, Utah), 1965.

784. GRIFFIN, CELESTE F. *The Prediction of College Graduation From Aptitude, Achievement and Personality Variables by Multiple Discriminant Analysis.* Master's thesis, Brown University (Providence, R.I.), 1965.

785. HALCOMB, CHARLES G., AND KIRK, ROGER E. "Organismic Variables as Predictors of Vigilance Behavior." *Percept & Motor Skills* 21:547–52 O '65. * *(PA* 40:2289)

786. HYDE, GLENNA GARFF. *Some Relationships Between Values and Self-Image and Academic Achievement.* Master's thesis, University of Utah (Salt Lake City, Utah), 1965.

787. TURLEY, DONNA LEE. *Psychological Need and Personality Trait Difference Comparisons Between Students With Positive Attitudes and Students With Negative Attitudes Toward Independent Study.* Master's thesis, Brigham Young University (Provo, Utah), 1965.

788. ADAMS, DARREL K.; HARVEY, O. J.; AND HESLIN, RICHARD E. Chap. 10, "Variation in Flexibility and Creativity as a Function of Hypnotically Induced Past Histories," pp. 217–34. In *Experience, Structure and Adaptability.* Edited by O. J. Harvey. New York: Springer Publishing Co., Inc., 1966. Pp. ix, 406. *

789. BIGELOW, GORDON SHOEMAKER. *Personality Correlates of Success and Satisfaction in Independent and Traditional Study.* Master's thesis, Brigham Young University (Provo, Utah), 1966.

790. CARNEY, RICHARD E., AND MCKEACHIE, WILBERT J. "Personality, Sex, Subject Matter and Student Ratings." *Psychol Rec* 16:137–44 Ap '66. * *(PA* 40:9211)

791. GRISWOLD, BARBARA B.; WILTSE, KERMIT T.; AND ROBERTS, ROBERT W. "Some Personality and Intellectual Correlates of Repeated Out-of-Wedlock Childbirth Among Welfare Recipients." *J Clin Psychol* 22:348–53 Jl '66. * *(PA* 40:11141)

792. HOYT, ROBERT L. *The Relationships Between Resident Counselor Personality Variables and Students' Perceived Communication Willingness.* Master's thesis, Northwestern University (Evanston, Ill.), 1966.

793. LARSEN, STIRLING D. *Personality Characteristics of Students With Varying Socio-Economic Status.* Master's thesis, Brigham Young University (Provo, Utah), 1966.

794. SEARS, NANCY JANE. *Fabric Preferences as Related to Selected Personality Characteristics of Delinquent and Non-delinquent Adolescent Girls.* Master's thesis, University of North Carolina (Greensboro, N.C.), 1966.

795. VINEY, LINDA L. "Congruence of Measures of Self-Regard." *Psychol Rec* 16:487–93 O '66. * *(PA* 41:1618)

796. WHITTEMORE, ROBERT G.; ECHEVERRIA, BEN P.; AND GRIFFIN, JOHN V. "Can We Use Existing Tests for Adult Basic Education?" *Adult Ed* 17:19–29 au '66. *

797. CARNEY, RICHARD E. "Sex Chromatin, Body Masculinity, Achievement Motivation and Smoking Behavior." *Psychol Rep* 20:859–66 Je '67. * *(PA* 41:13303)

798. FREEDMAN, MERVIN B. Chap. 5, "Personality Development After College," pp. 59–66. In his *The College Experience.* San Francisco, Calif.: Jossey Bass Inc., Publishers, 1967. Pp. xix, 202. *

799. HICKS, ROBERT A.; BRAMBLE, WILLIAM; AND ULSETH, SANDRA. "Socialization and Time Perception in Aged Ss." *Percept & Motor Skills* 24:1170 Je '67. * *(PA* 41:15079, title only)

800. VINGOE, FRANK J. "Self-Awareness, Self-Acceptance, and Hypnotizability." *J Abn Psychol* 72:454–6 O '67. * *(PA* 42:242)

801. BARRON, FRANK, AND ROSENBERG, MARVIN. "King Lear and His Fool: A Study of the Conception and Enactment of Dramatic Role in Relaltion to Self-Conception." Abstract. *Proc 76th Ann Conv Am Psychol Assn* 3:369–70 '68. * *(PA* 43:883, title only)

802. SHEBESTA, DONALD F. "What Tests Say About the 'Disadvantaged.'" *Wis J Ed* 101:13–5 D '68. *

803. VINGOE, FRANK J. "Rogers' Self Theory and Eysenck's Extraversion and Neuroticism." *J Consult & Clin Psychol* 32:618–20 O '68. * *(PA* 43:33)

804. BAJAJ, DEV RAJ. *The Relationship of Certain Personality Traits to Selected Professional and Social Attributes of Oklahoma Male County Field Extension Personnel.* Doctor's thesis, Oklahoma State University (Stillwater, Okla.), 1969. *(DAI* 31:3996A)

805. PARKINSON, LANALEE. *Personality, Self-Disclosure and Predicted Success.* Master's thesis, University of Alberta (Edmonton, Alta., Canada), 1969.

806. ROBINSON, DENNIS JAY. *A Study of Personality Characteristics of Volunteers Taken From Groups of Honor Students and Non-Honor Students of Equivalent General Ability at the*

University of Utah. Master's thesis, University of Utah (Salt Lake City, Utah), 1969.

807. RUCHTI, GARY EDWARD. *Achievement Motivation and Item Recall on Objective Examinations.* Doctor's thesis, Oklahoma State University (Stillwater, Okla.), 1969. *(DAI* 31:4560A)

808. SEVREN, MARION, AND MENDELSON, LLOYD. "Characteristics of Family Caretakers." *Hosp & Commun Psychiatry* 20(8):245–7 Ag '69. * *(PA* 47:3438)

809. TABAK, RHEA MALLINGER. *The Use of the California Psychological Inventory as a Possible Screening Device for the Identification of Competent Teachers for the Educable Mentally Retarded Child.* Master's thesis, California State College (Long Beach, Calif.), 1969.

810. TOMKO, TONY. *Personality Correlates of Home Disruption.* Master's thesis, University of Alberta (Edmonton, Alta., Canada), 1969.

811. ZDEP, S. M. "Intra Group Reinforcement and Its Effects on Leadership Behavior." *Organiz Behav & Hum Perfor* 4(3): 284–98 Ag '69. * *(PA* 43:17364)

812. ZIMMERMAN, DONALD DREW. *The Effects of Differentiated Community Placement Upon Attitudes and Personality Characteristics of College Juniors in a Laboratory Setting.* Doctor's thesis, Temple University (Philadelphia, Pa.), 1969. *(DAI* 32:1390A)

813. ABBOTT, KENNETH ALBERT. *Cultural Change, Psychological Functioning, and the Family: A Case Study in the Chinese-American Community of San Francisco.* Doctor's thesis, University of California (Berkeley, Calif.), 1970. *(DAI* 32:1077A)

814. AREND, PAUL JOSEPH. *The Relationships Between Selected Factors and the Rated Effectiveness of Teachers of Educable Mentally Handicapped Pupils.* Doctor's thesis, University of Virginia (Charlottesville, Va.), 1970. *(DAI* 31:4401A)

815. BECKER, CALVIN JAMES. *A Study of Selected Personality Variables Among Three Groups of Sophomore Women Elementary Education Students Classified According to Teacher Attitudes Following an Off Campus Sophomore Aide Experience.* Doctor's thesis, University of North Dakota (Grand Forks, N.D.), 1970. *(DAI* 31:4448A)

816. BENNETT, LAWRENCE A. "Test Taking 'Insight' of Prison Inmates and Subsequent Parole Adjustment." *Correct Psychologist* 4(1):27–34 Jl '70. * *(PA* 46:9308)

817. BERRICK, MARGARET LYN WILSON. *Patient Pre-Therapy Expectancies of Therapist Behaviors as Related to Certain Demographic, Personality and Value Variables.* Doctor's thesis, Pennsylvania State University (University Park, Pa.), 1970. *(DAI* 32:552B)

818. BROUGHTON, ANDREW. *The Exploration and Measurement of Trustworthiness.* Doctor's thesis, Pennsylvania State University (University Park, Pa.), 1970. *(DAI* 32:1234B)

819. BRUCE, GRADY D., AND WITT, ROBERT E. "Personality Correlates of Innovative Buying Behavior." *J Marketing Res* 7(2):259–60 My '70. * Criticism of 681.

820. CARNEY, EILEEN. *A Measurement Study of Passively Defensive Persons in Communication Workshops.* Doctor's thesis, United States International University (San Diego, Calif.), 1970. *(DAI* 31:7590B)

821. CARTWRIGHT, LILLIAN KAUFMAN. *Women in Medical School.* Doctor's thesis, University of California (Berkeley, Calif.), 1970. *(DAI* 31:6237B)

822. CHEN, SHIUM ANDREW. *The Differences and Relationships Between Amount of Psychology Courses and Certain Cognitive and Affective Behavior Patterns.* Doctor's thesis, University of Pittsburgh (Pittsburgh, Pa.), 1970. *(DAI* 31:3948A)

823. CULLIGAN, KEVIN G. *Personality Characteristics of Diocesan Priests in Middle-Adulthood: A Preliminary Study.* Master's thesis, Marquette University (Milwaukee, Wis.), 1970.

824. CURL, GERALD ALLEN. *A Comparison of Freshman Achievers and Non-Achievers From Economically Deprived Families.* Doctor's thesis, University of Illinois (Urbana, Ill.), 1970. *(DAI* 31:4455A)

825. DE COSTER, DON THEODORE. *A Comparison of Interpersonal Relationship Variables of Northwest Public Accountants With Selected Comparison Groups.* Doctor's thesis, University of Oregon (Eugene, Ore.), 1970. *(DAI* 31:5119A)

826. DODGENS, CLARENCE EDWARD. *A Comparison of College Resident and Commuter Students on Certain Psycho-Sociological Characteristics.* Doctor's thesis, North Carolina State University (Raleigh, N.C.), 1970. *(DAI* 31:6360A)

827. FELKER, SALLY ANNA. *The Relationship Between Communication and Discrimination Skills and Selected Factors of Personality, Intellect, and Experience in Counselor Trainees.* Doctor's thesis, Kent State University (Kent, Ohio), 1970. *(DAI* 31:5122A)

828. FLOM, PENELOPE KEGEL. *Performance in the Medical Internship.* Doctor's thesis, University of California (Berkeley, Calif.), 1970. *(DAI* 32:1188B)

829. GASTON, JOSEPH ALEXANDER. *A Comparison of the Personality Characteristics of Northern and Midwestern Urban Afro-American Freshmen, Southern Town and Rural Afro-American Freshmen, and Southern Afro-American College Stu-*

dent Personnel Staff. Doctor's thesis, Michigan State University (East Lansing, Mich.), 1970. (*DAI* 31:5843A)

830. GREENBERG, GARY. *Exploration of Personalities, Needs and Attitudes of Female Child-Care Workers*. Doctor's thesis, Illinois Institute of Technology (Chicago, Ill.), 1970. (*DAI* 31:7596B)

831. HARRINGTON, CHARLES CHRISTOPHER. *Errors in Sex-Role Behavior in Teen-Age Boys*. New York: Teachers College Press, 1970. Pp. viii, 109. * (*PA* 44:21190, title only)

832. HARRIS, LE BRONE CLAYTON. *A Comparison of the Personality Traits of Accounting Students, Students in Selected Majors, and Successful Accountants*. Doctor's thesis, Florida State University (Tallahassee, Fla.), 1970. (*DAI* 31:4324A)

833. ISLAM, A F M SERAJUL. *An Investigation of the Relationships Between Certain Personality Traits and Selected Professional and Socio-Economic Variables of Oklahoma Student Teaching Personnel in Vocational Agriculture*. Doctor's thesis, Oklahoma State University (Stillwater, Okla.), 1970. (*DAI* 31:5848A)

834. JEKEL, JEROME R. *A Study of the Effects of a Free Reading Program in Social Studies on the Self Image of a Selected Group of Eleventh Grade Core Students*. Doctor's thesis, University of North Dakota (Grand Forks, N.D.), 1970. (*DAI* 32:6780A)

835. LEHRER, MAXINE COILIE BROOKS. *Personality and Student Activism*. Doctor's thesis, Colorado State University (Ft. Collins, Colo.), 1970. (*DAI* 31:7602B)

836. LEVENTHAL, GERALD S. "Influence of Brothers and Sisters on Sex-Role Behavior." *J Pers & Social Psychol* 16(3): 452-65 N '70. * (*PA* 45:4058)

837. LOY, JOHN W., JR., AND SAGE, JOHN N. "The Effects of Formal Structure on Organizational Leadership: An Investigation of Interscholastic Baseball Teams," pp. 363-73. In *Contemporary Psychology of Sport*. Proceedings of the Second International Congress of Sport Psychology, Washington, D.C., 1968. Chicago, Ill.: Athletic Institute, 1970. Pp. xix, 878. *

838. MONSON, MARY ADELE GIBBS. *Relationships of Age With the California Psychological Inventory Scales for Female Registered Nurses*. Master's thesis, University of Utah (Salt Lake City, Utah), 1970.

839. ROBERTSON, THOMAS S., AND MYERS, JAMES H. "Personality Correlates of Innovative Buying Behavior: A Reply." *J Marketing Res* 7(2):260-1 My '70. * Reply to 819.

840. SCHENDEL, JACK S. "The Psychological Characteristics of High School Athletes and Nonparticipants in Athletics: A Three Year Longitudinal Study," pp. 79-96. In *Contemporary Psychology of Sport*. Proceedings of the Second International Congress of Sport Psychology, Washington, D.C., 1968. Chicago, Ill.: Athletic Institute, 1970. Pp. xix, 878. *

841. SMITH, DAN FAYE. *A Study of the Relationship of Teacher Sex to Fifth Grade Boys' Sex Role Preference, General Self Concept, and Scholastic Achievement in Science and Mathematics*. Doctor's thesis, University of Miami (Coral Gables, Fla.), 1970. (*DAI* 31:4563A)

842. STASSER, DOROTHY ANN. *Nonintellectual Factors in College Achievement at Bethany Nazarene College*. Doctor's thesis, Oklahoma State University (Stillwater, Okla.), 1970. (*DAI* 31:5139A)

843. TACCARINO, JOHN ROBERT. *The Relationship Between Value Inconsistency and Ineffective Social Adjustment*. Doctor's thesis, Northwestern University (Evanston, Ill.), 1970. (*DAI* 31:4978B)

844. TOMKO, LAWRENCE J. *Personality Factors in Mathematics Learning*. Master's thesis, University of Alberta (Edmonton, Alta., Canada), 1970.

845. VANDER LIND, JAMES ROBERT. *A Study of the Personality and Biographical Characteristics of Certain Campus Leaders and Nonleaders*. Doctor's thesis, Ohio University (Athens, Ohio), 1970. (*DAI* 31:3890A)

846. ABBOTT, ROBERT D. "A Factor Analysis of the CPI and EPI." *Ed & Psychol Meas* 31(2):549-53 su '71. *

847. ASCHER, GORDON. *Teacher Job Satisfaction: The Effects of Teacher Personality and the Educational Environment of the School*. Doctor's thesis, Rutgers—The State University (New Brunswick, N.J.), 1971. (*DAI* 32:2932A)

848. BAHNEMAN, CARL PHILLIP. *An Analysis of the Relationship Between Selected Personality Characteristics and the Verbal Behavior of Physical Education Teachers*. Doctor's thesis, University of Pittsburgh (Pittsburgh, Pa.), 1971. (*DAI* 32:4399A)

849. BARNETT, ROSALIND. "Personality Correlates of Vocational Planning." *Genetic Psychol Monogr* 83(2):309-56 My '71. * (*PA* 46:5539)

850. BARRO, ARLENE RING. *A Comparison of Two Approaches to Identifying Creativity in Graduate Student Writers*. Doctor's thesis, University of California (Los Angeles, Calif.), 1971. (*DAI* 32:809A)

851. BAST, BERNARD ARTHUR. *A Predictive Study of Employability Among the Visually Impaired With the California Psychological Inventory*. Doctor's thesis, University of Michigan (Ann Arbor, Mich.), 1971. (*DAI* 32:1817B)

852. BELFER, MYRON L.; SHADER, RICHARD I.; CARROLL, MARY; AND HARMATZ, JEROLD S. "Alcoholism in Women." *Arch Gen Psychiatry* 25(6):540-4 D '71. *

853. BERMAN, GRAHAM, AND EISENBERG, MILDRED. "Psycho-Social Aspects of Academic Achievement." *Am J Orthopsychiatry* 41(3):406-15 Ap '71. * (*PA* 46:7673)

854. BERWICK, PETER THOMAS. *The Relationship Between Self-Reinforcement, Self-Acceptance and External Reinforcement*. Doctor's thesis, Arizona State University (Tempe, Ariz.), 1971. (*DAI* 32:3628B)

855. BOYLE, BLAKE P., AND COOMBS, ROBERT H. "Personality Profiles Related to Emotional Stress in the Initial Year of Medical Training." *J Med Ed* 46(10):882-8 O '71. *

856. BROADWAY, CLIFFORD MONROE. *Personality Correlates of Imagery Ability*. Doctor's thesis, Texas Tech University (Lubbock, Tex.), 1971. (*DAI* 32:5433B)

857. BROWN, REX B. "Personality Characteristics Related to Injuries in Football." *Res Q* 42(2):133-8 My '71. * (*PA* 47:2964)

858. BYAS, WILLIAM HERBERT. *Non-Intellectual Factors of High Risk Students*. Doctor's thesis, University of Tennessee (Knoxville, Tenn.), 1971. (*DAI* 32:2476A)

859. CARDWELL, JESSE FRANKLIN. *A Comparative Study of Intellectually Able Students Who Completed and Who Did Not Complete an Honors and Advanced Placement Program*. Doctor's thesis, George Peabody College for Teachers (Nashville, Tenn.), 1971. (*DAI* 32:1939A)

860. CONE, JOHN D. "Social Desirability Scale Values and Ease of Responding to Personality Statements." Abstract. *Proc 79th Ann Conv Am Psychol Assn* 6(1):119-20 '71. * (*PA* 46:3082)

861. COOPER, JOEL, AND DUNCAN, BIRT L. "Cognitive Dissonance as a Function of Self-Esteem and Logical Inconsistency." *J Personality* 39(2):289-302 Je '71. * (*PA* 47:803)

862. COWDEN, JAMES E.; SCHROEDER, CHARLES R.; AND PETERSON, WILLIAM M. "The CPI vs. the 16 PF at a Reception Center for Delinquent Boys." *J Clin Psychol* 27(1):109-11 Ja '71. * (*PA* 46:1471)

863. CROSS, WILLIAM M., AND CORTEZ, JAMES C. "A Comparative Personality Study of Resigners at USMA," pp. 245-54. In *Second Annual Symposium: Psychology in the Air Force, 20-22 April 1971*. Edited by Hal W. Hendrick. Colorado Springs, Colo.: United States Air Force Academy, [1971]. Pp. x, 409. *

864. DAVIS, RUTH KALAIDJIAN. *A Study of the Factors Affecting Congruent or Incongruent College Choice Among Highly Gifted Girls*. Doctor's thesis, New York University (New York, N.Y.), 1971. (*DAI* 32:5543A)

865. DILLON, MICHAEL JAMES. *Helper Effectiveness on Hotline Telephone, Helper Personality and Offered Therapeutic Conditions*. Doctor's thesis, University of Florida (Gainesville, Fla.), 1971. (*DAI* 32:4942A)

866. DOMINO, GEORGE. "Cinematographic Creativity and Personality." Abstract. *Proc 79th Ann Conv Am Psychol Assn* 6(1):413-4 '71. * (*PA* 46:3070)

867. DOMINO, GEORGE. "Interactive Effects of Achievement Orientation and Teaching Style on Academic Achievement." *J Ed Psychol* 62(5):427-31 O '71. * (*PA* 47:5748)

868. DYER, ELAINE D.; MONSON, MARY A.; AND VAN DRIMMELEN, JENNIE B. "Are Administrative Level, Age and Educational Preparation Reflected in California Psychological Inventory Scores?" *Psychol Rep* 29(3):1111-20 D '71. * (*PA* 48:1041)

869. DYER, ELAINE D.; MONSON, MARY A.; AND VAN DRIMMELEN, JENNIE B. "Do Age, Education, and Administrative Position Reflect in CPI Scores?" Abstract. *Proc 79th Ann Conv Am Psychol Assn* 6(2):573-4 '71. * (*PA* 46:5036)

870. FENELON, JAMES R., AND MEGARGEE, EDWIN I. "Influence of Race on the Manifestation of Leadership." *J Appl Psychol* 55(4):353-8 Ag '71. * (*PA* 47:2828)

871. FOLSOM, CLYDE HILDRETH, JR. *The Validity of Holland's Theory of Vocational Choice*. Doctor's thesis, University of Maine (Orono, Me.), 1971. (*DAI* 32:4345A)

872. FRY, JOSEPH N. "Personality Variables and Cigarette Brand Choice." *J Marketing Res* 8(3):298-304 Ag '71. *

873. GARBER, JOHN RODNEY. *Characteristics of Students Enrolled in the Guided Studies Program at Rockingham Community College and Their Implications for Curriculum Development*. Doctor's thesis, North Carolina State University (Raleigh, N.C.), 1971. (*DAI* 32:3555A)

874. GARLIE, NORMAN WAYNE. *Characteristics of Teenagers With Alcohol Related Problems*. Doctor's thesis, University of Utah (Salt Lake City, Utah), 1971. (*DAI* 31:4544A)

875. GELSO, CHARLES J.; OSTERHOUSE, ROBERT; AND BODDEN, JACK L. "Nonintellective Factors in Improvement During an Educational Skills Course." Abstract. *J Counsel Psychol* 18(5): 503-4 S '71. * (*PA* 47:3784)

876. GLUSKINOS, URY, AND BRENNAN, THOMAS F. "Selection and Evaluation Procedure for Operating Room Personnel." *J Appl Psychol* 55(2):165-9 Ap '71. * (*PA* 46:3909)

877. GLUSKINOS, URY M. "Criteria for Student Engineering Creativity and Their Relationship to College Grades." *J Ed Meas* 8(3):189-95 f '71. *

878. GOUGH, HARRISON G. "Scoring High on an Index of Social Maturity." *J Abn Psychol* 77(3):236-41 Je '71. * (*PA* 46:6850)

879. GRAF, RICHARD G. "Induced Self-Esteem as a Determinant of Behavior." *J Social Psychol* 85(2):213-7 D '71. * (*PA* 47:8902)

880. HALL, JAY, AND WILLIAMS, MARTHA S. "Personality and Group Encounter Style: A Multivariate Analysis of Traits and Preferences." *J Pers & Social Psychol* 18(2):163–72 My '71. * (*PA* 46:4952)

881. HAMILTON, DAVID L. "A Comparative Study of Five Methods of Assessing Self-Esteem, Dominance, and Dogmatism." *Ed & Psychol Meas* 31(2):441–52 Su '71. * (*PA* 46:10888)

882. HARTMANN, ERNEST; BAEKELAND, FREDERICK; ZWILLING, GEORGE; AND HOY, PATRICK. "Sleep Need: How Much Sleep and What Kind?"*Am J Psychiatry* 127(8):1001–8 F '71. * (*PA* 47:121)

883. HEADRICK, EDWIN BRUCE. *A Comparison of Personality Traits of Experienced and Prospective Teachers of the Educable Mentally Retarded and Non-Retarded in Mississippi.* Doctor's thesis, Mississippi State University (State College, Miss.), 1971. (*DAI* 32:1916A)

884. HELSON, RAVENNA. "Women Mathematicians and the Creative Personality." *J Consult & Clin Psychol* 36(2):210–20 Ap '71. * (*PA* 46:3073)

885. HOGAN, ROBERT. "Personality Characteristics of Highly Rated Policemen." *Personnel Psychol* 24(4):679–86 w '71. *

886. HOUNTRAS, PETER T., AND HENSRUD, NEIL B. "Demographic Data, Aptitude, Personality Characteristics and Level of Manifest Anxiety." *Col Ed Rec Univ N Dak* 56(4):65–73 Ja '71. *

887. IMIG, DAVID RICHARD. *Masculinity-Femininity as Related to Family-Marital Adjustment.* Doctor's thesis, Michigan State University (East Lansing, Mich.), 1971. (*DAI* 32:3620B)

888. JACOBS, DANIEL ROBERT. *Effects of Number of Response Choices on Scale Validity.* Doctor's thesis, Wayne State University (Detroit, Mich.), 1971. (*DAI* 32:2798A)

889. KISH, GEORGE B. "CPI Correlates of Stimulus-Seeking in Male Alcoholics." *J Clin Psychol* 27(2):251–3 Ap '71. * (*PA* 46:7102)

890. KISH, GEORGE B., AND TIMMONS, FRANK. "CPI Descriptions of Alcoholics Differing in Alienation." *Percept & Motor Skills* 33(2):569–70 O '71. * (*PA* 47:7117)

891. KULIK, JAMES A.; SARBIN, THEODORE R.; AND STEIN, KENNETH B. "Language, Socialization, and Delinquency." *Develop Psychol* 4(3):434–9 My '71. * (*PA* 46:7142)

892. LASHLEY, KENT ADRIAN. *A Comparative Study of Negro and Caucasian Junior High School Boys on Selected Factors of Personality, Socioeconomic Status, and Physical Fitness.* Doctor's thesis, East Texas State University (Commerce, Tex.), 1971. (*DAI* 32:5022A)

893. LeMAISTRE, GRESS. "Computer as Psychologist: Who's Running the Show?" *J Ed Data Processing* 8(2–3):18–21 '71. *

894. LESSER, RICHARD ALLEN. *A Comparison of Police Science With Other College Students Using the Socialization Scale of the California Psychological Inventory.* Master's thesis, California State College (Long Beach, Calif.), 1971.

895. LEVIN, JOSEPH. "Spherical Model of Vector Extension for Determining the Factor Pattern of the California Psychological Inventory." *J Counsel Psychol* 18(6):579–82 N '71. * (*PA* 47:7560)

896. LEVIN, JOSEPH, AND KARNI, ELIEZER S. "A Comparative Study of the CPI Femininity Scale: Validation in Israel." *J Cross-Cultural Psychol* 2(4):387–91 D '71. * (*PA* 48:1018)

897. LEVONIAN, EDWARD. "Student Personality and Academic Achievement." *Personality* 1(1):25–39 sp '71. * (*PA* 47:9804)

898. LIN, YI-GUANG, AND McKEACHIE, WILBERT J. "Sex Similarity in Personality Correlates of Test Anxiety." *Psychol Rep* 29(2):515–20 O '71. * (*PA* 47:9616)

899. LYNCH, DENIS J. "Future Time Perspective and Impulsivity in Old Age." *J Genetic Psychol* 118(2):245–52 Je '71. * (*PA* 46:8803)

900. McCLANAHAN, L. D. "Social Maturity and Multivariate Discriminant Analysis Personality Descriptions of Conservatives, Activists, and Radicals." *Meas & Eval Guid* 4(3):135–44 O '71. * (*PA* 49:10099)

901. McGILLIGAN, ROBERT PATRICK. *Psychological Differentiation, Abilities and Personality.* Doctor's thesis, St. Louis University (St. Louis, Mo.), 1971. (*DAI* 33:1291B)

902. McKENZIE, SHEILA PEREIRA. *A Comparative Study of Feminine Role Perceptions, Selected Personality Characteristics, and Traditional Attitudes of Professional Women and Housewives.* Doctor's thesis, University of Houston (Houston, Tex.), 1971. (*DAI* 32:5615A)

903. McMILLEN, DAVID L. "Transgression, Self-Image, and Compliant Behavior." *J Pers & Social Psychol* 20(2):176–9 N '71. * (*PA* 47:6686)

904. MARTINDALE, DAVID A. "Territorial Dominance Behavior in Dyadic Verbal Interactions." Abstract. *Proc 79th Ann Conv Am Psychol Assn* 6(1):305–6 '71. * (*PA* 46:2918)

905. MASON, EVELYN P. "Stability of Differences in Personality Characteristics of Junior High Students From American Indian, Mexican, and Anglo Ethnic Background." *Psychol Sch* 8(1):86–9 Ja '71. * (*PA* 46:7455)

906. MATSUNAGA, ALLEN SADAO. *A Comparative Study of Ninth Grade Male Underachievers and Achievers on Selected Factors Related to Achievement.* Doctor's thesis, University of Illinois (Urbana, Ill.), 1971. (*DAI* 32:5614A)

907. MEGARGEE, EDWIN I.; PARKER, GEORGE V. C.; AND LEVINE, ROBERT V. "Relationship of Familial and Social Factors to Socialization in Middle-Class College Students." *J Abn Psychol* 77(1):76–89 F '71. * (*PA* 45:9605)

908. MUKHERJEE, SUBHASH CHANDRA. *A Comparative Study of the Parents of Low and High Achieving Students.* Doctor's thesis, Illinois Institute of Technology (Chicago, Ill.), 1971. (*DAI* 32:6624B)

909. OSTRAND, JANET LOUISE. *Change in Counselor Trainee Personality Variables After Practicum as Measured by the California Psychological Inventory and Subjects Most Amenable to Change According to Interests Measured by the Strong Vocational Interest Blank.* Master's thesis, University of Illinois (Urbana, Ill.), 1971.

910. PATTERSON, VIRGINIA; LEVENE, HOWARD; AND BREGER, LOUIS. "Treatment and Training Outcomes With Two Time-Limited Therapies." *Arch Gen Psychiatry* 25(2):161–7 Ag '71. *

911. PURANAJOTI, VANNA PIROONRAKS. *Relationship of Personality Characteristics to Counseling Success of Graduate Students in Counseling Practicum Courses.* Doctor's thesis, University of Northern Colorado (Greeley, Colo.), 1971. (*DAI* 32:3700A)

912. ROARK, GLENN E. "Psychosomatic Factors in the Epidemiology of Infectious Mononucleosis." *Psychosomatics* 12(6):402–11 N–D '71. * (*PA* 48:5515)

913. ROSENBERG, B. G., AND SUTTON-SMITH, B. "Sex-Role Identity and Sibling Composition." *J Genetic Psychol* 118(1):29–32 Mr '71. * (*PA* 46:8780)

914. SHEPPARD, NATHANIEL ALAN. *Educational-Vocational Decision and Indecision in College Freshmen.* Doctor's thesis, Ohio State University (Columbus, Ohio), 1971. (*DAI* 32:3040A)

915. SHERRICK, MICHAEL F.; DAVENPORT, CHARLES A.; AND COLINA, THOMAS L. "Flexibility and Satisfaction With College Major." *J Counsel Psychol* 18(5):487–9 S '71. * (*PA* 47:3615)

916. SILBER, DIANE BERMAN. *Adaptation-Level as a Function of Extraversion and Field Dependence.* Doctor's thesis, Washington University (St. Louis, Mo.), 1971. (*DAI* 32:1195B)

917. STEELE, CAROLYN I. "Sexual Identity Problems Among Adolescent Girls in Institutional Placement." *Adolescence* 6(24):509–22 w '71. * (*PA* 48:7393)

918. STEFIC, EDWARD C., AND LORR, MAURICE. "Analysis of Defensiveness in Relation to Psychopathology." *J Consult & Clin Psychol* 36(2):205–9 Ap '71. * (*PA* 46:3043)

919. STEIN, KENNETH B.; ROZYNKO, VITALI; AND PUGH, LAWRENCE A. "The Heterogeneity of Personality Among Alcoholics." *Brit J Social & Clin Psychol* 10(3):253–9 S '71. * (*PA* 47:11160)

920. STEIN, KENNETH B.; SARBIN, THEODORE R.; AND KULIK, JAMES A. "Further Validation of Antisocial Personality Types." *J Consult & Clin Psychol* 36(2):177–82 Ap '71. * (*PA* 46:3371)

921. SUTER, BARBARA ANN. *Masculinity-Femininity in Creative Women.* Doctor's thesis, Fordham University (New York, N.Y.), 1971. (*DAI* 32:2411B)

922. TITZE, PETER KLAUS. *The Effect of the Student Teacher's and the Supervising Teacher's Personality Traits on the Supervising Teacher's Evaluation of the Student Teacher: An Exploratory Study.* Doctor's thesis, University of Oregon (Eugene, Ore.), 1971. (*DAI* 32:3145A)

923. TOPPEN, J. T. "Underemployment: Economic or Psychological." *Psychol Rep* 28(1):111–22 F '71. * (*PA* 46:4762)

924. VELDHUIZEN, JOHN FRANCIS. *The Effect of Institutional Placement on Delinquent Adolescent Girls: An MMPI and CPI Sequence Testing Approach.* Doctor's thesis, Graduate Theological Union (Berkeley, Calif.), 1971. (*DAI* 32:4232B)

925. WAAG, WAYNE LESLIE. *The Prediction of Individual Differences in Monitoring Performance.* Doctor's thesis, Texas Tech University (Lubbock, Tex.), 1971. (*DAI* 32:5502B)

926. WALSH, W. BRUCE, AND BARROW, CYNTHIA A. "Consistent and Inconsistent Career Performances and Personality." *J Voc Behav* 1(3):271–8 Jl '71. * (*PA* 48:3771)

927. WHITE, JAMES ARTHUR. *The Relationships Between Selected Characteristics and Rated Effectiveness of Student Teachers of the Mentally Retarded.* Doctor's thesis, University of Virginia (Charlottesville, Va.), 1971. (*DAI* 32:4457A)

928. WIGGINS, JERRY S.; GOLDBERG, LEWIS R.; AND APPELBAUM, MARK. "MMPI Content Scales: Interpretative Norms and Correlations With Other Scales." *J Consult & Clin Psychol* 37(3):403–10 D '71. * (*PA* 47:8950)

929. WILCOX, ANNE H., AND FRETZ, BRUCE R. "Actual-Ideal Discrepancies and Adjustment." *J Counsel Psychol* 18(2):166–9 Mr '71. * (*PA* 46:1766)

930. WILSON, MARILYN L., AND GREENE, ROGER L. "Personality Characteristics of Female Homosexuals." *Psychol Rep* 28(2):407–12 Ap '71. * (*PA* 46:7151)

CUMULATIVE NAME INDEX

Howell, M. A.: 238, 286
Hoy, P.: 882
Hoy, W. K.: 358
Hoyt, R. L.: 792
Hunt, J. G.: 75
Hunter, K. J.: 258
Hyde, G. G.: 786
Ibrahim, H.: 654
Ihlanfeldt, W. I.: 729
Imig, D. R.: 887
Islam, A F M S.: 833
Ismir, A. A.: 451
Jackson, D. N.: 26, 62, 76, 369, 767
Jacobs, D. R.: 888
Jaffe, L. D.: 164, 467
James, G. R.: 171
Janssen, J. W.: 655
Jekel, J. R.: 834
Jenkins, C. D.: 656
Jentsch, R. C.: 412
Jerdee, T. H.: 79, 426
Jerome, W. C. F.: 657
Johannsen, W. J.: 200
Johnsgard, K. W.: 495
Johnson, D. E.: 201
Johnson, J. E.: 712
Johnson, R. C.: 202
Johnson, R. T.: 99
Johnston, D.: 506
Johnston, R. P.: 37
Jones, A. M.: 34a
Jones, I. A.: 658
Jones, R. L.: 124
Jones, R. R.: 336, 481
Josephs, P. O.: 713
Joshi, B. L.: 203
Judd, L. R.: 659
Jurjevich, R. M.: 287-8
Kahn, R. L.: 780
Kalis, B. L.: 99a
Karni, E. S.: 741, 896
Kasl, S. V.: 575, 730
Kassera, W. J.: 576, 731
Katter, R. V.: 34a
Kay, B.: 25, 40, 67, 406
Kay, B. A.: 411
Kayton, R.: 660
Kearney, D. L.: 519
Keimowitz, R. I.: 63
Keith-Spiegel, P.: 691
Kelley, S. L.: 661
Kelly, E. L.: 41; rev, 6:71
Kelly, F. J.: 260
Keogh, J.: 46
Keogh, J. F.: 416
Khanna, J. L.: 146 *
Kilburn, K. L.: 732
Kilcawley, M. P.: 577
King, F. J.: 109, 402
Kingsbury, W. T.: 578
Kinne, S.: 496
Kipnis, D.: 370
Kirchner, W. K.: 30-1, 239
Kirk, B. A.: 133, 204, 719, 721
Kirk, R. E.: 785
Kish, G. B.: 733-6, 889-90
Kleban, M. H.: 451
Klein, W. W.: 106
Kleman, M.: 592
Kliewer, V. D.: 452
Klugh, H. E.: 15, 17
Knafle, J. D.: 240
Knapp, R. R.: 134, 205
Koenig, K.: 47
Kohfeld, D. L.: 662
Korman, M.: 100, 371
Korn, H. A.: 101, 579
Krasner, L.: 217, 771
Kraus, W. A.: 737
Kriegsman, S. A.: 535, 610
Kulik, J. A.: 649, 891, 920
Kunert, K. M.: 738
Kurek, A.: 351
Kurland, H. D.: 172
LaCrosse, E. R.: 520
Lamb, A. L.: 289
Landers, D. M.: 739
Lange, G. W.: 290
Lanier, W. J.: 102
Lansky, L. M.: 356, 400, 425
Lanyon, R. I.: 740
Larimore, D.: 760

Larsen, S. D.: 793
Lashley, K. A.: 892
Lauer, L. W.: 96
Lawler, E. E.: 337
Lay, C. H.: 369
Lazarus, R. S.: 393
Leary, T.: 496
Lefcourt, H. M.: 372
Lehrer, M. C. B.: 835
LeMaistre, G.: 893
Lesser, R. A.: 894
Lessinger, L. M.: 77
Leton, D. A.: 103-4
Levene, H.: 910
Leventhal, A. M.: 291, 373
Leventhal, G. S.: 836
Levin, J.: 741, 895-6
Levin, J. L.: 438
Levine, R. V.: 907
Levonian, E.: 897
Lichtenstein, E.: 241, 292
Liddle, G.: 33
Liddle, G. P.: 450
Lim, D.: 202
Lin, Y. G.: 383, 688, 898
Lindzey, D.: 395
Linton, T. E.: 212, 338
Lipinski, B. G.: 497
Lipp, L.: 374
Lippmann, G. K.: 663
Lipsitt, P. D.: 542
Lister, J. L.: 328
Littlefield, D. H.: 620
Livson, N.: 533
Lorei, T. W.: 206
Lorr, M.: 918
Lovell, V. R.: 207
Loy, D. L.: 664
Loy, J. W.: 837
Lucas, D. H.: 339
Lunneborg, C. E.: 742
Lunneborg, P. W.: 742
Lynch, D. J.: 543, 899
McCarthy, D.: 743
McCaulley, M. H.: 482
McCauslin, J. A.: 453
McClain, E. W.: 454
McClaine, R. E.: 580
McClanahan, L. D.: 900
McClosky, H.: 8, 394
McClung, T. E.: 665
McConnel, H. F.: 666
McCormick, R. P.: 272
McDermid, C. D.: 242
McDole, G.: 732
McFadden, J. D.: 375, 498
McGilligan, R. P.: 901
McGovney, W. C.: 397
McGuire, E. C.: 582
McGurk, E.: 243
McGurk, E. L.: 483
McHenry, T. B.: 112, 441, 457
McKeachie, W. J.: 47, 124a, 790, 898
McKee, J. P.: 78
McKenzie, S. P.: 902
MacKinnon, D. W.: 105, 439, 648
McMillen, D. L.: 903
Madson, D. L.: 521
Magoon, T. M.: 221
Mahal, B. K.: 293
Mahboob, S. G.: 294
Mahoney, T. A.: 79, 426
Malley, P. B.: 744
Mankin, D.: 728
Mann, P. E.: 272
Marlowe, D.: 629
Marquis, D. G.: 41
Martin, C. V.: 522
Martin, L. W.: 371
Martin, P.: 610
Martindale, D. A.: 904
Martino, T. P.: 544
Martinson, R. A.: 77
Maruyama, Y.: 667
Mason, E. P.: 244, 295-6, 340, 583, 668, 905
Mathis, C.: 230
Matsch, P. L.: 545
Matsunaga, A. S.: 906
Matthews, C. V.: 450
Maxwell, M. J.: 64
May, M. B.: 584

Mazer, M.: 669
Meadow, A.: 417
Meehl, P. E.: 8, 394
Mees, H. L.: 208
Megargee, E. I.: 297-8, 484, 523, 670, 870, 907
Mehrens, W. A.: 745
Mendelson, L.: 346, 808
Mendelson, M.: 86
Merigold, F. A.: 671
Merriman, J. B.: 48, 65
Merritt, M. A.: 80
Messick, S.: 767
Mettee, D. R.: 557
Metzner, R.: 496
Michie, J.: 585
Milbrath, L. W.: 106
Miller, D. E.: 524
Miller, D. I.: 245, 299
Miller, D. L.: 151
Miller, J. G.: 41
Miller, J. M.: 376
Miller, J. O.: 546
Miller, M. B.: 746
Miller, R. E.: 672
Minium, E. W.: 344
Miranda, S. B.: 356
Mitchell, J. V.: 66, 109, 135, 430, 440, 586
Mitchell, L. H.: 499
Mittman, H.: 485
Mizushima, K.: 341, 366
Moeller, G.: 121
Monson, M. A.: 868-9
Monson, M. A. G.: 838
Moore, R. K.: 781
Morano, N. T.: 500
Mordkoff, A. M.: 300
Mordock, J. B.: 246
Morris, R. P.: 27, 209
Moses, J.: 525
Mosher, D. L.: 547
Moskovis, L. M.: 548, 747
Mottesheard, N.: 182
Mowrer, O. H.: 342
Mueller, D. J.: 673
Muench, G. A.: 495
Mukherjee, S. C.: 908
Mundy, J.: 152
Murray, E.: 402, 431, 766
Mussen, P.: 81
Mussen, P. H.: 401, 455
Muthard, J. E.: 674
Myers, J. H.: 681, 839
Nakamura, C. Y.: 153
Nash, A. N.: 79, 426
Neithercutt, M. G.: 587
Nelson, J. A.: 107
Nelson, J. W.: 456
Netsky, M. G.: 210
Neufeld, J. A.: 588
Nichols, R. C.: 87, 108, 112, 116, 136, 173, 247, 301-2, 427, 441
Niyekawa, A. M.: 21
Norfleet, M. A. W.: 377
Nugent, F. A.: 82, 589
Nussbaum, H.: 174
O'Brien, C. C.: 248
Obst, F.: 49
O'Connell, W. E.: 722
O'Donnell, J. A.: 428
Oettel, A. M.: 16
O'Gara, P. W.: 337
O'Kane, J. M.: 590
Olch, D.: 748
Olds, C. M.: 526
Oliver, W. A.: 547
Olsen, L. C.: 228
Opton, E. M.: 393
Osterhouse, R.: 875
Ostrand, J. L.: 909
Ouellette, E. G.: 429
Pacine, L.: 76
Pandya, D. N.: 549
Pappas, J. G.: 527, 591
Parker, C. A.: 273
Parker, G. V. C.: 907
Parkinson, L.: 805
Parloff, M. B.: 501, 592
Parnes, S. J.: 417, 750
Patterson, C. H.: 246, 343
Patterson, V.: 910
Payne, D. E.: 401

Peck, R. F.: 165, 175, 387
Pennell, L. A.: 676
Peskin, H.: 593, 639
Petersen, D. J.: 677
Peterson, D. R.: 7, 418
Peterson, R. S.: 550
Peterson, W. M.: 862
Pierce, J. V.: 83, 450
Pierce-Jones, J.: 66, 109, 218, 430
Piliavin, I.: 683
Pivik, T.: 378
Plant, W. T.: 249-50, 303, 344, 384
Pleck, J.: 714
Podell, H. A.: 137
Podshadley, D. W.: 320, 678
Poey, K.: 621
Polansky, N. A.: 164
Pouncey, A. T.: 145
Prentiss, R. J.: 704
Presnell, M.: 496
Pugh, L. A.: 919
Pumroy, D. K.: 110
Puranajoti, V. P.: 911
Purkey, W. W.: 211, 304, 675
Quan, J.: 248
Quay, H. C.: 418
Query, W. T.: 305
Quinn, A. W.: 749
Quinn, R. P.: 780
Ramey, J. W.: 768
Ramseyer, G.: 368
Rand, K. H.: 354
Rawls, D. J.: 379, 594
Rawls, J. R.: 594
Ray, J. B.: 570
Reckless, W. C.: 25, 40, 67, 89, 402, 406, 411, 431, 766
Redel, M. C.: 200
Reed, C. F.: 24, 407
Reese, H. W.: 750
Rehfisch, J. M.: 769
Rempel, P. P.: 72
Resnick, J. H.: 759
Reuter, M. W.: 679
Reutzel, E.: 229
Rexroat, M. E.: 306
Reynolds, C. M.: 680
Richardson, H.: 251-2
Richardson, I. F.: 34a
Richardson, J.: 368
Richek, H. G.: 387
Ridley, D. W.: 528
Rigney, F. J.: 84
Roark, G. E.: 912
Robbins, H.: 380
Roberts, H. E.: 772
Roberts, R. W.: 791
Robertson, T. S.: 681, 839
Robinson, D. J.: 806
Roden, A. H.: 408
Rodgers, D. A.: 307, 535, 610, 704
Roebuck, J.: 252
Roessler, R.: 529
Rogers, B. G.: 745
Rogers, M. I.: 595
Rogers, M. S.: 138, 253
Rohila, P. K.: 682
Rokeach, M.: 397
Rorer, L. G.: 187-8, 465
Rosenberg, A. M.: 112, 441, 457
Rosenberg, B. G.: 596, 913
Rosenberg, J. L.: 502
Rosenberg, L. A.: 111-2, 441, 457
Rosenberg, M.: 705, 801
Rosenfeld, H. M.: 551
Rosenhan, D.: 113
Rosenman, R. H.: 656
Rosenthal, R. A.: 780
Rosett, H. L.: 380
Ross, J.: 213, 487
Rothaus, P.: 722
Roundy, C. O.: 777
Rozynko, V.: 919
Rozynko, V. V.: 233
Rubinroit, C. I.: 751
Ruble, R. A.: 123, 778
Ruchti, G. E.: 807
Rudoff, A.: 23, 683
Rufe, C. P.: 226

[1122]

*[Re California Psychological Inventory] Behaviordyne Psychodiagnostic Lab Service. A computerized scoring and interpreting service for qualified users of the CPI or MMPI; 1969–72; formerly called OPTIMUM Psychodiagnostic Consultation Service; various types of interpretive reports are available: types OR (statistical report for researchers), 1 (for industrial psychologists and personnel counselors), 2 (for counselors and caseworkers), 3 (for correctional counselors), 4 (self-report to be given to patient by counselor or therapist), 5 (for physicians), 6 (standard report for psychiatrists and psychologists), 7 (comprehensive report for psychiatrists and psychologists); a penal option is available with the above reports; each type of report (except type 4) available in full or brief form; Joseph C. Finney, Charles Dwight Auvenshine, David Fulton Smith, and Donald E. Skeeters; Behaviordyne, Inc. *

For additional information, see 7:50; for a review of this scoring service for the MMPI, see 7:107 (9 references).

[1123]

California Test of Personality. Grades kgn–3, 4–8, 7–10, 9–14, adults; 1939–53; CTP; 15 scores: self-reliance, sense of personal worth, sense of personal freedom, feeling of belonging, withdrawing tendencies, nervous symptoms, total personal adjustment, social standards, social skills, anti-social tendencies, family relations, school relations or occupation relations (adult level), community relations, total social adjustment, total adjustment; Louis P. Thorpe, Willis W. Clark, and Ernest W. Tiegs; CTB/McGraw-Hill. *

For additional information, see P:29 (73 references); see also 6:73 (49 references); for a review by Verner M. Sims, see 5:38 (93 references); for reviews by Laurance F. Shaffer and Douglas Spencer and an excerpted review by Earl R. Gabler of the original edition, see 3:26 (27 references); for reviews by Raymond B. Cattell, Percival M. Symonds, and P. E. Vernon and an excerpted review by Marion M. Lamb of the elementary and secondary levels, see 2:1213.

REFERENCES THROUGH 1971

1–24. See 3:26.
25–117. See 5:38.
118–166. See 6:73.
167–239. See P:29.
240. WOOD, KENNETH SCOTT. "Parental Maladjustment and Functional Articulatory Defects in Children." J Speech Disorders 11:255–75 D '46. * (PA 21:1497)
241. RAMM, KATHERINE M. "Personality Maladjustment Among Monotones." Smith Col Studies Social Work 17:264–84 Je '47. * (PA 21:3590)

242. HOOD, PHILIP N.; SHANK, KENNON H.; AND WILLIAMSON, DORIS B. "Environmental Factors in Relation to the Speech of Cerebral Palsied Children." *J Speech & Hearing Disorders* 13:325–31 D '48. * (*PA* 23:3301)

243. WATT, GEORGE D. "An Evaluation of Non-Directive Counseling in the Treatment of Delinquents." *J Ed Res* 42:343–52 Ja '49. * (*PA* 23:3836)

244. ALPRIN, STANLEY I. "The Relationship of Self Adjustment to Pursuit Rotor Performance." *Motor Skills Res Exch* 2:36–9 S '50. * (*PA* 25:4317)

245. BEALS, LESTER. "A Study of Certain Home Factors and Their Relationship to the Personal Adjustment of Children." *Sch & Soc* 72:55–7 Je 22 '50. * (*PA* 26:3890)

246. ELIAS, GABRIEL. "Self-Evaluative Questionnaires as Projective Measures of Personality." *J Consult Psychol* 15:496–500 D '51. * (*PA* 26:6995)

247. ACKERMAN, GENE FRANKLIN. *A Comparative Study of Teacher and Pupil Ratings of Personality Traits of Boys and Girls of Stark County as Compared With Results of Objective Tests.* Doctor's thesis, Bradley University (Peoria, Ill.), 1952. (*DA* 13:696)

248. SEWELL, WILLIAM H., AND MUSSEN, PAUL H. "The Effects of Feeding, Weaning, and Scheduling Procedures on Childhood Adjustment and the Formation of Oral Symptoms." *Child Develop* 23:185–91 S '52. * (*PA* 27:7091)

249. ANDRIOLA, JOSEPH. *A Comparative Study of Non-Truant and Truant Children.* Doctor's thesis, University of Minnesota (Minneapolis, Minn.), 1953. (*DA* 14:564)

250. CARTER, ROBERT SCRIVEN. "Non-Intellectual Variables Involved in Teachers' Marks." *J Ed Res* 47:81–95 O '53. * (*PA* 28:6587)

251. MARTINSON, FLOYD M. *Some Personality Adjustment Differences of Rural Nonmigrants and Migrants.* Doctor's thesis, University of Minnesota (Minneapolis, Minn.), 1953. (*DA* 13:1291)

252. CHRISTIANSEN, JOHN R., AND BLACK, THEREL R. "Group Participation and Personality Adjustment." *Rural Sociol* 19:183–5 Je '54. * (*PA* 29:5363)

253. JENSEN, BARRY T. "Instruction and Personality as Factors in Student Performance." *J Ed Res* 47:529–35 Mr '54. * (*PA* 28:7977)

254. SPILKA, BERNARD. "Relationships Between Certain Aspects of Personality and Some Vocal Effects of Delayed Speech Feedback." *J Speech & Hearing Disorders* 19:491–503 D '54. * (*PA* 29:5326)

255. ANGELINO, HENRY, AND MECH, EDMUND V. "Factors Influencing Routine Performance Under Noise: 2, An Exploratory Analysis of the Influence of 'Adjustment.'" *J Psychol* 40:397–401 O '55. * (*PA* 30:7855)

256. BAUMANN, MARGARET LOUISE. *Behavior Anomalies and School Adjustment.* Doctor's thesis, Northwestern University (Evanston, Ill.), 1955. (*DA* 15:1549)

257. HAND, JACK, AND LEBO, DELL. "Predicting the Institutional Adjustment of Delinquent Boys." *J Crim Law Criminol & Police Sci* 45:694–6 Mr–Ap '55. * (*PA* 30:3157)

258. MARTINSON, FLOYD M. "Ego Deficiency as a Factor in Marriage." *Am Sociol R* 20:161–4 Ap '55. * (*PA* 31:912)

259. REYNOLDS, LYLE GORDON. "The School Adjustment of Children With Minimal Hearing Loss." *J Speech & Hearing Disorders* 20:380–4 D '55. * (*PA* 30:7632)

260. SOPCHAK, ANDREW L. "Projective Study of Peter and His Parents: Revealing the Necessary Therapeutic Limitations." *J Child Psychiatry* 3:149–200 Ag '56. * (*PA* 31:8363)

261. WILLIAMS, META FEINER. *Classmate Acceptance in Relation to the Performance of Intellectually Gifted Children in Certain Elementary Schools.* Doctor's thesis, New York University (New York, N.Y.), 1956. (*DA* 17:2889)

262. ALDRICH, ANITA. *A Comparison of Sectarian College Women and University Women in Motor Ability, Personality Adjustment, Scholastic Aptitude, and Background.* Doctor's thesis, Pennsylvania State University (University Park, Pa.), 1957. (*DA* 18:141)

263. BURCHINAL, LEE G.; HAWKES, GLENN R.; AND GARDNER, BRUCE. "Adjustment Characteristics of Rural and Urban Children." *Am Sociol R* 22:81–7 F '57. * (*PA* 32:303)

264. LEWIS, JAMES FRANKLIN. *Characteristics of Highly Gifted Children: An Experimental Analysis.* Doctor's thesis, State University of Iowa (Iowa City, Iowa), 1957. (*DA* 19:731)

265. LUFT, JOSEPH. "Monetary Value and the Perception of Persons." *J Social Psychol* 46:245–51 N '57. * (*PA* 34:3403)

266. TURNER, DANIEL. *A Study of Speech Effectiveness and Personal and Social Adjustment Among Ninth Grade Pupils.* Doctor's thesis, Boston University (Boston, Mass.), 1957. (*DA* 17:2902)

267. EPPLEY, MARY VINEITA (BOOTS). *The Relationship of Personal Factors and Reading Performance to Academic Achievement of Selected Oregon State College Students.* Doctor's thesis, Oregon State University (Corvallis, Ore.), 1958. (*DA* 19:730)

268. HALLOCK, GEORGE A. *Attitudinal Factors Affecting Achievement in Reading.* Doctor's thesis, Wayne State University (Detroit, Mich.), 1958. (*DA* 18:2061)

269. HENDERSON, EDWARD HENRY. *The Relationship of Certain Child Characteristics to Social Status in Group Process.*

Doctor's thesis, University of Wisconsin (Madison, Wis.), 1958. (*DA* 19:1672)

270. DOWLING, WILLIAM DEAN. *A Study of the Personal and Social Behavior of Boys and Girls in Reorganized and Non-Reorganized School Districts.* Doctor's thesis, University of Wisconsin (Madison, Wis.), 1959. (*DA* 20:2640)

271. DOLLINS, JOSEPH G.; ANGELINO, HENRY; AND MECH, EDMUND V. "With Words of Praise." *El Sch J* 60:446–50 My '60. * (*PA* 35:6993)

272. IRWIN, JACK MENZENWERTH. *A Study of Certain Personal and Social Factors Differentiating the Nonevidently Handicapped From the Physically Normal Adolescent.* Doctor's thesis, Cornell University (Ithaca, N.Y.), 1960. (*DA* 21:3852)

273. JACKSON, PHILIP W.; GETZELS, JACOB W.; AND XYDIS, GEORGE A. "Psychological Health and Cognitive Functioning in Adolescence: A Multivariate Analysis." *Child Develop* 31:285–98 Je '60. * (*PA* 36:3FH85J)

274. KENNEDY, WALLACE A.; SMITH, MARION; VAN DE RIET, HANNAH; VAN DE RIET, VERNON; SMITH, HERBERT; RAPP, DON; AND PAINE, R. W. "A Multidimensional Study of Mathematically Gifted Adolescents." *Child Develop* 31:655–66 D '60. * (*PA* 36:2FH55K)

275. SEAY, LESTEN CLARE. *A Study to Determine Some Relations Between Changes in Reading Skills and Self-Concepts Accompanying a Remedial Program for Boys With Low Reading Ability and Reasonably Normal Intelligence.* Doctor's thesis, North Texas State College (Denton, Tex.), 1960. (*DA* 21:2598)

276. CHRONISTER, GLENN MORRISON. *The Relationship of Certain Personality Variables to Fifth Grade Reading Achievement in a Selected Group of Pupils.* Doctor's thesis, University of Missouri (Columbia, Mo.), 1961. (*DA* 22:2680)

277. LINN, GEORGE WILLIAM. *An Exploratory Comparison of the Personal Social Adjustment of Selected Participants and Nonparticipants in Two Junior High School Athletic Programs.* Doctor's thesis, University of Michigan (Ann Arbor, Mich.), 1961. (*DA* 22:2281)

278. MOFFETT, ELEANOR WARD. *A Study of the Relationship Between Perception of Self and Achievement in Reading.* Doctor's thesis, University of North Carolina (Chapel Hill, N.C.), 1961. (*DA* 23:534)

279. RICHARDS, BERNA FLANDERS. *A Predictive Longitudinal Study of Intellective and Non-Intellective Factors Affecting School Achievement of Gifted Children.* Doctor's thesis, Ohio State University (Columbus, Ohio), 1961. (*DA* 22:3526)

280. SHECHTMAN, AUDREY M. *The Relationship of Variability in Children's Verbal and Non-Language Test Performance to Current and Later Behavioral Functions.* Doctor's thesis, University of Minnesota (Minneapolis, Minn.), 1961. (*DA* 22:2065)

281. TIEMAN, NORMAN. *A Multi-Dimensional Evaluation of the Effect of Formal Classroom Guidance on Adjustment: An Experimental Study of the Ability of a School Guidance Program to Produce Changes in the Behavior and Attitudes of Seventh Grade Pupils as Measured by Teacher Ratings of Classroom Behavior and a Standardized Test of Personality.* Doctor's thesis, New York University (New York, N.Y.), 1961. (*DA* 22:4276)

282. TOBIAS, MILTON, AND MICHAEL, WILLIAM B. "An Exploration Into Child Ecology: Physiological and Maturational Indices as Predictors of Measures of Achievement, Aptitude, and Adjustment." *Ed & Psychol Meas* 21:967–74 w '61. *

283. CAPPS, LELON R. "A Comparison of Superior Achievers and Underachievers in Arithmetic." *El Sch J* 63:141–5 D '62. *

284. DAVIS, MARIE LEONORA FARANDA. *Prattville: A Study of Adolescent Values and Self-Concepts.* Doctor's thesis, University of Connecticut (Storrs, Conn.), 1962. (*DA* 23:1602)

285. HAVIGHURST, ROBERT J.; BOWMAN, PAUL HOOVER; LIDDLE, GORDON P.; MATTHEWS, CHARLES V.; AND PIERCE, JAMES V. *Growing Up in River City.* New York: John Wiley & Sons, Inc., 1962. Pp. xiii, 189. * (*PA* 37:4762)

286. POWELL, MARVIN, AND BERGEM, JERRY. "An Investigation of the Differences Between Tenth-, Eleventh-, and Twelfth-Grade 'Conforming' and 'Nonconforming' Boys." *J Ed Res* 56:184–90 D '62. *

287. PRASAD, CHANDRIKA. *A Comparison of Personal and Social Development and Interest Patterns Between Matched Groups of Ninth Grade 4-H and Non-4-H Members in Ten Wisconsin Rural Communities.* Doctor's thesis, University of Wisconsin (Madison, Wis.), 1962. (*DA* 22:3328)

288. WOLCOTT, CLARISSA M. *A Comparison and Analysis of the Attitudes of Negro and White Elementary Students as Revealed by the California Test of Personality.* Master's thesis, Millersville State College (Millersville, Pa.), 1962.

289. ANDERSON, LINNEA MAE. *Factors Affecting High and Low Achievement Among Adolescents Enrolled in Special Classes for the Mentally Handicapped.* Doctor's thesis, Wayne State University (Detroit, Mich.), 1963. (*DA* 25:279)

290. BRUNDIDGE, ARTHUR DuBOIS. *Rehabilitation Therapy and Psychosocial Adjustment: An Investigation of the Effects of Rehabilitation Therapy Upon Certain Aspects of the Behavior and Self Concept of Hospitalized Tuberculous Patients.* Doctor's thesis, New York University (New York, N.Y.), 1963. (*DA* 26:517)

291. FUSTER, JOACHIM M. "The Self Concept Approach to

Personal Adjustment." *J Social Psychol* 59:239–46 Ap '63. * (*PA* 38:1037)

292. HERMSEN, LEON PAUL. *A Comparative Study of the Background Data, Academic Achievement and the Persistence of Students Electing Business Teacher Education With Those in Other Subject Fields at Wisconsin State College, Whitewater.* Doctor's thesis, University of Wisconsin (Madison, Wis.), 1963. (*DA* 24:1492)

293. JOHNSON, KENNETH EDWIN. *Personal Religious Growth Through Small Group Participation: A Psychological Study of Personality Changes and Shifts in Religious Attitudes Which Result From Participation in a Spiritual Growth Group.* Doctor's thesis, Pacific School of Religion (Berkeley, Calif.), 1963. (*DA* 25:628)

294. STERN, NANCY WERNICK. *Maternal Personality, Attitudes, and Child-Rearing Practices, and Their Relation to Child Adjustment.* Doctor's thesis, Northwestern University (Evanston, Ill.), 1963. (*DA* 25:635)

295. TOBIAS, MILTON, AND MICHAEL, WILLIAM B. "Dimensions of Biological and Psychological Function in Two Samples of Children in the Third Grade." *Psychol Rep* 12:759–62 Je '63. * (*PA* 38:5756)

296. TUTTLE, LAURA L. *A Comparative Study of Ohio University Freshman Women Physical Education Majors and Non-Majors in Scholastic Aptitude, General Motor Ability, and Personality.* Master's thesis, Ohio University (Athens, Ohio), 1963.

297. CAUBLE, BEN LEROY. *Anxiety in Intermediate Grade Children and Its Relationship With Their Scores on Measures of Intelligence, Academic Achievement, and Several Personality Factors.* Doctor's thesis, Southern Illinois University (Carbondale, Ill.), 1964. (*DA* 25:5150)

298. COCHRAN, NORMAN A. *The Influences of Elementary School Physical Education on Selected Physical and Psychological Tests.* Doctor's thesis, University of Maryland (College Park, Md.), 1964. (*DA* 26:3146)

299. CRIDER, MILDRED MURRAY. *A Study of the Effectiveness of Group Guidance Upon Personality Conflict and Reading Retardation.* Doctor's thesis, University of Southern Mississippi (Hattiesburg, Miss.), 1964. (*DA* 26:4438)

300. GOODISON, JULES M., AND ADAMS, JAMES F. "Personality Factors and Academic Achievement." *Sch Counselor* 11:144–8 Mr '64. *

301. HAGEN, REED HARRY. *A Comparative Study of Underachieving and Overachieving Boys in Grade 4B-Detroit Public Schools.* Doctor's thesis, Wayne State University (Detroit, Mich.), 1964. (*DA* 25:5015)

302. HUBER, WILLIAM GEORGE. *The Relationship of Anxiety and of Adjustment to the Academic Performance of Institutionalized Retardates.* Doctor's thesis, Ohio State University (Columbus, Ohio), 1964. (*DA* 25:1006)

303. JARRETT, WILLIAM H., AND HALLER, ARCHIBALD O. "Situational and Personal Antecedents of Incipient Alienation: An Exploratory Study." *Genetic Psychol Monogr* 69:151–91 F '64. * (*PA* 39:1352)

304. KENNEDY, KIERAN, AND KATES, SOLIS L. "Conceptual Sorting and Personality Adjustment in Children." *J Abn & Social Psychol* 68:211–3 F '64. * (*PA* 38:5786)

305. LOCKHART, HAZEL SHIERRY. *The Relationship of Personality With Reading Readiness.* Master's thesis, Illinois State University (Normal, Ill.), 1964.

306. RYAN, MARY ANN. *Personality: Relationship With Reading and Spelling of Intermediate-Grade Pupils.* Master's thesis, Illinois State University (Normal, Ill.), 1964.

307. SUMNER, JOSEPH WILLIAM. *A Comparison of the Personal and Social Adjustment of Some Negro and White Children in Special Education Classes for the Educable Retarded.* Master's thesis, North Carolina State College (Raleigh, N.C.), 1964.

308. YEE, GEORGE FONG. *The Influences of Problem-Solving Instruction and Personal-Social Adjustment Upon Creativity Test Scores of Twelfth Grade Students.* Doctor's thesis, Pennsylvania State University (University Park, Pa.), 1964. (*DA* 26:916)

309. HALLER, A. O., AND WOLFF, CAROLE ELLIS. "A Note on 'Personality Orientations of Farm, Village, and Urban Boys.'" *Rural Sociol* 30:338–40 S '65. * (*PA* 39:14903, title only)

310. LAMBERT, PHILIP; GOODWIN, WILLIAM L.; AND WIERSMA, WILLIAM. "A Comparison of Pupil Adjustment in Team and Self-Contained Organizations." *J Ed Res* 58:311–4 Mr '65. *

311. MEEKS, DOROTHY A. *A Comparison of Physically Fit and Physically Unfit Junior High School Girls.* Master's thesis, Arkansas State College (State College, Ark.), 1965.

312. PATRICK, M "Identifying the Emotionally Disturbed." *Cath Sch J* 65:47–8 O '65. * (*PA* 40:1426)

313. RAPHAEL, SHARON. *The Relationship of Intelligence and Personality on the Reading Achievement of Culturally Deprived Second-Grade Students.* Master's thesis, Central Connecticut State College (New Britain, Conn.), 1965.

314. WHITE, DARRELL K. *The Relationship of Certain Personality Variables to Achievement in Programed Instruction.* Master's thesis, Utah State University (Logan, Utah), 1965.

315. WINTERS, ARTHUR WAYNE. *The Identification of Early Delinquent Tendencies in Preadolescent Children in Umatilla*

and Union Counties of Oregon. Doctor's thesis, Oregon State University (Corvallis, Ore.), 1965. (*DA* 27:3645A)

316. ANDERSON, LOUIS VALENTINE. *The Effects of Desegregation on the Achievement and Personality Patterns of Negro Children.* Doctor's thesis, George Peabody College for Teachers (Nashville, Tenn.), 1966. (*DA* 27:1529A)

317. ASHFORD, ZELODIOUS WILLIAMS. *Personality: Reading and Spelling Achievement of Mentally Retarded Pupils.* Master's thesis, Illinois State University (Normal, Ill.), 1966.

318. BELCHER, MARY S. *An Investigative Study of Certain Personality Characteristics and Achievement Differences of Children From Broken and Normal Homes in Grade Six, at W. H. Councill High School, Huntsville, Alabama.* Master's thesis, Alabama A & M College (Normal, Ala.), 1966.

319. BRIGGS, L. D. *The Impact of Failure on Elementary School Pupils.* Doctor's thesis, North Texas State University (Denton, Tex.), 1966. (*DA* 27:2719A)

320. DICKEY, BILLY ALBERT. *Little League Baseball and Its Effect on Social and Personal Adjustment.* Doctor's thesis, University of Arkansas (Fayetteville, Ark.), 1966. (*DA* 27:656A)

321. GROVES, WILLIAM CONERLY. *Rhythmic Training and Its Relationship to the Synchronization of Motor-Rhythmic Responses.* Doctor's thesis, University of Arkansas (Fayetteville, Ark.), 1966. (*DA* 27:702A)

322. MAW, WALLACE H., AND MAW, ETHEL W. *Personal and Social Variables Differentiating Children With High and Low Curiosity.* An unpublished report to the U.S. Office of Education, Cooperative Research Project No. 1511, University of Delaware, 1966. Pp. xii, 181. * (ERIC ED 003 274)

323. MEYER, KATHERINE CHARLOTTE. *Personality: Relationship of Junior High School Students' Scholastic Achievement.* Master's thesis, Illinois State University (Normal, Ill.), 1966.

324. STARK, THOMAS F. *Pupil Adjustment Among Seventh Graders in Schools Organized Under Different Plans: 8-4, 6-6, 6-3-3, and 5-3-4.* Doctor's thesis, Michigan State University (East Lansing, Mich.), 1966. (*DA* 27:1611A)

325. TELFORD, NANCY J. *Personality Maladjustment and Reading Disability Among Sixth Grade Children.* Master's thesis, Northern Illinois University (DeKalb, Ill.), 1966.

326. BAKER, LUTHER GALLOWAY, JR. *A Comparison of the Personal and Social Adjustment of 38 Never-Married Women and 38 Married Women.* Doctor's thesis, Oregon State University (Corvallis, Ore.), 1967. (*DA* 28:775A)

327. BINKLEY, MARVIN EDWARD. *First Grade Entrance Variables Related to Achievement and Personality: A Study of Culturally Deprived Fourth Graders.* Doctor's thesis, University of Tennessee (Knoxville, Tenn.), 1967. (*DA* 28:2065A)

328. CLEVELAND, GERALD ARTHUR, AND BOSWORTH, DOROTHY L. "A Study of Certain Psychological and Sociological Characteristics as Related to Arithmetic Achievement." *Arith Teach* 14:383–7 My '67. *

329. COURY, VICTOR MICHAEL. *The Validity of Teacher Ratings of Pupil Adjustment.* Doctor's thesis, University of Georgia (Athens, Ga.), 1967. (*DA* 28:2550A)

330. DAVIDSON, RICHARD ALLEN. *A Study of Personality Traits and Value Systems of High School Athletes and Non-athletes.* Doctor's thesis, University of Kentucky (Lexington, Ky.), 1967. (*DAI* 30:3777A)

331. FLETCHER, ROBERT E. *The Effects of a Guidance Oriented Psychology Course on the Personality Adjustment of High School Seniors as Indicated by the California Test of Personality and a Course Evaluation Report.* Master's thesis, University of South Carolina (Columbia, S.C.), 1967.

332. NICKORE, AMRIT, AND DESHPANDE, M. V. "Anxiety Levels and Personality Patterns." *J Ed & Psychol* (India) 24:215–8 Ja '67. *

333. PANEY, HENRY, AND HORROCKS, CAROL. "Creativity in a Troop of Low Average Intelligent Boy Scouts." *Adolescence* 2:231–41 su '67. * (*PA* 42:3962)

334. SPAIGHTS, ERNEST. "Effects of Social Reinforcement as a Technique in Counseling." *J Col Stud Personnel* 8:116–20 Mr '67. *

335. THOMAS, ELIZABETH NOALL. *A Comparison of the Results of a Personality Test With the Results of a Reading Achievement Test in the First Grade.* Master's thesis, University of Utah (Salt Lake City, Utah), 1967.

336. WALLACE, DONNEL GENE. *Group Loyalty, Communication, and Trust in a Mixed-Motive Game.* Doctor's thesis, University of Houston (Houston, Tex.), 1967. (*DA* 27:4569B)

337. ADEN, ROBERT C. "Correlation Between Personality and Number of Siblings." *Peabody J Ed* 46:88–9 S '68. *

338. BAKER, BETTY SUE. *A Study of Social Status, Personality Characteristics, and Motor Ability of Mentally Handicapped Girls.* Doctor's thesis, University of Alabama (University, Ala.), 1968. (*DA* 29:3439A)

339. BAKER, LUTHER G., JR. "The Personal and Social Adjustment of the Never-Married Woman." *J Marriage & Family* 30:473–9 Ag '68. * (*PA* 43:17722)

340. CHARETTE, ANNE. *Personality and Study Habits Correlates of Achievement Among Lower Socio-Economic Class Boys.* Master's thesis, University of Alberta (Edmonton, Alta., Canada), 1968.

341. CLAPPER, INEZ WILLIAMS. *Personality: Relationship With Reading and Spelling Achievement of Intermediate-Grade*

California Test of Personality

Pupils. Master's thesis, Illinois State University (Normal, Ill.), 1968.

342. CRUMLEY, FRANCES S. *The Relationship of Personal-Social Adjustment and Intellectual Capacity to the Academic Achievement of Ninety-Three Junior High School Students.* Master's thesis, East Tennessee State University (Johnson City, Tenn.), 1968.

343. FEEZEL, BETTY FLOE. *A Study of the Interrelationship Between Personality With Special Reference to Self Concept and Achievement in Reading.* Master's thesis, Eastern Illinois University (Charleston, Ill.), 1968.

344. HEISEY, MARION J. *An Investigation of Self-Perceptions of Oral Communication Skills Among Fifth Grade School Children.* Doctor's thesis, Kent State University (Kent, Ohio), 1968. (*DA* 29:4326A)

345. LANDAU, DALE; ERICSON-MUSSIG, CARYL; AND WAITE, MELINDA. "Personality Variables Related to Subliminal Perception." *J Psychol & Behav Sci* 3:3–9 My '68. *

346. LEIGHTY, DORIS LEE. *Relationship of a Planned Program in Physical Education to Personality Development in the Kindergarten Child.* Doctor's thesis, George Peabody College for Teachers (Nashville, Tenn.), 1968. (*DAI* 30:1338A)

347. LOCKHART, HAZEL M. "A Comparison of Personality and Reading Scores of Fourth Grade Pupils: A Follow-Up." *Ill Sch Res* 5:8–10 N '68. *

348. MAJESKY, STANLEY W. *A Follow-Up Study of the Permanence of Institutional Changes in Certain Personality Characteristics in Female Delinquents From the Youth Development Center at Waynesburg, Pennsylvania.* Master's thesis, California State College (California, Pa.), 1968.

349. PETTEWAY, SAMUEL BRUCE. *A Comparison of College Resident and Commuter Students on Selected Psycho-Sociological Characteristics.* Doctor's thesis, North Carolina State University (Raleigh, N.C.), 1968. (*DA* 29:1413A)

350. PETTY, COLLEEN ANN. *An Investigation of Handwriting Traits.* Master's thesis, Eastern Illinois University (Charleston, Ill.), 1968.

351. PONDER, VIRGINIA BREAZEALE. *An Investigation of the Effects of Bibliotherapy and Teachers' Self-Others Acceptance on Pupils' Self-Acceptance and Reading Achievement Scores.* Doctor's thesis, University of Southern Mississippi (Hattiesburg, Miss.), 1968. (*DA* 29:2900A)

352. RADER, BLAINE BURDETTE. *Identification of Selected Personality Characteristics Which Make for Effectiveness in Pastoral Care.* Doctor's thesis, Drew University (Madison, N.J.), 1968. (*DA* 29:1849B)

353. REINERT, HENRY ROBERT. *Decision Making in the Educationally Handicapped and Normal Child: A Comparative Study.* Doctor's thesis, Colorado State College (Greeley, Colo.), 1968. (*DA* 29:1137A)

354. STAPLES, MARK WHITAKER. *The Effect of Authoritarian Teachers on the Personality Growth of Fifth-Grade Students.* Master's thesis, Brigham Young University (Provo, Utah), 1968.

355. SUTARIA, SAROJ DAHYABHAI. *A Study to Determine the Relationship Between Teachers' Preparation and Achievement of Educable Mentally Retarded Children Placed in Special Classes.* Doctor's thesis, Syracuse University (Syracuse, N.Y.), 1968. (*DA* 29:4206A)

356. WILLOUGHBY, JAMES RONALD. *The Influence of Personality Factors and Type of Physics Course on High School Physics Students' Growth of Understanding of Science.* Doctor's thesis, University of Virginia (Charlottesville, Va.), 1968. (*DAI* 30:631A)

357. WILSON, ANAISE VICTORIANNE. *A Study of the Relationship of Selected Factors to the Academic Achievement of College Freshmen in the School of Education of Tuskegee Institute.* Doctor's thesis, New York University (New York, N.Y.), 1968. (*DAI* 30:144A)

358. WINTERROSE, HAZEL GENEVA. *A Comparison of High Achieving and Low Achieving Fourth Grade Culturally Disadvantaged Pupils.* Doctor's thesis, Utah State University (Logan, Utah), 1968. (*DA* 29:1382A)

359. APPLEBERRY, MARY HILTON. *A Study of the Effect of Bibliotherapy on Third-Grade Children Using a Master List of Titles From Children's Literature.* Doctor's thesis, University of Houston (Houston, Tex.), 1969. (*DAI* 30:2718A)

360. BERRY, GORDON LA VERN. *A Comparative Study of Selected Personality Characteristics of Educationally Disadvantaged Adolescents Enrolled in a Continuation School and Adolescents Enrolled in a Public High School.* Doctor's thesis, Marquette University (Milwaukee, Wis.), 1969. (*DAI* 31:140A)

361. BERRYMAN, BERLE WAYNE. *The Effects of Group Counseling Upon Visual Perception and Its Relationship to Other Forms of Perception.* Doctor's thesis, North Texas State University (Denton, Tex.), 1969. (*DAI* 30:2793A)

362. BOZARTH, DOROTHY CRAIG. *The Relationship of Intelligence Test Scatter and Self-Concept.* Master's thesis, Millersville State College (Millersville, Pa.), 1969.

363. BROWN, STEPHEN WILLIAM. *A Comparative Study of Maternal Employment and Non-Employment to Delinquency, Intelligence, Achievement, Personality Development, and Social Maladjustment Among Eighth and Ninth Grade Males in Five Junior High Schools of Dallas County, Texas.* Doctor's thesis, Mississippi State University (State College, Miss.), 1969. (*DAI* 30:4708A)

364. BUNNING, MADELINE JEANETTE. *The Relationship Between Children's Personal-Social Adjustment and Their Perception of Adults' Nonverbal Behavior: An Exploratory Study.* Doctor's thesis, University of the Pacific (Stockton, Calif.), 1969. (*DAI* 30:2323A)

365. CONDUFF, ELIZABETH. *Personality Characteristics and Adjustment of Adolescents With Regard to Vocational Maturity.* Master's thesis, University of Tennessee (Knoxville, Tenn.), 1969.

366. FEKRAT, MOHAMMAD AMIN. *A Correlational Study Between Self-Concept and Academic Achievement of College Freshmen and Seniors.* Doctor's thesis, Indiana University (Bloomington, Ind.), 1969. (*DAI* 30:5283A)

367. GREEN, MARGIE LOUISE. *Effects of Competitive Basketball Experiences of Girls in the Gainesville State Training School Upon Selected Personal and Social Behavior Patterns.* Master's thesis, North Texas State University (Denton, Tex.), 1969.

368. HAGEN, DEAN SMITH. *Group Counseling, Individual Counseling, and Teacher Consultation as Means of Modifying Self-Reports on Personality Inventory Items by Elementary School Children.* Doctor's thesis, Florida State University (Tallahassee, Fla.), 1969. (*DAI* 30:5236A)

369. HAMMOND, LONNIE L. *A Non-Linear Relationship Study of Personality and Intelligence.* Master's thesis, East Tennessee State University (Johnson City, Tenn.), 1969.

370. HAVLIN, NORMA JEAN. *The Relationship Between Teacher Expectancy and the Behavior of First and Second Grade Students Identified as Behavior Problems.* Doctor's thesis, Southern Illinois University (Carbondale, Ill.), 1969. (*DAI* 30:4276A)

371. HELBERG, DONALD HENRY. *The Effects of Educational-Vocational Group Guidance and Client-Centered Group Counseling on Personality Factors, Student Problems, and Vocational Direction of Junior College Students in a Developmental Program.* Doctors thesis, Colorado State College (Greeley, Colo.), 1969. (*DAI* 30:4222A)

372. HESS, TYLER. *A Comparison of Group Counseling With Individual Counseling in the Modification of Self-Adjustment and Social Adjustment of Fifteen Year Old Males Identified as Potential Dropouts.* Doctor's thesis, University of Virginia (Charlottesville, Va.), 1969. (*DAI* 31:998A)

373. KILLIAN, WILLIAM DAVID. *A Study of Persistence of Adult Students in the Fundamental Learning Laboratories of the North Carolina Community College System.* Doctor's thesis, North Carolina State University (Raleigh, N.C.), 1969. (*DAI* 30:5222A)

374. KOST, DENNIS R. *Relation of Individualized Instruction to Social Acceptance, Total Adjustment, Social Adjustment, and Personal Adjustment.* Doctor's thesis, University of North Dakota (Grand Forks, N.D.), 1969. (*DAI* 31:297A)

375. KUEHN, JUDITH PAULA. *A Study of Personality Factors and Academic Achievement in the Elementary School.* Master's thesis, Eastern Illinois University (Charleston, Ill.), 1969.

376. LANTZ, ALBERT WESLEY. *Relationship of Sensitivity Training to Change in Attitudes Held by Student Teachers.* Doctor's thesis, United States International University (San Diego, Calif.), 1969. (*DAI* 30:2402A)

377. MARASCIULLO, DAVID LOUIS. *The Self-Perception of Deviate Boys in Special Public School Classes and Its Relationship to Their Achievement and Adjustment.* Doctor's thesis, St. John's University (Jamaica, N.Y.), 1969. (*DAI* 30:1901B)

378. MELNICK, BARRY, AND HURLEY, JOHN R. "Distinctive Personality Attributes of Child-Abusing Mothers." *J Consult & Clin Psychol* 33(6):746–9 D '69. * (*PA* 44:3841)

379. PEDERSEN, DARHL M., AND STANFORD, GEORGE H. "Personality Correlates of Children's Self-Esteem and Parental Identification." *Psychol Rep* 25(1):41–2 Ag '69. * (*PA* 44:3418)

380. RUSK, MARIAN TERRY. *A Study of Delinquency Among Urban Mexican American Youth.* Doctor's thesis, University of Southern California (Los Angeles, Calif.), 1969. (*DAI* 30:1877A)

381. SAX, ARNOLD BERTON. *A Comparative Study of Personality Characteristics Between Seventh-Grade Students Classified as Educationally Deprived and Non-Educationally Deprived.* Doctor's thesis, University of Houston (Houston, Tex.), 1969. (*DAI* 30:4838A)

382. SCHREIBER, ELLIOTT H. "Personality Characteristics and Dental Disorders in Adolescents." *Psychol Rep* 24(2):626 Ap '69. * (*PA* 43:16056)

383. STANFORD, GEORGE H., AND PEDERSEN, DARHL M. "Correlation Between Self-Esteem, Level of Identification With Parents, and Adjustment of Parents and Children." *Interam J Psychol* (Mexico) 3(4):273–8 D '69. * (*PA* 44:16393)

384. STRANGES, RICHARD JAMES. *The Relationship Between Various Characteristics of Counselees and Their Selected Counselors.* Doctor's thesis, Ohio State University (Columbus, Ohio), 1969. (*DAI* 30:3289A)

385. SWANSON, BERNICE MARIAN. *Parent-Child Relations: A Child's Acceptance by Others, of Others, and of Self.* Doctor's thesis, University of Oklahoma (Norman, Okla.), 1969. (*DAI* 30:1890B)

386. VAN KIRK, HENRY ALLEN. *The Effect of Short Term*

Freeing Approach Counseling on Foster Children as Measured Through a Test of Self-Concept and an Index of Counseling Progress Stages. Doctor's thesis, Colorado State College (Greeley, Colo.), 1969. (*DAI* 30:1831A)

387. WILLIAMS, WARREN STEPHEN. *Measuring the Meaning of Personality Test Items to Fifth Grade Children From Different Socioeconomic Groups.* Doctor's thesis, University of Rochester (Rochester, N.Y.), 1969. (*DAI* 30:3338A)

388. ZANI, LEONARD P. *Intensive vs. Protracted Counselor Directed Group Counseling With Underachieving Secondary School Students.* Doctor's thesis, State University of New York (Buffalo, N.Y.), 1969. (*DAI* 30:1834A)

389. BARE, CAROLE E. "The Relationship Between Man-Machine Attitudes and Performance." *Programmed Learning* 7(1):1–6 Ja '70. *

390. BARNES, KEITH DAVID. *The School Counselor Preferences of Senior High School Students.* Doctor's thesis, Ohio State University (Columbus, Ohio), 1970. (*DAI* 31:1571A)

391. CARTER, HELEN LOUISE. *An Investigation of Two Methods of Short-Term Group Counseling With White Preadolescents Rated Low on Social Status by Their Peers.* Doctor's thesis, University of North Carolina (Chapel Hill, N.C.), 1970. (*DAI* 31:5757A)

392. CREEK, ROY JOHN. *Middle School Rationale: The Sixth Grade Component.* Doctor's thesis, University of Pittsburgh (Pittsburgh, Pa.), 1970. (*DAI* 32:663A)

393. DEFRAIN, DAVID MURRAY. *The Effects of Self-Concept and Selected Personal and Educational Variables Upon Attrition in a Non-Credit College Reading Improvement Program.* Doctor's thesis, Oklahoma State University (Stillwater, Okla.), 1970. (*DAI* 31:5195A)

394. DELPH, DONNA JEAN. *The Relationship of Personal and Social Adjustment and Academically Related Interests to the School Success of Sixth-Grade Children From Low-Income Homes.* Doctor's thesis, Ball State University (Muncie, Ind.), 1970. (*DAI* 31:5028A)

395. DEMING, ROMINE R. *A Study of the Association Between the Attraction to the Probation Officer-Client Relationship and Various Psycho-Social Attitudes of Juvenile Probationers.* Doctor's thesis, Iowa State University (Iowa City, Iowa), 1970. (*DAI* 31:1912A)

396. EDELMAN, FLORENCE. *The Selected Factors That May Distinguish the Successful Speaker From the Unsuccessful Speaker Following Laryngectomy.* Doctor's thesis, New York University (New York, N.Y.), 1970. (*DAI* 31:6972B)

397. EVANS, JAMES JOSEPH. *An Analysis of Academic Achievement and Educational Attitudes of Students in a Senior High School.* Doctor's thesis, Wayne State University (Detroit, Mich.), 1970. (*DAI* 31:3264A)

398. HARMESON, VERNON F. *A Comparative Study of Social Behavior of Children: Kindergarten Through Grade Three as Identified by Teacher Rankings, the California Test of Personality and the Hewlett Teacher Rating Scale.* Doctor's thesis, University of North Dakota (Grand Forks, N.D.), 1970. (*DAI* 31:6403A)

399. HOOPES, JANET L.; SHERMAN, EDMUND A.; LAWDER, ELIZABETH; ANDREWS, ROBERTA G.; AND LOWER, KATHERINE D. *A Follow-Up Study of Adoptions (Vol. II): Post-Placement Functioning of Adopted Children.* New York: Child Welfare League of America, Inc., 1970. Pp. v, 126. *

400. HOULIHAN, MARGARET BRIDGET. *A Comparison of Personality and Attitudes About Teachers, Classroom Peers, and Subject Matter as Found Between Eighth Grade Gifted High and Low Achievers.* Doctor's thesis, St. Louis University (St. Louis, Mo.), 1970. (*DAI* 31:3957A)

401. KALMAN, BARBARA ANNE. *Differences in the Emotional Adjustment and Self Concepts Among Institutionalized Delinquent Girls Relative to the Kinship System and Homosexuality.* Doctor's thesis, Ball State University (Muncie, Ind.), 1970. (*DAI* 31:6259B)

402. KEHAS, CHRIS D. "Grouping for Instruction and Self-Definition." *Meas & Eval Guid* 2(4):205–13 W '70. *

403. KRAUSE, MARILYN A. *A Comparison of Personality Factors of Women Intercollegiate Team and Individual Sports Participants.* Master's thesis, Lamar State College of Technology (Beaumont, Tex.), 1970.

404. MOORE, CHARLES H., AND ASCOUGH, JAMES C. "Self-Acceptance and Adjustment Revisited: A Replication." *Psychol Rep* 26(3):855–8 Je '70. * (*PA* 45:691)

405. MYERS, NORMAN KENT. *The Physical, Intellectual, Emotional and Social Maturity Levels of Eighth, Ninth and Tenth Grade Students With Implications for School Grade Organization.* Doctor's thesis, University of Missouri (Columbia, Mo.), 1970. (*DAI* 31:3832A)

406. PIPPIN, LOUIS DANNY. *The Relationships Between Personality Adjustment and Perceived Behavior of Teenage Boys at Boys Ranch, Texas.* Doctor's thesis, North Texas State University (Denton, Tex.), 1970. (*DAI* 31:3349A)

407. ROSENSHEIN, JOEL S. *A Study of the Emotional and Social Differences Between Homebound and School Attending Physically Handicapped Children.* Doctor's thesis, New York University (New York, N.Y.), 1970. (*DAI* 31:7610B)

408. SELLS, MARGALEE ANN. *A Correlational Study of a Semantic Differential Measure of Self-Concept and the California Test of Personality.* Doctor's thesis, Kansas State Teachers College (Emporia, Kan.), 1970.

409. STEWART, JAMES HENRY, JR. *A Study of Early Changes in Selected Personality Components of Students in an Institutional Home and School.* Doctor's thesis, North Texas State University (Denton, Tex.), 1970. (*DAI* 31:3241A)

410. TAYLOR, RALPH LEE. *A Comparison of the Self-Concept of Negro Students at the University of Alabama and Negro Students at Stillman College.* Doctor's thesis, University of Alabama (University, Ala.), 1970. (*DAI* 31:6355A)

411. TOWNSEL, CHARLES WILBERT. *Self-Concept and Mental Health as a Function of Academic Achievement.* Doctor's thesis, Michigan State University (East Lansing, Mich.), 1970. (*DAI* 32:1246A)

412. WISSER, ROBERT EDWARD. *A Comparison of the Effects of Three Types of Counseling Upon the Adjustment of Fifth Grade Boys.* Doctor's thesis, Lehigh University (Bethlehem, Pa.), 1970. (*DAI* 31:3284A)

413. YOUNG, MARY L. "Personal-Social Adjustment, Physical Fitness, Attitude Toward Physical Education of High School Girls by Socioeconomic Level." *Res Q* 41(4):593–9 D '70. * (*PA* 46:5455)

414. BAUER, NORMAN J. "Differences in Personality Traits Among Most Preferred and Least Preferred Students in Grades 10, 11, and 12." *J Ed Res* 65(2):65–70 O '71. * (*PA* 48:1592)

415. BERRY, GORDON L. "A Descriptive View of Personal and Social Adjustment Characteristic of Two Groups of Inner-City Adolescents." *Col Stud J* 5(3):96–103 N–D '71. *

416. BUCK, JOHN WILLIAM. *Relationship of Health Behavior to the Adjustment of Selected High School Seniors.* Doctor's thesis, University of Utah (Salt Lake City, Utah), 1971. (*DAI* 32:3073A)

417. BUSH, HAROLD. *Adolescents' Personality Correlates of Self- and Group-Ratings of Empathy.* Doctor's thesis, Illinois Institute of Technology (Chicago, Ill.), 1971. (*DAI* 33:1282B)

418. DOUGHTY, EARL. "Test Rankings and Selection Procedures for Identifying Gifted Intermediate Elementary Students." *Ill Sch Res* 8(1):29–32 f '71. *

419. EGELAND, BYRON, AND HALPERIN, SILAS. "A Factor Analysis of the Elementary Level of the California Test of Personality." *J Clin Psychol* 27(1):105–8 Ja '71. * (*PA* 46:1500)

420. FINNIGAN, DANIEL WILLIAM. *Relationship of Openmindedness/Closemindedness to Certain Personality Characteristics Involving Self-Regard.* Doctor's thesis, United States International University (San Diego, Calif.), 1971. (*DAI* 32:2376B)

421. GARTMAN, JAMES CARROLL. *An Investigation of Relationships Between Selected Personality Traits and Factors Associated With Change of Major in State Supported Colleges in Arkansas.* Doctor's thesis, Northeast Louisiana University (Monroe, La.), 1971. (*DAI* 32:4346A)

422. GOLDSTEIN, ALAN MAURICE. *Denial as a Function of Internal-External Control in Chronic Renal Failure.* Doctor's thesis, Fordham University (New York, N.Y.), 1971. (*DAI* 32:3001B)

423. GWALTNEY, WAYNE KEITH. *Reading in Upward Bound: An Evaluation of a Reading Improvement Course and an Analysis of Some Correlates of Reading Achievement.* Doctor's thesis, University of Georgia (Athens, Ga.), 1971. (*DAI* 32:3557A)

424. HARTH, ROBERT, AND GLAVIN, JOHN P. "Validity of Teacher Rating as a Subtest for Screening Emotionally Disturbed Children." *Excep Children* 37(8):605–6 Ap '71. * (*PA* 47:1635)

425. HEATH, DUDLEY DUTTON. *The Relationship Between School Size and Personal and Social Adjustment of High School Seniors.* Doctor's thesis, University of Pennsylvania (Philadelphia, Pa.), 1971. (*DAI* 32:1916A)

426. KING, HOLLIS HEATON. *An Investigation of Relationships Between Hypnotic Susceptibility, Manifest Dream Content and Personality Characteristics.* Doctor's thesis, Louisiana State University (Baton Rouge, La.), 1971. (*DAI* 33:442B)

427. LIEDTKE, WERNER. "Mathematics Learning and Pupil Characteristics." *Alberta J Ed Res* (Canada) 17(3):143–53 S '71. * (*PA* 48:1864)

428. MIHALOPOULOS, NICHOLAS GEORGE. *A Comparative Study of Normal Nuclear Families and Problem Nuclear Families.* Doctor's thesis, University of Utah (Salt Lake City, Utah), 1971. (*DAI* 32:3097A)

429. MORGAN, ROBERT. *Changes in Social and Personal Adjustment as Related to Academic and Social Functioning at the Upper Elementary School Level.* Doctor's thesis, Kent State University (Kent, Ohio), 1971. (*DAI* 32:3794A)

430. PURCELL, ELIZABETH WELLS. *The Relationship of Personality to Achievement in Reading Comprehension.* Doctor's thesis, St. Louis University (St. Louis, Mo.), 1971. (*DAI* 33:906A)

431. SALLADE, JACQUELINE B. ROZET. *A Comparison of the Psychological Adjustment of Obese vs. Nonobese Children.* Doctor's thesis, Pennsylvania State University (University Park, Pa.), 1971. (*DAI* 33:428B)

432. SEITHER, FRANCES GARDNER. *An Investigation of the Predictive Validity of Selected Admission Screening Measures Relative to Success in Practical Nursing.* Doctor's thesis, University of Maryland (College Park, Md.), 1971. (*DAI* 32:5890B)

433. SWANSON, BERNICE M., AND PARKER, HARRY J. "Parent-Child Relations: A Child's Acceptance by Others, of Others, and

California Test of Personality

of Self." *Child Psychiatry & Hum Develop* 1(4):243–54 su '71. * (*PA* 49:4872)

434. WILLIAMS, MARY JANET. *The Effect of Group Counseling Upon Selected Personality and Behavioral Variables in Delinquent Adolescents.* Doctor's thesis, North Texas State University (Denton, Tex.), 1971. (*DAI* 32:3710A)

435. WILLIAMS, WARREN S. "A Semantic Differential Study of the Meaning of Personality Test Items to Children From Different Socioeconomic Groups." *J Psychol* 79(2):179–88 N '71. * (*PA* 47:6523)

CUMULATIVE NAME INDEX

Pusey, H. C.: 4
Rader, B. B.: 352
Ramm, K. M.: 241
Raphael, S.: 313
Rapp, D.: 274
Rasor, F.: 34
Ratliff, J. A.: 122
Reinbold, E. J.: 129
Reinert, H. R.: 353
Reynolds, L. G.: 259
Ricciuti, E. A.: 57
Richards, B. F.: 279
Ringness, T. A.: 207
Robey, D. L.: 184
Robinson, C. A.: 58
Roffee, D. T.: 141
Ros, P. de M. M.: 93
Rosenshein, J. S.: 407
Rosenwald, A.: 5
Ross, D. R.: 203
Roth, R. M.: 155, 166
Ruch, F.: 14
Rusk, M. T.: 380
Ruter, M. D.: 232
Ryan, M. A.: 306
Sallade, J. B. R.: 431
Salyers, M. H.: 71
Santos, J. F.: 176
Sax, A. B.: 381
Scandrette, O. C.: 94
Schlueter, M. P.: 185
Schmotz, R. R.: 191
Schreiber, E. H.: 231, 234, 382
Schurr, E.: 227
Seay, L. C.: 275
Seeman, M.: 37
Seidenfeld, M. A.: 24, 44
Seither, F. G.: 432
Seitz, T. L.: 194
Sells, M. A.: 408
Semler, I. J.: 123, 149, 223
Serot, N. M.: 156
Serpento, S. T.: 118
Sewell, W. H.: 84, 121, 142, 248
Shaffer, L. F.: rev, 3:26
Shank, K. H.: 242
Shechtman, A. M.: 280
Sherman, E. A.: 399
Shreffler, J.: 131
Shuttlesworth, R. H.: 106
Simmons, M.: 9
Sims, V. M.: rev, 5:38
Singer, A.: 78
Skidmore, R. A.: 79
Smallenburg, H. W.: 7
Smith, H.: 274
Smith, J. T.: 232
Smith, L. M.: 107, 117
Smith, M.: 274
Smith, P. M.: 130, 157
Snellgrove, J. L.: 150
Snyder, B. J.: 45
Snyder, R.: 208
Snyder, R. T.: 195
Snyder, W. U.: 45
Sopchak, A. L.: 260
Spaights, E.: 334
Spencer, D.: rev, 3:26
Spilka, B.: 113, 254
Stanford, G. H.: 379, 383
Staples, M. W.: 354
Stark, T. F.: 324
Stennett, R. G.: 217
Stephens, H. B.: 196
Stern, N. W.: 294
Stewart, J. H.: 409

Stott, L. H.: 14a, 14b
Stranges, R. J.: 384
Straus, M. A.: 170, 172
Strauss, R.: 208
Struening, E. L.: 113
Sumner, J. W.: 307
Sutaria, S. D.: 355
Swanson, B. M.: 385, 433
Symonds, P. M.: rev, 2:1213
Taylor, C.: 85
Taylor, R. L.: 410
Teevan, R. C.: 156
Teigland, J. J.: 218
Telford, N. J.: 325
Terrell, G.: 131
Thomas, E. N.: 335
Thomas, S.: 160
Thompson, B. F.: 59
Thompson, C. E.: 10
Thompson, G. G.: 74
Thomsen, V. B.: 209
Thorpe, L. P.: 3
Tiegs, E. W.: 3, 7a
Tieman, N.: 281
Tindall, R. H.: 108
Tobias, M.: 282, 295
Townsel, C. W.: 411
Traweek, M. W.: 197
Turner, D.: 266
Tuttle, L. L.: 296
Twining, G. A.: 219
Tyler, L. E.: 152
Van De Riet, H.: 274
Van De Riet, V.: 274
Van Fleet, B.: 81
Van Kirk, H. A.: 386
Vegely, A. B.: 238
Vernon, P. E.: rev, 2:1213
Volberding, E.: 60
Waite, M.: 345
Walker, E. M.: 25
Wallace, D. G.: 336
Watt, G. D.: 243
Weiland, E. J.: 80
White, D. K.: 314
Wiersma, W.: 310
Williams, D. E.: 220
Williams, M. F.: 261
Williams, M. J.: 434
Williams, W. S.: 387, 435
Williamson, D. B.: 242
Willoughby, J. R.: 356
Wills, H. S.: 210
Wilson, A. V.: 357
Wilson, J. A. R.: 132, 143
Wilson, J. J.: 211
Wilson, P. B.: 175
Winkler, R. C.: 218
Winterrose, H. G.: 358
Winters, A. W.: 315
Wisser, R. E.: 412
Wolcott, C. M.: 288
Wolf, W.: 239
Wolff, C. E.: 159, 309
Wood, K. S.: 240
Woodward, R. H.: 72
Wrighter, J.: 40
Wrightstone, J. W.: 77
Xydis, G. A.: 273
Yee, G. F.: 308
Young, L. L.: 29
Young, M. L.: 413
Zakolski, F. C.: 61
Zani, L. P.: 388
Zelen, S. L.: 100
Zimmerman, I. L.: 212

REFERENCES THROUGH 1971

1–5. See 5:39.
6. See P:32.
7. JAQUES, ODILIA MARIE. "Predicting Juvenile Delinquency Proneness by Group Tests." *Personnel & Guid J* 36:489–92 Mr '58. * (*PA* 33:6598)
8. ROSENTHAL, ROBERT. "Perception of Success or Failure in Pictures of Others." *J Clin Psychol* 15:216–7 Ap '59. * (*PA* 35:5258)
9. SELDEN, EDWARD HARVEY. *A Study of Self-Structure and Level of Aspiration in Delinquent and Non-Delinquent Boys.* Doctor's thesis, University of Minnesota (Minneapolis, Minn.), 1960. (*DA* 21:2394)
10. RED, S. B.; MCCARY, J. L.; AND JOHNSON, BETTE. "A Study of the Relationship Between Aspirational Levels and Academic Achievement." *J Ed Res* 55:159–63 D–Ja '62. * (*PA* 37:2014)
11. EMERICK, LONNIE L. *An Evaluation of Three Psychological Variables in Tonic and Clonic Stutterers and in Non-stutterers.* Doctor's thesis, Michigan State University (East Lansing, Mich.), 1966. (*DA* 28:317A)
12. MAW, WALLACE H., AND MAW, ETHEL W. *Personal and Social Variables Differentiating Children With High and Low Curiosity.* An unpublished report to the U.S. Office of Education, Cooperative Research Project No. 1511, University of Delaware, 1966. Pp. xii, 181. * (ERIC ED 0033 274)
13. STAFFORD, BEVERLY LOUISE. *The Effects of Age and Sex on the Level of Aspiration in Selected Motor Tasks.* Doctor's thesis, Louisiana State University (Baton Rouge, La.), 1969. (*DAI* 30:2838A)
14. SISKIND, GEORGE. "Note on Level of Aspiration as a Selective Device for Psychiatric Aides." *Psychol Rep* 27(3):874 D '70. * (*PA* 45:11069)

CUMULATIVE NAME INDEX

Cassel, R. N.: 1–4
Dahlstrom, W. G.: rev, 5:39
Emerick, L. L.: 11
Gough, H. G.: rev, 5:39
Holt, R. R.: exc, 5:39
Jaques, O. M.: 7
Johnson, B.: 10
McCary, J. L.: 10
Maw, E. W.: 12
Maw, W. H.: 12

Niyekawa, A. M.: 5
Red, S. B.: 10
Rosenthal, R.: 8
Saugstad, R. G.: 1
Selden, E. H.: 9
Shaffer, L. F.: exc, 5:39
Siskind, G.: 6, 14
Stafford, B. L.: 13
Sutcliffe, J. P.: rev, 5:39
Van Vorst, R.: 3–4

[1125]

Chapin Social Insight Test. Ages 13 and over; 1967–68; CSIT; F. Stuart Chapin (test) and Harrison G. Gough (manual); Consulting Psychologists Press, Inc. *

For additional information and reviews by Richard I. Lanyon and David B. Orr, see 7:51; see also P:34 (3 references).

REFERENCES THROUGH 1971

1–3. See P:34.

CUMULATIVE NAME INDEX

Chapin, F. S.: 1
Gough, H. G.: 2
Lanyon, R. I.: rev, 7:51

McDermid, C. D.: 3
Orr, D. B.: rev, 7:51

[1126]

The Child Behavior Rating Scale. Grades kgn–3; 1960–62; CBRS; ratings by teachers or parents; 6 adjustment scores: self, home, social, school, physical, total; Russell N. Cassel; Western Psychological Services. *

For additional information and a review by James A. Dunn, see 7:52; see also P:35 (1 reference).

REFERENCES THROUGH 1971

1. See P:35.

CUMULATIVE NAME INDEX

Cassel, R. N.: 1   Dunn, J. A.: rev, 7:52

[1127]

*****Children's Embedded Figures Test.** Ages 5–12; 1963–71; CEFT; revision of the Goodenough-Eagle modification of the *Embedded Figures Test;* test by Stephen A. Karp and Norma Konstadt; combined manual (for this and two other embedded figures tests) by Herman A. Witkin, Philip K. Oltman, Eve-

[1124]

The Cassel Group Level of Aspiration Test. Grades 5–16 and adults; 1952–57; CGLAT; 7 scores: clinical difference, Hausmann, aspiration difference, first goal, psychological response to failure, physiological response to failure, level of aspiration quotient; Russell N. Cassel; Western Psychological Services. *

For additional information, see P:32 (1 reference); for reviews by W. Grant Dahlstrom, Harrison G. Gough, and J. P. Sutcliffe and excerpted reviews by Robert R. Holt and Laurance F. Shaffer, see 5:39 (5 references).

California Test of Personality

lyn Raskin, and Stephen A. Karp; Consulting Psychologists Press, Inc. *

For additional information and a review by Sheldon A. Weintraub, see 7:53 (15 references) ; see also P:36 (7 references) and 6:74b (2 references).

REFERENCES THROUGH 1971

1–2. See 6:74b.
3–9. See P:36.
10–24. See 7:53.
25. OKONJI, MICHAEL O. "The Differential Effects of Rural and Urban Upbringing on the Development of Cognitive Styles." *Int J Psychol* (France) 4(4):293–305 '69. * (*PA* 45:6137)
26. BLANTON, WILLIAM ELGIT. *The Interactive Effects of Perceptual Centration and Decentration on Reading Readiness and Reading Achievement at the First Grade Level.* Doctor's thesis, University of Georgia (Athens, Ga.), 1970. (*DAI* 31:5837A)
27. CARING, LILLIAN COTT. *The Relation of Cognitive Style, Sex and Intelligence to Moral Judgement in Children.* Doctor's thesis, New York University (New York, N.Y.), 1970. (*DAI* 31:7568B)
28. ESKA, BRUNHILDE ELSA. *"Cognitive Style" in Young School Age Children.* Doctor's thesis, Purdue University (Lafayette, Ind.), 1970. (*DAI* 31:6238B)
29. MEBANE, DONATA, AND JOHNSON, DALE L. "A Comparison of the Performance of Mexican Boys and Girls on Witkin's Cognitive Tasks." *Interam J Psychol* (Mexico) 4(3–4):227–39 '70. * (*PA* 47:2757)
30. ASSAWAMATIYANONT, SUREE. *The Relationship Between Psychological Differentiation and Egocentrism.* Doctor's thesis, Ohio State University (Columbus, Ohio), 1971. (*DAI* 32: 1816B)
31. BIGELOW, GORDON S. "Field Dependence-Field Independence in 5- to 10-Year-Old Children." *J Ed Res* 64(9):397–400 My–Je '71. * (*PA* 47:6507)
32. CAMPBELL, SUSAN B.; DOUGLAS, VIRGINIA I.; AND MORGENSTERN, GERT. "Cognitive Styles in Hyperactive Children and the Effect of Methylphenidate." *J Child Psychol & Psychiatry* (England) 12(1):55–67 Je '71. * (*PA* 47:5004)
33. DREYER, ALBERT S.; DREYER, CECILY A.; AND NEBELKOPF, EDWIN B. "Portable Rod-and-Frame Test as a Measure of Cognitive Style in Kindergarten Children." *Percept & Motor Skills* 33 (3):775–81 D '71. * (*PA* 48:710)
34. FERRELL, JACK GORDON, JR. *The Differential Performance of Lower Class, Preschool, Negro Children as a Function of the Sex of E, Sex of S, Reinforcement Condition, and Level of Field Dependence.* Doctor's thesis, University of Southern Mississippi (Hattiesburg, Miss.), 1971. (*DAI* 32:3028B)
35. KEOGH, BARBARA K., AND RYAN, STEPHAN R. "Use of Three Measures of Field Organization With Young Children." *Percept & Motor Skills* 33(2):466 O '71. * (*PA* 47:6511)
36. LEWIS, NEIL PHILLIP. *Cognitive Style, Cognitive Complexity, and Behavior Prediction in Process and Reactive Schizophrenia.* Doctor's thesis, Fordham University (New York, N.Y.), 1971. (*DAI* 32:1217B)
37. MARKUS, ELLIOT J. "Perceptual Field Dependence Among Aged Persons." *Percept & Motor Skills* 33(1):175–8 Ag '71. * (*PA* 47:2718)
38. RANDOLPH, LAWRENCE CLIFFORD. *A Study of the Effects of Praise, Criticism and Failure on the Problem Solving Performance of Field-Dependent and Field-Independent Individuals.* Doctor's thesis, New York University (New York, N.Y.), 1971. (*DAI* 32:3014B)

CUMULATIVE NAME INDEX

Assawamatiyanont, S.: 30
Bigelow, G. S.: 6, 31
Blanton, W. E.: 26
Blenkner, M.: 12
Bloom, M.: 12
Boersma, F. J.: 7
Bruininks, R. H.: 13
Campbell, D. R.: 7
Campbell, S. B.: 32
Caring, L. C.: 27
Carter, H. L.: 14
Clack, G. S.: 19
Corah, N. L.: 3
Degerman, R.: 5
Douglas, V. I.: 32
Dowley, E. M.: 5
Dreyer, A. S.: 15, 24, 33
Dreyer, C. A.: 15, 33
Dye, G. M.: 8
Dyer, F. N.: 7
Eagle, C. J.: 2
Elkind, S. N.: 10
Eska, B. E.: 28
Ferrell, J. G.: 34
Fiebert, M.: 9
Fiebert, M. S.: 4

Goodenough, D. R.: 1–2
Grossman, M.: 20
Hagen, J. W.: 5
Herron, W. G.: 17
Irving, D. D.: 21
Johnson, D. L.: 29
Karp, S. A.: 1
Keogh, B. K.: 35
Lewis, N. P.: 36
Lovano, J. J.: 22
Maccoby, E. E.: 5
Markus, E.: 12
Markus, E. J.: 37
Mebane, D.: 29
Miller, J. O.: 23
Morgenstern, G.: 32
Mumbauer, C. C.: 23
Nash, M. S.: 16
Nebelkopf, E.: 15, 33
Nebelkopf, E. B.: 24
Okonji, M. O.: 25
Randolph, L. C.: 38
Ryan, S. R.: 35
Scallon, R. J.: 11, 17
Watson, B. L.: 18
Weintraub, S. A.: *rev,* 7:53

[1128]
The Children's Hypnotic Susceptibility Scale. Ages 5–12, 13–16; 1963, c1962; CHSS; downward extension of *Stanford Hypnotic Susceptibility Scale,* on which its content is based; Perry London; Consulting Psychologists Press, Inc. *

For additional information, see P:37 (4 references) ; for reviews by C. Scott Moss and John G. Watkins and an excerpted review by André Weitzenhoffer, see 6:75 (2 references).

REFERENCES THROUGH 1971

1–2. See 6:75.
3–6. See P:37.
7. LONDON, PERRY, AND MADSEN, CHARLES H., JR. "Effect of Role Playing on Hypnotic Susceptibility in Children." *J Pers & Social Psychol* 10:66–8 S '68. * (*PA* 43:225)
8. LONDON, PERRY, AND COOPER, LESLIE M. "Norms of Hypnotic Susceptibility in Children." *Develop Psychol* 1(2): 113–24 Mr '69. * (*PA* 43:8134)
9. LONDON, PERRY, AND MADSEN, CHARLES H., JR. "Role Playing and Hypnotic Susceptibility in Children: 2, An Extension and Partial Replication." *Int J Clin & Exp Hyp* 17(1): 37–49 Ja '69. * (*PA* 43:9560)
10. COOPER, LESLIE M., AND LONDON, PERRY. "The Development of Hypnotic Susceptibility: A Longitudinal (Convergence) Study." *Child Develop* 42(2):487–503 Je '71. * (*PA* 47:595)

CUMULATIVE NAME INDEX

Cooper, L. M.: 4, 6, 8, 10
Lauer, L. W.: 2
London, P.: 1, 3–5, 7–10
Madsen, C. H.: 5, 7, 9

Moore, R. K.: 2, 6
Moss, C. S.: *rev,* 6:75
Watkins, J. G.: *rev,* 6:75
Weitzenhoffer, A.: *exc,* 6:75

[1129]
*Children's Personality Questionnaire.** Ages 8–12; 1959–72; CPQ; test booklet title is *What You Do and What You Think;* 14 scores: reserved vs. warmhearted (A), dull vs. bright (B), affected by feelings vs. emotionally stable (C), phlegmatic vs. excitable (D), obedient vs. dominant (E), sober vs. enthusiastic (F), expedient vs. conscientious (G), shy vs. venturesome (H), tough-minded vs. tender-minded (I), zestful vs. circumspect individualism (J), forthright vs. shrewd (N), self-assured vs. guilt-prone (O), undisciplined self-conflict vs. controlled (Q₃), relaxed vs. tense (Q₄) ; Rutherford B. Porter and Raymond B. Cattell ; Institute for Personality and Ability Testing. (South African adaptation: Standards 1–2 [ages 8–9], 3–5/6 [ages 10–13] ; 1973 ; adaptation by L. du Toit and E. M. Madge ; Human Sciences Research Council [South Africa].) *

For additional information, see P:38 (14 references) ; for reviews by Anne Anastasi, Wilbur L. Layton, and Robert D. Wirt, see 6:122 (2 references).

REFERENCES THROUGH 1971

1–2. See 6:122.
3–16. See P:38.
17. CATTELL, RAYMOND B., AND GRUEN, WALTER. "Primary Personality Factors in the Questionnaire Medium for Children Eleven to Fourteen Years Old." *Ed & Psychol Meas* 14:50–76 sp '54. * (*PA* 28:7212)
18. ORIOLE, RICHARD A. *A Comparison of Personality Factors Between Selected Highly Gifted and Moderately Gifted Elementary School Children.* Master's thesis, Kent State University (Kent, Ohio), 1963.
19. CATTELL, RAYMOND B., AND HOWARTH, EDGAR. "Verification of Objective Test Personality Factor Patterns in Middle Childhood." *J Genetic Psychol* 104:331–49 Je '64. *
20. HADDEN, HELEN JEAN. *Changing the Self Concepts of Physically Handicapped Children Through the Use of a Specific Curriculum Procedure.* Doctor's research study No. 1, Colorado State College (Greeley, Colo.), 1964. (*DA* 28:154A)
21. FLINT, FRIEDA SNYDOVER. *A Validation and Developmental Study of Some Interpretations of the Bender Gestalt Test.* Doctor's thesis, New York University (New York, N.Y.), 1965. (*DA* 27:608B)
22. LAWRENCE, JORDAN. *Some Social and Personal Variables Affecting Elementary School Guidance Practice.* Doctor's thesis, Catholic University of America (Washington, D.C.), 1965. (*DA* 26:2077)
23. BERGER, SUSAN ROBBINS. *The Effects of a Cross-Cultural Experience Upon the Personal and Social Adjustment of Selected*

American Elementary School Students. Doctor's thesis, Boston University (Boston, Mass.), 1966. (*DA* 27:3715A)

24. COOLEY, CLIFFORD EWING. *The Relationship Between Sociotele and Psychetele Status Discrepancy and Selected Personality Factors.* Doctor's thesis, North Texas State University (Denton, Tex.), 1966. (*DA* 27:251A)

25. JOHNSON, DAVID W. "Freedom School Effectiveness: Changes in Attitudes of Negro Children." *J Appl Behav Sci* 2:325–30 Jl–S '66. *

26. MAW, WALLACE H., AND MAW, ETHEL W. *Personal and Social Variables Differentiating Children With High and Low Curiosity.* An unpublished report to the U.S. Office of Education, Cooperative Research Project No. 1511, University of Delaware, 1966. Pp. xii, 181. * (ERIC ED 003 274)

27. LESSING, ELISE E., AND OBERLANDER, MARK. "Ordinal Position and Childhood Psychopathology as Evaluated From Four Perspectives." Abstract. *Proc 75th Ann Conv Am Psychol Assn* 2:179–80 '67. * (*PA* 41:13441)

28. NEWBERT, NANCY. *A Study of Certain Personality Correlates of the Middle Child in a Three-Child Family.* Doctor's thesis, Boston University (Boston, Mass.), 1967. (*DA* 29:4333A)

29. BERK, T. J. C. "An Analysis of Personality Traits in Two Groups Dyslectic Boys With a Multivariate Personality Test." *Proc Inter Congr Appl Psychol* 16:664–8 '68. *

30. BOND, NORMAN DAVID. *Correlates of Altruism in Elementary School Children.* Doctor's thesis, University of Texas (Austin, Tex.), 1968. (*DA* 29:3454A)

31. BRICKNER, CHARLOTTE ANN. *Experimental Analysis of Auditory Discrimination Skills in the Developmental Structure of Pre-School Children.* Doctor's thesis, University of Colorado (Boulder, Colo.), 1968. (*DA* 29:3454A)

32. HETRICK, SUZANNE H.; LILLY, ROY S.; AND MERRIFIELD, PHILIP R. "Figural Creativity, Intelligence, and Personality in Children." *Multiv Behav Res* 3:173–87 Ap '68. * (*PA* 42:15273)

33. HICKS, JOHN SIMPSON. *Introversion and Extraversion and Their Relationship to Academic Achievement Among Emotionally Disturbed Children.* Doctor's thesis, Columbia University (New York, N.Y.), 1968. (*DA* 29:3462A)

34. KIRKENDALL, DON RAYMOND. *The Relationships Among the Motor, Intellectual, and Personality Domains of Development in Preadolescent Children.* Doctor's thesis, Purdue University (Lafayette, Ind.), 1968. (*DA* 29:3860A)

35. LOWERY, DONELLA W. *An Analysis of the Relationship Between Personality Traits and Reading Comprehension Achievement of Students in Grades Four Through Seven.* Master's thesis, East Tennessee State University (Johnson City, Tenn.), 1968.

36. PUGH, RICHARD C. "Tests for Creative Thinking—Potential for School Testing Programs." *B Sch Ed Ind Univ* 44(6): 1–30 N '68. * (*PA* 46:5483)

37. SEDARAT, NASSIR. *Relationship of Achievement Motive, Ego Strength, and Certain Aspects of Word Association to the Reading Ability of Intellectually Superior Pupils.* Doctor's thesis, University of Wisconsin (Madison, Wis.), 1968. (*DA* 29:4202A)

38. TAYLOR, A. J. W. "Personality Factors of Extraversion and Anxiety in New Zealand's Persistent Offenders." *Austral & N Zeal J Criminol* (Australia) 1:243–8 D '68. *

39. VEHAR, MARY ANN. "Extraversion, Introversion, and Reading Ability." *Read Teach* 21:357–60 Ja '68. * (*PA* 42: 17818)

40. YLITALO, SUSAN H. *A Comparative Study of the Bower-Lambert Screening Scale and the Children's Personality Questionnaire.* Master's thesis, Indiana State University (Terre Haute, Ind.), 1968. (Abstract: *Cont Ed* 40:361)

41. BACHTOLD, LOUISE M. "Personality Differences Among High Ability Underachievers." *J Ed Res* 63(1):16–8 S '69. * (*PA* 46:5711)

42. GODSHALL, TRICIA A. *An Investigation of the Influence of Teacher Anxiety Upon the Anxiety Level of Students From the Lowest Socio-Economic Level.* Doctor's thesis, University of Miami (Coral Gables, Fla.), 1969. (*DAI* 30:3320A)

43. HAGEN, DEAN SMITH. *Group Counseling, Individual Counseling, and Teacher Consultation as Means of Modifying Self-Reports on Personality Inventory Items by Elementary School Children.* Doctor's thesis, Florida State University (Tallahassee, Fla.), 1969. (*DAI* 30:5236A)

44. KAPLAN, HARVEY A. *Relationships Among Cognitive Styles, Personality Traits and Reading Achievement at the Elementary School Level.* Doctor's thesis, Rutgers—The State University (New Brunswick, N.J.), 1969. (*DAI* 30:4278A)

45. LESSING, ELISE E., AND ZAGORIN, SUSAN W. "Correlation Between Lorge-Thorndike IQ and Factor B of the IPAT Children's Personality Questionnaire." *Psychol Rep* 24(2):569–70 Ap '69. * (*PA* 43:15590)

46. NAGEL, THOMAS SCOTT. *A Descriptive Study of Cognitive and Affective Variables Associated With Achievement in a Computer-Assisted Instruction Learning Situation.* Doctor's thesis, Michigan State University (East Lansing, Mich.), 1969. (*DAI* 30:5295A)

47. PURCELL, K.; MUSER, J.; MIKLICH, D.; AND DIETIKER, K. E. "A Comparison of Psychologic Findings in Variously Defined Asthmatic Subgroups." *J Psychosom Res* 13(1):67–75 Mr '69. * (*PA* 44:3896)

48. RICHES, RALF CLYDE. *A Two Year Study of Personality Adjustment and Achievement Gains of Fourth Grade Students*

in Self-Contained and Team Teaching Classroom Organizational Teaching Plans. Doctor's thesis, University of Utah (Salt Lake City, Utah), 1969. (*DAI* 30:1925A)

49. WERNER, EMMY E., AND BACHTOLD, LOUISE M. "Personality Factors of Gifted Boys and Girls in Middle Childhood and Adolescence." *Psychol Sch* 6(2):177–82 Ap '69. * (*PA* 43:14130)

50. YATER, ALLAN C. *Differentiation: A Psychological Construct.* Doctor's thesis, St. Louis University (St. Louis, Mo.), 1969. (*DAI* 30:3881B)

51. AHAMMER, INGE M., AND SCHAIE, K. WARNER. "Age Differences in the Relationship Between Personality Questionnaire Factors and School Achievement." *J Ed Psychol* 61(3): 193–7 Je '70. * (*PA* 44:13364)

52. CURRY, ROBERT ST. CLAIR. *Analysis of Selected Personality and Social Characteristics of Students Revealing Changes in Creativity.* Doctor's thesis, United States International University (San Diego, Calif.), 1970. (*DAI* 31:2734A)

53. DUNN, JOHN PATTERSON. *The Relationship Between Strength and Selected Social and Personality Factors.* Doctor's thesis, Texas A & M University (College Station, Tex.), 1970. (*DAI* 31:3318A)

54. ISMAIL, A. H., AND KIRKENDALL, D. R. "Personality and Motor Aptitude Variables as Discriminators in Preadolescent Children." *Am Correct Ther J* 24(6):159–63 N–D '70. *

55. KIRKENDALL, DON R., AND ISMAIL, A. H. "The Ability of Personality Variables in Discriminating Among Three Intellectual Groups of Preadolescent Boys and Girls." *Child Develop* 41(4):1173–81 D '70. * (*PA* 46:835)

56. NEAVES, ALISON I. "To Establish a Basis for Prognosis in Stammering." *Brit J Dis Commun* 5(1):46–58 Ap '70. * (*PA* 46:5319)

57. PANEPINTO, JOSEPH VINCENT. *The Interpersonal Style of Parents and Their Children.* Doctor's thesis, West Virginia University (Morgantown, W.Va.), 1970. (*DAI* 31:3001B)

58. PARIS, JOHN AUGUST. *The Relation of a Personality Trait and Game Conditions to Participant Learning.* Doctor's thesis, Syracuse University (Syracuse, N.Y.), 1970. (*DAI* 32:102A)

59. REDDING, JAMES FRANCIS. *Personality Factors and Family Variables Differentiating Emotionally Disturbed, Emotionally Handicapped and Emotionally Adjusted Pupils.* Doctor's thesis, St. John's University (Jamaica, N.Y.), 1970. (*DAI* 31:5006B)

60. RYCHLAK, JOSEPH F. "Personality Factors in Self- and Peer-Evaluations of WISC Performance Intelligence Among Middle-Class Children." *J Spec Ed* 4(3):269–77 su–f '70. * (*PA* 46:6585)

61. SMITH, DAN FAYE. *A Study of the Relationship of Teacher Sex to Fifth Grade Boys' Sex Role Preference, General Self Concept, and Scholastic Achievement in Science and Mathematics.* Doctor's thesis, University of Miami (Coral Gables, Fla.), 1970. (*DAI* 31:4563A)

62. STEWART, R. R.; WALKER, W.; AND SAVAGE, R. D. "A Developmental Study of Cognitive and Personality Characteristics Associated With Haemolytic Disease of the Newborn." *Develop Med & Child Neurol* (England) 12(1):16–26 F '70. * (*PA* 44:17249)

63. BOND, NORMAN D., AND PHILLIPS, BEEMAN N. "Personality Traits Associated With Altruistic Behavior of Children." *J Sch Psychol* 9(1):24–34 '71. * (*PA* 47:4574)

64. BROOKE, KATHRYN M. *The Children's Personality Questionnaire and the Picture Frustration Study as Predictors of Academic Achievement of Fifth Grade Elementary School Children.* Master's thesis, Ohio State University (Columbus, Ohio), 1971.

65. CACHA, FRANCES BLACKHALL. *A Study of the Relation of Creative Thinking Abilities to Personality Factors and Peer Nominations of Fifth Grade Children.* Doctor's thesis, New York University (New York, N.Y.), 1971. (*DAI* 32:1329A)

66. DAVIS, JOHN KENT. *Personality Factor Patterns of Children Who Manifest Behavioral and Emotional Problems.* Doctor's thesis, Syracuse University (Syracuse, N.Y.), 1971. (*DAI* 32: 6045B)

67. MORRIS, CARL EUGENE. *The Influence of Teacher Dogmatism on Student Alienation in the Middle Grades.* Doctor's thesis, Ohio State University (Columbus, Ohio) and Miami University (Oxford, Ohio), 1971. (*DAI* 32:2192A)

68. MYERS, KARIN RUTH. *A Study of the Self Concept of Students in Individually Prescribed Instruction.* Doctor's thesis, University of Illinois (Urbana, Ill.), 1971. (*DAI* 32:4247A)

69. PHIFER, MELVIN PRESTON. *A Comparison of the Problems, Personality Characteristics and Self Concept of Students Identified as Potential Dropouts and Non-Potential Dropouts in a Two County Area in Mississippi.* Doctor's thesis, Mississippi State University (State College, Miss.), 1971. (*DAI* 32:1864A)

70. PHILLIPS, BEEMAN N.; MARTIN, ROY P.; AND ZORMAN, LEON. "Factorial Structure of the Children's School Questionnaire in American and Slovenian Samples." *J Cross-Cultural Psychol* 2(1):65–76 Mr '71.*

71. SHIEK, DAVID A. *Sociometric Self-Ranking and Personality Structure.* Doctor's thesis, Indiana State University (Terre Haute, Ind.), 1971. (*DAI* 32:6225A)

72. THURLOW, BRUCE HERBERT. *A Comparative Analysis of the Elementary Counseling Role and the Elementary Consultant Role With Selected Anxious Fifth Grade Students.* Doctor's

Children's Personality Questionnaire

thesis, University of Maine (Orono, Me.), 1971. (*DAI* 32: 4362A)

73. VROEGH, KAREN. "Masculinity and Femininity in the Elementary and Junior High School Years." *Develop Psychol* 4(2):254–61 Mr '71. * (*PA* 45:9704)

74. WERNER, LAWRENCE KURT. *The Relationships Among the Psycho-Motor, Motor Coordination, Personality, and Intellectual Domains of Development in Preadolescent Children.* Doctor's thesis, Purdue University (Lafayette, Ind.), 1971. (*DAI* 32: 4435A)

75. WICKWIRE, PATRICIA JOANNE NELLOR. *The Academic Achievement and Language Development of American Children of Latin Heritage: Factors of Intellect, Home Educational Environment, and Personality.* Doctor's thesis, University of Texas (Austin, Tex.), 1971. (*DAI* 32:6232A)

76. WILSON, J. A. "Personality and Attainment in the Primary School: 1, Personality Structure of Ten-Year-Olds." *Res Ed* (England) 6:12–23 N '71. * (*PA* 48:12254)

CUMULATIVE NAME INDEX

Ahammer, I. M.: 51	Miklich, D.: 47
Anastasi, A.: *rev*, 6:122	Morris, C. E.: 67
Bachtold, L. M.: 4, 41, 49	Mundy, J. M.: 9
Berger, S. R.: 23	Muser, J.: 47
Berk, T. J. C.: 15, 29	Myers, K. R.: 68
Bernstein, L.: 1	Nagel, T. S.: 46
Berson, M. P.: 5	Neaves, A. I.: 56
Bond, N. D.: 30, 63	Newbert, N.: 28
Brickner, C. A.: 31	Oberlander, M.: 27
Brooke, K. M.: 64	Oriole, R. A.: 18
Cacha, F. B.: 65	Panepinto, J. V.: 57
Cattell, R. B.: 2, 16–7, 19	Paris, J. A.: 58
Collins, J. L.: 3, 8	Phifer, M. P.: 69
Cooley, C. E.: 24	Phillips, B. N.: 63, 70
Curry, R. St. C.: 52	Porter, R. B.: 8
Davis, J. K.: 66	Pugh, R. C.: 36
DeVault, M. V.: 12	Purcell, K.: 1, 47
Dietiker, K. E.: 47	Redding, J. F.: 59
Dunn, J. P.: 53	Riches, R. C.: 48
Flint, F. S.: 21	Rosenblatt, H. S.: 14
Frost, B. P.: 6	Rushton, J.: 10
Godshall, T. A.: 42	Rychlak, J. F.: 60
Gruen, W.: 17	Savage, R. D.: 62
Hadden, H. J.: 20	Schaie, K. W.: 51
Hagen, D. S.: 43	Sedarat, N.: 37
Hetrick, S. H.: 32	Shiek, D. A.: 71
Hicks, J. S.: 33	Smith, D. F.: 61
Howarth, E.: 19	Smouse, A. D.: 13
Hundleby, J. D.: 16	Stewart, R. R.: 62
Ismail, A. H.: 54–5	Taylor, A. J. W.: 38
Johnson, D. W.: 25	Thurlow, B. H.: 72
Kaplan, H.A.: 44	Turnbull, J. W.: 1
Karson, S.: 7	Vehar, M. A.: 39
Kirkendall, D. R.: 34, 54–5	Vroegh, K.: 73
Kosier, K. P.: 12	Walker, W.: 62
Lawrence, J.: 22	Werner, E. E.: 11, 49
Layton, W. L.: *rev*, 6:122	Werner, L. K.: 74
Lessing, E. E.: 13, 27, 45	Wickwire, P. J. N.: 75
Lilly, R. S.: 32	Wilson, J. A.: 76
Lowery, D. W.: 35	Wirt, R. D.: *rev*, 6:122
McIver, M. R.: 8	Yater, A. C.: 50
Martin, R. P.: 70	Ylitalo, S. H.: 40
Maw, E. W.: 26	Zagorin, S. W.: 45
Maw, W. H.: 26	Zorman, L.: 70
Merrifield, P. R.: 32	

[1130]

Client-Centered Counseling Progress Record. Adults and children undergoing psychotherapeutic counseling; 1950–60; form for rating progress in up to 40 counseling visits; Russell N. Cassel; Associated Publishers. *

For additional information, see P :39; for a review by William Schofield, see 6 :76.

[1131]

Clinical Analysis Questionnaire, Research Edition. Ages 18 and over; 1970–71; CAQ; 37 scores (listed below) : 28 primary factor scores and 9 second-order factor scores; 2 parts; Karl H. Delhees and Raymond B. Cattell; Institute for Personality and Ability Testing. *

a) PART 1 [THE CLINICAL 16PF]. Shortened version of the *Sixteen Personality Factor Questionnaire;* the regular version of the 16PF may be substituted; 16 primary factor scores: reserved vs. outgoing (A), less intelligent vs. more intelligent (B), affected by feelings vs. emotionally stable (C), humble vs. assertive (E), sober vs. happy-go-lucky (F), expedient vs. conscientious (G), shy vs. venturesome (H), tough-minded vs. tender-minded (I), trusting vs. suspicious (L), practical vs. imaginative (M), forthright vs. shrewd (N), self-assured vs. apprehensive (O), conservative vs. experimenting (Q₁), group-dependent vs. self-sufficient (Q₂), undisciplined self-conflict vs. controlled (Q₃), relaxed vs. tense (Q₄), plus 5 second-order factor scores: introversion vs. extraversion (I), low anxiety vs. high anxiety (II), tenderminded emotionality vs. tough poise (III), subduedness vs. independence (IV), broad superego vs. lack of self-sentiment (VIII).

b) PART 2 [THE PATHOLOGY SUPPLEMENT]. 12 primary factor scores : low hypochondriasis vs. high hypochondriasis (D₁), zestfulness vs. suicidal disgust (D₂), low brooding discontent vs. high brooding discontent (D₃), low anxious depression vs. high anxious depression (D₄), high energy euphoria vs. low energy depression (D₅), low guilt vs. high guilt (D₆), low bored depression vs. high bored depression (D₇), low paranoia vs. high paranoia (Pa), low psychopathic deviation vs. high psychopathic deviation (Pp), low schizophrenia vs. high schizophrenia (Sc), low psychasthenia vs. high psychasthenia (As), low general psychosis vs. high general psychosis (Ps), plus 4 second-order factor scores: general frustration depression (IX), restless depression (X), suicidal depression (XI), general maladjustment depression (XII).

For additional information, see 7 :54 (1 reference).

REFERENCES THROUGH 1971

1. See 7:54.
2. MAY, DAVID ROBERT. *Psychiatric Syndrome Classifications Checked by Taxonome and Discriminant Functions on the Clinical Analysis Questionnaire.* Doctor's thesis, University of Illinois (Urbana, Ill.), 1971. (*DAI* 32:6056B)

CUMULATIVE NAME INDEX

Cattell, R. B.: 1   May, D. R.: 2

[1132]

Clinical Behavior Check List and Rating Scale. Clinical clients; 1965; 10 ratings: cooperation, activity level, intelligence, disposition, persistence, sociability, emotional stability, attention, communicativeness, relaxation-tension; Psychological Research and Development Institute; Psychological Publications Press. *

For additional information, see P :40.

[1133]

College and University Environment Scales, Second Edition. College; 1962–69; CUES; an adaptation of the *College Characteristics Index;* students' conceptions of "the prevailing atmosphere or climate of the campus"; 7 scores: practicality, community, awareness, propriety, scholarship, campus morale, quality of teaching and faculty-student relationships; C. Robert Pace; Educational Testing Service. *

For additional information and reviews by Paul L. Dressel and James V. Mitchell, Jr., see 7 :56 (99 references) ; see also P :42 (40 references).

REFERENCES THROUGH 1971

1–40. See P:42.
41–139. See 7:56.
140. HARTNETT, RODNEY T., AND SELIGSOHN, HARRIET C. "The Effects of Varying Degrees of Anonymity on Responses to Different Types of Psychological Questionnaires." *J Ed Meas* 4:95–103 su '67. * (*PA* 42:3199)
141. WEISS, ROBERT F. Chap. 3, "The Environment for Learning on the Catholic College Campus," pp. 57–82. In *The Shape of Catholic Higher Education.* Edited by Robert Hassenger. Chicago, Ill.: University of Chicago Press, 1967. Pp. xviii, 378. *
142. WINNIMAN, HOWARD NOEL. *A Study of Environmental Press: Expectations of Incoming Freshmen Compared With Perceptions of Residence Hall Seniors at the University of*

Miami. Master's thesis, University of Miami (Coral Gables, Fla.), 1968.

143. MITCHELL, JAMES V., JR. "Education's Challenge to Psychology: The Prediction of Behavior From Person-Environment Interactions." *R Ed Res* 39(5):695–721 D '69. *

144. SPEEGLE, JAMES REED. *College Catalogs: An Investigation of the Congruence of Catalog Descriptions of College Environments With Student Perceptions of the Same Environments as Revealed by the College Characteristics Index.* Doctor's thesis, Syracuse University (Syracuse, N.Y.), 1969. (*DAI* 31:1026A)

145. BELL, CHARLENE ANN. *A Comparison of Environmental Perceptions and Other Variables Between Sorority, Fraternity and Residence Hall Students.* Doctor's thesis, University of South Dakota (Vermillion, S.D.), 1970. (*DAI* 31:5754A)

146. BROOKE, MARINEZ LAYFIELD. *An Investigation of Differences in Attitudes and Values Between Freshmen and Sophomore Women at the University of Alabama.* Doctor's thesis, University of Alabama (University, Ala.), 1970. (*DAI* 31:5117A)

147. BURLEY, WILLIAM WADE. *An Investigation and Comparison of Environmental Influences at the University of North Carolina at Chapel Hill as Perceived by the Student Body, the Faculty, and Various Student Groups.* Doctor's thesis, University of North Carolina (Chapel Hill, N.C.), 1970. (*DAI* 31:5192A)

148. BUTLER, ROBERT RAY. *Perception of Environmental Press by Students and Faculty in the College of Education, University of Missouri-Columbia.* Doctor's thesis, University of Missouri (Columbia, Mo.), 1970. (*DAI* 31:4453A)

149. CHRISTOFF, PATRICK LEO. *The Relationship Between Attendance at a Summer Orientation Program, Expectation-Press Congruence, and Selected Behavioral Correlates.* Doctor's thesis, University of Maryland (College Park, Md.), 1970. (*DAI* 31:4454A)

150. CHRYSLER, JAMES DALE. *A Measurement and Comparison of Environmental Perceptions of Students, Faculty, and Administrators, at the College of Santa Fe.* Doctor's thesis, University of New Mexico (Albuquerque, N.M.), 1970. (*DAI* 31:5757A)

151. GALLESSICH, JUNE. "Characteristics of Engineering Students." *Eng Ed* 60(10):980–3 Je '70. *

152. GILBERT, ALLISON EDWARD. *The Community College Environment as Perceived by Faculty and Students at Miracosta College.* Doctor's thesis, University of Southern California (Los Angeles, Calif.), 1970. (*DAI* 32:196A)

153. KLOEPPEL, PAMELA CUTHRELL. *The Difference Between Certain High School Seniors' Perceptions of the Community College.* Doctor's thesis, University of Virginia (Charlottesville, Va.), 1970. (*DAI* 31:4465A)

154. MCINTOSH, GERALD ALFRED. *A Study of the Perceptions of Black and White College Freshmen at Michigan State University Toward the University Environment.* Doctor's thesis, Michigan State University (East Lansing, Mich.), 1970. (*DAI* 32:1298A)

155. MONROE, CHARLES EUGENE. *An Analysis of the Campus Environment of a Church-Related Liberal Arts College, With Student Enrollment Implications.* Doctor's thesis, University of Southern California (Los Angeles, Calif.), 1970. (*DAI* 32:203A)

156. NEWCOMB, THEODORE M.; BROWN, DONALD R.; KULIK, JAMES A.; REIMER, DAVID J.; AND REVELLE, WILLIAM R. Chap. 6, "Self-Selection and Change," pp. 137–60. In *The Cluster College.* Edited by Jerry G. Gaff and Associates. San Francisco, Calif.: Jossey-Bass, Inc., Publishers, 1970. Pp. xix, 249. *

157. PITTS, GRIFF D. *Values, Attitudes, Opinions, and Concerns of Subcultures of Concerned Students in an Urban Commuter College.* Doctor's thesis, Northwestern University (Evanston, Ill.), 1970. (*DAI* 31:5152A)

158. POWELL, EDWARD MICHAEL. *School Purpose as Perceived by Teachers and Environmental Press as Perceived by High School Pupils in Schools Classified by Selected Demographic Characteristics.* Doctor's thesis, Purdue University (Lafayette, Ind.), 1970. (*DAI* 31:3836A)

159. SPENCE, CHARLES CALVIN, III. *Perceptions of Selected Faculty and Undergraduate Students of Three Different Environments at a Complex University Using the College and University Environment Scale: An Experimental Social Science Residential College, a Conventional Living-Learning Residence Hall and a College of Social Science.* Doctor's thesis, Michigan State University (East Lansing, Mich.), 1970. (*DAI* 31:5804A)

160. ABELL, JOHN MINOR. *The Relationship Between Students' Perception of a University Environment and Their Knowledge of Their Counseling Services.* Doctor's thesis, University of Houston (Houston, Tex.), 1971. (*DAI* 32:1842A)

161. ASTIN, ALEXANDER W. "Two Approaches to Measuring Students' Perceptions of Their College Environment." *J Col Stud Personnel* 12(3):169–72 My '71. * (*PA* 46:11458)

162. BASS, DONALD ANTHONY. *An Operational Process Integrating Environmental Perceptions, Factual Data, and Institutional Objectives to Obtain Management Information for Decision Making in a Small Church-Related College.* Doctor's thesis, University of Houston (Houston, Tex.), 1971. (*DAI* 33:1341A)

163. BERGER, JAY VARI. *Perceived Changes in a University Environment: The Study of a Freshman Class.* Doctor's thesis,

University of Southern California (Los Angeles, Calif.), 1971. (*DAI* 32:4367A)

164. BRAZIER, JEANNE FRANCES. *How Successful Students, Unsuccessful Students, and Faculty Members See Their College: A Multivariate Analysis of the Relationship of Environmental Perceptions to Academic Performance.* Doctor's thesis, Northwestern University (Evanston, Ill.), 1971. (*DAI* 32:3016A)

165. BURCKY, WILLIAM DEAN. *A Study of Resident Students' Perceptions of University Housing Goals.* Doctor's thesis, St. Louis University (St. Louis, Mo.), 1971. (*DAI* 33:888A)

166. CHICKERING, ARTHUR W. "Cultural Sophistication and College Experience." *Ed Rec* 52(2):125–8 sp '71. *

167. CLAPP, ROGER ROSS. *A Study of the College Environments of Two Selected Groups of Accredited, Interdenominational Bible Colleges.* Doctor's thesis, University of Tennessee (Knoxville, Tenn.), 1971. (*DAI* 32:5489A)

168. COPPOCK, GLENN STEPHEN. *Environmental Perceptual Influences of Student Retention at Southwest Baptist College.* Doctor's thesis, Southern Baptist Theological Seminary (Louisville, Ky.), 1971. (*DAI* 33:387A)

169. COPPOLA, VINCENT JAMES. *The Utilization of Student Perceptions of Environmental Press Towards Determining Conditions for Change in a Community College.* Doctor's thesis, State University of New York (Buffalo, N.Y.), 1971. (*DAI* 32:3653A)

170. DELANEY, JOHN F. *Change in Environmental Perceptions of College Freshmen as Related to Socioeconomic Status and Academic Achievement.* Doctor's thesis, Rutgers—The State University (New Brunswick, N.J.), 1971. (*DAI* 32:6188A)

171. FELDMAN, KENNETH A. "Measuring College Environments: Some Uses of Path Analysis." *Am Ed Res J* 8(1):51–70 Ja '71. *

172. FLOREY, HENRY EDWARD, JR. *A Study of the Relationship Between First-Semester Freshmen and Persistent Students at the University of Alabama on Selected Perceptions, Characteristics, and Attitudes.* Doctor's thesis, University of Alabama (University, Ala.), 1971. (*DAI* 32:4980A)

173. FOX, JULIA MARY VAN DEUSEN. *Actual and Desirable Campus Environment as Perceived by Allied Health Students Classified Into Four Creative Ability Groups.* Doctor's thesis, University of Southern California (Los Angeles, Calif.), 1971. (*DAI* 31:6361A)

174. GASSERT, LELAND CALVIN. *A Comparative Study of the Perceptions of the University Environment of Candidates for Student Government Positions and Other Students and the Effects of the Election Experience Upon Those Perceptions.* Doctor's thesis, Oregon State University (Corvallis, Ore.), 1971. (*DAI* 32:695A)

175. GELLOR, JAIME MENDEZ. *Student Perceptions of Campus Environment.* Doctor's thesis, University of British Columbia (Vancouver, B.C., Canada), 1971. (*DAI* 32:6758A)

176. GELSO, CHARLES J.; SIMS, DAVID M.; COTTINGHAM, W. T.; AND HARTSFIELD, KIRK. "The Process of Change in a College Environment." *Col & Univ* 46(2):108–14 w '71. *

177. GIFFORD, BRIAN MARSHALL. *The Effect of Different Residence Hall Administrative Structures on Students at the University of Missouri-Columbia.* Doctor's thesis, University of Missouri (Columbia, Mo.), 1971. (*DAI* 33:104A)

178. HODGES, LEWIS RILEY. *A Study of Campus Environment: A Study of the Perceptions of the Groups Affecting a Religiously Orientated Liberal Arts College.* Doctor's thesis, University of Utah (Salt Lake City, Utah), 1971. (*DAI* 32:3051A)

179. HOWARD, LARRY LADON. *Institutional Goal-Statement Evaluation Using an Environmental Assessment Approach: A Case Study.* Doctor's thesis, University of Missouri (Columbia, Mo.), 1971. (*DAI* 32:4986A)

180. HUNT, NORMAN JEROME. *A Study of Differences in Perceptions of University Environment by Selected Freshmen Classifications.* Doctor's thesis, Indiana State University (Terre Haute, Ind.), 1971. (*DAI* 32:6130A)

181. JIMERSON, PATRICK DENNIS. *How Selected Classifications of Pupils in Two City High Schools Perceive Various Dimensions of the School Environment.* Doctor's thesis, Purdue University (Lafayette, Ind.), 1971. (*DAI* 32:5106A)

182. KENNEDY, PATRICK JOSEPH. *Freshmen Expectations Contrasted With Upperclass Perceptions of the Campus Environment.* Doctor's thesis, United States International University (San Diego, Calif.), 1971. (*DAI* 32:3692A)

183. LACKEY, JOHN WESLEY. *A Study of the Institutional Environment of Northwest College as Perceived and Desired by Students, Faculty, and the Board of Directors.* Doctor's thesis, University of Washington (Seattle, Wash.), 1971. (*DAI* 32:3722A)

184. LANDON, ROBERT FULTON. *The Perceived Environments of Selected Church of Christ-Related Senior Colleges, Methodist-Related Senior Colleges, and Similar State Supported Senior Colleges.* Doctor's thesis, George Peabody College for Teachers (Nashville, Tenn.), 1971. (*DAI* 32:3723A)

185. LANCE, ARTHUR JOHN, JR. *A Descriptive Study of Differences Among College Freshman Subcultures on Selected Attitudes, Environmental Perceptions, Behaviors, and Attainment of Certain Goals.* Doctor's thesis, American University (Washington, D.C.), 1971. (*DAI* 32:1856A)

College and University Environment Scales

186. Lynch, Robert C., and Sedlacek, William E. "Differences Between Student and Student Affairs Staff Perceptions of a University." *J Col Stud Personnel* 12(3):173–6 My '71. * (*PA* 46:11478)

187. Merrill, Calvin Conrad. *A Study of the Image of the University of Alabama Held by Selected Junior College Students in the State.* Doctor's thesis, University of Alabama (University, Ala.), 1971. (*DAI* 32:4990A)

188. Metz, Joseph Farrow. *A Study of the Relationship Between Student Evaluation of Teaching and Selected Faculty Characteristics.* Doctor's thesis, University of Maryland (College Park, Md.), 1971. (*DAI* 32:2440A)

189. Mullis, Herman Thomas. *Clustering University Students: Its Psychological and Behavioral Effects on Perceptions of the University, Personality Variables, Interaction Patterns and Integration Into the University System.* Doctor's thesis, University of Utah (Salt Lake City, Utah), 1971. (*DAI* 31:4556A)

190. Pfeil, Robert Larry. *A Comparison of Environmental Perceptions and Other Selected Characteristics Between Male and Female, Married and Single Subjects Who Reside in University Housing.* Doctor's thesis, University of South Dakota (Vermillion, S.D.), 1971. (*DAI* 32:4964A)

191. Poppen, Donald Eugene. *The Physical Environment of the Residence Hall Room: Its Impact on Student Attitudes and Behavior.* Doctor's thesis, University of Northern Colorado (Greeley, Colo.), 1971. (*DAI* 32:5572A)

192. Resnick, Martin Neal. *A Study of the Educational Environment of the Main Campus of the University of Oklahoma.* Doctor's thesis, University of Oklahoma (Norman, Okla.), 1971. (*DAI* 32:103A)

193. Roberts, David Lee. *An Investigation of the Effects of Congruence Between Perceived Environment and Openness or Closedness of Belief Systems and Success of Freshmen in a Junior College.* Doctor's thesis, East Texas State University (Commerce, Tex.), 1971. (*DAI* 32:5553A)

194. Rossier, Barbara Jeanesse. *Student Perceptions of Institutional Environment and Counseling Services at Selected Community Colleges Utilizing Centralized and Decentralized Systems.* Doctor's thesis, University of Southern California (Los Angeles, Calif.), 1971. (*DAI* 32:2444A)

195. Scheel, William Preston. *Assessing and Creating the Community Environmental Press in Selected Independent Secondary Schools.* Doctor's thesis, University of Massachusetts (Amherst, Mass.), 1971. (*DAI* 32:1840A)

196. Self, Lee Vann. *A Study of Selected Environmental Factors of the Student Body at the University of Alabama, Tuscaloosa, 1970–71.* Doctor's thesis, University of Alabama (University, Ala.), 1971. (*DAI* 32:5574A)

197. Shelton, Harris White. *A Comparison of the Environments of Two Florida Junior Colleges and Their Relatedness to Student Activism.* Doctor's thesis, Florida State University (Tallahassee, Fla.), 1971. (*DAI* 32:6159A)

198. Shirley, Mack Garner. *A Study of Institutional Image: Analysis of Perceptions of Sub-Populations in a College Environment.* Doctor's thesis, University of Utah (Salt Lake City, Utah), 1971. (*DAI* 32:4308A)

199. Snead, Robert Floyd. *Analysis of Student Response to Alternative Advising Programs in the Two-Year College.* Doctor's thesis, University of Missouri (Columbia, Mo.), 1971. (*DAI* 32:4967A)

200. Stone, Thomas Kent. *Organizational Size and Member Behavior: A Study of the Relationship Between Campus Enrollment and Student Satisfaction in a Community College.* Doctor's thesis, Wayne State University (Detroit, Mich.), 1971. (*DAI* 32:2446A)

201. Taylor, Keith L. *The Environmental Image of a Church-Related Continuing Education Center: An Analysis of Perceptions of Selected Populations.* Doctor's thesis, University of Utah (Salt Lake City, Utah), 1971. (*DAI* 32:2380A)

202. Theriault, Donald Paul. *A Comparison of Groups of Students and Faculty at Oregon Technical Institute With Reference to Their Perception of the College Environment.* Doctor's thesis, Oregon State University (Corvallis, Ore.), 1971. (*DAI* 31:6289A)

203. Treece, Joe Max. *Comparisons of Environmental Perceptions of Students and Faculty at Otero Junior College, La Junta, Colorado.* Doctor's thesis, University of Northern Colorado (Greeley, Colo.), 1971. (*DAI* 32:3707A)

204. Underwood, Arthur Grant. *A Longitudinal Study of Selected Changes in the Perception of the University Environment as Held by Students Who Participate in Two Forms of University Governance.* Doctor's thesis, Oregon State University (Corvallis, Ore.), 1971. (*DAI* 31:5808A)

205. Wallace, Darlene Joan. *Campus Environment and Its Relationship to Personal Needs as Perceived by Selected Sophomores at Four Colorado Junior Colleges.* Doctor's thesis, University of Northern Colorado (Greeley, Colo.), 1971. (*DAI* 32:3733A)

206. Warren, Mary Jane. *Campus Environment as Viewed by Administrators, Faculty and Students.* Doctor's thesis, United States International University (San Diego, Calif.), 1971. (*DAI* 31:2750A)

207. Wildman, Louis Robert. *An Investigation of the Relationship Between Student Perceptions of a Collegiate Institu-tional Environment and the Phenomena of Student Transfer.* Doctor's thesis, University of Washington (Seattle, Wash.), 1971. (*DAI* 32:2448A)

208. Wilson, Jeremy Robert. *A Longitudinal Examination of the Undergraduate Student Environment at Northwestern University: 1965–1970.* Doctor's thesis, Northwestern University (Evanston, Ill.), 1971. (*DAI* 32:3063A)

CUMULATIVE NAME INDEX

Self, L. V.: 196
Seligman, R.: 103, 131
Seligsohn, H. C.: 140
Shearer, R. A.: 105
Shelton, H. W.: 197
Shemky, M. W.: 27, 50
Shirley, M. G.: 198
Sidles, C. W.: 69
Simmons, H. E.: 39
Sims, D. M.: 32, 176
Skelton, D. R.: 106
Snead, R. F.: 199
Speegle, J. R.: 144
Speerstra, B. T.: 70
Spence, C. C.: 159
Spradling, J. W.: 136
Stallings, W. M.: 51
Standing, G. R.: 2
Stanfiel, J. D.: 137
Stillion, G. W.: 71
Stone, T. K.: 200
Stover, R. M.: 138

Taylor, D. S.: 107
Taylor, K. L.: 201
Theriault, D. P.: 202
Treece, J. M.: 203
Trimble, M. G.: 108
Tucker, S. B.: 3
Underwood, A. G.: 204
Vanderhoof, T. J.: 109
Vander Wilt, R. B.: 110
Wallace, D. J.: 205
Walsh, W. B.: 88, 111
Warren, M. J.: 206
Watts, F. P.: 137
Weiss, R.: 11
Weiss, R. F.: 141
Wiese, H.: 72
Wildman, L. R.: 207
Wilson, J. R.: 208
Wilson, R. S.: 139
Winborn, B. B.: 33
Winniman, H. N.: 142
Yonge, G. D.: 40

[1134]

The College Inventory of Academic Adjustment.
College; 1949; CIAA; 7 scores: curriculur adjustment, maturity of goals and level of aspiration, personal
efficiency-planning and use of time, study skills and
practices, mental health, personal relations, total; Henry
Borow; Consulting Psychologists Press, Inc. *

For additional information, see P:43 (8 references);
for a review by Leonard D. Goodstein, see 6:77 (12
references); for reviews by Lysle W. Croft and Harrison G. Gough, see 4:34 (3 references).

REFERENCES THROUGH 1971

1-3. See 4:34.
4-15. See 6:77.
16-23. See P:43.
24. GRAFF, ROBERT WALTER. *The Relationship of the Opinion,
Attitude, and Interest Survey to College Achievement and Academic Adjustment Factors.* Doctor's thesis, State University of
New York (Buffalo, N.Y.), 1968. (*DA* 29:2959A)
25. GRAFF, ROBERT W., AND COOLEY, GARY R. "Adjustment
of Commuter and Resident Students." *J Col Stud Personnel*
11(1):54-6 Ja '70. *
26. HANSEN, JAMES C., AND WARNER, RICHARD W., JR. "Environmental Press, Student Needs, and Academic Adjustment."
J Ed Res 63(9):404-6 My-Je '70. * (*PA* 46:5427)
27. WILLIAMS, LILLIE EVALINE. *The Relationships Between
Dogmatism, Academic Adjustment, and Grade Point Averages
for American Indian College Students.* Doctor's thesis, Arizona
State University (Tempe, Ariz.), 1970. (*DAI* 31:2028A)
28. GELSO, CHARLES J.; OSTERHOUSE, ROBERT; AND BODDEN,
JACK L. "Nonintellective Factors in Improvement During an
Educational Skills Course." Abstract. *J Counsel Psychol* 18(5):
503-4 S '71. * (*PA* 47:3784)

CUMULATIVE NAME INDEX

Allen, R. J.: 13
Bodden, J. L.: 28
Bond, P. J.: 17
Borow, H.: 1-2, 21
Burgess, E.: 4, 7
Carmichael, J. J.: 19
Centi, P.: 14
Christensen, C. M.: 8
Cooley, G. R.: 25
Croft, L. W.: *rev*, 4:34
Curran, A. M.: 10
DeSena, P. A.: 20-2
Gelso, C. J.: 23, 28
Goodstein, L. D.: *rev*, 6:77
Gough, H. G.: *rev*, 4:34

Graff, R. W.: 24-5
Hansen, J. C.: 26
Jensen, V. H.: 16
Lanier, W. J.: 15
McCullough, C. A.: 5
Moore, M. R.: 9, 11-2
Osterhouse, R.: 28
Poor, F. A.: 18
Popham, W. J.: 11-2
Rowell, D.: 23
Spencer, G. M.: 6
Troxel, L. L.: 3
Warner, R. W.: 26
Williams, L. E.: 27

[1135]

*****College Student Questionnaires.** College entrants,
students; 1965-71; CSQ; for research use only; institutional self-study of student populations; 2 editions;
Richard E. Peterson (technical manual); Educational
Testing Service. *

a) PART 1. College entrants; 7 scores: motivation for
grades, family social status, family independence, peer
independence, liberalism, social conscience, cultural
sophistication.

b) PART 2. College students end of academic year; 11
scores: family independence, peer independence, liberal-

ism, social conscience, cultural sophistication, satisfaction with faculty, satisfaction with administration, satisfaction with major, satisfaction with students, study
habits, extracurricular involvement.

c) CONTROL TEST FOR ACADEMIC APTITUDE. CTAA; an
optional test; group measure of academic aptitude used
in tandem with CSQ; test booklet title is *Control Test
AA.*

For additional information and reviews by Paul L.
Dressel and Harrison G. Gough, see 7:57 (51 references); see also P:44 (2 references).

REFERENCES THROUGH 1971

1-2. See P:44.
3-53. See 7:57.
54. APOSTAL, ROBERT A. "Comparison of Counselees and Non-
counselees With Type of Problem Controlled." *J Counsel Psychol*
15:407-10 S '68. * (*PA* 42:19322)
55. BLACK, RICHARD W. *A Comparative Study of the Differences in Self-Concept and Other Variables Between Students
Choosing Terminal and Degree Programs.* Doctor's thesis, University of South Dakota (Vermillion, S.D.), 1970. (*DAI* 31:
5755A)
56. COVEY, DIXIE SCOWCROFT. *Politics and Personality: A
Multivariate Analysis of Student Attitudes Toward the New
Left Movement.* Doctor's thesis, University of Utah (Salt Lake
City, Utah), 1970. (*DAI* 31:4985B)
57. HARTNETT, RODNEY T. "Differences in Selected Attitudes
and College Orientations Between Black Students Attending
Traditionally Negro and Traditionally White Institutions."
Sociol Ed 43(4):419-36 f '70. * (*PA* 47:9611)
58. HURD, DONALD EUGENE. *The Relationship of Affective
Variables to College Achievement.* Doctor's thesis, Indiana University (Bloomington, Ind.), 1970. (*DAI* 31:5793A)
59. KANE, JOHN GALVIN. *A Comparative Study of Academic
Success and Other Selected Characteristics of Financial Aid and
Non-Financial Aid Recipients at Winona State College.* Doctor's
thesis, Oregon State University (Corvallis, Ore.), 1970. (*DAI*
31:3818A)
60. LORENZ, MARTHA KATHERINE. *A Descriptive Study of
the Backgrounds, Attitudes, and Values of Home Economics
Students at Michigan State University.* Doctor's thesis, Michigan
State University (East Lansing, Mich.), 1970. (*DAI* 32:1054B)
61. MILLER, LEONARD. *Distinctive Characteristics of Freshmen Fraternity Members at a Large Urban Private University.*
Doctor's thesis, University of Pennsylvania (Philadelphia, Pa.),
1970. (*DAI* 32:202A)
62. NEWCOMB, THEODORE M.; BROWN, DONALD R.; KULIK,
JAMES A.; REIMER, DAVID J.; AND REVELLE, WILLIAM R. Chap.
6, "Self-Selection and Change," pp. 137-60. In *The Cluster
College.* Edited by Jerry G. Gaff and Associates. San Francisco,
Calif.: Jossey-Bass, Inc., Publishers, 1970. Pp. xix, 249. *
63. ABELL, JOHN MINOR. *The Relationship Between Students' Perception of a University Environment and Their Knowledge of Their Counseling Services.* Doctor's thesis, University
of Houston (Houston, Tex.), 1971. (*DAI* 32:1842A)
64. BLANCHFIELD, W. C. "College Dropout Identification: A
Case Study." *J Exp Ed* 40(2):1-4 w '71. * (*PA* 48:1856)
65. BRAINARD, STEPHEN R., AND DOLLAR, ROBERT J. "Personality Characteristics of Leaders Identifying With Different
Student Subcultures." *J Col Stud Personnel* 12(3):200-3 My
'71. * (*PA* 46:11461)
66. CALVIN, RICHMOND EDWARD. *A Comparative Study of
Freshmen Students in a Selected Multicampus Junior College
District.* Doctor's thesis, North Texas State University (Denton, Tex.), 1971. (*DAI* 32:4369A)
67. CLEARY, MARY ELIZABETH LEAHY. *Student Evaluation
of Faculty at West Chester State College of Pennsylvania: An
Investigation of the Differential Effects of Selected Institutional
and Student Variables.* Doctor's thesis, George Washington
University (Washington, D.C.), 1971. (*DAI* 32:3048A)
68. FRY, JAMES SCOTT. *A Study of Negro and Caucasian
Undergraduate Students' Attitudes Toward Selected Components of University Environment.* Doctor's thesis, Memphis
State University (Memphis, Tenn.), 1971. (*DAI* 32:1220A)
69. GARTMAN, JAMES CARROLL. *An Investment of Relationships Between Selected Personality Traits and Factors Associated With Change of Major in State Supported Colleges in
Arkansas.* Doctor's thesis. Northeast Louisiana University
(Monroe, La.), 1971. (*DAI* 32:4346A)
70. GUIDO, STEPHEN MICHAEL. *The Validity and Reliability
of a New Ego Strength Sentence Completion Test.* Doctor's
thesis, St. John's University (Jamaica, N.Y.), 1971. (*DAI*
32:4213B)
71. HARVEY, RAYMOND CHESTERFIELD, JR. *The Relationship
of Study Habits and Attitudes to College Subcultures and to
Personality Types.* Doctor's thesis, East Texas State University
(Commerce, Tex.), 1971. (*DAI* 32:6030B)
72. HATCH, DELSA DIANE. *Differential Personal Change of
Males and Females in Two College Environments.* Doctor's

thesis, University of Michigan (Ann Arbor, Mich.), 1971. (*DAI* 32:4105A)

73. HENSLEY, MARJORIE. *An Analysis of Patterns of Transfer Students' Progress in an Urban University.* Doctor's thesis, Boston University (Boston, Mass.), 1971. (*DAI* 32:2435A)

74. JONES, JOHN D. "A Study of the Relationship Between the Student's Socio-Economic Background and His Freshman Year in College." *NASPA J* 8(4):234–6 Ap '71. *

75. LARKIN, CAROLINE MARIA. *A Longitudinal Analysis of Changes in Attitudes and Values During the Undergraduate Years as Measured by the College Student Questionnaires.* Doctor's thesis, University of Pennsylvania (Philadelphia, Pa.), 1971. (*DAI* 32:1880A)

76. LOUNSBURY, JERALD ELBERT. *An Analysis of the Satisfactions With College Experienced by Special Project Students, Primarily Inner-City and Negro, at a Non-Metropolitan University as Measured by the College Student Questionnaire.* Doctor's thesis, Michigan State University (East Lansing, Mich.), 1971. (*DAI* 32:4989A)

77. MORRISEY, ROBERT J. "Attrition in Probationary Freshmen." *J Col Stud Personnel* 12(4):279–85 Jl '71. *

78. OZAKI, ROGER HIROSHI. *A Comparative Study of Student Subcultures and Value Systems in Three State-Supported Institutions of Higher Education in Georgia.* Doctor's thesis, University of Georgia (Athens, Ga.), 1971. (*DAI* 32:3699A)

79. PASSONS, WILLIAM R. "Student Satisfaction as Perceived by Three Groups of University Personnel." *J Col Stud Personnel* 12(2):126–9 Mr '71. *

80. PICCARD, LEROY ALVIN. *A Comparison of Attitudes, by Sex, Ethnic, and Program Classifications, of Junior College Students Toward Higher Education.* Doctor's thesis, University of Missouri (Columbia, Mo.), 1971. (*DAI* 32:1281A)

81. POWERS, RICHARD J. *Selected Noncognitive Variables as Predictors of Academic Achievement.* Doctor's thesis, St. John's University (Jamaica, N.Y.), 1971. (*DAI* 32:4194B)

82. SMITH, JOHN STEPHEN. *A Multivariate Combination of Academic and Non-Academic Factors Related to Student Attrition.* Doctor's thesis, University of Pittsburgh (Pittsburgh, Pa.), 1971. (*DAI* 32:6786A)

83. STONE, THOMAS KENT. *Organizational Size and Member Behavior: A Study of the Relationship Between Campus Enrollment and Student Satisfaction in a Community College.* Doctor's thesis, Wayne State University (Detroit, Mich.), 1971. (*DAI* 32:2446A)

84. WATERMAN, ALAN S., AND WATERMAN, CAROLINE K. "A Cross-Institutional Study of Variables Relating to Satisfaction With College." *J Ed Res* 65(3):132–6 N '71. * (*PA* 48:1626)

85. WATERMAN, ALAN S., AND WATERMAN, CAROLINE K. "A Longitudinal Study of Changes in Ego Identity Status During the Freshman Year at College." *Develop Psychol* 5(1):167–73 Jl '71. * (*PA* 46:9562)

86. WILLSEY, ALAN DOUGLAS. *College Student Satisfaction and Academic Performance.* Doctor's thesis, State University of New York (Buffalo, N.Y.), 1971. (*DAI* 32:3063A)

CUMULATIVE NAME INDEX

Abell, J. M.: 63
Althouse, R.: 24
Apostal, R. A.: 14–5, 32–3, 54
Black, R. W.: 55
Blanchfield, W. C.: 64
Bors, A.: 5
Brainard, S. R.: 65
Brown, D. R.: 20, 62
Buescher, R. M.: 16
Burns, J. L.: 17
Calvert, S. G.: 9
Calvin, R. E.: 66
Centra, J. A.: 19
Cleary, M. E. L.: 67
Covey, D. S.: 56
Davis, J. A.: 50
Deiulio, R. S.: 34
Dollar, R. J.: 65
Dressel, P. L.: *rev*, 7:57
Dyer, P. T.: 35
Flores, P. V.: 36
Folsom, C. H.: 18, 37
Fry, J. S.: 68
Gartman, J. C.: 69
Gehman, W. S.: 50
Gough, H. G.: *rev*, 7:57
Griffen, W. L.: 1
Guido, S. M.: 70
Hartnett, R. T.: 10, 19, 38, 57
Harvey, R. C.: 71
Hatch, D. D.: 72
Hedegard, J. M.: 20
Hensley, M.: 73
Hummers, J. A.: 39
Hurd, D. E.: 58
Ihlanfeldt, W. I.: 40
Johnson, E.: 41
Jones, J. D.: 74

Kane, J. G.: 59
Kerpelman, L. C.: 21
Kidd, K. A. J.: 22
Kramer, H. C.: 42
Kuder, J. M.: 43
Kulik, J. A.: 62
LaBach, P. A.: 23
Larkin, C. M.: 75
Lindsay, C. A.: 24
Lorenz, M. K.: 60
Lounsbury, J. E.: 76
Lucy, W.: 37
Madson, D. L.: 3
Magrab, P. R.: 25
Majer, K.: 44
Miller, L.: 61
Morrisey, R. J.: 45, 77
Newcomb, T. M.: 62
Ozaki, R. H.: 78
Passons, W. R.: 79
Paulus, G. S.: 6
Peterson, A. V.: 46
Peterson, R. E.: 2, 10–1
Piccard, L. A.: 80
Powell, J.: 47
Powers, R. J.: 81
Reimer, D. J.: 62
Revelle, W. R.: 62
Richardson, T. E.: 12, 48
Riggs, R. O.: 49
Rogers, M. E. P.: 13
Romine, B. H.: 26, 50
Sandeen, A.: 27
Skelton, D. R.: 28
Smith, J. S.: 82
Sockloff, A. L.: 29
Stewart, M. A.: 30
Stone, T. K.: 83

Walker, J. R.: 7
Waterman, A. S.: 51–2, 84–5
Waterman, C. K.: 51–2, 84–5
White, R. A. M.: 53

Widmar, G. E.: 4
Willsey, A. D.: 86
Work, G. G.: 8
Zimmerman, J. J.: 31

[1136]

★College Student Satisfaction Questionnaire. College; 1971; CSSQ; 6 scores: working conditions, compensation, quality of education, social life, recognition, total; Ellen L. Betz, John W. Menne, John E. Klingensmith (test), and Ann M. Starr (manual); Central Iowa Associates, Inc. *

REFERENCES THROUGH 1971

1. BETZ, ELLEN L.; KLINGENSMITH, JOHN E.; AND MENNE, JOHN W. "The Measurement and Analysis of College Student Satisfaction." *Meas & Eval Guid* 3(2):110–8 su '70. * (*PA* 45:1274)

2. BETZ, ELLEN L.; MENNE, JOHN W.; STARR, ANN M.; AND KLINGENSMITH, JOHN E. "A Dimensional Analysis of College Student Satisfaction." *Meas & Eval Guid* 4(2):99–106 Jl '71. *

3. STURTZ, SUE ANN. "Age Differences in College Student Satisfaction." *J Col Stud Personnel* 12(3):220–2 My '71. * (*PA* 46:11488)

CUMULATIVE NAME INDEX

Betz, E. L.: 1–2
Klingensmith, J. E.: 1–2
Menne, J. W.: 1–2

Starr, A. M.: 2
Sturtz, S. A.: 3

[1137]

Community Adaptation Schedule. Normals and psychiatric patients; 1965–68; CAS; for research use only; self-report measure of subject's relationship to the world outside of himself; primarily intended for measuring groups; 45 scores: work (employment, housework, family care, work potential, unemployment, volunteer, wage history, total), family (general living, spouse, children, parents, other relatives, total), social (general social, friends, dating, peers at work, neighbors, total), larger community (recreation, religion, organizations, communications, education, moving, civic, total), commercial (finances, shopping, transportation, modern technology, housing, total), professional (social services, other services, individual professionals, schools, total), affect, behavior, cognition, common question total, total, consistency; Sheldon R. Roen and Alan J. Burnes; Behavioral Publications, Inc. *

For additional information and reviews by Julian J. Lasky and Lester M. Libo, see 7:58 (4 references); see also P:45 (2 references).

REFERENCES THROUGH 1971

1–2. See P:45.
3–6. See 7:58.

7. AMERSON, GEORGE THOMAS. *An Examination of the Social, Educational, and Economic Adaptation of an Isolate Population.* Doctor's thesis, University of Oregon (Eugene, Ore.), 1970. (*DAI* 31:5228A)

8. DONELAN, JOHN ROBERT, JR. *Socialization of the Older American in Three Modes of Health Care.* Doctor's thesis, Boston University (Boston, Mass.), 1970. (*DAI* 32:566A)

9. ROMO, BERTRAM EARL. *Attitudinal and Behavioral Correlates of Work Success Among Educable Mentally Retarded Young Adults in Oregon.* Doctor's thesis, University of Oregon (Eugene, Ore.), 1970. (*DAI* 32:1100A)

CUMULATIVE NAME INDEX

Amerson, G. T.: 7
Burnes, A.: 1
Burnes, A. J.: 2
Cook, P. E.: 6
Cooper, S.: 1
Donelan, J. R.: 8
Griffin, C. L.: 3
Hammarback, M. D.: 4

Josephs, P. O.: 6
Lasky, J. J.: *rev*, 7:58
Libo, L. M.: *rev*, 7:58
McDowell, R. L.: 5
Ottenstein, D.: 1
Roen, S. R.: 1–2
Romo, B. E.: 9

[1138]

Community Improvement Scale. Adults; 1955; CIS; community morale; Inez Fay Smith; Psychometric Affiliates. *

For additional information, see P:46; for a review by Wimburn L. Wallace, see 5:42.

[1139]

Comrey Personality Scales. Ages 16 and over; 1970; CPS; 10 scores: trust vs. defensiveness (T), orderliness vs. lack of compulsion (O), social conformity vs. rebelliousness (C), activity vs. lack of energy (A), emotional stability vs. neuroticism (S), extraversion vs. introversion (E), masculinity vs. femininity (M), empathy vs. egocentrism (P), validity check (V), response bias (R); Andrew L. Comrey; Educational and Industrial Testing Service. *

For additional information and reviews by R. G. Demaree and M. Y. Quereshi, see 7:59 (20 references).

REFERENCES THROUGH 1971

1–20. See 7:59.
21. BACKER, THOMAS E.; COMREY, ANDREW L.; AND HAHN, MILTON E. "Comparison of the Comrey Personality Scales and the California Life Goals Evaluation Schedules." *Psychol Rep* 29(2):513–4 O '71. * (*PA* 47:8935)
22. FABIAN, JUDITH JANARO, AND COMREY, ANDREW L. "Construct Validation of Factored Neuroticism Scales." *Multiv Behav Res* 6(3):287–99 Jl '71. * (*PA* 47:4817)
23. JAMISON, KAY. "British and American Personality Stereotyping." Abstract. *Proc 79th Ann Conv Am Psychol Assn* 6(1):349–50 '71. * (*PA* 46:2831)
24. JEFFERS, JAMES JOHN LYLE. *Effects of Marathon Encounter Groups on Personality Characteristics of Group Members and Group Facilitators.* Doctor's thesis, University of Colorado (Boulder, Colo.), 1971. (*DAI* 32:4153A)

CUMULATIVE NAME INDEX

Backer, T. E.: 19, 21
Bloom, M. H.: 16
Cohen, S.: 16
Comrey, A. L.: 1–2, 4, 6–8, 10–5, 18–9, 21–2
Demaree, R. G.: *rev, 7:59*
Duffy, K. E.: 10, 15
Edwards, A. E.: 3, 5, 9, 16
Fabian, J. J.: 17, 22
Hahn, M. E.: 21
Hill, R. A.: 9
Jamison, K.: 8, 11–3, 15, 18, 23
Jeffers, J. J. L.: 24
King, N.: 11
Kumar, S.: 20
Quereshi, M. Y.: *rev, 7:59*
Rosenberg, B.: 9
Wine, D. B.: 3, 5

[1140]

Concept Formation Test. Normal and schizophrenic adults; 1940; CFT; also called *Vigotsky Test;* Jacob Kasanin and Eugenia Hanfmann; Stoelting Co. *

For additional information, see P:47 (7 references); see also 6:78 (11 references); for a review by Kate Levine Kogan (with William S. Kogan), see 4:35 (8 references); for a review by O. L. Zangwill, see 3:27 (21 references). For excerpts from related book reviews, see 3:28 (12 excerpts).

REFERENCES THROUGH 1971

1–19. See 3:27.
20–27. See 4:35.
28–38. See 6:78.
39–45. See P:47.
46. PEARL, DAVID. *A Comparative Study by Means of the Vigotski Blocks of Conceptual Thinking in Individuals With and Without Brain Injury.* Master's thesis, University of Chicago (Chicago, Ill.), 1948.
47. BAGGALEY, ANDREW R. "Concept Formation and Its Relation to Cognitive Variables." *J General Psychol* 52:297–306 Ap '55. * (*PA* 30:4158)
48. BRUNK, LARRY. "Test Performance as an Involuntary Function of Interpersonal Relationships." *J Abn & Social Psychol* 51:699–701 N '55. * (*PA* 31:3011)
49. SIMMONS, AUDREY ANN. "Factors Related to Lipreading." *J Speech & Hearing Res* 2:340–52 D '59. * (*PA* 34:6510)
50. GATES, MAXINE FULLER. *A Comparison of the Learning Characteristics of Hyperactive and Hypoactive Children With Related Central Nervous System Dysfunctions.* Doctor's thesis, Ohio State University (Columbus, Ohio), 1968. (*DAI* 30:166A)
51. STEWIN, L. *The Nature of Rigidity as Determined by Vygotsky Test Performance.* Master's thesis, University of Alberta (Edmonton, Alta., Canada), 1968.
52. BROMLEY, D. B. "Studies of Intellectual Function in Relation to Age and Their Significance for Professional and Managerial Functions." *Interdiscipl Topics Gerontol* 4:103–26 '69. * (*PA* 44:7411, title only)
53. REED, G. F. " 'Under-Inclusion'—A Characteristic of Obsessional Personality Disorder: II." *Brit J Psychiatry* 115(524):787–90 Jl '69. * (*PA* 44:7020)
54. STONES, E. "Verbal Labelling and Concept Formation in Primary School Children." *Brit J Ed Psychol* 40(3):245–52 N '70. * (*PA* 45:6059)

CUMULATIVE NAME INDEX

Aldrich, C. K.: 15
Allison, R. N.: 41
Baggaley, A. R.: 47
Baker, C. A.: 27
Bolles, M. M.: 4
Bressler, M. B.: 33
Bromley, D. B.: 43, 52
Brown, J. F.: 9
Brunk, L.: 48
Cameron, N.: 6
Cook, C. H.: 22
Corter, H. M.: 29
Davidson, J. L.: 37
Des Lauriers, A.: 23
Diethelm, O.: *exc, 3:28*
Doehring, D. G.: 27
Draper, W. A.: 38
Dworsky, A.: 2
Edrington, T. C.: 34
Fisher, S.: 26
Fosberg, I. A.: 21, 24
French, T. M.: *exc, 3:28*
Gates, M. F.: 50
Gill, M.: 13, 17–8
Gillespie, W. H.: *exc, 3:28*
Goldstein, K.: *exc, 3:28*
Halpern, F.: 23
Hanfmann, E.: 3, 5, 5a, 7–8, 12, 20, 31
Hartmann, G. W.: *exc, 3:28*
Heslop, J. R.: 45
Kasanin, J.: 3, 5, 5a, 12
Kasanin, J. S.: 16
Knight, R. P.: 13
Kogan, K. L.: *rev, 4:35*
Kogan, W. S.: *rev, 4:35*
Kress, R. A.: 36
Laird, A. J.: 30
Landis, C.: 4
Lovibond, S. H.: 32
Lozoff, M.: 13
Maskin, M.: *exc, 3:28*
Mayman, M.: 19
Meece, R. S.: 42
Miller, E. O.: 35
Muncie, W.: *exc, 3:28*
Myden, W. D.: 39
Norman, R. D.: 27
O'Neill, J. J.: 37
Pearl, D.: 46
Penny, R.: 28
Pickford, A. S.: *exc, 3:28*
Pickford, R. W.: *exc, 3:28*
Rapaport, D.: 9, 12a, 13–4, 17–8
Reed, G. F.: 53
Reichard, S.: 14
Rosen, G. P.: 4
Rosenblum, S.: 42
Schafer, R.: 17–8, 25
Semeonoff, B.: 30
Sen, M.: 40
Sengstake, C. B.: 38
Simmons, A. A.: 49
Sonoda, B. C.: 38
Stewin, L.: 51
Stones, E.: 45, 54
Su, C. W.: 44
Thompson, C.: *exc, 3:28*
Thompson, J.: 10–1
Vigotsky, L. S.: 1
von Holt, H. W.: 38
Wright, D. G.: *exc, 3:28*
Zangwill, O. L.: *rev, 3:27*
Zubin, J.: 11

[1141]

★**Concept-Specific Anxiety Scale.** College and adults; 1972; CSAS; for research use only; 3 scores: physiological response, mood, total; 2 versions; stimuli to be determined locally; C. W. Cole and E. R. Oetting; Rocky Mountain Behavioral Science Institute, Inc. *
a) CAS 1. For use with printed verbal stimuli.
b) CAS 2. For use with pictorial stimuli.

REFERENCES THROUGH 1971

1. COLE, CHARLES W.; OETTING, E. R.; AND SHARP, BRENDA. "Measurement of Stimulus-Specific Anxiety." *Psychol Rep* 25(1):49–50 Ag '69. * (*PA* 44:3629)
2. BIRNEY, SHERMAN DARYL. *Effects of Verbal Feedback on Concept Specific-Anxiety.* Doctor's thesis, Colorado State University (Ft. Collins, Colo.), 1970. (*DAI* 32:1203B)
3. DINGES, NORMAN GERALD. *Interaction Distance Anxiety.* Doctor's thesis, Colorado State University (Ft. Collins, Colo.), 1970. (*DAI* 31:7593B)

CUMULATIVE NAME INDEX

Birney, S. D.: 2
Cole, C. W.: 1
Dinges, N. G.: 3
Oetting, E. R.: 1
Sharp, B.: 1

[1142]

★**Conceptual Systems Test.** Grades 7 and over; 1971; CST; concreteness-abstractness; 6 scores: divine fate control, need for structure order, need to help people, need for people, interpersonal aggression, anomie; no manual; O. J. Harvey and James K. Hoffmeister; Test Analysis and Development Corporation. *

REFERENCES THROUGH 1971

1. HARVEY, O. J.; WHITE, B. JACK; PRATHER, MISHA S.; ALTER, RICHARD D.; AND HOFFMEISTER, JAMES K. "Teachers' Belief Systems and Preschool Atmospheres." *J Ed Psychol* 57:373–81 D '66. * (*PA* 41:2003)
2. HARVEY, O. J.; PRATHER, MISHA; WHITE, B. JACK; AND HOFFMEISTER, JAMES K. "Teachers' Beliefs, Classroom Atmosphere and Student Behavior." *Am Ed Res J* 5:151–66 Mr '68. *
3. KAATS, GILBERT R. "Developmental Changes in Belief Systems During a Service Academy Education." Abstract. *Proc 77th Ann Conv Am Psychol Assn* 4(2):651–2 '69. * (*PA* 44:1235)
4. BOWER, A. C., AND ANDERSON, C. C. "A Study of the Construct Validity of the Conceptual Systems Test." *Can J Behav Sci* 2(4):279–93 O '70. * (*PA* 45:3259)
5. SCHMID, AL C. "Susceptibility to Social Influence and Retention of Opinion Change in Two Types of Delinquents." *J Abn Psychol* 76(1):123–9 Ag '70. * (*PA* 44:21223)

[1143]

The Conservatism Scale. Ages 12 and over; 1970; "general factor underlying social attitudes" variously labeled authoritarianism, fascism, dogmatism, rigidity, perseveration, and anti-scientific attitude; Glenn D. Wilson and John R. Patterson; NFER Publishing Co. Ltd. [England]. *

For additional information, see 7:60 (9 references).

REFERENCES THROUGH 1971

1–9. See 7:60.
10. WILSON, GLENN D. "Personality, GSR Conditioning and Response to Instructional Set." *Psychol Rep* 22:618 Ap '68. * (*PA* 42:11619)
11. BAGLEY, CHRISTOPHER. "Racial Prejudice and the 'Conservative' Personality: A British Sample." *Pol Stud* 18(1): 134–41 Mr '70. *
12. CLOUD, JONATHAN, AND VAUGHAN, GRAHAM M. "Using Balanced Scales to Control Acquiescence." *Sociometry* 33(2): 193–202 Je '70. * (*PA* 46:6886)
13. HARTLEY, JAMES, AND HOLT, JANET. "A Note on the Validity of the Wilson-Patterson Measure of Conservatism." *Brit J Social & Clin Psychol* 10(1):81–3 F '71. * (*PA* 46:1845)
14. INSEL, PAUL, AND WILSON, GLENN D. "Measuring Social Attitudes in Children." *Brit J Social & Clin Psychol* 10(1): 84–6 F '71. * (*PA* 46:830)
15. MIKESELL, RICHARD H., AND PERSENSKY, J. J. "Simulation of Liberal and Conservative Attitudes on the Conservatism Scale." *Brit J Social & Clin Psychol* 10(4):383–4 D '71. * (*PA* 47:10742)
16. ORPEN, CHRISTOPHER. "Relative Susceptibility of Catch-Phrase and Propositional Scales to Social Desirability." *Psychol Rep* 29(2):487–95 O '71. * (*PA* 8:8761)
17. RAY, JOHN J. " 'A New Measure of Conservatism': Its Limitations." *Brit J Social & Clin Psychol* 10(1):79–80 F '71. * (*PA* 46:1033)
18. THOMAS, D. R.; SHEA, J. D.; AND RIGBY, R. G. "Conservatism and Response to Sexual Humor." *Brit J Social & Clin Psychol* 10(2):185–6 Je '71. *

[1144]

Cornell Index. Ages 18 and over; 1944–49; CI; revision for civilian use of the *Cornell Selectee Index Form N* and the *Cornell Service Index;* title on test is *C.I. —Form N2;* psychosomatic and neuropsychiatric symptoms; Arthur Weider, Harold G. Wolff, Keeve Brodman, Bela Mittelmann, and David Wechsler; Psychological Corporation. *

For additional information, see P:48 (22 references); see also 5:43 (7 references); for reviews by Hans J. Eysenck, Nelson G. Hanawalt, and Laurance F. Shaffer, see 4:37 (41 references).

REFERENCES THROUGH 1971

1–41. See 4:37.
42–48. See 5:43.
49–70. See P:48.
71. DYNES, J. B., AND SPRINGER, N. N. "The Psychiatric Evaluation of Naval Personnel Returning From Combat and Overseas Duty." *J Nerv & Mental Dis* 102:564–70 D '45. * (*PA* 20:2037)
72. HARRIS, HAROLD J. "Functions of a Psychiatrist in a Navy Yard." *U S Naval Med B* 44:1036–41 My '45. * (*PA* 20:1100)
73. DYNES, JOHN B. "Mental Breaking Points." *New Engl J Med* 234:42–5 Ja 10 '46. * (*PA* 21:466)
74. MARKEY, OSCAR B., AND ZISSON, MILES M. "A Psychiatric

Screening Aid for Pre-Combat Troops." *Am J Psychiatry* 103:377–80 N '46. * (*PA* 21:1514)
75. WEIDER, ARTHUR. "Some Aspects of an Industrial Mental Hygiene Program." *J Appl Psychol* 35:383–5 D '51. * (*PA* 26:6560)
76. TUREEN, LOUIS L., AND PALMER, JAMES O. "Some Group Differences in Personal Values Between American Soldiers and German Prisoners of War." *J Social Psychol* 42:305–13 N '55. * (*PA* 31:801)
77. VAN ALPHEN DER VEER, M. R.; VAN ANDEL, G. A.; HOLST, W.; v. NORREN, C.; AND WILLEMS, P. J. "Psychosomatic Investigations on Patients With Heart Complaints, Respectively on a Physical and Non-Physical Basis." *Adv Psychosom Med* 1:298–306 '60. *
78. CAUFFMAN, WILLIAM J., AND PAULEY, WILLIAM G. "Obesity and Emotional Status." *Pa Med J* 64:505–7 Ap '61. *
79. SHNEIDMAN, EDWIN S. "The Case of El: Psychological Test Data." *J Proj Tech* 25:131–54 Je '61. * (*PA* 36:21K31S)
80. GUNTER, LAURIE M. "Psychopathology and Stress in the Life Experience of Mothers of Premature Infants." *Am J Obstet & Gynecol* 86:333–40 Je 1 '63. *
81. LEON, ROBERT L.; MARTIN, HARRY W.; GLADFELTER, JOHN H.; AND MAY, SOPHIA BELLE. "Use of the Cornell Index in Screening for Socially Inadequate Men." *Tex State J Med* 59:93–5 F '63. *
82. SHAPIRO, DAVID S., AND MAHOLICK, LEONARD T. *Opening Doors for Troubled People.* Springfield, Ill.: Charles C Thomas, Publishers, 1963. Pp. xi, 121. * (*PA* 38:8858)
83. WIENER, MARK L. "A Comparison of Personality Patterns of Individuals Requesting Contact Lenses and Those Rejecting Them." *Optom Weekly* 55:21–8 Ap 9 '64. *
84. EISENMAN, RUSSELL. "Birth Order, Anxiety, and Verbalizations in Group Psychotherapy." *J Consult Psychol* 30:521–6 D '66. * (*PA* 41:2985)
85. ELY, NEAL E., AND JOHNSON, MERLIN H. "Emotional Responses to Peptic Ulcer Management." *Am J Psychiatry* 122:1362–71 Je '66. * (*PA* 40:9762)
86–7. DELL, HELEN LUCILE DAVIS. *The Evaluation of Teaching Procedures Designed to Increase Empathic Ability.* Doctor's thesis, Ball State University (Muncie, Ind.), 1967. (*DA* 29: 1447A)
88. FRANKLE, A. H. "Indirect Measurement of Personal Adjustment by Use of a Conventional Industrial Aptitude Test." *Proc Inter Congr Appl Psychol* 16:284–90 '68. *
89. RAPONI, TEODORO. *A Study of the Relationships Between Personality Characteristics, Manifest Health, Academic Performance, and the Use of a Selected Personnel Service by Selected Incoming Freshmen at Kent State University.* Master's thesis, Kent State University (Kent, Ohio), 1968.
90. SMITH, RICHARD W., AND YOUNG, HARL H. "Symptom Patterns of Psychiatrically Diagnosed Veterans Who Request Treatment and Those Who Do Not." *Psychol Rep* 22:1001–5 Je '68. * (*PA* 42:14071)
91. CARR, JOHN E., AND WHITTENBAUGH, JOHN. "Sources of Disagreement in the Perception of Psychotherapy Outcomes." *J Clin Psychol* 25(1):16–21 Ja '69. * (*PA* 43:9864)
92. CHERRY, ADA LOU. *A Comparison of Selected Characteristics of Graduated Students and Academically Disqualified Students Who Were Admitted With Warning to Ball State University Autumns, 1963 and 1964.* Doctor's thesis, Ball State University (Muncie, Ind.), 1969. (*DAI* 30:4217A)
93. MINNICK, MICHAEL LINDEN. *An Analysis of the Interrelationship Between Selected Cornell Index Groups and Their Sixteen Personality Factor Questionnaire Scores.* Doctor's thesis, Ball State University (Muncie, Ind.), 1969. (*DAI* 30:3327A)
94. CARR, JOHN E. "Differentiation Similarity of Patient and Therapist and the Outcome of Psychotherapy." *J Abn Psychol* 76(3):361–9 D '70. * (*PA* 45:6473)
95. BAEKELAND, FREDERICK, AND HARTMANN, ERNEST. "Reported Sleep Characteristics: Effects of Age, Sleep Length and Psychiatric Impairment." *Comprehen Psychiatry* 12(2):141–7 Mr '71. * (*PA* 47:7185)
96. KIPLINGER, GLENN F.; MANNO, JOSEPH E.; RODDA, BRUCE E.; AND FORNEY, ROBERT B.; WITH THE TECHNICAL ASSISTANCE OF SUSAN E. HAINE, RITA EAST, AND ALICE B. RICHARDS. "Dose-Response Analysis of the Effects of Tetrahydrocannabinol in Man." *Clin Pharmacol & Therapeu* 12(4): 650–7 Jl–Ag '71. *
97. KORMAN, MAURICE, AND GILLER, DONALD W. "Psychological Factors in Early Release From Psychiatric Hospitalization." *Psychol Rep* 28(1):251–7 F '71. * (*PA* 46:5123)
98. TOPPEN, J. T. "Underemployment: Economic or Psychological." *Psychol Rep* 28(1):111–22 F '71. * (*PA* 46:4762)

[1145]

Cornell Medical Index—Health Questionnaire.

Ages 14 and over; 1949–56; CMI; a questionnaire for use by physicians in collecting medical and psychiatric information from patients; Keeve Brodman, Albert J. Erdmann, Jr., and Harold G. Wolff; Cornell University Medical College. *

For additional information and reviews by Eugene E. Levitt and David T. Lykken, see 7:61 (32 references); see also P:49 (77 references).

REFERENCES THROUGH 1971

1–77. See P:49.
78–109. See 7:61.
110. STEINHARDT, ROGER W.; ZEMAN, FREDERIC D.; TUCKMAN, JACOB; AND LORGE, IRVING. "Appraisal of Physical and Mental Health of the Elderly: Use of the Cornell Medical Index and Supplementary Health Questionnaire." J Am Med Assn 151:378–82 Ja 31 '53. *
111. TUCKMAN, JACOB; LORGE, IRVING; STEINHARDT, ROGER W.; AND ZEMAN, FREDERIC D. "Somatic and Psychological Complaints of Older People in Institutions and at Home." Geriatrics 8:274–9 My '53. * (PA 28:2384)
112. REZNIKOFF, MARVIN. "Motivational Factors in Persons Attending a Cancer-Detection Center." Cancer 8:454–8 Jl–Ag '55. * (PA 30:5064)
113. WEINER, HERBERT; THALER, MARGARET; REISER, MORTON F.; AND MIRSKY, I. ARTHUR. "Etiology of Duodenal Ulcer: I, Relation of Specific Psychological Characteristics to Rate of Gastric Secretion (Serum Pepsinogen)." Psychosom Med 19:1–10 Ja–F '57. * (PA 32:1913)
114. TUCKMAN, JACOB, AND LORGE, IRVING. "The Projection of Personal Symptom Into Stereotype About Aging." J Gerontol 13:70–3 Ja '58. * (PA 33:3479)

115. ABRAMSON, J. H. "Observations on the Health of Adolescent Girls in Relation to Cultural Change." Psychosom Med 23:156–65 Mr–Ap '61. * (PA 36:3FH56A)
116. IMBODEN, JOHN B.; CANTER, ARTHUR; AND CLUFF, LEIGHTON E. "Convalescence From Influenza: A Study of the Psychological and Clinical Determinants." Arch Intern Med 108:393–9 S '61. *
117. WHISKIN, FREDERICK E.; DIBNER, ANDREW S.; AND RHUDICK, PAUL J. "Psychological, Cultural, and Health Characteristics of Aging Smokers and Nonsmokers." J Gerontol 17:69–74 Ja '62. *
118. KAHN, ROBERT L.; WOLFE, DONALD M.; QUINN, ROBERT P.; AND SNOEK, J. DIEDRICH; IN COLLABORATION WITH ROBERT A. ROSENTHAL. Part 5, "Personality Processes in Role Stress," pp. 223–333. In their Organizational Stress: Studies in Role Conflict and Ambiguity. New York: John Wiley & Sons, Inc., 1964. Pp. xiii, 470. * (PA 39:8866)
119. AZAR, GORDON J.; BOND, JAMES O.; CHAPPELL, G. LINDSEY; AND LAWTON, ALFRED H. "Follow-up Studies of St. Louis Encephalitis in Florida: Health Questionnaire Findings." Ann Internal Med 63:212–20 Ag '65. *
120. COOPER, BRIAN. "A Study of One Hundred Chronic Psychiatric Patients Identified in General Practice." Brit J Psychiatry 111:595–605 Jl '65. * (PA 39:15940)
121. DENNEY, DUANE; KOLE, DELBERT M.; AND MATARAZZO, RUTH G. "The Relationship Between Age and the Number of Symptoms Reported by Patients." J Gerontol 20:50–3 Ja '65. *
122. PILOWSKY, I. "The Relation of Cornell Medical Index Responses to a Measure of Interview Behaviour." J Psychosom Res (England) 8:481–5 Mr '65. *
123. RAHE, RICHARD H., AND HOLMES, THOMAS H. "Social, Psychologic and Psychophysiologic Aspects of Inguinal Hernia." J Psychosom Res (England) 8:487–91 Mr '65. *
124. AZAR, GORDON J.; BOND, JAMES O.; AND LAWTON, ALFRED H. "St. Louis Encephalitis: Age Aspects of 1962 Epidemic in Pinellas County, Florida." J Am Geriatrics Soc 14:326–33 Ap '66. *
125. CANTER, ARTHUR; IMBODEN, JOHN B.; AND CLUFF, LEIGHTON. "The Frequency of Physical Illness as a Function of Prior Psychological Vulnerability and Contemporary Stress." Psychosom Med 28:344–50 Jl–Ag '66. *
126. PAYKEL, E. S. "Abnormal Personality and Thyrotoxicosis: A Follow-Up Study." J Psychosom Res (England) 10:143–50 S '66. * (PA 41:769)
127. WEISS, STEPHEN M. "Psychological Adjustment Following Open-Heart Surgery." J Nerv & Mental Dis 143:363–8 O '66. * (PA 41:7770)
128. BROWN, D. G. "Emotional Disturbance in Eczema: A Study of Symptom-Reporting Behaviour." J Psychosom Res (England) 11:27–40 Je '67. * (PA 42:4405)
129. MCDONALD, CARRICK. "Measures of Neuroticism in the Elderly." Austral & N Zeal J Psychiatry (Australia) 1:44–7 Mr '67. *
130. SCHAIE, K. W., AND STROTHER, C. R. "Limits of Optimal Functioning in Superior Old Adults." Discussion by Joseph H. Britton. Interdiscipl Topics Gerontol 1:132–53 '68. *
131. SCHAIE, K. WARNER, AND STROTHER, CHARLES R. "Cognitive and Personality Variables in College Graduates of Advanced Age," pp. 281–308. (PA 43:15628, title only) In Human Aging and Behavior: Recent Advances in Research and Theory. Edited by George A. Talland. New York: Academic Press Inc., 1968. Pp. xiii, 322. *
132. SILVERSTONE, J. TREVOR. "Psychosocial Aspects of Obesity." Proc Royal Soc Med (England) 61:371–5 Ap '68. *
133. CLUM, GEORGE A.; HOIBERG, ANNE; AND KOLE, DELBERT M. "Attitude Change in Marine Recruit Training." Psychol Rep 24(1):311–8 F '69. * (PA 43:14210)
134. BIANCHI, G. N.; CAWTE, J. E.; AND KILOH, L. G. "Cultural Identity and the Mental Health of Australian Aborigines." Social Sci & Med (England) 3(3):371–87 Ja '70. *
135. BIANCHI, G. N.; MCELWAIN, D. W.; AND CAWTE, J. E. "The Dispensary Syndrome in Australian Aborigines: Origins of Their Bodily Preoccupation and Sick Role Behavior." Brit J Med Psychol 43(4):375–82 D '70. *
136. CHERASKIN, E., AND RINGSDORF, W. M., JR. "Familial Clinical Patterns: I, Reported Symptoms and Signs in the Dentist and His Wife." Geriatrics 25(2):123–6 F '70. *
137. CHU, HUNG-MING, AND RIN, HSIEN. "The Distribution of Psychiatric Symptoms in a Chinese Community: An Application of a Modified Cornell Medical Index Health Questionnaire." J Formosan Med Assn (Taiwan) 69(2):89–104 F 28 '70. *
138. EASTWOOD, M. R. "Psychiatric Morbidity and Physical State in a General Practice Population," pp. 291–8. In Psychiatric Epidemiology. Proceedings of the International Symposium Held at Aberdeen University 22–5 July 1969, World Psychiatric Association and the Royal Medico-Psychological Association. Edited by E. H. Hare and J. K. Wing. London: Oxford University Press, 1970. Pp. xvi, 379. *
139. KIMBALL, CHASE P. "The Experience of Open Heart Surgery: 2, Determinants of Post-operative Behavior." Psychother & Psychosom (Switzerland) 18(1–6):259–74 '70. * (PA 47:5515)
140. LAWTON, A. H.; RICH, T. A.; MCLENDON, S.; GATES, E. H.; AND BOND, J. O. "Follow-up Studies of St. Louis Encephalitis in Florida: Reevaluation of the Emotional and

Health Status of the Survivors Five Years After Acute Illness." *South Med J* 63(1):66–71 Ja '70. *

141. VALEK, J., AND KUHN, E. "Stress-Induced Changes of Carbohydrate and Lipid Metabolism in Coronary Heart Disease (CHD)." *Psychother & Psychosom* (Switzerland) 18(1–6): 275–80 '70. * (*PA* 47:5524)

142. WOODFORDE, JOHN M., AND FIELDING, JENNIFER R. "Pain and Cancer." *J Psychosom Res* (England) 14(4):365–70 D '70. * (*PA* 47:1513)

143. BOND, M. R. "The Relation of Pain to the Eysenck Personality Inventory, Cornell Medical Index and Whiteley Index of Hypochondriasis." *Brit J Psychiatry* 119(553):671–8 D '71. *

144. JOHNS, M. W.; GAY, T. J. A.; MASTERTON, J. P.; AND BRUCE, D. W. "Relationship Between Sleep Habits, Adrenocortical Activity and Personality." *Psychosom Med* 33(6):499–508 N–D '71. * (*PA* 49:2474)

145. KIDSON, MALCOLM A. "Personality Factors in Hypertension." *Austral & N Zeal J Psychiatry* (Australia) 5(3): 139–45 S '71. *

146. KREITMAN, NORMAN; COLLINS, JOYCE; NELSON, BARBARA; AND TROOP, JANE. "Neurosis and Marital Interaction: 4, Manifest Psychological Interaction." *Brit J Psychiatry* 119(550):243–52 S '71. * (*PA* 47:9435)

147. PATTISON, E. MANSELL; RHODES, ROBERT J.; AND DUDLEY, DONALD L. "Response to a Group Treatment in Patients With Severe Chronic Lung Disease." *Int J Group Psychother* 21(2): 214–25 Ap '71. * (*PA* 48:1099)

148. PILOWSKY, I., AND SHARP, JEANETTE. "Psychological Aspects of Preeclamptic Toxaemia: A Prospective Study." *J Psychosom Res* (England) 15(2):193–7 Je '71. * (*PA* 49:7261)

149. POLLACK, M. R. "The Relationship Between Cornell Medical Index Scores and Attendance Rates." *J Royal Col Gen Pract* (England) 21(109):453–9 Ag '71. *

150. PRUESKE, ELEANOR C. "Relationship Between Hostility and Health Problems in College Students." *J Sch Health* 41(3): 142–6 Mr '71. *

151. TEMPLER, DONALD I. "Death Anxiety as Related to Depression and Health of Retired Persons." *J Gerontol* 26(4): 521–3 O '71. * (*PA* 49:6616)

[1146]

Cornell Word Form 2. Adults; 1946–55; title on test is *C.W.F.-2;* civilian edition of *Cornell Word Form* designed for use in military psychiatric screening; psychosomatic and neuropsychiatric symptoms; Arthur Weider, Bela Mittelmann, David Wechsler, and Harold Wolff; Cornell University Medical College. *

For additional information, see P:50 (2 references); for a review by S. B. Sells, see 6:80 (1 reference); see also 5:44 (11 references).

REFERENCES THROUGH 1971

1–11. See 5:44.
12. See 6:80.
13–14. See P:50.
15. WEIDER, ARTHUR. "Some Aspects of an Industrial Mental Hygiene Program." *J Appl Psychol* 35:383–5 D '51. * (*PA* 26:6560)

Wechsler, D.: 3, 11   Weider, N.: 1
Weider, A.: 1, 3, 11, 13, 15 Wolff, H. G.: 1, 4, 11, 13

[1147]

Cotswold Personality Assessment P.A.1. Ages 11–16; 1960; manual subtitle is *A Study of Preferences and Values for Use in Schools and Clubs;* 6 scores: 3 preference scores (things, people, ideas) and 3 attitude scores (using one's hands, being with other people, talking about school); C. M. Fleming; Robert Gibson & Sons (Glasgow), Ltd. [Scotland]. *

For additional information, see P:51; for reviews by Ralph D. Dutch and G. A. V. Morgan, see 6:81 (1 reference).

REFERENCES THROUGH 1971
1. See 6:81.

CUMULATIVE NAME INDEX
Dutch, R. D.: *rev,* 6:81 Morgan, G. A. V.: *rev,* 6:81
Fleming, C. M.: 1

[1148]

★Crawford Psychological Adjustment Scale. Psychiatric patients; 1968; CPAS; 7 scores based upon 25 behavior ratings: social-economic-environmental competence, derangement of thought processes and peculiar behavior, physical behavior, communications, social acceptability and moderation of behavior, management of hostility, total; Paul L. Crawford; the Author. *

REFERENCES THROUGH 1971
1. CRAWFORD, PAUL L. *Construction, Validation, and Factor Analysis of a Psychological Adjustment Scale.* Doctor's thesis, Ohio University (Athens, Ohio), 1967. (*DA* 27:4561B)

CUMULATIVE NAME INDEX
Crawford, P. L.: 1

[1149]

Cree Questionnaire. Industrial employees; 1957–59; CQ; creativity and inventiveness; Thelma Gwinn Thurstone (test), John Mellinger (test), and Measurement Research Division, Industrial Relations Center, University of Chicago (manual); the Center. *

For additional information, see P:53 (3 references); for reviews by Allyn Miles Munger and Theodor F. Naumann, see 6:84.

REFERENCES THROUGH 1971
1-3. See P:53.
4. BAEHR, MELANY E.; FURCON, JOHN E.; AND FROEMEL, ERNEST C. *Psychological Assessment of Patrolman Qualifications in Relation to Field Performance.* Washington, D.C.: United States Government Printing Office, 1969. Pp. vii, 246. *

CUMULATIVE NAME INDEX
Abrams, P.: 1   Furcon, J. E.: 4
Allred, R. C.: 3   Kerr, W. A.: 1
Baehr, M. E.: 4   Munger, A. M.: *rev,* 6:84
Boyce, R. W.: 2   Naumann, T. F.: *rev,* 6:84
Froemel, E. C.: 4   Paxson, R. C.: 2

[1150]

Current and Past Psychopathology Scales. Psychiatric patients and nonpatients; 1966–68; CAPPS; the *Psychiatric Evaluation Form—Diagnostic Version* and the *Psychiatric History Schedule* have been stapled together and given a new title (the 2 component parts are no longer available as separates); rating scale and optional interview guide for use in diagnosing or describing mental illness if any; judgments based upon various sources of information (subject, informant, case records, nurse's reports, etc.); the PEF-D section, which deals with the patient's current functioning over the past month, yields 8 summary scale scores: reality testing-social disturbance, depression-anxiety, impulse control, somatic concern-functioning, disorganization, obsessive-guilt-phobic, elation-grandiosity, summary; the PHS section, which deals with the patient's past functioning

Cornell Word Form 2

from age 12 up to the past month, yields 18 summary scale scores: depression-anxiety, impulse control, social-sexual relations, reality testing, dependency, somatic concern-functioning, obsessive-compulsive, anger-excitability, manic, sexual disturbance, memory-orientation, disorganized, organicity, neurotic childhood, phobia, retardation-stubborn, hysterical symptoms, intellectual performance; no manual; Robert L. Spitzer and Jean Endicott; Biometrics Research, New York State Psychiatric Institute. *

For additional information and reviews by William J. Eichman and Raymond D. Fowler, Jr., see 7:62 (3 references); see also P:53A (1 reference).

REFERENCES THROUGH 1971
1. See P:53A.
2-4. See 7:62.

CUMULATIVE NAME INDEX
Eichman, W. J.: *rev,* 7:62 Morrow, G. M.: 2
Endicott, J.: 1   Schachter, J.: 4
Fowler, R. D.: *rev,* 7:62 Spitzer, R. L.: 1
Glueck, B. C.: 3   Stroebel, C. F.: 3
Melrose, J. P.: 3

[1151]

DF Opinion Survey. Grades 12–16 and adults; 1954–56; DFOS; 10 scores: need for attention, liking for thinking, adventure vs. security, self-reliance vs. dependence, aesthetic appreciation, cultural conformity, need for freedom, realistic thinking, need for precision, need for diversion; J. P. Guilford, Paul R. Christensen, and Nicholas A. Bond, Jr.; Sheridan Psychological Services, Inc. *

For additional information, see P:54 (12 references); for reviews by Andrew R. Baggaley, John W. French, and Arthur W. Meadows, see 5:45.

REFERENCES THROUGH 1971
1-12. See P:54.
13. BECK, ISABEL HOLDERMAN HANDLEY. *A Study of Criteria of Social Perception and Some Related Variables.* Doctor's thesis, University of Southern California (Los Angeles, Calif.), 1959. (*DA* 20:2372)
14. OLSON, NORMAN. *An Investigation of Orality Among Schizophrenics, Psychoneurotics, and Normals.* Doctor's thesis, Temple University (Philadelphia, Pa.), 1959. (*DA* 20:3388)
15. BENTON, JOHN L.; MILLS, LLOYD, JR.; HARTMAN, KEN; AND CROW, JAMES T. "Auto Driver Fitness: An Evaluation of Useful Criteria: A Study of Records Kept on Individual Drivers and on Results of Physical, Psychological, Ophthalmological, and Reaction-Time Tests." *J Am Med Assn* 176:419–23 My 6 '61. * (*PA* 39:10936)
16. SCHUSTER, D. H., AND GUILFORD, J. P. "The Psychometric Prediction of Problem Drivers." *Hum Factors* 6:393–421 Ag '64. *
17. BRADFIELD, LLOYD EUGENE. *The Personal Characteristics Related to College Performance and Adjustment of Work-Study and Non-Work-Study Freshmen Males.* Doctor's thesis, University of North Dakota (Grand Forks, N.D.), 1966. (*DA* 27: 1626A)
18. LAHEY, HENRY CHARLES. *Personality Differentiation of Elevated Outdoor and Literary Kuder Preference Record Scales in an Urban Population.* Doctor's thesis, University of Connecticut (Storrs, Conn.), 1970. (*DAI* 31:1014A)
19. SIMMS, JEANNE THOMAS. *An Investigation of the Differences Between Creative High Socio-Economic College Freshmen and Creative Low-Socio-Economic College Freshmen on Measures of Vocational Interests and Certain Motivational Factors.* Doctor's thesis, Catholic University of America (Washington, D.C.), 1970. (*DAI* 31:2693A)

CUMULATIVE NAME INDEX
Abou-Ghorra, I. M.: 7 Knapp, R. R.: 5–6
Baggaley, A. R.: *rev,* 5:45 Lahey, H. C.: 18
Beck, I. H. H.: 13   Leep, A. G.: 8
Benton, J. L.: 15   Meadows, A. W.: *rev,* 5:45
Bradfield, L. E.: 10, 17 Mills, L.: 15
Cattell, R. B.: 12   Olson, N.: 14
Crow, J. T.: 15   Plittman, J. C.: 3
French, J. W.: *rev,* 5:45 Roby, T. B.: 11
Gibbons, B. D.: 9, 12 Schuster, D. H.: 16
Grangaard, G. H.: 4 Simms, J. T.: 19
Guilford, J. P.: 16   Singer, E.: 11
Hartman, K.: 15   Zoberi, H.: 1
Hetherington, E. L.: 2

[1152]

Defense Mechanism Inventory. Ages 16 and over; 1968–69; DMI; for research use only; 5 scores: turning against object, projection, principalization, turning against self, reversal; David Ihilevich and Goldine C. Gleser; Goldine C. Gleser. *

For additional information and a review by James A. Walsh, see 7 :63 (4 references).

REFERENCES THROUGH 1971

1–4. See 7:63.
5. COHEN, DAVID BENJAMIN. "Frequency of Dream Recall Estimated by Three Methods and Related to Defense Preference and Anxiety." *J Consult & Clin Psychol* 33(6):661–7 D '69. * (*PA* 43:12962, title only)
6. GOLDSTEIN, STEVEN R. *Differential Effects of Physical and Nonphysical Encounter Group Techniques on Dimensions of Self-Esteem, Interpersonal Relations and Defense.* Doctor's thesis, Temple University (Philadelphia, Pa.), 1970. (*DAI* 31:6257B)
7. DIXON, SAMUEL LEE. *The Relationship of Counselor Defense Mechanisms to Counseling Outcome.* Doctor's thesis, Iowa State University (Ames, Iowa), 1971. (*DAI* 32:1849A)
8. IHILEVICH, DAVID, AND GLESER, GOLDINE C. "Relationship of Defense Mechanisms to Field Dependence-Independence." *J Abn Psychol* 77(3):296–302 Je '71. * (*PA* 46:7179)
9. WEISSMAN, HERBERT N.; RITTER, KENNETH; AND GORDON, ROBERT M. "Reliability Study of the Defense Mechanism Inventory." *Psychol Rep* 29(3):1237–8 D '71. * (*PA* 48:1019)

CUMULATIVE NAME INDEX

Bogo, N.: 4	Ihilevich, D.: 2–3, 8
Cohen, D. B.: 1, 5	Ritter, K.: 9
Dixon, S. L.: 7	Walsh, J. A.: *rev,* 7:63
Gleser, G. C.: 3–4, 8	Weissman, H. N.: 9
Goldstein, S. R.: 6	Winget, C.: 4
Gordon, R. M.: 9	

[1153]

The Demos D Scale: An Attitude Scale for the Identification of Dropouts. Grades 7–12; 1965–70; DDS; also called *Demos Dropout Scale;* 5 attitude scores: teachers, education, peers and parents, school behavior, total; George D. Demos; Western Psychological Services. *

For additional information and reviews by John R. Braun and Leonard V. Gordon, see 7 :64.

REFERENCES THROUGH 1971

1. CHEDEKEL, DAVID SELWYN. *The Levels of Anxiety and Self-Actualization in Dropout-Prone Ninth Grade Boys.* Doctor's thesis, Boston University (Boston, Mass.), 1971. (*DAI* 32: 1847A)

CUMULATIVE NAME INDEX

Braun, J. R.: *rev,* 7:64	Gordon, L. V.: *rev,* 7:64
Chedekel, D. S.: 1	

[1154]

Depression Adjective Check Lists. Grades 9–16 and adults; 1967; DACL; Bernard Lubin; Educational and Industrial Testing Service. *

For additional information and reviews by Leonard D. Goodstein and Douglas M. McNair, see 7 :65 (3 references) ; see also P :57 (4 references).

REFERENCES THROUGH 1971

1–4. See P:57.
5–7. See 7:65.
8. LEVITT, EUGENE E.; KOOIKER, JOHN E.; AND NORTON, JAMES A. "Depression and Oral Contraception." *Curr Topics Clin & Commun Psychol* 2:157–82 '70. *
9. LO, SAMUEL NAI-MING. *Effects of Self-Reinforcement and Goal-Setting on the Affect and Personal Orientation of Housewives.* Doctor's thesis, Fuller Theological Seminary (Pasadena, Calif.), 1971. (*DAI* 32:7315B)

CUMULATIVE NAME INDEX

Atwood, G. E.: 7	Lewinsohn, P. M.: 7
Curtis, G. C.: 5	Lo, S. N. M.: 9
Dupre, V. A.: 3	Lubin, A. W.: 3
Fogel, M. L.: 5	Lubin, B.: 1, 3–4, 6
Goodstein, L. D.: *rev,* 7:65	McNair, D. M.: *rev,* 7:65
Holmes, J. S.: 2	Marone, J.: 4
Kooiker, J. E.: 8	Norton, J. A.: 8
Kordasz, F.: 5	Smith, W. G.: 5
Levitt, E. E.: 8	

[1155]

Detroit Adjustment Inventory. Ages 5–8, grades 3–6, 7–12; 1942–54, c1940–54; DAI; title on tests for grades 3–6 and 7–12 is *Telling What I Do;* Harry J. Baker; Bobbs-Merrill Co., Inc. *

For additional information, see P :58 (1 reference) ; for a review by Laurance F. Shaffer, see 5 :46 (1 reference) ; for a review by Albert Ellis of the form for grades 7–12, see 3 :31.

REFERENCES THROUGH 1971

1. See 5:46.
2. See P:58.
3. WOLF, S. J. "A Comparative Study of Two Groups of Girls of Relatively Equal Intelligence but Differing Markedly in Achievement." *J Appl Psychol* 21:304–10 Je '37. * (*PA* 11:4815)
4. CRAWFORD, RONALD EUGENE. *Teacher-Pupil Personality Relationships.* Doctor's thesis, New York University (New York, N.Y.), 1953. (*DA* 13:589)

CUMULATIVE NAME INDEX

Bouise, L. M.: 1	Shaffer, L. F.: *rev,* 5:46
Crawford, R. E.: 4	Wolf, S. J.: 2–3
Ellis, A.: *rev,* 3:31	

[1156]

Developmental Potential of Preschool Children. Handicapped children ages 2–6; 1958–62; DPPC; title on record form is *Educational Evaluation of Preschool Children;* subtitle on report form is *Inventory of Developmental Levels;* level and pattern of intellectual, sensory, and emotional functioning and "readiness to profit from an educational program"; Else Haeussermann; Grune & Stratton, Inc. *

For additional information, see P :59. For an excerpt from a related book review, see 6 :B230.

[1157]

Devereux Adolescent Behavior Rating Scale. Normal and emotionally disturbed children ages 13–18; 1967; DAB; problem behaviors; 12 factor scores (unethical behavior, defiant-resistive, domineering-sadistic, heterosexual interest, hyperactive expansive, poor emotional control, need approval and dependency, emotional distance, physical inferiority-timidity, schizoid withdrawal, bizarre speech and cognition, bizarre action), 3 cluster scores (inability to delay, paranoid thought, anxious self-blame), 11 item scores (persecution, plotting, bodily concern, external influences, compulsive acts, avoids competition, withdrawn, socialization, peer dominance, physical coordination, distraction) ; George Spivack, Jules Spotts, and Peter E. Haimes; Devereux Foundation Press. *

For additional information and a review by Carl F. Jesness, see 7 :66; see also P :60 (1 reference).

REFERENCES THROUGH 1971

1. See P:60.

CUMULATIVE NAME INDEX

Jesness, C. F.: *rev,* 7:66	Spotts, J.: 1
Spivack, G.: 1	

[1158]

Devereux Child Behavior Rating Scale. Emotionally disturbed and mentally retarded children ages 8–12; 1966; DCB; ratings by clinicians, child care workers, parents, house parents, or others who have had "intimate living arrangement with the child over a period of time"; 17 scores: distractibility, poor self care, pathological use of senses, emotional detachment, social isolation, poor coordination and body tonus, incontinence, messiness-sloppiness, inadequate need for independence, unresponsiveness to stimulation, proneness to emotional upset, need for adult contact, anxious-fearful ideation, "impulse" ideation, inability to delay, social aggression, unethical behavior; George Spivack and Jules Spotts; Devereux Foundation Press. *

For additional information and a review by Allan G. Barclay, see 7:67; see also P:61 (3 references).

REFERENCES THROUGH 1971

1–3. See P:61.
4. NELSON, C. MICHAEL. "Techniques for Screening Conduct Disturbed Children." *Excep Children* 37(7):501–7 Mr '71. * (*PA* 47:3609)

CUMULATIVE NAME INDEX

Barclay, A. G.: *rev, 7*:67	Nelson, C. M.: 4
Levine, M.: 1	Spivack, G.: 1–2
Nalven, F. B.: 3	Spotts, J.: 2

[1159]

Devereux Elementary School Behavior Rating Scale. Grades kgn–6; 1966–67; DESB; problem behaviors; 11 factor scores (classroom disturbance, impatience, disrespect-defiance, external blame, achievement anxiety, external reliance, comprehension, inattentive-withdrawn, irrelevant-responsiveness, creative initiative, need for closeness to the teacher), 3 item scores (unable to change, quits easily, slow work); George Spivack and Marshall Swift; Devereux Foundation Press. *

For additional information and a review by William M. Littell, see 7:68 (1 reference); see also P:62 (2 references).

REFERENCES THROUGH 1971

1–2. See P:62.
3. See 7:68.
4. HYING, JUDITH A. *A Comparison of the Behavior of Elementary Level Educationally Handicapped and Educable Mentally Retarded Children as Measured by the Devereux Elementary School Behavior Rating Scale.* Master's thesis, California State College (Long Beach, Calif.), 1970.
5. SPIVACK, GEORGE; SWIFT, MARSHALL; AND PREWITT, JUDITH. "Syndromes of Disturbed Behavior: A Behavioral Diagnostic System for Elementary Schools." *J Spec Ed* 5(3): 269–92 f '71. * (*PA* 49:12082)
6. TAYLOR, WINNIFRED FLETCHER. *Direct vs. Indirect Intervention in Elementary Group Counseling.* Doctor's thesis, University of Akron (Akron, Ohio), 1971. (*DAI* 32:1869A)

CUMULATIVE NAME INDEX

Hying, J. A.: 4	Spivack, G.: 1–3, 5
Littell, W. M.: *rev, 7*:68	Swift, M. S.: 1–3, 5
Prewitt, J.: 5	Taylor, W. F.: 6

[1160]

Diplomacy Test of Empathy. Business and industry; 1957–60; DTE; revision of *Primary Empathic Abilities;* test booklet title is *Diplomacy Test of Empathic Ability;* Willard A. Kerr; Psychometric Affiliates. *

For additional information, see P:64 (2 references); for reviews by Arthur H. Brayfield and Richard S. Hatch, see 6:85 (1 reference); for a review by Robert L. Thorndike of the earlier test, see 5:99.

REFERENCES THROUGH 1971

1. See 6:85.
2–3. See P:64.
4. CONNELLY, WILLIAM. "Empathy, Ego Drive and the Pharmaceutical Salesman." *Pharma Marketing & Media* 2:15+ D '67. *

CUMULATIVE NAME INDEX

Aderman, M.: 1	Kerr, W. A.: 3
Brayfield, A. H.: *rev, 6*:85	Melville, N. T.: 3
Connelly, W.: 4	Ross, P. F.: 2
Dunfield, N. M.: 2	Smouse, A. D.: 1
Hatch, R. S.: *rev, 6*:85	Thorndike, R. L.: *rev, 5*:99
Kelleher, E. J.: 3	VanBuskirk, C.: 1

[1161]

★**Discharge Readiness Inventory.** Psychiatric patients; 1968–72; DRI; ratings by social workers of patient's "potential for release and community adjustment"; 4 scores: community adjustment potential, psychosocial adequacy, belligerence, manifest psychopathology; Gerard E. Hogarty, Robert F. Prien (test),

Leonard R. Derogatis (test), Roland R. Bonato (test), Barbara Oliver (test), and Richard F. Ulrich (manual); published by National Educational Consultants, Inc. for Friends Medical Science Research Center, Inc. *

REFERENCES THROUGH 1971

1. HOGARTY, GERARD E. "Discharge Readiness: The Components of Casework Judgment." *Social Casework* 47:165–71 Mr '66. *
2. HOGARTY, GERARD E. "Hospital Differences in the Release of Discharge Ready Chronic Schizophrenics." *Arch Gen Psychiatry* 18:367–72 Mr '68. * (*PA* 42:12473)
3. PRIEN, ROBERT F., AND COLE, JONATHAN O. "High Dose Chlorpromazine Therapy in Chronic Schizophrenia: Report of National Institute of Mental Health—Psychopharmacology Research Branch Collaborative Study Group." *Arch Gen Psychiatry* 18:482–95 Ap '68. * (*PA* 42:12292)
4. MESSIER, MICHEL; FINNERTY, RICHARD; BOTVIN, CONSTANCE S.; AND GRINSPOON, LESTER. "A Follow-Up Study of Intensively Treated Chronic Schizophrenic Patients." *Am J Psychiatry* 125(8):1123–7 F '69. * (*PA* 43:10094)
5. RAVENSBORG, MILTON R. "Hospital and Community Ratings of Factors Related to Psychiatric Patient Discharge Readiness." *Psychol Rep* 24(3):719–20 Je '69. * (*PA* 44:1017)

CUMULATIVE NAME INDEX

Botvin, C. S.: 4	Hogarty, G. E.: 1–2
Cole, J. O.: 3	Messier, M.: 4
Finnerty, R.: 4	Prien, R. F.: 3
Grinspoon, L.: 4	Ravensborg, M. R.: 5

[1162]

Dynamic Personality Inventory. Ages 15 or 17 and over with IQ's of 80 and over; 1956–70; DPI; for research and experimental use only (not so labeled in distributor's catalog); 33 scores: hypocrisy, passivity, seclusion-introspection, orality, oral aggression, oral dependence, emotional independence, verbal aggression, impulsiveness, unconventionality, hoarding behavior, attention to details, conservatism, submissiveness, anal sadism, insularity, phallic symbol interest, narcissism, exhibitionism, active Icarus complex, passive Icarus complex, sensuality, Icarian exploits, sexuality, tactile impression enjoyment, creative interests, masculine sexual identification, feminine sexual identification, social role seeking, social activity interest, need to give affection, ego defense persistence, initiative; also available, in abbreviated form and without scores for orality, phallic symbol interest, and sexuality, under the title *Likes and Interests Test* for use with apprentices and employee applicants ages 15 and over; T. G. Grygier; distributed by NFER Publishing Co. Ltd. [England]. *

For additional information, see 7:70 (9 references); see also P:65 (6 references); for a review by S. B. Sells, see 6:86 (7 references).

REFERENCES THROUGH 1971

1–7. See 6:86.
8–13. See P:65.
14–22. See 7:70.
23. GRYGIER, TADEUSZ. "A Factorial Study of Insularity." *Psychol Rep* 3:613–4 D '57. * (*PA* 33:3838)
24. BISHOP, FRANCES V. "The Anal Character: A Rebel in the Dissonance Family." *J Pers & Social Psychol* 6:23–36 My '67. * (*PA* 41:8720)
25. GRYGIER, TADEUSZ. "Validity of the Dynamic Personality Inventory." *Brit J Proj Psychol & Pers Study* 15(2):25–9 D '70. * (*PA* 47:941)
26. HAMILTON, V., AND FREEMAN, P. "Academic Achievement and Student Personality Characteristics: Multivariate Study." *Brit J Sociol* 22(1):31–52 Mr '71. * (*PA* 47:3755)

CUMULATIVE NAME INDEX

Barron, F.: 1	Hamilton, V.: 20, 26
Beach, L.: 7	Hubbard, B. L.: 10
Bishop, F. V.: 14, 24	Kline, P.: 12, 21
Bromberg, P. M.: 17	Lish, J. A.: 18
Brown, D. G.: 8	Luparello, T. J.: 17
Freeman, P.: 26	Sells, S. B.: *rev, 6*:86
Glasberg, H. M.: 17	Springer, P.: 13
Gordon, C. M.: 9, 15	Stein, M.: 17
Grygier, P.: 2	Stringer, P.: 11, 16, 22
Grygier, T.: 5–6, 19, 23, 25	Tyson, M.: 13
Grygier, T. G.: 3–4	Young, A. J.: 8

[1163]

*Early School Personality Questionnaire. Ages 6–8; 1966–72, c1963–72; ESPQ; 13 first order factor scores (reserved vs. outgoing, less intelligent vs. more intelligent, affected by feelings vs. emotionally stable, phlegmatic vs. excitable, obedient vs. assertive, sober vs. happy-go-lucky, expedient vs. conscientious, shy vs. venturesome, self-reliant vs. dependent, vigorous vs. doubting, forthright vs. shrewd, placid vs. apprehensive, relaxed vs. tense), 2 second order factor scores (extraversion, anxiety); Richard W. Coan and Raymond B. Cattell; Institute for Personality and Ability Testing. *

For additional information and a review by Lovick C. Miller, see 7:71 (8 references); see also P:66 (7 references).

REFERENCES THROUGH 1971

1–7. See P:66.
8–15. See 7:71.
16. COAN, RICHARD W., AND CATTELL, RAYMOND B. "Reproducible Personality Factors in Middle Childhood." *J Clin Psychol* 14:339–45 O '58. * (*PA* 34:3391)
17. DIELMAN, T. E.; CATTELL, R. B.; AND LEPPER, CAROLYN. "Personality Correlates of Behavior Problems in Early Childhood." *Personality* 2(2):141–7 su '71. * (*PA* 47:7078)
18. VROEGH, KAREN. "Masculinity and Femininity in the Elementary and Junior High School Years." *Develop Psychol* 4(2):254–61 Mr '71. * (*PA* 45:9704)

CUMULATIVE NAME INDEX

Ahammer, I. M.: 15	Lal, J. N.: 10, 13–4
Baker, H. L.: 6	Lepper, C.: 17
Baker, R. R.: 9	Miller, L. C.: *rev*, 7:71
Boss, M. W.: 12	Newbert, N.: 8
Cattell, R. B.: 1–5, 16–7	Peterson, D. R.: 4
Coan, R. W.: 1–3, 5, 16	Rosenblatt, J. B.: 11
DeVault, M. V.: 7	Schaie, K. W.: 15
Dielman, T. E.: 17	Vroegh, K.: 18
Kosier, K. P.: 7	

[1164]

Edwards Personal Preference Schedule. College and adults; 1953–59; EPPS; 15 scores: achievement, deference, order, exhibition, autonomy, affiliation, intraception, succorance, dominance, abasement, nurturance, change, endurance, heterosexuality, aggression; Allen L. Edwards; Psychological Corporation. *

For additional information and reviews by Alfred B. Heilbrun, Jr. and Michael G. McKee, see 7:72 (391 references); see also P:67 (363 references); for reviews by John A. Radcliffe and Lawrence J. Stricker and an excerpted review by Edward S. Bordin, see 6:87 (284 references); for reviews by Frank Barron, Åke Bjerstedt, and Donald W. Fiske and excerpted reviews by John W. Gustad and Laurance F. Shaffer, see 5:47 (50 references).

REFERENCES THROUGH 1971

1–50. See 5:47.
51–326. See 6:87.
327–689. See P:67.
690–1080. See 7:72.
1081. CARMAN, PHILIP MCCELLAN. *The Relationship of Individual and Husband-Wife Patterns of Personality Characteristics to Marital Stability.* Doctor's thesis, University of Washington (Seattle, Wash.), 1955. (*DA* 15:113)
1082. FEY, WILLIAM F. "Correlates of Certain Subjective Attitudes Towards Self and Others." *J Clin Psychol* 13:44–9 Ja '57. * (*PA* 32:5231)
1083. HOYT, DONALD P., AND KENNEDY, CARROLL E. "Interest and Personality Correlates of Career-Motivated and Homemaking-Motivated College Women." Comment by Charles McArthur. *J Counsel Psychol* 5:44–9 sp '58. * (*PA* 33:6850)
1084. ZUCKERMAN, MARVIN; NORTON, JAMES; AND SPRAGUE, DAVID S. "Acquiescence, and Extreme Sets and Their Role in Tests of Authoritarianism and Parental Attitudes." Discussion by Marvin Zuckerman. *Psychiatric Res Rep* 10:28–51 D '58. * (*PA* 35:2305)
1085. GOERING, ORLANDO JAMES. *Marriage Among High School Girls in Iowa.* Doctor's thesis, Iowa State College (Ames, Iowa), 1959. (*DA* 20:409)
1086. HARWAY, NORMAN I. "Some Factors in Psychotherapists' Perception of Their Patients." *J Consult Psychol* 23:379–86 O '59. * (*PA* 34:5952)

1087. SCHONBAR, ROSALEA A. "Some Manifest Characteristics of Recallers and Nonrecallers of Dreams." *J Consult Psychol* 23:414–8 O '59. * (*PA* 34:6267)
1088. KOPONEN, ARTHUR. "Personality Characteristics of Purchasers." *J Adv Res* 1:6–12 S '60. * (*PA* 35:2858)
1089. LANG, GERHARD. "Motives in Selecting Elementary and Secondary School Teaching." *J Exp Ed* 29:101–4 S '60. * (*PA* 36:2KMo1L)
1090. EVANS, FRANKLIN B. "Reply: 'You Still Can't Tell a Ford Owner From a Chevrolet Owner.'" *J Bus* 34:67–73 Ja '61. *
1091. ROBBINS, PAUL R. "Immediate and Delayed Effects of Social Influence Upon Individual Opinion." *J Social Psychol* 53:159–67 F '61. * (*PA* 35:6325)
1092. SNYDER, WILLIAM U., AND SNYDER, B. JUNE. *The Psychotherapy Relationship.* New York: Macmillan Co., 1961. Pp. xiii, 418. *
1093. STEINER, GARY A. "Notes on Franklin B. Evans' 'Psychological and Objective Factors in the Prediction of Brand Choice.'" *J Bus* 34:57–60 Ja '61. * (*PA* 37:6590)
1094. WINICK, CHARLES. "The Relationship Among Personality Needs, Objective Factors, and Brand Choice: A Re-examination." *J Bus* 34:61–6 Ja '61. *
1095. EVANS, FRANKLIN B. "Correlates of Automobile Shopping Behavior." *J Marketing* 26:74–7 O '62. *
1096. MILLER, SUTHERLAND, JR. "Relationship of Personality to Occupation, Setting, and Function." *J Counsel Psychol* 9:115–21 su '62. * (*PA* 37:7237)
1097. SECORD, PAUL F.; BACKMAN, CARL W.; AND MEREDITH, HELEN E. "Cue-Dominance in Person Perception as a Function of Strength of Perceiver-Need." *J Social Psychol* 58:305–13 D '62. * (*PA* 37:6590)
1098. BULATAO, JAIME. "Personal Preferences of Filipino Students." *Philippine Sociol R* 11:168–78 Jl–O '63. *
1099. GOLDBERG, PHILIP A. "Varieties of Failure and Assumed Similarity." *Psychol Rep* 13:19–22 Ag '63. * (*PA* 38:5850)
1100. HEILBRUN, ALFRED B., JR. "Sex-Role Identity and Achievement Motivation." *Psychol Rep* 12:483–90 Ap '63. * (*PA* 38:4236)
1101. HUGHES, HERBERT H., AND WATERS, MAX L. "A Comparison of Scores on the Edwards' PPS Under Realistic, Faking, and Social Desirability Conditions." *J Res Services* 3:13–6 D '63. *
1102. HUGHES, HERBERT H.; SPARKS, JACK N.; AND WATERS, MAX L. "The Use of the EPPS in Analyzing Differences Between Special Subgroups at the College Level." *J Res Services* 2:3–7 My '63. *
1103. LEVITT, EUGENE E.; LUBIN, BERNARD; AND BRADY, JOHN PAUL. "Personality Correlates of Hypnotizability in Young Women: The Anxiety-Dependency Constellation." *Congreso Interamericano de Psicologia* (Mexico) 7:360–4 '63. *
1104. MURPHY, JOSEPH R. "Questionable Correlates for Automobile Shopping Behavior." *J Marketing* 27:71–2 O '63. * Comment on 1095.
1105. RUSH, ALLEN C. "Better Police Personnel Selection." *Police Chief* 30:18+ S '63. *
1106. RYCHLAK, JOSEPH F., AND BRAMS, JEROME M. "Personality Dimensions in Recalled Dream Content." *J Proj Tech & Pers Assess* 27:226–34 Je '63. * (*PA* 38:2643)
1107. STEVENSON, LESLIE, JR. *Personality Needs of Persevering and Non-Persevering Male Secondary Education Graduates.* Master's thesis, University of Utah (Salt Lake City, Utah), 1963.
1108. BURKET, GEORGE R. *A Study of Reduced Rank Models for Multiple Prediction.* Psychometric Monograph No. 12. Richmond, Va.: William Byrd Press, Inc., 1964. Pp. xi, 66. *
1109. EVANS, FRANKLIN B. "True Correlates of Automobile Shopping Behavior." *J Marketing* 28:65–6 Ja '64. * Reply to 1104.
1110. GAZDA, GEORGE M., AND FOLDS, JANELL H. "The Effects of Three Methods of Test Interpretation on the Recall of Test Scores and Change in Self Concept." *J Stud Pers Assn Teach Ed* 4:10–21 D '64. *
1111. HEWITT, MARJORIE L. *Personality Characteristics of School Counselors.* Master's thesis, University of Utah (Salt Lake City, Utah), 1964.
1112. HUTCHINS, EDWIN B. "The AAMC Longitudinal Study: Implications for Medical Education." *J Med Ed* 39:265–77 Mr '64. *
1113. JONES, G. B., AND CHRISTENSEN, C. M. "An Experimental Application of the Principle of Incongruity Tolerance to the Counseling Setting." *Alberta J Ed Res* (Canada) 10:158–69 S '64. * (*PA* 39:12135)
1114. KEMP, C. GRATTON. "A Comparative Study of the Need Structures of Administrators, Teachers, and Counselors." *J. Ed Res* 57:425–7 Ap '64. *
1115. RARDIN, MAX W. *Correlates of the Good Geriatric Aide.* Master's thesis, University of Utah (Salt Lake City, Utah), 1964.
1116. SECORD, PAUL F.; BACKMAN, CARL W.; AND EACHUS, H. TODD. "Effects of Imbalance in the Self-Concept on the Perception of Persons." *J Abn & Social Psychol* 68:442–6 Mr '64. * (*PA* 39:1685)

1117. TENNISON, JAMES C. *Some Relaltionships Between Attitudes Toward the Church and Certain Personality Characteristics.* Master's thesis, Ohio University (Athens, Ohio), 1964.

1118. VENEMA, WILLIAM HARRY. *A Comparison of Personality Traits Between Fraternity Pledge Candidates and Freshmen Residence Hall Men at Washington State University.* Master's thesis, Washington State University (Pullman, Wash.), 1964.

1119. WARD, WILLIAM D. "Opinion Change as Related to Sequence of Degrees of Change Suggested." Abstract. *Psychol Rep* 14:93–4 F '64. * (*PA* 39:1558)

1120. CLAYCAMP, HENRY J. "Characteristics of Owners of Thrift Deposits in Commercial Banks and Savings and Loan Associations." *J Marketing Res* 2:163–70 My '65. *

1121. LUBLIN, SHIRLEY CURRAN. "Reinforcement Schedules, Scholastic Aptitude, Autonomy Need, and Achievement in a Programmed Course." *J Ed Psychol* 56:295–302 D '65. * (*PA* 40:3352)

1122. OSBORNE, CLIFFORD R. *The Relationship Between Two Personality Variables and Job Success of Student Assistants in Men's Residence Halls.* Master's thesis, University of Wyoming (Laramie, Wyo.), 1965.

1123. PLOTNICK, HAROLD L. "The Attitudinal Orientation of the Worker and Accuracy in Predicting Client Behavior." *Social Service R* 39:23–30 Mr '65. *

1124. ROSENKRANTZ, PAUL S., AND O'HALLORAN, WILLIAM J. "Are Abasement Scores Predictive of Adjustment." *J Psychol* 61:33–7 S '65. * (*PA* 40:5472)

1125. SCHNEIDER, WILBUR F. "Comparative Achievement of Graduates of Public and Catholic High Schools in Their Freshman College Year." *J Ed Res* 59:115–20 N '65. * (*PA* 40:3345)

1126. STAFFORD, JAMES E., AND GREER, THOMAS V. "Consumer Preference for Types of Salesmen: A Study of Independence-Dependence Characteristics." *J Retail* 41:27–33 su '65. *

1127. TOLOR, ALEXANDER, AND KISSINGER, R. DAVID. "The Role of the Therapist's Interventions in a Simulated Therapy Situation." *J Clin Psychol* 21:442–5 O '65. * (*PA* 40:1660)

1128. TUCKMAN, BRUCE W. "Integrative Complexity and Attitudinal Orientation." *Percept & Motor Skills* 21:838 D '65. * (*PA* 40:4254)

1129. TURLEY, DONNA LEE. *Psychological Need and Personality Trait Difference Comparisons Between Students With Positive Attitudes and Students With Negative Attitudes Toward Independent Study.* Master's thesis, Brigham Young University (Provo, Utah), 1965.

1130. FISHER, SEYMOUR. "Body Attention Patterns and Personality Defenses." *Psychol Monogr* 80(9):1–31 '66. * (*PA* 40:10142)

1131. GRUENFELD, LEOPOLD W. "Personality Needs and Expected Benefits From a Management Development Program." *Occup Psychol* (England) 40:75–81 Ja–Ap '66. * (*PA* 41:854)

1132. MORGAN, RONALD R. *Prediction of Academic Achievement Using the Edwards Achievement Scale.* Master's thesis, Marshall University (Huntington, W.Va.), 1966.

1133. REICH, ROBIN D. *Personality and Value Differences Between a Group of Teacher-Trained Students and a Group of Non-Teacher-Trained Students Enrolled in the Guidance Program in Education at the Catholic University of America.* Master's thesis, Catholic University of America (Washington, D.C.), 1966.

1134. SALEH, SHOUKRY D., AND COUGHLAN, DANIEL W. "Characteristics of Successful Probation Officers: A Validation Study." *Pub Personnel R* 27:43–5 Ja '66. *

1135. BASUMALLIK, TAPAN, AND BANERJEE, DEBABRATA. "On the Relationship Between Achievement Motivation and Risk Taking." *Indian J Psychol* 42(1–4):93–6 '67. *

1136. DEMETRIADES, DESPINA G. *A Study to Identify Some Personality Characteristics of Freshmen Academic Underachievers at Appalachian State University.* Master's thesis, Appalachian State University (Boone, N.C.), 1967.

1137. DOTY, BARBARA A. "Teaching Method Effectiveness in Relation to Certain Student Characteristics." *J Ed Res* 60:363–5 Ap '67. *

1138. JENNINGS, CHARLES L. "The Use of Normative Data in the Psychological Evaluation of Flying Personnel." *Int Psychiatry Clinics* 4:37–51 w '67. *

1139. MILLER, AARON J., AND TWYMAN, J. PASCHAL. "Persistence in Engineering and Technical Institute Programs: A Study of Some Nonintellective Concomitants." *J Hum Resources* 2(2):254–62 sp '67. *

1140. WINCH, ROBERT F. "Another Look at the Theory of Complementary Needs in Mate-Selection." *J Marriage & Family* 29:756–62 N '67. * (*PA* 42:3859)

1141. BAKER, STEVEN WILBUR. *A Comparison of the Needs and Values of Graduating Prospective Teachers of Special Education and the Needs and Values of Graduating Prospective Teachers of Regular Education.* Master's thesis, Central Washington State College (Ellensburg, Wash.), 1968.

1142. BRUNO, FRANK BARTOLO. *Life Values, Manifest Needs, and Vocational Interests as Factors Influencing Professional Career Satisfaction Among Teachers of Emotionally Disturbed Children.* Doctor's thesis, Wayne State University (Detroit, Mich.), 1968. (*DAI* 31:3999A)

1143. DOLBY, JAMES R.; HANSON, CHARLES; AND STRAYER, RICHARD. "Personality Factors and Religious Attitude Change." *J Sci Study Relig* 7(2):283 f '68. *

1144. DUNKIN, M. J. "The Need Structure of Teachers Varying in Experience and Job Satisfaction." *J Ed Adm* 6:41–51 My '68. *

1145. EVANS, FRANKLIN B. "Ford Versus Chevrolet: Park Forest Revisited." *J Bus* 41:445–59 O '68. *

1146. HENRY, LYLE K.; MOORE, CHARLES; MOORE, NANCY; KESSLER, SHERYL; AND STONER, MILDRED. "An Analysis of the Attitudes of College Students Concerning the War in Vietnam." *Proc Iowa Acad Sci* 75:312–7 '68. *

1147. HOFFMANN, H. "Dimensions of Desirability Ratings in a German and Austrian Sample: A Cross-Cultural Study." *Proc Inter Congr Appl Psychol* 16:769–75 '68. *

1148. HORN, ROBERT M. *Personality Correlates of Heterosexual Somatic Preference.* Master's thesis, Pennsylvania State University (University Park, Pa.), 1968.

1149. JACOBS, LYDIA P. *A Study of the Relationship Between Values and Grade Point Average.* Master's thesis, Kent State University (Kent, Ohio), 1968.

1150. LANDMAN, STEPHEN H. *Prediction of College Grades From Measures of Manifest Anxiety, Achievement Motivation, Test Anxiety, Study Habits, and Scholastic Aptitude.* Master's thesis, Kent State University (Kent, Ohio), 1968.

1151. LAYTON, GEORGE. "Differences in Need Patterns Between Open and Closed Minded High School Students." *Grad Res Ed & Related Discip* 4:93 w '68. *

1152. MASSY, WILLIAM F.; FRANK, RONALD E.; AND LODAHL, THOMAS M. *Purchasing Behavior and Personal Attributes,* pp. 73–126, 146–63. Philadelphia, Pa.: University of Pennsylvania Press, 1968. Pp. iv, 175. *

1153. MERRICK, RICHARD A. *The Relationship of Assessed Need Achievement to Aggressive Behavior in Competition.* Master's thesis, Kent State University (Kent, Ohio), 1968.

1154. RODGERS, CHARLES W. *A Comparison of the Need for Achievement and Hypnotic Susceptibility.* Master's thesis, University of Wyoming (Laramie, Wyo.), 1968.

1155. SCHAIE, K. W., AND STROTHER, C. R. "Limits of Optimal Functioning in Superior Old Adults." Discussion by Joseph H. Britton. *Interdiscipl Topics Gerontol* 1:132–53 '68. *

1156. SCHAIE, K. WARNER, AND STROTHER, CHARLES R. "Cognitive and Personality Variables in College Graduates of Advanced Age," pp. 281–308. (*PA* 43:15628, title only) In *Human Aging and Behavior: Recent Advances in Research and Theory.* Edited by George A. Talland. New York: Academic Press Inc., 1968. Pp. xiii, 322. *

1157. SCOTT, WILLIAM A. "Comparative Validities of Forced-Choice and Single-Stimulus Tests." *Psychol B* 70:231–44 O '68. * (*PA* 43:117)

1158. FRANK, RONALD E.; MASSY, WILLIAM F.; AND LODAHL, THOMAS M. "Purchasing Behavior and Personal Attributes." *J Adv Res* 9(4):15–24 D '69. * (*PA* 45:3183)

1159. HOGAN, ROBERT A. "Academic Excellence and Its Philosophical Motivation." *Ill State Univ J* 31(4):25–30 Ap '69. *

1160. KINNICK, BERNARD C.; NELSON, THEODORE M.; AND QUINLAN, CLAIRE A. "Comparison of Psychological Needs of Counseled and Non-counseled Students." *J Stud Pers Assn Teach Ed* 8(1):14–21 f '69. * (*PA* 44:17422)

1161. MONSMA, THEODORE HENRY. *Therapists' Needs and Judgments of Patients' Needs.* Doctor's thesis, Columbia University (New York, N.Y.), 1969. (*DAI* 33:446B)

1162. NEWMAN, CARL. "A Study of Underachievement in an Average College Population," pp. 338–58. In *Professional School Psychology: Vol. 3.* Edited by Gloria B. Gottsegen and Monroe G. Gottsegen. New York: Grune & Stratton, Inc., 1969. Pp. xiii, 407. * (*PA* 44:2860)

1163. SNORTUM, JOHN R., AND MYERS, HECTOR F. "Intensity of T-Group Relationships as a Function of Interaction." Abstract. *Proc 77th Ann Conv Am Psychol Assn* 4(1):455–6 '69. * (*PA* 43:17355)

1164. WOTRUBA, RICHARD T. "Can Residence Hall Staff Be Selected Scientifically?" *NASPA* 7(2):107–11 O '69. *

1165. AUVENSHINE, C. D.; SMITH, DAVID F.; AND HENAGHAN, MARGARET B. "Need for Achievement: Relation to Academic Achievement and Inventoried Needs." *J Stud Pers Assn Teach Ed* 8(4):105–14 su '70. * (*PA* 45:2386)

1166. BIRD, EVELYN I. "Personality Structure of Canadian Intercollegiate Women Ice Hockey Players," pp. 149–56. In *Contemporary Psychology of Sport.* Proceedings of the Second International Congress of Sport Psychology, Washington, D.C., 1968. Chicago, Ill.: Athletic Institute, 1970. Pp. xix, 878. *

1167. BRICKNER, SALLY ANN MARY. *Observed Classroom Behaviors and Personality Types of 178 Beginning Teachers.* Doctor's thesis, Michigan State University (East Lansing, Mich.), 1970. (*DAI* 31:5898A)

1168. CARNOT, JOSEPH BARRY. *A Comparison of Role Expectations and Personality Variables: Ohio Migrant and Public School Administrators.* Doctor's thesis, Bowling Green State University (Bowling Green, Ohio), 1970. (*DAI* 31:4407A)

1169. FISHER, GARY, AND HOWELL, LEISLA M. "Psychological Needs of Homosexual Pedophiliacs." *Dis Nerv System* 31(9):623–5 S '70. * (*PA* 45:6637)

1170. FLETCHER, RAYMOND LEE. *Selected Personality Characteristics and Activity Participation of Male College Freshmen.*

Doctor's thesis, Texas A & M University (College Station, Tex.), 1970. (*DAI* 31:5176A)

1171. GALLESSICH, JUNE. "Characteristics of Engineering Students." *Eng Ed* 60(10):980–3 Je '70. *

1172. GOSINE, M., AND KEITH, M. V. "Bureaucracy, Teacher Personality Needs and Teacher Satisfaction." *Can Administrator* 10(1):1–5 O '70. *

1173. GRANDE, PETER P. "How Objective Are Measures of Campus Climate," pp. 41–7. In *The Challenge and Response of Institutional Research.* Proceedings of the Ninth Annual Forum on Institutional Research. Athens, Ga.: Association for Institutional Research (c/o Cameron Fincher, University of Georgia), 1970. Pp. vii, 182. *

1174. GUTERMAN, STANLEY S. *The Machiavellians: A Social Psychological Study of Moral Character and Organizational Milieu.* Lincoln, Neb.: University of Nebraska Press, 1970. Pp. xviii, 178. * (*PA* 44:19660)

1175. HILL, JAMES W.; BASS, ALAN R.; AND ROSEN, HJALMAR. "The Prediction of Complex Organizational Behavior: A Comparison of Decision Theory With More Traditional Techniques." *Organiz Behav & Hum Perfor* 5(5):449–62 S '70. * (*PA* 45:5120)

1176. HOLYFIELD, JAMES RAY. *A Study of Selective Personality Characteristics of Teachers for Children in Impoverished Areas.* Doctor's thesis, Ohio State University (Columbus, Ohio), 1970. (*DAI* 32:284A)

1177. HUGHES, LOIS JUNE. *Selected Factors as Related to Success in Student Teaching of Home Economics.* Doctor's thesis, University of Missouri (Columbia, Mo.), 1970. (*DAI* 31:5249A)

1178. HUTSLAR, JOHN LEE. *The Relationship Between Selected Personality Traits and Bicycle Ergometer Endurance.* Master's thesis, Pennsylvania State University (University Park, Pa.), 1970.

1179. HUTTER, JEFFREY IRA. *Interpersonal Themes in Encounter Group Process as a Function of Style of Leadership.* Doctor's thesis, University of Florida (Gainesville, Fla.), 1970. (*DAI* 32:1846B)

1180. INMAN, GERALD DUANE. *A Study of Expectations Held by Intern Teachers With Selected Personal Characteristics for Intern Consultant Role.* Doctor's thesis, Michigan State University (East Lansing, Mich.), 1970. (*DAI* 31:4007A)

1181. KIDD, JAMES EMMITT, JR. *The Influence of Selected Variables on the Reinforcement Rates of Educators Enrolled in a Three Week Workshop on Behavior Modification.* Doctor's thesis, University of Virginia (Charlottesville, Va.), 1970. (*DAI* 31:4599A)

1182. KNAPP, WILLIAM MARTIN. *A Study of Teacher Personality Characteristics and Rated Effectiveness.* Doctor's thesis, University of Southern Mississippi (Hattiesburg, Miss.), 1970. (*DAI* 31:5712A)

1183. KNOX, JAMES BERNARD. *Characteristics of Teachers of Institutionalized Delinquent Youth.* Doctor's thesis, Ohio State University (Columbus, Ohio), 1970. (*DAI* 32:286A)

1184. KOELLING, JOHN ALBERT. *A Differential Study of Prospective Elementary School Teachers at the University of Oregon: A Comparison of Those Preferring Lower and Upper Teaching Levels.* Doctor's thesis, University of Oregon (Eugene, Ore.), 1970. (*DAI* 31:5251A)

1185. LACAMERA, JOSEPH, JR. *The Effectiveness of Selected Intellectual and Non-Intellectual Variables in the Selection of Residence Hall Staff at the University of Colorado.* Doctor's thesis, University of Colorado (Boulder, Colo.), 1970. (*DAI* 32:753A)

1186. LUCERO, DONALD LAURO. *An Analysis of the Relationship of Values and Needs to Counselor Effectiveness in a Selected Group of Counselors in Training.* Doctor's thesis, University of New Mexico (Albuquerque, N.M.), 1970. (*DAI* 31:6346A)

1187. NAZZARI, RICHARD HAROLD. *The Relationship Between Selected Personality Characteristics of Elementary School Principals and Four Administrative Performance Factors.* Doctor's thesis, Rutgers—The State University (New Brunswick, N.J.), 1970. (*DAI* 31:3833A)

1188. O'CONNOR, CONSTANCE ANN. *A Study of Personality Needs Involved in the Selection of Specific Leisure Interest Groups.* Doctor's thesis, University of Southern California (Los Angeles, Calif.), 1970. (*DAI* 31:5865A)

1189. OGILVIE, BRUCE C., AND TUTKO, THOMAS. "Self-Perception as Compared With Measured Personality of Selected Male Physical Educators," pp. 73–7. In *Contemporary Psychology of Sport.* Proceedings of the Second International Congress of Sport Psychology, Washington, D.C., 1968. Chicago, Ill.: Athletic Institute, 1970. Pp. xix, 878. *

1190. QUELLO, DANIEL Y. "A Comparative Investigation of the Personality Profiles of CPE and Non-CPE Theological Students." *J Pastoral Care* 24(4):240–3 D '70. * (*PA* 47:758)

1191. REFICE, RONALD J. *A Study of the Relationship of Interest and Personality Variables Using a Multimethod Factor Analysis.* Doctor's thesis, University of Kansas (Lawrence, Kan.), 1970. (*DAI* 31:5777A)

1192. ROMINE, PHILIP GORDON. *The Combined Moderating Influences of Personality Variables on the Accuracy of Prediction of Academic Success.* Doctor's thesis, University of Alabama (University, Ala.), 1970. (*DAI* 31:5213A)

1193. SANDFORD, MAY DANIELS. *The Relationship Between Home Economics Teachers' Self-Awareness and Their Perception of Inner City Seventh- and Eighth-Grade Negro Girls' Coping Behavior Related to Problems With Boys.* Doctor's thesis, Columbia University (New York, N.Y.), 1970. (*DAI* 31:3790A)

1194. SHIPMAN, EDWIN ABRAHAM. *A Comparison of Selected Values and Needs of Employed and Non-Employed College Students at the University of Northern Colorado.* Doctor's thesis, University of Northern Colorado (Greeley, Colo.), 1970. (*DAI* 31:2791A)

1195. SLOCUM, JOHN W., JR.; MILLER, JAMES D.; AND MISSHANK, MICHAEL J. "Needs, Environmental Work Satisfaction and Job Performance." *Training & Develop J* 24(2):12–5 F '70. * (*PA* 44:19648)

1196. SMITH, MARIE ALLEN. *Menstrual Disorders: Incidence and Relationship to Attitudes, Manifest Needs, and Scholastic Achievement in College Freshman Women.* Doctor's thesis, University of Denver (Denver, Colo.), 1970. (*DAI* 31:6354A)

1197. SMITH, ROBERT CHARLES. *Self Esteem and the Relationship Between Manifest Need of Nurturance and Satisfaction.* Doctor's thesis, University of Maryland (College Park, Md.), 1970. (*DAI* 31:7615B)

1198. SNYDER, PHILLIP CARL. *A Comparative Analysis of the Expectations of Experienced Advisers and Experienced Administrators Toward the Personality Traits of a Secondary Education Adviser in a Developing Country.* Doctor's thesis, University (Athens, Ohio), 1970. (*DAI* 31:3842A)

1199. SORENSON, DAVID PETER. *Student Attitudes, Judgments, Usage, and Personal Characteristics in Regard to Marijuana and LSD at the University of Northern Colorado.* Doctor's thesis, University of Northern Colorado (Greeley, Colo.), 1970. (*DAI* 31:4268A)

1200. STASSER, DOROTHY ANN. *Nonintellectual Factors in College Achievement at Bethany Nazarene College.* Doctor's thesis, Oklahoma State University (Stillwater, Okla.), 1970. (*DAI* 31:5139A)

1201. STEVENSON, JOANNE SABOL. *Determining the Discriminatory Value of Selected Personal Variables as Predictors of Specialty Choice in Nursing.* Doctor's thesis, Ohio State University (Columbus, Ohio), 1970. (*DAI* 32:189A)

1202. SULLIVAN, BLOOMER DON. *The Correlates of Leadership Behavior of Chief Administrative Officers in Selected Junior Colleges.* Doctor's thesis, University of Missouri (Columbia, Mo.), 1970. (*DAI* 31:5736A)

1203. UTZ, VERNON RAY. *The Relation of Certain Personality, Value, and Interest Factors to a Choice of Elementary or Secondary Teaching Levels Among Women at the University of Oregon.* Doctor's thesis, University of Oregon (Eugene, Ore.), 1970. (*DAI* 31:5140A)

1204. WALTON, JOSEPH MOSES. *Predicting the Success of Prospective Teachers in an Urban Teacher Education Project.* Doctor's thesis, Ohio State University (Columbus, Ohio), 1970. (*DAI* 32:190A)

1205. ZURHELLEN, HENRY SCOTT. *A Study of Teacher Attitudes During an In-Service Education Program in Selected East Tennessee Schools.* Doctor's thesis, University of Tennessee (Knoxville, Tenn.), 1970. (*DAI* 31:4613A)

1206. ZURHELLEN, JOAN HARRIS. *An Evaluation of Attitude Changes Among Science Teachers During an ESCP In-Service Institute.* Doctor's thesis, University of Tennessee (Knoxville, Tenn.), 1970. (*DAI* 31:4613A)

1207. ADAMS, WESLEY J. "Sex Composition in Family Life Courses: How Important Is This?" *Family Coordinator* 20(1):55–62 Ja '71. *

1208. BAILEY, ROGER L. "Testing Holland's Theory." *Meas & Eval Guid* 4(2):107–14 Jl '71. *

1209. BAIRD, JOHN SANFORD, JR. *A Multivariate Developmental Study of Political Ideology and Intolerance.* Doctor's thesis, North Carolina State University (Raleigh, N.C.), 1971. (*DAI* 32:6633B)

1210. BALLARD, STANLEY NEWTON. *The Effects of Motivational Group Techniques Upon Selected Personality and Behavioral Variables.* Doctor's thesis, North Texas State University (Denton, Tex.), 1971. (*DAI* 32:1844A)

1211. BERNHARDSON, CLEMENS S., AND FISHER, RONALD J. "The Relationship Between Personal Desirability and Endorsement With a Forced-Choice Technique." *Multiv Behav Res* 6(1):63–73 Ja '71. * (*PA* 46:9073)

1212. BLACKBURN, LAURA FAIRFAX. *Intern Counseling Competence as a Function of Supervisor and Intern Personality Characteristics.* Doctor's thesis, University of Missouri (Kansas City, Mo.), 1971. (*DAI* 31:6338A)

1213. BOWDRE, JACK ROSS, III. *Some Personality Differences Between Undergraduates Female Volunteers and Non-Volunteers for an Hypnosis Experiment as Measured by the Edwards Personal Preference Schedule.* Master's thesis, Radford College (Radford, Va.), 1971.

1214. BURTON, D. A. "A Factor Analysis of the Edwards Personal Preference Schedule and 16 PF in a Psychiatric Population." *J Clin Psychol* 27(2):248–51 Ap '71. * (*PA* 46:7153)

1215. CAMPOS, PRISCILLA BERNADETTE. *Representative Personality Dimensions Characteristic of Different Occupational Choice in the Paramedical Field.* Doctor's thesis, University of the Pacific (Stockton, Calif.), 1971. (*DAI* 32:733A)

Edwards Personal Preference Schedule

1216. CENTERS, RICHARD. "Evaluating the Loved One: The Motivational Congruency Factor." *J Personality* 39(2):303–18 Je '71. * (*PA* 47:907)

1217. CHADIALLY, REHANA, AND FOSHEE, DONALD P. "Nationality, Attitude Similarity and Affiliation Need as Factors in Interpersonal Attraction." *Indian J Psychol* 46(2):125–34 Je '71. *

1218. CLAR, PHILIP NORMAN. *The Relationship of Psychological Differentiation to Client Behavior in Vocational Choice Counseling.* Doctor's thesis, University of Michigan (Ann Arbor, Mich.), 1971. (*DAI* 32:1837B)

1219. DHALIWAL, AMAR SINGH. "Achievement-Motive as a Non-Intellectual Predictor of Scholastic Attainment." *Indian J Psychol* 46(3):265–79 S '71. *

1220. DIEKER, RICHARD J.; CRANE, LOREN; AND BROWN, CHARLES T. "Repeated Self-Viewings on Closed-Circuit Television as It Affects Changes in the Self-Concept and Personality Needs of Student Speakers." *Speech Teach* 20(2):131–42 Mr '71. *

1221. DI GIUSEPPE, RAYMOND A. "Correlation of Locus of Control With Four EPPS Items." *Psychol Rep* 28(1):290 F '71. * (*PA* 4:946)

1222. DIXON, PAUL W.; FUKUDA, NOBUKO K.; AND BERENS, ANNE E. "A Factor Analysis of EPPS Scales, Ability, and Achievement Measures." *J Exp Ed* 39(4):31–41 su '71. * (*PA* 47:1723)

1223. DUKE, BILLY WAYNE. *A Study of Certain Socio-Psychological Differences Among Migratory and Nonmigratory Single Sophomores at the University of Missouri—Columbia.* Doctor's thesis, University of Missouri (Columbia, Mo.), 1971. (*DAI* 32:1268A)

1224. DUNN, BENJAMIN ALLEN. *Stress and Personal Distance: An Analysis of Stress and Personal Distance as Related to Personality and Recreational Preferences.* Doctor's thesis, University of Georgia (Athens, Ga.), 1971. (*DAI* 32:4181B)

1225. EPPERLY, EDGAR VERN. *A Study of Teachers' Expressed Preference for Levels of Pupil Contact Presented by Simulated Teaching Situations and Its Relationship to Patterns of Needs and Years of Teaching Experience.* Doctor's thesis, George Peabody College for Teachers (Nashville, Tenn.), 1971. (*DAI* 32:3859A)

1226. FEDERICO, PAT-ANTHONY. "Sanction Assignment in a Dyad as a Function of Aggression and Outcome Quality." *J Social Psychol* 85(1):127–36 O '71. * (*PA* 47:4742)

1227. FERGUSON, EVA D. "Relationship Between Ego-Involvement Instructions and Various Motivation and Performance Measures." *Psychol Rep* 29(2):547–56 O '71. * (*PA* 47:8123)

1228. FISHER, GARY, AND RIVLIN, EPHRAIM. "Psychological Needs of Rapists." *Brit J Criminol* 11(2):182–5 Ap '71. *

1229. FITZGERALD, BERNARD J., AND PASEWARK, RICHARD A. "Sex Differences on the Edwards Personal Preference Schedule." *Psychol Rep* 29(3):892 D '71. * (*PA* 47:8937)

1230. FLETCHER, R., AND DOWELL, L. "Selected Personality Characteristics of High School Athletes and Nonathletes." *J Psychol* 77(1):39–41 F '71. * (*PA* 45:8203)

1231. FLETCHER, RAYMOND. "Correlations of EPPS Personality Traits and Intramural Participation." *Percept & Motor Skills* 32(1):242 F '71. * (*PA* 46:3775)

1232. FLETCHER, RAYMOND. "Differences Between Civilian and Corps Intramural Participants in Selected Personality Characteristics." *Psychol* 8(2):41–2 My '71. * (*PA* 47:2943)

1233. FLETCHER, RAYMOND. "Differences in Selected Psychological Characteristics of Participants and Nonparticipants in Activity." *Percept & Motor Skills* 32(1):301–2 F '71. * (*PA* 46:5552)

1234. GABLE, ROBERT KEITH. *A Multivariate Study of Work Value Orientations.* Doctor's thesis, State University of New York (Albany, N.Y.), 1971. (*DAI* 32:1997A)

1235. GARFIELD, SOL L., AND BERGIN, ALLEN E. "Therapeutic Conditions and Outcome." *J Abn Psychol* 77(2):108–14 Ap '71. * (*PA* 46:3194)

1236. GEHRING, DONALD DAVID. *Need Characteristics of Students Who Voluntarily Enrolled in Independent Study Courses: A Comparative Analysis.* Doctor's thesis, University of Georgia (Athens, Ga.), 1971. (*DAI* 32:4981A)

1237. GENNARINO, ELIZABETH B. *An Analysis of Need-Structures and Attitudes Toward Teaching, Among Full-Time Community College Faculty Members.* Doctor's thesis, University of Colorado (Boulder, Colo.), 1971. (*DAI* 32:1876A)

1238. GEORGE, RICKEY L. "Resident or Commuter: A Study of Personality Differences." *J Col Stud Personnel* 12(3):216–9 My '71. * (*PA* 46:11440)

1239. GEORGE, RICKEY L., AND MARSHALL, JON C. "Personality of Young Adults: College Versus Noncollege." *J Col Stud Personnel* 12(6):438–44 N '71. * (*PA* 47:9760)

1240. GROSZ, HANUS J., AND WAGONER, ROBERT. "MMPI and EPPS Profiles of High and Low Verbal Interactors in Therapy Groups." *Psychol Rep* 28(3):951–5 Je '71. * (*PA* 46:10991)

1241. GWALTNEY, WAYNE KEITH. *Reading in Upward Bound: An Evaluation of a Reading Improvement Course and an Analysis of Some Correlates of Reading Achievement.* Doctor's thesis, University of Georgia (Athens, Ga.), 1971. (*DAI* 32:3557A)

1242. HAMILTON, V., AND FREEMAN, P. "Academic Achievement and Student Personality Characteristics: Multivariate Study." *Brit J Sociol* 22(1):31–52 Mr '71. * (*PA* 47:3755)

1243. HARPER, JACK A. *Personality Traits Exhibited by Individual and Team Sport Athletes as Measured by the Edwards Personal Preference Schedule.* Master's thesis, University of North Dakota (Grand Forks, N.D.), 1971.

1244. HINES, TODD FRANKLIN. *A Multitrait-Multimethod Analysis of the Internal-External Control Concept.* Doctor's thesis, Washington University (St. Louis, Mo.), 1971. (*DAI* 32:5442B)

1245. HOFFMANN, HELMUT, AND NELSON, PAUL C. "Personality Characteristics of Alcoholics in Relation to Age and Intelligence." *Psychol Rep* 29(1):143–6 Ag '71. * (*PA* 47:3292)

1246. HOHMAN, ROBERT JOSEPH. *The Use of Selected Personality Characteristics and Role Expectations as Determiners for Successful Student-Teaching Assignments.* Doctor's thesis, Bowling Green State University (Bowling Green, Ohio), 1971. (*DAI* 32:2529A)

1247. HORNADAY, JOHN A., AND ABOUD, JOHN. "Characteristics of Successful Entrepreneurs." *Personnel Psychol* 24(2):141–53 su '71. * (*PA* 49:3400)

1248. HOYT, MICHAEL F., AND CENTERS, RICHARD. "Ego Disjunction as a Factor in Intersexual Attraction." *J Pers Assess* 35(4):367–74 Ag '71. * (*PA* 47:4801)

1249. IVERS, KENNETH JOHN. *An Investigation of Holland's (S) Social and (A) Artistic Personality Types With Music and Art Education Majors, and Applied Music and Art Majors.* Doctor's thesis, University of Kansas (Lawrence, Kan.), 1971. (*DAI* 32:1854A)

1250. JEGHELIAN, ALICE. *Persistence in Adult Students and Its Relationship to Selected Psychological Factors.* Doctor's thesis, Boston College (Chestnut Hill, Mass.), 1971. (*DAI* 32:3691A)

1251. JOHNSON, FRANK NORRIS. *A Comparison of the Perceptions of Sixth-Grade Male Teachers, Sixth-Grade Female Teachers, Elementary School Principals, and School Psychologists Regarding Their Own Needs and Those of Their Pupils.* Doctor's thesis, University of Southern California (Los Angeles, Calif.), 1971. (*DAI* 32:241A)

1252. KANITZ, HUGO EDWARD. *Predicting Effectiveness in Potential Teachers.* Doctor's thesis, Ohio State University (Columbus, Ohio), 1971. (*DAI* 32:1855A)

1253. KAPLAN, MARTIN F. "Response Hierarchy, Information Reception, and the Process of Person Perception." *Hum Relations* (England) 24(3):189–99 Je '71. * (*PA* 50:939)

1254. KARASICK, BERNARD WOLFE. *Organizational Climate and Its Relationship to Managerial Behavior.* Doctor's thesis, Purdue University (Lafayette, Ind.), 1971. (*DAI* 32:1266B)

1255. KIRCHNER, ELIZABETH P. "Undergraduate Military Training and Measures of Aggression." *J Pers Assess* 35(4):350–8 Ag '71. * (*PA* 47:4790)

1256. KNOX, WILLIAM HUGH. *A Comparative Study of Fraternity and Non-Fraternity Members on Selected Personality Variables.* Doctor's thesis, University of North Carolina (Chapel Hill, N.C.), 1971. (*DAI* 32:2421A)

1257. KORMAN, ABRAHAM K.; ANTONELLI, MARIE B.; SINGER, ROBERT D.; AND FEKETE, ADELE F. "The Generality of the Characteristics of 'Competent' People." *J Voc Behav* 1(2):201–8 Ap '71. * (*PA* 47:11855)

1258. KOZMA, FREDERICK, JR. *Personality Change in Institutionalized Psychotic and Non-Psychotic Populations.* Doctor's thesis, Pennsylvania State University (University Park, Pa.), 1971. (*DAI* 32:5445B)

1259. LEATHERWOOD, HELEN WAUGH. *The Effectiveness of Small-Group Procedures in the Classroom as Aids in Movement Toward Self-Actualization in Junior College Students.* Doctor's thesis, East Texas State University (Commerce, Tex.), 1971. (*DAI* 32:4988A)

1260. LEMKE, ELMER A., AND KIRCHNER, JOHN H. "A Multivariate Study of Handwriting, Intelligence, and Personality Correlates." *J Pers Assess* 35(6):584–92 D '71. * (*PA* 47:10876)

1261. LEVITT, EUGENE E.; LUBIN, BERNARD; AND DEWITT, KATHRYN N. "An Attempt to Develop an Objective Test Battery for the Selection of Nursing Students." *Nursing Res* 20(3):255–8 My–Je '71. * (*PA* 51:3969)

1262. LINN, MOTT ROBERTSON. *Achievement, Aptitude, Interest, and Personality Variables as Predictors of Curriculum, Graduation, and Placement.* Doctor's thesis, University of Pennsylvania (Philadelphia, Pa.), 1971. (*DAI* 32:1857A)

1263. MCKINNEY, DAVID WAYNE. *A Comparison of Personality Profiles of Employees in Selected Job Classifications in a Textile Company.* Master's thesis, University of North Carolina (Greensboro, N.C.), 1971.

1264. MARSHALL, JON C., AND GEORGE, RICKEY L. "Personality Differences Between Persons Choosing to Attend College and Persons Choosing Not to Attend College." *Col Stud J* 5(2):41–4 S–O '71. *

1265. MEGGINSON, MARY JEAN HAYDOCK. *The Relationship of the Edwards Personal Preference Schedule Variables to the Academic Achievement of Selected University of Mississippi Female Students Within Five Ability Levels.* Doctor's thesis, University of Mississippi (University, Miss.), 1971. (*DAI* 32:3696A)

1266. MEHAFFEY, THOMAS DAVID. *The Effects of a T-Group*

Experience on Clients With Measured High and Low Dependency Needs. Doctor's thesis, Indiana State University (Terre Haute, Ind.), 1971. (*DAI* 33:3299A)

1267. MITCHELL, RUSSELL AUSTIN, JR. *The Effect of Group Counseling Experiences in a Didactic Classroom Setting on Selected Personality Variables and Counseling Effectiveness.* Doctor's thesis, North Texas State University (Denton, Tex.), 1971. (*DAI* 32:6765A)

1268. MURPHY, FINIAN JOSEPH. *Personality Characteristics as Predictors of Counselor-Trainee Success in Practicum.* Doctor's thesis, Northern Illinois University (DeKalb, Ill.), 1971. (*DAI* 32:3697A)

1269. MURSTEIN, BERNARD I. "Self—Ideal-Self Discrepancy and the Choice of Marital Partner." *J Consult & Clin Psychol* 37(1):47–52 Ag '71. * (*PA* 47:913)

1270. NAVRAN, LESLIE, AND KENDALL, LORNE M. "A Canonical Correlational Analysis of the Strong Vocational Interest Blank, the Holland Vocational Preference Inventory, and the Edwards Personal Preference Schedule." *J Counsel Psychol* 18(6):514–9 N '71. * (*PA* 47:7653)

1271. O'HARA, RONALD JOHN. *The Associations Between Attitudinal Predispositions Toward Child Management (Interpretive Versus Behavior Modification) and Personality Characteristics.* Doctor's thesis, Wayne State University (Detroit, Mich.), 1971. (*DAI* 32:6213A)

1272. O'KEEFE, BETH EGAN. *Attitudes Towards Women's Liberation: Relationships Between Cooperation, Competition, Personality, and Demographic Variables.* Doctor's thesis, St. Louis University (St. Louis, Mo.), 1971. (*DAI* 33:1293B)

1273. O'REILLY, LAWRENCE BICHE. *Educational Plans of Working-Class Youth: A Survey of Manifest Needs and Goal-Discrepant Behavior.* Doctor's thesis, State University of New York (Albany, N.Y.), 1971. (*DAI* 32:1863A)

1274. ORPEN, CHRISTOPHER. "The Fakability of the Edwards Personal Preference Schedule in Personnel Selection." *Personnel Psychol* 24(1):1–4 sp '71. * (*PA* 47:3309)

1275. ORPEN, CHRISTOPHER. "The Susceptibility of the EPPS to Faking in Simulated and Actual Employment Situations." *J Pers Assess* 35(5):480–5 O '71. * (*PA* 47:9766)

1276. PAGE, MARY JEAN. *A Descriptive Analysis of Selected Attitudes, Interests, and Personality Characteristics of Mature College Women.* Doctor's thesis, North Texas State University (Denton, Tex.), 1971. (*DAI* 32:3699A)

1277. PARRILLO, VINCENT NICHOLAS. *Predicting Academic Success in College for Disadvantaged Students.* Doctor's thesis, Rutgers—The State University (New Brunswick, N.J.), 1971. (*DAI* 32:3457A)

1278. PASEWARK, RICHARD A.; FITZGERALD, BERNARD J.; AND WATSON, RILEY L. "Associated Personality Differences in Delinquents and Non-Delinquents." *J Pers Assess* 35(2):159–61 Ap '71. * (*PA* 47:3309)

1279. PETERSEN, WALTER HAROLD. *The Relationship Between Client Personality and Demographic Characteristics and Classification by Problem Type and Cause.* Doctor's thesis, University of Missouri (Columbia, Mo.), 1971. (*DAI* 32:4963A)

1280. PETERSON, LARRY DALE. *Student Attitudes and Perceptions of the Edwards Personal Preference Schedule as Used by the Counseling Center of the University of Northern Colorado.* Doctor's thesis, University of Northern Colorado (Greeley, Colo.), 1971. (*DAI* 32:3700A)

1281. PIETROFESA, JOHN J., AND VAN HOOSE, WILLIAM H. "Participant Change During an EPDA Institute: Personality, Attitudinal, and Learning Dimensions." *Counselor Ed & Sup* 11(2):147–52 D '71. * (*PA* 47:9768)

1282. POPE, SHARON KAY. *Effects of Female Career Role Models on Occupational Aspirations, Attitude, and Personalities of High School Seniors.* Doctor's thesis, University of Missouri (Columbia, Mo.), 1971. (*DAI* 32:4964A)

1283. POSAVAC, EMIL J. "Dimensions of Trait Preferences and Personality Type." *J Pers & Social Psychol* 19(3):274–81 S '71. * (*PA* 47:2881)

1284. QUAGLIOTTI, CAROL A. *A Comparison Between Physical Characteristics and Personality Traits in Women.* Master's thesis, Appalachian State University (Boone, N.C.), 1971.

1285. RICHMAN, BRUCE JACK. *A Test of the Theme Interference Hypothesis in Mental Health Consultation.* Doctor's thesis, University of Texas (Austin, Tex.), 1971. (*DAI* 33:450B)

1286. ROBBINS, PAUL R.; TANCK, ROLAND H.; AND MEYERSBURG, HERMAN A. "Psychological Factors in Smoking, Drinking, and Drug Experimentation." *J Clin Psychol* 27(4):450–2 O '71. * (*PA* 47:8861)

1287. SCHWARTZ, RONALD ALAN. *The Sexual Behavior of Obese Women.* Doctor's thesis, Illinois Institute of Technology (Chicago, Ill.), 1971. (*DAI* 32:1226B)

1288. SHARPE, LOUIS K., AND PETERSON, ROBERT A. "A Comparison of Two Approaches to the Analysis of Personality Differences." *J Psychol* 79(2):257–62 N '71. * (*PA* 47:6811)

1289. SIMS, B. WAYNE. *The Effect of Edwards Personal Preference Schedule Variables Upon the Prediction of Academic Success for Low Performing College Students.* Master's thesis, Central Missouri State University (Warrensburg, Mo.), 1971.

1290. SLOCUM, JOHN W., JR., AND HAND, HERBERT H. "Prediction of Job Success and Employee Satisfaction for Executives

and Foremen." *Training & Develop J* 25(10):28–36 O '71. * (*PA* 48:3980)

1291. SMITH, NANETTE PATCHELL. *An Analysis of the Relationship of Counselor Characteristics and Behavior Exhibited in Group Experience With Counselor Effectiveness in a Selected Group of Counselor Trainees.* Doctor's thesis, University of New Mexico (Albuquerque, N.M.), 1971. (*DAI* 32:3704A)

1292. SNORTUM, JOHN R., AND MYERS, HECTOR F. "Intensity of T-Group Relationships as a Function of Interaction." *Int J Group Psychother* 21(2):190–201 Ap '71. * (*PA* 48:1105)

1293. SQUIER, ROGER W., JR. "The Effect of Feedback Information and Behavior Consistency on Accuracy of Social Prediction." *J Social Psychol* 83(2):255–64 Ap '71. * (*PA* 46:2982)

1294. STAIERT, PAUL JOHN. *Changes of Selected Attitudes, Values, Needs and Personality Traits of Participants in a Fellowship Program for Prospective Teachers of the Disadvantaged.* Doctor's thesis, University of Denver (Denver, Colo.), 1971. (*DAI* 32:3803A)

1295. WALLACE, DARLENE JOAN. *Campus Environment and Its Relationship to Personal Needs as Perceived by Selected Sophomores at Four Colorado Junior Colleges.* Doctor's thesis, University of Northern Colorado (Greeley, Colo.), 1971. (*DAI* 32:3733A)

1296. WEBERSINN, ALFRED LAURENCE. *Creativity and Personality Traits in College Students.* Doctor's thesis, Case Western Reserve University (Cleveland, Ohio), 1971. (*DAI* 32:3107A)

1297. WEICK, LUCINDA KATHRYN. *An Analysis of the Influence of Experience in Physical Activities on Certain Psychological-Social and Physical Needs of University Freshman and Sophomore Men and Women.* Doctor's thesis, University of Missouri (Columbia, Mo.), 1971. (*DAI* 32:3080A)

1298. WEIGEL, RICHARD G.; WEIGEL, VIRGINIA M.; AND HEBERT, JOHN A. "Non-Volunteer Subjects: Temporal Effects." *Psychol Rep* 28(1):191–2 F '71. * (*PA* 46: 5449)

1299. WIGGINS, JERRY S.; GOLDBERG, LEWIS R.; AND APPELBAUM, MARK. "MMPI Content Scales: Interpretative Norms and Correlations With Other Scales." *J Consult & Clin Psychol* 37(3):403–10 D '71. * (*PA* 47:8950)

1300. WILKINSON, ALMA EARL; PRADO, WILLIAM M.; WILLIAMS, WOODROW O.; AND SCHNADT, FREDERICK W. "Psychological Test Characteristics and Length of Stay in Alcoholism Treatment." *Q J Studies Alcohol* 32(1A):60–5 Mr '71. * (*PA* 46:7116)

1301. WILSON, MARILYN L., AND GREENE, ROGER L. "Personality Characteristics of Female Homosexuals." *Psychol Rep* 28(2):407–12 Ap '71. * (*PA* 46:7151)

1302. WOODY, ROBERT H. "Self-Understanding Seminars: The Effects of Group Psychotherapy in Counselor Training." *Counselor Ed & Sup* 10(2):112–9 w '71. * (*PA* 47:1384)

1303. WOODY, ROBERT H., AND DUBNER, MARY ANN P. "British and Commonwealth Counselors: An Investigation of Counselor Characteristics and Theoretical Views." *Counselor Ed & Sup* 10(3):233–41 sp '71. * (*PA* 47:1686)

1304. WUBBOLDING, ROBERT EDWARD. *The Relationship Between Pre-Measured Personality Variables and Counselor Behavior During Structured Interviews.* Doctor's thesis, University of Cincinnati (Cincinnati, Ohio), 1971. (*DAI* 32:3711A)

1305. YURA, MICHAEL THOMAS. *The Personality Traits and Vocational Interests of Guidance Students.* Doctor's thesis, Ohio State University (Columbus, Ohio), 1971. (*DAI* 32:3711A)

1306. ZACCARIA, LUCY, AND CREASER, JAMES. "Factors Related to Persistence in an Urban Commuter University." *J Col Stud Personnel* 12(4):286–91 Jl '71. * (*PA* 47:7550)

CUMULATIVE NAME INDEX

[1165]

Edwards Personality Inventory. Grades 11–16 and adults; 1966–67; EPI; 53 scores listed below; 5 booklets; Allen L. Edwards; Science Research Associates, Inc. *

a) BOOKLETS IA AND IB. 14 scores: plans and organizes things, intellectually oriented, persistent, self-confident, has cultural interests, enjoys being the center of attention, carefree, conforms, is a leader, kind to others, worries about making a good impression on others, seeks new experiences, likes to be alone, interested in the behavior of others.

b) BOOKLET 2. 11 scores: anxious about his performance, avoids facing problems, is a perfectionist, absentminded, sensitive to criticism, likes a set routine, wants sympathy, avoids arguments, conceals his feelings, easily influenced, feels misunderstood.

c) BOOKLET 3. 15 scores: motivated to succeed, impressed by status, desires recognition, plans work efficiently, cooperative, competitive, articulate, feels superior, logical, assumes responsibility, self-centered, makes friends easily, independent in his opinions, is a hard worker, neat in dress.

d) BOOKLET 4. 13 scores: self-critical, critical of others, active, talks about himself, becomes angry, helps others, careful about his possessions, understands himself, considerate, dependent, shy, informed about current affairs, virtuous.

For additional information, reviews by Lewis R. Goldberg and Warren T. Norman, and excerpted reviews by Thomas J. Bouchard, Jr. and Benjamin Kleinmuntz, see 7:73 (9 references); see also P:68 (2 references).

REFERENCES THROUGH 1971

1-2. See P:68.
3-11. See 7:73.
12. ABBOTT, ROBERT D. "A Factor Analysis of the CPI and EPI." *Ed & Psychol Meas* 31(2):549-53 su '71. *
13. BRAUN, JOHN R., AND FARRELL, ROBERT M. "Differential Reliability of Personality Inventory Scores Under Standard vs Faking Instructions." *Psychol Rep* 29(2):666 O '71. * (*PA* 47:8944)
14. GELLOR, JAIME MENDEZ. *Student Perceptions of Campus Environment.* Doctor's thesis, University of British Columbia (Vancouver, B.C., Canada), 1971. (*DAI* 32:6758A)
15. SMITH, DAVID JOHN. *A Comparison of the Effects of Short-Term Individual Counseling, Group Counseling, and Sensitivity Training on the Self-Concepts of Male College Students.* Doctor's thesis, Boston College (Chestnut Hill, Mass.), 1971. (*DAI* 32:1867A)

CUMULATIVE NAME INDEX

Abbott, R. D.: 12
Bouchard, T. J.: *exc*, 7:73
Braun, J. R.: 7, 13
Edwards, A. L.: 4
Farrell, R. M.: 13
Fowler, R. S.: 3
Gellor, J. M.: 14
Goldberg, L. R.: *rev*, 7:73
Kleinmuntz, B.: *exc*, 7:73
Lunneborg, P. W.: 2, 8
Norman, W. T.: *rev*, 7:73
Oakland, J. A.: 1, 5-6, 9
Pearson, P. H.: 10
Pfister, G. C.: 11
Smith, D. J.: 15

[1166]

The Ego-Ideal and Conscience Development Test. Ages 12-18; 1969; EICDT; 9 scores: home and family, inner development, community relations, rules and law, school and education, romance and psychosexual, economic sufficiency, self-actualization, total; R. N. Cassel; Monitor. *

For additional information, see 7:74 (5 references).

REFERENCES THROUGH 1971

1-5. See 7:74.

CUMULATIVE NAME INDEX

Blum, L. P.: 1
Cassel, R. N.: 1-2, 5
Chiu, A.: 3
Reise, M. W.: 4

[1167]

The Ego Strength Q-Sort Test. Grades 9-16 and adults; 1956-58; ESQST; 6 scores: ego-status, social status, goal setting and striving, good mental health, physical status, total; 1958 form essentially the same as form copyrighted 1956; Russell N. Cassel; Psychometric Affiliates. *

For additional information, see P:69; for reviews by Allen L. Edwards and Harrison G. Gough, see 6:88 (3 references).

REFERENCES THROUGH 1971

1-3. See 6:88.
4. SWEARINGEN, ARMELDA HARRIS. *Correlates of Non-Conforming Behavior of Domiciled Veterans.* Doctor's thesis, Ohio State University (Columbus, Ohio), 1963. (*DA* 24:4808)

CUMULATIVE NAME INDEX

Bailey, M. A.: 3
Cassel, R. N.: 1-2
Cohen, J.: 3
Edwards, A. L.: *rev*, 6:88
Gough, H. G.: *rev*, 6:88
Harriman, B. L.: 2
Swearingen, A. H.: 4
Warshaw, L.: 3

[1168]

Elizur Test of Psycho-Organicity: Children and Adults. Ages 6 and over, 10 and over; 1959-69; ETPO; brain injury; 3 scores: drawings, digits, blocks; Abraham Elizur; Western Psychological Services. *

For additional information, reviews by Joseph M. Wepman and Aubrey J. Yates, and an excerpted review by Muriel D. Lezak, see 7:75 (5 references).

REFERENCES THROUGH 1971

1-5. See 7:75.

CUMULATIVE NAME INDEX

Elizur, A.: 1-4
Kraus, J.: 5
Lezak, M. D.: *exc*, 7:75
Wepman, J. M.: *rev*, 7:75
Yates, A. J.: *rev*, 7:75

[1169]

*Embedded Figures Test. Ages 10 and over; 1950-71; EFT; test by Herman A. Witkin; combined manual (for this and two other embedded figures tests) by Herman A. Witkin, Philip K. Oltman, Evelyn Raskin, and Stephen A. Karp; Consulting Psychologists Press, Inc. *

For additional information, see P:71 (47 references); for reviews by Harrison G. Gough and Leona E. Tyler, see 6:89 (24 references); see also 5:49 (9 references).

REFERENCES THROUGH 1971

1-9. See 5:49.
10-33. See 6:89.
34-80. See P:71.
81. BOUND, MAE MATTHISEN. *A Study of the Relationship Between Witkin's Indices of Field Dependency and Eysenck's Indices of Neuroticism.* Doctor's thesis, Purdue University (Lafayette, Ind.), 1957. (*DA* 17:2062)
82. GRUEN, ARNO. "A Critique and Re-Evaluation of Witkin's Perception and Perception-Personality Work." *J General Psychol* 56:73-93 Ja '57. * (*PA* 33:2742)
83. JACKSON, DOUGLAS N. "Intellectual Ability and Mode of Perception." Abstract. *J Consult Psychol* 21:458 D '57. * (*PA* 33:2744, title only)
84. WERTHEIM, JACK, AND MEDNICK, SARNOFF A. "The Achievement Motive and Field Independence." *J Consult Psychol* 22:38 F '58. * (*PA* 33:5862)
85. CALLAWAY, ENOCH. "The Influence of Amobarbital (Amylobarbitone) and Methamphetamine on the Focus of Attention." *J Mental Sci* (England) 105:382-92 Ap '59. * (*PA* 34:4429)
86. WITKIN, HERMAN A.; KARP, STEPHEN A.; AND GOODENOUGH, DONALD R. "Dependence in Alcoholics." *Q J Studies Alcohol* 20:493-504 S '59. * (*PA* 34:6286)
87. YOUNG, HARL H., JR. "A Test of Witkin's Field-Dependence Hypothesis." *J Abn & Social Psychol* 59:188-92 S '59. * (*PA* 34:2798)
88. ELLIOTT, ROGERS. *Interrelationships Among Measures of Field Dependence Ability, and Personality Traits.* Doctor's thesis, University of Illinois (Urbana, Ill.), 1960. (*DA* 21:3163)
89. BRYANT, ARTHUR RUSSELL PAUL. *An Investigation of Process-Reactive Schizophrenia With Relation to Perception of Visual Space.* Doctor's thesis, University of Utah (Salt Lake City, Utah), 1961. (*DA* 22:2460)
90. GARDNER, RILEY W. "Cognitive Controls of Attention Deployment as Determinants of Visual Illusions." *J Abn & Social Psychol* 62:120-7 Ja '61. * (*PA* 36:3BD20G)
91. LINTON, HARRIET B.; EPSTEIN, LAWRENCE; AND HARTFORD, HUNTINGTON. "Personality and Perceptual Correlates of Secondary Beginning Strokes in Handwriting." *Percept & Motor Skills* 12:271-81 Je '61. * (*PA* 36:2HE71L)
92. FARROW, BOBBY J., AND SANTOS, JOHN F. "On Conditionability, Personality, and Perception." *Percept & Motor Skills* 15:578 D '62. * (*PA* 38:2620)
93. CANCRO, RALPH. *The Relation of Laterality of Brain Lesion to Intellectual Dysfunction.* Doctor's thesis, Columbia University (New York, N.Y.), 1963. (*DA* 24:2120)
94. WALLER, RONALD CHESTER. *The Effect of Hue Change on Judgment of Facial Expression.* Doctor's thesis, University of California (Los Angeles, Calif.), 1963. (*DA* 24:2128)
95. BROWN, SHIRLEY C. *Cognitive Style, as Preferential Organizing Tendency, in Serial Anticipation Learning and Free Recall.* Doctor's thesis, Wayne State University (Detroit, Mich.), 1964. (*DA* 28:4743B)
96. EGAN, GERARD VINCENT. *Antecedents and Consequents of Cross-Identification in Adolescent Females.* Doctor's thesis, St. Louis University (St. Louis, Mo.), 1964. (*DA* 25:4814)
97. HILL, EVELYN FOSTER. *Affect Aroused by Color, a Function of Stimulus Strength.* Doctor's thesis, Catholic University of America (Washington, D.C.), 1964. (*DA* 25:2611)
98. HUSTMYER, FRANK E., JR., AND KARNES, EDWARD. "Background Autonomic Activity and 'Analytic Perception.'" *J Abn & Social Psychol* 68:467-8 Ap '64. * (*PA* 39:2010)
99. JANNUCCI, GLORIA I. *Size Constancy in Schizophrenia: A Study of Subgroup Differences.* Doctor's thesis, Rutgers—The State University (New Brunswick, N.J.), 1964. (*DA* 26:503)
100. POWELL, BARBARA JOAN. *A Study of the Perceptual Field Approach of Normal Subjects and Schizophrenic Patients Under Conditions of an Aversive Stimulus.* Doctor's thesis, Washington University (St. Louis, Mo.), 1964. (*DA* 26:1173)
101. BLOOMBERG, MORTON. "Field Independence-Dependence and Susceptibility to Distraction." *Percept & Motor Skills* 20:805-13 Je '65. * (*PA* 39:13427)
102. BRUCE, DONALD KENNETH, JR. *The Effect of Field Dependence and Anxiety on the Perception of Social Stimuli.* Doctor's thesis, University of Utah (Salt Lake City, Utah), 1965. (*DA* 26:3475)
103. DYK, RUTH B., AND WITKIN, HERMAN A. "Family Experiences Related to the Development of Differentiation in Children." *Child Develop* 36:21-55 Mr '65. * (*PA* 39:11936)
104. FELDMAN, RUTH CAMM. *A Study of Cognitive Style*

and Some Personality Variables in Relation to the Conceptual Performance of Emotionally Disturbed Adolescents. Doctor's thesis, Temple University (Philadelphia, Pa.), 1965. (DA 26:1773)

105. GIBEAU, PHILIP JOSEPH. Field Dependency and the Process-Reactive Dimension in Schizophrenia. Doctor's thesis, Purdue University (Lafayette, Ind.), 1965. (DA 26:1775)

106. KARP, STEPHEN A.; WITKIN, HERMAN A.; AND GOODENOUGH, DONALD R. "Alcoholism and Psychological Differentiation: Effect of Achievement of Sobriety on Field Dependence." Q J Studies Alcohol 26:580–5 D '65. * (PA 40:4394)

107. KASWAN, JAQUES; HARALSON, SALLY; AND CLINE, RUTH. "Variables in Perceptual and Cognitive Organization and Differentiation." J Personality 33:164–77 Je '65. * (PA 40:2418)

108. OGDEN, WILLIAM EUGENE. Field Dependency in a Sample of University Counseling Center Clients. Doctor's thesis, University of Kansas (Lawrence, Kan.), 1965. (DA 27:679A)

109. SCHONBAR, ROSALEA ANN. "Differential Dream Recall Frequency as a Component of 'Life Style.'" J Consult Psychol 29:468–74 O '65. * (PA 40:105)

110. STEINGART, JOYCE N. An Experimental Investigation of the Relationship Between Field Articulation and Anxiety in Latency Children. Doctor's thesis, New York University (New York, N.Y.), 1965. (DA 26:1783)

111. MASSOTH, NEIL ALAN. The Relationship of Psychological Differentiation to Stimulus Generalization in Two Modalities. Doctor's thesis, Washington University (St. Louis, Mo.), 1966. (DA 27:4579B)

112. ROSETT, HENRY L.; NACKENSON, BURTON L.; ROBBINS, HERBERT; AND SAPIRSTEIN, MILTON R. "Personality and Cognitive Characteristics of Engineering Students: Implications for the Occupational Psychiatrist." Am J Psychiatry 122:1147–52 Ap '66. *

113. ZUCKERMAN, MARVIN; PERSKY, HAROLD; HOPKINS, T. ROBERT; MURTAUGH, THOMAS; BASU, G. K.; AND SCHILLING, MARY. "Comparison of Stress Effects of Perceptual and Social Isolation." Arch Gen Psychiatry 14:356–65 Ap '66. * (PA 40:6182)

114. BUZBY, DALLAS E. "Precognition and a Test of Sensory Perception." J Parapsychol 31:135–42 Je '67. * (PA 41:12705)

115. DAWSON, JOHN L. M. "Cultural and Physiological Influences Upon Spatial-Perceptual Processes in West Africa, Part I." Int J Psychol (France) 2(2):115–28 '67. * (PA 41:15125)

116. DAWSON, JOHN L. M. "Cultural and Physiological Influences Upon Spatial-Perceptual Processes in West Africa, Part II." Int J Psychol (France) 2(3):171–85 '67. * (PA 43:5194)

117. ELITCHER, HELENE. Children's Causal Thinking as a Function of Cognitive Style and Question Wording. Doctor's thesis, New York University (New York, N.Y.), 1967. (DA 28:1294A)

118. MAYER, ANNE DAVISON. Preferences in Level of Conceptualization as Related to Motor Inhibition and Field Dependence. Doctor's thesis, Columbia University (New York, N.Y.), 1967. (DA 28:2628B)

119. STEWART, RALPH H. "Birth Order and Dependency." J Pers & Social Psychol 6:192–4 Je '67. * (PA 41:10350)

120. STUART, IRVING R. "A Culture-Free Factor in Reading Grade Level: Perceptual Style." Abstract. Proc Interam Congr Psychol 10(1966):459 '67. *

121. WITKIN, HERMAN A.; AND OLTMAN, PHILIP K. "Cognitive Style." Int J Neurol (Uruguay) 6(2):119–37 '67. *

122. BUZBY, DALLAS E. "Precognition and Clairvoyance as Related to the Draw-a-Man Test." J Parapsychol 32:244–7 D '68. * (PA 43:12016)

123. CABE, PATRICK A. "The Relation Between the Rod-and-Frame Test and Witkin's Embedded Figures Test." Ed & Psychol Meas 28:1243–5 w '68. * (PA 44:5880)

124. CARROLL, LAWRENCE THOMAS. An Investigation of the Internal-External Control Construct in a Population of Patients Addicted to Narcotic Drugs. Doctor's thesis, University of Kentucky (Lexington, Ky.), 1968. (DAI 30:1893B)

125. COHN, MARVIN LESTER. Field Dependence-Independence and Reading Comprehension. Doctor's thesis, New York University (New York, N.Y.), 1968. (DA 29:476A)

126. CONKLIN, RODNEY C.; MUIR, WALTER; AND BOERSMA, FREDERIC J. "Field Dependency-Independency and Eye-Movement Patterns." Percept & Motor Skills 26:59–65 F '68. * (PA 42:9785)

127. DARLINGTON, MERRILL DEAN. An Actor-Reactor Concept of Internal-External Control and Articulated-Global Cognitive Style: A Construct Validity Test. Doctor's thesis, University of Oregon (Eugene, Ore.), 1968. (DAI 30:830B)

128. DAVIDOV, WILLIAM H. The Relationship of the Concept of Differentiation to the Structure of Verbal Behavior. Doctor's thesis, University of Florida (Gainesville, Fla.), 1968. (DAI 30:2414B)

129. DICKSTEIN, LOUIS S. "Field Independence in Concept Attainment." Percept & Motor Skills 27:635–42 O '68. * (PA 43:4803)

130. FINNIE, FRANCES RUTH. The Relationship Between Perceptual Field Articulation and Intellectual Functioning in Paranoid Male Schizophrenics. Doctor's thesis, George Washington University (Washington, D.C.), 1968.

131. FITZGIBBONS, DAVID JOSEPH. Task and Social Orientation: An Experimental Study of Field Dependence. "Arousal," and Memory for Incidental Material. Doctor's thesis, New York University (New York, N.Y.), 1968. (DAI 30:379B)

132. GREENWALD, EDDE R. Perceptual Style in Relation to Role Choices and Motivational Variables. Doctor's thesis, Yeshiva University (New York, N.Y.), 1968. (DA 29:2192B)

133. HOUSTON, B. KENT. "Inhibition and the Facilitating Effect of Noise on Interference Tasks." Percept & Motor Skills 27:947–50 D '68. * (PA 43:7659)

134. IHILEVICH, DAVID. The Relationship of Defense Mechanisms to Field Dependence-Independence. Doctor's thesis, University of Cincinnati (Cincinnati, Ohio), 1968. (DAI 29:1843B)

135. KERNALEGUEN, ANNE PAULE. Creativity Level, Perceptual Style and Peer Perception of Attitudes Towards Clothing. Doctor's thesis, Utah State University (Logan, Utah), 1968. (DA 29:2960B)

136. KISSIN, BENJAMIN; ROSENBLATT, SIDNEY M.; AND MACHOVER, SOLOMON. "Prognostic Factors in Alcoholism." Psychiatric Res Rep Am Psychiatric Assn 24:22–43 Mr '68. * (PA 43:1099)

137. LEWIS, LAURA H. "Acquiescence Response Set: Construct or Artifact?" J Proj Tech & Pers Assess 32:578–84 D '68. * (PA 43:9763)

138. MACARTHUR, RUSSELL. "Some Differential Abilities of Northern Canadian Native Youth." Int J Psychol (France) 3(1):43–50 '68. * (PA 42:15325)

139. McWHINNIE, HAROLD J. "Some Relationships Between Creativity and Perception in Sixth Grade Children (1)." Scientia Paedagogica Experimentalis (Belgium) 5(1):84–90 '68. * (PA 45:2137)

140. NASH, CATHERINE S., AND NASH, CARROLL B. "Effect of Target Selection, Field Dependence, and Body Concept on ESP Performance." J Parapsychol 32:248–57 D '68. * (PA 43:12019)

141. PRESSEY, ALEXANDER W., AND KOFFMAN, GOLDA. "Figural Aftereffects, Illusions and the Dimension of Field Dependence." Psychon Sci 10:279–80 Mr 15 '68. * (PA 42:8194)

142. SCHIMEK, J. G. "Cognitive Style and Defenses: A Longitudinal Study of Intellectualization and Field Independence." J Abn Psychol 73:575–80 D '68. * (PA 43:3996)

143. SILVERSTONE, STANLEY, AND KISSIN, BENJAMIN. "Field Dependence in Essential Hypertension and Peptic Ulcer." J Psychosom Res 12:157–61 Ag '68. * (PA 43:8520)

144. STELLE, WALTER WILLIAM. Field-Dependency and Process-Reactive Schizophrenia. Master's thesis, College of William and Mary (Williamsburg. Va.), 1968.

145. THORNTON, CARL L.; BARRETT, GERALD V.; AND DAVIS, JAMES A. "Field Dependence and Target Identification." Hum Factors 10:493–6 O '68. * (PA 43:8826)

146. WACHTEL, PAUL L. "Style and Capacity in Analytic Functioning." J Personality 36:202–12 Je '68. * (PA 42:17216)

147. ARBUTHNOT, JACK, AND GRUENFELD, LEOPOLD. "Field Independence and Educational-Vocational Interests." Abstract. J Consult & Clin Psychol 33(5):631 O '69. * (PA 44:2325)

148. BARRETT, MICHAEL JEROME. Some Behavioral Attributes of Professional Audit Independence. Doctor's thesis, University of Colorado (Boulder, Colo.), 1969. (DAI 30:4543A)

149. BLOOMBERG, MORTON. "Differences Between Field Independent and Field Dependent Persons on the Stroop Color-Word Test." J Clin Psychol 25(1):45 Ja '69. * (PA 43:9757)

150. BRESKIN, STEPHEN, AND GORMAN, BERNARD S. "On Rigidity and Field-Dependence." Percept & Motor Skills 29(2):541–2 O '69. * (PA 44:3651)

151. BRINTON, GEORGE, AND ROULEAU, ROBERT A. "Automating the Hidden and Embedded Figures Tests." Percept & Motor Skills 29(2):401–2 O '69. * (PA 44:3652)

152. BURDICK, J. ALAN. "A Field-Independent Alcoholic Population." J Psychol 73(2):163–6 N '69. * (PA 44:8769)

153. CANCRO, ROBERT, AND VOTH, HAROLD M. "Autokinesis and Psychological Differentiation." Percept & Motor Skills 28(1):99–103 F '69. * (PA 43:11297)

154. CULVER, CHARLES M., AND DUNHAM, FRANCES. "Birth Order and Spatial-Perceptual Ability: Negative Note." Percept & Motor Skills 28(1):301–2 F '69. * (PA 43:10568)

155. DeFAZIO, VICTOR J., AND MORONEY, WILLIAM F. "Performance Characteristics of Field Dependent and Independent Individuals on an Auditory Signal Detection Task." J Psychol 71(1):77–82 Ja '69. * (PA 43:4731)

156. DUKE, ROBERT B. "Relation of Field Dependence to the 'Philosophies of Human Nature.'" Psychol Rep 24(1):197–8 F '69. * (PA 43:14246)

157. GRUENFELD, LEOPOLD, AND ARBUTHNOT, JACK. "Field Independence as a Conceptual Framework for Prediction of Variability in Ratings of Others." Percept & Motor Skills 28(1):31–44 F '69. * (PA 43:11305)

158. HOUSTON, B. KENT. "Field Independence and Performance in Distraction." J Psychol 72(1):65–9 My '69. * (PA 43:15823)

159. KAPLAN, HARVEY A. Relationships Among Cognitive Styles, Personality Traits and Reading Achievement at the Elementary School Level. Doctor's thesis, Rutgers—The State University (New Brunswick, N.J.), 1969. (DAI 30:4278A)

160. KARP, STEPHEN A.; SILBERMAN, LESTER; AND WINTERS, STEPHEN. "Psychological Differentiation and Socioeconomic

Embedded Figures Test

Status." *Percept & Motor Skills* 28(1):55–60 F '69. * (*PA* 43:11306)

161. KARP, STEPHEN A.; WINTERS, STEPHEN; AND POLLACK, IRWIN W. "Field Dependence Among Diabetics." *Arch Gen Psychiatry* 21(1):72–6 Jl '69. * (*PA* 44:2723)

162. KAZELSKIS, RICHARD. *Serial Learning and Cognitive Style.* Doctor's thesis, University of Georgia (Athens, Ga.), 1969. (*DAI* 30:5287A)

163. LAPIDUS, LEAH BLUMBERG. "Cognitive Control and Re-actions to Stress: Conditions for Mastery in the Anticipatory Phase." Abstract. *Proc 77th Ann Conv Am Psychol Assn* 4(2):569–70 '69. * (*PA* 44:651)

164. McWHINNIE, HAROLD J. "Some Relationships Between Creativity and Perception in Fourth Grade Children." *Acta Psychologica* (Netherlands) 31(2):169–75 Ag '69. * (*PA* 44:14345)

165. MATTHEWS, LILLIAN B. "Fabric Preferences, Perceptual-Personality Characteristics, and Obesity." *J Home Econ* 61(3):177–82 Mr '69. *

166. MINARD, JAMES G., AND MOONEY, WILLIAM. "Psycho-logical Differentiation and Perceptual Defense: Studies of the Separation of Perception From Emotion." *J Abn Psychol* 74(2):131–9 Ap '69. * (*PA* 43:9715)

167. NAIMAN, DORIS WEINKLE. *The Relation of Verbal Language Ability to Psychological Differentiation in the Adult Deaf.* Doctor's thesis, New York University (New York, N.Y.), 1969. (*DAI* 31:2261B)

168. OKONJI, MICHAEL O. "The Differential Effects of Rural and Urban Upbringing on the Development of Cognitive Styles." *Int J Psychol* (France) 4(4):293–305 '69. * (*PA* 45:6137)

169. PANDE, C. G., AND KOTHARI, S. "Field Dependence and the Raven's Progressive Matrices." *Psychologia* (Japan) 12(1):49–51 Mr '69. * (*PA* 44:8457, title only)

170. RENEAR, KATHERINE ROBERTS. *Field Dependence and Parole Success.* Doctor's thesis, Claremont Graduate School (Claremont, Calif.), 1969. (*DAI* 30:5678B)

171. RUBIN, SUELLEN SAFIR. *An Investigation of Experimentally-Based Measures of Conformity and Independence.* Doctor's thesis, Johns Hopkins University (Baltimore, Md.), 1969. (*DAI* 30:2936B)

172. SCALLON, RICHARD J., AND HERRON, WILLIAM G. "Field Articulation of Enuretic Boys and Their Mothers." *Percept & Motor Skills* 28(2):407–13 Ap '69. * (*PA* 43:15604)

173. SCHAFFER, MARILYN CERCONE. *Parent-Child Similarity in Psychological Differentiation.* Doctor's thesis, Purdue University (Lafayette, Ind.), 1969. (*DAI* 30:1888B)

174. SOLAR, DIANA; DAVENPORT, GERALD; AND BRUEHL, DIETER. "Social Compliance as a Function of Field Dependence." *Percept & Motor Skills* 29(1):299–306 Ag '69. * (*PA* 44:2343)

175. STEELE, JAMES. "The Hysteria and Psychasthenia Constructs as an Alternative to Manifest Anxiety and Conflict-Free Ego Functions." *J Abn Psychol* 74(1):79–85 F '69. * (*PA* 43:8494)

176. WILNER, WARREN. *The Relationship of the Perceptual Styles of Field Dependency and Field Independency to Some Formal Features of Attitudes.* Doctor's thesis, City University of New York (New York, N.Y.), 1969. (*DAI* 30:4022A)

177. ZYTOWSKI, DONALD G.; MILLS, DAVID H.; AND PAEPE, CLAUDE. "Psychological Differentiation and the Strong Vocational Interest Blank." *J Counsel Psychol* 16(1):41–4 Ja '69. * (*PA* 43:5367)

178. ALEXANDER, SHIRLEY MAE. *A Study of Perceptual and Verbal Differentiation Among Male College Students.* Doctor's thesis, George Washington University (Washington, D.C.), 1970. (*DAI* 31:6887B)

179. BARRETT, S BARRE. *A Study of the Interrelationship and Influences of Scholastic Aptitude and Perception Upon Aesthetic Sensitivity in College Students.* Doctor's thesis, University of Kansas (Lawrence, Kan.), 1970. (*DAI* 31:5835A)

180. BOGO, NORMAN; WINGET, CAROLYN; AND GLESER, GOLDINE C. "Ego Defenses and Perceptual Styles." *Percept & Motor Skills* 30(2):599–605 Ap '70. * (*PA* 46:6842)

181. CAHOON, RICHARD L. "Vigilance Performance Under Hypoxia." *J Appl Psychol* 54(6):479–83 D '70. * (*PA* 45:5163)

182. DUBOIS, THOMAS E., AND COHEN, WALTER. "Relation-ship Between Measures of Psychological Differentiation and Intellectual Ability." *Percept & Motor Skills* 31(2):411–6 O '70. * (*PA* 45:6333)

183. FISK, CLAIRE BRACE. *Psychological Dependence, Perceptual Dependence and the Establishment of a Treatment Relationship Among Male Alcoholics.* Doctor's thesis, Boston University (Boston, Mass.), 1970. (*DAI* 31:2981B)

184. GOLDSTEIN, GERALD; NEURINGER, CHARLES; AND KLAPPERSACK, BERNARD. "Cognitive, Perceptual, and Motor Aspects of Field Dependency in Alcoholics." *J Genetic Psychol* 117(2):253–66 D '70. * (*PA* 45:6611)

185. GROSS, STEVEN J., AND MOORE, SAMUEL F. "The Portable Rod-and-Frame Test and the Short-Form Embedded-Figures Test: A Combined Index of the Field-Dependence Dimension." *Psychon Sci* 20(4):213–4 Ag 25 '70. * (*PA* 45:2409)

186. GROSSMAN, MARVIN. "Perceptual Style, Creativity, and Various Drawing Abilities." *Studies Art Ed* 11(2):51–4 W '70. *

187. HARANO, RICHARD M. "Relationship of Field Dependence

and Motor-Vehicle-Accident Involvement." *Percept & Motor Skills* 31(1):272–4 Ag '70. * (*PA* 45:7156)

188. HELGESON, RICHARD LEE. *An Investigation of Concept Learning as a Function of Cognitive Style, Stimulus Characteristics, and Training Procedure.* Doctor's thesis, Washington State University (Pullman, Wash.), 1970. (*DAI* 31:4995B)

189. JOHNSON, JANE COOK. *A Comparison of Two Personality Systems: The PAS and Witkin's Field Dependence-Independence.* Doctor's thesis, University of Missouri (Columbia, Mo.), 1970. (*DAI* 31:6241B)

190. KANGAS, BARBARA BROWNELL. *An Experimental Manipulation of Expressed Values.* Doctor's thesis, Washington State University (Pullman, Wash.), 1970. (*DAI* 31:4997B)

191. KARP, STEPHEN A.; KISSIN, BENJAMIN; AND HUSTMYER, FRANK E., JR. "Field Dependence as a Predictor of Alcoholic Therapy Dropouts." *J Nerv & Mental Dis* 150(1):77–83 Ja '70. * (*PA* 44:8778)

192. KURIE, GEORGE D., AND MORDKOFF, ARNOLD M. "Effects of Brief Sensory Deprivation and Somatic Concentration on Two Measures of Field Dependence." *Percept & Motor Skills* 31(3):683–7 D '70. * (*PA* 45:9278)

193. LAPIDUS, LEAH BLUMBERG. "Cognitive Control, Parental Practices, and Contemporary Social Problems." Abstract. *Proc 78th Ann Conv Am Psychol Assn* 5(1):427–8 '70. * (*PA* 44:18379)

194. McWHINNIE, HAROLD J. "A Third Study of Some Relationships Between Creativity and Perception in 6th Grade Children." *Calif J Ed Res* 21(1):35–42 Ja '70. *

195. McWHINNIE, HAROLD J. "A Third Study of the Effects of a Learning Experience Upon Preference for Complexity-Asymmetry in Fourth, Fifth, and Sixth Grade Children." *Calif J Ed Res* 21(5):216–25 N '70. * (*PA* 46:2721)

196. MARINO, DOMINIC R.; FITZGIBBONS, DAVID J.; AND MIRABILE, CHARLES S., JR. "Attention Deployment in Field Dependence and Autokinetic Movement." *Percept & Motor Skills* 31(1):155–8 Ag '70. * (*PA* 45:6292)

197. PANDE, C. G. "Sex Differences in Field-Dependence: Confirmation With Indian Sample." *Percept & Motor Skills* 31(1):70 Ag '70. * (*PA* 45:4287)

198. PHELAN, JOSEPH G.; BROOKS, RICHARD; AND BRASHEARS, GLADYS C. "Relationship of Kinesthetic Figural Aftereffect to Masculinity-Femininity and Expectation for Internal Versus External Control of Reinforcement." *Percept & Motor Skills* 31(3):863–6 D '70. * (*PA* 45:9967)

199. POWELL, BARBARA J. "Role of Verbal Intelligence in the Field Approach of Selected Groups of Psychotics." *J Abn Psychol* 76(1):47–9 Ag '70. * (*PA* 44:21246)

200. RENNELS, MAX RAYMOND. "The Effects of Instructional Methodology in Art Education Upon Achievement on Spatial Tasks by Disadvantaged Negro Youths." *J Negro Ed* 39(2):116–23 sp '70. * (*PA* 46:7841)

201. SMITH, JUNE MARGARET MAKINS. *Interpretation of the Field-Independence Dimension: The Effect of Variations in Stimulus Input on the Performance of Field-Independent, Intermediate and Field-Dependent Subjects.* Doctor's thesis, University of British Columbia (Vancouver, B.C., Canada), 1970. (*DAI* 31:7580B)

202. WELKOWITZ, JOAN, AND FELDSTEIN, STANLEY. "Relation of Experimentally Manipulated Interpersonal Perception and Psychological Differentiation to the Temporal Patterning of Conversation." Abstract. *Proc 78th Ann Conv Am Psychol Assn* 5(1):387–8 '70. * (*PA* 44:18582)

203. ZARA, RONALD CHARLES. *Expectations of Social Reaction Toward Self as Related to Cognitive Style and Locus of Control in Persons With Obvious and Hidden Physical Handicaps.* Doctor's thesis, University of Houston (Houston, Tex.), 1970. (*DAI* 31:404B)

204. BECKER, JOSEPH; DOCTOR, RONALD M.; MIRANDA, MANUEL; AND WALLACE, JEAN. "Analytic-Perceptual Style and Verbal Conditioning." *Percept & Motor Skills* 32(2):631–6 Ap '71. * (*PA* 46:10861)

205. BECKER-CARUS, CHRISTIAN. "Electrophysiological Correlates of a Cognitive Personality Variable (Automatization)." *Archiv für die Gesamte Psychologie* (West Germany) 123:171–85 '71. *

206. BERRY, J. W. "Ecological and Cultural Factors in Spatial Perceptual Development." *Can J Behav Sci* 3(4):324–36 O '71. * (*PA* 47:8577)

207. BRAUN, JOSEPH ADAMS. *The Empathic Ability of Psychotherapists as Related to Therapist Perceptual Flexibility and Professional Experience, Patient Insight, and Therapist-Patient Similarity.* Doctor's thesis, Fordham University (New York, N.Y.), 1971. (*DAI* 32:2391B)

208. CLAR, PHILIP NORMAN. *The Relationship of Psychological Differentiation to Client Behavior in Vocational Choice Counseling.* Doctor's thesis, University of Michigan (Ann Arbor, Mich.), 1971. (*DAI* 32:1837B)

209. DEL GAUDIO, ANDREW CHARLES. *Psychological Differentiation and Mobility as Related to Creativity.* Doctor's thesis, Fordham University (New York, N.Y.), 1971. (*DAI* 32:2393B)

210. DENMARK, FLORENCE L.; HAVLENA, ROBERT A.; AND MURGATROYD, DOROTHY. "Reevaluation of Some Measures of Cognitive Styles." *Percept & Motor Skills* 33(1):133–4 Ag '71. * (*PA* 47:3002)

211. DERSHOWITZ, ZACHARY. "Jewish Subcultural Patterns

Embedded Figures Test

and Psychological Differentiation." *Int J Psychol* (France) 6(3):223-31 '71. * (*PA* 49:672)

212. DeRussy, Edith A., and Futch, Emily. "Field Dependence-Independence as Related to College Curricula." *Percept & Motor Skills* 33(3):1235-7 D '71. * (*PA* 48:1888)

213. Holtzman, Wayne H.; Swartz, Jon D.; and Thorpe, Joseph S. "Artists, Architects, and Engineers—Three Contrasting Modes of Visual Experience and Their Psychological Correlates." *J Personality* 39(3):432-49 S '71. * (*PA* 47:6777)

214. Huckabee, Malcolm W., and Ferrell, Jack G., Jr. "The Tactual Embedded Figures Task as a Measure of Field Dependence-Independence in Blind Adolescents." *Ed Visually Handicapped* 3(2):37-40 My '71. *

215. Ihilevich, David, and Gleser, Goldine C. "Relationship of Defense Mechanisms to Field Dependence-Independence." *J Abn Psychol* 77(3):296-302 Je '71. * (*PA* 46:7179)

216. Langley, C. W. "Differentiation and Integration of Systems of Personal Constructs." *J Personality* 39(1):10-25 Mr '71. * (*PA* 46:4956)

217. Loewenstein, Arline Perry. *Cognitive Style and Empathic Behavior in Counseling.* Doctor's thesis, University of Miami (Coral Gables, Fla.), 1971. (*DAI* 32:3033A)

218. Magaro, Peter A., and Vojtisek, John E. "Embedded Figures Performance of Schizophrenics as a Function of Chronicity, Premorbid Adjustment, Diagnosis, and Medication." *J Abn Psychol* 77(2):184-91 Ap '71. * (*PA* 46:3447)

219. Moore, N. I. "Cognitive Styles and the Schizophrenias and Character Disorders." *Percept & Motor Skills* 33(2):475-82 O '71. * (*PA* 47:7200)

220. Moore, Telford Ira. *The Relationship Among Differentiated Cognitive Abilities, Field Dependency, Achievement, and Rated Classroom Behavior of Ninth Grade Junior High School Students.* Doctor's thesis, University of Southern California (Los Angeles, Calif.), 1971. (*DAI* 32:249A)

221. Mosher, Loren R.; Pollin, William; and Stabenau, James R. "Families With Identical Twins Discordant for Schizophrenia: Some Relationships Between Identification, Thinking Styles, Psychopathology and Dominance-Submissiveness." *Brit J Psychiatry* 118(542):29-42 Ja '71. * (*PA* 46:11248)

222. Nedd, Albert N. B. "The Simultaneous Effect of Several Variables on Attitudes Toward Change." *Adm Sci Q* 16(3):258-69 S '71. * (*PA* 47:11914)

223. Nevill, Dorothy Dobbins. *Experimental Manipulation of Dependency Motivation and Its Effects on Eye Contact and Measures of Field Dependency.* Doctor's thesis, University of Florida (Gainesville, Fla.), 1971. (*DAI* 32:7295B)

224. Nickel, Ted. "The Reduced Size Rod and Frame Test as a Measure of Psychological Differentiation." *Ed & Psychol Meas* 31(2):555-9 su '71. *

225. Offenbach, Stefan Gared. *A Multitrait-Multimethod Analysis of Witkin's Concept of Psychological Differentiation.* Doctor's thesis, Washington University (St. Louis, Mo.), 1971. (*DAI* 32:2406B)

226. Pérez, Raquel Lucia Cruz. *The Effect of Experimentally Induced Failure on Cognitive Differentiation of High and Low Self-Esteem Subjects.* Doctor's thesis, Wayne State University (Detroit, Mich.), 1971. (*DAI* 32:3012B)

227. Spears, Julia Buckner. *Field Dependence and Verbal Comprehension on Two Visual-Motor Verbal Tasks.* Doctor's thesis, New York University (New York, N.Y.), 1971. (*DAI* 32:6089B)

228. Wade, Estelle Betty. *Field-Independence, Authoritarianism, and Verbal Reinforcement in Anagram Solution.* Doctor's thesis, Columbia University (New York, N.Y.), 1971. (*DAI* 32:3625B)

229. Weissman, Hilda Jane. *Sex Differences in Perceptual Style in Junior High School in Relation to Nursery-School and Current Dependency and Sex Role Crystallization.* Doctor's thesis, Catholic University of America (Washington, D.C.), 1971. (*DAI* 32:2390B)

CUMULATIVE NAME INDEX

Rosett, H. L.: 112
Rouleau, R. A.: 151
Rubin, S. S.: 171
Santos, J. F.: 92
Sapirstein, M. R.: 112
Saucer, R. T.: 29
Scallon, R. J.: 172
Schaffer, M. C.: 173
Schilling, M.: 113
Schimek, J. G.: 142
Schonbar, R. A.: 109
Schwartz, D. W.: 67
Seitz, R.: 43
Severson, R. A.: 40
Silberman, L.: 160
Silverstone, S.: 143
Sinkeldam, C.: 41
Smith, J. M. M.: 201
Solar, D.: 174
Spears, J. B.: 227
Spence, D. P.: 14
Spotts, J. V.: 68
Stabenau, J. R.: 221
Steele, J.: 175
Steele, J. R.: 39
Stein, B.: 71
Steingart, J. N.: 110
Stelle, W. W.: 144
Stewart, H. F.: 27
Stewart, R. H.: 119
Stuart, I. R. 52–3, 69, 120

Sugarman, A. A.: 66
Swartz, J. D.: 213
Taylor, J. N.: 8
Thornton, C. L.: 70, 72, 145
Thorpe, J. S.: 54, 213
Tyler, L. E.: rev, 6:89
Vojtisek, J. E.: 218
Voth, H. M.: 153
Wachtel, P. L.: 146
Wade, E. B.: 228
Wallace, J.: 204
Waller, R. C.: 94
Wapner, S.: 2
Weiss, A. A.: 71
Weissenberg, P.: 58
Weissman, H. J.: 229
Welkowitz, J.: 202
Wertheim, J.: 84
Wilkins, L. G.: 44
Wilner, W.: 176
Winget, C.: 180
Winters, S.: 160–1
Witkin, H. A.: 1–2, 19, 24, 28, 59, 86, 103, 106, 121
Wolpoff, M.: 53
Yorioka, G. N.: 78
Young, H. H.: 87
Zara, R. C.: 203
Zoob, I.: 45
Zuckerman, M.: 45, 80, 113
Zytowski, D. G.: 177

[1170]

Emo Questionnaire. Adults; 1958–60; EQ; 14 scores: rationalization, inferiority feelings, fear and anxiety, N vector (total of preceding 3 scores), depression, projection, unreality, withdrawal, Z vector (total of preceding 4 scores), hostility, sex, organic response, total diagnostic, buffer score; George O. Baehr (test), Melany E. Baehr (test), and Measurement Research Division, Industrial Relations Center, University of Chicago (manual); the Center. * [The publisher has not replied to our four requests to check the accuracy of this entry.]

For additional information, see P :72; for reviews by Bertram D. Cohen and W. Grant Dahlstrom, see 6:90 (1 reference).

REFERENCES THROUGH 1971

1. See 6:90.
2. PACK, MARGARET E. *A Comparison of the Use of Four Specific Defense Mechanisms Among College Women Varsity Athletes and Non-Athletes.* Master's thesis, Texas Woman's University (Denton, Tex.), 1969.

CUMULATIVE NAME INDEX

Cohen, B. D.: rev, 6:90   Olson, L. O.: 1
Dahlstrom, W. G.: rev, 6:90   Pack, M. E.: 2
Jacobs, D. F.: 1   Pishkin, V.: 1

[1171]

The Empathy Test. Ages 13 and over; 1947–61; ET; Willard A. Kerr and Boris J. Speroff; Psychometric Affiliates. *

For additional information, see P :73 (1 reference); for a review by Wallace B. Hall, see 6:91 (9 references); for a review by Robert L. Thorndike, see 5:50 (20 references).

REFERENCES THROUGH 1971

1–20. See 5:50.
21–29. See 6:91.
30. See P:73.
31. BASS, BERNARD M. "Validity Information Exchange, No. 10–25; D.O.T. Code 1-85.22, Salesman, Foodstuffs." *Personnel Psychol* 10:343–4 au '57. *
32. MAHONEY, STANLEY C., AND AUSTON, CHARLES A. "The Empathy Test and Self-Awareness of Kuder Interest Pattern." *Psychol Rep* 4:422 S '58. * (PA 33:6265)
33. MAHONEY, T. A.; JERDEE, T. H.; AND NASH, A. N. "Predicting Managerial Effectiveness." *Personnel Psychol* 13:147–63 su '60. * (PA 36:2LI47M)
34. SPEAL, STANLEY ALLAN. *The Relationship of Phenomenological Empathy to Certain Personality and Interpersonal Variables.* Doctor's thesis, Vanderbilt University (Nashville, Tenn.), 1960. (DA 21:675)

35. SKELLY, CLYDE G. *Some Variables Which Differentiate the Highly Intelligent and Highly Divergent Thinking Adolescent.* Doctor's thesis, University of Connecticut (Storrs, Conn.), 1961. (DA 22:2699)
36. SCROGGS, JAMES RUDOLPH. *Empathy: Aesthetic and Interpersonal.* Doctor's thesis, Boston University (Boston, Mass.), 1963. (DA 24:825)
37. McALLISTER, JOHN GERALD. *Analyses of Selected Personality and Intellectual Attributes of Teenage Volunteer Counselor-Attendants Serving at a Residential Camp for the Dependent Cerebral Palsied.* Doctor's thesis, University of Denver (Denver, Colo.), 1966. (DA 27:3328A)
38. TITUS, H. EDWIN. "Prediction of Supervisory Success by Use of Standard Psychological Tests." *J Psychol* 72(1):35–40 My '69. * (PA 43:16503)
39. KALISCH, BEATRICE J. "An Experiment in the Development of Empathy in Nursing Students." *Nursing Res* 20(3): 202–11 My–Je '71. * (PA 51:3243)
40. LEVITT, EUGENE E.; LUBIN, BERNARD; AND DEWITT, KATHRYN N. "An Attempt to Develop an Objective Test Battery for the Selection of Nursing Students." *Nursing Res* 20(3): 255–8 My–Je '71. * (PA 51:3969)

CUMULATIVE NAME INDEX

Albright, L. E.: 22   McCullough, G.: 7
Alden, P. J.: 6   Mahoney, S. C.: 32
Auston, C. A.: 32   Mahoney, T. A.: 33
Bass, B. M.: 7, 31   Nash, A. N.: 33
Bell, G. B.: 3, 8, 13   Patterson, C. H.: 28–9
DeWitt, K. N.: 40   Pruitt, R. C.: 7
Dightman, C. R.: 27   Reed, K. E.: 25
Fahrion, S. L.: 27   Rich, J. M.: 23
Frankel, N.: 15   Rose, G.: 15
Giblette, J. F.: 24   Scroggs, J. R.: 36
Glennon, J. R.: 22   Siegel, A. I.: 10
Hall, H. E.: 8   Skelly, C. G.: 35
Hall, H. S.: 3   Smith, F. J.: 11
Hall, W. B.: rev, 6:91   Smith, W. J.: 22
Jarrard, L. E.: 14   Smith, W. R.: 26
Jerdee, T. H.: 33   Speal, S. A.: 34
Juliano, C. V.: 16   Speroff, B. J.: 4, 9, 12
Kalisch, B. J.: 39   Stolper, R.: 13
Karstendiek, B.: 7   Strunk, O.: 25
Kerr, W.: 15   Szpak, M. L.: 30
Kerr, W. A.: 1, 9, 16   Thorndike, R. L.: rev, 5:50
Levitt, E. E.: 40   Titus, H. E.: 38
Lubin, B.: 40   Tobolski, F. P.: 1, 16
McAllister, J. G.: 37   Van Zelst, R. H.: 2, 5
McCarty, J. J.: 17–20   Wolfson, B. N.: 21

[1172]

Evaluation Modality Test. Adults; 1956; EMT; 4 scores: realism, moralism, individualism, total; Hugo O. Engelmann; Psychometric Affiliates. *

For additional information, see P :74; for a review by Wilson H. Guertin, see 5:51.

[1173]

★**Experiential World Inventory.** Disturbed adolescents and adults; 1970; EWI; 8 scores: 5 perception scores (sensory, time, body, self, others), ideation, dysphoria, impulse regulation; A. Moneim El-Meligi and Humphry Osmond; Mens Sana Publishing Inc. *

REFERENCES THROUGH 1971

1. EL-MELIGI, A. MONEIM. "The Experiential World Inventory—A Non-Projective Aid for the Rorschach." *Int Congr Rorsch & Other Proj Tech* 7:744–58 '70. *

CUMULATIVE NAME INDEX

El-Meligi, A. M.: 1

[1174]

Eysenck Personality Inventory. Grades 9–16 and adults; 1963–69; EPI; revision of *Maudsley Personality Inventory;* 3 scores: extraversion, neuroticism, lie; 2 editions; H. J. Eysenck and Sybil B. G. Eysenck. *
a) UNITED STATES EDITION. Grades 9–16 and adults; 1963–69; Educational and Industrial Testing Service.
b) BRITISH EDITION. Adults; 1963–64; University of London Press Ltd. [England].

For additional information, reviews by Victor B. Cline and Richard I. Lanyon, and excerpted reviews by A. W. Heim and James Linden, see 7:76 (121 references); see also P :77 (52 references); for a review by James C. Lingoes, see 6:93 (1 reference).

Embedded Figures Test

REFERENCES THROUGH 1971

1. See 6:93.
2–53. See P:77.
54–174. See 7:76.
175. EYSENCK, H. J. "Personality and Reminiscence—An Experimental Study of the 'Reactive Inhibition' and the 'Conditioned Inhibition' Theories." Life Sci (England) 3:189–98 Mr '64. * (PA 39:565)
176. SCOTT, EARL D., AND WILKINSON, DAVID. "Adaptation as Related to the Introversion-Extroversion Dimension." Proc Iowa Acad Sci 71:420–4 '64. *
177. MCALLISTER, JAMES. "Trial of Oxypertine for Anxiety Neurosis." Letter. Brit J Psychiatry 111:1010–1 O '65. *
178. DAY, HY. "Looking Time as a Function of Stimulus Variables and Individual Differences." Percept & Motor Skills 22:423–8 Ap '66. * (PA 40:8320)
179. PAYKEL, E. S. "Abnormal Personality and Thyrotoxicosis: A Follow-Up Study." J Psychosom Res (England) 10:143–50 S '66. * (PA 41:769)
180. BROWN, D. G. "Emotional Disturbance in Eczema: A Study of Symptom-Reporting Behaviour." J Psychosom Res (England) 11:27–40 Je '67. * (PA 42:4405)
181. EYSENCK, SYBIL B. G., AND EYSENCK, H. J. "Physiological Reactivity to Sensory Stimulation as a Measure of Personality." Psychol Rep 20:45–6 F '67. * (PA 41:7368)
182. VINGOE, FRANK J. "Self-Awareness, Self-Acceptance, and Hypnotizability." J Abn Psychol 72:454–6 O '67. * (PA 42:242)
183. FARLEY, FRANK H. "Season of Birth, Intelligence and Personality." Brit J Psychol 59:281–3 Ag '68. * (PA 42:17018)
184. GOEDICKE, RITA. The Relation Between Academic Success and Personality Variables. Master's thesis, University of Alberta (Edmonton, Alta., Canada), 1968.
185. HALSTEAD, HERBERT, AND NEAL, C. DAVID. "Intelligence and Personality in Drug Addicts: A Pilot Study." Brit J Addict 63:237–40 D '68. *
186. JOHNSON, RONALD C.; ACKERMAN, J. MARK; FRANK, HARRY; AND FIONDA, A. JOSEPH. "Resistance to Temptation, Guilt Following Yielding, and Psychopathology." J Consult & Clin Psychol 32:169–75 Ap '68. * (PA 42:9024)
187. MCLAUGHLIN, ROBERT J. "Retention in Paired-Associate Learning Related to Extroversion and Neuroticism." Psychon Sci 13:333–4 D 25 '68. * (PA 43:6898)
188. RAMSAY, R. W., AND BROADHURST, ANNE. "The Non-Randomness of Attempts at Random Responses: Relationships With Personality Variables and Psychiatric Disorder." Brit J Psychol 59:299–304 Ag '68. * (PA 42:17210)
189. TAYLOR, P. J. "Personal Factors Associated With Sickness Absence: A Study of 194 Men With Contrasting Sickness Absence Experiences in a Refinery Population." Brit J Indus Med 25:106–18 Ap '68. *
190. VINGOE, FRANK J. "Rogers' Self Theory and Eysenck's Extraversion and Neuroticism." J Consult & Clin Psychol 32:618–20 O '68. * (PA 43:33)
191. WILSON, GLENN D. "Personality, GSR Conditioning and Response to Instructional Set." Psychol Rep 22:618 Ap '68. * (PA 42:11619)
192. BERRY, G. W. Personality Patterns and Delinquency. Master's thesis, University of Manchester (Manchester, England), 1969. (Abstract: Brit J Ed Psychol 41:221)
193. BHUSHAN, L. I. "A Hindi Version of Eysenck Personality Inventory (Form A)." Psychol Ann 3:27–30 Mr '69. * (PA 45:4293)
194. BROADHURST, ANNE. "Time Estimation Related to Personality, Cognitive Speed and Schizophrenia." Life Sci (England) 8(pt 2, 2):69–78 Ja 15 '69. * (PA 45:2722)
195. BROOKE, J. D.; HAMELY, E. J.; AND STONE, P. "Personality, Achievement in Physical Competition, Physique and Grip Strength in Female Physical Education Students." Med & Sci Sports 1(4):185–8 D '69. *
196. HASETH, KJELL; SHAGASS, CHARLES; AND STRAUMANIS, JOHN J. "Perceptual and Personality Correlates of EEG and Evoked Response Measures." Biol Psychiatry 1(1):49–60 Ja '69. * (PA 46:4440)
197. HAWARD, L. R. C. "Personality of Parachutists: Part 1, Neuroticism, Extraversion and Stress Tolerance." Flight Safety (England) 2(4):12–5 My '69. * (PA 46:7922)
198. KISSEN, DAVID M., AND RAO, L. G. S. "Steroid Excretion Patterns and Personality in Lung Cancer." Ann NY Acad Sci 164 (2):476–82 O '69. *
199. KISSEN, DAVID M.; BROWN, R. I. F.; AND KISSEN, MARGARET. "A Further Report on Personality and Psychosocial Factors in Lung Cancer." Ann NY Acad Sci 164(2):535–45 O 14 '69. *
200. MEHRABIAN, ALBERT, AND WILLIAMS, MARTIN. "Nonverbal Concomitants of Perceived and Intended Persuasiveness." J Pers & Social Psychol 13(1):37–58 S '69. * (PA 43:17375)
201. ROWE, ALAN J. "Mental Problems in Rheumatoid Arthritis." Letter. Brit Med J 4(5686):806–7 D 27 '69. *
202. VERGHESE, ABRAHAM. "Eysenck Personality Inventory N Scores in Different Diseases." Indian J Psychiatry 11(3–4):71–4 Jl–O '69. *
203. BANIKIOTES, PAUL GREGORY. Interpersonal Attraction in Simulated and Real Interactions. Doctor's thesis, Purdue University (Lafayette, Ind.), 1970. (DAI 31:4979B)

204. BECK, ROBERT CLIFFORD. Performance of Introverts and Extraverts on Various Tests of Cognitive Control. Doctor's thesis, Texas Tech University (Lubbock, Tex.), 1970. (DAI 31:6251B)
205. BHUSHAN, L. I. "Personality Factors and Leadership Preference." Thesis abstract. Indian Psychol R 6(2):125–6 Ja '70. * (PA 46:9028)
206. BOUCHER, MICHAEL LOUIS. Effect of Non-Verbal Communication on Attraction and Disclosure in a Psychotherapy Analogue. Doctor's thesis, Syracuse University (Syracuse, N.Y.), 1970. (DAI 31:6891B)
207. CHILD, DENNIS. "Social Attitudes of University Students." Durham Res R (England) 6(25):471–6 au '70. *
208. CLARK, T. J. H., AND COCHRANE, G. M. "Effect of Personality on Alveolar Ventilation in Patients With Chronic Airways Obstruction." Brit Med J 1(5691):273–5 Ja '70. * (PA 46:3647)
209. COVERDALE, HERBERT L., JR. Pupillary Response, Connotative Meaning and Personality. Doctor's thesis, Illinois Institute of Technology (Chicago, Ill.), 1970. (DAI 31:5045B)
210. CRISP, A. H.; STONEHILL, E.; AND FENTON, G. W. "An Aspect of the Biological Basis of the Mind-Body Apparatus: The Relationship Between Sleep, Nutritional State and Mood in Disorders of Weight." Psychother & Psychosom (Switzerland) 18(1–6):161–75 '70. * (PA 47:5246)
211. CROOKES, T. G., AND HUTT, S. J. "Perception of Hidden Figures by Neurotic and Schizophrenic Patients." Brit J Psychiatry 116(532):335–6 Mr '70. * (PA 45:1015)
212. FARLEY, FRANK H., AND TRUOG, ANTHONY L. "Individual Differences in Reading Comprehension." J Read Behav 3(1):29–35 w '70–71. *
213. GRAY, JEFFREY A. "The Psychophysiological Basis of Introversion-Extraversion." Behav Res & Ther (England) 8(3):249–66 Ag '70. * (PA 46:2499)
214. GRODEN, B. M., AND BROWN, R. I. F. "Differential Psychological Effects of Early and Late Mobilisation After Myocardial Infarction." Scand J Rehabil Med (Sweden) 2(2–3):60–4 '70. *
215. HEIM, ALICE. Intelligence and Personality: Their Assessment and Relationship, pp. 88–92. Harmondsworth, Middlesex, England: Penguin Books Ltd., 1970. Pp. 206. * (PA 48:936, title only)
216. KANEKAR, SURESH, AND SAHU, SATYANARAYAN. "Extraversion, Neuroticism, Authoritarianism and Mysogyny Among Male College Students." Indian Psychol R 7(1):30–4 Jl '70. *
217. KIMBALL, CHASE P. "The Experience of Open Heart Surgery: 2, Determinants of Post-operative Behavior." Psychother & Psychosom (Switzerland) 18(1–6):259–74 '70. * (PA 47:5515)
218. LEUNES, ARNOLD, AND CHRISTENSEN, LARRY. "Reliability and Inmate Test Results." Correct Psychologist 4(3):85–93 N–D '70. * (PA 49:2670)
219. MILLS, MICHAEL WILLIAM. Extraversion, Neuroticism, and the Critical Flicker Frequency Threshold in Antisocial Personalities. Doctor's thesis, Washington University (St. Louis, Mo.), 1970. (DAI 31:7604B)
220. NICELY, ROY EDWARD. An Empirical Study of the Relationship Between Extroversion and Sensitivity to Advertising. Doctor's thesis, Pennsylvania State University (University Park, Pa.), 1970. (DAI 32:603A)
221. OSWALD, N. C.; WALLER, R. E.; AND DRINKWATER, J. "Relationship Between Breathlessness and Anxiety in Asthma and Bronchitis: A Comparative Study." Brit Med J 2(5700):14–7 Ap 4 '70. Comments by A. K. Zealley and R. C. B. Aitken, 2(5705):363 My 9 '70; by D. R. Redman, 2(5710):672 Je 13 '70; and by H. Brian McNamee, 2(5712):791 Je 27 '70. *
222. PERRINE, M. W. "Identification of Personality, Attitudinal, and Biographical Characteristics of Drinking Drivers." Behav Res Highway Safety 1(4):207–26 w '70. *
223. SEAGER, C. P. "Treatment of Compulsive Gamblers by Electrical Aversion." Brit J Psychiatry 117(540):545–53 N '70. * (PA 45:10121)
224. SMITH, I. MACFARLANE. "The Use of Diagnostic Tests for Assessing the Abilities of Overseas Students Attending Institutions of Further Education, Part I." Voc Aspect Ed (England) 22(51):1–8 Mr '70. *
225. SMITHERS, ALAN. "What Do Students Expect of Lectures?" Univ Q (England) 24(3):330–6 su '70. *
226. STRELAU, JAN. "Nervous System Type and Extraversion-Introversion: A Comparison of Eysenck's Theory With Pavlov's Typology." Polish Psychol B 1(1):17–24 '70. * (PA 48:522)
227. VALEK, J., AND KUHN, E. "Stress-Induced Changes of Carbohydrate and Lipid Metabolism in Coronary Heart Disease (CHD)." Psychother & Psychosom (Switzerland) 18(1–6):275–80 '70. * (PA 47:5524)
228. AKHTAR, SYED NEHAL, AND KAFILUDDIN, S. R. "Relationship Among Neuroticism, Extraversion and Manifest Hostility." Manas (India) 18(1):37–44 My '71. * (PA 48:9149)
229. ANANT, SANTOKH S. "Belongingness and Mental Health: Cross Cultural, Sex and Marital Differences." Manas (India) 18(1):11–23 My '71. * (PA 48:9151)
230. ANDREWS, J. C. "Personality, Sporting Interest and Achievement." Ed R (England) 23(2):126–34 F '71. *
231. BANIKIOTES, PAUL G.; RUSSELL, JOHN M.; AND LINDEN, JAMES D. "Interpersonal Attraction Methodology: Oversimpli-

fied or Related to Real Interaction?" Abstract. *Proc 79th Ann Conv Am Psychol Assn* 6(1):279–80 '71. * (*PA* 46:2956)

232. BATES, HENRY D. "Toward the Development of a Screening Scale for Assertive Training." *Psychol Rep* 28(1):99–107 F '71. *

233. BERG, NORMAN L. "Effect of Alcoholic Intoxication of Self-Concept: Studies of Alcoholics and Controls in Laboratory Conditions." *Q J Studies Alcohol* 32(2):442–53 Je '71. *

234. BOND, M. R. "The Relation of Pain to the Eysenck Personality Inventory, Cornell Medical Index and Whiteley Index of Hypochondriasis." *Brit J Psychiatry* 119(553):671–8 D '71. *

235. BRADLEY, LORETTA JEAN DIXON. *An Analysis of Life History and Personality Correlates That Differentiate Effective and Ineffective School Counselor Predictors.* Doctor's thesis, Purdue University (Lafayette, Ind.), 1971. (*DAI* 32:4935A)

236. BULL, R. H. C., AND STRONGMAN, K. T. "Anxiety, Neuroticism and Extraversion." *Psychol Rep* 29(3):1101–2 D '71. * (*PA* 48:942)

237. CAMERON, PAUL. "Personality Differences Between Typical Urban Negroes and Whites." *J Negro Ed* 40(1):66–75 w '71. *

238. CARR, GORDON D. "Introversion-Extraversion and Vigilance Performance." Abstract. *Proc 79th Ann Conv Am Psychol Assn* 6(1):379–80 '71. * (*PA* 46:3049)

239. CASTELLOW, WILBUR ALLEN. *Relationships Between the Spiral After-Effect and Extraversion, Neuroticism, Sex, and Induced Arousal.* Doctor's thesis, University of North Carolina (Chapel Hill, N.C.), 1971. (*DAI* 32:7287B)

240. CHILD, DENNIS, AND SMITHERS, ALAN. "Some Cognitive and Affective Factors in Subjective Choice." *Res Ed* (England) 5:1–9 My '71. *

241. COLES, MICHAEL G. H.; GALE, ANTHONY; AND KLINE, PAUL. "Personality and Habituation of the Orienting Reaction: Tonic and Response Measures of Electrodermal Activity." *Psychophysiol* 8(1):54–63 Ja '71. * (*PA* 47:2469)

242. COLMAN, ANDREW M. "Social Rejection, Role Conflict, and Adjustment: Psychological Consequences of Orthopaedic Disability." *Percept & Motor Skills* 33(3):907–10 D '71. * (*PA* 48:1416)

243. COWELL, M. D., AND ENTWISTLE, N. J. "The Relationships Between Personality, Study Attitudes and Academic Performance in a Technical College." *Brit J Ed Psychol* 41(1):85–90 F '71. * (*PA* 46:9542)

244. CRISP, A. H., AND STONEHILL, EDWARD. "Aspects of the Relationship Between Psychiatric Status, Sleep, Nocturnal Motility and Nutrition." *J Psychosom Res* (England) 15(4):501–9 D '71. *

245. DEICH, RUTH F., AND EMAMI, JAVAD. "Computer Dating: An Investigation of Client Characteristics." *Psychol* 8(3):1–8 Ag '71. * (*PA* 48:970)

246. DI SCIPIO, WILLIAM J. "Divergent Thinking: A Complex Function of Interacting Dimensions of Extraversion-Introversion and Neuroticism-Stability." *Brit J Psychol* 62(4):545–50 N '71. * (*PA* 47:8899)

247. DI SCIPIO, WILLIAM J. "Divergent Thinking and Personality Measures of English and American Education Majors." *J Genetic Psychol* 119(1):99–107 S '71. * (*PA* 47:2752)

248. DI SCIPIO, WILLIAM J. "Psychomotor Performance as a Function of White Noise and Personality Variables." *Percept & Motor Skills* 33(1):82 Ag '71. * (*PA* 47:2079)

249. ENTWISTLE, N. J., AND BRENNAN, T. "The Academic Performance of Students: 2, Types of Successful Students." *Brit J Ed Psychol* 41(3):268–76 N '71. * (*PA* 47:11759)

250. ENTWISTLE, N. J.; NISBET, JENNIFER; ENTWISTLE, DOROTHY; AND COWELL, M. D. "The Academic Performance of Students: 1, Prediction From Scales of Motivation and Study Methods." *Brit J Ed Psychol* 41(3):258–67 N '71. * (*PA* 47:11781)

251. EYSENCK, H. J. "Hysterical Personality and Sexual Adjustment, Attitudes and Behaviour." *J Sex Res* 7(4):274–81 N '71. * (*PA* 48:5284)

252. EYSENCK, HANS J. "Relation Between Intelligence and Personality." *Percept & Motor Skills* 32(2):637–8 Ap '71. * (*PA* 46:10929)

253. EYSENCK, S. B. G., AND EYSENCK, H. J. "Attitudes to Sex Personality and Lie Scale Scores." *Percept & Motor Skills* 33(1):216–8 Ag '71. * (*PA* 47:2966)

254. FABIAN, JUDITH JANARO, AND COMREY, ANDREW L. "Construct Validation of Factored Neuroticism Scales." *Multiv Behav Res* 6(3):287–99 Jl '71. * (*PA* 47:4817)

255. FARLEY, FRANK H. Chap. 64, "Reminiscence, Performance and Personality," pp. 599–624. In *Readings in Extraversion-Introversion: Vol. 3, Bearings on Basic Psychological Processes.* Edited by H. J. Eysenck. London: Staples Press Ltd., 1971. Pp. xv, 640. *

256. FARLEY, FRANK H. "Some EPI Reliability Estimates." *J Pers Assess* 35(4):364–6 Ag '71. * (*PA* 47:4823)

257. FARLEY, FRANK H., AND MEALIEA, WALLACE L., JR. "Dissimulation and Social Desirability in the Assessment of Fears." *Behav Ther* 2(1):101–2 Ja '71. * (*PA* 47:9200)

258. FAULK, M. "Factors in the Treatment of Frigidity." *Brit J Psychiatry* 119(548):53–6 Jl '71. * (*PA* 47:7181)

259. FENZ, WALTER D. "Heart Rate Responses to a Stressor: A Comparison Between Primary and Secondary Psychopaths

and Normal Controls." *J Exp Res Personality* 5(1):7–13 Mr '71. * (*PA* 46:7159)

260. FRANSELLA, FAY. "A Personal Construct Theory and Treatment of Stuttering." *J Psychosom Res* (England) 15(4):433–8 D '71. *

261. GALE, ANTHONY; COLES, MICHAEL; KLINE, PAUL; AND PENFOLD, VALERIE. "Extraversion-Introversion, Neuroticism and the EEG: Basal and Response Measures During Habituation of the Orienting Response." *Brit J Psychol* 62(4):533–43 N '71. * (*PA* 47:8459)

262. GIBSON, H. B. "The Validity of the Eysenck Personality Inventory Studied by a Technique of Peer-rating Item by Item, and by Sociometric Comparisons." *Brit J Social & Clin Psychol* 10(3):213–20 S '71. * (*PA* 47:10893)

263. GORDON, RONALD DOUGLAS. *A Quantitative Investigation of Selected Dynamics and Outcomes of the Basic Encounter Group.* Doctor's thesis, University of Kansas (Lawrence, Kan.), 1971. (*DAI* 32:6046B)

264. GRAHAM, MALCOLM J., III. *The Effects of Introversion-Extroversion on the Scaling, Paired-Associate Learning and Paced Free Recall of Concrete and Abstract Nouns.* Doctor's thesis, University of Southern Mississippi (Hattiesburg, Miss.), 1971. (*DAI* 32:5477B)

265. HAZARI, ANANDI, AND THAKUR, GIRDHAR P. "Hindu Version of the Eysenck Personality Inventory (EPI)." *Indian Psychol R* 7(2):30–2 Ja '71. *

266. HEKMAT, HAMID. "Extraversion, Neuroticism, and Verbal Conditioning of Affective Self-Disclosures." *J Counsel Psychol* 18(1):64–9 Ja '71. * (*PA* 45:8218)

267. HERZBERG, BRENDA N.; DRAPER, KATHARINE C.; JOHNSON, ANTHONY L.; AND NICOL, GILLIAN C. "Oral Contraceptives, Depression, and Libido." *Brit Med J* 3(5773):495–500 Ag '71. * (*PA* 48:820)

268. HRITZUK, J. "A Comparative and Experimental Study of the Psychology of Set as Related to Personality." *Can J Behav Sci* 3(2):127–34 Ap '71. * (*PA* 46:9356)

269. JESSUP, GILBERT, AND JESSUP, HELEN. "Validity of the Eysenck Personality Inventory in Pilot Selection." *Occup Psychol* (England) 45(2):111–23 '71. * (*PA* 48:1963)

270. JOHNS, M. W.; GAY, T. J. A.; MASTERTON, J. P.; AND BRUCE, D. W. "Relationship Between Sleep Habits, Adrenocortical Activity and Personality." *Psychosom Med* 33(6):499–508 N–D '71. * (*PA* 49:2474)

271. KANEKAR, SURESH, AND MUKERJEE, SUMITRA. "Personality Variables Among Three Communities in India." *J Social Psychol* 84(2):305–6 Ag '71. * (*PA* 47:2948)

272. KIDSON, MALCOLM A. "Personality Factors in Hypertension." *Austral & N Zeal J Psychiatry* (Australia) 5(3):139–45 S '71. *

273. KLINE, P., AND GALE, A. "Extraversion, Neuroticism and Performance in a Psychology Examination." *Brit J Ed Psychol* 41(1):90–4 F '71. * (*PA* 46:9554)

274. KRUPSKI, ANTOINETTE; RASKIN, DAVID C.; AND BAKAN, PAUL. "Physiological and Personality Correlates of Commission Errors in an Auditory Vigilance Task." *Psychophysiol* 8(3):304–11 My '71. * (*PA* 47:2472)

275. KUMAR, K., AND WILKINSON, J. C. M. "Thought Stopping: A Useful Treatment in Phobias of 'Internal Stimuli.'" *Brit J Psychiatry* 119(550):305–7 S '71. * (*PA* 47:9089)

276. LIAKOS, A., AND CRISP, A. H. "Pupil Size in Psychoneurotic Patients: A Psychophysiological and Psychometric Investigation." *Psychother & Psychosom* (Switzerland) 19(1–2):104–10 '71. * (*PA* 47:5250)

277. LINDAUER, MARTIN S., AND REUKAUF, LYNN C. "Introversion-Extraversion and Figure-Ground Perception." *J Pers & Social Psychol* 19(1):107–13 Jl '71. * (*PA* 46:9043)

278. LUDVIGH, ELEK JOHN, III. *Extraversion and Preferred Level of Sensory Stimulation.* Doctor's thesis, Michigan State University (East Lansing, Mich.), 1971. (*DAI* 32:3642B)

279. McCOLL, I.; DRINKWATER, J. E.; HULME-MOIR, I.; AND DONNAN, S. P. B. "Prediction of Success or Failure of Gastric Surgery." *Brit J Surgery* 58(10):768–71 O '71. *

280. McCOLL, I.; DRINKWATER, J. E.; HULME-MOIR, I.; AND DONNAN, S. P. B. "Preoperative Prediction of Success or Failure of Gastric Surgery." Abstract. *Gut* (England) 12(10):856 O '71. *

281. McKERRACHER, D. W. "Psychological Aspects of a Sex Chromatin Abnormality." *Can Psychologist* 12(2):270–81 Ap '71. * (*PA* 46:9096)

282. MARKS, ISAAC; BOULOUGOURIS, JOHN; AND MARSET, PEDRO. "Flooding Versus Desensitization in the Treatment of Phobic Patients: A Crossover Study." *Brit J Psychiatry* 119(551):353–75 O '71. * (*PA* 47:9100)

283. MAYO, P. R., AND BELL, J. M. "Hostility and Personality in a Student-Teacher Population." *Brit J Social & Clin Psychol* 10(4):375–8 D '71. * (*PA* 48:1800)

284. MEARES, RUSSELL. "Features Which Distinguish Groups of Spasmodic Torticollis." *J Psychosom Res* (England) 15(1):1–11 Mr '71. * (*PA* 47:9396)

285. MEARES, RUSSELL. "Obsessionality, the Sandler-Hazari Scale and Spasmodic Torticollis." *Brit J Med Psychol* 44(2):181–2 Je '71. * (*PA* 47:5441)

286. MEARES, RUSSELL, AND LADER, MALCOLM. "Electromyographic Studies in Patients With Spasmodic Torticollis." *J Psychosom Res* (England) 15(1):13–8 Mr '71. * (*PA* 47:9468)

Eysenck Personality Inventory

287. MEHRABIAN, ALBERT. "Nonverbal Betrayal of Feeling." *J Exp Res Personality* 5(1):64–73 Mr '71. * *(PA* 46:6779)

288. MITCHELL, KENNETH R. "Effects of Neuroticism on Intra-Treatment Responsivity to Group Desensitization of Test Anxiety." *Behav Res & Ther* (England) 9(4):373–4 N '71. * *(PA* 48:3169)

289. MOWBRAY, R. M., AND DAVIES, BRIAN. "Personality Factors in Choice of Medical Specialty." *Brit J Med Ed* 5(2): 110–7 Je '71. *

290. NANCE, EVERETTE E. *The Effects of Human Relations Training on Selected Personality Variables.* Doctor's thesis, Western Michigan University (Kalamazoo, Mich.), 1971. *(DAI* 32:1861A)

291. OGSTON, DON, AND DRAKEFORD, GRANT C. "Note on the Costello-Comrey Anxiety Scale (CCAS)." *Psychol Rep* 28(1): 287–9 F '71. * *(PA* 46:4996)

292. ORENSTEIN, ALAN M. *Field-Dependence-Independence, Extraversion-Introversion, and Individual Differences in the Learning of a Serial Task Varying in Sequential Redundancy.* Doctor's thesis, West Virginia University (Morgantown, W.Va.), 1971. *(DAI* 32:2383B)

293. ORFORD, J. F. Chap. 7, "The Assessment of Personality and Its Influence on the Outcome of Treatment," pp. 133–55. In *Homosexual Behaviour: Therapy and Assessment.* By M. P. Feldman and M. J. MacCulloch. Oxford, England: Pergamon Press Ltd., 1971. Pp. ix, 288. *

294. ORPEN, CHRISTOPHER. "The Relationship Between Extraversion and Tough-Mindedness in a 'Tough-Minded' Culture." *J Psychol* 78(1):27–9 My '71. * *(PA* 46:4802)

295. PETERSON, ROGER LEE. *Interpersonal Attraction, Channels of Communication, and Extraversion and Neuroticism.* Doctor's thesis, Purdue University (Lafayette, Ind.), 1971. *(DAI* 32: 3649B)

296. PLATT, JEROME J.; POMERANZ, DAVID; AND EISENMAN, RUSSELL. "Validation of the Eysenck Personality Inventory by the MMPI and Internal-External Control Scale." *J Clin Psychol* 27(1):104–5 Ja '71. * *(PA* 46:1212)

297. POST, ALAN WILSON. *Deprivation of Opportunity: Industrial Mental Health and Job Behavior.* Doctor's thesis, Case Western Reserve University (Cleveland, Ohio), 1971. *(DAI* 32:5507B)

298. POWER, R. P., AND MACRAE, K. D. "Detectability of Items in the Eysenck Personality Inventory." *Brit J Psychol* 62(3):395–401 Ag '71. * *(PA* 47:6815)

299. RUMP, E. E., AND COURT, JOHN. "The Eysenck Personality Inventory and Social Desirability Response Set With Student and Clinical Groups." *Brit J Social & Clinical Psychol* 10(1):42–54 F '71. * *(PA* 46:1169)

300. SADLER, TIMOTHY G., AND MEFFERD, ROY B., JR. "The Interaction of Extraversion and Neuroticism in Human Operant Behavior." *J Exp Res Personality* 5(4):278–85 D '71. * *(PA* 48:980)

301. SADLER, TIMOTHY G.; MEFFERD, ROY B., JR.; AND HOUCK, ROBERT L. "The Interaction of Extraversion and Neuroticism in Orienting Response Habituation." *Psychophysiol* 8(3):312–8 My '71. * *(PA* 47:2473)

302. SEGRAVES, R. T. "Intercorrelations Between the Sjöbring and Eysenckian Personality Dimensions." *Acta Psychiatrica Scandinavica* (Denmark) 47(3):288–94 '71. *

303. SINGH, SOHBH NATH. "Influence of Intellectual Development on the Aggressive Attitude." Doctor's thesis abstract. *Indian Psychol R* 7(2):40–1 Ja '71. *

304. SIPOS, IVAN. "Operators' Personality Traits and Visual Vigilance." *Studia Psychologica* (Czechoslovakia) 13(4):318–25 '71. *

305. SMITH, I. MACFARLANE. "The Use of Diagnostic Tests for Assessing the Abilities of Overseas Students Attending Institutions of Further Education, Part II." *Voc Aspect Ed* (England) 23(54):39–48 Ap '71. *

306. STARR, DARTHA FAY. *Personality Characteristics and Learning Style: Phonics Achievement of Preservice Elementary Teachers Exposed to a Social or Isolated Learning Environment.* Doctor's thesis, St. Louis University (St. Louis, Mo.), 1971. *(DAI* 32:4434A)

307. VERGHESE, A.; MATHEW, P. M.; SENSEMAN, L. A.; AND KARAT, A. B. A. "Psychosomatic Aspects of Rehabilitation of Leprosy Patients." *Int J Leprosy* 39(4):842–7 O–D '71. *

308. VERGHESE, ABRAHAM. "Relationship Between the Psychogalvanic Reflex and the Eysenck Personality Inventory Score." *Austral & N Zeal J Psychiatry* (Australia) 5(4):277–9 D '71. *

309. WILLIAMS, ROBERT L. "Relationship of Class Participation to Personality, Ability, and Achievement Variables." *J Social Psychol* 83(2):193–8 Ap '71. * *(PA* 46:3721)

310. WILSON, GLENN D.; TUNSTALL, OLIVE A.; AND EYSENCK, H. J. "Individual Differences in Tapping Performance as a Function of Time on the Task." *Percept & Motor Skills* 33(2):375–8 O '71. * *(PA* 47:6073)

311. WILSON, J. D. "Predicting Levels of First Year University Performance." *Brit J Ed Psychol* 41(2):163–70 Je '71. * *(PA* 47:9821)

312. WILSON, MARILYN L., AND GREENE, ROGER L. "Personality Characteristics of Female Homosexuals." *Psychol Rep* 28(2):407–12 Ap '71. * *(PA* 46:7151)

313. ZEALLEY, A. K. "Bronchial Asthma: A Problem Attributable to Sampling When Establishing Its Psychopathology."

Psychother & Psychosom (Switzerland) 19(1–2):37–46 '71. * *(PA* 47:5375)

314. ZEALLEY, A. K.; AITKEN, R. C. B.; AND ROSENTHAL, S. V. "Personality and Bronchial Asthma." *Proc Royal Soc Med* (England) 64(8):825–9 Ag '71. *

CUMULATIVE NAME INDEX

Kline, P.: 17, 30, 241, 261, 273
Knapp, R. R.: 10
Knowles, J. B.: 11–2
Koller, K. M.: 110
Kramer, E.: 111, 154
Kreitman, N.: 11–2
Krupski, A.: 274
Kuhn, E.: 227
Kumar, K.: 275
Kumar, K. V.: 98
Lader, M.: 286
Lanyon, R. I.: rev, 7:76
Leith, G. O. M.: 155
LeUnes, A.: 218
Levey, A.: 9
Liakos, A.: 276
Lindauer, M. S.: 277
Linden, J.: exc, 7:76
Linden, J. D.: 231
Lingoes, J. C.: rev, 6:93
Loughnane, T.: 44
Lovell, R. R. H.: 31
Ludvigh, E. J.: 278
Lunghi, M.: 48, 112
Lynn, R.: 113–4
McAllister, J.: 12, 177
McCabe, O. L.: 70
McColl, I.: 279–80
McEvedy, C. P.: 18–9
McKerracher, D. W.: 44, 71, 156, 281
McLaughlin, R. J.: 32, 102, 187
McNamee, H. B.: 221
McNeely, J. B.: 157
MacRae, K. D.: 298
Mangan, G. L.: 115, 126, 133
Marks, I.: 282
Marks, I. M.: 33, 116
Marset, P.: 282
Martin, I.: 73, 116
Mascia, G. V.: 117
Masterton, J. P.: 270
Mathew, P. M.: 307
Mayo, P. R.: 283
Mealiea, W. L.: 257
Meares, R.: 284–6
Mefferd, R. B.: 300–1
Mehrabian, A.: 118, 200, 287
Mehryar, A. H.: 158–60
Metcalfe, M.: 83
Mills, M. W.: 219
Mitchell, K. R.: 288
Morgan, W. P.: 72
Morgenson, D. F.: 73
Morrish, R. B.: 126, 133
Moss, P. D.: 19
Mowbray, R.: f50
Mowbray, R. M.: 37, 45, 289
Mukerjee, S.: 271
Munro, H.: 46
Muthayya, B. C.: 74
Nance, E. E.: 290
Neal, D. C.: 185
Nicely, R. E.: 220
Nicol, G. C.: 267
Nisbet, J.: 250
O'Gorman, J. G.: 115
Ogston, D.: 291
Ogston, D. G.: 61
Orenstein, A. M.: 292
Orford, J. F.: 293
Orpen, C.: 294
Orwin, W.: 119
Oswald, N. C.: 221
Paykel, E. S.: 20, 179
Payne, R.: 24, 161
Pearson, I. B.: 86
Pearson, P. R.: 140
Penfold, V.: 261
Perrine, M. W.: 222
Peterson, R. L.: 295
Platman, S. R.: 162
Platt, J. J.: 296
Plutchik, R.: 162

Pomeranz, D.: 296
Post, A. W.: 297
Power, R. P.: 163, 298
Prabhu, G. G.: 164
Rajeswari, S.: 74
Ramsay, R. W.: 55, 120, 188
Rao, L. G. S.: 198
Raskin, D. C.: 274
Redman, D. R.: 221
Reukauf, L. C.: 277
Richardson, J. F.: 34, 36, 47, 50
Robinson, J. T.: 12
Robinson, L.: 165
Rosenberg, C. M.: 121–3
Rosenthal, S. V.: 81, 314
Rowe, A. J.: 201
Rump, E. E.: 299
Russell, J. M.: 231
Ryle, A.: 48, 112
Sadler, T. G.: 124, 300–1
Sahu, S.: 216
Salas, R. G.: 35–6, 49–50
Savage, R. D.: 21
Scott, E. D.: 176
Seager, C. P.: 223
Segraves, R. T.: 166, 302
Senseman, L. A.: 307
Shagass, C.: 196
Shaw, G. K.: 125
Siddle, D. A.: 133
Siddle, D. A. T.: 126
Singer, B. A.: 127
Singh, S. N.: 303
Šipos, I.: 304
Skinner, N. F.: 167
Škodackova, J.: 141
Smith, I. M.: 224, 305
Smith, S. L.: 75
Smithers, A.: 77, 169, 225, 240
Smithers, A. G.: 76, 168
Soueif, M. I.: 128, 134–5, 170
Stanley, G.: 129
Starr, D. F.: 306
Stephenson, G. M.: 53
Stone, P.: 195
Stonehill, E.: 210, 244
Straumanis, J. J.: 196
Strelau, J.: 226
Strongman, K. T.: 236
Taylor, P. J.: 189
Templer, D. I.: 93
Thakur, G. P.: 265
Thompson, W. T.: 163
Trown, E. A.: 171
Truog, A. L.: 212
Tunstall, O. A.: 310
Uherik, A.: 101, 130
Válek, J.: 227
Vando, A.: 131
Verghese, A.: 31, 56, 58, 172, 202, 307–8
Vingoe, F. J.: 13, 22, 51–2, 78, 182, 190
Waller, R. E.: 221
Warr, P. B.: 173
Watson, R. A.: 44, 71
Weinstein, F. T.: 79
Wells, B. W. P.: 132
White, J. H.: 53
White, K. D.: 126, 133
White, P. O.: 128, 134–5
Whitehill, R. P.: 174
Wilkinson, H.: 53
Wilkinson, J. C. M.: 275
Williams, C.: 136
Williams, M.: 200
Williams, R. L.: 309
Wilson, G. D.: 191, 310
Wilson, J. D.: 80, 145, 311
Wilson, M. L.: 312
Wisdom, B.: 155
Zealley, A. K.: 81, 221, 313–4
Zwirner, W.: 156

[1175]

The Eysenck-Withers Personality Inventory (For I.Q. 50–80 Range). Institutionalized subnormal adults; 1965–66; EWPI; more than two thirds of the items are from the *Junior Eysenck Personality Inven-*

Eysenck Personality Inventory

tory; 3 scores: extraversion, neuroticism, lie; Sybil B. G. Eysenck; University of London Press Ltd. [England]. *

For additional information and reviews by Paul Kline and Robert D. Wirt, see 7:77 (2 references); see also P:78 (1 reference).

REFERENCES THROUGH 1971
1. See P:78.
2–3. See 7:77.

CUMULATIVE NAME INDEX

Balaguer, A. B.: 1   Kline, P.: rev, 7:77
Bardecki, A.: 1   Thorpe, J. G.: 1
Eysenck, H. J.: 2   Wirt, R. D.: rev, 7:77
Eysenck, S. B. G.: 2–3

[1176]

*The FIRO Scales. Grades 4–8, 9–16 and adults; 1957–72; 7 tests, of which all but FIRO-B are experimental; William C. Schutz and Marilyn Wood (b); Consulting Psychologists Press, Inc. *

a) FIRO-B [FUNDAMENTAL INTERPERSONAL RELATIONS ORIENTATION—BEHAVIOR]. Grades 9–16 and adults; 1957–67; 6 scores of behavior toward others: inclusion (expressed, wanted), control (expressed, wanted), affection (expressed, wanted).

b) FIRO-BC. Grades 4–8; 1972, c1966; 6 scores: same as for FIRO-B; no manual.

c) FIRO-F [FUNDAMENTAL INTERPERSONAL RELATIONS ORIENTATION—FEELINGS]. Grades 9–16 and adults; 1957–67; 6 scores of feelings toward others: inclusion (expressed, wanted), control (expressed, wanted), affection (expressed, wanted).

d) LIPHE [LIFE INTERPERSONAL HISTORY ENQUIRY]. Grades 9–16 and adults; 1962–67; retrospective childhood relationships with parents; 12 scores (6 scores for each parent): inclusion (behavior, feelings), control (behavior, feelings), affection behavior-feeling, perceived parental approval.

e) COPE [COPING OPERATIONS PREFERENCE ENQUIRY]. Grades 9–16 and adults; 1962–67; 5 scores: denial, isolation, projection, regression-dependency, turning-against-self.

f) MATE [MARITAL ATTITUDES EVALUATION]. Grades 9–16 and adults; 1967; 5 scores: inclusion (behavior, feelings), control (behavior, feelings), affection.

g) VAL-ED [EDUCATIONAL VALUES]. Grades 9–16 and adults; 1967; 14 scores: importance, mind, school-child control, teacher-child (control, affection), teacher-community (inclusion, control, affection), administrator-teacher (inclusion, control, affection), administrator-community (inclusion, control, affection).

For additional information and a review by Bruce Bloxom, see 7:78 (70 references); see also P:79 (30 references) and 6:94 (15 references). For excerpts from related book reviews, see 6:B432 (2 excerpts).

REFERENCES THROUGH 1971
1–15. See 6:94.
16–45. See P:79.
46–115. See 7:78.
116. HUTCHERSON, DONALD. "Junior High School Social Studies Teacher-Pupil Compatibility—Its Relation to Pupil Sex, Social Level, and Indexes of Achievement." *J Ed Res* 59:39–44 S '65. *
117. WYETH, EZRA R. "Evaluation of the Effectiveness of the Leadership Training Program in the Area of the Deaf at San Fernando Valley State College." *Am Ann Deaf* 110:479–82 S '65. * (PA 40:5848)
118. BAUMGARTEL, HOWARD, AND GOLDSTEIN, JOEL W. "Need and Value Shifts in College Training Groups." *J Appl Behav Sci* 3:87–101 Ja–Mr '67. * (PA 43:1337)
119. EXLINE, RALPH V., AND MESSICK, DAVID. "The Effects of Dependency and Social Reinforcement Upon Visual Behaviour During an Interview." *Brit J Social & Clin Psychol* 6:256–66 D '67. * (PA 42:6618)
120. WINCH, ROBERT F. "Another Look at the Theory of Complementary Needs in Mate-Selection." *J Marriage & Family* 29:756–62 N '67. * (PA 42:3859)

121. FLEISHER, DANIEL S. "Composition of Small Learning Groups." *J Med Ed* 43:349–55 Mr '68. * (*PA* 43:12024)

122. ANASTASIOW, NICHOLAS J. "Teaching: The Interaction of Performance and Personality." *B Sch Ed Ind Univ* 45(4): 1–46 Jl '69. *

123. AUBRY, WILLIAM EDWARD. *An Analysis of a One-Week Workshop for Developing Self-Actualization and Effective Interpersonal Behavior.* Doctor's thesis, University of Arizona (Tucson, Ariz.), 1970. (*DAI* 31:4446A)

124. BARBEE, RUTH ELAINE. *Personality Variables Related to the Use of Interaction Analysis in a Counseling Practicum Experience.* Doctor's thesis, University of North Dakota (Grand Forks, N.D.), 1970. (*DAI* 31:6336A)

125. BLOCK, JOEL DAVID. *A Comparison of the Verbal Interaction in Counseling Groups Differing in Member Interpersonal Compatibility.* Doctor's thesis, Syracuse University (Syracuse, N.Y.), 1970. (*DAI* 32:780A)

126. BOUCHER, MICHAEL LOUIS. *Effect of Non-Verbal Communication on Attraction and Disclosure in a Psychotherapy Analogue.* Doctor's thesis, Syracuse University (Syracuse, N.Y.), 1970. (*DAI* 31:6891B)

127. CHURUKIAN, GEORGE ALLEN. *An Investigation of the Relationships Between the Compatibility of Supervisor-Supervisee Interpersonal Needs and the Quality of Their Interpersonal Relations and Productivity of Supervision.* Doctor's thesis, Syracuse University (Syracuse, N.Y.), 1970. (*DAI* 31:5656A)

128. COX, WALTER HAROLD. *Selected Non-Intellective Correlates of Academic Achievement for High School Seniors.* Doctor's thesis, Indiana University (Bloomington, Ind.), 1970. (*DAI* 31:5758A)

129. DeCOSTER, DON THEODORE. *A Comparison of Interpersonal Relationship Variables of Northwest Public Accountants With Selected Comparison Groups.* Doctor's thesis, University of Oregon (Eugene, Ore.), 1970. (*DAI* 31:5119A)

130. FLEISHER, DANIEL S., AND LEVIN, JOEL L. "A Second Study in Composition of Small Learning Groups in Medical Education." *J Med Ed* 45(11):929–38 N '70. * (*PA* 47:4877)

131. GOLDSTEIN, STEVEN R. *Differential Effects of Physical and Nonphysical Encounter Group Techniques on Dimensions of Self-Esteem, Interpersonal Relations and Defense.* Doctor's thesis, Temple University (Philadelphia, Pa.), 1970. (*DAI* 31:6257B)

132. GREENBERG, GARY. *Exploration of Personalities, Needs and Attitudes of Female Child-Care Workers.* Doctor's thesis, Illinois Institute of Technology (Chicago, Ill.), 1970. (*DAI* 31:7596B)

133. HARDWICK, MARK WILLIAM. *An Instrumented Self-Awareness Program for College Students: The Evaluation and Description of the Effects of Group Composition and Learning Climate on Selected Self-Concept and Group Experience Variables.* Doctor's thesis, Michigan State University (East Lansing, Mich.), 1970. (*DAI* 31:3900A)

134. HIPPLE, JOHN LeROY. *Effects of Differential Human Relations Laboratory Training Designs on the Interpersonal Behavior of College Students.* Doctor's thesis, University of Iowa (Iowa City, Iowa), 1970. (*DAI* 31:4463A)

135. HOOPER, DOUGLAS, AND SHELDON, ALAN. "A Study of Group Psychotherapy With Married Couples: Part 2, 'Evaluating the Changes.'" *Int J Social Psychiatry* (England) 16(4):299–305 au '70. * (*PA* 48:1092)

136. LEITERMAN, PEGGY HOROWITZ. *Attitudinal and Behavioral Changes in Self-Directed and Leader-Directed Personal Growth Groups.* Doctor's thesis, University of Kentucky (Lexington, Ky.), 1970. (*DAI* 32:741A)

137. LEVINGER, GEORGE; SENN, DAVID J.; AND JORGENSEN, BRUCE W. "Progress Toward Performance in Courtship: A Test of the Kerckhoff-Davis Hypothesis." *Sociometry* 33(4):427–43 D '70. * (*PA* 46:8930)

138. LIDDELL, WILLIAM WALLACE. *The Effects of Individual-Role Compatibility Upon Group Performance.* Doctor's thesis, Pennsylvania State University (University Park, Pa.), 1970. (*DAI* 32:1191B)

139. PEASE, DEAN A. *Player-Coach Compatibility: A Study of the Relationship of Interpersonal Relations Orientations to Athletic Exclusion in Junior High School Baseball Programs.* Doctor's thesis, University of New Mexico (Albuquerque, N.M.), 1970. (*DAI* 31:5829A)

140. TERLESKI, DONALD RICHARD. *The Relationship Between Unstructured and Structured Sensitivity Group Experiences and Self-Perceived Changes of Group Members.* Doctor's thesis, Purdue University (Lafayette, Ind.), 1970. (*DAI* 31:5139A)

141. WHITMORE, HAROLD LEE. *Group Satisfaction: A Function of the Client Selection Procedures, Using Interpersonal Needs.* Doctor's thesis, West Virginia University (Morgantown, W.Va.), 1970. (*DAI* 31:3891A)

142. WIESNER, CHRISTINE WHITE. *The FIRO-B as a Predictor of Friendship Choices Among College Freshmen Women.* Master's thesis, Cornell University (Ithaca, N.Y.), 1970.

143. ALLEE, L. DALE. *A Study of the Relationships Between Selected Interpersonal Variables and Perceived Need Satisfaction of Student Teachers.* Doctor's thesis, George Peabody College for Teachers (Nashville, Tenn.), 1971. (*DAI* 32:3829A)

144. ARONSON, STEPHEN ROGER. *A Comparison of Cognitive vs Focused-Activities Techniques in Sensitivity Group Training.*

Doctor's thesis, University of Connecticut (Storrs, Conn.), 1971. (*DAI* 32:548B)

145. BAUM, RONALD CHARLES. *Self-Disclosure in Small Groups as a Function of Group Composition.* Doctor's thesis, University of Cincinnati (Cincinnati, Ohio), 1971. (*DAI* 32:4200B)

146. BROWN, JACK E. *The Effects of Instant Visual Feedback of Congruence in Group Counseling.* Doctor's thesis, University of North Dakota (Grand Forks, N.D.), 1971. (*DAI* 33:436B)

147. CENTERS, RICHARD, AND GRANVILLE, ARTHUR C. "Reciprocal Need Gratification in Intersexual Attraction: A Test of the Hypotheses of Schutz and Winch." *J Personality* 39(1): 26–43 Mr '71. * (*PA* 46:4824)

148. COULTAS, MARY JOAN. *The Convergent and Discriminant Validation of the Fundamental Interpersonal Relations Orientation—Behavior (FIRO-B).* Doctor's thesis, Catholic University of America (Washington, D.C.), 1971. (*DAI* 32:1268A)

149. DAVIS, JAMES ROBERT. *A Study to Aid in the Selection of Linkers for the Educational Change Process.* Doctor's thesis, New Mexico State University (University Park, N.M.), 1971. (*DAI* 32:1776A)

150. EVANS, JAMES HAROLD. *The Influence of Teacher Personality and Pupil Misbehavior Upon Teacher Impressions of Pupils.* Doctor's thesis, Indiana University (Bloomington, Ind.), 1971. (*DAI* 32:235A)

151. FISHER, JAMES JOSEPH. *Effects of a Simulated Society Experience on Interpersonal Behavior of a Junior College Faculty.* Doctor's thesis, Arizona State University (Tempe, Ariz.), 1971. (*DAI* 31:4485A)

152. FULTINEER, JAMES DEAN. *School Principals Look at Leader Behavior: The Problem of Interpersonal Needs.* Doctor's thesis, West Virginia University (Morgantown, W.Va.), 1971. (*DAI* 32:6036A)

153. GANTZ, BENJAMIN S., JR.; ERICKSON, CLARA; AND STEPHENSON, ROBERT W. "Measuring the Motivation to Manage in a Research and Development Population." Abstract. *Proc 79th Ann Conv Am Psychol Assn* 6(1):129–30 '71. * (*PA* 46:3949)

154. GRAY, SANDRA LEE. *Eye Contact as a Function of Sex, Race, and Interpersonal Needs.* Doctor's thesis, Case Western Reserve University (Cleveland, Ohio), 1971. (*DAI* 32:1842B)

155. HOLBERT, WILLIAM M.; CORMIER, WILLIAM H.; AND FRIEDMAN, MARTIN I. "The Semantic Differential in Sensitivity Training: An Exploratory Study." *Comparative Group Studies* 2(1):36–42 F '71. * (*PA* 47:4715)

156. KLEIN, JOHN FRANCIS. *Compatibility and Satisfaction in the Adolescent Sibling Relationship.* Doctor's thesis, Case Western Reserve University (Cleveland, Ohio), 1971. (*DAI* 32:3455A)

157. KLEIN, THOMAS DICKER. *A Model for Planning Teacher Change Based on Demographic, Personality, Organizational and Pedagogical Measures of Fifty High School English Teachers.* Doctor's thesis, Northwestern University (Evanston, Ill.), 1971. (*DAI* 32:4469A)

158. MEHAFFEY, THOMAS DAVID. *The Effects of a T-Group Experience on Clients With Measured High and Low Dependency Needs.* Doctor's thesis, Indiana State University (Terre Haute, Ind.), 1971. (*DAI* 33:3299A)

159. MURILLO-ROHDE, ILDAURA MARIA. *The Relationship Between Puerto Rican Mother-Son Interpersonal Compatibility in the Area of Control Behavior and Adjustment in School.* Doctor's thesis, New York University (New York, N.Y.), 1971. (*DAI* 32:4030B)

160. POLLACK, HERBERT B. "Change in Homogeneous and Heterogeneous Sensitivity Training Groups." *J Consult & Clin Psychol* 37(1):60–6 Ag '71. * (*PA* 47:829)

161. POPIEL, ELDA S., AND WELCH, CHARLES E. "Intrapersonal Factors as Correlates of Interpersonal Awareness in Training Groups." *Nursing Res* 20(2):165–7 Mr–Ap '71. * (*PA* 47:3077)

162. RODGERS, ROBERT FLOYD. *The Relationship Between Personality and Style of Interpersonal Relationships and Effectiveness and Satisfaction as a Residence Hall Counselor.* Doctor's thesis, Ohio State University (Columbus, Ohio), 1971. (*DAI* 32:1282A)

163. ROSENFELD, LAWRENCE BERNARD. *A Critique of William Schutz's Three-Dimensional Theory of Interpersonal Behavior Using His Measuring Instrument FIRO-B.* Doctor's thesis, Pennsylvania State University (University Park, Pa.), 1971. (*DAI* 32:5427B)

164. SCHUBERT, PAUL WILLIAM. *Personality Type and Self-Perceived Change Resulting From Sensitivity Group Experience.* Doctor's thesis, Purdue University (Lafayette, Ind.), 1971. (*DAI* 32:4360A)

165. SINATRA, LEWIS JAMES. *The Organizational Climate Description Questionnaire and Interpersonal Compatibility.* Doctor's thesis, State University of New York (Buffalo, N.Y.), 1971. (*DAI* 32:2983A)

166. SMALLEGAN, MARIAN. "A Comparison of Two Training Formats for Persons With Varying Interpersonal Needs." *Adult Ed* 21(3):166–76 sp '71. * (*PA* 46:10771)

167. SNEAD, ROBERT FLOYD. *Analysis of Student Response to Alternative Advising Programs in the Two-Year College.* Doctor's thesis, University of Missouri (Columbia, Mo.), 1971. (*DAI* 32:4967A)

168. STRAWSER, ROY STANLEY. *Intensity of Interpersonal Needs as Measured by Schutz FIRO-B as a Predictor of a School*

Administrator's Choice of Job Setting, Choice of Role and Upward Mobility. Doctor's thesis, Utah State University (Logan, Utah), 1971. (*DAI* 33:3229A)

169. UNDERWOOD, WILLIAM JOE. *A Test of the FIRO Theory of Interpersonal Compatibility Among Managerial Dyads.* Doctor's thesis, Temple University (Philadelphia, Pa.), 1971. (*DAI* 32:1267B)

170. VRAA, CALVIN W. "Influence of Need for Inclusion on Group Participation." *Psychol Rep* 28(1):271-4 F '71. * (*PA* 46:4856)

171. VRAA, CALVIN W. "Predicting Academic Achievement of Canadian College Freshmen." *J Col Stud Personnel* 12(4): 303-8 Jl '71. *

172. WEISSMAN, HERBERT N.; SELDMAN, MARTIN; AND RITTER, KENNETH. "Changes in Awareness of Impact Upon Others as a Function of Encounter and Marathon Group Experiences." *Psychol Rep* 28(2):651-61 Ap '71. * (*PA* 46:6770)

173. WIENER, WILLIAM K. *Selected Perceptions and Compatibilities of Personnel in Innovative and Non-Innovative Schools.* Doctor's thesis, Syracuse University (Syracuse, N.Y.), 1971. (*DAI* 33:131A)

174. WITT, HENRY FREDERICK. *An Interpersonal Profile of Area School Instructors.* Doctor's thesis, Iowa State University (Ames, Iowa), 1971. (*DAI* 32:1823A)

CUMULATIVE NAME INDEX

[1177]

★**Fairview Development Scale: For the Infirm Mentally Retarded.** 1971-74; FDS; behavior rating scale yielding 11 scores: perceptual and motor skills (ambulation, total), self-help skills (toilet training, dressing, feeding, grooming, total), language, social interaction, self-direction, total; Robert T. Ross and Alan Boroskin; Research Department, Fairview State Hospital. *

[1178]

★**Fairview Problem Behavior Record.** Mentally retarded; 1971; FPBR; checklist of 29 problem behaviors in 5 areas (aggressive, hyperactive, sexual, covert, inappropriate) plus an adjective checklist; Robert T. Ross; Research Department, Fairview State Hospital. *

[1179]

★**Fairview Self-Help Scale.** Mentally retarded; 1969-70; FSHS; behavior rating scale yielding 11 scores: motor dexterity (ambulation, total), self-help skills (toilet training, dressing, eating, grooming, total), communication skills, social interaction, self-direction, total; Robert T. Ross; Research Department, Fairview State Hospital. *

REFERENCES THROUGH 1971

1. BOROSKIN, ALAN, AND GIAMPICCOLO, JAMES S. "Effect of Staff Ethnocentrism on the Rating of Self-Help Skills of Minority Group Mentally Retarded Patients." *Am J Mental Def* 76(2): 249-51 S '71. * (*PA* 47:9527)

2. PASQUAL, STANLEY; BOROSKIN, ALAN; AND ROSS, ROBERT T. "TMR Self-Help Skills: Public School vs. State Hospital." *Am J Mental Def* 76(2):261-2 S '71. *

3. ROSS, ROBERT T. "A Preliminary Study of Self-Help Skills and Age in Hospitalized Down's Syndrome Patients." *Am J Mental Def* 76(3):373-7 N '71. * (*PA* 48:3555)

CUMULATIVE NAME INDEX

[1180]

★**Fairview Social Skills Scale: For Mildly and Moderately Retarded.** Mentally retarded; 1971-74; FSSS; behavior rating scale yielding 11 scores: self-help skills (locomotion, toilet training, dressing, eating, grooming, total), communication, social interaction, occupation, self-direction, total; Robert T. Ross and James S. Giampiccolo, Jr.; Research Department, Fairview State Hospital. *

[1181]

Family Adjustment Test. Ages 12 and over; 1952–54; FAT; test booklet title is *Elias Family Opinion Survey;* 11 scores: attitudes toward mother, attitudes toward father, father-mother attitude quotient, oedipal, struggle for independence, parent-child friction-harmony, interparental friction-harmony, family inferiority-superiority, rejection of child, parental qualities, total; Gabriel Elias; Psychometric Affiliates. *

For additional information, see P:80 (1 reference); for a review by John Elderkin Bell, see 6:95; for a review by Albert Ellis, see 5:53 (6 references).

REFERENCES THROUGH 1971

1–6. See 5:53.
7. See P:80.
8. LANE, ROBERT C., AND SINGER, JEROME L. "Familial Attitudes in Paranoid Schizophrenics and Normals From Two Socioeconomic Classes." *J Abn & Social Psychol* 59:328–39 N '59. * *(PA* 34:6366)
9. WINER, FRANK. *The Relationship of Certain Attitudes Toward the Mother to Sex-Role Identity.* Doctor's thesis, New York University (New York, N.Y.), 1961. *(DA* 22:4416)
10. KRONENBERGER, EARL J., AND HECK, E. MARJORIE. "Child-Parent Identification Between Reading Ability Groups." *Psychol* 1:2–4 My '64. * *(PA* 39:1366)
11. RIDLEY, DAVID WENDELL. *Patterns of Dating Behavior Associated With Differences in Interpersonal Competence—A Twelfth Grade Sample.* Doctor's thesis, University of Oregon (Eugene, Ore.), 1966. *(DA* 27:2637A)
12. ANIFANT, DAVID C. *A Study of Perceived Family Adjustment and Personality Patterns Among Emotionally Disturbed Girls.* Master's thesis, Springfield College (Springfield, Mass.), 1967.
13. JANUS, SAMUEL. *Personality Factors and Their Relationship to Adjustment in a Camping Situation.* Doctor's thesis, New York University (New York, N.Y.), 1967. *(DA* 29:147A)
14. MAXWELL, JOSEPH WEBSTER, JR. *The Relationship of Family Adjustment to the Self Concept of Lower-Class Adolescent Males.* Doctor's thesis, Florida State University (Tallahassee, Fla.), 1967. *(DA* 28:1915A)
15. KLECKNER, JAMES HERBERT. *An Investigation Into the Personal Characteristics and Family Backgrounds of Psychedelic Drug Users.* Doctor's thesis, Columbia University (New York, N.Y.), 1968. *(DA* 29:4380B)
16. KELLER, JAMES F. *The Relationship Between Educational Aspirations and Factors That Affect Their Fulfillment Among Lower-Class Males.* Doctor's thesis, Florida State University (Tallahassee, Fla.), 1969. *(DAI* 31:1378B)
17. NASH, JOHN MORTON. *Prediction of Academic Achievement of Women at a Private Junior College Through Use of Certain Intellective and Family Relationships Measures.* Doctor's thesis, Boston University (Boston, Mass.), 1970. *(DAI* 31:2113A)
18. BRUHN, JOHN G.; HAMPTON, JAMES W.; AND CHANDLER, BETTY C. "Clinical Marginality and Psychological Adjustment in Hemophilia." *J Psychosom Res* (England) 15(2):207–13 Je '71. * *(PA* 49:7094)
19. BRUHN, JOHN G.; HAMPTON, JAMES W.; AND PHILIPS, BILLY U. "A Psycho-Social Study of Married Hemophiliacs and Their Wives and Hemophiliac Adolescents and Their Parents." *J Psychosom Res* (England) 15(2):293–303 Je '71. *

CUMULATIVE NAME INDEX

[1182]

Family Relations Test. Ages 3–7, 7–15, adults; 1957–65; 3 levels; distributed by NFER Publishing Co. Ltd. [England]. *

a) FAMILY RELATIONS TEST: AN OBJECTIVE TECHNIQUE FOR EXPLORING EMOTIONAL ATTITUDES IN CHILDREN. Ages 3–7, 7–15; 1957; Eva Bene and James Anthony.
b) ADULT VERSION OF THE FAMILY RELATIONS TEST: AN OBJECTIVE TECHNIQUE FOR EXPLORING RECOLLECTED CHILDHOOD FEELINGS. Adults; 1965; Eva Bene.

For additional information and an excerpted review by B. Semeonoff, see 7:79 (7 references); see also P:81 (12 references); for reviews by John E. Bell, Dale B. Harris, and Arthur R. Jensen of children's levels, see 5:132 (1 reference).

REFERENCES THROUGH 1971

1. See 5:132.
2–13. See P:81.
14–20. See 7:79.
21. HOUSTON, H. STEWART. "Familial Correlates of Sex-Role Development in Boys: An Exploratory Study." *Personality* 1(4):303–17 w '70. * *(PA* 47:8646)
22. KAUFFMAN, JAMES M. "Family Relations Test Responses of Disturbed and Normal Boys: Additional Comparative Data." *J Pers Assess* 35(2):128–38 Ap '71. * *(PA* 47:3037)
23. KAUFFMAN, JAMES M.; WEAVER, S. JOSEPH; AND WEAVER, ANN. "Age and Intelligence as Correlates of Perceived Family Relationships of Underachievers." *Psychol Rep* 28(2):522 Ap '71. * *(PA* 46:7758)
24. SWANSON, BERNICE M., AND PARKER, HARRY J. "Parent-Child Relations: A Child's Acceptance by Others, of Others, and of Self." *Child Psychiatry & Hum Develop* 1(4):243–54 su '71. * *(PA* 49:4872)

CUMULATIVE NAME INDEX

[1183]

Famous Sayings. Grades 9–16 and business and industry; 1958, c1957–58; FS; 4 scores: conventional mores, hostility, fear of failure, social acquiescence; Bernard M. Bass; Psychological Test Specialists. *

For additional information, see P:82 (4 references); for reviews by Wesley C. Becker and Robert L. Thorndike, see 6:96 (17 references).

REFERENCES THROUGH 1971

1–17. See 6:96.
18–21. See P:82.
22. BASS, BERNARD M. "Validity Information Exchange, No. 10–25: D.O.T. Code 1-85.22, Salesman, Foodstuffs." *Personnel Psychol* 10:343–4 au '57. *
23. HOFFMAN, PAUL J. "Social Acquiescence and Education." *Ed & Psychol Meas* 20:769–76 w '60. * *(PA* 35:3894)
24. BASS, BERNARD M. "Some Recent Studies in Social Acquiescence." *Psychol Rep* 9:447–8 O '61. *
25. EISENMAN, RUSSELL, AND PLATT, JEROME J. "Authoritarianism, Creativity, and Other Correlates of the Famous Sayings Test." *Psychol Rep* 26(1):267–71 F '70. * *(PA* 45:4279)
26. GREENBERG, ROGER P., AND FISHER, SEYMOUR. "Some Differential Effects of Music on Projective and Structured Psychological Tests." *Psychol Rep* 28(3):817–8 Je '71. * *(PA* 46:10869)
27. HALL, JAY, AND WILLIAMS, MARTHA S. "Personality and Group Encounter Style: A Multivariate Analysis of Traits and Preferences." *J Pers & Social Psychol* 18(2):163–72 My '71. * *(PA* 46:4952)
28. PLATT, JEROME J.; EISENMAN, RUSSELL; DeLISSER, OSWALD; AND DARBES, ALEX. "Temporal Perspective as a Personality Dimension in College Students: A Re-Evaluation." *Percept & Motor Skills* 33(1):103–9 Ag '71. * *(PA* 47:2956)
29. SCHMIDT, HAROLD-EDWIN. "Use of the 'Famous Sayings' Test in South Africa." *Percept & Motor Skills* 32(1):135–41 F '71. * *(PA* 46:3090)

CUMULATIVE NAME INDEX

[1184]

Fatigue Scales Kit. Adults; 1944-54; FSK; 3 scales; [Willard A. Kerr]; Psychometric Affiliates. *

a) INDUSTRIAL SUBJECTIVE FATIGUE AND EUPHORIA SCALES. Adults; 1944-54; 2 scores: fatigue, unpleasantness; 1954 scale identical with scale published 1944.

b) RETROSPECTIVE WORK CURVE FEELINGS FOR NATIONAL RESEARCH PROGRAM ON EMPLOYEE FEELINGS AT WORK. Adults; 1954.

c) STUDY OF DAY [MOTHER'S DAY FATIGUE SCALE]. Housewives; 1954.

For additional information, see P:83; for a review by Richard S. Barrett, see 6:97 (1 reference).

REFERENCES THROUGH 1971
1. See 6:97.

CUMULATIVE NAME INDEX

[1185]

Fear Survey Schedule. College and adults; 1964-69; FSS; self-ratings on 108 fears; Joseph Wolpe and Peter J. Lang; Educational and Industrial Testing Service. *

For additional information and a review by R. G. Demaree, see 7:80 (17 references).

REFERENCES THROUGH 1971

1-17. See 7:80.
18. REHM, LYNN P., AND MARSTON, ALBERT R. "Reduction of Social Anxiety Through Modification of Self-Reinforcement: An Instigation Therapy Technique." *J Consult & Clin Psychol* 32:565-74 O '68. * (*PA* 43:1018)
19. ADAMS, JERRY. "Change on the Fear Survey Schedule During Psychiatric Hospitalization." *J Clin Psychol* 27(4):533-5 O '71. * (*PA* 47:9166)
20. ADAMS, JERRY, AND ROTHSTEIN, WILLIAM. "The Relationship Between 16 Fear Factors and Psychiatric Status." *Behav Res & Ther* (England) 9(4):361-5 N '71. * (*PA* 48:3253)
21. BATES, HENRY D. "Factorial Structure and MMPI Correlates of a Fear Survey Schedule in a Clinical Population." *Behav Res & Ther* (England) 9(4):355-60 N '71. * (*PA* 48:3345)
22. FARLEY, FRANK H., AND MEALIEA, WALLACE L., JR. "Dissimulation and Social Desirability in the Assessment of Fears." *Behav Ther* 2(1):101-2 Ja '71. * (*PA* 47:9200)
23. FROST, BARRY P. "A Semantic Differential Analysis of the Leary Adjectival Check List." *J Clin Psychol* 27(3):372-5 Jl '71. * (*PA* 47:4824)
24. HEKMAT, HAMID, AND VANIAN, DANIEL. "Behavior Modification Through Covert Semantic Desensitization." *J Consult & Clin Psychol* 36(2):248-51 Ap '71. * (*PA* 46:3225)
25. HERSEN, MICHEL. "Fear Scale Norms for an In-Patient Population." *J Clin Psychol* 27(3):375-8 Jl '71. * (*PA* 47:5086)
26. HERSEN, MICHEL. "Personality Characteristics of Nightmare Sufferers." *J Nerv & Mental Dis* 153(1):27-31 Jl '71. * (*PA* 47:9334)
27. KUMAR, K., AND WILKINSON, J. C. M. "Thought Stopping: A Useful Treatment in Phobias of 'Internal Stimuli.'" *Brit J Psychiatry* 119(550):305-7 S '71. * (*PA* 47:9089)
28. KUTNER, S. JEROME. "A Survey of Fear of Pregnancy and Depression." *J Psychol* 79(2):263-72 N '71. * (*PA* 47:6631)
29. LANDY, FRANK J., AND GAUPP, LARRY A. "A Factor

Analysis of the Fear Survey Schedule—III." *Behav Res & Ther* (England) 9(2):89-93 My '71. * (*PA* 47:1165)
30. MERMIS, BERNIE, AND ROSS, DON. "Rater Agreement on the Reinforcement and Fear Survey Schedules." *Psychol Rep* 28(1):243-6 F '71. * (*PA* 46:5143)
31. SOLYOM, L.; HESELTINE, G. F. D.; McCLURE, D. J.; LEDWIDGE, B.; AND KENNY, F. "A Comparative Study of Aversion Relief and Systematic Desensitization in the Treatment of Phobias." *Brit J Psychiatry* 119(550):299-303 S '71. * (*PA* 47:9123)

CUMULATIVE NAME INDEX

[1186]

Fels Parent Behavior Rating Scales. 1937-49; FPBRS; "for the use of the trained home visitor in appraising certain aspects of parent-child relationships"; 30 scores: adjustment of home, activeness of home, discord in home, sociability of family, coordination of household, child-centeredness of home, duration of contact with mother, intensity of contact with mother, restrictiveness of regulation, readiness of enforcement, severity of actual penalties, justification of policy, democracy of policy, clarity of policy, effectiveness of policy, disciplinary friction, quantity of suggestion, coerciveness of suggestion, accelerational attempt, general babying, general protectiveness, readiness of criticism, direction of criticism, readiness of explanation, solicitousness for welfare, acceptance of child, understanding, emotionality toward child, affectionateness toward child, rapport with child; Alfred L. Baldwin, Joan Kalhorn, Fay Huffman Breese, and Horace Champney; Fels Research Institute. *

For additional information, see P:84 (8 references); for a review by Dale B. Harris, see 4:43 (15 references).

REFERENCES THROUGH 1971

1-15. See 4:43.
16-23. See P:84.
24. MEYER, CHARLENE TRUMBO. "The Assertive Behavior of Children as Related to Parent Behavior." *J Home Econ* 39: 77-80 F '47. * (*PA* 22:645)
25. HIGHBERGER, RUTH LEAH. *The Relationship Between Maternal Behavior and the Child's Early Adjustment to Nursery School.* Doctor's thesis, State University of Iowa (Iowa City, Iowa), 1953. (*DA* 13:732)
26. KOCH, HELEN L. "Attitudes of Young Children Toward Their Peers as Related to Certain Characteristics of Their Siblings." *Psychol Monogr* 70(19):1-41 '56. * (*PA* 31:7521)
27. SONTAG, LESTER W., AND BAKER, CHARLES T. "Personality, Familial, and Physical Correlates of Change in Mental Ability." *Monogr Soc Res Child Develop* 23(2):87-143 '58. * (*PA* 33:5729)
28. BARSKY, MARILYN LEE. *The Relationship of Some Aggressive Characteristics to Reading Achievement in Fifth and Sixth Grade Males and Females.* Doctor's thesis, Rutgers—The State University (New Brunswick, N.J.), 1966. (*DA* 27:1257A)
29. SCARR, SANDRA. "Social Introversion-Extraversion as a Heritable Response." *Child Develop* 40(3):823-32 S '69. * (*PA* 44:2201)

[1187]

*The Forty-Eight Item Counseling Evaluation Test, Revised. Adolescents and adults; 1963–71; ICET; 7 problem area scores: anxiety-tension-stress, compulsive-obsessive-rigid behavior, depressive-defeatist thoughts and feelings, friendship-socialization, religious-philosophical goals, inadequacy feelings and behavior, total; 1971 test identical with test copyrighted 1963 except for format and directions; Frank B. McMahon; Western Psychological Services. *

For additional information and a review by John O. Crites, see 7:81 (1 reference).

REFERENCES THROUGH 1971

1. See 7:81.
2. McMahon, Frank B., Jr., and Hunt, Raymond G. "A 'Contingent-Item' Method for Constructing a Short Personality Questionnaire." J Appl Psychol 48:197–200 Je '64. * (PA 39:5026)

[1188]

The Freeman Anxiety Neurosis and Psychosomatic Test. Mental patients; 1952–55; FANPT; test booklet title is *The Freeman AN and PS Test;* 9 scores: anxiety neurosis, psychosomatic syndrome, and 7 subscores; M. J. Freeman; Grune & Stratton, Inc. *

For additional information, see P:86; for reviews by Gerald A. Mendelsohn and Robert C. Nichols, see 6:99 (4 references); see also 5:55 (3 references).

REFERENCES THROUGH 1971

1–3. See 5:55.
4–7. See 6:99.

[1189]

★Frost Self Description Questionnaire. Ages 8–14; 1972–73; FSDQ; 14 scores: anxiety (test, social, worry and tension, concentration, separation from family, spatial separation, body damage, free floating), aggression (externalized, internalized, projective), denial, affiliation, submissiveness; Barry P. Frost; Alberta Behavioral Resource Consultants Ltd. [Canada]. *

REFERENCES THROUGH 1971

1. Frost, Barry P. "Anxiety and Educational Achievement." Brit J Ed Psychol 38:293–301 N '68. * (PA 43:7368)
2. Frost, Barry P. "Extraversion and Educational Achievement." West Psychologist 1(1):5–18 S '69. * (PA 45:8976)
3. Frost, Barry P. "A Note on Extraversion and Aggression." West Psychologist 1(3):111–2 My '70. * (PA 45:6313)

[1190]

Getting Along. Grades 7–9; 1964–65; GA; 4 scores: self acceptance, acceptance by others, facing reality, total; Trudys Lawrence; the Author. *

For additional information, see P:89 (2 references).

REFERENCES THROUGH 1971

1–2. See P:89.

[1191]

The Gibson Spiral Maze. Ages 8.5 and over; 1961–65; GSM; psychomotor performance associated with maladjustment, delinquency, mental illness, and accident proneness; 2 scores: time, error; H. B. Gibson; University of London Press Ltd. [England]. *

For additional information, a review by D. F. Clark, and excerpted reviews by C. H. Ammons and J. C. Raven, see 7:82 (4 references); see also P:90 (2 references).

REFERENCES THROUGH 1971

1–2. See P:90.
3–6. See 7:82.
7. Alexander, D. A. "Two Tests of Psychomotor Function in Detection of Organic Cerebral Damage in Elderly Psychiatric Patients." Percept & Motor Skills 33(3):1291–7 D '71. * (PA 48:3524)
8. McDonald, Kenneth G., and Parker, Adrian D. "Gibson Spiral Maze and MPI Scores: A Comparison Using Normal Adolescent Subjects." Brit J Social & Clin Psychol 10(2):191–2 Je '71. *
9. Martin, D. N., and Warde, Susan. "The Performance of Approved-School Boys on the Gibson Spiral Maze." Brit J Psychol 62(4):551–5 N '71. * (PA 47:9276)

[1192]

Goldstein-Scheerer Tests of Abstract and Concrete Thinking. Brain damaged adults; 1941–51; 5 tests; Kurt Goldstein, Martin Scheerer, and Louis Rosenberg (c, record booklet); Psychological Corporation. *

a) GOLDSTEIN-SCHEERER CUBE TEST. 1941–45.
b) GELB-GOLDSTEIN COLOR SORTING TEST. 1941–51.
c) GOLDSTEIN-SCHEERER OBJECT SORTING TEST. 1941–51.
d) WEIGL-GOLDSTEIN-SCHEERER COLOR FORM SORTING TEST. 1941–45.
e) GOLDSTEIN-SCHEERER STICK TEST. 1941–45.

For additional information, see P:91 (19 references); for a review by R. W. Payne, see 6:101 (23 references); see also 5:57 (21 references); for reviews by Kate Levine Kogan, C. R. Strother (with Ludwig Immergluck), and O. L. Zangwill, see 3:41 (28 references). For an excerpt from a related book review, see 3:42.

REFERENCES THROUGH 1971

1–28. See 3:41.
29–49. See 5:57.
50–72. See 6:101.
73–91. See P:91.
92. Scherer, Isidor W. "Prognoses and Psychological Scores in Electroconvulsive Therapy, Psychosurgery, and Spontaneous Remission." Am J Psychiatry 107:926–31 Je '51. * (PA 27:477)
93. Madonick, M. J., and Stein, J. M. "A Case of Amnesic Aphasia of Fifteen Years' Duration: Disturbances in Abstract Thinking." J Nerv & Mental Dis 117:251–61 Mr '53. * (PA 29:1182)
94. Silverman, Albert J., and Harris, Virgil W. "Electroencephalography and Psychometric Testing in Brain-Dam-

aged Patients." *J Nerv & Mental Dis* 120:31–5 Jl–Ag '54. * (*PA* 29:6111)

95. HOPKINS, BARBARA, AND POST, FELIX. "The Significance of Abstract and Concrete Behaviour in Elderly Psychiatric Patients and Control Subjects." *J Mental Sci* (England) 101: 841–50 O '55. * (*PA* 30:7000)

96. GLASS, BLANCHE. *A Study of Concept Formation in Schizophrenics and Non-Psychotics: A Comparison of the Concept Formation of Two Hospitalized Groups of Schizophrenics With Varying Durations of Illness and Non-Psychotics in Two Different Age Groups.* Doctor's thesis, New York University (New York, N.Y.), 1956. (*DA* 16:1945)

97. JAHODA, GUSTAV. "Assessment of Abstract Behavior in a Non-Western Culture." *J Abn & Social Psychol* 53:237–43 S '56. * (*PA* 32:2798)

98. KIRSCHNER, DAVID. *An Analysis of Certain Relationships Between "Abstract" and "Concrete" Attitude, Avoidance Behavior, and Stimulus Generalization.* Doctor's thesis, University of Pittsburgh (Pittsburgh, Pa.), 1957. (*DA* 17:2314)

99. PAYNE, R. W. "Some Aspects of Perception and Thought Disorder in Schizophrenic Subjects." *Schweizerische Zeitschrift für Psychologie und Ihre Anwendungen* (Switzerland) 17(4): 300–8 '58. * (*PA* 34:1791)

100. WEINBERG, NORRIS H. *Cognitive Development, Self-Orientation, and Piaget's Notion of Ego-Centricity.* Doctor's thesis, University of Pennsylvania (Philadelphia, Pa.), 1958. (*DA* 18:2222)

101. HUGHES, DOROTHY HALE. *A Study of Concept Formation in a Group of Superior, Average and Mentally Retarded Children of Similar Mental Age: A Comparison of the Concept Formation of Boys and Girls Whose Mental Ages Are Between 9-6 and 10-6, but Whose Intellectual Levels Vary From Superior to Mentally Retarded.* Doctor's thesis, New York University (New York, N.Y.), 1959. (*DA* 20:3378)

102. TALLAND, GEORGE A. "Psychological Studies of Korsakoff's Psychosis: 3, Concept Formation." *J Nerv & Mental Dis* 128:214–26 Mr '59. * (*PA* 34:3305)

103. JAN-TAUSCH, JAMES. *Concrete Thinking as a Factor in Reading Retardation.* Doctor's thesis, Rutgers University (New Brunswick, N.J.), 1960. (*DA* 21:2984)

104. MIRSKY, ALLEN F.; PRIMAC, DANIEL W.; MARSAN, COSIMO AJMONE; ROSVOLD, H. ENGER; AND STEVENS, JANICE R. "A Comparison of the Psychological Test Performance of Patients With Focal and Nonfocal Epilepsy." *Exp Neurol* 2:75–89 F '60. *

105. WODIN, MARTIN HENRY. *An Examination of Perceptual and Cognitive Rigidity in Deaf Adolescent Boys.* Doctor's thesis, New York University (New York, N.Y.), 1960. (*DA* 22:329)

106. PIERCY, MALCOLM M., AND SMYTH, V. O. G. "Right Hemisphere Dominance for Certain Non-Verbal Intellectual Skills." *Brain* (England) 85:775–90 D '62. *

107. SINGER, MARGARET THALER. Chap. 12, "Personality Measurements in the Aged," pp. 217–49. In *Human Aging: A Biological and Behavioral Study.* Edited by James E. Birren, Robert N. Butler, Samuel W. Greenhouse, Louis Sokoloff, and Marian R. Yarrow. National Institute of Mental Health, Public Health Service Publication No. 986. Washington, D.C.: United States Government Printing Office, 1963. Pp. xiii, 328. * (*PA* 38:5821)

108. SKLAR, MAURICE. "Relation of Psychological and Language Test Scores and Autopsy Findings in Aphasia." *J Speech & Hearing Res* 6:84–90 Mr '63. * (*PA* 38:1201)

109. WALLER, RONALD CHESTER. *The Effect of Hue Change on Judgment of Facial Expression.* Doctor's thesis, University of California (Los Angeles, Calif.), 1963. (*DA* 24:2128)

110. SMITH, AARON. "Mental Deterioration in Chronic Schizophrenia." *J Nerv & Mental Dis* 139:479–87 N '64. *

111. DE RENZI, E.; FAGLIONI, P.; SAVOIARDO, M.; AND VIGNOLO, L. A. "The Influence of Aphasia and of the Hemispheric Side of the Cerebral Lesion on Abstract Thinking." *Cortex* (Italy) 2:399–420 O '66. * (*PA* 41:7708)

112. MAY, A. E. "Anxiety and Overinclusion." *Brit J Psychiatry* 112:41–2 Ja '66. * (*PA* 40:5745)

113. NOLAN, JEREMIAH DENNIS. *Intradimensional and Extradimensional Shifts in Abstract and Concrete Schizophrenics.* Doctor's thesis, University of Maryland (College Park, Md.), 1966. (*DA* 27:4131B)

114. DELANY, FRANCES IMELDA. *An Investigation Into Certain Aspects of Visual and Visuo-Motor Perception in Children With Cerebral Palsy.* Doctor's thesis, Fordham University (New York, N.Y.), 1967. (*DA* 28:1293A)

115. JUDGE, CAROLE HESSE. *Thought Disorder in Parents of Schizophrenics.* Doctor's thesis, University of Minnesota (Minneapolis, Minn.), 1967. (*DA* 28:3473B)

116. ASKAR, A. M.; RAKHAWY, Y. T.; AND SHAALAN, M. "Conceptual Measurement as a Means of Assessing Therapeutic Changes in Schizophrenia." *J Egypt Med Assn* 51(1):1–17 '68. *

117. KELLAGHAN, THOMAS. "Abstraction and Categorization in African Children." *Int J Psychol* (France) 3(2):115–20 '68. * (*PA* 43:746)

118. PAYNE, R. W. "The Long Term Prognostic Implications of Overinclusive Thinking in Mental Patients: A Follow-Up Study Using Objective Tests." *Proc 4th World Congr Psychiatry* 1966(pt 4):2657–60 '68. *

119. JAMBOR, K. L. "Cognitive Functioning in Multiple Sclerosis." *Brit J Psychiatry* 115(524):765–75 Jl '69. * (*PA* 44:7136)

120. McDONALD, CARRICK. "Clinical Heterogeneity in Senile Dementia." *Brit J Psychiatry* 115(520):267–71 Mr '69. * (*PA* 43:13272)

121. VITALE, JOHN H.; STEINHELBER, JOHN C.; DRAKE, WILLIAM E., JR.; AND DAHLGREN, HELEN. "Psychological Dimensions of Cerebrovascular Insufficiency." *Percept & Motor Skills* 29(2): 555–63 O '69. * (*PA* 44:3996)

122. BOYD, M. EUNICE. *A Study to Determine the Effect of Science Inquiry on the Abstract Categorization Behavior of Deaf Children.* Doctor's thesis, University of Pennsylvania (Philadelphia, Pa.), 1970. (*DAI* 31:2213A)

123. CHOVAN, WILLIAM L. "Vocal Mediating Responses in Short-Term Memory of Severely and Profoundly Deaf Children." *Percept & Motor Skills* 31(2):539–44 O '70. * (*PA* 45:6826)

124. CRAIG, ROBERT J. "Relationship Between Severity of Illness and Overinclusive Thinking in Schizophrenia." *Psychol Rep* 26(1):251–4 F '70. * (*PA* 45:4646)

125. PAYNE, ROBERT W.; HOCHBERG, ARTHUR C.; AND HAWKS, DAVID V. "Dichotic Stimulation as a Method of Assessing Disorder of Attention in Overinclusive Schizophrenic Patients." *J Abn Psychol* 76(2):185–93 O '70. * (*PA* 45:2737)

126. BROMET, EVELYN JUNE. *Thought Disorder and Psycho-Social Factors in the Posthospital Adjustment of Psychiatric Patients.* Doctor's thesis, Yale University (New Haven, Conn.), 1971. (*DAI* 32:2982B)

127. HAWKS, D. V., AND PAYNE, R. W. "Overinclusive Thought Disorder and Symptomatology." *Brit J Psychiatry* 118 (547):663–70 Je '71. * (*PA* 47:7190)

CUMULATIVE NAME INDEX

[1193]

Gordon Personal Inventory. Grades 9–16 and adults; 1956–63, c1955–63; GPI; 4 scores: cautiousness, original thinking, personal relations, vigor; 1963 test identical with test copyrighted 1956 except for format and wording changes in directions; Leonard V. Gordon; Harcourt Brace Jovanovich, Inc. *

For additional information, see P:92 (13 references); for reviews by Charles F. Dicken and Alfred B. Heilbrun, Jr., see 6:102 (13 references); for reviews by Benno G. Fricke and John A. Radcliffe and excerpted reviews by Laurance F. Shaffer and Laurence Siegel, see 5:58.

REFERENCES THROUGH 1971

1–13. See 6:102.
14–26. See P:92.
27. SKELLY, CLYDE G. Some Variables Which Differentiate the Highly Intelligent and Highly Divergent Thinking Adolescent. Doctor's thesis, University of Connecticut (Storrs, Conn.), 1961. (DA 22:2699)
28. BECKER, PAUL W. Correlates of Psychopathic and Neurotic Delinquency Within a Federal Reformatory Population. Master's thesis, Ohio University (Athens, Ohio), 1964.
29. MEISGEIER, CHARLES. "The Identification of Successful Teachers of Mentally or Physically Handicapped Children." Excep Children 32:229–35 D '65. * (PA 40:3409)
30. PATTERSON, LEWIS EARL. Counselor Education as a Process of Adult Socialization. Doctor's thesis, Pennsylvania State University (University Park, Pa.), 1965. (DA 26:6451)
31. BARE, CAROLE E. "Counselor Sensitivity to the Counselor-Client Communication Process." Abstract. Proc 74th Ann Conv Am Psychol Assn 1:301–2 '66. * (PA 41:6145)
32. STROMNES, FRODE J. "Development and Differentiation of Acquaintance in Engaged and Married Couples." Scand J Psychol 7(1):34–42 '66. * (PA 40:6581)
33. ZELLER, EARNEST JEROME. A Short-Term Adult Program Experiment in a Correctional Institution. Doctor's thesis, Indiana University (Bloomington, Ind.), 1966. (DA 28:101A)
34. HAYS, BOB BURK. Student Teacher Expectations of the Leadership Role of the Principal. Doctor's thesis, North Texas State University (Denton, Tex.), 1967. (DA 28:3557A)
35. LYNCH, DENIS JOSEPH. Future Time Perspective and Impulsivity in Old Age. Doctor's thesis, Case Western Reserve University (Cleveland, Ohio), 1967. (DA 28:4296B)
36. POPE, ALLEN LAWRENCE. An Exploratory Study of Certain Aspects of the Personal-Social Relations of the Highly Creative Student as Compared to the Academically-Intelligent Student. Doctor's thesis, University of Montana (Missoula, Mont.), 1967. (DA 28:1629A)
37. ASHMORE, BETTIE JANE. An Investigation of Changes in Attitudes and Personality Characteristics Among Counselors in Three Types of Counselor Education Programs. Doctor's thesis, University of Alabama (University, Ala.), 1968. (DA 29:1416A)
38. BLANK, STANLEY S. "An Examination of the Usefulness of Various Psychological Instruments for Predicting Department Managers' Ratings of Clerical Sales Personnel." Can Counsellor 2:46–50 Ja '68. *
39. BRAUN, JOHN R., AND ASTA, PATRICIA. "Intercorrelations Between Personal Orientation Inventory and Gordon Personal Inventory Scores." Psychol Rep 23:1197–8 D '68. * (PA 43:8368)
40. CHIPMAN, LEROY P. A Comparison of Participants and Nonparticipants in Intercollegiate Athletics With Respect to Selected Personality Traits. Doctor's thesis, Springfield College (Springfield, Mass.), 1968.
41. GOLDMEIER, JOHN. "A Study of Selected Personality Attributes and Treatment Preferences of Caseworkers and Casework Students." Social Service R 42:231–40 Je '68. *

42. KERNAN, JEROME B. "Choice Criteria, Decision Behavior, and Personality." J Marketing Res 5:155–64 My '68. *
43. BALDWIN, WILLIAM R., AND LEVINE, NIRA R. "Personality Norms Characteristic of Optometrists." Am J Optom 46(8):616–27 Ag '69. *
44. DOYLE, JAMES RAYMOND. The Relationship of Direct and Indirect Teaching to Accurate Perceptions of Student Personality and Temperament Characteristics. Doctor's thesis, Wayne State University (Detroit, Mich.), 1969. (DAI 31:1506A)
45. SPARKS, DAVID LEE. An Analysis of the Relationship Between Product Use and Personality. Doctor's thesis, University of Texas (Austin, Tex.), 1969. (DAI 30:2675A)
46. WHEELER, MARY FLORENCE. A Study of Relationships Among Professional Attitudes, Personal Traits, and Attitudinal Change During Instruction in Perceptual Media. Doctor's thesis, East Texas State University (Commerce, Tex.), 1969. (DAI 30:2391A)
47. WOLLOWICK, HERBERT B., AND McNAMARA, W. J. "Relationship of the Components of an Assessment Center to Management Success." J Appl Psychol 53(5):348–52 O '69. * (PA 44:1448)
48. BARE, CAROLE E. "Personality and Self Concept Correlates of Occupational Aspirations." Voc Guid Q 18(4):297–305 Je '70. *
49. BERGEMANN, KAREN. "The Effects of Chronic Disability on Field Dependence-Independence." Grad Res Ed & Related Discip 5(2):109–23 sp '70. * (PA 46:9441)
50. DODD, WILLIAM E. "Will Management Assessment Centers Insure Selection of the Same Old Types?" Abstract. Proc 78th Ann Conv Am Psychol Assn 5(2):569–70 '70. * (PA 44:19658)
51. GOZA, JOHN THOMAS. An Investigation of the Academic Potential, Academic Achievement, and Personality of Participants in an Associate Degree Nursing Program. Doctor's thesis, East Texas State University (Commerce, Tex.), 1970. (DAI 31:5442B)
52. JOESTING, JOAN AXTELL. A Comparative Study of Activists and Nonactivists at a Southern Black College. Doctor's thesis, University of Georgia (Athens, Ga.), 1970. (DAI 31:3958A)
53. MORETZ, WALTER JENNINGS, JR. Selected Personality Traits of Negro Senior High School Pupils in Northern Florida, as Related to School Racial Composition and Sex of Pupils. Doctor's thesis, Florida State University (Tallahassee, Fla.), 1970. (DAI 31:5774A)
54. PRIEN, ERICH P. "Measuring Performance Criteria of Bank Tellers." J Indus Psychol 5(1):29–36 Mr '70. * (PA 45:7135)
55. SCHWAB, DONALD P. "Counterbalancing and Fakability of the Gordon Personal Inventory and Profile." Psychol Rep 26(2):671–5 Ap '70. * (PA 44:20994)
56. SHOCHAT, ELIMELECH. A Study of the Relationship Between Specified Personality Traits and Body-Cathexis of Male Participants and Non-Participants in High School Athletics. Doctor's thesis, University of Massachusetts (Amherst, Mass.), 1970. (DAI 31:2079A)
57. DONNELLY, MONA MARY. A Study of Elementary Teachers' Personality Traits and Attitudes Toward Teaching Selected Content Areas in the Elementary School. Doctor's thesis, University of Illinois (Urbana, Ill.), 1971. (DAI 32:5648A)
58. KORNFELD-JACOBS, GILA. A Study of Dimensions of Personality and Occupational Function. Doctor's thesis, State University of New York (Buffalo, N.Y.), 1971. (DAI 32:1274A)
59. LYNCH, DENIS J. "Future Time Perspective and Impulsivity in Old Age." J Genetic Psychol 118(2):245–52 Je '71. * (PA 46:8803)
60. PRISELAC, STEPHEN MICHAEL. A Study of Certain Personal Characteristics of Pennsylvania School Board and Teacher Negotiating Team Members. Doctor's thesis, West Virginia University (Morgantown, W.Va.), 1971. (DAI 32:1806A)
61. REID, JAYNE. The Relationship of Selected Aspects of Attitude, Personality, and Achievement to the Post-High School Employment of Senior Stenographic Students. Doctor's thesis, University of Cincinnati (Cincinnati, Ohio), 1971. (DAI 32:3570A)
62. SCHWAB, DONALD P. "Issues in Response Distortion Studies of Personality Inventories: A Critique and Replicated Study." Personnel Psychol 24(4):637–47 w '71. *
63. SPARKS, DAVID L., AND TUCKER, W. T. "A Multivariate Analysis of Personality and Product Use." J Marketing Res 8(1):67–70 F '71. * (PA 46:9898)
64. WUBBOLDING, ROBERT EDWARD. The Relationship Between Pre-Measured Personality Variables and Counselor Behavior During Structured Interviews. Doctor's thesis, University of Cincinnati (Cincinnati, Ohio), 1971. (DAI 32:3711A)

Daniel, K. laV.: 17
Dawson, R. I.: 8
Dicken, C. F.: *rev, 6*:102
Dodd, W. E.: 50
Donnelly, M. M.: 57
Doyle, J. R.: 44
Dugan, R. D.: 7
Fricke, B. G.: *rev,* 5:58
Goldmeier, J.: 41
Goza, J. T.: 51
Hays, B. B.: 34
Heilbrun, A. B.: *rev,* 6:102
Joesting, J. A.: 52
Jones, J. E.: 26
Jones, J. M.: 24
Kernan, J. B.: 42
Kornfeld-Jacobs, G.: 58
Kriedt, P. H.: 8
Levine, N. R.: 43
Locke, E. A.: 18
Lodato, F. J.: 14
Lynch, D. J.: 35, 59
McKinney, E. D.: 2
McNamara, W. J.: 47
Magaw, D. C.: 4
Meisgeier, C.: 29

Meisgeier, C. H.: 15
Moretz, W. J.: 53
Patterson, L. E.: 30
Phelan, J. G.: 16
Pope, A. L.: 36
Prien, E. P.: 21, 54
Priselac, S. M.: 60
Radcliffe, J. A.: *rev,* 5:58
Reid, J.: 61
Ried, B. R.: 9
Schoch, E. W.: 26
Schwab, D. P.: 55, 62
Shaffer, L. F.: *exc,* 5:58
Shochat, E.: 56
Siegel, L.: *exc,* 5:58
Skelly, C. G.: 27
Sparks, D. L.: 45, 63
Strømnes, F. J.: 32
Tucker, W. T.: 63
Weiss, R.: 6
Welsch, L. A.: 25
Wheeler, M. F.: 46
Willingham, W. W.: 13
Wollowick, H. B.: 47
Wubbolding, R. E.: 64
Zeller, E. J.: 33

[1194]

Gordon Personal Profile. Grades 9–16 and adults; 1953–63, ci951–63; GPP; 4 scores: ascendancy, responsibility, emotional stability, sociability; 1963 test identical with test copyrighted 1953 except for format and wording changes in directions; Leonard V. Gordon; Harcourt Brace Jovanovich, Inc. *

For additional information, see P:93 (23 references); for reviews by Charles F. Dicken and Alfred B. Heilbrun, Jr., see 6:103 (25 references); for reviews by Benno G. Fricke and John A. Radcliffe and an excerpted review by Laurance F. Shaffer, see 5:59 (16 references).

REFERENCES THROUGH 1971

1–16. See 5:59.
17–41. See 6:103.
42–64. See P:93.
65. BASS, BERNARD M. "Validity Information Exchange, No. 10–25: D.O.T. Code 1–85.22, Salesman, Foodstuffs." *Personnel Psychol* 10:343–4 au '57. *
66. GREENBERG, H.; STRAIGHT, B.; HASSENGER, W.; AND RASKA, W. "Personality and Attitudinal Differences Between Employed and Unemployed Married Women." *J Social Psychol* 53:87–96 F '61. *
67. PROCTOR, ROBERT ALLEN, JR. *A Study of Attitude Changes in Theological Students During One Year of Seminary Training.* Doctor's thesis, Temple University (Philadelphia, Pa.), 1961. (*DA* 22:343)
68. ELKIN, FREDERICK; HALPERN, GERALD; AND COOPER, ANTHONY. "Leadership in a Student Mob." *Can J Psychol* 16:199–201 S '62. * (*PA* 37:4890)
69. DIERMAN, FREDERICK G. *The Relationship Between Personality Traits and Aptitude for the Service in Naval ROTC Students.* Master's thesis, University of Utah (Salt Lake City, Utah), 1964.
70. BEST, GILMARY. *Transfer Effects of Directed Classroom Experience to an Elementary Methods Class and Student Teaching.* Doctor's thesis, Wayne State University (Detroit, Mich.), 1965. (*DA* 26:5120)
71. DOUGLAS, EARL D.; FIKE, DAVID; AND WIERZBINSKI, ERVIN J. "Effects of Group Counseling: An Experiment Evaluated by Objective Tests." *Crime & Del* 11:360–5 O '65. *
72. PATTERSON, LEWIS EARL. *Counselor Education as a Process of Adult Socialization.* Doctor's thesis, Pennsylvania State University (University Park, Pa.), 1965. (*DA* 26:6451)
73. BARE, CAROLE E. "Counselor Sensitivity to the Counselor-Client Communication Process." Abstract. *Proc 74th Ann Conv Am Psychol Assn* 1:301–2 '66. * (*PA* 41:6145)
74. SALEH, SHOUKRY D., AND COUGHLAN, DANIEL W. "Characteristics of Successful Probation Officers: A Validation Study." *Pub Personnel R* 27:43–5 Ja '66. *
75. STROMNES, FRODE J. "Development and Differentiation of Acquaintance in Engaged and Married Couples." *Scand J Psychol* (Sweden) 7(1):34–42 '66. * (*PA* 40:6581)
76. ZELLER, EARNEST JEROME. *A Short-Term Adult Program Experiment in a Correctional Institution.* Doctor's thesis, Indiana University (Bloomington, Ind.), 1966. (*DA* 28:101A)
77. ANDERSON, ELWOOD GRANT. *A Comparison of Emotional Stability in Stutterers and Non-Stutterers.* Doctor's thesis, Wayne State University (Detroit, Mich.), 1967. (*DA* 28:3511B)
78. HAYS, BOB BURK. *Student Teacher Expectations of the Leadership Role of the Principal.* Doctor's thesis, North Texas State University (Denton, Tex.), 1967. (*DA* 28:3557A)
79. ASHMORE, BETTIE JANE. *An Investigation of Changes in Attitudes and Personality Characteristics Among Counselors in Three Types of Counselor Education Programs.* Doctor's thesis, University of Alabama (University, Ala.), 1968. (*DA* 29:1416A)
80. BLANK, STANLEY S. "An Examination of the Usefulness of Various Psychological Instruments for Predicting Department Managers' Ratings of Clerical Sales Personnel." *Can Counsellor* 2:46–50 Ja '68. *
81. CHIPMAN, LEROY P. *A Comparison of Participants and Nonparticipants in Intercollegiate Athletics With Respect to Selected Personality Traits.* Doctor's thesis, Springfield College (Springfield, Mass.), 1968.
82. HOWELL, MARGARET A. "Medical Interns: A Study of Types." *Ed & Psychol Meas* 28:327–38 su '68. * (*PA* 42:18860)
83. HUNT, DAVID HERBERT. *A Comparison of Specific Aspects of Personality of Selected White Varsity Athletes and Nonathletes With Specific Aspects of Personality of Selected Negro Varsity Athletes and Nonathletes at the College Level Utilizing the Gordon Personal Profile.* Doctor's thesis, University of New Mexico (Albuquerque, N.M.), 1968. (*DA* 29:4186A)
84. KERNAN, JEROME B. "Choice Criteria, Decision Behavior, and Personality." *J Marketing Res* 5:155–64 My '68. *
85. KERPELMAN, LARRY C. "Student Activism, Ideology, and Personality." Abstract. *Proc 76th Ann Conv Am Psychol Assn* 3:377–8 '68. * (*PA* 43:895, title only)
86. McLEOD, JACK DONALD. *Prediction of Independent Study Performance in Secondary School.* Doctor's thesis, Stanford University (Stanford, Calif.), 1968. (*DA* 29:3044A)
87. MAULSBY, ANN. *Hewett's Theory of Educational Engineering of Emotionally Disturbed Children Adapted for Curriculum and Clinical Practice of Baccalaureate Student Nurses in a Pediatric Course.* Doctor's thesis, University of California (Los Angeles, Calif.), 1968. (*DA* 29:2571A)
88. RAPONI, TEODORO. *A Study of the Relationships Between Personality Characteristics, Manifest Health, Academic Performance, and the Use of a Selected Personnel Service by Selected Incoming Freshmen at Kent State University.* Master's thesis, Kent State University (Kent, Ohio), 1968.
89. BALDWIN, WILLIAM R., AND LEVINE, NIRA R. "Personality Norms Characteristic of Optometrists." *Am J Optom* 46(8):616–27 Ag '69. *
90. DOYLE, JAMES RAYMOND. *The Relationship of Direct and Indirect Teaching to Accurate Perceptions of Student Personality and Temperament Characteristics.* Doctor's thesis, Wayne State University (Detroit, Mich.), 1969. (*DAI* 31:1506A)
91. HINRICHS, J. R. "Comparison of 'Real Life' Assessments of Management Potential With Situational Exercises, Paper-and-Pencil Ability Tests, and Personality Inventories." *J Appl Psychol* 53(5):425–32 O '69. * (*PA* 44:1442)
92. HUNT, DAVID H. "A Cross Racial Comparison of Personality Traits Between Athletes and Nonathletes." *Res Q* 40(4):704–7 D '69. *
93. KERPELMAN, LARRY C. "Student Political Activism and Ideology: Comparative Characteristics of Activists and Non-activists." *J Counsel Psychol* 16(1):8–13 Ja '69. * (*PA* 43:5868)
94. SPARKS, DAVID LEE. *An Analysis of the Relationship Between Product Use and Personality.* Doctor's thesis, University of Texas (Austin, Tex.), 1969. (*DAI* 30:2675A)
95. WHEELER, MARY FLORENCE. *A Study of Relationships Among Professional Attitudes, Personal Traits, and Attitudinal Change During Instruction in Perceptual Media.* Doctor's thesis, East Texas State University (Commerce, Tex.), 1969. (*DAI* 30:2391A)
96. WHEELER, RICHARD WADE. *A Study of the Relationship Between Selected Interviewer Variables and the Interpretation of Interview Information.* Doctor's thesis, University of Houston (Houston, Tex.), 1969. (*DAI* 30:425B)
97. WOLLOWICK, HERBERT B., AND McNAMARA, W. J. "Relationship of the Components of an Assessment Center to Management Success." *J Appl Psychol* 53(5):348–52 O '69. * (*PA* 44:1448)
98. BARE, CAROLE E. "Personality and Self Concept Correlates of Occupational Aspirations." *Voc Guid Q* 18(4):297–305 Je '70. *
99. BERGEMANN, KAREN. "The Effects of Chronic Disability on Field Dependence-Independence." *Grad Res Ed & Related Discip* 5(2):109–23 sp '70. * (*PA* 46:9441)
100. DODD, W. E.; WOLLOWICK, H. B.; AND McNAMARA, W. J. "Task Difficulty as a Moderator of Long-Range Prediction." *J Appl Psychol* 54(3):265–70 Je '70. * (*PA* 44:13452)
101. DODD, WILLIAM E. "Will Management Assessment Centers Insure Selection of the Same Old Types?" Abstract. *Proc 78th Ann Conv Am Psychol Assn* 5(2):569–70 '70. * (*PA* 44:19658)
102. GOZA, JOHN THOMAS. *An Investigation of the Academic Potential, Academic Achievement, and Personality of Participants in an Associate Degree Nursing Program.* Doctor's thesis, East Texas State University (Commerce, Tex.), 1970. (*DAI* 31:5442B)
103. JOESTING, JOAN AXTELL. *A Comparative Study of Activists and Nonactivists at a Southern Black College.* Doctor's

thesis, University of Georgia (Athens, Ga.), 1970. (*DAI* 31: 3958A)

104. McBride, Robin S. "Prediction of Driving Behavior Following a Group Driver Improvement Session." *J Appl Psychol* 54(1):45–50 F '70. * (*PA* 44:5798)

105. Mason, Marion, and Rivers, Jerry. "Factors Influencing Plasma Ascorbic Acid Levels of Pregnant Women: 1, Predicting Second and Third Trimester Levels." *J Am Dietetic Assn* 56(4):313–20 Ap '70. *

106. Mason, Marion, and Rivers, Jerry. "Factors Influencing Plasma Ascorbic Acid Levels of Pregnant Women: 2, Predicting Change in Levels Following Dietary Instruction." *J Am Dietetic Assn* 56(4):321–6 Ap '70. *

107. Moretz, Walter Jennings, Jr. *Selected Personality Traits of Negro Senior High School Pupils in Northern Florida, as Related to School Racial Composition and Sex of Pupils.* Doctor's thesis, Florida State University (Tallahassee, Fla.), 1970. (*DAI* 31:5774A)

108. Prien, Erich P. "Measuring Performance Criteria of Bank Tellers." *J Indus Psychol* 5(1):29–36 Mr '70. * (*PA* 45:7135)

109. Schwab, Donald P. "Counterbalancing and Fakability of the Gordon Personal Inventory and Profile." *Psychol Rep* 26(2):671–5 Ap '70. * (*PA* 44:20994)

110. Shochat, Elimelech. *A Study of the Relationship Between Specified Personality Traits and Body-Cathexis of Male Participants and Non-Participants in High School Athletics.* Doctor's thesis, University of Massachusetts (Amherst, Mass.), 1970. (*DAI* 31:2079A)

111. Silverblank, Francine. *Sense of Responsibility, Level of Anxiety, and Sociability in Suburban Male High School Seniors Who Are Talented in Mathematics and Those Talented in English.* Doctor's thesis, New York University (New York, N.Y.), 1970. (*DAI* 31:6414A)

112. Athanassiades, John Constantine. *Distortion of Upward Communication as a Function of a Subordinate's Security Level, His Achievement Motive, and Organizational Authority-Structure.* Doctor's thesis, New York University (New York, N.Y.), 1971. (*DAI* 32:5937A)

113. Donnelly, Mona Mary. *A Study of Elementary Teachers' Personality Traits and Attitudes Toward Teaching Selected Content Areas in the Elementary School.* Doctor's thesis, University of Illinois (Urbana, Ill.), 1971. (*DAI* 32:5648A)

114. Horn, Jeraldine Frances Hooton. *Selected Personality Variables of Volunteers and Non-Volunteers for a Crisis Intervention Center.* Doctor's thesis, Ball State University (Muncie, Ind.), 1971. (*DAI* 32:5425B)

115. Mulder, Frans. "Characteristics of Violators of Formal Company Rules." *J Appl Psychol* 55(5):500–2 O '71. * (*PA* 47:7906)

116. Murdoch, George Wallace. *Values and Personal Profiles of Employed and Non-Employed College Students.* Doctor's thesis, George Washington University (Washington, D.C.), 1971. (*DAI* 32:3035A)

117. Priselac, Stephen Michael. *A Study of Certain Personal Characteristics of Pennsylvania School Board and Teacher Negotiating Team Members.* Doctor's thesis, West Virginia University (Morgantown, W.Va.), 1971. (*DAI* 32:1806A)

118. Reid, Jayne. *The Relationship of Selected Aspects of Attitude, Personality, and Achievement to the Post-High School Employment of Senior Stenographic Students.* Doctor's thesis, University of Cincinnati (Cincinnati, Ohio), 1971. (*DAI* 32:3570A)

119. Sparks, David L., and Tucker, W. T. "A Multivariate Analysis of Personality and Product Use." *J Marketing Res* 8(1):67–70 F '71. * (*PA* 46:9898)

120. Wubbolding, Robert Edward. *The Relationship Between Pre-Measured Personality Variables and Counselor Behavior During Structured Interviews.* Doctor's thesis, University of Cincinnati (Cincinnati, Ohio), 1971. (*DAI* 32:3711A)

CUMULATIVE NAME INDEX

[1195]

Gottschalk-Gleser Content Analysis Scales. Ages 14 and over; 1969; GGCAS; content analysis by 2 or more scorers of 5-minute verbal samples tape recorded and then typed; 13 scores: anxiety (death, mutilation, separation, guilt, shame, diffuse, total), hostility directed outward (overt, covert, total), hostility directed inward, ambivalent hostility, social alienation-personal disorganization (schizophrenic); Louis A. Gottschalk, Goldine C. Gleser, and Carolyn N. Winget (manual); University of California Press. *

For additional information, a review by S. B. Sells, and an excerpted review by Kurt Salzinger, see 7:83 (10 references). For excerpts from related book reviews, see 7:B252 (2 excerpts).

REFERENCES THROUGH 1971

1–10. See 7:83.

11. Gottschalk, Louis A., and Hambidge, Gove, Jr. "Verbal Behavior Analysis: A Systematic Approach to the Problem of Quantifying Psychologic Processes." *J Proj Tech* 19:387–409 D '55. * (*PA* 30:7167)

12. Gottschalk, Louis A.; Gleser, Goldine C.; and Hambidge, Gove, Jr. "Verbal Behavioral Analysis: Some Content and Form Variables in Speech Relevant to Personality Adjustment." *Arch Neurol & Psychiatry* 77:300–11 Mr '57. * (*PA* 32:2667)

13. Gottschalk, Louis A.; Gleser, Goldine C.; Daniels, Robert S.; and Block, Stanley L. "The Speech Patterns of Schizophrenic Patients: A Method of Assessing Relative Degree of Personal Disorganization and Social Alienation." *Psychiatric Res Rep* 10:141–71 '58. * (*PA* 35:2627)

14. Kaplan, Stanley M., and Gottschalk, Louis A. "Modifications of the Oropharyngeal Bacteria With Changes in the Psychodynamic State: 2, A Validation Study." *Psychosom Med* 20:314–30 Jl–Ag '58. *

15. Gleser, Goldine C.; Gottschalk, Louis A.; and John, Watkins. "The Relationship of Sex and Intelligence to Choice

of Words: A Normative Study of Verbal Behavior." *J Clin Psychol* 15:182–91 Ap '59. * *(PA* 35:4391)

16. GOTTSCHALK, LOUIS A.; GLESER, GOLDINE C.; SPRINGER, KAYLA J.; KAPLAN, STANLEY M.; SHANON, JAY; AND ROSS, W. DONALD. "Effects of Perphenazine on Verbal Behavior Patterns: A Contribution to the Problem of Measuring the Psychological Effects of Psychoactive Drugs." *Arch Gen Psychiatry* 2:632–9 Je '60. * *(PA* 35:507)

17. GLESER, GOLDINE C.; GOTTSCHALK, LOUIS A.; AND SPRINGER, KAYLA J. "An Anxiety Scale Applicable to Verbal Samples." *Arch Gen Psychiatry* 5:593–605 D '61. * *(PA* 36:4HB93G)

18. GOTTSCHALK, LOUIS A.; GLESER, GOLDINE C.; MAGLIOCCO, E. BRUNO; AND D'ZMURA, THOMAS L. "Further Studies on the Speech Patterns of Schizophrenic Patients: Measuring Inter-Individual Differences in Relative Degree of Personal Disorganization and Social Alienation." *J Nerv & Mental Dis* 132:101–13 F '61. * *(PA* 36:1JQ01G)

19. KAPLAN, STANLEY M.; GOTTSCHALK, LOUIS A.; MAGLIOCCO, E. BRUNO; ROHOVIT, D. DEAN; AND ROSS, W. DONALD. "Hostility in Verbal Productions and Hypnotic Dreams of Hypertensive Patients." *Psychosom Med* 23:311–22 Jl–Ag '61. * *(PA* 36:5JU11K)

20. GOTTSCHALK, LOUIS A.; KAPLAN, STANLEY M.; GLESER, GOLDINE C.; AND WINGET, CAROLYN N. "Variations in Magnitude of Emotion: A Method Applied to Anxiety and Hostility During Phases of the Menstrual Cycle." *Psychosom Med* 24:300–11 My–Je '62. * *(PA* 37:5109)

21. GOTTSCHALK, LOUIS A.; GLESER, GOLDINE C.; D'ZMURA, THOMAS; AND HANENSON, IRWIN B. "Some Psychophysiologic Relations in Hypertensive Women: Effect of Hydrochlorothiazide on the Relation of Affect to Blood Pressure." *Psychosom Med* 26:610–7 S–O '64. * *(PA* 39:10692)

22. GLESER, GOLDINE C.; GOTTSCHALK, LOUIS A.; FOX, ROBERT; AND LIPPERT, WALTER. "Immediate Changes in Affect With Chlordiazepoxide: Chlordiazepoxide Administration in Juvenile Delinquent Boys." *Arch Gen Psychiatry* 13:291–5 O '65. *

23. GOTTSCHALK, LOUIS A.; GLESER, GOLDINE C.; WYLIE, HAROLD W., JR.; AND KAPLAN, STANLEY M. "Effects of Imipramine on Anxiety and Hostility Levels." *Psychopharmacologia* (West Germany) 7(4):303–10 '65. *

24. MILLER, CLARENCE K. "Psychological Correlates of Coronary Artery Disease." *Psychosom Med* 27:257–65 My–Je '65. * *(PA* 39:16282)

25. GOTTLIEB, ANTHONY A.; GLESER, GOLDINE C.; AND GOTTSCHALK, LOUIS A. "Verbal and Physiological Responses to Hypnotic Suggestion of Attitudes." *Psychosom Med* 29:172–83 Mr–Ap '67. * *(PA* 41:11291)

26. GOTTSCHALK, LOUIS A. "Theory and Application of a Verbal Behavior Method of Measuring Transient Psychological States," pp. 299–325. In *Research in Verbal Behavior and Some Neurophysiological Implications.* Edited by Kurt Salzinger and Suzanne Salzinger. New York: Academic Press Inc., 1967. Pp. xvii, 510. *

27. GOTTSCHALK, LOUIS A.; GLESER, GOLDINE C.; STONE, WALTER N.; AND KUNKEL, ROBERT L. Chap. 5, "Studies on Psychoactive Drug Effects on Nonpsychiatric Patients: Measurement of Affective and Cognitive Changes by Content Analysis of Speech," pp. 162–88. In *The Psychopharmacology of the Normal Human.* Edited by Wayne O. Evans and Nathan S. Kline. Springfield, Ill.: Charles C Thomas, Publisher, 1968. Pp. xi, 252. *

28. GOTTSCHALK, L. A.; STONE, W. M.; GLESER, G. C.; AND IACONO, J. M. "Anxiety and Plasma Free Fatty Acids (FFA)." *Life Sci* (England) 8(pt 2, 2):61–8 Ja 15 '69. *

29. STONE, WALTER N.; GLESER, GOLDINE C.; GOTTSCHALK, LOUIS A.; AND IACONO, JAMES M. "Stimulus, Affect, and Plasma Free Fatty Acid." *Psychosom Med* 31(4):331–41 Jl–Ag '69. * *(PA* 44:12091)

30. OAKES, MERILEE R. *Pills, Periods, and Personality.* Doctor's thesis, University of Michigan (Ann Arbor, Mich.), 1970. *(DAI* 31:7577B)

31. GOTTSCHALK, LOUIS A.; BATES, DANIEL E.; WASKOW, IRENE E.; KATZ, MARTIN M.; AND OLSSON, JAMES. "Effect of Amphetamine or Chlorpromazine on Achievement Strivings Scores Derived From Content Analysis of Speech." *Comprehen Psychiatry* 12(5):430–6 S '71. * *(PA* 48:1260)

32. GOTTSCHALK, LOUIS A.; GLESER, GOLDINE C.; CLEGHORN, JOHN M.; STONE, WALTER N.; AND WINGET, CAROLYN M. Chap. 37, "Prediction of Changes in Severity of the Schizophrenic Syndrome With Discontinuation and Administration of Phenothiazines in Chronic Schizophrenic Patients: Language as a Predictor and Measure of Change in Schizophrenia," pp. 605–27. In *The Schizophrenic Syndrome: An Annual Review 1971.* Edited by Robert Cancro. New York: Brunner/Mazel, Inc., 1971. Pp. xv, 791. *

33. KRAMER, MILTON; WINGET, CAROLYN; AND WHITMAN, ROY M. "A City Dreams: A Survey Approach to Normative Dream Content." *Am J Psychiatry* 127(10):1350–6 Ap '71. *

34. PERLEY, JANICE; WINGET, CAROLYN; AND PLACCI, CARLOS. "Hope and Discomfort as Factors Influencing Treatment Continuance." *Comprehen Psychiatry* 12(6):557–63 N '71. * *(PA* 49:11714)

35. SILBERGELD, SAM; BRAST, NEIL; AND NOBLE, ERNEST P. "The Menstrual Cycle: A Double-Blind Study of Symptoms, Mood and Behavior, and Biochemical Variables Using Enovid and Placebo." *Psychosom Med* 33(5):411–28 S–O '71. * *(PA* 48:2416)

36. VINEY, LINDA L. "Anxiety as a Function of Self-Evaluation and Related Feedback." *Personality* 2(3):205–17 au '71. * *(PA* 47:6770)

CUMULATIVE NAME INDEX

[1196]

The Grassi Block Substitution Test: For Measuring Organic Brain Pathology. Mental patients; 1947–66; GBST; formerly called *The Fairfield Block Substitution Test;* manual out of print; Joseph R. Grassi; Scoptec Labs, Inc. *

For additional information, see P:94 (13 references); for excerpted reviews by J. G. McMurray and one other, see 5:60 (5 references). For an excerpt from a related book review, see 7:B254.

REFERENCES THROUGH 1971

1–5. See 5:60.
6–18. See P:94.

19. HIRT, MICHAEL. "Validation of the Grassi Block Substitution Test for Measuring Brain Pathology." *Proc Iowa Acad Sci* 63:627–33 '56. * *(PA* 32:4179)

20. DOERRING, PAUL LUTHER. *Psychological Deficits in Children as Sequelae of Western and St. Louis Encephalitis.* Doctor's thesis, Stanford University (Stanford, Calif.), 1962. *(DA* 23:2006)

21. McLEOD, HUGH N., AND QUARRINGTON, BRUCE J. "An Evaluation of the Grassi Test for Measuring Organic Brain Pathology." *Ont Psychol Assn Q* (Canada) 17:54–9 su '64. *

22. CRONHOLM, BÖRJE, AND SCHALLING, DAISY. "Cognitive Test Performances in Cerebrally Palsied Adults Without Mental Retardation." *Acta Psychiatrica Scandinavica* (Denmark) 44(1): 37–50 '68. * *(PA* 43:2937)

23. AFTANAS, M. S., AND ROYCE, J. R. "A Factor Analysis of Brain Damage Tests Administered to Normal Subjects With Factor Score Comparisons Across Ages." *Multiv Behav Res* 4(4):459–81 O '69. * *(PA* 44:11030)

24. KINGSLEY, LEONARD. "Functioning of Acute and Chronic Schizophrenics on Measures of Abstract Reasoning." *J Clin Psychol* 25(2):144–7 Ap '69. * *(PA* 43:14470)

25. GRASSI, JOSEPH R. *The Grassi Block Substitution Test for Measuring Organic Brain Pathology, Second Edition.* Springfield, Ill.: Charles C Thomas, Publisher, 1970. Pp. vii, 84. *

CUMULATIVE NAME INDEX

Stewart, K. D.: 8   Wepman, J. M.: 16–8
Stonesifer, F. A.: 6   Young, F. M.: 3
Thomas, C. A.: 15

[1197]
The Grayson Perceptualization Test. Detection of
cortical impairment; 1950–57; GPT; 2 scores: perceptualization rate (speed), quality of performance; Harry
M. Grayson; Western Psychological Services. *
For additional information, see P:95 (1 reference);
for reviews by D. Russell Davis and William Schofield,
see 5:61.

REFERENCES THROUGH 1971
1. See P:95.
2. AFTANAS, M. S., AND ROYCE, J. R. "A Factor Analysis of
Brain Damage Tests Administered to Normal Subjects With
Factor Score Comparisons Across Ages." *Multiv Behav Res*
4(4):459–81 O '69. * (*PA* 44:11030)

CUMULATIVE NAME INDEX
Aftanas, M. S.: 2   Royce, J. R.: 2
Davis, D. R.: rev, 5:61   Schofield, W.: rev, 5:61
Freed, E. X.: 1

[1198]
Grid Test of Schizophrenic Thought Disorder.
Adults; 1967; GTSTD; 2 scores: intensity, consist-
ency; D. Bannister and Fay Fransella; Psychological
Test Publications [England]. *
For additional information and a review by David
Jones, see 7:84 (7 references); see also P:96 (8 ref-
erences).

REFERENCES THROUGH 1971
1–8. See P:96.
9–15. See 7:84.
16. AL-ISSA, IHSAN, AND ROBERTSON, JAMES PATRICK S.
"Divergent Thinking Abilities in Chronic Schizophrenia." *J
Clin Psychol* 20:433–5 O '64. * (*PA* 39:12832)
17. MUNTZ, HILARY J., AND POWER, R. P. "Thought Disorder
in the Parents of Thought Disordered Schizophrenics." *Brit J
Psychiatry* 117(541):707–8 D '70. * (*PA* 46:11250)
18. BANNISTER, D.; FRANSELLA, FAY; AND AGNEW, JOYCE.
"Characteristics and Validity of the Grid Test of Thought
Disorder." *Brit J Social & Clin Psychol* 10(2):144–51 Je '71. *
19. FRANSELLA, FAY, AND JOYSTON-BECHAL, M. P. "An
Investigation of Conceptual Process and Pattern Change in a
Psychotherapy Group." *Brit J Psychiatry* 119(549):199–206 Ag
'71. * (*PA* 47:6925)
20. McPHERSON, F. M.; BUCKLEY, FELICITY; AND DRAFFAN,
JOAN. "'Psychological' Constructs, Thought-Process Disorder
and Flattening of Affect." *Brit J Social & Clin Psychol* 10(3):
267–70 S '71. * (*PA* 47:11284)
21. MELLSOP, G. W.; SPELMAN, M. S.; AND HARRISON, A. W.
"The Performance of Manic Patients on the 'Grid Test for
Schizophrenic Thought Disorder.'" *Brit J Psychiatry* 118(547):
671–3 Je '71. * (*PA* 47:7091)
22. SPELMAN, MICHAEL S.; HARRISON, ARTHUR W.; AND
MELLSOP, GRAHAM W. "Grid Test for Schizophrenic Thought
Disorder in Acute and Chronic Schizophrenia." *Psychol Med*
(England) 1(3):234–8 My '71. * (*PA* 47:11296)
23. WILLIAMS, EDERYN. "The Effect of Varying the Elements
in the Bannister-Fransella Grid Test of Thought Disorder."
Brit J Psychiatry 119(549):207–12 Ag '71. * (*PA* 47:7267)

CUMULATIVE NAME INDEX
Adams, B.: 9   Jones, D.: rev, 7:84
Agnew, J.: 18   Joyston-Bechal, M. P.: 19
Al-Issa, I.: 16   McPherson, F. M.: 10–1, 15,
Ashcroft, J. B.: 14   20
Bannister, D.: 1–7, 18   Mair, J. M. M.: 8
Boyd, P. R.: 8   Mayo, P. R.: 10–1
Bromley, E.: 14   Mellsop, G. W.: 21–2
Buckley, F.: 15, 20   Muntz, H. J.: 17
Draffan, J.: 20   Power, R. P.: 17
Foulds, G. A.: 10–1   Presly, A. S.: 12
Fransella, F.: 7, 9, 18–9 Robertson, J. P. S.: 16
Gathercole, C. E.: 14   Romney, D.: 13
Harrison, A. W.: 21–2   Spelman, M. S.: 21–2
Hope, K.: 10–1   Williams, E.: 23

[1199]
Group Cohesiveness: A Study of Group Morale.
Adults; 1958, c1957–58; GC; title on test is *A Study
of Group Morale*; 5 scores: satisfaction of individual
motives, satisfaction of interpersonal relations, homoge-

neity of attitude, satisfaction with leadership, total;
Bernard Goldman; Psychometric Affiliates. *
For additional information, see P:97; for reviews by
Eric F. Gardner and Cecil A. Gibb, see 6:104 (1 ref-
erence).

REFERENCES THROUGH 1971
1. See 6:104.
2. FROEBE, DORIS JEAN. *Effect of Leadership Turnover in
Nursing Upon Job Satisfaction and Cohesion of Head Nurses
and Registered Staff Nurses.* Doctor's thesis, University of
Maryland (College Park, Md.), 1970. (*DAI* 31:6301A)

CUMULATIVE NAME INDEX
Froebe, D. J.: 2   Gibb, C. A.: rev, 6:104
Gardner, E. F.: rev, 6:104 Goldman, B.: 1

[1200]
Group Dimensions Descriptions Questionnaire.
College and adult groups; 1956; GDDQ; for research
use only; 13 group dimensions scores: autonomy, control, flexibility, hedonic tone, homogeneity, intimacy,
participation, permeability, polarization, potency, stability, stratification, viscidity; John K. Hemphill and
Charles M. Westie; distributed by Educational Testing
Service (Atlanta Office). *
For additional information, see P:98 (2 references);
see also 6:105 (5 references). For an excerpt from a
review of the manual, see 5:B203.

REFERENCES THROUGH 1971
1–5. See 6:105.
6–7. See P:98.
8. GEKOSKI, NORMAN. "Predicting Group Productivity." *Personnel Psychol* 5:281–92 w '52. * (*PA* 27:6817)
9. RUSH, CARL HARRISON, JR. *Group Dimensions of Aircrews.*
Doctor's thesis, Ohio State University (Columbus, Ohio), 1953.
(*DA* 19:1847)
10. HEMPHILL, JOHN K. "Leadership Behavior Associated
With the Administrative Reputation of College Departments."
J Ed Psychol 46:385–401 N '55. * (*PA* 31:3837)
11. HEMPHILL, JOHN K. Chap. 7, "Leader Behavior Associated With the Administrative Reputations of College Departments," pp. 74–85. In *Leader Behavior: Its Description and
Measurement.* Edited by Ralph M. Stogdill and Alvin E. Coons.
Ohio State University, Bureau of Business Research, Research
Monograph No. 88. Columbus, Ohio: the Bureau, 1957. Pp. xv,
168. * (*PA* 32:1466)
12. RUSH, CARL H., JR. Chap. 6, "Leader Behavior and Group
Characteristics," pp. 69–73. In *Leader Behavior: Its Description
and Measurement.* Edited by Ralph M. Stogdill and Alvin E.
Coons. Ohio State University, Bureau of Business Research,
Research Monograph No. 88. Columbus, Ohio: the Bureau, 1957.
Pp. xv, 168. * (*PA* 32:1466)
13. LAW, LILLARD EUGENE. *The Identification of Informal
Groups and Informal Group Leadership in Selected Schools in
Ohio.* Doctor's thesis, Ohio State University (Columbus, Ohio),
1962. (*DA* 23:3207)
14. DECKARD, NOBLE SHERMAN. *An Investigation of the
Interrelationship of an Individual's Interaction Patterns in Two
Different Work Group Settings and His Task-Frame-of-Ref-
erence: An Empirical Case Study of Environmental Sanitarians.*
Doctor's thesis, University of Washington (Seattle, Wash.),
1966. (*DA* 27:823A)
15. FINDIKYAN, N., AND SELLS, S. B. "Organizational Structure and Similarity of Campus Student Organizations." *Organiz
Behav & Hum Perfor* 1:169–90 D '66. * (*PA* 41:4523)
16. CARTER, CECIL E., JR. *The Relation of Leader Behavior
Dimensions and Group Characteristics to County Extension
Advisory Committee Performance.* Doctor's thesis, Ohio State
University (Columbus, Ohio), 1967. (*DA* 28:3450A)
17. SLAUGHTER, KENNETH BROOKS. *A Study of Male Dropouts
From Selected Public Secondary Schools of Mississippi.* Doctor's
thesis, University of Southern Mississippi (Hattiesburg, Miss.),
1967. (*DA* 28:3443A)
18. CROGHAN, JOHN HENRY. *A Study of the Relationships
Between the Perceived Leadership Behavior of Elementary
Principals and Informal Group Dimensions and Composition in
Elementary Schools.* Doctor's thesis, Syracuse University (Syracuse, N.Y.), 1969. (*DAI* 30:3220A)
19. DAVIES, EVAN; WYNDHAM, JOHN; AND BINKS, NOEL.
"Psychological Changes in Sensitivity Training." *Austral Psychologist* 3(3):171–6 Mr '69. * (*PA* 45:7142)
20. OWENS, EUGENE. *The Effect of Disconfirmed Expectations
on Adjustment to Cadet Life at the United States Air Force
Academy.* Doctor's thesis, University of California (Los Angeles,
Calif.), 1970. (*DAI* 31:3717A)
21. PHEYSEY, DIANA C., AND PAYNE, ROY L. "The Hemphill
Group Dimensions Description Questionnaire: A British Indus-

trial Application." *Hum Relations* (England) 23(5):473–97 O '70. * (*PA* 47:1953, title only)

CUMULATIVE NAME INDEX

Binks, N.: 19	Klockars, A. J.: 7
Borgatta, E. F.: 3	Law, L. E.: 13
Carter, C. E.: 16	Meyer, H. J.: 3
Cottrell, L. S.: 3	Moran, G.: 7
Croghan, J. H.: 18	Owens, E.: 20
Davies, E.: 19	Payne, R. L.: 21
Deckard, N. S.: 14	Pheysey, D. C.: 21
Findikyan, N.: 15	Rush, C. H.: 9, 12
Gekoski, N.: 8	Sells, S. B.: 15
Hemphill, J. K.: 1–2, 4, 10–1	Slaughter, K. B.: 17
Hill, T. B.: 5–6	Westie, C. M.: 1
Jackson, J. M.: *exc,* 5:B203	Wyndham, J.: 19

[1201]

★**Group Embedded Figures Test.** Ages 10 and over; 1971; GEFT; adaptation of the individually administered *Embedded Figures Test;* Philip K. Oltman, Evelyn Raskin, Herman A. Witkin, and Stephen A. Karp (combined manual); Consulting Psychologists Press, Inc. *

For reference to reviews of the individual test, see 1169.

REFERENCES THROUGH 1971

1. MESSICK, SAMUEL, AND FRITZKY, FERDINAND J. "Dimensions of Analytic Attitude in Cognition and Personality." *J Personality* 31:346–70 S '63. * (*PA* 39:11345)
2. STEIN, FRANKLIN. *Consistency of Cognitive, Interest, and Personality Variables With Academic Mastery: A Study of Field-Dependence-Independence, Verbal Comprehension, Self-Perception, and Vocational Interest in Relation to Academic Performance Among Male Juniors Attending an Urban University.* Doctor's thesis, New York University (New York, N.Y.), 1968. (*DA* 29:1429A)
3. RICHARDS, TERRY D. *The Effects of Cognitive Style Sets of Flexibility Upon Counselor Perception: Field Dependence and Repression-Sensitization in Relation to Empathic Accuracy.* Doctor's thesis, New York University (New York, N.Y.), 1971. (*DAI* 32:1865A)

CUMULATIVE NAME INDEX

Fritzky, F. J.: 1	Richards, T. D.: 3
Messick, S.: 1	Stein, F.: 2

[1202]

Group Psychotherapy Suitability Evaluation Scale. Patients in group therapy; 1965–68; SES; also called *Suitability Evaluation Scale;* title on test is *Group Psychotherapy Evaluation Scale;* ratings by therapists; 6 ratings: amount of communication, quality of relatedness and communication, quality of content in relatedness, capacity for change and involvement, amount of therapist verbal activity, direction of therapist verbal activity; Clifton E. Kew; the Author. *

For additional information, see P:99 (1 reference).

REFERENCES THROUGH 1971

1. See P:99.

CUMULATIVE NAME INDEX

Kew, C. E.: 1

[1203]

*****Guidance Inventory.** High school; 1960–73; GI; identification of problems related to underachievement and need for counseling; 1973 manual is a condensation of manual copyrighted 1960; Ralph Gallagher; the Author. *

For additional information, see P:100; for a review by John W. M. Rothney, see 6:106.

[1204]

Guilford-Holley L Inventory. College and adults; 1953–63; GHLI; leadership behavior; 5 scores: benevolence, ambition, meticulousness, discipline, aggressiveness; J. P. Guilford and J. W. Holley; Sheridan Psychological Services, Inc. *

For additional information and reviews by Harrison

G. Gough and Warren T. Norman, see 7:85 (1 reference).

REFERENCES THROUGH 1971

1. See 7:85.
2. SCHUSTER, D. H., AND GUILFORD, J. P. "The Psychometric Prediction of Problem Drivers." *Hum Factors* 6:393–421 Ag '64. *

CUMULATIVE NAME INDEX

Gough, H. G.: *rev,* 7:85	Norman, W. T.: *rev,* 7:85
Guilford, J. P.: 2	Schuster, D. H.: 2
Holley, J. W.: 1	

[1205]

The Guilford-Martin Inventory of Factors GAMIN, Abridged Edition. Grades 12–16 and adults; 1943–48; GAMIN; 5 scores: general activity, ascendance-submission, masculinity-femininity, inferiority feelings, nervousness; J. P. Guilford and H. G. Martin; Sheridan Psychological Services, Inc. *

For additional information, see P:102 (14 references); see also 6:108 (11 references) and 5:63 (33 references); for a review by Hubert E. Brogden, see 4:47 (18 references); for a review by H. J. Eysenck, see 3:43 (7 references); for a review by R. A. Brotemarkle, see 3:45.

REFERENCES THROUGH 1971

1–7. See 3:43.
8–25. See 4:47.
26–58. See 5:63.
59–69. See 6:108.
70–83. See P:102.
84. WHITE, MELANY. "An Investigation of the Secondary-Order Domain of the Nine Primary Factors Described in 'The Dimensions of Temperament' by L. L. Thurstone." *B Nat Inst Personnel Res* (South Africa) 1:4–13 Mr '49. *
85. STORMENT, CHARLYNE TOWNSEND. "Personality and Heart Disease." *Psychosom Med* 13:304–13 S–O '51. * (*PA* 26:3584)
86. DAILEY, CHARLES A. "The Effects of Premature Conclusion Upon the Acquisition of Understanding of a Person." *J Psychol* 33:133–52 Ja '52. * (*PA* 26:6065)
87. HEALY, IRENE, AND BORG, WALTER R. "Personality and Vocational Interests of Successful and Unsuccessful Nursing School Freshmen." *Ed & Psychol Meas* 12:767–75 w '52. * (*PA* 27:6221)
88. BITNER, HAROLD MILLER. *Ethnic Inter-Group Differences in Personality, General Culture, Academic Ability, and Interests in a Geographically Restricted Area.* Doctor's thesis, Ohio State University (Columbus, Ohio), 1954. (*DA* 20:772)
89. HALPERN, HOWARD MARVIN. *Some Factors Involved in Empathy.* Doctor's thesis, Columbia University (New York, N.Y.), 1954. (*DA* 14:1458)
90. SHIRE, ALBERT. *Personality Correlates of Preferences Among Psychoanalytic Defense Mechanisms.* Doctor's thesis, University of Michigan (Ann Arbor, Mich.), 1954. (*DA* 14:715)
91. GETZELS, J. W., AND GUBA, E. G. "Role Conflict and Personality." *J Personality* 24:74–85 S '55. * (*PA* 30:5758)
92. JAYASWAL, SITA RAM. *Ascendance-Submission in the Preschool Child and in His Adult Personality.* Doctor's thesis, University of Michigan (Ann Arbor, Mich.), 1955. (*DA* 15:763)
93. JAYASWAL, SITA RAM, AND STOTT, LELAND H. "Persistence and Change in Personality From Childhood to Adulthood: 1, Ascendance-Submission in Nursery School Children." *Merrill-Palmer Q* 1:47–56 w '55. *
94. TRESSELT, M. E. "The Effects of Background Contrast Upon the Time-Error in Visual Extents and Certain Characteristics Related to the Judgments." *J General Psychol* 52:75–82 Ja '55. * (*PA* 30:2195)
95. HERRING, FRED H. "Response During Anesthesia and Surgery; Effect of Psychological Factors." *Psychosom Med* 18:243–51 My–Je '56. * (*PA* 31:5007)
96. THOMSEN, DONALD R. *An Analysis of Certain Objective Measures for the Prediction of the Community's Reaction to a Principal's Behavior.* Doctor's thesis, University of Florida (Gainesville, Fla.), 1956. (*DA* 16:2352)
97. LANGER, PHILIP. *Relation of Certain Selected Factors Among Connecticut School Teachers to Status Leader Role Expectations.* Doctor's thesis, University of Connecticut (Storrs, Conn.), 1957. (*DA* 18:1353)
98. OLSON, NORMAN. *An Investigation of Orality Among Schizophrenics, Psychoneurotics, and Normals.* Doctor's thesis, Temple University (Philadelphia, Pa.), 1959. (*DA* 20:3388)
99. SANFORD, ALPHEUS. *The Practice Teaching Experience and Its Effect on Cadet Teacher Attitudes Toward Pupils.* Doctor's thesis, Boston University (Boston, Mass.), 1959. (*DA* 20:3212)

100. LIBERTY, PAUL G., JR.; DOUGHTIE, EUGENE B., JR.; AND EMBREE, ROYAL B., JR. "Value and Trait Comparisons of Clinical and Counseling Students: An Exploratory Study." *Psychol Rep* 17:157–8 Ag '65. * (*PA* 40:846)

101. RYCHLAK, JOSEPH F. "The Similarity, Compatibility, or Incompatibility of Needs in Interpersonal Selection." *J Pers & Social Psychol* 2:334–40 S '65. * (*PA* 39:15059)

102. COHEN, DAVID B. "A Study of the Correlation Between the Use of Incidental Stimuli to Facilitate Learning and Selected Personality Traits." *J Psychol* 62:11–4 Ja '66. * (*PA* 40:6225)

103. BENTZ, V. JON. Chap. 7, "The Sears Experience in the Investigation, Description, and Prediction of Executive Behavior," pp. 147–205; critique by Ross Stagner, pp. 206–27. In *Measuring Executive Effectiveness*. Edited by Frederic R. Wickert and Dalton E. McFarland. New York: Appleton-Century-Crofts, 1967. Pp. xiii, 242. *

104. BENTZ, V. JON. Chap. 3, "The Sears Experience in the Investigation, Description and Prediction of Executive Behavior," pp. 59–152. In *Predicting Managerial Success*. Edited by John A. Myers, Jr. Ann Arbor, Mich.: Foundation for Research on Human Behavior, April 1968. Pp. v, 173. *

105. DOBELL, HELEN R. *A Comparison of Selected Temperament Traits Among Junior and Senior Women Majoring in Physical Education, Art, and History.* Master's thesis, Illinois State University (Normal, Ill.), 1968.

106. EYSENCK, H. J.; WHITE, P. O.; AND SOUEIF, M. I. Chap. 18, "Factors in the Guilford Personality Inventory," pp. 229–38. In *Personality Structure and Measurement*, see 107. *

107. EYSENCK, HANS J., AND EYSENCK, SYBIL B. G. *Personality Structure and Measurement.* San Diego, Calif.: Robert R. Knapp, Publisher, 1969. Pp. xiii, 365. *

108. SOUEIF, M. I.; EYSENCK, H. J.; AND WHITE, P. O. Chap. 15, "A Joint Factorial Study of the Guilford, Cattell and Eysenck Scales," pp. 171–93. In *Personality Structure and Measurement*, see 107. *

109. WHITE, P. O.; EYSENCK, H. J.; AND SOUEIF, M. I. Chap. 19, "Combined Analysis of Cattell, Eysenck and Guilford Factors," pp. 239–50. In *Personality Structure and Measurement*, see 107. *

110. LUNNEBORG, PATRICIA W., AND LUNNEBORG, CLIFFORD E. "Factor Structure of MF Scales and Items." *J Clin Psychol* 26(3):360–6 Jl '70. * (*PA* 45:707)

111. SMITH, KAY H. "Conformity as Related to Masculinity, Self, and Other Descriptions, Suspicion, and Artistic Preference by Sex Groups." *J Social Psychol* 80(1):79–88 F '70. * (*PA* 44:12572)

112. SELLS, S. B.; DEMAREE, R. G.; AND WILL, DONALD P., JR. "Dimensions of Personality: 2, Separate Factor Structures in Guilford and Cattell Trait Markers." *Multiv Behav Res* 6(2):135–85 Ap '71. * (*PA* 47:4821)

CUMULATIVE NAME INDEX

[1206]

The Guilford-Martin Personnel Inventory.
Adults; 1943–46; GMPI; 3 scores: objectivity, agreeableness, cooperativeness; J. P. Guilford and H. G. Martin; Sheridan Psychological Services, Inc. *

For additional information, see P:103 (6 references); see also 6:109 (9 references) and 5:64 (27 references); for a review by Neil Van Steenberg, see 4:48 (20 references); for a review by Benjamin Shimberg, see 3:44 (7 references); for a review by R. A. Brotemarkle, see 3:45.

REFERENCES THROUGH 1971

1–7. See 3:44.
8–27. See 4:48.
28–54. See 5:64.
55–63. See 6:109.
64–69. See P:103.

70. WHITE, MELANY. "An Investigation of the Secondary-Order Domain of the Nine Primary Factors Described in 'The Dimensions of Temperament' by L. L. Thurstone." *B Nat Inst Personnel Res* (South Africa) 1:4–13 Mr '49. *

71. GUEST, LESTER, AND NUCKOLS, ROBERT. "A Laboratory Experiment in Recording in Public Opinion Interviewing." *Int J Opin & Attitude Res* (Mexico) 4:336–52 f '50. * (*PA* 25:7387)

72. STORMENT, CHARLYNE TOWNSEND. "Personality and Heart Disease." *Psychosom Med* 13:304–13 S–O '51. * (*PA* 26:3584)

73. GRANT, DONALD LINDSAY. *An Exploratory Study of Halo Effect in Rating.* Doctor's thesis, Ohio State University (Columbus, Ohio), 1952. (*DA* 18:1096)

74. HEALY, IRENE, AND BORG, WALTER R. "Personality and Vocational Interests of Successful and Unsuccessful Nursing School Freshmen." *Ed & Psychol Meas* 12:767–75 w '52. * (*PA* 27:6221)

75. RICHARDSON, HAROLD WELLINGTON. *A Study of the Readiness of American Baptist Theological Students Holding Opposing "Fundamentalist" and "Modernist" Theological Views to Associate in Religious Groups With Those Differing From Themselves.* Doctor's thesis, University of Michigan (Ann Arbor, Mich.), 1952. (*DA* 12:525)

76. BITNER, HAROLD MILLER. *Ethnic Inter-Group Differences in Personality, General Culture, Academic Ability, and Interests in a Geographically Restricted Area.* Doctor's thesis, Ohio State University (Columbus, Ohio), 1954. (*DA* 20:772)

77. TRESSELT, M. E. "The Effects of Background Contrast Upon the Time-Error and Certain Extents and Certain Characteristics Related to the Judgments." *J General Psychol* 52:75–82 Ja '55. * (*PA* 30:2195)

78. EPPLEY, MARY VINEITA (BOOTS). *The Relationship of Personal Factors and Reading Performance to Academic Achievement of Selected Oregon State College Students.* Doctor's thesis, Oregon State University (Corvallis, Ore.), 1958. (*DA* 19:730)

79. MORELLO, MICHAEL. *A Study of the Adjustive Behavior of Prison Inmates to Incarceration.* Doctor's thesis, Temple University (Philadelphia, Pa.), 1958. (*DA* 19:2149)

80. PEDERSEN, DARHL M. "The Measurement of Individual Differences in Perceived Personality-Trait Relationships and Their Relation to Certain Determinants." *J Social Psychol* 65:233–58 Ap '65. * (*PA* 39:14976)

81. BENTZ, V. JON. Chap. 7, "The Sears Experience in the Investigation, Description, and Prediction of Executive Behavior," pp. 147–205; critique by Ross Stagner, pp. 206–27. In

Measuring Executive Effectiveness. Edited by Frederic R. Wickert and Dalton E. McFarland. New York: Appleton-Century-Crofts, 1967. Pp. viii, 242. *

82. BENTZ, V. JON. Chap. 3, "The Sears Experience in the Investigation, Description and Prediction of Executive Behavior," pp. 59-152. In *Predicting Managerial Success.* Edited by John A. Myers, Jr. Ann Arbor, Mich.: Foundation for Research on Human Behavior, April 1968. Pp. v, 173. *

83. EYSENCK, H. J.; WHITE, P. O.; AND SOUEIF, M. I. Chap. 18, "Factors in the Guilford Personality Inventory," pp. 229-38. In *Personality Structure and Measurement, see 84.* *

84. EYSENCK, HANS J., AND EYSENCK, SYBIL B. G. *Personality Structure and Measurement.* San Diego, Calif.: Robert R. Knapp, Publisher, 1969. Pp. xiii, 365. *

85. SOUEIF, M. I.; EYSENCK, H. J.; AND WHITE, P. O. Chap. 15, "A Joint Factorial Study of the Guilford, Cattell and Eysenck Scales," pp. 171-93. In *Personality Structure and Measurement, see 84.* *

86. WHITE, P. O.; EYSENCK, H. J.; AND SOUEIF, M. I. Chap. 19, "Combined Analysis of Cattell, Eysenck and Guilford Factors," pp. 239-50. In *Personality Structure and Measurement, see 84.* *

87. SELLS, S. B.; DEMAREE, R. G.; AND WILL, DONALD P., JR. "Dimensions of Personality: 2, Separate Factor Structures in Guilford and Cattell Trait Markers." *Multiv Behav Res* 6(2): 135-85 Ap '71. * (*PA* 47:4821)

CUMULATIVE NAME INDEX

[1207]

The Guilford-Zimmerman Temperament Survey. Grades 12-16 and adults; 1949-55; GZTS; revision and condensation of 3 still-in-print tests: *Guilford-Martin Inventory of Factors GAMIN, Guilford-Martin Personnel Inventory,* and *Inventory of Factors STDCR;* 10 scores: general activity, restraint, ascendance, sociability, emotional stability, objectivity, friendliness, thoughtfulness, personal relations, masculinity; 3 *Falsification Scales;* J. P. Guilford and Wayne S. Zimmerman; falsification scales by Alfred Jacobs and Allan Schlaff; Sheridan Psychological Services, Inc. *

For additional information, see P:104 (132 references); see also 6:110 (120 references); for a review

Guilford-Martin Personnel Inventory

by David R. Saunders, see 5:65 (48 references); for reviews by William Stephenson and Neil Van Steenberg and an excerpted review by Laurance F. Shaffer, see 4:49 (5 references).

REFERENCES THROUGH 1971

1-5. See 4:49.
6-53. See 5:65.
54-173. See 6:110.
174-305. See P:104.

306. BASS, BERNARD M.; McGEHEE, CHARLES R.; HAWKINS, WILLIAM C.; YOUNG, PAUL C.; AND GEBEL, ARNOLD S. "Personality Variables Related to Leaderless Group Discussion Behavior." *J Abn & Social Psychol* 48:120-8 Ja '53. * (*PA* 28:925)

307. BOYD, ROBERT DEAN. *Reading Retardation as Related to Personality Factors of Children and Their Parents.* Doctor's thesis, University of Michigan (Ann Arbor, Mich.), 1953. (*DA* 13:872)

308. McCARTHY, MARY VITERBO. "An Empirical Study of the Personality Profiles Characterizing Differential Quantitative and Linguistic Ability." *Studies Psychol & Psychiatry* 8(4): 1-45 Je '53. * (*PA* 28:4043)

309. BONSALL, MARCELLA RYSER, AND STEFFLRE, BUFORD. "The Temperament of Gifted Children." *Calif J Ed Res* 6:162-5 S '55. * (*PA* 30:5795)

310. COMREY, ANDREW L., AND STAATS, CAROLYN K. "Group Performance in a Cognitive Task." *J Appl Psychol* 39:354-6 O '55. * (*PA* 30:6887)

311. ROSENTHAL, SHELDON. *Correlates of Attitudes Among Clinical Psychology Students.* Doctor's thesis, Columbia University (New York, N.Y.), 1955. (*DA* 16:580)

312. VERNALLIS, FRANCIS F. "Teeth-Grinding: Some Relationships to Anxiety, Hostility, and Hyperactivity." *J Clin Psychol* 11:389-91 O '55. * (*PA* 30:6129)

313. KELLER, HORACE T., JR. *Personality Measures as Related to Performance Under Auditory Distraction.* Doctor's thesis, Temple University (Philadelphia, Pa.), 1956. (*DA* 16:994)

314. KNAAK, NANCY KATHERINE. *A Study of the Characteristics of Academically Successful and Unsuccessful Freshmen Women Who Entered Northwestern University in the Fall of 1954.* Doctor's thesis, Northwestern University (Evanston, Ill.), 1956. (*DA* 17:304)

315. STEVENS, PETER H. *An Investigation of the Relationship Between Certain Aspects of Self-Concept Behavior and Students' Academic Achievement.* Doctor's thesis, New York University (New York, N.Y.), 1956. (*DA* 16:2531)

316. CURRIE, CAROLINE. *The Relationship of Certain Selected Factors to Achievement in Freshman Composition.* Doctor's thesis, Northwestern University (Evanston, Ill.), 1957. (*DA* 18:884)

317. SIMONS, WESLEY STANLEY. *The Personality Characteristics of the Residence Hall Assistant as Related to Job Performance.* Doctor's thesis, Michigan State University (East Lansing, Mich.), 1957. (*DA* 18:135)

318. DARLING, HAROLD WILLIAM. *A Comparative Study of Persisting and Non-Persisting Ministerial Candidates in Evangelical Colleges.* Doctor's thesis, Purdue University (Lafayette, Ind.), 1958. (*DA* 20:586)

319. FREY, ALLAN H., AND BECKER, WESLEY C. "Some Personality Correlates of Subjects Who Fail to Appear for Experimental Appointments." Abstract. *J Consult Psychol* 22:164 Je '58. * (*PA* 35:4984)

320. GARFINKLE, MAX. *The Relationship Between General Self Concept, Role Self Concept and Role Behavior in High School.* Doctor's thesis, Columbia University (New York, N.Y.), 1958. (*DA* 19:897)

321. GELBMANN, FREDERICK JOHN. *Authoritarianism and Temperament: An Obverse Factor Analysis of 'Authoritarians' and 'Non Authoritarians' in Terms of a Well Defined Set of Personality Variables.* Washington, D.C.: Catholic University of America Press, Inc., 1958. Pp. vi, 63. * (*PA* 34:2765)

322. NASH, CARROLL B., AND NASH, CATHERINE S. "Checking Success and the Relationship of Personality Traits to ESP." *J Am Soc Psychical Res* 52:98-107 Jl '58. *

323. NUNNALLY, JUM, AND HUSEK, T. R. "'Semantic Clarity': One Standard for Factored Tests." *Ed & Psychol Meas* 18:761-7 w '58. * (*PA* 34:156)

324. WEBB, SAM C.; GOODLING, RICHARD A.; AND SHEPHERD, IRMA LEE. "The Prediction of Field Work Ratings in a Theological School." *Relig Ed* 53:534-8 N-D '58. * (*PA* 33:9362)

325. BECK, ISABEL HOLDERMAN HANDLEY. *A Study of Criteria of Social Perception and Some Related Variables.* Doctor's thesis, University of Southern California (Los Angeles, Calif.), 1959. (*DA* 20:2372)

326. HOFFMAN, L. RICHARD. "Homogeneity of Member Personality and Its Effect on Group Problem-Solving." *J Abn & Social Psychol* 58:27-32 Ja '59. * (*PA* 34:954)

327. LaBUE, ANTHONY C. "Teachers' Classroom Attitudes." *J Teach Ed* 10:433-4 D '59. * (*PA* 34:8420)

328. HAND, QUENTIN LAMOIN. *A Psychological Study of Thirty Prayer Group Participants.* Doctor's thesis, Boston University (Boston, Mass.), 1960. (*DA* 21:1270)

329. MYERS, BETTYE BLANCHE. *Evaluation of the Effectiveness of the University of Michigan's Summer Counselor Education Program at the National Music Camp.* Doctor's thesis, University of Michigan (Ann Arbor, Mich.), 1960. (*DA* 21:2196)

330. WAGNER, EDWIN E. "Predicting Success for Young Executives From Objective Test Scores and Personal Data." *Personnel Psychol* 13:181-6 su '60. * (*PA* 36:2LD81W)

331. ABOU-GHORRA, IBRAHIM MANSOUR. *A Study of Affective Sets: The Effects of Family and Non-Family Verbal Contexts on Word-Need Stimuli in a Word Association Experiment With Reference to Pleasant and Emotional Tones of Associated Verbal Responses.* Doctor's thesis, University of Southern California (Los Angeles, Calif.), 1961. (*DA* 22:3262)

332. BORGATTA, EDGAR F. "Role-Playing Specification, Personality and Performance." *Sociometry* 24:218-33 S '61. * (*PA* 36:3GE18B)

333. CAMPBELL, MARY GREGORY. *A Comparative Study of Mental Ability, Personality, and Interests of First-Year Nursing Students in the Diploma and the Baccalaureate Programs.* Doctor's thesis, Fordham University (New York, N.Y.), 1961. (*DA* 26:7152)

334. BEAMISH, JEROME J., AND MALFETTI, JAMES L. "A Psychological Comparison of Violator and Non-Violator Automobile Drivers in the 16 to 19 Year Age Group." *Traffic Safety Res R* 6:12-5 Mr '62. *

335. BEAUPRE, WALTER JOSEPH. *The Influence of Speech From Three Dialect Areas in the United States on Personality Ratings of Judges From Four Speech Regions.* Doctor's thesis, Columbia University (New York, N.Y.), 1962. (*DA* 23:1117)

336. LUBIN, BERNARD; BRADY, JOHN PAUL; AND LEVITT, EUGENE E. "A Comparison of Personality Characteristics of Volunteers and Nonvolunteers for Hypnosis Experiments." *J Clin Psychol* 18:341-3 Jl '62. * (*PA* 39:1811)

337. MARSH, STEWART H. "Validating the Selection of Deputy Sheriffs." *Pub Personnel R* 23:41-4 Jl '62. * (*PA* 37:2051)

338. PERRY, JAMES OLDEN. *A Study of a Selective Set of Criteria for Determining Success in Secondary Student Teaching at Texas Southern University.* Doctor's thesis, University of Texas (Austin, Tex.), 1962. (*DA* 23:1617)

339. ROBINSON, MARCELLE. *A Study of Recall Set Utilizing Early Childhood Recollections and Recent Recollections.* Doctor's thesis, University of Southern California (Los Angeles, Calif.), 1962. (*DA* 23:302)

340. DOLLAR, ROBERT JOSEPH. *A Study of Certain Psychosocial Differences Among Dormitory, Fraternity, and Off-Campus Freshman Men at Oklahoma State University.* Doctor's thesis, Oklahoma State University (Stillwater, Okla.), 1963. (*DA* 25:961)

341. LEVITT, EUGENE E.; LUBIN, BERNARD; AND BRADY, JOHN PAUL. "Personality Correlates of Hypnotizability in Young Women: The Anxiety-Dependency Constellation." *Congreso Interamericano de Psicologia* (Mexico) 7:360-4 '63. *

342. MARKS, ALVIN; MICHAEL, WILLIAM B.; AND KAISER, HENRY F. "Factors of Creativity and Temperament in the Assessment of Officers." *Psychol Rep* 12:851-4 Je '63. * (*PA* 38:6697)

343. NIELSEN, J. K. "Case Studies of Socially Isolated Males in Senior High School." *Alberta J Ed Res* (Canada) 9:247-53 D '63. *

344. RANKIN, EARL F., JR. "Reading Test Performance of Introverts and Extroverts." *Yearb Nat Read Conf* 12:158-66 '63. *

345. SHAFFER, JOHN W. Chap. 24, "Masculinity-Femininity and Other Personality Traits in Gonadal Aplasia (Turner's Syndrome)," pp. 219-32. (*PA* 39:8303) In *Advances in Sex Research: A Publication of the Society for the Scientific Study of Sex.* Edited by Hugo G. Beigel. New York: Harper & Row, Publishers, Inc., 1963. Pp. xiv, 261. *

346. KELLY, EMMET EUGENE. *Group Counseling Interaction and Member Personality.* Doctor's thesis, University of Texas (Austin, Tex.), 1964. (*DA* 25:5117)

347. REAVIS, LARRY D. *Delay of Gratification and Activity Level.* Master's thesis, University of Missouri (Columbia, Mo.), 1964. (*Masters Abstracts* 5:19)

348. SCHUSTER, D. H., AND GUILFORD, J. P. "The Psychometric Prediction of Problem Drivers." *Hum Factors* 6:393-421 Ag '64. *

349. DAVIS, LUTHER EDWARD, JR. *A Study of Selected Traits of St. Petersburg Junior College Students and Their Value in Predicting Academic Success in Certain Courses of Study at the Senior College Level.* Doctor's thesis, Auburn University (Auburn, Ala.), 1965. (*DA* 26:791)

350. EYNON, THOMAS G., AND SIMPSON, JON E. "The Boy's Perception of Himself in a State Training School for Delinquents." *Social Service R* 39:31-7 Mr '65. *

351. PIERCE, ROBERT ALLYN. *Response Sets as Personality Variables: An Attempt at Validation.* Doctor's thesis, University of Rochester (Rochester, N.Y.), 1965. (*DA* 26:3490)

352. RAPP, MAJORIE LEE. *Factors Related to the Impressions Made on One Another by Members of a Discussion Group.* Doctor's thesis, University of California (Los Angeles, Calif.), 1965. (*DA* 25:7087)

353. RITCHEY, RONALD E. "Predicting Success of Schizophrenics in Industrial Therapy." *J Counsel Psychol* 12:68-73 sp '65. * (*PA* 39:10413)

354. ROMANELLA, ALAN EUGENE. *Emotions in Adolescence and Response to Color on the Rorschach.* Doctor's thesis, St. John's University (Jamaica, N.Y.), 1965. (*DA* 28:344B)

355. ROSENFELD, HOWARD M., AND JACKSON, JAY. "Temporal Mediation of the Similarity-Attraction Hypothesis." *J Personality* 33:649-56 D '65. * (*PA* 40:4167)

356. TOLLEFSON, NONA FALMLEN. *Relationship of Counselor Need Orientation to Counselor Effectiveness and Counselor Personality.* Doctor's thesis, Purdue University (Lafayette, Ind.), 1965. (*DA* 27:122A)

357. TOOBERT, SAUL. *The Relation Between Personality and Interaction Behavior in Small Groups.* Doctor's thesis, University of Oregon (Eugene, Ore.), 1965. (*DA* 26:5574)

358. WILSON, NORMAN EDWARD. *Personality Correlates of Person Perception Patterns Among School Counselors in Two Advanced Programs of Counselor Education.* Doctor's thesis, University of Texas (Austin, Tex.), 1965. (*DA* 27:123A)

359. ALTLAND, N. RICHARD, AND WEITZMAN, ELLIS. "Personality Differentiation of Patients With Coronary Artery Disease." *Md State Med J* 15:63-5 Je '66. * (*PA* 40:10902)

360. CHARLES, LOUIS. *A Multiple Discriminant Analysis of the Effects of Personality Variables on Academic Achievement in a Dental Education Setting.* Doctor's thesis, University of Pittsburgh (Pittsburgh, Pa.), 1966. (*DA* 27:3303A)

361. ESPENSCHADE, ANNA S. "General Activity Measures of Women 35 to 80 Years of Age." *Percept & Motor Skills* 23:718 D '66. * (*PA* 41:7164)

362. GOLDEN, JAMES FRANKLIN. *Aspirations and Capabilities of Rural Youth in Selected Areas of Arkansas in Relation to Present and Projected Labor Market Requirements.* Doctor's thesis, University of Arkansas (Fayetteville, Ark.), 1966. (*DA* 27:1199A)

363. HANSON, ROBERT NELTON. *Visual Stimulus Versus Combined Audio-Visual Stimuli for Out-of-Class Practice in First-Semester College Gregg Shorthand.* Doctor's thesis, University of North Dakota (Grand Forks, N.D.), 1966. (*DA* 27:3224A)

364. HINTON, BERNARD LLOYD. *A Model of Creative Problem Solving Performance and the Effects of Frustration.* Doctor's thesis, Stanford University (Stanford, Calif.), 1966. (*DA* 27:2508B)

365. HOOVER, BASIL. *College Students Who Did Not Seek Counseling During a Period of Academic Difficulty.* Doctor's thesis, University of Florida (Gainesville, Fla.), 1966. (*DA* 28:1298A)

366. JONES, ROBERT KENNETH. *Social and Personal Orientation in Behavior Disorders.* Doctor's thesis, Purdue University (Lafayette, Ind.), 1966. (*DA* 27:609B)

367. KOPFF, RICHARD GARMS. *Manager Performance as Related to Goal Setting, Intelligence, and Selected Personality Characteristics.* Doctor's thesis, Columbia University (New York, N.Y.), 1966. (*DA* 27:677A)

368. MCALLISTER, JOHN GERALD. *Analyses of Selected Personality and Intellectual Attributes of Teenage Volunteer Counselor-Attendants Serving at a Residential Camp for the Dependent Cerebral Palsied.* Doctor's thesis, University of Denver (Denver, Colo.), 1966. (*DA* 27:3328A)

369. MEADOWS, MARK EUGENE. *A Comparative Study of Selected Characteristics of Counseled and Non-Counseled Students in a College Counseling Center.* Doctor's thesis, University of Georgia (Athens, Ga.), 1966. (*DA* 27:2404A)

370. PHILLIPS, MAURICE. *Trends in a Visual Satiation Effect in Relation to Extraversion.* Doctor's thesis, New York University (New York, N.Y.), 1966. (*DA* 27:4132B)

371. RUMBAUGH, DUANE M. "The Psychological Aspects." *J Rehabil* 32:56-8 Mr-Ap '66. * (*PA* 40:9082)

372. SHERIN, CAROLYN RICHARDS. *Some Relationships Among Popularity, Friendship Choice, and Personality Variables.* Doctor's thesis, University of Miami (Coral Gables, Fla.), 1966. (*DA* 27:1931A)

373. SMITH, KAY H.; PEDERSEN, DARHL M.; AND LEWIS, ROBERT E. "Dimensions of Interpersonal Perception in a Meaningful Ongoing Group." *Percept & Motor Skills* 22:867-80 Je '66. * (*PA* 40:11110)

374. TOOBERT, SAUL. "The Relation Between Personality and Interaction Behavior in Small Groups." *Calif Mental Health Res Dig* 4:152-4 au '66. *

375. ANDERSON, ELWOOD GRANT. *A Comparison of Emotional Stability in Stutterers and Non-Stutterers.* Doctor's thesis, Wayne State University (Detroit, Mich.), 1967. (*DA* 28:3511B)

376. ANIFANT, DAVID C. *A Study of Perceived Family Adjustment and Personality Patterns Among Emotionally Disturbed Girls.* Master's thesis, Springfield College (Springfield, Mass.), 1967.

377. BLUM, FRANK J., AND CHAGNON, MAURICE. "Extraversion and Subsequent Recidivism for a Selected Group of Young Adult Offenders." *Can J Correct* 9:94-8 Ja '67. *

378. BLUM, FRANK J., AND CHAGNON, MAURICE. "Some Parameters of Persistent Criminal Behaviour." *J Clin Psychol* 23:168-70 Ap '67. * (*PA* 41:9120)

379. BORG, WALTER R. "Teacher Effectiveness in Team Teaching." *J Exp Ed* 35:65-70 sp '67. *

380. BREIMEIER, KENNETH H. *Relationship Between Various Psychological Measures in Use at Theological Seminaries.* Com-

ments by James E. Dittes. Occasional Papers No. 1. Washington, D.C.: Ministry Studies Board, 1967. Pp. iii, 59. *

381. CANNON, FRANCES CLAIRE. *Selected Personal Characteristics of Undergraduate Recreation Majors Who Are Successful in a Recreation Curriculum.* Doctor's thesis, Columbia University (New York, N.Y.), 1967. (*DA* 28:3985A)

382. CONNERLY, ROBERT JESSE. *A Comparison of Personality Characteristics for Parents of Brain-Injured and Normal Children.* Doctor's thesis, University of Denver (Denver, Colo.), 1967. (*DA* 28:1291A)

383. DOTY, BARBARA A. "Teaching Method Effectiveness in Relation to Certain Student Characteristics." *J Ed Res* 60:363–5 Ap '67. *

384. HARTSOCK, WOODROW WILSON. *The Prediction of Academic Performance in a Seminary.* Master's thesis, Southern Methodist University (Dallas, Tex.), 1967.

385. MAHONEY, M. FRANCES. *An Investigation Into Temperament and Teacher Potentiality in Selected Groups of College Women Students.* Doctor's thesis, St. John's University (Jamaica, N.Y.), 1967. (*DA* 28:4284B)

386. MOORE, JOYCE HENDEE. *Self-Awareness of Personality Factors as Related to Occupational Satisfaction Among Male Junior High School Teachers.* Doctor's thesis, Michigan State University (East Lansing, Mich.), 1967. (*DA* 28:1680A)

387. MORGAN, JACK COLLINS. *A Study of the Observed Behaviors of Student Teachers in Secondary Social Studies as Correlates With Certain Personality Characteristics and Creativity.* Doctor's thesis, Purdue University (Lafayette, Ind.), 1967. (*DA* 28:519A)

388. NASH, CARROLL B., AND NASH, CATHERINE S. "Relations Between ESP Scoring Level and Personality Traits of the Guilford-Zimmerman Temperament Survey." *J Am Soc Psychical Res* 61:64–71 Ja '67. * (*PA* 41:2174)

389. NIBLOCK, MARJOIE W. *Personality Traits and Intelligence Level of Female Athletes and Nonparticipants From McNally High School.* Master's thesis, University of Washington (Seattle, Wash.), 1967.

390. ROWLEY, JOHN VAIL. *The Personality Characteristics of Team Teachers Selected by Their Peers for Team Membership.* Doctor's thesis, Rutgers—The State University (New Brunswick, N.J.), 1967. (*DA* 28:1251A)

391. WAGNER, HILMAR ERNEST. *A Study of Physical, Mental and Musical Characteristics of Selected Band Members.* Doctor's thesis, North Texas State University (Denton, Tex.), 1967. (*DA* 28:2285A) Reviewed by James M. Shugert, *Council Res Music Ed B* 24:27–35 sp '71. *

392. WICKS, JOHN H., AND NELSON, CALVIN C. "A Preliminary Investigation of Some Psychological Determinants of Consumption Propensity." *South Econ J* 33:383–7 Ja '67. *

393. BROWN, THOMAS O. *The Urban University Student: Selected Factors Related to Continuation and Withdrawal.* Doctor's thesis, Kent State University (Kent, Ohio), 1968. (*DA* 29:4318A)

394. CHABASSOL, DAVID J. "A Comparison of Measures of Masculinity-Femininity." *Meas & Eval Guid* 1:173–4 f '68. *

395. CURB, LAURA SOMERVILL. *Personality Traits of Elementary School Teachers Who Voted for or Against Sanctions.* Doctor's thesis, University of Oklahoma (Norman, Okla.), 1968. (*DA* 29:2559A)

396. ELDER, JAMES LYN. *A Differential Analysis of the Guilford-Zimmerman Temperament Survey as a Predictor of Leadership Effectiveness in the Ministry.* Master's thesis, San Francisco State College (San Francisco, Calif.), 1968.

397. EVANS, THOMAS PARKER. *An Exploratory Study of the Verbal and Non-Verbal Behaviors of Biology Teachers and Their Relationship to Selected Personality Traits.* Doctor's thesis, Ohio State University (Columbus, Ohio), 1968. (*DA* 29:1359A)

398. FURR, HENRY BEDFORD. *Some Influences of a Course in Business Speaking on Certain Personality Traits of College Students.* Doctor's thesis, North Texas State University (Denton, Tex.), 1968. (*DA* 29:3460A)

399. GRUENFELD, LEOPOLD, AND ARBUTHNOT, JACK. "Field Independence, Achievement Values and the Evaluation of a Competency Related Dimension on the Least Preferred Co-Worker (LPC) Means." *Percept & Motor Skills* 27:991–1002 D '68. * (*PA* 43:8813)

400. HESCH, GEORGE PETER. *A Study of the Relationship Between Counselor Trainee Attitudes Towards Adolescents and Preferences for Client Characteristics and Counseling Effectiveness.* Doctor's thesis, Purdue University (Lafayette, Ind.), 1968. (*DA* 29:2523A)

401. JACOBS, ALFRED, AND BARRON, ROBERT. "Falsification of the Guilford-Zimmerman Temperament Survey: 2, Making a Poor Impression." *Psychol Rep* 23:1271–7 D '68. * (*PA* 43:8372)

402. KASSEN, TEX LEO. *An Analysis of Temperament Traits of Selected High School Football Coaches and Varsity Football Teams as Measured by the Guilford-Zimmerman Temperament Survey.* Doctor's thesis, University of Houston (Houston, Tex.), 1968. (*DA* 29:4230A)

403. LAURENT, HARRY. Chap. 1, "Research on the Identification of Management Potential," pp. 1–34. In *Predicting Managerial Success.* Edited by John A. Myers, Jr. Ann Arbor,

Mich.: Foundation for Research on Human Behavior, April 1968. Pp. v, 173. *

404. SHEMBERG, K. M., AND LEVENTHAL, D. B. "Masculinity-Femininity and Need for Social Approval." *J Proj Tech & Pers Assess* 32:575–7 D '68. * (*PA* 43:9720)

405. SINDT, DORIS M. *An Investigation of the Relationship Between the Intolerance of Ambiguity Dimension of the Counselor's Personality and Counseling Behaviors and Certain Other Personality Dimensions.* Doctor's thesis, University of Kansas (Lawrence, Kan.), 1968. (*DA* 29:1759A)

406. SNAPP, MATTHEW. *A Comparison of Guilford-Zimmerman Temperament Survey Scores of Students on Academic Probation and Students in Good Academic Standing at Brigham Young University.* Master's thesis, Brigham Young University (Provo, Utah), 1968.

407. TALLMADGE, G. K. "Relationships Between Training Methods and Learner Characteristics." *J Ed Psychol* 59:32–6 F '68. * (*PA* 42:7932)

408. THRONEBERRY, CONNIE A. *An Investigation of Weight Change as Related to Personality Traits and Activity Programs.* Master's thesis, California State College (Long Beach, Calif.), 1968.

409. TIMMERMANS, HELEN M. "A Comparison Between Physical Education Majors and Nonmajors in Certain Personality Traits." *Res Q* 39:1088–93 D '68. *

410. WILSON, HAROLD LEWIS. *Temperament Patterns of Potential Teachers.* Doctor's thesis, University of Nebraska (Lincoln, Neb.), 1968. (*DA* 29:1796A)

411. WILSON, PHILIP KEITH. *Relationship Between Motor Achievement and Selected Personality Factors of Junior and Senior High School Boys.* Doctor's thesis, Colorado State College (Greeley, Colo.), 1968. (*DA* 29:1125A)

412. ARBUTHNOT, JACK, AND GRUENFELD, LEOPOLD. "Field Independence and Educational-Vocational Interests." Abstract. *J Consult & Clin Psychol* 33(5):631 O '69. * (*PA* 44:2325)

413. BECKER, GILBERT. "Ego-Defence Pattern, Extraversion-Introversion, and Sex-Role Adjustment." *Brit J Social & Clin Psychol* 8(3):275–86 S '69. * (*PA* 44:3598)

414. BISHOP, JOHN BYRON. *The Relation of Counselor Trainee Interview Behaviors to Selected Personality Traits and Clients' Ratings of Effectiveness.* Doctor's thesis, Ohio University (Athens, Ohio), 1969. (*DAI* 30:3715A)

415. BREDEMEIER, RICHARD ALAN. *An Exploration of Factors Associated With Students Who Are Successful Following Their Readmission to Purdue University.* Doctor's thesis, Purdue University (Lafayette, Ind.), 1969. (*DAI* 30:3716A)

416. BREWER, TED EUGENE. *Relationships Among Individual Short-term Counseling, Academic Achievement, Personality Factors, and College Persistence of Certain Junior College Students.* Doctor's thesis, North Texas State University (Denton, Tex.), 1969. (*DAI* 30:4765A)

417. ESPENSCHADE, ANNA S. "Role of Exercise in the Well-Being of Women in 35–80 Years of Age." *J Gerontol* 24(1):86–9 Ja '69. *

418. EVANS, THOMAS P. "Teacher Verbal and Nonverbal Behaviors and Their Relationship to Personality." *J Exp Ed* 38(1):38–47 f '69. * (*PA* 45:10847)

419. GEEN, RUSSELL G., AND GEORGE, ROBERT. "Relationship of Manifest Aggressiveness to Aggressive Word Associations." *Psychol Rep* 25(3):711–4 D '69. * (*PA* 44:18691)

420. GRACE, EVELYN RANDALL. *The Relationship Between Personality Traits and Vocational Interests in the Choice of Field of Study of Selected Junior College Students in Business Administration.* Doctor's thesis, North Texas State University (Denton, Tex.), 1969. (*DAI* 30:4827A)

421. HACKMAN, RAY C. *The Motivated Working Adult.* New York: American Management Association, Inc., 1969. Pp. 206. *

422. HARRELL, THOMAS W. "The Personality of High Earning MBA's in Big Business." *Personnel Psychol* 22(4):457–63 w '69. * (*PA* 44:13525)

423. HASKELL, ROGER WILLIAM. *Effect of Personality Characteristics Upon Learning via Selected Modes of Instruction—An Experimental Investigation.* Doctor's thesis, Purdue University (Lafayette, Ind.), 1969. (*DAI* 30:5355A)

424. HUSEMOLLER, KENNETH E. *The Prediction of Freshmen Academic Success at Eastern New Mexico University, Roswell, by Means of Selected Demographic and Standardized Tests Data.* Doctor's thesis, Colorado State College (Greeley, Colo.), 1969. (*DAI* 30:1467A)

425. KOOKER, EARL W., AND BELLAMY, ROY Q. "Some Psychometric Differences Between Graduates and Dropouts." *Psychol* 6(2):65–70 My '69. * (*PA* 43:14868)

426. KRATZ, GERALD BERNARD. *A Descriptive Analysis of the Personality Traits of Public School Negotiating Team Members in Selected Southeastern Michigan School Districts.* Doctor's thesis, Wayne State University (Detroit, Mich.), 1969. (*DAI* 30:3639A)

427. LAGRONE, C. W. "Sex and Personality Differences in Relation to Feeling for Direction." *J General Psychol* 81(1):23–33 Jl '69. * (*PA* 44:5150)

428. LAUBACHER, M. CORONATA. *The Relationship of Personality and Self-Concept to the Degree of Competency in the Student Teaching of a Selected Group of Marygrove College Seniors.* Doctor's thesis, Wayne State University (Detroit, Mich.), 1969. (*DAI* 30:4858A)

429. LEVENTHAL, D. B., AND SHEMBERG, K. M. "Sex Role Adjustment and Nonsanctioned Aggression." *J Exp Res Personality* 3(4):283–6 Ap '69. * (*PA* 43:14305)

430. LINDEN, KATHRYN W., AND LINDEN, JAMES D. "A Longitudinal Study of Teachers' Attitudes and Personality Characteristics." *J Teach Ed* 20(3):351–60 f '69. * (*PA* 44:11336)

431. LUNNEBORG, CLIFFORD E., AND LUNNEBORG, PATRICIA W. "Architecture School Performance Predicted From ASAT, Intellective, and Nonintellective Measures." *J Appl Psychol* 53(3):209–13 Je '69. * (*PA* 43:11928)

432. MCCARLEY, WALTER WILLIAM. *An Experimental Study to Evaluate the Effectiveness of an Individualized Instructional Method and the Lecture-Discussion Method for Teaching Vocational Agriculture Classes.* Doctor's thesis, Michigan State University (East Lansing, Mich.), 1969. (*DAI* 30:5323A)

433. MEHRABIAN, ALBERT. "Measures of Achieving Tendency." *Ed & Psychol Meas* 29(2):445–51 su '69. * (*PA* 44:17478)

434. MORGAN, JACK C., AND WOERDEHOFF, FRANK J. "Stability of Student Teacher Behaviors and Their Relationship to Personality and Creativity Factors." *J Ed Res* 62(6):251–4 F '69. *

435. MORRISON, JESSIE SYKES. *Characteristics of Students in Two-Year Post-High School Occupational Education Programs.* Doctor's thesis, Ohio State University (Columbus, Ohio), 1969. (*DAI* 30:4228A)

436. O'NEILL, MARION, AND KEMPLER, BERNHARD. "Approach and Avoidance Responses of the Hysterical Personality to Sexual Stimuli." *J Abn Psychol* 74(3):300–5 Je '69. * (*PA* 43:12986)

437. RUCKER, MARGARET HOWARD. *The Relationship of Perceived Locus of Control and Ascendancy to Reactions to a Manipulative and a Participative Problem-Solving Situation.* Doctor's thesis, Purdue University (Lafayette, Ind.), 1969. (*DAI* 30:4406B)

438. SHOUKSMITH, GEORGE. "Personality Attributes Associated With Two Measures of Cognitive Style." *Acta Psychologica* (Netherlands) 30(3) '69. * (*PA* 44:14589)

439. STRICKER, LAWRENCE J. " 'Test-Wiseness' on Personality Scales." *J Appl Psychol Monogr* 53(3, pt 2):1–18 Je '69. * (*PA* 43:11343)

440. SZABO, MICHAEL. *The Relationship of Intellective, Personality, and Biographical Variables to Success and Its Prediction in an Independent Study Science Course at the College Level.* Doctor's thesis, Purdue University (Lafayette, Ind.), 1969. (*DAI* 30:4845A)

441. THAI, THOMAS VU MINH. *An Investigation of Religious Attitudes, Ideals, and Personality Traits of Four Groups of Catholic College Students.* Doctor's thesis, Fordham University (New York, N.Y.), 1969. (*DAI* 30:1441A)

442. TITUS, H. EDWIN. "Prediction of Supervisory Success by Use of Standard Psychological Tests." *J Psychol* 72(1):35–40 My '69. * (*PA* 43:16503)

443. TITUS, H. EDWIN, AND GOSS, RICHARD G. "Psychometric Comparison of Old and Young Supervisors." *Psychol Rep* 24(3):727–33 Je '69. * (*PA* 44:1447)

444. TRUJILLO, CECILIA M. *Effects of Beginning Swimming Instruction on Selected Personality Traits.* Master's thesis, University of Washington (Seattle, Wash.), 1969.

445. VAN HALL, RICHARD. *The Relationship Between Personality Factors and the Choice of Selected Major Fields in Education.* Doctor's thesis, North Texas State University (Denton, Tex.), 1969. (*DAI* 30:548A)

446. WILEY, NANCY NEWELL. *A Comparison of Certain Personality Traits and Academic Performance in Freshman Students Who Do and Do Not Seek Counseling.* Master's thesis, Southern Methodist University (Dallas, Tex.), 1969.

447. WILSON, PHILIP K. "Relationship Between Motor Achievement and Selected Personality Factors of Junior and Senior High School Boys." *Res Q* 40(4):841–4 D '69. *

448. YOUNGER, JESSAMINE GRIMES. *The Effect of Vocational Choice Counseling on Vocational Maturity in Selected First Year University Students.* Master's thesis, Southern Methodist University (Dallas, Tex.), 1969.

449. ANDRUD, WESLEY E. *The Personality Traits of High School, College, and Professional Football Coaches as Measured by the Guilford-Zimmerman Temperament Survey.* Master's thesis, University of North Dakota (Grand Forks, N.D.), 1970.

450. BOTTGER, JOAN E. *A Study of the Relationship Between the Percentage of Buccal Cell Nuclei Containing Barr Bodies and the Psychological Masculinity-Femininity Indices of 100 Freshman and Sophomore College Women.* Doctor's thesis, Texas Woman's University (Denton, Tex.), 1970.

451. BRICKMAN, ROBERT LEE. *School Climate: A Reflection of the Principal's Personality.* Doctor's thesis, Claremont Graduate School (Claremont, Calif.), 1970. (*DAI* 31:6293A)

452. DIAMANT, LOUIS. "Attitude, Personality, and Behavior in Volunteers and Nonvolunteers for Sexual Research." Abstract. *Proc 78th Ann Conv Am Psychol Assn* 5(1):423–4 '70. * (*PA* 44:18499)

453. FURR, H. BEDFORD. "Influences of a Course in Speech-Communication on Certain Aspects of the Self-Concept of College Freshmen." *Speech Teach* 19(1):26–31 Ja '70. *

454. HARRELL, THOMAS W. "The Personality of High Earn-

ing MBA's in Small Business." *Personnel Psychol* 23(3):369–75 au '70. * (*PA* 45:9041)

455. HERDT, BERYL F. "The Human Movement Factor (M) in the Rorschach, Motor Activity, and Behavior." *J Motor Behav* 2(2):134–9 Je '70. *

456. HINTON, BERNARD L. "Personality Variables and Creative Potential." *J Creative Behav* 4(3):210–7 su '70. *

457. HUGHES, JEROME MICHAEL. *Big Brothers of Greater Flint: A History and Profile, Including an Evaluation of the Male Model in the Life of a Fatherless Boy.* Doctor's thesis, Wayne State University (Detroit, Mich.), 1970. (*DAI* 31:3215A)

458. HUTSLAR, JOHN LEE. *The Relationship Between Selected Personality Traits and Bicycle Ergometer Endurance.* Master's thesis, Pennsylvania State University (University Park, Pa.), 1970.

459. IBRAHIM, HILMI. "Recreation Preference and Temperament." *Res Q* 41(2):145–54 My '70. *

460. JANSEN, DAVID G.; ROBB, GEORGE P.; AND BONK, EDWARD C. "Characteristics of High-Rated and Low-Rated Master's Degree Candidates in Counseling and Guidance." *Counselor Ed & Sup* 9(3):162–70 sp '70. * (*PA* 46:5559)

461. JOHNSON, CLARICE WELLS. *Nonintellective Factors Related to College Achievement and Attrition.* Doctor's thesis, University of South Carolina (Columbia, S.C.), 1970. (*DAI* 31:5129A)

462. JONES, KENNETH J., AND JONES, PRISCILLA P. "Contribution of the Rorschach to Description of Personality Structure Defined by Several Objective Tests." *Psychol Rep* 26(1):35–45 F '70. * (*PA* 45:4281)

463. JORDAN, BRIAN T., AND KEMPLER, BERNHARD. "Hysterical Personality: An Experimental Investigation of Sex-Role Conflict." *J Abn Psychol* 75(2):172–6 Ap '70. * (*PA* 44:10820)

464. LAURENT, HARRY. "Cross-Cultural Cross-Validation of Empirically Validated Tests." *J Appl Psychol* 54(5):417–23 O '70. * (*PA* 45:3135)

465. McGOWAN, RAYMOND PETER. *Line Managers and College Business Students: A Differential Analysis of Personality Variables and Value Concepts.* Doctor's thesis, St. John's University (Jamaica, N.Y.), 1970. (*DAI* 31:3745B)

466. PETERSON, GARY WINSTON. *Interaction Between Energy Expenditure and Discharge Control With Respect to Academic and Non-Academic Productivity of College Males.* Doctor's thesis, Duke University (Durham, N.C.), 1970. (*DAI* 32:1281A)

467. PHELAN, JOSEPH G.; BROOKS, RICHARD; AND BRASHEARS, GLADYS C. "Relationship of Kinesthetic Figural Aftereffect to Masculinity-Femininity and Expectation for Internal Versus External Control of Reinforcement." *Percept & Motor Skills* 31(3):863–6 D '70. * (*PA* 45:9967)

468. ROSIER, F. N. G. "A Study of Juvenile Delinquents in a Remand Home." *Papers Psychol* (Northern Ireland) 4(1–2):54–5 Ap–O '70. *

469. ROUBERTOUX, PIERRE. "Personality Variables and Interest in Art." *J Pers & Social Psychol* 16(4):665–8 D '70. * (*PA* 45:6357)

470. SHIPMAN, WILLIAM G.; HEATH, HELEN A.; AND OKEN, DONALD. "Response Specificity Among Muscular and Autonomic Variables." *Arch Gen Psychiatry* 23(4):369–74 O '70. * (*PA* 45:2693)

471. SHIPMAN, WILLIAM G.; OKEN, DONALD; AND HEATH, HELEN A. "Muscle Tension and Effort at Self-Control During Anxiety." *Arch Gen Psychiatry* 23(4):359–68 O '70. * (*PA* 45:2694)

472. STARKS, WALTER LIVINGSTON. *The Relationship of Residence and Economic Factors to the First Semester Academic Achievement of College of Business Administration and College of Agriculture 1969 Freshmen, Male Students.* Doctor's thesis, Oklahoma State University (Stillwater, Okla.), 1970. (*DAI* 31:5805A)

473. STEWART, LINDA JOAN. *Characteristics of Students Attaining Different Achievement Levels at Northwestern State College.* Doctor's thesis, Oklahoma State University (Stillwater, Okla.), 1970. (*DAI* 31:5139A)

474. SZABO, MICHAEL, AND FELDHUSEN, JOHN F. "Personality and Intellective Predictors and Academic Success in an Independent Study Science Course at the College Level." *Psychol Rep* 26(2):493–4 Ap '70. * (*PA* 44:21622)

475. WEBB, P. A. "The Guilford-Zimmerman Temperament Survey: Australian Business Executives." *Austral Psychologist* 5(3):278–9 N '70. * (*PA* 46:4998)

476. ARBUTHNOT, JACK BRAEDEN. *Field Independence and Maturity of Moral Judgment, Critical Distinctive Feature Analysis, and Perceived Locus of Control.* Doctor's thesis, Cornell University (Ithaca, N.Y.), 1971. (*DAI* 32:2190A)

477. CALANDRA, GERALD NEIL. *Relationships Among Selected Traits of Cardiovascular Fitness and Selected Traits of Personality.* Doctor's thesis, University of Georgia (Athens, Ga.), 1971. (*DAI* 32:3777A)

478. CULL, JOHN G., JR., AND HARDY, RICHARD E. "Concurrent Validation Information on the Machover Draw-A-Person Test." *J Genetic Psychol* 118(2):211–5 Je '71. * (*PA* 46:9080)

479. DAVIS, WALTER NEWTON. *Authoritarianism and Selected Trait Patterns of School Administrators: Seventeen Case Studies.* Doctor's thesis, North Texas State University (Denton, Tex.), 1971. (*DAI* 32:1777A)

Guilford-Zimmerman Temperament Survey

480. DOBRUSZEK, ZBIGNIEW. "Leadership Attitudes Measured by the Bass Orientation Inventory." *Polish Psychol B* 2(1):31–5 '71. * (*PA* 48:1988)

481. GIESE, RONALD NORMAN. *An Analysis of Selected Aspects of the ISCS Model of Science Teaching: Part 1, Relationships of Selected Characteristics and Behaviors of Teachers Using the Intermediate Science Curriculum Study.* Doctor's thesis, Temple University (Philadelphia, Pa.), 1971. (*DAI* 32:4466A)

482. HASKELL, ROGER W. "Effect of Certain Individual Learner Personality Differences on Instructional Methods." *AV Commun R* 19(3):287–97 f '71. * (*PA* 47:7825)

483. HOUSER, RONALD L. *Development of Affective Scales to Predict Career Commitment to Education.* Doctor's thesis, Purdue University (Lafayette, Ind.), 1971. (*DAI* 32:788A)

484. JENNINGS, LILLIAN PEGUES. *Selected Case Studies of Students in a Teacher Education Field Experience Program.* Doctor's thesis, University of Pittsburgh (Pittsburgh, Pa.), 1971. (*DAI* 32:3051A)

485. JERNIGAN, LARRY R., AND DEMAREE, ROBERT G. "Item-Factor Analysis of the Guilford-Zimmerman Temperament Survey." Abstract. *Proc 79th Ann Conv Am Psychol Assn* 6(1): 111–2 '71. * (*PA* 46:3086)

486. KLOSS, MARIE G., AND DREGER, RALPH MASON. "Abstract Art Preferences and Temperament Traits: A Study in the Psychology of Aesthetics." *J Pers Assess* 35(4):375–8 Ag '71. * (*PA* 47:4802)

487. MASICA, DANIEL N.; MONEY, JOHN; AND EHRHARDT, ANKE A. "Fetal Feminization and Female Gender Identity in the Testicular Feminizing Syndrome of Androgen Insensitivity." *Arch Sex Behav* 1(2):131–42 '71. * (*PA* 48:1284)

488. MOZDZIERZ, GERALD J.; MACCHITELLI, FRANK J.; FLAHERTY, LAWRENCE; AND deVITO, ROBERT. "Temperament Characteristics of Chronic Alcoholics as Measured by the Guilford-Zimmerman Temperament Survey." *J Psychol* 79(1):97–102 S '71. * (*PA* 47:5137)

489. NEDD, ALBERT N. B. "The Simultaneous Effect of Several Variables on Attitudes Toward Change." *Adm Sci Q* 16(3):258–69 S '71. * (*PA* 47:11914)

490. NICKERSON, EILEEN T. "Some Correlates of Adjustment by Paraplegics." *Percept & Motor Skills* 32(1):11–23 F '71. * (*PA* 46:3538)

491. OFFENBACH, STEFAN GARED. *A Multitrait-Multimethod Analysis of Witkin's Concept of Psychological Differentiation.* Doctor's thesis, Washington University (St. Louis, Mo.), 1971. (*DAI* 32:2406B)

492. POPE, JOHN WINFRED. *A Comparison of Personality Traits Between College Students Reared Within a Selected Polar Region by Non-Native Parents and College Students Reared Within Non-Polar Regions by Native Parents.* Doctor's thesis, North Texas State University (Denton, Tex.), 1971. (*DAI* 32:7323B)

493. SELLS, S. B.; DEMAREE, R. G.; AND WILL, DONALD P., JR. "Dimensions of Personality: 2, Separate Factor Structures in Guilford and Cattell Trait Markers." *Multiv Behav Res* 6(2):135–85 Ap '71. * (*PA* 47:4821)

494. SZABO, MICHAEL, AND FELDHUSEN, JOHN F. "Success in an Independent Study Science Course at the College Level as Related to Intellective, Personality, and Biographical Variables." *J Res Sci Teach* 8(3):225–9 '71. *

CUMULATIVE NAME INDEX

[1208]

★[Hahn Self Psychoevaluation Materials.] Ages 40 and over; 1967–73; 11 self-study questionnaires and record forms available separately or as part of a booklet entitled *Planning Ahead After 40;* Milton E. Hahn; Western Psychological Services. *

a) PERSONAL INFORMATION: PAST, PRESENT, FUTURE.

b) AN ACTIVITY RECORD: AVOCATIONS AND RECREATIONS-PAST-PRESENT-FUTURE.

c) THE AUTOBIOGRAPHY AND LIFE HISTORY.

d) APTITUDES AND ABILITIES: A RATING PROCEDURE. 7 ratings: academic or school, mechanical, social (communication), clerical, musical, artistic, physical agility.

e) THE VALUING PROCESS AND SENTIMENTS. Ratings in 6 areas: patriotism, family, religion, occupation, mechanical-materialistic, play and recreation.

f) NEEDS: A RATING PROCEDURE. 2 rating scales.

g) THE DIMENSIONS OF SELF-ACTUALIZATION: A RATING PROCEDURE. 10 ratings: academic and other aptitudes and abilities, self-expression-independence-vocational satisfaction, leadership, performance vs. potential, social-political balance, social contribution, self-sufficiency, creativity, maturity, social-vocational multipotentiality.

h) INTERESTS: "PULLING" MOTIVATORS. 6 ratings: realistic, intellectual, social, conventional, enterprising, artistic.

i) LIFE GOALS: A "PULLING" MOTIVATOR. 10 ratings: esteem, profit, fame, power, leadership, security, social service, interesting experiences, self-expression, independence.

j) THE CALIFORNIA LIFE GOALS EVALUATION SCHEDULE. See 1118.

k) A SUMMARY OF YOUR SELF-STUDY: PROBLEM AREAS AND PERSONAL CONDITIONS.

[1209]

★**Hahnemann High School Behavior Rating Scale.** Grades 7–12; 1971–72; HHSB; ratings by teachers; 13 scores: reasoning ability, originality, verbal interaction, rapport with teacher, anxious producer, general anxiety, quiet-withdrawn, poor work habits, lack intellectual independence, dogmatic-inflexible, verbal negativism, disturbance-restless, expressed inability; George Spivack and Marshall Swift; Division of Research and Evaluation, Hahnemann Medical College and Hospital. *

[1210]

The Handicap Problems Inventory. Ages 16 and over with physical disabilities; 1960; HPI; 4 scores: personal, family, social, vocational; George N. Wright and H. H. Remmers; University Book Store. *

For additional information, see P:105 (2 references); for a review by Dorothy M. Clendenen, see 6:111.

REFERENCES THROUGH 1971

1–2. See P:105.

3. KOECHEL, JOHN W. *Perceptual Defence and Perceptual Vigilance in Individuals With Obvious and Hidden Disabilities.* Doctor's thesis, University of Houston (Houston, Tex.), 1964. (*DA* 26:1778)

4. BLASKOVICS, THOMAS LEE. *Measurement of the Impact of Disability Upon Handicapped Persons.* Doctor's thesis, University of Wisconsin (Madison, Wis.), 1965. (*DA* 26:5570)

5. MATHEWS, JOHN BURT. *The Psychological Impact of Physical Disability Upon Vocationally Handicapped Individuals.* Doctor's thesis, University of Wisconsin (Madison, Wis.), 1966. (*DA* 28:1204B)

6. HAUCK, WILLIAM EDWARD. *The Derivation of Item Weights and Additional Normative Data for the Handicap Problems Inventory.* Doctor's thesis, University of Wisconsin (Madison, Wis.), 1968. (*DA* 29:4325A)

7. HOLMAN, RICHARD JAY. *Change in Self Evaluation of Vocational Problems Among Physically, Mentally Culturally Handicapped Clients During the Vocational Rehabilitation Process.* Doctor's thesis, University of Wisconsin (Madison, Wis.), 1968. (*DAI* 30:133A)

8. ROSILLO, RONALD H., AND FOGEL, MAX L. "Emotional Support." *Psychosomatics* 11(3):194–6 My–Je '70. * (*PA* 45:2814)

9. LASKY, ROBERT G., AND SALOMONE, PAUL R. "A Modification of the Handicap Problems Inventory." *Rehabil Counsel B* 15(2):106–15 D '71. * (*PA* 48:5388)

CUMULATIVE NAME INDEX

Blaskovics, T. L.: 4
Clendenen, D. M.: *rev*, 6:111
Fogel, M. L.: 8
Hauck, W. E.: 6
Holman, R. J.: 7
Koechel, J. W.: 3
Lasky, R. G.: 9
Mathews, J. B.: 5
Meissner, A. L. W.: 2
Rosillo, R. H.: 8
Salomone, P. R.: 9
Wright, G. N.: 1

[1211]

*****The Hartman Value Profile.** Ages 12 and over; 1965–72; HVP; formerly called *The Hartman Value Inventory;* also called the *Axiometric Test;* test copyrighted 1970 same as 1966 test except for 1 revised item; "capacity to value"; 57 scores: 15 capacity to value the outside world scores, 15 capacity to value one's self scores, 7 scores resulting from both capacities, 2 retest scores, and 18 deviation scores; Robert S. Hartman and Mario Cardenas Trigos; Research Concepts. *

For additional information, see P:106 (2 references).

REFERENCES THROUGH 1971

1–2. See P:106.

3. LOHMAN, JAMES STANLEY. *The Professor's Influence on Students' "Capacity to Value."* Doctor's thesis, Boston University (Boston, Mass.), 1968. (*DAI* 30:68A)

4. ELLIOTT, BILLIE CANNON. *Factor and Cluster Analyses of the Hartman Inventory: A Study of Item Homogeneity and Factorial Invariance for Normative and Ipsative Scales.* Doctor's thesis, University of Tennessee (Knoxville, Tenn.), 1969. (*DAI* 30:3318A)

CUMULATIVE NAME INDEX

Elliott, B. C.: 4
Hartman, R. S.: 1–2
Lohman, J. S.: 3

[1212]

Harvard Group Scale of Hypnotic Susceptibility. College and adults; 1959–62; HGSHS; adaptation for group administration of Form A of *Stanford Hypnotic Susceptibility Scale;* Ronald E. Shor and Emily Carota Orne; Consulting Psychologists Press, Inc. *

For additional information, see P:107 (12 references); for a review by Seymour Fisher, see 6:112 (4 references).

REFERENCES THROUGH 1971

1–3. See 6:112.

4–15. See P:107.

16. COE, WILLIAM C., AND SARBIN, THEODORE R. "An Experimental Demonstration of Hypnosis as Role Enactment." *J Abn Psychol* 71:400–6 D '66. * (*PA* 41:1091)

17. KRAMER, ERNEST. "Group Induction of Hypnosis With Institutionalized Patients." *Int J Clin & Exp Hyp* 14:243–6 Jl '66. * (*PA* 40:11189)

18. RODGERS, CHARLES W. *A Comparison of the Need for Achievement and Hypnotic Susceptibility.* Master's thesis, University of Wyoming (Laramie, Wyo.), 1968.

19. VELTEN, EMMETT, JR. "A Laboratory Task for Induction of Mood States." *Behav Res & Ther* (England) 6:473–82 N '68. * (*PA* 43:9031)

20. KLEMP, RAYMOND H. "The Rotter I-E Scale and Hypnotic Susceptibility." *Psychol Rep* 24(2):660 Ap '69. * (*PA* 43:15116)

21. KRAMER, ERNEST. "Hypnotic Suggestibility and Previous Relationship With the Hypnotist." *Am J Clin Hyp* 11(3):175–7 Ja '69. * (*PA* 43:13652)

22. NOWLIS, DAVID P. "The Child-Rearing Antecedents of Hypnotic Susceptibility and of Naturally Occurring Hypnotic-Like Experience." *Int J Clin & Exp Hyp* 17(2):109–20 Ap '69. * (*PA* 44:1673)

23. RHOADES, CHRISTOPHER D., AND EDMONSTON, WILLIAM E., JR. "Personality Correlates of Hypnotizability: A Study Using the Harvard Group Scale of Hypnotic Susceptibility, the 16-PF and the IPAT." *Am J Clin Hyp* 11(4):228–33 Ap '69. *(*PA* 43:13654)

24. BALASCHAK, BARBARA; BLOCKER, KENT; ROSSITER, THOMAS; AND PERIN, C. T. "Influence of Race and Expressed Experience of the Hypnotist on Hypnotic Susceptibility." Abstract. *Proc 78th Ann Conv Am Psychol Assn* 5(2):835–6 '70. * (*PA* 44:17846)

25. BOWERS, KENNETH S., AND VAN DER MEULEN, SANDRA J. "Effect of Hypnotic Susceptibility on Creativity Test Performance." *J Pers & Social Psychol* 14(3):247–56 Mr '70. * (*PA* 44:8441)

26. KING, DAVID J. "Note on Suggestibility and Clustering." *Psychol Rep* 27(1):316 Ag '70. * (*PA* 45:5412)

27. MITCHELL, MEREDITH B. "Hypnotizability and Distractibility." *Am J Clin Hyp* 13(1):35–45 Jl '70. * (*PA* 45:129)

28. BOWERS, KENNETH S. "Sex and Susceptibility as Moderator Variables in the Relationship of Creativity and Hypnotic Susceptibility." *J Abn Psychol* 78(1):93–100 Ag '71. * (*PA* 47:2042)

29. BOWERS, KENNETH S., AND KEELING, KENNETH R. "Heart-Rate Variability in Creative Functioning." *Psychol Rep* 29(1):160–2 Ag '71. * (*PA* 47:2468)

30. GOEBEL, RONALD A., AND STEWART, CHARLES G. "Effects of Experimenter Bias and Induced Subject Expectancy on Hypnotic Susceptibility." *J Pers & Social Psychol* 18(2):263–72 My '71. * (*PA* 46:4151)

31. HOPKINSON, DANIEL DAVID. *Questionnaire and Behavioral Correlates of Hypnotic Susceptibility.* Doctor's thesis, University of Texas (Austin, Tex.), 1971. (*DAI* 32:6049B)

32. SHEEHAN, PETER W. "Countering Preconceptions About Hypnosis: An Objective Index of Involvement With the Hypnotist." *J Abn Psychol* 78(3):299–322 D '71. * (*PA* 47:8116)

33. SHOR, RONALD E. "Expectancies of Being Influenced and Hypnotic Performance." *Int J Clin & Exp Hyp* 19(3):154–66 Jl '71. * (*PA* 47:2046)

34. SVOBODA, MOJMIR. "Dimensions of Activity and Passivity in Hypnosis and Hypnotic Susceptibility." *Am J Clin Hyp* 14(1):44–7 Jl '71. * (*PA* 47:10139)

CUMULATIVE NAME INDEX

Balaschak, B.: 24
Belair, R. R.: 15
Bentler, P. M.: 1, 1a
Blocker, K.: 24
Bowers, K. S.: 25, 28–9
Coe, W. C.: 4, 16
Dermen, D.: 8
Edmonston, W. E.: 23
Evans, F. J.: 10, 13
Field, P. B.: 5, 9–10
Fisher, S.: *rev*, 6:112
Goebel, R. A.: 30
Hartman, B. J.: 11–2
Hilgard, E. R.: 1
Hopkinson, D. D.: 31
Keeling, K. R.: 29
King, D. J.: 26
Klemp, R. H.: 20
Kramer, E.: 17, 21
London, P.: 2, 8
Mitchell, M. B.: 14, 27
Nowlis, D.: 22
O'Connell, D. N.: 6
Orne, E. C.: 3
Orne, M. T.: 10
Perin, C. T.: 24
Rhoades, C. D.: 23
Roberts, M. R.: 1a

[1213]

The Hellenic Affiliation Scale: An Inventory of Student Behavior and Beliefs for Use by School Personnel, Experimental Form. College; 1967; HAS; title on test is *H.A.S.*; fraternity or sorority affiliation proneness; LeRoy A. Stone, Marlo A. Skurdal, and David R. Skeen; LeRoy A. Stone. *

For additional information, see P :108.

REFERENCES THROUGH 1971

1. STONE, LEROY A.; SKURDAL, MARLO A.; AND SKEEN, DAVID R. "Hellenic Affiliation Scale." *J Col Stud Personnel* 9:332–3 S '68. *

CUMULATIVE NAME INDEX

[1214]

Hill Interaction Matrix. Prospective members and members, leaders of psychotherapy groups; 1954–68; HIM; matrix of 4 columns (topics, groups, personal, relationship) and 4 rows (conventional, assertive, speculative, confrontive) produces 16 scores, 8 marginal total scores, grand total, and other derivative scores; 3 editions; Wm. Fawcett Hill; Sage Publications. *

a) HIM A AND B. Prospective and actual members of psychotherapy groups; 2 editions are the same except HIM-A has simpler language than HIM-B in 31 of the 64 items; 1954–68.

b) HIM-G. Observers and leaders of psychotherapy groups; 1967–68; no manual.

For additional information, see P :109.

REFERENCES THROUGH 1971

1. LIEBRODER, MALCOLM NEIL. *Effects of Therapist Style on Interaction in Psychotherapy Groups.* Doctor's thesis, University of Utah (Salt Lake City, Utah), 1962. (*DA* 23:3976)
2. RAVSTEN, LYNN ALLEN. *Mood-Judgment From Vocal Cues and Its Relationship to Personality Variables and Group Psychotherapy.* Doctor's thesis, University of Utah (Salt Lake City, Utah), 1966. (*DA* 27:2876B)
3. HILL, WM. FAWCETT; STOLLER, FREDERICK H.; AND STRAUB, CONSTANCE J. "Group Therapy for Social Impact: Innovation in Leadership Training." *Am Behav Sci* 9:1–49 S–O '67. *
4. YALOM, IRVIN D.; HOUTS, PETER S.; NEWELL, GARY; AND RAND, KENNETH H. "Preparation of Patients for Group Therapy: A Controlled Study." *Arch Gen Psychiatry* 17:416–27 O '67. * (*PA* 42:830)
5. AHEARN, THOMAS RICHARD. *An Interaction Process Analysis of Extended Group Counseling With Prospective Counselors.* Doctor's thesis, University of Georgia (Athens, Ga.), 1968. (*DA* 29:4271A)
6. HOUTS, PETER S., AND WITTNER, WILLIAM K. "Patients' Recognition Memory for Statements Made in Ward Community Meetings." *J Consult & Clin Psychol* 32:130–3 Ap '68. * (*PA* 42:9022)
7. STEFFEN, JOHN DAVID. *The Effects of Two Behavioral Models of Group Counseling on the Academic Performance of Selected College Women.* Doctor's thesis, University of Minnesota (Minneapolis, Minn.), 1968. (*DA* 29:3426A)
8. BOYD, ROBERT EMMETT. *Counselor Interests as a Factor in Counselor Effectiveness.* Doctor's thesis, University of Minnesota (Minneapolis, Minn.), 1969. (*DAI* 30:4785B)
9. COMEAUX, CHARLES RAY. *Intensity of Group Interaction as a Factor in Change in Self-Concept and Dogmatism.* Doctor's thesis, University of Arizona (Tuscon, Ariz.), 1969. (*DAI* 30:4218A)
10. GUTZMER, WILLARD ERNEST. *A Study in Structured Discussion.* Doctor's thesis, University of Utah (Salt Lake City, Utah), 1969. (*DAI* 30:1749A)
11. KOHLER, ADAM THOMAS. *Some Possible Effects of Leader-Member, Similarity-Dissimilarity in the Counseling Technique of Group Psychoevaluation.* Doctor's thesis, University of California (Los Angeles, Calif.), 1969. (*DAI* 30:5240B)
12. MERMIS, WILLIAM L., JR. *The Effect of Small Group Relationship Counseling on Professional Staff Communication and Counselor-Client Interaction in a Youth Opportunity Center.*

Doctor's thesis, Arizona State University (Tempe, Ariz.), 1969. (*DAI* 30:2340A)
13. ROFFERS, TONY. *Conditioning a Style of Interaction in Counseling Groups and Its Effects on Behavior and Attitude Changes in College Students.* Doctor's thesis, University of Minnesota (Minneapolis, Minn.), 1969. (*DAI* 30:2915B)
14. SELIGMAN, MILTON, AND STERNE, DAVID M. "Verbal Behavior in Therapist-Led, Leaderless, and Alternating Group Psychotherapy Sessions." *J Counsel Psychol* 16(4):325–8 Jl '69. * (*PA* 43:14420)
15. BLOCK, JOEL DAVID. *A Comparison of the Verbal Interaction in Counseling Groups Differing in Member Interpersonal Compatibility.* Doctor's thesis, Syracuse University (Syracuse, N.Y.), 1970. (*DAI* 32:780A)
16. BOYD, ROBERT E. "Whitehorn-Betz A-B Score as an Effector of Client-Counselor Interaction." *J Counsel Psychol* 17(3):279–83 My '70. * (*PA* 44:13057)
17. CONYNE, ROBERT KARLTON. *Facilitator-Directed and Self-Directed Sensitivity Models: Their Effect on Self-Perceptual Change.* Doctor's thesis, Purdue University (Lafayette, Ind.), 1970. (*DAI* 31:3868A)
18. GIBSON, DENNIS LEE. *Prediction of Verbal Behavior of Individuals in Small Counseling Groups.* Doctor's thesis, University of Minnesota (Minneapolis, Minn.), 1970. (*DAI* 32:559B)
19. PARKS, JAMES C., AND ANTENEN, W. W. "A Modified Marathon With Voluntarily Institutionalized Alcoholics: An Interaction Process Analysis." *Comparative Group Studies* 1(4):357–71 N '70. * (*PA* 47:6929)
20. PARKS, JAMES CLAYTON. *An Interaction Process Analysis of a Modified Marathon With Voluntarily Institutionalized Alcoholics.* Doctor's thesis, University of Georgia (Athens, Ga.), 1970. (*DAI* 31:3883A)
21. SISSON, PERRY JOE. *An Interaction Process Analysis of Extended Group Counseling With Psychiatry Residents.* Doctor's thesis, University of Georgia (Athens, Ga.), 1970. (*DAI* 31:3887A)
22. TERLESKI, DONALD RICHARD. *The Relationship Between Unstructured and Structured Sensitivity Group Experiences and Self-Perceived Changes of Group Members.* Doctor's thesis, Purdue University (Lafayette, Ind.), 1970. (*DAI* 31:5139A)
23. ACKLAND, VERGIE LEE BEHRENS. *A Comparison of Two Group Counseling Models in Facilitating Verbal Interaction Among Delinquent Girls.* Doctor's thesis, Arizona State University (Tempe, Ariz.), 1971. (*DAI* 31:5752A)
24. HILL, PRISCILLA SMITH. *Verbal Interaction Styles of Three Marathon Encounter Groups.* Doctor's thesis, University of Utah (Salt Lake City, Utah), 1971. (*DAI* 32:1845B)
25. HILL, WM. FAWCETT. "The Hill Interaction Matrix." Comment by Richard C. Rank. *Personnel & Guid J* 49(8):619–23 Ap '71. *
26. PAISLEY, JAMES DONALD. *Verbal Interaction and Member Acceptance of Associates and Non-Associates in Encounter Groups.* Doctor's thesis, Arizona State University (Tempe, Ariz.), 1971. (*DAI* 32:1757A)
27. SCHUBERT, PAUL WILLIAM. *Personality Type and Self-Perceived Change Resulting From Sensitivity Group Experience.* Doctor's thesis, Purdue University (Lafayette, Ind.), 1971. (*DAI* 32:4360A)
28. SISSON, CHARLES JIMMY, SR. *A Comparative Analysis of Extended Group Counseling With Psychiatry Residents Using the Hill Interaction Matrix and the Bonney Scale.* Doctor's thesis, University of Georgia (Athens, Ga.), 1971. (*DAI* 32:3704A)
29. STERNE, DAVID M., AND SELIGMAN, MILTON. "Further Comparisons of Verbal Behavior in Therapist-Led, Leaderless, and Alternating Group Psychotherapy Sessions." *J Counsel Psychol* 18(5):472–7 S '71. * (*PA* 47:3125)

CUMULATIVE NAME INDEX

[1215]

The Hoffer-Osmond Diagnostic Test. Mental patients; 1961–67; HOD; diagnosis of schizophrenia; 5 scores: perceptual, paranoid, depression, ratio, total; a short form score may also be determined; Abraham Hoffer, Humphry Osmond, and Harold Kelm (man-

ual) ; Northland Stationers Ltd. [Canada] (Card Form only). (United States distributor: Bell Therapeutic Supplies, Inc.) *

For additional information, see P:110 (22 references) ; for reviews by Maurice Lorr and William Schofield, see 6:114 (6 references).

REFERENCES THROUGH 1971

1-5. See 6:114.
6-27. See P:110.

28. HOFFER, A., AND OSMOND, H. "Malvaria: A New Psychiatric Disease." *Acta Psychiatrica Scandinavica* (Denmark) 39(2):335-66 '63. *
29. KLINE, N. S.; BARCLAY, G. L.; COLE, J. O.; ESSER, A. H.; LEHMANN, H.; WITTENBORN, J. R. "Controlled Evaluation of Nicotinamide Adenine Dinucleotide in the Treatment of Chronic Schizophrenic Patients." *Brit J Psychiatry* 113:731-42 Jl '67. * (*PA* 41:15559)
30. VOGEL, M. J. "Tests for Schizophrenia." Letter. *Can Med Assn J* 96:430 F 18 '67. * (*PA* 41:6119)
31. HAWKINS, DAVID R. "Treatment of Schizophrenia Based on the Medical Model." *J Schizophrenia* 2(1):3-10 '68. * (*PA* 43:10091)
32. KELM, H.; HALL, R. W.; AND HOFFER, A. "A Biochemical and Perceptual Measure Related to Length of Hospitalization." *Dis Nerv System* 29:844-5 D '68. * (*PA* 43:8511)
33. KOWALCHUK, MERVIN P. *The Hoffer-Osmond Diagnostic Test of Perceptual Disorders and the Academic Achievement of Indian and Metis Students in Northern Saskatchewan.* Master's thesis, University of Saskatchewan (Saskatoon, Sask., Canada), 1971.

CUMULATIVE NAME INDEX

[1216]

The Hooper Visual Organization Test. Ages 14 and over; 1957-66; HVOT; organic brain pathology; H. Elston Hooper; Western Psychological Services. *

For additional information, see P:111 (7 references) ; for reviews by Ralph M. Reitan and Otfried Spreen, see 6:116 (4 references).

REFERENCES THROUGH 1971

1-4. See 6:116.
5-11. See P:111.

12. DOERRING, PAUL LUTHER. *Psychological Deficits in Children as Sequelae of Western and St. Louis Encephalitis.* Doctor's thesis, Stanford University (Stanford, Calif.), 1962. (*DA* 23:2006)
13. AFTANAS, M. S., AND ROYCE, J. R. "A Factor Analysis of Brain Damage Tests Administered to Normal Subjects With Factor Score Comparisons Across Ages." *Multiv Behav Res* 4(4):459-81 O '69. * (*PA* 44:11030)
14. RUPP, L. GLENN. *A Comparative Study of Brain Damaged and Normal Children of Elementary School Age for the Purpose of Validating the Hooper Visual Organization Test.* Master's thesis, Millersville State College (Millersville, Pa.), 1969.
15. LOVE, HENRY G. I. "Validation of the Hooper Visual Organization Test on a New Zealand Psychiatric Hospital Population." *Psychol Rep* 27(3):915-7 D '70. * (*PA* 45:10217)
16. MUELLER, LOU E. *A Study of Usefulness of the Hooper Visual Organization Test With Elementary School Children.* Master's thesis, Millersville State College (Millersville, Pa.), 1971.

CUMULATIVE NAME INDEX

[1217]

Hospital Adjustment Scale. Mental patients; 1951-53; HAS; 4 ratings: communication and interpersonal relations, self-care and social responsibility, work and recreation, total; James T. Ferguson, Paul McReynolds, and Egerton L. Ballachey (test) ; Consulting Psychologists Press, Inc. *

For additional information, see P:112 (6 references) ; for a review by Wilson H. Guertin, see 6:117 (3 references) ; for a review by Maurice Lorr, see 5:67 (5 references).

REFERENCES THROUGH 1971

1-5. See 5:67.
6-8. See 6:117.
9-14. See P:112.

15. GUERTIN, WILSON H. "A Factor Analytic Study of the Adjustment of Chronic Schizophrenics." *J Clin Psychol* 11:174-7 Ap '55. * (*PA* 30:1344)
16. ELLSWORTH, ROBERT B. "Some Observations on Patient Government: Problems and Parameters." *J Clin Psychol* 12:353-7 O '56. * (*PA* 32:4290)
17. SEMON, RALPH G., AND GOLDSTEIN, NORMAN. "The Effectiveness of Group Psychotherapy With Chronic Schizophrenic Patients and an Evaluation of Different Therapeutic Methods." *J Consult Psychol* 21:317-22 Ag '57. * (*PA* 33:1492)
18. CONGDON, CLYDE S. *Self Theory and Chlorpromazine Treatment.* Doctor's thesis, Vanderbilt University (Nashville, Tenn.), 1958. (*DA* 19:2654)
19. DIGIOVANNI, PHILIP. *A Comparison Between Orthodox Group Psychotherapy and Activity-Group Therapy in the Treatment of Chronic Hospitalized Schizophrenics.* Doctor's thesis, University of Illinois (Urbana, Ill.), 1958. (*DA* 19:3361)
20. DIAMOND, LEON S., AND MARKS, JOHN B. "Discontinuance of Tranquilizers Among Chronic Schizophrenic Patients Receiving Maintenance Dosage." *J Nerv & Mental Dis* 131:247-51 S '60. * (*PA* 35:2332)
21. CORNETT, STEPHEN J., JR. *An Analysis of Variables in an Experimental Measurement of Attitudes of Psychiatric Patients.* Doctor's thesis, University of Kentucky (Lexington, Ky.), 1962. (*DAI* 30:1814)
22. LASKY, LORRAIN E. "Treatment Effects Associated With Personal Trait Preferences Shared by Schizophrenic Patients and Psychiatric Aide Trainees." *Nursing Res* 11:176-8 su '62. *
23. KHANNA, J. L.; PRATT, STEVE; BURDIZK, E. G.; AND CHADDHA, R. L. "A Study of Certain Effects of Tranylcypromine, a New Antidepressant." *J New Drugs* 3:227-32 Jl-Ag '63. * (*PA* 38:9786)
24. ROBACK, HOWARD B. *A Comparison of Hospitalized Mental Patients' Adjustment With Their Attitudes Toward Psychiatric Hospitals.* Master's thesis, Ohio University (Athens, Ohio), 1964.
25. MARKS, JOHN; SCHALOCK, ROBERT; AND SONODA, BEVERLY. "Reinforcement Versus Relationship Therapy for Schizophrenics." Abstract. *Proc 75th Ann Conv Am Psychol Assn* 2:237-8 '67.* (*PA* 42:17323)
26. GRINSPOON, LESTER; EWALT, JACK R.; AND SHADER, RICHARD. "Psychotherapy and Pharmacotherapy in Chronic Schizophrenia." *Am J Psychiatry* 124:1645-52 Je '68. * (*PA* 42:14206)
27. KANTOR, HERMAN I.; MICHAEL, CARMEN M.; SHORE, HERBERT; AND LUDVIGSON, H. WAYNE. "Administration of Estrogens to Older Women: A Psychometric Evaluation." *Am J Obstet & Gynecol* 101:658-61 Jl 1 '68. *
28. COCKBURN, KATHLEEN ANN. *Behavioral Responses of Schizophrenic Patients to Increased Awareness of Sensory Stimuli.* Doctor's thesis, Boston University (Boston, Mass.), 1969. (*DAI* 31:1816B)
29. COONS, W. H., AND PEACOCK, E. P. "Interpersonal Interaction and Personality Change in Group Psychotherapy." *Can Psychiatric Assn J* 15(4):347-55 Ag '70. * (*PA* 44:21108)
30. HARTLAGE, LAWRENCE C. "Subprofessional Therapists' Use of Reinforcement Versus Traditional Psychotherapeutic Techniques With Schizophrenics." *J Consult & Clin Psychol* 34(2):181-3 Ap '70. * (*PA* 44:10889)
31. MICHAEL, CARMEN M.; KANTOR, HERMAN I.; AND SHORE, HERBERT. "Further Psychometric Evaluation of Older Women—The Effects of Estrogen Administration." *J Gerontol* 25(4):337-41 O '70. *
32. LUDWIG, ARNOLD M., AND MARX, ARNOLD J. "The Response of Chronic Schizophrenics to Attention and Structure." *Brit J Psychiatry* 118(545):447-50 Ap '71. * (*PA* 47:1338)
33. McGEE, THOMAS F., AND WILLIAMS, MEYER. "Time-Limited and Time-Unlimited Group Psychotherapy: A Comparison With Schizophrenic Patients." *Comparative Group Studies* 2(1):71-84 F '71. * (*PA* 47:5339)

CUMULATIVE NAME INDEX

[1218]
Hostility and Direction of Hostility Questionnaire: Personality and Personal Illness Questionnaires. Mental patients and normals; 1967; HDHQ; test booklet title is *Personality Questionnaire*; all items from *Minnesota Multiphasic Personality Inventory*; 7 scores: intropunitive (self criticism, guilt), extrapunitive (urge to act out hostility, criticism of others, projected delusional hostility), total hostility, direction of hostility; T. M. Caine, G. A. Foulds, and K. Hope (diagrams and manual) ; University of London Press Ltd. [England]. *

For additional information and reviews by H. J. Eysenck and Maurice Lorr, see 7:86 (32 references).

REFERENCES THROUGH 1971

1–32. See 7:86.

33. Vinoda, K. S. "A Comparative Study of the Personality Characteristics of Attempted Suicides, Psychiatric Patients and Normals." *Trans All-India Inst Mental Health* 5:67–74 D '65. * (*PA* 40:7860)

34. Foulds, G. A. " 'Psychic:somatic' Symptoms and Hostility." *Brit J Social & Clin Psychol* 5:185–9 S '66. * (*PA* 40:13224)

35. Vinoda, K. S. "Personality Characteristics of Attempted Suicides." *Brit J Psychiatry* 112:1143–50 N '66. * (*PA* 41:4769)

36. Hassall, Elizabeth Christine. *Young Alcoholics: Personal and Social Characteristics Compared With Those of Older Alcoholics.* Master's thesis, University of Edinburgh (Edinburgh, Scotland), 1967.

37. Murthy, Vinoda Narayana. "Punitiveness and Personal Disturbance." *Trans All-India Inst Mental Health* 7:62–8 D '67. *

38. Hassall, Christine, and Foulds, G. A. "Hostility Among Young Alcoholics." *Brit J Addict* 63:203–8 D '68. *

39. Warder, John. "Two Studies of Violent Offenders." *Brit J Criminol* 9(4):389–93 O '69. * (*PA* 44:8811)

40. Anumonye, Amechi. "Personality Factors and Barbiturate Dependence." *Brit J Addict* 64(3–4):365–70 Ja '70. *

41. Ross, Elizabeth K., and Priest, Robert C. "The Effect of Hydroxyzine on Phenothiazine Therapy (A Method of Study)." *Dis Nerv System* 31(6):412–4 Je '70. * (*PA* 45:2568)

42. Banks, M. H., and Bolton, N. "The Personality Structure of a Delinquent Group." *Durham Res R* (England) 6(27):596–7 au '71. *

43. Foulds, G. A. "Personality Deviance and Personal Symptomatology." *Psychol Med* (England) 1(3):222–33 My '71. * (*PA* 47:11125)

44. Griffiths, A. W. "Prisoners of XYY Constitution: Psychological Aspects." *Brit J Psychiatry* 119(549):193–4 Ag '71. * (*PA* 47:7155)

45. Mayo, P. R., and Bell, J. M. "Hostility and Personality in a Student-Teacher Population." *Brit J Social & Clin Psychol* 10(4):375–8 D '71. * (*PA* 48:1800)

46. Mayo, P. R.; Walton, H. J.; and Littmann, S. K. "Relevance of Repression-Sensitization to Neurotic Patients in Milieu Treatment." *Psychol Rep* 28(3):794 Je '71. * (*PA* 46:11221)

47. Philip, Alistair E. "Psychometric Changes Associated With Response to Drug Treatment." *Brit J Social & Clin Psychol* 10(2):138–43 Je '71. *

48. Philip, Alistair E., and Cay, Lorna. "The Reliability and Utility of a Clinical Rating of Personality." *Brit J Med Psychol* 44(1):85–9 Mr '71. * (*PA* 46:11103)

49. Ritson, B. "Personality and Prognosis in Alcoholism." *Brit J Psychiatry* 118(542):79–82 Ja '71. * (*PA* 46:11133)

50. Ross, Christopher F. J. "Comparison of Hospital and Prison Alcoholics." *Brit J Psychiatry* 118(542):75–8 Ja '71. * (*PA* 46:11135)

51. Singh, S. N. "Hostility and Hystericism." *Indian Psychol R* 8(1):42–5 Jl '71. *

52. Singh, S. N. "Intelligence and Hostility." *Indian Psychol R* 7(2):10–4 Ja '71. *

53. Singh, Sobhh Nath. "Influence of Intellectual Development on the Aggressive Attitude." Doctor's thesis abstract. *Indian Psychol R* 7(2):40–1 Ja '71. *

54. Warder, J., and Ross, C. J. "Age and Alcoholism." *Brit J Addict* 66(1):45–51 Je '71. *

55. Zealley, A. K. "Bronchial Asthma: A Problem Attributable to Sampling When Establishing Its Psychopathology." *Psychother & Psychosom* (Switzerland) 19(1–2):37–46 '71. * (*PA* 47:5375)

56. Zealley, A. K.; Aitken, R. C. B.; and Rosenthal, S. V. "Personality and Bronchial Asthma" *Proc Royal Soc Med* (England) 64(8):825–9 Ag '71. *

CUMULATIVE NAME INDEX

[1219]
★How I See Myself Scale. Grades 3–6, 7–12; 1966–69; HISMS; 2 levels; Ira J. Gordon; test published by the Author, manual published by the Florida Educational Research and Development Council. *

a) ELEMENTARY FORM. Grades 3–6; 5 or 7 scores: teacher-school, physical appearance, autonomy, academic adequacy, interpersonal adequacy, attitudes toward boys (boys), attitudes toward girls (boys).

b) SECONDARY FORM. Grades 7–12; 7 or 8 scores in grades 7–9: teacher-school, physical appearance, autonomy, academic adequacy, physical adequacy, interpersonal adequacy, emotions (girls), attitudes toward peers (boys), body build (girls) ; 7 or 9 scores in grades 10–12: teacher-school, physical appearance, autonomy, academic adequacy, physical adequacy, interpersonal adequacy (girls), emotions, attitudes toward boys (boys), attitudes toward girls (boys), language adequacy (boys).

REFERENCES THROUGH 1971

1. Yeatts, Pearline Peters. *An Analysis of Developmental Changes in the Self-Report of Negro and White Children, Grades 3–12.* Doctor's thesis, University of Florida (Gainesville, Fla.), 1967. (*DA* 29:823A)

2. Killough, Curtis Banion. *An Investigation of the Effects of Abrupt Change in Educational Environment Upon the Reported Self-Concept of Third Grade Pupils.* Doctor's thesis, University of Southern Mississippi (Hattiesburg, Miss.), 1968. (*DA* 29:3003A)

3. Yeatts, Pearline P., and Gordon, Ira J. "Effects of Physical Education Taught by a Specialist on Physical Fitness and Self-Image." *Res Q* 39:766–70 O '68. *

4. Smith, Horace Lewis. *Predictive Ability of Elementary Teachers: The Relationship Between Selected Personality Variables and the Ability to Judge Ratings Pupils Make of Themselves and Others.* Doctor's thesis, Michigan State University (East Lansing, Mich.), 1969. (*DAI* 30:1439A)

5. Lomen, Donald Oscar. *Changes in Self-Concept Factors: A Comparison of Fifth-Grade Instrumental Music Participants and Non-Participants in Target and Non Target Schools in Des*

Moines, Iowa. Doctor's thesis, University of Northern Colorado (Greeley, Colo.), 1970. (*DAI* 31:3962A)
6. PETERSON, FRANCIS THOMAS. *Marijuana Smokers and Non-Smokers: A Self-Concept Study.* Doctor's thesis, University of Northern Colorado (Greeley, Colo.), 1971. (*DAI* 32:5619A)

CUMULATIVE NAME INDEX

Gordon, I. J.: 3	Peterson, F. T.: 6
Killough, C. B.: 2	Smith, H. L.: 4
Lomen, D. O.: 5	Yeatts, P. P.: 1, 3

[1220]
How Well Do You Know Yourself? High school, college, office and factory workers; 1959–61; HWDYKY; 19 scores: irritability, practicality, punctuality, novelty-loving, vocational assurance, cooperativeness, ambitiousness, hypercriticalness, dejection, general morale, persistence, nervousness, seriousness, submissiveness, impulsiveness, dynamism, emotional control, consistency, test objectivity; 1961 test identical with test copyrighted 1959 except for two interchanged items; Thomas N. Jenkins, John H. Coleman (manual), and Harold T. Fagin (manual); Executive Analysis Corporation. *

For additional information, see P:113; for reviews by Lee J. Cronbach and Harrison G. Gough and excerpted reviews by Edward S. Bordin and Laurence Siegel, see 6:118 (2 references).

REFERENCES THROUGH 1971
1–2. See 6:118.
3. KOROBOW, ALICE SCHUSTER. *Counseling: An Analysis of the Predisposing Variables. An Inquiry Into the Personal and Social Elements Related to the Acceptance of Counseling.* Doctor's thesis, New York University (New York, N.Y.), 1957. (*DA* 18:661)
4. BRACY, LEWIS FLETCHER. *An Exploration of the Relationship Between Personality Factors and Automobile Accident Proneness.* Doctor's thesis, University of Southern Mississippi (Hattiesburg, Miss.), 1970. (*DAI* 31:4967B)

CUMULATIVE NAME INDEX

Bordin, E. S.: *exc*, 6:118	Jenkins, T. N.: 1–2
Bracy, L. F.: 4	Korobow, A. S.: 3
Cronbach, L. J.: *rev*, 6:118	Siegel, L.: *exc*, 6:118
Gough, H. G.: *rev*, 6:118	

[1221]
Human Relations Inventory. Grades 9–16 and adults; 1954–59; HRI; social conformity; Raymond E. Bernberg; Psychometric Affiliates. *

For additional information, see P:114 (1 reference); see also 6:119 (6 references); for reviews by Raymond C. Norris and John A. Radcliffe, see 5:68.

REFERENCES THROUGH 1971
1–6. See 6:119.
7. See P:114.
8. SMITH, ALEXANDER B. *Analysis of Interaction Process and Sociometric Relations Developed During Group Therapy With Offenders on Probation.* Doctor's thesis, New York University (New York, N. Y.), 1959. (*DA* 20:406)
9. SMITH, ALEXANDER B.; BASSIN, ALEXANDER; AND FROEHLICH, ABRAHAM. "Change in Attitudes and Degree of Verbal Participation in Group Therapy With Adult Offenders." *J Consult Psychol* 24:247–9 Je '60. * (*PA* 35:6894)
10. SINGH, UDAI PRATAP. "Movement From One's Own Position Towards a Group Norm as a Function of Intellect." *Psychol Studies* (India) 14(2):88–93 Jl '69. *
11. BHUSHAN, RAJNISH. "Intolerance of Ambiguity in Conformists and Nonconformists." *Manas* (India) 17(1):35–9 My '70. * (*PA* 46:9040)

CUMULATIVE NAME INDEX

Adams, A. A.: 5	Gorfein, D. S.: 6
Anderson, L. M.: 6	Mundy, J.: 7
Bassin, A.: 9	Norris, R. C.: *rev*, 5:68
Bernberg, R. E.: 1–4	Radcliffe, J. A.: *rev*, 5:68
Bhushan, R.: 11	Singh, U. P.: 10
Froehlich, A.: 9	Smith, A. B.: 8–9

[1222]
The Humm-Wadsworth Temperament Scale. Adults; 1934–60; HWTS; 47 scores: normal (4 scores, total), hysteroid (6 scores, total), manic (4 scores,

total), depressive (5 scores, total), autistic (5 scores, total), paranoid (3 scores, total), epileptoid (4 scores, total), response bias (2 scores), self mastery (6 component control scores plus integration index); distribution restricted; Doncaster G. Humm and Kathryn A. Humm; Humm Personnel Consultants. *

For additional information, see P:115; for reviews by James R. Glennon and Floyd L. Ruch, see 6:120 (3 references); see also 5:69 (20 references); for reviews by H. J. Eysenck, H. Meltzer, and Lorenz Misbach, see 3:48 (34 references); for reviews by Forrest A. Kingsbury and P. E. Vernon, see 2:1223 (13 references); for a review by Daniel A. Prescott, see 1:920.

REFERENCES THROUGH 1971
1–13. See 2:1223.
14–44. See 3:48.
45–64. See 5:69.
65–67. See 6:120.
68. GROSS, BETHUEL, AND SEASHORE, ROBERT H. "Psychological Characteristics of Student and Professional Musical Composers." *J Appl Psychol* 25:159–70 Ap '41. * (*PA* 15:4297)
69. WITT, NORMAN ERNEST. *A Study of Significant Factors Which Tend to Predict Selection as a Candidate for the Position of Commercial Airline Pilot.* Doctor's thesis, University of California (Los Angeles, Calif.), 1969. (*DAI* 30:3291A)

CUMULATIVE NAME INDEX

Arnold, D. A.: 24	Jurgensen, C. E.: 49
Beales, B. B.: 42	Karlan, S. C.: 18
Bills, M. A.: 21a	Kingsbury, F. A.: *rev*, 2:1223
Bluett, C. G.: 42	Kruger, B. L.: 5
Caine, T. M.: 50	Marke, S.: 63–4, 66
Canning, W.: 56	Marshall, H.: 47
Cerf, A. Z.: 46	Meehl, P. E.: 38
Collins, J. H.: 19–21, 31	Meltzer, H.: *rev*, 3:48
Conrad, H. S.: 51, 65	Misbach, L.: *rev*, 3:48
Dorcus, R. M.: 32	Mosier, C. I.: 6
Dysinger, D. W.: 8	Newburn, H. K.: 25
Ellis, A.: 5, 65	Newman, S. E.: 61
Eysenck, H. J.: *rev*, 3:48	Paterson, D. G.: 7
Fortune, D. M.: 52	Poole, F. E.: 27
Fulton, J. L.: 36	Prescott, D. A.: *rev*, 1:920
Gilliland, A. R.: 59–61	Prudden, G. H.: 20a
Glennon, J. R.: *rev*, 6:120	Reed, P. H.: 28
Greenberg, P.: 60	Regelin, C.: 56
Grieder, C.: 25	Ruch, F. L.: *rev*, 6:120
Gross, B.: 68	Schneidler, G. G.: 7
Guilford, J. P.: 67	Seagoe, M. V.: 39–41
Hansen, A. V.: 29	Seashore, R. H.: 68
Harlow, G.: 56	Smith, G.: 63–4, 66
Harrell, T. W.: 53	Storment, R. C.: 12, 21
Hathaway, S. R.: 45	Super, D. E.: 44
Hemsath, M. E.: 9	Vernon, P. E.: *rev*, 2:1223
Houtchens, H. M.: 17	Viteles, M. S.: 23
Humm, D. G.: 1–2, 4, 10–2, 14–5, 19–20, 22, 26, 30–1, 33–5, 37, 43, 48, 54–5, 57–8, 62	Wadsworth, G. W.: 1–3, 14, 16, 22, 23a, 30
Humm, K. A.: 35, 43, 55, 57–8, 62	Wasson, M. M.: 13
	Williamson, E. G.: 7
Iorns, M. E.: 12	Witt, N. E.: 69
	Wittman, P.: 28

[1223]
*The Hunt-Minnesota Test for Organic Brain Damage.** Chronological ages 16–70 and mental ages 8 and over; 1943–66; 16 tests grouped in 3 divisions: the vocabulary test of *Stanford-Binet Intelligence Scale,* interpolated tests, learning and recall; 1966 manual identical with manual copyrighted 1943; Howard F. Hunt; Western Psychological Services, Inc. *

For additional information, see P:323 (5 references); for a review by Seymour G. Klebanoff, see 4:51 (8 references); for reviews by Margaret Ives and O. L. Zangwill, see 3:49 (11 references).

REFERENCES THROUGH 1971
1–11. See 3:49.
12–19. See 4:51.
20–24. See P:323.
25. CANTER, AARON HERMAN. "Direct and Indirect Measures of Psychological Deficit in Multiple Sclerosis: Part 1." *J General Psychol* 44:3–25 Ja '51. * (*PA* 25:7027)
26. CANTER, AARON HERMAN. "Direct and Indirect Measures of Psychological Deficit in Multiple Sclerosis: Part 2." *J General Psychol* 44:27–50 Ja '51. * (*PA* 25:7028)

27. BALDWIN, MARCELLA VIG. "A Clinico-Experimental Investigation Into the Psychological Aspects of Multiple Sclerosis." *J Nerv & Mental Dis* 115:299–342 Ap '52. * (*PA* 27: 2915)

[1224]

The Hysteroid-Obsessoid Questionnaire: Personality and Personal Illness Questionnaires.

Mental patients and normals; 1967; HOQ; test booklet title is *Self-Description Questionnaire;* T. M. Caine and K. Hope (manual); University of London Press Ltd. [England]. *

For additional information and reviews by H. J. Eysenck and Maurice Lorr, see 7 :87 (26 references).

REFERENCES THROUGH 1971

1–26. See 7:87.

27. VINODA, K. S. "A Comparative Study of the Personality Characteristics of Attempted Suicides, Psychiatric Patients and Normals." *Trans All-India Inst Mental Health* 5:67–74 D '65. * (*PA* 40:7860)

28. SEDMAN, G. "Depersonalization in a Group of Normal Subjects." *Brit J Psychiatry* 112:907–12 S '66. * (*PA* 41:592)

29. VINODA, K. S. "Personality Characteristics of Attempted Suicides." *Brit J Psychiatry* 112:1143–50 N '66. * (*PA* 41:4769)

30. KUMARIAH, V., AND MURTHY, NARAYANA. "Speed Accuracy Factors in Relation to Personality and Diagnosis." *Trans All-India Inst Mental Health* 8:35–41 D '68. * (*PA* 43:11379)

31. CHINNIAN, R. RAWLIN, AND MURTHY, VINODA NARAYANA. "Persistence and Personality." *Trans All-India Inst Mental Health* 9:51–8 D '69. * (*PA* 46:11213)

32. ANUMONYE, AMECHI. "Personality Factors and Barbiturate Dependence." *Brit J Addict* 64(3–4):365–70 Ja '70. *

33. FOULDS, G. A. "Personality Deviance and Personal Symptomatology." *Psychol Med* (England) 1(3):222–33 My '71. * (*PA* 47:11125)

34. PHILIP, ALISTAIR E. "Psychometric Changes Associated With Response to Drug Treatment." *Brit J Social & Clin Psychol* 10(2):138–43 Je '71. *

[1225]

*The IPAT Anxiety Scale Questionnaire.

Ages 14 and over; 1957–67; IPAT ASQ; also called *IPAT Anxiety Scale;* title on test is *IPAT Self Analysis Form;* 6 scores: lack of self-sentiment development, ego weakness, protension or paranoid trend, guilt proneness, ergic tension, total anxiety; Raymond B. Cattell and I. H. Scheier (manual); Institute for Personality and Ability Testing. (South African adaptation: Ages 15 and over; 1968; adaptation by Elizabeth M. Madge; Human Sciences Research Council [South Africa].) *

For additional information, see P:116 (45 references); for a review by Jacob Cohen, see 6:121 (23 references); for reviews by J. P. Guilford and E. Lowell Kelly and an excerpted review by Laurance F. Shaffer, see 5 :70.

REFERENCES THROUGH 1971

1–23. See 6:121.

24–68. See P:116.

69. SHAGASS, CHARLES, AND LIPOWSKI, ZBIGNIEW J. "Effect of Methedrine on Critical Flicker Fusion and Its Relation to Personality and Effect." *J Nerv & Mental Dis* 127:407–16 N '58. * (*PA* 34:1564)

70. QUINTAR, BADY. *An Investigation of the Effect of Initial Anxiety Level on Instrumental Act Regression in College Students.* Doctor's thesis, University of Kentucky (Lexington, Ky.), 1959. (*DA* 27:613B)

71. SCHONBAR, ROSALEA A. "Some Manifest Characteristics of Recallers and Nonrecallers of Dreams." *J Consult Psychol* 23:414–8 O '59. * (*PA* 34:6267)

72. BRADY, JOHN PAUL; LEVITT, EUGENE E.; AND LUBIN, BERNARD. "Expressed Fear of Hypnosis and Volunteering Behavior." *J Nerv & Mental Dis* 133:216–7 S '61. * (*PA* 36: 4II16B)

73. LUBIN, BERNARD; BRADY, JOHN PAUL; AND LEVITT, EUGENE E. "A Comparison of Personality Characteristics of Volunteers and Nonvolunteers for Hypnosis Experiments." *J Clin Psychol* 18:341–3 Jl '62. * (*PA* 39:1811)

74. WORKING, RUSSELL ANDREW. *Self Perceptual Change as a Function of Anxiety and Short-Term Group Therapy.* Doctor's thesis, Indiana University (Bloomington, Ind.), 1962. (*DA* 23:4236)

75. LEVITT, EUGENE E.; LUBIN, BERNARD; AND BRADY, JOHN PAUL. "Personality Correlates of Hypnotizability in Young Women: The Anxiety-Dependency Constellation." *Congreso Interamericano de Psicologia* (Mexico) 7:360–4 '63. *

76. LEVITT, EUGENE E.; PERSKY, HAROLD; BRADY, JOHN PAUL; AND FITZGERALD, JOSEPH A. "The Effect of Hydrocortisone Infusion on Hypnotically Induced Anxiety." *Psychosom Med* 25:158–61 Mr–Ap '63. * (*PA* 38:4347)

77. WEINER, SAMUEL; DORMAN, DANIEL; PERSKY, HAROLD; STARCH, THOMAS W.; NORTON, JAMES; AND LEVITT, EUGENE E. "Effect on Anxiety of Increasing the Plasma Hydrocortisone Level." *Psychosom Med* 25:69–77 Ja–F '63. * (*PA* 37:7705)

78. KAHN, ROBERT L.; WOLFE, DONALD M.; QUINN, ROBERT P.; AND SNOEK, J. DIEDRICK; IN COLLABORATION WITH ROBERT A. ROSENTHAL. Part 5, "Personality Processes in Role Stress," pp. 223–333. In their *Organizational Stress: Studies in Role Conflict and Ambiguity.* New York: John Wiley & Sons, Inc., 1964. Pp. xiii, 470. * (*PA* 39:8866)

79. CHANCE, WILLIAM GEORGE. *A Study of Selected Factors as They Relate to the Establishment of Interpersonal Relations by Student Teachers.* Doctor's thesis, Oklahoma State University (Stillwater, Okla.), 1965. (*DA* 27:47A)

80. GLESER, GOLDINE C.; GOTTSCHALK, LOUIS A.; FOX, ROBERT; AND LIPPERT, WALTER. "Immediate Changes in Affect With Chlordiazepoxide: Chlordiazepoxide Administration in Juvenile Delinquent Boys." *Arch Gen Psychiatry* 13:291–5 O '65. *

81. MCALLISTER, JAMES. "Trial of Oxypertine for Anxiety Neurosis." Letter. *Brit J Psychiatry* 111:1010–1 O '65. *

82. MARKS, SAMUEL B. *Some Factors Influencing the Ratings of Professional and Technical Personnel: An Exploratory Study.* Doctor's thesis, New York University (New York, N.Y.), 1965. (*DA* 26:2862)

83. ODOM, ROBERT R., AND ATTWELL, ARTHUR A. "Experimentally Induced Anxiety and Inhibition of College Students' Test Performances." *Calif J Ed Res* 16:151–7 S '65. * (*PA* 40:982)

84. ROBINSON, J. T.; DAVIES, L. S.; KREITMAN, NORMAN; AND KNOWLES, J. B. "A Double-Blind Trial of Oxypertine for Anxiety Neurosis." *Brit J Psychiatry* 111:527–9 Je '65. Criticism by James McAllister, 111:1010–1 O '65. *

85. STERN, GARY S.; LANA, ROBERT E.; AND PAULING, FREDERICK J. "Fear Arousal and Order of Presentation of Persuasive Communications." *Psychol Rep* 16:789–95 Je '65. * (*PA* 39: 14993)

86. WEINREB, ANITA CYRELE. *An Experimental Investigation of the Relationship Between Two Personality Variables (Anxiety and Neuroticism) and Perception of Non-Verbal Vocal Communication of Feeling.* Doctor's thesis, New York University (New York, N.Y.), 1965. (*DA* 27:307B)

87. CASSOTTA, LOUIS. *The Stability and Modification of the Vocal Behavior of Individuals in Stress and Nonstress Interviews.* Doctor's thesis, New York University (New York, N.Y.), 1966. (*DA* 27:2867B)

88. CATTELL, RAYMOND B. Chap. 2, "Anxiety and Motivation: Theory in Crucial Experiments," pp. 23–62. In *Anxiety and Behavior.* Edited by Charles D. Spielberger. New York: Academic Press, Inc., 1966. Pp. xv, 414. * (*PA* 40:12311, title only)

89. DEWOLFE, ALAN S.; BARRELL, ROBERT P.; AND CUMMINGS, JONATHAN W. "Parent Variables in Emotional Response to Hospitalization for Physical Illness." *J Consult Psychol* 30:68–72 F '66. * (*PA* 40:4358)

90. FISHER, WAYNE BURRELL, II. *Some Effects of Low,*

Average, and High Anxious Teachers on the Anxiety Levels and Achievement of Sixth Grade Students. Doctor's thesis, University of Tennessee (Knoxville, Tenn.), 1966. (*DA* 27:2876A)

91. KARBE, WOLFGANG WILHELM. *The Relationship of General Anxiety and Specific Anxiety Concerning the Learning of Swimming.* Doctor's thesis, New York University (New York, N.Y.), 1966. (*DA* 28:3489A)

92. McALLISTER, JOHN GERALD. *Analyses of Selected Personality and Intellectual Attributes of Teenage Volunteer Counselor-Attendants Serving at a Residential Camp for the Dependent Cerebral Palsied.* Doctor's thesis, University of Denver (Denver, Colo.), 1966. (*DA* 27:3328A)

93. MASON, MARIE. *Manifest Anxiety Level of Physically Disabled Rehabilitation Clients.* Doctor's thesis, University of Kentucky (Lexington, Ky.), 1966. (*DAI* 30:2443B)

94. NELSON, DALE O. "Leadership in Sports." *Res Q* 37:268-75 My '66. * (*PA* 40:8726)

95. TWOMEY, JOHN F. *Personality Patterns of Coronary Heart Patients.* Doctor's thesis, Boston University (Boston, Mass.), 1966. (*DA* 27:2866B)

96. WATMAN, WALTER ALAN. *The Capacity to Delay Gratification and Its Relationship to Perceptual Developmental Level, Ego Strength and Anxiety Level: A Study of Prisoners.* Doctor's thesis, Michigan State University (East Lansing, Mich.), 1966. (*DA* 28:354B)

97. JACKSON, ROBERT LEON. *An Investigation of the Creative Growth Curves of University Students.* Doctor's thesis, East Texas State University (Commerce, Tex.), 1967. (*DA* 28:3508A)

98. KANIA, WALTER. "Healthy Defensiveness in Theological Students." Comment by John J. Rooney. *Ministry Studies* 1:1-24 D '67. * (*PA* 42:18809)

99. MEINKE, DEAN L., AND KLAUSMEIER, HERBERT J. "Concept Attainment and Its Relation to Some Personality Variables." *Teach Col J* 39:106-9 D '67. *

100. POPEJOY, DOROTHY IMOGENE. *The Effects of a Physical Fitness Program on Selected Psychological and Physiological Measures of Anxiety.* Doctor's thesis, University of Illinois (Urbana, Ill.), 1967. (*DA* 28:4900A)

101. ABRAMS, AMANDA ULM. *Magic Thinking and Anxiety in Junior College Freshmen.* Doctor's thesis, University of Maryland (College Park, Md.), 1968. (*DA* 29:3450A)

102. ADAMS, NANCY MURPHY. *Changes in Pupil Size Under Conditions of Anxiety and Stress.* Doctor's thesis, George Washington University (Washington, D.C.), 1968. (*DA* 29:2625B)

103. CAMPBELL, GENE VIRGINIA. *A Descriptive Study of the Effects of Student Teaching Upon Attitudes, Anxieties, and Perceived Problems of Student Teachers.* Doctor's thesis, University of Houston (Houston, Tex.), 1968. (*DA* 29:3890A)

104. CHRISTENFELD, ROGER MICHAEL. *Pathology of the American Dream: The Relationship of Need for Achievement and Social Mobility to Coronary Disease Risk.* Doctor's thesis, University of Michigan (Ann Arbor, Mich.), 1968. (*DA* 29:958A)

105. CORELL, JOAN HELENE. *Comparison of Two Methods of Counseling With Academically Deteriorated University Upperclassmen.* Doctor's thesis, Indiana University (Bloomington, Ind.), 1968. (*DA* 29:1419A)

106. ELLIOTT, JERRY GORDON. *Factors Related to Inmate Participation in an Institutional Religious Program.* Doctor's thesis, School of Theology (Claremont, Calif.), 1968. (*DAI* 31:3016A)

107. EUBANK, JOHN YOUNG, JR. *The Relationship Between Preconception and Conception of Environment and Academic Achievement of High Ability Male Students.* Doctor's thesis, University of Tennessee (Knoxville, Tenn.), 1968. (*DA* 29:3871A)

108. HUGGAN, R. E. "Neuroticism and Anxiety Among Women With Cancer." *J Psychosom Res* (England) 12:215-21 O '68. * (*PA* 43:8627)

109. KEUTZER, CAROLIN S. "Sex Differences in a Smoking Treatment Program." *Dis Nerv System* 29:529-33 Ag '68. * (*PA* 43:5324)

110. McGOWAN, KENNETH. *The Effects of a Competitive Situation Upon the Motor Performance of High-Anxious and Low-Anxious Boys.* Master's thesis, Springfield College (Springfield, Mass.), 1968.

111. McLOONE, GERALD WILLIAM. *Relationships Between a Measure of Anxiety and Aspects of Self-Actualization, With Implications for Vocational Choice and Vocational Counseling.* Master's thesis, Catholic University of America (Washington, D.C.), 1968.

112. MUSLIN, HYMAN L.; SINGER, PAUL R.; MEUSER, MARY F.; AND LEAHY, JERRY P. "Research and Learning in Psychiatric Interviewing." *J Med Ed* 43:398-404 Mr '68. * (*PA* 43:12029)

113. PERSKY, HAROLD; ZUCKERMAN, MARVIN; AND CURTIS, GEORGE C. "Endocrine Function in Emotionally Disturbed and Normal Men." *J Nerv & Mental Dis* 146:488-97 Je '68. * (*PA* 42:16830)

114. SONG, RALPH HUNG SIK. *Selected Characteristics of Lincoln Hall Delinquents From Two Family Conditions.* Doctor's thesis, St. John's University (Jamaica, N.Y.), 1968. (*DAI* 30:855B)

115. VAN HANDEL, PETER J. *The Relationship Between Manifest Anxiety Level and Skill Performance in Stressful and Nonstressful Situations.* Master's thesis, Wisconsin State University (La Crosse, Wis.), 1968.

116. BARRATT, ERNEST S., AND WHITE, ROBERT. "Impulsiveness and Anxiety Related to Medical Students' Performance and Attitudes." *J Med Ed* 44(7):604-7 Jl '69. * (*PA* 45:4877)

117. BAUMAN, MILTON JAMES, AND STRAUGHAN, JAMES H. "BSR as a Function of Anxiety, Stress and Sex." *Psychol Rec* 19(2):339-44 Ap '69. * (*PA* 43:14300)

118. BLAIR, MAUDINE. *Divorcées' Adjustment and Attitudinal Changes About Life.* Doctor's thesis, Florida State University (Tallahassee, Fla.), 1969. (*DAI* 30:5541A)

119. COHEN, DAVID BENJAMIN. "Frequency of Dream Recall Estimated by Three Methods and Related to Defense Preference and Anxiety." *J Consult & Clin Psychol* 33(6):661-7 D '69. * (*PA* 43:12962, title only)

120. COMPTON, NORMA H. "Body Perception in Relation to Anxiety Among Women." *Percept & Motor Skills* 28(1):215-8 F '69. * (*PA* 43:11299)

121. DiBARTOLO, RUSSELL. *Self-Concept and the Attainment of Esophageal Speech.* Doctor's thesis, State University of New York (Buffalo, N.Y.), 1969. (*DA* 30:2890B)

122. GULATI, AVINASH. "A Study in Motivation Towards Unionization." *Indian J Indus Relations* 5(1):68-74 Jl '69. * (*PA* 47:7901)

123. LIPPMANN, GLENDA KATHRYN. *Personality Correlates of Differential Performance and Satisfaction in Self-Directed vs Teacher-Directed Instructional Strategies.* Doctor's thesis, University of Texas (Austin, Tex.), 1969. (*DAI* 31:1119A)

124. MATTHEWS, LILLIAN B. "Fabric Preferences, Perceptual-Personality Characteristics, and Obesity." *J Home Econ* 61(3):177-82 Mr '69. *

125. MILLER, JON P., AND HAGEDORN, ROBERT B. "The Relationship Between Self-Images and Anxiety and Neurosis." *Pac Sociol R* 12(2):109-17 f '69. *

126. MUKHERJEE, BISHWA NATH, AND SREEKUMAR, MENON A. "Personality Characteristics and Intra-Individual Variability in Industrial Output." *Indian J Indus Relations* 4(4):462-81 Ap '69. *

127. MUTHARD, JOHN E., AND SALOMONE, PAUL R. "The Roles and Functions of Rehabilitation Counselors." *Rehabil Counsel B* 13(1-SP):81-165 O '69. *

128. RHOADES, CHRISTOPHER D., AND EDMONSTON, WILLIAM E., JR. "Personality Correlates of Hypnotizability: A Study Using the Harvard Group Scale of Hypnotic Susceptibility, the 16-PF and the IPAT." *Am J Clin Hyp* 11(4):228-33 Ap '69. * (*PA* 43:13654)

129. ROSENBERG, C. M. "Determinants of Psychiatric Illness in Young People." *Brit J Psychiatry* 115(525):907-15 Ag '69. * (*PA* 44:10505)

130. ROSENBERG, C. M. "Young Alcoholics." *Brit J Psychiatry* 115(519):181-8 F '69. * (*PA* 43:13086)

131. ROSENBERG, CHAIM M. "Young Drug Addicts: Background and Personality." *J Nerv & Mental Dis* 148(1):65-73 Ja '69. * (*PA* 43:14491)

132. SCHMIDT, HERMANN O. "Relationship Between the IPAT Self-Analysis Scale and the Marlowe-Crowne Personal Reaction Inventory." *Psychol Rep* 24(2):361-2 Ap '69. * (*PA* 43:15828)

133. SCHREIBER, ELLIOTT H. "Personality Characteristics and Dental Disorders in Adolescents." *Psychol Rep* 24(2):626 Ap '69. * (*PA* 43:16050)

134. SMITH, CLYDE RAYMOND. *An Analysis of the Effectiveness of a College Preparatory Program for the Visually Impaired.* Doctor's thesis, University of Tennessee (Knoxville, Tenn.), 1969. (*DAI* 31:1653A)

135. WILLIAMS, JAMES G.; JONES, JOHN R.; AND WILLIAMS, BARBARA. "A Physiological Measure of Preoperative Anxiety." *Psychosom Med* 31(6):522-7 N-D '69. * (*PA* 44:12987)

136. BRUEGEL, MARY ANN. *Relationship of Preoperative Anxiety to Perception of Postoperative Pain.* Doctor's thesis, University of Northern Colorado (Greeley, Colo.), 1970. (*DAI* 31:3687B)

137. CAMPUS, NANCY RUTH. *A Study of Personality Characteristics Related to Trans-Situational Consistency of Self-Descriptions.* Doctor's thesis, New York University (New York, N.Y.), 1970. (*DAI* 31:7567B)

138. CURTIS, GEORGE; FOGEL, MAX; McEVOY, DONALD; AND ZARATE, CARLOS. "Urine and Plasma Corticosteroids, Psychological Tests, and Effectiveness of Psychological Defenses." *J Psychiatric Res* 7(4):237-47 Jl '70. * (*PA* 45:5859)

139. FARLEY, GAIL ANN. *An Investigation of Death Anxiety and the Sense of Competence.* Doctor's thesis, Duke University (Durham, N.C.), 1970. (*DAI* 31:7595B)

140. GOLDMAN, ROY DAVID. *Parameters in the Choice of Cognitive Strategies.* Doctor's thesis, University of California (Berkeley, Calif.), 1970. (*DAI* 31:7571B)

141. GRAFTON, TOMMY DOYLE. *The Relationship of General Anxiety to the Performance of Selected Motor Tasks.* Doctor's thesis, University of Southern Mississippi (Hattiesburg, Miss.), 1970. (*DAI* 31:5177A)

142. GREENLAW, RONALD WELLESLEY. *A Study of Speech and Selected Physiological Correlates in Young Adult Stutterers During Chemically Induced Anxiety.* Doctor's thesis, University of Utah (Salt Lake City, Utah), 1970. (*DAI* 31:3054B)

143. HACKLER, NICKIE LYNNE. *A Comparative Study of the IPAT Anxiety Scale Questionnaire and the Luscher Color Test.* Master's thesis, Radford College (Radford, Va.), 1970.

IPAT Anxiety Scale Questionnaire

144. HUNDAL, P. S.; SINGH, AGYAJIT; AND SINGH, MOHINDER. "Factor Analytical Study of Tests of Anxiety." *Psychol Rep* 26(3):875–8 Je '70. * (*PA* 45:706)

145. LEVITA, ERIC, AND RIKLAN, MANUEL. "Integrative Functions in Parkinsonism." *Percept & Motor Skills* 31(2):379–85 O '70. * (*PA* 45:6405)

146. OSWALD, N. C.; WALLER, R. E.; AND DRINKWATER, J. "Relationship Between Breathlessness and Anxiety in Asthma and Bronchitis: A Comparative Study." *Brit Med J* 2(5700): 14–7 Ap 4 '70. Comments by A. K. Zealley and R. C. B. Aitken, 2(5705):363 My 9 '70; by D. R. Redman, 2(5710):672 Je 13 '70; and by H. Brian McNamee, 2(5712):791 Je 27 '70. *

147. PERRY, ALICE K. *The Relationship Between Pre-Operative Anxiety and Two Post-Operative Physiological Responses in Male Herniorrhaphy Patients: An Investigation of the Relationship Between Pre-Operative Anxiety and Two Post-Operative Physiological Responses, Plasma 11-Hydroxycorticosteroid Levels and External Wound Healing, in Male Herniorrhaphy Patients.* Doctor's thesis, New York University (New York, N.Y.), 1970. (*DAI* 31:4158B)

148. ROUBERTOUX, PIERRE. "Personality Variables and Interest in Art." *J Pers & Social Psychol* 16(4):665–8 D '70. * (*PA* 45:6357)

149. SCHWAP, JOHN J.; McGINNIS, NANCY A.; AND WARHEIT, GEORGE J. "The Differential Perception of Anxiety in Medical Patients: Sociodemographic Aspects." *Psychiatry Med* 1(2):151–64 Ap '70. * (*PA* 47:9553)

150. SILVERBLANK, FRANCINE. *Sense of Responsibility, Level of Anxiety, and Sociability in Suburban Male High School Seniors Who Are Talented in Mathematics and Those Talented in English.* Doctor's thesis, New York University (New York, N.Y.), 1970. (*DAI* 31:6414A)

151. VIA, MURRAY EUGENE. *Changes in Personality Characteristics and Attitudes of Male College Freshmen.* Doctor's thesis, Claremont Graduate School (Claremont, Calif.), 1970. (*DAI* 31:1636A)

152. WADE, ARNOLD, AND SHERTZER, BRUCE. "Anxiety Reduction Through Vocational Counseling." *Voc Guid Q* 19(1):46–9 S '70. *

153. WALSH, JOAN EVELYN. *A Study of the Relationship Between Instruction in Psychiatric Nursing, Level of Anxiety, and Direction of Attitudes Toward the Mentally Ill.* Doctor's thesis, New York University (New York, N.Y.), 1970. (*DAI* 31:4162B)

154. WINK, RICHARD L. "The Relationship of Self-Concept and Selected Personality Variables to Achievement in Music Student Teaching." *J Res Music Ed* 18(3):234–41 f '70. * (*PA* 45:8972)

155. BELFER, MYRON L.; SHADER, RICHARD I.; CARROLL, MARY; AND HARMATZ, JEROLD S. "Alcoholism in Women." *Arch Gen Psychiatry* 25(6):540–4 D '71. *

156. BRUEGEL, MARY ANN. "Relationship of Preoperative Anxiety to Perception of Postoperative Pain." *Nursing Res* 20(1):26–31 Ja–F '71. * (*PA* 47:1488)

157. BULL, R. H. C., AND STRONGMAN, K. T. "Anxiety, Neuroticism and Extraversion." *Psychol Rep* 29(3):1101–2 D '71. * (*PA* 48:942)

158. CHEDEKEL, DAVID SELWYN. *The Levels of Anxiety and Self-Actualization in Dropout-Prone Ninth Grade Boys.* Doctor's thesis, Boston University (Boston, Mass.), 1971. (*DAI* 32: 1847A)

159. CLARK, SIDNEY LANIER. *A Study of the Relationship Between Secondary Student Teachers' Anxiety Levels and Their Assignation of Letter Grades Under Simulated Conditions.* Doctor's thesis, Columbia University (New York, N.Y.), 1971. (*DAI* 32:3834A)

160. DAVIS, SHARON FRANCES. *Correlates of Anxiety in Student Teachers in Microteaching.* Doctor's thesis, University of Illinois (Urbana, Ill.), 1971. (*DAI* 32:784A)

161. FAGAN, EULALIA CONNORS. *Personality Characteristics of Alcoholics, With Varying Degrees of Sobriety, and Those of Their Wives.* Doctor's thesis, Columbia University (New York, N.Y.), 1971. (*DAI* 32:1839B)

162. GIDDINGS, WILLIAM VANDUYN. *An Investigation of the Relationship Between the Self-Concepts and Anxiety Levels of Counselor-Candidates and Their Performance in Counseling Interviews.* Doctor's thesis, Northern Illinois University (DeKalb, Ill.), 1971. (*DAI* 32:174A)

163. GLASS, KENNETH D. "Denominational Differences in Religious Belief, Practice, Anxiety, and Dogmatism." *Relig Ed* 66(3):204–6 My '71. * (*PA* 47:10690)

164. GLASS, KENNETH D., AND SCHOCH, EUGENE W. "Religious Belief and Practice Related to Anxiety and Dogmatism in College Women." *J Nat Assn Women Deans & Counselors* 34(3):130–3 sp '71. *

165. HORNE, ARTHUR M. *A Comparative Study of Three Group Counseling Techniques for Reducing Test Anxiety.* Doctor's thesis, Southern Illinois University (Carbondale, Ill.), 1971. (*DAI* 32:4952A)

166. HUGHES, M. L., AND BONE, RONALD N. "The Effects of Anxiety on Simple and Complex Anagram Solutions Among College Students." *Proc W Va Acad Sci* 42(1970):233–6 '71. *

167. INGHAM, ROGER J., AND ANDREWS, GAVIN. "The Relation Between Anxiety Reduction and Treatment." *J Commun Disorders* (Netherlands) 4(4):289–301 D '71. * (*PA* 48:3499)

168. JAWA, SARLA. "Anxiety and Job Satisfaction." *Indian J Appl Psychol* 8(2):70–1 Jl '71. *

169. JOHNSON, JAMES H. "Note on the Validity of Machover's Indicators of Anxiety." *Percept & Motor Skills* 33(1):126 Ag '71. * (*PA* 47:3022)

170. JOHNSON, JAMES H. "Upper Left Hand Placement of Human Figure Drawings as an Indicator of Anxiety." *J Pers Assess* 35(4):336–7 Ag '71. * (*PA* 47:4833)

171. KAHN, MALCOLM, AND SCHILL, THOMAS. "Anxiety Report in Defensive and Nondefensive Repressors." Abstract. *J Consult & Clin Psychol* 36(2):300 Ap '71. * (*PA* 46:3055)

172. LEVITT, EUGENE E.; LUBIN, BERNARD; AND DEWITT, KATHRYN N. "An Attempt to Develop an Objective Test Battery for the Selection of Nursing Students." *Nursing Res* 20(3): 255–8 My–Je '71. * (*PA* 51:3969)

173. LOW, MORTON D., AND SWIFT, SHERRILL J. "The Contingent Negative Variation and the 'Resting' D.C. Potential of the Human Brain: Effects of Situational Anxiety." *Neuropsychologia* (England) 9(2):203–8 Je '71. * (*PA* 47:482)

174. McJULIEN, WESLEY JOSEPH. *The Effect of Modes of Presentation and Anxiety Levels on Individual Participant Achievement in an Educational Game.* Doctor's thesis, Syracuse University (Syracuse, N.Y.), 1971. (*DAI* 32:4491A)

175. MASTRATI, PETER SALVATORE. *Motivation as a Factor in Self-Congruence, Reported Anxiety, and Galvanic Skin Response Activation Among Hospitalized Mental Patients.* Doctor's thesis, Boston University (Boston, Mass.), 1971. (*DAI* 32:1858A)

176. MEANS, JAMES EDWARD. *An Empirical Study of the Relationship Between Anxiety-Proneness and Free Speech Attitudes.* Doctor's thesis, University of Denver (Denver, Colo.), 1971. (*DAI* 32:4748A)

177. MILLIKEN, ROBERT L., AND KIRCHNER, REGIS, JR. "Counselor's Understanding of Student's Communication as a Function of the Counselor's Perceptual Defense." *J Counsel Psychol* 18(1):14–8 Ja '71. * (*PA* 45:8696)

178. NIELD, MARGARET ANN. "The Effect of Health Teaching on the Anxiety Level of Patients With Chronic Obstructive Lung Disease." *Nursing Res* 20(6):537–41 N–D '71. *

179. PERSKY, HAROLD; SMITH, KEITH D.; AND BASU, GOPAL K. "Relation of Psychologic Measures of Aggression and Hostility to Testosterone Production in Man." *Psychosom Med* 33(3): 265–77 My–Je '71. * (*PA* 47:4310)

180. SCHLACHTER, LOUISE C. *The Relation Between Anxiety, Perceived Body and Personal Space and Actual Body Space Among Young Female Adults.* Doctor's thesis, New York University (New York, N.Y.), 1971. (*DAI* 32:3458B)

181. SCHREIBER, ELLIOTT H., AND SCALES, JAMES L. "Anxiety and Dental Health in Institutionalized Delinquent Adolescents." *J Am Dental Assn* 82(3):600–2 Mr '71. *

182. SELLINGER, STUART. *An Investigation of the Effects of Organizational Climate and Teacher Anxiety on Test Anxiety of Elementary School Students.* Doctor's thesis, New York University (New York, N.Y.), 1971. (*DAI* 32:5515A)

183. SINGH, AGYA JIT. "A Comparative Study of the Anxiety Level Among the Post Graduate Teachers and Post Graduate Students of the University." *Manas* (India) 18(2):81–4 N '71. * (*PA* 50:5853)

184. SOLYOM, L.; HESELTINE, G. F. D.; McCLURE, D. J.; LEDWIDGE, B.; AND KENNY, F. "A Comparative Study of Aversion Relief and Systematic Desensitization in the Treatment of Phobias." *Brit J Psychiatry* 119(550):299–303 S '71. * (*PA* 47:9123)

185. TEMPLER, A. J. "A Study of the Relationship Between Anxiety and Extraversion-Introversion." *Psychologia Africana* (South Africa) 14(1):20–31 My '71. * (*PA* 47:10869)

186. WALSH, JOAN E. "Instruction in Psychiatric Nursing, Level of Anxiety, and Direction of Attitude Change Toward the Mentally Ill." *Nursing Res* 20(6):522–9 N–D '71. * (*PA* 48:3091)

187. WIGGINS, CAROL ANN. *The Relationship of Anxiety and Tolerance of Ambiguity to the Curricular Choices of Female University Students.* Doctor's thesis, University of Connecticut (Storrs, Conn.), 1971. (*DAI* 33:5505A)

188. ZEDECK, SHELDON; CRANNY, C. J.; VALE, CAROL A.; AND SMITH, PATRICIA CAIN. "Comparison of 'Joint Moderators' in Three Prediction Techniques." *J Appl Psychol* 55(3):234–40 Je '71. * (*PA* 46:9774)

CUMULATIVE NAME INDEX

[1226]

IPAT Contact Personality Factor Test. High school and adults; 1954–56; title on test is *C.P.F.;* 2 scores: extroversion-introversion, distortion; Raymond B. Cattell, Joseph E. King, and A. K. Schuettler; Institute for Personality and Ability Testing. (Form A also published, under the title *Employee Attitude Series: C.P.F.,* by Industrial Psychology, Inc.) *

For additional information, see P:117 (1 reference); see also 6:123 (6 references); for reviews by Cecil D. Johnson and S. B. Sells, see 5:71.

REFERENCES THROUGH 1971

1–6. See 6:123.
7. See P:117.
8. SAXENA, P. C. "Attitudes, Intelligence and Personality Correlates of Competent Teachers." *Indian Psychol R* 5(2): 107–12 Ja '69. *
9. SRIVASTAVA, S. S. "The Contact Personality Factor Test (An Extraversion Scale in Indian Conditions)." *Indian Psychol R* 7(1):14–20 Jl '70. *

CUMULATIVE NAME INDEX

Braun, J. R.: 7　　　　　　　Johnson, C. D.: rev, 5:71
Brengelmann, J. C.: 6　　　　La Faro, D.: 7
Cattell, R. B.: 1　　　　　　Saxena, P. C.: 8
Claridge, G.: 2　　　　　　　Sells, S. B.: rev, 5:71
Eysenck, H. J.: 3　　　　　　Srivastava, S. S.: 9
Field, J. G.: 6　　　　　　　Willett, R. A.: 5
Holland, H. C.: 4

[1227]

*IPAT 8-Parallel-Form Anxiety Battery. Ages 14 or 15 and over; 1960–73; 8PFAB; 1973 tests identical with tests copyrighted 1960 except for slight changes in wording and sequence of items; Ivan H. Scheier and Raymond B. Cattell; Institute for Personality and Ability Testing. *

For additional information, see P:118 (8 references); for reviews by Jacob Cohen and Paul M. Kjeldergaard, see 6:124 (4 references).

REFERENCES THROUGH 1971

1–4. See 6:124.
5–12. See P:118.
13. BEDNAR, MARY ANN. *Changes in Social Perception in Adolescents During Group Psychotherapy.* Doctor's thesis, Washington University (St. Louis, Mo.), 1964. (*DA* 26:1166)
14. HENINGER, GEORGE; DIMASCIO, ALBERTO; AND KLERMAN, GERALD L. "Personality Factors in Variability of Response to Phenothiazines." *Am J Psychiatry* 121:1091–4 My '65. * (*PA* 39:12484)
15. SCHACHTER, JOSEPH; WILLIAMS, THOMAS A.; ROWE, RICHARD; SCHACHTER, JUDITH S.; AND JAMESON, JEAN. "Personality Correlates of Physiological Reactivity to Stress: A Study of Forty-Six College Males." *Am J Psychiatry* 121(sup): xii–xxiv My '65. * (*PA* 39:12246)
16. BAKER, JOHN WILLIAM, II. *The Effects of Four Types of Vicarious Aggression on Physiological and Psychological Arousal.* Doctor's thesis, West Virginia University (Morgantown, W.Va.), 1967. (*DA* 28:2132B)
17. NEWMAN, RICHARD E. *A Comparison of the Anxiety Measures and Match Performance Evaluations of High School Wrestlers.* Master's thesis, South Dakota State University (Brookings, S.D.), 1967.
18. PECK, ARDEN. *The Influence of Anxiety on Volleyball Skills.* Master's thesis, University of North Carolina (Greensboro, N.C.), 1967.

19. TURNER, WILLIAM J. "The Usefulness of Diphenyl-hydantoin in Treatment of Nonepileptic Emotional Disorders." *Int J Neuropsychiatry* 3(sup 2):S8–20 D '67. * (*PA* 42:14005)

20. DIMASCIO, ALBERTO; MEYER, ROGER E.; AND STIFLER, LAWRENCE. "Effects of Imipramine on Individuals Varying in Level of Depression." *Am J Psychiatry* 124(8, sup):55–8 F '68. * (*PA* 42:9111)

21. HOFFMAN, HARVEY E. "Effect of Stress on Scanning." *Percept & Motor Skills* 27:891–900 D '68. * (*PA* 43:7779)

22. REYNOLDS, JAMES CONRAD. *The Effect of Viewer Distance on Film Induced Anxiety.* Doctor's thesis, Indiana University (Bloomington, Ind.), 1968. (*DA* 29:3341A)

23. SHEPHERD, DAVID C., AND GOLDSTEIN, ROBERT. "Intra-subject Variability in Amplitude of Bekesy Tracings and Its Relation to Measures of Personality." *J Speech & Hearing Res* 11:523–35 S '68. * (*PA* 43:3372)

24. PAYTON, OTTO D. "A Study of the Dexterity and Coordination of Physical Therapy Students." *Physical Ther* 49(8):845–51 Ag '69. *

25. SIEVERS, FARRELL PATRICK. *A Study of Variables Differentiating Counselors.* Doctor's thesis, University of South Dakota (Vermillion, S.D.), 1969. (*DAI* 30:3740A)

26. STETTER, RICHARD. "A Group Guidance Technique for the Classroom Teacher." *Sch Counselor* 16(3):179–84 Ja '69. * (*PA* 44:7298)

27. BROOKS, FRED ORVILLE. *Effect of Personal Values and Open-Closed Mindedness on Student Teacher Anxiety.* Doctor's thesis, University of North Dakota (Grand Forks, N.D.), 1970. (*DAI* 31:6447A)

28. BUSH, JONE J. *Anxiety and Performance at Three Levels of Competition in Women's Intercollegiate Gymnastics.* Doctor's thesis, Springfield College (Springfield, Mass.), 1970.

29. CAPEL, W. C.; YOUNGBLOOD, DAVID; AND STEWART, G. T. "Note on Stress, Anxiety and Related Defenses in a Controlled Situation." *Psychol Rep* 27(2):351–5 O '70. * (*PA* 45:7151)

30. FORD, ROBERT M. *Anxiety in Non-Competitive and Pre-Competitive Situations Involving Intercollegiate Football Players.* Doctor's thesis, Springfield College (Springfield, Mass.), 1970.

31. MEYER, ROGER E.; DiMASCIO, ALBERTO; AND STIFLER, LAWRENCE. "Personality Differences in the Response to Stimulant Drugs Administered During a Sleep-Deprived State." *J Nerv & Mental Dis* 150(2):91–101 F '70. * (*PA* 44:12032)

32. MORGAN, WILLIAM P. "Psychological Effect of Weight Reduction in the College Wrestler." *Med & Sci Sports* 2(1):24–7 sp '70. *

33. PHILIP, ALISTAIR E. "Reliability and Equivalence in the Eight-Parallel Form Anxiety Battery." *Brit J Psychol* 61(4):517–20 N '70. * (*PA* 45:4288)

34. RATZLAFF, CLIFFORD NELSON. *Effects of Relaxation of Self-Report Measures of a Basic-Encounter Group Experience.* Doctor's thesis, Arizona State University (Tempe, Ariz.), 1970. (*DAI* 31:2116A)

35. SHEPPARD, CHARLES; O'NEIL, CAROLYN; FRACCHIA, JOHN; AND MERLIS, SYDNEY. "Levels of Personal Conflict Derived From Response to the Emotion Profile Index." *J Psychol* 74(2):143–8 Mr '70. * (*PA* 44:12658)

36. ZIMMERMAN, SAUNDRA F.; SMITH, KAY H.; AND PEDERSEN, DARHL M. "The Effect of Anticonformity Appeals on Conformity Behavior." *J Social Psychol* 81(1):93–103 Je '70. * (*PA* 44:18593)

37. HOFFMAN, HARVEY E. "Scanning, Stress, and the Defense Profile." *J Clin Psychol* 27(2):199–202 Ap '71. * (*PA* 46:6865)

38. VANDERSTOK, ANNIE ALETTA. *A Study of the Effect of Selected Biological, Psychological, and Sociological Factors on the Learning Rate of the Negro Male Beginning Swimmer.* Doctor's thesis, University of North Carolina (Greensboro, N.C.), 1971. (*DAI* 32:225A)

CUMULATIVE NAME INDEX

Baker, J. W.: 16
Bakker, C. B.: 10
Balfrey, W. R.: 9
Bednar, M. A.: 13
Bendig, A. W.: 2
Bortner, T. W.: 10
Brooks, F. O.: 27
Bruder, G.: 2
Bush, J. J.: 28
Capel, W. C.: 29
Cattell, R. B.: 1, 3, 5
Cohen, J.: *rev*, 6:124
Collins, L.: 12
Dimascio, A.: 14, 20, 31
Fiorentino, D.: 12
Fisher, W. P.: 11
Ford, R. M.: 30
Forrest, G. L.: 10
Fracchia, J.: 35
Goldstein, R.: 23
Heninger, G.: 14
Hoffman, H. E.: 21, 37
Jameson, J.: 15
Kjeldergaard, P. M.: *rev*, 6: 124
Klerman, G. L.: 14
Ladd, C. E.: 11
Langer, P.: 7
Merlis, S.: 12, 35
Meyer, R. E.: 20, 31
Miller, N. B.: 11
Morgan, W. P.: 32
Newman, R. E.: 17
O'Neil, C.: 35
Outridge, M.: 6
Payton, O. D.: 24
Peck, A.: 18
Pedersen, D. M.: 36
Petrusich, M. M.: 8
Philip, A. E.: 33
Rankin, J.: 9
Ratzlaff, C. N.: 34
Reynolds, J. C.: 22
Rickels, K.: 5
Rowe, R.: 15
Schachter, J.: 15
Schachter, J. S.: 15
Scheier, I. H.: 1, 4
Shepherd, D. C.: 23
Sheppard, C.: 12, 35

Sievers, F. P.: 25
Smith, K. H.: 36
Stetter, R.: 26
Stewart, G. T.: 29
Stifler, L.: 20, 31

Turner, W. J.: 19
Vanderstok, A. A.: 38
Williams, T. A.: 15
Youngblood, D.: 29
Zimmerman, S. F.: 36

[1228]

IPAT Humor Test of Personality. High school and adults; 1949–66; test booklet title is *The IPAT Humor Test;* 13 scores: anxious considerateness vs. debonair sexual and general uninhibitedness, dry wit vs. good-natured play, compensation vs. tough self-composure, flirtatious playfulness vs. gruesomeness, urbane pleasantness vs. hostile derogation, impudent defiance of decency vs. resignation, theatricalism vs. cold realism, neat and lighthearted wit vs. ponderous humor, damaging retort vs. unexpected off-beat humor, cheerful independence vs. mistreatment humor, anxious concern vs. evasion of responsibility, rebound against feminine aggression vs. scorn of ineffectual male, dullness vs. general intelligence; Raymond B. Cattell and Donald L. Tollefson; Institute for Personality and Ability Testing. *

For additional information, see P:119 (8 references); for reviews by W. Grant Dahlstrom, Ardie Lubin (with Frank M. Loos), and J. R. Wittenborn, see 4:61 (5 references).

REFERENCES THROUGH 1971

1–5. See 4:61.
6–13. See P:119.
14. TOLLEFSON, DONALD LLOYD. *Differential Responses to Humor and Their Relation to Personality and Motivation Measures.* Doctor's thesis, University of Illinois (Urbana, Ill.), 1961. (*DA* 22:1712)
15. PAWLIK, KURT, AND CATTELL, RAYMOND B. "The Relationship Between Certain Personality Factors and Measures of Cortical Arousal." *Neuropsychologia* (England) 3:129–51 My '65. *

CUMULATIVE NAME INDEX

Adcock, C. J.: 12
Berkeley, M. H.: 7
Cattell, R. B.: 1–3, 6, 15
Dahlstrom, W. G.: *rev*, 4:61
Fleigler, L.: 9
Griffith, R. M.: 10
Horowitz, J. Z.: 6
Howard, K. I.: 11
Lee, J. C.: 10
Loos, F. M.: *rev*, 4:61
Lubin, A.: *rev*, 4:61
Luborsky, L. B.: 2–3
Pawlik, K.: 15
Philippus, M. J.: 8–9
Schwartz, A. N.: 4
Smith, N. V. O.: 5
Taylor, A. J. W.: 13
Tollefson, D. L.: 14
Vinacke, W. E.: 5
Wittenborn, J. R.: *rev*, 4:61
Yarnold, J. K.: 7

[1229]

IPAT Neurotic Personality Factor Test. Grades 9–16 and adults; 1955; NPFT; for later version, see *Neuroticism Scale Questionnaire;* test booklet title is *N.P.F.;* 2 scores: neuroticism, distortion; R. B. Cattell, J. E. King, and A. K. Schuettler; published jointly by Institute for Personality and Ability Testing and Industrial Psychology, Inc. (Industrial Psychology, Inc. distributes the test under the title *Employee Attitude Series: N.P.F.*) *

For additional information, see P:121 (7 references); for reviews by S. B. Sells and William Stephenson, see 5:74.

REFERENCES THROUGH 1971

1–7. See P:121.

CUMULATIVE NAME INDEX

Bendig, A. W.: 1–3, 6
Cattell, R. B.: 4
Kear-Colwell, J. J.: 5
Kidd, C. B.: 7
Scheier, I. H.: 4
Sells, S. B.: *rev*, 5:74
Stephenson, W.: *rev*, 5:74
Watt, K. I. M.: 7

[1230]

Independent Activities Questionnaire. High school and college; 1965–67; IAQ; for research use only; non-academic achievement; 25 scores: 20 scale scores (agriculture, art and design, business, collecting, drama, electronics, exploring, games, handicraft, home responsibility, leadership, mathematics, mechanics, music, politics, public speaking, scholarship, science, sports, writing) and 5 derived scores (arts and crafts, speech, sciences, arts and sciences, social activities) ; Stephen P. Klein (manual) ; Educational Testing Service. *

For additional information, see P:122 (2 references).

REFERENCES THROUGH 1971

1-2. See P:122.
3. KLEIN, STEPHEN P., AND EVANS, FRANKLIN R. "Early Predictors of Later Creative Achievements." Abstract. *Proc 77th Ann Conv Am Psychol Assn* 4(1):153-4 '69. * (*PA* 43:17499)

CUMULATIVE NAME INDEX

Evans, F. R.: 3   Schultz, C. B.: 1-2
Klein, S. P.: 1-3   Skager, R. W.: 1-2

[1231]

★The Inferred Self-Concept Scale. Grades 1-6; ratings by teachers and counselors; 1969-73; ISCS; E. L. McDaniel; Western Psychological Services. *

REFERENCES THROUGH 1971

1. MCDANIEL, ELIZABETH ALICE LOGAN. *Relationships Between Self-Concept and Specific Variables in a Low-Income Culturally Different Population.* Doctor's thesis, University of Texas (Austin, Tex.), 1967. (*DAI* 28:4005A)

CUMULATIVE NAME INDEX

McDaniel, E. A. L.: 1

[1232]

Inpatient Multidimensional Psychiatric Scale. Hospitalized mental patients; 1953-67; IMPS; 10 scores based on ratings following an interview : excitement, hostile belligerence, paranoid projection, grandiose expansiveness, perceptual distortions, anxious intropunitiveness, retardation and apathy, disorientation, motor disturbances, conceptual disorganization; original materials by Maurice Lorr, C. James Klett, Douglas M. McNair (scale), and Julian J. Lasky (scale) ; Consulting Psychologists Press, Inc. *

For additional information and a review by Jerome D. Pauker, see 7:88 (27 references) ; see also P:124 (61 references) and 6:126 (26 references).

REFERENCES THROUGH 1971

1-26. See 6:126.
27-87. See P:124.
88-114. See 7:88.
115. JENKINS, RICHARD L., AND LORR, MAURICE. "Type-Tracking Among Psychotic Patients." *J Clin Psychol* 10:114-9 Ap '54. * (*PA* 29:1250)
116. GAITZ, CHARLES M.; ROY, H.; THOMPSON, W.; KIMBELL, I.; MULLEN, A. J.; AND POKORNY, A. D. "Evaluation of Chlorpromazine in Comparison With Other Methods of Treatment of Hospitalized Patients, Using the Lorr Multidimensional Scale for Rating Psychiatric Patients." *Psychiatric Res Rep* 1:84-94 Jl '55. * (*PA* 30:8305)
117. GARDNER, M. J.; HAWKINS, H. M.; JUDAH, L. N.; AND MURPHREE, O. D. "Objective Measurement of Psychiatric Changes Produced by Chlorpromazine and Reserpine in Chronic Schizophrenia." *Psychiatric Res Rep* 1:77-83 Jl '55. * (*PA* 30:8411)
118. LORR, MAURICE; HOLSOPPLE, JAMES Q.; JENKINS, RICHARD L.; AND O'CONNOR, JAMES P. "Factors of Change in Lobotomized Chronic Schizophrenic Patients." *J Consult Psychol* 19:39-43 F '55. * (*PA* 29:8805)
119. GUERTIN, WILSON H., AND JENKINS, RICHARD L. "A Transposed Factor Analysis of a Group of Schizophrenic Patients." *J Clin Psychol* 12:64-8 Ja '56. * (*PA* 30:4960)
120. PEARL, DAVID; VANDER KAMP, HARRY; OLSEN, ALBERT L.; GREENBERG, PAUL D.; AND ARMITAGE, STEWART G. "The Effects of Reserpine on Schizophrenic Patients." *Arch Neurol & Psychiatry* 76:198-204 Ag '56. * (*PA* 31:8494)
121. SWENSON, W. M.; GISLASON, SOLVIG; AND ANDERSON, D. E. "Behavioral Evaluation of Chronic Mental Hospital Patients Treated With Reserpine." *Arch Neurol & Psychiatry* 76:60-4 Jl '56. * (*PA* 31:6448)
122. GORDON, M. H.; LINDLEY, S. B.; AND MAY, R. B. "A Criterion Measure of Within-Hospital Change in Psychiatric Illness." *J Clin Psychol* 13:145-7 Ap '57. * (*PA* 32:3161)
123. RUBINSTEIN, ELI A., AND LORR, MAURICE. "Patient Types in Outpatient Psychotherapy." *J Clin Psychol* 13:356-61 O '57. * (*PA* 33:1484)

124. RUBINSTEIN, ELI A., AND LORR, MAURICE. "Self and Peer Personality Ratings of Psychotherapists." *J Clin Psychol* 13:295-8 Jl '57. * (*PA* 32:5576)
125. HANLON, THOMAS E.; KURLAND, ALBERT A.; ESQUIBEL, AUGUSTO J.; AND OTA, KAY Y. "A Comparative Study of Chlorpromazine and Trifluopromazine in the Management of the Chronic Hospitalized Psychotic Patient." *J Nerv & Mental Dis* 127:17-20 Jl '58. * (*PA* 33:10409)
126. HANLON, THOMAS E.; SHEETS, CAROLYN S.; AND KURLAND, ALBERT A. "Spontaneous Fluctuations in the Severity of Illness of Hospitalized Lobotomized Patients." *J Clin Psychol* 14:6-10 Ja '58. * (*PA* 33:6497)
127. ROSENTHAL, MELVIN, AND SCHWARTZ, LIONEL A. "Psychological Implications and Effects of Insulin Therapy." *J Nerv & Mental Dis* 127:232-7 S '58. * (*PA* 34:1555)
128. TANCK, ROLAND H. "Psychologic Changes Induced by Reserpine Therapy on a Group of Severely Disturbed Psychotics." *J Nerv & Mental Dis* 126:353-9 Ap '58. * (*PA* 33:8581)
129. GORHAM, DONALD R., AND OVERALL, JOHN E. "Drug-Action Profiles Based on an Abbreviated Psychiatric Rating Scale." *J Nerv & Mental Dis* 131:528-35 D '60. *
130. ADELSON, DANIEL. "Approaches to Rating the Mute Patient." *J Clin Psychol* 17:348-51 O '61. * (*PA* 38:8914)
131. ROOS, PHILIP. "Evaluation of Psychotherapy as an Adjunct to Insulin-Coma Therapy." *J Consult Psychol* 25:450-5 O '61. * (*PA* 37:3346)
132. ADELSON, DANIEL, AND EPSTEIN, LEON J. "A Study of Phenothiazines With Male and Female Chronically Ill Schizophrenic Patients." *J Nerv & Mental Dis* 134:543-54 Je '62. *
133. HONIGFELD, GILBERT. "Relationships Among Physicians' Attitudes and Response to Drugs." *Psychol Rep* 11:683-90 D '62. * (*PA* 38:2796)
134. CRUMPTON, EVELYN; BRILL, NORMAN Q.; EIDUSON, SAMUEL; AND GELLER, EDWARD. "The Role of Fear in Electroconvulsive Treatment." *J Nerv & Mental Dis* 136:29-33 Ja '63. * (*PA* 37:8054)
135. MARKS, JOHN. "Predrug Behavior as a Predictor of Response to Phenothiazines Among Schizophrenics." *J Nerv & Mental Dis* 137:597-601 D '63. * (*PA* 38:6187)
136. HOENIG, J. "Syndromes of Psychosis: A Review." *Brit J Psychiatry* 110:605-6 Jl '64. *
137. HOLLISTER, LEO E.; OVERALL, JOHN E.; JOHNSON, MERLIN; PENNINGTON, VERONICA; KATZ, GEORGE; AND SHELTON, JACK. "Controlled Comparison of Amitriptyline, Imipramine and Placebo in Hospitalized Depressed Patients." *J Nerv & Mental Dis* 139:370-5 O '64. *
138. MOSELEY, EDWARD C., AND KLETT, C. JAMES. "An Empirical Comparison of Factor Scoring Methods." *Psychol Rep* 14:179-84 F '64. * (*PA* 39:185)
139. DOWNING, ROBERT W.; EBERT, JOHN N.; BORUCHOW, JOAN K.; AND VALENTINE, JOHN H. "Temporal Changes in Handwriting Size, Level of Premorbid Social Functioning and Intellectual Level During Treatment in Acute Schizophrenics." *J Nerv & Mental Dis* 142:526-33 Je '66. * (*PA* 41:3129)
140. HOLLISTER, LEO E.; OVERALL, JOHN E.; JOHNSON, MERLIN H.; SHELTON, JACK; KIMBALL, ISHAM, JR.; AND BRUNSE, ANTHONY. "Amitriptyline Alone and Combined With Perphenazine in Newly Admitted Depressed Patients." *J Nerv & Mental Dis* 142:460-9 My '66. *
141. MARJERRISON, G.; HRYCHUK, W.; AND VARSANYI, E. I. "A Comparison of Two Butyrophenones With Trifluoperazine." *Can Psychiatric Assn J* 11:26-30 F '66. * (*PA* 40:4349)
142. RASKIN, ALLEN, AND GOLOB, RISA. "Occurrence of Sex and Social Class Differences in Premorbid Competence, Symptom and Outcome Measures in Acute Schizophrenics." *Psychol Rep* 18:11-22 F '66. * (*PA* 40:6889)
143. GOLDBERG, SOLOMON C., AND MATTSSON, NILS. "Symptom Changes Associated With Improvement in Schizophrenia." *J Consult Psychol* 31:175-80 Ap '67. * (*PA* 41:7579)
144. SHIMKUNAS, ALGIMANTAS M.; GYNTHER, MALCOLM D.; AND SMITH, KATHLEEN. "Schizophrenic Responses to the Proverbs Test: Abstract, Concrete, or Autistic?" *J Abn Psychol* 72:128-33 Ap '67. * (*PA* 41:7605)
145. CHAMBERS, J. L., AND WILSON, W. T. "Perception of Apparent Motion and Degree of Mental Pathology." *Percept & Motor Skills* 26:855-61 Je '68. * (*PA* 42:15503)
146. LORR, MAURICE. Chap. 22, "Syndromes of Deviation," pp. 1086-102. In *Handbook of Personality Theory and Research.* Edited by Edgar F. Borgatta and William W. Lambert. Chicago, Ill.: Rand McNally & Co., 1968. Pp. xiv, 1232. *
147. COCKBURN, KATHLEEN ANN. *Behavioral Responses of Schizophrenic Patients to Increased Awareness of Sensory Stimuli.* Doctor's thesis, Boston University (Boston, Mass.), 1969. (*DAI* 31:5441B)
148. LORR, MAURICE. Chap. 3, "A Typological Conception of the Behavior Disorders," pp. 101-16. In *New Approaches to Personality Classification.* Edited by Alvin R. Mahrer. New York: Columbia University Press, 1970. Pp. vii, 425. * (*PA* 45:6276)
149. LORR, MAURICE, AND KLETT, C. JAMES. "Life History Differentia of Five Acute Psychotic Types," pp. 147-57. In *Life History Research in Psychopathology.* Edited by Merrill

Roff and David F. Ricks. Minneapolis, Minn.: University of Minnesota Press, 1970. Pp. viii, 321. *

150. CAFFEY, EUGENE M.; GALBRECHT, CHARLES R.; AND KLETT, C. JAMES. "Brief Hospitalization and Aftercare in the Treatment of Schizophrenia." *Arch Gen Psychiatry* 24(1):81–6 Ja '71. * (*PA* 45:10394)

151. COPELAND, J. R. M.; COOPER, J. E.; KENDELL, R. E.; AND GOURLAY, A. J. "Differences in Usage of Diagnostic Labels Amongst Psychiatrists in the British Isles." *Brit J Psychiatry* 118(547):629–40 Je '71. * (*PA* 47:7073)

152. DEWOLFE, ALAN S.; BARRELL, ROBERT P.; LONDON, LESLIE; AND SPANER, FRED E. "Prolixin Enanthate and Thorazine-Stelazine Regimens in the Treatment of Schizophrenic Patients: An Experimental Evaluation." *Psychosomatics* 12(3): 186–90 My '71. * (*PA* 47:7273)

153. LORR, MAURICE. Chap. 10, "Dimensions and Categories for Assessment of Psychotics," pp. 198–215. In *Advances in Psychological Assessment, Vol. 2*. Edited by Paul McReynolds. Palo Alto, Calif.: Science and Behavior Books, Inc., 1971. Pp. xii, 395. *

154. LORR, MAURICE, AND HAMLIN, ROY M. "A Multimethod Factor Analysis of Behavioral and Objective Measures of Psychopathology." *J Consult & Clin Psychol* 36(1):136–41 F '71. * (*PA* 45:10358)

155. MCGEE, THOMAS F., AND WILLIAMS, MEYER. "Time-Limited and Time-Unlimited Group Psychotherapy: A Comparison With Schizophrenic Patients." *Comparative Group Studies* 2(1):71–84 F '71. * (*PA* 47:5339)

156. MOSHER, LOREN R.; POLLIN, WILLIAM; AND STABENAU, JAMES R. "Identical Twins Discordant for Schizophrenia: Neurologic Findings." *Arch Gen Psychiatry* 24(5):422–30 My '71. * (*PA* 47:9365)

157. PATTISON, E. MANSELL; RHODES, ROBERT J.; AND DUDLEY, DONALD L. "Response to a Group Treatment in Patients With Severe Chronic Lung Disease." *Int J Group Psychother* 21(2): 214–25 Ap '71. * (*PA* 48:1099)

158. RABINER, EDWIN L.; REISER, MORTON F.; BARR, HARRIET L.; AND GRALNICK, ALEXANDER. "Therapists' Attitudes and Patients' Clinical Status: A Study of 100 Psychotherapy Pairs." *Arch Gen Psychiatry* 25(6):555–69 D '71. *

159. RASKIN, ALLEN, AND MCKEON, JAMES J. "Super Factors of Psychopathology in Hospital Depressed Patients." *J Psychiatric Res* (England) 9(1):11–9 D '71. *

160. SCHOOLER, CARMI, AND SILVERMAN, JULIAN. "Differences Between Correlates of Perceptual Style and Petrie Task Performance in Chronic and Acute Schizophrenics." *Percept & Motor Skills* 32(2):595–601 Ap '71. * (*PA* 46:11261)

161. SHOPSIN, BARON; KIM, SUK SIK; AND GERSHON, SAMUEL. "A Controlled Study of Lithium vs. Chlorpromazine in Acute Schizophrenics." *Brit J Psychiatry* 119(551):435–40 O '71. * (*PA* 47:9388)

CUMULATIVE NAME INDEX

[1233]

Institute of Child Study Security Test. Grades 1–3, 4–8; 1957–68; 2 scores: consistency, security; 2 levels; Michael F. Grapko; distributed by Guidance Centre [Canada]. *

a) PRIMARY FORM. Grades 1–3; 1964–65; title on test is *The Story of Tommy.*

b) ELEMENTARY FORM. Grades 4–8; 1957–68; title on test is *The Story of Jimmy.*

For additional information, see P :125 (4 references); for a review by Laurance F. Shaffer, see 5 :75.

REFERENCES THROUGH 1971

1–4. See P :125.
5. MAW, WALLACE H., AND MAW, ETHEL W. *Personal and Social Variables Differentiating Children With High and Low Curiosity.* An unpublished report to the U.S. Office of Education, Cooperative Research Project No. 1511, University of Delaware, 1966. Pp. xii, 181. * (ERIC ED 003 274)

CUMULATIVE NAME INDEX

Fine, M. J.: 2–3   Maw, W. H.: 5
Grapko, M. F.: 1, 4   Shaffer, L. F.: *rev,* 5:75
Maw, E. W.: 5

[1234]

Institutional Functioning Inventory. College faculty and administrators; 1968–70; IFI; a measure of perceived institutional vitality; the first half of the inventory may be used with students; for research use only; 11 scores: intellectual-aesthetic extracurriculum, freedom, human diversity, concern for improvement of society, concern for undergraduate learning, democratic governance, meeting local needs, self-study and planning, concern for advancing knowledge, concern for innovation, institutional esprit; Richard E. Peterson, John A. Centra, Rodney T. Hartnett, and Robert L. Linn; Educational Testing Service. *

For additional information and reviews by Paul L. Dressel and Clifford E. Lunneborg, see 7 :89 (3 references).

REFERENCES THROUGH 1971

1–3. See 7 :89.
4. CENTRA, JOHN A. "Validation by the Multigroup-Multiscale Matrix: An Adaptation of Campbell and Fiske's Convergent and Discriminant Validational Procedure." *Ed & Psychol Meas* 31(3):675–83 au '71. * (*PA* 47:5961)
5. HARTNETT, RODNEY T. "A Note on the Comparability of Alternative Scoring Methods for the Institutional Functioning Inventory." *J Ed Meas* 8(4):311–5 w '71. * (*PA* 47:9649)

CUMULATIVE NAME INDEX

Centra, J. A.: 1–2, 4   Lunneborg, C. E.: *rev,* 7:89
Dressel, P. L.: *rev,* 7:89   Ogden, G. B.: 3
Hartnett, R. T.: 2, 5   Peterson, R. E.: 2

[1235]

★**Institutional Goals Inventory.** College faculty and students and other subgroups; 1972; IGI; "to help college communities delineate goals and establish priorities among them"; 3 scores (goal is, goal should be, discrepancy) for total group and each subgroup for each of 90 goal statements and each of 20 goal summary areas (based on 80 of the goal statements): academic development, intellectual orientation, individual personal development, humanism/altruism, cultural/aesthetic awareness, traditional religiousness, vocational preparation, advanced training, research, meeting local needs, public service, social egalitarianism, social criticism/activism, freedom, democratic governance, community, intellectual/aesthetic environment, innovation, off-campus learning, accountability/efficiency; Institutional Research Program for Higher Education; Educational Testing Service. *

REFERENCES THROUGH 1971

1. PETERSON, RICHARD E. *College Goals and the Challenge of Effectiveness.* Princeton, N.J.: Educational Testing Service, 1971. Pp. 17. *
2. PETERSON, RICHARD E. "Toward Institutional Goal-Consciousness." *West Reg Conf Testing Probl* 20:11–31 '71. *

CUMULATIVE NAME INDEX

Peterson, R. E.: 1–2

[1236]

The Institutional Self-Study Service Survey, College Student Form. College students; 1969–71; ISS; also called *The ISS Survey Questionnaire, College Stu-*

dent Form; designed to provide a college with student opinion concerning "its policies, practices, faculty, service, and programs" and to appraise student development; each "research report" consists of means, percentages, or correlations by sexes and total for 3 groups in the following 7 areas: *student goals and aspirations:* educational majors, vocational choices, vocational role preferences, educational aspirations, importance of college goals (academic, vocational, social, nonconventional); *student development:* intellectual pursuits outside of class (science-mathematics, humanities, social science), nonacademic achievements in college (leadership, social participation, art, social service, humanistic-cultural, religious, music, writing, dramatic arts, total), student ratings of progress in achieving selected college goals; *student evaluations of their collegiate experience:* instructors, college services, selected policies, practices, and facilities; *correlations between college grade point average and:* other measures of college progress, teacher characteristics, college services, policies, practices, and facilities; *cross tabulations between ACT scores and:* majors, intellectual pursuits outside of class, nonacademic achievements; *cross tabulations between college admission data and current status on:* major, vocational choice, aspirations, nonacademic achievements; *additional tabulations:* total nonacademic achievements for specific educational majors, responses to locally developed items; initial experimental form, entitled *Survey of Educational Status and Progress,* by Donald P. Hoyt; Oscar T. Lenning; American College Testing Program. *

For additional information and a review by James V. Mitchell, Jr., see 7 :90.

REFERENCES THROUGH 1971

1. CHRISTOFF, PATRICK LEO. *The Relationship Between Attendance at a Summer Orientation Program, Expectation-Press Congruence, and Selected Behavioral Correlates.* Doctor's thesis, University of Maryland (College Park, Md.), 1970. (*DAI* 31:4454A)
2. VANDER WELL, ALLEN R. "Influence of Financial Need on the Vocational Development of College Students." *ACT Res Rep* 36:1–29 S '70. * (*PA* 47:1845)
3. CARMODY, JAMES FRANCIS. *A Descriptive Analysis of Students Expressing a Proposed Future Vocation in an Area of Education and a Test of the Suitability of Holland's Personality Model to Describe Future Educators.* Doctor's thesis, University of Iowa (Iowa City, Iowa), 1971. (*DAI* 32:2477A)
4. DOLAN, ROBERT EDMUND. *An Environmental Assessment of Wilbur Wright College by Students in Differing Curricula Programs.* Doctor's thesis, Loyola University (Chicago, Ill.), 1971. (*DAI* 32:1875A)

CUMULATIVE NAME INDEX

Carmody, J. F.: 3   Mitchell, J. V.: *rev,* 7:90
Christoff, P. L.: 1   Vander Well, A. R.: 2
Dolan, R. E.: 4

[1237]

The Integration Level Test Series. Adults; 1965–66; ILTS; for research use only; 8 tests; no manual (except for *Sex Inventory* and *Ideological Survey*); Frederick C. Thorne; Clinical Psychology Publishing Co., Inc. *

a) PERSONAL HEALTH SURVEY. PHS; physical and mental symptoms related to mental health; 12 scores: general health, general development, gastro-intestinal system, cardio-vascular system, miscellaneous systems, central nervous system, neuro-muscular systems, anxiety-fear states, anger-frustration states, schizophrenia, affective psychoses, character disorders.

b) THE SEX INVENTORY. SI; 2 editions.

1) *Male Form.* 9 scores: sex drive and interest, sexual maladjustment and frustration, neurotic conflict associated with sex, sexual cathexes and fixations, repression of sexuality, loss of sex controls, homosexuality, sex role confidence, promiscuity and sociopathic tendency.

2) *Female Form.* 11 scores: sex drive and interest, sex maladjustment and frustration, neurotic conflict over sex, sexual cathexes and fixations, sexual repression, sex control, homosexuality, sex role confidence, sexual psychopathy, nymphomania, sexual frigidity.

c) THE IDEOLOGICAL SURVEY. IS; factors contributing to a person's conception of the place of man in the world; 13 scores: 5 scores reflecting individualism and capitalism (morality and reason, rational self-interest, self-sufficiency, self-responsibility, earning and creativity), 8 scores reflecting collectivism and socialism (altruism and morality, socialism, collectivism, insecurity and defensiveness, dependency, inadequacy, rationalizing failure, work attitudes).

d) SOCIAL STATUS STUDY. SSS; 10 role scores: citizen, social person, social class, parent and family, financial manager, sex partner, worker, marriage partner, leader-follower, political.

e) THE PERSONAL DEVELOPMENT STUDY. PDS; utilization of classical Freudian mechanisms in personality structure; 10 scores: repression, regression, projection, identification, rationalization, reaction formations, extrapunitiveness, intropunitiveness, impunitiveness, miscellaneous mechanisms.

f) THE EXISTENTIAL STUDY. EA; also called *Existential Analysis;* state of being in the world; 7 scores: self-status, self-actualization, existential morale, existential vacuum, humanistic identification, existence and destiny, suicide.

g) THE LIFE STYLE ANALYSIS. LSA; Adlerian life style patterns in relation to the Murray need systems; 30 scores: 10 characteristic life styles (normal coping, individual, exploitative, pampered-spoiled, defiant-resistive, domineering-authoritarian, conforming, escapist, oneupmanship, evasive-ignoring), 20 Murray needs (abasement, achievement, affiliation, aggression, autonomy, blame avoidance, counteraction, defendance, deference, dominance, exhibition, harm avoidance, inferiority avoidance, nurturance, order, play, rejection, sentience, succorance, understanding).

h) THE FEMININITY STUDY. FS; special situational problems of women in modern culture; 11 scores: feminine social role, female parent role, feminine career role, female homemaker role, female role confidence, female sex identification, development and maturation, sex drive and interests, promiscuity, homosexuality, health and neurotic conflict.

For additional information, see P:125A (12 references).

REFERENCES THROUGH 1971

1–12. See P:125A.
13. COWDEN, JAMES E., AND PACHT, ASHER R. "The Sex Inventory as a Classification Instrument for Sex Offenders." *J Clin Psychol* 25(1):53–7 Ja '69. * (*PA* 43:9998)
14. GALBRAITH, GARY G. "The Mosher Sex-Guilt Scale and the Thorne Sex Inventory: Intercorrelations." *J Clin Psychol* 25(3):292–4 Jl '69. * (*PA* 44:3603)
15. SCHOOLMAN, DAVID A. *Empirical Validity of the Thorne Sex Inventory and Sexual Perceptions on the Rorschach.* Master's thesis, Pennsylvania State University (University Park, Pa.), 1969.
16. COWDEN, JAMES E., AND MORSE, EDWIN L. "The Relationship of Defensiveness to Responses on the Sex Inventory." *J Clin Psychol* 26(4):505–9 O '70. * (*PA* 45:4607)
17. RADEN, BERNARD. *Personality Characteristics of Social Workers Working With Unwed Mothers.* Doctor's thesis, Illinois Institute of Technology (Chicago, Ill.), 1971. (*DAI* 32:1858B)

CUMULATIVE NAME INDEX

Allen, R. M.: 1–2	Pacht, A. R.: 13
Cowden, J. E.: 13, 16	Pishkin, V.: 8–12
Galbraith, G. G.: 7, 14	Raden, B.: 17
Haupt, T. D.: 1–2, 6	Schoolman, D. A.: 15
Higgins, J. D.: 7	Thorne, F. C.: 3–6, 8–12
Kaplan, B. E.: 7	Tuton, K.: 7
Morse, E. L.: 16	

[1238]

Interest Inventory for Elementary Grades: George Washington University Series. Grades 4–6; 1941; IIEG; 11 scores: reading, movies, radio, games and toys, hobbies, things to own, school subjects, people, occupations, activities, total; Mitchell Dreese and Elizabeth Mooney; Center for Psychological Service. *

For additional information, see P:126 (4 references); for reviews by Harold D. Carter and Lee J. Cronbach, see 3:52 (1 reference).

REFERENCES THROUGH 1971

1. See 3:52.
2–5. See P:126.
6. TYLER, LEONA E. "The Antecedents of Two Varieties of Vocational Interests." *Genetic Psychol Monogr* 70:177–227 N '64. * (*PA* 39:10878)

CUMULATIVE NAME INDEX

Carter, H. D.: *rev*, 3:52	Stewart, L. H.: 4–5
Cronbach, L. J.: *rev*, 3:52	Tyler, L. E.: 2–3, 6
Mooney, E.: 1	

[1239]

Inter-Person Perception Test. Ages 6–13, 14 and over; 1969; IPPT; F. K. Heussenstamm and R. Hoepfner; Monitor. *

For additional information, see 7:91.

[1240]

***Interpersonal Check List.** Adults; 1955–73; ICL; for research use only; 4 summary scores (dominance, love, average intensity, acquiescence) or 20 detail scores (managerial, self-confident, competitive, critical, hostile, resentful, distrustful, self-critical, submissive, dependent, trusting, agreeable, friendly, sympathetic, nurturant, impressive, 4 level of intensity scores) at 1–2 levels of personality: descriptions by others, descriptions by self (including ego ideal); mimeographed manual (1973) and single copies of Form 4 (uncopyrighted) are only materials currently available; Rolfe LaForge, Timothy Leary (test), Robert Suczek (test), and Mervin Freedman (test); Rolfe LaForge. *

For additional information, see P:127 (70 references); for a review by P. M. Bentler, see 6:127 (39 references). For excerpts from related book reviews, see 5:B261 (6 excerpts).

REFERENCES THROUGH 1971

1–39. See 6:127.
40–109. See P:127.
110. PERR, HERBERT M. "Criteria Distinguishing Parents of Schizophrenic and Normal Children: An Initial Study With the Interpersonal Diagnostic System." *Arch Neurol & Psychiatry* 79:217–24 F '58. * (*PA* 33:6274)
111. SCHOPLER, JOHN HENRY. *The Relation of Patient-Therapist Personality Similarity to the Outcome of Psychotherapy.* Doctor's thesis, University of Colorado (Boulder, Colo.), 1958. (*DA* 19:2659)
112. ALTROCCHI, JOHN. "Dominance as a Factor in Interpersonal Choice and Perception." *J Abn & Social Psychol* 59:303–8 N '59. * (*PA* 34:5595)
113. SHARP, WILLIAM HARRY. *An Investigation of Certain Aspects of the Interaction Between a Group of Delinquent Boys and Their Mother-Figures.* Doctor's thesis, Ohio State University (Columbus, Ohio), 1959. (*DA* 20:2391)
114. SPILKA, BERNARD, AND LEWIS, MARVIN. "Empathy, Assimilative Projection, and Disowning Projection." *Psychol Rec* 9:99–102 Jl '59. * (*PA* 34:2615)
115. BULATAO, JAIME CARLOS. *The Direction of Aggression in Clinically Depressed Women.* Doctor's thesis, Fordham University (New York, N.Y.), 1961. (*DA* 22:1249)
116. DeLANGE, WALTER H. *Conceptions of Patient Role by Patients and Staff in a State Mental Hospital.* Doctor's thesis, University of Houston (Houston, Tex.), 1961. (*DA* 22:2461)
117. GARWOOD, DOROTHY SEMENOW. *Some Personality Factors Related to Creativity in Young Scientists.* Doctor's thesis, Claremont Graduate School (Claremont, Calif.), 1961. (*DA* 22:3273)
118. KOGAN, KATE L., AND JACKSON, JOAN K. "Some Role Perceptions of Wives of Alcoholics." *Psychol Rep* 9:119–24 Ag '61. *
119. KOTLAR, SALLY LEE. *Middle-Class Marital Roles—Ideal and Perceived in Relation to Adjustment in Marriage.* Doctor's

thesis, University of Southern California (Los Angeles, Calif.), 1961. (*DA* 22:1734)

120. LAFFERTY, JAMES CLAYTON. *A Study of Changes in Self-Concepts of Teachers Following Participation in a Consulting Mental Health Program.* Doctor's thesis, University of Michigan (Ann Arbor, Mich.), 1961. (*DA* 22:489)

121. LANTZ, DONALD LEROY. *The Relationships Between Self Concepts and Teaching Behavior Among Elementary Student Teachers.* Doctor's thesis, University of Minnesota (Minneapolis, Minn.), 1961. (*DA* 22:1510)

122. LUCKEY, ELEANORE BRAUN. "Perceptual Congruence of Self and Family Concepts as Related to Marital Interaction." *Sociometry* 24:234–50 S '61. * (*PA* 36:3IQ34L)

123. SMELSER, WILLIAM T. "Dominance as a Factor in Achievement and Perception in Cooperative Problem-Solving Interactions." *J Abn & Social Psychol* 62:535–42 My '61. * (*PA* 36:4CN3SS)

124. KOGAN, KATE L. "Endorsement of Social Desirability as a Meaningful Dimension of Response." *J Clin Psychol* 18:348–9 Jl '62. * (*PA* 39:1808)

125. COTTINGHAM, ALICE LUISA. *Defensive Organization of Personality and Its Relation to the Prediction of Progress in Therapy.* Doctor's thesis, New York University (New York, N.Y.), 1963. (*DA* 25:1332)

126. HELLER, KENNETH; MYERS, ROGER A.; AND KLINE, LINDA VIKAN. "Interviewer Behavior as a Function of Standardized Client Roles." *J Consult Psychol* 27:117–22 Ap '63. * (*PA* 37:8065)

127. MCDONALD, ROBERT L., AND CHRISTAKOS, ARTHUR C. "Relationship of Emotional Adjustment During Pregnancy to Obstetric Complications." *Am J Obstet & Gynecol* 86:341–8 Je 1 '63. *

128. BEDNAR, MARY ANN. *Changes in Social Perception in Adolescents During Group Psychotherapy.* Doctor's thesis, Washington University (St. Louis, Mo.), 1964. (*DA* 26:1166)

129. GARWOOD, DOROTHY SEMENOW. "Personality Factors Related to Creativity in Young Scientists." *J Abn & Social Psychol* 68:413–9 Ap '64. * (*PA* 39:1729)

130. LEVINSON, ALMA. *A Comparison of Concepts of Self and Parental Figures in Selected Groups of Under-, Average and High Achieving High School Boys: A Comparison of a Group of Underachievers With Groups of Average and Above Average Achievers Selected for Intelligence, Age and Grade.* Doctor's thesis, New York University (New York, N.Y.), 1964. (*DA* 25:1320)

131. MOGAR, ROBERT E., AND SAVAGE, CHARLES. "Personality Change Associated With Psychedelic (LSD) Therapy: A Preliminary Report." *Psychother Theory Res & Prac* 1:154–62 f '64. * (*PA* 40:1700)

132. SMITH, CLIFFORD ORVIS. *Interpersonal Responsivity in a Free Responding Verbal Conditioning Situation as a Function of Need for Approval, Expectancy of Experimenter Congeniality, and Evaluation of Task Performance.* Doctor's thesis, Stanford University (Stanford, Calif.), 1964. (*DA* 25:6667)

133. CHRISTOPHER, SAMUEL ALLAN. *Perceived Strength of Interpersonal Relationships and Parental Value Orientation as Factors Related to Academic Achievement.* Doctor's thesis, University of Pittsburgh (Pittsburgh, Pa.), 1965. (*DA* 27:666A)

134. FRIEDMAN, ALICE LISA. *The Effect of Personality and Interest Variables on Learning by Linear and Scrambled Methods of Programmed Instruction.* Doctor's thesis, New York University (New York, N.Y.), 1965. (*DA* 27:390A)

135. HEWITT, JACK LEE. *A Communications Approach to the Prediction and Alteration of Hypnotic Susceptibility.* Doctor's thesis, University of Kansas (Lawrence, Kan.), 1965. (*DA* 26:4075)

136. KEEFE, JEFFREY FRANCIS. *A Study of Two Seminary and Two Non-Seminary High School Groups on Selected Aspects of Maturity.* Doctor's thesis, Fordham University (New York, N.Y.), 1965. (*DA* 26:4076)

137. LANTZ, DONALD L. "Relationship Between Classroom Emotional Climate and Concepts of Self, Others, and Ideal Among Elementary Student Teachers." *J Ed Res* 59:80–3 O '65. * (*PA* 40:3408)

138. SWARR, RALPH ROHRER. *An Exploratory Study of Masculinity and the Attribution of Dominance and Love to Parents.* Doctor's thesis, Michigan State University (East Lansing, Mich.), 1965. (*DA* 26:4818)

139. LAMONT, JAMES F. "Repressors and Sensitizers as Described by Themselves and Their Peers." *J Personality* 34:224–40 Je '66. *

140. LONGABAUGH, RICHARD. "The Structure of Interpersonal Behavior." *Sociometry* 29:441–60 D '66. * (*PA* 41:4461)

141. MILLER, LOUIS IRVING. *Familial Role Typology, Accuracy of Perception, and Mutual Needs Among Pre-Nuptial Partners.* Doctor's thesis, University of Southern California (Los Angeles, Calif.), 1966. (*DA* 27:265A)

142. PRESTON, CAROLINE E. "Traits Endorsed by Older Non-retired and Retired Subjects." *J Gerontol* 21:261–4 Ap '66. *

143. ROTH, HERBERT SAMUEL. *Personal and Demographic Characteristics Associated With L-I-D Response Bias of Domiciled Veterans on an Institutional Interest Inventory.* Doctor's thesis, University of Kansas (Lawrence, Kan.), 1966. (*DA* 28:1209B)

144. SHERIN, CAROLYN RICHARDS. *Some Relationships Among*

Popularity, Friendship Choice, and Personality Variables. Doctor's thesis, University of Miami (Coral Gables, Fla.), 1966. (*DA* 27:1931A)

145. VANDERHOST, LEONETTE LOUISE. *An Investigation of Displacement and Identification as Variables Affecting Academic Achievement.* Doctor's thesis, New York University (New York, N.Y.), 1966. (*DA* 27:971A)

146. FORSLEFF, LOUISE PETERSON. *A Study of Counselor-Supervisor and Counselor-Client Dyadic Relationships.* Doctor's thesis, Michigan State University (East Lansing, Mich.), 1967. (*DA* 28:1677A)

147. GRIFFIN, CAROL LEE. *Dominance in Marriage and the Post-Hospital Adjustment of Male Psychiatric Patients.* Doctor's thesis, Boston University (Boston, Mass.), 1967. (*DA* 28:2136B)

148. GUERNEY, BERNARD, JR., AND BURTON, JEAN L. "Comparison of Typical Peer, Self, and Ideal Percepts Related to College Achievement." *J Social Psychol* 73:253–9 D '67. * (*PA* 42:4568)

149. HILL, FREDERICK E. *The Attraction of Upper-Class and Under-Class Vocationally Undecided Male Students Towards a Counseling Relationship.* Doctor's thesis, Michigan State University (East Lansing, Mich.), 1967. (*DA* 29:122A)

150. KOTLAR, SALLY L. "Role Theory in Marriage Counseling." *Sociol & Social Res* 52:50–62 O '67. * (*PA* 42:1007)

151. LANTZ, DONALD L. "The Relationship of University Supervisors and Supervising Teachers' Ratings to Observed Student Teachers' Behavior." *Am Ed Res J* 4:279–88 My '67. * (*PA* 41:14210)

152. SEEGARS, JAMES E., JR. *Dogmatism and College Achievement.* Doctor's thesis, University of Kentucky (Lexington, Ky.), 1967. (*DAI* 30:1827A)

153. SIMMONS, DALE D. "Self Concept, Occupational Stereotype, and Engineering Career Plans." *Psychol Rep* 20:514 Ap '67. * (*PA* 41:9477)

154. STEWART, RALPH H. "Birth Order and Dependency." *J Pers & Social Psychol* 6:192–4 Je '67. * (*PA* 41:10350)

155. BROWN, ELEANOR JESSEN. *Some Psychological Differences Between Neglected and Delinquent Adolescent Girls.* Doctor's thesis, University of Oklahoma (Norman, Okla.), 1968. (*DA* 29:1503B)

156. CONLEY, SUSAN JANE. *Strategies of Maneuvers During the Acquaintance Process.* Doctor's thesis, Michigan State University (East Lansing, Mich.), 1968. (*DAI* 30:378B)

157. CRITES, KENNETH ROY. *Interpersonal Concerns as a Function of Perceived Parental Identification and Influence.* Doctor's thesis, Catholic University of America (Washington, D.C.), 1968. (*DA* 29:4842B)

158. DRUDGE, WALTER JOHN. *The Relationship Between Self-Spouse Perceptions and Marital Satisfaction.* Doctor's thesis, Case Western Reserve University (Cleveland, Ohio), 1968. (*DA* 29:4558A)

159. DUPONT, ROBERT L., JR., AND GRUNEBAUM, HENRY. "Willing Victims: The Husbands of Paranoid Women." *Am J Psychiatry* 125:151–9 Ag '68. * (*PA* 42:17437)

160. GILBERT, WAYNE MASON. *Toward the Development of an Animal Analog of the Leary Test.* Doctor's thesis, University of Kansas (Lawrence, Kan.), 1968. (*DA* 29:2632B)

161. GRAHAM, JACK ARNOLD. *The Effect of the Use of Counselor Positive Responses to Positive Perceptions of Mate in Marriage Counseling.* Doctor's thesis, Arizona State University (Tempe, Ariz.), 1968. (*DA* 28:3504A)

162. GUERNEY, BERNARD G., JR.; SHAPIRO, ELLEN B.; AND STOVER, LILLIAN. "Parental Perceptions of Maladjusted Children: Agreement Between Parents, and Relation to Mother-Child Interaction." *J Genetic Psychol* 113:215–25 D '68. * (*PA* 43:4207)

163. HAMILTON, DAVID LEWIS. *A Multivariate Analysis of Personological Differences in Response to Unfavorable Evaluations of One's Self.* Doctor's thesis, University of Illinois (Urbana, Ill.), 1968. (*DAI* 30:388A)

164. PESKIN, HARVEY. "The Duration of Normal Menses as a Psychosomatic Phenomenon." *Psychosom Med* 30:378–89 Jl–Ag '68. * (*PA* 43:2882)

165. POSAVAC, EMIL J., AND TRIANDIS, HARRY C. "Personality Characteristics, Race, and Grades as Determinants of Interpersonal Attitudes." *J Social Psychol* 76:227–42 D '68. * (*PA* 43:4035)

166. RHOLL, KEITH NORRIS. *A Study of Relationships Between Occupational and Marital Roles and Marital Adjustment.* Doctor's thesis, University of Southern California (Los Angeles, Calif.), 1968. (*DA* 29:2375A)

167. ROMANO, EDITH. *The Impact of Mental Retardation Upon the Self Concept of the Mother: A Comparative Study of the Self-Regarding Attitudes of Mothers of Trainable Retarded Children and Selected Mothers of Nonretarded Children.* Doctor's thesis, Syracuse University (Syracuse, N.Y.), 1968. (*DA* 29:1510B)

168. SCHEINER, SUZANNE BEATRICE. *Differential Perception of Personality Characteristics in Cross-Cultural Interaction.* Doctor's thesis, University of California (Los Angeles, Calif.), 1968. (*DAI* 30:477B)

169. SPENCER, ROBERT LOWELL. *The Interpersonal Check List as an Instrument in Person Perception.* Doctor's thesis,

University of Oklahoma (Norman, Okla.), 1968. (*DA* 29: 3922B)

170. Spero, Jeannette R. *A Study of the Relationship Between Selected Functional Menstrual Disorders and Interpersonal Conflict.* Doctor's thesis, New York University (New York, N.Y.), 1968. (*DA* 29:2905A)

171. Stabenau, James R., and Pollin, William. "Comparative Life History Differences of Families of Schizophrenics, Delinquents, and 'Normals.' " *Am J Psychiatry* 124:1526–34 My '68. * (*PA* 42:12507)

172. Alumbaugh, Richard V., and Brown, G. Duane. "A Comparison of Diagnostic and Interpersonal Labels as Perceived by the 'Criminally Insane' and Psychiatric Patients." *J Clin Psychol* 25(4):391–3 O '69. * (*PA* 44:10712)

173. Brown, Jerome Banks. *Some Factors in Response to Criticism in Group Therapy.* Doctor's thesis, University of Houston (Houston, Tex.), 1969. (*DAI* 30:376B)

174. Collier, Boy N., Jr. "Comparisons Between Adolescents With and Without Diabetes." *Personnel & Guid J* 47(7):679–84 Mr '69. * (*PA* 43:12806)

175. Collier, Boy N., Jr. "Interpersonal Traits of Secondary School Adolescents With and Without Diabetes." *Rehabil Counsel B* 13(2):190–6 D '69. *

176. Crandall, James E. "Self-Perception and Interpersonal Attraction as Related to Tolerance-Intolerance of Ambiguity." *J Personality* 37(1):127–40 Mr '69. * (*PA* 43:12963)

177. Doherty, Anne. *The Relationship of Dependency and Perception of Parents to the Development of Feminine Sex Role and Conscience.* Doctor's thesis, Catholic University of America (Washington, D.C.), 1969. (*DAI* 30:2415B)

178. Garner, Gwen Frances. *Patterns of Communication in a Training School for Adolescent Girls.* Doctor's thesis, University of Oklahoma (Norman, Okla.), 1969. (*DAI* 30:3866B)

179. Hamilton, David L. "Measures of Self-Esteem, Dominance, and Dogmatism: Convergent and Discriminant Validity." Abstract. *Proc 77th Ann Conv Am Psychol Assn* 4(1):127–8 '69. * (*PA* 43:17517)

180. Hamilton, David L. "Responses to Cognitive Inconsistencies: Personality, Discrepancy Level, and Response Stability." *J Pers & Social Psychol* 11(4):351–62 Ap '69. * (*PA* 43:11287)

181. Hull, Joshua Shelton, III. *An Investigation of Identification of Male College Students With Their Fathers as a Variable Influencing Vocational Interests and Vocational Counseling.* Doctor's thesis, Michigan State University (East Lansing, Mich.), 1969. (*DAI* 30:4775A)

182. Kamerschen, Karen Sue. *Multiple Therapy: Variables Relating to Co-Therapist Satisfaction.* Doctor's thesis, Michigan State University (East Lansing, Mich.), 1969. (*DAI* 31:915B)

183. Lomont, James F.; Gilner, Frank H.; Spector, Norman J.; and Skinner, Kathryn K. "Group Assertion Training and Group Insight Therapies." *Psychol Rep* 25(2):463–70 O '69. * (*PA* 44:5255)

184. Padover, Ann Feingold. *Impact on Attitudes, Personality Factors, and Behavior of an N.D.E.A. Summer Institute for Teachers and Other Professional School Personnel of Disadvantaged Youth.* Doctor's thesis, University of Michigan (Ann Arbor, Mich.), 1969. (*DAI* 30:4780B)

185. Park, James, and Eberlein, Larry. "Self-Ideal Congruence and Flexibility in Counselling." *West Psychologist* 1(1):39–45 S '69. * (*PA* 45:8954)

186. Rice, Patricia Lawgdon Kintner. *The Modification of Interpersonal Roles.* Doctor's thesis, West Virginia University (Morgantown, W.Va.), 1969. (*DAI* 30:4797B)

187. Salas, R. G., and Jones, P. R. "A Balanced Version of the Leary Interpersonal Checklist." *Austral Psychologist* 3(3): 181–5 Mr '69. * (*PA* 45:6365)

188. Smith, Horace Lewis. *Predictive Ability of Elementary Teachers: The Relationship Between Selected Personality Variables and the Ability to Judge Ratings Pupils Make of Themselves and Others.* Doctor's thesis, Michigan State University (East Lansing, Mich.), 1969. (*DAI* 30:1439A)

189. Beard, Bruce H., and Pishkin, Vladimir. "Self-Concept Changes in Training Medical and Nursing Students." *Dis Nerv System* 31(9):616–23 S '70. * (*PA* 45:6419)

190. Cumming, Gordon Hugh. *A Study of Adjustment to a Family Crisis in the Form of a Disability to the Male Wage Earner.* Doctor's thesis, University of Southern California (Los Angeles, Calif.), 1970. (*DAI* 31:3667A)

191. Curtis, George; Fogel, Max; McEvoy, Donald; and Zarate, Carlos. "Urine and Plasma Corticosteroids, Psychological Tests, and Effectiveness of Psychological Defenses." *J Psychiatric Res* 7(4):237–47 Jl '70. * (*PA* 45:5859)

192. Edmunds, Paul K., Jr. *Committee Chairmen and Doctoral Candidates: Their Expectations and Perceptions of the Role of Each.* Doctor's thesis, Arizona State University (Tempe, Ariz.), 1970. (*DAI* 31:2043A)

193. Hamilton, David L. "Personality Attributes Related to Response Preferences in Resolving Inconsistency." *J Personality* 38(1):134–45 Mr '70. * (*PA* 44:14597)

194. Huff, Frederick W. "The Desensitization of a Homosexual." *Behav Res & Ther* (England) 8(1):99–102 F '70. *

195. Kobos, Joseph C. *An Exploration of Aspects of the*

Client-Therapist Relationship in Group Psychotherapy. Doctor's thesis, Ohio University (Athens, Ohio), 1970. (*DAI* 31:7601B)

196. Lange, Donald E. "Validation of the Orthogonal Dimensions Underlying the ICL and the Octant Constellations Assumed To Be Their Measure." *J Proj Tech & Pers Assess* 34(6):519–27 D '70. * (*PA* 45:8245)

197. Lester, David, and Orloff, Lee F. "Personality Correlates of the Duration of Menses." *Psychol Rep* 26(2):650 Ap '70. * (*PA* 44:20443)

198. Murphy, Donald Clarence. *Verbal and Nonverbal Communication in High and Low Marital Adjustment.* Doctor's thesis, Florida State University (Tallahassee, Fla.), 1970. (*DAI* 31:4919A)

199. Nelson, Carol M. *The Relationship Between the Interpersonal Check List and a Self Report of Roommate Satisfaction in a Women's Residential Hall.* Master's thesis, University of Wyoming (Laramie, Wyo.), 1970.

200. Palmer, John, and Byrne, Donn. "Attraction Toward Dominant and Submissive Strangers: Similarity Versus Complementarity." *J Exp Res Personality* 4(2):108–15 F '70. * (*PA* 44:10293)

201. Stabenau, James R., and Pollin, William. "Experiential Differences for Schizophrenics as Compared With Their Non-Schizophrenic Siblings: Twin and Family Studies," pp. 94–126. In *Life History Research in Psychopathology.* Edited by Merrill Roff and David F. Ricks. Minneapolis, Minn.: University of Minnesota Press, 1970. Pp. viii, 321. *

202. Thommes, Martin John. *Changes in Values, Perceptions, and Academic Performance of College Freshmen Underachievers in a Remedial Program.* Doctor's thesis, United States International University (San Diego, Calif.), 1970. (*DAI* 31:2969B)

203. Valek, J., and Kuhn, E. "Stress-Induced Changes of Carbohydrate and Lipid Metabolism in Coronary Heart Disease (CHD)." *Psychother & Psychosom* (Switzerland) 18(1–6): 275–80 '70. * (*PA* 47:5524)

204. Wiener, Daniel J. "Failure of Personality Variables to Mediate Interpersonal Attraction." *Psychol Rep* 26(3):784–6 Je '70. * (*PA* 45:639)

205. Bain, Earle. "Values and Attitudes of Militia Officer Cadets," pp. 255–72. In *Second Annual Symposium: Psychology in the Air Force, 20–22 April 1971.* Edited by Hal W. Hendrick. Colorado Springs, Colo.: United States Air Force Academy, [1971]. Pp. x, 409. *

206. Cohen, Charles P.; Johnson, Dale L.; and Hanson, Philip G. "Interpersonal Changes Among Psychiatric Patients in Human Relations Training." *J Pers Assess* 35(5):472–9 O '71. * (*PA* 47:9040)

207. Cone, John D. "Social Desirability, Marital Satisfaction, and Concomitant Perceptions of Self and Spouse." *Psychol Rep* 28(1):173–4 F '71. * (*PA* 46:6673)

208. Counselman, Eleanor Frey. *A Comparison of the Self-Concepts, Self-Acceptance, Ideal Self-Concepts, and Career Woman Stereotypes of Career- and Non-Career-Oriented College Senior Women.* Doctor's thesis, Boston University (Boston, Mass.), 1971. (*DAI* 32:1996A)

209. Eberlein, Larry, and Park, James. "Self-Concept/Ideal-Self-Concept Congruence and Rated Effectiveness of Counselor Trainees." *Counselor Ed & Sup* 10(2):126–32 W '71. * (*PA* 47:1643)

210. Eberlein, Larry; Park, James; and Matheson, Wayne. "Self-Ideal Congruence in Five Occupational Groups." *Alberta J Ed Res* (Canada) 17(2):95–103 Je '71. * (*PA* 47: 4786)

211. Frost, Barry P. "A Semantic Differential Analysis of the Leary Adjectival Check List." *J Clin Psychol* 27(3):372–5 Jl '71. * (*PA* 47:4824)

212. Gynther, Malcolm D. "A Technique for Assessing Covert Interpersonal Perceptions." *Personality* 2(4):299–304 w '71. * (*PA* 48:7146)

213. Hamilton, David L. "A Comparative Study of Five Methods of Assessing Self-Esteem, Dominance, and Dogmatism." *Ed & Psychol Meas* 31(2):441–52 su '71. * (*PA* 46:10888)

214. Kinsinger, John Ray. *The Relationship Between Lethality of Suicidal Intentions and Assertive, Aggressive, and Hostile Traits.* Doctor's thesis, Southwestern Medical School (Dallas, Tex.), 1971. (*DAI* 31:7600B)

215. Lange, Donald E. "An EDP System Package for Scoring the Interpersonal Check List." *Ed & Psychol Meas* 31(3): 775–6 au '71. *

216. Liberman, Robert. "Reinforcement of Cohesiveness in Group Therapy: Behavioral and Personality Changes." *Arch Gen Psychiatry* 25(2):168–77 Ag '71. *

217. Liberman, Robert Paul. "Behavioural Group Therapy: A Controlled Clinical Study." *Brit J Psychiatry* 119(552):535–44 N '71. * (*PA* 48:3131)

218. McKenna-Hartung, Sheila; Hartung, Jurgen R.; and Baxter, James C. "Self and Ideal Self-Concept in a Drug-Using Subculture." *J Pers Assess* 35(5):463–71 O '71. * (*PA* 47:8859)

219. Rutan, James Scott, Jr. *Self Acceptance Change as a Function of a Short Term Small Group Experience.* Doctor's thesis, Boston University (Boston, Mass.), 1971. (*DAI* 32: 2194A)

220. SHEEHAN, PETER W. "Countering Preconceptions About Hypnosis: An Objective Index of Involvement With the Hypnotist." *J Abn Psychol* 78(3):299–322 D '71. * (*PA* 47:8116)

221. SILVER, ALBERT W., AND MOOD, DARLENE W. "Group Homogeneity, Conformity, and Flexibility of Interpersonal Perceptions." *Comparative Group Studies* 2(1):25–35 F '71. * (*PA* 47:4890)

222. TEASDALE, JOHN D., AND HINKSON, JUDY. "Stimulant Drugs: Perceived Effect on the Interpersonal Behavior of Dependent Patients." *Int J Addic* 6(3):407–17 S '71. * (*PA* 48:1232)

223. TRUCKENMILLER, JAMES LEROY. *Equivalence of Personality Structure in Leary's Interpersonal System of Diagnosis.* Doctor's thesis, West Virginia University (Morgantown, W.Va.), 1971. (*DAI* 32:6663B)

224. WALHOOD, DALE S., AND KLOPFER, WALTER G. "Congruence Between Self-Concept and Public Image." *J Consult & Clin Psychol* 37(1):148–50 Ag '71. * (*PA* 47:906)

CUMULATIVE NAME INDEX

[1241]

★**Interpersonal Communication Inventory.** Grades 9–16 and adults; 1969–71; ICI; Millard J. Bienvenu, Sr.; the Author. *

REFERENCES THROUGH 1971

1. BIENVENU, MILLARD J., SR. "An Interpersonal Communication Inventory." *J Commun* 21(4):381–8 D '71. * (*PA* 48:7171)

CUMULATIVE NAME INDEX

Bienvenu, M. J.: 1

[1242]

★**The Interpersonal Orientation Scale.** College and adults; 1965–71; IOS; 5 scores: general orientation, coercion, masking, coaxing, postponing; John Douglas Alcorn, Everett Duane Erb, and James Barrett Davis; John D. Alcorn. *

REFERENCES THROUGH 1971

1. ALCORN, JOHN, D. "Construct Validation of the Interpersonal Orientation Scale." *South J Ed Res* 1:105–20 Ap '67. *
2. ALCORN, JOHN D., AND ERB, EVERETT D. "Interpersonal Relationship Preferences of Educators." *Personnel & Guid J* 45:463–8 Ja '67. *
3. IGLINSKY, CLYDE LEE. *Intellectual and Non-Intellectual Factors Affecting Academic Success of College Freshmen.* Doctor's thesis, East Texas State University (Commerce, Tex.), 1968. (*DA* 29:1423A)
4. LOW, GARY ROY. *A Study of Counselor Trainee Changes in Two Types of Practicum.* Doctor's thesis, East Texas State University (Commerce, Tex.), 1969. (*DAI* 30:5240A)

5. Bost, David L. "Changes in Altruistic Orientations and Theory Preferences of Beginning Counselors." *Counselor Ed & Sup* 9(2):116–21 w '70. * (*PA* 46:9419)

6. Shafer, Bill Wayne. *A Study of Behavioral and Perceptual Changes in Counselor Trainees as a Result of Resident and Nonresident Practicum Programs.* Doctor's thesis, East Texas State University (Commerce, Tex.), 1970. (*DAI* 31: 4475A)

7. Stelter, Mervyn Walter. *Changes in Self-Perception, Interpersonal Orientation, and View of the Nature of Man of Residence Hall Personnel.* Doctor's thesis, East Texas State University (Commerce, Tex.), 1970. (*DAI* 31:4476A)

8. Iglinsky, Clyde Lee, and Wiant, Harry V., Jr. "Non-Intellectual Factors in Academic Success." *Improving Col & Univ Teach* 19(4):297–8 au '71. *

9. Johnson, Algot Robert. *An Investigation of the Relationship Among Selected Personality Traits in Beginning Counselors.* Doctor's thesis, Oklahoma State University (Stillwater, Okla.), 1971. (*DAI* 33:2105A)

CUMULATIVE NAME INDEX

Alcorn, J. D.: 1–2
Bost, D. L.: 5
Erb, E. D.: 2
Iglinsky, C. L.: 3, 8
Johnson, A. R.: 9
Low, G. R.: 4
Shafer, B. W.: 6
Stelter, M. W.: 7
Wiant, H. V.: 8

[1243]

Interpersonal Perception Method. Married couples and other 2-person or 2-group situations; 1966; IPM; 6 scores: interdependence and autonomy, warm concern and support, disparagement-disappointment, contentions, contradiction and confusion, extreme denial of autonomy; R. D. Laing, H. Phillipson, and A. R. Lee; distributed by NFER Publishing Co. Ltd. [England]. * (United States distributor: Springer Publishing Co., Inc.)

For additional information, reviews by Bernard I. Murstein and Norman D. Sundberg, and excerpted reviews by Michael Argyle, Inge Bergmann, Fay Fransella, and N. L. Gage, see 7:92 (1 reference); see also P:128 (1 reference).

REFERENCES THROUGH 1971

1. See P:128.
2. See 7:92.
3. Cardillo, Joseph P. "Effects of Teaching Communication Roles on Interpersonal Perception and Self-Concept in Disturbed Marriages." Abstract. *Proc 79th Ann Conv Am Psychol Assn* 6(1):441–2 '71. * (*PA* 46:5279)
4. Cardillo, Joseph Peter. *The Effects of Teaching Communication Roles on Interpersonal Perception and Self-Concept in Disturbed Marriages.* Doctor's thesis, George Peabody College for Teachers (Nashville, Tenn.), 1971. (*DAI* 32:2392B)

CUMULATIVE NAME INDEX

Argyle, M.: *exc,* 7:92
Bergmann, I.: *exc,* 7:92
Cardillo, J. P.: 3–4
Fransella, F.: *exc,* 7:92
Gage, N. L.: *exc,* 7:92
Kotkas, L. J.: 2
Laing, R. D.: 1
Lee, A. R.: 1
Murstein, B. I.: *rev,* 7:92
Phillipson, H.: 1
Sundberg, N. D.: *rev,* 7:92

[1244]

*The Inventory of College Activities. College; 1962–71; ICA; measure of characteristics of the college environment likely to have some influence upon student development; 33 scores: peer environment (competitiveness vs. cooperativeness, organized dating, independence, cohesiveness, informal dating, femininity, drinking vs. religiousness, musical and artistic activity, leisure time, career indecision, regularity of sleeping habits, use of the library, conflict with regulations, student employment, use of automobiles), classroom environment (involvement in the class, verbal aggressiveness, extraversion of the instructor, familiarity with the instructor, organization in the classroom, severity of grading), administrative environment (severity of administrative policy against drinking, against aggression, against heterosexual activity, against cheating), college image (academic competitiveness, concern for the individual student, school spirit, permissiveness, snobbishness, emphasis on athletics, flexibility of the curriculum,

emphasis on social life); Alexander W. Astin; NCS Interpretive Scoring Systems. *

For additional information and a review by James V. Mitchell, Jr., see 7:93 (7 references). For excerpts from related book reviews, see 7:B50 (2 excerpts).

REFERENCES THROUGH 1971

1–7. See 7:93.
8. Astin, Alexander W. "Two Approaches to Measuring Students' Perceptions of Their College Environment." *J Col Stud Personnel* 12(3):169–72 My '71. * (*PA* 46:11458)
9. Astin, Alexander W., and Bayer, Alan E. "Antecedents and Consequents of Disruptive Campus Protests." *Meas & Eval Guid* 4(1):18–30 Ap '71. *
10. Creager, John A. "Academic Achievement and Institutional Environments: Two Research Strategies." *J Exp Ed* 40(2):9–23 w '71. * (*PA* 47:11757)
11. Feldman, Kenneth A. "Measuring College Environments: Some Uses of Path Analysis." *Am Ed Res J* 8(1):51–70 Ja '71. *
12. Lange, Arthur John, Jr. *A Descriptive Study of Differences Among College Freshman Subcultures on Selected Attitudes, Environmental Perceptions, Behaviors, and Attainment of Certain Goals.* Doctor's thesis, American University (Washington, D.C.), 1971. (*DAI* 32:1856A)

CUMULATIVE NAME INDEX

Astin, A. W.: 1–5, 8–9
Bayer, A. E.: 9
Creager, J. A.: 10
Feldman, K. A.: 11
Friis, R. H.: 6
Hedegard, J. M.: *exc,* 7:B50
Katz, J.: *exc,* 7:B50
Lange, A. J.: 12
Madden, H. L.: 7
Mitchell, J. V.: *rev,* 7:93
Panos, R.: 1
Panos, R. J.: 5
Tupes, E. C.: 7

[1245]

An Inventory of Factors STDCR. Grades 9–16 and adults; 1934–45; STDCR; 5 scores: social introversion-extraversion, thinking introversion-extraversion, depression, cycloid disposition, rhathymia; J. P. Guilford; Sheridan Psychological Services, Inc. *

For additional information, see P:130 (10 references); see also 6:128 (17 references) and 5:78 (28 references); for a review by Hubert E. Brogden, see 4:59 (17 references); for a review by H. J. Eysenck, see 3:55 (10 references); for a review by R. A. Brotemarkle, see 3:45.

REFERENCES THROUGH 1971

1–10. See 3:55.
11–27. See 4:59.
28–55. See 5:78.
56–72. See 6:128.
73–82. See P:130.
83. Richardson, LaVange Hunt. "A Personality Study of Stutterers and Non-Stutterers." *J Speech Disorders* 9:152–60 Mr '44. * (*PA* 19:716)
84. White, Melany. "An Investigation of the Secondary-Order Domain of the Nine Primary Factors Described in 'The Dimensions of Temperament' by L. L. Thurstone." *B Nat Inst Personnel Res* (South Africa) 1:4–13 Mr '49. *
85. Storment, Charlyne Townsend. "Personality and Heart Disease." *Psychosom Med* 13:304–13 S–O '51. * (*PA* 26:3584)
86. Healy, Irene, and Borg, Walter R. "Personality and Vocational Interests of Successful and Unsuccessful Nursing School Freshmen." *Ed & Psychol Meas* 12:767–75 w '52. * (*PA* 27:6221)
87. Lorenz, Thomas H.; Calden, George; and Ousley, Joseph L. "A Study of Effects of Isoniazid on the Emotions of Tuberculous Patients." *Am R Tuberc* 68:523–34 O '53. * (*PA* 30:7579)
88. Shrock, John G. *Functions of Methodology in Adult Education Ceramics Courses.* Doctor's thesis, Stanford University (Stanford, Calif.), 1953. (*DA* 13:711)
89. Bitner, Harold Miller. *Ethnic Inter-Group Differences in Personality, General Culture, Academic Ability, and Interests in a Geographically Restricted Area.* Doctor's thesis, Ohio State University (Columbus, Ohio), 1954. (*DA* 20:772)
90. Spilka, Bernard. "Relationships Between Certain Aspects of Personality and Some Vocal Effects of Delayed Speech Feedback." *J Speech & Hearing Disorders* 19:491–503 D '54. * (*PA* 29:5326)
91. Denton, J. C., and Taylor, Calvin W. "A Factor Analysis of Mental Abilities and Personality Traits." *Psychometrika* 20:75–81 Mr '55. * (*PA* 29:8422)
92. Getzels, J. W., and Guba, E. G. "Role Conflict and Personality." *J Personality* 24:74–85 S '55. * (*PA* 30:5758)

93. Riggs, Margaret M., and Kaess, Walter. "Personality Differences Between Volunteers and Nonvolunteers." *J Psychol* 40:229–45 O '55. * (*PA* 30:6918)

94. Tresselt, M. E. "The Effects of Background Contrast Upon the Time-Error in Visual Extents and Certain Characteristics Related to the Judgments." *J General Psychol* 52:75–82 Ja '55. * (*PA* 30:2195)

95. Herring, Fred H. "Response During Anesthesia and Surgery; Effect of Psychological Factors." *Psychosom Med* 18:243–51 My–Je 56. * (*PA* 31:5007)

96. Seymour, John H. *Some Changes in Psychometric, Perceptual and Motor Performance as a Function of Sleep Deprivation.* Doctor's thesis, New York University (New York, N.Y.), 1956. (*DA* 16:2216)

97. Beach, Leslie Robert. *The Relationship Between Sociability, Satisfaction, and Academic Achievement in Various Types of Learning Situations.* Doctor's thesis, University of Michigan (Ann Arbor, Mich.), 1957. (*DA* 18:1334)

98. Beloff, Halla. "The Structure and Origin of the Anal Character." *Genetic Psychol Monogr* 55:141–72 My '57. * (*PA* 33:3387)

99. Diers, Helen A. *Factors in the Understanding of Others.* Doctor's thesis, Columbia University (New York, N.Y.), 1957. (*DA* 17:1594)

100. Eppley, Mary Vineita (Boots). *The Relationship of Personal Factors and Reading Performance to Academic Achievement of Selected Oregon State College Students.* Doctor's thesis, Oregon State University (Corvallis, Ore.), 1958. (*DA* 19:730)

101. Hildebrand, H. P. "A Factorial Study of Introversion-Extraversion." *Brit J Psychol* 49:1–11 F '58. * (*PA* 33:8632)

102. Laverty, S. G. "Sodium Amytal and Extraversion." *J Neurol Neurosurg & Psychiatry* (England) 21:50–4 F '58. * (*PA* 33:5760)

103. Levin, Gerald Richard. *Extraversion and Benefits From Spaced Practice.* Doctor's thesis, Columbia University (New York, N.Y.), 1958. (*DA* 18:1865)

104. Shagass, Charles, and Kerenyi, Albert B. "Neurophysiologic Studies of Personality." *J Nerv & Mental Dis* 126:141–7 F '58. * (*PA* 33:8565)

105. Shagass, Charles, and Lipowski, Zbigniew J. "Effect of Methedrine on Critical Flicker Fusion and Its Relation to Personality and Effect." *J Nerv & Mental Dis* 127:407–16 N '58. * (*PA* 34:1564)

106. Olson, Norman. *An Investigation of Orality Among Schizophrenics, Psychoneurotics, and Normals.* Doctor's thesis, Temple University (Philadelphia, Pa.), 1959. (*DA* 20:3388)

107. Sloane, R. B.; Habib, A.; Eveson, M. B.; and Payne, R. W. "Some Behavioural and Other Correlates of Cholesterol Metabolism." *J Psychosom Res* (England) 5:183–90 Je '61. * (*PA* 36:5HN83S)

108. Mogel, Steve. *A Comparison of Dysthymics and Hysterics in the Conditioning and Extinction of a Finger Withdrawal Response.* Doctor's thesis, University of Kentucky (Lexington, Ky.), 1963. (*DAI* 30:2932B)

109. Brown, D. G., and Young, A. J. "Body Image and Susceptibility to Contact Dermatitis." *Brit J Med Psychol* 38:261–7 S '65. *

110. Liberty, Paul G., Jr.; Doughtie, Eugene B., Jr.; and Embree, Royal B., Jr. "Value and Trait Comparisons of Clinical and Counseling Students: An Exploratory Study." *Psychol Rep* 17:157–8 Ag '65. * (*PA* 40:846)

111. Pedersen, Darhl M. "The Measurement of Individual Differences in Perceived Personality-Trait Relationships and Their Relation to Certain Determinants." *J Social Psychol* 65:233–58 Ap '65. * (*PA* 39:14976)

112. Bentz, V. Jon. Chap. 7, "The Sears Experience in the Investigation, Description, and Prediction of Executive Behavior," pp. 147–205; critique by Ross Stagner, pp. 206–27. In *Measuring Executive Effectiveness.* Edited by Frederic R. Wickert and Dalton E. McFarland. New York: Appleton-Century-Crofts, 1967. Pp. viii, 242. *

113. Goodstein, Michael A. "Relationship Between Verbal Operant Conditioning and Extraversion-Introversion." *Psychol Rep* 20:1036 Je '67. * (*PA* 41:14648, title only)

114. Sattler, Jerome M., and Brandon, Ronald A. "Early Recollections Related to Anxiety and Introversion-Extroversion." Abstract. *J Consult Psychol* 31:107 F '67. * (*PA* 41:4588, title only)

115. Bentz, V. Jon. Chap. 3, "The Sears Experience in the Investigation, Description and Prediction of Executive Behavior," pp. 59–152. In *Predicting Managerial Success.* Edited by John A. Myers, Jr. Ann Arbor, Mich.: Foundation for Research on Human Behavior, April 1968. Pp. v, 173. *

116. Abramowitz, Stephen I. "Locus of Control and Self-Reported Depression Among College Students." *Psychol Rep* 25(1):149–50 Ag '69. * (*PA* 44:3597)

117. Eysenck, H. J.; White, P. O.; and Soueiff, M. I. Chap. 18. "Factors in the Guilford Personality Inventory," pp. 229–38. In *Personality Structure and Measurement,* see 118. *

118. Eysenck, Hans J., and Eysenck, Sybil B. G. *Personality Structure and Measurement.* San Diego, Calif.: Robert R. Knapp, Publisher, 1969. Pp. xiii, 365. *

119. Pruit, Sherman A. *The Relationship Between Personality Factors and Football Ability.* Master's thesis, Texas Tech University (Lubbock, Tex.), 1969.

120. Rose, Norman Harold. *The Relationship Between Sociability and Type and Rate of Interaction.* Doctor's thesis, Florida State University (Tallahassee, Fla.), 1969. (*DAI* 30:1807A)

121. Soueiff, M. I.; Eysenck, H. J.; and White, P. O. Chap. 15, "A Joint Factorial Study of the Guilford, Cattell and Eysenck Scales," pp. 171–93. In *Personality Structure and Measurement,* see 118. *

122. White, P. O.; Eysenck, H. J.; and Soueiff, M. I. Chap. 19, "Combined Analysis of Cattell, Eysenck and Guilford Factors," pp. 239–50. In *Personality Structure and Measurement,* see 118. *

123. Blessing, Patton G. *Personality Factors STDCR and Its Relationship to Football Ability of High School Football Linebackers.* Master's thesis, Texas Tech University (Lubbock, Tex.), 1970.

124. Soueiff, M. I., and El-Sayed, A. M. "Curvilinear Relationships Between Creative Thinking Abilities and Personality Trait Variables." *Acta Psychologica* (Netherlands) 34(1):1–21 S '70. * (*PA* 45:2374)

125. Sells, S. B.; Demaree, R. G.; and Will, Donald P., Jr. "Dimensions of Personality: 2, Separate Factor Structures in Guilford and Cattell Trait Markers." *Multiv Behav Res* 6(2):135–85 Ap '71. * (*PA* 47:4821)

CUMULATIVE NAME INDEX

[1246]

★The "Is of Identity" Test. Grades 4–16; 1954–71; "social adjustment"; Thomas M. Weiss; International Society for General Semantics. *

REFERENCES THROUGH 1971

1. WEISS, THOMAS MICHAEL. An Experimental Study Applying Non-Aristotelian Principles in the Measurement of Adjustment and Maladjustment. Doctor's thesis, Michigan State College (East Lansing, Mich.), 1954. (DA 14:2264)
2. WEISS, THOMAS M. "An Experimental Study Applying Non-Aristotelian Principles in the Measurement of Adjustment and Maladjustment." Sci Ed 40:312–6 O '56. *
3. HOPKINS, ROBERT FLOYD. A Replication Study of an Experiment Applying Non-Aristotelian Principles in the Measurement of Adjustment and Maladjustment. Doctor's thesis, Michigan State University (East Lansing, Mich.), 1958. (DA 20:3628)
4. WEISS, THOMAS M. "The Construction and Validation of an 'Is of Identity' Test." Gen Semantics B 24–25:69–80 '59. *
5. WEISS, THOMAS M. "Discussion of the Rationale and Previous Findings of the 'Is of Identity' Test as a Basis for Furthering Research." Sci Ed 43:181–3 Mr '59. *
6. WEISS, THOMAS M. "Identification and False-to-Fact Notions." Sci Ed 43:185–7 Mr '59. *
7. WEISS, THOMAS M. "Identification Restricts Problem Solving." Sci Ed 43:184–5 Mr '59. *
8. WEISS, THOMAS M. "Additional Evidence Supporting Korzybskian Principles." Sci Ed 45:114–8 Mr '61. *
9. VELLANTI, JOSEPH T. "The Relation of Intelligence and Sex to the Use of the 'Is of Identity' for High School Students." Sci Ed 46:71–82 F '62. *

CUMULATIVE NAME INDEX

[1247]

It Scale for Children. Ages 5–6; 1956; ITSC; for research use only; sex role preference; Daniel G. Brown; Psychological Test Specialists. *

For additional information, see P:131 (7 references); for reviews by Philip L. Harriman and Boyd R. McCandless, see 6:129 (18 references).

REFERENCES THROUGH 1971

1–18. See 6:129.
19–25. See P:131.
26. EPSTEIN, RALPH. Verbal Conditioning in Children as a Function of Sex-Role Identification, Internal Control, and Need for Approval. Doctor's thesis, Ohio State University (Columbus, Ohio), 1961. (DA 22:2462)
27. BROIDA, HELEN. An Empirical Study of Sex-Role Identification and Sex-Role Preference in a Selected Group of Stuttering Male Children. Doctor's thesis, University of Southern California (Los Angeles, Calif.), 1962. (DA 23:2620)
28. LANSKY, LEONARD M., AND MCKAY, GERALD. "Sex Role Preferences of Kindergarten Boys and Girls: Some Contradictory Results." Psychol Rep 13:415–21 O '63. * (PA 38:8006)
29. MUSSEN, PAUL H., AND PARKER, ANN L. "Mother Nurturance and Girls' Incidental Imitative Learning." J Pers & Social Psychol 2:94–7 Jl '65. * (PA 39:12022)
30. BILLER, HENRY BURT. An Exploratory Investigation of Masculine Development in Kindergarten Age Boys. Doctor's thesis, Duke University (Durham, N.C.), 1967. (DA 28:4290B)
31. BENNETT, MARGARET COOPER. Exploratory Study of Masculine-Feminine Choices of Preschool Children. Doctor's thesis, Claremont Graduate School (Claremont, Calif.), 1968. (DA 29:2616B)
32. BILLER, HENRY B. "A Multiaspect Investigation of Masculine Development in Kindergarten Age Boys." Genetic Psychol Monogr 78:89–138 Ag '68. * (PA 42:18602)
33. BILLER, HENRY B. "A Note on Father Absence and Masculine Development in Lower-Class Negro and White Boys." Child Develop 39:1003–6 S '68. * (PA 43:3750)
34. LANSKY, LEONARD M. "Some Comments on Ward's (1968) 'Variance of Sex-Role Preferences Among Boys and Girls.'" Psychol Rep 23:649–50 O '68. * (PA 43:9512)
35. SHER, MONROE A., AND LANSKY, LEONARD M. "The IT Scale for Children: Effects of Variations in the Sex-Specificity of the IT Figure." Merrill-Palmer Q 14:321–30 O '68. * (PA 43:15843)
36. BILLER, HENRY B. "Maternal Salience and Feminine

Development in Young Girls." Abstract. Proc 77th Ann Conv Am Psychol Assn 4(1):259–60 '69. * (PA 43:17221)
37. BRAY, RUTH M. An Examination and Revision of the Brown, "It Scale for Children." Master's thesis, University of Toronto (Toronto, Ont., Canada), 1969.
38. JOSHI, ASHA K. Sex-Role Preferences in Preschool Children From Five Subcultures of the United States. Doctor's thesis, Iowa State University (Ames, Iowa), 1969. (DAI 30:5120B)
39. LANGFORD, EUGENE PRESTON. The Sex Role of the Female as Perceived by Anglo and Negro Children. Doctor's thesis, East Texas State University (Commerce, Tex.), 1969. (DAI 30:2803A)
40. LANSKY, LEONARD M., AND MCKAY, GERALD. "Independence, Dependence, Manifest and Latent Masculinity-Femininity: Some Complex Relationships Among Four Complex Variables." Psychol Rep 24(1):263–8 F '69. * (PA 43:14136)
41. MOTTE, CAROLE JEAN DELA. An Investigation of the Masculine Personality as Related to Varying Experiences With Family Consistency. Doctor's thesis, Case Western Reserve University (Cleveland, Ohio), 1969. (DAI 30:4378B)
42. BIGNER, JERRY JOE. The Effects of Sibling Influence on Sex-Role Development in Young Children. Doctor's thesis, Florida State University (Tallahassee, Fla.), 1970. (DAI 31:6093B)
43. HOUSTON, H. STEWART. "Familial Correlates of Sex-Role Development in Boys: An Exploratory Study." Personality 1(4):303–17 w '70. * (PA 47:8646)
44. SUMMERS, DARRYL L., AND FELKER, DONALD W. "Use of the It Scale for Children in Assessing Sex-Role Preference in Preschool Negro Children." Develop Psychol 2(3):330–4 My '70. * (PA 44:12348)
45. THOMPSON, NORMAN L., JR., AND MCCANDLESS, BOYD R. "It Score Variations by Instructional Style." Child Develop 41(2):425–36 Je '70. * (PA 44:14369)
46. BOOTH, DAVID WARREN. The Effect of Psychological Sexual Identity on Imitation of Aggression in Preschool Children. Doctor's thesis, University of Maine (Orono, Me.), 1971. (DAI 32:667 1B)
47. DIXIT, RAMESH C. "Sex-Role Preference in Children as a Function of Birth Space." Psychologia (Japan) 14(3–4):175–8 D '71. * (PA 49:589)
48. DOLL, PADDY A.; FAGOT, HACKER J.; AND HIMBERT, JOANNA D. "Experimenter Effect on Sex-Role Preference Among Black and White Lower-Class Male Children." Psychol Rep 29(3):1295–301 D '71. * (PA 48:709)
49. GROB, PAUL. The Relationship of Self Concept, Sex-Role Preference, and Religio-Cultural Background to the Academic Performance of Ten Year Olds of Predominantly Middleclass Backgrounds. Doctor's thesis, University of Virginia (Charlottesville, Va.), 1971. (DAI 32:4348A)
50. SUGAWARA, ALAN IWAO. Sex Role Discrimination and Preference in Preschool Aged Children. Doctor's thesis, Oregon State University (Corvallis, Ore.), 1971. (DAI 32:1830B)

CUMULATIVE NAME INDEX

[1248]

★Jesness Behavior Checklist. Ages 10 and over; 1970–71; JBC; ratings by observers and self-ratings in 14 areas: unobtrusiveness, friendliness, responsibility, considerateness, independence, rapport, enthusiasm, sociability, conformity, calmness, effective communication, insight, social control, anger control; Carl F. Jesness; Consulting Psychologists Press, Inc. *

[1249]

*The Jesness Inventory. Disturbed children and adolescents ages 8–18, adults; 1966–72, c1962–66; JI; adult form is experimental; 11 scores: social maladjustment, value orientation, immaturity, autism, alienation, manifest aggression, withdrawal, social anxiety, repression, denial, asocial index; Carl F. Jesness; Consulting Psychologists Press, Inc. *

For additional information and a review by Sheldon A. Weintraub, see 7:94 (10 references); see also P:133 (3 references). For an excerpt from a related book review, see 7:B436.

REFERENCES THROUGH 1971

1–3. See P:133.
4–13. See 7:94.
14. WHITE, MERVIN FORREST. *A Study of Pinehills Recidivism Rates as Related to Personality and Peer Association Changes.* Master's thesis, Brigham Young University (Provo, Utah), 1965.
15. EWING, DORLESA BARMETTLER. *The Relationship Between Anomie, Dogmatism, and Selected Personal-Social Factors Among Asocial Adolescent Boys.* Doctor's thesis, University of California (Berkeley, Calif.), 1970. (*DAI* 31:5197A)
16. WOYCHICK, TOM. "Asociability Index Scores' Relationship to Adjustment of Youthful Offenders." *Correct Psychologist* 4(2):68–72 S-O '70. * (*PA* 47:11198)
17. EWING, DORLESA B. "The Relations Among Anomie, Dogmatism, and Selected Personal-Social Factors in Asocial Adolescent Boys." *J Social Issues* 27(4):159–69 '71. * (*PA* 48:6984)
18. VALLANCE, R. C., AND FORREST, A. R. "A Study of the Jesness Personality Inventory With Scottish Children." *Brit J Ed Psychol* 41(3):338–44 N '71. * (*PA* 47:11195)

CUMULATIVE NAME INDEX

Baer, D. J.: 7
Baker, J. W.: 11
Butler, E. W.: 4
Clarke, R. V. G.: 8
Cowden, J. E.: 6
Davies, M.: 2
Ewing, D. B.: 15, 17
Fisher, R. M.: 3
Forrest, A. R.: 18
Gibson, H. B.: *exc,* 7:B436
Jesness, C. F.: 1
Joseph, J. J.: 12
Kelly, F. J.: 7.

Martin, D. N.: 8
Mott, J.: 9
Pacht, A. R.: 6
Peterson, W. M.: 6
Rochlin, M.: 5
Rothenberg, E.: 10
Speilberg, M. J.: 11
Vallance, R. C.: 18
Weintraub, S. A.: *rev,* 7:94
White, M. F.: 14
Woychick, J. T.: 13
Woychick, T.: 16

[1250]

*Job Analysis and Interest Measurement. Adults; 1957–72; JAIM; for research use only; personal qualities influencing job success or failure; 2 editions; specimen sets of *a* (with 1964 manual) available from Educational Testing Service (Atlanta Office); Regis Walther; the Author. *

a) [MACHINE SCORED EDITION.] 1957–72; 32 scores: orientations (optimism, self confidence, interpersonal trust, unconventional), self management (plan ahead, orderliness, perseverance, emotional control, schedule activities), interpersonal style (self assertive, supportive of others, take leadership, move toward aggressor, move away from aggressor, move against aggressor), cognitive style (concrete-practical, systematic-methodical), relationship to authority (act independently, work as an assistant), supervisory style (directive leadership, motivate by rewards, motivate by results), work preferences (social interaction, mechanical activities, group participation, activity-frequent change, job challenge), values (status attainment, social service, approval from others, intellectual achievement, role conformity).

b) [SELF-SCORED EDITION.] 1971; manual title is *Exercises in Self Understanding: A Workbook for Trainers;* 9 tests.

1) *Basic Beliefs Inventory.* 3 scores: optimism, self-confidence, basic trust.

2) *Activity Preference Inventory.* 4 scores: job challenge, social interaction, mechanical activities, activity-frequent change.

3) *Personal Values Inventory.* 5 scores: status attainment, social service, approval from others, intellectual achievement, dependability.

4) *Self Management Inventory.* 5 scores: plan ahead, orderliness, perseverance, emotional control, schedule activities.

5) *Relationship to Authority Inventory.* 5 scores: work as supervisor, work as an assistant, work with group, work alone, act independently.

6) *Reaction to Aggression Inventory.* 3 scores: move toward aggressor, move away from aggressor, move against aggressor.

7) *Leadership Style Inventory.* 4 scores: directive leadership, external controls, motivates by rewards, motivates by results.

8) *Information Processing Inventory.* 3 scores: systematic-methodical, concrete-practical, open system.

9) *Interpersonal Style Inventory.* 3 scores: self-assertiveness, supportive of others, take leadership.

For additional information concerning an earlier form, see 7:95 (14 references).

REFERENCES THROUGH 1971

1–14. See 7:95.
15. PETERSEN, PETER BARRON. *A Comparison of Behavioral Styles Between Entering and Graduating Students in Officer Candidate School.* Master's thesis, George Washington University (Washington, D.C.), 1967.
16. REIMER, DAVID JOHN. *The Relationship Between Childhood Experience and Certain Variables Correlated With Occupational Choice and Performance.* Master's thesis, George Washington University (Washington, D.C.), 1967.
17. CROSS, EDWARD M. "The Behavioral Styles of Computer Programmers." *Proc Ann Computer Personnel Res Conf* 8:69–91 '70. *
18. CROSS, EDWARD MEIER. *The Behavioral Styles, Work Preferences and Values of an Occupational Group: Computer Programmers.* Doctor's thesis, George Washington University (Washington, D.C.), 1970. (*DAI* 32:4273B)
19. KIRSCH, JOHN MITCHELL. *The Successful Police Educator: A Profile.* Master's thesis, George Washington University (Washington, D.C.), 1970.
20. CROSS, EDWARD M. "Behavioral Styles of Computer Programmers—Revisited." *Proc Ann Computer Personnel Res Conf* 9:140–66 '71. *
21. PETERSEN, PETER BARRON. *An Investigation of the Effect of Training.* Doctor's thesis, George Washington University (Washington, D.C.), 1971. (*DAI* 31:7661B)
22. TROJANOWICZ, ROBERT C. "The Contrasting Behavioral Styles of Policemen and Social Workers." *Pub Personnel R* 32(4):246–51 O '71. * (*PA* 48:3983)
23. TROJANOWICZ, ROBERT C. "The Policeman's Occupational Personality." *J Crim Law Criminol & Police Sci* 62(4):551–9 D '71. * (*PA* 48:7974)
24. WALD, MAX. *A Study of Selected Personal and Behavioral Characteristics of Public School Principals in the Commonwealth of Pennsylvania.* Doctor's thesis, Temple University (Philadelphia, Pa.), 1971. (*DAI* 32:2385A)

CUMULATIVE NAME INDEX

Cross, E. M.: 17–8, 20
Kirsch, J. M.: 19
Lippitt, G. L.: 10, 12
McCune, S. D.: 7–9, 11
Mills, E. W.: 11
Petersen, P. B.: 10, 12, 15, 21

Reeves, E. A.: 14
Reimer, D. J.: 16
Trojanowicz, R. C.: 13, 22–3
Wald, M.: 24
Walther, R. H.: 1–8

[1251]

Jones Personality Rating Scale. Grades 9–12 and adults; 1939; 8 ratings: dependability, cultural refinement, leadership, industriousness, mental alertness, thoroughness, personal appearance, ability to get along with others; Harold J. Jones; Jones Teaching Aids. *

For additional information, see P:134.

[1252]

Junior Eysenck Personality Inventory. Ages 7–15; 1963–70; JEPI; downward extension of *Eysenck Personality Inventory;* 3 scores: extraversion, neuroticism, lie; 2 editions (identical except for 2 words and directions); Sybil B. G. Eysenck. *

a) UNITED STATES EDITION. 1963–70; Educational and Industrial Testing Service.

b) BRITISH EDITION. 1965; University of London Press Ltd. [England].

For additional information, reviews by Maurice Chazan and Robert D. Wirt, and excerpted reviews by Gertrude H. Keir and B. Semeonoff, see 7:96 (19 references) ; see also P :135 (7 references).

REFERENCES THROUGH 1971

1–7. See P :135.
8–26. See 7 :96.
27. BROWN, G. "The Relationship of Extraversion With Two Aspects of Academic Attainment." *Durham Res R* (England) 5(23):399–402 au '69. *
28. BROWN, GEOFFREY. "An Investigation Into the Relationships Between Performance and Neuroticism." *Durham Res R* (England) 6(25):483–8 au '70. *
29. DUBNER, MARY ANN POLLACK. *Vicarious Reinforcement and Some Personality Factors in Imitation Learning.* Doctor's thesis, University of Maryland (College Park, Md.), 1970. (*DAI* 31:6895B)
30. EYSENCK, S. B. G., AND EYSENCK, H. J. "A Factor-Analytic Study of the Lie Scale of the Junior Eysenck Personality Inventory." *Personality* 1(1):3–10 sp '70. * (*PA* 47:8644)
31. CASEY, JOHN, AND MCMANIS, DONALD L. "Salivary Response to Lemon Juice as a Measure of Introversion in Children." *Percept & Motor Skills* 33(3):1059–65 D '71. * (*PA* 48:707)
32. ELLIOTT, COLIN D. "Noise Tolerance and Extraversion in Children." *Brit J Psychol* 62(3):375–80 Ag '71. * (*PA* 47:4563)
33. EYSENCK, SYBIL B. G.; NIAS, D. K. B.; AND EYSENCK, H. J. "The Interpretation of Children's Lie Scale Scores." *Brit J Ed Psychol* 41(1):23–31 F '71. * (*PA* 46:8757)
34. GUPTA, B. S. "Adaptation of a Hindi Version of the Junior Eysenck Personality Inventory." *Brit J Social & Clin Psychol* 10(2):189–90 Je '71. *
35. HARDY, C. A., AND NIAS, D. K. B. "An Investigation of Physical and Personality Factors Involved in Learning to Swim." *Personality* 2(1):1–7 sp '71. * (*PA* 47:8645)
36. JENSEN, ARTHUR R. "Do Schools Cheat Minority Children?" *Ed Res* (England) 14(1):3–28 N '71. * (*PA* 49:11953)
37. ORWIN, WILLIAM. "A Study of the Reliability Implications of Lie Scores in the Junior Eysenck Personality Inventory." *Brit J Social & Clin Psychol* 10(3):260–6 S '71. * (*PA* 47:10894)
38. RIM, Y., AND SEIDENROSS, H. "Personality and Response to Pressure From Peers vs. Adults." *Personality* 2(1):35–43 sp '71. * (*PA* 47:8718)
39. ROBINSON, C. D. "Personality Variables of Juvenile Delinquents Grouped According to the Type of Crime Committed." *Austral & N Zeal J Criminol* (Australia) 4(3):181–6 S '71. *
40. WILSON, J. A. "Personality and Attainment in the Primary School: 1, Personality Structure of Ten-Year-Olds." *Res Ed* (England) 6:12–23 N '71. * (*PA* 48:12254)

CUMULATIVE NAME INDEX

Brown, G.: 27–8
Casey, J.: 31
Chazan, M.: *rev,* 7:96
Cookson, D.: 11–2, 18–9
Cunningham, S.: 4
Dubner, M. A. P.: 29
Elliott, C. D.: 32
Entwistle, N. J.: 4, 10
Eysenck, H. J.: 3, 11–13, 19–20, 30, 33
Eysenck, S. B. G.: 1, 3, 5, 13–4, 20, 30, 33
Finlayson, D. S.: 21
Forrest, A. R.: 24
Frost, B. P.: 6, 15, 22
Gupta, B. S.: 34
Hall, E.: 16
Harbison, J. J. M.: 23
Hardy, C. A.: 35
Hoghughi, M. S.: 24
Jensen, A. R.: 36
Keir, G. H.: *exc,* 7:96

Laungani, D.: 8
McManis, D. L.: 31
Nias, D. K. B.: 33, 35
Orwin, W.: 37
Pickup, A. J.: 5
Rim, Y.: 2, 38
Robinson, C. D.: 39
Russell, T.: 20
Savage, R. D.: 25
Seidenross, H.: 38
Semeonoff, B.: *exc,* 7:96
Shamberg, N. S.: 7
Shepherd, J. E. D.: 17
Stewart, R. R.: 25
Syed, I. A.: 3
Walker, W.: 25
Waters, T. J.: 9
Welsh, J.: 10
Williams, J. G.: 26
Wilson, J. A.: 40
Wirt, R. D.: *rev,* 7:96

[1253]

*Jr.-Sr. High School Personality Questionnaire.
Ages 12–18; 1953–73; HSPQ; 14 scores: reserved vs. warmhearted (A), dull vs. bright (B), affected by feelings vs. emotionally stable (C), undemonstrative vs. excitable (D), obedient vs. assertive (E), sober vs. enthusiastic (F), disregards rules vs. conscientious (G), shy vs. adventurous (H), tough-minded vs. tender-minded (I), zestful vs. circumspect individualism

(J), self-assured vs. apprehensive (O), sociable group-dependent vs. self-sufficient (Q₂), uncontrolled vs. controlled (Q₃), relaxed vs. tense (Q₄) ; 2 editions. (British adaptation: Ages 13–15; 1973; manual by Peter Saville and Laura Finlayson; NFER Publishing Co. Ltd. [England]. South African adaptation: Ages 13–18; 1967; adaptation by E. M. Madge; Human Sciences Research Council [South Africa].) *

a) IPAT EDITION. 1953–73; Raymond B. Cattell and Mary D. L. Cattell; Institute for Personality and Ability Testing.

b) BOBBS-MERRILL EDITION. 1958–60; 1960 forms identical with out of print 1958 IPAT edition except for format, title, and directions; Raymond B. Cattell, Richard W. Coan, and Halla Beloff; Bobbs-Merrill Co., Inc.

For additional information and reviews by Robert Hogan and Douglas N. Jackson, see 7 :97 (53 references) ; see also P :136 (29 references) ; for reviews by C. J. Adcock and Philip E. Vernon of an earlier edition (the current Bobbs-Merrill edition), see 6 :131 (17 references) ; see also 5 :72 (4 references).

REFERENCES THROUGH 1971

1–4. See 5 :72.
5–21. See 6 :131.
22–51. See P :136.
52–104. See 7 :97.
105. CRARY, JAMES O., JR. *An Investigation of Personality and Socio-Economic Differences of Groups of Students Classified as Above Average, Average, and Below Average.* Master's thesis, Northern Illinois University (DeKalb, Ill.), 1963.
106. LOEHLIN, JOHN C. "A Heredity-Environment Analysis of Personality Inventory Data," pp. 163–70. In *Methods and Goals in Human Behavior Genetics.* Edited by Steven G. Vandenberg. New York: Academic Press Inc., 1965. Pp. xiii, 351. *
107. PECK, D. JANE. *Personality Adjustment of Emotionally Disturbed Children as Influenced by Music.* Master's thesis, Illinois State University (Normal, Ill.), 1965.
108. PIERSON, GEORGE R. "A Specification Equation for Predicting Treatment Response." *J Social Psychol* 65:59–62 F '65. * (*PA* 39:12809)
109. WEINER, A. S. "Blood Groups and Personality Traits." *Am J Hum Genetics* 17:369–70 Jl '65. *
110. POWER, MARY EUGENE FRANCIS. *An Investigation to Determine the Degree to Which Catholic School Pupils at the Eighth Grade Level Compare With Public School Pupils at the Same Level in Possessing Specific Character Traits Conducive to Leadership in American Society.* Master's thesis, Catholic University of America (Washington, D.C.), 1966.
111. YOUNG, HARBEN BOUTOURLINE, AND KNAPP, ROBERT. "Personality Characteristics of Converted Left Handers." *Percept & Motor Skills* 23:35–40 Ag '66. * (*PA* 40:12363)
112. AINSWORTH, MARJORIE E. "The Relationship Between Motivation, Personality, Intelligence and School Attainment in a Secondary Modern School." *Brit J Ed Psychol* 37:135–7 F '67. * Abstract of master's thesis, University of Manchester (Manchester, England), 1966.
113. VANDENBERG, STEVEN G. "Hereditary Factors in Normal Personality Traits (as Measured by Inventories)." *Recent Adv Biol Psychiatry* 9:65–104 '67. *
114. ZAHRAN, HAMED A. S. "The Self-Concept in the Psychological Guidance of Adolescents." *Brit J Ed Psychol* 37:225–40 Je '67. * (*PA* 41:15077)
115. TAYLOR, A. J. W. "Personality Factors of Extraversion and Anxiety in New Zealand's Persistent Offenders." *Austral & N Zeal J Criminol* (Australia) 1:243–8 D '68. *
116. BERRY, G. W. *Personality Patterns and Delinquency.* Master's thesis, University of Manchester (Manchester, England), 1969. (Abstract: *Brit J Ed Psychol* 41:221)
117. GROSZ, HANUS J.; STERN, HERBERT; AND FELDMAN, EDWARD. "A Study of Delinquent Girls Who Participated in and Who Abstained From Participating in a Riot." *Am J Psychiatry* 125(10):1370–9 Ap '69. * (*PA* 43:11606)
118. KOUL, LOKESH. "Personality Traits of High and Low Achievers in Mathematics." *Ed & Psychol R* (India) 9(3):122–8 Jl '69. *
119. RANDALL, LAURENCE H. *A Comparison of the Self Concept and Personality Characteristics of Deaf High School Students With Norms for the Hearing and With Norms for Delinquents.* Master's thesis, University of Tennessee (Knoxville, Tenn.), 1969.
120. HENNING, JOHN J., AND LEVY, RUSSELL H. "Personality Characteristics of White and Negro Adolescent Delinquents." *Correct Psychologist* 4(1):12–9 Jl '70. * (*PA* 46:9321)
121. MCDONALD, KAYE. *A Comparison of the Personality Traits of Participants and Nonparticipants in High School Interscholastic Tennis Programs for Girls.* Doctor's thesis,

122. NEAVES, ALISON I. "To Establish a Basis for Prognosis in Stammering." *Brit J Dis Commun* 5(1):46–58 Ap '70. * (*PA* 46:5319)

123. BARTON, K.; DIELMAN, T. E.; AND CATTELL, R. B. "The Prediction of School Grades From Personality and IQ Measures." *Personality* 2(4):325–33 w '71. * (*PA* 48:7878)

124. GREEN, MARY G.; BLAKE, BRIAN F.; CARBOY, JOHN J.; AND ZENHAUSERN, ROBERT J. "Personality Characteristics of the Middle-Class High School Drug User." Abstract. *Proc 79th Ann Conv Am Psychol Assn* 6(2):559–60 '71. * (*PA* 46:4925)

125. GREEN, MARY GRACE. *Adolescent Drug Users and Non-Users: A Differential Analysis of Personality Correlates.* Doctor's thesis, St. John's University (Jamaica, N.Y.), 1971. (*DAI* 33:1763B)

126. HOOKE, JAMES F. "Correlates of Delinquent Behavior." *Psychol Rep* 28(3):795–800 Je '71. * (*PA* 46:11174)

127. KANTHAMANI, B. K., AND RAO, K. RAMAKRISHNA. "Personality Characteristics of ESP Subjects: I, Primary Personality Characteristics and ESP." *J Parapsychol* 35(3):189–207 S '71. * (*PA* 48:2024)

128. KIRKENDALL, DON R., AND GRUBER, JOSEPH J. "Multivariate Relationships Between Motor and Personality Measures in Culturally Deprived High School Pupils." *J Motor Behav* 3(1):31–8 Mr '71. * (*PA* 47:11803)

129. KUCERA, GERALD ANTHONY. *Generalization Gradients and Response Cues in the Expression of Dependency.* Doctor's thesis, University of Arizona (Tucson, Ariz.), 1971. (*DAI* 32:5446B)

130. LESSING, ELISE E., AND HARROD, ALAN R. "Comparative Predictive Validity of the IPAT Jr.-Sr. High School Personality Questionnaire for White and Black Subsamples." Abstract. *Proc 79th Ann Conv Am Psychol Assn* 6(1):245–6 '71. * (*PA* 46:3087)

131. LEVONIAN, EDWARD. "Student Personality and Academic Achievement." *Personality* 1(1):25–39 sp '71. * (*PA* 47:9804)

132. MCKELVIE, WILLIAM HARRY. *An Evaluation of a Model to Train High School Students as Leaders of Adlerian Guidance Groups.* Doctor's thesis, West Virginia University (Morgantown, W.Va.), 1971. (*DAI* 32:3694A)

133. MARTIN, JOHN PHILMONT, JR. *A Comparative Study of Personality Profiles in Normal and Hemophilic Male Adolescents.* Doctor's thesis, University of Alabama (University, Ala.), 1971. (*DAI* 32:6251A)

134. NORTON, H. W. "Blood Groups and Personality Traits." Letter. *Am J Hum Genetics* 23(2):225 Mr '71. *

135. SAMPLE, DUANE, AND HOTCHKISS, SALLY M. "An Investigation of Relationships Between Personality Characteristics and Success in Instrumental Study." *J Res Music Ed* 19(3):307–13 f '71. * (*PA* 48:5871)

136. SCHLEUTER, STANLEY LEROY. *An Investigation of the Interrelation of Personality Traits, Musical Aptitude and Musical Achievement.* Doctor's thesis, University of Iowa (Iowa City, Iowa), 1971. (*DAI* 32:1556A)

137. SOARES, LOUISE M., AND SOARES, ANTHONY T. "Age Differences in the Personality Profiles of Disadvantaged Females." Abstract. *Proc 79th Ann Conv Am Psychol Assn* 6(1):163–4 '71. * (*PA* 46:2610, title only)

138. THAYER, ROBERT WILCOX. *An Investigation of the Interrelation of Personality Traits, Musical Achievement, and Different Measures of Musical Aptitude.* Doctor's thesis, University of Iowa (Iowa City, Iowa), 1971. (*DAI* 32:2734A)

139. TYLER, VERNON O., JR., AND KELLY, ROBERT F. "Predicting the Behavior of Institutionalized Delinquents With—and Without—Cattell's HSPQ." *Ed & Psychol Meas* 31(4):1019–24 w '71. * (*PA* 48:1273)

140. VROEGH, KAREN. "Masculinity and Femininity in the Elementary and Junior High School Years." *Develop Psychol* 4(2):254–61 Mr '71. * (*PA* 45:9704)

141. WARD, CHARLES ALTON. *An Investigation of Achievement Motivation of a Select Group of Emotionally Disturbed, Delinquent Children.* Doctor's thesis, Baylor University (Waco, Tex.), 1971. (*DAI* 32:2389B)

CUMULATIVE NAME INDEX

[1254]

KD Proneness Scale and Check List. Grades 7–12, ages 7 and over; 1950–56; William C. Kvaraceus; Western Psychological Services. *

a) KD PRONENESS SCALE. Grades 7–12; KDPS; also called *Delinquency Proneness Scale.*

b) KD PRONENESS CHECK LIST, REVISED. Ages 7 and over; KDPCL; ratings by teachers.

For additional information, see P:137 (22 references); for a review by John W. M. Rothney, see 5:79 (6 references); for reviews by Douglas Courtney and Dale B. Harris, see 4:64.

REFERENCES THROUGH 1971

1–6. See 5:79.
7–28. See P:137.
29. THURSTON, JOHN R.; BENNING, JAMES J.; AND FELDHUSEN, JOHN F. "Delinquency Proneness and Classroom Behavior." *Criminologica* 4(4):36–43 F '67. *
30. SPEEDIE, STUART; HOBSON, SANDRA; FELDHUSEN, JOHN; AND THURSTON, JOHN. "Evaluation of a Battery of Noncognitive Variables as Long-Range Predictors of Academic

Achievement." Abstract. *Proc 79th Ann Conv Am Psychol Assn* 6(2):517–8 '71. * (*PA* 46:5708)

CUMULATIVE NAME INDEX

[1255]

Katz Adjustment Scales. Normal and mentally disordered adults; 1961–64; KAS; adjustment and social behavior in the community; for research use only; test booklet title is *KAS Behavior Inventories;* Martin M. Katz, Samuel B. Lyerly (manual), M. Kathleen Herron (supplement), William W. Michaux (supplement), and Henri A. Lowery (supplement) ; Martin M. Katz. *

a) SCALES DESIGNED FOR RELATIVES RATINGS (R SCALES). 18 scores: 13 factor scores for Form R1, 1 score for each of Forms R2–R5 and 1 score (level of dissatisfaction with performance) based on differences between corresponding items on Forms R2 and R3; 5 scales.

1) *Form R1, Relative's Ratings of Patient's Symptoms and Social Behavior.* Primarily for use prior to hospitalization or following discharge; 13 factor scores: belligerence, verbal expansiveness, negativism, helplessness, suspiciousness, anxiety, withdrawal and retardation, general psychopathology, nervousness, confusion, bizarreness, hyperactivity, emotional stability.

2) *Form R2, Level of Performance of Socially Expected Activities.*

3) *Form R3, Level of Expectations for Performance of Social Activities.*

4) *Form RS4, Level of Free Time Activities.* Adaptation of *Your Activities and Attitudes.*

5) *Form R5, Level of Satisfaction With Free Time Activities.* Items are identical to those in Form RS4.

b) SCALES DESIGNED FOR PATIENT'S SELF-RATINGS (S SCALES). 6 scores: 1 score for each of Forms S1, S2, S3, RS4, S5 and 1 score (level of dissatisfaction with performance) based on differences between corresponding items on Forms S2 and S3; 5 scales.

1) *Form S1, Symptom Discomfort.* Adaptation of Johns Hopkins Symptom Distress Scale.

2) *Forms S2, S3, RS4, and S5.* Identical to the corresponding R scales except that they are adapted for self-rating.

For additional information, see P:138 (10 references).

REFERENCES THROUGH 1971

1–10. See P:138.
11. HOGARTY, GERARD E.; DENNIS, HELEN; GUY, WILLIAM; AND GROSS, GERTRUDE M. " 'Who Goes There?'—A Critical Evaluation of Admissions to a Psychiatric Day Hospital." *Am J Psychiatry* 124:934–44 Ja '68. * (*PA* 42:9143)
12. MICHAUX, MARY HELEN; MICHAUX, WILLIAM W.; ESSER, EUGENIE K.; AND OLIVER, BARBARA A. "Attitudes of Psychiatric Ex-Patients Toward a Study of Community Adjustment." *Psychol Rep* 23:567–72 O '68. *
13. SYDIAHA, DANIEL; STEWART, ALEX; AND LAFAVE, HUGH G. "A Study of Mail Questionnaire Technique With Discharged Psychiatric Patients." *Int J Social Psychiatry* (England) 14:135–40 sp '68. *

14. KATZ, MARTIN M.; GUDEMAN, HOWARD; AND SANBORN, KENNETH. Chap. 9, "Characterizing Differences in Psychopathology Among Ethnic Groups: A Preliminary Report on Hawaii-Japanese and Mainland-American Schizophrenics," pp. 148–63. In *Mental Health Research in Asia and the Pacific.* Edited by William Caudill and Tsung-yi Lin. Honolulu, Hawaii: East-West Center Press, 1969. Pp. xv, 487. *
15. KATZ, MARTIN M.; SANBORN, KENNETH O.; AND GUDEMAN, HOWARD. "Characterizing Differences in Psychopathology Among Ethnic Groups in Hawaii." *Res Publ Assn Res Nerv & Mental Dis* 47:139–53 '69. *
16. MICHAUX, WILLIAM W.; KATZ, MARTIN M.; KURLAND, ALBERT A.; AND GANSEREIT, KATHLEEN H. *The First Year Out: Mental Patients After Hospitalization.* Baltimore, Md.: Johns Hopkins Press, 1969. Pp. xvii, 299. *
17. SOSKIS, DAVID A., AND BOWERS, MALCOLM B. "The Schizophrenic Experience: A Follow-Up Study of Attitude and Posthospital Adjustment." *J Nerv & Mental Dis* 149(6):443–9 D '69. * (*PA* 44:8873)
18. STEWART, A.; SELKIRK, SHEENA A.; AND SYDIAHA, D. "Patterns of Adjustment of Discharged Psychiatric Patients as Measured by Mailed Questionnaires." *Commun Mental Health J* 5(4):314–9 Ag '69. * (*PA* 44:12663)
19. VESTRE, NORRIS D., AND ZIMMERMANN, ROBERT. "Validity of Informants' Ratings of the Behavior and Symptoms of Psychiatric Patients." *J Consult & Clin Psychol* 33(2):175–9 Ap '69. * (*PA* 43:10028)
20. KATZ, MARTIN M.; SANBORN, KENNETH O.; AND GUDEMAN, HOWARD. "Characterizing Differences in Psychopathology Among Ethnic Groups in Hawaii." *Schizophrenia B* 2:20–9 f '70. *
21. CAFFEY, EUGENE M.; GALBRECHT, CHARLES R.; AND KLETT, C. JAMES. "Brief Hospitalization and Aftercare in the Treatment of Schizophrenia." *Arch Gen Psychiatry* 24(1): 81–6 Ja '71. * (*PA* 45:10394)
22. HOGARTY, GERARD E., AND KATZ, MARVIN M. "Norms of Adjustment and Social Behavior." *Arch Gen Psychiatry* 25(5): 470–80 N '71. *

CUMULATIVE NAME INDEX

[1256]

Kuder Preference Record—Personal. Grades 9–16 and adults; 1948–63; KPR-P; 6 scores: group activity, stable situations, working with ideas, avoiding conflict, directing others, verification; G. Frederic Kuder; Science Research Associates, Inc. *

For additional information, see P:139 (9 references) ; for reviews by Dorothy M. Clendenen and Wilbur L. Layton, see 6:132 (11 references) ; for a review by Dwight L. Arnold, see 5:80 (5 references) ; for an excerpted review by Laurance F. Shaffer, see 4:65 (4 references).

REFERENCES THROUGH 1971

1–4. See 4:65.
5–9. See 5:80.
10–20. See 6:132.
21–29. See P:139.
30. SHROCK, JOHN G. *Functions of Methodology in Adult Education Ceramics Courses.* Doctor's thesis, Stanford University (Stanford, Calif.), 1953. (*DA* 13:711)
31. GORMAN, WILLIAM EDWARD. *The Effect of Occupational Information in English Classes on High School Juniors.* Doctor's thesis, Northwestern University (Evanston, Ill.), 1956. (*DA* 17:301)
32. SMITH, ARTHUR EDWARD. *Rapport and Social Perception in Mother-Adolescent Relationships.* Doctor's thesis, University of Illinois (Urbana, Ill.), 1957. (*DA* 17:2924)
33. COTE, THEODORE JOHN. *The Relationship Between Parents' Awareness of Their Adolescent Children's Problems and the*

Affective Adjustment of Those Children. Doctor's thesis, University of Connecticut (Storrs, Conn.), 1960. (*DA* 21:1842)

34. WAGNER, EDWIN E. "Predicting Success for Young Executives From Objective Test Scores and Personal Data." *Personnel Psychol* 13:181–6 su '60. * (*PA* 36:2LD81W)

35. BOHLANDER, BENNY LEE. *Personality Characteristics of Leaders in High School.* Master's thesis, Illinois State University (Normal, Ill.), 1963.

36. NIELSEN, J. K. "Case Studies of Socially Isolated Males in Senior High School." *Alberta J Ed Res* (Canada) 9:247–53 D '63. *

37. BURNS, ROBERT JOHN. *A Study of the Relationships of Certain Values, Personal Preferences, and Activities of Pre-Retired and Retired Professional Engineers.* Doctor's thesis, University of Michigan (Ann Arbor, Mich.), 1966. (*DA* 27:3717A)

38. HOYT, ROBERT L. *The Relationships Between Resident Counselor Personality Variables and Students' Perceived Communication Willingness.* Master's thesis, Northwestern University (Evanston, Ill.), 1966.

39. NUCHO, AINA OZOLINS. *The Problem of Psychological Similarity and the Process of Codification in Therapeutic Interaction.* Doctor's thesis, Bryn Mawr College (Bryn Mawr, Pa.), 1966. (*DA* 27:3678B)

40. BRABBLE, ELIZABETH WILLIAMS. *Student Teacher-Supervising Teacher Compatibility and Its Relation to Success in Student Teaching.* Doctor's thesis, Pennsylvania State University (University Park, Pa.), 1969. (*DAI* 31:660A)

41. HARRINGTON, JOSEPH ANDREW. *Multivariate Test Score Patterns on the KPR-V, the KPR-P, and Both Combined for College Women in Four Curriculum Groups and College Men in Five Curriculum Groups.* Doctor's thesis, Boston College (Chestnut Hill, Mass.), 1969. (*DAI* 30:3784A)

42. HAKANSON, IRVING STEARNS. *Influences of Parent Education and Occupation Upon Eventual Occupational Choice and Interest Patterns of Students.* Doctor's thesis, University of Oregon (Eugene, Ore.), 1970. (*DAI* 32:176A)

43. OBERLANDER, MARK I.; FRAUENFELDER, KENNETH J.; AND HEATH, HELEN. "Ordinal Position, Sex of Sibling, Sex, and Personal Preferences in a Group of Eighteen-Year-Olds." *J Consult & Clin Psychol* 35(1):122–5 Ag '70. * (*PA* 44:20691)

44. WILKINSON, A. EARL; PRADO, WILLIAM M.; WILLIAMS, WOODROW O.; AND SCHNADT, FREDERICK W. "Psychological Test Characteristics and Length of Stay in Alcoholism Treatment." *Q J Studies Alcohol* 32(1A):60–5 Mr '71. * (*PA* 46:7116)

CUMULATIVE NAME INDEX

Anderson, M. E.: 15	Iscoe, I.: 7
Armstrong, M. E.: 21	Kuder, G. F.: 1, 4
Arnold, D. L.: *rev*, 5:80	Layton, W. L.: *rev*, 6:132
Ash, P.: 14	Lee, M. C.: 22
Atkinson, G.: 28	Lucier, O.: 7
Birge, W. R.: 2	Lunneborg, C. E.: 28
Blocher, D. H.: 20	McGuire, F. L.: 18
Bohlander, B. L.: 35	Mosier, M. F.: 1
Brabble, E. W.: 40	Murray, L. E.: 8
Bruce, M. M.: 8	Nielsen, J. K.: 36
Burns, R. J.: 37	Nucho, A. O.: 39
Caine, T. M.: 24	Oberlander, M. I.: 43
Campbell, R. E.: 23	Prado, W. M.: 44
Clendenen, D. M.: *rev*, 6:132	Schnadt, F. W.: 44
Costello, C. G.: 15	Scholl, C. E.: 11
Cote, T. J.: 33	Schroeder, P.: 26
Crites, J. O.: 19	Shaffer, L. F.: *exc*, 4:65
Fjeld, H. A.: 5	Shrock, J. G.: 30
Flowers, J. F.: 10, 17	Silverman, P.: 25
Frauenfelder, K. J.: 43	Smith, A. E.: 32
Gorman, W. E.: 31	Smith, D. D.: 9, 12
Goshorn, W. M.: 3	Super, D. E.: 19
Greene, J. E.: 6	Wagner, E. E.: 16, 34
Hakanson, I. S.: 42	Ward, P. L.: 13
Harrington, J. A.: 41	Wardlow, M. E.: 6
Hartman, B. J.: 29	Whiteley, D. P.: 27
Heath, H.: 43	Wilkinson, A. E.: 44
Hoyt, R. L.: 38	Williams, W. O.: 44

[1257]

Kundu's Neurotic Personality Inventory. Adults; 1965; test booklet title is *K.N.P.I.;* KNPI; Ramanath Kundu; the Author [India]. *

For additional information, see P:140 (5 references).

REFERENCES THROUGH 1971

1–5. See P:140.
6. MUKHERJEE, BISHWA NATH, AND SREEKUMAR, MENON A. "Personality Characteristics and Intra-Individual Variability in Industrial Output." *Indian J Indus Relations* 4(4):462–81 Ap '69. *
7. MITRA, SADHNA. "Adaptation of Kundu's Neurotic Personality Inventory in Bengali." *Indian J Psychol* 45(4):369–71 D '70. *

CUMULATIVE NAME INDEX

Khanna, A.: 5	Mukherjee, B. N.: 6
Kundu, R.: 1–5	Sreekumar, M. A.: 6
Mitra, S.: 7	

[1258]

★**Kupfer-Detre System.** Psychiatric patients; 1971–73; KDS; also called *KDS System;* 9 questionnaires for "systematic interviewing and psychiatric history-taking"; 3 of the forms (*a, d, f*) are headed Western Psychiatric Institute and Clinic, University of Pittsburgh; David J. Kupfer, Thomas P. Detre (forms), and Jane Ingenito (manual); KDS Systems, Inc. *

a) [INITIAL CONTACT AND ADMISSION FORM.] 1973.

b) KDS-1. 1971–72; also called *Kupfer-Detre Self-Rating Scale;* self-administered checklist of psychological symptoms; 1972 form identical with form copyrighted 1971 except for format.

c) KDS-2. 1971; self-rating of somatic symptoms "covering complaints most commonly attributed to psychotropic drugs."

d) [KDS-3] HISTORY. 1971–73; self-administered patient history.

e) KDS-3A. 1971; personality-style part of an earlier edition of KDS-3; self-administered.

f) [KDS-4] CLINICAL INTERVIEW. 1971–73.

g) KDS-5, MENTAL STATUS. 1971; judgments by clinician of appearance and attitude, intellectual functioning, and behavior.

h) KDS-6, SUMMARY AND RECOMMENDATIONS. 1971.

i) KDS-7, PSYCHIATRIC SYMPTOM SCALE. 1971; for periodic follow-up examinations.

REFERENCES THROUGH 1971

1. KUPFER, DAVID J., AND DETRE, THOMAS P. "Development and Application of the KDSTM-1 in Patient and Outpatient Settings." *Psychol Rep* 29(2):607–17 O '71. * (*PA* 47:9204)
2. KUPFER, DAVID J., AND DETRE, THOMAS P. "Once More—On the Extraordinary Side Effects of Drugs." *Clin Pharmacol Therapeu* 12(4):575–82 Jl–Ag '71. *
3. KUPFER, DAVID J.; DETRE, THOMAS P.; SWIGAR, MARY E.; AND SOUTHWICK, WAYNE O. "Adjustment of Patients After Hip Surgery." *J Am Geriatrics Soc* 19(8):709–20 Ag '71. *

CUMULATIVE NAME INDEX

Detre, T. P.: 1–3	Southwick, W. O.: 3
Kupfer, D. J.: 1–3	Swigar, M. E.: 3

[1259]

The Leadership Ability Evaluation. Grades 9–16 and adults; 1961; LAE; social climate created in influencing others; 5 scores: laissez faire, democratic-cooperative, autocratic-submissive, autocratic-aggressive, decision pattern; Russell N. Cassel and Edward J. Stancik; Western Psychological Services. *

For additional information, see P:142; for reviews by John D. Black and Cecil A. Gibb, see 6:133 (4 references).

REFERENCES THROUGH 1971

1–4. See 6:133.
5. HILL, DUANE COLLINS. *Leadership and Test Performance Relationships as Determinants of Successful Progress in Doctoral Level Educational Administration Programs.* Doctor's thesis, University of Minnesota (Minneapolis, Minn.), 1968. (*DA* 29:4228A)
6. OTTE, ARLAND WAYNE. *Relationships Between Selected Personal and Professional Characteristics of School Principals and Propensities Toward Group Decision Making.* Doctor's thesis, University of Minnesota (Minneapolis, Minn.), 1968. (*DA* 29:1727A)
7. DAVIES, EVAN; WYNDHAM, JOHN; AND BINKS, NOEL. "Psychological Changes in Sensitivity Training." *Austral Psychologist* 3(3):171–6 Mr '69. * (*PA* 45:7142)

CUMULATIVE NAME INDEX

Binks, N.: 7	Gibb, C. A.: *rev*, 6:133
Black, J. D.: *rev*, 6:133	Haddox, G.: 1
Cassel, R.: 4	Hill, D. C.: 5
Cassel, R. N.: 1–3	Otte, A. W.: 6
Childers, K.: 4	Sanders, R. A.: 3
Davies, E.: 7	Wyndham, J.: 7

[1260]

The Leadership Q-Sort Test (A Test of Leadership Values). Adults; 1958; LQST; 7 scores: personal integrity, consideration of others, mental health, technical information, decision making, teaching and communication, total; Russell N. Cassel; Psychometric Affiliates. *

For additional information, see P:143; for reviews by Joel T. Campbell, Cecil A. Gibb, and William Stephenson, see 6:134 (6 references).

REFERENCES THROUGH 1971

1–6. See 6:134.

CUMULATIVE NAME INDEX

Campbell, J. T.: rev, 6:134
Carp, A.: 1–2
Cassel, R.: 1
Cassel, R. N.: 2–6
Gibb, C. A.: rev, 6:134
Haddox, G.: 4–5
Harriman, B. L.: 3
Sanders, R. A.: 6
Stephenson, W.: rev, 6:134

[1261]

The Level of Aspiration Board. Mental ages 12.5 and over; 1940–50; LAB; 2 scores: mean difference between performance and estimate, shifts; J. B. Rotter; distributed by Edward Butler. *

For additional information, see P:144 (9 references).

REFERENCES THROUGH 1971

1–9. See P:144.
10. ELKIN, VICTOR B. The Relationship Between Personality Characteristics and Efficiency in the Use of Aural Sensory Aids by a Group of Acoustically Handicapped Patients. Doctor's thesis, New York University (New York, N.Y.), 1952. (DA 13:202)
11. RAIFMAN, IRVING. An Investigation of the Personality Factors of Dependency and Overcompensatory Goal Striving Behavior Associated With the Development of Peptic Ulcer in a Group of Veteran Male Patients. Doctor's thesis, New York University (New York, N.Y.), 1952. (DA 12:539)
12. HARRIS, MYRON WILLARD. Protective Mechanisms Utilized in Reaction to Ego-Threatening Situations, as Evidenced by Performance on a Level of Aspiration Problem. Doctor's thesis, New York University (New York, N.Y.), 1954. (DA 15:116)
13. SHEEHAN, JOSEPH G., AND ZELEN, SEYMOUR L. "Level of Aspiration in Stutterers and Nonstutterers." J Abn & Social Psychol 51:83–6 Jl '55. * (PA 30:4889)
14. YORMAK, BERNARD B. An Investigation of Behavioral Changes Following General Semantic Training of Neuropsychiatric Patients. Doctor's thesis, Pennsylvania State University (University Park, Pa.), 1956. (DA 17:402)
15. RAIFMAN, IRVING. "Level of Aspiration in a Group of Peptic Ulcer Patients." J Consult Psychol 21:229–31 Je '57. * (PA 32:5794)
16. SUMMERS, LINDEN D., JR. Goal-Setting as a Problem in the Psychodynamics of Obesity. Doctor's thesis, Syracuse University (Syracuse, N.Y.), 1957. (DA 17:1817)
17. CORRIE, CHRISTOPHER C. Aspiration, Self Acceptance, and Acceptance of Others in Normal and Neuropsychiatric Groups. Doctor's thesis, Florida State University (Tallahassee, Fla.), 1958. (DA 18:1855)
18. MOSS, HOWARD ALAN. The Generality of Cautiousness as a Defense Behavior. Doctor's thesis, Ohio State University (Columbus, Ohio), 1958. (DA 19:879)
19. KRUGMAN, ARNOLD D. "A Note on Level-of-Aspiration Behavior and Aging." J Gerontol 14:222–5 Ap '59. * (PA 34:719)
20. WILLENSON, DAVID. Relationship of Adult Personality Characteristics to Perceived Parental Behavior: A Partial Validation of Ausubel's Theory of Ego Development. Doctor's thesis, University of Houston (Houston, Tex.), 1959. (DA 20:3393)
21. GOLDMAN, RONALD. Comparisons of the Goals That Parents of Stutterers and Parents of Non-Stutterers Set for Their Children. Doctor's thesis, University of Pittsburgh (Pittsburgh, Pa.), 1960. (DA 21:2405)
22. RAO, KUNAPULI U., AND RUSSELL, ROGER W. "Effects of Stress on Goal Setting Behavior." J Abn & Social Psychol 61:380–8 N '60. * (PA 36:2FH80R)
23. JENSEN, MILTON B., AND YANAGI, GARRET H. "Directive Treatment of Long-Term Closed Ward Schizophrenics." J Clin Psychol 17:139–41 Ap '61. *
24. EGAN, GERARD VINCENT. Antecedents and Consequents of Cross-Identification in Adolescent Females. Doctor's thesis, St. Louis University (St. Louis, Mo.), 1964. (DA 25:4814)
25. LEFCOURT, HERBERT M., AND LADWIG, GORDON W. "The American Negro: A Problem in Expectancies." J Pers & Social Psychol 1:377–80 Ap '65. * (PA 39:9917)
26. CROWNE, DOUGLAS P. "Family Orientation, Level of Aspiration, and Interpersonal Bargaining." J Pers & Social Psychol 3:641–5 Je '66. * (PA 40:7587)
27. NICOLAY, GLEN C. Relationship Between a Risk-Taking Questionnaire and Selected Personality Characteristics. Doctor's thesis, Fordham University (New York, N.Y.), 1966. (DA 27:2142B)
28. CAVA, ESTHER LADEN. Differences Between Interactions of Mothers With Their More Troublesome Children and Their Less Troublesome Children. Doctor's thesis, Ohio State University (Columbus, Ohio), 1967. (DA 28:2619B)
29. LEFCOURT, HERBERT M. "Effects of Cue Explication Upon Persons Maintaining External Control Expectancies." J Pers & Social Psychol 5:372–8 Mr '67. * (PA 41:5917)
30. AX, ALBERT F., AND BAMFORD, JACQUELINE L. "Validation of a Psychophysiological Test of Aptitude for Learning Social Motives." Psychophysiol 5:316–32 S '68. * (PA 43:3943)
31. CROWNE, DOUGLAS P.; CONN, LANE K.; MARLOWE, DAVID; AND EDWARDS, CARL N. "Some Developmental Antecedents of Level of Aspiration." J Personality 37(1):73–92 Mr '69. * (PA 43:12978)
32. EPPES, JOHN WILLIFORD. The Effect of Varying the Race of the Experimenter on the Level of Aspiration of Externally Controlled Inner City School Children. Doctor's thesis, Emory University (Atlanta, Ga.), 1969. (DAI 31:912B)
33. FINEMAN, CAROL ALSON. Goal Setting Strategies and the Avoidance of Evaluation in Schizophrenia. Doctor's thesis, University of Miami (Coral Gables, Fla.), 1970. (DAI 31:2278B)
34. LEFCOURT, HERBERT M., AND STEFFY, RICHARD A. "Level of Aspiration, Risk-Taking Behavior, and Projective Test Performance: A Search for Coherence." J Consult & Clin Psychol 34(2):193–8 Ap '70. * (PA 44:10528)
35. RIEDEL, WOLFGANG W., AND MILGRAM, NORMAN A. "Level of Aspiration, Locus of Control and n-Achievement in Retardates and Normal Children." Psychol Rep 27(2):551–7 O '70. * (PA 45:6890)
36. RABINDRADAS, L. D. "The Effect of Personality Rigidity on Level of Aspiration." Indian J Exp Psychol 5(1):1–6 Ja '71. *
37. STRICKLAND, BONNIE R. "Aspiration Responses Among Negro and White Adolescents." J Pers & Social Psychol 19(3):315–20 S '71. * (PA 47:2708)

CUMULATIVE NAME INDEX

Adams, H. B.: 6
Ax, A. F.: 30
Bamford, J. L.: 30
Cava, E. L.: 28
Cohen, L. D.: 6
Conn, L. K.: 31
Cooper, G. D.: 6
Corrie, C. C.: 17
Crowne, D. P.: 7, 26, 31
Edwards, C. N.: 31
Egan, G. V.: 24
Elkin, V. B.: 10
Eppes, J. W.: 32
Eshbaugh, R. N.: 5
Fineman, C. A.: 33
Friedman, S. R.: 5
Goldman, R.: 21
Harris, M. W.: 12
Jensen, M. B.: 23
Krugman, A. D.: 19
Ladwig, G. W.: 25
Lefcourt, H. M.: 9, 25, 29, 34
Lewis, L.: 9
Marlowe, D.: 31
Milgram, N. A.: 35
Moss, H. A.: 18
Nicolay, G. C.: 27
Rabindradas, L. D.: 36
Raifman, I.: 11, 15
Rajeswari, S.: 8
Rao, K. U.: 22
Riedel, W. W.: 35
Rotter, J. B.: 1–3
Russell, R. W.: 22
Sheehan, J. G.: 13
Silverman, I. W.: 9
Steffy, R. A.: 34
Strickland, B. R.: 37
Summers, L. D.: 16
Willenson, D.: 20
Worthington, A. M. L.: 4
Yanagi, G. H.: 23
Yormak, B. B.: 14
Zelen, S. L.: 13

[1262]

The Life Adjustment Inventory. High school; 1951; LAI; 14 scores: adjustment to curriculum, reading and study skills, communication and listening skills, social skills and etiquette, boy-girl relationships, religion-moral-ethics, functional citizenship, vocational orientation and preparation, physical and mental health, family living, orientation to science, consumer education, art appreciation and creativity, use of leisure time; J. Wayne Wrightstone and Ronald C. Doll; Psychometric Affiliates. *

For additional information, see P:145 (1 reference); for reviews by John W. M. Rothney and Helen Shacter, see 4:67.

REFERENCES THROUGH 1971

1. See P:145.

CUMULATIVE NAME INDEX

Rothney, J. W. M.: rev, 4:67
Rowley, I. F.: 1
Shacter, H.: rev, 4:67

[1263]

The Lüscher Color Test. Adults; 1947-69; LCT; an 8-color patch version (also called *Short Lüscher Test*) of the 73-color patch *Full Lüscher Test* available in German edition only; a personality test sold through bookstores for self-administration or administration to others; translated and edited by Ian A. Scott; Max Lüscher; Random House, Inc. *

For additional information, a review by S. G. Lee, and excerpted reviews by C. H. Ammons (with R. B. Ammons), Bernard I. Murstein, and David Sanford, see 7:98.

REFERENCES THROUGH 1971

1. MOGENSEN, ALAN, AND JUEL-NIELSEN, NIELS. "Factors Influencing Preference Rankings in a Special Picture Test and in Luscher's Colour Test: A Study of Uniovular Twins Brought Up Apart." *Acta Psychiatrica Scandinavica* (Denmark) 38:208–12 '62. * (*PA* 37:6307)
2. HACKLER, NICKIE LYNNE. *A Comparative Study of the IPAT Anxiety Scale Questionnaire and the Luscher Color Test.* Master's thesis, Radford College (Radford, Va.), 1970.

CUMULATIVE NAME INDEX

Ammons, C. H.: *exc, 7:98* Lee, S. G.: *rev, 7:98*
Ammons, R. B.: *exc, 7:98* Mogensen, A.: 1
Hackler, N. L.: 2 Murstein, B. I.: *exc, 7:98*
Juel-Nielsen, N.: 1 Sanford, D.: *exc, 7:98*

[1264]

*****The MACC Behavioral Adjustment Scale, Revised 1971.** Psychiatric patients; 1957-71; MACC; 5 scores: mood, cooperation, communication, social contact, total adjustment; same as the 1962 edition except for format and a few changes in wording; Robert B. Ellsworth; Western Psychological Services. *

For additional information, see P:147 (10 references); for a review by Wilson H. Guertin, see 6:135 (2 references); for a review by Maurice Lorr, see 5:82.

REFERENCES THROUGH 1971

1-2. See 6:135.
3-12. See P:147.
13. THOMPSON, JOHN RICHARD. *The Effects of Industrial Therapy Upon Personality and Behavior.* Doctor's thesis, University of Colorado (Boulder, Colo.), 1960. (*DA* 21:3170)
14. HANLON, THOMAS E.; NUSSBAUM, KURT; WITTIG, BARBARA; HANLON, DOLORES D.; AND KURLAND, ALBERT A. "The Comparative Effectiveness of Amitriptyline, Perphenazine, and Their Combination in the Treatment of Chronic Psychotic Female Patients." *J New Drugs* 4:52–60 Ja-F '64. *
15. MAY, PHILIP R. A., AND TUMA, A. HUSSAIN. "Choice of Criteria for the Assessment of Treatment Outcome." *J Psychiatric Res* (England) 2(3):199–209 '64. * (*PA* 39:15562)
16. GASSNER, SUZANNE MARIE. *The Relationship Between Patient-Therapist Compatibility and Treatment Effectiveness.* Doctor's thesis, Syracuse University (Syracuse, N.Y., 1968. (*DA* 29:4845B)
17. URBAN, THEODORE STANLEY. *Wives' Needs as Related to Perceptions of Their Husbands' Post-Mental Hospital Behavior.* Doctor's thesis, Pennsylvania State University (University Park, Pa.), 1968. (*DA* 29:3954B)
18. McDOWELL, RICHARD LANE. *An Evaluation of a Residential Treatment Program for Adolescents as Measured by Post-Hospital Adjustment: A Follow-Up Study.* Doctor's thesis, University of Kansas (Lawrence, Kan.), 1969. (*DAI* 30:2855A)
19. RAPPAPORT, JULIAN, AND CHINSKY, JACK M. "Behavior Ratings of Chronic Hospitalized Patients: Cross-Situational and Cross-Rater Agreement." *J Consult & Clin Psychol* 34(3): 394–7 Je '70. * (*PA* 44:14637)
20. RITTENHOUSE, JOAN DUNNE. "Endurance of Effect: Family Unit Treatment Compared to Identified Patient Treatment." Abstract. *Proc 78th Ann Conv Am Psychol Assn* 5(2): 535–6 '70. * (*PA* 44:18805)
21. SATO, FUMIKO. "A Study on the Staff-Patient Interaction in the Psychiatric Hospital: 1, Analysis of the Attendants' Ratings of the MACC Behavioral Adjustment Scale With Psychiatric Patients." *Tohoku Psychologica Folia* (Japan) 29(1–2): 21–32 '70. * (*PA* 49:7291)
22. CULMER, PHYLLIS ANNE. *Staff-Patient Goal Congruence and Changes in Three Measures of Improvement During Milieu Therapy.* Doctor's thesis, University of Texas (Austin, Tex.), 1971. (*DAI* 32:6638B)
23. SMITH, CHARLES E.; PRYER, MARGARET W.; AND DI-STEFANO, M. K., JR. "Internal-External Control and Severity of Emotional Impairment Among Psychiatric Patients." *J Clin Psychol* 27(4):449–50 O '71. * (*PA* 47:9303)

Lüscher Color Test

CUMULATIVE NAME INDEX

Abbott, P. S.: 7 Lorr, M.: *rev, 5:82*
Anker, J. M.: 3 Lyerly, S. B.: 7
Arthur, G.: 9–10, 12 Lyle, C.: 2
Childers, B.: 9–10, 12 McDowell, R. L.: 18
Chinsky, J. M.: 19 McKeever, W. F.: 6
Clayton, W. H.: 1 Marks, J.: 2
Culmer, P. A.: 22 May, P. R. A.: 6, 15
Distefano, M. K.: 11, 23 Nussbaum, K.: 14
Ellsworth, R.: 9–10 Pryer, M. W.: 11, 23
Ellsworth, R. B.: 1, 12 Rappaport, J.: 19
Foster, L.: 12 Rittenhouse, J. D.: 20
Gassner, S. M.: 16 Sato, F.: 21
Giedt, F. H.: 4 Smith, C. E.: 23
Goldstein, M. J.: 5 Stauffacher, J. C.: 2
Guertin, W. H.: *rev, 6:135* Thompson, J. R.: 13
Hanlon, D. D.: 14 Tuma, A. H.: 15
Hanlon, T. S.: 14 Urban, T. S.: 17
Jones, R. B.: 5 Walsh, R. P.: 3
Kroeker, D.: 9–10, 12 Weeks, L. E.: 8
Kurland, A. A.: 14 Wittig, B.: 14

[1265]

*****M-B History Record: Self-Administered Form.** Psychiatric patients and penal groups; 1957-72; MBHR; 7 scores: family disunity, conflict with parents, health awareness, introversion, school and job failure, social misfit, breakdowns and addiction; test by Peter F. Briggs; manual (reprint of *J Clin Psychol* 28(4):431–48 O '72) by Peter F. Briggs, David L. Rouzer, Ronald L. Hamberg, and Thomas R. Holman; Clinical Psychology Publishing Co., Inc. *

For additional information, see P:148 (3 references); see also 6:136 (2 references).

REFERENCES THROUGH 1971

1-2. See 6:136.
3-5. See P:148.
6. WIRT, ROBERT D., AND BRIGGS, PETER F. "Personality and Environmental Factors in the Development of Delinquency." *Psychol Monogr* 73(15):1–47 '59. * (*PA* 35:5219)
7. FULTON, JOHN R., AND LOREI, THEODORE W. "Predicting Length of Psychiatric Hospitalization From History Records." *J Clin Psychol* 23:218–21 Ap '67. * (*PA* 41:9047)
8. MACK, JAMES LEWIS. *An Objective Comparison of Parole Successes and Failures in Terms of Their History and Personality Adjustment.* Doctor's thesis, University of Minnesota (Minneapolis, Minn.), 1967. (*DA* 28:3475B)
9. TALBOT, AMY. *Differences Between Good and Poor Prognosis Schizophrenics in Defensive Behavior, Perceptual Organization, Concept Formation, and Development and Social Experiences.* Doctor's thesis, University of Houston (Houston, Tex.), 1968. (*DA* 29:4854B)
10. BARDEN, DONNA MARIE FARRELL. *A Comparison of the Histories of Delinquent Boys and Girls.* Doctor's thesis, University of Minnesota (Minneapolis, Minn.), 1969. (*DAI* 30: 3860B)
11. LOREI, THEODORE W., AND VESTRE, NORRIS D. "A Set of Factor Analytically Derived Scales for Scoring the M-B History Record." *Multiv Behav Res* 4(2):181–93 Ap '69. * (*PA* 43:16010)
12. ROUZER, DAVID LEE. *Construct Validation of the Minnesota-Briggs History Questionnaire: Age and Personality Correlates.* Doctor's thesis, University of Minnesota (Minneapolis, Minn.), 1970. (*DAI* 31:3006B)

CUMULATIVE NAME INDEX

Barden, D. M. F.: 10 Mack, J. L.: 8
Briggs, P. F.: 1–2, 6 Rouzer, D. L.: 12
Fulton, J. R.: 7 Talbot, A.: 9
Guertin, W. H.: 3 Vestre, N. D.: 5, 11
Holman, T. R.: 4 Wirt, R. D.: 6
Lorei, T. W.: 5, 7, 11

[1266]

*****M-Scale: An Inventory of Attitudes Toward Black/White Relations in the United States.** College and adults; 1968-69; MS; James H. Morrison; the Author. *

For additional information, see P:146.

REFERENCES THROUGH 1971

1. MORRISON, JAMES H. "M-Scale: Encounter With Reality." *Training & Develop J* 23(10):20–1 O '69. * (*PA* 44:19612)

CUMULATIVE NAME INDEX

Morrison, J. H.: 1

[1267]

★**Maferr Inventory of Feminine Values.** Older adolescents and adults; 1955–68; formerly called *Inventory of Feminine Values* and *Inventory of Female Values*; perception of sex role; 1968 tests identical with tests copyrighted 1966; a lower level version, entitled *Maferr Developmental Inventory of Feminine Values,* for younger adolescents in junior and senior high school is also available; 5 tests (consisting of basically the same 34 items with differing directions and scrambled order) : woman's self-perception (Form A), woman's ideal woman (B), woman's perception of man's ideal woman (C), man's ideal woman (BB, for men), man's perception of woman's ideal woman (G, for men) ; original inventory by Alexandra Botwin, revision by Anne Steinmann and David J. Fox; Maferr Foundation, Inc. *

REFERENCES THROUGH 1971

1. FAND, ALEXANDRA BOTWINIK. *Sex Role and Self-Concept: A Study of the Feminine Sex Role as Perceived by Eighty-Five College Women for Themselves, Thir Ideal Woman, the Average Woman and Men's Ideal Woman.* Doctor's thesis, Cornell University (Ithaca, N.Y.), 1955. (*DA* 15:1135)
2. STEINMANN, ANNE; LEVI, JOSEPH; AND FOX, DAVID J. "Feminine Role Perceptions of Women Physicians: Self-Perception of Women Physicians as Compared to Their Perception of Ideal Women and Men's Ideal Women." *J Am Med Women's Assn* 19:776–82 S '64. *
3. STEINMANN, ANNE; LEVI, JOSEPH; AND FOX, DAVID J. "Self-Concept of College Women Compared With Their Concept of Ideal Woman and Men's Ideal Woman." *J Counsel Psychol* 11:370–4 w '64. * (*PA* 39:7710)
4. STEINMANN, ANNE. "Guidance Personnel and the College Woman." *Personnel J* 45:294–9 My '66. * (*PA* 40:8101)
5. STEINMANN, ANNE, AND FOX, DAVID J. "Male-Female Perceptions of the Female Role in the United States." *J Psychol* 64:265–76 N '66. * (*PA* 41:1520)
6. STEINMANN, ANNE, AND FOX, DAVID J. "Male and Female Physicians' Perceptions of Ideal Feminine Roles." *J Am Med Women's Assn* 22:184–8 Mr '67. *
7. STEINMANN, ANNE, AND FOX, DAVID J. "Specific Areas of Agreement and Conflict in Women's Self-Perception and Their Perception of Men's Ideal Woman in Two South American Urban Communities and an Urban Community in the United States." *J Marriage & Family* 31(2):281–9 My '69. * (*PA* 44:20767)
8. RAPPAPORT, ALAN F.; PAYNE, DAVID; AND STEINMANN, ANNE. "Marriage as a Factor in the Dyadic Perception of the Female Sex Role." *Psychol Rep* 27(1):283–4 Ag '70. * (*PA* 45:6148)
9. RAPPAPORT, ALAN F.; PAYNE, DAVID; AND STEINMANN, ANNE. "Perceptual Differences Between Married and Single College Women for the Concepts of Self, Ideal Woman, and Man's Ideal Woman." *J Marriage & Family* 32(3):441–2 Ag '70. * (*PA* 46:6660)
10. STEINMANN, ANNE. "Female-Role Perception as a Factor in Counseling of High School and College Women." *J Nat Assn Women Deans & Counselors* 34(1):27–33 f '70. *
11. STEINMANN, ANNE; DOHERTY, MARY AUSTIN; AND FOX, DAVID J. "Perceptions of Women Religious Regarding the Female Role." *Nat Cath Guid Conf J* 15(1):43–54 f '70. * (*PA* 45:8152)

CUMULATIVE NAME INDEX

Doherty, M. A.: 11	Payne, D.: 8–9
Fand, A. B.: 1	Rappaport, A. F.: 8–9
Fox, D. J.: 2–3, 5–7, 11	Steinmann, A.: 2–11
Levi, J.: 2–3	

[1268]

★**Maferr Inventory of Masculine Values.** Older adolescents and adults; 1966–73; perception of sex role; a lower level version, entitled *Maferr Developmental Inventory of Masculine Values,* for younger adolescents in junior and senior high school is also available; 5 tests (consisting of basically the same 34 items with differing directions and scrambled order) : man's self perception (Form H), man's ideal man (D), man's perception of woman's ideal man (E), woman's ideal man (DD, for women), woman's perception of man's ideal man (F, for women) ; Anne Steinmann and David J. Fox; Maferr Foundation, Inc. *

REFERENCES THROUGH 1971

1. STEINMANN, ANNE; FOX, DAVID J.; AND FARKAS, RUTH. "Male and Female Perceptions of Male Sex Roles." Abstract. *Proc 76th Ann Conv Am Psychol Assn* 3:421–2 '68. * (*PA* 43:771, title only)

CUMULATIVE NAME INDEX

Farkas, R.: 1	Steinmann, A.: 1
Fox, D. J.: 1	

[1269]

The Manchester Scales of Social Adaptation. Ages 6–15; 1966; MSSA; adaptation of *Vineland Social Maturity Scale;* 13 scores: social perspective (general, sport, current affairs, aesthetic, scientific, total), self-direction (socialisation of play, freedom of movement, self-help, handling of money, responsibility in home, total), total; E. A. Lunzer; NFER Publishing Co. Ltd. [England]. *

For additional information, reviews by G. A. V. Morgan and M. L. Kellmer Pringle, and an excerpted review by Maurice Chazan, see 7:99 (1 reference).

REFERENCES THROUGH 1971

1. See 7:99.

CUMULATIVE NAME INDEX

Brennan, W. K.: 1	Morgan, G. A. V.: *rev,* 7:99
Chazan, M.: *exc,* 7:99	Pringle, M. L. K.: *rev,* 7:99

[1270]

Mandel Social Adjustment Scale. Psychiatric patients and others; 1959; MSAS; 8 scores: occupational, family life, economic, health, religion, residence, community and social, total; Nathan G. Mandel; the Author. *

For additional information, see P:151 (2 references).

REFERENCES THROUGH 1971

1–2. See P:151.

CUMULATIVE NAME INDEX

Briggs, P. F.: 2	Mandel, N.: 1
Golden, J. S.: 1	Silver, R. J.: 1

[1271]

The Manson Evaluation. Adults; 1948; ME; identification of alcoholics, potential alcoholics, and severely maladjusted adults; 8 scores: anxiety, depressive fluctuations, emotional sensitivity, resentfulness, incompleteness, aloneness, interpersonal relations, total; Morse P. Manson; Western Psychological Services. *

For additional information, see P:152 (1 reference) ; for a review by Dugal Campbell, see 6:137 (5 references) ; for reviews by Charles H. Honzik and Albert L. Hunsicker, see 4:68 (4 references).

REFERENCES THROUGH 1971

1–4. See 4:68.
5–9. See 6:137.
10. See P:152.
11. MOSES, KENNETH L. *A Psychometric Differentiation of Active Alcoholics From Alcoholics in Remission.* Master's thesis, Springfield College (Springfield, Mass.), 1968.
12. TOPPEN, J. T. "Underemployment: Economic or Psychological." *Psychol Rep* 28(1):111–22 F '71. * (*PA* 46:4762)

CUMULATIVE NAME INDEX

Campbell, D.: *rev,* 6:137	Moses, K. L.: 11
Clark, J. W.: 7	Murphy, D. G.: 5–6
Gavales, D.: 10	Seeley, J. R.: 8
Gibbins, R. J.: 8	Smart, R. G.: 8
Honzik, C. H.: *rev,* 4:68	Stotsky, B. A.: 9
Hunsicker, A. L.: *rev,* 4:68	Toppen, J. T.: 12
Manson, M. P.: 1–4	

[1272]

Martin S-D Inventory. Clients and patients; 1970; MSDI; William T. Martin; Psychologists and Educators, Inc. *

For additional information, see 7:100.

[1273]

Maryland Parent Attitude Survey. Parents; [1957–66]; MPAS; parental attitudes toward child rearing; for research use only; 4 scores: disciplinarian, indulgent, protective, rejecting; Donald K. Pumroy; the Author. *

For additional information, see P:160 (6 references).

REFERENCES THROUGH 1971

1–6. See P:160.
7. BRODY, GRACE F. "Maternal Child-Rearing Attitudes and Child Behavior." Abstract. *Develop Psychol* 1(1):66 Ja '69. * *(PA* 43:6767)
8. DAVIS, WILLIAM L., AND PHARES, E. JERRY. "Parental Antecedents of Internal-External Control of Reinforcement." *Psychol Rep* 24(2):427–36 Ap '69. * *(PA* 43:15598)
9. NASH, JOHN MORTON. *Prediction of Academic Achievement of Women at a Private Junior College Through Use of Certain Intellective and Family Relationships Measures.* Doctor's thesis, Boston University (Boston, Mass.), 1970. *(DAI* 31:2113A)
10. SWENSON, STEPHEN SHAILER. *Changing Expressed Parental Attitudes Toward Child-Rearing Practices and Its Effect on School Adaptation and Level of Adjustment Perceived by Parents.* Doctor's thesis, Boston University (Boston, Mass.), 1970. *(DAI* 31:2118A)

CUMULATIVE NAME INDEX

Allan, T. K.: 6   Phares, E. J.: 8
Baer, D. J.: 4   Pumroy, D. K.: 3
Brody, G. F.: 1–2, 7   Schwitzgebel, R. K.: 4
Davis, W. L.: 8   Swenson, S. S.: 10
Hodgson, E. W.: 6   Tolor, A.: 5
Nash, J. M.: 9

[1274]

★**Mathematics Anxiety Rating Scale.** College and adults; 1972; MARS; Richard M. Suinn; Rocky Mountain Behavioral Science Institute, Inc. *

[1275]

Maudsley Personality Inventory. College and adults; 1959–62; MPI; for revised edition, see *Eysenck Personality Inventory;* 2 scores: neuroticism, extraversion; H. J. Eysenck. *

a) BRITISH EDITION. 1959; University of London Press Ltd. [England].

b) UNITED STATES EDITION. 1962; test items identical with British edition; Robert R. Knapp (manual); Educational and Industrial Testing Service.

For additional information, see P:161 (149 references); for reviews by Arthur R. Jensen, James C. Lingoes, William Stephenson, and Philip E. Vernon and excerpted reviews by Edward S. Bordin, A. Bursill, and G. A. Foulds, see 6:138 (120 references).

REFERENCES THROUGH 1971

1–117. See 6:138.
118–266. See P:161.
267. BENDIG, A. W., AND HOFFMAN, JENNY L. "Bills' Index of Adjustment and the Maudsley Personality Inventory." *Psychol Rep* 3:507 D '57. * *(PA* 33:3304)
268. HARRIS, JOSEPH JERRY. *A Self Concept Measure for Prisoners and Its Relation to Certain Objective Indices of Criminality.* Doctor's thesis, University of Pittsburgh (Pittsburgh, Pa.), 1957. *(DA* 18:285)
269. ROBIN, A. A. "A Pilot Study as Suggested by 'Recidivism, Psychotherapy and Personality.' " *Brit J Delinq* 8:139–41 Jl '57. * *(PA* 33:1786)
270. BENDIG, A. W. "Extraversion, Neuroticism, Radicalism, and Tendermindedness." Abstract. *J Consult Psychol* 22:292 Ag '58. * *(PA* 33:1670, title only)
271. COPPEN, ALEC J. "Psychosomatic Aspects of Pre-Eclamptic Toxaemia." *J Psychosom Res* (England) 2(4):241–65 '58. * *(PA* 33:8835)
272. CALLAWAY, ENOCH. "The Influence of Amobarbital (Amylobarbitone) and Methamphetamine on the Focus of Attention." *J Mental Sci* (England) 105:382–92 Ap '59. * *(PA* 34:4429)
273. COPPEN, A. J. "Vomiting of Early Pregnancy: Psychological Factors and Body Build." *Lancet* (England) 1:172–3 Ja 24 '59. *
274. DOWDY, CHARLES DANIEL. *An Experimental Test of Eysenck's and Cattell's Theories of Extraversion-Introversion.* Doctor's thesis, University of Pittsburgh (Pittsburgh, Pa.), 1959. *(DA* 20:3376)

275. EVERSTINE, LOUIS. *The Conditioning of Neurotic Verbalizations.* Doctor's thesis, University of Pittsburgh (Pittsburgh, Pa.), 1960. *(DA* 21:3849)
276. KNOWLES, J. B., AND LUCAS, C. J. "Experimental Studies of the Placebo Response." *J Mental Sci* (England) 106:231–40 Ja '60. * *(PA* 35:6542)
277. LYNN, R. "Extraversion, Reminiscence, and Satiation Effects." *Brit J Psychol* 51:319–24 N '60. * *(PA* 35:2273)
278. SAINSBURY, P. "Neurosis and Psychosomatic Disorders in Out-Patients." *Adv Psychosom Med* 1:259–69 '60. *
279. CAIRD, W. K.; SLOANE, BRUCE; AND INGLIS, JAMES. "The Effects of Nialamide and Ethyl Alcohol on Some Personality, Cognitive and Psychomotor Variables in Normal Volunteers." *J Neuropsychiatry* 2:31–4 S–O '61. *
280. EYSENCK, H. J. "Personality and Social Attitudes." *J Social Psychol* 53:243–8 Ap '61. * *(PA* 36:1GD43E)
281. EYSENCK, S. B. G. "Personality, and Pain Assessment in Childbirth of Married and Unmarried Mothers." *J Mental Sci* (England) 107:417–30 My '61. * *(PA* 36:3JU17E)
282. INGLIS, J.; CAIRD, W. K.; AND SLOANE, R. B. "An Objective Assessment of the Effects of Nialamide on Depressed Patients." *Can Med Assn J* 84:1059–63 My 13 '61. *
283. LYNN, R. "Personality Characteristics of the Mothers of Aggressive and Unaggressive Children." *J Genetic Psychol* 99:159–64 S '61. * *(PA* 36:3FG59L)
284. LYNN, R., AND EYSENCK, H. J. "Tolerance for Pain, Extraversion and Neuroticism." *Percept & Motor Skills* 12:161–2 Ap '61. * *(PA* 36:1HJ61L)
285. SINGH, S. D., AND SINGH, V. "The Effect of Stimulant and Depressant Drugs on the Latency of Autokinetic Illusion." *Acta Psychologica* (Netherlands) 18(5):354–9 '61. * *(PA* 37:661)
286. VOGEL, MURIEL D. "The Relationship of Personality Factors to Drinking Patterns of Alcoholics." *Q J Studies Alcohol* 22:394–400 S '61. *
287. BRENGELMANN, JOHANNES C., AND LINDAHL, LESLIE E. H. "Personality, Task Difficulty, and Level of Memory Performance." *Archiv für die Gesamte Psychologie* (West Germany) 114:242–59 D '62. * *(PA* 38:1179)
288. DAS, J. P., AND MITRA, A. K. "Relative Effectiveness of Electric Shock and Praise and Reproof in Verbal Conditioning." *J General Psychol* 67:141–6 Jl '62. * *(PA* 37:2442)
289. HOWARTH, E. "Extroversion and Dream Symbolism: An Empirical Study." *Psychol Rep* 10:211–4 F '62. * *(PA* 37:1469)
290. KNOWLES, J. B., AND LUCAS, C. J. "The Contribution of Attitude and Personality to the Patient's Rating of Treatment." *Proc Royal Soc Med* (England) 55:778–80 S '62. *
291. LYNN, R., AND BUTLER, J. "Introversion and the Arousal Jag." *Brit J Social & Clin Psychol* 1:150–1 Je '62. * *(PA* 37:3261)
292. COPPEN, ALEC, AND METCALFE, MARYSE. "Cancer and Extraversion." *Brit Med J* 2(5348):18–9 Jl 6 '63. *
293. EDWARDS, GRIFFITH. "Duration of Post-Hypnotic Effect." *Brit J Psychiatry* 109:259–66 Mr '63. * *(PA* 38:2856)
294. FRANKS, CYRIL M., AND LINDAHL, L. E. H. "Extraversion and Rate of Fluctuation of the Necker Cube." *Percept & Motor Skills* 16:131–7 F '63. * *(PA* 38:136)
295. KNOWLES, J. B. "Rigidity, Extraversion and Verbal Conditioning Effects." *J Clin Psychol* 19:282–6 Jl '63. * *(PA* 39:6776)
296. PERRIS, CARLO, AND BRATTEMO, CARL-ERIK. "The Sedation Threshold as a Method of Evaluating Anti-Depressive Treatments: A Preliminary Report." *Acta Psychiatrica Scandinavica Supplementum* (Denmark) 169:111–9 '63. *
297. CHAPPLE, P. A. L., AND FURNEAUX, W. D. "Changes of Personality in Pregnancy and Labour." Abstract. *Practitioner* (England) 192:286 F '64. *
298. CHAPPLE, P. A. L., AND FURNEAUX, W. D. "Changes of Personality in Pregnancy and Labour." *Proc Royal Soc Med* (England) 57:260–1 Ap '64. *
299. COPPEN, A. J., AND METCALFE, M. "Cancer and Extraversion," pp. 30–4. In *Psychosomatic Aspects of Neoplastic Disease.* The Proceedings of the Third International Conference of the International Psychosomatic Cancer Study Group Held at Newnham College, Cambridge, England, 22nd to 26th July 1963. Edited by D. M. Kissen and L. L. Leshan. Philadelphia, Pa.: J. B. Lippincott Co., 1964. Pp. xii, 231. *
300. DAVIDSON, P. O.; PAYNE, R. W.; AND SLOANE, R. B. "Introversion, Neuroticism, and Conditioning." *J Abn & Social Psychol* 68:136–43 F '64. * *(PA* 38:5233)
301. EVANS, E. G. S. "Reasoning Ability and Personality Differences Among Student-Teachers." *Brit J Ed Psychol* 34:305–14 N '64. * *(PA* 39:8718)
302. FURNEAUX, W. D., AND CHAPPLE, P. A. L. "Hypnosis and Relaxation." Abstract. *Practitioner* (England) 192:287 F '64. *
303. FURNEAUX, W. D., AND CHAPPLE, P. A. L. "Some Objective and Subjective Characteristics of Labour Influenced by Personality, and Their Modification by Hypnosis or Relaxation." *Proc Royal Soc Med* (England) 57:261–2 Ap '64. *
304. JONSSON, CARL-OTTO; LIVDAHL, HANS F.; HENRYSSON, STEN; AND LINDÉN, ÅKE. "A Factor Analysis of a Neuroticism

Inventory." *Scand J Psychol* (Sweden) 5(2):108–16 '64. * (*PA* 39:1892)

305. KISSEN, D. M. "Lung Cancer, Inhalation and Personality," pp. 3–11. In *Psychosomatic Aspects of Neoplastic Disease.* The Proceedings of the Third International Conference of the International Psychosomatic Cancer Study Group Held at Newnham College, Cambridge, England, 22nd to 26th July 1963. Edited by D. M. Kissen and L. L. Leshan. Philadelphia, Pa.: J. B. Lippincott Co., 1964. Pp. xii, 231. *

306. KISSEN, DAVID M. "Personality and Lung Cancer." Letter. *Lancet* (England) 1:216–7 Ja 25 '64. *

307. KISSEN, DAVID M. "Relationship Between Lung Cancer, Cigarette Smoking, Inflation and Personality." *Brit J Med Psychol* 37:203–16 pt 3 '64. *

308. KRISHNAMOORTI, SINGA R., AND SHAGASS, CHARLES. "Some Psychological Test Correlates of Sedation Threshold." *Recent Adv Biol Psychiatry* 6:256–66 '64. *

309. LEIPOLD, WILLIAM D., AND KNUTSON, CLIFFORD S. "Differences in Social Desirability, Anxiety, and Introversion-Extraversion With Varying Lengths of Hospitalization." *Psychol Rep* 15:723–6 D '64. * (*PA* 39:7948)

310. REED, G. F., AND SEDMAN, G. "Personality and Depersonalization Under Sensory Deprivation Conditions." *Percept & Motor Skills* 18:659–60 Ap '64. * (*PA* 39:3615)

311. SAINSBURY, P. "Neuroticism and Hypertension in an Out-Patient Population." *J Psychosom Res* (England) 8:235–8 D '64. *

312. SPENCE, KENNETH W., AND SPENCE, JANET TAYLOR. "Relation of Eyelid Conditioning to Manifest Anxiety, Extraversion, and Rigidity." *J Abn & Social Psychol* 68:144–9 F '64. * (*PA* 38:5259)

313. SYKES, M. K., AND TREDGOLD, R. F. "Restricted Orbital Undercutting: A Study of Its Effects on 350 Patients Over the Ten Years 1951–1960." *Brit J Psychiatry* 110:609–40 S '64. * (*PA* 39:5329)

314. BROWN, D. G., AND YOUNG, A. J. "Body Image and Susceptibility to Contact Dermatitis." *Brit J Med Psychol* 38:261–7 S '65. *

315. DODGE, DAVID WILSON. *Contrasts and Similarities in the Orienting Responses of Extraverts and Introverts as Indicated by Long and Short Term Vasoconstrictive Reactions to Auditory Signals and Monotones.* Doctor's thesis, Purdue University (Lafayette, Ind.), 1965. (*DA* 27:301B)

316. EYSENCK, HANS J. "Extraversion and the Acquisition of Eyeblink and GSR Conditioned Responses." *Psychol B* 63:258–70 Ap '65. * (*PA* 39:10319)

317. GUTMAN, GLORIA M. "The Effects of Age and Extraversion on Pursuit Rotor Reminiscence." *J Gerontol* 20:346–50 Jl '65. *

318. HARE, E. H., AND SHAW, G. K. Chap. 8, "Correlates of Mental Health: 2, Personality and Physique," pp. 62–75, passim. In their *Mental Health on a New Housing Estate: A Comparative Study of Health in Two Districts of Croydon.* London: Oxford University Press, 1965. Pp. ix, 135. *

319. HARE, E. H., AND SHAW, G. K. "The Patient's Spouse and Concordance on Neuroticism." Letter. *Brit J Psychiatry* 111:102–3 Ja '65. *

320. HARE, E. H., AND SHAW, G. K. "A Study in Family Health: 1, Health in Relation to Family Size." *Brit J Psychiatry* 111:461–6 Je '65. * (*PA* 39:15893)

321. HARPER, MAX; GURNEY, CLAIR; SAVAGE, R. DOUGLASS; AND ROTH, MARTIN. "Forearm Blood Flow in Normal Subjects and Patients With Phobic Anxiety States." *Brit J Psychiatry* 111:723–31 Ag '65. * (*PA* 40:1242)

322. JOHNSTON, JAMES ORRIN. *Relationships Between Intelligence and Personality Variables.* Doctor's thesis, Oklahoma State University (Stillwater, Okla.), 1965. (*DA* 27:315B)

323. KREITMAN, NORMAN. "Familial Aspects of Neuroticism and Extraversion." Letter. *Brit J Psychiatry* 111:101–7 Ja '65. *

324. LEVINSON, FREDA, AND MEYER, VICTOR. "Personality Changes in Relation to Psychiatric Status Following Orbital Cortex Undercutting." *Brit J Psychiatry* 111:207–18 Mr '65. * (*PA* 39:9509)

325. LUCAS, C. J.; KELVIN, R. P.; AND OJHA, A. B. "The Psychological Health of the Pre-Clinical Medical Student." *Brit J Psychiatry* 111:473–8 Je '65. * (*PA* 39:15925)

326. MONTVILLE, PAUL R. *Introversion-Extraversion, Neuroticism, and Retino-Cortical Inhibition.* Doctor's thesis, University of Ottawa (Ottawa, Ont., Canada), 1965.

327. QUAY, HERBERT C., AND HUNT, WILLIAM A. "Psychopathy, Neuroticism, and Verbal Conditioning: A Replication and Extension." Abstract. *J Consult Psychol* 29:283 Je '65. * (*PA* 39:12656)

328. SHAGASS, CHARLES, AND SCHWARTZ, MARVIN. "Age, Personality, and Somatosensory Cerebral Evoked Responses." *Sci* 148:1359–61 Je 4 '65. * (*PA* 39:11532)

329. SHANMUGAM, T. E. "Personality Traits of Pupils Who Had Their Education Through the Medium of Their Mother Tongue and English." *J Ed Res & Exten* (India) 2:51–7 O '65. *

330. SINGH, AMAR J. *Interests, Values and Personality Traits of Students Specialising in Different Fields of Study in Univer-*

sity. Master's thesis, University of London (London, England), 1965. [Abstract: *Brit J Ed Psychol* 39(1):90–1 (*PA* 43:17900)]

331. BAGG, C. E., AND CROOKES, T. G. "Palmar Digital Sweating in Women Suffering From Depression." *Brit J Psychiatry* 112:1251–5 D '66. * (*PA* 41:6094)

332. BRADY, PAUL R. J. *The Relationship of Introversion-Extraversion to Physical Persistence.* Master's thesis, University of Alberta (Edmonton, Alta., Canada), 1966.

333. BROWN, L. B. "The Structure of Religious Belief." *J Sci Study Relig* 5:259–72 sp '66. * (*PA* 41:1465)

334. BURDICK, J. ALAN. "Autonomic Lability and Neuroticism." *J Psychosom Res* (England) 9:339–42 My '66. * (*PA* 40:10852)

335. DEVADASAN, K. "Ratiocination and Certain Selected Personality Variables." *Manas* (India) 13(1):5–9 '66. * (*PA* 40:12910)

336. ESTABROOK, MARINA, AND SOMMER, ROBERT. "Study Habits and Introversion-Extroversion." *Psychol Rep* 19:750 D '66. * (*PA* 41:4970)

337. FARLEY, F. H. "Individual Differences in Solution Time in Error-Free Problem Solving." *Brit J Social & Clin Psychol* 5:306–9 D '66. * (*PA* 41:3952)

338. FRANKS, CYRIL M., AND MANTELL, DAVID. "Introversion-Extraversion and the Verbal Conditioning and Generalization of Meaning Responses to Nonsense Syllables in Normal and Alcoholic Subjects." *Brit J Social & Clin Psychol* 5:299–305 D '66. * (*PA* 41:3889)

339. KISSEN, DAVID M. "The Significance of Personality in Lung Cancer in Men." *Ann N Y Acad Sci* 125:820–6 Ja 21 '66. * (*PA* 40:6900)

340. LEVINE, FREDERIC M.; TURSKY, BERNARD; AND NICHOLS, DAVID C. "Tolerance for Pain, Extraversion and Neuroticism: Failure to Replicate Results." *Percept & Motor Skills* 23:847–50 D '66. * (*PA* 41:7370)

341. MADDI, SALVATORE R., AND ANDREWS, SUSAN L. "The Need for Variety in Fantasy and Self-Description." *J Personality* 34:610–25 D '66. * (*PA* 41:10467)

342. PARKE, ROSS D., AND WALTERS, RICHARD H. "Alcoholism, Avoidance Learning and Emotional Responsiveness." *Brit J Social & Clin Psychol* 5:276–89 D '66. * (*PA* 41:3878)

343. SHAPIRO, EMANUEL. *An Investigation of the Utility of Two Dimensional Models for the Assessment of Personality.* Doctor's thesis, Purdue University (Lafayette, Ind.), 1966. (*DA* 27:2519B)

344. SHEPHARD, R. J. "Initial 'Fitness' and Personality as Determinants of the Response to a Training Regime." *Ergonomics* (England) 9:3–16 Ja '66. *

345. WEST, JOY, AND WEST, ERIC D. "The Electroencephalogram and Personality of Women With Headaches on Oral Contraceptives." *Lancet* (England) 1(7448):1180–2 My 28 '66. *

346. WILLIAMS, A. P. "The Selection of Maintenance Engineers for Data Processing Equipment." *Occup Psychol* (England) 40:53–65 Ja–Ap '66. * (*PA* 41:851)

347. ZUCKERMAN, MARVIN; PERSKY, HAROLD; HOPKINS, T. ROBERT; MURTAUGH, THOMAS; BASU, G. K.; AND SCHILLING, MARY. "Comparison of Stress Effects of Perceptual and Social Isolation." *Arch Gen Psychiatry* 14:356–65 Ap '66. * (*PA* 40:6182)

348. CLARIDGE, GORDON S. Chap. 5, "Causal and Descriptive Analysis of Dysthymia-Hysteria," pp. 98–115, passim. In his *Personality and Arousal: A Psychophysiological Study of Psychiatric Disorder.* Oxford, England: Pergamon Press Ltd., 1967. Pp. xviii, 274. *

349. CROOKES, T. G. "Yes- and No-Saying on the Maudsley Personality Inventory." *Papers Psychol* (Northern Ireland) 1:53–5 O '67. * (*PA* 42:3980)

350. GEORGE, E. I.; PILLAY, P. GOPALA; AND DHARMANGADAN, B. "Effect of Physical Disability on Personality Adjustment and Achievement of Secondary School Pupils." *J Ed & Psychol* (India) 24:180–7 Ja '67. *

351. MCDONALD, CARRICK. "Measures of Neuroticism in the Elderly." *Austral & N Zeal J Psychiatry* (Australia) 1:44–7 Mr '67. *

352. MAY, A. E., AND STIRRUP, W. "Neuroticism and Extraversion in ABO Blood Groups." *Brit J Psychiatry* 113:281–2 F '67. * (*PA* 41:9139)

353. SANATAN, R. N., AND WIG, N. N. "A Personality Study of Neurotics on Modified Hindi and Punjabi Version of the M.P.I." *Indian J Psychiatry* 9:49–52 Ja '67. *

354. STAVELEY, BRYAN. *The Abilities and Interests of Craft and Technician Students of Mechanical Engineering.* Master's thesis, University of Manchester (Manchester, England), 1967. (Abstract: *Brit J Ed Psychol* 38:324)

355. TAFT, RONALD. "The Role of Personality Traits in the Social Assimilation of Immigrants." *Austral & N Zeal J Sociol* (Australia) 3:19–31 Ap '67. * (*PA* 42:10447)

356. BENNETT, LAWRENCE A. *Sociopathy and Stress.* Doctor's thesis, Claremont Graduate School (Claremont, Calif.), 1968. (*DA* 29:2627B)

357. BETHE, DONALD RAY. *Success in Beginning Handball as a Function of the Theory of Achievement Motivation.* Doctor's thesis, Ohio State University (Columbus, Ohio), 1968. (*DA* 29:1769A)

358. BISHOP, TERENCE J. S. "An Investigation of the Effects of Visual and Auditory Distraction Upon an 'Intellectual' Task With Reference to Distraction Complexity and Extraversion-Introversion." Abstract. *Papers Psychol* (Northern Ireland) 2:66–7 O '68. *

359. BONE, RONALD N. "Extraversion, Neuroticism and Dream Recall." *Psychol Rep* 23:922 D '68. * (*PA* 43:9023)

360. CLUM, GEORGE ARTHUR. *The Relationships Between Measures of Classical and Operant Conditioning, Psychiatric Diagnoses and Statistically Derived Classificatory Groups.* Doctor's thesis, St. John's University (Jamaica, N.Y.), 1968. (*DA* 29:3899B)

361. CRICKMORE, LEON. "An Approach to the Measurement of Music Appreciation (II)." *J Res Music Ed* 16:291–301 w '68. * (*PA* 43:8756)

362. FA-YU, CHENG. "Reaction Time of Introverts vs Extroverts in Schizophrenics and Normals." *Acta Psychologica Taiwanica* (Taiwan) 10:45–51 Mr '68. * (*PA* 45:4650)

363. GLAZER, MICHAEL WARREN. *A Comparison of Interference and Reactive Inhibition in Extraversion-Introversion.* Doctor's thesis, University of Florida (Gainesville, Fla.), 1968. (*DAI* 30:381B)

364. GUPTA, B. S. "A Study of Extraversion and Phenobarbitone as Experimental Variables in Verbal Conditioning." *Indian J Exp Psychol* 2:18–20 Ja '68. *

365. HEBRON, MIRIAM E. "A Note on the Predictive Validity of the MPI as Tested by a Semantic Differential Technique." *Brit J Psychol* 59:473–4 N '68. * (*PA* 43:3324)

366. KANUNGO, RABINDRA N. "Retention of Affective Material: Role of Extraversion and Intensity of Affect." *J Pers & Social Psychol* 8:63–8 Ja '68. * (*PA* 42:5500)

367. KELLY, D. H. W., AND WALTER, C. J. S. "The Relationship Between Clinical Diagnosis and Anxiety, Assessed by Forearm Blood Flow and Other Measurements." *Brit J Psychiatry* 114:611–26 My '68. * (*PA* 42:19003)

368. KENYON, F. E. "Physique and Physical Health of Female Homosexuals." *J Neurol Neurosurg & Psychiatry* (England) 31:487–9 O '68. * (*PA* 44:3835)

369. KENYON, F. E. "Studies in Female Homosexuality: 6, The Exclusively Homosexual Group." *Acta Psychiatrica Scandinavica* (Denmark) 44(3):224–37 '68. * (*PA* 43:17634)

370. KONTTINEN, RAIMO. *Relationships Between Graphic Expansivity and Extraversion as a Function of Anxiety and Defensiveness.* Annals Academia Scientiarum Fennica, Series B, No. 159. Helsinki, Finland: Suomalainen Tiedeakatemia, Academia Scientiarum Fennica, 1968. Pp. 108. * (*PA* 43:11307)

371. MARKS, ISAAC. "Measurement of Personality and Attitude: Applications to Clinical Research." *Postgrad Med J* (England) 44:277–85 Ap '68. *

372. MOHAN, JITENDRA, AND CLAIRE, CUCKI. "Personality and Verbal Conditioning." *Manas* (India) 15:87–93 D '68. * (*PA* 43:10726)

373. MOHAN, JITENDRA, AND MOHAN, VIDHU. "Personality, Drive and Fluctuation of Attention." *Indian J Exp Psychol* 2:6–8 Ja '68. *

374. MUTHAYYA, B. C. "Personality Variables and Their Relation to Achievement Motive." *Psychol Studies* (India) 13:98–100 Jl '68. * (*PA* 43:5336)

375. NELSON, D., AND CHERRY, M. "Personality, Adjustment, and Work in a Nation-Wide Longitudinal Survey." *Proc Inter Congr Appl Psychol* 16:732–6 '68. *

376. PRICE, J. B. "Some Results on the Maudsley Personality Inventory From a Sample of Girls in a Borstal." *Brit J Criminol* 8:383–401 O '68. * (*PA* 43:5617)

377. REYNOLDS, EDWARD NEAL. *Interpersonal Risk and Self-Actualization in Four Religious Groups.* Doctor's thesis, Case Western Reserve University (Cleveland, Ohio), 1968. (*DAI* 30:4019A)

378. RIM, Y., AND COHEN, N. "Personality Variables in Making a Choice." *Psychologia* (Japan) 11:191–7 D '68. * (*PA* 44:6053)

379. SAVAGE, R. D., AND BOLTON, N. "A Factor Analysis of Learning Impairment and Intellectual Deterioration in the Elderly." *J Genetic Psychol* 113:177–82 D '68. * (*PA* 43:4391)

380. SHORKEY, CLAYTON THOMAS. *A Study of Variables Related to Conditionability of Verbal Behavior in Schizophrenics.* Doctor's thesis, University of Michigan (Ann Arbor, Mich.), 1968. (*DA* 29:3517B)

381. SINGH, UDAI PRATAP. "Neuroticism and Extraversion on an Indian Sample." *Indian Psychol R* 5:35–9 Jl '68. *

382. SINHA, AWADHESH KUMAR, AND KOCHAR, DINESH CHANDRA. "Worldmindedness: In Relation to Some Personality Variables." *Indian Psychol R* 5:7–12 Jl '68. *

383. WALLACH, MICHAEL A., AND BRANTLEY, HELEN T. "Relative Graphic Expansiveness as a Function of Gross Bodily Activity and the Level of Psychological Disturbance." *J Personality* 36:246–58 Je '68. * (*PA* 42:17219)

384. WALTON, H. J. "Sex Differences in Ability and Outlook of Senior Medical Students." *Brit J Med Ed* 2:156–62 Je '68. *

385. WARD, DOROTHY BALL. *Extraversion-Introversion and Neuroticism-Stability in Relation to Person Perception.* Doctor's thesis, University of Florida (Gainesville, Fla.), 1968. (*DAI* 30:394B)

386. WILLIS, JOE DON. *Achievement Motivation, Success, and Competitiveness in College Wrestling.* Doctor's thesis, Ohio State University (Columbus, Ohio), 1968. (*DA* 29:1443A)

387. ABE, K., AND COPPEN, ALEC. "Personality and Body Composition in Monozygotic Twins With an Affective Disorder." *Brit J Psychiatry* 115(524):777–80 Jl '69. * (*PA* 44:7008)

388. ANDERSSON, ALF L. "Adaptive Regulation of Visual After-Effect Duration and Social-Emotional Adjustment." *Acta Psychologica* (Netherlands) 29(1):1–34 F '69. * (*PA* 43:17450)

389. ASSO, DOREEN; CROWN, SIDNEY; RUSSELL, JOHN A.; AND LOGUE, VALENTINE. "Psychological Aspects of the Stereotactic Treatment of Parkinsonism." *Brit J Psychiatry* 115(522): 541–53 My '69. * (*PA* 44:3964)

390. BAEHR, MELANY E.; FURCON, JOHN E.; AND FROEMEL, ERNEST C. *Psychological Assessment of Patrolman Qualifications in Relation to Field Performance.* Washington, D.C.: United States Government Printing Office, 1969. Pp. vii, 246. *

391. BAILEY, JOHN E., AND METCALFE, MARYSE. "The MPI and the EPI: A Comparative Study on Depressive Patients." *Brit J Social & Clin Psychol* 8(1):50–4 F '69. * (*PA* 43:8483)

392. BELL, DURWARD LYNN. *Background and Personality Variables as Correlates of Attitudes Toward and Information About Mental Health and Mental Illness.* Doctor's thesis, University of Texas (Austin, Tex.), 1969. (*DAI* 30:3379B)

393. BESHAI, JIMMY A. *Behavioral Correlates of Cerebral Dysrhythmia in Delinquents.* Doctor's thesis, University of Kentucky (Lexington, Ky.), 1969. (*DAI* 30:2902B)

394. BILLINGTON, D. REX. *Methods of Determining Pain Tolerance and Relationships to Personality Traits.* Master's thesis, University of Iowa (Iowa City, Iowa), 1969.

395. BROADHURST, ANNE, AND GLASS, A. "Relationship of Personality Measures to the Alpha Rhythm of the Electroencephalogram." *Brit J Psychiatry* 115(519):199–204 F '69. * (*PA* 43:12596)

396. BURNS, B. H. "Chronic Chest Disease, Personality, and Success in Stopping Cigarette Smoking." *Brit J Prev & Social Med* 23(1):23–7 F '69. *

397. BUTT, DORCAS SUSAN, AND FISKE, DONALD W. "Differential Correlates of Dominance Scales." *J Personality* 37(3): 415–28 S '69. * (*PA* 44:6748)

398. CHOUNGOURIAN, A. "The Maudsley Personality Inventory: Extraversion and Neuroticism in the Middle East." *Brit J Social & Clin Psychol* 8(1):77–8 F '69. * (*PA* 43:8238)

399. CHOYNOWSKI, MIECZYSLAW. "The Development of the Polish Adaptation of the Eysenck's 'Maudsley Personality Inventory.'" *Acta Psychologica* (Netherlands) 31(1):45–65 Jl '69. * (*PA* 44:14643)

400. CLAEYS, WILLEM. "Zeigarnik Effect, 'Reversed Zeigarnik Effect,' and Personality." *J Pers & Social Psychol* 12(4): 320–7 Ag '69. * (*PA* 43:15223)

401. CLUM, GEORGE A. "A Correlational Analysis of the Relationships Between Personality and Perceptual Variables and Discriminant GSR Conditioning." *J Clin Psychol* 25(1):33–5 Ja '69. * (*PA* 43:9826)

402. COCHRANE, RAYMOND. "Neuroticism and the Discovery of High Blood Pressure." *J Psychosom Res* (England) 13(1): 21–5 Mr '69. * (*PA* 44:3890)

403. DANA, RICHARD H., AND COCKING, RODNEY R. "Repression-Sensitization and Maudsley Personality Inventory Scores: Response Sets and Stress Effects." *Brit J Social & Clin Psychol* 8(3):243–9 S '69. * (*PA* 44:3645)

404. DAS, J. P., AND DUTTA, TAPATI. "Some Correlates of Extreme Response Set." *Acta Psychologica* (Netherlands) 29(1):85–92 F '69. * (*PA* 43:16752)

405. DAVIDSON, P. O., AND McDOUGALL, C. EVALYNNE A. "The Generality of Pain Tolerance." *J Psychosom Res* (England) 13(1):83–9 Mr '69. * (*PA* 44:3320)

406. DAVIDSON, P. O., AND McDOUGALL, C. EVALYNNE A. "Personality and Pain Tolerance Measures." *Percept & Motor Skills* 28:787–90 Je '69. * (*PA* 43:17453)

407. EDWARDS, GRIFFITH. "The Role of Therapy in Meeting Complex Problems." *Proc 28th Inter Congr Alcohol & Alcoholism* 2(1968):212–22 '69. *

408. GINSBURG, NORMAN. "Extraversion and Adaptation to Intermittent Light." *Percept & Motor Skills* 28(1):195–201 F '69. * (*PA* 43:10897)

409. GUPTA, VED PARKASH. "A Study of Some Correlates of Superstition." *J Psychol Res* (India) 13(1):16–20 Ja '69. *

410. HASETH, KJELL; SHAGASS, CHARLES; AND STRAUMANIS, JOHN J. "Perceptual and Personality Correlates of EEG and Evoked Response Measures." *Biol Psychiatry* 1(1):49–60 Ja '69. * (*PA* 46:4440)

411. HESKIN, KENNETH J. "Some Factors Influencing Performance on a Motor Task and a Verbal Task." *Papers Psychol* (Northern Ireland) 3(1):32–3 Ap '69. *

412. HOGAN, ROBERT. "Development of an Empathy Scale." *J Consult & Clin Psychol* 33(3):307–16 Je '69. * (*PA* 43:12966)

413. IWAWAKI, SABURO, AND ZAX, MELVIN. "Personality Dimensions and Extreme Response Tendency." *Psychol Rep* 25(1):31–4 Ag '69. * (*PA* 44:3634)

414. JULIAN, THELMA; METCALFE, MARYSE; AND COPPEN, ALEC. "Aspects of Personality of Depressive Patients." *Brit J Psychiatry* 115(522):587–9 My '69. * (*PA* 44:3839)

415. KELLY, DESMOND, AND MARTIN, IRENE. "Autonomic Reactivity, Eyelid Conditioning and Their Relationship to

Maudsley Personality Inventory

Neuroticism and Extraversion." *Behav Res & Ther* (England) 7(3):233–44 S '69. * (*PA* 44:16666)

416. KELLY, DESMOND, AND WALTER, C. J. S. "A Clinical and Psychological Relationship Between Anxiety and Depression." *Brit J Psychiatry* 115(521):401–6 Ap '69. * (*PA* 44:861)

417. KELLY, DESMOND; BROWN, CLINTON; AND SHAFFER, JOHN W. "A Controlled Physiological, Clinical and Psychological Evaluation of Chlordiazepoxide." *Brit J Psychiatry* 115 (529):1387–92 D '69. * (*PA* 44:14811)

418. MEHRYAR, A. H. "Generality of Social Perception: Some Negative Results." *J Social Psychol* 78(1):91–8 Je '69. * (*PA* 43:15730)

419. O'DONOVAN, DENNIS. "An Historical Review of the Lie Scale—With Particular Reference to the Maudsley Personality Inventory." *Papers Psychol* (Northern Ireland) 3(1):13–9 Ap '69. *

420. OJHA, H., AND JHA, S. S. "Prestige Suggestion in High and Low Neurotic Subjects." *Manas* (India) 16(2):81–5 N '69. *

421. PIERS, ELLEN V., AND KIRCHNER, ELIZABETH P. "Eyelid Conditioning and Personality: Positive Results From Nonpartisans." *J Abn Psychol* 74(3):336–9 Je '69. * (*PA* 43:12987)

422. POWER, R. P. "The Effect on Norms for the M.P.I. of a Malingerer Scale." *Papers Psychol* (Northern Ireland) 3(1):22–3 Ap '69. *

423. POWER, R. P., AND O'DONOVAN, D. "Detection of Simulation on the MPI by Subjects Given the Rationale of the Lie Scale." *Brit J Psychiatry* 60(4):535–41 N '69. * (*PA* 44:5168)

424. PRICE, JOHN R. "Extroversion and Perspective Duration of a Three Dimensional Reversible Figure." *J Exp Res Personality* 3(3):228–32 Mr '69. * (*PA* 43:10596)

425. SHAMBERG, NEIL; BAKER, STANLEY; AND BURNS, JAMES. "Reminiscence and Pursuit Rotor Performance in Introverts, Extraverts, and Neurotics." *Brit J Social & Clin Psychol* 8(4):375–82 D '69. * (*PA* 44:6757)

426. SHOUKSMITH, GEORGE. "Personality Attributes Associated With Two Measures of Cognitive Style." *Acta Psychologica* (Netherlands) 31(4):353–64 D '69. * (*PA* 44:14589)

427. SWIHART, P. J.; DELEON, P. H.; AND SWENSEN, C. H. "Life History and Personality Correlates of Dominant-Submissive Behavior." *Percept & Motor Skills* 28(2):491–8 Ap '69. * (*PA* 43:15800)

428. TAFT, RONALD. "Peak Experiences and Ego Permissiveness: An Exploratory Factor Study of Their Dimensions in Normal Persons." *Acta Psychologica* (Netherlands) 29(1):35–64 F '69. * (*PA* 43:17526)

429. TUCKER, GARY; HARROW, MARTIN; DETRE, THOMAS; AND HOFFMAN, BROWNING. "Perceptual Experiences in Schizophrenic and Nonschizophrenic Patients." *Arch Gen Psychiatry* 20(2):159–66 F '69. * (*PA* 43:11659)

430. WALTON, H. F. "Personality Correlates of a Career Interest in Psychiatry." *Brit J Psychiatry* 115(519):211–9 F '69. * (*PA* 43:13021)

431. WETTERBERG, LENNART, AND OSTERBERG, ERIC. "Acute Intermittent Porphyria: A Psychometric Study of Twenty-Five Patients." *J Psychosom Res* (England) 13(1):91–3 Mr '69. * (*PA* 44:4088)

432. WHITTAKER, RONALD DUANE. *A Study of the Relationship Between Neuroticism, Extraversion, Internal Versus External Control of Reinforcement, Sex, and Grade Point Average for a Selected Sample of the Florida State University Students.* Doctor's thesis, Florida State University (Tallahassee, Fla.), 1969. (*DAI* 30:4289A)

433. ACHESON, E. D.; COWDELL, R. H.; AND JOLLES, B. "Breathlessness and Anxiety." Letter. *Brit Med J* 2(5712):791 Je 27 '70. *

434. ANDERSSON, ALF L.; NILSSON, ALF; AND HENRICKSSON, NILS-GUNNAR. "Personality Differences Between Accident-Loaded and Accident-Free Young Car Drivers." *Brit J Psychol* 61(3):409–21 Ag '70. * (*PA* 44:21720)

435. AOKI, TAKAYOSHI. "A Comparative Study of Personality Test Scores and Verbal Descriptions of Perceived Self." *Tohoku Psychologica Folia* (Japan) 29(1–2):38–44 '70. * (*PA* 49:6918)

436. BASU, AMIYA KUMAR. "Personality Factors and Academic Performance." *J Ed & Psychol* (India) 28(2):35–7 Jl '70. *

437. BIGGS, J. B. "Personality Correlates of Certain Dimensions of Study Behaviour." *Austral J Psychol* 22(3):287–97 D '70. * (*PA* 46:1843)

438. BLUM, DONNA M., AND VINCENT, M. O. "Personality Test Characteristics of Staff Physicians and Physicians as Psychiatric Patients." *J Clin Psychol* 26(3):389–90 Jl '70. * (*PA* 45:750)

439. BONE, RONALD N., AND MONTGOMERY, DOIL D. "Extraversion, Neuroticism, and Sensation Seeking." *Psychol Rep* 26(3):974 Je '70. * (*PA* 45:678)

440. BROWN, W. P. "Individual Differences in Associating to Neutral and Emotional Words." *J Consult & Clin Psychol* 34(1):33–6 F '70. * (*PA* 44:6747)

441. DEBRODER, GORDON WAYNE. *The Relationship of Improvement in Training of Musical Perception to Dimensions of the Personality.* Doctor's thesis, University of Denver (Denver, Colo.), 1970. (*DAI* 31:4197A)

442. DUCKWORTH, EDWIN. *Counseling Psychology Super-*

visors and Interns: An Analysis of Their Higher-Order Personality Dimensions, Performed Job-Tasks, and Preferred Job-Tasks. Doctor's thesis, University of Missouri (Columbia, Mo.), 1970. (*DAI* 31:5122A)

443. DUTT, N. K. "A Study of Anxiety and Some Correlates." *J Psychol Res* (India) 14(2):50–2 My '70. *

444. FARLEY, FRANK H. "Comparability of the MPI and EPI on Normal Subjects." *Brit J Social & Clin Psychol* 9(1):74–6 F '70. * (*PA* 44:12616)

445. FARLEY, FRANK H. "Moderating Effects of Psychopathology on the Independence of Extraversion and Neuroticism." *J Clin Psychol* 26(3):298–9 Jl '70. * (*PA* 45:927)

446. FREMONT, THEODORE; MEANS, GLADYS H.; AND MEANS, ROBERT S. "Anxiety as a Function of Task Performance Feedback and Extraversion-Introversion." *Psychol Rep* 27(2):455–8 O '70. * (*PA* 45:6312)

447. FREMONT, THEODORE STANTON. *Anxiety as a Function of Task Performance Feedback and Introversion-Extraversion.* Doctor's thesis, Oklahoma State University (Stillwater, Okla.), 1970. (*DAI* 31:6399A)

448. GARSIDE, R. F.; KAY, D. W. K.; ROY, J. R.; AND BEAMISH, PAMELA. "M.P.I. Scores and Symptoms of Depression." *Brit J Psychiatry* 116(533):429–32 Ap '70. * (*PA* 45:931)

449. GOORNEY, A. B. "MPI and MMPI Scores, Correlations and Analysis for a Military Aircrew Population." *Brit J Social & Clin Psychol* 9(2):164–70 Je '70. * (*PA* 44:16710)

450. GOORNEY, A. B. "Psychological Measures in Air Crew." *Aerospace Med* 41(1):87–91 Ja '70. *

451. GOORNEY, A. B. "Treatment of Aviation Phobias by Behaviour Therapy." *Brit J Psychiatry* 117(540):535–44 N '70. * (*PA* 45:10107)

452. GREENLAW, RONALD WELLESLEY. *A Study of Speech and Selected Physiological Correlates in Young Adult Stutterers During Chemically Induced Anxiety.* Doctor's thesis, University of Utah (Salt Lake City, Utah), 1970. (*DAI* 31:3054B)

453. GUPTA, VED PARKASH. "A Study of Personality, Intelligence and Social Adjustment Level, Differences Between the Teachers Under-Training in General and Physical Education." *J Ed Res & Exten* (India) 6(3):93–6 Ja '70. *

454. HAHN, P., AND LEISNER, R. "The Influence of Biographical Anamnesis and Group Psychotherapy on Postmyocardial Patients." *Psychother & Psychosom* (Switzerland) 18(1–6):299–306 '70. * (*PA* 47:5508)

455. HERZBERG, BRENDA, AND COPPEN, ALEC. "Changes in Psychological Symptoms in Women Taking Oral Contraceptives." *Brit J Psychiatry* 116(531):161–4 F '70. * (*PA* 44:18113)

456. HUNDAL, P. S.; SINGH, AGYAJIT; AND SINGH, MOHINDER. "Factor Analytical Study of Tests of Anxiety." *Psychol Rep* 26(3):875–8 Je '70. * (*PA* 45:706)

457. IWAWAKI, SABURO; OYAMA, TADASU; SUGIYAMA, YOSHIO; KIKUCHI, MICHIKO; AND KOMATSU, REIKO. "Development and Validation of the Japanese Version of the MPI (Maudsley Personality Inventory)." *Jap Psychol Res* 12(4):176–83 D '70. * (*PA* 49:5769)

458. KELLY, DESMOND; BROWN, CLINTON C.; AND SHAFFER, JOHN W. "A Comparison of Physiological and Psychological Measurements on Anxious Patients and Normal Controls." *Psychophysiol* 6(4):429–41 Ja '70. * (*PA* 44:20409)

459. KERR, T. A.; SCHAPIRA, KURT; ROTH, MARTIN; AND GARSIDE, R. F. "The Relationship Between the Maudsley Personality Inventory and the Course of Affective Disorders." *Brit J Psychiatry* 116(530):11–20 Ja '70. * (*PA* 44:21176)

460. KOELEGA, HENRY S. "Extraversion, Sex, Arousal and Olfactory Sensitivity." *Acta Psychologica* (Netherlands) 34(1):51–66 S '70. * (*PA* 45:2022)

461. KOPPEL, MARK A., AND SECHREST, LEE. "A Multitrait-Multimethod Matrix Analysis of Sense of Humor." *Ed & Psychol Meas* 30(1):77–85 sp '70. * (*PA* 44:18672)

462. KRAFT, TOM, AND WIJESINGHE, BRIAN. "Systematic Desensitization of Social Anxiety in the Treatment of Alcoholism: A Psychometric Evaluation of Change." *Brit J Psychiatry* 117(539):443–4 O '70. * (*PA* 45:10113)

463. KREITMAN, NORMAN; COLLINS, JOYCE; NELSON, BARBARA; AND TROOP, JANE. "Neurosis and Marital Interaction: 1, Personality and Symptoms." *Brit J Psychiatry* 117(536):33–46 Jl '70. * (*PA* 45:2702)

464. KRISHNA, K. P. "Further Validation of Comprehensive Test of Anxiety." *J Psychol Res* (India) 14(3):119–21 S '70. *

465. LAUTZ, ROBERT; MACLEAN, G. DONALD; VAUGHAN, ANDREW T.; AND OLIVER, THOMAS C. "Characteristics of Successful Students Following Academic Suspension." *Col & Univ* 45(2):192–202 w '70. *

466. McLEISH, JOHN. *Students' Attitudes and College Environments.* Cambridge, England: Cambridge Institute of Education, 1970. Pp. vii, 251. *

467. McNAMEE, H. BRIAN. "Breathlessness and Anxiety." Letter. *Brit Med J* 2(5712):791 Je 27 '70. *

468. MEHRYAR, A. H. "A Cross-Cultural Investigation of Eysenck's Hypothesis Regarding the Relationship Between Personality and Attitudes." *Brit J Social & Clin Psychol* 9(3):216–21 S '70. * (*PA* 45:2237)

469. MEIKLE, STEWART. "Drug Induced Sympathetic Arousal and Neuroticism." *Can Psychologist* 11(3):269–80 Jl '70. * (*PA* 44:20360)

470. MEISELS, MURRAY, AND CANTER, FRANCIS M. "Personal Space and Personality Characteristics: A Non-Confirmation." *Psychol Rep* 27(1):287–90 Ag '70. * (*PA* 45:6294)

471. MOHAN, JITENDRA. "Reminiscence, Personality and Disinhibition." *Studia Psychologica* (Czechoslovakia) 12(2):147–50 '70. * (*PA* 45:5542)

472. NELSON, BARBARA; COLLINS, JOYCE; KREITMAN, NORMAN; AND TROOP, JANE. "Neurosis and Marital Interaction: 2, Time Sharing and Social Activity." *Brit J Psychiatry* 117(536): 47–58 Jl '70. * (*PA* 45:2705)

473. OJHA, H. "An Experimental Study of Prestige Suggestion in Female Extraverts and Introverts." *Manas* (India) 17(1):1–5 My '70. * (*PA* 46:9045)

474. PASSINGHAM, R. E. "The Neurological Basis of Introversion-Extraversion: Gray's Theory." *Behav Res & Ther* (England) 8(4):353–66 N '70. * (*PA* 46:640)

475. PAYKEL, EUGENE S.; KLERMAN, GERALD L.; AND PRUSOFF, BRIGITTE A. "Treatment Setting and Clinical Depression." *Arch Gen Psychiatry* 22(1):11–21 Ja '70. * (*PA* 44:10686)

476. RAMSAY, R. W. "Introversion-Extraversion and Volunteering for Testing." *Brit J Social & Clin Psychol* 9(1):89 F '70. *

477. ROMINE, PHILIP GORDON. *The Combined Moderating Influences of Personality Variables on the Accuracy of Prediction of Academic Success.* Doctor's thesis, University of Alabama (University, Ala.), 1970. (*DAI* 31:5213A)

478. SCHULZ, HARTMUT, AND STROBACH, HANS. "Catecholamine Excretion as a Function of Personality." *Psychon Sci* 18(4):237–8 F 24 '70. * (*PA* 44:9969)

479. SINHA, L. N. K., AND KRISHNA, K. P. "Some Differential Personality Variables of Smokers and Non-Smokers." *J Psychol Res* (India) 14(3):95–7 S '70. *

480. SMITH, LEON E. "Relationship Between Muscular Fatigue, Pain Tolerance, Anxiety, Extraversion-Intraversion and Neuroticism Traits of College Men," pp. 259–74. In *Contemporary Psychology of Sport.* Proceedings of the Second International Congress of Sport Psychology, Washington, D.C., 1968. Chicago, Ill.: Athletic Institute, 1970. Pp. xix, 878. *

481. TER HOEVAN, B., AND NURCOMBE, B. "Characteristics of a Group of Male Schizoid Adolescent Offenders." *Austral & N Zeal J Psychiatry* (Australia) 4(4):196–200 D '70. *

482. TONKS, CLIVE M.; PAYKEL, EUGENE S.; AND KLERMAN, GERALD L. "Clinical Depressions Among Negroes." *Am J Psychiatry* 127(3):329–35 S '70. * (*PA* 45:8605)

483. WALKER, LARRY DALE. *The Effect of Reactive Inhibition and Extroversion on the Standardized Test Scores of Selected Groups of Students.* Doctor's thesis. Mississippi State University (State College, Miss.), 1970. (*DAI* 31:6249B)

484. WILLIS, JERRY; WILSON, WARNER; AND WILLIS, JOAN. "Religious Orientations of Three Samples of Graduate Students in Clinical Psychology, Social Work, and Counseling and Guidance." *Psychol Rep* 26(2):623–30 Ap '70. * (*PA* 44:21083)

485. WRETMARK, GERDT; ÅSTRÖM, JAN; AND ERIKSSON, MARGARETA. "The Maudsley Personality Inventory as a Prognostic Instrument." *Brit J Psychiatry* 116(530):21–6 Ja '70. * (*PA* 44:21186)

486. YOST, MURRAY A., JR., AND KIMBALL, CHASE PATTERSON. "Personality Factors in Preeclampsia of Pregnancy." *Obstet & Gynecol* 36(5):753–7 N '70. *

487. ALLEN, GEORGE J. "Effectiveness of Study Counseling and Desensitization in Alleviating Test Anxiety in College Students." *J Abn Psychol* 77(3):282–9 Je '71. * (*PA* 46:7536)

488. ANDREWS, J. C. "Personality, Sporting Interest and Achievement." *Ed R* (England) 23(2):126–34 F '71. *

489. BANKS, M. H., AND BOLTON, N. "The Personality Structure of a Delinquent Group." *Durham Res R* (England) 6(27): 596–7 au '71. *

490. BESHAI, JAMES A. "Behavioral Correlates of the EEG in Delinquents." Abstract. *Proc 79th Ann Conv Am Psychol Assn* 6(1):459–60 '71. * (*PA* 46:5187)

491. BESHAI, JAMES A. "Behavioral Correlates of the EEG in Delinquents." *J Psychol* 79(1):141–6 S '71. * (*PA* 47:5197)

492. BLACK, STEPHEN, AND WATTS, KENNETH. "Smoking, Personality and Oral Contraception." *Social Sci & Med* (England) 5(6):629–35 D '71. *

493. BOLLER, JON D. *Some Differential Effects of Two Training Group Styles.* Doctor's thesis, Arizona State University (Tempe, Ariz.), 1971. (*DAI* 31:6394A)

494. BOLTON, N., AND SAVAGE, R. D. "Neuroticism and Extraversion in Elderly Normal Subjects and Psychiatric Patients: Some Normative Data." *Brit J Psychiatry* 118(545):473–4 Ap '71. * (*PA* 47:3573)

495. BONE, RONALD N. "Interference, Extraversion and Paired-Associate Learning." *Brit J Social & Clin Psychol* 10(3):284–5 S '71. * (*PA* 47:10870)

496. BROWN, STEVEN R., AND HENDRICK, CLYDE. "Introversion, Extraversion and Social Perception." *Brit J Social & Clin Psychol* 10(4):313–9 D '71. * (*PA* 48:968)

497. BRUHN, JOHN G.; HAMPTON, JAMES W.; AND CHANDLER, BETTY C. "Clinical Marginality and Psychological Adjustment in Hemophilia." *J Psychosom Res* (England) 15(2):207–13 Je '71. * (*PA* 49:7094)

498. BRUHN, JOHN G.; HAMPTON, JAMES W.; AND PHILIPS, BILLY U. "A Psycho-Social Study of Married Hemophiliacs and Their Wives and Hemophiliac Adolescents and Their Parents." *J Psychosom Res* (England) 15(2):293–303 Je '71. *

499. CHANDLER, JANE; HENSMAN, CELIA; AND EDWARDS, GRIFFITH. "Determinants of What Happens to Alcoholics." *Q J Studies Alcohol* 32(2):349–63 Je '71. *

500. COCKBURN, J. J. "Spasmodic Torticollis: A Psychogenic Condition?" *J Psychosom Res* (England) 15(4):471–7 D '71. *

501. GUPTA, B. S., AND SINGH, S. D. "The Effect of Extraversion, Neuroticism and a Depressant Drug on Verbal Conditioning." *Indian J Exp Psychol* 5(1):15–7 Ja '71. *

502. GUPTA, V. P. "Body Build, Personality, Tension and Academic Achievement." *J Ed Res & Exten* (India) 8(1):25–32 Jl '71. *

503. GUPTA, VED PARKASH. "Personality, Motivation and Persistence on a Physical Task." *Psychol Studies* (India) 16(2): 49–54 Jl '71. *

504. GUPTA, VED PARKASH. "The Relation of Neuroticism, Extraversion, Intelligence and Persistence to Educational Attainment." *J Psychol Res* (India) 15(2):86–7 My '71. *

505. HAMILTON, LARRY KENDALL. *The Relationship Between Self-Disclosure and Neuroticism.* Doctor's thesis, Northwestern University (Evanston, Ill.), 1971. (*DAI* 32:3635B)

506. HENDRICK, CLYDE, AND BROWN, STEVEN R. "Introversion, Extraversion, and Interpersonal Attraction." *J Pers & Social Psychol* 20(1):31–6 O '71. * (*PA* 47:6715)

507. HINCHCLIFFE, RONALD. "Intercorrelation of MMPI and MPI Scales on Vertiginous Populations." *Personality* 2(4):315–23 w '71. * (*PA* 47:7284)

508. HINDELANG, MICHAEL J. "Extroversion, Neuroticism, and Self-Reported Delinquent Involvement." *J Res Crime & Del* 8(1):23–31 Ja '71. *

509. HOLMES, DAVID S. "Visual Aftermovement Effects, Pupillary Constriction and Personality Differences." *J Personality* 39(4):473–80 D '71. * (*PA* 48:519)

510. HORE, BRIAN D. "Factors in Alcoholic Relapse." *Brit J Addic* 66(2):89–96 S '71. * (*PA* 48:1241)

511. HUGHES, WILLIAM G., AND SHEAN, GLENN D. "Ability to Control GSR Amplitude." *Psychon Sci* 23(4):309–11 My 25 '71. * (*PA* 48:6670)

512. HUNDAL, P. S., AND SINGH, MOHINDER. "A Factor Analytical Study of Intellectual and Non-Intellectual Characteristics." *Multiv Behav Res* 6(4):503–14 O '71. * (*PA* 47: 11735)

513. JOHNSON, ALGOT ROBERT. *An Investigation of the Relationship Among Selected Personality Traits in Beginning Counselors.* Doctor's thesis, Oklahoma State University (Stillwater, Okla.), 1971. (*DAI* 33:2105A)

514. JONES, LAWRENCE KEITH. *Relationship Between Self-Disclosure and Positive Mental Health, Modeled Self-Disclosure, and Socioeconomic Status.* Doctor's thesis, University of Missouri (Columbia, Mo.), 1971. (*DAI* 32:4953A)

515. KOLVIN, I.; GARSIDE, R. F.; AND KIDD, J. S. H. "Parental Personality and Attitude and Childhood Psychoses: Studies in the Childhood Psychoses, IV." *Brit J Psychiatry* 118(545): 403–6 Ap '71. * (*PA* 47:1293)

516. KREITMAN, NORMAN; COLLINS, JOYCE; NELSON, BARBARA; AND TROOP, JANE. "Neurosis and Marital Interaction: 4, Manifest Psychological Interaction." *Brit J Psychiatry* 119(550): 243–52 S '71. * (*PA* 47:9435)

517. MCDONALD, KENNETH G., AND PARKER, ADRIAN D. "Gibson Spiral Maze and MPI Scores: A Comparison Using Normal Adolescent Subjects." *Brit J Social & Clin Psychol* 10(2):191–2 Je '71. *

518. MASSIE, J. F., AND SHEPHARD, ROY J. "Physiological and Psychological Effects of Training: A Comparison of Individual and Gymnasium Programs With a Characterization of the Exercise 'Drop-Out.'" *Med & Sci Sports* 3(3):110–7 f '71. *

519. MEHDI, S. G., AND SINHA, J. N. "A Study of Relationship Between Neuroticism and Job Satisfaction in School Teachers." *Indian J Appl Psychol* 8(1):46–7 Ja '71. *

520. MILLER, JEFFREY O. "Personality Factors and Perceptual Factors in Motor Performance." *ICHPER* 13:46–61 '71. *

521. MITCHELL, ROBERT EUGENE. *Personality Correlates of Frequent Marijuana and Alcohol Use in a College Male Population.* Doctor's thesis, Ohio State University (Columbus, Ohio), 1971. (*DAI* 32:6655B)

522. NANCE, EVERETTE E. *The Effects of Human Relations Training on Selected Personality Variables.* Doctor's thesis, Western Michigan University (Kalamazoo, Mich.), 1971. (*DAI* 32:1861A)

523. PAYKEL, E. S. "Classification of Depressed Patients: A Cluster Analysis Derived Grouping." *Brit J Psychiatry* 118(544): 275–88 Mr '71. * (*PA* 47:1281)

524. PAYKEL, EUGENE S.; PRUSOFF, BRIGITTE; AND KLERMAN, GERALD L. "The Endogenous-Neurotic Continuum in Depression: Rater Independence and Factor Distributions." *J Psychiatric Res* (England) 8(2):73–90 Je '71. * (*PA* 50:7467)

525. PERRIS, C. "Personality Patterns in Patients With Affective Disorders." *Acta Psychiatrica Scandinavica Supplementum* (Denmark) 221:43–51 '71. *

526. PERRY, JOHN WILLIAM, JR. *Arousal and Memory: Psychophysiological and Personality Factors.* Doctor's thesis, University of Texas (Austin, Tex.), 1971. (*DAI* 32:6693B)

527. PETERSEN, WALTER HAROLD. *The Relationship Between*

Maudsley Personality Inventory

Client Personality and Demographic Characteristics and Classi-fication by Problem Type and Cause. Doctor's thesis, University of Missouri (Columbia, Mo.), 1971. (*DAI* 32:4963A)

528. RUSSELL, G. W. "The Personality of Zambian Student Teachers in Relation to Their Social Behaviour and Teaching Ability." *Teach Ed New Countries* (England) 12(2):137–43 N '71. *

529. SINGH, U. P., AND AKHTAR, S. N. "Criminals and Non-criminals: A Comparative Study of Their Personality." *Indian J Psychol* 46(3):257–63 S '71. *

530. SNAITH, R. P.; McGUIRE, R. J.; AND FOX, K. "Aspects of Personality and Depression." *Psychol Med* (England) 1(3): 239–46 My '71. * (*PA* 47:11246)

531. SUND, ARNE. "Personality Inventories as Selective and Prognostic Criteria." *Mil Med* 136(2):97–104 F '71. * (*PA* 46:6894)

532. TEMPLER, A. J. "A Study of the Relationship Between Anxiety and Extraversion-Introversion." *Psychologia Africana* (South Africa) 14(1):20–31 My '71. * (*PA* 47:10869)

533. VERMA, S. K. "Short Scale of M.P.I." *Indian Psychol R* 8(1):37–8 Jl '71. *

534. WAAG, WAYNE LESLIE. *The Prediction of Individual Differences in Monitoring Performance.* Doctor's thesis, Texas Tech University (Lubbock, Tex.), 1971. (*DAI* 32:5502B)

535. WARD, DERMOT J. "Rheumatoid Arthritis and Per-sonality: A Controlled Study." *Brit Med J* 2(5757):297–9 My 8 '71. Comments by O. W. Hill, 2(5761):588 Je 5 '71. Reply by author, 3(5768):251 Jl 24 '71. *

536. WECKOWICZ, T. E.; YONGE, K. A.; CROPLEY, A. J.; AND MUIR, W. "Objective Therapy Predictors in Depression: A Multivariate Approach." *J Clin Psychol* 27(1):3–29 Ja '71. * (*PA* 46:1295)

537. WILLIAMS, JOHN L. "Personal Space and Its Relation to Extraversion-Introversion." *Can J Behav Sci* 3(2):156–60 Ap '71. * (*PA* 46:9053)

538. WINTER, ITZHAK. "The Evaluation of the Psychoanalytic Theory on Neurocirculatory-Asthenia by Experimental Methods." *Israel Ann Psychiatry* 9(3):233–51 D '71. * (*PA* 48:7542)

539. ZEDECK, SHELDON. "Identification of Moderator Variables by Discriminant Analysis in a Multipredictable Group Valida-tion Model." *J Appl Psychol* 55(4):364–71 Ag '71. * (*PA* 47:1947)

CUMULATIVE NAME INDEX

[1276]

Maxfield-Buchholz Scale of Social Maturity for Use With Preschool Blind Children. Infancy–6 years; 1958; revision of *Maxfield-Fjeld Adaptation of the Vineland Social Maturity Scale;* manual title is *A Social Maturity Scale for Blind Preschool Children;* Kathryn E. Maxfield and Sandra Buchholz; American Foundation for the Blind, Inc. *

For additional information, see P:162; see also 6:139 (2 references).

REFERENCES THROUGH 1971

1–2. See 6:139.

CUMULATIVE NAME INDEX

[1277]

Memory-For-Designs Test. Ages 8.5 and over; 1946–60; MFD; brain damage; Frances K. Graham and Barbara S. Kendall; Psychological Test Specialists. *

For additional information and a review by R. W. Payne, see 7:101 (26 references); see also P:163 (15 references); for a review by Otfried Spreen, see 6:140 (18 references); see also 4:69 (5 references).

REFERENCES THROUGH 1971

1–5. See 4:69.
6–23. See 6:140.

24–38. See P:163.
39–64. See 7:101.
65. GARDNER, M. J.; HAWKINS, H. M.; JUDAH, L. N.; AND MURPHREE, O. D. "Objective Measurement of Psychiatric Changes Produced by Chlorpromazine and Reserpine in Chronic Schizophrenia." *Psychiatric Res Rep* 1:77–83 Jl '55. * (*PA* 30:8411)
66. BLAIR, FRANCIS X. "A Study of the Visual Memory of Deaf and Hearing Children." *Am Ann Deaf* 102:254–63 Mr '57. * (*PA* 32:1952)
67. PRICE, A. COOPER; GARRETT, EPHRAIM S.; HARDY, MILES W.; AND HALL, HARRY E., JR. "Perception of Binaural Beats in Organic and Nonorganic Patients." *Arch Neurol & Psychiatry* 79:214–6 F '58. * (*PA* 33:6276)
68. NEWCOMBE, FREDA, AND STEINBERG, BENJAMIN. "Some Aspects of Learning and Memory Function in Older Psychiatric Patients." *J Gerontol* 19:490–3 O '64. *
69. SPREEN, OTFRIED, AND BENTON, ARTHUR L. "Comparative Studies of Some Psychological Tests for Cerebral Damage." *J Nerv & Mental Dis* 140:323–33 My '65. * (*PA* 40:700)
70. MACKIE, JAMES B., AND BECK, EDWARD C. "Relations Among Rigidity, Intelligence and Perception in Brain-Damaged and Normal Individuals." *J Nerv & Mental Dis* 142:310–7 Ap '66. * (*PA* 40:13429)
71. MEIER, MANFRED J., AND FRENCH, LYLE A. "Longitudinal Assessment of Intellectual Functioning Following Unilateral Temporal Lobectomy." *J Clin Psychol* 22:22–7 Ja '66. * (*PA* 40:4283)
72. DAVIES, ANN D. M. "Measurement of Mental Deterioration in Aging and Brain Damage." Discussion by Walter W. Surwillo. *Interdiscipl Topics Gerontol* 1:78–92 '68. *
73. WHITE, J. G. "The Clinical Measurement of Memory and Its Electrophysiological Correlates." *Proc Inter Congr Appl Psychol* 16:835–8 '68. *
74. CRONON, D.; BODLEY, P.; POTTS, L.; MATHER, MARCIA D.; GARDNER, R. K.; AND TOBIN, JEAN C. "Unilateral and Bilateral ECT: A Study of Memory Disturbance and Relief From Depression." *J Neurol Neurosurg & Psychiatry* (England) 33(5):705–13 O '70. * (*PA* 47:9139)
75. ASCOUGH, JAMES C.; STROUF, MICHAEL J.; COHN, CAROL S.; AND SMITH, RONALD E. "Differential Diagnosis of Brain Damage and Schizophrenia by the Memory-for-Designs Test." *J Clin Psychol* 27(4):471–2 O '71. * (*PA* 47:9191)
76. CLARKE, BRYAN R., AND LESLIE, PERRY T. "Visual-Motor Skills and Reading Ability of Deaf Children." *Percept & Motor Skills* 33(1):263–8 Ag '71. * (*PA* 47:3463)
77. CRARY, HELEN L., AND RIDGWAY, ROBERT W. "Relationships Between Visual Form Perception Abilities and Reading Achievement in the Intermediate Grades." *J Exp Ed* 40(1):17–22 f '71. * (*PA* 47:9796)
78. GLAISTER, BRIAN R. "An Ordinate Comparison Method of Calculating Brain Damage Probability." *Brit J Social & Clin Psychol* 10(4):367–74 D '71. * (*PA* 48:1489)
79. ROSEN, HAROLD. "A Comparison of Two Scoring Systems for the Memory-For-Designs Test." *J Clin Psychol* 27(1):79–81 Ja '71. * (*PA* 46:1681)
80. SINGH, SATISH C. P. "The Clinical Usefulness of the Memory for Designs Test." *Indian J Appl Psychol* 8(2):49–52 Jl '71. *

CUMULATIVE NAME INDEX

Adler, M. L.: 25
Aftanas, M. S.: 44
Ajax, E. T.: 60–1
Alexander, D. A.: 57
Andy, O. J.: 39
Anglin, R.: 29
Armstrong, R. G.: 6
Ascough, J. C.: 75
Bannatyne, A. D.: 45–6
Barclay, A.: 21
Beck, E. C.: 61, 70
Benton, A. L.: 69
Blair, F. X.: 66
Blumberg, S.: 22
Bodley, P.: 74
Bourestom, N. C.: 34
Brilliant, P. J.: 19
Bruininks, R. H.: 47
Burdus, J. A.: 11
Burgess, M. M.: 58–9
Butler, A. J.: 28
Chown, S.: 40
Clarke, B. R.: 76
Cohn, C. S.: 75
Craddick, R. A.: 20
Crary, H. L.: 77
Cronholm, B.: 42
Davies, A. D. M.: 33, 72
Deabler, H. L.: 10
Drake, W. E.: 55
Fjeld, S. P.: 31
Flick, G. L.: 56

Flynn, P. S.: 15
French, L. A.: 71
Friedman, E. C.: 21
Gallagher, J. J.: 24
Games, P.: 39
Gardner, M. J.: 65
Gardner, R. K.: 74
Garrett, E. S.: 10, 67
Gilliland, J.: 11
Glaister, B. R.: 78
Graham, F. K.: 1–2, 4, 12
Greenburg, H.: 59
Grundvig, J. L.: 60–1
Gynther, M. D.: 19
Hall, H. E.: 67
Hardy, M. W.: 67
Hawkins, H. M.: 65
Hayden, M. P.: 31
Heron, A.: 40
Hovey, H. B.: 13
Howard, A. R.: 9
Howard, M. T.: 34
Hunt, H. F.: 7
Judah, L. N.: 65
Jurko, M. F.: 39
Kendall, B. S.: 1–4, 12, 16, 32
Knox, W. J.: 26
Kodanaz, A.: 58–9
Korman, M.: 22
Lange, U. A.: 48
Leslie, P. T.: 76
Leton, D. A.: 17
Levita, E.: 62

Lilliston, L. G.: 49, 63
Lyle, J. G.: 35, 50
Mackie, J. B.: 27, 70
Mather, M. D.: 74
May, A. E.: 41, 64
Meier, M. J.: 71
Michaelson, S.: 41
Murphree, O. D.: 65
Murray, L. M. N.: 51
Needham, W. E.: 60–1
Newcombe, F.: 30, 68
Owens, R. T.: 52
Payne, R. W.: *rev*, 7:101
Potts, L.: 74
Price, A. C.: 10, 67
Pullen, M.: 29
Pustel, G.: 37
Quattlebaum, L. F.: 36, 53
Rappaport, S. R.: 8
Richie, J.: 28
Ridgway, R. W.: 77
Riklan, M.: 62
Rose, J. T.: 41
Rosen, H.: 79
Royce, J. R.: 44
Schalling, D.: 42
Scott, J. S.: 43
Shoemaker, D. J.: 9
Siegel, L.: 37

Singh, S. C. P.: 80
Small, I. F.: 31
Small, J. G.: 31
Smith, R. E.: 75
Spreen, O.: 69; *rev*, 6:140
Steinberg, B.: 68
Steinhard, M.: 54
Steinhelber, J. C.: 55
Stern, M. R.: 20
Sternlicht, M.: 37
Strouf, M. J.: 75
Surwillo, W. W.: 72
Taylor, F. R.: 18
Tobin, J. C.: 74
Tortorella, W. M.: 23
Turland, D. N.: 54
Urquhart, A.: 64
Vitale, J. H.: 55
Walters, C. E.: 14
Watson, C. G.: 38
Watson, R. I.: 5
Watts, R. E.: 64
Whaley, D.: 26
White, J. G.: 73
White, W. F.: 53
Wichiarajote, P.: 46
Wohlford, P.: 56
Ziegler, D. K.: 58–9

[1278]

Mental Status Schedule.

Psychiatric patients and nonpatients; 1964–66; MSS; standardized interview schedule and matching inventory of present-absent items descriptive of pathological behavior; 3 macro scores (feelings-concern, confusion-retardation, delusions-hallucinations), 13 factor scores (inappropriate-bizarre, belligerence-negativism, agitation-excitement, retardation-withdrawal, speech disorganization, suspicion-persecution-hallucinations, grandiosity, depression-anxiety, suicide-self mutilation, somatic concerns, social isolation, disorientation-memory, denial of illness), and 22 supplemental scores (anxiety, auditory hallucinations, conversion reaction, depression-suicide, dissociation, elated mood, grandiosity non-delusional, grandiose psychoticism, guilt non-delusional, inappropriate-bizarre, incoherence, schizophrenic, non-specific complaints, obsessions-compulsions, persecutory delusions, phobia, silliness, sociopath, somatic preoccupation, somatic delusions, somatic hallucinations, visual hallucinations); Robert L. Spitzer, Eugene I. Burdock (test), Anne S. Hardesty (test), Jean Endicott (manual), and George M. Cohen (manual); Biometrics Research, New York State Psychiatric Institute. *

For additional information and reviews by Sol L. Garfield and Julian J. Lasky, see 7:102 (9 references); see also P:164 (8 references).

REFERENCES THROUGH 1971

1–8. See P:164.
9–17. See 7:102.
18. HOGARTY, GERARD E.; DENNIS, HELEN; GUY, WILLIAM; AND GROSS, GERTRUDE M. " 'Who Goes There?'—A Critical Evaluation of Admissions to a Psychiatric Day Hospital." *Am J Psychiatry* 124:934–44 Ja '68. * (*PA* 42:9143)
19. GAITZ, CHARLES M., AND BAER, PAUL E. "Characteristics of Elderly Patients With Alcoholism." *Arch Gen Psychiatry* 24(4):372–8 Ap '71. * (*PA* 47:11155)
20. GOTTSCHALK, LOUIS A.; GLESER, GOLDINE C.; CLEGHORN, JOHN M.; STONE, WALTER N.; AND WINGET, CAROLYN N. Chap. 37, "Prediction of Changes in Severity of the Schizophrenic Syndrome With Discontinuation and Administration of Phenothiazines in Chronic Schizophrenic Patients: Language as a Predictor and Measure of Change in Schizophrenia," pp. 605–27. In *The Schizophrenic Syndrome: An Annual Review 1971.* Edited by Robert Cancro. New York: Brunner/Mazel, Inc., 1971. Pp. xv, 791. *

CUMULATIVE NAME INDEX

Baer, P. E.: 19
Baldwin, I. T.: 4
Brandon, S.: 12
Burdock, E. I.: 1–2, 9
Cleghorn, J. M.: 16, 20
Cohen, J.: 8
Cole, J. O.: 13

Copley, D.: 17
Denney, D.: 5
Dennis, H.: 18
Endicott, J.: 7–8
Fahy, T. J.: 12
Fleiss, J.: 4, 9
Fleiss, J. L.: 1–2, 7–8

Gaitz, C. M.: 19
Garfield, S. L.: *rev*, 7:102
Garside, R. F.: 12
Glesser, G. C.: 10, 16, 20
Gottschalk, L. A.: 10, 16, 20
Gross, G. M.: 18
Gudeman, H.: 14
Guy, W.: 18
Hardesty, A. S.: 1, 9
Headley, E. B.: 10
Hogarty, G. E.: 18
Holland, J.: 17
Katz, M. M.: 13–4
Kernohan, W.: 4

Lasky, J. J.: *rev*, 7:102
Lee, J. C.: 4
Lowery, H. A.: 13
Masling, J.: 17
Pattison, E. M.: 10
Quass, R. M.: 5
Rich, D. C.: 5
Sanborn, K.: 14
Spitzer, R. L.: 1–4, 6–8
Stone, W. N.: 6, 20
Thompson, J. K.: 5
Weinstock, C. S.: 15
Winget, C. N.: 16, 20
Zubin, J.: 11

[1279]

Middlesex Hospital Questionnaire. Ages 18 and over; 1970; MHQ; 7 scores: free-floating anxiety, phobic anxiety, obsessionality, somatic anxiety, depression, hysteria, total (neuroticism); A. H. Crisp and Sidney Crown; Psychological Test Publications [England]. *

For additional information and a review by D. F. Clark, see 7:103 (5 references).

REFERENCES THROUGH 1971

1–5. See 7:103.
6. CRISP, A. H., AND PRIEST, R. G. "Nature of Complaint in Relation to Social Class." *Psychother & Psychosom* (Switzerland) 18(1–6):216–25 '70. * (*PA* 47:5348)
7. CRISP, A. H.; STONEHILL, E.; AND FENTON, G. W. "An Aspect of the Biological Basis of the Mind-Body Apparatus: The Relationship Between Sleep, Nutritional State and Mood in Disorders of Weight." *Psychother & Psychosom* (Switzerland) 18(1–6):161–75 '70. * (*PA* 47:5246)
8. BANKS, M. H., AND BOLTON, N. "The Personality Structure of a Delinquent Group." *Durham Res R* (England) 6(27):596–7 au '71. *
9. CRISP, A. H., AND PRIEST, R. G. "Psychoneurotic Profiles in Middle Age: A Study of Persons Aged 40 to 65 Registered With a General Practitioner." *Brit J Psychiatry* 119(551):385–92 O '71. * (*PA* 47:8686)
10. CRISP, A. H., AND STONEHILL, EDWARD. "Aspects of the Relationship Between Psychiatric Status, Sleep, Nocturnal Motility and Nutrition." *J Psychosom Res* (England) 15(4):501–9 D '71. *
11. HOWELL, R. W., AND CROWN, SIDNEY. "Sickness Absence Levels and Personality Inventory Scores." *Brit J Indus Med* 28(2):126–30 Ap '71. *
12. LIAKOS, A., AND CRISP, A. H. "Pupil Size in Psychoneurotic Patients: A Psychophysiological and Psychometric Investigation." *Psychother & Psychosom* (Switzerland) 19(1–2):104–10 '71. * (*PA* 47:5250)
13. YOUNG, J. P. R.; FENTON, G. W.; AND LADER, M. H. "The Inheritance of Neurotic Traits: A Twin Study of the Middlesex Hospital Questionnaire." *Brit J Psychiatry* 119(551):393–8 O '71. * (*PA* 47:9327)

CUMULATIVE NAME INDEX

Banks, M. H.: 8
Bolton, N.: 8
Clark, D. F.: *rev*, 7:103
Cockett, R.: 3
Crisp, A. H.: 1, 4, 6–7, 9–10, 12
Crown, S.: 1, 5, 11
Duncan, K. P.: 5
Fenton, G. W.: 7, 13

Howell, R. W.: 5, 11
Lader, M. H.: 13
Liakos, A.: 12
Loughnane, T.: 2
McKerracher, D. W.: 2
Priest, R. G.: 6, 9
Stonehill, E.: 4, 7, 10
Watson, R. A.: 2
Young, J. P. R.: 13

[1280]

Minnesota Counseling Inventory. High school; 1953–57; MCI; based on *Minnesota Multiphasic Personality Inventory* and *Minnesota Personality Scale*; 9 scores: family relationships, social relationships, emotional stability, conformity, adjustment to reality, mood, leadership, validity, question; Ralph F. Berdie and Wilbur L. Layton; Psychological Corporation. *

For additional information, see P:165 (37 references); for reviews by Norman Frederiksen and John W. M. Rothney, see 6:142 (10 references); for an excerpted review by Laurance F. Shaffer, see 5:85.

REFERENCES THROUGH 1971

1–10. See 6:142.
11–47. See P:165.
48. AIKEN, LEWIS R., JR., AND DREGER, RALPH MASON. "The Effect of Attitudes on Performance in Mathematics." *J Ed Psychol* 52:19–24 F '61. * (*PA* 36:2KD19A)

49. SKELLY, CLYDE G. *Some Variables Which Differentiate the Highly Intelligent and Highly Divergent Thinking Adolescent.* Doctor's thesis, University of Connecticut (Storrs, Conn.), 1961. (*DA* 22:2699)
50. BEAMISH, JEROME J., AND MALFETTI, JAMES L. "A Psychological Comparison of Violator and Non-Violator Automobile Drivers in the 16 to 19 Year Age Group." *Traffic Safety Res R* 6:12–5 Mr '62. *
51. DVORAK, EDWARD JOHN. *Characteristics of University Students With Regard to Acceptance and Rejection of Polio Vaccination.* Doctor's thesis, University of Minnesota (Minneapolis, Minn.), 1962. (*DA* 23:3326)
52. BRODIE, THOMAS ADAMS, JR. *Factors Associated With Positive and Negative Attitudes Toward Senior High School.* Doctor's thesis, University of Minnesota (Minneapolis, Minn.), 1963. (*DA* 24:4537)
53. BROWN, ROBERT EARL. *The Relationship of the Acceptance of Scholastic Ability Data and Personal Adjustment.* Doctor's thesis, Rutgers—The State University (New Brunswick, N.J.), 1963. (*DA* 24:2777)
54. HINTON, MAXINE ARMSTRONG; EPPRIGHT, ERCEL S.; CHADDERDON, HESTER; AND WOLINS, LEROY. "Eating Behavior and Dietary Intake of Girls 12 to 14 Years Old." *J Am Dietetic Assn* 43:223–7 S '63. *
55. FORTNEY, HOWARD MARION. *Some Characteristics of Underachievers in Two Groups of Academically Talented Male High School Pupils.* Doctor's thesis, University of Alabama (University, Ala.), 1964. (*DA* 25:7025)
56. COLEMAN, KATHERINE ANN. *The Significance of Eye Responses on the Holtzman Inkblot Technique as Measured by the Minnesota Counseling Inventory.* Master's thesis, Springfield College (Springfield, Mass.), 1965.
57. BERDIE, RALPH F., AND STEIN, JUNE. "A Comparison of New University Students Who Do and Do Not Seek Counseling." *J Counsel Psychol* 13:310–7 f '66. * (*PA* 40:12631)
58. FILICETTI, PETER JAMES. *A Comparison of Selected Personality Characteristics of Upper Level High School Students From Catholic and Public High Schools Who Sought Vocational Guidance at an Out of School Agency.* Doctor's thesis, Fordham University (New York, N.Y.), 1966. (*DA* 27:389A)
59. McCRORY, MARGARET ANNE. *An Analysis of Mental Emotional and Social Factors Related to Success in Student Teaching.* Doctor's thesis, Boston University (Boston, Mass.), 1966. (*DA* 27:3318A)
60. WALSTER, ELAINE; ARONSON, VERA; ABRAHAMS, DARCY; AND ROTTMAN, LEON. "Importance of Physical Attractiveness in Dating Behavior." *J Pers & Social Psychol* 4:508–16 N '66. * (*PA* 41:536)
61. HOOD, ALBERT B. "Academic Achievement of Rebels and Introverts." *J Col Stud Personnel* 8:246–50 Jl '67. *
62. ZAHRAN, HAMED A. S. "The Self-Concept in the Psychological Guidance of Adolescents." *Brit J Ed Psychol* 37:225–40 Je '67. * (*PA* 41:15077)
63. BEAL, MARY ARTHUR. *A Comparative Study of Teacher Evaluation of Personality Traits and Pupil Self-Evaluation as Scored by the Minnesota Counseling Inventory.* Doctor's thesis, Fordham University (New York, N.Y.), 1968. (*DA* 29:3863A)
64. BECKERT, CHARLES BRENT. *Tattooing and Juvenile Delinquency: A Study of Relationships Between the Practice of Tattooing and Personality.* Master's thesis, Brigham Young University (Provo, Utah), 1968.
65. LEE, KEY TON. *A Study of the Nature and Correlates of Pupil Adjustment in Seventh-Day Adventist Secondary Schools.* Doctor's thesis, University of Oklahoma (Norman, Okla.), 1968. (*DA* 29:2569A)
66. McINTIRE, WALTER GORDON. *A Comparative Study of Selected Personality Characteristics of Students Who Cheat and Do Not Cheat in an Academic Situation.* Doctor's thesis, University of North Dakota (Grand Forks, N.D.), 1968. (*DA* 29:3079B)
67. NELSON, DEANE DALE. *A Study of School Achievement and Personality Adjustment Among Adolescent Children With Working and Nonworking Mothers.* Doctor's thesis, University of South Dakota (Vermillion, S.D.), 1968. (*DA* 29:153A)
68. BRAUN, JOHN R., AND ASTA, PATRICIA. "Faking and Faking Detection on the Minnesota Counseling Inventory." *Meas & Eval Guid* 2(1):25–31 sp '69. * (*PA* 44:10444)
69. COWDEN, JAMES E. "Prediction Enhancement Through the Use of Moderator Variables." *J Consult & Clin Psychol* 33(5):621–4 O '69. * (*PA* 44:2559)
70. COWDEN, JAMES E., AND MONSON, LARRY. "An Analysis of Some Relationships Between Personality Adjustment, Placement, and Post-Release Adjustment of Delinquent Boys." *J Res Crime & Del* 6(1):63–70 Ja '69. *
71. COWDEN, JAMES E.; BASSETT, H. THOMAS; AND COHEN, MICHAEL F. "An Analysis of Some Relationships Between Fantasy-Aggressive and Aggressive Behavior Among Institutionalized Delinquents." *J Genetic Psychol* 114(2):179–83 Je '69. * (*PA* 43:17631)
72. COWDEN, JAMES E.; PETERSON, WILLIAM M.; AND PACHT, ASHER R. "The MCI vs. the Jesness Inventory as a Screening and Classification Instrument at a Juvenile Correctional Institution." *J Clin Psychol* 25(1):57–60 Ja '69. * (*PA* 43:9996)
73. KAMMEIER, MARY LEO. *Biographic, Cognitive, Demographic and Personality Differences Between Adolescents From*

Mental Status Schedule

Families With Identifiable Alcohol Problems and From Families Without Identifiable Alcohol Problems. Doctor's thesis, University of North Dakota (Grand Forks, N.D.), 1969. (*DAI* 30:1398A)

74. McFARLAND, CHARLES JEROME. *The Relationship of the Minnesota Counseling Inventory With Academic Achievement and Intelligence in High School.* Master's thesis, University of New Brunswick (Fredericton, N.B., Canada), 1969.

75. MATTSSON, KENNETH DALE. *Relationships Between Certain Personality Factors of Student Teachers, Success in Student Teaching and Certain Responses From Dropout-Prone Pupils.* Doctor's thesis, University of Minnesota (Minneapolis, Minn.), 1969. (*DAI* 30:1899A)

76. PARNES, PHYLLIS SALLY. *Adolescent Daughters of Emotionally Ill Mothers: Their Psycho-Social and Physical Adaptive Behavior.* Doctor's thesis, Boston University (Boston, Mass.), 1969. (*DAI* 30:3251B)

77. PATROS, PHILIP GEORGE. *An Investigation of the Relationship Between Certain Non-Intellective Factors and Academic Performance of Academically Bright Junior High School Girls.* Doctor's thesis, Boston College (Chestnut Hill, Mass.), 1969. (*DAI* 30:3734A)

78. BERDIE, RALPH F.; LOEFFLER, DOROTHY R.; AND ROTH, JOHN D. "Intergeneration Communication." *J Col Stud Personnel* 11(5):348–54 S '70. *

79. BERDIE, RALPH F.; PILAPIL, BONIFACIO; AND IM, IN JAE. "Entrance Correlates of University Satisfaction." *Am Ed Res J* 7(2):251–66 Mr '70. *

80. COWDEN, JAMES E.; PACHT, ASHER R.; AND BODEMER, OTTMAR A. "The 16 PF vs. the MCI in a Group Testing Program of Reformatory Inmates." *J Clin Psychol* 26(4):510–3 O '70. * (*PA* 45:4586)

81. HANSON, GARY R., AND TAYLOR, RONALD G. "Interaction of Ability and Personality: Another Look at the Drop-Out Problem in an Institute of Technology." *J Counsel Psychol* 17(6):540–5 N '70. * (*PA* 45:3036)

82. HANSON, GARY RANDALL. *Empirical Exploration of the Correlates of Academic Predictability.* Doctor's thesis, University of Minnesota (Minneapolis, Minn.), 1970. (*DAI* 32:177A)

83. IM, IN JAE. *A Multivariate Analysis of the Relationship of Academic, Personality, and Family Background Variables to the Different Patterns of Collegiate Attendance.* Doctor's thesis, University of Minnesota (Minneapolis, Minn.), 1970. (*DAI* 32:240A)

84. JOHNSON, DUANE E. "Personality Characteristics in Relation to College Persistence." *J Counsel Psychol* 17(2):162–7 Mr '70. * (*PA* 44:9237)

85. O'SHEA, ARTHUR J. "Low-Achievement Syndrome Among Bright Junior High School Boys." *J Ed Res* 63(6):257–62 F '70. *

86. TRUAX, CHARLES B., AND LISTER, JAMES L. "Effects of Therapist Persuasive Potency in Group Psychotherapy." *J Clin Psychol* 26(3):396–7 Jl '70. * (*PA* 45:836)

87. BAKER, DONALD DOAN. *The Relationship Between Personality Development and Perception of Environmental Press During an Initial College Experience.* Doctor's thesis, University of Rochester (Rochester, N.Y.), 1971. (*DAI* 32:3083A)

88. NELSON, DEANE D. "A Study of Personality Adjustment Among Adolescent Children With Working and Nonworking Mothers." *J Ed Res* 64(7):328–30 Mr '71. * (*PA* 46:10633)

89. STERK, SAM. "Adolescent Personality Growth as a Function of a Counselor-in-Training Program." *Adolescence* 6(21):93–106 sp '71. * (*PA* 46:10641)

90. TRUAX, CHARLES B. "Counselor Focus on Client Anxiety Source and Client Outcome in Juvenile Delinquents." *Can Counselor* 5(1):57–61 Ja '71. *

91. TRUAX, CHARLES B. "Degree of Negative Transference Occurring in Group Psychotherapy and Client Outcome in Juvenile Delinquents." *J Clin Psychol* 27(1):132–6 Ja '71. * (*PA* 46:1325)

92. WASESCHA, BLAINE EUGENE. *Comparison of American-Indian, Eskimo, Spanish-American, and Anglo Youthful Offenders on the Minnesota Counseling Inventory.* Doctor's thesis, University of Utah (Salt Lake City, Utah), 1971. (*DAI* 32:1929A)

CUMULATIVE NAME INDEX

[1281]

Minnesota Multiphasic Personality Inventory. Ages 16 and over; 1942–67; MMPI; 14 scores: hypochondriasis (Hs, '43), depression (D, '43), hysteria (Hy, '43), psychopathic deviate (Pd, '43), masculinity-femininity (Mf, '43), paranoia (Pa, '43), psychasthenia (Pt, '43), schizophrenia (Sc, '43), hypomania (Ma, '43), social (Si, '51), question (?), lie (L), validity (F, '43), test taking attitude (K, '46); 3 editions; Starke R. Hathaway and J. Charnley McKinley; Psychological Corporation. * For computerized scoring and interpreting services, see 1282–5.

a) INDIVIDUAL FORM ("THE CARD SET"). 1942–67.

b) OLD GROUP FORM ("THE BOOKLET FORM"). 1943–67; items same as in individual form.

c) NEW GROUP FORM (FORM R). 1965–67, c1943–67; new sequence of items with the 399 items used to obtain the 14 scores appearing first and the 167 research items last; shortened versions consist of the first 399 items or if K and Si scales are not wanted, 366 items.

For additional information and reviews by Malcolm D. Gynther and David A. Rodgers, see 7:104 (831 references); see also P:166 (1066 references); for reviews by C. J. Adcock and James C. Lingoes, see 6:143 (626 references); for reviews by Albert Ellis and Warren T. Norman, see 5:86 (496 references); for a review by Arthur L. Benton, see 4:71 (211 references); for reviews by Arthur L. Benton, H. J. Eysenck, L. S. Penrose, and Julian B. Rotter, and an excerpted review, see 3:60 (76 references). For excerpts from related book reviews, see 7:B125 (2 excerpts), 7:B130 (1 excerpt), 7:B232 (1 excerpt), 7:B277 (2 excerpts), 7:B374 (3 excerpts), 7:B419 (1 excerpt), 6:B64 (1 excerpt), 6:B113 (1 excerpt), 6:B146 (1 excerpt), 6:B159 (3 excerpts), 6:B206 (1 excerpt), 6:B241 (2 excerpts), 6:B414 (1 excerpt), 5:B199 (2 excerpts), 5:B200 (5 excerpts), 5:B467 (6 excerpts), and 4:72 (2 excerpts).

REFERENCES THROUGH 1971

1–72. See 3:60.
73–283. See 4:71.
284–779. See 5:86.
780–1394. See 6:143.
1395–2460. See P:166.
2461–3291. See 7:104.
3292. BROZEK, JOSEF; GUETZKOW, HAROLD; KEYS, ANCEL; with the collaboration of R. B. Cattell, Mary R. Harrower, and

Starke R. Hathaway. "A Study of Personality of Normal Young Men Maintained on Restricted Intakes of Vitamins of the B Complex." *Psychosom Med* 8:98–109 Mr '46. * (*PA* 20:3205)

3293. ROSE, ANNELIES ARGELANDER. "A Study of Homesickness in College Freshmen." *J Social Psychol* 26:185–202 N '47. * (*PA* 22:4613)

3294. RUESCH, JURGEN; CHRISTIANSEN, CAROLE; PATTERSON, LLOYD C.; DEWEES, SALLY; JACOBSON, ANNEMARIE; AND IN COOPERATION WITH MAYO H. SOLEY. "Psychological Invalidism in Thyroidectomized Patients." *Psychosom Med* 9:77–91 Mr–Ap '47. * (*PA* 21:3483)

3295. ZWERLING, ISRAEL. "Psychological Factors in Susceptibility to Motion Sickness." *J Psychol* 23:219–39 Ap '47. * (*PA* 21:3534)

3296. PORTENIER, LILLIAN G. "Personality Tests in a University Guidance Program." *J Ed Psychol* 39:479–87 D '48. * (*PA* 23:3218)

3297. ALTUS, WILLIAM D., AND CLARK, JERRY H. "The Effect of Adjustment Patterns Upon the Intercorrelation of Intelligence Subtest Variables." *J Social Psychol* 30:39–48 Ag '49. * (*PA* 24:2362)

3298. WATT, GEORGE D. "An Evaluation of Non-Directive Counseling in the Treatment of Delinquents." *J Ed Res* 42:343–52 Ja '49. * (*PA* 23:3836)

3299. ALLERHAND, MELVIN E.; GOUGH, HARRISON G.; AND GRAIS, MELVIN L. "Personality Factors in Neurodermatitis: A Preliminary Study." *Psychosom Med* 12:386–90 N–D '50. * (*PA* 25:4752)

3300. DRAKE, FRANCIS E. "A Study of the Personality Traits of Students Interested in Acting." *Speech Monogr* 17:123–33 Je '50. * (*PA* 25:3386)

3301. BALDWIN, MARCELLA VIG. "A Clinico-Experimental Investigation Into the Psychological Aspects of Multiple Sclerosis." *J Nerv & Mental Dis* 115:299–342 Ap '52. * (*PA* 27:2915)

3302. BERAN, MARIANNE; PERKINS, JOHN C.; AND SCOLLON, ROBERT W. "Psychological Studies on Patients Undergoing Nonconvulsive Electric-Stimulation Treatment." *Am J Psychiatry* 109:367–74 N '52. * (*PA* 27:5168)

3303. LEVY, SOL, AND KENNARD, MARGARET. "A Study of Electroencephalogram as Related to Personality Structure in a Group of Inmates of a State Penitentiary." *Am J Psychiatry* 109:832–9 My '53. * (*PA* 28:2974)

3304. McCARTHY, MARY VITERBO. "An Empirical Study of the Personality Profiles Characterizing Differential Quantitative and Linguistic Ability." *Studies Psychol & Psychiatry* 8(4): 1–45 Je '53. * (*PA* 28:4043)

3305. ROSENBERG, B. G. "Compulsiveness as a Determinant in Selected Cognitive-Perceptual Performances." *J Personality* 21:506–16 Je '53. * (*PA* 28:4699)

3306. SEARS, RICHARD. "Leadership Among Patients in Group Therapy." *Int J Group Psychother* 3:191–7 Ap '53. * (*PA* 28:4471)

3307. WEBER, JOHN ROBERT. "Relationship of Physical Fitness to Success in College and to Personality." *Res Q* 24:471–4 D '53. * (*PA* 28:6524)

3308. BLUMBERG, EUGENE M.; WEST, PHILIP M.; AND ELLIS, FRANK W. "A Possible Relationship Between Psychological Factors and Human Cancer." *Psychosom Med* 16:277–86 Jl–Ag '54. * (*PA* 29:4488)

3309. CRAMOND, WILLIAM A. "Psychological Aspects of Uterine Dysfunction." *Lancet* (England) 267:1241–5 D 18 '54. * (*PA* 29:7722)

3310. DUNHAM, RALPH E. "Factors Related to Recidivism in Adults." *J Social Psychol* 39:77–91 F '54. * (*PA* 28:8866)

3311. SPILKA, BERNARD. "Relationships Between Certain Aspects of Personality and Some Vocal Effects of Delayed Speech Feedback." *J Speech & Hearing Disorders* 19:491–503 D '54. * (*PA* 29:5326)

3312. TYLER, FRED T. "Do University Women Think There Is a Teacher Stereotype?" *Calif J Ed Res* 5:195–201 N '54. * (*PA* 29:6307)

3313. UECKER, ALBERT E.; FRENCH, LYLE A.; AND JOHNSON, DAVID R. "Psychological Studies of Seven Epileptic Hemiparetics Before and After Hemispherectomy." *Arch Neurol & Psychiatry* 72:555–64 N '54. * (*PA* 29:6114)

3314. WATSON, GEORGE, AND COMREY, ANDREW L. "Nutritional Replacement for Mental Illness." *J Psychol* 38:251–64 O '54. * (*PA* 29:5879)

3315. WIEDER, GERALD S. "Group Procedures Modifying Attitudes of Prejudice in the College Classroom." *J Ed Psychol* 45:332–44 O '54. * (*PA* 29:5553)

3316. ALLEN, MARK KNIGHT. *Personality and Cultural Factors Related to Religious Authoritarianism.* Doctor's thesis, Stanford University (Stanford, Calif.), 1955. (*DA* 15:2324)

3317. ARCHIBALD, HERBERT C. "Referred Pain in Headache." *Calif Med* 82:186–7 Mr '55. *

3318. BROEN, WILLIAM E., JR. "Personality Correlates of Certain Religious Attitudes." Abstract. *J Consult Psychol* 19:64 F '55. * (*PA* 29:8426)

3319. BROZEK, JOSEF. "Nutrition and Behavior: Psychologic Changes in Acute Starvation With Hard Physical Work." *J Am Dietetic Assn* 31:703–7 Jl '55. * (*PA* 30:8071)

3320. CROSS, THEODORE RYLAND. *An Exploratory Investigation of the Personality and Background Factors Characterizing*

Entering College Men Who Possess a Low Intensity of Vocational Interests. Doctor's thesis, University of Minnesota (Minneapolis, Minn.), 1955. (*DA* 15:2467)

3321. DAVIDSON, M. A.; LEE, D.; PARNELL, R. W.; AND SPENCER, S. J. G. "The Detection of Psychological Vulnerability in Students." *J Mental Sci* (England) 101:810–25 O '55. * (*PA* 30:7161)

3322. GENGERELLI, J. A., AND BUTLER, BRUCE V. "A Method for Comparing the Profiles of Several Population Samples." *J Psychol* 40:247–68 O '55. * (*PA* 30:6534)

3323. HOLT, SHIRLEY MAE. *Prognostic Factors in Psychoneurosis, Mixed Type.* Doctor's thesis, University of Minnesota (Minneapolis, Minn.), 1955. (*DA* 15:1118)

3324. JOHNSON, RALPH HAAKON. *Factors Related to the Success of Disabled Veterans of World War II in the Rehabilitation Training Program Approved for Mechanics and Repairmen, Motor Vehicle.* Doctor's thesis, University of Minnesota (Minneapolis, Minn.), 1955. (*DA* 15:2460)

3325. MATHIAS, RUDOLF E. S. *An Experimental Investigation of the Personality Structure of Chronic Alcoholic, Alcoholics Anonymous, Neurotic and Normal Groups.* Doctor's thesis, University of Buffalo (Buffalo, N.Y.), 1955. (*DA* 16:156)

3326. SUNDBERG, NORMAN D. "The Acceptability of 'Fake' Versus 'Bona Fide' Personality Test Interpretations." *J Abn & Social Psychol* 50:145–7 Ja '55. * (*PA* 29:7325)

3327. TOMS, ESTHER CHRISTINE. *Personality Characteristics of Mothers of Schizophrenic Veterans.* Doctor's thesis, University of Minnesota (Minneapolis, Minn.), 1955. (*DA* 15:2580)

3328. VERNALLIS, FRANCIS F. "Teeth-Grinding: Some Relationships to Anxiety, Hostility, and Hyperactivity." *J Clin Psychol* 11:389–91 O '55. * (*PA* 30:6129)

3329. WARREN, ANNE BONNER, AND GRANT, DAVID A. "The Relation of Conditioned Discrimination to the MMPI Pd Personality Variable." *J Exp Psychol* 49:23–7 Ja '55. * (*PA* 29:8362)

3330. WECKOWITZ, T. E. "Psychological Factors in Frequency of Micturition." *Brit J Med Psychol* 28:257–63 pt 4 '55. * (*PA* 33:10608)

3331. APPLEBY, THOMAS LORING, AND HANER, CHARLES F. "MMPI Profiles of a College Faculty Group." *Proc Iowa Acad Sci* 63:605–9 '56. * (*PA* 32:4635)

3332. BURKE, MAURICE O. "A Search for Systematic Personality Differentiae of the Only Child in Young Adulthood." *J Genetic Psychol* 89:71–84 S '56. * (*PA* 33:3307)

3333. CARTWRIGHT, DESMOND S. "Note on 'Changes in Psychoneurotic Patients With and Without Psychotherapy.'" *J Consult Psychol* 20:403–4 O '56. * (*PA* 31:8521)

3334. FRAME, M. C., AND OSMOND, W. M. G. "Alcoholism: Psychopathic Personality and Psychopathic Reaction Type." *Med Proc* (South Africa) 2:257–61 My '56. *

3335. FREUDENBERG, R. K., AND ROBERTSON, J. P. S. "Symptoms in Relation to Psychiatric Diagnosis and Treatment." *Arch Neurol & Psychiatry* 76:14–22 Jl '56. * (*PA* 31:6248)

3336. KUBANY, A. J.; DANOWSKI, T. S.; AND MOSES, C. "The Personality and Intelligence of Diabetics." *Diabetes* 5:462–7 N–D '56. * (*PA* 33:9963)

3337. LEWINSOHN, PETER M. "Some Individual Differences in Physiological Reactivity to Stress." *J Comp & Physiol Psychol* 49:271–7 Je '56. * (*PA* 31:6485)

3338. McGUIRE, FREDERICK. "Psychological Comparison of Automobile Drivers: Accident- and Violation-Free Versus Accident-Violation-Incurring Drivers." *US Armed Forces Med J* 7:1741–8 D '56. * (*PA* 31:3949)

3339. PENMAN, ALLEN S., AND DREDGE, THOMAS E. "Effect of Reserpine and Open-Ward Privileges on Chronic Schizophrenics." *Arch Neurol & Psychiatry* 76:42–9 Jl '56. * (*PA* 31:6438)

3340. SOPCHAK, ANDREW L. "Projective Study of Peter and His Parents: Revealing the Necessary Therapeutic Limitations." *J Child Psychiatry* 3:149–200 Ag '56. * (*PA* 31:8363)

3341. ARNHOFF, FRANKLYN N. "Ethnocentrism and Stimulus Generalization: A Replication and Further Study." *J Abn & Social Psychol* 55:393–4 N '57. * (*PA* 33:940)

3342. CARPENTER, LEWIS G., JR. "Relation of Aggression in the Personality to Outcome With Electro-Convulsive Shock Therapy." *J General Psychol* 57:3–22 Jl '57. * (*PA* 33:8453)

3343. CHANCE, JUNE ELIZABETH. "Some Correlates of Affective Tone of Early Memories." *J Consult Psychol* 21:203–5 Je '57. * (*PA* 32:5094)

3344. DAANE, CALVIN J., AND SCHMIDT, LOUIS G. "Empathy and Personality Variables." *J Ed Res* 51:129–36 O '57. * (*PA* 33:6568)

3345. GREENFIELD, NORMAN S. "Neurosis and Problem-Solving Behavior." *J Clin Psychol* 13:375–7 O '57. * (*PA* 33:1925)

3346. HERR, VINCENT V., AND KOBLER, FRANK J. "Further Study of Psychogalvanometric Test for Neuroticism." *J Clin Psychol* 13:387–90 O '57. * (*PA* 33:1274)

3347. KEUTHE, JAMES L., AND ERIKSEN, CHARLES W. "Personality, Anxiety, and Muscle Tension as Determinants of Response Stereotypy." *J Abn & Social Psychol* 54:400–4 My '57. * (*PA* 33:5937)

3348. KORNETSKY, CONAN, AND HUMPHRIES, OGRETTA. "Relationship Between Effects of a Number of Centrally Acting

Minnesota Multiphasic Personality Inventory

Drugs and Personality." *Arch Neurol & Psychiatry* 77:325-7 Mr '57. * (*PA* 32:2903)

3349. MULDOON, JOHN F. "Some Psychological Concomitants of Tuberculosis and Hospitalization: A Preliminary Study." *Psychosom Med* 19:307-14 Jl-Ag '57. * (*PA* 33:1958)

3350. ROSEN, HJALMAR, AND ROSEN, R. A. HUDSON. "Personality Variables and Role in a Union Business Agent Group." *J Appl Psychol* 41:131-6 Ap '57. * (*PA* 33:2341)

3351. SILVERMAN, ROBERT E. "The Manifest Anxiety Scale as a Measure of Drive." *J Abn & Social Psychol* 55:94-7 Jl '57. * (*PA* 33:1318)

3352. SUCZEK, ROBERT F. "The Personality of Obese Women." *Am J Clin Nutr* 5:197-202 Mr-Ap '57. * (*PA* 32:4450)

3353. TRUAX, CHARLES B. "The Repression Response to Implied Failure as a Function of the Hysteria-Psychasthenia Index." *J Abn & Social Psychol* 55:188-93 S '57. * (*PA* 33:3076)

3354. ZUCKERMAN, MARVIN, AND MONASHKIN, IRWIN. "Self-Acceptance and Psychopathology." *J Consult Psychol* 21:145-8 Ap '57. * (*PA* 33:861)

3355. CALLAWAY, ENOCH, III, AND BAND, RAYMOND I. "Some Psychopharmacological Effects of Atropine: Preliminary Investigation of Broadened Attention." *Arch Neurol & Psychiatry* 79:91-102 Ja '58. * (*PA* 33:5502)

3356. DENBER, HERMAN C. B., AND VAN WEST, ALEXANDER. "Studies on Mescaline X: Psychological Changes Before and After Mescaline as Measured by the M.M.P.I." *Am J Psychiatry* 115:546 D '58. *

3357. DUMLER, MARVIN J. "A Study of Factors Related to Gains in the Reading Rate of College Students Trained With the Tachistoscope and Accelerator." *J Ed Res* 52:27-30 S '58. * (*PA* 33:10956)

3358. GREENFIELD, NORMAN S., AND ROESSLER, ROBERT. "Hypochondriasis: A Reevaluation." *J Nerv & Mental Dis* 126:482-4 My '58. * (*PA* 33:8838)

3359. JACKSON, DOUGLAS N. AND MESSICK, SAMUEL. "Content and Style in Personality Assessment." *Psychol B* 55:243-52 Jl '58. * (*PA* 33:7926)

3360. KING, GERALD F., AND SCHILLER, MARVIN. "Note on Ego-Strength, Defensiveness, and Acquiescence." *Psychol Rep* 4:434 S '58. * (*PA* 33:5755)

3361. LUNDY, RICHARD M. "Self-Perceptions Regarding Masculinity-Femininity and Descriptions of Same and Opposite Sex Sociometric Choices." *Sociometry* 21:238-46 S '58. * (*PA* 33:9967)

3362. MEHLMAN, BENJAMIN, AND KAPLAN, JANICE E. "A Comparison of Some Concepts of Psychological Health." *J Clin Psychol* 14:118-22 Ap '58. * (*PA* 33:6269)

3363. MONROE, JACK J., AND HILL, HARRIS E. "The Hill-Monroe Inventory for Predicting Acceptability for Psychotherapy in the Institutionalized Narcotic Addict." *J Clin Psychol* 14:31-6 Ja '58. * (*PA* 33:6271)

3364. PERR, HERBERT M. "Criteria Distinguishing Parents of Schizophrenic and Normal Children: An Initial Study With the Interpersonal Diagnostic System." *Arch Neurol & Psychiatry* 79:217-24 F '58. * (*PA* 33:6274)

3365. REHFISCH, JOHN M. "Some Scale and Test Correlates of a Personality Rigidity Scale." *J Consult Psychol* 22:372-4 O '58. * (*PA* 34:1050)

3366. SCHOFIELD, WILLIAM, AND BRIGGS, PETER F. "Criteria of Therapeutic Response in Hospitalized Psychiatric Patients." *J Clin Psychol* 14:227-32 Jl '58. * (*PA* 33:8397)

3367. SIMON, WERNER; WIRT, ROBERT D.; WIRT, ANNE L.; HALLORAN, ALDEN V.; HINCKLEY, ROBERT G.; LUND, J. BENJAMIN; AND HOPKINS, G. WENDELL. "A Controlled Study of the Short-Term Differential Treatment of Schizophrenia." *Am J Psychiatry* 114:1077-85 Je '58. * (*PA* 33:8568)

3368. ULLMANN, LEONARD P., AND HUNDRICH, WILLIAM A. "The Role of Anxiety in Psychodiagnosis: Replication and Extension." *J Clin Psychol* 14:276-9 Jl '58. * (*PA* 33:8416)

3369. WEBB, SAM C.; GOODLING, RICHARD A.; AND SHEPHERD, IRMA LEE. "The Prediction of Field Work Ratings in a Theological School." *Relig Ed* 53:534-8 N-D '58. * (*PA* 33:9362)

3370. CONGER, JOHN J.; GASKILL, HERBERT S.; GLAD, DONALD D.; HASSEL, LINDA; RAINEY, ROBERT V.; SAWREY, WILLIAM L.; AND TURRELL, EUGENE S. "Psychological and Psychophysiological Factors in Motor Vehicle Accidents." *J Am Med Assn* 169:1581-7 Ap 4 '59. *

3371. LUBY, ELLIOT D.; WARE, J. GARTH; SENF, RITA; AND FROHMAN, CHARLES E. "Stress and the Precipitation of Acute Intermittent Porphyria." *Psychosom Med* 21:34-9 Ja-F '59. * (*PA* 34:1853)

3372. ROMMEL, R. C. S. "Personality Characteristics and Attitudes of Youthful Accident-Repeating Drivers." *Traffic Safety Res R* 3:13-4 Mr '59. *

3373. STIEPER, DONALD R., AND WIENER, DANIEL N. "The Problem of Interminability in Outpatient Psychotherapy." *J Consult Psychol* 23:237-42 Je '59. * (*PA* 34:4496)

3374. BRIGGS, PETER F., AND WIRT, ROBERT D. "Intra-Q Deck Relationships as Influences and Realities in Personality Assessment." *J Consult Psychol* 24:61-6 F '60. * (*PA* 34:7835)

3375. GOWAN, J. C., AND DIBLE, ISABEL. "Age Effects on the Test Scores of Women Teaching Candidates." *Calif J Ed Res* 11:37-8 Ja '60. * (*PA* 34:8417)

3376. JOHNSON, MERLIN H.; FORDYCE, WILBERT E.; MASUDA, MINORU; AND DORPAT, THEODORE L. "The Abood and Akerfeldt Tests: Assessments of Their Reliability, Predictive Efficiency, and Relationship to the MMPI." *J Neuropsychiatry* 2:24-30 S-O '60. *

3377. KENNEDY, WALLACE A.; SMITH, MARION; VAN DE RIET, HANNAH; VAN DE RIET, VERNON; SMITH, HERBERT; RAPP, DON; AND PAINE, R. W. "A Multidimensional Study of Mathematically Gifted Adolescents." *Child Develop* 31:655-66 D '60. * (*PA* 36:2FH55K)

3378. KUETHE, JAMES L. "Acquiescent Response Set and the Psychasthenia Scale: An Analysis via the Aussage Experiment." *J Abn & Social Psychol* 61:319-22 N '60. * (*PA* 36:2HF19K)

3379. STRICKLAND, JOHN F., AND KUETHE, JAMES L. "An Experimental Investigation of the Relationship Between Psychasthenia and Ego-Strength." *J General Psychol* 60:245-52 Ap '60. * (*PA* 36:2HE45S)

3380. WATSON, GEORGE, AND CURRIER, W. D. "Intensive Vitamin Therapy in Mental Illness." *J Psychol* 49:67-81 Ja '60. * (*PA* 34:8211)

3381. EYSENCK, H. J. "A Note on 'Impulse Repression and Emotional Adjustment.'" *J Consult Psychol* 25:362-3 Ag '61. * (*PA* 37:1301)

3382. FINNEY, JOSEPH CLAUDE. "Some Maternal Influences on Children's Personality and Character." *Genetic Psychol Monogr* 63:199-278 My '61. * (*PA* 36:1FG99F)

3383. HAUN, KENNETH W., AND COHEN, DONNA J. "Prediction of Feminine Interest Scores by Picture Judgment." *Percept & Motor Skills* 13:378 D '61. *

3384. IMBODEN, JOHN B.; CANTER, ARTHUR; AND CLUFF, LEIGHTON E. "Convalescence From Influenza: A Study of the Psychological and Clinical Determinants." *Arch Intern Med* 108:393-9 S '61. *

3385. KRASNER, LEONARD; ULLMANN, LEONARD P.; WEISS, ROBERT L.; AND COLLINS, BEVERLY J. "Responsivity to Verbal Conditioning as a Function of Three Different Examiners." *J Clin Psychol* 17:411-5 O '61. * (*PA* 38:7295)

3386. PARKER, CLYDE A. ["Kleinmuntz's MMPI Maladjustment Scale."] Letter. *J Counsel Psychol* 8:88-9 sp '61. *

3387. SHNEIDMAN, EDWIN S. "The Case of El: Psychological Test Data." *J Proj Tech* 25:131-54 Je '61. * (*PA* 36:21K31S)

3388. SNYDER, WILLIAM U., AND SNYDER, B. JUNE. *The Psychotherapy Relationship.* New York: Macmillan Co., 1961. Pp. xiii, 418. *

3389. TUCK, JAMES A. "Wechsler Verbal Scale Propensity in Psychopathic Patients." *Ont Psychol Assn Q* (Canada) 14:12-3 Mr '61. *

3390. FISHER, SETHARD. "The MMPI: Assessing a Famous Personality Test." *Am Behav Sci* 6:20-1 O '62. *

3391. MILLER, SUTHERLAND, JR. "Relationship of Personality to Occupation, Setting, and Function." *J Counsel Psychol* 9:115-21 su '62. * (*PA* 37:7237)

3392. ROSENTHAL, ROBERT; PERSINGER, GORDON W.; AND FODE, KERMIT L. "Experimenter Bias, Anxiety, and Social Desirability." *Percept & Motor Skills* 15:73-4 Ag '62. * (*PA* 37:5017)

3393. SCHULTZ, CHARLES B.; KOGAN, WILLIAM S.; AND CHAPMAN, HARRY. "Favorability, Unfavorability, and Content Considerations in SD Scales." *Psychol Rep* 10:619-22 Je '62. * (*PA* 37:5018)

3394. TRANEL, NED. "Effects of Perceptual Isolation on Introverts and Extraverts." *J Psychiatric Res* (England) 1(3):185-92 '62. * (*PA* 39:1898)

3395. WHISKIN, FREDERICK E.; DIBNER, ANDREW S.; AND RHUDICK, PAUL J. "Psychological, Cultural, and Health Characteristics of Aging Smokers and Nonsmokers." *J Gerontol* 17:69-74 Ja '62. *

3396. WITTENBORN, J. R.; PLANTE, MARC; BURGESS, FRANCES; AND MAURER, HELEN. "A Comparison of Imipramine, Electroconvulsive Therapy and Placebo in the Treatment of Depressions." *J Nerv & Mental Dis* 135:131-7 Ag '62. * (*PA* 37:3329)

3397. ZUCKERMAN, MARVIN; ALBRIGHT, RICHARD J.; MARKS, CLIFFORD S.; AND MILLER, GERALD L. "Stress and Hallucinatory Effects of Perceptual Isolation and Confinement." *Psychol Monogr* 76(30):1-15 '62. * (*PA* 38:7226)

3398. BLATT, EVA FISHELL. "The Relationship Between Severity of Disease and Extent of Psychopathology in Psychosomatic Illness: A Test of Regression Theory." *Psychosomatics* 4:207-14 Jl-Ag '63. *

3399. DAHLKE, ARNOLD E., AND DANA, RICHARD H. "Intraindividual Verbal-Numerical Discrepancies and Personality." Abstract. *J Consult Psychol* 27:182 Ap '63. *

3400. DUBNO, PETER. "Decision Time Characteristics of Leaders and Group Problem-Solving Behavior." *J Social Psychol* 59:259-82 Ap '63. * (*PA* 38:883)

3401. FINE, BERNARD J. "Introversion-Extraversion and Motor Vehicle Driver Behavior." *Percept & Motor Skills* 16:95-100 F '63. * (*PA* 38:1514)

3402. FRYER, D. G. "A Trial of Imipramine (Tofranil) in Depressed Patients With Chronic Physical Disease." *J Chronic Dis* 16:173-8 F '63. *

3403. KHANNA, J. L.; PRATT, STEVE; BURDIZK, E. G.; AND

CHADDHA, R. L. "A Study of Certain Effects of Tranylcypromine, a New Antidepressant." *J New Drugs* 3:227–32 Jl–Ag '63. * (*PA* 38:9786)

3404. LaGRONE, C. W. "Sex and Personality Differences in Relation to Fantasy." *J Consult Psychol* 27:270–2 Je '63. * (*PA* 38:922)

3405. MILNER, G. "Ascorbic Acid in Chronic Psychiatric Patients—A Controlled Trial." *Brit J Psychiatry* 109:294–9 Mr '63. *

3406. OELKE, MERRITT C. "An Evaluation of the MMPI as a Screening Test for Teacher Interns." *J Stud Pers Assn Teach Ed* 2:19–24 w '63. *

3407. PENN, MARY P. *A Cross-Cultural Comparison Using MMPI Profiles From College Students.* Master's thesis, University of Arizona (Tucson, Ariz.), 1963.

3408. PERRIS, CARLO, AND BRATTEMO, CARL-ERIK. "The Sedation Threshold as a Method of Evaluating Anti-Depressive Treatments: A Preliminary Report." *Acta Psychiatrica Scandinavica Supplementum* (Denmark) 169:111–9 '63. *

3409. RUSH, ALLEN C. "Better Police Personnel Selection." *Police Chief* 30:18+ S '63. *

3410. RYCHLAK, JOSEPH F., AND BRAMS, JEROME M. "Personality Dimensions in Recalled Dream Content." *J Proj Tech & Pers Assess* 27:226–34 Je '63. * (*PA* 38:2643)

3411. SCHOENBERG, BERNARD, AND CARR, ARTHUR C. "An Investigation of Criteria for Brief Psychotherapy of Neurodermatitis." *Psychosom Med* 25:253–63 My–Je '63. * (*PA* 38:4425)

3412. SHAFFER, JOHN W.; FREINEK, WILFRIED R.; WOLF, SIDNEY; FOXWELL, NANCY H.; AND KURLAND, ALBERT A. "A Controlled Evaluation of Chlordiazepoxide (Librium) in the Treatment of Convalescing Alcoholics." *J Nerv & Mental Dis* 137:494–507 N '63. * (*PA* 39:5332)

3413. SHAPIRO, DAVID S., AND MAHOLICK, LEONARD T. *Opening Doors for Troubled People.* Springfield, Ill.: Charles C Thomas, Publishers, 1963. Pp. xi, 121. * (*PA* 38:8858)

3414. SMALL, J. J. "A Case Study Approach to Success and Failure Among First Year Students in New Zealand." *Austral J Higher Ed* 1:80–90 N '63. *

3415. TURK, HERMAN. "Norms, Persons, and Sentiments." *Sociometry* 26:163–77 Je '63. * (*PA* 38:4202)

3416. ULLMANN, LEONARD P.; WEISS, ROBERT L.; AND KRASNER, LEONARD. "The Effect of Verbal Conditioning of Emotional Words on Recognition of Threatening Stimuli." *J Clin Psychol* 19:182–3 Ap '63. * (*PA* 39:5162)

3417. WILSON, IAN C.; VERNON, J. TAYLOR; AND SANDIFER, MYRON G., JR. "A Controlled Study of Treatments of Depression." *J Neuropsychiatry* 4:331–7 My–Je '63. *

3418. YAMAMOTO, JOE; SEEMAN, WILLIAM; AND LESTER, BOYD K. "The Tattooed Man." *J Nerv & Mental Dis* 136:365–7 Ap '63. * (*PA* 38:4344)

3419. BAER, DANIEL J. "Factors in Perception and Rigidity." *Percept & Motor Skills* 19:563–70 O '64. * (*PA* 39:6290)

3420. BROD, DIANE; KERNOFF, PHYLLIS; AND TERWILLIGER, ROBERT F. "Anxiety and Semantic Differential Responses." *J Abn & Social Psychol* 68:570–4 My '64. * (*PA* 39:4647)

3421. EDWARDS, WARREN P., III. *An Investigation of Sex Area Maladjustment and Manifest Level of Psychosexual Development.* Master's thesis, Ohio University (Athens, Ohio), 1964.

3422. FOSTER, PHYLLIS. *The Susceptibility of Subtle and Obvious Items on the MMPI to Response Set With Normal College Students.* Master's thesis, University of Cincinnati (Cincinnati, Ohio), 1964.

3423. HETHERINGTON, E. MAVIS, AND KLINGER, ERIC. "Psychopathy and Punishment." *J Abn & Social Psychol* 69:113–5 Jl '64. * (*PA* 39:2383)

3424. HOLLISTER, LEO E.; OVERALL, JOHN E.; JOHNSON, MERLIN; PENNINGTON, VERONICA; KATZ, GEORGE; AND SHELTON, JACK. "Controlled Comparison of Amitriptyline, Imipramine and Placebo in Hospitalized Depressed Patients." *J Nerv & Mental Dis* 139:370–5 O '64. *

3425. KAHN, ROBERT L.; WOLFE, DONALD M.; QUINN, ROBERT P.; AND SNOEK, J. DIEDRICK; IN COLLABORATION WITH ROBERT A. ROSENTHAL. Part 5, "Personality Processes in Role Stress," pp. 223–333. In their *Organizational Stress: Studies in Role Conflict and Ambiguity.* New York: John Wiley & Sons, Inc., 1964. Pp. xiii, 470. * (*PA* 39:8866)

3426. KANFER, FREDERICK H., AND MARSTON, ALBERT R. "Characteristics of Interactional Behavior in a Psychotherapy Analogue." *J Consult Psychol* 28:456–67 O '64. * (*PA* 39:5351)

3427. MAY, PHILIP R. A., AND TUMA, A. HUSSAIN. "Choice of Criteria for the Assessment of Treatment Outcome." *J Psychiatric Res* (England) 2(3):199–209 '64. * (*PA* 39:15562)

3428. MOORE, ROSEMARIE K. "Susceptibility to Hypnosis and Susceptibility to Social Influence." *J Abn & Social Psychol* 68:282–94 Mr '64. * (*PA* 38:8193)

3429. MURTHY, HOSUR NARAYANA. "Development and Validation of a Schizophrenic Scale." *Trans All-India Inst Mental Health* 4:1–9 Jl '64. *

3430. PROBST, GARY K. *A Study of Personality Characteristics in Relation to Reading Difficulties.* Master's thesis, East Tennessee State University (Johnson City, Tenn.), 1964.

3431. RECHTSCHAFFEN, ALLAN, AND VERDONE, PAUL. "Amount of Dreaming: Effect of Incentive, Adaptation to Laboratory,

and Individual Differences." *Percept & Motor Skills* 19:947–58 D '64. * (*PA* 39:6631)

3432. SPEISMAN, JOSEPH C.; LAZARUS, RICHARD S.; DAVISON, LES; AND MORDKOFF, ARNOLD M. "Experimental Analysis of a Film Used as a Threatening Stimulus." *J Consult Psychol* 28:23–33 F '64. * (*PA* 38:8380)

3433. SPEISMAN, JOSEPH C.; LAZARUS, RICHARD S.; MORDKOFF, ARNOLD; AND DAVISON, LES. "Experimental Reduction of Stress Based on Ego-Defense Theory." *J Abn & Social Psychol* 68:367–80 Ap '64. * (*PA* 39:1450)

3434. SPIELBERGER, CHARLES D., AND WEITZ, HENRY. "Improving the Academic Performance of Anxious College Freshmen: A Group-Counseling Approach to the Prevention of Underachievement." *Psychol Monogr* 78(13):1–20 '64. * (*PA* 39:5919)

3435. WALLEN, NORMAN E.; SAMUELSON, CECIL O.; BREWER, JETTA J.; GERBER, STERLING K.; AND WOOLAVER, JOHN N. "A Comparison of Slightly and Severely Orthopedically Disabled and 'Normal' Adults on Several Psychological Tests." *Rehabil Counsel B* 8:50–7 D '64. *

3436. WITTENBORN, J. R.; DEMPSTER, ARTHUR; MAURER, HELEN; AND PLANTE, MARC. "Pretreatment Individual Differences as Potential Predictors of Response to Pharmacology." *J Nerv & Mental Dis* 139:186–94 Ag '64. *

3437. COLON, FERNANDO. "A Study of Response to Achromatic and Chromatic Stimuli." *J Consult Psychol* 29:571–6 D '65. * (*PA* 40:2894)

3438. DAVIS, RICHARD E., AND RUIZ, RENE A. "Infant Feeding Method and Adolescent Personality." *Am J Psychiatry* 122:673–8 D '65. * (*PA* 40:2653)

3439. EVANS, JAMES L. "Psychiatric Illness in the Physician's Wife." *Am J Psychiatry* 122:159–63 Ag '65. * (*PA* 39:16154)

3440. GILES, PHILIP GRAY, AND RYCHLAK, JOSEPH F. "The Validity of the Role Construct Repertory Test as a Measure of Sexual Identification." *J Proj Tech & Pers Assess* 29:7–11 Mr '65. * (*PA* 39:10110)

3441. GOLDBERG, PHILIP A., AND MILSTEIN, JUDITH T. "Perceptual Investigation of Psychoanalytic Theory Concerning Latent Homosexuality in Women." *Percept & Motor Skills* 21:645–6 O '65. * (*PA* 40:2771)

3442. GOTTESMAN, IRVING I. "Personality and Natural Selection," pp. 63–80. In *Methods and Goals in Human Behavior Genetics.* Edited by Steven G. Vandenberg. New York: Academic Press Inc., 1965. Pp. xiii, 351. *

3443. HAAS, KURT. "Direction of Hostility and Psychiatric Symptoms." *Psychol Rep* 16:555–6 Ap '65. * (*PA* 39:10639)

3444. HEATH, DOUGLAS H.; WITH THE ASSISTANCE OF HARRIET E. HEATH. *Explorations of Maturity: Studies of Mature and Immature College Men.* New York: Appleton-Century-Crofts, 1965. Pp. xv, 423. * (*PA* 39:12057)

3445. KRUEGER, BRIAN, AND FRUEHLING, W. G. "The Effect of Family Size, Sex of Siblings and Ordinal Position on Personality Characteristics." *Proc Iowa Acad Sci* 72:357–66 '65. *

3446. LEE-TENG, EVELYN. "Trance-Susceptibility, Induction-Susceptibility, and Acquiescence as Factors in Hypnotic Performance." *J Abn Psychol* 70:383–9 O '65. * (*PA* 40:110)

3447. MURTHY, H. N. "Development of the Paranoid, Depressive, Manic and Anxiety Scales." *Trans All-India Inst Mental Health* 5:50–9 D '65. * (*PA* 40:7201)

3448. PFAEHLER, G. T., AND ROESSLER, ROBERT. "Ego Strength and Intravenous Glucose Tolerance." *J Psychosom Res* (England) 8:431–9 Mr '65. *

3449. REDMAN, ROBERT S.; GORLIN, ROBERT J.; PEAGLER, FREDERICK D.; VANCE, FORREST L.; AND MESKIN, LAWRENCE H. "A Psychological Component in the Etiology of Geographic Tongue." Abstract. *Am J Psychiatry* 121:805–6 F '65. *

3450. SCHOTTSTAEDT, WILLIAM W. "Some Factors Affecting Performance in Medical School." *Trans Am Clin & Climatol Assn* 77:137–49 '65. *

3451. SILVERMAN, JULIAN; BERG, PAUL S. D.; AND KANTOR, ROBERT. "Some Perceptual Correlates of Institutionalization." *J Nerv & Mental Dis* 141:651–7 D '65. * (*PA* 40:7919)

3452. SWENSON, WENDELL M. "Psychometric Analysis of Personality Changes Through the Life Span." *Proc Int Congr Gerontol* 6:301–4 '65. *

3453. TECCE, JOSEPH J.; FRIEDMAN, STANFORD B.; AND MASON, JOHN W. "Anxiety, Defensiveness and 17-Hydroxycorticosteroid Excretion." *J Nerv & Mental Dis* 141:549–54 N '65. *

3454. WAGMAN, MORTON. "Daydreaming Frequency and Some Personality Measures." Abstract. *J Consult Psychol* 29:395 Ag '65. * (*PA* 39:15335, title only)

3455. BONNER, R. E. "Cluster Analysis." *Ann N Y Acad Sci* 128:972–83 Ja 31 '66. * (*PA* 40:9409)

3456. CANTER, ARTHUR; IMBODEN, JOHN B.; AND CLUFF, LEIGHTON. "The Frequency of Physical Illness as a Function of Prior Psychological Vulnerability and Contemporary Stress." *Psychosom Med* 28:344–50 Jl–Ag '66. *

3457. COLLINS, L. GLENN, AND STONE, LE ROY A. "Family Structure and Pain Reactivity." *J Clin Psychol* 22:33–9 Ja '66. * (*PA* 40:4247)

3458. CVETKOVICH, GEORGE T.; POPPLESTONE, JOHN A.; AND McPHERSON, MARION WHITE. "Exoskeletal Benefits of Membership in Elite Military Units." *Psychol Rec* 16:479–86 D '66. * (*PA* 41:1586)

3459. ELY, NEAL E., AND JOHNSON, MERLIN H. "Emotional Responses to Peptic Ulcer Management." *Am J Psychiatry* 122:1362–71 Je '66. * (*PA* 40:9762)

3460. GOTTESMAN, IRVING I., AND SHIELDS, JAMES. "Schizophrenia in Twins: 16 Years' Consecutive Admissions to a Psychiatric Clinic." *Brit J Psychiatry* 112:809–18 Ag '66. * (*PA* 40:13372)

3461. GRISWOLD, BARBARA B.; WILTSE, KERMIT T.; AND ROBERTS, ROBERT W. "Some Personality and Intellectual Correlates of Repeated Out-of-Wedlock Childbirth Among Welfare Recipients." *J Clin Psychol* 22:348–53 Jl '66. * (*PA* 40:11141)

3462. KOLLAR, EDWARD J., AND ATKINSON, ROLAND M. "Responses of Extremely Obese Patients to Starvation." *Psychosom Med* 28:227–46 My–Je '66. * (*PA* 40:12522)

3463. MENDELSOHN, GERALD A.; GRISWOLD, BARBARA B.; AND ANDERSON, MILTON L. "Individual Differences in Anagram-Solving Ability." *Psychol Rep* 19:799–809 D '66. * (*PA* 41:3943)

3464. PARKE, ROSS D., AND WALTERS, RICHARD H. "Alcoholism, Avoidance Learning and Emotional Responsiveness." *Brit J Social & Clin Psychol* 5:276–89 D '66. * (*PA* 41:3878)

3465. ROSSI, A. MICHAEL, AND SOLOMON, PHILIP. "Effects of Sensory Deprivation on Introverts and Extraverts: A Failure to Find Reported Differences." *J Psychiatric Res* (England) 4:115–25 N '66. * (*PA* 41:3820)

3466. SMITH, EARL JAY. *A Study of Selected Students in the Oquirrh Manpower Project, Using Twelve Measures Consisting of Six Standardized Variables and Six Behavioral Variables.* Master's thesis, University of Utah (Salt Lake City, Utah), 1966.

3467. WEISS, STEPHEN M. "Psychological Adjustment Following Open-Heart Surgery." *J Nerv & Mental Dis* 143:363–8 O '66. * (*PA* 41:7770)

3468. WILSON, IAN C.; RABON, ARCHIE M.; MERRICK, HOWARD A.; KNOX, A. E.; TAYLOR, JOHN P.; AND BUFFALOE, W. J. "Imipramine Pamoate in the Treatment of Depression." *Psychosomatics* 7:251–3 Jl–Ag '66. *

3469. YAMAMOTO, JOE, AND GOIN, MARCIA KRAFT. "Social Class Factors Relevant for Psychiatric Treatment." *J Nerv & Mental Dis* 142:332–9 Ap '66. *

3470. ZUCKERMAN, MARVIN; PERSKY, HAROLD; HOPKINS, T. ROBERT; MURTAUGH, THOMAS; BASU, G. K.; AND SCHILLING, MARY. "Comparison of Stress Effects of Perceptual and Social Isolation." *Arch Gen Psychiatry* 14:356–65 Ap '66. * (*PA* 40:6182)

3471. ARNETTE, JOHNNY L. "The Effect of Short Term Group Counseling on Anxiety and Hostility of Newly Incarcerated Prison Inmates." *J Correct Ed* 19:18–22 Jl '67. *

3472. BIASE, D. VINCENT, AND ZUCKERMAN, MARVIN. "Sex Differences in Stress Responses to Total and Partial Sensory Deprivation." *Psychosom Med* 29:380–90 Jl–Ag '67. * (*PA* 42:1602)

3473. BIXENSTINE, V. EDWIN, AND DOUGLAS, JOAN. "Effect of Psychopathology on Group Consensus and Cooperative Choice in a Six-Person Game." *J Pers & Social Psychol* 5:32–7 Ja '67. * (*PA* 41:4783)

3474. ERICKSON, RALPH J. "Programmed Learning and Personality Styles at the College Level." *J Ed Res* 60:330–3 Mr '67. *

3475. FORT, DONALD JAMES. *Personality Correlates of Good and Poor Judges of Others.* Master's thesis, University of Utah (Salt Lake City, Utah), 1967.

3476. FRAS, IVAN; LITIN, EDWARD M.; AND PEARSON, JOHN S. "Comparison of Psychiatric Symptoms in Carcinoma of the Pancreas With Those in Some Other Intra-abdominal Neoplasms." *Am J Psychiatry* 123:1553–62 Je '67. * (*PA* 41:12432)

3477. FREEDMAN, MERVIN B. Chap. 5, "Personality Development After College," pp. 59–66. In his *The College Experience.* San Francisco, Calif.: Jossey Bass Inc., Publishers, 1967. Pp. xix, 202. *

3478. HANLEY, CHARLES. "Individual Responses and Social Desirability." *J Appl Psychol* 51:167–9 Ap '67. * (*PA* 41:7338)

3479. HINCHCLIFFE, R. "Personality Profile in Menière's Disease." *J Laryng & Otol* (England) 81:477–81 My '67. *

3480. JACKSON, DOUGLAS N. "A Review of *The Challenge of Response Sets* by Jack Block." *Ed & Psychol Meas* 27:207–19 sp '67. * Block, Jack. "Remarks on Jackson's 'Review' of Block's *Challenge of Response Sets.*" 27:49–501 su '67. * Jackson, Douglas. "Balanced Scales, Item Overlap and the Stables of Augeas." 27:502–7 su '67. *

3481. JENNINGS, CHARLES L. "The Use of Normative Data in the Psychological Evaluation of Flying Personnel." *Int Psychiatry Clinics* 4:37–51 w '67. *

3482. KIESLER, DONALD J.; KLEIN, MARJORIE H.; MATHIEU, PHILIPPA; AND SCHOENINGER, DOUGLAS. Chap. 11, "Constructive Personality Change for Therapy and Control Patients," pp. 251–94. In *The Therapeutics Relationship and Its Impact: A Study of Psychotherapy With Schizophrenics.* Edited by Carl R. Rogers. Madison, Wis.: University of Wisconsin Press, 1967. Pp. xix, 625. *

3483. KOZMA, ALBERT. "Deconditioning a Phobia." *Atlantic Psychologist* (Canada) 16:37–40 f '67. * (*PA* 43:2845)

3484. KURLAND, ALBERT A.; UNGER, SANFORD; SHAFFER, JOHN W.; AND SAVAGE, CHARLES. "Psychedelic Therapy Utilizing LSD in the Treatment of the Alcoholic Patient: A Preliminary Report." *Am J Psychiatry* 123:1202–9 Ap '67. * (*PA* 41:9027)

3485. MITCHELL, DORIS, AND WILSON, WARNER. "Relationship of Father Absence to Masculinity and Popularity of Delinquent Boys." *Psychol Rep* 20:1173–4 Je '67. * (*PA* 41:15509)

3486. ROSEN, ALBERT. "Limitations of Personality Inventories for Assessment of Deaf Children and Adults as Illustrated by Research With the Minnesota Multiphasic Personality Inventory." *J Rehabil Deaf* 1:47–52 Jl '67. *

3487. SEGAL, BERNARD E., AND PHILLIPS, DEREK L. "Work, Play, and Emotional Disturbance: An Examination of Environment and Disturbance." *Arch Gen Psychiatry* 16:173–9 F '67. *

3488. SIMON, NATHAN M.; SENTURIA, AUDREY G.; AND ROTHMAN, DAVID. "Psychiatric Illness Following Therapeutic Abortion." *Am J Psychiatry* 124:59–65 Jl '67. * (*PA* 41:13945)

3489. SULLIVAN, THOMAS M.; FROHMAN, CHARLES E.; BECKETT, PETER G. S.; AND GOTTLIEB, JACQUES S. "Clinical and Biochemical Studies of Families of Schizophrenic Patients." *Am J Psychiatry* 123:947–52 F '67. * (*PA* 41:7613)

3490. TAYLOR, A. J. W., AND VAUGHAN, GRAHAM M. "Clinical Depression and Conformity." *Percept & Motor Skills* 25:257–60 Ag '67. * (*PA* 42:2735)

3491. THURSTON, JOHN R.; BRUNCLIK, HELEN L.; AND FELDHUSEN, JOHN F. *The Prediction of Success in Nursing Education: Phase I and II, 1959–67; A Manual for the Luther Hospital Sentence Completions and the Nursing Sentence Completions.* An unpublished report to the Division of Nursing, National Institutes of Health, Research Grant NU 00018-07, Luther Hospital (Eau Claire, Wis.), 1967. Pp. xvi, 265. *

3492. VANDENBERG, STEVEN G. "Hereditary Factors in Normal Personality Traits (as Measured by Inventories)." *Recent Adv Biol Psychiatry* 9:65–104 '67. *

3493. VAN DER VEEN, FERDINAND. "Basic Elements in the Process of Psychotherapy: A Research Study." *J Consult Psychol* 31:295–303 Je '67. * (*PA* 41:10595)

3494. WILLERMAN, LEE. *Temporal Integration of Rewards and Punishments as a Function of Delay of Punishment and Psychopathic Tendency.* Doctor's thesis, Wayne State University (Detroit, Mich.), 1967. (*DAI* 31:6886B)

3495. WOHLFORD, PAUL, AND JONES, MARSHALL R. "Ordinal Position, Age, Anxiety, and Defensiveness in Unwed Mothers." Abstract. *Proc 75th Ann Conv Am Psychol Assn* 2:177–8 '67. * (*PA* 41:13510)

3496. YAMASHITA, TSUNEO. "Predicting the Direction of Selective Memory From Personality Variables." *Jap Psychol Res* 9:111–8 S '67. * (*PA* 42:11687)

3497. BOHRNSTEDT, GEORGE W.; BORGATTA, EDGAR F.; AND EVANS, ROBERT R. "Religious Affiliation, Religiosity, and MMPI Scores." *J Sci Study Relig* 7(2):255–8 f '68. * (*PA* 45:579)

3498. BOLDING, O. THOMAS, AND WILLCUTT, HERMAN C. "Weight Loss and Psychological Observations of Gynecological Patients." *Ala J Med Sci* 5:158–63 Ap '68. *

3499. DIMASCIO, ALBERTO; MEYER, ROGER E.; AND STIFLER, LAWRENCE. "Effects of Imipramine on Individuals Varying in Level of Depression." *Am J Psychiatry* 124(8, sup):55–8 F '68. * (*PA* 42:9111)

3500. DUPONT, ROBERT L., JR., AND GRUNEBAUM, HENRY. "Willing Victims: The Husbands of Paranoid Women." *Am J Psychiatry* 125:151–9 Ag '68. * (*PA* 42:17437)

3501. FISCHER, ROLAND; MARKS, PHILIP A.; HILL, RICHARD M.; AND ROCKEY, MARSHA A. "Personality Structure as the Main Determinant of Drug Induced (Model) Psychoses." *Nature* (England) 218(5138):296–8 Ap 20 '68. * (*PA* 42:16799)

3502. GNAGEY, WILLIAM J. "Parental Acceptance and the Professional Attitudes of Students in Teacher Education." *J Ed Res* 61:234–7 Ja '68. *

3503. GOLDSTEIN, NORMAN P.; EWERT, JOSEPHINE C.; RANDALL, RAYMOND V.; AND GROSS, JOHN B. "Psychiatric Aspects of Wilson's Disease (Hepatolenticular Degeneration): Results of Psychometric Tests During Long-Term Therapy." *Am J Psychiatry* 124:1555–61 My '68. * (*PA* 42:12656)

3504. GOTTESMAN, IRVING I., AND SHIELDS, JAMES. Chap. 6, "In Pursuit of the Schizophrenic Genotype," pp. 67–103. In *Progress in Human Behavior Genetics.* Edited by Steven G. Vandenberg. Baltimore, Md.: Johns Hopkins Press, 1968. Pp. xi, 356. *

3505. HOFFMAN, PAUL J. Chap. 3, "Cue-Consistency and Configurality in Human Judgment," pp. 53–90. In *Formal Representation of Human Judgment.* Edited by Benjamin Kleinmuntz. New York: John Wiley & Sons, Inc., 1968. Pp. xiii, 273. *

3506. KLEINMUNTZ, BENJAMIN. Chap. 6, "The Processing of Clinical Information by Man and Machine," pp. 149–86. In his *Formal Representation of Human Judgment.* New York: John Wiley & Sons, Inc., 1968. Pp. xiii, 273. *

3507. MURTHY, H. N., AND LAKSHMINARAYAN, C. S. "A Note on the Development of the Hysteria Scale." *Trans All-India Inst Mental Health* 8:42–5 D '68. * (*PA* 43:11385)

3508. PERSKY, HAROLD; ZUCKERMAN, MARVIN; AND CURTIS, GEORGE C. "Endocrine Function in Emotionally Disturbed and Normal Men." *J Nerv & Mental Dis* 146:488–97 Je '68. * (*PA* 42:16830)

3509. RHEAD, CLIFTON; ABRAMS, ARNOLD; TROSMAN, HARRY; AND MARGOLIS, PHILIP. "The Psychological Assessment of Police Candidates." *Am J Psychiatry* 124:1575–80 My '68. * (*PA* 42:12365)

3510. SAVAGE, CHARLES. "Psychedelic Therapy." *Res Psychother* 3:512–20 '68. *

3511. STEVENS, CAROL JEANNE. *A Comparison of Certain Creativity and Personality Variables.* Master's thesis, Central Washington State College (Ellensburg, Wash.), 1968.

3512. TAYLOR, A. J. W. "Personality Factors of Extraversion and Anxiety in New Zealand's Persistent Offenders." *Austral & N Zeal J Criminol* (Australia) 1:243–8 D '68. *

3513. UNGER, SANFORD; KURLAND, ALBERT A.; SHAFFER, JOHN W.; SAVAGE, CHARLES; WOLF, SIDNEY; LEIHY, ROBERT; McCABE, O. LEE; AND SHOCK, HARRY. "LSD-Type Drugs and Psychedelic Therapy." *Res Psychother* 3:521–35 '68. *

3514. BOLDING, O. THOMAS, AND WILLCUTT, HERMAN C. "Physiological and Personality Evaluation of the Estrogen Deprived Patient." *J Med Assn State Ala* 39(5):459–63 N '69. *

3515. COLLIER, HERBERT L. "Psychometric Considerations in Patient Selection for Pain Control Procedures." *Ariz Med* 26(12):1046–9 D '69. *

3516. FISCHER, R. "On Creative, Psychotic and Ecstatic States." *Psychiatry & Art* 2:33–65 '69. *

3517. HEATH, DOUGLAS H. "Secularization and Maturity of Religious Beliefs." *J Relig & Health* 8(4):335–58 O '69. * (*PA* 44:14436)

3518. HIRSCH, IRWIN, AND WALDER, LEOPOLD. "Training Mothers in Groups as Reinforcement Therapists for Their Own Children." Abstract. *Proc 77th Ann Conv Am Psychol Assn* 4(2):561–2 '69. * (*PA* 44:753)

3519. KLEINMUNTZ, BENJAMIN. "Personality Assessment by Computer." *Sci J* 5(2):59–64 F '69. * (*PA* 44:20989)

3520. MacKENZIE, K. ROY; MARTIN, MAURICE J.; AND HOWARD, FRANK M., JR. "Myasthenia Gravis: Psychiatric Concomitants." *Can Med Assn J* 100(21):988–91 Je 7 '69. * (*PA* 44:17245)

3521. RAKHAWY, Y. T.; SHAHEEN, O.; AND GAWAD, M. S. "Assessment of Behavioural Effect of Drug Therapy by the Use of Personality Testing." *J Egypt Med Assn* 52(11/12):954–68 '69. *

3522. ANGRIST, SHIRLEY S. "Personality Maladjustment and Career Aspirations of College Women." *Sociological Symposium* 5:1–8 f '70. * (*PA* 47:10857)

3523. ARNOLD, PAUL DERWOOD. *Marriage Counselee MMPI Profile Characteristics With Objective Signs That Discriminate Them From Married Couples in General.* Doctor's thesis, University of Minnesota (Minneapolis, Minn.), 1970. (*DAI* 32:548B)

3524. ASKAR, A. M.; RAKHAWY, Y. T.; AND SHAHEEN, O. "The Quantitative Assessment of the Therapeutic Effect of Methamphetamine on Psychiatric Patients." *J Egypt Med Assn* 53(7/8):563–77 '70. *

3525. BARCUS, CAROLYN G. *Personality and Sports Preference in Women Majoring in Physical Education in Utah and Idaho.* Master's thesis, Utah State University (Logan, Utah), 1970.

3526. BAUKOL, JACK H. *A Comparative Study of Male and Female Alcoholics in Treatment as Measured by the MMPI.* Master's thesis, University of North Dakota (Grand Forks, N.D.), 1970.

3527. BAUMAN, MARTIN H., AND KRAMER, HOWARD C. "Characteristics of Male Undergraduate Registrants of Firearms." *J Am Col Health Assn* 18(4):317–9 Ap '70. *

3528. BENNETT, LAWRENCE A. "Test Taking 'Insight' of Prison Inmates and Subsequent Parole Adjustment." *Correct Psychologist* 4(1):27–34 Jl '70. * (*PA* 46:9308)

3529. BOLDING, O. THOMAS, AND WILLCUTT, HERMAN C. "Weight Loss and Psychological Observations of Gynecological Patients II." *Ala J Med Sci* 7(1):87–91 Ja '70. *

3530. BOWEN, GEORGE RONALD. *MMPI Scales and Personal History Items as Indices of Prognosis.* Master's thesis, San Diego State College (San Diego, Calif.), 1970.

3531. CLAGHORN, JAMES. "The Anxiety-Depression Syndrome." *Psychosomatics* 11(5):438–41 S–O '70. * (*PA* 45:6677)

3532. DEAN, KATHERINE IMOGENE. *Father Absence, Feminine Identification, and Assertive-Aggressiveness—A Test of Compulsive Masculinity Among Institutionalized Negro Juvenile Delinquents.* Doctor's thesis, Florida State University (Tallahassee, Fla.), 1970. (*DAI* 31:4912A)

3533. DE VITO, ROBERT A.; FLAHERTY, LAWRENCE A.; AND MOZDZIERZ, GERALD J. "Toward a Dynamic Theory of Alcoholism." *Dis Nerv System* 31(1):43–9 Ja '70. * (*PA* 44:12860)

3534. DODD, JACK. "A Retrospective Analysis of Variables Related to Duration of Treatment in a University Psychiatric Clinic." *J Nerv & Mental Dis* 151(2):75–84 Ag '70. * (*PA* 45:10054)

3535. DOTY, BARBARA A. "Predictions of Teaching Effectiveness of Women Who Begin Teaching After Age Thirty-Five." *J Teach Ed* 21(4):519–25 w '70. *

3536. EASTON, ZELDA FAITH. *Relationship of Hypnotic Susceptibility to Personality Variables as Shown by MMPI and California Q-Set Scores.* Doctor's thesis, Louisiana State University (Baton Rouge, La.), 1970. (*DAI* 31:5618B)

3537. FALEK, ARTHUR; CRADDICK, RAY; AND COLLUM, JULIUS. "An Attempt to Identify Prisoners With an XYY Chromosome Complement by Psychiatric and Psychological Means." *J Nerv & Mental Dis* 150(3):165–70 Mr '70. * (*PA* 45:8539)

3538. FORREST, GARY GRAN. *Transparency as a Prognostic Variable in Psychotherapy.* Doctor's thesis, University of North Dakota (Grand Forks, N.D.), 1970. (*DAI* 31:4457A)

3539. FRANK, COLIN HUGHES. *The Prediction of Recidivism Among Young Adult Offenders by the Recidivism-Rehabilitation Scale and Index.* Doctor's thesis, University of Oklahoma (Norman, Okla.), 1970. (*DAI* 32:557B)

3540. GAY, RICHARD LEE. *The Relationship Between Psychopathology and Cancer.* Doctor's thesis, Michigan State University (East Lansing, Mich.), 1970. (*DAI* 31:4992B)

3541. HAHN, P., AND LEISNER, R. "The Influence of Biographical Anamnesis and Group Psychotherapy on Postmyocardial Patients." *Psychother & Psychosom* (Switzerland) 18(1–6):299–306 '70. * (*PA* 47:5508)

3542. HANSEN, CARL S. *MMPI Characteristics of Students Showing Conduct Infractions at Utah State University.* Master's thesis, Utah State University (Logan, Utah), 1970.

3543. HARRIS, EILEEN M. KOERBER. *A Measurement of Alienation in College Student Marijuana Users and Non-Users.* Doctor's thesis, Southern Illinois University (Carbondale, Ill.), 1970. (*DAI* 31:4788B)

3544. HATHAWAY, STARKE R.; MONACHESI, ELIO; AND SALASIN, SUSAN. "A Follow-Up Study of MMPI High 8, Schizoid, Children," pp. 171–88. In *Life History Research in Psychopathology.* Edited by Merrill Roff and David F. Ricks. Minneapolis, Minn.: University of Minnesota Press, 1970. Pp. viii, 321. *

3545. HINCKLEY, ROBERT G.; MESSENHEIMER, MYRON G.; BARDON, EDWARD J.; PENNINGTON, MARY H.; DREDGE, THOMAS E., SR.; DVORAK, EDWARD E.; REYNOLDS, PHYLLIS C.; AND RUPPRECHT, PAUL. "Nonmedical Drug Use Among College Student Psychiatric Patients." *J Am Col Health Assn* 18(5):333–41 Je '70. *

3546. HOEY, HENRY PATRICK. *The Interpersonal Behavior of Suicidal Individuals.* Doctor's thesis, Ohio University (Athens, Ohio), 1970. (*DAI* 31:7598B)

3547. HOLLAND, PAUL LaVERNE. *A Study of Factors Predictive of Persistence in the Parish Ministry of United Presbyterian Clergymen.* Doctor's thesis, University of Illinois (Urbana, Ill.), 1970. (*DAI* 31:6426A)

3548. HUFFER, VIRGINIA; LEVIN, LEON; AND ARONSON, HARRIET. "Oral Contraceptives: Depression and Frigidity." *J Nerv & Mental Dis* 151(1):35–41 Jl '70. * (*PA* 45:8079)

3549. JACKSON, GEORGE DANIEL. *Personality Characteristics of Narcotics Users.* Doctor's thesis, New York University (New York, N.Y.), 1970. (*DAI* 32:3638B)

3550. JOSHI, MOHAN C., AND SINGH, BEER. "Neurotic and Psychopathic Tendencies of Habitual Liars." *Indian Psychol R* 6(2):113–7 Ja '70. * (*PA* 46:9341)

3551. KERRY, R. J.; ORME, J. E.; AND WILKES, E. "Personality Testing: A New Diagnostic Aid." *Practitioner* (England) 205(1226):217–21 Ag '70. *

3552. KODMAN, FRANK, JR., AND HOPKINS, ROBERT W. "Correlates of Ego-Strength in a Sample of Kentucky Prison Inmates." *Correct Psychologist* 4(1):20–6 Jl '70. * (*PA* 46:9311)

3553. KODMAN, FRANK, JR., AND HOPKINS, ROBERT W. "MMPI Profile Characteristics of Kentucky Prison Inmates." *Correct Psychologist* 4(1):7–11 Jl '70. * (*PA* 46:9312)

3554. KRAFT, TOM, AND WIJESINGHE, BRIAN. "Systematic Desensitization of Social Anxiety in the Treatment of Alcoholism: A Psychometric Evaluation of Change." *Brit J Psychiatry* 117(539):443–4 O '70. * (*PA* 45:10113)

3555. KURTZ, ROBERT ROGER. *A Comparison of Different Approaches to the Measurement of Counselor Empathy in Personal Counseling.* Doctor's thesis, Michigan State University (East Lansing, Mich.), 1970. (*DAI* 31:5768A)

3556. LABIB, M. A.; ABBOUD, I.; AND SHAHEEN, O. "Primary Glaucoma Profile on the Minnesota Multiphasic Personality Inventory." *B Ophthalmol Soc Egypt* 63:127–37 '70. *

3557. LASZLO, JOHN P., AND ROSENTHAL, ROBERT. "Subject Dogmatism, Experimenter Status, and Experimenter Expectancy Effects." *Personality* 1(1):11–23 sp '70. * (*PA* 47:8908)

3558. LESTER, DAVID. "Personality Correlates Associated With Choice of Method of Committing Suicide." *Personality* 1(3):261–4 au '70. * (*PA* 45:6618)

3559. LeUNES, ARNOLD, AND CHRISTENSEN, LARRY. "Reliability and Inmate Test Results." *Correct Psychologist* 4(3):85–93 N–D '70. * (*PA* 49:2670)

3560. LEVENTHAL, GERALD S. "Influence of Brothers and Sisters on Sex-Role Behavior." *J Pers & Social Psychol* 16(3):452–65 N '70. * (*PA* 45:4058)

3561. LYNCH, WILLIAM JOHN. *The Performance of LSD Users on Certain Neuropsychological Tests.* Doctor's thesis, University of Tennessee (Knoxville, Tenn.), 1970. (*DAI* 31:5630B)

3562. McDANIEL, SYLVIA PARNELL. *The Effects of Selected Teacher Personality Variables on Reading Readiness, Self-Concept, and Changes in IQ in Culturally Deprived Five-Year-Olds.*

Minnesota Multiphasic Personality Inventory

Doctor's thesis, University of Alabama (University, Ala.), 1970. (*DAI* 31:6409A)

3563. MALMQUIST, CARL P. "Depression and Object Loss in Acute Psychiatric Admissions." *Am J Psychiatry* 126(12): 1782–7 Je '70. * (*PA* 47:5229)

3564. MEAD, PHILIP G. "The Effect of Orientation Passages on Patient Stress Prior to Dentistry." *Psychol Rec* 20(4):479–88 f '70. * (*PA* 46:638)

3565. MEGARGEE, EDWIN I. "The Prediction of Violence With Psychological Tests." *Curr Topics Clin & Commun Psychol* 2:97–156 '70. *

3566. MENSH, IVAN N. "Orientation of Social Values in Medical Student Assessment." *Social Sci & Med* (England) 3(3):339–48 Ja '70. *

3567. MIGNONE, R. J.; DONNELLY, E. F.; AND SADOWSKY, DORIS. "Psychological and Neurological Comparisons of Psychomotor and Non-Psychomotor Epileptic Patients." *Epilepsia* (Netherlands) 11(4):345–59 D '70. *

3568. MONE, LOUIS C. "Short-Term Group Psychotherapy With Postcardiac Patients." *Int J Group Psychother* 20(1):99–108 '70. * (*PA* 44:10619)

3569. MUCHA, THEODORE F., AND REINHARDT, ROGER F. "Conversion Reactions in Student Aviators." *Am J Psychiatry* 127(4):493–7 O '70. * (*PA* 47:1260)

3570. MURAWSKI, BENJAMIN J.; CHAZAN, BERNARD I.; BALODIMOS, MARIOS C.; AND RYAN, JEROME R. "Personality Patterns in Patients With Diabetes Mellitus of Long Duration." *Diabetes* 19(4):259–63 Ap '70. *

3571. NAOR, NEHAMA KLIBAN. *Configurational Analysis of the Strong Vocational Interest Blank (SVIB) and Concomitant Personality Correlates.* Doctor's thesis, University of North Carolina (Chapel Hill, N.C.), 1970. (*DAI* 31:6908B)

3572. NICHOLS, DAVID S. *Form-Level and the MMPI: A Construct Validational Study of Mayman's Form-Level Scoring Method.* Master's thesis, San Diego State College (San Diego, Calif.), 1970.

3573. NICOL, DONALD D., AND WARD, GEORGE, II. "A Canonical Correlation Analysis of the Minnesota Multiphasic Personality Inventory and the Kuder Preference Record." *Proc W Va Acad Sci* 41(1969):214–8 '70. *

3574. PAITICH, DANIEL. "The Clarke Automated Psychological Examination and Report (CAPER)." *Ont Psychologist* (Canada) 2(5):304–14 '70. *

3575. PEARCE, K. I. "A Comparison of Care Given by Family Practitioners and Psychiatrists in a Teaching Hospital Psychiatric Unit." *Am J Psychiatry* 127(6):835–40 D '70. * (*PA* 47:5048)

3576. PRAGER, RICHARD ANTHONY. *The Relationship of Certain Client Characteristics to Therapist-Offered Conditions and Therapeutic Outcome.* Doctor's thesis, Columbia University (New York, N.Y.), 1970. (*DAI* 31:5634B)

3577. QUELLO, DANIEL Y. "A Comparative Investigation of the Personality Profiles of CPE and Non-CPE Theological Students." *J Pastoral Care* 24(4):240–3 D '70. * (*PA* 47:758)

3578. ROUTH, DONALD K. "MMPI Responses of Mothers and Fathers as a Function of Mental Retardation of the Child." *Am J Mental Def* 75(3):376–7 N '70. *

3579. RUSKIN, H. D.; STEIN, L. L.; SHELSKY, I. M.; AND BAILEY, M. A.; WITH THE COLLABORATION OF G. ELIZABETH JEFFERSON, E. I. BRAVERMAN, AND J. A. ZATZKIN. "MMPI: Comparison Between Patients With Coronary Heart Disease and Their Spouses Together With Other Demographic Data: A Preliminary Report." *Scand J Rehabil Med* (Sweden) 2(2–3): 99–104 '70. *

3580. SHAHEEN, O.; LABIB, M. A.; ABBOUD, I.; AND EL-RIFAI, M. "Some Ophthalmological Factors Affecting the Personality Patterns in Primary Glaucoma Patients as Determined by the Minnesota Multiphasic Personality Inventory." *B Ophthalmol Soc Egypt* 63:139–40 '70. *

3581. SHANNON, ANNA MARIAN. *Differences Between Depressives and Schizophrenics in the Recognition of Facial Expression of Emotion.* Doctor's thesis, University of California (San Francisco, Calif.), 1970. (*DAI* 32:2822B)

3582. SIMON, WERNER, AND LUMRY, GAYLE K. "Suicide of the Spouse as a Divorce Substitute." *Dis Nerv System* 31(9): 608–12 S '70. * (*PA* 45:6624)

3583. SPEER, DAVID C. "Effects of Marathon Group Therapy: Short-Term MMPI Changes." *Comparative Group Studies* 1(4):397–404 N '70. * (*PA* 47:6934)

3584. STEINBOOK, RICHARD M., AND CHAPMAN, A. BRADLEY. "Lithium Responders: An Evaluation of Psychological Test Characteristics." *Comprehen Psychiatry* 11(6):524–30 N '70. * (*PA* 47:1123)

3585. STROEBEL, CHARLES F., AND GLUECK, BERNARD C., JR. "Computer Derived Global Judgments in Psychiatry." *Am J Psychiatry* 126(8):1057–66 F '70. * (*PA* 44:12844)

3586. SWENSON, WENDELL M. "Automated Personality Assessment in Medical Practice." *Med Clinics N Am* 54(4):835–49 Jl '70. *

3587. TALLANT, WELDON J. *Changes in Pre-Service Teachers Involved in a Multi-Cultural Training Program Utilizing Formal Presentations, Sensitivity Training, Planned Social Activities, and a Cooperative Living Arrangement.* Doctor's thesis, East Texas State University (Commerce, Tex.), 1970. (*DAI* 31:4608A)

3588. TUFT, L. H., AND BERMAN, M. I. "The Use of the MMPI in Describing an Inpatient Population of Merchant Seamen." *N Zeal Med J* 71(452):26–9 Ja '70. *

3589. VERNALLIS, FRANCIS F.; SHIPPER, JOHN C.; BUTLER, DONALD C.; AND TOMLINSON, T. M. "Saturation Group Psychotherapy in a Weekend Clinic: An Outcome Study." *Psychother Theory Res & Prac* 7(3):144–52 f '70. * (*PA* 45:4416)

3590. WEISMAN, SIDNEY. "The Significance of Diagnosis in the Treatment of Narcotic Addicts." *Int J Addic* 5(4):717–30 D '70. *

3591. WHITE, WILLIAM CLINTON, JR. *Selective Modeling in Youthful Offenders With High and Low O-H (Overcontrolled-Hostility) Personality Types.* Doctor's thesis, Florida State University (Tallahassee, Fla.), 1970. (*DAI* 31:5648B)

3592. AARONSON, BERNARD S. "Hypnosis, Depth Perception and Schizophrenia." *Percept & Motor Skills* 32(1):271–5 F '71. * (*PA* 46:3477)

3593. ADAMS, JERRY. "Defensiveness on the MMPI as a Function of the Warmth of Test Introduction." Abstract. *J Consult & Clin Psychol* 36(3):444 Je '71. * (*PA* 46:9272)

3594. AIKEN, LINDA H., AND HENRICHS, THEODORE F. "Systematic Relaxation as a Nursing Intervention Technique With Open Heart Surgery Patients." *Nursing Res* 20(3):212–7 My-Je '71. * (*PA* 51:3670)

3595. ANANT, SANTOKH S. "Belongingness and Mental Health: Cross Cultural, Sex and Marital Differences." *Manas* (India) 18(1):11–23 My '71. * (*PA* 48:9151)

3596. ANDREWS, DONALD. *Relationships of Various Elements to Successful Completion of Training in a Manpower Skills Center.* Doctor's thesis, University of Nebraska (Lincoln, Neb.), 1971. (*DAI* 32:3650A)

3597. ANTHONY, NICHOLAS. "Comparison of Clients' Standard, Exaggerated, and Matching MMPI Profiles." *J Consult & Clin Psychol* 36(1):100–3 F '71. * (*PA* 45:10208)

3598. APFELDORF, MAX; HUNLEY, PHYLLIS J.; AND COOPER, G. David. "Differences Between Older Institutionalized Offenders and Nonoffenders on MMPI Hostility and Control Scales." *J Clin Psychol* 27(3):370–2 Jl '71. * (*PA* 47:5066)

3599. APOSTAL, ROBERT A. "Personality Descriptions of Mental Health Center Patients for Use as Pre-Therapy Information." *Mental Hyg* 55(1):119–20 Ja '71. * (*PA* 46:3307)

3600. ARNOLD, KRISTIN ELLEN OKERLUND. *Language in Schizophrenics and Their Twins.* Doctor's thesis, University of Minnesota (Minneapolis, Minn.), 1971. (*DAI* 32:6632B)

3601. ARNOLD, RICHARD RUSSELL. *The Relationships Among Ego Characteristics and Self Constructs in Delinquent Boys.* Doctor's thesis, University of North Carolina (Chapel Hill, N.C.), 1971. (*DAI* 32:2994B)

3602. ATWOOD, ROBERT W., AND HOWELL, ROBERT J. "Pupillometric and Personality Test Score Differences of Female Aggressing Pedophiliacs and Normals." *Psychon Sci* 22(2):115–6 Ja 25 '71. * (*PA* 48:7473)

3603. BALANCE, WILLIAM D. G.; SANDBERG, SONNY S.; AND BRINGMANN, WOLFGANG G. "Acceptance of Trait-Descriptive vs 'Medical Model' Oriented Feedback Statements." *Psychol Rep* 29(2):539–44 O '71. * (*PA* 47:9193)

3604. BARKER, HARRY R.; FOWLER, RAYMOND D.; AND PETERSON, LARS P. "Factor Analytic Structure of the Short Form MMPI Items in a VA Hospital Population." *J Clin Psychol* 27(2):228–33 Ap '71. * (*PA* 46:7069)

3605. BATES, HENRY D. "Factorial Structure and MMPI Correlates of a Fear Survey Schedule in a Clinical Population." *Behav Res & Ther* (England) 9(4):355–60 N '71. * (*PA* 48: 3345)

3606. BATES, HENRY D. "Toward the Development of a Screening Scale for Assertive Training." *Psychol Rep* 28(1): 99–107 F '71. *

3607. BEARDSLEY, JAMES V., AND PULETTI, FLAVIO. "Personality (MMPI) and Cognitive (WAIS) Changes After Levodopa Treatment: Occurrence in Patients With Parkinson's Disease." *Arch Neurol* 25(2):145–50 Ag '71. * (*PA* 48:1446)

3608. BELFER, MYRON L.; SHADER, RICHARD I.; CARROLL, MARY; AND HARMATZ, JEROLD S. "Alcoholism in Women." *Arch Gen Psychiatry* 25(6):540–4 D '71. *

3609. BENTLER, P. M.; JACKSON, DOUGLAS N.; AND MESSICK, SAMUEL. "Identification of Content and Style: A Two-Dimensional Interpretation of Acquiescence." *Psychol B* 76(3):186–204 S '71. * (*PA* 47:3014)

3610. BERGER, EMANUEL M. "MMPI Item Differences Between Smoker and Nonsmoker College Freshmen Males." Abstract. *J Consult & Clin Psychol* 36(3):446 Je '71. * (*PA* 46: 9019)

3611. BERNHARDSON, CLEMENS S. "Social Desirability, Endorsement and Judged Frequency of Occurrence on the Items From Four Social Desirability Scales." *Percept & Motor Skills* 33(3):1007–12 D '71. * (*PA* 48:888)

3612. BERRY, DAVID FREDERICK. *A Comparison of Multivariate Procedures for Grouping MMPI Profile Data.* Doctor's thesis, Ohio State University (Columbus, Ohio), 1971. (*DAI* 32:2995B)

3613. BERZINS, JURIS I.; ROSS, WESLEY F.; AND MONROE, JACK J. "A Multivariate Study of the Personality Characteristics of Hospitalized Narcotic Addicts on the MMPI." *J Clin Psychol* 27(2):174–81 Ap '71. * (*PA* 46:7086)

3614. BETZ, ROGER CHARLES. *Predicting Rehabilitation Out-*

comes Through Selected Personal, Psychological and Program Variables. Doctor's thesis, University of Northern Colorado (Greeley, Colo.), 1971. (DAI 32:3681A)

3615. BIER, WILLIAM C. "A Modified Form of the Minnesota Multiphasic Personality Inventory for Religious Personnel." Theol Ed 7(2):121-33 W '71. *

3616. BLACK, JOHN MITCHELL. The Marathon as an Adjunct to Ongoing Group Process. Doctor's thesis, Southern Illinois University (Carbondale, Ill.), 1971. (DAI 32:4852B)

3617. BLACKBURN, R. "Personality Types Among Abnormal Homicides." Brit J Criminol 11(1):14-31 Ja '71. * (PA 46:11149)

3618. BLACKBURN, RONALD. "MMPI Dimensions of Sociability and Impulse Control." Abstract. J Consult & Clin Psychol 37(1):166 Ag '71. * (PA 47:1217)

3619. BLOCK, JACK. "On Further Conjectures Regarding Acquiescence." Psychol B 76(3):205-10 S '71. * (PA 47:3015)

3620. BLUM, DONNA M. "Educational and Diagnostic MMPI Characteristics of a Private Hospital Population." Psychol Rep 28(3):724-6 Je '71. * (PA 46:11090)

3621. BRAATZ, GORDON A.; LUMRY, GAYLE K.; AND WRIGHT, M. SUZANNE. "The Young Veteran as a Psychiatric Patient in Three Eras of Conflict." Mil Med 136(5):455-7 My '71. * (PA 47:1246)

3622. BREWSTER, EDWARD THOMAS. Personality Characteristics of Giving- Versus Receiving-Oriented Individuals. Doctor's thesis, University of Arizona (Tucson, Ariz.), 1971. (DAI 32:2476A)

3623. BRILL, NORMAN Q.; CRUMPTON, EVELYN; AND GRAYSON, HARRY M. "Personality Factors in Marihuana Use: A Preliminary Report." Arch Gen Psychiatry 24(2):163-5 F '71. * (PA 46:4922)

3624. BRINGMANN, WOLFGANG G.; BALANCE, WILLIAM D. G.; AND SANDBERG, SONNY S. "Self-Validation of Programmed Feedback Statements." Psychol Rep 29(3):733-4 D '71. * (PA 47:8945)

3625. BRISTER, DAVID MICHAEL. Discrimination of Alcoholics With Configural MMPI Scaling Procedures. Doctor's thesis, University of Alabama (University, Ala.), 1971. (DAI 32:1204B)

3626. BROSKOWSKI, ANTHONY; SILVERMAN, RITA; AND HINKEL, HELEN. "Actuarial Assessment of Criminality in Women." Criminol 9(2-3):166-84 Ag-N '71. *

3627. BROWN, DAVID JEFFREY. The Fear of Death and the Western-Protestant Ethic Personality Identity. Doctor's thesis, Ohio State University (Columbus, Ohio), 1971. (DAI 32:7302B)

3628. BRUHN, JOHN G.; WOLF, STEWART; AND PHILIPS, BILLY U. "A Psycho-Social Study of Surviving Male Coronary Patients and Controls Followed Over Nine Years." J Psychosom Res (England) 15(2):305-13 Je '71. *

3629. BURNES, KAY; BROWN, WALTER A.; AND KEATING, GORDON W. "Dimensions of Control: Correlations Between MMPI and I-E Scores." Abstract. J Consult & Clin Psychol 36(2):301 Ap '71. * (PA 46:3022)

3630. BUTLER, PAMELA ELLEN. The Relaltionship of Depression to Aggressive Response Intensity and State-Trait Anxiety. Doctor's thesis, University of Alabama (University, Ala.), 1971. (DAI 32:5433B)

3631. CANTER, FRANCIS M. "Authoritarian Attitudes, Degree of Pathology and Preference for Structured Versus Unstructured Psychotherapy in Hospitalized Mental Patients." Psychol Rep 28(1):231-4 F '71. * (PA 46:5047)

3632. CARROLL, JAMES L., AND FULLER, GERALD B. "An MMPI Comparison of Three Groups of Criminals." J Clin Psychol 27(2):240-2 Ap '71. * (PA 46:7124)

3633. CHEIFETZ, DAVID I.; GARRON, DAVID C.; LEAVITT, FRANK; KLAWANS, HAROLD L.; AND GARVIN, JOHN S. "Emotional Disturbance Accompanying the Treatment of Parkinsonism With L-Dopa." Clin Pharmacol & Therapeu 12(1):56-61 Ja-F '71. *

3634. CLARK, CARL G., AND MILLER, HOWARD I. "Validation of Gilberstadt and Duker's 8-6 Profile Type on a Black Sample." Psychol Rep 29(1):259-64 Ag '71. * (PA 47:3264)

3635. CLINE, DAVID W., AND ROUZER, DAVID L. "The Nonphysician as Primary Therapist in Hospital Psychiatry." Am J Psychiatry 128(4):407-11 O '71. * (PA 47:9170)

3636. COHEN, CHARLES P.; JOHNSON, DALE L.; AND HANSON, PHILIP G. "Interpersonal Changes Among Psychiatric Patients in Human Relations Training." J Pers Assess 35(5):472-9 O '71. * (PA 47:9040)

3637. COOKE, GERALD, AND ROBEY, AMES. "The MMPI: A Case Study in Dissimulation." J Consult & Clin Psychol 36(3):355-9 Je '71. * (PA 46:9335)

3638. CORSSEN, GUENTER; OGET, SOLMAZ; AND REED, PERCY C. "Computerized Evaluation of Psychic Effects of Kelamine." Anesth & Analg 50(3):397-401 My-Je '71. *

3639. COSTELLO, RAYMOND MICHAEL. Racial Comparisons on the Minnesota Multiphasic Personality Inventory. Doctor's thesis, University of Tennessee (Knoxville, Tenn.), 1971. (DAI 32:4855B)

3640. COUNTS, PERRY DALMOND. A Study of the Relationship Between Academic Achievement and Creativity. Doctor's thesis, University of Tennessee (Knoxville, Tenn.), 1971. (DAI 32:4342A)

3641. CRIDER, ANDREW, AND LUNN, ROBERT. "Electrodermal Lability as a Personality Dimension." J Exp Res Personality 5(2):145-50 Je '71. *

3642. CRUMPTON, EVELYN, AND BRILL, NORMAN Q. "Personality Factors Associated With Frequency of Marijuana Use." Calif Med 115(3):11-5 S '71. *

3643. DAVIES, JOHN G. V., AND MALIPHANT, RODNEY. "Refractory Behaviour at School in Normal Adolescent Males in Relation to Psychopathy and Early Experience." J Child Psychol & Psychiatry (England) 12(1):35-41 Je '71. * (PA 47:7522)

3644. DAVIS, GLENN C., AND BREHM, MARY L. "Juvenile Prisoners: Motivational Factors in Drug Use." Abstract. Proc 79th Ann Conv Am Psychol Assn 6(1):333-4 '71. * (PA 46:3363)

3645. DAVIS, KENNETH R., AND SINES, JACOB O. "An Antisocial Behavior Pattern Associated With a Specific MMPI Profile." J Consult & Clin Psychol 36(2):229-34 Ap '71. * (PA 46:3311)

3646. DAVIS, KENNETH RUST. The Actuarial Development of a Female 4'3 MMPI Profile. Doctor's thesis, St. Louis University (St. Louis, Mo.), 1971. (DAI 32:1207B)

3647. DAVIS, LEO J., JR.; OSBORNE, DAVID; SIEMENS, PETER J.; AND BROWN, JOE R. "MMPI Correlates With Disability in Multiple Sclerosis." Psychol Rep 28(3):700-2 Je '71. * (PA 46:11353)

3648. DAVIS, WILLIAM E., AND DEWOLFE, ALAN S. "Premorbid Adjustment and Affective Expression in Schizophrenia." J Abn Psychol 78(2):198-201 O '71. * (PA 47:9347)

3649. DELHEES, KARL H., AND CATTELL, RAYMOND B. "The Dimensions of Pathology: Proof of Their Projection Beyond the Normal 16PF Source Traits." Personality 2(2):149-73 su '71. * (PA 47:7076)

3650. DODGE, GORDON R., AND KOLSTOE, RALPH H. "The MMPI in Differentiating Early Multiple Sclerosis and Conversion Hysteria." Psychol Rep 29(1):155-9 Ag '71. * (PA 47:3265)

3651. DUPONT, ROBERT L.; RYDER, ROBERT G.; AND GRUNEBAUM, HENRY U. "An Unexpected Result of Psychosis in Marriage." Discussion by John S. Kafka. Am J Psychiatry 128(6):735-9 D '71. * (PA 48:1333)

3652. EMANUELSON, MARGARET SELLS. Parental Personality Variables as Predictors of Specific Behavioral Disorders in Children. Doctor's thesis, University of Virginia (Charlottesville, Va.), 1971. (DAI 32:4856B)

3653. EVERETT, ROYICE B., AND SCHECHTER, MARSHALL D. "A Comparative Study of Prenatal Anxiety in the Unwed Mother." Child Psychiatry & Hum Develop 2(2):84-91 w '71. *

3654. EWING, DOUGLAS RHEA. Psychiatric Patient Self-Description Via Self-Report and the MMPI. Doctor's thesis, University of Missouri (Columbia, Mo.), 1971. (DAI 32:1839B)

3655. FARLEY, FRANK H.; HATCH, ROBERT; MURPHY, PATRICK; AND MILLER, KENNETH. "Sibling Structure and Masculinity-Femininity in Male Adolescents." Adolescence 6(24):441-50 w '71. * (PA 48:6985)

3656. FENZ, WALTER D. "Heart Rate Responses to a Stressor: A Comparison Between Primary and Secondary Psychopaths and Normal Controls." J Exp Res Personality 5(1):7-13 Mr '71. * (PA 46:7159)

3657. FINN, JANE ANN. Reactions to Pain in Psychopathic Criminals. Doctor's thesis, University of Kansas (Lawrence, Kan.), 1971. (DAI 32:4209B)

3658. FINNEY, JOSEPH C.; SMITH, DAVID F.; SKEETERS, DONALD E.; AND AUVENSHINE, C. DWIGHT. "MMPI Alcoholism Scales: Factor Structure and Content Analysis." Q J Studies Alcohol 32(4):1055-60 D '71. *

3659. FISHMAN, DANIEL B., AND PETTY, THOMAS L. "Physical, Symptomatic and Psychological Improvement in Patients Receiving Comprehensive Care for Chronic Airway Obstruction." J Chronic Dis 24(11):775-85 D '71. *

3660. FLEISS, JOSEPH L.; LAWLOR, WILLIAM; PLATMAN, STANLEY R.; AND FIEVE, RONALD R. "On the Use of Inverted Factor Analysis for Generating Typologies." J Abn Psychol 77(2):127-32 Ap '71. * (PA 46:3315)

3661. FLICK, GRAD L., AND EDWARDS, KENNETH R. "Prediction of Organic Brain Dysfunction With the MMPI: A Discriminant Function Analysis." Newsl Res Psychol 13(4):18-9 N '71. *

3662. FLYNN, JAMES DUNN. An Analysis of Feasibility and Nonfeasibility of Vocational Rehabilitation Applicants as Measured by the Projective Occupational Attitudes Test. Doctor's thesis, Washington State University (Pullman, Wash.), 1971. (DAI 32:1210B)

3663. FORD, CHARLES V.; CASTELNUOVO-TEDESCO, PIETRO; AND LONG, KAHLILA D. "Abortion: Is It a Therapeutic Procedure in Psychiatry?" J Am Med Assn 218(8):1173-8 N 22 '71. * (PA 47:10721)

3664. FOWLER, RAYMOND D., JR., AND ATHEY, ELIZABETH B. "A Cross-Validation of Gilberstadt and Duker's 1-2-3-4 Profile Type." J Clin Psychol 27(2):238-40 Ap '71. * (PA 46:7074)

3665. FROMHART, MICHAEL V. "Characteristics of Male Homosexual College Students." J Am Col Health Assn 19(4):247-52 Ap '71. *

3666. GARFIELD, SOL L., AND BERGIN, ALLEN E. "Personal

Therapy, Outcome and Some Therapist Variables." *Psychother Theory Res & Prac* 8(3):251–3 f '71. * (*PA* 47:10982)

3667. GARFIELD, SOL L., AND BERGIN, ALLEN E. "Therapeutic Conditions and Outcome." *J Abn Psychol* 77(2):108–14 Ap '71. * (*PA* 46:3194)

3668. GARFIELD, SOL L.; PRAGER, RICHARD A.; AND BERGIN, ALLEN E. "Evaluating Outcome in Psychotherapy: A Hardy Perennial." *J Consult & Clin Psychol* 37(3):320–2 D '71.. *

3669. GARFIELD, SOL L.; PRAGER, RICHARD A.; AND BERGIN, ALLEN E. "Evaluation of Outcome in Psychotherapy." *J Consult & Clin Psychol* 37(3):307–13 D '71. * (*PA* 47:9011)

3670. GAYTON, WILLIAM F., AND WILSON, WINSTON T. "Utility of the Mini-Mult in a Child Guidance Clinic Setting." *J Pers Assess* 35(6):569–75 D '71. * (*PA* 47:11126)

3671. GEIST, HAROLD. "Emotional Aspects of Dermatitis." Abstract. *Proc 79th Ann Conv Am Psychol Assn* 6(2):627–8 '71. * (*PA* 46:5380)

3672. GENDREAU, PAUL, AND SUBOSKI, MILTON D. "Classical Discrimination Eyelid Conditioning in Primary Psychopaths." *J Abn Psychol* 77(3):242–6 Je '71. * (*PA* 46:7126)

3673. GILBERSTADT, HAROLD. "Computerized Scoring, Interpretation and Cross-Validation of Objective Tests." *Newsl Res Psychol* 13(2):44–5 My '71. *

3674. GOLDSTEIN, ALAN MAURICE. *Denial as a Function of Internal-External Control in Chronic Renal Failure.* Doctor's thesis, Fordham University (New York, N.Y.), 1971. (*DAI* 32:3001B)

3675. GOLIN, SANFORD; SOLKOFF, NORMAN; AND GOLIN, ANNE K. "Distractibility as a Function of MMPI Hy and Pt Scores." *J Clin Psychol* 27(4):491–2 O '71. * (*PA* 47:8948)

3676. GOZALI, JOAV, AND SLOAN, JACK. "Control Orientation as a Personality Dimension Among Alcoholics." *Q J Studies Alcohol* 32(1A):159–61 Mr '71. * (*PA* 46:7096)

3677. GRAHAM, JOHN R. "Feedback and Accuracy of Clinical Judgments From the MMPI." *J Consult & Clin Psychol* 36(2):286–91 Ap '71. * (*PA* 46:3316)

3678. GRAHAM, JOHN R. "Feedback and Accuracy of Predictions of Hospitalization From the MMPI." *J Clin Psychol* 27(2):243–5 Ap '71. * (*PA* 46:7077)

3679. GRAHAM, JOHN R.; SCHROEDER, HAROLD E.; AND LILLY, ROY S. "Factor Analysis of Items on the Social Introversion and Masculinity-Femininity Scales of the MMPI." *J Clin Psychol* 27(3):367–70 Jl '71. * (*PA* 47:4825)

3680. GRAVITZ, MELVIN A. "Declination Rates on the MMPI Validity and Clinical Scales." *J Clin Psychol* 27(1):103 Ja '71. * (*PA* 46:1208)

3681. GREAVES, GEORGE. "MMPI Correlates of Chronic Drug Abuse in Hospitalized Adolescents." *Psychol Rep* 29(3):1222 D '71. * (*PA* 48:1221)

3682. GROSZ, HANUS J., AND WAGONER, ROBERT. "MMPI and EPPS Profiles of High and Low Verbal Interactors in Therapy Groups." *Psychol Rep* 28(3):951–5 Je '71. * (*PA* 46:10991)

3683. GUINDON, JOSEPH ERNEST. *Paradox, Schizophrenia and the Double Bind Hypothesis: An Exploratory Study.* Doctor's thesis, University of Washington (Seattle, Wash.), 1971. (*DAI* 32:3002B)

3684. GUPTA, V. P. "Physiological Changes in Relation to Personality Traits as Measured by MMPI." *Indian J Exp Psychol* 5(1):18–9 Ja '71. *

3685. GYNTHER, MALCOLM D.; FOWLER, RAYMOND D.; AND ERDBERG, PHILIP. "False Positives Galore: The Application of Standard MMPI Criteria to a Rural, Isolated, Negro Sample." *J Clin Psychol* 27(2):234–7 Ap '71. * (*PA* 46:6891)

3686. HAMA, HARUYO. "A Personality Scale for Susceptibility to Conflict." *Jap Psychol Res* 13(1):34–44 My '71. * (*PA* 49:4496)

3687. HARRIS, EILEEN M. "A Measurement of Alienation in College Student Marijuana Users and Non-Users." *J Sch Health* 41(3):130–3 Mr '71. * (*PA* 46:10841)

3688. HARTMANN, ERNEST; BAEKELAND, FREDERICK; ZWILLING, GEORGE; AND HOY, PATRICK. "Sleep Need: How Much Sleep and What Kind?" *Am J Psychiatry* 127(8):1001–8 F '71. * (*PA* 47:121)

3689. HEILBRUN, ALFRED B., JR. "Prediction of Rehabilitation Outcome in Chronic Court-Case Alcoholics." *Q J Studies Alcohol* 32(2):328–33 Je '71. *

3690. HEILIZER, FRED, AND CUTTER, HENRY S. G. "Anxiety and Arousal." *J General Psychol* 85(1):63–70 Jl '71. * (*PA* 46:10075)

3691. HEILIZER, FRED, AND CUTTER, HENRY S. G. "Generality and Correlates of Risks Taking." *J General Psychol* 85(2):259–83 O '71. * (*PA* 47:4800)

3692. HELSON, RAVENNA. "Women Mathematicians and the Creative Personality." *J Consult & Clin Psychol* 36(2):210–20 Ap '71. * (*PA* 46:3073)

3693. HENDRICHS, THEODORE F.; MACKENZIE, JAMES W.; AND ALMOND, CARL H. "Psychological Adjustment and Psychiatric Complications Following Open Heart Surgery." *J Nerv & Mental Dis* 152(5):332–45 My '71. * (*PA* 46:11404)

3694. HERRELL, JAMES M. "Administrative Variables Affecting the Utility of an MMPI Atlas." *J Consult & Clin Psychol* 37(2):302–3 O '71. * (*PA* 47:9203)

3695. HERSEN, MICHEL, AND SUDIK, ELLEN. "Verbal Conditioning as Related to Awareness, Paranoia, and Suspiciousness." *J Clin Psychol* 27(1):43–7 Ja '71. * (*PA* 46:1175)

3696. HINCHCLIFFE, RONALD. "Intercorrelation of MMPI and MPI Scales on Vertiginous Populations." *Personality* 2(4):315–23 w '71. * (*PA* 48:7284)

3697. HOERL, JEAN BOKA. *Objections to Selected MMPI Items as a Function of Sex, Internal Versus External Locus of Control and Procedures for Objecting.* Doctor's thesis, St. Louis University (St. Louis, Mo.), 1971. (*DAI* 32:4859B)

3698. HOFFMANN, HELMUT, AND NELSON, PAUL C. "Personality Characteristics of Alcoholics in Relation to Age and Intelligence." *Psychol Rep* 29(1):143–6 Ag '71. * (*PA* 47:3292)

3699. HOLLE, ERVIN F. *Teacher Effectiveness: A Study of the Relationship Between Teacher Personality Characteristics and Anxiety in Elementary Pupils.* Doctor's thesis, University of New Mexico (Albuquerque, N.M.), 1971. (*DAI* 32:6269A)

3700. HOOKE, JAMES F., AND KRAUSS, HERBERT H. "Personality Characteristics of Successful Police Sergeant Candidates." *J Crim Law Criminol & Police Sci* 62(1):104–6 Mr '71. * (*PA* 46:11787)

3701. HOOVER, EVE BLAND. *An Investigation of the Role of MMPI Personality Variables and Rated Effectiveness of Public School Counselors.* Doctor's thesis, University of North Carolina (Chapel Hill, N.C.), 1971. (*DAI* 32:738A)

3702. HOPKINS, NEIL ROBERT. *Student Activism and Techniques of Persuasive Communications as Related to Selected Personality Variables.* Doctor's thesis, University of Maryland (College Park, Md.), 1971. (*DAI* 32:2954A)

3703. HOUSTON, B. KENT. "Anxiety, Defensiveness, and Differential Prediction of Performance in Stress and Nonstress Conditions." *J Pers & Social Psychol* 17(1):66–8 Ja '71. * (*PA* 45:9960)

3704. HOUSTON, B. KENT. "Sources, Effects, and Individual Vulnerability of Psychological Problems for College Students." *J Counsel Psychol* 18(2):157–65 Mr '71. * (*PA* 46:1820)

3705. HOUSTON, B. KENT. "Trait and Situational Denial and Performance Under Stress." *J Pers & Social Psychol* 18(3):289–93 Je '71. * (*PA* 46:6866)

3706. HOUTS, DONALD C. "Ego Identity and Professional Preparation for the Ministry." *J Pastoral Care* 25(1):12–23 Mr '71. * (*PA* 46:8839)

3707. HUGO, JOHN ADAM, II. *Abbreviation of the Minnesota Multiphasic Personality Inventory Through Multiple Regression.* Doctor's thesis, University of Alabama (University, Ala.), 1971. (*DAI* 32:1213B)

3708. JACKSON, DOUGLAS N. "The Dynamics of Structured Personality Tests: 1971." *Psychol R* 78(3):229–48 My '71. * (*PA* 46:4995)

3709. JAMES, REUBEN J. *Traits Associated With the Initial and Persistent Interest in the Study of College Science.* Doctor's thesis, State University of New York (Buffalo, N.Y.), 1971. (*DAI* 32:1296A)

3710. JENKINS, C. DAVID. "Psychologic and Social Precursors of Coronary Disease (First of Two Parts)." *New Engl J Med* 284(5):244–55 F 4 '71. * (*PA* 46:7366)

3711. JOHNS, M. W.; GAY, T. J. A.; MASTERTON, J. P.; AND BRUCE, D. W. "Relationship Between Sleep Habits, Adrenocortical Activity and Personality." *Psychosom Med* 33(6):499–508 N–D '71. * (*PA* 49:2474)

3712. JOHNSON, GEORGE; FOX, JACK; SCHAEFER, HALMUTH H.; AND ISHIKAWA, WESLEY. "Predicting Rehospitalization From Community Placement." *Psychol Rep* 29(2):475–8 O '71. * (*PA* 47:9357)

3713. JONES, BEN MORGAN. "Verbal and Spatial Intelligence in Short and Long Term Alcoholics." *J Nerv & Mental Dis* 153(4):292–7 O '71. * (*PA* 47:11157)

3714. KADRI, Z. N. "The Use of the MMPI for Personality Study of Singapore Students." *Brit J Social & Clin Psychol* 10(1):90–1 F '71. * (*PA* 46:1209)

3715. KASTE, CAROL MAE MADSEN. *A Ten-Year Follow-Up of Children Diagnosed in a Child Guidance Clinic as Having Cerebral Dysfunction.* Doctor's thesis, University of Minnesota (Minneapolis, Minn.), 1971. (*DAI* 33:1797B)

3716. KENDALL, RICHARD F., AND PITTEL, STEPHEN M. "Three Portraits of the Young Drug User: Comparison of MMPI Group Profiles." *J Psychedelic Drugs* 3(2):63–6 sp '71. * (*PA* 48:4954)

3717. KIESLER, DONALD J. "Patient Experiencing and Successful Outcome in Individual Psychotherapy of Schizophrenics and Psychoneurotics." *J Consult & Clin Psychol* 37(3):370–85 D '71. * (*PA* 47:9013)

3718. KILPATRICK, DEAN G.; CAUTHEN, NELSON R.; AND ROITZSCH, JOHN C. "Psychopathy, Repression-Sensitization, and Anxiety." *Psychol Rep* 28(2):615–8 Ap '71. * (*PA* 46:7130)

3719. KING, HOLLIS HEATON. *An Investigation of Relationships Between Hypnotic Susceptibility, Manifest Dream Content and Personality Characteristics.* Doctor's thesis, Louisiana State University (Baton Rouge, La.), 1971. (*DAI* 33:442B)

3720. KINSINGER, JOHN RAY. *The Relationship Between Lethality of Suicidal Intentions and Assertive, Aggressive, and Hostile Traits.* Doctor's thesis, Southwestern Medical School (Dallas, Tex.), 1971. (*DAI* 31:7600B)

3721. KLETT, WILLIAM. "The Utility of Computer Interpreted MMPI's at St. Cloud VA Hospital." *Newsl Res Psychol* 13(2):45–7 My '71. *

3722. KLINEDINST, JAMES KARL. *Relationships Between Minnesota Multiphasic Personality Inventory and Personality Inventory for Children Data From Mothers of Disturbed Children.* Doctor's thesis, University of Minnesota (Minneapolis, Minn.), 1971. (*DAI* 32:4860B)

3723. KOKOSH, JOHN. "Two-Point MMPI Code Types and Academic Achievement." *Psychol Rep* 28(2):671-6 Ap '71. * (*PA* 46:7709)

3724. KOZMA, FREDERICK, JR. *Personality Change in Institutionalized Psychotic and Non-Psychotic Populations.* Doctor's thesis, Pennsylvania State University (University Park, Pa.), 1971. (*DAI* 32:5445B)

3725. LeMAISTRE, GRESS. "Computer as Psychologist: Who's Running the Show?" *J Ed Data Processing* 8(2-3):18-21 '71. *

3726. LESTER, DAVID. "MMPI Scores of Old and Young Completed Suicides." *Psychol Rep* 28(1):146 F '71. * (*PA* 46:5176)

3727. LEVITT, EUGENE E.; LUBIN, BERNARD; AND DeWITT, KATHRYN N. "An Attempt to Develop an Objective Test Battery for the Selection of Nursing Students." *Nursing Res* 20(3):255-8 My-Je '71. * (*PA* 51:3969)

3728. LEWIS, JERRY M.; KRAUS, WILLIAM L.; GOSSETT, JOHN T.; AND PHILLIPS, VIRGINIA AUSTIN. "Chest Pain, Personality and Coronary Arteriography: A Preliminary Study." *South Med J* 64(4):467-71 Ap '71. *

3729. LIBB, J. WESLEY, AND TAULBEE, EARL S. "Psychotic-Appearing MMPI Profiles Among Alcoholics." *J Clin Psychol* 27(1):101-2 Ja '71. * (*PA* 46:1452)

3730. LIEBERMAN, LEWIS R., AND WALTERS, SUSAN M. "Self-Ratings and Inventory Scores in the Measurement of Social Introversion." *J Clin Psychol* 27(3):363-6 Jl '71. * (*PA* 47:4826)

3731. LISTIAK, RICHARD L., AND STONE, LeROY A. "Psychophysical Approach to Clinical Judgment of Low *T* Scores on the MMPI." Abstract. *J Consult & Clin Psychol* 36(3):447 Je '71. * (*PA* 46:9282)

3732. LISTIAK, RICHARD LANCE. *A Psychophysical Approach to Clinical Judgment on the MMPI.* Doctor's thesis, University of North Dakota (Grand Forks, N.D.), 1971. (*DAI* 32:7315B)

3733. LO, SAMUEL NAI-MING. *Effects of Self-Reinforcement and Goal-Setting on the Affect and Personal Orientation of Housewives.* Doctor's thesis, Fuller Theological Seminary (Pasadena, Calif.), 1971. (*DAI* 32:7315B)

3734. LONEY, JAN. "An MMPI Measure of Maladjustment in a Sample of 'Normal' Homosexual Men." *J Clin Psychol* 27(4):486-8 O '71. * (*PA* 47:9285)

3735. LORD, JESS R. *Marijuana and Personality Change.* Lexington, Mass.: Heath-Lexington Books, 1971. Pp. xv, 125. * (*PA* 49:1905, title only)

3736. LUBORSKY, LESTER. "Perennial Mystery of Poor Agreement Among Criteria for Psychotherapy Outcome." *J Consult & Clin Psychol* 37(3):316-9 D '71. * (*PA* 47:9016)

3737. McCLANAHAN, L. D. "Social Maturity and Multivariate Discriminant Analysis Personality Descriptions of Conservatives, Activists, and Radicals." *Meas & Eval Guid* 4(3):135-44 O '71. * (*PA* 49:10999)

3738. McCORMICK, CLARENCE C.; KLAPPAUF, JEANNIE; SCHNOBRICH, JANICE N.; AND HARVEY, JOHN. "Relationships Among Arrow-Dot IES Scores and Wechsler IQs and MMPI Scales for Hospitalized, Disturbed Adolescents." *Percept & Motor Skills* 33(3):1227-34 D '71. * (*PA* 48:3263)

3739. MANNING, HORACE M. "Programmed Interpretation of the MMPI." *J Pers Assess* 35(2):162-76 Ap '71. * (*PA* 47:3018)

3740. MANOSEVITZ, MARTIN. "Education and MMPI *Mf* Scores in Homosexual and Heterosexual Males." *J Consult & Clin Psychol* 36(3):395-9 Je '71. * (*PA* 46:9328)

3741. MARTRAY, CARL RICHARD. *An Empirical Investigation Into the Learning Styles and Retention Patterns of Various Personality Types.* Doctor's thesis, University of Alabama (University, Ala.), 1971. (*DAI* 32:5043A)

3742. MASTERSON, MICHAEL LYNN. *Correlates of Intrafamilial Body-Contact.* Doctor's thesis, University of Nevada (Reno, Nev.), 1971. (*DAI* 32:4863B)

3743. MELNICK, BARRY, AND PIERCE, RICHARD M. "Client Evaluation of Therapist Strength and Positive-Negative Evaluation as Related to Client Dynamics, Objective Ratings of Competency and Outcome." *J Clin Psychol* 27(3):408-10 Jl '71. * (*PA* 47:4915)

3744. MICHAEL, WILLIAM B.; HANEY, RUSSELL; LEE, YOUNG B.; AND MICHAEL, JOAN J. "The Criterion-Related Validities of Cognitive and Noncognitive Predictors in a Training Program for Nursing Candidates." *Ed & Psychol Meas* 31(4):983-7 w '71. * (*PA* 48:1866)

3745. MILLER, ALAN R.; STEWART, ROBERT A.; STEELE, RICHARD E.; WATSON, RICHARD A. R.; NEWHAUSER, DAVID; AND KIKER, VERNON. "Psychopathology and Perception of Physiques." *Percept & Motor Skills* 32(2):475-8 Ap '71. * (*PA* 46:11164)

3746. MONROE, JACK J.; ROSS, WESLEY F.; AND BERZINS, JURIS I. "The Decline of the Addict as 'Psychopath': Implications for Community Care." *Int J Addic* 6(4):601-8 D '71. * (*PA* 49:5138)

3747. MORF, MARTIN E. "Examination of the Clarke Auto-mated Psychological Examination and Report." *Ont Psychologist* (Canada) 3(2):96-102 '71. *

3748. MOSHER, LOREN R.; POLLIN, WILLIAM; AND STABENAU, JAMES R. "Families With Identical Twins Discordant for Schizophrenia: Some Relationships Between Identification, Thinking Styles, Psychopathology and Dominance-Submissiveness." *Brit J Psychiatry* 118(542):29-42 Ja '71. * (*PA* 46:11248)

3749. MULLEN, JOHN, AND ABELES, NORMAN. "Relationship of Liking, Empathy, and Therapist's Experience to Outcome of Therapy." *J Counsel Psychol* 18(1):39-43 Ja '71. * (*PA* 45:8362)

3750. NADEAU, GILLES GUY. *Predictive Validity of Data on Application and Responses to MMPI Items for Discriminating Among Certain Education Graduates and Non-Graduates' Occupational Activities.* Doctor's thesis, University of Minnesota (Minneapolis, Minn.), 1971. (*DAI* 32:2535A)

3751. NEUBECK, ROBERT CHARLES. *Variables Affecting Ratings of Pathology on Test Protocols.* Doctor's thesis, Southern Illinois University (Carbondale, Ill.), 1971. (*DAI* 32:4865B)

3752. NEWMARK, CHARLES S. "MMPI: Comparison of the Oral Form Presented by a Live Examiner and the Booklet Form." *Psychol Rep* 29(3):797-8 D '71. * (*PA* 47:9210)

3753. NEWTON, JOSEPH R. "A Comparison of Studies of the Mini-Mult." *J Clin Psychol* 27(4):489-90 O '71. * (*PA* 47:9249)

3754. NORTON, FRANCIS E., JR. "Demographic and Personality Variables Associated With Airmen Court-Martialed for Involvement With Marijuana," pp. 228-32. In *Second Annual Symposium: Psychology in the Air Force, 20-22 April 1971.* Edited by Hal W. Hendrick. Colorado Springs, Colo.: United States Air Force Academy, [1971]. Pp. x, 409. *

3755. OLCZAK, PAUL V.; DONNERSTEIN, EDWARD; HERSHBERGER, THOMAS J.; AND KAHN, IRWIN. "Group Hysteria and the MMPI." *Psychol Rep* 28(2):413-4 Ap '71. * (*PA* 46:7182)

3756. ORLOFF, HENRY. *Physiological and Psychological Factors in Stress.* Texas Christian University (Ft. Worth, Tex.), 1971. (*DAI* 32:3040B)

3757. OSBORNE, DAVID. "Age and Sex Differences on MMPI Factor Scales *ER-0* and *EC-5* in a Medical Population." *J Clin Psychol* 27(2):245-6 Ap '71. * (*PA* 46:7372)

3758. OSBORNE, DAVID. "An MMPI Index of Disturbed Marital Interaction." *Psychol Rep* 29(3):852-4 D '71. * (*PA* 47:11356)

3759. PAIGE, PAUL E.; LA POINTE, WILLIAM; AND KRUEGER, ANN. "The Marital Dyad as a Diagnostic and Treatment Variable in Alcohol Addiction." *Psychol* 8(1):64-73 F '71. * (*PA* 46:5165)

3760. PARTINGTON, JOHN T., AND CLARKE, LOUISE. "Personality Impression Formation: A Correlational-Experimental Design." *Can J Behav Sci* 3(1):47-54 Ja '71. * (*PA* 46:1129)

3761. PASNAU, ROBERT O., AND BAYLEY, STEPHEN J. "Personality Changes in the First Year of Psychiatric Residency Training." Discussion by Gerald H. Flamm. *Am J Psychiatry* 128(1):79-84 Jl '71. * (*PA* 47:6870)

3762. PAUKER, JEROME D. "Fathers of Children Conceived Out of Wedlock: Prepregnancy, High School, Psychological Test Results." *Develop Psychol* 4(2):215-8 Mr '71. * (*PA* 45:9747)

3763. PEARSON, JOHN S., AND STEINHILBER, RICHARD M. "Psychological Assessment of Therapy in Coronary Artery Disease." *J Am Med Assn* 217(1):72-4 Jl 5 '71. *

3764. PEREZ, FRANCISCO, AND SATZ, PAUL. "Effects of Feedback on Clinical Prediction." Abstract. *Proc 79th Ann Conv Am Psychol Assn* 6(1):465-6 '71. * (*PA* 46:5148)

3765. PERSKY, HAROLD; SMITH, KEITH D.; AND BASU, GOPAL K. "Relation of Psychologic Measures of Aggression and Hostility to Testosterone Production in Man." *Psychosom Med* 33(3):265-77 My-Je '71. * (*PA* 47:4310)

3766. PERSONS, ROY W., AND MARKS, PHILIP A. "The Violent 4-3 MMPI Personality Type." *J Consult & Clin Psychol* 36(2):189-96 Ap '71. * (*PA* 46:3358)

3767. PHILIP, ROBERT, AND SCHILL, THOMAS. "MMPI Social Introversion-Extroversion and Hypnotic Previous Existence Fantasies." *Psychol Rep* 29(1):247-50 Ag '71. * (*PA* 47:2972)

3768. PINO, CHRISTOPHER J. "Relation of a Trainability Index to T-Group Outcomes." *J Appl Psychol* 55(5):439-42 O '71. * (*PA* 47:7874)

3769. PITTEL, STEPHEN M. "Psychological Aspects of Heroin and Other Drug Dependence." *J Psychedelic Drugs* 4(1):40-5 f '71. * (*PA* 49:4813)

3770. PLATT, JEROME J.; POMERANZ, DAVID; AND EISENMAN, RUSSELL. "Validation of the Eysenck Personality Inventory by the MMPI and Internal-External Control Scale." *J Clin Psychol* 27(1):104-5 Ja '71. * (*PA* 46:1212)

3771. PORIER, GARY W., AND SMITH, ROGER C. "MMPI 'Cookbooks': Are Rule Relaxation and System Combination Procedures an Answer to Low Classification Rates?" *J Clin Psychol* 27(1):96-101 Ja '71. * (*PA* 46:1432)

3772. PRYOR, ANTONE B. *Relationships of the Minnesota Multiphasic Personality Inventory and the Bipolar Psychological Inventory to Each Other and to Incarceration.* Doctor's thesis, University of Utah (Salt Lake City, Utah), 1971. (*DAI* 32:3798A)

3773. PULVERMACHER, GERALD D., AND BRINGMANN, WOLFGANG G. "The Mini-Mult Used With French-Canadian College Students." *Psychol Rep* 29(1):134 Ag '71. * (*PA* 47:3020)

3774. QUAGLIOTTI, CAROL A. *A Comparison Between Physical*

Characteristics and Personality Traits in Women. Master's thesis, Appalachian State University (Boone, N.C.), 1971.

3775. REDDY, MICHAEL JOSEPH. *Interaction Testing in the Measurement of Marital Disturbance.* Doctor's thesis, Ohio State University (Columbus, Ohio), 1971. (*DAI* 32:6659B)

3776. RICHEK, HERBERT G. "Attitudes Toward Authority and Mental Health in Adolescent College Students." *Psychiatric Q* 45(3):357–62 '71. * (*PA* 48:7719)

3777. RICHEK, HERBERT G., AND REID, BRAXTON. "Religious Authoritarianism and Psychopathology in College Students." *Psychiatric Q* 45(3):363–71 '71. * (*PA* 48:7720)

3778. RICHEK, HERBERT GEORGE. *Personality and Mental Health Concomitants of Religiousness in Late Adolescent College Students.* Doctor's thesis, University of Texas (Austin, Tex.), 1971. (*DAI* 32:5620A)

3779. ROBBINS, PAUL R., AND TANCK, ROLAND H. "MMPI Scales and Dream Recall: A Failure to Confirm." *Percept & Motor Skills* 33(2):473–4 O '71. * (*PA* 47:6046)

3780. ROBBINS, PAUL R.; TANCK, ROLAND H.; AND MEYERSBURG, HERMAN A. "Psychological Factors in Smoking, Drinking, and Drug Experimentation." *J Clin Psychol* 27(4):450–2 O '71. * (*PA* 47:8861)

3781. ROBINSON, ELIZABETH BEACH. *Women on Parole: Reintegration of the Female Offender.* Doctor's thesis, Ohio State University (Columbus, Ohio), 1971. (*DAI* 32:2816A)

3782. ROHLF, RICHARD J. "A Higher-Order Alpha Factor Analysis of Interest, Personality, and Ability Variables, Including an Evaluation of the Effect of Scale Interdependency." *Ed & Psychol Meas* 31(2):381–96 su '71. * (*PA* 46:11516)

3783. RORISON, JOHN ROBERT. *Scores on the Minnesota Multiphasic Personality Inventory and Their Relationship to Completion of the Program of Intern Teaching for College Graduates for a Selected Group at Temple University.* Doctor's thesis, Temple University (Philadelphia, Pa.), 1971. (*DAI* 32:826A)

3784. ROSEN, M.; BERGMAN, MARILYN; AND TELFER, MARY A. "MMPI Profiles of Males With Abnormal Sex Chromosome Complements." *J Mental Def Res* (England) 15(3):169–76 S '71. * (*PA* 49:11477)

3785. ROTH, LOREN H.; ROSENBERG, NATHAN; AND LEVINSON, ROBERT B. "Prison Adjustment of Alcoholic Felons." *Q J Studies Alcohol* 32(2):382–92 Je '71. *

3786. ROTHSTEIN, ARNOLD. *Depression in Pregnancy as It Relates to Feminine Identification Conflict and Perceived Environmental Support.* Doctor's thesis, Smith College (Northampton, Mass.), 1971. (*DAI* 32:5347A)

3787. ROUSELL, CHARLES H., AND EDWARDS, CARL N. "Some Developmental Antecedents of Psychopathology." *J Personality* 39(3):362–77 S '71. * (*PA* 47:7204)

3788. ROUTH, DONALD K. "Instructional Effects on Word Association Commonality in High and Low 'Schizophrenic' College Students." *J Pers Assess* 35(2):139–47 Ap '71. * (*PA* 47:2975)

3789. RYBACK, RALPH S.; LEWIS, OLIVER F.; AND LESSARD, CHARLES S. "Psychobiologic Effects of Prolonged Bed Rest (Weightless) in Young Healthy Volunteers (Study II)." *Aerospace Med* 42(5):529–35 My '71. *

3790. SAFER, DANIEL J., AND ALLEN, RICHARD P. "The Effect of Fluphenazine in Psychologically Normal Volunteers: Some Temporal, Performance, and Biochemical Relationships." *Biol Psychiatry* 3(3):237–49 '71. * (*PA* 47:8363)

3791. SANBORN, DONALD E., III; CASEY, THOMAS M.; AND NISWANDER, G. DONALD. "Drug Abusers, Suicide Attempters, and the MMPI." *Dis Nerv System* 32(3):183–7 Mr '71. *

3792. SCAGNELLI, JOAN MARIE. *A Study of the Etiology and Symptomatology of the Paranoid Syndrome.* Doctor's thesis, University of North Carolina (Chapel Hill, N.C.), 1971. (*DAI* 32:7324B)

3793. SCHILDHAUS, ANDREW FRANK. *Student Nurse Attitudes Toward Mental Illness Following a Psychiatric Training Program.* Doctor's thesis, Columbia University (New York, N.Y.), 1971. (*DAI* 32:3801A)

3794. SCHMALE, A. H., AND IKER, H. "Hopelessness as a Predictor of Cervical Cancer." *Social Sci & Med* (England) 5(2): 95–100 Ap '71. * (*PA* 48:1555)

3795. SCHWARTZ, MARK S., AND KRUPP, NEAL E. "The MMPI 'Conversion V' Among 50,000 Medical Patients: A Study of Incidence, Criteria, and Profile Elevation." *J Clin Psychol* 27(1):89–95 Ja '71. * (*PA* 46:1436)

3796. SCHWARTZ, MARK S.; KRUPP, NEAL E.; AND BYRNE, DONN. "Repression-Sensitization and Medical Diagnosis." *J Abn Psychol* 78(3):286–91 D '71. * (*PA* 47:9554)

3797. SCHWARTZ, MELVIN L., AND CAHILL, ROBERT. "Psychopathology Associated With Myasthenia Gravis and Its Treatment by Psychotherapeutically Oriented Group Counseling." *J Chronic Dis* 24(9):543–52 O '71. *

3798. SCHWENDIMAN, GARY. *Machiavellianism as a Predictor of Success in Bargaining Under High and Low Incentive Conditions.* Doctor's thesis, Brigham Young University (Provo, Utah), 1971. (*DAI* 31:6881B)

3799. SCURA, WILLIAM C., AND EISENMAN, RUSSELL. "Punishment Learning in Psychopaths With Social and Nonsocial Reinforcers." *Correct Psychiatry & J Social Ther* 17(1):58–64 '71. * (*PA* 47:5192)

3800. SHOENBERG, BERNARD; CARR, ARTHUR C.; KUTSCHER, AUSTIN H.; AND ZEGARELLI, EDWARD V. "Chronic Idiopathic

Orolingual Pain: Psychogenesis of Burning Mouth." *N Y State J Med* 71(15):1832–7 Ag '71. * (*PA* 47:11245)

3801. SMITH, ROGER C., AND PORIER, GARY W. "Factors Influencing Administrative Disposition of Psychiatric Patients." *J Clin Psychol* 27(1):54–9 Ja '71. * (*PA* 46:1437)

3802. SNORTUM, JOHN R., AND LOEWE, ALLAN P. "The Relationship of Pd and MAS Scores to Approach-Avoidance Behavior Under Immediate Versus Delayed Punishment." *J Clin Psychol* 27(3):321–4 Jl '71. * (*PA* 47:5193)

3803. SOLYOM, L.; HESELTINE, G. F. D.; McCLURE, D. J.; LEDWIDGE, B.; AND KENNY, F. "A Comparative Study of Aversion Relief and Systematic Desensitization in the Treatment of Phobias." *Brit J Psychiatry* 119(550):299–303 S '71. * (*PA* 47:9123)

3804. SOMASUNDARAM, C. P.; KALIAPPAN, K. V.; AND POLNAYA, MEERA. "A Psychometric Study of Patients Disabled by Cerebrovascular Disease (A Preliminary Study of 54 Cases)." *Neurol India* 19(1):34–7 Mr '71. *

3805. STACK, JAMES THOMAS. *Performance of Acute Paranoid and Non-Paranoid Schizophrenic Patients on the Halstead-Reitan Battery Using Two Levels of Symptomatology.* Doctor's thesis, Louisiana State University (Baton Rouge, La.), 1971. (*DAI* 32:3018B)

3806. STEFIC, EDWARD C., AND LORR, MAURICE. "Analysis of Defensiveness in Relation to Psychopathology." *J Consult & Clin Psychol* 36(2):205–9 Ap '71. * (*PA* 46:3043)

3807. STEIN, KENNETH B., AND BEALL, LYNNETTE. "Externalizing-Internalizing Symptoms and Psychotherapeutic Outcome." *Psychother Theory Res & Prac* 8(4):269–75 w '71. * (*PA* 50:1633)

3808. STEIN, KENNETH B.; ROZYNKO, VITALI; AND PUGH, LAWRENCE A. "The Heterogeneity of Personality Among Alcoholics." *Brit J Social & Clin Psychol* 10(3):253–9 S '71. * (*PA* 47:11160)

3809. STONE, LEROY A.; COLES, GARY J.; SINNETT, E. ROBERT; AND SHERMAN, GAIL L. "Multidimensional Scaling Used to Evaluate Students Residing in a Rehabilitation Unit." *Psychol Rep* 28(3):879–86 Je '71. * (*PA* 47:11306)

3810. STRAUSS, MILTON E.; GYNTHER, MALCOLM D.; AND KNEFF, DENNIS. "Psychiatric Patients' Responses to MMPI Religion Items." *J Pers Assess* 35(3):282–4 Je '71. * (*PA* 47:3364)

3811. SUTER, BARBARA ANN. *Masculinity-Femininity in Creative Women.* Doctor's thesis, Fordham University (New York, N.Y.), 1971. (*DAI* 32:2411B)

3812. SUTKER, PATRICIA B. "Personality Differences and Sociopathy in Heroin Addicts and Nonaddict Prisoners." *J Abn Psychol* 78(3):247–51 D '71. * (*PA* 47:9270)

3813. SUTKER, PATRICIA B., AND GIL, SANDRA H. "Sociopathy and Serial Learning of CVC Combinations With High and Low Social Content Ratings." *J Pers & Social Psychol* 17(2):158–62 F '71. * (*PA* 45:8521)

3814. SVILAND, MARY ANN PETRICH. *Factors of Adaptation and Rehabilitation in Home Hemodialysis.* Doctor's thesis, University of Southern California (Los Angeles, Calif.), 1971. (*DAI* 32:4230B)

3815. TAUFER, FLORENCE JOY. *Personality Change in Teachers After Participating in Human Relations Interaction Groups.* Master's thesis, California State College (Long Beach, Calif.), 1971.

3816. TEMPLER, DONALD I. "Death Anxiety as Related to Depression and Health of Retired Persons." *J Gerontol* 26(4):521–3 O '71. * (*PA* 49:6616)

3817. THAYER, ROBERT E. "Personality and Discrepancies Between Verbal Reports and Physiological Measures of Private Emotional Experience." *J Personality* 39(1):57–69 Mr '71. * (*PA* 46:4963)

3818. THORNE, GAYLORD L. "Sensation Seeking Scale With Deviant Populations." *J Consult & Clin Psychol* 37(1):106–10 Ag '71. * (*PA* 47:964)

3819. THUMIN, FRED J. "A Comparative Study of the MMPI Profiles of Salesmen and Technical Managers." *Personnel Psychol* 24(3):481–7 au '71. *

3820. THURLOW. H. JOHN. "Illness in Relation to Life Situation and Sick-Role Tendency." *J Psychosom Res* (England) 15(1):73–88 Mr '71. * (*PA* 47:11540)

3821. TRIESCHMANN, ROBERTA B., AND SAND, PATRICIA L. "WAIS and MMPI Correlates of Increasing Renal Failure in Adult Medical Patients." *Psychol Rep* 29(3):1251–62 D '71. * (*PA* 48:1559)

3822. TRUAX, CHARLES B. "The Initial Status of the Client and the Predictability of Psychotherapeutic Change." *Comparative Group Studies* 2(1):3–16 F '71. * (*PA* 47:4953)

3823. TRUAX, CHARLES B. "Normalization of Verbal Productivity and Improvement in Depressive Status in Schizophrenics." *J Clin Psychol* 27(4):537–9 O '71. * (*PA* 47:9325)

3824. TRUAX, CHARLES B., AND WITTMER, JOE. "Self-Disclosure and Personality Adjustment." *J Clin Psychol* 27(4): 535–7 O '71. * (*PA* 47:8887)

3825. TRUAX, CHARLES B.; WITTMER, JOE; AND WARGO, DONALD G. "Effects of the Therapeutic Conditions of Accurate Empathy, Non-Possessive Warmth, and Genuineness on Hospitalized Mental Patients During Group Therapy." *J Clin Psychol* 27(1):137–42 Ja '71. * (*PA* 46:1326)

3826. VAN ATTA, RALPH E., AND RUPPEL, RODNEY W. "H

Group Method of Profile Analysis." *J Clin Psychol* 27(3):327–33 Jl '71. * (*PA* 47:5106)

3827. VAUGHAN, JAMES LELAND. *Measurement and Analysis of Values Pertaining to Psychotherapy and Mental Health.* Doctor's thesis, Columbia University (New York, N.Y.), 1971. (*DAI* 32:3655B)

3828. VEGA, ARTHUR. "Cross-Validation of Four MMPI Scales for Alcoholism." *Q J Studies Alcohol* 32(1A):791–7 S '71. *

3829. VELDHUIZEN, JOHN FRANCIS. *The Effect of Institutional Placement on Delinquent Adolescent Girls: An MMPI and CPI Sequence Testing Approach.* Doctor's thesis, Graduate Theological Union (Berkeley, Calif.), 1971. (*DAI* 32:4232B)

3830. VELLUTINO, FRANK R. "Verbal Response Stereotypy as a Function of Psychological and Physiological Drive." *Percept & Motor Skills* 33(3):851–8 D '71. * (*PA* 48:165)

3831. WATSON, CHARLES G. "An MMPI Scale to Separate Brain-Damaged From Schizophrenic Men." *J Consult & Clin Psychol* 36(1):121–5 F '71. * (*PA* 45:10226)

3832. WEBB, JAMES T. "Regional and Sex Differences in MMPI Scale High-Point Frequencies of Psychiatric Patients." *J Clin Psychol* 27(4):483–6 O '71. * (*PA* 47:9219)

3833. WHITELOCK, PAUL R.; OVERALL, JOHN E.; AND PATRICK, JERRY H. "Personality Patterns and Alcohol Abuse in a State Hospital Population." *J Abn Psychol* 78(1):9–16 Ag '71. * (*PA* 47:3299)

3834. WIESEN, LAWRENCE EVAN. *An Examination of Motivation Hygiene Inversion in a Clinical Population.* Doctor's thesis, Case Western Reserve University (Cleveland, Ohio), 1971. (*DAI* 32:1895B)

3835. WIGGINS, JERRY S.; GOLDBERG, LEWIS R.; AND APPELBAUM, MARK. "MMPI Content Scales: Interpretative Norms and Correlations With Other Scales." *J Consult & Clin Psychol* 37(3):403–10 D '71. * (*PA* 47:8950)

3836. WIGGINS, NANCY. "Individual Differences in Diagnostic Judgments of Psychosis and Neurosis From the MMPI." *Ed & Psychol Meas* 31(1):199–214 sp '71. * (*PA* 46:11109)

3837. WILKINSON, A. EARL; PRADO, WILLIAM M.; WILLIAMS, WOODROW O.; AND SCHNADT, FREDERICK W. "Psychological Test Characteristics and Length of Stay in Alcoholism Treatment." *Q J Studies Alcohol* 32(1A):60–5 Mr '71. * (*PA* 46:7116)

3838. WOLFF, WIRT M., AND MORRIS, LARRY A. "Intellectual and Personality Characteristics of Parents of Autistic Children." *J Abn Psychol* 77(2):155–61 Ap '71. * (*PA* 46:3465)

3839. ZELIN, MARTIN L. "Validity of the MMPI Scales for Measuring Twenty Psychiatric Dimensions." *J Consult & Clin Psychol* 37(2):286–90 O '71. * (*PA* 47:9221)

3840. ZUNG, WILLIAM W. K., AND GIANTURCO, JUDITH A. "Personality Dimension and the Self-Rating Depression Scale." *J Clin Psychol* 27(2):247–8 Ap '71. * (*PA* 46:7084)

CUMULATIVE NAME INDEX

Peters, J.: 1546
Peters, P. G.: 1876
Petersen, K. H.: 2041
Peterson, C. A.: 2082
Peterson, D. R.: 372, 521-2
Peterson, H. C.: 3006
Peterson, H. W.: 1954
Peterson, L. P.: 3604
Peterson, M. E.: 917
Peterson, R. S.: 2712
Petty, T. L.: 3659
Petzel, T. P.: 2205, 3007
Pfaehler, G. T.: 3448
Phelan, J. G.: 2463
Philip, A. E.: 2215
Philip, F. J.: 1810
Philip, R.: 3767
Philippus, M. J.: 1136, 2083
Philips, B. U.: 3628
Phillips, A. R.: 1471
Phillips, C. E.: 2713, 3217
Phillips, D. L.: 3487
Phillips, E. L.: 69, 150
Phillips, M.: 2319
Phillips, R. L.: 1079
Phillips, V. A.: 3728
Pierce, C. M.: 2281
Pierce, K. K.: 523
Pierce, R. M.: 2418, 3218, 3743
Pierce, W. E.: 3064
Pierce-Jones, J.: 524, 769, 827
Pierson, J. S.: 1839
Pigg, E. E.: 1547
Pihkanen, T. A.: 812
Pilapil, B.: 3091
Pile, E. N.: 2503
Pilling, L. F.: 2280, 3030
Pinchard, A. G.: 2242
Pinneau, S. R.: 764, 1427
Pino, C. J.: 3008, 3768
Pinto, A.: 2790, 3242
Piotrowski, Z.: 68a
Piotrowski, Z. A.: 2714
Pishkin, V.: 2281
Pittel, S. M.: 3716, 3769
Pivik, T.: 2419
Plante, M.: 1392, 3396, 3436
Platman, S. R.: 3219, 3660
Platt, J. J.: 3220, 3770
Plotnik, R. J.: 1563
Plumeau, F.: 905
Plummer, J. M.: 3009
Plyler, S. A.: 1877
Podell, H. A.: 1356
Podolnick, E. E.: 1064
Poe, R.: 3221
Pokorny, A. D.: 2407
Polcari, A. R.: 2392
Pollack, D.: 1878
Polley, H. F.: 3222
Pollin, W.: 3748
Pollock, E.: 808
Polnaya, M.: 3804
Pomeranz, D.: 3220, 3770
Pomeranz, D. M.: 1357
Pool, D. A.: 1701-2, 1879
Pool, K. B.: 700
Pope, B.: 1901, 2282
Popplestone, J. A.: 1358, 3458
Porier, G. W.: 3771, 3801
Portenier, L.: 134
Portenier, L. G.: 3296
Porter, K. D.: 1548
Poshek, N. A.: 2290
Postema, L. J.: 2283
Pothast, M. D.: 649
Potter, C. S.: 228
Powell, B. J.: 3181
Powell, J. A.: 3010
Powell, J. O.: 162, 250
Powell, R. K.: 2135
Powers, J. H.: 1495
Prado, W. M.: 3837
Prager, R. A.: 3576, 3668-9
Prange, A. J.: 968, 3074
Pratt, S.: 3403
Prell, A. E.: 2504
Prentiss, R. J.: 3080
Presnell, M.: 2616
Price, J. R.: 1496, 2051
Price, R. V.: 2284
Probst, G. K.: 3430
Probst, K. A.: 34

Pruitt, W. A.: 1268
Pryor, A. B.: 3772
Pryor, F. A.: 3011
P'Simer, C.: 2505
Ptasnik, J. A.: 2420
Pugh, L. A.: 3808
Puletti, F.: 3607
Pulvermacher, G. D.: 3773
Pumroy, D. K.: 765
Purcell, C. K.: 373
Purcell, K.: 1026
Purdom, G. A.: 837
Puryear, H. B.: 1549, 2985, 3230
Pustell, T. E.: 766
Puzzo, F. S.: 905
Quagliotti, C. A.: 3774
Quarrington, B.: 2326
Quast, W.: 2121, 2932-3
Quay, H.: 463, 525, 586-7
Quello, D. Y.: 3577
Quenk, N. L.: 2661
Quesnell, J. G.: 1857
Quevillon, N. M.: 1449
Quinn, L. W.: 2579
Quinn, R. P.: 1119, 1880, 3425
Quinn, S. B.: 712
Rabon, A. M.: 2727, 2843, 3468
Race, R.: 822
Rachiele, L. D.: 1425
Rae, J. B.: 2084
Raftery, F. M.: 2715
Rainey, R. V.: 799, 3370
Rakhawy, Y. T.: 3521, 3524
Rand, M. A.: 2808
Rand, M. E.: 838, 1018
Randall, R. V.: 3503
Randolph, M. H.: 1137
Rankin, R. J.: 2421
Rapaport, G. M.: 839, 1269
Rapoport, J. L.: 1881
Rapp, D.: 3377
Rappaport, H.: 2379, 2422
Rasch, P. J.: 1027
Rashkis, H. A.: 50
Ratnoff, O. D.: 2847
Ratzeburg, F.: 411
Ravensborg, M. R.: 3012
Ravsten, L. A.: 2662
Ray, E.: 1581
Raygor, A. L.: 1703
Raygor, B. R.: 3223
Raymaker, H.: 651
Raynor, G. H.: 2520
Rechtschaffen, A.: 1623, 3431
Reddy, M. J.: 3775
Reding, G. R.: 2423
Redlo, M.: 314, 370-1
Redman, R. S.: 3449
Reed, M. R.: 713, 2488
Reed, P. C.: 2363, 3638
Reed, R. L.: 3013
Rees, M. B.: 2152
Rees, M. E.: 1138
Reese, P. M.: 2424-5
Regal, J.: 448
Regal, L. H.: 1359
Regelin, C.: 201
Rehfisch, J. M.: 3365
Reid, A. R.: 588
Reid, B.: 3777
Reid, L. L.: 782
Reiff, C.: 2367
Reilley, R. R.: 3224
Reilly, H. E.: 1882
Reineck, L.: 2198
Reinhardt, R. F.: 3569
Reitan, R. M.: 589, 591, 970, 3225
Reiter, M.: 2663
Rempel, P. P.: 590, 767, 1028
Renaud, H. R.: 229
Renzaglia, G. A.: 2467
Reschke, S. E.: 2716
Resh, M. G.: 3226-8
Resnick, J. H.: 3261
Resnick, R. W.: 2285
Resnikoff, A.: 2426
Rettig, S.: 1704
Reynolds, P. C.: 2664, 2936, 3545

Reznikoff, M.: 1787, 1883, 2286, 2379, 2422, 2887
Rhead, C.: 3509
Rheinstrom, D.: 840
Rhode, J. F.: 1550
Rhodes, F.: 2976
Rhodes, J. M.: 1435
Rhodes, R. J.: 3014
Rhudick, P. J.: 1139, 3395
Rice, D.: 2395
Rice, D. G.: 2427, 3015, 3229
Rice, P. J.: 841
Rich, C. C.: 3016
Richards, C. B.: 1947
Richards, T. W.: 374
Richardson, C. E.: 1140
Richardson, H.: 1137, 1596, 1884, 1982
Richardson, R. L.: 1885
Richek, H. G.: 2985, 3230, 3776-8
Richer, H. M.: 1563
Rickard, H. C.: 3126
Ricks, D. F.: 2683
Rieck, E. C.: 918, 1141
Riedel, R. G.: 3067
Riedel, W. W.: 1956
Ries, H. A.: 2085
Riffel, P. A.: 2287
Rigney, F. J.: 1142
Riley, G. L.: 543
Rim, Y.: 1705
Ringrose, C. A. D.: 1472-3
Ringuette, E. L.: 2136
Rinkel, M.: 897a
Rinne, K. W.: 449
Rippy, M. L.: 1029
Ritchey, R. E.: 2428
Rittenhouse, C. H.: 375-6
Rittenhouse, J. D.: 3231
Ritter, R. M.: 1121a
Rivoire, J. L.: 1657, 1676, 1826
Rizzo, G. B.: 1144
Roa, C. D.: 2622
Robb, G. P.: 3166
Robbins, P. R.: 3779-80
Roberts, A. H.: 1992
Roberts, F. J.: 2623
Roberts, L. K.: 3042
Roberts, R. W.: 3461
Robertson, J. M.: 2798
Robertson, J. P. S.: 3335
Robertson, M. H.: 1948
Robertson, P. C.: 1027
Robertson, Y.: 43a
Robey, A.: 3637
Robinowitz, R.: 1030
Robinson, B. W.: 2086
Robinson, E. B.: 3781
Rockey, M. A.: 3501
Rodgers, D. A.: 1886, 2087, 2684, 2846, 3080; rev, 7:104
Roebuck, J.: 1884
Roessel, F. P.: 527
Roessler, R.: 1434, 1506, 1528-9, 1551, 2665, 3358, 3448
Rogal, R. A.: 3286
Rogers, A. H.: 919
Rogers, M. S.: 1900
Rogge, H. J.: 920
Rohan, W. P.: 3017
Rohila, P. K.: 3018
Rohlf, R. J.: 2817, 3782
Roitzsch, J. C.: 3718
Roman, P. M.: 3051
Rome, H. P.: 1497-8, 1552, 1722, 1874-5, 1887, 1922
Rommel, R. C. S.: 842, 3372
Rooney, J. J.: 2703
Rorabaugh, M. E.: 450
Rorer, L. G.: 1360, 1525, 1629, 1888-90, 2570
Rorison, J. R.: 3783
Rose, A. A.: 3293
Rose, R.: 1538
Rose, R. M.: 3221
Rosecrans, C. J.: 3019
Rosen, A.: 377-8, 451, 528, 768, 843, 921, 1270, 1361, 2088, 3486
Rosen, A. C.: 1031

Rosen, E.: 230, 274, 379, 652-3, 1143-4, 1362
Rosen, H.: 13, 3350
Rosen, I. C.: 380
Rosen, M.: 3784
Rosen, R. A. H.: 3350
Rosenbaum, G.: 2429
Rosenberg, B. G.: 1381, 1920, 3305
Rosenberg, L. A.: 1217
Rosenberg, N.: 3785
Rosenman, M. F.: 3232
Rosenstein, A. J.: 1450
Rosenthal, R.: 3392, 3557
Rosenthal, R. A.: 3425
Rosenthal, T. L.: 1553, 2666
Rosenzweig, S.: 51, 182
Rosman, R. R.: 2089
Rosmarin, M. S.: 2667
Ross, A. T.: 591
Ross, J.: 2604
Ross, W. F.: 3613, 3746
Rossi, A. M.: 676, 1059, 3465
Rossillon, J. P.: 2668
Roston, R. A.: 1891
Roth, H. S.: 2288, 2669
Roth, L. H.: 3785
Roth, R. H.: 1957, 2145
Rothaus, P.: 2291, 3149
Rothenberg, P. J.: 3184
Rothman, D.: 3488
Rothman, I.: 1476
Rothstein, A.: 3786
Rotman, S. R.: 1706, 3017, 3044
Rotter, J. B.: 62; rev, 3:60
Rottman, L.: 2680
Rousell, C. H.: 3787
Routh, D. K.: 3578, 3788
Rouzer, D. L.: 3083, 3233, 3635
Rowe, F. B.: 1414
Rowe, J.: 2968
Rowell, J. T.: 587
Rowley, V. N.: 1100, 1271, 1377, 2104
Roy, H. L.: 59
Rozynko, V.: 3808
Rozynko, V. V.: 1794
Rubin, H.: 135, 231, 529
Rubin, R. T.: 2964
Rubin, S. B.: 315
Ruch, F. L.: 2289
Ruch, W. W.: 2289
Ruderman, V.: 2474
Ruebush, B. K.: 1032
Ruesch, J.: 3294
Ruhling, R. O.: 2670
Ruiz, R. A.: 2234-5, 2290, 3438
Rumrill, C.: 937
Rundquist, E. A.: 2671
Ruppel, R. W.: 3826
Rupprecht, P.: 3545
Rush, A. C.: 3409
Rushton, J. G.: 3030
Ruskin, H. D.: 3579
Rust, R. M.: 1630
Rutherford, R. C.: 1970
Rutledge, J. A.: 596
Ryan, C. W.: 1851
Ryan, J. R.: 3570
Ryback, R. S.: 3789
Rychlak, J. F.: 3410, 3440
Ryder, R. G.: 3651
Rytel, M. W.: 3064
Sadowsky, D.: 3567
Safer, D. J.: 3790
Sainz, A.: 897a
Sako, Y.: 2192
Salasin, S.: 3544
Salcines, R. A.: 779
Salmon, P.: 1892
Salop, P.: 1061
Salzman, L. F.: 1208
Samuels, S. D.: 784
Samuelson, C. O.: 3435
Sanborn, D. E.: 3791
Sand, P. L.: 3821
Sandberg, S. S.: 3603, 3624
Sanders, M. W.: 232
Sanders, W. B.: 647
Sanderson, J. W.: 381, 452
San Diego, E. A.: 3020

Sternitzke, V. L.: 2516
Stevens, C. J.: 3511
Stevens, E.: 2409
Stevens, J. R.: 1276a
Stevens, R. R.: 2303
Stevens, S. S.: 2357
Stevens, T. G.: 2304
Stewart, B. M.: 549, 598
Stewart, D. J.: 3261
Stewart, G. T.: 3064
Stewart, H. F.: 1281
Stewart, P.: 2380
Stewart, R. A.: 3745
Stewart, R. A. C.: 3037
Stiavelli, R. E.: 1151
Stieper, D. R.: 1376, 3373
Stier, S. A.: 2721
Stifler, J.: 3499
Stix, D. L.: 2305, 2677
Stoffer, S. S.: 3038
Stoler, N.: 2629, 2678
Stone, D. R.: 251, 660-1
Stone, F. B.: 1271, 1377,
   2104
Stone, G. V.: 3262
Stone, L. A.: 1717-8, 1912-9,
   2105, 3457, 3731, 3809
Storms, L. H.: 648
Stortroen, M.: 1391
Stotland, E.: 2166
Stoup, D. D.: 2212
Stout, M.: 186
Stover, D. O.: 2916
Straight, G. H.: 662
Straits, B. C.: 1378
Strang, B.: 1986
Straughan, J. H.: 3039
Strauss, M. E.: 3147, 3810
Strauss, R. S.: 2306
Strenger, S. B.: 3040
Stricker, G.: 1152, 3041
Stricker, L. J.: 2604, 3263
Strickland, J. F.: 3379
Stroebel, C. F.: 2920, 3585
Strommen, E.: 1153
Struening, E. L.: 658
Suboski, M. D.: 3672
Suczek, R. F.: 3352
Sudik, E.: 3695
Sullivan, D. F.: 743
Sullivan, F. W.: 2307
Sullivan, P. F.: 3042
Sullivan, P. L.: 386, 772
Sullivan, T. M.: 3489
Sulzer, E. S.: 930, 1153a,
   1282
Sundberg, N. D.: 387, 663-4,
   3326
Super, D. E.: 187, 1283
Suslak, K. V.: 2830
Suter, B. A.: 3811
Sutker, P. B.: 3264, 3812-3
Sutterer, J. R.: 3019
Sutton, M. L.: 388
Sutton-Smith, B.: 1920
Sviland, M. A. P.: 3814
Swan, R. J.: 462, 718
Swanson, E. O.: 2798
Swarr, R. R.: 2627
Sweeney, D. R.: 2353
Sweeney, R. H.: 1719-20
Sweetland, A.: 143, 463, 525
Swensen, C.: 2004
Swenson, W. M.: 273, 848,
   1154, 1498, 1721-2, 1874-
   5, 1921-2, 2106, 2279-80,
   2523, 2728, 3222, 3452,
   3586
Swickard, D. L.: 1155
Swope, A. J.: 3043
Swords, I. R.: 2107
Sydow, D. W.: 464
Syme, L.: 719
Szmyd, L.: 1121a, 2256
Taaffe, G.: 389
Tafejian, T. T.: 316, 403
Taft, R.: 720-1, 1156
Taggart, M.: 2308, 2559
Tait, A. T.: 446
Takala, M.: 812
Talland, G. A.: exc, 5:B467
Tallant, W. J.: 3587
Tallent, N.: 3044

Tamkin, A. S.: 722-3, 931,
   1157, 2108-9, 2442, 3045
Tanck, R. H.: 3779-80
Tanner, W. C.: 2486
Tarnapol, L.: 773
Tart, C. T.: 1284
Tartaglia, C. R.: 2860
Tarter, R. E.: 3265
Tatro, R. L.: 3017
Taufer, F. J.: 3815
Taulbee, E. S.: 629, 724,
   774-5, 1158, 2443, 3729
Tausig, T. N.: 1173
Taylor, A. J. W.: 1379,
   2309, 3490, 3512
Taylor, D. A.: 3046
Taylor, G. P.: 2722, 3266
Taylor, H. L.: 1418
Taylor, J. A.: 465
Taylor, J. B.: 932
Taylor, J. P.: 3468
Taylor, K. E.: 390
Taylor, R. E.: 1988
Tecce, J. J.: 3453
Teel, S. K.: 2186
Teeter, B.: 1362
Telfer, M. A.: 3784
Tellegen, A.: 1723, 1923,
   1969, 2149, 3047
Templer, D. I.: 2723, 3048,
   3267, 3816
Terwilliger, R. F.: 1724,
   3420
Tesseneer, R.: 665
Teter, J. T.: 1725
Tew, B. O.: 1726
Thaler, V. H.: 2310
Thaller, J. L.: 1409
Thatcher, K.: 3268
Thayer, K. H.: 1435
Thayer, R. E.: 3817
Thelen, M. H.: 3269
Thiele, W. B.: 111
Thomas, H.: 545
Thomas, M. H.: 892
Thomas, R. W.: 781, 2455
Thomason, O. B.: 2139
Thomassen, P. R.: 1226a
Thompson, C. W.: 1054; exc,
   5:B199
Thompson, G.: 144
Thompson, G. M.: 145
Thompson, J. S.: 666
Thompson, L. W.: 2148
Thomson, M.: 2869
Thoreson, R. W.: 1955
Thorn, K. F.: 236
Thorne, F. C.: 276
Thorne, G. L.: 3818
Thornton, D. R.: 1173
Thorpe, J. G.: 1502
Thumin, F. J.: 1727, 1924,
   2444, 2831, 3049-50, 3819
Thurlow, H. J.: 3820
Thurston, D. R.: 599
Thurston, H. I.: 2290
Thurston, J.: 584
Thurston, J. R.: 549, 1159,
   2445, 3491
Tiege, E.: 477
Tierney, R. W.: 1199a
Tocchini, J. J.: 1226a
Tollefson, N. F.: 2628
Tollman, G. A.: 1743
Tomita, M.: 2655
Tomlinson, T. M.: 3589
Toms, E. C.: 1160, 3327
Tonningsen, E. L.: 466
Toobert, S.: 933
Toomey, L. C.: 1883
Topetzes, N. J.: 725
Townsend, J. C.: 1293
Townsend, J. K.: 2832
Tranel, N.: 3394
Trapp, E. P.: 1243
Traxler, A. E.: 33
Treadway, C. R.: 3074
Treece, R. R.: 391
Tremaine, D. L.: 1146a
Trever, R. W.: 1436
Trice, H. M.: 3051
Trieschmann, R. B.: 3821
Trosman, H.: 3509
Troxel, W. D.: 1728

Truax, C. B.: 1925-6, 2446,
   3052, 3270, 3353, 3822-5
Truax, W. E.: 359, 578
Truelove, J. W.: 849
Trumbull, R.: 467
Trumm, O.: 794
Tryon, R. C.: 2110, 2311-2,
   2447, 3271
Tsubouchi, K.: 3053
Tuck, J. A.: 3389
Tuddenham, R. D.: 1477
Tuft, L. H.: 3272-3, 3588
Tuma, A. H.: 1852, 3427
Turbovsky, J. M.: 533
Turk, H.: 3415
Turner, J.: 997
Turner, L. N.: 1557
Turrell, E. S.: 799, 3370
Tuthill, E. W.: 2313
Twomey, J. F.: 2679, 3054
Tydlaska, M.: 468, 665
Tyler, D. W.: 2914, 3132
Tyler, F. T.: 271, 277, 469-
   70, 534, 3312
Uecker, A. E.: 2468, 2833,
   3055-8, 3274, 3313
Uhr, L.: 831
Ullmann, L. P.: 1285, 1380,
   1503, 1678, 3368, 3385,
   3416
Unger, B. L.: 3184
Unger, S.: 3484, 3513
Upper, D.: 2448
Upshaw, H. S.: 749
Urbach, N.: 1831
Urmer, A. H.: 1040
Uyeno, E.: 1782
Vacchiano, R. B.: 1949
Vadum, A. C.: 3257
Valles, J.: 1902-3
Van Atta, R. E.: 3826
Vance, F. L.: 3449
Van Dalsem, E. L.: 2506
Van de Castle, R. L.: 1268,
   2834, 2948
Vandenberg, S. G.: 3492
Vanderhoof, E.: 2111
Van De Riet, H.: 3377
Van De Riet, V.: 3377
van der Veen, F.: 2629, 3493
Vandiveer, J. M.: 1560
Vando, A.: 3059
Van Dyke, P.: 535
Vaness, N. L.: 2748
Van Evra, J. P.: 1381
Van Pelt, J.: 2165, 2859
Van Praag, J.: 650
Van Vorst, R. B.: 10
Van West, A.: 3356
Varble, D.: 3269
Varva, F.: 188
Vaughan, G. M.: 3490
Vaughan, J. A.: 1382
Vaughan, J. L.: 3827
Vaughan, R. P.: 1383-4,
   1927, 2112, 2314, 2449,
   3275
Veal, L. R.: 2605
Vega, A.: 3828
Veldhuizen, J. F.: 3829
Veldman, D. J.: 2531
Vellutino, F. R.: 3830
Verdone, P.: 3431
Vernallis, F. F.: 3328, 3589
Verniaud, W. M.: 31, 53
Vernon, J. T.: 3417
Vertein, L. D.: 1161, 1452
Very, P. S.: 2450
Vesprani, G. J.: 2724, 3060
Vestre, N. D.: 1309, 1390,
   1706, 2231, 2315, 2388,
   3061-3
Vialle, H. D.: 1558
Vidor, M.: 278
Vincent, M. O.: 3095
Vincent, N. M. P.: 2113
Vineberg, S. E.: 549, 598
Visotsky, H. M.: 1012
Vitale, J. H.: 2476
Vitola, B. M.: 1839
Vitz, P. C.: 1928
Voas, R. B.: 667, 726-7, 776
Vodde, T. W.: 2961
Vogel, J. L.: 1385

Vogel, R. B.: 2725
Vogel, W.: 1245, 1286, 1386
Vogler, R. E.: 3168
Voldseth, E. V.: 850
Volkman, A. P.: 1428
Vollmar, J.: 938
Vondracek, F. W.: 2835
Voors, A. W.: 3064
Wadsworth, H. M. M.: 600
Wagman, M.: 2451, 3454
Wagner, E. E.: 2316
Wagner, P. D.: 2693, 2755
Wagner, R. F.: 1162
Wagoner, R.: 3682
Wahba, M.: 1504
Wahler, H. J.: 557, 1163,
   1929, 2452
Wainwright, B. B.: 3276
Waite, R. R.: 1032
Walch, A. E.: 90
Walder, L.: 3518
Waldo, G. P.: 2726
Wales, B.: 2453, 3065
Wales, M. E.: 2836
Walike, B. C.: 2114
Walker, A.: 2569
Walker, C. E.: 2317, 3066
Walker, G.: 2532
Walker, J. N.: 1083-5, 1164,
   1193, 1287
Walker, R. E.: 2630, 2640,
   2837, 3067
Wallach, M. A.: 1041
Wallach, M. S.: 1387, 1930
Wallen, N. E.: 3435
Walnut, F.: 536
Walsh, J.: 1824
Walsh, J. A.: 1307-8, 1610,
   3068
Walsh, T. M.: 919, 2673
Walster, E.: 2680
Walter, P. B.: 851
Walters, R. H.: 3464; exc,
   5:B467
Walters, S. M.: 3730
Walters, W. M.: 2398
Waltmann, R. H.: 1931, 2170
Walton, D.: 934
Ward, D. B.: 2838
Ward, G.: 2806, 3573
Ward, J.: 935, 3066
Ware, J. G.: 3371
Wargo, D. G.: 2446, 3052,
   3825
Wark, D. M.: 1703
Warman, R. E.: 1641, 1932
Warren, A. B.: 3329
Warren, L. W.: 3069
Warren, S. A.: 1177, 1296
Wasman, M.: 2847
Waterfall, R. A.: 1729
Waters, T. J.: 1020
Watley, D. J.: 1933, 2115
Watman, W. A.: 2681
Watson, C. G.: 1934, 2318,
   2454-5, 3070, 3277, 3831
Watson, G.: 728, 3314, 3380
Watson, R. A. R.: 3745
Watt, G. D.: 3298
Wattron, J. B.: 777, 1388
Wauck, L.: 795
Wauck, L. A.: 237, 2980
Webb, C. E.: 2810
Webb, J. T.: 2424-5, 3071,
   3278-80, 3832
Webb, R. A.: 1743
Webb, S. C.: 852, 3369
Weber, J. R.: 3307
Weber, R. J.: 2469
Webster, A. S.: 786
Webster, H.: 559, 625, 796,
   809
Weckowitz, T. E.: 3330
Wehmer, G. M.: 2682
Weick, D. V.: 157
Weigel, R. G.: 2319
Weil, G.: 2616
Weinbaum, L.: 2839
Weinberg, S. L.: 3090
Weiner, I. W.: 668
Weinstein, B.: 3219
Weinstein, J.: 2840
Weinstein, M. R.: 2550
Weintraub, W.: 2134

[1282]

*[Re Minnesota Multiphasic Personality Inventory] Behaviordyne Psychodiagnostic Lab Service. A computerized scoring and interpreting service for qualified users of the MMPI or the *California Psychological Inventory;* 1969–72; formerly called *OPTIMUM Psychodiagnostic Consultation Service;* various types of interpretive reports are available: types OR (statistical report for researchers), 1 (for industrial psychologists and personnel counselors), 2 (for counselors and caseworkers), 3 (for correctional counselors), 4 (self-report to be given to patient by counselor or therapist), 5 (for physicians), 6 (standard report for psychiatrists and psychologists), 7 (comprehensive report for psychiatrists and psychologists) ; a penal option is available with the above reports; each type of report (except type 4) available in full or brief form; Joseph C. Finney, Charles Dwight Auvenshine, David Fulton Smith, and Donald E. Skeeters; Behaviordyne, Inc. *

For additional information and reviews by William J. Eichman, see 7:105 and 7:107 (9 references).

REFERENCES THROUGH 1971

1–9. See 7:107.
10. LeMaistre, Gress. "Computer as Psychologist: Who's Running the Show?" *J Ed Data Processing* 8(2–3):18–21 '71. *
11. Manning, Horace M. "Programmed Interpretation of the MMPI." *J Pers Assess* 35(2):162–76 Ap '71. * (*PA* 47:3018)

CUMULATIVE NAME INDEX

[1283]

*[Re Minnesota Multiphasic Personality Inventory] MMPI-ICA Computer Report. A computerized scoring and interpreting service for physicians, psychiatrists, and psychologists; 1963–72; the interpretive report is a 5 or 6 page computer printout presenting an emotional disturbance score (called *Multiphasic Index,* MI), probability of significant disturbance, descriptive and interpretative statements (regarding MI interpretation, summary, validity, personality description, suggestions for improving coping, special coping problems, positive traits, most frequent diagnosis, salient clinical features with critical items), scores on 4 validity scales, 10 clinical scales, and 101 research scales grouped in 24 categories (validity, anxiety, phobias, depression, guilt and intropunitiveness, overactivity, authority conflict, anticonformity, thinking disturbance, oversensitivity, introversion-extroversion, social imperturbability, hostility and aggression, inhibition of aggression, passive/feminine interest, alcohol and drugs, family conflict, sexual problems, general category, social responsibility, social desirability, need for social approval, excessive moral virtue, general defenses and somatic complaints), and a profile of the

validity and clinical scores; Edwin Dunlop (manual);
Institute of Clinical Analysis. *

For additional information and reviews by William
J. Eichman, see 7:105 and 7:106 (3 references); see
also P:167 (2 references).

REFERENCES THROUGH 1971

1–2. See P:167.
3–5. See 7:106.

CUMULATIVE NAME INDEX

Birds, V. G.: 1   Spiegel, D.: 4–5
Dunlop, E.: 2–3   Waltmann, R. H.: 1–2
Eichman, W. J.: *rev,* 7:105–6

[1284]

[Re Minnesota Multiphasic Personality Inventory] The Psychological Corporation MMPI Reporting Service. A computerized scoring and interpreting service for qualified users of the MMPI; 1967; the interpretive report is a 1 page computer printout presenting 6 to 15 interpretive statements (selected from a population of 73 statements), scores on 4 validity scales, 10 clinical scales, and 13 special scales [first factor (A), second factor (R), ego strength (Es), low back pain (Lb), caudality (Ca), dependency (Dy), dominance (Do), social responsibility (Re), prejudice (Pr), status (St), control (Cn), tired housewife (Th), worried breadwinner (Wb)], and a profile of the validity and clinical scores; program and manual by John S. Pearson and Wendell M. Swenson; Psychological Corporation. *

For additional information and reviews by William J. Eichman, see 7:105 and 7:108 (1 reference); see also P:168 (8 references).

REFERENCES THROUGH 1971

1–8. See P:168.
9. See 7:108.
10. SWENSON, WENDELL M. "Automated Personality Assessment in Medical Practice." *Med Clinics N Am* 54(4):835–49 Jl '70. *
11. MANNING, HORACE M. "Programmed Interpretation of the MMPI." *J Pers Assess* 35(2):162–76 Ap '71. * (*PA* 47:3018)

CUMULATIVE NAME INDEX

Brannick, T. L.: 6   Nahum, L. H.: 9
Eichman, W. J.: *rev,* 7:105,   Pearson, J. S.: 4–8
7:108   Rome, H. P.: 1, 3, 5–6
Gastineau, C. F.: 2   Swenson, W. M.: 4–5, 7–8,
Manning, H. M.: 11   10
Mataya, P.: 6

[1285]

*[Re Minnesota Multiphasic Personality Inventory] Roche MMPI Computerized Interpretation Service.** A computerized scoring and interpreting service for qualified users of the MMPI (clinical psychologists and physicians for use in clinical practice and research); 1966–72; the interpretive report is a 3 page computer printout presenting a narrative report, scores on 4 validity scales, 10 clinical scales, and 14 special scales [first factor (A), second factor (R), ego strength (Es), low back pain (Lb), caudality (Ca), dependency (Dy), dominance (Do), responsibility (Re), prejudice (Pr), social status (St), control (Cn), manifest anxiety (At), social desirability (So-R), maladjustment (Mt)], reproduction of critical items with responses, and a profile of the validity and clinical scores; only 5 (A, Es, Ca, Do, Pr) of the 14 special scales are utilized in the computerized narrative report; program and manual by Raymond D. Fowler, Jr.; programmed learning text for primary physicians, entitled *Clinical Use of the Automated MMPI,* by Raymond D. Fowler and Dempsey F. Pennington, Jr.; Roche Psychiatric Service Institute. *

For additional information and reviews by William

J. Eichman and Benjamin Kleinmuntz, see 7:105 and 7:109 (6 references); see also P:169 (9 references).

REFERENCES THROUGH 1971

1–9. See P:169.
10–15. See 7:109.
16. CORSSEN, GUENTER; OGET, SOLMAZ; AND REED, PERCY C. "Computerized Evaluation of Psychic Effects of Kelamine." *Anesth & Analg* 50(3):397–401 My–Je '71. *
17. MANNING, HORACE M. "Programmed Interpretation of the MMPI." *J Pers Assess* 35(2):162–76 Ap '71. * (*PA* 47:3018)

CUMULATIVE NAME INDEX

Cahill, C. A.: 2   Kleinmuntz, B.: *rev,* 7:109
Corssen, G.: 16   Manning, H. M.: 17
Coyle, F. A.: 6–7   Marlowe, G. H.: 8
Eichman, W. J.: *rev,* 7:105,   Mason, D. J.: 9
7:109   Miller, M. L.: 12–3, 15
Fowler, R. D.: 1, 3–8, 10–3, Oget, S.: 16
15   Reed, P. C.: 16
Herring, F. H.: 9   Webb, J. T.: 13–5

[1286]

Minnesota Rating Scale for Personal Qualities and Abilities. College and adults; 1925–38; revision of Part 2 of *Rating Scale for Teachers of Home Economics;* Clara M. Brown; University of Minnesota Press. *

For additional information, see P:170; for a review by Dorothy M. Clendenen, see 5:88 (1 reference).

REFERENCES THROUGH 1971

1. See 5:88.

CUMULATIVE NAME INDEX

Brown, C. M.: 1   Clendenen, D. M.: *rev,* 5:88

[1287]

★The Missouri Children's Picture Series. Ages 5–16; 1971, c1963–64; MCPS; 8 scores: conformity, masculinity-femininity, maturity, aggression, inhibition, activity level, sleep disturbance, somatization; Jacob O. Sines, Jerome D. Pauker, and Lloyd K. Sines; Jacob O. Sines. *

REFERENCES THROUGH 1971

1. BAKER, EUGENE A., AND OWEN, DAVID R. "Negro-White Personality Differences in Integrated Classrooms." Abstract. *Proc 77th Ann Conv Am Psychol Assn* 4(2):539–40 '69. * (*PA* 44:1217)
2. CANNELL, ROBERT THOMAS, III. *Effects of Physical Disorders on the Adjustment of Hospitalized Children.* Doctor's thesis, University of Missouri (Columbia, Mo.), 1970. (*DAI* 31:3987A)
3. OWEN, DAVID R., AND SINES, JACOB O. "Heritability of Personality in Children." *Behav Genetics* 1(3–4):235–48 Ag–N '70. * (*PA* 47:10446)
4. VEGELY, ANN B. "Performance of Hearing-Impaired Children on a Non-Verbal Personality Test." *Am Ann Deaf* 116(4):427–33 Ag '71. * (*PA* 47:11383)

CUMULATIVE NAME INDEX

Baker, E. A.: 1   Sines, J. O.: 3
Cannell, R. T.: 2   Vegely, A. B.: 4
Owen, D. R.: 1, 3

[1288]

★Mood Altering Substances: A Behavior Inventory. High school and college; 1971, c1967–71; MAS; Marion Pollock; Mejor Associates. *

[1289]

Mooney Problem Check List. Grades 7–9, 9–12, 13–16, adults; 1941–50; MPCL; 4 levels; Ross L. Mooney and Leonard V. Gordon (manuals, c and d); Psychological Corporation. *
a) JUNIOR HIGH SCHOOL FORM. Grades 7–9; 1942–50; 7 scores: health and physical development, school, home and family, money-work-the future, boy and girl relations, relations to people in general, self-centered concerns.
b) HIGH SCHOOL FORM. Grades 9–12; 1941–50; 11 scores: health and physical development, finances-liv-

ing conditions-employment, social and recreational activities, social-psychological relations, personal-psychological relations, courtship-sex-marriage, home and family, morals and religion, adjustment to school work, the future—vocational and educational, curriculum and teaching procedures.

c) COLLEGE FORM. Grades 13–16; 1941–50; 11 scores: same as for High School Form.

d) ADULT FORM. Adults; 1950; 9 scores: health, economic security, self-improvement, personality, home and family, courtship, sex, religion, occupation.

For additional information, see P:173 (55 references); for a review by Thomas C. Burgess, see 6:145 (25 references); see also 5:89 (26 references); for reviews by Harold E. Jones and Morris Krugman, see 4:73 (13 references); for reviews by Ralph C. Bedell and Theodore F. Lentz, see 3:67 (17 references).

REFERENCES THROUGH 1971

1–17. See 3:67.
18–30. See 4:73.
31–56. See 5:89.
57–81. See 6:145.
82–136. See P:173.
137. DAVIS, MALCOLM ADKINS. *A Study of the Personalities and Social Interests of a Group of Negro College Freshmen as Revealed in Their Compositions.* Doctor's thesis, New York University (New York, N.Y.), 1952. (*DA* 15:206)
138. HENZE, ARTHUR LOUIS. *Relation of Parental Authoritarianism to the Adjustment of Home-Resident College Students.* Doctor's thesis, University of Michigan (Ann Arbor, Mich.), 1952. (*DA* 12:511)
139. HILL, PAUL LEROY. *Personal Problems of Junior High School Children in Relation to Intelligence, Socioeconomic Status, Sex and School Grade.* Doctor's thesis, Northwestern University (Evanston, Ill.), 1953. (*DA* 14:395)
140. MARTIN, RICHARD PANTALL. *The Adjustment of Latin-American Male Students in Selected Private Secondary Schools in the United States.* Doctor's thesis, Northwestern University (Evanston, Ill.), 1954. (*DA* 14:1605)
141. EHRHARDT, MARYANN. *A Sociometric Study of the Friendship Status of College Women.* Doctor's thesis, Indiana University (Bloomington, Ind.), 1955. (*DA* 15:1663)
142. JONES, WORTH ROOSEVELT. *A Study of the Affective Tolerance and the Typical Problems of Married and Unmarried Undergraduate College Students.* Doctor's thesis, Indiana University (Bloomington, Ind.), 1955. (*DA* 15:2325)
143. MORTON, ROBERT B. "An Experiment in Brief Psychotherapy." *Psychol Monogr* 69(1):1–17 '55. * (*PA* 30:1112)
144. SLINGER, GEORGE EDWARD. *Freshman Problems and Academic Achievement.* Doctor's thesis, University of Florida (Gainesville, Fla.), 1955. (*DA* 15:2474)
145. WALTHALL, NANCY. *A Study of the Effectiveness of the Resident Counselor in the Adjustment of a Selected Group of Freshmen Women.* Doctor's thesis, Northwestern University (Evanston, Ill.), 1957. (*DA* 17:2944)
146. EPPLEY, MARY VINEITA (BOOTS). *The Relationship of Personal Factors and Reading Performance to Academic Achievement of Selected Oregon State College Students.* Doctor's thesis, Oregon State University (Corvallis, Ore.), 1958. (*DA* 19:730)
147. FRANKEL, EDWARD. *A Comparative Study of Achieving and Underachieving High School Boys of High Intellectual Ability.* Doctor's thesis, Yeshiva University (New York, N.Y.), 1958. (*DA* 20:956)
148. PARROTT, LESLIE. *A Study of Student Personnel Services in Six Liberal Arts Church Colleges.* Doctor's thesis, Michigan State University (East Lansing, Mich.), 1958. (*DA* 20:189)
149. SMITH, EDWARD JAMES. *An Experimental Study of the Problems and Attitudes of High School Athletes.* Doctor's thesis, University of Colorado (Boulder, Colo.), 1958. (*DA* 19:2516)
150. COX, RICHARD HENRY. *A Comparison of Male Freshmen at Northwestern University From Public and Private Secondary Schools Relative to Adjustmental, Personality, Academic, and Socio-Economic Factors.* Doctor's thesis, Northwestern University (Evanston, Ill.), 1959. (*DA* 20:2141)
151. LEVINSON, BORIS M. "The Problems of Jewish Religious Youth." *Genetic Psychol Monogr* 60:309–48 N '59. * (*PA* 34:5850)
152. OVERSTREET, PHOEBE LUCILLE. *Factors Associated With the Quality of Self-Evaluations.* Doctor's thesis, Columbia University (New York, N.Y.), 1959. (*DA* 20:761)
153. COTE, THEODORE JOHN. *The Relationship Between Parents' Awareness of Their Adolescent Children's Problems and the Affective Adjustment of Those Children.* Doctor's thesis, University of Connecticut (Storrs, Conn.), 1960. (*DA* 21:1842)
154. ELSHIEKH, YOUSEF MAHMOUD. *A Comparative Study of Adjustment Problems of Undergraduate Students in Egyptian and American Teachers Colleges, With Implications for College*

Counseling. Doctor's thesis, Indiana University (Bloomington, Ind.), 1960. (*DA* 21:3356)
155. FRANKEL, EDWARD. "A Comparative Study of Achieving and Underachieving High School Boys of High Intellectual Ability." *J Ed Res* 53:172–80 Ja '60. * (*PA* 35:7115)
156. HARVEY, LESTER JAMES. *A Study of the Guidance Resources of Students in High Schools Affiliated With the National Union of Christian Schools in Michigan and Illinois.* Doctor's thesis, Michigan State University (East Lansing, Mich.), 1960. (*DA* 22:153)
157. RATHBURN, IONE JEAN ALOHILANI. *Teachers' and Pupils' Perceptions of Pupil Problems in Honolulu Public High Schools.* Doctor's thesis, Stanford University (Stanford, Calif.), 1960. (*DA* 21:2597)
158. LEVIN, JACOB LOUIS. *An Analysis of Certain Characteristics of Youthful Offenders in the Cook County Jail (Chicago, Illinois).* Doctor's thesis, Northwestern University (Evanston, Ill.), 1961. (*DA* 22:2692)
159. McCAUSLIN, JACK ALFRED. *Differences Between College Students Motivated to Seek Help With Their Problems and Those Who Are Not and Changes in the Attitudes of the Latter Following a Counseling Interview.* Doctor's thesis, University of Maryland (College Park, Md.), 1962. (*DA* 23:1583)
160. GAWRONSKI, DANIEL ANTHONY. *A Comparative Study of Differences Existing Among Overachieving, Normal Achieving and Underachieving High School Seniors.* Doctor's thesis, Northwestern University (Evanston, Ill.), 1963. (*DA* 25:292)
161. GREENE, JAMES E., SR. "Factors Associated With Absenteeism Among Students in Two Metropolitan High Schools." *J Exp Ed* 31:389–94 su '63. *
162. PARKS, ANNE B. *A Study of Factors Related to Underachievement of Ninth Grade Students of Cadillac Junior High School, Detroit, Michigan.* Doctor's thesis, University of Michigan (Ann Arbor, Mich.), 1963. (*DA* 23:4576)
163. SHAPIRO, DAVID S., AND MAHOLICK, LEONARD T. *Opening Doors for Troubled People.* Springfield, Ill.: Charles C Thomas, Publishers, 1963. Pp. xi, 121. * (*PA* 38:8858)
164. STEPHENS, STEPHEN LEE. *The Personal Problems of Athletes and Non-Athletes as Seen by Themselves and Their Parents.* Master's thesis, University of Wisconsin (Madison, Wis.), 1963.
165. CORTNER, FREDERICK DALE. *Personality Characteristics in Adolescents as Related to Length of Residence in a New School System.* Doctor's thesis, University of North Carolina (Chapel Hill, N.C.), 1964. (*DA* 26:3149)
166. DOLEYS, ERNEST J. "Differences Between Clients and Non-Clients on the Mooney Problem Check List." *J Col Stud Personnel* 6:21–4 O '64. *
167. HORNE, DONALD LEVON. *An Experimental Study of the Change in Activities of Selected Counselors Subsequent to Receiving Information About Themselves and Their Students.* Doctor's thesis, Auburn University (Auburn, Ala.), 1964. (*DA* 25:5737)
168. MITTMAN, HOWARD. *The Adjustment of Twins: An Evaluation of the Relationship Between Twinship, Patterns of Identification, and Adjustment.* Doctor's thesis, Yeshiva University (New York, N.Y.), 1964. (*DA* 25:3678)
169. ALLEN, DIXIE JEAN. *An Analysis of the Relationship Between Maturational Status and Psychological Status in Certain Adolescent Girls.* Doctor's thesis, University of Florida (Gainesville, Fla.), 1965. (*DA* 26:5856)
170. CLEMENTS, HUBERT MADISON. *A Study of the Relationship Between Certain Variables and the Reported Problems of Selected White High School Students in Georgia.* Doctor's thesis, University of Georgia (Athens, Ga.), 1965. (*DA* 27:385A)
171. DUNCAN, JACKIE ALBERT. *The Effects of Short-Term Group Counseling on Selected Characteristics of Culturally Deprived Ninth Grade Students.* Doctor's thesis, University of Georgia (Athens, Ga.), 1965. (*DA* 27:387A)
172. GAY, JAMES DONALD. *Personality Changes Associated With Workshop Participation.* Doctor's thesis, University of Kentucky (Lexington, Ky.), 1965. (*DAI* 30:2436B)
173. PERRONE, PHILIP A.; WEIKING, MARY L.; AND NAGEL, ELWYN H. "The Counseling Function as Seen by Students, Parents and Teachers." *J Counsel Psychol* 12:148–52 su '65. * (*PA* 39:13006)
174. STARK, MATTHEW. "Commuter and Residence Hall Students Compared." *Personnel & Guid J* 44:277–81 N '65. * (*PA* 40:4597)
175. WEAVER, HAZEL STEWART. *Characteristics of High School Girls Which May Lead to Early Marriage.* Doctor's thesis, North Texas State University (Denton, Tex.), 1965. (*DA* 25:7094)
176. PEPIN, ROBERT ROLAND. *A Study of Scholastic Achievements and Personal Adjustments of Military and Non-Military Transitory High School Students.* Doctor's thesis, University of Connecticut (Storrs, Conn.), 1966. (*DA* 28:403A)
177. WAKEFIELD, WILLIAM MAXWELL. *Awareness, Affection, and Perceived Similarity in the Parent-Child Relationship.* Doctor's thesis, Columbia University (New York, N.Y.), 1966. (*DA* 27:401A)
178. DAHLIN, DONALD DALE. *Developing Holding Power in the Public School for Potential Dropouts.* Doctor's thesis, University of Nebraska (Lincoln, Neb.), 1967. (*DA* 28:4371A)

Mooney Problem Check List

179. HUSTON, BEATRICE MOORE. *A Normative Survey of the Personal and Academic Characteristics of the Freshmen Women Students Enrolled in Mary Hardin-Baylor College, 1966-1967.* Doctor's thesis, Baylor University (Waco, Tex.), 1967. (*DA* 28:1209A)

180. McMILLAN, ALTA ANN. *Student Personnel Service for a Small, Church-Related, Women's Liberal Arts College.* Doctor's thesis, University of Mississippi (University, Miss.), 1967. (*DA* 28:4824A)

181. NELSON, ORAL DEAN. *A Study of the Understanding of Youth Problems on the Part of Community Workers With Adolescents.* Doctor's thesis, Northwestern University (Evanston, Ill.), 1967. (*DA* 28:2518A)

182. PETERSON, RONALD SKEEN. *A Longitudinal Study of Nonintellective Characteristics of College Dropouts.* Doctor's thesis, University of Oregon (Eugene, Ore.), 1967. (*DA* 28:2076A)

183. WEBB, WAYNE DWIGHT. *The Effects of Teacher Sensitivity on Insecure, School-Problem, and Problem-Free Students.* Doctor's thesis, Stanford University (Stanford, Calif.), 1967. (*DA* 28:108A)

184. ANDERSON, GRADY LEE. *A Study of the Relationship Between Certain Variables and the Reported Problems of Selected Negro High School Students in Georgia.* Doctor's thesis, University of Georgia (Athens, Ga.), 1968. (*DA* 29:3410A)

185. BERCEGEAY, WELMAN JOSEPH. *Use of the Mooney Problem Check List to Measure the Effectiveness of Guidance Oriented Group Discussions.* Master's thesis, Xavier University (New Orleans, La.), 1968.

186. EL-GAWHARY, FARAH HANNA. *A Study of the Personal Problems of United Arab Republic High School Adolescents With Implications for the Gradual Establishment of a Guidance Program.* Doctor's thesis, Florida State University (Tallahassee, Fla.), 1968. (*DAI* 30:985A)

187. FAZEL, MOHAMMED K. *Child's Perception of Parental Attitude and Its Relationship to Academic Achievement and Problem Awareness.* Doctor's thesis, Utah State University (Logan, Utah), 1968. (*DA* 29:3084B)

188. MORAN, SHEILA MAUREEN. *Some Applications of the Mooney Problem Check List to the Guidance of Mentally Handicapped Children.* Master's thesis, Cardinal Stritch College (Milwaukee, Wis.), 1968.

189. MUKERJI, KAMAL, AND BANERJEE, DEBABRATA. "Relationship Between the Direction of Aggression and Self-Perceived Problem-Variables Among a Group of Offenders." *Indian J Psychol* 43(1-4):37-40 '68. *

190. RIVERS, LINDA S. "Self-Report Correlates of the Process Scale." *Proc W Va Acad Sci* 40:196-200 '68. *

191. WILLNER, ERIC. "Problems of Adjustment of All-Day School Pupils and Their Guidance Implications." *Jewish Ed* 37:188-98 Jl '68. *

192. AUSTIN, CATHERINE J. *An Investigation of the Problems of Seventh Grade Students as Indicated by the Mooney Problem Check List.* Master's thesis, Glassboro State College (Glassboro, N.J.), 1969.

193. GINGRICH, DOUGLAS DAVID. *Adolescent Problems: Relationships Between Adolescent and Adult Perceptions in a Rural Community.* Doctor's thesis, Colorado State College (Greeley, Colo.), 1969. (*DAI* 30:4221A)

194. HELBERG, DONALD HENRY. *The Effects of Educational-Vocational Group Guidance and Client-Centered Group Counseling on Personality Factors, Student Problems, and Vocational Direction of Junior College Students in a Developmental Program.* Doctor's thesis, Colorado State College (Greeley, Colo.), 1969. (*DAI* 30:4222A)

195. HENDRICKSON, DONALD EUGENE. *Personal Problems of Junior High School, Senior High School, and Young Adult Delinquents in State Correctional Institutions.* Doctor's thesis, Indiana University (Bloomington, Ind.), 1969. (*DAI* 30:1822A)

196. JACOBS, JAMES ROGER. *Characteristics of Students Who Seek Counseling.* Doctor's thesis, University of Wisconsin (Madison, Wis.), 1969. (*DAI* 30:5238A)

197. MONTGOMERY, MARY ANN. *An Investigation of Students Who Succeed Academically and Those Who Do Not Succeed Academically in a Community College.* Doctor's thesis, University of Pittsburgh (Pittsburgh, Pa.), 1969. (*DAI* 31:1578A)

198. MORGAN, JACK C. "Adolescent Problems and the Mooney Problem Check List." *Adolescence* 4(13):111-26 sp '69. * (*PA* 43:12812)

199. NELSEN, HART M., AND STOREY, STUART E. "Personality Adjustment of Rural and Urban Youth: The Formation of a Rural Disadvantaged Subculture." *Rural Sociol* 34(1):43-55 Mr '69. * (*PA* 45:576)

200. PANDEY, JAGDISH. "Problems of Adjustment of Adolescents in Relation to Their Personality Variables." Doctoral thesis abstract. *Indian Psychol R* 5(2):212-4 Ja '69. *

201. SAX, ARNOLD BERTON. *A Comparative Study of Personality Characteristics Between Seventh-Grade Students Classified as Educationally Deprived and Non-Educationally Deprived.* Doctor's thesis, University of Houston (Houston, Tex.), 1969. (*DAI* 30:4838A)

202. SINGH, SHIVA NATH. "Adjustment Problems During Pre-Adolescence." *Indian Psychol R* 5(2):184-91 Ja '69. *

203. WALKER, RONALD E.; NICOLAY, ROBERT C.; KLUCZNY, RITA; AND RIEDEL, ROBERT G. "Psychological Correlates of Smoking." *J Clin Psychol* 25(1):42-4 Ja '69. * (*PA* 43:9698)

204. WALSH, W. BRUCE, AND RUSSEL, JOHN H., III. "College Major Choice and Personal Adjustment." *Personnel & Guid J* 47(7):685-8 Mr '69. * (*PA* 43:13297)

205. WATSON, PATRICIA A. *Residence Hall Student Counselors: The Blurred Image.* Doctor's thesis, Marquette University (Milwaukee, Wis.), 1969. (*DAI* 31:1583A)

206. AKERS, STEPHEN JAY. *An Analysis of Student Academic and Personal Concerns and Awareness of Counseling Services at Purdue University.* Doctor's thesis, Purdue University (Lafayette, Ind.), 1970. (*DAI* 31:1570A)

207. BAILEY, ROBERT EDWARD. *Differences in the Personal-Social Problems of Negro and Caucasian Secondary School Students.* Doctor's thesis, University of Florida (Gainesville, Fla.), 1970. (*DAI* 31:3326A)

208. BLATT, MARTIN ROBERT. *An Investigation of Intervention as It Relates to Motivation for Counseling.* Doctor's thesis, Temple University (Philadelphia, Pa.), 1970. (*DAI* 31:6889B)

209. BUTCOFSKY, DONALD LAMAR. *Effects of a Secondary School Humanities Program Upon Selected Aspects of Student Personal-Social Adjustment.* Doctor's thesis, University of Pennsylvania (Philadelphia, Pa.), 1970. (*DAI* 31:6465A)

210. CURL, GERALD ALLEN. *A Comparison of Freshman Achievers and Non-Achievers From Economically Deprived Families.* Doctor's thesis, University of Illinois (Urbana, Ill.), 1970. (*DAI* 31:4455A)

211. ERICKSON, DOUGLAS EUGENE. *Differential Personality, Academic, and Biographical Characteristics of International Graduate Students at the University of North Dakota.* Doctor's thesis, University of North Dakota (Grand Forks, N.D.), 1970. (*DAI* 32:6756A)

212. McIVOR, MARILYN YVONNE HOFFMAN. *Graduate Students' Perceptions of Guidance Services in Three Iowa Universities.* Doctor's thesis, University of Iowa (Iowa City, Iowa), 1970. (*DAI* 31:4468A)

213. MUKERJI, KAMAL, AND RAYCHAUDHURI, MANAS. "Assessment Equivalence of Clinical Ratings, Structured and Projective Measures of Personality." *Manas* (India) 17(2):67-76 N '70. * (*PA* 47:9277)

214. PAYNE, LINDA M. *A Comparative Study of Problems of a Selected Group of Students as Revealed by the Mooney Problem Check List.* Master's thesis, East Tennessee State University (Johnson City, Tenn.), 1970.

215. POWELL, JOANN. *An Analysis of Factors Relating to Decisions to Transfer From Northwestern University By Freshman Women.* Doctor's thesis, Northwestern University (Evanston, Ill.), 1970. (*DAI* 31:3277A)

216. SEEVERS, CHARLES J. *Problems and Psychological Needs of Lutheran Confirmands.* Doctor's thesis, University of Notre Dame (Notre Dame, Ind.), 1970. (*DAI* 31:4572A)

217. SHETTERLY, HENRY TITUS. *Self and Social Perceptions and Personal Characteristics of a Group of Suburban High School Marijuana Users.* Doctor's thesis, University of Denver (Denver, Colo.), 1970. (*DAI* 31:3279A)

218. THOMAS, "D" CORNELL. *A Comparative Study of Absenteeism at Kennedy and Olympus Junior High Schools.* Doctor's thesis, University of Utah (Salt Lake City, Utah), 1970. (*DAI* 31:3847A)

219. VAN LANDINGHAM, ROBERT W. *An Analysis of the Problems of Junior High School Boys Attending Southern California Military Academy as Expressed on the Junior High Form of the Mooney Problem Check List.* Master's thesis, Chapman College (Orange, Calif.), 1970.

220. BREWSTER, HOYT WILLIAM, JR. *The Problems of Jr. College Freshmen and the Development of the Jr. College Problem Check List.* Doctor's thesis, University of Southern California (Los Angeles, Calif.), 1971. (*DAI* 32:3017A)

221. CARR, WILLIAM LUTHER. *The Personal Problems of Graduate Students at a Private University as Perceived by Their Faculty Advisors.* Doctor's thesis, University of Pennsylvania (Philadelphia, Pa.), 1971. (*DAI* 32:6119A)

222. EVANS, ARTHUR JAMES. *Perceptions of Personal Problems by Students of Different Ethnic Groups in a Large Suburban High School.* Doctor's thesis, University of Pittsburgh (Pittsburgh, Pa.), 1971. (*DAI* 33:2612A)

223. GARBER, JOHN RODNEY. *Characteristics of Students Enrolled in the Guided Studies Program at Rockingham Community College and Their Implications for Curriculum Development.* Doctor's thesis, North Carolina State University (Raleigh, N.C.), 1971. (*DAI* 32:3555A)

224. GILBERT, JOSEPH. "Insight Acquisition and Counseling With Group Test Data—A Negative Outcome With Some Wry Reflections on Certain Imperatives of Research in the Clinical Area." *Psychol* 8(3):9-14 Ag '71. * (*PA* 48:1398)

225. GROSS, WILLIAM F.; CARPENTER, LINDA L.; AND ALDER, LINDA O. "Problems of Adjustment Reported by Alcoholics Prior to Leaving a Hospital Treatment Program." *Q J Studies Alcohol* 32(2):454-6 Je '71. *

226. KNOX, WILLIAM HUGH. *A Comparative Study of Fraternity and Non-Fraternity Members on Selected Personality Variables.* Doctor's thesis, University of North Carolina (Chapel Hill, N.C.), 1971. (*DAI* 32:2421A)

Mooney Problem Check List

227. PHIFER, MELVIN PRESTON. *A Comparison of the Problems, Personality Characteristics and Self Concept of Students Identified as Potential Dropouts and Non-Potential Dropouts in a Two County Area in Mississippi.* Doctor's thesis, Mississippi State University (State College, Miss.), 1971. (*DAI* 32:1864A)

228. ROLAND, NATHAN LEWIS. *A Study of the Prevalence of Health Problems as Reported by Advantaged and Disadvantaged, Black and White, Junior High School Girls on the Mooney Problem Check List and Through Medical Examinations.* Doctor's thesis, University of South Carolina (Columbia, S.C.), 1971. (*DAI* 33:163A)

CUMULATIVE NAME INDEX

[1290]

The Mother-Child Relationship Evaluation. Mothers; 1961; MCRE; experimental form; 5 scores: 4 direct scores (acceptance, overprotection, overindulgence, rejection) and 1 derived score (confusion-dominance); Robert M. Roth; Western Psychological Services. *

For additional information, see P:174; for reviews by John Elderkin Bell and Dale B. Harris, see 6:146.

[1291]

Motivation Analysis Test. Ages 17 and over; 1959–70; MAT; for a downward extension, see 1367; 45 scores: 4 motivation scores (integrated, unintegrated, total, conflict) for each of 5 drives (mating, assertiveness, fear, narcism-comfort, pugnacity-sadism) and each of 5 sentiment structures (superego, self-sentiment, career, home-parental, sweetheart-spouse), plus 5 optional scores (total integration, total personal interest, total conflict, autism-optimism, information-intelligence); Raymond B. Cattell, John L. Horn, and Arthur B. Sweney, with the assistance of John A. Radcliffe; Institute for Personality and Ability Testing. *

For additional information, reviews by Henry A. Alker and Andrew L. Comrey, and an excerpted review by Gilbert E. Mazer, see 7:110 (18 references); see also P:175 (6 references).

REFERENCES THROUGH 1971

1–6. See P:175.

7–24. See 7:110.

25. VINEY, LINDA L. "Congruence of Measures of Self-Regard." *Psychol Rec* 16:487–93 O '66. * (*PA* 41:1618)

26. AINSWORTH, MARJORIE E. "The Relationship Between Motivation, Personality, Intelligence and School Attainment in a Secondary Modern School." *Brit J Ed Psychol* 37:135–7 F '67. * Abstract of master's thesis, University of Manchester (Manchester, England), 1966.

27. FOGEL, MARVIN EDWARD. *Conflict, Stress Response and Stress Adaptation in Sensitizers, Neutrals and Repressors: A Construct Validity Study.* Doctor's thesis, Texas Tech University (Lubbock, Tex.), 1970. (*DAI* 31:6255B)

28. JOHNSON, CARL I. *A Descriptive Study of the Relationship of Certain Critical Values and Motivational Achievement of Self-Concept in Reticent and Non-Reticent Speakers.* Doctor's

thesis, University of Denver (Denver, Colo.), 1970. (*DAI* 31:6757A)

29. CATTELL, RAYMOND B., AND BARTLETT, HAROLD W. "An R-dR-Technique Operational Distinction of the States of Anxiety, Stress, Fear, Etc." *Austral J Psychol* 23(2):105–23 Ag '71. * (*PA* 47:10889)

30. CORDINER, CONSTANCE M., AND HALL, DAVID J. "The Use of the Motivational Analysis Test in the Selection of Scottish Nursing Students." *Nursing Res* 20(4):357–62 Jl-Ag '71. *

31. GOODWIN, NANCY-LEE. *The Prediction of Artistic Performance From Cognitive and Non-Cognitive Measures*. Doctor's thesis, University of Illinois (Urbana, Ill.), 1971. (*DAI* 32:4419A)

32. JEGHELIAN, ALICE. *Persistence in Adult Students and Its Relationship to Selected Psychological Factors*. Doctor's thesis, Boston College (Chestnut Hill, Mass.), 1971. (*DAI* 32:3691A)

33. LAWLIS, G. FRANK. "Motivational Factors Reflecting Employment Instability." *J Social Psychol* 84(2):215–23 Ag '71. * (*PA* 47:1869)

34. LAWLIS, G. FRANK. "A Psychological View of the Chronically Unemployed: Personality and Motivation." *Psychol Rep* 28(3):838 Je '71. * (*PA* 46:11295)

35. PILCH, ARTHUR, AND ZELHART, PAUL F., JR. "Motivational Correlates of University Athletes and Exercising and Non-exercising Middle-Aged Subjects." *Res Q* 42(2):229–23 My '71. *

36. STAUFFER, ROBERT WAYNE. *The Effects of Sleep Deprivation on Dynamic Strength and Stamina*. Doctor's thesis, Temple University (Philadelphia, Pa.), 1971. (*DAI* 33:1496A)

37. WAAG, WAYNE LESLIE. *The Prediction of Individual Differences in Monitoring Performance*. Doctor's thesis, Texas Tech University (Lubbock, Tex.), 1971. (*DAI* 32:5502B)

CUMULATIVE NAME INDEX

[1292]

The Multidimensional Maturity Scale. Grades kgn–12; 1968; MMS; ratings (based upon records, interviews, observations, and tests) in 6 areas: physiological, emotional, psychosexual, mental, educational, social; Barnard J. Hartman; Priority Innovations, Inc. *

For additional information, see 7:111.

[1293]

Multiple Affect Adjective Check List. Grades 8–16 and adults; 1960–67; MAACL; extension of *Affect Adjective Check List*; 3 scores: anxiety, depression, hostility; Marvin Zuckerman and Bernard Lubin; Educational and Industrial Testing Service. *

For additional information and reviews by E. Lowell Kelly and Edwin I. Megargee, see 7:112 (60 references); see also P:176 (28 references).

REFERENCES THROUGH 1971

1–28. See P:176.
29–88. See 7:112.

89. PERSKY, HAROLD; MAROC, JAMES; CONRAD, EVERETT; AND DEN BREEIJEN, ARIE. "Blood Corticotropin and Adrenal Weight-Maintenance Factor Levels of Anxious Patients and Normal Subjects." *Psychosom Med* 21:379–86 S–O '59. * (*PA* 34:6442)

90. LEVITT, EUGENE E.; PERSKY, HAROLD; BRADY, JOHN PAUL; FITZGERALD, JOSEPH; AND DEN BREEIJEN, ARIE. "Evi-

dence for Hypnotically Induced Amnesia as an Analog of Repression." *J Nerv & Mental Dis* 133:218–21 S '61. * (*PA* 36:4118L)

91. HANKOFF, LEON D.; RUDORFER, LEON; AND PALEY, HERBERT M. "The Psychiatric Use of Pyrbenziondole: A Double Blind Outpatient Study." *J New Drugs* 2:167–72 My-Je '62. *

92. HANKOFF, LEON D.; RUDORFER, LEON; AND PALEY, HERBERT M. "A Reference Study of Ataraxics: A Two-Week Double Blind Outpatient Evaluation." *J New Drugs* 2:173–8 My-Je '62. *

93. LEVITT, EUGENE E., AND PERSKY, HAROLD. "Experimental Evidence for the Validity of the IPAT Anxiety Scale." *J Clin Psychol* 18:458–61 O '62. * (*PA* 39:5076)

94. ZUCKERMAN, MARVIN; ALBRIGHT, RICHARD J.; MARKS, CLIFFORD S.; AND MILLER, GERALD L. "Stress and Hallucinatory Effects of Perceptual Isolation and Confinement." *Psychol Monogr* 76(30):1–15 '62. * (*PA* 38:7226)

95. LEVITT, EUGENE E.; PERSKY, HAROLD; BRADY, JOHN PAUL; AND FITZGERALD, JOSEPH A. "The Effect of Hydrocortisone Infusion on Hypnotically Induced Anxiety." *Psychosom Med* 25:158–61 Mr-Ap '63. * (*PA* 38:4347)

96. WEINER, SAMUEL; DORMAN, DANIEL; PERSKY, HAROLD; STARCH, THOMAS W.; NORTON, JAMES; AND LEVITT, EUGENE E. "Effect on Anxiety of Increasing the Plasma Hydrocortisone Level." *Psychosom Med* 25:69–77 Ja-F '63. * (*PA* 37:7705)

97. ZUCKERMAN, MARVIN; LEVINE, SHELDON; AND BIASE, D. VINCENT. "Stress Response in Total and Partial Perceptual Isolation." *Psychosom Med* 26:250–60 My-Je '64. * (*PA* 39:4231)

98. HARROW, MARTIN; COLBERT, JOHN; DETRE, THOMAS; AND BAKEMAN, ROGER. "Symptomatology and Subjective Experiences in Current Depressive States." *Arch Gen Psychiatry* 14:203–12 F '66. * (*PA* 40:5763)

99. KATKIN, EDWARD S. "The Relationship Between a Measure of Transitory Anxiety and Spontaneous Autonomic Activity." *J Abn Psychol* 71:142–6 Ap '66. * (*PA* 40:6201)

100. PERSKY, HAROLD; ZUCKERMAN, MARVIN; BASU, GOPAL K.; AND THORNTON, DORIS. "Psycho-Endocrine Effects of Perceptual and Social Isolation." *Arch Gen Psychiatry* 15:499–505 N '66. * (*PA* 41:2563)

101. WILLIAMS, ALLAN F. "Social Drinking, Anxiety and Depression." *J Pers & Social Psychol* 3:689–93 Je '66. * (*PA* 40:7715)

102. ZUCKERMAN, MARVIN; PERSKY, HAROLD; HOPKINS, T. ROBERT; MURTAUGH, THOMAS; BASU, G. K.; AND SCHILLING, MARY. "Comparison of Stress Effects of Perceptual and Social Isolation." *Arch Gen Psychiatry* 14:356–65 Ap '66. * (*PA* 40:6182)

103. BIASE, D. VINCENT, AND ZUCKERMAN, MARVIN. "Sex Differences in Stress Responses to Total and Partial Sensory Deprivation." *Psychosom Med* 29:380–90 Jl-Ag '67. * (*PA* 42:1602)

104. HODGES, WILLIAM FITZGERALD. *The Effects of Success, Threat of Shock and Failure on Anxiety*. Doctor's thesis, Vanderbilt University (Nashville, Tenn.), 1967. (*DA* 28:4296B)

105. ARMIGER, BERNADETTE. *Pain Perception and Reaction: Response to Carisoprodol and Meprobamate*. Doctor's thesis, St. John's University (Jamaica, N.Y.), 1968. (*DA* 29:4858B)

106. FIEVE, RONALD R.; PLATMAN, STANLEY R.; AND PLUTCHIK, ROBERT R. "The Use of Lithium in Affective Disorders: 2, Prophylaxis of Depression in Chronic Recurrent Affective Disorder." *Am J Psychiatry* 125:492–8 O '68. * (*PA* 43:2721)

107. PERSKY, HAROLD; ZUCKERMAN, MARVIN; AND CURTIS, GEORGE C. "Endocrine Function in Emotionally Disturbed and Normal Men." *J Nerv & Mental Dis* 146:488–97 Je '68. * (*PA* 42:16830)

108. VELTEN, EMMETT, JR. "A Laboratory Task for Induction of Mood States." *Behav Res & Ther* (England) 6:473–82 N '68. * (*PA* 43:9031)

109. GOUAUX, VICTOR CHARLES. *Interpersonal Attraction as a Function of Induced Affect and Social Dependence*. Master's thesis, University of Texas (Austin, Tex.), 1969.

110. ZUCKERMAN, MARVIN; PERSKY, HAROLD; AND LINK, KATHRYN E. "The Influence of Set and Diurnal Factors on Automatic Responses to Sensory Deprivation." *Psychophysiol* 5(6):612–24 My '69. * (*PA* 43:15424)

111. BECKER, CALVIN JAMES. *A Study of Selected Personality Variables Among Three Groups of Sophomore Women Elementary Education Students Classified According to Teacher Attitudes Following an Off Campus Sophomore Aide Experience*. Doctor's thesis, University of North Dakota (Grand Forks, N.D.), 1970. (*DAI* 31:4448A)

112. ELLNER, MELVYN R. *The Effects of Experimentally Induced Frustration Upon Depressed and Nondepressed College Students*. Doctor's thesis, City University of New York (New York, N.Y.), 1970. (*DAI* 31:5619B)

113. KIMBALL, CHASE P. "The Experience of Open Heart Surgery: 2, Determinants of Post-operative Behavior." *Psychother & Psychosom* (Switzerland) 18(1–6):259–74 '70. * (*PA* 47:5515)

114. MEAD, PHILIP G. "The Effect of Orientation Passages on Patient Stress Prior to Dentistry." *Psychol Rec* 20(4):479–88 f '70. * (*PA* 46:638)

115. RUTSTEIN, ELEANOR H. *The Effects of Aggressive Stimulation on Suicidal Patients: An Experimental Study of the*

Psychoanalytic Theory of Suicide. Doctor's thesis, New York University (New York, N.Y.), 1970. (*DAI* 31:7611B)

116. WHITE, HELEN MURIEL. *An Investigation of Some Characteristics of High and Low Self-Actualization and Their Relationship to Alienation From Self and Society.* Doctor's thesis, University of California (Berkeley, Calif.), 1970. (*DAI* 31:5142A)

117. ABRAMSON, EDWARD ERIC. *The Effects of Neurotic Anxiety and Objective Fear on the Eating Behavior of Obese and Normal Weight Individuals.* Doctor's thesis, Catholic University of America (Washington, D.C.), 1971. (*DAI* 32:1201B)

118. ALSIP, JONATHAN E., AND WARD, GEORGE, II. "A Validity Study of Three Group Measures of Hostility and Anxiety Among College Students." *Proc W Va Acad Sci* 42(1970):252–6 '71. *

119. BIASE, D. VINCENT. "Adolescent Heroin Abusers in a Therapeutic Community: Use of MAACL to Assess Emotional Traits and Splitting From Treatment." *J Psychedelic Drugs* 4(2):145–7 w '71. * (*PA* 49:9534)

120. CHEIFETZ, DAVID I.; GARRON, DAVID C.; LEAVITT, FRANK; KLAWANS, HAROLD L.; AND GARVIN, JOHN S. "Emotional Disturbance Accompanying the Treatment of Parkinsonism With L-Dopa." *Clin Pharmacol & Therapeu* 12(1):56–61 Ja–F '71. *

121. CHESS, STEPHEN B.; NEURINGER, CHARLES; AND GOLDSTEIN, GERALD. "Arousal and Field Dependency in Alcoholics." *J General Psychol* 85(1):93–102 Jl '71. * (*PA* 46:11121)

122. CLARK, W. CRAWFORD, AND GREENBERG, DAVID B. "Effect of Stress, Knowledge of Results, and Proactive Inhibition on Verbal Recognition Memory (*d'*) and Response Criterion (*Lx*)." *J Pers & Social Psychol* 17(1):42–7 Ja '71. * (*PA* 45:9336)

123. COWEN, LEON. "Achievement of Specific Treatment Goals Through Day Hospital." *Psychol Rep* 29(3):1206 D '71. * (*PA* 48:1174)

124. DAVIDSON, PARK O., AND WATKINS, ROBERT E. "Repressor-Sensitizer Differences in Psychiatric Patients on Repeated Exposures to Film Induced Stress." *Psychol Rep* 28(1): 159–62 F '71. * (*PA* 46:7155)

125. FLEISS, JOSEPH L.; LAWLOR, WILLIAM; PLATMAN, STANLEY R.; AND FIEVE, RONALD R. "On the Use of Inverted Factor Analysis for Generating Typologies." *J Abn Psychol* 77(2):127–32 Ap '71. * (*PA* 46:3315)

126. GOUAUX, CHARLES. "Induced Affective States and Interpersonal Attraction." *J Pers & Social Psychol* 20(1):37–43 O '71. * (*PA* 47:6713)

127. GOUAUX, CHARLES, AND LAMBERTH, JOHN. "Interpersonal Attraction as a Function of Izard's FIRS Evaluations and Affective States." *Personality* 2(4):289–97 w '71. * (*PA* 48:7145)

128. GRIM, PAUL F. "Anxiety Change Produced by Self-Induced Muscle Tension and by Relaxation With Respiration Feedback." *Behav Ther* 2(1):11–7 Ja '71. * (*PA* 47:9081)

129. HOLMES, DAVID S., AND HOUSTON, B. KENT. "The Defensive Function of Projection." *J Pers & Social Psychol* 20(2):208–13 N '71. * (*PA* 47:6762)

130. HOUSTON, B. KENT. "Trait and Situational Denial and Performance Under Stress." *J Pers & Social Psychol* 18(3):289–93 Je '71. * (*PA* 46:6866)

131. KNOTTS, JAMES DONALD. *A Study of Changes in Self Concepts and Feelings of Graduate Education Students Following Participation in an Encounter Laboratory Training Experience of One Term Duration.* Doctor's thesis, Wayne State University (Detroit, Mich.), 1971. (*DAI* 32:6744A)

132. LAGINA, SUZANNE MAREK. "A Computer Program to Diagnose Anxiety Levels." *Nursing Res* 20(6):484–92 N–D '71. * (*PA* 48:3262)

133. LEHERISSEY, BARBARA L.; O'NEIL, HAROLD F., JR.; HEINRICH, DARLENE L.; AND HANSEN, DUNCAN N. "Effect of Anxiety, Response Mode, Subject Matter Familiarity, and Learning Times on Achievement in Computer-Assisted Learning." Abstract. *Proc 79th Ann Conv Am Psychol Assn* 6(2):537–8 '71. * (*PA* 46:5784)

134. NIELD, MARGARET ANN. "The Effect of Health Teaching on the Anxiety Level of Patients With Chronic Obstructive Lung Disease." *Nursing Res* 20(6):537–41 N–D '71. *

135. PERSKY, HAROLD; SMITH, KEITH D.; AND BASU, GOPAL K. "Relation of Psychologic Measures of Aggression and Hostility to Testosterone Production in Man." *Psychosom Med* 33(3):265–77 My–Je '71. * (*PA* 47:4310)

136. PLATMAN, S. R.; PLUTCHIK, R.; AND WEINSTEIN, BETTE. "Psychiatric, Physiological, Behavioral and Self-Report Measures in Relation to a Suicide Attempt." *J Psychiatric Res* (England) 8(2):127–37 Je '71. * (*PA* 50:7080)

137. PLUTCHIK, R.; PLATMAN, S. R.; AND FIEVE, R. R. "Evaluation of Manic-Depressive States With an Affect Adjective Check List." *J Clin Psychol* 27(3):310–4 Jl '71. * (*PA* 47:5271)

138. RYBACK, RALPH S.; LEWIS, OLIVER F.; AND LESSARD, CHARLES S. "Psychological Effects of Prolonged Bed Rest (Weightless) in Young Healthy Volunteers (Study II)." *Aerospace Med* 42(5):529–35 My '71. *

139. RYBACK, RALPH S.; TRIMBLE, RALPH W.; LEWIS, OLIVER F.; AND JENNINGS, CHARLES L. "Psychobiologic Effects

of Prolonged Weightlessness (Bed Rest) in Young Healthy Volunteers." *Aerospace Med* 42(4):408–15 Ap '71. *

140. TEASDALE, JOHN D., AND BEAUMONT, J. GRAHAM. "The Effect of Mood on Performance on the Modified New Word Learning Test (Walton-Black)." *Brit J Social & Clin Psychol* 10(4):342–5 D '71. * (*PA* 48:1231)

141. TOLOR, ALEXANDER. "Are the Alienated More Suggestible?" *J Clin Psychol* 27(4):441–2 O '71. * (*PA* 47:8886)

142. TOLOR, ALEXANDER, AND LEBLANC, RICHARD F. "Personality Correlates of Alienation." Abstract. *J Consult & Clin Psychol* 37(3):444 D '71. * (*PA* 47:8919)

143. WOODS, DONALD JOSEPH. *Repression-Sensitization, Attitude Towards Emotionality, and Response to a Threatening and Non-Threatening Film.* Doctor's thesis, Northwestern University (Evanston, Ill.), 1971. (*DAI* 32:5464B)

144. ZEDECK, SHELDON. "Identification of Moderator Variables by Discriminant Analysis in a Multipredictable Group Validation Model." *J Appl Psychol* 55(4):364–71 Ag '71. * (*PA* 47:1947)

CUMULATIVE NAME INDEX

O'Neil, H. F.: 133
Opton, E. M.: 46
Paley, H. M.: 91–2
Persky, H.: 6, 22–3, 28, 55, 72, 88–90, 93, 95–6, 100, 102, 107, 110, 135
Piper, W. E.: 82
Platman, S. R.: 70, 83, 106, 125, 136–7
Plutchik, R.: 70, 136–7
Plutchik, R. R.: 106
Price, L.: 7
Ransom, R.: 4
Robins, S.: 10
Roessler, R.: 81, 84
Roscoe, D. L.: 20
Rose, A.: 63
Rosen, H.: 27
Rosmarin, M. S.: 39
Rudorfer, L.: 91–2
Rutstein, E. H.: 115
Ryback, R. S.: 138–9
Schilling, M.: 102
Siller, J.: 3
Smith, K. D.: 135
Smith, W. G.: 15
Smouse, A. D.: 52
Spielberger, C. D.: 36, 45, 51, 67

Starch, T. W.: 96
Stern, R.: 85
Teasdale, J. D.: 140
Thornton, D.: 100
Tolor, A.: 18, 141–2
Trimble, R. W.: 139
Turteltaub, A.: 43
Unger, B. L.: 86
Valerius, E.: 8
Vandiveer, J. M.: 5
Velten, E.: 108
Vogel, L.: 8
Ward, G.: 118
Watkins, R. E.: 124
Weaver, T. T.: 34
Weiner, S.: 96
Weinstein, B.: 83, 136
White, H. M.: 116
Williams, A. F.: 101
Winter, W. D.: 4
Wogan, M.: 82
Woods, D. J.: 143
Zedeck, S.: 144
Zimmerman, W. S.: 20
Zoob, I.: 7
Zuckerman, M.: 1–2, 5, 7–10, 21–3, 28, 40, 53–5, 69, 71–2, 87–8, 94, 97, 100, 102–3, 107, 110

[1294]

Myers-Briggs Type Indicator. Grades 9–16 and adults; 1943–62; MBTI; 4 scores: extraversion vs. introversion, sensation vs. intuition, thinking vs. feeling, judgment vs. perception; Katharine C. Briggs (test) and Isabel Briggs Myers; Educational Testing Service (Atlanta Office). *

For additional information, see P:177 (56 references); for reviews by Gerald A. Mendelsohn and Norman D. Sundberg and an excerpted review by Laurence Siegel, see 6:147 (10 references).

REFERENCES THROUGH 1971

1–10. See 6:147.
11–66. See P:177.
67. HOWARTH, E. "Extroversion and Dream Symbolism: An Empirical Study." *Psychol Rep* 10:211–4 F '62. * (*PA* 37:1469)
68. OWEN, CRAMER. "An Investigation of Creative Potential at the Junior High Level." *Studies Art Ed* 3:16–33 sp '62. *
69. TRANEL, NED. "Effects of Perceptual Isolation on Introverts and Extraverts." *J Psychiatric Res* (England) 1(3):185–92 '62. * (*PA* 39:1898)
70. ISAAC, STEPHEN WILLIAM. *Patterns of Aptitude, Motivation, and Achievement in Mathematics Students.* Doctor's thesis, Claremont Graduate School (Claremont, Calif.), 1963. (*DA* 24:2573)
71. WHITTEMORE, ROBERT GEORGE, JR. *Modification of Originality Responses in Academically Talented, Male University Freshmen.* Doctor's thesis, Arizona State University (Tempe, Ariz.), 1963. (*DA* 25:6403)
72. KNAPP, ROBERT H. "An Experimental Study of a Triadic Hypothesis Concerning the Sources of Aesthetic Imagery." *J Proj Tech & Pers Assess* 28:49–54 Mr '64. * (*PA* 39:1641)
73. BARBEROUSSE, ELEANOR H. *An Investigation of the Variability of Eighth Grade Students' Behavioral Responses on Creativity Criteria, Intelligence, and Sociometric Choices in Relation to Their Jungian Psychological Types.* Doctor's thesis, Auburn University (Auburn, Ala.), 1965. (*DA* 26:5219)
74. COLLINS, JAMES ALBERT. *Individual Personality and Organizational Climate.* Doctor's thesis, Claremont Graduate School (Claremont, Calif.), 1965. (*DA* 27:623A)
75. MCGLOTHLIN, WILLIAM H., AND COHEN, SIDNEY. "The Use of Hallucinogenic Drugs Among College Students." *Am J Psychiatry* 122:572–4 N '65. *
76. PLAXTON, ROBERT P. *Personality of the Principal and School Organizational Climate.* Master's thesis, University of Alberta (Edmonton, Alta., Canada), 1965.
77. WYETH, EZRA R. "Evaluation of the Effectiveness of the Leadership Training Program in the Area of the Deaf at San Fernando Valley State College." *Am Ann Deaf* 110:479–82 S '65. * (*PA* 40:5848)
78. BARRY, ALAN J.; STEINMETZ, JOHN R.; PAGE, HENRY F.; AND RODAHL, KAARE. "The Effects of Physical Conditioning on Older Individuals: 2, Motor Performance and Cognitive Function." *J Gerontol* 21:192–9 Ap '66. *
79. BENNETT, DEWEY EUGENE. *Myers-Briggs Validation of Rorschach Experience Balance.* Master's thesis, San Diego State College (San Diego, Calif.), 1966.
80. BLANTON, WARREN BRADLEY. *Interrelationships Between Selected Aspects of Cognitive Organization of the Social World,*

Self Perception and Overall Mental Health. Doctor's thesis, University of Texas (Austin, Tex.), 1966. (*DA* 27:2868A)
81. BOUCHARD, THOMAS JOSEPH, JR. *Personality, Problem Solving Procedure, and Performance in Small Groups.* Doctor's thesis, University of California (Berkeley, Calif.), 1966. (*DA* 27:3685B)
82. FRETZ, BRUCE R., AND SCHMIDT, LYLE D. "Effects of Teacher-Student Similarity in an Educational Skills Program." Abstract. *Proc 74th Ann Conv Am Psychol Assn* 1:271–2 '66. * (*PA* 41:6264)
83. HELSON, RAVENNA. "Personality of Women With Imaginative and Artistic Interests: The Role of Masculinity, Originality, and Other Characteristics in Their Creativity." *J Personality* 34:1–25 Mr '66. * (*PA* 40:8830)
84. MEYER, PAUL GERHARDT. *Factors Related to Adherence to Denominational Patterns Among Missouri Synod Lutheran College Students.* Doctor's thesis, University of Pittsburgh (Pittsburgh, Pa.), 1966. (*DA* 27:1679A)
85. PHILLIPS, MAURICE. *Trends in a Visual Satiation Effect in Relation to Extraversion.* Doctor's thesis, New York University (New York, N.Y.), 1966. (*DA* 27:4132B)
86. POE, CHARLES ALFRED. *Placement in Heath's Model of Personality: Reliability and Assessment.* Doctor's thesis, University of Missouri (Columbus, Mo.), 1966. (*DA* 27:3276B)
87. QUENK, NAOMI LITT. *Fantasy and Personal Outlook: A Study of Daydreaming as a Function of Optimism, Pessimism, Realism, and Anxiety.* Doctor's thesis, University of California (Berkeley, Calif.), 1966. (*DA* 27:970B)
88. ROSSI, A. MICHAEL, AND SOLOMON, PHILIP. "Effects of Sensory Deprivation on Introverts and Extraverts: A Failure to Find Reported Differences." *J Psychiatric Res* (England) 4:115–25 N '66. * (*PA* 41:3820)
89. STANFIEL, JAMES DONALD. *The Jungian Typology, Neuroticism, and Field-Dependence.* Doctor's thesis, Duke University (Durham, N.C.), 1966. (*DA* 27:618B)
90. AHNELL, INGEMAR V. *A Study of Relationships Between the Personal Characteristics of Elementary School Principals and Their Evaluations of Teachers.* Doctor's thesis, University of Kansas (Lawrence, Kan.), 1967. (*DA* 28:3395A)
91. BREIMEIER, KENNETH H. *Relationship Between Various Psychological Measures in Use at Theological Seminaries.* Comments by James E. Dittes. Occasional Papers No. 1. Washington, D.C.: Ministry Studies Board, 1967. Pp. iii, 59.*
92. CONNELLY, WILLIAM. "Empathy, Ego Drive and the Pharmaceutical Salesman." *Pharma Marketing & Media* 2:15+ D '67. *
93. GOODELL, JUDITH ANNE. *An Investigation of Personality Characteristics of Psychotherapists According to Jungian Theory.* Master's thesis, Sacramento State College (Sacramento, Calif.), 1967.
94. MEARA, NAOMI MARIE. *A Factor Analytic Study of the Relationship Between Attitudinal Variables and Academic Learning.* Doctor's thesis, Ohio State University (Columbus, Ohio), 1967. (*DA* 28:3468A)
95. SIMMONS, JUDY ROBERSON. *An Investigation of the Interrelationships of Jungian Personality Types Within Families.* Master's thesis, Auburn University (Auburn, Ala.), 1967.
96. VANDENBERG, STEVEN G. "Hereditary Factors in Normal Personality Traits (as Measured by Inventories)." *Recent Adv Biol Psychiatry* 9:65–104 '67. *
97. WEBB, SAM C. *The Relations of College Grades and Personal Qualities Considered Within Two Frames of Reference.* Multivariate Behavioral Research Monographs, No. 67–2. Ft. Worth, Tex.: Texas Christian University Press, 1967. Pp. 53. * (*PA* 42:9511)
98. BURT, ROGER BIVENS. *An Exploratory Study of Personality Manifestations in Paintings.* Doctor's thesis, Duke University (Durham, N.C.), 1968. (*DA* 29:1493B)
99. BUSH, MARSHALL. *A Study of Reality-Closeness-Reality-Distance: A Directional Determinant of Attention Deployment.* Doctor's thesis, University of Michigan (Ann Arbor, Mich.), 1968. (*DA* 29:1168B)
100. CARLSON, RAE, AND LEVY, NISSIM. "Brief Method for Assessing Social-Personal Orientation." *Psychol Rep* 23:911–4 D '68. * (*PA* 43:9702)
101. GREENFIELD, MURRAY. *The Typologies of Pulpit and Nonpulpit Rabbis.* Doctor's thesis, Rutgers—The State University (New Brunswick, N.J.), 1968. (*DA* 29:2114A)
102. HATFIELD, ROBERT C. *A Study of the Relationships of Selected Components of Creativity, Cognitive Style, and Self-Concept Identified in a Random Sample of Twelfth Grade Students in One High School With Their Learning of Selected Information in the Social Studies.* Doctor's thesis, Wayne State University (Detroit, Mich.), 1968. (*DAI* 30:1334A)
103. HELSON, RAVENNA. "Effects of Sibling Characteristics and Parental Values on a Creative Interest and Achievement." *J Personality* 36:589–607 D '68. * (*PA* 43:6923)
104. JONES, HENRY TWYMAN. *The Relationship of Counselor-Client Personality Similarity to Counseling Process and Outcome.* Doctor's thesis, University of Missouri (Columbia, Mo.), 1968. (*DA* 29:2962A)
105. KING, STANLEY H. "Characteristics of Students Seeking Psychiatric Help During College." *J Am Col Health Assn* 17:150–6 D '68. *

106. Mehrotra, Chandra Mohan Nath. *Behavioral Cognition as Related to Interpersonal Perception and Some Personality Traits of College Students.* Doctor's thesis, Ohio State University (Columbus, Ohio), 1968. (*DAI* 30:372B)

107. Rader, Blaine Burdette. *Identification of Selected Personality Characteristics Which Make for Effectiveness in Pastoral Care.* Doctor's thesis, Drew University (Madison, N.J.), 1968. (*DA* 29:1849B)

108. Reddy, Michael Joseph. *Accuracy, Assimilation and Sterotyping in Married Couples' Predictions of Each Others' Responses on the Myers-Briggs Type Indicator.* Master's thesis, Ohio State University (Columbus, Ohio), 1968.

109. Schmidt, Lyle D., and Fretz, Bruce R. "Teacher-Student Similarity in an Educational Skills Course." *J Exp Ed* 36:78–83 su '68. *

110. Sigmund, Carol Brown. *Personality Traits of Nurses Who Give Nursing Care to Children.* Master's thesis, Ohio State University (Columbus, Ohio), 1968.

111. Sindt, Doris M. *An Investigation of the Relationship Between the Intolerance of Ambiguity Dimension of the Counselor's Personality and Counseling Behaviors and Certain Other Personality Dimensions.* Doctor's thesis, University of Kansas (Lawrence, Kan.), 1968. (*DA* 29:1759A)

112. Spare, Geraldine Hallam. *A Study of the Law of Enantiadromia, as It Relates to the Attitudes of Introversion-Extraversion.* Doctor's thesis, Washington State University (Pullman, Wash.), 1968. (*DA* 29:1850B)

113. Sutch, Marjorie Anne. *Personality Characteristics of a Group of Freshmen Home Economics Students as Measured by the Myers-Briggs Type Indicator.* Master's thesis, Cornell University (Ithaca, N.Y.), 1968.

114. Barrett, Michael Jerome. *Some Behavioral Attributes of Professional Audit Independence.* Doctor's thesis, University of Colorado (Boulder, Colo.), 1969. (*DAI* 30:4543A)

115. Bouchard, Thomas J., Jr. "Personality, Problem-Solving Procedure, and Performance in Small Groups." *J Appl Psychol Monogr* 53(1, pt 2):1–29 F '69. * (*PA* 43:6351)

116. Bown, Oliver H., and Richek, Herbert G. "Teachers-To-Be: Extraversion/Introversion and Self-Perceptions." *El Sch J* 70(3):164–70 D '69. * (*PA* 48:1783)

117. Caine, T. M., and Smail, D. J. "The Effects of Personality and Training on Attitudes to Treatment: Preliminary Investigations." *Brit J Med Psychol* 42(3):277–82 Ag '69. * (*PA* 44:6850)

118. Carlson, Rae, and Parker, Janet. "Personality and Esthetic Sensitivity." *J Proj Tech & Pers Assess* 33(6):530–4 D '69. * (*PA* 44:6749)

119. Clark, Agnes Lorraine Howard. *The Relationship of Selected Physiological Factors to Interpersonal Encounters.* Doctor's thesis, East Texas State University (Commerce, Tex.), 1969. (*DAI* 30:5228A)

120. Davis, Corrine Ray. *Personality Type Discrepancies and Student Teacher—Cooperating Teacher Relationships.* Doctor's thesis, East Texas State University (Commerce, Tex.), 1969. (*DAI* 31:260A)

121. Dobyns, Zipporah Pottenger. *A Comparison of Hippies and College Students With Respect to Beliefs, Attitudes, and Personality.* Doctor's thesis, University of Arizona (Tucson, Ariz.), 1969. (*DAI* 30:2415B)

122. Eigenbrod, Frederick A., Jr. *The Effects of Territory and Personality Compatability on Identity and Security.* Doctor's thesis, Michigan State University (East Lansing, Mich.), 1969. (*DAI* 30:2329A)

123. Fitzgerald, Owen Ray. *Psychodynamics of Volunteers Serving Overseas: Religious Vocation Workers and Peace Corps Volunteers in a North African Country.* Doctor's thesis, Boston University (Boston, Mass.), 1969. (*DAI* 30:2126A)

124. Greenfield, Murray. "Typologies of Persisting and Nonpersisting Jewish Clergymen." *J Counsel Psychol* 16(4): 368–72 Jl '69. * (*PA* 43:14193)

125. Hall, Wallace B., and MacKinnon, Donald W. "Personality Inventory Correlates of Creativity Among Architects." *J Appl Psychol* 53(4):322–6 Ag '69. * (*PA* 43:15815)

126. Hogan, Robert. "Development of an Empathy Scale." *J Consult & Clin Psychol* 33(3):307–16 Je '69. * (*PA* 43:12966)

127. Kooyumjian, Mary Louise Van Heule. *Cognitive Achievement Through Independent Study in Summer Programs in Continuing Education.* Doctor's thesis, University of Illinois (Urbana, Ill.), 1969. (*DAI* 30:3349A)

128. Penfold, D. M., and Meldon, R. P. "Social Sensitivity in Relation to Teaching Competence." *Ed Res* (England) 12(1): 64–6 N '69. *

129. Praul, Judith Ann. *The Relationship of Personality Variables to Selected Outcomes of the Counselor Training Process.* Doctor's thesis, Indiana University (Bloomington, Ind.), 1969. (*DAI* 31:161A)

130. Richek, Herbert G. "Jung's Typology and Psychological Adjustment in Prospective Teachers: A Preliminary Investigation." *Alberta J Ed Res* (Canada) 15(4):235–43 D '69. * (*PA* 46:1846)

131. Richek, Herbert G. "A Note on Differentiating Prospective Elementary and Secondary School Teachers." *Alberta J Ed Res* (Canada) 15(3):159–63 S '69. * (*PA* 44:9331)

132. Richek, Herbert G. "Note on Intercorrelations of

Scales of the Myers-Briggs Type Indicator." *Psychol Rep* 25(1): 28–30 Ag '69. * (*PA* 44:3640)

133. Shapiro, Kenneth J., and Alexander, Irving E. "Extraversion-Introversion, Affiliation, and Anxiety." *J Personality* 37(3):387–406 S '69. * (*PA* 44:6758)

134. Terrill, Jerry Lee. *Correlates of Counselor Role Perception.* Doctor's thesis, University of Colorado (Boulder, Colo.), 1969. (*DAI* 31:166A)

135. Thompson, Charles L. "The Secondary School Counselor's Ideal Client." *J Counsel Psychol* 16(1):69–74 Ja '69. * (*PA* 43:5929)

136. Wotruba, Richard T. "Can Residence Hall Staff Be Selected Scientifically?" *NASPA* 7(2):107–11 O '69. *

137. Asbury, Frank R.; Ball, Robert L.; and Constantino, Nicholas V. "Some General Effects of a Foundations of Education Course on Selected Personality Variables of Teacher Candidates." *J Stud Pers Assn Teach Ed* 9(1):23–32 f '70. * (*PA* 46:5604)

138. Blank, Logan Fink. *Relationship Between Student Instructional Ratings and Student-Faculty Psychological Types.* Doctor's thesis, Michigan State University (East Lansing, Mich.), 1970. (*DAI* 31:2123A)

139. Cohn, Rebecca Roddey. *The Tennessee Self Concept Scale as a Differentiator of Delinquent Female Subgroups.* Doctor's thesis, University of Oklahoma (Norman, Okla.), 1970. (*DAI* 31:2979B)

140. Dunning, James E. *Values and Humanities Study: An Operational Analysis of the Humanities Using the Myers-Briggs Type Indicator.* Doctor's thesis, Claremont Graduate School (Claremont, Calif.), 1970. (*DAI* 32:785A)

141. Erickson, Clara; Gantz, Benjamin S.; and Stephenson, Robert W. "Logical and Construct Validation of a Short-Form Biographical Inventory Predictor of Scientific Creativity." Abstract. *Proc 78th Ann Conv Am Psychol Assn* 5(1):151–2 '70. * (*PA* 44:18715)

142. Fischer, Roland; Kappeler, Thomas; Wisecup, Philip; and Thatcher, Karen. "Personality Trait Dependent Performance Under Psilocybin." *Dis Nerv System* 31(2):91–101 F '70. * (*PA* 44:12634)

143. Garrison, Nelson. *Instructor-Student Compatibility: A Study of the Effects of Personality Similarity on Academic Performance.* Doctor's thesis, Duke University (Durham, N.C.), 1970. (*DAI* 31:5199A)

144. Gaston, Joseph Alexander. *A Comparison of the Personality Characteristics of Northern and Midwestern Urban Afro-American Freshmen, Southern Town and Rural Afro-American Freshmen, and Southern Afro-American College Student Personnel Staff.* Doctor's thesis, Michigan State University (East Lansing, Mich.), 1970. (*DAI* 31:5843A)

145. Grant, W. Harold, and Eigenbrod, Frederick A., Jr. "Behavioral Change Influenced by Structured Peer Group Activities." *J Col Stud Personnel* 11(4):291–5 Jl '70. * (*PA* 45: 4885)

146. Grass, Paul Louis. *Differential Effects of Short-Term Small-Group Interaction on the Behavioral Development of College Freshmen According to Personality Type.* Doctor's thesis, Michigan State University (East Lansing, Mich.), 1970. (*DAI* 32:196A)

147. Helson, Ravenna, and Crutchfield, Richard S. "Creative Types in Mathematics." *J Personality* 38(2):177–97 Je '70. * (*PA* 44:18669)

148. Hill, David Oliver. *Extraversion-Introversion: An Investigation of Typological Theory.* Doctor's thesis, Texas Tech University (Lubbock, Tex.), 1970. (*DAI* 31:6257B)

149. Hogan, Robert. "A Dimension of Moral Judgement." *J Consult & Clin Psychol* 35(2):205–12 O '70. * (*PA* 45:4239)

150. Jensen, John A., and Schmitt, John A. "The Influence of Test Title on Test Response." *J Ed Meas* 7(4):241–5 w '70. * (*PA* 45:8244)

151. Klavetter, Robert E.; Mogar, Robert E.; and Watt, James. "Changes on the Myers-Briggs Following Psychedelic Therapy: A Pilot Study." *Psychol Rep* 26(2):510 Ap '70. * (*PA* 44:21140)

152. Lahey, Henry Charles. *Personality Differentiation of Elevated Outdoor and Literary Kuder Preference Record Scales in an Urban Population.* Doctor's thesis, University of Connecticut (Storrs, Conn.), 1970. (*DAI* 31:1014A)

153. Lordahl, Josephine Ann. *The Effect in a Counseling Analog of Manipulated Client-Counselor Similarity on Three Outcome Measures.* Doctor's thesis, Florida State University (Tallahassee, Fla.), 1970. (*DAI* 31:4466A)

154. Marshall, Nancy Jean Chapman. *Orientations Toward Privacy: Environmental and Personality Components.* Doctor's thesis, University of California (Berkeley, Calif.), 1970. (*DAI* 31:4315B)

155. Ohnmacht, Fred W. "Personality and Cognitive Referents of Creativity: A Second Look." *Psychol Rep* 26(1):336–8 F '70. * (*PA* 45:4267)

156. Pellegrin, Victor Bruce Holker. *A Descriptive Study of a Midwestern Sample of Episcopal Clergy and Seminarians Categorized According to Various Criteria.* Doctor's thesis, University of Kansas (Lawrence, Kan.), 1970. (*DAI* 31:2690A)

157. Reekie, Elagrace. *Personality Factors and Biographical Characteristics Associated With Criterion Behaviors of Success*

in Professional Nursing. Doctor's thesis, University of Washington (Seattle, Wash.), 1970. (*DAI* 31:5212A)

158. REIFF, DELBERT JOHN. *Some Effects of Personality Type and Certain Selected Characteristics on the Interpersonal Relationships Between Doctoral Advisers and Advisees at the University of Northern Colorado.* Doctor's thesis, University of Northern Colorado (Greeley, Colo.), 1970. (*DAI* 31:6367A)

159. REYNOLDS, RICHARD J., AND HOPE, AMY G. "Typology as a Moderating Variable in Success in Science." *Psychol Rep* 26(3):711-6 Je '70. * (*PA* 45:1363)

160. RICHEK, HERBERT G. "A Comparison of Characteristics of Prospective Secondary School Teachers Enrolled in Two Different Degree Programs." *Calif J Ed Res* 21(5):204-7 N '70. * (*PA* 46:3812)

161. SMITH, EARL PEARSON. *An Investigation Into the Relationship Between Selected Personal and Professional Characteristics of Teachers and Their Preferences for Behavioral Objectives.* Doctor's thesis, Syracuse University (Syracuse, N.Y.), 1970. (*DAI* 31:2798A)

162. SMITH, RONALD AUBREY. *The Relationship Between the Type Theory and the Personality Growth Theory of Carl Jung and the Helping Relationship Theory of Carl Rogers.* Doctor's thesis, University of California (Los Angeles, Calif.), 1970. (*DAI* 31:4344B)

163. THATCHER, KAREN; KAPPELER, THOMAS; WISECUP, PHILIP; AND FISCHER, ROLAND. "Personality Trait Dependent Performance Under Psilocybin, Part II." *Dis Nerv System* 31(3):181-92 Mr '70. * (*PA* 44:12034)

164. TSCHRITTER, RICHARD E. *A Comparison of Personality Characteristics of Prospective and Practicing Elementary Teachers.* Master's thesis, University of Victoria (Victoria, B.C., Canada), 1970.

165. WALTON, JOSEPH MOSES. *Predicting the Success of Prospective Teachers in an Urban Teacher Education Project.* Doctor's thesis, Ohio State University (Columbus, Ohio), 1970. (*DAI* 32:190A)

166. BISSIRI, GERALD RICHARD. *Adolescent Negativism, Field-Independence and the Development of Integrated Structures.* Doctor's thesis, Claremont Graduate School (Claremont, Calif.), 1971. (*DAI* 32:2981B)

167. BRAUN, JOSEPH ADAMS. *The Empathic Ability of Psychotherapists as Related to Therapist Perceptual Flexibility and Professional Experience, Patient Insight, and Therapist-Patient Similarity.* Doctor's thesis, Fordham University (New York, N.Y.), 1971. (*DAI* 32:2391B)

168. DURFEE, RICHARD. "Personality Characteristics and Attitudes Toward the Disabled of Students in the Health Professions." *Rehabil Counsel B* 15(1):35-44 S '71. * (*PA* 47:8980)

169. GANTZ, BENJAMIN S., JR.; ERICKSON, CLARA; AND STEPHENSON, ROBERT W. "Measuring the Motivation to Manage in a Research and Development Population." Abstract. *Proc 79th Ann Conv Am Psychol Assn* 6(1):129-30 '71. * (*PA* 46:3949)

170. HARVEY, RAYMOND CHESTERFIELD, JR. *The Relationship of Study Habits and Attitudes to College Subcultures and to Personality Types.* Doctor's thesis, East Texas State University (Commerce, Tex.), 1971. (*DAI* 32:6030B)

171. KANITZ, HUGO EDWARD. *Predicting Effectiveness in Potential Teachers.* Doctor's thesis, Ohio State University (Columbus, Ohio), 1971. (*DAI* 32:1855A)

172. LESSIG, V. PARKER, AND TOLLEFSON, JOHN O. "Market Segmentation Through Taxonomy." *J Marketing Res* 8(4):480-7 N '71. *

173. LIVINGSTON, GAYLE BORDEN. *A Correlational Analysis of Modes of Perception and Judgment and Measures of Self-Concept.* Doctor's thesis, Washington State University (Pullman, Wash.), 1971. (*DAI* 32:182A)

174. LUCASSE, PHILIP ROGER. *The Effect of Certain Personality Variables Within the Student Teacher-Cooperating Teacher Dyad on the Outcomes of the Student Teaching Experience.* Doctor's thesis, University of Michigan (Ann Arbor, Mich.), 1971. (*DAI* 32:6272A)

175. MCGLOTHLIN, WILLIAM H., AND ARNOLD, DAVID O. "LSD Revisited: A Ten-Year Follow-Up of Medical LSD Use." *Arch Gen Psychiatry* 24(1):35-49 Ja '71. * (*PA* 45:9496)

176. MACKINNON, DONALD W. "Creativity and Transliminal Experience." *J Creative Behav* 5(4):227-41 '71. * (*PA* 48:7233)

177. MARTRAY, CARL RICHARD. *An Empirical Investigation Into the Learning Styles and Retention Patterns of Various Personality Types.* Doctor's thesis, University of Alabama (University, Ala.), 1971. (*DAI* 32:5043A)

178. NEVILLE, WILLIAM GORDON. *An Analysis of Personality Types and Their Differential Response to Marital Enrichment Groups.* Doctor's thesis, University of Florida (Gainesville, Fla.), 1971. (*DAI* 32:6766A)

179. NORTON, WILLIAM KIRK, JR. *Empathic Ability and Adjustment in Marriage.* Doctor's thesis, Florida State University (Tallahassee, Fla.), 1971. (*DAI* 32:6571A)

180. SMITH, DOUGLAS DUANE. *A Study of Learner Characteristics and Computer Assisted Instruction Decision Making.* Doctor's thesis, Ohio State University (Columbus, Ohio), 1971. (*DAI* 32:6018A)

181. STROOPS, SYLVIA LYNN. *Personality Types and Vocational Interests of Women Students Majoring in Two Different Areas of Teacher Education.* Doctor's thesis, University of Alabama (University, Ala.), 1971. (*DAI* 32:5027A)

182. TAUFER, FLORENCE JOY. *Personality Change in Teachers After Participating in Human Relations Interaction Groups.* Master's thesis, California State College (Long Beach, Calif.), 1971.

183. VEACH, TRACY L., AND TOUHEY, JOHN C. "Personality Correlates of Accurate Time Perception." *Percept & Motor Skills* 33(3):765-6 D '71. * (*PA* 48:984)

184. WILSON, JACK THOMAS. *The Relationship Between Personality Type and Student Perception of Head Resident Effectiveness.* Doctor's thesis, University of Northern Colorado (Greeley, Colo.), 1971. (*DAI* 32:3735A)

185. WITTMEYER, ALMA L.; CAMISCIONI, JOHN S.; AND PURDY, PATRICIA A. "A Longitudinal Study of Attrition and Academic Performance in a Collegiate Nursing Program." *Nursing Res* 20(4):339-47 Jl-Ag '71. *

186. YURA, MICHAEL THOMAS. *The Personality Traits and Vocational Interests of Guidance Students.* Doctor's thesis, Ohio State University (Columbus, Ohio), 1971. (*DAI* 32:3711A)

CUMULATIVE NAME INDEX

Richardson, R. L.: 34
Richek, H. G.: 40, 64, 116, 130–2, 160
Richter, R. H.: 44
Rodahl, K.: 78
Ross, J.: 5, 7, 9–10, 36, 45
Rossi, A. M.: 35, 88
Schiffman, H.: 36
Schmidt, L. D.: 50, 82, 109
Schmitt, J. A.: 150
Sease, W. A.: 20
Shapiro, K. J.: 133
Siegel, L.: exc, 6:147
Sigmund, C. B.: 110
Simmons, J. R.: 95
Sindt, D. M.: 111
Smail, D. J.: 117
Smith, D. D.: 180
Smith, E. P.: 161
Smith, R. A.: 162
Solomon, P.: 35, 88
Spare, G. H.: 112
Splaver, C.: 49
Stalcup, D. L. K.: 57
Stanfiel, J. D.: 89
Steele, F. I.: 65
Steinmetz, J. R.: 78
Stephenson, R. W.: 141, 169
Stevens, T. G.: 58

Stricker, L. J.: 7, 9–10, 36
Stroops, S. L.: 181
Sundberg, N. D.: rev, 6:147
Sutch, M. A.: 113
Taufer, F. J.: 182
Taylor, R. E.: 66
Terrill, J. L.: 134
Thatcher, K.: 142, 163
Thompson, C. L.: 135
Tollefson, J. O.: 172
Touhey, J. C.: 183
Tranel, N.: 69
Tschritter, R. E.: 164
Vandenberg, S. G.: 96
Vaughan, J. A.: 8
Veach, T. L.: 183
Walter, J. I.: 59
Walton, J. M.: 165
Watt, J.: 151
Webb, S. C.: 21–2, 97
Whittemore, R. G.: 37, 71
Wilson, J. T.: 184
Winter, W. D.: 44
Wisecup, P.: 49, 142, 163
Wittmeyer. A. L.: 185
Wotruba, R. T.: 136
Wright, J. A.: 46
Wyeth, E. R.: 77
Yura, M. T.: 186

[1295]

The Neuroticism Scale Questionnaire. Ages 13
and over; 1961; NSQ; test booklet title is *NSQ*; the
still-in-print *IPAT Neurotic Personality Factor Test*
is "an earlier version" of this test; 5 scores: depres-
siveness, submissiveness, overprotection, anxiety, total;
Ivan H. Scheier and Raymond B. Cattell; Institute for
Personality and Ability Testing. *

For additional information, see P:178 (10 references) ; for reviews by E. Lowell Kelly and Jerome D.
Pauker and an excerpted review by John O. Crites (reply by Ivan H. Scheier), see 6:148 (1 reference).

REFERENCES THROUGH 1971

1. See 6:148.
2–11. See P:178.
12. Puttick, Winston Hugh. *A Factor Analytic Study of Positive Modes of Experiencing and Behaving in a Teacher College Population.* Doctor's thesis, University of Florida (Gainesville. Fla.), 1964. (*DA* 29:817A)
13. Weinreb, Anita Cyrele. *An Experimental Investigation of the Relationship Between Two Personality Variables (Anxiety and Neuroticism) and Perception of Non-Verbal Vocal Communication of Feeling.* Doctor's thesis. New York University (New York, N.Y.), 1965. (*DA* 27:307B)
14. Colwell, J. J. Kear. "The Consistency of Measurement of the N.S.Q. in Normal and Patient Populations." Abstract. *B Brit Psychol Soc* 19:A3–4 Ap '66. *
15. Harris, George Alexander. *Interpersonal Sensitivity in the Counselor-Client Relationship.* Doctor's thesis, University of Southern Mississippi (Hattiesburg, Miss.), 1967. (*DA* 28:3462A)
16. Popejoy, Dorothy Imogene. *The Effects of a Physical Fitness Program on Selected Psychological and Physiological Measures of Anxiety.* Doctor's thesis, University of Illinois (Urbana, Ill.), 1967. (*DA* 28:4900A)
17. Ax, Albert F., and Bamford, Jacqueline L. "Validation of a Psychophysiological Test of Aptitude for Learning Social Motives." *Psychophysiol* 5:316–32 S '68. * (*PA* 43:3943)
18. Bottrill, John H. "Effectiveness of an Adjustment Course for Those Recently Rendered Blind." *Percept & Motor Skills* 26:366 Ap '68. * (*PA* 42:12569)
19. Cooper, Alan J. "'Neurosis' and Disorders of Sexual Potency in the Male." *J Psychosom Res* (England) 12:141–4 Ag '68. * (*PA* 43:8478)
20. Huggan, R. E. "Neuroticism and Anxiety Among Women With Cancer." *J Psychosom Res* (England) 12:215–21 O '68. * (*PA* 43:8627)
21. Bottrill, John H. "Personality Change in LSD Users." *J General Psychol* 80(2):157–61 Ap '69. * (*PA* 43:11280)
22. Cooper, Alan J. "Some Personality Factors in Frigidity." *J Psychosom Res* (England) 13(2):149–56 Je '69. * (*PA* 44:12563)
23. Fabian, Judith Janaro. *Comparison of Theoretical Viewpoints and Empirical Measures of Neuroticism.* Doctor's thesis, University of California (Los Angeles, Calif.), 1969. (*DAI* 30:4369B)
24. Jarrahi-Zadeh, Ali; Kane, F. J., Jr.; Van de Castle, R. L.; Lachenbruch, P. A.; and Ewing, J. A. "Emotional and Cognitive Changes in Pregnancy and Early Puerperium." *Brit J Psychiatry* 115(524):797–805 Jl '69. * (*PA* 44:6605)
25. Kear-Colwell, J. J. "Neuroticism (Cattell) and Its Relationship to the Presence of Neurotic Symptomatology." *Multiv Behav Res* 4(2):223–33 Ap '69. * (*PA* 43:16005)
26. Mihalick, Ronald Eugene. *Values and Psychotherapy.* Doctor's thesis, Ohio University (Athens, Ohio), 1969. (*DAI* 30:4377B)
27. Miller, Jon P., and Hagedorn, Robert B. "The Relationship Between Self-Images and Anxiety and Neurosis." *Pac Sociol R* 12(2):109–17 f '69. *
28. Parnes, Phyllis Sally. *Adolescent Daughters of Emotionally Ill Mothers: Their Psycho-Social and Physical Adaptive Behavior.* Doctor's thesis, Boston University (Boston, Mass.), 1969. (*DAI* 30:3251B)
29. Alp, M. H.; Court, J. H.; and Grant, A. Kerr. "Personality Pattern and Emotional Stress in the Genesis of Gastric Ulcer." *Gut* (England) 11(9):773–7 S '70. *
30. Anumonye, Amechi. "Personality Factors and Barbiturate Dependence." *Brit J Addict* 64(3–4):365–70 Ja '70. *
31. Gerstein, Offra Bilha. *The Relationship Between Perception of Parental Behavior, Level of Dependency, and Vocational Interest Pattern in Hemophilic Young Adults.* Doctor's thesis, New York University (New York, N.Y.), 1970. (*DAI* 31:6401A)
32. Philip, Alistair E., and McCulloch, J. W. "Test-Retest Characteristics of a Group of Attempted Suicide Patients." *J Consult & Clin Psychol* 34(2):144–7 Ap '70. * (*PA* 44:10778)
33. Fabian, Judith Janaro, and Comrey, Andrew L. "Construct Validation of Factored Neuroticism Scales." *Multiv Behav Res* 6(3):287–99 Jl '71. * (*PA* 47:4817)
34. Hamilton, Larry Kendall. *The Relationship Between Self-Disclosure and Neuroticism.* Doctor's thesis, Northwestern University (Evanston, Ill.), 1971. (*DAI* 32:3635B)
35. Kane, Francis J.; Lachenbruch, Peter A.; Lokey, Lee; Chafetz, Neil; Auman, Richard; Pocuis, Leo; and Lipton, Morris A. "Post-Partum Depression in Southern Black Women." *Dis Nerv System* 32(7):486–9 Jl '71. * (*PA* 47:7224)
36. Liakos, A., and Crisp, A. H. "Pupil Size in Psychoneurotic Patients: A Psychophysiological and Psychometric Investigation." *Psychother & Psychosom* (Switzerland) 19(1–2): 104–10 '71. * (*PA* 47:5250)
37. Philip, Alistair E. "Psychometric Changes Associated With Response to Drug Treatment." *Brit J Social & Clin Psychol* 10(2):138–43 Je '71. *
38. Schneider, L. Ronald, and Stevens, Nancy D. "Personality Characteristics Associated With Job-Seeking Behavior Patterns." *Voc Guid Q* 19(3):194–200 Mr '71. * (*PA* 48:1959)

CUMULATIVE NAME INDEX

[1296]

The New Junior Maudsley Inventory. Ages 9–16;
1961–67; NJMI; 3 scores: neuroticism, extraversion,
lie; 2 editions; W. D. Furneaux and H. B. Gibson. *
a) british edition. 1961–66; University of London
Press Ltd. [England].
b) united states edition. 1966–67; for research use
only; Educational and Industrial Testing Service. *Out
of print.*

For additional information and reviews by Philip E.
Vernon and Robert D. Wirt, see 7:113 (9 references) ;
see also P:179 (17 references).

REFERENCES THROUGH 1971

1–17. See P:179.
18–26. See 7:113.
27. COSTELLO, C. G., AND EYSENCK, H. J. "Persistence, Personality, and Motivation." *Percept & Motor Skills* 12:169–70 Ap '61. * (*PA* 36:1HJ69C)
28. REED, G. F., AND FRANCIS, T. R. "Drive, Personality, and Audiometric Response Consistency." *Percept & Motor Skills* 15:681–2 D '62. * (*PA* 38:1673)
29. ZAHRAN, HAMED A. S. "A Study of Personality Differences Between Blind and Sighted Children." *Brit J Ed Psychol* 35:329–38 N '65. * (*PA* 40:3278)
30. SLEE, F. W. "The Feminine Image Factor in Girls' Attitudes to School Subjects." *Brit J Ed Psychol* 38:212–4 Je '68. * (*PA* 42:17636)
31. WILSON, J. A. "Personality and Attainment in the Primary School: 1, Personality Structure of Ten-Year-Olds." *Res Ed* (England) 6:12–23 N '71. * (*PA* 48:12254)

CUMULATIVE NAME INDEX

Anderson, C. C.: 11
Brachman, H. M.: 3, 5
Callard, M. P.: 2
Child, D.: 6, 12
Clarke, R. V. G.: 23
Costello, C. G.: 3, 5, 27
Cropley, A. J.: 8, 11
D'Aoust, B. R.: 8
Eysenck, H. J.: 27
Forrest, A. R.: 25
Francis, T. R.: 28
Furneaux, W. D.: 1
Gibson, H. B.: 1, 4, 7, 13, 20–1
Goodfellow, C. L.: 2
Harbison, J. J. M.: 24
Hoghughi, M. S.: 25
Lytton, H.: 19

McAllister, J.: 22
Marshall, T. F.: 22
Martin, D. N.: 23
Mehryar, A. H.: 14, 26
Reed, G. F.: 28
Regan, G.: 15
Shamberg, N. S.: 16
Shapiro, M. A.: 17
Shapurian, R.: 26
Slee, F. W.: 30
Stembridge, D. E.: 9
Vernon, P. E.: *rev*, 7:113
Whiting, H. T. A.: 9
Wilson, J. A.: 31
Wirt, R. D.: *rev*, 7:113
Yates, A. J.: 18
Young, G. C.: 10
Zahran, H. A. S.: 29

[1297]
Northampton Activity Rating Scale. Mental patients; 1951; NARS; "behavior exhibited by mental patients in rehabilitation and activity therapies of the hospital environment"; Isidor W. Scherer; the Author. *

For additional information, see P:180.

[1298]
Nurses' Observation Scale for Inpatient Evaluation. Mental patients; 1965–66; NOSIE; manual title is *NOSIE-30: A Treatment-Sensitive Ward Behavior Scale;* 7 scores: social competence, social interest, personal neatness, irritability, manifest psychosis, retardation, total; Gilbert Honigfeld, Roderic D. Gillis, and C. James Klett (manual); Behavior Arts Center. *

For additional information, see 7:114 (24 references).

REFERENCES THROUGH 1971

1–24. See 7:114.
25. BEARD, MARGARET T., AND BIDUS, DONALD R. "A Study of the Effects of Remotivation on Social Competence, Social Interest and Personal Neatness." *J Psychiatric Nursing* 6:197–201 Jl–Ag '68. * (*PA* 45:6931)
26. NEEDHAM, R. F. H., AND BLIGNAULT, W. J. "A Comparison of an Acridan Derivative (Smith Kline and French 14336) and Trifluoperazine in the Treatment of Chronic Schizophrenia." *Med J Austral* 2(11):550–3 S 13 '69. * (*PA* 45:1068)
27. RAVENSBORG, MILTON ROBERT. *An Operant Conditioning Approach to Increasing Interpersonal Awareness Among Chronic Schizophrenics.* Doctor's thesis, University of Minnesota (Minneapolis, Minn.), 1970. (*DAI* 32:569B)
28. WOLPERT, A.; WHITE, L.; DANA, J.; SUGERMAN, A. A.; ARENGO, A. D.; SIMPSON, G. M.; BISHOP, M. P.; AND GALLANT, D. M. "Clinical Pharmacological Trial of Loxapine Succinate." *J Clin Pharmacol* 10(3):175–81 My–Je '70. * (*PA* 45:4664)
29. CLARK, MERVIN L.; HUBER, WOLFGANG K.; CHARALAMPOUS, KANELLOS D.; SERAFETINIDES, EUSTACE A.; TROUSDALE, WILLIAM; AND COLMORE, JOHN P. "Drug Treatment in Newly Admitted Schizophrenic Patients." *Arch Gen Psychiatry* 25(5):404–9 N '71. *
30. LENTZ, ROBERT J., AND PAUL, GORDON L. " 'Routine' vs 'Therapeutic' Transfer of Chronic Mental Patients." *Arch Gen Psychiatry* 25(2):187–91 Ag '71. *
31. LENTZ, ROBERT J.; PAUL, GORDON L.; AND CALHOUN, JAMES F. "Reliability and Validity of Three Measures of Functioning With 'Hard-Core' Chronic Mental Patients." *J Abn Psychol* 78(1):69–76 Ag '71. * (*PA* 47:3362)

32. LUDWIG, ARNOLD M., AND MARX, ARNOLD J. "The Response of Chronic Schizophrenics to Attention and Structure." *Brit J Psychiatry* 118(545):447–50 Ap '71. * (*PA* 47:1338)
33. PATTISON, E. MANSELL; RHODES, ROBERT J.; AND DUDLEY, DONALD L. "Response to a Group Treatment in Patients With Severe Chronic Lung Disease." *Int J Group Psychother* 21(2):214–25 Ap '71. * (*PA* 48:1099)
34 SHOPSIN, BARON; KIM, SUK SIK; AND GERSHON, SAMUEL. "A Controlled Study of Lithium vs. Chlorpromazine in Acute Schizophrenics." *Brit J Psychiatry* 119(551):435–40 O '71. * (*PA* 47:9388)
35. SPIEGEL, DON; KEITH-SPIEGEL, PATRICIA; ZIRGULIS, JUSTINE; AND WINE, DAVID B. "Effects of Student Visits on Social Behavior of Regressed Schizophrenic Patients." *J Clin Psychol* 27(3):396–400 Jl '71. * (*PA* 47:5343)

CUMULATIVE NAME INDEX

Angus, J. W. S.: 16
Arengo, A. D.: 28
Ban, T. A.: 23
Beard, M. T.: 25
Bidus, D. R.: 25
Bishop, M. P.: 28
Blignault, W. J.: 26
Blumenthal, I. J.: 3
Calhoun, J. F.: 31
Charalampous, K. D.: 29
Clark, M. L.: 29
Cole, J. O.: 15
Colmore, J. P.: 29
Dana, L.: 28
Dudley, D. L.: 33
Fabrega, H.: 11–12
Francis, R. W.: 13
Frederick, A. N. D.: 18
Freeman, H.: 18
Gallant, D. M.: 28
Gershon, S.: 34
Gillis, R.: 7
Gillis, R. D.: 5
Grayson, H. M.: 6, 9
Honigfeld, G.: 1–2, 5, 7
Honigfeld, H.: 3
Huber, W. K.: 29
Kales, A.: 19
Keith-Lee, P.: 4
Keith-Spiegel, P.: 6, 9, 35
Kim, S. S.: 34
Kish, G. B.: 14, 22
Klett, C. J.: 1–2, 5
Klett, W. G.: 24
Kollar, E. J.: 19
Lambert, H. L.: 3
Lehmann, H. E.: 23

Lentz, R. J.: 30–1
Lorei, T. W.: 24
Ludwig, A. M.: 32
Marx, A. J.: 32
Miller, A. G.: 8
Naitoh, P.: 19
Needham, R. F. H.: 26
Pasnau, R. O.: 19
Pattison, E. M.: 33
Paul, G. L.: 30–1
Prien, R. F.: 15
Ravensborg, M. R.: 20–1, 27
Rhodes, R. J.: 33
Roberts, A. J.: 3
Rosenblum, M. P.: 3
Rubin, R. T.: 19
Saxena, B. M.: 23
Serafetinides, E. A.: 29
Shopsin, B.: 34
Simpson, G. M.: 16, 28
Slater, G. G.: 19
Spiegel, D.: 35
Spiegel, D. E.: 4, 6, 9
Sterlin, C.: 23
Stier, S. A.: 10
Stolberg, H.: 16, 28
Sugerman, A. A.: 16
Swartz, J. D.: 11–12
Trousdale, W.: 29
Wallace, C. A.: 11–12
Watson, G. C.: 24
Wendt, M. J.: 17
White, L.: 28
Willenson, D.: 21
Wine, D. B.: 35
Wolpert, A.: 28
Zirgulis, J.: 35

[1299]
Object Sorting Scales. Adults; 1966; OSS; modification of *Goldstein-Scheerer Object Sorting Test;* 2 scores: schizotypy, brain damage; S. H. Lovibond; Australian Council for Educational Research [Australia]. *

For additional information, see P:181

REFERENCES THROUGH 1971

1. LOVIBOND, S. H. "The Object Sorting Test and Conceptual Thinking in Schizophrenia." *Austral J Psychol* 6:52–70 Je '54. * (*PA* 29:6035)
2. MCCONAGHY, N. "The Use of an Object Sorting Test in Elucidating the Hereditary Factor in Schizophrenia." *J Neurol Neurosurg & Psychiatry* (England) 22:243–6 Ag '59. * (*PA* 34:8166)
3. LIDZ, THEODORE; WILD, CYNTHIA; SCHAFER, SARAH; ROSMAN, BERNICE; AND FLECK, STEPHEN. "Thought Disorders in the Parents of Schizophrenic Patients: A Study Utilizing the Object Sorting Test." *J Psychiatric Res* (England) 1:193–200 D '62. * (*PA* 39:2695)
4. LOVIBOND, S. H. "Conceptual Thinking, Personality and Conditioning." *Brit J Social & Clin Psychol* 2:100–11 Je '63. * (*PA* 38:3654)
5. ROSMAN, BERNICE; WILD, CYNTHIA; RICCI, JUDITH; FLECK, STEPHEN; AND LIDZ, THEODORE. "Thought Disorders in the Parents of Schizophrenic Patients: A Further Study Utilizing the Object Sorting Test." *J Psychiatric Res* (England) 2:211–21 O '64. * (*PA* 39:16236)
6. WILD, CYNTHIA; SINGER, MARGARET; ROSMAN, BERNICE; RICCI, JUDITH; AND LIDZ, THEODORE. "Measuring Disordered Styles of Thinking: Using the Object Sorting Test on Parents of Schizophrenic Patients." *Arch Gen Psychiatry* 13:471–6 N '65. * (*PA* 40:1831)
7. LOVIBOND, S. H., AND HOLLOWAY, I. "Differential Sorting Behavior of Schizophrenics and Organics." *J Clin Psychol* 24:307–11 Jl '68. * (*PA* 42:17388)

New Junior Maudsley Inventory

8. ROMNEY, DAVID. "Psychometrically Assessed Thought Disorder in Schizophrenic and Control Patients and in Their Parents and Siblings." *Brit J Psychiatry* 115(526):999–1002 S '69. * (*PA* 44:10875)

9. ROMNEY, DAVID. "The Validity of Certain Tests of Over-inclusion." *Brit J Psychiatry* 115(522):591–2 My '69. * (*PA* 44:3689)

10. SCHOPLER, ERIC, AND LOFTIN, JULIE. "Thinking Disorders in Parents of Young Psychotic Children." *J Abn Psychol* 74(3):281–7 Je '69. * (*PA* 43:13123)

11. SCHOPLER, ERIC, AND LOFTIN, JULIE. "Thought Disorders in Parents of Psychotic Children: A Function of Test Anxiety." *Arch Gen Psychiatry* 20(2):174–81 F '69. * (*PA* 43:11572)

CUMULATIVE NAME INDEX

[1300]

Objective-Analytic (O-A) Anxiety Battery. Ages 14 and over; 1955–67; OAAB; revision of anxiety-to-achieve battery (U. I. 24) of *Objective-Analytic Personality Test Batteries;* Raymond B. Cattell and Ivan H. Scheier; Institute for Personality and Ability Testing. *

For additional information and a review by Andrew L. Comrey, see 7:115 (2 references) ; see also P:182 (6 references) ; for a review by Harold Borko and an excerpted review by Gordon V. Anderson, see 6:149 (5 references).

REFERENCES THROUGH 1971

1–5. See 6:149.
6–11. See P:182.
12–13. See 7:115.

14. SLOANE, R. B.; HABIB, A.; EVESON, M. B.; AND PAYNE, R. W. "Some Behavioural and Other Correlates of Cholesterol Metabolism." *J Psychosom Res* (England) 5:183–90 Je '61. * (*PA* 36:5HN83S)

15. McGLOTHLIN, WILLIAM H.; COHEN, SIDNEY; AND McGLOTHLIN, MARCELLA S. "Short-Term Effects of LSD on Anxiety, Attitudes, and Performance." *J Nerv & Mental Dis* 139:266–73 S '64. * (*PA* 39:7046)

16. SAYER, KAREN E., AND TORRES, AURELIO A. "Effect of Anxiety on Alpha Responsiveness to Light Stimulation." *Psychol Rep* 19:1143–6 D '66. * (*PA* 41:4077)

17. RUBY, THOMAS MARVIN. *Performance on the Wechsler Adult Intelligence Scale by High and Low Anxious College Students.* Master's thesis, Southern Methodist University (Dallas, Tex.), 1967.

18. DELHEES, KARL H., AND CATTELL, RAYMOND B. "Differences of Personality Factors, by the O-A Battery, in Paranoid and Non-Paranoid Schizophrenics, Manic-Depressives, Psychoneurotics, and the Personality Disorders." *Archiv für die Gesamte Psychologie* (West Germany) 123(1):35–48 O '71. *

19. FABIAN, JUDITH JANARO, AND COMREY, ANDREW L. "Construct Validation of Factored Neuroticism Scales." *Multiv Behav Res* 6(3):287–99 Jl '71. * (*PA* 47:4817)

20. GUIDO, STEPHEN MICHAEL. *The Validity and Reliability of a New Ego Strength Sentence Completion Test.* Doctor's thesis, St. John's University (Jamaica, N.Y.), 1971. (*DAI* 32:4213B)

CUMULATIVE NAME INDEX

[1301]

Ohio College Association Rating Scale. High school; no date; ratings by teachers; [Herbert A. Toops] ; distributed by Wilbur L. Layton. *

For additional information, see P:183.

[1302]

Omnibus Personality Inventory. College; 1968, c1959–68; OPI; 15 scores: thinking introversion (TI), theoretical orientation (TO), estheticism (Es), complexity (Co), autonomy (Au), religious orientation (RO), social extroversion (SE), impulse expression (IE), personal integration (PI), anxiety level (AL), altruism (Am), practical outlook (PO), masculinity-femininity (MF), response bias (RB), intellectual disposition category (IDC) based on the first 6 scores; Paul Heist, George Yonge, T. R. McConnell (test), and Harold Webster (test) ; Psychological Corporation. *

For additional information and reviews by Richard W. Coan and Paul McReynolds, see 7:116 (82 references) ; see also P:184 (60 references) ; for reviews by Paul M. Kjeldergaard and Norman E. Wallen and an excerpted review by Laurence Siegel of earlier forms, see 6:150 (11 references).

REFERENCES THROUGH 1971

1–11. See 6:150.
12–70. See P:184.
71–152. See 7:116.

153. STEWART, LAWRENCE H. "Modes of Response on the Strong Blank and Selected Personality Variables." *J Counsel Psychol* 7:127–31 su '60. * (*PA* 35:3461)

154. WARREN, JONATHAN R. "Self Concept, Occupational Role Expectation, and Change in College Major." *J Counsel Psychol* 8:164–9 su '61. * (*PA* 36:3KD64W)

155. OLESEN, VIRGINIA L., AND WHITTAKER, ELVI W. *The Silent Dialogue: A Study in the Social Psychology of Professional Socialization,* pp. 92–3, 132–5. San Francisco, Calif.: Jossey-Bass Inc., Publishers, 1968. Pp. xvi, 312. *

156. WALTON, H. J. "Sex Differences in Ability and Outlook of Senior Medical Students." *Brit J Med Ed* 2:156–62 Je '68. *

157. PIERCE, ROBERT A. "Athletes in Psychotherapy: How Many, How Come?" *J Am Col Health Assn* 17(3):244–9 F '69. *

158. SNYDER, BENSON R., AND KAHNE, MERTON J. "Stress in Higher Education and Student Use of University Psychiatrists." *Am J Orthopsychiatry* 39(1):23–35 Ja '69. * (*PA* 45:1324)

159. AUSTIN, ROY LESLIE. *The Effect of Faculty Training on Student Attitude.* Doctor's thesis, East Texas State University (Commerce, Tex.), 1970. (*DAI* 32:730A)

160. BONNIN, ROBERT MILTON. *An Assessment of Relationships Between Certain Personality Variables and Teacher Performance in Teaching Assignments of Higher and Lower Difficulty.* Doctor's thesis, University of California (Berkeley, Calif.), 1970. (*DAI* 31:6446A)

161. BURGESS, WILLIAM VANDER. *The Analysis of Teacher Creativity, Pupil Age, and Pupil Sex as Sources of Variation Among Elementary Pupils' Performances on Pre- and Post-Tests of Creative Thinking.* Doctor's thesis, University of California (Berkeley, Calif.), 1970. (*DAI* 32:747A)

162. CAZZELLE, JACKIE GENE. *A Study of Non-Intellective Variables Related to the Academic Success and Adjustment of College Freshmen From Low Socioeconomic Backgrounds.* Doctor's thesis, Oklahoma State University (Stillwater, Okla.), 1970. (*DAI* 31:5118A)

163. GRASS, PAUL LOUIS. *Differential Effects of Short-Term Small-Group Interaction on the Behavioral Development of College Freshmen According to Personality Type.* Doctor's thesis, Michigan State University (East Lansing, Mich.), 1970. (*DAI* 32:196A)

164. HEIST, PAUL, AND BILORUSKY, JOHN. Chap. 4, "A Special Breed of Student," pp. 71–104. In *The Cluster College.* Edited by Jerry G. Gaff and Associates. San Francisco, Calif.: Jossey-Bass Inc., Publishers, 1970. Pp. xix, 247. *

165. HUNGERMAN, J. MICHAEL. *The Relationship of Sensitivity to Others to Certain Selected Personality Characteristics.* Doctor's thesis, Kent State University (Kent, Ohio), 1970. (*DAI* 31:5128A)

166. KNAPP, DAVID MAYNARD. *The Effect of Ego Therapy on Personality Integration.* Doctor's thesis, University of California (Santa Barbara, Calif.), 1970. (*DAI* 31:7600B)

167. KUGLER, JEAN E. *The Impact of a New Women's College on Its First Graduating Class.* Doctor's thesis, Claremont Graduate School (Claremont, Calif.), 1970. (*DAI* 31:7575B)

168. LACHER, MAURY. *The Life Styles of Underachieving, Overachieving and Normally Achieving College Students.* Doctor's thesis, University of Michigan (Ann Arbor, Mich.), 1970. (*DAI* 31:4999B)

169. LINDEMAN, ROBERT PAUL. *A Study of Selected Non-Intellectual Variables Among Classes of Students in a College of Engineering.* Doctor's thesis, Oklahoma State University (Stillwater, Okla.), 1970. (*DAI* 31:5852A)

170. NEWCOMB, THEODORE M.; BROWN, DONALD R.; KULIK, JAMES A.; REIMER, DAVID J.; AND REVELLE, WILLIAM R. Chap. 6, "Self-Selection and Change," pp. 137–60. In *The Cluster College*. Edited by Jerry G. Gaff and Associates. San Francisco, Calif.: Jossey-Bass Inc., Publishers, 1970. Pp. xix, 249. *

171. OSWALD, ROBERT MATHEAS. *The Relationships Between Certain Personality Variables and Conservative, Moderate, and Liberal Theological Beliefs*. Doctor's thesis, North Texas State University (Denton, Tex.), 1970. (*DAI* 32:251A)

172. PASSMORE, WYNOKA SUE JAY. *An Investigation of the Relationship of Self-Concept and Selected Personal Characteristics of Student Teachers to Success in Student Teaching*. Doctor's thesis, North Texas State University (Denton, Tex.), 1970. (*DAI* 31:5254A)

173. PITTS, GRIFF D. *Values, Attitudes, Opinions, and Concerns of Subcultures of Concerned Students in an Urban Commuter College*. Doctor's thesis, Northwestern University (Evanston, Ill.), 1970. (*DAI* 31:5152A)

174. THOMPSON, DELL NORMAN. *The Impact of a University on Selected Personality Measures of Transfer Students From Two-Year Colleges*. Doctor's thesis, State University of New York (Albany, N.Y.), 1970. (*DAI* 32:1869A)

175. TRENT, JAMES W. Chap. 2, "Revolution, Reformation, and Revolution," pp. 23–59. In *Student Activism and Protest*. Edited by Edward F. Sampson, Harold A. Korn, and Associates. San Francisco, Calif.: Jossey-Bass Inc., Publishers, 1970. Pp. xix, 265. *

176. ALPERT, ELIZABETH, AND SUCZEK, ROBERT F. "Personality Development and Cultural Change." *J Higher Ed* 42(1):21–6 Ja '71. *

177. BRAINARD, STEPHEN RICHARD. *Correlates of Leadership Effectiveness in Personnel Assistants*. Doctor's thesis, University of Missouri (Columbia, Mo.), 1971. (*DAI* 32:2542A)

178. CARTER, KENNETH WARD. *An Assessment of the Impact of Various College Characteristics on Change in Student Personality*. Doctor's thesis, Ohio State University (Columbus, Ohio), 1971. (*DAI* 32:1873A)

179. DeVECCHIO, RICHARD CHARLES. *Scholastic Aptitudes, Academic Motivation, Personality and Biographical Characteristics of Non-Returning and Returning Community College Freshmen*. Doctor's thesis, University of Virginia (Charlottesville, Va.), 1971. (*DAI* 32:4371A)

180. DUTT, LOUISE ELIZABETH GETTYS. *Student Persistence in College: An Analysis*. Doctor's thesis, University of Kentucky (Lexington, Ky.), 1971. (*DAI* 32:4943A)

181. ELTON, CHARLES F. "Interaction of Environment and Personality: A Test of Holland's Theory." *J Appl Psychol* 55(2):114–8 Ap '71. * (*PA* 46:3772)

182. ELTON, CHARLES F., AND ROSE, HARRIETT A. "A Longitudinal Study of the Vocationally Undecided Male Student." *J Voc Behav* 1(1):85–92 Ja '71. * (*PA* 47:3682)

183. ELTON, CHARLES F., AND ROSE, HARRIETT A. "Students Who Leave Engineering." *Eng Ed* 62(1):30–2 S–O '71. *

184. ELTON, CHARLES F., AND SMART, JOHN C. "Many Are Rushed, But Who Will Pledge?" *J Col Stud Personnel* 12(3):204–7 My '71. *

185. FELLOWS, MARGUERITE ANN. *Personality Traits Related to Rating Self and Others by Viewing Videotape of a Motor Performance*. Doctor's thesis, State University of New York (Buffalo, N.Y.), 1971. (*DAI* 32:770A)

186. FENSTEMACHER, WILLIAM PROCTOR. *A Study of the Relationship of Instrumental and Intellectual Orientations to the Educational Experiences of Black Students at the University of Michigan*. Doctor's thesis, University of Michigan (Ann Arbor, Mich.), 1971. (*DAI* 32:1291A)

187. FINNEY, HENRY C. "Political Libertarianism at Berkeley: An Application of Perspectives From the New Student Left." *J Social Issues* 27(1):35–61 '71. *

188. GOLDBERG, ROBERT WOLF. *Cognitive Flexibility: Its Relationship to Personality Style and Its Generality as a Thought Process*. Doctor's thesis, University of Michigan (Ann Arbor, Mich.), 1971. (*DAI* 32:4210B)

189. HANNAH, WILLIAM. "Personality Differentials Between Lower Division Dropouts and Stay-ins." *J Col Stud Personnel* 12(1):16–9 Ja '71. * (*PA* 46:1757)

190. HATCH, DELSA DIANE. *Differential Personal Change of Males and Females in Two College Environments*. Doctor's thesis, University of Michigan (Ann Arbor, Mich.), 1971. (*DAI* 32:4105A)

191. HAUSELMAN, ALBERT J. *Personality and the Choice of Undergraduate Major: A Test of Holland's Theory*. Doctor's thesis, University of Kentucky (Lexington, Ky.), 1971. (*DAI* 32:4948A)

192. HJELLE, LARRY A., AND LOMASTRO, JAMES. "Personality Differences Between High and Low Dogmatism Groups of Catholic Seminarians and Religious Sisters." *J Sci Study Relig* 10(1):49–50 sp '71. * (*PA* 47:6596)

193. HORN, BARBARA JEAN. *An Evaluation of an Independent Study Course and Personality Correlates of Selection of the Independent Study Option*. Doctor's thesis, University of Michigan (Ann Arbor, Mich.), 1971. (*DAI* 32:1337A)

194. KEES, DONALD J., AND McDOUGALL, WILLIAM P. "A

Validation Study of the Clark-Trow College Subculture Typology." *J Col Stud Personnel* 12(3):193–9 My '71. *

195. KENNEDY, WILLIAM ROBERT. *The Relationship of Selected Student Characteristics to Components of Teacher/Course Evaluations Among Freshman English Students at Kent State University*. Doctor's thesis, Kent State University (Kent, Ohio), 1971. (*DAI* 32:5038A)

196. KINZER, SUZANNE MARIE. *A Study of the Development of Experimental Behavior in a Teacher Education Seminar Group*. Doctor's thesis, University of Rochester (Rochester, N.Y.), 1971. (*DAI* 32:3139A)

197. McWILLIAMS, ROBERT H. *An Investigation of the Counseling Process Utilizing a Systems Analysis Model*. Doctor's thesis, University of North Dakota (Grand Forks, N.D.), 1971. (*DAI* 33:160A)

198. MANN, PHILIP A. "Effects of Anxiety and Defensive Style on Some Aspects of Friendship." *J Pers & Social Psychol* 18(1):55–61 Ap '71. * (*PA* 46:2917)

199. MILLER, JOHN K., AND FARR, S. DAVID. "Bimultivariate Redundancy: A Comprehensive Measure of Interbattery Relationship." *Multiv Behav Res* 6(3):313–24 Jl '71. * (*PA* 47:3955)

200. MITCHELL, ROBERT EUGENE. *Personality Correlates of Frequent Marijuana and Alcohol Use in a College Male Population*. Doctor's thesis, Ohio State University (Columbus, Ohio), 1971. (*DAI* 32:6655B)

201. MOCK, KATHLEEN RANLETT. "The Potential Activist and His Perception of the University." *J Appl Behav Sci* 7(1):3–13 Ja '71. * (*PA* 46:9558)

202. MULLIS, HERMAN THOMAS. *Clustering University Students: Its Psychological and Behavioral Effects on Perceptions of the University, Personality Variables, Interaction Patterns and Integration Into the University System*. Doctor's thesis, University of Utah (Salt Lake City, Utah), 1971. (*DAI* 31:4556A)

203. RICHARDSON, LEROY, AND SOUCAR, EMIL. "Comparison of Cognitive Complexity With Achievement and Adjustment: A Convergent-Discriminant Study." *Psychol Rep* 29(3):1087–90 D '71. * (*PA* 48:1011)

204. ROSE, HARRIETT A., AND ELTON, CHARLES F. "Attrition and the Vocationally Undecided Student." *J Voc Behav* 1(1):99–103 Ja '71. * (*PA* 47:3709)

205. ROSE, HARRIETT A., AND ELTON, CHARLES F. "Sex and Occupational Choice." *J Counsel Psychol* 18(5):456–61 S '71. * (*PA* 47:3710)

206. ROSE, HARRIETT A., AND ELTON, CHARLES F. "Sorority Dropout." *J Col Stud Personnel* 12(6):460–3 N '71. *

207. SHAPIRO, STEWART B., AND KNAPP, DAVID M. "The Effect of Ego Therapy on Personality Integration." *Psychother Theory Res & Prac* 8(3):208–12 f '71. * (*PA* 47:11052)

208. SMART, JOHN CARSON, III. *Personality and Voting Behavior: A Study of Voting and Non-Voting College Students*. Doctor's thesis, University of Kentucky (Lexington, Ky.), 1971. (*DAI* 32:1887A)

209. STEWART, L. H. "Relationships Between Interests and Personality Scores of Occupation-Oriented Students." *J Counsel Psychol* 18(1):31–8 Ja '71. * (*PA* 45:8248)

210. WALIZER, MICHAEL H., AND HERRIOTT, ROBERT E. "The Impact of College on Students' Competence to Function in a Learning Society." *ACT Res Rep* 47:1–42 D '71. * (*PA* 48:1625)

211. WALKER, BETTY ANN. *Effects of Short-Term Group Counseling on Changes in Attitudes of Flexibility, Tolerance, and Nonauthoritarianism*. Doctor's thesis, University of Southern California (Los Angeles, Calif.), 1971. (*DAI* 32:3708A)

212. WHITTAKER, DAVID. "The Psychological Adjustment of Intellectual, Nonconformist, Collegiate Dropouts." *Adolescence* 6(24):415–24 w '71. * (*PA* 48:7723)

213. WONNEBERG, GARY R., AND KAATS, GILBERT R. "Self, In-Group, and Out-Group Stereotypes of Air Academy and Civilian College Students," pp. 111–4. In *First Annual Symposium: Psychology in the Air Force 31 March–2 April 1970*. Edited by Hal W. Hendrick. Colorado Springs, Colo.: United States Air Force Academy, [1971]. Pp. vii, 200. *

214. WRIGHT, WILBERT. "Vocational and Learning Attitudes of Black Students." *J Col Stud Personnel* 12(4):253–8 Jl '71. * (*PA* 47:7674)

CUMULATIVE NAME INDEX

Omnibus Personality Inventory

[1303]

Opinion, Attitude, and Interest Survey. High school seniors and college students; 1962–68, c1955–65; OAIS; factors related to academic success and educational interest; 14 scores: 3 response bias scores (set for true, infrequent response, social undesirability), 3 academic promise scores (achiever personality, intellectual quality, creative personality), 3 adjustment scores (social, emotional, masculine orientation), and 5 interest scores (business, humanities, social science, physical science, biological science); 1964 test identical with test copyrighted 1955 except for format and directions; Benno G. Fricke; OAIS Testing Program. *

For additional information, see P:185 (19 references); for reviews by John O. Crites and Harold Webster, see 6:151 (4 references).

REFERENCES THROUGH 1971

1–4. See 6:151.
5–23. See P:185.
24. KRUMBOLTZ, JOHN D., AND FARQUHAR, WILLIAM W. "The Effect of Three Teaching Methods on Achievement and Motivational Outcomes in a How-to-Study Course." *Psychol Monogr* 71(14):1–26 '57. * (*PA* 33:4700)
25. KRUMBOLTZ, JOHN D., AND FARQUHAR, WILLIAM W. "Reliability and Validity of the n-Achievement Test." *J Consult Psychol* 21:226–8 Je '57. * (*PA* 32:5966)
26. BOAZ, MARY EVELYN. *Identification and Evaluation of Creative Abilities of Students in the Area of Textiles and Clothing.* Doctor's thesis, Oklahoma State University (Stillwater, Okla.), 1965. (*DA* 27:219B)
27. BURKE, RONALD J., AND MAIER, NORMAN R. F. "Attempts to Predict Success on an Insight Problem." *Psychol Rep* 17:303–10 Ag '65. * (*PA* 40:1115)
28. WENBERG, BURNESS G., AND INGERSOLL, RALPH W. "Medical Dietetics: Part 2, The Development of Evaluative Techniques." *J Am Dietetic Assn* 47:298–300 O '65. *
29. BURKE, RONALD J. "The Relationship of Some Interest, Intellectual Ability, and Nonintellectual Ability Tests to Problem-Solving Success and Effective Use of Hints in Individual Problem-Solving." *Mich Acad Sci Arts & Letters* 51:353–60 '66. * (*PA* 41:14722)
30. EVANS, LLOYD R.; INGERSOLL, RALPH W.; AND SMITH, EDWIN JAY. "The Reliability, Validity, and Taxonomic Structure of the Oral Examination." *J Med Ed* 41:651–7 Jl '66. *
31. GINLEY, THOMAS J. "Present Status and Future Plans of the Dental Aptitude Testing Program." *J Dental Ed* 30:163–74 Je '66. *
32. HENRY, JOAN LOUISE. *Student Characteristics and Perceptions of Indiana University.* Doctor's thesis, Indiana University (Bloomington, Ind.), 1966. (*DA* 27:1544A)
33. RIEGEL, KLAUS F.; RIEGEL, RUTH M.; AND LEVINE, ROBERT S. "An Analysis of Associative Behavior and Creativity." *J Pers & Social Psychol* 4:50–6 Jl '66. * (*PA* 40:10102)
34. HAUENSTEIN, FREDERICK B. "Predictive Validity of the OAIS With Junior College Grades." *Mich Col Personnel Assn J* 4:15–9 f '67. *
35. JOHNSON, THOMAS HATCHER. *A Comparison of Male Maximum Participants and Male Non-Participants in a College Intramural Program.* Doctor's thesis, University of North Carolina (Chapel Hill, N.C.), 1967. (*DA* 28:3488A)
36. WHARTON, WILLIAM P. "Beyond the Two R's—What Further Responsibilities in College Admissions." *J Assn Col Adm Counselors* 12(2):20–2 '67. *
37. BUSH, MARSHALL. *A Study of Reality-Closeness-Reality-Distance: A Directional Determinant of Attention Deployment.* Doctor's thesis, University of Michigan (Ann Arbor, Mich.), 1968. (*DA* 29:1168B)
38. DONNAN, HUGH. "Personality Factors Related to College Achievement and Attrition." *J Col Stud Personnel* 9:116–9 Mr '68. *
39. GRAFF, ROBERT WALTER. *The Relationship of the Opinion, Attitude, and Interest Survey to College Achievement and Academic Adjustment Factors.* Doctor's thesis, State University of New York (Buffalo, N.Y.), 1968. (*DA* 29:2959A)
40. HASKINS, MARY JANE. "Characteristics of Professional Women Students in Physical Education as Indicated by the Opinion, Attitude, and Interest Survey." *Percept & Motor Skills* 27:875–9 D '68. * (*PA* 43:8663)
41. JAMES, NEWTON E., AND BRONSON, LOUISE. "The OAIS—An Evaluation." *J Col Stud Personnel* 9:120–5 Mr '68. *
42. MANN, WILLIAM RAY. *Changes in the Level of Attitude Sophistication of College Students as a Measure of Teacher Effectiveness.* Doctor's thesis, University of Michigan (Ann Arbor, Mich.), 1968. (*DA* 29:2443A). Reviewed by Edwin L. Simpson, *Council Res Music Ed B* 24:57–60 sp '71. *
43. ARBUTHNOT, JACK, AND GRUENFELD, LEOPOLD. "Field Independence and Educational-Vocational Interests." Abstract. *J Consult & Clin Psychol* 33(5):631 O '69. * (*PA* 44:2325)
44. BRAUN, JOHN R., AND TINLEY, JOHN J. "Comment on Fricke's Approach to Controlling Social Desirability in the Forced-Choice Format." *Psychol Rep* 25(1):93–4 Ag '69. * (*PA* 44:3628)
45. CORL, SAMUEL SHIREY, III. *The Relationships Between Student Teacher Innovative Behaviors and Selected Attitudes, Perceptions and Personality Characteristics.* Doctor's thesis,

University of Michigan (Ann Arbor, Mich.), 1969. (*DAI* 31:661A)

46. DOHNER, CHARLES W. "The OAIS as Related to Academic Performance." *J Col Stud Personnel* 10(4):254-7 Jl '69. *

47. HOEHN, JEANNETTE G. *Relationship of the Achiever Personality and the OAIS to Academic Success and to the Self Concept.* Doctor's thesis, Oklahoma State University (Stillwater, Okla.), 1969. (*DAI* 31:3956A)

48. MILLER, DORIS METZGER, AND O'CONNOR, PATRICIA. "Achiever Personality and Academic Success Among Disadvantaged College Students." *J Social Issues* 25(3):103-16 su '69. * (*PA* 47:1750)

49. SCHWAB, FRANCIS JOSEPH. *A Comparison of Personality Profiles of Over- and Under-Achieving Students at South Dakota State University.* Doctor's thesis, University of South Dakota (Vermillion, S.D.), 1969. (*DAI* 30:2343A)

50. SHERRON, RONALD HOMER. *A Study of Academic and Nonacademic Predictors and Criteria of Success Among the Morehead Scholars at the University of North Carolina at Chapel Hill.* Doctor's thesis, University of North Carolina (Chapel Hill, N.C.), 1969. (*DAI* 30:3287A)

51. SOCKLOFF, ALAN LEONARD. *The Analysis of Student Characteristics Associated With Grades for Varying Levels of College Freshman Grade Complexity.* Doctor's thesis, Emory University (Atlanta, Ga.), 1969. (*DAI* 31:903B)

52. STONE, MICHAEL HORACE. *A Study of the Relationships Between Selected Variables and the Differential Academic Achievement of Freshmen in the University of Michigan School of Music.* Doctor's thesis, University of Michigan (Ann Arbor, Mich.), 1969. (*DAI* 30:1881A)

53. VINCENT, VERONA. *Personality Factors of Competitors and Noncompetitors in Athletic Activities.* Master's thesis, Lamar State College of Technology (Beaumont, Tex.), 1969.

54. WENBERG, BURNESS G.; INGERSOLL, RALPH W.; AND DOHNER, CHARLES W. "Evaluation of Dietetic Interns." *J Am Dietetic Assn* 54(4):297-301 Ap '69. *

55. WIGGINS, NANCY; BLACKBURN, MARGARET; AND HACKMAN, J. RICHARD. "Prediction of First-Year Graduate Success in Psychology: Peer Ratings." *J Ed Res* 63(2):81-5 O '69. * (*PA* 46:5710)

56. BATEMAN, JOHN KEITH. *A Multivariate and Univariate Validity Study of the OAIS.* Doctor's thesis, University of Kansas (Lawrence, Kan.), 1970. (*DAI* 31:5753A)

57. CHASE, CLINTON I., AND HEMMETER, JOHN T. *A Characterization of Honors Students.* Indiana Studies in Prediction No. 14. Bloomington, Ind.: Bureau of Educational Studies and Testing, 1970. Pp. vii, 26. *

58. DELAURETIS, ROBERT J.; LEBOLD, WILLIAM K.; AND MOLNAR, GEORGE E. "A Multiple-Regressional Analysis of the Complementary Roles of Cognitive and Noncognitive Measures of Engineering Behavior." Abstract. *Proc 78th Ann Conv Am Psychol Assn* 5(2):607-8 '70. * (*PA* 44:19532)

59. FRICKE, BENNO G. "Creative Writing Course Grades, OAIS Creative Personality Test Scores, and Other Assessment Measures." Abstract. *Proc 78th Ann Conv Am Psychol Assn* 5(2):617-8 '70. * (*PA* 44:19533)

60. FRICKE, BENNO G. "OAIS Scores of University of Amsterdam Students: Invalidity of High Infrequent Response Scale Scores." Abstract. *Proc 78th Ann Conv Am Psychol Assn* 5(1):173-4 '70. * (*PA* 44:18727)

61. GRAFF, ROBERT W., AND HANSEN, JAMES C. "Relationship of OAIS Scores to College Achievement and Adjustment." *J Col Stud Personnel* 11(2):129-34 Mr '70. *

62. HOFLAND, DEAN MYRON. *A Study of Selected Characteristics of Freshman Male Students Who Choose a Major and Those Who Do Not Choose a Major Upon Matriculation.* Doctor's thesis, University of South Dakota (Vermillion, S.D.), 1970. (*DAI* 31:3269A)

63. MANN, WILLIAM R., AND FUSFELD, DANIEL R. "Attitude Sophistication and Effective Teaching in Economics." *J Econ Ed* 1(2):111-29 sp '70. *

64. PENNSCOTT, WILLIAM W., AND SORENSEN, MOURITS A. "OAIS Achiever Personality and Desire for Improvement in Reading and Study Skills." *Meas & Eval Guid* 3(1):25-7 sp '70. * (*PA* 45:2953)

65. SHERRON, RONALD H. "A Study of Academic and Nonacademic Predictors and Criteria of Success Among Scholarship Recipients." *J Exp Ed* 38(3):72-82 sp '70.*

66. BLASCHAK, VERONICA MACRINA. *An Exploration of the Relationship Between Selected Characteristics of First Grade Reading Teachers and Pupil Growth in Reading.* Doctor's thesis, University of Michigan (Ann Arbor, Mich.), 1971. (*DAI* 32:3549A)

67. BLOOMBERG, MORTON. "Creativity as Related to Field Independence and Mobility." *J Genetic Psychol* 118(1):3-12 Mr '71. * (*PA* 46:9065)

68. BRAUN, JOHN R.; SEAMON, JOHN; AND BILL, J. CHRISTOPHER. "Faking and Faking Detection on the OAIS." *Psychol Rep* 29(2):672 O '71. * (*PA* 47:9604)

69. BURKE, RONALD J. "Correlates of the Ability to Fragment and Reorganize Stored Information." *J General Psychol* 84(2):183-9 Ap '71. * (*PA* 46:4255)

70. CLAR, PHILIP NORMAN. *The Relationship of Psychological Differentiation to Client Behavior in Vocational Choice Coun-*

seling. Doctor's thesis, University of Michigan (Ann Arbor, Mich.), 1971. (*DAI* 32:1837B)

71. COHEN, ROBERT MICHAEL. *Effects of Feedback on Test Anxiety and Performance as a Function of Certain Personal Characteristics.* Doctor's thesis, New York University (New York, N.Y.), 1971. (*DAI* 32:6094B)

72. GRAFF, ROBERT W.; BEGGS, DONALD L.; AND SPANER, STEVEN D. "The Use of the OAIS in Admission Selection and Counseling." *Col & Univ* 46(2):115-21 w '71. *

73. HEMMETER, JOHN T.; CHASE, CLINTON I.; AND GRIFFIN, NANCY L. *Majors for Honor Students: Their Predictability.* Indiana Studies in Prediction No. 16. Bloomington, Ind.: Bureau of Educational Studies and Testing, Indiana University, 1971. Pp. iv, 15. *

74. MENTLEY, MARC CHARLES. *Some Relationships Between Personality, Class Selection Characteristics and Teacher Attitude Change of Secondary Teaching Methods Students, Michigan State University, Winter Term, 1971.* Doctor's thesis, Michigan State University (East Lansing, Mich.), 1971. (*DAI* 32:5093A)

75. NELSON, BARBARA. "Predicting Success in the College Physical Education Major Program." *Physical Educator* 28(4):196-7 D '71. *

76. PERNELL, EUGENE, JR. *Predictions of Individual Student Teacher Behavior in Classrooms for Emotionally Disturbed Children.* Doctor's thesis, University of Michigan (Ann Arbor, Mich.), 1971. (*DAI* 32:6013A)

77. SCHOBEL, JAMES ALLAN. *The Use of the OAIS Psychological Test, the ACT Achievement Test and High School Rank in a Discriminant Analysis to Predict Freshmen Attrition at a Midwestern State College.* Doctor's thesis, Ohio University (Athens, Ohio), 1971. (*DAI* 32:4995A)

78. SMITH, ROSEMARY. "Repression-Sensitization Related to a Measure of Self-Actualization." *Proc W Va Acad Sci* 42(1970):262-6 '71. *

CUMULATIVE NAME INDEX

[1304]

★**Opinions Toward Adolescents.** College and adults; 1971-72; OTA; 8 scores: liberal-conservative, punitive-permissive, morally restrictive-morally accepting, authoritarian-democratic, mistrust-trust, prejudice-acceptance, understanding-misunderstanding, skepticism-sincerity (test taking attitude); William T. Martin; Psychologists and Educators, Inc. *

[1305]

Organic Integrity Test. Ages 5 and over; 1960-67; OIT; form perception as an indication of brain deficit unrelated to intelligence; H. C. Tien; Psychodiagnostic Test Co. *

For additional information and reviews by Ralph M. Reitan and Joseph M. Wepman, see 7:117 (8 references) ; see also P:186 (12 references).

REFERENCES THROUGH 1971

1. Same as reference 2.
2–13. See P:186.
14–21. See 7:117.
22. "Cumulative Bibliography on the Organic Integrity Test." *World J Psychosynthesis* 1(3):56–7 N '69. *
23. HAWARD, L. R. C. "Organic Integrity Test (OIT) in Phenytoin Autogenic Training." *World J Psychosynthesis* 1(4):47–50 D '69. *
24. ANDRADE, CLARA PAWLIKOWSKI. "The Use of the Organic Integrity Test (OIT) in Peru." *World J Psychosynthesis* 2(11):37–40 N '70. *
25. HAWARD, L. R. C. "Organic Integrity Test (OIT) in Phenytoin Autogenic Training: Tables and Summary." *World J Psychosynthesis* 2(1):52 Ja '70. *
26. SUWANLERT, SOMSONG; CHUPRAYOON, LO-IAD; THEPHASADIN, ROCHANA; AYUDHAYA, NA; AND SIRISAWAT, SUMANA. "Diagnosis of Brain Diseases With the OIT in Thailand." *World J Psychosynthesis* 2(4):41–4 Ap '70. *
27. THOMPSON, MARGARET ADELAIDE. "An Investigation Into the Validity of the Organic Integrity Test." *World J Psychosynthesis* 2(10):44–8 O '70. *
28. TIEN, H. C. "Organic Integrity Test (OIT) and Electroencephalography (EEG)." *World J Psychosynthesis* 2(5):41–6 My '70. *
29. LARRAGOITI, RAFAEL J. "Applications of the Organic Integrity Test (OIT) in Psychiatry." *World J Psychosynthesis* 3(1):45 Ja '71. *
30. NEDELCU, ADRIAN. "Diagnosis of Brain Disease in Romania With the Organic Integrity Test (OIT)." *World J Psychosynthesis* 3(4):44–6 Ap '71. *
31. ZAPPARDINO, PAMELA H., AND VERNON, McCAY. "Organic Integrity Test (OIT) With a Deaf Sample." *World J Psychosynthesis* 3(11):42–4 N '71. *

CUMULATIVE NAME INDEX

Aftanas, M. S.: 14
Alvis, H. J.: 15–6
Andrade, C. P.: 24
Ayudhaya, N.: 26
Chuprayoon, L.: 26
Clark, G. D.: 3, 9
Drdkova, S.: 19
Engelsmann, F.: 19
Golightly, C.: 10
Haerer, A. F.: 21
Haward, L. R. C.: 23, 25
Jacobs, E. A.: 15–6
Larragoiti, R. J.: 29
Lin, J. Y.: 5
Nedelcu, A.: 30
Paul, G. T.: 6
Reinehr, R. C.: 10
Reitan, R. M.: *rev*, 7:117
Royce, J. R.: 14
Schwaab, E. L.: 11
Sherman, L. J.: 11
Sirisawat, S.: 26
Small, S. M.: 15–6
Snelbecker, G. E.: 11
Suwanlert, S.: 26
Thephasadin, R.: 26
Thompson, M. A.: 27
Tien, H. C.: 2–4, 7–9, 12–3, 17–8, 20, 28
Vernon, M.: 31
Watts, C. C.: 21
Wepman, J. M.: *rev*, 7:117
Williams, M. W.: 4
Winter, P. M.: 15–6
Zappardino, P. H.: 31

[1306]

The Orientation Inventory. College and industry; 1962; OI; kinds of satisfactions and rewards sought in jobs; 3 scores: self-orientation, interaction-orientation, task-orientation; Bernard M. Bass; Consulting Psychologists Press, Inc. *

For additional information, see P:187 (13 references) ; for reviews by Richard S. Barrett and H. Bradley Sagen, see 6:153 (2 references).

REFERENCES THROUGH 1971

1–2. See 6:153.
3–15. See P:187.
16. GURMAN, ERNEST B., JR. *The Effect of Self, Task and Interaction Orientation on Brainstorming.* Doctor's thesis, Louisiana State University (Baton Rouge, La.), 1962. (*DA* 24:380)
17. BASS, BERNARD M., AND DUNTEMAN, GEORGE. "Behavior in Groups as a Function of Self-Interaction, and Task Orientation." *J Abn & Social Psychol* 66:419–28 My '63. * (*PA* 38:2579)
18. CRAIG, KENNETH DENTON. *Partner Competency and Prior Success-Failure Experiences as Determinants of Manding in Dyadic Interactions.* Doctor's thesis, Purdue University (Lafayette, Ind.), 1964. (*DA* 25:1333)
19. HARRISON, LAWRENCE BRIGHT. *The Relationship Between Ordinal Position and Dependency, Dominance, Affiliation, Affection, and Task-Orientation.* Doctor's thesis, University of Oklahoma (Norman, Okla.), 1964. (*DA* 25:3688)

20. KANFER, FREDERICK H., AND MARSTON, ALBERT R. "Characteristics of Interactional Behavior in a Psychotherapy Analogue." *J Consult Psychol* 28:456–67 O '64. * (*PA* 39:5351)
21. KNAPP, DEANNE ERMA. *Interrelationships Among Measures of Affiliation Motivation.* Doctor's thesis, Purdue University (Lafayette, Ind.), 1964. (*DA* 25:6053)
22. LUPFER, MICHAEL BURKE. *Role Enactment as a Function of Orientation, Expectations, and Duration of Interaction.* Doctor's thesis, University of Miami (Coral Gables, Fla.), 1964. (*DA* 25:5376)
23. DUNTEMAN, GEORGE H. "Self, Interaction, and Task Orientation Scores and Their Relationship to Promotability Ratings." *J Indus Psychol* 4(1):20–6 '65. *
24. FRYE, ROLAND L.; SOUTH, DONALD R.; AND VEGAS, OLGA V. "The Effect of Parental Orientation on the Development of the Child's Orientation." *J Genetic Psychol* 106:315–8 Je '65. * (*PA* 39:14747)
25. KORMAN, ABRAHAM K. "Self-Esteem Variable in Vocational Choice." *J Appl Psychol* 50:479–86 D '66. * (*PA* 41:3499)
26. ROTHAUS, PAUL; JOHNSON, DALE L.; HANSON, PHILIP G.; BROWN, JEROME B.; AND LYLE, FRANCIS A. "Sentence-Completion Test Prediction of Autonomous and Therapist-Led Group Behavior." *J Counsel Psychol* 14:28–34 Ja '67. * (*PA* 41:4688)
27. STINNETT, NICK, JR. *Marital Competence.* Doctor's thesis, Florida State University (Tallahassee, Fla.), 1967. (*DA* 28:3280A)
28. BASS, BERNARD M. "How to Succeed in Business According to Business Students and Managers." *J Appl Psychol* 52:254–62 Je '68. * (*PA* 42:12889)
29. CAMPBELL, JOHN P. "Individual Versus Group Problem Solving in an Industrial Sample." *J Appl Psychol* 52:205–10 Je '68. * (*PA* 42:11696)
30. GURMAN, ERNEST B. "Creativity as a Function of Orientation and Group Participation." *Psychol Rep* 22:471–8 Ap '68. * (*PA* 42:12099)
31. RIM, Y., AND COHEN, N. "Personality Variables in Making a Choice." *Psychologia* (Japan) 11:191–7 D '68. * (*PA* 44:6053)
32. RYAN, PETER LEIGHTON. *A Comparison of Three Theories of Group Behavior and Their Relationship to Behavioral Variables.* Doctor's thesis, University of California (Berkeley, Calif.), 1968. (*DAI* 30:1367B)
33. TAYLOR, LUCY C., AND COMPTON, NORMA H. "Personality Correlates of Dress Conformity." *J Home Econ* 60:653–6 O '68. *
34. WEAVER, FRANCES JEAN. *Selected Aspects of Father-Daughter Interaction and Daughter's Instrumentalness in Late Adolescence.* Doctor's thesis, Pennsylvania State University (University Park, Pa.), 1968. (*DA* 29:3690A)
35. CARRON, THEODORE J. "Validity of Tests for Chemical Plant Personnel." *Personnel Psychol* 22(3):307–12 au '69. * (*PA* 44:9414)
36. DISTEFANO, M. K., JR. "Changes in Work Related Attitudes With Age." *J Genetic Psychol* 114(1):127–34 Mr '69. * (*PA* 43:9493)
37. JAWA, SARALA. "Creativity and Orientation Type." *Psychol Ann* 4:45–8 Mr '70. * (*PA* 46:3074)
38. LYSAUGHT, JEROME P., AND PIERLEONI, ROBERT G. "Predicting Individual Success in Programing Self-Instructional Materials." *AV Commun R* 18(1):5–24 sp '70. * (*PA* 44:13334)
39. DOBRUSZEK, ZBIGNIEW. "Leadership Attitudes Measured by the Bass Orientation Inventory." *Polish Psychol B* 2(1):31–5 '71. * (*PA* 48:1988)
40. HECHLIK, JOHN EDWARD. *A Study of Factors Related to Job Satisfaction of Secondary School Counselors.* Doctor's thesis, University of Michigan (Ann Arbor, Mich.), 1971. (*DAI* 32:5546A)
41. SHYBUT, JOHN, AND UHES, MICHAEL J. "Self, Interaction, and Task Orientation of High- and Low-Rated Peace Corps Trainees." *Psychol Rep* 29(1):183–6 Ag '71. * (*PA* 47:3847)

CUMULATIVE NAME INDEX

Barrett, R. S.: *rev*, 6:153
Barry, J. R.: 13
Bass, B. M.: 1–2, 11, 17, 28
Braun, J. R.: 6, 14
Brown, J. B.: 26
Cagle, B. G.: 7
Campbell, J. P.: 29
Carron, T. J.: 35
Cohen, N.: 31
Compton, N. H.: 33
Craig, K. D.: 18
Distefano, M. K.: 3, 9, 12, 15, 36
Dobruszek, Z.: 39
Dubé, C. S.: 6
Dunteman, G.: 1–2, 17
Dunteman, G. H.: 13, 23
Frye, R.: 1
Frye, R. L.: 24
Gurman, E. B.: 16, 30
Hanson, P. G.: 26
Harrison, L. B.: 19
Hechlik, J. E.: 40
Jawa, S.: 37
Johnson, D. L.: 26
Kanfer, F. H.: 20
Knapp, D.: 10
Knapp, D. E.: 10, 21
Korman, A. K.: 25
Levine, E. M.: 5
Lupfer, M. B.: 22
Lyle, F. A.: 26
Lysaught, J. P.: 38
McGehearty, L. I. D.: 8
Marston, A. R.: 4–5, 20
Pierleoni, R. G.: 38
Pryer, M. W.: 3, 9, 15
Rice, D. P.: 9
Rim, Y.: 31
Rothaus, P.: 26
Ryan, P. L.: 32
Sagen, H. B.: *rev*, 6:153

Orientation Inventory

Shybut, J.: 41
South, D. R.: 24
Stinnett, N.: 27
Taylor, L. C.: 33
Uhes, M. J.: 41
Vegas, O. V.: 24

Vidulich, R.: 1
Wambach, H.: 1
Weaver, F. J.: 34
Webb, M. W.: 13
Weick, K.: 10

[1307]

★**Ottawa School Behavior Check List.** Ages 6–12; 1967–69; OSBCL; total score and 7 optional scores: deviance, probability of disorder, probability of non-disorder, immaturity, overactivity, conduct problem, personality problem; June B. Pimm and Gordon Mc-Clure; Pimm Consultants Ltd. [Canada]. *

REFERENCES THROUGH 1971

1. PIMM, JUNE B., AND McCLURE, GORDON. "A Screening Device for Early Detection of Emotional Disturbance in a Public School Setting." *Excep Children* 33:647–8 My '67. * (*PA* 41:9637)
2. PIMM, JUNE B.; QUAY, HERBERT; AND WERRY, JOHN S. "Dimensions of Problem Behavior in First Grade Children." *Psychol Sch* 4:155–7 Ap '67. * (*PA* 41:9373)
3. COWEN, EMORY L.; DORR, DARWIN A.; AND ORGEL, ARTHUR R. "Interrelations Among Screening Measures for Early Detection of School Dysfunction." *Psychol Sch* 8(2):135–9 Ap '71. * (*PA* 46:11496)

CUMULATIVE NAME INDEX

Cowen, E. L.: 3
Dorr, D. A.: 3
McClure, G.: 1
Orgel, A. R.: 3

Pimm, J. B.: 1–2
Quay, H.: 2
Werry, J. S.: 2

[1308]

*PHSF Relations Questionnaire.** Standards 6–10 and college and adults; 1969–71; PHSF; 12 scores: personal (self-confidence, self-esteem, self-control, nervousness, health), home (family influences, personal freedom), social (sociability—group, sociability—specific person, moral sense), formal relations, validity scale; F. A. Fouché and P. E. Grobbelaar; Human Sciences Research Council [South Africa]. *

For additional information, see 7:118.

[1309]

PRADI Autobiographical Form. Clinical clients; 1966; PAF; Psychological Research and Development Institute and Sheldon J. Lachman (manual); Psychological Publications Press. *

For additional information, see P:190.

[1310]

Parent-Adolescent Communication Inventory. High school and adults; 1968–69; PACI; Millard J. Bienvenu, Sr.; Family Life Publications, Inc. *

For additional information and a review by David B. Orr, see 7:119 (3 references).

REFERENCES THROUGH 1971

1–3. See 7:119.
4. LARSON, ROBERT ERNEST. *Adolescent Perceptions of Parent-Youth Communication: Patterns, Processes, and Correlates.* Doctor's thesis, Florida State University (Tallahassee, Fla.), 1970. (*DAI* 31:4918A)

CUMULATIVE NAME INDEX

Bienvenu, M. J.: 1
Larson, R. E.: 4
Love, N. W.: 3

Orr, D. B.: *rev*, 7:119
Taylor, D. H.: 2

[1311]

*The Perceptual Maze Test.** Ages 6–16, adults; 1955–73; PMT; brain damage; 2 levels; Alick Elithorn, Janice Smith (manual), and David Jones (manual); Medical Research Council [England]. *

a) CHILDREN'S EDITION. Ages 6–16; 1969–73.
b) ADULT EDITION. Adults; 1955–68.
c) RECTANGULAR VERSION. Adults; 1955–67; "while this version. . . . has some advantages it has in general been superseded by the triangular version" (b above).

For additional information and reviews by Manfred J. Meier and Aubrey J. Yates, see 7:120 (3 references); see also P:190A (23 references).

REFERENCES THROUGH 1971

1–23. See P:190A.
24–26. See 7:120.
27. DAVIES, ANN D. M. "Measurement of Mental Deterioration in Aging and Brain Damage." Discussion by Walter W. Surwillo. *Interdiscipl Topics Gerontol* 1:78–92 '68. *

CUMULATIVE NAME INDEX

Archibald, Y. M.: 18–9, 22
Beard, R. M.: 9
Benton, A. L.: 3
Buckingham, R. A.: 4
Chown, S.: 20
Colonna, A.: 16
Davies, A. D. M.: 10–2, 27
Davies, M. G.: 11–2
Elithorn, A.: 1–8, 13–4, 17, 23, 25
Faglioni, P.: 16
Fogel, M. L.: 3
Gross, M. L.: 24
Heron, A.: 20

Jagoe, J. R.: 17
Jahoda, G.: 26
Jones, D.: 5, 8
Jones, L. V.: 18–9
Kerr, M.: 2–3, 5, 8
Lee, D.: 8
Lee, D. N.: 4, 15, 17, 21
Meier, M. J.: *rev*, 7:120
Nixon, W. L. B.: 4
Surwillo, W. W.: 27
Telford, A.: 25
Wepman, J. M.: 18–9, 22
Yates, A. J.: *rev*, 7:120

[1312]

*Personal Adjustment Index: ETSA Test 8A.** Job applicants; 1960–73, c1957–59; revision of *Personal Adjustability Test;* 8 scores: community spirit, attitude toward cooperation, attitude toward health, attitude toward authority, nervous tendencies, leadership, job stability, total; manual and technical handbook by S. Trevor Hadley and George A. W. Stouffer, Jr.; test by Psychological Services Bureau; Educators'-Employers' Tests & Services Associates. * For the complete battery entry, see 2106.

For reviews of the complete battery, see 6:1025 (2 reviews).

[1313]

Personal Adjustment Inventory. Ages 9–13; 1931–61; PAI; formerly called *Test of Personality Adjustment;* test booklet title is *P. A. Inventory;* 5 scores: personal inferiority, social maladjustment, family maladjustment, daydreaming, total; 1961 tests identical with tests copyrighted 1931 except for four wording changes; 1961 manual identical with 1931 manual except for introduction and minor revisions; Carl R. Rogers; Association Press. *

For additional information, see P:191 (2 references); for reviews by Norman D. Sundberg and Robert D. Wirt, see 6:154 (6 references); for reviews by Dan L. Adler and Harrison G. Gough, see 5:117 (19 references); for a review by C. M. Louttit, see 2:1258.

REFERENCES THROUGH 1971

1–19. See 5:117.
20–25. See 6:154.
26–27. See P:191.
28. WATSON, GOODWIN, AND FORLANO, GEORGE. "Prima Facie Validity in Character Tests." *J Ed Psychol* 26:1–16 Ja '35. * (*PA* 9:2874)
29. BRUNSCHWIG, LILY. "Study of Some Personality Aspects of Deaf Children." *Teach Col Contrib Ed* 687:1–143 '36. * (*PA* 10:5861)
30. MOTT, SINA M. "Mother-Father Preference." *Char & Pers* 5:302–4 Je '37. * (*PA* 11:4859)
31. WOLF, S. J. "A Comparative Study of Two Groups of Girls of Relatively Equal Intelligence but Differing Markedly in Achievement." *J Appl Psychol* 21:304–10 Je '37. * (*PA* 11:4815)
32. MORGAN, JOHN J. B., AND BANKER, MARY H. "The Relation of Mental Stamina to Parental Protection." *J Genetic Psychol* 52:347–60 Je '38. * (*PA* 13:608)
33. FRANKLIN, MARY LELIA. *A Study of Personality Maladjustment Among Elementary School Children.* Master's thesis, University of Colorado (Boulder, Colo.), 1939. (Abstract: *Univ Colo Studies* 26:56)
34. HENKE, MILO W., AND KUHLEN, RAYMOND G. "Changes in Social Adjustment in a Summer Camp: A Preliminary Report." *J Psychol* 15:223–31 Ap '43. * (*PA* 17:2791)
35. JONES, HAROLD E. "Physical Ability as a Factor in Social

Adjustment in Adolescence." *J Ed Res* 40:287–301 D '46. * (*PA* 21:1695)

36. GRACE, GLORIA LAUER. "The Relation of Personality Characteristics and Response to Verbal Approval in a Learning Task." *Genetic Psychol Monogr* 37:73–103 F '48. * (*PA* 22:4825)

37. CRAWFORD, RONALD EUGENE. *Teacher-Pupil Personality Relationships.* Doctor's thesis, New York University (New York, N.Y.), 1953. (*DA* 13:589)

38. BURCHINAL, LEE GARWOOD. *The Relation of Parental Acceptance to Adjustment of Children.* Doctor's thesis, Ohio State University (Columbus, Ohio), 1956. (*DA* 16:1528)

39. KOPPITZ, ELIZABETH MUNSTERBERG. "Relationships Between Some Background Factors and Children's Interpersonal Attitude." *J Genetic Psychol* 91:119–29 S '57. * (*PA* 36:1FF19K)

40. NUDD, ELLEN. "Perception of Pictured Social Interactions by Brain-Injured and Non-Brain-Injured Children of Normal Intelligence." *Excep Children* 24:242–8+ F '58. * (*PA* 33:6755)

41. GRUPE, AUDREY JEAN. *Adjustment and Acceptance of Mentally Superior Children in Regular and Special Fifth Grade Classes in a Public School System.* Doctor's thesis, University of Illinois (Urbana, Ill.), 1961. (*DA* 22:1508)

42. LEREA, LOUIS, AND KOHUT, SUZANNE. "A Comparative Study of Monolinguals and Bilinguals in a Verbal Task Performance." *J Clin Psychol* 17:49–52 Ja '61. * (*PA* 37:2480)

43. LINN, GEORGE WILLIAM. *An Exploratory Comparison of the Personal Social Adjustment of Selected Participants and Nonparticipants in Two Junior High School Athletic Programs.* Doctor's thesis, University of Michigan (Ann Arbor, Mich.), 1961. (*DA* 22:2281)

44. DAVIS, MARIE LEONORA FARANDA. *Prattville: A Study of Adolescent Values and Self-Concepts.* Doctor's thesis, University of Connecticut (Storrs, Conn.), 1962. (*DA* 23:1602)

45. GREENE, JAMES E., SR. "Factors Associated With Absenteeism Among Students in Two Metropolitan High Schools." *J Exp Ed* 31:389–94 su '63. *

46. BERGER, SUSAN ROBBINS. *The Effects of a Cross-Cultural Experience Upon the Personal and Social Adjustment of Selected American Elementary School Students.* Doctor's thesis, Boston University (Boston, Mass.), 1966. (*DA* 27:3715A)

47. TURBERG, JESSIE. *An Investigation of the Association of Maternal Attitudes and Childhood Obesity and the Self-Concept of the Obese Child.* Doctor's thesis, New York University (New York, N.Y.), 1966. (*DA* 28:243B)

CUMULATIVE NAME INDEX

Adler, D. L.: *rev,* 5:117	Kohut, S.: 42
Babcock, M. E.: 2	Koppitz, E. M.: 39
Banker, M. H.: 32	Kuhlen, R. G.: 34
Berger, S. R.: 46	L'Abate, L.: 24–5
Boynton, P. L.: 3	Leibman, O. B.: 11
Brunschwig, L.: 29	Lerea, L.: 42
Burchinal, L. G.: 16, 18, 20, 38	Linn, G. W.: 43
Christy, W. J.: 7	Louttit, C. M.: *rev,* 2:1258
Clarke, H. J.: 5	Mason, E. P.: 9
Clements, S. D.: 23	Mensh, I. N.: 9
Cramer, W. F.: 26	Morgan, J. J. B.: 32
Crawford, R. E.: 37	Mott, S. M.: 30
Davis, M. L. F.: 44	Norris, N. P.: 27
Dorfman, E.: 21	Nowell, A.: 12
Epstein, H. L.: 6	Nudd, E.: 40
Forlano, G.: 28	Oxford, N. C.: 22
Franklin, M. L.: 33	Prickett, F. S.: 13
Gardner, E.: 16–8	Rogers, C. R.: 1
Gibson, R. L.: 8	Satterlee, R. L.: 14
Gough, H. G.: *rev,* 5:117	Schwartz, A.: 6
Grace, G. L.: 36	Smith, L. M.: 15, 19
Greene, J. E.: 45	Spaeth, C. F.: 10
Gruen, E. W.: 4	Sundberg, N. D.: *rev,* 6:154
Grupe, A. J.: 41	Turberg, J.: 47
Hawkes, G. R.: 16–8	Walsworth, B. M.: 3
Henke, M. W.: 34	Watson, G.: 28
Jones, H. E.: 35	Wirt, R. D.: *rev,* 6:154
	Wolf, S. J.: 31

[1314]

Personal Audit. Grades 9–16 and adults; 1941–45; PA; emotional adjustment; 2 editions; Clifford R. Adams and William M. Lepley; Science Research Associates, Inc. *

a) FORM SS (SHORT FORM). 6 scores: seriousness, firmness, frankness, tranquility, stability, tolerance.

b) FORM LL (LONG FORM). 9 scores: 6 scores same as for short form plus steadiness, persistence, contentment.

For additional information, see P:192 (6 references); for a review by William Seeman, see 4:75 (3 references); for a review by Percival M. Symonds, see 3:64 (10 references).

REFERENCES THROUGH 1971

1–9. See 3:64.
10–12. See 4:75.
13–18. See P:192.
19. PHILLIPS, DAVID C. "Factors of Effective and Ineffective Conversation." *Speech Monogr* 16:203–13 S '49. * (*PA* 24:4582)
20. JONES, WORTH ROOSEVELT. *A Study of the Affective Tolerance and the Typical Problems of Married and Unmarried Undergraduate College Students.* Doctor's thesis, Indiana University (Bloomington, Ind.), 1955. (*DA* 15:2325)
21. SMITH, WENDELL I.; POWELL, ELIZABETH K.; AND ROSS, SHERMAN. "Food Aversions: Some Additional Personality Correlates." *J Consult Psychol* 19:145–9 Ap '55. * (*PA* 30:1270)
22. HUCKABEE, MALCOM W. "Response Style in a Personality Inventory With Multiple Choice Format: The Stability-Emotionality Scale of the Personal Audit." *South J Ed Res* 3(3):167–74 Jl '69. *

CUMULATIVE NAME INDEX

Adams, C. R.: 2, 7	Powell, E. K.: 21
Adams, E. L.: 5a	Reppert, H. C.: 6
Becker, J. A.: 18	Ross, S.: 21
Cerf, A. Z.: 10	Sawyer, J.: 16
Giese, W. J.: 11	Seeman, W.: *rev,* 4:75
Gilliard, S. B.: 3	Smith, W. I.: 21
Huckabee, M. W.: 22	Spaney, B.: 15
Jones, W. R.: 17, 20	Super, D. E.: 8
Lepley, W. M.: 4	Symonds, P. M.: *rev,* 3:64
Lifton, W. M.: 12	Thompson, C. E.: 9
O'Shea, J. V.: 14	Tubbs, W. R.: 1, 5
Phillips, D. C.: 19	Walcher, H. R.: 13

[1315]

Personal Orientation Inventory. Grades 9–16 and adults; 1962–68; POI; 12 scores: time competent, inner directed, self-actualizing value, existentiality, feeling reactivity, spontaneity, self regard, self acceptance, nature of man, synergy, acceptance of aggression, capacity for intimate contact; Everett L. Shostrom; Educational and Industrial Testing Service. *

For additional information and reviews by Bruce Bloxom and Richard W. Coan, see 7:121 (97 references); see also P:193 (26 references).

REFERENCES THROUGH 1971

1–26. See P:193.
27–123. See 7:121.
124. WEIS, SUSAN F. *An Exploratory Study of the Nature of the Occurrence of Creativity and Self Actualization Among College Students Making Vocational Selections in Home Economics Fields.* Master's thesis, Pennsylvania State University (University Park, Pa.), 1966.
125. GRATER, M. R. *Effects of Knowledge of Characteristics of Self-Actualization and Faking of a Self-Actualized Response on Shostrom's Personal Orientation Inventory.* Master's thesis, University of Toledo (Toledo, Ohio), 1968.
126. MCLOONE, GERALD WILLIAM. *Relationships Between a Measure of Anxiety and Aspects of Self-Actualization, With Implications for Vocational Choice and Vocational Counseling.* Master's thesis, Catholic University of America (Washington, D.C.), 1968.
127. AUBRY, WILLIAM EDWARD. *An Analysis of a One-Week Workshop for Developing Self-Actualization and Effective Interpersonal Behavior.* Doctor's thesis, University of Arizona (Tucson, Ariz.), 1970. (*DAI* 31:4446A)
128. BLAIR, CHARLES EDWARD. *An Examination of the Relationship of the POI to Rated Success of Superintendents.* Doctor's thesis, Indiana University (Bloomington, Ind.), 1970. (*DAI* 31:5688A)
129. BOEHME, LINDA CAROLYN. *Persuasibility and Visual Perception of a Dress Design as Related to Selected Personality Characteristics.* Doctor's thesis, Pennsylvania State University (University Park, Pa.), 1970. (*DAI* 32:578B)
130. BOSBYSHELL, WILLIAM A. *Some Correlates of Empathic Counseling Behavior of Episcopal Clergymen.* Doctor's thesis, University of Florida (Gainesville, Fla.), 1970. (*DAI* 32:168A)
131. BOUVERAT, ROBERTA ANN. *A Study of Self-Actualization and Perceptions of Teaching Roles of Prospective Teachers of Young Children.* Doctor's thesis, Ohio State University (Columbus, Ohio), 1970. (*DAI* 32:85A)
132. BRENDEN, HERBERT ALLEN. *A Study of the Effects of Induced Anxiety and Induced Relaxation Upon the Performance of Subjects on the Personal Orientation Inventory.* Doctor's thesis, Ball State University (Muncie, Ind.), 1970. (*DAI* 31:7589B)
133. DAVIES, MICHAEL MARTIN. *A Comparison of the Effects of Sensitivity Training and Programmed Instruction on the Development of Human Relations Skills of Beginning Nursing Students in an Associate Degree Program.* Doctor's thesis, St. Louis University (St. Louis, Mo.), 1970. (*DAI* 32:734A)

134. DUNCAN, CLARENCE WALLACE. *A Comparison of Certain Experiences by Life Stages of Selected Groups of Self-Actualized, Modal, and Low-Functioning College Students.* Doctor's thesis, University of Florida (Gainesville, Fla.), 1970. (*DAI* 32:172A)

135. GREY, DAVID FRANCIS. *A Study of Terminators and Remainers in Treatment at a Community Mental Health Day Center.* Doctor's thesis, United States International University (San Diego, Calif.), 1970. (*DAI* 31:5622B)

136. HURD, DONALD EUGENE. *The Relationship of Affective Variables to College Achievement.* Doctor's thesis, Indiana University (Bloomington, Ind.), 1970. (*DAI* 31:5793A)

137. KLEINER, FREDRIC BARRY. *Personality and Training: Their Effects on the Communication of Empathy.* Doctor's thesis, Ohio State University (Columbus, Ohio), 1970. (*DAI* 32:563B)

138. KROUNER, PAUL JOSEPH. *The Relationship Between Teacher Psychological Health and Acceptance of the Paraprofessional.* Doctor's thesis, Syracuse University (Syracuse, N.Y.), 1970. (*DAI* 31:5671A)

139. McCLAIN, EDWIN W. "Personal Growth for Teachers in Training Through Self-Study." *J Teach Ed* 21(3):372–7 f '70. * (*PA* 45:8967)

140. MACE, RICHARD EDWARD. *Factors Influencing the Decisions of Teachers to Become Administrators: A Study of the Differences in Self-Actualization and Job Satisfaction Occurring Between Future Administrators and Career Teachers.* Doctor's thesis, Syracuse University (Syracuse, N.Y.), 1970. (*DAI* 32:132A)

141. MAUL, TERRY LEE. *An Investigation of the Relationships Between Self-Actualization and Creative Thinking Processes.* Doctor's thesis, University of California (Berkeley, Calif.), 1970. (*DAI* 32:793A)

142. OLIVER, CHARLES MICHAEL. *A Study of the Effects of Behavioral Group Counseling on Self-Actualization.* Doctor's thesis, University of Southern Mississippi (Hattiesburg, Miss.), 1970. (*DAI* 31:3881A)

143. PITTS, GRIFF D. *Values, Attitudes, Opinions, and Concerns of Subcultures of Concerned Students in an Urban Commuter College.* Doctor's thesis, Northwestern University (Evanston, Ill.), 1970. (*DAI* 31:5152A)

144. PROVOST, RICHARD LEON. *A Follow-Up Study of Beginning Teachers in Multi-Cultural Schools Who Have Attended a Pre-Service Institute Dealing With Problems of School Desegregation.* Doctor's thesis, East Texas State University (Commerce, Tex.), 1970. (*DAI* 31:4472A)

145. REEKIE, ELAGRACE. *Personality Factors and Biographical Characteristics Associated With Criterion Behaviors of Success in Professional Nursing.* Doctor's thesis, University of Washington (Seattle, Wash.), 1970. (*DAI* 31:5212A)

146. RUTSCHMANN, DONALD FREDERICK. *Affective Versus Cognitive Groups With Pre-College Blind Youth.* Doctor's thesis, University of Illinois (Urbana, Ill.), 1970. (*DAI* 32:1283A)

147. SCHMIDT, MONICA MARIE. *Effects of Group Interaction on the Self-Perceptions of Women in Religious Life.* Doctor's thesis, University of Illinois (Urbana, Ill.), 1970. (*DAI* 31:6353A)

148. SCHROEDER, BETTY LOU FOSTER. *An Examination of the Characteristics of Students and Faculty in a Small, Black, Denominational College.* Doctor's thesis, University of Texas (Austin, Tex.), 1970. (*DAI* 32:3703A)

149. SHAFER, BILL WAYNE. *A Study of Behavioral and Perceptual Changes in Counselor Trainees as a Result of Resident and Nonresident Practicum Programs.* Doctor's thesis, East Texas State University (Commerce, Tex.), 1970. (*DAI* 31:4475A)

150. STOUT, ROBERT J. *A Study of Alienation on Three Diverse Ohio College Campuses.* Doctor's thesis, Bowling Green State University (Bowling Green, Ohio), 1970. (*DAI* 31:6324A)

151. TALLANT, WELDON J. *Changes in Pre-Service Teachers Involved in a Multi-Cultural Training Program Utilizing Formal Presentations, Sensitivity Training, Planned Social Activities, and a Cooperative Living Arrangement.* Doctor's thesis, East Texas State University (Commerce, Tex.), 1970. (*DAI* 31:4608A)

152. TUCKER, FLOYD C., JR. *A Study of the Relationships Between: (1) Teachers' Level of Self-Actualization and Their Teaching Behavioral Styles, and (2) Teachers' Teaching Behavioral Styles and the Gratifications They Derive From Interacting With Their Students.* Doctor's thesis, Syracuse University (Syracuse, N.Y.), 1970. (*DAI* 31:5739A)

153. UHLIG, GEORGE E.; TROTTER, ANN B.; GOZALI, JOAV; AND TESCH, MARY JANE. "Self-Actualization in Hospitalized Disabled and Non-Hospitalized Adults as Measured by the Personal Orientation Inventory." *Psychol Aspects Disability* 17(2):83–5 Jl '70. * (*PA* 45:8709)

154. WESCH, JERRY EDWARD. *Self-Actualization and the Fear of Death.* Doctor's thesis, University of Tennessee (Knoxville, Tenn.), 1970. (*DAI* 31:6270B)

155. WHITE, HELEN MURIEL. *An Investigation of Some Characteristics of High and Low Self-Actualization and Their Relationship to Alienation From Self and Society.* Doctor's thesis, University of California (Berkeley, Calif.), 1970. (*DAI* 31:5142A)

156. BARNETT, LUCILE CATHERINE FECHTER. *The Effect of Silent Communications Upon Counseling Processes: An Experimental Study. The Relevance of Nonverbal Behavior and Self-Actualization for Counselor Empathy and Genuineness and Client Self-Exploration.* Doctor's thesis, University of Missouri (Kansas City, Mo.), 1971. (*DAI* 31:6336A)

157. BISHOP, HOWARD CLAY. *The Relationship Organizational Climate to Psychological Health of School Administrators in Selected Black and White Elementary Schools of Florida.* Doctor's thesis, Syracuse University (Syracuse, N.Y.), 1971. (*DAI* 32:4267A)

158. BROCKOPP, GENE W., AND LESTER, DAVID. "Time Competence and Suicidal History." *Psychol Rep* 28(1):80 F '71 * (*PA* 46:5174)

159. CHEDEKEL, DAVID SELWYN. *The Levels of Anxiety and Self-Actualization in Dropout-Prone Ninth Grade Boys.* Doctor's thesis, Boston University (Boston, Mass.), 1971. (*DAI* 32:1847A)

160. COBLE, CHARLES RAY. *An Analysis of the Relationship Between the Biology Teacher's Level of Self-Actualization and Student Progress.* Doctor's thesis, University of North Carolina (Chapel Hill, N.C.), 1971. (*DAI* 32:2503A)

161. COHEN, ALAN WARREN. *Some Factors Relating to the Attrition of Beginning Teachers From Inner City Schools: Predictors for Improved Recruitment.* Doctor's thesis, University of Connecticut (Storrs, Conn.), 1971. (*DAI* 32:1330A)

162. COOPER, CARY L. "T-Group Training and Self-Actualization." *Psychol Rep* 28(2):391–4 Ap '71. * (*PA* 46:7870)

163. DAVIS, JAMES BARRETT. *An Investigation of the Utility of Sixteen Personality Factor Questionnaire Scores in Predicting Counseling Effectiveness.* Doctor's thesis, University of Southern Mississippi (Hattiesburg, Miss.), 1971. (*DAI* 32:4939A)

164. FISHER, GARY. "Self-Actualization of 'Paranormals.'" *J Pers Assess* 35(5):486–91 O '71. * (*PA* 47:7944)

165. FOULDS, MELVIN L. "Measured Changes in Self-Actualization as a Result of Growth Group Experience." *Psychother Theory Res & Prac* 8(4):338–41 w '71. * (*PA* 50:910)

166. FOULDS, MELVIN L., AND WAREHIME, ROBERT G. "Effects of a 'Fake Good' Response Set on a Measure of Self-Actualization." *J Counsel Psychol* 18(3):279–80 My '71. * (*PA* 46:4948)

167. FOULDS, MELVIN L., AND WAREHIME, ROBERT G. "Relationship Between Repression-Sensitization and a Measure of Self-Actualization." *J Consult & Clin Psychol* 36(2):257–9 Ap '71. * (*PA* 46:3024)

168. FREEMAN, HARVEY R., AND BRUBAKER, PAUL. "Personality Characteristics of Campus Demonstrators Compared to Non-demonstrators." *J Counsel Psychol* 18(5):462–4 S '71. * (*PA* 47:3600)

169. GORDON, RONALD DOUGLAS. *A Quantitative Investigation of Selected Dynamics and Outcomes of the Basic Encounter Group.* Doctor's thesis, University of Kansas (Lawrence, Kan.), 1971. (*DAI* 32:6046B)

170. GRAFF, ROBERT W., AND LADD, CLAYTON E. "POI Correlates of a Religious Commitment Inventory." *J Clin Psychol* 27(4):502–4 O '71. * (*PA* 47:8903)

171. HAMILTON, JAMES T. "Educational Administrators and Their Level of Self-Actualization." *Ed Leadership* 28(6):633–5 Mr '71. *

172. HAYES, PRESLEY LEANDER, III. *A Study of the Relationship of a Measure of Self-Actualization to Resident Counselor Effectiveness.* Doctor's thesis, University of Virginia (Charlottesville, Va.), 1971. (*DAI* 32:4349A)

173. HEATON, JEAN MOSSMAN. *Adolescent Orientation, Achievement and Family Interaction.* Doctor's thesis, Florida State University (Tallahassee, Fla.), 1971. (*DAI* 32:6486B)

174. HEKMAT, HAMID, AND THEISS, MICHAEL. "Self-Actualization and Modification of Affective Self-Disclosures During a Social Conditioning Interview." *J Counsel Psychol* 18(2):101–5 Mr '71. * (*PA* 46:1331)

175. INSKO, W. ROBERT. "Developing Family Actualization: The Frankfort Project." *Family Coordinator* 20(1):17–22 Ja '71. *

176. JACKSON, ARTHUR MELLS. *The Effects of Three Group Approaches in Effecting Change Among Black Students.* Doctor's thesis, Indiana University (Bloomington, Ind.), 1971. (*DAI* 32:4351A)

177. JEFFERS, JAMES JOHN LYLE. *Effects of Marathon Encounter Groups on Personality Characteristics of Group Members and Group Facilitators.* Doctor's thesis, University of Colorado (Boulder, Colo.), 1971. (*DAI* 32:4153A)

178. JONES, LAWRENCE KEITH. *Relationship Between Self-Disclosure and Positive Mental Health, Modeled Self-Disclosure, and Socioeconomic Status.* Doctor's thesis, University of Missouri (Columbia, Mo.), 1971. (*DAI* 32:4953A)

179. KLINGBERG, HADDON E., JR. *An Evaluation of Sensitivity Training Effects on Self-Actualization, Purpose in Life, and Religious Attitudes of Theological Students.* Doctor's thesis, Fuller Theological Seminary (Pasadena, Calif.), 1971. (*DAI* 32:7312B)

180. LEATHERWOOD, HELEN WAUGH. *The Effectiveness of Small-Group Procedures in the Classroom as Aids in Movement Toward Self-Actualization in Junior College Students.* Doctor's thesis, East Texas State University (Commerce, Tex.), 1971. (*DAI* 32:4988A)

181. LO, SAMUEL NAI-MING. *Effects of Self-Reinforcement*

Personal Orientation Inventory

and *Goal-Setting on the Affect and Personal Orientation of Housewives.* Doctor's thesis, Fuller Theological Seminary (Pasadena, Calif.), 1971. (*DAI* 32:7315B)

182. MARGULIS, MARTIN. *Perceptual and Cognitive Correlates of Self-Actualization.* Doctor's thesis, University of Maine (Orono, Me.), 1971. (*DAI* 32:6055B)

183. MAZER, GILBERT E., AND ENGLE, KENNETH B. "Personality and Attitude Change in Counselor Trainees: An Evaluation." *Counselor Ed & Sup* 10(3):273–81 sp '71. * (PA 47:1379)

184. MELCHERS, EARL EARNEST. *The Value of the Personal Orientation Inventory in Predicting Counselor Effectiveness and the Value of a Counseling Practicum in Promoting Self-Actualization.* Doctor's thesis, University of Northern Colorado (Greeley, Colo.), 1971. (*DAI* 32:3696A)

185. MULLOZZI, ANTHONY, JR., AND SPEES, EMIL R. "Factors in Selecting Residence Hall Fellows." *J Nat Assn Women Deans & Counselors* 34(4):185–90 su '71. *

186. MUNDEN, J. R. *An Analysis of a Master of Education Program in Counseling and Guidance Through a Follow-Up of Graduates for the Period of 1965 Through 1969.* Doctor's thesis, St. Louis University (St. Louis, Mo.), 1971. (*DAI* 32:742A)

187. OHLBAUM, JUDY SUE. *Self-Concepts, Value Characteristics and Self-Actualization of Professional and Non-Professional Women.* Doctor's thesis, United States International University (San Diego, Calif.), 1971. (*DAI* 32:1221B)

188. PENNER, CLIFFORD LEVIS. *The Effectiveness of a Theologically Oriented Approach to Lay Counselor Training.* Doctor's thesis, Fuller Theological Seminary (Pasadena, Calif.), 1971. (*DAI* 32:6658B)

189. POE, BOBBY JOE. *The Effect of Sensitivity Training on the Relationship Between Risk Taking and Other Selected Behavioral Factors.* Doctor's thesis, East Texas State University (Commerce, Tex.), 1971. (*DAI* 32:6637B)

190. POST, ALAN WILSON. *Deprivation of Opportunity: Industrial Mental Health and Job Behavior.* Doctor's thesis, Case Western Reserve University (Cleveland, Ohio), 1971. (*DAI* 32:5507B)

191. ROHALY, KATHLEEN ALICE. *The Relationships Between Movement Participation, Movement Satisfaction, Self-Actualization, and Trait Anxiety in Selected College Freshmen Women.* Doctor's thesis, Ohio State University (Columbus, Ohio), 1971. (*DAI* 32:3766A)

192. ROWE, WAYNE. *The Effect of Short-Term Group Counseling and Cognitive Learning on a Measure of Self-Actualization of Counselors in Training.* Doctor's thesis, Michigan State University (East Lansing, Mich.), 1971. (*DAI* 32:4965A)

193. RUBIN, HOWARD STANLEY. *The Prevention of Student Attrition in Nursing Education: A Community Psychology Approach.* Doctor's thesis, Illinois Institute of Technology (Chicago, Ill.), 1971. (*DAI* 33:1296B)

194. SANDS, BILLIE LOU. "Relationship Between Family Life Teachers' Self-Actualization and Self-Perception of Competency." *J Home Econ* 63(2):113–5 F '71. *

195. SMITH, ROSEMARY. "Repression-Sensitization Related to a Measure of Self-Actualization." *Proc W Va Acad Sci* 42(1970):262–6 '71. *

196. STEPHENSON, GERALD HARRIS. *Group Counseling Experience for Elementary Education Majors: Effects on Selected Personality Characteristics and Interrelationships Between Selected Counselor and Client Variables.* Doctor's thesis, North Texas State University (Denton, Tex.), 1971. (*DAI* 32:6771A)

197. TROTTER, ANN B.; UHLIG, GEORGE E.; AND FARGO, GLENN E. "Self-Actualization as a Predictor of Rehabilitation Counselor Success." *Rehabil Counsel B* 15(1):58–67 S '71. * (PA 47:9411)

198. TUELLER, REX LAMAR. *The Use of Personality Traits in Predicting Doctoral Student Success at Utah State University.* Doctor's thesis, Utah State University (Logan, Utah), 1971. (*DAI* 32:3723A)

199. UHES, MICHAEL J., AND SHYBUT, JOHN. "Personal Orientation Inventory as a Predictor of Success in Peace Corps Training." *J Appl Psychol* 55(5):498–9 O '71. * (PA 47:7883)

200. VANDER WILT, ROBERT B., AND KLOCKE, RONALD A. "Self-Actualization of Females in an Experimental Orientation Program." *J Nat Assn Women Deans & Counselors* 34(3):125–9 sp '71. *

201. VAUGHAN, JAMES LELAND. *Measurement and Analysis of Values Pertaining to Psychotherapy and Mental Health.* Doctor's thesis, Columbia University (New York, N.Y.), 1971. (*DAI* 32:3655B)

202. WAREHIME, ROBERT G., AND FOULDS, MELVIN L. "Perceived Locus of Control and Personal Adjustment." *J Consult & Clin Psychol* 37(2):250–2 O '71. * (PA 47:8921)

203. WEBSTER, ALAN C. "Factor Analysis of Family Attitudes, Cooperation, Personality, and Personal Orientation in a Small New Zealand Sample." *Personality* 2(3):249–66 au '71. * (PA 47:6618)

CUMULATIVE NAME INDEX

Vance, E. M. B.: 18
Vander Wilt, R. B.: 200
Vaughan, J. L.: 201
Walker, N. P.: 66
Wall, J. B.: 121
Warehime, R. G.: 166–7, 202
Webster, A. C.: 120, 203
Weir, W.: 97
Weir, W. R.: 19

Weis, S. F.: 124
Wesch, J. E.: 154
White, H. M.: 155
Whitsett, D. A.: 40
Yeager, J. C.: 98
Young, E. R.: 122
Zaccaria, J. S.: 19
Zimmerman, S. F.: 99, 123

[1316]

The Personal Preference Scale. Ages 15 and over;
1947–54; PPS; 10 scores: active-inactive, sociable-
individualistic, permissive-critical, consistent-inconsistent, efficient-inefficient, self effacing-egocentric, mascu-
line-effeminoid, feminine-masculinoid, emotionally
mature-emotionally immature, socially mature-socially
immature; Maurice H. Krout and Johanna Krout;
[Johanna Krout Tabin]. *

For additional information, see P:194 (5 references); see also 5:93 (2 references).

REFERENCES THROUGH 1971

1–2. See 5:93.
3–7. See P:194.
8. STAGNER, ROSS, AND MOFFITT, J. WELDON. "A Statistical
Study of Freud's Theory of Personality Types." *J Clin Psychol*
12:72–4 Ja '56. * (*PA* 30:4201)
9. HAWARD, L. R. C. "Personality of Parachutists: Part 2,
Psychosexual Profiles of American and British Paratroops."
Flight Safety (England) 2(4):16–7 My '69. * (*PA* 46:6887)

CUMULATIVE NAME INDEX

Cohler, J. R.: 3
Haward, L. R. C.: 6, 9
Krout, M. H.: 1
Lawson, E. D.: 2
Littman, R. A.: 7
McNeil, E. B.: 3
Moffitt, J. W.: 2, 8

Nidorf, L.: 4
Nidorf, L. J.: 7
Snider, M.: 5
Stagner, R.: 2, 8
Sundberg, N. D.: 7
Tabin, J. K.: 1

[1317]

★**Personal Values Abstract.** Ages 13 and over;
1972, c1956–70; PVA; 3-scale abstract of *California
Psychological Inventory;* 3 scores: modernity (My,
composite of CPI scales Do, Cs, Sy, Sp, Sa, Wb),
socialization (Sn), femininity (Fy); Harrison G.
Gough; Consulting Psychologists Press, Inc. *

[1318]

Personal Values Inventory. Grades 12–13; 1941–69;
PVI; for predicting academic achievement; 12 scores:
high school self report, need for achievement, direction
of aspirations, socioeconomic status, peer influence,
home influence, planning, persistence, self control, total
of persistence and self control, faking, self insight; separate editions for men and women; George E. Schlesser, John A. Finger, and Thomas Lynch (manual);
Colgate University Testing Service. *

For additional information and reviews by Henry A.
Alker and Robert R. Knapp, see 7:122 (2 references);
see also P:195 (15 references).

REFERENCES THROUGH 1971

1–15. See P:195.
16–17. See 7:122.
18. PRATT, EARLE W. *A Validation Study of Self-Control
and Deliberateness Scale of the Personal Values Inventory.*
Master's thesis, Colgate University (Hamilton, N.Y.), 1964.
19. PINTO, PHYLLIS. *The Personal Values Inventory and
Elementary School Academic Performance.* Master's thesis,
Adelphi University (Garden City, N.Y.), 1966.
20. WRIGHT, DONALD LELLAND. *Non-Intellective Factors
Differentiating Academic Warning Students From General
College Students, Humanities and Social Science Students, and
Honor Roll Students as Measured by the Personal Values
Inventory.* Master's thesis, Brigham Young University (Provo,
Utah), 1966.

CUMULATIVE NAME INDEX

Alker, H. A.: *rev,* 7:122
Bidgood, F. E.: 6
d'Heurle, A.: 2
Finegan, A.: 13

Finger, J. A.: 4, 7, 10–2
Foresman, C. S.: 5
Grande, P. P.: 14–6
Haggard, E. A.: 2

Knapp, R. R.: *rev,* 7:122
McCord, C. G.: 3
Mellinger, J. C.: 2
Pallone, N. J.: 15
Pinto, P.: 19
Pratt, E. W.: 18
Rivera, E.: 17

Schlesser, G. E.: 1, 4, 7
Silverman, M.: 12
Simons, J. B.: 14–5
Smith, C. L.: 8
Stone, D. B.: 9
Wright, D. L.: 20

[1319]

**The Personality Evaluation Form: A Technique
for the Organization and Interpretation of Personality Data.** Ages 2 and over; 1955; PEF; Charlotte Buhler and Gertrude Howard; Western Psychological Services. *

For additional information, see P:197; for a review
by Dorothy H. Eichorn and an excerpted review by
Laurance F. Shaffer, see 5:94.

[1320]

The Personality Inventory. Grades 9–16 and adults;
1931–38; PI, also BPI; commonly called *Bernreuter
Personality Inventory;* 6 scores: neurotic tendency,
self-sufficiency, introversion-extroversion, dominance-
submission, confidence, sociability; Robert G. Bernreuter; Consulting Psychologists Press, Inc. *

For additional information, see P:198 (20 references); for reviews by Wesley C. Becker and Donald
J. Veldman, see 6:157 (22 references); see also 5:95
(39 references); for a review by Leona E. Tyler, see
4:77 (188 references); for reviews by Charles I. Mosier and Theodore Newcomb, see 2:1239 (72 references). For excerpts from related book reviews, see
1:B358 (2 excerpts).

REFERENCES THROUGH 1971

1–71. See 2:1239.
72–259. See 4:77.
260–299. See 5:95.
300–321. See 6:157.
322–341. See P:198.
342. CARROLL, HERBERT A. "A Preliminary Report on a Study
of the Relationship Between Ability in Art and Certain
Personality Traits." *Sch & Soc* 36:285–8 Ag 27 '32. * (*PA*
7:230)
343. DOWNEY, JUNE E. "Familial Trends in Personality."
Char & Pers 1:35–47 S '32. * (*PA* 7:124)
344. HOFFEDITZ, E. LOUISE. *Family Resemblances in Personality Traits.* Master's thesis, Pennsylvania State University
(University Park, Pa.), 1932.
345. McMURRY, ROBERT N. "Efficiency, Work-Satisfaction
and Neurotic Tendency: A Study of Bank Employees." *Personnel
J* 11:201–10 D '32. * (*PA* 7:1086)
346. ALLEN, GRACE E. "Plane Geometry and Character Education." *J Ed Sociol* 7:254–8 D '33. * (*PA* 8:2254)
347. McLELLAND, MAY. *A Study of the Relationship of the
Traits Measured by the Bernreuter Inventory to the Adjustment
Problems of a Group of Junior College Students.* Master's thesis,
North Carolina State College (Raleigh, N.C.), 1933.
348. MILES, C. C. "Age and Certain Personality Traits of
Adults." Abstract. *Psychol B* 30:570 O '33. * (*PA* 8:1191,
title only)
349. PALMER, IRENE. "Personal Qualities of Women Teachers
of Physical Education: Their Relation to the Problem of the
Guidance of the Prospective Teacher." *Res Q* 4:31–8 D '33. *
350. PINTNER, RUDOLF. "Emotional Stability of the Hard of
Hearing." *J Genetic Psychol* 43:293–311 D '33. * (*PA* 8:3661)
351. DEXTER, EMILY S., AND OMWAKE, KATHARINE T. "The
Relation Between Pitch Discrimination and Accent in Modern
Languages." *J Appl Psychol* 18:267–71 Ap '34. * (*PA* 8:5221)
352. ENGLE, T. L. "A Personality Study of a Group of High
School Honor Society Pupils." *J Appl Psychol* 18:293–6 Ap
'34. * (*PA* 8:5090)
353. HARTMANN, GEORGE W. "Personality Traits Associated
With Variations in Happiness." *J Abn & Social Psychol* 29:
202–12 Jl–S '34. * (*PA* 9:1287)
354. HOFFEDITZ, E. LOUISE. "Family Resemblances in Personality Traits." *J Social Psychol* 5:214–27 My '34. * (*PA*
8:5996)
355. OMWAKE, KATHARINE T.; DEXTER, EMILY S.; AND
LEWIS, L. WAYNE. "The Inter-Relations of Certain Physiological
Measurements and Aspects of Personality." *Char & Pers* 3:64–71
S '34. * (*PA* 9:291)
356. ROTHNEY, JOHN WATSON MURRAY. *Interests in Relation
to School Success at the High School Level.* Doctor's thesis,
Harvard University (Cambridge, Mass.), 1934.
357. STONE, CALVIN P., AND BARKER, ROGER G. "On the
Relationships Between Menarcheal Age and Certain Aspects of

Personality, Intelligence and Physique in College Women." *J Genetic Psychol* 45:121–35 S '34. * *(PA* 9:463)

358. BERNARD, JESSIE. "Some Biological Factors in Personality and Marriage." *Hum Biol* 7:430–6 S '35. * *(PA* 10:2580)

359. BERNHOLZ, ELNA. *Independence of Traits and Consistency of Measurement in the Bernreuter Personality Inventory.* Master's thesis, Columbia University (New York, N.Y.), 1935.

360. BROWN, RALPH H. "Drug Addiction in Its Relation to Extraversion, Ambiversion and Introversion." *J Appl Psychol* 19:555–63 O '35. * *(PA* 10:1989)

361. CARTER, HAROLD D. "Twin-Similarities in Emotional Traits." *Char & Pers* 4:61–78 S '35. * *(PA* 10:320)

362. DAVIS, FREDERICK B., AND RULON, PHILLIP J. "Gossip and the Introvert." *J Abn & Social Psychol* 30:17–21 Ap–Je '35. * *(PA* 9:5763)

363. GOLDSTEIN, HYMAN. "The Biochemical Variability of the Individual in Relation to Personality and Intelligence." *J Exp Psychol* 18:348–71 Je '35. * *(PA* 9:4677)

364. HUNTER, ARIA DANIEL. "A Comparison of Introverted and Extroverted High School Speakers." *Speech Monogr* 2:50–3 S '35. * *(PA* 13:2761, title only)

365. MOORE, GLENN E. "Personality Changes Resulting From Training in Speech Fundamentals." *Speech Monogr* 2:56–9 S '35. * *(PA* 13:2639, title only)

366. NEWMAN, DERWOOD AUSTIN. *Curriculum Differentiation in Engineering: A Study of Statistical Differences as an Aid to Guidance in Engineering Colleges.* Doctor's thesis, Harvard University (Cambridge, Mass.), 1935.

367. OLDHAM, ERNESTINE VIVIAN. "The Socio-Economic Status and Personality of Negro Adolescent Girls." *J Negro Ed* 4:514–22 O '35. * *(PA* 10:1255)

368. SWARD, KEITH, AND FRIEDMAN, MEYER B. "The Family Resemblance in Temperament." *J Abn & Social Psychol* 30:256–61 Jl–S '35. * *(PA* 10:1978)

369. TRACY, JAMES A. "A Study of Personality Traits of Mature Actors and Mature Public Speakers." *Speech Monogr* 2:53–6 S '35. * *(PA* 13:2611, title only)

370. DUGGAN, ANNE SCHLEY. "A Comparative Study of Undergraduate Women Majors and Non-Majors With Respect to Certain Personality Traits." *Teach Col Contrib Ed* 682:1–117 '36. * *(PA* 10:5862)

371. HEILMAN, J. D., AND ARMENTROUT, W. D. "The Rating of College Teachers on Ten Traits by Their Students." *J Ed Psychol* 27:197–216 Mr '36. * *(PA* 10:3710)

372. MURRAY, ELWOOD. "A Study of Factors Contributing to the Maldevelopment of the Speech Personality." *Speech Monogr* 3:95–108 S '36. * *(PA* 13:3799)

373. ROYER, ELMER B. "A Formula for Intercorrelations Among Multi-Scores." *J Ed Psychol* 27:457–66 S '36. * *(PA* 11:35)

374. STAGNER, ROSS, AND KATZOFF, E. T. "Personality as Related to Birth Order and Family Size." *J Appl Psychol* 20:340–6 Je '36. * *(PA* 10:5462)

375. KENDIG, ISABEL. "Studies in Perseveration: 2, Determining Factors in the Development of Compulsive Activity." *J Psychol* 3:231–46 Ja '37. * *(PA* 11:4201)

376. MATHEWS, C. O. "Factors Which Contribute to Undesirable Overt Behavior." *J Consult Psychol* 1:41–8 My–Je '37. * *(PA* 11:3836)

377. NOLLEN, MARION. *The Relationship Between Certain Personality Traits and Religious Adjustment.* Master's thesis, Purdue University (Lafayette, Ind.), 1937.

378. NOTTINGHAM, RUTH D. "A Psychological Study of Forty Unmarried Mothers." *Genetic Psychol Monogr* 19:157–228 My '37. * *(PA* 11:4670)

379. SPEER, GEORGE S. "The Measurement of Emotions Aroused in Response to Personality Test Items." *J Psychol* 3:445–61 Ap '37. * *(PA* 11:5184)

380. STONE, C. P., AND BARKER, R. G. "Aspects of Personality and Intelligence in Post Menarcheal and Premenarcheal Girls of the Same Chronological Age." *J Comp Psychol* 23:439–45 Je '37. * *(PA* 11:4871)

381. YOUNG, KIMBALL; DROUGHT, NEAL; AND BERGSTRESSER, JOHN. "Social and Emotional Adjustments of Freshmen at the University of Wisconsin." *Am Sociol R* 2:166–77 Ap '37. * *(PA* 11:4377)

382. CABOT, P. S. DE Q. "The Relationship Between Characteristics of Personality and Physique in Adolescents." *Genetic Psychol Monogr* 20:3–120 F '38. * *(PA* 12:3592)

383. CLARKE, FRANCES M., AND SKULLY, JAMES H. "Guidance Problems in Connecticut C.C.C. Camps." *J Ed Res* 32:131–7 O '38. * *(PA* 13:390)

384. EAGLESON, ORAN W. "A Racial Comparison of Personality Traits." *J Appl Psychol* 22:271–4 Je '38. * *(PA* 12:6499)

385. HORSCH, ALFRED C., AND DAVIS, ROBERT A. "Personality Traits and Conduct of Institutionalized Delinquents." *J Am Inst Crim Law & Criminol* 29:241–4 Jl–Ag '38. * *(PA* 12:6561)

386. MESSER, A. L.; HINCKLEY, E. D.; AND MOSIER, C. I. "Suggestibility and Neurotic Symptoms in Normal Subjects." *J General Psychol* 19:391–9 O '38. * *(PA* 13:967)

387. REMMLEIN, MADALINE KINTER. "Analysis of Leaders

Among High-School Seniors." *J Exp Ed* 6:413–22 Je '38. * *(PA* 12:6533)

388. BENDER, JAMES F. *The Personality Structure of Stuttering,* pp. 69–106. New York: Pitman Publishing Corp., 1939. Pp. xvi, 189. * *(PA* 14:1953)

389. DENNIS, FLAVIUS ELIAS. *An Investigation of the Mental Ability, Educational Achievement, and Neurotic Tendencies of a Group of Partially Seeing Pupils.* Master's thesis, University of Colorado (Boulder, Colo.), 1939. (Abstract: *Univ Colo Studies* 26:48)

390. DOUGLASS, LOWELL N. "A Study of Certain Factors Influencing Academic Achievement With Special Reference to the Health Factor." *J Exp Ed* 7:235–44 Mr '39. * *(PA* 13:5911)

391. MOORE, WILBUR E. "Personality Traits and Voice Quality Deficiencies." *J Speech Disorders* 4:33–6 Mr '39. * *(PA* 13:4216)

392. TURNER, WILLIAM D., AND CARL, GEORGE P. "Temporary Changes in Affect and Attitude Following Ingestion of Various Amounts of Benzedrine Sulfate (Amphetamine Sulfate)." *J Psychol* 8:415–82 O '39. * *(PA* 14:1818)

393. ABERNETHY, ETHEL MARY. "Further Data on Personality and Family Position." *J Psychol* 10:303–7 O '40. * *(PA* 15:917)

394. ADAMS, CLIFFORD ROSE. *Individual Differences in Behavior Resulting From Experimentally Induced Frustration.* Doctor's thesis, Pennsylvania State University (University Park, Pa.), 1940.

395. LAYMAN, JAMES W. "A Quantitative Study of Certain Changes in Schizophrenic Patients Under the Influence of Sodium Amytal." *J General Psychol* 22:67–86 Ja '40. * *(PA* 14:2439)

396. MIDDLETON, WARREN C., AND MOFFETT, DONOVAN C. "The Relation of Height and Weight Measurements to Intelligence and to Dominance-Submission Among a Group of College Freshmen." *Res Q* 11:53–9 D '40. * *(PA* 15:1699)

397. TURNEY, AUSTIN H., AND COLLINS, FLOYD I. "An Experiment in Improving the Personality of High School Seniors." *J Ed Psychol* 31:550–3 O '40. * *(PA* 15:1988)

398. VAN DYNE, E. VIRGINIA. "Personality Traits and Friendship Formation in Adolescent Girls." *J Social Psychol* 12:291–303 N '40. * *(PA* 15:1843)

399. BILLIG, ALBERT LeROY. "Finger Nail-Biting: Its Incipience, Incidence, and Amelioration." *Genetic Psychol Monogr* 24:123–218 Ag '41. * *(PA* 16:795)

400. BOWN, MAX DUANE. "Variability as a Function of Ability and Its Relation to Personality and Interests." *Arch Psychol* 262:1–45 Jl '41. * *(PA* 16:493)

401. FAY, PAUL J., AND MIDDLETON, WARREN C. "The Ability to Judge Sociability From the Voice as Transmitted Over a Public Address System." *J Social Psychol* 13:303–9 My '41. * *(PA* 15:4704)

402. JOHANNSEN, DOROTHEA E. "The Effect of Neuroticism Upon the Capacity to Observe the Emotional Reactions of Friends." *J Social Psychol* 13:291–302 My '41. * *(PA* 15:4708)

403. LAZARSFELD, PAUL F., AND GAUDET, HAZEL. "Who Gets a Job?" *Sociometry* 4:64–77 F '41. * *(PA* 15:3514)

404. MIDDLETON, WARREN C. "The Ability of Untrained Subjects to Judge Neuroticism, Self-Confidence, and Sociability From Handwriting Samples." *Char & Pers* 9:227–34 Mr '41. * *(PA* 15:3476)

405. ROACH, JAMES H. L. "An Experimental Study of Suggestibility in Extroverts and Introverts." *J Appl Psychol* 25:458–68 Ag '41. * *(PA* 15:5109)

406. WRENN, C. GILBERT, AND CRANDALL, ELIZABETH B. "Behavior Ratings and Scholarship Among College Freshmen." *J Ed Res* 34:259–64 D '41. * *(PA* 15:2396)

407. FAY, PAUL J., AND MIDDLETON, WARREN C. "Judgment of Introversion From the Transcribed Voice." *Q J Speech* 28:226–8 Ap '42. * *(PA* 16:2725)

408. LOCKET, BERNARD. "Various Factors in a Penal Population." *J Crim Law & Criminol* 33:316–20 N–D '42. * *(PA* 17:1289)

409. DEXTER, EMILY S. "Relation of Imagination to Certain Other Factors." *J General Psychol* 28:139–41 Ja '43. * *(PA* 17:1106)

410. McCANN, WILLIS H. "Nostalgia: A Descriptive and Comparative Study." *J Genetic Psychol* 62:97–104 Mr '43. * *(PA* 17:2324)

411. MOORE, WILBUR E. "Factors Related to Achievement and Improvement in Public Speaking." *Q J Speech* 29:213–7 Ap '43. *

412. FISKE, DONALD W. "A Study of Relationships to Somatotype." *J Appl Psychol* 28:504–19 D '44. * *(PA* 19:1263)

413. COMBS, ARTHUR W. "Follow-Up of a Counseling Case Treated by the Non-Directive Method." *J Clin Psychol* 1:147–54 Ap '45. * *(PA* 20:134)

414. HELLFRITZSCH, A. G. "A Factor Analysis of Teacher Abilities." *J Exp Ed* 14:166–99 D '45. * *(PA* 20:2075)

415. SEAGOE, MAY V. "Permanence of Interest in Teaching." *J Ed Res* 38:678–84 My '45. * *(PA* 19:3183)

416. SUMNER, F. C., AND CLARK, K. B. "Some Factors Influencing a Group of Negroes in Their Estimation of the Intelligence and Personality-Wholesomeness of Negro Subjects." *J Psychol* 19:75–8 Ja '45. * *(PA* 19:1272)

417. WOOD, KENNETH SCOTT. "Parental Maladjustment and

Personality Inventory

Functional Articulatory Defects in Children." *J Speech Disorders* 11:255–75 D '46. * (*PA* 21:1497)

418. GUEST, LESTER. "A Study of Interviewer Competence." *Int J Opin & Attitude Res* (Mexico) 1:17–30 S '47. * (*PA* 22:4361)

419. HOUSTON, THOMAS J., AND SUMNER, F. C. "Measurement of Neurotic Tendency in Women With Uncommon Given Names." *J General Psychol* 39:289–92 O '48. * (*PA* 23:3651)

420. MULL, HELEN K. "Myopia and Introversion." *Am J Psychol* 61:575–6 O '48. * (*PA* 23:4135)

421. PORTENIER, LILLIAN G. "Personality Tests in a University Guidance Program." *J Ed Psychol* 39:479–87 D '48. * (*PA* 23:3218)

422. TRESSELT, M. E., AND BECKER, MAXWELL. "Scales of Judgment and Personality Correlates." *J General Psychol* 43:221–30 O '50. * (*PA* 25:6005)

423. ADAMSON, DERYCK. "Selection and Appraisal of Engineering Graduates: A Case Study." *Personnel* 29:175–93 S '52. * (*PA* 27:3797)

424. BRUCE, MARTIN MARC. *The Importance of Certain Personality Characteristics, Skills and Abilities in Effectiveness as a Factory Foreman.* Doctor's thesis, New York University (New York, N.Y.), 1952. (*DA* 13:116)

425. COOLEY, JOHN CHRISTOPHER. *A Study of the Relation Between Certain Mental and Personality Traits and Ratings of Musical Abilities.* Doctor's thesis, Michigan State College (East Lansing, Mich.), 1952. (*DA* 13:240)

426. MIDDLETON, CHARLES E., AND SUMNER, F. C. "Season of Birth as Related to Seasonal Preference and Personality Traits." *J Psychol* 36:423–5 O '53. * (*PA* 28:4045)

427. GAYEN, A. K., AND SAHA, R. P. "Factors in the Study of Personality." *Indian J Psychol* 29:87–96 pts 1–2 '54. * (*PA* 29:8637)

428. RUBIN-RABSON, GRACE. "Correlates of the Non-Committal Test-Item Response." *J Clin Psychol* 10:93–5 Ja '54. * (*PA* 28:7546)

429. TATE, MILDRED THUROW, AND MUSICK, VIRGINIA ANNE. "Adjustment Problems of College Students." *Social Forces* 33:182–5 D '54. * (*PA* 29:6206)

430. DEXTER, EMILY S., AND STEIN, BETTY. "The Measurement of Leadership in White and Negro Students." *J Abn & Social Psychol* 51:219–21 S '55. * (*PA* 30:5185)

431. BEACH, LESLIE ROBERT. *The Relationship Between Sociability, Satisfaction, and Academic Achievement in Various Types of Learning Situations.* Doctor's thesis, University of Michigan (Ann Arbor, Mich.), 1957. (*DA* 18:1334)

432. DOUGLASS, ROBERT RAYMOND. *Personality of the Librarian.* Doctor's thesis, University of Chicago (Chicago, Ill.), 1957.

433. GREENBERG, HERBERT, AND JORDAN, SIDNEY. "Differential Effects of Total Blindness and Partial Sight on Several Personality Traits." *Excep Children* 24:123–4 N '57. * (*PA* 33:2097)

434. JAEGER, MARTHA. *Some Aspects of Relationship Between Motor Coordination and Personality in a Group of College Women.* Doctor's thesis, Columbia University (New York, N.Y.), 1957. (*DA* 17:2065)

435. MARTIN, R. M., AND MARCUSE, F. L. "Characteristics of Volunteers and Non-Volunteers for Hypnosis." *J Clin & Exp Hyp* 5:176–80 O '57. * (*PA* 36:3I176M)

436. ROGERS, MARY ELAINE. *The Attitude of College Sophomores and Seniors Toward Counseling Procedure With Reference to Certain Personality Factors and Personal Problem Frequency.* Doctor's thesis, St. Louis University (St. Louis, Mo.), 1957. (*DA* 18:503)

437. MALLORY, EDITH B., AND MILLER, VIRGINIA B. "A Possible Basis for the Association of Voice Characteristics and Personality Traits." *Speech Monogr* 25:255–60 N '58. * (*PA* 33:9969)

438. MARTIN, R. M., AND MARCUSE, F. L. "Characteristics of Volunteers and Nonvolunteers in Psychological Experimentation." *J Consult Psychol* 22:475–9 D '58. * (*PA* 33:9973)

439. SAGUIGUIT, GIL FRANCO. *The Maximum Separation of Students Into Two Programs of Course Work in a College of Agriculture by Discriminant Analysis Involving Certain Selected Measurements.* Doctor's thesis, Pennsylvania State University (University Park, Pa.), 1959. (*DA* 20:2986)

440. MURPHY, RAYMOND ORIN. *Non-Intellectual Factors in Early Discontinuances of the 1959–1960 Freshman Class in Engineering of the Pennsylvania State University.* Doctor's thesis, Pennsylvania State University (University Park, Pa.), 1960. (*DA* 21:2536)

441. MARKS, EDMOND; VAIRO, JOHN D.; AND ZEIGLER, MARTIN L. "Scholastic Aptitudes, Vocational Interests, and Personality Characteristics of Journalism Students." *J Ed Res* 56:37–40 S '62. *

442. LYSAUGHT, JEROME P. "An Analysis of Factors Related to Success in Constructing Programed Learning Sequences." *J Programed Instr* 2:35–42 f '63. * (*PA* 38:10415)

443. EVANS, E. G. S. "Reasoning Ability and Personality Differences Among Student-Teachers." *Brit J Ed Psychol* 34:305–14 N '64. * (*PA* 39:8718)

444. LYSAUGHT, JEROME P. "Further Analysis of Success Among Auto-Instructional Programmers." *Teaching Aid News* 4:6–11 O 15 '64. *

445. LYSAUGHT, JEROME P. "Selecting Instructional Programmers: New Research Into Characteristics of Successful Programmers." *Training Directors J* 18:8–14 Je '64. *

446. HEATH, DOUGLAS H.; WITH THE ASSISTANCE OF HARRIET E. HEATH. *Explorations of Maturity: Studies of Mature and Immature College Men.* New York: Appleton-Century-Crofts, 1965. Pp. xv, 423. * (*PA* 39:12057)

447. KAHRS, KAROL ANNE. *Group Differences of Various Personality Qualities Among Physical Education Major Students, Dance Major Students, Physical Education Faculty, and General College Freshmen.* Master's thesis, Ohio State University (Columbus, Ohio), 1965.

448. MAHANTA, D. "Assessmet of Personality (A Study on the Bernreuter Personality Inventory)." *B Council Social & Psychol Res* (India) 4:17–23 Ja '65. * (*PA* 40:2942)

449. ANANT, SANTOKH S. "Belongingness and Mental Health: Some Research Findings." *Acta Psychologica* (Netherlands) 26:391–6 N '67. * (*PA* 42:5892)

450. DENOVA, CHARLES CULLOTTE. *An Assessment of the Effect on Self-Confidence by the Acquisition of New Skills.* Doctor's thesis, University of California (Los Angeles, Calif.), 1968. (*DA* 29:2882A)

451. DHILLON, P. K. "A Comparative Study of a Few Major Traits of Personality Between Two Cultural Groups With Distinctive Religious Base." *J Ed & Psychol* (India) 26:136–48 Jl '68. *

452. DHILLON, P. K. "A Study on the Attitudinal Difference on Family Planning of Two Cultural Groups." *Manas* (India) 15(1):25–36 '68. * (*PA* 43:11171)

453. KHANNA, ASHA, AND KUNDU, RAMANATH. "A Comparison of Bernreuter Personality Inventory and Kundu Neurotic Personality Inventory." *Psychol Studies* (India) 13:101–4 Jl '68. * (*PA* 43:5372)

454. BIRD, RICHARD B. *The Relationship of Size and Slant of Handwriting to Introversion-Extroversion and Sociability Characteristics of College Students.* Master's thesis, Brigham Young University (Provo, Utah), 1969.

455. BUTT, DORCAS SUSAN, AND FISKE, DONALD W. "Differential Correlates of Dominance Scales." *J Personality* 37(3):415–28 S '69. * (*PA* 44:6748)

456. PICKETT, WARREN WHEELER. *An Experiment in Response by Different Temperament Types to Different Styles of Set Design.* Doctor's thesis, University of Michigan (Ann Arbor, Mich.), 1969. (*DAI* 31:2539A)

457. BERGEMANN, KAREN. "The Effects of Chronic Disability on Field Dependence-Independence." *Grad Res Ed & Related Discip* 5(2):109–23 sp '70. * (*PA* 46:9441)

458. DEB, MAYA. "Achievement in Engineering College and Neuroticism." *J Ed & Psychol* (India) 27(4):378–9+ Ja '70. *

459. LYSAUGHT, JEROME P., AND PIERLEONI, ROBERT G. "Predicting Individual Success in Programing Self-Instructional Materials." *AV Commun R* 18(1):5–24 sp '70. * (*PA* 44:13334)

460. NIELSEN, WINNIFRED. "Relationships Between Precognition Scoring Level and Mood." *J Parapsychol* 34(2):93–116 Je '70. * (*PA* 46:3975)

461. SOUEIF, M. I., AND EL-SAYED, A. M. "Curvilinear Relationships Between Creative Thinking Abilities and Personality Trait Variables." *Acta Psychologica* (Netherlands) 34(1):1–21 S '70. * (*PA* 45:2374)

462. STEVENS, HOWARD LAMAR. *A Study of Creative and Causal Thinking Skills and Student-Faculty Perceptions in a Mexican Institution.* Doctor's thesis, University of Georgia (Athens, Ga.), 1970. (*DAI* 31:6416A)

463. STEVENS, NORMA YOUNG. *A Longitudinal Study of Biographical, Intelligence, and Personality Variables in Predicting Achievement of Mexican Theological Students.* Doctor's thesis, University of Georgia (Athens, Ga.), 1970. (*DAI* 31:4564A)

464. ANANT, SANTOKH S. "Belongingness and Mental Health: Cross Cultural, Sex and Marital Differences." *Manas* (India) 18(1):11–23 My '71. * (*PA* 48:9151)

465. RICHARDS, WILLIAM S., AND MERRENS, MATTHEW R. "Student Evaluation of Generalized Personality Interpretations as a Function of Method of Assessment." *J Clin Psychol* 27(4):457–9 O '71. * (*PA* 47:8942)

CUMULATIVE NAME INDEX

[1321]

Personality Rating Scale. Grades 4–12; 1944–62; PRS; identical with *Child Personality Scale* ('51) except for format; originally called *22-Trait Personality Rating Scale;* modification for use with children of E. Lowell Kelly's *36-Trait Personality Rating Scale* (see *19* below); ratings by classmates and teachers or self-ratings; 22 ratings: pep, intelligence, sociability, nervousness-calmness, popularity, religiousness, punctuality, courtesy, cooperation, generosity, persistence, honesty, neatness, patience, interests, disposition, good sport, boisterous-quiet, entertaining, thoughtfulness, sense of humor, dependability; S. Mary Amatora; Educators'-Employers' Tests & Services Associates. *

For additional information, see P:199; for a review by Laurance F. Shaffer, see 6:158 (4 references); for reviews by Robert H. Bauernfeind and Dale B. Harris, see 5:41 (18 references).

REFERENCES THROUGH 1971

1–18. See 5:41.
19–22. See 6:158.
23. BURNS, MIKE H. "Use of a Personality Rating Scale in Identifying Cooperation and Noncooperative Orthodontic Patients." Abstract. *Am J Orthodontics* 57(4):418 Ap '70. *
24. SWENSON, STEPHEN SHAILER. *Changing Expressed Parental Attitudes Toward Child-Rearing Practices and Its Effect on School Adaptation and Level of Adjustment Perceived by Parents.* Doctor's thesis, Boston University (Boston, Mass.), 1970. (*DAI* 31:2118A)

CUMULATIVE NAME INDEX

Amatora, M.: 8, 11, 13–8, 21
Bauernfeind, R. H.: rev, 5:41
Burns, M. H.: 23
Harris, D. B.: rev, 5:41
Kelly, E. L.: 19
Shaffer, L. F.: rev, 6:158
Swenson, S. S.: 24
Tschechtelin, M. A.: 1–7, 9–10, 12, 20, 22

[1322]

Personality Research Form. College; 1965–68; PRF; 2 editions; Douglas N. Jackson; Research Psychologists Press, Inc. *

a) STANDARD EDITION. 1965–68; 15 scores: achievement, affiliation, aggression, autonomy, dominance, endurance, exhibition, harm avoidance, impulsivity, nurturance, order, play, social recognition, understanding, infrequency.

b) LONG EDITION. 1965–67; 22 scores: same as for Standard Edition plus abasement, change, cognitive structure, defendence, sentience, succorance, desirability.

For additional information, reviews by Anne Anastasi, E. Lowell Kelly, and Jerry S. Wiggins, and excerpted reviews by John O. Crites, Lonnie D. Valentine, Jr., and Ruth Wessler (with Jane Loevinger), see 7:123 (27 references); see also P:201 (13 references).

REFERENCES THROUGH 1971

1–13. See P:201.
14–40. See 7:123.
41. GENTILE, J. RONALD, AND SCHIPPER, LOWELL M. "Personality Variables in Probability-Learning, Decision-Making, and Risk-Taking." *Percept & Motor Skills* 22:583–91 Ap '66. * (*PA* 40:8492)
42. MEHRABIAN, ALBERT, AND WILLIAMS, MARTIN. "Nonverbal Concomitants of Perceived and Intended Persuasiveness." *J Pers & Social Psychol* 13(1):37–58 S '69. * (*PA* 43:17375)
43. PIERCE, ROBERT A. "Athletes in Psychotherapy: How Many, How Come?" *J Am Col Health Assn* 17(3):244–9 F '69. *
44. REITZ, WILLIARD E., AND ROBINSON, NANCY. "Effect of Social Desirability on Interpersonal Attraction." Abstract. *Proc 77th Ann Conv Am Psychol Assn* 4(1):339–40 '69. * (*PA* 43:17354)
45. BIRD, EVELYN I. "Personality Structure of Canadian Intercollegiate Women Ice Hockey Players," pp. 149–56. In *Contemporary Psychology of Sport.* Proceedings of the Second International Congress of Sport Psychology, Washington, D.C., 1968. Chicago, Ill.: Athletic Institute, 1970. Pp. xix, 878. *
46. JACKSON, DOUGLAS N. "A Sequential System for Personality Scale Development." *Curr Topics Clin & Commun Psychol* 2:61–96 '70. *
47. PIERCE, ROBERT A. "Need Similarity and Complementarity as Determinants of Friendship Choice." *J Psychol* 76(2):231–8 N '70. * (*PA* 45:4136)
48. BALANCE, WILLIAM D. G.; SANDBERG, SONNY S.; AND BRINGMANN, WOLFGANG G. "Acceptance of Trait-Descriptive vs 'Medical Model' Oriented Feedback Statements." *Psychol Rep* 29(2):539–44 O '71. * (*PA* 47:9193)
49. BERZINS, JURIS I.; BARNES, DANIEL F.; COHEN, DANIEL I.; AND ROSS, WESLEY F. "Reappraisal of the A-B Therapist 'Type' Distinction in Terms of the Personality Research Form." *J Consult & Clin Psychol* 36(3):360–9 Je '71. * (*PA* 46:9163)
50. BRINGMANN, WOLFGANG G.; BALANCE, WILLIAM D. G.; AND SANDBERG, SONNY S. "Self-Validation of Programmed Feedback Statements." *Psychol Rep* 29(3):733–4 D '71. * (*PA* 47:8945)
51. FRY, JOSEPH N. "Personality Variables and Cigarette Brand Choice." *J Marketing Res* 8(3):298–304 Ag '71. *
52. FRYMAN, NANCY, AND ROSS, WALTER L. "A Study of Personality Correlates of Task-Oriented and Participation-Oriented Leaders." *Proc W Va Acad Sci* 42(1970):273–5 '71. *
53. GIDDINGS, JOHN WINTHROP. *Operant Conditioning of Visual Acuity.* Doctor's thesis, University of Pittsburgh (Pittsburgh, Pa.), 1971. (*DAI* 32:1841B)
54. HALEY, GRAHAM A. "Effects of Personality Factors and Increased Eye Movement on a Size-Matching Measure of Scanning." *J Abn Psychol* 77(3):303–7 Je '71. * (*PA* 46:6863)
55. HOFFMANN, HELMUT. "Personality Changes of Hospitalized Alcoholics After Treatment." *Psychol Rep* 29(3):948–50 D '71. * (*PA* 47:9244)
56. HOFFMANN, HELMUT, AND NELSON, JANET I. "Desirability Responses in the Personality Research Form by a Sample of Alcoholics." *Psychol Rep* 29(2):559–62 O '71. * (*PA* 47:9245)
57. NARDI, ANNE HIGGINBOTHAM. *Autoperception and Heteroperception of Personality Traits in Adolescents, Adults and the Aged.* Doctor's thesis, West Virginia University (Morgantown, W.Va.), 1971. (*DAI* 32:6624B)
58. PARTINGTON, JOHN T., AND CLARKE, LOUISE. "Personality Impression Formation: A Correlational-Experimental Design." *Can J Behav Sci* 3(1):47–54 Ja '71. * (*PA* 46:1129)
59. PIERCE, ROBERT A., AND SCHWARTZ, ALLAN J. "Personality Styles of Student Activists." *J Psychol* 79(2):221–31 N '71. * (*PA* 47:7534)
60. RANDOLPH, DANIEL LEE. *A Comparison of Personality Needs of Doctoral Students in Counselor Education Who Prefer the Administrator or the Practitioner Functional Specialty.* Doctor's thesis, Florida State University (Tallahassee, Fla.), 1971. (*DAI* 33:2722A)
61. SIESS, THOMAS F., AND JACKSON, DOUGLAS N. Chap. 6, "The Personality Research Form and Vocational Interest Research," pp. 109–32. In *Advances in Psychological Assessment,* Vol. 2. Edited by Paul McReynolds. Palo Alto, Calif.: Science and Behavior Books, Inc., 1971. Pp. xii, 395. *
62. WAAG, WAYNE LESLIE. *The Prediction of Individual Differences in Monitoring Performance.* Doctor's thesis, Texas Tech University (Lubbock, Tex.), 1971. (*DAI* 32:5502B)
63. WATSON, DAVID. "Reinforcement Theory of Personality and Social System: Dominance and Position in a Group Power

Structure." *J Pers & Social Psychol* 20(2):180–5 N '71. * (*PA* 47:6702)

CUMULATIVE NAME INDEX

Acker, M. B.: 3
Adinolfi, A. A.: 27–8
Anastasi, A.: *rev,* 7:123
Asta, P.: 19
Balance, W. D. G.: 48, 50
Barnes, D. F.: 49
Bentler, P. M.: 1, 17
Berzins, J. I.: 49
Bevan, A. R.: 24
Bird, E. I.: 45
Bither, S. W.: 18
Braun, J. R.: 19, 29
Bringmann, W. G.: 48, 50
Butt, D. S.: 20
Clarke, L.: 58
Cohen, D. I.: 49
Costantini, A.: 29
Crites, J. O.: *exc,* 7:123
Fiske, D. W.: 20–1
Flowers, J. F.: 39
Fry, J. N.: 51
Fryman, N.: 52
Gentile, J. R.: 41
Giddings, J. W.: 53
Greenwood, D. E.: 33
Guthrie, G. M.: 7
Haley, G. A.: 54
Hoffmann, H.: 15, 30–2, 55–6
Holtzman, W. H.: 22
Jackson, D. N.: 2, 5–9, 11–2, 23–5, 36, 40, 46, 61
Johnson, G. W.: 16
Kelly, E. L.: *rev,* 7:123

Kusyszyn, I.: 4, 10–2, 33
Lay, C. H.: 8, 9, 25
Loevinger, J.: *exc,* 7:123
Marks, E.: 13, 34
Mehrabian, A.: 42
Merrens, M. R.: 26, 35
Nardi, A. H.: 57
Neill, J. A.: 24, 36
Nelson, J. I.: 56
Osborne, W. J.: 14
Partington, J. T.: 58
Pearson, P. H.: 37
Pierce, R. A.: 38, 43, 47, 59
Prince, C.: 17
Randolph, D. L.: 60
Reitz, W. E.: 44
Richards, W. S.: 35
Robinson, N.: 44
Ross, W. F.: 49
Ross, W. L.: 52
Rothman, A. I.: 39
Sandberg, S. S.: 48, 50
Schipper, L. M.: 41
Schwartz, A. J.: 59
Siess, T. F.: 5, 40, 61
Trott, D. M.: 6
Valentine, L. D.: *exc,* 7:123
Waag, W. L.: 62
Watson, D.: 63
Wessler, R.: *exc,* 7:123
Wiggins, J. S.: *rev,* 7:123
Williams, M.: 42

[1323]

*The Personnel Reaction Blank, Revised Edition.
Adults; 1954–72; PRB; worker dependability and conscientiousness; Harrison G. Gough; Consulting Psychologists Press, Inc. *

For additional information, see P:202.

REFERENCES THROUGH 1971

1. Gough, Harrison G. "The Assessment of Wayward Impulse by Means of the Personnel Reaction Blank." *Personnel Psychol* 24(4):669–77 w '71. *

CUMULATIVE NAME INDEX

Gough, H. G.: 1

[1324]

The Philo-Phobe. Ages 10 and over; 1943–50; PP; interview form for obtaining and analyzing data in 4 areas: aspiration, emotion, judgment and insight, ethicomoral development; John N. Buck; Western Psychological Services. *

For additional information, see P:203; for a review by Parker Davis, Jr., see 3:66 (3 references).

REFERENCES THROUGH 1971

1–3. See 3:66.

CUMULATIVE NAME INDEX

Buck, J. N.: 1
Davis, P.: *rev,* 3:66

French, V. V.: 2
Landisberg, S.: 3

[1325]

Pictorial Study of Values: Pictorial Allport-Vernon. Ages 14 and over; 1957; PSV; test booklet title is *The Pictorial Study;* 7 scores: aesthetic, economic, political, religious, social, theoretical, strength of liking things in general; Charles Shooster; Psychometric Affiliates. *

For additional information, see P:204 (1 reference); for reviews by Andrew R. Baggaley and Harrison G. Gough, see 5:96.

REFERENCES THROUGH 1971

1. See P:204.
2. Davidson, Richard Allen. *A Study of Personality Traits and Value Systems of High School Athletes and Nonathletes.* Doctor's thesis, University of Kentucky (Lexington, Ky.), 1967. (*DAI* 30:3777A)

CUMULATIVE NAME INDEX

Baggaley, A. R.: *rev,* 5:96
Davidson, R. A.: 2
Gough, H. G.: *rev,* 5:96

Kelleher, E. J.: 1
Kerr, W. A.: 1
Melville, N. T.: 1

[1326]

The Piers-Harris Children's Self Concept Scale (The Way I Feel About Myself). Grades 3–12; 1969; CSCS; Ellen V. Piers and Dale B. Harris (test); Counselor Recordings and Tests. *

For additional information and a review by Peter M. Bentler, see 7:124 (8 references).

REFERENCES THROUGH 1971

1–8. See 7:124.
9. Guardo, Carol J. "Sociometric Status and Self-Concept in Sixth Graders." *J Ed Res* 62(7):320–2 Mr '69. *
10. Combs, Roland Gerry. *An Investigation of the Effect of One-to-One Interpersonal Relationships on the Self-Concept and Sociometric Status of Fourth Grade Students in Cheyenne, Wyoming.* Doctor's thesis, University of Wyoming (Laramie, Wyo.), 1970. (*DAI* 33:153A)
11. Creek, Roy John. *Middle School Rationale: The Sixth Grade Component.* Doctor's thesis, University of Pittsburgh (Pittsburgh, Pa.), 1970. (*DAI* 32:663A)
12. Brady, Robert Paul. *An Examination of Selected Variables Affecting the Vocational Development of Elementary School Children.* Doctor's thesis, University of Cincinnati (Cincinnati, Ohio), 1971. (*DAI* 32:3681A)
13. Felker, Donald W., and Stanwyck, Douglas J. "General Self-Concept and Specific Self-Evaluations After an Academic Task." *Psychol Rep* 29(1):60–2 Ag '71. * (*PA* 47:3752)
14. Felker, Donald W., and Thomas, Susan Bahlke. "Self-Initiated Verbal Reinforcement and Positive Self-Concept." *Child Develop* 42(4):1285–7 O '71. * (*PA* 48:2704)
15. Harris, Susan, and Braun, John R. "Self-Esteem and Racial Preference in Black Children." Abstract. *Proc 79th Ann Conv Am Psychol Assn* 6(1):259–60 '71. * (*PA* 46:2735)
16. Jensen, Olive Marie Jacobson. *Differences in Perception Through Teaching Drawing in Contrasting Groups of Fifth Grade Students.* Doctor's thesis, University of Minnesota (Minneapolis, Minn.), 1971. (*DAI* 32:3156A)
17. Roberts, Albert. *The Self-Esteem of Disadvantaged Third and Seventh Graders.* Doctor's thesis, Emory University (Atlanta, Ga.), 1971. (*DAI* 32:1924A)
18. Wagener, Ruth Elaine Hoffman. *An Experimental Study of the Effects of a Program of Oral Reading of Children's Literature About Negroes on the Self-Concept of Negro Fourth Grade Children.* Doctor's thesis, University of Tennessee (Knoxville, Tenn.), 1971. (*DAI* 32:4336A)

CUMULATIVE NAME INDEX

Ashby, M. L.: 6
Bentler, P. M.: *rev,* 7:124
Brady, R. P.: 12
Braun, J. R.: 15
Combs, R. G.: 10
Cox, S. H.: 2
Creek, R. J.: 11
Farls, R. J.: 5
Felker, D. W.: 13–4
Guardo, C. J.: 9
Harris, S.: 15

Hugo, M. J.: 7
Jensen, O. M. J.: 16
Mayer, C. L.: 1
Millen, L.: 3
Roberts, A.: 17
Sisenwein, M.: 8
Stanwyck, D. J.: 13
Thomas, S. B.: 14
Wagener, R. E. H.: 18
Wing, S. W.: 4

[1327]

Polarity Scale, Fourth Edition. College and adults; 1954–66; PS; 4 scores: humanistic, normative, both, neither; Silvan S. Tomkins; Springer Publishing Co., Inc. *

For additional information, see P:205 (1 reference).

REFERENCES THROUGH 1971

1. See P:205.
2. Cayley, William E. *Authoritarianism, Dogmatism, and Ideological Polarity: A Correlational Study.* Master's thesis, Southern Methodist University (Dallas, Tex.), 1967.
3. Suedfeld, Peter; Tomkins, Silvan S.; and Tucker, William H. "On Relations Among Perceptual and Cognitive Measures of Information Processing." *Percept & Psychophysics* 6(1):45–6 Jl '69. * (*PA* 43:15811)

CUMULATIVE NAME INDEX

Cayley, W. E.: 2
Suedfeld, P.: 3

Tomkins, S. S.: 1, 3
Tucker, W. H.: 3

[1328]

Polyfactorial Study of Personality. Adults; 1959; PSP; 11 scores: hypochondriasis, sexual identification, anxiety, social distance, sociopathy, depression, compulsivity, repression, paranoia, schizophrenia, hyperaffectivity; Ronald H. Stark; Martin M. Bruce, Ph.D., Publishers. *

For additional information, see P :206; for reviews by Bertram D. Cohen and Donald R. Peterson and an excerpted review by Edward S. Bordin, see 6:160.

[1329]

The Power of Influence Test. Grades 2–13; 1958; POIT; seating preference sociometric test; Roy Cochrane and Wesley Roeder; Psychometric Affiliates. *

For additional information, see P :209; for reviews by Ake Bjerstedt and Eric F. Gardner, see 6:162 (1 reference).

REFERENCES THROUGH 1971
1. See 6:162.

CUMULATIVE NAME INDEX
Bjerstedt, A.: *rev,* 6:162   Gardner, E. F.: *rev,* 6:162
Cochrane, R.: 1

[1330]

Practical Policy Test. Adults; 1948; PPT; also called *Test of Cynicism;* no manual; Martin F. Fritz and Charles O. Neidt; Martin F. Fritz. *

For additional information, see P :210; see also 5 :98 (9 references).

REFERENCES THROUGH 1971
1–9. See 5:98.
10. NELSON, ARNOLD E. "Measuring Cynicism With the Opinion Check List." *Proc W Va Acad Sci* 33:127–9 N '61. * (*PA* 36:5GD27N)

CUMULATIVE NAME INDEX
Fritz, M. F.: 1, 3, 6–9   Nelson, A. E.: 10
Neidt, C. O.: 2, 4–5, 8

[1331]

★**Preschool Embedded Figures Test.** Ages 3–5; 1972; PEFT; downward extension of *Children's Embedded Figures Test;* Susan W. Coates; Consulting Psychologists Press, Inc. *

REFERENCES THROUGH 1971
1. SEITZ, ELAINE KELLER. *The Relationship Between Cognitive Abilities and Impulse Control in Project Headstart Children.* Doctor's thesis, New York University (New York, N.Y.), 1971. (*DAI* 32:6061B)

CUMULATIVE NAME INDEX
Seitz, E. K.: 1

[1332]

Preschool Self-Concept Picture Test. Ages 4–5; 1966–68; PSCPT; comparison of self-concept and ideal self-concept; Rosestelle B. Woolner; the Author. *

For additional information, see P :212 (1 reference).

REFERENCES THROUGH 1971
1. See P:212.

CUMULATIVE NAME INDEX
Woolner, R. B.: 1

[1333]

The Press Test. Industrial employees; 1961–65; PT; ability to work under stress; 5 scores: reading speed, color-naming speed, color-naming speed with distraction, difference between color-naming speed with and without distraction, difference between reading speed and color-naming speed; 1965 test identical with test copyrighted 1961 except for slight modification in directions; Melany E. Baehr, Raymond J. Corsini, Richard Renck (manual), and Measurement Research Division, Industrial Relations Center, University of Chicago (manual) ; the Center. * [The publisher has not replied

to our four requests to check the accuracy of this entry.]

For additional information, see P :213 (1 reference) ; for reviews by William H. Helme and Allyn Miles Munger, see 6:163.

REFERENCES THROUGH 1971
1. See P:213.
2. BAEHR, MELANY E.; FURCON, JOHN E.; AND FROEMEL, ERNEST C. *Psychological Assessment of Patrolman Qualifications in Relation to Field Performance.* Washington, D.C.: United States Government Printing Office, 1969. Pp. vii, 246. *

CUMULATIVE NAME INDEX
Baehr, M. E.: 2   Kerr, W. A.: 1
Froemel, E. C.: 2   McGehee, E. M.: 1
Furcon, J. E.: 2   Munger, A. M.: *rev,* 6:163
Helme, W. H.: *rev,* 6:163

[1334]

★**Primary Self-Concept Inventory.** Grades kgn–4; 1973; PSCI; self-concept relevant to school success; 10 scores: personal self (physical size, emotional state, total), social self (peer acceptance, helpfulness, total), intellectual self (success, student self, total), total; separate forms for boys, girls; directions in English and Spanish; Douglas G. Muller and Robert Leonetti; Learning Concepts. *

[1335]

Problem Check List: Form for Rural Young People. Ages 16–30; 1946–48; adaptation of an earlier edition of *Mooney Problem Check List, 1950 Revision,* College Form; 10 scores: health and physical, relationship with people, citizenship, education, vocation and economic, morals and religion, personal temperament, courtship-sex-marriage, social and recreational, home and family; Ralph E. Bender, Mary Alice Price, and Ross L. Mooney; Bureau of Educational Research, Ohio State University; distributed by University Publications Sales. *

For additional information, see P :214 (1 reference) ; see also 4 :81 (2 references).

REFERENCES THROUGH 1971
1–2. See 4:81.
3. See P:214.

CUMULATIVE NAME INDEX
Bender, R. E.: 1–2   Waters, E. W.: 3

[1336]

A Process for In-School Screening of Children With Emotional Handicaps. Grades kgn–3, 3–7, 7–12; 1961–62; for research use only; 3 ratings: teacher, peer, and self; Nadine M. Lambert and Eli M. Bower; distributor in California: Fiscal Office, State Department of Education; distributor in all other states: Educational Testing Service (Atlanta Office). *
a) BEHAVIOR RATINGS OF PUPILS. Grades kgn–12; ratings by teachers.
b) [PEER RATINGS.] Grades kgn–3, 3–7, 7–12; 3 levels.
    1) *The Class Pictures.* Grades kgn–3.
    2) *A Class Play.* Grades 3–7.
    3) *Student Survey.* Grades 7–12.
c) [SELF-RATINGS.] Grades kgn–3, 3–7, 7–12; 3 levels.
    1) *A Picture Game.* Grades kgn–3.
    2) *Thinking About Yourself.* Grades 3–7.
    3) *A Self Test.* Grades 7–12.
For additional information, see P :215 (1 reference) ; for reviews by Alan O. Ross and J. Robert Williams, see 6:164 (3 references). For excerpts from related book reviews, see 7:B99 (2 excerpts) and 6:B93 (1 excerpt).

REFERENCES THROUGH 1971
1–3. See 6:164.
4. See P:215.

5. HENRY, MARIE, AND RUDDER, JAMES. "An Evaluation of a Process for Screening School Children With Emotional Handicaps." *J Sch Psychol* 1:28–32 Ja '63. * (*PA* 39:8644)

6. OGDEN, JOHN ALLEN. *A Study of the Interrelationships of High Creativity, Curiosity, Intelligence and Achievement and Emotional Handicap.* Doctor's research study No. 1, Colorado State College (Greeley, Colo.), 1963. (*DA* 24:1887)

7. RAUTIO, EDWIN ARTHUR. *A Comparison of Intelligence and Academic Achievement With Ratings on a Classroom Method for Screening Children for Emotional Handicaps.* Doctor's thesis, University of Nebraska (Lincoln, Neb.), 1966. (*DA* 27:602B)

8. NORTON, JUDITH BURTON. *A Study of the Correlation Between Visual Perception and Social Perception in Educable Mentally Retarded Children.* Master's thesis, Utah State University (Logan, Utah), 1967.

9. YLITALO, SUSAN H. *A Comparative Study of the Bower-Lambert Screening Scale and the Children's Personality Questionnaire.* Master's thesis, Indiana State University (Terre Haute, Ind.), 1968. (Abstract: *Cont Ed* 40:361)

10. BOWER, ELI M. *Early Identification of Emotionally Handicapped Children in School, Second Edition.* Springfield, Ill.: Charles C Thomas, Publisher, 1969. Pp. viii, 261. *

CUMULATIVE NAME INDEX

Allen, F. H.: *exc,* 6:B93
Bower, E. M.: 1, 3, 10; *exc,* 7:B99
Henry, M.: 5
King, J. D.: 4
Norton, J. B.: 8
Ogden, J. A.: 6
Rautio, E. A.: 7
Ross, A. O.: *rev,* 6:164
Rudder, J.: 5
Weisbrod, K. C.: 2
Wilderson, F. B.: *exc,* 7:B99
Williams, J. R.: *rev,* 6:164
Ylitalo, S. H.: 9

[1337]

★**Profile of Mood States.** College and psychiatric outpatients; 1971; POMS; earlier experimental forms called *Lorr Outpatient Mood Scale* and *Psychiatric Outpatient Mood Scale;* 6 scores: tension-anxiety, depression-dejection, anger-hostility, vigor-activity, fatigue-inertia, confusion-bewilderment; Douglas M. McNair, Maurice Lorr, and Leo F. Droppleman; Educational and Industrial Testing Service. *

REFERENCES THROUGH 1971

1. LORR, MAURICE; McNAIR, DOUGLAS M.; AND WEINSTEIN, G. J. "Early Effects of Chlordiazepoxide (Librium) Used With Psychotherapy." *J Psychiatric Res* (England) 1:257–70 D '63. *

2. McNAIR, DOUGLAS M., AND LORR, MAURICE. "An Analysis of Mood in Neurotics." *J Abn & Social Psychol* 69:620–7 D '64. * (*PA* 39:8539)

3. McNAIR, DOUGLAS M.; GOLDSTEIN, ARNOLD P.; LORR, MAURICE; CIBELLI, LOUIS A.; AND ROTH, IRVIN. "Some Effects of Chlordiazepoxide and Meprobamate With Psychiatric Outpatients." *Psychopharmacologia* (West Germany) 7(4):256–65 '65. *

4. LORR, MAURICE, AND McNAIR, DOUGLAS M. Chap. 33, "Methods Relating to Evaluation of Therapeutic Outcome," pp. 573–94. In *Methods of Research in Psychotherapy.* Edited by Louis A. Gottshalk and Arthur H. Auerbach. New York: Appleton-Century-Crofts, 1966. Pp. xvii, 654. *

5. LORR, MAURICE; DASTON, PAUL; AND SMITH, IOLA R. "An Analysis of Mood States." *Ed & Psychol Meas* 27:89–96 sp '67. * (*PA* 41:8280)

6. PILLARD, RICHARD C., AND FISHER, SEYMOUR. "Effects of Chlordiazepoxide and Secobarbital on Film-Induced Anxiety." *Psychopharmacologia* (West Germany) 12(1):18–23 '67. * (*PA* 42:8561)

7. PILLARD, RICHARD C.; ATKINSON, KIM WELLS; AND FISHER, SEYMOUR. "The Effect of Different Preparations on Film-Induced Anxiety." *Psychol Rec* 17:35–41 Ja '67. * (*PA* 41:8282)

8. WENDT, MIRIAM JANE. *The Conditioning of Defensive Verbal Constructs in Schizophrenic Patients.* Doctor's thesis, Case Western Reserve University (Cleveland, Ohio), 1968. (*DA* 29:4857B)

9. FRANCIS, BARRY SHERWOOD. *The Psychological Measurement of Affect: A Comparison of Two Measurement Models.* Doctor's thesis, University of Arizona (Tucson, Ariz.), 1969. (*DAI* 30:4370B)

10. HASKELL, DAVID; PUGATCH, DONALD; AND McNAIR, DOUGLAS M. "Time-Limited Psychotherapy for Whom." *Arch Gen Psychiatry* 21(5):546–52 N '69. * (*PA* 44:8586)

11. NATHAN, PETER E.; TITLER, NILES S.; LOWENSTEIN, LEAH M.; SOLOMON, PHILIP; AND ROSSI, A. MICHAEL. "Behavioral Analysis of Chronic Alcoholism: Interaction of Alcohol and Human Contact." *Arch Gen Psychiatry* 22(5):419–30 My '70. * (*PA* 44:14884)

12. PILLARD, RICHARD C., AND FISHER, SEYMOUR. "Aspects of Anxiety in Dental Patients." *J Am Dental Assn* 80(6):1331–4 Je '70. *

13. STEPHENS, JOSEPH H., AND SHAFFER, JOHN W. "A Controlled Study of the Effects of Diphenylhydantoin on Anxiety, Irritability, and Anger in Neurotic Outpatients." *Psychopharmacologia* (West Germany) 17(2):169–81 '70. * (*PA* 45:880)

14. MIRIN, STEVEN M.; SHAPIRO, LEO M.; MEYER, ROGER E.; PILLARD, RICHARD C.; AND FISHER, SEYMOUR. "Casual Versus Heavy Use of Marijuana: A Redefinition of the Marijuana Problem." *Am J Psychiatry* 127(9):1134–40 Mr '71. * (*PA* 47:891)

15. ROTHSTEIN, ARNOLD. *Depression in Pregnancy as It Relates to Feminine Identification Conflict and Perceived Environmental Support.* Doctor's thesis, Smith College (Northampton, Mass.), 1971. (*DAI* 32:5347A)

16. TEASDALE, JOHN D., AND BEAUMONT, J. GRAHAM. "The Effect of Mood on Performance on the Modified New Word Learning Test (Walton-Black)." *Brit J Social & Clin Psychol* 10(4):342–5 D '71. * (*PA* 48:1231)

CUMULATIVE NAME INDEX

Atkinson, K. W.: 7
Beaumont, J. G.: 16
Cibelli, L. A.: 3
Daston, P.: 5
Fisher, S.: 6–7, 12, 14
Francis, B. S.: 9
Goldstein, A. P.: 3
Haskell, D.: 10
Lorr, M.: 1–5
Lowenstein, L. M.: 11
McNair, D. M.: 1–4, 10
Meyer, R. E.: 14
Mirin, S. M.: 14
Nathan, P. E.: 11
Pillard, R. C.: 6–7, 12, 14
Pugatch, D.: 10
Rossi, A. M.: 11
Roth, I.: 3
Rothstein, A.: 15
Shaffer, J. W.: 13
Shapiro, L. M.: 14
Smith, I. R.: 5
Solomon, P.: 11
Stephens, J. H.: 13
Teasdale, J. D.: 16
Titler, N. A.: 11
Weinstein, G. J.: 1
Wendt, M. J.: 8

[1338]

***Progress Assessment Chart of Social Development.** Mentally handicapped children, mentally handicapped adults; 1962–73; behavior checklist for assessing progress in 4 areas: self-help, communication, socialisation, occupation; 4 levels; H. C. Gunzburg; SEFA (Publications) Ltd. [England]. *

a) PRIMARY PROGRESS ASSESSMENT CHART, SIXTH EDITION. Profoundly handicapped children and adults; 1966–69; PPAC: norms and record folder entitled *Primary Progress Evaluation Index.*

b) PROGRESS ASSESSMENT CHART I, ELEVENTH EDITION. Severely mentally handicapped children; 1962–73; PAC 1; norms and record folder entitled *Progress Evaluation Index 1;* 1973 test identical with test copyrighted 1965 except for format, remarks, and minor revisions in 3 items; an adaptation for mongol children, M/PAC 1, is also available.

c) PROGRESS ASSESSMENT CHART IA, EXPERIMENTAL EDITION NO. 1. "Pupils and trainees who have been fairly successful in attaining competence in the more demanding skills of the PAC 1"; 1972; PAC 1A.

d) PROGRESS ASSESSMENT CHART 2, EIGHTH EDITION. Older mentally handicapped trainees; 1963–69; PAC 2; norms and record folder entitled *Progress Evaluation Index 2.*

For additional information, see 7:125 (1 reference); see also P:216 (5 references).

REFERENCES THROUGH 1971

1–5. See P:216.
6. See 7:125.
7. GUNZBURG, H. C. "Assessing Social Competence." *Spec Ed* 57:11–4 Je '68. *
8. SCHIPHORST, BERNARD. "Social Education of the Subnormal." *Spec Ed* 57:26–9 Mr '68. *
9. ELLIOTT, R., AND MacKAY, D. N. "Social Competence of Subnormal and Normal Children Living Under Different Types of Residential Care." *Brit J Mental Subnormal* 17(32):48–53 Je '71. * (*PA* 47:11471)

CUMULATIVE NAME INDEX

Elliott, R.: 9
Gunzburg, H. C.: 1–5, 7
MacKay, D. N.: 9
Marshall, A.: 6
Schiphorst, B.: 8

[1339]

Psychiatric Evaluation Form. Psychiatric patients and nonpatients; 1967–68; PEF; interview guide and rating scale for recording scaled judgments (based upon various sources of information: subject, inform-ant, case records, nurses' notes, etc.) of a person's functioning over a one week period in 19 psychopathological dimensions and role impairment in 3 occupational roles and 2 social roles; Robert L. Spitzer, Jean Endicott, Alvin Mesnikoff, and George Cohen; Biometrics Research, New York State Psychiatric Institute. * [The Diagnostic Version, PEF-D (same as regular edition except for the addition of 12 scales and the coverage of a person's functioning over the past month) is available only as a part of *Current and Past Psychopathology Scales.*]

For additional information and reviews by Goldine C. Gleser and Jerome D. Pauker, see 7:126 (1 reference).

REFERENCES THROUGH 1971

1. See 7:126.
2. FIEVE, RONALD R.; PLATMAN, STANLEY R.; AND PLUTCHIK, ROBERT R. "The Use of Lithium in Affective Disorders: 2, Prophylaxis of Depression in Chronic Recurrent Affective Disorder." *Am J Psychiatry* 125:492–8 O '68. * (*PA* 43:2721)
3. FLEISS, JOSEPH L.; LAWLOR, WILLIAM; PLATMAN, STANLEY R.; AND FIEVE, RONALD R. "On the Use of Inverted Factor Analysis for Generating Typologies." *J Abn Psychol* 77(2): 127–32 Ap '71. * (*PA* 46:3315)
4. HERZ, MARVIN I.; ENDICOTT, JEAN; SPITZER, ROBERT L.; AND MESNIKOFF, ALVIN. "Day Versus Inpatient Hospitalization: A Controlled Study." Discussion by Jack F. Wilder. *Am J Psychiatry* 127(10):1371–82 Ap '71. *
5. PLATMAN, S. R.; PLUTCHIK, R.; AND WEINSTEIN, BETTE. "Psychiatric, Physiological, Behavioral and Self-Report Measures in Relation to a Suicide Attempt." *J Psychiatric Res* (England) 8(2):127–37 Je '71. * (*PA* 50:7080)

CUMULATIVE NAME INDEX

Endicott, J.: 1, 4	Pauker, J. D.: *rev*, 7:126
Fieve, R. R.: 2–3	Platman, S. R.: 2–3, 5
Fleiss, J. L.: 1, 3	Plutchik, T.: 2
Gleser, G. C.: *rev*, 7:126	Plutchik, R. R.: 2
Herz, M. I.: 4	Spitzer, R. L.: 1, 4
Lawlor, W.: 3	Weinstein, B.: 5
Mesnikoff, A.: 4	Wilder, J. F.: 4

[1340]
The Psychiatric Status Schedules: Subject Form, Second Edition. Psychiatric patients and nonpatients; 1966–68; PSS; a standardized interview schedule for gathering from a subject information needed to fill out a matching inventory designed to evaluate social and role functioning as well as mental status; most of the sections dealing with signs and symptoms of psychiatric disorder are from the *Mental Status Schedule;* 18 symptom scores (inappropriate affect-appearance-behavior, interview belligerence–negativism, agitation-excitement, retardation–lack of emotion, speech disorganization, grandiosity, suspicion-persecution-hallucinations, reported overt anger, depression-anxiety, suicide–self-mutilation, somatic concerns, social isolation, daily routine–leisure time impairment, antisocial impulses or acts, alcoholic abuse, drug abuse, disorientation memory, denial of illness), 5 role functioning scores (wage earner, housekeeper, student or trainee, mate, parent), 5 summary symptom and role scales (subjective distress, behavioral disturbance, impulse control disturbance, reality testing disturbance, summary role), and 20 supplemental scores (anxiety, auditory hallucinations, catatonic behavior, conversion reaction, delusions-hallucinations, depression-suicide, disassociation, elated mood, guilt, lack of emotion, obsessions-compulsions, persecutory delusions, phobia, psychomotor retardation, sex deviation, silliness, somatic delusions or hallucinations, visual hallucinations, miscellaneous, validity check); Robert L. Spitzer, Jean Endicott, and George Cohen; Biometrics Research, New York State Psychiatric Institute. *

For additional information and a review by Hans H. Strupp, see 7:127 (5 references).

REFERENCES THROUGH 1971

1–5. See 7:127.
6. SPITZER, ROBERT L., AND ENDICOTT, JEAN. "DIAGNO: A Computer Program for Psychiatric Diagnosis Utilizing the Differential Diagnostic Procedure." *Arch Gen Psychiatry* 18: 746–56 Je '68. * (*PA* 42:17400)
7. COOPER, J. E. "The Use of a Procedure for Standardizing Psychiatric Diagnosis," pp. 109–31. In *Psychiatric Epidemiology*. Proceedings of the International Symposium Held at Aberdeen University 22–5 July 1969, World Psychiatric Association and the Royal Medico-Psychological Association. Edited by E. H. Hare and J. K. Wing. London: Oxford University Press, 1970. Pp. xvi, 379. *
8. DOHRENWEND, BRUCE P. "Psychiatric Disorder in General Populations: Problem of the Untreated 'Case.' " *Am J Pub Health* 60(6):1052–64 Je '70. *
9. DOHRENWEND, BRUCE P.; CHIN-SHONG, EDWIN T.; EGRI, GLADYS; MENDELSOHN, FREDERICK S.; AND STOKES, JANET. "Measures of Psychiatric Disorder in Contrasting Class and Ethnic Groups: A Preliminary Report of On-Going Research," pp. 159–209. Discussion by K. Rawnsley and Robert J. Kleiner. In *Psychiatric Epidemiology*. Proceedings of the International Symposium Held at Aberdeen University 22–5 July 1969, World Psychiatric Association and the Royal Medico-Psychological Association. Edited by E. H. Hare and J. K. Wing. London: Oxford University Press, 1970. Pp. xvi, 379. *
10. FLEISS, JOSEPH L.; GURLAND, BARRY J.; AND COOPER, JOHN E. "Some Contributions to the Measurement of Psychopathology." *Brit J Psychiatry* 119(553):647–56 D '71. *
11. HERZ, MARVIN I.; ENDICOTT, JEAN; SPITZER, ROBERT L.; AND MESNIKOFF, ALVIN. "Day Versus Inpatient Hospitalization: A Controlled Study." Discussion by Jack F. Wilder. *Am J Psychiatry* 127(10):1371–82 Ap '71. *

CUMULATIVE NAME INDEX

Chin-Shong, E. T.: 9	Kleiner, R. J.: 9
Cohen, G.: 3	Mendelsohn, F. S.: 9
Cohen, J.: 5	Mesnikoff, A.: 11
Cooper, J. E.: 2, 7, 10	Miller, J. D.: 3
Dohrenwend, B. P.: 8–9	Platman, S. R.: 4
Egri, G.: 9	Rawnsley, K.: 9
Endicott, J.: 1, 3, 5–6, 11	Sartorius, N.: 2
Farkas, T.: 2	Spitzer, R. L.: 1, 3, 5–6, 11
Fleiss, J. L.: 1, 5, 10	Stokes, J.: 9
Gurland, B. J.: 2, 10	Strupp, H. H.: *rev*, 7:127
Herz, M. I.: 11	Weinstein, B.: 4
Kendell, R. E.: 2	Wilder, J. F.: 11

[1341]
Psychological Audit for Interpersonal Relations, Revised Edition. Marriage counselees and industrial personnel; 1964–65; PAIR; also called *The "PAIR" Test;* 20 scores: social status, intellectual rigidity, family cohesiveness, social extraversion, political conservatism, self-rejection, aggressive hostility, physical affection, monetary concern, change and variety, dominant leadership, nurturant helpfulness, order and routine, esthetic pleasures, submissive passivity, psychological support, emotional control, dependent suggestibility, health concern or outdoor interest, self-acceptance; Richard R. Stephenson; the Author. *

For additional information, see P:218.

[1342]
★**Psychological Screening Inventory.** Ages 16 and over; 1973, c1968–73; PSI; "a brief mental health screening device in situations where time and professional manpower may be at a premium"; 5 scores: alienation, social nonconformity, discomfort, expression, defensiveness; Richard I. Lanyon; Research Psychologists Press, Inc. *

REFERENCES THROUGH 1971

1. LANYON, RICHARD I. "Development and Validation of a Psychological Screening Inventory." *J Consult & Clin Psychol Monogr* 35(1, pt 2):1–24 Ag '70. * (*PA* 44:18915)
2. SCHOON, CRAIG GERALD. *A Study of the Psychological Screening Inventory: How It Relates to Other Counseling Variables and How It Discriminates Between Different Types of Clients.* Master's thesis, University of Iowa (Iowa City, Iowa), 1970.
3. BROSKOWSKI, ANTHONY; SILVERMAN, RITA; AND HINKEL, HELEN. "Actuarial Assessment of Criminality in Women." *Criminol* 9(2–3):166–84 Ag–N '71. *
4. BUTCHER, JAMES N. "Psychological Screening Inventory." Review. *Prof Psychol* 2(4):416–8 f '71. *
5. ORPEN, CHRISTOPHER. "Susceptibility to Faking of the

Psychological Screening Inventory." *J Clin Psychol* 27(4):
463–5 O '71. * (*PA* 47:8949)

6. OSBORN, MICHAEL ERNEST. *Factors Associated With the Classification of Clients in a University Counseling Service.* Doctor's thesis, University of Iowa (Iowa City, Iowa), 1971. (*DAI* 32:2423A)

7. SCHOON, CRAIG G., AND STAHMANN, ROBERT F. "Use of the Psychological Screening Inventory in a University Counseling Service." *J Counsel Psychol* 18(4):367–8 Jl '71. * (*PA* 46:11593)

CUMULATIVE NAME INDEX

Broskowski, A.: 3   Osborn, M. E.: 6
Butcher, J. N.: 4   Schoon, C. G.: 2, 7
Hinkel, H.: 3   Silverman, R.: 3
Lanyon, R. I.: 1   Stahmann, R. F.: 7
Orpen, C.: 5

[1343]

Psychometric Behavior Checklist. Adults; 1960; PBC; also called *Maryland Test Behavior Checklist;* for recording unusual test taking behavior; Bernard G. Berenson, Kathryn C. Biersdorf, Thomas M. Magoon, Martha J. Maxwell, Donald K. Pumroy, and Marjorie H. Richey; University Counseling Center. *

For additional information, see P:219; see also 6:166 (1 reference).

REFERENCES THROUGH 1971

1. See 6:166.

CUMULATIVE NAME INDEX

Berenson, B. G.: 1   Maxwell, M. J.: 1
Biersdorf, K. C.: 1   Pumroy, D. K.: 1
Magoon, T. M.: 1   Richey, M. H.: 1

[1344]

Psycho-Somatic Inventory. Late adolescents and adults; 1938; PSI; 3 scores: physiological, psychological, total; title on test is *P-S Experience Blank;* Ross A. McFarland and Clifford P. Seitz; Ross A. McFarland. *

For additional information, see P:220 (11 references); for reviews by Doncaster G. Humm and Charles I. Mosier, see 2:1234 (2 references).

REFERENCES THROUGH 1971

1–2. See 2:1234.
3–13. See P:220.
14. DARLING, C. D., AND SUMMERSKILL, JOHN. "Emotional Factors in Obesity and Weight Reduction." *J Am Dietetic Assn* 29:1204–7 D '53. *
15. ZEMLICK, MAURICE J., AND WATSON, ROBERT I. "Maternal Attitudes of Acceptance and Rejection During and After Pregnancy." *Am J Orthopsychiatry* 23:570–84 Jl '53. * (*PA* 28:3109)
16. SMITH, WENDELL I.; POWELL, ELIZABETH K.; AND ROSS, SHERMAN. "Food Aversions: Some Additional Personality Correlates." *J Consult Psychol* 19:145–9 Ap '55. * (*PA* 30:1270)
17. DAVIDS, ANTHONY. "The Influence of Ego-Involvement on Relations Between Authoritarianism and Intolerance of Ambiguity." *J Consult Psychol* 20:179–84 Je '56. * (*PA* 31:6071)
18. BONIER, RICHARD J., AND HANLEY, CHARLES. "Relationship Among PGR Indices." *J Psychosom Res* (England) 9:285–9 D '65. * (*PA* 40:7928)
19. STRÜMPFER, D. J. W. "The Relation of Draw-A-Person Test Variables to Psychometric and Inventory Measures." *J Social Res* (South Africa) 15(1):1–9 '66. * (*PA* 42:2613)

CUMULATIVE NAME INDEX

Bonier, R. J.: 18   Pildner, H.: 11
Brown, D. G.: 12   Powell, E. K.: 16
Cauffiel, P. W.: 6–7   Prentice, N. M.: 13
Darling, C. D.: 14   Ross, S.: 16
Davids, A.: 9–11, 17   Seitz, C. P.: 1
Eriksen, C. W.: 10   Smith, W. I.: 16
French, V. V.: 4   Snyder, W. U.: 7
Hanley, C.: 18   Strumpfer, D. J. W.: 19
Humm, D. G.: *rev*, 2:1234 Summerskill, J.: 14
Klugman, S. F.: 5   Watson, R. I.: 15
McFarland, R. A.: 1   Williams, M. E.: 8
Mosier, C. I.: 2; *rev*, 2:1234 Zemlick, M. J.: 15
Page, H. E.: 3

[1345]

Psychotic Inpatient Profile. Mental patients; 1961–68; PIP; ratings by nurses and psychiatric aides; revision of still-in-print *Psychotic Reaction Profile;* 12

scores: excitement, hostile belligerence, paranoid projection, anxious depression, retardation, seclusiveness, care needed, psychotic disorganization, grandiosity, perceptual disorganization, depressive mood, disorientation; 10 of the scores are "essentially equivalent" to the 10 scores obtained on the *Inpatient Multidimensional Psychiatric Scale,* the 2 new scores are seclusiveness and care needed; Maurice Lorr and Norris D. Vestre; Western Psychological Services. *

For additional information and a review by Goldine C. Gleser, see 7:128 (4 references). For reference to a review of the original edition, see 1346.

REFERENCES THROUGH 1971

1–4. See 7:128.
5. LORR, MAURICE, AND HAMLIN, ROY M. "A Multimethod Factor Analysis of Behavioral and Objective Measures of Psychopathology." *J Consult & Clin Psychol* 36(1):136–41 F '71. * (*PA* 45:10358)

CUMULATIVE NAME INDEX

Gleser, G. C.: *rev*, 7:128   Schiele, B. C.: 1
Hall, W. B.: 1   Vestre, N. D.: 1–3
Hamlin, R. M.: 5   Watson, C. G.: 4
Klett, W. G.: 4   Zimmermann, R.: 3
Lorei, T. W.: 4   Zimmermann, R. A.: 1
Lorr, M.: 2, 5

[1346]

The Psychotic Reaction Profile: An Inventory of Patient Behavior for Use by Hospital Personnel. Mental patients; 1961; PRP; for revised edition, see 1345; ratings by nurses or psychiatric aides; 4 scores: withdrawal, thinking disorganization, paranoid belligerence, agitated depression; Maurice Lorr, James P. O'Connor (test), and John W. Stafford (test); Western Psychological Services. *

For additional information, see P:221A (18 references); for a review by Wilson H. Guertin, see 6:167 (4 references).

REFERENCES THROUGH 1971

1–4. See 6:167.
5–22. See P:221A.
23. KURLAND, ALBERT A.; HANLON, THOMAS E.; TATOM, MARY H.; OTA, KAY Y.; AND SIMOPOULOS, ARIS M. "The Comparative Effectiveness of Six Phenothiazine Compounds, Phenobarbital and Inert Placebo in the Treatment of Acutely Ill Patients: Global Measures of Severity of Illness." *J Nerv & Mental Dis* 133:1–18 Jl '61. * (*PA* 38:6183)
24. HONIGFELD, GILBERT. "Relationships Among Physicians' Attitudes and Response to Drugs." *Psychol Rep* 11:683–90 D '62. * (*PA* 38:2796)
25. HANLON, THOMAS E., NUSSBAUM, KURT; WITTIG, BARBARA; HANLON, DOLORES D.; AND KURLAND, ALBERT A. "The Comparative Effectiveness of Amitriptyline, Perphenazine, and Their Combination in the Treatment of Chronic Psychotic Female Patients." *J New Drugs* 4:52–60 Ja–F '64. *
26. GERBER, IRWIN. *Behavioral Characteristics of Patients as Perceived by the Staff of a Mental Hospital.* Doctor's thesis, New York University (New York, N.Y.), 1965. (*DA* 27:533A)
27. KLETT, WILLIAM G. "The Effect of Historically Based Inferences on the Behavior of Withdrawn Psychiatric Patients." *J Clin Psychol* 22:427–9 O '66. * (*PA* 41:2987)
28. MARJERRISON, G.; HRYCHUK, W.; AND VARSANYI, E. I. "A Comparison of Two Butyrophenones With Trifluoperazine." *Can Psychiatric Assn J* 11:26–30 F '66. * (*PA* 40:4349)
29. CARDONE, SAMUEL STEVE. *The Effect of Chlorpromazine on the Body Image of Chronic Schizophrenics.* Doctor's thesis, Illinois Institute of Technology (Chicago, Ill.), 1967. (*DA* 28:4291B)
30. BISHOP, M. P.; GALLANT, D. M.; AND THOMPSON, R. D. "A Preliminary Evaluation of Magnesium Pemoline in Chronic Schizophrenic Patients." *Am J Psychiatry* 124:982–6 Ja '68. * (*PA* 42:8523)
31. FENZ, WALTER D., AND STEFFY, RICHARD A. "Electrodermal Arousal of Chronically Ill Psychiatric Patients Undergoing Intensive Behavioral Treatment." *Psychosom Med* 30: 423–36 Jl–Ag '68. * (*PA* 43:2685)
32. HALL, WILSON D.; VESTRE, NORRIS D.; SCHIELE, BURTRUM C.; AND ZIMMERMANN, ROBERT A. "A Controlled Comparison of Haloperidol and Fluphenazine in Chronic Treatment-Resistant Schizophrenics." *Dis Nerv System* 29:405–8 Je '68. * (*PA* 42:15606)
33. ABENSON, M. H. "Drug Withdrawal in Male and Female Chronic Schizophrenics." *Brit J Psychiatry* 115(525):961–2 Ag '69. * (*PA* 44:10858)

34. CARDONE, SAMUEL S., AND OLSON, RONALD E. "Chlor-promazine and Body Image: Effects on Chronic Schizophrenics." *Arch Gen Psychiatry* 20(5):576–82 My '69. * (*PA* 43:16118)

35. CARTER, ROSS EDWARD. *Rorschach Signs, Thinking Disorganization, and Withdrawal in Process and Reactive Schizophrenics.* Doctor's thesis, Michigan State University (East Lansing, Mich.), 1969. (*DAI* 31:1531B)

36. LORR, MAURICE, AND VESTRE, NORRIS D. "The Psychotic Impatient Profile: A Nurse's Observation Scale." *J Clin Psychol* 25(2):137–40 Ap '69. * (*PA* 43:14474)

37. VESTRE, NORRIS D., AND ZIMMERMANN, ROBERT. "Validity of Informants' Ratings of the Behavior and Symptoms of Psychiatric Patients." *J Consult & Clin Psychol* 33(2):175–9 Ap '69. * (*PA* 43:10028)

38. CRAIG, ROBERT J. "Relationship Between Severity of Illness and Overinclusive Thinking in Schizophrenia." *Psychol Rep* 26(1):251–4 F '70. * (*PA* 45:4646)

39. LAPUC, PAUL S., AND HARMATZ, MORTON G. "Verbal Conditioning and Therapeutic Change." *J Consult & Clin Psychol* 35(1):70–8 Ag '70. * (*PA* 44:21116)

40. ROSENZWEIG, STANLEY P., AND HARFORD, THOMAS. "Correlates of the Psychotic Reaction Profile in an Outpatient Psychiatric Sample." *J Consult & Clin Psychol* 35(2):244–7 O '70. * (*PA* 45:4549)

CUMULATIVE NAME INDEX

[1347]

Pupil Behavior Inventory. Grades 7–12; 1966; PBI; ratings by teachers; 5 scores: classroom conduct, academic motivation, socio-emotional, teacher dependence, personal behavior; manual out of print; Robert D. Vinter, Rosemary C. Sarri, Darrel J. Vorwaller, and Walter E. Schafer; Campus Publishers. *

For additional information and a review by John W. M. Rothney, see 7:129.

[1348]

The Purdue Master Attitude Scales. Grades 7–16; 1934–60; PMAS; formerly listed as *Generalized Attitude Scales; a–h* have space for insertion of any 5 attitude variables; 15 scales; H. H. Remmers (editor and manual author); University Book Store. *

a) A SCALE FOR MEASURING ATTITUDE TOWARD ANY SCHOOL SUBJECT. 1934–60; original forms by Ella B. Silance.

b) A SCALE FOR MEASURING ATTITUDES TOWARD ANY VOCATION. 1934–60; original forms by Harold E. Miller.

c) A SCALE FOR MEASURING ATTITUDE TOWARD ANY INSTITUTION. 1934–60; original forms by Ida B. Kelley.

d) A SCALE FOR MEASURING ATTITUDE TOWARD ANY DEFINED GROUP. 1934–60; revision of *A Scale for Measuring Attitude Toward Races and Nationalities*; original forms by H. H. Grice.

e) A SCALE FOR MEASURING ATTITUDES TOWARD ANY PROPOSED SOCIAL ACTION. 1935–60; original forms by Dorothy M. Thomas.

f) A SCALE FOR MEASURING ATTITUDES TOWARD ANY PRACTICE. 1934–60; original forms by H. W. Bues.

g) A SCALE FOR MEASURING ATTITUDE TOWARD ANY HOME-MAKING ACTIVITY. 1934–60; original forms by Beatrix Kellar.

h) A SCALE FOR MEASURING INDIVIDUAL AND GROUP "MORALE." 1936–60; original forms by Laurence Whisler.

i) HIGH SCHOOL ATTITUDE SCALE. 1935–60; original forms by F. H. Gillespie.

j) A SCALE FOR MEASURING ATTITUDE TOWARD ANY DISCIPLINARY PROCEDURE. 1936; V. R. Clouse. *Out of print.*

k) A SCALE FOR MEASURING ATTITUDE TOWARD ANY TEACHER. 1935; L. D. Hoshaw. *Out of print.*

l) A SCALE FOR MEASURING ATTITUDE TOWARD ANY PLAY. 1935; Mildred Dimmitt. *Out of print.*

m) A SCALE FOR MEASURING ATTITUDE TOWARD ANY SELECTION OF POETRY. 1935; J. E. Hadley. *Out of print.*

n) A SCALE FOR MEASURING ATTITUDE TOWARD ANY SOCIAL SITUATION. 1938; Elna Huffman. *Out of print.*

o) A SCALE TO MEASURE ATTITUDE TOWARD ANY ADVERTISEMENT. 1938; Ruth E. Henion. *Out of print.*

For additional information, see P:223 (1 reference); for a review by Donald T. Campbell, see 6:168; for reviews by Donald T. Campbell and Kenneth E. Clark of the original forms, see 4:46 (37 references); for reviews by W. D. Commins and Theodore Newcomb, see 2:1202 (9 references); for a review by Stephen M. Corey, see 1:897; for a review by Lee J. Cronbach of earlier forms of the High School Attitude Scale, see 3:46. For excerpts from related book reviews, see 2:B1050 (2 excerpts).

REFERENCES THROUGH 1971

1–9. See 2:1202.

10–46. See 4:46.

47. See P:223.

48. REMMERS, H. H.; BRANDENBURG, G. C.; AND GILLESPIE, F. H. "Measuring Attitude Toward the High School." *J Exp Ed* 2:60–4 S '33. * (*PA* 8:623)

49. NOLLEN, MARION. *The Relationship Between Certain Personality Traits and Religious Adjustment.* Master's thesis, Purdue University (Lafayette, Ind.), 1937.

50. REMMERS, H. H., AND WHISLER, LAURENCE. "The Effect of the President's Speech on Pupils' Attitudes Towards the Proposed Supreme Court Changes." *Sch & Soc* 46:64 Jl 10 '37. * (*PA* 11:5266)

51. WHISLER, L. D., AND REMMERS, H. H. "Liberalism, Optimism, and Group Morale: A Study of Student Attitudes." *J Social Psychol* 9:451–67 N '38. * (*PA* 13:1613)

52. WHISLER, LAURENCE. "Changes in Attitudes Towards Social Issues Accompanying a One-Year Freshman Social Science Course." *J Social Psychol* 10:387–96 O '40. * (*PA* 15:1441)

53. BOLTON, EURI BELLE, AND ENGLISH, MILDRED. "Morale of a Group of Senior High-School Girls." *J Psychol* 17:117–35 Ja '44. * (*PA* 18:1464)

54. BOLLINGER, RUSSELL V. "The Social Impact of the Teacher on the Pupil." *J Exp Ed* 13:153–73 Je '45. * (*PA* 19:3483)

55. BOLTON, EURI BELLE, AND ENGLISH, MILDRED. "Further Study of Attitudes of High School Seniors Toward Problems of the War and the Peace." *J Psychol* 20:157–82 Jl '45. * (*PA* 19:3416)

56. PROTHRO, E. TERRY, AND JENSEN, JOHN A. "Group Differences in Ethnic Attitudes of Louisiana College Students." *Sociol & Social Res* 34:252–8 Mr–Ap '50. * (*PA* 25:1262)

57. GLASNER, SAMUEL. "Two Experiments in the Modification of Attitude by the Use of Hypnotic and Waking Suggestion." *J Clin & Exp Hyp* 1:71–5 Ja '53. * (*PA* 27:6483)

58. PROTHRO, E. TERRY. "The Effect of Strong Negative Attitudes on the Placement of Items in a Thurstone Scale." *J Social Psychol* 41:11–7 F '55. * (*PA* 30:841)

59. ALBRIGHT, LEWIS E.; KIRSCH, ARTHUR D.; LAWSHE, C. H.; AND REMMERS, H. H. "A Longitudinal Comparison of Student Attitudes Toward Minorities." *J Ed Psychol* 47:372–9 O '56. * (*PA* 32:4535)

60. BLEDSOE, JOSEPH C., AND BROWN, IVA D. "Role Perceptions of Secondary Teachers as Related to Pupils' Perceptions of Teacher Behavioral Characteristics." *J Ed Res* 61:422–9 My–Je '68. *

61. MOAN, CHARLES E., AND FLICK, GRAD L. "Support and

Refutation of a Threat-Inducing Communication in Change of Attitude Toward Cigarette Smoking." *Psychol Rep* 22:1054 Je '68. * (*PA* 42:18720)

62. LYONS, RICHARD ALAN, SR. *A Comparison of the Effect of Conceptually and Non-Conceptually Oriented Tests Upon Student Achievement and Attitude in Basic Electronics at the College Level.* Doctor's thesis, University of Missouri (Columbia, Mo.), 1969. (*DAI* 30:4254A)

63. WESTBROOK, JOSEPH WILSON. *An Assessment of the Attitudes of Selected Negro Students Toward School and Some Factors That Influence These Attitudes.* Doctor's thesis, University of Tennessee (Knoxville, Tenn.), 1970. (*DAI* 31:3249A)

64. GENNARINO, ELIZABETH B. *An Analysis of Need-Structures and Attitudes Toward Teaching, Among Full-Time Community College Faculty Members.* Doctor's thesis, University of Colorado (Boulder, Colo.), 1971. (*DAI* 32:1876A)

CUMULATIVE NAME INDEX

Albright, L. E.: 59
Bateman, R. M.: 44
Bledsoe, J. C.: 60
Bollinger, R. V.: 54
Bolton, E. B.: 53, 55
Brandenburg, G. C.: 48
Brown, I. D.: 60
Bues, H. W.: 12
Campbell, D. T.: *rev*, 4:46, 6:168
Clark, K. E.: *rev*, 4:46
Clouse, V. R.: 36
Cohen, L. K.: 47
Commins, W. D.: *rev*, 2:1202
Corey, S. M.: *rev*, 1:897
Cronbach, L. J.: *rev*, 3:46
Davidoff, M. D.: 45
Dimmitt, M.: 27–8
Dunlap, J. W.: 9, 37
English, M.: 53, 55
Flick, G. L.: 61
Gennarino, E. B.: 64
Gillespie, F. H.: 48
Glasner, S.: 57
Grice, H. H.: 13–4
Hadley, E.: 33
Hadley, E.: 29
Hancock, J.: 30
Hancock, J. W.: 38
Hoshaw, L. D.: 24, 31
Huffman, E. S.: 39
Jensen, J. A.: 46, 56

Karslake, R. H.: 43
Kellar, B.: 15–6
Kelley, I. B.: 17–8
Kirsch, A. D.: 59
Kroll, A.: 9, 37
Lawshe, C. H.: 59
Likert, R.: 1
Lyons, R. A.: 62
Miller, F. D.: 19–20
Miller, H. E.: 10, 21
Moan, C. E.: 61
Newcomb, T.: *rev*, 2:1202
Nollen, M.: 49
Paterson, D. G.: 7
Prothro, E. T.: 46, 56, 58
Ramseyer, L. L.: *exc*, 2:B1050
Remmers, H. H.: 2–6, 8, 22–3, 32–3, 40, 48, 50–1, 59
Schmidt, A. G.: *exc*, 2:B1050
Schneider, E. B.: 7
Sigerfoos, C. C.: 25, 34
Silance, E. B.: 3, 11, 23
Snow, A.: 47
Thomas, D. M.: 26
Thomas-Baines, D. M.: 35
Tussing, L.: 41
Westbrook, J. W.: 63
Whisler, L.: 6, 50, 52
Whisler, L. D.: 40, 42, 51
Williamson, E. G.: 7

[1349]

The Purdue Rating Scale for Administrators and Executives. Administrators and executives; 1950–51; 36 ratings plus factor scores; 3 profile folders; H. H. Remmers and R. L. Hobson; University Book Store. *

a) REPORT FORM A. College administrators; 3 factor scores: fairness to subordinates, administrative achievement, democratic orientation.

b) REPORT FORM B. Business executives; 2 factor scores: social responsibility for subordinates and society, executive achievement.

c) REPORT FORM C. School administrators.

For additional information, see P:224; for reviews by John P. Foley, Jr. and Herbert A. Tonne, see 5:101 (1 reference); for a review by Kenneth L. Heaton, see 4:83 (7 references).

REFERENCES THROUGH 1971

1–7. See 4:83.
8. See 5:101.
9. BAICH, HENRY. *A Study of the Use of Value Analysis to Differentiate Between High and Low Scoring Administrators on the Purdue Rating Scale.* Doctor's thesis, University of Oregon (Eugene, Ore.), 1965. (*DA* 26:4434)

CUMULATIVE NAME INDEX

Baich, H.: 9
Elliott, D. N.: 8
Foley, J. P.: *rev*, 5:101
Heaton, K. L.: *rev*, 4:83
Hobson, R. L.: 1–3

Kirk, B.: 4
Remmers, H. H.: 8
Rupe, J. C.: 5–7
Tonne, H. A.: *rev*, 5:101

[1350]

The Purpose in Life Test. Adults; 1962–69; PIL; James C. Crumbaugh and Leonard T. Maholick; Psychometric Affiliates. *

For additional information and reviews by John R. Braun and George Domino, see 7:130 (7 references).

REFERENCES THROUGH 1971

1–7. See 7:130.
8. DOERRIES, LEE E. "Purpose in Life and Social Participation." *J Indiv Psychol* 26(1):50–3 My '70. * (*PA* 45:2927)
9. RICHMOND, BERT O., AND TISDEL, LINWOOD D. "Existential Frustration of Graduate and Undergraduate Students." *J Hum Relations* 19(4):506–11 f '71. *
10. SHEAN, GLENN D., AND FECHTMANN, FREDDIE. "Purpose in Life Scores of Student Marihuana Users." *J Clin Psychol* 27(1):112–3 Ja '71. * (*PA* 46:1159)
11. YARNELL, THOMAS D. "Purpose-in-Life Test: Further Correlates." *J Indiv Psychol* 27(1):76–9 My '71. * (*PA* 46:11273)

CUMULATIVE NAME INDEX

Ballard, R. E.: 2
Braun, J. R.: *rev*, 7:130
Butler, A. C.: 4
Carr, L.: 4
Crumbaugh, J. C.: 1, 5, 7
Doerries, L. E.: 8
Domino, G.: *rev*, 7:130
Fechtmann, F.: 10
Maholick, L. T.: 1
Mason, R. L.: 6

Raphael, M.: 7
Richmond, B. O.: 6, 9
Shean, G. D.: 10
Shrader, R. R.: 7
Smith, V.: 6
Strom, K. R.: 3
Tisdel, L. D.: 9
Tranel, N. N.: 3
Yarnell, T. D.: 11

[1351]

The Q-Tags Test of Personality. Ages 6 and over, 12 and over; 1967–69; QTTP; 2 forms; Arthur G. Storey and Louis I. Masson (manual); Institute of Psychological Research, Inc. [Canada]. *

a) [BIOGRAPHICAL FORM.] Ages 6 and over; 13 scores: 6 factor scores (affective, assertive, effective, hostility, reverie, social) in each of 2 areas (he or she is, he or she should be), correlation of self and idealself.

b) [AUTOBIOGRAPHICAL FORM.] Ages 12 and over; 13 scores: 6 factor scores (same as *a* above) in each of 2 areas (I am, I wish I were), correlation of self and idealself.

For additional information and a review by Joan Preston, see 7:131 (2 references); see also P:225 (5 references).

REFERENCES THROUGH 1971

1–5. See P:225.
6–7. See 7:131.
8. DOOLEY, LILY B. "Self-Concept of English and French Speaking High School Canadians: A Comparative Study." *Can Counselor* 4(2):107–12 Ap '70. *
9. SAINTY, GEOFFREY E. "Predicting Drop-Outs in Adult Education Courses." *Adult Ed* 21(4):223–30 su '71. *

CUMULATIVE NAME INDEX

Clark, R. B.: 5
Dooley, L. B.: 2, 8
Gough, J. W.: 3
Masson, L. I.: 3

Preston, J.: *rev*, 7:131
Sainty, G. E.: 4, 9
Sainty, J. E.: 6
Storey, A. G.: 1, 5–7

[1352]

★Reactions to Everyday Situations. Ages 16 and over; 1970–72; RES; anxiety; Sheena M. A. Waterhouse (test) and Valerie J. Fairbairn (manual); National Institute for Personnel Research [South Africa]. *

[1353]

★Reid Report. Job applicants; 1969–72; RR; for predicting the likelihood of employee theft; no manual; John E. Reid and Associates. *

For additional information, see 7:132 (1 reference).

REFERENCES THROUGH 1971

1. See 7:132.
2. ASH, PHILIP. "Screening Employment Applicants for Attitudes Toward Theft." *J Appl Psychol* 55(2):161–4 Ap '71. * (*PA* 46:3907)

CUMULATIVE NAME INDEX

Ash, P.: 1–2

[1354]

The Richardson Emergency Psychodiagnostic Summary. Mental patients; 1966; REP; checklist for making immediate reports of findings, impressions, and suggestions following diagnostic testing; O. Roderick Richardson; Western Psychological Services. *

For additional information, see P :228.

[1354A]

★Risk-Taking-Attitude-Values Inventory. Ages 3 and over; 1972; RTAVI; developmental editions called *Risk-Taking Attitude Questionnaire* and *Behavioral Values Inventory;* although originally constructed for use in "drug-abuse prevention programs," the author states that the inventory is "a general-purpose instrument" for use "whenever information about values and behavior is desired"; ratings of self and others (only *e* below); importance and nearness ratings for each of 8 value goals (affection, respect, skill, enlightenment, power, wealth, well-being, rectitude) and ratings in 4 areas (usefulness, expectancy, ways of changing, frequency) for several specific behaviors; 5 levels; Richard E. Carney; Educators Assistance Institute. *
a) PRIMARY FORM. Ages 3–8.
b) ELEMENTARY LEVEL. Grades 4–7.
c) SECONDARY LEVEL. Grades 7–12 and adults.
d) POST HIGH SCHOOL LEVEL. College.
e) ADULT LEVEL GROUP COMPARISON FORM. Adults.

REFERENCES THROUGH 1971
1. CARNEY, RICHARD E. Chap. 7, "Attitudes Toward Risk," pp. 96–128. In *Risk-Taking Behavior: Concepts, Methods, and Applications in Smoking and Drug Abuse.* Edited by Richard E. Carney. Springfield, Ill.: Charles C Thomas, Publisher, 1971. Pp. xii, 211. *

CUMULATIVE NAME INDEX
Carney, R. E.: 1

[1355]

★Rokeach Value Survey. Grades 7–16 and adults; 1967–73; RVS; test booklet title is *Value Survey;* manual title is *The Nature of Human Values;* Milton Rokeach; Free Press (manual); Halgren Tests (test). *

REFERENCES THROUGH 1971
1. PENNER, LOUIS; HOMANT, ROBERT; AND ROKEACH, MILTON. "Comparison of Rank-Order and Paired-Comparison Methods for Measuring Value Systems." *Percept & Motor Skills* 27:417–8 O '68. * *(PA* 43:5246)
2. PICHE, MARY. *Value Survey Among Women in Religious Orders Throughout Alberta.* Master's thesis, University of Alberta (Edmonton, Alta., Canada), 1968.
3. ROKEACH, MILTON. "The Role of Values in Public Opinion Research." *Pub Opinion Q* 32(4):547–59 w '68–69. * *(PA* 44: 16520)
4. GORSUCH, RICHARD L. "Rokeach's Approach to Value Systems and Social Compassion." *R Relig Res* 11(2):139–43 w '69. *
5. HILL, SAMUEL S., JR. "A Theologian's Response." *R Relig Res* 11(2):143–5 w '69. *
6. HOMANT, ROBERT. "Semantic Differential Ratings and the Rank-Ordering of Values." *Ed & Psychol Meas* 29(4):885–9 w '69. * *(PA* 44:19746)
7. LARSON, DONALD N. "Rokeach in Linguistic Perspective." *R Relig Res* 11(2):146–8 w '69. *
8. ROKEACH, MILTON. "Commentary on the Commentaries." *R Relig Res* 11(2):155–62 w '69. *
9. ROKEACH, MILTON. "Religious Values and Social Compassion." *R Relig Res* 11(2):24–39 f '69. *
10. ROKEACH, MILTON. "Value Systems and Religion." *R Relig Res* 11(1):3–23 f '69. *
11. SPILKA, BERNARD. "Religious Values and Social Compassion: A Problem in Theory and Measurement." *R Relig Res* 11(2):149–51 w '69. *
12. STARK, RODNEY. "Rokeach, Religion, and Reviewers: Keeping an Open Mind." *R Relig Res* 11(2):151–4 w '69. *
13. BERRICK, MARGARET LYN WILSON. *Patient Pre-Therapy Expectancies of Therapist Behaviors as Related to Certain Demographic, Personality and Value Variables.* Doctor's thesis, Pennsylvania State University (University Park, Pa.), 1970. *(DAI* 32:552B)
14. COCHRANE, RAYMOND, AND ROKEACH, MILTON. "Rokeach's Value Survey: A Methodological Note." *J Exp Res Personality* 4(2):159–61 F '70. * *(PA* 44:10241)
15. CROSS, HERBERT J.; DOOST, RAINER M.; AND TRACY, JAMES J. "A Study of Values Among Hippies." Abstract. *Proc*

78th Ann Conv Am Psychol Assn 5(1):449–50 '70. * *(PA* 44: 18491)
16. FEATHER, N. T. "Educational Choice and Student Attitudes in Relation to Terminal and Instrumental Values." *Austral J Psychol* 22(2):127–44 Ag '70. * *(PA* 45:4882)
17. FEATHER, N. T. "Value Systems in State and Church Schools." *Austral J Psychol* 22(3):299–313 D '70. * *(PA* 46: 1756)
18. HOMANT, ROBERT. "Denotative Meaning of Values." *Personality* 1(3):213–9 f '70. * *(PA* 47:8752)
19. KASHEFI-ZIHAGH, MOJTABA. *An Empirical Investigation of the Relationship Between Value Systems and Organizational Effectiveness.* Doctor's thesis, Michigan State University (East Lansing, Mich.), 1970. *(DAI* 32:3494A)
20. LORENZ, MARTHA KATHERINE. *A Descriptive Study of the Backgrounds, Attitudes, and Values of Home Economics Students at Michigan State University.* Doctor's thesis, Michigan State University (East Lansing, Mich.), 1970. *(DAI* 32:1054B)
21. MCCARY, PATRICK WELLINGTON. *The Effects of Small Self-Understanding Groups on the Self-Concept and Anxiety Level When Group Composition Has Been Varied.* Doctor's thesis, Michigan State University (East Lansing, Mich.), 1970. *(DAI* 31:2112A)
22. RIM, Y. "Values and Attitudes." *Personality* 1(3):243–50 au '70. * *(PA* 47:8879)
23. ROKEACH, MILTON. "Faith, Hope, and Bigotry." *Psychol Today* 3(11):33–7 Ap '70. * *(PA* 46:4769)
24. ROKEACH, MILTON, AND PARKER, SEYMOUR. "Values as Social Indicators of Poverty and Race Relations in America." *Ann Am Acad Pol & Social Sci* 388:97–111 Mr '70. *
25. ROKEACH, MILTON; HOMANT, ROBERT; AND PENNER, LOUIS. "A Value Analysis of the Disputed Federalist Papers." *J Pers & Social Psychol* 16(2):245–50 O '70. * *(PA* 45:2360)
26. SHOTLAND, R. LANCE, AND BERGER, WALLACE G. "Behavioral Validation of Several Values From the Rokeach Value Scale as an Index of Honesty." *J Appl Psychol* 54(5):433–5 O '70. * *(PA* 45:2384)
27. SIKULA, ANDREW FRANK. *A Study of the Values and Value Systems of College Roommates in Conflict and Nonconflict Situations, and an Investigation to Determine Whether Roommate Conflict Can Be Attributed to Differing Values and Value Systems.* Doctor's thesis, Michigan State University (East Lansing, Mich.), 1970. *(DAI* 32:26A)
28. BAIN, EARLE. "Values and Attitudes of Militia Officer Cadets," pp. 255–72. In *Second Annual Symposium: Psychology in the Air Force, 20–22 April 1971.* Edited by Hal W. Hendrick. Colorado Springs, Colo.: United States Air Force Academy, [1971]. Pp. x, 409. *
29. CANTEY, DORIS STEVENS. *Attitudes Toward University Authority and Personal Values of Undergraduates at Florida State University, 1970–1971.* Doctor's thesis, Florida State University (Tallahassee, Fla.), 1971. *(DAI* 32:6145A)
30. COCHRANE, RAYMOND. "The Structure of Value Systems in Male and Female Prisoners." *Brit J Criminol* 11(1):73–9 Ja '71. * *(PA* 46:11152)
31. FEATHER, N. T. "Similarity of Value Systems as a Determinant of Educational Choice at University Level." *Austral J Psychol* 23(2):201–11 Ag '71. * *(PA* 47:11697)
32. FEATHER, N. T. "Test-Retest Reliability of Individual Values and Value Systems." *Austral Psychologist* 6(3):181–8 N '71. * *(PA* 48:8111)
33. FEATHER, N. T. "Value Differences in Relation to Ethnocentrism, Intolerance of Ambiguity, and Dogmatism." *Personality* 2(4):349–66 w '71. * *(PA* 48:7224)
34. RIM, Y. "Values in Leadership Group Discussions." *Archivio di Psicologia Neurologia e Psichiatria* (Italy) 32(1–2):131–6 Ja–Ap '71. *
35. ROKEACH, MILTON. "Long-Range Experimental Modification of Values, Attitudes, and Behavior." *Am Psychologist* 26(5):453–9 My '71. * *(PA* 47:2815)
36. ROKEACH, MILTON. "The Measurement of Values and Value Systems," pp. 20–39. In *Social Psychology and Political Behavior: Problems and Prospects.* Edited by Gilbert Abcarian and John W. Soule. Columbus, Ohio: Charles E. Merrill Publishing Co., 1971. Pp. x, 209. *
37. ROKEACH, MILTON. "Persuasion That Persists." *Psychol Today* 5(4):68–71+ S '71. * *(PA* 47:8772)
38. ROKEACH, MILTON; MILLER, MARTIN G.; AND SNYDER, JOHN A. "The Value Gap Between Police and Policed." *J Social Issues* 27(2):155–71 '71. * *(PA* 47:8762)
39. TATE, EUGENE D., AND MILLER, GERALD R. "Differences in Value Systems of Persons With Varying Religious Orientations." *J Sci Study Relig* 10(4):357–69 w '71. * *(PA* 48:2817)

CUMULATIVE NAME INDEX
Bain, E.: 28   Hill, S. S.: 5
Berger, W. G.: 26   Homant, R.: 1, 6, 18, 25
Berrick, M. L. W.: 13   Kashefi-Zihagh, M.: 19
Cantey, D. S.: 29   Larson, D. N.: 7
Cochrane, R.: 14, 30   Lorenz, M. K.: 20
Cross, H. J.: 15   McCary, P. W.: 21
Doost, R. M.: 15   Miller, G. R.: 39
Feather, N. T.: 16–7, 31–3   Miller, M. G.: 38
Gorsuch, R. L.: 4   Parker, S.: 24

Penner, L.: 1, 25
Piche, M.: 2
Rim, Y.: 22, 34
Rokeach, M.: 1, 3, 8–10, 14,
  23–5, 35–8
Shotland, R. L.: 26

Sikula, A. F.: 27
Snyder, J. A.: 38
Spilka, B.: 11
Stark, R.: 12
Tate, E. D.: 39
Tracy, J. J.: 15

[1356]

★Runner Studies of Attitude Patterns: Interview Form, 1970 Revision. Job applicants; 1964–73; RSAP; 14 scores in 4 areas: control oriented (need for definition, emphasis on efficiency, need for established authority, wariness of people), freedom oriented (emphasis on personal feelings, need for new experience, resistance to social pressure, pleasure in tool skills), affiliation oriented (need for affectional acceptance, feelings of pressure, avoidance of confrontation, feelings of disappointment), recognition oriented (desire to direct activities, need for public acclaim); Kenyon Runner; Runner Associates. *

REFERENCES THROUGH 1971

1. RUNNER, KENYON R. *A Pattern Analytic Approach to the Prediction of Rated Personality Characteristics.* Doctor's thesis, University of Denver (Denver, Colo.), 1959.
2. STORLIE, THEODORE RUDOLPH. *Selected Characteristics of Teachers Whose Verbal Behavior Is Influenced by an In-Service Course in Interaction Analysis.* Doctor's thesis, University of Minnesota (Minneapolis, Minn.), 1961. (*DA* 22:3941)
3. MILLER, ARLYN HOCHBERG. *A Study of Personality Differences of Achieving and Underachieving Eleventh Grade Students.* Doctor's thesis, Temple University (Philadelphia, Pa.), 1965. (*DA* 26:4454)
4. TORRANCE, E. PAUL, AND DAUW, DEAN C. "Aspirations and Dreams of Three Groups of Creatively Gifted High School Seniors and a Comparable Unselected Group." *Gifted Child Q* 9:177–82 w '65. * (*PA* 40:5281)
5. GUTH, ROBERT OTTO. *Creativity, Competitive Drive, and Interest Patterns Associated With Success in a Program for Academically Talented High School Students.* Doctor's thesis, Temple University (Philadelphia, Pa.), 1966. (*DA* 27:3692A)
6. LOGUE, JOHN JOSEPH. *A Comparison of Interest and Personality Variables in Two Job Categories.* Doctor's thesis, Temple University (Philadelphia, Pa.), 1966. (*DA* 27:1282B)
7. NEWCOMER, CHARLES ALFRED, JR. *The Relationship Between Certain Types of Aggressive Behavior and Selected Attitudes and Values.* Doctor's thesis, Temple University (Philadelphia, Pa.), 1966. (*DA* 27:3697A)
8. STIX, DANIEL LOUIS. *Overachievement in College as a Function of Anxiety, Repression and Attitudes.* Doctor's thesis, Temple University (Philadelphia, Pa.), 1966. (*DA* 27:969A)
9. TORRANCE, E. PAUL, AND DAUW, DEAN C. "Attitude Patterns of Creatively Gifted High School Seniors." *Gifted Child Q* 10:53–7 su '66. * (*PA* 41:788)
10. TORRANCE, E. PAUL, AND WITT, GEORGE. "Experimental Grouping on the Basis of Creative Abilities and Motivations." *Gifted Child Q* 10:9–14 sp '66. * (*PA* 40:11158)
11. GENSEMER, IRA BENNETT. *A Study of Psychometric Measures of Creativity and Their Relationship to Field-Dependency, Teacher Proficiency and Attitudes.* Doctor's thesis, Temple University (Philadelphia, Pa.), 1967. (*DA* 29:1128A)
12. GERSHENFELD, MATTI KIBRICK. *Factors Affecting Responsible Behavior Under Conditions of Threat and Non-Threat.* Doctor's thesis, Temple University (Philadelphia, Pa.), 1967. (*DA* 28:4269A)
13. MARQUETTE, GEORGE REYNOLDS. *The Relationship of Measurement and Estimated Attitudes to Academic Achievement.* Doctor's thesis, Temple University (Philadelphia, Pa.), 1967. (*DA* 28:2098A)
14. BRADLEY, WILLIAM R. "A Preliminary Study of the Effect of Verbalization and Personality Orientation on Art Quality." *Studies Art Ed* 9:31–7 w '68. *
15. HAUCK, JEAN MOSEBAR. *Perception and Coalition as a Function of Creativity in Triadic Groups.* Doctor's thesis, University of Georgia (Athens, Ga.), 1968. (*DA* 29:4325A)
16. ABERMAN, HUGH M. *An Investigation Into the Relationship Between Individual Personality Characteristics and Perceived Behavior in Small Groups.* Doctor's thesis, Temple University (Philadelphia, Pa.), 1969. (*DAI* 31:1062A)
17. APPEL, MARILYN BAKER. *The Use of the Runner Studies of Attitude Patterns in the Prediction of Teacher Failure.* Doctor's thesis, Temple University (Philadelphia, Pa.), 1969. (*DAI* 31:1677A)
18. REYNOLDS, CHRISTOPHER MACDONALD. *Personality Traits of Approving and Disapproving Responders to Controversial Theatre Material.* Doctor's thesis, University of Michigan (Ann Arbor, Mich.), 1969. (*DAI* 31:853A)
19. SCHEIBNER, RUTH MARTIN. *Field Dependence-Independence as a Basic Variable in the Measurement of Interest and*

Personality. Doctor's thesis, Temple University (Philadelphia, Pa.), 1969. (*DAI* 30:3375B)
20. ABERMAN, HUGH M., AND CHANSKY, NORMAN. "Factor Analysis of Two Personality Tests With Differing Conceptual Frameworks." *Psychol Rep* 27(2):475–80 O '70. * (*PA* 45:6344)
21. BAGGALEY, ANDREW R.; ISARD, ELEANORE S.; AND SHERWOOD, EMILY J. "Discrimination of Academic Curricula by the Runner Studies of Attitude Patterns—College Form." *Meas & Eval Guid* 3(1):41–4 sp '70. * (*PA* 45:2938)
22. BEAN, ANDREW GEORGE. *Personality Measures as Multiple Moderators in the Prediction of College Student Attrition.* Doctor's thesis, University of Pennsylvania (Philadelphia, Pa.), 1970. (*DAI* 32:229A)
23. DeRENZIS, JOSEPH JOHN. *An Investigation Into the Attitude Patterns and Their Relationship to Prescription Writing Procedures of Teachers Using the IPI Instructional System in Elementary Mathematics.* Doctor's thesis, Temple University (Philadelphia, Pa.), 1970. (*DAI* 31:6398A)
24. MARRINGTON, DAVID JAMES. *A Study of the Attitude Patterns of Certain Junior and Senior High School Teachers.* Doctor's thesis, Temple University (Philadelphia, Pa.), 1970. (*DAI* 31:5716A)
25. KHATENA, JOE, AND TORRANCE, E. PAUL. "Attitude Patterns and the Production of Original Verbal Images: A Study in Construct Validity." *Gifted Child Q* 15(2):117–22 su '71. * (*PA* 47:9614)
26. WESTLER, LORETTA, AND CHANSKY, NORMAN M. "Social Desirability of the Runner Studies of Attitude Patterns." *Psychol Rep* 28(3):930 Je '71. * (*PA* 46:10724)

CUMULATIVE NAME INDEX

Aberman, H. M.: 16, 20
Appel, M. B.: 17
Baggaley, A. R.: 21
Bean, A. G.: 22
Bradley, W. R.: 14
Chansky, N.: 20
Chansky, N. M.: 26
Dauw, D. C.: 4, 9
DeRenzis, J. J.: 23
Gensemer, I. B.: 11
Gershenfeld, M. K.: 12
Guth, R. O.: 5
Hauck, J. M.: 15
Isard, E. S.: 21
Khatena, J.: 25

Logue, J. J.: 6
Marquette, G. R.: 13
Marrington, D. J.: 24
Miller, A. H.: 3
Newcomer, C. A.: 7
Reynolds, C. M.: 18
Runner, K. R.: 1
Scheibner, R. M.: 19
Sherwood, E. J.: 21
Stix, D. L.: 8
Storlie, T. R.: 2
Torrance, E. P.: 4, 9–10, 25
Westler, L.: 26
Witt, G.: 10

[1357]

Rutgers Social Attribute Inventory. Adults; 1959; RSAI; perception of others (either real persons or generalized classes); 24 trait ratings: good natured-stubborn, intelligent-unintelligent, tense-relaxed, strong-weak, childish-mature, old fashioned-modern, dominating-submissive, thin-fat, adventurous-cautious, lazy-ambitious, optimistic-pessimistic, masculine-feminine, young-old, responsible-irresponsible, crude-refined, tall-short, suspicious-trusting, talkative-quiet, thrifty-wasteful, dependent-self reliant, unsympathetic-sympathetic, good looking-plain, conventional-unconventional, rich-poor; William D. Wells; Psychometric Affiliates. *

For additional information, see P:231; for reviews by David B. Orr and John Pierce-Jones, see 6:169.

[1358]

SAQS Chicago Q Sort. College and adults; 1956–57; SAQS; Raymond Corsini; Psychometric Affiliates. *

For additional information, see P:232 (2 references); for reviews by William Stephenson and Clifford H. Swensen, Jr., see 5:103 (2 references).

REFERENCES THROUGH 1971

1–2. See 5:103.
3–4. See P:232.
5. OAKES, RALPH H., AND CORSINI, RAYMOND J. "Social Perceptions of One Other Self." *J Social Psychol* 53:235–42 Ap '61. * (*PA* 36:1HE350)
6. CARROLL, JAMES L., AND FULLER, GERALD B. "The Self and Ideal-Self Concept of the Alcoholic as Influenced by Length of Sobriety and/or Participation in Alcoholics Anonymous." *J Clin Psychol* 25(4):363–4 O '69. * (*PA* 44:10756)
7. EBY, JANE M. *The Relationship Between Selected Factors Concerning Elementary Education Majors and Their Achievements in Specified Music Fundamentals Classes.* Doctor's thesis, Indiana University (Bloomington, Ind.), 1969. (*DAI* 30:750A)
8. ROTHENBERG, EUGENIA. *The Effect of Self-Disclosure and Pseudo-Self-Disclosure on Social Adjustment of Institutionalized*

Delinquent Girls. Doctor's thesis, University of New Mexico (Albuquerque, N.M.), 1969. (*DAI* 30:5246A)

9. BERG, NORMAN L. "Effect of Alcoholic Intoxication of Self-Concept: Studies of Alcoholics and Controls in Laboratory Conditions." *Q J Studies Alcohol* 32(2):442–53 Je '71. *

CUMULATIVE NAME INDEX

Berg, N. L.: 9	Oakes, R. H.: 5
Carroll, J. L.: 6	Rector, W.: 4
Corsini, R. J.: 1–2, 5	Rothenberg, E.: 8
Eby. J. M.: 7	Stephenson, W.: *rev*, 5:103
Foulkes. D.: 3	Swensen, C. H.: *rev*, 5:103
Fuller, G. B.: 6	Van Dusen, W.: 4
Heaxt, S.: 3	

[1359]

S-D Proneness Checklist. Clients and patients; 1970; SDPC; 3 ratings: suicidal, depressive, total; William T. Martin; Psychologists and Educators, Inc. *

For additional information, see 7:133.

[1360]

STS Junior Inventory. Grades 4–8; 1957–72; problems checklist; revision of *SRA Junior Inventory* with deletion of items construed by some as invading the personal privacy of the student and his family; H. H. Remmers and Robert H. Bauernfeind; Scholastic Testing Service, Inc. *

For additional information, see P:232A; for a review by Warren R. Baller and excerpted reviews by Laurance F. Shaffer and Laurence Siegel of the original edition, see 5:104 (5 references); for a review by Dwight L. Arnold, see 4:90.

REFERENCES THROUGH 1971

1–5. See 5:104.

6. BOMSE, GERARD C. *A Study to Determine the Degree of Similarity of Personality Problem Awareness Between Normal and Mentally Retarded Children.* Doctor's thesis, New York University (New York, N.Y.), 1957. (*DA* 18:1844)

7. BILLINGER, LOIS WHITE. *Relation of Empathy, Self Image, and Social Acceptance Among Gifted and Average Children of the Sixth Grade.* Doctor's thesis, University of Connecticut (Storrs, Conn.), 1959. (*DA* 20:1222)

8. CLARKE, H. HARRISON, AND GREENE, WALTER H. "Relationships Between Personal-Social Measures Applied to 10-Year-Old Boys." *Res Q* 34:288–98 O '63. * (*PA* 38:5727)

9. HOWARD, DOUGLAS PIERRE. *The Relationship Between the Needs and Problems of Socially Disadvantaged Urban Children as Perceived by the Children and by Public School Personnel.* Doctor's thesis, Syracuse University (Syracuse, N.Y.), 1966. (*DA* 27:4040A)

10. HOWARD, DOUGLAS P. "The Needs and Problems of Socially Disadvantaged Children as Perceived by Students and Teachers." *Excep Children* 34:327–35 Ja '68. * (*PA* 42:9410)

11. CANNELL, ROBERT THOMAS, III. *Effects of Physical Disorders on the Adjustment of Hospitalized Children.* Doctor's thesis, University of Missouri (Columbia, Mo.), 1970. (*DAI* 31:3987A)

CUMULATIVE NAME INDEX

Arnold, D. L.: *rev*, 4:90	Greene, W. H.: 8
Baller, W. R.: *rev*, 5:104	Hernández, C.: 5
Bauernfeind, R. H.: 1, 4	Howard, D. P.: 9–10
Billinger, L. W.: 7	Nixon, W. W.: 3
Bomse, G. C.: 6	Rabinovitch, V.: 2
Cannell, R. T.: 11	Shaffer, L. F.: *exc*, 5:104
Clarke, H. H.: 8	Siegel, L.: *exc*, 5:104

[1361]

STS Youth Inventory. Grades 7–12; 1956–71; problems checklist; revision of *SRA Youth Inventory* with deletion of items construed by some as invading the personal privacy of the student and his family; 5 scores: my school, after high school, about myself, getting along with others, things in general; Hermann H. Remmers and Benjamin Shimberg; Scholastic Testing Service, Inc. *

For additional information, see P:233 (2 references); for a review by Forrest L. Vance and an excerpted review by Laurence Siegel of the original edition, see 6:170 (12 references); see also 5:105 (12 references); for reviews by Kenneth E. Clark and Frank S. Freeman, see 4:91 (7 references).

REFERENCES THROUGH 1971

1–7. See 4:91.
8–19. See 5:105.
20–31. See 6:170.
32–33. See P:233.

34. GORMAN, WILLIAM EDWARD. *The Effect of Occupational Information in English Classes on High School Juniors.* Doctor's thesis, Northwestern University (Evanston, Ill.), 1956. (*DA* 17:301)

35. STILLMAN, NATHAN. *A Study of the Relationship Between Parent Empathy and the School Adjustment of Seventh- and Eighth-Grade Male Children.* Doctor's thesis, New York University (New York, N.Y.), 1957. (*DA* 19:272)

36. CHILMAN, CATHERINE STREET. *A Comparative Study of Measured Personality Needs and Self-Perceived Problems of Ninth and Tenth Grade Students: Half of the Group Possessing Characteristics Associated With Early School Leaving and the Other Half Not Possessing Such Characteristics.* Doctor's thesis, Syracuse University (Syracuse, N.Y.), 1959. (*DA* 20:3190)

37. DARTER, CLARENCE LESLIE, JR. *A Comparative Study of Over-Achieving and Under-Achieving Ninth-Grade Students.* Doctor's thesis, Texas Technological College (Lubbock, Tex.), 1961. (*DA* 22:1462)

38. NIELSEN, J. K. "Case Studies of Socially Isolated Males in Senior High School." *Alberta J Ed Res* (Canada) 9:247–53 D '63. *

39. HOLMES, JACK A., AND SINGER, HARRY. *Speed and Power of Reading in High School.* Cooperative Research Monograph No. 14. Washington, D.C.: United States Government Printing Office, 1966. Pp. xii, 183. *

40. KAPLAN, MARVIN S., AND SPRUNGER, BENJAMIN. "Psychological Evaluations and Teacher Perceptions of Students." *J Sch Psychol* 5:287–91 su '67. * (*PA* 42:1091)

41. CHIASSON, JOSEPH WILBERT. *The Change in Concerns During the 1967–1968 School Year Among Seventh and Eighth Grade Students Under Two School Organizational Patterns.* Doctor's thesis, Wayne State University (Detroit, Mich.), 1968. (*DAI* 30:945A)

42. MITCHELL, JAMES V. "The Identification of Student Personality Characteristics Related to Perceptions of the School Environment." *Sch R* 76:50–9 Mr '68. * (*PA* 43:3006)

43. BOSWORTH, DOROTHY LONGLEY. *The Sociology of the School Community: Some Aspects of the Psychological Meaning of Relative Social Class Within and Between Schools.* Doctor's thesis, Syracuse University (Syracuse, N.Y.), 1970. (*DAI* 32:537B)

44. BROWN, SHARON LEE. *A Factor Analytic and Comparative Study of the Perceived Problems of Adolescents.* Doctor's thesis, Northern Illinois University (DeKalb, Ill.), 1971. (*DAI* 32:231A)

45. DIBENNARDO, FRANK RICHARD. *The Effect of Problem Locus and Problem Focus Upon Self-Relevant Content and Rapport in Relation to Interview Sequence: An Investigation of Dynamics of Communication in the Counseling Interview.* Doctor's thesis, New York University (New York, N.Y.), 1971. (*DAI* 32:2999B)

CUMULATIVE NAME INDEX

Barragan, M. F.: 21	Kulkarni, S. S.: 28
Beckwith, A. V.: 22	Meyer, J. K.: 6
Bosworth, D. L.: 43	Milburn, D. J.: 29
Brown, C. P.: 8	Mitchell, J. V.: 42
Brown, S. L.: 44	Musselman, D. L.: 23
Chiasson, J. W.: 41	Nielsen, J. K.: 38
Chiles, D. R.: 32	Nixon, W. W.: 20
Chilman, C. S.: 36	Overn, A. V.: 2
Clark, K. E.: *rev*, 4:91	Paisios, J. P.: 16
Clarke, H. H.: 31	Pam, E.: 33
Coombs, R. W.: 15	Pauley, B.: 19
Darter, C. L.: 37	Remmers, H. H.: 7, 9–10,
de Lopategui, M. N.: 17	16, 30
DiBennardo, F. R.: 45	Rice, D. L.: 24
Drucker, A. J.: 9–10	Shimberg, B.: 1, 3–4
Eugene, C. J.: 2	Siegel, L.: *exc*, 6:170
Fick, R. L.: 11	Singer, H.: 39
Freeman, F. S.: *rev*, 4:91	Smith, L. M.: 25
Gorman, W. E.: 34	Spivak, M. L.: 18
Greene, J. E.: 12	Sprunger, B.: 40
Greene, W. H.: 31	Stillman, N.: 35
Hackett, C. G.: 7	Taliana, L. E.: 26
Holmes, J. A.: 39	Vance, F. L.: *rev*, 6:170
Hudgins, B. B.: 25	Wardlow, M. E.: 12
Jacobs, R.: 5	Weimer, L. B.: 14
Kaplan, M. S.: 40	Weisbrodt, J. A.: 27
Keislar, E. R.: 13	

[1362]

Scale of Socio-Egocentrism. Grades 7–16; 1964; SSE; also called *S-E Scale;* 8 scores: 7 relationship scores (self, primary, peer group, boy-girl, secondary authority, impersonal, generalized), total; James S. Peters, II; Peters & Associates. *

For additional information, see P:234.

[1363]
A Scale to Measure Attitudes Toward Disabled Persons. Disabled and nondisabled adults; 1957–66; ATDP; title on test is *ATDP Scale;* Harold E. Yuker, J. R. Block, and Janet H. Younng; Human Resources Center. *

For additional information, see P:235 (14 references).

REFERENCES THROUGH 1971
1–14. See P:235.
15. SILLER, JEROME. "Reactions to Physical Ability." *Rehabil Counsel B* 7:12–6 S '63. *
16. EHRLE, RAYMOND A., AND PAUZA, JOSEPH A. "A Pilot Study Using the Attitudes Toward Disabled Persons Scale." *Rehabil Counsel B* 7:87–91 Mr '64.*
17. PETERSON, ADRIAN GORDON. *A Study of the Relationship of Rehabilitation Client Behavior to Both Counselor Predictions and Scores on the ATDP Scale.* Master's thesis, University of Utah (Salt Lake City, Utah), 1964.
18. SILLER, JEROME. "Personality Determinants of Reaction to the Physically Disabled." *Am Found Blind Res B* 7:37–52 D '64. * *(PA* 39:9978)
19. STIFF, ROBERT H., AND PHIPPS, GRANT T. "Attitudes of Dental Students Toward Chronically Ill, Aged, and Disabled Persons." *J Dental Ed* 28:149–54 Je '64. *
20. FELTY, JOHN ERNEST. *Attitudes Toward Physical Disability in Costa Rica and Their Determinants: A Pilot Study.* Doctor's thesis, Michigan State University (East Lansing, Mich.), 1965. *(DA* 26:4442)
21. FEINBERG, LAWRENCE BERNARD. *The Influence of Social Desirability on Measured Attitudes Toward the Disabled.* Doctor's thesis, State University of New York (Buffalo, N.Y.), 1966. *(DA* 27:1926A)
22. CESSNA, WILLIAM CONRAD, JR. *The Psychosocial Nature and Determinants of Attitudes Toward Education and Toward Physically Disabled Persons in Japan.* Doctor's thesis, Michigan State University (East Lansing, Mich.), 1967. *(DA* 28:1674A)
23. GREEN, JAMES HARLEN. *Attitudes of Special Educators Versus Regular Teachers Toward the Physically Handicapped and Toward Education in Michigan.* Doctor's thesis, Michigan State University (East Lansing, Mich.), 1967. *(DA* 28:4872A)
24. MADER, JOHN BUCKINGHAM. *Attitudes of Special Educators Toward the Physically Handicapped and Toward Education.* Doctor's thesis, Michigan State University (East Lansing, Mich.), 1967. *(DA* 28:1624A)
25. NEUHAUS, MAURY. *The Relationship Between Parental Attitudes and the Emotional Adjustment of Deaf Children in Early Childhood, Late Childhood, and Adolescence.* Doctor's thesis, New York University (New York, N.Y.), 1967. *(DA* 28:4299B)
26. PALMERTON, KEITH E. *A Study of the Nature and Determinants of Attitudes of College Counselors Toward Physically Disabled Persons.* Doctor's thesis, Michigan State University (East Lansing, Mich.), 1967. *(DA* 28:4828A)
27. WEBSTER, JOHN DANIEL. *The Attitudes of Non-Disabled Adolescents Toward Disabled Adolescents.* Doctor's thesis, University of Maryland (College Park, Md.), 1967. *(DA* 28:2466A)
28. CONINE, TALI ALBORZ. *Teachers' Attitudes Toward Disabled Persons.* Doctor's thesis, Indiana University (Bloomington, Ind.), 1968. *(DA* 29:4102A)
29. JORDAN, JOHN E., AND FRIESEN, EUGENE W. "Attitudes of Rehabilitation Personnel Toward Physically Disabled Persons in Colombia, Peru, and the United States." *J Social Psychol* 74:151–61 Ap '68. * *(PA* 42:10471)
30. PENZER, WILLIAM NORMAN. *Attitudinal Predictors of Judged Vocational Potential Among Vocationally Disabled Individuals.* Doctor's thesis, New York University (New York, N.Y.), 1968. *(DAI* 30:424B)
31. ANTHONY, WILLIAM A. "The Effects of Contact on an Individual's Attitude Toward Disabled Persons." *Rehabil Counsel B* 12(3):168–71 Mr '69. *
32. CORDARO, LUCIANO L., AND SHONTZ, FRANKLIN C. "Psychological Situations as Determinants of Self-Evaluations." *J Counsel Psychol* 16(6):575–8 N '69. * *(PA* 44:3934)
33. FORADER, ALVIN THOMAS. *Modifying Social Attitudes Toward the Physically Disabled Through Three Different Modes of Instruction.* Doctor's thesis, University of Massachusetts (Amherst, Mass.), 1969. *(DAI* 30:4360B)
34. HEACOCK, DELBERT D. *The Reliability of the Action Tendency Attitude Scale and Its Relationship to the Attitudes Toward Disabled Persons Scale.* Master's thesis, University of Utah (Salt Lake City, Utah), 1969.
35. JAQUES, MARCELINE E.; LINKOWSKI, DONALD C.; AND SIEKA, FRANK L. "Cultural Attitudes Toward Disability: Denmark, Greece, and the United States." *Int J Social Psychiatry* (England) 16(1):54–62 w '69. * *(PA* 47:6609)
36. PALMERTON, KEITH E., AND FRUMKIN, R. M. "College Counselor Knowledge About and Attitudes Toward Disabled Persons." *Percept & Motor Skills* 28(2):657–8 Ap '69. * *(PA* 43:15882)

37. PALMERTON, KEITH E., AND FRUMKIN, R. M. "College Counselors' Attitudes Toward Education Considered a Determinant of Attitudes Toward Disabled Persons." *Percept & Motor Skills* 28(2):441–2 Ap '69. * *(PA* 43:15883)
38. PALMERTON, KEITH E., AND FRUMKIN, R. M. "Contact With Disabled Persons and Intensity of Counselors' Attitudes." *Percept & Motor Skills* 28(2):434 Ap '69. * *(PA* 43:15884)
39. PALMERTON, KEITH E., AND FRUMKIN, R. M. "Type of Contact as a Factor in Attitudes of College Counselors Toward the Physically Disabled." *Percept & Motor Skills* 28(2):489–90 Ap '69. * *(PA* 43:15885)
40. SAUNDERS, FRANKLIN FAY. *Attitudes Toward Handicapped Persons: A Study of the Differential Effects of Five Variables.* Doctor's thesis, Florida State University (Tallahassee, Fla.), 1969. *(DAI* 30:3818A)
41. WILSON, EARL D., AND ALCORN, DEWAINE. "Disability Simulation and Development of Attitudes Toward the Exceptional." *J Spec Ed* 3(3):303–7 f '69. * *(PA* 44:14477)
42. NOONAN, J. ROBERT; BARRY, JOHN R.; AND DAVIS, HUGH C. "Personality Determinants in Attitudes Toward Visible Disability." *J Personality* 38(1):1–15 Mr '70. * *(PA* 44:14600)
43. SAUNA, VICTOR D. "A Cross Cultural Study of Cerebral Palsy." *Social Sci & Med* (England) 4(5):461–512 O '70. *
44. SHERR, ROSE LYNN. *Dogmatism as a Factor in Preprofessionals' Evaluations of Persons With Physical Disabilities.* Doctor's thesis, University of Kansas (Lawrence, Kan.), 1970. *(DAI* 31:6164A)
45. ANTHONY, WILLIAM A. "A Methodological Investigation of the 'Minimally Facilitative Level of Interpersonal Functioning.'" *J Clin Psychol* 27(1):156–7 Ja '71. * *(PA* 46:1607)
46. DURFEE, RICHARD. "Personality Characteristics and Attitudes Toward the Disabled of Students in the Health Professions." *Rehabil Counsel B* 15(1):35–44 S '71. * *(PA* 47:8980)
47. ENGLISH, R. WILLIAM, AND OBERLE, JUDSON B. "Toward the Development of New Methodology for Examining Attitudes Toward Disabled Persons." *Rehabil Counsel B* 15(2):88–96 D '71. * *(PA* 48:5342)
48. FEINBERG, LAWRENCE B. "Intolerance of Ambiguity as a Variable in Attitudes Toward the Disabled." *Psychol Aspects Disability* 18(3):117–21 N '71. * *(PA* 48:3462)
49. FEINBERG, LAWRENCE B. "Nonimmediacy in Verbal Communication as an Indicator of Attitudes Toward the Disabled." *J Social Psychol* 84(1):135–40 Je '71. * *(PA* 46:8876)
50. GOZALI, JOAV. "The Relationship Between Age and Attitude Toward Disabled Persons." *Gerontologist* 11(4, pt 1): 289–91 w '71. * *(PA* 48:3463)
51. HIGGS, REGINALD WAYNE. *Attitudes Toward Persons With Physical Disabilities as a Function of Information Level and Degree of Contact.* Doctor's thesis, University of Minnesota (Minneapolis, Minn.), 1971. *(DAI* 32:4450A)
52. LAZAR, ALFRED L.; GENSLEY, JULIANA T.; AND ORPET, RUSSELL E. "Changing Attitudes of Young Mentally Gifted Children Toward Handicapped Persons." *Excep Children* 37(8): 600–2 Ap '71. * *(PA* 47:1598)
53. LINKOWSKI, DONALD C. "A Scale to Measure Acceptance of Disability." *Rehabil Counsel B* 14(4):236–44 Je '71. * *(PA* 48:3466)
54. SMITS, STANLEY J.; CONINE, TALI ALBOREZ; AND EDWARDS, LARRY D. "Definitions of Disability as Determinants of Scores on the Attitude Toward Disabled Persons Scale." *Rehabil Counsel B* 14(4):227–35 Je '71. * *(PA* 48:3471)

CUMULATIVE NAME INDEX

[1364]

★**The School Attitude Survey: Feelings I Have About School.** Grades 3–6; 1970; SAS; 4 areas: about the things we learn, about the teacher and me, about the other children and me, about me and my classroom; Harold F. Burks; Arden Press. *

REFERENCES THROUGH 1971

1. GUTHERY, GEORGE H. "Differences in Attitude of Educationally Handicapped, Mentally Retarded and Normal Students: A Study of Attitudes Toward School, Teachers and Academics." *J Learn Dis* 4(6):330–2 Je-Jl '71. * (*PA* 47:9726)

CUMULATIVE NAME INDEX

Guthery, G. H.: 1

[1365]

School Interest Inventory. Grades 7–12; 1966, c1959–66; SII; revision of *Life Adjustment Scale, Number 1* ('58) ; for identifying potential dropouts who "should receive counseling"; William C. Cottle; Houghton Mifflin Co. *

For additional information, reviews by Gene V Glass and Leonard V. Gordon and an excerpted review by William L. Goodwin, see 7:134 (7 references) ; see also P:236 (9 references).

REFERENCES THROUGH 1971

1–9. See P:236.
10–16. See 7:134.
17. FOLEY, PATRICIA M. *Differences Between Delinquents and Nondelinquents on the School Interest Inventory.* Doctor's thesis, Boston College (Chestnut Hill, Mass.), 1971. (*DAI* 32:1851A)

CUMULATIVE NAME INDEX

Childers, R. D.: 8	Gordon, L. V.: *rev*, 7:134
Cottle, W. C.: 3–6	Havens, N. H.: 1
Das, A. K.: 7	Herrman, L.: 4
Davenport, C. M.: 12	Herrman, W. L.: 2
Epps, M. W.: 3	Newbury, D. N.: 10
Foley, P. M.: 17	O'Shea, A. J.: 9, 16
Gaetano, C. R.: 13	Patros, P. G.: 14
Glass, G. V: *rev*, 7:134	Renfrow, O. W.: 11
Goodwin, W. L.: *exc*, 7:134	Uber, T. B.: 15

[1366]

The School Inventory. High school; 1936; SI; attitudes toward teachers and school; Hugh M. Bell; Consulting Psychologists Press, Inc. *

For additional information, see P:237 (2 references) ; for a review by Ross W. Matteson, see 4:84 (3 references) ; for reviews by Robert G. Bernreuter and J. B. Maller, see 2:1252 (4 references). For excerpts from related book reviews, see 2:B842 (4 excerpts) and 1:B309 (1 excerpt).

REFERENCES THROUGH 1971

1–4. See 2:1252.
5–7. See 4:84.
8–9. See P:237.
10. TRAXLER, ARTHUR E. "The Reliability of the Bell Inventories and Their Correlation With Teachers' Judgment." *J Appl Psychol* 25:672–8 D '41. * (*PA* 16:1576)
11. GREENE, JAMES E., SR. "Factors Associated With Absenteeism Among Students in Two Metropolitan High Schools." *J Exp Ed* 31:389–94 su '63. *

CUMULATIVE NAME INDEX

Bell, H. M.: 1, 3	Ryans, D. G.: 4, 6–7
Bernreuter, R. G.: *rev*, 2: 1252	Salley, R. E.: *exc*, 2:B842
Greene, J. E.: 8, 11	Schmidt, A. G.: *exc*, 36:B30, 2:B842
Kimball, C. S.: *exc*, 1:B309	Speer, S. C.: 9
McAndrew, W.: *exc*, 36:B30	Traxler, A. E.: 10
Maller, J. B.: *rev*, 2:1252	Tyler, H. T.: 2
Matteson, R. W.: *rev*, 4:84	Walters, J. E.: *exc*, 36:B30
Peters, E. F.: 4–7	Wardlow, M. E.: 8

[1367]

School Motivation Analysis Test, Research Edition. Ages 12–17; 1961–70; SMAT; downward extension of *Motivation Analysis Test;* 40 scores: 4 motivation scores (unintegrated, integrated, total, difference [conflict]) for each of 6 drives (assertiveness, mating,

fear, narcism, pugnacity-sadism, protectiveness) and each of 4 sentiments (self-sentiment, superego, school, home) ; Arthur B. Sweney, Raymond B. Cattell, and Samuel E. Krug; Institute for Personality and Ability Testing. *

For additional information, see 7:135 (10 references).

REFERENCES THROUGH 1971

1–10. See 7:135.
11. BERNTSEN, DONALD ARNE. *Motivational Differences in the Music and Non-Music Student.* Doctor's thesis, University of North Dakota (Grand Forks, N.D.), 1971. (*DAI* 32:6804A)
12. DIELMAN, T. E.; BARTON, K.; AND CATTELL, R. B. "The Prediction of Junior High School Achievement From Objective Motivation Tests." *Personality* 2(4):279–87 w '71. * (*PA* 48:7881)

CUMULATIVE NAME INDEX

Barton, K.: 12	Hundleby, J. D.: 9
Barton, V.: 6	Johnson, H. S.: 4
Bell, D. B.: 10	Pierson, G. R.: 5–6
Berntsen, D. A.: 11	Radcliffe, J. A.: 1–3
Cattell, R. B.: 3, 7, 9, 12	Roach, A. J.: 8
Dielman, T. E.: 12	Sealy, A. P.: 7
Hey, G.: 6	Sweney, A. B.: 1–3, 7

[1368]

The Science Research Temperament Scale. Grades 12–16 and adults; 1955; SRTS; test booklet title is *SRT Scale;* William C. Kosinar; Psychometric Affiliates. *

For additional information, see P:238 (4 references) ; for reviews by John D. Black and David R. Saunders, see 5:106 (1 reference).

REFERENCES THROUGH 1971

1. See 5:106.
2–5. See P:238.
6. MACKAY, LINDSAY D. "Creativity and Performance in Science Examinations." *Austral J Ed* 14(1):76–83 Mr '70. *

CUMULATIVE NAME INDEX

Abrams, P.: 3	McGehee, E. M.: 5
Black, J. D.: *rev*, 5:106	Mackay, L. D.: 6
Kerr, W. A.: 3, 5	Mansfield, N. S.: 2
Kosinar, W. C.: 1	Saunders, D. R.: *rev*, 5:106
Locke, E. A.: 4	

[1369]

★**Secondary School Research Program.** High school students, teachers and administrators; 1971–72; SSRP; school environment; 2 questionnaires; interpretive manual by Leonard L. Baird and Frederick A. Peterson; Educational Testing Service. *

a) QUESTIONNAIRE FOR NEW STUDENTS (QUESTA I). Entering students in grades 9–12; administered in September at participating secondary schools; 178 item percentage scores for 3–7 groups (boys, girls, total, 1–4 optional additional subgroups) in 5 areas: background data (9 scores), how the student sees himself (53 scores), parent attitudes as seen by the student (14 scores), reasons for choosing the school (31 scores), expectations of the school (71 scores).
b) QUESTIONNAIRE FOR STUDENTS, TEACHERS, AND ADMINISTRATORS [QUESTA II]. Administered in December–January or May–June at participating secondary schools; 254–259 item percentage scores for 6–10 groups (boys, girls, student total, teachers, administrators, nonstudent total, 1–4 optional additional subgroups) in 18 areas: background data (14 scores), general satisfaction level (3 scores), opinions about purposes of the school (33 scores), effects of the school on the student (17 scores), personal values and life goals (15 scores), personal relations and communications (10 scores), governance of the school (10 scores), perceptions of change (16 scores), teachers in the classroom (17 scores), grading (12 scores), curriculum (4 scores), the arts (14 scores), extra curricular (8 scores), counseling (31 scores), relations between racial and ethnic groups, pressures on the student (14 scores),

opinions about tobacco–alcohol–drugs (11 scores), rules and regulations (24–29 scores).

[1370]

Security-Insecurity Inventory. Grades 9–16 and adults; 1945–52; SII; test booklet title is *The S-I Inventory;* A. H. Maslow, E. Birsh, I. Honigmann, F. McGrath, A. Plason, and M. Stein; Consulting Psychologists Press, Inc. *

For additional information, see P:239 (16 references) ; for reviews by Nelson G. Hanawalt and Harold Webster, see 5:107 (10 references).

REFERENCES THROUGH 1971

1–10. See 5:107.
11–26. See P:239.
27. ELIAS, GABRIEL. "Self-Evaluative Questionnaires as Projective Measures of Personality." *J Consult Psychol* 15:496–500 D '51. * (*PA* 26:6995)
28. SECORD, PAUL F., AND JOURARD, SIDNEY M. "The Appraisal of Body-Cathexis: Body-Cathexis and the Self." *J Consult Psychol* 17:343–7 O '53. * (*PA* 28:5683)
29. JOURARD, SIDNEY M., AND REMY, RICHARD M. "Perceived Parental Attitudes, the Self, and Security." *J Consult Psychol* 19:364–6 O '55. * (*PA* 30:5761)
30. BENNETT, CARSON MAHAN. *The Relationships Between Responses to Pupil Aggression and Selected Personality Characteristics of Student Teachers.* Doctor's thesis, University of Michigan (Ann Arbor, Mich.), 1957. (*DA* 18:1335)
31. MEHLMAN, BENJAMIN, AND KAPLAN, JANICE E. "A Comparison of Some Concepts of Psychological Health." *J Clin Psychol* 14:118–22 Ap '58. * (*PA* 33:6269)
32. WEINBERG, JON R. "A Further Investigation of Body-Cathexis and the Self." Abstract. *J Consult Psychol* 24:277 Je '60. *
33. LYNCH, HILLQUIT. *The Romantic Complex and the Adolescent: An Analysis of Basic Assumptions in Family Sociology.* Doctor's thesis, University of Texas (Austin, Tex.), 1963. (*DA* 24:885)
34. SHELL, STANLEY A., JR.; O'MALLY, JAMES M.; AND JOHNSGARD, KEITH W. "The Semantic Differential and Inferred Identification." *Psychol Rep* 14:547–58 Ap '64. * (*PA* 39:2768)
35. GAY, JAMES DONALD. *Personality Changes Associated With Workshop Participation.* Doctor's thesis, University of Kentucky (Lexington, Ky.), 1965. (*DAI* 30:2436B)
36. MCALLISTER, JOHN GERALD. *Analyses of Selected Personality and Intellectual Attributes of Teenage Volunteer Counselor-Attendants Serving at a Residential Camp for the Dependent Cerebral Palsied.* Doctor's thesis, University of Denver (Denver, Colo.), 1966. (*DA* 27:3328A)
37. VINCENT, MARY JANE PARKS. *A Study of Construct Validity in Self Concept Measurement.* Doctor's thesis, University of Idaho (Moscow, Idaho), 1966. (*DA* 27:3741A)
38. MEINKE, DEAN L., AND KLAUSMEIER, HERBERT J. "Concept Attainment and Its Relation to Some Personality Variables." *Teach Col J* 39:106–9 D '67. *
39. GILL, NEWELL T.; KING, ROY; AND WILBURN, RON G. "A Helping Relationship Experience in Teacher Education." *J Exp Ed* 37:24–33 w '68. *
40. SINHA, AWADHESH KUMAR. "Psychology and Non-Psychology College Women: A Comparison on Some Personality Traits." *Psychol Studies* (India) 13:94–7 Jl '68. * (*PA* 43:5342)
41. SINHA, AWADHESH KUMAR, AND KOCHAR, DINESH CHANDRA. "Worldmindedness: In Relation to Some Personality Variables." *Indian Psychol R* 5:7–12 Jl '68. *
42. WILLNER, ERIC. "Problems of Adjustment of All-Day School Pupils and Their Guidance Implications." *Jewish Ed* 37:188–98 Jl '68. *
43. DOUCE, PEARL D. M. *Selected Aspects of Personality Related to Social Acceptance and Clothing Oriented Variables.* Doctor's thesis, Utah State University (Logan, Utah), 1969. (*DAI* 30:3730B)
44. GOLDSTEIN, JOEL W., AND ROSENFELD, HOWARD M. "Insecurity and Preference for Persons Similar to Oneself." *J Personality* 37(2):253–68 Je '69. * (*PA* 48:892)
45. MATTHEWS, LILLIAN B. "Fabric Preferences, Perceptual-Personality Characteristics, and Obesity." *J Home Econ* 61(3):177–82 Mr '69. *
46. MISRA, S. L. "Effect of Birth Order, Education and Rank Status on Insecurity." *Psychol Ann* 3:17–9 Mr '69. * (*PA* 46:7164)
47. MISRA, S. L. "Insecurity as a Cause of Mental Illness." *Indian J Appl Psychol* 6(1):1–7 Ja '69. * (*PA* 47:7199)
48. SPIEGEL, DON, AND KEITH-SPIEGEL, PATRICIA. "Factor Analysis of 78 Variables From Nine Personality Tests and Scales." *J Proj Tech & Pers Assess* 33(2):160–7 Ap '69. * (*PA* 43:11352)
49. TORRETA, DELFINA MARQUEZ. *Somesthetic Perception of Clothing Fabrics in Relation to Body Image and the Psychological Security.* Doctor's thesis, Utah State University (Logan, Utah), 1969. (*DAI* 30:3731B)
50. VARMA, K., AND SINHA, J. N. "Sex Difference and Educational Level in the Influence of Prestige-Suggestion on 'Secure' and 'Insecure' Persons." *Psychol Studies* (India) 14(2):140–2 Jl '69. *
51. VERMA, K., AND SINHA, J. N. "An Experimental Study of Prestige-Suggestion in Secured and Insecured Persons." *Psychologia* (Japan) 12(2):121–3 Je '69. * (*PA* 44:12459)
52. HANNEN, CHARLES D. *An Examination of the Appropriateness of Maslow's Security-Insecurity Inventory for a Ninth Grade Population.* Master's thesis, University of Illinois (Urbana, Ill.), 1970.
53. JHA, SHEO SHANKAR, AND SINGH, R. I. P. "Prestige Suggestion in Secure and Insecure Subjects." *Manas* (India) 17(2):95–101 N '70. * (*PA* 47:10776)
54. SCHLUDERMANN, SHIRIN, AND SCHLUDERMANN, EDUARD. "Personality Correlations of Adolescent Self-Concepts and Security-Insecurity." *J Psychol* 74(1):85–90 Ja '70. * (*PA* 44:10162)
55. WHITE, BARBARA A. *A Comparison of Selected Perceptual and Personality Variables Among College Women, Deviant and Non-Deviant in Clothing Appearance.* Master's thesis, Utah State University (Logan, Utah), 1970.
56. ATHANASSIADES, JOHN CONSTANTINE. *Distortion of Upward Communication as a Function of a Subordinate's Security Level, His Achievement Motive, and Organizational Authority-Structure.* Doctor's thesis, New York University (New York, N.Y.), 1971. (*DAI* 32:5937A)
57. BAKKE, LARRY H. *A Study of the Relationship of Aesthetic Judgment to Self-Esteem and Security in University Women.* Doctor's thesis, Syracuse University (Syracuse, N.Y.), 1971. (*DAI* 32:4410A)
58. BHAN, RAJ NATH. "Factors in Social Environment as Related to Emotional Security-Insecurity Syndrome." *Psychol Studies* (India) 16(1):29–34 Ja '71. *
59. BISHOP, JOSEPH LAYTON. *The Relationship of Faculty Members' Perceived Sense of Security/Insecurity to Instructional Innovation in the Community College.* Doctor's thesis, Claremont Graduate School (Claremont, Calif.), 1971. (*DAI* 32:2520A)
60. JONES, LAWRENCE KEITH. *Relationship Between Self-Disclosure and Positive Mental Health, Modeled Self-Disclosure, and Socioeconomic Status.* Doctor's thesis, University of Missouri (Columbia, Mo.), 1971. (*DAI* 32:4953A)
61. KRISHNA, K. P., AND PRASAD, S. C. "Authoritarianism as a Function of Security-Insecurity and Anxiety." *Manas* (India) 18(2):85–9 N '71. * (*PA* 50:4925)
62. OWENS, CHARLES EDWARD. *An Investigation of the Relationship of Values and Security-Insecurity to Student Activism.* Doctor's thesis, University of New Mexico (Albuquerque, N.M.), 1971. (*DAI* 32:4994A)
63. SINGH, R. M. P., AND KRISHNA, K. P. "Prejudice of College Students Towards Caste." *Indian J Psychol* 46(3):219–25 S '71. *
64. SPIEGEL, DON, AND KEITH-SPIEGEL, PATRICIA. "Multiple Predictors of Course Grades for College Men and Women." *J Col Stud Personnel* 12(1):44–8 Ja '71. * (*PA* 46:1871)
65. WHITE, BARBARA O., AND KERNALEGUEN, ANNE P. "Comparison of Selected Perceptual and Personality Variables Among College Women Deviant and Non-Deviant in Their Appearance." *Percept & Motor Skills* 32(1):87–92 F '71. * (*PA* 46:3060)

CUMULATIVE NAME INDEX

Spilka, B.: 21
Stein, M.: 3
Stewart, H. F.: 15
Sutherland, B. V.: 21
Sweetland, A.: 6
Torreta, D. M.: 49
Varma, K.: 50
Verma, K.: 51

Vincent, J.: 26
Vincent, M. J. P.: 37
Webster, H.: rev, 5:107
Weinberg, J. R.: 32
White, B. A.: 55
White, B. O.: 65
Wilburn, R. G.: 39
Willner, E.: 17, 42

[1371]

Self-Analysis Inventory. Adults; 1945; SAI; test booklet title is *"How'm I Doin'?"*; interviewing aid for locating maladjustment in 37 problem areas; Harry J. Baker; Bobbs-Merrill Co., Inc. *

For additional information, see P:240; for reviews by Warren R. Baller and John W. Gustad, see 5:108.

[1372]

★Self-Concept Adjective Checklist. Grades kgn–8; 1971; SCAC; Alan J. Politte; Psychologists and Educators, Inc. *

[1373]

★The Self-Concept and Motivation Inventory: What Face Would You Wear? Age 4–kgn, grades 1–3, 3–6, 7–12; 1967–68; SCAMIN; 4 levels; George A. Farrah, Norman J. Milchus, and William Reitz; Person-O-Metrics, Inc. *

a) PRE-SCHOOL/KINDERGARTEN FORM. Age 4–kgn; 3 scores: motivation (goal and achievement needs, achievement investment), self-concept.

b) EARLY ELEMENTARY FORM. Grades 1–3; 4 scores: motivation (goal and achievement needs, achievement investment), self-concept (role expectations, self-adequacy).

c) LATER ELEMENTARY FORM. Grades 3–6; 4–10 scores: same as for early elementary form plus 6 optional sources of support climate scores (parents, teachers, peers and siblings, academic self, academic activity climate, school climate).

d) SECONDARY FORM. Grades 7–12; 4–20 scores: same as for early elementary form plus 16 optional scores: sources of support climate (parents, teachers, peers, academic self, physical and social self, adults and counselors, academic activity climate, school climate), immediate-intrinsic orientation (evaluated competition, tasks and projects, discovery and creativity, skills), fulfillment orientation (aspiration, cooperation and conformity, responsibility, acceptance and praise).

[1374]

★Self-Esteem Questionnaire. Ages 9 and over; 1971; SEQ; 2 scores: self-esteem, self-other satisfaction; James K. Hoffmeister; Test Analysis and Development Corporation. *

[1375]

Self-Interview Inventory. Adult males; 1958; SII; 10 scores: current complaints, emotional insecurity, guilt feelings, composite neurotic (based on first 3 scores), prepsychotic or psychotic, behavior problems, childhood illness, composite maladjustment (based on previous 3 scores), validation (lack of carefulness, lack of truthfulness); H. Birnet Hovey; Psychometric Affiliates. *

For additional information, see P:241; for reviews by Andrew R. Baggaley and David T. Lykken, see 6:172 (1 reference).

REFERENCES THROUGH 1971
1. See 6:172.

CUMULATIVE NAME INDEX
Baggaley, A. R.: rev, 6:172
Hovey, H. B.: 1
Lykken, D. T.: rev, 6:172

Security-Insecurity Inventory

[1376]

Self Perception Inventory. Ages 12 and over; 1967–69; SPI; 12 scores: general adjustment (consistency, self-actualization, supervision, total), general maladjustment (uncommon response, rigidity-dogmatism, authoritarianism, anxiety, depression, paranoia, total), time; William T. Martin; Psychologists and Educators, Inc. *

For additional information, see 7:136 (3 references).

REFERENCES THROUGH 1971
1–3. See 7:136.

CUMULATIVE NAME INDEX
Braun, J. R.: 2   Tinley, J. J.: 2
Martin, W. T.: 1, 3

[1377]

Self-Rating Depression Scale. Adults; 1965–67; SDS; intensity of depression regardless of diagnosis; William W. K. Zung; the Author. *

For additional information and a review by Leonard D. Goodstein, see 7:137 (16 references); see also P:242 (8 references).

REFERENCES THROUGH 1971

1–8. See P:242.
9–24. See 7:137.
25. PORTERFIELD, AUSTIN L. "Education and Race Attitudes." *Sociol & Social Res* 21:538–43 Jl–Ag '37. * (PA 12:5451)
26. RICKELS, KARL; GORDON, PAUL E.; MECKELNBURG, ROBERT; SABLOSKY, LESTER; WHALEN, EDWARD M.; AND DION, HARRY. "Iprindole in Neurotic Depressed General Practice Patients: A Controlled Study." *Psychosomatics* 9:208–14 Jl–Ag '68. * (PA 43:11625)
27. ZUNG, WILLIAM W. K. "Evaluating Treatment Methods for Depressive Disorders." *Am J Psychiatry* 124(11, sup):40–8 My '68. *
28. RYBACK, RALPH S. "Alcohol the Euphoric Agent?" *Psychol* 6(4):7–12 N '69. * (PA 44:8790)
29. HINCHLIFFE, MARY; LANCASHIRE, MEREDITH; AND ROBERTS, F. J. "Eye-Contact and Depression: A Preliminary Report." *Brit J Psychiatry* 117(540):571–2 N '70. * (PA 45:10317)
30. KELLY, DESMOND; BROWN, CLINTON C.; AND SHAFFER, JOHN W. "A Comparison of Physiological and Psychological Measurements in Anxious Patients and Normal Controls." *Psychophysiol* 6(4):429–41 Ja '70. * (PA 44:20409)
31. PRANGE, ARTHUR J., JR.; WILSON, IAN C.; KNOX, ANGELINE; McCLANE, THOMAS K.; AND LIPTON, MORRIS A. "Enhancement of Imipramine by Thyroid Simulating Hormone: Clinical and Theoretical Implications." *Am J Psychiatry* 127(2):191–9 Ag '70. *
32. BIRTCHNELL, JOHN, AND ALARCON, JOSÉ. "Depression and Attempted Suicide: A Study of 91 Cases Seen in a Casualty Department." *Brit J Psychiatry* 118(544):289–96 Mr '71. * (PA 47:1290)
33. BUTTERWORTH, A. T., AND WATTS, ROBERT D. "Treatment of Hospitalized Alcoholics With Doxepin and Diazepam: A Controlled Study." *Q J Studies Alcohol* 32(1A):78–81 Mr '71. * (PA 46:7020)
34. FRANSELLA, FAY, AND JOYSTON-BECHAL, M. P. "An Investigation of Conceptual Process and Pattern Change in a Psychotherapy Group." *Brit J Psychiatry* 119(549):199–206 Ag '71. * (PA 47:6925)
35. HIBEL, DORIS ETHEL. *The Relationship Between Reminiscence and Depression Among Thirty Selected Institutionalized Aged Males.* Doctor's thesis, Boston University (Boston, Mass.), 1971. (DAI 32:2253B)
36. LO, SAMUEL NAI-MING. *Effects of Self-Reinforcement and Goal-Setting on the Affect and Personal Orientation of Housewives.* Doctor's thesis, Fuller Theological Seminary (Pasadena, Calif.), 1971. (DAI 32:7315B)
37. RYBACK, RALPH S.; TRIMBLE, RALPH W.; LEWIS, OLIVER F.; AND JENNINGS, CHARLES L. "Psychobiologic Effects of Prolonged Weightlessness (Bed Rest) in Young Healthy Volunteers." *Aerospace Med* 42(4):408–15 Ap '71. *
38. SELKIN, JAMES, AND MORRIS, JOLINE. "Some Behavioral Factors Which Influence the Recovery Rate of Suicide Attempters." *B Suicidol* 8:29–38 f '71. *
39. SNAITH, R. P.; AHMED, N.; MEHTA, S.; AND HAMILTON, MAX. "Assessment of the Severity of Primary Depressive Illness: Wakefield Self-Assessment Depression Inventory." *Psychol Med* (England) 1(2):143–9 F '71. * (PA 49:1541)
40. ZUNG, WILLIAM W. K. "Depression in the Normal Adult Population." *Psychosomatics* 12(3):164–7 My–Je '71. * (PA 47:7232)
41. ZUNG, WILLIAM W. K. "The Differentiation of Anxiety and Depressive Disorders: A Biometric Approach." *Psychosomatics* 12(6):380–4 N–D '71. * (PA 48:5210)

42. ZUNG, WILLIAM W. K., AND GIANTURCO, JUDITH A. "Personality Dimension and the Self-Rating Depression Scale." *J Clin Psychol* 27(2):247-8 Ap '71. * (*PA* 46:7084)

CUMULATIVE NAME INDEX

[1378]

★Self-Report Inventory. College; 1959–67; SRI; for research use only; Form R-3; 10 scores: self, others, children, authority, work, reality, parents, hope, total, intensity; Oliver H. Bown and Donald J. Veldman (preliminary manual); distributed by Research and Development Center for Teacher Education, University of Texas. *

REFERENCES THROUGH 1971

1. McCLAIN, EDWIN WAYNE. *The Relationship Between Student Teachers' Self-Reported Perceptions and Pupil Evaluations.* Doctor's thesis, University of Texas (Austin, Tex.), 1962. (*DA* 23:154)
2. VELDMAN, DONALD J., AND PECK, ROBERT F. "Student-Teacher Characteristics From the Pupils' Viewpoint." *J Ed Psychol* 54:346–55 D '63. * (*PA* 38:6670)
3. McLENDON, BILLYE BURRELL. *Patterns of Phenomenological Perceptions of Student Teachers as Predictors of Supervisor-Judged Teaching Effectiveness.* Doctor's thesis, University of Texas (Austin, Tex.), 1965. (*DA* 26:2056)
4. VELDMAN, D. J., AND KELLY, F. J. "Personality Correlates of a Composite Criterion of Teaching Effectiveness." *Alberta J Ed Res* (Canada) 11:102–7 Je '65. * (*PA* 39:16482)
5. BLOOM, WALLACE. "Effectiveness of a Cooperative Special Education Vocational Rehabilitation Program." *Am J Mental Def* 72:393–403 N '67. * (*PA* 42:7625)
6. BOWN, OLIVER H., AND RICHEK, HERBERT G. "The Bown Self-Report Inventory (SRI): A Quick Screening Instrument for Mental Health Professionals." *Comprehen Psychiatry* 8:45–52 F '67. * (*PA* 41:9628)
7. BOWN, OLIVER H.; FULLER, FRANCES F.; AND RICHEK, HERBERT G. "A Comparison of Self-Perceptions of Prospective Elementary and Secondary School Teachers." *Psychol Sch* 4:21–4 Ja '67. * (*PA* 41:5039)
8. BOWN, OLIVER H., AND RICHEK, HERBERT G. "The Mental Health of Commuter College Students: A Partial Test of Kysar's Hypothesis." *Mental Hyg* 52(3):354–9 Jl '68. *
9. RICHEK, HERBERT G., AND BOWN, OLIVER H. "Phenomenological Correlates of Jung's Typology." *J Anal Psychol* 13:57–65 Ja '68. * (*PA* 42:9728)
10. VELDMAN, DONALD J. "Effects of Sex, Aptitudes, and Attitudes on the Academic Achievement of College Freshmen." *J Ed Meas* 5:245–9 f '68. * (*PA* 44:11403)
11. VELDMAN, DONALD J., AND BOWN, OLIVER H. "Relationships of Cigarette Smoking to Academic Achievement, Cognitive Abilities, and Attitudes Toward Authority." *Multiv Behav Res* 3:513–7 O '68. * (*PA* 43:8333)
12. VELDMAN, DONALD J.; PECK, ROBERT F.; AND RICHEK, HERBERT G. "Personality Correlates of the High School Experi-

ences of Prospective Teachers." *Personnel & Guid J* 46:473–7 Ja '68. * (*PA* 42:9489)

13. BOWN, OLIVER H., AND RICHEK, HERBERT G. "Teachers-to-Be: Extraversion/Introversion and Self-Perceptions." *El Sch J* 70(3):164–70 D '69. * (*PA* 48:1783)
14. CONNELLY, RICHARD JOSEPH. *The Relationship Between Role Adaptation of Student Teachers, Its Attitudinal and Academic Correlates, and Supervisor and Peer Evaluations.* Doctor's thesis, University of Texas (Austin, Tex.), 1969. (*DAI* 30:2877A)
15. GREEN, MARY FRANCES FULFORD. *Attitudes, as Measured by the Bown Self Report Inventory, of Selected Junior College Freshmen Toward the Phenomenal World and Their Correlation With Achievement, Attrition and the Changes Which Occur After One Year.* Doctor's thesis, Florida State University (Tallahassee, Fla.), 1969. (*DAI* 30:4243A)
16. RICHEK, HERBERT G. "Jung's Typology and Psychological Adjustment in Prospective Teachers: A Preliminary Investigation." *Alberta J Ed Res* (Canada) 15(4):235–43 D '69. * (*PA* 46:1846)
17. RICHEK, HERBERT G. "Phenomenal Correlates of Marital Status in Junior College Students." *Psychol Rep* 24(3):795–8 Je '69. * (*PA* 44:545)
18. BARTON, ROBERT ERNEST. *Self-Reported Perceptions as Predictors of Entry Into a Teaching Career by Elementary and Secondary Prospective Teachers.* Master's thesis, University of Texas (Austin, Tex.), 1970.
19. RICHEK, HERBERT G. "A Comparison of Characteristics of Prospective Secondary School Teachers Enrolled in Two Different Degree Programs." *Calif J Ed Res* 21(5):204–7 N '70. * (*PA* 46:3812)
20. VELDMAN, DONALD J., AND PARKER, GEORGE V. C. "Adjective Rating Scales for Self Description." *Multiv Behav Res* 5(3):295–302 Jl '70. * (*PA* 45:710)
21. MURPHY, MURIEL EVA. *Behavioral, Self-Report, and Projective Factors Related to Birth Order.* Doctor's thesis, University of Texas (Austin, Tex.), 1971.
22. RUPPEL, RODNEY WAYNE. *Correlates of University Students' Counseling Approach Preferences.* Doctor's thesis, University of Texas (Austin, Tex.), 1971. (*DAI* 32:6137A)
23. SLAVIK, FRANK HENRY, JR. *The Relationship Between Attitudinal Similarity and Peer Evaluations of Prospective Teachers.* Doctor's thesis, University of Texas (Austin, Tex.), 1971. (*DAI* 32:6628B)

CUMULATIVE NAME INDEX

[1379]

The Sherman Mental Impairment Test. Adults; 1955–57; SMIT; 2 scores: letter finding, reaction time; Murray H. Sherman; Western Psychological Services. *

For additional information, see P:243 (1 reference); for reviews by D. Russell Davis and William Schofield, see 5:110 (1 reference).

REFERENCES THROUGH 1971

1. See 5:110.
2. See P:243.
3. OBRZUT, JOHN E., AND THWEATT, ROGER C. "An Investigation of the Sherman Mental Impairment Test: A Normative Study." *J Clin Psychol* 27(2):224–5 Ap '71. * (*PA* 46:7307)

CUMULATIVE NAME INDEX

[1380]

Shipley-Institute of Living Scale for Measuring Intellectual Impairment. Adults; 1939–46; SILS; formerly called *Shipley-Hartford Retreat Scale for Measuring Intellectual Impairment;* 4 scores: vocabulary, abstractions, total, conceptual quotient; 1946 manual identical with manual copyrighted 1940 except for title; Walter C. Shipley; distributed by Mrs. John H. Boyle. *

For additional information and a review by Aubrey

J. Yates, see 7:138 (21 references) ; see also P:244 (38 references), 6:173 (13 references), and 5:111 (23 references) ; for reviews by E. J. G. Bradford, William A. Hunt, and Margaret Ives, see 3:95 (25 references).

REFERENCES THROUGH 1971

1–25. See 3:95.
26–48. See 5:111.
49–61. See 6:173.
62–99. See P:244.
100–120. See 7:138.

121. WAGGONER, R. W., AND ZEIGLER, THORNTON WOODWARD. "Psychiatric Factors in Medical School Students Who Fail." *Am J Psychiatry* 103:369–76 N '46. * (*PA* 21:1671)

122. GARBER, W. F. "Evaluation of Psychometric Tests for Optometry." *Optom Weekly* 40:1927–32+, 1953–7 D 22, 29 '49. * (*PA* 24:3477)

123. REITMAN, F., AND ROBERTSON, J. P. S. "Reitman's Pin-Man Test: A Means of Disclosing Impaired Conceptual Thinking." *J Nerv & Mental Dis* 112:498–510 D '50. * (*PA* 25:4588)

124. CANTER, AARON HERMAN. "Direct and Indirect Measures of Psychological Deficit in Multiple Sclerosis: Part 1." *J General Psychol* 44:3–25 Ja '51. * (*PA* 25:7027)

125. CANTER, AARON HERMAN. "Direct and Indirect Measures of Psychological Deficit in Multiple Sclerosis: Part 2." *J General Psychol* 44:27–50 Ja '51. * (*PA* 25:7028)

126. BALDWIN, MARCELLA VIG. "A Clinico-Experimental Investigation Into the Psychological Aspects of Multiple Sclerosis." *J Nerv & Mental Dis* 115:299–342 Ap '52. * (*PA* 27:2915)

127. ROBIN, ASHLEY A., AND HARRISON, E. J. "Some Clinical and Aetiological Aspects of Depersonalization With a Case Report of Identical Twins." *J Mental Sci* (England) 98:469–76 Jl '52. * (*PA* 27:3656)

128. PLAUT, ERIKA, AND CRANNELL, C. W. "The Ability of Clinical Psychologists to Discriminate Between Drawings by Deteriorated Schizophrenics and Drawings by Normal Subjects." *Psychol Rep* 1:153–8 S '55. * (*PA* 30:5477)

129. MOOS, RUDOLPH, AND MUSSEN, PAUL. "Sexual Symbolism, Personality Integration, and Intellectual Functioning." *J Consult Psychol* 23:521–3 D '59. * (*PA* 34:5587)

130. FRYER, DAVID G., AND RICH, MARGARET P. "Denial of Illness in Relation to Intellectual Function." *J Nerv & Mental Dis* 131:523–7 D '60. * (*PA* 35:4955)

131. JARVIE, HUGH. "Problem-Solving Deficits Following Wounds of the Brain." *J Mental Sci* (England) 106:1377–82 O '60. * (*PA* 35:5145)

132. KRUGMAN, ARNOLD D.; ROSS, SHERMAN; VICINO, FRANK L.; AND CLYDE, DEAN J. "A Research Note: Effects of Dextro-Amphetamine and Meprobamate on Problem-Solving and Mood of Aged Subjects." *J Gerontol* 15:419–20 O '60. * (*PA* 35:1812)

133. SASTRY, M. N. C., AND KASTURI, H. Y. "Conceptual Error, Vocabulary and Level of Abstraction." *Trans All-India Inst Mental Health* 2:107–14 D '61. * (*PA* 37:5502)

134. SHNEIDMAN, EDWIN S. "The Case of El: Psychological Test Data." *J Proj Tech* 25:131–54 Je '61. * (*PA* 36:21K31S)

135. MAY, PHILIP R. A., AND TUMA, A. HUSSAIN. "Choice of Criteria for the Assessment of Treatment Outcome." *J Psychiatric Res* (England) 2(3):199–209 '64. * (*PA* 39:15562)

136. DIXON, JAMES C. "Cognitive Structure in Senile Conditions With Some Suggestions for Developing a Brief Screening Test of Mental Status." *J Gerontol* 20:41–9 Ja '65. *

137. SALZMAN, LEONARD F.; GOLDSTEIN, ROBERT H.; ATKINS, ROBERT; AND BABIGIAN, HAROUTUN. "Conceptual Thinking in Psychiatric Patients." *Arch Gen Psychiatry* 14:55–9 Ja '66. * (*PA* 40:4443)

138. GOLDSTEIN, ROBERT H., AND SALZMAN, LEONARD F. "Cognitive Functioning in Acute and Remitted Psychiatric Patients." *Psychol Rep* 21:24–6 Ag '67. * (*PA* 42:2738)

139. TURNER, WILLIAM J. "The Usefulness of Diphenylhydantoin in Treatment of Nonepileptic Emotional Disorders." *Int J Neuropsychiatry* 3(sup 2):S8–20 D '67. * (*PA* 41:4005)

140. GOLDSTEIN, NORMAN P.; EWERT, JOSEPHINE C.; RANDALL, RAYMOND V.; AND GROSS, JOHN B. "Psychiatric Aspects of Wilson's Disease (Hepatolenticular Degeneration): Results of Psychometric Tests During Long-Term Therapy." *Am J Psychiatry* 124:1555–61 My '68. * (*PA* 42:12656)

141. HALSTEAD, HERBERT, AND NEAL, C. DAVID. "Intelligence and Personality in Drug Addicts: A Pilot Study." *Brit J Addict* 63:237–40 D '68. *

142. MEHRABIAN, ALBERT, AND WILLIAMS, MARTIN. "Nonverbal Concomitants of Perceived and Intended Persuasiveness." *J Pers & Social Psychol* 13(1):37–58 S '69. * (*PA* 43:17375)

143. PAGE, STEWART. "Examiner Effect, Expertise, and Intelligence Testing." *Ont Psychologist* (Canada) 2(3):181–4 '70. * (*PA* 42:12656)

144. EISENTHAL, SHERMAN, AND HARFORD, THOMAS. "Correlation Between the Raven Progressive Matrices Scale and the Shipley Institute of Living Scale." *J Clin Psychol* 27(2):213–5 Ap '71. * (*PA* 46:7158)

145. EISNER, DONALD A., AND APFELDORF, MAX. "Verbal Intelligence and Susceptibility to Visual Illusions." *Percept & Motor Skills* 33(3):1298 D '71. * (*PA* 48:2744)

146. HOFFMANN, HELMUT, AND NELSON, PAUL C. "Personality Characteristics of Alcoholics in Relation to Age and Intelligence." *Psychol Rep* 29(1):143–6 Ag '71. * (*PA* 47:3292)

147. JONES, BEN MORGAN. "Verbal and Spatial Intelligence in Short and Long Term Alcoholics." *J Nerv & Mental Dis* 153(4):292–7 O '71. * (*PA* 47:11157)

148. MILLHAM, JIM; JACOBSON, LEONARD I.; AND BERGER, STEPHEN E. "Effects of Intelligence, Information Processing, and Mediation Conditions on Conceptual Learning." *J Ed Psychol* 62(4):293–9 Ag '71. * (*PA* 47:220)

149. PAGE, STEWART. "On Wessler's 'Estimating IQ: Expertise or Examiner Effect?': Research and Discussion." *Percept & Motor Skills* 33(2):435–8 O '71. * (*PA* 47:7094)

150. PRINGLE, ROGER K., AND HAANSTAD, MARTIN. "Estimating WAIS IQs From Progressive Matrices and Shipley-Hartford Scores." *J Clin Psychol* 27(4):479–81 O '71. * (*PA* 47:8929)

151. REISS, DAVID, AND ELSTEIN, ARTHUR S. "Perceptual and Cognitive Resources of Family Members: Contrasts Between Families of Paranoid and Nonparanoid Schizophrenics and Non-schizophrenic Psychiatric Patients." *Arch Gen Psychiatry* 24(2):121–34 F '71. * (*PA* 46:5217)

152. SPIEGEL, DON, AND KEITH-SPIEGEL, PATRICIA. "Multiple Predictors of Course Grades for College Men and Women." *J Col Stud Personnel* 12(1):44–8 Ja '71. * (*PA* 46:1871)

153. TARTER, RALPH E., AND JONES, BEN M. "Absence of Intellectual Deterioration in Chronic Alcoholics." *J Clin Psychol* 27(4):453–4 O '71. * (*PA* 47:9254)

154. WILKINSON, A. EARL; PRADO, WILLIAM M.; WILLIAMS, WOODROW O.; AND SCHNADT, FREDERICK W. "Psychological Test Characteristics and Length of Stay in Alcoholism Treatment." *Q J Studies Alcohol* 32(1A):60–5 Mr '71. * (*PA* 46:7116)

CUMULATIVE NAME INDEX

Mehrabian, A.: 142
Millham, J.: 148
Monroe, H. J.: 44
Monroe, K. L.: 80
Moos, R.: 129
Murray, M. D.: 118
Mussen, P.: 38, 129
Nathanson, I. A.: 78
Neal, C. D.: 141
Nelson, P. C.: 146
Nelson, S. E.: 40
Nichols, R. C.: 56, 67, 88
Nosik, W. A.: 6
Olson, R. W.: 83
Page, J.: 118
Page, S.: 143, 149
Palmer, J. O.: 69
Parker, J. W.: 47
Paulson, M. J.: 119
Phelps, H. B.: 100
Phillips, J. E.: 71
Plaut, E.: 128
Pollack, D.: 5
Pope, B.: 73
Prado, W. M.: 72, 81, 95, 154
Pringle, R. K.: 150
Pulos, L.: 56
Rabinovitz, A.: 21
Ramer, J. C.: 77
Randall, R. V.: 140
Reiss, D.: 151
Reitan, R. M.: 21
Reitman, F.: 123
Rich, M. P.: 130
Riley, G. L.: 50
Ritchey, R. E.: 96
Robertson, J. P. S.: 123
Robin, A. A.: 127
Robles, A. G.: 101
Ross, S.: 132
Ross, W. D.: 12
Ruiz, R. A.: 86, 90
Salzman, L. F.: 137–8
Sastry, M. N. C.: 133

Schalock, R. L.: 97
Scherer, I. W.: 35
Schnadt, F. W.: 154
Shaw, D. J.: 82
Shipley, W. C.: 1–2, 4, 41
Shneidman, E. S.: 134
Siegman, A. W.: 73
Simmons, H.: 51
Simpson, M.: 28
Simpson, M. M.: 31
Sines, L. K.: 48, 51
Sklar, M.: 57
Slater, P.: 11, 15, 26
Solomon, J. C.: 32
Spano, R. M.: 89
Spiegel, J.: 152
Stone, L. A.: 74–7
Stotland, E.: 118
Suinn, R. M.: 53
Sydow, D. W.: 42
Tarter, R. E.: 153
Taub, D. V.: 81
Tuma, A. H.: 70, 135
Turner, W. J.: 71, 139
Vicino, F. L.: 132
Vincent, M. O.: 113
Waggoner, R. W.: 121
Wahler, H. J.: 58, 97
Watson, C. G.: 98–9
Watson, L. S.: 58
Webb, M. W.: 91
Weingold, H. P.: 106
Wesley, E. L.: 33
Wheeler, E. T.: 13, 29
Wiener, D. N.: 55
Wiens, A. N.: 54
Wilkinson, A. E.: 120, 154
Williams, M.: 142
Williams, S. B.: 25
Williams, W. O.: 154
Winfield, D. L.: 43
Wright, M. E.: 20
Yates, A. J.: 49; rev, 7:138
Zelen, S. L.: 83
Ziegler, T. W.: 121

[1381]

★Situational Attitude Scale. College; 1972, c1969–72; SAS; "attitudes of whites toward blacks"; 11 scores: 10 situations scores, total; William E. Sedlacek and Glenwood C. Brooks, Jr.; Natresources, Inc. *

REFERENCES THROUGH 1971

1. SEDLACEK, WILLIAM E., AND BROOKS, GLENWOOD C., JR. "Development of a Measure of Racial Attitudes." Abstract. *Proc 78th Ann Conv Am Psychol Assn* 5(1):161–2 '70. * (*PA* 44:18523)
2. SEDLACEK, WILLIAM E., AND BROOKS, GLENWOOD C., JR. "Measuring Racial Attitudes in a Situational Context." *Psychol Rep* 27(3):971–80 D '70. * (*PA* 45:9830)
3. SEDLACEK, WILLIAM E., AND BROOKS, GLENWOOD C., JR. "Social Acceptability in the Measurement of Racial Attitudes." *Psychol Rep* 29(1):17–8 Ag '71. * (*PA* 47:2802)

CUMULATIVE NAME INDEX

Brooks, G. C.: 1–3   Sedlacek, W. E.: 1–3

[1382]

★Situational Preference Inventory. Grades 9–16 and adults; 1968–73; SPI; "individual styles of social interaction"; 3 scores: cooperational, instrumental, analytic; Carl N. Edwards; the Author. *

REFERENCES THROUGH 1971

1. EDWARDS, CARL N. "Characteristics of Volunteers and Nonvolunteers for a Sleep and Hypnotic Experiment." *Am J Clin Hyp* 11:26–9 Jl '68. * (*PA* 43:912)
2. EDWARDS, CARL N. "Defensive Interaction and the Volunteer Subject: An Heuristic Note." *Psychol Rep* 22:1305–9 Je '68. * (*PA* 42:18820)

CUMULATIVE NAME INDEX

Edwards, C. N.: 1–2

[1383]

*Sixteen Personality Factor Questionnaire. Ages 16 and over; 1949–73; 16PF; 22 scores: 16 primary factor scores: reserved vs. outgoing (A), less intelligent vs. more intelligent (B), affected by feelings vs.

emotionally stable (C), humble vs. assertive (E), sober vs. happy-go-lucky (F), expedient vs. conscientious (G), shy vs. venturesome (H), tough-minded vs. tender-minded (I), trusting vs. suspicious (L), practical vs. imaginative (M), forthright vs. shrewd (N), self-assured vs. apprehensive (O), conservative vs. experimenting (Q_1), group-dependent vs. self-sufficient (Q_2), undisciplined self-conflict vs. controlled (Q_3), relaxed vs. tense (Q_4), plus 6 second-order factor scores: introversion vs. extraversion (I), low anxiety vs. high anxiety (II), tenderminded emotionality vs. tough poise (III), subduedness vs. independence (IV), naturalness vs. discreetness (V), cool realism vs. prodigal subjectivity (VI); 3 levels; Raymond B. Cattell, Herbert W. Eber, and Maurice M. Tatsuoka (handbook); Institute for Personality and Ability Testing. (British norms supplement for Forms A and B: 1972; Peter Saville; NFER Publishing Co. Ltd. [England].) *

a) FORMS A AND B, 1967–68 EDITION. 1949–73; authors recommend administration of both forms (total of 374 items).

b) FORMS C AND D, 1969 EDITION. Reading levels grades 6 and over; 1954–73; short forms (105 items each) using less difficult vocabulary; authors recommend administration of both forms; administration of all four forms (A, B, C, and D making a total of 584 items) is recommended for important research; industrial edition of Form C (1956 edition), entitled *Employee Attitude Series: 16 P.F.*, published by Industrial Psychology, Inc.

c) FORM E. Reading levels grades 3–5; 1965–73; experimental edition.

For additional information and reviews by Thomas J. Bouchard, Jr. and Leonard G. Rorer, see 7:139 (295 references); see also P:245 (249 references); for a review by Maurice Lorr of an earlier edition, see 6:174 (81 references); for a review by C. J. Adcock, see 5:112 (21 references); for reviews by Charles M. Harsh, Ardie Lubin, and J. Richard Wittenborn, see 4:87 (8 references).

REFERENCES THROUGH 1971

1–8. See 4:87.
9–29. See 5:112.
30–108. See 6:174.
109–357. See P:245.
358–652. See 7:139.
653. CATTELL, R. B., AND WENIG, P. W. "Dynamic and Cognitive Factors Controlling Misperception." *J Abn & Social Psychol* 47:797–809 O '52. * (*PA* 27:5000)
654. McCARTHY, MARY VITERBO. "An Empirical Study of the Personality Profiles Characterizing Differential Quantitative and Linguistic Ability." *Studies Psychol & Psychiatry* 8(4):1–45 Je '53. * (*PA* 28:4043)
655. DREVDAHL, JOHN E. "Factors of Importance for Creativity." *J Clin Psychol* 12:21–6 Ja '56. * (*PA* 30:4160)
656. MONROE, JACK J., AND HILL, HARRIS E. "The Hill-Monroe Inventory for Predicting Acceptability for Psychotherapy in the Institutionalized Narcotic Addict." *J Clin Psychol* 14:31–6 Ja '58. * (*PA* 33:6271)
657. NUNNALLY, JUM, AND HUSEK, T. R. " 'Semantic Clarity': One Standard for Factored Tests." *Ed & Psychol Meas* 18:761–7 W '58. * (*PA* 34:156)
658. WILLIAMS, J. ROBERT. "A Test of the Validity of the P-Technique in the Measurement of Internal Conflict." *J Personality* 27:418–37 S '59. * (*PA* 34:6059)
659. BHAGOLIWAL, B. S. "The Personality Profile of a Sample of Indian M.Sc. Students on the Sixteen Personality Factor Questionnaire." *J Ed & Psychol* (India) 18:322–36 Jl '60. * (*PA* 35:2216)
660. SLOANE, R. B.; HABIB, A.; EVESON, M. B.; AND PAYNE, R. W. "Some Behavioural and Other Correlates of Cholesterol Metabolism." *J Psychosom Res* (England) 5:183–90 Je '61. * (*PA* 36:5HN83S)
661. DENNIS, ISOBEL G. "Faking on the Sixteen Personality Factor Questionnaire." *Ont Psychol Assn Q* (Canada) 15:43–6 Je '62. *
662. WILLIAMS, J. R., AND KNECHT, WALTER W. "Teachers' Ratings of High-School Students on 'Likability' and Their Relation to Measures of Ability and Achievement." *J Ed Res* 56:152–5 N '62. *

663. BUTT, DORCAS S. *The Relationship of Personality Factors to Conceived Values in University Male Students.* Master's thesis, University of British Columbia (Vancouver, B.C., Canada), 1963.

664. GOWER, JERRY MAURICE. *Identification of Personality Traits of Various Academic Interests.* Master's thesis, Central Washington College of Education (Ellensburg, Wash.), 1964.

665. KAHN, ROBERT L.; WOLFE, DONALD M.; QUINN, ROBERT P.; AND SNOEK, J. DIEDRICK; IN COLLABORATION WITH ROBERT A. ROSENTHAL. Part 5, "Personality Processes in Role Stress," pp. 223–333. In their *Organizational Stress: Studies in Role Conflict and Ambiguity.* New York: John Wiley & Sons, Inc., 1964. Pp. xiii, 470. * (*PA* 39:8866)

666. SCHAFER, TED. *Motivational Distortion and Its Relation to the Scales of a Factored Personality Questionnaire.* Master's thesis, University of Ottawa (Ottawa, Ont., Canada), 1964.

667. ADCOCK, C. J. "A Comparison of the Concepts of Cattell and Eysenck." *Brit J Ed Psychol* 35:90–7 F '65. * (*PA* 39:9004)

668. HALLER, A. O., AND WOLFF, CAROLE ELLIS. "A Note on 'Personality Orientations of Farm, Village, and Urban Boys.'" *Rural Sociol* 30:338–40 S '65. * (*PA* 39:14903, title only).

669. SAUNDERS, CHARLES B., AND DEEBLE, CHARLES T. "The Personality Structure of Chain Store Buyers, With Implications for Management." *J Retail* 41:39–47+ w '65–66 ['65]. *

670. WARBURTON, F. W. "Observations on a Sample of Psychopathic American Criminals." *Behav Res & Ther* (England) 3:129–35 S '65. * (*PA* 40:3148)

671. WOODFORD, DONALD PAUL. *Identification and Analysis of Art Preference and Personality Relationships.* Master's thesis, Illinois State University (Normal, Ill.), 1965.

672. FINN, FRANCES; MULCAHY, RISTEARD; AND O'DOHERTY, E. F. "The Psychological Assessment of Patients With Coronary Heart Disease: A Preliminary Communication." *Irish J Med Sci* 6:399–404 S '66. *

673. FROSTAD, ALVIN L.; FORREST, GARY L.; AND BAKKER, CORNELIS B. "Influence of Personality Type on Drug Response." *Am J Psychiatry* 122:1153–8 Ap '66. * (*PA* 40:7798)

674. GETZELS, J. W., AND CSIKSZENTMIHALYI, M. Chap. 15, "The Study of Creativity in Future Artists: The Criterion Problem," pp. 349–68. In *Experience, Structure and Adaptability.* Edited by O. J. Harvey. New York: Springer Publishing Co., Inc., 1966. Pp. ix, 406. *

675. KANE, J. "The Description of High Level Sporting Ability by Use of the 16PF Questionnaire." Abstract. *B Brit Psychol Soc* 19:A4 Ap '66. *

676. KANE, J. E. "Personality and Physical Ability, pp. 201–8. In *Proceedings of International Congress of Sport Sciences, 1964.* Edited by Kitsuo Kato. Tokyo, Japan: University of Tokyo Press, 1966. Pp. xii, 624. *

677. McALLISTER, J. "Personality Profiles of the 16PF and Diagnostic Categories." Abstract. *B Brit Psychol Soc* 19:A4 Ap '66. *

678. NELSON, DALE O. "Leadership in Sports." *Res Q* 37:268–75 My '66. * (*PA* 40:8726)

679. VINEY, LINDA L. "Congruence of Measures of Self-Regard." *Psychol Rec* 16:487–93 O '66. * (*PA* 41:1618)

680. GREENBERG, GLORIA U., AND FRANK, GEORGE H. "Personality Correlates of Attitude Change: The Tendency to Alter Attitudes Toward Self in Other-Directed and Inner-Directed People." *J General Psychol* 76:85–90 Ja '67. * (*PA* 41:4554)

681. TURNER, WILLIAM J. "The Usefulness of Diphenylhydantoin in Treatment of Nonepileptic Emotional Disorders." *Int J Neuropsychiatry* 3(sup 2):S8–20 D '67. * (*PA* 42:14005)

682. WHITE, KENNETH D., AND VAUGHAN, GRAHAM M. "Some Sex Differences in Relating Trans-Situational Conformity to Personality." Abstract. *Percept & Motor Skills* 24:190 F '67. * (*PA* 41:8912)

683. WHITE, WILLIAM F. "Personality Determinants of the Effects of Praise and Reproof in Classroom Achievement." Abstract. *Proc 75th Ann Conv Am Psychol Assn* 2:323–4 '67. * (*PA* 41:14228)

684. BREEDING, KEMPER A. *Relationships Among Academic Aptitude, Academic Achievement, Anxiety Level, and Personality Traits for Male and Female College Juniors and Seniors.* Master's thesis, East Tennessee State University (Johnson City, Tenn.), 1968.

685. CATTELL, RAYMOND B., AND HUNDLEBY, JOHN H. "Conceptual and Experimental Requirements in Relating Independence (U.I. 19) and Field Independence in L- and Q-Data Media: A Comment on Dr. Ohnmacht's Research." *Percept & Motor Skills* 27:733–4 D '68. * (*PA* 43:7483)

686. FRANCIS, R. D., AND TAYLOR, A. J. W. "Extraversion and Anxiety Among Certain Groups of Australian Offenders." *Austral & N Zeal J Criminol* (Australia) 1:249–51 D '68. *

687. HONN, MAX MICHAEL. *Relationship Between Inter-Test Variability on the ACT and Personality Characteristics.* Master's thesis, Illinois State University (Normal, Ill.), 1968.

688. LOY, JOHN W., JR. "Sociopsychological Attributes Associated With the Early Adoption of a Sport Innovation." *J Psychol* 70:141–7 N '68. * (*PA* 43:3914)

689. MAJESKY, STANLEY W. *A Follow-Up Study of the Permanence of Institutional Changes in Certain Personality Characteristics in Female Delinquents From the Youth Develop-*

ment Center at Waynesburg, Pennsylvania. Master's thesis, California State College (California, Pa.), 1968.

690. MEYER, ROBERT G. "Chronic High Blood Pressure, Essential Hypertension, and the Inhibition of Agression." Abstract. *Proc 76th Ann Conv Am Psychol Assn* 3:535–6 '68. * (*PA* 43:1114, title only)

691. SHARP, FRANKLIN D. *A Study of the Personality Traits and Characteristics of Different Kinds of Public School Teachers.* Master's thesis, University of Tennessee (Knoxville, Tenn.), 1968.

692. TAYLOR, A. J. W. "Personality Factors of Extraversion and Anxiety in New Zealand's Persistent Offenders." *Austral & N Zeal J Criminol* (Australia) 1:243–8 D '68. *

693. WURMSER, JEANNE H. *Personality Development in Douglass College Undergraduates.* Master's thesis, Rutgers—The State University (New Brunswick, N.J.), 1968.

694. ALEXANDER, FRANK D. "The Personality of 4-H Leaders." *J Coop Exten* 7(2):104–14 su '69. *

695. CATTELL, RAYMOND B. "The Profile Similarity Coefficient, rp, in Vocational Guidance and Diagnostic Classification." *Brit J Ed Psychol* 39(2):131–42 Je '69. * (*PA* 44:5862)

696. GREENWOOD, KATHRYN B. *A Study of Personality Traits and Interest of Prospective Teachers.* Master's thesis, University of Tennessee (Knoxville, Tenn.), 1969.

697. MONROE, NANCY C. *A Comparison of Selected Personality Traits of College Women With an Interest in Sports Activities and College Women With an Interest in Modern Dance.* Master's thesis, University of Tennessee (Knoxville, Tenn.), 1969.

698. NAGALAKSHMI, S. V., AND MURTHY, H. N. "Relation of Conditioned Response Strength to Anxiety in Normals, Neurotics and Psychotics." *Trans All-India Inst Mental Health* 9:65–73 D '69. * (*PA* 46:11203)

699. RISLEY, LINDA V. *Relationship of Certain Clothing Behaviors, Clothing Interest, and the Personality Traits of Masculinity-Femininity of a Select Group of College Men.* Master's thesis, University of Tennessee (Knoxville, Tenn.), 1969.

700. ROSENBROCK, PATRICIA A. *A Description of the Personality Structure of Women Physical Education Majors at San Diego State College.* Master's thesis, San Diego State College (San Diego, Calif.), 1969.

701. RUSHTON, JAMES, AND WARD, JAMES. "American and British Teachers' Attitudes to Education." *Durham Res R* (England) 5(23):403–5 au '69. *

702. STARR, J. W. "Attitudes to Corporal Punishment Among Student Teachers." *Ed Res* (England) 12(1):51–5 N '69. *

703. VANDERGRIFF, JERRY C. *A Study of the Relationship of Certain Personality Characteristics in Producing High School Quarterbacks.* Master's thesis, Texas Tech University (Lubbock, Tex.), 1969.

704. WARD, J., AND RUSHTON, JAMES. "Teacher Personality Related to Job Satisfaction, Attitudes to Education and Perception of School Environment." *Durham Res R* (England) 5(22):358–64 sp '69. *

705. WITTMER, JOE, AND HENRY, MARVIN. "Teacher Corps Interns in Disadvantaged Schools and Regular Teacher Trainees: A Personality Comparison." *J Stud Pers Assn Teach Ed* 8(1):1–8 '69. * (*PA* 44:17453)

706. BECK, ROBERT CLIFFORD. *Performance of Introverts and Extraverts on Various Tests of Cognitive Control.* Doctor's thesis, Texas Tech University (Lubbock, Tex.), 1970. (*DAI* 31:6251B)

707. BRADY, EVELYN I. "Personality Structure of Canadian Intercollegiate Women Ice Hockey Players," pp. 149–56. In *Contemporary Psychology of Sport.* Proceedings of the Second International Congress of Sport Psychology, Washington, D.C., 1968. Chicago, Ill.: Athletic Institute, 1970. Pp. xix, 878. *

708. BOOTHROYD, GREGORY WILLIAM. *An Exploratory Investigation Into Some Characteristics Associated With High and Low Ranked Resident Advisors.* Doctor's thesis, University of Michigan (Ann Arbor, Mich.), 1970. (*DAI* 31:3866A)

709. BRACY, LEWIS FLETCHER. *An Exploration of the Relationship Between Personality Factors and Automobile Accident Proneness.* Doctor's thesis, University of Southern Mississippi (Hattiesburg, Miss.), 1970. (*DAI* 31:4967B)

710. BRYAN, THOMAS CLARK. *A Study to Profile and Compare Personality Characteristics of Full-Time Ministers and Those Who Have Withdrawn From the Full-Time Pastoral Ministry.* Doctor's thesis, University of Southern Mississippi (Hattiesburg, Miss.), 1970. (*DAI* 31:3867A)

711. DIEHM, WILLIAM JOHN, JR. *The Relationship of Sense of Guilt Criminal Behavior and Legal Guilt.* Doctor's thesis, University of California (Los Angeles, Calif.), 1970. (*DAI* 32:272A)

712. DUTHLER, BERNARD THOMAS. *A Study of the Prediction of Transfer Students' Academic Success in a College of Education.* Doctor's thesis, University of Toledo (Toledo, Ohio), 1970. (*DAI* 31:4457A)

713. FLOCKEN, JOYCE MARY. *An Analysis of Selected Presage Criteria of Reciprocal Student and Teacher Ratings in Beginning College Speech Classes.* Doctor's thesis, University of Southern California (Los Angeles, Calif.), 1970. (*DAI* 31:6196A)

714. FRANCIS, R. D. "Recidivism, Types of Crime and Extra-

Sixteen Personality Factor Questionnaire

version." *Austral & N Zeal J Criminol* (Australia) 3(2):92–4 Je '70. *

715. GERSTEIN, OFFRA BILHA. *The Relationship Between Perception of Parental Behavior, Level of Dependency, and Vocational Interest Pattern in Hemophilic Young Adults.* Doctor's thesis, New York University (New York, N.Y.), 1970. (*DAI* 31:6401A)

716. GREEN, PAUL C., JR. *The Effectiveness of Supervisory Style When Leader, Group and Situational Variables Are Considered.* Doctor's thesis, Memphis State University (Memphis, Tenn.), 1970. (*DAI* 31:7659B)

717. HILL, DAVID OLIVER. *Extraversion-Introversion: An Investigation of Typological Theory.* Doctor's thesis, Texas Tech University (Lubbock, Tex.), 1970. (*DAI* 31:6257B)

718. HUTSLAR, JOHN LEE. *The Relationship Between Selected Personality Traits and Bicycle Ergometer Endurance.* Master's thesis, Pennsylvania State University (University Park, Pa.), 1970.

719. JOSHI, MEERA M. "Study of Ego-Ideals as Measures of Values in Relation to Personality Variables Among College Students." *Indian Psychol R* 7(1):77–9 Jl '70. *

720. KALEHOFF, DOROTHY W. *Selected Personal Characteristics of the Adult Basic Education Student in Mississippi.* Doctor's thesis, Mississippi State University (State College, Miss.), 1970. (*DAI* 31:5109A)

721. KANE, JOHN E. "Personality and Physical Abilities," pp. 131–41. In *Contemporary Psychology of Sport.* Proceedings of the Second International Congress of Sport Psychology, Washington, D.C., 1968. Chicago, Ill.: Athletic Institute, 1970. Pp. xix, 878. *

722. KHAN, JANET ADRIENNE GRIFFITH. *A Descriptive Comparison of the Personality, Life Experiences and Counseling Behaviors of the Typical and Creative School Counselors.* Doctor's thesis, University of Michigan (Ann Arbor, Mich.), 1970. (*DAI* 32:1274A)

723. KNAPP, WILLIAM MARTIN. *A Study of Teacher Personality Characteristics and Rated Effectiveness.* Doctor's thesis, University of Southern Mississippi (Hattiesburg, Miss.), 1970. (*DAI* 31:5712A)

724. KNAPSTEIN, JOHN WILLIAM. *A Cross-Cultural Study of Certain Personality Features of Tuberculous Alcoholic Patients.* Doctor's thesis, Texas Tech University (Lubbock, Tex.), 1970. (*DAI* 31:6260B)

725. KROLL, WALTER, AND CRENSHAW, WILLIAM. "Multivariate Personality Profile Analysis of Four Athletic Groups," pp. 97–106. In *Contemporary Psychology of Sport.* Proceedings of the Second International Congress of Sport Psychology, Washington, D.C., 1968. Chicago, Ill.: Athletic Institute, 1970. Pp. xix, 878. *

726. KULIS, JOSEPH CHESTER. *General Testing Factors, Person-Item Distance, and the Repeated Testings Effect.* Doctor's thesis, Northwestern University (Evanston, Ill.), 1970. (*DAI* 31:6260B)

727. LAMB, RONALD WRIGHT. *Factors Affecting Cooperating Teacher Influence Upon Student Teacher Attitude and Role Perception.* Doctor's thesis, University of Arizona (Tucson, Ariz.), 1970. (*DAI* 31:4600A)

728. LEASE, SHARON A. *Masculine and Feminine Personality Traits of Counselor Trainees and Recent Graduates in Counselor Education.* Master's thesis, Millersville State College (Millersville, Pa.), 1970.

729. LeUNES, ARNOLD, AND CHRISTENSEN, LARRY. "Reliability and Inmate Test Results." *Correct Psychologist* 4(3):85–93 N–D '70. * (*PA* 49:2670)

730. LITVAK, STUART BRUCE. *The Contribution of Non-Specific Variables to Outcome of Systematic Desensitization Therapy.* Doctor's thesis, Arizona State University (Tempe, Ariz.), 1970. (*DAI* 31:5629B)

731. LONG, ROGER L. *The Relationships Between Certain Personality Factors and the Behavioral Characteristics of Elementary School Principals.* Doctor's thesis, University of Virginia (Charlottesville, Va.), 1970. (*DAI* 31:4422A)

732. McGRAIL, RICHARD FRANCIS. *The Relationships Between the Organizational Climate of Schools and the Personality Characteristics of Teachers: A Puerto Rican Sample.* Doctor's thesis, Boston College (Chestnut Hill, Mass.), 1970. (*DAI* 31:5085A)

733. McHUGH, MARY-MARGARET. *Personality Traits of Varsity Lettermen of Illinois State University.* Master's thesis, Illinois State University (Normal, Ill.), 1970.

734. McLEISH, JOHN. *Students' Attitudes and College Environments.* Cambridge, England: Cambridge Institute of Education, 1970. Pp. vii, 251. *

735. NEWNAM, BOYD LEE. *A Study of the Personality of Male College Freshmen Students in Adaptive Physical Education.* Doctor's thesis, University of North Carolina (Chapel Hill, N.C.), 1970. (*DAI* 31:5828A)

736. OLIVER, CHARLES MICHAEL. *A Study of the Effects of Behavioral Group Counseling on Self-Actualization.* Doctor's thesis, University of Southern Mississippi (Hattiesburg, Miss.), 1970. (*DAI* 31:3881A)

737. PAITICH, DANIEL. "The Clarke Automated Psychological Examination and Report (CAPER)." *Ont Psychologist* (Canada) 2(5):304–14 '70. *

738. PARLETT, T. A. A. *The Modification of Criminal Personality Through Massed Learning by Programmed Instruction.* Master's thesis, University of Victoria (Victoria, B.C., Canada), 1970.

739. PHILLIPS, MORTON. *Response to "Double-Bind" Messages in Relation to Four Dimensions of Personality and to Two Maternal Child Rearing Attitudes.* Doctor's thesis, New York University (New York, N.Y.), 1970. (*DAI* 31:6299B)

740. RHODES, ROY GEORGE. *Measuring Change in Short-Term Psychotherapy Using the Sixteen Personality Factor Questionnaire as the Instrument.* Doctor's thesis, Indiana University (Bloomington, Ind.), 1970. (*DAI* 31:6412A)

741. ROTHWELL, ELIZABETH ANN. *The Relationship of Personality Traits, Teacher Attitude, Anxiety Level, and Academic Achievement to Ratings of Teacher Interns.* Doctor's thesis, Auburn University (Auburn, Ala.), 1970. (*DAI* 31:4021A)

742. ROTHWELL, WADE BROWNELL. *The Relationship of Certain Predictive Factors Including Personality Traits to Job Success of Graduates of Stenographic and Secretarial Programs of Public Supported Technical Institutes and Junior Colleges in the State of Alabama.* Doctor's thesis, Auburn University (Auburn, Ala.), 1970. (*DAI* 31:4055A)

743. RUSHALL, BRENT S. "An Evaluation of the Relationship Between Personality and Physical Performance Categories," pp. 157–65. In *Contemporary Psychology of Sport.* Proceedings of the Second International Congress of Sport Psychology, Washington, D.C., 1968. Chicago, Ill.: Athletic Institute, 1970. Pp. xix, 878. *

744. RUSHALL, BRENT S. "Some Practical Applications of Personality Information to Athletes," pp. 167–73. In *Contemporary Psychology of Sport.* Proceedings of the Second International Congress of Sport Psychology, Washington, D.C., 1968. Chicago, Ill.: Athletic Institute, 1970. Pp. xix, 878. *

745. SCHAEFER, JOSEPH HENRY. *Personality Factors and Teaching Influence.* Doctor's thesis, St. Louis University (St. Louis, Mo.), 1970. (*DAI* 31:4021A)

746. SMITH, ANITA MAXINE WILSON. *The Relationship of Selected Personality Characteristics in Teachers of Culturally Disadvantaged Children and Reading Achievement.* Doctor's thesis, Ohio State University (Columbus, Ohio), 1970. (*DAI* 32:105A)

747. TALLANT, WELDON J. *Changes in Pre-Service Teachers Involved in a Multi-Cultural Training Program Utilizing Formal Presentations, Sensitivity Training, Planned Social Activities, and a Cooperative Living Arrangement.* Doctor's thesis, East Texas State University (Commerce, Tex.), 1970. (*DAI* 31:4608A)

748. TIRPAK, RICHARD DANIEL. *Relationship Between Organizational Climate of Elementary Schools and Personal Characteristics of the Schools' Principals.* Doctor's thesis, University of Akron (Akron, Ohio), 1970. (*DAI* 32:145A)

749. VAN GALDER, ROBERT BRUCE. *Somatotype Groups and Their Relationship to Personality, Heart Rate Recovery, and Selected Motor Ability Variables in College Men.* Doctor's thesis, University of Northern Colorado (Greeley, Colo.), 1970. (*DAI* 31:3943A)

750. WILLIAMS, CONSTANCE MARIE DiSIPIO. *Personality Factors, Value Patterns, and Occupational Choices of Male Graduate Students.* Doctor's thesis, University of North Dakota (Grand Forks, N.D.), 1970. (*DAI* 31:6357A)

751. ZALEZNIK, ABRAHAM; DALTON, GENE W.; AND BARNES, LOUIS B.; WITH PIERRE LAURIN. Chap. 8, "Personality Characteristics," pp. 153–87, passim. In *Orientation and Conflict in Career,* see 752. *

752. ZALEZNIK, ABRAHAM; DALTON, GENE W.; AND BARNES, LOUIS B.; WITH PIERRE LAURIN. *Orientation and Conflict in Career.* Boston, Mass.: Division of Research, Harvard University, Graduate School of Business Administration, 1970. Pp. xxiii, 508. *

753. ZIMMERMAN, ROBERT EDGAR. *Teacher Perceptions and Personality Characteristics Associated With Innovation.* Doctor's thesis, University of North Dakota (Grand Forks, N.D.), 1970. (*DAI* 31:6462A)

754. ADCOCK, C. J., AND WEBBERLEY, M. "Primary Mental Abilities." *J General Psychol* 84(2):229–43 Ap '71. * (*PA* 46:4979)

755. ADCOCK, NGAIRE. "Skin Conductance Responses and Personality Dimensions." *Personality* 2(1):15–22 sp '71. * (*PA* 47:8458)

756. ANDREWS, J. C. "Personality, Sporting Interest and Achievement." *Ed R* (England) 23(2):126–34 F '71. *

757. BACHTOLD, LOUISE M., AND WERNER, EMMY E. "Personality Profiles of Women Psychologists: Three Generations." *Develop Psychol* 5(2):273–8 S '71. * (*PA* 47:2996)

758. BAIRD, JOHN SANFORD, JR. *A Multivariate Developmental Study of Political Ideology and Intolerance.* Doctor's thesis, North Carolina State University (Raleigh, N.C.), 1971. (*DAI* 32:6633B)

759. BANKS, M. H., AND BOLTON, N. "The Personality Structure of a Delinquent Group." *Durham Res R* (England) 6(27):596–7 au '71. *

760. BARILE, PETER ANTHONY, JR. *Properties of Organizational Structure, Teacher Personality Characteristics, and Their*

Relationship to Teacher Role Behavior. Doctor's thesis, New York University (New York, N.Y.), 1971. (*DAI* 32:2932A)

761. BERTOU, PATRICK, AND CLASEN, ROBERT E. "An Analysis of a Spanish Translation of the Sixteen Personality Factors Tests." *J Exp Ed* 39(4):13–21 su '71. *

762. BEYER, DARRELL ERICK. *An Analysis of Selected Intellectual and Nonintellectual Characteristics of Dropouts and Survivors in a Private College.* Doctor's thesis, Baylor University (Waco, Tex.), 1971. (*DAI* 32:3773A)

763. BREWSTER, EDWARD THOMAS. *Personality Characteristics of Giving- Versus Receiving-Oriented Individuals.* Doctor's thesis, University of Arizona (Tucson, Ariz.), 1971. (*DAI* 32:2476A)

764. BREWSTER, ELIZABETH S. GREEN. *Personality Factors Relevant to Intensive Audio-Lingual Foreign Language Learning.* Doctor's thesis, University of Texas (Austin, Tex.), 1971. (*DAI* 33:68A)

765. BROADWAY, CLIFFORD MONROE. *Personality Correlates of Imagery Ability.* Doctor's thesis, Texas Tech University (Lubbock, Tex.), 1971. (*DAI* 32:5433B)

766. BURDESHAW, DOROTHY. "Personality Profiles on Non-Swimmers Among University Women." *J Sports Med & Phys Fitness* (Italy) 11(2):80–6 Je '71. *

767. BURTON, D. A. "A Factor Analysis of the Edwards Personal Preference Schedule and 16 PF in a Psychiatric Population." *J Clin Psychol* 27(2):248–51 Ap '71. * (*PA* 46:7153)

768. CALLIOTTE, JAMES ANTHONY. *The Effect of Basic Encounter Groups on Student Teachers' Personality Traits and Subsequent Teaching Behaviors.* Doctor's thesis, St. Louis University (St. Louis, Mo.), 1971. (*DAI* 32:4462A)

769. CAROTHERS, CHARLES. *A Discriminatory Analysis of Personality Characteristics of the Intemperate and the Rehabilitated Alcoholic.* Doctor's thesis, Texas Tech University (Lubbock, Tex.), 1971. (*DAI* 32:2393B)

770. CARR, RONALD J. "Personality Test Scores (16 P.F.) of Male P.E. Students." *Brit J Phys Ed* 2(6):xlv–xlvii N '71. *

771. CATTELL, RAYMOND B., AND BARTLETT, HAROLD W. "An R-dR-Technique Operational Distinction of the States of Anxiety, Stress, Fear, Etc." *Austral J Psychol* 23(2):105–23 Ag '71. * (*PA* 47:10889)

772. CHUNG, KAE H., AND FERRIS, MICHAEL J. "An Inquiry of the Nominal Group Process." *Acad Mgmt J* 14(4):520–4 D '71. *

773. CLARK, MARION NORCROSS. *Characteristics Associated With Innovative Behavior in Specified Organizational Climates.* Doctor's thesis, Rutgers—The State University (New Brunswick, N.J.), 1971. (*DAI* 32:2902A)

774. COFFMAN, PHILLIP HUDSON. *A Comparison of Selected Personality Characteristics of Doctoral Students Majoring in Higher Education and Other Doctoral Students.* Doctor's thesis, University of Toledo (Toledo, Ohio), 1971. (*DAI* 32:3715A)

775. COWDEN, JAMES E.; SCHROEDER, CHARLES R.; AND PETERSON, WILLIAM M. "The CPI vs. the 16 PF at a Reception Center for Delinquent Boys." *J Clin Psychol* 27(1):109–11 Ja '71. * (*PA* 46:1471)

776. COX, WRAY KENT. *Personality, Intelligence, and Work Performance of Disadvantaged Adolescents.* Doctor's thesis, University of Missouri (Columbia, Mo.), 1971. (*DAI* 32:4939A)

777. DAVIS, JAMES BARRETT. *An Investigation of the Utility of Sixteen Personality Factor Questionnaire Scores in Predicting Counseling Effectiveness.* Doctor's thesis, University of Southern Mississippi (Hattiesburg, Miss.), 1971. (*DAI* 32:4939A)

778. DAVIS, JAMES ROBERT. *A Study to Aid in the Selection of Linkers for the Educational Change Process.* Doctor's thesis, New Mexico State University (University Park, N.M.), 1971. (*DAI* 32:1776A)

779. DAVISON, K.; BRIERLEY, H.; AND SMITH, C. "A Male Monozygotic Twinship Discordant for Homosexuality: A Repertory Grid Study." *Brit J Psychiatry* 118(547):675–82 Je '71. * (*PA* 47:7180)

780. DEBLASSIE, RICHARD R. "A Comparative Study of the Personality Structures of Persistent and Prospective Teachers." *J Ed Res* 64(7):331–3 Mr '71. * (*PA* 46:11615)

781. DELHEES, KARL H., AND CATTELL, RAYMOND B. "The Dimensions of Pathology: Proof of Their Projection Beyond the Normal 16PF Source Traits." *Personality* 2(2):149–73 su '71. * (*PA* 47:7076)

782. EDWARDS, STEPHEN FRANCIS. *The Repression-Sensitization Dimension: Personality, Adjustment, Defenses, Self-Ideal Discrepancy.* Doctor's thesis, Texas Tech University (Lubbock, Tex.), 1971. (*DAI* 32:5437B)

783. ELLIOTT, RONALD E. *Cattell's Sixteen Personality Factor Questionnaire as a Predictor of Successful Practice Teaching.* Master's thesis, University of New Brunswick (Fredericton, N.B., Canada), 1971.

784. EVANS, ROBERT LEWIS. *Nurse Refresher Course—Predicting Effectiveness.* Doctor's thesis, Georgia State University (Atlanta, Ga.), 1971. (*DAI* 32:1695A)

785. FAGAN, EULALIA CONNORS. *Personality Characteristics of Alcoholics, With Varying Degrees of Sobriety, and Those of Their Wives.* Doctor's thesis, Columbia University (New York, N.Y.), 1971. (*DAI* 32:1839B)

786. FLEISHMAN, JOSEPH J., AND FINE, BERNARD J. "Note

on Cognitive Factors Related to Factor B of the 16 PF Test." *Psychol Rep* 29(3):1075–7 D '71. * (*PA* 48:988)

787. FOZARD, JAMES L., AND NUTTALL, RONALD L. "Effects of Age and Socioeconomic Status Differences on the Sixteen Personality Factor Questionnaire Scores." Abstract. *Proc 79th Ann Conv Am Psychol Assn* 6(2):597–8 '71. * (*PA* 46:4949)

788. GALLOP, ROY. "Value Patterns, Personality, and Social Attitudes of Foundation Students at Bournemouth College of Art." *Voc Aspect Ed* (England) 23(54):29–37 Ap '71. *

789. GEORGE, JULIUS R., AND BISHOP, LLOYD K. "Relationship of Organizational Structure and Teacher Personality Characteristics to Organizational Climate." *Adm Sci Q* 16(4):467–75 D '71. * (*PA* 47:11723)

790. GILLIS, JOHN S., AND KINSELLA, NOEL A. "Some Personality Factors of Matched Groups of New Brunswick Blacks and Whites." *Can J Behav Sci* 3(1):66–71 Ja '71. * (*PA* 46:1195)

791. GOODMAN, GAY. *A Study of the Relationship of Student Teacher Effectiveness and Personality Characteristics Measured by the Sixteen Personality Factor Questionnaire.* Doctor's thesis, University of Iowa (Iowa City, Iowa), 1971. (*DAI* 32:5086A)

792. GOODWIN, NANCY-LEE. *The Prediction of Artistic Performance From Cognitive and Non-Cognitive Measures.* Doctor's thesis, University of Illinois (Urbana, Ill.), 1971. (*DAI* 32:4419A)

793. GOTTSCHALK, LOUIS A.; GLESER, GOLDINE C.; CLEGHORN, JOHN M.; STONE, WALTER N.; AND WINGET, CAROLYN N. Chap. 37, "Prediction of Changes in Severity of the Schizophrenic Syndrome With Discontinuation and Administration of Phenothiazines in Chronic Schizophrenic Patients: Language as a Predictor and Measure of Change in Schizophrenia," pp. 605–27. In *The Schizophrenic Syndrome: An Annual Review 1971.* Edited by Robert Cancro. New York: Brunner/Mazel, Inc., 1971. Pp. xv, 791. *

794. GROSS, WILLIAM F., AND CARPENTER, LINDA L. "Alcoholic Personality: Reality or Fiction?" *Psychol Rep* 28(2):375–8 Ap '71. * (*PA* 46:7097)

795. HEADRICK, EDWIN BRUCE. *A Comparison of Personality Traits of Experienced and Prospective Teachers of the Educable Mentally Retarded and Non-Retarded in Mississippi.* Doctor's thesis, Mississippi State University (State College, Miss.), 1971. (*DAI* 32:1916A)

796. HEDDENDORF, RUSSELL "Professionalism and Personality Types Among Student Teachers." *J Teach Ed* 22(3):310–3 f '71. * (*PA* 47:11732)

797. HEINTZEN, ERICH HUGO, III. *The Religious Attitudes and Interests of Seminary Students and Clergymen of the Lutheran Church-Missouri Synod.* Doctor's thesis, University of North Dakota (Grand Forks, N.D.), 1971. (*DAI* 32:7078A)

798. HERITAGE, LENA JEANNETTE GREER. *A Study of Selected Factors and Their Effect on Postdivorce Adjustment.* Doctor's thesis, University of Southern Mississippi (Hattiesburg, Miss.), 1971. (*DAI* 32:4950A)

799. HOLTZ, RUTH RICHARDS. *A Study of Selected Creative Thinking Tests in Conjunction With Measures of Intelligence and Personality.* Doctor's thesis, University of California (Berkeley, Calif.), 1971. (*DAI* 32:4185B)

800. HOWARTH, EDGAR, AND BROWNE, JAMES A. "An Item-Factor-Analysis of the 16PF." *Personality* 2(2):117–39 su '71. * (*PA* 47:6813)

801. HUGHES, HENRY MICHAEL, JR. *Vocational Choice Level, and Consistency: A Test of Holland's Theory on an Employed Sample.* Doctor's thesis, State University of New York (Albany, N.Y.), 1971. (*DAI* 32:1999A)

802. HUNDAL, P. S., AND SINGH, MOHINDER. "A Factor Analytical Study of Intellectual and Non-Intellectual Characteristics." *Multiv Behav Res* 6(4):503–14 O '71. * (*PA* 47:11735)

803. JENKINS, C. DAVID. "Psychologic and Social Precursors of Coronary Disease (First of Two Parts)." *New Engl J Med* 284(5):244–55 F 4 '71. * (*PA* 46:7366)

804. JOHNSON, PETER JAMES. *Personality Characteristics of Unsuccessful Student Teachers.* Doctor's thesis, University of North Dakota (Grand Forks, N.D.), 1971. (*DAI* 32:6837A)

805. JOHNSTON, JOHN ALEXANDER. *A Comparison of the Difference in the Effects of Trust on Learning Between Character-Disorder Delinquent and Nondelinquent Boys, as Viewed in Three Learning Situations.* Doctor's thesis, Boston University (Boston, Mass.), 1971. (*DAI* 32:1829A)

806. KARDAK, VISHNU. "Cognitive Ability and Personality Measures of Probationary Officers Selected by Psychological Tests and Traditional Examination." *Indian J Psychol* 46(3):247–55 S '71. *

807. KARSON, SAMUEL, AND O'DELL, JERRY W. "Performance Ratings and Personality Factors in Radar Controllers." *J Clin Psychol* 27(3):339–42 Jl '71. * (*PA* 47:5888)

808. KELLER, CHARLES WILLIAM. *Characteristics of Rorschach Interpreter Types: An Exploratory Study.* Doctor's thesis, Texas Tech University (Lubbock, Tex.), 1971. (*DAI* 32:2400B)

809. KENNEDY, THOMAS G. "Crow-Northern Cheyenne Selected for Study." *J Am Indian Ed* 11(1):27–31 O '71. *

810. KIDSON, MALCOLM A. "Personality Factors in Hypertension." *Austral & N Zeal J Psychiatry* (Australia) 5(3):139–45 S '71. *

811. KLUKKEN, PHILIP GARY. *Personality and Interpersonal*

Distance. Doctor's thesis, University of Florida (Gainesville, Fla.), 1971. (*DAI* 32:6033B)

812. KORELLA, KARL. *Teen-Age Suicidal Gestures: A Study of Suicidal Behavior Among High School Students.* Doctor's thesis, University of Oregon (Eugene, Ore.), 1971. (*DAI* 32:5039A)

813. KRAVAS, KONSTANTINOS JAMES. *A Study of the Relative Effectiveness of Two Forms of a Counseling Practicum in Reducing the Level of Dogmatism and Rigidity in Counselor Trainees.* Doctor's thesis, University of Michigan (Ann Arbor, Mich.), 1971. (*DAI* 32:6132A)

814. LASHER, IVAN WARD. *A Study of Personality Characteristics of Elementary and Secondary Teachers in Relation to Identifying Administrative Leadership Qualities.* Doctor's thesis, Utah State University (Logan, Utah), 1971. (*DAI* 32:3619A)

815. LAURY, PATRICK DAVID. *Philosophies of Education and Personality Correlates.* Doctor's thesis, St. Louis University (St. Louis, Mo.), 1971. (*DAI* 32:4490A)

816. LAWLIS, G. FRANK. "The Hard-Core Unemployed: Unidimensional or Multidimensional Personality?" *Rehabil Counsel B* 15(1):13–8 S '71. * (*PA* 47:9409)

817. LAWLIS, G. FRANK. "Motivational Factors Reflecting Employment Instability." *J Social Psychol* 84(2):215–23 Ag '71. * (*PA* 47:1869)

818. LAWLIS, G. FRANK. "A Psychological View of the Chronically Unemployed: Personality and Motivation." *Psychol Rep* 28(3):838 Je '71. * (*PA* 46:11295)

819. LAWLIS, G. FRANK, AND RUBIN, STANFORD E. "16-PF Study of Personality Patterns in Alcoholics." *Q J Studies Alcohol* 32(2):318–27 Je '71. *

820. LEE, JAMES L. "Seminary Persisters and Leavers." *Counsel & Values* 16(1):39–45 f '71. * (*PA* 49:2262)

821. LEMKE, ELMER A., AND KIRCHNER, JOHN H. "A Multivariate Study of Handwriting, Intelligence, and Personality Correlates." *J Pers Assess* 35(6):584–92 D '71. * (*PA* 47:10876)

822. LEWIS, JUDITH A., AND LEWIS, MICHAEL D. "Some Still Can Smile—and Some Cannot." *Sch Counselor* 19(1):18–24 S '71. *

823. LIBBY, WM. L., JR. "Sociometric Task Leadership and the Perception of Deviance and Subsequent Conformity, as Functions of Personality." *Genetic Psychol Monogr* 84(2):254–73 N '71. * (*PA* 49:782)

824. LIN, YI-GUANG, AND MCKEACHIE, WILBERT J. "Sex Similarity in Personality Correlates of Test Anxiety." *Psychol Rep* 29(2):515–20 O '71. * (*PA* 47:9616)

825. LOCKHART, BARBARA DAY. *Personality Factors of University Women in Relation to Their Attitudes Toward Physical Education and Physical Activity.* Doctor's thesis, Brigham Young University (Provo, Utah), 1971. (*DAI* 32:3077A)

826. LOWE, BENJAMIN. *The Aesthetic Sensitivity of Athletes.* Doctor's thesis, University of Wisconsin (Madison, Wis.), 1971. (*DAI* 32:773A)

827. MCCONAUGHY, JOHN B., AND PALMER, J. DAVID. "Personality and Performance of State Executives in South Carolina." *Pub Personnel R* 32(1):44–8 Ja '71. *

828. MCCULLOCH, MAX PRESTON. *The Effectiveness of Selected Personality Variables in Predicting Performance of Secondary Social Studies Teachers.* Doctor's thesis, Texas Tech University (Lubbock, Tex.), 1971. (*DAI* 32:1962A)

829. MCEWEN, WILLIAM E. *Some Personality Traits of Athletes at the University of Tennessee.* Master's thesis, University of Tennessee (Knoxville, Tenn.), 1971.

830. MAHONEY, JOHN MILTON. *The Effect of Reality Orientation and Impulse Control on the Preference for Frivolous, Social and Existential Humor.* Doctor's thesis, State University of New York (Buffalo, N.Y.), 1971. (*DAI* 32:5426B)

831. MAIN, CECIL LOCKWOOD, JR. *A Comparative Study of Personality and Behavior of Selected Secondary Science and Non-Science Teachers.* Doctor's thesis, University of North Carolina (Chapel Hill, N.C.), 1971. (*DAI* 32:2507A)

832. MARTIN, WILLIAM A. "Word Fluency—Intellect or Personality?" *J Genetic Psychol* 118(1):17–24 Mr '71. * (*PA* 46:8848)

833. MARZOLF, STANLEY S., AND KIRCHNER, JOHN H. "Color in House-Tree-Person Drawings by College Men and Women." *J Clin Psychol* 27(4):504–9 O '71. * (*PA* 47:8953)

834. MICHAEL, WILLIAM B.; HANEY, RUSSELL; LEE, YOUNG B.; AND MICHAEL, JOAN J. "The Criterion-Related Validities of Cognitive and Noncognitive Predictors in a Training Program for Nursing Candidates." *Ed & Psychol Meas* 31(4):983–7 w '71. * (*PA* 48:1866)

835. MILLER, JAMES HOWARD. *Sensitivity Training With Incarcerated Criminals: Personality Correlates of Participant Duration and an Assessment of Therapeutic Value.* Doctor's thesis, Auburn University (Auburn, Ala.), 1971. (*DAI* 32:3794A)

836. MILLER, JEFFREY O. "Personality Factors and Perceptual Factors in Motor Performance." *ICHPER* 13:46–61 '71. *

837. MOLDOFSKY, HARVEY, AND ROTHMAN, ARTHUR I. "Personality, Disease Parameters and Medication in Rheumatoid Arthritis." *J Chronic Dis* 24(6):363–72 Ag '71. *

838. MORF, MARTIN E. "Examination of the Clarke Automated Psychological Examination and Report." *Ont Psychologist* (Canada) 3(2):96–102 '71. *

839. MORRIS, MARVIN LEON. *Relationships Among Sociometric Status, Prognosis, and Selected Personality Variables of State Hospital Patients.* Doctor's thesis, North Texas State University (Denton, Tex.), 1971. (*DAI* 32:6058B)

840. MURPHY, FINIAN JOSEPH. *Personality Characteristics as Predictors of Counselor-Trainee Success in Practicum.* Doctor's thesis, Northern Illinois University (DeKalb, Ill.), 1971. (*DAI* 32:3697A)

841. NELSON, JOHN CLEMENT. *Relating Student and Teacher Personality and Cognitive Characteristics With School Achievement of Educable Mentally Retarded Children.* Doctor's thesis, George Peabody College for Teachers (Nashville, Tenn.), 1971. (*DAI* 32:1948A)

842. NULL, ELDON J. "Relationships Between Personal Variables of Teachers and Their Perception of the Behavior of School Personnel." *J Ed Res* 64(8):351–4 Ap '71. * (*PA* 46:11627)

843. NUTTALL, RONALD L.; FOZARD, JAMES L.; ROSE, CHARLES L.; AND BURNEY, SPENCER W. "Ages of Man: Ability Age, Personality Age, and Biochemical Age." Abstract. *Proc 79th Ann Conv Am Psychol Assn* 6(2):605–6 '71. * (*PA* 46:4729)

844. O'DELL, JERRY W. "Method for Detecting Random Answers on Personality Questionnaires." *J Appl Psychol* 55(4):380–3 Ag '71. * (*PA* 47:3008)

845. ORFORD, J. F. Chap. 7, "The Assessment of Personality and Its Influence on the Outcome of Treatment," pp. 133–55. In *Homosexual Behaviour: Therapy and Assessment.* By M. P. Feldman and M. J. MacCulloch. New York: Pergamon Press Inc., 1971. Pp. ix, 288. *

846. O'TUEL, FRANCES SETTLE. *A Study of Attitude and Personality Changes in Teachers and Teacher Aides in Williamsburg County, South Carolina as Related to Formal Training and Experience.* Doctor's thesis, University of South Carolina (Columbia, S.C.), 1971. (*DAI* 32:2489A)

847. PARLETT, T. A. A., AND AYERS, J. D. "The Modification of Criminal Personality Through Massed Learning by Programmed Instruction." *Can J Criminol & Correct* 13(2):155–65 Ap '71. *

848. PENN, LAVERN. *Relationships Between Level of Interpersonal Skill Scores of Counselors as Rated by Their Counselees and Personality Questionnaire Scores.* Doctor's thesis, University of Arkansas (Fayetteville, Ark.), 1971. (*DAI* 32:2490A)

849. PERCY, RICHARD LYLE. *The Relationships Between Selected Counselor Interview Behaviors and Certain Personality Factors of Counselor Trainees.* Doctor's thesis, University of Virginia (Charlottesville, Va.), 1971. (*DAI* 32:4359A)

850. PHILIP, ALISTAIR E., AND CAY, LORNA. "The Reliability and Utility of a Clinical Rating of Personality." *Brit J Med Psychol* 44(1):85–9 Mr '71. * (*PA* 46:11103)

851. PILOWSKY, I., AND SHARP, JEANETTE. "Psychological Aspects of Preeclamptic Toxaemia: A Prospective Study." *J Psychosom Res* (England) 15(2):193–7 Je '71. * (*PA* 49:7261)

852. POWER, D. J. "Characteristics of Successful Student Teachers of the Deaf." *Volta R* 73(9):529–37 D '71. * (*PA* 47:11741)

853. PREEDEDILOK, KITIMA PHANICH. *An Analysis of Personality Characteristics of the Teachers in Bangkok, Thailand Related to Educational Innovative Attitude.* Doctor's thesis, Utah State University (Logan, Utah), 1971. (*DAI* 33:3220A)

854. PULLEN, JAMES RALPH. *A Comparative Study of Personality Factors and Certain Other Variables of Army ROTC Cadets Terminating With the Basic Program and Those Electing to Continue in the Advanced Program.* Doctor's thesis, University of South Dakota (Vermillion, S.D.), 1971. (*DAI* 32:2491A)

855. PUM, ROBERT JOSEPH. *Differential Characteristics of Art-Teaching Majors and Elementary-Education Majors in College; as Measured by Selected Attitude, Value, and Personality Factors.* Doctor's thesis, Ball State University (Muncie, Ind.), 1971. (*DAI* 32:5659A)

856. RAJ, JACOB SELVA. *A Comparative Study of Homeless and Domiciled Alcoholic Men.* Doctor's thesis, Yeshiva University (New York, N.Y.), 1971. (*DAI* 32:1858B)

857. REITER, HENRY. "Relationships Among Four Measures of Anxiety." *Psychol Rep* 28(3):761–2 Je '71. * (*PA* 46:10896)

858. ROBINSON, HARRY; KIRK, ROBERT F., JR.; AND FRYE, ROLAND L. "A Psychological Study of Rheumatoid Arthritis and Selected Controls." *J Chronic Dis* 23(10–11):791–801 Ap–My '71. *

859. RODE, A.; SHEPHARD, ROY J.; AND ROSS, ROY. "Smoking and Personality." *Am R Resp Dis* 104(6):929–32 D '71. *

860. ROSS, CHRISTOPHER F. J. "Comparison of Hospital and Prison Alcoholics." *Brit J Psychiatry* 118(542):75–8 Ja '71. * (*PA* 46:11135)

861. ROUBERTOUX, P.; CARLIER, M.; AND CHAQUIBOFF, J. "Preference for Non-Objective Art: Personal and Psychological Determiners." *Brit J Psychol* 62(1):105–10 F '71. * (*PA* 46:1201)

862. RUSSELL, G. W. "The Personality of Zambian Student Teachers in Relation to Their Social Behaviour and Teaching Ability." *Teach Ed New Countries* (England) 12(2):137–43 N '71. *

863. SALAS, R. G. "Letter Regarding the 16PF." *Austral Psychologist* 6(3):201–2 N '71. *

864. SANDERS, WILLIAM FRED, JR. *The Relationship Between*

Personality Variables and Conception of the Teacher's Role.
Doctor's thesis, University of Utah (Salt Lake City, Utah),
1971. (*DAI* 33:1028A)

865. SCHACKOW, CARL F. *Selected Personality Characteristics
of the American Overseas Teacher.* Doctor's thesis, Miami
University (Oxford, Ohio), 1971. (*DAI* 32:6694A)

866. SEELEY, MARK STANLEY. *An Experimental Evaluation of
Sociodrama as a Social Habilitation Technique for Mentally
Retarded Adolescents.* Doctor's thesis, University of Wisconsin
(Madison, Wis.), 1971. (*DAI* 32:3040A)

867. SELLS, S. B.; DEMAREE, R. G.; AND WILL, DONALD P.,
JR. "Dimensions of Personality: 2, Separate Factor Structures
in Guilford and Cattell Trait Markers." *Multiv Behav Res*
6(2):135–85 Ap '71. * (*PA* 47:4821)

868. SEMPER, LOUIS THOMAS. *The Effects of Motivation on
Performance of Individuals Possessing Selected Personality
Characteristics.* Doctor's thesis, Texas A & M University (College
Station, Tex.), 1971. (*DAI* 32:5026A)

869. SHELTON, JUDITH E. *A Comparison of Selected Personality Variables and the Effectiveness of Counselors Serving
Economically Disadvantaged and Economically Advantaged
Youth.* Doctor's thesis, University of Wyoming (Laramie, Wyo.),
1971. (*DAI* 33:164A)

870. SHIBUYA, RUTH RURIKO. *Differentiating Traits Among
LSD Abusers, Marihuana Abusers and Nonusers.* Doctor's thesis,
Purdue University (Lafayette, Ind.), 1971. (*DAI* 32:5427B)

871. SINGH, AMARJIT. "Norms for First-Year Student Nurses:
General Intelligence and Personality." *Nursing Times* (England)
67(30, sup):117–9 Jl 29 '71. *

872. SINGH, AMARJIT. "The Student Nurse on Experimental
Courses: 2, Personality Patterns." *Int J Nursing Studies* 8(3):
189–205 Ag '71. *

873. SIPOS, IVAN. "Operators' Personality Traits and Visual
Vigilance." *Studia Psychologica* (Czechoslovakia) 13(4):318–25
'71. *

874. SMITH, RICHARD LEE. *A Factor-Analytic Study of
Critical Reading/Thinking, Influenceability, and Related Factors.*
Doctor's thesis, University of Maine (Orono, Me.), 1971. (*DAI*
32:6229A)

875. SNELL, LYNN EVERETT. *Personality Traits Contributing
to the Success of Arkansas Superintendents.* Doctor's thesis,
University of Arkansas (Fayetteville, Ark.), 1971. (*DAI* 32:
799A)

876. SOARES, LOUISE M., AND SOARES, ANTHONY T. "Age
Differences in the Personality Profiles of Disadvantaged Females." Abstract. *Proc 79th Ann Conv Am Psychol Assn* 6(1):
163–4 '71. * (*PA* 46:2610, title only)

877. STAIERT, PAUL JOHN. *Changes of Selected Attitudes,
Values, Needs and Personality Traits of Participants in a
Fellowship Program for Prospective Teachers of the Disadvantaged.* Doctor's thesis, University of Denver (Denver, Colo.),
1971. (*DAI* 32:3803A)

878. STRAUB, WILLIAM F., AND DAVIS, STANLEY W. "Personality Traits of College Football Players Who Participated at
Different Levels of Competition." *Med & Sci Sports* 3(1):252–60
sp '71. *

879. TERRY, ROGER L., AND HOWARD, ERIC. "Anxiety Reactions
of Extraverts and Introverts to Experienced and Anticipated
Sensory Redundancy." *Percept & Motor Skills* 32(3):919–22 Je
'71. * (*PA* 47:919)

880. TRUCHSES, RICHARD ELMER. *Personality Characteristics
of Ministers and Their Social Change Activity.* Doctor's thesis,
Ohio University (Athens, Ohio), 1971. (*DAI* 32:3654B)

881. TURES, ROBERT STEPHEN. *The Analysis of Sex Differences in Intelligence, Achievement, Behavior, and Personality
of the Same Student Sample at the Third and Tenth Grade
Levels: A Longitudinal Study.* Doctor's thesis, West Virginia
University (Morgantown, W.Va.), 1971. (*DAI* 32:4363A)

882. VAN KOEVERING, THOMAS E. "The Distinguishing Characteristics of High Schools With High and Low Enrollments in
Physics." *J Res Sci Teach* 8(1):37–9 '71. *

883. VERGHESE, A.; MATHEW, P. M.; SENSEMAN, L. A.;
AND KARAT, A. B. A. "Psychosomatic Aspects of Rehabilitation
of Leprosy Patients." *Int J Leprosy* 39(4):842–7 O–D '71. *

884. VEST, THOMAS JOSEPH. *Selected Personality Characteristics of the Successful Overseas School Administrator.* Doctor's
thesis, Miami University (Coral Gables, Fla.), 1971. (*DAI*
32:2384A)

885. WAAG, WAYNE LESLIE. *The Prediction of Individual
Differences in Monitoring Performance.* Doctor's thesis, Texas
Tech University (Lubbock, Tex.), 1971. (*DAI* 32:5502B)

886. WALKER, JOHN EDWARD. *The Relationships Between the
Personality Characteristics, Personal Factors, and Effectiveness
of Community School Directors.* Doctor's thesis, Utah State
University (Logan, Utah), 1971. (*DAI* 32:3644A)

887. WEBSTER, ALAN C. "Factor Analysis of Family Attitudes,
Cooperation, Personality, and Personal Orientation in a Small
New Zealand Sample." *Personality* 2(3):249–66 au '71. * (*PA*
47:6618)

888. WENNERGREN, JOHN ANDERSON. *The Relationship Be-
tween Personality Factors of School Building Principals in
Monterey County and Effective Leadership as Perceived by Their
Subordinates.* Doctor's thesis, Utah State University (Logan,
Utah), 1971. (*DAI* 33:3236A)

889. WILLETT, ELIZABETH A.; RIFFEL, P. A.; BREEN, LAW-
RENCE J.; AND DICKSON, ELINOR J. "Selection and Success of
Students in a Hospital School of Nursing." *Can Nurse* 67(1):
41–5 Ja '71. *

890. WITTMER, JOE. "Old Order Amish and Non-Amish
Youth: A Personality Comparison Utilizing the 16 PF." *Personality* 2(4):305–13 w '71. * (*PA* 48:7267)

891. WITTMER, JOE, AND LISTER, JAMES L. "The Graduate
Record Examination, 16 PF Questionnaire, and Counseling Effectiveness." *Counselor Ed & Sup* 10(3):293 sp '71. *

892. WITTMER, JOE, AND LISTER, JAMES L. "Rehabilitation and
Nonrehabilitation Counselor Candidates: Comparison of Interview
Behavior and Personality Techniques." *Counselor Ed & Sup*
10(4):324–9 su '71. *

893. WITTMEYER, ALMA L.; CAMISCIONI, JOHN S.; AND
PURDY, PATRICIA A. "A Longitudinal Study of Attrition and
Academic Performance in a Collegiate Nursing Program."
Nursing Res 20(4):339–47 Jl–Ag '71. *

894. WOODARD, GEORGE. *Excitation and Inhibition as Measured by the Movement of a Concept in Semantic Space.* Doctor's
thesis, New York University (New York, N.Y.), 1971. (*DAI*
32:2497A)

895. YONCE, CLARENCE WALTER, JR. *Personality Correlates of
Description and Evaluation in Verbal Behavior.* Doctor's thesis,
University of South Carolina (Columbia, S.C.), 1971. (*DAI*
32:2993B)

896. ZIMMERMAN, ROBERT E., AND WILLIAMS, JOHN D.
"Personality Characteristics of Innovative and Non-Innovative
Teachers." *Psychol Rep* 29(2):343–6 O '71. * (*PA* 47:9790)

CUMULATIVE NAME INDEX

Sixteen Personality Factor Questionnaire

Tatsuoka, M. M.: 597, 646
Taylor, A. J. W.: 312, 582, 686, 692
Taylor, H. L.: 111
Taylor, P. A.: 541
Terry, R. L.: 879
Thaler, V. H.: 313
Thelen, M. H.: 350
Thomas, S.: 58, 91
Thompson, S. A.: 481, 512
Thorndike, R. L.: 125
Tilker, H. A.: 314
Tillman, K.: 209
Tillman, K. G.: 169
Tirpak, R. D.: 748
Titus, H. E.: 583–4
Tollefson, D. L.: 366
Townes, B. D.: 247, 315
Trent, S. J.: 482
Trice, H. M.: 585
Trousdale, W. W.: 302
Truchses, R. E.: 880
Tseng, M. S.: 647
Tsujioka, B.: 210–1
Tucker, W. V.: 351
Tuma, J. W.: 361
Tumampos, R. S.: 426
Tures, R. S.: 881
Turner, A. J.: 258
Turner, M. M.: 483
Turner, W. J.: 681
Udry, J. R.: 316
Uhr, L.: 36
Vacchiano, R. B.: 352
Vandergriff, J. C.: 703
Van Galder, R. B.: 749
Van Koevering, T. E.: 882
Vaughan, G. M.: 682
Verghese, A.: 883
Vernier, C. M.: 80
Vest, T. J.: 884
Vincent, J.: 353
Vincent, M. J. P.: 248
Viney, L. L.: 679
Volksdorf, N. R.: 586
Waag, W. L.: 885
Waggoner, B. E.: 389
Wagner, N. N.: 247, 315
Waldfogel, S.: 358
Walker, J. E.: 886
Walker, R. E.: 396
Walker, W. L.: 249, 472
Walter, J. I.: 484
Walton, H. J.: 354, 648
Warburton, F. W.: 67, 108, 670
Ward, J.: 701, 704

Wash, J. A.: 491
Waxman, B. D.: 360
Weaver, W. W.: 318, 355, 587
Webberley, M.: 754
Weber, J. C.: 302
Webster, A. C.: 887
Weiant, E. A.: 649
Weitzenhoffer, A. M.: 38
Weitzenhoffer, G. B.: 38
Weitzner, M.: 317
Wells, H. P.: 39
Wenig, P. W.: 653
Wennergren, J. A.: 888
Werner, A. C.: 250
Werner, E. E.: 594, 757
Wessman, A. E.: 405
White, K.: 212, 356
White, K. D.: 682
White, P. O.: 517, 578, 588
White, W. F.: 170, 213, 215, 229, 280–1, 304, 318–9, 321, 355, 427, 587, 683
Wilkins, L. G.: 171
Will, D. P.: 867
Willett, E. A.: 889
Williams, C. M. D.: 750
Williams, F. E.: 322
Williams, H. Y.: 390
Williams, J. D.: 896
Williams, J. M.: 650
Williams, J. R.: 112, 658, 662
Williams, R. C.: 251, 485
Willis, C. H.: 263, 270–1
Wilson, A. P.: 651
Wilson, P. K.: 357, 589
Winborn, B. B.: 320
Winget, C. N.: 610, 793
Wittenborn, J. R.: rev, 4:87
Wittmer, J.: 652, 705, 890–2
Wittmeyer, A. L.: 893
Wolfe, D. M.: 665
Wolff, C. E.: 90, 668
Wood, R. L.: 110
Woodard, G.: 894
Woodbury, M. A.: 64
Woodford, D. P.: 671
Workman, S. N.: 537
Worsham, J. W.: 590
Wright, S.: 18
Wurmser, J. H.: 693
Yonce, C. W.: 895
Yuhasz, M. S.: 420
Zaleznik, A.: 751–2
Zielonka, A. W.: 319
Zimmerman, R. E.: 753, 896
Zwirner, W.: 628

[1384]

Slosson Drawing Coordination Test for Children and Adults. Ages 1.5 and over; 1962–67; SDCT; brain dysfunction and perceptual disorders; Richard L. Slosson; Slosson Educational Publications, Inc. *

For additional information and reviews by Arthur L. Benton and James C. Reed, see 7 :140.

[1385]

[Social Competence Inventories.] Adults; 1951–68; behavior checklist; 2 editions; Katharine M. Banham; Family Life Publications, Inc. *

a) A SOCIAL COMPETENCE INVENTORY FOR ADULTS. Adults (physically handicapped, mentally retarded, or senile); 1951–60; SCIA.

b) SOCIAL COMPETENCE INVENTORY FOR OLDER PERSONS. Ages 50 and over; 1951–68; SCIOP; 5 scores: motor skills and control, perception and memory, self-care and self-help, social relationships and emotional control, total.

For additional information, see P:249; for reviews by William J. Eichman and Jerome D. Pauker of a, see 6:175.

[1386]

Social Intelligence Test: George Washington University Series. Grades 9–16 and adults; 1930–55; SIT; 3 editions; F. A. Moss, Thelma Hunt, K. T.

Omwake, and L. G. Woodward (a and manual); Center for Psychological Service. *

a) SECOND EDITION. 1930–55; 6 scores: judgment in social situations, recognition of the mental state of the speaker, memory for names and faces, observation of human behavior, sense of humor, total.

b) SHORT EDITION. 1944–55; 5 scores: same as for Second Edition except for omission of memory for names and faces.

c) SP (SPECIAL) EDITION. 1947–55; 3 scores: judgment in social situations, observation of human behavior, total.

For additional information, see P:250 (3 references); see also 6:176 (14 references) and 4:89 (7 references); for reviews by Glen U. Cleeton and Howard R. Taylor, see 3:96 (9 references); for a review by Robert L. Thorndike, see 2:1253 (20 references).

REFERENCES THROUGH 1971

1–20. See 2:1253.
21–29. See 3:96.
30–36. See 4:89.
37–50. See 6:176.
51–53. See P:250.
54. GARRETT, HENRY E. "Jews and Others: Some Group Differences in Personality, Intelligence, and College Achievement." *Personnel J* 7:341–8 F '29. * (*PA* 3:2299)
55. OLIVER, R. A. C. "The Traits of Extroverts and Introverts." *J Social Psychol* 1:345–66 Ag '30. * (*PA* 5:308)
56. MOSS, FRED A. "Preliminary Report of Social Intelligence and Executive Ability." *Pub Personnel Studies* 9:2–9 Ja–F '31. *
57. ULLMAN, ROY ROLAND. *The Prognostic Value of Certain Factors Related to Teaching Success.* Ashland, Ohio: A. L. Garber Co., 1931. Pp. xiv, 133. * (*PA* 5:4316)
58. FLEMMING, EDWIN G. "Testing Some Aspects of Personality." *J Social Psychol* 3:376–84 Ag '32. * (*PA* 7:920)
59. STAGNER, ROSS. "Differential Factors in the Testing of Personality: 1, Sex Differences; 2, Differences in Maturity." *J Social Psychol* 3:477–87 N '32. * (*PA* 7:1382)
60. VREELAND, FRANCIS M., AND COREY, STEPHEN M. "A Study of College Friendships." *J Abn & Social Psychol* 30:220–36 Jl–S '35. * (*PA* 10:2153)
61. SHEDDAN, BOYD R., AND WITMER, LOUISE R. "Employment Tests for Relief Visitors." *J Appl Psychol* 23:270–9 Ap '39. * (*PA* 13:4837)
62. BRUCE, MARTIN MARC. *The Importance of Certain Personality Characteristics, Skills and Abilities in Effectiveness as a Factory Foreman.* Doctor's thesis, New York University (New York, N.Y.), 1952. (*DA* 13:116)
63. DI VESTA, FRANCIS J. "Instructor-Centered and Student-Centered Approaches in Teaching a Human Relations Course." *J Appl Psychol* 38:329–35 O '54. * (*PA* 29:6161)
64. WITRYOL, SAM L., AND KAESS, WALTER A. "Sex Differences in Social Memory Tasks." *J Abn & Social Psychol* 54:343–6 My '57. * (*PA* 33:5685)
65. THIESSEN, IRMGARD; WRIGHT, MORGAN W.; AND SISLER, GEORGE C. "A Comparison of Personality Characteristics of Mennonites With Non-Mennonites." *Can Psychologist* 10(2):129–37 Ap '69. * (*PA* 43:15654)
66. TITUS, H. EDWIN. "Prediction of Supervisory Success by Use of Standard Psychological Tests." *J Psychol* 72(1):35–40 My '69. * (*PA* 43:16503)
67. TITUS, H. EDWIN, AND GOSS, RICHARD G. "Psychometric Comparison of Old and Young Supervisors." *Psychol Rep* 24(3):727–33 Je '69. * (*PA* 44:1447)
68. WEVRICK, L. "Evaluation of the Personnel Test Battery," pp. 1–5. In *Applied Research in Public Personnel Administration.* By L. Wevrick and Others. Personnel Report No. 702. Chicago, Ill.: Public Personnel Association, 1970. Pp. 29. *

CUMULATIVE NAME INDEX

Abt, L. E.: 34
Aron, J.: 47
Bass, B. M.: 38
Becker, G. J.: 51
Bottrill, J.: 52
Broom, M. E.: 5, 8
Bruce, M. M.: 37, 39–40, 42–5, 62
Burks, F. W.: 18
Cleeton, G. U.: rev, 3:96
Corey, S. M.: 60
Crane, W. J.: 48
DiVesta, F. J.: 63
Eimicke, V. W.: 33, 36
Fish, H. L.: 33
Flemming, C. W.: 29
Flemming, E. G.: 29, 58

Garrett, H. E.: 30, 54
Goss, R. G.: 67
Grosvenor, E. L.: 1
Harrell, W.: 27
Hartman, B. J.: 53
Hecht, R.: 45, 47
Herbert, N.: 50
Huddleston, E.: 32
Human Engineering Laboratory: 15, 20
Hunt, T.: 2–3, 6, 16, 22
Jackson, V. D.: 28
Juergenson, E. M.: 46
Kaess, W. A.: 41, 64
Karstendiek, B.: 38
Kellogg, W. W.: 30
McClatchy, V. R.: 7

McCullough, G.: 38
Moss, F. A.: 3, 21–2, 56
Oliver, R. A. C.: 55
Pintner, R.: 4
Pruitt, R. C.: 38
Randolph, J. M.: 25
Raubenheimer, A. S.: 31
Rhinehart, J. B.: 13
Scudder, C. R.: 31
Sheddan, B. R.: 61
Sisler, G. C.: 65
Smith, H. C.: 35
Stagner, R.: 11, 14, 24, 59
Stein, S.: 19, 26
Strang, R.: 9–10, 12

Taylor, H. R.: *rev,* 3:96
Thiessen, I.: 65
Thorndike, R. L.: 17, 19; *rev,* 2:1253
Titus, H. E.: 66–7
Turnbull, G. H.: 50
Ullman, R. R.: 57
Upshall, C. C.: 4
Vreeland, F. M.: 60
Wang, C. K. A.: 23
Wevrick, L.: 68
Witmer, L. R.: 61
Witryol, S. L.: 41, 64
Wright, M. W.: 65

[1387]

Spiral Aftereffect Test. Ages 5 and over; 1958; SAT; brain damage; Psychological Research & Development Corporation. * [Many variations of the spiral aftereffect are in use. The references listed below relate to the procedure in general as well as to the specific test apparatus and accessories.]

For additional information, see P:251 (17 references); for reviews by William J. Eichman and Ralph M. Reitan, see 6:177 (43 references).

REFERENCES THROUGH 1971

1–43. See 6:177.
44–60. See P:251.
61. STANDLEE, LLOYD S. "Validity of Archimedes Spiral in Discriminating Memory Ability of Psychotics and of Normals." *Arch Neurol & Psychiatry* 71:648–50 My '54. * (*PA* 29:2839)
62. PRICE, A. COOPER; GARRETT, EPHRAIM S.; HARDY, MILES W.; AND HALL, HARRY E., JR. "Perception of Binaural Beats in Organic and Nonorganic Patients." *Arch Neurol & Psychiatry* 79:214–6 F '58. * (*PA* 33:6276)
63. BURKS, HAROLD F. "The Hyperkinetic Child." *Excep Children* 27:18–26 S '60. *
64. LYNN, R. "Extraversion, Reminiscence, and Satiation Effects." *Brit J Psychol* 51:319–24 N '60. * (*PA* 35:2273)
65. BUTLER, ALFRED J., AND CONRAD, W. GLENN. "Psychological Correlates of Abnormal Electroencephalographic Patterns in Familial Retardates." *J Clin Psychol* 20:338–43 Jl '64. * (*PA* 39:10572)
66. JURKO, M. F., AND ANDY, O. J. "Psychological Aspects of Diencephalotomy." *J Neurol Neurosurg & Psychiatry* (England) 27:516–21 D '64. * (*PA* 39:9508)
67. KRISHNAMOORTI, SINGA R., AND SHAGASS, CHARLES. "Some Psychological Test Correlates of Sedation Threshold." *Recent Adv Biol Psychiatry* 6:256–66 '64. *
68. MANN, LESTER; ALVORD, AGNES; RICHARDSON, PAUL C.; AND WASSERMAN, JOSEPH. "Relationships Between Spiral After Effect Reports and Measures of Intelligence in Fifth Grade Children." *Psychol Sch* 1:305–8 Jl '64. *
69. PINCKNEY, GEORGE A. "Reliability of Duration as a Measure of the Spiral Aftereffect." *Percept & Motor Skills* 18:375–6 Ap '64. * (*PA* 39:3493)
70. JALAVISTO, EEVA. "On the Interdependence of Circulatory-Respiratory and Neural-Mental Variables." *Gerontologia* (Switzerland) 10(1):31–7 '65. * (*PA* 39:14791)
71. ALBRIGHT, MARY JOAN. *Visual Perception in Children of Retarded and Normal Reading Ability.* Doctor's thesis, Fordham University (New York, N.Y.), 1966. (*DA* 27:2128B)
72. CLARIDGE, G. S.; WAWMAN, R. J.; DAVIES, M. H.; AND BURNS, B. H. "Sedation Threshold, Spiral After-Effect and Overinclusion." *Brit J Social & Clin Psychol* 5:63–70 F '66. * (*PA* 40:6845)
73. COLMAN, P. G. "A Comparative Study of the Test Performances of Brain-Injured Children." *S Afric Med J* 40:945–50 O 22 '66. *
74. EFSTATHIOU, AGLAIA, AND MORANT, RICARDO B. "Persistence of the Waterfall Illusion After-Effect as a Test of Brain Damage." *J Abn Psychol* 71:300–3 Ag '66. * (*PA* 40:11410)
75. GARNER, FRANCES E.; NEURINGER, CHARLES; AND GOLDSTEIN, GERALD. "The Spiral Aftereffect, Extraneous Stimulation and Brain Damage." *Cortex* (Italy) 2:385–98 O '66. * (*PA* 41:7709)
76. DAMODAR, VIJAYA N., AND MURTHY, H. N. "Spiral After-Effect and Introversion-Extraversion." *Trans All-India Inst Mental Health* 7:79–84 D '67. *
77. HERON, ALASTAIR, AND CHOWN, SHEILA. *Age and Function.* London: J. & A. Churchill Ltd., 1967. Pp. x, 182. *
78. CLUM, GEORGE ARTHUR. *The Relationships Between Measures of Classical and Operant Conditioning, Psychiatric Diagnoses and Statistically Derived Classificatory Groups.* Doctor's thesis, St. John's University (Jamaica, N.Y.), 1968. (*DA* 29:3899B)
79. DAVIES, ANN D. M. "Measurement of Mental Deterioration in Aging and Brain Damage." Discussion by Walter W. Surwillo. *Interdiscipl Topics Gerontol* 1:78–92 '68. *
80. GILBERSTADT, HAROLD. "Relationships Among Scores of

Tests Suitable for the Assessment of Adjustment and Intellectual Functioning." *J Gerontol* 23:483–7 O '68. *
81. MILLIGAN, W. LLOYD, AND SCOTT, THOMAS R. "Spiral Aftereffect: Rate, Duration, and Amount." *Percept & Motor Skills* 28(3):935–8 Je '69. * (*PA* 43:16663)
82. ANDERSSON, ALF L.; NILSSON, ALF; AND HENRICKSSON, NILS-GUNNAR. "Personality Differences Between Accident-Loaded and Accident-Free Young Car Drivers." *Brit J Psychol* 61(3):409–21 Ag '70. * (*PA* 44:21720)
83. OBRZUT, JOHN E., AND THWEATT, ROGER C. "Clinical Differentiation With the Spiral Aftereffect Technique." *Percept & Motor Skills* 31(3):995–9 D '70. * (*PA* 46:1429)
84. REILLY, THOMAS. "Some Normative Data for the Spiral Aftereffect." *Percept & Motor Skills* 31(1):211–7 Ag '70. * (*PA* 45:3319)
85. UPADHYAYA, S., AND MURTHY, H. N. "Conditionability as Related to Introversion-Extroversion and Not to Neuroticism." *Trans All-India Inst Mental Health* 10:117–25 D '70. * (*PA* 48:1310)
86. ANDERSSON, ALF L., AND RUUTH, EGIL. "Relation Between Spiral Aftereffect Duration and Rod-and-Frame Test Performance in Early Childhood." *Percept & Motor Skills* 32(3):843–9 Je '71. * (*PA* 47:2657)
87. CASTELLOW, WILBUR ALLEN. *Relationships Between the Spiral After-Effect and Extraversion, Neuroticism, Sex, and Induced Arousal.* Doctor's thesis, University of North Carolina (Chapel Hill, N.C.), 1971. (*DAI* 32:7287B)
88. MONTGOMERY, NOEL PAUL. *The Effects of Distance and Retinal Velocity on the Duration of the Spiral After-Effect.* Doctor's thesis, University of Southern Mississippi (Hattiesburg, Miss.), 1971. (*DAI* 32:3038B)

CUMULATIVE NAME INDEX

Aaronson, B. S.: 13
Adam, J.: 59
Albright, M. J.: 71
Allen, R. M.: 22
Alvord, A.: 42, 68
Andersson, A. L.: 46, 82, 86
Andy, O. J.: 66
Baumeister, A.: 50
Beech, H. R.: 17
Berger, D.: 14
Blau, T. H.: 23
Blumberg, S.: 41
Bragg, R. A.: 43
Bryan, J. H.: 18, 27, 74
Burks, H. F.: 63
Burns, B. H.: 72
Butler, A. J.: 65
Castellow, W. A.: 87
Chown, S.: 77
Claridge, G. S.: 39, 72
Clum, G. A.: 78
Colman, P. G.: 73
Conrad, W. G.: 65
Coons, W. H.: 29
Damodar, V. N.: 76
Davids, A.: 6
Davies, A. D. M.: 79
Davies, M. H.: 72
Day, R. H.: 24
Deabler, H. L.: 3, 5, 8
Efstathiou, A.: 56, 74
Eichman, W. J.: *rev,* 6:177
Elliott, J. J.: 51
Everson, R.: 14
Eysenck, H. J.: 7, 25–6
Eysenck, S. B. G.: 25
Freeman, E.: 1
Freud, S. L.: 35, 40, 58
Frisk, G. C.: 48
Gallese, A. J.: 4
Garner, F. E.: 75
Garrett, E. S.: 8, 62
Gertz, B.: 12
Gilberstadt, H.: 15, 80
Gilbert, J. G.: 52, 57
Glassman, S.: 9
Goldberg, L. R.: 16
Goldenberg, L.: 6
Goldstein, G.: 75
Gynther, M. D.: 12
Hall, H. E.: 62
Harding, G. F.: 9
Hardy, M. W.: 62
Helz, W. C.: 9
Henricksson, N. G.: 82
Heron, A.: 77
Herrington, R. N.: 39
Hildt, M. T.: 53
Holland, H.: 7, 26
Holland, H. C.: 17
Honigfeld, G. H.: 45

Jalavisto, E.: 70
Josey, W. E.: 1
Jurko, M. F.: 66
Kaplan, H. K.: 10
Kaskoff, Y. D.: 14
Knowles, J. B.: 54
Korman, M.: 41
Krasner, L.: 54
Krishnamoorti, S. R.: 67
Kurtzke, J. F.: 38
Laufer, M. W.: 6
Levee, R. F.: 52, 57
Levine, M.: 11, 21, 36
Loder, E.: 34
London, P.: 18, 27
Lynn, R.: 64
McDonough, J. M.: 28
Mann, L.: 42, 68
Mayer, E.: 29
Medlin, R. E.: 37
Metwally, A.: 33
Milligan, W. L.: 81
Minard, J. G.: 60
Montgomery, N. P.: 88
Morant, R. B.: 56, 74
Murthy, H. N.: 76, 85
Neuringer, C.: 75
Nilsson, A.: 82
Obrzut, J. E.: 83
Page, H. A.: 45
Philbrick, E. B.: 20
Pinckney, G. A.: 69
Price, A. C.: 3, 8, 62
Price, H.: 42
Rakita, G.: 10
Reilly, T.: 84
Reitan, R. M.: *rev,* 6:177
Richardson, P. C.: 68
Ring, M.: 59
Ripke, R. J.: 31
Roehrig, W. C.: 47
Rosen, A.: 15
Rutledge, L.: 14
Rutschmann, J.: 47
Ruuth, E.: 86
Sappenfield, B. R.: 31
Saucer, R. T.: 5
Schaffer, R. E.: 23
Schein, J.: 15
Schein, J. D.: 19, 30
Scott, T. R.: 37, 43, 81
Shagass, C.: 67
Sindberg, R. M.: 32
Smarr, R. G.: 43
Smith, J. P.: 55
Smith, N. B.: 10
Smith, P. A.: 16
Smith, T. E.: 50
Snyder, R. T.: 58
Soueif, M. I.: 33
Spivack, G.: 11, 21, 36

Standlee, L. S.: 2, 61
Stern, A.: 44
Stilson, D. W.: 12
Suehs, J. E.: 49
Surwillo, W. W.: 79
Thweatt, R. C.: 83
Trouton, D. S.: 7

Truss, C. V.: 22
Upadhyaya, S.: 85
Urquhart, D.: 50
VanLiere, D. E.: 53
Wasserman, J.: 68
Wawman, R. J.: 72
Whitmyre, J. W.: 38

[1388]

*Stamp Behaviour Study Technique. Preschool–kgn; 1968–72; BST; checklist for recording teacher's observation of behavior in 12 areas: people, selfhood, demands of others, demands on others, frustration, stress, realistic fears, need for approval, communication, physical health, use of powers, general behaviour; Isla M. Stamp; Australian Council for Educational Research [Australia]. *

For additional information, see P:252.

[1389]

Stanford Hypnotic Susceptibility Scale. College and adults; 1959–62; SHSS; for a downward extension, see 1128; André M. Weitzenhoffer and Ernest R. Hilgard; Consulting Psychologists Press, Inc. *

For additional information, see P:253 (18 references); for reviews by Milton V. Kline and C. Scott Moss, see 6:178 (17 references).

REFERENCES THROUGH 1971

1–17. See 6:178.
18–35. See P:253.
36. HATFIELD, ELAINE C. "The Validity of the LeCron Method of Evaluating Hypnotic Depth." *Int J Clin & Exp Hyp* 9:215–21 O '61. * (*PA* 36:4I115H)
37. ÅS, ARVID. "Non-Hypnotic Experiences Related to Hypnotizability in Male and Female College Students." *Scand J Psychol* (Sweden) 3(2):112–21 '62. * (*PA* 37:3382)
38. LEVITT, EUGENE E.; LUBIN, BERNARD; AND BRADY, JOHN PAUL. "Personality Correlates of Hypnotizability in Young Women: The Anxiety-Dependency Constellation." *Congreso Interamericano de Psicologia* (Mexico) 7:360–4 '63. *
39. LEVITT, EUGENE E., AND BRADY, JOHN PAUL. "Expectation and Performance in Hypnotic Phenomena." *J Abn & Social Psychol* 69:572–4 N '64. * (*PA* 39:8151)
40. HEWITT, JACK LEE. *A Communications Approach to the Prediction and Alteration of Hypnotic Susceptibility.* Doctor's thesis, University of Kansas (Lawrence, Kan.), 1965. (*DA* 26:4075)
41. HILGARD, ERNEST R., AND COOPER, LESLIE M. "Spontaneous and Suggested Posthypnotic Amnesia." *Int J Clin & Exp Hyp* 13:261–73 O '65. * (*PA* 40:109)
42. LEE-TENG, EVELYN. "Trance-Susceptibility, Induction-Susceptibility, and Acquiescence as Factors in Hypnotic Performance." *J Abn Psychol* 70:383–9 O '65. * (*PA* 40:110)
43. LEVITT, EUGENE E., AND OVERLEY, TONER M. "Experience of the Hypnotist as a Factor in Hypnotic Behavior." *Int J Clin & Exp Hyp* 13:34–8 Ja '65. * (*PA* 39:8153)
44. SHOR, RONALD E.; ORNE, MARTIN T.; AND O'CONNELL, DONALD N. "Psychological Correlates of Plateau Hypnotizability in a Special Volunteer Sample." *J Pers & Social Psychol* 3:80–95 Ja '66. * (*PA* 40:2262)
45. EDMONSTON, WILLIAM E., JR., AND ROBERTSON, THOMAS G., JR. "A Comparison of the Effects of Task Motivational and Hypnotic Induction Instructions on Responsiveness to Hypnotic Suggestibility Scales." *Am J Clin Hyp* 9:184–7 Je '67. * (*PA* 42:1612)
46. FIELD, PETER B., AND PALMER, ROBERT D. "Factor Analysis of an Inventory of Hypnotic Experiences." *Newsl Res Psychol* 10:3–4 N '68. *
47. GOSS, ALLEN, AND MOROSKO, TOM. "Stanford Hypnotic Susceptibility Scale, Form A: Score Distribution of Volunteer Subjects." *Int J Clin & Exp Hyp* 16:237–42 O '68. * (*PA* 43:1856)
48. NOWLIS, DAVID P., AND RHEAD, JOHN C. "Relation of Eyes-Closed Resting EEG Alpha Activity to Hypnotic Susceptibility." *Percept & Motor Skills* 27:1047–50 D '68. * (*PA* 43:9284)
49. FIELD, PETER B., AND PALMER, ROBERT D. "Factor Analysis: Hypnosis Inventory." *Int J Clin & Exp Hyp* 17(1):50–61 Ja '69. * (*PA* 43:9028)
50. GREENE, JAMES T. "Hypnotizability of Hospitalized Psychotics." *Int J Clin & Exp Hyp* 17(2):103–8 Ap '69. * (*PA* 44:2574)
51. KINNEY, JILL CLAIRE MCCLEAVE. *Modification of Hypnotic Susceptibility.* Doctor's thesis, Stanford University (Stanford, Calif.), 1969. (*DAI* 30:5675B)
52. WEITZENHOFFER, ANDRE M. "Eye-Blink Rate and Hypnosis: Preliminary Findings." *Percept & Motor Skills* 28(2):671–6 Ap '69. * (*PA* 43:15120)

53. WEITZENHOFFER, ANDRE M. "Hypnosis and Eye Movements: 1, Preliminary Report on a Possible Slow Eye Movement Correlate of Hypnosis." *Am J Clin Hyp* 11(4):221–7 Ap '69. * (*PA* 43:13655)
54. WICKRAMASEKERA, IAN. "Norms on the Stanford Hypnotic Susceptibility Scale, Form A, for Prison Volunteers." *Int J Clin & Exp Hyp* 17(2):99–102 Ap '69. * (*PA* 44:1677)
55. MORGAN, ARLENE H.; HILGARD, ERNEST R.; AND DAVERT, EDNA C. "The Heritability of Hypnotic Susceptibility of Twins: A Preliminary Report." *Behav Genetics* 1(3–4):213–24 Ag–N '70. * (*PA* 47:10444)
56. NACE, EDGAR P., AND ORNE, MARTIN T. "Fate of an Uncompleted Posthypnotic Suggestion." *J Abn Psychol* 75(3):278–85 Je '70. * (*PA* 44:13729)
57. SPANOS, NICHOLAS P., AND CHAVES, JOHN F. "Hypnosis Research: A Methodological Critique of Experiments Generated by Two Alternative Paradigms." *Am J Clin Hyp* 13(2):108–27 O '70. * (*PA* 45:7335)
58. SUTCLIFFE, J. P.; PERRY, C. W.; AND SHEEHAN, P. W. "Relation of Some Aspects of Imagery and Fantasy to Hypnotic Susceptibility." *J Abn Psychol* 76(2):279–87 O '70. * (*PA* 45:3389)
59. HILGARD, ERNEST R. "Hypnosis and Childlikeness," pp. 29–51. In *Minnesota Symposia on Child Psychology, Vol. 5.* Edited by John P. Hill. Minneapolis, Minn.: University of Minnesota Press, 1971. Pp. xiii, 216. *
60. HOWELL, ROBERT J., AND CARLISLE, A. LINDSAY. "The Effect of Hypnotically Induced and Nonhypnotic Mood Changes on the Rorschach Test." *Int J Clin & Exp Hyp* 19(1):28–36 Ja '71. * (*PA* 46:1217)
61. LEVITT, EUGENE E., AND OVERLEY, TONER M. "A Comparison of the Performance of Hypnotic Subjects and Simulators on a Variety of Measures: A Pilot Study." *Int J Clin & Exp Hyp* 19(4):234–42 O '71. * (*PA* 47:4064)
62. PALMER, ROBERT D., AND FIELD, PETER B. "Cognitive Factors in Hypnotic Susceptibility." Abstract. *J Consult & Clin Psychol* 37(1):165 Ag '71. * (*PA* 47:132)
63. RUCH, JOHN C., AND MORGAN, ARLENE H. "Subject Posture and Hypnotic Susceptibility: A Comparison of Standing, Sitting, and Lying-Down Subjects." *Int J Clin & Exp Hyp* 19(2):100–8 Ap '71. * (*PA* 46:8091)
64. SILVER, MAURICE JOSEPH. *Hypnotizability as a Function of Adaptive Regression, Repression and Mood.* Doctor's thesis, Boston University (Boston, Mass.), 1971. (*DAI* 32:2409B)
65. SPANOS, NICHOLAS P. "Goal-Directed Fantasy and the Performance of Hypnotic Test Suggestions." *Psychiatry* 34(1):86–96 F '71. * (*PA* 46:8093)
66. WEITZENHOFFER, ANDRE M. "Ocular Changes Associated With Passive Hypnotic Behavior." *Am J Clin Hyp* 14(2):102–21 O '71. * (*PA* 47:8118)

CUMULATIVE NAME INDEX

Anderson, W. L.: 33
Ås, A.: 37
Beier, E. G.: 35
Bentler, P. M.: 11–4
Brady, J. P.: 38–9
Brennan, E. P.: 21
Carlisle, A. L.: 60
Chaves, J. F.: 57
Cooper, G. W.: 19
Cooper, L. M.: 9, 27, 41
Dana, R. H.: 19
Davert, E. C.: 55
Edmonston, W. E.: 45
Evans, F. J.: 20, 29
Field, P. B.: 34, 46, 49, 62
Fisher, S.: 18
Fuhrer, M.: 3
Goss, A.: 47
Gough, P.: 1
Greene, J. T.: 50
Hatfield, E. C.: 36
Hewitt, J. L.: 40
Hilgard, E. R.: 1–2, 5–6, 12, 14, 22, 25, 41, 55, 59
Hilgard, J. R.: 26
Howell, R. J.: 60
Johnson, H. J.: 9
Kinney, J. C. M.: 51
Kline, M. V.: *rev*, 6:178
Kramer, E.: 21
Kramer, E. F.: 31
Landes, J.: 2
Lang, P. J.: 7
Lauer, L. W.: 6
Lazovik, A. D.: 7
Lee-Teng, E.: 42
Levitt, E. E.: 38–9, 43, 61

London, P.: 3, 8–9, 15
Lubin, B.: 38
Melei, J. P.: 22
Moore, R. K.: 2
Morgan, A. H.: 55, 63
Morosko, T.: 47
Moss, C. S.: *rev*, 6:178
Nace, E. P.: 56
Nowlis, D. P.: 48
O'Connell, D. N.: 23, 30, 44
Orne, E. C.: 16
Orne, M. T.: 30, 44, 56
Overley, T. M.: 43, 61
Palmer, R. D.: 32, 34, 46, 49, 62
Pedersen, D. M.: 27
Perry, C. W.: 58
Rhead, J. C.: 48
Roberts, M. J. R.: 24
Roberts, M. R.: 13
Robertson, T. G.: 45
Ruch, J. C.: 63
Sachs, L. B.: 33
Schmeidler, D.: 20, 29
Schulman, R. E.: 15
Sheehan, P. W.: 58
Shor, R. E.: 16, 30, 44
Silver, M. J.: 64
Sjoberg, B. M.: 4
Spanos, N. P.: 57, 65
Sutcliffe, J. P.: 58
Thorne, D. E.: 35
Vingoe, F. J.: 28, 31
Weitzenhoffer, A. M.: 1–2, 4, 10, 17, 52–3, 66
Wickramasekera, I.: 54

[1390]

Stanford Profile Scales of Hypnotic Susceptibility, Revised Edition. College and adults; 1963–67;

SPSHS; 25 scores: agnosia and cognitive distortion (4 item scores plus total), positive hallucinations (4 item scores plus total), negative hallucinations (4 item scores plus total), dreams and regressions (4 item scores plus total), amnesia and post-hypnotic compulsions (3 item scores plus total), total susceptibility; one of the item scores for amnesia and post-hypnotic compulsions is derived from Form A of the *Stanford Hypnotic Susceptibility Scale* and provision is also made for profiling 3 additional scores (loss of motor coordination and 2 subscores) from this scale; Ernest R. Hilgard and André M. Weitzenhoffer (test), (revised standardization data by Ernest R. Hilgard, Leslie M. Cooper, Lillian W. Lauer, and Arlene H. Morgan); Consulting Psychologists Press, Inc. *

For additional information, see P:254 (4 references); for reviews by Seymour Fisher and Eugene E. Levitt of the original edition, see 6:179.

REFERENCES THROUGH 1971

1–4. See P:254.
5. LAUER, LILLIAN FAE WILLIAMSON. *Factorial Components of Hypnotic Susceptibility.* Doctor's thesis, Stanford University (Stanford, Calif.), 1966. (*DA* 26:7461)
6. KINNEY, JILL CLAIRE McCLEAVE. *Modification of Hypnotic Susceptibility.* Doctor's thesis, Stanford University (Stanford, Calif.), 1969. (*DAI* 30:5675B)
7. SPANOS, NICHOLAS P., AND CHAVES, JOHN F. "Hypnosis Research: A Methodological Critique of Experiments Generated by Two Alternative Paradigms." *Am J Clin Hyp* 13(2):108–27 O '70. * (*PA* 45:7335)

CUMULATIVE NAME INDEX

Banford, S. A.: 4   Kinney, J. C. M.: 6
Chaves, J. F.: 7   Lauer, L. F. W.: 5
Cooper, L. M.: 4   Levitt, E. E.: *rev, 6*:179
Fisher, S.: *rev, 6*:179 Schubot, E.: 4
Hilgard, E. R.: 1–2   Spanos, N. P.: 7
Hilgard, J. R.: 3   Tart, C. T.: 4

[1391]

State-Trait Anxiety Inventory. Grades 9–16 and adults; 1968–70; STAI; for a downward extension, see 1392; title on test is *Self-Evaluation Questionnaire;* 2 scores: state anxiety, trait anxiety; C. D. Spielberger, R. L. Gorsuch, and R. Lushene; Consulting Psychologists Press, Inc. *

For additional information, see 7:141 (20 references).

REFERENCES THROUGH 1971

1–20. See 7:141.
21. EDWARDS, KENNETH ROBERT, JR. *Psychological Changes Associated With Pregnancy and Obstetric Complications.* Doctor's thesis, University of Miami (Coral Gables, Fla.), 1969. (*DAI* 30:3864B)
22. GORSUCH, RICHARD L. "Changes in Trait Anxiety as a Function of Recent States of Anxiety." Abstract. *Proc 77th Ann Conv Am Psychol Assn* 4(1):329–30 '69. * (*PA* 43:17460)
23. O'NEIL, HAROLD F., JR. *Effects of Stress on State Anxiety and Performance in Computer-Assisted Learning.* Doctor's thesis, Florida State University (Tallahassee, Fla.), 1969. (*DAI* 31:1568B)
24. PARRINO, JOHN JOSEPH. *The Effects of Pre-Therapy Information on Learning in Psychotherapy.* Doctor's thesis, Louisiana State University (Baton Rouge, La.), 1969. (*DAI* 31:400B)
25. DeLONG, RIEVA DARLENE. *Individual Differences in Patterns of Anxiety Arousal, Stress-Relevant Information and Recovery From Surgery.* Doctor's thesis, University of California (Los Angeles, Calif.), 1970. (*DAI* 32:554B)
26. KELLY, CAROL HILGEMAN. *Stress, Trait-Anxiety, and Type of Coping Process.* Doctor's thesis, University of Colorado (Boulder, Colo.), 1970. (*DAI* 31:5627B)
27. LITVAK, STUART BRUCE. *The Contribution of Non-Specific Variables to Outcome of Systematic Desensitization Therapy.* Doctor's thesis, Arizona State University (Tempe, Ariz.), 1970. (*DAI* 31:5629B)
28. LUSHENE, ROBERT EDWARD. *The Effects of Physical and Psychological Threat on the Autonomic, Motoric, and Ideational Components of State Anxiety.* Doctor's thesis, Florida State University (Tallahassee, Fla.), 1970. (*DAI* 31:5630B)
29. McADOO, WILLIAM GEORGE. *The Effects of Success, Mild Failure, and Strong Failure Feedback on A-State for Subjects Who Differ in A-Trait.* Doctor's thesis, Florida State University (Tallahassee, Fla.), 1970. (*DAI* 31:6263B)

30. MARTIN, ROY PAUL. *The Development of Anxiety in Persons Anticipating a Highly Stressful Event.* Doctor's thesis, University of Texas (Austin, Tex.), 1970. (*DAI* 31:5854A)
31. MOTE, THOMAS ALLAN, JR. *Student Grade Perception and the Prediction of Academic Achievement.* Doctor's thesis, University of Texas (Austin, Tex.), 1970. (*DAI* 32:3794A)
32. NOYES, ROBERT C. *The Effects of Success and Failure in Physical Performance Upon State Anxiety and Bodily Concern of College Students Varying in Anxiety Proneness.* Doctor's thesis, Florida State University (Tallahassee, Fla.), 1970. (*DAI* 31:4529A)
33. ALLEN, GEORGE J. "Effectiveness of Study Counseling and Desensitization in Alleviating Test Anxiety in College Students." *J Abn Psychol* 77(3):282–9 Je '71. * (*PA* 46:7536)
34. AUERBACH, STEPHEN MICHAEL. *The Effects of Surgery-Induced Stress on State and Trait Anxiety.* Doctor's thesis, Florida State University (Tallahassee, Fla.), 1971. (*DAI* 33:434B)
35. BURTON, ELSIE CARTER. "State and Trait Anxiety, Achievement Motivation and Skill Attainment in College Women." *Res Q* 42(2):139–44 My '71. * (*PA* 47:3745)
36. BUTLER, PAMELA ELLEN. *The Relationship of Depression to Aggressive Response Intensity and State-Trait Anxiety.* Doctor's thesis, University of Alabama (University, Ala.), 1971. (*DAI* 32:5433B)
37. CLARK, NEWTON CECIL, JR. *Test Anxiety, Locus of Control, and Feedback in Self-Instruction.* Doctor's thesis, George Peabody College for Teachers (Nashville, Tenn.), 1971. (*DAI* 32:1912A)
38. COCO, HAROLD BYRD. *The Relationship Between Trait and State Anxiety and a Projective Personality Test.* Doctor's thesis, Louisiana State University (Baton Rouge, La.), 1971. (*DAI* 32:4204B)
39. EDER, SIDNEY CHARLES. *The Effect of Group Counseling Upon the Classroom Behavior and on the Manifest Anxiety of Elementary School Student Teachers.* Doctor's thesis, Arizona State University (Tucson, Ariz.), 1971. (*DAI* 32:2524A)
40. ETTKIN, LARRY F. *Anxiety in Original Persons.* Doctor's thesis, Arizona State University (Tempe, Ariz.), 1971. (*DAI* 32:3617B)
41. EVERETT, ROYICE B., AND SCHECHTER, MARSHALL D. "A Comparative Study of Prenatal Anxiety in the Unwed Mother." *Child Psychiatry & Hum Develop* 2(2):84–91 w '71. *
42. FORREST, MARVIN, AND KROTH, JEROME A. "Psychometric and Physiological Indices of Anxiety." *J Clin Psychol* 27(1):40–2 Ja '71. * (*PA* 46:633)
43. GRIFFIN, MARY ROLAND. *An Analysis of State and Trait Anxiety Experienced in Sports Competition by Women at Different Age Levels.* Doctor's thesis, Louisiana State University (Baton Rouge, La.), 1971. (*DAI* 32:3758A)
44. HEDL, JOHN J., JR.; O'NEIL, HAROLD F., JR.; AND HANSEN, DUNCAN N. "Affective Nature of Computer-Based Testing Procedures." Abstract. *Proc 79th Ann Conv Am Psychol Assn* 6(2):535–6 '71. * (*PA* 46:5468)
45. HENNEBERRY, JOHN KEVIN. *The Effects of Situational and Dispositional Factors Upon Digit Span Performance and the Arousal of Anxiety-State.* Doctor's thesis, Syracuse University (Syracuse, N.Y.), 1971. (*DAI* 32:6031B)
46. KAMEN, GARY B. "A Second Look at the Effects of a Stress-Producing Film on Adult Test Performance." *J Clin Psychol* 27(4):465–7 O '71. * (*PA* 47:8126)
47. LEHERISSEY, BARBARA L.; O'NEIL, HAROLD F., JR.; AND HANSEN, DUNCAN N. "Effects of Memory Support on State Anxiety and Performance in Computer-Assisted Learning." *J Ed Psychol* 62(5):413–20 O '71. * (*PA* 47:5855)
48. LEHERISSEY, BARBARA L.; O'NEIL, HAROLD F., JR.; HEINRICH, DARLENE L.; AND HANSEN, DUNCAN N. "Effect of Anxiety, Response Mode, Subject Matter Familiarity, and Learning Times on Achievement in Computer-Assisted Learning." Abstract. *Proc 79th Ann Conv Am Psychol Assn* 6(2):537–8 '71. * (*PA* 46:5784)
49. McAMMOND, DIANE M.; DAVIDSON, PARK O.; AND KOVITZ, DAVID M. "A Comparison of the Effects of Hypnosis and Relaxation Training on Stress Reactions in a Dental Situation." *Am J Clin Hyp* 13(4):233–42 Ap '71. * (*PA* 46:11022)
50. MERRILL, PAUL F., AND TOWLE, NELSON J. "Interaction of Abilities and Anxiety With Availability of Objectives and/or Test Items on Computer-Based Task Performance." Abstract. *Proc 79th Ann Conv Am Psychol Assn* 6(2):539–40 '71. * (*PA* 46:5790)
51. MILLER, HAROLD JOHN. *The Relationship of Self-Concept and Anxiety.* Doctor's thesis, University of Northern Colorado (Greeley, Colo.), 1971. (*DAI* 32:6036B)
52. MONKE, ROBERT H. "Effect of Systematic Desensitization on the Training of Counselors." *J Counsel Psychol* 18(4):320–3 Jl '71. * (*PA* 46:10935)
53. MORRIS, LARRY WAYNE. *Effects of Threat of Failure, Threat of Shock, and Level of Trait Anxiety on the Arousal of Worry and Emotionality.* Doctor's thesis, Vanderbilt University (Nashville, Tenn.), 1971. (*DAI* 32:1219B)
54. MOTE, THOMAS A., JR.; NATALICIO, LUIZ F. S.; AND RIVAS, FERNANDO. "Comparability of the Spanish and English Editions of the Spielberger State-Trait Anxiety Inventory." *J Cross-Cultural Psychol* 2(2):205–6 Je '71. * (*PA* 47:4827)

55. NELSON, DAVID ALEXANDER. *Trait Anxiety as an Individual Factor in Prediction and as It Correlates With Other Variables in Predicting Academic Achievement.* Doctor's thesis, University of Northern Colorado (Greeley, Colo.), 1971. (*DAI* 32:3699A)

56. NEWMARK, CHARLES STEPHEN. *Systematic Stimulus Control of Noncontent Verbal Behavior as a Function of State and Trait Anxiety.* Doctor's thesis, University of Alabama (University, Ala.), 1971. (*DAI* 32:1220B)

57. RAY, WILLIAM J.; KATAHN, MARTIN; AND SNYDER, C. R. "Effects of Test Anxiety on Acquisition, Retention, and Generalization of a Complex Verbal Task in a Classroom Situation." *J Pers & Social Psychol* 20(2):147–54 N '71. * (*PA* 47:7743)

58. ROARK, GLENN E. "Psychosomatic Factors in the Epidemiology of Infectious Mononucleosis." *Psychosomatics* 12(6): 402–11 N–D '71. * (*PA* 48:5515)

59. ROHALY, KATHLEEN ALICE. *The Relationships Between Movement Participation, Movement Satisfaction, Self-Actualization, and Trait Anxiety in Selected College Freshmen Women.* Doctor's thesis, Ohio State University (Columbus, Ohio), 1971. (*DAI* 32:3766A)

60. SNYDER, C. R., AND RAY, WILLIAM J. "Observed Body Movement in the College Test-Taking Situation and Scores on the Scholastic Aptitude Test." *Percept & Motor Skills* 32(1): 265–6 F '71. * (*PA* 46:3733)

61. TENNYSON, ROBERT D., AND WOOLLEY, F. ROSS. "Interaction of Anxiety With Performance on Two Levels of Task Difficulty." Abstract. *Proc 79th Ann Conv Am Psychol Assn* 6(1):377–8 '71. * (*PA* 46:4977)

62. TENNYSON, ROBERT D., AND WOOLLEY, F. ROSS. "Interaction of Anxiety With Performance on Two Levels of Task Difficulty." *J Ed Psychol* 62(6):463–7 D '71. * (*PA* 47:8165)

63. TOBIASON, ROLF VAN COTT. *The Relative Effectiveness of Individual and Group Desensitization in Reducing Student Nurses' Anxiety.* Doctor's thesis, Arizona State University (Tempe, Ariz.), 1971. (*DAI* 32:3707A)

64. VINES, ROLAND HAROLD. *The Influence of Race and Anxiety Level Upon Performance of Novel Motor Tasks Under Varying Stressful Conditions.* Doctor's thesis, Louisiana State University (Baton Rouge, La.), 1971. (*DAI* 32:3770A)

65. WEINSTEIN, P.; SMITH, T.; AND PACKER, M. "Method for Evaluating Patient Anxiety and the Interpersonal Effectiveness of Dental Personnel: An Exploratory Study." *J Dental Res* 50(5):1324–6 S–O '71. *

CUMULATIVE NAME INDEX

Allen, G. J.: 15, 33
Altman, I.: 4
Auerbach, S. M.: 34
Barton, K.: 5
Burton, E. C.: 35
Butler, P. E.: 36
Clark, N. C.: 37
Coco, H. B.: 38
Davidson, P. O.: 49
DeLong, R. D.: 25
Diblin, J. E.: 6
Edelman, R. I.: 16
Eder, S. C.: 39
Edwards, K. R.: 21
Eigenbrod, F. A.: 7
Ettkin, L. F.: 40
Everett, R. B.: 41
Felling, J. P.: 17
Forrest, M.: 42
Gorsuch, R. L.: 2, 22
Griffin, M. R.: 43
Grippaldi, R.: 19
Hansen, D. N.: 12, 44, 47–8
Hedl, J. J.: 44
Heinrich, D. L.: 48
Henneberry, J. K.: 45
Hodges, W. F.: 17
Johnson, D. T.: 3
Kamen, G. B.: 18, 46
Kass, E. L.: 8
Katahn, M.: 57
Kelly, C. H.: 26
Knox, W. J.: 19
Kovitz, D. M.: 49
Kroth, J. A.: 42
Lamb, D. H.: 9
Leherissey, B. L.: 47–8
Litvak, S. B.: 27

Lushene, R. E.: 28
McAdoo, W. G.: 29
McAmmond, D. M.: 49
Martin, R. P.: 30
Merrill, P. F.: 50
Miller, H. J.: 51
Monke, R. H.: 10, 52
Morris, L. W.: 53
Mote, T. A.: 31, 54
Natalicio, L. F. S.: 54
Nelson, D. A.: 55
Newmark, C. S.: 56
Nixon, G. F.: 11
Noyes, R. C.: 32
O'Neil, H. F.: 12, 23, 44, 47–8
Packer, M.: 65
Parrino, J. J.: 24
Ratzlaff, C. N.: 20
Ray, W. J.: 57, 60
Rivas, F.: 54
Roark, G. E.: 58
Rohaly, K. A.: 59
Schechter, M. D.: 41
Smith, T.: 65
Snyder, C. R.: 57, 60
Spielberger, C. D.: 1–2, 12
Stoudenmire, J. A.: 13
Taylor, D. A.: 4
Tennyson, R. D.: 61–2
Tobiason, R. V. C.: 63
Towle, N. J.: 50
Vines, R. H.: 64
Weinstein, P.: 65
Wheeler, L.: 4
Woolley, F. R.: 61–2
Worth, J. W.: 14

[1392]

★**State-Trait Anxiety Inventory for Children.** Grades 4–8; 1970–73; STAIC; downward extension of *State-Trait Anxiety Inventory;* title on test is *How-I-Feel Questionnaire;* 2 scores: state anxiety, trait anxiety; Charles D. Spielberger in collaboration with C. Drew Edwards, Robert E. Lushene, Joseph Montu-

ori, and Denna Platzek; Consulting Psychologists Press, Inc. *

REFERENCES THROUGH 1971

1. GAUDRY, ERIC. "Anxiety and Ability Grouping: A Review of Some Non-Experimental and Some Experimental Studies." *Austral J Ed* 15(3):244–52 O '71. *
2. MONTUORI, JOSEPH JOHN. *The Effects of Stress and Anxiety on Verbal Conditioning in Children.* Doctor's thesis, Florida State University (Tallahassee, Fla.), 1971. (*DAI* 32: 7319B)

CUMULATIVE NAME INDEX

Gaudry, E.: 1   Montuori, J. J.: 2

[1393]

[**Stereopathy-Acquiescence Schedule.**] College; [1960]; test booklet title is *SSRC S-A Schedule;* for research use only; 2 parts, 13 scores for each: stereopathic (violent categorical, violent qualified, moderate categorical, moderate qualified, total), nonstereopathic (violent categorical, violent qualified, moderate categorical, moderate qualified, antiviolent categorical, antiviolent qualified, total), total; George Stern, Nevitt Sanford, Hugh Lane, Harold Webster, and Richard Christie; distributed by Psychological Research Center. *

a) FORM I [IDEOLOGICAL].

b) FORM P [PERSONALITY].

REFERENCES THROUGH 1971

1. CROSS, HERBERT J., AND KAWASH, GEORGE F. "A Short Form of PARI to Assess Authoritarian Attitudes Toward Child Rearing." *Psychol Rep* 23:91–8 Ag '68. * (*PA* 43:6818)
2. OSKAMP, STUART, AND THOMPSON, GENEVIEVE. "Internal Inconsistency in the Stereopathy-Acquiescence Scales: A Warning Note." *J Social Psychol* 81(1):73–7 Je '70. * (*PA* 44: 18732)

CUMULATIVE NAME INDEX

Cross, H. J.: 1   Oskamp, S.: 2
Kawash, G. F.: 1   Thompson, G.: 2

[1394]

★**Stern Activities Index.** Grades 7–16 and adults; 1950–72; SAI; personal needs (see 1395 for related tests of environmental press covering the same areas); 2 editions; George G. Stern; Psychological Research Center. *

a) [FORM 1158.] 1950–70; 48 scores: 30 need scores (abasement-assurance, achievement, adaptability-defensiveness, affiliation, aggression-blame avoidance, change-sameness, conjunctivity-disjunctivity, counteraction, deference-restiveness, dominance-tolerance, ego achievement, emotionality-placidity, energy-passivity, exhibitionism-inferiority avoidance, fantasied achievement, harm avoidance-risk taking, humanities and social science, impulsiveness-deliberation, narcissism, nurturance, objectivity-projectivity, order-disorder, playwork, practicalness-impracticalness, reflectiveness, science, sensuality-puritanism, sexuality-prudishness, supplication-autonomy, understanding), 12 factor scores (self-assertion, audacity-timidity, intellectual interests, motivation, applied interests, orderliness, submissiveness, closeness, sensuousness, friendliness, expressiveness-constraint, egoism-diffidence), 4 second-order factor scores (achievement orientation, dependency needs, emotional expression, educability), 1 validity score, 1 academic aptitude score; also 5 composite culture factor scores (expressive, intellectual, protective, vocational, collegiate) based on combinations of needs scores with environmental press scores.

b) FORM 1158-SHORT FORM. 1972; 18 scores: same as for *a* except for omission of 30 need scores.

For additional information and reviews by Wilbur L. Layton and Rodney W. Skager of *a*, see 7:142 (61 references); see also P:255 (41 references) and 6:180

(*27* references). For excerpts from related book reviews, see 7:B594 (3 excerpts).

REFERENCES THROUGH 1971

1–27. See 6:180.
28–68. See P:255.
69–129. See 7:142.
130. TAYLOR, MARVIN. *The Effects of Three Cue Conditions, Interpersonal Relations Attitudes and Ideology of Judges on the Formation and Modification of First Impressions.* Doctor's thesis, Syracuse University (Syracuse, N.Y.), 1955. (*DA* 15:2476)
131. HARING, NORRIS G.; STERN, GEORGE G.; AND CRUICKSHANK, W. M. *Attitudes of Educators Toward Exceptional Children.* Syracuse, N.Y.: Syracuse University Press, 1958. Pp. xv, 238. * (*PA* 32:3312)
132. BEHRING, DANIEL W. *The Prediction of Academic Success From an Inventory of Student Preferences for Activities.* Master's thesis, Ohio University (Athens, Ohio), 1964.
133. MILLER, PEGGY ARLENE. *A Comparative Analysis of Motor Ability, Personality Needs, and Academic Achievement of Women Health and Physical Education Majors and Non-Majors at Tennessee Technological University.* Master's thesis, Tennessee Technological University (Cookeville, Tenn.), 1966.
134. BARTON, DONNA ROGERS. *An Analysis of the Perceived Personality Needs of Selected Students Participating in a Program for Junior High School Aged Rural Mountain Youth.* Master's thesis, Tennessee Technological University (Cookeville, Tenn.), 1967.
135. GILBREATH, STUART H. "Group Counseling, Dependence, and College Male Underachievement." *J Counsel Psychol* 14:449–53 S '67. * (*PA* 41:15845)
136. HASSENGER, ROBERT. Chap. 4, "Portrait of a Catholic Women's College," pp. 83–100. In his *The Shape of Catholic Higher Education.* Chicago, Ill.: University of Chicago Press, 1967. Pp. xviii, 378. *
137. VANDENBERG, STEVEN G. "Hereditary Factors in Normal Personality Traits (as Measured by Inventories)." *Recent Adv Biol Psychiatry* 9:65–104 '67. *
138. GILBREATH, STUART H. "Appropriate and Inappropriate Group Counseling With Academic Underachievers." *J Counsel Psychol* 15:506–11 N '68. * (*PA* 43:1505)
139. LEWIS, RUTH BENELLA. *A Need-Press Comparison of Australian and United States College Groups.* Doctor's thesis, University of Alabama (University, Ala.), 1970. (*DAI* 31:5133A)
140. MUHICH, DOLORES. *Multivariable Prediction of Selected Measures of College Success.* Doctor's thesis, Southern Illinois University (Carbondale, Ill.), 1970. (*DAI* 31:5209A)
141. PACE, WALTER T. "On Congruence and Dissonance in the Perceptions of Negro Teacher Trainees." *Ed* 90(4):315–8 Ap–My '70. *
142. PULVINO, CHARLES JOSEPH. *A Study of Individual "Needs" and Environmental "Press" as They Relate to Alienation, Anxiety, and Students' Grade Point Average.* Doctor's thesis, State University of New York (Buffalo, N.Y.), 1970. (*DAI* 31:4472A)
143. ALSING, EDWIN JOSEPH. *Organizational Climate in a Public Utility.* Doctor's thesis, New York University (New York, N.Y.), 1971. (*DAI* 32:2326A)
144. BRAINARD, STEPHEN R., AND DOLLAR, ROBERT J. "Personality Characteristics of Leaders Identifying With Different Student Subcultures." *J Col Stud Personnel* 12(3):200–3 My '71. * (*PA* 46:11461)
145. HERR, EDWIN L. "Student Needs, College Expectations, and 'Reality' Perceptions." *J Ed Res* 65(2):51–6 O '71. * (*PA* 48:1610)
146. PIERCE, ROBERT A., AND SCHWARTZ, ALLAN J. "Personality Styles of Student Activists." *J Psychol* 79(2):221–31 N '71. * (*PA* 47:7534)
147. ROBERSON, J. KAREN. *A Study of the Relationship Between Personality Needs and Attitudes Towards Drugs.* Master's thesis, Wake Forest University (Winston-Salem, N.C.), 1971.
148. ROBINSON, THOMAS C. *The Interaction of Student Personality Factors With the University Environmental Press as Related to Student Attrition.* Doctor's thesis, State University of New York (Buffalo, N.Y.), 1971. (*DAI* 32:3731A)
149. SHERRILL, DAVID, AND DRUGER, MARVIN. "Relationships Among Student Variables in an Audio-Tutorial Biology Course." *J Res Sci Teach* 8(2):191–4 '71. *
150. STAFFORD, MARGARET PARKER. *Freshman Expectations and Socialization in the College Environment.* Doctor's thesis, Syracuse University (Syracuse, N.Y.), 1971. (*DAI* 32:4434A)
151. STERN, GEORGE G. "Self-Actualizing Environments for Students." *Sch R* 80(1):1–25 N '71. *
152. WALLACE, CHARLES WILLIAM. *An Investigation of the Relationships Among Selected Attitudinal–Personality Characteristics and Success of Teachers in Installing an Innovative Elementary Science Curriculum.* Doctor's thesis, Syracuse University (Syracuse, N.Y.), 1971. (*DAI* 32:5064A)

CUMULATIVE NAME INDEX

Ager, J.: 4
Alsing, E. J.: 143

Andrews, S. L.: 86
Barton, D. R.: 134

Bauer, G. R.: 109
Behring, D. W.: 132
Bennett, J. W.: 95
Bloom, B. S.: 2
Brainard, S. R.: 144
Brewer, J. H.: 28
Briggs, D. A.: 3, 8
Brown, J. M.: 110
Buhl, A. J.: 122
Califf, S. N.: 52
Callihan, D. J. G.: 83
Campbell, P. S.: 31
Cassell, W.: 117
Chambliss, C. A.: 123
Chilman, C. S.: 70
Cohen, R. D.: 89
Cole, D. A.: 71
Cosby, B. W.: 19
Cox, L.: 13
Crist, R. L.: 12
Crowder, T. H.: 96
Cruickshank, W. M.: 131
Cureton, C. B.: 32
D'Amico, D. J.: 53, 67
Davis, W. R.: 84
DiVesta, F. J.: 13
Dollar, R. J.: 144
Donoian, G.: 76
Druger, M.: 149
Ducanis, A. J.: 73
Dworkin, S. F.: 90
Edens, F. N.: 111
Eschenfelder, W.: 1
Eubank, J. Y.: 97
Feldman, K. A.: 112
Furst, E. J.: 47
Gardner, P. L.: 72
Gilbreath, S. H.: 78, 135, 138
Gillis, J.: 33
Godbold, D. H.: 91
Goodrich, A. H.: 63
Gradel, D. V.: 41
Grady, M. J.: 34
Graham, L. E.: 54
Greene, J. E.: 55
Griffin, W. M.: 35
Haefner, D. A.: 56
Hamaty, G. G.: 57
Hamm, B. H.: 98
Hansen, J. C.: 58, 124
Haring, N. G.: 131
Harvey, D.: 4
Hassenger, R.: 136
Healy, M. M. I.: 48
Hedley, W. H.: 99
Herman, S.: 74
Herr, E. L.: 58, 145
Hiner, E. S.: 82
Hiscox, E. A. W.: 69
Hunt, W. O.: 113
Jambura, J. W.: 59
Keith, J. A.: 36
Kelly, J. G.: *exc,* 7:B594
Kight, H. R.: 58
King, S. H.: 100
Kirkland, M. C.: 85
Kirkpatrick, P. R.: 101
Klein, J. W.: 114
Lachica, G. M.: 115
Landis, H. L.: 29
Lawlor, G. F.: 125
Layton, W. L.: *rev,* 7:142
Lewis, R. B.: 139
Loree, M. R.: 129
Lorr, M.: 23

Loveless, E. J.: 37
Lukens, L. E.: 38
Lukens, L. G.: 42, 79
McCormick, F. C.: 49
McFee, A.: 11
McGuire, C.: 5
McKeel, J. T.: 102
McLaughlin, R. J.: 50
McNair, D. M.: 23
Maddi, S. R.: 86
Marshall, J. F.: 116
Matis, E. E.: 103
Merritt, W. R.: 60
Miller, P. A.: 133
Mitchell, J. V.: 104
Mueller, W. J.: 24, 30, 51
Muhich, D.: 140
Myers, J. W.: 43
Naugle, F.: 4, 6
Naugle, F. W.: 1
Newport, D. L.: 92
Norred, R. G.: 80
Olson, G. F.: 61
Ouzts, D. H.: 93
Pace, W. T.: 17, 141
Parker, H. J.: 68
Pearson, P. H.: 126
Peck, R. F.: 5, 14
Pierce, R. A.: 146
Pulvino, C. J.: 142
Raab, W. E.: 25
Richman, J.: 117
Riddle, L.: 105
Roberson, J. K.: 147
Robinson, T. C.: 148
Sagen, H. B.: 20
Saunders, D. R.: 118
Scanlon, J. C.: 9–10
Schultz, D.: 6
Schwartz, A. J.: 146
Schwartz, R. M.: 39
Sells, S. B.: *exc,* 7:B594
Sherrill, D.: 149
Shockley, V. L.: 127
Siegelman, M.: 5, 14
Simmons, M. D.: 62, 68
Sinco, E. D.: 106
Skager, R. W.: *rev,* 7:142
Soldahl, T. A.: 75
Spuhler, L.: 44
Stabler, J. R.: 63
Stafford, M. P.: 150
Stegman, W. N.: 64
Stein, M. I.: 2
Steinhoff, C. R.: 87
Stellwagen, W.: 7
Stern, G. G.: 1–2, 4, 6–7, 10, 15–6, 18, 21–2, 26, 45, 65, 81, 128, 131, 151
Stone, L. A.: 27
Stricker, G.: 46, 66
Tatham, D. F.: 7
Taylor, M.: 130
Tiller, T. C.: 107
Trimble, M. D.: 119
VanBuskirk, C.: 77
Vandenberg, S. G.: 137
Voss, D. H.: 88
Wallace, C. W.: 152
Walsh, W. B.: *exc,* 7:B594
Warner, R. W.: 124
Webb, S. C.: 40, 94
Weisberg, M.: 120
Whisenton, J. T.: 108, 129
Yufit, R. I.: 77, 121

[1395]

*Stern Environment Indexes. Grades 7 through graduate school and adults; 1957–72; SEI; environmental press (see 1394 for a related test of personal needs covering the same areas); 30 press scores (abasement-assurance, achievement, adaptability-defensiveness, affiliation, aggression-blame avoidance, change-sameness, conjunctivity-disjunctivity, counteraction, deference-restiveness, dominance-tolerance, ego achievement, emotionality-placidity, energy-passivity, exhibitionism-inferiority avoidance, fantasied achievement, harm avoidance-risk taking, humanities and social science, impulsiveness-deliberation, narcissism, nurturance, objectivity-projectivity, order-disorder, play-work, practicalness-impracticalness, reflectiveness, science, sensuality-puritanism, sexuality-prudishness, supplication-autonomy, understanding) for each index plus press factor scores and composite culture factor scores based on combinations of environmental press scores with needs scores specific to each edition as listed below; 6 editions; Psychological Research Center. *

a) CLASSROOM ENVIRONMENT INDEX. Grades 7 through graduate school; 1971; CEI; 38 scores: 30 press scores listed above, 6 factor scores (humanistic-intellectual climate, group intellectual life, achievement standards, personal dignity, orderliness, science) based on combinations of the press scores, and 2 second-order factor scores (development press, control press); George G. Stern and William J. Walker.

b) HIGH SCHOOL CHARACTERISTICS INDEX. Grades 9–13; 1960–70; HSCI; 40 scores: 30 press scores listed above, 7 factor scores (intellectual climate, expressiveness, group life, personal dignity, achievement standards, orderliness, practicalness) based on combinations of the press scores, and 3 second-order factor scores (development press, orderliness, practicalness); George G. Stern.

c) COLLEGE CHARACTERISTICS INDEX. Grades 13–16; 1957–70; CCI; 49 scores: 30 press scores listed above, 11 factor scores (aspiration level, intellectual climate, student dignity, academic climate, academic achievement, self-expression, group life, academic organization, social form, play-work, vocational climate) based on combinations of the press scores, 3 second-order factor scores (intellectual climate, non-intellectual climate, impulse control), and 5 composite culture factor scores (expressive, intellectual, protective, vocational, collegiate) based on combinations of needs scores with press scores; George G. Stern and C. Robert Pace.

d) COLLEGE CHARACTERISTICS INDEX—SHORT FORM. Grades 13–16; 1972; CCI–SF; 19 scores: same as for c except for omission of 30 press scores; George G. Stern.

e) EVENING COLLEGE CHARACTERISTICS INDEX. Adults; 1961–70; ECCI; for research use only; 30 press scores listed above; George G. Stern, Clifford L. Winters, Jr., N. Sidney Archer, and Donald L. Meyer.

f) ORGANIZATIONAL CLIMATE INDEX. Employees; 1958–70; OCI; 3 norm groups; school districts: 47 scores: 30 press scores listed above, 6 factor scores (intellectual climate, achievement standards, practicalness, supportiveness, orderliness, impulse control) based on combinations of the press scores, 2 second-order factor scores (development press, control press), 6 composite culture factor scores (protective, achievement, development, emotional, friendliness, submissiveness) based on combinations of the need and press scores, 3 second-order composite culture factor scores (conventional, expressive, warmth); Peace Corps: 38 scores: 30 press scores listed above, 6 factor scores (group life vs. isolation, intellectual climate, personal dignity, achievement standards, orderliness, impulse control) based on combinations of the press scores, 2 second-order factor scores (development press, control press); industrial sites: 38 scores: 30 press scores listed above, 6 factor scores (intellectual climate, organizational effectiveness, personal dignity, orderliness, work, impulse control) based on combinations of the press scores, 2 second-order factor scores (development press, control press); George G. Stern and Carl R. Steinhoff.

For additional information and reviews by Wilbur L. Layton and Rodney W. Skager of b–f, see 7:143 (59 references); see also P:256 (65 references) and 6:92 (19 references). For excerpts from related book reviews, see 7:B594 (3 excerpts).

REFERENCES THROUGH 1971

1–19. See 6:92.
20–84. See P:256.
85–143. See 7:143.
144. LARSON, ARDIS I. A Study of Environmental Press Upon Selected Groups of Women Students at a State University. Master's thesis, Ohio University (Athens, Ohio), 1964.
145. WEISS, ROBERT F. Chap. 3, "The Environment for Learning on the Catholic College Campus," pp. 57–82. In The Shape of Catholic Higher Education. Edited by Robert Hassenger. Chicago, Ill.: University of Chicago Press, 1967. Pp. xviii, 378. *
146. GOTTHEIL, EDWARD; HASSENFELD, IRWIN N.; AND GRONKIEWICZ, ELIZABETH. "Students' Perceptions of Medical Schools and Their Attitudes Towards Patients." Brit J Med Ed 3(4):355–8 D '69. *
147. HERR, EDWIN L., AND MOORE, GILBERT D. "English and American Student Expectations of College: Some Comparisons." NASPA 7(1):35–9 Jl '69. *
148. KATZ, F. M., AND KATZ, N. "Great Expectations." Univ Q (England) 23(4):420–30 au '69. *
149. MITCHELL, JAMES V., JR. "Education's Challenge to Psychology: The Prediction of Behavior From Person-Environment Interactions." R Ed Res 39(5):695–721 D '69. *
150. STERN, GEORGE G. Chap. 16, "Campus Environments and Student Unrest," pp. 123–35. In Agony and Promise: Current Issues in Higher Education 1969. Edited by G. Kerry Smith. San Francisco, Calif.: Jossey-Bass Inc., Publishers, 1969. Pp. xix, 282. *
151. BONNER, ROSS WAYNE. Student, Parent, and Teacher Perception of College Environments. Doctor's thesis, North Texas State University (Denton, Tex.), 1970. (DAI 32:732A)
152. DONATO, DONALD JOHN. The Effect of Expectation-Press Incongruency on Junior College Transfer Student Achievement. Doctor's thesis, University of Missouri (Columbia, Mo.), 1970. (DAI 31:5121A)
153. KELLEY, EDGAR ALAN. Case Studies and an Analysis of the Role of Morale, Organizational Climate, and Conflict in the Study of Secondary School Environments. Doctor's thesis, Michigan State University (East Lansing, Mich.), 1970. (DAI 31:6306A)
154. LEWIS, RUTH BENELLA. A Need-Press Comparison of Australian and United States College Groups. Doctor's thesis, University of Alabama (University, Ala.), 1970. (DAI 31:5133A)
155. McGRAIL, RICHARD FRANCIS. The Relationships Between the Organizational Climate of Schools and the Personality Characteristics of Teachers: A Puerto Rican Sample. Doctor's thesis, Boston College (Chestnut Hill, Mass.), 1970. (DAI 31:5085A)
156. PACE, WALTER T. "On Congruence and Dissonance in the Perceptions of Negro Teacher Trainees." Ed 90(4):315–8 Ap–My '70. *
157. PULVINO, CHARLES JOSEPH. A Study of Individual "Needs" and Environmental "Press" as They Relate to Alienation, Anxiety, and Students' Grade Point Average. Doctor's thesis, State University of New York (Buffalo, N.Y.), 1970. (DAI 31:4472A)
158. SCHNEE, RONALD GENE. A Method for Describing and Comparing the Environments of Selected High Schools. Doctor's thesis, Oklahoma State University (Stillwater, Okla.), 1970. (DAI 31:5780A)
159. SPEEGLE, JAMES R. "College Catalog—Tell It Like It Is or More Than You Really Need to Know." Col & Univ 45(4):724–38 su '70. *
160. ALSING, EDWIN JOSEPH. Organizational Climate in a Public Utility. Doctor's thesis, New York University (New York, N.Y.), 1971. (DAI 32:2326A)
161. BUCKLEY, H. DONALD. "A Comparison of Freshman and Transfer Expectations." J Col Stud Personnel 12(3):186–8 My '71. * (PA 46:11464)
162. COWAN, WILLIAM JOSEPH. An Investigation of Teacher Perceptions of School Organizational Climate Before and After the Court-Ordered Transfer of Teachers in the Atlanta Public Schools. Doctor's thesis, Georgia State University (Atlanta, Ga.), 1971. (DAI 32:3598A)
163. DRESSER, DAVID LELAND. The Relationship Between Personality Needs, College Expectations, Environmental Press and Undergraduate Attrition in a University College of Liberal Arts. Doctor's thesis, Syracuse University (Syracuse, N.Y.), 1971. (DAI 32:4979A)
164. ELLIOTT, BURTON LAMAR. Comparative Analysis of the Results of the High School Characteristics Index Administered at Two Vocational and Two General High Schools. Doctor's thesis, University of Arkansas (Fayetteville, Ark.), 1971. (DAI 32:2339A)
165. FELDMAN, KENNETH A. "Measuring College Environments: Some Uses of Path Analysis." Am Ed Res J 8(1):51–70 Ja '71. *
166. HERR, EDWIN L. "Student Needs, College Expectations, and 'Reality' Perceptions." J Ed Res 65(2):51–6 O '71. * (PA 48:1610)
167. IVEY, ALLEN E., AND WILSON, RAY. "Perceptions of College Environment: A Four-Year Longitudinal Study." J Col Stud Personnel 12(3):177–8 My '71. * (PA 46:11472)

168. KIEVIT, MARY BACH. "Environmental Press: Two Year Occupational Programs in a Community College and a Technical Institute." *J Indus Teach Ed* 8(4):48–58 su '71. *

169. KING, JOSEPH HAROLD. *Perceptions of Some Environmental Press Characteristics of the College of Education, University of Illinois (Urbana).* Doctor's thesis, University of Illinois (Urbana, Ill.), 1971. (*DAI* 32:702A)

170. McCART, PATRICIA ANN. *Effects of an Independent School Merger on Boys' and Girls' Perceptions of Environmental Press.* Doctor's thesis, University of Minnesota (Minneapolis, Minn.), 1971. (*DAI* 33:84A)

171. MERRILL, CALVIN CONRAD. *A Study of the Image of the University of Alabama Held by Selected Junior College Students in the State.* Doctor's thesis, University of Alabama (University, Ala.), 1971. (*DAI* 32:4990A)

172. PAYNE, R. L., AND PHEYSEY, D. C. "G. G. Stern's Organizational Climate Index: A Reconceptualization and Application to Business Organizations." *Organiz Behav & Hum Perfor* 6(1):77–98 Ja '71. * (*PA* 46:1962)

173. PIERCE, ROBERT A., AND SCHWARTZ, ALLAN J. "Personality Styles of Student Activists." *J Psychol* 79(2):221–31 N '71. * (*PA* 47:7534)

174. RAINALDI, FRANKLIN DELANO. *A Comparative Study of the Perceived Institutional Environment of a High School Under Two Organizational Plans: Traditional Versus Modular.* Doctor's thesis, University of Minnesota (Minneapolis, Minn.), 1971. (*DAI* 32:2367A)

175. ROBINSON, THOMAS C. *The Interaction of Student Personality Factors With the University Environmental Press as Related to Student Attrition.* Doctor's thesis, State University of New York (Buffalo, N.Y.), 1971. (*DAI* 32:3731A)

176. SCOTT, JACK CARTER. *A Study of the Relationship Between Students' Personal Perception of Environmental Press and Attrition at a Two Year College.* Doctor's thesis, University of Missouri (Columbia, Mo.), 1971. (*DAI* 32:4965A)

177. STAFFORD, MARGARET PARKER. *Freshman Expectations and Socialization in the College Environment.* Doctor's thesis, Syracuse University (Syracuse, N.Y.), 1971. (*DAI* 32:4434A)

178. STERN, GEORGE G. "Self-Actualizing Environments for Students." *Sch R* 80(1):1–25 N '71. *

179. TOLSMA, ROBERT JAMES. *Measurement of Group Responses to Assess the Environmental Press of Secondary Schools.* Doctor's thesis, Iowa State University (Ames, Iowa), 1971. (*DAI* 32:5557A)

180. WALLACE, CHARLES WILLIAM. *An Investigation of the Relationships Among Selected Attitudinal—Personality Characteristics and Success of Teachers in Installing an Innovative Elementary Science Curriculum.* Doctor's thesis, Syracuse University (Syracuse, N.Y.), 1971. (*DAI* 32:5064A)

181. WESTLAKE, EUGENE JOSEPH. *The Relationship Between Students' Perception of the High School Environment and Academic Achievement.* Doctor's thesis, Fordham University (New York, N.Y.), 1971. (*DAI* 32:746A)

CUMULATIVE NAME INDEX

[1396]

Stockton Geriatric Rating Scale. Hospital or nursing home patients 65 and over; 1964–66; SGRS; prediction of improvement; 5 scores: physical disability, apathy, communication failure, socially irritating behavior, total; Bernard Meer and Janet A. Baker; Department of Research, Stockton State Hospital. *

For additional information, see P:257 (2 references).

REFERENCES THROUGH 1971

1–2. See P:257.
3. MEER, BERNARD, AND KRAG, CLETUS L. "Correlates of Disability in a Population of Hospitalized Geriatric Patients." *J Gerontol* 19:440–6 O '64. *

CUMULATIVE NAME INDEX

[1397]

★**Structured and Scaled Interview to Assess Maladjustment.** Mental patients; 1974; SSIAM; social adjustment; 11 ratings (5 deviant behavior, friction with others, 3 distress, 2 inferential) in each of 5 areas (work, social-leisure, family, marriage, sex) plus 11 overall ratings; Barry J. Gurland, Neil J. Yorkston, Anthony R. Stone, and Jerome D. Frank; Springer Publishing Co., Inc. *

[1398]

Structured Clinical Interview. Mental patients; 1963–69; SCI; 11 scores: anger-hostility, conceptual dysfunction, fear-worry, incongruous behavior, incongruous ideation, lethargy-dejection, perceptual dysfunction, physical complaints, self depreciation, sexual problems, total; Eugene I. Burdock and Anne S. Hardesty; Springer Publishing Co., Inc. *

For additional information, reviews by Douglas M. McNair and S. B. Sells, and an excerpted review by J. R. M. Copeland, see 7:144 (7 references).

REFERENCES THROUGH 1971

1-7. See 7:144

8. GERSHON, SAMUEL; HEKIMIAN, LEON J.; AND FLOYD, ARTHUR, JR. "Evaluation of a New Antidepressant: A-10749." *J Clin Pharmacol* 7:348-53 N-D '67. * (*PA* 42:4114)

9. FLEISS, JOSEPH L.; LAWLOR, WILLIAM; PLATMAN, STANLEY R.; AND FIEVE, RONALD R. "On the Use of Inverted Factor Analysis for Generating Typologies." *J Abn Psychol* 77(2): 127-32 Ap '71. * (*PA* 46:3315)

10. JOHNSON, GORDON; GERSHON, SAMUEL; BURDOCK, EUGENE I.; FLOYD, ARTHUR; AND HEKIMIAN, LEON. "Comparative Effects of Lithium and Chlorpromazine in the Treatment of Acute Manic States." *Brit J Psychiatry* 119(550):267-76 S '71. * (*PA* 47:9154)

11. MENSH, IVAN. "Structured Clinical Interview: A Review." *Prof Psychol* 2(1):92-3 w '71. *

12. SHOPSIN, BARON; KIM, SUK SIK; AND GERSHON, SAMUEL. "A Controlled Study of Lithium vs. Chlorpromazine in Acute Schizophrenics." *Brit J Psychiatry* 119(551):435-40 O '71. * (*PA* 47:9388)

13. SIMON, ROBERT J.; FISHER, BERNICE; FLEISS, JOSEPH L.; GURLAND, BARRY J.; AND SHARPE, LAWRENCE. "Relationship Between Psychopathology and British- or American-Oriented Diagnosis." *J Abn Psychol* 78(1):26-9 Ag '71. * (*PA* 47:3391)

CUMULATIVE NAME INDEX

Burdock, E. I.: 1-3, 5, 10
Copeland, J. R. M.: *exc,* 7:144
Fieve, R. R.: 9
Fisher, B.: 13
Fleiss, J. L.: 9, 13
Floyd, A.: 8, 10
Gershon, S.: 8, 10, 12
Gurland, B. J.: 13
Hardesty, A. S.: 1-3, 5
Hekimian, L. J.: 8, 10
Johnson, G.: 6

Kim, S. S.: 12
Lawlor, W.: 9
McNair, D. M.: *rev,* 7:144
Mensh, I.: 11
Platman, S. R.: 7, 9
Sells, S. B.: *rev,* 7:144
Sharpe, L.: 13
Shopsin, B.: 12
Simon, R. J.: 13
Weinstein, B.: 7
Zubin, J.: 4

[1399]

Student Attitude Inventory. College; 1967; formerly called *Study of Professional Education Attitude Inventory;* for research purposes only; 7 scales: academic, intellectual, political-economic liberalism, social liberalism, pragmatism, dogmatism, cynicism; D. S. Anderson and J. S. Western; Australian Council for Educational Research [Australia]. *

For additional information, see 7:145 (2 references).

REFERENCES THROUGH 1971

1-2. See 7:145.

CUMULATIVE NAME INDEX

Anderson, D. S.: 1-2   Western, J. S.: 1-2

[1400]

Student Description Form. Grades 9-12; 1964; SDF; ratings by teachers to be used on *Secondary-School Record—Student Description Summary;* 8 ratings: participation in discussion, involvement in classroom activities, pursuit of independent study, evenness of performance, critical and questioning attitude, depth of understanding, personal responsibility, consideration for others; National Association of Secondary-School Principals. *

For additional information, see P:258.

[1401]

★**Student Evaluation Scale.** Grades 1-12; 1970; SES; ratings by teachers; 3 scores: educational response, social-emotional response, total; William T. Martin and Sue Martin; Psychologists and Educators, Inc. *

[1402]

A Study of Choices. Ages 16 and over; 1948; 16 scores: 12 value scores (intellectual activity, home life, social service, personal improvement, friends, security, political power, comfort, excitement, wealth, society, religion) and 4 derived scores; Asahel D. Woodruff; the Author. *

REFERENCES THROUGH 1971

1. WOODRUFF, ASAHEL D., AND DiVESTA, FRANCIS J. "The Relationship Between Values, Concepts, and Attitudes." *Ed & Psychol Meas* 8:645-59 w '48. * (*PA* 24:1470)

CUMULATIVE NAME INDEX

DiVesta, F. J.: 1   Woodruff, A. D.: 1

[1403]

Study of Values: A Scale for Measuring the Dominant Interests in Personality, Third Edition. Grades 10-16 and adults; 1931-70; SV, also AVL; for British adaptation, see 1404; 6 scores: theoretical, economic, aesthetic, social, political, religious; 1960 test identical with test copyrighted 1951; Gordon W. Allport, Philip E. Vernon, and Gardner Lindzey; Houghton Mifflin Co. *

For additional information and a review by Robert Hogan, see 7:146 (212 references); see also P:259 (195 references); for reviews by John D. Hundleby and John A. Radcliffe, see 6:182 (137 references); for a review by N. L. Gage of the second edition, see 5:114 (57 references); for reviews by Harrison G. Gough and William Stephenson and an excerpted review by Laurance F. Shaffer, see 4:92 (25 references); for a review by Paul E. Meehl of the original edition, see 3:99 (61 references).

REFERENCES THROUGH 1971

1-61. See 3:99.
62-86. See 4:92.
87-143. See 5:114.
144-280. See 6:182.
281-475. See P:259.
476-687. See 7:146.

688. HARTMANN, GEORGE W. "Personality Traits Associated With Variations in Happiness." *J Abn & Social Psychol* 29: 202-12 Jl-S '34. * (*PA* 9:1287)

689. TRACY, JAMES A. "A Study of Personality Traits of Mature Actors and Mature Public Speakers." *Speech Monogr* 2:53-6 S '35. * (*PA* 13:2611, title only)

690. SCHOOLEY, MARY. "Personality Resemblances Among Married Couples." *J Abn & Social Psychol* 31:340-7 O-D '36. * (*PA* 11:1854)

691. THOMSON, WILLIAM A. "An Inventory for Measuring Socialization—Self-Seeking and Its Relationship to the Study of Values Test, the ACE Psychological Examination, and the Strong Vocational Interest Blank." *J Appl Psychol* 25:202-12 Ap '41. * (*PA* 15:4285)

692. SPERLING, ABRAHAM P. "A Comparison Between Jews and Non-Jews With Respect to Several Traits of Personality." *J Appl Psychol* 26:828-40 D '42. * (*PA* 17:2819)

693. SPERLING, ABRAHAM P. "The Relationship Between Personality Adjustment and Achievement in Physical Education Activities." *Res Q* 13:351-63 O '42. * (*PA* 17:600)

694. TODD, J. E. "Measurement in the Continuous Selection and Counseling of Students in a College of Physical Education and Social Work." *Ed & Psychol Meas* 4:233-43 au '44. * (*PA* 19:1810)

695. PORTENIER, LILLIAN G. "Personality Tests in a University Guidance Program." *J Ed Psychol* 39:479-87 D '48. * (*PA* 23:3218)

696. LANDIS, PAUL H. "Personality Differences of Girls From Farm, Town, and City." *Rural Sociol* 14:10-20 Mr '49. *

697. DRAKE, FRANCIS E. "A Study of the Personality Traits of Students Interested in Acting." *Speech Monogr* 17:123-33 Je '50. * (*PA* 25:3386)

698. McGINNIES, ELLIOTT. "Personal Values as Determinants of Word Association." *J Abn & Social Psychol* 45:28-36 Ja '50. * (*PA* 24:4580)

699. KLINE, MILTON V., AND CUMINGS, RUTH. "A Study of the Learning Characteristics of Public Health Nurses in Relation to Mental Health Education and Consultation: 3, Comparative Study of Some Aspects of Personality and Learning Skill in Relation to In-Service Educational Performance." *J Social Psychol* 42:43-60 Ag '55. * (*PA* 30:7149)

700. RIGGS, MARGARET M., AND KAESS, WALTER. "Personality

Differences Between Volunteers and Nonvolunteers." *J Psychol* 40:229-45 O '55. * (*PA* 30:6918)

701. GRZIWOK, RUDOLF, AND SCODEL, ALVIN. "Some Psychological Correlates of Humor Preferences." Abstract. *J Consult Psychol* 20:42 F '56. * (*PA* 31:2594, title only)

702. LUNDY, RICHARD M. "Assimilative Projection and Accuracy of Prediction in Interpersonal Perceptions." *J Abn & Social Psychol* 52:33-8 Ja '56. * (*PA* 31:2560)

703. VAN KREVELEN, ALICE. "Relationships Between Number of Verbal Associations to Value Words and Subjective Ratings of Values." *Proc Iowa Acad Sci* 63:576-80 '56. * (*PA* 32:4054)

704. DAANE, CALVIN J., AND SCHMIDT, LOUIS G. "Empathy and Personality Variables." *J Ed Res* 51:129-36 O '57. * (*PA* 33:6568)

705. THOMPSON, J. W. "A Factorial Study of the Values and Attitudes of Graduate Teachers in Training." Abstract. *Brit J Ed Psychol* 28:182-3 Je '58. *

706. GOWAN, J. C., AND DIBLE, ISABEL. "Age Effects on the Test Scores of Women Teaching Candidates." *Calif J Ed Res* 11:37-8 Ja '60. * (*PA* 34:8417)

707. KENNEDY, WALLACE A.; SMITH, MARION; VAN DE RIET, HANNAH; VAN DE RIET, VERNON; SMITH, HERBERT; RAPP, DON; AND PAINE, R. W. "A Multidimensional Study of Mathematically Gifted Adolescents." *Child Develop* 31:655-66 D '60. * (*PA* 36:2FH55K)

708. KLEYENSTEUBER, CARL J. "Evaluative Attitudes and Behaviors of School Administrators." *J Ed Res* 53:352-4 My '60. *

709. STEWART, LAWRENCE H. "Modes of Response on the Strong Blank and Selected Personality Variables." *J Counsel Psychol* 7:127-31 su '60. * (*PA* 35:3461)

710. SHNEIDMAN, EDWIN S. "The Case of El: Psychological Test Data." *J Proj Tech* 25:131-54 Je '61. * (*PA* 36:21K31S)

711. RUSH, ALLEN C. "Better Police Personnel Selection." *Police Chief* 30:18+ S '63. *

712. WEBER, ROBERT GENE. *Leadership Characteristics of Public School Business Administrators.* Doctor's research study No. 1, Colorado State College (Greeley, Colo.), 1963. (*DA* 25:259)

713. BARTH, ROBERT E. *A Study of the Values of Fraternity Men and Non-Fraternity Men.* Master's thesis, Ohio University (Athens, Ohio), 1964.

714. HUTCHINS, EDWIN B. "The AAMC Longitudinal Study: Implications for Medical Education." *J Med Ed* 39:265-77 Mr '64. *

715. KNAPP, ROBERT H. "An Experimental Study of a Triad:c Hypothesis Concerning the Sources of Aesthetic Imagery." *J Proj Tech & Pers Assess* 28:49-54 Mr '64. * (*PA* 39:1641)

716. LYSAUGHT, JEROME P. "Selecting Instructional Programmers: New Research Into Characteristics of Successful Programmers." *Training Directors J* 18:8-14 Je '64. *

717. PEYTON, PATRICIA. *A Comparison of Values, Self Concept, and Success in College of Negro and White College Students.* Master's thesis, Ohio University (Athens, Ohio), 1964.

718. SCHUSTER, D. H., AND GUILFORD, J. P. "The Psychometric Prediction of Problem Drivers." *Hum Factors* 6:393-421 Ag '64. *

719. SMITH, WILLIAM G.; ENGLISH, JOSEPH T.; AND HANSELL, NORRIS. "Mental Illness and Values in a College Population." *J Nerv & Mental Dis* 138:156-62 F '64. *

720. TURO, JOANN K. *The Relationship of Differential Value and Interest Patterns to Authoritarian Attitudes.* Master's thesis, Ohio University (Athens, Ohio), 1964.

721. ADAMS, PAUL L.; SCHWAB, JOHN J.; AND APONTE, JOSEPH F. "Authoritarian Parents and Disturbed Children." *Am J Psychiatry* 121:1162-7 Je '65. * (*PA* 39:14742)

722. HAVEN, GEORGE A., JR. "Creative Thought, Productivity, and the Self-Concept." *Psychol Rep* 16:750-2 Je '65. * (*PA* 39:15291)

723. HEATH, DOUGLAS H.; WITH THE ASSISTANCE OF HARRIET E. HEATH. *Explorations of Maturity: Studies of Mature and Immature College Men.* New York: Appleton-Century-Crofts, 1965. Pp. xv, 423. * (*PA* 39:12057)

724. PERL, MARY L. *A Comparative Study of the Dominant Personality Interests of Religious and Lay Teachers in Selected Schools.* Master's thesis, St. John College (Cleveland, Ohio), 1965.

725. SICURO, NATALE A. "A Comparison of Academic Aptitudes, Certain Values, and Personal and Background Characteristics of Students in Off-Campus Centers and on Central Campus of the Same University." *J Ed Res* 58:229-32 Ja '65. *

726. SMITH, WILLIAM G.; HANSELL, NORRIS; AND ENGLISH, JOSEPH T. "Values and Mental Health in a College Population: A Follow-Up Report." *J Nerv & Mental Dis* 140:92-5 Ja '65. *

727. TISDALE, JOHN R. "Value Patterns in Three Midwest Colleges." *Proc Iowa Acad Sci* 72:389-95 '65. *

728. BARE, CAROLE E. "Counselor Sensitivity to the Counselor-Client Communication Process." Abstract. *Proc 74th Ann Conv Am Psychol Assn* 1:301-2 '66. * (*PA* 41:6145)

729. COOK, THOMAS E. "The Influence of Client-Counselor Value Similarity on Change in Meaning During Brief Counseling." *J Counsel Psychol* 13:77-81 sp '66. * (*PA* 40:5802)

730. DUNFORD, G. GARY. *A Study of Value Differences Between Freshman and Senior Students at Brigham Young University.* Master's thesis, Brigham Young University (Provo, Utah), 1966.

731. GETZELS, J. W., AND CSIKSZENTMIHALYI, M. Chap. 15, "The Study of Creativity in Future Artists: The Criterion Problem," pp. 349-68. In *Experience, Structure and Adaptability.* Edited by O. J. Harvey. New York: Springer Publishing Co., Inc., 1966. Pp. ix, 406. *

732. NEURINGER, CHARLES; MYERS, ROGER A.; AND NORDMARK, TORBERG, JR. "The Transfer of a Verbally Conditioned Response Class." *J Counsel Psychol* 13:208-13 su '66. * (*PA* 40:8433)

733. SCHMITT, RAYMOND L. "Major Role Change and Self Change." *Sociol Q* 7:311-22 su '66. *

734. ZUCKERMAN, MARVIN; PERSKY, HAROLD; HOPKINS, T. ROBERT; MURTAUGH, THOMAS; BASU, G. K.; AND SCHILLING, MARY. "Comparison of Stress Effects of Perceptual and Social Isolation." *Arch Gen Psychiatry* 14:356-65 Ap '66. * (*PA* 40:6182)

735. BENTZ, V. JON. Chap. 7, "The Sears Experience in the Investigation, Description, and Prediction of Executive Behavior," pp. 147-205; critique by Ross Stagner, pp. 206-27. In *Measuring Executive Effectiveness.* Edited by Frederic R. Wickert and Dalton E. McFarland. New York: Appleton-Century-Crofts, 1967. Pp. viii, 242. *

736. BIASE, D. VINCENT, AND ZUCKERMAN, MARVIN. "Sex Differences in Stress Responses to Total and Partial Sensory Deprivation." *Psychosom Med* 29:380-90 Jl-Ag '67. * (*PA* 42:1602)

737. JORDAN, MARCELLA JULIE. *The Relationship of Life Values and Work Values of College Women to Their Vocational Preferences.* Master's thesis, Catholic University of America (Washington, D.C.), 1967.

738. KESSEL, PAUL, AND McBREARTY, JOHN F. "Verbal Behavior as a Function of Social Reinforcement, Awareness of the Response-Reinforcement Contingency, Value Similarity, and Need for Social Approval." Abstract. *Proc 75th Ann Conv Am Psychol Assn* 2:255-6 '67. * (*PA* 41:13545)

739. MILLER, AARON J., AND TWYMAN, J. PASCHAL. "Persistence in Engineering and Technical Institute Programs: A Study of Some Nonintellective Concomitants." *J Hum Resources* 2(2):254-62 sp '67. *

740. WILLERSCHEIDT, MARY MARGARET. *Personal Values and Factors Influencing the Decision of Mankato State College Women to Major in Physical Education.* Master's thesis, Mankato State College (Mankato, Minn.), 1967.

741. ATHELSTAN, GARY T. *The Vocational Interests, Values, and Career Development of Specialists in Physical Medicine and Rehabilitation.* CEPM&R Bulletin 9. Minneapolis, Minn.: Commission on Education in Physical Medicine and Rehabilitation, 1968. Pp. vii, 63. *

742. BAKER, STEVEN WILBUR. *A Comparison of the Needs and Values of Graduating Prospective Teachers of Special Education and the Needs and Values of Graduating Prospective Teachers of Regular Education.* Master's thesis, Central Washington State College (Ellensburg, Wash.), 1968.

743. BASS, BERNARD M. "Ability, Values, and Concepts of Equitable Salary Increases in *Exercise Compensation.*" *J Appl Psychol* 52:299-303 Ag '68. * (*PA* 42:16239)

744. BASS, BERNARD M. "How to Succeed in Business According to Business Students and Managers." *J Appl Psychol* 52:254-62 Je '68. * (*PA* 42:12889)

745. BOURQUE, LINDA BROOKOVER, AND BACK, KURT W. "Values and Transcendental Experiences." *Social Forces* 47:34-8 S '68. * (*PA* 44:4312)

746. BRUNO, FRANK BARTOLO. *Life Values, Manifest Needs, and Vocational Interests as Factors Influencing Professional Career Satisfaction Among Teachers of Emotionally Disturbed Children.* Doctor's thesis, Wayne State University (Detroit, Mich.), 1968. (*DAI* 31:3999A)

747. CAMPBELL, DOUGLAS F., AND MAGILL, DENNIS W. "Religious Involvement and Intellectuality Among University Students." *Sociol Analysis* 29:79-93 su '68. *

748. GETZELS, J. W., AND CSIKSZENTMIHALYI, M. "On the Roles, Values, and Performance of Future Artists: A Conceptual and Empirical Exploration." *Sociol Q* 9:516-30 au '68. *

749. HOWELL, MARGARET A. "Medical Interns: A Study of Types." *Ed & Psychol Meas* 28:327-38 su '68. * (*PA* 42:18860)

750. KHARE, P. G. "Occupational Differences in Life-Values." *Indian Psychol R* 4:104-9 Ja '68. * (*PA* 43:11161)

751. PICHE, MARY. *Value Survey Among Women in Religious Orders Throughout Alberta.* Master's thesis, University of Alberta (Edmonton, Alta., Canada), 1968.

752. SCOTT, WILLIAM A. "Comparative Validities of Forced-Choice and Single-Stimulus Tests." *Psychol B* 70:231-44 O '68. * (*PA* 43:117)

753. TAGIURI, RENATO, AND BARNETT, ROSALIND. "Perception of Values and Self-Presentation." Abstract. *Proc 76th Ann Conv Am Psychol Assn* 3:419-20 '68. * (*PA* 43:829, title only)

754. APOSTAL, ROBERT A. "Clinical Observations of High Aesthetic Counselees." *Col Ed Rec Univ N Dak* 55(1):11-3 O '69. *

755. DIXIT, RAMESH C., AND SHARMA, DEO DUTT. "Incorporation by Students of Teachers' Values: A Study of the Student-Teacher Relationship." *Indian Ed R* 4(2):89-96 Jl '69. *

Study of Values

756. HEATH, DOUGLAS H. "Secularization and Maturity of Religious Beliefs." *J Relig & Health* 8(4):335–58 O '69. * (*PA* 44:14436)

757. HOGAN, ROBERT A. "Academic Excellence and Its Philosophical Motivation." *Ill State Univ J* 31(4):25–30 Ap '69. *

758. BENDER, HENRY ELIAS. *Emotional Components of Value Orientations: A Study of Relationships Between Emotion Dimensions and Value Orientations as a Function of Maladjustment.* Doctor's thesis, New York University (New York, N.Y.), 1970. (*DAI* 31:6888B)

759. BENSON, WAYNE WALTON. *A Study of Personal-Professional Factor Constellations as Revealed by the Administrative Decisions of Secondary School Principals.* Doctor's thesis, University of Wisconsin (Madison, Wis.), 1970. (*DAI* 31:5058A)

760. BOOTHROYD, GREGORY WILLIAM. *An Exploratory Investigation Into Some Characteristics Associated With High and Low Ranked Resident Advisors.* Doctor's thesis, University of Michigan (Ann Arbor, Mich.), 1970. (*DAI* 31:3866A)

761. BROOKE, MARINEZ LAYFIELD. *An Investigation of Differences in Attitudes and Values Between Freshmen and Sophomore Women at the University of Alabama.* Doctor's thesis, University of Alabama (University, Ala.), 1970. (*DAI* 31:5117A)

762. BROOKS, FRED ORVILLE. *Effect of Personal Values and Open-Closed Mindedness on Student Teacher Anxiety.* Doctor's thesis, University of North Dakota (Grand Forks, N.D.), 1970. (*DAI* 31:6447A)

763. CATELLIER, ELAINE. *Nurses' Dominant Value-Profiles and Identification of Priority Patient Needs.* Doctor's thesis, University of California (Berkeley, Calif.), 1970. (*DAI* 32:1040B)

764. CHEN, SHIUM ANDREW. *The Differences and Relationships Between Amount of Psychology Courses and Certain Cognitive and Affective Behavior Patterns.* Doctor's thesis, University of Pittsburgh (Pittsburgh, Pa.), 1970. (*DAI* 31:3948A)

765. DIXIT, RAMESH C., AND SHARMA, DEO DUTTA. "Transformation of Social and Religious Values of Different Castes." *Psychologia* (Japan) 13(2–3):117–9 S '70. * (*PA* 46:10669)

766. ERICKSON, DOUGLAS EUGENE. *Differential Personality, Academic, and Biographical Characteristics of International Graduate Students at the University of North Dakota.* Doctor's thesis, University of North Dakota (Grand Forks, N.D.), 1970. (*DAI* 32:6756A)

767. FRIEMAN, BARRY B. *A Comparison of the Values of Prospective Teachers in Early Childhood Education With the Values of a Criterion Group of Exemplary Teachers of Afro-American Urban Poverty Children.* Doctor's thesis, University of Maryland (College Park, Md.), 1970. (*DAI* 31:5903A)

768. HARRIS, JODY MERRITT. *An Investigation of the Applicability of the Allport, Vernon, and Lindzey Revised Study of Values Scale for Identifying and Selecting Teachers to Staff the Inner-City School, Grades 7 and 8.* Doctor's thesis, Pennsylvania State University (University Park, Pa.), 1970. (*DAI* 31:4598A)

769. HEIM, ALICE. *Intelligence and Personality: Their Assessment and Relationship,* pp. 92–6. Harmondsworth, Middlesex, England: Penguin Books Ltd., 1970. Pp. 206. * (*PA* 48:936, title only)

770. KANGAS, BARBARA BROWNELL. *An Experimental Manipulation of Expressed Values.* Doctor's thesis, Washington State University (Pullman, Wash.), 1970. (*DAI* 31:4997B)

771. KHAN, ABDUL RASHID. *Relationship Between the Personal Values of Teachers and Their Pupils.* Doctor's thesis, Purdue University (Lafayette, Ind.), 1970. (*DAI* 31:3819A)

772. KNOX, JAMES BERNARD. *Characteristics of Teachers of Institutionalized Delinquent Youth.* Doctor's thesis, Ohio State University (Columbus, Ohio), 1970. (*DAI* 32:286A)

773. LeUNES, ARNOLD, AND CHRISTENSEN, LARRY. "Reliability and Inmate Test Results." *Correct Psychologist* 4(3):85–93 N–D '70. * (*PA* 49:2670)

774. LINDEMAN, ROBERT PAUL. *A Study of Selected Non-Intellectual Variables Among Classes of Students in a College of Engineering.* Doctor's thesis, Oklahoma State University (Stillwater, Okla.), 1970. (*DAI* 31:5852A)

775. LUCERO, DONALD LAURO. *An Analysis of the Relationship of Values and Needs to Counselor Effectiveness in a Selected Group of Counselors in Training.* Doctor's thesis, University of New Mexico (Albuquerque, N.M.), 1970. (*DAI* 31:6346A)

776. LYSAUGHT, JEROME P., AND PIERLEONI, ROBERT G. "Predicting Individual Success in Programing Self-Instructional Materials." *AV Commun R* 18(1):5–24 sp '70. * (*PA* 44:13334)

777. McDANIEL, SYLVIA PARNELL. *The Effects of Selected Teacher Personality Variables on Reading Readiness, Self-Concept, and Changes in IQ in Culturally Deprived Five-Year-Olds.* Doctor's thesis, University of Alabama (University, Ala.), 1970. (*DAI* 31:6409A)

778. NELSON, EMOGENE ANITA. *Value Patterns of Physical Educators in Colleges and Universities of the United States.* Doctor's thesis, University of Minnesota (Minneapolis, Minn.), 1970. (*DAI* 31:5182A)

779. NYBLADE, ORVILLE WESLEY. *Factors Related to Persistence in the Protestant Missionary Vocation in Sub-Saharan Africa: 1961–1967.* Doctor's thesis, University of Pittsburgh (Pittsburgh, Pa.), 1970. (*DAI* 31:6426A)

780. OHIKHENA, TITUS OFUOVO. *Values and Perception of Educational Objectives as Factors in Preferential Behaviour.* Doctor's thesis, University of Toronto (Toronto, Ont., Canada), 1970. (*DAI* 32:5512A)

781. OLIVER, GEORGE MICHAEL. *Organizational Climate and the Personal Values of Managers: An Exploratory Field Study.* Doctor's thesis, Rensselaer Polytechnic Institute (Troy, N.Y.), 1970. (*DAI* 31:3716A)

782. PATRYLOW, SARAH SNYDER. *The Relation of the Dominant Values of Senior Associate Degree Nursing Students to Their Attitudes Toward Caring for the Dying.* Doctor's thesis, New York University (New York, N.Y.), 1970. (*DAI* 31:7390B)

783. PEARL, HARVEY. *Comparison of the Personal Values and Worker Assessments of Work Evaluators in Rehabilitation and Industrial Work Settings.* Doctor's thesis, Syracuse University (Syracuse, N.Y.), 1970. (*DAI* 31:6349A)

784. PITTS, GRIFF D. *Values, Attitudes, Opinions, and Concerns of Subcultures of Concerned Students in an Urban Commuter College.* Doctor's thesis, Northwestern University (Evanston, Ill.), 1970. (*DAI* 31:5152A)

785. STATMAN, JAMES MARVIN. *The Role of Value-Orientations in the Resolution of Moral Dilemmas.* Doctor's thesis, Yeshiva University (New York, N.Y.), 1970. (*DAI* 31:4889A)

786. TOM, VICTOR R. *The Role of Personality and Organizational Images in the Recruiting Process.* Doctor's thesis, University of California (Berkeley, Calif.), 1970. (*DAI* 31:7662B)

787. UTZ, VERNON RAY. *The Relation of Certain Personality, Value, and Interest Factors to a Choice of Elementary or Secondary Teaching Levels Among Women at the University of Oregon.* Doctor's thesis, University of Oregon (Eugene, Ore.), 1970. (*DAI* 31:5140A)

788. WILLIAMS, CONSTANCE MARIE DiSIPIO. *Personality Factors, Value Patterns, and Occupational Choices of Male Graduate Students.* Doctor's thesis, University of North Dakota (Grand Forks, N.D.), 1970. (*DAI* 31:6357A)

789. ZALEZNIK, ABRAHAM; DALTON, GENE W.; AND BARNES, LOUIS B.; WITH PIERRE LAURIN. *Orientation and Conflict in Career.* Boston, Mass.: Division of Research, Harvard University, Graduate School of Business Administration, 1970. Pp. xxiii, 508. *

790. ADCOCK, C. J., AND WEBBERLEY, M. "Primary Mental Abilities." *J General Psychol* 84(2):229–43 Ap '71. * (*PA* 46:4979)

791. BARRO, ARLENE RING. *A Comparison of Two Approaches to Identifying Creativity in Graduate Student Writers.* Doctor's thesis, University of California (Los Angeles, Calif.), 1971. (*DAI* 32:809A)

792. BHATNAGAR, JOTI K. "A Cross-Cultural Study of Values." *Psychol Studies* (India) 16(1):22–8 Ja '71. *

793. BIGLIN, RONALD JOSEPH. *A Comparison of Opinions About Performance Appraisal Among Faculty and Administrators in Institutions of Higher Education in Baltimore, Maryland.* Doctor's thesis, George Washington University (Washington, D.C.), 1971. (*DAI* 32:6605A)

794. COLBERT, AUSTIN MICHAEL. *A Study of Values of Educators in Oregon's Correctional Institutions.* Doctor's thesis, Oregon State University (Corvallis, Ore.), 1971. (*DAI* 32:1741A)

795. CROMPTON, T. E. "Teachers' Attitudes to Educational Controversies." *Ed Res* (England) 13(3):204–9 Je '71. * (*PA* 49:11872)

796. DAVIS, WALTER NEWTON. *Authoritarianism and Selected Trait Patterns of School Administrators: Seventeen Case Studies.* Doctor's thesis, North Texas State University (Denton, Tex.), 1971. (*DAI* 32:1777A)

797. ENTWISTLE, N. J., AND BRENNAN, T. "The Academic Performance of Students: 2, Types of Successful Students." *Brit J Ed Psychol* 41(3):268–76 N '71. * (*PA* 47:11759)

798. GAERTNER, SAMUEL L., AND SEIDENBERG, BERNARD. "Familiarity and Value Effects Upon Stereoscopic Word Recognition." *Percept & Motor Skills* 32(3):703–8 Je '71. * (*PA* 47:1993)

799. GALLOP, ROY. "Value Patterns, Personality, and Social Attitudes of Foundation Students at Bournemouth College of Art." *Voc Aspect Ed* (England) 23(54):29–37 Ap '71. *

800. GARBER, JOYCE AUDREY. *The Relationship Between Power Motivation and Some Experimental Variables in a Gambling Situation.* Doctor's thesis, New York University (New York, N.Y.), 1971. (*DAI* 32:1822B)

801. GELLER, E. SCOTT; WHITMAN, CHARLES P.; AND BEAMON, WILLIAM S. "Effects of Expressed and Measured Value Preference on Decision Speed." *Psychon Sci* 24(2):84–6 Jl 25 '71. * (*PA* 48:8367)

802. GILLILAND, STEVE FOSTER. *Some Effects of a Human Relations Laboratory on Moral Orientation.* Doctor's thesis, Boston University (Boston, Mass.), 1971. (*DAI* 32:1828A)

803. GREENFIELD, NORMAN. "A Study of Student Values." *J Psychol* 79(1):85–9 S '71. * (*PA* 47:5578)

804. HALEY, HAROLD B.; JUAN, ISABEL R.; AND PAIVA, ROSALIA E. A. "MCAT Scores in Relation to Personality Measures and Biographical Variables." *J Med Ed* 46(11):947–58 N '71. *

805. HEREDERO, J. M. "Motivation Courses and College Students." *Indian Ed R* 6(2):165–81 Jl '71. *

806. HOOKE, JAMES F., AND KRAUSS, HERBERT H. "Personality Characteristics of Successful Police Sergeant Candidates." *J Crim Law Criminol & Police Sci* 62(1):104–6 Mr '71. * (*PA* 46:11787)

807. HUANG, DAVID DARMING. *An Investigation of Probationary and Non-Probationary Engineering Students' Self Perceived Versus Measured Temperaments, Values and Vocational Preferences.* Doctor's thesis, Purdue University (Lafayette, Ind.), 1971. (*DAI* 32:3030A)

808. HUNDAL, P. S., AND SINGH, MOHINDER. "A Factor Analytical Study of Intellectual and Non-Intellectual Characteristics." *Multiv Behav Res* 6(4):503–14 O '71. * (*PA* 47:11735)

809. JACOBY, JACOB, AND MATELL, MICHAEL S. "Three-Point Likert Scales Are Good Enough." *J Marketing Res* 8(4):495–500 N '71. * (*PA* 48:11405)

810. KAKKAR, S. B. "Value Scores of Teacher Trainees and College Teachers." *Indian J Appl Psychol* 8(2):77–80 Jl '71. *

811. LANDON, ROBERT FULTON. *The Perceived Environments of Selected Church of Christ-Related Senior Colleges, Methodist-Related Senior Colleges, and Similar State Supported Senior Colleges.* Doctor's thesis, George Peabody College for Teachers (Nashville, Tenn.), 1971. (*DAI* 32:3723A)

812. MACFIE, JESSIE LOUISE. *Characteristic Values of Participants of the Georgia Governor's Honors Program and Valued Aspects of the Program as Judged by Participants, With Implications for Program Improvement.* Doctor's thesis, Florida State University (Tallahassee, Fla.), 1971. (*DAI* 32:3124A)

813. MITCHELL, RUSSELL AUSTIN, JR. *The Effect of Group Counseling Experiences in a Didactic Classroom Setting on Selected Personality Variables and Counseling Effectiveness.* Doctor's thesis, North Texas State University (Denton, Tex.), 1971. (*DAI* 32:6765A)

814. MUKHERJEE, SUBHASH CHANDRA. *A Comparative Study of the Parents of Low and High Achieving Students.* Doctor's thesis, Illinois Institute of Technology (Chicago, Ill.), 1971. (*DAI* 32:6624B)

815. MURDOCH, GEORGE WALLACE. *Values and Personal Profiles of Employed and Non-Employed College Students.* Doctor's thesis, George Washington University (Washington, D.C.), 1971. (*DAI* 32:3035A)

816. OZAKI, ROGER HIROSHI. *A Comparative Study of Student Subcultures and Value Systems in Three State-Supported Institutions of Higher Education in Georgia.* Doctor's thesis, University of Georgia (Athens, Ga.), 1971. (*DAI* 32:3699A)

817. PAGE, MARY JEAN. *A Descriptive Analysis of Selected Attitudes, Interests, and Personality Characteristics of Mature College Women.* Doctor's thesis, North Texas State University (Denton, Tex.), 1971. (*DAI* 32:3699A)

818. PAIVA, ROSALIA E. A., AND HALEY, HAROLD B. "Intellectual, Personality, and Environmental Factors in Career Specialty Preferences." *J Med Ed* 46(4):281–9 Ap '71. * (*PA* 46:6947)

819. PLUTCHIK, ROBERT; CONTE, HOPE; AND KANDLER, HENRY. "Variables Related to the Selection of Psychiatric Residents." *Am J Psychiatry* 127(11):1503–8 My '71. * (*PA* 47:4883)

820. PUM, ROBERT JOSEPH. *Differential Characteristics of Art-Teaching Majors and Elementary-Education Majors in College; as Measured by Selected Attitude, Value, and Personality Factors.* Doctor's thesis, Ball State University (Muncie, Ind.), 1971. (*DAI* 32:5659A)

821. RICHARDS, ELIZABETH A., AND HAWTHORNE, RUTH E. "Values, Body Cathexis, and Clothing of Male University Students." *J Home Econ* 63(3):190–4 Mr '71. *

822. RICHMOND, BERT O., AND TISDEL, LINWOOD D. "Existential Frustration of Graduate and Undergraduate Students." *J Hum Relations* 19(4):506–11 f '71. *

823. ROTH, NEIL CHARLES. *An Investigation of the Effects of Cognitive Dissonance Upon the Variables: Basic Values, Vocational Interest, and Vocational Choice.* Doctor's thesis, University of Idaho (Moscow, Idaho), 1971. (*DAI* 32:3039A)

824. RYAN, PAUL MICHAEL. *An Empirical Study of the Relationship of Personal Values, News Content, and Media Credibility Perception.* Doctor's thesis, Southern Illinois University (Carbondale, Ill.), 1971. (*DAI* 32:4549A)

825. SMITH, DONALD LEWIS. *The Relationship of the Six Basic Interests of Personality as Measured by the Allport-Vernon-Lindzey Study of Values and Driving Record of Michigan Civilian Drivers as Determined by Accident Involvement and Traffic Violations.* Doctor's thesis, Michigan State University (East Lansing, Mich.), 1971. (*DAI* 32:3106A)

826. SMITH, NANETTE PATCHELL. *An Analysis of the Relationship of Counselor Characteristics and Behavior Exhibited in Group Experience With Counselor Effectiveness in a Selected Group of Counselor Trainees.* Doctor's thesis, University of New Mexico (Albuquerque, N.M.), 1971. (*DAI* 32:3704A)

827. STAIERT, PAUL JOHN. *Changes of Selected Attitudes, Values, Needs and Personality Traits of Participants in a Fellowship Program for Prospective Teachers of the Disadvantaged.* Doctor's thesis, University of Denver (Denver, Colo.), 1971. (*DAI* 32:3803A)

828. SZABO, CHARLES CARL, JR. *A Comparative Study of the Dominant Value Patterns of Students Majoring in Education.* Doctor's thesis, Ohio State University (Columbus, Ohio), 1971. (*DAI* 32:3706A)

829. TOM, VICTOR R. "The Role of Personality and Organizational Images in the Recruiting Process." *Organiz Behav & Hum Perfor* 6(5):573–92 S '71. * (*PA* 47:9882)

830. TRANG, MYRON LEE. *The Effects of a Small Group Leadership Experience Upon Selected Upper Division Education Students at Washington State University.* Doctor's thesis, Washington State University (Pullman, Wash.), 1971. (*DAI* 32:4386A)

831. UNDERWOOD, HAROLD LEE. *An Evaluation of Certain Aspects of the Auburn University 1970–71 Junior College Leadership Program.* Doctor's thesis, Auburn University (Auburn, Ala.), 1971. (*DAI* 32:3061A)

832. VERMA, I. B. "Sex Differences in the Impact of Training on the Values and Attitudes of Student Teachers." *J Ed Res & Exten* (India) 7(4):233–7 Ap '71. *

833. WALTER, JAMES EDGAR. *Relationships Between Selected Values of Students and Their Perception of a University Instructor.* Doctor's thesis, Purdue University (Lafayette, Ind.), 1971. (*DAI* 32:4387A)

834. WHITTAKER, DAVID. "The Psychological Adjustment of Intellectual, Nonconformist, Collegiate Dropouts." *Adolescence* 6(24):415–24 w '71. * (*PA* 48:7723)

835. WILDMAN, LOUIS ROBERT. *An Investigation of the Relationship Between Student Perceptions of a Collegiate Institutional Environment and the Phenomena of Student Transfer.* Doctor's thesis, University of Washington (Seattle, Wash.), 1971. (*DAI* 32:2448A)

836. WILKINSON, A. EARL; PRADO, WILLIAM M.; WILLIAMS, WOODROW O.; AND SCHNADT, FREDERICK W. "Psychological Test Characteristics and Length of Stay in Alcoholism Treatment." *Q J Studies Alcohol* 32(1A):60–5 Mr '71. * (*PA* 46:7116)

CUMULATIVE NAME INDEX

[1404]

Study of Values: British Edition, 1965. College and adults; 1965; adaptation of *Study of Values: A Scale for Measuring the Dominant Interests in Personality, Third Edition;* 6 scores: theoretical, economic, aesthetic, social, political, religious; original test by Gordon W. Allport, Philip E. Vernon, and Gardner Lindzey; adaptation by Sylvia Richardson; NFER Publishing Co. Ltd. [England]. *

For additional information, see P:259A.

REFERENCES THROUGH 1971

1. MEHRYAR, A. H. "Generality of Social Perception: Some Negative Results." *J Social Psychol* 78(1):91–8 Je '69. * (*PA* 43:15730)
2. KAKKAR, S. B. "Influence of Teacher Training on Student's Values." *Psychologia* (Japan) 13(4):192–202 D '70. * (*PA* 46:11624)
3. MEHRYAR, A. H. "A Cross-Cultural Investigation of Eysenck's Hypothesis Regarding the Relationship Between Personality and Attitudes." *Brit J Social & Clin Psychol* 9(3):216–21 S '70. * (*PA* 45:2237)
4. CROMPTON, T. E. "Teachers' Attitudes to Educational Controversies." *Ed Res* (England) 13(3):204–9 Je '71. * (*PA* 49:11872)

CUMULATIVE NAME INDEX

[1405]

Style of Mind Inventory: Trait, Value and Belief Patterns in Greek, Roman and Hebrew Perspectives. College and adults; 1958–61, c1957–61; SMI; formerly called *Fetler Self-Rating Test;* 3 scores (Greek, Roman, Judeo-Christian) in each of 3 areas (traits, values, beliefs); Daniel Fetler; the Author. *

For additional information, see P:260.

[1406]

★Suinn Test Anxiety Behavior Scale. College and adults; 1971; STABS; Richard M. Suinn; Rocky Mountain Behavioral Science Institute, Inc. *

REFERENCES THROUGH 1971

1. SUINN, RICHARD M. "The STABS, a Measure of Test Anxiety for Behavior Therapy: Normative Data." *Behav Res & Ther* 7(3):335–40 S '69. * (*PA* 44:16707)
2. HALL, ROGER ALLEN. *Desensitization of Test Anxiety.* Doc-

tor's thesis, Colorado State University (Ft. Collins, Colo.), 1970. (*DAI* 31:4338B)
3. WISOCKI, PATRICIA ANNE. *An Application of Covert Reinforcement for the Treatment of Test Anxiety.* Doctor's thesis, Boston College (Chestnut Hill, Mass.), 1971. (*DAI* 32:1229B)

CUMULATIVE NAME INDEX

[1407]

Survey of Interpersonal Values. Grades 9–16 and adults; 1960–63; SIV; 6 scores: support, conformity, recognition, independence, benevolence, leadership; Leonard V. Gordon; Science Research Associates, Inc. *

For additional information, see P:261 (48 references); for reviews by Lee J. Cronbach, Leonard D. Goodstein, and John K. Hemphill and an excerpted review by Laurence Siegel, see 6:184 (12 references).

REFERENCES THROUGH 1971

1–12. See 6:184.
13–60. See P:261.
61. SNELBECKER, GLENN EUGENE. *Factors Influencing College Students' Person-Perceptions of Psychotherapists in a Laboratory Analog.* Doctor's thesis, Cornell University (Ithaca, N.Y.), 1961. (*DA* 22:3928)
62. DOLLAR, ROBERT JOSEPH. *A Study of Certain Psychosocial Differences Among Dormitory, Fraternity, and Off-Campus Freshman Men at Oklahoma State University.* Doctor's thesis, Oklahoma State University (Stillwater, Okla.), 1963. (*DA* 25:961)
63. LITZINGER, WILLIAM DAVID. *Entrepreneurial Prototype in Bank Management: A Comparative Study of Branch Bank Managers.* Doctor's thesis, University of Southern California (Los Angeles, Calif.), 1963. (*DA* 24:127)
64. SWEARINGEN, ARMELDA HARRIS. *Correlates of Non-Conforming Behavior of Domiciled Veterans.* Doctor's thesis, Ohio State University (Columbus, Ohio), 1963. (*DA* 24:4808)
65. FELTY, JOHN ERNEST. *Attitudes Toward Physical Disability in Costa Rica and Their Determinants: A Pilot Study.* Doctor's thesis, Michigan State University (East Lansing, Mich.), 1965. (*DA* 26:4442)
66. GORDON, LEONARD V., AND MEDLAND, FRANCIS F. "Values Associated With Intentions of Cuban Refugees to Remain in the U.S. Army." *Psychol Rep* 17:15–8 Ag '65. * (*PA* 40:1502)
67. HARARI, HERBERT. *An Experimental Evaluation of Heider's Balance Theory With Respect to Situational and Predispositional Factors.* Doctor's thesis, University of Miami (Coral Gables, Fla.), 1965. (*DA* 26:1183)
68. LITZINGER, WILLIAM D. "Interpersonal Values and Leadership Attitudes of Branch Bank Managers." *Personnel Psychol* 18:193–8 su '65. * (*PA* 39:16587)
69. McFADDEN, JACK DONALD. *The Relationship of Values, Attitude and Personality Characteristics of Student Teachers to Ratings by Their Supervisors.* Doctor's thesis, Northwestern University (Evanston, Ill.), 1965. (*DA* 26:7169)
70. ASHBURN, FRANKLIN GLENDON. *A Study of Differential Role Expectations of Police Patrolmen in the Manila Police Department, Republic of the Philippines.* Doctor's thesis, Florida State University (Tallahassee, Fla.), 1966. (*DA* 27:2611A)
71. BARE, CAROLE E. "Counselor Sensitivity to the Counselor-Client Communication Process." Abstract. *Proc 74th Ann Conv Am Psychol Assn* 1:301–2 '66.* (*PA* 41:6145)
72. FRIESEN, EUGENE WESLEY. *Nature and Determinants of Attitudes Toward Education and Toward Physically Disabled Persons in Colombia, Peru, and the United States.* Doctor's thesis, Michigan State University (East Lansing, Mich.), 1966. (*DA* 27:1655A)
73. NEEDHAM, WALTER EVANS. *Intellectual, Personality and Biographical Characteristics of Southern Negro and White College Students.* Doctor's thesis, University of Utah (Salt Lake City, Utah), 1966. (*DA* 27:1609B)
74. TARWATER, JESSE W. "Chinese and American Students' Interpersonal Values: A Cross-Cultural Comparison." *J Col Stud Personnel* 7:351–4 N '66. *
75. CESSNA, WILLIAM CONRAD, JR. *The Psychosocial Nature and Determinants of Attitudes Toward Education and Toward Physically Disabled Persons in Japan.* Doctor's thesis, Michigan State University (East Lansing, Mich.), 1967. (*DA* 28:1674A)
76. DEAN, JOHN TEMPLE. *An Analysis of Attitudes Toward Education, Theological Orientations, Interpersonal Values, and Educational Experience.* Doctor's thesis, Michigan State University (East Lansing, Mich.), 1967. (*DA* 28:1701A)
77. DICKIE, ROBERT FRANCIS. *An Investigation of Differential Attitudes Toward the Physically Handicapped, Blind Persons, and Attitudes Toward Education and Their Determinants Among Various Occupational Groups in Kansas.* Doctor's thesis, Michigan State University (East Lansing, Mich.), 1967. (*DA* 28:1702A)

78. GREEN, JAMES HARLEN. *Attitudes of Special Educators Versus Regular Teachers Toward the Physically Handicapped and Toward Education in Michigan.* Doctor's thesis, Michigan State University (East Lansing, Mich.), 1967. (*DA* 28:4872A)

79. LASSON, MORRIS S. *Personality Aspects of Secondary School Guidance Counselors.* Doctor's thesis, Catholic University of America (Washington, D.C.), 1967. (*DA* 28:2072A)

80. MADER, JOHN BUCKINGHAM. *Attitudes of Special Educators Toward the Physically Handicapped and Toward Education.* Doctor's thesis, Michigan State University (East Lansing, Mich.), 1967. (*DA* 28:1624A)

81. PANG, HENRY, AND FROST, LINDA. "Relatedness of Creativity, Values, and ESP." *Percept & Motor Skills* 24:650 Ap '67. * (*PA* 41:9549)

82. ROHDE, ROBERT HENRY. *The Relationship of Values, Biographical Data, and Product Use to Perceptions of Advertising Offensiveness.* Doctor's thesis, Purdue University (Lafayette, Ind.), 1967. (*DA* 28:1251B)

83. WHITE, HAZEL WILMA. *A Descriptive Analysis of a Group of AFDC (Aid to Families With Dependent Children) Recipients.* Doctor's thesis, University of New Mexico (Albuquerque, N.M.), 1967. (*DA* 28:3472A)

84. GORDON, LEONARD V., AND HOFMANN, RICHARD J. "The Forced-Choice Test as a Structured Q-Sort." *Ed & Psychol Meas* 28:1103–10 w '68. * (*PA* 44:5881)

85. JORDAN, JOHN E., AND FRIESEN, EUGENE W. "Attitudes of Rehabilitation Personnel Toward Physically Disabled Persons in Colombia, Peru, and the United States." *J Social Psychol* 74:151–61 Ap '68. * (*PA* 42:10471)

86. KERPELMAN, LARRY C. "Student Activism, Ideology, and Personality." Abstract. *Proc 76th Ann Conv Am Psychol Assn* 3:377–8 '68. * (*PA* 43:895, title only)

87. McCLAINE, RICHARD EARL. *Factors in Executive Promotion and Demotion: An Empirical Study.* Doctor's thesis, Ohio State University (Columbus, Ohio), 1968. (*DA* 29:1326A)

88. RIM, Y., AND COHEN, N. "Personality Variables in Making a Choice." *Psychologia* (Japan) 11:191–7 D '68. * (*PA* 44:6053)

89. TAYLOR, GEORGE JOSIAH. *An Analysis of Teacher's Attitudes Toward Education in Costa Rica.* Doctor's thesis, Michigan State University (East Lansing, Mich.), 1968. (*DAI* 30:1408A)

90. BACHTOLD, LOUISE M. "Changes in Interpersonal Values of Gifted Adolescents." *Psychol Sch* 6(3):303–6 Jl '69. * (*PA* 44:4157)

91. FINCH, CURTIS R. "The Trade and Industrial Education Teacher's Background, Values, and Attitude Toward Teaching." *J Indus Teach Ed* 6(2):55–64 w '69. *

92. GORDON, LEONARD V. "Q-Typing: An Exploration in Personality Measurement." *J Social Psychol* 78(1):121–36 Je '69. * (*PA* 43:15822)

93. KERPELMAN, LARRY C. "Student Political Activism and Ideology: Comparative Characteristics of Activists and Nonactivists." *J Counsel Psychol* 16(1):8–13 Ja '69. * (*PA* 43:5868)

94. McCULLAH, ROBERT DOUGLAS. *Prediction of Academic Performance in the U.S. Navy Hospital Corps School Vocational Training Programs.* Doctor's thesis, University of Maryland (College Park, Md.), 1969. (*DAI* 30:5677B)

95. MEEKER, DAVID LEWIS. *Measuring Attitude and Value Changes in Selected Humanities and Human Relations Programs.* Doctor's thesis, Kent State University (Kent, Ohio), 1969. (*DAI* 30:5292A)

96. RAVENSBORG, MILTON R. "Psychiatric Technicians' Ranking of Five Potential Employment Screening Tests." *Personnel J* 48(1):39–41 Ja '69. * (*PA* 44:2910)

97. SHERMAN, CHARLES EVANS. *Differences in the Personal and Interpersonal Values of Negro and White College Freshmen.* Doctor's thesis, Northern Illinois University (DeKalb, Ill.), 1969. (*DAI* 30:3800A)

98. STEIN, SANDRA LOU. *The Interrelationships Among Self-Esteem, Personal Values, and Interpersonal Values.* Doctor's thesis, Northern Illinois University (DeKalb, Ill.), 1969. (*DAI* 30:3803A)

99. WHIGHAM, BARNEY R., AND MATTSON, BRUCE D. "Attitudes Influencing Employment of the Handicapped." *J Employ Counsel* 6(2):72–8 Je '69. * (*PA* 47:3441)

100. ZIMMERMAN, SAUNDRA F.; PEDERSEN, DARHL M.; AND SMITH, KAY H. "The Factorial Determination of Types of Conforming Individuals." *J Psychol* 72(1):101–7 My '69. * (*PA* 43:15688)

101. BELLUCCI, JOSEPH T. *The Contribution of Values in Predicting Success in Practical Nursing Training Programs.* Doctor's thesis, Lehigh University (Bethlehem, Pa.), 1970. (*DAI* 31:2731A)

102. CARLETON, FREDERICK O. "Relationships Between Follow-Up Evaluations and Information Developed in a Management Assessment Center." Abstract. *Proc 78th Ann Conv Am Psychol Assn* 5(2):565–6 '70. * (*PA* 44:19655)

103. DE MARTINO, ALICE J. *The Relations Among Adaptive Regression, Independence, and Creativity in Adolescents.* Doctor's thesis, New York University (New York, N.Y.), 1970. (*DAI* 32:539B)

104. DODD, WILLIAM E. "Will Management Assessment Centers Insure Selection of the Same Old Types?" Abstract. *Proc 78th Ann Conv Am Psychol Assn* 5(2):569–70 '70. * (*PA* 44:19658)

105. DOLLAR, ROBERT J. "Interpersonal Values and College Persistence." *J Col Stud Personnel* 11(3):200–2 My '70. *

106. FENNELL, NANCY WILMINK, AND KENTON, ROBERT WILLIAM. *Some Effects on Personality of a Basic Encounter Group in a Community College Class.* Doctor's thesis, United States International University (San Diego, Calif.), 1970. (*DAI* 31:2493A)

107. FLOCKEN, JOYCE MARY. *An Analysis of Selected Presage Criteria of Reciprocal Student and Teacher Ratings in Beginning College Speech Classes.* Doctor's thesis, University of Southern California (Los Angeles, Calif.), 1970. (*DAI* 31:6196A)

108. GORDON, LEONARD V., AND KIKUCHI, AKIO. "The Comparability of the Forced-Choice and Q-Sort Measurement Approaches: An Other-Cultural Study." *J Social Psychol* 81(2):137–44 Ag '70. * (*PA* 44:20760)

109. HORNADAY, JOHN A., AND BUNKER, CHARLES S. "The Nature of the Entrepreneur." *Personnel Psychol* 23(1):47–54 sp '70. * (*PA* 44:17555)

110. JOHNSON, CARL I. *A Descriptive Study of the Relationship of Certain Critical Values and Motivational Achievement of Self-Concept in Reticent and Non-Reticent Speakers.* Doctor's thesis, University of Denver (Denver, Colo.), 1970. (*DAI* 31:6757A)

111. JUAN, ISABEL R., AND HALEY, HAROLD B. "High and Low Levels of Dogmatism in Relation to Personality, Intellectual, and Environmental Characteristics of Medical Students." *Psychol Rep* 26(2):535–44 Ap '70. * (*PA* 44:20939)

112. KAKKAR, S. B. "Teacher Attitude Change and Value Structure." *Manas* (India) 17(2):103–9 N '70. * (*PA* 47:9784)

113. KIKUCHI, AKIO, AND GORDON, LEONARD V. "Japanese and American Personal Values: Some Cross-Cultural Findings." *Int J Psychol* 5(3):183–7 '70. * (*PA* 46:4774)

114. KIRCHNER, ELIZABETH P. "Values and Value Changes During and After Graduate Study in Psychology." *J Clin Psychol* 26(2):252–6 Ap '70. * (*PA* 44:13586)

115. KNIGHT, JAMES HENRY. *The Interpersonal Values and Aspiration Levels of Negro Seniors in Totally Integrated and Segregated Southern High Schools.* Doctor's thesis, University of North Carolina (Chapel Hill, N.C.), 1970. (*DAI* 31:2110A)

116. MENSH, IVAN N. "Orientation of Social Values in Medical Student Assessment." *Social Sci & Med* (England) 3(3):339–48 Ja '70. *

117. STARKS, WALTER LIVINGSTON. *The Relationship of Residence and Economic Factors to the First Semester Academic Achievement of College of Business Administration and College of Agriculture 1969 Freshmen, Male Students.* Doctor's thesis, Oklahoma State University (Stillwater, Okla.), 1970. (*DAI* 31:5805A)

118. THOMMES, MARTIN JOHN. *Changes in Values, Perceptions, and Academic Performance of College Freshmen Underachievers in a Remedial Program.* Doctor's thesis, United States International University (San Diego, Calif.), 1970. (*DAI* 31:2969B)

119. ZIMMERMAN, SAUNDRA F.; SMITH, KAY H.; AND PEDERSEN, DARHL M. "The Effect of Anticonformity Appeals on Conformity Behavior." *J Social Psychol* 81(1):93–103 Je '70. * (*PA* 44:18593)

120. ABRAHAM, CAROL. *The Relationship of Authoritarianism to Independence and Creativity Among College Students.* Doctor's thesis, New York University (New York, N.Y.), 1971. (*DAI* 32:6023B)

121. BREAKSTONE, JACK. *Interpersonal Values of Personnel in Children's Institutions.* Doctor's thesis, Temple University (Philadelphia, Pa.), 1971. (*DAI* 32:733A)

122. DUKE, BILLY WAYNE. *A Study of Certain Socio-Psychological Differences Among Migratory and Nonmigratory Single Sophomores at the University of Missouri-Columbia.* Doctor's thesis, University of Missouri (Columbia, Mo.), 1971. (*DAI* 32:1268A)

123. GABLE, ROBERT KEITH. *A Multivariate Study of Work Value Orientations.* Doctor's thesis, State University of New York (Albany, N.Y.), 1971. (*DAI* 32:1997A)

124. GOODEY, DARWIN JOSEPH. *A Study of Interpersonal Values of Indian Adolescents.* Doctor's thesis, University of Oregon (Eugene, Ore.), 1971. (*DAI* 32:6128A)

125. GORDON, LEONARD V. "Are There Two Extremeness Response Sets?" *Ed & Psychol Meas* 31(4):867–73 w '71. * (*PA* 48:1005)

126. HAVENS, JANET M. *Relationship Between Some Intellective and Nonintellective Factors of Disadvantaged High Risk Students and Their Success in College.* Doctor's thesis, Rutgers —The State University (New Brunswick, N.J.), 1971. (*DAI* 32:6201A)

127. HELWEG, GREGORY CHARLES. *The Relationships Between Selected Personality Characteristics and Perceptions of Directive and Nondirective Psychotherapeutic Approaches.* Doctor's thesis, University of Maryland (College Park, Md.), 1971. (*DAI* 32:2396B)

128. HORNADAY, JOHN A., AND ABOUD, JOHN. "Characteristics of Successful Entrepreneurs." *Personnel Psychol* 24(2):141–53 su '71. * (*PA* 49:3400)

129. JACKSON, ARTHUR MELLS. *The Effects of Three Group Approaches in Effecting Change Among Black Students.* Doctor's thesis, Indiana University (Bloomington, Ind.), 1971. (*DAI* 32:4351A)

130. KEDZUF, MARY ANN. *Self-Esteem, Personal and Interpersonal Values of Nursing Students in Diploma, Associate Degree, and Baccalaureate Programs.* Doctor's thesis, Northern Illinois University (DeKalb, Ill.), 1971. (*DAI* 32:4030B)

131. KORNFELD-JACOBS, GILA. *A Study of Dimensions of Personality and Occupational Function.* Doctor's thesis, State University of New York (Buffalo, N.Y.), 1971. (*DAI* 32:1274A)

132. MEEKER, DAVID L. "Measuring Attitude and Value Changes in Selected Humanities and Human Relations Programs." *J Res Music Ed* 19(4):467–73 w '71. * (*PA* 48:5860)

133. PAIVA, ROSALIA E. A., AND HALEY, HAROLD B. "Intellectual, Personality, and Environmental Factors in Career Specialty Preferences." *J Med Ed* 46(4):281–9 Ap '71. * (*PA* 46:6947)

134. REED, JOSEPH C. *A Comparison of Measured Self Concept of Kansas High School Graduates Who Begin Their Higher Education in Kansas Junior Colleges and Those Who Begin in Kansas Four-Year Colleges.* Doctor's thesis, University of Wyoming (Laramie, Wyo.), 1971. (*DAI* 33:976A)

135. SCHUBERT, PAUL WILLIAM. *Personality Type and Self-Perceived Change Resulting From Sensitivity Group Experience.* Doctor's thesis, Purdue University (Lafayette, Ind.), 1971. (*DAI* 32:4360A)

136. SHERMAN, CHARLES E. "An Investigation of the Interpersonal Values of Negro and White Junior College Students." *J Negro Ed* 40(4):356–60 f '71. * (*PA* 48:7037)

137. STEIN, SANDRA LOU. "The Interrelationships Among Self-Esteem, Personal Values, and Interpersonal Values." *J Ed Res* 64(10):448–50 Jl–Ag '71. * (*PA* 47:8682)

138. WIERSTEINER, S. R. "Perception of Vocational Teaching as Held by Two Groups of Two-Year Community College Students." *J Indus Teach Ed* 8(4):41–7 su '71. *

CUMULATIVE NAME INDEX

[1408]

Survey of Personal Attitude "SPA" (With Pictures): Individual Placement Series. Adults; 1960–66; SPA; 3 scores: social attitude, personal frankness, aggressiveness; J. H. Norman; Personnel Research Associates, Inc. *

For additional information and reviews by Harold Borko and Wayne S. Zimmerman, see 7:147.

[1409]

Survey of Personal Values. Grades 11–16 and adults; 1964–67; SPV; 6 scores: practical mindedness, achievement, variety, decisiveness, orderliness, goal orientation; Leonard V. Gordon; Science Research Associates, Inc. *

For additional information and a review by Gene V Glass, see 7:148 (6 references); see also P:263 (3 references).

REFERENCES THROUGH 1971

1–3. See P:263.
4–9. See 7:148.
10. FLOCKEN, JOYCE MARY. *An Analysis of Selected Presage Criteria of Reciprocal Student and Teacher Ratings in Beginning College Speech Classes.* Doctor's thesis, University of Southern California (Los Angeles, Calif.), 1970. (*DAI* 31:6196A)
11. GORDON, LEONARD V. "Are There Two Extremeness Response Sets?" *Ed & Psychol Meas* 31(4):867–73 w '71. * (*PA* 48:1005)
12. KEDZUF, MARY ANN. *Self-Esteem, Personal and Interpersonal Values of Nursing Students in Diploma, Associate Degree, and Baccalaureate Programs.* Doctor's thesis, Northern Illinois University (DeKalb, Ill.), 1971. (*DAI* 32:4030B)
13. KORNFELD-JACOBS, GILA. *A Study of Dimensions of Personality and Occupational Function.* Doctor's thesis, State University of New York (Buffalo, N.Y.), 1971. (*DAI* 32:1274A)
14. STEIN, SANDRA LOU. "The Interrelationships Among Self-Esteem, Personal Values, and Interpersonal Values." *J Ed Res* 64(10):448–50 Jl–Ag '71. * (*PA* 47:8682)

CUMULATIVE NAME INDEX

[1410]

Symptom Sign Inventory: Personality and Personal Illness Questionnaires. Mental patients; 1968; 2 editions; G. A. Foulds and K. Hope (manual); University of London Press Ltd. [England]. *

a) [REGULAR EDITION.] SSI; differential diagnosis among 8 categories (anxiety state, neurotic depression, hysteria, obsessional state, non-paranoid schizophrenia, paranoid schizophrenia, mania, psychotic depression) and 2 scales (personal disturbance, psychotic vs. neurotic).

b) SHORT VERSION. SSI/PD; consists of the 20 items of the personal disturbance scale of regular edition; may be used as a screening device.

For additional information, reviews by H. J. Eysenck and Maurice Lorr, and an excerpted review by D. J. Small, see 7:149 (31 references).

REFERENCES THROUGH 1971

1–31. See 7:149.
32. VINODA, K. S. "A Comparative Study of the Personality Characteristics of Attempted Suicides, Psychiatric Patients and

Normals." *Trans All-India Inst Mental Health* 5:67–74 D '65. * (*PA* 40:7860)

33. FOULDS, G. A. " 'Psychic:somatic' Symptoms and Hostility." *Brit J Social & Clin Psychol* 5:185–9 S '66. * (*PA* 40:13224)

34. VINODA, K. S. "Personality Characteristics of Attempted Suicides." *Brit J Psychiatry* 112:1143–50 N '66. * (*PA* 41:4769)

35. MURTHY, VINODA NARAYANA. "Punitiveness and Personal Disturbance." *Trans All-India Inst Mental Health* 7:62–8 D '67. *

36. KUMARIAH, V., AND MURTHY, NARAYANA. "Speed Accuracy Factors in Relation to Personality and Diagnosis." *Trans All-India Inst Mental Health* 8:35–41 D '68. * (*PA* 43:11379)

37. WARDER, JOHN. "Two Studies of Violent Offenders." *Brit J Criminol* 9(4):389–93 O '69. * (*PA* 44:8811)

38. ANUMONYE, AMECHI. "Personality Factors and Barbiturate Dependence." *Brit J Addict* 64(3–4):365–70 Ja '70. *

39. FOULDS, G. A. "The Personal Illness Continuum." *Brit J Social & Clin Psychol* 10(4):387 D '71. * (*PA* 48:1200)

40. FOULDS, G. A. "Personality Deviance and Personal Symptomatology." *Psychol Med* (England) 1(3):222–33 My '71. * (*PA* 47:11125)

41. GREGSON, R. A. M., AND GORDON, A. V. "A Comment on Foulds on Continua." *Brit J Social & Clin Psychol* 10(4):388 D '71. * (*PA* 48:1200)

42. MAYO, P. R.; WALTON, H. J.; AND LITTMANN, S. K. "Relevance of Repression-Sensitization to Neurotic Patients in Milieu Treatment." *Psychol Rep* 28(3):794 Je '71. * (*PA* 46:11221)

43. ROSS, CHRISTOPHER F. J. "Comparison of Hospital and Prison Alcoholics." *Brit J Psychiatry* 118(542):75–8 Ja '71. * (*PA* 46:11135)

CUMULATIVE NAME INDEX

Adams, A.: 1, 3, 8, 10	McCulloch, J. W.: 14, 16, 29
Anumonye, A.: 38	McPherson, F. M.: 19, 22
Caine, T. M.: 10, 17, 25	Mayo, P. R.: 12–3, 19, 23, 42
Eysenck, H. J.: rev, 7:149	Murthy, N.: 36
Foulds, G. A.: 1–12, 15, 18–9, 31, 33, 39–40	Murthy, V. N.: 24, 35
Giel, R.: 26	Owen, A.: 4, 6, 9–10
Gordon, A. V.: 27, 41	Philip, A. E.: 14, 16, 28–9
Gregson, R. A. M.: 27, 41	Presly, A. S.: 31
Hall-Smith, P.: 20	Ross, C. F. J.: 43
Hope, K.: 18–9	Ryle, A.: 20
Kear-Colwell, J. J.: 21	Smail, D. J.: 17, 30; exc, 7: 149
Kumariah, V.: 36	Vinoda, K. S.: 32, 34
Littmann, S. K.: 31, 42	Walton, H. J.: 31, 42
Lorr, M.: rev, 7:149	Warder, J.: 37

[1411]

Systematic Interview Guides. Mothers; 1967; SIG; for gathering information from mothers about the early development of their children; 2 guides; D. H. Stott; University of London Press Ltd. [England]. *

a) NO. 1—BIRTH TO 5 YEARS. 9 scores: physical abnormality, behavior disturbance, birth complication, condition at birth, epidemic illness, functional impairment, adverse health conditions, retardation in development, trauma.

b) NO. 2—PRENATAL. 8 scores: adverse health conditions, mental stress, nervous condition, reproductive abnormality, smoking habits, trauma, unwanted pregnancy, working conditions.

For additional information and an excerpted review by Michael Rutter, see 7:150.

[1412]

★T.M.R. Performance Profile for the Severely and Moderately Retarded. Ages 4 and over; 1963–67; 7 scores: social behavior, self-care, communication, basic knowledge, practical skills, body usage, total; Alfred J. DiNola, Bernard P. Kaminsky, and Allan E. Sternfeld; Educational Performance Associates, Inc. *

REFERENCES THROUGH 1971

1. SELLIN, DONALD F. "The Usefulness of the IQ in Predicting the Performance of Moderately Mentally Retarded Children." *Am J Mental Def* 71:561–2 Ja '67. * (*PA* 41:6193)

CUMULATIVE NAME INDEX
Sellin, D. F.: 1

[1413]

Temperament Comparator. Adults; 1958–61; TC; identical with *Paired Comparison Temperament Sched-*

ule except for format; 24 scores: 18 trait scores (calm, cautious, decisive, demonstrative, emotionally stable, energetic, enthusiastic, even-tempered, lively, persevering, prompt starter, quick worker, seeks company, self-confident, serious, socially at ease, steady worker, talkative), 5 factor scores (controlled vs. outgoing, stable vs. unstable, self-reliant vs. dependent, excitable vs. placid, sociable vs. solitary), and consistency; Melany E. Baehr and R. W. Pranis; Industrial Relations Center, University of Chicago. * [The publisher has not replied to our four requests to check the accuracy of this entry.]

For additional information, see P:265; for reviews by Lawrence J. Stricker and Robert L. Thorndike, see 6:187 (1 reference).

REFERENCES THROUGH 1971

1. See 6:187.
2. BAEHR, MELANY E.; FURCON, JOHN E.; AND FROEMEL, ERNEST C. *Psychological Assessment of Patrolman Qualifications in Relation to Field Performance.* Washington, D.C.: United States Government Printing Office, 1969. Pp. vii, 246. *

CUMULATIVE NAME INDEX

Baehr, M. E.: 1–2	Stricker, L. J.: rev, 6:187
Froemel, E. C.: 2	Thorndike, R. L.: rev, 6:187
Furcon, J. E.: 2	

[1414]

★Temperament Questionnaire. Standards 8 and over; 1964–68; primary-secondary functioning; no manual; J. M. Schepers; National Institute for Personnel Research [South Africa]. *

REFERENCES THROUGH 1971

1. TEMPLER, A. J. "A Study of the Relationship Between Anxiety and Extraversion-Introversion." *Psychologia Africana* (South Africa) 14(1):20–31 My '71. * (*PA* 47:10869)

CUMULATIVE NAME INDEX
Templer, A. J.: 1

[1415]

Tennessee Self Concept Scale. Ages 12 and over; 1964–65; TSCS; 2 scoring systems referred to as Counseling Form and Clinical and Research Form; William H. Fitts; Counselor Recordings and Tests. *

a) COUNSELING FORM. 14 profiled scores: self criticism, 9 self esteem scores (identity, self satisfaction, behavior, physical self, moral-ethical self, personal self, family self, social self, total), 3 variability of response scores (variation across the first 3 self esteem scores, variation across the last 5 self esteem scores, total), distribution score.

b) CLINICAL AND RESEARCH FORM. 29 profiled scores: the 14 scores in *a* above and the following 15: response bias, net conflict, total conflict, 6 empirical scales (defensive positive, general maladjustment, psychosis, personality disorder, neurosis, personality integration), deviant signs, 5 scores consisting of counts of each type of response made.

For additional information, reviews by Peter M. Bentler and Richard M. Suinn, and an excerpted review by John O. Crites, see 7:151 (88 references); see also P:266 (30 references).

REFERENCES THROUGH 1971

1–30. See P:266.
31–118. See 7:151.
119. LINDLEY, MICHAEL R. *A Study of the Relationship Between Self-Concept and Reading Ability.* Master's thesis, Furman University (Greenville, S.C.), 1966.
120. DEMETRIADES, DESPINA G. *A Study to Identify Some Personality Characteristics of Freshmen Academic Underachievers at Appalachian State University.* Master's thesis, Appalachian State University (Boone, N.C.), 1967.
121. GREENBERG, GLORIA U., AND FRANK, GEORGE H. "Personality Correlates of Attitude Change: The Tendency to Alter Attitudes Toward Self in Other-Directed and Inner-Directed People." *J General Psychol* 76:85–90 Ja '67. * (*PA* 41:4554)
122. ALFORD, BARBARA ANN. *The Self-Concept of Gifted*

Students in the Secondary School in Relation to Creativity and Achievement. Master's thesis, Brigham Young University (Provo, Utah), 1968.

123. BECKERT, CHARLES BRENT. Tattooing and Juvenile Delinquency: A Study of Relationships Between the Practice of Tattooing and Personality. Master's thesis, Brigham Young University (Provo, Utah), 1968.

124. GROOM, HARRY DEE. Predicting Achievement Behavior of Academic Probation Students at Brigham Young University. Master's thesis, Brigham Young University (Provo, Utah), 1968.

125. UNDERWOOD, JOHN R., JR. Exploration of Self Concept, Dogmatism, and Grade-Point-Average Relationships. Master's thesis, Brigham Young University (Provo, Utah), 1968.

126. BAILEY, HOWARD CLARK. The Kuder Preference Record as an Instrument for Diagnosing Maladjustment in Prospective Members of the Helping Professions. Doctor's thesis, Florida State University (Tallahassee, Fla.), 1969. (DAI 32:550B)

127. COLEMAN, MARGARET, AND GLOFKA, PETER T. "Effect of Group Therapy on Self-Concept of Senior Nursing Students." Nursing Res 18(3):274–5 My '69. * (PA 47:973)

128. FITTS, WILLIAM H., AND HAMNER, WILLIAM T. The Self Concept and Delinquency. Nashville, Tenn.: Counselor Recordings and Tests, 1969. Pp. vii, 96. *

129. HOEHN, JEANNETTE G. Relationship of the Achiever Personality and the OAIS to Academic Success and to the Self Concept. Doctor's thesis, Oklahoma State University (Stillwater, Okla.), 1969. (DAI 31:3956A)

130. PASSONS, WILLIAM R., AND OLSON, LEROY C. "Relationship of Counselor Characteristics and Empathic Sensitivity." J Counsel Psychol 16(5):440–5 S '69. * (PA 43:17717)

131. RANDALL, LAURENCE H. A Comparison of the Self Concept and Personality Characteristics of Deaf High School Students With Norms for the Hearing and With Norms for Delinquents. Master's thesis, University of Tennessee (Knoxville, Tenn.), 1969.

132. BLACK, RICHARD W. A Comparative Study of the Differences in Self-Concept and Other Variables Between Students Choosing Terminal and Degree Programs. Doctor's thesis, University of South Dakota (Vermillion, S.D.), 1970. (DAI 31:5755A)

133. BROOKS, JAMES BRYAN. An Analysis of Community College Faculty Morale and Selected Factors. Doctor's thesis, North Carolina State University (Raleigh, N.C.), 1970. (DAI 31:5744A)

134. CARTER, HELEN LOUISE. An Investigation of Two Methods of Short-Term Group Counseling With White Preadolescents Rated Low on Social Status by Their Peers. Doctor's thesis, University of North Carolina (Chapel Hill, N.C.), 1970. (DAI 31:5757A)

135. COLLINS, HARDIN A.; BURGER, GARY K.; AND DOHERTY, DANIEL. "Self-Concept of Mentally Retarded Adolescents." Am J Mental Def 75(3):285–9 N '70. * (PA 46:3594)

136. FAHRNER, BONITA GULLETTE. Perspectives on Psychotherapy: Drive Expressions and Self-Esteem as Related to Outcome. Doctor's thesis, Michigan State University (East Lansing, Mich.), 1970. (DAI 31:6895B)

137. GASTON, JOSEPH ALEXANDER. A Comparison of the Personality Characteristics of Northern and Midwestern Urban Afro-American Freshmen, Southern Town and Rural Afro-American Freshmen, and Southern Afro-American College Student Personnel Staff. Doctor's thesis, Michigan State University (East Lansing, Mich.), 1970. (DAI 31:5843A)

138. GREENSPAN, BARNEY. Differences in Self-Concept Identification by a Schizophrenic and Non-Schizophrenic Prison Population. Doctor's thesis, Michigan State University (East Lansing, Mich.), 1970. (DAI 31:6901B)

139. HARDWICK, MARK WILLIAM. An Instrumented Self-Awareness Program for College Students: The Evaluation and Description of the Effects of Group Composition and Learning Climate on Selected Self-Concept and Group Experience Variables. Doctor's thesis, Michigan State University (East Lansing, Mich.), 1970. (DAI 31:3900A)

140. JAMES, DOYLE HILL. The Effect of Desegregation on the Self-Concept of Negro High School Students. Doctor's thesis, University of Southern Mississippi (Hattiesburg, Miss.), 1970. (DAI 31:4464A)

141. JOHNSON, JOSEPH BENJAMIN. A Comparison of Physical Fitness and Self-Concept Between Junior High Negro and White Male Students. Doctor's thesis, University of Alabama (University, Ala.), 1970. (DAI 31:5180A)

142. KALMAN, BARBARA ANNE. Differences in the Emotional Adjustment and Self Concepts Among Institutionalized Delinquent Girls Relative to the Kinship System and Homosexuality. Doctor's thesis, Ball State University (Muncie, Ind.), 1970. (DAI 31:6259B)

143. KURTZ, ROBERT ROGER. A Comparison of Different Approaches to the Measurement of Counselor Empathy in Personal Counseling. Doctor's thesis, Michigan State University (East Lansing, Mich.), 1970. (DAI 31:5768A)

144. MOORE, ALLEN BURNELL. Noncognitive Attributes of Participants and Nonparticipants in Selected Adult Basic Education Programs. Doctor's thesis, North Carolina State University (Raleigh, N.C.), 1970. (DAI 32:154A)

145. MORAVEK, MARJORY. The Relationship of Self Concept of the Beginning Teachers to Selected Aspects of Their Verbal Behavior as a Basis for Recommendations for Home Economics Education. Doctor's thesis, Oklahoma State University (Stillwater, Okla.), 1970. (DAI 31:6725B)

146. PASSMORE, WYNOKA SUE JAY. An Investigation of the Relationship of Self-Concept and Selected Personal Characteristics of Student Teachers to Success in Student Teaching. Doctor's thesis, North Texas State University (Denton, Tex.), 1970. (DAI 31:5254A)

147. PEGG, JOANNE L. The Personality Integration of Early Adolescents. Doctor's thesis, George Peabody College for Teachers (Nashville, Tenn.), 1970. (DAI 31:5003B)

148. SHAFER, BILL WAYNE. A Study of Behavioral and Perceptual Changes in Counselor Trainees as a Result of Resident and Nonresident Practicum Programs. Doctor's thesis, East Texas State University (Commerce, Tex.), 1970. (DAI 31:4475A)

149. STELTER, MERVYN WALTER. Changes in Self-Perception, Interpersonal Orientation, and View of the Nature of Man of Residence Hall Personnel. Doctor's thesis, East Texas State University (Commerce, Tex.), 1970. (DAI 31:4476A)

150. STEWART, LINDA JOAN. Characteristics of Students Attaining Different Achievement Levels at Northwestern State College. Doctor's thesis, Oklahoma State University (Stillwater, Okla.), 1970. (DAI 31:5139A)

151. WARNER, RICHARD W., JR., AND HANSEN, JAMES C. "The Relationship Between Alienation and Other Demographic Variables Among High School Students." H Sch J 54(3):202–10 D '70. *

152. ADAMS, JENNIE L., AND FITTS, WILLIAM H. Chap. 3, "The Development of the Self Concept," pp. 27–38. In The Self Concept and Self-Actualization. By William H. Fitts and Others. Nashville, Tenn.: Counselor Recordings and Tests, 1971. Pp. v, 108. *

153. ALEXANDER, ROBERT LEE. The Effects of a Job Training Program on the Self-Concept of Non-Skilled Youthful Offenders. Doctor's thesis, Rutgers—The State University (New Brunswick, N.J.), 1971. (DAI 32:2895A)

154. ANKENBRAND, RALPH JAMES. An Investigation of the Relationship Between Achievement and Self Concept of High Risk Community College Freshmen. Doctor's thesis, St. Louis University (St. Louis, Mo.), 1971. (DAI 32:4338A)

155. ARNEKLEV, BRUCE LEON. The Use of Defensiveness as a Covariate of Self-Report in the Assessment of Self-Concept Among Navajo Adolescents. Doctor's thesis, Utah State University (Logan, Utah), 1971. (DAI 32:3772A)

156. ARNOLD, RICHARD RUSSELL. The Relationships Among Ego Characteristics and Self Constructs in Delinquent Boys. Doctor's thesis, University of North Carolina (Chapel Hill, N.C.), 1971. (DAI 32:2994B)

157. BALLARD, STANLEY NEWTON. The Effects of Motivational Group Techniques Upon Selected Personality and Behavioral Variables. Doctor's thesis, North Texas State University (Denton, Tex.), 1971. (DAI 32:1844A)

158. BARON, REUBEN M.; BASS, ALAN R.; AND VIETZE, PETER M. "Type and Frequency of Praise as Determinants of Favorability of Self-Image: An Experiment in a Field Setting." J Personality 39(4):493–511 D '71. * (PA 48:731)

159. BOYCE, ROBERT DESMOND. Predicting Success of Urban Corps Interns Based Upon the Perceptual Basis of Behavior. Doctor's thesis, University of Michigan (Ann Arbor, Mich.), 1971. (DAI 32:3591A)

160. BROWN, DAVID JEFFREY. The Fear of Death and the Western-Protestant Ethic Personality Identity. Doctor's thesis, Ohio State University (Columbus, Ohio), 1971. (DAI 32:7302B)

161. BROWN, JACK E. The Effects of Instant Visual Feedback of Congruence in Group Counseling. Doctor's thesis, University of North Dakota (Grand Forks, N.D.), 1971. (DAI 33:436B)

162. BROWN, VENIE EDWARD. Obesity as a Factor in Self Concept and Attitude Toward Physical Fitness and Exercise. Doctor's thesis, University of Mississippi (University, Miss.), 1971. (DAI 32:2462A)

163. CARDILLO, JOSEPH P. "Effects of Teaching Communication Roles on Interpersonal Perception and Self-Concept in Disturbed Marriages." Abstract. Proc 79th Ann Conv Am Psychol Assn 6(1):441–2 '71. * (PA 46:5279)

164. CARDILLO, JOSEPH PETER. The Effects of Teaching Communication Roles on Interpersonal Perception and Self-Concept in Disturbed Marriages. Doctor's thesis, George Peabody College for Teachers (Nashville, Tenn.), 1971. (DAI 32:2392B)

165. CARGILE, LEE LANE. The Relationship of Counselor Self-Acceptance to Counselor Effectiveness as Found in Secondary School Counselors Employed in Four Counties of Northwest Arkansas. Doctor's thesis, University of Arkansas (Fayetteville, Ark.), 1971. (DAI 32:2414A)

166. CLARKE, RAY VARNADO. A Study of Self-Concepts as Characteristics of Effective Teachers of Adult Basic Education. Doctor's thesis, Florida State University (Tallahassee, Fla.), 1971. (DAI 32:6731A)

167. DIETZEL, CLEASON S., AND ABELES, NORMAN. "Thematic Drive Expression and Self-Esteem." J Pers Assess 35(5):442–7 O '71. * (PA 47:8951)

Tennessee Self Concept Scale

168. EARL, ROBERT BARRY. *A Study of the Relationship Between Frequency of Use of Independent Study Behaviors and Student Self-Concept.* Doctor's thesis, University of Oregon (Eugene, Ore.), 1971. (*DAI* 32:4918A)

169. FITTS, WILLIAM H. Chap. 2, "A Conceptualization of the Self Concept," pp. 11–26. In *The Self Concept and Self-Actualization.* By William H. Fitts and Others. Nashville, Tenn.: Counselor Recordings and Tests, 1971. Pp. v, 108. *

170. FITTS, WILLIAM H., AND RICHARD, WAYNE C. Chap. 1, "The Self Concept, Self-Actualization, and Rehabilitation: An Overview," pp. 1–10. In *The Self Concept and Self-Actualization.* By William H. Fitts and Others. Nashville, Tenn.: Counselor Recordings and Tests, 1971. Pp. v, 108. *

171. FRYETT, HOWARD LESLIE. *An Interpretation of Student Self Concept and Analysis of Relationships Between the Self and Selected Characteristics of Business Education Students Enrolled in Minnesota Area Vocational-Technical Schools.* Doctor's thesis, University of North Dakota (Grand Forks, N.D.), 1971. (*DAI* 33:76A)

172. GARRISON, CLIFFORD BEVERLY. *A Comparative Investigation of Behavioral Counseling Group Techniques Used to Modify Study Skills, Attitudes and Achievement of Selected High School Pupils.* Doctor's thesis, State University of New York (Buffalo, N.Y.), 1971. (*DAI* 32:1271A)

173. GROSS, W. F. "Self-Concepts of Alcoholics Before and After Treatment." *J Clin Psychol* 27(4):539–41 O '71. * (*PA* 47:9243)

174. GROSS, WILLIAM F. "Self Concepts of Alcoholics Before and After Treatment." *Newsl Res Psychol* 13(2):13–5 My '71. *

175. HARRINGTON, JOHN JOSEPH. *The Relationship of Self Concept Measures to Selected Characteristics of Air Force Officers.* Doctor's thesis, George Washington University (Washington, D.C.), 1971. (*DAI* 32:2421A)

176. IGLINSKY, CLYDE LEE, AND WIANT, HARRY V., JR. "Non-Intellectual Factors in Academic Success." *Improving Col & Univ Teach* 19(4):297–8 au '71. *

177. KNOX, WILLIAM HUGH. *A Comparative Study of Fraternity and Non-Fraternity Members on Selected Personality Variables.* Doctor's thesis, University of North Carolina (Chapel Hill, N.C.), 1971. (*DAI* 32:2421A)

178. KROPP, W.; CALHOON, B.; AND VERRIER, R. "Modification of the 'Self-Concept' of Emotionally Disturbed Children by Covert Reinforcement." *Behav Ther* 2(2):201–4 Ap '71. * (*PA* 47:9088)

179. LATHEY, ROBERT KNOWLTON. *A Comparison of Change Toward Self-Actualization in Marathon Group Counseling and Traditional Group Counseling.* Doctor's thesis, North Texas State University (Denton, Tex.), 1971. (*DAI* 32:3692A)

180. LEFEBVRE, ANDRÉ. *The Relationship Between Self-Concept and Level of Aspiration With Negro and White Children.* Doctor's thesis, Loyola University (Chicago, Ill.), 1971. (*DAI* 32:3036B)

181. LEWIS, RAYMOND LEE. *The Effect of Self Concept and Various Conceptual and Physical Practice Methods Upon the Performance of a Selected Basketball Motor Skill.* Doctor's thesis, North Texas State University (Denton, Tex.), 1971. (*DAI* 32:1902A)

182. LITTLE, FRANK WILLIAM. *The Effect of a Personal Growth Group Experience Upon Measured Self Concept of a Selected Group of Black College Freshmen.* Doctor's thesis, Purdue University (Lafayette, Ind.), 1971. (*DAI* 32:4957A)

183. LIVINGSTON, LOVELESS BENJAMIN. *Self-Concept Change of Black College Males as a Result of a Weekend Black Experience Encounter Workshop.* Doctor's thesis, Arizona State University (Tempe, Ariz.), 1971. (*DAI* 32:2423B)

184. MILLER, HAROLD JOHN. *The Relationship of Self-Concept and Anxiety.* Doctor's thesis, University of Northern Colorado (Greeley, Colo.), 1971. (*DAI* 32:6036B)

185. PENDERGRASS, PRESLEY WADE. *The Relationship of Perceived Threat to Adolescent Students' Feelings of Adequacy in the Classroom.* Doctor's thesis, University of Florida (Gainesville, Fla.), 1971. (*DAI* 32:6814A)

186. PERNELL, EUGENE, JR. *Predictions of Individual Student Teacher Behavior in Classrooms for Emotionally Disturbed Children.* Doctor's thesis, University of Michigan (Ann Arbor, Mich.), 1971. (*DAI* 32:6013A)

187. POE, BOBBY JOE. *The Effect of Sensitivity Training on the Relationship Between Risk Taking and Other Selected Behavioral Factors.* Doctor's thesis, East Texas State University (Commerce, Tex.), 1971. (*DAI* 32:6037B)

188. RADFORD, GLADYS; THOMPSON, WARREN; AND FITTS, WILLIAM H. Chap. 4, "The Measurement of the Self Concept," pp. 39–64. In *The Self Concept and Self-Actualization.* By William H. Fitts and Others. Nashville, Tenn.: Counselor Recordings and Tests, 1971. Pp. v, 108. *

189. RAMSEY, MARL EDGAR. *Self Concept Among Selected Iowa School Teachers and Administrators as Measured by a Self Report.* Doctor's thesis, Iowa State University (Ames, Iowa), 1971. (*DAI* 32:3631A)

190. SCHALL, ROBERT PHILIP. *A Study of the Effect of the Allegheny College Off-Campus Student Teaching Program Upon Student Teacher Self-Concept and Attitude Toward Teacher-Pupil Relations.* Doctor's thesis, George Peabody College for Teachers (Nashville, Tenn.), 1971. (*DAI* 32:1966A)

191. THOMAS, ALFRED ERVIN. *An Analysis of Self Perceptions According to Types and Dimensions of Personality: A Test of Holland's Theory of Vocational Choice.* Doctor's thesis, University of North Carolina (Chapel Hill, N.C.), 1971. (*DAI* 32:745A)

192. THOMAS, BARBARA K.; THOMAS, MURPHY M.; AND FITTS, WILLIAM H. Chap. 5, "Self Concept and Personality Integration," pp. 65–100. In *The Self Concept and Self-Actualization.* By William H. Fitts and Others. Nashville, Tenn.: Counselor Recordings and Tests, 1971. Pp. v, 108. *

193. WHATLEY, ARTHUR ALLEN. *The Relationship Between Dogmatism and Neuroticism and Supervisors of Sheltered Workshops and Changes in the Self-Concept of Handicapped Employees.* Doctor's thesis, North Texas State University (Denton, Tex.), 1971. (*DAI* 32:4113A)

194. WHITE, KINNARD, AND ALLEN, RICHARD. "Art Counseling in an Educational Setting: Self-Concept Change Among Pre-Adolescent Boys." *J Sch Psychol* 9(2):218–25 '71. * (*PA* 47:7673)

195. WILLIAMS, ROBERT L. "Relationship of Class Participation to Personality, Ability, and Achievement Variables." *J Social Psychol* 83(2):193–8 Ap '71. * (*PA* 46:3721)

196. WILLINGHAM, MARY ELIZABETH. *The Relationship Between Self Concept, Self Disclosure, and Peer Selection.* Doctor's thesis, George Washington University (Washington, D.C.), 1971. (*DAI* 32:4365A)

197. WOODARD, BARBARA CHARLENE CHESNEY. *The Effects of Group Interaction on Sociometric Status, Self-Concept, and Group Perceptions of Nursing Personnel.* Doctor's thesis, North Texas State University (Denton, Tex.), 1971. (*DAI* 32:3710A)

198. WOODY, ROBERT H. "Self-Understanding Seminars: The Effects of Group Psychotherapy in Counselor Training." *Counselor Ed & Sup* 10(2):112–9 w '71. * (*PA* 47:1384)

CUMULATIVE NAME INDEX

Tennessee Self Concept Scale

[1416]

Test for Developmental Age in Girls. Girls ages 8–18; 1933–34; social maturity; also called *A Scale for Measuring Developmental Age in Girls;* Celestine Sullivan; Catholic University of America Press. *

For additional information, see P:267 (1 reference). For an excerpt from a related book review, see 1:B495.

REFERENCES THROUGH 1971

1. See P:267.
2. Stone, C. P., and Barker, R. G. "Aspects of Personality and Intelligence in Post Menarcheal and Premenarcheal Girls of the Same Chronological Age." *J Comp Psychol* 23:439–45 Je '37. * (*PA* 11:4871)
3. Thorndike, Robert L. "Performance of Gifted Children on Tests of Developmental Age." *J Psychol* 9:337–43 Ap '40. * (*PA* 14:3824)

CUMULATIVE NAME INDEX

[1417]

Test of Basic Assumptions. Adults; 1959–68, c1957–59; TBA; for experimental and research use only; 12 scores: 3 attitude scores (realist, idealist, pragmatist) for each of 4 "life areas" (organization of effort and problem solving, human abilities and the individual, general philosophy of life, economics and business); James H. Morrison and Martin Levit (test); James H. Morrison. *

For additional information, see P:268.

[1418]

Test of Behavioral Rigidity, Research Edition. Ages 21 and over; 1960, c1956–60; TBR; 4 scores:

motor-cognitive rigidity, personality-perceptual rigidity, psychomotor speed, total; K. Warner Schaie; Consulting Psychologists Press, Inc. *

For additional information, see P:269 (4 references); for reviews by Douglas P. Crowne and Benjamin Kleinmuntz, see 6:189 (9 references).

REFERENCES THROUGH 1971

1–9. See 6:189.
10–13. See P:269.
14. Mackie, James Benjamin. *A Comparative Study of Brain Damaged and Normal Individuals on Tests of Intelligence, Perception and Rigidity.* Doctor's thesis, University of Utah (Salt Lake City, Utah), 1963. (*DA* 24:1700)
15. Baer, Daniel J. "Factors in Perception and Rigidity." *Percept & Motor Skills* 19:563–70 O '64. * (*PA* 39:6290)
16. Mackie, James B., and Beck, Edward C. "Relations Among Rigidity, Intelligence and Perception in Brain-Damaged and Normal Individuals." *J Nerv & Mental Dis* 142:310–7 Ap '66. * (*PA* 40:13429)
17. Lewis, Laura H. "Acquiescence Response Set: Construct or Artifact?" *J Proj Tech & Pers Assess* 32:578–84 D '68. * (*PA* 43:9763)
18. Schaie, K. W., and Strother, C. R. "Limits of Optimal Functioning in Superior Old Adults." Discussion by Joseph H. Britton. *Interdiscipl Topics Gerontol* 1:132–53 '68. *
19. Schaie, K. Warner, and Strother, Charles R. "Cognitive and Personality Variables in College Graduates of Advanced Age," pp. 281–308. (*PA* 43:15628, title only) In *Human Aging and Behavior: Recent Advances in Research and Theory.* Edited by George A. Talland. New York: Academic Press Inc., 1968. Pp. xiii, 322. *
20. Schaie, K. Warner, and Strother, Charles R. "A Cross-Sequential Study of Age Changes in Cognitive Behavior." *Psychol B* 70:671–80 D '68. * (*PA* 43:6779)
21. Breskin, Stephen; Gorman, Bernard S.; and Hochman, Sidney H. "Nonverbal Rigidity and Perseveration." *J Psychol* 75(2):239–42 Jl '70. * (*PA* 44:20980)
22. Baltes, Paul B.; Schaie, K. Warner; and Nardi, Anne H. "Age and Experimental Mortality in a Seven-Year Longitudinal Study of Cognitive Behavior." *Develop Psychol* 5(1):18–26 Jl '71. * (*PA* 46:8800)

CUMULATIVE NAME INDEX

[1419]

Test of Social Insight. Grades 6–12, 13–16 and adults; 1959–63; TSI; 6 scores: withdrawal, passivity, cooperation, competition, aggression, total; Russell N. Cassel; Martin M. Bruce, Ph.D., Publishers. *

For additional information, see P:270; for reviews by John D. Black and John Pierce-Jones and an excerpted review by Edward S. Bordin, see 6:190 (4 references).

REFERENCES THROUGH 1971

1–4. See 6:190.
5. Cassel, R. N., and Clayton, Julia. "A Preliminary Analysis of Certain Social Self Concepts of Women in a Correctional Institution." *Sociol & Social Res* 45:316–9 Ap '61. * (*PA* 36:3J016C)
6. Baehr, Melany E.; Furcon, John E.; and Froemel, Ernest C. *Psychological Assessment of Patrolman Qualifications in Relation to Field Performance.* Washington, D.C.: United States Government Printing Office, 1969. Pp. vii, 246. *
7. Wohl, Julian; Horowitz, Irwin A.; Tapingkae, Amnuay; and Pardthaisong, Thieng. "Some Personality Characteristics of Thai and American University Students." *Psychol Rep* 27(1):45–6 Ag '70. * (*PA* 45:6144)

CUMULATIVE NAME INDEX

[1420]

Test of Work Competency and Stability. Ages 21 and over; 1960–61, c1959–60; TWCS; for predicting work capacity and identifying persons psychologically incapable of work; 1 form consisting of an interview questionnaire (1 or 2 scores: ego strength and, optionally, occupational stability) and 4–6 tests: 2 perceptual tests of intelligence (digits backward, picture arrangement), 2 psychomotor tests (tapping, steadiness), and (optionally) stress test (mirror drawing), digit symbol; A. Gaston Leblanc; Institute of Psychological Research, Inc. [Canada]. *

For additional information, see P :271; see also 6 :191 (2 references).

REFERENCES THROUGH 1971

1–2. See 6 :191.
3. Lesh, Terry V. "Prediction of Vocational Rehabilitation Success." *Rehabil Counsel B* 12 :9–13 S '68. *

CUMULATIVE NAME INDEX

Leblanc, A. G.: 1–2　　　　　Weil, P. G.: 2
Lesh, T. V.: 3

[1421]

Tests of Social Intelligence. High school and adults; 1965–66; TSI; 6 tests; 5 scores: implications (test *a*), classes (test *b*), systems (tests *c, d*), transformations (tests *e, f*), composite (tests *a, b, c, f*); J. P. Guilford, Maureen O'Sullivan, and R. deMille (*c, d, e*); Sheridan Psychological Services, Inc. *
a) CARTOON PREDICTIONS.
b) EXPRESSION GROUPING.
c) MISSING CARTOONS.
d) MISSING PICTURES.
e) PICTURE EXCHANGE.
f) SOCIAL TRANSLATIONS.

For additional information and a review by Douglas N. Jackson, see 7 :152 (2 references); see also P :272 (1 reference).

REFERENCES THROUGH 1971

1. See P :272.
2–3. See 7 :152.
4. Mehrotra, Chandra Mohan Nath. *Behavioral Cognition as Related to Interpersonal Perception and Some Personality Traits of College Students.* Doctor's thesis, Ohio State University (Columbus, Ohio), 1968. (*DAI* 30 :372B)
5. Khan, Janet Adrienne Griffith. *A Descriptive Comparison of the Personality, Life Experiences and Counseling Behaviors of the Typical and Creative School Counselors.* Doctor's thesis, University of Michigan (Ann Arbor, Mich.), 1970. (*DAI* 32 :1274A)
6. Mehrotra, C. M. N. "Behavioral Cognition as Related to Interpersonal Perception and Some Personality Traits of College Students." *Ed & Psychol Meas* 31(1) :145–53 sp '71. * (*PA* 46 :11446)
7. Shanley, Luke A.; Walker, Ronald E.; and Foley, Jeanne M. "Social Intelligence: A Concept in Search of Data." *Psychol Rep* 29(3) :1123–32 D '71. * (*PA* 48 :1661)

CUMULATIVE NAME INDEX

Clark, L. F.: 3　　　　　　　Mehrotra, C. M. N.: 4, 6
Foley, J. M.: 7　　　　　　　O'Sullivan, M.: 1
Hoepfner, A.: 1　　　　　　　Shanley, L. A.: 7
Jackson, D. N.: *rev*, 7 :152　Tenopyr, M. L.: 2
Khan, J. A. G.: 5　　　　　　Walker, R. E.: 7

[1422]

Thorndike Dimensions of Temperament. Grades 11–16 and adults; 1963–66; TDOT; 10 scores: sociable, ascendant, cheerful, placid, accepting, tough-minded, reflective, impulsive, active, responsible; Robert L. Thorndike; Psychological Corporation. *

For additional information, reviews by C. J. Adcock and Alfred B. Heilbrun, Jr., and excerpted reviews by Kenneth B. Stein, Lawrence J. Stricker, and Donald J. Veldman, see 7 :154 (6 references); see also P :276 (2 references).

REFERENCES THROUGH 1971

1–2. See P :276.
3–8. See 7 :154.

9. LeUnes, Arnold, and Christensen, Larry. "Reliability and Inmate Test Results." *Correct Psychologist* 4(3) :85–93 N–D '70. * (*PA* 49 :2670)

CUMULATIVE NAME INDEX

Adcock, C. J.: *rev*, 7 :154　　LeUnes, A.: 9
Braun, J. R.: 2, 4　　　　　　Sappenfield, B. R.: 6–7
Christensen, L.: 9　　　　　　Stein, K. B.: *exc*, 7 :154
Colquhoun, D. R.: 3　　　　　Stricker, L. J.: *exc*, 7 :154
Heilbrun, A. B.: *rev*, 7 :154　Thorndike, R. L.: 5
Horn, D. M.: 1　　　　　　　Tinley, J.: 4
LaFaro, D.: 2　　　　　　　　Veldman, D. J.: *exc*, 7 :154
Lederman, E.: 8

[1423]

Thurstone Temperament Schedule. Grades 9–16 and adults; 1949–53; TTS; 7 scores: active, vigorous, impulsive, dominant, stable, sociable, reflective; L. L. Thurstone; Science Research Associates, Inc. *

For additional information, see P :277 (20 references); see also 6 :192 (17 references); for a review by Neil J. Van Steenberg, see 5 :118 (12 references); for reviews by Hans J. Eysenck, Charles M. Harsh, and David G. Ryans and an excerpted review by Laurance F. Shaffer, see 4 :93.

REFERENCES THROUGH 1971

1–12. See 5 :118.
13–28. See 6 :192.
29–48. See P :277.
49. McNulty, John Patrick. *The Superior Old Person: Case Studies and Furthering Conditions.* Doctor's thesis, Ohio State University (Columbus, Ohio), 1954. (*DA* 20 :738)
50. Martin, Richard Pantall. *The Adjustment of Latin-American Male Students in Selected Private Secondary Schools in the United States.* Doctor's thesis, Northwestern University (Evanston, Ill.), 1954. (*DA* 14 :1605)
51. Barratt, Ernest S. "The Space-Visualization Factors Related to Temperament Traits." *J Psychol* 39 :279–87 Ap '55. * (*PA* 29 :8424)
52. Hofstaetter, Peter R.; O'Connor, James P.; and Suziedelis, Antanas. "Sequences of Restricted Associative Responses and Their Personality Correlates." *J General Psychol* 57 :219–27 O '57. * (*PA* 33 :9818)
53. Talmadge, Max. *A Study of Expressive Graphic Motor Movements and Their Relationship to Temperament Factors.* Doctor's thesis, University of Utah (Salt Lake City, Utah), 1957. (*DA* 17 :2073)
54. Nunnally, Jum, and Husek, T. R. " 'Semantic Clarity': One Standard for Factored Tests." *Ed & Psychol Meas* 18 :761–7 w '58. * (*PA* 34 :156)
55. Schor, Theodore. *Some Variables Among Elementary School Teachers That Affect the Utilization of Audio-Visual Materials.* Doctor's thesis, Rutgers University (New Brunswick, N.J.), 1959. (*DA* 20 :2662)
56. Pauk, Walter J. "Are Present Reading Tests Valid for Both Girls and Boys?" *J Ed Res* 53 :279–80 Mr '60. *
57. Powell, Marvin, and Bergem, Jerry. "An Investigation of the Differences Between Tenth-, Eleventh-, and Twelfth-Grade 'Conforming' and 'Nonconforming' Boys." *J Ed Res* 56 :184–90 D '62. *
58. Nielsen, J. K. "Case Studies of Socially Isolated Males in Senior High School." *Alberta J Ed Res* (Canada) 9 :247–53 D '63. *
59. Richardson, John Francis, III. *A Comparison of Certain Characteristics of a Group of Negro Education and Non-Education College Students: An Investigation to Determine the Nature and Significance of the Differences in Various Characteristics Between Negro College Students Who Select Teaching and Those Who Choose Other Vocational Goals.* Doctor's thesis, New York University (New York, N.Y.), 1963. (*DA* 24 :2789)
60. Baer, Daniel J. "Factors in Perception and Rigidity." *Percept & Motor Skills* 19 :563–70 O '64. * (*PA* 39 :6290)
61. Randles, Harry Edward. *The Effects of Organizational Climate on Beginning Elementary Teachers.* Doctor's thesis, Ohio State University (Columbus, Ohio), 1964. (*DA* 25 :7049)
62. Servis, Margery Ann. *Qualities Related to Success in Women's Physical Education Professional Preparation Program.* Doctor's thesis, Springfield College (Springfield, Mass.), 1964.
63. Kirsh, Jack Lorin. *Relationship Between Certain Teacher Personality Traits and Background Experiences and Teacher Preference for Working With Children Who Exhibit a High Degree of Originality.* Doctor's thesis, University of Florida (Gainesville, Fla.), 1965. (*DA* 27 :704A)
64. Loehlin, John C. "A Heredity-Environment Analysis of Personality Inventory Data," pp. 163–70. In *Methods and Goals in Human Behavior Genetics.* Edited by Steven G. Vandenberg. New York: Academic Press Inc., 1965. Pp. xiii, 351. *
65. Marks, Samuel B. *Some Factors Influencing the Ratings of Professional and Technical Personnel: An Exploratory Study.*

Doctor's thesis, New York University (New York, N.Y.), 1965. (*DA* 26:2862)

66. MEISGEIER, CHARLES. "The Identification of Successful Teachers of Mentally or Physically Handicapped Children." *Excep Children* 32:229–35 D '65. * (*PA* 40:3409)

67. WILSON, RICHARD K. *An Analysis of the Personality Traits of the Successful School Administrator.* Master's thesis, Northern Illinois University (DeKalb, Ill.), 1965.

68. FREDERIKSEN, NORMAN. "Validation of a Simulation Technique." *Organiz Behav & Hum Perfor* 1:87–109 S '66. * (*PA* 41:862)

69. ROSETT, HENRY L.; NACKENSON, BURTON L.; ROBBINS, HERBERT; AND SAPIRSTEIN, MILTON R. "Personality and Cognitive Characteristics of Engineering Students: Implications for the Occupational Psychiatrist." *Am J Psychiatry* 122:1147–52 Ap '66. *

70. BENTZ, V. JON. Chap. 7, "The Sears Experience in the Investigation, Description, and Prediction of Executive Behavior," pp. 147–205; critique by Ross Stagner, pp. 206–27. In *Measuring Executive Effectiveness.* Edited by Frederic R. Wickert and Dalton E. McFarland. New York: Appleton-Century-Crofts, 1967. Pp. viii, 242. *

71. VANDENBERG, STEVEN G. "Hereditary Factors in Normal Personality Traits (as Measured by Inventories)." *Recent Adv Biol Psychiatry* 9:65–104 '67. *

72. WILLIAMS, JACK, AND FOX, A. M. "Prediction of Performance in Student Teaching." *Ed & Psychol Meas* 27:1169–70 w '67. * (*PA* 42:9491)

73. LANNON, JOHN ROBERT. *Personality Characteristics and Environmental Perceptions of Political and Social Activists and Nonactivists at a Large Urban Liberal Arts College.* Doctor's thesis, New York University (New York, N.Y.), 1968. (*DAI* 30:587A)

74. TURNER, CASTELLANO B., AND FISKE, DONALD W. "Item Quality and Appropriateness of Response Processes." *Ed & Psychol Meas* 28:297–315 su '68. * (*PA* 42:18111)

75. BUTT, DORCAS SUSAN, AND FISKE, DONALD W. "Differential Correlates of Dominance Scales." *J Personality* 37(3): 415–28 S '69. * (*PA* 44:6748)

76. CHANG, CHUN-HSING. "EEG Alpha Frequency Correlate of Emotional Stability in Normal Adult Subjects." *Psychol & Ed* (Taiwan) 3:49–56 D '69. *

77. ALSPAUGH, CAROL ANN. *A Study of the Relationships Between Student Characteristics and Proficiency in Symbolic and Algebraic Computer Programming.* Doctor's thesis, University of Missouri (Columbia, Mo.), 1970. (*DAI* 31:4627B)

78. SCHMIDT, GENE L. "Temperament, Ability, and Achievement of High School Athletes as Compared to Non-Athletes." *Ill Sch Res* 6(2):16–22 F '70. *

79. FARR, JAMES L.; O'LEARY, BRIAN S.; AND BARTLETT, C. J. "Ethnic Group Membership as a Moderator of the Prediction of Job Performance." *Personnel Psychol* 24(4):609–36 w '71. *

80. GILBERT, ALBIN R. "Latency-Weighted Testing of Police Applicants." *Proc W Va Acad Sci* 42(1970):241–6 '71. *

[1424]

Trait Evaluation Index. College and adults; 1967–68; TEI; 22 scores (social orientation, compliance, benevolence, elation, ambition, motivational drive, self confidence, dynamism, independence, personal adequacy, caution, self organization, responsibility, propriety, courtesy, verbal orientation, intellectual orientation, perception, self control, fairmindedness, adaptability, sincerity), plus 4 general supplementary scores (overall adjustment, masculinity, femininity, consistency) and 3 supplementary scores for engineers (employment stability, productivity-creativity, job satisfaction); Alan R. Nelson; Martin M. Bruce, Ph.D., Publishers. *

For additional information and reviews by Harold Borko and Jacob Cohen, see 7:155 (1 reference).

REFERENCES THROUGH 1971

1. See 7:155.
2. LEONARD, SKIPTON, AND WEITZ, JOSEPH. "Task Enjoyment and Task Perseverance in Relation to Task Success and Self-Esteem." *J Appl Psychol* 55(5):414–21 O '71. * (*PA* 47:6779)

[1425]

Triadal Equated Personality Inventory. Adult males; 1960–63; TEPI; 22 scores: dominance, self confidence, decisiveness, independence, toughness, suspiciousness, conscientiousness, introversion, restlessness, solemnity, foresight, industriousness, warmth, enthusiasm, conformity, inventiveness, persistence, sex drive, recognition drive, cooperativeness, humility-tolerance, self control; Research Staff, United Consultants; Psychometric Affiliates. *

For additional information and a review by Jacob Cohen, see 7:156.

[1426]

★**Tri-Cultural Attitude Scale.** Grades kgn–6; 1973; recommended for group measurement only; 3 scales which may be administered alone or in combination; 2 scores for each scale: cultural attitudes, cultural knowledge; directions in English and Spanish; Perry A. Zirkel; Learning Concepts. *

a) ANGLO AMERICAN CULTURAL ATTITUDE SCALE.
b) BLACK AMERICAN CULTURAL ATTITUDE SCALE.
c) PUERTO RICAN CULTURAL ATTITUDE SCALE.

[1427]

Tulane Factors of Liberalism-Conservatism. Social science students; 1946–55; TFLC; 5 scores: political, economic, religious, social, aesthetic; Willard A. Kerr; Psychometric Affiliates. *

For additional information, see P:280; for reviews by Donald T. Campbell and C. Robert Pace, see 5:119 (2 references).

REFERENCES THROUGH 1971
1–2. See 5:119.
3. HICKS, JACK M., AND WRIGHT, JOHN H. "Convergent-
Discriminant Validation and Factor Analysis of Five Scales of
Liberalism-Conservatism." *J Pers & Social Psychol* 14(2):114–
20 F '70. * *(PA 44:6741)*

CUMULATIVE NAME INDEX

[1428]

Vineland Social Maturity Scale. Birth to maturity;
1935–65; VSMS; 1965 test identical with test copyrighted 1936 except for format; Edgar A. Doll; American Guidance Service, Inc. * (Australian edition: Australian Council for Educational Research [Australia].)
For additional information, see P:281 (21 references) ; see also 6:194 (20 references) and 5:120 (15
references) ; for reviews by William M. Cruickshank
and Florence M. Teagarden, see 4:94 (21 references) ;
for reviews by C. M. Louttit and John W. M. Rothney
and an excerpted review, see 3:107 (58 references) ;
for reviews by Paul H. Furfey, Elaine F. Kinder, and
Anna S. Starr, see 1:1143. For excerpts from related
book reviews, see 5:B121 (7 excerpts).

REFERENCES THROUGH 1971
1–58. See 3:107.
59–79. See 4:94.
80–94. See 5:120.
95–114. See 6:194.
115–135. See P:281.
136. SKEELS, HAROLD M.; UPDEGRAFF, RUTH; WELLMAN,
BETH L.; AND WILLIAMS, HAROLD M. *A Study of Environmental Stimulation: An Orphanage Preschool Project*, pp. 129–45.
University of Iowa Studies in Child Welfare, Vol. 15, No. 4.
Iowa City, Iowa: the University, 1938. Pp. 191. * *(PA 13:*
1758)
137. WILE, IRA S., AND DAVIS, ROSE M. "Behavior Differentials of Children With IQ's 120 and Above and IQ's 79 and
Below, With Some Reference to Socio-Economic Status." *Am J
Orthopsychiatry* 9:529–40 Jl '39. * *(PA 13:6159)*
138. AVERY, CHARLOTTE B. "The Social Competence of Pre-
School Acoustically Handicapped Children." *Volta R* 50:256–7+
Je '48. * *(PA 23:6089)*
139. BOYD, ROBERT DEAN. *Reading Retardation as Related to
Personality Factors of Children and Their Parents.* Doctor's
thesis, University of Michigan (Ann Arbor, Mich.), 1953. *(DA
13:872)*
140. BERKO, MARTIN J. "Measurement of Behavioral Development in Cerebral Palsy." *Cereb Palsy R* 15:16–7 Je–Jl '54.
* *(PA 29:6088)*
141. MASON, EVELYN P. "Some Correlates of Self-Judgments
of the Aged." *J Gerontol* 9:324–37 Jl '54. * *(PA 29:5429)*
142. UECKER, ALBERT E.; FRENCH, LYLE A.; AND JOHNSON,
DAVID R. "Psychological Studies of Seven Epileptic Hemiparetics Before and After Hemispherectomy." *Arch Neurol &
Psychiatry* 72:555–64 N '54. * *(PA 29:6114)*
143. WERNER, EMMY ELISABETH. *Social Competence of Kindergarten and Fifth Grade Children as Evaluated by the Vineland Scale.* Doctor's thesis, University of Nebraska (Lincoln,
Neb.), 1955. *(DA 15:2108)*
144. GOLDSTEIN, HERBERT. "Lower Limits of Eligibility for
Classes for Trainable Children." *Excep Children* 22:226–8 Mr
'56. * *(PA 31:3723)*
145. SMITH, WALTER D., AND LEBO, DELL. "Some Changing
Aspects of the Self-Concept of Pubescent Males." *J Genetic
Psychol* 88:61–75 Mr '56. * *(PA 31:4443)*
146. GARRISON, MORTIMER, JR. "A Comparison of Psychological Measures in Mentally Retarded Boys Over a Three-Year
Period as a Function of Etiology." *Training Sch B* 55:54–60 N
'58. * *(PA 34:1664)*
147. TRACHTMAN, GILBERT M. *Personality and Developmental Characteristics of Children Rated Most and Least Ready for
First Grade by Their Kindergarten Teachers.* Doctor's thesis,
New York University (New York, N.Y.), 1958. *(DA 19:3028)*
148. GORDON, JESSE E. "Relationships Among Mothers' *n*
Achievement, Independence Training Attitudes, and Handicapped Children's Performance." *J Consult Psychol* 23:207–12
Je '59. * *(PA 34:4764)*
149. KRIPPNER, STANLEY. "Correlates of Reading Improvement." *J Develop Read* 7:29–39 au '63. *
150. BIERMAN, JESSIE M.; CONNOR, ANGIE; VAAGE, MARILYN;
AND HONZIK, MARJORIE P. "Pediatricians' Assessments of the
Intelligence of Two-Year-Olds and Their Mental Test Scores."
Pediatrics 34:680–90 N '64. *

151. WERNER, EMMY; SIMONIAN, KENNETH; BIERMAN,
JESSIE M.; AND FRENCH, FERN E. "Cumulative Effect of Perinatal Complications and Deprived Environment on Physical, Intellectual, and Social Development of Preschool Children."
Pediatrics 39:490–505 Ap '67. *
152. BONACCORSI, MARIE-THÉRÈSE; GAGNON, JACQUES; DES-
TROOPER, JOHAN; AND TOUSIGNANT, FRANCINE. "The Relationship Between Mongoloid Phenotype and Genotype: A Comparative Study of the Psychological and Social Developments of
Diplo 21/Triplo 21 Mosaic and Standard Trisomy 21." *Proc
4th World Congr Psychiatry* 1966(pt 3):1584–6 '68. *
153. WERNER, EMMY E.; HONZIK, MARJORIE P.; AND SMITH,
RUTH S. "Prediction of Intelligence and Achievement at Ten
Years From Twenty Months Pediatric and Psychologic Examinations." *Child Develop* 39:1063–75 D '68. * *(PA 43:8145)*
154. BARCLAY, A. "Longitudinal Changes in Intellectual and
Social Development of Non-Institutionalized Retardates." *Am J
Mental Def* 73(5):831–7 Mr '69. * *(PA 43:10216)*
155. CASSE, ROBERT MACPHERSON. *A Comparison of Mothers'
and Teachers' Perceptions of Normal and Retarded Preschool
and Adolescent Children.* Doctor's thesis, University of Southern Mississippi (Hattiesburg, Miss.), 1969. *(DAI 30:2324A)*
156. CONGDON, DAVID M. "The Vineland and Cain-Levine: A
Correlational Study and Program Evaluation." *Am J Mental
Def* 74(2):231–4 S '69. * *(PA 44:5594)*
157. CORNWELL, ANNE C., AND BIRCH, HERBERT C. "Psychological and Social Development in Home-Reared Children
With Down's Syndrome (Mongolism)." *Am J Mental Def*
74(3):341–50 N '69. * *(PA 44:5539)*
158. HALPERN, ANDREW S., AND EQUINOZZI, ARTHUR M.
"Verbal Expressivity as an Index of Adaptive Behavior." *Am J
Mental Def* 74(2):180–6 S '69. * *(PA 44:5551)*
159. LOCKYER, LINDA, AND RUTTER, MICHAEL. "A Five-to
Fifteen-Year Follow-up Study of Infantile Psychosis: 3, Psychological Aspects." *Brit J Psychiatry* 115(525):865–82 Ag
'69. * *(PA 44:10847)*
160. McINTOSH, ERANELL I., AND WARREN, SUE ALLEN.
"Adaptive Behavior in the Retarded: A Semi-Longitudinal
Study." *Training Sch B* 66(1):12–22 My '69. * *(PA 44:4049)*
161. ARENA, THOMAS. "Social Maturity in the Prediction of
Academic Achievement." *J Ed Res* 64(1):21–2 S '70. *
162. CANNELL, ROBERT THOMAS, III. *Effects of Physical Disorders on the Adjustment of Hospitalized Children.* Doctor's
thesis, University of Missouri (Columbia, Mo.), 1970. *(DAI
31:3987A)*
163. COMSTOCK, JOHN ALLAN. *The Relationship Between
Clinically Derived Scores of Employability and Employability
Scores Predicted by an Employability Model for Mentally Retarded Adolescents.* Doctor's thesis, University of Minnesota
(Minneapolis, Minn.), 1970. *(DAI 32:271A)*
164. DAVIS, BETTY JOE. "Differential Language Behavior
Patterns and Diagnostic Evaluation." *J Learn Dis* 3(5):264–75
My '70. * *(PA 47:5075)*
165. EAVES, LINDA C.; NUTTALL, J. C.; KLONOFF, H.; AND
DUNN, H. G. "Developmental and Psychological Test Scores in
Children of Low Birth Weight." *Pediatrics* 45(1):9–20 Ja '70. *
Correction: 45(5):886–7 My '70. *
166. ERICKSON, MARILYN T.; JOHNSON, NANCY M.; AND
CAMPBELL, FRANCES A. "Relationships Among Scores on Infant
Tests for Children With Developmental Problems." *Am J Men-
tal Def* 75(1):102–4 Jl '70. * *(PA 45:926)*
167. ESTES, ROBERT E., AND MORRIS, HUGHLETT L. "Relationship Among Intelligence, Speech Proficiency, and Hearing
Sensitivity in Children With Cleft Palates." *Cleft Palate J*
7(9):763–73 Jl '70. *
168. GUTSCH, KENNETH URIAL, AND CASSE, ROBERT M., JR.
"A Comparison of Mothers' and Teachers' Perception of Normal
and Retarded Preschool and Adolescent Children." *South J Ed
Res* 4(1):1–17 Ja '70. *
169. KRIPPNER, STANLEY. "Reading Improvement and Its
Correlates." *Percept & Motor Skills* 31(3):727–31 D '70. * *(PA
45:10694)*
170. LEATH, JACK R., AND FLOURNOY, RICHARD L. "Three
Year Follow-Up of Intensive Habit-Training Program." *Mental
Retard* 8(3):32–4 Je '70. * *(PA 47:11515)*
171. LOCKYER, LINDA, AND RUTTER, MICHAEL. "A Five- to
Fifteen-Year Follow-Up Study of Infantile Psychosis: 4, Patterns of Cognitive Ability." *Brit J Social & Clin Psychol* 9(2):
152–63 Je '70. * *(PA 44:16983)*
172. MARTIN, EILEEN, AND POTTER, ROBERT E. "A Compara-
tive Investigation of Speech and Language Development and
Social Maturity of E.M.R. Children." *J Spec Educators Mental
Handicap* 6(2):74–9 w '70. *
173. ROSENSHEIN, JOEL S. *A Study of the Emotional and
Social Differences Between Homebound and School Attending
Physically Handicapped Children.* Doctor's thesis, New York
University (New York, N.Y.), 1970. *(DAI 31:7610B)*
174. ROSENZWEIG, STANLEY P., AND HARTFORD, THOMAS.
"Correlates of the Psychotic Reaction Profile in an Outpatient
Psychiatric Sample." *J Consult & Clin Psychol* 35(2):244–7 O
'70. * *(PA 45:4549)*·
175. WARREN, SUE ALLEN, AND McINTOSH, ERANELL IRENE.
"Reported Skills of Chosen Children." *Excep Children* 37(1):
31–6 S '70. *

176. DUROJAIYE, M. O. A., AND SUCH, M. "Predicting Educational Suitability of Children in an Assessment Unit." *J Exp Ed* 40(2):27–36 w '71 * (*PA* 47:11608)

177. ELLIOTT, R., AND MACKAY, D. N. "Social Competence of Subnormal and Normal Children Living Under Different Types of Residential Care." *Brit J Mental Subnormal* 17(32):48–53 Je '71. * (*PA* 47:11471)

178. FALK, LIBBY JANET. *A Profile of Learning Abilities and Behavioral Characteristics of Elementary School-Age Children With Phenylketonuria.* Doctor's thesis, Temple University (Philadelphia, Pa.), 1971. (*DAI* 32:1913A)

179. GARDNER, JAMES M., AND GIAMPA, FRANKLYN L. "Utility of Three Behavioral Indices for Studying Severely and Profoundly Retarded Children." *Am J Mental Def* 76(3):352–6 N '71. * (*PA* 48:1509)

180. GREEN, JOSEPH B., AND HARTLAGE, LAWRENCE C. "Comparative Performance of Epileptic and Nonepileptic Children and Adolescents." *Dis Nerv System* 32(6):418–21 Je '71. * (*PA* 48:3530)

181. HORSLEY, JO ANNE. *Token Expenditure of a Predictor of the Social Competence of Chronically Ill Mental Patients.* Doctor's thesis, University of Michigan (Ann Arbor, Mich.), 1971. (*DAI* 32:1846B)

182. LITTLE, JASPER WESLEY. *A Comparative Study of the Social Maturity of Kindergarten Age Children.* Doctor's thesis, University of Arkansas (Fayetteville, Ark.), 1971. (*DAI* 32:822A)

183. PARKER, HARRY J.; STERNLOF, RICHARD E.; AND McCOY, JOHN F. "Objective Versus Individual Mental Ability Tests With Former Head Start Children in the First Grade." *Percept & Motor Skills* 32(1):287–92 F '71. * (*PA* 46:3868)

184. SILVERSTEIN, A. B. "Deviation Social Quotients for the Vineland Social Maturity Scale." *Am J Mental Def* 76(3):348–51 N '71. * (*PA* 48:1525)

185. WEINER, PAUL S. "The Cognitive Functioning of Language Deficient Children." *Cognitive Studies* 2:338–63 '71. *

CUMULATIVE NAME INDEX

[1429]

The Visual-Verbal Test: A Measure of Conceptual Thinking. Schizophrenic patients; 1959–60; VVT; Marvin J. Feldman and James Drasgow; Western Psychological Services. *

For additional information, see P:282; for reviews by R. W. Payne and Donald R. Peterson, see 6:195 (8 references).

REFERENCES THROUGH 1971

1–8. See 6:195.

CUMULATIVE NAME INDEX

[1430]

Vocational Preference Inventory, Sixth Revision. Grades 12–16 and adults; 1953–65; VPI; "a personality test employing occupational item content"; formerly called *Holland Vocational Preference Inventory;* 11 scores: realistic, intellectual, social, conventional, enterprising, artistic, self-control, masculinity, status, infrequency, acquiescence; John L. Holland; Consulting Psychologists Press, Inc. *

For additional information and reviews by Joseph A. Johnston and Paul R. Lohnes, see 7:157 (39 references) ; see also P:283 (31 references) ; for reviews by Robert L. French and H. Bradley Sagen of an earlier edition, see 6:115 (13 references).

REFERENCES THROUGH 1971

1–13. See 6:115.
14–44. See P:283.

45–83. See 7:157.

84. ABE, CLIFFORD; HOLLAND, JOHN L.; LUTZ, SANDRA W.; AND RICHARDS, JAMES M., JR. "A Description of American College Freshmen." *ACT Res Rep* 1:1–65 Mr '65. *

85. COLE, NANCY S., AND COLE, JAMES W. L. "An Analysis of Spatial Configuration and Its Application to Research in Higher Education." *ACT Res Rep* 35:1–15 Ag '70. * (*PA* 45: 9167)

86. LACEY, DAVID WILLIAM. *Holland's Vocational Models: A Study of Work Groups and Need Satisfaction.* Doctor's thesis, Ohio State University (Columbus, Ohio), 1970. (*DAI* 31: 6316B)

87. LEE, DAVID LAWRENCE. *Selected Interest Factors Related to Academic Achievement at the University of North Dakota.* Doctor's thesis, University of North Dakota (Grand Forks, N.D.), 1970. (*DAI* 32:6762A)

88. MORROW, JAMES MACK, JR. *Satisfaction With Choice of College Major: A Test of Holland's Theory of Vocational Choice.* Doctor's thesis, University of North Carolina (Chapel Hill, N.C.), 1970. (*DAI* 31:5774A)

89. PECK, ISAAC DAN. *A Test of Holland's Theory: Personality Type and Vocational Choice With Community College Students.* Doctor's thesis, University of Oregon (Eugene, Ore.), 1970. (*DAI* 31:5775A)

90. POWELL, WILLIAM DONALD, II. *A Study of Alienation in Resident Students on Selected State University Campuses in the Southeastern United States.* Doctor's thesis, University of Georgia (Athens, Ga.), 1970. (*DAI* 31:5776A)

91. SALIER, MAX N. *A Comparison of the Vocational Preference Profiles of Deprived and Non-Deprived Rural High School Students.* Master's thesis, Glassboro State College (Glassboro, N.J.), 1970.

92. SCHULDT, DAVID L. *Men Leaving the Pastorate: Social and Psychological Factors Involved in Change of United Methodist Ministers.* Master's thesis, University of Iowa (Iowa City, Iowa), 1970.

93. SMITH, ADA MAE BLANTON. *The Relationship of Ninth and Twelfth Grade Rural High School Students' Perceived Parent-Child Attitudes and Their Vocational Preferences.* Doctor's thesis, University of Texas (Austin, Tex.), 1970. (*DAI* 31:6414A)

94. WILLIAMS, CONSTANCE MARIE DiSIPIO. *Personality Factors, Value Patterns, and Occupational Choices of Male Graduate Students.* Doctor's thesis, University of North Dakota (Grand Forks, N.D.), 1970. (*DAI* 31:6357A)

95. ANDREWS, HANS ARTHUR. *Personality Patterns and Vocational Choice: A Test of Holland's Theory With Adult Part-Time Community College Students.* Doctor's thesis, University of Missouri (Columbia, Mo.), 1971. (*DAI* 32:3014A)

96. BLASI, DONALD THOMAS. *A Test of Certain Aspects of Holland's Occupational Choice-Personality Theory and of Its Applicability to VA Educational and Vocational Counseling.* Doctor's thesis, University of Oklahoma (Norman, Okla.), 1971. (*DAI* 32:1845A)

97. BRUCE, ELDON J.; ENGEN, HAROLD B.; AND MAXEY, E. JAMES. "How Do Community College Transfer and Occupational Students Differ?" *ACT Res Rep* 41:1–33 F '71. * (*PA* 47:1775)

98. COLE, NANCY S., AND HANSON, GARY R. "An Analysis of the Structure of Vocational Interests." *ACT Res Rep* 40:1–17 Ja '71. * (*PA* 47:1843)

99. COLE, NANCY S., AND HANSON, GARY R. "An Analysis of the Structure of Vocational Interests." *J Counsel Psychol* 18(5):478–86 S '71. * (*PA* 47:3679)

100. COLE, NANCY S.; WHITNEY, DOUGLAS R.; AND HOLLAND, JOHN L. "A Special Configuration of Occupations." *J Voc Behav* 1(1):1–9 Ja '71. * (*PA* 47:3834)

101. COX, STEVEN G. "Do Educational Measures Predict Vocational Success?" *Voc Guid Q* 19(4):271–4 Je '71. * (*PA* 48:1981)

102. CRABTREE, PAUL DOUGLAS. *A Test of Holland's Hexagonal Model of Occupational Classification Using a Rural High School Population.* Doctor's thesis, Ohio University (Athens, Ohio), 1971. (*DAI* 32:2565A)

103. DANEK, THOMAS ARNOLD. *A Test of Predictions Based on the Consistency and Homogeneity Dimensions of Holland's Personality Theory.* Doctor's thesis, University of North Carolina (Chapel Hill, N.C.), 1971. (*DAI* 32:2414A)

104. FINLEY, MURRAY HAMILTON, JR. *Assessing the Relationship Between Student Environment Fit and Academic Success and Satisfaction for Nine Iowa Four-Year Colleges.* Doctor's thesis, University of Iowa (Iowa City, Iowa), 1971. (*DAI* 32: 4945A)

105. FOLSOM, CLYDE HILDRETH, JR. *The Validity of Holland's Theory of Vocational Choice.* Doctor's thesis, University of Maine (Orono, Me.), 1971. (*DAI* 32:4345A)

106. GREEN, LENNIS HARRIS. *An Investigation of Factors Which Influence the Vocational Classification of Career Oriented and Home Oriented Women.* Doctor's thesis, Ohio State University (Columbus, Ohio), 1971. (*DAI* 32:2377B)

107. HAAKENSTAD, KENNETH W., AND APOSTAL, ROBERT A. "Acquiescence and Nonoccupational Interests." Abstract. *J Counsel Psychol* 18(5):501–2 S '71. * (*PA* 47:3602)

108. HAASE, RICHARD F. "Canonical Analysis of the Vocational Preference Inventory and the Strong Vocational Interest Blank." *J Counsel Psychol* 18(2):182–3 Mr '71. * (*PA* 46:1819)

109. HARVEY, DAVID WATSON HAWKINS. *The Validity of Holland's Vocational Preference Inventory for Adult Women.* Doctor's thesis, University of Connecticut (Storrs, Conn.), 1971. (*DAI* 32:6129A)

110. HUGHES, HENRY MICHAEL, JR. *Vocational Choice Level, and Consistency: A Test of Holland's Theory on an Employed Sample.* Doctor's thesis, State University of New York (Albany, N.Y.), 1971. (*DAI* 32:1999A)

111. IVERS, KENNETH JOHN. *An Investigation of Holland's (S) Social and (A) Artistic Personality Types With Music and Art Education Majors, and Applied Music and Art Majors.* Doctor's thesis, University of Kansas (Lawrence, Kan.), 1971. (*DAI* 32:1854A)

112. JARY, PAUL WINSTON. *The Relationship Between Job Satisfaction of High School Principals and Their Vocational Interests as Measured by the Holland Vocational Preference Inventory.* Doctor's thesis, University of Maryland (College Park, Md.), 1971. (*DAI* 32:5502A)

113. JOHNSON, DALE MITCHELL. *An Investigation of Holland's Theory of Vocational Psychology.* Doctor's thesis, University of New Mexico (Albuquerque, N.M.), 1971. (*DAI* 32:4421A)

114. KERNEN, PHYLLIS JASPER. *An Investigation of Personality Characteristics of Counselees and Non-Counselees as Related to Holland's Theory.* Doctor's thesis, University of North Carolina (Chapel Hill, N.C.), 1971. (*DAI* 32:6761A)

115. KOSS, ALLEN B. *The Use of the Vocational Preference Inventory With a North Dakota Indian Population.* Doctor's thesis, University of North Dakota (Grand Forks, N.D.), 1971. (*DAI* 32:6761A)

116. LACEY, DAVID W. "Holland's Vocational Models: A Study of Work Groups and Need Satisfaction." *J Voc Behav* 1(2): 105–22 Ap '71. * (*PA* 47:11890)

117. LEWIS, ROBERT WILLIAM, JR. *The Effects of a Planned Group Guidance Program for College-Bound High School Seniors on Selected Guidance Program Variables.* Doctor's thesis, University of Maine (Orono, Me.), 1971. (*DAI* 32:2421A)

118. LUCY, WILLIAM TRUDELL. *A Study Designed to Test the Validity of Selected Formulations From John Holland's Theory of Vocational Choice.* Doctor's thesis, University of Maine (Orono, Me.), 1971. (*DAI* 32:2422A)

119. MORGAN, ROBERT EARLE. *A Study of the Choices of Majors of Gardner-Webb College's Senior Class 1970–1971.* Doctor's thesis, University of North Carolina (Chapel Hill, N.C.), 1971. (*DAI* 32:4991A)

120. MORROW, JAMES M., JR. "A Test of Holland's Theory of Vocational Choice." *J Counsel Psychol* 18(5):422–5 S '71. * (*PA* 47:3608)

121. MOSIER, JACK ARTHUR. *A Study of Parent Occupational Expectations for Gifted and Average Children Compared With the Child's Occupational Goals and Creativity.* Doctor's thesis, Brigham Young University (Provo, Utah), 1971. (*DAI* 32: 4297A)

122. NAVRAN, LESLIE, AND KENDALL, LORNE M. "A Canonical Correlational Analysis of the Strong Vocational Interest Blank, the Holland Vocational Preference Inventory, and the Edwards Personal Preference Schedule." *J Counsel Psychol* 18(6):514–9 N '71. * (*PA* 47:7653)

123. NELSON, A. GORDON. "Discrepancy Between Expressed and Inventoried Vocational Interests." *Voc Guid Q* 20(1):21–4 S '71. * (*PA* 48:1755)

124. NICHOLS, WILLIAM RANDOLPH. *Relationship Between Holland's Personality Types and Consistent-Inconsistent Personality Patterns and Educational Decisions.* Doctor's thesis, University of Virginia (Charlottesville, Va.), 1971. (*DAI* 32:4356A)

125. OLSON, RICHARD ROGER. *Career Patterns and Job Satisfaction as Related to the Selection of Postsecondary Technology Instructors.* Doctor's thesis, Pennsylvania State University (University Park, Pa.), 1971. (*DAI* 33:1087A)

126. SCHMIDT, MARLIN R. "Relationship Between Sorority Membership and Changes in Selected Personality Variables and Attitudes." *J Col Stud Personnel* 12(3):208–13 My '71. * (*PA* 46:11486)

127. SCHULDT, DAVID L., AND STAHMANN, ROBERT F. "Interest Profiles of Clergymen as Indicated by the Vocational Preference Inventory." *Ed & Psychol Meas* 31(4):1025–8 W '71. * (*PA* 48:1012)

128. THOMAS, ALFRED ERVIN. *An Analysis of Self Perceptions According to Types and Dimensions of Personality: A Test of Holland's Theory of Vocational Choice.* Doctor's thesis, University of North Carolina (Chapel Hill, N.C.), 1971. (*DAI* 32:745A)

129. WALSH, W. BRUCE, AND BARROW, CYNTHIA A. "Consistent and Inconsistent Career Performances and Personality." *J Voc Behav* 1(3):271–8 Jl '71. * (*PA* 48:3771)

130. WEINSTEIN, P.; SMITH, T.; AND PACKER, M. "Method for Evaluating Patient Anxiety and the Interpersonal Effectiveness of Dental Personnel: An Exploratory Study." *J Dental Res* 50(5):1324–6 S–O '71. *

131. WHITTLESEY, RICHARD ROLLAN. *The Effect of Client-Counselor Similarity on Selected Measures of Counseling Outcome: An Application of Holland's Hexagonal Configuration.*

Vocational Preference Inventory

Doctor's thesis, University of Iowa (Iowa City, Iowa), 1971. (*DAI* 32:4973A)

CUMULATIVE NAME INDEX

[1431]

WLW Personal Attitude Inventory. Business and industry; 1954–69; 6 scores: emotional stability, friendliness, aggressiveness, humility and insight, reliability, leadership; Robert W. Henderson; third edition by W. E. Brown, T. L. Chappell, L. D. Edmonson, W. H. E. Geiger, R. L. Kaiser, L. C. Steckle, and L. E. Saddler; William, Lynde & Williams. *

For additional information and a review by James E. Kennedy, see 7:158.

[1432]

★**Wahler Physical Symptoms Inventory.** Psychiatric patients and counselees; 1973; WPSI; H. J. Wahler; Western Psychological Services. *

REFERENCES THROUGH 1971

1. WAHLER, H. J. "The Physical Symptoms Inventory: Measuring Levels of Somatic Complaining Behavior." *J Clin Psychol* 24:207–11 Ap '68. * (*PA* 42:12127)

CUMULATIVE NAME INDEX

Wahler, H. J.: 1

[1433]

★**Wahler Self-Description Inventory.** Grades 7 and over and psychiatric patients; 1971; WSDI; 2 scores:

favorable attributes, unfavorable attributes; H. J. Wahler; Western Psychological Services. *

REFERENCES THROUGH 1971

1. WAHLER, H. J. "The Self-Description Inventory: Measuring Levels of Self-Evaluative Behavior in Terms of Favorable and Unfavorable Personality Attributes." *J Clin Psychol* 24: 40–5 Ja '68. * (*PA* 42:8974)
2. WAHLER, H. J. "Self-Evaluation With Favorable-Unfavorable Response Patterns: Reliability, Discriminative Validity and Changes With Instructions." *J Clin Psychol* 24:319–23 Jl '68. * (*PA* 42:17403)
3. WAHLER, H. J., AND BIRCHLER, G. R. "Duration of Hospitalization and Changes in Responses to Favorable and Unfavorable Scales With Typical- and Best-Period Instructions." *Psychol Rep* 22:579–85 Ap '68. * (*PA* 42:12370)

CUMULATIVE NAME INDEX

Birchler, G. R.: 3   Wahler, H. J.: 1–3

[1434]

Walker Problem Behavior Identification Checklist. Grades 4–6; 1970; WPBIC; ratings by teachers; 6 scores: acting-out, withdrawal, distractability, disturbed peer relations, immaturity, total; Hill M. Walker; Western Psychological Services. *

For additional information, see 7:159 (1 reference).

REFERENCES THROUGH 1971

1. See 7:159.

CUMULATIVE NAME INDEX

Walker, H. M.: 1

[1435]

Ward Behavior Inventory. Mental patients; 1959–68; WBI; revision of *Ward Behavior Rating Scale;* ratings by ward nurses and attendants; Eugene I. Burdock, Anne S. Hardesty, Gad Hakerem (test), Joseph Zubin (test), and Yvonne M. Beck (test); Springer Publishing Co., Inc. *

For additional information, see P:285 (14 references).

REFERENCES THROUGH 1971

1–14. See P:285.
15. BURDOCK, E. I., AND HARDESTY, ANNE S. "The Reliability of Judgments of Ward Behavior." Abstract. *Am Psychologist* 15:469 Jl '60. *
16. HARDESTY, ANNE S., AND BURDOCK, E. I. "Predictive Validity of the Ward Behavior Rating Scale for Hospitalized Mental Patients." Abstract. *Am Psychologist* 16:377–8 Jl '61. *
17. BURDOCK, EUGENE I., AND HARDESTY, ANNE S. "Quantitative Techniques for the Evaluation of Psychiatric Treatment." *Proc Am Psychopath Assn* 52:58–74 '64. *
18. BALDWIN, I. TRYON. "Selected Interpersonal Interactions for Regressed Schizophrenics." *J Clin Psychol* 21:73–5 Ja '65. * (*PA* 39:12833)
19. RASKIN, ALLEN, AND GOLOB, RISA. "Occurrence of Sex and Social Class Differences in Premorbid Competence, Symptom and Outcome Measures in Acute Schizophrenics." *Psychol Rep* 18:11–22 F '66. * (*PA* 40:6889)
20. GOLDBERG, SOLOMON C., AND MATTSSON, NILS. "Symptom Changes Associated With Improvement in Schizophrenia." *J Consult Psychol* 31:175–80 Ap '67. * (*PA* 41:7579)
21. GOLDBERG, SOLOMON C., AND MATTSSON, NILS B. "Schizophrenic Subtypes Defined by Response to Drugs and Placebo." *Dis Nerv System* 29(5, sup):153–8 My '68. * (*PA* 42:15603)
22. GOLDSTEIN, B. J.; BRAUZER, B.; CLYDE, D. J.; AND CALDWELL, J. M. "The Differential Prediction of Response to Two Anti-Psychotic Drugs." *Psychosomatics* 10(3):193–7 My–Je '69. *
23. RASKIN, ALLEN; SCHULTERBRANDT, JOY; REATIG, NATALIE; AND MCKEON, JAMES J. "Replication of Factors of Psychopathology in Interview, Ward Behavior and Self-Report Ratings of Hospitalized Depressives." *J Nerv & Mental Dis* 148(1): 87–98 Ja '69. * (*PA* 43:14444)
24. HENINGER, GEORGE R.; FRENCH, NANCY H.; SLAVINSKY, ANN T.; DAVIS, LINDA; AND MUELLER, PETER S. "A Short Clinical Rating Scale for Use by Nursing Personnel: 2, Reliability, Validity, and Application." *Arch Gen Psychiatry* 23(3): 241–8 S '70. * (*PA* 45:4538)
25. SELLERS, LOIS BELLE. *The Effect of Nursing Management on Patients at Eastern State Hospital.* Doctor's thesis, Columbia University (New York, N.Y.), 1970. (*DAI* 31:6716B)
26. RASKIN, ALLEN, AND MCKEON, JAMES J. "Super Factors of Psychopathology in Hospital Depressed Patients." *J Psychiatric Res* (England) 9(1):11–9 D '71. *

[1436]

A Weighted-Score Likability Rating Scale. Ages 6 and over; 1946; 10 ratings: honesty, cooperation, courtesy, responsibility, initiative, industry, attentiveness, enthusiasm, perseverance, willingness; A. B. Carlile; the Author. *

For additional information, see P :286.

[1437]

Welsh Figure Preference Test, Research Edition. Ages 6 and over; 1959, c1949–59; WFPT; 27 scores: don't like total, repeat, conformance, *Barron-Welsh Art Scale*, revised art scale, male-female, neuropsychiatric, children, movement, 5 sex symbol scores, and 13 figure-structure preference scores; George S. Welsh; Consulting Psychologists Press, Inc. *

For additional information, see P :287 (24 references) ; for a review by Harold Borko and an excerpted review by Gordon V. Anderson, see 6 :197 (20 references).

REFERENCES THROUGH 1971

1–20. See 6 :197.
21–44. See P :287.
45. ROSENBERG, B. G., AND ZIMET, CARL N. "Authoritarianism and Aesthetic Choice." *J Social Psychol* 46:293–7 N '57. * (*PA* 34:3412)
46. JOHNSON, NANCY MARIMON. *The Relation of Training and Other Variables to the Content and Accuracy of Predictions Made From Thematic Test Materials.* Doctor's thesis, University of North Carolina (Chapel Hill, N.C.), 1961. (*DA* 23:702)
47. OWEN, CRAMER. "An Investigation of Creative Potential at the Junior High Level." *Studies Art Ed* 3:16–33 sp '62. *
48. SMITH, GAIL VEERHOFF. *Welsh Figure Preference Test Performance of Preschool Children.* Master's thesis, University of North Carolina (Chapel Hill, N.C.), 1962.
49. CASHDAN, SHELDON. *Personality and Creativity: A Study of Talented High School Students.* Doctor's thesis, University of North Carolina (Chapel Hill, N.C.), 1965. (*DA* 27:290B)
50. McWHINNIE, HAROLD JAMES. *The Effects of a Learning Experience Upon the Preference for Complexity and Asymmetry.* Doctor's thesis, Stanford University (Stanford, Calif.), 1965. (*DA* 26:874)
51. MORANO, NICHOLAS THOMAS. *Complexity-Simplicity: An Investigation of Cognitive, Motivational and Personality Correlates.* Doctor's thesis, Fordham University (New York, N.Y.), 1965. (*DA* 26:4079)
52. VINT, VIRGINIA HOLLISTER. *The Effect of Prior Convergent or Divergent Art Training on Subsequent Art Activity.* Doctor's thesis, Stanford University (Stanford, Calif.), 1965. (*DA* 26:914)
53. HAMPTON, CAROL DEAN. *An Analysis of Pupil Progress as Related to Selected Teacher Behaviors: A Study of the Senior High School Associate Teachers Enrolled in the Fifth-Year Program in Teacher Education at the University of North Carolina, 1964–1965.* Doctor's thesis, University of North Carolina (Chapel Hill, N.C.), 1966. (*DA* 27:3755A)
54. LaCROSSE, EDWIN ROBERT, JR. *The Relationship of Biological Sex, Psychological Sex, Intelligence, and Perceptual Rigidity to Visual Exploratory Behavior in Second and Sixth Grade, White, Southern Rural Children.* Doctor's thesis, University of North Carolina (Chapel Hill, N.C.), 1966. (*DA* 27:2860B)
55. MENDELSOHN, GERALD A., AND GRISWOLD, BARBARA B. "Assessed Creative Potential, Vocabulary Level, and Sex as Predictors of the Use of Incidental Cues in Verbal Problem

Solving." *J Pers & Social Psychol* 4:423–31 O '66. * (*PA* 40:12919)
56. AIKEN, LEWIS R., JR. *A Review of Research on the Welsh Figure Preference Test.* Greensboro, N.C.: Creativity Research Institute of the Richardson Foundation, Inc., June 1967. Pp. i, 31. *
57. BRIDGMAN, JOHN NORTHAN, JR. *Selected Teacher Characteristics and Their Relationships With Certain Behavior Patterns and Teaching Effectiveness.* Doctor's thesis, University of North Carolina (Chapel Hill, N.C.), 1967. (*DA* 28:3524A)
58. McWHINNIE, HAROLD J. "Some Relationships Between Creativity and Perception in Sixth-Grade Children." *Percept & Motor Skills* 25:979–80 D '67. * (*PA* 42:8733)
59. McWHINNIE, HAROLD JAMES. "A Study of the Relationships Between Figure Preferences for Complexity-Asymmetry and Preferences in Works of Art in Fourth, Fifth, and Sixth Grade Children." *Int J Exp Res Ed* (Belgium) 4(2):207–30 '67. * (*PA* 42:13508)
60. GOOD, RONALD GLENN. *An Analysis of the Self-Perceptions and Other Selected Characteristics of Effective and Ineffective Teachers: A Study Based on the Educational Philosophy of the Fifth-Year Program in Teacher Education at the University of North Carolina.* Doctor's thesis, University of North Carolina (Chapel Hill, N.C.), 1968. (*DA* 29:4373A)
61. KARNES, LUCIA ROONEY. *The Comparison of Scores of Eighth-Grade Reading and Nonreading Boys on the Lorge-Thorndike Tests, Wechsler Intelligence Scale for Children, the D48 Test, and the Welsh Figure Preference Test, GW Scale.* Doctor's thesis, University of North Carolina (Chapel Hill, N.C.), 1968. (*DAI* 30:585A)
62. McWHINNIE, HAROLD J. "Some Relationships Between Creativity and Perception in Sixth Grade Children (1)." *Scientia Paedagogica Experimentalis* (Belgium) 5(1):84–90 '68. * (*PA* 45:2137)
63. MITCHELL, MARLYS MARIE. *The Revised Art Scale of the Welsh Figure Preference Test as a Personality Assessment Instrument With Educable Mentally Handicapped Children.* Doctor's thesis, University of North Carolina (Chapel Hill, N.C.), 1968. (*DA* 29:4851B)
64. RAYCHAUDHURI, MANAS, AND MAITRA, AMAL K. "Relationship Between Level of Creativity and Projection of Movement Responses as Measured by Rorschach M, Welsh Mv and a Drawing Completion Task." *Indian J Psychol* 43(1–4):30–6 '68. *
65. BLAKEY, JAMES. *Relationship Among Measures of Perceptual Rigidity and Aspects of Religion.* Doctor's thesis, Rutgers—The State University (New Brunswick, N.J.), 1969. (*DAI* 31:1066A)
66. CORNWELL, HENRY G. "Figure Preference and Personality." *Percept & Motor Skills* 29(3):812–4 D '69. * (*PA* 46:4081)
67. WELSH, GEORGE S. *Gifted Adolescents: A Handbook of Test Results.* Greensboro, N.C.: Prediction Press, June 1969. Pp. viii, 89. *
68. WELSH, GEORGE S. "Preferences for Basic Geometric Shapes by American and Egyptian Subjects." *Int J Symbol* 1(1):58–66 Ag '69. * (*PA* 45:4056)
69. WIGGINS, NANCY; HOFFMAN, PAUL J.; AND TABER, THOMAS. "Types of Judges and Cue Utilization in Judgments of Intelligence." *J Pers & Social Psychol* 12(1):52–9 My '69. * (*PA* 43:11266)
70. CARLETON, FREDERICK O. "Relationships Between Follow-Up Evaluations and Information Developed in a Management Assessment Center." Abstract. *Proc 78th Ann Conv Am Psychol Assn* 5(2):565–6 '70. * (*PA* 44:19655)
71. EISENBERG, MYRON GAIL. *An Examination of a Procedure for Determining Personality Correlates to Independence of Judgment in Male University Students.* Doctor's thesis, Northwestern University (Evanston, Ill.), 1970. (*DAI* 31:4309B)
72. JOHNSON, GERALD, AND BRADLEY, WILLIAM. "Some Correlational Aspects of Performance on the Art Scale of the WFPT Among Certain Variables in a Deaf Population." *J Exp Ed* 39(1):59–62 f '70. *
73. McWHINNIE, HAROLD J. "A Third Study of Some Relationships Between Creativity and Perception in 6th Grade Children." *Calif J Ed Res* 21(1):35–42 Ja '70. *
74. MAHLMANN, JOHN JAMES. *The Effect of Various Visual Stimuli on the Drawings of College Students.* Doctor's thesis, Pennsylvania State University (University Park, Pa.), 1970. (*DAI* 32:792A)
75. NAOR, NEHAMA KLIBAN. *Configurational Analysis of the Strong Vocational Interest Blank (SVIB) and Concomitant Personality Correlates.* Doctor's thesis, University of North Carolina (Chapel Hill, N.C.), 1970. (*DAI* 31:6908B)
76. ZUCKERMAN, MARVIN; NEARY, RICHARD S.; AND BRUSTMAN, BARBARA A. "Sensation-Seeking Scale Correlates in Experience (Smoking, Drugs, Alcohol, 'Hallucinations,' and Sex) and Preference for Complexity (Designs)." Abstract. *Proc 78th Ann Conv Am Psychol Assn* 5(1):317–8 '70. * (*PA* 44:18705)
77. DICK, ROBERT MARCUS, II. *Screening Identification of First Grade Problems in an American Indian Population.* Doctor's thesis, University of North Carolina (Chapel Hill, N.C.), 1971. (*DAI* 32:1209B)

Ward Behavior Inventory

78. HOLTZMAN, WAYNE H.; SWARTZ, JON D.; AND THORPE, JOSEPH S. "Artists, Architects, and Engineers—Three Contrasting Modes of Visual Experience and Their Psychological Correlates." *J Personality* 39(3):432–49 S '71. * (*PA* 47:6777)

CUMULATIVE NAME INDEX

Aiken, L. R.: 56
Anderson, G. V.: *exc*, 6:197
Barron, F.: 2, 4, 19
Blakey, J.: 65
Block, J.: 29
Boelling, G. M.: 14
Borko, H.: *rev*, 6:197
Bradley, W.: 72
Bridgman, J. N.: 57
Brown, G. I.: 25, 27
Brustman, B. A.: 76
Caracena, P. F.: 12
Carleton, F. O.: 70
Cashdan, S.: 31, 49
Chang, T.: 37
Cornwell, H. G.: 66
Dana, R. H.: 35
Dick, R. M.: 77
Dollard, J.: 3
Edwards, E. S.: 8
Eisenberg, M. G.: 71
Golann, S. E.: 9, 13
Good, R. G.: 60
Griswold, B. B.: 55
Hampton, C. D.: 53
Harris, T. L.: 10
Hawthorne, R. E.: 39
Heimann, R. A.: 30
Hoffman, P. J.: 69
Holtzman, W. H.: 78
Howell, M. A.: 32
Hutton, R. D.: 14
Jackson, D. N.: 17
James, G. R.: 22
Johnson, G.: 72
Johnson, N. M.: 46
Karnes, L. R.: 61
Keith, B. W.: 33
King, G. F.: 12
Knapp, W. E.: 7
Kroger, R. O.: 40, 44
L'Abate, L.: 14
LaCrosse, E. R.: 54

Littlejohn, M. T.: 34, 41
Lucas, F. H.: 35
McDermid, C. D.: 28
MacKinnon, D. W.: 3, 11, 15
McWhinnie, H. J.: 36, 50, 58–9, 62, 73
Mahlmann, J. J.: 74
Maitra, A. K.: 42, 64
Mathews, D. L.: 14
Mendelsohn, G. A.: 55
Millman, M.: 37
Mitchell, M. M.: 63
Morano, N. T.: 51
Moyles, E. W.: 29
Mukherji, K.: 42
Naor, N. K.: 75
Neary, R. S.: 76
Norman, W. T.: 20
Owen, C.: 47
Pepper, L. J.: 6
Pine, F.: 16
Puryear, H. B.: 23
Raychaudhuri, M.: 24, 42, 64
Rosen, J. C.: 5
Rosenberg, B. G.: 45
Schaefer, C. E.: 43
Schultz, K. V.: 7
Sechrest, L.: 17
Smith, G. V.: 48
Swartz, J. D.: 78
Tabor, T.: 69
Thorpe, J. S.: 78
Tuddenham, R. D.: 29
Van De Castle, R. L.: 18
Vint, V. H.: 52
Wahba, M.: 21
Watson, W. G.: 26
Welsh, G. S.: 1–2, 31, 38, 67–8
Whittemore, R. G.: 30
Wiggins, N.: 69
Zimet, C. N.: 45
Zuckerman, M.: 76

[1438]

The Western Personality Inventory. Adults; 1948–63; WPI; a combination in one booklet of *The Alcadd Test* and *The Manson Evaluation;* identification of alcoholics and potential alcoholics; Morse P. Manson; Western Psychological Services. *

For additional information, see P:288. For reference to reviews of *The Alcadd Test* and *The Manson Evaluation*, see 1098 and 1271.

[1439]

What I Like to Do: An Inventory of Children's Interests. Grades 4–7; 1954–58; WILD; 8 scores: art, music, social studies, active play, quiet play, manual arts, home arts, science; Louis P. Thorpe, Charles E. Meyers, and Marcella Ryser Sea [Bonsall]; Science Research Associates, Inc. *

For additional information, see P:289 (4 references); for reviews by John W. M. Rothney and Naomi Stewart and an excerpted review by Laurance F. Shaffer, see 5:122.

REFERENCES THROUGH 1971

1–4. See P:289.
5. LEWIS, JAMES FRANKLIN. *Characteristics of Highly Gifted Children: An Experimental Analysis.* Doctor's thesis, State University of Iowa (Iowa City, Iowa), 1957. (*DA* 19:731)
6. BIRKEMEYER, FLORENCE WELK. *A Comparative Study of Four Methods for Discovering Children's Interests.* Doctor's thesis, University of Arizona (Tucson, Ariz.), 1962. (*DA* 23:1229)
7. BOWMAN, DANIEL OLIVER. *A Longitudinal Study of Selected Facets of Children's Self Concepts as Related to Achievement, Intelligence, and Interests.* Doctor's thesis, University of Georgia (Athens, Ga.), 1963. (*DA* 24:4536)
8. LAMKIN, FLOYD DUANE. *Masculinity-Femininity of Preadolescent Youth in Relation to Behavior Acceptability, Tested and Graded Achievement, Inventoried Interests and General In-*

telligence. Doctor's thesis, University of Virginia (Charlottesville, Va.), 1967. (*DA* 28:2558A)
9. DZIUBAN, CHARLES D., AND ELLIOTT, JESS P. "A Factor Analysis of Urban Disadvantaged Children's Interests." *Ed Leadership* 26:161–3 N '68. *
10. LYNDE, ROBERT E. *Longitudinal Analysis of Interest Scores of Boys Ten to Twelve Years of Age as Related to Selected Physical Measures.* Master's thesis, University of Oregon (Eugene, Ore.), 1968.
11. ANDRE, VIRGIE, AND BROWN, DUANE. "Children's Interests and Their Mothers' Perceptions of These Interests." *Meas & Eval Guid* 2(3):168–73 f '69. * (*PA* 44:12351)
12. DELPH, DONNA JEAN. *The Relationship of Personal and Social Adjustment to Academically Related Interests to the School Success of Sixth-Grade Children From Low-Income Homes.* Doctor's thesis, Ball State University (Muncie, Ind.), 1970. (*DAI* 31:5028A)

CUMULATIVE NAME INDEX

Andre, V.: 11
Birkemeyer, F. W.: 6
Bledsoe, J. C.: 3
Bowman, D. O.: 7
Brown, D.: 11
Brown, I. D.: 3
Claypool, A. M.: 4
Delph, D. J.: 12
Dziuban, C. D.: 9

Elliott, J. P.: 9
Henze, M. V.: 1
Lamkin, F. D.: 8
Lewis, J. F.: 5
Loudon, M. L. (S): 2
Lynde, R. E.: 10
Rothney, J. W. M.: *rev*, 5:122
Shaffer, L. F.: *exc*, 5:122
Stewart, N.: *rev*, 5:122

[1440]

★Whitaker Index of Schizophrenic Thinking. Mental patients; 1973; WIST; Leighton C. Whitaker; Western Psychological Services. *

[1441]

*William, Lynde & Williams Analysis of Personal Values, Second Edition. Business and industry; 1958–71; 6 scores: theoretical, practical, social, personal power, aesthetic, religious; R. W. Henderson; William, Lynde & Williams. *

For additional information and a review by Wayne S. Zimmerman, see 7:160.

[1442]

★Work Environment Preference Schedule. Grades 11–16 and adults; 1973; WEPS; "bureaucratic orientation"; Leonard V. Gordon; Psychological Corporation. *

REFERENCES THROUGH 1971

1. GORDON, LEONARD V. "Validity of Scoring Methods for Bipolar Scales." *Ed & Psychol Meas* 27:1099–1106 w '67. * (*PA* 42:8094)
2. BRONZO, ANTHONY F., AND BAER, DANIEL J. "Leadership and Bureaucratic Tendency Measures as Predictors of Freshman Dropouts From AFROTC." *Psychol Rep* 22:232 F '68. * (*PA* 42:11233)
3. GORDON, L. V. "Correlates of Bureaucratic Orientation." *Proc Inter Congr Appl Psychol* 16:291–7 '68. *
4. McCULLAH, ROBERT DOUGLAS. *Prediction of Academic Performance in the U.S. Navy Hospital Corps School Vocational Training Programs.* Doctor's thesis, University of Maryland (College Park, Md.), 1969. (*DAI* 30:5677B)
5. GORDON, LEONARD V. "Bureaucratic Values and ROTC Re-Enrollment." *Psychol Rep* 26(2):570 Ap '70. * (*PA* 44:21517)
6. GORDON, LEONARD V. "Measurement of Bureaucratic Orientation." *Personnel Psychol* 23(1):1–11 sp '70. * (*PA* 44:17545)
7. GORDON, LEONARD V., AND KIKUCHI, AKIO. "The Measurement of Bureaucratic Orientation in Japan." *Int R Appl Psychol* 19(2):133–40 O '70. * (*PA* 45:11089)
8. GORDON, LEONARD V. "Weber in the Classroom." *J Ed Psychol* 62(1):60–6 F '71. * (*PA* 46:3710)

CUMULATIVE NAME INDEX

Baer, D. J.: 2
Bronzo, A. F.: 2
Gordon, L. V.: 1, 3, 5–8

Kikuchi, A.: 7
McCullah, R. D.: 4

[1443]

★Y.E.M.R. Performance Profile for the Young Moderately and Mildly Retarded. Ages 5–9; 1967; 11 scores: social behavior, self-help, safety, communication, motor skills, manipulative skills, perceptual and intellectual development, academics, imagination and

creative expression, emotional behavior, total ; Alfred J. DiNola, Bernard P. Kaminsky, and Allan E. Sternfeld ; Educational Performance Associates, Inc. *

[Out of Print Since TIP I]

Adjustment Questionnaire, P :292A, 5 :31

Affectivity Interview Blank, P :293, 4 :29 (2 reviews, 3 references)

Aspects of Personality, P :294 (2 reviews, 1 excerpt, 15 references), 2 :1201

BEC Personality Rating Schedule, P :297 (2 reviews, 1 reference), 1 :915

Behavior Preference Record: What Would You Do?, P :302 (2 reviews, 1 excerpt, 3 references), 5 :32

Billett-Starr Youth Problems Inventory, P :304 (3 reviews, 4 references), 6 :66

Biographical Inventory for Students, 7 :43 (1 review, 6 references), P :17

Bonney-Fessenden Sociograph, P :18, 5 :33 (2 reviews)

Book About Me, P :19, 5 :34 (1 review)

California Q-Set, P :28 (2 reviews, 3 excerpts, 3 references), 6 :72

Cardiac Adjustment Scale, P :30 (1 reference)

Cassel Psychotherapy Progress Record, P :33, 6 :74 (1 review)

Clyde Mood Scale, 7 :55 (1 review, 25 references), P :41

Constant-Choice Perceptual Maze Attitude of Responsibility Test, P :309, 6 :79

Cowell Personal Distance Scale, P :311 (4 references), 6 :82

Cowell Social Behavior Trend Index, P :312 (4 references), 6 :83

Differential Value Profile (status unknown), 7 :69 (1 review, 5 references), P :63

Every-Day Life, P :75, 4 :41 (2 reviews, 6 references)

Friend-Critic Statement (status unknown), 5 :56

G.C. Personality Development Record, P :88, 6 :100

Haggerty-Olson-Wickman Behavior Rating Schedules, P :321 (1 review, 22 references), 2 :1222

Heston Personal Adjustment Inventory, P :322 (3 reviews, 1 excerpt, 31 references), 6 :113

IPAT Music Preference Test of Personality, P :120, 6 :125 (4 reviews, 11 references)

Illinois Opinion Inventories, P :324 (1 review, 4 references), 4 :52

Interaction Chronograph, P :326 (1 review, 36 references), 5 :76

Inventory of Affective Tolerance, P :129 (3 reviews, 7 references), 3 :54

Life Experience Inventory, P :337 (2 reviews, 2 references), 5 :81

Mental Health Analysis, P :339 (6 reviews, 1 excerpt, 22 references), 6 :141

Minnesota T-S-E Inventory, P :171 (2 reviews, 12 references), 6 :144

New York Rating Scale for School Habits, T :232

Objective-Analytic Personality Test Batteries, P :344 (1 review, 23 references), 5 :90

Personal and Social Development Program, P :350, 5 :92 (2 reviews)

Personal Index, P :353 (2 reviews, 8 references), 2 :1237

Personal Qualities Inventory, P :355, 6 :155 (1 reference)

Personality and Interest Inventory: Elementary Form, P :356, 6 :156 (2 reviews, 3 references)

Personality Index, P :357, 3 :65 (1 review)

Personality Record, P :200 (1 review, 5 references), 4 :78

Personality Report, T :249

Personality Schedule, P :360, 6 :159 (1 review, 66 references)

Y.E.M.R. Performance Profile

Pre-Counseling Inventory, P :211 (1 review, 2 references), 4 :80

Primary Empathic Abilities, P :364, 5 :99 (1 review)

Problem Check List: Form for Schools of Nursing, P :365 (2 references), 4 :82

Psychiatric History Schedule, P :365A

Pupil Adjustment Inventory, P :366, 5 :100 (2 reviews, 1 excerpt)

Rating Scale for Pupil Adjustment, P :226 (2 reviews, 4 references), 5 :102

Report Form on Temperament and Social Behavior, P :370, 2 :1247 (1 reference)

Russell Sage Social Relations Test, P :230 (3 references)

Schrammel-Gorbutt Personality Adjustment Scale, P : 376, 3 :92 (2 reviews)

Self-Perception Inventory, P :379, 5 :109 (1 review)

Sense of Humor Test, P :380, 3 :94

16 PF Computer Analysis and Reporting Service, P : 246

Social Personality Inventory for College Women, P : 384 (1 review, 15 references), 3 :97

Straus Rural Attitudes Profile, P :386, 6 :181 (1 reference, 1 excerpt)

Syracuse Scales of Social Relations, P :390 (2 reviews, 1 excerpt, 23 references), 6 :186

Temperament and Character Test, P :392, 5 :115

Thomas Self-Concept Values Test (status unknown), 7 :153 (2 reviews), P :274

Washburne Social-Adjustment Inventory, P :399 (2 reviews, 2 excerpts, 34 references), 4 :95

Wilson Scales of Stability and Instability, P :405, 3 :112 (2 reviews)

Wishes and Fears Inventory, P :291 (1 reference)

Wittenborn Psychiatric Rating Scales, P :408 (2 reviews, 1 excerpt, 31 references), 5 :123

PROJECTIVE

[1444]

The African T.A.T. Urban African adults ; 1960–61 ; no manual ; J. C. de Ridder ; Industrial Psychological Services [South Africa]. *

For additional information, see P :412 (1 reference) ; see also 6 :200 (1 reference). For excerpts from related book reviews, see 6 :B153 (3 excerpts).

REFERENCES THROUGH 1971

1. See 6 :200.
2. See P :412.
3. Spangenberg, H. H. "The Use of Projective Tests in the Selection of Bus Drivers." *Traffic Safety Res R* 12 :118–21 D '68. *
4. Shaw, Lynette, and Sichel, Herbert S. *Accident Proneness: Research in the Occurrence, Causation, and Prevention of Road Accidents,* pp. 299–371. Oxford, England: Pergamon Press Ltd., 1971. Pp. xiv, 476. * (*PA* 47 :5920, title only)

CUMULATIVE NAME INDEX

de Ridder, J. C.: 1   Shaw, L.: 2, 4
Doob, L. W.: *exc,* 6 :B153   Sichel, H. S.: 4
Lee, S. G.: *exc,* 6 :B153   Spangenberg, H. H.: 3
LeVine, R. A.: *exc,* 6 :B153

[1445]

Association Adjustment Inventory. Normal and institutionalized adults ; 1959 ; AAI ; adaptation of *Kent-Rosanoff Free Association Test*; 13 scores : juvenility, psychotic responses, depressed-optimistic, hysteric-non-hysteric, withdrawal-sociable, paranoid-naive, rigid-flexible, schizophrenic-objective, impulsive-restrained, sociopathic-empathetic, psychosomapathic-physical contentment, anxious-relaxed, total ; Martin M. Bruce ; Martin M. Bruce, Ph.D., Publishers. *

For additional information, see P:413; for reviews by W. Grant Dahlstrom and Bertram R. Forer and an excerpted review by Edward S. Bordin, see 6:201.

[1446]
The Auditory Apperception Test. Grades 9 and over; 1953; AAT; Western Psychological Services. *

For additional information, see P:414; for reviews by Kenneth L. Bean and Clifford H. Swensen, Jr., see 5:124 (3 references).

REFERENCES THROUGH 1971
1-3. See 5:124.

CUMULATIVE NAME INDEX

[1447]
[Bender-Gestalt Test.] Ages 4 and over; 1938-70; the original Bender-Gestalt is listed as *a* below; the modifications listed as *b-g* consist primarily of alterations in administration procedure, new scoring systems, or expanded interpretive procedures, rather than changes in the test materials; *b-f* use essentially the same administration procedure as the basic testing procedure; *c* and *d* provide, in addition, for use of the materials as projective stimuli for associations.

a) VISUAL MOTOR GESTALT TEST. Ages 4 and over; 1938-46; VMGT; Lauretta Bender; American Orthopsychiatric Association, Inc. *

b) THE BENDER GESTALT TEST. Ages 4 and over; 1951; BGT; Gerald R. Pascal and Barbara J. Suttell; Grune & Stratton, Inc. *

c) THE HUTT ADAPTATION OF THE BENDER-GESTALT TEST. Ages 7 and over; 1944-69; HABGT; formerly called *Revised Bender-Gestalt Test;* Max L. Hutt; Grune & Stratton, Inc. *

d) THE BENDER VISUAL MOTOR GESTALT TEST FOR CHILDREN. Ages 7-12; 1962; utilizes same test cards as *a;* Aileen Clawson; Western Psychological Services. *

e) THE BENDER GESTALT TEST FOR YOUNG CHILDREN. Ages 5-10; 1964; a developmental scoring system; Elizabeth Munsterberg Koppitz; Grune & Stratton, Inc. *

f) ★THE CANTER BACKGROUND INTERFERENCE PROCEDURE FOR THE BENDER GESTALT TEST. Ages 4 and over; 1966-70; BIP; also called *BIP Bender Test;* Arthur Canter; the Author. *

g) THE VISUAL MOTOR GESTALT TEST TWO-COPY DRAWING FORM. Ages 4 and over; 1964; Western Psychological Services. *

For additional information and a review by Philip M. Kitay, see 7:161 (192 references); see also P:415 (170 references); for a review by C. B. Blakemore and an excerpted review by Fred Y. Billingslea, see 6:203 (99 references); see also 5:172 (118 references); for reviews by Arthur L. Benton and Howard R. White, see 4:144 (34 references); see also 3:108 (8 references). For excerpts from related book reviews, see 7:B320 (2 excerpts), 7:B321 (1 excerpt), 7:B363 (2 excerpts), 6:B268 (2 excerpts), 6:B297 (1 excerpt), 6:B487 (2 excerpts), 5:B330 (3 excerpts), 4:145 (3 excerpts), 3:109 (2 excerpts), and 2:B843 (10 excerpts).

REFERENCES THROUGH 1971
1-8. See 3:108.
9-42. See 4:144.
43-160. See 5:172.
161-259. See 6:203.
260-429. See P:415.
430-621. See 7:161.
622. ORENSTEIN, LEO L., AND SCHILDER, PAUL. "Psychological Considerations of the Insulin Treatment in Schizophrenia." *J Nerv & Mental Dis* 88:397-413, 644-60 O, N '38. * (*PA* 13:2550)

623. WAYNE, DAVID M.; ADAMS, M.; AND ROWE, LILLIAN A. "A Study of Military Prisoners at a Disciplinary Barracks Suspected of Homosexual Activities." *Mil Surg* 101:499-504 D '47. * (*PA* 22:5498)

624. FREUDENBERG, R. K., AND ROBERTSON, J. P. S. "Investigation Into Intellectual Changes Following Prefrontal Leucotomy." *J Mental Sci* (England) 95:826-41 O '49. * (*PA* 24:3833)

625. WILCOX, KATHERINE W. "Perceptual-Motor Changes Following Electroconvulsive Therapy." *Confinia Neurologica* (Switzerland) 12(5-6):337-42 '52. * (*PA* 27:6586)

626. GUREVITZ, SAUL, AND HELME, WILLIAM H. "Effects of Electroconvulsive Therapy on Personality and Intellectual Functioning of the Schizophrenic Child." *J Nerv & Mental Dis* 120:213-26 S-O '54. * (*PA* 29:7650)

627. KAPLAN, ARTHUR, AND SAKHEIM, GEORGE. "Manic-Depressive Psychosis in a 13-Year-Old Boy: Psychological Test Findings." *J Nerv & Mental Dis* 121:140-54 F '54. * (*PA* 29:7657)

628. KARLSEN, BJÖRN. *A Comparison of Some Educational and Psychological Characteristics of Successful and Unsuccessful Readers at the Elementary School Level.* Doctor's thesis, University of Minnesota (Minneapolis, Minn.), 1954. (*DA* 15:456)

629. PAZEIAN, BESSIE. "Classification and Treatment Problems in a Case of Encephalopathy." *J Clin Psychol* 10:149-55 Ap '54. * (*PA* 29:1376)

630. SILVERMAN, ALBERT J., AND HARRIS, VIRGIL W. "Electroenephalography and Psychometric Testing in Brain-Damaged Patients." *J Nerv & Mental Dis* 120:31-5 Jl-Ag '54. * (*PA* 29:6111)

631. TATERKA, JOHN H., AND KATZ, JOSEPH. "Study of Correlations Between Electroencephalographic and Psychological Patterns in Emotionally Disturbed Children." *Psychosom Med* 17:62-72 Ja-F '55. * (*PA* 29:7565)

632. GAYLORD, HELEN C. *The Visual Motor Gestalt Test as a Measure of Intelligence and Personality Variation.* Master's thesis, University of Arizona (Tucson, Ariz.), 1956.

633. NIEBUHR, HERMAN, JR., AND COHEN, DAVID. "The Effect of Psychopathology on Visual Discrimination." *J Abn & Social Psychol* 53:173-7 S '56. * (*PA* 32:2912)

634. OKINO, HIROSHI. "Studies on the Bender-Gestalt Test." *Folia Psychiatrica et Neurologica Japonica* (Japan) 9:314-28 Mr '56. * (*PA* 31:7954)

635. PEYMAN, D. A. R. "An Investigation of the Effects of Group Psychotherapy on Chronic Schizophrenic Patients." *Group Psychother* 9:35-9 Ap '56. * (*PA* 33:4391)

636. GARRISON, MORTIMER, JR. "A Comparison of Psychological Measures in Mentally Retarded Boys Over a Three-Year Period as a Function of Etiology." *Training Sch B* 55:54-60 N '58. * (*PA* 34:1664)

637. LEBO, DELL; TOAL, ROBERT A.; AND BRICK, HARRY. "Manifest Anxiety in Prisoners Before and After CO_2." *J Consult Psychol* 22:51-5 F '58. * (*PA* 33:6255)

638. SPIELBERGER, CHARLES D.; GOODSTEIN, LEONARD D.; AND DAHLSTROM, W. GRANT. "Complex Incidental Learning as a Function of Anxiety and Task Difficulty." *J Exp Psychol* 56:58-61 Jl '58. * (*PA* 33:9874)

639. BECK, HARRY S. "A Comparison of Convulsive Organic, Non-Convulsive Organic, and Non-Organic Public School Children." *Am J Mental Def* 63:866-75 Mr '59. * (*PA* 34:1656)

640. RIKLAN, MANUEL; WEINER, HERMAN; AND DILLER, LEONARD. "Somato-Psychologic Studies in Parkinson's Disease." *J Nerv & Mental Dis* 129:263-72 S '59. * (*PA* 34:6482)

641. SCHACTER, FRANCES F., AND APGAR, VIRGINIA. "Perinatal Asphyxia and Psychologic Signs of Brain Damage in Childhood." *Pediatrics* 24:1016-25 D '59. *

642. FISH, FRANK; FORREST, ALISTAIR; AND MACPHERSON, E. "Hallucinations as a Disorder of Gestalt Function." *J Mental Sci* (England) 106:523-30 Ap '60. * (*PA* 35:6906)

643. BERKOWITZ, PEARL H. "Some Psychophysical Aspects of Mental Illness in Children." *Genetic Psychol Monogr* 63:103-48 F '61. * (*PA* 35:6452)

644. SEGAL, STANLEY J. "A Psychoanalytic Analysis of Personality Factors in Vocational Choice." *J Counsel Psychol* 8:202-10 f '61. * (*PA* 36:5HG02S)

645. VINODA, K. S. "The Bender-Gestalt Performance of Epileptics." *Trans All-India Inst Mental Health* 2:62-9 D '61. * (*PA* 37:5371)

646. SACKS, LENORA; FEINSTEIN, ALVAN R.; AND TARANTA, ANGELO. "A Controlled Psychologic Study of Sydenham's Chorea." *J Pediatrics* 61:714-22 N '62. *

647. KRAL, V. A., AND WIGDOR, B. T. "Clinical and Psychological Observations in a Group of Well-Preserved Aged People." *Med Services J Can* 19:1-11 Ja '63. *

648. MACKAY, G. W. S., AND VERNON, P. E. "The Measurement of Learning Ability." *Brit J Ed Psychol* 33:177-86 Je '63. * (*PA* 38:4067)

649. MULERO, RICARDO; IN COLLABORATION WITH J. WHITNEY KELLEY AND DONALD L. FAUTH. "The Effects of Valium on Psychological Testing." *Neb Med J* 48:499-505 S '63. *

650. TOBIAS, MILTON, AND MICHAEL, WILLIAM B. "Dimensions of Biological and Psychological Function in Two Samples

of Children in the Third Grade." *Psychol Rep* 12:759–62 Je '63. * (*PA* 38:5756)

651. KRAL, V. A.; GRAD, B.; CRAMER-AZIMA, F.; AND RUSSELL, L. "Biologic, Psychologic, and Sociological Studies in Normal Aged Persons and Patients With Senile Psychosis." *J Am Geriatrics Soc* 12:21–37 Ja '64. *

652. KRISHNAMOORTI, SINGA R., AND SHAGASS, CHARLES. "Some Psychological Test Correlates of Sedation Threshold." *Recent Adv Biol Psychiatry* 6:256–66 '64. *

653. TAYLOR, JAMES BENTLEY. "The Structure of Ability in the Lower Intellectual Range." *Am J Mental Def* 68:766–74 My '64. * (*PA* 39:1793)

654. WRIGHT, HELEN C. *The Analysis of WISC Profiles and Bender-Gestalt Protocols of a Sample of Elementary School Children With Reading Disability.* Master's thesis, University of Arizona (Tucson, Ariz.), 1964.

655. BROWN, FRED. Chap. 28, "The Bender Gestalt and Acting Out," pp. 320–32. In *Acting Out: Theoretical and Clinical Aspects.* By Lawrence Edwin Abt and Stuart L. Weissman. New York: Grune & Stratton, Inc., 1965. Pp. xiii, 336. *

656. LAWRENCE, RONALD M., AND LEICHMAN, NATHAN S. "Comparison of the Effects of Heparin Sodium, Xanthinol Niacinate (Complamin) and 2-Dimethyl-Aminoethanol (Deaner) in Institutionalized Geriatric Groups." *J Am Geriatrics Soc* 13:325–42 Ap '65. *

657. RIKLAN, MANUEL; LEVITA, ERIC; AND COOPER, IRVING S. "Psychological Effects of Bilateral Subcortical Surgery for Parkinson's Disease." *J Nerv & Mental Dis* 141:403–9 O '65. * (*PA* 40:5052)

658. SPREEN, OTFRIED, AND BENTON, ARTHUR L. "Comparative Studies of Some Psychological Tests for Cerebral Damage." *J Nerv & Mental Dis* 140:323–33 My '65. * (*PA* 40:700)

659. STILLWELL, LILLIAN M. *The Bender-Gestalt Test and Male Delinquency: A Comparison of the Pascal and Suttell Quantitative Score Performance in Delinquent and Nondelinquent Males.* Master's thesis, Sacramento State College (Sacramento, Calif.), 1965.

660. EVVARD, EVELYN. "Results of the Bender Gestalt Visual Motor Test Given in a Beginners' Class and First and Second Grades." *J Am Indian Ed* 5:6–10 My '66. *

661. MARJERRISON, GORDON. "The Effects of Pheniprazine on Visual Imagery in Perceptual Deprivation." *J Nerv & Mental Dis* 142:254–64 Mr '66. * (*PA* 40:10667)

662. SHANAN, JOEL; COHEN, MARGALITH; AND ADLER, EMIL. "Intellectual Functioning in Hemiplegic Patients After Cerebrovascular Accidents." *J Nerv & Mental Dis* 143:181–9 Ag '66. * (*PA* 41:4893)

663. FIONDO, JOHN PHILLIP. *Toward the Development of an Economical, Valid Test Battery for the Identification of Emotional Disturbance in Children.* Doctor's thesis, Wayne State University (Detroit, Mich.), 1967. (*DAI* 31:6897B)

664. GOLDMAN, JACQUELIN, AND PLOTNICK, MICHAELENE M. "Aging: The Criterion Problem in Diagnosis of Brain Dysfunction." *J Gerontol* 22:14–6 Ja '67. *

665. JENNINGS, CHARLES L. "The Use of Normative Data in the Psychological Evaluation of Flying Personnel." *Int Psychiatry Clinics* 4:37–51 w '67. *

666. MOTANYK, GUY U.; ZAKS, MISHA S.; AND GROVES, MARION H. "The Role of Pre-Morbid Psychological and Social Characteristics in Behavioral Reactions Following Acute Brain Damage." *Bulletin de l'Association Internationale de Psychologie Appliquée* (England) 16:124–30 au '67. *

667. PASCAL, G. R., AND THOROUGHMAN, J. C. "Psychological Studies of Surgical Intractability in Duodenal Ulcer Patients." *Psychosomatics* 8:11–5 Ja–F '67. * (*PA* 41:6461)

668. GIEBINK, JOHN W., AND MARDEN, MARY L. "Verbal Expression, Verbal Fluency, and Grammar Related to Cultural Experience." *Psychol Sch* 5:365–8 O '68. * (*PA* 43:5912)

669. GOLDSTEIN, NORMAN P.; EWERT, JOSEPHINE C.; RANDALL, RAYMOND V.; AND GROSS, JOHN B. "Psychiatric Aspects of Wilson's Disease (Hepatolenticular Degeneration): Results of Psychometric Tests During Long-Term Therapy." *Am J Psychiatry* 124:1555–61 My '68. * (*PA* 42:12656)

670. LOISELLE, ROBERT H.; YOUNG, KATHLEEN M.; AND McDONALD, MARGARET A. "Four Common Tests of Brain Damage Compared." *Psychiatric Commun* 10(2):41–4 '68. *

671. LOVELL, K., AND GORTON, A. "A Study of Some Differences Between Backward and Normal Readers of Average Intelligence." *Brit J Ed Psychol* 38:240–8 N '68. * (*PA* 43:7398)

672. OBERSTEIN, RITA M. *Reading Achievement: Its Relationship to Visual Motor Perception and Mental Age in First and Third Grade Students.* Master's thesis, Adelphi University (Garden City, N.Y.), 1968.

673. SKORE, MARVIN LEONARD. *The Use of the Bender Gestalt in Assessing Latent Intellectual Ability of Culturally Disadvantaged Children.* Doctor's thesis, Wayne State University (Detroit, Mich.), 1968. (*DAI* 31:3972A)

674. VORMELAND, ODDVAR. "The Bender Gestalt Test as a Group Test With Young Children." *Scand J Ed Res* (Norway) 1:21–38 '68. * (*PA* 42:17820)

675. GRANDOVIC, MARGARET CLARK. *A Study of the Usefulness of the Bender Gestalt Test With Young Educable Retarded Children Using the Koppitz Procedures.* Doctor's thesis, Temple University (Philadelphia, Pa.), 1969. (*DAI* 32:1335A)

676. GROSS, MORRIS. "Learning Readiness in Two Groups: A Study in 'Cultural Deprivation.'" *Jewish Ed* 39(1):36–48 Ja '69. *

677. KLINE, CARL L., AND LEE, NORMA. "A Transcultural Study of Dyslexia: Analysis of Reading Disabilities in 425 Chinese Children Simultaneously Learning to Read and Write in English and in Chinese: A Preliminary Report." *B Orton Soc* 19:67–81 '69. * (*PA* 47:1622)

678. LIS, STANISLAWA. "Visuo-Motor Development and Its Disturbances in a Sample of Prematures Born With the Weight Below 1250 Grams." *Slow Learning Child* (Australia) 16(2): 73–84 Jl '69. * (*PA* 44:17150)

679. MEYER, WILLIAM J. "Measuring Perceptual Motor Ability in Preschool Children." Abstract. *CEC Selected Conv Papers* 1969:8–9 '69. *

680. MULLER, ELSIE FERRAR. "Case Study: An Autistic Child and His Drawings." *Psychiatry & Art* 2:145–53 '69. *

681. SONG, A. Y., AND SONG, R. H. "Visual Memory and Reading Ability of Mental Retardates." *Am J Mental Def* 73(6):942–5 My '69. * (*PA* 43:13331)

682. CAMPBELL, WILLIAM A., III; WEISSMAN, MARTIN; AND LUPP, JANE. "Bender-Gestalt Test and the Urodynamics of Enuresis." *J Urology* 104(6):934–9 D '70. *

683. DIELMAN, T. E., AND FURUNO, SETSU. "Interrelationships Among Selected Environmental, Cognitive, and Achievement Variables: A Further Analysis of the Ten-Year Follow-Up of the Children of the Kauai Pregnancy Study." *Personality* 1(3):185–99 au '70. * (*PA* 47:9797)

684. DuBOIS, NELSON FREDERICK. *Selected Relationships Between Reading Achievement and Visual Perceptual, Visual Motor and Intersensory Integration Abilities in a 2nd and 4th Grade Population.* Doctor's thesis, University of Maryland (College Park, Md.), 1970. (*DAI* 32:3858A)

685. EAVES, LINDA C.; NUTTALL, J. C.; KLONOFF, H.; AND DUNN, H. G. "Developmental and Psychological Test Scores in Children of Low Birth Weight." *Pediatrics* 45(1):9–20 Ja '70. * Correction: 45(5):886–7 My '70. *

686. FRETZ, BRUCE R.; JOHNSON, WARREN R.; AND JOHNSON, JULIA A. "Intellectual and Perceptual Motor Development as a Function of Therapeutic Play," pp. 475–80. In *Contemporary Psychology of Sport.* Proceedings of the Second International Congress of Sport Psychology, Washington, D.C., 1968. Chicago, Ill.: Athletic Institute, 1970. Pp. xix, 878. *

687. HARTMAN, ROBERT KINTZ. *An Investigation of the Incremental Validity of Human Figure Drawings in the Diagnosis of Learning Disabilities.* Doctor's thesis, University of Connecticut (Storrs, Conn.), 1970. (*DAI* 31:6403A)

688. HOCKER, MARY ELSA MURPHY. *Visual-Motor Characteristics of Retarded Readers and the Relationship to Their Classroom Behavior.* Doctor's thesis, University of Virginia (Charlottesville, Va.), 1970. (*DAI* 31:4383A)

689. KEOGH, BARBARA K., AND VORMELAND, ODDVAR. "Performance of Norwegian Children on the Bender Gestalt and Draw-A-Person Tests." *Scand J Ed Res* (Norway) 14(3):105–11 '70. * (*PA* 47:10628)

690. NORDÉN, K. "The Structure of Abilities in a Group of Deaf Adolescents." *Ed & Psychol Interactions* (Sweden) 32:1–22 '70. * (*PA* 44:15094)

691. PEDDER, DONALD. *Discrimination Abilities and Motor Skills in Relation to Reading.* Doctor's thesis, Case Western Reserve University (Cleveland, Ohio), 1970. (*DAI* 32:252A)

692. REYNOLDS, SUSAN CORNELIA. *The Relationship Between Ability to Read and the Meaning and Expression of Emotion: A Study of Lower Class, Institutionalized Boys With Anti-Social Behavior Problems.* Doctor's thesis, Columbia University (New York, N.Y.), 1970. (*DAI* 31:5636B)

693. ROCHE, DERMOT. "On the Concurrent Validity of the Goodenough-Harris Draw-A-Person Test." *Papers Psychol* (Northern Ireland) 4(1–2):5–7 Ap–O '70. * (*PA* 46:9059)

694. SILBERBERG, NORMAN, AND FELDT, LEONARD S. "Intellectual and Perceptual Correlates of Reading Disabilities." *Skolepsykologi* (Denmark) 7(2):67–81 '70. * (*PA* 46:5502)

695. TARNOPOL, LESTER. "Delinquency and Minimal Brain Dysfunction." *J Learn Dis* 3(4):200–7 Ap '70. * (*PA* 47:3517)

696. TEGNELL, JEAN E. *The Use of the Bender Gestalt Test in the Prediction of First Grade Reading Achievement.* Master's thesis, Towson State College (Baltimore, Md.), 1970.

697. ACKERMAN, PEGGY T.; PETERS, JOHN E.; AND DYKMAN, ROSCOE A. "Children With Specific Learning Disabilities: Bender Gestalt Test Findings and Other Signs." *J Learn Dis* 4(8): 437–46 O '71. * (*PA* 47:9714)

698. ADAMS, JERRY. "Comparison of Task-Central and Task-Peripheral Forms of the Canter-BIP in Diagnosing Brain Damage in Adults." *Percept & Motor Skills* 33(3):1259–67 D '71. * (*PA* 48:3523)

699. ALBOTT, WILLIAM L., AND GUNN, HARRY E. "Bender-Gestalt Performance by Culturally Disadvantaged First Graders." *Percept & Motor Skills* 33(1):247–50 Ag '71. * (*PA* 47:5599)

700. ALLEN, ROBERT M.; ADAMO, CYNTHIA; ALKER, LESLIE N.; AND LEVINE, MARTIN N. "A Study of Recognition and Reproduction of Bender Gestalt Figures by Children of Average and Below Intelligence." *J Genetic Psychol* 119(1):75–8 S '71. * (*PA* 47:3528)

Bender-Gestalt Test

701. BAIN, BRUCE. "Further Information on the Bender-Gestalt as a Group Test for Screening School Children." *Percept & Motor Skills* 33(3):1204 D '71. * (*PA* 48:3658)

702. BARRY, LAWRENCE CONRAD. *Development of Norms for an Educable Mentally Retarded Sample and Evaluation of the Plenk Scoring System Including Exploration of the Relationship of the Bender Gestalt Test to Intelligence.* Doctor's thesis, University of Utah (Salt Lake City, Utah), 1971. (*DAI* 31:7587B)

703. BAT-ZION, NAOMI. *A Developmental Study of Sequence in the Bender Gestalt Test: Circular Versus Linear Sequence.* Doctor's thesis, Boston University (Boston, Mass.), 1971. (*DAI* 32:2375B)

704. BAUMAN, EDWARD, AND ST. JOHN, JOAN. "The Clinical Usefulness of Some Tests of Visual Perception." *Psychol Sch* 8(3):247–9 Jl '71. * (*PA* 47:9635)

705. BECKER, JOHN T., AND SABATINO, DAVID A. "Reliability of Individual Tests of Perception Administered Utilizing Group Techniques." *J Clin Psychol* 27(1):86–8 Ja '71. * (*PA* 46:895)

706. BELLAMY, EDWARD ELLSWORTH. *A Study of Productive Thinking in Mentally Retarded Children.* Doctor's thesis, University of Illinois (Urbana, Ill.), 1971. (*DAI* 32:4411A)

707. BEYEL, VIRGINIA; FRACCHIA, JOHN; SHEPPARD, CHARLES; AND MERLIS, SIDNEY. "Relationships Among Raven Progressive Matrices Avoidable and Atypical Errors and Bender Gestalt Errors." *Percept & Motor Skills* 33(3):1269–70 D '71. * (*PA* 48:3366)

708. BLAKSLEE, ROBERT WAYNE. *The Relationship Between the Bender Gestalt Test and Reading Achievement in First Grade Children.* Doctor's thesis, University of New Mexico (Albuquerque, N.M.), 1971. (*DAI* 32:4934A)

709. BRAUN, JEAN S., AND BRANE, MARIA. "Comparison of the Performance of Children With Dysrhythmia Grade 1 and Normal EEG on Psychological Tests." Abstract. *Proc 79th Ann Conv Am Psychol Assn* 6(1):457–8 '71. * (*PA* 46:5135)

710. CANTER, ARTHUR. "A Comparison of the Background Interference Procedure Effect in Schizophrenic, Nonschizophrenic and Organic Patients." *J Clin Psychol* 27(4):473–4 O '71. * (*PA* 47:9195)

711. CERBUS, GEORGE, AND OZIEL, L. JEROME. "Correlation of the Bender-Gestalt and WISC for Negro Children." *Percept & Motor Skills* 32(1):276 F '71. * (*PA* 46:2703)

712. CLARKE, BRYAN R., AND LESLIE, PERRY T. "Visual-Motor Skills and Reading Ability of Deaf Children." *Percept & Motor Skills* 33(1):263–8 Ag '71. * (*PA* 47:3463)

713. CLAYMAN, DEBORAH P. GOLDWEBER. *The Relationship of Error and Correction of Error in Oral Reading to Visual-Form Perception and Word Attack Skills.* Doctor's thesis, Columbia University (New York, N.Y.), 1971. (*DAI* 32:5033A)

714. CRARY, HELEN L., AND RIDGWAY, ROBERT W. "Relationships Between Visual Form Perception Abilities and Reading Achievement in the Intermediate Grades." *J Exp Ed* 40(1):17–22 f '71. * (*PA* 47:9796)

715. DEMERS, ROBERT G., AND HENINGER, GEORGE R. "Visual-Motor Performance During Lithium Treatment—A Preliminary Report." *J Clin Pharmacol* 11(4):274–9 Jl '71. * (*PA* 47:3169)

716. DICK, ROBERT MARCUS. *Screening Identification of First Grade Problems in an American Indian Population.* Doctor's thesis, University of North Carolina (Chapel Hill, N.C.), 1971. (*DAI* 32:1209B)

717. EDWARDS, R. PHILIP; ALLEY, GORDON R.; AND SNIDER, WILLIAM. "Academic Achievement and Minimal Brain Dysfunction." *J Learn Dis* 4(3):134–8 Mr '71. * (*PA* 47:9671)

718. FARMER, CORNELIA REYNOLDS, AND GARFIELD, SOL L. "The Relationship Between Ability to Read and the Meaning and Expression of Emotion." *J Learn Dis* 4(10):558–62 D '71. * (*PA* 47:11232)

719. GEIS, ROBLEY. *The Prediction and Prevention of Reading Failure.* Doctor's thesis, University of Southern California (Los Angeles, Calif.), 1971. (*DAI* 32:5611A)

720. GOEBEL, ALICE KATHRINE. *A Comparison of Visual Perceptual Abilities Between Learning Disabled Kindergarten Children and Non-Learning Disabled Kindergarten Children.* Doctor's thesis, University of Oklahoma (Norman, Okla.), 1971. (*DAI* 32:6618B)

721. GOFFENEY, BARBARA; HENDERSON, NORMAN B.; AND BUTLER, BRUCE V. "Negro-White, Male-Female Eight-Month Developmental Scores Compared With Seven-Year WISC and Bender Test Scores." *Child Develop* 42(2):595–604 Je '71. * (*PA* 47:651)

722. GOLDSMITH, R. W., AND BRENGELMANN, J. C. "Rotation of Brain-Damaged and Schizophrenic Subjects." *Archiv für die Gesamte Psychologie* (West Germany) 123:164–70 '71. *

723. GORDON, GEORGE, AND HYMAN, IRWIN. "The Measurement of Perceptual-Motor Abilities of Head Start Children." *Psychol Sch* 8(1):41–8 Ja '71. * (*PA* 46:7777)

724. HANDLER, LEONARD, AND McINTOSH, JERRY. "Predicting Aggression and Withdrawal in Children With the Draw-A-Person and Bender Gestalt." *J Pers Assess* 35(4):331–5 Ag '71. * (*PA* 47:4564)

725. HARTLAGE, LAWRENCE C., AND LUCAS, DAVID G. "Scaled Score Transformations of Bender Gestalt Expectancy Levels for Young Children." *Psychol Sch* 8(1):76–8 Ja '71. * (*PA* 46:7448)

726. HASAZI, JOSEPH E.; ALLEN, ROBERT M.; AND WOHLFORD, PAUL. "Effects of Mode of Administration on Bender-Gestalt Test Performance of Familial Retardates." *J Clin Psychol* 27(3):360–2 Jl '71. * (*PA* 47:5085)

727. HOLROYD, RICHARD G. "On the Translation of Koppitz's Normative Data Into Standard Scores: A Response to Furr." *J Clin Psychol* 27(1):88 Ja '71. * (*PA* 46:52)

728. ISAAC, BLANCHE K. *Perceptual-Motor Development of First-Graders as Related to Class, Race, and Factors of Motivation, Personality, and Visual Discrimination.* Doctor's thesis, Rutgers—The State University (New Brunswick, N.J.), 1971. (*DAI* 32:3092A)

729. JACOBS, JON C. "Group Administration of the Bender Gestalt." *Psychol Sch* 8(4):345–6 O '71. * (*PA* 47:9652)

730. JOHNSON, JAMES E.; HELLKAMP, DAVID T.; AND LOTTMAN, THOMAS J. "The Relationship Between Intelligence, Brain Damage, and Hutt-Briskin Errors on the Bender-Gestalt." *J Clin Psychol* 27(1):84–5 Ja '71. * (*PA* 46:1680)

731. JONES, MARTHA A. *Comparison of Consistency of Errors on the Bender-Gestalt Test Between Brain Injured and Severely Emotionally Disturbed Children.* Master's thesis, Millersville State College (Millersville, Pa.), 1971.

732. KENNY, THOMAS J. "Background Interference Procedure: A Means of Assessing Neurologic Dysfunction in School-Age Children." *J Consult & Clin Psychol* 37(1):44–6 Ag '71. * (*PA* 47:1435)

733. KILLIAN, L. R. "WISC, Illinois Test of Psycholinguistic Abilities, and Bender Visual-Motor Gestalt Test Performance of Spanish-American Kindergarten and First-Grade School Children." *J Consult & Clin Psychol* 37(1):38–43 Ag '71. * (*PA* 47:1738)

734. KO, YUNG-HO. "The Frequency of Eye-Movement on the Bender-Gestalt Test as a Measure of Attention Breadth." *Acta Psychologica Taiwanica* (Taiwan) 13:65–74 Mr '71. * (*PA* 48:11820)

735. KOPPITZ, ELIZABETH MUNSTERBERG. *Children With Learning Disabilities: A Five Year Follow-Up Study.* New York: Grune & Stratton, Inc., 1971. Pp. xv, 218. *

736. LAMBERT, NADINE M. "An Item Analysis and Validity Investigation of Bender Visual Motor Gestalt Test Score Items." *Psychol Sch* 8(1):78–85 Ja '71. * (*PA* 46:7454)

737. MOORE, MARY, AND WELCHER, DORIS W. "A Descriptive Analysis of the Seven-Year Psychological Data." *Johns Hopkins Med J* 128(6):332–46 Je '71. *

738. OLIVER, RONALD A., AND KRONENBERGER, EARL J. "Testing the Applicability of Koppitz's Bender-Gestalt Scores to Brain-Damaged, Emotionally Disturbed and Normal Adolescents." *Psychol Sch* 8(3):250–3 Jl '71. * (*PA* 47:9681)

739. OWEN, FREYA WEAVER; ADAMS, PAULINE AUSTIN; FORREST, THOMAS; STOLTZ, LOIS MEEK; AND FISHER, SARA. "Learning Disorders in Children: Sibling Studies." *Monogr Soc Res Child Develop* 36(4):1–77 N '71. * (*PA* 48:12196)

740. PARSONS, LOWELL B.; McLEROY, NANCY; AND WRIGHT, LOGAN. "Validity of Koppitz's Developmental Score as a Measure of Organicity." *Percept & Motor Skills* 33(3):1013–4 D '71. * (*PA* 48:1493)

741. PATE, ROBERT H., JR., AND NICHOLS, WILLIAM R. "A Scoring Guide for the Koppitz System of Evaluating Children's Human Figure Drawings." *Psychol Sch* 8(1):55–6 Ja '71. * (*PA* 46:6565)

742. PAUL, LEONARD MARC. *WISC and Bender as Predictors of Reading Performance in Children With Learning Disabilities.* Doctor's thesis, University of Pennsylvania (Philadelphia, Pa.), 1971. (*DAI* 32:1923A)

743. PELC, ROBERT E. "Advancement Along a Complexity Gradient in Perceptual Level and Brain Damage." *Percept & Motor Skills* 32(1):251–4 F '71. * (*PA* 46:3322)

744. RAJ, JACOB SELVA. *A Comparative Study of Homeless and Domiciled Alcoholic Men.* Doctor's thesis, Yeshiva University (New York, N.Y.), 1971. (*DAI* 32:1858B)

745. RICE, JAMES A. "Head Start Screening: Effectiveness of a Teacher-Administered Battery." *Percept & Motor Skills* 32(2):675–8 Ap '71. * (*PA* 46:11733)

746. RICHARDSON, WAYNE, AND RUBINO, CARL. "The Purdue Perceptual Motor Survey and the Bender Gestalt as Measures of Perceptual Motor Abilities in Children." *Ont Psychologist* (Canada) 3(4):243–7 '71. * (*PA* 48:1035)

747. SABATINO, DAVID A., AND BECKER, JOHN T. "Relationship Between Lateral Preference and Selected Behavioral Variables for Children Failing Academically." *Child Develop* 42(6):2055–60 D '71. * (*PA* 48:9861)

748. SAPIR, SELMA G. "Learning Disability and Deficit Centered Classroom Training." *Cognitive Studies* 2:324–38 '71. * (*PA* 49:1359, title only)

749. SIEBEL, CYNTHIA C.; FAUST, WILLIAM L.; AND FAUST, MARGARET S. "Administration of Design Copying Tests to Large Groups of Children." *Percept & Motor Skills* 32(2):355–60 Ap '71. * (*PA* 46:11518)

750. SIMOS, ALEXANDER THOMAS. *Imitation and Grapho-Motor Performance of Mentally Retarded Boys.* Doctor's thesis, New York University (New York, N.Y.), 1971. (*DAI* 32:6062B)

751. SNYDER, ROBERT T.; HOLOWENZAK, STEPHEN P.; AND HOFFMAN, NORMA. "A Cross-Cultural Item-Analysis of Bender-Gestalt Protocols Administered to Ghetto and Suburban Chil-

dren." *Percept & Motor Skills* 33(3):791–6 D '71. * (*PA* 48:696)

752. SOMASUNDARAM, C. P.; KALIAPPAN, K. V.; AND POLNAYA, MEERA. "A Psychometric Study of Patients Disabled by Cerebrovascular Disease (A Preliminary Study of 54 Cases)." *Neurol India* 19(1):34–7 Mr '71. *

753. SPIEGEL, ARLENE R. *An Evaluation of an Experimental Form of the Bender Visual Motor Gestalt Test.* Master's thesis, Pennsylvania State University (University Park, Pa.), 1971.

754. STAVRIANOS, BERTHA K. "Can Projective Test Measures Aid in the Detection and Differential Diagnosis of Reading Deficit?" *J Pers Assess* 35(1):80–91 F '71. * (*PA* 46:7527)

755. SWALLOW, ROSE-MARIE. *Automatic Processing of Perceptual-Linguistic Stimuli in Second Grade Achieving and Non-Achieving Readers.* Doctor's thesis, University of Southern California (Los Angeles, Calif.), 1971. (*DAI* 32:3827A)

756. SWIGGUM, SANFORD C. *A Functional Correlate of the Bender Gestalt Test: The Wide Range Achievement Test.* Master's thesis, University of Wisconsin (LaCrosse, Wis.), 1971.

757. WEINER, PAUL S. "The Cognitive Functioning of Language Deficient Children." *Cognitive Studies* 2:338–63 '71. *

758. WEISS, A. A. "Directionality in Four Bender-Gestalt Figures: II." *Percept & Motor Skills* 32(2):412–4 Ap '71. * (*PA* 46:10584)

759. WEISS, A. A. "Incidence of Rotations of Bender-Gestalt Figures in Three Age Groups of Normal Israeli School Children." *Percept & Motor Skills* 32(3):691–4 Je '71. * (*PA* 47:672)

760. WEISS, A. A. "The Influence of Sheet Position on Placement of Bender-Gestalt Figures." *Israel Ann Psychiatry* 9(1):63–7 Ap '71. * (*PA* 47:2656)

761. WELCHER, DORIS W.; MELLITS, E. DAVID; AND HARDY, JANET B. "A Multivariate Analysis of Factors Affecting Psychological Performance." *Johns Hopkins Med J* 129(1):19–35 Jl '71. *

762. WETZEL, KARL H.; WELCHER, DORIS W.; AND MELLITS, E. DAVID. "The Possibility of Overdiagnosing Brain Dysfunction From a Single Administration of the Bender Gestalt Test." *Johns Hopkins Med J* 129(1):6–9 Jl '71. *

763. WILSON, GERALDINE O. *The Difference in Approach to the Block Subtest of the Wechsler Intelligence Scale for Children and the Bender Visual-Motor Gestalt Test by Subjects With Organic Brain Dysfunction and Normal Subjects.* Master's thesis, Southern Connecticut State College (New Haven, Conn.), 1971.

764. WILSON, LONNY R. "Successive Discrimination Learning of Children With and Without Perceptual-Motor Handicaps." *Percept & Motor Skills* 33(3):935–42 D '71. * (*PA* 48:1718)

765. WRIGHT, LOGAN, AND JIMMERSON, STEVE. "Intellectual Sequelae of Hemophilus Influenzae Meningitis." *J Abn Psychol* 77(2):181–3 Ap '71. * (*PA* 46:3584)

CUMULATIVE NAME INDEX

[1448]

The Blacky Pictures: A Technique for the Exploration of Personality Dynamics. Ages 5 and over; 1950–67; BP; psychosexual development; Gerald S. Blum; scoring blanks by Earl S. Taulbee and David E. Stenmark; Psychodynamic Instruments. *

For additional information, see P:416 (39 references); for a review by Bert R. Sappenfield, see 6:204 (34 references); for a review by Kenneth R. Newton and an excerpted review by Samuel J. Beck, see 5:125 (38 references); for a review by Albert Ellis and excerpted reviews by M. M. Genn, Ephriam Rosen, and Laurance F. Shaffer, see 4:102 (7 references).

REFERENCES THROUGH 1971

1–7. See 4:102.
8–45. See 5:125.
46–79. See 6:204.
80–118. See P:416.
119. GOLDSTEIN, STANLEY. *A Projective Study of Psycho-analytic Mechanisms of Defense.* Doctor's thesis, University of Michigan (Ann Arbor, Mich.), 1952. (*DA* 12:218)
120. BLOCK, WILLIAM ELLIS. *A Study of Somatopsychological*

Relationships in Cerebral Palsy Children. Doctor's thesis, New York University (New York, N.Y.), 1953. (*DA* 13:1254)

121. BOYD, ROBERT DEAN. *Reading Retardation as Related to Personality Factors of Children and Their Parents.* Doctor's thesis, University of Michigan (Ann Arbor, Mich.), 1953. (*DA* 13:872)

122. FRANKEL, ESTHER BRINA. *An Experimental Study of Psychoanalytic Theories of Humor.* Doctor's thesis, University of Michigan (Ann Arbor, Mich.), 1953. (*DA* 13:1257)

123. WATSON, DOROTHY JEANNE. *Some Social Psychological Correlates of Personality: A Study of Usefulness of Psychoanalytic Theory in Predicting to Social Behavior.* Doctor's thesis, University of Michigan (Ann Arbor, Mich.), 1953. (*DA* 13:447)

124. BERNHARDT, ROGER BURTON. *Personality Conflict and the Act of Stuttering.* Doctor's thesis, University of Michigan (Ann Arbor, Mich.), 1954. (*DA* 14:709)

125. SHIRE, ALBERT. *Personality Correlates of Preferences Among Psychoanalytic Defense Mechanisms.* Doctor's thesis, University of Michigan (Ann Arbor, Mich.), 1954. (*DA* 14:715)

126. VERNALLIS, FRANCIS F. "Teeth-Grinding: Some Relationships to Anxiety, Hostility, and Hyperactivity." *J Clin Psychol* 11:389–91 O '55. * (*PA* 30:6129)

127. WEISS, JUSTIN LEON. *An Experimental Study of the Psychodynamics of Humor.* Doctor's thesis, University of Michigan (Ann Arbor, Mich.), 1955. (*DA* 15:873)

128. COHEN, ARTHUR R. "Experimental Effects of Ego-Defense Preference on Interpersonal Relations." *J Abn & Social Psychol* 52:19–27 Ja '56. * (*PA* 31:2539)

129. SHELLOW, ROBERT SCOTT. *Perceptual Distortion in the Spatial Localization of Emotionally Meaningful Stimuli.* Doctor's thesis, University of Michigan (Ann Arbor, Mich.), 1956. (*DA* 16:2529)

130. MERRITT, ROGER KING. *The Measurement of Parent-Child Relationships in Deviant and Normal Groups.* Doctor's thesis, University of Houston (Houston, Tex.), 1957. (*DA* 18:1867)

131. POLLIE, DONALD MITCHELL. *Conflict and Defense in Three Psychosomatic Syndromes.* Doctor's thesis, University of Michigan (Ann Arbor, Mich.), 1957. (*DA* 18:1499)

132. WEINER, HERBERT; THALER, MARGARET; REISER, MORTON F.; AND MIRSKY, I. ARTHUR. "Etiology of Duodenal Ulcer: 1, Relation of Specific Psychological Characteristics to Rate of Gastric Secretion (Serum Pepsinogen)." *Psychosom Med* 19:1–10 Ja–F '57. * (*PA* 32:1913)

133. ADAMS, ABBY BONIME. *The Relationship Between Prenatal Choice of Infant Feeding Technique (Breast or Bottle) and Maternal Personality.* Doctor's thesis, Columbia University (New York, N.Y.), 1958. (*DA* 19:168)

134. AMCHIN, ABRAHAM. *Personality Patterns of Adolescent Delinquent Enuretics: A Comparative Analysis Between Adolescent Delinquents Who Are Known To Be Enuretic and Adolescent Delinquents Who Are Known Not To Be Enuretic.* Doctor's thesis, New York University (New York, N.Y.), 1958. (*DA* 19:2652)

135. ADAMS, ABBY BONIME. "Choice of Infant Feeding Technique as a Function of Maternal Personality." *J Consult Psychol* 23:143–6 Ap '59. * (*PA* 34:991)

136. LINDZEY, GARDNER. "On the Classification of Projective Techniques." *Psychol B* 56:158–68 Mr '59. * (*PA* 34:1389)

137. YOUNG, MAXIM F. *An Investigation of Narcissism and Correlates of Narcissism in Schizophrenics, Neurotics, and Normals.* Doctor's thesis, Temple University (Philadelphia, Pa.), 1959. (*DA* 20:3394)

138. PEDERSEN, FRANK, AND MARLOWE, DAVID. "Capacity and Motivational Differences in Verbal Recall." *J Clin Psychol* 16:219–22 Ap '60. * (*PA* 36:2HJ19P)

139. WHITE, JOSEPH LEWIS, JR. *Attitudes Toward Child Rearing as Related to Some Psychodynamic Factors in Mothers.* Doctor's thesis, Michigan State University (East Lansing, Mich.), 1961. (*DA* 22:4414)

140. GRANT, CHARLES O. *A Study of Personality Characteristics of Clients Self-Referred and Other-Referred to a Student Counseling Center.* Doctor's thesis, University of Buffalo (Buffalo, N.Y.), 1962. (*DA* 23:2204)

141. PRYOR, DAVID BRUCE. *Regression in the Service of the Ego: Psychosexual Development and Ego Functions.* Doctor's thesis, Michigan State University (East Lansing, Mich.), 1962. (*DA* 23:3982)

142. BERGER, LESLIE. "Interrelationship Between Blood Pressure Responses to Mecholyl and Personality Variables." *Psychophysiol* 1:115–8 O '64. * (*PA* 41:5684)

143. BLATT, SIDNEY J. "An Attempt to Define Mental Health." *J Consult Psychol* 28:146–53 Ap '64. * (*PA* 39:2352)

144. EDWARDS, WARREN P., III. *An Investigation of Sex Area Maladjustment and Manifest Level of Psychosexual Development.* Master's thesis, Ohio University (Athens, Ohio), 1964.

145. KARON, BERTRAM P. "An Experimental Study of Parental Castration Phantasies in Schizophrenia." *Brit J Psychiatry* 110:67–73 Ja '64. * (*PA* 39:2690)

146. ZUBIN, JOSEPH; ERON, LEONARD D.; AND SCHUMER, FLORENCE. *An Experimental Approach to Projective Techniques,* pp. 497–502. New York: John Wiley & Sons, Inc., 1965. Pp. xxi, 645. * (*PA* 39:15432)

147. FISHER, SEYMOUR. "Body Attention Patterns and Person-

ality Defenses." *Psychol Monogr* 80(9):1–31 '66. * (*PA* 40:10142)

148. MIGDOLE, SAMUEL MARK. *An Investigation of Orality, Depression, and Denial in Obese and Non-Obese Adolescent Females.* Doctor's thesis, Boston University (Boston, Mass.), 1967. (*DA* 29:4850B)

149. ROBINSON, SANDRA AUSTIN. *A Comparison of Expressed Acceptance of Self and of Others and Responses on the Blacky Pictures of Two Adolescent Groups.* Doctor's thesis, University of California (Los Angeles, Calif.), 1967. (*DA* 28:1311A)

150. GROSS, STEVEN JAY; HIRT, MICHAEL; AND SEEMAN, WILLIAM. "Psychosexual Conflicts in Asthmatic Children." *J Psychosom Res* 11:315–7 Mr '68. * (*PA* 42:15936)

151. HEDEGARD, SHEILA ANNE GALLIVAN. *A Molecular Analysis of Psychological Defense Mechanisms.* Doctor's thesis, University of Michigan (Ann Arbor, Mich.), 1968. (*DAI* 30:369B)

152. SCHAEFFER, DIRK L. "Addenda to an Annotated Bibliography of the Blacky Test (1949–1967)." *J Proj Tech & Pers Assess* 32:550–5 D '68. * (*PA* 43:9802)

153. SCHAEFFER, DIRK L. "Blacky the Cat: 1, Semantic Differential Ratings." *J Proj Tech & Pers Assess* 32:542–9 D '68. * (*PA* 43:9803)

154. FALK, HILDA B. *Developmental Crisis, Perceived Family Relations and College Achievement.* Doctor's thesis, Yeshiva University (New York, N.Y.), 1969. (*DAI* 30:2906B)

155. KLINE, PAUL, AND GALE, ANTHONY. "An Objective Method of Administering a Projective Test—The Blacky Pictures." *Brit J Proj Psychol & Pers Study* 14(2):12–6 D '69. * (*PA* 46:5010)

156. MARUYAMA, YOSHIO. *The Sense of Competence in Middle Adolescent Boys.* Doctor's thesis, Boston University (Boston, Mass.), 1969. (*DAI* 30:2405B)

157. PODOLNICK, EDWARD E. *Oral Anxiety and Hypnotic Susceptibility.* Doctor's thesis, New York University (New York, N.Y.), 1969. (*DAI* 30:3873B)

158. WEISS, LILLIE RABIE. "Effects of Subject, Experimenter and Task Variables on Compliance With the Experimenter's Expectation." *J Proj Tech & Pers Assess* 33(3):247–56 Je '69. * (*PA* 43:14309)

159. KARON, BERTRAM P. "An Experimental Study of Parental Castration Phantasies." *Brit J Psychiatry* 117(536):69–73 Jl '70. * (*PA* 45:2590)

160. KLINE, PAUL. "A Projective and Psychometric Study of the Oral Character." *Int Congr Rorsch & Other Proj Tech* 7:506–12 '70. *

161. AGUADO, ROBERT STANLEY. *An Investigation of the Psychodynamics of Black Junior College Freshmen With Reading Disabilities Utilizing the Rotter Incomplete Sentences Blank and Psychoanalytic Theory as Psychodiagnostic Tools for Counseling.* Doctor's thesis, University of Southern California (Los Angeles, Calif.), 1971. (*DAI* 32:3081A)

162. BLUM, GERALD S., AND GRAEF, JED R. "The Detection Over Time of Subjects Simulating Hypnosis." *Int J Clin & Exp Hyp* 19(4):211–24 O '71. * (*PA* 47:4059)

163. COOPERMAN, MARC, AND CHILD, IRVIN L. "Differential Effects of Positive and Negative Reinforcement on Two Psychoanalytic Character Types." *J Consult & Clin Psychol* 37(1):57–9 Ag '71. * (*PA* 47:908)

164. GALINSKY, M. DAVID. "Relationships Among Personality, Defense, and Academic Failure." *J Pers Assess* 35(4):359–63 Ag '71. * (*PA* 47:4799)

165. KLINE, PAUL, AND TREJDOSIEWICZ, L. "The I.E.S. Test and the Blacky Pictures." *Brit J Proj Psychol & Pers Study* 16(2):19–21 D '71. *

Graef, J. R.: 162
Granick, S.: 44
Grant, C. O.: 140
Grayden, C.: 84
Gross, S. J.: 150
Hammer, E.: 7
Hart, R. D.: 8
Hedegard, S. A. G.: 151
Hendrix, V. L.: 109
Hilgeman, L. M. B.: 9
Hirt, M.: 150
Hogan, V.: 26
Hunt, H. F.: 11
Irwin, T. C.: 77
Jacobs, M. O.: 42
Karon, B. P.: 145, 159
Kaufman, J. B.: 12
Kimeldorf, C.: 108
King, D. C.: 99
King, F. W.: 99
Klehr, H.: 4, 15
Kline, P.: 116, 155, 160, 165
Lasky, J. J.: 60
Lawton, M. J.: 71
Leichty, M. M.: 53, 88
Lindner, H.: 10, 21
Lindzev, G.: 136
Logan, N. P.: 89
Lutzky, H. L.: 93
Lyon, B.: 49
Machover, S.: 61-2
McNeil, E. B.: 16
Maes, J. L.: 94
Magnussen, M. G.: 63
Marcus, M. M.: 95
Margolis, M.: 91
Margolis, M. O.: 64
Marlowe, D.: 138
Marquis, D. P.: 48
Martin, J. O.: 54
Maruyama, Y.: 156
Mendelsohn, G. A.: 69
Merritt, R. K.: 130
Michal-Smith, H.: 7
Migdole, S. M.: 148
Miller, D. R.: 13
Minkowich, A.: 69, 86
Mirsky, I. A.: 132
Molish, H. B.: 49
Neuman, G. G.: 55
Newton, K. R.: rev, 5:125
Noblin, C. D.: 79, 105
Normington, C. J.: 100
Orbach, C. H.: 90
Pedersen, F.: 138
Perloe, S. I.: 67, 69, 87
Podolnick, E. E.: 157
Pollie, D. M.: 101, 131
Powell, E. K.: 39
Pryor, D. B.: 141
Puzzo, F. S.: 61-2
Rabin, A. I.: 45, 107
Redmond, J.: 52

Reed, W. W.: 31
Reiser, M. F.: 132
Robinson, S. A.: 109, 117, 149
Rosen, E.: exc, 4:102
Rosen, I. C.: 17
Rossi, A. M.: 72
Salvatore, J. C.: 55
Sappenfield, B. R.: rev, 6:204
Schaeffer, D. L.: 152-3
Scheflen, N. A.: 44
Schill, T.: 110
Schmeidler, G. R.: 93
Schumer, F.: 146
Seeman, W.: 150
Segal, A. S. B.: 80
Seward, J. P.: 5
Shaffer, L. F.: exc, 4:102
Sharma, S. L.: 81
Shellow, R. S.: 129
Shire, A.: 125
Silverman, A. J.: 70
Sinnett, E. R.: 22, 48
Sirota, L. M.: 82
Smith, W.: 39
Smock, C. D.: 27
Solomon, P.: 72
Spitz, H.: 7
Stenmark, D. E.: 118
Streitfield, H. S.: 50
Stricker, G.: 78, 112
Swanson, G. E.: 46
Taulbee, E. S.: 118
Taylor, K. E.: 18
Teevan, R. C.: 28
Thaler, M.: 132
Thelen, M. H.: 102, 113
Thomas, R. W.: 47
Thompson, G. F.: 27
Timmons, E. O.: 79, 105
Tober, L. H.: 23
Trejdosiewicz, L.: 165
Trent, R. D.: 43
Trippe, M. J.: 85
Vernallis, F. F.: 126
Vroom, A. L.: 69
Vroom, A. L. W.: 68
Waddell, W.: 70
Watson, D. J.: 123
Weiner, H.: 132
Weingarten, L. L.: 96
Weiss, J. L.: 69, 127
Weiss, L. R.: 158
White, J. L.: 139
Winter, L. M.: 40
Winter, W. D.: 29, 32, 48
Wolf, I. W.: 69
Wolff, F.: 41
Wolfson, W.: 41
Yelsky, M.: 103
Young, M. F.: 137
Zubin, J.: 146
Zuidema, G. D.: 70

[1449]

Braverman-Chevigny Auditory Projective Test.
Ages 4 and over; 1955-64; BCAPT; for research use
only; intended to be an auditory equivalent of *Thematic Apperception Test;* Sydell Braverman and Hector Chevigny; American Foundation for the Blind,
Inc. *

For additional information, see P:417 (2 references).

REFERENCES THROUGH 1971

1-2. See P:417.
3. BREGER, ILANA. "Some Structural Variables in Auditory
Projective Testing." *J Proj Tech & Pers Assess* 33(5):414-8 O
'69. * (*PA* 44:3650)
4. LAX, BERNARD. *The Effects of Environmental Conditions
on Blind and Sighted Children as Measured by Structured
Sound Situations.* Doctor's thesis, University of Texas (Austin,
Tex.), 1970. (*DAI* 31:5851A)

CUMULATIVE NAME INDEX

Abramson, L. S.: 1   Kramer, E.: 2
Aronovitch, C. D.: 2   Lax, B.: 4
Breger, I.: 3

[1450]

**Buttons: A Projective Test for Pre-Adolescent
and Adolescent Boys and Girls.** Grades 7-9; maladjustment; 1963; 3 scores: initial, content, total;

Blacky Pictures

Esther P. Rothman and Pearl H. Berkowitz; Western
Psychological Services. *

For additional information and a review by Willard
E. Reitz, see 7:162.

[1451]

***Children's Apperception Test.** Ages 3-10; 1949-
74; CAT; 3 editions; Leopold Bellak, Sonya Sorel
Bellak, Mary R. Haworth (checklist), and Marvin S.
Hurvich (manual for c); C.P.S., Inc. *

a) CHILDREN'S APPERCEPTION TEST. 1949-74; 1959 test
picture cards same as cards published 1949 and 1951
except for finish.

b) CHILDREN'S APPERCEPTION TEST—SUPPLEMENT. 1952-
55; 10 pictures, one or more of which may be presented
in addition to the regular CAT.

c) CHILDREN'S APPERCEPTION TEST (HUMAN FIGURES).
1965; designed to be "equivalent" to the regular CAT
cards.

For additional information, see P:419 (18 refer-
ences); for reviews by Bernard I. Murstein and Robert
D. Wirt, see 6:206 (19 references); for reviews by
Douglas T. Kenny and Albert I. Rabin, see 5:126 (15
references); for reviews by John E. Bell and L. Joseph
Stone and excerpted reviews by M. M. Genn, Herbert
Herman, Robert R. Holt, Laurance F. Shaffer, and
Adolf G. Woltmann, see 4:103 (2 references). For
excerpts from related book reviews, see 7:B280 (2
excerpts) and 5:B63 (8 excerpts).

REFERENCES THROUGH 1971

1-2. See 4:103.
3-17. See 5:126.
18-36. See 6:206.
37-54. See P:419.
55. BENNETT, EDWARD M., AND JOHANNSEN, DOROTHEA E.
"Psychodynamics of the Diabetic Child." *Psychol Monogr*
68(11):1-23 '54. * (*PA* 29:6072)
56. FITZSIMONS, RUTH. *Some Developmental, Psycho-Social,
and Educational Variables Among Children With Normal Speech
and Children With Functional Articulation Problems.* Doctor's
thesis, Boston University (Boston, Mass.), 1955. (*DA* 16:404)
57. KOCH, HELEN L. "The Relation of Certain Family Constellation Characteristics and the Attitudes of Children Toward
Adults." *Child Develop* 26:13-40 Mr '55. * (*PA* 30:2546)
58. SOPCHAK, ANDREW L. "Projective Study of Peter and
His Parents: Revealing the Necessary Therapeutic Limitations."
J Child Psychiatry 3:149-200 Ag '56. * (*PA* 31:8363)
59. SCHULMAN, DORIS. *A Study of the Relationships Between
Mothers' Attitudes Toward Their Children, and the Personality
Adjustment and School Behavior of These Children.* Doctor's
thesis, New York University (New York, N.Y.), 1958. (*DA*
19:734)
60. POWELL, KATHRYN SUMMERS. *Maternal Employment in
Relation to Family Life.* Doctor's thesis, Florida State University
(Tallahassee, Fla.), 1960. (*DA* 21:2269)
61. SIEGEL, GERALD M. "Interexaminer Reliability for Mean
Length of Response." *J Speech & Hearing Res* 5:91-5 Mr '62. *
(*PA* 37:1937)
62. BOURISSEAU, WHITFIELD. *A Study of Non-Intellectual
Factors in Relation to School Achievement of Primary-Grade
Pupils.* Master's thesis, Kent State University (Kent, Ohio),
1964.
63. TSUJI, SHOZO. "Some Investigations of Parental Preference in Early Childhood." *Rorsch Newsl* 10:37-41 Je '65. *
(*PA* 40:2706)
64. ZUBIN, JOSEPH; ERON, LEONARD D.; AND SCHUMER,
FLORENCE. *An Experimental Approach to Projective Techniques,*
pp. 502-8. New York: John Wiley & Sons, Inc., 1965. Pp. xxi,
645. * (*PA* 39:15432)
65. KOOLS, JOSEPH ANTHONY. *Adaptation, Consistency, and
Loci of Disfluency in Young Children.* Doctor's thesis, University of Iowa (Iowa City, Iowa), 1966. (*DA* 27:1648B)
66. FRANCIS-WILLIAMS, JESSIE. Chap. 9, "A Serial Study of
an Institutionalised Child Showing the Comparative Contribution to Rorschach Findings of Two Other Projective Techniques
—The Children's Apperception Test and the Family Relations
Test," pp. 110-23. In her *Rorschach With Children: A Comparative Study of the Contribution Made by the Rorschach and
Other Projective Techniques to Clinical Diagnosis in Work
With Children.* London: Pergamon Press Ltd., 1968. Pp. xi,
168. *
67. RYMSZA, JANUSZKA SOFIA DE LILIO. *Factors Analysis of
Measures of Divergent Thinking Obtained From the Children's
Apperception Test and Measures of Intelligence Obtained From
the Wechsler Intelligence Scale for Children.* Doctor's thesis,

Florida State University (Tallahassee, Fla.), 1968. (*DAI* 30: 831B)

68. Silverman, Ellen-Marie, and Williams, Dean E. "A Comparison of Stuttering and Nonstuttering Children in Terms of Five Measures of Oral Language Development." *J Commun Disorders* (Netherlands) 1:305–9 O '68. * (*PA* 43:15553)

69. Tiwari, J. G., and Shukla, S. N. "P-F and C.A.T. Responses of the Over- and Under-Chosen in Municipal Primary Schools of Aligarh." *Indian J Social Work* 28:467–70 Ja '68. * (*PA* 42:14495)

70. Bose, Sukumar, and Benerjee, Surendra N. "A Resolution on the Personality Make-Up of Some Institutionalised Physically Handicapped Children by the Children's Apperception Test." *J Psychol Res* (India) 13(1):32–6 Ja '69. * (*PA* 45:4696)

71. Porterfield, Charles L. "Adaptive Mechanisms of Young Disadvantaged Stutterers and Nonstutterers." *J Proj Tech & Pers Assess* 33(4):371–5 Ag '69. * (*PA* 44:2144)

72. Garrish, Eunice. *The Relationship of Violence to the Ability, Achievement, and Adjustment of Sixth-Grade Children.* Doctor's thesis, North Texas State University (Denton, Tex.), 1970. (*DAI* 31:5199A)

73. Hirsch, Ernest A. *The Troubled Adolescent: As He Emerges From Psychological Tests.* New York: International Universities Press, Inc., 1970. Pp. xv, 645. *

74. Neuringer, Charles, and Livesay, Robert C. "Projective Fantasy on the CAT and CAT-H." *J Proj Tech & Pers Assess* 34(6):487–91 D '70. * (*PA* 45:7939)

75. Scott, Edward. "Social Value Acquisition in Preschool Aged Children: 3, Internalization of Institutionalized Value Expectations." *Sociol Q* 11(1):14–31 w '70. *

76. Singh, Udai Pratap, and Akhtar, Syed Nehal. "The Children's Apperception Test in the Study of Orphans." *Psychol Ann* 4:1–6 Mr '70. * (*PA* 46:2744)

77. Bellak, Leopold; with the assistance of Ann Noll and Lynn Lustbader. *The Thematic Apperception Test and the Children's Apperception Test in Clinical Use, Second Edition.* New York: Grune & Stratton, Inc., 1971. Pp. xvi, 328. *

CUMULATIVE NAME INDEX

Adelman, C.: 24
Ainsworth, M. D.: 3
Akhtar, S. N.: 76
Armstrong, M. A. S.: 18
Arthur, B.: *exc,* 7:B280
Barbour, R. F.: *exc,* 7:B280
Bell, J. E.: *rev,* 4:103
Bellak, L.: 1, 9, 24, 44, 50, 77
Bellak, S. S.: 1
Benerjee, S. N.: 70
Bennett, E. M.: 55
Biersdorf, K. R.: 6
Bose, S.: 70
Boston, M.: 3
Bourisseau, W.: 62
Budoff, M.: 25, 34
Butler, R. L.: 29
Byrd, E.: 10
Cain, A. C.: 30
Catalano, F. L.: *exc,* 5:B63
d'Heurle, A.: 38
Edwards, A. S.: *exc,* 5:B63
Eron, L. D.: 64
FitzSimons, R.: 37, 56
Foster, H. C.: 33
Francis-Williams, J.: 66
Furuya, K.: 16
Garrish, E.: 72
Genn, M. M.: *exc,* 4:103
Ginsparg, H. T.: 17
Golias, G. A.: 26
Good, J. A.: 43
Gross, S. Z.: 35
Gunn, R. C.: 40
Gurevitz, S.: 2
Haggard, E. A.: 38
Haworth, M. R.: 32, 36, 41, 45, 51
Herman, H.: *exc,* 4:103
Hirsch, E. A.: 73
Holden, R. H.: 14
Holt, R. R.: *exc,* 4:103
Hurvich, M. S.: 44
Hutt, M. L.: *exc,* 5:B63
Johannsen, D. E.: 55
Kagan, M. G.: 13
Kato, N.: 47
Kelley, D. M.: *exc,* 5:B63
Kenny, D. T.: *rev,* 5:126
Klapper, Z. S.: 2
Koch, H. L.: 57
Kools, J. A.: 65
Kosier, K. P.: 42

Kumar, B.: 48
Lawton, M. J.: 46
Lehmann, I. J.: 21
Light, B. H.: 11
Livesay, R. C.: 74
Lustbader, L.: 77
Lyle, J. G.: *exc,* 5:B63
Lyles, W. K.: 19
Lynn, D. B.: 8
Magnusson, D.: 27
Mainord, F. R.: 12
Marcuse, F. L.: 6, 12
Mathur, S.: 48
Mellinger, J. C.: 38
Millar, M.: 4
Moriarty, A. E.: 52
Murstein, B. I.: *rev,* 6:206
Neuringer, C.: 74
Nolan, R. D.: 22
Noll, A.: 77
Porterfield, C. L.: 71
Powell, K. S.: 39, 60
Rabin, A. I.: 53; *rev,* 5:126
Reddy, P. V.: 28
Rosenblatt, M. S.: 20
Rymsza, J. S. D.: 67
Schulman, D.: 59
Schumer, F.: 64
Scott, E.: 75
Semeonoff, B.: *exc,* 5:B63
Shaffer, L. F.: *exc,* 4:103, 5:B63
Shneidman, E. S.: 7; *exc,* 5:B63
Shukla, S. N.: 69
Siegel, G. M.: 61
Silverman, E. M.: 68
Simmons, D. D.: 49
Singh, U. P.: 76
Sopchak, A. L.: 58
Stone, L. J.: *rev,* 4:103
Tiwari, J. G.: 69
Toppelstein, S.: 5
Tsuji, S.: 47, 63
Walton, D.: 23
Weisskopf-Joelson, E.: 33
Weisskopf-Joelson, E. A.: 8
Wheeler, W. M.: 15
Williams, D. E.: 68
Williams, J. M.: 31
Wirt, R. D.: *rev,* 6:206
Witherspoon, R. L.: 10, 54
Woltmann, A. G.: *exc,* 4:103
Zubin, J.: 64

[1452]

Color Pyramid Test. Ages 6 and over; 1951–65 (English edition, 1964–65); CPT; nonverbal "technique for the study of the role of emotion and affect"; English revision of *Der Farbpyramiden-Test nach Max Pfister* (1951) by Robert Heiss and Hildegard Hiltmann; K. Warner Schaie and Robert Heiss; Hans Huber [Switzerland]. * (United States distributor: Grune & Stratton, Inc.)

For additional information, reviews by S. G. Lee and Albert I. Rabin, and excerpted reviews by C. H. Ammons, L. J. Clements, and Moyra Williams, see 7:163 (1 reference); see also P:420 (9 references).

REFERENCES THROUGH 1971

1–9. See P:420.
10. See 7:163.
11. O'Reilly, P. O.; Holzinger, Rudolf; and Blewett, Duncan. "The Pfister Colored Pyramid Test." *J Nerv & Mental Dis* 125:385–7 Jl–S '57. * (*PA* 33:3858)
12. Bjerstedt, Åke. "Warm-Cool Color Preferences as Potential Personality Indicators: Preliminary Note." *Percept & Motor Skills* 10:31–4 F '60. * (*PA* 34:7369)
13. O'Reilly, P. O., and Harrison, K. "Experimentation With an Objective Test Battery." *Can Psychiatric Assn J* 5:108–23 Ap '60. *
14. Oo, M.; Csirszka, J.; and Hegedus, J. "Psychological Tests in Leukaemia Patients," pp. 18–29. In *Psychosomatic Aspects of Neoplastic Disease.* The Proceedings of the Third International Conference of the International Psychosomatic Cancer Study Group Held at Newnham College, Cambridge, England, 22nd to 26th July 1963. Edited by D. M. Kissen and L. L. Leshan. Philadelphia, Pa.: J. B. Lippincott Co., 1964. Pp. xii, 231. *
15. Greene, William J. *Differentiation of Schizophrenics From Other Mental Institution Patients by the Pfister Color Pyramid Test.* Master's thesis, Sacramento State College (Sacramento, Calif.), 1969.
16. Hooke, James F. "Correlates of Delinquent Behavior." *Psychol Rep* 28(3):795–800 Je '71. * (*PA* 46:11174)

CUMULATIVE NAME INDEX

Ammons, C. H.: *exc,* 7:163
Bjerstedt, A.: 12
Blewett, D.: 11
Burdick, J. A.: 7
Clements, L. J.: *exc,* 7:163
Csirszka, J.: 14
Dilts, M.: 3
Greene, W. J.: 15
Harrison, K.: 13
Hegedus, J.: 14
Heiss, R.: 4

Holanchock, G. M.: 5
Holzinger, R.: 11
Hooke, J. F.: 8, 16
Lee, S. G.: *rev,* 7:163
Oo, M.: 14
O'Reilly, P. O.: 11, 13
Rabin, A. I.: *rev,* 7:163
Schaie, K. W.: 1–2, 4, 6, 8–10
Taylor, R. E.: 3
Williams, M.: *exc,* 7:163

[1453]

The Columbus: Picture Analysis of Growth Towards Maturity. Ages 5–20; 1969; M. J. Langeveld; S. Karger AG [Switzerland]. *

For additional information and excerpted reviews by C. H. Ammons (with R. B. Ammons) and Steven G. Vandenberg, see 7:164 (1 reference).

REFERENCES THROUGH 1971

1. See 7:164.

CUMULATIVE NAME INDEX

Ammons, C. H.: *exc,* 7:164   Langeveld, M. J.: 1
Ammons, R. B.: *exc,* 7:164   Vandenberg, S. G.: *exc,* 7:164

[1454]

Curtis Completion Form. Grades 11–16 and adults; 1950–68; CCF; emotional maturity and adjustment; James W. Curtis; Western Psychological Services. *

For additional information, see P:421 (3 references); for reviews by Irwin G. Sarason and Laurance F. Shaffer, see 6:208 (2 references); for a review by Alfred B. Heilbrun, Jr., see 5:128.

REFERENCES THROUGH 1971

1–2. See 6:208.
3–5. See P:421.
6. Hampton, Peter J. "A Study of Hidden Motives and Conflicts in University Counseling." *Congreso Interamericano de Psicologia* (Mexico) 7:437–41 '63. *

[1455]

The Draw-A-Person. Ages 5 and over; 1963; DAP; William H. Urban; Western Psychological Services. *

For additional information and reviews by Dale B. Harris and Philip M. Kitay, see 7:165.

[1456]

Draw-A-Person Quality Scale. Ages 16–25; 1955–65; DPQS; level of intellectual functioning; Mazie Earle Wagner and Herman J. P. Schubert; Herman J. P. Schubert. *

For additional information, see P:423 (3 references) ; for a review by Philip L. Harriman, see 5:129 (3 references).

REFERENCES THROUGH 1971

1–3. See 5:129.
4–6. See P:423.

[1457]

The Driscoll Play Kit. Ages 2–10; 1952; DPK; personality development and adjustment; Gertrude P. Driscoll; Psychological Corporation. *

For additional information, see P:424; see also 6:210 (2 references).

REFERENCES THROUGH 1971

1–2. See 6:210.
3. PEIXOTTO, HELEN E., AND HILL, EVELYN F. "Phantasy in Asthmatic Children With Special Reference to Driscoll Doll Play." *J Asthma Res* 2:199–204 Mr '65. *

[1458]

★Education Apperception Test. Preschool and elementary school; 1973; EAT; photographs attempting to evoke phantasy in 4 areas : reaction toward authority, reaction toward learning, peer relationship, home attitude toward school; no scores; Jack M. Thompson and Robert A. Sones; Western Psychological Services. *

REFERENCES THROUGH 1971

1. THOMPSON, JACK M., AND SONES, ROBERT A. "The Education Apperception Test: A Preliminary Development." *Calif J Ed Res* 19:101–11 My '68. * (*PA* 42:14733)

[1459]

The Family Relations Indicator, Revised Edition. Emotionally disturbed children and their parents; 1962–67; FRI; intra-family relationships; John G. Howells and John R. Lickorish; Brunner/Mazel, Inc. *

For additional information, a review by Paul Kline, and excerpted reviews by R. F. Barbour and Alistair Munro, see 7:166 (2 references) ; see also P:427 (1 reference) ; for reviews by C. B. Blakemore and Walter Katkovsky of the original edition, see 6:212 (1 reference).

REFERENCES THROUGH 1971

1. See 6:212.
2. See P:427.
3–4. See 7:166.

[1460]

The Five Task Test: A Performance and Projective Test of Emotionality, Motor Skill and Organic Brain Damage. Ages 8 and over; 1955; FTT; Charlotte Buhler and Kathryn Mandeville; Western Psychological Services. *

For additional information, see P:428; for reviews by Dorothy H. Eichorn and Bert R. Sappenfield and an excerpted review by Laurance F. Shaffer, see 5:133.

[1461]

*The Forer Structured Sentence Completion Test. Ages 10–18, adults; 1957–67; FSSCT; Bertram R. Forer; Western Psychological Services. *

For additional information, see P:429 (4 references) ; for reviews by Charles N. Cofer and Percival M. Symonds, see 5:134 (5 references).

REFERENCES THROUGH 1971

1–5. See 5:134.
6–9. See P:429.
10. SHNEIDMAN, EDWIN S. "The Case of El: Psychological Test Data." *J Proj Tech* 25:131–54 Je '61. * (*PA* 36:21K31S)
11. GOLDBERG, PHILIP A. "A Review of Sentence Completion Methods in Personality Assessment." *J Proj Tech & Pers Assess* 29:12–45 Mr '65. * (*PA* 39:10112)
12. CARR, ARTHUR C. "Psychological Testing and Reporting." *J Proj Tech & Pers Assess* 32:513–21 D '68. * (*PA* 43:9995)

[1462]

The Forer Vocational Survey. Adolescents and adults; 1957; FVS; vocational adjustment; Bertram R. Forer; Western Psychological Services. *

For additional information, see P:430; for reviews by Benjamin Balinsky and Charles N. Cofer and an excerpted review by Laurence Siegel, see 5:135.

[1463]

Franck Drawing Completion Test. Ages 6 and over; 1951–52; FDCT; masculinity-femininity; Kate Franck; Australian Council for Educational Research [Australia]. *

For additional information, see P:432 (5 references) ; for a review by Arthur W. Meadows, see 5:136 (5 references).

REFERENCES THROUGH 1971

1–5. See 5:136.
6–10. See P:432.
11. REED, MAX RODNEY. *A Study of the Masculinity-Femininity Dimension of Personality in "Normal" and "Pathological" Groups: An Investigation of Differences in MF Test Productions of Hospitalized and Non-Hospitalized Women.* Doctor's thesis, Washington University (St. Louis, Mo.), 1955. (*DA* 15:1442)
12. LANSKY, LEONARD MARVIN. *Patterns of Defense Against Conflict.* Doctor's thesis, University of Michigan (Ann Arbor, Mich.), 1956. (*DA* 16:2539)
13. WEITZENHOFFER, ANDRÉ MULLER. *Hypnotic Susceptibility as Related to Masculinity-Femininity.* Doctor's thesis, University of Michigan (Ann Arbor, Mich.), 1956. (*DA* 17:1397)
14. ALTUCHER, NATHAN. *Conflict in Sex Identification in Boys.* Doctor's thesis, University of Michigan (Ann Arbor, Mich.), 1957. (*DA* 18:1487)
15. LANSKY, LEONARD M. Chap. 12, "Mechanisms of Defense: 5, Sex Identity and Defenses Against Aggression," pp. 272–88. In *Inner Conflict and Defense.* By Daniel R. Miller and Others. New York: Henry Holt & Co., Inc., 1960. Pp. x, 452. *
16. WINER, FRANK. *The Relationship of Certain Attitudes*

Toward the Mother to Sex-Role Identity. Doctor's thesis, New York University (New York, N.Y.), 1961. (*DA* 22:4416)

17. JASKAR, RAINO O., AND REED, MAX R. "Assessment of Body Image Organization of Hospitalized and Non-Hospitalized Subjects." *J Proj Tech & Pers Assess* 27:185–90 Je '63. * (*PA* 38:2627)

18. STRASSBURGER, FRED. *Perception and Fantasy: A Study of Sex Differences and Personality Correlates.* Doctor's thesis, Stanford University (Stanford, Calif.), 1963. (*DA* 24:3417)

19. MCCAULLEY, MARY H. *Dimensions of Masculinity-Femininity in Relation to Field Dependence, Dogmatism, and Other Estimates of Perceptual-Cognitive Differentiation.* Doctor's thesis, Temple University (Philadelphia, Pa.), 1964. (*DA* 25:4259)

20. FELDMAN, RUTH CAMM. *A Study of Cognitive Style and Some Personality Variables in Relation to the Conceptual Performance of Emotionally Disturbed Adolescents.* Doctor's thesis, Temple University (Philadelphia, Pa.), 1965. (*DA* 26:1773)

21. LIPINSKI, BEATRICE GRACE. *Sex-Role Conflict and Achievement Motivation in College Women.* Doctor's thesis, University of Cincinnati (Cincinnati, Ohio), 1965. (*DA* 26:4077)

22. PRESTON, GRACE ANN. *Parental Role Perceptions and Identification in Adolescent Girls.* Doctor's thesis, University of Michigan (Ann Arbor, Mich.), 1965. (*DA* 27:612B)

23. VINT, VIRGINIA HOLLISTER. *The Effect of Prior Convergent or Divergent Art Training on Subsequent Art Activity.* Doctor's thesis, Stanford University (Stanford, Calif.), 1965. (*DA* 26:914)

24. COLSON, DONALD BERNARD. *The Interaction of Sex-Role Conflict With the Experimental Manipulation of Masculinity-Femininity Test Scores of College Students.* Doctor's thesis, University of Cincinnati (Cincinnati, Ohio), 1966. (*DA* 27:2131B)

25. LIPSITT, PAUL D., AND STRODTBECK, FRED L. "Defensiveness in Decision Making as a Function of Sex-Role Identification." *J Pers & Social Psychol* 6:10–5 My '67. * (*PA* 41:8396)

26. ROSENFELD, HERBERT MICHAEL. *Delinquent Acting-Out in Adolescent Males and Its Relationship to the Task of Sexual Identification.* Doctor's thesis, Smith College (Northhampton, Mass.), 1967. (*DA* 28:4301B)

27. COTTLE, THOMAS J. "Family Perceptions, Sex Role Identity and the Prediction of School Performance." *Ed & Psychol Meas* 28:861–86 au '68. * (*PA* 43:4515)

28. LANDAU, DALE; ERICSON-MUSSIG, CARYL; AND WAITE, MELINDA. "Personality Variables Related to Subliminal Perception." *J Psychol & Behav Sci* 3:3–9 My '68. *

29. RAYCHAUDHURI, MANAS, AND MAITRA, AMAL K. "Relationship Between Level of Creativity and Projection of Movement Responses as Measured by Rorschach M, Welsh Mv and a Drawing Completion Task." *Indian J Psychol* 43(1–4):30–6 '68. *

30. BOMBARD, JAMES ARTHUR. *An Experimental Examination of Penis Envy.* Doctor's thesis, Wayne State University (Detroit, Mich.), 1969. (*DAI* 32:2996B)

31. BONIFACIO, PHILIP P., AND SCHAEFER, CHARLES E. "Creativity and the Projection of Movement Responses." *J Proj Tech & Pers Assess* 33(4):380–4 Ag '69. * (*PA* 44:2360)

32. FELLOWS, ROBERT, AND CERBUS, GEORGE. "HTP and DCT Indicators of Sexual Identification in Children." *J Proj Tech & Pers Assess* 33(4):376–9 Ag '69. * (*PA* 44:2136)

33. LANSKY, LEONARD M., AND MCKAY, GERALD. "Independence, Dependence, Manifest and Latent Masculinity-Femininity: Some Complex Relationships Among Four Complex Variables." *Psychol Rep* 24(1):263–8 F '69. * (*PA* 43:14136)

34. SCHAEFER, CHARLES E. "The Prediction of Creative Achievement From a Biographical Inventory." *Ed & Psychol Meas* 29(2):431–7 su '69. * (*PA* 44:17333)

35. BEZDEK, WILLIAM, AND STRODTBECK, FRED L. "Sex-Role Identity and Pragmatic Action." *Am Sociol R* 35(3):491–502 Je '70. * (*PA* 46:4943)

36. BLANE, HOWARD T., AND YAMAMOTO, KAZUO. "Sexual Role Identity Among Japanese and Japanese-American High School Students." *J Cross-Cultural Psychol* 1(4):345–54 D '70. * (*PA* 45:9789)

37. COTTLE, THOMAS J.; EDWARDS, CARL N.; AND PLECK, JOSEPH. "The Relationship of Sex Role Identity and Social and Political Attitudes." *J Personality* 38(3):435–52 S '70. * (*PA* 45:4071)

38. HARRINGTON, CHARLES CHRISTOPHER. *Errors in Sex-Role Behavior in Teen-Age Boys.* New York: Teachers College Press, 1970. Pp. viii, 109. * (*PA* 21190, title only)

39. MCCARTHY, DOROTHEA; ANTHONY, ROBERT J.; AND DOMINO, GEORGE. "A Comparison of the CPI, Franck, MMPI, and WAIS Masculinity-Femininity Indexes." *J Consult & Clin Psychol* 35(3):414–6 D '70. * (*PA* 45:4284)

40. SCHAEFER, CHARLES E. "Development of an Originality Scale for the Franck Drawing Completion Test." *Percept & Motor Skills* 31(2):402 O '70. * (*PA* 45:6342)

41. URBINA, SUSANA; HARRISON, JOAN B.; SCHAEFER, CHARLES E.; AND ANASTASI, ANNE. "Relationship Between Masculinity-Femininity and Creativity as Measured by the Franck Drawing Completion Test." *Psychol Rep* 26(3):799–804 Je '70. * (*PA* 45:717)

42. ANASTASI, ANNE, AND SCHAEFER, CHARLES E. "The Franck Drawing Completion Test as a Measure of Creativity." *J Genetic Psychol* 119(1):3–12 S '71. * (*PA* 47:2989)

43. BILLER, HENRY B., AND BARRY, WILLIAM. "Sex-Role Patterns, Paternal Similarity, and Personality Adjustment in College Males." Abstract. *Develop Psychol* 4(1):107 Ja '71. * (*PA* 45:8201)

44. GREENE, GERALD MICHAEL. *Somato-Psychological Indicants of Schizophrenia: A Partial Validation of the Penetration-Barrier Index.* Doctor's thesis, University of Oklahoma (Norman, Okla.), 1971. (*DAI* 32:4212B)

45. MUNROE, ROBERT L., AND MUNROE, RUTH H. "Male Pregnancy Symptoms and Cross-Sex Identity in Three Societies." *J Social Psychol* 84(1):11–25 Je '71. * (*PA* 46:8849)

46. ROTHSTEIN, ARNOLD. *Depression in Pregnancy as It Relates to Feminine Identification Conflict and Perceived Environmental Support.* Doctor's thesis, Smith College (Northampton, Mass.), 1971. (*DAI* 32:5347A)

47. SUTER, BARBARA ANN. *Masculinity-Femininity in Creative Women.* Doctor's thesis, Fordham University (New York, N.Y.), 1971. (*DAI* 32:2411B)

48. THOMPSON, NORMAN LEE, JR. *Family Background and Sexual Identity in Male and Female Homosexuals.* Doctor's thesis, Emory University (Atlanta, Ga.), 1971. (*DAI* 32:1863B)

CUMULATIVE NAME INDEX

[1464]

★**The Gerontological Apperception Test.** Ages 66 and over; 1971; GAT; no scores; Robert L. Wolk and Rochelle B. Wolk; Behavioral Publications, Inc. *

REFERENCES THROUGH 1971

1. WOLK, ROBERT L.; RUSTIN, STANLEY L.; AND SEIDEN, ROCHELLE. "A Custom-Made Projective Technique for the Aged: The Gerontological Apperception Test." *J Long Island Consul Center* 4(1):7–21 f '66. *

2. OBERLEDER, MURIEL. "Adapting Current Psychological Techniques for Use in Testing the Aging." *Gerontologist* 7(3, pt 1):188–91 S '67. * (*PA* 42:3801)

CUMULATIVE NAME INDEX

[1465]

The Graphoscopic Scale: A Projective Psychodiagnostic Method.
Ages 5–16, 15 and over; 1953–69; author uses acronym PGS, denoting *Pikunas Graphoscopic Scale;* drawing completion technique; 5 scores: self-expressive balance, intelligence, creativity index, adjustment, total (called diagnostic and prognostic rating); Justin Pikunas; the Author. *

For additional information, see P:433 (8 references).

REFERENCES THROUGH 1971

1–8. See P:433.

9. BARNWELL, ADRIENNE. "Responses of Brazilian Children to the Pikunas Graphoscopic Scale." *Am Anthrop* 68:748–52 Je '66. *

CUMULATIVE NAME INDEX

[1466]

The Group Personality Projective Test. Ages 11 and over; 1956–61; GPPT; formerly called *Kahn Stick Figure Personality Test;* 7 scores: tension reduction quotient, nurturance, withdrawal, neuroticism, affiliation, succorance, total; Russell N. Cassel and Theodore C. Kahn; Psychological Test Specialists. *

For additional information and reviews by Edwin I. Megargee, Stuart Oskamp, and Marvin Reznikoff, see 7:167 (5 references); see also P:434 (2 references) and 6:214 (7 references).

REFERENCES THROUGH 1971

1–7. See 6:214.
8–9. See P:434.
10–14. See 7:167.
15. BATY, MARTHA ALDRIDGE. *A Comparison of Three Methods of Recording TAT Protocols.* Doctor's thesis, Louisiana State University (Baton Rouge, La.), 1970. (*DAI* 31:5613B)
16. BOUDREAUX, RONALD FELIX. *An Investigation of Hypothesized Item Content of the Group Personality Projective Test: A Validity Study.* Doctor's thesis, Louisiana State University (Baton Rouge, La.), 1971. (*DAI* 32:4201B)
17. KORELLA, KARL. *Teen-Age Suicidal Gestures: A Study of Suicidal Behavior Among High School Students.* Doctor's thesis, University of Oregon (Eugene, Ore.), 1971. (*DAI* 32:5039A)
18. NEWTON, JOYCE A. *Experimental Study of the Effects of a Pictorial Version of the Group Personality Projective Test With High School Students.* Master's thesis, University of Southern California (Los Angeles, Calif.), 1971.
19. OGSTON, DON, AND THOMPSON, ANGUS. "Influence of Social Desirability Upon the Group Personality Projective Test." *Psychol Rep* 28(2):677–8 Ap '71. * (*PA* 46:6903)

CUMULATIVE NAME INDEX

[1467]

Group Projection Sketches for the Study of Small Groups. Groups of 3–40 people (ages 16 and over); 1949; manual out of print; William E. Henry and Harold Guetzkow; William E. Henry. *

For additional information, see P:435; for a review by Cecil A. Gibb, see 5:138 (1 reference); for reviews by Robert R. Holt and N. W. Morton, see 4:106.

REFERENCES THROUGH 1971

1. See 5:138.
2. TORRANCE, E. PAUL. "Perception of Group Functioning as a Predictor of Group Performance." *J Social Psychol* 42:271–82 N '55. * (*PA* 31:799)

CUMULATIVE NAME INDEX

[1468]

HFD Test. Ages 5–12; 1968; HFDT; human figure drawing test, drawing of a whole person; level of mental ability score and 30 emotional indicator signs; Elizabeth Munsterberg Koppitz; Grune & Stratton, Inc. *

For additional information and a review by Dale B. Harris, see 7:168 (7 references); see also P:436 (8

references). For excerpts from related book reviews, see 7:B364 (3 excerpts).

REFERENCES THROUGH 1971

1–8. See P:436.
9–15. See 7:168.
16. CAMPBELL, WILLIAM A., III. "Psychometric Testing With the Human Figure Drawing in Chronic Cystitis." *J Urology* 104(6):930–3 D '70. *
17. GOLDMAN, ROANETE T-N. *A Gross Diagnosis of Minimal Cerebral Dysfunction in Children by Means of the Human Figure Drawing: A Validation of the Koppitz Method.* Doctor's thesis, University of Cincinnati (Cincinnati, Ohio), 1971. (*DAI* 32:4211B)
18. HANDLER, LEONARD, AND McINTOSH, JERRY. "Predicting Aggression and Withdrawal in Children With the Draw-A-Person and Bender Gestalt." *J Pers Assess* 35(4):331–5 Ag '71. * (*PA* 47:4564)
19. KOPPITZ, ELIZABETH MUNSTERBERG. *Children With Learning Disabilities: A Five Year Follow-Up Study.* New York: Grune & Stratton, Inc., 1971. Pp. xv, 218. *
20. LINGREN, RONALD H. "An Attempted Replication of Emotional Indicators in Human Drawings by Shy and Aggressive Children." *Psychol Rep* 29(1):35–8 Ag '71. * (*PA* 47:2671)

CUMULATIVE NAME INDEX

[1469]

H-T-P: House-Tree-Person Projective Technique. Ages 3 and over; 1946–66; John N. Buck and Isaac Jolles (children's interrogation folder); Western Psychological Services. *

For additional information, see P:437 (24 references); for a review by Mary R. Haworth, see 6:215 (32 references); for a review by Philip L. Harriman, see 5:139 (61 references); for reviews by Albert Ellis and Ephraim Rosen and an excerpted review, see 4:107 (14 references); for reviews by Morris Krugman and Katherine W. Wilcox, see 3:47 (5 references). For excerpts from related book reviews, see 5:B234 (2 excerpts).

REFERENCES THROUGH 1971

1–5. See 3:47.
6–19. See 4:107.
20–80. See 5:139.
81–112. See 6:215.
113–136. See P:437.
137. SCHNECK, JEROME M., AND KLINE, MILTON V. "Clinical Psychiatric Status and Psychological Test Alterations Following Hypnotherapy." *Brit J Med Hyp* 2:30–41 Ag '50. * (*PA* 25:3913)
138. FREED, HERBERT, AND PASTOR, JOYCE T. "Evaluation of the 'Draw-A-Person' Test (Modified) in Thalamotomy With Particular Reference to the Body Image." *J Nerv & Mental Dis* 114:106–20 Ag '51. * (*PA* 26:1610)
139. WAXENBERG, SHELDON EDWARD. *Psychosomatic Patients and Other Physically Ill Persons: A Comparative Study.* Doctor's thesis, Columbia University (New York, N.Y.), 1954. (*DA* 14:1818)
140. P'SIMER, CHRISTINE. *An Experimental Study of the Effects of Counseling in Freshmen Halls.* Doctor's thesis, Florida State University (Tallahassee, Fla.), 1956. (*DA* 17:317)
141. HOMMA, MASAYASU. "Studies on the H-T-P (Buck)." *Folia Psychiatrica et Neurologica Japonica* (Japan) 11:1–26 Je '57. * (*PA* 33:3841)
142. GARRISON, MORTIMER, JR. "A Comparison of Psychological Measures in Mentally Retarded Boys Over a Three-Year Period as a Function of Etiology." *Training Sch B* 55:54–60 N '58. * (*PA* 34:1664)
143. MURRAY, DAVID C., AND DEABLER, HERDIS L. "Drawings, Diagnoses, and the Clinician's Learning Curve." *J Proj Tech* 22:415–20 D '58. * (*PA* 34:1400)
144. FAULS, JOHN THOMAS. *Superior Readers Versus Mediocre Readers: A Comparison of Ego Organizations.* Doctor's thesis, Florida State University (Tallahassee, Fla.), 1959. (*DA* 20:3376)

145. GIER, JAMES DALE. *The Relationship of Physical Ability to Certain Psychological Scores and Ratings Among Mentally Retarded Boys.* Master's thesis, University of Washington (Seattle, Wash.), 1959.

146. BROWN, FRED; KATZ, HARRIET; AND KAUFMAN, M. RALPH. "The Patient Under Study for Cancer: A Personality Evaluation." *Psychosom Med* 23:166–71 Mr–Ap '61. * (*PA* 36: 3JU66B)

147. SACKS, LENORA; FEINSTEIN, ALVAN R.; AND TARANTA, ANGELO. "A Controlled Psychologic Study of Sydenham's Chorea." *J Pediatrics* 61:714–22 N '62. *

148. SHELLEY, ERNEST L. V., AND TOCH, HANS H. "The Perception of Violence as an Indicator of Adjustment in Institutionalized Offenders." *J Crim Law Criminol & Police Sci* 53: 463–9 D '62. * (*PA* 37:8184)

149. BAUER, JOHN. "A Vestibular Technique in the Teaching of Psychology." *Percept & Motor Skills* 17:679–85 D '63. * (*PA* 38:4889)

150. BERNERT, RAYMOND M., SR. *The Relationship Between H-T-P I.Qs. and Personality Variables.* Master's thesis, Xavier University (Cincinnati, Ohio), 1964.

151. FIONDO, JOHN PHILLIP. *Toward the Development of an Economical, Valid Test Battery for the Identification of Emotional Disturbance in Children.* Doctor's thesis, Wayne State University (Detroit, Mich.), 1967. (*DAI* 31:6897B)

152. FLEMING, JEAN McKEY. *Body Image and Learning of Deaf and Hearing Boys.* Doctor's thesis, University of Florida (Gainesville, Fla.), 1967. (*DA* 29:144A)

153. WOLK, ROBERT L., AND GOLDFARB, ALVIN I. "The Response to Group Psychotherapy of Aged Recent Admissions Compared With Long-Term Mental Hospital Patients." *Am J Psychiatry* 123:1251–7 Ap '67. * (*PA* 41:8996)

154. ZUTTERMAN, PAUL C. *H-T-P Drawings, Their Meaning and Levels Hypothesis.* Doctor's thesis, University of Ottawa (Ottawa, Ont., Canada), 1967.

155. GORDING, E. J., AND MATCH, ELMER. "Personality Changes of Certain Contact Lens Patients." *J Am Optom Assn* 39:266–9 Mr '68. * (*PA* 42:15492)

156. KONTTINEN, RAIMO. *Relationships Between Graphic Expansivity and Extraversion as a Function of Anxiety and Defensiveness.* Annals Academic Scientiarum Fennica, Series B, No. 159. Helsinki, Finland: Suomalainen Tiedeakatemia, Academia Scientiarum Fennica, 1968. Pp. 108. * (*PA* 43:11307)

157. REXROAD, WALLACE WARREN. *Correlational Analysis of First-Grade Reading Achievement, With Objective and Projective Measures.* Doctor's thesis, University of Oklahoma (Norman, Okla.), 1968. (*DA* 29:2126A)

158. SALLERY, ROBERT D. H. "Artistic Expression and Self-Description With Arabs and Canadian Students." *J Social Psychol* 76:273–4 D '68. * (*PA* 43:4024)

159. BARNOUW, VICTOR. Chap. 18, "Cross-Cultural Research With the House-Tree-Person Test," pp. 417–47. In *Advances in the House-Tree-Person Technique: Variations and Applications*, see 162. *

160. BUCK, JOHN N. Chap. 15, "The Use of the H-T-P in the Investigation of the Dynamics of Intra-Familial Conflict," pp. 347–79. In *Advances in the House-Tree-Person Technique: Variations and Applications*, see 162. *

161. BUCK, JOHN N. "Chronological Milestones in the Development of the H-T-P," pp. ix–xiii. In *Advances in the House-Tree-Person Technique: Variations and Applications*, see 162. *

162. BUCK, JOHN N., AND HAMMER, EMANUEL F., EDITORS. *Advances in the House-Tree-Person Technique: Variations and Applications.* Los Angeles, Calif.: Western Psychological Services, 1969. Pp. xiv, 464. *

163. COOPER, LOWELL, AND CASTON, JOSEPH. "Size of Human Figures Drawn Before and After Stress." *Percept & Motor Skills* 29(1):57–8 Ag '69. * (*PA* 44:2362)

164. DAVIS, CLIFFORD E. Chap. 16, "Uses of the H-T-P Technique by and in the Church," pp. 381–401. In *Advances in the House-Tree-Person Technique: Variations and Applications*, see 162. *

165. DEABLER, HERDIS L. Chap. 7, "The H-T-P in Group Testing and as a Screening Device," pp. 171–7. In *Advances in the House-Tree-Person Technique: Variations and Applications*, see 162. *

166. DIAMOND, SOLOMON. Chap. 4, "The House, Tree, and Person in Verbal Fantasy," pp. 85–99. In *Advances in the House-Tree-Person Technique: Variations and Applications*, see 162. *

167. FELLOWS, ROBERT, AND CERBUS, GEORGE. "HTP and DCT Indicators of Sexual Identification in Children." *J Proj Tech & Pers Assess* 33(4):376–9 Ag '69. * (*PA* 44:2136)

168. FUKADA, NAOHIKO. Chap. 17, "Japanese Children's Tree Drawings," pp. 403–15. In *Advances in the House-Tree-Person Technique: Variations and Applications*, see 162. *

169. HAMMER, EMANUEL F. Chap. 1, "Hierarchal Organization of Personality and the H-T-P, Achromatic and Chromatic," pp. 1–35. In *Advances in the House-Tree-Person Technique: Variations and Applications*, see 162. *

170. HAMMER, EMANUEL F. Chap. 12, "The Use of the H-T-P in a Criminal Court: Predicting Acting-Out," pp. 267–92. In *Advances in the House-Tree-Person Technique: Variations and Applications*, see 162. *

171. JACKS, IRVING. Chap. 13, "The Clinical Application of the H-T-P in Criminological Settings," pp. 295–312. In *Advances in the House-Tree-Person Technique: Variations and Applications*, see 162. *

172. JOLLES, ISAAC. Chap. 10, "The Use of the H-T-P in a School Setting," pp. 223–41. In *Advances in the House-Tree-Person Technique: Variations and Applications*, see 162. *

173. KING, FRANCIS W. Chap. 19, "The H-T-P as an Adjunct in Psychotherapy," pp. 449–60. In *Advances in the House-Tree-Person Technique: Variations and Applications*, see 162. *

174. LANDISBERG, SELMA. Chap. 5, "The Use of the H-T-P in a Mental Hygiene Clinic for Children," pp. 101–32. In *Advances in the House-Tree-Person Technique: Variations and Applications*, see 162. *

175. LEVINE, ABRAHAM, AND SAPOLSKY, ALLAN. Chap. 8, "The Use of the H-T-P as an Aid in the Screening of Hospitalized Patients," pp. 179–93. In *Advances in the House-Tree-Person Technique: Variations and Applications*, see 162. *

176. MAXWELL, ELIZABETH S. Chap. 11, "The Use of the House-Tree-Person Technique With Elementary School Underachievers," pp. 243–65. In *Advances in the House-Tree-Person Technique: Variations and Applications*, see 162. *

177. MICHAL-SMITH, HAROLD, AND MORGENSTERN, MURRY. Chap. 6, "The Use of the H-T-P With the Mentally Retarded Child in a Hospital Clinic," pp. 135–69. In *Advances in the House-Tree-Person Technique: Variations and Applications*, see 162. *

178. MULLER, ELSIE FERRAR. "Case Study: An Autistic Child and His Drawings." *Psychiatry & Art* 2:145-53 '69. *

179. MURSELL, GEORGE REX. Chap. 9, "The Use of the H-T-P With the Mentally Deficient," pp. 195–221. In *Advances in the House-Tree-Person Technique: Variations and Applications*, see 162. *

180. PHILO, THOMAS F. *House-Tree-Person Responses and Measured Personality Characteristics of Delinquents.* Master's thesis, Illinois State University (Normal, Ill.), 1969.

181. PRYOR, FELICIA A., AND BUTLER, JOEL R. "Test of the Unimportance of Particular Item Content Using the HTP and the MMPI." *Psychol Rep* 24(3):989–90 Je '69. * (*PA* 44:667)

182. RUSK, MARIAN TERRY. *A Study of Delinquency Among Urban Mexican American Youth.* Doctor's thesis, University of Southern California (Los Angeles, Calif.), 1969. (*DAI* 30: 1877A)

183. SPENCER, VERLIN. Chap. 2, "The Use of Watercolors to Increase Chromatic H-T-P Productivity," pp. 37–72. In *Advances in the House-Tree-Person Technique: Variations and Applications*, see 162. *

184. TOPPER, ROBERT C., AND BORING, RANDOLPH O. Chap. 3, "The Topper-Boring H-T-P Variation," pp. 75–83. In *Advances in the House-Tree-Person Technique: Variations and Applications*, see 162. *

185. WOLK, ROBERT L. Chap. 14, "Projective Drawings (H-T-P-P) of Aged People," pp. 315–45. In *Advances in the House-Tree-Person Technique: Variations and Applications*, see 162. *

186. BECKER, BRUCE. "The Projective Approach to the Study of Multiple Personality—A Case Study." *Int Congr Rorsch & Other Proj Tech* 7:423–38 '70. *

187. JORDAN, SIDNEY. "Projective Drawings in a Cerebellar Disorder Due to Chicken Pox Encephalitis." *J Proj Tech & Pers Assess* 34(3):256–8 Je '70. * (*PA* 44:18910)

188. McWHINNIE, HAROLD J. "A Third Study of Some Relationships Between Creativity and Perception in 6th Grade Children." *Calif J Ed Res* 21(1):35–42 Ja '70. *

189. MARZOLF, STANLEY S., AND KIRCHNER, JOHN H. "Characteristics of House-Tree-Person Drawings by College Men and Women." *J Proj Tech & Pers Assess* 34(2):138–45 Ap '70. * (*PA* 44:16720)

190. SAUNDERS, MAUDERIE HANCOCK, AND TESKA, PERCY T. "An Analysis of Cultural Differences on Certain Projective Techniques." *J Negro Ed* 39(2):109–15 sp '70. *

191. STAVRIANOS, BERTHA K. "Emotional and Organic Characteristics in Drawings of Deficient Readers." *J Learn Dis* 3(10):488–501 O '70. *

192. UHLIN, DONALD M., AND DICKSON, JAMES D. "The Effect of Figure-Ground Reversal in H-T-P Drawings by Spastic Cerebral Palsied Children." *J Clin Psychol* 26(1):87–8 Ja '70. * (*PA* 44:11025)

193. WAGNER, EDWIN E. "Results of Psychological Testing on a Child With Gilles De La Tourette's Disease." *J Clin Psychol* 26(1):52–7 Ja '70. * (*PA* 44:10955)

194. LYNN, BARBARA. *Potential of the H-T-P Test for Diagnosing Organicity and Retardation.* Doctor's thesis, Illinois Institute of Technology (Chicago, Ill.), 1971. (*DAI* 32:1850B)

195. MARZOLF, STANLEY S., AND KIRCHNER, JOHN H. "Color in House-Tree-Person Drawings by College Men and Women." *J Clin Psychol* 27(4):504–9 O '71. * (*PA* 47:8953)

196. PUSTEL, G., STERNLICHT, M., AND DeRESPINIS, M. "Tree Drawings of Institutionalized Retardates: Seasonal and Color Effects." *J Genetic Psychol* 118(2):217–22 Je '71. * (*PA* 46:9487)

197. STAVRIANOS, BERTHA K. "Can Projective Test Measures

H-T-P: House-Tree-Person Projective Technique

Aid in the Detection and Differential Diagnosis of Reading Deficit?" *J Pers Assess* 35(1):80–91 F '71. * (*PA* 46:7527)

CUMULATIVE NAME INDEX

[1470]

*The Hand Test. Ages 6 and over; 1959–71; HT; 1971 manual identical to manual copyrighted 1969 except for addition of 4 pages; 10 scores: interpersonal, environmental, maladjustive, withdrawal, affection-dependence-communication, direction-aggression, total responses, average initial response time, highest minus lowest response time, pathological; Edwin E. Wagner; Western Psychological Services. *

For additional information, see P:438 (12 references); for a review by Goldine C. Gleser and an excerpted review by Irving R. Stone, see 6:216 (6 references). For an excerpt from a related book review, see 6:B95.

REFERENCES THROUGH 1971

1–6. See 6:216.
7–18. See P:438.
19. VIERS, ROGER F. *Normative Data on the Hand Test for Children at Four Grade Levels.* Master's thesis, Kent State University (Kent, Ohio), 1966.
20. MUSSER, CHARLES E., JR. *The Role of Hazard Expectancy in Mediating Behavior.* Doctor's thesis, University of Akron (Akron, Ohio), 1968. (*DA* 29:2622B)
21. SARBIN, THEODORE R.; WENK, ERNST ALBERT; AND SHERWOOD, DAVID W. "An Effort to Identify Assault-Prone Offenders." *J Res Crime & Del* 5:66–71 Ja '68. *
22. ABRAM, HARRY S.; ALLAN, J. HAMILTON; HUGHES, DEANNA; SMITH, BURKE M.; HALL, WILLIAM E.; AND LEWIS, DAVID W. "A Multidisciplinary Computerized Approach to the Study of Adjustment to Lower Limb Amputation." *South Med J* 62(9):1072–6 S '69. *
23. ATWOOD, ROBERT WILLIAM. *A Study of Pedophilia.* Doctor's thesis, Brigham Young University (Provo, Utah), 1969. (*DAI* 30:4367B)
24. AZCARATE, EDUARDO, AND GUTIERREZ, MANUEL. "Differentiation of Institutional Adjustment of Juvenile Delinquents With the Hand Test." *J Clin Psychol* 25(2):200–3 Ap '69. * (*PA* 43:14460)
25. BAEHR, MELANY E.; FURCON, JOHN E.; AND FROEMEL, ERNEST C. *Psychological Assessment of Patrolman Qualifications in Relation to Field Performance.* Washington, D.C.: United States Government Printing Office, 1969. Pp. vii, 246. *
26. SINGER, MYRON M., AND DAWSON, JOSEPH G. "Experimental Falsification of the Hand Test." *J Clin Psychol* 25(2): 204–5 Ap '69. * (*PA* 43:14336)
27. TAYLOR, JOHN F. "Group Administration of the Hand Test: Effects on Card Pull and Responses." *J Proj Tech & Pers Assess* 33(3):243–6 Je '69. * (*PA* 43:14348)
28. THORNTON, CARL L. "Evaluation of Roe's Theory Using the Hand Test." *Percept & Motor Skills* 28(1):95–8 F '69. * (*PA* 43:11362)
29. WILLIAMS, RUSSELL A. *The Use of the Hand Test for the Study of the Personality Structure of Individuals Whose Performance IQ Is Significantly Above Their Verbal IQ.* Master's thesis, Brigham Young University (Provo, Utah), 1969.
30. NEUBER, JACK L. *Suitability of the Hand Test for Use With Guamanian Populations.* Master's thesis, University of Guam (Agana, Guam), 1970.
31. ROBERTS, BONNIE BETH KLECKNER. *Development of Norms for Mentally Retarded and Bright Children on the Hand Test.* Doctor's thesis, University of Oklahoma (Norman, Okla.), 1971. (*DAI* 32:2516A)
32. WAGNER, EDWIN E. "Structural Analysis: A Theory of Personality Based on Projective Techniques." *J Pers Assess* 35(5):422–35 O '71. * (*DA* 47:8870)
33. WELLS, HOWARD E. *Hand Test and Rorschach Indicators of Aggressive Behavior.* Master's thesis, Central Michigan University (Mt. Pleasant, Mich.), 1971.

CUMULATIVE NAME INDEX

Gutierrez, M.: 24
Hall, W. E.: 22
Hawkins, R.: 9
Hodge, J. R.: 11
Huberman, J.: 7
Hughes, D.: 22
Jordan, D. C.: 18
Lewis, D. W.: 22
Linden, J. D.: 8
Loftus, A. P.: 15
Medvedeff, E.: 6
Musser, C. E.: 20
Neuber, J. L.: 30
Oswald, M. O.: 15
Piotrowski, Z. A.: 2
Roberts, B. B. K.: 31
Sarbin, T. R.: 21

Schreiner, F.: 11
Shapiro, R. J.: 16
Shaw, D. J.: 8
Sherwood, D. W.: 21
Singer, M. M.: 26
Smith, B. M.: 22
Stone, I. R.: exc, 6:216
Taylor, J. F.: 27
Thornton, C. L.: 28
Viers, R. F.: 19
Wagner, E. E.: 1–6, 9, 11–3, 16, 32
Wells, H. E.: 33
Wenk, E. A.: 21
Wetsel, H.: 16
Williams, R. A.: 29
Zucker, K. B.: 18

[1471]

The Holtzman Inkblot Technique. Ages 5 and over; 1958–66; HIT; 22 scores: reaction time, rejections, location, space, form definiteness, form appropriateness, color, shading, movement, pathognomic verbalization, integration, content (human, animal, anatomy, sex, abstract), anxiety, hostility, barrier, penetration, balance, popular; 2 formats; Wayne H. Holtzman, Joseph S. Thorpe (manual), Jon D. Swartz (manual), and E. Wayne Herron (manual); Psychological Corporation. *

a) [INDIVIDUAL TEST.] 1958–61.

b) [GROUP TEST.] 1958–66; Donald R. Gorham (record form).

For additional information and excerpted reviews by Raymond J. McCall and David G. Martin, see 7:169 (106 references); see also P:439 (90 references); for reviews by Richard W. Coan, H. J. Eysenck, Bertram R. Forer, and William N. Thetford, see 6:217 (22 references). For excerpts from reviews of the manual, see 6:B264 (2 excerpts).

REFERENCES THROUGH 1971

1–22. See 6:217.
23–112. See P:439.
113–218. See 7:169.
219. ROCKETT, FREDERICK C. "Speed of Form Recognition as a Function of Stimulus Factors and Test Anxiety." *J Abn & Social Psychol* 53:197–202 S '56. * *(PA* 32:2918)
220. HOLTZMAN, WAYNE H. "A New Approach to Personality Through Inkblot Perception." *Congreso Interamericano di Psicologia* (Mexico) 7:306–10 '63. *
221. MORTON, JOYCE C. *The Relationship Between Inkblot Barrier Scores and Sociometric Status in Adolescents.* Master's thesis, University of British Columbia (Vancouver, B.C., Canada), 1964.
222. SPREEN, OTFRIED, AND BENTON, ARTHUR L. "Comparative Studies of Some Psychological Tests for Cerebral Damage." *J Nerv & Mental Dis* 140:323–33 My '65. * *(PA* 40:700)
223. GORHAM, DONALD R. "Computer Use in Psychological Testing." *Inter-Am Congr Psychol* (Mexico) 9(paper 93):1–7 '67. *
224. NICHOLS, DAVID C., AND TURSKY, BERNARD. "Body Image, Anxiety, and Tolerance for Experimental Pain." *Psychosom Med* 29:103–10 Mr–Ap '67. * *(PA* 41:11277)
225. SWARTZ, JON D.; WITZKE, DONALD B.; AND SWARTZ, CAROL J. "Culture, Age, Sex, Socioeconomic Level, and Trial as Sources of Variation in Responses to the Holtzman Inkblot Technique." *Inter-Am Congr Psychol* (Mexico) 9(paper 51):1–14 '67. *
226. LEVY, LEON H. "Originality as Role-Defined Behavior." *J Pers & Social Psychol* 9:72–8 My '68. * *(PA* 42:10583)
227. PERSKY, HAROLD; ZUCKERMAN, MARVIN; AND CURTIS, GEORGE C. "Endocrine Function in Emotionally Disturbed and Normal Men." *J Nerv & Mental Dis* 146:488–97 Je '68. * *(PA* 42:16830)
228. HILL, DAVID OLIVER. *Extraversion-Introversion: An Investigation of Typological Theory.* Doctor's thesis, Texas Tech University (Lubbock, Tex.), 1970. *(DAI* 31:6257B)
229. LAVIT, RONALD J. *Effects of Levels of Anxiety on Holtzman Inkblot Responses.* Doctor's thesis, Oklahoma State University (Stillwater, Okla.), 1970. *(DAI* 31:6261B)
230. LAVIT, RONALD J. "Variables Underlying the Perception of Inkblots by High Test Anxious Students." *Psychol* 7(4): 58–60 N '70. * *(PA* 46:3096)
231. LAVIT, RONALD J., AND GARMS, JOE D. "Factors in Inkblot Perception of College Students." *Psychol* 7(4):27–9 N '70. * *(PA* 46:3098)
232. LAVIT, RONALD J., AND GARMS, JOE D. "Factors in the

Perception of Inkblots for Female College Students." *Psychol* 7(4):38–40 N '70. * *(PA* 46:3099)
233. LAVIT, RONALD J., AND GARMS, JOE D. "Factors in the Perception of Inkblots for Male College Students." *Psychol* 7(4):48–50 N '70. * *(PA* 46:3097)
234. MEGARGEE, EDWIN I. "The Prediction of Violence With Psychological Tests." *Curr Topics Clin & Commun Psychol* 2:97–156 '70. *
235. RICE, MARC. *A Psychological Study of the Effects of Chlorpromazine (Thorazine).* Doctor's thesis, Yeshiva University (New York, N.Y.), 1970. *(DAI* 31:7609B)
236. STITT, JANE DUPUY. *Family and Social Background Factors as They Influence Cognitive and Perceptual Development in Children.* Doctor's thesis, University of Texas (Austin, Tex.), 1970. *(DAI* 31:5860A)
237. VELEZ-DIAZ, ANGEL G. *The Holtzman Inkblot Technique and the Assessment of Organic Brain Damage.* Doctor's thesis, Florida State University (Tallahassee, Fla.), 1970. *(DAI* 31: 6915B)
238. BOWERS, KENNETH S. "Sex and Susceptibility as Moderator Variables in the Relationship of Creativity and Hypnotic Susceptibility." *J Abn Psychol* 78(1):93–100 Ag '71. * *(PA* 47:2042)
239. BOWERS, KENNETH S., AND KEELING, KENNETH R. "Heart-Rate Variability in Creative Functioning." *Psychol Rep* 29(1):160–2 Ag '71. * *(PA* 47:2468)
240. FERNALD, PETER S., AND STOLUROW, KATHERINE ANN. "Projected 'Eye' Responses and Sensitivity to the Opinions of Others." *J Clin Psychol* 27(2):258–9 Ap '71. * *(PA* 46:6897)
241. FISHER, SEYMOUR. "Boundary Effects of Persistent Inputs and Messages." *J Abn Psychol* 77(3):290–5 Je '71. * *(PA* 46:6847)
242. HANSSEN, SVEIN GRÖNNER, AND TEIGEN, KARL HALVOR. "Sex Differences on the Group Version of the HIT." *J Clin Psychol* 27(3):378–82 Jl '71. * *(PA* 47:4830)
243. HAWKINS, DAVID B., AND HOROWITZ, HERBERT. "Variations in Body Image as a Function of Achievement Level in School Performance." *Percept & Motor Skills* 33(3):1299–302 D '71. * *(PA* 48:1875)
244. HIRT, MICHAEL; SCHROEDER, HAROLD; AND KAPLAN, MARVIN S. "A Failure to Provide Construct Validity for Psychological Differentiation." *Personality* 2(3):267–9 au '71. * *(PA* 47:6761)
245. HOLTZMAN, WAYNE H.; SWARTZ, JON D.; AND THORPE, JOSEPH S. "Artists, Architects, and Engineers—Three Contrasting Modes of Visual Experience and Their Psychological Correlates." *J Personality* 39(3):432–49 S '71. * *(PA* 47:6777)
246. IRIZARRY, RAYMOND. "Anxiety, Repression and Varieties of Anti-Social Behavior in Psychopaths." *J Pers Assess* 35(1): 56–61 F '71. * *(PA* 46:7161)
247. IVES, RITA KLEIN. *The Development of a Psycho-Social Assessment Scale: A Methodological Investigation of an Instrument for Attitude Measurement as It Relates to the Preparation of Teachers.* Doctor's thesis, George Washington University (Washington, D.C.), 1971. *(DAI* 32:2530A)
248. KAMEN, GARY B. "A Second Look at the Effects of a Stress-Producing Film on Adult Test Performance." *J Clin Psychol* 27(4):465–7 O '71. * *(PA* 47:8126)
249. KIDD, ALINE H., AND KIDD, ROBERT M. "Relation of Holtzman Scores to Rigidity." *Percept & Motor Skills* 32(3): 1003–10 Je '71. * *(PA* 47:2970)
250. KRIPPNER, STANLEY. "Scores Made by Retarded Readers on the Holtzman Inkblot Technique." *Percept & Motor Skills* 33(3):1089–90 D '71. * *(PA* 48:1693)
251. LAVIT, RONALD J. "A Validational Study of the Test Anxiety Questionnaire With College Students." *Psychol* 8(1): 2–3 F '71. * *(PA* 46:5004)
252. LAVIT, RONALD J. "Variables Underlying the Perception of Inkblots by Low Test Anxious College Students." *Psychol* 8(1):16–8 F '71. * *(PA* 46:5011)
253. LEHMAN, ELYSE BRAUCH, AND LEVY, BERNARD I. "Discrepancies in Estimates of Children's Intelligence: WISC and Human Figure Drawings." *J Clin Psychol* 27(1):74–6 Ja '71. * *(PA* 46:1427)
254. LUHN, CAROL LITTRELL. *Effects of Differing Stimulation Techniques on Body Boundary in Schizophrenics.* Doctor's thesis, University of Arkansas (Fayetteville, Ark.), 1971. *(DAI* 32: 3010B)
255. MATTSSON, AKE; GROSS, SAMUEL; AND HALL, THOMAS W. "Psychoendocrine Study of Adaptation in Young Hemophiliacs." *Psychosom Med* 33(3):215–25 My–Je '71. * *(PA* 47:5518)
256. MEGARGEE, EDWIN I., AND VELEZ-DIAZ, ANGEL. "A Profile Sheet for the Clinical Interpretation of the Holtzman Inkblot Technique." *J Pers Assess* 35(6):545–60 D '71. * *(PA* 47:11128)
257. PENK, W. E. "Developmental Patterns of Conceptual Styles." *Psychol Rep* 29(2):635–49 O '71. * *(PA* 47:8621)
258. SELKIN, JAMES, AND MORRIS, JOLINE. "Some Behavioral Factors Which Influence the Recovery Rate of Suicide Attempters." *B Suicidol* 8:29–38 f '71. *
259. SWARTZ, JON D.; CLELAND, CHARLES C.; DREW, CLIFFORD J.; AND WITZKE, DONALD B. "The Holtzman Inkblot Technique as a Measure of Perceptual Development in Mental Retardation." *J Pers Assess* 35(4):320–5 Ag '71. * *(PA* 47:5488)

260. WITZKE, DONALD B.; SWARTZ, JON D.; AND DREW, CLIFFORD J. "Level of Perceptual Development of Normal Adults as Measured by the Holtzman Inkblot Technique." Abstract. *Proc 79th Ann Conv Am Psychol Assn* 6(2):609–10 '71. * (PA 46:4731)

CUMULATIVE NAME INDEX

[1472]

[Re Holtzman Inkblot Technique] Computer Scoring Service for the Holtzman Inkblot Technique. A computerized scoring and statistical service for qualified users of HIT; 1966–68; primarily for research and screening purposes where large numbers of subjects are being tested using the group method of administration developed by Donald R. Gorham; report consists of a printout listing subject's identification number, sex, age and 17 scores (compared with the 22 scores on the individually administered HIT): location, rejection, form definiteness, color, shading, movement, integration, human, animal, anatomy, sex, abstract, anxiety, hostility, barrier, penetration, popular; program by Donald R. Gorham; ARBEC, Inc. *

For additional information, see P:440 (5 references).

REFERENCES THROUGH 1971

1–5. See P:440.
6. MOSELEY, EDWARD C. "Some Results of Cross-Cultural Computer Scoring of Mexican, Panamanian, Chinese, and American Students." *Proc Interam Congr Psychol* 9(1964):277–81 ['65]. *
7. GORHAM, DONALD R. "Computer Use in Psychological Testing." *Inter-Am Congr Psychol* (Mexico) 9(paper 93):1–7 '67. *
8. GORHAM, DONALD R. "Validity and Reliability of a Computer Scoring System for Inkblot Responses." *Proc Interam Congr Psychol* 10(1966):276–90 '67. *
9. MOSELEY, EDWARD C. "Multivariate Comparison of Seven Cultures: Argentina, Colombia (Bogota), Colombia (Cartagena), Mexico, Panama, United States and Venezuela." *Proc Interam Congr Psychol* 10(1966): 291–304 '67. *

[1473]

The Howard Ink Blot Test. Adults; 1953–60;
HIBT; James W. Howard; Clinical Psychology Publishing Co., Inc. *

For additional information and an excerpted review
by John Graham White, see 7:170; see also P:442 (1
reference); for reviews by Jesse G. Harris, Jr. and
Bernard I. Murstein and an excerpted review by H. R.
Wideman, see 6:219 (1 reference); for a review by
C. R. Strother and an excerpted review by Walter G.
Klopfer, see 5:141 (3 references).

REFERENCES THROUGH 1971

1–3. See 5:141.
4. See 6:219.
5. See P:442.

[1474]

Human Figure Drawing Techniques. This is a
dummy entry to serve as a catchall for references on
the use of human figure drawings in general. References
dealing with specific tests are listed under the relevant
tests: *Goodenough-Harris Drawing Test*, see 381 (388
references); *Draw-A-Person Quality Scale*, see 1456
(6 references); *HFD Test*, see 1468 (20 references);
H-T-P: House-Tree-Person Projective Technique,
see 1469 (197 references); *Machover Draw-A-Person
Test*, see 1481 (304 references); and *Eight Card Redrawing Test*, see P:425 (7 references).

See P:442A (181 references).

REFERENCES THROUGH 1971

1–181. See P:442A.
182. GOODENOUGH, FLORENCE L. "Studies in the Psychology of
Children's Drawings." *Psychol B* 25:272–83 My '28. * (*PA* 2:
3675)
183. APPEL, KENNETH E. "Drawings by Children as Aids to
Personality Studies." *Am J Orthopsychiatry* 1:129–44 Ja '31. *
(*PA* 5:2485)
184. ANASTASI, ANNE, AND FOLEY, JOHN P., JR. "A Survey
of the Literature on Artistic Behavior in the Abnormal: 3,
Spontaneous Productions." *Psychol Monogr* 52(6):1–71 '40. *
(*PA* 15:3387)
185. SPOERL, DOROTHY TILDEN. "A Note on the Anastasi-
Foley Cultural Interpretation of Children's Drawings." *J Social
Psychol* 13:187–92 F '41. * (*PA* 15:2428)
186. GOODENOUGH, FLORENCE L., AND HARRIS, DALE B.
"Studies in the Psychology of Children's Drawings: 2, 1928–49."
Psychol B 47:369–433 S '50. * (*PA* 25:2456)
187. ABEL, THEODORA M. "Personality Characteristics of the
Facially Disfigured." *Trans N Y Acad Sci* 14:325–9 Je '52. *
(*PA* 27:3739)
188. GORDON, MYRON H. *A Clinical Study of Personality
Patterns in Children With Reading Disability.* Doctor's thesis,
New York University (New York, N.Y.), 1952. (*DA* 13:68)
189. KNOPF, IRWIN J., AND RICHARDS, T. W. "The Child's
Differentiation of Sex as Reflected in Drawings of the Human
Figure." *J Genetic Psychol* 81:99–112 S '52. * (*PA* 27:3378)
190. KOSSEFF, JEROME WILLIAM. *A Study of Changes in Body
Image During Psychotherapy.* Doctor's thesis, New York University (New York, N.Y.), 1952. (*DA* 12:383)
191. KRASNER, JACK DANIEL. *The Psychological Effects of
Regressive Electroshock Therapy.* Doctor's thesis, New York
University (New York, N.Y.), 1952. (*DA* 12:591)
192. SINGER, HARRY. *Validity of the Projection of Sexuality
in Drawing the Human Figure.* Master's thesis, Western Reserve University (Cleveland, Ohio), 1952.
193. KATZ, WILLIAM D. *A Study of the Changes in Personality Structure in Depression by Means of Psychological Tests.*
Doctor's thesis, New York University (New York, N.Y.), 1953.
(*DA* 13:592)
194. CLEVELAND, SIDNEY E., AND FISHER, SEYMOUR. "Behavior and Unconscious Fantasies of Patients With Rheumatoid

Arthritis." *Psychosom Med* 16:327–33 Jl–Ag '54. * (*PA* 29:
4495)
195. HARROWER, MOLLY. "Clinical Aspects of Failures in the
Projective Techniques." *J Proj Tech* 18:294–302 S '54. * (*PA*
29:4059)
196. KATZ, MELVYN MYRON. "Psychodynamics of Peptic Ulcer
Pathogenesis in Hospitalized Schizophrenic Patients." *Psychosom Med* 16:47–55 Ja–F '54. * (*PA* 28:7826)
197. KELLER, HORACE T., JR. *Personality Measures as Related
to Performance Under Auditory Distraction.* Doctor's thesis,
Temple University (Philadelphia, Pa.), 1956. (*DA* 16:994)
198. ROSENBLATT, BERNARD PHILIP. *The Influence of Affective States Upon the Body-Image and Upon the Perceptual Organization of External Space.* Doctor's thesis, Clark University
(Worcester, Mass.), 1956. (*DA* 16:1721)
199. SHONTZ, FRANKLIN C. "Body-Concept Disturbances of
Patients With Hemiplegia." *J Clin Psychol* 12:293–5 Jl '56. *
(*PA* 31:6528)
200. SMITH, WALTER D., AND LEBO, DELL. "Some Changing
Aspects of the Self-Concept of Pubescent Males." *J Genetic
Psychol* 88:61–75 Mr '56. * (*PA* 31:4443)
201. SOPCHAK, ANDREW L. "Projective Study of Peter and
His Parents: Revealing the Necessary Therapeutic Limitations."
J Child Psychiatry 3:149–200 Ag '56. * (*PA* 31:8363)
202. BERENBERG, ALBERT N. *A Study of the Relationship
Between Skills in Certain Cognitive Areas and Certain Patterns
Involving Attitudes, Interests and Identifications in Eighth
Grade Students.* Doctor's thesis, New York University (New
York, N.Y.), 1957. (*DA* 18:651)
203. GOODENOUGH, EVELYN WILTSHIRE. "Interest in Persons
as an Aspect of Sex Difference in the Early Years." *Genetic
Psychol Monogr* 55:287–323 My '57. * (*PA* 33:3403)
204. RAWN, MOSS L. "Degree of Disturbance in Figure Drawings as Related to Mode of Approach to Problem Solving." *J
Genetic Psychol* 91:191–6 D '57. * (*PA* 33:1H191R)
205. TALKOFF, ALVIN ROY. *The Consistency of Control Function in Non-Patient and Patient Populations: An Evaluation of
Intra-Individual Control in the Self, the Ego, and Behavior in
Non-Hospitalized Persons and in Groups of Patients Diagnosed
as Paranoid Schizophrenia.* Doctor's thesis, New York University (New York, N.Y.), 1957. (*DA* 18:670)
206. JOHNSON, STEWART R., AND GLOYE, EUGENE E. "A Critical Analysis of Psychological Treatment of Children's Drawings
and Paintings." *J Aesthet Art Crit* 17:242–50 D '58. * (*PA*
34:1074)
207. KIMMEL, JAMES. *A Comparison of Children With Congenital and Acquired Orthopedic Handicaps on Certain Personality Characteristics: An Evaluation of Self-Concept, Anxiety,
Defense Mechanisms, and Adjustment in Children With Orthopedic Handicaps.* Doctor's thesis, New York University (New
York, N.Y.), 1958. (*DA* 19:3023)
208. LAKIN, MARTIN. "Affective Tone in Human Figure
Drawings by Institutionalized Aged and by Normal Children."
J Am Geriatrics Soc 6:495–500 Je '58. * (*PA* 33:2747)
209. MURSTEIN, BERNARD I. "Personality and Intellectual
Changes in Leukemia: A Case Study." *J Proj Tech* 22:421–6
D '58. * (*PA* 34:1401)
210. RILL, HERBERT J. *Effects of Sparine and a Total-Push
Program on the Psychopathological Functions of Paranoid
Schizophrenics.* Doctor's thesis. Temple University (Philadelphia, Pa.), 1958. (*DA* 19:3371)
211. SILVERSTEIN, ARTHUR B., AND KLEE, GERALD D. "A
Psychopharmacological Test of the 'Body Image' Hypothesis."
J Nerv & Mental Dis 127:323–9 O '58. * (*PA* 33:10364)
212. WARMAN, ROY ELTON, JR. *Differential Perceptions of
the Counseling Role of a University Counseling Center.* Doctor's
thesis, Ohio State University (Columbus, Ohio), 1958. (*DA*
19:874)
213. MARLENS, HANNA S. *A Study of the Effect of Hospitalization on Children in a Metropolitan Municipal Institution: A
Comparative Study of Emotional Attitudes Toward Self and
the Environment of Children Hospitalized and Those Non-Hospitalized With Similar Physical Complaints.* Doctor's thesis,
New York University (New York, N.Y.), 1959. (*DA* 20:3385)
214. HARDY, MILES W. *The Interaction of Patients' Intelligence and Other Factors With Clinicians' Skill in the Diagnostic
Use of Human Figure Drawings.* Doctor's thesis, Florida State
University (Tallahassee, Fla.), 1960. (*DA* 20:4438)
215. KATZ, JOSEPH. "A New Figure Drawing Technique for
Diagnosis and Evaluation." *Psychoanalysis & Psychoanalytic
R* 47:103–5 su '60. * (*PA* 35:3395)
216. KRAGH, ULF. "Pathogenesis in Dipsomania: An Illustration of the Actual-Genetic Model of Perception-Personality:
Part 1, Theoretical Frame, Anamnesis." *Acta Psychiatrica et
Neurologica Scandinavica* (Denmark) 35(2):207–22 '60. * (*PA*
35:3799)
217. KRAGH, ULF. "Pathogenesis in Dipsomania: An Illustration of the Actual-Genetic Model of Perception-Personality: Part
2, Presentation and Analysis of the Actual-Genetic Series."
Acta Psychiatrica et Neurologica Scandinavica (Denmark)
35(3):261–88 '60. * (*PA* 35:2577)
218. KRAGH, ULF. "Pathogenesis in Dipsomania: An Illustration of the Actual-Genetic Model of Perception-Personality: Part
3. The Retest Series, the Pathogenic Transformations, Repres-

sion and Regression." *Acta Psychiatrica et Neurologica Scandinavica* (Denmark) 35(4):480–97 '60. * (*PA* 35:6864)

219. LERNER, MILDRED SHERWOOD. *The Relationship of Certain Aspects of the Body Image of Female Schizophrenic Patients to Therapeutic Success or Failure.* Doctor's thesis, New York University (New York, N.Y.), 1960. (*DA* 22:4408)

220. CRADDICK, RAY A. "Size of Santa Claus Drawings as a Function of Time Before and After Christmas." *J Psychol Studies* 12:121–5 Mr '61. * (*PA* 39:10257)

221. GASSER, EDITH STRIETER. *An Investigation of the Body Image of Boys as Expressed in Self Drawings: An Intercultural Study.* Doctor's thesis, New York University (New York, N.Y.), 1961. (*DA* 22:4425)

222. HULEK, JANE ELIZABETH. *Peer Relations and Body-Image Maturity in Children.* Doctor's thesis, Boston University (Boston, Mass.), 1961. (*DA* 22:1252)

223. TUCKMAN, JACOB; LORGE, IRVING; AND ZEMAN, FREDERIC D. "The Self-Image in Aging." *J Genetic Psychol* 99:317–21 D '61. * (*PA* 36:3F117T)

224. AINSWORTH, LEONARD H., AND AINSWORTH, MARY D. "Acculturation in East Africa: I, Political Awareness and Attitudes Towards Authority." *J Social Psychol* 57:391–9 Ag '62. * (*PA* 37:4802)

225. HOLDEN, RAYMOND H. "Changes in Body Image of Physically Handicapped Children Due to Summer Camp Experience." *Merrill-Palmer Q* 8:19–26 Ja '62. * (*PA* 37:1595)

226. PAUKER, JEROME D. "A Simple Method for Measuring the Area of a Figure Drawing." *J Proj Tech* 26:237–8 Je '62. *

227. RIKLAN, MANUEL; JOHN, THOMAS P.; AND DILLER, LEONARD. "Human Figure Drawings Before and After Chemosurgery of the Basal Ganglia in Parkinsonism." *J Nerv & Mental Dis* 135:500–6 D '62. *

228. DRAINER, BARBARA ADELINE. *A Study of Children's Self-Feelings Through the Draw-a-Family Technique and Spontaneous Paintings.* Doctor's thesis, Columbia University (New York, N.Y.), 1963. (*DA* 24:3433)

229. LEWINSOHN, PETER M., AND MAY, JACK G., JR. "A Technique for the Judgement of Emotion From Figure Drawings." *J Proj Tech* 27:79–85 Mr '63. * (*PA* 38:925)

230. BAHNSON, C. B., AND BAHNSON, M. B. "Denial and Repression of Primitive Impulses and of Disturbing Emotions in Patients With Malignant Neoplasms," pp. 42–62. In *Psychosomatic Aspects of Neoplastic Disease.* The Proceedings of the Third International Conference of the International Psychosomatic Cancer Study Group Held at Newnham College. Cambridge, England, 22nd to 26th July 1963. Edited by D. M. Kissen and L. L. Leshan. Philadelphia, Pa.: J. B. Lippincott Co., 1964. Pp. xii, 231. *

231. BURTON, ARTHUR, AND SJOBERG, BERNARD, JR. "The Diagnostic Validity of Human Figure Drawings in Schizophrenia." *J Psychol* 57:3–18 Ja '64. *

232. COCHRAN, NORMAN A. *The Influences of Elementary School Physical Education on Selected Physical and Psychological Tests.* Doctor's thesis, University of Maryland (College Park, Md.), 1964. (*DA* 26:3146)

233. FISHER, HARWOOD. "Similarity, Consistency, and Dissociation in Figure Drawings With the Nondominant Hand: Preliminary Report." *Percept & Motor Skills* 18:711–2 Je '64. * (*PA* 39:4247)

234. HUNT, JAMES WILLIAM. *Children's Drawings as an In-School Screening Process for Mentally Retarded Children.* Doctor's thesis, University of Mississippi (University, Miss.), 1964. (*DA* 26:2013)

235. LEFKOWITZ, MONROE M. "Aggression and Size of Human Figure Drawings." *Psychol Sch* 1:312–4 Jl '64. *

236. MARCUS, JOSEPH. "Temporary Vicissitudes in Children's Drawings: Their Importance in Diagnostic Evaluations (A Brief Communication)." *Israel Ann Psychiatry* 1:217–24 O '64. * (*PA* 39:7399)

237. SUGERMAN, A. ARTHUR, AND HARONIAN, FRANK. "Body Type and Sophistication of Body Concept." *J Personality* 32: 380–94 S '64. *

238. HAMMER, EMANUEL F. Chap. 27, "Acting Out and Its Prediction by Projective Drawing Assessment," pp. 288–319. In *Acting Out: Theoretical and Clinical Aspects.* By Lawrence Edwin Abt and Stuart L. Weissman. New York: Grune & Stratton, Inc., 1965. Pp. xiii, 336. *

239. RIKLAN, MANUEL; LEVITA, ERIC; AND COOPER, IRVING S. "Psychological Effects of Bilateral Subcortical Surgery for Parkinson's Disease." *J Nerv & Mental Dis* 141:403–9 O '65. * (*PA* 40:5052)

240. SHAPIRO, THEODORE, AND STINE, JOHN. "The Figure Drawings of Three-Year-Old Children: A Contribution to the Early Development of Body Image." *Psychoanalytic Study Child* 20:298–309 '65. *

241. EISENMAN, RUSSELL. "Birth Order, Anxiety, and Verbalizations in Group Psychotherapy." *J Consult Psychol* 30: 521–6 D '66. * (*PA* 41:2985)

242. EISENMAN, RUSSELL, AND SMITH, JAMES FRANKLIN. "Moral Judgment and Effort in Human Figure Drawings." *Percept & Motor Skills* 23:951–4 D '66. * (*PA* 41:7355)

243. HIRSCHENFANG, SAMUEL, AND BENTON, JOSEPH G. "Assessment of Phantom Limb Sensation Among Patients With

Lower Extremity Amputation." *J Psychol* 63:197–9 Jl '66. * (*PA* 40:10150)

244. MONEY, JOHN; ALEXANDER, DUANE; AND EHRHARDT, ANKE. "Visual-Constructional Deficit in Turner's Syndrome." *J Pediatrics* 69:126–7 Jl '66. *

245. SIMMONS, ALLAN DAVID. *A Test of the Body Image Hypothesis in Human Figure Drawings.* Doctor's thesis, University of Texas (Austin, Tex.), 1966. (*DA* 27:3682B)

246. STRÜMPFER, D. J. W. "The Relation of Draw-A-Person Test Variables to Psychometric and Inventory Measures." *J Social Res* (South Africa) 15(1):1–9 '66. * (*PA* 42:2613)

247. MOTANKY, GUY U.; ZAKS, MISHA S.; AND GROVES, MARION H. "The Role of Pre-Morbid Psychological and Social Characteristics in Behavioral Reactions Following Acute Brain Damage." *Bulletin de l'Association Internationale de Psychologie Appliquée* (England) 16:124–30 au '67. *

248. OBERLEDER, MURIEL. "Adapting Current Psychological Techniques for Use in Testing the Aging." *Gerontologist* 7(3, pt 1):188–91 S '67. * (*PA* 42:3801)

249. WILLIAMS, CHARLES R. *Predicting Reading Readiness From Human Figure Drawings.* Master's thesis, Central Washington College of Education (Ellensburg, Wash.), 1967.

250. WITKIN, HERMAN A., AND OLTMAN, PHILIP K. "Cognitive Style." *Int J Neurol* (Uruguay) 6(2):119–37 '67. *

251. BILLER, HENRY B. "A Multiaspect Investigation of Masculine Development in Kindergarten Age Boys." *Genetic Psychol Monogr* 78:89–138 Ag '68. * (*PA* 42:18602)

252. BUZBY, DALLAS E. "Precognition and Clairvoyance as Related to the Draw-a-Man Test." *J Parasychol* 32:244–7 D '68. * (*PA* 43:12016)

253. CHASE, JOAN B., AND RAPAPORT, IRENE N. "A Verbal Adaptation of the Draw-A-Person Techniques for Use With Blind Subjects: A Preliminary Report." *Int J Ed Blind* 18:113–5 D '68. * (*PA* 43:8547)

254. CONNOLLY, CHRISTOPHER GEORGE. *The Psychosocial Adjustment of Children With Dyslexia.* Doctor's thesis, Northwestern University (Evanston, Ill.), 1968. (*DA* 29:3456A)

255. DENNIS, WAYNE. "Racial Change in Negro Drawings." *J Psychol* 69:129–30 My '68. * (*PA* 42:12069)

256. FREDMAN, NORMAN JACOB. *The Measurement of Pupil Attitudes Toward School.* Doctor's thesis, Northwestern University (Evanston, Ill.), 1968. (*DA* 29:3458A)

257. GILLIES, JOHN. "Variations in Drawings of 'a Person' and 'Myself' by Hearing-Impaired and Normal Children." *Brit J Ed Psychol* 38:86–9 F '68. * (*PA* 42:12750)

258. GORDON, MARY J. *The Figure Drawings of Pre-School Children.* Master's thesis, Emory University (Atlanta, Ga.), 1968.

259. KISSIN, BENJAMIN; ROSENBLATT, SIDNEY M.; AND MACHOVER, SOLOMON. "Prognostic Factors in Alcoholism." *Psychiatric Res Rep Am Psychiatric Assn* 24:22–43 Mr '68. * (*PA* 43:1099)

260. KUEFFER, EDWARD ALBERT. *The Haworth Sexual Differentiation Scale: A Validation Study.* Doctor's thesis, University of California (Berkeley, Calif.), 1968. (*DAI* 30:170A)

261. NASH, CATHERINE S., AND NASH, CARROLL B. "Effect of Target Selection, Field Dependence, and Body Concept on ESP Performance." *J Parapsychol* 32:248–57 D '68. * (*PA* 43:12019)

262. RUNDE, RAYMOND EDWARD. *The Effects of Intelligence and Residence on Educably Retarded Boys' Concept of God and Their Parents, as Indicated by the Projective "Draw A Person" Technique.* Doctor's thesis, Catholic University of America (Washington, D.C.), 1968. (*DA* 29:3881A)

263. THOMAS, CAROLINE BEDELL; JONES, LEONA WISE; AND ROSS, DONALD CLARE. "Studies on Figure Drawings: Biological Implications of Structural and Graphic Characteristics." *Psychiatric Q Sup* 42(2):223–51 '68. * (*PA* 46:2503, 50:3094)

264. ABRAM, HARRY S.; ALLAN, J. HAMILTON; HUGHES, DEANNA; SMITH, BURKE M.; HALL, WILLIAM E.; AND LEWIS, DAVID W. "A Multidisciplinary Computerized Approach to the Study of Adjustment to Lower Limb Amputation." *South Med J* 62(9):1072–6 S '69. *

265. BAR, A., AND JAKAB, IRENE. "Graphic Identification of the Stuttering Episode as Experienced by Stutterers." *Psychiatry & Art* 2:2–15 '69. *

266. BELLAMY, EDWARD, AND DALY, WILLIAM C. "The Height of Figure Drawings Related to IQ, Sex and CA in Mental Retardates." *J Clin Psychol* 25(2):206–7 Ap '69. * (*PA* 43:14731)

267. BILLER, HENRY B. "Maternal Salience and Feminine Development in Young Girls." Abstract. *Proc 77th Ann Conv Am Psychol Assn* 4(1):259–60 '69. * (*PA* 43:17221)

268. CRADDICK, RAY A. "Identification With the Aggressor Through Figure Drawing." *Percept & Motor Skills* 28(2):547–50 Ap '69. * (*PA* 43:15838)

269. FATERSON, HANNA F.; MOLDOWSKI, EDWARD W.; AND MOLDOWSKI, LESLIE H. K. "The Human Figure Drawing Test and Academic Outcome in Medical School." *J Med Ed* 44(10):929–33 O '69. * (*PA* 45:3059)

270. GARDINER, HARRY W. "A Cross-Cultural Comparison of Hostility in Children's Drawings." *J Social Psychol* 79(2):261–3 D '69. * (*PA* 44:10213)

271. GARDNER, JAMES M. "Indicators of Homosexuality in the Human Figure Drawings of Heroin- and Pill-Using Addicts." *Percept & Motor Skills* 28(3):705–6 Je '69. * (*PA* 43:17620)

Human Figure Drawing Techniques

272. GOLDSTEIN, HARRIS S., AND FATERSON, HANNA F. "Shading as an Index of Anxiety in Figure Drawings." *J Proj Tech & Pers Assess* 33(5):454–6 O '69. * (*PA* 44:3654)

273. GOLOMB, CLAIRE. "Children's Representation of the Human Figure: Syncretism or Invention." Abstract. *Proc 77th Ann Conv Am Psychol Assn* 4(1):479–80 '69. * (*PA* 43:17150)

274. GRAVITZ, MELVIN A. "Direction of Psychosexual Interest and Figure Drawing Choice." *J Clin Psychol* 25(3):311 Jl '69. * (*PA* 44:3655)

275. HAMMER, EMANUEL F. "DAP: Back Against the Wall?" *J Consult & Clin Psychol* 33(2):151–6 Ap '69. * (*PA* 43:10005)

276. HARDI, I. "Confrontation in Dynamic Drawing Tests." *Psychiatry & Art* 2:66–71 '69. *

277. HUTTER, ADELIA. *The Predictive Value of the Draw-A-Person Technique With First Graders.* Doctor's thesis, Kansas State Teachers College (Emporia, Kan.), 1969.

278. MCELHANEY, MARK. *Clinical Psychological Assessment of the Human Figure Drawing.* Springfield, Ill.: Charles C Thomas, Publisher, 1969. Pp. xi, 256. * (*PA* 44:16910, title only)

279. MINARD, JAMES G., AND MOONEY, WILLIAM. "Psychological Differentiation and Perceptual Defense: Studies of the Separation of Perception From Emotion." *J Abn Psychol* 74(2): 131–9 Ap '69. * (*PA* 43:9715)

280. RUTTER, WINONA A. *Exploring an Objective Method of Scoring the Draw-A-Person Test for Power Versus Powerlessness.* Master's thesis, Newark State College (Union, N.J.), 1969.

281. SCHNALL, MELVYN. "Representations and Reproductions in Children's Drawings and Descriptions of Events." Abstract. *Proc 77th Ann Conv Am Psychol Assn* 4(1):481–2 '69. * (*PA* 43:17164)

282. SONDHEIMER, RUTH. *Field Dependency and Rehabilitation Therapy in Physically Disabled Patients.* Doctor's thesis, City University of New York (New York, N.Y.), 1969. (*DAI* 30:3878B)

283. SUINN, RICHARD M., AND OSKAMP, STUART. *The Predictive Validity of Projective Measures: A Fifteen-Year Evaluative Review of Research,* pp. 85–91, 128–30. Springfield, Ill.: Charles C Thomas, Publisher, 1969. Pp. xv, 161. * (*PA* 44:10455, title only)

284. WANDERER, ZEV WILLIAM. "Validity of Clinical Judgments Based on Human Figure Drawings." *J Consult & Clin Psychol* 33(2):143–50 Ap '69. * (*PA* 43:10029)

285. WHITE, WILLIAM J. *Relationship Between Degree of Difficulty of Drawing for Various Body Parts and Rated Disturbance in the Draw-A-Person Test.* Master's thesis, Loyola University (Chicago, Ill.), 1969.

286. ADLER, PETER T. "Evaluation of the Figure Drawing Technique: Reliability, Factorial Structure, and Diagnostic Usefulness." *J Consult & Clin Psychol* 35(1):52–7 Ag '70. * (*PA* 44:21164)

287. AZANCOT, C. A. "A New Approach to the Human Figure Drawing Test." *Int Congr Rorsch & Other Proj Tech* 7:418–22 '70. *

288. BECK, MICHAEL, AND BART, LEONARD. "Inter-Rater and Test-Retest Reliability of a Proportionality Measure for the D-A-P." *Percept & Motor Skills* 30(1):89–90 F '70. * (*PA* 46:9079)

289. BOGO, NORMAN; WINGET, CAROLYN; AND GLESER, GOLDINE C. "Ego Defenses and Perceptual Styles." *Percept & Motor Skills* 30(2):599–605 Ap '70. * (*PA* 46:6842)

290. BRITAIN, SUSAN D. "Effect of Manipulation of Children's Affect on Their Family-Drawings." *J Proj Tech & Pers Assess* 34(3):234–7 Je '70. * (*PA* 44:18362)

291. CLODFELDER, D. LEON, AND CRADDICK, RAY A. "Variance in Size of Drawing in a Psychotic Population." *Percept & Motor Skills* 30(1):110 F '70. * (*PA* 46:9369)

292. CRADDICK, RAY A.; LEIPOLD, WILLIAM D.; AND LEIPOLD, VAL. "Effect of Role-Empathy on Height of Human Figures Drawn by Male Alcoholics." *Percept & Motor Skills* 30(3):747–52 Je '70. * (*PA* 44:16921)

293. DANWITZ, MARY WINIFRED. *A Study of the Human Figure Drawings of Children With Language Disorders.* Doctor's thesis, City University of New York (New York, N.Y.), 1970. (*DAI* 31:3749B)

294. DEPPE, A. H. "Body Image Disturbance in Air Scuba Diving." *Psychologia Africana* (South Africa) 13(2–3):248–51 O '70. *

295. ENGLE, PATRICIA L., AND SUPPES, JOAN SIEBER. "The Relation Between Human Figure Drawing and Test Anxiety in Children." *J Proj Tech & Pers Assess* 34(3):223–31 Je '70. * (*PA* 44:18745)

296. FATERSON, HANNA F., AND WITKIN, HERMAN A. "Longitudinal Study of Development of the Body Concept." *Develop Psychol* 2(3):429–38 My '70. * (*PA* 44:12238)

297. FRAAS, LOUIS A. "Sex of Figure Drawing in Identifying Practicing Male Homosexuals." *Psychol Rep* 27(1):172–4 Ag '70. * (*PA* 45:6638)

298. GOZALI, JOAV, AND JOHNSON, LOUIS B. "A Comparison of the Chromatic and Achromatic Figure Drawings of Adult Psychiatric Patients." *J Proj Tech & Pers Assess* 34(3):232–3 Je '70. * (*PA* 44:18907)

299. HANDLER, LEONARD, AND REYHER, JOSEPH. "Comment on 'Shading as an Index of Anxiety in Figure Drawings.'" *J Proj Tech & Pers Assess* 34(4):340–1 Ag '70. * (*PA* 44: 21008)

300. HARROWER, MOLLY. Chap. 5, "Projective Classification," pp. 139–64. In *New Approaches to Personality Classification.* Edited by Alvin R. Mahrer. New York: Columbia University Press, 1970. Pp. vii, 425. * (*PA* 45:6276)

301. IRVING, DOUGLAS DORSET. *The Field-Dependence Hypothesis in Cross-Cultural Perspective.* Doctor's thesis, Rice University (Houston, Tex.), 1970. (*DAI* 31:3691B)

302. JERNIGAN, A. J. "Judging Whether a Patient Is White or Black by His Draw-A-Person Test." *J Proj Tech & Pers Assess* 34(6):503–6 D '70. * (*PA* 45:8255)

303. KAPLAN, MARVIN L.; COLARELLI, NICK J.; GROSS, RUTH BRILL; LEVENTHAL, DONALD B.; AND SIEGAL, SAUL M. *The Structural Approach to Psychological Testing.* New York: Pergamon Press, Inc., 1970. Pp. xi, 195. *

304. MCKAY, DOROTHY. "An Examination of the Differences Between the Paintings and Figure Drawings of a Group of Institutionalized Mentally Retarded Children and a Group of 'Family-Reared' Mentally Retarded Children." *Austral Occup Ther J* 17(1):13–24 Ja–Mr '70. * (*PA* 46:5352)

305. NEIDIG, PETER HARPER. *Controls for Demand Characteristics Applied to Psychological Stress Assessment Research.* Doctor's thesis, University of Tennessee (Knoxville, Tenn.), 1970. (*DAI* 32:567B)

306. SHIPMAN, WILLIAM G.; OKEN, DONALD; AND HEATH, HELEN A. "Muscle Tension and Effort at Self-Control During Anxiety." *Arch Gen Psychiatry* 23(4):359–68 O '70. * (*PA* 45:2694)

307. SMITH, WARREN C., AND FIGETAKIS, NICK. "Some Effects of Isometric Exercise on Muscular Strength, Body-Image Perception, and Psychiatric Symptomatology in Chronic Schizophrenics." *Am Correct Ther J* 24(4):100–4 Jl–Ag '70. *

308. VROEGH, KAREN. "Lack of Sex-Role Differentiation in Preschoolers' Figure Drawings." *J Proj Tech & Pers Assess* 34(1):38–40 F '70. * (*PA* 44:8216)

309. WAINWRIGHT, BRUCE B. *Quantitative Scales for Scoring Human Figure Drawings.* Doctor's thesis, University of California (Los Angeles, Calif.), 1970. (*DAI* 31:1637A)

310. ZIV, AVNER, AND SHECHORI, HANNAH. "Human Figure Drawing as a Measure of Social Adjustment in School." *J Sch Psychol* 8(2):152–3 Ag–Je '70. * (*PA* 45:15282)

311. ADLER, PETER T. "Ethnic and Socioeconomic Status Differences in Human Figure Drawings." *J Consult & Clin Psychol* 36(3):344–54 Je '71. * (*PA* 46:9331)

312. CUMMINS, SHIRLEY; GARMS, NANCY; AND ZUSNE, LEONARD. "Another Note to Santa Claus." *Percept & Motor Skills* 32(2):510 Ap '71. * (*PA* 46:10601)

313. DEL GAUDIO, ANDREW CHARLES. *Psychological Differentiation and Mobility as Related to Creativity.* Doctor's thesis, Fordham University (New York, N.Y.), 1971. (*DAI* 32:2393B)

314. DREYER, ALBERT S.; HULAC, VALERIE; AND RIGLER, DAVID. "Differential Adjustment to Pubescence and Cognitive Style Patterns." *Develop Psychol* 4(3):456–62 My '71. * (*PA* 46:6611)

315. EICHENBAUM, IRVING W., AND DUNN, NAOMI A. "Projective Drawings by Children Under Repeated Dental Stress." *J Dentistry Children* 38(3):164–74 My–Je '71. *

316. GRAVITZ, MELVIN A. "Nudity and Amount of Clothing on the Figure Drawings of Normal Adults." *J Genetic Psychol* 118(1):141–5 Mr '71. * (*PA* 46:9082)

317. GREENBERG, ROGER P., AND FISHER, SEYMOUR. "Some Differential Effects of Music on Projective and Structured Psychological Tests." *Psychol Rep* 28(3):817–8 Je '71. * (*PA* 46: 10869)

318. HENDERSON, NORMAN B.; BUTLER, BRUCE V.; GOFFENEY, BARBARA; SAITO, CARRIE H.; AND CLARKSON, QUENTIN D. "Sex of Person Drawn by Japanese, Navajo, American White, and Negro Seven-Year-Olds." *J Pers Assess* 35(3):261–4 Je '71. * (*PA* 47:2668)

319. JALOTA, S., AND MISHRA, A. N. "Human Figure Drawing Test or Draw-A-Man Test: Item Analysis and Item Discrimination." *Indian J Psychom & Ed* 2(1–2):1–10 Je–D '71. *

320. JOHNSON, JAMES H. "Upper Left Hand Placement of Human Figure Drawings as an Indicator of Anxiety." *J Pers Assess* 35(4):336–7 Ag '71. * (*PA* 47:4833)

321. LEMESHNIK, SHIRLEY. *Children's Projections of Rejection and Hostility Onto Teachers Assessed by the Draw-A-Teacher Technique.* Doctor's thesis, Columbia University (New York, N.Y.), 1971. (*DAI* 32:792A)

322. MCWHINNIE, HAROLD J. "Review of Recent Literature on Figure Drawing Tests as Related to Research Problems in Art Education." *R Ed Res* 41(2):131–42 Ap '71. * (*PA* 47: 3794)

323. MCWHINNIE, HAROLD J., AND LASCARIDES-MORGAN, VASSILIKI CELIA. "A Correlational Study of Perceptual Behavior and Perceptual Learning in Four and Five Year Old Children." *Int J Exp Res Ed* (Belgium) 8(1):38–61 '71. * (*PA* 48:702)

324. OLCH, DORIS. "Personality Characteristics of Hemophiliacs." *J Pers Assess* 35(1):72–9 F '71. * (*PA* 46:7371)

325. PUSTEL, G.; STERNLICHT, M.; AND DEUTSCH, M. "Feminine Tendencies in Figure Drawings by Male Homo-

sexual Retarded Dyads." *J Clin Psychol* 27(2):260–1 Ap '71. *
(*PA* 46:7149)

326. ROITMAN, RAYMOND T. *A Pilot Study: The Use of the
Human Figure Drawing Test for Self-Concept on Junior High
School Educable Mentally Handicapped Students.* Master's
thesis, Northern Illinois University (DeKalb, Ill.), 1971.

327. VERMA, S. K. "Disturbance of Body Image in Psychiatric Patients." *Manas* (India) 18(2):111–5 N '71. * (*PA*
50:5200)

328. VERMA, S. K.; SHAH, D. K.; AND VERMA, H. C. "The
Body Image Concept of Schoolgoing Children in India: A Study
of 294 Children." *Manas* (India) 18(1):59–64 My '71. * (*PA*
48:8843)

329. WATSON, CHARLES G.; LALIBERTE, MICHAEL; AND SELL-
ERS, HOWARD. "Personality Correlates of DAP Facial Expression." *J Clin Psychol* 27(1):115–7 Ja '71. * (*PA* 46:1439)

330. WELLER, LEONARD, AND SHARAN (SINGER), SHLOMO.
"Articulation of the Body Concept Among First Grade Children." *Child Develop* 42(5):1553–9 N '71. * (*PA* 48:4662)

331. WIRLS, CHARLES J., AND PLOTKIN, ROSALIE R. "A Com-
parison of Children With Cleft Palate and Their Siblings on
Projective Test Personality Factors." *Cleft Palate J* 8:399–408
O '71. *

CUMULATIVE NAME INDEX

Human Figure Drawing Techniques

[1475]

The IES Test. Ages 10 and over and latency period girls; 1956–58; 14 scores: 3 scores each for a–c (impulses, ego, superego) plus 5 scores listed in d below; 4 tests; Lawrence A. Dombrose and Morton S. Slobin; Psychological Test Specialists. *

a) ARROW-DOT TEST. 1957–58; reaction to goal barriers.

b) PICTURE STORY COMPLETION TEST. 1956–58; conception of outside world.

c) PHOTO-ANALYSIS TEST. 1956–58; desired self-gratifications.

d) PICTURE TITLE TEST. 1956–58; recognition and acceptance of ego pressures; 5 scores: impulse, ego, superego, defense, superego plus defense.

For additional information, see P:443 (26 references); for reviews by Douglas P. Crowne and Walter Katkovsky and an excerpted review by John O. Crites, see 6:220 (15 references).

REFERENCES THROUGH 1971

1–15. See 6:220.
16–41. See P:443.
42. LYNCH, DENIS JOSEPH. *Future Time Perspective and Impulsivity in Old Age.* Doctor's thesis, Case Western Reserve University (Cleveland, Ohio), 1967. (*DA* 28:4296B)
43. RIGGS, SHELDON KENNETH. *Manifestations of Impulse, Ego, and Superego in Boys Identified for Remedial Reading Instruction in a Public School System.* Doctor's thesis, University of Maryland (College Park, Md.), 1967. (*DA* 28:4492A)
44. STERLING, ELLEN SEGAL. *The Comparative Personality Integration of Lower Class and Middle Class Delinquent and Nondelinquent Males.* Doctor's thesis, Case Western Reserve University (Cleveland, Ohio), 1968. (*DAI* 30:4383B)
45. BAEHR, MELANY E.; FURCON, JOHN E.; AND FROEMEL, ERNEST C. *Psychological Assessment of Patrolman Qualifications in Relation to Field Performance.* Washington, D.C.: United States Government Printing Office, 1969. Pp. vii, 246. *
46. GARDINER, HARRY W. "Use of the IES Test in Thailand: Responses of Female College Students." *Percept & Motor Skills* 28(3):858 Je '69. * (*PA* 43:17280)
47. MCCORMICK, CLARENCE C., AND SCHNOBRICH, JANICE N. "IES Arrow-Dot Performance in Two Montessori Preschools." *Percept & Motor Skills* 29(1):235–9 Ag '69. * (*PA* 44:2200)

48. WARFEL, CHARLES I. *A Study Using the IES Test for Discrimination of Differences in Impulse, Ego and Superego Functioning of Delinquent and Non-Delinquent Adolescents.* Master's thesis, Millersville State College (Millersville, Pa.), 1969.
49. MCCORMICK, CLARENCE C., AND SCHNOBRICH, JANICE N. "Longitudinal Corroboration of a Cross-Sectional Study of Development of Preschool Children With the Arrow-Dot Test." *Percept & Motor Skills* 30(1):269–70 F '70. * (*PA* 46:9798)
50. SINGH, SATISH CHANDRA PRASAD. "A Study of the Relative Strength of Impulse, Ego and Superego in Normal Group, Neurotic Group and Paranoid Group on IES Test." *Psychol Studies* (India) 15(2):90–4 Jl '70. *
51. GAUTAM, R. P. "Relationship Between Personal & Social Variables and Sociometric Status in Classroom Situation." *J Psychol Res* (India) 15(3):91–5 S '71. *
52. KLINE, PAUL, AND TREJDOSIEWICZ, L. "The I.E.S. Test and the Blacky Pictures." *Brit J Proj Psychol & Pers Study* 16(2):19–21 D '71. *
53. KLINE, PAUL, AND TREJDOSIEWICZ, LUDWIK. "IES Test Scores of Students in Great Britain." *Percept & Motor Skills* 33(3):1209–10 D '71. * (*PA* 48:1007)
54. LYNCH, DENIS J. "Future Time Perspective and Impulsivity in Old Age." *J Genetic Psychol* 118(2):245–52 Je '71. * (*PA* 46:8803)
55. MCCORMICK, CLARENCE C., AND SCHNOBRICH, JANICE N. "Perceptual-Motor Training and Improvement in Concentration in a Montessori Preschool." *Percept & Motor Skills* 32(1):71–7 F '71. * (*PA* 46:3865)
56. MCCORMICK, CLARENCE C.; KLAPPAUF, JEANNIE; SCHNOBRICH, JANICE N.; AND HARVEY, JOHN. "Relationships Among Arrow-Dot IES Scores and Wechsler IQs and MMPI Scales for Hospitalized, Disturbed Adolescents." *Percept & Motor Skills* 33(3):1227–34 D '71. * (*PA* 48:3263)
57. ZIVKOVIC, MOMCILO. "Influence of Deafness on the Structure of Personality." *Percept & Motor Skills* 33(3):863–6 D '71. * (*PA* 48:1426)

CUMULATIVE NAME INDEX

[1476]

An Incomplete Sentence Test. Employees, college; 1949–53; 2 editions; George Spache; Reading Laboratory and Clinic. *

a) AN INCOMPLETE SENTENCE TEST FOR INDUSTRIAL USE. Employees; 1949.

b) AN INCOMPLETE SENTENCE TEST [COLLEGE EDITION]. College; 1953; no manual.

For additional information, see P:444; for a review by Benjamin Balinsky, see 5:142.

[1477]

The Industrial Sentence Completion Form. Employee applicants; 1963; ISCF; experimental form; no manual; Martin M. Bruce; Martin M. Bruce, Ph.D., Publishers. *

For additional information, see P:445.

[1478]

Kahn Test of Symbol Arrangement. Ages 6 and over; 1949–60; KTSA; Theodore C. Kahn; Psychological Test Specialists. *

For additional information, see P:447 (36 references) ; see also 6:224 (10 references) ; for reviews by Cherry Ann Clark and Richard Jessor and an excerpted review by Laurance F. Shaffer, see 5:145 (16 references) ; for a review by Edward Joseph Shoben, Jr., see 4:110 (2 references).

REFERENCES THROUGH 1971

1–2. See 4:110.
3–18. See 5:145.
19–28. See 6:224.
29–64. See P:447.
65. HERRON, WILLIAM G. "Abstract Ability in the Process-Reactive Classification of Schizophrenia." *J General Psychol* 67:147–54 Jl '62. * (*PA* 37:3691)
66. RUBIN, EDMUND JOSEPH. *Performance of Totally-Blind and Sighted Subjects on Tests of Abstraction.* Doctor's thesis, Fordham University (New York, N.Y.), 1963. (*DA* 24:2989)
67. WHITE, P. OWEN, AND MCLEOD, HUGH N. "A Multiple Discriminant Analysis Comparing Psychotic, Neurotic, and Character-Disorder Patients on the Kahn Test of Symbol Arrangement." *Ont Psychol Assn Q* (Canada) 16:2–5 f '63. *
68. SCHILLER, JEANNE RUBIN. *The Kahn Test of Symbol Arrangement as a Predictor of Success in College.* Master's thesis, Richmond Professional Institute (Richmond, Va.), 1964.
69. BALLO, G. R. *The Kahn Test of Symbol Arrangement as a Possible Predictor of Academic Achievement.* Master's thesis, Eastern Washington State College (Cheney, Wash.), 1966.
70. GUERIN, A. J. *A Comparison of Normal and Emotionally Disturbed Children on the KTSA.* Master's thesis, Trinity University (San Antonio, Tex.), 1966.
71. AUCUTT, J. P. *The Effect of Perceptual Set on the Numerical Element of the Kahn Test of Symbol Arrangement.* Master's thesis, Eastern Washington State College (Cheney, Wash.), 1967.
72. BOHN, SUZANNE ERBE. *Normal- and Simulated-Murder Responses to the Kahn Test of Symbol Arrangement.* Master's thesis, Washington University (St. Louis, Mo.), 1967.
73. AFTANAS, M. S., AND ROYCE, J. R. "A Factor Analysis of Brain Damage Tests Administered to Normal Subjects With Factor Score Comparisons Across Ages." *Multiv Behav Res* 4(4):459–81 O '69. * (*PA* 44:11030)
74. CHAWLA, TILAK R. "An Evaluative Study of New Culture-Free Intelligence Test (Kit:Exp)." *J Psychol Res* 13(2):74–6 My '69. * (*PA* 45:4248)
75. KELLY, WILLIAM L. "The Group Kahn Test of Symbolic Arrangement." *Int J Symbol* 1(2):15–29 D '69. * (*PA* 45:10001)
76. L'ABATE, LUCIANO, AND GALE, ELLIOT N. "Neurological Status and Psychological Functioning." *Percept & Motor Skills* 29(3):999–1007 D '69. * (*PA* 46:5330)
77. MANN, EDWARD T. "Male Drug Addiction and the Kahn Test of Symbol Arrangement." *Percept & Motor Skills* 29(3):875–80 D '69. * (*PA* 46:5154)
78. MANN, EDWARD T. "Use of the KTSA as a Technique for Assessing Intelligence and Psychodynamics in Drug Addicts." *Int J Symbol* 1(2):57–66 D '69. * (*PA* 45:10218)
79. NAKANISHI, NOBUO. "Symbol Perception of the Kahn Test of Symbol Arrangement Among Four Cultures." *Int J Symbol* 1(1):20–4 Ag '69. * (*PA* 45:4051)
80. SILVERS, DAMON L., III. *The Meanings of Symbols on the Kahn Test of Symbol Arrangement as Determined by a Semantic Differential.* Master's thesis, Millersville State College (Millersville, Pa.), 1969.
81. THEINER, ERIC C. "Current Approaches to Symbolization: The Kahn Test of Symbol Arrangement." *Int J Symbol* 1(1):52–8 Ag '69. * (*PA* 45:4055)
82. WAGNER, RUDOLPH F. "Levels of Symbolization in Adolescent Adjustment Patterns." *Int J Symbol* 1(1):67–74 Ag '69. * (*PA* 45:4005)
83. ABIDIN, RICHARD R., JR. "KTSA Interscorer Reliability for Children's Protocols." *Int J Symbol* 1(3):37–9 Ap '70. * (*PA* 45:7231)
84. GUTBRODT, ERIKA J.; LYMAN, ROGER C.; AND JERRY, MARIAN B. "Suicide Attempts and Suicide in Psychiatric Patients: A Risk Assessment With Psychological Techniques." Abstract. *Proc 78th Ann Conv Am Psychol Assn* 5(2):559–60 '70. * (*PA* 44:18943)
85. KELLY, WILLIAM L. "Normative Data on the Group-KTSA." *Int J Symbol* 1(3):41–50 Ap '70. * (*PA* 45:7235)
86. PLUMMER, JACK. "A Pilot Study for the Differential Diagnosis of Frontal and Parietal Lobe Brain Damage." *Int J Symbol* 1(3):27–36 Ap '70. *
87. SILVERS, DAMON, AND WIRLS, C. J. "A Determination of the Symbolic Meanings of the Kahn Test of Symbol Arrangement Objects." *J Proj Tech & Pers Assess* 34(5):401–8 O '70. * (*PA* 45:4305)
88. WAGNER, RUDOLPH F. "Form Symbolization in Normal

Readers and Dyslexics Based on a Modified Pattern Recognition Theory." *Int J Symbol* 1(3):51–6 Ap '70. * (*PA* 45:8945)
89. KELLY, WILLIAM L. "Analysis of Covariance for Certain Symbolic Functions." *Int J Symbol* 2(3):26–39 N '71. * (*PA* 48:10077)
90. KIPPER, DAVID A. "Identifying Habitual Criminals by Means of the Kahn Test of Symbol Arrangement." *J Consult & Clin Psychol* 37(1):151–4 Ag '71. * (*PA* 47:1164)
91. WIRLS, CHARLES J., AND PLOTKIN, ROSALIE R. "A Comparison of Children With Cleft Palate and Their Siblings on Projective Test Personality Factors." *Cleft Palate J* 8:399–408 O '71. *

CUMULATIVE NAME INDEX

[1479]

Ka-Ro Inkblot Test. Ages 3 and over ; 1970 ; designed as "a Rorschach parallel series" ; Yasufumi Kataguchi and the Ka-Ro Research Group (manual and record booklet) ; Kaneko Shobo Publisher [Japan]. *

For additional information, see 7:171 (1 reference).

REFERENCES THROUGH 1971

1. See 7:171.

CUMULATIVE NAME INDEX

[1480]

Kent-Rosanoff Free Association Test. Ages 4 and over ; 1910 ; K-R ; for an adaptation, see 1445 ; G. H. Kent and A. J. Rosanoff ; Stoelting Co. *

For additional information, see P:448 (34 references) ; for a review by Jerry S. Wiggins, see 6:226 (82 references).

REFERENCES THROUGH 1971

1–82. See 6:226.
83–116. See P:448.
117. FRANZ, SHEPHERD IVORY. *Handbook of Mental Examination Methods, Second Edition*, pp. 113–26. New York: Macmillan Co., 1919. Pp. vii, 193. *
118. MATEER, FLORENCE; FITZGERALD, FLORENCE; AND DAVISON, MARGARET. "The Clinical Significance of the Kent-Rosanoff Association Tests." Abstract. *Psychol B* 18:84–5 F '21. *
119. FREYD, MAX. "The Personalities of the Socially and the Mechanically Inclined." *Psychol Monogr* 33(4):1–101 '24. *
120. BRIDGES, J. W. "Emotional Instability of College Students." *J Abn & Social Psychol* 22:227–34 O–D '27. * (*PA* 2:856)

121. McDowell, Elizabeth Dickinson. "Educational and Emotional Adjustments of Stuttering Children." *Teach Col Contrib Ed* 314:1–59 '28. * (*PA* 3:299)

122. Weber, C. Oliver, and Maijgren, Ruth. "The Experimental Differentia of Introversion and Extraversion." *J Genetic Psychol* 36:571–80 D '29. * (*PA* 4:932)

123. Graham, James L. "A Quantitative Comparison of Certain Mental Traits of Negro and White College Students." *J Social Psychol* 1:97–121, 267–85 F, My '30. * (*PA* 5:503)

124. Oliver, R. A. C. "The Traits of Extroverts and Introverts." *J Social Psychol* 1:345–66 Ag '30. * (*PA* 5:308)

125. Vetter, George B. "The Measurement of Social and Political Attitudes and the Related Personality Factors." *J Abn & Social Psychol* 25:149–89 Jl–S '30. * (*PA* 5:1899)

126. McElwee, Edna Willis. "Association in Normal and Sub-Normal Adolescents." *Am J Psychiatry* 88:311–8 S '31. * (*PA* 6:4548)

127. McElwee, Edna Willis. "A Comparison of the Personality Traits of 300 Accelerated, Normal, and Retarded Children." *J Ed Res* 26:31–4 S '32. * (*PA* 6:5053)

128. Cason, Hulsey. "Association in Relation to Feeling and Gross Bodily Movement." *Am J Psychol* 46:207–28 Ap '34. * (*PA* 8:3953)

129. Ferguson, Henry H. "An Association Scale: A Preliminary Investigation." *Austral J Psychol & Philos* 13:232–4 S '35. * (*PA* 10:145)

130. Kephart, Newell C., and Houtchens, H. Max. "The Specificity of Response Obtained on the Association-Motor Test." *Proc Iowa Acad Sci* 43:333–5 '36. *

131. Nottingham, Ruth D. "A Psychological Study of Forty Unmarried Mothers." *Genetic Psychol Monogr* 19:157–228 My '37. * (*PA* 11:4670)

132. Bentley, Madison. "Oxygen-Tension and 'the Higher Mental Processes.'" *Am J Psychol* 52:72–82 Ja '39. * (*PA* 13:2430)

133. Graham, Virginia Taylor. "Psychological Studies of Hypoglycemia Therapy." *J Psychol* 10:327–58 O '40. * (*PA* 15:1337)

134. Keir, Gertrude. "An Experiment in Mental Testing Under Hypnosis." *J Mental Sci* (England) 91:346–52 Jl '45. * (*PA* 20:425)

135. Jenkins, James J., and Russell, Wallace A. "Associative Clustering During Recall." *J Abn & Social Psychol* 47:818–21 O '52. * (*PA* 27:4944)

136. Russell, Wallace A., and Storms, Lowell H. "Implicit Verbal Chaining in Paired-Associate Learning." *J Exp Psychol* 49:287–93 Ap '55. * (*PA* 30:555)

137. Smith, Jean Judson. *Semantic Generalization as a Function of Connotative Similarity and Awareness of Stimulus Relationships.* Doctor's thesis, Michigan State University (East Lansing, Mich.), 1956. (*DA* 19:1838)

138. Rosen, Ephraim, and Russell, Wallace A. "Frequency-Characteristics of Successive Word-Association." *Am J Psychol* 70:120–2 Mr '57. * (*PA* 33:1305)

139. Jenkins, James J.; Mink, Walter D.; and Russell, Wallace A. "Associative Clustering as a Function of Verbal Association Strength." *Psychol Rep* 4:127–36 Mr '58. * (*PA* 33:3150)

140. Milgram, Norman Alvin. *Cognitive and Empathic Factors in the Role Attitudes of Schizophrenic and Brain-Damaged Patients.* Doctor's thesis, Boston University (Boston, Mass.), 1958. (*DA* 19:878)

141. Maltzman, Irving; Seymore, Simon; and Licht, Leonard. "Verbal Conditioning of Common and Uncommon Word Associations." *Psychol Rep* 10:363–9 Ap '62. * (*PA* 37:2450)

142. Kurcz, Ida. "Inter-Language Comparison of Word-Association Responses." *Int J Psychol* (France) 1(2):151–61 '66. * (*PA* 41:563)

143. Lambert, Wallace E., and Moore, Nancy. "Word Association Responses: Comparisons of American and French Monolinguals With Canadian Monolinguals and Bilinguals." *J Pers & Social Psychol* 3:313–20 Mr '66. * (*PA* 40:5428)

144. Dyer, Alice Mildred. *Cognitive Style of Levelers Versus Sharpeners as Related to Frequency of Original Responses to the Kent-Rosanoff List.* Master's thesis, California State College (Fullerton, Calif.), 1967. (*Masters Abstracts* 6:101)

145. Foley, Lawrence Joseph. *A Study of the Word Associations of Schizophrenic Dimensions With Varied Instructions.* Doctor's thesis, Rutgers—The State University (New Brunswick, N.J.), 1967. (*DA* 28:1190B)

146. Nunnally, Jum C.; Koplin, James H.; Blanton, Richard L.; and Shaw, Robert E. "Individual Differences in Word Association in Relation to Paired-Associate Learning." *J Verbal Learning & Verbal Behav* 6:107–11 F '67. * (*PA* 41:8348)

147. Ries, Harold A., and Johnson, Monty H. "Commonality of Word Associations and Good and Poor Premorbid Schizophrenia." *J Abn Psychol* 72:487–8 D '67. * (*PA* 42:4293)

148. Belcher, Leon H., and Campbell, Joel T. "An Exploratory Study of Word Associations of Negro College Students." *Psychol Rep* 23:119–34 Ag '68. * (*PA* 43:6946)

149. Dokecki, Paul R. *Commonality of Word Association Responses in Schizophrenics and Normals of Two Levels of Social Adequacy.* Doctor's thesis, George Peabody College for Teachers (Nashville, Tenn.), 1968. (*DA* 29:1839B)

150. Fuller, George D., and Kates, Solis L. "Word Association Repertoires of Schizophrenics and Normals." *J Consult & Clin Psychol* 33(4):497–500 Ag '69. * (*PA* 43:16075)

151. Kahana, B.; Stern, J. A.; and Clack, G. S. "Age-Related Differences in Logical Responses to the Word Association Test." Abstract. *Proc 77th Ann Conv Am Psychol Assn* 4(1):281–2 '69. * (*PA* 43:17206)

152. Mintz, Sanford. "Effect of Actual Stress on Word Associations." *J Abn Psychol* 74(3):293–5 Je '69. * (*PA* 43:13003)

153. Buckey, Harold M.; Muench, George A.; and Sjoberg, Bernard M. "Effects of a College Student Visitation Program on a Group of Chronic Schizophrenics." *J Abn Psychol* 75(3):242–4 Je '70. * (*PA* 44:14961)

154. Deckner, C. William, and Cromwell, Rue L. "Commonality of Word Association Response in Schizophrenia as a Function of Premorbid Adjustment, Chronicity, and Paranoid Status." *Psychol Rep* 26(2):503–9 Ap '70. * (*PA* 44:21252)

155. Jenkins, James J. Chap. 1, "The 1952 Minnesota Word Association Norms," pp. 1–38. In *Norms of Word Association.* Edited by Leo Postman and Geoffrey Keppel. New York: Academic Press Inc., 1970. Pp. vii, 467. *

156. Miller, Kenneth M. Chap. 2, "Free-Association Responses of English and Australian Students to 100 Words From the Kent-Rosanoff Word Association Test," pp 39–52. In *Norms of Word Association.* Edited by Leo Postman and Geoffrey Keppel. New York: Academic Press Inc., 1970. Pp. vii, 467. *

157. Rosenzweig, Mark R. Chap. 4, "International Kent-Rosanoff Word Association Norms, Emphasizing Those of French Male and Female Students and French Workmen," pp. 95–176. In *Norms of Word Association.* Edited by Leo Postman and Geoffrey Keppel. New York: Academic Press Inc., 1970. Pp. vii, 467. *

158. Russell, Wallace A. Chap. 3, "The Complete German Language Norms for Responses to 100 Words From the Kent-Rosanoff Word Association Test," pp. 53–94. In *Norms of Word Association.* Edited by Leo Postman and Geoffrey Keppel. New York: Academic Press Inc., 1970. Pp. vii, 467. *

159. Arthur, Artur Z. "A Comparison of Queen's and Minnesota Kent-Rosanoff Word Association Norms." *Can J Behav Sci* 3(3):291–7 Jl '71. * (*PA* 47:2891)

160. Yaryura-Tobias, Jose A.; Diamond, Bruce; and Merlis, Sidney. "Verbal Communication With L-Dopa Treatment." *Nature* (England) 234(5326):224–5 N 26 '71. * (*PA* 48:1170)

CUMULATIVE NAME INDEX

Maijgren, R.: 122
Maltzman, I.: 141
Marlowe, D.: 76
Martin, J. G.: 89
Mateer, F.: 14, 118
Mayzner, M. S.: 51, 81
Merlis, S.: 160
Meyers, R.: 33
Milgram, N. A.: 84, 140
Miller, K. M.: 156
Mink, W. D.: 139
Mintz, S.: 152
Mitchell, I.: 13
Moore, N.: 143
Muench, G. A.: 41, 153
Murphy, G. M.: 15-6
Nottingham, R. D.: 131
Nunnally, J. C.: 108, 112, 146
O'Connor, J.: 22
Odom, P. B.: 112
Oliver, R. A. C.: 124
Oschrin, E.: 12
Osipow, S. H.: 90, 97
Osmond, H.: 66-7
Otis, M.: 8
Palermo, D. S.: 74, 79-80, 86, 96, 98-9
Peterson, M. S.: 54
Polidoro, L. G.: 93
Restaino, L. C. R.: 100
Riegel, K. F.: 101-2
Ries, H. A.: 115, 147
Robbins, H.: 116
Rosanoff, A. J.: 1, 4, 6, 13, 19
Rosanoff, I. R.: 6, 13
Rosen, E.: 138
Rosen, H.: 36
Rosenzweig, M. R.: 69, 91, 157
Rosett, H. L.: 116

Rothkopf, E. Z.: 70-1
Russell, W. A.: 47, 64, 135-6, 138-9, 158
Sarason, I. G.: 59
Schellenberg, P. E.: 24
Schiffman, H.: 105, 113
Schnack, G. F.: 37-8
Seymore, S.: 141
Shakow, D.: 37-8, 103
Shaw, R. E.: 146
Shlaudeman, K. W.: 30
Silverstein, A. B.: 92, 109
Sjoberg, B. M.: 153
Smith, H. C.: 43
Smith, J. J.: 137
Sommer, R.: 66-7
Spoerl, D. T.: 35
Stern, J. A.: 151
Stroms, L. H.: 136
Strong, E. K.: 7
Symonds, P. M.: 26
Tendler, A. D.: 28, 39
Thorndike, E. L.: 27
Tresselt, M. E.: 45-6, 48-51, 57, 60, 68, 81
Vetter, G. B.: 125
Volsky, T. C.: 83
Watson, W. S.: 116
Weber, C. O.: 122
Wells, F. L.: 2-3, 5, 20
Wexler, N.: 113
Whipple, G. M.: 9
White, R. K.: 32
Wiggins, J. S.: rev, 6:226
Wolff, C.: 104
Woodrow, H.: 10, 21
Woodworth, R. S.: 3
Wynne, R. D.: 82, 105, 113
Yaryura-Tobias, J. A.: 160

[1481]

Machover Draw-A-Person Test. Ages 2 and over; 1949; MDAP; also called *Machover Figure Drawing Test;* Karen Machover; Charles C Thomas, Publisher. *

For additional information, see P:451 (85 references) ; for a review by Philip M. Kitay, see 6:229 (84 references) ; see also 5:148 (39 references) ; for reviews by Philip L. Harriman and Naomi Stewart, see 4:111 (13 references). For excerpts from related book reviews, see 4:112 (14 excerpts).

REFERENCES THROUGH 1971

1-13. See 4:111.
14-52. See 5:148.
53-136. See 6:229.
137-221. See P:451.

222. COOK, MURRAY. "A Preliminary Study of the Relationship of Differential Treatment of Male and Female Head Size in Figure Drawing to the Degree of Attribution of Social Function to the Female." *Psychol Newsl* 34:1-5 D '51. * (PA 26:6258)
223. FREED, HERBERT, AND PASTOR, JOYCE T. "Evaluation of the 'Draw-A-Person' Test (Modified) in Thalamotomy With Particular Reference to the Body Image." *J Nerv & Mental Dis* 114:106-20 Ag '51. * (PA 26:1610)
224. DOZIER, JUSTIN P., AND GETZ, S. B. "Problems Involved in the Placement of a Deaf Puerto Rican Child in an Educational Environment in the United States." *Am Ann Deaf* 98: 260-7 Mr '53. * (PA 28:3253)
225. KAPLAN, ARTHUR, AND SAKHEIM, GEORGE. "Manic-Depressive Psychosis in a 13-Year-Old Boy: Psychological Test Findings." *J Nerv & Mental Dis* 121:140-54 F '54. * (PA 29:7657)
226. SILVERMAN, ALBERT J., AND HARRIS, VIRGIL W. "Electroencephalography and Psychometric Testing in Brain-Damaged Patients." *J Nerv & Mental Dis* 120:31-5 Jl-Ag '54. * (PA 29:6111)
227. FERRACUTI, F., AND RIZZO, G. B. "Psychological Patterns in Terminal Cancer Cases." *Ed & Psychol* (India) 2:26-36 Ja-Mr '55. * (PA 31:3531)
228. GETZ, STEVEN B. "A Psychological Aid in the Diagnosis of Deafness of Emotional Origin." *Arch Otolaryng* 61:217-9 F '55. * (PA 30:1453)
229. REED, MAX RODNEY. *A Study of the Masculinity-Femininity Dimension of Personality in "Normal" and "Pathological" Groups: An Investigation of Differences in MF Test Productions of Hospitalized and Non-Hospitalized Women.* Doctor's thesis, Washington University (St. Louis, Mo.), 1955. (DA 15:1442)

230. TATERKA, JOHN H., AND KATZ, JOSEPH. "Study of Correlations Between Electroencephalographic and Psychological Patterns in Emotionally Disturbed Children." *Psychosom Med* 17:62-72 Ja-F '55. * (PA 29:7565)
231. VERNIER, CLAIRE M. Chap. 18, "Predictability in Treatment of Tuberculosis Patients," pp. 344-52. In *Personality, Stress and Tuberculosis.* Edited by Phineas J. Sparer. New York: International Universities Press, Inc., 1956. Pp. xviii, 629. * (PA 31:1535)
232. ASCH, MORTON JAY. *Negative Response Bias and Personality Adjustment.* Doctor's thesis, Syracuse University (Syracuse, N.Y.), 1957. (DA 17:1704)
233. CLANCY, DAVID DANA. *The Relationship of Positive Response Bias or Acquiescence to Psychopathology.* Doctor's thesis, Syracuse University (Syracuse, N.Y.), 1957. (DA 17:2054)
234. ISHAM, A. CHAPMAN. "Use of a Brief Psychological Battery in Psychiatric Practice." *Am J Psychother* 11:790-802 O '57. * (PA 33:6241)
235. KISSIN, BENJAMIN; GOTTSFELD, HARRY; AND DICKES, ROBERT. "Inhibition and Tachistoscopic Thresholds for Sexually Charged Words." *J Psychol* 43:333-9 Ap '57. * (PA 33:6249)
236. PONZO, EZIO. "An Experimental Variation of the Draw-A-Person Technique." *J Proj Tech* 21:278-85 S '57. * (PA 33:1300)
237. PHILIPPOPOULOS, G. S.; WITTKOWER, E. D.; AND COUSINEAU, A. "The Etiologic Significance of Emotional Factors in Onset and Exacerbations of Multiple Sclerosis: A Preliminary Report." *Psychosom Med* 20:458-74 N-D '58. * (PA 33:10888)
238. RIKLAN, MANUEL; WEINER, HERMAN; AND DILLER, LEONARD. "Somato-Psychologic Studies in Parkinson's Disease." *J Nerv & Mental Dis* 129:263-72 S '59. * (PA 34:6482)
239. YOUNG, HARL H., JR. "A Test of Witkins Field-Dependence Hypothesis." *J Abn & Social Psychol* 59:188-92 S '59. * (PA 34:2798)
240. ROSEN, MORTON HAROLD. *The Relationship Between Unevenness of Cognitive Functioning as Derived From Verbal-Spatial Discrepancy Scores and Measures of Personality Functioning.* Doctor's thesis, New York University (New York, N.Y.), 1960. (DA 20:4724)
241. WACHS, HIRSH, AND KATZ, MISHA S. "Studies of Body Image in Men With Spinal Cord Injury." *J Nerv & Mental Dis* 131:121-7 Ag '60. * (PA 35:2527)
242. LINTON, HARRIET B.; EPSTEIN, LAWRENCE; AND HARTFORD, HUNTINGTON. "Personality and Perceptual Correlates of Secondary Beginning Strokes in Handwriting." *Percept & Motor Skills* 12:271-81 Je '61. * (PA 36:2HE71L)
243. SILVERMAN, ALBERT J.; COHEN, SANFORD I.; SHMAVONIAN, BARRY M.; AND GREENBERG, GEORGE. "Psychophysiological Investigations in Sensory Deprivation." Discussion by Philip Solomon. *Psychosom Med* 23:48-62 Ja-F '61. * (PA 36:3HN48S)
244. YANAGI, GARRET HONORU. *An Appraisal of Psychologic Deficit in Children With Cerebral Palsy.* Doctor's thesis, University of Tennessee (Knoxville, Tenn.), 1961. (DA 22:4088)
245. BROIDA, HELEN. *An Empirical Study of Sex-Role Identification and Sex-Role Preference in a Selected Group of Stuttering Male Children.* Doctor's thesis, University of Southern California (Los Angeles, Calif.), 1962. (DA 23:2620)
246. GUERRANT, JOHN; ANDERSON, WILLIAM W.; FISCHER, AMES; WEINSTEIN, MORTON R.; JAROS, R. MARY; AND DESKINS, ANDREW. Chap 5, "Psychological Considerations," pp. 66-92. In their *Personality in Epilepsy.* Springfield, Ill.: Charles C Thomas, Publisher, 1962. Pp. xii, 112. *
247. HOWARD, STEPHEN JAMES. *Determinants of Sex-Role Identifications of Homosexual Female Delinquents.* Doctor's thesis, University of Southern California (Los Angeles, Calif.), 1962. (DA 23:2588)
248. GREENE, ROBERT J., AND JOHNSTONE, EDWARD R. "Prediction of Runaway Behavior From Drawings of the Human Figure." *Correct Psychiatry & J Social Ther* 9(3):146-8 '63. *
249. GROSS, MARTIN; HITCHMAN, IRENE; REEVES, WALTER P.; LAWRENCE, JORDAN; AND BACON, E. FAYE. "The Repetitive Administration of Two Psychological Tests During Withdrawal From Ataractic Drugs." *J Nerv & Mental Dis* 137:574-6 D '63. * (PA 38:6181)
250. KENDIG, ISABELLE V. Chap. 16, "The Draw-A-Person Test," pp. 257-68. In *The Genain Quadruplets.* Edited by David Rosenthal. New York: Basic Books, Inc., 1963. Pp. xv, 609. * (PA 38:9070)
251. BOURISSEAU, WHITFIELD. *A Study of Non-Intellectual Factors in Relation to School Achievement of Primary-Grade Pupils.* Master's thesis, Kent State University (Kent, Ohio), 1964.
252. EDENS, LESTER WILLIAM. *An Analysis of Certain Socio-Psychological Characteristics of Unwed Mothers Referred to Private Agencies in Washington and Idaho.* Doctor's thesis, University of Idaho (Moscow, Idaho), 1964. (DA 25:5730)
253. ESLER, HAROLD DEAN. *An Investigation of the Causes of Suicide in Patients Diagnosed as Schizophrenic.* Doctor's thesis, Michigan State University (East Lansing, Mich.), 1964. (DA 26:1169)
254. GERDINE, PHILIP VAN HORN, JR. *Patterns of Ego Function in Psychophysiological Skin Disorders.* Doctor's thesis, Boston University (Boston, Mass.), 1964. (DA 25:3108)

Kent-Rosanoff Free Association Test

255. HUFF, FREDEDICK WARE. *Reliability of Clinical, Psychological Judgment as a Function of Information Presentation and Response Classification.* Doctor's thesis, University of Georgia (Athens, Ga.), 1964. (*DA* 25:3110)

256. POGUE, BETTY CASKEY. *An Exploration of the Interrelationship Among Creativity, Self-Esteem and Race.* Doctor's thesis, Ball State Teachers College (Muncie, Ind.), 1964. (*DA* 26:3155)

257. REITMAN, E. EDWARD, AND CLEVELAND, SIDNEY E. "Changes in Body Image Following Sensory Deprivation in Schizophrenic and Control Groups." *J Abn & Social Psychol* 68:168–76 F '64. * (*PA* 38:5172)

258. SCHON, MARTHA. "Hypothyroidism: A Psychoendocrinological Evaluation." *Psychosomatics* 5:203–12 Jl–Ag '64. *

259. CORAH, NORMAN L. "Differentiation in Children and Their Parents." *J Personality* 33:300–8 Je '65. * (*PA* 40:2895)

260. PERKINS, CHARLES W., AND SHANNON, DONALD T. "Three Techniques for Obtaining Self-Perceptions in Preadolescent Boys." *J Pers & Social Psychol* 2:443–7 S '65. * (*PA* 39:15196)

261. SEWARD, GEORGENE H.; WAGNER, PHILIP S.; HEINRICH, JEROME F.; BLOCK, SAUL K.; AND MYERHOFF, H. LEE. "The Question of Psychophysiologic Infertility: Some Answers." *Psychosom Med* 27:533–45 N–D '65. * (*PA* 40:5774)

262. DONINI, GERALD PETER. "An Evaluation of Sex-Role Identification Among Father-Absent and Father-Present Boys." *Psychol* 4:13–6 Ag '67. * (*PA* 41:16582)

263. FELZ, GERALD ANTHONY. *Group Process as an Enabling Activity in an Elementary Teacher Preparation Curriculum.* Doctor's thesis, Arizona State University (Tempe, Ariz.), 1967. (*DA* 27:2913A)

264. GOODMAN, ELLEN. *A Study of Certain Aspects of the Social-Emotional Adjustment of Nonpromoted Elementary School Children.* Doctor's thesis, Lehigh University (Bethlehem, Pa.), 1967. (*DA* 28:3997A)

265. GRAYSON, HENRY TATE, JR. *Psychosexual Conflict in Adolescent Girls Who Experienced Early Parental Loss by Death.* Doctor's thesis, Boston University (Boston, Mass.), 1967. (*DA* 28:2136B)

266. KAPUR, MALAVIKA, AND KAPUR, R. L. "Study of Impotence Through Projective Tests." *Indian J Psychiatry* 9:208–12 Jl '67. *

267. VOGEL, FRANCIS XAVIER. *The Relationship of the Form of School Organization to Selected Classroom Behaviors of Pupils.* Doctor's thesis, Northwestern University (Evanston, Ill.), 1967. (*DA* 28:3957A)

268. GILBERSTADT, HAROLD. "Relationships Among Scores of Tests Suitable for the Assessment of Adjustment and Intellectual Functioning." *J Gerontol* 23:483–7 O '68. *

269. KONTTINEN, RAIMO. *Relationships Between Graphic Expansivity and Extraversion as a Function of Anxiety and Defensiveness.* Annales Academia Scientiarum Fennica, Series B, No. 159. Helsinki, Finland: Suomalainen Tiedeakatemia, Academia Scientiarum Fennica, 1968. Pp. 108. * (*PA* 43:11307)

270. SANDMAN, CURT A.; CAUTHEN, NELSON R.; KILPATRICK, DEAN G.; AND DEABLER, HERDIS L. "Size of Figure Drawing in Relation to Depression." *Percept & Motor Skills* 27:945–6 D '68. * (*PA* 43:8447)

271. CAUTHEN, NELSON R.; SANDMAN, CURT A.; KILPATRICK, DEAN G.; AND DEABLER, HERDIS L. "DAP Correlates of Sc Scores on the MMPI." *J Proj Tech & Pers Assess* 33(3):262–4 Je '69. * (*PA* 43:14346)

272. DANIELS, LLOYD KEITH. *The Relation Between the Self Concept, Perceived Parental Behavior, and Vocational Adjustment for Mentally Retarded Young Adults.* Doctor's thesis, Boston University (Boston, Mass.), 1969. (*DAI* 31:378B)

273. GRAVITZ, MELVIN A. "Figure Drawing Size as an Index of Depression and MMPI Depression Scores in Normal Adults." *J Clin Psychol* 25(1):77–9 Ja '69. * (*PA* 43:10003)

274. GRAVITZ, MELVIN A. "Marital Status and Figure Drawing Choice in Normal Older Americans." *J Social Psychol* 77(1):143–4 F '69. * (*PA* 43:6947)

275. LUDWIG, DAVID J. "Self-Perception and the Draw-a-Person Test." *J Proj Tech & Pers Assess* 33(3):257–61 Je '69. * (*PA* 43:14347)

276. MARINOW, A. "Mental Illness as Reflected in Machover's Drawing Test." *Psychiatry & Art* 2:133–6 '69. *

277. MELIKIAN, LEVON H., AND WAHAB, A. ZAHER. "First-Drawn Picture: A Cross-Cultural Investigation of the DAP." *J Proj Tech & Pers Assess* 33(6):539–41 D '69. * (*PA* 44:6792)

278. OWENS, RICHARD THOMAS. *A Study of the Performance of Minimally Brain-Damaged and Emotionally Disturbed Boys on Six Selected Psychological Tests.* Doctor's thesis, University of Nebraska (Lincoln, Neb.), 1969. (*DAI* 31:383B)

279. REZNIKOFF, MARVIN, AND DIES, ROBERT R. "The Use of Clothing in Human Figure Drawings." *J Clin Psychol* 25(1):80–1 Ja '69. * (*PA* 43:10018)

280. WELSH, ROBERT JOSEPH, AND WHITE, WILLIAM JOSEPH, III. *Relationship Between Degree of Difficulty of Drawing for Various Body Parts and Rated Disturbance in the Draw-A-Person Test.* Master's thesis, Loyola University (Chicago, Ill.), 1969.

281. WISE, JAMES H. "Self-Reports by Negro and White Adolescents to the Draw-A-Person." *Percept & Motor Skills* 28(1):193–4 F '69. * (*PA* 43:11363)

282. BAILEY, WILLIAM L.; SHINEDLING, MARTIN M.; AND PAYNE, I. REED. "Obese Individuals' Perception of Body Image." *Percept & Motor Skills* 31(2):617–8 O '70. * (*PA* 45:5857)

283. DANIELS, LLOYD K., AND STEWART, JAMES A. "Mentally Retarded Adults' Perceptions of Self and Parent Related to Their Vocational Adjustment." *Training Sch B* 66(4):164–71 F '70. * (*PA* 44:13172)

284. HIRSCH, ERNEST A. *The Troubled Adolescent: As He Emerges From Psychological Tests.* New York: International Universities Press, Inc., 1970. Pp. xv, 645. *

285. KRALL, VITA. "Personality Factors in Nursing School Success and Failure." *Nursing Res* 19(3):265–8 My–Je '70. * (*PA* 47:10931, title only)

286. MEBANE, DONATA F., AND DIE, JERRY G. "A Scoring System for Human Figure Drawings as a Measure of Personality at Level III of the Leary Interpersonal Diagnostic System." *Percept & Motor Skills* 30(2):385–6 Ap '70. * (*PA* 46:6902)

287. MURSTEIN, BERNARD I., AND WOLF, STEVEN R. "An Empirical Test of the 'Levels' Hypothesis With Five Projective Techniques." *Int Congr Rorsch & Other Proj Tech* 7:558–72 '70. *

288. MURSTEIN, BERNARD I., AND WOLF, STEVEN R. "Empirical Test of the 'Levels' Hypothesis With Five Projective Techniques." *J Abn Psychol* 75(1):38–44 F '70. * (*PA* 44:6794)

289. SOLAR, DIANA; BRUEHL, DIETER; AND KOVACS, JOHN. "The Draw-A-Person Test: Social Conformity or Artistic Ability?" *J Clin Psychol* 26(4):524–5 O '70. * (*PA* 45:4306)

290. SOPCHAK, ANDREW L. "Anxiety Indicators on the Draw-A-Person Test for Clinic and Nonclinic Boys and Their Parents." *J Psychol* 76(2):251–60 N '70. * (*PA* 45:4552)

291. STEWART, JAMES A., AND DANIELS, LLOYD K. "A Modified Scoring Procedure for the Machover Draw-A-Person Test in Assessing the Self Concept of Mentally Retarded Subjects." *Training Sch B* 67(3):178–82 N '70. * (*PA* 45:8822)

292. CANCRO, ROBERT. "Sophistication of Body Concept in Process-Reactive Schizophrenia." *Percept & Motor Skills* 32(2):567–70 Ap '71. * (*PA* 46:11240)

293. CARLSON, KATHLEEN; TUCKER, G.; HARROW, M.; AND QUINLAN, D. "Body Image and Mental Illness: A Study of the Human Figure Drawings of Psychiatric Patients." *Psychiatry & Art* 3:162–9 '71. *

294. CHAPMAN, LOREN J. Chap. 3, "Studies of Psychodiagnostic Errors of Observation as a Contribution Toward a Nondynamic Psychopathology of Everyday Life," pp. 123–61. In *Advances in Experimental Clinical Psychology.* Edited by Henry E. Adams and William K. Boardman. New York: Pergamon Press, Inc., 1971. Pp. x, 219. *

295. CHAPMAN, LOREN J., AND CHAPMAN, JEAN. "Test Results Are What You Think They Are." *Psychol Today* 5(6):18+ N '71. * (*PA* 47:11122)

296. CULL, JOHN G., JR., AND HARDY, RICHARD E. "Concurrent Validation Information on the Machover Draw-A-Person Test." *J Genetic Psychol* 118(2):211–5 Je '71. * (*PA* 46:9080)

297. CUNNINGHAM, DIANA P. *An Investigation of the Relationship of Anxiety and Children's Performance on the Draw-A-Person Test.* Master's thesis, Texas Woman's University (Denton, Tex.), 1971.

298. GEIST, HAROLD. "Emotional Aspects of Dermatitis." Abstract. *Proc 79th Ann Conv Am Psychol Assn* 6(2):627–8 '71. * (*PA* 46:5380)

299. JENSEN, DIANA E.; PRANDONI, JOGUES R.; AND ABUDABBEH, NUHA N. "Figure Drawings by Sex Offenders and a Random Sample of Offenders." *Percept & Motor Skills* 32(1):295–300 F '71. * (*PA* 46:3356)

300. JOHNSON, JAMES H. "Note on the Validity of Machover's Indicators of Anxiety." *Percept & Motor Skills* 33(1):126 Ag '71. * (*PA* 47:3022)

301. KING, HOLLIS HEATON. *An Investigation of Relationships Between Hypnotic Susceptibility, Manifest Dream Content and Personality Characteristics.* Doctor's thesis, Louisiana State University (Baton Rouge, La.), 1971. (*DAI* 33:442B)

302. MASICA, DANIEL N.; MONEY, JOHN; AND EHRHARDT, ANKE A. "Fetal Feminization and Female Gender Identity in the Testicular Feminizing Syndrome of Androgen Insensitivity." *Arch Sex Behav* 1(2):131–42 '71. * (*PA* 48:1284)

303. NEUBECK, ROBERT CHARLES. *Variables Affecting Ratings of Pathology on Test Protocols.* Doctor's thesis, Southern Illinois University (Carbondale, Ill.), 1971. (*DAI* 32:4865B)

304. WINTER, ITZHAK. "The Evaluation of the Psychoanalytic Theory on Neurocirculatory-Asthenia by Experimental Methods." *Israel Ann Psychiatry* 9(3):233–51 D '71. * (*PA* 48:7542)

CUMULATIVE NAME INDEX

[1482]

Make A Picture Story. Ages 6 and over; 1947–52; MAPS; Edwin S. Shneidman; Psychological Corporation. *

For additional information, see P:452 (4 references); for a review by Arthur R. Jensen, see 6:230 (10 references); see also 5:149 (18 references); for reviews by Albert I. Rabin and Charles R. Strother, see 4:113 (19 references). For excerpts from related book reviews, see 4:114 (2 excerpts).

REFERENCES THROUGH 1971

1–19. See 4:113.
20–38. See 5:149.
39–48. See 6:230.
49–52. See P:452.
53. WORDEN, FREDERIC G., AND MARSH, JAMES T. "Psychological Factors in Men Seeking Sex Transformation: A Preliminary Report." *J Am Med Assn* 157:1292–8 Ap 9 '55. *
54. MOSS, HOWARD ALAN. *The Generality of Cautiousness as a Defense Behavior.* Doctor's thesis, Ohio State University (Columbus, Ohio), 1958. (*DA* 19:879)
55. HOZIER, ANN. "On the Breakdown of the Sense of Reality: A Study of Spatial Perception in Schizophrenia." *J Consult Psychol* 23:185–94 Je '59. * (*PA* 34:4680)
56. LINDZEY, GARDNER. "On the Classification of Projective Techniques." *Psychol B* 56:158–68 Mr '59. * (*PA* 34:1389)
57. SHNEIDMAN, EDWIN S. "The Case of El: Psychological Test Data." *J Proj Tech* 25:131–54 Je '61. * (*PA* 36:21K31S)
58. ZUBIN, JOSEPH; ERON, LEONARD D.; AND SCHUMER, FLORENCE. *An Experimental Approach to Projective Techniques,* pp. 482–7. New York: John Wiley & Sons, Inc., 1965. Pp. xxi, 645. * (*PA* 39:15432)
59. NEURINGER, CHARLES. "Clinical Psychologists' Ratings of MAPS Figures Along a Social Withdrawal Scale." *J Proj Tech & Pers Assess* 23(1):30–3 F '69. * (*PA* 43:10017)
60. TOLOR, ALEXANDER, AND ORANGE, SUSAN. "An Attempt to Measure Psychological Distance in Advantaged and Disadvantaged Children." *Child Develop* 40(2):407–20 Je '69. * (*PA* 43:15605)
61. BAXTER, JAMES C., AND DEANOVICH, BETTYE F. "Anxiety Arousing Effects of Inappropriate Crowding." *J Consult & Clin Psychol* 35(2):174–8 O '70. * (*PA* 45:4106)
62. WEISSKOPF-JOELSON, EDITH; ZIMMERMAN, JAY; AND MCDANIEL, MAX. "Similarity Between Subject and Stimulus as an Influence on Projection." *J Proj Tech & Pers Assess* 34(4):328–31 Ag '70. * (*PA* 44:21011)

[1483]

The Measurement of Self Concept in Kindergarten Children. Kgn; 1967; MSCKC; experimental form; projective drawing technique; 3 scores: self concept, non-self concept, discrepancy; Lucienne Y. Levine and J. Clayton Lafferty; Research Concepts. *

For additional information, see P:454.

[1484]

Miner Sentence Completion Scale. Managers and management trainees; 1961–64; MSCS; motivation; item and rare scores in 7 areas (authority figures, competitive games, competitive situations, masculine role, imposing wishes, standing out from group, routine administrative functions), total, and popularity level; John B. Miner; Springer Publishing Co., Inc. *

For additional information and a review by C. J. Adcock, see 7:172 (2 references); see also P:456 (3 references) and 6:230a (2 references).

REFERENCES THROUGH 1971

1–2. See 6:230a.
3–5. See P:456.
6–7. See 7:172.
8. CAIN, LEWIS ALBERT. *The Significance of Paternal Education and Occupation as Contributing Factors in the Identification of Managerial Motivation in the High School Senior Boy.* Doctor's thesis, Oregon State University (Corvallis, Ore.), 1971. (*DAI* 31:5587A)
9. GANTZ, BENJAMIN S., JR.; ERICKSON, CLARA; AND STEPHENSON, ROBERT W. "Measuring the Motivation to Manage in a Research and Development Population." Abstract. *Proc 79th Ann Conv Am Psychol Assn* 6(1):129–30 '71. * (*PA* 46:3949)
10. MINER, JOHN B. "Changes in Student Attitudes Toward Bureaucratic Role Prescriptions During the 1960s." *Adm Sci Q* 16(3):351–64 S '71. * (*PA* 47:10755)
11. MINER, JOHN B. "Personality Tests as Predictors of Consulting Success." *Personnel Psychol* 24(2):191–204 su '71. * (*PA* 49:3422)

[1485]

*Minnesota Percepto-Diagnostic Test (Revised). Ages 5–16; 1962–69; MPDT; brain damage and emotional disturbances; G. B. Fuller and J. T. Laird (test); Clinical Psychology Publishing Co., Inc. *

For additional information, see P:457 (19 references); for reviews by Richard W. Coan and Eugene E. Levitt of the original edition, see 6:231 (2 references).

REFERENCES THROUGH 1971

1–2. See 6:231.
3–21. See P:457.
22. FULLER, GERALD B. "Perceptual Considerations in Children With a Reading Disability." *Psychol Sch* 1:314–7 Jl '64. *
23. ALBRIGHT, MARY JOAN. *Visual Perception in Children of Retarded and Normal Reading Ability.* Doctor's thesis, Fordham University (New York, N.Y.), 1966. (*DA* 27:2128B)
24. HASTINGS, MARGARET R. *The Construction and Testing of a Syndromic Instrument for Detecting Minimal Organic Brain Damage in Children.* Master's thesis, Southern Methodist University (Dallas, Tex.), 1966.
25. GREDLER, GILBERT R. "Performance on a Perceptual Test With Children From a Culturally Disadvantaged Background." *Proc Ann Conv Int Read Assn* 12(4):86–91 '68. *
26. AFTANAS, M. S., AND ROYCE, J. R. "A Factor Analysis of Brain Damage Tests Administered to Normal Subjects With Factor Score Comparisons Across Ages." *Multiv Behav Res* 4(4):459–81 O '69. * (*PA* 44:11030)
27. FRIEDRICH, DOUGLAS; FULLER, GERALD B.; AND HAWKINS, WILLIAM F. "Relationship Between Perception (Input) and Execution (Output)." *Percept & Motor Skills* 29(3):923–34 D '69. * (*PA* 46:5346)
28. FULLER, GERALD B. *The Minnesota Percepto-Diagnostic Test (Revised).* Journal of Clinical Psychology Monograph Supplement No. 28, July 1969. Brandon, Vt.: Clinical Psychology Publishing Co., Inc., 1969. Pp. 84. *
29. FULLER, GERALD B. "Perceptual Behaviors and Reading Disabilities: Emphasis on the Neurological Impaired." *CEC Selected Conv Papers* 1969:280–90 '69. *

30. FULLER, GERALD B., AND HAWKINS, WILLIAM F. "Differentiation of Organic From Nonorganic Retarded Children." *Am J Mental Def* 74(1):104–10 Jl '69. * (*PA* 43:17807)

31. PRABHU, G. G. "The Clinical Utility of Bender-Gestalt and Minnesota Percepto Diagnostic Tests." *Indian J Appl Psychol* 6(2):69–73 Jl '69. *

32. BURGESS, MICHAEL M.; KODANAZ, ALTAN; AND ZIEGLER, DEWEY K. "Prediction of Brain Damage in a Neurological Population With Cerebrovascular Accidents." *Percept & Motor Skills* 31(2):595–601 O '70. * (*PA* 45:6841)

33. BURGESS, MICHAEL M.; KODANAZ, ALTAN; ZIEGLER, DEWEY; AND GREENBURG, HOWARD. "Prediction of Brain Damage in Two Clinical Populations." *Percept & Motor Skills* 30(2):523–32 Ap '70. * (*PA* 46:7299)

34. CHARLESWORTH, WILLIAM J. *Differences in Performance on the Minnesota Percepto-Diagnostic Test by Brain Damaged and Psychotic Adults.* Master's thesis, Central Michigan University (Mt. Pleasant, Mich.), 1970.

35. LEVINE, MAUREEN. *Psychological, Neuropsychological, and Educational Correlates of Reading Deficit: Etiological and Normative Comparison.* Master's thesis, Central Michigan University (Mt. Pleasant, Mich.), 1970.

36. SCHWARTZ, MELVIN L., AND DENNERLL, RAYMOND D. "Neuropsychological Assessment of Children With, Without, and With Questionable Epileptogenic Dysfunction." *Percept & Motor Skills* 30(1):111–21 F '70. * (*PA* 46:11105)

37. STEWART, R. R.; WALKER, W.; AND SAVAGE, R. D. "A Developmental Study of Cognitive and Personality Characteristics Associated With Haemolytic Disease of the Newborn." *Develop Med & Child Neurol* (England) 12(1):16–26 F '70. * (*PA* 44:17249)

38. BAUMAN, EDWARD, AND ST. JOHN, JOAN. "The Clinical Usefulness of Some Tests of Visual Perception." *Psychol Sch* 8(3):247–9 Jl '71. * (*PA* 47:9635)

CUMULATIVE NAME INDEX

Aftanas, M. S.: 26
Albright, M. J.: 23
Bauman, E.: 38
Blum, D. M.: 16
Burgess, M. M.: 32–3
Burnett, A.: 8
Chagnon, J. G.: 10, 16
Charlesworth, W. J.: 34
Coan, R. W.: *rev*, 6:231
Coberly, L. M.: 3
Dennerll, R. D.: 36
Ende, R.: 18
Ende, R. S.: 17
Friedrich, D.: 27
Fuller, G.: 6
Fuller, G. B.: 1, 4–5, 8–9, 18–9, 21–2, 27–30
Gredler, G. R.: 25
Greenburg, H.: 33
Harrison, D. M.: 10
Hastings, M. R.: 24
Hawkins, W. F.: 19, 27, 30
Kodanaz, A.: 32–3

Kreitman, L.: 11
Krippner, S.: 12
L'Abate, L.: 13
Laird, J. T.: 1
Levine, M.: 35
Levitt, E. E.: *rev*, 6:231
Lunney, G. H.: 5
Noak, J. R.: 20
Paul, S. K.: 14
Prabhu, G. G.: 31
Royce, J. R.: 26
St. John, J.: 38
Savage, R. D.: 37
Schwartz, M. L.: 36
Sharp, H.: 19
Stewart, R. R.: 37
Swaney, C. W.: 7
Uecker, A. E.: 15
Uyeno, E.: 2, 6
Walker, W.: 37
Watson, C. G.: 15
Ziegler, D.: 33
Ziegler, D. K.: 32

[1486]

***The Object Relations Technique.** Ages 11 and over; 1955–73; ORT; Herbert Phillipson; distributed by NFER Publishing Co. Ltd. [England]. *

For additional information, see P:458 (5 references); for a review by H. R. Beech and an excerpted review by Leopold Bellak, see 6:233 (7 references); for a review by George Westby, see 5:151 (6 references). For excerpts from reviews of the manual, see 5:B338 (9 excerpts).

REFERENCES THROUGH 1971

1–6. See 5:151.
7–13. See 6:233.
14–18. See P:458.

19. COLEMAN, J. C. "The Perception of Interpersonal Relationships During Adolescence." *Brit J Ed Psychol* 39(3):253–60 N '69. * (*PA* 44:8231)

20. ASTON, P. JEAN. "Predicting Amount of Verbal Participation in a Newly-Formed Therapy Group From Picture-Thematic Stories." *Brit J Proj Psychol & Pers Study* 15(2):19–20 D '70. *

21. ASTON, P. JEAN. "Predicting Verbal Participation in Group Therapy." *Brit J Psychiatry* 116(530):45–50 Ja '70. * (*PA* 44:21106)

22. COLEMAN, JOHN C.; ELKAN, GEOFFREY; AND SHOOTER, ANTONIA. "The Perception of People and of Relationships: A Study of Four Clinical Groups Using the Object Relations Technique." *Int Congr Rorsch & Other Proj Tech* 7:760–81 '70. *

23. ASTON, P. JEAN. "Predicting Participation Length in

Minnesota Percepto-Diagnostic Test

Group Therapy." *Brit J Psychiatry* 119(548):57–8 Jl '71. * (*PA* 47:6919)

CUMULATIVE NAME INDEX

Alcock, A. T.: 5
Amado-Haguenauer, G.: 10
Aston, P. J.: 20–1, 23
Beech, H. R.: *rev*, 6:233
Bellak, L.: *exc*, 6:233
Coleman, J. C.: 19, 22
Davis, H.: 18
Elkan, G.: 22
Gladston, E. R.: 10
Hahn, H.: 16
Haskell, R. J.: 11
Hetherington, R.: *exc*, 5:B338
Hopkins, J.: 14–5
Keir, G.: *exc*, 5:B338
Kutash, S. B.: *exc*, 5:B338
McMahon, D.: *exc*, 5B338

Meyer, M. M.: *exc*, 5:B338
Nevis, E. C.: *exc*, 5:B338
O'Kelly, E.: 2, 6–7
Orme, J. E.: 9
Phillipson, H.: 1, 3, 5, 8, 14–5
Rayner, E. H.: 16
Sells, S. B.: *exc*, 5:B338
Semeonoff, B.: *exc*, 5:B338
Shaffer, L. F.: *exc*, 5:B338
Shooter, A.: 22
Staunton, G. J.: 4
Takala, K.: 17
Vernon, M. D.: 12
Viitamaki, R. O.: 13
Westby, G.: *rev*, 5:151

[1487]

PRADI Draw-A-Person Test. Clinical clients; 1966; DAPT; Psychological Research and Development Institute; Psychological Publications Press. *

For additional information, see P:459.

[1488]

***Pain Apperception Test.** Adults; 1973, c1956–73; PAT; 10 scores: 3 scores (intensity, duration, total) in each of 3 areas (felt pain sensation, anticipation of pain vs. felt-sensation, self-inflicted vs. other-inflicted pain), total; Donald V. Petrovich; Western Psychological Services. *

REFERENCES THROUGH 1971

1. PETROVICH, DONALD V. "The Pain Apperception Test: A Preliminary Report." *J Psychol* 44:339–46 O '57. * (*PA* 33:9249)

2. PETROVICH, DONALD V. "The Pain Apperception Test: Psychological Correlates of Pain Perception." *J Clin Psychol* 14:367–74 O '58. * (*PA* 34:3019)

3. PETROVICH, DONALD V. "A Survey of Painfulness Concepts." *J Clin Psychol* 14:288–91 Jl '58. * (*PA* 33:7460)

4. PETROVICH, DONALD V. "The Pain Apperception Test: An Application to Sex Differences." *J Clin Psychol* 15:412–4 O '59. * (*PA* 36:1HG12P)

5. MOSS, C. SCOTT, AND WATERS, THOMAS J. "Intensive Longitudinal Investigation of Anxiety in Hospitalized Juvenile Patients." *Psychol Rep* 7:379–80 O '60. * (*PA* 35:2278)

6. PETROVICH, DONALD V. "The Apperceptive Study of Psychological Aspects of Pain." *Percept & Motor Skills* 11:57 Ag '60. * (*PA* 35:3437)

7. PETROVICH, DONALD V. "Pain Apperception in Chronic Schizophrenics." *J Proj Tech* 24:21–7 Mr '60. * (*PA* 35:1141)

8. SILVERSTEIN, A. B., AND OWENS, EARL P. "Pain Apperception in the Mentally Retarded." *J Proj Tech* 25:352–5 S '61. * (*PA* 36:3JI52S)

9. SILVERSTEIN, A. B. "Age Differences in Pain Apperception." *Percept & Motor Skills* 16:169–70 F '63. * (*PA* 38:193)

10. BLITZ, BERNARD; DINNERSTEIN, ALBERT J.; AND LOWENTHAL, MILTON. "Performance on the Pain Apperception Test and Tolerance for Experimental Pain: A Lack of Relationship." *J Clin Psychol* 24:73 Ja '68. * (*PA* 42:8986)

CUMULATIVE NAME INDEX

Blitz, B.: 10
Dinnerstein, A. J.: 10
Lowenthal, M.: 10
Moss, C. S.: 5

Owens, E. P.: 8
Petrovich, D. V.: 1–4, 6–7
Silverstein, A. B.: 8–9
Waters, T. J.: 5

[1489]

Pickford Projective Pictures. Ages 5–15; 1963; PPP; R. W. Pickford with the assistance of Ruth Bowyer and John Struthers; NFER Publishing Co. Ltd. [England]. *

For additional information and excerpted reviews by R. F. Barbour and Albert I. Rabin, see 7:173; for a review by Stanley J. Segal and excerpted reviews by R. Hetherington and two others, see 6:234 (5 references).

REFERENCES THROUGH 1971

1–5. See 6:234.

[1490]

*Picture Identification Test. High school and college; 1959–71; PIT; 3 scores (judgment, attitude, association) and an effectiveness rating for each of 22 needs (abasement, achievement, affiliation, aggression, autonomy, blame avoidance, counteraction, defendance, deference, dominance, exhibition, gratitude, harm avoidance, inferiority avoidance, nurturance, order, play, rejection, sentience, sex, succorance, understanding), average; no manual for examiners; Jay L. Chambers; the Author. *

For additional information, see P:463 (17 references).

REFERENCES THROUGH 1971

1–17. See P:463.
18. PLUMMER, NOEL ARTHUR. *Patient-Therapist Need Compatibility and Expectation of Psychotherapeutic Outcome.* Doctor's thesis, University of Florida (Gainesville, Fla.), 1966. (*DA* 27:1628B)
19. CHAMBERS, JAY, AND WILSON, WINSTON T. "Need Associations to Acquisition Modes, Education, and Adjustment." *Percept & Motor Skills* 33(3):911–7 D '71. * (*PA* 48:943)

[1491]

The Picture Impressions Test. Adolescents and adults; 1956–69; PIT; for investigating the patient-therapist relationship; Lester M. Libo; Consulting Psychologists Press, Inc. *

For additional information and a review by Eugene E. Levitt, see 7:174 (2 references); see also P:464 (1 reference); for an excerpted review by Steven G. Vandenberg, see 5:152 (1 reference).

REFERENCES THROUGH 1971

1. See 5:152.
2. See P:464.
3–4. See 7:174.

[1492]

*Picture Situation Test. Adult males; 1971; PST; "reaction to aggression provoking stimuli in a social situation"; 4 scores: type of aggression (direct, denial), effect of response (constructive, destructive); A. J. Templer (manual); National Institute for Personnel Research [South Africa]. *

[1493]

The Picture Story Test Blank. Clinical clients; 1965–66; PSTB; manual title is *Picture Story Test Booklet;* for recording protocols of picture story tests; Psychological Research and Development Institute; Psychological Publications Press. *

For additional information, see P:465.

[1494]

The Picture World Test. Ages 6 and over; 1955–65; PWT; 1965 manual identical with 1956 manual except

for format, slight changes in wording, and the addition of 2 illustrative protocols; Charlotte Buhler and Morse P. Manson; Western Psychological Services. *

For additional information, see P:466 (1 reference); for a review by Walter Kass and an excerpted review by Laurance F. Shaffer, see 5:153.

REFERENCES THROUGH 1971

1. See P:466.

[1495]

★Politte Sentence Completion Test. Grades 1–8, 7–12; 1970–71; PSCT; no scores; 2 levels; Alan J. Politte; Psychologists and Educators, Inc. *

a) ELEMENTARY SCHOOL FORM. Grades 1–8; 1970–71.
b) INTERMEDIATE AND SECONDARY FORM. Grades 7–12; 1971.

[1496]

Psychiatric Attitudes Battery. Adults; 1955–61; PAB; attitudes toward mental hospitals, psychiatrists, and psychiatric treatment; 5 parts; Marvin Reznikoff, John Paul Brady, William W. Zeller, and Omneya Souelem (*d*); Fordham University. *

a) PICTURE ATTITUDES TEST. 1959.
b) SENTENCE COMPLETION ATTITUDES TEST. 1959–61; 4 attitude scores: psychiatrists, hospitals, treatment, outcome.
c) MULTIPLE CHOICE ATTITUDES QUESTIONNAIRE. 1959.
d) SOUELEM ATTITUDES SCALE. 1955–59.
e) DEGREE OF IMPROVEMENT RATING SCALE. 1959; ratings by psychiatrists.

For additional information, see P:467 (2 references); see also 6:235 (10 references).

REFERENCES THROUGH 1971

1–10. See 6:235.
11–12. See P:467.

[1497]

Rock-A-Bye, Baby: A Group Projective Test for Children. Ages 5–10; 1959, c1951–56; sibling rivalry; 6 scores: self concept, jealousy index, aggression to parents, guilt index, anxiety index, index of obsessive trends; Mary R. Haworth and Adolf G. Woltmann; Audio-Visual Services, Pennsylvania State University. *

For additional information, see P:468; see also 6:236 (4 references).

REFERENCES THROUGH 1971

1–4. See 6:236.
5. HAWORTH, MARY ROBBINS. *An Exploratory Study to Determine the Effectiveness of a Filmed Puppet Show as a Group Projective Technique for Use With Children.* Doctor's thesis, Pennsylvania State University (University Park, Pa.), 1956. (*DA* 17:304)

[1498]

Rohde Sentence Completions Test. Ages 12 and over; 1940–57; RSCT; revision of *Payne Sentence Completion Blank* ('29); Amanda R. Rohde; Western Psychological Services. *

For additional information, see P:469 (5 references); see also 5:158 (1 reference); for reviews by

Charles N. Cofer and Charles R. Strother and an excerpted review by Laurance F. Shaffer of an earlier edition, see 4:131 (3 references). For an excerpt from a related book review, see 5:B358.

REFERENCES THROUGH 1971

1-3. See 4:131.
4. See 5:158.
5-9. See P:469.
10. GOLDBERG, PHILIP A. "A Review of Sentence Completion Methods in Personality Assessment." *J Proj Tech & Pers Assess* 29:12-45 Mr '65. * (*PA* 39:10112)
11. GREEN, EMMANUEL BERT. *Dependent Behavior in the Blind Adult.* Doctor's thesis, Boston University (Boston, Mass.), 1966. (*DA* 27:1606B)

CUMULATIVE NAME INDEX

Cofer, C. N.: *rev*, 4:131
English, R. H.: 6
Goldberg, P. A.: 10
Green, E. B.: 11
Ives, M.: *exc*, 5:B358
Krugman, A. D.: 5
Levitt, E. E.: 7
Lubin, B.: 7
Rohde, A. R.: 1-2, 4
Shaffer, L. F.: *exc*, 4:131
Smith, R. M.: 8
Stafford, J. W.: 5
Stein, M. I.: 3
Strother, C. R.: *rev*, 4:131
Vaughan, R. P.: 9
Vernier, C. M.: 5
Zuckerman, M.: 7

[1499]

Rorschach. Ages 3 and over; 1921-66; variously referred to by such titles as Rorschach Method, Rorschach Test, Rorschach Ink Blot Test, Rorschach Psychodiagnostics; many variations and modifications are in use with no one method of scoring and interpreting generally accepted; unless otherwise indicated, the word Rorschach may be interpreted as referring to the use of the Psychodiagnostic Plates listed as *f* below.
a) BEHN-RORSCHACH TEST. 1941-56; BRT; a parallel set of inkblots; also called *The Bero-Test;* Hans Zulliger; Hans Huber [Switzerland]. (United States distributor: Grune & Stratton, Inc.) *
b) THE DAVIS RORSCHACH MINIATURE LOCATION CHARTS IN COLOR (BRUNO KLOPFER SCORING AREAS). 1966; Julian C. Davis; Western Psychological Services. *
c) HARROWER'S GROUP RORSCHACH. Ages 12 and over; 1941-45; HGR; M. R. Harrower; distributed by Psychological Corporation. *
d) HARROWER'S MULTIPLE CHOICE TEST. Ages 12 and over; 1943-45; HMCT; M. R. Harrower; distributed by Psychological Corporation. *
e) HARROWER'S PSYCHODIAGNOSTIC INKBLOT TEST. Ages 16 and over; 1945-66; HPIT; a parallel set of inkblots; formerly called *Psychodiagnostic Inkblots;* 1966 cards identical with set copyrighted 1945 except for finish; Molly R. Harrower; Western Psychological Services. *
f) PSYCHODIAGNOSTIC PLATES, FIFTH EDITION. 1921-54; 1954 cards identical with original edition copyrighted 1921; Hermann Rorschach; Hans Huber [Switzerland]. (United States distributor: Grune & Stratton, Inc.) *
g) THE REVISED RORSCHACH EVALOGRAPH. 1954-65; Morse P. Manson and George A. Ulett; Western Psychological Services. *
h) RORSCHACH COMBINED LOCATION AND RECORD FORM. 1957; Nicholas De Palma; the Author. *
i) THE RORSCHACH CONCEPT EVALUATION TECHNIQUE. Adults; 1965; CET; 3 conceptual scores: precision (J), conformity (V), deviance (C); Paul McReynolds; Western Psychological Services. *
j) RORSCHACH LOCATION CHARTS (BECK'S SCORING AREAS). 1951-54; 1954 cards identical with set copyrighted 1951; Julian C. Davis; Hans Huber [Switzerland]. (United States distributor: Grune & Stratton, Inc.) *
k) RORSCHACH METHOD OF PERSONALITY DIAGNOSIS: INDIVIDUAL RECORD BLANK, REVISED EDITION. 1942-60; Bruno Klopfer and Helen H. Davidson; Harcourt Brace Jovanovich, Inc. *

l) THE RORSCHACH MINIATURE INKBLOTS IN COLOR: A LOCATION AND RECORD FORM. 1955-64; Morse P. Manson; Western Psychological Services. *
m) STRUCTURED-OBJECTIVE RORSCHACH TEST: PRELIMINARY EDITION. See 1513.

For additional information and reviews by Alvin G. Burstein, John F. Knutson, Charles C. McArthur, Albert I. Rabin, and Marvin Reznikoff, see 7:175 (455 references); see also P:470 (719 references); for reviews by Richard H. Dana, Leonard D. Eron, and Arthur R. Jensen, see 6:237 (734 references); for reviews by Samuel J. Beck, H. J. Eysenck, Raymond J. McCall, and Laurance F. Shaffer, see 5:154 (1078 references); for a review by Helen Sargent, see 4:117 (621 references); for reviews by Morris Krugman and J. R. Wittenborn, see 3:73 (452 references); see also 2:1246 (147 references). For excerpts from related book reviews, see 7:B33 (3 excerpts), 7:B37 (2 excerpts); see also 7:B69 (2 excerpts), 7:B70 (2 excerpts), 7:B196 (2 excerpts), 7:B221 (3 excerpts), 7:B373 (2 excerpts), 7:B383 (2 excerpts), 7:B487 (1 excerpt), 7:B521 (4 excerpts), 7:B612 (1 excerpt), 7:B613 (2 excerpts), 6:B40 (2 excerpts), 6:B52 (2 excerpts), 6:B72 (4 excerpts), 6:B73 (3 excerpts), 6:B91 (3 excerpts), 6:B129 (2 excerpts), 6:B152 (2 excerpts), 6:B260 (2 excerpts), 6:B295 (2 excerpts), 6:B306 (3 excerpts), 6:B307 (3 excerpts), 6:B344 (1 excerpt), 6:B398 (2 excerpts), 6:B409 (3 excerpts), 6:B452 (2 excerpts), 6:B526 (2 excerpts), 5:B32 (3 excerpts), 5:B34 (3 excerpts), 5:B40 (1 excerpt), 5:B41 (2 excerpts), 5:B60 (7 excerpts), 5:B73 (3 excerpts), 5:B79 (2 excerpts), 5:B190 (4 excerpts), 5:B247 (6 excerpts), 5:B248 (4 excerpts), 5:B337 (4 excerpts), 5:B369 (6 excerpts), 5:B372 (6 excerpts), 5:B402 (2 excerpts), 4:118 (3 excerpts), 4:119 (9 excerpts), 4:120 (6 excerpts), 4:121 (6 excerpts), 4:122 (2 excerpts), 4:123 (1 excerpt), 4:124 (1 excerpt), 4:125 (5 excerpts), 4:126 (14 excerpts), 4:127 (3 excerpts), 4:128 (6 excerpts), 3:74 (1 excerpt), 3:75 (11 excerpts), 3:76 (6 excerpts), 3:77 (2 excerpts), 3:78 (17 excerpts), 3:79 (7 excerpts), 3:80 (5 excerpts), 3:81 (4 excerpts), 3:82 (13 excerpts), 3:82a (2 excerpts), 3:83 (1 excerpt), 3:84 (13 excerpts), 3:86 (2 excerpts), 3:87 (4 excerpts), 3:88 (1 excerpt), 3:89 (3 excerpts), 3:89a (1 excerpt), 3:90 (4 excerpts), and 3:91 (1 excerpt).

REFERENCES THROUGH 1971

1-147. See 2:1246.
148-598. See 3:73.
599-1219. See 4:117.
1220-2297. See 5:154.
2298-3030. See 6:237.
3031-3749. See P:470.
3750-4204. See 7:175.
4205. STUMBERG, DORRITT. "A Study of Poetic Talent." *J Exp Psychol* 11:219-34 Je '28. * (*PA* 3:1622)
4206. GRAHAM, VIRGINIA TAYLOR. "Psychological Studies of Hypoglycemia Therapy." *J Psychol* 10:327-58 O '40. * (*PA* 15:1337)
4207. LAYMAN, JAMES W. "A Quantitative Study of Certain Changes in Schizophrenic Patients Under the Influence of Sodium Amytal." *J General Psychol* 22:67-86 Ja '40. * (*PA* 14:2439)
4208. KALLMANN, FRANZ J.; BARRERA, S. EUGENE; HOCH, PAUL H.; AND KELLEY, DOUGLAS M. "The Role of Mental Deficiency in the Incidence of Schizophrenia." *Am J Mental Def* 45:514-39 Ap '41. * (*PA* 15:4226)
4209. SELIGER, ROBERT V., AND ROSENBERG, SEYMOUR J. "Personality of the Alcoholic." *Med Rec* 154:418-21 D 3 '41. * (*PA* 16:1025)
4210. ROSE, ANNELIES ARGELANDER, AND STAVRIANOS, BERTHA K. "Sex Differences in the Perceptual Attitude of Children." *J Psychol* 16:129-43 Jl '43. * (*PA* 17:4318)
4211. FISKE, DONALD W. "A Study of Relationships to Somatotype." *J Appl Psychol* 28:504-19 D '44. * (*PA* 19:1263)
4212. RICHARDSON, LAVANGE HUNT. "A Personality Study of Stutterers and Non-Stutterers." *J Speech Disorders* 9:152-60 Mr '44. * (*PA* 19:716)

4213. FRENKEL-BRUNSWIK, ELSE, AND SANFORD, R. NEVITT. "Some Personality Factors in Anti-Semitism." *J Psychol* 20: 271–91 O '45. * *(PA* 20:475)

4214. KARDINER, ABRAHAM; LINTON, RALPH; DU BOIS, CORA; AND WEST, JAMES. *The Psychological Frontiers of Society,* pp. 240–52. New York: Columbia University Press, 1945. Pp. xxiv, 475. * *(PA* 19:2675)

4215. KEIR, GERTRUDE. "An Experiment in Mental Testing Under Hypnosis." *J Mental Sci* (England) 91:346–52 Jl '45. * *(PA* 20:425)

4216. RUESCH, JURGEN. "Personality Structure, Lactic Acid Production, and Work Performance in Psychiatric Patients." *J Psychol* 20:381–90 O '45. * *(PA* 20:827)

4217. SELIGER, ROBERT V., AND CRANFORD, VICTORIA. Chap. 3, "The Rorschach Analysis Technique as a Means of Determining Therapy for the Patient With an Alcoholic Problem," pp. 34–55. In their *A Guide on Alcoholism for Social Workers.* Baltimore, Md.: Alcoholism Publications, 1945. Pp. 94. * *(PA* 22:262)

4218. BROZEK, JOSEF; GUETZKOW, HAROLD; KEYS, ANCEL; WITH THE COLLABORATION OF R. B. CATTEL, MARY R. HARROWER, AND STARKE R. HATHAWAY. "A Study of Personality of Normal Young Men Maintained on Restricted Intakes of Vitamins of the B Complex." *Psychosom Med* 8:98–109 Mr '46. * *(PA* 20:3205)

4219. KRAUSS, STEPHEN. "Post-Choreic Personality and Neurosis." *J Mental Sci* (England) 92:75–95 Ja '46. * *(PA* 20: 3215)

4220. WAGGONER, R. W., AND ZEIGLER, THORNTON WOODWARD. "Psychiatric Factors in Medical School Students Who Fail." *Am J Psychiatry* 103:369–76 N '46. * *(PA* 21:1671)

4221. EBAUGH, FRANKLIN G., AND HOEKSTRA, CLARENCE S. "Psychosomatic Relationships in Acute Anterior Poliomyelitis." *Am J Med Sci* 213:115–21 Ja '47. *

4222. GRAVES, WINIFRED SIBLEY. "Factors Associated With Children's Taking Music Lessons, Including Some Parent-Child Relationships: 1, History and Procedures; 2, Results and Conclusions." *J Genetic Psychol* 70:65–89, 91–125 Mr '47. * *(PA* 21:3495–6)

4223. RAMM, KATHERINE M. "Personality Maladjustment Among Monotones." *Smith Col Studies Social Work* 17:264–84 Je '47. * *(PA* 21:3590)

4224. WAYNE, DAVID M.; ADAMS, M.; AND ROWE, LILLIAN A. "A Study of Military Prisoners at a Disciplinary Barracks Suspected of Homosexual Activities." *Mil Surg* 101:499–504 D '47. * *(PA* 22:5498)

4225. ZIMMERMAN, FREDERIC T.; BURGEMEISTER, BESSIE B.; AND PUTNAM, TRACY J. "A Group Study of the Effect of Glutamic Acid Upon Mental Functioning in Children and Adolescents." *Psychosom Med* 9:175–83 My–Je '47. * *(PA* 21:3474)

4226. BOOTH, GOTTHARD. "Psychodynamics in Parkinsonism." *Psychosom Med* 10:1–14 Ja–F '48. * *(PA* 22:5085)

4227. HUTTON, E. L., AND BASSETT, M. "The Effect of Leucotomy on Creative Personality." *J Mental Sci* (England) 94: 332–8 Ap '48. * *(PA* 23:1189)

4228. McANDREW, HELTON. "Rigidity and Isolation: A Study of the Deaf and the Blind." *J Abn & Social Psychol* 43:476–94 O '48. * *(PA* 23:1903)

4229. SEVRINGHAUS, ELMER L. "A Psychomotor Syndrome Associated With a Heterotopic Pancreatic Adenoma." *Psychosom Med* 10:109–10 Mr '48. * *(PA* 22:5081)

4230. GIBB, CECIL A. "Some Tentative Comments Concerning Group Rorschach Pointers to the Personality Traits of Leaders." *J Social Psychol* 30:251–63 Ag '49. * *(PA* 24:4277)

4231. OHWAKI, YOSHIKAZU; KURODA, M.; KATO, K.; AND ABE, J. "Experimental Investigation on the Local Character of People in North-Eastern Japan." *Tohoku Psychologica Folia* (Japan) 11:37–56 '49. * *(PA* 25:1729)

4232. REES, LINFORD. "Electronarcosis in the Treatment of Schizophrenia." *J Mental Sci* (England) 95:625–37 Jl '49. * *(PA* 24:2007)

4233. ABRAHAMSEN, DAVID, AND PALM, ROSE. "Family Role in Diagnosis and Treatment of Offenders." *J Nerv & Mental Dis* 112:311–21 O '50. * *(PA* 25:2575)

4234. BECKHAM, ALBERT S. "A Rorschach Study of High School Failures." Abstract. *Am Psychologist* 5:346 Jl '50. *

4235. FISHER, SEYMOUR, AND FISHER, RHODA. "Value of Isolation Rigidity in Maintaining Integration in Seriously Disturbed Personalities." *J Personality* 19:41–7 S '50. * *(PA* 25: 6323)

4236. PROUT, CURTIS T., AND WHITE, MARY ALICE. "A Controlled Study of Personality Relationships in Mothers of Schizophrenic Male Patients." *Am J Psychiatry* 107:251–6 O '50. * *(PA* 25:3911)

4237. SCHNECK, JEROME M., AND KLINE, MILTON V. "Clinical Psychiatric Status and Psychological Test Alterations Following Hypnotherapy." *Brit J Med Hyp* 2:30–41 Ag '50. * *(PA* 25:3913)

4238. SMITH, JOYCE L. *Multiple-Choice Rorschach Responses of Over and Under Achievers Among College Women.* Master's thesis, Catholic University of America (Washington, D.C.), 1950.

4239. WALLACE, ANTHONY F. C. "A Possible Technique for Recognizing Psychological Characteristics of the Ancient Maya

From an Analysis of Their Art." *Am Imago* 7:239–58 N '50. * *(PA* 25:7404)

4240. CALABRESI, RENATA A. "Repression and Control in Psychological Tests: Illustrative Cases." *Case Rep Clin Psychol* 2:42–51 S '51. * *(PA* 27:4244)

4241. FREED, HERBERT, AND PASTOR, JOYCE T. "Evaluation of the 'Draw-A-Person' Test (Modified) in Thalamotomy With Particular Reference to the Body Image." *J Nerv & Mental Dis* 114:106–20 Ag '51. * *(PA* 26:1610)

4242. HIMMELWEIT, HILDE T., AND SUMMERFIELD, ARTHUR. "Student Selection—An Experimental Investigation: II." *Brit J Sociol* 2:59–75 Mr '51. * *(PA* 26:542)

4243. KAHN, ROBERT L., AND SCHLESINGER, BENNO. "Preoperative and Postoperative Personality Changes Accompanying Frontal Lobe Meningioma." *J Nerv & Mental Dis* 114:492–510 D '51. * *(PA* 26:5031)

4244. KRAL, V. A., AND DÖRKEN, HERBERT, JR. "Comparative Psychological Study of Hyperkinetic and Akinetic Extrapyramidal Disorders." *Arch Neurol & Psychiatry* 66:431–42 O '51. * *(PA* 26:2937)

4245. MERCER, MARGARET, AND HECKER, ARTHUR O. "The Use of Tolserol (Myanesin) in Psychological Testing." *J Clin Psychol* 7:263–6 Jl '51. * *(PA* 26:926)

4246. ROE, ANNE. "A Study of Imagery in Research Scientists." *J Personality* 19:459–70 Je '51. * *(PA* 26:3680)

4247. SCHERER, ISIDOR W. "Prognoses and Psychological Scores in Electroconvulsive Therapy, Psychosurgery, and Spontaneous Remission." *Am J Psychiatry* 107:926–31 Je '51. * *(PA* 27:477)

4248. ABEL, THEODORA M. "Personality Characteristics of the Facially Disfigured." *Trans NY Acad Sci* 14:325–9 Je '52. * *(PA* 27:3739)

4249. ALLISON, HARRY W., AND ALLISON, SARAH G. "Personality Changes Following Transorbital Lobotomy." *Proc Okla Acad Sci* 33:265–71 '52. * *(PA* 29:7631)

4250. BERAN, MARIANNE; PERKINS, JOHN C.; AND SCOLLON, ROBERT W. "Psychological Studies on Patients Undergoing Nonconvulsive Electric-Stimulation Treatment." *Am J Psychiatry* 109:367–74 N '52. * *(PA* 27:5168)

4251. CALDWELL, BETTYE McDONALD, AND WATSON, ROBERT I. "An Evaluation of Psychologic Effects of Sex Hormone Administration in Aged Women: 1, Results of Therapy After Six Months." *J Gerontol* 7:228–44 Ap '52. * *(PA* 27:1874)

4252. GAIER, EUGENE L. "Selected Personality Variables and the Learning Process." *Psychol Monogr* 66(17):1–28 '52. * *(PA* 27:7028)

4253. GLUECK, ELEANOR T. "Predicting Juvenile Delinquency." *Brit J Delinq* 2:275–86 Ap '52. * *(PA* 27:2862)

4254. JACKMAN, A. J., AND SCHORR, C. A. "Evaluation of Carbon Dioxide Therapy of the Neuroses." *J Clin & Exp Psychopathol* 13:17–30 Mr '52. * *(PA* 27:2147)

4255. KALDEGG, A. "Migraine Patients: A Discussion of Some Test Results." *J Mental Sci* (England) 98:672–82 O '52. * *(PA* 27:6067)

4256. LIDZ, THEODORE; CARTER, JAMES D.; LEWIS, BERNARD I.; AND SURRATT, CAROLYN. "Effect of ACTH and Cortisone on Mood and Mentation." *Psychosom Med* 14:363–77 S–O '52. * *(PA* 27:4457)

4257. MENSH, IVAN N.; SCHWARTZ, HENRY G.; MATARAZZO, RUTH G.; AND MATARAZZO, JOSEPH D. "Psychological Functioning Following Cerebral Hemispherectomy in Man." *Arch Neurol & Psychiatry* 67:787–96 Je '52. * *(PA* 27:2167)

4258. REUNING, H., AND ROSEN, J. "Temperament Assessment by Observation of Behavior in Test Situations." *B Nat Inst Pers Res* (South Africa) 4:91–109 D '52. * *(PA* 28:2668)

4259. ROBIN, ASHLEY A., AND HARRISON, E. J. "Some Clinical and Aetiological Aspects of Depersonalization With a Case Report of Identical Twins." *J Mental Sci* (England) 98:469–76 Jl '52. * *(PA* 27:3656)

4260. TOWBIN, ALAN P., AND SMALHEISER, IRWIN. "The Rorschach Method: A New Conceptualization." *Complex* 8:3–27 sp '52. * *(PA* 27:3565)

4261. BASS, BERNARD M.; McGEHEE, CHARLES R.; HAWKINS, WILLIAM C.; YOUNG, PAUL C.; AND GEBEL, ARNOLD S. "Personality Variables Related to Leaderless Group Discussion Behavior." *J Abn & Social Psychol* 48:120–8 Ja '53. * *(PA* 28: 925)

4262. GEORGE, CLAY E. *Rorschach Color and Form Variables: A Validation Study.* Master's thesis, University of Arizona (Tucson, Ariz.), 1953.

4263. GLADWIN, THOMAS. "The Role of Man and Woman on Truk: A Problem in Personality and Culture." *Trans NY Acad Sci* 15:305–9 Je '53.* *(PA* 28:4195)

4264. KAIM, S. C.; SCHEINBERG, P.; AND STENGER, C. "Correlation of the EEG With the Rorschach and Cerebral Metabolic Tests in Multiple Sclerosis." Abstract. *EEG Clin Neuro-Physiol* 3(sup):29 '53. * *(PA* 29:4554, title only)

4265. McLAUGHLIN, JAMES T.; ZABARENKO, RALPH N.; DIANA, PEARL BUTLER; AND QUINN, BEATTA. "Emotional Reactions of Rheumatoid Arthritis to ACTH." *Psychosom Med* 15: 187–99 My–Je '53. * *(PA* 28:3088)

4266. REITAN, RALPH M. "Intellectual and Affective Functions in Chronic Brucellosis." *Am J Psychiatry* 110:19–28 Jl '53. * *(PA* 28:3093)

4267. VAN LENNEP, J. E. "Some Considerations Regarding the Clinical-Psychological Examination of Paranoid States." *Folia Psychiatrica Neurologica et Neurochirurgica Neerlandica* (Netherlands) 56:769–78 '53. *

4268. BENNETT, EDWARD M., AND JOHANNSEN, DOROTHEA E. "Psychodynamics of the Diabetic Child." *Psychol Monogr* 68 (11):1–23 '54. * (*PA* 29:6072)

4269. BOWER, WARREN CORNELL. *Rorschach Patterns Among Groups of College Majors at Two New England Universities.* Doctor's thesis, Boston University (Boston, Mass.), 1954.

4270. CADMAN, WILLIAM H.; MISBACH, LORENZ; AND BROWN, DONALD V. "An Assessment of Round-Table Psychotherapy." *Psychol Monogr* 68(13):1–48 '54. * (*PA* 29:7345)

4271. CALDWELL, BETTYE McDONALD, AND WATSON, ROBERT I. "An Evaluation of Sex Hormone Replacement in Aged Women." *J Genetic Psychol* 85:181–200 D '54. * (*PA* 29:7046)

4272. CHANCE, JUNE; LOTSOF, ERWIN J.; PINE, IRVING; PATTERSON, RALPH M.; AND CRAIG, JAMES. "Effects of Cortisone on Psychiatric Patients." *Psychosom Med* 16:516–25 N–D '54. * (*PA* 29:6020)

4273. CLEVELAND, SIDNEY E., AND FISHER, SEYMOUR. "Behavior and Unconscious Fantasies of Patients With Rheumatoid Arthritis." *Psychosom Med* 16:327–33 Jl–Ag '54. * (*PA* 29:4495)

4274. ERIKSEN, CHARLES W. "Needs in Perception and Projective Techniques." *J Proj Tech* 18:435–40 D '54. * (*PA* 29:7272)

4275. KAPLAN, ARTHUR, AND SAKHEIM, GEORGE. "Manic-Depressive Psychosis in a 13-Year-Old Boy: Psychological Test Findings." *J Nerv & Mental Dis* 121:140–54 F '54. * (*PA* 29:7657)

4276. KARLSEN, BJÖRN. *A Comparison of Some Educational and Psychological Characteristics of Successful and Unsuccessful Readers at the Elementary School Level.* Doctor's thesis, University of Minnesota (Minneapolis, Minn.), 1954. (*DA* 15:456)

4277. KUTASH, SAMUEL B. "The Impact of Projective Techniques on Basic Psychological Science." *J Proj Tech* 18:453–69 D '54. * (*PA* 29:6473)

4278. LUFT, JOSEPH. "An Exercise in Personality Assessment." *J Social Psychol* 39:293–7 My '54. * (*PA* 29:3340)

4279. McADAM, W., AND ORME, J. E. "Personality Traits and the Normal Electro-Encephalogram." *J Mental Sci* (England) 100:913–21 O '54. * (*PA* 29:6933)

4280. MILES, HENRY H. W.; WALDFOGEL, SAMUEL; BARRABEE, EDNA L.; AND COBB, STANLEY. "Psychosomatic Study of 46 Young Men With Coronary Artery Disease." *Psychosom Med* 16:455–77 N–D '54. * (*PA* 29:6080)

4281. PISULA, DOROTHY HELEN. *A Study of Mental Maturity and Personality Structure at the Eight Year Level.* Washington, D.C.: Catholic University of America, 1954. Pp. vi, 34. *

4282. ROGERS, LAWRENCE S., AND TAYLOR, JAMES W. "Case Report on a Mental Hygiene Clinic Patient Tested Before and After Frontal Lobe Injury." *J Clin Psychol* 10:75–9 Ja '54. * (*PA* 28:7908)

4283. ROSENBERG, SELIG. "The Relationship of Certain Personality Factors to Prognosis in Psychotherapy." *J Clin Psychol* 10:341–5 O '54. * (*PA* 29:4164)

4284. SCHAFER, ROY. "Some Applications of Contemporary Psychoanalytic Theory to Projective Testing." *J Proj Tech* 18:441–7 D '54. * (*PA* 29:7315)

4285. SHAPIRO, DAVID. "Special Problems of Testing Borderline Psychotics." *J Proj Tech* 18:387–94 S '54. * (*PA* 29:4448)

4286. SILVERMAN, ALBERT J., AND HARRIS, VIRGIL W. "Electroencephalography and Psychometric Testing in Brain-Damaged Patients." *J Nerv & Mental Dis* 120:31–5 Jl–Ag '54. * (*PA* 29:6111)

4287. STEIN, MORRIS I., AND MEER, BERNARD. "Perceptual Organization in a Study of Creativity." *J Psychol* 37:39–43 Ja '54. * (*PA* 28:7204)

4288. SYMONDS, PERCIVAL M. "Are Projective Test Data Valid Bases for Prediction?" *J Proj Tech* 18:515–9 D '54. * (*PA* 29:7327)

4289. BARRATT, ERNEST S. "The Space-Visualization Factors Related to Temperament Traits." *J Psychol* 39:279–87 Ap '55. * (*PA* 29:8424)

4290. BECKER, WESLEY CLEMENCE. *The Relation of Severity of Thinking Disorder to the Process-Reactive Concept of Schizophrenia.* Doctor's thesis, Stanford University (Stanford, Calif.), 1955. (*DA* 15:1894)

4291. CHARLES, HARVEY, AND MECH, EDMUND. "Performance in an Operational 'Stress' Situation Related to a Projective Technique." *J Ed Res* 48:569–19 Mr '55. * (*PA* 30:769)

4292. FERRACUTI, F., AND RIZZO, G. B. "Psychological Patterns in Terminal Cancer Cases." *Ed & Psychol* (India) 2:26–36 Ja–Mr '55. * (*PA* 31:3531)

4293. FINE, HAROLD J.; FULKERSON, SAMUEL C.; AND PHILLIPS, LESLIE. "Maladjustment and Social Attainment." *J Abn & Social Psychol* 50:33–5 Ja '55. * (*PA* 29:7068)

4294. GARDNER, M. J.; HAWKINS, H. M.; JUDAH, L. N.; AND MURPHREE, O. D. "Objective Measurement of Psychiatric Changes Produced by Chlorpromazine and Reserpine in Chronic Schizophrenia." *Psychiatric Res Rep* 1:77–83 Jl '55. * (*PA* 30:8411)

4295. HANDELMAN, NORMAN SIDNEY. *The Relationship Between Certain Personality Factors and Speechreading Proficiency: An Investigation of the Differences in Personality Between a Group of Good Speechreaders and a Matched Group of Poor Speechreaders.* Doctor's thesis, New York University (New York, N.Y.), 1955. (*DA* 15:1899)

4296. HERTZMAN, MAX; SEITZ, CLIFFORD P.; AND ORLANSKY, JESSE. "Stability of Personality Structure Under Anoxia." *J General Psychol* 52:65–73 Ja '55. * (*PA* 30:2460)

4297. KERR, MADELINE. "The Study of Personality Deprivation Through Projection Tests." *Social & Econ Studies* (Jamaica) 4:83–94 Mr '55. * (*PA* 30:2773)

4298. MATHIAS, RUDOLF E. S. *An Experimental Investigation of the Personality Structure of Chronic Alcoholic, Alcoholics Anonymous, Neurotic and Normal Groups.* Doctor's thesis, University of Buffalo (Buffalo, N.Y.), 1955. (*DA* 16:156)

4299. MILLER, WILFRED THEODORE. *Perception of Apparent Depth as a Function of Illumination Intensity in the Case of Relatively Unstructured Stimulus.* Doctor's thesis, University of Oklahoma (Norman, Okla.), 1955. (*DA* 15:2312)

4300. MILLS, EUGENE S. "Personality Adjustment and the Study of Abnormal Psychology." *J Appl Psychol* 39:358–61 O '55. * (*PA* 30:6917)

4301. NAGELBERG, LEO, AND ROSENTHAL, LESLIE. "Validation of Selection of Patients for Activity Group Therapy Through the Rorschach and Other Tests." *Int J Group Psychother* 5:380–91 O '55. * (*PA* 30:7293)

4302. REZNIKOFF, MARVIN. "Motivational Factors in Persons Attending a Cancer-Detection Center." *Cancer* 8:454–8 Jl–Ag '55. * (*PA* 30:5064)

4303. SCHEIDE, ELIZABETH JOHNSTON. *Anxiety: Its Relationship to Self-Evaluation.* Doctor's thesis, University of Pittsburgh (Pittsburgh, Pa.), 1955. (*DA* 15:880)

4304. TATERKA, JOHN H., AND KATZ, JOSEPH. "Study of Correlations Between Electroencephalographic and Psychological Patterns in Emotionally Disturbed Children." *Psychosom Med* 17:62–72 Ja–F '55. * (*PA* 29:7565)

4305. TOW, P. MACDONALD. Chap. 25, "Ink-Blot Test of Imaginative Response," pp. 190–203. In his *Personality Changes Following Frontal Leucotomy.* London: Oxford University Press, 1955. Pp. xv, 262. * (*PA* 30:8319)

4306. VON FELSINGER, JOHN M.; LASAGNA, LOUIS; AND BEECHER, HENRY K. "Drug-Induced Mood Changes in Man: 2, Personality and Reactions to Drugs." *J Am Med Assn* 157:1113–9 Mr 26 '55. *

4307. WHEELER, JOHN I., JR., AND CALDWELL, BETTYE McDONALD. "Psychological Evaluation of Women With Cancer of the Breast and of the Cervix." *Psychosom Med* 17:256–68 Jl–Ag '55. * (*PA* 30:5074)

4308. WORDEN, FREDERIC G., AND MARSH, JAMES T. "Psychological Factors in Men Seeking Sex Transformation: A Preliminary Report." *J Am Med Assn* 157:1292–8 Ap 9 '55. *

4309. ASTHANA, HARI SHANKER. "Some Aspects of Personality Structuring in Indian (Hindu) Social Organization." *J Social Psychol* 44:155–63 Ag '56. * (*PA* 33:8142)

4310. BURKE, MAURICE O. "A Search for Systematic Personality Differentiae of the Only Child in Young Adulthood." *J Genetic Psychol* 89:71–84 S '56. * (*PA* 33:3307)

4311. DAI, BINGHAM. "Intensive Personality Study as a Method of Training in Psychotherapy." *Psychol Newsl* 7:59–63 Mr–Ap '56. * (*PA* 31:3109)

4312. DAVIDS, ANTHONY. "The Influence of Ego-Involvement on Relations Between Authoritarianism and Intolerance of Ambiguity." *J Consult Psychol* 20:179–84 Je '56. * (*PA* 31:6071)

4313. DAVIDSON, HELEN H., AND BALDUCCI, DEAN. "Class and Sex Differences in Verbal Facility of Very Bright Children." *J Ed Psychol* 47:476–80 D '56. * (*PA* 32:4590)

4314. EYSENCK, H. J. "The Inheritance of Extraversion-Introversion." *Acta Psychologica* (Netherlands) 12(2):95–110 '56. * (*PA* 31:4378)

4315. FISHER, SEYMOUR, AND CLEVELAND, SIDNEY E. "Body-Image Boundaries and Style of Life." *J Abn & Social Psychol* 52:373–9 My '56. * (*PA* 31:4379)

4316. GLUECK, SHELDON, AND GLUECK, ELEANOR T. "Early Detection of Future Delinquents." *J Crim Law Criminol & Police Sci* 47:174–82 Jl–Ag '56. * (*PA* 31:6369)

4317. HERRING, FRED H. "Response During Anesthesia and Surgery; Effect of Psychological Factors." *Psychosom Med* 18:243–51 My–Je '56. * (*PA* 31:5007)

4318. JORDAN, THOMAS E. "Psychological Findings in a Case of Von Recklinghausen's Disease and Hyperpituitarism." *J Clin Psychol* 12:389–91 O '56. * (*PA* 32:4470)

4319. KIRKPATRICK, JAMES J. "Validation of a Test Battery for the Selection and Placement of Engineers." *Personnel Psychol* 9:211–27 su '56. * (*PA* 31:8964)

4320. MENDELL, DAVID, AND FISHER, SEYMOUR. "An Approach to Neurotic Behavior in Terms of a Three Generation Family Model." *J Nerv & Mental Dis* 123:171–80 F '56. * (*PA* 31:8537)

4321. PEYMAN, D. A. R. "An Investigation of the Effects of Group Psychotherapy on Chronic Schizophrenic Patients." *Group Psychother* 9:35–9 Ap '56. * (*PA* 33:4391)

4322. RICHARDS, T. W., AND HOOPER, SARA. "Brain-Injury at

Rorschach

Birth (Cerebral Palsy) and Perceptual Responses During Childhood and Adolescence." *J Nerv & Mental Dis* 123:117–24 F '56. * (*PA* 31:8608)

4323. SOPCHAK, ANDREW L. "Projective Study of Peter and His Parents: Revealing the Necessary Therapeutic Limitations." *J Child Psychiatry* 3:149–200 Ag '56. * (*PA* 31:8363)

4324. STEIN, MARIE D. "Bibliography: Part One, Alphabetical Bibliography to 1945; Part Two, Classified Bibliography, 1945 to 1955," pp. 659–776. In *Developments in the Rorschach Technique, Vol. 2: Fields of Application.* Edited by Bruno Klopfer. New York: Harcourt, Brace & World, Inc., 1956. Pp. xx, 828. * (*PA* 30:7202)

4325. STRAUS, MURRAY A., AND STRAUS, JACQUELINE H. "Personal Insecurity and Sinhalese Social Structure: Rorschach Evidence for Primary School Children." *Eastern Anthropologist* (India) 10(2):97–111 D '56–F '57. *

4326. WIRT, ROBERT D. "Ideational Expression of Hostile Impulses." *J Consult Psychol* 20:185–9 Je '56. * (*PA* 31:6149)

4327. BARENDREGT, J. T. "A Cross-Validation Study of the Hypothesis of Psychosomatic Specificity, With Special Reference to Bronchial Asthma." *J Psychosom Res* (England) 2(2):109–14 '57. * (*PA* 33:1935)

4328. BARENDREGT, J. T. "A Psychological Investigation of the Effect of Group Psychotherapy in Patients With Bronchial Asthma." *J Psychosom Res* (England) 2(2):115–9 '57. * (*PA* 33:1354)

4329. BECK, SAMUEL J., AND MOLISH, H. B. "Course in the Individual Patient as Traced in the Six Schizophrenias." *J Nerv & Mental Dis* 125:403–11 Jl–S '57. * (*PA* 33:4332)

4330. CORMIER, B. M., AND WITTKOWER, E. D.; WITH THE ASSISTANCE OF YVES MARCOTTE AND FRANCOISE FORGET. "Psychological Aspects of Rheumatoid Arthritis." *Can Med Assn J* 77:533–41 S 1 '57. *

4331. EPSTEIN, SEYMOUR, AND SMITH, RICHARD. "Thematic Apperception, Rorschach Content, and Ratings of Sexual Attractiveness of Women as Measures of the Sex Drive." *J Consult Psychol* 21:473–8 O '57. * (*PA* 33:3832)

4332. HONIGMANN, JOHN J., AND CARRERA, RICHARD. "Another Experiment in Sample Reliability." *Southw J Anthrop* 13:99–102 sp '57. * (*PA* 32:4181)

4333. ISHAM, A. CHAPMAN. "Use of a Brief Psychological Battery in Psychiatric Practice." *Am J Psychother* 11:790–802 O '57. * (*PA* 33:6241)

4334. KISSIN, BENJAMIN; GOTTESFELD, HARRY; AND DICKES, ROBERT. "Inhibition and Tachistoscopic Thresholds for Sexually Charged Words." *J Psychol* 43:333–9 Ap '57. * (*PA* 33:6249)

4335. LALITHA, M. S. "A Study of the Development of Imagination in Children." *J Psychol Res* (India) 1:39–48 My '57. * (*PA* 33:3257)

4336. MINTZ, ELIZABETH EMMONS. "Personal Problems and Diagnostic Errors in Clinical Psychologists." *J Proj Tech* 21:123–8 Je '57. * (*PA* 33:1292)

4337. MOLISH, HERMAN B.; HANLON, THOMAS E.; AND KURLAND, ALBERT A. "A Prognostic Indicator of Treatment Failure in Schizophrenia." *Arch Neurol & Psychiatry* 78:177–93 Ag '57. * (*PA* 33:1870)

4338. ORME, J. E. "Initial Psychiatric Illness in Involutional Women: 2, Psychological Aspects." *J Mental Sci* (England) 103:227–39 Ja '57. * (*PA* 32:3182)

4339. POWERS, WILLIAM T., AND HAMLIN, ROY M. "The Validity, Bases, and Process of Clinical Judgment, Using a Limited Amount of Projective Test Data." *J Proj Tech* 21:286–93 S '57. * (*PA* 33:1301)

4340. STENBACK, ASSER; VIITAMAKI, R. OLAVI; AND KUKKONEN, SIMO. "Personality Changes in Electroconvulsive Treatment. A Study of the Effect of Three Successive Electroconvulsive Treatments With Special Reference to Spacing of Treatments." *Acta Psychiatrica et Neurologica Scandinavica* (Denmark) 32(3):345–59 '57. * (*PA* 33:1500)

4341. THALER, MARGARET; WEINER, HERBERT; AND REISER, MORTON F. "Exploration of the Doctor-Patient Relationship Through Projective Techniques." *Psychosom Med* 19:228–39 My–Je '57. * (*PA* 33:1974)

4342. WEINER, HERBERT; THALER, MARGARET; REISER, MORTON F.; AND MIRSKY, I. ARTHUR. "Etiology of Duodenal Ulcer: 1, Relation of Specific Psychological Characteristics to Rate of Gastric Secretion (Serum Pepsinogen)." *Psychosom Med* 19:1–10 Ja–F '57. * (*PA* 32:1913)

4343. HILER, E. WESLEY. "An Analysis of Patient-Therapist Compatibility." *J Consult Psychol* 22:341–7 O '58. * (*PA* 34:1493)

4344. MURSTEIN, BERNARD I. "Personality and Intellectual Changes in Leukemia: A Case Study." *J Proj Tech* 22:421–6 D '58. * (*PA* 34:1401)

4345. MURSTEIN, BERNARD I. "Some Determinants of the Perception of Hostility." *J Consult Psychol* 22:65–9 F '58. * (*PA* 33:6273)

4346. ORME, J. E. "Rorschach Performances in Normal Old Age, Elderly Depression and Senile Dementia." *Zeitschrift für Diagnostische Psychologie und Persönlichkeitsforschung* (Switzerland) 6(2):132–41 '58. * (*PA* 33:10354)

4347. PHILIPPOPOULOS, G. S.; WITTKOWER, E. D.; AND COUSINEAU, A. "The Etiologic Significance of Emotional Factors in Onset and Exacerbations of Multiple Sclerosis: A Preliminary Report." *Psychosom Med* 20:458–74 N–D '58. * (*PA* 33:10888)

4348. SPINDLER, LOUISE, AND SPINDLER, GEORGE. "Male and Female Adaptations in Culture Change." *Am Anthrop* 60:217–33 Ap '58. * (*PA* 33:10184)

4349. TANCK, ROLAND H. "Psychologic Changes Induced by Reserpine Therapy on a Group of Severely Disturbed Psychotics." *J Nerv & Mental Dis* 126:353–9 Ap '58. * (*PA* 33:8581)

4350. ULLMANN, LEONARD P., AND HUNDRICHS, WILLIAM A. "The Role of Anxiety in Psychodiagnosis: Replication and Extension." *J Clin Psychol* 14:276–9 Jl '58. * (*PA* 33:8416)

4351. BECKER, WESLEY C. "The Process-Reactive Distinction: A Key to the Problem of Schizophrenia?" *J Nerv & Mental Dis* 129:442–9 N '59. * (*PA* 34:6342)

4352. BUTLER, EDWARD S. *Hostility Conflict and Certain Cognitive Processes.* Doctor's thesis, University of Buffalo (Buffalo, N.Y.), 1959. (*DA* 20:372)

4353. FINK, MAX; KAHN, ROBERT L.; AND POLLACK, MAX. "Psychological Factors Affecting Individual Differences in Behavioral Response to Convulsive Therapy." *J Nerv & Mental Dis* 128:243–8 Mr '59. * (*PA* 34:3059)

4354. FISHER, SEYMOUR. "Body Image Boundaries in the Aged." *J Psychol* 48:315–8 O '59. * (*PA* 35:706)

4355. KAMIYA, MIYEKO. "Psychiatric Studies on Leprosy." *Folia Psychiatrica et Neurologica Japonica* (Japan) 13:143–73 Jl '59. * (*PA* 34:6433)

4356. KHANNA, J. L., AND KHANNA, PRABHA. "The Reliability and Validity of the Rorschach Test." *J Ed & Psychol* (India) 17:4–10 Ap '59. *

4357. MINDLIN, DOROTHEE F. "The Characteristics of Alcoholics as Related to Prediction of Therapeutic Outcome." *Q J Studies Alcohol* 20:604–19 S '59. * (*PA* 34:6257)

4358. RAY, P. C. "The Children of the Abor and Gallong: A Psycho-Cultural Study by the Rorschach Technique." *Ed & Psychol* (India) 6(1–2):1–72 '59. *

4359. RIKLAN, MANUEL; WEINER, HERMAN; AND DILLER, LEONARD. "Somato-Psychologic Studies in Parkinson's Disease." *J Nerv & Mental Dis* 129:263–72 S '59. * (*PA* 34:6482)

4360. SANUA, VICTOR D. Chap. 20, "Differences in Personality Adjustment Among Different Generations of American Jews and Non-Jews," pp. 443–66. (*PA* 37:1011) In *Culture and Mental Health: Cross-Cultural Studies.* Edited by Marvin K. Opler. New York: Macmillan, 1959. Pp. xxi, 533. *

4361. SHELDON, PAUL M. "Isolation as a Characteristic of Highly Gifted Children." *J Ed Sociol* 32:215–21 Ja '59. * (*PA* 34:2737)

4362. DOOB, LEONARD W. *Becoming More Civilized: A Psychological Exploration,* passim. New Haven, Conn.: Yale University Press, Inc., 1960. Pp. xii, 333. * (*PA* 36:1GB33D)

4363. HSU, FRANCIS L. K.; WATROUS, BLANCHE G.; AND LORD, EDITH M. "Culture Pattern and Adolescent Behavior." *Int J Social Psychiatry* (England) 7:33–53 w '60–61. * (*PA* 36:4FH33H)

4364. JACKSON, PHILIP W.; GETZELS, JACOB W.; AND XYDIS, GEORGE A. "Psychological Health and Cognitive Functioning in Adolescence: A Multivariate Analysis." *Child Develop* 31:285–98 Je '60. * (*PA* 36:3FH85J)

4365. ORCHINIK, C. W. "Some Psychological Aspects of Circumscribed Lesions of the Diencephalon." *Confinia Neurologica* (Switzerland) 20:292–310 '60. * (*PA* 35:2522)

4366. STRICKLAND, JOHN F., AND KUETHE, JAMES L. "An Experimental Investigation of the Relationship Between Psychasthenia and Ego-Strength." *J General Psychol* 60:245–52 Ap '60. * (*PA* 36:2HE45S)

4367. VAN ALPHEN DER VEER, M. R.; VAN ANDEL, G. A.; HOLST, W.; V. NORREN, C.; AND WILLEMS, P. J. "Psychosomatic Investigations on Patients With Heart Complaints, Respectively on a Physical and Non-Physical Basis." *Adv Psychosom Med* 1:298–306 '60. *

4368. ALEXANDER, FRANZ; FLAGG, GLENN W.; FOSTER, SUSAN; CLEMENS, THEODORE; AND BLAHD, WILLIAM. "Experimental Studies of Emotional Stress: 1, Hyperthyroidism." *Psychosom Med* 23:104–14 Mr–Ap '61. * (*PA* 36:3JU04A)

4369. BOWYER, RUTH. "Individual Differences in Stress at the Eleven-Plus Examination." *Brit J Ed Psychol* 31:268–80 N '61. *

4370. EPSTEIN, SEYMOUR. "Food-Related Responses to Ambiguous Stimuli as a Function of Hunger and Ego Strength." *J Consult Psychol* 25:463–9 D '61. * (*PA* 37:5025)

4371. FISHER, SEYMOUR. "Front-Back Differentiations in Body Image and Body Reactivity." *J General Psychol* 64:373–9 Ap '61. * (*PA* 36:1HE73F)

4372. LINTON, HARRIET B.; EPSTEIN, LAWRENCE; AND HARTFORD, HUNTINGTON. "Personality and Perceptual Correlates of Secondary Beginning Strokes in Handwriting." *Percept & Motor Skills* 12:271–81 Je '61. * (*PA* 36:2HE71L)

4373. McCONNELL, OWEN L., AND DASTON, PAUL G. "Body Image Changes in Pregnancy." *J Proj Tech* 25:451–6 D '61. *

4374. McGHIE, ANDREW. "A Comparative Study of the Mother-Child Relationship in Schizophrenia: 2, Psychological Testing." *Brit J Med Psychol* 34:209–21 pt 3–4 '61. * (*PA* 37:1800)

4375. MURSTEIN, BERNARD I. "Assumptions, Adaptation-Level,

and Projective Techniques." *Percept & Motor Skills* 12:107–25 Ap '61. * (*PA* 36:1HG07M)

4376. SEGAL, STANLEY J. "A Psychoanalytic Analysis of Personality Factors in Vocational Choice." *J Counsel Psychol* 8:202–10 f '61. * (*PA* 36:5HG02S)

4377. SHNEIDMAN, EDWIN S. "The Case of El: Psychological Test Data." *J Proj Tech* 25:131–54 Je '61. * (*PA* 36:21K31S)

4378. TRAMER, L., AND BENTOVIM, L. "Clinical Psychological Study on Eastern Drug Addicts." *Confinia Psychiatrica* (Switzerland) 4(3–4):194–213 '61. * (*PA* 37:1729)

4379. ABRAMS, S. "A Refutation of Eriksen's Sensitization: Defense Hypotheses." *J Proj Tech* 26:259–65 S '62. * (*PA* 37:3286)

4380. DOWNING, R. W., AND RICKELS, K. "Personality and Attitudinal Correlates of Response to Drug Treatment in Psychiatric Outpatients: 2, Preliminary Investigation and Implications for Further Research." *J Psychol* 54:345–61 O '62. * (*PA* 37:6820)

4381. LAPKIN, BENJAMIN. "The Relation of Primary-Process Thinking to the Recovery of Subliminal Material." *J Nerv & Mental Dis* 135:10–25 Jl '62. * (*PA* 37:3368)

4382. LINTON, HARRIET B.; EPSTEIN, LAWRENCE; AND HARTFORD, HUNTINGTON. "Personality and Perceptual Correlates of Primary Beginning Strokes in Handwriting." *Percept & Motor Skills* 15:159–70 Ag '62. * (*PA* 37:4987)

4383. MURPHY, DONALD B., AND MYERS, THOMAS I. "Occurrence, Measurement and Experimental Manipulation of Visual 'Hallucinations.'" *Percept & Motor Skills* 15:47–54 Ag '62. * (*PA* 37:4281)

4384. SACKS, LENORA; FEINSTEIN, ALVAN R.; AND TARANTA, ANGELO. "A Controlled Psychologic Study of Sydenham's Chorea." *J Pediatrics* 61:714–22 N '62. *

4385. SHELLEY, ERNEST L. V., AND TOCH, HANS H. "The Perception of Violence as an Indicator of Adjustment in Institutionalized Offenders." *J Crim Law Criminol & Police Sci* 53:463–9 D '62. * (*PA* 37:8184)

4386. APPELBAUM, STEPHEN A. "The Masochistic Character as a Self-Saboteur (With Special Reference to Psychological Testing)." *J Proj Tech* 27:35–46 Mr '63. * (*PA* 38:911)

4387. BAXTER, JAMES C.; BECKER, JOSEPH; AND HOOKS, WALTER. "Defensive Style in the Families of Schizophrenics and Controls." *J Abn & Social Psychol* 66:512–8 My '63. * (*PA* 38:3041)

4388. BLATT, EVA FISHELL. "The Relationship Between Severity of Disease and Extent of Psychopathology in Psychosomatic Illness: A Test of Regression Theory." *Psychosomatics* 4:207–14 Jl–Ag '63. *

4389. CASSELL, WILFRED A., AND FISHER, SEYMOUR. "Body-Image Boundaries and Histamine Flare Reaction." *Psychosom Med* 25:344–50 Jl–Ag '63. * (*PA* 38:7435)

4390. DAVIDSON, HELEN H.; GREENBERG, JUDITH W.; AND GERVER, JOAN M. "Rorschach Patterns of Good and Poor School Achievers From Deprived Environments." *Congreso Interamericano de Psicologia* (Mexico) 7:276–9 '63. *

4391. EVANS, RAY B., AND MARMORSTON, JESSIE. "Improved Mental Functioning With Premarin Therapy in Atherosclerosis." *Proc Soc Exp Biol & Med* 113:698–703 Jl '63. *

4392. FISHER, SEYMOUR. "Further Appraisal of the Body Boundary Concept." *J Consult Psychol* 27:62–74 F '63. * (*PA* 37:8029)

4393. GINSBERG, ANIELA MEYER. "Personality Variables Seen in the Rorschach Test Compared With Different Types of Social Adjustment of Immigrants." *Congreso Interamericano de Psicologia* (Mexico) 7:394–6 '63. *

4394. JASKAR, RAINO O., AND REED, MAX R. "Assessment of Body Image Organization of Hospitalized and Non-Hospitalized Subjects." *J Proj Tech & Pers Assess* 27:185–90 Je '63. * (*PA* 38:2627)

4395. JOHNSON, DALE L. "Projective Test Responses of Psychiatric Patients From Three American Sub-Cultures." *Congreso Interamericano de Psicologia* (Mexico) 7:171–7 '63. *

4396. KRAL, V. A., AND WIGDOR, B. T. "Clinical and Psychological Observations in a Group of Well-Preserved Aged People." *Med Services J Can* 19:1–11 Ja '63. *

4397. LEVITT, EUGENE E.; LUBIN, BERNARD; AND BRADY, JOHN PAUL. "Personality Correlates of Hypnotizability in Young Women: The Anxiety-Dependency Constellation." *Congreso Interamericano de Psicologia* (Mexico) 7:360–4 '63. *

4398. MATKOM, ANTHONY J. "Impression Formation as a Function of Adjustment." *Psychol Monogr* 77(5):1–19 '63. * (*PA* 38:4341)

4399. SATO, ISAO, AND OYAMA, MASAHIRO. "Studies on Sensory Deprivation: I, Preliminary Studies: Part 3, Rorschach Performance in Sensory Deprivation." *Tohoku Psychologica Folia* (Japan) 22(1–2):15–34 '63. * (*PA* 38:5173)

4400. SCHOENBERG, BERNARD, AND CARR, ARTHUR C. "An Investigation of Criteria for Brief Psychotherapy of Neurodermatitis." *Psychosom Med* 25:253–63 My–Je '63. * (*PA* 38:4425)

4401. SHUVAL, R., AND KRASILOWSKY, D. "A Study of Hospitalized Male Alcoholics." *Israel Ann Psychiatry* 1:277–92 O '63. * (*PA* 39:8402)

4402. WEINER, SAMUEL; DORMAN, DANIEL; PERSKY, HAROLD; STARCH, THOMAS W.; NORTON, JAMES; AND LEVITT, EUGENE E.

"Effect on Anxiety of Increasing the Plasma Hydrocortisone Level." *Psychosom Med* 25:69–77 Ja–F '63. * (*PA* 37:7705)

4403. BAHNSON, C. B., AND BAHNSON, M. B. "Denial and Repression of Primitive Impulses and of Disturbing Emotions in Patients With Malignant Neoplasms," pp. 42–62. In *Psychosomatic Aspects of Neoplastic Disease.* The Proceedings of the Third International Conference of the International Psychosomatic Cancer Study Group Held at Newnham College, Cambridge, England, 22nd to 26th July 1963. Edited by D. M. Kissen and L. L. Leshan. Philadelphia, Pa.: J. B. Lippincott Co., 1964. Pp. xii, 231. *

4404. CARR, ARTHUR C. "Psychological Defect and Psychological Testing." *Int Psychiatry Clinics* 1:773–98 O '64. *

4405. HAMMER, EMANUEL F. "Creativity and Feminine Ingredients in Young Male Artists." *Percept & Motor Skills* 19:414 O '64. * (*PA* 39:7817)

4406. JUEL-NIELSEN, NIELS. "Individual and Environment: A Psychiatric-Psychological Investigation of Monozygotic Twins Reared Apart." *Acta Psychiatrica Scandinavica Supplementum* (Denmark) 183:1–292 '64. *

4407. KRAL, V. A.; GRAD, B.; CRAMER-AZIMA, F.; AND RUSSELL, L. "Biologic, Psychologic, and Sociologic Studies in Normal Aged Persons and Patients With Senile Psychosis." *J Am Geriatrics Soc* 12:21–37 Ja '64. *

4408. McCULLY, ROBERT S. "Vampirism: Historical Perspective and Underlying Process in Relation to a Case of Auto-Vampirism." *J Nerv & Mental Dis* 139:440–52 N '64. * (*PA* 39:8174)

4409. NEMETH, G., AND MEZEI, A. "Personality Traits of Cancer Patients Compared With Benign Tumour Patients on the Basis of the Rorschach Test," pp. 12–7. In *Psychosomatic Aspects of Neoplastic Disease.* The Proceedings of the Third International Conference of the International Psychosomatic Cancer Study Group Held at Newnham College, Cambridge, England, 22nd to 26th July 1963. Edited by D. M. Kissen and L. L. Leshan. Philadelphia, Pa.: J. B. Lippincott Co., 1964. Pp. xii, 231. *

4410. OBERLEDER, MURIEL. "Effects of Psycho-Social Factors on Test Results of the Aging." *Psychol Rep* 14:383–7 Ap '64. * (*PA* 39:1390)

4411. OO, M.; CSIRSZKA, J.; AND HEGEDUS, J. "Psychological Tests in Leukaemia Patients," pp. 18–29. In *Psychosomatic Aspects of Neoplastic Disease.* The Proceedings of the Third International Conference of the International Psychosomatic Cancer Study Group Held at Newnham College, Cambridge, England, 22nd to 26th July 1963. Edited by D. M. Kissen and L. L. Leshan. Philadelphia, Pa.: J. B. Lippincott Co., 1964. Pp. xii, 231. *

4412. RIKLAN, MANUEL, AND LEVITA, ERIC. "Psychological Effects of Lateralized Basal Ganglia Lesions: A Factorial Study." *J Nerv & Mental Dis* 138:233–40 Mr '64. * (*PA* 39:4087)

4413. STEISEL, IRA M. "Note on 'Personality Variables and Response to Color.'" *Psychol Rep* 61:399 My '64. * (*PA* 39:1686)

4414. BERGAN, JOHN R. "Pitch Perception, Imagery, and Regression in the Service of the Ego." *J Res Music Ed* 13:15–32 sp '65. * (*PA* 39:12224)

4415. BROWN, D. G., AND YOUNG, A. J. "Body Image and Susceptibility to Contact Dermatitis." *Brit J Med Psychol* 38:261–7 S '65. *

4416. HAAS, KURT. "Direction of Hostility and Psychiatric Symptoms." *Psychol Rep* 16:555–6 Ap '65. * (*PA* 39:10639)

4417. HEATH, DOUGLAS H.; WITH THE ASSISTANCE OF HARRIET E. HEATH. *Explorations of Maturity: Studies of Mature and Immature College Men.* New York: Appleton-Century-Crofts, 1965. Pp. xv, 423. * (*PA* 39:12057)

4418. HERTZ, MARGUERITE R. Chap. 25, "Detection of Suicidal Risks With the Rorschach," pp. 257–70. In *Acting Out: Theoretical and Clinical Aspects.* By Lawrence Edwin Abt and Stuart L. Weissman. New York: Grune & Stratton, Inc., 1965. Pp. xiii, 336. *

4419. KANTOR, ROBERT E., AND HERRON, WILLIAM G. "Perceptual Learning in the Reactive-Process Schizophrenias." *J Proj Tech & Pers Assess* 29:58–70 Mr '65. * (*PA* 39:10659)

4420. LASKOWITZ, DAVID, AND JONES, FERDINAND. "A Comparison of the Rorschach Behavior of Adolescent Addicts Who Have Died of an Overdose With Addict Controls," pp. 99–106. In *Drug Addiction in Youth.* Edited by Ernest Harms. London: Pergamon Press, 1965. Pp. xi, 210. *

4421. LEVI, JOSEPH. Chap. 24, "Acting Out Indicators on the Rorschach," pp. 252–6. In *Acting Out: Theoretical and Clinical Aspects.* By Lawrence Edwin Abt and Stuart L. Weissman. New York: Grune & Stratton, Inc., 1965. Pp. xiii, 336. *

4422. RIKLAN, MANUEL; LEVITA, ERIC; AND COOPER, IRVING S. "Psychological Effects of Bilateral Subcortical Surgery for Parkinson's Disease." *J Nerv & Mental Dis* 141:403–9 O '65. * (*PA* 40:5052)

4423. THEILGAARD, A. "Psychological Testing of Patients With Anorexia Nervosa," pp. 122–8. (*PA* 40:3170) In *Anorexia Nervosa: Symposium am 24.125 April 1965 in Göttingen.* Edited by J.-E. Meyer and H. Feldman. Stuttgart, Germany: Georg Thieme Verlag, 1965. Pp. vi, 168. *

4424. WILLIAMS, HERBERT H., AND WILLIAMS, JUDITH R. "The Definition of the Rorschach Test Situation: A Cross-Cultural Illustration," pp. 338–54. In *Context and Meaning in Cultural Anthropology*. Edited by Melford E. Spiro in honor of A. Irving Hallowell. New York: Free Press, 1965. Pp. xxii, 442. *

4425. GUNDERSON, E. K. ERIC, AND KAPFER, E. L. "The Predictability of Clinicians' Evaluations From Biographical Data." *J Clin Psychol* 22:144–50 Ap '66. * (*PA* 40:7682)

4426. GUNDERSON, E. K. ERIC, AND KAPFER, E. L. "The Predictive Validity of Clinical Ratings for an Extreme Environment." *Brit J Psychiatry* 112:405–12 Ap '66. * (*PA* 40:10105)

4427. KAHN, PAUL. "Time Orientation and Perceptual and Cognitive Organization." *Percept & Motor Skills* 23:1059–66 D '66. * (*PA* 41:5333)

4428. KOHN, MARTIN, AND LEVENSON, EDGAR A. "Differences Between Accepted and Rejected Patients in a Treatment Project of College Dropouts." *J Psychol* 63:143–56 My '66. * (*PA* 40:10355)

4429. MURTHY, HOSUR NARAYANA. "A Factorial Study of a Battery of Psychological Tests Used in Student Selection." *J Ed & Psychol* (India) 24:9–12 Ap '66. *

4430. RICKELS, KARL; DOWNING, ROBERT W.; AND DOWNING, MILDRED H. "Personality Differences Between Somatically and Psychologically Oriented Neurotic Patients." *J Nerv & Mental Dis* 142:10–8 Ja '66. * (*PA* 40:10269)

4431. SIDDIQUI, MASUD HUSSAIN. *A Comparative Study of Rorschach Responses of Pakistani and Thai Adolescents.* Doctor's thesis, University College, University of London (London, England), 1966.

4432. SILVERMAN, LLOYD H. "A Technique for the Study of Psychodynamic Relationships: The Effects of Subliminally Presented Aggressive Stimuli on the Production of Pathological Thinking in a Schizophrenic Population." *J Consult Psychol* 30: 103–11 Ap '66. * (*PA* 40:6881)

4433. STRICKER, GEORGE, AND ZAX, MELVIN. "Intelligence and Semantic Differential Discriminability." *Psychol Rep* 18:775–8 Je '66. * (*PA* 40:9929)

4434. BRENNER, LEON O., AND THOMPSON, RICHARD E. "The Use of Projective Techniques in Personality Evaluation of Deaf Adults." *J Rehabil Deaf* 1:17–30 Jl '67. *

4435. FIONDO, JOHN PHILLIP. *Toward the Development of an Economical, Valid Test Battery for the Identification of Emotional Disturbance in Children.* Doctor's thesis, Wayne State University (Detroit, Mich.), 1967. (*DAI* 31:6897B)

4436. GOLDMAN, JACQUELIN, AND PLOTNICK, MICHAELENE M. "Aging: The Criterion Problem in Diagnosis of Brain Dysfunction." *J Gerontol* 22:14–6 Ja '67. *

4437. HAYASHI, SHUZO. "A Study of Juvenile Delinquency in Twins." *B Osaka Med Sch Sup* (Japan) 12:373–8 '67. *

4438. JENNINGS, CHARLES L. "The Use of Normative Data in the Psychological Evaluation of Flying Personnel." *Int Psychiatry Clinics* 4:37–51 w '67. *

4439. KAPUR, MALAVIKA, AND KAPUR, R. L. "Study of Impotence Through Projective Tests." *Indian J Psychiatry* 9:208–12 Jl '67. *

4440. MORSE, HOWARD N. "The Rorschach Test in Clinical Psychology and Law." *J Am Med Assn* 200:285–6 Je 5 '67. *

4441. MOTANKY, GUY U.; ZAKS, MISHA S.; AND GROVES, MARION H. "The Role of Pre-Morbid Psychological and Social Characteristics in Behavioral Reactions Following Acute Brain Damage." *Bulletin de l'Association Internationale de Psychologie Appliquée* (England) 16:124–30 au '67. *

4442. NASH, DENNISON, AND HEISS, JEROLD. "Sources of Anxiety in Laboratory Strangers." *Sociol Q* 8:215–21 sp '67. *

4443. OTSUKA, FUMIO; TSUDA, KIYOSHIGE; OKI, TADAHIKO; OTSUKA, YOSHITAKA; AND YAMAMOTO, SHOJIRO. "Case Studies of Homicide in Children." *B Osaka Med Sch Sup* (Japan) 12: 385–93 '67. *

4444. VERNON, PHILIP E. "A Cross-Cultural Study of 'Creativity Tests' With 11-Year Boys." *New Res Ed* (England) 1: 135–46 Je '67. *

4445. CARR, ARTHUR C. "Psychological Testing and Reporting." *J Proj Tech & Pers Assess* 32:513–21 D '68. * (*PA* 43: 9995)

4446. DE-NOUR, ATARA K.; SHALTIEL, JUDITH; AND CZACZKES, J. W. "Emotional Reactions of Patients on Chronic Hemodialysis." *Psychosom Med* 30:521–33 S–O '68. * (*PA* 43:8624)

4447. GINSBERG, A. "Problems of Validation of Some Projective Methods in Personality Assessment." *Proc Inter Congr Appl Psychol* 16:810–4 '68. *

4448. GLUCKSMAN, MYRON L.; HIRSCH, JULES; McCULLY, ROBERT S.; BARRON, BRUCE A.; AND KNITTLE, JEROME L. "The Response of Obese Patients to Weight Reduction: 2, A Quantitative Evaluation of Behavior." *Psychosom Med* 30:359–73 Jl–Ag '68. * (*PA* 43:2314)

4449. LOEWER, H. D. "The Dependence of the Factorial Structure of Intelligence From the Level of Intelligence and From the Brain State." *Proc Inter Congr Appl Psychol* 16:707–12 '68. *

4450. NORDAN, ROBERT WARREN. *The Relation Between Cognitive Style and Rorschach M Responses.* Doctor's thesis, University of Chicago (Chicago, Ill.), 1968.

4451. RAYCHAUDHURI, MANAS, AND MAITRA, AMAL K. "Relationship Between Level of Creativity and Projection of Movement Responses as Measured by Rorschach M, Welsh Mv and a

Drawing Completion Task." *Indian J Psychol* 43(1–4):30–6 '68. *

4452. SHAPIRO, ARTHUR K.; WILENSKY, HAROLD; AND STRUENING, ELMER L. "Study of the Placebo Effect With a Placebo Test." *Comprehen Psychiatry* 9:118–37 Mr '68. * (*PA* 43:2745)

4453. CHATTERJEE, TARIT K. "A Study of the Personality of Parents of the Schizophrenics." *Samikas* (India) 23(1):22–48 '69. * (*PA* 45:8622)

4454. COBERT, WILLA. *Schizophrenic Patients and Their Siblings: A Rorschach Study of Thought Disorder.* Doctor's thesis, Adelphi University (Garden City, N.Y.), 1969.

4455. DOSEY, MICHAEL A., AND MEISELS, MURRAY. "Personal Space and Self-Protection." *J Pers & Social Psychol* 11(2):93–7 F '69. * (*PA* 43: 8297)

4456. HOLMES, DAVID S., AND SHALLOW, JOHN R. "Reduced Recall After Ego Threat: Repression or Response Competition?" *J Pers & Social Psychol* 13(2):145–52 O '69. *

4457. KUNDU, C. L. "The Ink Blot Responses of Some Tribal Delinquents." *J Ed Res & Exten* (India) 5(3):127–35 Ja '69. *

4458. KUTTNER, ROBERT E.; LORINCZ, ALBERT B.; AND HICKEY, ROBERT E. "Constellations of the Zodiac: A Cultural Rorschach Test?" *Percept & Motor Skills* 29(3):919–21 D '69. * (*PA* 46:4745)

4459. LUDWIG, ALFRED O.; MURAWSKI, BENJAMIN J.; AND STURGIS, SOMERS H. *Psychosomatic Aspects of Gynecological Disorders: Seven Psychoanalytic Case Studies,* pp. 95–116. Cambridge, Mass.: Harvard University Press, 1969. Pp. vii, 119. *

4460. RAYCHAUDHURI, MANAS; MUKERJI, KAMAL; AND RAYCHAUDHURI, SIBANI. "Rorschach Indices of Aggression and Maladjustment: A Comparative Study With Normal and Indisciplined Boys." *Arch Child Health* 11(1):31–8 Mr–My '69. *

4461. ACKERMAN, MARC JAMES. *Alcoholism as Predicted by the Rorschach: A Critical View.* Master's thesis, Marquette University (Milwaukee, Wis.), 1970.

4462. BAKER, GERTRUDE. Chap. 8, "Post-Diagnostic Use of the Rorschach." pp. 321–84. In *Developments in the Rorschach Technique, Vol. 3, see 4475.*

4463. BARKER, G. B. "The Female Homosexual in Hospital." *Brit J Proj Psychol & Pers Study* 15(2):2–6 D '70. * (*PA* 47: 3314)

4464. BRAWER, FLORENCE B. Chap. 9, "The Rorschach in Academic and Vocational Research: A Review," pp. 385–437. In *Developments in the Rorschach Technique, Vol. 3, see 4475.* *

4465. CUTTER, FRED, AND FARBEROW, NORMAN L. Chap. 6, "The Consensus Rorschach," pp. 209–61. In *Developments in the Rorschach Technique, Vol. 3, see 4475.* *

4466. DE MARTINO, ALICE J. *The Relations Among Adaptive Regression, Independence, and Creativity in Adolescents.* Doctor's thesis, New York University (New York, N.Y.), 1970. (*DAI* 32:539B)

4467. EWERT, LAWRENCE DONALD. *Individual Difference Models for Studying Rorschach Perception: An "Indirect" Approach to Personality Assessment.* Doctor's thesis, University of Illinois (Urbana, Ill.), 1970. (*DAI* 31:7594B)

4468. HARROWER, MOLLY. Chap. 5, "Projective Classification," pp. 139–64. In *New Approaches to Personality Classification.* Edited by Alvin R. Mahrer. New York: Columbia University Press, 1970. Pp. vii, 425. * (*PA* 45:6276)

4469. HARTY, MICHAEL KIMBROUGH. *The Capacity for Adaptive Regression as a Component of Empathic Ability.* Doctor's thesis, University of Michigan (Ann Arbor, Mich.), 1970. (*DAI* 31:7598B)

4470. HOLT, ROBERT R. Chap. 7, "Artistic Creativity and Rorschach Measures of Adaptive Regression," pp. 263–320. In *Developments in the Rorschach Technique, Vol. 3, see 4475.* *

4471. HOPKINS, JUNE H. "Lesbian Signs on the Rorschach." *Brit J Proj Psychol & Pers Study* 15(2):7–14 D '70. * (*PA* 47:3316)

4472. JOHNSTON, WADE W. "A Questionable Case of Multiple Personalities." *Brit J Proj Psychol & Pers Study* 15(2):21–4 D '70. * (*PA* 47:1162)

4473. JONES, SARA JARVIS. *A Comparison of Defensive Behavior in Schizophrenic, Neurotic and Normal Subjects.* Doctor's thesis, University of Houston (Houston, Tex.), 1970. (*DAI* 32: 3638B)

4474. KHORANA, SUMAN. "Pattern of Rorschach Responses in Schizophrenic and Normal Male Children." *Indian J Psychiatry* 12(3):185–9 Jl '70. *

4475. KLOPFER, BRUNO; MEYER, MORTIMER M.; BRAWER, FLORENCE B.; AND KLOPFER, WALTER G. *Developments in the Rorschach Technique: Vol. 3, Aspects of Personality Structure.* New York: Harcourt Brace Jovanovich, Inc., 1970. Pp. xviii, 446. *

4476. McARTHUR, CHARLES. "Vocational Guidance in the Ivy League," pp. 105–11. *Int Psychiatric Clinic* 7(3):83–131 '70. *

4477. McDONAGH, JOHN MICHAEL. *The Relationship Between Familial Characteristics and Two Measures of Dependency.* Doctor's thesis, University of Oklahoma (Norman, Okla.), 1970. (*DAI* 32:542B)

4478. MAYMAN, MARTIN. Chap. 1, "Reality Contact, Defense Effectiveness, and Psychopathology in Rorschach Form-Level Scores," pp. 11–46. In *Developments in the Rorschach Technique, Vol. 3, see 4475.* *

4479. MEGARGEE, EDWIN I. "The Prediction of Violence With

Psychological Tests." *Curr Topics Clin & Commun Psychol* 2: 97–156 '70. *

4480. MEYER, MORTIMER M., AND CARUTH, ELAINE. Chap. 2, "Rorschach Indices of Ego Processes," pp. 47–81. In *Developments in the Rorschach Techniques, Vol. 3*, see *4475.* *

4481. MINDESS, HARVEY. Chap. 3, "The Symbolic Dimension," pp. 83–98. In *Developments in the Rorschach Technique, Vol. 3*, see *4475.* *

4482. MUKERJI, KAMAL, AND RAYCHAUDHURI, MANAS. "Assessment Equivalence of Clinical Ratings, Structured and Projective Measures of Personality." *Manas* (India) 17(2):67–76 N '70. * (*PA* 47:9277)

4483. NATHAN, SUSAN, AND PISULA, DOROTHY. "Psychological Observations of Obese Adolescents During Starvation Treatment." *J Am Acad Child Psychiatry* 9(4):722–40 O '70. * (*PA* 45:8849)

4484. PRABHU, G. G. "Clinical Utility of Piotrowski's Alpha Diagnostic Formula." *Indian Psychol R* 6(2):110–2 Ja '70. * (*PA* 46:9289)

4485. RUTSTEIN, ELEANOR H. *The Effects of Aggressive Stimulation on Suicidal Patients: An Experimental Study of the Psychoanalytic Theory of Suicide.* Doctor's thesis, New York University (New York, N.Y.), 1970. (*DAI* 31:7611B)

4486. SHEVRIN, HOWARD, AND SMITH, WILLIAM H. "Subliminally Stimulated Brain and Verbal Responses of Twins Differing in Repressiveness." *J Abn Psychol* 76(1):39–46 Ag '70. * (*PA* 44:20437)

4487. SOLIMAN, PIERRE L. "Some Remarks on the Expression of Anxiety, Libido and Counter-Cathexis in the Rorschach Test." *Brit J Proj Psychol & Pers Study* 15(2):15–8 D '70. * (*PA* 47:949)

4488. WÜRSTEN, HELMUT. Chap. 4, "The Relationship Between Piaget's Developmental Theory and the Rorschach Method." pp. 99–142. In *Developments in the Rorschach Technique, Vol. 3*, see *4475.* *

4489. ZABARENKO, LUCY; BADGER, GEORGE F., JR.; AND WILLIAMS, ELLEN B. "TABRA: A Projective Test for Computer Personnel Research: Preliminary Report." *Proc Ann Computer Personnel Res Conf* 8:92–107 '70. *

4490. ZELEN, SEYMOUR L. Chap. 5, "Rorschach Patterns in Three Generations of a Family," pp. 143–205. In *Developments in the Rorschach Technique, Vol. 3*, see *4475.* *

4491. ACKERMAN, MARC J. "Alcoholism and the Rorschach." *J Pers Assess* 35(3):224–8 Je '71. * (*PA* 47:3286)

4492. AMES, LOUISE BATES; MÉTRAUX, RUTH W.; AND WALKER, RICHARD N. *Adolescent Rorschach Responses: Developmental Trends From Ten to Sixteen Years, Second Edition.* New York: Brunner/Mazel, Inc., 1971. Pp. xvi, 319. *

4493. ARONOW, EDWARD, AND REZNIKOFF, MARVIN. "Application of Projective Tests to Psychotherapy: A Case Study." *J Pers Assess* 35(4):379–93 Ag '71. * (*PA* 47:5067)

4494. BAGADIA, V. N.; ANAND, SHASHI; SARAF, K. R.; AND SHAH, L. P. "Analysis of Rorschach Test of 250 Cases of Schizophrenia." *Indian J Psychiatry* 13(4):248–52 O '71. *

4495. BECKER, JOSEPH; DOCTOR, RONALD M.; MIRANDA, MANUEL; AND WALLACE, JEAN. "Analytic-Perceptual Style and Verbal Conditioning." *Percept & Motor Skills* 32(2):631–6 Ap '71. * (*PA* 46:10861)

4496. BIEDERMAN, LINDA, AND CERBUS, GEORGE. "Changes in Rorschach Teaching." *J Pers Assess* 35(6):524–6 D '71. * (*PA* 47:10896)

4497. BOROFSKY, GERALD LEWIS. *Regression and Ego Functioning in Creative Normals and Psychotics.* Doctor's thesis, Michigan State University (East Lansing, Mich.), 1971. (*DAI* 32:7301B)

4498. BROMET, EVELYN JUNE. *Thought Disorder and Psycho-Social Factors in the Posthospital Adjustment of Psychiatric Patients.* Doctor's thesis, Yale University (New Haven, Conn.), 1971. (*DAI* 32:2982B)

4499. BROWN, FRED. "Changes in Sexual Identification and Role Over a Decade and Their Implications." *J Psychol* 77(2): 229–51 Mr '71. * (*PA* 46:1227)

4500. CAMPO, VERA. "Scoring and Perception." *Brit J Proj Psychol & Pers Study* 16(1):7–20 Je '71. * (*PA* 48:1196)

4501. CAMPO, VERA, AND DE SANTOS, DIANA R. "A Critical Review of the Shading Responses in the Rorschach: 1. Scoring Problems." *J Pers Assess* 35(1):3–21 F '71. * (*PA* 46:6908)

4502. CARLSON, KATHLEEN; TUCKER, G.; HARROW, M.; AND QUINLAN, D. "Body Image and Mental Illness: A Study of the Human Figure Drawings of Psychiatric Patients." *Psychiatry & Art* 3:162–9 '71. *

4503. CARNES, G. D., AND BATES, ROBERT E. "Rorschach Anatomy Response Correlates in Rehabilitation Failure Subjects." *J Pers Assess* 35(6):527–37 D '71. * (*PA* 47:11334)

4504. CAUTHEN, NELSON R., AND BOARDMAN, WILLIAM K. "Body Boundary and Stimulus Enhancement." *Percept & Motor Skills* 32(2):559–63 Ap '71. * (*PA* 46:10863)

4505. CUTLER, ROBERT. *An Examination of the Cognitive Control of Scanning: An Exploration of Its Adaptative and Defensive Significance With Particular Reference to Myopia.* Doctor's thesis, New York University (New York, N.Y.), 1971. (*DAI* 32:6044B)

4506. DEKONINCK, JOSEPH-M., AND CRABBÉ-DECLÈVE, GENE-VIÈVE. "Field Dependence and Rorschach White-Space Figure-Ground Reversal Responses." *Percept & Motor Skills* 33(3): 1191–4 D '71. * (*PA* 48:3036)

4507. DUBLIN, JAMES E. "The Physiognomic Icon as Unconscious Symbol." *Int J Symbol* 2(2):13–9 Mr '71. * (*PA* 27:3254)

4508. DUDEK, STEPHANIE Z. "Portrait of the Artist as a Rorschach Reader." *Psychol Today* 4(12):46–7+ My '71. * (*PA* 46:10901)

4509. EKEHAMMAR, BO. "A Psychophysical Approach to the Study of Individuals' Perceptions of Rorschach Cards." *Percept & Motor Skills* 33(3):951–65 D '71. * (*PA* 48:1024)

4510. FARMER, R. G., AND WRIGHT, J. M. C. "Muscular Reactivity and Systematic Desensitization." *Behav Ther* 2(1):1–10 Ja '71. * (*PA* 47:9075)

4511. FOX, HAYWARD MICHAEL. *Muscle Potential and Rorschach Movement.* Doctor's thesis, Ohio University (Athens, Ohio), 1971. (*DAI* 32:5438B)

4512. FRAZIER, ROY WOODROW, JR. *Differential Perception of Individuals Subgrouped on the Basis of Biodata Responses.* Doctor's thesis, University of Georgia (Athens, Ga.), 1971. (*DAI* 32:6045B)

4513. GEIST, HAROLD. "Emotional Aspects of Dermatitis." Abstract. *Proc 79th Ann Conv Am Psychol Assn* 6(2):627–8 '71. * (*PA* 46:5380)

4514. GLATT, CHARLES THOMAS. *Some Rorschach Correlates of Change in Clinical Status: An Investigation of Ego Regression in Schizophrenia.* Doctor's thesis, Michigan State University (East Lansing, Mich.), 1971. (*DAI* 32:7309B)

4515. GOLDFRIED, MARVIN R.; STRICKER, GEORGE; AND WEINER, IRVING B. *Rorschach Handbook of Clinical Research Applications.* Englewood Cliffs, N.J.: Prentice-Hall, Inc., 1971. Pp. xii, 436. *

4516. GREENBERG, NATHAN; RAMSAY, MARIA; SEGAL, PERRY; WEISS, ABRAHAM; AND EVANS, HARVEY. "Changes in Primary Process Thinking of a Prepsychotic Adolescent in Psychotherapy." *J Pers Assess* 35(6):538–44 D '71. * (*PA* 47:10983)

4517. GREENE, GERALD MICHAEL. *Somato-Psychological Indicants of Schizophrenia: A Partial Validation of the Penetration-Barrier Index.* Doctor's thesis, University of Oklahoma (Norman, Okla.), 1971. (*DAI* 32:4212B)

4518. GRUTTNER, TILO. "Teaching the Rorschach." Letter. *Brit J Proj Psychol & Pers Study* 16(2):22 D '71. *

4519. HAMILTON, J.; BLEWETT, D.; AND SYDIAHA, D. "Ink-Blot Responses of Identical and Fraternal Twins." *J Genetic Psychol* 119(1):37–41 S '71. * (*PA* 47:2461)

4520. HANNINEN, HELENA. "Psychological Picture of Manifest and Latent Carbon Disulphide Poisoning." *Brit J Indus Med* 28(4):374–81 O '71. *

4521. HARROWER, MOLLY. "Koffka's Rorschach Experiment." *J Pers Assess* 35(2):103–21 Ap '71. * (*PA* 47:3024)

4522. HERSEN, MICHEL, AND GREAVES, SALLY T. "Rorschach Productivity as Related to Verbal Reinforcement." *J Pers Assess* 35(5):436–41 O '71. * (*PA* 47:8954)

4523. HIRSCH, STEVEN R., AND LEFF, JULIAN P. "Parental Abnormalities of Verbal Communication in the Transmission of Schizophrenia." *Psychol Med* (England) 1(2):118–27 F '71. * (*PA* 49:2641)

4524. HOWELL, ROBERT J., AND CARLISLE, A. LINDSAY. "The Effect of Hypnotically Induced and Nonhypnotic Mood Changes on the Rorschach Test." *Int J Clin & Exp Hyp* 19(1):28–36 Ja '71. * (*PA* 46:1217)

4525. JACOBS, JOHN C. "Rorschach Studies Reveal Possible Misinterpretations of Personality Traits of the Gifted." *Gifted Child Q* 15(3):195–200 au '71. * (*PA* 47:11650)

4526. JACOBS, JON C. "A Projective Assessment of the Development of Personality Characteristics of Average and Gifted Children." *Mich Academician* 4(1):37–42 su '71. * (*PA* 47:9690)

4527. KAHN, MARVIN W. "Murderers Who Plead Insanity: A Descriptive Factor-Analytic Study of Personality, Social, and History Variables." *Genetic Psychol Monogr* 84(2):275–360 N '71. * (*PA* 49:990)

4528. KELLER, CHARLES WILLIAM. *Characteristics of Rorschach Interpreter Types: An Exploratory Study.* Doctor's thesis, Texas Tech University (Lubbock, Tex.), 1971. (*DAI* 32:2400B)

4529. KING, HOLLIS HEATON. *An Investigation of Relationships Between Hypnotic Susceptibility, Manifest Dream Content and Personality Characteristics.* Doctor's thesis, Louisiana State University (Baton Rouge, La.), 1971. (*DAI* 33:442B)

4530. McCULLY, ROBERT S. "The Rorschach in a New Key." *Brit J Proj Psychol & Pers Study* 16(2):15–8 D '71. *

4531. McCULLY, ROBERT S. *Rorschach Theory and Symbolism: A Jungian Approach to Clinical Material.* Baltimore, Md.: William & Wilkins Co., 1971. Pp. xxi, 271. *

4532. MAHAL, A. S., AND PRABHU, G. G. "Irritable Bowel Syndrome—A Psychological Study." *Indian J Appl Psychol* 8(1):1–4 Ja '71. *

4533. MARWIT, SAMUEL J. "Further Notes on the Effect of Pretest Expectancies on the Psychological Test Report." *J Pers Assess* 35(4):303–6 Ag '71. * (*PA* 47:4835)

4534. MEARES, RUSSELL. "'Ego Boundary' and the 'Barrier Score.'" *Brit J Med Psychol* 44(2):179–80 Je '71. * (*PA* 47:4793)

Rorschach

4535. MILLER, DELBERT G. *A Comparative Study of the Rorschach F+ Per Cent to the General Aptitude Test Battery Subtests S, Spatial Aptitude and P, Form Perception.* Master's thesis, University of Idaho (Moscow, Idaho), 1971.

4536. MITCHELL, STEPHEN J. *A Multiple-Criterion Approach to Rorschach Validity.* Master's thesis, California State College (Fullerton, Calif.), 1971.

4537. MOLISH, H. BARRY; KRAFT, IRVIN A.; AND WIGGINS, P. Y. "Psychodiagnostic Evaluation of the Heart Transplant Patient." *Seminars Psychiatry* 3(1):46–57 F '71. * (PA 49: 7577)

4538. MOOCHHALA, NAFISA Y., AND SHAH, NALINI M. "Behavioural Correlates of Color in Rorschach and Drawings of Schizophrenics." *Indian J Psychiatry* 13(4):237–42 O '71. *

4539. MURAWSKI, BENJAMIN J. "Genetic Factors in Tests of Perception and the Rorschach." *J Genetic Psychol* 119(1):43–52 S '71. * (PA 47:2463)

4540. NICHOLLS, JOHN G. "Movement Responses and Originality." *Percept & Motor Skills* 33(3):698 D '71. * (PA 48: 1001)

4541. PAPAJOHN, JOHN C., AND SPIEGEL, JOHN P. "The Relationship of Culture Value Orientation Change and Rorschach Indices of Psychological Development." *J Cross-Cultural Psychol* 2(3):257–72 S '71. * (PA 47:6582)

4542. PHILLIPSON, H. "Rorschach: Its Heritage in Prospect." *Brit J Proj Psychol & Pers Study* 16(2):10–4 D '71. *

4543. PIOTROWSKI, ZYGMUNT A., AND SMOLINSKY, HAROLD J. "The Computerized Perceptanalytic Rorschach." *Newsl Res Psychol* 13(2):47–8 My '71. *

4544. POTKAY, CHARLES R. *The Rorschach Clinician: A New Research Approach and Its Application.* New York: Grune & Stratton, Inc., 1971. Pp. xiv, 223. *

4545. POTKAY, CHARLES R. "Sources of Utility in Rorschach Interpretation." Abstract. *Proc 79th Ann Conv Am Psychol Assn* 6(1):469–70 '71. * (PA 46:5017)

4546. RAJ, JACOB SELVA. *A Comparative Study of Homeless and Domiciled Alcoholic Men.* Doctor's thesis, Yeshiva University (New York, N.Y.), 1971. (DAI 32:1858B)

4547. RAYCHAUDHURI, MANAS. "Relation of Creativity and Sex to Rorschach M Responses." *J Pers Assess* 35(1):27–31 F '71. * (PA 46:6911)

4548. RAYCHAUDHURI, MANAS, AND MUKERJI, KAMAL. "Rorschach Differentials of Homosexuality in Male Convicts: An Examination of Wheeler and Schafer Signs." *J Pers Assess* 35(1):22–6 F '71. * (PA 46:7131)

4549. REDMOND, NEIL JOSEPH. *Rorschach Correlates of Underachievement and Cognitive Deficits of Underachievers.* Doctor's thesis, St. John's University (Jamaica, N.Y.), 1971. (DAI 32:3015B)

4550. RICHARDS, WILLIAM S., AND MERRENS, MATTHEW R. "Student Evaluation of Generalized Personality Interpretations as a Function of Method of Assessment." *J Clin Psychol* 27(4): 457–9 O '71. * (PA 47:8942)

4551. ROSEN, MARCIA SHORR. *Trust, Orality and Openness to Sensory Experience: A Study of Some Personality Correlates of Creativity.* Doctor's thesis, New York University (New York, N.Y.), 1971. (DAI 32:6060B)

4552. RYAN, BRUCE A.; BOERSMA, FREDERICK J.; AND MILLS, DAVID H. "A Note on Eye Movements as a Measure of Emotional Reactivity to Chromatic Elements in Rorschach Stimuli." *J Abn Psychol* 78(3):245–6 D '71. * (PA 47:8955)

4553. RYBACK, RALPH S.; LEWIS, OLIVER F.; AND LESSARD, CHARLES S. "Psychobiologic Effects of Prolonged Bed Rest (Weightless) in Young Healthy Volunteers (Study II)." *Aerospace Med* 42(5):529–35 My '71. *

4554. RYBACK, RALPH S.; TRIMBLE, RALPH W.; LEWIS, OLIVER F.; AND JENNINGS, CHARLES L. "Psychobiologic Effects of Prolonged Weightlessness (Bed Rest) in Young Healthy Volunteers." *Aerospace Med* 42(4):408–15 Ap '71. *

4555. SCHACHTER, M. "Card Turning in Rorschach Interpretation—Notes Referring to the Contribution by Celia Williams to the June 1970 Issue of This Journal." *Brit J Proj Psychol & Pers Study* 16(1):6 Je '71. *

4556. SEMEONOFF, BORIS. "Rorschach and the Development of Projective Psychology: A Personal View." *Brit J Proj Psychol & Pers Study* 16(2):5–10 D '71. *

4557. SETHI, B. B.; GUPTA, S. C.; RAJ, A.; AND NATHAWAT, S. S. "Rorschach as a Measure of Psychopathology in Murder." *Indian J Psychiatry* 13(4):243–7 O '71. *

4558. SHEEHAN, PETER W. "Task Structure as a Limiting Condition of the Occurrence of the Treatment Effects of Simulation Instruction in Application of the Real-Simulating Model of Hypnosis." *Int J Clin & Exp Hyp* 19(4):260–76 O '71. * (PA 47:4066)

4559. SHERE, EUGENIA S., AND TEICHMAN, YONA. "Evaluation of Group Therapy With Preadolescent Girls: Assessment of Therapeutic Effects Based on Rorschach Records." *Int J Group Psychother* 21(1):99–104 Ja '71. * (PA 46:6995)

4560. SHIVADASANI, H. K. "Rorschach Hostility Content and Its Relation With Various Forms of Aggression-Hostility." *Psychol Studies* 16(1):15–8 Ja '71. * (PA 47:948)

4561. SILVER, MAURICE JOSEPH. *Hypnotizability as a Function of Adaptive Regression, Repression and Mood.* Doctor's

thesis, Boston University (Boston, Mass.), 1971. (DAI 32: 2409B)

4562. SINHA, AWADHESH KUMAR, AND SHARAN, MITHILA BEHARI. "Some Extra-Content Indicators of Maladjustment in TAT and Rorschach." *Indian J Psychol* 46(2):115–24 Je '71. *

4563. SMITH, GARY GRAGG. *Experimenter-Subject Acquaintance, Rorschach Barrier Score, and Attitude Toward the Experiment: An Experimental Analysis.* Master's thesis, University of Florida (Gainesville, Fla.), 1971.

4564. SOLOMON, DANIEL, AND GOODSON, DIANE F. "Hypnotic Age Regression Evaluated Against a Criterion of Prior Performance." *Int J Clin & Exp Hyp* 19(4):243–59 O '71. * (PA 47:4067)

4565. SOMASUNDARAM, C. P.; MATHAI, K. V.; AND JESUDIAN, G. "The Application of the Rorschach Technique in Patients Disabled by Convulsive Disorders, Part 1." *Neurol India* 19(2): 64–72 Je '71. *

4566. SOMASUNDARAM, C. P.; MATHAI, K. V.; AND JESUDIAN, G. "The Rorschach Popular Responses in Patients With Epilepsy, Part 2." *Neurol India* 19(2):73–6 Je '71. *

4567. SOMODEVILLA, SANTIAGO ALBERTO. *A Comparative Study of Drug Abusers and Non-Users: Body Image as Measured by the Rorschach.* Doctor's thesis, Texas Tech University (Lubbock, Tex.), 1971. (DAI 32:5460B)

4568. STARK, STANLEY. "An Essay in Rorschach Revisionism, With Special Reference to the Maslowian Self-Actualizer: 1, Innovation *vs* Imagination, Idealism, Mysticism, Romanticism." *Percept & Motor Skills* 33(2):343–57 O '71. * (PA 47:6825)

4569. STAVRIANOS, BERTHA K. "Can Projective Test Measures Aid in the Detection and Differential Diagnosis of Reading Deficit?" *J Pers Assess* 35(1):80–91 F '71. * (PA 46:7527)

4570. STRAUSS, MILTON E. "Note on Rosenthal's 'Unintended Effects of the Clinician in Clinical Interaction.' " *Austral J Psychol* 23(1):53–7 Ap '71. * (PA 46:9084)

4571. THAKUR, G. P., AND THAKUR, MANJU. "Symbolic Meaning of Rorschach Cards II, IV and VII." *Percept & Motor Skills* 32(1):190 F '71. * (PA 46:3104)

4572. THOMAS, MURPHY, AND SEEMAN, JULIUS. "Criterion Measures for Therapy Outcome: A Study in Personality Integration." *Psychother Theory Res & Prac* 8(1):26–30 sp '71. * (PA 49:3055, title only)

4573. TRACHTMAN, JOAN P. "Socio-Economic Class Bias in Rorschach Diagnosis: Contributing Psychosocial Attributes of the Clinician." *J Pers Assess* 35(3):229–40 Je '71. * (PA 47: 3279)

4574. VITALE, JOHN. "Comments on the Computerized Perceptanalytic Rorschach." *Newsl Res Psychol* 13(2):48–9 My '71. *

4575. WAGNER, EDWIN E. "Structural Analysis: A Theory of Personality Based on Projective Techniques." *J Pers Assess* 35(5):422–35 O '71. * (PA 47:8870)

4576. WAGNER, EDWIN E., AND HOOVER, THOMAS O. "Exhibitionistic M in Drama Majors: A Validation." *Percept & Motor Skills* 32(1):125–6 F '71. * (PA 46:3105)

4577. WELLS, HOWARD E. *Hand Test and Rorschach Indicators of Aggressive Behavior.* Master's thesis, Central Michigan University (Mt. Pleasant, Mich.), 1971.

4578. WILLIAMS, CELIA, AND HADZIENESTI, NELLIE. "Projective Assessment of Brain Damage in a Maladjusted Child: Dora." *Brit J Proj Psychol & Pers Study* 16(2):23–30 D '71. *

4579. WIMMERS, DICK. *The Stability of Projective Interpretations.* Doctor's thesis, University of Missouri (Columbia, Mo.), 1971. (DAI 32:1865B)

4580. WIRLS, CHARLES J., AND PLOTKIN, ROSALIE R. "A Comparison of Children With Cleft Palate and Their Siblings on Projective Test Personality Factors." *Cleft Palate J* 8:399–408 O '71. *

CUMULATIVE NAME INDEX

Brady, J. P.: 2986, 3274, 3850, 4397
Brams, J. M.: 2757
Branston, W. T.: 1494
Brar, H. S.: 4113
Brawer, F. B.: 2856, 3231-3, 3451, 3876, 4464, 4475
Brecher, S.: 1854, 2019
Breda, R.: 3793
Breiger, B.: 2077
Bremner, E. A.: 1551
Brener, R.: 678
Brenman, M.: 301
Brenner, B.: 3302
Brenner, L. O.: 4434
Breslow, A. K.: 3639
Bresnahan, T. J.: 914
Brewer, E. J.: 3336
Brewer, J.: 4014
Brick, H.: 2665
Bricklin, B.: 2438, 2492, 2758-9, 2825, 2857, 2958
Briggs, L. D.: 3899
Brigham, B. W.: 3926
Bristol, M.: 2086, 2571
Brockway, A. L.: 1669
Brodie, R. E.: 3639
Brodsky, M.: 4014
Brody, A. B.: 913
Brody, C. M. H.: 1855
Brody, G. G.: 1495
Brody, H.: 3095
Brody, J. R.: 2072
Broedel, J. W.: 3575
Broekmann, N. C.: 4114
Broida, D. C.: 1670-1
Bromet, E. J.: 4498
Brooks, M.: 2166
Brooks, M. O.: 2255
Broomhead, E.: 612
Brosin, H.: 679
Brosin, H. W.: 129, 241
Brower, D.: 556, 615, 680, 737
Brown, B. H.: 2020
Brown, C. C.: 1097
Brown, D. G.: 2493, 3335, 4415; exc, 6:B91
Brown, D. V.: 3798, 4270
Brown, E.: 2141
Brown, F.: 1316, 1496, 1507, 2038, 2055, 2167, 2760, 3722, 4499
Brown, F. T.: 349
Brown, G. G.: 935
Brown, J.: 1699
Brown, L. B.: 2021, 3561
Brown, M.: 914, 1085
Brown, R. A.: 3552
Brown, R. R.: 242, 302, 681; exc, 3:78
Brown, T. E.: 2761
Brozek, J.: 1374, 4218
Bruce, J. M.: 1497
Brudo, C. S.: 1498
Bruell, J. H.: 3171
Bruner, J. S.: 561, 682
Brussel, J. A.: 243-4, 631
Bryan, V.: 3956
Bryn, D.: 46
Buckle, D. F.: 303, 1086, 1672
Buel, W. D.: exc, 7:B487
Bugental, J. F. T.: 2312
Buhler, C.: 304, 444, 557, 632, 683-4, 786-7, 915, 1317, 1499
Buhler, K.: 683
Buker, S. L.: 865, 1087, 1318, 1319; exc, 4:126
Burchard, E. M. L.: 123, 486, 1319, 2858, 4225
Burgemeister, B. B.: 419, 1219, 2858, 4225
Burgess, E.: 1500, 2022
Burke, M.: 2859
Burke, M. O.: 4310
Burnand, G.: 2610-1, 2762, 2860, 2868, 2959-60, 3562
Burnham, C. A.: 788
Burnham, R. K.: 2378
Burstein, A. G.: 2763; rev, 7:175
Burton, A.: 789
Buss, A. H.: 2861
Butcher, T.: 3662

Butler, E. S.: 4352
Button, A. D.: 2023
Cadman, W. H.: 4270
Cahen, E. R.: 1130, 1363
Calabresi, R. A.: 685, 1242, 4240
Calden, G.: 1088, 1320, 1501-2
Caldwell, B. M.: 1321, 1673, 4251, 4271, 4307
Caliman, A. W.: 3760
Callahan, R.: 1089
Calogeras, R. C.: 3657
Calvin, A. D.: 1715
Cambier, L.: 3662
Cameron, D. C.: 245
Campbell, E. F.: 1322
Campbell, F. A.: 2494
Campo, V.: 4015, 4115-6 4500-1
Candee, B.: 391
Canter, A.: 1090, 2168, 2172, 2398
Canter, F. M.: 1503
Capone, T. A.: 3597
Caracena, P. F.: 2862
Cardin, P. J.: 4024
Cardone, S. S.: 3927, 4016
Carlisle, A. L.: 4524
Carlson, K.: 4502
Carlson, R.: 1323, 4017
Carlson, V. R.: 1324, 1504
Carnes, G. D.: 4503
Carp, A.: 686, 1088
Carp, A. L.: 916
Carp, F. M.: 687, 917
Carr, A. C.: 790, 1674, 2024, 2399, 4400, 4404, 4445
Carrera, R.: 4332
Carrera, R. N.: 2949; exc, 7: B383
Carrigan, P. M.: 2612
Carrison, D.: 477
Carstairs, G. M.: 2613
Carter, H. D.: 1665, 2015
Carter, J. D.: 4256
Carter, R. E.: 4018
Cartwright, D. S.: 3867
Cartwright, R. D.: 2256, 3144
Cartwright, R. W.: 822, 4480
Caruth, E.: 3387
Casella, C. F.: 3190
Caspari, I. E.: 2863
Cass, W. A.: 918, 1091
Cassel, R. N.: 919
Cassell, W. A.: 3234, 3452, 3877, 4389
Castelnuovo-Tedesco, P.: 688, 4117
Castro, P. N.: 2400
Castrogiovanni, P.: 4118
Cattell, R. B.: 608, 4218
Caudill, W.: 1895, 2342
Cauthen, N. R.: 4504
Centers, L.: 4061
Cerbus, G.: 2961, 4496
Ceres, M.: 1385
Cerf, A. Z.: 633
Chalke, F. C. R.: 456, 487, 914, 1085
Challman, R. C.: 420; exc, 3:82
Chambers, G. S.: 1675, 2169-70
Chance, J.: 1747, 4272
Chandra, S.: 3550
Chang, S.: 2455
Chapman, A. H.: 1505-6
Chapman, J. P.: 4019
Chapman, K. W.: 274-5
Chapman, L. J.: 4019
Chapman, M. V.: 3957
Charen, S.: 1507, 2025, 2171, 2348
Charles, H.: 1325, 4291
Charny, I. W.: 2401, 2495
Chase, J.: 2760
Chatterjee, T. K.: 4453
Chelnek, I.: 834
Chen, W.: 3435
Cherry, N.: 3535
Chesrow, E. J.: 791
Chipman, C. E.: 488
Christ, A. E.: 3997

Christensen, A. H.: 1092
Christenson, J. A.: 689
Christiansen, C.: 499
Chu-chang, C.: 2407
Chung, B. M.: 2764
Chute, E.: 358
Claeys, W.: 3563
Clancy, D. D.: 3809
Clapp, H. S.: 86
Clardy, E. R.: 189
Clark, J. H.: 690-1
Clark, K. B.: 811
Clark, M.: 1767
Clark, R. W.: 483
Clark, S. G.: 2257
Clark, V.: exc, 3:79
Clark, W. D.: 3453
Clarke, H. J.: 489
Clarke, J. I. C.: 1856
Clarke, N. B.: 3741
Class, L.: 3547
Clayton, T. E.: 920
Clemens, T.: 4368
Clemes, S.: 2962
Cleveland, S. E.: 921, 990, 1606, 2026, 2039, 2409, 2496, 2864, 3336-7, 4030-1, 4273, 4315
Clifton, J. A.: 2497, 2765, 3154
Cliggett, D. P.: 3810
Clyde, R. J.: 1412, 2027
Coan, R.: 2028
Coan, R. W.: 2498
Coates, S.: 2148, 2865
Cobb, B.: 3172
Cobb, S.: 4280
Cobert, W.: 4454
Cobrinik, L.: 2766
Cocking, R. R.: 3670, 4020, 4122
Cofer, C. N.: 634
Coffin, M.: 665-6
Coffin, T. E.: 2298
Cohart, M. S.: 1508
Cohen, A. M.: 3451
Cohen, B. D.: 2029
Cohen, D.: 1676
Cohen, G.: 3761
Cohen, H.: 3173
Cohen, I.: 4119
Cohen, I. H.: 2614
Cohen, I. S.: 2441
Cohen, J.: 2902; exc, 4:126
Cohen, L. B.: 1326, 1502
Cohen, L. D.: 3338
Cohen, M.: 3634
Cohen, M. L.: 2113, 2219
Cohen, R.: 3372
Cohen, S.: 2767
Colarelli, N. J.: 4157
Cole, D. A.: 3832
Cole, D. L.: 2768
Cole, J. K.: 3608
Cole, S.: 3564, 3663, 4021
Coleman, J. C.: 2125, 3565, 3664
Collet, G. M.: 698, 1509
Collin, A. G.: 305
Colm, H.: 692-3
Colson, D. B.: 3652
Compton, N. H.: 3235, 3928
Comrey, A.: 2275
Conkey, R. C.: 927
Connolly, C. G.: 3958
Conrad, D. C.: 1031
Consalvi, C.: 2030, 2172
Cook, B. F.: 3566
Cook, P. H.: 246-7, 303, 616
Cooley, W. W.: 2963
Coons, W. H.: 4120
Cooper, A.: 3162
Cooper, G. D.: 2742, 2848, 2866, 2949, 3338
Cooper, G. W.: 3339
Cooper, I. S.: 4422
Cooper, J. G.: 792, 1093, 1857
Cooper, L.: 4022
Cooper, M.: 1510
Cooper, S.: 2519, 3959
Coopersmith, S.: 2867
Corke, P. P.: 3315
Cormier, B. M.: 4330
Cornelison, A. R.: 2230

Cornett, S. J.: 3846
Corrigan, H. G.: 485
Corsini, R. J.: 1677, 1858
Corter, H. M.: 1327
Cortner, R. H.: 1859
Costello, C. G.: 2258
Counts, R. M.: 922
Cousineau, A.: 4347
Covey, D. S.: 3567
Cowen, E. L.: 1094, 3028
Cowin, M.: 421; exc, 3:89
Cox, F. N.: 1678
Cox, K. J.: 255, 694
Cox, R. D.: 1679, 2031
Cox, S. M.: 923, 1095
Coyle, F. A.: 4078
Crabbé-Declève, G.: 4506
Craddick, R. A.: 3236
Craft, M.: 2868, 3340
Craig, J.: 4272
Cramer-Azima, F.: 4407
Cranford, V.: 365-6, 466, 4217
Crasilneck, H. B.: 1680
Crawford, C. S.: 3486
Creager, J. A.: 1654
Crites, J. O.: 2938
Crokes, T. G.: 3838
Cromwell, R. L.: 2945
Cronbach, L. J.: 793-5, 924, 4121; exc, 3:80, 5:B60, 5: B247, 5:B337
Crookes, T. G.: 2173, 2615, 3838
Crosby, M. J.: 925
Crowell, D. H.: 3080
Crown, S.: 3069
Crowne, D. P.: 3866
Cruickshank, W. M.: 2226; exc, 5:B32
Crumpton, E.: 1860, 2032, 2869, 3454-5
Csirszka, J.: 4411
Cucciare, S.: 4023
Cummings, S. T.: 926, 1681, 2308
Curnutt, R. H.: 3089
Curtis, H. S.: 1096
Curtis, J. M.: 2402
Cutler, R.: 4505
Cutter, F.: 2174, 3665-8, 4465
Cutts, R. A.: 695
Czaczkes, J. W.: 4446
Dai, B.: 4311
Daingerfield, M.: 765
Damarin, F.: 3172
Dana, J. M.: 4020, 4122
Dana, R. H.: 1682, 1861, 2499, 2870, 3313, 3456, 3669-70, 4020, 4063, 4122; rev, 6:237
Dancey, T. E.: 349
D'Andrade, R. G.: exc, 6: B129
Darbonne, A. R.: 4131
Darby, J.: 3568
Daroff, R. B.: 3970
Daston, P. G.: 1835, 2616, 2871, 3174, 3569, 4373
Datel, W. E.: 1862-3
David, H. P.: exc, 6:B91, 7: B373
Davids, A.: 2033, 2964-5, 3237, 4024, 4312
Davidson, G. M.: 927
Davidson, H.: 141
Davidson, H. H.: 87-8, 382, 518-9, 928, 1328, 1562, 1666, 1864, 2316, 2895, 3457, 4313, 4390
Davidson, K.: 2288
Davidson, K. S.: 1683
Davidson, N.: 1227
Davidson, W.: 628, 675
Davies, R.: 3341
Davis, A. D.: 2617, 3127
Davis, H. B.: 2770
Davis, H. S.: 2500, 2769
Davis, R. W.: 4123
Daw, R. P.: 3238
Dawes, R. M.: 3239
Dawson, J. G.: 3024, 3749
Day, F.: 169

Rorschach

[1500]

*Rosenzweig Picture-Frustration Study. Ages 4–13, 12–18, 14 and over; 1944–64; also called *Rosenzweig P-F Study;* 15 scores: direction of aggression (extrapunitive, intropunitive, impunitive), type of aggression (obstacle-dominance, ego-defense, need-persistence), 9 combinations of the preceding categories; 3 levels; Saul Rosenzweig; the Author. *

a) FORM FOR CHILDREN. Ages 4–13; 1948–60.

b) REVISED FORM FOR ADOLESCENTS. Ages 12–18; 1964; no manual.

c) REVISED FORM FOR ADULTS. Ages 14 and over; 1944–49.

For additional information regarding *a* and *c*, see P:471 (63 references); for a review by Åke Bjerstedt, see 6:238 (61 references); for reviews by Richard H. Dana and Bert R. Sappenfield, see 5:155 (109 references); for reviews by Robert C. Challman and Percival M. Symonds, see 4:129 (77 references). For excerpts from related book reviews, see 7:B473 (2 excerpts).

REFERENCES THROUGH 1971

1–77. See 4:129.
78–186. See 5:155.
187–247. See 6:238.
248–310. See P:471.
311. HAYES, MARGARET L. "Personality and Cultural Factors in Intergroup Attitudes: I." *J Ed Res* 43:122–8 O '49. * (*PA* 24:2507)
312. HAYES, MARGARET L. "Personality and Cultural Factors in Intergroup Attitudes: II." *J Ed Res* 43:197–204 N '49. * (*PA* 24:3691)
313. GATLING, FRANK P. "Frustration Reactions of Delin-

quents Using Rosenzweig's Classification System." *J Abn & Social Psychol* 45:749–52 O '50. * (*PA* 25:2438)
314. LINDZEY, GARDNER. "Differences Between the High and Low in Prejudice and Their Implications for a Theory of Prejudice." *J Personality* 19:16–40 Je '50. * (*PA* 25:6161)
315. WINSLOW, CHARLES N., AND BRAINERD, JAMES E. "A Comparison of the Reactions of Whites and Negroes to Frustration as Measured by the Rosenzweig Picture-Frustration Test." Abstract. *Am Psychologist* 5:297 Jl '50. * (*PA* 25:1048)
316. COX, F. N. "Some Effects of Frustration: I, A Methodical Programme." *Austral J Psychol* 4:94–106 D '52. * (*PA* 28:4558)
317. JUNKEN, ELIZABETH M. *A Comparison of the Reactions to Frustration of Children Academically Advanced With Those of Children Academically Retarded.* Doctor's thesis, New York University (New York, N.Y.), 1952. (*DA* 13:583)
318. LOWINGER, LOUIS. *The Psychodynamics of Stuttering: An Evaluation of the Factors of Aggression and Guilt Feelings in a Group of Institutionalized Children.* Doctor's thesis, New York University (New York, N.Y.), 1952. (*DA* 12:725)
319. EFRON, HERMAN YALE. *Some Personality Correlates of the Learning of the Galvanic Skin Response.* Doctor's thesis, New York University (New York, N.Y.), 1953. (*DA* 14:404)
320. SEITZ, PHILIP F. D.; GOSMAN, JAMES S.; AND CROTON, JEAN. "Super-Ego and Aggression in Circumscribed Neurodermatitis." *J Invest Derm* 20:263–9 Ap '53. *
321. BENNETT, EDWARD M., AND JOHANNSEN, DOROTHEA E. "Psychodynamics of the Diabetic Child." *Psychol Monogr* 68(11):1–23 '54. * (*PA* 29:6072)
322. FERGUSON, ROBERT G. "Some Developmental Factors in Childhood Aggression." *J Ed Res* 48:15–27 S '54. * (*PA* 29:4294)
323. HARRIS, MYRON WILLARD. *Protective Mechanisms Utilized in Reaction to Ego-Threatening Situations, as Evidenced by Performance on a Level of Aspiration Problem.* Doctor's thesis, New York University (New York, N.Y.), 1954. (*DA* 15:116)
324. SCHMEIDLER, GERTRUDE R. "Picture-Frustration Ratings and ESP Scores for Subjects Who Showed Moderate Annoyance at the ESP Task." *J Parapsychol* 18:137–52 S '54. * (*PA* 29:6641)
325. ZUCKERMAN, MARVIN. *The Effect of Frustration on the Perception of Neutral and Aggressive Words.* Doctor's thesis, New York University (New York, N.Y.), 1954. (*DA* 17:2694)
326. FERRACUTI, F., AND RIZZO, G. B. "Psychological Patterns in Terminal Cancer Cases." *Ed & Psychol* (India) 2:26–36 Ja–Mr '55. * (*PA* 31:3531)
327. GETZELS, J. W., AND GUBA, E. G. "Role Conflict and Personality." *J Personality* 24:74–85 S '55. * (*PA* 30:5758)
328. WEISS, WALTER, AND FINE, BERNARD J. "Opinion Change as a Function of Some Intrapersonal Attributes of the Communicatees." *J Abn & Social Psychol* 51:246–53 S '55. * (*PA* 30:4206)
329. JEFFERSON, FREDERICA YOUNG. *Fostering Cooperative Attitudes in Children Through an Action Program.* Doctor's thesis, Cornell University (Ithaca, N.Y.), 1956. (*DA* 16:1731)
330. McGUIRE, FREDERICK. "Psychological Comparison of Automobile Drivers: Accident- and Violation-Free Versus Accident-Violation-Incurring Drivers." *U S Armed Forces Med J* 7:1741–8 D '56. * (*PA* 31:3949)
331. SOPCHAK, ANDREW L. "Projective Study of Peter and His Parents: Revealing the Necessary Therapeutic Limitations." *J Child Psychiatry* 3:149–200 Ag '56. * (*PA* 31:8363)
332. BENNETT, CARSON MAHAN. *The Relationships Between Responses to Pupil Aggression and Selected Personality Characteristics of Student Teachers.* Doctor's thesis, University of Michigan (Ann Arbor, Mich.), 1957. (*DA* 18:1335)
333. BRANSON, BERNARD DAVID. *An Investigation of Manifest Anxiety and the Role of Discrimination of Self-Ideal Discrepancy and Complex Tasks.* Doctor's thesis, Syracuse University (Syracuse, N.Y.), 1957. (*DA* 17:2063)
334. CARPENTER, LEWIS G., JR. "Relation of Aggression in the Personality to Outcome With Electro-Convulsive Shock Therapy." *J General Psychol* 57:3–22 Jl '57. * (*PA* 33:8453)
335. LEWIS, JAMES FRANKLIN. *Characteristics of Highly Gifted Children: An Experimental Analysis.* Doctor's thesis, State University of Iowa (Iowa City, Iowa), 1957. (*DA* 19:731)
336. NEIBERG, NORMAN A. *The Effects of Induced Stress on the Management of Hostility in Essential Hypertension.* Doctor's thesis, Boston University (Boston, Mass.), 1957. (*DA* 17:1597)
337. BESWICK, D. G., AND COX, F. N. "Reputed Aggression and Dependence in Children." *Austral J Psychol* 10:144–50 S '58. *
338. DIAMOND, M. DAVID. "Role-Taking Ability and Schizophrenia." *J Clin Psychol* 14:321–4 Jl '58. * (*PA* 33:8770)
339. MORELLO, MICHAEL. *A Study of the Adjustive Behavior of Prison Inmates to Incarceration.* Doctor's thesis, Temple University (Philadelphia, Pa.), 1958. (*DA* 19:2149)
340. PAREEK, UDAI. "Studying Cultural Differences in Personality Development With the Help of Rosenzweig P-F Study." *J All-India Inst Mental Health* 1:115–23 Jl '58. * (*PA* 35:720)
341. ROBERTS, ALAN H., AND JESSOR, RICHARD. "Authoritarianism, Punitiveness, and Perceived Social Status." *J Abn & Social Psychol* 56:311–4 My '58. * (*PA* 33:9987)

342. KAMIYA, MIYEKO. "Psychiatric Studies on Leprosy." *Folia Psychiatrica et Neurologica Japonica* (Japan) 13:143–73 Jl '59. * (*PA* 34:6433)

343. LESSER, GERALD S. "Population Differences in Construct Validity." *J Consult Psychol* 23:60–5 F '59. * (*PA* 34:1039)

344. BREITHAUPT, JACK F. *The Effects of Intelligence and Orthopedic Handicap Upon Selected Personality Variables.* Doctor's thesis, Indiana University (Bloomington, Ind.), 1960. (*DA* 21:545)

345. CHOROST, SHERWOOD BRUCE. *Parental Child-Rearing Attitudes and Their Correlates in Adolescent Aggression.* Doctor's thesis, University of Texas (Austin, Tex.), 1960. (*DA* 21:2782)

346. BULATAO, JAIME CARLOS. *The Direction of Aggression in Clinically Depressed Women.* Doctor's thesis, Fordham University (New York, N.Y.), 1961. (*DA* 22:1249)

347. CUTTER, HENRY STURGIS GREW. *Aggressive Response Strength as a Function of Interference With Goal-Oriented Responses Near to and Far From Their Goal.* Doctor's thesis, Boston University (Boston), 1962. (*DA* 23:2608)

348. NATHAN, PETER. *A Comparative Investigation of Conceptual Ability in Relation to Frustration Tolerance.* Doctor's thesis, Washington University (St. Louis, Mo.), 1962. (*DA* 24:394)

349. CUTTER, HENRY S. G. "Aggressive Response Strength as a Function of Interference With Goal-Oriented Responses Near to and Far From Their Goal." *Psychol Rep* 12:855–61 Je '63. * (*PA* 38:6012)

350. GOLDBERG, PHILIP A. "Varieties of Failure and Assumed Similarity." *Psychol Rep* 13:19–22 Ag '63. * (*PA* 38:5850)

351. MONOSOFF, HARRIS. *The Comparative Effects of Rewarding, Punishing and Counterconditioning Verbal Aggressive Behavior.* Doctor's thesis, Stanford University (Stanford, Calif.), 1963. (*DA* 24:3423)

352. McGLOTHLIN, WILLIAM H.; COHEN, SIDNEY; AND McGLOTHLIN, MARCELLA S. "Short-Term Effects of LSD on Anxiety, Attitudes and Performance." *J Nerv & Mental Dis* 139:266–73 S '64. * (*PA* 39:7046)

353. MAISEL, RICHARD N. *Psychological Concomitants of Chronic Disease: A Study of Hansen's Disease and Pulmonary Tuberculosis Patients Who Are Fast and Slow Recoverers.* Doctor's thesis, University of Miami (Coral Gables, Fla.), 1964. (*DA* 25:5385)

354. MEGARGEE, EDWIN INGLEE. *Undercontrol and Overcontrol in Assaultive and Homicidal Adolescents.* Doctor's thesis, University of California (Berkeley, Calif.), 1964. (*DA* 25:2614)

355. VAN VURST, RAYNER. *An Investigation Into the Relationship Between Selected Personality Traits and Reactions to Frustration Among Religious Seminarians and Lay Students.* Master's thesis, University of Detroit (Detroit, Mich.), 1964.

356. WALLEN, NORMAN E.; SAMUELSON, CECIL O.; BREWER, JETTA J.; GERBER, STERLING K.; AND WOOLAVER, JOHN N. "A Comparison of Slightly and Severely Orthopedically Disabled and 'Normal' Adults on Several Psychological Tests." *Rehabil Counsel B* 8:50–7 D '64. *

357. WITTENBORN, J. R.; DEMPSTER, ARTHUR; MAURER, HELEN; AND PLANTE, MARC. "Pretreatment Individual Differences as Potential Predictors of Response to Pharmacology." *J Nerv & Mental Dis* 139:186–94 Ag '64. *

358. MARKS, SAMUEL B. *Some Factors Influencing the Ratings of Professional and Technical Personnel: An Exploratory Study.* Doctor's thesis, New York University (New York, N.Y.), 1965. (*DA* 26:2862)

359. WILLIAMS, STEPHEN GUION. *Temporal Experience and Schizophrenia: A Study of Time Orientation, Attitude, and Perspective.* Doctor's thesis, University of Houston (Houston, Tex.), 1965. (*DA* 26:6862)

360. WRIGHT, JACK M., AND HARVEY, O. J. "Attitude Change as a Function of Authoritarianism and Punitiveness." *J Pers & Social Psychol* 1:177–81 F '65. * (*PA* 39:7629)

361. ZUBIN, JOSEPH; ERON, LEONARD D.; AND SCHUMER, FLORENCE. *An Experimental Approach to Projective Techniques,* pp. 487–96. New York: John Wiley & Sons, Inc., 1965. Pp. xxi, 645. * (*PA* 39:15432)

362. BACHELIS, FAITH G. *Regional Origin, Personality, and Mothers' Attitudes of Jewish Day School Students.* Doctor's thesis, Yeshiva University (New York, N.Y.), 1966. (*DA* 28:1154B)

363. BROWN, L. B. "The Structure of Religious Belief." *J Sci Study Relig* 5:259–72 sp '66. * (*PA* 41:1465)

364. EMERICK, LONNIE A. *An Evaluation of Three Psychological Variables in Tonic and Clonic Stutterers and in Nonstutterers.* Doctor's thesis, Michigan State University (East Lansing, Mich.), 1966. (*DA* 28:317A)

365. MEGARGEE, EDWIN I. "Undercontrolled and Overcontrolled Personality Types in Extreme Antisocial Aggression." *Psychol Monogr* 80(3):1–29 '66. *

366. MISA, KENNETH FRANKLIN. *Cognitive, Personality, and Familial Correlates of Children's Occupational Preferences.* Doctor's thesis, St. John's University (Jamaica, N.Y.), 1966. (*DA* 28:1170B)

367. ROSANES, MARILYN BLITZER. *Psychological Correlates to Myopia Compared to Hyperopia and Emmetropia.* Doctor's thesis, Yeshiva University (New York, N.Y.), 1966. (*DA* 27:2125B)

368. SHOR, RONALD E.; ORNE, MARTIN T.; AND O'CONNELL, DONALD N. "Psychological Correlates of Plateau Hypnotizability in a Special Volunteer Sample." *J Pers & Social Psychol* 3:80–95 Ja '66. * (*PA* 40:2262)

369. WESSMAN, ALDEN E., AND RICKS, DAVID F. *Mood and Personality.* New York: Holt, Rinehart & Winston, Inc., 1966. Pp. xiii, 317. *

370. HARDY, MARY JOHNSTON. *A Study of Frustration and Height-Weight Classifications of College Women.* Master's thesis, Texas Woman's University (Denton, Tex.), 1967.

371. COETSIER, L.; LIEVENS, S.; AND VAN BAVINCKHOVE-OSSOLA. "Empirical Investigation Into the Reaction-Types to Frustration." *Proc Inter Congr Appl Psychol* 16:721–3 '68. *

372. CONNOLLY, CHRISTOPHER GEORGE. *The Psychosocial Adjustment of Children With Dyslexia.* Doctor's thesis, Northwestern University (Evanston, Ill.), 1968. (*DA* 29:3456A)

373. DVONCH, PATRICIA. *Anomie and Physical Disability: An Application of the Concept of Anomie to the Psychology of the Disabled.* Doctor's thesis, New York University (New York, N.Y.), 1968. (*DA* 29:478A)

374. HWANG, CHIEN-HOU. "Reactions of Chinese University Students to Rosenzweig's Picture-Frustration Study." *Psychol & Ed* (Taiwan) 2:37–48 D '68. *

375. LIEBERMAN, MARTHA. *Projective Responses of Retarded and Adequate Readers to Frustrating Academic vs. Nonacademic Situations.* Doctor's thesis, University of California (Berkeley, Calif.), 1968. (*DA* 29:3004A)

376. MIKAWA, JAMES K., AND BOSTON, JOHN A., JR. "Psychological Characteristics of Adopted Children." *Psychiatric Q Sup* 42(2):274–81 '68. * (*PA* 46:2740, 50:3077)

377. MINTZ, MARTIN MURRAY. *An Investigation of the Relationship Between Test Anxiety and Dependency Needs in Children.* Doctor's thesis, New York University (New York, N.Y.), 1968. (*DA* 29:2206B)

378. MUKERJI, KAMAL, AND BANERJEE, DEBABRATA. "Relationship Between the Direction of Aggression and Self-Perceived Problem-Variables Among a Group of Offenders." *Indian J Psychol* 43(1–4):37–40 '68. *

379. SPIVA, PHILIP GENESKY. *The Loser Syndrome in Juvenile Delinquents.* Doctor's thesis, University of Oklahoma (Norman, Okla.), 1968. (*DA* 29:2641B)

380. TIWARI, J. G., AND SHUKLA, S. N. "P-F and C.A.T. Responses of the Over- and Under-Chosen in Municipal Primary Schools of Aligarh." *Indian J Social Work* 28:467–70 Ja '68. * (*PA* 42:14495)

381. VARIAKOJIS, SUSAN J. *A Comparative Study of the Relationship Between Four Factors: Race, Sex, Intelligence, and Socio-Economic Class and the Extent to Which They Are Associated With the Rosenzweig P-F Study for Children.* Master's thesis, Kent State University (Kent, Ohio), 1968.

382. DUNLAP, EVA LOVELACE. *The Relationship Between Frustration Reaction and Occupational Training Success in a Group of Mentally Retarded Adolescents.* Doctor's thesis, Auburn University (Auburn, Ala.), 1969. (*DAI* 30:1863A)

383. EDWARDS, ALLAN E.; BLOOM, MARSHALL H.; AND COHEN, SIDNEY. "The Psychedelics: Love or Hostility Potion?" *Psychol Rep* 24(3):843–6 Je '69. * (*PA* 44:627)

384. HWANG, CHIEN-HOU. "Parent-Child Resemblance in Psychological Characteristics." *Psychol & Ed* (Taiwan) 3:29–36 D '69. *

385. KOSKI, MAIJA-LIISA. "The Coping Process in Childhood Diabetes." *Acta Paediatrica Scandinavica Supplement* (Sweden) 198:1–56 '69. *

386. KUMAR, PRAMOD. "Reaction to Frustration and Student Leadership." *J Psychol Res* (India) 13(1):12–5 Ja '69. *

387. MARTIN, LAWRENCE A. *The Effects of Competition Upon the Aggressive Responses of Basketball Players and Wrestlers.* Doctor's thesis, Springfield College (Springfield, Mass.), 1969.

388. MARUYAMA, YOSHIO. *The Sense of Competence in Middle Adolescent Boys.* Doctor's thesis, Boston University (Boston, Mass.), 1969. (*DAI* 30:2405B)

389. MUTHAYYA, B. C. "A Study of the Relationship Between Level of Aspiration and Reactions to Frustration." *Psychol Ann* 3:3–9 Mr '69. * (*PA* 46:6618)

390. O'CONNELL, WALTER E. "Creativity in Humor." *J Social Psychol* 78(2):237–41 Ag '69. * (*PA* 44:6948)

391. PERCZEL, J., AND PERCZEL, T. "Description and Measurement of Personality Traits by a Projective Technique and an Auto-Definition Questionnaire With Production Engineering Inspectors." *Brit J Proj Psychol & Pers Study* 14(1):27–9 Je '69. * (*PA* 46:5837)

392. PIERLOOT, ROLAND A., AND VAN ROY, JULIENNE. "Asthma and Aggression." *J Psychosom Res* (England) 13(4):333–7 D '69. * (*PA* 44:12652)

393. RECK, JON J.; McCARY, JAMES L.; AND WEATHERLY, J. K. "Intra-Familial Comparisons of Frustration-Aggression Patterns." *Psychol Rep* 25(2):356 O '69. * (*PA* 44:5177)

394. SARKAR, S. N. "Reactions of the Tribal Hindu and Tribal Christian Girls to Common Stress-Producing Situations." *Indian Psychol R* 5(2):146–9 Ja '69. *

395. SCHILL, THOMAS, AND BLACK, JOHN. "Differences in Reactions to Rosenzweig's P-F Study by Defensive and Nondefensive Repressors and Sensitizers." *Psychol Rep* 25(3):929–30 D '69. * (*PA* 44:18750)

Rosenzweig Picture-Frustration Study

396. WRIGHT, MARY RUTH, AND McCARY, J. L. "Positive Effects of Sex Information on Emotional Patterns of Behavior." *J Sex Res* 5(3):162-9 Ag '69. *

397. ADAR, LEA D. *An Investigation of the Relationship of Some Aspects of Frustration to Pulmonary Tuberculosis.* Doctor's thesis, New York University (New York, N.Y.), 1970. (*DAI* 31:4322B)

398. FARMELANT, MARSHA C. S. *An Investigation Into the Personality Characteristics and Family Relationships of Accident Prone Children.* Master's thesis, Smith College (Northampton, Mass.), 1970.

399. HAYASHI, KATSUZO, AND ICHITANI, TSUYOSHI. "Factorial Patterns of the Rosenzweig P-F Study." *Psychologia* (Japan) 13(4):181-91 D '70. * (*PA* 46:11173)

400. HINKLE, JOHN EDWARD. *A Study of Attitudes Toward Anger and the Expression or Inhibition of Anger in a Religious and Non-Religious Population.* Doctor's thesis, Northwestern University (Evanston, Ill.), 1970. (*DAI* 31:4256A)

401. LESTER, DAVID. "Attempts to Predict Suicidal Risk Using Psychological Tests." *Psychol B* 74(1):1-17 Jl '70. * (*PA* 44:16905)

402. LEVENSON, MARVIN, AND NEURINGER, CHARLES. "Intropunitiveness in Suicidal Adolescents." *J Proj Tech & Pers Assess* 34(5):409-11 O '70. * (*PA* 45:6621)

403. LUDWIG, DAVID J. "Evidence of Construct and Criterion-Related Validity for the Self-Concept." *J Social Psychol* 80(2):213-23 Ap '70. * (*PA* 44:14585)

404. NISENSON, R. *Aggressive Reactions to Frustration in Relation to the Individual Level of Extrapunitiveness.* Master's thesis, University of Pittsburgh (Pittsburgh, Pa.), 1970.

405. ROSENZWEIG, SAUL, AND BRAUN, STEPHEN H. "Adolescent Sex Differences in Reactions to Frustration as Explored by the Rosenzweig P-F Study." *J Genetic Psychol* 116(1):53-61 Mr '70. * (*PA* 44:14393)

406. WHITE, WILLIAM CLINTON, JR. *Selective Modeling in Youthful Offenders With High and Low O-H (Overcontrolled-Hostility) Personality Types.* Doctor's thesis, Florida State University (Tallahassee, Fla.), 1970. (*DAI* 31:5648B)

407. BAIRD, JOHN SANFORD, JR. *A Multivariate Developmental Study of Political Ideology and Intolerance.* Doctor's thesis, North Carolina State University (Raleigh, N.C.), 1971. (*DAI* 32:6633B)

408. HINES, TODD FRANKLIN. *A Multitrait-Multimethod Analysis of the Internal-External Control Concept.* Doctor's thesis, Washington University (St. Louis, Mo.), 1971. (*DAI* 32:5442B)

409. SCHWARTZBURD, LEONARD. *Reliability and Validity of the Timed Multiple Response Method of Administering the Rosenzweig Picture-Frustration Study.* Doctor's thesis, University of Oklahoma (Norman, Okla.), 1971. (*DAI* 32:4228B)

410. SELKIN, JAMES, AND MORRIS, JOLINE. "Some Behavioral Factors Which Influence the Recovery Rate of Suicide Attempters." *B Suicidol* 8:29-38 f '71. *

411. SINHA, RUBY. "Direction of Aggression and Reaction-Type in Relation to Personality Adjustment." *J Psychol Res* (India) 15(2):71-2 My '71. *

412. SIVANANDAM, CHANDRA. "A Study of Frustration-Reaction in Delinquent and Non-Delinquent Children." *Indian J Social Work* 32(2):151-4 Jl '71. * (*PA* 48:7472)

413. SPEEDIE, STUART; HOBSON, SANDRA; FELDHUSEN, JOHN; AND THURSTON, JOHN. "Evaluation of a Battery of Noncognitive Variables as Long-Range Predictors of Academic Achievement." Abstract. *Proc 79th Ann Conv Am Psychol Assn* 6(2):517-8 '71. * (*PA* 46:5708)

414. SVILAND, MARY ANN PETRICH. *Factors of Adaptation and Rehabilitation in Home Hemodialysis.* Doctor's thesis, University of Southern California (Los Angeles, Calif.), 1971. (*DAI* 32:4230B)

415. TAFT, RONALD. "Creativity: Hot and Cold." *J Personality* 39(3):345-61 S '71. * (*PA* 47:6804)

416. TEICHMAN, MEIR. "Ego Defense, Self-Concept and Image of Self Ascribed to Parents by Delinquent Boys." *Percept & Motor Skills* 32(3):819-23 Je '71. * (*PA* 47:3313)

CUMULATIVE NAME INDEX

[1501]

The Rotter Incomplete Sentences Blank. Grades 9-12, 13-16, adults; 1950; RISB; test booklet title is *Incomplete Sentences Blank;* Julian B. Rotter and Janet E. Rafferty (manual); Psychological Corporation. *

For additional information, see P:472 (35 references); see also 6:239 (17 references) and 5:156 (18 references); for reviews by Charles N. Cofer and William Schofield and an excerpted review by Adolf G. Woltmann, see 4:130 (6 references).

REFERENCES THROUGH 1971

1-6. See 4:130.
7-24. See 5:156.
25-41. See 6:239.
42-76. See P:472.
77. GLICK, HOWARD LEE. *Some Comparisons Between Narcotic Addicts, Schizophrenics, and Normal Individuals on the Basis of Rotter's Sentence Incomplete Blanks.* Master's thesis, Texas Christian University (Ft. Worth, Tex.), 1952.
78. BLYTH, DAVID DeWALLER. *Dependence, Independence, and Other Factors Related to Veterans' Reactions to an Offer of Psychotherapy.* Doctor's thesis, Ohio State University (Columbus, Ohio), 1953. (*DA* 20:2899)
79. MORTON, ROBERT B. "An Experiment in Brief Psychotherapy." *Psychol Monogr* 69(1):1-17 '55. * (*PA* 30:1112)
80. NEFF, JOHN WILLARD. *Individual Differences in Resistance to Extinction as a Function of Generalized Expectancy.* Doctor's thesis, Ohio State University (Columbus, Ohio), 1956. (*DA* 16:2213)
81. ESSRIG, HARRY. *The Nature of Chauvinism Among Jewish Adolescents.* Doctor's thesis, University of Michigan (Ann Arbor, Mich.), 1957. (*DA* 18:1335)
82. MASLING, JOSEPH M. "The Effects of Warm and Cold Interaction on the Interpretation of a Projective Protocol." *J Proj Tech* 21:377-83 D '57. * (*PA* 33:3852)
83. SHAFFER, JACOB ABRAHAM. *Parental Reinforcement, Parental Dominance, and Therapist Preference.* Doctor's thesis, Ohio State University (Columbus, Ohio), 1957. (*DA* 17:2310)
84. DUBIN, WILLIAM. *Toward a Definition of Effective Functioning.* Doctor's thesis, Columbia University (New York, N.Y.), 1958. (*DA* 18:1858)
85. GIER, JAMES DALE. *The Relationship of Physical Ability to Certain Psychological Scores and Ratings Among Mentally Retarded Boys.* Master's thesis, University of Washington (Seattle, Wash.), 1959.
86. OVERSTREET, PHOEBE LUCILLE. *Factors Associated With the Quality of Self-Evaluations.* Doctor's thesis, Columbia University (New York, N.Y.), 1959. (*DA* 20:761)
87. JOHNSON, LYNN ERIC. *Personality Changes in Emotionally Disturbed Students During Counseling.* Doctor's thesis, University of Utah (Salt Lake City, Utah), 1962. (*DA* 24:2985)
88. ANKENBRAND, RALPH J. *Identifying Students in the Junior High School Who Have Emotional, Social, and Educational Handicaps.* Master's thesis, Eastern Illinois University (Charleston, Ill.), 1963.
89. NICHOLSON, RICHARD C. *A Correlation Study of the Parole Behavior of Youth Offenders and Their Scores Made on the Rotter Incomplete Sentences Blank, High School Form.*

Master's thesis, Sacramento State College (Sacramento, Calif.), 1963.

90. TUTKO, THOMAS ARTHUR. *Need for Social Approval and Its Effect on Responses to Projective Tests.* Doctor's thesis, Northwestern University (Evanston, Ill.), 1963. (*DA* 24:3429)

91. CROWNE, DOUGLAS P., AND MARLOWE, DAVID. *The Approval Motive: Studies in Evaluative Dependence*, pp. 171–85. New York: John Wiley & Sons, Inc., 1964. Pp. xiii, 233. *

92. ROSE, HARRIETT ABRAHAM. *Prediction and Prevention of Freshman Attrition.* Doctor's thesis, University of Kentucky (Lexington, Ky.), 1964. (*DAI* 31:2264B)

93. SHELL, STANLEY A., JR.; O'MALLY, JAMES M.; AND JOHNSGARD, KEITH W. "The Semantic Differential and Inferred Identification." *Psychol Rep* 14:547–58 Ap '64. * (*PA* 39:2768)

94. GAY, JAMES DONALD. *Personality Changes Associated With Workshop Participation.* Doctor's thesis, University of Kentucky (Lexington, Ky.), 1965. (*DAI* 30:2436B)

95. GOLDBERG, PHILIP A. "A Review of Sentence Completion Methods in Personality Assessment." *J Proj Tech & Pers Assess* 29:12–45 Mr '65. * (*PA* 39:10112)

96. HIRSCHENFANG, SAMUEL, AND BENTON, JOSEPH G. "Assessment of Phantom Limb Sensation Among Patients With Lower Extremity Amputation." *J Psychol* 63:197–9 Jl '66. * (*PA* 40: 10150)

97. COHEN, STUART JORDAN. *Effects of Situational Stress and Failure Expectancies on College Examination Performance.* Doctor's thesis, University of Connecticut (Storrs, Conn.), 1967. (*DA* 28:3468B)

98. THURSTON, JOHN R.; BRUNCLIK, HELEN L.; AND FELDHUSEN, JOHN F. *The Prediction of Success in Nursing Education: Phase I and II, 1959–67; A Manual for the Luther Hospital Sentence Completions and the Nursing Sentence Completions.* An unpublished report to the Division of Nursing, National Institutes of Health, Research Grant NU 00018–07, Luther Hospital (Eau Claire, Wis.), 1967. Pp. xvi, 265. *

99. ATCHISON, CALVIN O. "Relationships Between Some Intellectual and Non-Intellectual Factors of High Anxiety and Low Anxiety Negro College Students." *J Negro Ed* 37:174–8 sp '68. *

100. BOHM, KENNETH HERBERT. *Group Behavior and Freedom of Movement as Measured by Locus of Reinforcement Control and Time Orientation.* Doctor's thesis, St. Louis University (St. Louis, Mo.), 1968. (*DAI* 30:3381B)

101. BURT, ROGER BIVENS. *An Exploratory Study of Personality Manifestations in Paintings.* Doctor's thesis, Duke University (Durham, N.C.), 1968. (*DA* 29:1493B)

102. SPIVA, PHILIP GENESKY. *The Loser Syndrome in Juvenile Delinquents.* Doctor's thesis, University of Oklahoma (Norman, Okla.), 1968. (*DA* 29:2641B)

103. FITZGERALD, OWEN RAY. *Psychodynamics of Volunteers Serving Overseas: Religious Vocation Workers and Peace Corps Volunteers in a North African Country.* Doctor's thesis, Boston University (Boston, Mass.), 1969. (*DAI* 30:2126A)

104. McCARTHY, BARRY WAYNE. *Effect of Need for Approval and Self-Concept Scores on the Measurement of Adjustment.* Doctor's thesis, Southern Illinois University (Carbondale, Ill.), 1969. (*DAI* 30:4817B)

105. SCHLICHT, WILLIAM J., JR.; CARLSON, HILMER J.; SKEEN, DAVID R.; AND SKURDAL, MARLO A. "Self-Images Without Awareness and Projective Methods of Personality Assessment." *J Proj Tech & Pers Assess* 33(5):419–21 O '69. * (*PA* 44:3658)

106. SCHWARZ, J. CONRAD. "Contribution of Generalized Expectancy to Stated Expectancy Under Conditions of Success and Failure." *J Pers & Social Psychol* 11(2):157–64 F '69. * (*PA* 43:7656)

107. WOOD, FRANK A. "An Investigation of Methods of Presenting Incomplete Sentence Stimuli." *J Abn Psychol* 74(1): 71–4 F '69. * (*PA* 43:8465)

108. ALBERT, GERALD. "Sentence Completions as a Measure of Progress in Therapy." *J Cont Psychother* 3(1):31–4 su '70. * (*PA* 46:1417)

109. BAKER, ROBERT P., AND KING, HOLLIS H. "The Relationship Between the Repression-Sensitization Scale and the Incomplete Sentences Blank." *J Proj Tech & Pers Assess* 34(6): 492–6 D '70. * (*PA* 45:8253)

110. CARPENTER, JAMES CLINTON. *Patterns of Self-Disclosure and Confirmation in Mother-Daughter Communication.* Doctor's thesis, Ohio State University (Columbus, Ohio), 1970. (*DAI* 31:4331B)

111. CHAWLA, TILAK R. "Adjustment and Academic Achievement." *Psychol Studies* (India) 15(1):13–6 Ja '70. *

112. KATKOVSKY, WALTER. "Denial Reactions and Maladjustment." Abstract. *Proc 78th Ann Conv Am Psychol Assn* 5(1): 345–6 '70. * (*PA* 44:18671)

113. MURSTEIN, BERNARD I., AND WOLF, STEVEN R. "Empirical Test of the 'Levels' Hypothesis With Five Projective Techniques." *J Abn Psychol* 75(1):38–44 F '70. * (*PA* 44:6794)

114. STEPHENS, MARK W. "Stimulus Pull as a Determinant of Individual Differences in Sentence Completion Responses." *J Proj Tech & Pers Assess* 34(4):332–9 Ag '70. * (*PA* 44:21010)

115. VERNALLIS, FRANCIS F.; SHIPPER, JOHN C.; BUTLER, DONALD C.; AND TOMLINSON, T. M. "Saturation Group Psychotherapy in a Weekend Clinic: An Outcome Study." *Psychother Theory Res & Prac* 7(3):144–52 f '70. * (*PA* 45:4416)

116. AGUADO, ROBERT STANLEY. *An Investigation of the Psychodynamics of Black Junior College Freshmen With Reading Disabilities Utilizing the Rotter Incomplete Sentences Blank and Psychoanalytic Theory as Psychodiagnostic Tools for Counseling.* Doctor's thesis, University of Southern California (Los Angeles, Calif.), 1971. (*DAI* 32:3081A)

117. BAEKELAND, FREDERICK, AND HARTMANN, ERNEST. "Reported Sleep Characteristics: Effects of Age, Sleep Length and Psychiatric Impairment." *Comprehen Psychiatry* 12(2):141–7 Mr '71. * (*PA* 47:7185)

118. BANIKIOTES, PAUL G.; RUSSELL, JOHN M.; AND LINDEN, JAMES D. "Social Desirability, Adjustment and Effectiveness." *Psychol Rep* 29(2):581–2 O '71. * (*PA* 47:8896)

119. JENNINGS, LILLIAN PEGUES. *Selected Case Studies of Students in a Teacher Education Field Experience Program.* Doctor's thesis, University of Pittsburgh (Pittsburgh, Pa.), 1971. (*DAI* 32:3051A)

120. KORELLA, KARL. *Teen-Age Suicidal Gestures: A Study of Suicidal Behavior Among High School Students.* Doctor's thesis, University of Oregon (Eugene, Ore.), 1971. (*DAI* 32:5039A)

121. McCARTHY, BARRY W., AND RAFFERTY, JANET E. "Effect of Social Desirability and Self-Concept Scores on the Measurement of Adjustment." *J Pers Assess* 35(6):576–83 D '71. * (*PA* 47:10891)

122. NEUBECK, ROBERT CHARLES. *Variables Affecting Ratings of Pathology on Test Protocols.* Doctor's thesis, Southern Illinois University (Carbondale, Ill.), 1971. (*DAI* 32:4865B)

123. PETERSON, VERNON OLIF. *A Clinical and Longitudinal Study of Anxiety and Attitudinal Trends in College Students Using a Projective Test as a Disguised Technique.* Doctor's thesis, University of Wisconsin (Madison, Wis.), 1971. (*DAI* 32:4868B)

124. RICHARDSON, LEROY, AND SOUCAR, EMIL. "Comparison of Cognitive Complexity With Achievement and Adjustment: A Convergent-Discriminant Study." *Psychol Rep* 29(3):1087–90 D '71. * (*PA* 48:1011)

CUMULATIVE NAME INDEX

Peterson, V. O.: 123
Prentice, N. M.: 33
Pruitt, R. C.: 12
Rafferty, J. E.: 6, 11, 13, 121
Reid, J. W.: 15
Renner, K. E.: 37
Richardson, L.: 124
Rose, H. A.: 54, 58, 92
Rotter, J. B.: 2–4, 6, 11, 13
Russell, J. M.: 118
Sarason, I. G.: 50
Schachtitz, E.: 6
Scheibe, K. E.: 64
Schlicht, W. J.: 75, 105
Schmitt, J. A.: 27
Schofield, W.: rev, 4:130
Schwarz, J. C.: 106
Sechrest, L.: 41
Sechrest, L. B.: 14
Shaffer, J. A.: 83
Shell, S. A.: 93
Shipper, J. C.: 115
Skeen, D. R.: 75, 105
Skurdal, M. A.: 75, 105
Smith, A.: 40
Smith, W. E.: 8
Sohler, D. T.: 23

Soucar, E.: 124
Spiva, P. G.: 102
Stack, J. J.: 48
Stark, M. J.: 52
Stephens, M. W.: 32, 114
Stricker, G.: 59
Sutker, A. R.: 19
Theiner, E. C.: 38
Thurston, J. R.: 76, 98
Tindall, R. H.: 18
Tomlinson, T. M.: 115
Tutko, T. A.: 90
Vernallis, F. F.: 115
Walker, C. E.: 68
Wallace, J.: 41
Walsh, J.: 53
Walter, D.: 50
Walter, V. A.: 9, 21
Webb, M. W.: 70
Weiss, S. D.: 72
Willerman, B.: 3
Wischner, G. J.: 4
Wolf, S. R.: 113
Woltmann, A. G.: exc, 4:130
Wood, F. A.: 69, 107
Worthington, A. M. L.: 44
Yoshpe, S. R.: 28

[1502]

The Ruth Fry Symbolic Profile. Ages 14 and over; 1959–61; RFSP; no manual; Ruth Thacker Fry; C. G. Jung Educational Center. *

[1503]

School Apperception Method. Grades kgn–9; 1968; SAM; Irving L. Solomon and Bernard D. Starr; Springer Publishing Co., Inc. *
For additional information and reviews by Willard E. Reitz and Norman D. Sundberg, see 7:176 (1 reference); see also P:473 (2 references).

REFERENCES THROUGH 1971
1–2. See P:473.
3. See 7:176.

CUMULATIVE NAME INDEX
Klein, M. I.: 1
Reitz, W. E.: rev, 7:176
Solomon, I. L.: 1–2
Starr, B. D.: 1–3
Sundberg, N. D.: rev, 7:176

[1504]

The Self Explorations Inventory. College and adults; 1966; SEI; for research use only; no scores, 12 questions allowing for "projective-type" responses; Sheldon J. Lachman; Psychological Publications Press. *
For additional information, see 7:177.

[1505]

Self Valuation Test. Ages 7–15, adults; 1957; test booklet title is *S.V.T.*; verbal and nonverbal projective test employing several stimuli simultaneously; 2 levels; John Liggett; J. & P. Bealls Ltd. [England]. *
a) [FORM FOR CHILDREN.] Ages 7–15.
b) [FORMS FOR ADULTS.] Adults; forms also available under the title *Faces Test.*
For additional information, see P:473A (3 references); see also 5:157 (2 references).

REFERENCES THROUGH 1971
1–2. See 5:157.
3–5. See P:473A.
6. LIGGETT, JOHN. "10 Years Research With the Self Valuation Test: Validity, Reliability and Factor Analytical Studies." *Int Congr Rorsch & Other Proj Tech* 7:651–2 '70. *

CUMULATIVE NAME INDEX
Liggett, J.: 1–6

[1506]

Sentence Completion Blank. College and adults; 1955–66; SCB; Sheldon J. Lachman; Psychological Publications Press. *
For additional information, see 7:178.

[1507]

★Sentence Completion Test. High school and college; 1972; SCT; 35 item scores in 6 areas: self concept, parental attitude, peer attitude, need for achievement, learning attitude, body image; Floyd S. Irvin; Psychologists and Educators, Inc. *

REFERENCES THROUGH 1971
1. IRVIN, FLOYD S. "Adjective Check List Correlates of Positive and Negative Sentence Completion Responses." *J Clin Psychol* 23:419–21 O '67. * (*PA* 42:2582)
2. IRVIN, FLOYD S. "Sentence-Completion Responses and Scholastic Success or Failure." *J Counsel Psychol* 14:269–71 My '67. * (*PA* 41:9367)
3. LAPLANTE, MARGARET J. *An Investigation of the Relation of Sentence Completion Scales to Academic Aptitude and Achievement.* Master's thesis, Loyola University (Chicago, Ill.), 1969.
4. IRVIN, FLOYD S., AND JOHNSON, MARIE L. "Effect of Differential Instructional Set on Sentence Completion Responses." *J Consult & Clin Psychol* 34(3):319–22 Je '70. * (*PA* 44:14633)
5. LAPLANTE, MARGARET J., AND IRVIN, FLOYD S. "Sentence-Completion Responses and Academic Performance Re-Examined." *J Proj Tech & Pers Assess* 34(3):219–22 Je '70. * (*PA* 44:19342)

CUMULATIVE NAME INDEX
Irvin, F. S.: 1–2, 4–5
Johnson, M. L.: 4
LaPlante, M. J.: 3, 5

[1508]

Seven Squares Technique. Ages 5 and over; 1952–68; SST; also called *7-Squares Test;* no set scoring or interpretation procedures; Heinz Hector; English translation of manual by Daniel James Bradley; Skandinaviska Testförlaget AB [Sweden]. *
For additional information, see 7:179 (18 references).

REFERENCES THROUGH 1971
1–18. See 7:179.

CUMULATIVE NAME INDEX
Bradley, D. J.: 8, 12, 14, 16–7
Dana, R. H.: 10, 15
Dlodlo, M. S.: 9
Du Plessis, C. F.: 9
Fabian, H.: 3
Hector, H.: 4–5, 9, 11, 13, 18
Hudson, W.: 5
Ichimura, K.: 6
Morgan, P.: 7
Shmukler, D.: 13
Voigt, W. H.: 10
Yssel, G. J.: 1–2

[1509]

Social Relations Test. Adult males; 1960–66; test booklet title is *S.R.T.*; no manual; [J. C. de Ridder and Lynette Shaw]; Industrial Psychological Services [South Africa]. *
For additional information, see P:473B (1 reference).

REFERENCES THROUGH 1971
1. See P:473B.
2. SPANGENBERG, H. H. "The Use of Projective Tests in the Selection of Bus Drivers." *Traffic Safety Res R* 12:118–21 D '68. *
3. SHAW, LYNETTE, AND SICHEL, HERBERT S. *Accident Proneness: Research in the Occurrence, Causation, and Prevention of Road Accidents,* pp. 299–371. Oxford, England: Pergamon Press Ltd., 1971. Pp. xiv, 476. * (*PA* 47:5920, title only)

CUMULATIVE NAME INDEX
Shaw, L.: 1, 3
Sichel, H. S.: 3
Spangenberg, H. H.: 2

[1510]

The Sound-Apperception Test. Ages 16 and over; 1965; "unstructured sounds much like auditory equivalents of ink blots" and 16 "semi-structured sound effects that reveal fantasy and dynamics of interpersonal situations"; 10 scores: reality orientation, like-indifferent-dislike, loss of life, physical aggression, nonphysical aggression, internalized emotional stress, positive reassurance, total, failure, success; Kenneth L. Bean; Sound Apperception Test Distributor. *
For additional information, see P:474 (3 references).

REFERENCES THROUGH 1971
1–3. See P:474.

CUMULATIVE NAME INDEX
Bean, K. L.: 1–3
Moore, J. R.: 1

[1511]

The South African Picture Analysis Test. Ages 5–13; 1960, c1959; SAPAT; 8 interpretive categories: condition of hero, environmental pressure, needs, reactions, characteristics of stories (4 categories); B. F. Nel and A. J. K. Pelser; Swets & Zeitlinger [The Netherlands]. *

For additional information, see P :475; for reviews by S. G. Lee and Johann M. Schepers and an excerpted review by Wilson H. Guertin, see 6 :240.

[1512]

Structured Doll Play Test. Ages 2–6; 1959–60; SDPT; family and peer relationships; 2 forms; David B. Lynn; Test Developments. *
a) [SERIES 1.] 1959.
b) [SERIES 2.] 1959–60; for research use only.

For additional information, see P :476; for reviews by Terence Moore and Alan O. Ross, see 6 :241 (6 references).

REFERENCES THROUGH 1971

1–6. See 6 :241.
7. LYNN, DAVID B., AND SAWREY, WILLIAM L. "Sex Differences in the Personality Development of Norwegian Children." *J Genetic Psychol* 101 :367–74 D '62. * (*PA* 37 :6473)

CUMULATIVE NAME INDEX

Lynn, D. B.: 1–2, 4–5, 7   Ross, A. O.: *rev,* 6 :241
Lynn, R.: 3, 5–6   Sawrey, W. L.: 7
Moore, T.: *rev,* 6 :241

[1513]

Structured-Objective Rorschach Test: Preliminary Edition. Adults; 1958; SORT; also called *S-O Rorschach Test;* 15 scores (for deriving 26 traits): whole-blot (W), major details (D), minor details (Dd), white space (S), form resemblance (F), poor form resemblance (F–), human movement (M), animal movement (FM), color and form resemblance (FC), color and poor form resemblance (CF), shading (Fch), animal figure (A), human figure (H), modal responses (P), rare responses (O); Joics B. Stone; [S-O Publishers]. *

For additional information, see P :477 (33 references); for reviews by Jesse G. Harris, Jr. and Boris Semeonoff and excerpted reviews by Edward S. Bordin and Laurence Siegel, see 6 :242 (16 references).

REFERENCES THROUGH 1971

1–16. See 6 :242.
17–49. See P :477.
50. CHANSKY, NORMAN M. "Report Cards and Teacher Personality." *J Ed Res* 57 :492–4 My–Je '64. *
51. JOHNSTON, JAMES ORRIN. *Relationships Between Intelligence and Personality Variables.* Doctor's thesis, Oklahoma State University (Stillwater, Okla.), 1965. (*DA* 27 :315B)
52. WICAS, EDWARD A., AND MAHAN, THOMAS W., JR. "Characteristics of Counselors Rated Effective by Supervisors and Peers." *Counselor Ed & Sup* 6 :50–6 f '66. * (*PA* 42 :63)
53. MAHONEY, M. FRANCES. *An Investigation Into Temperament and Teacher Potentiality in Selected Groups of College Women Students.* Doctor's thesis, St. John's University (Jamaica, N.Y.), 1967. (*DA* 28 :4284B)
54. STONE, JOICS B. "Data Congruent With Weinlander's Analysis." *Percept & Motor Skills* 24 :204 F '67. * (*PA* 41 :8937)
55. HARTNELL, AGNES ALBERY. *An Assessment of Attitude and Personality Correlations of Title I Inservice Teachers.* Doctor's thesis, Arizona State University (Tempe, Ariz.), 1968. (*DA* 29 :1464A)
56. BLAKEY, JAMES. *Relationship Among Measures of Perceptual Rigidity and Aspects of Religion.* Doctor's thesis, Rutgers—The State University (New Brunswick, N.J.), 1969. (*DAI* 31 :1066A)
57. SCHLICHT, WILLIAM J., JR.; CARLSON, HILMER J.; SKEEN, DAVID R.; AND SKURDAL, MARLO A. "Self-Images Without Awareness and Projective Methods of Personality Assessment." *J Proj Tech & Pers Assess* 33(5) :419–23 O '69. * (*PA* 44 :3658)
58. MOHR, KENT EDWARD. *An Evaluation of Marathon Group Procedures and Leaders as Measured by the Structured Objective Rorschach Test (S.O.R.T.).* Doctor's thesis, Indiana University (Bloomington, Ind.), 1970. (*DAI* 31 :2741A)

59. NAU, LOUIS YEHLING. *A Projective Analysis of Adult Learner Personality Attributes.* Doctor's thesis, Arizona State University (Tempe, Ariz.), 1971. (*DAI* 31 :6332A)

CUMULATIVE NAME INDEX

Angelino, H.: 2   Lewis, J. N.: 35
Bailey, R. W.: 19   Little, E. L.: 12
Bellrose, B.: 33   McKain, C. W.: 21
Blakey, J.: 56   Mahan, T. W.: 22, 52
Bordin, E. S.: *exc,* 6 :242   Mahoney, M. F.: 53
Bradberry, R. D.: 47   Mink, O. G.: 5
Broe, J. R.: 17   Mohr, K. E.: 58
Buchan, L. G.: 33   Nau, L. Y.: 59
Carlisle, A. L.: 14   Norton, J. L.: 11
Carlson, H. J.: 57   Norton, R.: 29
Chansky, N. M.: 20, 23, 50   Ortiz, J. D.: 33
Cooke, N. B.: 24   Osborne, R. T.: 6
Downs, H. S.: 18   Perry, M. L.: 16
Gallagher, R. P.: 48   Phillips, B. N.: 36
Goetzinger, C. P.: 33   Rankin, R. J.: 37
Hall, R. L.: 2   Schlicht, W. J.: 57
Hammes, J. A.: 6   Segel, R. H.: 41
Hampton, P. J.: 3   Semeonoff, B.: *rev,* 6 :242
Harris, F. E.: 40   Sharp, H. C.: 15
Harris, J. G.: *rev,* 6 :242   Siegel, L.: *exc,* 6 :242
Hartnell, A. A.: 55   Skeen, D. R.: 57
Hayes, W. G.: 14–5   Skurdal, M. A.: 57
Hick, T. L.: 25, 27–8, 34   Steinberg, M.: 41
Hicks, J. A.: 7   Stone, J. B.: 7, 54
Hosford, P. M.: 4   Thompson, K.: 37
Johnston, J. O.: 51   Vinson, D. B.: 13
Khan, L.: 1, 8   Weinlander, A. A.: 38, 49
Kirchner, W. K.: 26   Weinlander, M. M.: 31–2, 39,
Langer, P.: 9–10, 14–5, 21,   42–6
  27–30, 34   Wicas, E. A.: 22, 52
Law, D. H.: 11   Wood, C. G.: 30
Levine, H. D.: 41

[1514]

Symbol Elaboration Test. Ages 6 and over; 1950–53; SET; Johanna Krout; [Johanna Krout Tabin]. *

For additional information, see P :478; for a review by Richard H. Dana, see 5 :160 (1 reference).

REFERENCES THROUGH 1971

1. See 5 :160.

CUMULATIVE NAME INDEX

Dana, R. H.: *rev,* 5 :160   Krout, J.: 1

[1515]

Symonds Picture-Story Test. Grades 7–12; 1948; SPST; Percival M. Symonds; Teachers College Press. *

For additional information, see P :479 (5 references); for reviews by Walter Kass and Kenneth R. Newton, see 5 :161 (2 references); for a review by E. J. G. Bradford and an excerpted review by Robert R. Holt, see 4 :132 (2 references). For excerpts from related book reviews, see 4 :133 (11 excerpts).

REFERENCES THROUGH 1971

1–2. See 4 :132.
3–4. See 5 :161.
5–9. See P :479.
10. FIELDING, BENJAMIN BLUMENFELD. "A 'Story Completion' for Use With the Physically Handicapped." *J Proj Tech* 15 :299–306 S '51. * (*PA* 26 :4168)
11. GELFOND, ABRAHAM. *The Relationship of the Onset of Pubescence to Certain Interpersonal Attitudes in Girls.* Doctor's thesis, New York University (New York, N.Y.), 1952. (*DA* 12 :721)
12. FEINER, ARTHUR H. *A Study of Certain Aspects of the Perception of Parental Figures and Sexual Identifications of an Obese Adolescent Female Group.* Doctor's thesis, New York University (New York, N.Y.), 1954. (*DA* 14 :868)
13. HYATT, ISADORE. *Apperceptive Values and Adjustments Differentiating Delinquents and Non-Delinquents.* Doctor's thesis, Temple University (Philadelphia, Pa.), 1958. (*DA* 19 :362)
14. SILVER, ALBERT W., AND DERR, JOHN. "A Comparison of Selected Personality Variables Between Parents of Delinquent and Non-Delinquent Adolescents." *J Clin Psychol* 22 :49–50 Ja '66. * (*PA* 40 :4414)
15. HUMES, CHARLES WARREN, JR. *Group Counseling With Educable Mentally Retarded Adolescents in a Public School Setting: A Description of the Process and a Quantitative Assessment of Its Effectiveness.* Doctor's thesis, University of Massachusetts (Amherst, Mass.), 1968. (*DA* 29 :1105A)

16. Spiva, Philip Genesky. *The Loser Syndrome in Juvenile Delinquents.* Doctor's thesis, University of Oklahoma (Norman, Okla.), 1968. *(DA* 29:2641B)
17. Hall, Lincoln H. "Selective Variables in the Academic Achievement of Junior College Students From Different Socioeconomic Backgrounds." *J Ed Res* 63(2):60–2 O '69. *
18. Rosenquist, Carl M., and Megargee, Edwin I. *Delinquency in Three Cultures,* pp. 334–74. Austin, Tex.: University of Texas Press, 1969. Pp. xvi, 554. *

CUMULATIVE NAME INDEX

Ansari, A.: 9
Arthur, H.: *exc,* 4:133
Balken, E. R.: *exc,* 4:133
Bentley, M.: *exc,* 4:133
Blake, R. R.: *exc,* 4:133
Bradford, E. J. G.: *rev,* 4:132
Derr, J.: 14
Farrell, J. R.: 6
Feiner, A. H.: 12
Fielding, B. B.: 10
Fine, H. J.: 3
Gelfond, A.: 11
Gorlow, L.: 3
Grimshaw, J. A.: *exc,* 4:133
Hall, L. H.: 17
Holt, R. R.: *exc,* 4:132
Houlahan, F. J.: *exc,* 4:133

Humes, C. W.: 15
Hyatt, I.: 13
Jensen, A. R.: 4, 8
Kanner, L.: 4:133
Kass, W.: *rev,* 5:161
Lippman, H. S.: *exc,* 4:133
Megargee, E. I.: 18
Newton, K. R.: *rev,* 5:161
Powell, M.: *exc,* 4:133
Rosenquist, C. M.: 18
Shaffer, L. F.: *exc,* 4:133
Sherman, R. L.: 5
Silver, A. W.: 14
Spiva, P. G.: 16
Stickler, J. I.: 7
Symonds, P. M.: 1–2, 4, 8
Zimet, C. N.: 3

[1516]

Szondi Test. Ages 5 and over; 1937–65; ST; 8 factors, 4 vectors (each vector is a total of 2 factors): homosexual, sadistic, sexual vector, epileptic, hysteric, paroxysmal vector, catatonic, paranoic, schizophrenic vector, depressive, manic, contact vector; 2 editions; Lipot Szondi; Hans Huber [Switzerland]. *
a) [INDIVIDUAL] SZONDI TEST. 1937–65; English translation of manual by Gertrude Aull is out of print. (United States distributor: Grune & Stratton, Inc.)
b) THE GROUP SZONDI TEST. 1961; adapted for group administration by A. Friedemann. (United States distributor: Williams & Wilkins Co.)

For additional information, see P:480 (24 references); see also 6:243 (21 references) and 5:162 (74 references); for reviews by Ardie Lubin and Albert I. Rabin, see 4:134 (67 references); for a review by Susan K. Deri, see 3:100. For excerpts from related book reviews, see 7:B95 (1 excerpt), 6:B474 (3 excerpts), 6:B501 (2 excerpts), 5:B418 (3 excerpts), and 4:135 (9 excerpts).

REFERENCES THROUGH 1971

1–64. See 4:134.
65–138. See 5:162.
139–159. See 6:243.
160–183. See P:480.
184. Jansic, Anthony. "The Szondi Technique." *Persona* 1:7–9 w '48–49. * *(PA* 24:187)
185. Holt, Robert R. "An Approach to the Validation of the Szondi Test Through a Systematic Study of Unreliability." Abstract. *Am Psychologist* 4:269 Jl '49. * *(PA* 23:6211, title only)
186. Calabresi, Renata A. "Repression and Control in Psychological Tests: Illustrative Cases." *Case Rep Clin Psychol* 2:42–51 S '51. * *(PA* 27:4244)
187. Metsky, Marvin. *The Effects of Photographic Clarity on the Choice of Szondi Pictures.* Doctor's thesis, New York University (New York, N.Y.), 1953. *(DA* 13:723)
188. Starer, Emanuel. "A Study of Preferences for Photographs of Men in Different Professions." *J Proj Tech* 18:510–4 D '54. * *(PA* 29:7323)
189. Bendel, R. "The Modified Szondi Test in Male Homosexuality." *Int J Sexol* 8:226–7 My '55. * *(PA* 30:3085)
190. Smith, G., and Kragh, U. "Do Micro-Genetic Sequences Reflect Life History? An Illustration." *Acta Psychologica* (Netherlands) 11(4):504–12 '55. * *(PA* 30:7180)
191. Stumper, E. "The Modified Szondi Test in Male Homosexuality." *Int J Sexol* 8:228–9 My '55. * *(PA* 30:3128)
192. Fleishman, Martin. "The Investigation of Changes in Directional Reactions on the Szondi Test." *J General Psychol* 54:197–202 Ap '56. * *(PA* 33:1262)
193. Shipman, William G. "Similarity of Personality in the Sociometric Preferences of Mental Patients." *J Clin Psychol* 13:292–4 Jl '57. * *(PA* 32:5754)
194. Van Krevelen, Alice. "Judgments of Personality Traits in the Self and Others." *J Clin Psychol* 14:178–9 Ap '58. * *(PA* 33:5798)

195. Lindzey, Gardner. "On the Classification of Projective Techniques." *Psychol B* 56:158–68 Mr '59. * *(PA* 34:1389)
196. Cottingham, Alice Luisa. *Defensive Organization of Personality and Its Relation to the Prediction of Progress in Therapy.* Doctor's thesis, New York University (New York, N.Y.), 1963. *(DA* 25:1332)
197. Deri, Susan K. "Genotropism in the Framework of a Unified Theory of Choice." *Schweizerische Zeitschrift für Psychologie und Ihre Anwendungen* (Switzerland) 47:39–74 '63. *
198. Krass, Alvin. *A Comparative Study of Attitude Towards Authority Among Parents of Institutionalized Antisocial Boys and Parents of Non-Antisocial Boys.* Doctor's thesis, New York University (New York, N.Y.), 1965. *(DA* 27:396A)
199. Webb, M. W. "Predicting Surgical Results in Intractable Duodenal Ulcer." *Schweizerische Zeitschrift für Psychologie und Ihre Anwendungen* (Switzerland) 51:252–72 '66. *
200. Benincasa, Benjamin D. "Szondi-Diagnostic and Electro-Encephalographic Correlation Studies in Paroxysmal Cerebral Dysrhythmia in School Children." *Psychol* 5:74–80 N '68. * *(PA* 43:5774)
201. Borg, Jaakko G. *On Perception of Photoportraits of Abnormal Individuals: A Study of the Szondi Collection by Parallel Series.* Acta Universitatis Tamperensis, Series A, Vol. 21. Tampere, Finland: University of Tampere, 1968. Pp. 171. *
202. Borg, Jaakko G. *Apprehension of Abnormality: "Semantic Differential" Studies With the Szondi Portraits.* Reports From the Department of Psychology, University of Tampere, No. 39. Tampere, Finland: University of Tampere, 1969. Pp. 20. *
203. Suinn, Richard M., and Oskamp, Stuart. *The Predictive Validity of Projective Measures: A Fifteen-Year Evaluative Review of Research,* pp. 101–5, 132–3. Springfield, Ill.: Charles C Thomas, Publisher, 1969. Pp. xv, 161. *
204. Köhle, K., and Simons, C. "Psychodynamic Aspects in Young Patients Suffering From Peripheral Vascular Occlusions." *Psychother & Psychosom* (Switzerland) 18(1–6):313–20 '70. * *(PA* 47:5516)
205. Painton, Max Bennett. *A Clinical Validation of the Szondi Test.* Doctor's thesis, University of Oklahoma (Norman, Okla.), 1970. *(DAI* 31:3712B)
206. Thorén, A. "The Statistical Analysis of the Valence Quality of the Szondi-Pictures." *Schweizerische Zeitschrift für Psychologie und Ihre Anwendungen—Szondiana VIII* (Switzerland) 54:247–58 '71. *
207. Webb, M. "A Comparison of Electrocorticographic and Electromyographic Activity With Behavioral Patterns Portrayed in the Szondi Test During Normal States and During Regression in the Hypnotic State." *Schweizerische Zeitschrift für Psychologie und Ihre Anwendungen—Szondiana VIII* (Switzerland) 54:129–46 '71. *

CUMULATIVE NAME INDEX

Abel, T. M.: 140
Aumack, L.: 128
Balint, M.: 4
Ball, M. T.: 68
Balogh, B.: 174
Baratz, S. S.: 148
Barraclough, P.: 71
Beardsley, K.: 149
Bedford, G. S.: 16
Beeli, A.: 150
Bell, J. E.: 5, 7
Bendel, R.: 189
Benincasa, B. D.: 200
Bennett, G. K.: *exc,* 4:135
Best, H. L.: 62, 89
Blazsanyik, J.: 141, 151
Blessing, H. D.: 16
Blumer, D.: 176
Booth, G.: 161
Borg, J. G.: 201–2
Borstelmann, L. J.: 17–8, 30, 39–40, 90
Cahill, R. F.: 41
Calabresi, R. A.: 6, 8, 186
Campos, L. P.: 182
Caston, V. T.: 98
Chaney, J. W.: 72
Cohen, J.: 42–3, 99
Cole, D.: 19, 44, 71
Conway, R.: 152
Cortner, R. H.: 114
Cottingham, A.: 177
Cottingham, A. L.: 196
Coulter, W. M.: 142
David, H. P.: 9, 20–1, 45–7, 73, 91, 100; *exc,* 5:B418
Davidson, W. N.: 10
Davis, N. E.: 74
Deri, O.: 3
Deri, S.: 11, 166, 172, 178
Deri, S. K.: 1, 2d, 12–3, 22,

75, 101–2, 168, 197; *rev,* 3: 100
Dudek, F. J.: 76–7
Elonen, A. S.: 50
Fancher, E. C.: 120–1, 158
Feamster, J. H.: 160
Feigenbaum, L.: 48, 99
Ferracuti, F.: *exc,* 6:B501
Fleishman, M.: 92, 103–4, 192
Fosberg, I. A.: 23, 49
Friedman, B.: 137
Friedman, E.: 163
Fromm, E. O.: 50
Gallagher, J. J.: 24
Geers, J. B.: 65
Gill, M.: 2c
Glad, D. D.: 16
Goldman, G. D.: 25, 78
Gordon, L. V.: 93, 105
Grant, R. A.: 122
Guertin, W. H.: 26–7, 51–3, 79
Hamilton, J. T.: 143
Harrower, M.: 80, 138, 167
Helme, W. H.: 8
Hill, V.: 94, 96, 106
Holmqvist, S.: 153
Holt, R. R.: 28, 185
Hurley, J. R.: 129
Irving, R. W.: 169, 175
Jackson, V. A.: 81
Jacobs, D.: 117
Jansic, A.: 184
Juel-Nielsen, N.: 155
Kaldegg, A.: 54
Kass, W.: *exc,* 4:135
Katz, J.: 55
Keltner, D.: 66
Klein, A.: 115
Klopfer, W. G.: 14, 18, 29–30, 40, 90, 168; *exc,* 6:B474

[1517]

*Tasks of Emotional Development Test. Ages 6–11, adolescents; 1960–71; TED; 2 levels; Haskel Cohen and Geraldine Rickard Weil; D. C. Heath & Co. *

a) LATENCY. Ages 6–11; 5 scores (perception, outcome, affect, motivation, spontaneity) in each of 12 areas (peer socialization, trust, aggression toward peers, attitudes for learning, respect for property of others, separation from mother figure, identification with same-sex parent, acceptance of siblings, acceptance of need-frustration, acceptance of parents' affection to one another, orderliness and responsibility, self-image).

b) ADOLESCENCE. 5 scores in each of 13 areas: same as for latency level plus heterosexual socialization.

For additional information, see P:481 (1 reference).

REFERENCES THROUGH 1971

1. See P:481.
2. COHEN, HASKEL, AND WEIL, GERALDINE RICKARD. *Tasks of Emotional Development: A Projective Test for Children and Adolescents.* Lexington, Mass.: D. C. Heath and Co., 1971. Pp. xx, 361. *
3. SCRUGGS, ALLIE W. *The Effect of the Fall River and Lowell Head Start Programs on Behavioral Characteristics Associated With Lower Socio-Economic Class Preschool Children.* Doctor's thesis, Boston University (Boston, Mass.), 1971. (*DAI* 32:1949A)

CUMULATIVE NAME INDEX

[1518]

A Test of Family Attitudes. Ages 6–12; 1952–66; Lydia Jackson; Editest [Belgium]. *

For additional information, see 7:180; see also P:504 (2 references); for a review by John E. Bell, see 5:163 (2 references).

REFERENCES THROUGH 1971

1–2. See 5:163.
3–4. See P:504.

CUMULATIVE NAME INDEX

[1519]

Thematic Apperception Test. Ages 4 and over; 1935–43; TAT; Henry A. Murray; Harvard University Press. * Related materials are listed below.

a) ANALYSIS SHEET FOR THE THEMATIC APPERCEPTION TEST. Ages 4 and over; 1970; a form for "summarizing TAT data"; no manual; John A. Blazer; Psychologists and Educators, Inc. *

b) *BELLAK TAT AND CAT BLANK, SHORT FORM. Ages 3–10; 1955–70; for recording and analyzing responses to the TAT and the CAT (see 1451); Leopold Bellak; C.P.S., Inc. *

c) *BELLAK TAT BLANK. Ages 7 and over; 1947–73; for recording and analyzing responses to the TAT; Leopold Bellak; Psychological Corporation. *

For additional information and reviews by Richard H. Dana and Leonard D. Eron, see 7:181 (297 references); see also P:484 (339 references); for a review by C. J. Adcock, see 6:245 (287 references); for reviews by Leonard D. Eron and Arthur R. Jensen, see 5:164 (311 references); for a review by Arthur L. Benton, see 4:136 (198 references); for an excerpted review of *c*, see 4:137; for reviews by Arthur L. Benton, Julian B. Rotter, and J. R. Wittenborn and an excerpted review, see 3:103 (102 references). For excerpts from related book reviews, see 7:B438 (2 excerpts), 6:B60 (2 excerpts), 6:B326 (1 excerpt), 5:B63 (8 excerpts), 5:B204 (5 excerpts), 5:B395 (7 excerpts), 4:139 (3 excerpts), 4:140 (7 excerpts), 4:141 (14 excerpts), 3:104 (1 excerpt), and 3:104a (1 excerpt).

REFERENCES THROUGH 1971

1–101. See 3:103.
102–299. See 4:136.
300–610. See 5:164.
611–897. See 6:245.
898–1236. See P:484.
1237–1533. See 7:181.
1534. KEPECS, JOSEPH G. "Neurotic Reactions in Parachutists." *Psychoanalytic Q* 13:273–99 Jl '44. * (*PA* 19:135)
1535. RICHARDSON, LAVANGE HUNT. "A Personality Study of Stutterers and Non-Stutterers." *J Speech Disorders* 9:152–60 Mr '44. * (*PA* 19:716)
1536. FRENKEL-BRUNSWIK, ELSE, AND SANFORD, R. NEVITT. "Some Personality Factors in Anti-Semitism." *J Psychol* 20:271–91 O '45. * (*PA* 20:475)
1537. RUESCH, JURGEN. "Personality Structure, Lactic Acid Production, and Work Performance in Psychiatric Patients." *J Psychol* 20:381–90 O '45. * (*PA* 20:827)
1538. RENAUD, HAROLD. "Group Differences in Fantasies: Head Injuries, Psychoneurotics, and Brain Diseases." *J Psychol* 21:327–46 Ap '46. * (*PA* 20:3188)
1539. WOOD, KENNETH SCOTT. "Parental Maladjustment and Functional Articulatory Defects in Children." *J Speech Disorders* 11:255–75 D '46. * (*PA* 21:1497)
1540. WAYNE, DAVID M.; ADAMS, M.; AND ROWE, LILLIAN A. "A Study of Military Prisoners at a Disciplinary Barracks Suspected of Homosexual Activities." *Mil Surg* 101:499–504 D '47. * (*PA* 22:5498)
1541. HOOD, PHILIP N.; SHANK, KENNON H.; AND WILLIAMSON, DORIS B. "Environmental Factors in Relation to the Speech of Cerebral Palsied Children." *J Speech & Hearing Disorders* 13:325–31 D '48. * (*PA* 23:3301)

1542. HUTTON, E. L., AND BASSETT, M. "The Effect of Leucotomy on Creative Personality." *J Mental Sci* (England) 94:332–8 Ap '48. * (*PA* 23:1189)

1543. WARNER, W. LLOYD, AND HENRY, WILLIAM E. "The Radio Day Time Serial: A Symbolic Analysis." *Genetic Psychol Monogr* 37:3–71 F '48. * (*PA* 22:4937)

1544. WHITEHOUSE, ELIZABETH. "Norms for Certain Aspects of the Thematic Apperception Test on a Group of Nine and Ten Year Old Children." *Persona* 1:12–5 f '49. * (*PA* 24:1210)

1545. LINDZEY, GARDNER. "Differences Between the High and Low in Prejudice and Their Implications for a Theory of Prejudice." *J Personality* 19:16–40 Je '59. * (*PA* 25:6161)

1546. FRENKEL-BRUNSWIK, ELSE. "Patterns of Social and Cognitive Outlook in Children and Parents." *Am J Orthopsychiatry* 21:543–58 Jl '51. * (*PA* 26:3320)

1547. GELLERMAN, SAUL W. "The Relation Between Social Attitudes and a Projected Thema of Frustration by Parents." *J Social Psychol* 34:183–90 Ag '51. * (*PA* 26:5474)

1548. ROE, ANNE. "A Study of Imagery in Research Scientists." *J Personality* 19:459–70 Je '51. * (*PA* 26:3680)

1549. ROGERS, CARL R. "Studies in Client-Centered Psychotherapy: 3, The Case of Mrs. Oak—A Research Analysis." *Psychol Service Center J* 3:47–165 Mr–Je '51. * (*PA* 27:1220)

1550. SARNOFF, IRVING. "Identification With the Aggressor: Some Personality Correlates of Anti-Semitism Among Jews." *J Personality* 20:199–218 D '51. * (*PA* 27:1103)

1551. ALEXANDER, THERON, AND ALEXANDER, MARIE. "A Study of Personality and Social Status." *Child Develop* 23:207–13 S '52. * (*PA* 27:7045)

1552. CALDWELL, BETTYE MCDONALD, AND WATSON, ROBERT I. "An Evaluation of Psychologic Effects of Sex Hormone Administration in Aged Women: 1, Results of Therapy After Six Months." *J Gerontol* 7:228–44 Ap '52. * (*PA* 27:1874)

1553. COX, F. N. "Some Effects of Frustration: I, A Methodical Programme." *Austral J Psychol* 4:94–106 D '52. * (*PA* 28:4558)

1554. GOODMAN, LEO A. "An Application of Sequential Analysis to Problems Relative to the Use of Qualitative Tests." *Am Sociol R* 17:223–6 Ap '52. * (*PA* 27:5081)

1555. ROBIN, ASHLEY A., AND HARRISON, E. J. "Some Clinical and Aetiological Aspects of Depersonalization With a Case Report of Identical Twins." *J Mental Sci* (England) 98:469–76 Jl '52. * (*PA* 27:3656)

1556. GLADWIN, THOMAS. "The Role of Man and Woman on Truk: A Problem in Personality and Culture." *Trans NY Acad Sci* 15:305–9 Je '53. * (*PA* 28:4195)

1557. HAMZA, MUKHTAR. "The Dynamic Forces in the Personalities of Juvenile Delinquents in the Egyptian Environment." *Brit J Psychol* 44:330–8 N '53. * (*PA* 28:6301)

1558. LORENZ, MARIA, AND COBB, STANLEY. "Language Behavior in Psychoneurotic Patients." *Arch Neurol & Psychiatry* 69:684–94 My '53. * (*PA* 28:3059)

1559. ROE, ANNE. "A Psychological Study of Eminent Psychologists and Anthropologists, and a Comparison With Biological and Physical Scientists." *Psychol Monogr* 67(2):1–55 '53. * (*PA* 28:1956)

1560. VAN LENNEP, J. E. "Some Considerations Regarding the Clinical-Psychological Examination of Paranoid States." *Folia Psychiatrica Neurologica et Neurochirurgica Neerlandica* (Netherlands) 56:769–78 '53. *

1561. ZEMLICK, MAURICE J., AND WATSON, ROBERT I. "Maternal Attitudes of Acceptance and Rejection During and After Pregnancy." *Am J Orthopsychiatry* 23:570–84 Jl '53. * (*PA* 28:3109)

1562. AULD, FRANK, JR. "Contributions of Behavior Theory to Projective Testing." *J Proj Tech* 18:421–6 D '54. * (*PA* 29:7255)

1563. CHANCE, JUNE; LOTSOF, ERWIN J.; PINE, IRVING; PATTERSON, RALPH M.; AND CRAIG, JAMES. "Effects of Cortisone on Psychiatric Patients." *Psychosom Med* 16:516–25 N–D '54. * (*PA* 29:6020)

1564. CLEVELAND, SIDNEY E., AND FISHER, SEYMOUR. "Behavior and Unconscious Fantasies of Patients With Rheumatoid Arthritis." *Psychosom Med* 16:327–33 Jl–Ag '54. * (*PA* 29:4495)

1565. ERIKSEN, CHARLES W. "Needs in Perception and Projective Techniques." *J Proj Tech* 18:435–40 D '54. * (*PA* 29:7272)

1566. KATZ, MELVYN MYRON. "Psychodynamics of Peptic Ulcer Pathogenesis in Hospitalized Schizophrenic Patients." *Psychosom Med* 16:47–55 Ja–F '54. * (*PA* 28:7826)

1567. LIPKIN, STANLEY. "Clients' Feelings and Attitudes in Relation to the Outcome of Client-Centered Therapy." *Psychol Monogr* 68(1):1–30 '54. * (*PA* 29:2537)

1568. PARRISH, JOHN, AND RETHLINGSHAFER, DOROTHY. "A Study of the Need to Achieve in College Achievers and Non-Achievers." *J General Psychol* 50:209–26 Ap '54. * (*PA* 29:4654)

1569. ROBINSON, JAMES T., AND COHEN, LOUIS D. "Individual Bias in Psychological Reports." *J Clin Psychol* 10:333–6 O '54. * (*PA* 29:3998)

1570. SCHAFER, ROY. "Some Applications of Contemporary Psychoanalytic Theory to Projective Testing." *J Proj Tech* 18:441–7 D '54. * (*PA* 29:7315)

1571. SHAPIRO, DAVID. "Special Problems of Testing Borderline Psychotics." *J Proj Tech* 18:387–94 S '54. * (*PA* 29:4448)

1572. SYMONDS, PERCIVAL M. "Are Projective Test Data Valid Bases for Prediction?" *J Proj Tech* 18:515–9 D '54. * (*PA* 29:7327)

1573. VARGAS, MANUEL J. Chap. 10, "Changes in Self-Awareness During Client-Centered Therapy," pp. 145–66. (*PA* 29:4182) In *Psychotherapy and Personality Change.* Edited by Carl R. Rogers and Rosalind F. Dymond. Chicago, Ill.: University of Chicago Press, 1954. Pp. x, 447. *

1574. DYMOND, ROSALIND F. "Adjustment Changes in the Absence of Psychotherapy." *J Consult Psychol* 19:103–7 Ap '55. * (*PA* 30:1088)

1575. FERRACUTI, F., AND RIZZO, G. B. "Psychological Patterns in Terminal Cancer Cases." *Ed & Psychol* (India) 2:26–36 Ja–Mr '55. * (*PA* 31:3531)

1576. FOULDS, G. A. "The Reliability of Psychiatric, and the Validity of Psychological, Diagnoses." *J Mental Sci* (England) 101:851–62 O '55. * (*PA* 30:7165)

1577. FRIEDMAN, IRA. "Phenomenal, Ideal, and Projected Conceptions of Self." *J Abn & Social Psychol* 51:611–5 N '55. * (*PA* 31:2547)

1578. GOTTSCHALK, LOUIS A., AND HAMBIDGE, GOVE, JR. "Verbal Behavior Analysis: A Systematic Approach to the Problem of Quantifying Psychologic Processes." *J Proj Tech* 19:387–409 D '55. * (*PA* 30:7167)

1579. HANDELMAN, NORMAN SIDNEY. *The Relationship Between Certain Personality Factors and Speechreading Proficiency: An Investigation of the Differences in Personality Between a Group of Good Speechreaders and a Matched Group of Poor Speechreaders.* Doctor's thesis, New York University (New York, N.Y.), 1955. (*DA* 15:1890)

1580. KERRICK, JEAN S. "The Influence of Captions on Picture Interpretation." *Journalism Q* 32:177–82 sp '55. * (*PA* 31:1045)

1581. MORTON, ROBERT B. "An Experiment in Brief Psychotherapy." *Psychol Monogr* 69(1):1–17 '55. * (*PA* 30:1112)

1582. ORBACH, CHARLES E.; SUTHERLAND, ARTHUR M.; AND BOZEMAN, MARY F. "Psychological Impact of Cancer and Its Treatment: 3, The Adaptation of Mothers to the Threatened Loss of Their Children Through Leukemia: Part 2." *Cancer* 8:20–33 Ja–F '55. * (*PA* 29:7744)

1583. REZNIKOFF, MARVIN. "Psychological Factors in Breast Cancer: A Preliminary Study of Some Personality Trends in Patients With Cancer of the Breast." *Psychosom Med* 17:96–108 Mr–Ap '55. * (*PA* 30:1405)

1584. RIGGS, MARGARET M., AND KAESS, WALTER. "Personality Differences Between Volunteers and Nonvolunteers." *J Psychol* 40:229–45 O '55. * (*PA* 30:6918)

1585. SCHWARTZ, BERNARD J. "The Measurement of Castration Anxiety and Anxiety Over Loss of Love." *J Personality* 24:204–19 D '55. * (*PA* 30:7453)

1586. SMITH, G., AND KRAGH, U. "Do Micro-Genetic Sequences Reflect Life History? An Illustration." *Acta Psychologica* (Netherlands) 11(4):504–12 '55. * (*PA* 30:7180)

1587. TOMS, ESTHER CHRISTINE. *Personality Characteristics of Mothers of Schizophrenic Veterans.* Doctor's thesis, University of Minnesota (Minneapolis, Minn.), 1955. (*DA* 15:2580)

1588. WEISS, WALTER, AND FINE, BERNARD J. "Opinion Change as a Function of Some Intrapersonal Attributes of the Communicatees." *J Abn & Social Psychol* 51:246–53 S '55. * (*PA* 30:4206)

1589. WINCH, ROBERT F. "The Theory of Complementary Needs in Mate Selection: A Test of One Kind of Complementariness." *Am Sociol R* 20:52–6 F '55. * (*PA* 31:938)

1590. WINCH, ROBERT F. "The Theory of Complementary Needs in Mate-Selection: Final Results on the Test of the General Hypothesis." *Am Sociol R* 20:552–5 O '55. * (*PA* 31:937)

1591. WORDEN, FREDERIC G., AND MARSH, JAMES T. "Psychological Factors in Men Seeking Sex Transformation: A Preliminary Report." *J Am Med Assn* 157:1292–8 Ap 9 '55. *

1592. FISHER, SEYMOUR, AND CLEVELAND, SIDNEY E. "Body-Image Boundaries and Style of Life." *J Abn & Social Psychol* 52:373–9 My '56. * (*PA* 31:4379)

1593. GRZIWOK, RUDOLF, AND SCODEL, ALVIN. "Some Psychological Correlates of Humor Preferences." Abstract. *J Consult Psychol* 20:42 F '56. * (*PA* 31:2594, title only)

1594. HERRING, FRED H. "Response During Anesthesia and Surgery; Effect of Psychological Factors." *Psychosom Med* 18:243–51 My–Je '56. * (*PA* 31:5007)

1595. KELLER, HORACE T., JR. *Personality Measures as Related to Performance Under Auditory Distraction.* Doctor's thesis, Temple University (Philadelphia, Pa.), 1956. (*DA* 16:994)

1596. MEADOW, LLOYD. "A Study of Dyadic Relationships in the French Family." *J Proj Tech* 20:196–206 Je '56. * (*PA* 31:4564)

1597. MENDELL, DAVID, AND FISHER, SEYMOUR. "An Approach to Neurotic Behavior in Terms of a Three Generation Family Model." *J Nerv & Mental Dis* 123:171–80 F '56. * (*PA* 31:8537)

1598. MILLS, THEODORE M. "Development Processes in Three-

Person Groups." *Hum Relations* 9(3):343–55 '56. * (*PA* 32:2764)

1599. SCHWARTZ, BERNARD J. "An Empirical Test of Two Freudian Hypotheses Concerning Castration Anxiety." *J Personality* 24:318–27 Mr '56. * (*PA* 31:1346)

1600. SOPCHAK, ANDREW L. "Projective Study of Peter and His Parents: Revealing the Necessary Therapeutic Limitations." *J Child Psychiatry* 3:149–200 Ag '56. * (*PA* 31:8363)

1601. WINCH, ROBERT F., AND MORE, DOUGLAS M. "Quantitative Analysis of Qualitative Data in the Assessment of Motivation: Reliability, Congruence, and Validity." *Am J Sociol* 61:445–52 Ja '56. * (*PA* 31:2763)

1602. CARPENTER, LEWIS G., JR. "Relation of Aggression in the Personality to Outcome With Electro-Convulsive Shock Therapy." *J General Psychol* 57:3–22 Jl '57. * (*PA* 33:8453)

1603. CARTWRIGHT, DESMOND S., AND ROTH, IRVIN. "Success and Satisfaction in Psychotherapy." *J Clin Psychol* 13:20–6 Ja '57. * (*PA* 32:5544)

1604. FINK, HOWARD H. "The Relationship of Time Perspective to Age, Institutionalization, and Activity." *J Gerontol* 12:414–7 O '57. * (*PA* 33:3470)

1605. GOTTSCHALK, LOUIS A.; GLESER, GOLDINE C.; AND HAMBIDGE, GOVE, JR. "Verbal Behavioral Analysis: Some Content and Form Variables in Speech Relevant to Personality Adjustment." *Arch Neurol & Psychiatry* 77:300–11 Mr '57. * (*PA* 32:2667)

1606. KAFKA, JOHN S. "A Note on the Therapeutic and Teaching Use of Projective Techniques With Groups." *Am J Psychother* 11:839–40 O '57. * (*PA* 36:6244)

1607. KOPPITZ, ELIZABETH MUNSTERBERG. "Relationships Between Some Background Factors and Children's Interpersonal Attitude." *J Genetic Psychol* 91:119–29 S '57. * (*PA* 36:1FF19K)

1608. MALMO, ROBERT B.; BOAG, THOMAS J.; AND SMITH, A. ARTHUR. "Physiological Study of Personal Interaction." *Psychosom Med* 19:105–19 Mr–Ap '57. * (*PA* 32:3222)

1609. MINTZ, ELIZABETH EMMONS. "Personal Problems and Diagnostic Errors in Clinical Psychologists." *J Proj Tech* 21:123–8 Je '57. * (*PA* 33:1292)

1610. MORE, DOUGLAS M. "The Congruence of Projective Instruments in Personnel Assessment." *J Appl Psychol* 41:137–40 Je '57. * (*PA* 33:2240)

1611. MUSSEN, PAUL HENRY, AND JONES, MARY COVER. "Self-Conceptions, Motivations, and Interpersonal Attitudes of Late- and Early-Maturing Boys." *Child Develop* 28:243–56 Je '57. * (*PA* 33:912)

1612. ORME, J. E. "Initial Psychiatric Illness in Involutional Women: 2, Psychological Aspects." *J Mental Sci* (England) 103:227–39 Ja '57. * (*PA* 32:3182)

1613. SUCZEK, ROBERT F. "The Personality of Obese Women." *Am J Clin Nutr* 5:197–202 Mr–Ap '57. * (*PA* 32:4450)

1614. ULLMANN, LEONARD P. "Selection of Neuropsychiatric Patients for Group Psychotherapy." *J Consult Psychol* 21:277–80 Je '57. * (*PA* 32:5587)

1615. FRIEDMAN, IRA. "A Critique of Shneidman and Farberow's 'TAT Heroes of Suicidal and Non-Suicidal Subjects.'" *J Proj Tech* 22:281–3 S '58. * (*PA* 33:10328)

1616. LONG, ROBERT T.; LAMONT, JOHN H.; WHIPPLE, BABETTE; BANDLER, LOUISE; BLOM, GASTON E.; BURGIN, LEO; AND JESSNER, LUCIE. "A Psychosomatic Study of the Allergic and Emotional Factors in Children With Asthma." *Am J Psychiatry* 114:890–9 Ap '58. * (*PA* 33:6721)

1617. MUSSEN, PAUL H., AND NEWMAN, DAVID K. "Acceptance of Handicap, Motivation, and Adjustment in Physically Disabled Children." *Excep Children* 24:255–60+ F '58. * (*PA* 33:6782)

1618. MUSSEN, PAUL HENRY, AND KAGAN, JEROME. "Group Conformity and Perceptions of Parents." *Child Develop* 29:57–60 Mr '58. * (*PA* 33:8095)

1619. PERR, HERBERT M. "Criteria Distinguishing Parents of Schizophrenic and Normal Children: An Initial Study With the Interpersonal Diagnostic System." *Arch Neurol & Psychiatry* 79:217–24 F '58. * (*PA* 33:6274)

1620. SHRUT, SAMUEL D. "Attitudes Toward Old Age and Death." *Mental Hyg* 42:259–66 Ap '58. * (*PA* 33:8044)

1621. ZUCKERMAN, MARVIN; NORTON, JAMES; AND SPRAGUE, DAVID S. "Acquiescence, and Extreme Sets and Their Role in Tests of Authoritarianism and Parental Attitudes." Discussion by Marvin Zuckerman. *Psychiatric Res Rep* 10:28–51 D '58. * (*PA* 35:2305)

1622. GLADWIN, THOMAS, AND SARASON, SEYMOUR B. Chap. 7, "Culture and Individual Personality Integration on Truk," pp. 173–210. In *Culture and Mental Health: Cross-Cultural Studies.* Edited by Marvin K. Opler. New York: Macmillan, 1959. Pp. xxi, 553. * (*PA* 34:7593)

1623. GORDON, JESSE E. "Relationships Among Mothers' *n* Achievement, Independence Training Attitudes, and Handicapped Children's Performance." *J Consult Psychol* 23:207–12 Je '59. * (*PA* 34:4764)

1624. KLABER, MAX MICHAEL. *Manifestations of Hostility in Neurodermatitis.* Doctor's thesis, Columbia University (New York, N.Y.), 1959. (*DA* 20:375)

1625. MURRAY, EDWARD J. "Conflict and Repression During Sleep Deprivation." *J Abn & Social Psychol* 59:95–101 Jl '59. * (*PA* 34:4567)

1626. MURSTEIN, BERNARD I. "A Conceptual Model of Projective Techniques Applied to Stimulus Variations With Thematic Techniques." *J Consult Psychol* 23:3–14 F '59. * (*PA* 1627. BOBROFF, ALLEN. "The Stages of Maturation in Socialized Thinking and in the Ego Development of Two Groups 34:1403)

of Children." *Child Develop* 31:321–38 Je '60. * (*PA* 36:3JI21B)

1628. CARTWRIGHT, ROSALIND DYMOND, AND VOGEL, JOHN L. "A Comparison of Changes in Psychoneurotic Patients During Matched Periods of Therapy and No Therapy." *J Consult Psychol* 24:121–7 Ap '60. * (*PA* 34:8198)

1629. HEILIZER, FRED. "An Exploration of the Relationship Between Hypnotizability and Anxiety and/or Neuroticism." *J Consult Psychol* 24:432–6 O '60. * (*PA* 35:5101)

1630. KLABER, M. MICHAEL. "Manifestations of Hostility in Neurodermatitis." *J Consult Psychol* 24:116–20 Ap '60. * (*PA* 34:8048)

1631. KRAGH, ULF. "Pathogenesis in Dipsomania: An Illustration of the Actual-Genetic Model of Perception-Personality: Part 1, Theoretical Frame, Anamnesis." *Acta Psychiatrica et Neurologica Scandinavica* (Denmark) 35(2):207–22 '60. * (*PA* 35:3799)

1632. KRAGH, ULF. "Pathogenesis in Dipsomania: An Illustration of the Actual-Genetic Model of Perception-Personality: Part 2, Presentation and Analysis of the Actual-Genetic Series." *Acta Psychiatrica et Neurologica Scandinavica* (Denmark) 35(3):261–88 '60. * (*PA* 35:2577)

1633. KRAGH, ULF. "Pathogenesis in Dipsomania: An Illustration of the Actual-Genetic Model of Perception-Personality: Part 3, The Retest Series, the Pathogenic Transformations, Repression and Regression." *Acta Psychiatrica et Neurologica Scandinavica* (Denmark) 35(4):480–97 60. * (*PA* 35:6864)

1634. LEVITT, EUGENE E.; DEN BREEIJEN, ARDIE; AND PERSKY, HAROLD. "The Induction of Clinical Anxiety by Means of a Standardized Hypnotic Technique." *Am J Clin Hyp* 2:206–14 Ap '60. * (*PA* 35:3623)

1635. SMITH, ALEXANDER B.; BASSIN, ALEXANDER; AND FROEHLICH, ABRAHAM. "Change in Attitudes and Degree of Verbal Participation in Group Therapy With Adult Offenders." *J Consult Psychol* 24:247–9 Je '60. * (*PA* 35:6894)

1636. HOKANSON, JACK E. "The Effects of Guilt Arousal and Severity of Discipline on Adult Aggressive Behavior." *J Clin Psychol* 17:29–32 Ja '61. * (*PA* 37:3146)

1637. MURSTEIN, BERNARD I. "Assumptions, Adaptation-Level, and Projective Techniques." *Percept & Motor Skills* 12:107–25 Ap '61. * (*PA* 36:1HG07M)

1638. RAO, S. K. RAMACHANDRA. "Studies With the Thematic Apperception Test." *Trans All-India Inst Mental Health* 2:84–106 D '61. *

1639. SHNEIDMAN, EDWIN S. "The Case of El: Psychological Test Data." *J Proj Tech* 25:131–54 Je '61. * (*PA* 36:21K31S)

1640. BARWICK, JANICE M., AND ARBUCKLE, DUGALD S. "A Study of the Relationship Between Parental Acceptance and the Academic Achievement of Adolescents." *J Ed Res* 56:148–51 N '62. *

1641. BAXTER, JAMES C., AND BECKER, JOSEPH. "Anxiety and Avoidance Behavior in Schizophrenics in Response to Parental Figures." *J Abn & Social Psychol* 64:432–7 Je '62. * (*PA* 38:1310)

1642. DAVIDS, ANTHONY, AND DeVAULT, SPENCER. "Maternal Anxiety During Pregnancy and Childbirth Abnormalities." *Psychosom Med* 24:464–70 S–O '62. * (*PA* 37:5522)

1643. DAVIDS, ANTHONY, AND ROSENGREN, WILLIAM R. "Social Stability and Psychological Adjustment During Pregnancy." *Psychosom Med* 24:579–83 N–D '62. * (*PA* 37:8122)

1644. SACKS, LENORA; FEINSTEIN, ALVAN R.; AND TARANTA, ANGELO. "A Controlled Psychologic Study of Sydenham's Chorea." *J Pediatrics* 61:714–22 N '62. * (*PA*)

1645. SHELLEY, ERNEST L. V., AND TOCH, HANS H. "The Perception of Violence as an Indicator of Adjustment in Institutionalized Offenders." *J Crim Law Criminol & Police Sci* 53:463–9 D '62. * (*PA* 37:8184)

1646. BLATT, EVA FISHELL. "The Relationship Between Severity of Disease and Extent of Psychopathology in Psychosomatic Illness: A Test of Regression Theory." *Psychosomatics* 4:207–14 Jl–Ag '63. *

1647. BOTHA, ELIZABETH, AND KÖPER, C. "An Investigation Into Some Patterns of Motivation of Soft Drink Salesmen." *Psychologia Africana* (South Africa) 10:123–6 '63. * (*PA* 38:9301)

1648. CRUMPTON, EVELYN; BRILL, NORMAN Q.; EIDUSON, SAMUEL; AND GELLER, EEWARD. "The Role of Fear in Electroconvulsive Treatment." *J Nerv & Mental Dis* 136:29–33 Ja '63. * (*PA* 37:8054)

1649. GUNTER, LAURIE M. "Psychopathology and Stress in the Life Experience of Mothers of Premature Infants." *Am J Obstet & Gynecol* 86:333–40 Je 1 '63. *

1650. JOHNSON, DALE L. "Projective Test Responses of Psychiatric Patients From Three American Sub-Cultures." *Congreso Interamericano de Psicologia* (Mexico) 7:171–7 '63. *

1651. LASKOWITZ, DAVID. "Degree of Pictorial Ambiguity and Fantasy Evocation: An Appraisal of the Non-Monotonic Hy-

Thematic Apperception Test

pothesis." *Percept & Motor Skills* 16:187–93 F '63. * (*PA* 38: 923)

1652. McCully, Robert S. "Fantasy Productions of Children With a Progressively Crippling and Fatal Illness." *J Genetic Psychol* 102:203–16 Je '63. * (*PA* 38:4058)

1653. Schoenberg, Bernard, and Carr, Arthur C. "An Investigation of Criteria for Brief Psychotherapy of Neurodermatitis." *Psychosom Med* 25:253–63 My–Je '63. * (*PA* 38:4425)

1654. Singer, Robert D. "A Cognitive View of Rationalized Projection." *J Proj Tech & Pers Assess* 27:235–43 Je '63. * (*PA* 38:2758)

1655. Hammer, Emanuel F. "Creativity and Feminine Ingredients in Young Male Artists." *Percept & Motor Skills* 19:414 O '64. * (*PA* 39:7817)

1656. Morrison, Denton E. "Achievement Motivation of Farm Operators: A Measurement Study." *Rural Sociol* 29:367–84 D '64. * (*PA* 39:7524)

1657. Oo, M.; Csirszka, J.; and Hegedus, J. "Psychological Tests in Leukaemia Patients," pp. 18–29. In *Psychosomatic Aspects of Neoplastic Disease*. The Proceedings of the Third International Conference of the International Psychosomatic Cancer Study Group Held at Newnham College, Cambridge, England, 22nd to 26th July 1963. Edited by D. M. Kissen and L. L. Leshan. Philadelphia, Pa.: J. B. Lippincott Co., 1964. Pp. xii, 231. *

1658. Rao, S. K. Ramachandra. "Studies With the Thematic Apperception Test: Study IV, Projected Aggression." *Trans All-India Inst Mental Health* 4:24–32 Jl '64. *

1659. Rothaus, Paul, and Worchel, Philip. "Ego-Support, Communication, Catharsis, and Hostility." *J Personality* 32:296–312 Je '64. * (*PA* 39:7870)

1660. Botha, E., and Close, A. "Achievement Motivation and Speed of Perception in Relation to Reading Skill." *J Social Res* (South Africa) 14:63–8 D '64. * (*PA* 41:15768)

1661. Goldberg, Philip A., and Milstein, Judith T. "Perceptual Investigation of Psychoanalytic Theory Concerning Latent Homosexuality in Women." *Percept & Motor Skills* 21:645–6 O '65. * (*PA* 40:2771)

1662. Haas, Kurt. "Direction of Hostility and Psychiatric Symptoms." *Psychol Rep* 16:555–6 Ap '65. * (*PA* 39:10639)

1663. Heath, Douglas H.; with the assistance of Harriet E. Heath. *Explorations of Maturity: Studies of Mature and Immature College Men*. New York: Appleton-Century-Crofts, 1965. Pp. xv, 423. * (*PA* 39:12057)

1664. Miller, David, and Lieberman, Morton A. "The Relationship of Affect State and Adaptive Capability to Reactions to Stress." *J Gerontol* 20:492–7 O '65. *

1665. Piotrowski, Zygmunt A. Chap. 26, "Predicting Acting Out by Means of the Thematic Apperception Test," pp. 271–87. In *Acting Out: Theoretical and Clinical Aspects*. By Lawrence Edwin Abt and Stuart L. Weissman. New York: Grune & Stratton, Inc., 1965. Pp. xiii, 336. *

1666. Shore, Milton F.; Massimo, Joseph L.; and Mack, Ronald. "Changes in the Perception of Interpersonal Relationships in Successfully Treated Adolescent Delinquent Boys." *J Consult Psychol* 29:213–7 Je '65. * (*PA* 39:12518)

1667. Silverman, Lloyd H. "Further Data on the Relationship Between Aggressive Drive Activation and Impairments in Thinking: The Effects of Blocking of Aggressive Discharge of the Thought Processes." *J Nerv & Mental Dis* 141:61–7 Jl '65. * (*PA* 40:3169)

1668. Theilgaard, A. "Psychological Testing of Patients With Anorexia Nervosa," pp. 122–8. (*PA* 40:3170) In *Anorexia Nervosa: Symposium am 24.125 April 1965 in Göttingen*. Edited by J.-E. Meyer and H. Feldman. Stuttgart, Germany: Georg Thieme Verlag, 1965. Pp. vi, 118. *

1669. Williams, Redford B., Jr., and McKegney, F. Patrick. "Psychological Aspects of Hypertension: 1, The Influence of Experimental Interview Variables on Blood Pressure." *Yale J Biol Med* 38:265–72 D '65. *

1670. Edlow, Donald W., and Kiesler, Charles A. "Ease of Denial and Defensive Projection." *J Exp Social Psychol* 2:56–69 Ja '66. * (*PA* 40:6619)

1671. Carlson, Hilmer Jon. *Validity of Word-Count Scoring for the Thematic Apperception Test*. Master's thesis, Northern Illinois University (DeKalb, Ill.), 1966.

1672. Handel, Gerald. Chap. 7, "Analysis of Correlative Meaning: The TAT in the Study of Families," pp. 104–24. In his *The Psychosocial Interior of the Family: A Sourcebook for the Study of Whole Families*. Chicago, Ill.: Aldine Publishing Co., 1967. Pp. xiii, 560. *

1673. Jennings, Charles L. "The Use of Normative Data in the Psychological Evaluation of Flying Personnel." *Int Psychiatry Clinics* 4:37–51 w '67. *

1674. Kapur, Malavika, and Kapur, R. L. "Study of Impotence Through Projective Tests." *Indian J Psychiatry* 9:208–12 Jl '67. *

1675. Klineberg, Stephen L. "Changes in Outlook on the Future Between Childhood and Adolescence." *J Pers & Social Psychol* 7:185–93 O '67. * (*PA* 41:16459)

1676. McKegney, F. Patrick, and Williams, Redford B., Jr. "Psychological Aspects of Hypertension: 2, The Differential Influence of Interview Variables on Blood Pressure." *Am J Psychiatry* 123:1539–45 Je '67. * (*PA* 41:12236)

1677. Meisels, Murray. "Test Anxiety, Stress, and Verbal Behavior." *J Consult Psychol* 31:577–82 D '67. * (*PA* 42:1632)

1678. Peskin, Harvey. "Pubertal Onset and Ego Functioning." *J Abn Psychol* 72:1–15 F '67. * (*PA* 41:4738)

1679. Press, Irwin. "Maya Aging: Cross-Cultural Projective Techniques and the Dilemma of Interpretation." *Psychiatry* 30:197–202 My '67. * (*PA* 41:15320)

1680. Schaefer, Judith B., and Norman, Martin. "Punishment and Aggression in Fantasy Responses of Boys With Antisocial Character Traits." *J Pers & Social Psychol* 6:237–40 Je '67. * (*PA* 41:10677)

1681. Carr, Arthur C. "Psychological Testing and Reporting." *J Proj Tech & Pers Assess* 32:513–21 D '68. * (*PA* 43: 9995)

1682. Elliott, Rosalie Calhoun. *Creativity and the Handling of Conflict in Bright Sixth Graders*. Doctor's thesis, Claremont Graduate School (Claremont, Calif.), 1968. (*DAI* 31: 7621B)

1683. Heilbrun, Alfred B., Jr., and Tiemeyer, Elizabeth Brown. "Relationships Between Perceived Maternal Childrearing Experiences and Projective Responses to Censure-Control Cues in Normal Males." *J Genetic Psychol* 112:3–14 Mr '68. * (*PA* 42:10414)

1684. Mandell, Edward R. *Measurement of Personality Characteristics of Clients in a Rehabilitation Setting: Construction of a Sentence Completion Test*. Master's thesis, Wayne State University (Detroit, Mich.), 1968.

1685. Martin, James G. "Two Psychological Mechanisms Specified by Hesitation in Spontaneous Speech." Abstract. *Proc 76th Ann Conv Am Psychol Assn* 3:17–8 '68. * (*PA* 43:856, title only)

1686. Persky, Harold; Zuckerman, Marvin; and Curtis, George C. "Endocrine Function in Emotionally Disturbed and Normal Men." *J Nerv & Mental Dis* 146:488–97 Je '68. * (*PA* 42:16830)

1687. Shapiro, Arthur K.; Wilensky, Harold; and Struening, Elmer L. "Study of the Placebo Effect With a Placebo Test." *Comprehen Psychiatry* 9:118–37 Mr '68. * (*PA* 43:2745)

1688. Brand, Judith. "The Effect of Highly Aggressive Content in Comic Books on Seventh Grade Children." *Grad Res Ed & Related Discip* 5(1):46–61 f '69. * (*PA* 46:8783)

1689. Chatterjee, Tarit K. "A Study of the Personality of Parents of the Schizophrenics." *Samikas* (India) 23(1):22–48 '69. * (*PA* 45:8622)

1690. Clark, Edward T., and Propper, Martin M. "Alienation Syndrome Among Catholic Male Undergraduates." *Psychol Rep* 25(1):167–72 Ag '69. * (*PA* 44:4159)

1691. Edwards, Carl N. "The Student Nurse: A Study in Sex Role Transition." *Psychol Rep* 25(3):975–90 D '69. * (*PA* 44: 19584)

1692. Ellinwood, Charlotte Grace. *Age-Development of Verbal Expressions of Feeling in Psychotherapy Interviews and TAT Protocols*. Doctor's thesis, University of Chicago (Chicago, Ill.), 1969.

1693. Weems, Luther B., Jr., and Wolowitz, Howard M. "The Relevance of Power Themes Among Male, Negro and White. Paranoid and Non-Paranoid Schizophrenics." *Int J Social Psychiatry* 15(3):189–96 su '69. * (*PA* 44:18925)

1694. Baty, Martha Aldridge. *A Comparison of Three Methods of Recording TAT Protocols*. Doctor's thesis, Louisiana State University (Baton Rouge, La.), 1970. (*DAI* 31:5613B)

1695. Bohn, Suzanne Erbe. *Temporal Perspective, Inner Responsivity, and External Responsivity in Schizophrenics and Normals*. Doctor's thesis, Washington University (St. Louis, Mo.), 1970. (*DAI* 31:6890B)

1696. Campus, Nancy Ruth. *A Study of Personality Characteristics Related to Trans-Situational Consistency of Self-Descriptions*. Doctor's thesis. New York University (New York, N.Y.), 1970. (*DAI* 31:7567B)

1697. Culligan, Kevin G. *Personality Characteristics of Diocesan Priests in Middle-Adulthood: A Preliminary Study*. Master's thesis, Marquette University (Milwaukee, Wis.), 1970.

1698. Harty, Michael Kimbrough. *The Capacity for Adaptive Regression as a Component of Empathic Ability*. Doctor's thesis, University of Michigan (Ann Arbor, Mich.), 1970. (*DAI* 31:7598B)

1699. Hoopes, Janet L.; Sherman, Edmund A.; Lawder, Elizabeth; Andrews, Roberta G.; and Lower, Katherine D. *A Follow-Up Study of Adoptions (Vol. II): Post-Placement Functioning of Adopted Children*. New York: Child Welfare League of America, Inc., 1970. Pp. v, 126. *

1700. Köhle, K., and Simons, C. "Psychodynamic Aspects in Young Patients Suffering From Peripheral Vascular Occlusions." *Psychother & Psychosom* (Switzerland) 18(1–6):313–20 '70. * (*PA* 47:5516)

1701. Mebane, Donata F., and Die, Jerry G. "A Scoring System for Human Figure Drawings as a Measure of Personality at Level III of the Leary Interpersonal Diagnostic System." *Percept & Motor Skills* 30(2):385–6 Ap '70. * (*PA* 46: 6902)

1702. Megargee, Edwin I. "The Prediction of Violence With Psychological Tests." *Curr Topics Clin & Commun Psychol* 2:97–156 '70. *

1703. Murphy, Donald Clarence. *Verbal and Nonverbal*

Communication in High and Low Marital Adjustment. Doctor's thesis, Florida State University (Tallahassee, Fla.), 1970. (*DAI* 31:4919A)

1704. OBUCHOWSKI, K.; ZIENKIEWICZ, H.; AND GRACZYKOWSKA-KOCZOROWSKA, A. "Psychological Studies in Pituitary Dwarfism." *Polish Med J* 9(5):1229–35 '70. * (*PA* 48:1554)

1705. POSTEMA, LEONARD JAMES. *Reminiscing, Time Orientation, and Self-Concept in Aged Men.* Doctor's thesis, Michigan State University (East Lansing, Mich.), 1970. (*DAI* 31:6880B)

1706. ROSSEL, ROBERT D. "Fantasy in Interracial Groups." *Sociol Q* 11(1):50–66 w '70. *

1707. SAUNA, VICTOR D. "A Cross Cultural Study of Cerebral Palsy." *Social Sci & Med* (England) 4(5):461–512 O '70. *

1708. SELVEY, CAROLE LIGHT. *Concerns About Death in Relation to Sex, Dependency, Guilt About Hostility, and Feelings of Powerlessness.* Doctor's thesis, Columbia University (New York, N.Y.), 1970. (*DAI* 31:5641B)

1709. WACHTEL, PAUL L., AND SCHIMEK, JEAN G. "An Exploratory Study of the Effects of Emotionally Toned Incidental Stimuli." *J Personality* 38(4):467–81 D '70. * (*PA* 46:1216)

1710. WINTER, SARA K. "Mother and Child: Fantasies at Breast Feeding Time." *Psychol Today* 3(8):30–2 Ja '70. * (*PA* 46:2766)

1711. ZALEZNIK, ABRAHAM. Chap. 12, "The Psychodynamics of Career Orientation and Conflict," pp. 281–383. In *Orientation and Conflict in Career,* see 1712. *

1712. ZALEZNIK, ABRAHAM; DALTON, GENE W.; AND BARNES, LOUIS B.; WITH PIERRE LAURIN. *Orientation and Conflict in Career.* Boston, Mass.: Division of Research, Harvard University, Graduate School of Business Administration, 1970. Pp. xxiii, 508. *

1713. AARON, P. G.; MARIHAL, V. G.; AND MALATESHA, R. N. "Standardization of a TAT Instrument to Measure n-Achievement of High School Boys in South India." *Indian J Appl Psychol* 8(1):30–2 Ja '71. *

1714. ARONOW, EDWARD, AND REZNIKOFF, MARVIN. "Application of Projective Tests to Psychotherapy: A Case Study." *J Pers Assess* 35(4):379–93 Ag '71. * (*PA* 47:5067)

1715. BELLAK, LEOPOLD; WITH THE ASSISTANCE OF ANN NOLL AND LYNN LUSTBADER. *The Thematic Apperception Test and the Children's Apperception Test in Clinical Use, Second Edition.* New York: Grune & Stratton, Inc., 1971. Pp. xvi, 328. *

1716. CHIRIBOGA, DAVID, AND LOWENTHAL, MARJORIE FISKE. "Psychological Correlates of Perceived Well-Being." Abstract. *Proc 79th Ann Conv Am Psychol Assn* 6(2):603–4 '71. * (*PA* 46:4945)

1717. DE RIOS, MARLENE DOBKIN. "A Note on the Use of 'Ethno-Tests' and Western Projective Tests in a Peruvian Amazon Slum." *Hum Org* 30(1):89–94 sp '71. *

1718. DHAPOLA, T. S. "The Effectiveness of TAT as a Measure of Aggression: A Review." *Indian J Psychol* 46(4):319–28 D '71. * (*PA* 50:3038)

1719. DIETZEL, CLEASON S., AND ABELES, NORMAN. "Thematic Drive Expression and Self-Esteem." *J Pers Assess* 35(5):442–7 O '71. * (*PA* 47:8951)

1720. ENNIS, RONALD FREDERICK. *A Typology for the Development of the Achievement Syndrome in Black College Students.* Doctor's thesis, Vanderbilt University (Nashville, Tenn.), 1971. (*DAI* 32:1102A)

1721. ENTIN, ELLIOT E. "Effect of Achievement-Oriented Tendencies and Extrinsic Tendencies on Performance." Abstract. *Proc 79th Ann Conv Am Psychol Assn* 6(1):383–4 '71. * (*PA* 46:3051)

1722. FRIED, CHRISTOPHER. "Icarianism, Masochism, and Sex Differences in Fantasy." *J Pers Assess* 35(1):38–55 F '71. * (*PA* 46:6898)

1723. GIFFIN, KIM, AND GILHAM, SHIRLEY MASTERSON. "Relationships Between Speech Anxiety and Motivation." *Speech Monogr* 38(1):70–3 Mr '71. *

1724. GREENBERG, ROGER P., AND FISHER, SEYMOUR. "Some Differential Effects of Music on Projective and Structured Psychological Tests." *Psychol Rep* 28(3):817–8 Je '71. * (*PA* 46:10869)

1725. HARTMAN, A. ARTHUR, AND NICOLAY, ROBERT C. "The Effect of Black-White Reversal on the TAT." *J Clin Psychol* 27(3):383–4 Jl '71. * (*PA* 47:4831)

1726. HEREDERO, I. M. "Motivation Courses and College Students." *Indian Ed R* 6(2):165–81 Jl '71. *

1727. HERSEN, MICHEL. "Sexual Aspects of TAT Administration: A Failure at Replication With an Inpatient Population." *J Consult & Clin Psychol* 36(1):20–2 F '71. * (*PA* 45:10000)

1728. HOLZMAN, PHILIP S., AND ROUSEY, CLYDE. "Disinhibition of Communicated Thought: Generality and Role of Cognitive Style." *J Abn Psychol* 77(3):263–74 Je '71. * (*PA* 46:6158)

1729. HONOR, STEPHEN H. *TAT and Direct Methods of Obtaining Educational Attitudes of High and Low Achieving High School Boys.* Doctor's thesis, Hofstra University (Hempstead, N.Y.), 1971. (*DAI* 32:1213B)

1730. IRIZARRY, RAYMOND. "Anxiety, Repression and Varieties of Anti-Social Behavior in Psychopaths." *J Pers Assess* 35(1):56–61 F '71. * (*PA* 46:7161)

1731. IRVIN, FLOYD S., AND VANDER WOUDE, KENNETH. "Empirical Support for a Basic TAT Set." *J Clin Psychol* 27(4):514–6 O '71. * (*PA* 47:8952)

1732. JACOBS, SUSAN LYNNE. *Achievement Motivation and Relevant Achievement Contexts: A Revised Methodology.* Doctor's thesis, University of Nebraska (Lincoln, Neb.), 1971. (*DAI* 32:2798A)

1733. KADUSHIN, PHINEAS; WAXENBERG, SHELDON E.; AND SAGER, CLIFFORD J. "Family Story Technique Changes in Interactions and Affects During Family Therapy." *J Pers Assess* 35(1):62–71 F '71. * (*PA* 46:7253)

1734. KEEPERS, TERRY D. "Conceptual Relationships Between Test Protocols and Clinical Report." *J Pers Assess* 35(3):241–7 Je '71. * (*PA* 47:3270)

1735. McKIE, ROBERT RAILTON. *A Clinical Study: Relationships of Anger and Fear to Aggression, in Murderers and in Non-Violent Offenders.* Doctor's thesis, Michigan State University (East Lansing, Mich.), 1971. (*DAI* 32:7317B)

1736. MEISELS, MURRAY, AND DOSEY, MICHAEL A. "Personal Space, Anger-Arousal, and Psychological Defense." *J Personality* 39(3):333–44 S '71. * (*PA* 47:6783)

1737. MOLISH, H. BARRY; KRAFT, IRVIN A.; AND WIGGINS, P. Y. "Psychodiagnostic Evaluation of the Heart Transplant Patient." *Seminars Psychiatry* 3(1):46–57 F '71. * (*PA* 49:7577)

1738. MUNDY, JEAN. "An Addition to Hartman's 'Basic TAT Set.'" *J Pers Assess* 35(4):307–8 Ag '71. * (*PA* 47:4834)

1739. MUNDY, JEAN. "Content Analysis: TAT Card 12BG—The Rowboat as a Symbol for Female Body Image and Sexual Activity." *Psychol Rep* 28(1):219–22 F '71. * (*PA* 46:5214)

1740. NAWAS, M. MIKE. "Change in Efficiency of Ego Functioning and Complexity From Adolescence to Young Adulthood." *Develop Psychol* 4(3):412–5 My '71. * (*PA* 46:6620)

1741. OLCH, DORIS. "Personality Characteristics of Hemophiliacs." *J Pers Assess* 35(1):72–9 F '71. * (*PA* 46:7371)

1742. PERKINS, KENNETH A., AND REYHER, JOSEPH. "Repression, Psychopathology and Drive Representation: An Experimental Hypnotic Investigation of Impulse Inhibition." *Am J Clin Hyp* 13(4):249–58 Ap '71. * (*PA* 46:11025)

1743. RADEN, BERNARD. *Personality Characteristics of Social Workers Working With Unwed Mothers.* Doctor's thesis, Illinois Institute of Technology (Chicago, Ill.), 1971. (*DAI* 32:1858B)

1744. RAJ, JACOB SELVA. *A Comparative Study of Homeless and Domiciled Alcoholic Men.* Doctor's thesis, Yeshiva University (New York, N.Y.), 1971. (*DAI* 32:1858B)

1745. RAWLS, DONNA J.; RAWLS, JAMES R.; AND HARRISON, C. WADE. "An Investigation of Six- to Eleven-Year-Old Children With Allergic Disorders." *J Consult & Clin Psychol* 36(2):260–4 Ap '71. * (*PA* 46:3655)

1746. ROLSTON, RICHARD HUMMEL. *The Effect of Prior Physical Abuse on the Expression of Overt and Fantasy Aggressive Behavior in Children.* Doctor's thesis, Louisiana State University (Baton Rouge, La.), 1971. (*DAI* 32:3016B)

1747. SCHAEFER, CHARLES E. "Imaginative Elements in the Thematic Fantasies of Creative Young Women." Abstract. *Proc 79th Ann Conv Am Psychol Assn* 6(1):417–8 '71. * (*PA* 46:3078)

1748. SCHAEFER, CHARLES E. "Primary-Process Thinking in Thematic Fantasies of Creative Adolescents." *Personality* 2(3):219–25 au '71. * (*PA* 47:6550)

1749. SCHULMAN, DAVID, AND SHONTZ, FRANKLIN C. "Body Posture and Thinking." *Percept & Motor Skills* 32(1):27–33 F '71. * (*PA* 46:2323)

1750. SHAPIRO, KENNETH JOEL. *The Concept of Introversion: Theoretical, Empirical, and Descriptive Considerations.* Doctor's thesis, Duke University (Durham, N.C.), 1971. (*DAI* 32:1830B)

1751. SINHA, AWADHESH KUMAR, AND SHARAN, MITHILA BEHARI. "Some Extra-Content Indicators of Maladjustment in TAT and Rorschach." *Indian J Psychol* 46(2):115–24 Je '71. *

1752. SMITH, R. BOB, III. "Coercive Influence as a Function of Frustration and Fantasy Aggression." Abstract. *Proc 79th Ann Conv Am Psychol Assn* 6(1):231–2 '71. * (*PA* 46:2952)

1753. STEELE, CAROLYN I. "Sexual Identity Problems Among Adolescent Girls in Institutional Placement." *Adolescence* 6(24):509–22 w '71. * (*PA* 48:7393)

1754. STOLOROW, ROBERT D. "Causality-Interpretation and the Precipitation of Distress." *J Pers Assess* 35(2):122–7 Ap '71. * (*PA* 47:2978)

1755. TAFT, RONALD. "Creativity: Hot and Cold." *J Personality* 39(3):345–61 S '71. * (*PA* 47:6804)

1756. TAYLOR, LINDA L.; CATFORD, JOHN C.; GUIORA, ALEXANDER Z.; AND LANE, HARLAN L. "Psychological Variables and Ability to Pronounce a Second Language." *Lang & Speech* (England) 14(2):146–57 Ap–Je '71. * (*PA* 47:4762)

1757. TRUCKENMILLER, JAMES LEROY. *Equivalence of Personality Structure in Leary's Interpersonal System of Diagnosis.* Doctor's thesis, West Virginia University (Morgantown, W.Va.), 1971. (*DAI* 32:6663B)

1758. VANDENBOS, GARY R., AND KARON, BERTRAM P. "Pathogenesis: A New Therapist Personality Dimension Related to Therapeutic Effectiveness." *J Pers Assess* 35(3):252–60 Je '71. * (*PA* 47:3113)

1759. VARBLE, DUANE L. Chap. 11, "Current Status of the Thematic Apperception Test," pp. 216–35. In *Advances in Psychological Assessment, Vol. 2.* Edited by Paul McReynolds. Palo

Thematic Apperception Test

Alto, Calif.: Science and Behavior Books, Inc., 1971. Pp. xii, 395. *

1760. VAVRIK, JULIE, AND JURICH, ANTHONY P. "Self-Concept and Attitude Toward Acceptance of Females: A Note." *Family Coordinator* 20(2):151–2 Ap '71. * (*PA* 46:10722)

1761. WAGNER, KATHRYN McJILTON. *Psychological Variables in Pre-Eclampsia: A Study in Three Parts.* Doctor's thesis, Purdue University (Lafayette, Ind.), 1971. (*DAI* 32:3626B)

1762. WIMMERS, DICK. *The Stability of Projective Interpretations.* Doctor's thesis, University of Missouri (Columbia, Mo.), 1971. (*DAI* 32:1865B)

1763. WOLK, STEPHEN, AND DUCETTE, JOSEPH. "Locus of Control and Achievement Motivation: Theoretical Overlap and Methodological Divergence." *Psychol Rep* 29(3):755–8 D '71. * (*PA* 47:8893)

1764. ZWEBEN, JOAN ELLEN. *Psychological and Psychosomatic Responses to the Oral Contraceptive.* Doctor's thesis, University of Michigan (Ann Arbor, Mich.), 1971. (*DAI* 32:6666B)

CUMULATIVE NAME INDEX

Aaron, N. S.: 1145
Aaron, P. G.: 1713
Abegglen, J. C.: 632
Abel, T. M.: 46, 955
Abeles, N.: 1719
Abram, H. S.: 1423
Abramson, L. S.: 857
Adams, M.: 1540
Adcock, C. J.: *rev*, 6:245
Adelman, G.: *exc*, 6:B60
Adrian, R. J.: 1184, 1235
Agrawal, K. G.: 1042
Ahmed, S. N.: 1146
Ainsworth, L. H.: 957
Ainsworth, M. D.: 957
Albrecht, K. J.: 586
Alexander, I. E.: 1468
Alexander, M.: 1551
Alexander, T.: 188, 1551
Alker, H. A.: 1424
Allan, J. H.: 1423
Allison, J.: 1189
Allison, R. B.: 985
Alper, T. G.: 1358; *exc*, 5: B395
Amen, E. W.: 11
Ammons, C. H.: 825; *exc*, 6: B326
Ammons, R. B.: 549, 825
Anastasi, A.: 750
Anderson, D. E.: 633
Anderson, H. H.: 367
Anderson, L. R.: 986, 1330
Andrews, R. G.: 1699
Apfelbaum, A.: 623
Applezweig, M. H.: 518
Arbuckles, D. S.: 1640
Arffa, M. S.: 969
Armand, A.: 1493
Armstrong, M. A. S.: 426
Arnold, M.: 290
Arnold, M. B.: 153, 811–2
Aron, B.: 118, 154, 189, 290
Aronow, E.: 1714
Arthur, B.: 970
Asher, E. J.: 586
Atkinson, J. W.: 119, 170, 302, 406, 427, 634, 775, 932, 942
Auld, F.: 428, 438, 468, 477, 1562
Avila, D. L.: 813
Axel, G. R.: 1043
Bachrach, A. J.: 294
Baker, C. T.: 591
Balcombe, J. K.: 1532
Balken, E. R.: 3, 6–7, 15, 25–6, 38, 47
Bandler, L.: 1616
Barclay, A.: 1425
Barclay, A. M.: 1359, 1426
Bard, M.: 469, 1242
Barnes, D. J.: 1044
Barnes, L. B.: 1712
Barnouw, V.: 858
Barrington, B. L.: 1360
Barron, F.: 618, 859, 1292
Barroso, M. A.: 1190
Barsky, M. L.: 1331
Barthol, R. P.: 719
Barwick, J. M.: 1274, 1640
Bassett, M.: 1542
Bassin, A.: 1635
Baty, M. A.: 1694

Baughman, E. E.: 933
Baxter, J. C.: 1641
Beardslee, D. C.: 925
Bechtel, R. B.: 1093
Becker, B.: 1485
Becker, G. J.: 987
Becker, J.: 1641
Beggs, J. J.: 1147
Behring, D. W.: 1427
Beier, E. G.: 249
Beigel, H. G.: 319
Bell, A.: 376
Bell, J. E.: 120, 155
Bellak, L.: 16, 39, 79, 156, 190–4, 290, 320, 429–30, 519, 751, 1715
Bennett, G.: 12, 17
Benton, A. L.: *rev*, 3:103, 4: 136
Benton, J. A.: 1297
Bentsen, I. B.: 520
Berenberg, A. N.: 1255
Berg, P. S. D.: 860
Bergman, M.: 377
Bergmann, M. S.: 64, 113
Berk, N.: 157
Berkowitz, H.: 916, 1016
Berkun, M. M.: 988
Berlew, D. E.: 943
Berne, N.: 1306
Bernstein, L.: 521, 697, 861, 1045
Berntson, R. K.: 378
Berthold, M. C.: 1191
Bethe, D. R.: 1379
Bettelheim, B.: 80
Bialick, I.: 306
Bijou, S. W.: 250, 398
Bills, N.: 379
Bills, R. E.: 195–6
Blackham, G. J.: 905
Blank, L.: 1046
Blatt, E. F.: 1646
Blatt, S. J.: 1189
Blek, L.: 331
Blendstrup, U.: 752
Block, S. K.: 1325
Blom, G. E.: 1616
Blondheim, S. H.: 1170
Bluhm, P. M.: 1298
Blum, G. S.: 321
Boag, T. J.: 1608
Bobroff, A.: 1627
Bock, C.: 158
Bodarky, C. J.: 821
Bohn, S. E.: 1695
Boileau, V.: 287
Bolgar, H.: *exc*, 5:B395
Bolton, R. J.: 620
Boone, J. N.: 1278
Borenstein, B. A.: 470
Borstein, I. J.: 1486
Botha, E.: 1647, 1660
Boyd, I.: 669
Bozeman, M. F.: 1582
Brackbill, B. J.: 252
Brackbill, G. A.: 251–2
Bradford, J.: 684
Bradford, J. L.: 1192
Bradley, M. O.: 566
Bradt, K. H.: 307
Brady, J. P.: 831, 1009
Bramel, D.: 862
Bramlette, C. A.: 380

Brand, J.: 1688
Braverman, S.: 79, 156
Bray, D. W.: 1161
Brayer, R.: 753
Breger, L.: 863, 1279
Brender, W. J.: 1148
Brener, E. M.: 1428
Brenman, M.: 18
Brenner, M. S.: 754
Brenner, R.: 1243
Brice, B. C.: 304
Briggs, D. L.: 431
Brill, N. Q.: 1648
Britton, J. H.: 864
Brodsky, S. L.: 1380
Brody, H.: 907
Brody, J. R.: 546
Broida, D. C.: 432
Broota, A.: 1193
Broota, K. D.: 989, 1193
Brower, D.: 121, 253
Brower, E.: 105, 281
Brown, J.: 1149
Brown, L. B.: **865**
Brown, W. T.: 291, 1381
Bryant, J. E.: 953
Bucher, S.: 381
Budnoff, C. K.: 662
Buhler, C.: 53
Buirski, P.: 1487
Burdick, H.: 518
Burdick, H. A.: 988
Burgess, E.: 382, 522
Burgin, L.: 1616
Burkard, M. I.: 814
Burnstein, E.: 971
Burrows, B.: 1433
Burton, A.: 159
Burton, L.: 1382
Butler, G. A.: 1194
Butler, O. P.: 122
Byrne, D.: 944–5, 972
Cahen, E. R.: 271
Caine, T. M.: 708
Caldwell, B. M.: 1552
Caligor, L.: 197, 254
Callahan, R.: 206
Calogeras, R. C.: 567, 635
Calvin, J. S.: 198
Cameron, N.: 335
Campbell, M. M.: 608
Campus, N. R.: 1696
Cansever, G.: 1383
Canter, F. M.: 383
Cardin, P. J.: 1436
Carlile, J. S. H.: 308, 322
Carlsen, N.: 323
Carlson, H. B.: 255
Carlson, H. J.: 1671
Carney, R. E.: 1094
Carpenter, L. G.: 1602
Carr, A. C.: 433, 523, 636, 1653, 1681
Carroll, J. F. X.: 1384
Carruth, B.: 395
Carter, A. R.: 1527
Cartwright, D. S.: 866, 1302, 1603
Cartwright, R. D.: 621, 1628
Castelnuovo-Tedesco, P.: 1488
Catalano, F. L.: *exc*, 5:B63
Catford, J. C.: 1756
Cattell, R. B.: 324
Caudill, W.: 325, 622
Cerf, A. Z.: 110
Cervantes, L. F.: 1311, 1425
Chakrabarti, P. K.: 1095
Chance, J.: 1563
Chapin, N.: 384
Chapman, G. O.: 1195
Chappell, M. C.: 879
Charlens, A. M.: 1096, 1287
Chatham, L. R.: 1179
Chatterjee, T. K.: 973, 1689
Chaubey, N. P.: 1385
Child, I. L.: 524
Chipman, C. E.: 59
Chiriboga, D.: 1716
Chorny, H. H.: 974
Chowdhury, U.: 709
Christ, A. E.: 1419
Christensen, A. H.: 309
Christenson, J. A.: 27
Christiansen, K.: 667

Christy, E. G.: 847
Chu, C.: 1047
Chu, C. P.: 1386–7
Clapperton, G.: 1150
Clark, E. T.: 1429, 1690
Clark, R. A.: 170, 326, 406, 471, 525–6
Clark, R. M.: 40, 59a
Cleland, C. C.: 1430
Clements, W. H.: 1388, 1480
Cleveland, S. E.: 527, 643, 663, 755, 815, 867, 1407, 1564, 1592
Clifford, P. I.: 637
Cline, V. B.: 568
Close, A.: 1660
Coale, J. M.: 701
Cobb, B.: 958
Cobb, S.: 1558
Coburn, T. E.: 1259
Coelho, G. V.: 821
Coffey, H. S.: 447
Cohen, A. F.: 1299
Cohen, H.: 959
Cohen, H. A.: 1431
Cohen, I.: 1489
Cohen, L. D.: 1569
Cohen, W. J.: 199, 257
Cohler, J. R.: 629, 931
Colarelli, N. J.: 1504
Coleman, J. C.: 853, 1151, 1389, 1432
Coleman, W.: 81
Collier, H. L.: 835
Combs, A. W.: 60–3, 82
Congdon, R. G.: 990
Conners, C. K.: 868
Conrad, W. K.: 756
Cook, P. E.: 1172
Cook, R. A.: 327, 385
Cooley, W. W.: 869
Cooper, G. W.: 992
Copple, R.: 1504
Cornelison, A. R.: 584
Cottingham, A.: 232, 286
Courtless, T. F.: 1228
Cowan, G.: 1152
Cowden, R. C.: 472
Cox, B.: 201
Cox, B. F.: 123, 200
Cox, F. N.: 816–7, 1553; *exc*, 5:B204
Cox, R. D.: 434, 528
Cox, S. H.: 1179
Craig, C.: 753
Craig, J.: 1563
Crandall, V.: 367
Crandall, V. J.: 258
Crasilneck, H. B.: 435
Crawford, A. E.: 1153
Cronbach, L. J.: 1490; *exc*, 5: B395
Crotty, W. F.: 1015
Crouch, R. G.: 580
Crowne, D. P.: 1300
Cruickshank, W.: 395
Crumpton, E.: 818, 1648
Csirszka, J.: 1657
Culligan, K. G.: 1697
Cummin, P. C.: 1154
Cumming, E.: 757
Cummings, S. T.: 1433
Curtis, G. C.: 1686
Cutler, C.: 1444
Dachowski, M. M.: 1097, 1280
Dahlin, G.: 1434
Dalack, J. D.: 991
Dalton, G. W.: 1712
Damarin, F.: 958
Dana, R. H.: 436, 473–4, 529–31, 569, 664–7, 710–1, 758, 861, 992, 1045, 1048, 1056, 1098–9, 1196; *rev*, 7:181
Danesino, A.: 1435
Danowski, T. S.: 802
Dass, S. L.: 1100
Davenport, B. F.: 328–9
David, C.: 788
Davids, A.: 475, 532, 587, 638, 686, 712, 759, 1436, 1642–3
Davison, A. H.: 202, 386
Day, C. W.: 993
Deabler, H. L.: 83, 472

Thematic Apperception Test

Thematic Apperception Test

Zimring, F. M.: 1532
Zubin, J.: 1092, 1204
Zuckerman, M.: 661, 810, 1188, 1621, 1686

Zuk, G. H.: 627
Zwanziger, M. D.: 985
Zweben, J. E.: 1764

[1520]

Thematic Apperception Test for African Subjects. Ages 10 and over; 1953; S. G. Lee; University of Natal Press [South Africa]. *

For additional information, see P:485 (1 reference); for a review by Mary D. Ainsworth, see 5:165 (1 reference).

REFERENCES THROUGH 1971
1. See 5:165.
2. See P:485.

CUMULATIVE NAME INDEX
Ainsworth, M. D.: *rev,* 5:165   Lee, S. G.: 1
de Ridder, J. C.: 2

[1521]

★This I Believe Test. Grades 9 and over; 1971; TIB; sentence completion; "concreteness-abstractness of conceptual or belief systems"; no manual; O. J. Harvey; the Author. *

REFERENCES THROUGH 1971
1. WHITE, JACK, AND HARVEY, O. J. "Effects of Personality and Own Stand on Judgment and Production of Statements About a Central Issue." *J Exp Social Psychol* 1:334–47 N '65. *
2. ADAMS, DARREL K.; HARVEY, O. J.; AND HESLIN, RICHARD E. Chap. 10, "Variation in Flexibility and Creativity as a Function of Hypnotically Induced Past Histories," pp. 217–34. In *Experience, Structure and Adaptability.* Edited by O. J. Harvey. New York: Springer Publishing Co., Inc., 1966. Pp. ix, 406. *
3. HARVEY, O. J. Chap. 4, "System Structure, Flexibility and Creativity," pp. 39–63. In his *Experience, Structure and Adaptability.* New York: Springer Publishing Co., Inc., 1966. Pp. ix, 406. *
4. HARVEY, O. J.; WHITE, B. JACK; PRATHER, MISHA S.; ALTER, RICHARD D.; AND HOFFMEISTER, JAMES K. "Teachers' Belief Systems and Preschool Atmospheres." *J Ed Psychol* 57:373–81 D '66. * (*PA* 41:2003)
5. MARCANTONIO, CHARLES. *Performance Expectancy as a Determinant of Actual Performance: With Particular Reference to Individual Difference Variables.* Doctor's thesis, State University of New York (Buffalo, N.Y.), 1966. (*DA* 28:785A)
6. HARVEY, O. J., AND WARE, ROBERT. "Personality Differences in Dissonance Resolution." *J Pers & Social Psychol* 7:227–30 O '67. * (*PA* 41:16679)
7. WARE, ROBERT, AND HARVEY, O. J. "A Cognitive Determinant of Impression Formation." *J Pers & Social Psychol* 5:38–44 Ja '67. * (*PA* 41:4519)
8. HARVEY, O. J.: PRATHER, MISHA; WHITE, B. JACK; AND HOFFMEISTER, JAMES K. "Teachers' Beliefs, Classroom Atmosphere and Student Behavior." *Am Ed Res J* 5:151–66 Mr '68. *
9. MATSUURO, LARY NOBUO. *The Relationship of Effective Counseling to Conceptual Systems Orientation.* Doctor's thesis, University of Northern Colorado (Greeley, Colo.), 1970. (*DAI* 31:5002B)
10. GREAVES, GEORGE. "Harvey's 'This I Believe' Test: Studies of Reliability." *Psychol Rep* 28(2):387–90 Ap '71. * (*PA* 46:6877)
11. PENRY, IRENE FREES. *Conceptual Systems and Self-Exploration.* Doctor's thesis, University of Florida (Gainesville, Fla.), 1971. (*DAI* 32:6767A)

CUMULATIVE NAME INDEX
Adams, D. K.: 2
Alter, R. D.: 4
Greaves, G.: 10
Harvey, O. J.: 1–4, 6–8
Heslin, R. E.: 2
Hoffmeister, J. K.: 4, 8
Marcantonio, C.: 5

Matsuuro, L. N.: 9
Penry, I. F.: 11
Prather, M.: 8
Prather, M. S.: 4
Ware, R.: 6–7
White, B. J.: 4, 8
White, J.: 1

[1522]

The Tomkins-Horn Picture Arrangement Test. Ages 10 and over; 1942–59; PAT; Silvan S. Tomkins, Daniel Horn, and John B. Miner (manuals); Springer Publishing Co., Inc. *

For additional information, see P:487 (4 references); for a review by Robert C. Nichols and excerpted reviews by Sidney E. Cleveland, H. Phillipson, and Leonard P. Ullmann, see 6:246 (7 references); for reviews by Donald W. Fiske, John W. Gittinger,

and Wayne H. Holtzman and an excerpted review by Leonard D. Goodstein, see 5:167 (6 references).

REFERENCES THROUGH 1971
1–6. See 5:167.
7–13. See 6:246.
14–17. See P:487.
18. MINER, JOHN B., AND CULVER, JOHN E. "Some Aspects of the Executive Personality." *J Appl Psychol* 39:348–53 O '55. * (*PA* 30:7809)
19. ALEXANDER, VALAVUCHIRACKAL K. *An Experimental Study of Some Determinants of Defensive Behavior.* Doctor's thesis, Princeton University (Princeton, N.J.), 1957. (*DA* 18:291)
20. FREDERIKSEN, NORMAN, AND GILBERT, ARTHUR C. F. "Replication of a Study of Differential Predictability." *Ed & Psychol Meas* 20:759–67 w '60. * (*PA* 35:7953)
21. MINER, JOHN B. "Conformity Among University Professors and Business Executives." *Adm Sci Q* 7:96–109 Je '62. * (*PA* 37:3016)
22. STOESS, ALFRED WILLIAM. *Conformity Behavior of Managers and Wives of Managers in Wife-Oriented and Non-Wife-Oriented Companies.* Doctor's thesis, University of Oregon (Eugene, Ore.), 1967. (*DA* 28:1940A)
23. MINER, JOHN B. "Personality Tests as Predictors of Consulting Success." *Personnel Psychol* 24(2):191–204 su '71. * (*PA* 49:3422)

CUMULATIVE NAME INDEX
Alexander, V. K.: 19
Cleveland, S. E.: *exc,* 6:246
Culver, J. E.: 18
Davis, M.: 14
Fiske, D. W.: *rev,* 5:167
Foster, P. B.: 17
Frederiksen, N.: 20
Gilbert, A. C. F.: 20
Gittinger, J. W.: *rev,* 5:167
Goodstein, L. D.: *exc,* 5:167
Higashimachi, W. H.: 13
Holtzman, W. H.: *rev,* 5:167
Karon, B. P.: 6

McCarter, R. E.: 9
Miner, J. B.: 4–5, 7–8, 10, 12, 15, 18, 21, 23
Nichols, R. C.: *rev,* 6:246
Pate, K. D.: 11
Phillipson, H.: *exc,* 6:246
Schiffman, H. M.: 9
Sjostedt, E. M.: 2
Stoess, A. W.: 22
Tomkins, S. S.: 1, 3–5, 7, 9, 16
Ullmann, L. P.: *exc,* 6:246

[1523]

The Toy World Test. Ages 2 and over; 1941–55; TWT; formerly called *The World Test;* Charlotte Buhler; Centre de Psychologie Appliquee [France]. *

For additional information, see P:488 (1 reference); for a review by L. Joseph Stone, see 5:168 (11 references); see also 4:147 (6 references).

REFERENCES THROUGH 1971
1–6. See 4:147.
7–17. See 5:168.
18. See P:488.
19. WENAR, CHARLES. "The Effects of a Motor Handicap on Personality: 2, The Effects of Integrative Ability." *Child Develop* 25:287–94 D '54. * (*PA* 29:7813)

CUMULATIVE NAME INDEX
Bell, J. E.: 3
Bolgar, H.: 7
Buhler, C.: 2, 5–6, 10–3, 15
Carrol, H. S.: 5–6, 13
Fischer, L. K.: 7–9
Kogan, K. L.: 4
Lowenfeld, M.: 7

Lumry, G. K.: 5–6, 14
Michael, J. C.: 2
Pascal, G. R.: 16
Rosenzweig, S.: 4
Sharma, S. N.: 18
Stone, L. J.: *rev,* 5:168
Wenar, C.: 17, 19

[1524]

The Tree Test. Ages 9 and over; 1949–52; Charles Koch; Hans Huber [Switzerland]. * (United States distributor: Grune & Stratton, Inc.)

For additional information, see P:489 (3 references); see also 5:170 (2 references). For excerpts from related book reviews, see 5:B251 (2 excerpts).

REFERENCES THROUGH 1971
1–2. See 5:170.
3–5. See P:489.

CUMULATIVE NAME INDEX
Forer, B. R.: *exc,* 5:B251
Gleser, G. C.: *exc,* 5:B251
Koch, C.: 1
Kunke, T.: 4

Straub, R. R.: 3
Tolor, A.: 2
Welman, A. J.: 5

[1525]

Twitchell-Allen Three-Dimensional Personality Test. Ages 3 and over (sighted and sightless); 1948–60; TA3DPT; formerly called *Twitchell-Allen Three-*

Dimensional Apperception Test; Doris Twitchell-Allen; the Author. *

For additional information, see P:490 (2 references); see also 5:171 (3 references); for a review by Edward Joseph Shoben, Jr., see 4:143.

REFERENCES THROUGH 1971
1–3. See 5:171.
4–5. See P:490.

CUMULATIVE NAME INDEX

Allen, D. T.: 3   Starer, E.: 2
Fein, L. G.: 3–5   Twitchell-Allen, D.: 1
Shoben, E. J.: *rev,* 4:143

[1526]
Visual Apperception Test '60. Ages 6 and over; 1960–62; VAT '60; prevalent mood and clinical diagnosis; Rafi Z. Khan; Midwest Psychological Services. *

For additional information, see P:491 (2 references); for reviews by Bert R. Sappenfield and Stanley J. Segal, see 6:247.

REFERENCES THROUGH 1971
1–2. See P:491.
3. CLARK, EDWARD T. "Culturally Disadvantaged Boys' and Girls' Aspirations to and Knowledge of White-Collar and Professional Occupations." *Urban Ed* 1:164–74 sp '65. * (*PA* 39: 14638)
4. KHAN, RAFI ZAMAN. "Perceptual Regression in Mental Illness as Revealed by Visual Apperception Test '60 (VAT '60)." *Int Congr Rorsch & Other Proj Tech* 7:330–42 '70. *

CUMULATIVE NAME INDEX

Clark, E. T.: 3   Sappenfield, B. R.: *rev,* 6:247
Khan, R. Z.: 1, 4   Segal, S. J.: *rev,* 6:247
Mons, W. E. R.: 2

[1527]
Washington University Sentence Completion Test. Ages 12 and over; 1962–70; WUSCT; various titles used by authors; ego development; Jane Loevinger, Ruth Wessler, and Carolyn Redmore (scoring manual); Jossey-Bass Inc., Publishers. *

For additional information, see 7:182 (5 references). For an excerpt from a related book review, see 7:B395.

REFERENCES THROUGH 1971
1–5. See 7:182.
6. BLASI, AUGUSTO. *A Developmental Approach to Responsibility Training.* Doctor's thesis, Washington University (St. Louis, Mo.), 1971. (*DAI* 32:1233B)

CUMULATIVE NAME INDEX

Bednar, M. A.: 1   Rafferty, J.: *exc,* 7:B395
Blasi, A.: 6   Redmore, C.: 5
Hezel, J. D.: 2   Wessler, R.: 4–5
Loevinger, J.: 3–5

[1528]
The Zulliger Individual and Group Test. Ages 3 and over; 1948–69; ZT; formerly called *Z-Test;* Hans Zulliger; English manual edited by Fritz Salomon, translated by Dusya T. Dubrovsky; Hans Huber [Switzerland]. (United States distributor: International Universities Press, Inc.) *

For additional information and excerpted reviews

by Margaret Mercer and Bernard I. Murstein, see 7: 183 (13 references); for an excerpted review by Boris Semenoff, see 7:B664.

REFERENCES THROUGH 1971
1–13. See 7:183.

CUMULATIVE NAME INDEX

Amado-Haguenauer, G.: 2–3   Lefkowitz, M. M.: 7
Bash, K. W.: 12   Mercer, M.: *exc,* 7:183
Bash-Liechti, J.: 12   Murstein, B. I.: *exc,* 7:183
Besijn, J. W.: 13   Salomon, F.: 11
Boeke, P. E.: 13   Schmid, F. W.: 8
Eble, S. J.: 5   Schut, D.: 13
Fernald, L. D.: 5   Semenoff, B.: 6, 9–10; *exc,*
Gladston, E. R.: 2–4   7:B664
Graziano, A. M.: 5   Uleman, A. L.: 13
Haguenauer, G.: 4   Zulliger, H.: 11
Kraus, A. R.: 1

[Out of Print Since TIP I]

Behavioral Complexity Test, P:494, 6:202 (1 review, 4 references)
Buhler-Lefever Rorschach Diagnostic Sign List, 6:237b
Controlled Projection for Children, P:495, 6:207 (3 reviews, 8 excerpts, 8 references)
Drawing-Completion Test, P:496 (4 excerpts, 19 references), 5:130
Eight Card Redrawing Test (status unknown), P:425 (2 reviews, 5 excerpts, 7 references), 6:211
Four Picture Test (1930), P:431 (5 reviews, 1 excerpt, 9 references), 6:213
Graphomotor Projection Technique, P:499, 5:137 (1 review, 2 excerpts, 7 references)
Horn-Hellersberg Test (status unknown), P:441 (2 reviews, 7 references), 6:218
Insight Test, P:500 (1 review, 12 references), 5:143
Interpersonal Diagnosis of Personality, P:446 (1 review, 28 references), 6:223
Kell-Hoeflin Incomplete Sentence Blank, P:501 (3 references), 6:225
Lowenfeld Kaleidoblocs (status unknown), P:449, 6: 227 (2 reviews, 3 references)
Lowenfeld Mosaic Test (status unknown), P:450 (3 reviews, 98 references), 6:228
Michigan Picture Test, P:455 (2 reviews, 2 excerpts, 18 references), 5:150
Myokinetic Psychodiagnosis, P:502 (2 reviews, 11 references), 6:232
Percept and Concept Cognition Test (status unknown), P:460
Ten Silhouettes (status unknown), P:482, 6:244 (4 references)
Test of Subjective and Objective Factors in Relationship to Communication Skills (status unknown), P: 483
Thematic Apperception Test: Thompson Modification, P:486 (1 review, 3 excerpts, 10 references), 5:166
Travis Projective Pictures, P:505 (2 reviews, 5 references), 5:169

READING

[1529]
A.C.E.R. Lower Grades Reading Test: Level 1, Second Edition. Grade 1; 1962–64; for schools in

New South Wales; M. L. Clark, N. E. Morison, and J. L. A. Russell; Australian Council for Educational Research [Australia]. *

[1530]

★**ACER Primary Reading Survey Tests.** Grades 3, 4, 5, 6; 1971–72; 2 parts: word knowledge, comprehension; interim manual prepared by G. P. Withers in collaboration with M. L. Clark, W. T. Renehan, and B. Rechter; Australian Council for Educational Research [Australia]. *

[1531]

A.C.E.R. Silent Reading Tests: Standardized for Use in New Zealand. Ages 9–12; 1955; 3 parts; tests identical with corresponding parts of Form B (Part 2) and Form C (Parts 1 and 3) of *A.C.E.R. Silent Reading Tests;* A. E. Fieldhouse (manual); New Zealand Council for Educational Research [New Zealand]. *
a) PART 1, WORD KNOWLEDGE.
b) PART 2, SPEED OF READING.
c) PART 3, READING FOR MEANING.
For additional information, see 5:618.

REFERENCES THROUGH 1971
1. FOSTER, MARION E. "A Comparison of Reading Achievement of Christchurch, New Zealand and Edmonton Alberta Public School Students of the Same Age and Number of Years of Schooling." *Alberta J Ed Res* (Canada) 11:21–31 Mr '65. * (*PA* 39:16455)
2. McCREARY, J. R. "Reading Tests With Maori Children." *N Zeal J Ed Studies* 1(1–2):40–50 '66. *

CUMULATIVE NAME INDEX
Foster, M. E.: 1   McCreary, J. R.: 2

[1532]

American School Achievement Tests: Part 1, Reading. Grades 2–3, 4–6, 7–9; 1941–63; 3 scores: sentence and word meaning, paragraph meaning, total; 1955–57 tests essentially the same as tests copyrighted 1941–43; Willis E. Pratt, Robert V. Young, and Clara E. Cockerille; Bobbs-Merrill Co., Inc. * For the complete battery entry, see 4.
For additional information, see 6:783; for reviews by Russell G. Stauffer and Agatha Townsend, see 5:620. For reviews of the complete battery, see 6:2 (2 reviews), 5:1 (2 reviews), 4:1 (1 review), and 3:1 (2 reviews).

[1533]

American School Reading Tests. Grades 10–13; 1955; 3 scores: vocabulary, reading rate, comprehension; Willis E. Pratt and Stanley W. Lore; Bobbs-Merrill Co., Inc. *
For additional information and reviews by Henry S. Dyer and Donald E. P. Smith, see 5:621.

[1534]

Buffalo Reading Test for Speed and Comprehension. Grades 9–16; 1933–41; 3 scores: speed, comprehension, total; 1965 tests identical with tests copyrighted 1941; 1965 manual reprinted from 1936 manual; Mazie Earle Wagner and Daniel S. P. Schubert (1965 manual); Mazie Earle Wagner. *
For additional information and reviews by Holland Roberts and William W. Turnbull, see 3:477.

REFERENCES THROUGH 1971
1. GREENWOOD, ROBERT LEROY. *The Prediction of Academic Success in the Technical Curricula of Community Colleges: An Investigation of the Prediction of Academic Success in the Chemical, Electrical, and Mechanical Curricula of Three Community Colleges in New York State.* Doctor's thesis, New York University (New York, N.Y.), 1962. (*DA* 23:898)

CUMULATIVE NAME INDEX
Greenwood, R. L.: 1   Turnbull, W. W.: *rev*, 3:477
Roberts, H.: *rev*, 3:477

[1535]

Burnett Reading Series: Survey Test. Grades 1.5–2.4, 2.5–3.9, 4.0–6.9, 7.0–9.9, 10.0–12.9; 1966–70; 5

levels; Richard W. Burnett; Scholastic Testing Service, Inc. *
a) PRIMARY 1. Grades 1.5–2.4; 1966–69; 4 scores: word identification, word meaning, comprehension, total.
b) PRIMARY 2. Grades 2.5–3.9; 1966–69; scores same as for Primary 1; 1967 test identical with test published 1966.
c) INTERMEDIATE. Grades 4.0–6.9; 1966–69; scores same as for Primary 1; 1967 test identical with test published 1966.
d) ADVANCED. Grades 7.0–9.9; 1967; 4 scores: vocabulary, comprehension, total, rate and accuracy.
e) SENIOR. Grades 10.0–12.9; 1968–70; scores same as for Advanced.
For additional information and a review by Roger Farr, see 7:682.

[1536]

*****California Achievement Tests: Reading.** Grades 1–14; 1933–72; earlier editions called *Progressive Reading Tests;* 3 scores: vocabulary, comprehension, total; 2 editions; Ernest W. Tiegs and Willis W. Clark; CTB/McGraw-Hill. * For the complete battery entry, see 7.
a) 1957 EDITION WITH 1963 NORMS. Grades 1–2, 2.5–4.5, 4–6, 7–9, 9–14; 1933–63; test booklet title is *California Reading Test;* 1963 tests identical with tests copyrighted 1957 except for profile and revision of Form X (grades 7–9).
b) 1970 EDITION. Grades 1.5–2.5, 2.5–4.5, 4–6, 6–9, 9–12; 1933–72.
For additional information concerning the 1970 edition, see 7:683 (29 references); see also 6:784 (13 references) and 5:622 (5 references); for reviews by John C. Flanagan and James R. Hobson and an excerpted review by Laurance F. Shaffer of an earlier edition, see 4:530; for a review by Frederick B. Davis, see 2:1563; for reviews by Ivan A. Booker and Joseph C. Dewey, see 1:1110. For reviews of the complete battery, see 6:3 (2 reviews), 5:2 (1 review), 4:2 (3 reviews), 3:15 (1 review), 2:1193 (2 reviews), and 1:876 (1 review, 1 excerpt).

REFERENCES THROUGH 1971
1–5. See 5:622.
6–18. See 6:784.
19–47. See 7:683.
48. WILSON, FRANK Y.; BURKE, AGNES; AND FLEMMING, CECILE WHITE. "Sex Differences in Beginning Reading in a Progressive School." *J Ed Res* 32:570–82 Ap '39. * (*PA* 13:4386)
49. AUKERMAN, ROBERT C., JR. "Differences in the Reading Status of Good and Poor Eleventh Grade Students." *J Ed Res* 41:498–515 Mr '48. * (*PA* 22:4599)
50. SCHUBERT, DELWYN G. "A Comparative Study of the Hearing and Reading Vocabularies of Retarded College Readers." *J Ed Res* 46:555–8 Mr '53. * (*PA* 28:3219)
51. MORRISON, IDA E., AND PERRY, IDA F. "Spelling and Reading Relationships With Incidence of Retardation and Acceleration." *J Ed Res* 52:222–7 F '59. * (*PA* 34:2012)
52. McBEE, GEORGE, AND DUKE, RALPH L. "Relationship Between Intelligence, Scholastic Motivation, and Academic Achievement." *Psychol Rep* 6:3–8 F '60. * (*PA* 34:8404)
53. POWELL, MARVIN, AND BERGEM, JERRY. "An Investigation of the Differences Between Tenth-, Eleventh-, and Twelfth-Grade 'Conforming' and 'Nonconforming' Boys." *J Ed Res* 56:184–90 D '62. *
54. KITTELL, JACK E. "Intelligence-Test Performance of Children From Bilingual Environments." *El Sch J* 64:76–83 N '63. *
55. PARSLEY, KENNETH M., JR.; POWELL, MARVIN; O'CONNOR, HENRY A.; AND DEUTSCH, MURRAY. "Are There Really Sex Differences in Achievement?" *J Ed Res* 57:210–2 D '63. *
56. SCHNEIDERHAN, ROSEMARY MALMGREN. *A Correlation of Individual and Group Reading Tests.* Master's thesis, St. Cloud State College (St. Cloud, Minn.), 1963.
57. KATZ, STANLEY S. "Selection and Evaluation of Students in Medical Technology Degree Programs." *Am J Med Technol* 30:51–63 Ja '64. *
58. NEVILLE, MARY H., AND FROST, BARRY P. "Differential Achievement in Reading and Arithmetic." *Alberta J Ed Res* (Canada) 10:192–200 D '64. *

59. FOSTER, MARION E. "A Comparison of Reading Achievement of Christchurch, New Zealand and Edmonton Alberta Public School Students of the Same Age and Number of Years of Schooling." *Alberta J Ed Res* (Canada) 11:21–31 Mr '65. * (*PA* 39:16455)

60. SINKS, NAOMI B., AND POWELL, MARVIN. "Sex and Intelligence as Factors in Achievement in Reading in Grades 4 Through 8." *J Genetic Psychol* 106:67–79 Mr '65. * (*PA* 39: 12952)

61. THOMPSON, EVA LUCILE. *Relationship of Standardized Reading Test Findings for Primary Grade Children.* Master's thesis, Illinois State University (Normal, Ill.), 1965.

62. KNIGHT, DAVID, AND ALCORN, JOHN D. "Comparisons of the Performance of Educationally Disadvantaged Adults and Elementary Children on Selected Measures of Reading Performance." *South J Ed Res* 4(4):262–72 O '70. *

63. SMITH, I. MACFARLANE. "The Use of Diagnostic Tests for Assessing the Abilities of Overseas Students Attending Institutions of Further Education, Part I." *Voc Aspect Ed* (England) 22(51):1–8 Mr '70. *

64. BURKE, LEE A. *Reading Habits and Reading Background and How They Effect a Student's Performance on the Interpretative Section of the California Reading Test.* Master's thesis, Jersey City State College (Jersey City, N.J.), 1971.

65. DAVIS, BOBBIE, AND MCNINCH, GEORGE. "A Comparison of Three Standardized Reading Tests in a Fifth Grade Sample." *South J Ed Res* 5(2):101–12 Ap '71. *

66. FARR, ROGER, AND ROELKE, PATRICIA. "Measuring Subskills of Reading: Intercorrelations Between Standardized Reading Tests, Teachers' Ratings, and Reading Specialists' Ratings." *J Ed Meas* 8(1):27–32 sp '71. * (*PA* 46:5464)

67. KNIGHT, DAVID, AND ALCORN, JOHN D. "Comparisons of the Performance of Educationally Disadvantaged Adults and Elementary Children on Selected Measures of Reading Performance." *Yearb Nat Read Conf* 19(2):113–7 '71. *

68. MICHAEL, WILLIAM B.; HANEY, RUSSELL; LEE, YOUNG B.; AND MICHAEL, JOAN J. "The Criterion-Related Validities of Cognitive and Noncognitive Predictors in a Training Program for Nursing Candidates." *Ed & Psychol Meas* 31(4):983–7 w '71. * (*PA* 48:1866)

69. PARKER, DEWEY L. *Relationships Among the Keystone Visual Survey Telebinocular With Reading Achievement and the Diagnoses of a Vision Clinic.* Doctor's thesis, University of Oklahoma (Norman, Okla.), 1971. (*DAI* 32:2316A)

70. PURCELL, ELIZABETH WELLS. *The Relationship of Personality to Achievement in Reading Comprehension.* Doctor's thesis, St. Louis University (St. Louis, Mo.), 1971. (*DAI* 33:906A)

71. SEITHER, FRANCES GARDNER. *An Investigation of the Predictive Validity of Selected Admission Screening Measures Relative to Success in Practical Nursing.* Doctor's thesis, University of Maryland (College Park, Md.), 1971. (*DAI* 32:5890B)

72. SMITH, I. MACFARLANE. "The Use of Diagnostic Tests for Assessing the Abilities of Overseas Students Attending Institutions of Further Education, Part II." *Voc Aspect Ed* (England) 23(54):39–48 Ap '71. *

73. WETHERELL, RICHARD H. *A Study of the Relationship Between Visual Perception and School Achievement.* Doctor's thesis, University of Southern Mississippi (Hattiesburg, Miss.), 1971. (*DAI* 32:2324A)

74. WINEMAN, JOHN H. "Cognitive Style and Reading Ability." *Calif J Ed Res* 22(2):74–9 Mr '71. * (*PA* 46:9762)

CUMULATIVE NAME INDEX

Alcorn, J. D.: 62, 67
Anastasiow, N.: 42
Anderson, H. E.: 11–12
Aukerman, R. C.: 49
Bergem, J.: 53
Black, D. B.: 6
Bobbe, C.: 28
Booker, I. A.: *rev,* 1:1110
Botel, M.: 41
Brown, S. R.: 25
Brown, S. W.: 34
Buck, J. R.: 27
Burke, A.: 48
Burke, J. D.: 37
Burke, L. A.: 64
Campbell, W.: 28
Campbell, W. J.: 18
Carmichael, A.: 1
Cooper, B.: 29
Coull, W. H.: 2
Davis, B.: 65
Davis, F. B.: *rev,* 2:1563
Davis, W. Q.: 38
Deutsch, M.: 55
Dewey, J. C.: *rev,* 1:1110
Duke, R. L.: 52
Eggers, P. M.: 39
Farr, R.: 40, 42, 66
Flanagan, J. C.: *rev,* 4:530
Flemming, C. W.: 48
Foster, M. E.: 59
Frost, B. P.: 58

Gaddis, L. W.: 10
Gershon, A.: 16–7
Gettinger, T.: 15
Gosnell, E. S.: 43
Haney, R.: 7, 9–10, 16–17, 34, 68
Hobson, J. R.: *rev,* 4:530
Hodges, J. D.: 15
Jolly, H.: 33
Jones, R. A.: 7, 9–10, 13–15, 30
Kaplan, R.: 30
Karlin, R.: 33
Katz, S. S.: 57
Kittel, J. E.: 54
Knight, D.: 62, 67
Kolesnik, P. E.: 15
Krippner, S.: 46
Lamberti, E.: 28
Lee, Y. B.: 68
Long, J. R.: 4
Lopez, D. C.: 24
Lovett, C. J.: 44
McBee, G.: 52
McCullough, R. O.: 21
McNinch, G.: 65
Makley, M.: 8
Mars, P. A.: 47
Michael, J. J.: 68
Michael, W. B.: 7, 9–10, 13–17, 30, 34, 68
Moe, I. L.: 19

Morrison, I. E.: 51
Neville, M. H.: 58
O'Connor, H. A.: 55
Parker, D. L.: 69
Parsley, K. M.: 55
Perry, I. F.: 51
Petty, E. L.: 31
Powell, M.: 53, 55, 60
Purcell, E. W.: 70
Rakes, T.: 45
Rees, R. E.: 1
Roelke, P.: 66
Scheck, R. R.: 32
Schneiderhan, R. M.: 56
Schubert, D. G.: 50
Seay, L. C.: 22
Seither, F. G.: 71

Seppala, J.: 15
Shaffer, L. F.: *exc,* 4:530
Sheppard, C.: 18, 28
Sinks, N. B.: 60
Sipay, E. R.: 23
Smith, I. M.: 63, 72
Sopchak, A. L.: 5
Sutherland, S. P.: 36
Thompson, E. L.: 61
Turner, D.: 20
Wetherell, R. H.: 73
Williams, J. L.: 26
Wilson, F. Y.: 48
Wilson, J. J.: 35
Wineman, J. H.: 74
Young, C.: 3

[1537]

*****The Carver-Darby Chunked Reading Test.** Grades 9–16 and adults; 1970–72; CDCRT; 3 scores: efficiency, accuracy, rate; Ronald P. Carver and Charles A. Darby, Jr.; American Institutes for Research; distributed by Revrac Publications. *

For additional information and reviews by Arlen R. Gullickson and Richard Rystrom, see 7:684.

REFERENCES THROUGH 1971

1. CARVER, RONALD P. "Criterion Referenced Aspects of the Carver-Darby Chunked Reading Test." *Yearb Nat Read Conf* 20:182–6 '71. *
2. CARVER, RONALD P. "What Is Reading Comprehension and How Should It Be Measured?" *Yearb Nat Read Conf* 19(1): 99–106 '71. *
3. CARVER, RONALD P., AND DARBY, C. A. "Development and Evaluation of a Test of Information Storage During Reading." *J Ed Meas* 8(1):33–44 sp '71. * (*PA* 46:5461)
4. SWALLOW, ROSE-MARIE. *Automatic Processing of Perceptual-Linguistic Stimuli in Second Grade Achieving and Non-Achieving Readers.* Doctor's thesis, University of Southern California (Los Angeles, Calif.), 1971. (*DAI* 32:3827A)

CUMULATIVE NAME INDEX

Carver, R. P.: 1–3
Darby, C. A.: 3
Gullickson, A. R.: *rev,* 7:684

Rystrom, R.: *rev,* 7:684
Swallow, R. M.: 4

[1538]

Commerce Reading Comprehension Test. Grades 12–16 and adults; 1956–58; Irma T. Halfter and Raymond J. McCall; Department of Psychological Testing, DePaul University. *

For additional information, see 5:624.

REFERENCES THROUGH 1971

1. HALFTER, IRMA T., AND DOUGLASS, FRANCES M. "Measurement of College Level Reading Competence in a Content Area." *J Ed Res* 53:223–30 F '60. *

CUMULATIVE NAME INDEX

Douglass, F. M.: 1

Halfter, I. T.: 1

[1539]

Comprehension Test for Training College Students. Training college students and applicants for admission; 1962; E. L. Black; distributed by NFER Publishing Co. Ltd. [England]. *

For additional information, see 6:785.

[1540]

Comprehensive Primary Reading Scales. Grade 1; 1956–60; 4 parts; M. J. Van Wagenen, Mary A. Van Wagenen (Part 1), and Maximilian L. G. Klaeger (Part 2); Van Wagenen Psycho-Educational Research Laboratories. *

a) PART 1, READING COMPREHENSION SCALE.
b) PART 2, PICTURE READING VOCABULARY SCALE.
c) PART 3, MEANING READING VOCABULARY SCALE.
d) PART 4, WORD RECOGNITION VOCABULARY SCALE.

[1541]

Comprehensive Reading Scales. Grades 4, 5, 6, 7, 8, 9–10, 11–12; 1948–53; M. J. Van Wagenen; Van Wagenen Psycho-Educational Research Laboratories. *

[1542]

*Comprehensive Tests of Basic Skills: Reading.
Grades kgn–12; 1968–73; 2 editions; CTB/McGraw-
Hill. * For the complete battery entry, see 11.
a) FORMS Q AND R. Grades 2.5–4, 4–6, 6–8, 8–12; 1968–
71; 3 scores: vocabulary, comprehension, total.
b) EXPANDED EDITION, FORM S. Grades kgn.5–1.9,
1.5–2.9, 2.5–4.9, 4.5–6.9, 6.5–8.9, 8.5–12.9; 1968–73; 2
tests.
 1) *Reading.* Grades kgn.5–1.9, 1.5–2.9; 2 levels.
  (*a*) Level B. Grades kgn.5–1.9; 5 scores: letter
  sounds, word recognition (2 scores), reading comprehension, total.
  (*b*) Level C. Grades 1.5–2.9; 4 scores: vocabulary, sentences, passages, total.
 2) *Reading and Reference Skills.* Grades 2.5–4.9,
 4.5–6.9, 6.5–8.9, 8.5–12.9; 4 scores: reading (vocabulary, comprehension, total), reference skills.
For additional information and a review by Earl F.
Rankin of *a*, see 7:685. For reviews of the complete
battery, see 7:9 (2 reviews, 3 excerpts).

REFERENCES THROUGH 1971

1. KIDD, LOR RHEBA R. *A Comparison of the Wide Range
Achievement Test With the Stanford Achievement Test and
Comprehensive Tests of Basic Skills as a Measurement of Read-
ing Achievement.* Master's thesis, California State College (Hay-
ward, Calif.), 1970.
2. DAVIS, BOBBIE, AND MCNINCH, GEORGE. "A Comparison of
Three Standardized Reading Tests in a Fifth Grade Sample."
South J Ed Res 5(2):101–12 Ap '71. *
3. DAVIS, BOBBIE SUE. *A Comparative Analysis of Three
Widely Used Standardized Reading Achievement Tests for a
Selected Group of Elementary School Children.* Doctor's thesis,
University of Southern Mississippi (Hattiesburg, Miss.), 1971.
(*DAI* 32:4831A)

CUMULATIVE NAME INDEX

[1543]

Cooperative Primary Tests: Reading. Grades
1.5–2.5, 2.5–3; 1965–67; Cooperative Tests and Services. * For the complete battery entry, see 12.
For reviews of the complete battery, see 7:10 (2
excerpts).

[1544]

**Cooperative Reading Comprehension Test, Form
Y.** Secondary forms 5–6 and university; 1948–64
(Australian edition, 1960–64); Australian adaptation
(spelling only) of Form Y of *Reading Comprehension:
Cooperative English Test, Higher Level C2;* 4 scores:
vocabulary, speed of comprehension, level of comprehension, total; Frederick B. Davis, Clarence Derrick,
Jeanne M. Bradford, and Geraldine Spaulding; Australian Council for Educational Research [Australia]. *

REFERENCES THROUGH 1971

1. ANDERSON, A. W. "Personality Traits in Reading Ability
of Western Australian University Freshmen." *J Ed Res* 54:234–
7 F '61. *
2. LEE, STUART E.; WITH THE ASSISTANCE OF COLETTE M.
ROSEN AND DOUGLAS MCNALLY. "Report on the Administration
and Standardization of the Co-operative Reading Comprehension
Test Higher Level C2 Form Y." *Forum Ed* (Australia) 22:90–
117 S '63. *
3. ANDERSON, A. W. "Reading and English Scores of a Group
of Foreign Students Entering the University of Western Australia in 1964." *Austral J Higher Ed* 2:84–90 N '64. *
4. POND, L. "A Study of High-Achieving and Low-Achieving
University Freshmen." *Austral J Higher Ed* 2:73–8 N '64. *
5. ANDERSON, A. W. "Intelligence and Reading Scores of
Entrants to the University of Western Australia 1954–65."
Austral J Higher Ed 2:177–82 N '65. *
6. SILCOCK, ANNE. "An Investigation Into Possible Relationships Between Reading Ability Scores and University First Year
Examination Results." *Austral J Higher Ed* 2:113–8 N '65. *

CUMULATIVE NAME INDEX

[1545]

**Cooperative Reading Comprehension Test,
Forms L and M.** Secondary forms 2–4 (ages 14–16);
1960–67 (Australian edition, 1964–73); Australian
adaptations (spelling only) of Forms 2A, 2B, and 2C
of *Reading Comprehension: Cooperative English Test,
1960 Revision;* 3 scores: vocabulary, level of comprehension, speed of comprehension; Clarence Derrick,
David P. Harris, and Biron Walker; Australian
Council for Educational Research [Australia]. *

[1546]

Davis Reading Test. Grades 8–11, 11–13; 1956–62;
2 scores: level of comprehension, speed of comprehension; Frederick B. Davis and Charlotte Croon Davis;
Psychological Corporation. *
For additional information and reviews by William
E. Coffman and Alton L. Raygor, see 6:786 (2 references); for a review by Benjamin Rosner of the
lower level, see 5:625.

REFERENCES THROUGH 1971

1–2. See 6:786.
3. ALSHAN, LEONARD M. *A Factor Analytic Study of Items
Used in the Measurement of Some Fundamental Factors of Reading Comprehension.* Doctor's thesis, Columbia University (New
York, N.Y.), 1964. (*DA* 25:5101)
4. GLIDDEN, GEORGE WAYNE. *Factors That Influence Achievement in Senior High School American History.* Doctor's thesis,
University of Nebraska (Lincoln, Neb.), 1964. (*DA* 25:3429)
5. MCGUIRE, FREDERICK L., AND SCOTT, WYNELLE. "The Davis
Reading Test, Hr Scale, MCAT, and Undergraduate Grades as
Predictors of Success in Medical School." Abstract. *J Med Ed*
39:886 S '64. *
6. RADCLIFFE, ROBERTA D. *An Analysis of Junior High School
Standardized Reading Tests Employing the Davis Reading Comprehension Scale.* Master's thesis, Glassboro State College (Glassboro, N.J.), 1965.
7. ALEXAKOS, C. E. "Predictive Efficiency of Two Multivariate
Statistical Techniques in Comparison With Clinical Predictions."
J Ed Psychol 57:297–306 O '66. * (*PA* 40:12756)
8. DAVIS, FREDERICK B. "Experimental Use of the Davis Reading Test in Independent Schools." *Ed Rec B* 89:46–50 F '66. *
(*PA* 40:7048, title only)
9. GOLDEN, JAMES FRANKLIN. *Aspirations and Capabilities of
Rural Youth in Selected Areas of Arkansas in Relation to Present
and Projected Labor Market Requirements.* Doctor's thesis, University of Arkansas (Fayetteville, Ark.), 1966. (*DA* 27:1199A)
10. CLAWAR, HARRY J. "A Comparison of the Davis Reading
Test and the Survey Section of the Diagnostic Reading Test
When Used With Independent-School Pupils." *Ed Rec B* 92:
39–42 Jl '67. * (*PA* 42:1126)
11. HOLLENBECK, GEORGE P. "Predicting High School Biology
Achievement With the Differential Aptitude Tests and the Davis
Reading Test." *Ed & Psychol Meas* 27:439–42 su '67. * (*PA*
41:14218)
12. HARDESTY, D. L., AND JONES, W. S. "Characteristics of
Judged High Potential Management Personnel—The Operations
of an Industrial Assessment Center." *Personnel Psychol* 21:85–
98 sp '68. * (*PA* 42:16197)
13. FEUERS, STELLE. *The Relationship Between General Reading Skills and Junior College Academic Achievement.* Doctor's
thesis, University of California (Los Angeles, Calif.), 1969.
(*DAI* 30:3186A)
14. WEAVER, WENDELL W.; KINGSTON, ALBERT J.; BICKLEY,
A. C.; AND WHITE, WILLIAM F. "Information-Flow Difficulty in
Relation to Reading Comprehension." *J Read Behav* 1(3):41–9
su '69. * (*PA* 45:2355)
15. CARLETON, FREDERICK O. "Relationships Between Follow-
Up Evaluations and Information Developed in a Management
Assessment Center." Abstract. *Proc 78th Ann Conv Am Psychol
Assn* 5(2):565–6 '70. * (*PA* 44:19655)
16. JOHNS, DANIEL JAY. *Correlates of Academic Success in a
Predominantly Black, Open-Door, Public, Urban Community
College.* Doctor's thesis, University of Virginia (Charlottesville,
Va.), 1970. (*DAI* 31:4464A)
17. BRADLEY, RICHARD W., AND SANBORN, MARSHALL P.
"Using Tests to Predict Four-Year Patterns of College Grade
Point." *J Col Stud Personnel* 12(2):138–42 Mr '71. * (*PA* 46:
5699)
18. HOLZMAN, PHILIP S., AND ROUSEY, CLYDE. "Disinhibition
of Communicated Thought: Generality and Role of Cognitive
Style." *J Abn Psychol* 77(3):263–74 Je '71. * (*PA* 46:6158)
19. KLINDIENST, DAVID HARVEY. *Predicting the Accommoda-
tion and Progressive Retention of Selected Freshmen at Clarion
State College.* Doctor's thesis, Pennsylvania State University
(University Park, Pa.), 1971. (*DAI* 33:988A)
20. SYKES, KIM CRISPIN. *A Comparison of the Effectiveness*

of *Standard Print and Large Print in Facilitating the Reading Skills of Visually Impaired Students.* Doctor's thesis, Michigan State University (East Lansing, Mich.), 1971. (*DAI* 32:3128A)

CUMULATIVE NAME INDEX

Alexakos, C. E.: 7	Jones, W. S.: 12
Alshan, L. M.: 3	Ketcham, H. E. (Mrs.): 1
Bickley, A. C.: 14	Kingston, A. J.: 2, 14
Bradley, R. W.: 17	Klindienst, D. H.: 19
Carleton, F. O.: 15	McGuire, F. L.: 5
Clawar, H. J.: 10	Radcliffe, R. D.: 6
Coffman, W. E.: *rev*, 6:786	Raygor, A. L.: *rev*, 6:786
Davis, F. B.: 8	Rosner, B.: *rev*, 5:625
Feuers, S.: 13	Rousey, C.: 18
Glidden, G. W.: 4	Sanborn, M. P.: 17
Golden, J. F.: 9	Scott, W.: 5
Hardesty, D. L.: 12	Sykes, K. C.: 20
Hollenbeck, G. P.: 11	Weaver, W. W.: 2, 14
Holzman, P. S.: 18	White, W. F.: 14
Johns, D. J.: 16	

[1547]

Delaware County Silent Reading Test, Second Edition. Grades 1^2, 2^1, 2^2, 3^1, 3^2, 4, 5, 6, 7, 8; 1965; 5 scores: interpretation, organization, vocabulary, structural analysis, total; no manual; Judson E. Newburg and Nicholas A. Spennato; Delaware County Reading Council. *

For additional information and a review by Allen Berger, see 7:686.

[1548]

★Edinburgh Reading Tests. Ages 8.5–10.5, 10–12.5; 1972–73; ERT; 2 levels; University of London Press Ltd. [England]. *

a) STAGE 2. Ages 8.5–10.5; 7 scores: vocabulary, comprehension of sequences, retention of significant details, use of context, reading rate, comprehension of essential ideas, total; test by Godfrey Thomson Unit, University of Edinburgh, in association with Scottish Education Department and Educational Institute of Scotland; manual by M. J. Hutchings and E. M. J. Hutchings.

b) STAGE 3. Ages 10–12.5; 6 scores: reading for facts, comprehension of sequences, retention of main ideas, comprehension of points of view, vocabulary, total; test by Moray House College of Education in association with Scottish Education Department and Educational Institute of Scotland; manual by J. F. McBride and P. C. McNaught.

[1549]

Emporia Reading Tests. Grades 1, 2–3, 4–6, 7–8; 1962–64; first published in the Every Pupil Scholarship Test series; 4 tests; M. W. Sanders, Marjorie Barnett (*a–b*), Donald E. Carline (*c–d*), Ed. L. Eaton (*d*), Angie Seybold (*c*), and Stafford E. Studer (*d*); Bureau of Educational Measurements. *

a) EMPORIA PRIMARY READING TEST. 1, 2 semesters grade 1.

b) EMPORIA ELEMENTARY READING TEST. 1, 2 semesters grades 2–3.

c) EMPORIA INTERMEDIATE READING TEST. 1, 2 semesters grades 4–6.

d) EMPORIA JUNIOR HIGH SCHOOL READING TEST. 1, 2 semesters grades 7–8.

For additional information and a review by Ronald W. Mitchell, see 7:687.

[1550]

GAP Reading Comprehension Test. Grades 2–7; 1965–70; GAP; cloze technique with approximately every tenth word omitted; 2 editions; J. McLeod. *

a) AUSTRALIAN EDITION. 1965–67; for an upward extension, see 1551; Heinemann Educational Australia Pty Ltd. [Australia].

b) BRITISH EDITION. 1965–70; manual edited by Derick Unwin; Heinemann Educational Books Ltd. [England].

For additional information and reviews by Donald B. Black and Earl F. Rankin, see 7:688.

REFERENCES THROUGH 1971

1. McLeod, J., AND Anderson, J. "Readability Assessment and Word Redundancy of Printed English." *Psychol Rep* 18:35–8 F '66. * (*PA* 40:7051)
2. Cochrane, R. G.; Elkins, J.; AND Richmond, Dawn M. "Analysis of Fourth Grade Testing." *Slow Learning Child* (Australia) 16(3):131–42 N '69. * (*PA* 44:18351)
3. Elkins, J. "Some Recent Queensland Norms for Widely Used Standardized Tests." *Slow Learning Child* (Australia) 18(3):142–7 N '71. *

CUMULATIVE NAME INDEX

Anderson, J.: 1	McLeod, J.: 1
Black, D. B.: *rev*, 7:688	Rankin, E. F.: *rev*, 7:688
Cochrane, R. G.: 2	Richmond, D. M.: 2
Elkins, J.: 2–3	

[1551]

★GAPADOL. Ages 10 and over; 1972; upward extension for "adolescent children" of *GAP Reading Comprehension Test;* cloze technique; J. McLeod and J. Anderson; Heinemann Educational Australia Pty Ltd. [Australia]. *

[1552]

*Gates-MacGinitie Reading Tests. Grades 1, 2, 3, 2.5–3, 4–6, 7–9; 1926–72; GMRT; Primary A is a revision of *Gates Primary Reading Tests;* Primary B is a revision of *Gates Advanced Primary Reading Tests;* the other tests in this series are revisions of *Gates Reading Survey;* 6 levels; Arthur I. Gates and Walter H. MacGinitie; Teachers College Press. *

a) PRIMARY A. Grade 1; 1926–72; 2 scores: vocabulary, comprehension. (British adaptation of Form 1: Ages 6-10 to 8-0; 1971–73; norms supplement by Peter Saville and Stephen Blinkhorn; NFER Publishing Co. Ltd. [England]).

b) PRIMARY B. Grade 2; 1926–72; 2 scores: same as for Primary A.

c) PRIMARY C. Grade 3; 1939–72; 2 scores: same as for Primary A.

d) PRIMARY CS. Grades 2.5–3; 1926–72; speed and accuracy.

e) SURVEY D. Grades 4–6; 1939–72; 3 scores: speed and accuracy, vocabulary, comprehension.

f) SURVEY E. Grades 7–9; 1939–72; 3 scores: same as for Survey D.

For additional information, reviews by Carolyn L. Burke and Byron H. Van Roekel, and an excerpted review by William R. Powell, see 7:689. For reviews by William Eller and Coleman Morrison of the *Gates Primary Reading Tests,* see 6:792 (1 reference); see also 5:632 (2 references); for reviews by William S. Gray and George D. Spache of an earlier edition, see 3:486 (7 references). For a review by Kenneth D. Hopkins of the *Gates Advanced Primary Reading Tests,* see 6:790 (1 reference); see also 5:630 (3 references); for reviews by Virginia Seavey and George D. Spache of an earlier edition, see 3:484. For reviews by George D. Spache and Morey J. Wantman of the *Gates Reading Survey,* see 6:793 (7 references); for reviews by Dorothy E. Holberg and Herbert F. Spitzer of an earlier edition, see 3:487.

REFERENCES THROUGH 1971

1. Davis, William Quinby. *A Study of Test Score Comparability Among Five Widely Used Reading Survey Tests.* Doctor's thesis, Southern Illinois University (Carbondale, Ill.), 1968. (*DA* 29:4370A)
2. Beyer, Donald A. *A Comparative Study of the Reading Performance of Third Grade Children Measured by the Reading Eye Camera and the Gates MacGinitie Reading Tests.* Master's thesis, Cardinal Stritch College (Milwaukee, Wis.), 1969.

3. FARR, ROGER, AND ANASTASIOW, NICHOLAS. *Tests of Reading Readiness and Achievement: A Review and Evaluation,* pp. 30–4. Newark, Del.: International Reading Association, 1969. Pp. iv, 51. *

4. RODGERS, DENIS CYRIL. *An Investigation of the Auditory Memory Abilities of Grade 2 Retarded-Underachieving Readers and Competent-Achieving Readers Under Conditions of Reinforcement and Non-Reinforcement.* Doctor's thesis, University of Toronto (Toronto, Ont., Canada), 1969. (*DAI* 31:2196A)

5. ROELKE, PATRICIA LYNN. *Reading Comprehension as a Function of Three Dimensions of Word Meaning.* Doctor's thesis, Indiana University (Bloomington, Ind.), 1969. (*DAI* 30:5300A)

6. WALLACE, GERALD. *A Study of the Relationship of Selected Visual Perceptual Capabilities and Intelligence to Achievement in Reading of Educable Mentally Retarded Children.* Doctor's thesis, University of Oregon (Eugene, Ore.), 1969. (*DAI* 30:3336A)

7. ALLEN, JOHN EDWARD. *A Survey of Third Grade Reading in the State of Utah.* Doctor's thesis, University of Utah (Salt Lake City, Utah), 1970. (*DAI* 31:2165A)

8. GAULKE, MARY FLORENCE. *A Longitudinal Two-Generation Study of Parent-Child Relationships on Selected Reading Skills and Aptitudes.* Doctor's thesis, University of Oregon (Eugene, Ore.), 1970. (*DAI* 31:3371A)

9. PAYNE, PATSY P. *A Comparison of the Performance of Third Grade Pupils Who Were Reading Below Grade Level on Two Test Formats of the Gates-MacGinitie Reading Test: Primary C Vocabulary and Comprehension.* Master's thesis, University of Texas (Austin, Tex.), 1970.

10. SMITH, CHARLES LEROY. *A Comparison of Selected Standardized Reading Test Scores and Informal Reading Inventory Results at Intermediate Grade Levels.* Doctor's thesis, University of Northern Colorado (Greeley, Colo.), 1970. (*DAI* 31:4046A)

11. CALVERT, KENNEITH CAROL HARBISON. *An Investigation of Relationships Between the Syntactic Maturity of Oral Language and Reading Comprehension Scores.* Doctor's thesis, University of Alabama (University, Ala.), 1971. (*DAI* 32:4828A)

12. COMPTON, MARY ELIZABETH. *A Study of the Relationship Between Oral Language Facility and Reading Achievement of Selected First-Grade Children.* Doctor's thesis, University of North Carolina (Chapel Hill, N.C.), 1971. (*DAI* 32:6848A)

13. FARR, ROGER, AND ROELKE, PATRICIA. "Measuring Subskills of Reading: Intercorrelations Between Standardized Reading Tests, Teachers' Ratings, and Reading Specialists' Ratings." *J Ed Meas* 8(1):27–32 sp '71. * (*PA* 46:5464)

14. GIRARD, JUDITH ANDERSON FUNK. *A Study of the Correlations Between the Gates-MacGinitie Reading Comprehension Test and Various Subtests From the Analysis of Learning Potential.* Doctor's thesis, University of Northern Colorado (Greeley, Colo.), 1971. (*DAI* 32:5468A)

15. GORMLY, JOHN, AND NITTOLI, MICHAEL J. "Rapid Improvement of the Reading Skills in Juvenile Delinquents." *J Exp Ed* 40(2):45–8 w '71. * (*PA* 48:1688)

16. JOHNSON, THEOLA GAE. *Influence of Selected Factors on the Ability of Fourth, Fifth, and Sixth Graders to Read Graphs.* Doctor's thesis, University of Southern California (Los Angeles, Calif.), 1971. (*DAI* 32:726A)

17. MYKLEBUST, HELMER R.; BANNOCHIE, MARGARET N.; AND KILLEN, JAMES R. Chap. 9, "Learning Disabilities and Cognitive Processes," pp. 213–51. In *Progress in Learning Disabilities, Vol. 2.* Edited by Helmer R. Myklebust. New York: Grune & Stratton, Inc., 1971. Pp. ix, 404. *

18. WADE, VERN JOSEPH. *A Comparison of Selected Standardized Reading Test Scores and Informal Reading Inventory Results at Eighth Grade Level.* Doctor's thesis, University of Northern Colorado (Greeley, Colo.), 1971. (*DAI* 32:3853A)

CUMULATIVE NAME INDEX

[1553]

Gates-MacGinitie Reading Tests: Survey F. Grades 10–12; 1969–70; 3 scores: speed and accuracy, vocabulary, comprehension; Arthur I. Gates and Walter H. MacGinitie; Teachers College Press. *

For additional information and a review by Jason Millman, see 7:690.

[1554]

Group Reading Assessment. End of first year junior school; 1964, c1962–64; Frank A. Spooncer; University of London Press Ltd. [England]. *

[1555]

Group Reading Test. Ages 6–10; 1968–69; D. Young; University of London Press Ltd. [England]. *

For additional information, see 7:691.

[1556]

High School Reading Test: National Achievement Tests. Grades 7–12; 1939–52; 6 scores: vocabulary, word discrimination, sentence meaning, noting details, interpreting paragraphs, total; 1951–52 tests identical with tests copyrighted 1939–40 except for minor changes; Robert K. Speer and Samuel Smith; Psychometric Affiliates. *

For additional information and a review by Victor H. Noll, see 5:634; for a review by Holland Roberts, see 4:536; for a review by Robert L. McCaul, see 3:488.

[1557]

Individual Reading Test. Ages 6-0 to 9-9; 1935–36; 3 scores: oral word reading, comprehension, speed; L. W. Allen; Australian Council for Educational Research [Australia]. *

For additional information and a review by R. W. McCulloch, see 5:663.

[1558]

★**Informal Reading Assessment Tests.** Grades 1–3; 1971; IRAT; 7 nonstandardized tests which may be used with the publisher's reading program or independently; Margaret Gerrard and Elinor Beard; Thomas Nelson & Sons (Canada) Ltd. [Canada]. *

a) TEST 1. 6 scores: vocabulary, comprehension, phonics (consonants, rhyme), oral reading (vocabulary, comprehension).

b) TEST 2. 6 scores: vocabulary, comprehension, word attack (word structure, phonics), oral reading (vocabulary, comprehension).

c) TEST 3. 6 scores: same as for Test 2.

d) TEST 4. 6 scores: same as for Test 2.

e) TEST 5. 6 scores: same as for Test 2.

f) TEST 6. 6 scores: same as for Test 2.

g) TEST 7. 6 scores: same as for Test 2.

[1559]

★**Inventory-Survey Tests.** Grades 4–6, 7–8; 1968–69; IST; 6 scores: word meaning, sentence meaning, paragraph meaning, word analysis, dictionary skills, total; 2 levels; Marion Monroe; Scott, Foresman & Co. *

a) INVENTORY-SURVEY TEST FOR INTERMEDIATE GRADES. Grades 4–6.

b) INVENTORY-SURVEY TEST FOR UPPER GRADES. Grades 7–8.

[1560]

*Iowa Silent Reading Tests.** Grades 4–16; 1927–73; ISRT; 2 editions; Harcourt Brace Jovanovich, Inc. *

a) 1939–42 EDITION. Grades 4–8, 9–14; 1927–56; 2 levels; H. A. Greene, A. N. Jorgensen, and V. H. Kelley.

1) *Elementary Test.* Grades 4–8; 1933–56; 9 scores: rate, comprehension, directed reading, word meaning, paragraph comprehension, sentence meaning, alphabetizing, use of index, total.

2) *Advanced Test.* Grades 9–14; 1927–43; 10 scores: rate, comprehension, directed reading, poetry comprehension, word meaning, sentence meaning, paragraph comprehension, use of index, selection of key words, total.

b) 1973 EDITION. Grades 6–9, 9–14, 11–16; 1927–73; 3 levels; coordinating editor: Roger Farr.

1) *Level 1.* Grades 6–9; 5 scores: vocabulary, reading comprehension, total, directed reading, reading efficiency.

2) *Level 2.* Grades 9–14; 5 scores: same as for Level 1.

3) *Level 3.* Grades 11–16; 4 scores: vocabulary, reading comprehension, total, reading efficiency.

For additional information and a review by Worth R. Jones of *a*, see 6:794 (40 references); for reviews by Frederick B. Davis and William W. Turnbull and excerpted reviews by Earl R. Gabler and Margaret Pankaskie, see 3:489 (21 references); for reviews by Ivan A. Booker and Holland D. Roberts of an earlier edition, see 2:1547 (6 references).

REFERENCES THROUGH 1971

1–6. See 2:1547.
7–27. See 3:489.
28–67. See 6:794.
68. LITTERER, OSCAR F. "An Experimental Study of Visual Apprehension in Reading." *J Appl Psychol* 17:266–76 Je '33. * (*PA* 8:496)
69. ROBINSON, F. P., AND McCOLLOM, F. H. "Reading Rate and Comprehension Accuracy as Determinants of Reading Test Scores." *J Ed Psychol* 25:154–7 F '34. * (*PA* 8:2703)
70. KELLEY, VICTOR H. "The Reading Abilities of Spanish and English Speaking Pupils." *J Ed Res* 29:209–11 N '35. * (*PA* 10:1621)
71. ANDERSON, VERNA L., AND TINKER, MILES A. "The Speed Factor in Reading Performance." *J Ed Psychol* 27:621–4 N '36. * (*PA* 11:1386)
72. ANDERSON, IRVING H., AND SWANSON, DONALD E. "Common Factors in Eye Movements in Silent and Oral Reading." *Psychol Monogr* 48(3):61–9 '37. * (*PA* 11:3319)
73. FAIRBANKS, GRANT. "The Relation Between Eye Movements and Voice in the Oral Reading of Good and Poor Silent Readers." *Psychol Monogr* 48(3):78–107 '37. * (*PA* 11:3325)
74. KENNAH, CATHERINE J. *A Comparison of Reading Grades Made on the Iowa Silent Reading Test With Scores Made in the Final Examination by Pupils in the Albany Senior High School.* Master's thesis, New York State College for Teachers (Albany, N.Y.), 1937.
75. SCHMITZ, SYLVESTER B. "Predicting Success in College: A Study of Various Criteria." *J Ed Psychol* 28:465–73 S '37. * (*PA* 12:538)
76. SWANSON, DONALD E. "Common Elements in Silent and Oral Reading." *Psychol Monogr* 48(3):36–60 '37. * (*PA* 11:3369)
77. READ, CECIL B. "The Prediction of Scholastic Success in a Municipal University." *Sch & Soc* 48:187–8 Ag 6 '38. * (*PA* 12:6645)
78. SMITH, MARJORIE A. *The Correlation Between Intelligence and Reading Ability.* Master's thesis, Fordham University (New York, N.Y.), 1938.
79. BEAR, ROBERT M., AND IMUS, HENRY A. "Changes in Reading Performance During the Freshman Year of College." *J Ed Psychol* 30:667–73 D '39. * (*PA* 14:3190)
80. DOUGLASS, LOWELL N. "A Study of Certain Factors Influencing Academic Achievement With Special Reference to the Health Factor." *J Exp Ed* 7:235–44 Mr '39. * (*PA* 13:5911)
81. BEAR, ROBERT M., AND ODBERT, HENRY S. "Experimental Studies of the Relation Between Rate of Reading and Speed of Association." *J Psychol* 10:141–7 Jl '40. * (*PA* 14:6188)
82. POND, FREDERICK L. "Influence of Reading Abilities on School Success in Grade IX." *Sch R* 48:437–44 Je '40. *
83. OSBORNE, AGNES ELIZABETH. "The Relationship Between Certain Psychological Tests and Shorthand Achievement." *Teach Col Contrib Ed* 873:1–58 '43. *
84. JONES, MARY M. WILCOX. "Relationship Between Reading Deficiencies and Left-Handedness." *Sch & Soc* 60:238–9 O 7 '44. * (*PA* 19:1055)
85. BERRY, GEORGE S. "An Experiment in Self-Analysis." *J Ed Psychol* 37:111–24 F '46. * (*PA* 20:2061)
86. MOORE, CHARLES E. A. "Reading and Arithmetic Abilities Associated With Speech Defects." *J Speech Disorders* 12:85–6 Mr '47. * (*PA* 21:3582)
87. FREEBURNE, CECIL MAX. "A Study of the Relationship Between Figural After-Effect and Reading-Test Performance." *J Ed Psychol* 43:309–12 My '52. * (*PA* 27:3752)
88. ADAMS, SAM, AND GARRETT, H. L. "Scholastic Background

as Related to Success in College Physics." *J Ed Res* 47:545–9 Mr '54. * (*PA* 28:7951)
89. WHEELER, LESTER R., AND WHEELER, VIOLA D. "A Study of the Relationship of Auditory Discrimination to Silent Reading Abilities." *J Ed Res* 48:103–13 O '54. * (*PA* 29:6186)
90. MANN, HELENE POWNER. "Some Hypotheses on Perceptual and Learning Processes With Their Applications to the Process of Reading: A Preliminary Note." *J Genetic Psychol* 90:167–202 Je '57. * (*PA* 35:1187)
91. TURNER, DANIEL. *A Study of Speech Effectiveness and Personal and Social Adjustment Among Ninth Grade Pupils.* Doctor's thesis, Boston University (Boston, Mass.), 1957. (*DA* 17:2902)
92. OLANDER, HERBERT T., AND KLEYLE, HELEN M. "Differences in Personal and Professional Characteristics of a Selected Group of Elementary Teachers With Contrasting Success Records." *Ed Adm & Sup* 45:191–8 Jl '59. * (*PA* 34:6582)
93. SIMMONS, AUDREY ANN. "Factors Related to Lipreading." *J Speech & Hearing Res* 2:340–52 D '59. * (*PA* 34:6510)
94. DARTER, CLARENCE LESLIE, JR. *A Comparative Study of Over-Achieving and Under-Achieving Ninth-Grade Students.* Doctor's thesis, Texas Technological College (Lubbock, Tex.), 1961. (*DA* 22:1462)
95. ROTHMAN, ARTHUR I. *The Determination of Criteria for the Selection of Students for the PSSC Physics Course.* Master's thesis, University of Maine (Orono, Me.), 1965.
96. JENKINS, ALICE CRAWFORD. *The Relationship of Certain Measurable Factors to Academic Success in Freshman Biology.* Doctor's thesis, New York University (New York, N.Y.), 1966. (*DA* 27:2274A)
97. KARP, ROBERT EUGENE. *An Analysis of Aptitudes, Abilities, and High School Class Rank and Their Relation to the Academic Success of First-Year Private Business School Students.* Doctor's thesis, Northern Illinois University (DeKalb, Ill.), 1966. (*DA* 27:3289A)
98. WHITTEMORE, ROBERT G.; ECHEVERRIA, BEN P.; AND GRIFFIN, JOHN V. "Can We Use Existing Tests for Adult Basic Education?" *Adult Ed* 17:19–29 au '66. *
99. HUFF, BETTY. *The Predictive Value of Standardized Testing in Relation to Mathematical Achievement at Virginia High School.* Master's thesis, East Tennessee State University (Johnson City, Tenn.), 1967.
100. JANSEN, DAVID G. "Verbal and Reading Skills of Students Participating in a University Reading and Study Skills Program." *J Col Stud Personnel* 8:181–4 My '67. *
101. KUSHINKA, MICHAEL. *The Predictive Components of Pupil Performance in Senior High School.* Doctor's thesis, Yeshiva University (New York, N.Y.), 1967. (*DA* 28:434A)
102. FARR, ROGER, AND ANASTASIOW, NICHOLAS. *Tests of Reading Readiness and Achievement: A Review and Evaluation,* pp. 34–6. Newark, Del.: International Reading Association, 1969. Pp. iv, 51. *
103. HALL, LUCIEN TALMAGE, JR. *The Prediction of Success in Each of Six Four-Year Selections of Secondary Mathematics Courses.* Doctor's thesis, University of Virginia (Charlottesville, Va.), 1969. (*DAI* 30:4141A)
104. HAYES, EDWARD MAJELLA. *The Relationship of Race and Sex to Academic Achievement in Selected Rural Elementary and High Schools Before and After Desegregation.* Doctor's thesis, University of Virginia (Charlottesville, Va.), 1969. (*DAI* 31:149A)
105. SUTHERLAND, KELLEY. *The Predictive Value of School and College Ability Test, Sequential Test of Educational Progress, Differential Aptitude Test, Iowa Silent Reading Test, and California Test of Mental Maturity Scores at Clintwood High School, Clintwood, Virginia.* Master's thesis, East Tennessee State University (Johnson City, Tenn.), 1969.
106. HALL, LUCIEN T., JR. "The Prediction of Success in Each of Six Four-Year Selections of Secondary Mathematics Courses." *Sch Sci & Math* 71(8):693–6 N '71. *
107. HARRIS, JOHN A. *A Study of Selected Graduate Students' Performances on Graduate Record Examination, Iowa Silent Reading Test, and Grade-Point Average.* Master's thesis, Fort Valley State College (Ft. Valley, Ga.), 1971.
108. HAYNES, ELIZABETH FINGER. *An Analysis of the Relationships Between Pupil Performance in the Learning of Transformational Grammar and Intelligence Test Scores.* Doctor's thesis, University of Virginia (Charlottesville, Va.), 1971. (*DAI* 32:4591A)
109. TAYLOR, ALTON L. "Regression Analysis of Antecedent Measures of Slow Sections in High School Biology." *Sci Ed* 55(3):395–402 Jl–S '71. *

CUMULATIVE NAME INDEX

Davis, F. B.: *rev*, 3:489
Dearborn, W. F.: 3, 10
Donnelly, M. C.: 9
Douglass, L. N.: 80
Dungan, E. W.: 56
Eaton, M. T.: 20, 25
Echeverria, B. P.: 98
Fairbanks, G.: 73
Farr, R.: 102
Freeburne, C. M.: 87
Gabler, E. R.: *exc*, 3:489
Garrett, H. L.: 88
Garrett, W. S.: 64
Garrison, K. C.: 30
Giesecke, G. E.: 36
Gladfelter, M. E.: 40
Gores, H. B.: 3
Gowan, J. C.: 60
Greene, H. A.: 27
Griffin, J. V.: 98
Grilk, W.: 51
Hall, L. T.: 103, 106
Harris, J. A.: 107
Havighurst, R. J.: 37, 41
Hayes, E. M.: 104
Haynes, E. F.: 108
Holcomb, G. W.: 7
Huff, B.: 99
Humber, W. J.: 38
Imus, H. A.: 79
Janke, L. L.: 37, 41
Jansen, D. G.: 100
Jenkins, A. C.: 96
Jones, K. J.: 67
Jones, M. M. W.: 84
Jones, W. R.: *rev*, 6:794
Jorgensen, A. N.: 1
Karp, R. E.: 97
Kelley, V. H.: 27, 70
Kennah, C. J.: 74
Kilby, R. W.: 23
Kleyle, H. M.: 92
Kushinka, M.: 101
Landry, H.: 4
Langsam, R. S.: 11, 34
Larsen, R. P.: 36
Laslett, H. R.: 7
Lindquist, E. F.: 18
Litterer, O. F.: 68
McCollom, F. H.: 69
Madigan, M. E.: 14
Mann, H. P.: 90
Manson, W. Y.: 50
Miles, T. A.: 21

Moore, C. E. A.: 86
Moore, J. E.: 32
Morgan, C. L.: 16
Norton, D. P.: 63
Odbert, H. S.: 81
Olander, H. T.: 92
Osborne, A. E.: 83
Pankaskie, M.: 12; *exc*, 3: 489
Pflieger, E. F.: 46
Pond, F. L.: 82
Preische, W. A.: 19
Preston, R. C.: 43, 52
Pugh, G. S.: 24
Rainier, R. N.: 14
Read, C. B.: 77
Rehfeld, F. W.: 14
Ridley, W. N.: 53
Roberts, H. D.: *rev*, 2:1547
Robinson, F. P.: 69
Rothman, A. I.: 95
Scarborough, R. L.: 65
Schmitz, S. B.: 75
Shaw, G. S.: 59
Sherman, O.: 31
Simmons, A. A.: 93
Slocum, R. L.: 33
Smith, F. F.: 42
Smith, H. L.: 20, 25
Smith, J. M.: 13
Smith, M. A.: 78
Solomon, L. E.: 39
Steinman, C. C.: 16
Strang, R.: 2
Stuit, D. B.: 8–9
Sullivan, B. A.: 48
Sutherland, K.: 105
Swanson, D. E.: 72, 76
Taylor, A. L.: 109
Terry, P. W.: 28
Tinker, M. A.: 21, 71
Townsend, A.: 22
Traxler, A. E.: 5–6, 29, 47, 49
Treumann, M. J.: 48
Tuft, E. N.: 43
Turnbull, W. W.: *rev*, 3:489
Turner, D.: 91
Wheeler, L. R.: 89
Wheeler, V. D.: 89
Whittemore, R. G.: 98
Wilking, S. V.: 15
Wittenborn, J. R.: 36

[1561]
Kelvin Measurement of Reading Ability. Ages 8–12; 1933; C. M. Fleming; Robert Gibson & Sons, Glasgow, Ltd. [Scotland]. *
For additional information, see 1:1103.

[1562]
The Kingston Test of Silent Reading. Ages 7–11; 1953–54; M. E. Hebron (formerly M. E. Highfield); George G. Harrap & Co. Ltd. [England]. *
For additional information and reviews by Neil Gourlay and Magdalen D. Vernon, see 5:637.

[1563]
Lee-Clark Reading Test. Grades 1, 1–2; 1931–65; 2 levels; J. Murray Lee and Willis W. Clark; CTB/McGraw-Hill. *
a) PRIMER. Grade 1; 1931–58; 4 scores: auditory stimuli, visual stimuli, following directions, total.
b) FIRST READER. Grades 1–2; 1931–65; 6 scores: auditory stimuli, visual stimuli, following directions, completion, inference, total.
For additional information and reviews by Thomas C. Barrett and Coleman Morrison, see 6:795; for a review by Ruth Lowes of an earlier edition of the primer level, see 3:490.

REFERENCES THROUGH 1971
1. DURKIN, DOLORES. "A Case-Study Approach Toward an Identification of Factors Associated With Success and Failure in Learning to Read." *Calif J Ed Res* 11:26–33 Ja '60. * (*PA* 34:8336)

2. MATTICK, WILLIAM E. "Predicting Success in the First Grade." *El Sch J* 63:273–6 F '63. *

CUMULATIVE NAME INDEX
Barrett, T. C.: *rev*, 6:795   Mattick, W. E.: 2
Durkin, D.: 1   Morrison, C.: *rev*, 6:795
Lowes, R.: *rev*, 3:490

[1564]
McGrath Test of Reading Skills, Second Edition. Grades 1–13; 1965–67; 4 scores: oral word recognition, oral paragraph reading, silent reading vocabulary, oral reading rate; Joseph E. McGrath; McGrath Publishing Co. *
For additional information and a review by Byron H. Van Roekel, see 7:692.

[1565]
McMenemy Measure of Reading Ability. Grades 3, 5–6, 7–8; 1964–68; Richard A. McMenemy; the Author. *
For additional information and reviews by Marvin D. Glock and Ronald W. Mitchell, see 7:693.

[1566]
Maintaining Reading Efficiency Tests. Grades 7–16 and adults; 1966–70; MRET; 3 scores: rate, comprehension accuracy, reading efficiency; 5 forms; no manual; Lyle L. Miller; Developmental Reading Distributors. *
a) TEST 1, HISTORY OF BRAZIL, 1970 REVISION. 1966–70.
b) TEST 2, HISTORY OF JAPAN, 1970 REVISION. 1966–70.
c) TEST 3, HISTORY OF INDIA. 1970.
d) TEST 4, HISTORY OF NEW ZEALAND. 1970.
e) TEST 5, HISTORY OF SWITZERLAND. 1970.
For additional information, see 7:694.

[1567]
*****Metropolitan Achievement Tests: Reading Tests.** Grades 2–9; 1932–71; catalog uses the title *Metropolitan Reading Tests;* 2 editions; Walter N. Durost, Harold H. Bixler, J. Wayne Wrightstone, Gertrude H. Hildreth (*a*), Kenneth W. Lund (*a*), George A. Prescott (*b*), and Irving H. Balow (*b*); Harcourt Brace Jovanovich, Inc. * For the complete battery entry, see 22.
a) 1958 EDITION. Grades 2, 3–4, 5–6, 7–9; 1932–62; 2 or 3 scores: word knowledge, word discrimination (grade 2 only), reading.
b) 1970 EDITION. Grades 2.5–3.4, 3.5–4.9, 5.0–6.9, 7.0–9.5; 1932–71; 3 scores: word knowledge, reading, total.
For additional information concerning the 1970 edition, see 7:696 (16 references); for a review by H. Alan Robinson of the 1958 edition, see 6:797 (4 references); for reviews by James R. Hobson and Margaret G. McKim of an earlier edition, see 4:543; for a review by D. A. Worcester, see 2:1551; for reviews by Ivan A. Booker and Joseph C. Dewey, see 1:1105. For reviews of an earlier edition of the complete battery, see 6:15 (2 reviews), 4:18 (1 review), 2:1189 (2 reviews), and 1:874 (3 reviews).

REFERENCES THROUGH 1971
1–4. See 6:797.
5–20. See 7:696.
21. JUSTMAN, JOSEPH. "Academic Aptitude and Reading Test Scores of Disadvantaged Children Showing Varying Degrees of Mobility." *J Ed Meas* 2:151–5 D '65. * (*PA* 40:5943)
22. RAPHAEL, SHARON. *The Relationship of Intelligence and Personality on the Reading Achievement of Culturally Deprived Second-Grade Students.* Master's thesis, Central Connecticut State College (New Britain, Conn.), 1965.
23. SAMTUR, SUSAN JOY. "The Effects of Noise on a Complex Task." *Grad Res Ed & Related Discip* 4(2):63–81 sp '69. * (*PA* 46:11670)
24. FELDHUSEN, HAZEL J.; LAMB, POSE; AND FELDHUSEN, JOHN. "Prediction of Reading Achievement Under Programmed and Traditional Instruction." *Read Teach* 23(5):446–54 F '70. * (*PA* 45:1382)

25. BALOW, BRUCE; FULTON, HELEN; AND PEPLOE, ELLA. "Reading Comprehension Skills Among Hearing Impaired Adolescents." *Volta R* 73(2):113–9 F '71. *

26. CROWLEY, HARRY L., AND ELLIS, BESSIE. "Cross Validation of a Method for Selecting Children Requiring Special Services in Reading." *Read Teach* 24(4):312–9 Ja '71. *

27. DAVIS, BOBBIE SUE. *A Comparative Analysis of Three Widely Used Standardized Reading Achievement Tests for a Selected Group of Elementary School Children.* Doctor's thesis, University of Southern Mississippi (Hattiesburg, Miss.), 1971. (*DAI* 32:4831A)

28. FLEISCHMAN, HOWARD L.; ORR, DAVID B.; AND STRASEL, H. C. "Relationships Between the Subtests of Six Achievement Test Batteries." Abstract. *Proc 79th Ann Conv Am Psychol Assn* 6(1):109–10 '71. * (*PA* 46:3727)

29. FLEISCHMANN, LILLIAN S. *A Comparison of the Gilmore Oral Reading Test and the Metropolitan Achievement Test in Reading for Grade Placement.* Master's thesis, Sacramento State College (Sacramento, Calif.), 1971.

30. HOPKINS, KENNETH D., AND BRACHT, GLENN H. "A Longitudinal Study of Constancy of Reading Performance," pp. 103–12. In *Diagnostic Viewpoints in Reading.* Edited by Robert E. Leibert. Newark, Del.: International Reading Association, 1971. Pp. viii, 133. *

31. SMITH, CAROLYN M. "The Relationship of Reading Method and Reading Achievement to ITPA Sensory Modalities." *J Spec Ed* 5(2):143–9 su '71. * (*PA* 48:9854)

32. SOLOMON, ALAN. "The Effect of Answer Sheet Format on Test Performance by Culturally Disadvantaged Fourth Grade Elementary School Pupils." *J Ed Meas* 8(4):289–90 w '71. * (*PA* 47:11632)

CUMULATIVE NAME INDEX

[1568]

Minnesota Reading Examination for College Students. Grades 9–16; 1930–35; 2 scores: vocabulary, paragraph reading; Melvin E. Haggerty and Alvin C. Eurich; University of Minnesota Press. *

For additional information and a review by James M. McCallister, see 3:491 (3 references); for a review by W. C. McCall, see 2:1554 (3 references); for a review by Ruth Strang, see 1:1106.

REFERENCES THROUGH 1971

1–3. See 2:1554.

4–6. See 3:491.

7. EURICH, ALVIN C. "The Relation of Speed of Reading to Comprehension." *Sch & Soc* 32:404–6 S 20 '30. * (*PA* 5:764)

8. LITTERER, OSCAR F. "An Experimental Study of Visual Apprehension in Reading." *J Appl Psychol* 17:266–76 Je '33. * (*PA* 8:496)

9. SORENSON, HERBERT. "Mental Ability Over a Wide Range of Adult Ages." *J Appl Psychol* 17:729–41 D '33. * (*PA* 8:3830)

10. RIZZO, NICHOLAS D. *The Predictive Value of the Minnesota Reading Examination.* Master's thesis, University of Kansas (Lawrence, Kan.), 1935.

11. PACE, C. ROBERT. "Handedness and Reading Ability in High School and College Students." *J Ed Res* 31:205–10 N '37. * (*PA* 12:952)

12. LANGSAM, ROSALIND STREEP. *A Factorial Analysis of Reading Ability.* Doctor's thesis, New York University (New York, N.Y.), 1941.

13. SOLOMON, LEWIS E. *Some Relationships Between Reading Ability and Degree of Academic Success in College.* Doctor's thesis, University of Colorado (Boulder, Colo.), 1944.

CUMULATIVE NAME INDEX

[1569]

Monroe's Standardized Silent Reading Test. Grades 3–5, 6–8, 9–12; 1919–59; 2 scores: rate, comprehension; Walter S. Monroe; Bobbs-Merrill Co., Inc. *

For additional information and reviews by Charles R. Langmuir and Agatha Townsend, see 6:798 (5 references).

REFERENCES THROUGH 1971

1–5. See 6:798.

6. MONROE, WALTER SCOTT. *Measuring the Results of Teaching,* pp. 22–9, *passim.* Boston, Mass.: Houghton Mifflin Co., 1918. Pp. xviii, 297. *

7. WEBB, L. W. "Ability in Mental Tests in Relation to Reading Ability." *Sch & Soc* 11:567–70 My 8 '20. *

8. WILSON, G. M., AND HOKE, KREMER J. *How to Measure,* pp. 111–8. New York: Macmillan Co., 1920. Pp. vii, 285. *

9. GATES, ARTHUR I. "An Experimental and Statistical Study of Reading and Reading Tests." *J Ed Psychol* 12:303–14, 378–91, 445–64 S, O, N '21. *

10. MADSEN, I. N. "Some Results From a Testing Program in Idaho." *Sch & Soc* 13:668–71 Je 11 '21. *

11. MONROE, WALTER S. Chap. 2, "Tentative Grade Norms," pp. 19–24, 58–9. In his *Report of Division of Educational Tests for '19–20.* University of Illinois Bulletin, Vol. 18, No. 21; Bureau of Educational Research Bulletin No. 5. Urbana, Ill.: the Bureau, 1921. Pp. 64. *

12. MONROE, WALTER S. *The Illinois Examination.* University of Illinois Bulletin, Vol. 19, No. 9; Bureau of Educational Research Bulletin No. 6. Urbana, Ill.: the Bureau, 1921. Pp. 70. *

13. PRESSEY, L. W., AND PRESSEY, S. C. "A Critical Study of the Concept of Silent Reading." *J Ed Psychol* 12:25–32 Ja '21. *

14. WYMAN, J. BENSON, AND WENDLE, MIRIAM. "What Is Reading Ability?" *J Ed Psychol* 12:518–31 D '21. *

15. FRANZEN, RAYMOND. "Attempts at Test Validation." *J Ed Res* 6:145–58 S '22. *

16. HARLAN, CHAS. L. "The Age-Grade Status as an Index of School Achievement." *Ed Adm & Sup* 8:413–23 O '22. *

17. MADSEN, I. N. "Tests and Measurements in the Schools of Idaho." *J Ed Res* 5:175–8 F '22. *

18. BROOKS, FOWLER D. "The Reliability of Silent Reading Tests." *Sch & Soc* 19:652 My 31 '24. *

19. GATES, ARTHUR I. "A Critique of Methods of Estimating and Measuring the Transfer of Training." *J Ed Psychol* 15:545–58 D '24. *

20. HULTEN, C. E. "A Study of the Speed of Upper Grade Reading." *J Ed Res* 10:141–8 S '24. *

21. KATHLEEN, M. "A Comparative Study of Certain Silent Reading Tests." *Cath Ed R* 22:589–95 D '24. *

22. MONROE, WALTER SCOTT; DEVOSS, JAMES CLARENCE; AND KELLY, FREDERICK JAMES. *Educational Tests and Measurements, Revised Edition,* pp. 99–106. Boston, Mass.: Houghton Mifflin Co., 1924. Pp. xxvii, 521. *

23. RITTER, B. T., AND LOFLAUD, W. T. "The Relation Between Reading Ability as Measured by Certain Standard Tests and the Ability Required in the Interpretation of Printed Matter Involving Reason." *El Sch J* 24:529–46 Mr '24. *

24. JONES, A. M. "An Analytical Study of One Hundred Twenty Superior Children." *Psychol Clinic* 16:19–76 Ja–F '25. * (*PA* 3:1656)

25. FORAN, T. G. "The Present Status of Silent Reading Tests: Part 1, The Measurement of Rate of Reading." *Cath Univ Am Ed Res B* 2(2):1–27 F '27. * (*PA* 2:2609)

26. MOSHER, RAYMOND M. "A Further Note on the Reliability of Reading Tests." *J Ed Psychol* 19:272–4 Ap '28. * (*PA* 2:2623)

27. SIMS, VERNER MARTIN. "The Relative Influence of Two Types of Motivation on Improvement." *J Ed Psychol* 19:480–4 O '28. * (*PA* 3:583)

28. EURICH, ALVIN C. "The Relation of Speed of Reading to Comprehension." *Sch & Soc* 32:404–6 S 20 '30. * (*PA* 5:764)

29. WERNER, OSCAR H. Chap. 2, "The Influence of the Study of Modern Foreign Languages on the Development of Desirable Abilities in English," pp. 97–145. (*PA* 4:2847) In *Studies in Modern Language Teaching.* By E. W. Bagster-Collins and Others. New York: Macmillan Co., 1930. Pp. xxxi, 491. *

30. HUDSON, ALVA. "Reading Achievement, Interests and Habits of Negro Women." *J Negro Ed* 1:367–73 O '32. * (*PA* 8:3690)

31. CROOKS, KENNETH B. M. "Entrance Examinations for Negro Colleges." *J Negro Ed* 3:593–7 O '34. * (*PA* 8:6093)

32. FEINBERG, HENRY, AND REED, CLYDE L. "Reading Level of a Group of Socially Maladjusted Boys." *J Social Psychol* 12:31–8 Ag '40. * (*PA* 15:424)

CUMULATIVE NAME INDEX

[1570]

N.B. Silent Reading Tests (Beginners): Reading Comprehension Test. Substandard B (grade 2); 1961; Human Sciences Research Council [South Africa]. *

For additional information, see 6:799.

[1571]

*National Teacher Examinations: Reading Specialist. College seniors and teachers; 1969–73; formerly entitled *National Teacher Examinations: Reading Specialist—Elementary School;* an inactive form (1969) entitled *Reading Specialist—Elementary School* is available to school systems for local use as part of the program entitled *School Personnel Research and Evaluation Services;* Educational Testing Service. *
For the testing program entry, see 869.

For additional information concerning earlier forms, see 7:731. For reviews of the testing program, see 7:582 (2 reviews), 6:700 (1 review), 5:538 (3 reviews), and 4:802 (1 review).

[1572]

The Nelson-Denny Reading Test. Grades 9–16 and adults; 1929–73; NDRT; 4 scores: vocabulary, comprehension, total, rate; original edition by M. J. Nelson and E. C. Denny; revision by James I. Brown; Houghton Mifflin Co. *
For additional information, reviews by David B. Orr and Agatha Townsend, and an excerpted review by John O. Crites, see 6:800 (13 references); for a review by Ivan A. Booker of an earlier edition, see 4:544 (17 references); for a review by Hans C. Gordon, see 2:1557 (6 references).

REFERENCES THROUGH 1971

1–6. See 2:1557.
7–23. See 4:544.
24–36. See 6:800.
37. NELSON, M. J. "Some Data From Freshman Tests." *Sch & Soc* 31:772–4 Je 7 '30. * (*PA* 4:3694)
38. JOHNSON, DONALD M., AND REYNOLDS, FLOYD. "A Factor Analysis of Verbal Ability." *Psychol Rec* 4:183–95 Ja '41. * (*PA* 15:3315)
39. SPOERL, DOROTHY TILDEN. "The Academic and Verbal Adjustment of College Age Bilingual Students." *J Genetic Psychol* 64:139–57 Mr '44. * (*PA* 18:2275)
40. WAGGONER, R. W., AND ZEIGLER, THORNTON WOODWARD. "Psychiatric Factors in Medical School Students Who Fail." *Am J Psychiatry* 103:369–76 N '46. * (*PA* 21:1671)
41. McCLANAHAN, WALTER R., AND MORGAN, DAVID H. "Use of Standard Tests in Counseling Engineering Students in College." *J Ed Psychol* 39:491–501 D '48. * (*PA* 23:3448)
42. BELLOWS, CAROL S., AND RUSH, CARL H., JR. "Reading Abilities of Business Executives." *J Appl Psychol* 36:1–4 F '52. * (*PA* 26:7286)
43. McCOLLUM, CLIFFORD G. "The Performance of Prospective Elementary School Teachers in a General Physical Science Course." *J Ed Res* 45:695–704 My '52. * (*PA* 27:2963)
44. OTTMAN, ROBERT WILLIAM. *A Statistical Investigation of the Influence of Selected Factors on the Skill of Sight-Singing.* Doctor's thesis, North Texas State College (Denton, Tex.), 1956. (*DA* 16:763)
45. CURRIE, CAROLINE. *The Relationship of Certain Selected Factors to Achievement in Freshman Composition.* Doctor's thesis, Northwestern University (Evanston, Ill.), 1957. (*DA* 18:884)
46. HAAS, MARY GERALDINE. *A Comparative Study of Critical Thinking, Flexibility of Thinking, and Reading Ability Involving Religious and Lay College Seniors.* Doctor's thesis, Fordham University (New York, N.Y.), 1963. (*DA* 24:622)
47. BLANTON, WINCIE L., AND PECK, ROBERT F. "College Student Motivation and Academic Performance." *Ed & Psychol Meas* 24:897–912 w '64. * (*PA* 39:8695)
48. PABST, ROBERT LEROY. *A Validation Study of the Relationship of Size of High School and Certain Intellective Factors to Academic Achievement in College.* Doctor's thesis, Indiana University (Bloomington, Ind.), 1965. (*DA* 27:331A)
49. TROY, ELIZABETH McGOLDRICK. *A Study of the Predictive Value of Eleven Variables Used at King's College to Determine General Scholastic Achievement of Two Hundred Forty-Three Entering Students.* Master's thesis, Marywood College (Scranton, Pa.), 1965.
50. LINDLEY, MICHAEL R. *A Study of the Relationship Between Self-Concept and Reading Ability.* Master's thesis, Furman University (Greenville, S.C.), 1966.
51. McCORMICK, ALBERT GRANT. *An Investigation of Reading Skills, General Mental Ability and Personality Variables Used in the Selection of Practical Nursing Students.* Doctor's thesis, Oklahoma State University (Stillwater, Okla.), 1966. (*DA* 27:4136A)
52. MOGHRABI, KAMEL M. *An Analysis of Factors That Influence the Degree of Success or Failure of Foreign Students at Texas A & M University.* Doctor's thesis, Texas A & M University (College Station, Tex.), 1966. (*DA* 27:3232A)
53. SHRADER, EDWARD FRANKLYN. *A Descriptive Study of Students in the Precollege Summer Session Program, the University of Maryland, 1964–1965.* Doctor's thesis, George Washington University (Washington, D.C.), 1966. (*DA* 27:4104A)
54. ADAMS, EFFIE KAYE. "Reading Performance of Elementary Student Teachers in a Developing Institution." *Yearb Nat Read Conf* 16:47–57 '67. *
55. WELCH, JOYCE. *The Effects of Timing on the Reliability and Validity of the Nelson-Denny Reading Test in Establishing Shasta Junior College Norms.* Master's thesis, Chico State College (Chico, Calif.), 1967.
56. BRADSHAW, OTTIE LEON. *The Relationship of Selected Measures of Aptitude, Interest, and Personality to Academic Achievement in Engineering and Engineering Technology.* Doctor's thesis, Oklahoma State University (Stillwater, Okla.), 1968. (*DAI* 30:979A)
57. FARR, ROGER. "The Convergent and Discriminant Validity of Several Upper Level Reading Tests." *Yearb Nat Read Conf* 17:181–91 '68. *
58. GREEN, JOHNNIE HENDERSON. *An Analysis of Academic Proficiency of the 1965–66 Beginning Freshman Class, School of Business, Texas Southern University, Houston, Texas.* Doctor's thesis, University of Houston (Houston, Tex.), 1968. (*DA* 29:3323A)
59. MARSHALL, JOSEPH JEMERSON. *Non-Cognitive Variables as a Predictor of Academic Achievement Among Freshmen, Sophomores, and Juniors at Abilene Christian College.* Doctor's thesis, Baylor University (Waco, Tex.), 1968. (*DA* 29:3833A)
60. MUNDAY, LEO. "Correlations Between ACT and Other Predictors of Academic Success in College." *Col & Univ* 44:67–76 f '68. *
61. REID, RONALD H. "Grammatical Complexity and Comprehension of Compressed Speech." *J Commun* 18:236–42 S '68. * (*PA* 43:3969)
62. REID, RONALD HENRY. *Comprehension of Compressed Speech as a Function of Difficulty of Material.* Doctor's thesis, Indiana University (Bloomington, Ind.), 1968. (*DA* 29:1689A)
63. SPURLIN, MELVIN DAVID. *A Study of the Relationship of Sex, Ability Level and Biology Preparation to Achievement in Freshman Biology at Metropolitan State College.* Doctor's thesis, University of Colorado (Boulder, Colo.), 1968. (*DA* 29:1173A)
64. STOUGH, KENNETH FRANCIS. *An Analysis of Selected Factors as Predictors of Success in Vocational Industrial Certification Courses.* Doctor's thesis, University of Maryland (College Park, Md.), 1968. (*DA* 29:2595A)
65. CLINE, RUTH K. J. "Reading Ability and Selection for Teacher Education Programs." *J Read* 12(8):634–8+ My '69. *
66. FEUERS, STELLE. *The Relationship Between General Reading Skills and Junior College Academic Achievement.* Doctor's thesis, University of California (Los Angeles, Calif.), 1969. (*DAI* 30:3186A)
67. JOHNSON, JOSEPH CARLTON, II, AND JACOBSON, MILTON D. "An Investigation of the Interrelationships Among Certain Specific Predictor Variables and Two College Bound High School Student Reading Enhancement Classes." *Yearb Nat Read Conf* 18:240–5 '69. *
68. PIERCE, DAVID RANDALL. *A Comparison of the Conventional, Printed-Programed and Audio-Programed Methods of Teaching Remediation-Oriented Mathematics.* Doctor's thesis, Purdue University (Lafayette, Ind.), 1969. (*DAI* 30:4692A)
69. TASCHOW, HORST GERARD. "A Comparison of Individual Reading Improvement Scores on a Group of Community College

Freshmen as Measured by the Crude Gain Method and the Residual Gain Method." *Yearb Nat Read Conf* 18:27–37 '69. *

70. WILLIAMS, VERNON. *A Multi-Predictive Measure to Predict Success at Two Levels in Freshman College Mathematics.* Doctor's thesis, Oklahoma State University (Stillwater, Okla.), 1969. (*DAI* 31:4026A)

71. CARVER, RONALD P. "Analysis of 'Chunked' Test Items as Measures of Reading and Listening Comprehension." *J Ed Meas* 7(3):141–50 f '70. * (*PA* 45:4913)

72. CREASER, JAMES; JACOBS, MITCHELL; ZACCARIA, LUCY; AND CARSELLO, CARMEN. "Effects of Shortened Time Limits on the Nelson-Denny Reading Test." *J Read* 14(3):167–70 D '70. * (*PA* 48:3667)

73. DEFRAIN, DAVID MURRAY. *The Effects of Self-Concept and Selected Personal and Educational Variables Upon Attrition in a Non-Credit College Reading Improvement Program.* Doctor's thesis, Oklahoma State University (Stillwater, Okla.), 1970. (*DAI* 31:5195A)

74. FOLLMAN, J. C.; LOWE, A. J.; AND BURLEY, W. W. "Relationship of Two Matching Item Test Formats to the Nelson-Denny Reading Test." *Fla J Ed Res* 12(1):103–8 Ja '70. *

75. RUSSELL, WENDELL PHILLIPS. *Intellectual and Non-Intellectual Factors Affecting the Attrition Rate of Students Entering Virginia Union University in 1965.* Doctor's thesis, University of Virginia (Charlottesville, Va.), 1970. (*DAI* 31:4474A)

76. CARVER, RONALD P., AND DARBY, CHARLES A., JR. "Development and Evaluation of a Test of Information Storage During Reading." *J Ed Meas* 8(1):33–44 sp '71. * (*PA* 46:5461)

77. FARR, ROGER, AND SMITH, CARL B. "The Effects of Test Item Validity on Total Test Reliability and Validity." *Yearb Nat Read Conf* 19(1):122–34 '71. *

78. FOLLMAN, JOHN; LOWE, A. J.; AND WILEY, RUSSELL. "Correlational and Factor Analysis of Critical Reading and Thinking Test Scores—Twelfth Grade." *Yearb Nat Read Conf* 20:128–36 '71. *

79. GIBSON, WALTER DANA. *Relationship Between Difficulty Levels of Assigned English Texts and Reading Ability of Community College Students.* Doctor's thesis, University of Southern California (Los Angeles, Calif.), 1971. (*DAI* 31:6362A)

80. JOHNSON, ROGER; FOLLMAN, JOHN; WILEY, RUSSELL; LOWE, A. J.; AND MILLER, WILLIAM. "Canonical and Partial Correlation of Critical Reading and Critical Thinking Test Scores—Twelfth Grade." *Yearb Nat Read Conf* 20:137–41 '71. *

81. KIRBY, BARBARA JANE. *An Analysis of the Relationships Between Academic Performance and Scores on Licensure Examinations of Mortuary Science Students at Miami-Dade Junior College 1966–1969.* Doctor's thesis, University of Miami (Coral Gables, Fla.), 1971. (*DAI* 32:3122A)

82. LOWE, A. J.; FOLLMAN, JOHN; BURLEY, WADE; AND FOLLMAN, JOHNNY. "Psychometric Analysis of Critical Reading and Critical Thinking Test Scores—Twelfth Grade." *Yearb Nat Read Conf* 20:142–7 '71. *

CUMULATIVE NAME INDEX

[1573]
The Nelson Reading Test, Revised Edition. Grades 3–9; 1931–62; revision of *The Nelson Silent Reading Test: Vocabulary and Paragraph;* 3 scores: vocabulary, paragraph comprehension, total; M. J. Nelson; Houghton Mifflin Co. *

For additional information and a review by H. Alan Robinson, see 6:802; for a review by William D. Sheldon of the original edition, see 4:545 (1 reference); for a review by Constance M. McCullough, see 3:492; for an excerpted review by Albert Grant, see 2:1558.

REFERENCES THROUGH 1971

1. See 4:545.
2. COLBY, ARCHIE N., AND TIFFIN, JOSEPH. "The Reading Ability of Industrial Supervisors." *Personnel* 27:156–9 S '50. * (*PA* 25:3437)
3. HALL, JODY C. "The Effect of Background Music on the Reading Comprehension of 278 Eighth and Ninth Grade Students." *J Ed Res* 45:451–8 F '52. * (*PA* 27:2195)
4. FREEHILL, MAURICE F. "The Prediction of Teaching Competence." *J Exp Ed* 31:307–11 Mr '63. *
5. FARR, ROGER. "The Convergent and Discriminant Validity of Several Upper Level Reading Tests." *Yearb Nat Read Conf* 17:181–91 '68. *
6. GEESLIN, ROBERT H., AND YORK, PATRICIA W. "Literacy Skills as a Barrier to Inservice Training." *J Read Behav* 3(3): 9–12 su '70–71 ['71]. *

CUMULATIVE NAME INDEX

[1574]
New Developmental Reading Tests. Grades 1–2.5, 2.5–3, 4–6; 1955–68; revision of *Developmental Reading Tests;* Guy L. Bond, Bruce Balow, and Cyril J. Hoyt; Lyons & Carnahan, Inc. *

a) PRIMARY TESTS. Grades 1–2.5, 2.5–3; 1955–65; 4 scores: word recognition, comprehending significant ideas, comprehending specific instructions, average grade score. *Out of print.*

b) INTERMEDIATE TESTS. Grades 4–6; 1959–68; 5 basic scores: (1) vocabulary, (2) reading for information, (3) reading for relationships, (4) reading for interpretation, (5) reading for appreciation, plus 3 combination scores—literal comprehension (2 and 3), creative comprehension (4 and 5), and general comprehension (2, 3, 4, and 5).

For additional information and reviews by Frederick B. Davis and Arthur E. Traxler, see 7:697 (4 references); for reviews by Edward B. Fry and Agatha Townsend of the original edition, see 6:787.

REFERENCES THROUGH 1971

1–4. See 7:697.
5. ROSEN, CARL L. "An Experimental Study of Visual Perceptual Training and Reading Achievement in First Grade." *Percept & Motor Skills* 22:979–86 Je '66. * (*PA* 40:11008)
6. BALOW, BRUCE; FULTON, HELEN; AND PEPLOE, ELLA. "Reading Comprehension Skills Among Hearing Impaired Adolescents." *Volta R* 73(2):113–9 F '71. *

CUMULATIVE NAME INDEX

[1575]

OISE Achievement Tests in Silent Reading: Advanced Primary Battery. Grade 2; 1969–71; 5 scores: words in use, multiple word meanings, Part A comprehension, Part B comprehension, total; Ontario Institute for Studies in Education and Patricia Tracy (handbook); distributed by Guidance Centre [Canada]. *

For additional information, see 7:698.

[1576]

Pressey Diagnostic Reading Tests. Grades 3–9; 1929; 4 scores: speed, vocabulary, paragraph meaning, total; S. L. Pressey and L. C. Pressey; Bobbs-Merrill Co., Inc. *

REFERENCES THROUGH 1971

1. FORAN, T. G., AND ROCK, ROBERT J., JR. "The Reliability of Some Silent Reading Tests." *Cath Univ Am Ed Res B* 5(6): 1–23 Je '30. * (*PA* 5:2921)
2. BARNARD, WILLIAM H. "An Analysis of a Sixth Grade Vocabulary Test." *Ed* 61:285–7 Ja '41. *
3. HARRIS, CHESTER W. "An Exploration of Language Skill Patterns." *J Ed Psychol* 39:321–36 O '48. * (*PA* 23:1755)

CUMULATIVE NAME INDEX

Barnard, W. H.: 2   Harris, C. W.: 3
Foran, T. G.: 1   Rock, R. J.: 1

[1577]

★**[Primary Reading Survey Tests.]** Grades 2, 3; 1973; subtest of *Primary Survey Tests;* 2 levels; Kenneth S. Goodman, John C. Manning, Marion Monroe, Andrew Schiller, Joseph M. Wepman, and E. Glenadine Gibb (handbooks); Scott, Foresman & Co. * For the complete battery entry, see 27.

a) EARLY PRIMARY READING SURVEY TEST. Grade 2.
b) LATE PRIMARY READING SURVEY TEST. Grade 3.

[1578]

Primary Reading Test: Acorn Achievement Tests. Grades 2–3; 1943–57; 5 scores: word recognition, words-similar meaning, word meaning-opposites, story-paragraph-sentence meaning, total; Winifred E. Stayton, Frances C. Ranson, and Roland L. Beck; Psychometric Affiliates. *

For additional information, see 5:642; for a review by Alice N. Jameson, see 3:495.

[1579]

Progressive Achievement Tests of Reading. Standards 2–4 and Forms I–IV (ages 8–14); 1969–70; PATR; 2 tests; manual by Warwick B. Elley and Neil A. Reid; New Zealand Council for Educational Research [New Zealand]. (Australian edition: Grades 3–9; 1970–73; manual by M. L. Clark; Australian Council for Educational Research [Australia].) *

a) READING COMPREHENSION.
b) READING VOCABULARY.

For additional information and excerpted reviews by Milton L. Clark and J. Elkins, see 7:699.

REFERENCES THROUGH 1971

1. MARSH, R. W. "Notes on Sampling in the Standardization of the Progressive Achievement Tests." *N Zeal J Ed Studies* 4(1):69–73 My '69. * (*PA* 46:11513)

CUMULATIVE NAME INDEX

Clark, M. L.: *exc,* 7:699   Marsh, R. W.: 1
Elkins, J.: *exc,* 7:699

[1580]

RBH Basic Reading and Word Test. Disadvantaged adults; 1968–69; Richardson, Bellows, Henry & Co., Inc. *

For additional information and a review by Thorsten R. Carlson, see 7:700.

[1581]

RBH Test of Reading Comprehension. Business and industry; 1951–63; Richardson, Bellows, Henry & Co., Inc. *

For additional information and reviews by Thorsten R. Carlson and Willard A. Kerr, see 7:701.

[1582]

*****Reading Comprehension: Canadian English Achievement Test, Part 1.** Grades 8.5–9.0; 1959–68; subtest of *Canadian Test Battery, Grades 8–9;* Ontario Institute for Studies in Education; distributed by Guidance Centre [Canada]. * For the complete battery entry, see 1047.

For additional information and reviews of the complete test, see 6:253 (2 reviews).

[1583]

Reading Comprehension: Cooperative English Tests. Grades 9–12, 13–14; 1940–60; separate booklet edition of reading subtest of *Cooperative English Tests;* 4 scores: vocabulary, level of comprehension, speed of comprehension, total; revision by Clarence Derrick, David P. Harris, and Biron Walker; Cooperative Tests and Services. * For the complete battery entry, see 69.

For additional information and reviews by W. V. Clemans and W. G. Fleming, see 6:806 (12 references); see also 5:645 (21 references) and 4:547 (20 references); for reviews by Robert Murray Bear and J. B. Stroud of an earlier edition, see 3:497 (15 references); see also 2:1564 (2 references). For reviews of the complete battery, see 6:256 (2 reviews, 1 excerpt) and 3:120 (3 reviews).

REFERENCES THROUGH 1971

1–2. See 2:1564.
3–17. See 3:497.
18–37. See 4:547.
38–58. See 5:645.
59–70. See 6:806.
71. ARTLEY, A. S. "The Appraisal of Reading Comprehension." *J Ed Psychol* 34:55–60 Ja '43. * (*PA* 17:3236)
72. ARTLEY, A. STERL. "A Study of Certain Relationships Existing Between General Reading Comprehension and Reading Comprehension in a Specific Subject Matter Area." *J Ed Res* 37:464–73 F '44. * (*PA* 18:2556)
73. COOLEY, JOHN CHRISTOPHER. *A Study of the Relation Between Certain Mental and Personality Traits and Ratings of Musical Abilities.* Doctor's thesis, Michigan State College (East Lansing, Mich.), 1952. (*DA* 13:240)
74. SOMMERFELD, ROY ELMER. *The Relationship of Reading Ability to Measures of Perceptual Span With Special Reference to Tachistoscopic Span for Digits.* Doctor's thesis, University of Michigan (Ann Arbor, Mich.), 1952. (*DA* 12:527)
75. BREEN, LELWYN CLYDE. *The Relation of Reading Ability to College Mortality of Certain Entering Freshmen at the University of Washington in the Year 1950–1951.* Doctor's thesis, University of Washington (Seattle, Wash.), 1953. (*DA* 14:483)
76. BRUCE, WILLIAM JOHN. *The Contribution of Eleven Variables to the Prognosis of Academic Success in Eight Areas at the University of Washington.* Doctor's thesis, University of Washington (Seattle, Wash.), 1953. (*DA* 13:505)
77. HUNT, JACOB TATE. "The Relation Among Vocabulary, Structural Analysis, and Reading." *J Ed Psychol* 44:193–202 Ap '53. * (*PA* 28:3205)
78. PHILLIPS, CLARENCE. "Achievement, Aptitude, and Background of Liberal Arts and Science Students (General Curriculum) Deficient in High School Mathematics." *J Ed Res* 47: 169–80 N '53. * (*PA* 28:6515)
79. SMITH, ALLAN B. *The Prediction of Scholastic Success for Freshman Entrants to the University of Connecticut 1933–1951.* Doctor's thesis, University of Connecticut (Storrs, Conn.), 1953. (*DA* 13:1121)
80. WHEELER, D. K. "Reading Ability of Students Entering the University of Western Australia." *Educand* (Australia) 1: 37–46 N '53. *
81. HYMAN, SIDNEY ROBERT. *The Development of Criteria of Research Competence in Psychology and Their Prediction From Certain Intellectual and Achievement Measures.* Doctor's thesis, University of Pittsburgh (Pittsburgh, Pa.), 1954. (*DA* 14:2395)
82. LA BUE, ANTHONY CHARLES. *An Analysis of Some Factors Associated With Persistence of Interest in Teaching as a Voca-*

tional Choice. Doctor's thesis, Syracuse University (Syracuse, N.Y.), 1954. (*DA* 14:2001)

83. Lebsack, Jacob Robert. *Specific Reading Ability as Associated With Subject Matter Achievement.* Doctor's thesis, University of Nebraska (Lincoln, Neb.), 1954. (*DA* 14:1995)

84. Hao, Peter Te Yuan. *An Analysis of Certain Learning Difficulties of Chinese Students in New York City.* Doctor's thesis, New York University (New York, N.Y.), 1955. (*DA* 15:1551)

85. Lins, L. J., and Pitt, H. "Comparison of Ability and Background of University of Wisconsin Freshmen According to Distance From Home to the University or Another College." *J Ed Res* 48:333–44 Ja '55. * (*PA* 29:8951)

86. Sanders, William B.; Osborne, R. Travis; and Greene, J. E. "Intelligence and Academic Performance of College Students of Urban, Rural, and Mixed Backgrounds." *J Ed Res* 49:185–93 N '55. * (*PA* 30:7774)

87. Chahbazi, Parviz. "Use of Projective Tests in Predicting College Achievement." *Ed & Psychol Meas* 16:538–42 w '56. * (*PA* 32:939)

88. Hendricks, Richard. *Relationships Among Tests of Intelligibility, Word-Reception, and Other Measures of Symbolic Formulation.* Doctor's thesis, Ohio State University (Columbus, Ohio), 1956. (*DA* 16:2239)

89. Anderson, A. W. "Reading Ability and Intelligence of Students: A Study of New Admissions to the University of Western Australia in 1957." *Educand* (Australia) 3:108–12 Mr '57. *

90. Farnum, Hollis B. "A Comparison of the Academic Aptitude of University Extension Degree Students and Campus Students." *J Appl Psychol* 41:63–5 F '57. * (*PA* 32:942)

91. Mann, Helene Powner. "Some Hypotheses on Perceptual and Learning Processes With Their Applications to the Process of Reading: A Preliminary Note." *J Genetic Psychol* 90:167–202 Je '57. * (*PA* 35:1187)

92. Fletcher, Junior Eugene. *A Study of the Relationships Between Ability to Use Context as an Aid in Reading and Other Verbal Abilities.* Doctor's thesis, University of Washington (Seattle, Wash.), 1959. (*DA* 20:2675)

93. Frederiksen, Norman, and Gilbert, Arthur C. F. "Replication of a Study of Differential Predictability." *Ed & Psychol Meas* 20:759–67 w '60. * (*PA* 35:7953)

94. Gunderson, Doris Virginia. *The Influence of College Reading Instruction Upon Academic Achievement.* Doctor's thesis, University of Minnesota (Minneapolis, Minn.), 1960. (*DA* 21:1806)

95. Anderson, A. W. "School of Entry and First-Year Academic Performance in the University of Western Australia." *Austral J Higher Ed* 1:20–3 N '61. *

96. Obst, Frances. "A Study of Abilities of Women Students Entering the Colleges of Letters and Science and Applied Arts at the University of California, Los Angeles." *J Ed Res* 57:84–6 O '63. *

97. Rankin, Earl F., Jr. "Reading Test Performance of Introverts and Extroverts." *Yearb Nat Read Conf* 12:158–66 '63. *

98. Callis, Robert, and Prediger, Dale J. "Predictors of Achievement in Counseling and Guidance Graduate Study." *Counselor Ed & Sup* 3:63–9 w '64. *

99. Chansky, Norman M. "A Note on the Validity of Reading Test Scores." *J Ed Res* 58:90 O '64. *

100. Hogben, D. "School of Entry and First Year Performance of Medical Students in the University of Western Australia." *Austral J Higher Ed* 2:79–83 N '64. *

101. Preston, Ralph C. "Ability of Students to Identify Correct Responses Before Reading." *J Ed Res* 58:181–3 D '64. *

102. Anderson, A. W. "Intelligence and Reading Scores of Entrants to the University of Western Australia 1954–65." *Austral J Higher Ed* 2:177–82 N '65. *

103. Chase, Clinton I. *The University Freshman Dropout.* Indiana University, Monograph of the Bureau of Educational Studies and Testing, Indiana Studies in Prediction, No. 6. Bloomington, Ind.: the Bureau, 1965. Pp. 36. *

104. Davis, Luther Edward, Jr. *A Study of Selected Traits of St. Petersburg Junior College Students and Their Value in Predicting Academic Success in Certain Courses of Study at the Senior College Level.* Doctor's thesis, Auburn University (Auburn, Ala.), 1965. (*DA* 26:791)

105. Hogben, D. "The Prediction of Academic Success in Relation to Student Selection in Medicine at the University of Western Australia." *Austral J Higher Ed* 2:152–60 N '65. *

106. Roulette, Thomas Grier. *An Investigation of Response Style Effects in an Objective Test of Achievement.* Doctor's thesis, Western Reserve University (Cleveland, Ohio), 1965. (*DA* 27:1611B)

107. Cashman, Jerome Patrick. *A Study of the Relationship Between Organic Factors, Certain Selected Variables and Progress in a Reading Improvement Program.* Doctor's thesis, Fordham University (New York, N.Y.), 1966. (*DA* 27:1648A)

108. Friedman, Stuart M. *Predicting Students' Success in a Comprehensive Junior College.* Doctor's thesis, University of Southern California (Los Angeles, Calif.), 1966. (*DA* 26:7112)

109. Guilliams, Clark Irvin. *Predicting Creative Productivity in College Classes Where Creative Thinking Is Empha-*

sized. Doctor's thesis, University of Arkansas (Fayetteville, Ark.), 1966. (*DA* 27:675A)

110. Lins, L. Joseph; Abell, Allan P.; and Hutchins, H. Clifton. "Relative Usefulness in Predicting Academic Success of the ACT, the SAT, and Some Other Variables." *J Exp Ed* 35:1–29 w '66. *

111. Hartsock, Woodrow Wilson. *The Prediction of Academic Performance in a Seminary.* Master's thesis, Southern Methodist University (Dallas, Tex.), 1967.

112. Rengstorff, Roy H. "The Types and Incidence of Hand-Eye Preference and Its Relationship With Certain Reading Abilities." *Am J Optom* 44:233–8 Ap '67. * (*PA* 41:10908)

113. Farr, Roger. "The Convergent and Discriminant Validity of Several Upper Level Reading Tests." *Yearb Nat Read Conf* 17:181–91 '68. *

114. McDonald, Andrew A. *Relationship Between Subtest Scores of Cooperative Reading and Grade Point Averages in Certain General Education Courses at Howard University.* Master's thesis, Howard University (Washington, D.C.), 1968.

115. Thumin, Fred J. "Ability Scores as Related to Age Among Male Job Applicants." *J Gerontol* 23:390–2 Jl '68. *

116. Howlett, John L. "A Study of Placement Methods for Entering College Freshmen in the Proper Mathematics Sequence at Michigan Technological University." *Math Teach* 62(8):651–9 D '69. *

117. Biggs, J. B. "Personality Correlates of Certain Dimensions of Study Behaviour." *Austral J Psychol* 22(3):287–97 D '70. * (*PA* 46:1843)

118. Singer, Carroll Rosenfeld. *Eye Movements, Reading Comprehension, and Vocabulary as Effected by Varying Visual and Auditory Modalities in College Students.* Doctor's thesis, New Mexico State University (University Park, N.M.), 1970. (*DAI* 31:164A)

119. Wile, Marcia Ziskind. *Sex Knowledge and Reading Ability of Selected Graduate Professional School Students.* Doctor's thesis, Case Western Reserve University (Cleveland, Ohio), 1970. (*DAI* 31:3307A)

120. Dielman, T. E.; Barton, K.; and Cattell, R. B. "The Prediction of Junior High School Achievement From Objective Motivation Tests." *Personality* 2(4):279–87 w '71. * (*PA* 48:7881)

121. Ross, Louis. "Forecasting the Academic Achievement of Engineering Freshmen." *J Ed Res* 64(7):307–10 Mr '71. *

CUMULATIVE NAME INDEX

Reading Comprehension: Cooperative English Tests

Stancik, E. J.: 62
Stroud, J. B.: *rev,* 3:497
Stucky, M. O.: 59–60
Thumin, F. J.: 115
Thurstone, L. L.: 14
Traxler, A.: 2

Traxler, A. E.: 15, 28, 34, 36
Van Der Jagt, E. R.: 54
Votaw, D. F.: 16
Wallace, W. L.: 37
Wheeler, D. K.: 80
Wile, M. Z.: 119

[1584]
Reading Comprehension Test. College entrants; 1963–68; William A. McCartney; the Author. *

[1585]
*Reading Comprehension Test DE. Ages 10–12.5; 1963–71; formerly called *Reading Comprehension Test 1;* E. L. Barnard; published for the National Foundation for Educational Research in England and Wales; Ginn & Co. Ltd. [England]. *
  For additional information, see 7:702.

[1586]
Reading Comprehension Test: National Achievement Tests [Crow, Kuhlmann, and Crow]. Grades 4–9; 1953–57; 1957 test identical with test copyrighted 1953; Lester D. Crow, Martha J. Kuhlmann, and Alice Crow; Psychometric Affiliates. *
  For additional information, see 5:647.

[1587]
Reading Comprehension Test: National Achievement Tests [Speer and Smith]. Grades 3–8; 1938–57; 4 scores: following directions, sentence meaning, paragraph meaning, total; 1957 test identical with test copyrighted 1938; Robert K. Speer and Samuel Smith; Psychometric Affiliates. *
  For additional information, see 5:646; for a review by James R. Hobson, see 3:498.

[1588]
*Reading for Understanding Placement Test. Grades 3–8, 8–12, 5–16; 1959–69; designed for use with the self-teaching reading exercises prepared by the same author; 3 levels; Thelma Gwinn Thurstone; Science Research Associates, Inc. *
a) JUNIOR EDITION. Grades 3–8; 1963.
b) SENIOR EDITION. Grades 8–12; 1963–65.
c) GENERAL EDITION. Grades 5–16; 1959–69.
  REFERENCES THROUGH 1971
1. FULLER, GERALD B., AND ENDE, RUSSELL. "The Effectiveness of Visual Perception, Intelligence and Reading Understanding in Predicting Reading Achievement in Junior High School Children." *J Ed Res* 60:280–2 F '67. *
2. ENDE, RUSSELL S. "Reading for Understanding in Grades 7, 8, and 9." *Ill Sch Res* 7(2):32–7 w '71. *
  CUMULATIVE NAME INDEX
Ende, R.: 1   Fuller, G. B.: 1
Ende, R. S.: 2

[1589]
★The Reading Progress Scale. Grades 3–12; 1970–71; RPS; Ronald P. Carver; Revrac Publications. *

[1590]
Reading: Public School Achievement Tests. Grades 3–8; 1928–59; Jacob S. Orleans; Bobbs-Merrill Co., Inc. * For the complete battery entry, see 28.
  For additional information, see 6:807. For reviews of the complete battery, see 2:1194 (2 reviews).

[1591]
Reading Test AD. Ages 7-6 to 11-1; 1956–70; formerly called *Sentence Reading Test 1;* 1960 test identical with test published 1956 except for format; 1970 manual identical with manual published 1956 except for title; A. F. Watts; published for the

National Foundation for Educational Research in England and Wales; Ginn & Co. Ltd. [England]. *
  For additional information, see 7:703; for reviews by Reginald R. Dale and Stephen Wiseman, see 5:652.
  REFERENCES THROUGH 1971
1. LOVELL, K.; SHAPTON, D.; AND WARREN, N. S. "A Study of Some Cognitive and Other Disabilities in Backward Readers of Average Intelligence as Assessed by a Non-Verbal Test." *Brit J Ed Psychol* 34:58–64 F '64. * (*PA* 38:9233)
2. YOUNG, J. A., AND JENKINSON, M. D. "An Objective Comparison of Achievement in the Basic Subjects for Matched Groups of Children in Manchester, England and Edmonton, Alberta." *Alberta J Ed Res* (Canada) 10:59–66 Je '64. * (*PA* 39:12096)
3. SAVAGE, R. D., AND O'CONNOR, D. J. "The Assessment of Reading and Arithmetic Retardation in the School." *Brit J Ed Psychol* 36:317–8 N '66. *
  CUMULATIVE NAME INDEX
Dale, R. R.: *rev,* 5:652   Shapton, D. 1
Jenkinson, M. D.: 2   Warren, N. S.: 1
Lovell, K.: 1   Wiseman, S.: *rev,* 5:652
O'Connor, D. J.: 3   Young, J. A.: 2
Savage, R. D.: 3

[1592]
Reading Test (Comprehension and Speed): Municipal Tests: National Achievement Tests. Grades 3–6, 6–8; 1938–57; subtest of *Municipal Battery;* 5 scores: following directions, sentence meaning, paragraph meaning, reading speed, total; 1950–55 tests identical with tests copyrighted 1938–39; Robert K. Speer and Samuel Smith; Psychometric Affiliates. *
  For additional information, see 5:648. For reviews of the complete battery, see 5:18 (1 review), 4:20 (1 review), and 2:1191 (2 reviews).

[1593]
Reading Test: McGraw-Hill Basic Skills System. Grades 11–14; 1970; also called *MHBSS Reading Test;* although designed for use with the MHBSS instructional program, the test may be used independently; 7 scores: 2 reading rates (recreational, study), flexibility, retention, skimming and scanning, paragraph comprehension, total; Alton L. Raygor; McGraw-Hill Book Co., Inc. *
  For additional information and a review by Donald B. Black, see 7:704.

[1594]
*Reading Tests A and BD. 1, 2–4 years primary school; 1967–73; 2 levels; published for the National Foundation for Educational Research in England and Wales; Ginn & Co. Ltd. [England]. *
a) READING TEST A. 1 year primary school; 1968–73; formerly called *Primary Reading Test 1.*
b) READING TEST BD. 2–4 years primary school; 1967–69; formerly called *Primary Reading Test 2.*
  For additional information, see 7:705.

[1595]
Reading Tests EH 1–3. First 4 years of secondary school; 1961–66; formerly called *Secondary Reading Tests 1–3;* 3 tests; S. M. Bate; published for the National Foundation for Educational Research in England and Wales; Ginn & Co. Ltd. [England]. *
a) TEST 1, VOCABULARY.
b) TEST 2, COMPREHENSION.
c) TEST 3, CONTINUOUS PROSE. Reading speed.

[1596]
SRA Achievement Series: Reading. Grades 1–2, 2–4, 4–9; 1954–69; Forms C and D; more recent Forms E and F are not available as separates; Louis P. Thorpe, D. Welty Lefever, and Robert A. Naslund; Science Research Associates, Inc. * For the complete battery entry, see 29.

a) HAND SCORED EDITION. Grades 1–2, 2–4; 1954–68; 2 levels. *Out of print.*

   1) *Grades 1–2.* 5 scores: verbal-pictorial association, language perception, comprehension, vocabulary, total.

   2) *Grades 2–4.* 3 scores: comprehension, vocabulary, total.

b) MULTILEVEL EDITION. Grades 4–9; 1963–69; 3 scores: comprehension, vocabulary, total.

For additional information and a review by John T. Guthrie, see 7:706 (6 references); for a review by Edward B. Fry of earlier forms, see 6:808; for a review by N. Dale Bryant and Clarence Derrick, see 5:649. For reviews of the complete battery, see 7:18 (2 reviews), 6:21 (1 review), and 5:21 (2 reviews).

REFERENCES THROUGH 1971
1–6. See 7:706.
   7. BUSWELL, G. T. "The Relationship Between Rate of Thinking and Rate of Reading." *Sch R* 59:339–46 S '51. *
   8. FLEISCHMAN, HOWARD L.; ORR, DAVID B.; AND STRASEL, H. C. "Relationships Between the Subtests of Six Achievement Test Batteries." Abstract. *Proc 79th Ann Conv Am Psychol Assn* 6(1):109–10 '71. * (*PA* 46:3727)

CUMULATIVE NAME INDEX

Anastasiow, N. J.: 5	Jolly, H.: 1
Bryant, N. D.: *rev*, 5:649	Karlin, R.: 1
Buswell, G. T.: 7	Orr, D. B.: 8
Davis, W. Q.: 4	Powell, K.: 6
Derrick, C.: *rev*, 5:649	Strasel, H. C.: 8
Fleischman, H. L.: 8	Sutherland, S. P.: 2
Fry, E. B.: *rev*, 6:808	Weaver, W. W.: 6
Guthrie, J. T.: *rev*, 7:706	Zeman, S. S.: 3
Hafner, L. E.: 6	

[1597]

SRA Reading Record. Grades 6–12; 1947–59; 5 scores: reading rate, comprehension, everyday reading skills, vocabulary, total; Guy T. Buswell; Science Research Associates, Inc. *

For additional information and a review by William W. Turnbull, see 4:550 (2 references); for a review by Frances Oralind Triggs and an excerpted review, see 3:502.

REFERENCES THROUGH 1971
1–2. See 4:550.
   3. KERN, DONALD WARREN. *The Prediction of Academic Success of Freshmen in a Community College.* Doctor's thesis, New York University (New York, N.Y.), 1953. (*DA* 15:85)

CUMULATIVE NAME INDEX

Budrow, G. F.: 1	Triggs, F. O.: *rev*, 3:502
Kern, D. W.: 3	Turnbull, W. W.: *rev*, 4:550
Selders, G. R. W.: 2	

[1598]

Schrammel-Gray High School and College Reading Test. Grades 7–16; 1940–42; 3 scores: gross-comprehension, comprehension-efficiency, rate; H. E. Schrammel and W. H. Gray; Bobbs-Merrill Co., Inc. *

For additional information, reviews by James M. McCallister and Robert L. McCaul, and an excerpted review by William J. Jones, see 3:500.

REFERENCES THROUGH 1971
   1. ANDERSON, MARY R., AND STEGMAN, ERWIN J. "Predictors of Freshman Achievement at Fort Hays Kansas State College." *Ed & Psychol Meas* 14:722–3 w '54. * (*PA* 29:7952)
   2. YOUNG, LEIL L. "Comparisons Between Eighth Grade Students and a Select Group of Adult Males on a Standardized Reading Test." *Calif J Ed Res* 8:129 My '57. *

CUMULATIVE NAME INDEX

Anderson, M. R.: 1	McCaul, R. L.: *rev*, 3:500
Jones, W. J.: *exc*, 3:500	Stegman, E. J.: 1
McCallister, J. M.: *rev*, 3:500	Young, L. L.: 2

[1599]

*Sequential Tests of Educational Progress: Reading. Grades 4–6, 7–9, 10–12, 13–14; 1956–72;

2 editions; Cooperative Tests and Services. * For the complete battery entry, see 35.

a) ORIGINAL SERIES [70 MINUTE TESTS]. 1956–63; Braille and large type editions (grades 4–12) are available from American Printing House for the Blind, Inc.

b) SERIES 2 [45 MINUTE TESTS]. 1956–72.

For additional information and reviews by Emmett Albert Betts and Paul R. Lohnes of *a*, see 6:810 (6 references); for reviews by Eric F. Gardner, James R. Hobson, and Stephen Wiseman, see 5:653. For reviews of the original edition of the complete battery, see 6:25 (2 reviews) and 5:24 (2 reviews, 1 excerpt).

REFERENCES THROUGH 1971
1–6. See 6:810.
   7. TRIMBLE, W. EUGENE. "A Study Using STEP Reading Scores to Predict Students Likely to Experience Academic Difficulty in the Freshman Year." *J Res Services* 3:9–12 D '63. *
   8. MICHAEL, WILLIAM B.; CATHCART, ROBERT; AND ZIMMERMAN, WAYNE S. "Linguistic Factors in Various Measures of Communication Skills for College Students With Implications for Predictive Validity." *Ed & Psychol Meas* 24:363–7 su '64. * (*PA* 39:3192)
   9. SCHECK, ROSE RAYNOR. *An Investigation of Children's Knowledge of Single and of Multiple Meanings of Words and Reading Comprehension.* Doctor's thesis, Temple University (Philadelphia, Pa.), 1964. (*DA* 25:6057)
   10. ELLIOTT, MERLE H., AND BADAL, ALDEN W. "Achievement and Racial Composition of Schools." *Calif J Ed Res* 16:158–66 S '65. * (*PA* 40:1478)
   11. MACGILLIVRAY, MARGARET C. *A Critical Analysis of the Item Content of the STEP Reading Test in Terms of Bloom's Taxonomy, Cognitive Domain.* Master's thesis, Catholic University of America (Washington, D.C.), 1965.
   12. MILLER, DORIS KOTEEN. *A Study of Differences Between Auditory and Visual Learners in Respect to Extraversion-Introversion.* Doctor's thesis, New York University (New York, N.Y.), 1965. (*DA* 26:4078)
   13. LUNDSTEEN, SARA W., AND MICHAEL, WILLIAM B. "Validation of Three Tests of Cognitive Style in Verbalization for the Third and Sixth Grades." *Ed & Psychol Meas* 26:449–61 su '66. * (*PA* 40:12763)
   14. PHELPS, ARTHUR M. *Predicting First Semester Grades in the Junior College Two-Year Terminal Vocational-Technical Programs.* Master's thesis, Stetson University (DeLand, Fla.), 1966.
   15. SUTHERLAND, SAMUEL PHILIP. *A Factor Analytic Study of Tests Designed to Measure Reading Ability.* Doctor's thesis, University of Southern California (Los Angeles, Calif.), 1966. (*DA* 27:4141A)
   16. HAYWARD, PRISCILLA. "A Comparison of Test Performance on Three Answer Sheet Formats." *Ed & Psychol Meas* 27:997–1004 w '67. * (*PA* 42:9420)
   17. HEATH, ROBERT W.; JANSSEN, DAVID R.; FORTNA, RICHARD O.; BIANCHINI, JOHN C.; AND YOUNG, MAURICE R. "The Use of Achievement and Ability Test Averages." *J Ed Meas* 4:81–6 su '67. *
   18. LIOTTI, ANTHONY R. *A Factor Analytic Study of Items Measuring Reading Comprehension in the STEP Reading Test.* Master's thesis, City College (New York, N.Y.), 1967.
   19. NICHOLLS, J. G. "Anxiety, Defensiveness, Self-Esteem, and Responsibility for Intellectual Achievement: Their Relation to Intelligence and Reading Achievement Test Score." *N Zeal J Ed Studies* 2:125–35 N '67. *
   20. TENOPYR, MARY L. "Social Intelligence and Academic Success." *Ed & Psychol Meas* 27:961–5 w '67. * (*PA* 42:9509)
   21. TRELA, THADDEUS M. "Comparing Achievement on Tests of General and Critical Reading." *J Read Specialist* 6:140–2 My '67. * (*PA* 41:14190)
   22. ORR, DAVID B., AND GRAHAM, WARREN R. "Development of a Listening Comprehension Test to Identify Educational Potential Among Disadvantaged Junior High School Students." *Am Ed Res J* 5:167–80 Mr '68. *
   23. STOREY, ARTHUR G. "The Versatile Multiple-Choice Item." *J Ed Res* 62:169–72 D '68. *
   24. ANASTASIOW, NICHOLAS J. "Fourth Through Sixth Grade Student Performance Differences on STEP and SRA Achievement Tests." *Meas & Eval Guid* 2(3):149–52 f '69. * (*PA* 44:13276)
   25. BOTEL, MORTON. "A Comparative Study of the Validity of the Botel Reading Inventory and Selected Standardized Tests." *Proc Ann Conv Int Read Assn* 13(1):721–7 '69. *
   26. SARUK, ALEC, AND GULUTSAN, METRO. "Academic Performance of Students and the Cultural Orientation of Their Parents." *Alberta J Ed Res* (Canada) 16(3):189–95 S '70. * (*PA* 45:8988)
   27. BRADLEY, RICHARD W., AND SANBORN, MARSHALL P. "Using Tests to Predict Four-Year Patterns of College Grade Point." *J Col Stud Personnel* 12(2):138–42 Mr '71. * (*PA* 46:5699)

28. FLEISCHMAN, HOWARD L.; ORR, DAVID B.; AND STRASEL, H. C. "Relationships Between the Subtests of Six Achievement Test Batteries." Abstract. *Proc 79th Ann Conv Am Psychol Assn* 6(1):109–10 '71. * (*PA* 46:3727)

29. JEFFERSON, GEORGE L., JR. "Lexical and Structural Items as Predictors of Readability for High and Low Ability Readers." *Yearb Nat Read Conf* 19(1):172–8 '71. *

30. SHAVER, JAMES P., AND NUHN, DEE. "The Effectiveness of Tutoring Underachievers in Reading and Writing." *J Ed Res* 65(3):107–12 N '71. * (*PA* 48:1878)

31. TUINMAN, J. JAAP. "Assessment of the Acquisition of Information From Reading Prose Passages." *Yearb Nat Read Conf* 20:198–205 '71. *

For additional references, see the bibliography for the series, 35.

CUMULATIVE NAME INDEX

Anastasiow, N. J.: 24
Badal, A. W.: 10
Betts, E. A.: *rev*, 6:810
Bianchini, J. C.: 17
Botel, M.: 25
Bradley, R. W.: 27
Cathcart, R.: 6, 8
Elliott, M. H.: 10
Endler, N. S.: 5
Fleischman, H. L.: 28
Fortna, R. O.: 17
Gardner, E. F.: *rev*, 5:653
Graham, W. R.: 22
Gulutsan, M.: 26
Hayward, P.: 16
Heath, R. W.: 17
Hobson, J. R.: *rev*, 5:653
Janssen, D. R.: 17
Jefferson, G. L.: 29
Liotti, A. R.: 18
Lohnes, P. R.: *rev*, 6:810
Lundsteen, S. W.: 13
MacGillivray, M. C.: 11
Mayer, R. W.: 1

Michael, W. B.: 6, 8, 13
Milfs, M.: 6
Miller, D. K.: 12
Nicholls, J. G.: 19
Nuhn, D.: 30
Orr, D. B.: 22, 28
O'Shaughnessy, M. M.: 2
Phelps, A. M.: 14
Rudd, J. P.: 3
Sanborn, M. P.: 27
Saruk, A.: 26
Scheck, R. R.: 9
Shaver, J. P.: 30
Steinberg, D.: 5
Storey, A. G.: 23
Strasel, H. C.: 28
Sutherland, S. P.: 15
Tenopyr, M. L.: 20
Trela, T. M.: 4, 21
Trimble, W. E.: 7
Tuinman, J. J.: 31
Wiseman, S.: *rev*, 5:653
Young, M. R.: 17
Zimmerman, W. S.: 6, 8

[1600]

Silent Reading Tests. Standards 1–3 (ages 7–10), 3–8 (ages 10–15), 6–10 (ages 13–17) ; 1947–63 ; 3 levels ; Human Sciences Research Council [South Africa]. *

a) SILENT READING TEST (ELEMENTARY). Standards 1–3 ; 4 tests.

1) *Paragraphs.* 1951 and 1963 tests essentially the same as tests copyrighted 1947.

2) *Sentences.* 1951 tests essentially the same as tests copyrighted 1947.

3) *Vocabulary.* 1961 tests essentially the same as tests copyrighted 1947–51.

4) *Speed.*

b) SILENT READING TESTS (REVISED EDITION). Standards 3–8, 6–10 ; 3 or 4 scores : vocabulary, paragraphs, sentences (standards 3–8 only), language usage.

For additional information, see 6:811.

[1601]

Southgate Group Reading Tests. Ages 6–7.5, 7–8 ; 1960–62, c1959–62 ; 2 tests ; Vera Southgate ; University of London Press Ltd. [England]. *

a) TEST 1—WORD SELECTION. Ages 6–7.5 ; 1960–61, c1959.

b) TEST 2—SENTENCE COMPLETION TEST. Ages 7–8 ; 1962.

For additional information, reviews by M. L. Kellmer Pringle and Magdalen D. Vernon, and an excerpted review by P. E. Vernon of Test 1, see 6:812.

[1602]

Stanford Achievement Test: High School Reading Test. Grades 9–12 ; 1965–66 ; catalog uses the title *Stanford High School Reading Test;* subtest of *Stanford Achievement Test: High School Basic Battery;* Eric F. Gardner, Jack C. Merwin, Robert Callis, and Richard Madden ; Harcourt Brace Jovanovich, Inc. * For the complete battery entry, see 37.

For additional information and reviews by Robert

H. Bauernfeind and H. Alan Robinson, see 7:707. For reviews of the complete battery, see 7:27 (2 reviews).

REFERENCES THROUGH 1971

1. KAY, PATRICIA M.; TITTLE, CAROL J.; AND WEINER, MAX. "Selecting Tests to Predict the Need for Remediation in a University Open Admissions Population." *Meas & Eval Guid* 4(3):154–9 O '71. * (*PA* 49:11964)

CUMULATIVE NAME INDEX

Kay, P. M.: 1
Tittle, C. J.: 1
Weiner, M.: 1

[1603]

Stanford Achievement Test: Reading Tests. Grades 1.5–9 ; 1922–74 ; 2 editions ; Richard Madden, Eric F. Gardner, Herbert C. Rudman, Truman L. Kelley (*a*), Bjorn Karlsen (*b*), and Jack C. Merwin (*b*) ; Harcourt Brace Jovanovich, Inc. * For the complete battery entry, see 36.

a) 1964 EDITION. Grades 1.5–2.4, 2.5–3.9, 4.0–5.4, 5.5–6.9, 7.0–9.9 ; 1922–68 ; catalog uses the title *Stanford Reading Tests;* 5 levels ; Braille and large type editions available from American Printing House for the Blind, Inc.

1) *Primary 1 Reading Tests.* Grades 1.5–2.4 ; 4 scores : word reading, paragraph meaning, vocabulary, word study skills.

2) *Primary 2 Reading Tests.* Grades 2.5–3.9 ; 3 scores : word meaning, paragraph meaning, word study skills.

3) *Intermediate 1 Reading Tests.* Grades 4.0–5.4 ; 2 scores : word meaning, paragraph meaning.

4) *Intermediate 2 Reading Tests.* Grades 5.5–6.9 ; 2 scores : word meaning, paragraph meaning.

5) *Advanced Paragraph Meaning Test.* Grades 7.0–9.9.

b) 1973 EDITION. Grades 1.5–2.4, 2.5–3.4, 3.5–4.4, 4.5–5.4, 5.5–6.9, 7.0–9.5 ; 1923–74 ; 6 levels.

1) *Primary Level 1.* Grades 1.5–2.4 ; 6 scores : reading (word, comprehension, word plus comprehension), word study skills, total, vocabulary.

2) *Primary Level 2.* Grades 2.5–3.4 ; 6 scores : same as for primary level 1.

3) *Primary Level 3.* Grades 3.5–4.4 ; 4 scores : comprehension, word study skills, total, vocabulary.

4) *Intermediate Level 1.* Grades 4.5–5.4 ; 4 scores : same as for primary level 3.

5) *Intermediate Level 2.* Grades 5.5–6.9 ; 4 scores : same as for primary level 3.

6) *Advanced.* Grades 7.0–9.5 ; 3 scores : vocabulary, comprehension, total.

For additional information and a review by Arthur E. Traxler of the 1964 edition, see 7:708 (16 references) ; see also 6:813 (1 reference) ; for reviews by Helen M. Robinson and Agatha Townsend of an earlier edition, see 5:656 ; for a review by James R. Hobson, see 4:555 (4 references) ; for a review by Margaret G. McKim, see 3:503. For reviews of the complete battery, see 7:25 (1 excerpt), 6:26 (1 review, 1 excerpt), 5:25 (1 review), 4:25 (2 reviews), and 3:18 (2 reviews).

REFERENCES THROUGH 1971

1–4. See 4:555.
5. See 6:813.
6–21. See 7:708.
22. GOODENOUGH, F. L. "The Reading Tests of the Stanford Achievement Scale and Other Variables." *J Ed Psychol* 16:523–31 N '25. *
23. FORAN, T. G. "The Present Status of Silent Reading Tests: Part 2, The Measurement of Comprehension." *Cath Univ Am Ed Res B* 2(3):1–51 Mr '27. * (*PA* 2:2610)
24. MOSHER, RAYMOND M. "A Further Note on the Reliability of Reading Tests." *J Ed Psychol* 19:272–4 Ap '28. * (*PA* 2:2623)
25. GIFFORD, CELIA ALLEN. *An Evaluation of Six Primary Reading Tests.* Master's thesis, University of California (Berkeley, Calif.), 1929.

26. MANUEL, H. T., AND WRIGHT, CARRIE E. "The Language Difficulty of Mexican Children." *J Genetic Psychol* 36:458–68 S '29. * (*PA* 4:304)

27. BOUSFIELD, MAUDELLE B. "The Intelligence and School Achievement of Negro Children." *J Negro Ed* 1:338–95 O '32. * (*PA* 8:3671)

28. ENGELHART, MAX D. "The Relative Contribution of Certain Factors to Individual Differences in Arithmetical Problem Solving Ability." *J Exp Ed* 1:19–27 S 15 '32. * (*PA* 7:1126)

29. CALDWELL, FLOYD F. "Speed as a Factor With Children of Superior and Inferior Intelligence." *J Ed Res* 26:522–4 Mr '33. * (*PA* 7:3046)

30. KNIPE, CHESTER S. *Correlation Between Reading Ages of Three Standard Reading Tests.* Master's thesis, Temple University (Philadelphia, Pa.), 1933.

31. LONG, HOWARD HALE. "Test Results of Third-Grade Negro Children Selected on the Basis of Socio-Economic Status." *J Negro Ed* 4:192–212, 523–52 Ap, O '35. * (*PA* 10:1089)

32. MANUEL, H. T. "A Comparison of Spanish-Speaking and English-Speaking Children in Reading and Arithmetic." *J Appl Psychol* 19:189–202 Ap '35. * (*PA* 9:5346)

33. WILSON, FRANK Y.; BURKE, AGNES; AND FLEMMING, CECILE WHITE. "Sex Differences in Beginning Reading in a Progressive School." *J Ed Res* 32:570–82 Ap '39. * (*PA* 13:4386)

34. ASHFORD, ZELODIOUS WILLIAMS. *Personality: Reading and Spelling Achievement of Mentally Retarded Pupils.* Master's thesis, Illinois State University (Normal, Ill.), 1966.

35. GADZELLA, BERNADETTE M., AND BENTALL, GRACE. "Differences in Mental Ability and Academic Achievement of Two Groups of High School Graduates." *J Ed Res* 60:104–6 N '66. *

36. McCRACKEN, ROBERT A. "A Two-Year Study of the Reading Achievement of Children Who Were Reading When They Entered First Grade." *J Ed Res* 59:207–10 Ja '66. * (*PA* 40:6506)

37. TRIEGLAFF, ANNETTE LOUISE. *The Relationship Between the Wechsler Intelligence Scale for Children and Reading Scores for the Stanford Achievement Test.* Master's thesis, Sacramento State College (Sacramento, Calif.), 1967.

38. LOWERY, DONELLA W. *An Analysis of the Relationship Between Personality Traits and Reading Comprehension Achievement of Students in Grades Four Through Seven.* Master's thesis, East Tennessee State University (Johnson City, Tenn.), 1968.

39. HAMMERMEISTER, FRIEDA K. "The Stability of Reading Achievement in Deaf Adults." *CEC Selected Conv Papers* 1969:467–76 '69. *

40. PAGE, BEN H. *Predicting Performance in Seventh Grade Advanced Mathematics at Kearns Junior High School.* Master's thesis, University of Utah (Salt Lake City, Utah), 1969.

41. KIDD, LOR RHEBA R. *A Comparison of the Wide Range Achievement Test With the Stanford Achievement Test and Comprehensive Tests of Basic Skills as a Measurement of Reading Achievement.* Master's thesis, California State College (Hayward, Calif.), 1970.

42. PLUMLEIGH, GEORGE ELWOOD, JR. *The Relationship of Selected Variables to the Ability of First-Grade Children to Read and Interpret Maps.* Doctor's thesis, University of Southern California (Los Angeles, Calif.), 1970. (*DAI* 31:5946A)

43. BORNSTEIN, HARRY, AND KANNAPELL, BARBARA. "More on the Effects of Verbal Load on Achievement Tests." *Am Ann Deaf* 116(6):575–9 D '71. * (*PA* 48:7769)

44. CALLENBACH, CARL ANTON. *The Effects of Instruction and Practice in Non-Substantive Test-Taking Techniques Upon the Standardized Reading Test Scores of Selected Second Grade Students.* Doctor's thesis, Pennsylvania State University (University Park, Pa.), 1971. (*DAI* 32:6183A)

45. DAVIS, BOBBIE, AND McNINCH, GEORGE. "A Comparison of Three Standardized Reading Tests in a Fifth Grade Sample." *South J Ed Res* 5(2):101–12 Ap '71. *

46. DAVIS, BOBBIE SUE. *A Comparative Analysis of Three Widely Used Standardized Reading Achievement Tests for a Selected Group of Elementary School Children.* Doctor's thesis, University of Southern Mississippi (Hattiesburg, Miss.), 1971. (*DAI* 32:4831A)

47. FLEISCHMAN, HOWARD L.; ORR, DAVID B.; AND STRASEL, H. C. "Relationships Between the Subtests of Six Achievement Test Batteries." Abstract. *Proc 79th Ann Conv Am Psychol Assn* 6(1): 109–10 '71. * (*PA* 46:3727)

48. GREEN, RICHARD B., AND ROHWER, WILLIAM D., JR. "SES Differences on Learning and Ability Tests in Black Children." *Am Ed Res J* 8(4):601–9 N '71. * (*PA* 47:11611)

49. HAMMERMEISTER, FRIEDA K. "Reading Achievement in Deaf Adults." *Am Ann Deaf* 116(1):25–8 F '71. *

50. JOHNSON, GARY L., AND HUMMEL, THOMAS J. "Effects of Three Modes of Test Administration on the Reading Achievement Scores of Fifth Graders." *El Sch Guid & Counsel* 6(1):21–6 O '71. * (*PA* 49:7853)

51. LIEDTKE, WERNER. "Mathematics Learning and Pupil Characteristics." *Alberta J Ed Res* (Canada) 17(3):143–53 S '71. * (*PA* 18:1864)

52. NEWMAN, ANABEL POWELL. *Longitudinal Study of Pupils Who Were Underachieving in Reading in First Grade.* Doctor's

thesis, State University of New York (Buffalo, N.Y.), 1971. (*DAI* 32:2313A)

53. TRIDER, MARY S. "The Right to Read and Standardized Testing: A Necessary Dimension." *Read Teach* 24(4):320–30 Ja '71. * (*PA* 46:11521)

CUMULATIVE NAME INDEX

[1604]

★**Sucher-Allred Reading Placement Inventory.** Reading level grades 1–9; 1968–71; SARPI; subtests referred to as *Sucher-Allred Word-Recognition Test* and *Sucher-Allred Oral Reading Paragraph Test;* 3 major scores: independent, instructional, and frustrational grade reading levels; Floyd Sucher and Ruel A. Allred; Brigham Young University Press. *

REFERENCES THROUGH 1971

1. KUEHN, JOHN ARTHUR. *A Word Recognition Test as a Placement Tool for Reading Instruction and the Relationship Between Reading Scores Received by Elementary Students on a Battery of Standardized and Informal Reading Tests.* Master's thesis, Brigham Young University (Provo, Utah), 1969.

CUMULATIVE NAME INDEX

[1605]

Survey of Primary Reading Development. Grades 1–2, 2–4; 1957–64; SPRD; J. Richard Harsh and Dorothy Soeberg; Educational Testing Service (Berkeley Office). *

For additional information and a review by Allen Berger, see 7:709; for reviews by Thomas C. Barrett and Russell G. Stauffer of the test for grades 1–2, see 6:814.

[1606]

Survey of Reading Achievement: California Survey Series. Grades 7–9, 9–12; 1959; all items from *California Reading Test;* Ernest W. Tiegs and Willis W. Clark; CTB/McGraw-Hill. *

For additional information and reviews by Clarence Derrick and J. Raymond Gerberich, see 6:815.

[1607]

Survey Tests of Reading. Grades 3–6, 7–13; 1931–32; 2 tests; L. J. O'Rourke; O'Rourke Publications. *
a) CENTRAL THOUGHT TEST. Grades 3–6, 7–13; 1931–32.
b) POWER TEST. Grades 3–13; 1931.

[1608]

Tests of Academic Progress: Reading. Grades 9–12; 1964–66; Dale P. Scannell and Henry P. Smith; Houghton Mifflin Co. * For the complete battery entry, see 44.

For additional information and a review by Marvin D. Glock, see 7:710 (2 references). For a review of the complete battery, see 7:31.

REFERENCES THROUGH 1971

1–2. See 7:710.

CUMULATIVE NAME INDEX

Caldwell, J. R.: 1   Meyers, C. E.: 1
Glock, M. D.: *rev*, 7:710   Michael, W. B.: 1
Goolsby, T. M.: 2   Schrader, D. R.: 1

[1609]

Tests of Reading: Inter-American Series. Grades 1, 2–3, 4–6, 7–9, 10–13; 1950–73; revision of *Tests of Reading: Cooperative Inter-American Tests;* parallel editions in English and Spanish; 5 levels; Herschel T. Manuel; Guidance Testing Associates. *
a) LEVEL 1, PRIMARY. Grade 1; 1966–73; 3 scores: vocabulary, comprehension, total.
b) LEVEL 2, PRIMARY. Grades 2–3; 1962–73; 5 scores: vocabulary, comprehension (level, speed, total), total.
c) LEVEL 3, ELEMENTARY. Grades 4–6; 1962–73; 5 scores: same as for Level 2.
d) LEVEL 4, INTERMEDIATE. Grades 7–9; 1962–73; 5 scores: same as for Level 2.
e) LEVEL 5, ADVANCED. Grades 10–13; 1962–67; 5 scores: same as for Level 2.

For additional information and a review by Georgia S. Adams, see 7:711 (4 references); see also 6:818 (4 references); for reviews by Jacob S. Orleans and Frederick L. Westover of the earlier edition, see 4:557 (4 references).

REFERENCES THROUGH 1971

1–4. See 4:557.
5–8. See 6:818.
9–12. See 7:711.

CUMULATIVE NAME INDEX

Adams, G. S.: *rev*, 7:711   McCranie, J.: 2
Arnold, R. D.: 12   Manuel, H. T.: 4, 6, 10–1
Bou, I. R.: 1   Martin, R. P.: 9
Chenault, V. M.: 5   Orleans, J. S.: *rev*, 4:557
Einspahr, M. H.: 7   Westover, F. L.: *rev*, 4:557
Fife, R. H.: 4   Zimmerer, A. M.: 8
Kelley, F.: 3

[1610]

Traxler High School Reading Test, Revised. Grades 10–12; 1938–67; 5 scores: rate, story comprehension, main ideas, total comprehension, total; 1966 tests identical with tests copyrighted 1938–39 except for minor changes in 12 items; Arthur E. Traxler; Bobbs-Merrill Co., Inc. *

For additional information and a review by Robert A. Forsyth, see 7:712; for a review by Harold D. Carter, see 4:559 (4 references); for reviews by Alvin C. Eurich, Constance M. McCullough, and C. Gilbert Wrenn, and excerpted reviews by E. L. Abell and J. Wayne Wrightstone, see 2:1578.

REFERENCES THROUGH 1971

1–4. See 4:559.
5. AUKERMAN, ROBERT C., JR. "Differences in the Reading Status of Good and Poor Eleventh Grade Students." *J Ed Res* 41:498–515 Mr '48. * (*PA* 22:4599)
6. SMITH, DONALD E. P. "A Note on 'Equivalent Forms.' " *J Develop Read* 1:62–3 su '58. *
7. THALBERG, STANTON P. "Reading Rate and Immediate Versus Delayed Retention." *J Ed Psychol* 58:373–8 D '67. * (*PA* 42:3379)

CUMULATIVE NAME INDEX

Abell, E. L.: *exc*, 2:1578   Blommers, P.: 3
Aukerman, R. C.: 5   Carter, H. D.: *rev*, 4:559

Eurich, A. C.: *rev*, 2:1578   Thalberg, S. P.: 7
Forsyth, R. A.: *rev*, 7:712   Traxler, A. E.: 1–2
Lindquist, E. F.: 3   Tuft, E. N.: 4
McCullough, C. M.: *rev*, 2:   Wrenn, C. G.: *rev*, 2:1578
1578   Wrightstone, J. W.: *exc*, 2:
Preston, R. C.: 4   1578
Smith, D. E. P.: 6

[1611]

Traxler Silent Reading Test. Grades 7–10; 1934–69; 6 scores: reading rate, story comprehension, word meaning, paragraph meaning, total comprehension, total; 1969 tests identical with tests copyrighted 1934 except for conversion of all items to multiple choice form; Arthur E. Traxler; Bobbs-Merrill Co., Inc. *

For additional information and a review by William E. Coffman, see 7:713; for a review by J. Thomas Hastings, see 4:560 (2 references); for reviews by Robert L. McCaul and Miles A. Tinker and an excerpted review by J. Wayne Wrightstone, see 2:1579 (3 references); for reviews by Frederick B. Davis and Spencer Shank, see 1:1114.

REFERENCES THROUGH 1971

1–3. See 2:1579.
4–5. See 4:560.
6. TRAXLER, ARTHUR. "Sex Differences in Comprehension Among Junior High School Students." *Ed* 89(4):312–4 Ap–My '69. *

CUMULATIVE NAME INDEX

Blanchard, H. L.: 4   Stoddard, G. D.: 1
Coffman, W. E.: *rev*, 7:713   Tinker, M. A.: *rev*, 2:1579
Davis, F. B.: *rev*, 1:1114   Traxler, A.: 6
Hastings, J. T.: *rev*, 4:560 Traxler, A. E.: 2–3, 5
McCaul, R. L.: *rev*, 2:1579   Wrightstone, J. W.: *exc*, 2:
Ruch, G. M.: 1   1579
Shank, S.: *rev*, 1:1114

[1612]

Van Wagenen Analytical Reading Scales. Grades 4–6, 7–9, 10–12; 1953–54; 6 or 7 scores: central thought, simple details, complex ideas, inferences, interpretation, total, word meaning (Form M only); Part 3 of *Diagnostic Examination of Silent Reading Abilities;* 3 levels; M. J. Van Wagenen; Van Wagenen Psycho-Educational Laboratories. *
a) INTERMEDIATE DIVISION. Grades 4–6; 1953.
b) JUNIOR DIVISON. Grades 7–9; 1953.
c) SENIOR DIVISION. Grades 10–12; 1953–54.

For reference to reviews of the *Diagnostic Examination of Silent Reading Abilities*, see 1622.

[1613]

W.A.L. English Comprehension Test. High school; 1962–65; 4 scores: recognition vocabulary, recall vocabulary, reading comprehension, total; Australian Council for Educational Research [Australia]. *

For additional information, see 6:819.

[1614]

★Wide-span Reading Test. Ages 7–15; 1972; Alan Brimer (incorporating material by Herbert Gross); Thomas Nelson & Sons Ltd. [England]. *

[1615]

Williams Primary Reading Test. Grades 1, 2–3; 1926–55; Allan J. Williams; Bobbs-Merrill Co., Inc.*

For additional information, see 5:658; for a review by Alice N. Jameson of the original edition, see 3:508.

REFERENCES THROUGH 1971

1. GIFFORD, CELIA ALLEN. *An Evaluation of Six Primary Reading Tests*. Master's thesis, University of California (Berkeley, Calif.), 1929.
2. BAKER, FLORENCE, AND BROOM, M. E. "Concerning One Criterion for the Choice of Primary Reading Tests." *J Appl Psychol* 16:419–20 Ag '32. * (*PA* 7:4098)

[1616]

Williams Reading Test for Grades 4–9. 1929; Allan J. Williams; Bobbs-Merrill Co., Inc. *

REFERENCES THROUGH 1971

1. FORAN, T. G., AND ROCK, ROBERT J., JR. "The Reliability of Some Silent Reading Tests." *Cath Univ Am Ed Res B* 5(6): 1–23 Je '30. * (*PA* 5:2921)

[Out of Print Since TIP I]

A.C.E.R. Silent Reading Tests, Forms A and B, R:2, 5:616 (1 review); Forms C and D, R:3, 6:782 (2 reviews, 1 reference)

Achievement Test in Silent Reading: Dominion Tests, R:5, 5:619 (4 reviews)

Ballard's Reading Tests, R:88

Burt's Reading Tests, R:9

Chapman Reading Comprehension Test, R:91, 5:623 (1 review)

Detroit Reading Test, T:1399

Detroit Word Recognition Test, R:20

Diagnostic Paragraph Comprehension: Group Achievement Tests: Niagara Edition, R:31, 5:13b

Elementary Reading: Every Pupil Scholarship Test, 6:788

Elementary Reading: Every Pupil Test, R:94, 6:789

Emporia Silent Reading Test, R:28, 2:1534 (2 reviews)

Gates Advanced Primary Reading Tests, 6:790 (3 reviews, 4 references); for a revision, see the Primary B level of the *Gates-MacGinitie Reading Tests,* 1552

Gates Basic Reading Tests, R:98, 6:791 (8 reviews, 1 excerpt, 9 references)

Gates Primary Reading Tests, 6:792 (4 reviews, 10 references); for a revision, see the Primary A level of the *Gates-MacGinitie Reading Tests,* 1552

Gates Reading Survey, 6:793 (4 reviews, 7 references); for a revision, see the grades 3–9 levels of the *Gates-MacGinitie Reading Tests,* 1552

General Reading Test: Ohio Senior Survey Tests, R:99, 4:534

Kansas Primary Reading Test, R:102, 4:539 (2 reviews)

Kelley-Greene Reading Comprehension Test, R:35, 5:636 (2 reviews, 1 reference)

Los Angeles Elementary Reading Test, R:39, 4:541 (1 review)

Manchester Reading Comprehension Test (Sen.) 1, 7:695 (2 reviews, 1 reference), R:42

Nelson-Lohmann Reading Test, R:104, 6:801 (1 review)

Primary Reading: Every Pupil Scholarship Test, 6:803

Primary Reading: Every Pupil Test, R:105, 6:804 (2 reviews)

Primary Reading Test, R:106, 3:494 (1 review, 1 reference)

Purdue Reading Test, R:55, 5:643 (1 review)

Reading: Seven Plus Assessment, R:63, 4:548

Sangren-Woody Reading Test, R:107, 4:551 (2 reviews, 7 references)

Silent Reading Comprehension: Iowa Every-Pupil Tests of Basic Skills, R:71, 4:554 (2 reviews)

Stone-Webster Test in Beginning Reading, R:109, 3:504 (1 review, 1 reference)

Techniques in Reading Comprehension: Every Pupil Test, R:110, 6:816 (2 reviews)

DIAGNOSTIC

[1617]

California Phonics Survey. Grades 7–12 and college; 1956–63; CPS; shortened version of *Stanford Diagnostic Phonics Survey, Research Edition;* 9 error analysis scores for Form 1 (Form 2 yields total score only): long-short vowel confusion, other vowel confusion, consonants-confusion with blends and digraphs, consonant-vowel reversals, configuration, endings, negatives-opposites-sight words, rigidity, total; Grace M. Brown and Alice B. Cottrell; CTB/McGraw-Hill. *

For additional information and a review by Constance M. McCullough, see 7:714 (1 reference); for a review by Thomas E. Culliton, Jr., see 6:820 (1 reference).

REFERENCES THROUGH 1971

1. See 6:820.
2. See 7:714.
3. ILIKA, JOSEPH. "The Third Annual Report of the Phonetic Skills of Teachers." *Yearb Nat Read Conf* 19(2):95–105 '71. *

[1618]

*Classroom Reading Inventory, Second Edition. Grades 2–10; 1965–73; CRI; 6 scores: word recognition, independent reading level, instructional reading level, frustration level, hearing capacity level, spelling; Nicholas J. Silvaroli; Wm. C. Brown Co. Publishers. *

For additional information and an excerpted review by Donald L. Cleland of an earlier edition, see 7:715.

REFERENCES THROUGH 1971

1. POWELL, WILLIAM R., AND DUNKELD, COLIN G. "Validity of the IRI Reading Levels." *El Engl* 48(6):637–42 O '71. *

[1619]

★The Cooper-McGuire Diagnostic Word-Analysis Test. Grades 1–5 and over; 1970–72; 32 overlapping tests (spirit masters for local duplicating) with 1 to 13 tests administered at a given reader level; J. Louis Cooper and Marion L. McGuire; Croft Educational Services, Inc. *

[1620]

Cooperative Primary Tests: Word Analysis. Grades 1.5–3; 1965–67; Cooperative Tests and Services. * For the complete battery entry, see 12.

For reviews of the complete battery, see 7:10 (2 excerpts).

[1621]

The Denver Public Schools Reading Inventory. Grades 1–8; 1965–68; 3 scores (instructional level, independent level, capacity level) and ratings of areas of both strength and weakness; based upon the Sheldon Basic Reading Series; Department of Instructional Services, Denver Public Schools. *

For additional information, see 7:716.

[1622]

Diagnostic Examination of Silent Reading Abilities. Grades 4–6, 7–9, 10–12; 1939–54; 4 parts, parts 2 and 3 are in 1 booklet; 1952–54 edition entitled *Dvorak-Van Wagenen Diagnostic Examination of Silent Reading Abilities;* August Dvorak and M. J. Van Wagenen; Van Wagenen Psycho-Educational Laboratories. *

a) PART I, VAN WAGENEN RATE OF COMPREHENSION SCALE. 1939–53; 1953 test identical with test copyrighted 1939.

b) PART 2. 1939–52; 4 scores: perception of relations, vocabulary (context, isolation), information.

c) PART 3. 1939–54; also published separately under the title *Van Wagenen Analytical Reading Scales* (see 1612); 6 scores: central thought, single details, related ideas, inferences, interpretation, total; 1954 test identical with test copyrighted 1939.

d) PART 4, READING FOR IDEAS. 1952–53; rate of reading.

For additional information and reviews by Frederick B. Davis, W. E. Hall, and J. B. Stroud, see 3:480 (2 references); for an excerpted review by Worth J. Osburn, see 2:1532.

REFERENCES THROUGH 1971

1–2. See 3:480.

3. TREACY, JOHN P. "The Relationship of Reading Skills to the Ability to Solve Arithmetic Problems." *J Ed Res* 38:86–96 O '44. * (*PA* 19:809)

4. BROMLEY, ANN, AND CARTER, GERALD C. "Predictability of Success in Mathematics." *J Ed Res* 44:148–50 O '50. * (*PA* 25:5630)

5. BUSWELL, G. T. "The Relationship Between Rate of Thinking and Rate of Reading." *Sch R* 59:339–46 S '51. *

6. HOLMES, JACK A. "Factors Underlying Major Reading Disabilities at the College Level." *Genetic Psychol Monogr* 49:3–95 F '54. * (*PA* 28:8982)

7. MUNRO, JAMES JACKSON RUTHERFORD. *The Predictive Value of Entrance Reading Test Scores at the University of Washington.* Doctor's thesis, University of Washington (Seattle, Wash.), 1954. (*DA* 14:1179)

8. FLETCHER, JUNIOR EUGENE. *A Study of the Relationships Between Ability to Use Context as an Aid in Reading and Other Verbal Abilities.* Doctor's thesis, University of Washington (Seattle, Wash.), 1959. (*DA* 20:2675)

9. HOLMES, JACK A., AND SINGER, HARRY. *Speed and Power of Reading in High School.* Cooperative Research Monograph No. 14. Washington, D.C.: United States Government Printing Office, 1966. Pp. xii, 183. *

CUMULATIVE NAME INDEX

Bromley, A.: 4
Buswell, G. T.: 5
Carter, G. C.: 4
Davis, F. B.: *rev*, 3:480
Fletcher, J. E.: 8
Hall, W. E.: *rev*, 3:480
Hayter, W. H.: 1
Holmes, J. A.: 6, 9
Munro, J. J. R.: 7
Osburn, W. J.: *exc*, 2:1532
Singer, H.: 9
Stroud, J. B.: *rev*, 3:480
Traxler, A. E.: 2
Treacy, J. P.: 3

[1623]

Diagnostic Reading Examination for Diagnosis of Special Difficulty in Reading. Grades 1–4; [1928–29]; a combination of assessment procedures consisting of the *Revised Stanford-Binet Scales,* Gray's *Standardized Oral Reading Paragraphs, Monroe's Standardized Silent Reading Tests,* an adaptation of *Ayres Spelling Scale,* the arithmetic computation subtest of *Stanford Achievement Test: Arithmetic,* and 9 additional tests: alphabet repeating and reading, *Iota Word Test,* letter naming, recognition of orientation, mirror reading, mirror writing, number reversals, word discrimination, sounding; Marion Monroe; Stoelting Co. *

REFERENCES THROUGH 1971

1. DELLA-PIANA, GABRIEL. "Analysis of Oral Reading Errors: Standardization, Norms and Validity." *Reading Teach* 15:254–7 Ja '62. *

2. HERLIN, WAYNE RICHARD. *A Comparison of Oral Reading Errors on the Monroe Diagnostic Reading Examination and the Durrell Analysis of Reading Difficulty.* Doctor's thesis, University of Utah (Salt Lake City, Utah), 1963. (*DA* 24:4084)

3. FLYNN, PAULINE T., AND BYRNE, MARGARET C. "Relationship Between Reading and Selected Auditory Abilities of Third-Grade Children." *J Speech & Hearing Res* 13(4):731–40 D '70. *

4. LARSEN, STEPHEN. "Performance of Achieving and Underachieving Second, Third, and Fourth Grade Children on Tests of Auditory Ability and Oral Form Discrimination." *Kan Studies Ed* 21(1–2): 53–9 sp–su '71. *

CUMULATIVE NAME INDEX

Byrne, M. C.: 3
Della-Piana, G.: 1
Flynn, P. T.: 3
Herlin, W. R.: 2
Larsen, S.: 4

[1624]

*Diagnostic Reading Scales, Revised Edition. Grades 1–6 and retarded readers in grades 7–12; 1963–72; DRS; 12 or 13 scores: word recognition, instructional level (oral reading), independent level (silent reading), rate of silent reading (optional), potential level (auditory comprehension), and 8 phonics scores (consonant sounds, vowel sounds, consonant blends, common syllables, blends, letter sounds, initial consonants, auditory discrimination); George D. Spache; CTB/McGraw-Hill. *

For additional information and a review by Rebecca C. Barr, see 7:717 (7 references); for a review by N. Dale Bryant, see 6:821.

REFERENCES THROUGH 1971

1–7. See 7:717.

8. DAHLKE, ANITA B. "Predicting True Reading Gains After Remedial Tutoring," pp. 81–102. In *Diagnostic Viewpoints in Reading.* Edited by Robert E. Leibert. Newark, Del.: International Reading Association, 1971. Pp. viii, 133. *

9. MERLIN, SHIRLEY B. *The Psycholinguistic and Reading Abilities of Educable Mentally Retarded Readers.* Doctor's thesis, West Virginia University (Morgantown, W.Va.), 1971. (*DAI* 32:1921A)

10. POWELL, WILLIAM R., AND DUNKELD, COLIN G. "Validity of the IRI Reading Levels." *El Engl* 48(6):637–42 O '71. *

11. RIGGLE, RICHARD RAY. *Correlations of Articulatory Disability With Various Aspects of Reading for Selected Modalities.* Doctor's thesis, University of Oregon (Eugene, Ore.), 1971. (*DAI* 32:2922A)

CUMULATIVE NAME INDEX

Attea, M.: 2
Barr, R. C.: *rev*, 7:717
Botel, M.: 7
Bradley, J.: 7
Bryant, N. D.: *rev*, 6:821
Dahlke, A. B.: 4, 8
Dunkeld, C. G.: 10
Glaser, N. A.: 1
Kashuba, M.: 7
Mann, G. T.: 6
Merlin, S. B.: 9
Powell, W. R.: 10
Rainwater, H. G.: 5
Riggle, R. R.: 11
Trela, T. M.: 3

[1625]

Diagnostic Reading Test: Pupil Progress Series. Grades 1.9–2.1, 2.2–3, 4–6, 7–8; 1956–70; DRT; various titles used by publisher; catalog uses the title *Pupil Progress Series Reading;* 4 levels; Oliver F. Anderhalter, R. Stephen Gawkoski, and Ruth Colestock; Scholastic Testing Service, Inc. *

a) PRIMARY LEVEL 1. Grades 1.9–2.1; 1956–68; 9 scores: vocabulary (word recognition, word to content relation, words in use, total), rate of reading for meaning, comprehension (recalling information, locating information, reading for descriptions, total).

b) PRIMARY LEVEL 2. Grades 2.2–3; 1956–68; 10 scores: vocabulary (words in use, word meaning, total), rate of reading for meaning, comprehension (recalling information, locating information, reading for meaning, following directions, reading for descriptions, total).

c) ELEMENTARY LEVEL. Grades 4–6; 1956–70; 13 scores: knowledge and use of sources (functions, best sources, use of index, use of table of contents, total), rate of reading for meaning, comprehension (word meaning, reading for recall of information, reading for meaning, reading to locate information, reading for directions or procedures, reading for descriptions, total).

d) ADVANCED LEVEL. Grades 7–8; 1956–70; 13 scores: same as for *c*.

For additional information and reviews by Lawrence M. Kasdon and Gus P. Plessas, see 7:718; for a review by Agatha Townsend, see 6:822.

REFERENCES THROUGH 1971

1. GOSNELL, EMMA SUE. *An Analysis of Questions Contained in Selected Intermediate Standardized Reading Tests.* Master's thesis, Eastern Illinois University (Charleston, Ill.), 1969.

CUMULATIVE NAME INDEX

Gosnell, E. S.: 1
Kasdon, L. M.: *rev*, 7:718
Plessas, G. P.: *rev*, 7:718
Townsend, A.: *rev*, 6:822

[1626]
*Diagnostic Reading Tests. Grades kgn–13; 1947–72; DRT; 3 levels; Committee on Diagnostic Reading Tests, Inc. *

a) DIAGNOSTIC READING TESTS: KINDERGARTEN THROUGH FOURTH GRADES. Grades kgn–4; 1957–66; 2 sections.

1) *Survey Section.* Grades kgn–1, 1, 2, 3–4; 1957–66; 4 levels.

(a) Reading Readiness Booklet. Grades kgn–1; 5 scores: relationships, eye-hand coordination, visual discrimination, auditory discrimination, vocabulary.

(b) Booklet 1. Grade 1; 12 scores: visual discrimination, auditory discrimination (3 subscores plus total), vocabulary (3 subscores plus total), story reading (2 subscores plus total).

(c) Booklet 2. Grade 2; 3 scores: word recognition, comprehension, total.

(d) Booklet 3. Grades 3–4; 3 scores: same as for (c) above.

2) *Section 4: Word Attack, Part 1: Oral.* Grades 1–8; 1958.

b) DIAGNOSTIC READING TESTS: LOWER LEVEL. Grades 4–8; 1947–72; 2 sections.

1) *Survey Section.* Grades 4–8; 1952–72; 3 parts in 2 booklets; Forms A and B also distributed by Science Research Associates, Inc.; Braille edition available from American Printing House for the Blind, Inc.

(a) Booklet 1: Part 1, Word Recognition and Comprehension. 2 scores: word recognition, comprehension.

(b) Booklet 2: Parts 2 and 3, Vocabulary-Story Reading. 3 scores: vocabulary, rate of reading, story comprehension.

2) *Section 4: Word Attack.* Grades 1–8, 4–13; 1947–69; 2 parts.

(a) Part 1, Oral. Grades 1–8; see a2 above.

(b) Part 2, Silent. Grades 4–13; 1947–69; 3 scores: identification of sounds, syllabication, total.

c) DIAGNOSTIC READING TESTS: [UPPER LEVEL]. Grades 7–13; 1947–71; 5 sections.

1) *Survey Section.* 1947–71; 5 scores: rate of reading, comprehension check, vocabulary, total comprehension, total; Forms A and B also distributed by Science Research Associates, Inc.; Braille edition available from American Printing House for the Blind, Inc.

2) *Section 1: Vocabulary (Revised).* 1947–66; 5 scores: English, mathematics, science, social studies, total.

3) *Section 2: Comprehension: Silent and Auditory.* 1947–66; may be administered as a listening comprehension test.

4) *Section 3: Rates of Reading: Part 1, General.* 1947–63; 4 scores: normal rate of reading, comprehension at normal rate, maximum rate of reading, comprehension at maximum rate.

5) *Section 4: Word Attack.* 1947–63; 2 parts.

(a) Part 1, Oral. 1948–58.

(b) Part 2, Silent. Grades 4–13; see b2(b) above.

For additional information and reviews by Albert J. Kingston and B. H. Van Roekel, see 6:823 (21 references); for reviews by Frederick B. Davis, William W. Turnbull, and Henry Weitz, see 4:531 (19 references).

REFERENCES THROUGH 1971

1–19. See 4:531.
20–40. See 6:823.
41. WRIGHT, JAMES CLYDE. *An Investigation of the Nature of Comprehension Gained Through Reading and Its Relationship to Other Aspects of Reading and to Academic Achievement.* Doctor's thesis, Ohio State University (Columbus, Ohio), 1954. (*DA* 20:2686)

42. PETERSON, MARGARET JEAN. "Comparison of Flesch Readability Scores With a Test of Reading Comprehension." *J Appl Psychol* 40:35–6 F '56. * (*PA* 31:3654)
43. STONER, WILLIAM GERALD. *Factors Related to the Underachievement of High School Students.* Doctor's thesis, Stanford University (Stanford, Calif.), 1956. (*DA* 17:96)
44. AINSWORTH, LABAN LINTON, JR. *An Exploratory Study of the Academic Achievement of Arab Students.* Doctor's thesis, University of Texas (Austin, Tex.), 1957. (*DA* 17:1702)
45. REED, JAMES C., AND PEPPER, ROGER S. "The Interrelationship of Vocabulary, Comprehension and Rate Among Disabled Readers." *J Exp Ed* 25:331–7 Je '57. * (*PA* 33:6840)
46. EPPLEY, MARY VINEITA (BOOTS). *The Relationship of Personal Factors and Reading Performance to Academic Achievement of Selected Oregon State College Students.* Doctor's thesis, Oregon State University (Corvallis, Ore.), 1958. (*DA* 19:730)
47. ROBERTSON, MALCOLM H. "Test Scores and Self-Estimates of Two Curricula Groups." *Personnel & Guid J* 38:746–50 My '60. * (*PA* 35:2767)
48. ALLMAN, REVA WHITE. "A Study of the Vocabulary Needs of a Class of Juniors and Seniors at the Alabama State College." *J Ed Res* 55:228–31 F '62. *
49. HAYDEN, LILLIAN A. "The Effect of Physical Fatigue on Reading Rate and Comprehension of College Athletes." *Yearb Nat Read Conf* 12:202–5 '63. *
50. DREW, ALFRED S. "The Relationship of General Reading Ability and Other Factors to School and Job Performance of Machine Apprentices." *J Indus Teach Ed* 2:47–60 f '64. *
51. LONG, JOHN M. "Sex Differences in Academic Prediction Based on Scholastic, Personality and Interest Factors." *J Exp Ed* 32:239–48 sp '64. * (*PA* 39:6058)
52. GERSTEIN, ALVIN I. "Development of a Selection Program for Nursing Candidates." *Nursing Res* 14:254–7 su '65. *
53. LEUTENEGGER, RALPH R.; MUELLER, THEODORE H.; AND WERSHOW, IRVING R. "Auditory Factors in Foreign Language Acquisition." *Mod Lang J* 49:22–31 Ja '65. *
54. EMANS, ROBERT; URBAS, RAYMOND; AND DUMMETT, MARJORIE. "The Meaning of Reading Tests." *J Read* 9:406–9 My '66. * (*PA* 40:10459)
55. CLAWAR, HARRY J. "A Comparison of the Davis Reading Test and the Survey Section of the Diagnostic Reading Test When Used With Independent-School Pupils." *Ed Rec B* 92:39–42 Jl '67. * (*PA* 42:1126)
56. COATES, LESLIE F. "The Enigma of the Survey Section of the Diagnostic Reading Tests." *Yearb Nat Read Conf* 17:70–8 '68. *
57. LITTRELL, J. HARVEY. "Teacher Estimates Versus Reading Test Results." *J Read* 12:18–23 O '68. *
58. ERNEST, DAVID J. "The Predication of Academic Success of College Music Majors." *J Res Music Ed* 18(3):273–6 f '70. * (*PA* 45:8994)
59. LLEWELLYN, HOWARD CHARLES. *The Relationship Between Selected Silent Word Perception Skills and Achievement in First-Year High School Typewriting.* Doctor's thesis, University of North Dakota (Grand Forks, N.D.), 1970. (*DAI* 31:6454A)
60. MAXON, LLOYD MELVIN. *The Relationship of Certain Mental Factors, Reading Factors, Aptitudes, and Situational Factors to Achievement in Selected Air Force Technical Courses.* Doctor's thesis, North Texas State University (Denton, Tex.), 1970. (*DAI* 31:3437A)
61. PEPPER, ROGER S. "The Study Skills and Academic Achievement of Marginal Admission Students." *Yearb Nat Read Conf* 19(1):248–53 '71. *

CUMULATIVE NAME INDEX

Wall, C. F.: 28   Wershow, I. R.: 53
Ward, L. R.: 26   Wright, J. C.: 41
Weitz, H.: *rev,* 4:531

[1627]

*Doren Diagnostic Reading Test of Word Recognition Skills, 1973 Edition.** Grades 1–4; 1956–73; 13 scores: letter recognition, beginning sounds, whole word recognition, words within words, speech consonants, ending sounds, blending, rhyming, vowels, discriminate guessing, spelling, sight words, total; Margaret Doren; American Guidance Service, Inc. *

For additional information and reviews by B. H. Van Roekel and Verna L. Vickery of an earlier edition, see 5:659.

REFERENCES THROUGH 1971

1. HACKNEY, BEN H., JR. "Reading Achievement and Word Recognition Skills." *Read Teach* 21:515–8 Mr '68. * (*PA* 42: 17789)
2. McCALL, ROZANNE A., AND McCALL, ROBERT B. "Comparative Validity of Five Reading Diagnostic Tests." *J Ed Res* 62(7):329–33 Mr '69. *

CUMULATIVE NAME INDEX

Hackney, B. H.: 1   Van Roekel, B. H.: *rev,* 5:659
McCall, R. A.: 2   Vickery, V. L.: *rev,* 5:659
McCall, R. B.: 2

[1628]

Durrell Analysis of Reading Difficulty, New Edition. Grades 1–6; 1937–55, c1933–55; 7 scores: reading (oral, silent), listening, flash words, word analysis, spelling, handwriting; Donald D. Durrell; Harcourt Brace Jovanovich, Inc. *

For additional information and reviews by James Maxwell and George D. Spache, see 5:660; for a review by Helen M. Robinson of the original edition, see 4:561 (2 references); for reviews by Guy L. Bond and Miles A. Tinker, see 2:1533; for a review by Marion Monroe, see 1:1098.

REFERENCES THROUGH 1971

1–2. See 4:561.
3. DUFFY, GERTRUDE BERCHMANS. *A Diagnostic Study of Reading Difficulties in a Third Grade.* Master's thesis, Boston University (Boston, Mass.), 1934.
4. BURNS, BARBARA. *A Diagnostic Study of Reading Difficulties in Fourth Grade.* Master's thesis, Boston University (Boston, Mass.), 1938.
5. SHELDON, WILLIAM D., AND HATCH, SHIRLEY. "Strengths and Weaknesses in Reading of a Group of Third-Grade Children." *El Sch J* 50:445–52 Ap '50. * (*PA* 24:6514)
6. LONG, DONNA JANET. *An Analysis of the Reading Difficulties of Retarded Readers in Second, Fourth, and Sixth Grades.* Doctor's thesis, State University of Iowa (Iowa City, Iowa), 1959. (*DA* 20:924)
7. MITCHELL, MARY K. *The Development of Proficiency in Marking the Oral Reading Section of the Durrell Analysis of Reading Difficulty by the Use of Tape Recordings.* Master's thesis, University of Kansas (Lawrence, Kan.), 1959.
8. DELLA-PIANA, GABRIEL. "Analysis of Oral Reading Errors: Standardization, Norms and Validity." *Read Teach* 15:254–7 Ja '62. *
9. HERLIN, WAYNE RICHARD. *A Comparison of Oral Reading Errors on the Monroe Diagnostic Reading Examination and the Durrell Analysis of Reading Difficulty.* Doctor's thesis, University of Utah (Salt Lake City, Utah), 1963. (*DA* 24:4084)
10. KRIPPNER, STANLEY. "Sociopathic Tendencies and Reading Retardation in Children." *Excep Children* 29:258–66 F '63. *
11. ATTEA, MARY. *A Comparison of Three Diagnostic Reading Tests.* Doctor's thesis, State University of New York (Buffalo, N.Y.), 1966. (*DA* 27:1530A)
12. FLOWER, RICHARD M.; VIEHWEG, RICHARD; AND RUZICKA, WILLIAM R. "The Communicative Disorders of Children With Kernicteric Athetosis: 2, Problems in Language Comprehension and Use." *J Speech & Hearing Disorders* 31:60–8 F '66. * (*PA* 40:9108)
13. OLSON, ARTHUR V. "Relation of Achievement Test Scores and Specific Reading Abilities to the Frostig Test of Visual Perception." *Optom Weekly* 57:31–4 Jl 14 '66. *
14. OLSON, ARTHUR V. "Relation of Achievement Test Scores and Specific Reading Abilities to the Frostig Developmental Test of Visual Perception." *Percept & Motor Skills* 22:179–84 F '66. * (*PA* 40:4750)
15. TRELA, THADDEUS M. "What Do Diagnostic Reading Tests Diagnose?" *El Engl* 43:370–2 Ap '66. *

16. MAXEY, EARL JAMES. *An Investigation of the Rasch Probability Model for Speed in an Oral Reading Test.* Doctor's thesis, University of Iowa (Iowa City, Iowa), 1967. (*DA* 28:3075A)
17. EARLY, GEORGE H., AND SHARPE, THEODORE M. "Developing Perceptual-Motor Skills: Perceptual-Motor Training and Basic Abilities." *Acad Ther* 5(3):235–40+ sp '70. * (*PA* 44: 19036)
18. EUBANKS, JOHN LLOYD. *The Relationship of Mental Age to Visual Memory and Word Analysis in Eight, Nine, and Ten Year Old Children of Selected Intellectual Levels.* Doctor's thesis, University of Alabama (University, Ala.), 1970. (*DAI* 31:5196A)
19. LEWIS, FRANKLIN D.; BELL, D. BRUCE; AND ANDERSON, ROBERT P. "Reading Retardation: A Bi-Racial Comparison." *J Read* 13(6):433–6, 474–8 Mr '70. *
20. POWELL, WILLIAM R., AND DUNKELD, COLIN G. "Validity of the IRI Reading Levels." *El Engl* 48(6):637–42 O '71. *

CUMULATIVE NAME INDEX

Anderson, R. P.: 19   Long, D. J.: 6
Attea, M.: 11   Maxey, E. J.: 16
Bell, D. B.: 19   Maxwell, J.: *rev,* 5:660
Bond, G. L.: *rev,* 2:1533 Mitchell, M. K.: 7
Burns, B.: 4   Monroe, M.: *rev,* 1:1098
Della-Piana, G.: 8   Olson, A. V.: 13–4
Duffy, G. B.: 3   Powell, W. R.: 20
Dunkeld, C. G.: 20   Robinson, H. M.: *rev,* 4:561
Durrell, D. D.: 1   Ruzicka, W. R.: 12
Early, G. H.: 17   Sharpe, T. M.: 17
Eubanks, J. L.: 18   Sheldon, W. D.: 5
Flower, R. M.: 12   Spache, G. D.: 2; *rev,* 5:660
Hatch, S.: 5   Tinker, M. A.: *rev,* 2:1533
Herlin, W. R.: 9   Trela, T. M.: 15
Krippner, S.: 10   Viehweg, R.: 12
Lewis, F. D.: 19

[1629]

Gates-McKillop Reading Diagnostic Tests. Grades 2–0 to 6–0; 1926–62; revision of *Gates Reading Diagnostic Tests;* 28 scores: omissions, additions, repetitions, mispronunciation (reversals, partial reversals, total reversals, wrong beginnings, wrong middle, wrong ending, wrong in several parts, total), oral reading total, words–flash presentation, words–untimed presentation, phrases–flash presentation, recognizing and blending common word parts, giving letter sounds, naming capital letters, naming lower-case letters, recognizing the visual form of sounds (nonsense words, initial letters, final letters, vowels), auditory blending, spelling, oral vocabulary, syllabication, auditory discrimination; Arthur I. Gates and Anne S. McKillop; Teachers College Press. *

For additional information and reviews by N. Dale Bryant and Gabriel M. Della-Piana, see 6:824 (2 references); for a review by George D. Spache of the earlier edition, see 5:662; for a review by Worth J. Osburn, see 4:563 (2 references); for a review by T. L. Torgerson, see 3:510 (3 references). For excerpts from related book reviews, see 4:564 (2 excerpts).

REFERENCES THROUGH 1971

1–3. See 3:510.
4–5. See 4:563.
6–7. See 6:824.
8. WILSON, FRANK Y.; BURKE, AGNES; AND FLEMMING, CECILE WHITE. "Sex Differences in Beginning Reading in a Progressive School." *J Ed Res* 32:570–82 Ap '39. * (*PA* 13: 4386)
9. RUSSELL, DAVID H. "A Diagnostic Study of Spelling Readiness." *J Ed Res* 37:276–83 D '43. * (*PA* 18:1534)
10. MURRAY, CAROL-FAITH. *A Concurrent Validity Study of the Silent Reading Diagnostic Tests and the Gates Reading Diagnostic Tests.* Master's thesis, San Diego State College (San Diego, Calif.), 1959.
11. ATTEA, MARY. *A Comparison of Three Diagnostic Reading Tests.* Doctor's thesis, State University of New York (Buffalo, N.Y.), 1966. (*DA* 27:1530A)
12. TRELA, THADDEUS M. "What Do Diagnostic Reading Tests Diagnose?" *El Engl* 43:370–2 Ap '66. *
13. BOND, GUY L., AND DYKSTRA, ROBERT. "The Cooperative Research Program in First-Grade Reading Instruction." *Read Res Q* 2:5–142 su '67. * (*PA* 42:4557)
14. BOEHNLEIN, MARY MAHER. *A Structure-of-Intellect Analysis of Two Diagnostic Reading Tests.* Doctor's thesis, Kent State University (Kent, Ohio), 1969. (*DAI* 31:212A)

15. Nurss, Joanne R. "A Diagnostic Comparison of Two Third Grade Reading Classes," pp. 42–54. In *Reading Difficulties: Diagnosis, Correction, and Remediation.* Edited by William K. Durr. Newark, Del.: International Reading Association, 1970. Pp. vii, 276. *

16. Horn, William Anthony. *An Investigation of Language and Reading Abilities of Educable Mentally Retarded and Normal Students in Rural and Urban Areas.* Doctor's thesis, West Virginia University (Morgantown, W.Va.), 1971. (*DAI* 32:6249A)

17. Myklebust, Helmer R.; Bannochie, Margaret N.; and Killen, James R. Chap. 9, "Learning Disabilities and Cognitive Processes," pp. 213–51. In *Progress in Learning Disabilities, Vol. 2.* Edited by Helmer R. Myklebust. New York: Grune & Stratton, Inc., 1971. Pp. ix, 404. *

18. Powell, William R., and Dunkeld, Colin G. "Validity of the IRI Reading Levels." *El Engl* 48(6):637–42 O '71. *

CUMULATIVE NAME INDEX

Attea, M.: 11	Horn, W. A.: 16
Bannochie, M. N.: 17	Karlsen, B.: 7
Boehnlein, M. M.: 14	Killen, J. R.: 17
Bond, E.: 2	Murray, C. F.: 7, 10
Bond, G. L.: 13	Myklebust, H. R.: 17
Bryant, N. D.: *rev,* 6:824	Nurss, J. R.: 15
Burke, A.: 8	Osburn, W. J.: *rev,* 4:563
Collins, E. M.: 4	Powell, W. R.: 18
Della-Piana, G. M.: *rev,* 6: 824	Russell, D. H.: 2, 6, 9
	Shaffer, L. F.: *exc,* 4:564
Dunkeld, C. G.: 18	Spache, G. D.: *rev,* 5:662
Dykstra, R.: 13	Tinker, M. A.: *exc,* 4:564
Flemming, C. W.: 8	Torgerson, T. L.: *rev,* 3:510
Gates, A. I.: 1–3, 5	Trela, T. M.: 12
Halpin, A.: 2	Wilson, F. Y.: 8
Horan, K.: 2	

[1630]

★**Gillingham-Childs Phonics Proficiency Scales.** Grades 1–12; 1966–73; GCPPS; for use in a phonics training program, especially programs using the book entitled *Remedial Training for Children With Specific Disability in Reading, Spelling, and Penmanship;* 2 series; Educators Publishing Service, Inc. *

a) SERIES I: BASIC READING AND SPELLING. 1966–70; 17 subtest scores in each of 2 areas: reading, spelling; Anna Gillingham, Bessie W. Stillman, and Sally B. Childs.

b) SERIES II: ADVANCED READING. 1970–73; 20 subtest scores; Sally B. Childs and Ralph de S. Childs.

[1631]

Group Diagnostic Reading Aptitude and Achievement Tests. Grades 3–9; 1939; 15 scores: reading (paragraph understanding, speed), word discrimination (vowels, consonants, reversals, additions and omissions), arithmetic, spelling, visual ability (letter memory, form memory), auditory ability (letter memory, discrimination and orientation), motor ability (copying text, crossing out letters), vocabulary; Marion Monroe and Eva Edith Sherman; C. H. Nevins Printing Co. *

For additional information, see 6:825.

REFERENCES THROUGH 1971

1. Witherspoon, Y. T. "The Measurement of Indian Children's Achievement in the Academic Tool Subjects."*J Am Indian Ed* 1:5–9 My '62. *

2. Golden, Nancy E., and Steiner, Sharon R. "Auditory and Visual Functions in Good and Poor Readers." *J Learn Dis* 2(9):476–81 S '69. * (*PA* 45:6666)

3. Kline, Carl L., and Lee, Norma. "A Transcultural Study of Dyslexia: Analysis of Reading Disabilities in 425 Chinese Children Simultaneously Learning to Read and Write in English and in Chinese: A Preliminary Report." *B Orton Soc* 19:67–81 '69. * (*PA* 47:1622)

CUMULATIVE NAME INDEX

Golden, N. E.: 2	Steiner, S. R.: 2
Kline, C. L.: 3	Witherspoon, Y. T.: 1
Lee, N.: 3	

[1632]

★**Group Phonics Analysis.** Reading level grades 1–3; 1971; GPA; no scores, 11 areas: numbers, letters, consonants, alphabetization, vowels, short sounds, long vowel sounds in words, vowel digraph rule, final e

rule, open and closed syllables, syllabification; Edward Fry; Dreier Educational Systems, Inc. *

[1633]

★**LRA Standard Mastery Tasks in Language.** Grades 1, 2; 1970; 2 levels; Donald E. P. Smith, Judith M. Smith, and Raymond Cabot (*a*); Learning Research Associates, Inc. *

a) PRIMARY 1. Grade 1; 2 scores: letter matching, sound matching.

b) PRIMARY 2. Grade 2; 5 scores: letter naming, letter writing, word naming, word writing, word attack.

[1634]

McCullough Word-Analysis Tests. Grades 4–6; 1962–63, c1960–63; MWAT; 10 scores: phonetic (initial blends and digraphs, phonetic discrimination, matching letters to vowel sounds, sounding whole words, interpreting phonetic symbols, total), structural (dividing words into syllables, root words in affixed forms, total), total; Constance M. McCullough; Personnel Press. *

For additional information and a review by Larry A. Harris, see 7:719 (2 references); for reviews by Emery P. Bliesmer and Albert J. Harris, see 6:826.

REFERENCES THROUGH 1971

1–2. See 7:719.

3. Farr, Roger, and Roelke, Patricia. "Measuring Subskills of Reading: Intercorrelations Between Standardized Reading Tests, Teachers' Ratings, and Reading Specialists' Ratings." *J Ed Meas* 8(1):27–32 sp '71. * (*PA* 46:5464)

CUMULATIVE NAME INDEX

Benson, J. P.: 1	Harris, L. A.: *rev,* 7:719
Bliesmer, E. P.: *rev,* 6:826	McCall, R. A.: 2
Farr, R.: 3	McCall, R. B.: 2
Harris, A. J.: *rev,* 6:826	Roelke, P.: 3

[1635]

★**The McGuire-Bumpus Diagnostic Comprehension Test.** Reading levels grades 2.5–3, 4–6; 1971–72; MBDCT; although designed as part of the Croft Inservice Program: Reading Comprehension Skills, the test may be used independently; 4 tests (spirit masters for local duplicating), 12 scores listed below; "mastery" (defined as 2 or fewer errors on each 12-item test) on previous test required before administering Tests B, C, and D; Marion L. McGuire and Marguerite J. Bumpus; Croft Educational Services, Inc. *

a) TEST A, LITERAL READING. 4 scores: recognizing stated details, translation of details, recognizing pattern words, recognizing the main idea.

b) TEST B, INTERPRETIVE READING. 3 scores: getting implied details, finding pattern clues, inferring the main idea.

c) TEST C, ANALYTIC READING. 3 scores: determining the main question, selecting a suitable hypothesis, distinguishing relevant and irrelevant details.

d) TEST D, CRITICAL READING. 2 scores: selecting a criterion as a basis for evaluation, making a judgment based on the criterion.

[1636]

★**Phonics Criterion Test.** Reading level grades 1–3; 1971; PCT; no scores, 99 phoneme grapheme correspondences in 14 areas: easy consonants, short vowels, long and silent vowels, difficult consonants, consonant digraphs, consonant second sounds, schwa sounds, long vowel digraphs, vowel plus r, broad o, diphthongs, difficult vowels, consonant blends, consonant exceptions; Edward Fry; Dreier Educational Systems, Inc. *

[1637]

Phonics Knowledge Survey. Grades 1–6; 1964; PKS; no scores other than item scores in 15 areas: names of letters, consonant sounds, vowels, vowel generalizations, sounds of c and g, sounds of y, consonant blends, digraphs, vowel combinations, vowels followed by r, sounds of qu, sounds of oo, sounds of x, beginning consonant combinations, syllabication; Dolores Durkin and Leonard Meshover; Teachers College Press. *

For additional information and reviews by Ira E. Aaron and Edward B. Fry, see 7:720.

[1638]

Phonovisual Diagnostic Test. Grades 3–12; 1949–58; formerly called *Phonovisual Diagnostic Spelling Test;* a spelling test "designed to discover phonetic weaknesses"; 13 scores: words incorrect, consonant errors (initial, final, 9 blends), vowel errors; Lucille D. Schoolfield and Josephine B. Timberlake; Phonovisual Products, Inc. *

For additional information and reviews by Charles M. Brown and George D. Spache, see 6:829.

[1639]

★**Prescriptive Reading Inventory.** Grades 1.5–2.5, 2.0–3.5, 3.0–4.5, 4.0–6.5; 1972; PRI; 34 to 42 scores (mastery, needs review, non-mastery) covering 90 reading objectives; 84 percent of the scores based on 3 and 4 item tests; mastery interpreted as 66⅔ and 75 percent correct on 3 and 4 item tests, respectively; also identifies "students who have failed to show mastery of 60 per cent of the objectives" in any of the following categories: recognition of sounds and symbols (grades 1.5–3.5 only), phonic analysis, structural analysis, translation, literal comprehension, interpretive comprehension (2 categories), critical comprehension; 4 levels; CTB/McGraw-Hill. *

a) RED BOOK, LEVEL A. Grades 1.5–2.5; 34 scores (each score based on 3–5 items): recognition of sounds and symbols (2 scores), phonic analysis (4 scores), structural analysis (9 scores), translation (7 scores), literal comprehension (3 scores), interpretive comprehension (7 scores), critical comprehension (2 scores).

b) GREEN BOOK, LEVEL B. Grades 2.0–3.5; 41 scores (each score based on 3–6 items): recognition of sounds and symbols (2 scores), phonic analysis (8 scores), structural analysis (8 scores), translation (7 scores), literal comprehension (3 scores), interpretive comprehension (12 scores), critical comprehension (1 score).

c) BLUE BOOK, LEVEL 3. Grades 3.0–4.5; 42 scores (each score based on 3–8 items): phonic analysis (4 scores), structural analysis (8 scores), translation (8 scores), literal comprehension (5 scores), interpretive comprehension (13 scores), critical comprehension (4 scores).

d) ORANGE BOOK, LEVEL 4. Grades 4.0–6.5; 38 scores (each score based on 3–6 items): phonic analysis (3 scores), structural analysis (5 scores), translation (6 scores), literal comprehension (3 scores), interpretive comprehension (12 scores), critical comprehension (9 scores).

[1640]

★**Prescriptive Reading Inventory Interim Tests.** Grades 1.5–2.5, 2.0–3.5, 3.0–4.5, 4.0–6.5; 1973; experimental edition; primarily for use after study of a behavior prescribed by the *Prescriptive Reading Inventory;* 163 scores (mastery, needs review, non-mastery) covering 90 reading objectives; mastery interpreted as 80 percent correct; also identifies "students who failed to show mastery of at least 60% of the objec-

tives" in any of the following categories: recognition of sounds and symbols (grades 1.5–3.5 only), phonic analysis, structural analysis, translation, literal comprehension, interpretive comprehension, critical comprehension; 4 levels; CTB/McGraw-Hill. *

a) A (RED) LEVEL. Grades 1.5–2.5; 25 skills tests, 10 comprehension tests in 3 booklets; no manual.

b) B (GREEN) LEVEL. Grades 2.0–3.5; 25 skills tests, 19 comprehension tests in 6 booklets.

c) C (BLUE) LEVEL. Grades 3.0–4.5; 20 skills tests, 27 comprehension tests in 8 booklets.

d) D (ORANGE) LEVEL. Grades 4.0–6.5; 14 skills tests, 28 comprehension tests in 8 booklets.

[1641]

Primary Reading Profiles. Grades 1–2, 2–3; 1953–68; PRP; 6 scores: reading aptitude, auditory association, word recognition, word attack, reading comprehension, total; James B. Stroud, Albert N. Hieronymus, and Paul McKee; Houghton Mifflin Co. *

For additional information and reviews by James R. Hobson and Verna L. Vickery, see 5:665.

REFERENCES THROUGH 1971

1. BREEN, JOSEPH MICHAEL. *Differential Prediction of Intermediate Grade Skills Achievement From Primary Grade Aptitude and Achievement Measures.* Doctor's thesis, University of Connecticut (Storrs, Conn.), 1965. (*DA* 26:5260)
2. BARZ, ANITA I. *Prediction of Secondary School Achievement From Primary Grade Aptitude and Achievement Measures.* Doctor's thesis, St. John's University (Jamaica, N.Y.), 1969. (*DAI* 30:3271A)

CUMULATIVE NAME INDEX

[1642]

★**Reading Diagnostic Probes.** Grades 2–5, 3–9; 1970; also called SARA (Systems Approach to Reading Analysis); 2 tests; manuals by Stella B. Warner and William R. Myers; American Testing Co. *

a) READING DIAGNOSTIC PROBE I: PROBES INTO AUDITORY DISCRIMINATION, PHONETIC ANALYSIS. Grades 2–5; SARA I; 9 scores: consonants (initial, final), rhyming elements, blends (initial, digraphs, final), vowels (long, short, digraph); test by the Diagnostic Reading Committee, revision by Stella B. Warner.

b) READING DIAGNOSTIC PROBE II: PROBE INTO STRUCTURAL ANALYSIS. Grades 3–9; SARA II; 12 scores: inflectional endings (3 scores), compound words, contractions, inflectional changes (3 scores), alphabetical order, prefixes, suffixes, syllabication; test by Ronald A. Herbert and William R. Myers, revision by Stella B. Warner.

[1643]

Roswell-Chall Diagnostic Reading Test of Word Analysis Skills. Grades 2–6; 1956–59; no scores, 6 areas: single consonant sounds, consonant combinations, short vowels, rule of silent e, vowel combinations, syllabication; 1959 tests identical with tests copyrighted 1956; 1959 manual essentially the same as 1956 manual; Florence G. Roswell and Jeanne S. Chall; Essay Press, Inc. *

For additional information and reviews by Ira E. Aaron and Emmett Albert Betts, see 6:831 (1 reference); for a review by Byron H. Van Roekel, see 5:667.

REFERENCES THROUGH 1971

1. See 6:831.
2. McCALL, ROZANNE A., AND McCALL, ROBERT B. "Comparative Validity of Five Reading Diagnostic Tests." *J Ed Res* 62(7):329–33 Mr '69. *
3. CLAYMAN, DEBORAH P. GOLDWEBER. *The Relationship of Error and Correction of Error in Oral Reading to Visual-Form*

Perception and Word Attack Skills. Doctor's thesis, Columbia University (New York, N.Y.), 1971. (*DAI* 32:5033A)

CUMULATIVE NAME INDEX

Aaron, I. E.: *rev*, 6:831   McCall, R. A.: 2
Betts, E. A.: *rev*, 6:831   McCall, R. B.: 2
Chall, J. S.: 1   Van Roekel, B. H.: *rev*, 5:667
Clayman, D. P. G.: 3

[1644]

Reading Skills Diagnostic Test. Grades 2–8; 1967; 9 scores: letter identification, letter-sound identification, phonetic sounds, phonetic words, inconsistent words, consistent phrases, inconsistent phrases, letters in context, words in context; Richard H. Bloomer; Brador Publications, Inc. *

REFERENCES THROUGH 1971

1. BLOOMER, RICHARD H. "Reading Patterns of the Rejected Child." *Read Teach* 22(4):320–4+ Ja '69. *

CUMULATIVE NAME INDEX

Bloomer, R. H.: 1

[1645]

★**SPIRE Individual Reading Evaluation.** Grades 1–6, 4–10; 1969–71; SPIRE (Student Problem Individual Reading Evaluation); 2 tests: diagnostic reading evaluation, quick placement test; 8 scores: 3 diagnostic scores (individual word recognition, oral reading, silent reading), 2 quick placement scores (individual word recognition, reading) and 3 derived scores (instructional level, frustration level, independent level); 2 levels; Harvey Alpert and Alvin Kravitz; New Dimensions in Education, Inc. *
a) [SPIRE 1.] Grades 1–6; 1969–70.
b) SPIRE 2. Grades 4–10; 1971.

[1646]

The Schonell Reading Tests. Ages 5–15, 6–9, 7–11, 9–13; 1942–55; 7 tests; Fred J. Schonell; Oliver & Boyd [Scotland]. *
a) TEST R1, GRADED WORD READING TEST. Ages 5–15; also called *Graded Reading Vocabulary Test.*
b) TEST R2, SIMPLE PROSE READING TEST. Ages 6–9; also called *My Dog Test.*
c) TEST R3, SILENT READING TEST A. Ages 7–11.
d) TEST R4, SILENT READING TEST B. Ages 9–13.
e) TEST R5, TEST OF ANALYSIS AND SYNTHESIS OF WORDS CONTAINING COMMON PHONIC UNITS. *Out of print.*
f) TEST R6, TEST OF DIRECTIONAL ATTACK ON WORDS. *Out of print.*
g) TEST R7, VISUAL WORD DISCRIMINATION TEST. *Out of print.*

For additional information and a review by R. W. McCulloch, see 5:651 (4 references); for a review by M. L. Kellmer Pringle, see 4:552 (3 references); for a review by Edith I. M. Thomson, see 3:499.

REFERENCES THROUGH 1971

1–3. See 4:552.
4–7. See 5:651.
8. JONES, W. R. "The Influence of Reading Ability in English on the Intelligence Test Scores of Welsh-Speaking Children." *Brit J Ed Psychol* 23:114–20 F '53. * (*PA* 28:4835)
9. PITTS, R., AND SIMON, A. "A Psychological and Educational Study of a Group of Male Prisoners." *Brit J Ed Psychol* 24: 106–21 Je '54. * (*PA* 29:2748)
10. SCHMIDT, W. H. O., AND MILLER, W. B. "A Standardisation of Three Reading Tests and a Survey of Reading Abilities in Primary Schools in Durban and Pietermaritzburg." *J Social Res* (South Africa) 6:99–111 D '55. *
11. KEATS, J. A. "The Difficulty of Available Word Recognition Tests for Queensland Children." *Austral J Ed* 2:168–70 N '58. *
12. MEDDLETON, G. "Overlap in Test Scores and Its Relation to Remedial Reading." *Slow Learning Child* (Australia) 6:68–76 N '59. *
13. CURR, W., AND GOURLAY, N. "The Effect of Practice on Performance in Scholastic Tests." *Brit J Ed Psychol* 30:155–67 Je '60. *

14. LEWIS, D. G. "Differences in Attainment Between Primary-Schools in Mixed-Language Areas: Their Dependence on Intelligence and Linguistic Background." *Brit J Ed Psychol* 30:63–70 F '60. *
15. POTTS, ERIC. "A Factorial Study of the Relationship Between the Child's Vocabulary and His Reading Progress at the Infants' Stage." Abstract. *Brit J Ed Psychol* 30:84–6 F '60. *
16. LOVELL, K.; JOHNSON, E.; AND PLATTS, D. "A Summary of a Study of the Reading Ages of Children Who Had Been Given Remedial Teaching." *Brit J Ed Psychol* 32:66–71 F '62. * (*PA* 37:1955)
17. ANDREWS, R. J. "Some Comments on the Use of Standardised Word Reading Tests." *Slow Learning Child* (Australia) 11:176–84 Mr '65. * (*PA* 39:15207)
18. FRANSELLA, FAY, AND GERVER, DAVID. "Multiple Regression Equations for Predicting Reading Age From Chronological Age and WISC Verbal I.Q." *Brit J Ed Psychol* 35:86–9 F '65. * (*PA* 39:10818)
19. LINFOOT, K. W. "An Investigation of the Word Order and Difficulty Level in Schonell's Graded Word Recognition Test (R.1)." *Slow Learning Child* (Australia) 13:158–63 Mr '67. * (*PA* 42:14500)
20. COCHRANE, R. G.; ELKINS, J.; AND RICHMOND, DAWN M. "Analysis of Fourth Grade Testing." *Slow Learning Child* (Australia) 16(3):131–42 N '69. * (*PA* 44:18351)
21. LOCKYER, LINDA, AND RUTTER, MICHAEL. "A Five- to Fifteen-Year Follow-up Study of Infantile Psychosis: 3, Psychological Aspects." *Brit J Psychiatry* 115(525):865–82 Ag '69. * (*PA* 44:10847)
22. BOOKBINDER, G. E. "Variations in Reading Test Norms." *Ed Res* (England) 12(2):99–105 F '70. *
23. O'KELLY, E. "A Method for Detecting Slow Learning Juniors." *Ed Res* (England) 12(2):135–9 F '70. *
24. ELKINS, J. "Some Recent Queensland Norms for Widely Used Standardized Tests." *Slow Learning Child* (Australia) 18(3):142–7 N '71. *
25. YOUNG, DENNIS, AND STIRTON, MARGARET E. "G.W.R. Test Equivalences and Reading Ages." *Remedial Ed* (England) 6(3):7–8 N '71. *

CUMULATIVE NAME INDEX

Andrews, R. J.: 17   Miller, W. B.: 10
Bookbinder, G. E.: 22   Neale, M. D.: 7
Cochrane, R. G.: 20   O'Kelly, E.: 23
Curr, W.: 13   Pitts, R.: 9
Elkins, J.: 20, 24   Platts, D.: 16
Fransella, F.: 18   Potts, E.: 15
Gerver, D.: 18   Pringle, M. L. K.: 7; *rev*, 4:
Gourlay, N.: 13   552
Johnson, E.: 16   Richmond, D. M.: 20
Jones, W. R.: 8   Rutter, M.: 21
Keats, J. A.: 11   Schmidt, W. H. O.: 10
Lewis, D. G.: 14   Schonell, F. E.: 3, 6
Linfoot, K. W.: 19   Schonell, F. J.: 1–6
Lockyer, L.: 21   Simon, A.: 9
Lovell, K.: 16   Stirton, M. E.: 25
McCulloch, R. W.: *rev*, 5:   Thomson, E. I. M.: *rev*, 3:499
   651   Young, D.: 25
Meddleton, G.: 12

[1647]

Silent Reading Diagnostic Tests. Grades 2–6; 1955–70; SRDT; 17 scores based upon 8 tests: words in isolation (test 1), words in context (2), total right (1, 2), initial errors (1, 2), middle errors (1, 2), ending errors (1, 2), orientation errors (1, 2), total errors (1, 2), total omitted (1, 2), visual-structural (3), syllabication (4), word synthesis (5), total right (3, 4, 5), beginning sounds (6), ending sounds (7), vowel and consonant sounds (8), total right (6, 7, 8); Guy L. Bond, Bruce Balow, and Cyril J. Hoyt; Lyons & Carnahan. *

For additional information and reviews by N. Dale Bryant and Roy A. Kress, see 7:722 (7 references); for reviews by Emery P. Bliesmer and Albert J. Kingston of the original edition, see 6:832 (1 reference).

REFERENCES THROUGH 1971

1. See 6:832.
2–8. See 7:722.
9. REYNOLDS, MAYNARD CLINTON. "A Study of the Relationships Between Auditory Characteristics and Specific Silent Reading Abilities." *J Ed Res* 46:439–49 F '53. * (*PA* 28:1492)
10. GLORFELD, PATRICIA. *The Relationship of Word Recognition Deficiencies as Measured by the Silent Reading Diagnostic Tests to the Reading Achievement of Seventh Graders.* Master's thesis, Northern Illinois University (DeKalb, Ill.), 1966.
11. SAMPLE, MELVIN LEON. *A Study of the Relationship of*

Visual Discrimination to the Recall of Words Taught by Visual Method Among Thirty Elementary School Children. Master's thesis, East Tennessee State University (Johnson City, Tenn.), 1966.

CUMULATIVE NAME INDEX

[1648]

★**Sipay Word Analysis Tests.** Grades 2–12; 1974, c1973–74; SWAT; designed to measure oral reading decoding skills in 1 or more of 3 areas: visual analysis, phonic analysis, visual blending; 2 types of scores based on following criteria: "specific strengths and weaknesses" scores (can or probably can perform the skill [68–100% correct], may be able to [51–67% correct], cannot or probably cannot [0–50% correct]), "performance objective" scores (based on at least 95% correct [some examiners may choose to use a lower standard]); 17 tests; Edward R. Sipay; Educators Publishing Service, Inc. *

a) SURVEY TEST. May be administered to help decide which of following tests to administer.

b) TEST 1: LETTER NAMES.

c) TEST 2: SYMBOL-SOUND ASSOCIATION: SINGLE LETTERS.

d) TEST 3: SUBSTITUTION: SINGLE LETTERS.

e) TEST 4: CONSONANT-VOWEL-CONSONANT TRIGRAMS.

f) TEST 5: INITIAL CONSONANT BLENDS AND DIGRAPHS.

g) TEST 6: FINAL CONSONANT BLENDS AND DIGRAPHS.

h) TEST 7: VOWEL COMBINATIONS.

i) TEST 8: OPEN-SYLLABLE GENERALIZATION.

j) TEST 9: FINAL SILENT E GENERALIZATION.

k) TEST 10: VOWEL VERSATILITY.

l) TEST 11: VOWELS PLUS R.

m) TEST 12: SILENT CONSONANTS.

n) TEST 13: VOWEL SOUNDS OF Y.

o) TEST 14: VISUAL ANALYSIS.

p) TEST 15: VISUAL BLENDING.

q) TEST 16: CONTRACTIONS.

[1649]

Standard Reading Inventory. Grades 1–7; 1966, c1963–66; SRI; 4 scores (independent reading level, minimum instructional level, maximum instructional level, frustration level), 6–9 subtest scores (vocabulary in isolation, vocabulary in context, oral word recognition errors, total oral errors, recall after oral reading, recall after silent reading, total comprehension, oral speed, silent speed) at each of 11 reading levels (pre-primer, 1^1, 1^2, 2^1, 2^2, 3^1, 3^2, 4, 5, 6, 7), and various ratings and checklists; Robert A. McCracken; Klamath Printing Co. *

For additional information and a review by H. Alan Robinson, see 7:723 (8 references).

REFERENCES THROUGH 1971

1–8. See 7:723.
9. FROESE, VICTOR. "Word Recognition Tests: Are They Useful Beyond Grade Three." *Read Teach* 24(5):432–8 F '71. * (*PA* 47:11610)
10. POWELL, WILLIAM R., AND DUNKELD, COLIN G. "Validity of the IRI Reading Levels." *El Engl* 48(6):637–42 O '71. *

CUMULATIVE NAME INDEX

[1650]

The Standard Reading Tests. Reading ages up to 9–0; 1958; SRT; 12 tests; J. C. Daniels and Hunter Diack; Hart-Davis Educational Ltd. [England]. *

a) TEST 1, THE STANDARD TEST OF READING SKILL.

b) TEST 2, COPYING ABSTRACT FIGURES.

c) TEST 3, COPYING A SENTENCE.

d) TEST 4, VISUAL DISCRIMINATION AND ORIENTATION TEST.

e) TEST 5, LETTER-RECOGNITION TEST.

f) TEST 6, AURAL DISCRIMINATION TEST.

g) TEST 7, DIAGNOSTIC WORD-RECOGNITION TESTS.

h) TEST 8, ORAL WORD-RECOGNITION TEST.

i) TEST 9, PICTURE WORD-RECOGNITION TEST.

j) TEST 10, SILENT PROSE-READING AND COMPREHENSION TEST.

k) TEST 11, GRADED SPELLING TEST.

l) TEST 12, GRADED TEST OF READING EXPERIENCE.

For additional information and a review by M. L. Kellmer Pringle, see 7:724; for a review by L. B. Birch, see 6:833 (1 reference).

REFERENCES THROUGH 1971

1. See 6:833.
2. McCRACKEN, ROBERT A. "A Two-Year Study of the Reading Achievement of Children Who Were Reading When They Entered First Grade." *J Ed Res* 59:207–10 Ja '66. * (*PA* 40:6506)

CUMULATIVE NAME INDEX

[1651]

★**Stanford Diagnostic Reading Test.** Grades 2.5–4.5, 4.5–8.5; 1966–71; SDRT; 2 levels; Bjorn Karlsen, Richard Madden, and Eric F. Gardner; Harcourt Brace Jovanovich, Inc. *

a) LEVEL 1. Grades 2.5–4.5; 1966–71; 7 scores: comprehension, vocabulary, auditory discrimination, syllabication, beginning and ending sounds, blending, sound discrimination.

b) LEVEL 2. Grades 4.5–8.5; 1966–68; 8 scores: comprehension (literal, inferential, total), vocabulary, syllabication, sound discrimination, blending, rate.

For additional information and a review by Lawrence M. Kasdon, see 7:725 (3 references).

REFERENCES THROUGH 1971

1–3. See 7:725.
4. HANNI, DONALD. *The Efficacy of a Classroom Reading Program Predicted Upon the Stanford Diagnostic Reading Test.* Master's thesis, Sonoma State College (Rohnert Park, Calif.), 1971.
5. MAHR, ILA RUTH. *An Investigation of the Empirical Validity of the Group Categories of the Stanford Diagnostic Reading Test Instructional Placement Report.* Doctor's thesis, University of Georgia (Athens, Ga.), 1971. (*DAI* 32:3792A)

CUMULATIVE NAME INDEX

[1652]

★**Swansea Test of Phonic Skills, Experimental Version.** Reading ages below 7.5; 1970–71; 6 scores: short vowels, long vowels, initial letter blends, final letter blends, miscellaneous, total; Phillip Williams assisted by Peter Congdon, Margaret Holder, and Norman Sims; published for the Schools Council Research and Development Project in Compensatory Education; Basil Blackwell, Publisher [England]. *

[1653]

★**Test of Individual Needs in Reading, Seventh Edition.** Grades 1–6; 1961–71; TINR; test booklet title is *John Bidwell and the Trail to California;* 20

scores: oral reading, comprehension, rate, word analysis (use of context, words beginning alike, beginning consonants, ending consonants, consonant substitutions, speech consonants, consonant blends, reversals, long and short vowels, vowel blends, blending letter sounds, prefixes, suffixes, compound words, recognizing syllables, syllabication, total); the 1970 test involves changes in 5 items but no change in norms; Hap Gilliland; Montana Reading Publications. *

For additional information and reviews by Larry A. Harris and George D. Spache, see 7:726.

[1654]

★**Test of Phonic Skills.** Reading level grades kgn–3; 1971; TPS; no scores, 19 areas: phone discrimination, print discrimination, initial consonants, final consonants, initial clusters, final clusters, consonant digraphs, selected spelling patterns, long vowels, short vowels, silent -e, vowel digraphs, vocalic/ʒ/ and -r as a vowel, -r controllers, -l and -w controllers, soft or hard -c, soft or hard -g, diphthongs, syllabication principles; taped *Phone Discrimination Test* to be administered if child makes 3 or more errors on phone discrimination subtest; Kenneth J. Smith and Henry M. Truby; Harper & Row, Publishers, Inc. *

[1655]

★**Wisconsin Tests of Reading Skill Development: Word Attack.** Grades kgn–2, 1, 1–3, 2–4, 3–6; 1970–72; WTRSD:WA; part of the Wisconsin Design for Reading Skill Development; 6–16 "single-skill" scores at each of 5 levels; 80% mastery criterion suggested for each subtest with retesting at next higher level if a child fails not more than one subtest and retesting at next lower level if a child passes not more than one subtest; handbook and planning guide by Wayne Otto (principal investigator) and Eunice Askov; tests and manuals by Karlyn Kamm, Pamela J. Miles, Deborah M. Stewart, Virginia L. Van Blaricom (tests), and Margaret L. Harris (tests); NCS Interpretive Scoring Systems. *
a) LEVEL A. Grades kgn–2; "early readiness" level; 6 scores: rhyming words, rhyming phrases, shapes, letters and numbers, words and phrases, initial consonants.
b) TRANSITION LEVEL A-B. Grade 1; "advanced readiness or preprimer" level; selected items from Levels A and B; 7 scores: rhyming words, rhyming phrases, words and phrases, initial consonants, beginning consonants, ending consonants, consonant blends.
c) LEVEL B. Grades 1–3; "primer or first reader" level; 11 scores: beginning consonants, ending consonants, consonant blends, rhyming elements, short vowels, consonant digraphs, compound words, contractions, base words and endings, plurals, possessives.
d) LEVEL C. Grades 2–4; "second reader" level; 16 scores: consonant variants, consonant blends, long vowels, vowel plus *r–a* plus *l–a* plus *w*, diphthongs, long and short *oo*, middle vowel, 2 vowels separated, 2 vowels together, final vowel, consonant digraphs, base words, plurals, homonyms, synonyms and antonyms, multiple meanings.
e) LEVEL D. Grades 3–6; "third reader" level; 6 scores: 3-letter consonant blends, silent letters, syllabication, accent, unaccented schwa, possessives.

REFERENCES THROUGH 1971
1. MOE, ALDEN JOHN. *An Investigation of the Uniqueness of Selected Auditory Discrimination Skills Among Kindergarten Children Enrolled in Two Types of Reading Readiness Programs.* Doctor's thesis, University of Minnesota (Minneapolis, Minn.), 1971. (*DAI* 32:6295A)

CUMULATIVE NAME INDEX
Moe, A. J.: 1

Test of Individual Needs in Reading

[1656]

★**Woodcock Reading Mastery Tests.** Grades kgn–12; 1972–73; WRMT; 6 scores (letter identification, word identification, word attack, word comprehension, passage comprehension, total) plus derived scores in these same 6 areas at each of 4 levels (easy reading level [96% mastery], reading grade score [90% mastery], failure reading level [75% mastery], relative mastery of grade level); Richard W. Woodcock; American Guidance Service, Inc. *

[Out of Print Since TIP I]

McGuffey Diagnostic Reading Test, R:143, 5:664
Reading Diagnostic Record for High School and College Students, R:144, 5:666 (5 reviews, 3 excerpts)
Scholastic Diagnostic Reading Test, R:146, 5:650 (2 reviews)
Stanford Diagnostic Phonics Survey, 5:670

MISCELLANEOUS

[1657]

Basic Sight Word Test. Grades 1–2; 1942; Edward W. Dolch; Garrard Publishing Co. *

REFERENCES THROUGH 1971
1. DOLCH, E. W. "A Basic Sight Vocabulary." *El Sch J* 36: 456–60 F '36. * (*PA* 10:3164)
2. HAMMILL, BETH A. *A Comparison of Reader Levels of a First Grade Group of Children With Reading Grade Equivalents on a Standardized Reading Test.* Master's thesis, State University of Iowa (Iowa City, Iowa), 1941.
3. ECKSTEIN, CATHERINE. *Use of the Dolch Basic Sight Word List as a Measure to Determine Reader Level.* Master's thesis, State University of Iowa (Iowa City, Iowa), 1944.
4. SPARROW, JULIA. *Accomplishment on the Dolch Basic Sight Word Test as a Measure of Reader-Level.* Master's thesis, State University of Iowa (Iowa City, Iowa), 1944.
5. McBROOM, MAUDE; SPARROW, JULIA L.; AND ECKSTEIN, CATHERINE G. *A Scale for Determining the Child's Reader Level.* University of Iowa Extension Bulletin, College of Education Series, No. 35. Iowa City, Iowa: State University of Iowa, 1947. Pp. 14. *

CUMULATIVE NAME INDEX
Dolch, E. W.: 1   McBroom, M.: 5
Eckstein, C.: 3   Sparrow, J.: 4
Eckstein, C. G.: 5   Sparrow, J. L.: 5
Hammill, B. A.: 2

[1658]

Botel Reading Inventory. Grades 1–4, 1–6, 1–12; 1961–70; BRI; 4 tests; 9 scores: frustrational, instructional (placement), and free reading grade score for each of tests *a, b,* and *d;* Morton Botel; Follett Publishing Co. *
a) WORD RECOGNITION TEST. Grades 1–4; 1961–70; oral reading fluency; 8 "graded" 20-word lists described as samples of reading materials at 8 levels (PP, P, 1^2, 2^1, 2^2, 3^1, 3^2, 4+); 3 grade scores: frustration level (0–65%), instructional level (70–90%), free reading level (95–100%).
b) WORD OPPOSITES TEST. Grades 1–12; 1961–70; a vocabulary test described as "an estimate of reading comprehension"; 10 "graded" 10-word lists described as samples of reading materials at 10 levels (1, 2^1, 2^2, 3^1, 3^2, 4, 5, 6, 7–8, 9–12); 3 grade scores: frustration level (0–60%), instructional level (70–80%), free reading level (90–100%).
c) PHONICS MASTERY TEST. Grades 1–4; 1961–70; "knowledge of key word perception skills"; 3 levels of phonic skills, each level to be mastered 100% before going on to the next.
d) SPELLING PLACEMENT TEST. Grades 1–6; 1970; 5 "graded" 20-word lists described as samples from the

author's *Spelling and Writing Patterns* at 5 levels (1–2, 3, 4, 5, 6) ; 3 grade scores : frustration level (0–80%), instructional level (85–90%), independent level (95–100%).

For additional information, see 7 :727 (5 references) ; for reviews by Ira E. Aaron and Charles M. Brown, see 6 :834.

REFERENCES THROUGH 1971

1–5. See 7 :727.
6. SCHNEIDERHAN, ROSEMARY MALMGREN. *A Correlation of Individual and Group Reading Tests*. Master's thesis, St. Cloud State College (St. Cloud, Minn.), 1963.
7. FINNEGAN, SHIRLEY BOOHER. *Relationships Between Certain Auditory Tasks and the Ability to Recode Nonsense Words*. Doctor's thesis, University of California (Berkeley, Calif.), 1971. (*DAI* 32 :2400A)

CUMULATIVE NAME INDEX

Aaron, I. E.: *rev*, 6 :834	Kashuba, M.: 4
Botel, M.: 3–4	McCracken, R. A.: 5
Bradley, J.: 4	Mullen, N. D.: 5
Brown, C. M.: *rev*, 6 :834	Schneiderhan, R. M.: 6
Davis, M. C. E.: 1	Trela, T. M.: 2
Finnegan, S. B.: 7	

[1659]

Cumulative Reading Record, 1956 Revision. Grades 9–12 ; 1933–56 ; revision of a record by Margaret M. Skinner ; National Council of Teachers of English. *

[1660]

Durrell Listening-Reading Series. Grades 1–2, 3–6, 7–9 ; 1969–70 ; 9 scores : listening (vocabulary, sentences or paragraphs, total—these scores are referred to as "potential reading grade equivalents"), reading (vocabulary, sentences or paragraphs, total—these scores are referred to as "actual reading grade equivalents"), potential minus actual reading grade equivalents (vocabulary, sentences or paragraphs, total—these scores are referred to as "differential" scores) ; 3 levels ; Donald D. Durrell, Mary T. Hayes (*a*), and Mary B. Brassard (*b*) ; Harcourt Brace Jovanovich, Inc. *
a) PRIMARY LEVEL. Grades 1–2.
b) INTERMEDIATE LEVEL. Grades 3–6.
c) ADVANCED LEVEL. Grades 7–9.

For additional information and reviews by John R. Bormuth and George D. Spache, see 7 :728 (3 references).

REFERENCES THROUGH 1971

1–3. See 7 :728.
4. SMITH, CHARLES LEROY. *A Comparison of Selected Standardized Reading Test Scores and Informal Reading Inventory Results at Intermediate Grade Levels*. Doctor's thesis, University of Northern Colorado (Greeley, Colo.), 1970. (*DAI* 31 :4046A)
5. BROUSSEAU, PAULA JOAN. *A Study of the Interrelationships of Reading Ability, Listening Ability and Intelligence of Ninth and Tenth Grade Students*. Doctor's thesis, Southern Illinois University (Carbondale, Ill.), 1971. (*DAI* 32 :4828A)
6. WADE, VERN JOSEPH. *A Comparison of Selected Standardized Reading Test Scores and Informal Reading Inventory Results at Eighth Grade Level*. Doctor's thesis, University of Northern Colorado (Greeley, Colo.), 1971. (*DAI* 32 :3853A)

CUMULATIVE NAME INDEX

Bormuth, J. R.: *rev*, 7 :728	Hayes, M. T.: 1
Brassard, M. B.: 2	Smith, C. L.: 4
Brousseau, P. J.: 5	Spache, G. D.: *rev*, 7 :728
Durrell, D. D.: 3	Wade, V. J.: 6

[1661]

Durrell-Sullivan Reading Capacity and Achievement Tests. Grades 2.5–4.5, 3–6 ; 1937–45 ; 3–5 scores : word meaning, paragraph meaning, total, spelling (optional), written recall (optional) ; 2 tests ; Donald D. Durrell and Helen Blair Sullivan ; Harcourt Brace Jovanovich, Inc. *
a) READING CAPACITY TEST.
b) READING ACHIEVEMENT TEST.

For additional information and a review by James Maxwell, see 5 :661 (5 references) ; for a review by Helen M. Robinson, see 4 :562 (4 references) ; for reviews by William S. Gray and Marion Monroe and an excerpted review of the original edition, see 1 :1099.

REFERENCES THROUGH 1971

1–4. See 4 :562.
5–9. See 5 :661.
10. WELSH, GEORGE BYRON. *An Investigation of Some Predictive Factors in Auding Ability*. Doctor's thesis, University of Pittsburgh (Pittsburgh, Pa.), 1954. (*DA* 14 :2407)
11. CARROW, MARY ARTHUR. "Linguistic Functioning of Bilingual and Monolingual Children." *J Speech & Hearing Disorders* 22 :371–80 S '57. * (*PA* 33 :4258)
12. RUSSELL, DAVID H. "Auditory Abilities and Achievement in Spelling in the Primary Grades." *J Ed Psychol* 49 :315–9 D '58. * (*PA* 36 :2KL15R)
13. HARVEY, JOHN C. *Study of the Durrell-Sullivan Reading Capacity Test as a Measure of Intelligence*. Master's thesis, Sacramento State College (Sacramento, Calif.), 1961.
14. TOUSSAINT, ISABELLA HASTIE. *Interrelationships of Reading, Listening, Arithmetic, and Intelligence and Their Implications*. Doctor's thesis, University of Pittsburgh (Pittsburgh, Pa.), 1961. (*DA* 22 :819)
15. CLELAND, DONALD L., AND TOUSSAINT, ISABELLA H. "The Interrelationships of Reading, Listening, Arithmetic Computation and Intelligence." *Read Teach* 15 :228–31 Ja '62. *
16. YOUNG, FRANCIS A. "Reading, Measures of Intelligence and Refractive Errors." *Am J Optom* 40 :257–64 My '63. *
17. SINGER, HARRY. "Validity of the Durrell-Sullivan Reading Capacity Test." *Ed & Psychol Meas* 25 :479–91 su '65. * (*PA* 39 :15268)
18. WENGER, THELMA WOOD. *A Study of the Effect on Listening Test Scores of Change in Methods of Presentation*. Doctor's thesis, University of Virginia (Charlottesville, Va.), 1967. (*DA* 28 :2466A)
19. WILLIAMS, FERN C. *A Comparison of Scores on the Durrell-Sullivan Reading Capacity Test and Auditory Comprehension Paragraphs of the Diagnostic Reading Scales*. Master's thesis, University of Texas (Austin, Tex.), 1967.
20. BRAGG, JANE K. *Six Predictive Reading Capacity Formulas With Actual Reading Achievement for Children in Grades 3–6*. Master's thesis, Rutgers—The State University (New Brunswick, N.J.), 1971.
21. GRUEN, RONALD STEVEN. *Prediction of End-of-Year Reading Achievement for First and Third Grade Pupils*. Doctor's thesis, Pennsylvania State University (University Park, Pa.), 1971. (*DAI* 32 :6198A)

CUMULATIVE NAME INDEX

Alden, C. L.: 3	Owen, J. C.: 9
Bliesmer, E. P.: 6, 8	Pugh, G. S.: 4
Bond, G. L.: 7	Robinson, H. M.: *rev*, 4 :562
Bragg, J. K.: 20	Russell, D. H.: 12
Carrow, M. A.: 11	Singer, H.: 17
Cleland, D. L.: 15	Sullivan, H. B.: 1, 3
Clymer, T. W.: 7	Tireman, L. S.: 2
Durrell, D. D.: 3	Toussaint, I. H.: 14–5
Gray, W. S.: *rev*, 1 :1099	Welsh, G. B.: 10
Gruen, R. S.: 21	Wenger, T. W.: 18
Harvey, J. C.: 13	Williams, F. C.: 19
Maxwell, J.: *rev*, 5 :661	Woods, V. E.: 2
Miller, V. J.: 5	Young, F. A.: 16
Monroe, M.: *rev*, 1 :1099	

[1662]

Dyslexia Schedule. Children having reading difficulties and first grade entrants ; 1968–69 ; an 89-item questionnaire to be completed by parents ; score based on 23 discriminating items, 21 of which are published separately under the title *School Entrance Check List* (SECL) for screening use ; John McLeod ; Educators Publishing Service, Inc. *

For additional information and a review by Martin Kling, see 7 :729 (3 references).

REFERENCES THROUGH 1971

1–3. See 7 :729.

CUMULATIVE NAME INDEX

Kling, M.: *rev*, 7 :729	McLeod, J.: 1–3

[1663]

Individual Reading Placement Inventory, Field Research Edition. Youths and adults with reading levels up to grade 7 ; 1969 ; IRPI ; 7 grade level scores : independent reading (words, paragraphs), instructional reading (words, paragraphs), frustration (words, paragraphs), present language potential; Edwin H. Smith and Weldon G. Bradtmueller; Follett Publishing Co. *

For additional information and reviews by Edward B. Fry and Albert J. Kingston, see 7:730.

REFERENCES THROUGH 1971

1. Wunderlich, Elaine, and Bradtmueller, Mary. "Teacher Estimates of Reading Levels Compared With IRPI Instructional Level Scores." *J Read* 14(5):303–8 F '71. *

CUMULATIVE NAME INDEX

Bradtmueller, M.: 1   Kingston, A. J.: *rev*, 7:730
Fry, E. B.: *rev*, 7:730   Wunderlich, E.: 1

[1664]

★The Instant Word Recognition Test. Reading level grades 1–4; 1971; IWRT; Edward Fry; Dreier Educational Systems, Inc. *

[1665]

★Inventory of Teacher Knowledge of Reading. Elementary school teachers and college students in methods courses; 1972, c1971; A. Sterl Artley and Veralee B. Hardin; Lucas Brothers Publishers. *

[1666]

Learning Methods Test. Grades kgn, 1, 2, 3; 1954–55; LMT; comparative effectiveness of four methods of teaching new words: visual, phonic, kinesthetic, combination; Robert E. Mills; Mills School. *

For additional information and reviews by Thomas E. Culliton, Jr. and William Eller, see 6:836 (1 reference).

REFERENCES THROUGH 1971

1. See 6:836.
2. Mills, Esther Brownell. *Relationships Between Psycholinguistic Abilities of Educable Mentally Retarded Pupils and the Effectiveness of Four Instructional Approaches in the Language Arts.* Doctor's thesis, University of Maryland (College Park, Md.), 1965. (*DA* 27:145A)
3. Sample, Melvin Leon. *A Study of the Relationship of Visual Discrimination to the Recall of Words Taught by Visual Method Among Thirty Elementary School Children.* Master's thesis, East Tennessee State University (Johnson City, Tenn.), 1966.
4. Long, Ruby Davidson. *Learning Mode Preference of Educable Mentally Retarded Children.* Doctor's thesis, University of Missouri (Columbia, Mo.), 1967. (*DA* 29:151A)

CUMULATIVE NAME INDEX

Coleman, J. C.: 1   Long, R. D.: 4
Culliton, T. E.: *rev*, 6:836   Mills, E. B.: 2
Eller, W.: *rev*, 6:836   Sample, M. L.: 3

[1667]

★National Test of Basic Words. Grades 1–5; 1970; NTBW; "service words" from preprimer to first reader difficulty arranged in 9 levels; next higher level administered when child has 4 or less errors in a 20-item set; 80% mastery suggested for entire test before instruction in second grade reader; manual by Sue Harrison Halpern; American Testing Co. *

[1668]

OC Diagnostic Syllabizing Test. Grades 4–6; 1960–62; formerly called *OC Diagnostic Syllable Test;* Katherine O'Connor; O'Connor Reading Clinic Publishing Co. *

For additional information, see 6:827.

[1669]

Phonics Test for Teachers. Reading methods courses; 1964; PTT; no scores other than item scores in 10 areas: syllabication, vowels, vowel generalizations, sounds of c and g, sounds of y, digraphs, diphthongs, sounds of oo, sounds of qu, sounds of x; Dolores Durkin; Teachers College Press. *

For additional information and reviews by Ira E. Aaron and Gerald G. Duffy, see 7:721 (2 references).

REFERENCES THROUGH 1971

1–2. See 7:721.

CUMULATIVE NAME INDEX

Aaron, I. E.: *rev*, 7:721   Gibson, G. C.: 1
Duffy, G. G.: *rev*, 7:721   Tyre, B. B.: 2

[1670]

The Reader Rater With Self-Scoring Profile. Ages 15 and over; 1959–65; self-administered survey of reading skills; designed for use either with the Rapid Reading Kit or separately; 12 scores: speed, comprehension, reading habits, reading for details, reading for inferences, reading for main ideas and adjusting speed, summarizing, skimming, recall of information read, unspeeded vocabulary, speeded vocabulary, total; Better Reading Program, Inc. *

For additional information, see 6:837.

[1671]

The Reader's Inventory. Entrants to a reading improvement course for secondary and college students and adults; 1963; information concerning a student's reading interests, attitudes, habits, visual conditions, educational and vocational background, and what he expects to gain from a reading course; George D. Spache and Stanford E. Taylor; Educational Developmental Laboratories, Inc. *

For additional information and reviews by John J. Geyer and David M. Wark, see 7:733.

[1672]

Reading Eye II. Grades 1, 2, 3, 4, 5, 6, 7–8, 9–16 and adults; 1959–69; a portable electronic eye-movement recorder with test materials; 5 reading component scores (fixations, regressions, average span of recognition, average duration of fixation, rate with comprehension), 3 ratings (grade level of reading, relative efficiency, directional attack), and 2 diagnostic categories (visual adjustment, general adjustment to reading); Stanford E. Taylor, Helen Frackenpohl, and James L. Pettee; Educational Developmental Laboratories, Inc. *

For additional information and a review by John J. Geyer, see 7:734 (9 references); for reviews by Arthur S. McDonald and George D. Spache of an earlier model, see 6:838 (3 references). For an excerpt from a related book review, see 6:B478.

REFERENCES THROUGH 1971

1–3. See 6:838.
4–12. See 7:734.
13. Smith, Peter B. "Eye Movements and Rapid Reading Reconsidered." *Yearb Nat Read Conf* 14:203–9 '65. *
14. Taylor, Stanford E. "Rebuttal to 'Eye Movements and Reading Reconsidered.'" *Yearb Nat Read Conf* 14:210–7 '65. *
15. Mann, Gloria T. "Eye Movements of Children in Reading English and Hebrew." *J Exp Ed* 36:60–8 su '68. *
16. Dizney, Henry; Rankin, Richard; and Johnston, James. "Eye-Movement Fixations in Reading as Related to Anxiety in College Females." *Percept & Motor Skills* 28:851–4 Je '69. * (*PA* 43:17454)
17. Hannah, Betty Rupard. *Visual Behavior of Children With Nystagmus While Reading Orally.* Doctor's thesis, University of Arizona (Tucson, Ariz.), 1971. (*DAI* 32:3821A)

CUMULATIVE NAME INDEX

Beyer, D. A.: 9   Mann, G. T.: 15
Brickner, C. A.: 10   Mickish, V. L.: 11
Bryant, N. D.: *exc*, 6:B478   Rankin, R.: 16
Dizney, H.: 16   Ryan, H. J. L.: 8
Erdley, R. R.: 5   Seifert, J. G.: 6
Evans, R. M.: 7   Singer, C. R.: 12
Geyer, J. J.: *rev*, 7:734   Smith, P. B.: 13
Hannah, B. R.: 17   Spache, G. D.: 2; *rev*, 6:838
Johnston, J.: 16   Taylor, S. E.: 1, 3–4, 14
McDonald, A. S.: *rev*, 6:838

[1673]

Reading Versatility Test. Grades 5–8, 8–12, 12–16; 1961–68; RVT; 7 scores: rate and comprehension (fiction, nonfiction, skimming, scanning) and 3 reading rate ratios (fiction/nonfiction, skimming/fiction, scanning/fiction); Arthur S. McDonald, M. Alodia, Harold M. Nason, George Zimny, and James A. Byrne; Educational Developmental Laboratories, Inc. *

For additional information and a review by John J. Geyer, see 7:735.

REFERENCES THROUGH 1971

1. See 6:839.
2. McDonald, Arthur S. "Reading Versatility Twelve Years Later." *Yearb Nat Read Conf* 20:168–73 '71. *

CUMULATIVE NAME INDEX

Geyer, J. J.: *rev,* 7:735   Theophemia, M.: 1
McDonald, A. S.: 2

[1674]

Roswell-Chall Auditory Blending Test. Grades 1–4; 1963; Florence G. Roswell and Jeanne S. Chall; Essay Press, Inc. *

For additional information and reviews by Ira E. Aaron and B. H. Van Roekel, see 6:830 (2 references).

REFERENCES THROUGH 1971

1–2. See 6:830.
3. Brown, Lily. *Auditory Blending Ability as a Perceptual Process and Its Relationship to Reading Success.* Master's thesis, Bank Street College of Education (New York, N.Y.), 1964.
4. Alshan, Leonard M. "Reading Readiness and Reading Achievement." *Proc Ann Conv Int Read Assn* 10:312–3 '65. *
5. Hanesian, Helen. *The Relationship of Auditory Abilities to First Grade Reading Achievement.* Doctor's thesis, Columbia University (New York, N.Y.), 1966. (*DA* 27:2883A)
6. Bruininks, Robert H. "Auditory and Visual Perceptual Skills Related to the Reading Performance of Disadvantaged Boys." *Percept & Motor Skills* 29(1):179–86 Ag '69. * (*PA* 44:2835)
7. McNinch, George Haas Wiley. *The Relationships Between Selected Perceptual Factors and Measured First Grade Reading Achievement.* Doctor's thesis, University of Georgia (Athens, Ga.), 1970. (*DAI* 31:3965A)
8. Goldman, Ronald, and Dixon, Sarah D. "The Relationship of Vocal-Phonic and Articulatory Abilities." *J Learn Dis* 4(5):251–6 My '71. * (*PA* 47:9457)
9. McNinch, George. "Auditory Perceptual Factors and Measured First-Grade Reading Achievement." *Read Res Q* 6(4):472–92 su '71. * (*PA* 47:11769)

CUMULATIVE NAME INDEX

Aaron, I. E.: *rev,* 6:830   Goldman, R.: 8
Alshan, L. M.: 4   Hanesian, H.: 5
Blumenthal, S. H.: 2   Huset, M. K.: 1
Brown, L.: 3   McNinch, G.: 9
Bruininks, R. H.: 6   McNinch, G. H. W.: 7
Chall, J.: 2   Roswell, F. G.: 2
Dixon, S. D.: 8   Van Roekel, B. H.: *rev,* 6:830

[1675]

Word Discrimination Test. Grades 1–8; 1958; WDT; no manual; Chas. B. Huelsman, Jr.; Miami University Alumni Association. *

For additional information, see 7:736 (2 references).

REFERENCES THROUGH 1971

1–2. See 7:736.

CUMULATIVE NAME INDEX

Huelsman, C. B.: 1   Robinson, H. A.: 2

[1676]

★Word Recognition Test. Preschool to age 8.5; 1970; WRT; Clifford Carver; University of London Press Ltd. [England]. *

[Out of Print Since TIP I]

Eye Movement Camera, T:1686
Functional Readiness Questionnaire for School and College Students (status unknown), R:151, 6:835
SRA Reading Checklist, R:158

ORAL

[1677]

★Concise Word Reading Tests. Ages 7–12; 1969; R. J. Andrews; Teaching and Testing Resources [Australia]. *

[1678]

Flash-X Sight Vocabulary Test. Grades 1–2; 1961; 2 scores: sight vocabulary, experience vocabulary; George D. Spache and Stanford E. Taylor; Educational Developmental Laboratories, Inc. *

For additional information, see 6:841.

[1679]

Gilmore Oral Reading Test. Grades 1–8; 1951–68; 3 scores: accuracy, comprehension, rate; John V. Gilmore and Eunice C. Gilmore; Harcourt Brace Jovanovich, Inc. *

For additional information and reviews by Albert J. Harris and Kenneth J. Smith, see 7:737 (17 references); for reviews by Lydia A. Duggins and Maynard C. Reynolds of the original edition, see 5:671.

REFERENCES THROUGH 1971

1–17. See 7:737.
18. Carrow, Mary Arthur. "Linguistic Functioning of Bilingual and Monolingual Children." *J Speech & Hearing Disorders* 22:371–80 S '57. * (*PA* 33:4258)
19. Corah, Norman L.; Anthony, E. James; Painter, Paul; Stern, John A.; and Thurston, Donald. "Effects of Perinatal Anoxia After Seven Years." *Psychol Monogr* 79(3):1–34 '65. * (*PA* 39:9776)
20. Mumpower, D. L., and Riggs, Sharon. "Overachievement in Word Accuracy as a Result of Parental Pressure." *Read Teach* 23(8):741–7 My '70. * (*PA* 45:3073)
21. Fleischmann, Lillian S. *A Comparison of the Gilmore Oral Reading Test and the Metropolitan Achievement Test in Reading for Grade Placement.* Master's thesis, Sacramento State College (Sacramento, Calif.), 1971.
22. Powell, William R., and Dunkeld, Colin G. "Validity of the IRI Reading Levels." *El Engl* 48(6):637–42 O '71. *

CUMULATIVE NAME INDEX

Anthony, E. J.: 19   Kirby, C. L.: 13
Bond, G. L.: 9   Kirby, C. L. L.: 10
Brown, J. L.: 11   Ladd, E. M.: 2
Carrow, M. A.: 18   Means, C. E.: 12
Clark, H. C.: 4   Mumpower, D. L.: 20
Corah, N. L.: 19   Painter, P.: 19
Dollarhide, R. S.: 6   Patty, D. L.: 7
Duggins, L. A.: *rev,* 5:671 Powell, W. R.: 22
Dunkeld, C. G.: 22   Reynolds, M. C.: *rev,* 5:671
Dykstra, R.: 9   Riddle, W. T.: 3
Fleischmann, L. S.: 21   Riggs, S.: 20
Garlock, J.: 6   Sabatino, D. A.: 14–6
Gilmore, J. V.: 1   Simpson, R. L.: 17
Harris, A. J.: *rev,* 7:737 Smith, K. J.: *rev,* 7:737
Hayden, D. L.: 14–6   Stern, J. A.: 19
Higgins, C.: 5   Thurston, D.: 19
Hopkins, K. D.: 6   Trela, T. M.: 8

[1680]

Graded Word Reading Test. Ages 5 and over; 1921–67; GWRT; pronunciation; 2 tests; 1967 manual identical with manual copyrighted 1938 except for addition of revised norms ['54] for *a*; P. E. Vernon; University of London Press Ltd. [England]. *

a) THE BURT (REARRANGED) WORD READING TEST. 1921–67; adaptation for Scottish schools of *Burt's Graded Word Reading Test* ('21).
b) GRADED WORD READING TEST. 1938; for use in Scottish schools.

For additional information, see 7:738 (3 references).

REFERENCES THROUGH 1971

1–3. See 7:738.
4. Vernon, P. E. "A Study of the Norms and the Validity of Certain Mental Tests at a Child Guidance Clinic: Part II." *Brit J Ed Psychol* 7:115–37 Je '37. * (*PA* 11:4827)
5. Vernon, Philip E. *The Standardization of a Graded Word Reading Test.* Publications of the Scottish Council for Research in Education, No. 12. London: University of London Press Ltd., 1938. Pp. 43. * (*PA* 18:2282)

6. Schmidt, W. H. O., and Miller, W. B. "A Standardisation of Three Reading Tests and a Survey of Reading Abilities in Primary Schools in Durban and Pietermaritzburg." *J Social Res* (South Africa) 6:99–111 D '55 *

7. Keats, J. A. "The Difficulty of Available Word Recognition Tests for Queensland Children." *Austral J Ed* 2:168–70 N '58. *

8. Potts, Eric. "A Factorial Study of the Relationship Between the Child's Vocabulary and His Reading Progress at the Infants' Stage." Abstract. *Brit J Ed Psychol* 30:84–6 F '60. *

9. Lovell, K.; Johnson, E.; and Platts, D. "A Summary of a Study of the Reading Ages of Children Who Had Been Given Remedial Teaching." *Brit J Ed Psychol* 32:66–71 F '62. * (*PA* 37:1955)

10. Young, Dennis, and Stirton, Margaret E. "G.W.R. Test Equivalences and Reading Ages." *Remedial Ed* (England) 6(3):7–8 N '71. *

CUMULATIVE NAME INDEX

Bannon, W. J.: 2	Platts, D.: 9
Johnson, E.: 9	Potts, E.: 8
Keats, J. A.: 7	Schmidt, W. H. O.: 6
Lovell, K.: 9	Stirton, M. E.: 10
Miller, W. B.: 6	Vernon, P. E.: 1, 4–5
Payne, J. F.: 3	Young, D.: 10
Phillips, C. J.: 2	

[1681]

Gray Oral Reading Test. Grades 1–16 and adults; 1963–67; GORT; William S. Gray; edited by Helen M. Robinson; Bobbs-Merrill Co., Inc. *

For additional information and reviews by Emery P. Bliesmer, Albert J. Harris, and Paul R. Lohnes, see 6:842.

REFERENCES THROUGH 1971

1. Patty, Delbert Lee. *A Comparison of Standardized Oral Reading Test Scores and Informal Reading Inventory Scores.* Doctor's thesis, Ball State University (Muncie, Ind.), 1965. (*DA* 26:5302)

2. Kirby, Clara Lou Laughlin. *A Comparison of Scores Obtained on Standardized Oral and Silent Reading Tests and a Cloze Test.* Doctor's thesis, Ball State University (Muncie, Ind.), 1967. (*DA* 28:4512A)

3. Stafford, Clarice M. Salli. *An Analysis of the Types of Oral Reading Errors in a Sample of Fourth Grade Pupils.* Doctor's thesis, Wayne State University (Detroit, Mich.), 1967. (*DA* 29:1375A)

4. Kasdon, Lawrence M. "Oral Versus Silent-Oral Diagnosis." *Proc Ann Conv Int Read Assn* 13(4):86–92 '68. *

5. Cotler, Sheldon. "The Effects of Positive and Negative Reinforcement and Test Anxiety on the Reading Performance of Male Elementary School Children." *Genetic Psychol Monogr* 80(1):29–50 Ag '69. * (*PA* 44:5700)

6. Hardin, Veralee B., and Ames, Wilbur S. "A Comparison of the Results of Two Oral Tests." *Read Teach* 22(4):329–34 Ja '69. *

7. Kasdon, Lawrence M. "Oral Versus Silent-Oral Diagnosis," pp. 86–92. In *Reading Diagnosis and Evaluation.* Edited by Dorothy L. De Boer. Newark, Del.: International Reading Association, 1970. Pp. vi, 138. *

8. Kirby, Clara L. "Using the Cloze Procedure as a Testing Technique," pp. 68–77. In *Reading Diagnosis and Evaluation.* Edited by Dorothy L. De Boer. Newark, Del.: International Reading Association, 1970. Pp. vi, 138. *

9. Clayman, Deborah P. Goldweber. *The Relationship of Error and Correction of Error in Oral Reading to Visual-Form Perception and Word Attack Skills.* Doctor's thesis, Columbia University (New York, N.Y.), 1971. (*DAI* 32:5033A)

10. Hardy, Miriam P.; Mellits, David; and Willig, Sharon N. "Reading: A Function of Language Usage." *Johns Hopkins Med J* 129(1):43–53 Jl '71. *

11. Powell, William R., and Dunkeld, Colin G. "Validity of the IRI Reading Levels." *El Engl* 48(6):637–42 O '71. *

CUMULATIVE NAME INDEX

Ames, W. S.: 6	Kirby, C. L.: 8
Bliesmer, E. P.: *rev,* 6:842	Kirby, C. L. L.: 2
Clayman, D. P. G.: 9	Lohnes, P. R.: *rev,* 6:842
Cotler, S.: 5	Mellits, D.: 10
Dunkeld, C. G.: 11	Patty, D. L.: 1
Hardin, V. B.: 6	Powell, W. R.: 11
Hardy, M. P.: 10	Stafford, C. M. S.: 3
Harris, A. J.: *rev,* 6:842	Willig, S. N.: 10
Kasdon, L. M.: 4, 7	

[1682]

Holborn Reading Scale. Ages 5.5–11.0; 1948; 2 scores: word recognition, comprehension; A. F. Watts; George G. Harrap & Co. Ltd. [England]. *

For additional information and a review by Stanley

Graded Word Reading Test

Nisbet, see 5:635 (1 reference); for a review by C. M. Fleming, see 4:537.

REFERENCES THROUGH 1971

1. See 5:635.

2. Sampson, Olive C. "Written Composition at 10 Years as an Aspect of Linguistic Development." *Brit J Ed Psychol* 34: 143–50 Je '64. * (*PA* 39:4958)

3. Parker, D. H. H. "Musical Perception and Backwardness in Reading." *Ed Res* (England) 12(3):244–6 Je '70. * (*PA* 47: 1754)

CUMULATIVE NAME INDEX

Fleming, C. M.: *rev,* 4:537	Sampson, O. C.: 2
Nisbet, S.: *rev,* 5:635	Watts, A. F.: 1
Parker, D. H. H.: 3	

[1683]

*Neale Analysis of Reading Ability, Second Edition. Ages 6–13; 1957–66; NARA; 3 scores (accuracy, comprehension, rate of reading) plus 3 optional supplementary tests (names and sounds of letters, auditory discrimination through simple spelling, blending and recognition of syllables); Marie D. Neale; Macmillan Education Ltd. [England]. *

For additional information, reviews by M. Alan Brimer and Magdalen D. Vernon, and an excerpted review, see 6:843.

REFERENCES THROUGH 1971

1. Sampson, Olive C. "Reading Skill at Eight Years in Relation to Speech and Other Factors." *Brit J Ed Psychol* 32:12–7 F '62. *

2. Netley, C.; Rachman, S.; and Turner, R. K. "The Effect of Practice on Performance in a Reading Attainment Test." *Brit J Ed Psychol* 35:1–8 F '65. * (*PA* 39:10837)

3. Levy, Philip. "The Reliability of a Difference Between Two Scores: A Re-Examination of Assumptions." *J Clin Psychol* 22:357–9 Jl '66. * (*PA* 40:10632)

4. Gooch, Stan; Levy, Philip; and Pringle, M. L. Kellmer. "The Interaction of Four Status Variables and Measured Intelligence and Their Effect on Attainment in Two Junior Schools." *Ed Sci* (England) 2:37–46 O '67. *

5. Yule, William. "Predicting Reading Ages on Neale's Analysis of Reading Ability." *Brit J Ed Psychol* 37:252–5 Je '67. * (*PA* 41:15822)

6. Bookbinder, G. E. "Variations in Reading Test Norms." *Ed Res* (England) 12(2):99–105 F '70. *

7. Andrews, R. J., and Elkins, J. "The Use of the Neale Analysis of Reading Ability With Lower Grade Primary School Children." *Slow Learning Child* (Australia) 18(1):3–7 Mr '71. * (*PA* 47:1571)

CUMULATIVE NAME INDEX

Andrews, R. J.: 7	Pringle, M. L. K.: 4
Bookbinder, G. E.: 6	Rachman, S.: 2
Brimer, M. A.: *rev,* 6:843	Sampson, O. C.: 1
Elkins, J.: 7	Turner, R. K.: 2
Gooch, S.: 4	Vernon, M. D.: *rev,* 6:843
Levy, P.: 3–4	Yule, W.: 5
Netley, C.: 2	

[1684]

★Oral Reading Criterion Test. Reading level grades 1–7; 1971; ORCT; 3 reading level scores: independent, instructional, frustration; Edward Fry; Dreier Educational Systems, Inc. *

[1685]

Oral Word Reading Test. Ages 7–11; 1952; A. E. Fieldhouse; New Zealand Council for Educational Research [New Zealand]. *

For additional information and reviews by S. A. Rayner and D. K. Wheeler, see 5:674.

REFERENCES THROUGH 1971

1. Keats, J. A. "The Difficulty of Available Word Recognition Tests for Queensland Children." *Austral J Ed* 2:168–70 N '58. *

2. McCreary, J. R. "Reading Tests With Maori Children." *N Zeal J Ed Studies* 1(1–2):40–50 '66. *

CUMULATIVE NAME INDEX

Keats, J. A.: 1	Rayner, S. A.: *rev,* 5:674
McCreary, J. R.: 2	Wheeler, D. K.: *rev,* 5:674

[1686]

★**Reading Miscue Inventory.** Grades 1–7; 1972; RMI; "deviations" (errors) are called *"miscues* to suggest that they are not random errors but, in fact, are cued by the thought and language of the reader"; tape recorder must be used to record the examinee's reading of a 15–20 minute selection (difficult enough to produce at least 25 errors) and the immediate retelling of what he read; 6 scores: retelling score, percentage breakdown of oral reading errors with comprehension loss (none, partial, total), percentage breakdown of oral reading errors (excluding omissions) with sound similarity (high, some, none) to text, percentage breakdown of oral reading errors (excluding omissions) with graphic similarity (high, some, none) to text, percentage breakdown of oral reading errors (excluding omissions) with grammatical function similarity (identical, indeterminate, different) to text, percentage breakdown of 18 possible oral reading error patterns—corrected, grammatically acceptable, semantically acceptable—characterizing the examinee's ability (strength, partial strength, weakness, overcorrection) in "using the grammatical and meaning cueing systems"; Yetta M. Goodman and Carolyn L. Burke; Macmillan Publishing Co., Inc. *

REFERENCES THROUGH 1971

1. HITTLEMAN, DANIEL RICHARD. *The Readability of Subject Matter Material Re-Written on the Basis of Students' Oral Reading Mis-Cues.* Doctor's thesis, Hofstra University (Hempstead, N.Y.), 1971. (*DAI* 32:5534A)

CUMULATIVE NAME INDEX

Hittleman, D. R.: 1

[1687]

★**St. Lucia Graded Word Reading Test.** Grades 2–7; 1969; R. J. Andrews; Teaching and Testing Resources [Australia]. *

[1688]

Slosson Oral Reading Test. Grades 1–8 and high school; 1963; SORT; no manual; Richard L. Slosson; Slosson Educational Publications, Inc. *

For additional information, see 6:844.

REFERENCES THROUGH 1971

1. DUGGAN, MARY DIONYSIA. *A Study of the Relation Between the Slosson Reading and Intelligence Tests and Other Standardized Tests at the Second Grade Level.* Master's thesis, Cardinal Stritch College (Milwaukee, Wis.), 1968.
2. KEANY, MARY. *A Study of the Relation Between the Slosson Reading and Intelligence Tests and Other Standardized Tests at the Sixth Grade Level.* Master's thesis, Cardinal Stritch College (Milwaukee, Wis.), 1968.
3. KILDUFF, CAROL T. *A Study of the Relation Between the Slosson Reading and Intelligence Tests and Other Standardized Tests at the Fourth Grade Level.* Master's thesis, Cardinal Stritch College (Milwaukee, Wis.), 1969.
4. BRADDOCK, BETTY J., AND ROBINSON, RUTH V. *A Correlation of Slosson Oral Reading Test With the McCracken Word Recognition Subtest.* Master's thesis, Glassboro State College (Glassboro, N.J.), 1970.
5. STUHLER, AGNES M. *An Experimental Study of the Relation Between the Slosson Reading and Intelligence Tests and Other Standardized Tests at the First Grade Level.* Master's thesis, Cardinal Stritch College (Milwaukee, Wis.), 1970.

CUMULATIVE NAME INDEX

Braddock, B. J.: 4   Kilduff, C. T.: 3
Duggan, M. D.: 1   Robinson, R. V.: 4
Keany, M.: 2   Stuhler, A. M.: 5

[1689]

Standardized Oral Reading Check Tests. Grades 1–2, 2–4, 4–6, 6–8; 1923–55; 2 scores: rate, accuracy; William S. Gray; Bobbs-Merrill Co., Inc. *

For additional information and reviews by David H. Russell and Clarence R. Stone, see 2:1570 (1 reference).

REFERENCES THROUGH 1971

1. See 2:1570.
2. STONE, CLARENCE R. "Validity of Tests in Beginning Reading." *El Sch J* 43:361–5 F '43. * (*PA* 18:2605)
3. MACLATCHY, JOSEPHINE H. "An Oral-Reading Test as an Appraisal of Progress." *Ed Res B* 28:230–9 D 7 '49. *
4. ROBINSON, HELEN M. Chap. 5, "Visual Efficiency and Reading," pp. 90–112. In *Clinical Studies in Reading, I.* University of Chicago, Supplementary Educational Monographs, No. 68. Chicago, Ill.: University of Chicago Press, June 1949. Pp. xiv, 173. *
5. SPACHE, GEORGE. "A Comparison of Certain Oral Reading Tests." *J Ed Res* 43:441–52 F '50. * (*PA* 25:562)
6. ROBINSON, HELEN M. "Factors Related to Monocular and Binocular Reading Efficiency." *Am J Optom* 28:337–46 Jl '51. * (*PA* 26:2977)
7. SHEPHERD, EDWIN M. "Reading Efficiency of 809 Average School Children: The Effect of Reversal on Their Performance." *Am J Ophthal* 41:1029–39 Je '56. * (*PA* 31:5081)
8. HARTE, MARY LABOURE. *Anxiety and Defensiveness as Related to Measurable Intelligence and Scholastic Achievement of Selected Institutionalized Children.* Doctor's thesis, Fordham University (New York, N.Y.), 1966. (*DA* 27:2884A)

CUMULATIVE NAME INDEX

Allen, C. H.: 1   Russell, D. H.: *rev,* 2:1570
Camp, C.: 1   Shepherd, E. M.: 7
Harte, M. L.: 8   Spache, G.: 5
Maclatchy, J. H.: 3   Stone, C. R.: 2; *rev,* 2:1570
Robinson, H. M.: 4, 6

[1690]

Standardized Oral Reading Paragraphs. Grades 1–8; 1915; SORP; William S. Gray; Bobbs-Merrill Co., Inc. *

For additional information and reviews by David Kopel and Clarence R. Stone, see 2:1571 (7 references).

REFERENCES THROUGH 1971

1–7. See 2:1571.
8. GRAY, WILLIAM S. "A Co-operative Study in Reading in Eleven Cities of Northern Illinois." *El Sch J* 17:250–65 D '16. *
9. GRAY, WILLIAM S. "A Study of the Emphasis on Various Phases of Reading Instruction in Two Cities." *El Sch J* 17:178–86 N '16. *
10. GRAY, WILLIAM SCOTT. "Methods of Testing Reading, II." *El Sch J* 16:281–98 F '16. *
11. JUDD, CHARLES HUBBARD. *Measuring the Work of the Public Schools,* pp. 124–61, 255–74. Cleveland, Ohio: The Survey Committee of the Cleveland Foundation, 1916. Pp. 290. *
12. UHL, W. L. "The Use of the Results of Reading Tests as Bases for Planning Remedial Work." *El Sch J* 17:266–75 D '16. *
13. GRAY, CLARENCE TRUMAN. *Types of Reading Ability as Exhibited Through Tests and Laboratory Experiments,* pp. 17–32. Supplementary Educational Monographs, Vol. 1, No. 5. Chicago, Ill.: University of Chicago Press, 1917. Pp. xiv, 196. *
14. WHITE, CECILE W. "A Study in Reading (Gray Oral and Silent Reading Tests) in Indiana Cities." *Ann Conf Ed Meas* 4:102–13 '17. *
15. GRAY, W. S. "A Cooperative Study of Reading in Sixteen Cities in Indiana." *Indiana Univ Studies* 5(37):1–43 Je '18. *
16. McLEOD, L. S. "The Influence of Increasing Difficulty of Reading Material Upon Rate, Errors, and Comprehension in Oral Reading." *El Sch J* 18:523–32 Mr '18. *
17. MONROE, WALTER SCOTT. *Measuring the Results of Teaching,* pp. 39–41, *passim.* Boston, Mass.: Houghton Mifflin Co., 1918. Pp. xviii, 297. *
18. WILSON, G. M., AND HOKE, KREMER J. *How to Measure,* pp. 133–43. New York: Macmillan Co., 1920. Pp. vii, 285. *
19. GATES, ARTHUR I. "An Experimental and Statistical Study of Reading and Reading Tests." *J Ed Psychol* 12:303–14, 378–91, 445–64 S, O, N '21. *
20. WALLIN, J. E. WALLACE. *The Achievement of Subnormal Children in Standardized Educational Tests.* Miami University Bulletin Series 20, No. 7. Miami, Ohio: the University, 1922. Pp. 97. *
21. MONROE, WALTER SCOTT; DeVOSS, JAMES CLARENCE; AND KELLY, FREDERICK JAMES. *Educational Tests and Measurements, Revised Edition,* pp. 135–43. Boston, Mass.: Houghton Mifflin Co., 1924. Pp. xxvii, 521. *
22. HUDSON, ALVA. "Reading Achievement, Interests and Habits of Negro Women." *J Negro Ed* 1:367–73 O '32. * (*PA* 8:3690)
23. WEISENBURG, THEODORE; ROE, ANNE; AND McBRIDE, KATHARINE E. *Adult Intelligence: A Psychological Study of Test Performances.* New York: Commonwealth Fund, 1936. Pp. xiii, 155. * (*PA* 10:3771)
24. LAWSON, JOHN R., AND AVILA, DONALD. "Comparison of Wide Range Achievement Test and Gray Oral Reading Para-

graphs Reading Scores of Mentally Retarded Adults." *Percept & Motor Skills* 14:474 Je '62. * (*PA* 37:3581)

25. DENNEHY, JOHN N. *An Experimental Study of the Influence of the Time Factor Upon the Magnitude of Score on Diagnostic Oral Reading Inventories.* Master's thesis, Central Connecticut State College (New Britain, Conn.), 1966.

26. ELDER, RICHARD D. "Oral Reading Achievement of Scottish and American Children." *El Sch J* 71(4):216–30 Ja '71. *

CUMULATIVE NAME INDEX

Avila, D.: 24	Kopel, D.: *rev*, 2:1571
Buckingham, B. R.: 6	Lawson, J. R.: 24
Dennehy, J. N.: 25	McBride, K. E.: 23
DeVoss, J. C.: 21	McLeod, L. S.: 16
Dolch, E. W.: 6	Monroe, W. S.: 3, 17, 21
Elder, R. D.: 26	Payne, C. S.: 4
Gates, A. I.: 5, 19	Roe, A.: 23
Gray, C. T.: 13	Stone, C. R.: 7; *rev*, 2:1571
Gray, W. S.: 1–2, 8–10, 15	Uhl, W. L.: 12
Hoke, K. J.: 18	Wallin, J. E. W.: 20
Hudson, A.: 22	Weisenburg, T.: 23
Judd, C. H.: 11	White, C. W.: 14
Kelly, F. J.: 21	Wilson, G. M.: 18

[Out of Print Since TIP I]

Graded Word Reading Test, Test 1, R:176
Leavell Analytical Oral Reading Test, R:179, 5:672 (2 reviews)
Oral Diagnostic Test of Word-Analysis Skills, R:170, 5:673 (2 reviews)

READINESS

[1691]

The ABC Inventory to Determine Kindergarten and School Readiness. Entrants to kgn and grade 1; 1965; Normand Adair and George Blesch; Research Concepts. *

For additional information and a review by David P. Weikart, see 7:739 (2 references).

REFERENCES THROUGH 1971
1–2. See 7:739.
3. MANSON, PAUL DIRK. *Pre-Kindergarten Readiness Testing Program Characteristics in Southern Michigan School Districts Using the ABC Inventory.* Doctor's thesis, Michigan State University (East Lansing, Mich.), 1971. (*DAI* 32:5507A)
4. SCRANTON, GARY B. *A Comparison Study of the Hess School Readiness Scale With the ABC Inventory.* Master's thesis, Millersville State College (Millersville, Pa.), 1971.

CUMULATIVE NAME INDEX

Knoll, D. B.: 1	Scranton, G. B.: 4
Lee, R. E.: 2	Weikart, D. P.: *rev*, 7:739
Manson, P. D.: 3	

[1692]

The APELL Test: Assessment Program of Early Learning Levels. Ages 4.5–7; 1969; program for identifying educational deficiencies, suggesting remedial instruction, and retesting; 16 scores: 4 pre-reading (visual discrimination, auditory discrimination, letter names, total), 4 pre-math (attributes, number concepts, number facts, total), 7 language (nouns, pronouns, verbs, adjectives, plurals, prepositions, total), total; Eleanor V. Cochran and James L. Shannon; Edcodyne Corporation. *

For additional information, see 7:740.

REFERENCES THROUGH 1971
1. PROGER, BARTON B. "The APELL Test: A Review: Assessment Program of Early Learning Levels: A Review." *J Spec Ed* 5(2):195–8 su '71. *

CUMULATIVE NAME INDEX
Proger, B. B.: 1

[1693]

Academic Readiness and End of First Grade Progress Scales. Beginning of first grade, end of first grade; 1968–69; ratings by teachers in 14–15 areas:

motor, perceptual-motor (2 scores), persistence, memory, attention, number recognition (*a*) or computational arithmetic (*b*), counting, word recognition, comprehension (*b*), vocabulary, interest in curriculum, social, humor, emotional; 2 levels; Harold F. Burks; Arden Press. *

a) ACADEMIC READINESS SCALE: END OF KINDERGARTEN OR BEGINNING FIRST GRADE. 1968; ARS.

b) END OF FIRST GRADE PROGRESS SCALE. 1969; EFGPS; no manual.

For additional information, see 7:741.

REFERENCES THROUGH 1971
1. MONAHAN, MICHAEL TIMOTHY. *Prediction of First Grade Reading Scores Utilizing Burks' Academic Readiness Scale.* Master's thesis, California State University (Long Beach, Calif.), 1971.

CUMULATIVE NAME INDEX
Monahan, M. T.: 1

[1694]

American School Readiness Test, Revised. First grade entrants; 1941–64; 1964 test identical with tests copyrighted 1941 and 1955 except for changes in titles and sequence of subtests and slight changes in format and drawings; Willis E. Pratt, George W. Stouffer (1964 form), Robert V. Young (1941 and 1955 forms), and Carroll A. Whitmer (1941 and 1955 forms); Bobbs-Merrill Co., Inc. *

For additional information and reviews by Joan Bollenbacher and Helen M. Robinson, see 5:675 (3 references); for reviews by David H. Russell and Paul A. Witty, see 3:513.

REFERENCES THROUGH 1971
1–3. See 5:675.

CUMULATIVE NAME INDEX

Bollenbacher, J.: *rev*, 5:675	Robinson, H. M.: *rev*, 5:675
Delancy, E. O.: 3	Russell, D. H.: *rev*, 3:513
Pratt, W. E.: 1–2	Witty, P. A.: *rev*, 3:513

[1695]

★**Analysis of Readiness Skills: Reading and Mathematics.** Grades kgn–1; 1972, c1969–72; 6 scores: visual perception of letters, letter identification, mathematics (identification, counting, total), total; directions in English and Spanish; Mary C. Rodrigues, William H. Vogler, and James F. Wilson; Houghton Mifflin Co. *

[1696]

The Anton Brenner Developmental Gestalt Test of School Readiness. Ages 5–6; 1964; BGT; also called *Brenner Gestalt Test;* an optional rating scale provides 2 scores: achievement-ability, social-emotional; Anton Brenner; Western Psychological Services. *

For additional information and a review by Dennis J. Deloria, see 7:742 (8 references); see also 6:844a (8 references).

REFERENCES THROUGH 1971
1–8. See 6:844a.
9–16. See 7:742.

CUMULATIVE NAME INDEX

Brenner, A.: 1, 4, 9	Luttgen, G.: 6
Bushey, J. T.: 13	Ralph, J.: 7
Chasey, W. C.: 15	Ralph, J. S.: 5
Deloria, D. J.: *rev*, 7:742	Sandhu, S. S.: 8
Donnelly, F.: 11	Scandary, E. J.: 12
Falik, L. H.: 14	Svagr, V. B.: 10
Hepburn, A. W.: 11	Viewag, W. E.: 3
Hofmann, H.: 2	Worthington, J. D.: 16

[1697]

The Basic Concept Inventory, Field Research Edition. Preschool and kgn; 1967; BCI; school readiness; 4 scores: basic concepts, statement repetition and comprehension, pattern awareness, total; Siegfried E. Engelmann; Follett Publishing Co. *

For additional information and reviews by Boyd R. McCandless and James J. McCarthy, see 7:743 (2 references).

REFERENCES THROUGH 1971

1-2. See 7:743.

CUMULATIVE NAME INDEX

Espeseth, V. K.: 2 | McCarthy, J. J.: rev, 7:743
Hofmeister, A.: 2 | Sears, C. R.: 1
McCandless, B. R.: rev, 7:743

[1698]

Binion-Beck Reading Readiness Test for Kindergarten and First Grade. Grades kgn–1; 1945; Harriet Seay Binion and Roland L. Beck; Psychometric Affiliates. *

For additional information and reviews by Irving H. Anderson and Paul A. Witty, see 3:514 (1 reference).

REFERENCES THROUGH 1971

1. See 3:514.

CUMULATIVE NAME INDEX

Anderson, I. H.: rev, 3:514   Witty, P. A.: rev, 3:514
Binion, H. S.: 1

[1699]

Clymer-Barrett Prereading Battery. First grade entrants; 1966–69; CBPB; 4 scores: visual discrimination, auditory discrimination, visual-motor, total; short screening form consisting of 2 of the 6 subtests yields a single score; 1967 tests identical with tests copyrighted 1966; Theodore Clymer and Thomas C. Barrett; Personnel Press. *

For additional information and reviews by Roger Farr and Kenneth J. Smith, see 7:744 (2 references).

REFERENCES THROUGH 1971

1-2. See 7:744.
3. HALL, FRANCES POULSON. A Re-Evaluation of the Predictive Validity of the Clymer-Barrett Pre-Reading Battery. Master's thesis, University of Texas (Austin, Tex.), 1971.
4. MOE, ALDEN JOHN. An Investigation of the Uniqueness of Selected Auditory Discrimination Skills Among Kindergarten Children Enrolled in Two Types of Reading Readiness Programs. Doctor's thesis, University of Minnesota (Minneapolis, Minn.), 1971. (DAI 32:6295A)

CUMULATIVE NAME INDEX

Farr, R.: rev, 7:744   Moe, A. J.: 4
Hall, F. P.: 3   Smith, K. J.: rev, 7:744
Johnson, R. E.: 1-2

[1700]

The Contemporary School Readiness Test. First grade entrants; 1970; CSRT; Clara Elbert Sauer; Montana Reading Publications. *

For additional information and a review by Gerald G. Duffy, see 7:745.

[1701]

★Delco Readiness Test. First grade entrants; 1970; DRT; 3 scores: visual-motor, visual discrimination, total; Walter M. Rhoades; Delco Readiness Test. *

[1702]

Gates-MacGinitie Reading Tests: Readiness Skills. Grades kgn–1; 1939–69; revision of Gates Reading Readiness Tests; catalog uses the title Gates-MacGinitie Readiness Skills Test; 9 scores: listening comprehension, auditory discrimination, visual discrimination, following directions, letter recognition, visual-motor coordination, auditory blending, total, word recognition; Arthur I. Gates and Walter H. MacGinitie; Teachers College Press. *

For additional information and reviews by Paul Conrad Berg and Robert Dykstra, see 7:749 (17 references); see also 6:845 (1 reference); for a review by F. J. Schonell of the original edition, see 4:566; for reviews by Marion Monroe Cox and Paul A. Witty, see 3:516 (3 references); for excerpted reviews by Austin G. Schmidt and one other, see 2:1537 (6 references).

REFERENCES THROUGH 1971

1-5. See 2:1537.
6-8. See 3:516.
9. See 6:845.
10-26. See 7:749.
27. MILLER, FLORENCE BRESSON. Reading Readiness Tests: Predictors of Reading Achievement. Master's thesis, Illinois State University (Normal, Ill.), 1964.
28. MOE, ALDEN JOHN. An Investigation of the Uniqueness of Selected Auditory Discrimination Skills Among Kindergarten Children Enrolled in Two Types of Reading Readiness Programs. Doctor's thesis, University of Minnesota (Minneapolis, Minn.), 1971. (DAI 32:6295A)

CUMULATIVE NAME INDEX

Althouse, R. E.: 21   Jansky, J. J.: 16
Anastasiow, N.: 25   Johnson, C. I.: 26
Balow, I. H.: 9-10   Kerfoot, J. F.: 14
Barrett, T. C.: 12   Langford, W. S.: 16
Berg, P. C.: rev, 7:749   Loper, D. J.: 15
Bond, E.: 5   Miller, F. B.: 27
Bond, G. L.: 1, 5   Miller, W. D.: 19
Burke, A.: 2   Moe, A. J.: 28
Cox, M. M.: rev, 3:516   Norris, R. C.: 19
de Hirsch, K.: 16   Ohnmacht, F. W.: 22-3
Dykstra, R.: 13, 17; rev, 7: Olson, A. V.: 22-3
    749   Russell, D. H.: 5
Everhart, R. W.: 11   Schmidt, A. G.: exc, 2:1537
Farr, R.: 25   Schonell, F. J.: rev, 4:566
Flemming, C. W.: 2   Silberberg, M.: 20, 24
Furbee, C.: 11   Silberberg, M. C.: 18
Garrison, C. G.: 2   Silberberg, N.: 20, 24
Gates, A. I.: 1, 3-6, 8 Weaver, C. H.: 11
Halpin, A.: 5   Wilson, F. T.: 2, 7
Horan, K.: 5   Witty, P. A.: rev, 3:516
Iversen, I.: 20, 24

[1703]

★The Gesell Developmental Tests. Ages 5-10; 1964-71; GDT; readiness to start school; Frances L. Ilg, Louise Bates Ames, and Jacqueline Haines (Copy Form cards); Programs for Education. *

For additional information and excerpted reviews by L. J. Borstelmann and Edith Meyer Taylor, see 7:750 (5 references).

REFERENCES THROUGH 1971

1-5. See 7:750.
6. KIMBELL, VALERIE W., AND KNIGHT, DAVID W. "The Performance of Two Populations on Selected Readiness Tests." South J Ed Res 4(3):186-92 Jl '70. *
7. ANDREWS, ANN M. The Gesell Developmental Test as a Predictor of School Readiness. Doctor's thesis, University of Pennsylvania (Philadelphia, Pa.), 1971. (DAI 32:3082A)
8. JENSEN, ARTHUR R. "Do Schools Cheat Minority Children?" Ed Res (England) 14(1):3-28 N '71. * (PA 49:11953)
9. KAUFMAN, ALAN S. "Piaget and Gesell: A Psychometric Analysis of Tests Built From Their Tasks." Child Develop 42(5):1341-60 N '71. * (PA 48:4592)

CUMULATIVE NAME INDEX

Ames, L. B.: 1-3   Jensen, A. R.: 8
Andrews, A. M.: 7   Kaufman, A. S.: 5, 9
Apell, R. J.: 1   Kimbell, V. W.: 6
Borstelmann, L. J.: exc, 7:750   Knight, D. W.: 6
Hirst, W. E.: 4   Taylor, E. M.: exc, 7:750
Ilg, F. L.: 1-2

[1704]

Group Test of Reading Readiness: The Dominion Tests. Grades kgn, kgn–1; 1949-59; 2 editions; Ontario Institute for Studies in Education; distributed by Guidance Centre [Canada]. *

a) [LONG FORM.] Grades kgn–1; 1949-59; 6 scores: discrimination of objects-symbols-words, listening-remembering-observing, familiarity with word forms, memory for word forms, motor coordination, total.

b) [SHORT FORM.] Kgn; 1954-55. Out of print.

For additional information and a review by N. Dale Bryant, see 5:676.

REFERENCES THROUGH 1971

1. SAVAGE, H. W. "Validity of the Dominion Group Test of Reading Readiness—Short Form, and Differences Among Groups of Pupils Tested." *Ont J Ed Res* 2:63–70 O '59. *

CUMULATIVE NAME INDEX

Bryant, N. D.: *rev*, 5:676   Savage, H. W.: 1

[1705]

The Harrison-Stroud Reading Readiness Profiles.
Grades kgn–1; 1949–56; 7 scores: using symbols, making visual discriminations (2 scores), using the context, making auditory discriminations, using context and auditory clues, giving the names of letters; M. Lucile Harrison and James B. Stroud; Houghton Mifflin Co. *

For additional information and a review by S. S. Dunn, see 5:677 (2 references); for a review by William S. Gray, see 4:568.

REFERENCES THROUGH 1971

1–2. See 5:677.
3. DURKIN, DOLORES. "A Case-Study Approach Toward an Identification of Factors Associated With Success and Failure in Learning to Read." *Calif J Ed Res* 11:26–33 Ja '60. * (*PA* 34:8336)
4. RALPH, JEAN. "The Brenner-Gestalt Test as a Measure of Readiness for School," pp. 87–101. In *The Inter-Institutional Seminar in Child Development: Collected Papers, 1960.* Greenfield Village, Mich.: Education Department, Henry Ford Museum, [1961]. Pp. vi, 272. *
5. DYKSTRA, ROBERT. *The Relationship Between Selected Reading Readiness Measures of Auditory Discrimination and Reading Achievement at the End of First Grade.* Doctor's thesis, University of Minnesota (Minneapolis, Minn.), 1962. (*DA* 24:195)
6. RANDECKER, HELEN. *A Study to Determine if Chronological Age, Mental Age Scores, and Reading Readiness Tests Predict the Probable Achievement in Reading of First Grade Pupils.* Master's thesis, Wisconsin State University (Whitewater, Wis.), 1963.
7. KERFOOT, JAMES FLETCHER. *The Relationship of Selected Auditory and Visual Reading Readiness Measures to First Grade Reading Achievement and Second Grade Reading and Spelling Achievement.* Doctor's thesis, University of Minnesota (Minneapolis, Minn.), 1964. (*DA* 25:1747)
8. MILLER, FLORENCE BRESSON. *Reading Readiness Tests: Predictors of Reading Achievement.* Master's thesis, Illinois State University (Normal, Ill.), 1964.
9. THACKRAY, D. V. *The Relationship Between Reading Readiness and Reading Progress.* Master's thesis, University of London (London, England), 1964. (Abstract: *Brit J Ed Psychol* 35:252–4)
10. DYKSTRA, ROBERT. "Auditory Discrimination Abilities and Beginning Reading Achievement." *Read Res Q* 1:5–34 sp '66. * (*PA* 40:11011)
11. ASHWORTH, MARY G. *An Empirical Study of the Predictive Validity of the Harrison-Stroud Reading Readiness Profiles With First Grade Pupils in the Warwick Public Schools.* Master's thesis, University of Rhode Island (Kingston, R.I.), 1967.
12. BAGFORD, JACK. "Reading Readiness Scores and Success in Reading." *Read Teach* 21:324–8 Ja '68. * (*PA* 42:17640)
13. MIEZITIS, SOLVEIGA AUSMA. *An Exploratory Study of Divergent Production in Preschoolers.* Doctor's thesis, University of Toronto (Toronto, Ont., Canada), 1968. (*DAI* 30:589A)
14. REHMSTEDT, HELEN. *The Characteristics of Underachievers in Reading According to Potentials as Indicated by Reading Readiness Scores.* Master's thesis, Wisconsin State University (Platteville, Wis.), 1968.
15. SLOBODZIAN, EVELYN BIRDSALL. *The Relationship Between Certain Readiness Measures and Reading Achievement at Level One.* Doctor's thesis, Temple University (Philadelphia, Pa.), 1968. (*DA* 29:1053A)
16. FARR, ROGER, AND ANASTASIOW, NICHOLAS. *Tests of Reading Readiness and Achievement: A Review and Evaluation,* pp. 13–5. Newark, Del.: International Reading Association, 1969. Pp. iv, 51. *
17. EGELAND, BYRON; DI NELLO, MARIO; AND CARR, DONALD. "The Relationship of Intelligence, Visual-Motor, Psycholinguistic and Reading-Readiness Skills With Achievement." *Ed & Psychol Meas* 30(2):451–8 su '70. * (*PA* 45:3056)
18. MCNINCH, GEORGE. "Auditory Perceptual Factors and Measured First-Grade Reading Achievement." *Read Res Q* 6(4):472–92 su '71. * (*PA* 47:11769)
19. MOE, ALDEN JOHN. *An Investigation of the Uniqueness of Selected Auditory Discrimination Skills Among Kindergarten Children Enrolled in Two Types of Reading Readiness Programs.* Doctor's thesis, University of Minnesota (Minneapolis, Minn.), 1971. (*DAI* 32:6295A)

Group Test of Reading Readiness

CUMULATIVE NAME INDEX

Anastasiow, N.: 16   McNinch, G.: 18
Ashworth, M. G.: 11   Miezitis, S. A.: 13
Bagford, J.: 12   Miller, F. B.: 8
Carr, D.: 17   Moe, A. J.: 19
Di Nello, M.: 17   Mosbo, A. O.: 1
Dunn, S. S.: *rev*, 5:667 Ralph, J.: 4
Durkin, D.: 3   Randecker, H.: 6
Dykstra, R.: 5, 10   Rehmstedt, H.: 14
Egeland, B.: 17   Slobodzian, E. B.: 15
Farr, R.: 16   Spaulding, G.: 2
Gray, W. S.: *rev*, 4:568 Thackray, D. V.: 9
Kerfoot, J. F.: 7

[1706]

★**Initial Survey Test.** First grade entrants; 1970–72; IST; skills for "success in beginning primary learning"; 7 scores: language meanings, auditory ability, visual ability, letter recognition, sound-letter relationships, mathematics, total; first five subtests originally published under the title *Initial Reading Survey Test;* Marion Monroe, John C. Manning, Joseph M. Wepman, and E. Glenadine Gibb; Scott, Foresman & Co. *

[1707]

★**An Inventory of Primary Skills.** Grades kgn–1; 1970; IPS; administered by parent; 20 scores: self information, body identification, body spatial relations, copying designs, alphabet printing, writing numbers, symbol matching, sentence copying, counting, basic arithmetic, copying house, draw-a-man, sight vocabulary, paragraph reading, alphabet knowledge, number knowledge, class concepts, position in space concepts, descriptive concepts, total; no manual; Robert E. Valett; Lear Seigler Inc./Fearon Publishers. *

[1708]

★**Kindergarten Behavioural Index: A Screening Technique for Reading Readiness.** Grades kgn–1; 1972; KBI; behavior checklist; 38 scores: self identity, handedness, directionality (3 scores), visual-motor coordination (7 scores), rhythm, speech, language structure (2 scores), language sequencing (5 scores), sequential memory (4 scores), language association, behaviour (8 scores), attention (3 scores), total; Enid M. Banks; Australian Council for Educational Research [Australia]. *

[1709]

Kindergarten Evaluation of Learning Potential.
Kgn; 1963–69; KELP; prediction of school success based upon the learning performance on KELP items presented as regular instructional activities throughout the kindergarten year; 4 scores: association learning, conceptualization, creative self-expression, total; John A. R. Wilson and Mildred C. Robeck; Webster Division, McGraw-Hill Book Co., Inc. *

For additional information and an excerpted review by Walter R. Borg, see 7:751 (5 references).

REFERENCES THROUGH 1971

1–5. See 7:751.

CUMULATIVE NAME INDEX

Blackman, C. T.: 4   Meredith, W. V.: 5
Borg, W. R.: *exc*, 7:751   Robeck, M. C.: 1–3
Coffey, L. W.: 5   Wilson, J. A. R.: 1–3

[1710]

★**LRS Seriation Test.** Ages 4–6; 1968; may be used alone or with instructional materials in The Learning Readiness System: Classification and Seriation Kit; 6 scores: 5 factor scores, total; Ralph Scott, Jerald Nelson, and Ann Mary Dunbar; Harper & Row, Publishers, Inc. *

REFERENCES THROUGH 1971

1. SCOTT, RALPH. "Perceptual Readiness as a Predictor of Success in Reading." *Read Teach* 22:36–9 O '68. *

2. SCOTT, RALPH. "Ceiling Level as a Factor in Assessing Disadvantaged Children's Abilities." *Psychol Sch* 6(3):279–82 Jl '69. * (*PA* 44:4172)
3. SCOTT, RALPH. "Perceptual Skills, General Intellectual Ability, Race, and Later Reading Achievement." *Read Teach* 23(7):660–8 Ap '70. * (*PA* 45:3069)

CUMULATIVE NAME INDEX

Scott, R.: 1–3

[1711]

Lee-Clark Reading Readiness Test. Grades kgn–1; 1931–62; LCRRT; 4 scores: letter symbols, concepts, word symbols, total; 1962 test identical with tests copyrighted 1943 and 1951 except for format and, in concepts subtest, revision of all art work and one-half of items; J. Murray Lee and Willis W. Clark; CTB/McGraw-Hill. *

For additional information and a review by Paul Conrad Berg, see 7:752 (15 references) ; see also 6:846 (9 references) ; for a review by James R. Hobson of an earlier edition, see 5:678; for reviews by Marion Monroe Cox and David H. Russell, see 3:517.

REFERENCES THROUGH 1971

1–9. See 6:846.
10–24. See 7:752.
25. PETTY, MARY CLARE. "An Experimental Study of Certain Factors Influencing Reading Readiness." *J Ed Psychol* 30:215–30 Mr '39. * (*PA* 13:4885)
26. PECK, L., AND MCGLOTHLIN, L. E. "Children's Information and Success in First-Grade Reading." *J Ed Psychol* 31:653–64 D '40. * (*PA* 15:2804)
27. POTTER, MURIEL CATHERINE. "Perception of Symbol Orientation and Early Reading Success." *Teach Col Contrib Ed* 939:1–69 '49. * (*PA* 24:6511)
28. MILLER, FLORENCE BRESSON. *Reading Readiness Tests: Predictors of Reading Achievement.* Master's thesis, Illinois State University (Normal, Ill.), 1964.
29. FIFE, JANICE. *A Longitudinal Study of Relationships Among Reading Readiness Test Scores, Reading and Over-All Achievement Test Scores, and Intelligence Quotients.* Master's thesis, Brigham Young University (Provo, Utah), 1965.
30. AVRIL, DOROTHY VERNON. *An Investigation of the Relationship Between Reading Readiness Test Scores and Reading Achievement in First Grade.* Master's thesis, Glassboro State College (Glassboro, N.J.), 1966.
31. REHMSTEDT, HELEN. *The Characteristics of Underachievers in Reading According to Potentials as Indicated by Reading Readiness Scores.* Master's thesis, Wisconsin State University (Platteville, Wis.), 1968.
32. GUENTHER, GEORGIA S. *A Comparative Analysis of the Predictive Validity of Two Reading Readiness Tests and Their Subtests.* Master's thesis, Indiana University of Pennsylvania (Indiana, Pa.), 1969.
33. BLANTON, WILLIAM ELGIT. *The Interactive Effects of Perceptual Centration and Decentration on Reading Readiness and Reading Achievement at the First Grade Level.* Doctor's thesis, University of Georgia (Athens, Ga.), 1970. (*DAI* 31:5837A)
34. DICK, ROBERT MARCUS, II. *Screening Identification of First Grade Problems in an American Indian Population.* Doctor's thesis, University of North Carolina (Chapel Hill, N.C.), 1971. (*DAI* 32:1209B)
35. FRIEDRICHS, THOMAS DONNELLY. *Prediction of First Grade Teachers' Ratings and Objective Achievement From Ability and Biographical Data.* Doctor's thesis, University of North Carolina (Chapel Hill, N.C.), 1971. (*DAI* 32:1211B)
36. LOWELL, ROBERT E. "Reading Readiness Factors as Predictors of Success in First Grade Reading." *J Learn Dis* 4(10):563–7 D '71. * (*PA* 47:11782)
37. SCRUGGS, ALLIE W. *The Effect of the Fall River and Lowell Head Start Programs on Behavioral Characteristics Associated With Lower Socio-Economic Class Preschool Children.* Doctor's thesis, Boston University (Boston, Mass.), 1971. (*DAI* 32:1949A)

CUMULATIVE NAME INDEX

Anastasiow, N.: 21
Avril, D. V.: 30
Barkley, M. J.: 16
Berg, P. C.: *rev,* 7:752
Blanton, W. E.: 33
Bridges, J. S.: 23
Clark, W. W.: 1
Cox, M. M.: *rev,* 3:517
Cunningham, W.: 11
Dick, R. M.: 34
Dobson, J. C.: 8–9
Farr, R.: 21
Fife, J.: 29
Fitzgibbon, N. H.: 18
Friedrichs, T. D.: 35
Gale, D. F.: 12
Guenther, G. S.: 32
Henig, M. S.: 3
Hernandez, P. E.: 10
Hobson, J. R.: *rev,* 5:678
Hopkins, K. D.: 9, 22
Koppitz, E. M.: 5
Lee, D. M.: 1
Lee, J. M.: 1
Lessler, K.: 23
Lindy, J.: 24
Lloyd, B. A.: 13
Lloyd, R.: 13
Lowell, R. E.: 36
McGlothlin, L. E.: 26
Mardis, V.: 5
Merrill, J. D.: 17
Miller, F. B.: 28
Moreau, M.: 4
Olson, A. V.: 18
Olson, N. H.: 14, 19
Panther, E. E.: 15
Parsley, K. M.: 6–7
Peck, L.: 26
Petty, M. C.: 25
Potter, M. C.: 27
Powell, M.: 6–7
Rehmstedt, H.: 31
Russell, D. H.: *rev,* 3:517
Schoeninger, D. W.: 23
Schrager, J.: 24
Scruggs, A. W.: 37
Seidel, H. E.: 16
Sitkei, E. G.: 22
Slobodzian, E. B.: 20
Stephens, T.: 5
Stith, D.: 16
Wilmore, W. W.: 2

[1712]

Lippincott Reading Readiness Test (Including Readiness Check List). Grades kgn–1; 1965–73; 1973 test identical with test copyrighted 1965 except for typeface and cover page; Pierce H. McLeod; J. B. Lippincott Co. *

For additional information and a review by Edward R. Sipay, see 7:753 (1 reference).

REFERENCES THROUGH 1971

1. See 7:753.

CUMULATIVE NAME INDEX

Norfleet, M. A.: 1   Sipay, E. S.: *rev,* 7:753

[1713]

McHugh-McParland Reading Readiness Test. Grades kgn–1; 1966–68; 5 scores: rhyming words, beginning sounds, visual discrimination, identifying letters, total; 1968 test identical with test copyrighted 1966; Walter J. McHugh and Myrtle McParland; Cal-State Bookstore. *

For additional information and reviews by Rebecca C. Barr and Edward R. Sipay, see 7:754.

[1714]

The Macmillan Reading Readiness Test, Revised Edition. First grade entrants; 1965–70; 6 or 7 scores: rating scale, visual discriminaton, auditory discrimination, vocabulary and concepts, letter names, total for tests 1–5; visual-motor (optional), total for tests 1–6; Albert J. Harris and Edward R. Sipay; Macmillan Publishing Co., Inc. *

For additional information, see 7:755.

[1715]

Maturity Level for School Entrance and Reading Readiness. Grades kgn–1; 1950–59; revision of *School Readiness Inventory;* behavior checklist completed by teachers; 1959 test is essentially a combination of items from the two forms of the original 1950 edition; 2 scores: maturity level, reading readiness; Katharine M. Banham; American Guidance Service, Inc. *

For additional information, see 6:847; for a review by David H. Russell of the original edition, see 4:572.

REFERENCES THROUGH 1971

1. BANHAM, KATHARINE M. "Maturity Level for Reading Readiness: A Check List for the Use of Teachers and Parents as a Supplement to Reading Readiness Tests." *Ed & Psychol Meas* 18:371–5 su '58. * (*PA* 33:11013)
2. TENHOFF, MARVIN LE ROY. *Conditions Associated With Readiness for School Entrance at Selected Ages.* University of Minnesota (Minneapolis, Minn.), 1962. (*DA* 24:150)
3. BILKA, LOISANNE PFEIFER. *An Evaluation of the Predictive Value of Certain Reading Readiness Measures as Related to Method of Instruction, Sex, and Mental Age.* Doctor's thesis, University of Pittsburgh (Pittsburgh, Pa.), 1970 (*DAI* 31:5922A)

CUMULATIVE NAME INDEX

Banham, K. M.: 1   Russell, D. H.: *rev,* 4:572
Bilka, L. P.: 3   Tenhoff, M. L.: 2

[1716]

Metropolitan Readiness Tests. Grades kgn–1; 1933–69; MRT; 7 or 8 scores: word meaning, listening, matching, alphabet, numbers, copying, total, draw-a-man (optional); Gertrude H. Hildreth, Nellie L. Griffiths, and Mary E. McGauvran; Harcourt Brace Jovanovich, Inc. *

For additional information and reviews by Robert Dykstra and Harry Singer, see 7:757 (124 references); for a review by Eric F. Gardner and an excerpted review by Fay Griffith, see 4:570 (3 references); for a review by Irving H. Anderson of the original edition, see 3:518 (5 references); for a review by W. J. Osburn, see 2:1552 (10 references).

REFERENCES THROUGH 1971

1–10. See 2:1552.
11–15. See 3:518.
16–18. See 4:570.
19–142. See 7:757.
143. WILSON, FRANK T. "Correlation of Information With Other Abilities and Traits in Grade I." *El Sch J* 37:295–301 D '36. * (*PA* 11:2478)
144. GRANT, ALBERT. "An Analysis of the Number Knowledge of First-Grade Pupils According to Levels of Intelligence." *J Exp Ed* 7:63–6 S '38. * (*PA* 13:1672)
145. WILMORE, WALDO W. *Relative Validity of Three Group Readiness Tests in Predicting Reading Achievement.* Master's thesis, University of Kansas (Lawrence, Kan.), 1939. (Abstract: *Univ Kan B Ed* 4:68)
146. HAMMOND, SARAH LOU, AND SKIPPER, DORA S. "Factors Involved in the Adjustment of Children Entering First Grade." *J Ed Res* 56:89–95 O '62. *
147. LOCKHART, HAZEL SHIERRY. *The Relationship of Personality With Reading Readiness.* Master's thesis, Illinois State University (Normal, Ill.), 1964.
148. MILLER, FLORENCE BRESSON. *Reading Readiness Tests: Predictors of Reading Achievement.* Master's thesis, Illinois State University (Normal, Ill.), 1964.
149. DICKERSON, MARJORIE KRAFT. *Readiness Test: Predictor of Reading Achievement in the Primary Grades.* Master's thesis, Illinois State University (Normal, Ill.), 1965.
150. DITTMAR, NANCY SIZEMORE. *Auditory Discrimination: Its Relation to Reading Achievement and Intelligence.* Master's thesis, Illinois State University (Normal, Ill.), 1965.
151. OSBORNE, AARON. *Predicting the Success of First Grade Children.* Master's thesis, East Tennessee State University (Johnson City, Tenn.), 1965.
152. ADAMS, MAMIE JOSEPHINE CUSTER. *Reading Readiness Factors and Reading Achievement of First-Grade Children.* Master's thesis, Illinois State University (Normal, Ill.), 1966.
153. FOSTER, JERRY D. *Academic Readiness and Physical Fitness of Kindergarten Boys and Girls.* Master's thesis, Northern Illinois University (DeKalb, Ill.), 1966.
154. GARRISON, THERESA MAE. *Reading Readiness Factors: Relationship to Reading Achievement.* Master's thesis, Illinois State University (Normal, Ill.), 1966.
155. HADLEY, BONNIE D. *Prediction of Third Grade Arithmetic Achievement Based on First Grade Readiness Tests.* Master's thesis, University of Louisville (Louisville, Ky.), 1966.
156. HAMMOND, FRANCES VIRGINIA. *Reading Readiness: Relationship in Kindergarten With Beginning First-Grade.* Master's thesis, Illinois State University (Normal, Ill.), 1966.
157. COHEN, ISABELLA. "Reading Readiness and Head Start Graduate." *Grad Res Ed & Related Discip* 4:66–80 w '68. *
158. GOOLSBY, THOMAS M. "Culturally Deprived Head Start Subjects' Reading Readiness After Training in Listening." *J Learn Dis* 1:561–4 O '68. * (*PA* 45:3079)
159. GORALSKI, PATRICIA J., AND KERL, JOYCE M. "Kindergarten Teacher Aides and Reading Readiness Minneapolis Public Schools." *J Exp Ed* 37:34–8 w '68. *
160. SPOMER, ESTHER E. *The Comparative Ability of a Test of Visual Perception and Measures of a Readiness Test of Kindergarten Children.* Master's thesis, Fort Hays Kansas State College (Hays, Kan.), 1968.
161. BUTLER, EVELYN AHLEEN (WINETEER). *The Prediction of Success in Reading by Sixth Grade With the Use of the Reading Readiness Test.* Master's thesis, University of Idaho (Moscow, Idaho), 1969.
162. GUENTHER, GEORGIA S. *A Comparative Analysis of the Predictive Validity of Two Reading Readiness Tests and Their Subtests.* Master's thesis, Indiana University of Pennsylvania (Indiana, Pa.), 1969.
163. KELLY, DENNIS E. *Predicting Reading Readiness Using Questionnaires.* Master's thesis, Glassboro State College (Glassboro, N.J.), 1969.
164. BENTZ, DARRELL DEAN. *A Study of the Effect of Perceptual and Language Training Upon Kindergarten Children Reading Readiness Performance.* Doctor's thesis, Oklahoma State University (Stillwater, Okla.), 1970. (*DAI* 31:5922A)

165. BILKA, LOISANNE PFEIFER. *An Evaluation of the Predictive Value of Certain Reading Readiness Measures as Related to Method of Instruction, Sex, and Mental Age.* Doctor's thesis, University of Pittsburgh (Pittsburgh, Pa.), 1970. (*DAI* 31:5922A)
166. BORDEAUX, ELIZABETH ANN. *Auditory and Visual Readiness Factors Related to Reading Achievement in First Grade Based on Three Methods of Instruction.* Doctor's thesis, University of North Carolina (Chapel Hill, N.C.), 1970. (*DAI* 31:5924A)
167. BUDDE, ELAINE HELEN. *The Relationship Between Performance of Kindergarten Children on Selected Motor Tests and the Metropolitan Readiness Tests—Otis-Lennon Mental Ability Test.* Doctor's thesis, University of Wisconsin (Madison, Wis.), 1970. (*DAI* 31:5820A)
168. COULTHARD, DOROTHY BLAKE. *Metropolitan Readiness Tests as Predictor for Success in Reading Achievement.* Master's thesis, Drake University (Des Moines, Iowa), 1970.
169. FRESHOUR, FRANK W. *The Effects of a Parent Education Program on Reading Readiness and Achievement of Disadvantaged First Grade Negro Children.* Doctor's thesis, University of Florida (Gainesville, Fla.), 1970. (*DAI* 32:91A)
170. HIERS, MARGARET HANES. *A Comparison of the Readiness Test Performance of a Group of Primary-Level Educable Mentally Retarded Children Instructed on Visual-Motor Perceptual Tasks and a Comparable Group Receiving No Prescribed Instruction.* Doctor's thesis, University of Georgia (Athens, Ga.), 1970. (*DAI* 31:6440A)
171. MITCHELL, KATHARINE E. *An Early Predictive Test and Its Relationship to Junior High School Achievement.* Doctor's thesis, Syracuse University (Syracuse, N.Y.), 1970. (*DAI* 32:97A)
172. RAGSDALE, NANCY L. *Relationship of Reading Readiness and the Frostig Visual Perception Test.* Master's thesis, Illinois State University (Normal, Ill.), 1970.
173. SLAUGHTER, DIANA T. "Parental Potency and the Achievements of Inner-City Black Children." *Am J Orthopsychiatry* 40(3):433–40 Ap '70. * (*PA* 45:8989)
174. WALKER, PAUL RANDOLPH. *The Validity of Syntax as a Predictor of Reading Success.* Doctor's thesis, University of Maine (Orono, Me.), 1970. (*DAI* 32:682A)
175. WOOD, MILDRED HOPE. *A Longitudinal Study of the Effectiveness of Certain Kindergarten Tests in Predicting Reading Achievement, School Failure, and the Need for Special Services.* Doctor's thesis, Indiana University (Bloomington, Ind.), 1970. (*DAI* 31:5683A)
176. ANDREWS, ANN M. *The Gesell Developmental Test as a Predictor of School Readiness.* Doctor's thesis, University of Pennsylvania (Philadelphia, Pa.), 1971. (*DAI* 32:3082A)
177. ASPRIDY, CHRISOULA. *Kindergarten Block Building Ratings Compared to Self-Concept and Readiness Scores as Predictors of First Grade Reading Achievement.* Doctor's thesis, University of Rochester (Rochester, N.Y.), 1971. (*DAI* 32:2997A)
178. BICKLEY, A. C.; DINNAN, JAMES A.; AND JONES, J. P. "Oral Associates and Reading Readiness." *Yearb Nat Read Conf* 20:14–6 '71. *
179. BLACK, BOB GENE. *Determining the Predictive Value of Selected Measures for First Grade Reading Success.* Doctor's thesis, North Texas State University (Denton, Tex.), 1971. (*DAI* 32:3548A)
180. BURTON, JANICE H. *The Predictive Value of the Metropolitan Readiness Tests for First Grade Readiness for Selected Groups of Children in the Johnson City, Tenn., Public Schools.* Master's thesis, East Tennessee State University (Johnson City, Tenn.), 1971.
181. CLAPP, BEECHER E. *A Study of the Relationships Between a Measure of School Readiness and Subsequent Performance on Reading Tests.* Master's thesis, University of Tennessee (Knoxville, Tenn.), 1971.
182. EVANS, MILDRED MAY BAILEY. *The Effects of a Physical Education Program on Auditory Discrimination Ability, Verbal and Non-Verbal, of Kindergarten Children.* Doctor's thesis, Michigan State University (East Lansing, Mich.), 1971. (*DAI* 32:3073A)
183. FRIEDRICHS, THOMAS DONNELLY. *Prediction of First Grade Teachers' Ratings and Objective Achievement From Ability and Biographical Data.* Doctor's thesis, University of North Carolina (Chapel Hill, N.C.), 1971. (*DAI* 32:1211B)
184. FULK, BARBARA F. *Correlations Between Scores of the Metropolitan Readiness Tests of Matching and Copying and the Stanford Achievement Tests Primary I Battery of Word Reading, Paragraph Meaning, Vocabulary, and Word Study Skills.* Master's thesis, Texas Woman's University (Denton, Tex.), 1971.
185. GAMSKY, NEAL R., AND LLOYD, FAYE WILLIAMS. "A Longitudinal Study of Visual Perceptual Training and Reading Achievement." *J Ed Res* 64(10):451–4 Jl–Ag '71. * (*PA* 47:9831)
186. GEIS, ROBLEY. *The Prediction and Prevention of Reading Failure.* Doctor's thesis, University of Southern California (Los Angeles, Calif.), 1971. (*DAI* 32:5611A)
187. HAMMILL, DONALD, AND WIEDERHOLT, J. LEE. "Appropriateness of the Metropolitan Tests in an Economically De-

prived, Urban Neighborhood." *Psychol Sch* 8(1):49–50 Ja '71. * (*PA* 46:7446)

188. LOWELL, ROBERT E. "Reading Readiness Factors as Predictors of Success in First Grade Reading." *J Learn Dis* 4(10): 563–7 D '71. * (*PA* 47:11782)

189. MCKINNEY, JAMES D. "Factor Analytic Study of the Developmental Test of Visual Perception and the Metropolitan Readiness Test." *Percept & Motor Skills* 33(3):1331–4 D '71. * (*PA* 48:1653)

190. MASON, GEORGE E., AND BLANTON, WILLIAM E. "Semantic Constructs and Beginning Reading." *Yearb Nat Read Conf* 19(1):39–45 '71. *

191. PROGER, BARTON B.; McGOWAN, JOHN R.; BAYUK, ROBERT J., JR.; MANN, LESTER; TREVORROW, RUTH L.; AND MASSA, EDWARD. "The Relative Predictive and Construct Validities of the Otis-Lennon Mental Ability Test, the Lorge-Thorndike Intelligence Test, and the Metropolitan Readiness Test in Grades Two and Four: A Series of Multivariate Analyses." *Ed & Psychol Meas* 31(2):529–38 su '71. *

192. SEDA, MARIA S. A., AND MICHAEL, JOAN J. "The Concurrent Validity of the Sprigle School Screening Readiness Test for a Sample of Preschool and Kindergarten Children." *Ed & Psychol Meas* 31(4):995–7 w '71. * (*PA* 48:1660)

193. SHELDON, HARRY JAY. *An Investigation of Syntactical Ability and Vocabulary Knowledge of First Graders as Related to Reading and Vocabulary Achievement as Measured by the Stanford Achievement Test.* Doctor's thesis, University of Iowa (Iowa City, Iowa), 1971. (*DAI* 32:1201A)

194. SPENCE, ALLYN G.; MISHRA, SHITALA P.; AND GHOZEIL, SUSAN. "Home Language and Performance on Standardized Tests." *El Sch J* 71(6): 309–13 Mr '71. * (*PA* 47:2655)

195. STEVENS, FRANCES ANN BENNETT. *Predicting Third Grade Reading Achievement for Mexican-American Students From Lower Socioeconomic Levels.* Doctor's thesis, New Mexico State University (University Park, N.M.), 1971. (*DAI* 32: 5480A)

196. WHITCRAFT, CAROL JONES. *Levels of Generative Syntax and Linguistic Performance of Young Children From Standard and Non-Standard English Language Environments.* Doctor's thesis, University of Texas (Austin, Tex.), 1971. (*DAI* 32: 5644A)

197. WILLIAMS, ROBERT. "Testing for Number Readiness: Application of the Piagetian Theory of the Child's Development of the Concept of Number." *J Ed Res* 64(9):394–6 My–Je '71. * (*PA* 47:6489)

CUMULATIVE NAME INDEX

[1717]

Murphy-Durrell Reading Readiness Analysis. First grade entrants; 1949–65, c1947–65; revision of *Murphy-Durrell Diagnostic Reading Readiness Test;* 6 scores: phonemes, letter names (capitals, lower case, total), learning rate, total; Helen A. Murphy and Donald D. Durrell; Harcourt Brace Jovanovich, Inc. *

For additional information and reviews by Rebecca C. Barr and Harry Singer, see 7:758 (10 references); for reviews by Joan Bollenbacher and S. S. Dunn of the earlier edition, see 5:679 (2 references); see also 4:571 (2 references).

REFERENCES THROUGH 1971

1–2. See 4:571.
3–4. See 5:679.
5–14. See 7:758.
15. BILKA, LOISANNE PFEIFER. *An Evaluation of the Predictive Value of Certain Reading Readiness Measures as Related to Method of Instruction, Sex, and Mental Age.* Doctor's thesis,

University of Pittsburgh (Pittsburgh, Pa.), 1970. (*DAI* 31: 5922A)

16. BORDEAUX, ELIZABETH ANN. *Auditory and Visual Readiness Factors Related to Reading Achievement in First Grade Based on Three Methods of Instruction.* Doctor's thesis, University of North Carolina (Chapel Hill, N.C.), 1970. (*DAI* 31: 5924A)

17. MOTTOLA, RICHARD ALBERT. *The Development of Auditory Discrimination Skills in Kindergarten Children.* Doctor's thesis, University of Connecticut (Storrs, Conn.), 1970. (*DAI* 31: 6284A)

18. GRUEN, RONALD STEVEN. *Prediction of End-of-Year Reading Achievement for First and Third Grade Pupils.* Doctor's thesis, Pennsylvania State University (University Park, Pa.), 1971. (*DAI* 32:6198A)

19. LOWELL, ROBERT E. "Reading Readiness Factors as Predictors of Success in First Grade Reading." *J Learn Dis* 4(10): 563–7 D '71. * (*PA* 47:11782)

20. NEWMAN, ANABEL POWELL. *Longitudinal Study of Pupils Who Were Underachieving in Reading in First Grade.* Doctor's thesis, State University of New York (Buffalo, N.Y.), 1971. (*DAI* 32:2313A)

21. O'PIELA, JOAN MARIE. *Identification of Predictor Variables of Success in First Grade Reading in Culturally Disadvantaged Inner-City Children Who Have Had a Preschool Experience.* Doctor's thesis, Wayne State University (Detroit, Mich.), 1971. (*DAI* 32:6109A)

CUMULATIVE NAME INDEX

Anastasiow, N.: 13	Kerfoot, J. F.: 7
Barr, R. C.: *rev*, 7:758	Lowell, R. E.: 19
Beauchamp, J. M.: 10	Mitchell, B. C.: 12
Biggy, M. V.: 2	Mottola, R. A.: 17
Bilka, L. P.: 15	Murphy, H. A.: 1
Bollenbacher, J.: *rev*, 5:679	Newman, A. P.: 20
Bond, G. L.: 11	Nicholson, A.: 3–4
Bordeaux, E. A.: 16	Noonan, J. D.: 5
Dunn, S. S.: *rev*, 5:679	O'Piela, J. M.: 21
Dykstra, R.: 6, 9, 11	Singer, H.: *rev*, 7:758
Farr, R.: 13	Ward, B. J.: 14
Gruen, R. S.: 18	Weeks, E. E.: 8

[1718]

Parent Readiness Evaluation of Preschoolers. Ages 3–9 to 5–8; 1968–69; PREP; administered by parent; 17 scores: verbal (general information, comprehension, opposites, identification, verbal association, verbal description, listening, language, total), performance (concepts, motor co-ordination, visual-motor association, visual interpretation, auditory memory, visual memory, total), total; A. Edward Ahr and Benita Simons (handbook); Priority Innovations, Inc. *

For additional information and reviews by S. Alan Cohen, Robert E. Valett, and David P. Weikart, see 7:759.

[1719]

★**Pre-Reading Assessment Kit.** Grades kgn–1; 1971–72; PRAK; 18 tests in 4 areas; Ontario Institute for Studies in Education; CTB/McGraw-Hill Ryerson Ltd. [Canada]. *
a) LISTENING UNIT. 6 tests: Rhyming (2 tests), Beginning Sounds (2 tests), Ending Sounds (2 tests).
b) SYMBOL PERCEPTION UNIT. 4 tests: Visual Discrimination (2 tests), Recognition of Letters, Recognition of Words.
c) EXPERIENCE VOCABULARY UNIT. 2 tests.
d) COMPREHENSION UNIT. 6 tests: Classification (2 tests), Emotional Response (2 tests), Cause-Effect and Prediction (2 tests).

[1720]

★**Prereading Expectancy Screening Scales.** First grade entrants; 1973; PRESS; predicting reading problems in beginning readers; 4 scores: visual sequencing, visual/auditory spatial, auditory sequencing, letter identification; Lawrence C. Hartlage and David G. Lucas; Psychologists and Educators, Inc. *

[1721]

Pre-Reading Screening Procedures. First grade entrants of average or superior intelligence; 1968–69;

PSP; identification of children "who make errors in perception and recall of language symbols which often indicate a Specific Language Disability, or dyslexia"; 7 or 8 scores: visual (discrimination of letter forms, discrimination of word forms, visual perception memory), visual-motor (copying, visual perception memory), auditory discrimination, letter knowledge, individual auditory tests (optional); Beth H. Slingerland; Educators Publishing Service, Inc. *

For additional information and reviews by Colleen B. Jamison and Roy A. Kress, see 7:732 (1 reference).

REFERENCES THROUGH 1971

1. See 7:732.
2. OLIPHANT, GENEVIEVE G. *A Study of Factors Involved in Early Identification of Specific Language Disability (Dyslexia).* Doctor's thesis, United States International University (San Diego, Calif.), 1969. (*DAI* 31:305A)

CUMULATIVE NAME INDEX

Jamison, C. B.: *rev*, 7:732	Oliphant, G. G.: 2
Kress, R. A.: *rev*, 7:732	Slingerland, B. H.: 1

[1722]

★**Preschool and Kindergarten Performance Profile.** Preschool and kgn; 1970; PKPP; ratings by teachers; 11 scores: social (interpersonal relations, emotional behavior, safety), intellectual (communication, basic concepts, perceptual development, imagination and creative expression), physical (self-help, gross motor skills, fine visual motor skills), total; Alfred J. DiNola, Bernard P. Kaminsky, and Allan E. Sternfeld; Educational Performance Associates. *

[1723]

Primary Academic Sentiment Scale. Ages 4–4 to 7–3; 1968; PASS; motivation for learning and level of maturity and parental independence; 2 scores: sentiment, dependency; Glen Robbins Thompson; Priority Innovations, Inc. *

For additional information and a review by Jerome Rosner, see 7:760.

[1724]

Reading Aptitude Tests. Grades kgn–1; 1935; also called *Monroe Reading Aptitude Tests;* 5 scores: visual, auditory, motor, articulation, language; Marion Monroe; Houghton Mifflin Co. *

For additional information and a review by Irving H. Anderson, see 3:519 (5 references).

REFERENCES THROUGH 1971

1–5. See 3:519.
6. CURRENT, W. F., AND RUCH, G. M. "Further Studies on the Reliability of Reading Tests." *J Ed Psychol* 17:476–81 O '26. * (*PA* 1:196)
7. CARROLL, MARJORIE WIGHT. "Sex Differences in Reading Readiness at the First Grade Level." *El Engl* 25:370–5 O '48. *
8. WELSH, GEORGE BYRON. *An Investigation of Some Predictive Factors in Auding Ability.* Doctor's thesis, University of Pittsburgh (Pittsburgh, Pa.), 1954. (*DA* 14:2407)
9. BRENNER, ANTON, AND MORSE, NANCY C. "The Measurement of Children's Readiness for School." *Papers Mich Acad Sci Arts & Letters* 41:333–40 '56. * (*PA* 37:6453)
10. DYKSTRA, ROBERT. *The Relationship Between Selected Reading Readiness Measures of Auditory Discrimination and Reading Achievement at the End of First Grade.* Doctor's thesis, University of Minnesota (Minneapolis, Minn.), 1962. (*DA* 24: 195)
11. MEYERS, E.; ORPET, R. E.; ATTWELL, A. A.; AND DINGMAN, H. F. *Primary Abilities at Mental Age Six.* Monographs of the Society for Research in Child Development, Vol. 27, No. 1, Serial No. 82. Lafayette, Ind.: Child Development Publications, 1962. Pp. 40. * (*PA* 38:8462)
12. NASTRI, LETITIA S. *An Experimental Study Investigating the Relationship Between the Articulation Subtest of the Monroe Reading Aptitude Tests and the Mendelson and Robinson Standard Speech Diagnostic Test.* Master's thesis, Southern Connecticut State College (New Haven, Conn.), 1962.
13. PELZ, KURT; PIKE, FRANCES; AND AMES, LOUISE B. "A Proposed Battery of Childhood Tests for Discriminating Between Different Levels of Intactness of Function in Elderly Subjects." *J Genetic Psychol* 100:23–40 Mr '62. * (*PA* 37:975)

14. Ames, Louise B., and Ilg, Frances L. "Sex Differences in Test Performance of Matched Girl-Boy Pairs in the Five-to-Nine-Year-Old Age Range." *J Genetic Psychol* 104:25–34 Mr '64. * (*PA* 39:4582)

15. Kerfoot, James Fletcher. *The Relationship of Selected Auditory and Visual Reading Readiness Measures to First Grade Reading Achievement and Second Grade Reading and Spelling Achievement.* Doctor's thesis, University of Minnesota (Minneapolis, Minn.), 1964. (*DA* 25:1747)

16. Dykstra, Robert. "Auditory Discrimination Abilities and Beginning Reading Achievement." *Reading Res Q* 1:5–34 sp '66. * (*PA* 40:11011)

17. Nerlove, Mary Ellen. *Some Factors Affecting Monroe Reading Aptitude Test Scores of Culturally Disadvantaged Kindergarteners.* Master's thesis, Southern Connecticut State College (New Haven, Conn.), 1968.

18. Bushey, James Thomas. *The Relationships Between a Preschool Measure of Readiness and Subsequent Test Performances Among a Group of Private Elementary School Children.* Doctor's thesis, Wayne State University (Detroit, Mich.), 1969. (*DAI* 30:3816A)

19. Kimbell, Valerie W., and Knight, David W. "The Performance of Two Populations on Selected Readiness Tests." *South J Ed Res* 4(3):186–92 Jl '70. *

20. Goldman, Ronald, and Dixon, Sarah D. "The Relationship of Vocal-Phonic and Articulatory Abilities." *J Learn Dis* 4(5):251–6 My '71. * (*PA* 47:9457)

21. Strainge, Renee Evelyn. *An Analysis of the Results Obtained on the Monroe Reading Aptitude Test for the Kindergarten Classes of the Bridgeport Public School System.* Master's thesis, Southern Connecticut State College (New Haven, Conn.), 1971.

CUMULATIVE NAME INDEX

Ames, L. B.: 13–4
Anderson, I. H.: *rev*, 3:519
Attwell, A. A.: 11
Brenner, A.: 9
Bushey, J. T.: 18
Carroll, M. W.: 7
Current, W. F.: 6
Dean, C. D.: 2
Dingman, H. F.: 11
Dixon, S. D.: 20
Dykstra, R.: 10, 16
Goldman, R.: 20
Ilg, F. L.: 14
Kerfoot, J. F.: 15
Kimbell, V. W.: 19

Kirk, S. A.: 3
Knight, D. W.: 19
Meyers, E.: 11
Morse, N. C.: 9
Nastri, L. S.: 12
Nerlove, M. E.: 17
Orpet, R. E.: 11
Pelz, K.: 13
Pike, F.: 13
Roslow, S.: 4
Ruch, G. M.: 6
Spache, G.: 5
Strainge, R. E.: 21
Welsh, G. B.: 8
Wylie, A. E.: 1

[1725]

★**Reading Inventory Probe 1.** Grades 1–2; 1970–73; also called READI (Reading Evaluation and Diagnostic Inventory); 17 scores: auditory discrimination (3 scores), visual discrimination (9 scores), vocabulary (2 scores), comprehension skills (3 scores); test by the Diagnostic Reading Committee, revision and manual by Stella Warner and Williams Myers; American Testing Co. *

[1726]

Reversal Test. Grade 1 entrants; 1954; Åke W. Edfeldt; Skandinaviska Testförlaget AB [Sweden]. *

[1727]

Riley Preschool Developmental Screening Inventory. Ages 3–5; 1969; RPDSI; school readiness; 2 scores: design, make-a-boy (girl); Clara M. D. Riley; Western Psychological Services. *
For additional information, see 7:761.

[1728]

The School Readiness Checklist. Ages 5–6; 1963–68; booklet title is *Ready or Not;* checklist to be used by parents; John J. Austin, J. Clayton Lafferty, Frederick Leaske (manual), and Fred Cousino (manual); Research Concepts. *
For additional information and a review by Dennis J. Deloria, see 7:762.

[1729]

School Readiness Survey. Ages 4–6; 1967–69; to be administered and scored by parents with school supervision; 8 scores: number concepts, discrimination

of form, color naming, symbol matching, speaking vocabulary, listening vocabulary, general information, total; F. L. Jordan and James Massey; Consulting Psychologists Press, Inc. *
For additional information and excerpted reviews by Dale E. Bennett and Byron Egeland, see 7:763.

[1730]

Screening Test of Academic Readiness. Ages 4–0 to 6–5; 1966; STAR; 9 scores: picture vocabulary, letters, picture completion, copying, picture description, human figure drawing, relationships, numbers, total (IQ); A. Edward Ahr; Priority Innovations, Inc. *
For additional information, a review by Mildred H. Huebner, and an excerpted review by Jon Magoon (with Richard C. Cox), see 7:765 (5 references).

REFERENCES THROUGH 1971
1–5. See 7:765.

CUMULATIVE NAME INDEX

Ahr, A. E.: 1–3
Cox, R. C.: 4; *exc*, 7:765
Huebner, M. H.: *rev*, 7:765

Hutton, J. B.: 5
Magoon, J.: 4; *exc*, 7:765

[1731]

Sprigle School Readiness Screening Test. Ages 4–6 to 6–9; 1965; SSRST; distribution restricted to physicians and psychologists; Herbert A. Sprigle; Learning to Learn School, Inc. *
For additional information and reviews by Nicholas Anastasiow and Alice Moriarty, see 7:766 (4 references).

REFERENCES THROUGH 1971
1–4. See 7:766.
5. Seda, Maria S. *A Validation Study of the Sprigle School Screening Readiness Test.* Master's thesis, California State College (Long Beach, Calif.), 1971.
6. Seda, Maria S. A., and Michael, Joan J. "The Concurrent Validity of the Sprigle School Screening Readiness Test for a Sample of Preschool and Kindergarten Children." *Ed & Psychol Meas* 31(4):995–7 w '71. * (*PA* 48:1660)

CUMULATIVE NAME INDEX

Anastasiow, N.: *rev*, 7:766
Bottrill, J. H.: 1
Hutton, J. B.: 3–4
Lanier, J.: 2
Michael, J. J.: 6

Moriarty, A. E.: *rev*, 7:766
Seda, M. S.: 5
Seda, M. S. A.: 6
Sprigle, H. A.: 2

[1732]

The Steinbach Test of Reading Readiness. Grades kgn–1; 1965–66; STRR; 5 scores: letter identification, word memory, auditory discrimination, language comprehension, total; M. Nila Steinbach; Scholastic Testing Service, Inc. *

REFERENCES THROUGH 1971
1. Steinbach, Mary Nila. *An Experimental Study of Progress in First-Grade Reading.* Doctor's thesis, Catholic University of America (Washington, D.C.), 1940.

CUMULATIVE NAME INDEX
Steinbach, M. N.: 1

[1733]

Van Wagenen Reading Readiness Scales. First grade entrants; 1933–58; 2 parts; Van Wagenen Psycho-Educational Research Laboratories. *
a) PART 1, LISTENING VOCABULARY. 1954–58; Maximilian L. G. Klaeger and M. J. Van Wagenen.
b) PART 2. 1933–58; 1954 test items same as in earlier edition published 1938 under the title *Reading Readiness Test;* 7 scores: range of information, perception of information, opposites, memory span for ideas, word discrimination, word learning, verbal IQ; M. J. Van Wagenen.
For additional information and a review by David H. Russell of an earlier edition of Part 2, see 3:520 (4 references).

REFERENCES THROUGH 1971

1-4. See 3:520.

5. WILSON, FRANK T. "Correlation of Information With Other Abilities and Traits in Grade I." *El Sch J* 37:295-301 D '36. * (*PA* 11:2478)

6. LOPER, DORIS JEAN. *Auditory Discrimination, Intelligence, Achievement, and Background of Experience and Information in a Culturally Disadvantaged First-Grade Population.* Doctor's thesis, Temple University (Philadelphia, Pa.), 1965. (*DA* 26: 5873)

7. CHARRY, LAWRENCE BERNARD. *The Relationship Between Prereading and First Grade Reading Performances and Subsequent Achievement in Reading and Other Specified Areas.* Doctor's thesis, Temple University (Philadelphia, Pa.), 1967. (*DA* 28:960A)

CUMULATIVE NAME INDEX

Bond, E.: 3
Bond, G. L.: 3
Burke, A.: 1
Charry, L. B.: 7
Gates, A. I.: 3
Halpin, A.: 3
Horan, K.: 3
Huggett, A. J.: 2
Johnson, N. E.: 4
Loper, D. J.: 6
Russell, D. H.: 3; *rev*, 3:520
Wilson, F. T.: 1, 5

[1734]

Watson Reading-Readiness Test. Grades kgn–1; 1960; 3 scores: subjective test (teacher's ratings of physical, social, emotional, and psychological readiness), objective test, total; G. Milton Watson; Book Society of Canada Ltd. [Canada]. *

For additional information, see 6:851.

[Out of Print Since TIP I]

Classification Test for Beginners in Reading, R:202, 3:515 (2 reviews, 2 references)

Early Detection Inventory, 7:746 (2 reviews), R:183

Evanston Early Identification Scale, 7:747 (1 review, 1 reference), P:426

Reading Readiness Test, R:203, 6:849 (1 review, 1 reference)

Scholastic Reading Readiness Test, R:204, 6:850 (1 review)

Webster Reading-Readiness Test, R:206, 5:682

SPECIAL FIELDS

[1735]

***ANPA Foundation Newspaper Test, 1972 Edition.** Grades 7–9, 10–12; 1969–72; newspaper reading ability; 1972 tests identical with experimental tests published 1969; sponsored by National Council for the Social Studies and developed in cooperation with American Newspaper Publishers Association Foundation; Cooperative Tests and Services. *

For additional information, see 7:768.

[1736]

The Adult Basic Reading Inventory. Functionally illiterate adolescents and adults; 1966; ABRI; test booklets with the title *Basic Reading Inventory* (BRI) are available for school use; scores in 5 areas: sight words, sound and letter discrimination, word meaning (reading), word meaning (listening), context reading; Richard W. Burnett; Scholastic Testing Service, Inc. *

For additional information and a review by Albert J. Kingston, see 7:769.

[1737]

***The Iowa Tests of Educational Development: Test 6, Ability to Interpret Reading Materials the Social Studies.** Grades 9–12; 1942–67; Forms X–4 and Y–4; more recent Forms X5 and Y5 are not available as separates; prepared under the direction of E. F. Lindquist and Leonard S. Feldt; Science

Research Associates, Inc. * For the complete battery entry, see 20.

For additional information concerning earlier forms, see 6:852. For reviews of the complete battery, see 6:14 (2 reviews), 5:17 (2 reviews), 4:17 (1 review), and 3:12 (3 reviews).

REFERENCES THROUGH 1971

1. LEBSACK, JACOB ROBERT. *Specific Reading Ability as Associated With Subject Matter Achievement.* Doctor's thesis, University of Nebraska (Lincoln, Neb.), 1954. (*DA* 14:1995)

2. COVELL, HAROLD MANFRED. *A Study of the Characteristics of Good and Poor Readers of Social Studies Materials at the Eleventh Grade Level.* Doctor's thesis, Florida State University (Tallahassee, Fla.), 1955. (*DA* 15:1570)

CUMULATIVE NAME INDEX

Covell, H. M.: 2   Lebsack, J. R.: 1

[1738]

***The Iowa Tests of Educational Development: Test 6, Ability to Interpret Reading Materials in the Natural Sciences.** Grades 9–12; 1942–67; Forms X–4 and Y–4; more recent Forms X5 and Y5 are not available as separates; prepared under the direction of E. F. Lindquist and Leonard S. Feldt; Science Research Associates, Inc. * For the complete battery entry, see 20.

For additional information concerning earlier forms, see 6:853. For reviews of the complete battery, see 6:14 (2 reviews), 5:17 (2 reviews), 4:17 (1 review), and 3:12 (3 reviews).

REFERENCES THROUGH 1971

1. LEBSACK, JACOB ROBERT. *Specific Reading Ability as Associated With Subject Matter Achievement.* Doctor's thesis, University of Nebraska (Lincoln, Neb.), 1954. (*DA* 14:1995)

2. JOHNSON, JENNINGS O. "The Relationship Between Science Achievement and Selected Student Characteristics." *Sci Ed* 53(4):307-18 O '69. *

CUMULATIVE NAME INDEX

Johnson, J. O.: 2   Lebsack, J. R.: 1

[1739]

Purdue Reading Test for Industrial Supervisors. Supervisors; 1955; Joseph Tiffin and Roy Dunlap; University Book Store. *

For additional information and reviews by Jerome E. Doppelt and Louis C. Nanassy, see 5:644 (1 reference).

REFERENCES THROUGH 1971

1. See 5:644.

2. SCHUCKER, RAYMOND E. *Validity and Reliability of the Purdue Reading Test for Industrial Supervisors.* Master's thesis, Purdue University (Lafayette, Ind.), 1957.

3. KIRCHNER, WAYNE; HANSON, RICHARD; AND BENSON, DALE. "Selecting Foremen With Psychological Tests." *Personnel Adm* 23:27-30 N–D '60. *

4. GRUENFELD, LEOPOLD W. "Selection of Executives for a Training Program." *Personnel Psychol* 14:421-31 w '61. * (*PA* 37:3922)

CUMULATIVE NAME INDEX

Benson, D.: 3
Doppelt, J. E.: *rev*, 5:644
Dunlap, R. D.: 1
Gruenfeld, L. W.: 4
Hanson, R.: 3
Kirchner, W.: 3
Nanassy, L. C.: *rev*, 5:644
Schucker, R. E.: 2

[1740]

RBH Scientific Reading Test. Employees in technical companies; 1950–69; Richardson, Bellows, Henry & Co., Inc. *

For additional information and a review by Samuel T. Mayo, see 7:772.

[1741]

Reading Adequacy "READ" Test: Individual Placement Series. Adults in industry; 1961–66; 3 scores: reading rate, per cent of comprehension, corrected reading rate; J. H. Norman; Personnel Research Associates, Inc. *

Van Wagenen Reading Readiness Scales

For additional information and a review by Samuel T. Mayo, see 7:773.

[1742]

[Reading: Adult Basic Education Student Survey, Parts 1 and 2.] Poorly educated adults; 1966–67; 2 scores: comprehension, vocabulary; Elvin Rasof and Monroe C. Neff; Follett Publishing Co. *

[1743]

Reading Comprehension Test for Personnel Selection. Applicants for technical training programs with high verbal content; 1965–66; L. R. C. Haward; University of London Press Ltd. [England]. *

For additional information and reviews by M. A. Brimer and Douglas A. Pidgeon, see 7:774 (3 references).

REFERENCES THROUGH 1971
1–3. See 7:774.

CUMULATIVE NAME INDEX
Brimer, M. A.: *rev*, 7:774   Pidgeon, D. A.: *rev*, 7:774
Haward, L. R. C.: 1–3

[1744]

★Reading/Everyday Activities in Life. High school and "adults at basic education levels"; 1972; R/EAL; functional literacy; Marilyn Lichtman; CAL Press, Inc. *

[1745]

[Robinson-Hall Reading Tests.] College; 1940–49; 4 tests; Francis P. Robinson and Prudence Hall; University Publications Sales, Ohio State University. *
a) A TEST OF READING ABILITY FOR ART.
b) A TEST OF READING ABILITY FOR GEOLOGY.
c) A TEST OF READING ABILITY FOR HISTORY.
d) A TEST OF READING ABILITY FOR FICTION.

For additional information and a review by Robert Murray Bear, see 4:575 (2 references); see also 3:533 (3 references).

REFERENCES THROUGH 1971
1–3. See 3:533.
4–5. See 4:575.
6. TAYLOR, JEANNE K. *Establishment of Norms for University of Wyoming Freshmen for the Robinson Reading Tests and the Development of a Comparable Reading Test.* Master's thesis, University of Wyoming (Laramie, Wyo.), 1954.
7. MAXWELL, MARTHA J. "An Experimental Investigation of the Effect of Instructional Set and Information on Reading Rate." *Yearb Nat Read Conf* 14:181–7 '65. *

CUMULATIVE NAME INDEX
Bear, R. M.: *rev*, 4:575   Maxwell, M. J.: 7
Edgerton, H. A.: 4   Robinson, F. P.: 1–3, 5
Hall, P.: 2   Taylor, J. K.: 6
Hall, W. E.: 5   Thomson, K. F.: 4

[1746]

SRA Reading Index. Job applicants with poor educational backgrounds; 1968; Science Research Associates, Inc. *

For additional information and a review by Dorothy C. Adkins of this test and the *SRA Arithmetic Index*, see 7:20.

[1747]

Understanding Communication (Verbal Comprehension). Industrial employees at the skilled level or below; 1959, c1956–59; Thelma G. Thurstone and Measurement Research Division, Industrial Relations Center, University of Chicago; the Center. * [The publisher has not replied to our four requests to check the accuracy of this entry.]

For additional information and reviews by C. E. Jurgensen and Donald E. P. Smith, see 6:840.

REFERENCES THROUGH 1971
1. BAEHR, MELANY E.; FURCON, JOHN E.; AND FROEMEL, ERNEST C. *Psychological Assessment of Patrolman Qualifications in Relation to Field Performance.* Washington, D.C.: United States Government Printing Office, 1969. Pp. vii, 246. *

CUMULATIVE NAME INDEX
Baehr, M. E.: 1   Jurgensen, C. E.: *rev*, 6:840
Froemel, E. C.: 1   Smith, D. E. P.: *rev*, 6:840
Furcon, J. E.: 1

[Out of Print Since TIP I]

Interpretation of Reading Materials in the Natural Sciences, 7:770, R:210; now available only as a subtest of *Tests of General Educational Development,* 48
Interpretation of Reading Materials in the Social Studies, 7:771 (2 reviews, 1 reference), R:211; now available only as a subtest of *Tests of General Educational Development,* 48
SRA Reading Progress Test, 7:775 (1 review), R:220
Tests of Natural Sciences: Vocabulary and Interpretation of Reading Materials: Cooperative Inter-American Tests, R:221, 4:576 (1 review, 4 references)
Tests of Social Studies: Vocabulary and Interpretation of Reading Materials: Cooperative Inter-American Tests, R:222, 4:577 (4 references)

SPEED

[1748]

＊Basic Reading Rate Scale. Grades 3–12; 1971, c1947–71; BRRS; the two forms consist of the first 97 or 98 items in the corresponding 450-item forms of *Tinker Speed of Reading Test* ('55); Ronald P. Carver (manual) and Miles A. Tinker (test); Revrac Publications. *

For additional information and a review by Leonard S. Feldt of the full length test, see 5:687.

[1749]

Minnesota Speed of Reading Test for College Students. Grades 12–16; 1936; Alvin C. Eurich; University of Minnesota Press. *

For additional information and a review by J. R. Gerberich, see 2:1555 (2 references); for reviews by Frederick B. Davis and Ruth Strang, see 1:1107.

REFERENCES THROUGH 1971
1–2. See 2:1555.
3. EURICH, ALVIN C. "The Relation of Speed of Reading to Comprehension." *Sch & Soc* 32:404–6 S 20 '30. * (*PA* 5:764)
4. LITTERER, OSCAR F. "An Experimental Analysis of Reading Performance." *J Exp Ed* 1:28–33 S 15 '32. * (*PA* 7:1137)
5. LITTERER, OSCAR F. "An Experimental Study of Visual Apprehension in Reading." *J Appl Psychol* 17:266–76 Je '33. * (*PA* 8:496)
6. PACE, C. ROBERT. "Handedness and Reading Ability in High School and College Students." *J Ed Res* 31:205–10 N '37. * (*PA* 12:952)
7. SEASHORE, R. H.; STOCKFORD, L. B. O.; AND SWARTZ, B. K. "A Correlational Analysis of Factors in Speed of Reading Tests." *Sch & Soc* 46:187–92 Ag 7 '37. * (*PA* 11:5346)
8. GREENE, PAUL C. "Some Relationships Between Placement Scores and Scholastic Rating." *Proc Iowa Acad Sci* 48:361–6 '41. * (*PA* 16:2867)
9. BLOMMERS, PAUL, AND LINDQUIST, E. F. "Rate of Comprehension of Reading: Its Measurement and Its Relation to Comprehension." *J Ed Psychol* 35:449–73 N '44. * (*PA* 19:1035)
10. SUTHERLAND, JEAN. "The Relationship Between Perceptual Span and Rate of Reading." *J Ed Psychol* 37:373–80 S '46. * (*PA* 21:1665)
11. LANIGAN, MARY A. "The Effectiveness of the Otis, the A.C.E. and the Minnesota Speed of Reading Tests for Predicting Success in College." *J Ed Res* 41:289–96 D '47. * (*PA* 22:2748)
12. PRESTON, RALPH C., AND TUFT, EDWIN N. "The Reading Habits of Superior College Students." *J Exp Ed* 16:196–202 Mr '48. * (*PA* 20:5126)
13. HOLMES, JACK A. "Factors Underlying Major Reading Disabilities at the College Level." *Genetic Psychol Monogr* 49: 3–95 F '54. * (*PA* 28:8982)

14. KERSH, BERT Y. "An Investigation of the Interpretation of Written Problems Among College Students." *Calif J Ed Res* 5:13–9 Ja '54. * (*PA* 28:7198)
15. SWEENEY, FRANCIS J. "Intelligence, Vocational Interests and Reading Speed of Senior Boys in Catholic High Schools of Los Angeles." *Calif J Ed Res* 5:159–65 S '54. * (*PA* 29:4656)

CUMULATIVE NAME INDEX

Blommers, P.: 9	Paterson, D. G.: 2
Davis, F. B.: *rev,* 1:1107	Preston, R. C.: 12
Eurich, A. C.: 1, 3	Schneidler, D. G.: 2
Gerberich, J. R.: *rev,* 2:1555	Seashore, R. H.: 7
Greene, P. C.: 8	Stockford, L. B. O.: 7
Holmes, J. A.: 13	Strang, R.: *rev,* 1:1107
Kersh, B. Y.: 14	Sutherland, J.: 10
Lanigan, M. A.: 11	Swartz, B. K.: 7
Lindquist, E. F.: 9	Sweeney, F. J.: 15
Litterer, O. F.: 4–5	Tuft, E. N.: 12
Pace, C. R.: 6	Williamson, E. G.: 2

[Out of Print Since TIP I]

Chapman-Cook Speed of Reading Test, R:232, 3:522 (1 review, 1 reference)
Reading Speed and Comprehension: Ohio Senior Survey Tests, R:234, 3:524 (2 reviews)
Tinker Speed of Reading Test, R:231, 5:687 (1 review)

STUDY SKILLS

[1750]

Bristol Achievement Tests: Study Skills. Ages 8–9, 9–10, 10–11, 11–12, 12–13; 1969; 6 scores: properties, structures, processes, explanations, interpretations, total; Alan Brimer, Margaret Fidler, Wynne Harlen, and John Taylor; Thomas Nelson & Sons Ltd. [England]. * For the complete battery entry, see 5.
For additional information and a review by Elizabeth J. Goodacre, see 7:776. For reviews of the complete battery, see 7:4 (2 reviews).

[1751]

College Adjustment and Study Skills Inventory. College; 1968; CASSI; 6 scores: time distribution, attitude and personal adjustment, reading and class participation, taking notes, taking examinations, total; Frank A. Christensen; Personal Growth Press, Inc. *
For additional information and reviews by William A. Mehrens and Walter Pauk, see 7:777.

[1752]

*Comprehensive Tests of Basic Skills: Study Skills.** Grades 2.5–4, 4–6, 6–8, 8–12; 1968–71; CTB/McGraw-Hill. * For the complete battery entry, see 11.
For additional information and a review by Walter Pauk, see 7:778. For reviews of the complete battery, see 7:9 (2 reviews, 3 excerpts).

[1753]

★**The Cornell Class-Reasoning Test.** Grades 4–12; 1964; deductive logic; no manual; Robert H. Ennis, William L. Gardiner, Richard Morrow, Dieter Paulus, and Lucille Ringel; Critical Thinking Project, University of Illinois. *

REFERENCES THROUGH 1971

1. ENNIS, ROBERT H., AND PAULUS, DIETER H. *Critical Thinking Readiness in Grades 1–12 (Phase 1, Deductive Logic in Adolescence).* An unpublished report to the U.S. Office of Education, Cooperative Research Project No. 1680, Cornell University, 1965. Pp. 348. * (ERIC ED003818)

CUMULATIVE NAME INDEX

Ennis, R. H.: 1   Paulus, D. H.: 1

[1754]

★**The Cornell Conditional-Reasoning Test.** Grades 4–12; 1964; deductive logic; no manual; Robert H. Ennis, William L. Gardiner, John Guzzetta, Richard Morrow, Dieter Paulus, and Lucille Ringel; Critical Thinking Project, University of Illinois. *

REFERENCES THROUGH 1971

1. ENNIS, ROBERT H., AND PAULUS, DIETER H. *Critical Thinking Readiness in Grades 1–12 (Phase 1, Deductive Logic in Adolescence).* An unpublished report to the U.S. Office of Education, Cooperative Research Project No. 1680, Cornell University, 1965. Pp. 348. * (ERIC ED003818)

CUMULATIVE NAME INDEX

Ennis, R. H.: 1   Paulus, D. H.: 1

[1755]

The Cornell Critical Thinking Test. Grades 7–12, 13–16; 1961–71; CCTT; 1971 tests identical with tests copyrighted 1961 except for format; Robert H. Ennis and Jason Millman; Critical Thinking Project, University of Illinois. *
For additional information, see 7:779 (10 references).

REFERENCES THROUGH 1971

1–10. See 7:779.
11. FOLLMAN, JOHN; MILLER, WILLIAM; AND BURG, ELDON. "Statistical Analysis of Three Critical Thinking Tests." *Ed & Psychol Meas* 31(2):519–20 su '71. *
12. TOLMAN, RICHARD. "Student Performance in Lower Division Collegiate General Biology Programs in Selected Community Colleges and Four-Year Institutions in Oregon." *J Res Sci Teach* 8(2):105–12 '71. *

CUMULATIVE NAME INDEX

Brown, L.: 9	Follman, J.: 4–6, 8–11
Brown, T. R.: 3	Follman, J. C.: 7
Burg, E.: 9, 11	Hernandez, D.: 5–6, 10
Craven, G. F.: 2	Miller, W.: 5–6, 10–1
Ennis, R. H.: 1	Tolman, R.: 12

[1756]

★**The Cornell Learning and Study Skills Inventory.** Grades 7–12, 13–16; 1970; CLSSI; 9 scores: goal orientation, activity structure, scholarly skills, lecture mastery, textbook mastery, examination mastery, self mastery, total, reading validity index; Walter Pauk and Russell Cassel; Psychologists and Educators, Inc. *

REFERENCES THROUGH 1971

1. CASSEL, RUSSELL, AND PAUK, WALTER. "Validation of Self-Concept of Typical Student as Substitute for Student's Own Self-Concept." *J Psychol* 73(1):111–4 S '69. * (*PA* 44:5142)
2. CASSEL, RUSSELL N., AND PAUK, WALTER. "Comparing Scores on the Cornell Learning and Study Skills Inventory With GPA and Age." *Cont Ed* 43(1):44–7 O '71. *

CUMULATIVE NAME INDEX

Cassel, R.: 1   Pauk, W.: 1–2
Cassel, R. N.: 2

[1757]

Evaluation Aptitude Test. Candidates for college and graduate school entrance; 1951–52; 5 scores: neutral syllogisms, emotionally toned syllogisms, total, emotional bias, indecision; DeWitt E. Sell; Psychometric Affiliates. *
For additional information and reviews by J. Thomas Hastings and Walker H. Hill, see 5:691.

[1758]

*The Iowa Tests of Educational Development: Test 9, Use of Sources of Information.** Grades 9–12; 1942–67; Forms X-4 and Y-4; more recent Forms X5 and Y5 are not available as separates; prepared under the direction of E. F. Lindquist and Leonard S. Feldt; Science Research Associates, Inc. * For the complete battery entry, see 20.
For additional information concerning earlier forms,

see 6:858. For reviews of the complete battery, see 6:14 (2 reviews), 5:17 (2 reviews), 4:17 (1 review), and 3:12 (3 reviews).

REFERENCES THROUGH 1971

1. MOELLER, VERNON E. *A Study of Relationships Between Measures of Academic Achievement. Study Habits and Attitudes, the Ability to Use Reference Materials, and Academic Aptitude in a Large Suburban Illinois High School.* Master's thesis, Northern Illinois University (DeKalb, Ill.), 1963.

CUMULATIVE NAME INDEX

Moeller, V. E.: 1

[1759]

A Library Orientation Test for College Freshmen. Grade 13; 1950–61; Ethel M. Feagley, Dorothy W. Curtiss, Mary V. Gaver, and Esther Greene; Teachers College Press. *

For additional information and a review by Morey J. Wantman, see 6:859 (1 reference); for reviews by Janet G. Afflerbach (with Lois Grimes Afflerbach) and J. Wayne Wrightstone, see 5:693.

REFERENCES THROUGH 1971

1. See 6:859.
2. LEE, CHI HO. *The Library Skills of Prospective Teachers at the University of Georgia.* Doctor's thesis, University of Georgia (Athens, Ga.), 1971. (*DAI* 32:5089A)

CUMULATIVE NAME INDEX

Afflerbach, J. G.: *rev, 5*:693   Wantman, M. J.: *rev, 6*:859
Afflerbach, L. G.: *rev, 5*:693   Wrightstone, J. W.: *rev, 5*:
Joyce, W. D.: 1   693
Lee, C. H.: 2

[1760]

★**Library Tests.** College; 1967–72; 3 tests; no manual; Perfection Form Co. *
a) TEST 1: LIBRARY SURVEY TEST. General knowledge of library.
b) TEST 2: LIBRARY SOURCES AND SKILLS TEST. More detailed knowledge of library.
c) TEST 3: LIBRARY SOURCES AND USES OF INFORMATION. Thorough knowledge of library and research techniques.

[1761]

Logical Reasoning. Grades 9–16 and adults; 1955; Alfred F. Hertzka and J. P. Guilford; Sheridan Psychological Services, Inc. *

For additional information and reviews by Duncan Howie and Charles R. Langmuir, see 5:694 (1 reference).

REFERENCES THROUGH 1971

1. See 5:694.
2. GUILFORD, J. P. *Personality.* New York: McGraw-Hill Book Co., Inc., 1959. Pp. xiii, 562. *
3. MERRIFIELD, P. R.; GUILFORD, J. P.; CHRISTENSEN, P. R.; AND FRICK, J. W. "The Role of Intellectual Factors in Problem Solving." *Psychol Monogr* 76 (10):1–21 '62. *
4. LEMKE, ELMER A.; KLAUSMEIER, HERBERT J.; AND HARRIS, CHESTER W. "Relationship of Selected Cognitive Abilities to Concept Attainment and Information Processing." *J Ed Psychol* 58:27–35 F '67. * (*PA* 41:3959)
5. VERY, PHILIP S. "Differential Factor Structures in Mathematical Ability." *Genetic Psychol Monogr* 75:169–207 My '67. * (*PA* 41:10451)
6. BERGER, RAYMOND M. "Selection of Systems Analysts and Programmer Trainees." *Proc Ann Computer Personnel Res Conf* 6:44–63 '68. *
7. FOLLMAN, JOHN. "Factor Analysis of Three Critical Thinking Tests, One Logical Reasoning Test, and One English Test." *Yearb Nat Read Conf* 18:154–60 '69. *
8. FOLLMAN, JOHN COSGROVE. *A Factor Analytic Study of Three Critical Thinking Tests, One English Test, and One Logical Reasoning Test.* Doctor's thesis, Indiana University (Bloomington, Ind.), 1969. (*DAI* 30:1015A)
9. VANDENBERG, STEVEN G. "A Twin Study of Spatial Ability." *Multiv Behav Res* 4(3):273–94 Jl '69. * (*PA* 44:356)
10. FOLLMAN, JOHN. "Correlational and Factor Analysis of Critical Thinking, Logical Reasoning, and English Total Test Scores." *Fla J Ed Res* 12(1):91–4 Ja '70. *
11. FOLLMAN, JOHN; BROWN, LAURENCE; AND BURG, ELDON. "Factor Analysis of Critical Thinking, Logical Reasoning, and English Subtests." *J Exp Ed* 38(4):11–6 su '70. *

CUMULATIVE NAME INDEX

Berger, R. M.: 6   Hills, J. R.: 1
Brown, L.: 11   Howie, D.: *rev, 5*:694
Burg, E.: 11   Klausmeier, H. J.: 4
Christensen, P. R.: 3   Langmuir, C. R.: *rev, 5*:694
Follman, J.: 7, 10–1   Lemke, E. A.: 4
Follman, J. C.: 8   Merrifield, P. R.: 3
Frick, J. W.: 3   Vandenberg, S. G.: 9
Guilford, J. P.: 2–3   Very, P. S.: 5
Harris, C. W.: 4

[1762]

★**National Test of Library Skills.** Grades 2–4, 4–12; 1967–71; NTLS; 2 levels; Frances Hatfield, Irene Gullette, and William Myers; American Testing Co. *
a) LEVELS 2 TO 4. Grades 2–4; 1971; 4 scores: arrangement of books, parts of a book, card catalog, reference books.
b) LEVELS 4 TO 12. Grades 4–12; 1967–71; 5 scores: same as for level 2–4 plus indexes.

[1763]

Nationwide Library Skills Examination. Grades 4–12; 1962–63; no manual; [Donald R. Honz]; Educational Stimuli. *

For additional information, see 6:860.

[1764]

OC Diagnostic Dictionary Test. Grades 5–8; 1960; Katherine O'Connor; O'Connor Reading Clinic Publishing Co. *

For additional information, see 6:861.

[1765]

SRA Achievement Series: Work-Study Skills. Grades 4–9; 1955–69; an optional supplement to Forms C and D of the series; 3 scores: references, charts, total; Louis P. Thorpe, D. Welty Lefever, and Robert A. Naslund; Science Research Associates, Inc. * For the complete battery entry, see 29.

For additional information, see 7:780; for reviews by Robert L. Ebel and Ruth M. Strang of earlier forms, see 5:696. For reviews of the complete battery, see 7:18 (2 reviews), 6:21 (1 review), and 5:21 (2 reviews).

[1766]

★**Study Attitudes and Methods Survey.** High school and college; 1972; SAMS; 6 scores: academic interest, academic drive, study methods, study anxiety, manipulation, alienation toward authority; William B. Michael, Joan J. Michael, and Wayne S. Zimmerman; Educational and Industrial Testing Service. *

REFERENCES THROUGH 1971

1. MICHAEL, WILLIAM B., AND REEDER, DOUGLAS E. "The Development and Validation of a Preliminary Form of a Study-Habits Inventory." *Ed & Psychol Meas* 12:236–47 su '52. * (*PA* 27:6156)
2. MICHAEL, WILLIAM B.; JONES, ROBERT A.; AND TREMBLY, W. A. "The Factored Dimensions of a Measure of Motivation for College Students." *Ed & Psychol Meas* 19:667–71 w '59. * (*PA* 34:6550)
3. ZIMMERMAN, WAYNE S.; MICHAEL, JOAN J.; AND MICHAEL, WILLIAM B. "The Factored Dimensions of the Study Attitudes and Methods Survey Test—Experimental Form." *Ed & Psychol Meas* 30(2):433–6 su '70. * (*PA* 45:2960)
4. MICHAEL, WILLIAM B.; LEE, YOUNG B.; MICHAEL, JOAN J.; HOOKE, ORA; AND ZIMMERMAN, WAYNE S. "A Partial Redefinition of the Factorial Structure of the Study Attitudes and Methods Survey (SAMS) Test." *Ed & Psychol Meas* 31(2):545–7 su '71. *

CUMULATIVE NAME INDEX

Hooke, O.: 4   Michael, W. B.: 1–4
Jones, R. A.: 2   Reeder, D. E.: 1
Lee, Y. B.: 4   Trembly, W. A.: 2
Michael, J. J.: 3–4   Zimmerman, W. S.: 3–4

Study Attitudes and Methods Survey

[1767]

Study Habits Checklist. Grades 9–14; 1957–67; also published as a pretest and posttest in the authors' booklet entitled *How to Study;* Ralph C. Preston and Morton Botel; Science Research Associates, Inc. *

REFERENCES THROUGH 1971

1. PRESTON, RALPH C. "Improving the Item Validity of Study Habits Inventories." *Ed & Psychol Meas* 21:129–31 sp '61. * (*PA* 36:1KI29P)
2. BROWN, SARA MAE. *Variables Associated With Overachievement and Underachievement.* Doctor's thesis, University of Pennsylvania (Philadelphia, Pa.), 1964.
3. BUTCOFSKY, DON. "Any Learning Skills Taught in High School?" *J Read* 15(3):195–8 D '71. *

CUMULATIVE NAME INDEX

Brown, S. M.: 2   Preston, R. C.: 1
Butcofsky, D.: 3

[1768]

Study Habits Inventory, Revised Edition. Grades 12–16; 1934–41; C. Gilbert Wrenn; Consulting Psychologists Press, Inc. *

For additional information and a review by Douglas E. Scates, see 3:540 (8 references); for reviews by Edward S. Jones and William A. McCall, see 2:1574.

REFERENCES THROUGH 1971

1–8. See 3:540.
9. DOUGLASS, LOWELL N. "A Study of Certain Factors Influencing Academic Achievement With Special Reference to the Health Factor." *J Exp Ed* 7:235–44 Mr '39. * (*PA* 13:5911)
10. SHEFFIELD, EDWARD F. "Achievement of Evening College Students." *J Am Assn Col Reg* 17:319–24 Ap '42. *
11. WAGGONER, R. W., AND ZEIGLER, THORNTON WOODWARD. "Psychiatric Factors in Medical School Students Who Fail." *Am J Psychiatry* 103:369–76 N '46. * (*PA* 21:1671)
12. PORTENIER, LILLIAN G. "Predicting Success in Introductory Psychology." *Ed & Psychol Meas* 8:117–26 sp '48. * (*PA* 22:3730)
13. PRESTON, RALPH C., AND TUFT, EDWIN N. "The Reading Habits of Superior College Students." *J Exp Ed* 16:196–202 Mr '48. * (*PA* 20:5126)
14. GARBER, W. F. "Evaluation of Psychometric Tests for Optometry." *Optom Weekly* 41:7–9 Ja '50. * (*PA* 24:5533)
15. ESHLEMAN, DAWN FORRESTER. *The Relationship of the Wrenn Study Habits Inventory to Personality Adjustment and Achievement of High School Seniors.* Master's thesis, Pennsylvania State College (State College, Pa.), 1951.
16. GEHMAN, WINFIELD SCOTT, JR. *Analysis of a Program Involving Required Psychological Counseling and Other Services for a College Population Having Serious Scholastic Difficulties.* Doctor's thesis, Pennsylvania State College (State College, Pa.), 1951.
17. MUNGER, PAUL F. "Factors Related to Persistence in College of Students Who Ranked in the Lower Third of Their High School Class." *J Counsel Psychol* 1:132–6 f '54. * (*PA* 29:6258)
18. GEHMAN, W. SCOTT. "Problems of College Sophomores With Serious Scholastic Difficulties." *J Counsel Psychol* 2:137–41 su '55. * (*PA* 30:3406)
19. RASMUS, CAROLYN A. *Predictive Value of the Wrenn Study-Habits Inventory in Predicting the Success of Miami University Freshmen.* Master's thesis, Miami University (Oxford, Ohio), 1955.
20. SLAYTON, WILFRED GEORGE. *A Comparison of Successful and Unsuccessful Bible College Students With Respect to Selected Personality Factors.* Doctor's thesis, University of Arizona (Tucson, Ariz.), 1965. (*DA* 26:1487)
21. LIGHT, LOUISE L., AND ALEXAKOS, C. E. "Effect of Individual and Group Counseling on Study Habits." *J Ed Res* 63(10):450–4 Jl–Ag '70. * (*PA* 46:7571)
22. ZEDECK, SHELDON; CRANNY, C. J.; VALE, CAROL A.; AND SMITH, PATRICIA CAIN. "Comparison of 'Joint Moderators' in Three Prediction Techniques." *J Appl Psychol* 55(3):234–40 Je '71. * (*PA* 46:9774)

CUMULATIVE NAME INDEX

Alexakos, C. E.: 21   McCall, W. A.: *rev*, 2:1574
Cranny, C. J.: 22   Munger, P. F.: 17
Douglass, L. N.: 9   Musselman, J. W.: 7
Eshleman, D. F.: 15   Portenier, L. G.: 12
Garber, W. F.: 14   Preston, R. C.: 13
Gehman, W. S.: 16, 18   Rasmus, C. A.: 19
Gordon, H. P.: 3   Reeder, C. W.: 1
Greene, J. E.: *rev*, 3:540   Scates, D. E.: *rev*, 3:540
Humber, W. J.: 4   Sheffield, E. F.: 10
Johnson, A. P.: 5–6   Slayton, W. G.: 20
Jones, E. S.: *rev*, 2:1574   Smith, P. C.: 22
Light, L. L.: 21   Staton, T. F.: 2

Traxler, A. E.: 8   Wrenn, C. G.: 4
Tuft, E. N.: 13   Zedeck, S.: 22
Vale, C. A.: 22   Zeigler, T. W.: 11
Waggoner, R. W.: 11

[1769]

Study Performance Test. High school and college; 1934–43; Herbert A. Toops, Grace Shover, and others; Wilbur L. Layton. *

[1770]

The Study Skills Counseling Evaluation. High school and college; 1962; George Demos; Western Psychological Services. *

For additional information and reviews by Stanley E. Davis and W. G. Fleming, see 6:865.

[1771]

Study Skills Test: McGraw-Hill Basic Skills System. Grades 11–14; 1970; also called *MHBSS Study Skills Test;* although designed for use with the MHBSS instructional program, the test may be used independently; 6 scores: problem solving, underlining, library information, study skills information, total, inventory of study habits and attitudes; Alton L. Raygor; McGraw-Hill Book Co., Inc. *

For additional information and a review by Walter Pauk, see 7:781.

[1772]

Survey of Study Habits and Attitudes. Grades 7–12, 12–14; 1953–67; SSHA; original edition called *Brown-Holtzman Survey of Study Habits and Attitudes;* 7 scores: study habits (delay avoidance, work methods, total), study attitudes (teacher approval, education acceptance, total), total; William F. Brown and Wayne H. Holtzman; Psychological Corporation. *

For additional information, a review by Carleton B. Shay, and excerpts by Martin J. Higgins and Albert E. Roark (with Scott A. Harrington), see 7:782 (69 references); see also 6:856 (12 references); for reviews by James Deese and C. Gilbert Wrenn (with Roy D. Lewis) of the original edition, see 5:688 (14 references).

REFERENCES THROUGH 1971

1–14. See 5:688.
15–26. See 6:856.
27–95. See 7:782.
96. PAUK, WALTER J. "Are Present Reading Tests Valid for Both Girls and Boys?" *J Ed Res* 53:279–80 Mr '60. *
97. DAR, RIFAAT JEHAN, AND ZIA-UL-HAQ, M. "A Study of Actual Study Habits Among IX Class Boys and Girls of Lahore Area in West Pakistan." *B Ed & Res* (Pakistan) 2:45–56 w '63. *
98. SCHNEYER, J. WESLEY. "Factors Associated With the Progress of Students Enrolled in a College Reading Program." *J Ed Res* 56:340–5 Mr '63. *
99. GIBBONS, K. C., AND SAVAGE, R. D. "Intelligence Study Habits and Personality Factors in Academic Success—A Preliminary Report." *Durham Res R* (England) 5:8–12 S '65. *
100. KEISTER, RUTH V. *The Relationship of Study Habits and Attitudes to Predicted and Achieved Grade Point Average and Reading Skills.* Master's thesis, West Virginia University (Morgantown, W.Va.), 1965.
101. HAYNES, CAROLYN R. *The Relationships of Performances of Seventh Grade Students on Measures of Creativity, Study Habits and Attitudes, Expressed Need for Counseling and Achievement.* Master's thesis, Texas A & M University (College Station, Tex.), 1966.
102. LAMMI, ELEANOR HEINZ. *An Investigation of the Relationship of Interests in Forestry and Study Habits and Attitudes to Grade-point Average.* Master's thesis, North Carolina State University (Raleigh, N.C.), 1966.
103. GROOM, HARRY DEE. *Predicting Achievement Behavior of Academic Probation Students at Brigham Young University.* Master's thesis, Brigham Young University (Provo, Utah), 1968.
104. HASLAM, WARREN L., AND BROWN, WILLIAM F. "Effectiveness of Study-Skills Instruction for High School Sophomores." *J Ed Psychol* 59:223–6 Ag '68. * (*PA* 42:16153)
105. COOPER, B., AND FOY, J. M. "Students' Study Habits,

Attitudes and Academic Attainment." *Univ Q* (England) 23(2): 203–12 sp '69. *

106. BRAUN, PETER H. *Subjective and Psychometric Non-Cognitive Scales in Relation to Over- and Under-Achievement.* Master's thesis, University of Alberta (Edmonton, Alta., Canada), 1970.

107. CAZZELLE, JACKIE GENE. *A Study of Non-Intellective Variables Related to the Academic Success and Adjustment of College Freshmen From Low Socioeconomic Backgrounds.* Doctor's thesis, Oklahoma State University (Stillwater, Okla.), 1970. (*DAI* 31:5118A)

108. CURL, GERALD ALLEN. *A Comparison of Freshman Achievers and Non-Achievers From Economically Deprived Families.* Doctor's thesis, University of Illinois (Urbana, Ill.), 1970. (*DAI* 31:4455A)

109. JOHNS, DANIEL JAY. *Correlates of Academic Success in a Predominantly Black, Open-Door, Public, Urban Community College.* Doctor's thesis, University of Virginia (Charlottesville, Va.), 1970. (*DAI* 31:4464A)

110. MOTE, THOMAS ALLAN, JR. *Student Grade Perception and the Prediction of Academic Achievement.* Doctor's thesis, University of Texas (Austin, Tex.), 1970. (*DAI* 32:3794A)

111. STARKS, WALTER LIVINGSTON. *The Relationship of Residence and Economic Factors to the First Semester Academic Achievement of College of Business Administration and College of Agriculture 1969 Freshmen, Male Students.* Doctor's thesis, Oklahoma State University (Stillwater, Okla.), 1970. (*DAI* 31:5805A)

112. BENGEL, JAMES ELWOOD. *The Relationship Between Self-Attitudes, Academic Performance and Student-Centered Teaching for First Semester Agricultural Institute Students at North Carolina State University.* Doctor's thesis, University of North Carolina (Chapel Hill, N.C.), 1971. (*DAI* 32:2412A)

113. BEYER, DARRELL ERICK. *An Analysis of Selected Intellectual and Nonintellectual Characteristics of Dropouts and Survivors in a Private College.* Doctor's thesis, Baylor University (Waco, Tex.), 1971. (*DAI* 32:3773A)

114. CARDWELL, JESSE FRANKLIN. *A Comparative Study of Intellectually Able Students Who Completed and Who Did Not Complete an Honors and Advanced Placement Program.* Doctor's thesis, George Peabody College for Teachers (Nashville, Tenn.), 1971. (*DAI* 32:1939A)

115. COWELL, M. D., AND ENTWISTLE, N. J. "The Relationships Between Personality, Study Attitudes and Academic Performance in a Technical College." *Brit J Ed Psychol* 41(1):85–90 F '71. * (*PA* 46:9542)

116. DISPENZIERI, ANGELO; GINIGER, SEYMOUR; REICHMAN, WALTER; AND LEVY, MARGUERITE. "College Performance of Disadvantaged Students as a Function of Ability and Personality." *J Counsel Psychol* 18(4):298–305 Jl '71. * (*PA* 46:11687)

117. ENTWISTLE, N. J., AND BRENNAN, T. "The Academic Performance of Students: 2, Types of Successful Students." *Brit J Ed Psychol* 41(3):268–76 N '71. * (*PA* 47:11759)

118. ENTWISTLE, N. J.; NISBET, JENNIFER; ENTWISTLE, DOROTHY; AND COWELL, M. D. "The Academic Performance of Students: 1, Prediction From Scales of Motivation and Study Methods." *Brit J Ed Psychol* 41(3):258–67 N '71. * (*PA* 47:11781)

119. GARRISON, CLIFFORD BEVERLY. *A Comparative Investigation of Behavorial Counseling Group Techniques Used to Modify Study Skills, Attitudes and Achievement of Selected High School Pupils.* Doctor's thesis, State University of New York (Buffalo, N.Y.), 1971. (*DAI* 32:1271A)

120. HARVEY, RAYMOND CHESTERFIELD, JR. *The Relationship of Study Habits and Attitudes to College Subcultures and to Personality Types.* Doctor's thesis, East Texas State University (Commerce, Tex.), 1971. (*DAI* 32:6030B)

121. JOHNSON, LEONARD ROSS. *A Comparative Investigation of Achievement Motivation in Vocational-Technical and Transfer Students in Selected Texas Junior Colleges.* Doctor's thesis, Baylor University (Waco, Tex.), 1971. (*DAI* 32:3790A)

122. LEWIS, ROBERT WILLIAM, JR. *The Effects of a Planned Group Guidance Program for College-Bound High School Seniors on Selected Guidance Program Variables.* Doctor's thesis, University of Maine (Orono, Me.), 1971. (*DAI* 32:2421A)

123. MOTE, THOMAS A., JR. "Uncontrolled vs. Controlled Administration of the SSHA." *Interam J Psychol* (Mexico) 5(3–4):159–61 '71. * (*PA* 48:12167)

124. PEPPER, ROGER S. "The Study Skills and Academic Achievement of Marginal Admission Students." *Yearb Nat Read Conf* 19(1):248–53 '71. *

125. PHILLIPS, GEORGE O., SR. "Study Habits and Attitudes of Disadvantaged Students in a College Reading and Study Skills Program." *Yearb Nat Read Conf* 19(2):152–7 '71. *

126. SHEPPS, FLORENCE P., AND SHEPPS, R. RONALD. "Relationship of Study Habits and School Attitudes to Achievement in Mathematics and Reading." *J Ed Res* 65(2):71–3 O '71. * (*PA* 48:1841, title only)

127. WEIGEL, RICHARD G.; WEIGEL, VIRGINIA M.; AND HEBERT, JOHN A. "Non-Volunteer Subjects: Temporal Effects." *Psychol Rep* 28(1):191–2 F '71. * (*PA* 46:5449)

128. ZEDECK, SHELDON. "Identification of Moderator Variables by Discriminant Analysis in a Multipredictable Group Validation Model." *J Appl Psychol* 55(4):364–71 Ag '71. * (*PA* 47:1947)

[1773]

A Test on Use of the Dictionary. High school and college; 1955–63; 6 scores: pronunciation, meaning, spelling, derivation, usage, total; George D. Spache; Reading Laboratory and Clinic. *

For additional information, see 6:866.

[1774]

★The Uncritical Inference Test. College; 1955–67; UIT; no manual; William V. Haney; International Society for General Semantics. *

REFERENCES THROUGH 1971

1. HANEY, WILLIAM VALENTINE. *Measurement of the Ability to Discriminate Between Inferential and Descriptive Statements.*

Doctor's thesis, Northwestern University (Evanston, Ill.), 1953. (*DA* 14:405)

2. HANEY, WILLIAM V. "Are Accident-Prone Drivers Unconscious-Inference Prone?" *Gen Semantics B* 20–21:79–80 '57. *

3. HANEY, WILLIAM V. "Police Experience and Uncritical Inference Behavior." *Gen Semantics B* 22–23:51–4 '58. *

4. HANEY, WILLIAM V. "The Uncritical Inference Test: Applications." *Gen Semantics B* 28–29:26 '61–62. *

5. KOTTMAN, E. JOHN. "Intension and Uncritical Inference Behavior." *ETC* 26(1):53–7 Mr '69. *

CUMULATIVE NAME INDEX

Haney, W. V.: 1–4   Kottman, E. J.: 5

[1775]

Watson-Glaser Critical Thinking Appraisal.
Grades 9–16 and adults; 1942–64; formerly called *Watson-Glaser Tests of Critical Thinking;* Goodwin Watson and Edward M. Glaser; Harcourt Brace Jovanovich, Inc. *

For additional information and excerpted reviews by John O. Crites and G. C. Helmstadter, see 7:783 (74 references); see also 6:867 (24 references); for reviews by Walker H. Hill and Carl I. Hovland of an earlier edition, see 5:700 (8 references); for a review by Robert H. Thouless and an excerpted review by Harold P. Fawcett, see 3:544 (3 references).

REFERENCES THROUGH 1971

1–3. See 3:544.
4–11. See 5:700.
12–35. See 6:867.
36–109. See 7:783.

110. SHNEIDMAN, EDWIN S. "The Case of El: Psychological Test Data." *J Proj Tech* 25:131–54 Je '61. * (*PA* 36:21K31S)

111. D'AOUST, THÉRÈSE. *Predictive Validity of Four Psychometric Tests in a Selected School of Nursing.* Master's thesis, Catholic University of America (Washington, D.C.), 1963.

112. OBST, FRANCES. "A Study of Abilities of Women Students Entering the Colleges of Letters and Science and Applied Arts at the University of California, Los Angeles." *J Ed Res* 57:84–6 O '63. *

113. LYSAUGHT, JEROME P. "Further Analysis of Success Among Auto-Instructional Programmers." *Teaching Aid News* 4:6–11 O 15 '64. *

114. LYSAUGHT, JEROME P. "Selecting Instructional Programmers: New Research Into Characteristics of Successful Programmers." *Training Directors J* 18:8–14 Je '64. *

115. COYLE, F. A., JR., AND BERNARD, J. L. "Logical Thinking and Paranoid Schizophrenia." *J Psychol* 60:283–9 Jl '65. *

116. KROCKOVER, GERALD H. "The Development of Critical Thinking Through Science Instruction." *Proc Iowa Acad Sci* 72:402–4 '65. *

117. LIVINGSTON, HOWARD. "An Investigation of the Effect of Instruction in General Semantics on Critical Reading Ability." *Calif J Ed Res* 16:93–6 Mr '65. * (*PA* 39:10787)

118. QUINN, PATRICK V. "Critical Thinking and Openmindedness in Pupils From Public and Catholic Secondary Schools." *J Social Psychol* 66:23–30 Je '65. * (*PA* 39:14915)

119. STALNAKER, ASHFORD W. "The Watson-Glaser Critical Thinking Appraisal as a Predictor of Programming Performance." *Proc Ann Computer Personnel Res Conf* 3:75–7 '65. *

120. WENBERG, BURNESS G., AND INGERSOLL, RALPH W. "Medical Dietetics: Part 2, The Development of Evaluative Techniques." *J Am Dietetic Assn* 47:298–300 O '65. *

121. ALEXAKOS, C. E. "Predictive Efficiency of Two Multivariate Statistical Techniques in Comparison With Clinical Predictions." *J Ed Psychol* 57:297–306 O '66. * (*PA* 40:12756)

122. STEPHENS, JAMES ALBERT. *A Study of the Correlation Between Critical Thinking Abilities and Achievement in Algebra Involving Advanced Placement.* Master's thesis, North Carolina State University (Raleigh, N.C.), 1966.

123. CROSSON, ROBERT F. "An Investigation Into Certain Personality Variables Among Capital Trial Jurors." Abstract. *Proc 76th Ann Conv Am Psychol Assn* 3:371–2 '68. * (*PA* 43:887, title only)

124. GRACE, JAMES L., JR. "Critical Thinking Ability of Students in Catholic and Public High Schools." *Nat Cath Ed Assn B* 65:49–57 N '68. *

125. PILLAI, N. P., AND NAYAR, P. P. "The Role of Critical Thinking in Science Achievement." *J Ed Res & Exten* (India) 5:1–8 Jl '68. *

126. BROADHURST, NORMAN A. "A Measure of Some Learning Outcomes in Matriculation Chemistry in South Australia." *Austral Sci Teach J* 15(3):67–70 N '69. *

127. WENBERG, BURNESS G.; INGERSOLL, RALPH W.; AND DOHNER, CHARLES W. "Evaluation of Dietetic Interns." *J Am Dietetic Assn* 54(4):297–301 Ap '69. *

128. LA FOREST, JAMES RENE. *Relation of Critical Thinking*

Uncritical Inference Test

to Program Planning. Doctor's thesis, North Carolina State University (Raleigh, N.C.), 1970. (*DAI* 32:1253A)

129. PARSLEY, JAMES FRANCIS, JR. *A Comparison of the Ability of Ninth Grade Students to Apply Several Critical Thinking Skills to Problematic Content Presented Through Two Different Media.* Doctor's thesis, Ohio University (Athens, Ohio), 1970. (*DAI* 31:4629A)

130. POEL, ROBERT HERMAN. *Critical Thinking as Related to PSSC and Non-PSSC Physics Programs.* Doctor's thesis, Western Michigan University (Kalamazoo, Mich.), 1970. (*DAI* 31:3983A)

131. SKINNER, SAMUEL BALLOU. *A Study of the Effect of the St. Andrews Presbyterian College Natural Science Course Upon Critical Thinking Ability.* Doctor's thesis, University of North Carolina (Chapel Hill, N.C.), 1970. (*DAI* 31:3984A)

132. BETRES, JAMES JOHN. *A Study in the Development of the Critical Thinking Skills of Preservice Elementary Teachers.* Doctor's thesis, Ohio University (Athens, Ohio), 1971. (*DAI* 32:2520A)

133. DAVIS, WALTER NEWTON. *Authoritarianism and Selected Trait Patterns of School Administrators: Seventeen Case Studies.* Doctor's thesis, North Texas State University (Denton, Tex.), 1971. (*DAI* 32:1777A)

134. DISPENZIERI, ANGELO; GINIGER, SEYMOUR; REICHMAN, WALTER; AND LEVY, MARGUERITE. "College Performance of Disadvantaged Students as a Function of Ability and Personality." *J Counsel Psychol* 18(4):298–305 Jl '71. * (*PA* 46:11687)

135. FOLLMAN, JOHN; MILLER, WILLIAM; AND BURG, ELDON. "Statistical Analysis of Three Critical Thinking Tests." *Ed & Psychol Meas* 31(2):519–20 su '71. *

136. HJELMHAUG, NOEL NELS. *Context Instruction and the Ability of College Students to Transfer Learning.* Doctor's thesis, Indiana University (Bloomington, Ind.), 1971. (*DAI* 32:1356A)

137. JAMES, REUBEN J. *Traits Associated With the Initial and Persistent Interest in the Study of College Science.* Doctor's thesis, State University of New York (Buffalo, N.Y.), 1971. (*DAI* 32:1296A)

138. KOOKER, EARL W. "The Relationship Between Performance in a Graduate Course in Statistics and the Miller Analogies Test and the Watson-Glaser Critical Thinking Appraisal." *J Psychol* 77(2):165–9 Mr '71. * (*PA* 46:1772)

139. LEWIS, DARRELL R., AND DAHL, TOR. "The Test of Understanding in College Economics and Its Construct Validity." *J Econ Ed* 2(2):155–66 sp '71. *

140. LOWE, A. J.; FOLLMAN, JOHN; BURLEY, WADE; AND FOLLMAN, JOHNNY. "Psychometric Analysis of Critical Reading and Critical Thinking Test Scores—Twelfth Grade." *Yearb Nat Read Conf* 20:142–7 '71. *

141. O'TOOLE, DENNIS MARTIN. *An Accountability Evaluation of an In-Service Economic Education Experience.* Doctor's thesis, Ohio University (Athens, Ohio), 1971. (*DAI* 32:2315A)

142. RADEBAUGH, BYRON F., AND JOHNSON, JAMES A. "Excellent Teachers: What Makes Them Outstanding? Phase 2." *Ill Sch Res* 7(3):12–20 sp '71. *

143. SMITH, RICHARD LEE. *A Factor-Analytic Study of Critical Reading/Thinking, Influenceability, and Related Factors.* Doctor's thesis, University of Maine (Orono, Me.), 1971. (*DAI* 32:6229A)

144. WILLIAMS, BILLY RICHARD. *Critical Thinking Ability as Affected by a Unit on Symbolic Logic.* Doctor's thesis, Arizona State University (Tempe, Ariz.), 1971. (*DAI* 31:6434A)

CUMULATIVE NAME INDEX

Alexakos, C. E.: 121	Cousins, J. E.: 39
Alspaugh, C. A.: 95	Coyle, F. A.: 115
Alston, D. N.: 78	Crane, W. J.: 29
Armstrong, N. A.: 96	Crawford, C. D.: 14
Barker, L. L.: 72	Crites, J. O.: *exc,* 7:783
Bass, J. C.: 18	Crosson, R. F.: 123
Beckman, V. E.: 36	Dahl, T.: 139
Bergman, L. M. E.: 23	D'Aoust, T.: 111
Bernard, J. L.: 115	Davis, W. N.: 133
Bessent, E. W.: 26	De Graaf, C.: 10
Betres, J. J.: 132	De Martino, H. A.: 99
Bledsoe, J. C.: 8	Denney, L. L.: 69
Bostrom, E. A.: 79	Dirr, P. M.: 51
Bradberry, R. D.: 65	Dispenzieri, A.: 134
Brakken, E.: 47	Dohner, C. W.: 127
Braun, J. R.: 80	Duckworth, J. B.: 70
Brembeck, W. L.: 4–5	Ennis, R. H.: 11
Broadhurst, N. A.: 81, 97, 126	Fawcett, H. P.: *exc,* 3:544
Brouillette, O. J.: 66	Flora, L. D.: 52
Brown, L.: 101	Follman, J.: 84–6, 100–1, 105,
Brownell, J. A.: 7	135, 140
Burg, E.: 101, 135	Follman, J. C.: 87
Burley, W.: 140	Frank, A. D.: 55, 88
Burton, A.: 3	Friend, C. M.: 15
Canter, R. R.: 6	Geckler, J. W.: 48
Carleton, F. O.: 98	George, K. D.: 71
Carnes, D. D.: 82	Gibson, J. W.: 72
Chang, E. C. F.: 83	Giniger, S.: 134
Combs, C. M.: 67	Glaser, E. M.: 1
Cook, J.: 9	Glidden, G. W.: 43
Corell, J. H.: 68	Goss, R. G.: 93

[1776]

★**Wisconsin Tests of Reading Skill Development: Study Skills.** Grades kgn–1, 1–2, 2–3, 3–4, 4–5, 5–6, 6–7; 1970–73; WTRSD:SS; part of the Wisconsin Design for Reading Skill Development; 2–14 "single-skill" scores at each of 7 levels; 80% mastery criterion suggested for each subtest, with retesting at next higher level if a child fails not more than one subtest and retesting at next lower level if a child passes not more than one subtest; handbook and planning guide by Wayne Otto (principal investigator), Eunice Askov, and Robert D. Chester; manuals by Deborah M. Stewart, Karlyn Kamm, James Allen, and Diane K. Sals (*c–e*); NCS Interpretive Scoring Systems. *

a) LEVEL A. Grades kgn–1; 2 scores: position of objects, measurement (size); test by Karlyn Kamm, Deborah M. Stewart, and Virginia L. Van Blaricom.
b) LEVEL B. Grades 1–2; 4 scores: picture symbols, picture grids, measurement (distance), graphs (relative amounts); test by Karlyn Kamm, Deborah M. Stewart, and Virginia L. Van Blaricom.

c) LEVEL C. Grades 2–3; 10 scores: nonpictorial symbols, color keys, number-letter grids, measurement (size, distance), graphs (exact amounts, differences), tables (relative amounts, one cell), alphabetizing; test by Karlyn Kamm, Deborah M. Stewart, Virginia L. Van Blaricom, James Allen, and Mary L. Ramberg.
d) LEVEL D. Grades 3–4; 12 scores: point and line symbols, scale (whole units), graphs (differences, approximate amounts), tables (differences), indexes, tables of contents, alphabetizing, guide words, headings and subheadings, selecting sources, facts or opinions; test by Karlyn Kamm, Deborah M. Stewart, Virginia L. Van Blaricom, Evelyn Weible, James Allen, J. Laird Marshall, Mary L. Ramberg, and Diane K. Sals.
e) LEVEL E. Grades 4–5; 14 scores: point-line-area symbols, intermediate directions, scale (multiple whole units), graphs (differences, purpose and summary), tables (multiplicative differences, purpose and summary), indexes, dictionary meanings, cross references, guide words, guide cards, specialized references, fact checking.
f) LEVEL F. Grades 5–6; 12 scores: maps (analysis), map projections, inset maps, different scales, graphs (differences), schedules (relationship), *Subject Index*, dictionary pronunciation, card filing rules, Dewey Decimal System, outlining, catalog cards.
g) LEVEL G. Grades 6–7; 10 scores: maps (synthesis), latitude and longitude, meridians and parallels, scale (fractional units), graphs (multiplicative differences, projecting and relating), schedules (problem solving), *Reader's Guide*, card catalogs, outlining.

[Out of Print Since TIP I]

Ability to Learn (Exploratory and Corrective Inventory), T:1519
Application of Certain Principles of Logical Reasoning, R:256, 2:1528 (4 references)
Bennett Use of Library Test, R:258, 4:578 (1 review)
California Study Methods Survey, R:236, 6:857 (2 reviews, 2 excerpts, 9 references)
Cooperative Dictionary Test, R:259, 5:690 (1 review)
Edmiston How to Study Test, R:262, 4:580
Library Usage Test, R:268, 3:537 (1 review)
Peabody Library Information Test, R:241, 3:538 (1 review, 2 excerpts, 2 references)
Senior High School Library and Reference Skills Test, R:274, 6:863
Special Reading Test: Ohio Senior Survey Tests, R:275, 3:539 (1 review)
Spitzer Study Skills Test, R:244, 6:864 (2 reviews, 1 reference)
Stanford Achievement Test: Study Skills, R:276, 5:698 (2 reviews)
Survey of Study Habits, R:249, 4:583 (1 review, 1 reference)
Test of Critical Thinking, R:279, 4:584
Test of Study Skills, R:280, 5:699 (2 reviews)
Tyler-Kimber Study Skills Test, R:251, 2:1580 (4 reviews, 1 reference)
Work-Study Skills: Iowa Every-Pupil Tests of Basic Skills, R:254, 4:588 (1 review)

SCIENCE

[1777]
Adkins-McBride General Science Test. High school; 1969; Leona Adkins and Richard McBride; Psychometric Affiliates. *
For additional information and a review by Clarence H. Nelson, see 7:784.

[1778]
Borman-Sanders Elementary Science Test. 1, 2 semesters in grades 5–8; 1964; BSEST; Ina M. Borman and M. W. Sanders; Bureau of Educational Measurements. *
For additional information and a review by Carl J. Olson, see 7:785.

[1779]
CLEP General Examinations: Natural Sciences. 1–2 years of college or equivalent; 1964–73; for college accreditation of nontraditional study, advanced placement, or assessment of educational attainment; a retired subtest of the *College-Level Examination Program General Examinations* published as a separate for local administration through the *Testing Academic Achievement* program (see 1061); 3 scores: biological, physical, total; program administered for the College Entrance Examination Board by Educational Testing Service. * For the testing program entry, see 1050.
For additional information concerning earlier forms, see 7:8b. For reviews of the testing program, see 7:664 (3 reviews).

[1780]
Cooperative Science Tests: Advanced General Science. Grades 8–9; 1962–65; Cooperative Tests and Services. *
For additional information and a review by Carl J. Olson, see 7:788 (1 reference). For excerpted reviews by Irvin J. Lehmann (with Clarence H. Nelson) and William Mehrens of the series, see 7:787.
REFERENCES THROUGH 1971
1. See 7:788.
CUMULATIVE NAME INDEX
Lehmann, I. J.: *exc*, 7:787   Olson, C. J.: *rev*, 7:788
Mehrens, W.: *exc*, 7:787   Olstad, R. G.: 1
Nelson, C. H.: *exc*, 7:787

[1781]
Cooperative Science Tests: General Science. Grades 7–9; 1962–65; Cooperative Tests and Services. *
For additional information and a review by Clarence H. Nelson, see 7:789 (1 reference). For excerpted reviews by Irvin J. Lehmann (with Clarence H. Nelson) and William Mehrens of the series, see 7:787.
REFERENCES THROUGH 1971
1. See 7:789.
2. DIELMAN, T. E.; BARTON, K.; AND CATTELL, R. B. "The Prediction of Junior High School Achievement From Objective Motivation Tests." *Personality* 2(4):279–87 w '71. * (PA 48:7881)

CUMULATIVE NAME INDEX
Barton, K.: 2   Mehrens, W.: *exc*, 7:787
Cattell, R. B.: 2   Nelson, C. H.: *rev*, 7:789; *exc*,
Dielman, T. E.: 2   7:787
Lehmann, I. J.: *exc*, 7:787   Underwood, S. S.: 1

[1782]
Elementary Science Test: National Achievement Tests. Grades 4–6; 1948–58; 6 scores: practical applications, cause and effect relationships, miscellaneous facts, simple identifications, evaluation of statements, total; 1955 test identical with test copyrighted 1948 except for minor change in 1 item; Lester D. Crow and W. L. Shuman; Psychometric Affiliates. *
For additional information and a review by William Harrison Lucow, see 5:707.
REFERENCES THROUGH 1971
1. CHARLES, C. M. "Bicultural Children and Science Achievement." *Sci Ed* 48:93–6 F '64. *
CUMULATIVE NAME INDEX
Charles, C. M.: 1   Lucow, W. H.: *rev*, 5:707

[1783]
Emporia General Science Test. 1, 2 semesters high school; 1962–64; first published 1962–63 in the Every Pupil Scholarship Test series; Donald Cross and M. W. Sanders; Bureau of Educational Measurements. *
For additional information and a review by Barbara F. Esser, see 7:791.

[1784]
★General Science Test. Matriculants and higher; 1955(?)–70; GST; revision of *Test A/12: Technical and Scientific Knowledge Test* and *Test A/13: Technical Reading Comprehension;* 2 scores: technical and scientific knowledge, technical reading comprehension; National Institute for Personnel Research [South Africa]. *
REFERENCES THROUGH 1971
1. GIESEKE, MARTHA. "Predicting the Ability to Learn a Foreign Language." *Psychologia Africana* (South Africa) 13(2–3):218–21 O '70. * (PA 46:6812)
CUMULATIVE NAME INDEX
Gieseke, M.: 1

[1785]
General Science Test: National Achievement Tests. Grades 7–9; 1936–50; 7 scores: general concepts, identifications, men of science, definitions, use of objects, miscellaneous facts, total; 1950 tests identical with tests copyrighted 1936 and 1939 except for minor changes; Robert K. Speer, Lester D. Crow, and Samuel Smith; Psychometric Affiliates. *
For additional information and a review by Robert M. W. Travers, see 5:712; for reviews by Francis D. Curtis and G. W. Hunter, see 2:1602.

[1786]
General Science III: Achievement Examinations for Secondary Schools. High school; 1951–54; Form 4 ('54) of the grade 9 level of a series of tests, currently (1973) entitled *Science: Minnesota High School*

Achievement Examinations (see 1791), issued annually for May testing; Victor C. Smith; Bobbs-Merrill Co., Inc. *

For additional information concerning later and earlier forms, see 1791, 7:798, 6:875, and 5:710–1.

[1787]

*The Iowa Tests of Educational Development: Test 2, General Background in the Natural Sciences.** Grades 9–12; 1942–67; Forms X-4 and Y-4; more recent Forms X5 and Y5 are not available as separates; prepared under the direction of E. F. Lindquist and Leonard S. Feldt; Science Research Associates, Inc. * For the complete battery entry, see 20.

For additional information and reviews by Lloyd H. Heidgerd and Jacqueline V. Mallinson of earlier forms, see 6:876 (1 reference). For reviews of the complete battery, see 6:14 (2 reviews), 5:17 (2 reviews), 4:17 (1 review), and 3:12 (3 reviews).

REFERENCES THROUGH 1971
1. See 6:876.
2. TWEETEN, PAUL WILLIAM. *Correlative Relationships Between Student Achievement and Selected Evaluative Measures of High School Science Programs.* Doctor's thesis, University of Iowa (Iowa City, Iowa), 1968. (*DA* 29:2045A)
3. JOHNSON, JENNINGS O. "The Relationship Between Science Achievement and Selected Student Characteristics." *Sci Ed* 53(4):307–18 O '69. *

CUMULATIVE NAME INDEX
French, J. L.: 1   Mallinson, J. V.: *rev,* 6:876
Heidgerd, L. H.: *rev,* 6:876   Tweeten, P. W.: 2
Johnson, J. O.: 3

[1788]

*National Teacher Examinations: Biology and General Science.** College seniors and teachers; 1940–73; an inactive form (1966) entitled *Teacher Education Examination Program: Biology and General Science* is available to colleges for local administration; another inactive form (1968) entitled *Specialty Examinations: Biology and General Science* is available to school systems for local use as part of the program entitled *School Personnel Research and Evaluation Services;* Educational Testing Service. * For the testing program entry, see 869.

For additional information concerning earlier forms, see 7:793. For reviews of the testing program, see 7:582 (2 reviews), 6:700 (1 review), 5:538 (3 reviews), and 4:802 (1 review).

[1789]

*National Teacher Examinations: Chemistry, Physics and General Science.** College seniors and teachers; 1940–73; an inactive form (1966) entitled *Teacher Education Examination Program: Chemistry, Physics and General Science* is available to colleges for local administration; another inactive form (1968) entitled *Specialty Examinations: Chemistry, Physics and General Science* is available to school systems for local use as part of the program entitled *School Personnel Research and Evaluation Services;* Educational Testing Service. * For the testing program entry, see 869.

For additional information concerning earlier forms, see 7:794. For reviews of the testing program, see 7:582 (2 reviews), 6:700 (1 review), 5:538 (3 reviews), and 4:802 (1 review).

[1790]

SRA Achievement Series: Science. Grades 4–9; 1963–69; Forms C and D; more recent Forms E and F are not available as separates; Louis P. Thorpe, D. Welty Lefever, and Robert A. Naslund; Science

Research Associates, Inc. * For the complete battery entry, see 29.

For additional information and a review by Clarence H. Nelson, see 7:797. For reviews of the complete battery, see 7:18 (2 reviews), 6:21 (1 review), and 5:21 (2 reviews).

[1791]

*Science: Minnesota High School Achievement Examinations.** Grades 7, 8, 9; 1951–70; a new, revised, or previously inactive form issued each May; Achievement Examinations for Secondary Schools, High School Achievement Examinations, and Midwest High School Achievement Examinations have also been used as series titles; Form GJ Rev ('70) used in 1970 and 1973 testings; 3 levels; edited by V. L. Lohmann; American Guidance Service, Inc. *
a) SCIENCE GRADE 7 (LIFE SCIENCE). 1962–70.
b) SCIENCE GRADE 8 (EARTH SCIENCE). 1962–70.
c) SCIENCE GRADE 9 (PHYSICAL SCIENCE). 1951–70; 1963 and earlier forms called *General Science;* Form 4 ('54), entitled *General Science III: Achievement Examinations for Secondary Schools* (see 1786), is available from another publisher.

For additional information concerning out of print and inactive forms, see 7:798, 6:875, and 5:710–1; for reviews by Elizabeth Hagen and Jacqueline V. Mallinson of Form E (1962) and Form F (1963) for grades 7 and 8, see 6:881.

[1792]

Science Tests: Content Evaluation Series. Grades 8–9; 1969; 2 tests in 1 booklet; Ernestine O'Connell; Houghton Mifflin Co. *
a) PHYSICAL SCIENCE TEST: CONTENT EVALUATION SERIES.
b) EARTH SCIENCE TEST: CONTENT EVALUATION SERIES.
For additional information and a review by Jacqueline V. Mallinson, see 7:799.

[1793]

Scientific Knowledge and Aptitude Test. High school; 1964; SKAT; S. Chatterji and M. Mukerjee; S. Chatterji [India]. *

For additional information, see 7:800 (1 reference).

REFERENCES THROUGH 1971
1. See 7:800.
2. MITRA, SUBIR KUMAR; CHATTERJI, S.; AND MUKERJEE, M. "Prediction of Success in Technical Stream at the Higher Secondary Level by Using Aptitude Tests." *Manas* (India) 17(2):85–94 N '70. * (*PA* 47:9819)

CUMULATIVE NAME INDEX
Chatterji, S.: 1–2   Mukerjee, M.: 1–2
Mitra, S. K.: 2

[1794]

*Sequential Tests of Educational Progress: Science.** Grades 4–6, 7–9, 10–12, 13–14; 1956–72; 2 editions; Cooperative Tests and Services. * For the complete battery entry, see 35.
a) ORIGINAL SERIES [70 MINUTE TESTS]. 1956–63; Braille and large type editions (grades 4–12) are available from American Printing House for the Blind, Inc.
b) SERIES 2 [40 MINUTE TESTS (GRADES 4–9) AND 60 MINUTE TESTS (GRADES 10–14)]. 1956–72.
For additional information and reviews by John C. Flanagan and George G. Mallinson of *a*, see 6:882 (2 references); for reviews by Palmer O. Johnson, Julian C. Stanley (with M. Jacinta Mann), and Robert M. W. Travers, see 5:716. For reviews of the original edition of the complete battery, see 6:25 (2 reviews) and 5:24 (2 reviews, 1 excerpt).

REFERENCES THROUGH 1971

1-2. See 6:882.

3. McBee, George, and Duke, Ralph L. "Relationship Between Intelligence, Scholastic Motivation, and Academic Achievement." *Psychol Rep* 6:3-8 F '60. * (*PA* 34:8404)

4. Sharefkin, Belle Drucker. *A Study of the Possession of the Science Abilities by Student Teachers in a Liberal Arts College Preparing to Teach in Grades Four Through Six.* Doctor's thesis, New York University (New York, N.Y.), 1960. (*DA* 21:3008)

5. McGuire, Carson. "Sex Role and Community Variability in Test Performances." *J Ed Psychol* 52:61-73 Ap '61. * (*PA* 38:3207)

6. Hukins, Austin Adolphus. *A Factorial Investigation of Measures of Achievement of Objectives in Science Teaching.* Doctor's thesis, University of Alberta (Edmonton, Alta., Canada), 1963.

7. Russell, James William. *An Analysis of the Academic Performance of Transfer and Native Students and Their Major Fields in the College of Arts and Sciences at the University of Georgia.* Doctor's thesis, University of Georgia (Athens, Ga.), 1963. (*DA* 25:1668)

8. Jones, Kenneth J. "Interest, Motivation, and Achievement in Science." *J Exp Ed* 33:41-53 f '64. * (*PA* 39:6097)

9. Roberts, John Byron. *A Study of the Problem Solving Processes of Successful and Nonsuccessful Problem Solvers in Ninth Grade Science.* Doctor's thesis, University of Alabama (University, Ala.), 1964. (*DA* 25:7088)

10. Bae, Agnes Young-Ok. *The Prediction of the Learning of Chemistry Among Eleventh Grade Girls.* Doctor's thesis, Catholic University of America (Washington, D.C.), 1965. (*DA* 25:487A)

11. Rowland, George William. *A Study of the Relationship Between Socio-Economic Status and Elementary School Science Achievement.* Doctor's thesis, University of Missouri (Columbia, Mo.), 1965. (*DA* 26:5306)

12. Boney, J. Don. "Predicting the Academic Achievement of Secondary School Negro Students." *Personnel & Guid J* 44:700-3 Mr '66. * (*PA* 40:8064)

13. Jenkins, Alice Crawford. *The Relationship of Certain Measurable Factors to Academic Success in Freshman Biology.* Doctor's thesis, New York University (New York, N.Y.), 1966. (*DA* 27:2279A)

14. Jones, Franklin McGehee. *A Controlled Comparison of the Academic Performance of Native and Transfer Students at the University of Georgia.* Doctor's thesis, University of Georgia (Athens, Ga.), 1966. (*DA* 27:3227A)

15. Senter, Donald Russell. *An Appraisal of an Elementary School Science Program.* Doctor's thesis, Wayne State University (Detroit, Mich.), 1966. (*DA* 28:882A)

16. Bae, Agnes Y. "The Prediction of the Learning of Chemistry Among Eleventh Grade Girls Through the Use of the Stepwise and Doolittle Techniques." *Ed & Psychol Meas* 27:1131-6 w '67. * (*PA* 42:9494)

17. Denney, Loren L. *The Relationships Between Teaching Method, Critical Thinking and Other Selected Teacher Traits.* Doctor's thesis, University of Missouri (Columbia, Mo.), 1968. (*DA* 29:2586A)

18. Underwood, Stephen Sharp. *A Study of the Relative Performance of Selected Sixth-Grade Children and Elementary School Student Teachers on Two Standardized Science Tests.* Doctor's thesis, University of Alabama (University, Ala.), 1969. (*DAI* 30:4865A)

19. Hinerman, Charles Ovalee. *The Level of Achievement of Graduating Missouri High School Seniors on Two Referents of Scientific Literacy.* Doctor's thesis, University of Wisconsin (Madison, Wis.), 1971. (*DAI* 31:6430A)

20. Stockwell, Keith William. *The Identification and Analysis of Selected Factors Contributing to High Achievement in Elementary School Science.* Doctor's thesis, Wayne State University (Detroit, Mich.), 1971. (*DAI* 32:3012A)

For additional references, see the bibliography for the series, 35.

CUMULATIVE NAME INDEX

Bae, A. Y.: 16	Liggitt, W. A.: 2
Bae, A. Y. O.: 10	McBee, G.: 3
Boney, J. D.: 12	McGuire, C.: 5
Denney, L. L.: 17	Mallinson, G. G.: *rev*, 6:882
Duke, R. L.: 3	Mann, M. J.: *rev*, 5:716
Flanagan, J. C.: *rev*, 6:882	Roberts, J. B.: 9
Gega, P. C.: 1	Rowland, G. W.: 11
Hinerman, C. O.: 19	Russell, J. W.: 7
Hukins, A. A.: 6	Senter, D. R.: 15
Jenkins, A. C.: 13	Sharefkin, B. D.: 4
Johnson, P. O.: *rev*, 5:716	Stanley, J. C.: *rev*, 5:716
Jones, F. M.: 14	Stockwell, K. W.: 20
Jones, K. J.: 8	Travers, R. M. W.: *rev*, 5:716
Karlsen, B.: 1	Underwood, S. S.: 18

[1795]

Stanford Achievement Test: High School Science Test. Grades 9-12; 1965-66; catalog uses the title *Stanford High School Science Test;* subtest of

---

Stanford Achievement Test: High School Basic Battery; 2 scores: Part A (basic), total (basic and advanced) ; Eric F. Gardner, Jack C. Merwin, Robert Callis, and Richard Madden; Harcourt Brace Jovanovich, Inc. * For the complete battery entry, see 37.

For additional information and reviews by Robert G. Brigham and Robert L. Ebel, see 7:801. For reviews of the complete battery, see 7:27 (2 reviews).

[1796]

Stanford Achievement Test, 1964 Edition: Science. Grades 5.5-6.9, 7.0-9.9; 1940-68; catalog uses the title *Stanford Science Tests;* not available as a separate in the 1973 edition of the battery; Braille editions are available from American Printing House for the Blind, Inc.; Truman L. Kelley, Richard Madden, Eric F. Gardner, and Herbert C. Rudman; Harcourt Brace Jovanovich, Inc. * For the complete battery entry, see 36.

For additional information and a review by Jacqueline V. Mallinson, see 7:802 (1 reference); for reviews by Bertram Epstein and Paul E. Kambly of an earlier edition, see 4:593. For reviews of the complete battery, see 7:25 (1 excerpt), 6:26 (1 review, 1 excerpt), 5:25 (1 review), 4:25 (2 reviews), and 3:18 (2 reviews).

REFERENCES THROUGH 1971

1. See 7:802.

CUMULATIVE NAME INDEX

Epstein, B.: *rev*, 4:593	Mallinson, J. V.: *rev*, 7:802
Kambly, P. E.: *rev*, 4:593	Story, W. E.: 1

[1797]

*Teacher Education Examination Program: Biology and General Science. College seniors preparing to teach secondary school; 1957-72; formerly called *Teacher Education Examination Program: Biological Science;* reprinting of inactive 1966 form of *National Teacher Examinations: Biology and General Science;* test available to colleges for local administration; Educational Testing Service. * For the testing program entry, see 898.

For additional information concerning an earlier form, see 6:887. For a review of the testing program, see 5:543.

[1798]

*Teacher Education Examination Program: Chemistry, Physics and General Science. College seniors preparing to teach secondary school; 1957-72; formerly called *Teacher Education Examination Program: Physical Science;* reprinting of inactive 1966 form of *National Teacher Examinations: Chemistry, Physics and General Science;* test available to colleges for local administration; Educational Testing Service. * For the testing program entry, see 898.

For additional information concerning an earlier form, see 6:878. For a review of the testing program, see 5:543.

[1799]

Tests of Academic Progress: Science. Grades 9-12; 1964-66; Dale P. Scannell and William B. Reiner; Houghton Mifflin Co. * For the complete battery entry, see 44.

For additional information and a review by Irvin J. Lehmann, see 7:805 (1 reference). For a review of the complete battery, see 7:31.

REFERENCES THROUGH 1971

1. See 7:805.

CUMULATIVE NAME INDEX

Goolsby, T. M.: 1	Lehmann, I. J.: *rev*, 7:805

Sequential Tests of Educational Progress: Science

[Out of Print Since TIP I]

Ability for Science: Fife Tests of Ability, 3:546 (2 references)

Cooperative General Achievement Tests: Natural Science [General Proficiency Series], 6:870 (1 review, 4 references)

Cooperative General Science Test, 4:623 (4 reviews, 1 reference)

Cooperative Science Test for Grades 7, 8, and 9, 4:624 (3 reviews)

Coordinated Scales of Attainment: Science, 5:704

Elementary Science and Health: Every Pupil Test, 6:872

Elementary Science: Every Pupil Scholarship Test, 6:871

General Science: Every Pupil Scholarship Test, 6:873

General Science: Every Pupil Test, 6:874

General Science Scales, T:1559

General Science Test: State High School Tests for Indiana, 4:592

McDougal General Science Test, 3:576 (2 reviews)

Metropolitan Achievement Tests: High School Science Tests, 7:792 (2 reviews)

Metropolitan Achievement Tests: Science, 6:877 (2 reviews)

Physical Science Aptitude Examination, 3:547 (2 reviews)

Processes of Science Test, 7:795 (1 review, 1 reference)

Purdue Physical Science Aptitude Test, 6:879 (1 review, 8 references)

Read General Science Test, 7:796 (4 reviews, 2 references)

Science Aptitude Examination, see 6:765

Science Background, 6:880

Survey Test in Introductory Science, 6:884 (2 reviews)

Survey Test in Physical Science, 6:885 (1 review)

T. C. General Science Test, 6:886

Test of Science Knowledge, 7:803 (1 review)

BIOLOGY

[1800]

*Advanced Placement Examination in Biology. High school students desiring credit for college level courses or admission to advanced courses; 1956–73; available to secondary schools for annual administration on specified days in May; inactive forms are available to colleges for local administration in the *Testing Academic Achievement* program; program administered for the College Entrance Examination Board by Educational Testing Service. * For the testing program entry, see 1045.

For additional information concerning earlier forms, see 7:807 (1 reference); for a review by Clarence H. Nelson, see 6:893 (1 reference); for a review by Clark W. Horton, see 5:724. For reviews of the testing program, see 7:662 (2 reviews).

REFERENCES THROUGH 1971
1. See 6:893.
2. See 7:807.

CUMULATIVE NAME INDEX
Horton, C. W.: *rev,* 5:724   Nelson, C. H.: *rev,* 6:893
Moore, M. R.: 2   Valley, J. R.: 1

[1801]

*BSCS Achievement Tests. Grade 10; 1962–70; 3 versions, each containing 4 quarterly achievement tests and a comprehensive final; prepared by Biological Sciences Curriculum Study. *

a) BLUE VERSION—BIOLOGICAL SCIENCE: MOLECULES TO MAN. 1962–68; 2 editions; for use with the BSCS text of the same title; Houghton Mifflin Co.
   1) [*Original Edition*]: *Forms R and S.* 1962–65.
   2) *Revised Edition: Forms T and U.* 1962–68; experimental edition; no manual.

b) YELLOW VERSION—BIOLOGICAL SCIENCE: AN INQUIRY INTO LIFE, SECOND EDITION. 1962–70; for use with the BSCS text of the same title; distributed by Harcourt Brace Jovanovich, Inc.

c) BSCS GREEN VERSION HIGH SCHOOL BIOLOGY, SECOND EDITION. 1962–70; for use with the BSCS text of the same title; Rand McNally & Co.

For additional information, see 7:808.

[1802]

*Biological Science: Interaction of Experiments and Ideas, Revised Edition. Grades 10–12; 1963–70; intended for use with the BSCS text of the same title; Biological Sciences Curriculum Study; Educational Programs Improvement Corporation. *

For additional information, see 7:809.

[1803]

*Biology: Minnesota High School Achievement Examinations. High school; 1951–70; a new, revised, or previously inactive form issued each May; Achievement Examinations for Secondary Schools, High School Achievement Examinations, and Midwest High School Achievement Examinations have also been used as series titles for tests now out of print; Form GJ Rev ('70) used in 1970 and 1973 testings; edited by V. L. Lohmann; American Guidance Service, Inc. *

For additional information concerning out of print and inactive forms, see 7:811, 5:719, and 5:722; for a review by Barbara F. Esser of Form E (1962) and Form F (1963), see 6:890.

[1804]

*CLEP Subject Examination in Biology. 1 year or equivalent; 1970–73; for college accreditation of nontraditional study, advanced placement, or assessment of educational achievement; tests administered monthly at centers throughout the United States; program administered for the College Entrance Examination Board by Educational Testing Service. * For the testing program entry, see 1050.

For additional information, see 7:812. For reviews of the testing program, see 7:664 (3 reviews).

[1805]

*College Board Achievement Test in Biology. Candidates for college entrance; 1915–73; test administered on specified dates at centers established by the publisher; inactive forms, entitled *College Placement Test in Biology,* are available to colleges for local administration; program administered for the College Entrance Examination Board by Educational Testing Service. * For the testing program entry, see 1048.

For additional information, see 7:813 (2 references); see also 6:892 (3 references); for a review by Elizabeth Hagen of an earlier form, see 5:723; for a review by Clark W. Horton, see 4:600. For reviews of the testing program, see 6:760 (2 reviews).

REFERENCES THROUGH 1971
1–3. See 6:892.
4–5. See 7:813.

CUMULATIVE NAME INDEX

Bleifeld, M.: 3
College Entrance Examination
  Board: 1
Evenson, A. B.: 2
Hagen, E.: *rev*, 5:723
Horton, C. W.: *rev*, 4:600
Kastrinos, W.: 4

Ludlow, H. G.: 5
Mayer, W. V.: *exc*, 7:B86
Morgan, J. M.: 5
Pugh, R. C.: 5
Smith, D. E.: 2
Voss, B.: 4

[1806]

*College Placement Test in Biology. Entering college freshmen; 1962–72, c1961–72; reprintings of inactive 1962 and 1963 forms of *College Board Achievement Test in Biology;* test available to colleges for local administration; program administered for the College Entrance Examination Board by Educational Testing Service. * For the testing program entry, see 1051.

For additional information, see 7:814. For a review of the testing program, see 7:665. For reference to reviews of the *College Board Achievement Test in Biology,* see 1805.

[1807]

*Cooperative Biology Test: Educational Records Bureau Edition. High school; 1941–70; Committee on Biology Tests of the Educational Records Bureau; Educational Records Bureau. *

For additional information concerning earlier forms, see 6:895; see also 5:725 (1 reference) and 4:602 (2 references).

REFERENCES THROUGH 1971

1–2. See 4:602.
3. See 5:725.
4. TRAXLER, ARTHUR E. "The 1964 ERB Edition of the Cooperative Biology, Chemistry, and Physics Tests: Difficulty, Reliability, and Correlation With School Marks." *Ed Rec B* 86:67–70 Jl '64. *

CUMULATIVE NAME INDEX

Traxler, A. E.: 1–4

[1808]

Cooperative Science Tests: Biology. Grades 10–12; 1963–65; 3 scores: general and human biology, the diversity of life, total; Cooperative Tests and Services. *

For additional information and a review by Clarence J. Goodnight, see 7:816. For excerpted reviews by Irvin J. Lehmann (with Clarence H. Nelson) and William Mehrens of the series, see 7:787.

[1809]

Emporia Biology Test. 1, 2 semesters high school; 1962–64; first published 1962–63 in the Every Pupil Scholarship Test series; Ted F. Andrews and M. W. Sanders; Bureau of Educational Measurements. *
For additional information, see 7:817.

[1810]

General Biology Test: National Achievement Tests. High school; 1951; 4 scores: uses-processes-results, biologists, miscellaneous facts, total; Lester D. Crow and James G. Murray; Psychometric Affiliates. *

For additional information and reviews by Elizabeth Hagen and Clark W. Horton, see 5:726.

[1811]

*The Graduate Record Examinations Advanced Biology Test. Graduate school candidates; 1939–73; 4 scores: cellular and subcellular, organismal, population, total; Educational Testing Service. * For the testing program entry, see 1053.
For additional information concerning earlier forms, see 7:818; for a review by Clark W. Horton, see

5:727. For reviews of the testing program, see 7:667 (1 review) and 5:601 (1 review).

[1812]

Nelson Biology Test, Revised Edition. Grades 9–13; 1950–65; Clarence H. Nelson; Harcourt Brace Jovanovich, Inc. *

For additional information, reviews by Barbara F. Esser and Arnold B. Grobman and an excerpted review by Joseph D. Novak, see 7:819 (3 references); for reviews by Clark W. Horton and Leland P. Johnson of the original edition, see 4:605.

REFERENCES THROUGH 1971

1–3. See 7:819.
4. SCHOCK, NORVILLE H. *An Analysis of the Relationship Which Exists Between Cognitive and Affective Educational Objectives in Selected Biology Classrooms of Wayne County, Michigan.* Doctor's thesis, Wayne State University (Detroit, Mich.), 1971. (*DAI* 32:6016A)

CUMULATIVE NAME INDEX

Esser, B. F.: *rev*, 7:819
Grobman, A. B.: *rev*, 7:819
Horton, C. W.: *rev*, 4:605
Johnson, L. P.: *rev*, 4:605
Kastrinos, W.: 2
Maberly, N. C.: 3

MacKinney, A. C.: 1
Novak, J. D.: *exc*, 7:819
Schock, N. H.: 4
Stephans, P.: 1
Wolins, L.: 1

[1813]

*The Undergraduate Program Field Tests: Biology Test. College; 1969–73; formerly called *The Undergraduate Record Examinations: Biology Test;* test available to colleges for local administration; Educational Testing Service. * For the testing program entry, see 1062.

For additional information, see 7:820. For reviews of the testing program, see 7:671 (2 reviews).

[Out of Print Since TIP I]

Biological Science: Patterns and Processes, 7:810 (1 excerpt)
Biology: Every Pupil Scholarship Test, 6:888
Biology: Every Pupil Test, 6:889
Biology Test: Affiliation Testing Program for Catholic Secondary Schools, 6:891 (1 review)
Biology Test: State High School Tests for Indiana, 4:598
Biology: 20th Century Test, 4:599; for a revision, see *Semester Test in Biology,* T:1593
Comprehensive Final Examination in First Year Biology, 7:815 (1 review, 1 reference)
Cooperative Biology Test, 4:601 (5 reviews, 1 reference)
First Year High School Biology: Manchester Semester-End Achievement Tests, T:1582, 36:549
Survey Test in Biological Science, 6:897 (2 reviews)
Williams Biology Test, 2:1589 (3 reviews, 1 reference)

CHEMISTRY

[1814]

ACS Cooperative Examination Brief Course in Organic Chemistry. 1 semester college; 1956–70; Examinations Committee, American Chemical Society. *

For additional information, see 7:821 (1 reference); for an excerpted review by LeRoy D. Johnson of an earlier form, see 6:905.

REFERENCES THROUGH 1971

1. See 7:821.

CUMULATIVE NAME INDEX

Johnson, L. D.: *exc*, 6:905

[1815]

*ACS Cooperative Examination in Analytical Chemistry, Graduate Level. Entering graduate students; 1961–73; an earlier edition called *A.C.S. Cooperative Examination for Graduate Placement in Analytical Chemistry;* Examinations Committee, American Chemical Society. *

For additional information, see 7:822 (1 reference); see also 6:899 (1 reference).

REFERENCES THROUGH 1971

1. See 6:899.
2. See 7:822.
3. "Condensed Norms: ACS Cooperative Examinations." *J Chem Ed* 47(4):321 Ap '70. *

[1816]

*ACS Cooperative Examination in Biochemistry. College; 1947–72; first part of test suitable for short survey courses; Examinations Committee, American Chemical Society. *

For additional information, see 7:823 (1 reference); for an excerpted review by Wilhelm R. Frisell of an earlier form, see 6:898 (2 references).

REFERENCES THROUGH 1971

1–2. See 6:898.
3. See 7:823.

CUMULATIVE NAME INDEX

Frisell, W. R.: *exc,* 6:898

[1817]

ACS Cooperative Examination in Brief Physical Chemistry. 1 semester college; 1968; Examinations Committee, American Chemical Society. *

For additional information, see 7:824.

REFERENCES THROUGH 1971

1. "Condensed Norms: ACS Cooperative Examinations." *J Chem Ed* 47(4):321 Ap '70. *

[1818]

*ACS Cooperative Examination in Brief Qualitative Analysis. College; 1961–73; Examinations Committee, American Chemical Society. *

For additional information, see 7:825; for an excerpted review by W. H. Waggoner of an earlier form, see 6:906 (4 references).

REFERENCES THROUGH 1971

1–2. See 4:608. For 4 additional references, see 6:906.
3. Hovey, Nelson W. "The Present and Future of Qualitative Analysis: Report of a Survey." *J Chem Ed* 40:410–2 Ag '63. *
4. "Condensed Norms: ACS Cooperative Examinations." *J Chem Ed* 42:170–1 Mr '65. *
5. "Condensed Norms: ACS Cooperative Examinations." *J Chem Ed* 45:273–4 Ap '68. *
6. "Condensed Norms: ACS Cooperative Examinations." *J Chem Ed* 48(7):487–8 Jl '71. *

CUMULATIVE NAME INDEX

Ashford, T. A.: 2
Calandra, A.: 1
Cortelyou, W. P.: 1
Frank, R. E.: *exc,* 6:906
Hovey, N. W.: 3
Meldrum, W. B.: *rev,* 3:562
Reed, R. D.: 1
Rieman, W.: *rev,* 3:562, 4:608
Waggoner, W. H.: *exc,* 6:906

[1819]

*ACS Cooperative Examination in General Chemistry. 1 year college; 1934–73; Examinations Committee, American Chemical Society. *

For additional information, see 7:826 (5 references); for reviews by J. A. Campbell and William Hered and an excerpted review by S. L. Burson, Jr. of earlier forms, see 6:902 (3 references); for reviews by Frank P. Cassaretto and Palmer O. Johnson, see 5:732 (2 references); for a review by Kenneth E. Anderson, see 4:610 (1 reference); for reviews by

Sidney J. French and Florence E. Hooper, see 3:557 (3 references); see also 2:1593 (5 references).

REFERENCES THROUGH 1971

1–5. See 2:1593.
6–8. See 3:557.
9. See 4:610.
10–11. See 5:732.
12–14. See 6:902.
15–19. See 7:826.
20. "Condensed Norms: ACS Cooperative Examinations." *J Chem Ed* 48(7):487–8 Jl '71. *

CUMULATIVE NAME INDEX

Allen, F. J.: 5
American Chemical Society, Division Chemical Education, Committee on Examinations and Tests: 1
Anderson, K. E.: *rev,* 4:610
Ashford, T. A.: 7, 9
Braun, J. R.: 18
Burson, S. L.: *exc,* 6:902
Calandra, A.: 8
Campbell, J. A.: *rev,* 6:902
Cassaretto, F. P.: *rev,* 5:732
Foster, L. S.: 6
French, S. J.: *rev,* 3:557
Hered, W.: *rev,* 6:902
Hooper, F. E.: *rev,* 3:557
Johnson, P. O.: *rev,* 5:732
Martin, F. D.: 4–5
Norton, B. M.: 11
Phelan, E. W.: 2
Reed, R. D.: 3
Rice, C. L.: 10
Snider, C. F. B.: 19
Troxel, V. A.: 19
Vinton, K. W.: 10

[1820]

*ACS Cooperative Examination in Inorganic Chemistry. College juniors and seniors; 1961–72; 3 scores: part 1 (objective type questions), part 2 (essay type questions), total; Examinations Committee, American Chemical Society. *

For additional information, see 7:827 (2 references); for a review by Frank J. Fornoff and an excerpted review by George B. Kauffman of an earlier form, see 6:903 (1 reference).

REFERENCES THROUGH 1971

1. See 6:903.
2–3. See 7:827.
4. "Condensed Norms: ACS Cooperative Examinations." *J Chem Ed* 47(4):321 Ap '70. *

[1821]

ACS Cooperative Examination in Inorganic Chemistry, Graduate Level. Entering graduate students; 1965–70; Examinations Committee, American Chemical Society. *

For additional information, see 7:828.

REFERENCES THROUGH 1971

1. "Condensed Norms: ACS Cooperative Examinations." *J Chem Ed* 48(7):487–8 Jl '71. *

[1822]

*ACS Cooperative Examination in Inorganic-Organic-Biological Chemistry (for Paramedical Programs). 1–2 semesters of chemistry for nursing, home economics, and other paramedical students; 1970–72; 4 scores: inorganic, organic, biological, total; Examinations Committee, American Chemical Society. *

For additional information, see 7:829.

[1823]

*ACS Cooperative Examination in Instrumental Analysis. College juniors and seniors; 1966–72; Examinations Committee, American Chemical Society. *

For additional information, see 7:830 (1 reference).

REFERENCES THROUGH 1971

1. See 7:830.

[1824]

*ACS Cooperative Examination in Organic Chemistry. 1 year college; 1942–71; earlier tests called *A.C.S. Cooperative Organic Chemistry Test;* Examinations Committee, American Chemical Society. *

For additional information, see 7:831 (3 references) ; see also 6:905 (4 references) ; for a review by Shailer Peterson of an earlier form, see 3:558.

REFERENCES THROUGH 1971

1-4. See 6:905.
5-7. See 7:831.

CUMULATIVE NAME INDEX

Heindel, N. D.: 7   Lepley, A. R.: 7
Johnson, L. D.: exc, 6:905   Peterson, S.: rev, 3:558

[1825]

ACS Cooperative Examination in Organic Chemistry, Graduate Level. Entering graduate students; 1961-71; an earlier edition called A.C.S. Cooperative Examination for Graduate Placement in Organic Chemistry; Examinations Committee, American Chemical Society. *

For additional information, see 7:832 (1 reference) ; see also 6:900 (1 reference).

REFERENCES THROUGH 1971

1. See 6:900.
2. See 7:832.

[1826]

*ACS Cooperative Examination in Physical Chemistry. 1 year college; 1946-73; 1973 form consists of 3 parts (thermodynamics, chemical dynamics, quantum chemistry) which may be administered separately or together; Examinations Committee, American Chemical Society. *

For additional information, see 7:833 (2 references) ; see also 6:904 (1 reference) ; for a review by Alfred S. Brown of an earlier form, see 3:559.

REFERENCES THROUGH 1971

1. See 6:904.
2-3. See 7:833.
4. "Condensed Norms: ACS Cooperative Examinations." J Chem Ed 47(4):321 Ap '70. *
5. "Condensed Norms: ACS Cooperative Examinations." J Chem Ed 48(7):487-8 Jl '71. *

CUMULATIVE NAME INDEX

Brown, A. S.: rev, 3:559   Lepley, A. R.: 3
Heindel, N. D.: 3

[1827]

*ACS Cooperative Examination in Physical Chemistry, Graduate Level. Entering graduate students; 1961-72; an earlier edition called A.C.S. Cooperative Examination for Graduate Placement in Physical Chemistry; Examinations Committee, American Chemical Society. *

For additional information, see 7:834 (2 references) ; see also 6:901 (1 reference).

REFERENCES THROUGH 1971

1. See 6:901.
2-3. See 7:834.

[1828]

ACS Cooperative Examination in Qualitative Analysis. College; 1939-69; formerly called A.C.S. Cooperative Chemistry Test in Qualitative Analysis; Examinations Committee, American Chemical Society. *

For additional information, see 7:835; for an excerpted review by Richard E. Frank of an earlier form, see 6:906 (4 references) ; for a review by William Rieman III, see 4:608; for reviews by William B. Meldrum and William Rieman III, see 3:562.

REFERENCES THROUGH 1971

1-4. See 6:906.

CUMULATIVE NAME INDEX

Frank, R. E.: exc, 6:906   Rieman, W.: rev, 3:562, 4:608
Meldrum, W. B.: rev, 3:562

[1829]

*ACS Cooperative Examination in Quantitative Analysis. College; 1944-74; Examinations Committee, American Chemical Society. *

For additional information, see 7:836 (1 reference) ; see also 6:907 (1 reference) ; for an excerpted review by H. E. Wilcox of an earlier form, see 5:735; for reviews by William B. Meldrum and William Rieman III, see 3:563.

REFERENCES THROUGH 1971

1. See 6:907.
2. See 7:836.

CUMULATIVE NAME INDEX

Meldrum, W. B.: rev, 3:563   Wilcox, H. E.: exc, 5:735
Rieman, W.: rev, 3:563

[1830]

*ACS-NSTA Cooperative Examination in High School Chemistry. 1 year high school; 1957-73; for an upper level test in the same area, see 1831; sponsored jointly with the National Science Teachers Association; Examinations Committee, American Chemical Society. *

For additional information and reviews by William R. Crawford and Irvin J. Lehmann, see 7:837 (9 references) ; for reviews by Frank J. Fornoff and William Hered and excerpted reviews by Christine Jansing and Joseph Schmuckler of earlier forms, see 6:908 (5 references) ; for reviews by Edward G. Rietz and Willard G. Warrington, see 5:729.

REFERENCES THROUGH 1971

1-5. See 6:908.
6-14. See 7:837.
15. "Condensed Norms: ACS Cooperative Examinations." J Chem Ed 47(4):321 Ap '70. *
16. "Condensed Norms: ACS Cooperative Examinations." J Chem Ed 48(7):487-8 Jl '71. *
17. DENNY, RITA T. "The Mathematics Skill Test (MAST) for Chemistry." J Chem Ed 48(12):845-6 D '71. *

CUMULATIVE NAME INDEX

Crawford, W. R.: rev, 7:837   Judge, A. J.: 12, 14
Denny, R. T.: 17   Larson, G. R.: 13
Edwin, H.: 2   Lehmann, I. J.: rev, 7:837
Fornoff, F. J.: rev, 6:908   Marie, J.: 2
Hendrickson, C. W.: 9-11, 14   Martin, A. M.: 2
Hered, W.: rev, 6:908   Rietz, E. G.: rev, 5:729
Jansing, C.: exc, 6:908   Schmuckler, J.: exc, 6:908
Jones, K. J.: 5   Sieveking, N. A.: 13
Judge, A.: 11   Warrington, W. G.: rev, 5:729

[1831]

*ACS-NSTA Cooperative Examination in High School Chemistry [Advanced Level]. Advanced high school classes; 1963-72; for a lower level test in the same area, see 1830; sponsored jointly with the National Science Teachers Association; Examinations Committee, American Chemical Society. *

For additional information and a review by Irvin J. Lehmann, see 7:838 (3 references) ; for reviews by Frank J. Fornoff and William Hered of the 1963 form, see 6:909.

REFERENCES THROUGH 1971

1-3. See 7:838.

CUMULATIVE NAME INDEX

Fornoff, F. J.: rev, 6:909   Lehmann, I. J.: rev, 7:838
Hered, W.: rev, 6:909   Morrison, R. T.: 2

[1832]

*Advanced Placement Examination in Chemistry. High school students desiring credit for college level courses or admission to advanced courses; 1954-73; available to secondary schools for annual administration on specified days in May; inactive forms are available to colleges for local administration in the Testing Academic Achievement program; program administered for the College Entrance Examination Board by Educational Testing Service. * For the testing program entry, see 1045.

For additional information concerning earlier forms, see 7:839; see also 6:915 (1 reference); for a review by Theo. A. Ashford, see 5:743. For reviews of the testing program, see 7:662 (2 reviews).

REFERENCES THROUGH 1971
1. See 6:915.
2. GILBERT, ARTHUR C. F. "Predicting Graduation From an Engineering School." J Psychol Studies 11:229-31 Jl-Ag '60. * (PA 35:7045)

CUMULATIVE NAME INDEX
Ashford, T. A.: rev, 5:743   Valley, J. R.: 1
Gilbert, A. C. F.: 2

[1833]
*CLEP Subject Examination in General Chemistry. 1 year or equivalent; 1964-73; for college accreditation of nontraditional study, advanced placement, or assessment of educational achievement; tests administered monthly at centers throughout the United States; program administered for the College Entrance Examination Board by Educational Testing Service. * For the testing program entry, see 1050.

For additional information, see 7:841. For reviews of the testing program, see 7:664 (3 reviews).

[1834]
Chemistry: Achievement Examinations for Secondary Schools. High School; 1951-54; Form 4 ('54) of a series of tests, currently (1973) entitled Chemistry: Minnesota High School Achievement Examinations (see 1836), issued annually for May testing; Harry E. Pulver; Bobbs-Merrill Co., Inc. *

For additional information concerning later and earlier forms, see 1836, 7:843, 6:912, 5:738, and 5:741 (1 review).

[1835]
Chemistry Achievement Test for CHEM Study or Equivalent. High school; 1968-69; no manual; George C. Whiteley, Jr., Harold W. Ferguson, William Allan Jacobs, and Kenneth Jackman; Educational Records Bureau. *

For additional information, see 7:842.

[1836]
*Chemistry: Minnesota High School Achievement Examinations. High school; 1955-73; a new, revised, or previously inactive form issued each May; Achievement Examinations for Secondary Schools, High School Achievement Examinations, and Midwest High School Achievement Examinations have also been used as series titles; Form GJ Rev ('70) used in 1970 and 1973 testings; Form 4 ('54) entitled Chemistry: Achievement Examinations for Secondary Schools (see 1834), is available from another publisher; edited by V. L. Lohmann; American Guidance Service, Inc. *

For additional information concerning out of print and inactive forms, see 7:843, 6:912, and 5:738; for a review by Edward G. Rietz of Form A (1955) and Form B (1957), see 5:741.

[1837]
*College Board Achievement Test in Chemistry. Candidates for college entrance; 1901-73; test administered on specified dates at centers established by the publisher; inactive forms, entitled College Placement Test in Chemistry, are available to colleges for local administration; program administered for the College Entrance Examination Board by Educational Testing Service. * For the testing program entry, see 1048.

For additional information, see 7:844 (3 references); for a review by William Hered of earlier forms, see 6:914 (4 references); for a review by Max D. Engelhart, see 5:742 (2 references); for a review by Evelyn Raskin, see 4:617 (4 references). For reviews of the testing program, see 6:760 (2 reviews).

REFERENCES THROUGH 1971
1-4. See 4:617.
5-6. See 5:742.
7-10. See 6:914.
11-13. See 7:844.

CUMULATIVE NAME INDEX
Black, D. B.: 7, 9   Jones, K. J.: 10
College Entrance Examination   Ludlow, H. G.: 13
  Board: 5   Morgan, J. M.: 13
Dickason, D. G.: 12   Pugh, R. C.: 13
Engelhart, M. D.: rev, 5:742   Raskin, E.: rev, 4:617
Evenson, A. B.: 6   Smith, D. E.: 6
Foster, L. F.: 1   Weber, C. O.: 4
Gilbert, A. C. F.: 8   Willingham, W. W.: 11
Hered, W.: rev, 6:914

[1838]
*College Placement Test in Chemistry. Entering college freshmen; 1962-72, c1956-72; reprintings of inactive 1964 and 1965 forms of College Board Achievement Test in Chemistry; test available to colleges for local administration; program administered for the College Entrance Examination Board by Educational Testing Service. * For the testing program entry, see 1051.

For additional information, see 7:845. For a review of the testing program, see 7:665. For reference to reviews of the College Board Achievement Test in Chemistry, see 1837.

[1839]
*Cooperative Chemistry Test: Educational Records Bureau Edition. High school; 1941-70; 3 scores: concepts, problems, total; Committee on Chemistry Tests of the Educational Records Bureau; Educational Records Bureau. *

For additional information and a review by Kenneth J. Jones of earlier forms, see 6:917; see also 5:745 (1 reference) and 4:619 (2 references).

REFERENCES THROUGH 1971
1-2. See 4:619.
3. See 5:745.
4. TRAXLER, ARTHUR E. "The 1964 ERB Edition of the Cooperative Biology, Chemistry, and Physics Tests: Difficulty, Reliability, and Correlation With School Marks." Ed Rec B 86:67-70 Jl '64. *

CUMULATIVE NAME INDEX
Jones, K. J.: rev, 6:917   Traxler, A. E.: 1-4

[1840]
Cooperative Science Tests: Chemistry. Grades 10-12; 1963-65; 3 scores: general concepts and principles, laboratory, total; Cooperative Tests and Services. *

For additional information, see 7:846. For excerpted reviews by Irvin J. Lehmann (with Clarence H. Nelson) and William Mehrens of the series, see 7:787.

[1841]
Emporia Chemistry Test. 1, 2 semesters high school; 1962-64; first published 1962-63 in the Every Pupil Scholarship Test series; A. T. Ericson and M. W. Sanders; Bureau of Educational Measurements. *

For additional information, see 7:847.

[1842]
General Chemistry Test: National Achievement Tests. Grades 10-16; 1958-59; 4 scores: uses-processes-results, formulae and valence, miscellaneous

facts, total; no manual; Lester D. Crow and Roy S. Cook; Psychometric Affiliates. *

For additional information and a review by J. A. Campbell, see 6:918.

[1843]

*The Graduate Record Examinations Advanced Chemistry Test.** Graduate school candidates; 1939–73; Educational Testing Service. * For the testing program entry, see 1053.

For additional information concerning earlier forms, see 7:848 (1 reference); for a review by Max D. Engelhart, see 6:919. For reviews of the testing program, see 7:667 (1 review) and 5:601 (1 review).

REFERENCES THROUGH 1971
1. See 7:848.

CUMULATIVE NAME INDEX

Engelhart, M. D.: *rev*, 6:919   Marco, G. L.: 1
Lannholm, G. V.: 1   Schrader, W. B.: 1

[1844]

Iowa Placement Examinations: Chemistry Aptitude. Grades 12–13; 1925–44; 2 editions; G. D. Stoddard, Jacob Cornog, L. W. Miller (*b*), and D. B. Stuit (*b*); Bureau of Educational Research and Service. *
a) SERIES CAI, REVISED. 1925–26.
b) NEW SERIES CA2, REVISED. 1925–44.

For additional information and a review by Kenneth E. Anderson, see 4:621 (5 references); for a review by Theodore A. Ashford, see 3:566 (15 references).

REFERENCES THROUGH 1971
1–15. See 3:566.
16–20. See 4:621.
21. HAMMOND, H. P., AND STODDARD, GEORGE DINSMORE. "A Study of Placement Examinations." *Univ Iowa Studies Ed* 4(7): 1–59 '28. * (*PA* 3:2069)
22. BRAY, WILLIS J. "Aptitude and Its Relation to Achievement in General Chemistry." *Sci Ed* 16:439–42 D '32. *
23. PERRY, ROBERT D. *Prediction Equations for Success in College Mathematics.* Contribution to Education No. 122. Nashville, Tenn.: George Peabody College for Teachers, 1934. Pp. xiii, 58. * (*PA* 8:3277)
24. McCLANAHAN, WALTER R., AND MORGAN, DAVID H. "Use of Standard Tests in Counseling Engineering Students in College." *J Ed Psychol* 39:491–501 D '48. * (*PA* 23:3448)
25. RALPH, SALLY. *The Prediction of Success in the College of Pharmacy at the University of Utah.* Master's thesis, University of Utah (Salt Lake City, Utah), 1948.
26. BARNETTE, W. LESLIE, JR. "Occupational Aptitude Pattern Research." *Occupations* 29:5–12 O '50. * (*PA* 25:3239)
27. JEX, FRANK B. *University of Utah Studies in the Prediction of Academic Success.* University of Utah Research Monographs in Education, Vol. 1, No. 1. Salt Lake City, Utah: the University, July 1957. Pp. ix, 51. *
28. HORNYAK, DOLORES J. *A Study of the Predictive Value of the Iowa Placement Examination—Chemistry Aptitude in a Freshman Chemistry Class.* Master's thesis, Bowling Green State University (Bowling Green, Ohio), 1961.
29. BAE, AGNES YOUNG-OK. *The Prediction of the Learning of Chemistry Among Eleventh Grade Girls.* Doctor's thesis, Catholic University of America (Washington, D.C.), 1965. (*DA* 28:487A)
30. OTA, YOSHIKO KAY. *Prediction of the Learning of Chemistry Among Eleventh Grade Boys.* Doctor's thesis, Catholic University of America (Washington, D.C.), 1965. (*DA* 26:4455)
31. BAE, AGNES Y. "The Prediction of the Learning of Chemistry Among Eleventh Grade Girls Through the Use of the Stepwise and Doolittle Techniques." *Ed & Psychol Meas* 27:1131–6 w '67. * (*PA* 42:9494)

CUMULATIVE NAME INDEX

Anderson, K. E.: *rev*, 4:621   Frank, G.: 13
Ashford, T. A.: *rev*, 3:566   Hammond, H. P.: 21
Bae, A. Y.: 31   Hornyak, D. J.: 28
Bae, A. Y. O.: 29   Jex, F. B.: 27
Barnette, W. L.: 17, 19, 26   Krathwohl, W. C.: 20
Bird, K. L.: 10   Langlie, T. A.: 4–5, 7–8
Bray, W. J.: 22   McClanahan, W. R.: 24
Brinegar, V.: 13   Miller, L. W.: 11
Cook, G. A.: 12   Moore, M. E.: 15
Cornog, J.: 1, 3   Morgan, D. H.: 24
Fisher, H. R.: 14   Ota, Y. K.: 30

Perry, R. D.: 23   Stalnaker, J. M.: 16
Ralph, S.: 25   Stoddard, G. D.: 1–3, 6, 21
Reusser, W. C.: 13   Trimble, H. M.: 9
Smith, O. M.: 9   Uhrbrock, R. S.: 18

[1845]

Iowa Placement Examinations: Chemistry Training: Series CT1, Revised. Grades 12–13; 1925–26; G. D. Stoddard and J. Cornog; Bureau of Educational Research and Service. *

For additional information and a review by Kenneth E. Anderson, see 4:622 (1 reference); for a review by Theodore A. Ashford, see 3:567 (14 references).

REFERENCES THROUGH 1971
1–14. See 3:567.
15. See 4:622.
16. HAMMOND, H. P., AND STODDARD, GEORGE DINSMORE. "A Study of Placement Examinations." *Univ Iowa Studies Ed* 4(7): 1–59 '28. * (*PA* 3:2069)
17. BRAY, WILLIS J. "A Study of the Achievements of Students of General Chemistry in College." *Sch Sci & Math* 32:19–29 Ja '32. *

CUMULATIVE NAME INDEX

Anderson, K. E.: *rev*, 4:622   McGehee, W.: 14
Ashford, T. A.: *rev*, 3:567   MacPhail, A. H.: 12–3
Bray, W. J.: 17   Miller, L. W.: 10
Brinegar, V.: 11   Moffie, D. J.: 14
Cornog, J.: 1, 3, 8   Reusser, W. C.: 11
Foster, L. S.: 12–3   Smith, O. M.: 9
Frank, G.: 11   Stoddard, G. D.: 1–3, 6, 8, 16
Hammond, H. P.: 16   Trimble, H. M.: 9
Langlie, T. A.: 4–5, 7   Uhrbrock, R. S.: 15

[1846]

RBH Test of Chemical Comprehension. Employee applicants and applicants for nurses training; 1951–68; "chemical facts" of an "everyday nature"; Richardson, Bellows, Henry & Co., Inc. *

For additional information, see 7:849.

[1847]

*Toledo Chemistry Placement Examination.** College entrants; 1959–67; TCPE; 7 scores: arithmetic and algebra, general knowledge, formulas and nomenclature, equations, algebraic formulations, chemical problems, total; Albertine Krohn and Nelson W. Hovey (Form 1963); Examinations Committee, American Chemical Society. *

For additional information and reviews by Kenneth E. Anderson and William R. Crawford of the 1959 and 1963 forms, see 6:920 (1 reference).

REFERENCES THROUGH 1971
1. See 6:920.
2. LEMBECK, MICHAEL. *Predicting Academic Success in Freshman Chemistry.* Master's thesis, San Diego State College (San Diego, Calif.), 1967.
3. NICHOLS, WILLIAM A. *An Evaluation of the Predictive Validity of the Toledo Chemistry Placement Examination at Northeast Missouri State College.* Master's thesis, Northeast Missouri State College (Kirksville, Mo.), 1968.

CUMULATIVE NAME INDEX

Anderson, K. E.: *rev*, 6:920   Krohn, A.: 1
Crawford, W. R.: *rev*, 6:920   Lembeck, M.: 2
Hovey, N. W.: 1   Nichols, W. A.: 3

[1848]

*The Undergraduate Program Field Tests: Chemistry Test.** College; 1969–73; formerly called *The Undergraduate Record Examinations: Chemistry Test;* test available to colleges for local administration; Educational Testing Service. * For the testing program entry, see 1062.

For additional information concerning an earlier form, see 7:850. For reviews of the testing program, see 7:671 (2 reviews).

General Chemistry Test: National Achievement Tests

[Out of Print Since TIP I]

Anderson-Fisk Chemistry Test, 7:840 (3 reviews, 1 excerpt, 4 references) ; original edition called *Anderson Chemistry Test,* 4:613

Chemistry: Every Pupil Scholarship Test, 6:910

Chemistry: Every Pupil Test, 6:911

Chemistry Test: Affiliation Testing Program for Catholic Secondary Schools, 6:913 (1 review)

Chemistry Test: State High School Tests for Indiana, 4:616 (1 review)

Cooperative Chemistry Test, 5:744 (7 reviews) ; see also 4:618 (4 references)

Cooperative Objective Unit Tests in Organic Chemistry (status unknown), T:1616, 2:1595

First Year High School Chemistry: Manchester Semester-End Achievement Tests, T:1617, 36:575

Junior Chemistry Test, 5:747 (2 reviews)

Kirkpatrick Chemistry Test, 3:568 (1 review, 1 reference)

Qualitative Analysis Supplement for General Chemistry, 5:732c (2 reviews)

GEOLOGY

[1849]

*CLEP Subject Examination in Geology. 1 year or equivalent; 1965–73; for college accreditation of nontraditional study, advanced placement, or assessment of educational achievement; tests administered monthly at centers throughout the United States; program administered for the College Entrance Examination Board by Educational Testing Service. * For the testing program entry, see 1050.

For additional information, see 7:851. For reviews of the testing program, see 7:664 (3 reviews).

[1850]

*The Graduate Record Examinations Advanced Geology Test. Graduate school candidates; 1939–73; 4 scores: stratigraphy-paleontology-geomorphology, structural geology and geophysics, mineralogy-petrology-geochemistry, total; Educational Testing Service. * For the testing program entry, see 1053.

For additional information concerning earlier forms, see 7:852 (1 reference). For reviews of the testing program, see 7:667 (1 review) and 5:601 (1 review).

REFERENCES THROUGH 1971

1. See 7:852.

CUMULATIVE NAME INDEX

Gruber, E. C.: 1

[1851]

*The Undergraduate Program Field Tests: Geology Test. College; 1969–73; formerly called *The Undergraduate Record Examinations: Geology Test;* test available to colleges for local administration; Educational Testing Service. * For the testing program entry, see 1062.

For additional information, see 7:853. For reviews of the testing program, see 7:671 (2 reviews).

MISCELLANEOUS

[1852]

The Butler Life Science Concept Test. Grades 1–6; 1965–69; LSCT; all 1969 materials identical with those copyrighted 1965 except for format; D. F. Butler; Psychometric Affiliates. *

For additional information and a review by Victor H. Noll, see 7:786.

[1853]

Dubins Earth Science Test. Grades 8–12; 1969; M. Ira Dubins; Harcourt Brace Jovanovich, Inc. *

For additional information and a review by Floyd V. Monaghan, see 7:790.

[1854]

★**NM Concepts of Ecology Test.** Grades 6–8, 9–12; 1973; NMCET; Monitor. *

[1855]

★**Science Attitude Questionnaire.** Secondary school; 1970–71; SAQ; also called *Attitudes to Science Questionnaire;* for research use only; 5 scores: science interest, social implications of science, learning activities, science teachers, schools; test by Larry S. Skurnik and Patricia M. Jeffs with a contribution by Taysir Kawa; manual by Desmond Nuttall; National Foundation for Educational Research in England and Wales [England]. *

[1856]

Test on Understanding Science. Grades 9–12; 1961; TOUS; for research use only; 4 understanding scores: the scientific enterprise, scientists, methods and aims of science, total; W. W. Cooley and L. E. Klopfer; Educational Testing Service (Atlanta Office). *

For additional information and reviews by Hulda Grobman and Victor H. Noll, see 7:804 (30 references) ; see also 6:925 (3 references).

REFERENCES THROUGH 1971

1–3. See 6:925.

4–33. See 7:804.

34. FIELD, T. W., AND CROPLEY, A. J. "Structure of Thought Among Senior Students: Science and Non-Science." *Austral Sci Teach J* 14:27–32 Ag '68. *

35. BROADHURST, NORMAN A. "A Measure of Some Learning Outcomes in Matriculation Chemistry in South Australia." *Austral Sci Teach J* 15(3):67–70 N '69. *

36. KLOPFER, LEOPOLD E., AND MCCANN, DONALD C. "Evaluation in Unified Science: Measuring the Effectiveness of the Natural Science Course at the University of Chicago High School." *Sci Ed* 53(2):155–64 Mr '69. *

37. LAVACH, JOHN F. "Organization and Evaluation of an In-Service Program in the History of Science." *J Res Sci Teach* 6(2):166–70 '69. *

38. JERDONEK, AGNES CLARE. *Correlates of School-Average Science Achievement in the Secondary Schools of the Catholic Diocese of Cleveland.* Doctor's thesis, Case Western Reserve University (Cleveland, Ohio), 1970. (*DAI* 32:268A)

39. MACKAY, LINDSAY D. "Development of Understanding of the Nature of Science in Some Victorian Students." *Austral Sci Teach J* 16(1):57–67+ My '70. *

40. CHAPMAN, HAROLD LEROY. *The Effect of an In-Service Summer Elementary School Science Education Institute on Attitudes Toward Science and Science Understandings of Elementary School Teachers.* Doctor's thesis, University of Connecticut (Storrs, Conn.), 1971. (*DAI* 32:2503A)

41. FUHRMANN, EARL FRED ALBERT. *Understanding and Support of Science on the Part of Clergy, Seminarians, and Youth of the Lutheran Church-Missouri Synod.* Doctor's thesis, University of Colorado (Boulder, Colo.), 1971. (*DAI* 32:6680A)

42. MACKAY, LINDSAY D. "Development of Understanding About the Nature of Science." *J Res Sci Teach* 8(1):57–66 '71. *

43. STANGL, GEORGE RONALD. *An Assessment of Introductory Physical Science Using the Test on Understanding Science.* Doctor's thesis, University of Michigan (Ann Arbor, Mich.), 1971. (*DAI* 32:1362A)

44. WILLIAMSON, TROY LEE. *Social Attitudes Toward Science of Freshmen at Hinds Junior College Relative to Their Understanding of Science.* Doctor's thesis, Mississippi State University (State College, Miss.), 1971. (*DAI* 32:3816A)

CUMULATIVE NAME INDEX

Abegg, G. L.: 15	Combs, C. M.: 16
Ahlgren, A.: 32	Cooley, W. W.: 1–2
Anderson, G. J.: 18, 30	Craven, G. F.: 9
Bae, A. Y.: 5, 12	Cropley, A. J.: 34
Broadhurst, N. A.: 22, 35	Crumb, G. H.: 6
Chapman, H. L.: 40	Field, T. W.: 34

Fuhrmann, E. F. A.: 41
Grobman, H.: *rev*, 7:804
Hukins, A. A.: 4
Jerdonek, A. C.: 38
Jerkins, K. F.: 23–4
Jones, K. M.: 25
Klopfer, L. E.: 1–2, 36
Lavach, J. F.: 37
McCann, D. C.: 36
Mackay, L. D.: 39, 42
Merkin, M.: 13
Noll, V. H.: *rev*, 7:804
Olstad, R. G.: 26
Rothman, A. I.: 19, 27–8
Schmidt, D. J.: 14

Schmidt, R. H.: 17
Senter, D. R.: 10
Smith, P. M.: 3
Snider, C. F. B.: 31
Stangl, G. R.: 43
Trent, J.: 7
Trent, J. H.: 8
Troxel, V. A.: 31
Wachs, S. R.: 11
Walberg, H. J.: 18, 28, 32
Waltz, M. F.: 33
Welch, W. W.: 19, 28–9
Williamson, T. L.: 44
Willoughby, J. R.: 20
Yager, R. E.: 21

[1857]

*Tests of Basic Experiences: Science. Prekgn–kgn, kgn–grade 1; 1970–72; Margaret H. Moss; CTB/McGraw-Hill. * For the complete battery entry, see 47.
For additional information, see 7:806. For a review of the complete battery, see 7:33.

[Out of Print Since TIP I]

Facts About Science Test, 6:921
Measurement of Observation and Understanding of Physical Phenomena and Life Processes, 4:631
Test of Reasoning in Conservation, 6:924 (1 reference)

PHYSICS

[1858]

*Advanced Placement Examination in Physics. High school students desiring credit for college level courses or admission to advanced courses; 1954–73; available to secondary schools for annual administration on specified days in May; inactive forms are available to colleges for local administration in the *Testing Academic Achievement* program; 2 levels; program administered for the College Entrance Examination Board by Educational Testing Service. * For the testing program entry, see 1045.
a) PHYSICS B. Equivalent of 1 year terminal course in college physics.
b) PHYSICS C. Equivalent of 1 year nonterminal course in college physics.
For additional information concerning earlier forms, see 7:854; see also 6:927 (2 references); for a review by Leo Nedelsky, see 5:750. For reviews of the testing program, see 7:662 (2 reviews).

REFERENCES THROUGH 1971
1–2. See 6:927.

CUMULATIVE NAME INDEX
Gilbert, A. C. F.: 2   Valley, J. R.: 1
Nedelsky, L.: *rev*, 5:750

[1859]

*College Board Achievement Test in Physics. Candidates for college entrance; 1901–73; test administered on specified dates at centers established by the publisher; inactive forms, entitled *College Placement Test in Physics,* are available to colleges for local administration; program administered for the College Entrance Examination Board by Educational Testing Service. * For the testing program entry, see 1048.
For additional information, see 7:855 (2 references); see also 6:926 (4 references); for a review by Theodore G. Phillips of an earlier form, see 5:749 (2 references); for a review by Palmer O. Johnson, see 4:633 (3 references). For reviews of the testing program, see 6:760 (2 reviews).

Test on Understanding Science

REFERENCES THROUGH 1971
1–3. See 4:633.
4–5. See 5:749.
6–9. See 6:926.
10–11. See 7:855.

CUMULATIVE NAME INDEX
Black, D. B.: 6, 8
College Entrance Examination Board: 4
Dickason, D. G.: 10
Evenson, A. B.: 5
Gewirtz, H.: 9
Gilbert, A. C. F.: 7
Johnson, P. O.: *rev*, 4:633
Phillips, T. G.: *rev*, 5:749
Schwarz, G.: 11
Smith, D. E.: 5
Thompson, R. E.: 11
Turnbull, W. W.: 3
Weber, C. O.: 2

[1860]

*College Placement Test in Physics. Entering college freshmen; 1962–72, c1954–72; reprintings of inactive 1964 forms of *College Board Achievement Test in Physics;* test available to colleges for local administration; program administered for the College Entrance Examination Board by Educational Testing Service. * For the testing program entry, see 1051.
For additional information, see 7:856. For a review of the testing program, see 7:665. For reference to reviews of the *College Board Achievement Test in Physics,* see 1859.

[1861]

*Cooperative Physics Test: Educational Records Bureau Edition. High school; 1941–70; 3 scores: concepts, problems, total; Committee on Physics Tests of the Educational Records Bureau; Educational Records Bureau. *
For additional information concerning earlier forms, see 6:929; see also 5:752 (1 reference) and 4:635 (2 references).

REFERENCES THROUGH 1971
1–2. See 4:635.
3. See 5:752.
4. TRAXLER, ARTHUR E. "The 1964 ERB Edition of the Cooperative Biology, Chemistry, and Physics Tests: Difficulty, Reliability, and Correlation With School Marks." *Ed Rec B* 86:67–70 Jl '64. *

CUMULATIVE NAME INDEX
Traxler, A. E.: 1–4

[1862]

Cooperative Science Tests: Physics. Grades 10–12; 1963–65; 3 scores: general concepts and principles, laboratory, total; Cooperative Tests and Services. *
For additional information and a review by Alexander Even, see 7:857. For excerpted reviews by Irvin J. Lehmann (with Clarence H. Nelson) and William Mehrens of the series, see 7:787.

[1863]

Dunning-Abeles Physics Test. Grades 10–13; 1950–67; revision of *Dunning Physics Test;* Gordon M. Dunning and Sigmund Abeles; Harcourt Brace Jovanovich, Inc. *
For additional information and a review by Theodore G. Phillips, see 7:858 (2 references); for a review by Robert M. W. Travers of the original edition, see 5:753; for a review by G. P. Cahoon, see 4:636.

REFERENCES THROUGH 1971
1–2. See 7:858.

CUMULATIVE NAME INDEX
Bannon, C. J.: 1
Brakken, E.: 2
Cahoon, G. P.: *rev*, 4:636
Phillips, T. G.: *rev*, 7:858
Travers, R. M. W.: *rev*, 5:753

[1864]

Emporia Physics Test. 1, 2 semesters high school; 1962–64; first published 1962–63 in the Every Pupil

Scholarship Test series; Gerald L. Witten and M. W. Sanders; Bureau of Educational Measurements. *

For additional information and a review by Theodore G. Phillips, see 7:859.

[1865]

General Physics Test: National Achievement Tests. Grades 10–16; 1958–62; 3 scores: uses and application of principles, miscellaneous facts and scientists, total; no manual; Lester D. Crow and Roy S. Cook; Psychometric Affiliates. *

For additional information and a review by Theodore G. Phillips, see 6:930.

[1866]

*The Graduate Record Examinations Advanced Physics Test. Graduate school candidates; 1939–73; Educational Testing Service. * For the testing program entry, see 1053.

For additional information concerning earlier forms, see 7:860; for a review by Theodore G. Phillips, see 6:931; for a review by Leo Nedelsky, see 5:754. For reviews of the testing program, see 7:667 (1 review) and 5:601 (1 review).

[1867]

Iowa Placement Examinations: Physics Aptitude. Grades 12–13; 1925–44; 2 editions; test by G. D. Stoddard, C. J. Lapp, and D. B. Stuit (b); Bureau of Educational Research and Service. *
a) SERIES PA-1, REVISED. 1925–26.
b) NEW SERIES PA-2, REVISED. 1925–44.

For additional information and a review by John W. French, see 4:638 (2 references); for a review by Robert M. W. Travers, see 3:587 (4 references).

REFERENCES THROUGH 1971
1–4. See 3:587.
5–6. See 4:638.
7. HAMMOND, H. P., AND STODDARD, GEORGE DINSMORE. "A Study of Placement Examinations." *Univ Iowa Studies Ed* 4(7): 1–59 '28. * (*PA* 3:2069)

CUMULATIVE NAME INDEX

Bear, R. M.: 2	Stoddard, G. D.: 1, 7
French, J. W.: *rev*, 4:638	Stuit, D. B.: 3–4
Hammond, H. P.: 7	Travers, R. M. W.: *rev*, 3:587
Lapp, C. J.: 4	Uhrbrock, R. S.: 6
Stalnaker, J. M.: 5	

[1868]

Iowa Placement Examinations: Physics Training: Series PT1, Revised. Grades 12–13; 1925–26; test by C. J. Lapp and G. D. Stoddard; Bureau of Educational Research and Service. *

For additional information and a review by G. P. Cahoon, see 4:639 (2 references).

REFERENCES THROUGH 1971
1–2. See 4:639.
3. HAMMOND, H. P., AND STODDARD, GEORGE DINSMORE. "A Study of Placement Examinations." *Univ Iowa Studies Ed* 4(7): 1–59 '28. * (*PA* 3:2069)

CUMULATIVE NAME INDEX

Cahoon, G. P.: *rev*, 4:639	Stoddard, G. D.: 1, 3
Hammond, H. P.: 3	Uhrbrock, R. S.: 2

[1869]

★Objective Tests in Physics. High school; 1971; OTP; 8 tests; Gwen M. Mossop, H. J. Ritchie, and E. J. Matthews; English Universities Press Ltd. [England]. *
a) 1, FUNDAMENTALS OF MATTER, ENERGY AND WAVES.
b) 2, FUNDAMENTALS OF MATTER, ENERGY AND WAVES.
c) 3, HEAT AND OPTICS.
d) 4, HEAT AND OPTICS.
e) 5, ELECTRICITY AND ATOMIC PHYSICS.

f) 6, ELECTRICITY AND ATOMIC PHYSICS.
g) 7, COMPLETE SYLLABUS.
h) 8, COMPLETE SYLLABUS.

[1870]

Physics: Achievement Examinations for Secondary Schools. High school; 1951–54; Form 4 ('54) of a series of tests, currently (1973) entitled *Physics: Minnesota High School Achievement Examinations* (see 1871), issued annually for May testing; Kenneth A. Berg; Bobbs-Merrill Co., Inc. *

For additional information concerning later and earlier forms, see 1871, 7:861, 6:934 (1 review), 5: 756, and 5:759.

[1871]

*Physics: Minnesota High School Achievement Examinations. High school; 1951–70; a new, revised, or old inactive form issued each May; Achievement Examinations for Secondary Schools, High School Achievement Examinations, and Midwest High School Achievement Examinations have been used as series titles; Form GJ Rev ('70) used in 1970 and 1973 testings; Form 4 ('54), entitled *Physics: Achievement Examinations for Secondary Schools* (see 1870), is available from another publisher; edited by V. L. Lohmann; American Guidance Service, Inc. *

For additional information concerning out of print and inactive forms, see 7:861, 5:756, and 5:759; for a review by Irvin J. Lehmann of Form E (1962) and Form F (1963), see 6:934.

[1872]

Tests of the Physical Science Study Committee. High school; 1959–67; based upon the secondary school physics course prepared by the Physical Science Study Committee; Cooperative Tests and Services. *
a) TESTS FOR BASIC COURSE. 1959–64; 10 tests: 8 unit tests and a test covering each half of the course.
b) FINAL EXAMINATION FOR BASIC COURSE. 1967; no manual.
c) ADVANCED TOPICS. 1967; 4 unit tests.

For additional information and an excerpted review by Haym Kruglak, see 7:862; for reviews by George G. Mallinson and Leo Nedelsky of a, see 6:936 (1 reference).

REFERENCES THROUGH 1971
1. See 6:936.
2. BRAUND, ROBERT A. "Pilot Study of a Cognitive Restructuring Paradigm." *Psychol Rep* 20:275–9 F '67. * (*PA* 41:7919)

CUMULATIVE NAME INDEX

Braund, R. A.: 2	Mallinson, G. G.: *rev*, 6:936
Fornoff, F. J.: 1	Nedelsky, L.: *rev*, 6:936
Kruglak, H.: *exc*, 7:862	

[1873]

*The Undergraduate Program Field Tests: Physics Test. College; 1969–73; formerly called *The Undergraduate Record Examinations: Physics Tests;* test available to colleges for local administration; Educational Testing Service. * For the testing program entry, see 1062.

For additional information concerning an earlier form, see 7:863. For reviews of the testing program, see 7:671 (2 reviews).

[Out of Print Since TIP I]

College Entrance Examination Board Achievement Test in PSSC Physics, T:1629
Cooperative Physics Test, 5:751 (7 reviews, 3 references)

Fulmer-Schrammel Physics Test, 2:1610 (2 reviews)
High School Physics: Manchester Semester-End Achievement Tests, T:1645, 36:795
Junior Physics Test, 5:755 (2 reviews)
Physics: Every Pupil Scholarship Test, 6:932
Physics: Every Pupil Test, 6:933

Physics Test: State High School Tests for Indiana, 4:642 (1 review)
Physics Test (Traditional and PSSC): Affiliation Testing Program for Catholic Secondary Schools, 6:935 (1 review)
Physics: 20th Century Test, 4:643

SENSORY-MOTOR

[1874]
The D-K Scale of Lateral Dominance. Grades 2–6; 1969; DKSLD; 6 dominance scores: hand, foot, visual, auditory, intermodal, intramodal; Russell A. Dusewicz and Keith M. Kershner; Foundation for Research in Mental Development. *
For additional information and a review by Donald A. Leton, see 7:865 (2 references).

REFERENCES THROUGH 1971
1–2. See 7:865.

CUMULATIVE NAME INDEX
Dusewicz, R. A.: 1–2   Leton, D. A.: *rev,* 7:865
Kershner, K. M.: 1–2

[1875]
Developmental Test of Visual-Motor Integration. Ages 2–8, 2–15; 1967; VMI; Keith E. Beery and Norman A. Buktenica (test); Follett Publishing Co. *
For additional information and a review by Brad S. Chissom, see 7:867 (5 references).

REFERENCES THROUGH 1971
1–5. See 7:867.
6. BUKTENICA, NORMAN A. "Perceptual Mode Dominance: An Approach to Assessment of First Grade Reading and Spelling." Abstract. *Proc 76th Ann Conv Am Psychol Assn* 3:585–6 '68. * (*PA* 43:1459, title only)
7. BROWN, LISA SABLE. *Good and Retarded Readers Compared According to Performance on Visual-Motor, Simulated Language Learning and Memory Tasks.* Doctor's thesis, University of Northern Colorado (Greeley, Colo.), 1970. (*DAI* 31:7566B)
8. COURTNEY, JOHN A. *Correlation of Performance on the Developmental Test of Visual-Motor Integration With Academic Success.* Master's thesis, Southern Connecticut State College (New Haven, Conn.), 1971.
9. FALK, LIBBY JANET. *A Profile of Learning Abilities and Behavorial Characteristics of Elementary School-Age Children With Phenylketonuria.* Doctor's thesis, Temple University (Philadelphia, Pa.), 1971. (*DAI* 32:1913A)
10. RYCKMAN, DAVID B., AND RENTFROW, ROBERT K. "The Beery Developmental Test of Visual-Motor Integration: An Investigation of Reliability." *J Learn Dis* 4(6):333–4 Je–Jl '71. * (*PA* 47:9662)
11. STEPSIS, JOAN ARLENE. *A Follow-Up Investigation of the Effects of a Program That Significantly Improved Perceptual Ability (Non-Verbal Intellectual Maturity) in Young School Children.* Doctor's thesis, University of Michigan (Ann Arbor, Mich.), 1971. (*DAI* 32:3803A)

CUMULATIVE NAME INDEX
Beery, K. E.: 2   Georgas, J. G.: 3
Brown, L. S.: 7   Giles, M. T.: 4
Bryant, D. H.: 5   Papadopoulou, E.: 3
Buktenica, N. A.: 1, 6   Rentfrow, R. K.: 10
Chissom, B. S.: *rev,* 7:867   Ryckman, D. B.: 10
Courtney, J. A.: 8   Stepsis, J. A.: 11
Falk, L. J.: 9

[1876]
★**Frostig Movement Skills Test Battery, Experimental Edition.** Ages 6–12; 1972; FMSTB; 6 scores: hand-eye coordination, strength, balance, visually guided movement, flexibility, composite; R. E. Orpet; Consulting Psychologists Press, Inc. *

[1877]
Harris Tests of Lateral Dominance. Ages 7 and over; 1947–58; 13–15 scores: knowledge of right and left, hand dominance (7 scores, 1 optional), eye dominance (4 scores, 1 optional), foot dominance (3 scores); Albert J. Harris; distributed by Psychological Corporation. *
For additional information, see 5:761 (1 reference); for reviews by William G. Peacher and Miles A. Tinker of an earlier edition, see 4:644; for an excerpted review, see 3:466.

REFERENCES THROUGH 1971
1. See 5:761.
2. STORCH, HERBERT R. *Retinal Rivalry: Its Relation to Reading Disability, ETE Movements in Reading, Ocular Dominance, and Visual Acuity.* Doctor's thesis, Yeshiva University (New York, N.Y.), 1957. (*DA* 19:578)
3. BALOW, IRVING H. *The Relationship of Lateral Dominance Characteristics to Reading Achievement in the First Grade.* Doctor's thesis, University of Minnesota (Minneapolis, Minn.), 1959. (*DA* 20:2138)
4. BALOW, IRVING H. "Lateral Dominance Characteristics and Reading Achievement in the First Grade." *J Psychol* 55:323–8 Ap '63. * (*PA* 38:1407)
5. PAYNE, JOE DEAN. *The Effect of Hand and Eye Dominance on Horizontal and Vertical Reading.* Doctor's thesis, Texas Technological College (Lubbock, Tex.), 1963. (*DA* 24:5205)
6. BALOW, IRVING H., AND BALOW, BRUCE. "Lateral Dominance and Reading Achievement in the Second Grade." *Am Ed Res J* 1:139–43 My '64. * (*PA* 39:7100)
7. COLEMAN, RICHARD I., AND DEUTSCH, CYNTHIA P. "Lateral Dominance and Right-Left Discrimination: A Comparison of Normal and Retarded Readers." *Percept & Motor Skills* 19:43–50 Ag '64. * (*PA* 39:4245)
8. MCDONALD, ANGUS, JR. *Differences Between High Ability Underachieving Students and High Ability Achieving Students in Relation to Self-Concept, Anxiety, and Lateral Dominance.* Doctor's thesis, University of Maryland (College Park, Md.), 1964. (*DA* 26:200)
9. TINKER, KAREN J. "The Role of Laterality in Reading Disability." *Proc Ann Conv Int Read Assn* 10:300–3 '65. *
10. BOONE, DANIEL R., AND LATAS, WILLIAM J. "Left-Right Discrimination Problems in Neurologically Impaired Children." *Univ Kan B Ed* 21:12–8 N '66. *
11. CASHMAN, JEROME PATRICK. *A Study of the Relationship Between Organic Factors, Certain Selected Variables and Progress in a Reading Improvement Program.* Doctor's thesis, Fordham University (New York, N.Y.), 1966. (*DAI* 27:1648A)
12. COHEN, ALICE. *Relationship Between Factors of Dominance and Reading Ability With Selected First and Fourth Grade Children.* Master's thesis, Adelphi University (Garden City, N.Y.), 1966.
13. ANTHONY, GEORGE A. *Cerebral Dominance as an Etiological Factor in Dyslexia (Severe Reading Disability).* Doctor's thesis, New York University (New York, N.Y.), 1968. (*DAI* 30:1425A)
14. WHATLEY, CLEVELAND EARL. *The Relationship Between Handedness and Selected Cognitive and Social Variables Among Culturally Disadvantaged Preschool Children.* Doctor's thesis, University of Alabama (University, Ala.), 1968. (*DA* 29:3477A)
15. COHEN, ALICE. "Relationship Between Factors of Domi-

nance and Reading Ability." *Proc Ann Conv Int Read Assn* 13(3):38–45 '69. *

16. GARRISON, ROBERTA ANN. *A Study of the Relationship Between Certain Traits of Laterality and the Take-Off Foot in Selected Skills of Locomotion.* Master's thesis, Texas Woman's University (Denton, Tex.), 1969.

17. MEWES, GORDEN EUGENE. *An Attempt to Determine the Association, if Any, Between Crossed Dominance and Achievement Levels in Instrumental Music Reading.* Doctor's thesis, University of Oklahoma (Norman, Okla.), 1969. (*DAI* 31:416A)

18. FORNESS, STEVEN R., AND WEIL, MARVIN C. "Laterality in Retarded Readers With Brain Dysfunction." *Excep Children* 36(9):684–5 My '70. * (*PA* 46:5518)

19. KNOX, ALBERT W., AND BOONE, DANIEL R. "Auditory Laterality and Tested Handedness." *Cortex* (Italy) 6(2):164–73 Je '70. *

20. ORLANDO, CHARLES PHILLIP. *Relationships Between Language Laterality and Handedness in Eight and Ten Year Old Boys.* Doctor's thesis, University of Connecticut (Storrs, Conn.), 1971. (*DAI* 32:2489A)

21. SAPIR, SELMA G. "Learning Disability and Deficit Centered Classroom Training." *Cognitive Studies* 2:324–38 '71. * (*PA* 49:1359, title only)

CUMULATIVE NAME INDEX

Anthony, G. A.: 13	Latas, W. J.: 10
Balow, B.: 6	McDonald, A.: 8
Balow, I. H.: 3–4, 6	Mewes, G. E.: 17
Boone, D. R.: 10, 19	Orlando, C. P. 20
Cashman, J. P.: 11	Payne, J. D.: 5
Cohen, A.: 12, 15	Peacher, W. G.: *rev*, 4:644
Coleman, R. I.: 7	Sapir, S. G.: 21
Deutsch, C. P.: 7	Storch, H. R.: 2
Forness, S. R.: 18	Tinker, K. J.: 9
Garrison, R. A.: 16	Tinker, M. A.: *rev*, 4:644
Harris, A. J.: 1	Weil, M. C.: 18
Knox, A. W.: 19	Whatley, C. E.: 14

[1878]

*Leavell Hand-Eye Coordinator Tests. Ages 8–14; 1958–61; for determining need for training on the Delacato Stereo-Reader; 7 scores: hand-foot preference, eye-ear preference, hand dexterity preference, visual imagery (3 scores), total; Ullin W. Leavell; Keystone View. *

For additional information, see 6:937.

[1879]

MKM Picture Arrangement Test. Grades kgn–6; 1963–65; "directionality"; Leland D. Michael and James W. King; MKM, Inc. *

For additional information, see 7:870.

[1880]

*Moore Eye-Hand Coordination and Color-Matching Test. Ages 2–6, 7 and over; 1949–68; 2 levels; Joseph E. Moore; Joseph E. Moore and Associates. *

a) THE MOORE EYE-HAND COORDINATION TEST: PRESCHOOL FORM. Ages 2–6.

b) MOORE EYE-HAND COORDINATION AND COLOR-MATCHING TEST. Ages 7 and over; 2 scores: eye-hand coordination, color matching.

For additional information, see 5:872 (1 reference); for reviews by Norman Frederiksen and Jay L. Otis, see 4:750 (6 references).

REFERENCES THROUGH 1971

1–6. See 4:750.
7. See 5:872.
8. JENSEN, MILTON B., AND SCHMID, JOHN. "An Analysis of Some Clinical Judgments on Male Basic Airmen Who Failed the Group Psychological Tests." *J Clin Psychol* 10:325–32 O '54. * (*PA* 29:4753)
9. ROBERTS, ARTHUR JAMES. *The Relationship Between Kindergarten Experience and Fine-Muscle Eye-Hand Coordination Abilities of First Grade Children.* Doctor's thesis, Oregon State University (Corvallis, Ore.), 1970. (*DAI* 31:2019A)

CUMULATIVE NAME INDEX

Frederiksen, N.: *rev*, 4:750	Roberts, A. J.: 9
Jensen, M. B.: 8	Schmid, J.: 8
Moore, J. E.: 1–6	Williams, W. A.: 7
Otis, J. L.: *rev*, 4:750	

[1881]

Perceptual Forms Test. Ages 5–6, 6–8; 1955–69; PFT; revision of *Children's Perceptual Achievement Forms;* visual-motor coordination in copying 7 or 8 geometric figures and completing incomplete forms of the same figures; Charles W. McQuarrie (teacher's guide), Florence E. Sutphin (handbooks), and Genevieve I. Curry (handbooks); Winter Haven Lions Research Foundation, Inc. *

For additional information and reviews by Lester Mann and Helen M. Robinson, see 7:872 (8 references); for a review by Mary C. Austin, see 6:848 (6 references).

REFERENCES THROUGH 1971

1–6. See 6:848.
7–14. See 7:872.
15. CLARK, CHARLES M., AND DODD, BYRON E. "Auditory Factor in Visual Motor Testing and Training." *J Learn Dis* 4(10): 582–5 D '71. * (*PA* 47:11642)

CUMULATIVE NAME INDEX

Austin, M. C.: *rev*, 6:848	Lowder, R. G.: 1
Bennett, R. M.: 11	Lyder, W.: 12
Bosworth, M. H.: 9	McQuarrie, C. W.: 8
Chasey, W. C.: 13	Manas, L.: 5
Clark, C. M.: 15	Mann, L.: *rev*, 7:872
DiMeo, K. P.: 10	Mozzi, L.: 2, 4
Dodd, B. E.: 15	Robinson, H. M.: 2, 4; *rev*, 7:
Harvey, J.: 6	872
Hill, P. J.: 14	Rosenbloom, A. A.: 2, 4
Kagerer, R. L.: 3	Sutphin, F. E.: 7
Kampsen, A.: 12	Wittick, M. L.: 4
Letton, M. C.: 2	Wyrick, W.: 13

[1882]

The Primary Visual Motor Test. Ages 4–8; 1964–70; PVMT; Mary R. Haworth; Grune & Stratton, Inc. *

For additional information, a review by Dale B. Harris, and an excerpted review by A. Barclay, see 7:873 (1 reference).

REFERENCES THROUGH 1971

1. See 7:873.

CUMULATIVE NAME INDEX

Barclay, A.: *exc*, 7:873	Haworth, M. R.: 1
Harris, D. B.: *rev*, 7:873	

[1883]

The Purdue Perceptual-Motor Survey. Ages 6–10; 1966; PPMS; to identify those children lacking perceptual-motor abilities necessary for acquiring academic success; 22 scores: balance and posture (walking board [3 scores], jumping), body image and differentiation (identification of body parts, imitation of movements, obstacle course, Krauss-Weber, angels in the snow), perceptual-motor match (chalkboard [4 scores], rhythmic writing [3 scores]), ocular control (4 scores), form perception (2 scores); Eugene G. Roach and Newell C. Kephart; Charles E. Merrill Publishing Co. *

For additional information and reviews by Colleen B. Jamison and Daniel Landis, see 7:874 (25 references).

REFERENCES THROUGH 1971

1–25. See 7:874.
26. CHARLTON, NORMAN WOOD, II. *An Investigation of Selected Visual-Perceptual and Motor Parameters of Young Trainable Mentally Retarded Children.* Doctor's thesis, University of Houston (Houston, Tex.), 1970. (*DAI* 32:271A)
27. KALAKIAN, LEONARD HARRIS. *Predicting Academic Achievement From Perceptual-Motor Efficiency in Educable Mentally Retarded Children.* Doctor's thesis, University of Utah (Salt Lake City, Utah), 1971. (*DAI* 32:3122A)
28. MECKLER, ROY STEWART. *The Effects of Perceptual-Motor Training on the Development of Fine Motor Proficiency of Trainable Mentally Retarded Adolescents.* Doctor's thesis, George Peabody College for Teachers (Nashville, Tenn.), 1971. (*DAI* 32: 1946A)

29. MUSGROVE, DOLORES MARIA. *A Factor Analytic Study of Perceptual Motor Attributes as Measured by Selected Test Batteries.* Doctor's thesis, University of Northern Colorado (Greeley, Colo.), 1971. *(DAI* 32:1904A)

30. NEEMAN, RENATE L. "Manipulative Dexterity and Perceptual-Motor Abilities of Mentally Retarded Adolescents and Young Adults: Perceptual-Motor Attributes of Mental Retardates, Part II." *Am J Occup Ther* 25(6):309–12 S '71. * *(PA* 49:10347)

31. NEEMAN, RENATE L. "Perceptual-Motor Attributes of Mental Retardates: A Factor Analytic Study." *Percept & Motor Skills* 33(3):927–34 D '71. * *(PA* 48:1519)

32. NEEMAN, RENATE L., AND PHILLIPS, HERBERT E. "Perceptual-Motor Attributes of Mental Retardates: Part 1, Perceptual-Motor Evaluation of Mental Retardates." *Am J Occup Ther* 25(5):253–8 Jl–Ag '71. *

33. RICHARDSON, WAYNE, AND RUBINO, CARL. "The Purdue Perceptual Motor Survey and the Bender Gestalt as Measures of Perceptual Motor Abilities in Children." *Ont Psychologist* (Canada) 3(4):243–7 '71. * *(PA* 48:1035)

34. RIGGLE, RICHARD RAY. *Correlations of Articulatory Disability With Various Aspects of Reading for Selected Modalities.* Doctor's thesis, University of Oregon (Eugene, Ore.), 1971. *(DAI* 32:2922A)

CUMULATIVE NAME INDEX

August, I.: 20
Baker, G. A. P.: 14
Ball, T. S.: 23
Bengston, G. M.: 10
Bibace, R.: 15
Campanaro, M. F.: 12
Charlton, N. W.: 26
Crittenden, J. B.: 16
Dunsing, J. D.: 17
Edgar, C. L.: 23
Gillion, H. E. J.: 21
Hancock, K.: 15
Heriot, J. T.: 2
Jamison, C. B.: *rev,* 7:874
Kalakian, L. H.: 27
Kephart, N. C.: 1
Knigge, K. R.: 11
Landis, D.: *rev,* 7:874
Lietz, E. S.: 13
Little, H. A.: 7
Little, S. J.: 22
Maloney, M. P.: 23
Meckler, R. S.: 28
Middleton, W. H.: 3
Musgrove, D. M.: 29
Neeman, R. L.: 24, 30–2
Pace, C. R.: *rev,* 7:666
Pardon, C. D.: 18
Phillips, H. E.: 24, 32
Richardson, W.: 33
Riggle, R. R.: 34
Roach, E. G.: 4
Rubino, C.: 33
Schadler, M. M.: 8
Schroeder, R.: 25
Sevilla, S. A.: 5
Swanson, E. M.: 6
Weddell, J. M.: 9
Wharry, R. E.: 19

[1884]

★Rosner Perceptual Survey, Experimental Edition. Ages 5–12; 1968; RPS; to be administered by an optometrist; a shortened version (omitting the optometric items and those which require special equipment), called the *Rosner-Richman Perceptual Survey,* is intended for use by teachers as "a gross screening device"; Jerome Rosner, Vivien Richman, and Russell H. Scott; Learning Research and Development Center. *

[1885]

Southern California Kinesthesia and Tactile Perception Tests. Ages 4–8; 1966; SCKT; also available as a subtest of *Southern California Sensory Integration Tests* (see 1887); dysfunction in somesthetic perception; 6 scores: kinesthesia, manual form perception, finger identification, graphesthesia, localization of tactile stimuli, double tactile stimuli perception; A. Jean Ayres; Western Psychological Services. *

For additional information and a review by Newell C. Kephart, see 7:877 (2 references).

REFERENCES THROUGH 1971

1–2. See 7:877.

3. FRETZ, BRUCE R.; JOHNSON, WARREN R.; AND JOHNSON, JULIA A. "Intellectual and Perceptual Motor Development as a Function of Therapeutic Play," pp. 475–80. In *Contemporary Psychology of Sport.* Proceedings of the Second International Congress of Sport Psychology, Washington, D.C., 1968. Chicago, Ill.: Athletic Institute, 1970. Pp. xix, 878. *

4. GREIF, SUSAN ANN. *A Study of the Relationship Between Auditory, Visual, and Haptic Perception and Selected Parameters of Language and Articulation in Children With Central Processing Dysfunction.* Doctor's thesis, Wayne State University (Detroit, Mich.), 1971. *(DAI* 32:6717B)

CUMULATIVE NAME INDEX

Ayres, A. J.: 1
Clapp, R. K.: 2
Fretz, B. R.: 3
Greif, S. A.: 4
Johnson, J. A.: 3
Johnson, W. R.: 3
Kephart, N. C.: *rev,* 7:877

[1886]

Southern California Perceptual-Motor Tests. Ages 4–8; 1965–69; SCPMT; also available as a subtest of *Southern California Sensory Integration Tests* (see 1887); 6 tests: imitation of postures (IP), crossing mid-line of body (CML), bilateral motor coordination (BMC), right-left discrimination (RLD), standing balance—eyes open (SBO), standing balance—eyes closed (SBC); A. Jean Ayres; Western Psychological Services. *

For additional information, a review by Daniel Landis, and an excerpted review by Barton B. Proger, see 7:879 (5 references).

REFERENCES THROUGH 1971

1–5. See 7:879.

6. AYRES, A. JEAN. "Interrelationships Among Perceptual-Motor Functions in Children." *Am J Occup Ther* 20:68–71 Mr–Ap '66. * *(PA* 40:8678)

7. AYRES, A. JEAN. "Deficits in Sensory Integration in Educationally Handicapped Children." *J Learn Dis* 2(3):160–8 Mr '69. * *(PA* 45:6978)

CUMULATIVE NAME INDEX

Ayres, A. J.: 1–7
Landis, D.: *rev,* 7:879
Proger, B. B.: *exc,* 7:879

[1887]

*Southern California Sensory Integration Tests. Ages 4–10 with learning problems; 1972; SCSIT; a battery of tests (1962–72) consisting of *The Ayres Space Test, Southern California Figure-Ground Visual Perception Test, Southern California Kinesthesia and Tactile Perception Tests, Southern California Motor Accuracy Test,* and *Southern California Perceptual-Motor Tests* with the addition of 2 new tests (position in space, design copying); 17 scores: *[The Ayres Space Test]* space visualization (ages 4–10), *[Southern California Figure-Ground Visual Perception Test]* figure-ground perception (ages 4–10), *[Southern California Kinesthesia and Tactile Perception Tests]* kinesthesia (ages 4–8), manual form perception (ages 4–8), finger identification (ages 4–8), graphesthesia (ages 6–8), localization of tactile stimuli (ages 4–8), double tactile stimuli perception (ages 4–8), *[Southern California Motor Accuracy Test]* motor accuracy (ages 4–8), *[Southern California Perceptual-Motor Tests]* imitation of postures (ages 4–8), crossing midline of body (ages 4–8), bilateral motor coordination (ages 4–8), right-left discrimination (ages 6–8), standing balance with eyes open (ages 4–8), standing balance with eyes closed (ages 4–8), [new tests] position in space (ages 4–10), design copying (ages 4–10); A. Jean Ayres; Western Psychological Services. *

For reference to reviews of *The Ayres Space Test,* see 1104; *Southern California Figure-Ground Visual Perception Tests,* see 1928; *Southern California Kinesthesia and Tactile Perception Tests,* see 1885; *Southern California Motor Accuracy Test,* see 1902; *Southern California Perceptual-Motor Tests,* see 1886.

REFERENCES THROUGH 1971

1. AYRES, A. JEAN. *Space Perception and Visualization in Cerebral Dysfunction.* Doctor's thesis, University of Southern California (Los Angeles, Calif.), 1961. *(DA* 22:1708)

2. SLEEPER, MILDRED L. *Correlation of Body Balance and Space Perception in Cerebral Palsied Individuals.* Master's thesis, University of Southern California (Los Angeles, Calif.), 1962.

3. AYRES, A. JEAN. "Patterns of Perceptual-Motor Dysfunction in Children: A Factor Analytic Study." *Percept & Motor Skills* 20:335–68 Ap '65. * *(PA* 39:12639)

4. AYRES, A. JEAN. "Interrelationships Among Perceptual-Motor Abilities in a Group of Normal Children." *Am J Occup Ther* 20:288–92 N–D '66. * *(PA* 41:5813)

5. AYRES, A. JEAN. "Interrelationships Among Perceptual-Motor Functions in Children." *Am J Occup Ther* 20:68–71 Mr–Ap '66. * *(PA* 40:8678)

6. AYRES, A. JEAN, AND REID, WILLIAM. "The Self-Drawing as an Expression of Perceptual-Motor Dysfunction." *Cortex* (Italy) 2:254–65 Ap '66. * (*PA* 41:665)

7. DOUDLAH, ANNA MAY. *The Perceptual-Motor Performance of Kindergarten Children With Low Scores on Selected Physical Tasks*. Doctor's thesis, University of Wisconsin (Madison, Wis.), 1967. (*DA* 28:4893A)

8. FOX, FRANK HEWITT. *A Description of Language and Perceptual Function of Culturally Deprived Children*. Doctor's thesis, University of Wisconsin (Madison, Wis.), 1968. (*DA* 29:4323A)

9. SABATINO, DAVID A.; ASSISTED BY R. L. JONES, CURTISS BROWN, AND W. M. GIBSON. "The Relationship Between Twenty-Three Learning Disability Behavorial Variables," pp. 149–61. In *CEC Selected Convention Papers*. 46th Annual International Convention, 1968. Washington, D.C.: Council for Exceptional Children, [1968]. Pp. xii, 346. *

10. SABATINO, DAVID A.; WICKHAM, WILLIAM, JR.; AND BURNETT, CALVIN W. "The Psychoeducational Assessment of Learning Disabilities." *Cath Ed R* 66:327–41 My '68. *

11. AYRES, A. JEAN. "Deficits in Sensory Integration in Educationally Handicapped Children." *J Learn Dis* 2(3):160–8 Mr '69. * (*PA* 45:6978)

12. AYRES, A. JEAN. "Relation Between Gesell Developmental Quotients and Later Perceptual-Motor Performance." *Am J Occup Ther* 23(1):11–7 Ja–F '69. * (*PA* 44:439)

13. CLAPP, ROBERT KENNETH. *The Body Schema of Normal and Mentally Retarded Children*. Doctor's thesis, University of Massachusetts (Amherst, Mass.), 1969. (*DAI* 30:841B)

14. FRETZ, BRUCE R.; JOHNSON, WARREN R.; AND JOHNSON, JULIA A. "Intellectual and Motor Development as a Function of Therapeutic Play," pp. 475–80. In *Contemporary Psychology of Sport*. Proceedings of the Second International Congress of Sport Psychology, Washington, D.C., 1968. Chicago, Ill.: Athletic Institute, 1970. Pp. xix, 878. *

15. PUNWAR, ALICE. "Spatial Visualization, Reading, Spelling, and Mathematical Abilities in Second- and Third-Grade Children." *Am J Occup Ther* 24(7):495–9 O '70. *

16. BOGARD, DOLORES ANN. *Visual Perception of Static and Dynamic Two-Dimensional Objects: A Cross-Sectional Study*. Doctor's thesis, University of Southern California (Los Angeles, Calif.), 1971. (*DAI* 32:2461A)

17. BROOKS, CLARENCE R., AND CLAIR, THEODORE NAT. "Relationships Among Visual Figure-Ground Perception, Word Recognition, IQ, and Chronological Age." *Percept & Motor Skills* 33(1):59–62 Ag '71. * (*PA* 47:3534)

18. GREIF, SUSAN ANN. *A Study of the Relationship Between Auditory, Visual, and Haptic Perception and Selected Parameters of Language and Articulation in Children With Central Processing Dysfunction*. Doctor's thesis, Wayne State University (Detroit, Mich.), 1971. (*DAI* 32:6717B)

CUMULATIVE NAME INDEX

[1888]

★**Spatial Orientation Memory Test, Preliminary Edition.** Ages 5–8; 1971; SOMT; Joseph M. Wepman and Dainis Turaids; Language Research Associates, Inc. *

[1889]

★**Symbol Digit Modalities Test.** Ages 8 and over; 1973; SDMT; "early screening of apparently normal children and adults for possible covert manual motor, visual, learning and/or other cerebral defects"; Aaron Smith; Western Psychological Services. *

REFERENCES THROUGH 1971

1. SMITH, AARON. "Consistent Sex Differences in a Specific (Decoding) Test Performance." *Ed & Psychol Meas* 27:1077–83 w '67. * (*PA* 42:9429)

2. SMITH, AARON. "The Symbol-Digit Modalities Test: A Neuropsychologic Test for Economic Screening of Learning and Other Cerebral Dysfunction," pp. 83–91. In *Learning Disorders, Vol. 3*. Edited by Jerome Hellmuth. Seattle, Wash.: Special Child Publications, 1968. Pp. 605. *

3. LANGE, UNA ANN. *Differential Performances of Minimally Brain-Damaged Boys and of Non-Brain-Damaged Boys on Selected Tests*. Doctor's thesis, University of Nebraska (Lincoln, Neb.), 1969. (*DAI* 30:2852A)

4. OWENS, RICHARD THOMAS. *A Study of the Performance of Minimally Brain-Damaged and Emotionally Disturbed Boys on Six Selected Psychological Tests*. Doctor's thesis, University of Nebraska (Lincoln, Neb.), 1969. (*DAI* 31:383B)

CUMULATIVE NAME INDEX

[1890]

Trankell's Laterality Tests: A Battery of Diagnostic Tests for the Determination of Degree of Left-Hand Preference and Asymmetry of Motor Skill. Left-handed children in grades 1–2; [1951]; 3 tests; Arne Trankell; Skandinaviska Testförlaget AB [Sweden]. *

a) IMPULSE SCALE. 3 scores: hand, foot, eye.
b) TAPPING. 3 scores: right, left, asymmetry index.
c) TRACING. 3 scores: same as for *b* above.

[1891]

★**Wold Digit-Symbol Test.** Ages 6–16; 1967–70; WDST; perceptual-motor speed; Robert M. Wold; Academic Therapy Publications. *

[1892]

★**Wold Sentence Copying Test.** Grades 2–8; 1967–70; WSCT; Robert M. Wold; Academic Therapy Publications. *

[1893]

★**Wold Visuo-Motor Test.** Ages 6–16; 1967–70; WVMT; 3 coordination scores: vertical, short horizontal, longer horizontal; Robert M. Wold; Academic Therapy Publications. *

[Out of Print Since TIP I]

Pre-Tests of Vision, Hearing, and Motor Coordination, 4:645

Standardized Road-Map Test of Direction Sense, 7:880
(1 review, 2 excerpts, 6 references)

MOTOR

[1894]

★**Devereux Test of Extremity Coordination.** Emotionally handicapped and neurologically impaired ages 4–10; 1971–73; DTEC; available only as part of the Individual Motor Achievement Guided Education (IMAGE) program; title on profile booklet is *Devereux IMAGE Profile;* 5 scores: sequential motor ability, fine motor ability, static balance, perceptual motor activity, total; George E. DeHaven, James D. Bruce, Franklin W. Dale (profile), and Jon E. Olexy (profile); Devereux Foundation. *

REFERENCES THROUGH 1971

1. DEHAVEN, GEORGE E.; MORDOCK, JOHN B.; AND LOYKOVICH, JOAN M. "Evaluation of Coordination Deficits in Children With Minimal Cerebral Dysfunction." *Physical Ther* 49(2):153–7 F '69. *

CUMULATIVE NAME INDEX

[1895]

The Lincoln-Oseretsky Motor Development Scale. Ages 6–14; 1948–56; revision of *Oseretsky Tests of Motor Proficiency;* William Sloan; Stoelting Co. *

For additional information and a review by Anna Espenschade, see 5:767 (10 references).

REFERENCES THROUGH 1971

1–10. See 5:767.

11. DISTEFANO, MICHAEL K., JR.; ELLIS, NORMAN R.; AND SLOAN, WILLIAM. "Motor Proficiency in Mental Defectives." *Percept & Motor Skills* 8:231–4 S '58. * (*PA* 33:5438)

12. MALPASS, LESLIE F. "Motor Proficiency in Institutionalized and Non-Institutionalized Retarded Children and Normal Children." *Am J Mental Def* 64:1012–5 My '60. * (*PA* 35:6839)

13. SMITH, JUDITH ROSER, AND HURST, JOHN G. "The Relationship of Motor Abilities and Peer Acceptance of Mentally Retarded Children." *Am J Mental Def* 66:81–5 Jl '61. * (*PA* 36:3J181S)

14. BUCK, ROBERT JAMES, JR. *An Investigation of Motor Ability and Articulatory Proficiency of Elementary School Pupils as Measured by the Lincoln-Oseretsky Motor Development Scale.* Master's thesis, Ohio University (Athens, Ohio), 1964.

15. VANDENBERG, STEVEN G. "Factor Analytic Studies of the Lincoln Oseretsky Test of Motor Proficiency." *Percept & Motor Skills* 19:23–41 Ag '64. * (*PA* 39:5105)

16. BIHLMEYER, EARL WALTER. *A Study of the Relationships Between Motor Ability and the Performance of Male Fourth Grade Pupils in Selected School Skills.* Doctor's thesis, University of South Dakota (Vermillion, S.D.), 1965. (*DA* 26:4436)

17. LILLIE, DAVID LEO. *The Effects of Motor Development Lessons on the Motor Proficiency of Preschool Culturally Deprived Children.* Doctor's thesis, Indiana University (Bloomington, Ind.), 1966. (*DA* 27:3317A)

18. TRUSSELL, ELLA MAY. *The Relation of Performance of Selected Physical Skills to Perceptual Aspects of Reading Readiness in Elementary School Children.* Doctor's thesis, University of California (Berkeley, Calif.), 1966. (*DA* 28:134A)

19. WEBER, MARYLOU ADAM. *The Motor Behavior Characteristics of Children With Operant Language Disorder.* Doctor's thesis, University of Arizona (Tucson, Ariz.), 1966. (*DA* 27:2381A)

20. DUDEK, S. Z.; LESTER, L. P.; AND HARRIS, B. R. "Variability on Tests of Cognitive and Perceptual-Motor Development in Kindergarten Children." *J Clin Psychol* 23:461–4 O '67. * (*PA* 42:2400)

21. HAFNER, MARGARET SMITH. *Motor Control and First Grade Reading Difficulties.* Doctor's thesis, Syracuse University (Syracuse, N.Y.), 1968. (*DA* 29:3913A)

22. LAUTEN, DORIS ANNE HIGGINS. *The Relationship Between Intelligence and Motor Proficiency in the Intellectually Gifted Child.* Doctor's thesis, University of North Carolina (Greensboro, N.C.), 1968. (*DAI* 31:1521B)

23. LILLIE, DAVID L. "The Effects of Motor Development Lessons on Mentally Retarded Children." *Am J Mental Def* 72:803–8 My '68. * (*PA* 42:14522)

24. PEARMAN, ROGER. *An Analysis of the Lincoln-Oseretsky Motor Development Scale With an Emphasis on the Reduction of Total Test Items.* Master's thesis, Western Kentucky University (Bowling Green, Ky.), 1968.

25. WILSECK, ROBERT F. *The Effects of a Patterning Program of Physical Activity on the Motor Ability Performance of the Educable Mentally Retarded.* Doctor's thesis, Colorado State College (Greeley, Colo.), 1968. (*DA* 29:2556A)

26. DUDEK, S. Z.; LESTER, E. P.; GOLDBERG, J. S.; AND DYER, G. B. "Relationship of Piaget Measures to Standard Intelligence and Motor Scales." *Percept & Motor Skills* 28(2):351–62 Ap '69. * (*PA* 43:15587)

27. GILES, MARIAN TAYLOR. *Fine Motor Development of Retarded and Nonretarded Children.* Doctor's thesis, Colorado State College (Greeley, Colo.), 1969. (*DAI* 30:1890A)

28. HOFMEISTER, ALAN. "Motor Proficiency and Other Variables in Educable Mentally Retarded Children." *Am J Mental Def* 74(2):264–8 S '69. * (*PA* 44:5585)

29. JURGENS, GRACE. "The Effect of Motor Development Lessons on Trainable Mentally Retarded Children." *Grad Res Ed & Related Discip* 5(1):62–77 f '69. * (*PA* 46:9492)

30. CHARLTON, NORMAN WOOD, II. *An Investigation of Selected Visual-Perceptual and Motor Parameters of Young Trainable Mentally Retarded Children.* Doctor's thesis, Univeristy of Houston (Houston, Tex.), 1970. (*DAI* 32:271A)

31. LESTER, EVA P.; MUIR, R.; AND DUDEK, STEPHANIE Z. "Cognitive Structure and Achievement in the Young Child." *Can Psychiatric Assn J* 15(3):279–87 Je '70. * (*PA* 45:5058)

32. LEWIS, FRANKLIN D.; BELL, D. BRUCE; AND ANDERSON, ROBERT P. "Reading Retardation: A Bi-Racial Comparison." *J Read* 13(6):433–6, 474–8 Mr '70. *

33. LEWIS, FRANKLIN D.; BELL, D. BRUCE; AND ANDERSON, ROBERT P. "Relationship of Motor Proficiency and Reading Retardation." *Percept & Motor Skills* 31(2):395–401 O '70. * (*PA* 45:7008)

34. STEWART, R. R.; WALKER, W.; AND SAVAGE, R. D. "A Developmental Study of Cognitive and Personality Characteristics Associated With Haemolytic Disease of the Newborn." *Develop Med & Child Neurol* (England) 12(1):16–26 F '70. * (*PA* 44:17249)

35. HOLLINGSWORTH, JACK DAREL. *A Comparison of Motor Ability of Mentally Retarded Children of Specific Mental and Chronological Ages and Normal Children.* Doctor's thesis, University of Georgia (Athens, Ga.), 1971. (*DAI* 32:3760A)

36. MECKLER, ROY STEWART. *The Effects of Perceptual-Motor Training on the Development of Fine Motor Proficiency of Trainable Mentally Retarded Adolescents.* Doctor's thesis, George Peabody College for Teachers (Nashville, Tenn.), 1971. (*DAI* 32:1946A)

37. UPCHURCH, WINIFRED BROOK. *The Relationship Between Perceptual-Motor Skills and Word Recognition Achievement at the Kindergarten Level.* Doctor's thesis, Syracuse University (Syracuse, N.Y.), 1971. (*DAI* 32:4497A)

CUMULATIVE NAME INDEX

[1896]

★**Manual Accuracy and Speed Test.** Ages 4 and over; 1971; MAST; also called *Minnesota MAST;* 10 scores: 2 scores (best hand, worst hand) for 5 subtests (alternate tapping, large peg placement, small peg placement, nails transfer, steadiness); Peter F. Briggs and Auke Tellegen; Lafayette Instrument Co. *

REFERENCES THROUGH 1971

1. BRIGGS, PETER F., AND TELLEGEN, AUKE. "Development of the Manual Accuracy and Speed Test (MAST)." *Percept & Motor Skills* 32(3):923–43 Je '71. * (*PA* 47:1958)

CUMULATIVE NAME INDEX

[1897]

★**Motor Problems Inventory.** Preschool–grade 5; 1972; MPI; Glyndon D. Riley; Western Psychological Services. *

[1898]

Oseretsky Tests of Motor Proficiency: A Translation From the Portuguese Adaptation. Ages 4–16; 1946; original test by N. Oseretsky published in Russian in 1923; Portuguese adaptation by Maria Irene Leite da Costa published in 1943; English translation by Elizabeth Joan Fosa; American Guidance Service, Inc. * For the revised edition entry, see 1895.

For additional information and a review by Anna Espenschade, see 4:650 (10 references); for an excerpted review, see 3:472 (6 references). For an excerpt from a related book review, see 4:651.

REFERENCES THROUGH 1971

1–6. See 3:472.

7–16. See 4:650.

17. FRENCH, JOSEPH L. *A Pilot Study With the Manual Dynamic Coordination Section of the Oseretsky Test.* Master's thesis, Illinois State Normal University (Normal, Ill.), 1950.

18. GARNERO, JOSEPH. *A Pilot Study With the General Static Coordination Section of the Oseretsky Test.* Master's thesis, Illinois State Normal University (Normal, Ill.), 1950.

19. HOLBROOK, SARAH FITCH. *A Study of the Development of Motor Abilities Between the Ages of Four and Twelve, Using a*

Modification of the Oseretsky Scale. Doctor's thesis, University of Minnesota (Minneapolis, Minn.), 1953. (*DA* 13:875)

20. FINKELSTEIN, PHYLLIS, AND WEISBERGER, STANLEY E. "The Motor Proficiency of Stutterers." *J Speech & Hearing Disorders* 19:52–8 Mr '54. * (*PA* 29:1179)

21. BERK, ROBERT LLOYD. *A Comparison of Performance of Subnormal, Normal, and Gifted Children on the Oseretsky Tests of Motor Proficiency.* Doctor's thesis, Boston University (Boston, Mass.), 1957. (*DA* 17:1947)

22. LEVINSON, BORIS M., AND BLOCK, ZELICK. "A Research Note on Some Motor Abilities of Children Attending Day (Yeshiva) Schools." *J Clin Psychol* 18:231 Ap '62. * (*PA* 38:9264)

23. JENKINS, EDNA, AND LOHR, FRANCES E. "Severe Articulation Disorders and Motor Ability." *J Speech & Hearing Disorders* 29:286–92 Ag '64. * (*PA* 39:5606)

24. HOLROYD, JEAN, AND WRIGHT, FRANCIS. "Neurological Implications of WISC Verbal-Performance Discrepancies in a Psychiatric Setting." *J Consult Psychol* 29:206–12 Je '65. * (*PA* 39:12690)

25. STOTT, D. H. "A General Test of Motor Impairment for Children." *Develop Med & Child Neurol* 8:523–31 D '66. * (*PA* 41:3214)

26. WILSON, GERALD E. *An Investigation of the Relationship of Mental Ability to Manual Dexterity and Coordination in Adolescents.* Master's thesis, California State College (Long Beach, Calif.), 1966.

27. DUDEK, S. Z.; GOLDBERG, J. S.; LESTER, E. P.; AND HARRIS, B. R. "The Validity of Cognitive, Perceptual-Motor and Personality Variables for Prediction of Achievement in Grade 1 and Grade 2." *J Clin Psychol* 25(2):165–70 Ap '69. * (*PA* 43:14874)

28. TRUSSELL, ELLA M. "Relation of Performance of Selected Physical Skills to Perceptual Aspects of Reading Readiness in Elementary School Children." *Res Q* 40(2):383–90 My '69. *

29. NEAVES, ALISON I. "To Establish a Basis for Prognosis in Stammering." *Brit J Dis Commun* 5(1):46–58 Ap '70. * (*PA* 46:5319)

30. TARNOPOL, LESTER. "Delinquency and Minimal Brain Dysfunction." *J Learn Dis* 3(4):200–7 Ap '70. * (*PA* 47:3517)

31. CHASEY, WILLIAM C., AND WYRICK, WANEEN. "Effects of a Physical Developmental Program on Psychomotor Ability of Retarded Children." *Am J Mental Def* 75(5):566–70 Mr '71. * (*PA* 46:5515)

CUMULATIVE NAME INDEX

Baldwin, B. J.: 11
Berk, R. L.: 21
Block, Z.: 22
Cassel, R. H.: 12–3
Chasey, W. C.: 31
da Costa, M. I. L.: 1–4
Doll, E. A.: 5
Dudek, S. Z.: 27
Espenschade, A.: *rev*, 4:650
Finkelstein, P.: 20
French, J. L.: 17
Garnero, J.: 18
Goldberg, J. S.: 27
Harris, B. R.: 27
Holbrook, S. F.: 19
Holroyd, J.: 24
Jenkins, E.: 23

Kopp, H.: 6–8
Lassner, R.: 9
Lester, E. P.: 27
Levinson, B. M.: 22
Lohr, F. E.: 23
Neaves, A. I.: 29
Phelps, W.: 14
Shaffer, L. F.: *exc*, 4:651
Sloan, W.: 10, 15–6
Stott, D. H.: 25
Tarnopol, L.: 30
Trussell, E. M.: 28
Weisberger, S. E.: 20
Wilson, G. E.: 26
Wright, F.: 24
Wyrick, W.: 31

[1899]

Perrin Motor Coordination Test. Adults; [1921]; F. A. C. Perrin; Stoelting Co. *

[1900]

The Rail-Walking Test. Ages 5 and over; 1941–44; locomotor coordination and general motor control; specifications for making rails and directions for administration, scoring, and interpretation are presented in *Am J Psychol* 57:482–99 O '44; S. Roy Heath, Jr.; norms may be obtained from the Author. *

For additional information and a review by William Sloan, see 4:652 (7 references).

REFERENCES THROUGH 1971

1–7. See 4:652.

8. O'CONNOR, N. "The Prediction of Psychological Stability and Anxiety-Aggressiveness From a Battery of Tests Administered to a Group of High Grade Male Mental Defectives." *J General Psychol* 46:3–17 Ja '52. * (*PA* 27:2055)

9. HEATH, S. ROY, JR. "The Relation of Rail-Walking and Other Motor Performances of Mental Defectives to Mental Age and Etiologic Type." *Training Sch B* 50:119–27 O '53. * (*PA* 28:6210)

10. HEATH, SAMUEL ROY, JR. *The Relation of Rail-Walking and Other Motor Performances of Mental Defectives to Mental*

Age and Etiological Type. Doctor's thesis, University of Pennsylvania (Philadelphia, Pa.), 1953. (*DA* 13:260)

11. DISTEFANO, MICHAEL K., JR.; ELLIS, NORMAN R.; AND SLOAN, WILLIAM. "Motor Proficiency in Mental Defectives." *Percept & Motor Skills* 8:231–4 S '58. * (*PA* 33:5438)

12. GOETZINGER, CORNELIUS P. "A Re-Evaluation of the Heath Railwalking Test." *J Ed Res* 54:187–91 Ja '61. * (*PA* 35:6187)

13. HOAG, RALPH LYNN. *A Comparative Study of Certain Motor Skills of Deaf and Hearing Mentally Retarded Children.* Doctor's thesis, University of Arizona (Tucson, Ariz.), 1961. (*DA* 22:488)

14. BUTLER, ALFRED J., AND CONRAD, W. GLENN. "Psychological Correlates of Abnormal Electroencephalographic Patterns in Familial Retardates." *J Clin Psychol* 20:338–43 Jl '64. * (*PA* 39:10572)

15. SCANLON, STANLEY L. *A Study of the Heath Rail-Walking Test and the Fukuda Vestibular Tests With Deaf and Hearing Subjects.* Master's thesis, University of Kansas (Lawrence, Kan.), 1966.

CUMULATIVE NAME INDEX

Butler, A. J.: 14
Conrad, W. G.: 14
Crawford, J. M.: 6
Distefano, M. K.: 11
Ellis, N. R.: 11
Goetzinger, C. P.: 12
Heath, S. R.: 1–4, 9–10

Hoag, R. L.: 13
Myklebust, H. R.: 5
O'Connor, N.: 6–8
Scanlon, S. L.: 15
Sloan, W.: 11; *rev*, 4:652
Tizard, J.: 6–7

[1901]

Smedley Hand Dynamometer. Ages 6–18; [1920 (?)–53]; strength of grip; F. Smedley; Stoelting Co. *

REFERENCES THROUGH 1971

1. WHIPPLE, GUY MONTROSE. *Manual of Mental and Physical Tests: Part 1, Simpler Processes,* pp. 100–10. Baltimore, Md.: Warwick & York, Inc., 1914. Pp. xvi, 365. *

2. WESTPHAL, GRENAFORE. "An Experimental Study of Certain Motor Abilities of Stutterers." *Child Develop* 4:214–21 S '33. * (*PA* 8:536)

3. FISHER, M. BRUCE, AND BIRREN, JAMES E. "Standardization of a Test of Hand Strength." *J Appl Psychol* 30:380–7 Ag '46. * (*PA* 21:81)

4. FISHER, M. BRUCE, AND BIRREN, JAMES E. "Age and Strength." *J Appl Psychol* 31:490–7 O '47. * (*PA* 22:1994)

5. WEINLAND, JAMES D. "A Five Month Strength Curve." *J Appl Psychol* 31:498–501 O '47. * (*PA* 22:2002)

6. MOORE, JOSEPH E., AND STURM, NORMAN H. "Relation of Hand Strength to Personality Measures." *Am J Psychol* 65:111 Ja '52. * (*PA* 27:2749)

7. JEANNERET, PAUL R., AND WEBB, WILSE B. "Strength of Grip on Arousal From Full Night's Sleep." *Percept & Motor Skills* 17:759–61 D '63. * (*PA* 38:4946)

8. MOSTOFSKY, DAVID, AND SHURTLEFF, DONALD. "The Dynamometer as a Human Response Manipulandum." *Percept & Motor Skills* 18:509–12 Ap '64. * (*PA* 39:3322)

9. WATSON, CHARLES G.; THOMAS, RICHARD W.; FELLING, JAMES; AND ANDERSEN, DENNIS. "Differentiation of Organics From Schizophrenics With the Trail Making, Dynamometer, Critical Flicker Fusion, and Light-Intensity Matching Tests." *J Clin Psychol* 25(2):130–3 Ap '69. * (*PA* 43:14489)

10. REITAN, RALPH M. "Sensorimotor Functions in Brain-Damaged and Normal Children of Early School Age." *Percept & Motor Skills* 33(2):655–64 O '71. * (*PA* 47:7385)

CUMULATIVE NAME INDEX

Andersen, D.: 9
Birren, J. E.: 3–4
Felling, J.: 9
Fisher, M. B.: 3–4
Jeanneret, P. R.: 7
Moore, J. E.: 6
Mostofsky, D.: 8
Reitan, R. M.: 10

Shurtleff, D.: 8
Sturm, N. H.: 6
Thomas, R. W.: 9
Watson, C. G.: 9
Webb, W. B.: 7
Weinland, J. D.: 5
Westphal, G.: 2
Whipple, G. M.: 1

[1902]

Southern California Motor Accuracy Test. Ages 4–7 with nervous system dysfunction; 1964; SCMAT; also available as a subtest of *Southern California Sensory Integration Tests;* test consists of tracing a line design; 2 scores: accuracy, adjusted (accuracy and speed); A. Jean Ayres; Western Psychological Services. *

For additional information, a review by Newell C. Kephart, and an excerpted review by C. H. Ammons, see 7:878 (9 references).

REFERENCES THROUGH 1971

1–9. See 7:878.
10. FOX, FRANK HEWITT. *A Description of Language and Perceptual Function of Culturally Deprived Children.* Doctor's thesis, University of Wisconsin (Madison, Wis.), 1968. (*DA* 29:4323A)
11. AYRES, A. JEAN. "Deficits in Sensory Integration in Educationally Handicapped Children." *J Learn Dis* 2(3):160–8 Mr '69. * (*PA* 45:6978)

CUMULATIVE NAME INDEX

Ammons, C. H.: *exc,* 7:878	Gibson, W. M.: 6
Ayres, A. J.: 1–3, 8–9, 11	Jones, R. L.: 6
Brown, C.: 6	Kephart, N. C.: *rev,* 7:878
Burnett, C. W.: 7	Reid, W.: 3
Doudlah, A. M.: 4	Sabatino, D. A.: 6–7
Fox, F. H.: 5, 10	Wickham, W.: 7

[1903]

★**The Teaching Research Motor-Development Scale.** Moderately and severely retarded (preschool-grade 12); 1972; 74 scores: standing and crouching on tiptoes (3 scores), standing heel to toe and on one foot (6 scores), jumping (4 scores), walking (5 scores), imitations of movements, touching nose and fingertips (3 scores), close and open hands, tapping with feet and fingers, stepping over, ducking under, passing between, placing matchsticks and coins in a box (4 scores), winding thread (4 scores), tapping and drawing lines (4 scores), mazes (4 scores), cutting (6 scores), catching and bouncing and throwing a ball (13 scores), pull-up (3 scores), sit-up (2 scores), push-up (3 scores), running (3 scores), total; H. D. Fredericks, Victor L. Baldwin, Philip Doughty, and L. James Walter; Charles C Thomas, Publisher. *

[1904]

★**Test of Motor Impairment.** Ages 5–14; 1972; TMI; D. H. Stott, F. A. Moyes, and S. E. Henderson; Brook Educational Publishing Ltd. [Canada]. * (United States distributor: Wardell Associates Inc.)

REFERENCES THROUGH 1971

1. STOTT, D. H. "A General Test of Motor Impairment for Children." *Develop Med & Child Neurol* 8:523–31 O '66. * (*PA* 41:3214)
2. LOVELL, K., AND GORTON, A. "A Study of Some Differences Between Backward and Normal Readers of Average Intelligence." *Brit J Ed Psychol* 38:240–8 N '68. * (*PA* 43:7398)
3. WHITING, H. T. A.; CLARKE, T. A.; AND MORRIS, P. R. "A Clinical Validation of the Stott Test of Motor Impairment." *Brit J Social & Clin Psychol* 8(3):270–4 S '69. * (*PA* 44:3813)
4. MOYES, FREDERICK ARCHIBALD. *A Validational Study of a Test of Motor Impairment.* Master's thesis, University of Leicester (Leicester, England), 1970.

CUMULATIVE NAME INDEX

Clarke, T. A.: 3	Moyes, F. A.: 4
Gorton, A.: 2	Stott, D. H.: 1
Lovell, K.: 2	Whiting, H. T. A.: 3
Morris, P. R.: 3	

[Out of Print Since TIP I]

Edmiston Motor Capacity Test, 4:649

VISION

[1905]

A-B-C Vision Test for Ocular Dominance. Ages 5 or 6 and over; 1927–46; Walter R. Miles; Psychological Corporation. *
For additional information and a review by Miles A. Tinker, see 4:654; see also 3:459 (5 references).

REFERENCES THROUGH 1971

1–5. See 3:459.
6. WOLFE, LILLIAN S. "Differential Factors in Specific Reading Disability: 1, Laterality of Function." *J Genetic Psychol* 58:45–56 Mr '41. * (*PA* 15:4036)

7. MINTZ, ALEXANDER. "Lateral Preferences of a Group of Mentally Subnormal Boys." *J Genetic Psychol* 71:75–84 S '47. * (*PA* 22:1739)
8. SMITH, BERTRAM JOSEPH. *Validation of Certain Tests of Ocular Dominance Against a Criterion of Bombsight Design Preference.* Doctor's thesis, University of Minnesota (Minneapolis, Minn.), 1954. (*DA* 14:1001)
9. WAY, EUNICE ELLEN. *An Investigation of the Relationships of Laterality to Success in Certain Physical Education Activities Among University of Washington Women Students.* Doctor's thesis, University of Washington (Seattle, Wash.), 1956. (*DA* 16:1837)
10. RIEGEL, ROBERT H., AND CALDWELL, WILLARD E. "The Influence of Stimulus, Set, and Subject Variables on Binocular Dominance in Normal and Schizophrenic Subjects." *J General Psychol* 78:247–65 Ap '68. * (*PA* 42:12493)

CUMULATIVE NAME INDEX

Caldwell, W. E.: 10	Smith, B. J.: 8
Faison, C.: 5	Tinker, M. A.: *rev,* 4:654
Miles, W.: 1	Updegraff, R.: 4
Miles, W. R.: 2–3	Washburn, M. R.: 5
Mintz, A.: 7	Way, E. E.: 9
Riegel, R. H.: 10	Wolfe, L. S.: 6
Scott, R.: 5	

[1906]

AO Sight Screener. Adults; 1945–56; targets are available for both readers and nonreaders of English letters and numbers; American Optical Corporation. *
For additional information, see 5:770 (8 references); for reviews by Henry A. Imus and F. Nowell Jones, see 3:460 (7 references).

REFERENCES THROUGH 1971

1–7. See 3:460.
8–15. See 5:770.
16. IMUS, H. A. "Visual Testing Technics." *Trans Am Acad Ophthal & Otol* 52:370–85 Mr–Ap '48. *
17. COUNCIL ON PHYSICAL MEDICINE AND REHABILITATION. "Sight-Screener, Model 1235, Accepted." *J Am Med Assn* 143: 440 Je 3 '50. *
18. SLOAN, LOUISE L., AND ROWLAND, WILLIAM M. "Comparison of Ortho-Rater and Sight Screener Tests of Heterophoria With Standard Clinical Tests." *Am J Ophthal* 34:1363–75 O '51. *
19. MORGAN, A. LLOYD; CRAWFORD, JOHN; PASHBY, THOMAS J.; AND GABY, JOHN B. "A Survey of Methods Used to Reveal Eye Defects in School Children." *Can Med Assn J* 67:29–34 Jl '52. *
20. ROBINSON, HELEN M. "An Analysis of Four Visual Screening Tests at Grades Four and Seven." *Am J Optom* 30: 177–87 Ap '53. * (*PA* 28:361)
21. WILSON, REX H., AND McCORMICK, WILLIAM E. "Visual Acuity—Results of a Survey of 10,000 Persons." *Indus Med & Surg* 23:64–72 F '54. *
22. MAIRE, F. "Validity Information Exchange, No. 15–01: D.O.T. Code 6.72.126, Jewel Setter; 6.72.111, Staking Machine Operator." *Personnel Psychol* 15:105–6 sp '62. *
23. RYAN, VERNON I., AND ROBERTS, JEAN. "Sight-Screener Calibration Study." *Am J Optom* 40:185–204 Ap '63. *

CUMULATIVE NAME INDEX

Bartlett, N. R.: 4–5, 7, 11	McCormick, W. E.: 21
Bemis, H. A.: 6	Maire, F.: 22
Cook, E. B.: 4–5, 7, 11	Morgan, A. L.: 19
Council, on Physical Medicine and Rehabilitation: 17	Oliver, J. R.: 14
	Pashby, T. J.: 19
Crane, M. M.: 12–3	Roberts, J.: 23
Crawford, J.: 19	Robinson, H. M.: 20
Department of the Army, the Adjutant General's Office, Personnel Research Section: 9	Rowland, W. M.: 18
	Ryan, V.: 15
	Ryan, V. I.: 23
Foote, F. M.: 12–3	Scobee, R. G.: 12
Freeman, E.: 1	Sloan, L. L.: 18
Gaby, J. B.: 19	Stack, H. J.: 10
Green, E. L.: 12	Staubach, F. W.: 2–3
Imus, H. A.: 16; *rev,* 3:460	Sulzman, J. H.: 4–5, 7, 11
Jones, F. N.: *rev,* 3:460	Wherry, R. J.: 8
Lauer, A. R.: 14	Wilson, R. H.: 21

[1907]

The Atlantic City Eye Test. Grades 1 and over; 1953–61; Samuel M. Diskan; Freund Brothers. *
For additional information, see 6:954 (1 reference).

REFERENCES THROUGH 1971

1. See 6:954.
2. DISKAN, SAMUEL M. "A New Visual Screening Test for

Children: A Preliminary Test of 799 School Children." *Am J Ophthal* 39:369–74 Mr '55. * (*PA* 30:304)

CUMULATIVE NAME INDEX

Diskan, S. M.: 1–2

[1908]

Basic Screen Test—Vision: Measurement of Skill Test 12. Job applicants; 1963–69; MOS 12; 10 scores: acuity (right, left eye), color (gray, red, orange, yellow, green, blue, purple, total); Walter V. Clarke Associates, Inc.; AVA Publications, Inc. *

For additional information, see 7:864.

[1909]

Burnham-Clark-Munsell Color Memory Test. Adults; 1955–56; also called *Test of Hue Memory;* Robert W. Burnham and Joyce R. Clark; Munsell Color Co. *

For additional information, see 5:771 (1 reference).

REFERENCES THROUGH 1971

1. See 5:771.
2. BURNHAM, ROBERT W., AND CLARK, JOYCE R. "A Color Memory Test." *J Opt Soc Am* 44:658–9 Ag '54. * (*PA* 29:3440)
3. LAKOWSKI, R. "Theory and Practice of Colour Vision Testing: A Review, Parts 1 and 2." *Brit J Indus Med* 26(3–4):173–89, 265–88 Jl, O '69. *

CUMULATIVE NAME INDEX

Burnham, R. W.: 1–2   Lakowski, R.: 3
Clark, J. R.: 1–2

[1910]

Dennis Visual Perception Scale. Grades 1–6; 1969, c1964–69; DVPS; identification of perceptually handicapped children; Royce Dennis and Margaret Dennis; Western Psychological Services. *

For additional information and a review by Carl L. Rosen, see 7:866 (1 reference).

REFERENCES THROUGH 1971

1. See 7:866.

CUMULATIVE NAME INDEX

Edson, L. N.: 1   Rosen, C. L.: *rev,* 7:866

[1911]

Dvorine Pseudo-Isochromatic Plates, Second Edition. Ages 3 and over; 1944–58; revision of *Dvorine Color Perception Testing Charts; also called Dvorine Color Vision Test;* 2 scores: nomenclature, color perception; Israel Dvorine; Harcourt Brace Jovanovich, Inc. *

For additional information, see 6:955 (12 references); for excerpted reviews by Elsie Murray, Laurance F. Shaffer, and Miles A. Tinker, see 5:773 (13 references); for excerpted reviews by Knight Dunlap, Carel C. Koch, Elsie Murray (reply by Israel Dvorine), and Miles A. Tinker, see 3:462 (4 references).

REFERENCES THROUGH 1971

1–4. See 3:462.
5–17. See 5:773.
18–29. See 6:955.
30. BOWLES, J. W., JR.; PRONKO, N. H.; ALLEN, G. W.; AND SNYDER, F. W. "Another Experiment in Pursuit of 'Color-Blindness.'" *J Psychol* 28:265–71 O '49. * (*PA* 24:2304)
31. PETERS, GEORGE A. "A Color-Blindness Test for Use in Vocational Guidance." *Optom Weekly* 48:1171–3 Je 13 '57. * (*PA* 33:417)
32. KETTELL, MARJORIE EDYTHE. *Integrity of Ego Processes in Aged Females.* Doctor's thesis, Boston University (Boston, Mass.), 1964. (*DA* 25:3111)
33. WILKINS, LEE GERTRUDE. *Some Correlates of Cognitive Controls, Personality Trait Factors, and n Achievement Motivation.* Doctor's thesis, New York University (New York, N.Y.), 1964. (*DA* 25:1327)
34. LAKOWSKI, R. "Testing of Colour Vision in Prospective Printers' Apprentices and the Problems This Presents in Selection." *Brit J Physiol Optics* 22(1):10–32 '65. *
35. SEEFELT, EDWARD R. "A Comparison of the AOC and the

Dvorine Pseudo-Isochromatic Tests in Color Vision Testing." *Am J Optom* 42:250–5 Ap '65. *
36. LAKOWSKI, R. "A Critical Evaluation of Colour Vision Tests." *Brit J Physiol Optics* 23(3):186–209 '66. *
37. SHERMAN, DAVID. "A Comparative Review of the Ishihara and Dvorine Tests for Colorblindness." *Manasa* 2:13–4 sp '67. *
38. KAPLAN, HARVEY A. *Relationships Among Cognitive Styles, Personality Traits and Reading Achievement at the Elementary School Level.* Doctor's thesis, Rutgers—The State University (New Brunswick, N.J.), 1969. (*DAI* 30:4278A)
39. SALVIA, JOHN. "Four Tests of Color Vision: A Study of Diagnostic Accuracy With the Mentally Retarded." *Am J Mental Def* 74(3):421–7 N '69. * (*PA* 44:5567)
40. FREY, ROGER M., AND KRAUSE, IRL BROWN. "The Incidence of Color Blindness Among Deaf Children." *Excep Children* 37(5):393–4 Ja '71. *
41. FREY, ROGER M., AND KRAUSE, IRL BROWN, JR. "Colour Perception Among Deaf Students: An Evaluation of the Educational Implications." *Slow Learning Child* (Australia) 18(1):42–7 Mr '71. * (*PA* 47:1605)
42. SALVIA, JOHN, AND YSSELDYKE, JAMES. "The Dvorine Color Blindness Test With Retarded Boys." *Excep Children* 38(3):263–4 N '71. *

CUMULATIVE NAME INDEX

Allen, G. W.: 30	Murray, E.: 6; *exc,* 3:462, 5:
Belcher, S. J.: 21	773
Bowles, J. W.: 8, 30	Peters, G.: 13, 19
Chapanis, A.: 10	Peters, G. A.: 14–18, 31
Crawford, A.: 11	Price, A. C.: 24
Dunlap, K.: *exc,* 3:462	Pronko, N. H.: 8–9, 30
Dvorine, I.: 1, 1a, 2–3, 5, 12,	Salvia, J.: 39, 42
25–7; *exc,* 3:462	Seefelt, E. R.: 35
Frey, R. M.: 40–1	Shaffer, L. F.: *exc,* 5:773
Greenshields, K. W.: 21	Sherman, D.: 37
Gross, H.: 15, 17	Sloan, L. L.: 7, 20
Habel, A.: 20	Snyder, F. W.: 8, 30
Harvey, J.: 28	Synolds, D. L.: 8–9
Harvey, J. E.: 23	Tinker, M. A.: *exc,* 3:462, 5:
Kaplan, H. A.: 38	773
Kettell, M. E.: 32	White, H. I.: 24
Koch, C. C.: *exc,* 3:462	Wilkins, L. G.: 33
Krause, I. B.: 40–1	Wilson, J. M.: 29
Lakowski, R.: 22, 34, 36	Wolfensberger, W.: 29
McCord, F.: 4	Wright, W. D.: 21
	Ysseldyke, J.: 42

[1912]

Farnsworth Dichotomous Test for Color Blindness: Panel D-15. Ages 12 and over; 1947; Dean Farnsworth; Psychological Corporation. *

For additional information and a review by Elsie Murray, see 4:656 (2 references); for an excerpted review, see 3:464.

REFERENCES THROUGH 1971

1–2. See 4:656.
3. HARDY, L. H.; RAND, G.; AND RITTLER, M. C. "H-R-R Polychromatic Plates." *J Opt Soc Am* 44:509–23 Jl '54. *
4. HARDY, LEGRAND H.; RAND, GERTRUDE; AND RITTLER, M. CATHERINE. "The H-R-R Polychromatic Plates: 2, Comparison of Qualitative and Quantitative Classifications by H-R-R Plates and Other Tests." *Arch Ophthal* 52:353–68 S '54. * (*PA* 29:3462)
5. SLOAN, LOUISE L. "Congenital Achromatopsia: A Report of 19 Cases." *J Opt Soc Am* 44:117–28 F '54. * (*PA* 28:7021)
6. COX, JENNIFER. "Colour Vision Defects Acquired in Diseases of the Eye, Part 1." *Brit J Physiol Optics* 17:195–216 O '60. *
7. COX, JENNIFER. "Colour Vision Defects Acquired in Diseases of the Eye, Parts 2 and 3." *Brit J Physiol Optics* 18:3–32, 67–84 Ja, Ap '61. *
8. CRONE, R. A. "Quantitative Diagnosis of Defective Color Vision: A Comparative Evaluation of the Ishihara Test, the Farnsworth Dichotomous Test and the Hardy-Rand-Rittler Polychromatic Plates." *Am J Opththal* 51:298–305 F '61. *
9. FRANCOIS, J., AND VERRIEST, G. "On Acquired Deficiency of Colour Vision, With Special Reference to Its Detection and Classification by Means of the Tests of Farnsworth." *Vision Res* (England) 1:201–19 O '61. *
10. SLOAN, LOUISE L. "Testing for Deficient Color Perception in Children," pp. 697–705. In *Diagnostic Procedures in Pediatric Ophthalmology.* International Ophthalmology Clinics, Vol. 3, No. 4. Edited by Leonard Apt. Boston, Mass.: Little, Brown & Co. (Inc.), December 1963. Pp. xv, 697–1051. *
11. WILSON, JOHN M., AND WOLFENSBERGER, WOLF. "Color-Blindness Testing as an Aid in the Etiological Diagnosis of Mental Retardation." *Am J Mental Def* 67:914–5 My '63. * (*PA* 38:1284)
12. COLLINS, H. BARRY. "Recognition of Acquired Colour Defects Using the Panel D-15." *Austral J Optom* 49:342–7 D '66. *
13. LINKSZ, ARTHUR. "The Farnsworth Panel D-15 Test." *Am J Ophthal* 62:27–37 Jl '66. *

14. LAXAR, KEVIN. "Performance of the Farnsworth Lantern Test as Related to Type and Degree of Color Vision Defect." *Mil Med* 132:726–31 S '67. * (*PA* 42:1525)

15. SALVIA, JOHN. "Four Tests of Color Vision: A Study of Diagnostic Accuracy With the Mentally Retarded." *Am J Mental Def* 74(3):421–7 N '69. * (*PA* 44:5567)

16. SASSOON, HUMPHREY F., AND WISE, JAMES B. "Diagnosis of Colour-Vision Defects in Very Young Children." Letter. *Lancet* (England) 1(7643):419–20 F 21 '70. *

17. PINCKERS, A. "Combined Panel D-15 and 100 Hue Recording." *Ophthalmologica* (Switzerland) 163(4):232–4 '71. *

18. RICHARDS, OSCAR W.; TACK, TERENCE O.; AND THOME, CARL. "Fluorescent Lights for Color Vision Testing." *Am J Optom* 48(9):747–53 S '71. *

CUMULATIVE NAME INDEX

[1913]

The Farnsworth-Munsell 100-Hue Test for the Examination of Color Discrimination. Mental ages 12 and over; 1942–57; Dean Farnsworth; Munsell Color Co. *

For additional information, see 5:775 (1 reference); for a review by Elsie Murray, see 4:657 (2 references).

REFERENCES THROUGH 1971

1–2. See 4:657.

3. See 5:775.

4. JOLLY, V. G. "The Selection of Colour Matchers." *J Oil & Colour Chem Assn* (England) 37:666–9 D '54. *

5. COX, JENNIFER. "Colour Vision Defects Acquired in Diseases of the Eye, Part 1." *Brit J Physiol Optics* 17:195–216 O '60. *

6. COX, JENNIFER. "Colour Vision Defects Acquired in Diseases of the Eye, Parts 2 and 3." *Brit J Physiol Optics* 18:3–32, 67–84 Ja, Ap '61. *

7. FRANCOIS, J., AND VERRIEST, G. "On Acquired Deficiency of Colour Vision, With Special Reference to Its Detection and Classification by Means of the Tests of Farnsworth." *Vision Res* (England) 1:201–19 O '61. *

8. LENNEBERG, ERIC H. "Color Naming, Color Recognition, Color Discrimination: A Re-Appraisal." *Percept & Motor Skills* 12:375–82 Je '61. * (*PA* 36:2BH75L)

9. KRILL, ALEX E., AND SCHNEIDERMAN, ARLENE. "A Hue Discrimination Defect in So-called Normal Carriers of Color Vision Defects." *Invest Ophthal* 3:445–50 Ag '64. *

10. LAKOWSKI, R. "A Critical Evaluation of Colour Vision Tests." *Brit J Physiol Optics* 23(3):186–209 '66. *

11. FORSIUS, H.; ERIKSSON, A. W.; AND FELLMAN, J. "Colour Blindness in Finland." *Acta Ophthalmologica* (Denmark) 46(3):542–52 '68. *

12. CHISHOLM, I. A. "An Evaluation of the Farnsworth-Munsell 100 Hue Test as a Clinical Tool in the Investigation and Management of Ocular Neurological Deficit." *Trans Ophthal Soc UK* (England) 89:243–50 '69. *

13. DREYER, V. "Occupational Possibilities of Colour Defectives." *Acta Ophthalmologica* (Denmark) 47(3):523–34 '69. *

14. LAKOWSKI, R. "Theory and Practice of Colour Vision Testing: A Review, Parts 1 and 2." *Brit J Indus Med* 26(3–4):173–89, 265–88 Jl, O '69. *

15. VARELA, ANIBAL; RIVERA, LUCIA; MARDENES, JORGE; AND CRUZ-COKE, RICARDO. "Color Vision Defects in Non-Alcoholic Relatives of Alcoholic Patients." *Brit J Addict* 64(1):67–73 My '69. *

16. AINLEY, R. G. "The Farnsworth-Munsell 100 Hue Test in Tobacco Amblyopia." *Trans Ophthal Soc UK* (England) 90:765–72 '70. *

17. BRONTE-STEWART, JOAN M., AND CRAIG, J. OMAN. "The Detection of Early Visual Loss in Young Diabetics." *Proc Royal Soc Med* (England) 63(8):786–8 Ag '70. *

18. CHISHOLM, A.; BRONTE-STEWART, J.; AND AWDUCHE, E. O. "Colour Vision in Tobacco Amblyopia." *Acta Ophthalmologica* (Denmark) 48(6):1145–56 '70. *

19. CRUZ-COKE, RICARDO. Chap. 5, "Diagnosis," pp. 57–78. In his *Color Blindness: An Evolutionary Approach*. Springfield, Ill.: Charles C Thomas, Publisher, 1970. Pp. xvi, 156. *

20. KINNEAR, P. R. "Proposals for Scoring and Assessing the 100-Hue Test." *Vision Res* (England) 10:423–33 My '70. *

21. SCOTTI, GIUSEPPE, AND SPINNLER, HANS. "Colour Imperception in Unilateral Hemisphere-Damaged Patients." *J Neurol Neurosurg & Psychiatry* (England) 33(1):22–8 F '70. * (*PA* 46:1682)

22. KRILL, ALEX E., AND FISHMAN, GERALD A. "Acquired Color Vision Defects." *Trans Am Acad Ophthal & Otol* 75(5):1095–111 S–O '71. *

23. PINCKERS, A. "Combined Panel D-15 and 100 Hue Recording." *Ophthalmologica* (Switzerland) 163(4):232–4 '71. *

24. RICHARDS, OSCAR W.; TACK, TERENCE O.; AND THOME, CARL. "Fluorescent Lights for Color Vision Testing." *Am J Optom* 48(9):747–53 S '71. *

25. SMITH, JAMES W., AND LAYDEN, THOMAS A. "Color Vision Defects in Alcoholism—II." *Brit J Addict* 66(1):31–7 Je '71. *

26. TAYLOR, DOROTHY B. *Modifications in Presentation of the Farnsworth-Munsell 100-Hue Test for Use in the Elementary Schools*. Master's thesis, University of British Columbia (Vancouver, B.C., Canada), 1971.

CUMULATIVE NAME INDEX

[1914]

★Guy's Colour Vision Test for Young Children. Ages 3–5 and handicapped; 1972; Peter A. Gardiner; Keeler Instruments Ltd. [England]. * (United States distributor: Keeler Optical Products, Inc.)

[1915]

*Inter-Society Color Council Color Aptitude Test, 1964 Edition. Adults; 1944–64; 1964 test identical with 1953 test; Color Aptitude Test Committee, Inter-Society Color Council; Federation of Societies for Paint Technology. *

For additional information, see 5:779 (5 references).

REFERENCES THROUGH 1971

1–5. See 5:779.

6. JOLLY, V. G. "The Selection of Colour Matchers." *J Oil & Colour Chem Assn* (England) 37:666–9 D '54. *

7. OUELLETTE, L. A. *Age Differences in Color Discrimination*. Master's thesis, Fordham University (New York, N.Y.), 1956.

8. GILBERT, JEANNE G. "Age Changes in Color Matching." *J Gerontol* 12:210–5 Ap '57. * (*PA* 32:2449)

9. HESS, M. "Personal Experience With the I.-S.C.C. Colour-Aptitude Test." Discussion, pp. 143–56. *J Oil & Colour Chem Assn* (England) 40:136–56 F '57. *

10. ADAMS, J. M. "Some Results Obtained With the I.-S.C.C. Colour-Aptitude Test." *J Oil & Colour Chem Assn* (England) 41:807–13 N '58. *

11. TILLEARD, D. L. "Colour-Aptitude Test: Analysis of Scores." *J Oil & Colour Chem Assn* (England) 41:797–806 N '58. *

12. COLLINS, WILLIAM E.; CASOLA, ALFRED S.; AND ZEGERS, RICHARD T. "The Performance of Color-Blind Subjects on the Color Aptitude Test." *J General Psychol* 64:245–50 Ap '61. * (*PA* 36:1BH45C)

13. LAKOWSKI, R. "A Critical Evaluation of Colour Vision Tests." *Brit J Physiol Optics* 23(3):186–209 '66. *

14. LAKOWSKI, R. "Theory and Practice of Colour Vision Testing: A Review, Parts 1 and 2." *Brit J Indus Med* 26(3–4):173–89, 265–88 Jl, O '69. *

15. BARRETT, S BARRE. *A Study of the Interrelationship and Influences of Scholastic Aptitude and Perception Upon Aesthetic Sensitivity in College Students*. Doctor's thesis, University of Kansas (Lawrence, Kan.), 1970. (*DAI* 31:5835A)

16. RICHARDS, OSCAR W.; TACK, TERENCE O.; AND THOME, CARL. "Fluorescent Lights for Color Vision Testing." *Am J Optom* 48(9):747–53 S '71. *

CUMULATIVE NAME INDEX

Croup, A. H.: 4
Dimmick, F. L.: 1, 3, 5
Gilbert, J. G.: 8
Hess, M.: 9
Jolly, V. G.: 6
Lakowski, R.: 13–4
Ouellette, L. A.: 7

Parsons, J. L.: 4
Richards, O. W.: 16
Tack, T. O.: 16
Thomas, G. J.: 2
Thome, C.: 16
Tilleard, D. L.: 11
Zegers, R. T.: 12

[1916]
Keystone Ready-to-Read Tests. School entrants; 1954; visual readiness "to read books at the usual distance"; 7 pass-fail scores: near point fusion, lateral posture, vertical posture, usable vision (4 scores); Keystone Telebinocular required for administration; no manual; Keystone View. *

[1917]
Keystone Tests of Binocular Skill. Grades 1, 2–3, 4–5, 8 and over; 1938–49; adaptation of *Standardized Oral Reading Check Tests* for use with the Keystone Telebinocular to identify children who can read better with one eye than with both eyes together; 2 scores (time, errors) for both eyes, left eye, right eye; Keystone View. *

For additional information, see 6:957 (1 reference).

REFERENCES THROUGH 1971
1. See 6:957.

CUMULATIVE NAME INDEX
Robinson, H. M.: 1

[1918]
*****[Keystone Visual Screening Tests.]** Preschool and over; 1933–71; visual screening tests which can be administered by lay personnel as a basis for referrals to eye specialists; basic instrument used is the Keystone Telebinocular; an attachment, the Keystone Periometer, can be added to any of the three models for measuring the extent of the lateral field of vision; Keystone View. *

a) KEYSTONE VISUAL SURVEY TESTS. Grades 1 (2 or 4 for some tests) and over; 1933–61; screening tests for use in referring students to eye specialists on the basis of failures made on both of two successive testings a week or so apart, preferably administered by different persons; revision of the *Betts Ready to Read Tests* (see 1:1097); "the regular tests for acuity both far and near should not be used until the end of the second grade"; the color tests should not be used below grade 4; low scores for children under 7 may represent visual immaturity rather than visual deficiency; Keystone Telebinocular No. 1103 required for administration; 15 tests: simultaneous vision, vertical posture, lateral posture (2 scores), fusion (2 scores), usable vision (6 scores), depth perception, color perception (2 scores); 10 additional tests for use with the Keystone Telebinocular No. 1103 are listed below.

1) *Keystone Massachusetts School Vision Test.* Grades 1 and over; 1962; 5 scores: visual acuity at a distance, hyperopia (far, near), phoria (far, near); no manual; not to be confused with out of print *Massachusetts Vision Test* (see 5:781).

2) *Keystone Michigan School Vision Test.* Grades 1 and over; 1959; 5 scores: visual acuity at a distance, hyperopia (far, near), phoria (far, near); no manual.

3) *Keystone New York School Vision Test.* Grades kgn–8; 1958; 5 scores: visual acuity at a distance (each eye), farsightedness, lateral phoria (far, near).

4) *Keystone Plus-Lens Test.* Ages 5 and over; 1957–71; farsightedness; referral to an eye specialist on the basis of this test alone is not warranted.

5) *Keystone Preschool Test.* Ages 4–6; 1956; "gross visual acuity" at far point; no manual.

6) *Keystone Ready-to-Read Tests.* See 1916.

7) *Keystone Tests of Binocular Skill.* See 1917.

8) *Keystone Rapid Screening Test.* Grades 1 and over; 1967; students failing to pass all tests should be administered the longer *Keystone Visual Survey Tests;* 9 pass-fail scores: fusion (2 scores), hyperphoria, depth perception, color perception, usable vision (4 scores).

9) *Near-Point Visual Acuity Test.* Nonreaders; 1967; usable vision of each eye and both eyes together at reading distance; no manual.

10) *Spache Binocular Reading Test.* See 1929.

b) KEYSTONE OCCUPATIONAL VISUAL SERVICE TESTS. Employees; 1935–61; screening tests for "determining an employee's visual status so that an appropriate job placement may be made" and for referring employees to eye specialists; Keystone Telebinocular No. 1102 is required for administration; 15 scores: vertical balance (2 scores), lateral balance (2 scores), fusion (2 scores), usable vision (6 scores), depth perception, color vision (2 scores); an additional test for use with the Keystone Telebinocular No. 1102 follows:

1) *Keystone Industrial Short Tests.* Employees; 1948; 12 pass-fail scores: hyperphoria (2 scores), fusion (2 scores), depth perception, color perception, usable vision (6 scores); "failure of any test indicates the need for examination on the complete battery of tests."

c) KEYSTONE DRIVER VISION TESTS. Driver applicants; 1950–70; 11 scores: vertical balance, lateral balance, fusion, usable vision (3 scores), depth perception, color perception (2 scores), tunnel vision (2 scores); Keystone Telebinocular No. 1101; periometer attachment necessary for tunnel vision test.

For additional information, see 5:780 (18 references); for a review by F. Nowell Jones and an excerpted review of an earlier model of the occupational telebinocular, see 3:467 (43 references).

REFERENCES THROUGH 1971
1–43. See 3:467.
44–61. See 5:780.
62. WAGNER, GUY WESLEY. *The Maturation of Certain Visual Functions and Their Relationship to Success in Reading and Arithmetic.* Doctor's thesis, University of Iowa (Iowa City, Iowa), 1935.
63. SLOCUM, ROGER LEON. *Reading Status of University of Wisconsin Freshmen.* Doctor's thesis, University of Wisconsin (Madison, Wis.), 1940.
64. IMUS, H. A. "Visual Testing Technics." *Trans Am Acad Ophthal & Otol* 52:370–85 Mr–Ap '48. *
65. SHAFFER, THOMAS E. "Study of Vision Testing Procedures." *Am J Pub Health* 38:1141–6 Ag '48. * (*PA* 23:1127) Correction of 52.
66. MORGAN, A. LLOYD; CRAWFORD, JOHN; PASHBY, THOMAS J.; AND GABY, JOHN B. "A Survey of Methods Used to Reveal Eye Defects in School Children." *Can Med Assn J* 67:29–34 Jl '52. *
67. ROBINSON, HELEN M. "An Analysis of Four Visual Screening Tests at Grades Four and Seven." *Am J Optom* 30: 177–87 Ap '53. * (*PA* 28:361)
68. FOOTE, FRANKLIN M., AND CRANE, MARIAN M. "An Evaluation of Vision Screening." *Excep Child* 20:153–61+ Ja '54. * (*PA* 28:6975)
69. TYLER, VIOLA. *A Comparative Evaluation of Massachusetts Test of Vision Versus Telebinocular Test of Vision, Short Form, as a Visual Screening Device.* Master's thesis, University of Texas (Austin, Tex.), 1957.
70. SLATON, PAUL, AND JORGENSEN, DONALD. "Visual Screening in a County School for Delinquent Boys." *Am J Optom* 35:369–72 Jl '58. * (*PA* 34:1760)
71. BLUM, HENRIK L.; PETERS, HENRY B.; AND BETTMAN, JEROME W. *Vision Screening for Elementary Schools: The Orinda Study.* Berkeley, Calif.: University of California Press, 1959. Pp. xi, 146.
72. BLUM, HENRIK L.; PETERS, HENRY B.; BETTMAN, JEROME W.; FELLOWS, VICTOR, JR.; AND JOHNSON, FRANK. "Design and Evaluation of a Vision Screening Program for Elementary School Children." *Am J Pub Health* 49:1670–81 D '59. *
73. HARVEY, JASPER ELLIOTT. *The Evaluation and Development of Techniques for Testing the Visual Acuity of Trainable*

Mentally Retarded Children. Doctor's thesis, University of Texas (Austin, Tex.), 1960. (*DA* 20:4587)

74. ZILLEY, ELVERA C. *A Comparison of the Snellen Chart and the Telebinocular Battery of Visual Tests in Vision Screening of Selected Pupils in Sioux Falls Schools.* Master's thesis, University of South Dakota (Vermillion, S.D.), 1961.

75. HARVEY, JASPER. "Evaluation and Development of Techniques for Testing Visual Acuity of Trainable Mentally Retarded Children." *Am J Optom* 40:745–54 D '63. *

76. MALMQUIST, EVE J. TH. "A Study of Vision Defects in Relation to Reading Disabilities, and a Test of the Validity of Certain Vision-Screening Programmes in Elementary Schools." *Slow Learning Child* 12:38–48 Jl '65. *

77. CASHMAN, JEROME PATRICK. *A Study of the Relationship Between Organic Factors, Certain Selected Variables and Progress in a Reading Improvement Program.* Doctor's thesis, Fordham University (New York, N.Y.), 1966. (*DA* 27:1648A)

78. BRIGHAM, BRUCE W. *A Study of the Reading Achievement and Certain Characteristics of Adult Males Convicted of Felonies.* Doctor's thesis, Temple University (Philadelphia, Pa.), 1967. (*DA* 28:4279B)

79. SANTORO, ROSEANN MARIE. *The Relationship of Reading Achievement to Specific Measures of Visual Perception, Visual-Motor Perception and Intelligence.* Doctor's thesis, Fordham University (New York, N.Y.), 1967. (*DA* 28:4010A)

80. WAGNER, HILMAR ERNEST. *A Study of Physical, Mental and Musical Characteristics of Selected Band Members.* Doctor's thesis, North Texas State University (Denton, Tex.), 1967. (*DA* 28:2285A)

81. WARTENBERG, HERBERT. *The Relationship Between Success in Beginning Reading and Various Predictive Measures.* Doctor's thesis, Temple University (Philadelphia, Pa.), 1967. (*DA* 28:979A)

82. HEIMERER, ELSA M. *A Study of the Relationship Between Visual Depth Perception and General Tennis Ability.* Master's thesis, University of North Carolina (Greensboro, N.C.), 1968.

83. ROBINSON, HELEN M. "Visual Efficiency and Reading Status in the Elementary School." *Sup Ed Monogr* 97:49–65 Ag '68. *

84. WILHELM, ROWENA. "Evaluating Score Differences on a Visual Acuity Test." *Percept & Motor Skills* 27:419–23 O '68. * (*PA* 43:5896)

85. WALTON, HOWARD N., and SCHUBERT, DELWYN G. "Vision-Perception Testing and Training Program: Clerical Operations." *Am J Optom* 46(11):840–7 N '69. * (*PA* 45:7119)

86. WILHELM, ROWENA MAY. *Modification of the Keystone Telebinocular Visual Acuity Sub-Test as a Means of Increasing Test Reliability.* Doctor's thesis, University of Michigan (Ann Arbor, Mich.), 1970. (*DAI* 32:262A)

87. PARKER, DEWEY L. *Relationships Among the Keystone Visual Survey Telebinocular With Reading Achievement and the Diagnoses of a Vision Clinic.* Doctor's thesis, University of Oklahoma (Norman, Okla.), 1971. (*DAI* 32:2316A)

88. WETHERELL, RICHARD H. *A Study of the Relationship Between Visual Perception and School Achievement.* Doctor's thesis, University of Southern Mississippi (Hattiesburg, Miss.), 1971. (*DAI* 32:2324A)

CUMULATIVE NAME INDEX

[1919]

MKM Binocular Preschool Test. Preschool; 1963–65; "near point performance"; Leland D. Michael and James W. King; MKM, Inc. *

For additional information, see 7:868.

[1920]

MKM Monocular and Binocular Reading Test. Grades 1–2, 3 and over; 1963–64; "to detect children who are likely to have reading problems associated with poor binocular coordination and macular suppression"; Leland D. Michael and James W. King; MKM, Inc. *

For additional information, see 7:869.

REFERENCES THROUGH 1971

1. FATE, WILLIAM HENRY. *A Study of the Effect of Nearpoint Lens Power on the Visual Tracking Performance of Perceptually Impaired Children.* Doctor's thesis, University of Idaho (Moscow, Idaho), 1971. (*DAI* 32:3120A)

CUMULATIVE NAME INDEX

Fate, W. H.: 1

[1921]

Marianne Frostig Developmental Test of Visual Perception, Third Edition. Ages 3–8; 1961–66; DTVP; 7 scores: eye-motor coordination, figure-ground discrimination, form constancy, position in space, spatial relations, total, perceptual quotient; Marianne Frostig in collaboration with D. Welty Lefever, John R. B. Whittlesey, and Phyllis Maslow (monograph); Consulting Psychologists Press, Inc. *

For additional information and reviews by Brad S. Chissom, Newell C. Kephart, and Lester Mann, see 7:871 (117 references); for reviews by James M. Anderson and Mary C. Austin, see 6:553 (7 references).

REFERENCES THROUGH 1971

1–7. See 6:553.
8–124. See 7:871.

125. ALLEN, ROBERT M.; JONES, R. WAYNE; AND HAUPT, THOMAS D. "Note of Caution on the Research Use of the Frostig Test With Mentally Retarded Children." *Percept & Motor Skills* 21:237–8 Ag '65. * (*PA* 40:708)

126. BENGER, KATHLYN. *A Study of the Relationships Between Perception, Personality, Intelligence and Grade One Reading Achievement.* Master's thesis, University of Alberta (Edmonton, Alta., Canada), 1966.

127. FROSTIG, MARIANNE. "The Relationship of Diagnosis to Remediation in Learning Problems." *Selected Papers Learn Disabilities* 3:45–66 '66. *

128. ROSEN, CARL L. "An Experimental Study of Visual Perceptual Training and Reading Achievement in First Grade." *Percept & Motor Skills* 22:979–86 Je '66. * (*PA* 40:11008)

129. NORTON, JUDITH BURTON. *A Study of the Correlation Between Visual Perception and Social Perception in Educable Mentally Retarded Children.* Master's thesis, Utah State University (Logan, Utah), 1967.

130. GILL, NEWELL T.; HERDTNER, THOMAS J.; AND LOUGH, LINDA. "Selected Perceptual and Socio-Economic Variables, Body-Orientation, and Predicted Academic Success in Young Children." *Childh Ed* 45:52–4 S '68. *

131. IRVINE, JAMES. *Correlates of Grade One Achievement.* Master's thesis, University of Alberta (Edmonton, Alta., Canada), 1968.

132. KORNOVICH, JAMES J. *A Study on the Relationship of Visual-Motor Dysfunction and Articulation Proficiency to Progress in Speech Therapy.* Master's thesis, St. Cloud State College (St. Cloud, Minn.), 1968.

133. SPOMER, ESTHER E. *The Comparative Ability of a Test of Visual Perception and Measures of a Readiness Test of Kindergarten Children.* Master's thesis, Fort Hays Kansas State College (Hays, Kan.), 1968.

134. ARCIERI, LIBERE; MARCUS, MICHAEL; AND SLAVIN, ROBERTA. "The Developmental Learning Program at P.S. 78." *J Learn Dis* 3(11):553–62 N '70. *

135. CHARLTON, NORMAN WOOD, II. *An Investigation of Selected Visual-Perceptual and Motor Parameters of Young Trainable Mentally Retarded Children.* Doctor's thesis, University of Houston (Houston, Tex.), 1970. (*DAI* 32:271A)

136. DuBOIS, NELSON FREDERICK. *Selected Relationships Between Reading Achievement and Visual Perceptual, Visual Motor and Intersensory Integration Abilities in a 2nd and 4th Grade Population.* Doctor's thesis, University of Maryland (College Park, Md.), 1970. (*DAI* 32:3858A)

137. FRETZ, BRUCE R.; JOHNSON, WARREN R.; AND JOHNSON, JULIA A. "Intellectual and Perceptual Motor Development as a Function of Therapeutic Play," pp. 475–80. In *Contemporary Psychology of Sport.* Proceedings of the Second International Congress of Sport Psychology, Washington, D.C., 1968. Chicago, Ill.: Athletic Institute, 1970. Pp. xix, 878. *

138. HASAZI, JOSEPH E. *The Relationship of Attentional, Motivational, and Visual-Perceptual Variables to Response Latency in Developmental Retardates.* Doctor's thesis, University of Miami (Coral Gables, Fla.), 1970. (*DAI* 31:5623B)

139. IRELAND, EVELYN CRAIG. *The Relationship Between Performance in Visual Perception and Maladjustment in Elementary School Boys.* Doctor's thesis, University of Maryland (College Park, Md.), 1970. (*DAI* 32:1847B)

140. LEIBERT, ROBERT E., AND SHERK, JOHN K. "Three Frostig Visual Perception Sub-Tests and Specific Reading Tasks for Kindergarten, First, and Second Grade Children." *Read Teach* 24(2):130–7 N '70. * (*PA* 45:10923)

141. PEDDER, DONALD. *Discrimination Abilities and Motor Skills in Relation to Reading.* Doctor's thesis, Case Western Reserve University (Cleveland, Ohio), 1970. (*DAI* 32:252A)

142. RAGSDALE, NANCY L. *Relationship of Reading Readiness and the Frostig Visual Perception Test.* Master's thesis, Illinois State University (Normal, Ill.), 1970.

143. SINCLAIR, WILLIAM ANDREW. *The Effect of Motor Skill Learning Upon Specific Dyslexia.* Doctor's thesis, University of New Mexico (Albuquerque, N.M.), 1970. (*DAI* 31:5830A)

144. WELLS, CLINTON GEORGE. *A Comparative Study of Children Grouped by Three Basic Score Patterns on the Wechsler Intelligence Scale for Children.* Doctor's thesis, University of Northern Colorado (Greeley, Colo.), 1970. (*DAI* 31:6444A)

145. ARMENTROUT, JAMES A. "Effects of Perceptual Training on Children's Human Figure Drawings." *J Genetic Psychol* 119(2):281–7 D '71. * (*PA* 47:11789)

146. BAUMAN, EDWARD, AND ST. JOHN, JOAN. "The Clinical Usefulness of Some Tests of Visual Perception." *Psychol Sch* 8(3):247–9 Jl '71. * (*PA* 47:9635)

147. BRAUN, JEAN S., AND BRANE, MARIA. "Comparison of the Performance of Children With Dysrhythmia Grade 1 and Normal EEG on Psychological Tests." Abstract. *Proc 79th Ann Conv Am Psychol Assn* 6(1):457–8 '71. * (*PA* 46:5135)

148. CHISSOM, BRAD S., AND THOMAS, JERRY R. "Comparison of Factor Structures for the Frostig Developmental Test of Visual Perception." *Percept & Motor Skills* 33(3):1015–9 D '71. * (*PA* 48:1634)

149. DOYLE, MARGARET Q. *Effects of the Frostig Program on First Grade Achievement.* Doctor's thesis, Boston College (Chestnut Hill, Mass.), 1971. (*DAI* 32:1331A)

150. GAMSKY, NEAL R., AND LLOYD, FAYE WILLIAMS. "A Longitudinal Study of Visual Perceptual Training and Reading Achievement." *J Ed Res* 64(10): 451–4 Jl–Ag '71. * (*PA* 47:9831)

151. GAMSKY, NEAL RICHARD, AND LLOYD, FAYE W. "Relationship of Child Behavior to Visual Perception Deficiencies." *Psychol Sch* 8(1):60–1 Ja '71. * (*PA* 46:7552)

152. GIBSON, RICHARD E. *Perceptual Difficulties of the Mentally Retarded in Five Areas of Vision as Measured by the Frostig Developmental Test of Visual Perception.* Master's thesis, East Tennessee State University (Johnson City, Tenn.), 1971.

153. GORDON, GEORGE, AND HYMAN, IRWIN. "The Measurement of Perceptual-Motor Abilities of Head Start Children." *Psychol Sch* 8(1):41–8 Ja '71. * (*PA* 46:7777)

154. GROSSMAN, MARVIN. "Motor Coordination and Young Children's Drawing Abilities." *Child Study J* 1(4):213–5 su '71. * (*PA* 48:6940)

155. GUTKNECHT, BRUCE ARTHUR. *A Psycholinguistic Analysis of the Oral Reading Behavior of Selected Children Identified as Perceptually Handicapped.* Doctor's thesis, Wayne State University (Detroit, Mich.), 1971. (*DAI* 32:6101A)

156. HAMMILL, DONALD; GOODMAN, LIBBY; AND WIEDERHOLT, J. LEE. "Use of the Frostig DTVP With Economically Disadvantaged Children." *J Sch Psychol* 9(4):430–5 w '71. * (*PA* 48:1643)

157. HOLOVKA, EDWARD ANDREW. *The Frostig Developmental Program: Prediction and Follow-Up of First Grade Remediation With Later Reading.* Doctor's thesis, Wayne State University (Detroit, Mich.), 1971. (*DAI* 32:6249A)

158. McKINNEY, JAMES D. "Factor Analytic Study of the Developmental Test of Visual Perception and the Metropolitan Readiness Test." *Percept & Motor Skills* 33(3):1331–4 D '71. * (*PA* 48:1653)

159. ROBINSON, HALBERT B., AND ROBINSON, NANCY M. "Longitudinal Development of Very Young Children in a Comprehensive Day Care Program: The First Two Years." *Child Develop* 42(6):1673–83 D '71. * (*PA* 48:8827)

160. SAPIR, SELMA G. "Learning Disability and Deficit Centered Classroom Training." *Cognitive Studies* 2:324–38 '71. * (*PA* 49:1359, title only)

161. SCRUGGS, ALLIE W. *The Effect of the Fall River and Lowell Head Start Programs on Behavorial Characteristics Associated With Lower Socio-Economic Class Preschool Children.* Doctor's thesis, Boston University (Boston, Mass.), 1971. (*DAI* 32:1949A)

162. SILOAC, KENNETH THOMAS. *An Investigation of Selected Perceptual Abilities in Educable Retarded and Normal Children.* Doctor's thesis, Wayne State University (Detroit, Mich.), 1971. (*DAI* 32:6719B)

163. STEWART, JOE GLENN. *The Relationship of Selected Abilities to Gross Motor Performance of Educable Mentally Retarded Students.* Doctor's thesis, North Texas State University (Denton, Tex.), 1971. (*DAI* 32:6799A)

164. VAN ZYL, F. J., AND IVES, L. A. "Visual Perception and Eye-Motor Co-ordination in a Group of Young Deaf Children." *Develop Med & Child Neurol* (England) 13(3):373–9 Je '71. * (*PA* 47:7345)

165. WALSH, JOHN F., AND D'ANGELO, RITA. "Effectiveness of the Frostig Program for Visual Perceptual Training With Head Start Children." *Percept & Motor Skills* 32(3):944–6 Je '71. * (*PA* 47:3806)

166. WIEDERHOLT, J. LEE, AND HAMMILL, DONALD D. "Use of the Frostig-Horne Visual Perception Program in the Urban School." *Psychol Sch* 8(3):268–74 Jl '71. * (*PA* 47:9862)

167. WRIGHT, LOGAN, AND JIMMERSON, STEVE. "Intellectual Sequelae of Hemophilus Influenzae Meningitis." *J Abn Psychol* 77(2):181–3 Ap '71. * (*PA* 46:3584)

CUMULATIVE NAME INDEX

[1922]

★**Motor-Free Visual Perception Test.** Ages 4–8; 1972; MVPT; Ronald P. Colarusso and Donald D. Hammill; Academic Therapy Publications. *

[1923]

Ortho-Rater. Adults; 1942–58; 12 scores for each model: binocular action of the eyes (4 tests), fineness of visual discrimination (6 tests), perception of depth, color discrimination; 2 models; Bausch & Lomb, Inc. *
a) MASTER ORTHO-RATER. 1942–58.
b) MODIFIED ORTHO-RATER. 1952–58.

For additional information, see 5:783 (59 references); for reviews by Henry A. Imus and F. Nowell Jones, see 3:471 (41 references).

REFERENCES THROUGH 1971

1–30. See 3:471.
31–89. See 5:783.
90. IMUS, H. A. "Visual Testing Technics." *Trans Am Acad Ophthal & Otol* 52:370–85 Mr–Ap '48. *
91. KEPHART, NEWELL C., AND BESNARD, GUY G. "Visual Differentiation of Moving Objects." *J Appl Psychol* 34:50–3 F '50. * (*PA* 24:6105)
92. SLOAN, LOUISE L., AND ROWLAND, WILLIAM M. "Comparison of Ortho-Rater and Sight Screener Tests of Heterophoria With Standard Clinical Tests." *Am J Ophthal* 34:1363–75 O '51. *
93. KEPHART, N. C., AND OLIVER, JAMES E. "A Study of the Relationship Between Lateral Phoria and Age." *Am J Optom* 29:423–9 Ag '52. * (*PA* 27:4004)
94. MORGAN, A. LLOYD; CRAWFORD, JOHN; PASHBY, THOMAS J.; AND GABY, JOHN B. "A Survey of Methods Used to Reveal Eye Defects in School Children." *Can Med Assn J* 67:29–34 Jl '52. *
95. KEPHART, NEWELL C. "Visual Skills and Their Relation to School Achievement." *Am J Ophthal* 36:794–9 Je '53. * (*PA* 28:3208)
96. ROBINSON, HELEN M. "An Analysis of Four Visual Screening Tests at Grades Four and Seven." *Am J Optom* 30: 177–87 Ap '53. * (*PA* 28:361)

97. GORDON, D. A.; ZEIDNER, J.; ZAGORSKI, H. J.; AND UHLANER, J. E. "A Psychometric Evaluation of Ortho-Rater and Wall Chart Tests." *Am J Ophthal* 37:699–705 My '54. * (*PA* 29:1976)
98. "Visual Screening of Applicants for Illinois Drivers Licenses." *Optom Weekly* 47:291–3 F 16 '56. * (*PA* 31:3933)
99. GRUBBS, ROBERT LOWELL. *The Relationship Between Speed of Visual Perception and Basic Skill in Typewriting.* Doctor's thesis, University of Pittsburgh (Pittsburgh, Pa.), 1956. (*DA* 17:62)
100. OVERTON, ELEAZER C. "Factors That Influence Personality Behavior of High School Students." *Optom Weekly* 48: 583–6 Mr 28 '57. * (*PA* 32:2464)
101. BOURASSA, G. LEE, AND GUION, ROBERT M. "A Factorial Study of Dexterity Tests." *J Appl Psychol* 43:199–204 Je '59. * (*PA* 34:6585)
102. BURG, ALBERT, AND HULBERT, SLADE. "Dynamic Visual Acuity as Related to Age, Sex, and Static Acuity." *J Appl Psychol* 45:111–6 Ap '61. * (*PA* 36:3LK11B)
103. SOLOMON, LILLIAN GREENBERG. *An Investigation of Visual Defect and Certain Cultural and Personality Factors in Juvenile Delinquency.* Doctor's thesis, University of Texas (Austin, Tex.), 1962. (*DA* 25:2617)
104. SPACHE, GEORGE D., AND TILLMAN, CHESTER E. "A Comparison of the Visual Profiles of Retarded and Non-Retarded Readers." *J Develop Read* 5:101–9 w '62. *
105. BEERY, KEITH EDMOND. *Behavorial Correlates of Visual Deficiencies in Sixth Grade Children.* Doctor's thesis, Purdue University (Lafayette, Ind.), 1963. (*DA* 24:1691)
106. CUTLER, G. H., AND DAVEY, J. B. "Some Comments on the Mavis and Ortho-Rater Vision Screeners (Made as a Result of the Screening at the Motor Show, 1961 and Racing Car Show, 1962)." *Brit J Physiol Optics* 22(1):53–6 '65. *
107. CUTLER, G. H., AND DAVEY, J. B. "Visual Screening: Motor Show 1961, Racing Car Show 1961/62: 1, The Vision of the Two Groups of Drivers." *Brit J Physiol Optics* 22(2):114–9 '65. *
108. GUION, ROBERT M. *Personnel Testing*, pp. 281–8. New York: McGraw-Hill Book Co., 1965. Pp. xiii, 585. *
109. MUSKOPF, A., AND ROBINSON, A. ALAN. "Screening the Visual Efficiency of Culturally Deprived 1st Grade Children." *Optom Weekly* 56:21–4 F 4 '65. *
110. TIFFIN, JOSEPH, AND McCORMICK, ERNEST J. *Industrial Psychology, Fifth Edition*, pp. 178–83. Englewood Cliffs, N.J.: Prentice-Hall, Inc., 1965. Pp. xv, 682. *
111. BURG, ALBERT. "Visual Acuity as Measured by Dynamic and Static Tests: A Comparative Evaluation." *J Appl Psychol* 50:460–6 D '66. * (*PA* 41:2299)
112. ROBINSON, H. ALAN. "Reliability of Measures Related to Reading Success of Average, Disadvantaged, and Advantaged Kindergarten Children." Comments by Samuel Weintraub. *Read Teach* 20:203–9 D '66. * (*PA* 41:3344)
113. MILLER, VIRGINIA S. "The Instrument Effect of Acuity Tests in the Ortho-Rater." *Sup Ed Monogr* 97:66–7 Ag '68. *
114. ROBINSON, H. ALAN, AND HANSON, EARL. "Reliability of Measures of Reading Achievement." *Read Teach* 21:307–13+ Ja '68. * (*PA* 42:17652)
115. ROBINSON, HELEN M. "Visual Efficiency and Reading Status in the Elementary School." *Sup Ed Monogr* 97:49–65 Ag '68. *
116. HORNE, E. P., AND HINES, DAVID A. "Changes in Visual Acuity in Repeated Measurement." *J General Psychol* 80(1): 93–7 Ja '69. * (*PA* 43:6170)
117. NASH, MARY SAUNDERS. *The Development of Depth Perception in Intermediate Age Children.* Doctor's thesis, University of Kentucky (Lexington, Ky.), 1969. (*DAI* 30:3894B)
118. VAN DER MERWE, R., AND SCHAUDER, D. E. "The Evaluation of a Simple Vision Screening Device." *Psychologia Africana* (South Africa) 13(1):28–33 O '69. * (*PA* 44:17794)
119. ROBERTS, JEAN, AND DUYAN, KENNETH R. "Visual Acuity in Children: United States." *Vital & Health Stat* Series 11 (101): 1–35 F '70. *
120. SHICK, JACQUELINE. "Relationship Between Depth Perception and Hand-Eye Dominance and Free-Throw Shooting in College Women." *Percept & Motor Skills* 33(2):539–42 O '71. * (*PA* 47:6072)

CUMULATIVE NAME INDEX

[1924]

*Pseudo-Isochromatic Plates for Testing Color Perception. Ages 7 and over; 1940-65; red-green deficiency; originally published in 1940 as a 46-plate test including 14 plates from Ishihara's *Test for Colour-Blindness* and 31 plates from Stilling's original pseudo-isochromatic diagrams; an 18-plate selection of the 46-plate edition was prepared in 1947 as suggested by LeGrand H. Hardy, Gertrude Rand, and M. Catherine Rittler; the current 1965 edition is a 14-plate selection—11 plates from the 18-plate edition and 3 plates from the 46-plate edition; not to be confused with the 21-plate *AO H-R-R Pseudoisochromatic Plates* (1957) now out of print; American Optical Corporation. *

For additional information, see 4:661 (8 references); for an excerpted review of the 46-plate test, see 3:473 (9 references).

REFERENCES THROUGH 1971

1-9. See 3:473.
10-17. See 4:661.
18. LOKEN, ROBERT D. "The Color-Meter: A Quantitative Color-Vision Test." *Am J Psychol* 55:563-8 O '42. * (*PA* 17:1481)
19. THOMAS, GARTH J. "Visual Sensitivity to Color: A Comparative Study of Four Tests." *Am J Psychol* 56:583-91 O '43. * (*PA* 18:422)
20. REED, J. D. "The Effect of Illumination in Changing the Stimuli in Pseudo-Isochromatic Plates." Abstract. *J Opt Soc Am* 34:350 Je '44. * (*PA* 18:3406, title only)
21. RICHARDSON, J. A., AND KINARD, F. W. "Effect of Vitamin A Administration Upon Defective Color Vision." *South Med J* 39:811-3 O '46. * (*PA* 21:1414)
22. SLOAN, LOUISE L. "Selection of Color Vision Tests for the Army Air Forces: A Summary of Studies Made at the Army Air Forces School of Aviation Medicine." *Arch Ophthal* 36:263-83 S '46. * (*PA* 21:389)
23. GALLAGHER, J. ROSWELL; LUDVIGH, ELEK J.; MARTIN, S. FORREST; AND GALLAGHER, CONSTANCE D. "Effect of Training Methods on Color Vision." *Arch Ophthal* 37:572-82 My '47. * (*PA* 21:3417)
24. VAN DEN AKKER, J. A.; TODD, J. EDWARD; NOLAN, PHILIP; AND WINK, WILLMER A. "Use of a Monochromatic Colorimeter

for the Study of Color Blindness." *J Opt Soc Am* 37:363-87 My '47. * (*PA* 21:2909)
25. BOICE, MARY L.; TINKER, MILES A.; AND PATERSON, DONALD G. "Color Vision and Age." *Am J Psychol* 61:520-6 O '48. * (*PA* 23:4053)
26. ROSS, SHERMAN, AND MUELLER, C. G. "A Note on the Memorization of Color Plates by a Color Deficient Individual." *J General Psychol* 40:269-74 Ap '49. * (*PA* 24:3039)
27. CHAPANIS, ALPHONSE. "Relationships Between Age, Visual Acuity and Color Vision." *Human Biol* 22:1-33 F '50. * (*PA* 24:5045)
28. KEPHART, NEWELL C., AND TIESZEN, MELVIN J. "Ortho-Rater Color Vision Test Compared With the Ishihara and the Pseudo-Isochromatic Plates." *J Appl Psychol* 35:127-9 Ap '51. * (*PA* 25:7862)
29. ROSS, SHERMAN, AND FLETCHER, JOHN L. "Response Time as an Indicator of Color Deficiency." *J Appl Psychol* 37:211-3 Je '53. * (*PA* 28:2113)
30. HARDY, L. H.; RAND, G.; AND RITTLER, M. C. "H-R-R Polychromatic Plates." *J Opt Soc Am* 44:509-23 Jl '54. *
31. MAYER, JACK J., AND ZACCARIA, MICHAEL A. "The Evaluation of a Color-Naming Test for Color Blindness." *J Appl Psychol* 39:160-3 Je '55. * (*PA* 30:2168)
32. OVERTON, RICHARD K., AND BROWN, W. LYNN. "Unrecognized Weakness and Compensatory Learning." *Am J Psychol* 70:126-7 Mr '57. * (*PA* 33:708)
33. GOLDSTEIN, ALVIN G., AND BROOKS, RICHARD. "A Red-Green Color Vision Test Employing Transparencies." *Percept & Motor Skills* 11:229-30 O '60. * (*PA* 35:1596)
34. SILVERMAN, STANLEY M.; BERGMAN, PHILIP S.; BATTERSBY, WILLIAM S.; AND BENDER, MORRIS B. "Pseudoisochromatic Plates: Use as a Test of Visual Field Deficit After Brain Damage." *Arch Neurol* 4:499-509 My '61. *
35. GALLAGHER, J. ROSWELL, AND GALLAGHER, CONSTANCE D. "Color Vision Screening of Pre-School and First Grade Children." *Arch Ophthal* 72:200-11 Ag '64. *
36. SEEFELT, EDWARD R. "An Evaluation of the Validity and Reliability of the AOC 15-Plate Pseudo-Isochromatic Test in Routine Testing." *Am J Optom* 41:371-81 Je '64. *
37. SEEFELT, EDWARD R. "A Comparison of the AOC and the Dvorine Pseudo-Isochromatic Tests in Color Vision Testing." *Am J Optom* 42:250-5 Ap '65. *
38. SALVIA, JOHN A., AND YSSELDYKE, JAMES E. "Validity and Reliability of the Red-Green AO H-R-R Pseudoisochromatic Plates With Mentally Retarded Children." *Percept & Motor Skills* 33(3):1071-4 D '71. * (*PA* 48:1523)

CUMULATIVE NAME INDEX

[1925]

School Vision Tester. Grades kgn and over; 1957-74; 6 tests: tumbling E acuity (each eye), farsightedness (each eye), muscle balance (far, near); the instrument is the same as the *Ortho-Rater* except for the test slides; the standard *Ortho-Rater* may be used to extend testing; Bausch & Lomb, Inc. *

For additional information and a review by Carl L. Rosen, see 7:875 (1 reference); for a review by Helen M. Robinson, see 6:958 (2 references).

REFERENCES THROUGH 1971

1-2. See 6:958.
3. See 7:875.

[1926]

★**Sheridan Gardiner Test of Visual Acuity.** Ages 5 and over; 1970; Mary D. Sheridan and Peter A. Gardiner; Keeler Instruments Ltd. [England]. * (United States distributor: Keeler Optical Products, Inc.)

REFERENCES THROUGH 1971

1. SHERIDAN, MARY D., AND GARDINER, PETER A. "Sheridan-Gardiner Test for Visual Acuity." *Brit Med J* 2(5701):108–9 Ap 11 '70. *

[1927]

★**Sloan Achromatopsia Test.** Individuals suspected of total color blindness; 1955–61; Louise L. Sloan; Munsell Color Co. *

[1928]

Southern California Figure-Ground Visual Perception Test. Ages 4–10; 1966; SCFG; also available as a subtest of *Southern California Sensory Integration Tests;* visual perception of a foreground figure on a rival background; A. Jean Ayres; Western Psychological Services. *

For additional information and a review by Rosslyn Gaines, see 7:876 (2 references).

REFERENCES THROUGH 1971

1–2. See 7:876.
3. FOX, FRANK HEWITT. *A Description of Language and Perceptual Function of Culturally Deprived Children.* Doctor's thesis, University of Wisconsin (Madison, Wis.), 1968. (*DA* 29:4323A)
4. BOGARD, DOLORES ANN. *Visual Perception of Static and Dynamic Two-Dimensional Objects: A Cross-Sectional Study.* Doctor's thesis, University of Southern California (Los Angeles, Calif.), 1971. (*DAI* 32:2461A)
5. BROOKS, CLARENCE R., AND CLAIR, THEODORE NAT. "Relationships Among Visual Figure-Ground Perception, Word Recognition, IQ, and Chronological Age." *Percept & Motor Skills* 33(1):59–62 Ag '71. * (*PA* 47:3534)
6. GREIF, SUSAN ANN. *A Study of the Relationship Between Auditory, Visual, and Haptic Perception and Selected Parameters of Language and Articulation in Children With Central Processing Dysfunction.* Doctor's thesis, Wayne State University (Detroit, Mich.), 1971. (*DAI* 32:6717B)

[1929]

Spache Binocular Reading Test. Nonreaders and grade 1, grades 1.5–2, 3 and over; 1943–55; eye preference in reading; 3 levels; George D. Spache; Keystone View. *
a) TEST 1. Nonreaders and grade 1.
b) TEST 2, MY BIG RED CAR. Grades 1.5–2.
c) TEST 3, THE QUEEN. Grades 3 and over.

For additional information and a review by Helen M. Robinson, see 6:959; see also 5:784 (4 references); for a review by Albert J. Harris of Test 3, see 3:461 (4 references).

REFERENCES THROUGH 1971

1–4. See 3:461.
5–8. See 5:784.
9. SPACHE, GEORGE. "One-Eyed and Two-Eyed Reading." *J Ed Res* 37:616–8 Ap '44. * (*PA* 18:3306)
10. ROSENBLOOM, ALFRED A., JR. "The Relationship Between Aniseikonia and Achievement in Reading." *Sup Ed Monogr* 97:109–16 Ag '68. *

[1930]

★**Speed of Color Discrimination Test.** College; 1964; SCDT; for research use only; group administered version of Stroop Color-Word Test; 2 scores: color discrimination, conflicting color discrimination; no manual; Educational Testing Service (Atlanta Office). *

REFERENCES THROUGH 1971

1. EPSTEIN, MARVIN. *An Investigation of Certain Aspects of Cognitive Controls and Reading Comprehension.* Doctor's thesis, Temple University (Philadelphia, Pa.), 1965. (*DA* 26:1764)

[1931]

Stycar Vision Tests. Normal and handicapped children ages 6 months to 2.5 years, 3–5, 5–7; 1958–70; SVT; 3 levels; Mary D. Sheridan; distributed by NFER Publishing Co. Ltd. [England]. *
a) GRADED BALLS TEST. Ages 6 months to 2.5 years; 1968–70.
b) AGES 3–5. 1958–70.
c) AGES 5–7. 1958–70.

For additional information, see 7:881.

REFERENCES THROUGH 1971

1. SHERIDAN, MARY D. "Diagnosis of Visual Defect in Early Childhood." *Brit Orthoptic J* 20:29–36 '63. *
2. SAVITZ, ROBERTA A.; VALADIAN, ISABELLE; AND REED, ROBERT B. "Vision Screening of Preschool Children at Home." *Am J Pub Health* 55:1555–62 O '65. *
3. LIPPMANN, OTTO. "Vision of Young Children." *Arch Ophthal* 81(6):763–75 Je '69. *
4. SHERIDAN, MARY D., AND GARDINER, PETER A. "Sheridan-Gardiner Test for Visual Acuity." *Brit Med J* 2(5701):108–9 Ap 11 '70. *
5. LIPPMANN, OTTO. "Vision Screening of Young Children." *Am J Pub Health* 61(8):1586–1601 Ag '71. *

[1932]

Test for Colour-Blindness. Ages 4 and over; 1917–70; congenital color vision deficiency; Shinobu Ishihara; Kanehara Shuppan Co., Ltd. [Japan]. * (United States distributor: Graham-Field Surgical Co., Inc.)

For additional information, see 7:882 (13 references); see also 6:962 (58 references).

REFERENCES THROUGH 1971

1–58. See 6:962.
59–71. See 7:882.
72. MILES, W. R., AND BEAUMONT, H. "Monocular Testing of the Color Blind." *Am J Ophthal* 14:636–9 Jl '31. * (*PA* 6:4681)
73. MILES, W. R., AND CRAIG, HOMER, JR. "Color Blindness in Dry Goods Salesmen." *Personnel J* 9:437–49 Ap '31. * (*PA* 5:3222)
74. LENNON, LAWRENCE JOSEPH. *The Constancy of Hypochromatic Vision Over a Period of Nine Months.* Master's thesis, Pennsylvania State University (University Park, Pa.), 1933.
75. COPELAND, HERMAN A. "Occupational Differences in Color-Blindness." *J Appl Psychol* 19:490–2 Ag '35. * (*PA* 10:740)
76. HSIAO, HSIAO HUNG. "A Study of Color-Blindness Among Chinese Children." *J Appl Psychol* 19:641–6 D '35. * (*PA* 10:3312)
77. LORENZ, ALICE B., AND McCLURE, WILLIAM E. "The Influence of Color Blindness on Intelligence and Achievement of College Men." *J Appl Psychol* 19:320–30 Je '35. * (*PA* 10:85)
78. MILLARD, MARY S., AND SHAKOW, DAVID. "A Note on Color-Blindness in Some Psychotic Groups." *J Social Psychol* 6:252–6 F '35. * (*PA* 10:1531)
79. PATERSON, DONALD G.; SCHNEIDLER, GWENDOLEN G.; AND WILLIAMSON, EDMUND G. *Student Guidance Techniques,* pp. 247–50. New York: McGraw-Hill Book Co., Inc., 1938. Pp. xviii, 316. * (*PA* 12:2131)
80. ERICKSON, MILTON H. "The Induction of Color Blindness

by a Technique of Hypnotic Suggestion." *J General Psychol* 20:61–89 Ja '39. * *(PA* 13:3643)

81. GRETHER, WALTER F. "A Comment on 'The Induction of Color Blindness by a Technique of Hypnotic Suggestion.'" *J General Psychol* 23:207–10 Jl '40. * *(PA* 15:87)

82. BATES, GEORGE N. "A Further Study in the Field of Color Vision." *McGill Med J* (Canada) 10:55–6+ F '41. * *(PA* 19: 2474)

83. SLOAN, LOUISE L. "The Use of Pseudo-Isochromatic Charts in Detecting Central Scotomas Due to Lesions in the Conducting Pathways." *Am J Ophthal* 25:1352–6 N '42. *

84. HAMILTON, W. F.; BRIGGS, A. P.; AND BUTLER, R. E. "The Testing of Color Vision in Relation to Vitamin A Administration." *Am J Physiol* 140:578–82 Ja '44. * *(PA* 19:62)

85. GEDDES, W. R. "The Colour Sense of Fijian Natives." *Brit J Psychol* 37:30–6 S '46. * *(PA* 21:38)

86. GALLAGHER, J. ROSWELL; LUDVIGH, ELEK J.; MARTIN, S. FORREST; AND GALLAGHER, CONSTANCE D. "Effect of Training Methods on Color Vision." *Arch Ophthal* 37:572–82 My '47. * *(PA* 21:3417)

87. CHAPANIS, ALPHONSE. "The Stability of 'Improvement' in Color Vision Due to Training—A Report of Three Cases." *Am J Optom* 26:251–9 Je '49. * *(PA* 24:473)

88. CHAN, EUGENE, AND MAO, WINIFRED S. "Colour-Blindness Among the Chinese." *Brit J Ophthal* 34:744–6 D '50. * *(PA* 25: 7246)

89. FETTER, MARION C. "Colorimetric Tests Read by Color-Blind People." *Am J Med Technol* 29:349–55 N–D '63. *

90. LAKOWSKI, R. "Colorimetric and Photometric Data for the 10th Edition of the Ishihara Plates." *Brit J Physiol Optics* 22(4): 195–207 '65. *

91. LAKOWSKI, R. "Testing of Colour Vision in Prospective Printers' Apprentices and the Problems This Presents in Selection." *Brit J Physiol Optics* 22(1):10–32 '65. *

92. FIALKOW, PHILIP J.; THULINE, HORACE C.; AND FENSTER, L. FREDERICK. "Lack of Association Between Cirrhosis and the Common Types of Color Blindness." *New Engl J Med* 275:584–7 S 15 '66. *

93. LAKOWSKI, R. "A Critical Evaluation of Colour Vision Tests." *Brit J Physiol Optics* 23(3):186–209 '66. *

94. GORRELL, G. J. "Inheritance of Alcoholism." Letter. *Lancet* (England) 1(7484):274 F 4 '67. *

95. THULINE, H. C. "Inheritance of Alcoholism." Letter. Reply by R. Cruz-Coke. *Lancet* (England) 1(7484):274–5 F 4 '67. *

96. CRUZ-COKE, RICARDO. Chap. 5, "Diagnosis," pp. 57–78. In his *Color Blindness: An Evolutionary Approach.* Springfield, Ill.: Charles C Thomas, Publisher, 1970. Pp. xvi, 156. *

97. COX, BRIAN J. "Validity of a Preschool Colour Vision Test." *J Sch Health* 41(3):163–5 Mr '71. * *(PA* 46:11439)

98. HENDERSON, S. T.; MORLEY, D. I.; AND HALSTEAD, M. B. "Colour Discrimination Tests on Visitors to a Scientific Exhibition." *Color Eng* 9(6):15–9 N–D '71. * *(PA* 48:109)

99. SALVIA, JOHN, AND YSSELDYKE, JAMES. "An Analysis of the Reliability and Validity of the Ishihara Color Plates With Mentally Retarded Males." *Percept & Motor Skills* 33(1):243–6 Ag '71. * *(PA* 47:3544)

100. SMITH, JAMES W., AND BRINTON, GEORGE A. "Color-Vision Defects in Alcoholism." *Q J Studies Alcohol* 32(1A):41–4 Mr '71. * *(PA* 46:7113)

CUMULATIVE NAME INDEX

[1933]

★**The 3-D Test of Visualization Skill.** Ages 3–8; 1972; Grace Petitclerc; Academic Therapy Publications. *

[1934]

Titmus Vision Tester. Ages 3 and over; 1958–69; TVT; formerly called *T/O Vision Tester;* 7 units; Titmus Optical Co., Inc. *

a) SCHOOL UNIT. Grades 1–5; 1959–66; duplicates the *Massachusetts Vision Test.*

b) PEDIATRIC UNIT. Ages 3–9, grades kgn–5; 1960–66; duplicates the *Michigan Pre-School Vision Test* and the *Massachusetts Vision Test.*

c) GENERAL TESTING UNIT. Ages 3–5, grades 1–12, grades 1–16 and adults; 1959–69; includes the *Michigan Pre-School Vision Test* and the *Massachusetts Vision Test.*

d) INDUSTRIAL-OCCUPATIONAL UNIT. Industry; 1959.

e) AEROMEDICAL UNIT. Pilots; 1959–68.

f) DRIVER EDUCATION UNIT. 1959–61; no manual.

g) DRIVER LICENSING UNIT. 1959–60; no manual.

For additional information and a review by Carl L. Rosen of the school unit, see 7:883.

REFERENCES THROUGH 1971

1. SCHRIER, MELVIN. "Freshman Visual Screening Program at Columbia University." *Am J Optom* 37:245–53 My '60. *

2. FORBES, T. W., JR.; PAIN, R. F.; BLOOMQUIST, D. W.; AND VANOSDALL, F. E. "Low Contrast and Standard Visual Acuity Under Mesopic and Photopic Illumination." *J Safety Res* 1(1): 5–12 Mr '69. * *(PA* 45:9222)

3. LIPPMANN, OTTO. "Vision of Young Children." *Arch Ophthal* 81(6):763–75 Je '69. *

4. SHERMAN, REUEL A. "Eyes for the Job." *Indus Med & Surg* 39(4):201–4 Ap '70. *

5. CAPLAN, BELLA, AND MONTGOMERY, LETHA A. "Results of Vision Screening at Seven Years in the Johns Hopkins Collaborative Perinatal Project." *Johns Hopkins Med J* 128(5):261–4 My '71. *

6. LIPPMANN, OTTO. "Vision Screening of Young Children." *Am J Pub Health* 61(8):1586–1601 Ag '71. *

CUMULATIVE NAME INDEX

[1935]

★**Visualization Test of Three Dimensional Orthographic Shape.** High school and college; 1971; E. C. Biewald; Chas. A. Bennett Co., Inc. *

[Out of Print Since TIP I]

AO H-R-R Pseudoisochromatic Plates, 5:768 (1 excerpt, 1 reference, 27; other references are for another color vision test)

AO School Vision Screening Test, 5:769 (4 references)
Color Aptitude Test, 5:772
Dvorine Animated Fusion Training Charts (status unknown), T:1683
Eames Eye Test, 6:956 (2 reviews, 8 references)
Freeman Acuity-Tester (status unknown), 5:776
Freeman Protometer (status unknown), 5:777

Illuminant-Stable Color Vision Test, 5:778 (4 references)
Massachusetts Vision Test, 5:781 (19 references, 1 excerpt)
New Test for the Detection of Colorblindness, 3:469 (2 excerpts)
Test of Color Blindness, 3:474

SOCIAL STUDIES

[1936]

American History—Government—Problems of Democracy: Acorn Achievement Tests. Grades 9–16; 1942–53; 6 scores: growth of a national spirit, growth of democracy, the Constitution, foreign policy, problems of American democracy, total; 1953 test identical with test copyrighted 1942 except for minor changes; Vincent McGarrett; Psychometric Affiliates. *

For additional information and a review by Richard E. Gross, see 5:785; for a review by Howard R. Anderson, see 3:590.

[1937]

American School Achievement Tests: Part 4, Social Studies and Science. Grades 4–6, 7–9; 1941–63; 2 scores: social studies, science; Willis E. Pratt, Robert V. Young (manuals), and Clara E. Cockerille; Bobbs-Merrill Co., Inc. * For the complete battery entry, see 4.

For additional information, see 6:963. For reviews of the complete battery, see 6:2 (2 reviews), 5:1 (2 reviews), 4:1 (1 review), and 3:1 (2 reviews).

[1938]

***CLEP General Examinations: Social Sciences and History.** 1–2 years of college or equivalent; 1964–73; for college accreditation of nontraditional study, advanced placement, or assessment of educational attainment; a retired subtest of the *College-Level Examination Program General Examinations* published as a separate for local administration through the *Testing Academic Achievement* program (see 1061); 3 scores: social sciences, history, total; program administered for the College Entrance Examination Board by Educational Testing Service. * For the testing program entry, see 1050.

For additional information concerning earlier forms, see 7:8b. For reviews of the testing program, see 7:664 (3 reviews).

[1939]

***College Board Achievement Test in American History and Social Studies.** Candidates for college entrance; 1901–73; test administered on specified dates at centers established by the publisher; inactive forms, entitled *College Placement Test in American History and Social Studies,* are available to colleges for local administration; program administered for the College Entrance Examination Board by Educational Testing Service. * For the testing program entry, see 1048.

For additional information, see 7:884; for a review

by Howard R. Anderson of earlier forms, see 6:966; for a review by Ralph W. Tyler, see 5:786 (3 references); for a review by Robert L. Thorndike, see 4:662 (6 references). For reviews of the testing program, see 6:760 (2 reviews).

REFERENCES THROUGH 1971

1–6. See 4:662.
7–9. See 5:786.
10. PUGH, RICHARD C.; MORGAN, JAMES M.; AND LUDLOW, H. GLENN. *Predicting Success for Indiana University Freshmen Using the CEEB Achievement Tests, the CEEB Scholastic Aptitude Test, and High School Rank.* Indiana Studies in Prediction, No. 13. Bloomington, Ind.: Bureau of Educational Studies and Testing, Indiana University, April 1970. Pp. xi, 39. *

CUMULATIVE NAME INDEX

Anderson, H. R.: *rev,* 6:966
Bobbitt, J. M.: 8
Bragdon, H. W.: 7
Chauncey, H.: 4
College Entrance Examination
  Board: 9
French, J. W.: 8
Ludlow, H. G.: 10
Morgan, J. M.: 10
Newman, S. H.: 8
Pargellis, S.: 2
Pugh, R. C.: 10
Stalnaker, J. M.: 5
Stalnaker, R. C.: 5
Thorndike, R. L.: *rev,* 4:662
Tyler, R. W.: *rev,* 5:786
Warr, C. F.: 1–3
Weber, C. O.: 6

[1940]

***College Board Achievement Test in European History and World Cultures.** Candidates for college entrance; 1901–73; test administered on specified dates at centers established by the publisher; inactive forms, entitled *College Placement Test in European History and World Cultures,* are available to colleges for local administration; program administered for the College Entrance Examination Board by Educational Testing Service. * For the testing program entry, see 1048.

For additional information, see 7:885; for a review by David K. Heenan of earlier forms, see 6:967. For reviews of the testing program, see 6:760 (2 reviews).

[1941]

***College Placement Test in American History and Social Studies.** Entering college freshmen; 1962–72; reprintings of inactive 1962 and 1964 forms of *College Board Achievement Test in American History and Social Studies;* test available to colleges for local administration; program administered for the College Entrance Examination Board by Educational Testing Service. * For the testing program entry, see 1051.

For additional information, see 7:886. For a review of the testing program, see 7:665. For reference to reviews of the *College Board Achievement Test in American History and Social Studies,* see 1939.

[1942]

College Placement Test in European History and World Cultures. Entering college freshmen; 1963–72; reprinting of inactive 1963 form of *College Board Achievement Test in European History and World Cultures;* test available to colleges for local administration; program administered for the College Entrance Examination Board by Educational Testing Service. * For the testing program entry, see 1051.

For additional information, see 7:887. For a review of the testing program, see 7:665. For reference to a review of the *College Board Achievement Test in European History and World Cultures,* see 1940.

[1943]

History and Civics Test: Municipal Tests: National Achievement Tests. Grades 3–6, 6–8; 1938–55; subtest of *Municipal Battery;* 3 scores: lessons of history, historical facts, total; 1948–55 tests identical with tests copyrighted 1938–39 except for minor changes; Robert K. Speer and Samuel Smith; Psychometric Affiliates. *

For additional information and a review by Howard R. Anderson, see 5:790; for a review by Harry D. Berg, see 4:664. For reviews of the complete battery, see 5:18 (1 review), 4:20 (1 review), and 2:1191 (2 reviews).

[1944]

The Iowa Tests of Educational Development: Test 1, Understanding of Basic Social Concepts. Grades 9–12; 1942–67; Forms X-4 and Y-4; more recent Forms X5 and Y5 are not available as separates; prepared under the direction of E. F. Lindquist and Leonard S. Feldt; Science Research Associates, Inc. * For the complete battery entry, see 20.

For additional information and a review by Morey J. Wantman of earlier forms, see 6:969. For reviews of the complete battery, see 6:14 (2 reviews), 5:17 (2 reviews), 4:17 (1 review), and 3:12 (3 reviews).

REFERENCES THROUGH 1971
1. HART, RICHARD LAVERNE. *An Analysis of Factors Related to High and Low Achievement in Understanding Basic Social Concepts.* Doctor's thesis, University of Nebraska (Lincoln, Neb.), 1960. (*DA* 21:2159)

CUMULATIVE NAME INDEX
Hart, R. L.: 1   Wantman, M. J.: *rev,* 6:969

[1945]

National Teacher Examinations: Social Studies. College seniors and teachers; 1940–73; an inactive form (1966) entitled *Teacher Education Examination Program: Social Studies* is available to colleges for local administration; another inactive form (1968) entitled *Specialty Examinations: Social Studies* is available to school systems for local use as part of the program entitled *School Personnel Research and Evaluation Services;* Educational Testing Service. * For the testing program entry, see 869.

For additional information concerning earlier forms, see 7:889; for a review by Harry D. Berg, see 6:974. For reviews of the testing program, see 7:582 (2 reviews), 6:700 (1 review), 5:538 (3 reviews), and 4:802 (1 review).

[1946]

Primary Social Studies Test. Grades 1–3; 1967; PSST; Ralph C. Preston and Robert V. Duffey; Houghton Mifflin Co. *

For additional information and a review by Virginia M. Rogers, see 7:890.

[1947]

SRA Achievement Series: Social Studies. Grades 4–9; 1963–69; Forms C and D; more recent Forms E and F are not available as separates; Louis P. Thorpe, D. Welty Lefever, and Robert A. Naslund; Science Research Associates, Inc. * For the complete battery entry, see 29.

For additional information, see 7:891. For reviews of the complete battery, see 7:18 (2 reviews), 6:21 (1 review), and 5:21 (2 reviews).

[1948]

Sequential Tests of Educational Progress: Social Studies. Grades 4–6, 7–9, 10–12, 13–14; 1956–72; 2 editions; Cooperative Tests and Services. * For the complete battery entry, see 35.

a) ORIGINAL SERIES [70 MINUTE TESTS]. 1956–63; Braille and large type editions (grades 4–12) are available from American Printing House for the Blind, Inc.

b) SERIES 2 [45 MINUTE TESTS (GRADES 4–9) AND 60 MINUTE TESTS (GRADES 10–14)]. 1956–72.

For additional information and reviews by Jonathon C. McLendon and Donald W. Oliver of *a,* see 6:971 (1 reference); for reviews by Richard E. Gross, S. A. Rayner, and Ralph W. Tyler, see 5:792. For reviews of the original edition of the complete battery, see 6:25 (2 reviews) and 5:24 (2 reviews, 1 excerpt).

REFERENCES THROUGH 1971
1. See 6:971.
2. MCBEE, GEORGE, AND DUKE, RALPH L. "Relationship Between Intelligence, Scholastic Motivation, and Academic Achievement." *Psychol Rep* 6:3–8 F '60. * (*PA* 34:8404)
3. MCGUIRE, CARSON. "Sex Role and Community Variability in Test Performances." *J Ed Psychol* 52:61–73 Ap '61. * (*PA* 38:3207)
4. RUSSELL, JAMES WILLIAM. *An Analysis of the Academic Performance of Transfer and Native Students and Their Major Fields in the College of Arts and Sciences at the University of Georgia.* Doctor's thesis, University of Georgia (Athens, Ga.), 1963. (*DA* 25:1668)
5. PEAKE, RONALD EDWARD. *An Examination of the Differences in Problem-Solving Processes of Successful and Nonsuccessful Students Taking Ninth Grade Social Studies.* Doctor's thesis, University of Alabama (University, Ala.), 1964. (*DA* 25:7111)
6. MARTIN, LOUIS. *An Examination of the Test and Item Validity of the Sequential Tests of Educational Progress, Social Studies—Level II, Form B.* Master's thesis, Catholic University of America (Washington, D.C.), 1965.
7. BONEY, J. DON. "Predicting the Academic Achievement of Secondary School Negro Students." *Personnel & Guid J* 44:700–3 Mr '66. * (*PA* 40:8064)
8. CHANDLER, JOSEPH DOUGLAS. *An Analysis of Competence in the Social Sciences by Elementary Education Majors at the University of Tennessee.* Doctor's thesis, University of Tennessee (Knoxville, Tenn.), 1966. (*DA* 27:3246A)
9. MICHAEL, JOAN JOHNSON. *An Experimental Analysis of the Relationship Between the Reliability of a Multiple-Choice Examination and Various Test-Scoring Procedures.* Doctor's thesis, University of Southern California (Los Angeles, Calif.), 1967. (*DA* 28:2561A)
10. MICHAEL, JOAN J. "The Reliability of a Multiple-Choice Examination Under Various Test-Taking Instructions." *J Ed Meas* 5:307–14 w '68. * (*PA* 44:11225)
11. BORNSTEIN, HARRY, AND CHAMBERLAIN, KAREN. "An Investigation of the Effects of 'Verbal Load' in Achievement Tests." *Am Ed Res J* 7(4):597–604 N '70. *
12. PARSLEY, JAMES FRANCIS, JR. *A Comparison of the Ability of Ninth Grade Students to Apply Several Critical Thinking Skills to Problematic Content Presented Through Two Different Media.* Doctor's thesis, Ohio University (Athens, Ohio), 1970. (*DAI* 31:4629A)
13. BORNSTEIN, HARRY. "Some Effects of Verbal Load on Achievement Tests." *Am Ann Deaf* 116(1):44–8 F '71. * (*PA* 47:1603)
14. BORNSTEIN, HARRY, AND KANNAPELL, BARBARA. "More on the Effects of Verbal Load on Achievement Tests." *Am Ann Deaf* 116(6): 575–9 D '71. * (*PA* 48:7769)
For additional references, see the bibliography for the series, 35.

CUMULATIVE NAME INDEX
Boney, J. D.: 7   Chandler, J. D.: 8
Bornstein, H.: 11, 13–4   Duke, R. L.: 2
Chamberlain, K.: 11   Gross, R. E.: *rev,* 5:792

Kannapell, B.: 14
Liggitt, W. A.: 1
McBee, G.: 2
McGuire, C.: 3
McLendon, J. C.: *rev, 6:971*
Martin, L.: 6
Michael, J. J.: 9–10

Oliver, D. W.: *rev, 6:971*
Parsley, J. F.: 12
Peake, R. E.: 5
Rayner, S. A.: *rev, 5:792*
Russell, J. W.: 4
Tyler, R. W.: *rev, 5:792*

[1949]

*Social Studies: Minnesota High School Achievement Examinations. Grades 7, 8, 9; 1961–70; a new, revised, or previously inactive form issued each May; Midwest High School Achievement Examinations used as series title through 1962; Form GJ Rev ('70, with 1973 copyright for grade 8) used in 1970 and 1973 testings; 3 levels; edited by V. L. Lohmann; American Guidance Service, Inc. *
a) SOCIAL STUDIES GRADE 7. 1961–70.
b) SOCIAL STUDIES GRADE 8. 1962–70.
c) SOCIAL STUDIES GRADE 9. 1962–70.
For additional information concerning out of print and inactive forms, see 7:892 and 6:973.

[1950]

Social Studies Test: Acorn National Achievement Tests. Grades 7–9; 1946–50; 5 scores: human relations and life situations, products and places, social ideas and facts, application of knowledge, total; Lester D. Crow and Everett F. Augspurger; Psychometric Affiliates. *
For additional information and a review by Edgar B. Wesley, see 4:666.

[1951]

Social Studies Test: National Achievement Tests. Grades 4–6, 7–9; 1937–57; 1945 and 1955–57 tests identical with tests copyrighted 1939 and 1945, respectively, except for minor changes; 2 levels; Robert K. Speer and Samuel Smith; Psychometric Affiliates. *
a) GRADES 4–6. 6 scores: human relations, life situations, social problems, products and peoples, meaning of events, total.
b) GRADES 7–9. 7 scores: human relations, life situations, social interpretations, values of products, social ideas, miscellaneous facts, total.
For additional information, see 5:798; for a review by Ray G. Wood, see 3:594.

[1952]

Stanford Achievement Test: High School Social Studies Test. Grades 9–12; 1965–66; catalog uses the title *Stanford High School Social Studies Test;* subtest of *Stanford Achievement Test: High School Basic Battery;* Eric F. Gardner, Jack C. Merwin, Robert Callis, and Richard Madden; Harcourt Brace Jovanovich, Inc. * For the complete battery entry, see 37.
For additional information, see 7:894. For reviews of the complete battery, see 7:27 (2 reviews).

REFERENCES THROUGH 1971
1. SMITH, I. LEON. "Validity of Taxonomic Tests." *Ed & Psychol Meas* 31(2):475–6 su '71. *
CUMULATIVE NAME INDEX
Smith, I. L.: 1

[1953]

Stanford Achievement Test, 1964 Edition: Social Studies Tests. Grades 5.5–6.9, 7.0–9.9; 1940–68; catalog uses the title *Stanford Social Studies Test;* not available as a separate in the 1973 edition of the battery; Braille editions are available from American Printing House for the Blind, Inc.; Truman L. Kelley, Richard Madden, Eric F. Gardner, and Herbert C.

Rudman; Harcourt Brace Jovanovich, Inc. * For the complete battery entry, see 36.
For additional information and a review by Virginia M. Rogers, see 7:895; for a review by Harry D. Berg of an earlier edition, see 5:799; for a review by Ray G. Wood, see 3:595. For reviews of the complete battery, see 7:25 (1 excerpt), 6:26 (1 review, 1 excerpt), 5:25 (1 review), 4:25 (2 reviews), and 3:18 (2 reviews).

[1954]

*Teacher Education Examination Program: Social Studies. College seniors preparing to teach secondary school; 1957–72; reprinting of inactive 1966 form of *National Teacher Examinations: Social Studies;* test available to colleges for local administration; Educational Testing Service. * For the testing program entry, see 808.
For additional information concerning an earlier form, see 6:975. For a review of the testing program, see 5:543. For reference to a review of the *National Teacher Examinations: Social Studies,* see 1945.

[1955]

Tests of Academic Progress: Social Studies. Grades 9–12; 1964–66; Dale P. Scannell and Alvin H. Schild; Houghton Mifflin Co. * For the complete battery entry, see 44.
For additional information and a review by Harry D. Berg, see 7:896 (1 reference). For a review of the complete battery, see 7:31.
REFERENCES THROUGH 1971
1. See 7:896.
CUMULATIVE NAME INDEX
Berg, H. D.: *rev, 7:896*   Goolsby, T. M.: 1

[1956]

*Tests of Basic Experiences: Social Studies. Prekgn–kgn, kgn–grade 1; 1970–72; Margaret H. Moss; CTB/McGraw-Hill. * For the complete battery entry, see 47.
For additional information, see 7:897. For a review of the complete battery, see 7:33.

[1957]

Zimmerman-Sanders Social Studies Test. 1, 2 semesters in grades 7–8; 1962–64; first published 1962–63 in the Every Pupil Scholarship Test series; John J. Zimmerman and M. W. Sanders; Bureau of Educational Measurements. *
For additional information, see 7:898.

[Out of Print Since TIP I]

Christian Democracy Test (Civics, Sociology, Economics): Affiliation Testing Program for Catholic Secondary Schools, 6:964 (1 review)
Citizenship: Every Pupil Scholarship Test, 6:965
Cooperative General Achievement Tests: Social Studies [General Proficiency Series], 6:968 (1 review), 4:668 (3 references)
Cooperative Social Studies Test for Grades 7, 8, and 9. 4:663 (3 reviews)
Graduate Record Examinations Advanced Anthropology Test, 7:546
Greig Social Studies Test, 5:788 (1 review)
Introduction to Social Studies: Achievement Examinations for Secondary Schools, 5:789
Metropolitan Achievement Tests: High School Social Studies Test, 7:888 (2 reviews)
Shearer Social Studies Test, 5:793 (1 review, 1 reference)
Social Studies: Every Pupil Scholarship Test, 6:972
T. C. Social Studies Test, 6:978

Sequential Tests of Educational Progress: Social Studies

CONTEMPORARY AFFAIRS

[1958]

*Current News Test. Grades 9–12; 1951–74; formerly called *Newsweek Current News Test;* 2 new tests issued annually: spring term review (covering mid December–mid April) issued each May, fall term review (covering September–mid December) issued each January; available only as part of the Newsweek Educational Program; no manual; Newsweek Educational Division. *

For additional information, see 6:985.

[1959]

*Newsweek NewsQuiz. Grades 9–12; 1951–74; formerly called *Newsweek Monthly Objective Test;* 6 tests (spirit masters for local duplicating) issued annually during school year (October, November, December, February, March, and April); available only as part of the Newsweek Educational Program; no manual; Newsweek Educational Division. *

For additional information, see 6:986.

[1960]

*School Weekly News Quiz. High school; 1947–74; revision of *New York Times Current Affairs Test;* although title implies weekly publication, 8 tests (spirit masters for local duplicating) issued annually during school year (October–May); available only as part of the New York Times Daily School Service Program; no manual; New York Times. *

For additional information concerning the earlier edition, see 6:983.

[1961]

*Time Current Affairs Test. Grades 9–12 and adults; 1935–74; formerly called *Current Affairs Test;* new test issued annually in January; available only as part of the Time Education Program; no manual; Time, Inc. *

[1962]

★The Time Monthly News Quiz. Grades 9–12 and adults; 1969–74; 9 tests (spirit masters for local duplicating) in each of 2 areas, issued annually in August (Summer Review Quiz), September, October, November, December–January, February, March, April, and May; available only as part of the Time Education Program; no manual; Time, Inc. *

a) ENGLISH REVIEW. 1973–74.

b) NEWS QUIZ. 1969–74.

[Out of Print Since TIP I]

Contemporary Affairs: Every Pupil Test, 6:979
Cooperative Test on Foreign Affairs, 6:980 (1 review, 1 excerpt, 1 reference)
Current Affairs: Every Pupil Scholarship Test, 6:981
Nationwide Current Events Examination, 6:982
New York Times Current Affairs Test for Colleges, 6:984

ECONOMICS

[1963]

*CLEP Subject Examination in Introductory Economics. 1 year or equivalent; 1964–73; for college accreditation of nontraditional study, advanced placement, or assessment of educational achievement; tests administered monthly at centers throughout the United States; program administered for the College Entrance Examination Board by Educational Testing Service. * For the testing program entry, see 1050.

For additional information, see 7:899. For reviews of the testing program, see 7:664 (3 reviews).

[1964]

★[Economics/Objective Tests.] 1 semester high school; 1970; 5 tests; no manual; Perfection Form Co. *

a) CONCEPTS IN ECONOMICS.

b) PRICE, INCOME AND PERSONAL GROWTH.

c) MONEY, BANKING AND INSURANCE.

d) INTERNATIONAL TRADE.

e) FINAL TEST.

[1965]

*The Graduate Record Examinations Advanced Economics Test. Graduate school candidates; 1939–73; Educational Testing Service. * For the testing program entry, see 1053.

For additional information concerning earlier forms, see 7:900; see also 6:987 (1 reference). For reviews of the testing program, see 7:667 (1 review) and 5:601 (1 review).

REFERENCES THROUGH 1971

1. See 6:987.

CUMULATIVE NAME INDEX

[1966]

★Modern Economics Test: Content Evaluation Series. Grades 10–12; 1971; Morris G. Sica, Sylvia Lane, and John D. Lafky; Houghton Mifflin Co. *

[1967]

★Primary Test of Economic Understanding. Grades 2–3; 1971; PTEU; Donald G. Davison and John H. Kilgore; Bureau of Business and Economic Research, University of Iowa; distributed by Joint Council on Economic Education. *

REFERENCES THROUGH 1971

1. DAVISON, DONALD G., AND KILGORE, JOHN H. "A Model for Evaluating the Effectiveness of Economic Education in Primary Grades." *J Econ Ed* 3(1):17–25 f '71. *

CUMULATIVE NAME INDEX

[1968]

Test of Economic Understanding. High school and college; 1963–64; TEU; test by Committee for Measurement of Economic Understanding, Joint Council on Economic Education; manual by George Leland Bach, Walter R. Jones, and Suzanne R. Meyer; Science Research Associates, Inc. *

For additional information, reviews by Edward J. Furst and Christine H. McGuire, and an excerpted review by Robert L. Ebel, see 7:901 (10 references).

REFERENCES THROUGH 1971

1–10. See 7:901.
11. CAMPBELL, MORRIS W. *Measurement of Economic Understandings of Grade Twelve Students.* Master's thesis, University of Alberta (Edmonton, Alta., Canada), 1964.
12. BACH, G. L., AND SAUNDERS, PHILLIP. "Economic Education: Aspirations and Achievements." *Am Econ R* 55:329–56 Je '65. *
13. BACH, G. L., AND SAUNDERS, PHILLIP. "Lasting Effects of Economics Courses at Different Types of Institutions." *Am Econ R* 56:505–11 Je '66. *
14. MOYER, M. E., AND PADEN, D. W. "On the Efficiency of the High School Economics Course." *Am Econ R* 58:870–7 S '68. *
15. GARMAN, E. THOMAS. *Economic Literacy of Prospective Business Education Teachers.* Doctor's thesis, Texas Tech University (Lubbock, Tex.), 1969. (*DAI* 31:264A)
16. MAHER, JOHN E. "DEEP: Strengthening Economics in the Schools." *Am Econ R* 59(2):230–8 My '69. *

17. VILLARD, HENRY H. "Where We Now Stand." *J Econ Ed* 1(1):60–6 f '69. *
18. WELSH, ARTHUR L., AND FELS, RENDIGS. "Performance on the New Test of Understanding in College Economics." *Am Econ R* 59(2):224–9 My '69. *
19. GARMAN, E. THOMAS. "Economic Literacy of Prospective Business Education Teachers." *Bus Ed Forum* 24(4):35 Ja '70. *
20. GERY, FRANK W. "Mathematics and the Understanding of Economic Concepts." Letter. *J Econ Ed* 2(1):100–4 f '70. *
21. MOYER, M. EUGENE, AND PADEN, DONALD W. "Economics Achievement and Mathematics Training." Letter. *J Econ Ed* 2(1):104–6 f '70. *
22. SAUNDERS, PHILLIP. "Does High School Economics Have a Lasting Impact?" *J Econ Ed* 2(1):39–55 f '70. *
23. GARMAN, E. THOMAS. "College Level Use of the 'Test of Economic Understanding.' " *Ill Sch Res* 7(2):53–5 w '71. *
24. JONES, ROLAND ODELL. *A Study of the Relationship Between Economic Understanding, Business Education Curricula and Certain Personal Factors of Business Education Seniors in Selected Delaware High Schools.* Doctor's thesis, Pennsylvania State University (University Park, Pa.), 1971. (*DAI* 32:4923A)
25. MCKENZIE, RICHARD B. "An Exploratory Study of the Economic Understanding of Elementary School Teachers." *J Econ Ed* 3(1):26–31 f '71. *
26. MORTON, JOHN S., AND REZNY, RONALD R. "Some Teaching Techniques." *J Econ Ed* 3(1):11–6 f '71. *
27. O'TOOLE, DENNIS MARTIN. *An Accountability Evaluation of an In-Service Economic Education Experience.* Doctor's thesis, Ohio University (Athens, Ohio), 1971. (*DAI* 32:2315A)
28. PHILLIPS, JAMES ARTHUR. *The Effects of Instructional Objectives Treatment on Economics Achievement Scores of Students in Selected Community Colleges.* Doctor's thesis, University of Southern California (Los Angeles, Calif.), 1971. (*DAI* 33:992A)
29. WALL, CARLTON DEWEY. *Contributing Factors to the Economic Understanding of High School Seniors.* Doctor's thesis, Ohio State University (Columbus, Ohio), 1971. (*DAI* 32:3581A)

CUMULATIVE NAME INDEX

Alexander, L. A.: 7	Kastner, H. H.: 3
Bach, G. L.: 12–3	McGuire, C. H.: *rev*, 6:901
Campbell, M. W.: 11	McKenzie, R. B.: 25
Daughtrey, A. S.: 2	Maher, J. E.: 16
Ebel, R. L.: *exc*, 6:901	Morton, J. S.: 26
Fels, R.: 18	Moyer, M. E.: 14, 21
Furst, E. J.: *rev*, 6:901	O'Toole, D. M.: 27
Gable, M.: 9	Paden, D. W.: 14, 21
Ganser, C. J.: 10	Paul, J. H.: 1
Garman, E. T.: 15, 19, 23	Phillips, J. A.: 28
Gentry, A. D.: 8	Rezny, R. R.: 26
Gery, F. W.: 20	Saunders, P.: 12–3, 22
Hopkins, C. R.: 5	Smith, A. J.: 4
Hunt, E. H.: 6	Villard, H. H.: 17
Jackson, H. D.: 3	Wall, C. D.: 29
Jones, R. O.: 24	Welsh, A. L.: 18

[1969]

★Test of Elementary Economics, Revised Experimental Edition. Grades 4–6; 1971; TEE; developed by Economic Education Enrichment Program, West Springfield Public Schools, West Springfield, Mass.; Joint Council on Economic Education. *

[1970]

Test of Understanding in College Economics. 1, 2 semesters college; 1967–68; TUCE; Committee for a College-Level Test of Economic Understanding, Joint Council on Economic Education; Psychological Corporation; distributed by the Council. *
For additional information and a review by Christine H. McGuire, see 7:902.

REFERENCES THROUGH 1971

1. FELS, RENDIGS. "A New 'Test of Understanding in College Economics.' " *Am Econ R* 57:660–6 My '67. *
2. FELS, RENDIGS. "Hard Research on a Soft Subject: Hypothesis-Testing in Economic Education." *South Econ J* 36(1):1–9 Jl '69. *
3. VILLARD, HENRY H. "Where We Now Stand." *J Econ Ed* 1(1):60–6 f '69. *
4. GERY, FRANK W. "Mathematics and the Understanding of Economic Concepts." Letter. *J Econ Ed* 2(1):100–4 f '70. *
5. HEALEY, RUTH M. "Economic Understandings of Junior College Students." *Bus Ed Forum* 24(7):32–4 Ap '70. *
6. BUCKLES, STEPHEN G., AND MCMAHON, MARSHALL E. "Further Evidence on the Value of Lectures in Elementary Economics." *J Econ Ed* 2(2):138–41 sp '71. *
7. LEWIS, DARRELL R., AND DAHL, TOR. "The Test of Understanding in College Economics and Its Construct Validity." *J Econ Ed* 2(2):155–66 sp '71. *

Test of Economic Understanding

8. MEINKOTH, MARIAN R. "Teachers of Economic Principles: Effect on Student Achievement and Attitudes." *J Exp Ed* 40(2):66–72 w '71. * (*PA* 47:11806)
9. MEINKOTH, MARIAN R. "Textbooks and the Teaching of Economic Principles." *J Econ Ed* 2(2):127–30 sp '71. *
10. O'TOOLE, DENNIS MARTIN. *An Accountability Evaluation of an In-Service Economic Education Experience.* Doctor's thesis, Ohio University (Athens, Ohio), 1971. (*DAI* 32:2315A)

CUMULATIVE NAME INDEX

Buckles, S. G.: 6	McGuire, C. H.: *rev*, 7:902
Dahl, T.: 7	McMahon, M. E.: 6
Fels, R.: 1–2	Meinkoth, M. R.: 8–9
Gery, F. W.: 4	O'Toole, D. M.: 10
Healey, R. M.: 5	Villard, H. H.: 3
Lewis, D. R.: 7	

[1971]

★Test of Understanding in Personal Economics. High school; 1971; TUPE; Joint Council on Economic Education. *

[1972]

*The Undergraduate Program Field Tests: Economics Test. College; 1969–73; formerly called *The Undergraduate Record Examinations: Economics Test;* test available to colleges for local administration; Educational Testing Service. * For the testing program entry, see 1062.
For additional information, see 7:903. For reviews of the testing program, see 7:671 (2 reviews).

[Out of Print Since TIP I]

Economics Test: State High School Tests for Indiana, 4:670
High School Economics: Manchester Semester-End Achievement Tests, T:1738
Hills Economics Test, 4:673
Standard Achievement Test in Economic Understanding for Secondary Schools, 6:988
Test of Economic Information, T:1971

GEOGRAPHY

[1973]

Brandywine Achievement Test in Geography for Secondary Schools. Grades 7–12; 1962; no manual; John A. Bonham and Harry R. Martini; [Brandywine Achievement Test]. *
For additional information, see 6:990.

[1974]

*Economic Geography: Achievement Examinations for Secondary Schools. High school; 1951–61; a new, revised, or previously inactive form was issued each May from 1951 through 1961; Form 4 ('54) is the only form in print; High School Achievement Examinations and Midwest High School Achievement Examinations have also been used as series titles; Helen Haberman; Bobbs-Merrill Co., Inc. *
For additional information concerning earlier forms, see 5:802.

[1975]

Geography Test: Municipal Tests: National Achievement Tests. Grades 3–6, 6–8; 1938–52; subtest of *Municipal Battery;* 3 scores: geographical ideas and comparisons, miscellaneous facts, total; 1949 and 1952 tests identical with tests copyrighted 1939 and 1938, respectively, except for minor changes; Robert K. Speer and Samuel Smith; Psychometric Affiliates. *
For additional information, see 5:806; for a review by Edwin H. Reeder, see 4:676. For reviews of the

complete battery, see 5:18 (1 review), 4:20 (1 review), and 2:1191 (2 reviews).

[1976]

Geography Test: National Achievement Tests.
Grades 6–8; 1938–49; 6 scores: geographical ideas, locating products, uses of products and instruments, economic and human relations, miscellaneous problems, total; Robert K. Speer, Lester D. Crow, and Samuel Smith; Psychometric Affiliates. *

For additional information, see 4:677; for a review by Elaine Forsyth, see 3:600.

[1977]

*The Graduate Record Examinations Advanced Geography Test. Graduate school candidates; 1966–73; 3 scores: human geography, physical geography, total; Educational Testing Service. * For the testing program entry, see 1053.

For additional information concerning earlier forms, see 7:905. For reviews of the testing program, see 7:667 (1 review) and 5:601 (1 review).

[1978]

Hollingsworth-Sanders Geography Test. 1, 2 semesters in grades 5–7; 1962–64; first published 1962–63 in the Every Pupil Scholarship Test series; Leon Hollingsworth and M. W. Sanders; Bureau of Educational Measurements. *

For additional information and a review by Dana G. Kurfman, see 7:906.

[1979]

*The Undergraduate Program Field Tests: Geography Test. College; 1969–73; formerly called *The Undergraduate Record Examinations: Geography Test;* test available to colleges for local administration; Educational Testing Service. * For the testing program entry, see 1062.

For additional information, see 7:907. For reviews of the testing program, see 7:671 (2 reviews).

[Out of Print Since TIP I]

Coordinated Scales of Attainment: Geography, 5:801
Emporia Geography Test, 3:598 (2 reviews)
Geography Achievement Test for Beginning High School Students, 7:904
Geography: Every Pupil Scholarship Test, 6:991
Geography of the Americas: Every Pupil Test, 6:992a1
Geography of the Eastern Hemisphere: Every Pupil Test, 6:992a2
Geography of the World: Every Pupil Test, 6:992b
Physical Geography: Every Pupil Scholarship Test, 6:993
Survey Test in Geography, 6:994 (1 review)
Tate Economic Geography Test, 3:601 (1 review)
World Geography: Every Pupil Scholarship Test, 6:995

HISTORY

[1980]

*Advanced Placement Examination in American History. High school students desiring credit for college level courses or admission to advanced courses; 1956–73; available to secondary schools for annual administration on specified days in May; inactive forms are available to colleges for local administration in the *Testing Academic Achievement* program; program administered for the College Entrance Examina-

tion Board by Educational Testing Service. * For the testing program entry, see 1045.

For additional information concerning earlier forms, see 7:908; for a review by Harry D. Berg, see 6:1000 (1 reference); for reviews by James A. Field, Jr. and Christine McGuire, see 5:812. For reviews of the testing program, see 7:662 (2 reviews).

REFERENCES THROUGH 1971
1. See 6:1000.
2. PARTIN, RONALD L. *The Value of Four Selected Test Scores in Predicting Advanced Placement American History Test Scores.* Master's thesis, Bowling Green State University (Bowling Green, Ohio), 1970.

CUMULATIVE NAME INDEX
Berg, H. D.: *rev, 6:1000*   McGuire, C.: *rev, 5:812*
Field, J. A.: *rev, 5:812*   Partin, R. L.: 2
Graff, H. F.: 1

[1981]

*Advanced Placement Examination in European History. High school students desiring credit for college level courses or admission to advanced courses; 1956–73; available to secondary schools for annual administration on specified days in May; inactive forms are available to colleges for local administration in the *Testing Academic Achievement* program; program administered for the College Entrance Examination Board by Educational Testing Service. * For the testing program entry, see 1045.

For additional information concerning earlier forms, see 7:909; see also 6:1001 (2 references). For reviews of the testing program, see 7:662 (2 reviews).

REFERENCES THROUGH 1971
1–2. See 6:1001.

CUMULATIVE NAME INDEX
Winkler, H. R.: 2

[1982]

★American History: Junior High—Objective. 1, 2 semesters in grades 7–9; 1963–70; revision of *Objective Tests in American History—Jr. H. S.* by John Barrett; 12 tests; no manual; Perfection Form Co. *
a) EXPLORATION AND COLONIZATION.
b) REVOLUTIONARY AMERICA.
c) FOUNDATION OF A STRONG GOVERNMENT.
d) THE DEVELOPMENT OF DEMOCRACY.
e) WESTWARD EXPANSION.
f) FIRST SEMESTER TEST.
g) DIVISION AND REUNION.
h) A MODERN AMERICA.
i) AMERICA BECOMES A WORLD POWER.
j) POST WORLD WAR II.
k) SECOND SEMESTER TEST.
l) FINAL TEST.

[1983]

*American History: Senior High—Objective. 1, 2 semesters high school; 1960–70; revision of *Objective Tests in American History* by Earl Bridgewater; 13 tests; no manual; Perfection Form Co. *
a) THE HERITAGE OF COLONIAL AMERICA.
b) BACKGROUND OF THE REVOLUTIONARY WAR, THE REVOLUTIONARY WAR AND ESTABLISHING A NEW GOVERNMENT (1763–1789).
c) THE UNITED STATES CONSTITUTION.
d) WASHINGTON'S ADMINISTRATION THROUGH THE WAR OF 1812.
e) EXPANSION WESTWARD AND THE JACKSONIAN ERA (1815 THRU 1841).
f) EXPANSION, WAR AND RECONSTRUCTION (1841–1868).
g) FIRST SEMESTER EXAMINATION.
h) THE EMERGENCE OF MODERN AMERICA.

i) THE UNITED STATES BECOMES A WORLD POWER (SPAN-ISH-AMERICAN WAR, WORLD WAR I, AND SETTLEMENT 1896–1921).

j) PROSPERITY AND DEPRESSION (1920 THRU 1940).

k) WORLD LEADERSHIP (1940–PRESENT).

l) SECOND SEMESTER EXAMINATION.

m) FINAL EXAMINATION.

For additional information concerning the earlier tests, see 6:1006.

[1984]

American History Test: National Achievement Tests. Grades 7–8; 1937–56; 5 scores: lessons of history, time concepts, historical associations, miscellaneous problems, total; 1945 and 1956 tests identical with tests copyrighted 1938 and 1939–49, respectively, except for minor changes; Robert K. Speer, Lester D. Crow, and Samuel Smith; Psychometric Affiliates. *

For additional information, see 5:811; for reviews by Jacob S. Orleans and Wallace Taylor, see 2:1630.

[1985]

★**CLEP Subject Examination in Afro-American History.** 1 semester or equivalent; 1973, c1972–73; for college accreditation of nontraditional study, advanced placement, or assessment of educational achievement; tests administered monthly at centers throughout the United States; program administered for the College Entrance Examination Board by Educational Testing Service. * For the testing program entry, see 1050.

For reviews of the testing program, see 7:664 (3 reviews).

[1986]

CLEP Subject Examination in American History. 1 year or equivalent; 1970–73; for college accreditation of nontraditional study, advanced placement, or assessment of educational achievement; tests administered monthly at centers throughout the United States; program administered for the College Entrance Examination Board by Educational Testing Service. * For the testing program entry, see 1050.

For additional information, see 7:910. For reviews of the testing program, see 7:664 (3 reviews).

[1987]

CLEP Subject Examination in Western Civilization. 1 year or equivalent; 1964–73; for college accreditation of nontraditional study, advanced placement, or assessment of educational achievement; tests administered monthly at centers throughout the United States; program administered for the College Entrance Examination Board by Educational Testing Service. * For the testing program entry, see 1050.

For additional information, see 7:911. For reviews of the testing program, see 7:664 (3 reviews).

[1988]

Cooperative Social Studies Tests: American History. Grades 7–8, 10–12; 1964–65; Cooperative Tests and Services. *

For additional information and a review by William J. Webster, see 7:912.

REFERENCES THROUGH 1971

1. DIELMAN, T. E.; BARTON, K.; AND CATTELL, R. B. "The Prediction of Junior High School Achievement From Objective Motivation Tests." *Personality* 2(4):279–87 w '71. * (*PA* 48:7881)

CUMULATIVE NAME INDEX

Barton, K.: 1   Dielman, T. E.: 1
Cattell, R. B.: 1   Webster, W. J.: *rev*, 7:912

[1989]

Cooperative Social Studies Tests: Modern European History. Grades 10–12; 1964–65; Cooperative Tests and Services. *

For additional information and a review by John Manning, see 7:913.

[1990]

Cooperative Social Studies Tests: World History. Grades 10–12; 1964–65; Cooperative Tests and Services. *

For additional information, see 7:914.

[1991]

Cooperative Topical Tests in American History. High school; 1963–65; CTTAH; 8 tests; Cooperative Tests and Services. *

a) TEST 1, EXPLORATION, COLONIZATION, AND INDEPENDENCE: 1450–1783.

b) TEST 2, FOUNDATIONS OF AMERICAN GOVERNMENT: 1781–1801.

c) TEST 3, GROWTH OF NATIONALISM AND DEMOCRACY: 1801–1840.

d) TEST 4, EXPANSION, CIVIL WAR, AND RECONSTRUCTION: 1840–1877.

e) TEST 5, DEVELOPMENT OF INDUSTRIAL AMERICA: 1865–1898.

f) TEST 6, IMPERIALISM, DOMESTIC REFORM, AND THE FIRST WORLD WAR: 1898–1920.

g) TEST 7, PROSPERITY, DEPRESSION, AND THE NEW DEAL: 1920–1940.

h) TEST 8, THE SECOND WORLD WAR AND AFTER.

For additional information and a review by Richard E. Gross, see 7:915.

[1992]

Crary American History Test, Revised Edition. Grades 10–13; 1950–65; Ryland W. Crary; Harcourt Brace Jovanovich, Inc. *

For additional information and a review by Richard E. Gross, see 7:916; for a review by Frederick H. Stutz of the original edition, see 5:816 (2 references); for a review by Edgar B. Wesley, see 4:688.

REFERENCES THROUGH 1971

1–2. See 5:816.
3. SCOTT, OWEN. "A Comparison of Summer School and Regular Session Achievement in Eleventh Grade American History." *J Ed Res* 59:235–7 Ja '66. * (*PA* 40:7014)

CUMULATIVE NAME INDEX

Cowne, L.: 2   Stutz, F. H.: *rev*, 5:816
Gross, R. E.: *rev*, 7:916   Townsend, A.: 1
Scott, O.: 3   Wesley, E. B.: *rev*, 4:688

[1993]

Emporia American History Test. 1, 2 semesters high school; 1962–64; first published 1062–63 in the Every Pupil Scholarship Test series; Shirley Meares and M. W. Sanders; Bureau of Educational Measurements. *

For additional information and a review by Howard R. Anderson, see 7:918.

[1994]

The Graduate Record Examinations Advanced History Test. Graduate school candidates; 1939–73; 3 scores: European history, American history, total; Educational Testing Service. * For the testing program entry, see 1053.

For additional information concerning earlier forms, see 7:919 (1 reference); for a review by Robert H. Ferrell, see 5:818. For reviews of the testing program, see 7:667 (1 review) and 5:601 (1 review).

American History: Senior High—Objective

REFERENCES THROUGH 1971
1. See 7:919.

CUMULATIVE NAME INDEX

Ferrell, R. H.: *rev*, 5:818   Marco, G. L.: 1
Lannholm, G. V.: 1   Schrader, W. B.: 1

[1995]

Hollingsworth-Sanders Intermediate History Test. 1, 2 semesters in grades 5–6; 1962–64; first published 1962–63 in the Every Pupil Scholarship Test series; Leon Hollingsworth and M. W. Sanders; Bureau of Educational Measurements. *
For additional information, see 7:920.

[1996]

Meares-Sanders Junior High School History Test. 1, 2 semesters in grades 7–8; 1962–64; first published 1962–63 in the Every Pupil Scholarship Test series; Shirley Meares and M. W. Sanders; Bureau of Educational Measurements. *
For additional information, see 7:921.

[1997]

Modern World History: Achievement Examinations for Secondary Schools. High school; 1951–54; Form 4 ('54) of a series of tests, currently ('73) entitled *Social Studies Grade 11 (World History): Minnesota High School Achievement Examinations* (see 2000), issued annually for May testing; M. J. Haggerty; Bobbs-Merrill Co., Inc. *
For additional information concerning later and earlier forms, see 2000, 7:924, 6:1009, and 5:821–2.

[1998]

Sanders-Buller World History Test. 1, 2 semesters high school; 1962–64; first published 1962–63 in the Every Pupil Scholarship Test series; M. W. Sanders and Robert Buller; Bureau of Educational Measurements. *
For additional information and a review by John Manning, see 7:922.

[1999]

***Social Studies Grade 10 (American History): Minnesota High School Achievement Examinations.** Grade 10; 1951–70; a new, revised, or previously inactive form issued each May; Achievement Examinations for Secondary Schools, High School Achievement Examinations, and Midwest High School Achievement Examinations have also been used as series titles; called *American History* through 1957; Form GJ Rev ('70, some tests have 1973 copyright) used in 1970 and 1973 testings; edited by V. L. Lohmann; American Guidance Service, Inc. *
For additional information concerning out of print and inactive forms, see 7:923, 6:1008, and 5:807; for a review by Howard R. Anderson of Form A (1955) and Form B (1957), see 5:810.

[2000]

***Social Studies Grade 11 (World History): Minnesota High School Achievement Examinations.** Grade 11; 1951–70; a new, revised, or previously inactive form issued each May; Achievement Examinations for Secondary Schools, High School Achievement Examinations, and Midwest High School Achievement Examinations have also been used as series titles; various titles have been used such as *Modern World History* and *World History;* Form GJ Rev ('70, some tests have 1973 copyright) used in 1970 and 1973 testings; Form 4 ('54), entitled *Modern World History: Achievement Examinations for Secondary Schools* (see 1997), is available from another publisher; edited by V. L. Lohmann; American Guidance Service, Inc. *
For additional information concerning out of print and inactive forms, see 7:924, 6:1009, and 5:821–2.

[2001]

***The Undergraduate Program Field Tests: History Test.** College; 1969–73; formerly called *The Undergraduate Record Examinations: History Test;* test available to colleges for local administration; Educational Testing Service. * For the testing program entry, see 1062.
For additional information, see 7:925. For reviews of the testing program, see 7:671 (2 reviews).

[2002]

***World History/Objective Tests.** 1, 2 semesters high school; 1961–70; revision of *Objective Tests in World History* by Earl Bridgewater; 16 tests: 13 unit tests, 2 semester tests, and a final examination; no manual; Perfection Form Co. *
For additional information concerning the earlier tests, see 6:1007.

[2003]

World History Test: Acorn National Achievement Tests. High school and college; 1948–57; 6 scores: social studies terms, world geography, contributions of world peoples to civilization, political history, economic-social-cultural history, total; 1957 direction sheet identical with sheet copyrighted 1948; Vincent McGarrett and Edward H. Merrill; Psychometric Affiliates. *
For additional information and a review by John Manning, see 5:825.

[Out of Print Since TIP I]

World History: Every Pupil Scholarship Test, 6:1011
World History: Every Pupil Test, 6:1012
World History Test: Affiliation Testing Program for Catholic Secondary Schools, 6:1013 (1 review)
World History Test: Manchester Semester-End Achievement Tests, T:1791
World History Test: State High School Tests for Indiana, 4:696
World History: 20th Century Test, 4:697

POLITICAL SCIENCE

[2004]

*CLEP Subject Examination in American Government. 1 semester or equivalent; 1965–73; for college accreditation of nontraditional study, advanced placement, or assessment of educational achievement; tests administered monthly at centers throughout the United States; program administered for the College Entrance Examination Board by Educational Testing Service. * For the testing program entry, see 1050.

For additional information concerning an earlier form, see 7:926. For reviews of the testing program, see 7:664 (3 reviews).

[2005]

Cooperative Social Studies Tests: American Government. Grades 10–12; 1964–65; Cooperative Tests and Services. *

For additional information and a review by Howard D. Mehlinger, see 7:927.

[2006]

Cooperative Social Studies Tests: Civics. Grades 8–9; 1964–65; Cooperative Tests and Services. *

For additional information and a review by Vincent N. Campbell, see 7:928.

[2007]

Cooperative Social Studies Tests: Problems of Democracy. Grades 10–12; 1964–65; Cooperative Tests and Services. *

For additional information and a review by Hulda Grobman, see 7:929 (1 reference).

REFERENCES THROUGH 1971
1. See 7:929.

CUMULATIVE NAME INDEX
Farnen, R. F.: 1   Wills, G. R.: 1
Grobman, H.: *rev*, 7:929

[2008]

★[Government/Objective Tests.] 1 semester in grades 11–12; 1970; 6 tests; no manual; Perfection Form Co. *
a) FUNDAMENTALS OF GOVERNMENT.
b) THE EXECUTIVE BRANCH (POLITICAL PARTIES AND ELECTION).
c) THE LEGISLATIVE BRANCH.
d) THE AMERICAN JUDICIARY SYSTEM AND CIVIL LIBERTIES.
e) AMERICAN GOVERNMENT—STATE AND LOCAL GOVERNMENT.
f) FINAL TEST.

[2009]

*The Graduate Record Examinations Advanced Political Science Test. Graduate school candidates; 1939–73; formerly called *The Graduate Record Exam-*

inations *Advanced Tests: Government;* Educational Testing Service. * For the testing program entry, see 1053.

For additional information concerning earlier forms, see 7:930; for a review by Christine McGuire, see 5:835. For reviews of the testing program, see 7:667 (1 review) and 5:601 (1 review).

[2010]

★National Teacher Examinations: Texas Government. College seniors and teachers; 1972–73; Educational Testing Service. * For the testing program entry, see 869.

For reviews of the testing program, see 7:582 (2 reviews), 6:700 (1 review), 5:538 (3 reviews), and 4:802 (1 review).

[2011]

Patterson Test or Study Exercises on the Constitution of the United States. Grades 9–16 and adults; 1931–53; 1953 test identical with test copyrighted 1937 except for minor changes; Raymond G. Patterson; Bobbs-Merrill Co., Inc. *

For additional information, see 5:838.

[2012]

Principles of Democracy Test. Grades 9–12; 1961, c1960–61; Nathaniel L. Gage, Neil F. Garvey, Charles B. Hagan, and Roland Payette; Science Research Associates, Inc. *

For additional information and reviews by William C. Bingham and John H. Haefner, see 6:1020.

[2013]

Sare-Sanders American Government Test. High school and college; 1962–64; first published 1962–63 in the Every Pupil Scholarship Test series; Harold V. Sare and M. W. Sanders; Bureau of Educational Measurements. *

For additional information and a review by Howard D. Mehlinger, see 7:931.

[2014]

Sare-Sanders Constitution Test. High school and college; 1962–64; first published 1962–63 in the Every Pupil Scholarship Test series; Harold V. Sare and M. W. Sanders; Bureau of Educational Measurements. *

For additional information, see 7:932.

[2015]

*Social Studies Grade 12 (American Problems): Minnesota High School Achievement Examinations. Grade 12; 1951–70; a new, revised, or previously inactive form issued each May; Achievement Examinations for Secondary Schools, High School Achievement Examinations, and Midwest High School Achievement Examinations have also been used as series titles; *Introduction to Social Science, Introduction to Social Studies,* and *Social Studies* were used as titles through 1962; within past 9 years an alternate subtitle, *Introduction to Social Science,* has been used every third year; Form GJ Rev ('70, some tests have 1973 copyright) used in 1970 and 1973 testings with the subtitle *Introduction to Social Science;* edited by V. L. Lohmann; American Guidance Service, Inc. *

For additional information concerning out of print and inactive forms, see 7:893, 6:976, 5:789, and 5:795.

[2016]

*The Undergraduate Program Field Tests: Political Science Test.** College; 1969–73; formerly called *The Undergraduate Record Examinations: Political Science Test;* test available to colleges for local administration; Educational Testing Service. * For the testing program entry, see 1062.

For additional information concerning an earlier form, see 7:933. For reviews of the testing program, see 7:671 (2 reviews).

[Out of Print Since TIP I]

American Civics and Government Tests for High Schools and Colleges, 6:1013a (1 review)
American Government and Citizenship: Every Pupil Test, 6:1014 (1 review)
American Government: Every Pupil Scholarship Test, 6:1015
Bear Test on United States Constitution, T:1798
Civic Vocabulary Test, 5:830 (1 review, 1 reference)
Civics: 20th Century Test, 4:701
Constitution: Every Pupil Scholarship Test, 6:1016
Cooperative American Government Test, 4:702 (1 review)
Dimond-Pflieger Problems of Democracy Test, 5:833 (2 reviews, 1 reference)
Duke University Political Science Information Test (American Government), 6:1017
Junior High School Civics Test: State High School Tests for Indiana, 4:704
Kansas Constitution Test, 5:836 (1 review)
Mordy-Schrammel American Government Test, T:1807
Patterson Test or Study Exercises on the Declaration of Independence, 5:839
Patterson's Tests on the Federal Constitution, 4:705
Peltier-Durost Civics and Citizenship Test, 6:1019 (2 reviews)
Senior High School Civics Tests: State High School Tests for Indiana, 4:706–7
United States Government Test: Manchester Semester-End Achievement Tests, T:1815, 36:848

SOCIOLOGY

[2017]

*CLEP Subject Examination in Introductory Sociology.** 1 year or equivalent; 1965–73; for college accreditation of nontraditional study, advanced placement, or assessment of educational achievement; tests administered monthly at centers throughout the United States; program administered for the College Entrance Examination Board by Educational Testing Service. * For the testing program entry, see 1050.

For additional information, see 7:934. For reviews of the testing program, see 7:664 (3 reviews).

[2018]

*The Graduate Record Examinations Advanced Sociology Test.** Graduate school candidates; 1939–73; Educational Testing Service. * For the testing program entry, see 1053.

For additional information concerning earlier forms, see 7:935; for a review by J. Richard Wilmeth, see 6:1021. For reviews of the testing program, see 7:667 (1 review) and 5:601 (1 review).

[2019]

Sare-Sanders Sociology Test.** High school and college; 1958; Harold Sare and Merritt W. Sanders; Bureau of Educational Measurements. *

For additional information and a review by J. Richard Wilmeth, see 6:1022.

[2020]

*The Undergraduate Program Field Tests: Sociology Test.** College; 1969–73; formerly called *The Undergraduate Record Examinations: Sociology Test;* test available to colleges for local administration; Educational Testing Service. * For the testing program entry, see 1062.

For additional information, see 7:936. For reviews of the testing program, see 7:671 (2 reviews).

[Out of Print Since TIP I]

Sociology: Every Pupil Scholarship Test, 5:844

SPEECH AND HEARING

[2021]

★Diagnostic Test of Speechreading.** Deaf children ages 4–9; 1970; DTS; 5 scores: words, phrases, sentences, subtotal for phrases and sentences, total; Helmer R. Myklebust and Arthur I. Neyhus; Grune & Stratton, Inc. *

[2022]

★Multiple-Choice Intelligibility Test.** College; 1963; MIT; 2 scores: speaking, listening; John W. Black and C. Hess Haagen; Interstate Printers & Publishers, Inc. *

REFERENCES THROUGH 1971

1. HENDRICKS, RICHARD. *Relationships Among Tests of Intelligibility, Word-Reception, and Other Measures of Symbolic Formulation.* Doctor's thesis, Ohio State University (Columbus, Ohio), 1956. (*DA* 16:2239)

2. PETERS, ROBERT W. "Effect of Acoustic Environment Upon Speaker Intelligibility." *J Speech & Hearing Disorders* 21:88–93 Mr '56. * (*PA* 31:978)
3. WORTHINGTON, ANNA MAY LANGE. *An Investigation of the Relationship Between the Lipreading Ability of Congenitally Deaf High School Students and Certain Personality Factors.* Doctor's thesis, Ohio State University (Columbus, Ohio), 1956. (*DA* 16:2241)
4. BLACK, JOHN W. "Multiple-Choice Intelligibility Tests." *J Speech & Hearing Disorders* 22:213–35 Je '57. * (*PA* 32:2839)
5. BAER, SHERWIN HYER. *An Analysis of the Responses in Word Intelligibility Testing.* Doctor's thesis, Ohio State University (Columbus, Ohio), 1958. (*DA* 19:3410)
6. BLACK, JOHN W., AND HAAGEN, C. HESS. "Multiple-Choice Intelligibility Tests, Forms A and B." *J Speech & Hearing Disorders* 28:77–86 F '63. * (*PA* 38:2606)

CUMULATIVE NAME INDEX

Baer, S. H.: 5
Black, J. W.: 4, 6
Haagen, C. H.: 6
Hendricks, R.: 1
Peters, R. W.: 2
Worthington, A. M. L.: 3

[2023]

★**The Ohio Tests of Articulation and Perception of Sounds.** Ages 5–8; 1973; OTAPS; 8 scores: articulation (sounds in words, sounds in phrases, nonsense words in context, stimulability of nonsense words), listening (identification of sounds by self, by examiner, comparator perception of sounds by self, by examiner) ; Ruth Beckey Irwin and Marcia Stevenson Abbate (test) ; Stanwix House, Inc. * (Canadian publisher: J. M. Dent & Sons (Canada) Ltd. [Canada].)

REFERENCES THROUGH 1971

1. IRWIN, RUTH BECKEY, AND MUSSELMAN, BARBARA WILSON. "A Compact Picture Articulation Test." *J Speech & Hearing Disorders* 27:36–9 F '62. * (*PA* 36:5JE36I)
2. STEVENSON, MARCIA LYNN. *The Development and Standardization of a Short Three-Part Picture Articulation Test for Screening and Diagnostic Purposes.* Master's thesis, Ohio State University (Columbus, Ohio), 1966.
3. MYERS, ANN KIMBALL. *A Prognostic and Normative Study of the Articulatory Proficiency of First Grade Children.* Master's thesis, Ohio State University (Columbus, Ohio), 1967.
4. SCHALK, MARY CAROL. *A Prognostic and Normative Study of the Articulatory Proficiency of Kindergarten Children.* Master's thesis, Ohio State University (Columbus, Ohio), 1967.

CUMULATIVE NAME INDEX

Irwin, R. B.: 1   Schalk, M. C.: 4
Musselman, B. W.: 1   Stevenson, M. L.: 2
Myers, A. K.: 3

[2024]

Preschool Language Scale. Ages 2–6; 1969; PLS; 3 scores: auditory comprehension, verbal ability, total, plus an articulation section; Irla Lee Zimmerman, Violette G. Steiner, and Roberta L. Evatt; Charles E. Merrill Publishing Co. *

For additional information, a review by Joel Stark, and an excerpted review by C. H. Ammons, see 7:965.

REFERENCES THROUGH 1971

1. PROGER, BARTON B. "The Preschool Language Scale: A Review." *J Spec Ed* 5(1):86–8 w–sp '71. *

CUMULATIVE NAME INDEX

Ammons, C. H.: *exc*, 7:965   Stark, J.: *rev*, 7:965
Proger, B. B.: 1

[2025]

Reynell Developmental Language Scales, Experimental Edition. Children ages 1–5 with delayed or deviant language development; 1969; RDLS; 3 scales; Joan Reynell; NFER Publishing Co. Ltd. [England]. *
a) VERBAL COMPREHENSION SCALE A.
b) VERBAL COMPREHENSION SCALE B. Adaptation of Scale A for use with children unable to use their hands.
c) EXPRESSIVE LANGUAGE SCALE. 4 scores: language structure, vocabulary, content, total.

For additional information, see 7:966.

REFERENCES THROUGH 1971

1. GILES, ANTHONY SNOWDEN. *The Verbal Environment of Institutionalized Mentally Retarded Children.* Doctor's thesis, Syracuse University (Syracuse, N.Y.), 1971. (*DAI* 32:6099B)
2. JEFFREE, D. M., AND CASHDAN, A. "Severely Subnormal Children and Their Parents: An Experiment in Language Improvement." *Brit J Ed Psychol* 41(2):184–94 Je '71. * (*PA* 47:9728)
3. REYNELL, JOAN, AND HUNTLEY, R. M. C. "New Scales for the Assessment of Language Development in Young Children." *J Learn Dis* 4(10):549–57 D '71. * (*PA* 47:10605)

CUMULATIVE NAME INDEX

Cashdan, A.: 2   Jeffree, D. M.: 2
Giles, A. S.: 1   Reynell, J.: 3
Huntley, R. M. C.: 3

[2026]

★**The Undergraduate Program Field Tests: Speech Pathology and Audiology Test.** College; 1969–73; formerly called *The Undergraduate Record*

Examinations: Speech and Hearing Test; test available to colleges for local administration; Educational Testing Service. * For the testing program entry, see 1062.

For additional information concerning an earlier form, see 7:937. For reviews of the testing program, see 7:671 (2 reviews).

HEARING

[2027]

★**Ambco Audiometers.** Ages 10 and over; 1954–70; Ambco Electronics. *
a) OTOMETER. 1954–70; for screening and threshold testing in schools, industry, and physicians' offices; 2 models (battery operated portable units): Models 601-S (single earphone), 601-D (double earphones).
b) OTO-CHEK AUDITORY SCREENER. 1956; for two-frequency air conduction screening; 2 models (transistorized, battery operated portable units): Models 700-S (single earphone), 700-D (double earphones); Howard P. House and Aram Glorig.
c) DIAGNOSTIC AUDIOMETER. 1958–70; for pure tone air and bone conduction threshold and screening testing; 6 models (transistorized, AC operated): Models 1150-S (portable unit, air conduction only), 1150-D (portable unit, air and bone conduction), 1150-D2 (desk model, air and bone conduction), A-15S (desk model, air conduction only), A-15D (desk model, air and bone conduction), A-15M (desk model, air and bone conduction plus microphone talk back).
d) SPEECH AUDIOMETER. 1961; for pure tone air and bone conduction testing using live or recorded voice; Model A-17 (transistorized, AC operated desk model).
e) "SCREEN-EAR" SCREENING AUDIOMETER. 1960–70; for pure tone air conduction screening and threshold testing in schools and industry; 2 models (transistorized, AC operated portable units): Models 1122, 1122F (permits fingertip operation of tone presentation).

For additional information, see 6:939.

[2027A]

Ambco Speech Test Record. Ages 3 and over; [1958]; for use with a speech audiometer for testing speech reception thresholds and discrimination; Ambco Electronics. *

[2028]

★**Auditory Discrimination Test (Revised 1973).** Ages 5–8; 1958–73; ADT; "ability to recognize the fine differences that exist between the phonemes used in English speech"; 1973 revision identical with test copyrighted 1958 except for use of a correct score rather than an error score; Joseph M. Wepman; Language Research Associates, Inc. *

For additional information and a review by Louis M. DiCarlo, see 6:940 (2 references).

REFERENCES THROUGH 1971

1–2. See 6:940.
3. GOETZINGER, C. P.; DIRKS, D. D.; AND BAER, C. J. "Auditory Discrimination and Visual Perception in Good and Poor Readers." *Ann Otol Rhinol & Laryngol* 69:121–36 Mr '60. *
4. THOMPSON, BERTHA BOYA. *The Relation of Auditory Discrimination and Intelligence Test Scores to Success in Primary Reading.* Doctor's thesis, Indiana University (Bloomington, Ind.), 1961. (*DA* 22:785)
5. LOVE, HAROLD D. "Bilingualism in Southwest Louisiana." *J Ed Res* 56:144–7 N '62. *
6. REID, RUTH L. *Auditory Aspects of Reading Readiness.* Master's thesis, University of Alberta (Edmonton, Alta., Canada), 1962.
7. PRINS, DAVID. "Relations Among Specific Articulatory Deviations and Responses to a Clinical Measure of Sound Dis-

crimination Ability." *J Speech & Hearing Disorders* 28:382–8 N '63. * (*PA* 38:8920)

8. BROWN, EDNA COOMER. *Auditory Discrimination: Its Relationship With Reading and Spelling Achievement of Primary-Grade Pupils.* Master's thesis, Illinois State University (Normal, Ill.), 1964.

9. CHRISTINE, DOROTHY, AND CHRISTINE, CHARLES. "The Relationship of Auditory Discrimination to Articulatory Defects and Reading Retardation." *El Sch J* 65:97–100 N '64. *

10. DEUTSCH, CYNTHIA P. "Auditory Discrimination and Learning: Social Factors." *Merrill-Palmer Q* 10:277–96 Jl '64. *

11. GOLDMARK, BERNICE. *The Relation of Visual Perception, Auditory Perception and One Aspect of Conceptualization to Word Recognition.* Doctor's thesis, University of Arizona (Tucson, Ariz.), 1964. (*DA* 25:186)

12. ALSHAN, LEONARD M. "Reading Readiness and Reading Achievement." *Proc Ann Conv Int Read Assn* 10:312–3 '65. *

13. LOPER, DORIS JEAN. *Auditory Discrimination, Intelligence, Achievement, and Background of Experience and Information in a Culturally Disadvantaged First-Grade Population.* Doctor's thesis, Temple University (Philadelphia, Pa.), 1965. (*DA* 26:5873)

14. RABBITT, PATTI HILL. *An Experimental Investigation of the Auditory Discrimination Ability of Four-, Five-, and Six-Year-Old Middle-Class and Socially Disadvantaged Children.* Master's thesis, University of California (Los Angeles, Calif.), 1965.

15. BENGER, KATHLYN. *A Study of the Relationships Between Perception, Personality, Intelligence and Grade One Reading Achievement.* Master's thesis, University of Alberta (Edmonton, Alta., Canada), 1966.

16. CLARK, ANN D., AND RICHARDS, CHARLOTTE J. "Auditory Discrimination Among Economically Disadvantaged Preschool Children." *Excep Children* 33:259–62 D '66. * (*PA* 41:2319)

17. DE HIRSCH, KATRINA; JANSKY, JEANETTE JEFFERSON; AND LANGFORD, WILLIAM S. *Predicting Reading Failure.* New York: Harper & Row, Publishers, Inc., 1966. Pp. xv, 144. *

18. HANESIAN, HELEN. *The Relationship of Auditory Abilities to First Grade Reading Achievement.* Doctor's thesis, Columbia University (New York, N.Y.), 1966. (*DA* 27:2883A)

19. HERMAN, ROSALEE S. *The Relationship Between Auditory Discrimination and the Reading Performance of a Group of Fourth Grade Children in the Jefferson County, Kentucky Public Schools.* Master's thesis, University of Louisville (Louisville, Ky.), 1966.

20. MCLEOD, JOHN. *Some Psychological and Psycholinguistic Aspects of Severe Reading Disability in Children.* Doctor's thesis, University of Queensland (Brisbane, Australia), 1966.

21. ROBINSON, H. ALAN. "Reliability of Measures Related to Reading Success of Average, Disadvantaged, and Advantaged Kindergarten Children." Comments by Samuel Weintraub. *Read Teach* 20:203–9 D '66. * (*PA* 41:3344)

22. SCHLANGER, BERNARD B., AND GALANOWSKY, GLORIA I. "Auditory Discrimination Tasks Performed by Mentally Retarded and Normal Children." *J Speech & Hearing Res* 9:434–40 S '66. *

23. BERLIN, CHARLES I., AND DILL, ANNE C. "The Effects of Feedback and Positive Reinforcement on the Wepman Auditory Discrimination Test Scores of Lower-Class Negro and White Children." *J Speech & Hearing Res* 10:384–9 Je '67. * (*PA* 41:14628)

24. DAVIS, ALICE FAY. *Auditory-Discrimination Skills: Effect on Reading Achievement.* Master's thesis, Illinois State University (Normal, Ill.), 1967.

25. FROSTIG, MARIANNE. "Testing as a Basis for Educational Therapy." *J Spec Ed* 2:15–34 f '67. * (*PA* 42:7770)

26. GROSS, REUBEN E. *Dialect Pronunciation, Auditory Discrimination, and Reading.* Doctor's thesis, Yeshiva University (New York, N.Y.), 1967. (*DA* 28:2124B)

27. HENDRIX, LELAND JACOB. *Auditory Discrimination Differences Between Culturally Deprived and Nondeprived Preschool Children.* Doctor's thesis, Brigham Young University (Provo, Utah), 1967. (*DA* 28:2556A)

28. MCLEOD, JOHN. "Some Psycholinguistic Correlates of Reading Disability in Young Children." *Read Res Q* 2:5–31 sp '67. * (*PA* 41:11883)

29. OAKLAND, THOMAS DAVID. *Social Class and Performance on Phonemic and Nonphonemic Auditory Discrimination Tests.* Doctor's thesis, Indiana University (Bloomington, Ind.), 1967. (*DA* 28:4490A)

30. TAUBER, ROSALYN. "Identification of Potential Learning Disabilities." *Acad Ther Q* 2:116–9+ w '67. * (*PA* 41:5004)

31. WARTENBERG, HERBERT. *The Relationship Between Success in Beginning Reading and Various Predictive Measures.* Doctor's thesis, Temple University (Philadelphia, Pa.), 1967. (*DA* 28:979A)

32. BAKER, MERLE E., AND LUCHS, ARTHUR F. "Visual Discrimination Handicaps in Kindergarten Pupils—An Experiment in the Discovery and Assistance of Kindergarten Pupils With Handicaps in Visual Discrimination." *Ill Sch Res* 4:44–8 F '68. *

33. BENGER, KATHLYN. "The Relationships of Perception, Per-

sonality, Intelligence, and Grade One Reading Achievement." *Proc Ann Conv Int Read Assn* 12(4):112–23 '68. *

34. BLANK, MARION. "Cognitive Processes in Auditory Discrimination in Normal and Retarded Readers." *Child Develop* 39:1091–101 D '68. * (*PA* 43:8182)

35. BUKTENICA, NORMAN A. "Perceptual Mode Dominance: An Approach to Assessment of First Grade Reading and Spelling." Abstract. *Proc 76th Ann Conv Am Psychol Assn* 3:585–6 '68. * (*PA* 43:1459, title only)

36. GATES, MAXINE FULLER. *A Comparison of the Learning Characteristics of Hyperactive and Hypoactive Children With Related Central Nervous System Dysfunctions.* Doctor's thesis, Ohio State University (Columbus, Ohio), 1968. (*DAI* 30:166A)

37. GELHART, ROBERT PRESTON. *Auditory Discrimination in the Educable Mentally Retarded.* Doctor's thesis, University of Southern California (Los Angeles, Calif.), 1968. (*DA* 29:833A)

38. GOTTESMAN, RUTH LEVY. *Auditory Discrimination Ability in Standard English Speaking and Negro Dialect Speaking Children.* Doctor's thesis, Columbia University (New York, N.Y.), 1968. (*DAI* 30:1358B)

39. HUTCHINSON, BARBARA B. "Self-Monitoring of Articulation Responses in Sound Discrimination Tests." *J Commun Disorders* 1:297–304 O '68. * (*PA* 43:15545)

40. HUTCHINSON, BARBARA B., AND CLARK, DOROTHY W. "Auditory and Visual Discrimination Skills of Normal and Articulation-Defective Children." *Percept & Motor Skills* 26:259–65 F '68. * (*PA* 42:10964)

41. IRVINE, JAMES. *Correlates of Grade One Achievement.* Master's thesis, University of Alberta (Edmonton, Alta., Canada), 1968.

42. KINNISON, ANN LOUISE. *An Investigation of the Relationship Between Auditory Discrimination Ability and Reading Achievement and Auditory Memory Ability and Reading Achievement.* Master's thesis, Sacramento State College (Sacramento, Calif.), 1968.

43. KOPPITZ, ELIZABETH MUNSTERBERG. Chap. 9, "Using HFD's in Combination With Other Psychological Tests," pp. 177–87. In her *Psychological Evaluation of Children's Human Figure Drawings.* New York: Grune & Stratton, Inc., 1968. Pp. x, 341. *

44. MORENCY, ANNE. "Auditory Modality, Research and Practice." *Proc Ann Conv Int Read Assn* 12(4):17–21 '68. *

45. ROBINSON, H. ALAN, AND HANSON, EARL. "Reliability of Measures of Reading Achievement." *Read Teach* 21:307–13+ Ja '68. * (*PA* 42:17652)

46. SANZONE, JEAN FAY FOWLS. *A Comparative Study of Two Approaches to the Teaching of Auditory Discrimination to Culturally Disadvantaged Educable Mentally Retarded Children With Implications for Exceptional Child Educational Centers.* Doctor's thesis, Florida State University (Tallahassee, Fla.), 1968. (*DAI* 30:1891A)

47. WOOLF, GERALD, AND MYERS, MARY JANE. "The Effect of Two Ear Training Procedures on the Improvement of Auditory Discrimination and Articulation." *Excep Children* 34:659–65 My '68. *

48. AYRES, A. JEAN. "Deficits in Sensory Integration in Educationally Handicapped Children." *J Learn Dis* 2(3):160–8 Mr '69. * (*PA* 45:6978)

49. BLAND, ROSA BEATRICE. *Relation of Auditory Discrimination to Reading Achievement.* Doctor's thesis, University of Virginia (Charlottesville, Va.), 1969. (*DAI* 31:1655A)

50. BRUININKS, ROBERT H. "Auditory and Visual Perceptual Skills Related to the Reading Performance of Disadvantaged Boys." *Percept & Motor Skills* 29(1):179–86 Ag '69. * (*PA* 44:2835)

51. CLARK, ANN D. *A Longitudinal Investigation of Selected Characteristics in an Economically Disadvantaged and Nondisadvantaged Headstart Population.* Doctor's thesis, University of Wisconsin (Madison, Wis.), 1969. (*DAI* 30:5310A)

52. CRITTENDEN, JERRY BLICKMAN. *An Empirical Investigation of the Behavioral Dimensions of Four Tests of Learning Disabilities.* Doctor's thesis, Michigan State University (East Lansing, Mich.), 1969. (*DAI* 30:5310A)

53. CURRY, DAL ROY. *The Effect of Two Types of Auditory Discrimination Training on Language Performance and Acquisition in a Culturally Deprived Preschool Population.* Doctor's thesis, University of Kansas (Lawrence, Kan.), 1969. (*DAI* 30:5281A)

54. LINGREN, RONALD H. "Performance of Disabled and Normal Readers on the Bender-Gestalt, Auditory Discrimination Test, and Visual-Motor Matching." *Percept & Motor Skills* 29(1):152–4 Ag '69. * (*PA* 44:2803)

55. NEVILLE, DONALD, AND BUCKE, BARBARA. "The Effect of Meaning on the Measurement of the Ability to Auditorially Discriminate Sounds Contained in Words." *Proc Ann Conv Int Read Assn* 13(1):650–4 '69. *

56. OAKLAND, THOMAS D. "Auditory Discrimination and Socioeconomic Status as Correlates of Reading Ability." *J Learn Dis* 2(6):324–9 Je '69. * (*PA* 45:7067)

57. OKADA, DORIS MAMIYA. *The Effects of Perceptual and Perceptual-Motor Training on the Visual Perception, Auditory Perception, and Language Performance of Institutionalized Educable Mental Retardates.* Doctor's thesis, New York University (New York, N.Y.), 1969. (*DAI* 30:2857A)

Auditory Discrimination Test

58. RODGERS, DENIS CYRIL. *An Investigation of the Auditory Memory Abilities of Grade 2 Retarded-Underachieving Readers and Competent-Achieving Readers Under Conditions of Reinforcement and Non-Reinforcement.* Doctor's thesis, University of Toronto (Toronto, Ont., Canada), 1969. (*DAI* 31:2196A)

59. SANZONE, JEAN F. "Two Approaches to the Teaching of Auditory Discrimination to Culturally Disadvantaged, Educable Mentally Retarded Children: A Comparative Study." *Ed & Train Mental Retard* 4(4):158–67 D '69. *

60. FLYNN, PAULINE T., AND BYRNE, MARGARET C. "Relationship Between Reading and Selected Auditory Abilities of Third-Grade Children." *J Speech & Hearing Res* 13(4):731–40 D '70. *

61. HAFNER, LAWRENCE E.; WEAVER, WENDELL W.; AND POWELL, KATHRYN. "Psychological and Perceptual Correlates of Reading Achievement Among Fourth Graders." *J Read Behav* 2(4):281–90 f '70. * (*PA* 46:5663)

62. LOWRY, LAURA M. "Differences in Visual Perception and Auditory Discrimination Between American Indian and White Kindergarten Children." *J Learn Dis* 3(7):359–63 Jl '70. *

63. MOTTOLA, RICHARD ALBERT. *The Development of Auditory Discrimination Skills in Kindergarten Children.* Doctor's thesis, University of Connecticut (Storrs, Conn.), 1970. (*DAI* 31:6284A)

64. SNYDER, ROBERT T., AND POPE, PEGGY. "New Norms for and an Item Analysis of the Wepman Test at the First Grade, Six-Year-Level." *Percept & Motor Skills* 31(3):1007–10 D '70. * (*PA* 46:910)

65. TOMA, ROBERTA J. *The Efficiency of Auditory and Visual Discrimination Tasks in the Reading Process.* Doctor's thesis, Fordham University (New York, N.Y.), 1970. (*DAI* 31:3357A)

66. UHL, NORMAN P., AND NURSS, JOANNE R. "Socio-Economic Level Styles in Solving Reading-Related Tasks." *Read Res Q* 5(3):452–85 sp '70. *

67. VAN CAMP, SARAH STREET. *An Auditory and Visual Discrimination Test for Kindergarten and First Grade Children: A New Approach.* Doctor's thesis, University of Massachusetts (Amherst, Mass.), 1970. (*DAI* 31:5680A)

68. ZBINDEN, WILLIAM ROSS. *Psycholinguistic and Perceptual Correlates of Spelling in Educable Mentally Handicapped Children.* Doctor's thesis, University of Illinois (Urbana, Ill.), 1970. (*DAI* 31:2765AAA)

69. AMDUR, JEANETTE LORRAINE READ. *Oral Language Abilities in a Low Socio-Economic Status Kindergarten Spanish-Surnamed Population Varying in Reading Achievement.* Doctor's thesis, University of Denver (Denver, Colo.), 1971. (*DAI* 32:779A)

70. EVANS, MILDRED MAY BAILEY. *The Effects of a Physical Education Program on Auditory Discrimination Ability, Verbal and Non-Verbal, of Kindergarten Children.* Doctor's thesis, Michigan State University (East Lansing, Mich.), 1971. (*DAI* 32:3073A)

71. FALK, LIBBY JANET. *A Profile of Learning Abilities and Behavorial Characteristics of Elementary School-Age Children With Phenylketonuria.* Doctor's thesis, Temple University (Philadelphia, Pa.), 1971. (*DAI* 32:1913A)

72. FREER, FRANK J. *Visual and Auditory Perceptual Modality Differences as Related to Success in First Grade Reading Word Recognition.* Doctor's thesis, Rutgers—The State University (New Brunswick, N.J.), 1971. (*DAI* 32:6193A)

73. GORDON, GEORGE, AND HYMAN, IRWIN. "The Measurement of Perceptual-Motor Abilities of Head Start Children." *Psychol Sch* 8(1):41–8 Ja '71. * (*PA* 46:7777)

74. GREIF, SUSAN ANN. *A Study of the Relationship Between Auditory, Visual, and Haptic Perception and Selected Parameters of Language and Articulation in Children With Central Processing Dysfunction.* Doctor's thesis, Wayne State University (Detroit, Mich.), 1971. (*DAI* 32:6717B)

75. LARSEN, STEPHEN. "Performance of Achieving and Underachieving Second, Third, and Fourth Grade Children on Tests of Auditory Ability and Oral Form Discrimination." *Kan Studies Ed* 21(1–2):53–9 sp–su '71. *

76. MARGOLESE, ARTHUR. *The Relationship of Hyperacusis to Hyperkinesis Among Regular Classroom Pupils as Compared to Educationally Handicapped Pupils.* Doctor's thesis, University of Southern California (Los Angeles, Calif.), 1971. (*DAI* 32:1945A)

77. MORGAN, ARTHUR T., JR. *An Analysis of Auditory Abilities as Predictors of First-Grade Reading Achievement.* Doctor's thesis, University of Houston (Houston, Tex.), 1971. (*DAI* 32:3125A)

78. RIGGLE, RICHARD RAY. *Correlations of Articulatory Disability With Various Aspects of Reading for Selected Modalities.* Doctor's thesis, University of Oregon (Eugene, Ore.), 1971. (*DAI* 32:2922A)

79. STEWART, JOE GLENN. *The Relationship of Selected Abilities to Gross Motor Performance of Educable Mentally Retarded Students.* Doctor's thesis, North Texas State University (Denton, Tex.), 1971. (*DAI* 32:6799A)

80. STRAG, GERALD ANTHONY. *Auditory Discrimination Techniques Useful With Culturally Disadvantaged Children.* Doctor's thesis, University of Georgia (Athens, Ga.), 1971. (*DAI* 32:3804A)

81. SWALLOW, ROSE-MARIE. *Automatic Processing of Perceptual-Linguistic Stimuli in Second Grade Achieving and Non-Achieving Readers.* Doctor's thesis, University of Southern California (Los Angeles, Calif.), 1971. (*DAI* 32:3827A)

82. UPCHURCH, WINIFRED BROOK. *The Relationship Between Perceptual-Motor Skills and Word Recognition Achievement at the Kindergarten Level.* Doctor's thesis, Syracuse University (Syracuse, N.Y.), 1971. (*DAI* 32:4497A)

83. VALDES, ALICE LAURA. *The Effects of Training in Auditory and Visual Discrimination Skills on Reading Readiness and Intelligence in the Disadvantaged Child.* Doctor's thesis, Lehigh University (Bethlehem, Pa.), 1971. (*DAI* 32:2496A)

84. WEINER, PAUL S. "The Cognitive Functioning of Language Deficient Children." *Cognitive Studies* 2:338–63 '71. *

CUMULATIVE NAME INDEX

[2029]

★**Auditory Memory Span Test.** Ages 5–8; 1973; "ability to recall single syllable spoken words in progressively increasing series"; Joseph M. Wepman and Anne Morency; Language Research Associates, Inc. *

[2030]

★**Auditory Sequential Memory Test.** Grades 5–8; 1973; digit recall; Joseph M. Wepman and Anne Morency; Language Research Associates, Inc. *

[2031]

Auditory Tests. Grades 2 and over; 1951–56; also called *C.I.D. Auditory Tests;* 3 tests on 2 sets of records; Central Institute for the Deaf; Technisonic Studios, Inc. *

a) AUDITORY TESTS W-1 AND W-2: SPONDAIC WORD LISTS. Recorded adaptation of *Auditory Test No. 9* developed by Harvard University Psycho-Acoustic Laboratory; threshold for speech; 2 tests.

1) *Test W-1.* A "constant level" test in which sound intensity must be attenuated by examiner.

2) *Test W-2.* A "descending level" test in which sound intensity has been attenuated on the record in downward steps of 3 decibels.

b) AUDITORY TEST W-22: PHONETICALLY-BALANCED WORD LISTS. Words selected in part from lists developed by Harvard University Psycho-Acoustic Laboratory; discrimination for speech at levels above threshold.

For additional information, see 6:941 (20 references).

REFERENCES THROUGH 1971

1-20. See 6:941.

21. FALCONER, G. A., AND DAVIS, H. "The Intelligibility of Connected Discourse as a Test for the 'Threshold for Speech.'" *Laryngoscope* 57:581-95 S '47. * (*PA* 22:1026)

22. HIRSH, I. J. "Clinical Application of Two Harvard Auditory Tests." *J Speech Disorders* 12:151-8 Je '47. * (*PA* 22:1461)

23. GOETZINGER, C. P.; DIRKS, D. D.; AND BAER, C. J. "Auditory Discrimination and Visual Perception in Good and Poor Readers." *Ann Otol Rhinol & Laryngol* 69:121-36 Mr '60. *

24. BOROS, VILMA. *Refinement of Selected Speech Discrimination Tests.* Doctor's thesis, University of Michigan (Ann Arbor, Mich.), 1964. (*DA* 25:7418)

25. BROOKS, ROBERT S. *The Relationship of Semantic Variables, Auditory Discrimination and Other Language Skills.* Doctor's thesis, University of Kansas (Lawrence, Kan.), 1964. (*DA* 26:539)

26. SCHULTZ, MARTIN C. "Suggested Improvement in Speech Discrimination Testing." *J Auditory Res* 4:1-14 Ja '64. * (*PA* 39:13628)

27. CAMPBELL, RICHARD A. "Discrimination Test Word Difficulty." *J Speech & Hearing Res* 8:13-22 Mr '65. * (*PA* 39:10071)

28. HAHN, JEAN MARIE. *An Evaluation of Five Speech Discrimination Tests.* Doctor's thesis, University of Pittsburgh (Pittsburgh, Pa.), 1965. (*DA* 27:1316B)

29. GIOLAS, THOMAS G. "Effectiveness of the Social Adequacy Index." *Ann Otol Rhinol & Laryngol* 75:1111-7 D '66. *

30. JERGER, JAMES; MALMQUIST, CAROLYN; AND SPEAKS, CHARLES. "Comparison of Some Speech Intelligibility Tests in the Evaluation of Hearing Aid Performance." *J Speech & Hearing Res* 9:253-8 Je '66. * (*PA* 40:10706)

31. FULTON, ROBERT T. "Task Adaptation and Word Familiarity of W-22 Discrimination Lists With Retarded Children." *J Auditory Res* 7:353-8 O '67. *

32. NACKES, MARY. *An Examination of the Relationship Between Speech Discrimination Performance and Hearing Handicap.* Master's thesis, Kent State University (Kent, Ohio), 1967.

33. THOMPSON, GARY. *Relationship of Performance on Selected Auditory Distortion Tests to the Discrimination of Speech Through Flat vs. Selective Amplifying Systems for a High-Frequency Hearing-Loss Population.* Doctor's thesis, University of Minnesota (Minneapolis, Minn.), 1967. (*DA* 28:3513B)

34. BELT, DONALD ALLEN. *A Study of the Auditory Intelligibility of CID W-22 List One as a Known vs. Unknown Message Set.* Doctor's thesis, University of Washington (Seattle, Wash.), 1968. (*DA* 29:3957B)

35. EPSTEIN, AUBREY; GIOLAS, THOMAS G.; AND OWENS, ELMER. "Familiarity and Intelligibility of Monosyllabic Word Lists." *J Speech & Hearing Res* 11:435-8 Jl '68. * (*PA* 42:16511)

36. HALEY, MARGARET JACKSON. *The Influence of Two Amplified Telephones on the Speech Discrimination of Hard-of-Hearing Patients.* Master's thesis, Southern Methodist University (Dallas, Tex.), 1968.

37. KOPRA, LENNART L.; BLOSSER, DENNIS; AND WALDRON, DARYLE L. "Comparison of Fairbanks Rhyme Test and CID Auditory Test W-22 in Normal and Hearing-Impaired Listeners." *J Speech & Hearing Res* 11:735-9 D '68. * (*PA* 45:4714)

38. LOVRINIC, JEAN HAHN; BURGI, ERNEST J.; AND CURRY, E. THAYER. "A Comparative Evaluation of Five Speech Discrimination Measures." *J Speech & Hearing Res* 11:372-81 Je '68. * (*PA* 42:17502)

39. KURGER, BARBARA. *The Systematic Selection of 25 Monosyllables Which Predict the CID W-22 Speech Discrimination Score.* Master's thesis, Queens College (Flushing, N.Y.), 1969.

40. OMER, JANE L. "Investigation of Speech Discrimination Ability of Children Selected for Learning Disability." *Kan Studies Ed* 19(3):25-8 Ag '69. *

41. THOMPSON, GARY, AND LASSMAN, FRANK. "Relationship of Auditory Distortion Test Results to Speech Discrimination vs. Selective Amplifying Systems." *J Speech & Hearing Res* 12(3):594-606 S '69. *

42. ELKINS, EARLEEN F. "Analyses of the Phonetic Composition and Word Familiarity Attributes of CNC Intelligibility Word Lists." *J Speech & Hearing Disorders* 35(2):156-60 My '70. * (*PA* 44:17832)

43. JIRSA, ROBERT EDWIN. *The Study of the Effects of Harmonic Distortion in Hearing Aids on the Intelligibility of Four Discrimination Tests in Normal and Hearing Impaired*

Listeners. Doctor's thesis, University of Kansas (Lawrence, Kan.), 1970. (*DAI* 31:3751B)

44. KEITH, ROBERT W., AND TALIS, HILARY P. "The Use of Speech in Noise in Diagnostic Audiometry." *J Auditory Res* 10(3):201-4 Jl '70. * (*PA* 49:9644)

45. PERLER, HELENE. *The Effects of Simultaneous Background Voices Upon the CID W-2 Test for Auditory Discrimination.* Master's thesis, Boston University (Boston, Mass.), 1970.

46. MARGOLIS, ROBERT H., AND MILLIN, JOSEPH P. "An Item Difficulty Based Speech Discrimination Test." *J Speech & Hearing Res* 14(4):865-73 D '71. *

47. NEFF, BROOKS E., JR. *Comparison of Speech Discrimination Scores on Three Monosyllabic Word Intelligibility Tasks and a Task Representing Everyday Speech Under Conditions of Low-Pass Filtering.* Doctor's thesis, University of Southern Mississippi (Hattiesburg, Miss.), 1971. (*DAI* 32:5512B)

48. PORTER, THOMAS A. *An Investigation of Inverted Frequency Masking of Monaural Test Material and Dichotic Test Results.* Doctor's thesis, University of Kansas (Lawrence, Kan.), 1971. (*DAI* 32:2248B)

49. SANBORN, E. SUE. *Speech Discrimination in Hypoacusics and Normals With Artificial Hearing Loss.* Doctor's thesis, University of Washington (Seattle, Wash.), 1971. (*DAI* 32:1901B)

50. SWAIN, CHARLES EUGENE, JR. *The Modified Rhyme Test: The Effects of Sensation Level on Discrimination Scores on an Adult Sensorineural Population.* Doctor's thesis, University of Illinois (Urbana, Ill.), 1971. (*DAI* 32:6105B)

CUMULATIVE NAME INDEX

[2032]

*Beltone Audiometers. Grades kgn and over; 1954–73; 6 models; Beltone Electronics Corporation. *

a) BELTONE PORTABLE AUDIOMETERS. 1955–67; 3 models (solid state), each available in portable (D) or desktop (DW) styling.

1) *Models 9-D and 9-DW.* 1967; for air conduction screening and threshold testing in schools and industry.

2) *Models 10-D and 10-DW.* 1967; for use in schools, industry, clinics, and physicians' offices; for pure tone air and bone conduction testing with masking.

3) *Models 12-D and 12-DW.* 1967; for use by otologists and clinical audiologists; for pure tone (air and bone conduction) and speech testing.

b) BELTONE CLINICAL AUDIOMETERS. 1958–73; for pure tone (air and bone conduction) and live, recorded, and taped speech testing; 3 models.

1) *Model 200-C (AC operated).* 1973; for clinical and general diagnostic procedures.

2) *Clinical Research Audiometers.* 1969; for use by audiological scientists; 2 models (solid state):

Models CR-4000, CR-5000 (similar to CR-4000 but with additional flexibility of signal routing between the 2 channels).

For additional information concerning earlier models, see 6:943. For comments by Louis M. DiCarlo on screening audiometers in general and specific comments on an earlier Beltone portable model and three other portable audiometers, see 6:942.

REFERENCES THROUGH 1971

1. LLOYD, LYLE L., AND MELROSE, JAY. "Reliability of Selected Auditory Responses of Normal Hearing Mentally Retarded Children." *Am J Mental Def* 71:133–43 Jl '66. * (*PA* 40:11439)

CUMULATIVE NAME INDEX

Lloyd, L. L.: 1   Melrose, J.: 1

[2033]

Comprehension of Oral Language: Inter-American Series. Grade 1; 1968; experimental form; parallel editions in English and Spanish; Herschel T. Manuel; Guidance Testing Associates. *

For additional information, see 7:950.

[2034]

*Eckstein Audiometers. Grades kgn and over; 1959–72; 8 models (solid state); Eckstein Bros., Inc. *
a) PORTABLE AUDIOMETERS. 1961–1972; 6 models.
  1) *EB Tetra-Tone Audiometer.* 1968–69; for screening in schools and medical offices; Model 46.
  2) *EB Miniature Audiometer.* 1961; for air conduction screening and threshold testing in schools and medical offices; Model 60.
  3) *EB Audiometer Model 350-I.* 1965–72; air conduction threshold testing in industry.
  4) *EB Full Range Portable Audiometers.* 1970–72; 3 models (may be AC operated).
    (*a*) Model 390. For pure tone air conduction testing.
    (*b*) Model 390G. Same as Model 390 with group output.
    (*c*) Model 390MB. Diagnostic model for pure tone air and bone conduction testing.
b) EB DIAGNOSTIC AUDIOMETER. 1969; for pure tone (air and bone conduction) and live or recorded speech testing; Model 400.
c) EB CLINICAL AUDIOMETER. 1970; for use by otologists and clinical audiologists; for pure tone (air and bone conduction) and live or recorded speech testing; Model 500-A.

For additional information, see 6:945.

[2035]

★Flowers-Costello Tests of Central Auditory Abilities, Experimental Edition. Grades kgn–6; 1970; 3 scores: low pass filtered speech, competing messages, total; Arthur Flowers, Mary Rose Costello, and Victor Small; Perceptual Learning Systems. *

REFERENCES THROUGH 1971

1. LEE, CONRAD EUGENE. *Relationships Between Central Auditory Abilities, I.Q. and Reading Achievement in Students Referred for Diagnosis.* Doctor's thesis, United States International University (San Diego, Calif.), 1971. (*DAI* 32:1919A)
2. MORGAN, ARTHUR T., JR. *An Analysis of Auditory Abilities as Predictors of First-Grade Reading Achievement.* Doctor's thesis, University of Houston (Houston, Tex.), 1971. (*DAI* 32:3125A)

CUMULATIVE NAME INDEX

Lee, C. E.: 1   Morgan, A. T.: 2

[2036]

★Four Tone Screening for Older Children and Adults. Ages 8 and over; 1973; for the detection of hearing impairments; Zenith Hearing Instrument Corporation. *

[2037]

Goldman-Fristoe-Woodcock Test of Auditory Discrimination. Ages 4 and over; 1970; GFW; speech-sound discrimination scores under 2 conditions: quiet, background noise; Ronald Goldman, Macalyne Fristoe, and Richard W. Woodcock; American Guidance Service, Inc. *

For additional information, reviews by Eugene C. Sheeley and Ralph L. Shelton, and an excerpted review by Barton B. Proger, see 7:938.

REFERENCES THROUGH 1971

1. GOLDMAN, RONALD, AND FRISTOE, MACALYNE. "Another Approach to Evaluating Speech Sound Discrimination." *Excep Children* 35(9):745–7 My '69. * (*PA* 44:18358)
2. CRUMP, WILLIAM DONALD. *Auditory Discrimination Among Disadvantaged Elementary School Children and Effects of Speech Sound Training on School-Related Language Skills.* Doctor's thesis, George Peabody College for Teachers (Nashville, Tenn.), 1971. (*DAI* 32:3820A)
3. GOLDMAN, RONALD; FRISTOE, MACALYNE W.; AND WOODCOCK, RICHARD W. "A New Dimension in the Assessment of Speech Sound Discrimination." *J Learn Dis* 4(7):364–8 Ag–S '71. * (*PA* 47:9673)
4. MCCOULSKEY, MILTON MACK. *Sentence Repetition Ability of Children With Language and/or Learning Disabilities.* Doctor's thesis, University of Texas (Austin, Tex.), 1971. (*DAI* 32:6830A)

CUMULATIVE NAME INDEX

Crump, W. D.: 2   Proger, B. B.: *exc*, 7:938
Fristoe, M.: 1   Sheeley, E. C.: *rev*, 7:938
Fristoe, M. W.: 3   Shelton, R. L.: *rev*, 7:938
Goldman, R.: 1, 3   Woodcock, R. W.: 3
McCoulskey, M. M.: 4

[2038]

*Grason-Stadler Audiometers. Ages 6 and over; 1950–73; 6 audiometers (AC operated); Grason-Stadler Co., Inc. *
a) DIAGNOSTIC AND SPEECH AUDIOMETERS. 1950–72; for pure tone (air and bone conduction) and speech testing in clinics and research; permits Békésy audiometry (except for manual model of 1701).
  1) *1701 Audiometer.* 1969–71; 3 sweep-frequency models: manual, automatic (117V, 234V).
  2) *1702 Audiometer.* 1972; fixed-frequency automatic and manual model.
  3) *1704 Audiometer.* 1972; fixed-frequency manual model.
b) SCREENING AUDIOMETERS. 1971–73.
  1) *1703 Recording Audiometer.* 1971; for pure tone air conduction testing in employment screening and hearing conservation programs; permits Békésy audiometry; 4 models: desk top (50HZ, 60HZ), portable (50HZ, 60HZ).
  2) *1707 Audiometer.* 1973; for use in schools and industry; portable manual model.
c) 1720 OTOADMITTANCE METER. 1971; for testing of middle ear pathologies in clinics and research; automatic model.

For additional information concerning earlier models, see 6:946 (6 references).

REFERENCES THROUGH 1971

1–6. See 6:946.
7. RINTELMANN, WILLIAM F., AND CARHART, RAYMOND. "Loudness Tracking by Normal Hearers via Bekesy Audiometers." *J Speech & Hearing Res* 7:79–93 Mr '64. * (*PA* 39:306)
8. WATSON, JOHN E., AND VOOTS, RICHARD J. "A Report on the Use of the Békésy Audiometer in the Performance of the Stenger Test." *J Speech & Hearing Disorders* 29:36–46 F '64. * (*PA* 39:518)
9. CODY, ROBERT C. "Instrumentation: SAL Technique With a Grason-Stadler Speech Audiometer." *J Speech & Hearing Disorders* 31:257–8 Ag '66. * (*PA* 41:135)
10. HOPKINSON, NORMA TROZZO. "Modifications of the Four Types of Békésy Audiograms." *J Speech & Hearing Disorders* 31:79–82 F '66. * (*PA* 40:9114)
11. FELDMAN, ALAN S.; ZELDNER, IRIS B.; AND GRIMES, CHARLES T. "A Modification of the Bing Test Utilizing Békésy

Audiometry." *J Speech & Hearing Disorders* 32:263–7 Ag '67. *
(*PA* 42:1571)

12. FULTON, ROBERT T. "Standard Puretone and Békésy
Audiometric Measures With the Mentally Retarded." *Am J
Mental Def* 72:60–73 Jl '67. * (*PA* 41:15716)

13. TOKAY, F. HARRY. *Validity and Reliability of Békésy
Audiometry With Preschool Age Children.* Doctor's thesis, Michigan State University (East Lansing, Mich.), 1967. (*DA* 28:
5229B)

14. SHEPHERD, DAVID C., AND GOLDSTEIN, ROBERT. "Intra-
subject Variability in Amplitude of Békésy Tracings and Its
Relation to Measures of Personality." *J Speech & Hearing Res*
11:523–35 S '68. * (*PA* 45:3372)

15. YOUNG, C. E. *An Investigation of Intra and Inter Testing
Relationships Between Selected Auditory Measures on Normal
Hearing, Mentally Retarded Adults.* Doctor's thesis, Oklahoma
State University (Stillwater, Okla.), 1968.

16. FULTON, ROBERT T., AND REID, MICHAEL J. "Békésy
Audiometry With the Retarded." *Am J Mental Def* 74(2):223–
30 S '69. * (*PA* 44:5545)

17. GRANITZ, DAVID WARREN. *An Evaluation of Diagnostic
Parameters of Békésy Audiometry.* Doctor's thesis, Louisiana
State University (Baton Rouge, La.), 1971. (*DAI* 32:4279B)

CUMULATIVE NAME INDEX

Carhart, R.: 7	Jerger, J. F.: 1–2
Cody, R. C.: 9	Price, L. L.: 5–6
Falck, V. T.: 6	Reid, M. J.: 16
Feldman, A. S.: 11	Rintelmann, W. F.: 7
Fulton, R. T.: 12, 16	Rose, D. E.: 4
Goldstein, R.: 14	Shepherd, D. C.: 14
Granitz, D. W.: 17	Tokay, F. H.: 13
Grimes, C. T.: 11	Voots, R. J.: 8
Herer, G.: 2	Watson, J. E.: 8
Hopkinson, N. T.: 10	Young, C. E.: 15
Jerger, J.: 3	Zeldner, I. B.: 11

[2039]

[Hearing of Speech Tests.] Ages 3–12; 1966; "administered live voice over speech audiometry test
equipment in standard audiological test rooms"; 2
tests; Bruce M. Siegenthaler and George S. Haspiel;
Speech and Hearing Clinic, Pennsylvania State University. *

a) THRESHOLD BY IDENTIFICATION OF PICTURES. TIP.
b) DISCRIMINATION BY IDENTIFICATION OF PICTURES.
DIP.

For additional information and a review by Eugene
C. Sheeley, see 7:939 (7 references).

REFERENCES THROUGH 1971

1–7. See 7:939.
8. SIEGENTHALER, BRUCE M.; PEARSON, JACK; AND LEZAK,
RAYMOND J. "A Speech Reception Threshold Test for Children."
J Speech & Hearing Disorders 19:360–6 S '54. * (*PA* 29:5156)

CUMULATIVE NAME INDEX

Bar-Or, O.: 6	Mullen, W. E.: 1
Bergstein, V.: 6	Pearson, J.: 8
Buskirk, E.: 6	Shearburn, C.: 6
Dahle, A. J.: 4	Sheeley, E. C.: *rev*, 7:939
Haas, J.: 6	Siegenthaler, B. M.: 3, 5, 7–8
Haspiel, G. S.: 2–3, 5	Skinner, J.: 6
Lezak, R. J.: 8	

[2040]

Hollien-Thompson Group Hearing Test. Grades
1 and over; 1968; HTGHT; pure tone screening test
requiring a standard audiometer equipped with multiple earphones; Harry Hollien and Carl L. Thompson; Language Research Associates, Inc. *

For additional information, see 7:940 (3 references).

REFERENCES THROUGH 1971

1–3. See 7:940.

CUMULATIVE NAME INDEX

Hollien, H.: 1–3	Wepman, J. M.: 3
Thompson, C. L.: 1–3	

[2041]

★Kindergarten Auditory Screening Test. Grades
kgn–1; 1971; KAST; 3 scores: speech in environmental noise, phonemic synthesis, same/different; Jack
Katz; Follett Publishing Co. *

[2042]

★Lindamood Auditory Conceptualization Test.
Grades kgn–12; 1971; LACT; 3 scores: isolated
sounds in sequence, sounds within syllable pattern,
total; Charles H. Lindamood and Patricia C. Lindamood; Teaching Resources Corporation. *

[2043]

★Maico Audiometers. Grades kgn and over; 1936–
72; 5 models; Maico Hearing Instruments. *
a) DIAGNOSTIC AND SPEECH AUDIOMETERS. 1962–70;
for pure tone (air and bone conduction) and speech
testing; 2 models (AC operated).

1) *Model MA-17.* 1969.
2) *Model MA-18.* 1970; professional model for use
by otologists and audiologists.

b) PORTABLE AUDIOMETERS. 1956–72; for testing in
schools and industry; 2 models (solid state).

1) *Model MA-19.* 1972; for air conduction testing.
2) *Model MA-20.* 1972; for air and bone conduction
testing.

c) DUAL CHANNEL RESEARCH AND DIAGNOSTIC AUDI-
OMETER. 1959–64; for pure tone (air and bone conduc-
tion) and speech testing in clinical and research work;
Model MA-24 (AC operated).

For additional information concerning earlier models, see 6:947 (2 references); see also 5:763 (4 references). For comments by Louis M. DiCarlo on
screening audiometers in general and specific comments on an earlier Maico portable model and three
other portable audiometers, see 6:942.

REFERENCES THROUGH 1971

1–4. See 5:763.
5–6. See 6:947.
7. ROBINSON, H. ALAN, AND HANSON, EARL. "Reliability of
Measures of Reading Achievement." *Read Teach* 21:307–13+
Ja '68. * (*PA* 42:17652)

CUMULATIVE NAME INDEX

Chase, H. C.: 4	Henry, S.: 1–2
Gaddie, B. G.: 6	Miller, V. R.: 3
Geyer, M. L.: 4	Robinson, H. A.: 7
Hanley, C. N.: 6	Williams, H. N.: 5
Hanson, E.: 7	Yankauer, A.: 4
Hegarty, I. E.: 3	

[2044]

★Maico Hearing Impairment Calculator. 1959–
65; for calculating percent of single-ear or binaural
impairment from hearing levels tested at frequencies
of 500, 1,000, and 2,000 cps; Maico Hearing Instruments. *

For additional information, see 6:948.

[2045]

The Massachusetts Hearing Test. Grades 1–16
and adults; 1948; method of group screening using
prescribed forms of scoring, signal presentation, and
calibration with any pure tone audiometer; method of
testing and instructions for scoring and interpretation
are presented in *J Acoust Soc Am* 20:697–703 S '48;
Philip W. Johnston; standardized instructions for
administering available from Massachusetts Department of Public Health, Division of Maternal and
Child Health. *

For additional information, see 6:949 (10 references).

REFERENCES THROUGH 1971

1–10. See 6:949.
11. FRIEDLANDER, GEORGE HARRIS. *Screening Tests of Hearing: An Investigation of the Relative Value of Four Screening
Tests of Hearing in Detecting Hearing Impairment.* Doctor's
thesis, New York University (New York, N.Y.), 1960. (*DA*
21:1288)

[2046]

Modified Rhyme Hearing Test. Grades 4 and over; 1963–68; MRHT; revision of Modified Rhyme Test ('63) by A. S. House and others; "for speech discrimination testing in audiology clinics"; E. James Kreul, James C. Nixon, Karl D. Kryter, Donald W. Bell, Janna S. Lang, and Earl D. Schubert; E. James Kreul. *

For additional information, see 7:941 (7 references).

REFERENCES THROUGH 1971

1–7. See 7:941.
8. ELKINS, EARLEEN F. "Evaluation of Modified Rhyme Test Results From Impaired- and Normal-Hearing Listeners." *J Speech & Hearing Res* 14(3):589–95 S '71. * (*PA* 48:3484)
9. NEFF, BROOKS E., JR. *Comparison of Speech Discrimination Scores on Three Monosyllabic Word Intelligibility Tasks and a Task Representing Everyday Speech Under Conditions of Low-Pass Filtering.* Doctor's thesis, University of Southern Mississippi (Hattiesburg, Miss.), 1971. (*DAI* 32:5512B)
10. PEREZ, EMILIO. *The Effects of Selected Frequency Distortion Upon the Perception of Speech by Hard-of-Hearing and Normal-Hearing Listeners.* Doctor's thesis, Ohio State University (Columbus, Ohio), 1971. (*DAI* 32:2830A)
11. SWAIN, CHARLES EUGENE, JR. *The Modified Rhyme Test: The Effects of Sensation Level on Discrimination Scores on an Adult Sensorineural Population.* Doctor's thesis, University of Illinois (Urbana, Ill.), 1971. (*DAI* 32:6105B)

[2047]

*National Teacher Examinations: Audiology. College seniors and teachers; 1970–73; Educational Testing Service. * For the testing program entry, see 869.

For additional information, see 7:942. For reviews of the testing program, see 7:582 (2 reviews), 6:700 (1 review), 5:538 (3 reviews), and 4:802 (1 review).

[2048]

New Group Pure Tone Hearing Test. Grades 1 and over; 1952–58; procedure for testing 10 children using a sweep check hearing test with any pure tone audiometer; directions for administering are presented in *J Speech & Hearing Disorders* 17:8–12 Mr '52; Philip W. Johnston; standardized instructions for administering available from Massachusetts Department of Public Health, Division of Maternal and Child Health. *

For additional information, see 6:950 (3 references).

REFERENCES THROUGH 1971

1–3. See 6:950.

[2049]

★Oliphant Auditory Discrimination Memory Test. Grades 2–6; 1971; OADMT; Genevieve Oliphant; Educators Publishing Service, Inc. *

REFERENCES THROUGH 1971

1. OLIPHANT, GENEVIEVE G. "A Study of Factors Involved in Early Identification of Specific Language Disability." *B Orton Soc* 20:81–92 '70. *

[2050]

★Oliphant Auditory Synthesizing Test. Grade 1; 1971; OAST; Genevieve Oliphant; Educators Publishing Service, Inc. *

REFERENCES THROUGH 1971

1. OLIPHANT, GENEVIEVE G. "A Study of Factors Involved in Early Identification of Specific Language Disability." *B Orton Soc* 20:81–92 '70. *

[2051]

The Pritchard-Fox Phoneme Auditory Discrimination Tests: Test Four. Grades kgn and over; 1970; PADT; 13 scores: 4 scores (initial, terminal, medial, total) in each of 3 categories (consonants, vowels, total), total; Alan S. Pritchard and Barbara S. Fox; Alpha Educational Associates. *

For additional information, see 7:943.

[2052]

Robbins Speech Sound Discrimination and Verbal Imagery Type Tests. Ages 4–8, 8 and over; 1948–58; 2 levels; Samuel D. Robbins and Rosa Seymour Robbins; Expression Co. *

a) [SPEECH SOUND DISCRIMINATION TESTS FOR YOUNG CHILDREN.] Ages 4–8; 1948–58; 2 tests.

1) *Verbal Imagery Test for Young Children.*

2) *Picture Speech Sound Discrimination Test for Young Children.*

b) SPEECH SOUND DISCRIMINATION TESTS FOR OLDER CHILDREN. Ages 8 and over; 1948.

For additional information and a review by Louis M. DiCarlo, see 6:938.

[2053]

[Rush Hughes (PB 50): Phonetically Balanced Lists 5–12.] Grades 2 and over; 1951; auditory discrimination; 8 lists on two records; no manual; [Central Institute for the Deaf]; [Technisonic Studios, Inc.]. *

For additional information, see 6:951 (6 references).

REFERENCES THROUGH 1971

1–6. See 6:951.
7. GOETZINGER, C. P.; DIRKS, D. D.; AND BAER, C. J. "Auditory Discrimination and Visual Perception in Good and Poor Readers." *Ann Otol Rhinol & Laryngol* 69:121–36 Mr '60. *
8. BOROS, VILMA. *Refinement of Selected Speech Discrimination Tests.* Doctor's thesis, University of Michigan (Ann Arbor, Mich.), 1964. (*DA* 25:7418)
9. BROOKS, ROBERT S. *The Relationship of Semantic Variables, Auditory Discrimination and Other Language Skills.* Doctor's thesis, University of Kansas (Lawrence, Kan.), 1964. (*DA* 26:539)
10. GIOLAS, THOMAS G. "Effectiveness of the Social Adequacy Index." *Ann Otol Rhinol & Laryngol* 75:1111–7 D '66. *
11. EPSTEIN, AUBREY; GIOLAS, THOMAS G.; AND OWENS, ELMER. "Familiarity and Intelligibility of Monosyllabic Word Lists." *J Speech & Hearing Res* 11:435–8 Jl '68. * (*PA* 42:16511)
12. LOVRINIC, JEAN HAHN; BURGI, ERNEST J.; AND CURRY, E. THAYER. "A Comparative Evaluation of Five Speech Discrimination Measures." *J Speech & Hearing Res* 11:372–81 Je '68. * (*PA* 42:17502)

[2054]

Screening Test for Auditory Perception, Experimental Edition. Grades 2–6; 1969; STAP; 6 scores: vowels, consonants, rhyming words, sound patterns, word differences, total; Geraldine M. Kimmell and Jack Wahl; Academic Therapy Publications. *

For additional information and reviews by Ann Brickner and Rosslyn Gaines, see 7:944 (1 reference).

REFERENCES THROUGH 1971

1. See 7:944.

CUMULATIVE NAME INDEX

Brickner, A.: *rev*, 7:944　　Kimmell, G. M.: 1
Gaines, R.: *rev*, 7:944　　Wahl, J.: 1

[2055]

Stycar Hearing Tests. Ages 6 months to 7 years (normal and mentally retarded); 1958–68; SHT; Mary D. Sheridan; distributed by NFER Publishing Co. Ltd. [England]. *

For additional information, see 7:945.

[2056]

Test of Listening Accuracy in Children. Ages 5–9; 1962–69; TLAC; formerly called *Picture Speech Discrimination Test;* 1969 picture cards identical with cards copyrighted 1962; Merlin J. Mecham, J. Lorin Jex, and J. Dean Jones; Brigham Young University Press. *

For additional information and reviews by Ann Brickner and Richard E. Shine, see 7:946.

REFERENCES THROUGH 1971

1. KINDER, LARAE M. *Relationships Between Listening Accuracy and Silent and Oral Reading Achievement of Remedial Reading Pupils.* Master's thesis, Brigham Young University (Provo, Utah), 1970.
2. MECHAM, MERLIN J. "Measurement of Verbal Listening Accuracy in Children." *J Learn Dis* 4(5):257–9 My '71. * (*PA* 47:8638)

CUMULATIVE NAME INDEX

Brickner, A.: *rev*, 7:946　　Mecham, M. J.: 2
Kinder, L. M.: 1　　Shine, R. E.: *rev*, 7:946

[2057]

★Test of Non-Verbal Auditory Discrimination, Experimental Edition. Ages 6–8; 1968; TENVAD; 6 scores: pitch, loudness, rhythm, duration, timbre, total; Norman A. Buktenica; the Author. *

REFERENCES THROUGH 1971

1. BUKTENICA, NORMAN A. *Relative Contributions of Auditory and Visual Perception to First-Grade Language Learning.* Doctor's thesis, University of Chicago (Chicago, Ill.), 1966.
2. BUKTENICA, NORMAN A. "Perceptual Mode Dominance: An Approach to Assessment of First Grade Reading and Spelling." Abstract. *Proc 76th Ann Conv Am Psychol Assn* 3:585–6 '68. * (*PA* 43:1459, title only)
3. DAVIS, JOAN CAROLYN. *Auditory Discrimination in Culturally Disadvantaged Children.* Master's thesis, Vanderbilt University (Nashville, Tenn.), 1970.
4. HORD, CHARLCIE LEE. *Effects of Preschool Language Instruction on Auditory Discrimination Skills.* Master's thesis, Vanderbilt University (Nashville, Tenn.), 1970.
5. HUTSON, KATHY. *Non-Verbal Auditory Discrimination in Culturally Disadvantaged Children.* Master's thesis, Vanderbilt University (Nashville, Tenn.), 1970.
6. MCBRIDE, GUY M. *Optimal Discriminative Differences in Loudness and Duration Between High and Low Performers in the Primary Grades: A Revision of the Buktenica Test of Non-Verbal Auditory Discrimination.* Master's thesis, George Peabody College (Nashville, Tenn.), 1970.
7. BUKTENICA, NORMAN A. "Auditory Discrimination: A New Assessment Procedure." *Excep Children* 38(3):237–40 N '71. * (*PA* 49:7743)
8. RENZULLI, JOSEPH S., AND HARTMAN, ROBERT K. "Scale for Rating Behaviorial Characteristics of Superior Students." *Excep Children* 38(3):243–8 N '71. * (*PA* 49:7940)
9. TINSLEY, DAVID GLOVER. *An Investigation of the Relationship Between the Test of Non-Verbal Auditory Discrimination and Certain Specific Reading Skills.* Master's thesis, George Peabody College (Nashville, Tenn.), 1971.

CUMULATIVE NAME INDEX

Buktenica, N. A.: 1–2, 7　　Hutson, K.: 5
Davis, J. C.: 3　　McBride, G. M.: 6
Hartman, R. K.: 8　　Renzulli, J. S.: 8
Hord, C. L.: 4　　Tinsley, D. G.: 9

[2058]

★Tracor Audiometers. Infants, grades kgn and over; 1955[?]–73; Tracor, Inc. *

a) RUDMOSE WARBLET 3000. Infants; 1965–67; for screening in newborn nurseries; Model RA-109 (battery operated).

b) BÉKÉSY RECORDING AUDIOMETERS. Grades kgn and over; 1966–72; for pure tone air conduction threshold testing in industrial and other mass testing; 2 audiometers (AC operated, individual and group models available for each).

　1) *Rudmose ARJ-4A.* 1966–69; automatic or manual.

　2) *Tracor Rudmose ARJ-4B.* 1972; automatic.

c) TRACOR RA-115 CLINICAL AUDIOMETER. Grades kgn and over; 1968–69; for pure tone (air and bone conduction) and live or recorded speech testing in hospitals, clinics, and medical offices; 2 models (AC operated): RA-115A (table model), RA-115AC (console).

d) TRACOR RUDMOSE CLINICAL BÉKÉSY AUDIOMETER. Grades kgn and over; 1972–73; for pure tone air and bone conduction testing in clinics and medical offices; Model RA-206 (AC operated).

e) TRACOR RUDMOSE MANUAL AUDIOMETERS. Grades kgn and over; 1972–73; for use in clinics, industry, and schools; 2 models (AC operated).

　1) *Model RA214.* 1972–73; for air conduction testing.

　2) *Model RA215.* 1973; for air and bone conduction testing.

f) ALLISON MODEL 22 CLINICAL AND RESEARCH AUDIOMETER. Grades kgn and over; 1964–72; for pure tone (air and bone conduction) and speech testing; Model 22A (solid state).

[2059]

Verbal Auditory Screening for Children. Ages 3–8; 1964–71; VASC; for the detection of preschool children requiring "more specialized diagnostic testing"; Zenith Hearing Instrument Corporation. *

For additional information, see 7:947 (6 references).

REFERENCES THROUGH 1971

1–6. See 7:947.
7. TEEL, JERRY RAY. *Verbal Auditory Screening With the Trainable Mentally Retarded.* Doctor's thesis, St. Louis University (St. Louis, Mo.), 1971. (*DAI* 33:1051A)

CUMULATIVE NAME INDEX

Dansinger, S.: 3　　Madow, A. A.: 3
Elshtain, E. L.: 6　　March, C.: 6
Garry, V.: 6　　Mencher, G. T.: 5
Griffing, T. S.: 1, 4　　Schaefer, T.: 6
Hartman, E. E.: 2　　Simonton, K. M.: 1, 4
Hedgecock, L. D.: 1, 4　　Teel, J. R.: 7
McCulloch, B. F.: 5　　Wannemacher, J. T.: 6

[2060]

★Washington Speech Sound Discrimination Test. Ages 3–5; 1971, c1969–71; WSSDT; Elizabeth Prather, Adah Miner, Margaret Anne Addicott, and Linda Sunderland; Interstate Printers & Publishers, Inc. *

[2061]

★Word Intelligibility by Picture Identification. Hearing impaired children ages 5–13; 1971; WIPI; speech discrimination; Mark Ross and Jay Lerman; Stanwix House, Inc. *

REFERENCES THROUGH 1971

1. MYATT, BETTY D., AND LANDES, BERNARD A. "Assessing Discrimination Loss in Children: A New Approach Toward a Picture Test." *Arch Otolaryng* 77:359–62 Ap '63. *
2. LERMAN, J. W.; ROSS, M.; AND McLAUCHLIN, R. M. "A Picture-Identification Test for Hearing-Impaired Children." *J Auditory Res* 5:273–8 O '65. *
3. ROSS, MARK, AND LERMAN, JAY. "A Picture Identification Test for Hearing-Impaired Children." *J Speech & Hearing Res* 13(1):44–53 Mr '70. * (*PA* 47:11382)

CUMULATIVE NAME INDEX

Landes, B. A.: 1   McLauchlin, R. M.: 2
Lerman, J.: 3   Myatt, B. D.: 1
Lerman, J. W.: 2   Ross, M.: 2, 3

[2062]

★ZECO Pure Tone Screening for Children. Ages 3–8; 1972; ZECO; Zenith Hearing Instrument Corporation. *

[2063–4]

*Zenith Audiometers. Preschool, grades kgn and over; 1959–73; 3 models; Zenith Hearing Instrument Corporation. *

a) ZENITH SPEECH SCREENING AUDIOMETER. Preschool; 1971; for speech tests using programmed cassettes; Model ZA-111.

b) ZENITH PURE TONE SCREENING AUDIOMETER. Grades kgn and over; 1972; for use in schools and industry; for pure tone air conduction testing; optional talkover module; Model ZA-112A.

c) ZENITH DIAGNOSTIC AUDIOMETER. Grades kgn and over; 1961–73; for use in schools, industry, clinics, and physicians' offices; for pure tone air and bone conduction testing with masking; optional speech module for live and recorded testing; Model ZA-113A.

For additional information concerning earlier models, see 6:953. For comments by Louis M. DiCarlo on screening audiometers in general and specific comments on an earlier Zenith portable model and three other portable audiometers, see 6:942.

[Out of Print Since TIP I]

Audivox Audiometers, 6:942 (1 review)
Children's Auditory Test, 6:944
How Well Can You Read Lips? (status unknown), 5: 579 (2 references)
Pressurelog Hearing Chart (status unknown), T:1663
Sonotone Pure-Tone Audiometers, 6:951a

SPEECH

[2065]

The Arizona Articulation Proficiency Scale, Revised. Mental ages 2–14 and over; 1963–70; AAPS; 1970 cards identical with cards copyrighted 1963 except for format and 3 new items; Janet Barker Fudala; Western Psychological Services. *

For additional information, see 7:948 (2 references) ; see also 6:307a (2 references).

REFERENCES THROUGH 1971

1–2. See 6:307a.
3–4. See 7:948.
5. GRAFF, JUDITH R. *A Study of the Articulation Abilities of a Group of Educable Familial Mentally Retarded Children.* Master's thesis, Ohio University (Athens, Ohio), 1964.
6. KING, SUSAN HOFMAN. *The Relationships Between Mental Age, Level of Language Functioning and Social Acceptability in the Trainable Mentally Retarded.* Doctor's thesis, Louisiana State University (Baton Rouge, La.), 1970. (*DAI* 31:5691B)

CUMULATIVE NAME INDEX

Barker, J.: 2   Jackson, B. R.: 3–4
Barker, J. O.: 1   King, S. H.: 6
England, G.: 2   Shanks, S. J.: 3–4
Graff, J. R.: 5   Sharpe, M. R.: 3–4

Word Intelligibility by Picture Identification

[2066]

★Boston Diagnostic Aphasia Examination. Aphasic patients; 1972; BDAE; 44 scores: severity rating, fluency (articulation rating, phrase length, verbal agility), auditory comprehension (word discrimination, body part identification, commands, complex material), naming (responsive, confrontation, animal, body part), oral reading (word reading, oral sentence), repetition (words, high-probability sentences, low-probability sentences), paraphasia (neologistic distortion, literal, verbal, extended), automatized speech (sequences, reciting), reading comprehension (symbol discrimination, word recognition, oral spelling, word picture matching, sentences and paragraphs), writing (mechanics, serial writing, primer-level dictation, written confrontation naming, spelling to dictation, sentences to dictation, narrative writing), music (singing, rhythm), parietal (drawing to command, stick memory, total fingers, right-left, arithmetic, clock setting, 3-dimensional blocks) plus 7 ratings: melodic line, phrase length, articulatory agility, grammatical form, paraphasia in running speech, word finding, auditory comprehension; Harold Goodglass with the collaboration of Edith Kaplan; Lea & Febiger. *

[2067]

★The Bzoch-League Receptive-Expressive Emergent Language Scale: For the Measurement of Language Skills in Infancy. Birth to age 3; 1970–71; also called *REEL Scale;* 3 scores: receptive, expressive, combined; Kenneth R. Bzoch and Richard League; Tree of Life Press. *

REFERENCES THROUGH 1971

1. BZOCH, KENNETH R., AND LEAGUE, RICHARD. *Assessing Language Skills in Infancy: A Handbook for the Multidimensional Analysis of Emergent Language.* Gainesville, Fla.: Tree of Life Press, 1971. Pp. 56. *
2. PROGER, BARTON B. "The Bzoch-League Receptive-Expressive Emergent Language Scale: A Review." *J Spec Ed* 5(4): 383–8 w '71. *

CUMULATIVE NAME INDEX

Bzoch, K. R.: 1   Proger, B. B.: 2
League, R.: 1

[2068]

Communicative Evaluation Chart From Infancy to Five Years. 1963–64; CEC; for "early detection of childhood communicative disabilities"; no manual; Ruth M. Anderson, Madeline Miles, and Patricia A. Matheny; Educators Publishing Service, Inc. *

For additional information, see 7:949.

[2069]

A Deep Test of Articulation. Reading levels grade 2 and under, grade 3 and over; 1964; DTA; for a screening deep test, see 2090; Eugene T. McDonald; Stanwix House, Inc. *

For additional information and reviews by Edgar R. Garrett and Harold A. Peterson, see 7:951 (6 references). For an excerpt from a related book review, see 7:B408.

REFERENCES THROUGH 1971

1–6. See 7:951.
7. WEIDNER, WILLIAM EDGAR. *The McDonald Deep Test: A Validity Study.* Doctor's thesis, Case Western Reserve University (Cleveland, Ohio), 1971. (*DAI* 32:1904B)
8. WOOLF, GERALD, AND PILBERG, ROCHELLE. "A Comparison of Three Tests of Auditory Discrimination and Their Relationship to Performance on a Deep Test of Articulation." *J Commun Disorders* (Netherlands) 3(4):239–49 Ja '71. * (*PA* 47:1424)

CUMULATIVE NAME INDEX

Appleton, P.: 5   Morris, H. L.: *exc,* 7:B408
Aungst, L. F.: 3   Palasek, J. R.: 6
Beaver, M. L.: 4   Peterson, H. A.: *rev,* 7:951
Dorsey, A. J.: 1   Pilberg, R.: 8
Garrett, E. R.: *rev,* 7:951   Weidner, W. E.: 7
McDonald, E. T.: 2   Woolf, G.: 8

[2070]

★**The Edinburgh Articulation Test.** Ages 3-0 to 6-0; 1971; EAT; T. T. S. Ingram, A. Anthony, D. Bogle, and M. W. McIsaac; Churchill Livingstone [Scotland]. * (United States distributor: Longman Inc.)

REFERENCES THROUGH 1971

1. ANTHONY, NAN, AND McISAAC, MARY W. "Notes on Patterns of Development Found by Using the Qualitative Phonetic Assessment Sheet of the Edinburgh Articulation Test." *Brit J Dis Commun* 5(2):148–64 O '70. *

CUMULATIVE NAME INDEX

Anthony, N.: 1   McIsaac, M. W.: 1

[2071]

Examining for Aphasia, Revised Edition. Adolescents and adults; 1946–54; Jon Eisenson; Psychological Corporation. *

For additional information, see P:76 (2 references); for a review by T. R. Miles and excerpted reviews by Louis M. DiCarlo and Laurance F. Shaffer, see 5:52 (3 references); for a review by D. Russell Davis and excerpted reviews by Nolan D. C. Lewis and one other, see 4:42; for a review by C. R. Strother and an excerpted review, see 3:39.

REFERENCES THROUGH 1971

1–3. See 5:52.
4–5. See P:76.
6. MIRON, MURRAY S. Appendix B, "A Psycholinguistic Analysis of Some Frequently Used Tests for Aphasia," pp. 176–99. In *Approaches to the Study of Aphasia: A Report of an Interdisciplinary Conference on Aphasia.* Edited by Charles E. Osgood and Murray S. Miron. Urbana, Ill.: University of Illinois Press, 1963. Pp. vii, 210. * (*PA* 38:4504)
7. MALPHURS, OJUS, JR. *Dyslexia in Adult Aphasics.* Doctor's thesis, University of Virginia (Charlottesville, Va.), 1970. (*DAI* 31:5691B)
8. FLICK, GRAD L., AND EDWARDS, KENNETH R. "Prediction of Lateralized Organic Brain Dysfunction With a Neuropsychological Test Battery: A Discriminant Function Analysis." *Newsl Res Psychol* 13(2):16–7 My '71. *

CUMULATIVE NAME INDEX

Blatt, B.: 1   Malphurs, O.: 7
Davis, D. R.: *rev,* 4:42   Miles, T. R.: *rev,* 5:52
DiCarlo, L. M.: *exc,* 5:52   Miron, M. S.: 6
Edwards, K. R.: 8   Nelson, L. A.: 5
Eisenson, J.: 2   Shaffer, L. F.: *exc,* 5:52
Feldman, L. P.: 3   Strother, C. R.: *rev,* 3:39
Flick, G. L.: 8   Tikofsky, R. S.: 4
Lewis, N. D. C.: *exc,* 4:42

[2072]

★**Fairview Language Evaluation Scale.** Mentally retarded; 1971; FLES; rating scale of language age 0–72 months; Alan Boroskin; Research Department, Fairview State Hospital. *

[2073]

★**The Fisher-Logemann Test of Articulation Competence.** Preschool to adult, grade 3 to adult; 1971; FLTAC; Hilda B. Fisher and Jerilyn A. Logemann; Houghton Mifflin Co. *

[2074]

Forms From Diagnostic Methods in Speech Pathology. Children and adults with speech problems; 1952–63; 20 forms consisting of coordination forms, rating scales, attitude surveys, and biographical questionnaires; Wendell Johnson, Frederic L. Darley, and D. C. Spriestersbach; Interstate Printers & Publishers, Inc. *

a) FORM 1, CHART OF SIGNIFICANT VARIATIONS IN SEVERITY OF THE STUTTERING PROBLEM SINCE ONSET.
b) FORM 2, GENERAL SPEECH BEHAVIOR RATING.
c) FORM 3, ARTICULATION TEST. Special printing of combined record and analysis sheets of *Templin-Darley Screening and Diagnostic Tests of Articulation.*

d) FORM 4, SPEECH MECHANISM EXAMINATION.
e) FORM 5, GENERAL VOICE QUALITY EXAMINATION.
f) FORM 6, SUPPLEMENTARY EXAMINATION FOR BREATHINESS.
g) FORM 7, SUPPLEMENTARY EXAMINATION FOR HARSHNESS.
h) FORM 8, SUPPLEMENTARY EXAMINATION FOR NASALITY.
i) FORM 9, MEASURES OF SPEECH AND LANGUAGE DEVELOPMENT.
j) FORM 10, MEASURES OF RATE OF SPEAKING AND ORAL READING.
k) FORM 11, MEASURES OF DISFLUENCY OF SPEAKING AND ORAL READING.
l) FORM 12, SPEAKING-TIME LOG.
m) FORM 13, CHECK LIST OF STUTTERING REACTIONS.
n) FORM 14, SCALE FOR RATING SEVERITY OF STUTTERING.
o) FORM 15, IOWA SCALE OF ATTITUDE TOWARD STUTTERING.
p) FORM 16, STUTTERER'S SELF-RATINGS OF REACTIONS TO SPEECH SITUATIONS.
q) FORM 17, MEASURES OF ADAPTATION OF STUTTERING AND ORAL READING RATE.
r) FORM 18, MEASURES OF STUTTERING CONSISTENCY.
s) FORM 19, IOWA UNIMANUAL HAND USAGE QUESTIONNAIRE.
t) FORM 20, IOWA PERFORMANCE TEST OF SELECTED MANUAL ACTIVITIES.

For additional information, see 6:308 (1 reference). For an excerpted review of the manual, see 6:B281.

REFERENCES THROUGH 1971

1. See 6:308.

CUMULATIVE NAME INDEX

Darley, F. L.: 1   Johnson, W.: 1
Hollien, H.: *exc,* 6:B281   Spriestersbach, D. C.: 1

[2075]

*****Goldman-Fristoe Test of Articulation.** Ages 2 and over; 1969–72; GFTA; 3 subtests: sounds in words, sounds in sentences, stimulability; subtest and total scores not recommended; Ronald Goldman and Macalyne Fristoe; American Guidance Service, Inc. *

For additional information, reviews by Margaret C. Byrne and Ralph L. Shelton, and an excerpted review by Dorothy Sherman, see 7:952 (4 references).

REFERENCES THROUGH 1971

1–4. See 7:952.

CUMULATIVE NAME INDEX

Byrne, M. C.: *rev,* 7:952   Shelton, R. L.: *rev,* 7:952
Fristoe, M.: 2–4   Sherman, D.: *exc,* 7:952
Fristoe, M. W.: 1   Thomas, L. S.: 1
Goldman, R.: 1–4

[2076]

Halstead Aphasia Test. Adults; 1949–55; HAT; pocket-size version of the out of print *Halstead-Wepman Aphasia Screening Test;* item responses grouped under 5 overlapping categories: agnosias (12 subcategories), aphaxias (7), anomia, dysarthria, paraphasia (2); Ward C. Halstead in cooperation with Joseph M. Wepman (test), Ralph M. Reitan (test), and Robert F. Heimburger (test); Industrial Relations Center, University of Chicago. *

For additional information, see 7:953 (10 references).

REFERENCES THROUGH 1971

1–10. See 7:953.
11. WHEELER, LAWRENCE. "Complex Behavorial Indices Weighted by Linear Discriminant Functions for the Prediction of Cerebral Damage." *Percept & Motor Skills* 19:907–23 D '64. * (*PA* 39:8357)
12. GOLDSTEIN, GERALD, AND SHELLY, CAROLYN H. "Field Dependence and Cognitive, Perceptual and Motor Skills in

Alcoholics." *Q J Studies Alcohol* 32(1A):29–40 Mr '71. * (*PA* 46:7095)

CUMULATIVE NAME INDEX

Cleeland, C. S.: 10
Davis, L. J.: 8
Goldstein, G.: 12
Halstead, W. C.: 1
Hopper, C. L.: 10
Maresca, V. K.: 5
Matthews, C. G.: 10
Miron, M. S.: 6

Reed, J. C.: 9
Reitan, R. M.: 4, 7–8
Shelly, C. H.: 12
Stock, J. C.: 3
Tikofsky, R. S.: 2
Wepman, J. M.: 1
Wheeler, L.: 4, 11

[2077]

The Houston Test for Language Development.
Ages 6 months to 3 years, 3–6 years; 1958–63; HTLD; Margaret Crabtree; Houston Test Co. *
For additional information, reviews by Margaret C. Byrne and Lawrence J. Turton, and an excerpted review by C. H. Ammons, see 7:954; see also 6:310 (1 reference).

REFERENCES THROUGH 1971
1. See 6:310.

CUMULATIVE NAME INDEX

Ammons, C. H.: *exc,* 7:954
Byrne, M. C.: *rev,* 7:954

Crabtree, M. C.: 1
Turton, L. J.: *rev,* 7:954

[2078]

Language Facility Test. Ages 3 and over; 1965–68; LFT; oral language facility independent of vocabulary, information, pronunciation, and grammar; John T. Dailey; Allington Corporation. *
For additional information and a review by Nicholas Anastasiow, see 7:955 (1 reference).

REFERENCES THROUGH 1971
1. See 7:955.

CUMULATIVE NAME INDEX

Anastasiow, N.: *rev,* 7:955   Lichtman, M. V.: 1

[2079]

Language Modalities Test for Aphasia. Adults; 1961; LMTA; Joseph M. Wepman and Lyle V. Jones; Industrial Relations Center, University of Chicago. *
For additional information and a review by Seymour Rigrodsky, see 7:956 (4 references); see also P:141 (8 references); for a review by T. R. Miles, see 6:312.

REFERENCES THROUGH 1971
1–8. See P:141.
9–12. See 7:956.
13. LOVELL, K., AND GORTON, A. "A Study of Some Differences Between Backward and Normal Readers of Average Intelligence." *Brit J Ed Psychol* 38:240–8 N '68. * (*PA* 43:7398)
14. BAR-DAVID, DAHLIA. "Adaptation of the Wepman-Jones Language Modalities Test for Aphasia Into Hebrew." *J Commun Disorders* (Netherlands) 4(1):44–50 Mr '71. * (*PA* 47:3473)

CUMULATIVE NAME INDEX

Archibald, Y. M.: 6–8
Bar-David, D.: 14
Carter, J. F.: 12
Fingerle, C. O.: 10
Goodfellow, R. L.: 2
Gorton, A.: 13
Jenkins, J. J.: 1
Jones, L. V.: 1, 3, 5–7
Kafes, P.: 3
Keenan, J. S.: 11

Lovell, K.: 13
Miles, T. R.: *rev,* 6:312
Miron, M. S.: 9
Radus, L.: 4
Rigrodsky, S.: *rev,* 7:956
Schuell, H.: 1
Spiegel, D. K.: 5
Wepman, J. M.: 1, 5–8
Zigler, E.: 3

[2080]

*Minnesota Test for Differential Diagnosis of Aphasia. Adults; 1965–73, c1948–73; MTDDA; used to classify subjects into 5 major and 2 minor categories of aphasia; 47 tests (9 auditory, 9 visual and reading, 15 speech and language, 10 visuomotor and writing, and 4 numerical relations and arithmetic processes); Hildred Schuell and Joyce W. Sefer (technical manual); University of Minnesota Press. *
For additional information and reviews by David

Jones and Seymour Rigrodsky, see 7:958 (7 references); see also P:172 (8 references).

REFERENCES THROUGH 1971
1–8. See P:172.
9–15. See 7:958.
16. KATSUKI, SHIBANOSUKE; NAGAE, KAZUHISA; OMAE, TERUO; AND KUROIWA, YOSHIGORO. "Minnesota Short Examination for Aphasia Modified for the Japanese: Preliminary Report With C.V.A. Cases." *Kyushu J Med Sci* (Japan) 14:257–70 O '63. *
17. MCPHAIL, FAY L. *A Comparison Between Selected Items on the Minnesota Test for Differential Diagnosis of Aphasia and the Token Test With Mild Adult Aphasics.* Master's thesis, University of North Dakota (Grand Forks, N.D.), 1970.
18. FELSENSTEIN, BERNARD. *Verbal Associative Strength as a Factor in Aphasia.* Doctor's thesis, Columbia University (New York, N.Y.), 1971. (*DAI* 32:3688B)
19. NABORS, MARTHA G. *A Study of the Effect of Temporal Redundancy on Aphasic Subjects' Performance on the Seashore Measures of Musical Talents.* Master's thesis, University of Tennessee (Knoxville, Tenn.), 1971.

CUMULATIVE NAME INDEX

Carroll, J. B.: 6
Carroll, V. B.: 3
Felsenstein, B.: 18
Fingerle, C. O.: 11
Freedheim, D. K.: 4
Hohman, L. B.: 4
Jenkins, J. J.: 6, 10
Jiménez-Pabón, E.: 10
Jones, D.: *rev,* 7:958
Katsuki, S.: 16
Keenan, J. S.: 12
Knapp, M. E.: 5

Kuroiwa, Y.: 16
McPhail, F. L.: 17
Massengill, J.: 13
Minear, D. J.: 14
Miron, M. S.: 9
Nabors, M. G.: 19
Nagae, K.: 16
Omae, T.: 16
Pettit, J. M.: 15
Rigrodsky, S.: *rev,* 7:958
Schuell, H.: 1–2, 6–8, 10

[2081]

*National Teacher Examinations: Speech-Communication and Theatre. College seniors and teachers; 1970–73; Educational Testing Service. * For the testing program entry, see 869.
For additional information concerning earlier forms, see 7:959. For reviews of the testing program, see 7:582 (2 reviews), 6:700 (1 review), 5:538 (3 reviews), and 4:802 (1 review).

[2082]

*National Teacher Examinations: Speech Pathology. College seniors and teachers; 1970–73; Educational Testing Service. * For the testing program entry, see 869.
For additional information concerning an earlier form, see 7:960. For reviews of the testing program, see 7:582 (2 reviews), 6:700 (1 review), 5:538 (3 reviews), and 4:802 (1 review).

[2083]

Nationwide Speech Examination. Grades 4–12; 1959–63; [Donald R. Honz]; Educational Stimuli. *
For additional information, see 6:313.

[2084]

★Northwestern Syntax Screening Test. Ages 3–7; 1969; NSST; 2 scores: receptive, expressive; [Laura Lee]; Northwestern University Press. *

REFERENCES THROUGH 1971
1. LEE, LAURA L. "A Screening Test for Syntax Development." *J Speech & Hearing Disorders* 35(2):103–12 My '70. * (*PA* 44:18339)
2. WARNER, JANET K. *Performance of a Group of Pre-School Children on the Northwestern Syntax Screening Test.* Master's thesis, Sacramento State College (Sacramento, Calif.), 1970.
3. HEIN, LADONA LOU. *Responses of Hard-of-Hearing Children to the Northwestern Syntax Screening Test.* Master's thesis, Sacramento State College (Sacramento, Calif.), 1971.

CUMULATIVE NAME INDEX

Hein, L. L.: 3
Lee, L. L.: 1

Warner, J. K.: 2

[2085]

The Orzeck Aphasia Evaluation. Mental and brain damaged patients; 1964–66; OAE; clinical interview form for recording presence of pathology (severe, moderate, mild, none) in 3 areas: apraxia, agnosia, sensory suppression; Arthur Z. Orzeck; Western Psychological Services. *

For additional information and reviews by Manfred J. Meier and Ralph M. Reitan, see 7:961.

[2086]

Photo Articulation Test. Ages 3–12; 1969; PAT; 4 scores: tongue sounds, lip sounds, vowel sounds, total; Kathleen Pendergast, Stanley E. Dickey, John W. Selmar, and Anton L. Soder; Interstate Printers & Publishers, Inc. *

For additional information, see 7:962 (2 references).

REFERENCES THROUGH 1971

1–2. See 7:962.

CUMULATIVE NAME INDEX

Jackson, B. R.: 1–2   Sharpe, M. R.: 1–2
Shanks, S. J.: 1–2

[2087]

***Porch Index of Communicative Ability.** Adults; 1967–71; PICA; aphasia; 22 scores: gestural (8 unnamed subtest scores and total), verbal (4 unnamed subtest scores and total), graphic (6 unnamed subtest scores and total), total; Bruce E. Porch; Consulting Psychologists Press, Inc. *

For additional information and a review by Daniel R. Boone, see 7:963 (1 reference).

REFERENCES THROUGH 1971

1. See 7:963.
2. BOLLINGER, RICK LEONARD. *Communication Abilities of "Chronic Brain Syndrome" Patients.* Doctor's thesis, University of Washington (Seattle, Wash.), 1970. (*DAI* 32:610B)
3. PORCH, BRUCE E. "Multidimensional Scoring in Aphasia Testing." *J Speech & Hearing Res* 14(4):776–92 D '71. *

CUMULATIVE NAME INDEX

Bollinger, R. L.: 2   Johnson, C. L.: 1
Boone, D. R.: *rev,* 7:963   Porch, B. E.: 3

[2088]

Predictive Screening Test of Articulation. Grade 1; 1968; PSTA; identification of children unlikely to master normal articulation by end of grade 2 without speech therapy; Charles Van Riper and Robert L. Erickson; Continuing Education Office, Western Michigan University. *

For additional information, see 7:964 (1 reference).

REFERENCES THROUGH 1971

1. See 7:964.
2. KIBBEY, STANLEY. *A Validation Study of the Predictive Screening Test of Articulation.* Master's thesis, Central Washington State College (Ellensburg, Wash.), 1970.
3. STOCKMAN, IDA MAE JONES. *Heterogeneity as a Confounding Factor When Predicting Change in Articulation Development.* Doctor's thesis, Pennsylvania State University (University Park, Pa.), 1971. (*DAI* 33:483B)

CUMULATIVE NAME INDEX

Erickson, R.: 1   Stockman, I. M. J.: 3
Kibbey, S.: 2   Van Riper, C.: 1

[2089]

***The Riley Articulation and Language Test, Revised.** Grades kgn–2; 1966–71; RALT; for rapid screening of children most in need of speech therapy; 4 scores: language proficiency, intelligibility, articulation function, language function; Glyndon D. Riley; Western Psychological Services. *

For additional information and a review by Raphael M. Haller of the original edition, see 7:967 (1 reference).

REFERENCES THROUGH 1971

1. See 7:967.

Haller, R. M.: *rev,* 7:967   Potter, R. E.: 1
Martin, E.: 1

[2090]

A Screening Deep Test of Articulation. Grades kgn and over; 1968; SDTA; for a lengthier deep test, see 2069; Eugene T. McDonald; Stanwix House, Inc. *

For additional information and reviews by Edgar R. Garrett and Harold A. Peterson, see 7:968 (2 references). For an excerpt from a related book review, see 7:B408.

REFERENCES THROUGH 1971

1–2. See 7:968.
3. STOCKMAN, IDA MAE JONES. *Heterogeneity as a Confounding Factor When Predicting Change in Articulation Development.* Doctor's thesis, Pennsylvania State University (University Park, Pa.), 1971. (*DAI* 33:483B)

CUMULATIVE NAME INDEX

Appleton, P.: 2   Morris, H. L.: *exc,* 7:B408
Garrett, E. R.: *rev,* 7:968 Peterson, H. A.: *rev,* 7:968
McDonald, E. T.: 1   Stockman, I. M. J.: 3

[2091]

***Screening Speech Articulation Test.** Ages 3.5–8.5; 1955–70; revision of *Speech Articulation Test for Young Children;* Merlin J. Mecham, J. Lorin Jex, and J. Dean Jones; Communication Research Associates. *

For additional information concerning the earlier edition, see 6:314.

[2092]

***Sklar Aphasia Scale, Revised 1973.** Brain damaged adults; 1966–73; SAS; 5 scores: auditory verbal comprehension, reading comprehension, oral expression, graphic production, total; Maurice Sklar; Western Psychological Services. *

For additional information and reviews by Arthur L. Benton and Daniel R. Boone of the original edition, see 7:970; see also P:247 (2 references).

REFERENCES THROUGH 1971

1–2. See P:247.

CUMULATIVE NAME INDEX

Benton, A. L.: *rev,* 7:970   Reeve, R. R.: 2
Boone, D. R.: *rev,* 7:970   Sklar, M.: 1

[2093]

Speech Defect Questionnaire. Ages 6 and over; 1933; Samuel D. Robbins; Expression Co. *

[2094]

Speech Diagnostic Chart. Grades 1–8; 1937–51; test words and sentences contained in the author's book entitled *Better Speech and Better Reading: A Practice Book;* Lucille D. Schoolfield; Expression Co. *

[2095]

Templin-Darley Tests of Articulation. Ages 3 and over; 1960–69; TDTA; 2 editions; Mildred C. Templin and Frederic L. Darley; Bureau of Educational Research and Service. *

a) TEMPLIN-DARLEY SCREENING AND DIAGNOSTIC TESTS OF ARTICULATION. Ages 3–8; 1960; 2 tests: screening test, total diagnostic test.

b) TEMPLIN-DARLEY TESTS OF ARTICULATION, [SECOND EDITION]. Ages 3 and over; 1960–69; 10 scores: screening test, consonant singles–initial and final, vowels, diphthongs and combination, clusters (4 scores), Iowa Pressure Articulation Test, total diagnostic test.

For additional information and a review by Raphael M. Haller of *b*, see 7:972 (16 references); for excerpted reviews by Harry Hollien and Al Knox of *a*, see 6:315 (9 references).

REFERENCES THROUGH 1971

1–9. See 6:315.

10–25. See 7:972.

26. TEMPLIN, MILDRED C. "A Note on a Screening Test of Articulation." *J Pediatrics* 45:443–5 O '54. * (*PA* 29:5989)

27. SPRIESTERSBACH, DUANE C., AND POWERS, GENE R. "Articulation Skills, Velopharyngeal Closure, and Oral Breath Pressure of Children With Cleft Palates." *J Speech & Hearing Res* 2:318–25 D '59. * (*PA* 34:6307)

28. WINITZ, HARRIS. "Language Skills of Male and Female Kindergarten Children." *J Speech & Hearing Res* 2:377–86 D '59. * (*PA* 34:5895)

29. GREIF, SUSAN ANN. *A Study of the Relationship Between Auditory, Visual, and Haptic Perception and Selected Parameters of Language and Articulation in Children With Central Processing Dysfunction.* Doctor's thesis, Wayne State University (Detroit, Mich.), 1971. (*DAI* 32:6717B)

30. KOOLS, JOSEPH A.; WILLIAMS, AMANDA F.; VICKERS, MARJORIE JO; AND COELL, ANN. "Oral and Limb Apraxia in Mentally Retarded Children With Deviant Articulation." *Cortex* (Italy) 7(4):387–400 D '71. * (*PA* 49:11425)

31. LEONARD, LAURENCE B., AND RITTERMAN, STUART I. "Articulation of /s/ as a Function of Cluster and Word Frequency of Occurrence." *J Speech & Hearing Res* 14(3):476–85 S '71. * (*PA* 48:3503)

32. RIGGLE, RICHARD RAY. *Correlations of Articulatory Disability With Various Aspects of Reading for Selected Modalities.* Doctor's thesis, University of Oregon (Eugene, Ore.), 1971. (*DAI* 32:2922A)

33. WOOLF, GERALD, AND PILBERG, ROCHELLE. "A Comparison of Three Tests of Auditory Discrimination and Their Relationship to Performance on a Deep Test of Articulation." *J Commun Disorders* (Netherlands) 3(4):239–49 Ja '71. * (*PA* 47:1424)

CUMULATIVE NAME INDEX

Betts, C. E.: 9
Coell, A.: 30
Darley, F. L.: 4, 7
Evans, J.: 11
Familant, R. P.: 18
Galanowsky, G. I.: 17
Gilmore, S. I.: 18
Greif, S. A.: 29
Haller, R. M.: *rev*, 7:972
Hollien, H.: *exc*, 6:315
Jackson, B. R.: 24–5
Jordan, E. P.: 6
Knox, A.: *exc*, 6:315
Kools, J. A.: 30
Krippner, S.: 13
Leonard, L. B.: 31
Morris, H. L.: 7, 16
Neal, W. R.: 15
Nichols, A. C.: 19–20
Nober, E. H.: 21
Pilberg, R.: 33

Pitzner, J. C.: 16
Powers, G. R.: 27
Rechner, J.: 23
Riggle, R. R.: 32
Ritterman, S. I.: 31
Rouse, V.: 4
Schlanger, B. B.: 17
Shanks, S. J.: 24–5
Sharpe, M. R.: 24–5
Siegel, G. M.: 8
Smith, P. B.: 22
Sprague, A. L.: 12
Spriestersbach, D. C.: 4, 7, 27
Templin, M. C.: 1–3, 5, 26
Trapp, E. P.: 11
Ufford, M. S.: 14
Vickers, M. J.: 30
Williams, A. F.: 30
Wilson, B. A.: 23
Winitz, H.: 10, 28
Woolf, G.: 33

[2096]

★**The Undergraduate Program Field Tests: Drama and Theatre Test.** College; 1971–73; test available to colleges for local administration; Educational Testing Service. * For the testing program entry, see 1062.

For reviews of the testing program, see 7:671 (2 reviews).

[2097]

Utah Test of Language Development, Revised Edition. Ages 1.5 to 14.5; 1958–67; UTLD; formerly called *Utah Verbal Language Development Scale*; a "direct-test" revision of the still-in-print "informant-interview" *Verbal Language Development Scale*; Merlin J. Mecham, J. Lorin Jex, and J. Dean Jones; Communication Research Associates, Inc. *

For additional information and reviews by Katharine G. Butler and William H. Perkins, see 7:973.

REFERENCES THROUGH 1971

1. MECHAM, MERLIN J., AND CASE, JAMES L. "Comparison of Two Approaches to the Assessment of Verbal Language Development of Mentally Retarded Children: A Review." *Dig Mental Retard* 5:29–32 f '68. *

2. GREIF, SUSAN ANN. *A Study of the Relationship Between Auditory, Visual, and Haptic Perception and Selected Parameters of Language and Articulation in Children With Central Processing Dysfunction.* Doctor's thesis, Wayne State University (Detroit, Mich.), 1971. (*DAI* 32:6717B)

3. MECHAM, MERLIN J. "Differential Evaluation of Verbal Language Disabilities in Children." *Calif J Commun Disorders* 1(2):81–5 My '71. *

4. SILOAC, KENNETH THOMAS. *An Investigation of Selected Perceptual Abilities in Educable Retarded and Normal Children.* Doctor's thesis, Wayne State University (Detroit, Mich.), 1971. (*DAI* 32:6719B)

CUMULATIVE NAME INDEX

Butler, K. G.: *rev*, 7:973
Case, J. L.: 1
Greif, S. A.: 2

Mecham, M. J.: 1, 3
Perkins, W. H.: *rev*, 7:793
Siloac, K. T.: 4

[2098]

***Verbal Language Development Scale.** Birth to age 15; 1958–71; VLDS; extension of the communication section of *Vineland Social Maturity Scale*; behavior checklist for use in interviewing adult informants; for a "direct-test" version of this scale, see 2097; Merlin J. Mecham; American Guidance Service, Inc. *

For additional information and reviews by Katharine G. Butler and William H. Perkins, see 7:974 (1 reference) ; see also 6:316 (7 references).

REFERENCES THROUGH 1971

1–7. See 6:316.

8. See 7:974.

9. MECHAM, MERLIN J., AND CASE, JAMES L. "Comparison of Two Approaches to the Assessment of Verbal Language Development of Mentally Retarded Children: A Review." *Dig Mental Retard* 5:29–32 f '68. *

10. GREEN, JOSEPH B., AND HARTLAGE, LAWRENCE C. "Comparative Performance of Epileptic and Nonepileptic Children and Adolescents." *Dis Nerv System* 32(6):418–21 Je '71. * (*PA* 48:3530)

11. JORDAN, THOMAS E. "Early Developmental Adversity and the First Two Years of Life." *Multiv Behav Res Monogr* 6(1):1–80 '71. * (*PA* 49:2132)

12. WEINER, PAUL S. "The Cognitive Functioning of Language Deficient Children." *Cognitive Studies* 2:338–63 '71. *

CUMULATIVE NAME INDEX

Barnard, L. W.: 4
Bown, J. C.: 7
Butler, K. G.: *rev*, 7:974
Case, J. L.: 9
Green, J. B.: 10
Hartlage, L. C.: 10

Jordan, T. E.: 11
Mecham, M. J.: 1–2, 5, 7, 9
Perkins, W. H.: *rev*, 7:974
Tauber, R.: 8
Weiner, P. S.: 12
Williams, W. G.: 3, 6

[2099]

Weidner-Fensch Speech Screening Test. Grades 1–3; 1955; William E. Weidner and Edwin A. Fensch; Psychometric Affiliates. *

For additional information and a review by Robert S. Cathcart (with Louise B. Scott), see 5:221.

[Out of Print Since TIP I]

Evaluating the Effectiveness of Oral English, T:522
Graduate Record Examinations Advanced Tests: Speech, 6:309 (1 reference)
Integrated Articulation Test for Use With Children With Cerebral Palsy, 6:311 (9 references)
Laradon Articulation Scale, 7:957 (1 review)
Speech Correction Records, T:526

VOCATIONS

[2100]

★ACT Assessment of Career Development. Grades 8–11; 1973, c1972–73; ACD; "career development behavior generally thought to be of practical significance in evaluating and modifying school career guidance programs"; "interpretation of ACD scores to individual students is not recommended"; 11 scores: occupational knowledge (occupational characteristics, occupational preparation requirements), exploratory occupational experiences (social-health-personal services, business sales and management, business operations, technologies and trades, natural-social-medical sciences, creative and applied arts, total), career planning (knowledge, involvement), plus statistical summaries of responses to 42 specific items and up to 19 locally developed items; Dale Prediger in conjunction with Bert Westbrook and John Roth; American College Testing Program. *

[2101]

★ACT Career Planning Program. Entrants to postsecondary educational institutions; 1970–73; CPP; test booklet title is *Career Planning Profile;* a battery of interest, ability, and background measures which may be administered by participating institutions; in addition to the scores and biographical details listed below, the Student Report lists ratings of interests, competencies, abilities, and expectancies of educational success in each of the 8 vocational interest areas; optional institutional summary available; colleges which administer the *Student Follow-Up Questionnaire* at the end of the first term may also receive an optional institutional report presenting local validity data on the CPP; 3 parts; American College Testing Program. *
a) VOCATIONAL INTEREST PROFILE. 8 scores: trades, technical, science, health, arts, social service, business contact, business detail.
b) ABILITY MEASURES. 8 scores: mechanical reasoning, numerical computation, mathematics usage, space relations, reading skills, language usage, clerical skills, nonverbal reasoning.
c) STUDENT INFORMATION SECTION. Background, educational plans, student concerns, work orientation, and career-related competencies.

REFERENCES THROUGH 1971
1. *Handbook for the ACT Career Planning Profile, 1970–71 Edition.* Iowa City, Iowa: ACT Publications, 1970. Pp. viii, 52. *
2. *Career Planning Profile National Norms for Vocational-Technical Students Beyond High School.* Iowa City, Iowa: American College Testing Program, Inc., 1971. Pp. vii, 31, plus unnumbered appendices. *
3. COLE, NANCY S., AND HANSON, GARY R. "An Analysis of the Structure of Vocational Interests." *ACT Res Rep* 40:1–17 Ja '71. * (*PA* 47:1843)
4. COLE, NANCY S., AND HANSON, GARY R. "An Analysis of the Structure of Vocational Interests." *J Counsel Psychol* 18(5): 478–86 S '71. * (*PA* 47:3679)

CUMULATIVE NAME INDEX
Cole, N. S.: 3–4   Hanson, G. R.: 3–4

[2102]

*[Aptitude Inventory.] Employee applicants; 1957–71; 1 test published in the same form under 3 titles; 4 scores for each test: intelligent job performance,

leadership qualities, proper job attitude, relations with others; John C. Denton; Psychological Business Research. *
a) MANAGEMENT APTITUDE INVENTORY. Applicants for management and supervisory positions; 1957–71; MAI.
b) EMPLOYMENT APTITUDE INVENTORY. Applicants for office and factory positions; 1957–61; EAI.
c) SALES APTITUDE INVENTORY. Applicants for sales positions; 1957–63; SAI.
For additional information, reviews by Leonard W. Ferguson and C. E. Jurgensen, and an excerpted review by Laurence Siegel, see 6:1024 (1 reference).

REFERENCES THROUGH 1971
1. See 6:1024.
2. GUION, ROBERT M. "Synthetic Validity in a Small Company: A Demonstration." *Personnel Psychol* 18:49–63 sp '65. * (*PA* 39:16490)

CUMULATIVE NAME INDEX
Denton, J. C.: 1   Jurgensen, C. E.: *rev,* 6:1024
Ferguson, L. W.: *rev,* 6:1024   Siegel, L.: *exc,* 6:1024
Guion, R. M.: 2

[2103]

★Career Maturity Inventory. Grades 6–12; 1973; CMI; formerly called *Vocational Development Inventory;* 2 tests; John O. Crites; CTB/McGraw-Hill. *
a) ATTITUDE SCALE.
b) COMPETENCE TEST, RESEARCH EDITION. 5 scores: self-appraisal, occupational information, goal selection, planning, problem solving.

REFERENCES THROUGH 1971
1. DAS, AJIT KUMAR. *The Effect of Counseling on the Vocational Maturity of a Group of Potential Drop-Outs From High School.* Doctor's thesis, State University of Iowa (Iowa City, Iowa), 1962. (*DA* 23:2788)
2. HALL, DONALD W. "The Vocational Development Inventory: A Measure of Vocational Maturity in Adolescence." *Personnel & Guid J* 41:771–5 My '63. *
3. JESSEE, BILLY EUGENE. *The Effects of Individual Counseling and Group Guidance With Eighth Grade Boys on Their Vocational Maturity the Following Year.* Doctor's thesis, Arizona State University (Tempe, Ariz.), 1963. (*DA* 25:6389)
4. HARLAN, GRADY EDWARD. *A Comparison of Differences in Selected Characteristics Among High School Seniors, College Freshmen, Trade School Students, Technical School Students, and Business School Students.* Doctor's thesis, State University of Iowa (Iowa City, Iowa), 1964. (*DA* 25:5016)
5. CRITES, JOHN O. "Measurement of Vocational Maturity in Adolescence: 1, Attitude Test of the Vocational Development Theory." *Psychol Monogr* 79(2):1–36 '65. * (*PA* 39:10869)
6. DRAHOZAL, EDWARD CHARLES. *A Study of Selected Characteristics of Senior High School Students and Their Perceptions of Their Counselor's Role in the Post High School Decision.* Doctor's thesis, State University of Iowa (Iowa City, Iowa), 1965. (*DA* 26:2544)
7. JESSEE, BILL E., AND HEINMANN, ROBERT A. "The Effects of Counseling and Group Guidance on the Vocational Maturity of Ninth Grade Boys." *J Ed Res* 59:68–72 O '65. * (*PA* 40: 3397)
8. HARRIS, JOHN WILLIAM, JR. *The Effect of Vocational Development and Family Social Status on the Academic Performance of Male Freshmen at Middle Tennessee State University.* Doctor's thesis, University of Tennessee (Knoxville, Tenn.), 1966. (*DA* 27:2828A)
9. MALONE, FRANCIS EDWARD, JR. *A Study of Students Enrolled in Post-High School Public Vocational Education Programs in Iowa During the 1964–1965 School Year.* Doctor's thesis, University of Iowa (Iowa City, Iowa), 1966. (*DA* 27: 678A)
10. MYERS, WAYNE PRUITT. *The Effect of Neighborhood Youth Corps Upon Vocational Development Variables of Rural Southern*

Appalachian Youth. Doctor's thesis, University of Tennessee (Knoxville, Tenn.), 1966. (*DA* 27:650A)

11. BARTLETT, WILLIS EDWARD. *Psychological Needs and Vocational Maturity of Manpower Trainees.* Doctor's thesis, Ohio State University (Columbus, Ohio), 1967. (*DA* 28:3456A)

12. CRITES, JOHN O., AND SEMLER, IRA J. "Adjustment, Educational Achievement, and Vocational Maturity as Dimensions of Development in Adolescence." *J Counsel Psychol* 14:489–96 N '67. * (*PA* 42:3783)

13. WILLIAMS, RODNEY HOWE. *The Relationship Between the Vocational Development and Scholastic Achievement of Male College Students: A Correlational Analysis and Evaluation of the Relationship Between Scores of Vocational Maturity, Vocational Maladjustment, Intellectual Capacity, and Scholastic Index.* Doctor's thesis, New York University (New York, N.Y.), 1967. (*DA* 28:1318A)

14. ASHBURY, FRANK A. "Vocational Development of Rural Disadvantaged Eighth-Grade Boys." *Voc Guid Q* 17:109–13 D '68. *

15. BARTLETT, WILLIS E. "Vocational Maturity and Personality Variables of Manpower Trainees." *Voc Guid Q* 17:104–8 D '68. *

16. COX, STEVEN GRAHN. *A Study of Relationships Between Student Scores on Various Predictor Measures and Vocational Success of Students Who Were Followed Up One and Five Years Following Training in Selected Private Trade, Technical, and Business Schools.* Doctor's thesis, University of Iowa (Iowa City, Iowa), 1968. (*DA* 29:3827A)

17. OSIPOW, SAMUEL H., AND ALDERFER, RICHARD D. "The Effects of a Vocationally Oriented Speech Course on the Vocational Planning Behavior of High School Students." *Personnel & Guid J* 47:244–8 N '68. *

18. SHIRTS, ROBERT GARRY. *Response Style in the Vocational Development Inventory.* Doctor's thesis, University of Utah (Salt Lake City, Utah), 1968. (*DA* 29:761B)

19. CONDUFF, ELIZABETH. *Personality Characteristics and Adjustment of Adolescents With Regard to Vocational Maturity.* Master's thesis, University of Tennessee (Knoxville, Tenn.), 1969.

20. NICHOL, JOHN STEWART. *The Use of Vocational Discussion in Small Groups to Increase Vocational Maturity.* Doctor's thesis, Arizona State University (Tempe, Ariz.), 1969. (*DAI* 30:3733A)

21. ANSELL, EDGAR MERLE. *An Assessment of Vocational Maturity of Lower-Class Caucasians, Lower-Class Negroes and Middle-Class Caucasians in Grades Eight Through Twelve.* Doctor's thesis, State University of New York (Buffalo, N.Y.), 1970. (*DAI* 31:2094A)

22. DOMENICHETTI, MADONNA. *Work Values in Adolescence as a Function of Vocational Maturity.* Doctor's thesis, Catholic University of America (Washington, D.C.), 1970. (*DAI* 31:1574A)

23. HANLEY, DENNIS EUGENE. *The Effects of Short-Term Counseling Upon High School Underachievers' Measured Self-Concepts, Academic Achievement, and Vocational Maturity.* Doctor's thesis, Purdue University (Lafayette, Ind.), 1970. (*DAI* 31:5125A)

24. JALKANEN, ARTHUR WILHELM. *A Comparison of Vocational Attitudes and Job Aspirations of Urban and Suburban School Students.* Doctor's thesis, Wayne State University (Detroit, Mich.), 1970. (*DAI* 31:4464A)

25. MAYNARD, PETER E., AND HANSEN, JAMES C. "Vocational Maturity Among Inner-City Youths." *J Counsel Psychol* 17(5):400–4 S '70. * (*PA* 45:3005)

26. MAYNARD, PETER ELWOOD. *Assessing the Vocational Maturity of Inner-City Youths.* Doctor's thesis, State University of New York (Buffalo, N.Y.), 1970. (*DAI* 31:4468A)

27. MUNSON, PAUL JONATHAN. *An Investigation of the Relationship of Values, and Curriculum Selection to Vocational Maturity.* Doctor's thesis, University of Virginia (Charlottesville, Va.), 1970. (*DAI* 31:4470A)

28. SCHRADER, CHARLES HENRY. *Vocational Choice Problems: Indecision vs. Indecisiveness.* Doctor's thesis, University of Iowa (Iowa City, Iowa), 1970. (*DAI* 31:3694B)

29. COX, STEVEN G. "Do Educational Measures Predict Vocational Success?" *Voc Guid Q* 19(4):271–4 Je '71. * (*PA* 48:1981)

30. CRITES, JOHN O. "Acquiescence Response Style and the Vocational Development Inventory." *J Voc Behav* 1(2):189–200 Ap '71. * (*PA* 47:11693)

31. CRITES, JOHN O. *The Maturity of Vocational Attitudes in Adolescence.* APGA Inquiry Series Number 2. Washington, D.C.: American Personnel and Guidance Association, 1971. Pp. 112. *

32. DONAHUE, MICHAEL A. *College Placement: An Exploratory Investigation of the Employment Selection Process and Certain Correlates of Vocational Development.* Doctor's thesis, Purdue University (Lafayette, Ind.), 1971. (*DAI* 32:735A)

33. KAPES, JEROME THEODORE. *The Relationship Between Selected Characteristics of Ninth Grade Boys and Curriculum Selection and Success in Tenth Grade.* Doctor's thesis, Pennsylvania State University (University Park, Pa.), 1971. (*DAI* 32:6131A)

34. MEERBACH, JOHN CALVIN. *A Study of the Relationship of Creativity, Vocational Maturity and Vocational Choice Among Eighth Grade Students.* Doctor's thesis, University of Toledo (Toledo, Ohio), 1971. (*DAI* 32:3695A)

35. STENSON, ORVIS J. *The Effect of Multi-Type Short Term Counseling on the Vocational Maturity of Male Tenth Grade Vocational Students.* Doctor's thesis, University of Montana (Missoula, Mont.), 1971. (*DAI* 32:2425A)

CUMULATIVE NAME INDEX

Alderfer, R. D.: 17
Ansell, E. M.: 21
Ashbury, F. A.: 14
Bartlett, W. E.: 11, 15
Conduff, E.: 19
Cox, S. G.: 16, 29
Crites, J. O.: 5, 12, 30–1
Das, A. K.: 1
Domenichetti, M.: 22
Donahue, M. A.: 32
Drahozal, E. C.: 6
Hall, D. W.: 2
Hanley, D. E.: 23
Hansen, J. C.: 25
Harlan, G. E.: 4
Harris, J. W.: 8

Heinmann, R. A.: 7
Jalkanen, A. W.: 24
Jessee, B. E.: 3, 7
Kapes, J. T.: 33
Malone, F. E.: 9
Maynard, P. E.: 25–6
Meerbach, J. C.: 34
Munson, P. J.: 27
Myers, W. P.: 10
Nichol, J. S.: 20
Osipow, S. H.: 17
Schrader, C. H.: 28
Semler, I. J.: 12
Shirts, R. G.: 18
Stenson, O. J.: 35
Williams, R. H.: 13

[2104]

★**Classification Test Battery.** Illiterate and semiliterate applicants for unskilled and semiskilled mining jobs; 1970–71; CTB; replaces *General Adaptability Battery;* nonverbal reasoning and spatial ability; tests administered at centers established by firms employing the publisher's consultation and training services; 4 tests, 4 scores: 3 scores listed below (*b, c, d*), total; pre-test instructions in any of 9 African languages or in English, all test instructions presented by silent motion pictures; National Institute for Personnel Research [South Africa]. *
a) COLOURED PEG BOARD. Unscored "buffer test."
b) PATTERN REPRODUCTION TEST.
c) CIRCLES TEST.
d) FORM SERIES TEST.

[2105]

The Dailey Vocational Tests. Grades 8–12 and adults; 1964–65; DVT; 3 tests; John T. Dailey and Kenneth B. Hoyt (manual); Houghton Mifflin Co. *
a) TECHNICAL AND SCHOLASTIC TEST. See 974.
b) SPATIAL VISUALIZATION TEST. See 2270.
c) BUSINESS ENGLISH TEST. See 57.
For additional information, reviews by Thomas S. Baldwin and Benjamin Shimberg, and excerpted reviews by Betty W. Ellis and Jack C. Merwin, see 7:976 (5 references).

REFERENCES THROUGH 1971

1–5. See 7:976.
6. COX, STEVEN G. "Do Educational Measures Predict Vocational Success?" *Voc Guid Q* 19(4):271–4 Je '71. * (*PA* 48:1981)

CUMULATIVE NAME INDEX

Baldwin, T. S.: *rev,* 7:976
Cox, S. G.: 3, 6
Doerr, J. J.: 2
Ellis, B. W.: *exc,* 7:976
Malone, F. E.: 1

Merwin, J. C.: *exc,* 7:976
Passmore, J. L.: 4
Shimberg, B.: *rev,* 7:976
Stone, T. C.: 5

[2106]

*****ETSA Tests.** Job applicants; 1960–73, c1957–66; formerly called *Aptitest;* 8 tests; publisher recommends use of Tests 1A, 8A, and one other; manual and technical handbook by S. Trevor Hadley and George A. W. Stouffer, Jr.; tests by Psychological Services Bureau; Educators'-Employers' Tests & Services Associates. *
a) ETSA TEST 1A, GENERAL MENTAL ABILITY TEST. See 378.
b) ETSA TEST 2A, OFFICE ARITHMETIC TEST. See 726.
c) ETSA TEST 3A, GENERAL CLERICAL ABILITY TEST. See 2128.

d) ETSA TEST 4A, STENOGRAPHIC SKILLS TEST. See 2160.
e) ETSA TEST 5A, MECHANICAL FAMILIARITY TEST. See 2417.
f) ETSA TEST 6A, MECHANICAL KNOWLEDGE TEST. See 2419.
g) ETSA TEST 7A, SALES APTITUDE TEST. See 2405.
h) ETSA TEST 8A, PERSONAL ADJUSTMENT INDEX. See 1312.

For additional information and reviews by Marvin D. Dunnette and Raymond A. Katzell, see 6:1025.

[2107]

*Flanagan Industrial Tests. Business and industry; 1960–70; FIT; adaptation for business use of the *Flanagan Aptitude Classification Tests;* 2 series; John C. Flanagan; Science Research Associates, Inc. *
a) FORM A SERIES. Job applicants and employees; 1960–65; 18 tests.
  1) *Arithmetic.*
  2) *Assembly.*
  3) *Components.*
  4) *Coordination.*
  5) *Electronics.*
  6) *Expression.*
  7) *Ingenuity.*
  8) *Inspection.*
  9) *Judgment and Comprehension.*
  10) *Mathematics and Reasoning.*
  11) *Mechanics.*
  12) *Memory.*
  13) *Patterns.*
  14) *Planning.*
  15) *Precision.*
  16) *Scales.*
  17) *Tables.*
  18) *Vocabulary.*
b) FORM AA SERIES. Entry level job applicants; 1960–70; 7 tests; this revision of the Form A series involves changes in time limits and directions and the rewording, rearrangement, and omission of items to make the tests more suitable for entry level job applicants; no manual.
  1) *Assembly.*
  2) *Components.*
  3) *Electronics.*
  4) *Ingenuity.*
  5) *Inspection.*
  6) *Memory.*
  7) *Scales.*
For additional information, reviews by C. J. Adcock and Robert C. Droege, and an excerpted review by John L. Horn, see 7:977 (1 reference).

REFERENCES THROUGH 1971
1. See 7:977.

CUMULATIVE NAME INDEX
Adcock, C. J.: *rev,* 7:977   Horn, J. L.: *exc,* 7:977
Droege, R. C.: *rev,* 7:977   Penfield, R. V.: 1

[2108]

Individual Placement Series. High school (*h* only) and adults; 1957–66; 8 tests, also listed separately; J. H. Norman: Personnel Research Associates, Inc. *
a) ACADEMIC ALERTNESS "AA." 1957–66; 7 scores: general knowledge, arithmetic, vocabulary, reasoning ability, logical sequence, accuracy, total.
b) PERFORMANCE ALERTNESS "PA" (WITH PICTURES). 1961–66.
c) READING ADEQUACY "READ" TEST. 1961–66; 3 scores: reading rate, comprehension, corrected reading rate.
d) SURVEY OF CLERICAL SKILLS "SOCS." 1959–66; 5 scores: spelling, office math, office terms, filing, grammar.

e) TYPING TEST. 1959–66.
f) SHORTHAND TEST. 1960–66.
g) SURVEY OF PERSONAL ATTITUDE "SPA" (WITH PICTURES). 1960-66; 3 scores: social attitude, personal frankness, aggressiveness.
h) OCCUPATIONAL INTEREST SURVEY "OIS" (WITH PICTURES). High school and adults; 1959–66; 9 scores: scientific, social service, literary, agricultural, business, mechanical, musical, clerical, artistic.

For additional information, see 7:979. For reviews of the personal attitude test, see 7:147 (2 reviews); the academic alertness test, see 7:332 (1 review); the performance alertness test, see 7:372 (1 review); the reading adequacy test, see 7:773 (1 review); the typing test, see 7:1008 (1 review); and the occupational interest test, see 7:1028 (2 reviews).

[2109]

*New Mexico Career Education Test Series. Grades 9–12; 1973; "designed to assess specific learner objectives in the area of career education"; 6 tests; Charles C. Healy and Stephen P. Klein; Monitor. *
a) NM ATTITUDE TOWARD WORK TEST.
b) NM CAREER PLANNING TEST.
c) NM CAREER ORIENTED ACTIVITIES CHECKLIST.
d) NM KNOWLEDGE OF OCCUPATIONS TEST.
e) NM JOB APPLICATION PROCEDURES TEST.
f) NM CAREER DEVELOPMENT TEST.

[2110]

Personal History Index. Job applicants; 1963–67; PHI; for research use only; 8 scores: school achievement, higher educational achievement, drive, leadership and group participation, financial responsibility, early family responsibility, parental family adjustment, stability; Melany E. Baehr, Robert K. Burns, and Robert N. McMurry; Industrial Relations Center, University of Chicago. *

For additional information and a review by John K. Hemphill, see 7:981 (5 references).

REFERENCES THROUGH 1971
1–5. See 7:981.

CUMULATIVE NAME INDEX
Baehr, M. E.: 1–3   Huber, N. A.: 4
Froemel, E. C.: 3   Marks, L. G.: 5
Furcon, J. E.: 3   Williams, G. B.: 1–2
Hemphill, J. K.: *rev,* 7:981

[2111]

Steward Basic Factors Inventory (1960 Edition). Applicants for sales and office positions; 1957–63; revision of *Steward Sales Aptitude Inventory;* originally called *Steward Vocational Fitness Inventory;* 14 scores: business knowledge (vocabulary, arithmetic, total), dominance, personal adjustment, occupational interests (clerical, artistic, supervisory, accounting, writing, selling, mechanical, total), total; Verne Steward; Steward-Mortensen & Associates. *

For additional information and reviews by Leonard V. Gordon and Lyman W. Porter, see 6:1182.

[2112]

Steward Personnel Tests (Short Form), 1958 Edition. Applicants for sales and office positions; 1957–58; abbreviated version of *Steward Sales Aptitude Inventory* and *Steward Vocational Fitness Inventory;* 10 scores: business knowledge, arithmetic, occupational interests (clerical, artistic, supervisory, accounting, writing, selling, mechanical, selling activities); Verne Steward; Steward-Mortensen & Associates. *

For additional information and reviews by Leonard V. Gordon and Lyman W. Porter, see 6:1029.

[2113]

TAV Selection System. Adults; 1963–68; TAV; vocational selection and counseling; 7 tests; R. R. Morman; TAV Selection System. *

a) TAV ADJECTIVE CHECKLIST. 1963–68; 3 scores: toward people (T), away from people (A), versus people (V).

b) TAV JUDGMENTS. 1964–68; 3 scores: same as in *a.*

c) TAV PERSONAL DATA. 1964–68; 3 scores: same as in *a.*

d) TAV PREFERENCES. 1963–68; 3 scores: same as in *a.*

e) TAV PROVERBS AND SAYINGS. 1966–68; 3 scores: same as in *a.*

f) TAV SALESMAN REACTIONS. 1967–68; 3 scores: same as in *a.*

g) TAV MENTAL AGILITY. 1965–68; 3 scores: follow directions and carefulness, weights and balances, verbal comprehension.

For additional information and an excerpted review by John O. Crites, see 7:983 (1 reference); see also P:263A (11 references).

REFERENCES THROUGH 1971

1–11. See P:263A.
12. See 7:983.
13. MORMAN, ROBERT R.; HANKEY, R. O.; JONES, E.; AND LIDDLE, L. R. "Adjuster Selection by Prediction." *Best's Insur News (Fire & Cas)* 68:38+ Je '67. *
14. BRAUN, JOHN R. "Effects of Faking Instructions on the TAV Adjective Check List." *Psychol Rep* 29(2):496 O '71. * (PA 47:8943)
15. LIDDLE, L. ROGERS; HEYWOOD, HAROLD L.; HANKEY, RICHARD O.; AND MORMAN, ROBERT R. "Predicting Baccalaureate Degree Attainment for Nursing Students: A Theoretical Study Using the TAV Selection System." *Nursing Res* 20(3): 258–61 My–Je '71. * (PA 51:3250)

CUMULATIVE NAME INDEX

Braun, J. R.: 14
Crites, J. O.: *exc,* 7:983
Duvlick, J.: 4
Goldwhite, M.: 9
Hankey, R. O.: 1–4, 7–9, 11–3, 15
Heywood, H.: 3, 10
Heywood, H. C.: 12
Heywood, H. L.: 1–2, 4–7, 9, 11, 15
Jones, E.: 13
Jones, E. M.: 8
Kennedy, P.: 1–2
Kennedy, P. K.: 3, 5, 8, 12
Liddle, L. R.: 4–7, 9–11, 13, 15
Morman, R.: 10
Morman, R. R.: 1–9, 11–3, 15

[2114]

Vocational Planning Inventory. Vocational students in grades 8–10, 11–12 and grade 13 entrants; 1968–70, c1954–70; VPI; the battery consists of the *SRA Arithmetic Index, SRA Pictorial Reasoning Test, SRA Verbal Form, Survey of Interpersonal Values, Survey of Personal Values,* Mechanics subtest of the *Flanagan Aptitude Classification Test,* and the following subtests of the *Flanagan Industrial Tests:* Arithmetic, Assembly (*a*), Expression (*a*), Memory (*a*), Scales (*b*), and Tables (*b*); tests cannot be scored locally; the student's copy of his test report presents predicted grades in 9 or 10 areas: agriculture (*a* only), business, construction trades, drafting and design, electronics and electrical trades, home economics and health, mechanics and mechanical maintenance, metal trades, general academic, general vocational; the counselor's copy of an individual test report also presents national percentile rank norms for the component tests: single scores for the 7 (or 8) nonpersonality tests and 12 value scores (practical mindedness, achievement, variety, decisiveness, orderliness, goal orientation, support, conformity, recognition, independence, benevolence, leadership) on the 2 personality tests; 2 levels; Science Research Associates, Inc. *

a) HIGH SCHOOL PREDICTION PROGRAM. Vocational students in grades 8–10; 1968–70, c1954–70; for predicting success in grades 9–12 in areas listed above.

b) POST-HIGH SCHOOL PREDICTION PROGRAM. Vocational students in grades 11–12 and grade 13 entrants; 1968,

c1954–68; for predicting success in grade 13 in areas listed above.

For additional information, see 7:984.

[2115]

WLW Employment Inventory, Short Form. Adults; 1957–64; 4 scores: general knowledge, emotional stability, humility, friendliness; manual by Robert W. Henderson; William, Lynde & Williams. *

For additional information, see 7:985.

[2116]

★Wide Range Employment Sample Test. Ages 16–35 (normal and handicapped); 1973; WREST; manual refers to the test as *The Jastak-King Work Samples;* originally developed for use with "mentally and physically handicapped" persons enrolled in a rehabilitation workshop; 12 scores: folding, stapling, bottle packaging, rice measuring, screw assembly, tag stringing, swatch pasting, collating, color and shade matching, pattern matching, total performance, total errors; J. F. Jastak and Dorothy E. King; Guidance Associates of Delaware, Inc. *

[Out of Print Since TIP I]

Airman Qualifying Examination, 6:1023 (1 reference)
General Adaptability Battery, 6:1026 (1 reference)
Personnel Selection and Classification Test, 3:690 (3 reviews)
RBH Industrial Questionnaire, 7:982
Screening Tests for Apprentices, 6:1028
Vocational Aptitude Examination, 3:695 (4 reviews, 4 references)

CLERICAL

[2117]

ACER Short Clerical Test—Form C. Ages 13 and over; 1953–67; 2 scores: checking, arithmetic; 1966 form essentially the same as form copyrighted 1956 except for conversion to decimal currency; Australian Council for Educational Research [Australia]. *

For additional information, see 7:986.

[2118]

A.C.E.R. Speed and Accuracy Tests. Ages 13.5 and over; 1942–62; 2 scores: number checking, name checking; revised manual by T. M. Whitford; Australian Council for Educational Research [Australia]. *

For additional information, see 6:1031 (2 references); for a review by D. W. McElwain of an earlier form, see 4:719.

REFERENCES THROUGH 1971

1–2. See 6:1031.
3. BILES, DAVID. "Test Performance and Imprisonment." *Austral & N Zeal J Criminol* (Australia) 1:46–58 Mr '68. *

CUMULATIVE NAME INDEX

Biles, D.: 3
Bucklow, M.: 2
Doughty, P.: 2
Hohne, H. H.: 1
McElwain, D. W.: *rev,* 4:719

[2119]

APT Dictation Test. Stenographers; 1955; Associated Personnel Technicians, Inc. *

For additional information, see 6:40.

[2120]

★Appraisal of Occupational Aptitudes. High school and adults; 1971; AOA; "for predicting success in . . . . office occupations"; 8 scores: checking letters, checking numbers, filing names, filing numbers, posting names, posting numbers, arithmetical computation and reasoning, desk calculator (norms for women only); Aurelius A. Abbatiello; Houghton Mifflin Co. *

[2121]

Clerical Skills Series. Clerical workers and applicants; 1966–69; CSS; 10 tests; Martin M. Bruce; Martin M. Bruce, Ph.D., Publishers. *
a) ALPHABETIZING-FILING. 1966.
b) ARITHMETIC. 1966–69; 1969 test identical with test copyrighted 1966.
c) CLERICAL SPEED AND ACCURACY. 1966.
d) CODING. 1966.
e) EYE-HAND ACCURACY. 1966.
f) GRAMMAR AND PUNCTUATION. 1966.
g) SPELLING. 1966–69; 1969 test identical with test copyrighted 1966.
h) SPELLING-VOCABULARY. 1966.
i) VOCABULARY. 1966.
j) WORD FLUENCY. 1966.
For additional information and a review by Robert Fitzpatrick, see 7:988.

[2122]

Clerical Tests. Applicants for clerical positions; 1951–66; 6 tests; no manual; Stevens, Thurow & Associates, Inc. *
a) INVENTORY J, ARITHMETICAL REASONING. 1966.
b) INVENTORY K, ARITHMETICAL PROFICIENCY. 1951–66.
c) INVENTORY M, INTERPRETATION OF TABULATED MATERIAL. 1951–66.
d) INVENTORY R, INTERPRETATION OF TABULATED MATERIAL. 1951–66.
e) INVENTORY S, ALPHABETICAL FILING. 1951–66.
f) INVENTORY Y, GRAMMAR. 1951–66.
For additional information, see 7:989.

[2123]

Clerical Tests, Series N. Applicants for clerical positions not involving frequent use of typewriter or verbal skill; 1940–59; 5 scores: comparing names and numbers, copying names, copying numbers, addition and multiplication, mental ability; 5 tests and 1 application form; Stevens, Thurow & Associates, Inc. *
a) INVENTORY E, COMPARING NAMES AND NUMBERS.
b) INVENTORY F, COPYING NUMBERS.
c) INVENTORY G, ADDITION AND MULTIPLICATION.
d) INVENTORY H, COPYING NAMES.
e) INVENTORY NO. 2. Mental ability. See 393.
f) APPLICATION FOR POSITION. See 2318.
For additional information, see 6:1036.

[2124]

Clerical Tests, Series V. Applicants for typing and stenographic positions; 1940–59; 5 scores: grammar, spelling, vocabulary, typing (words per minute), mental ability; 5 tests and 1 application form; Stevens, Thurow & Associates, Inc. *
a) INVENTORY A, GRAMMAR.
b) INVENTORY B, SPELLING.
c) INVENTORY C, VOCABULARY.
d) TEST OF TYPEWRITING ABILITY.
e) INVENTORY NO. 2. Mental ability. See 393.
f) APPLICATION FOR POSITION. See 2318b.
For additional information, see 6:1037.

[2125]

Clerical Worker Examination. Clerical workers; 1962–63; test booklet title is *Clerical Worker;* 5 scores: clerical speed and accuracy, verbal ability, quantitative ability, total ability, total; McCann Associates. *
For additional information, see 6:1038.

[2126]

Cross Reference Test. Clerical job applicants; 1959; James W. Curtis; Psychometric Affiliates. *
For additional information and a review by Philip H. Kriedt, see 6:1039.

[2127]

Curtis Verbal-Clerical Skills Tests. Applicants for clerical positions; 1963–65; 4 tests: computation, checking, comprehension, logical reasoning ability; James W. Curtis; Psychometric Affiliates. *
For additional information, see 7:990.

[2128]

*General Clerical Ability Test: ETSA Test 3A. Job applicants; 1960–72, c1957–59; manual and technical handbook by S. Trevor Hadley and George A. W. Stouffer, Jr.; test by Psychological Services Bureau; Educators'-Employers' Tests & Services Associates. * For the complete battery entry, see 2106.
For reviews of the complete battery, see 6:1025 (2 reviews).

[2129]

*General Clerical Test. Grades 9–16 and clerical job applicants; 1944–72; formerly called *Psychological Corporation General Clerical Test;* 4 scores: clerical speed and accuracy, numerical ability, verbal facility, total; Psychological Corporation. (British adaptation: NFER Publishing Co. Ltd. [England].) *
For additional information and reviews by Edward E. Cureton and G. A. Satter, see 4:730 (4 references); for reviews by Edward N. Hay, Thelma Hunt, Raymond A. Katzell, and E. F. Wonderlic, see 3:630.

REFERENCES THROUGH 1971

1–4. See 4:730.
5. BARNETTE, W. LESLIE, JR. "Occupational Aptitude Pattern Research." *Occupations* 29:5–12 O '50. * (*PA* 25:3239)
6. KERNAN, JOHN P. *An Empirical Determination of Test Reliability by Different Experimental Designs.* Master's thesis, Fordham University (New York, N.Y.), 1951.
7. BENNETT, GEORGE K. "Research Upon Item Types and Its Implications for Test Improvement." *Yearb Nat Council Meas Used Ed* 9:114–5 '52. *
8. HANNA, JOSEPH V. "Use of Speed Tests in Guidance." *Occupations* 30:329–31 F '52. * (*PA* 26:6355)
9. WESMAN, ALEXANDER G., AND KERNAN, JOHN P. "An Experimental Comparison of Test-Retest and Internal Consistency Estimates of Reliability with Speeded Tests." *J Ed Psychol* 43:292–8 My '52. * (*PA* 27:3154)
10. SEASHORE, HAROLD G. "Validation of Clerical Testing in Banks." *Personnel Psychol* 6:45–56 sp '53. * (*PA* 28:1670)
11. HUGHES, J. L., AND McNAMARA, W. J. "Relationship of Short Employment Tests and General Clerical Tests." *Personnel Psychol* 8:331–7 au '55. * (*PA* 30:7828)
12. MISKO, ALOYSIUS EDWARD. *An Investigation Into the Validity of Three Employment Tests of a Clerical Personnel Selection Program.* Doctor's thesis, University of Michigan (Ann Arbor, Mich.), 1962. (*DA* 23:3170)
13. DICKEN, CHARLES F., AND BLACK, JOHN D. "Predictive Validity of Psychometric Evaluations of Supervisors." *J Appl Psychol* 49:34–47 F '65. * (*PA* 39:8793)
14. PARRY, MARY ELLEN. "Ability of Psychologists to Estimate Validities of Personnel Tests." *Personnel Psychol* 21:139–47 su '68. * (*PA* 42:14727)
15. WILLE, GLENN R. *An Investigation of the Relationship Between the Wonderlic Personnel Test, Form I, and the General Clerical Test; the Relationship Between the Wonderlic Personnel Test, Form I, and Employee Job Performance.* Master's thesis, Wisconsin State University (Oshkosh, Wis.), 1969.

CUMULATIVE NAME INDEX

Bair, J. T.: 3	Giese, W. J.: 2
Barnette, W. L.: 1, 4–5	Hanna, J. V.: 8
Bennett, G. K.: 7	Hay, E. N.: *rev,* 3:630
Black, J. D.: 13	Hughes, J. L.: 11
Cureton, E. E.: *rev,* 4:730	Hunt, T.: *rev,* 3:630
Dicken, C. F.: 13	Katzell, R. A.: *rev,* 3:630

Kernan, J. P.: 6, 9
McNamara, W. J.: 11
Misko, A. E.: 12
Parry, M. E.: 14
Satter, G. A.: rev, 4:730

Seashore, H. G.: 10
Wesman, A. G.: 9
Wille, G. R.: 15
Wonderlic, E. F.: rev, 3:630

[2130]
*Group Test 20. Ages 15 and over; 1936–72; checking of names and numbers; 2 scores: speed, accuracy; National Institute of Industrial Psychology; NFER Publishing Co. Ltd. [England]. *

For additional information and a review by E. G. Chambers, see 4:723 (2 references).

REFERENCES THROUGH 1971
1–2. See 4:723.
3. LEE, TERENCE. "The Selection of Student Nurses: A Revised Procedure." Occup Psychol (England) 33:209–16 O '59. *

CUMULATIVE NAME INDEX
Chambers, E. G.: rev, 4:723
Kerr, G.: 1

Lee, T.: 3
Shuttleworth, C. W.: 2

[2131]
*Group Tests 61A, 64, and 66A. Clerical applicants; 1956–72; 1972 manual identical with manual copyrighted 1971 except for revised norms for c; 3 tests; National Institute of Industrial Psychology; NFER Publishing Co. Ltd. [England]. *

a) GROUP TEST 61A. 1956–71; decimalized version of Group Test 61; filing, classification, and checking; 2 scores: speed, accuracy.

b) GROUP TEST 64. 1957–71; spelling.

c) GROUP TEST 66A. 1957–72; decimalized version of Group Test 66; arithmetic; 2 scores: basic operations, problems.

For additional information, see 7:991.

[2132]
*[Hay Clerical Test Battery.] Applicants for clerical positions; 1941–72; formerly called Hay Tests for Clerical Aptitude; 4 tests; 1971 tests identical with tests copyrighted 1947–55; Edward N. Hay; Aptitude Test Service, Inc. *

a) TEST 1: THE WARM UP. 1945–72.

b) NUMBER PERCEPTION TEST. 1947–72.

c) NAME FINDING TEST. 1941–72.

d) NUMBER SERIES COMPLETION TEST. 1941–72.

For additional information, see 5:849 (2 references); for reviews by Reign H. Bittner and Edward E. Cureton, see 4:725 (8 references).

REFERENCES THROUGH 1971
1–8. See 4:725.
9–10. See 5:849.
11. MACKINNEY, ARTHUR C., AND WOLINS, LEROY. "Validity Information Exchange, No. 12–19: D.O.T. Code 1-36.05, Coding Clerk; 1-17.02, File Clerk II, Circulation Clerk." Personnel Psychol 12:482–3 au '59. *
12. HARKER, JOHN B. "Cross-Validation of an IBM Proof Machine Test Battery." J Appl Psychol 44:237–40 Ag '60. * (PA 35:4055)

CUMULATIVE NAME INDEX
Bittner, R. H.: rev, 4:725
Blakemore, A.: 7
Cureton, E. E.: rev, 4:725
Doub, B. A.: 2
Harker, J. B.: 12

Hay, E. N.: 1, 3–5, 8, 10
MacKinney, A. C.: 11
Miller, R. B.: 6
Seashore, H. G.: 9
Wolins, L.: 11

[2133]
[L & L Clerical Tests.] Applicants for office positions; 1964; 5 tests; no manual; distribution restricted to business firms; L & L Associates. *

a) ARITHMETIC REVIEW.

b) CHECK LIST REVIEW.

c) OFFICE ABILITY REVIEW. 6 scores: spelling, grammar and punctuation, arithmetic, filing, business terms, total.

d) SPELLING REVIEW.

e) TYPING REVIEW.

For additional information, see 7:992.

[2134]
[McCann Typing Tests.] Applicants for typing positions; 1961–64; 3 scores: speed, accuracy, total; McCann Associates. *

For additional information, see 6:50.

[2135]
Minnesota Clerical Test. Grades 8–12 and adults; 1933–59; formerly called Minnesota Vocational Test for Clerical Workers; 2 scores: number comparison, name comparison; Dorothy M. Andrew, Donald G. Paterson, and Howard P. Longstaff (test); Psychological Corporation. *

For additional information, see 6:1040 (10 references); for a review by Donald E. Super, see 5:850 (46 references); for reviews by Thelma Hunt, R. B. Selover, Erwin K. Taylor, and E. F. Wonderlic, see 3:627 (22 references); for a review by W. D. Commins, see 2:1664 (18 references).

REFERENCES THROUGH 1971
1–18. See 2:1664.
19–40. See 3:627.
41–86. See 5:850.
87–96. See 6:1040.
97. QUAYLE, MARGARET SIDNEY. "A Study of Some Aspects of Satisfaction in the Vocation of Stenography." Teach Col Contrib Ed 659:1–121 '35. * (PA 10:2644)
98. BRENTLINGER, W. H. "The Abilities and Occupational History of Transients: A Preliminary Study." J Appl Psychol 20:105–13 F '36. * (PA 10:3673)
99. OTIS, JAY L. "The Prediction of Success in Power Sewing Machine Operating." J Appl Psychol 22:350–66 Ag '38. * (PA 13:1688)
100. SUPER, DONALD E.; BRAASCH, WILLIAM F., JR.; AND SHAY, JOSEPH B. "The Effect of Distractions on Test Results." J Ed Psychol 38:373–7 O '47. * (PA 22:2159)
101. CARRUTHERS, JOHN B. "Tabular Summary Showing Relation Between Clerical Test Scores and Occupational Performance." Occupations 29:40–50 O '50. * (PA 25:3450)
102. GUEST, LESTER, AND NUCKOLS, ROBERT. "A Laboratory Experiment in Recording in Public Opinion Interviewing." Int J Opin & Attitude Res (Mexico) 4:336–52 f '50. * (PA 25:7387)
103. DUNHAM, RALPH E. "Factors Related to Recidivism in Adults." J Social Psychol 39:77–91 F '54. * (PA 28:8866)
104. STOREY, JOHN STUART. The Validity of Counseling Variables Considered in the Advisement of Disabled Veterans Entering Terminal Business Training. Doctor's thesis, Michigan State University (East Lansing, Mich.), 1955. (DA 15:1019)
105. BAIR, JOHN T.; LOCKMAN, ROBERT F.; AND MARTOCCIA, CHARLES T. "Validity and Factor Analyses of Naval Air Training Predictor and Criterion Measures." J Appl Psychol 40:213–9 Ag '56. * (PA 31:6701)
106. HABER, WILFRED. The Contribution of Selected Variables to Success or Failure in a Vocational Rehabilitation Evaluation. Doctor's thesis, New York University (New York, N.Y.), 1959. (DA 20:4171)
107. MATTHEWS, ROMINE ELLWOOD. Certain Personality Variables Related to Success in Veterans' Rehabilitation Training in Clerical Occupations. Doctor's thesis, University of Minnesota (Minneapolis, Minn.), 1960. (DA 21:127)
108. EDINGTON, EVERETT D. Abilities and Characteristics of Young Adult Dairy Farmers in Pennsylvania Which Are Associated With Successful Farm Management. Doctor's thesis, Pennsylvania State University (University Park, Pa.), 1961. (DA 22:3791)
109. LOCKE, EDWIN A. "Some Correlates of Classroom and Out-of-Class Achievement in Gifted Science Students." J Ed Psychol 54:238–48 O '63. * (PA 38:4649)
110. MORRISON, WILLIAM E. The Effectiveness of the Minnesota Clerical Test and the Wonderlic Personnel Test in the Selection of Clerk Typists and File Clerks. Master's thesis, Springfield College (Springfield, Mass.), 1963.
111. HAFEEZ, A., AND YAKUB, SYED. "A Study of Clerical Ability." J Indian Acad Appl Psychol 1:77–80 S '64. * (PA 39:8781)
112. DICKEN, CHARLES F., AND BLACK, JOHN D. "Predictive Validity of Psychometric Evaluations of Supervisors." J Appl Psychol 49:34–47 F '65. * (PA 39:8793)
113. STEIGELMAN, GEORGE W. The Effect of Controlled Distractions Upon the Minnesota Clerical Test Results of Eighth

Graders in Charleston, Illinois. Master's thesis, Eastern Illinois University (Charleston, Ill.), 1966.

114. MOSKOVIS, LEFTERIE MICHAEL. *An Identification of Certain Similarities and Differences Between Successful and Unsuccessful College Level Beginning Shorthand Students and Transcription Students.* Doctor's thesis, Michigan State University (East Lansing, Mich.), 1967. (*DA* 28:4826A)

115. BLANK, STANLEY S. "An Examination of the Usefulness of Various Psychological Instruments for Predicting Department Managers' Ratings of Clerical Sales Personnel." *Can Counsellor* 2:46–50 Ja '68. *

116. GEORGAS, JAMES G.; BRAMOS, IRENE; AND BAKIRDGIS, IOANNA. "The Minnesota Clerical Test in Greece: A Validation Study." *Personnel Psychol* 21:79–83 sp '68. * (*PA* 42:16172)

117. RAFFEL, SHERMAN C.; SWINK, RICHARD; AND LAMPTON, T. D. "The Influence of Chlorphenesin Carbamate and Carisoprodol on Psychological Test Scores." *Curr Ther Res* 11(9): 553–60 S '69. *

118. LLEWELLYN, HOWARD CHARLES. *The Relationship Between Selected Silent Word Perception Skills and Achievement in First-Year High School Typewriting.* Doctor's thesis, University of North Dakota (Grand Forks, N.D.), 1970. (*DAI* 31: 6454A)

119. MOSKOVIS, L. MICHAEL. "Similarities and Differences of College-Level Successful and Unsuccessful Shorthand Students." *Delta Pi Epsilon J* 12(2):12–6 F '70. *

CUMULATIVE NAME INDEX

Achard, F. H.: 44
American Gas Association, Personnel Committee: 70
Anderson, R. G.: 72
Anderson, R. N.: 30
Andrew, D. M.: 2–3, 9
Bair, J. T.: 50, 65, 105
Bakirdgis, I.: 116
Barnette, W. L.: 18
Barrett, D. M.: 38
Beamer, G. C.: 49
Beldo, L. A.: 86
Bellows, R. M.: 42
Bender, W. R. G.: 88
Bennett, G. K.: 39
Bergen, G. L.: 4
Berkshire, R.: 58
Berman, I. R.: 8
Bingham, W. V. D.: 10
Black, J. D.: 112
Black, M. H.: 51
Blakemore, A.: 66
Blakemore, A. M.: 27, 32
Blanchard, H. L.: 52
Blank, S. S.: 115
Blum, M.: 11
Blum, M. L.: 21
Bond, G. L.: 62
Borg, W. R.: 59
Braasch, W. F.: 100
Bramos, I.: 116
Brayfield, A. H.: 73
Brentlinger, W. H.: 98
Candee, B.: 11, 21
Capwell, D. F.: 53
Carpenter, E. K.: 46
Carruthers, J. B.: 101
Carter, L.: 54
Cass, J. C.: 93
Champion, J. M.: 89
Clarke, F. H.: 44
Commins, W. D.: *rev,* 2:1664
Cooper, J. H.: 42
Copeland, H. A.: 7, 12
Cox, K. J.: 45
Coyle, F. P.: 76
Crane, W. J.: 95
Crissey, O. L.: 43
Crites, J. O.: 96
Davidson, C. M.: 13–4
Dicken, C. F.: 112
Dodge, A. F.: 5
Dudycha, G. J.: 17
Dunham, R. E.: 103
Dvorak, B. J.: 6, 42
Edington, E. D.: 108
Edmonson, L. D.: 49
Endler, O. L.: 42
Engelhardt, O. E. de C.: 60
Erickson, I. P.: 20
Fife, I. E.: 40
Fleet, D.: 58
Forster, C. R.: 83
Garrett, W. S.: 94
Georgas, J. G.: 116
Ghiselli, E. E.: 22, 25–6

Graham, W. R.: 77
Green, H. J.: 8
Guest, L.: 102
Haber, W.: 106
Hackman, R. C.: 41
Hafeez, A.: 111
Hahn, M. E.: 47
Hales, W. M.: 15
Hay, E. N.: 27, 31–2, 61, 67
Hunt, T.: *rev,* 3:627
Jackson, J.: 55
Jenkins, J. J.: 74
Johnson, R. H.: 62
Kendall, W. E.: 47
Kirkpatrick, D. L.: 84
Klugman, S. F.: 33–4, 36
Kolbe, L. E.: 42
Lampton, T. D.: 117
Lee, M. C.: 63, 71
Lee, P. J.: 78
Llewellyn, H. C.: 118
Locke, E. A.: 109
Lockman, R. F.: 105
Loevinger, J.: 19
Longstaff, H. P.: 79, 86
Loveless, H. E.: 88
Lowe, L. M.: 80
McGehee, W.: 28
Maher, H.: 40
Martin, F.: 81
Martoccia, C. T.: 105
Matthews, R. E.: 107
Miller, R. B.: 64
Moffie, D. J.: 28
Morrison, W. E.: 110
Morrow, R. S.: 23
Moskovis, L. M.: 114, 119
Nixon, M.: 54
Nuckols, R.: 102
Osborne, H. F.: 42
Otis, J. L.: 42, 99
Paterson, D. G.: 2, 8, 16, 29
Petrie, A.: 68
Petro, P. K.: 87
Pond, M.: 1
Powell, M. B.: 68
Purdy, B. F.: 69
Quayle, M. S.: 97
Raffel, S. C.: 117
Rusmore, J.: 81
Sawyer, J.: 85
Schneidler, G. G.: 16, 24, 29
Seashore, H. G.: 75
Selover, R. B.: *rev,* 3:627
Shartle, C. L.: 42
Shay, J. B.: 100
Shore, R. P.: 90–2
Shuman, J. T.: 35
Stead, W. H.: 42
Steigelman, G. W.: 113
Storey, J. S.: 104
Strong, E. K.: 48
Strother, G. B.: 49
Super, D. E.: 56, 96, 100; *rev,* 5:850
Swem, B. R.: 37

Swink, R.: 117
Taylor, E. K.: *rev,* 3:627
Tiedeman, D. V.: 93
Trabue, M. R.: 8
Ward, R. S.: 42
Wesman, A. G.: 39

Wightwick, B.: 57
Williamson, E. G.: 16
Wonderlic, E. F.: *rev,* 3:627
Yakub, S.: 111
Young, M. B.: 82

[2136]

Office Skills Achievement Test. Employees; 1962–63; 7 scores: business letter, grammar, checking, filing, arithmetic, written directions, total; Paul L. Mellenbruch; Psychometric Affiliates. *

For additional information and reviews by Douglas G. Schultz and Paul W. Thayer, see 6:1043.

[2137]

***Office Worker Test.** Office workers; 1956–72; 11 scores: reading, vocabulary, reasoning, arithmetic, checking, filing, spelling, punctuation, usage, information, total; distribution restricted to member public personnel agencies and nonmember agencies approved by the publisher; International Personnel Management Association. *

For additional information and reviews by Ray G. Price and Douglas G. Schultz, see 6:1044.

[2138]

O'Rourke Clerical Aptitude Test, Junior Grade. Applicants for clerical positions; 1926–58; 2 parts; no manual; L. J. O'Rourke; O'Rourke Publications. *

a) CLERICAL PROBLEMS. 1926–35.

b) REASONING TEST. 1926–58; 1958 test essentially the same as test copyrighted 1936 except for changes in a few items.

For additional information, see 5:851 (1 reference); for a review by Raymond A. Katzell, see 3:629 (3 references).

REFERENCES THROUGH 1971

1–3. See 3:629.
4. See 5:851.
5. WOODY, CLIFFORD. *Aptitudes, Achievements and Interests of High School Pupils.* University of Michigan, Bureau of Educational Reference and Research Bulletin No. 157. Ann Arbor, Mich.: School of Education, the University, 1945. Pp. vi, 159. *

CUMULATIVE NAME INDEX

Anderson, R. N.: 2
Bair, J. T.: 4
Copeland, H. A.: 1

Katzell, R. A.: *rev,* 3:629
Woody, C.: 3, 5

[2139]

[Personnel Institute Clerical Tests.] Clerical personnel and typists-stenographers-secretaries; 1922–67; 12 tests; Personnel Institute, Inc. *

a) PRELIMINARY SCREENING INTERVIEW. 1957–67.

b) CONFIDENTIAL PERSONAL HISTORY INVENTORY. 1957–67.

c) DIAGNOSTIC INTERVIEWER'S GUIDE. 1956–67.

d) WORK REFERENCE INVESTIGATION. 1957–67.

e) MENTAL ALERTNESS TEST. 1922; formerly called *EM-AY Inventory;* reprint of the *Otis Employment Test.*

f) VOCABULARY TEST. 1954–67; 1967 test identical with tests copyrighted 1954 and 1956.

g) COMPARING NAMES TEST. 1957–67; 1967 test identical with test copyrighted 1957.

h) COPYING NUMBERS TEST. 1957–67; 1967 test identical with tests copyrighted 1957 and 1962.

i) ARITHMETIC TEST. 1957–67; 1967 test identical with tests copyrighted 1957 and 1963.

j) GRAMMAR TEST. 1957–67; 1967 test identical with tests copyrighted 1957 and 1960.

k) SPELLING TEST. 1957–67; 1967 test identical with tests copyrighted 1957 and 1963.

l) TYPING TEST. 1957–67; 1967 test identical with tests copyrighted 1957 and 1960.

For additional information, see 7:993.

[2140]

[Personnel Research Institute Clerical Battery.]
Applicants for clerical positions; 1945–48; 7 tests;
Personnel Research Institute. *
a) NUMBER COMPARISON TEST FOR CLERICAL AND IN-
DUSTRIAL INSPECTION OPERATIONS. 1945–46; Jay L.
Otis and Louise W. Garman.
b) NAME COMPARISON TEST FOR CLERICAL AND INDUS-
TRIAL INSPECTION OPERATIONS. 1945–46; Jay L. Otis
and Louise W. Garman.
c) TABULATION TEST. 1947; Jay L. Otis and David J.
Chesler.
d) FILING TEST. 1947; Jay L. Otis and David J. Chesler.
e) ALPHABETIZING TEST. 1947; David J. Chesler.
f) ARITHMETIC REASONING TEST. See 699.
g) SPELLING TEST FOR CLERICAL WORKERS. See 159.
For additional information and reviews by Louise
Witmer Cureton and Albert K. Kurtz, see 4:729. For
reference to a review of the spelling test, see 159.

REFERENCES THROUGH 1971
1. HILTON, ANDREW C.; BOLIN, STANLEY F.; PARKER, JAMES
W., JR.; TAYLOR, ERWIN K.; AND WALKER, WILLIAM B. "The
Validity of Personnel Assessments by Professional Psycholo-
gists." *J Appl Psychol* 39:287–93 Ag '55. * (*PA* 30:5294)
2. CAMPBELL, JOEL T., AND PRIEN, ERICH P., JR. "Normative
Data Information Exchange, Nos. 11–19, 11–20." *Personnel
Psychol* 11:449–50 au '58. *
3. CAMPBELL, JOEL T., AND PRIEN, ERICH P., JR. "Normative
Data Information Exchange, Nos. 11–21, 11–22." *Personnel
Psychol* 11:451–2 au '58. *
4. CAMPBELL, JOEL T., AND PRIEN, ERICH P., JR. "Normative
Data Information Exchange, Nos. 11–29, 11–30." *Personnel
Psychol* 11:595–6 w '58. *
5. CAMPBELL, JOEL T., AND PRIEN, ERICH P., JR. "Normative
Data Information Exchange, Nos. 11–31, 11–32." *Personnel
Psychol* 11:597–8 w '58. *
6. CAMPBELL, JOEL T.; PRIEN, ERICH P.; AND BRAILEY,
LESTER B. "Predicting Performance Evaluations." *Personnel
Psychol* 13:435–40 w '60. * (*PA* 36:1LD35C)

CUMULATIVE NAME INDEX
Bixler, H. H.: *rev,* 4:211   Kurtz, A. K.: *rev,* 4:729
Bolin, S. F.: 1   Parker, J. W.: 1
Brailey, L. B.: 6   Prien, E. P.: 2–6
Campbell, J. T.: 2–6   Taylor, E. K.: 1
Cureton, L. W.: *rev,* 4:729   Walker, W. B.: 1
Hilton, A. C.: 1

[2141]

**Personnel Research Institute Test of Shorthand
Skills.** Stenographers; 1951–54; title on test is *Otis
and Laurent Test of Shorthand Skills;* 2 scores: trans-
literation, transcription; Jay L. Otis and Harry
Laurent; Personnel Research Institute. *
For additional information and a review by Irol
Whitmore Balsley, see 6:43.

[2142]

**Purdue Clerical Adaptability Test, Revised Edi-
tion.** Applicants for clerical positions; 1949–56; 6
scores: spelling, computation, checking, word meaning, copying, reasoning; C. H. Lawshe, Joseph Tiffin,
and Herbert Moore; distributed by University Book
Store. *
For additional information and reviews by Mary
Ellen Oliverio and Donald Spearritt, see 5:853 (2
references); for reviews by Edward N. Hay, Joseph
E. Moore, and Alec Rodger of an earlier edition, see
4:731.

REFERENCES THROUGH 1971
1–2. See 5:853.
3. RAUBENHEIMER, I. VAN W. "Influence of Group and
Situational Differences on the Applicability of a Personnel Test."
J Appl Psychol 54(3):214–6 Je '70. * (*PA* 44:13464)
4. RAUBENHEIMER, I. VAN W., AND TIFFIN, JOSEPH. "Personnel Selection and the Prediction of Error." *J Appl Psychol*
55(3):229–33 Je '71. * (*PA* 46:9844)

CUMULATIVE NAME INDEX
Hay, E. N.: *rev,* 4:731   Rodger, A.: *rev,* 4:731
Lawshe, C. H.: 2   Sinclair, G. R.: 1
Moore, J. E.: *rev,* 4:731   Spearritt, D.: *rev,* 5:853
Oliverio, M. E.: *rev,* 5:853 Steinberg, M. D.: 2
Raubenheimer, I. van W.: 3–   Tiffin, J.: 4
4

[2143]

RBH Checking Test. Applicants for clerical and
stenographic positions; 1948–63; catalog uses the title
The RBH Coding Test; Richardson, Bellows, Henry
& Co., Inc. *
For additional information and a review by Douglas
G. Schultz, see 7:994.

[2144]

RBH Classifying Test. Business and industry;
1950–63; 3 scores: speed, accuracy, rights minus
wrongs; 1961 test identical with test copyrighted 1950
except for cover; Richardson, Bellows, Henry & Co.,
Inc. *
For additional information and a review by Douglas
G. Schultz, see 7:995.

[2145]

RBH Number Checking Test. Business and industry; 1957–63; 2 scores: checking forward, checking
backward; Richardson, Bellows, Henry & Co., Inc. *
For additional information and a review by Douglas
G. Schultz, see 7:997.

[2146]

*RBH Test of Dictation Speed. Stenographers;
1958–63; no manual; Richardson, Bellows, Henry & Co.,
Inc. *
For additional information, see 6:48.

[2147]

RBH Test of Typing Speed. Applicants for cleri-
cal positions; 1958–63; 2 scores: net speed, accuracy;
Richardson, Bellows, Henry & Co., Inc. *
For additional information, see 6:53.

[2148]

**The Seashore-Bennett Stenographic Proficiency
Test: A Standard Recorded Stenographic Worksample.** Adults; 1946–56; Harold Seashore and
George K. Bennett; Psychological Corporation. *
For additional information, see 5:519 (2 references);
for a review by Harold F. Rothe, see 4:455 (1 reference); for a review by Ann Brewington, see 3:386.

REFERENCES THROUGH 1971
1. See 4:455.
2–3. See 5:519.

CUMULATIVE NAME INDEX
Bennett, G. K.: 1   Rothe, H. F.: *rev,* 4:455
Brewington, A.: *rev,* 3:386   Seashore, H. G.: 1
McCarty, J. J.: 3

[2149]

Secretarial Performance Analysis. Employees;
1969; SPA; ratings by supervisors; 4 scores: basic
skills, executive skills, personal attributes, total; William T. Martin; Psychologists and Educators, Inc. *
For additional information, see 7:998.

[2150]

Selection Tests for Office Personnel. Insurance
office workers and applicants; 1962–64; STOP; 10
tests; Walter A. Eggert and Albert H. Malo; distributed by Kemper Psychological Services. *
a) LANGUAGE SKILLS 1A.
b) DATA PERCEPTION 2A.
c) ARITHMETIC 3A.

d) CODING 4A.
e) RATING 5A.
f) PERSONALITY 6A.
g) FILING 7A.
h) STENOGRAPHY 8A.
i) SPELLING 9A.
j) TYPING 10A.
For additional information, see 7:999.

[2151]

*The Short Employment Tests. Applicants for clerical positions; 1951–72; SET; 3 tests; distribution of Form 1 restricted to banks which are members of the American Bankers Association; George K. Bennett and Marjorie Gelink; Psychological Corporation. *
a) V [VERBAL].
b) N [NUMERICAL].
c) CA [CLERICAL].
For additional information and a review by Leonard W. Ferguson, see 6:1045 (9 references); for a review by P. L. Mellenbruch, see 5:854 (16 references).

REFERENCES THROUGH 1971
1–16. See 5:854.
17–25. See 6:1045.
26. MILLER, MARTIN M. *A Validation of the Short Employment Test on Secretarial Personnel at the University of Tennessee.* Master's thesis, University of Tennessee (Knoxville, Tenn.), 1964.
27. KIRCHNER, WAYNE K. "Analysis Prediction of Performance of Experienced Key-Punch Operators." *J Indus Psychol* 4(2):48–52 '66. *
28. THUMIN, FRED J., AND BOERNKE, CAROL. "Ability Scores as Related to Age Among Female Job Applicants." *J Gerontol* 21:369–71 Jl '66. *
29. KIRKPATRICK, JAMES J.; EWEN, ROBERT B.; BARRETT, RICHARD S.; AND KATZELL, RAYMOND A. *Testing and Fair Employment: Fairness and Validity of Personnel Tests for Different Ethnic Groups,* pp. 17, 25–7, 43–50. New York: New York University Press, 1968. Pp. x, 145. *
30. THUMIN, F., AND GOLDMAN, SUE. "Comparative Test Performance of Negro and White Job Applicants." *J Clin Psychol* 24:455–7 O '68. * (*PA* 43:4565)
31. PRIEN, ERICH P. "Measuring Performance Criteria of Bank Tellers." *J Indus Psychol* 5(1):29–36 Mr '70. * (*PA* 45:7135)

CUMULATIVE NAME INDEX

Ash, P.: 23
Banas, P.: 25
Barrett, R. S.: 29
Bennett, G. K.: 1, 9
Boernke, C.: 28
Buel, W. D.: 21
Doppelt, J. E.: 9
Dunnette, M. D.: 16
Ewen, R. B.: 29
Ferguson, L. W.: *rev,* 6:1045
Fitzpatrick, E. D.: 4–7, 10
Gelink, M.: 1
Goldman, S.: 30
Harker, J. B.: 24
Hughes, J. L.: 8
Katzell, R. A.: 29
Kirchner, W. K.: 16, 25, 27

Kirkpatrick, J. J.: 29
McCarty, J. J.: 4–7, 10, 12–5
McNamara, W. J.: 8
Martin, F.: 3
Mellenbruch, P. L.: *rev,* 5: 854
Miller, M. M.: 26
Prien, E. P.: 31
Rusmore, J.: 3
Shore, R. P.: 17–20, 22
Stevens, S. N.: 21
Thumin, F.: 30
Thumin, F. J.: 28
Walker, F. C.: 11
Westberg, W. C.: 4–6
Wilkinson, B.: 2

[2152]

Short Occupational Knowledge Test for Bookkeepers. Job applicants; 1970; score is pass, fail, or unclassifiable; Bruce A. Campbell and Suellen O. Johnson; Science Research Associates, Inc. *
For additional information, see 7:1000.

[2153]

Short Occupational Knowledge Test for Office Machine Operators. Job applicants; 1970; score is pass, fail, or unclassifiable; Bruce A. Campbell and Suellen O. Johnson; Science Research Associates, Inc. *
For additional information, see 7:1001.

[2154]

Short Occupational Knowledge Test for Secretaries. Job applicants; 1969–70; score is pass, fail, or unclassifiable; Bruce A. Campbell and Suellen O. Johnson; Science Research Associates, Inc. *
For additional information, see 7:1002.

[2155]

Short Tests of Clerical Ability. Applicants for office positions; 1959–60; 7 tests; Jean Maier; Science Research Associates, Inc. *
a) CODING.
b) CHECKING.
c) FILING.
d) DIRECTIONS—ORAL AND WRITTEN.
e) ARITHMETIC. 3 scores: computation, business arithmetic, total.
f) BUSINESS VOCABULARY.
g) LANGUAGE.
For additional information and reviews by Philip H. Kriedt and Paul W. Thayer, see 6:1046.

[2156]

Shorthand Test: Individual Placement Series. Adults; 1960–66; J. H. Norman; Personnel Research Associates, Inc. *
For additional information, see 7:1003.

[2157]

Skill in Typing: Measurement of Skill Test 9. Job applicants; 1966–68; MOS 9; Walter V. Clarke Associates, Inc.; AVA Publications, Inc. *
For additional information, see 7:1004.

[2158]

Stenographic Dictation Test. Applicants for stenographic positions; 1962–64; McCann Associates. *
For additional information, see 6:46.

[2159]

*Stenographic Skill-Dictation Test. Applicants for stenographic positions; 1950–73; formerly called *Test for Stenographic Skill;* 1972 test essentially the same as test copyrighted 1950 except for title and deletion from manual of one paragraph and a sample application-scoring sheet; Edward N. Hay; Aptitude Test Service, Inc. *
For additional information and reviews by Reign H. Bittner and Clifford E. Jurgensen, see 4:459.

[2160]

*Stenographic Skills Test: ETSA Test 4A. Job applicants; 1960–72, c1957–59; manual and technical handbook by S. Trevor Hadley and George A. W. Stouffer, Jr.; test by Psychological Services Bureau; Educators'-Employers' Tests & Services Associates. *
For the complete battery entry, see 2106.
For reviews of the complete battery, see 6:1025 (2 reviews).

[2161]

Survey of Clerical Skills: Individual Placement Series. Adults; 1959–66; SOCS; 5 scores: spelling, office math, office terms, filing, grammar; J. H. Norman; Personnel Research Associates, Inc. *
For additional information, see 7:1006.

[2162]

Thurstone Employment Tests. Applicants for clerical and typing positions; 1922; 2 tests, 3 scores for each test: speed, accuracy, total; L. L. Thurstone; Harcourt Brace Jovanovich, Inc. *

a) EXAMINATION IN CLERICAL WORK.
b) EXAMINATION IN TYPING.

For additional information and reviews by John M. Willits and E. F. Wonderlic of *a*, see 3:632 (6 references).

REFERENCES THROUGH 1971

1–6. See 3:632.
7. STEDMAN, MELISSA BRANSON. "A Study of the Possibility of Prognosis of School Success in Typewriting." *J Appl Psychol* 13:505–15 O '29. * (*PA* 4:891)
8. CARRUTHERS, JOHN B. "Tabular Summary Showing Relation Between Clerical Test Scores and Occupational Performance." *Occupations* 29:40–50 O '50. * (*PA* 25:3450)

CUMULATIVE NAME INDEX

Carruthers, J. B.: 8	Stedman, M. B.: 2, 7
Davidson, C. M.: 4–5	Thurstone, L. L.: 1
Hales, W. M.: 6	Willits, J. M.: *rev*, 3:632
Jorgensen, C.: 3	Wonderlic, E. F.: *rev*, 3:632

[2163]
*Typing Skill. Typists; 1952–71; formerly called *Test for Typing Skill;* Edward N. Hay; Aptitude Test Service, Inc. *

For additional information and a review by Bernadine Meyer, see 5:523.

[2164]
Typing Test for Business. Applicants for typing positions; 1967–68; TTB; 5 tests plus practice test (*a*); distribution restricted to personnel departments; Psychological Corporation (test), Jerome E. Doppelt (manual), Arthur D. Hartman (manual), and Fay B. Krawchick (manual); Psychological Corporation. *
a) PRACTICE COPY.
b) STRAIGHT COPY. 2 scores: speed, accuracy.
c) LETTERS.
d) REVISED MANUSCRIPT.
e) NUMBERS.
f) TABLES.
For additional information and reviews by Mary T. Harrison and Leonard J. West, see 7:1007.

[2165]
Typing Test: Individual Placement Series. Adults; 1959–66; J. H. Norman; Personnel Research Associates, Inc. *
For additional information and a review by Mary T. Harrison, see 7:1008.

[2166]
USES Clerical Skills Tests. Applicants for clerical positions; 1968; 6 tests; distribution restricted to State Employment Services affiliated with the United States Employment Service; published by United States Employment Service and distributed by United States Government Printing Office. *
a) TYPING TEST. 2 scores: speed, accuracy.
b) DICTATION TEST.
c) SPELLING TEST.
d) STATISTICAL TYPING TEST. 2 scores: speed, accuracy.
e) MEDICAL SPELLING TEST.
f) LEGAL SPELLING TEST.
For additional information, see 7:1009 (1 reference).

REFERENCES THROUGH 1971

1. See 7:1009.

CUMULATIVE NAME INDEX

Crambert, A. C.: 1

[Out of Print Since TIP I]

Beginner's Clerical Test, 6:1032 (2 reviews)
Business Career Aptitude Test (status unknown), 7:987
Cardall Test of Clerical Perception (status unknown), 6:1033

Clerical Perception Test, 3:624 (4 reviews, 1 excerpt)
Clerical Test D (status unknown), 3:625 (2 reviews)
Group Test 25 (*Clerical*), 4:724 (1 review, 1 reference)
Martin Office Aptitude Tests (status unknown), 4:726 (2 reviews)
National Institute of Industrial Psychology Clerical Test, 6:1041 (3 reviews, 6 references)
RBH Language Skills and Dictation Test, 7:996
Spot-the-Error Test, 7:1005
Stenogauge (status unknown), 3:389 (1 review)
Survey of Working Speed and Accuracy, 3:631 (3 reviews)
Turse Clerical Aptitudes Test, 5:855 (2 reviews, 1 reference)

INTERESTS

[2167]
The ACT Guidance Profile, Two-Year College Edition. Junior college; 1965–69; GP; the occupational interests section is the same as the *Vocational Preference Inventory;* self-administered inventory in 5 areas of which 3 (*c-e*) are profiled; Research and Development Division, American College Testing Program; the Program. *
a) AMBITIONS AND PLANS.
b) SELF-ESTIMATES.
c) OCCUPATIONAL INTERESTS. 7 scores: technical-realistic, scientific-intellectual, artistic, social, enterprising, clerical-conventional, infrequency.
d) POTENTIALS. 8 scores: technical, scientific, artistic, musical, literary, dramatic, social-enterprising, clerical.
e) COMPETENCIES. 10 SCORES: skilled trades (technical), home economics (technical), scientific, artistic, social (community service), business (enterprising), leadership (enterprising), clerical, sports, language.
For additional information and a review by Richard W. Watkins, see 7:1010 (2 references).

REFERENCES THROUGH 1971

1–2. See 7:1010.
3. McCLUNG, RAY O. *Differences in Student Characteristics and Perceptions of the College Environment Between Junior College Students Classified by Level of Satisfaction With Environment, Educational Classification and Sex.* Doctor's thesis, North Texas State University (Denton, Tex.), 1970. (*DAI* 31:5770A)
4. BRUE, ELDON J.; ENGEN, HAROLD B.; AND MAXEY, E. JAMES. "How Do Community College Transfer and Occupational Students Differ?" *ACT Res Rep* 41:1–33 F '71. * (*PA* 47:1775)

CUMULATIVE NAME INDEX

Brue, E. J.: 4	McClung, R. O.: 3
Engen, H. B.: 4	Maxey, E. J.: 4
Kee, B. E.: 2	Watkins, R. W.: *rev*, 7:1010
Lutz, S. W.: 1	

[2168]
A.P.U. Occupational Interests Guide: Intermediate Version. Ages 14–18; 1966–69; OIG; 8 scores: scientific, social service, clerical/sales, literary, artistic, computational, practical, outdoor; S. J. Closs, W. T. G. Bates (manual), M. C. Killcross (manual), and D. McMahon (manual); University of London Press Ltd. [England]. *
For additional information and reviews by David P. Campbell and David G. Hawkridge, see 7:1011 (1 reference).

REFERENCES THROUGH 1971

1. See 7:1011.
2. BATES, W. T. G.; KILLCROSS, M. C.; AND McMAHON, D. "Some Aspects of the Validation of a Measure of Occupa-

tional Interest." *Proc Inter Congr Appl Psychol* 16:717–20 '68. *

3. PRESTON, L. R.; OPENSHAW, JOAN M.; AND STOCKBRIDGE, H. C. W. "Measurement of Army Interests With APU Occupational Interests Guide." *Occup Psychol* (England) 45(3–4):243–51 '71. * (*PA* 48:12318)

CUMULATIVE NAME INDEX

Bates, W. T. G.: 1–2	McMahon, D.: 2
Campbell, D. P.: *rev*, 7:1011	Openshaw, J. M.: 3
Hawkridge, D. G.: *rev*, 7: 1011	Preston, L. R.: 3
Killcross, M. C.: 1–2	Stockridge, H. C. W.: 3

[2169]

The Applied Biological and Agribusiness Interest Inventory. Grade 8; 1965–71; revision of *Vocational Agriculture Interest Inventory;* 5 scores: animals, plants, mechanics, business, total; Robert W. Walker and Glenn Z. Stevens; Interstate Printers & Publishers, Inc. *

For additional information and a review by David P. Campbell of the original edition, see 7:1038 (4 references).

REFERENCES THROUGH 1971

1–4. See 7:1038.

CUMULATIVE NAME INDEX

Campbell, D. P.: *rev*, 7:1038	Robinson, W. A.: 3
McCarley, W. W.: 4	Walker, R. W.: 1–2

[2170]

*California Occupational Preference Survey. Grades 9–16 and adults; 1966–71; COPS; 14 scores: science professional, science skilled, technical professional, technical skilled, outdoor, business professional, business skilled, clerical, linguistic professional, linguistic skilled, aesthetic professional, aesthetic skilled, service professional, service skilled; Robert R. Knapp, Bruce Grant, and George D. Demos; Educational and Industrial Testing Service. *

For additional information, reviews by Jack L. Bodden and John W. French, and an excerpted review by Robert H. Bauernfeind, see 7:1012 (1 reference).

REFERENCES THROUGH 1971

1. See 7:1012.
2. SEDER, ROBIN WALTER. *An Investigation of the Relationship Between Inventoried Interest and Academic Major.* Master's thesis, California State College (Long Beach, Calif.), 1969.
3. HUANG, DAVID DARMING. *An Investigation of Probationary and Non-Probationary Engineering Students' Self Perceived Versus Measured Temperaments, Values and Vocational Preferences.* Doctor's thesis, Purdue University (Lafayette, Ind.), 1971. (*DAI* 32:3030A)

CUMULATIVE NAME INDEX

Bauernfeind, R. H.: *exc*, 7: 1012	French, J. W.: *rev*, 7:1012
Bodden, J. L.: *rev*, 7:1012	Huang, D. D.: 3
Freeberg, N. E.: 1	Seder, R. W.: 2

[2171]

California Pre-Counseling Self-Analysis Protocol Booklet. Student counselees; 1965; unscored survey of information and interests to be completed by student prior to counseling; no manual; George D. Demos and Bruce Grant; Western Psychological Services. *

For additional information, see 7:1013.

[2172]

★Career Guidance Inventory. Grades 7–13 students interested in trades, services and technologies; 1972; CGI; 25 scores: 14 engineering related trades (carpentry and woodworking, masonry, mechanical repair, painting and decorating, plumbing and pipefitting, printing, tool and die making, sheet metal and welding, drafting and design, mechanical engineering, in-

dustrial production, civil and architectural engineering, electrical engineering, chemical and laboratory) and 11 nonengineering related services (environmental health, agriculture and forestry, business management, communications, data processing, sales, transportation services, protective services, medical laboratory, nursing, food service); James E. Oliver; Educational Guidance, Inc. *

[2173]

Chatterji's Non-Language Preference Record. Ages 11–16; 1962; 10 scores: fine arts, literary, scientific, medical, agricultural, mechanical, crafts, outdoor, sports, household work; S. Chatterji; distributed by Manasayan [India]. *

For additional information, see 6:1050.

REFERENCES THROUGH 1971

1. CHATTERJI, S., AND MUKERJEE, MANJULA. "Stability of Measured Interests." *J Voc & Ed Guid* (India) 10:10–4 F '64. * (*PA* 39:1722)
2. ROHILA, PRITAM; SHANKHDHAR, S. C.; AND SHARMA, VIJAY. "Comparison of a Non-Verbal Interest Inventory With Its Verbal Equivalent." *J Psychol Res* (India) 10:32–6 Ja '66. * (*PA* 40:7719)
3. BAYTI, JAMNA LAL. "A Study of Vocational Preferences, Job Values and Occupational Choices of Secondary School Leavers." *J Ed Res & Exten* (India) 3:131–5 Ap '67. *
4. BANERJEE, CHHABI; DUTTA, ANATH; CHATTERJI, S.; AND MUKERJEE, M. "An Investigation Into the Interest Patterns of Deaf Children." *Psychol Ann* 4:40–4 Mr '70. * (*PA* 46:3545)
5. BOSE, UTPALA; SINHA, S.; CHATTERJI, S.; AND MUKERJEE, MANJULA. "An Investigation Into the Interest Patterns of the Students in Science, Humanities and Commerce Streams at the Higher Secondary Level." *J Psychol Res* (India) 14(1):14–21 Ja '70. *
6. CHATTERJI, S.; MUKERJEE, MANJULA; MITRA, SADHANA; AND DUTTA, A. "A Comparative Study of the Interest Patterns of the Inmates of the House of Detention, Normal School Children and Children Living in a Slum Area." *Indian J Appl Psychol* 7(2):56–62 Jl '70. *

CUMULATIVE NAME INDEX

Banerjee, C.: 4	Mukerjee, M.: 1, 4–6
Bayti, J. L.: 3	Rohila, P.: 2
Bose, U.: 5	Shankhdhar, S. C.: 2
Chatterji, S.: 1, 4–6	Sharma, V.: 2
Dutta, A.: 4, 6	Sinha, S.: 5
Mitra, S.: 6	

[2174]

College Interest Inventory. Grades 11–16; 1967; CII; 16 scores: agriculture, home economics, literature and journalism, fine arts, social science, physical science, biological science, foreign language, business administration, accounting, teaching, civil engineering, electrical engineering, mechanical engineering, law, total; Robert W. Henderson; Personal Growth Press. *

For additional information and reviews by John W. French and David A. Payne, see 7:1014.

[2175]

Connolly Occupational Interests Questionnaire. Ages 15 and over; 1967–70; COIQ; 7 scores: scientific, social welfare, persuasive, literary, artistic, clerical-computational, practical; T. G. Connolly and Joshua Fox (supplementary manual); Careers Research and Advisory Centre [England]. *

For additional information and a review by David G. Hawkridge, see 7:1015 (2 references).

REFERENCES THROUGH 1971

1–2. See 7:1015.

CUMULATIVE NAME INDEX

Connolly, T. G.: 1	Morea, P. C.: 2
Hawkridge, D. G.: *rev*, 7:1015	

[2176]

*Crowley Occupational Interests Blank. Ages 13 and over of average ability or less; 1970–72; COIB;

10 scores: 5 interest areas (active-outdoor, office, social, practical, artistic) and 5 sources of job satisfaction (financial gain, stability-security, companionship, working conditions, interest); A. D. Crowley; Careers Research and Advisory Centre [England]. *

For additional information, see 7:1016.

[2177]

Curtis Interest Scale. Grades 9–16 and adults; 1959; 10 scores (business, mechanics, applied arts, direct sales, production, science, entertainment, interpersonal, computation, farming) and 1 rating (desire for responsibility); James W. Curtis; Psychometric Affiliates. *

For additional information and reviews by Warren T. Norman and Leona E. Tyler, see 6:1052.

REFERENCES THROUGH 1971

1. KELLEHER, EDWARD J.; KERR, WILLARD A.; AND MELVILLE, NORBERT T. "The Prediction of Subprofessional Nursing Success." *Personnel Psychol* 21:379–88 au '68. * (*PA* 43:4063)

CUMULATIVE NAME INDEX

Kelleher, E. J.: 1   Norman, W. T.: *rev*, 6:1052
Kerr, W. A.: 1   Tyler, L. E.: *rev*, 6:1052
Melville, N. T.: 1

[2178]

Educational Interest Inventory. Grades 11–13 and adults; 1962–71; EII; 18 (females) or 19 (males) scores: literature, music, art, communication, education, business administration (males), engineering (males), industrial arts (males), agriculture (males), secretarial arts (females), nursing (females), library arts (females), home economics (females), botany, zoology, physics, chemistry, earth science (males), history and political science, sociology, psychology, economics, mathematics; James E. Oliver, Thomas C. Oliver (validity report), and Warren K. Willis (validity report); Educational Guidance, Inc. *

For additional information, see 7:1017 (6 references).

REFERENCES THROUGH 1971

1–6. See 7:1017.
7. WANDZEK, FRANK P. "Effects of Positive Verbal Reinforcements on Interest Selections." *Psychol Rep* 24(2):407–12 Ap '69. * (*PA* 43:15178)

CUMULATIVE NAME INDEX

Meisgeier, C. H.: 2   Thomas, D. L.: 4
Miller, C. D.: 4–6   Thomas, L. E.: 5–6
Morrill, W. H.: 5–6   Wandzek, F. P.: 7
Rishel, D. F.: 1   Weiser, J. C.: 3

[2179]

The Factorial Interest Blank. Ages 11–16; 1967; FIB; 8 scores: rural-practical, sociable, humanitarian, entertainment, physical, literate, aesthetic, scientific-mechanical; P. H. Sandall; distributed by NFER Publishing Co. Ltd. [England]. *

For additional information and reviews by David P. Campbell and Hugh F. Priest, see 7:1018 (1 reference).

REFERENCES THROUGH 1971

1. See 7:1018.
2. ZAHRAN, HAMED A. S. "The Self-Concept in the Psychological Guidance of Adolescents." *Brit J Ed Psychol* 37:225–40 Je '67. * (*PA* 41:15077)

CUMULATIVE NAME INDEX

Campbell, D. P.: *rev*, 7:1018   Sandall, P. H.: 1
Priest, H. F.: *rev*, 7:1018   Zahran, H. A. S.: 2

[2180]

The Geist Picture Interest Inventory. Grades 8–16 and adults; 1959–71; GPII; 18 (males) or 19 (females) scores: 11 or 12 interest scores (persuasive, clerical, mechanical, musical, scientific, outdoor,

literary, computational, artistic, social service, dramatic, personal service—females only) and 7 motivation scores (family, prestige, financial, intrinsic and personality, environmental, past experience, could not say); Harold Geist; Western Psychological Services. *

For additional information, reviews by Milton E. Hahn and Benjamin Shimberg, and an excerpted review by David V. Tiedeman, see 6:1054 (12 references).

REFERENCES THROUGH 1971

1–12. See 6:1054.
13. MONTESANO, NICHOLAS RAYMOND. *Interest Bases Differentials Between Ninth and Twelfth Grade Boys.* Doctor's thesis, Stanford University (Stanford, Calif.), 1962. (*DA* 23:4228)
14. GEIST, HAROLD. "Socio-Economic Status and Culture, and Occupational Aspiration and Choice." *Congreso Interamericano de Psicologia* (Mexico) 7:284–7 '63. *
15. MONTESANO, NICHOLAS, AND GEIST, HAROLD. "Differences in Occupational Choice Between Ninth and Twelfth Grade Boys." *Personnel & Guid J* 43:150–4 O '64. * (*PA* 39:9851)
16. BURG, BILLIE WALCUTT, AND BARRETT, ALBERT M. "Interest Testing With the Mentally Retarded: A Bi-Sensory Approach." *Am J Mental Def* 69:548–52 Ja '65. * (*PA* 39:10571)
17. CONNORS, MAUREEN. *A Comparative Study of the Occupational Interests of Negro and White Adolescent Boys.* Doctor's thesis, Catholic University of America (Washington, D.C.), 1965. (*DA* 26:6508)
18. GEIST, HAROLD. "Vocational Interests in Different Countries." Abstract. *Congr Inter-Am Soc Psychol* 9(1964):633–4 ['65]. *
19. HAYES, MARY P. *The Variability of Occupational Interest Patterns of Catholic, Public, and Training School Girls as Measured by the Geist Picture Interest Inventory.* Master's thesis, Catholic University of America (Washington, D.C.), 1965.
20. BLAKE, RICHARD HALEY. *A Comparison of the Test-Retest Reliability of Picture and Verbal Forms of Occupational Interest Inventories.* Doctor's thesis, University of Missouri (Columbia, Mo.), 1966. (*DA* 27:2868A)
21. KENNEDY, LEO THOMAS. *A Study of the Vocational Interest Differences Between Hearing and Non-Hearing Secondary School Students as Determined by the Geist Picture Interest Inventory.* Master's thesis, Catholic University of America (Washington, D.C.), 1967.
22. GEIST, H. "A Comparison of Occupational Choice in Various Cultures." *Proc Inter Congr Appl Psychol* 16:724–31 '68. *
23. GEIST, HAROLD. "A Comparison of Occupational Choice in Various Cultures." *Int J Exp Res Ed* 5(2):200–12 '68. *
24. GEIST, HAROLD. "A 10 Year Follow-Up of the Geist Picture Interest Inventory." *Calif J Ed Res* 19:198–206 S '68. * (*PA* 43:5924)
25. KRONENBERGER, EARL J., AND QUATMAN, GERALD L. "Performance of Institutionalized Juvenile Delinquents on the Geist Picture Interest Inventory." *Psychol Rep* 22:185–6 F '68. * (*PA* 42:10756)
26. BLAKE, RICHARD. "Comparative Reliability of Picture Form and Verbal Form Interest Inventories." *J Appl Psychol* 53(1):42–4 F '69. * (*PA* 43:7416)
27. GEIST, HAROLD. "A Comparison of Vocation Interests in Various Countries in Latin America." *Interam J Psychol* (Mexico) 3(3):169–76 S '69. * (*PA* 44:9293)
28. GEIST, HAROLD. "A Comparison of Vocational Interests at Different Levels in Schools in Japan and a Comparison With United States Counterparts." *Psychologia* (Japan) 12(3–4):227–31 D '69. * (*PA* 45:2998)
29. GEIST, HAROLD, AND GULATI, KRISHNA. "A Comparison of Vocation Interests in India and the United States." *Indian Psychol R* 7(1):67–70 Jl '70. *
30. MORRIS, J. L., AND PARKINSON, M. "Vocational Interests of Computer Programmers." *Austral Computer J* 2(3):139–42 Ag '70. *

CUMULATIVE NAME INDEX

Abdel-Meguid, S. G. M.: 1   Kennedy, L. T.: 21
Barrett, A. M.: 16   Kronenberger, E. J.: 25
Blake, R.: 26   McDaniel, H. B.: 2
Blake, R. H.: 20   Magary, J. F.: 7
Burg, B. W.: 16   Montesano, N.: 15
Clarke, C. T.: 3   Montesano, N. R.: 13
Connors, M.: 17   Morris, J. L.: 30
Geist, H.: 2, 4–6, 8–12, 14–5, Parkinson, M.: 30
   18, 22–4, 27–9; *exc*, 6:1054 Quatman, G. L.: 25
Gulati, K.: 29   Shimberg, B.: *rev*, 6:1054
Hahn, M. E.: *rev*, 6:1054   Tiedeman, D. V.: *exc*, 6:1054
Hayes, M. P.: 19

[2181]

Geist Picture Interest Inventory: Deaf Form: Male. Deaf and hard of hearing males (grades 7–16 and adults) ; 1962; adaptation of *Geist Picture Interest Inventory;* 10 scores: persuasive, clerical, mechanical, scientific, outdoor, literary, computational, artistic, social service, dramatic; Harold Geist; Western Psychological Services. *

For additional information, see 6:1055 (1 reference).

REFERENCES THROUGH 1971

1. See 6:1055.
2. BOLTON, BRIAN. "A Critical Review of the Geist Picture Interest Inventory: Deaf Form: Male." *J Rehabil Deaf* 5(2): 21–9 O '71. *

CUMULATIVE NAME INDEX

Bolton, B.: 2　　　　　　　Geist, H.: 1

[2182]

Gordon Occupational Check List. High school students not planning to enter college; 1961–67; 5 or 11 scores: business, outdoor, arts, technology, service, and 6 optional response summarization scores (preceding 5 areas and total) ; Leonard V. Gordon; Harcourt Brace Jovanovich, Inc. *

For additional information and reviews by John N. McCall and Bert W. Westbrook, see 7:1019; for reviews by John O. Crites and Kenneth B. Hoyt, see 6:1056.

[2183]

Gregory Academic Interest Inventory. Grades 13–16; 1946; 28 scores: agriculture, architecture, biological sciences, business administration, chemistry, civil engineering, commercial arts, electrical engineering, elementary education, English, fine arts, geology, history, home economics, journalism, languages, mathematics, mechanical engineering, military science, music, physics, physical education, psychology, public service engineering, religion, secondary education, sociology, speech; W. S. Gregory; Sheridan Psychological Services, Inc. *

For additional information and reviews by Paul S. Burnham, Lysle W. Croft, and Herbert A. Toops, see 3:636 (1 reference).

REFERENCES THROUGH 1971

1. See 3:636.
2. RICHARD, WILMA A. *Effectiveness of the Gregory Academic Interest Inventory in the Prediction of Academic Success of Home Economics Freshmen.* Master's thesis, University of Nebraska (Lincoln, Neb.), 1952.
3. SHAPPELL, DEAN L.; ARNOLD, FRANK C.; AND GREGORY, WILBUR S. "Differentiation of Academic Interests." *Ed & Psychol Meas* 29(2):473–8 su '69. * (*PA* 44:17427)

CUMULATIVE NAME INDEX

Arnold, F. C.: 3　　　　　　Richard, W. A.: 2
Burnham, P. S.: *rev,* 3:636　Shappell, D. L.: 3
Croft, L. W.: *rev,* 3:636　　Toops, H. A.: *rev,* 3:636
Gregory, W. S.: 1, 3

[2184]

The Guilford-Shneidman-Zimmerman Interest Survey. Grades 9–16 and adults; 1948; 18 scores: artistic (appreciative, expressive), linguistic (appreciative, expressive), scientific (investigatory, theoretical), mechanical (manipulative, designing), outdoor (natural, athletic), business-political (mercantile, leadership), social activity (persuasive, gregarious), personal assistance (personal service, social welfare), office work (clerical, numerical) ; J. P. Guilford, Edwin Shneidman, and Wayne S. Zimmerman; Sheridan Psychological Services, Inc. *

For additional information and reviews by George K. Bennett and Wilbur L. Layton, see 4:739 (2 references).

REFERENCES THROUGH 1971

1–2. See 4:739.
3. McCARTHY, MARY VITERBO. "An Empirical Study of the Personality Profiles Characterizing Differential Quantitative

and Linguistic Ability." *Studies Psychol & Psychiatry* 8(4):1–45 Je '53. * (*PA* 28:4043)
4. SHNEIDMAN, EDWIN S. "The Case of El: Psychological Test Data." *J Proj Tech* 25:131–54 Je '61. * (*PA* 36:21K31S)

CUMULATIVE NAME INDEX

Bennett, G. K.: *rev,* 4:739　　McCarthy, M. V.: 3
Foster, K. E.: 1　　　　　　Shneidman, E. S.: 2, 4
Guilford, J. P.: 2　　　　　Zimmerman, W. S.: 2
Layton, W. L.: *rev,* 4:739

[2185]

The Guilford-Zimmerman Interest Inventory. Grades 10–16 and adults; 1962–63; 10 scores: mechanical, natural, aesthetic, service, clerical, mercantile, leadership, literary, scientific, creative; Joan S. Guilford and Wayne S. Zimmerman; Sheridan Psychological Services, Inc. *

For additional information and a review by Kenneth B. Hoyt, see 6:1057.

REFERENCES THROUGH 1971

1. GUILFORD, J. P.; CHRISTENSEN, PAUL R.; BOND, NICHOLAS A., JR.; AND SUTTON, MARCELLA A. "A Factor Analysis Study of Human Interests." *Psychol Monogr* 68(4):1–38 '54. * (*PA* 29:4727)
2. GITLIN, SIDNEY. *A Study of the Interrelationships of Parents' Measured Interest Patterns and Those of Their Children.* Doctor's thesis, Temple University (Philadelphia, Pa.), 1958. (*DA* 19:3352)
3. GUILFORD, J. P. *Personality.* New York: McGraw-Hill Book Co., Inc., 1959. Pp. xiii, 562. *
4. ABDEL-GHAFFAR, ABDEL-SALAM ABDEL-KADER. *Relationships Between Selected Creativity Factors and Certain Non-Intellectual Factors Among High School Students.* Doctor's thesis, University of Denver (Denver, Colo.), 1963. (*DA* 25:1728)
5. FLAX, MORTON LEWIS. *The Stability of Relationships Between Creativity and Personality Variables.* Doctor's research study No. 1, Colorado State College (Greeley, Colo.), 1966. (*DA* 27:2857B)
6. BLANKENSHIP, KARL RICHARD. *The Relationship of Divergent Production Ability to the Interests of Selected Male Junior High School Students.* Doctor's thesis, University of Denver (Denver, Colo.), 1968. (*DA* 29:3761A)
7. SIMMS, JEANNE THOMAS. *An Investigation of the Differences Between Creative High Socio-Economic College Freshmen and Creative Low-Socio-Economic College Freshmen on Measures of Vocational Interests and Certain Motivational Factors.* Doctor's thesis, Catholic University of America (Washington, D.C.), 1970. (*DAI* 31:2693A)

CUMULATIVE NAME INDEX

Abdel-Ghaffar, A. S. A. K.: 4　Gitlin, S.: 2
Blankenship, K. R.: 6　　　　Guilford, J. P.: 1, 3
Bond, N. A.: 1　　　　　　　Hoyt, K. B.: *rev,* 6:1057
Christensen, P. R.: 1　　　　Simms, J. T.: 7
Flax, M. L.: 5　　　　　　　Sutton, M. A.: 1

[2186]

Hackman-Gaither Vocational Interest Inventory: Standard Edition. Grades 9–12 and adults; 1962–68; HGVII; positive (like), negative (dislike), and total scores for each of 8 areas: business contact, artistic, scientific-technical, health and welfare, business-clerical, mechanical, service, outdoor; 1968 form identical with form copyrighted 1965; Roy B. Hackman and James W. Gaither; Psychological Service Center of Philadelphia. *

For additional information and a review by Henry Weitz, see 7:1020 (21 references); see also 6:1058 (4 references).

REFERENCES THROUGH 1971

1–4. See 6:1058.
5–25. See 7:1020.

CUMULATIVE NAME INDEX

Arns, J.: 1　　　　　　　　Gash, I. A.: 15
Berrier, J. G.: 2　　　　　Hess, A. W.: 10
Buckalew, R. J.: 5　　　　Jeremias, H. I.: 16
Cohen, L. M.: 4　　　　　Kline, G. R.: 11
Cook, K. L.: 20　　　　　Llana, A.: 12
Creamer, W.: 18　　　　　Logue, J. J.: 17
DeCencio, D. V.: 14　　　Lubetkin, A. I.: 7
Dressler, R. M.: 21　　　Miller, J.: 8
Eddins, E. L.: 6　　　　　Reiter, R. G.: 13
Gaither, J. W.: 3　　　　Sherr, R. D.: 22

Silverman, E. H.: 9   Sullivan, J. W.: 24
Smith, J. A.: 19   Weitz, H.: rev, 7:1020
Spergel, P.: 23   Ziegler, D. J.: 25

[2187]

*Hall Occupational Orientation Inventory, Second Edition.** Grades 7–16 and adults; 1968–71, c1965–71; HOOI; 22 scores: creativity-independence, risk, information-knowledge, belongingness, security, aspiration, esteem, self-actualization, personal satisfaction, routine-dependence, data orientation, things orientation, people orientation, location concern, aptitude concern, monetary concern, physical abilities concern, environment concern, co-worker concern, qualifications concern, time concern, defensiveness; L. G. Hall, R. B. Tarrier (manual), and D. L. Shappell (manual); Scholastic Testing Service, Inc. *

For additional information and a review by Donald G. Zytowski of the earlier edition, see 7:1021 (4 references).

REFERENCES THROUGH 1971

1–4. See 7:1021.
5. YOUNGER, JESSAMINE GRIMES. *The Effect of Vocational Choice Counseling on Vocational Maturity in Selected First Year University Students.* Master's thesis, Southern Methodist University (Dallas, Tex.), 1969.
6. DIXON, DANA H. *A Comparison of the Personality Adjustment and the Occupational Needs of Black College Women.* Master's thesis, Wake Forest University (Winston-Salem, N.C.), 1971.
7. SHAPPELL, DEAN L.; HALL, LACY G.; AND TARRIER, RANDOLPH B. "Perceptions of the World of Work: Inner-City Versus Suburbia." *J Counsel Psychol* 18(1):55–9 Ja '71. * (*PA* 45: 8956)

CUMULATIVE NAME INDEX

Dixon, D. H.: 6   Tarrier, R. B.: 2, 4, 7
Hall, L. G.: 1, 4, 7   Younger, J. G.: 5
Shappell, D. L.: 3–4, 7   Zytowski, D. G.: rev, 7:1021

[2188]

Henderson Analysis of Interest, [Second Edition]. Grades 9–16 and adults; 1950; occupational preferences in 14 areas: business service, clerical, accounting and statistics, persuasive, managerial, social science, physical science, biological science, engineering, art and music, teaching, writing, mechanical, manual; Robert W. Henderson; [Personal Growth Press]. *

For additional information and reviews by Wilbur L. Layton and Donald E. Super, see 4:740.

[2189]

How Well Do You Know Your Interests. High school, college, adults; 1957–70; 54 scores: numerical, clerical, retail selling, outside selling, selling real estate, one-order selling, sales complaints, selling intangibles, buyer, labor management, production supervision, business management, machine operation, repair and construction, machine design, farm or ranch, gardening, hunting, adventure, social service, teaching service, medical service, nursing service, applied chemistry, basic chemical problems, basic biological problems, basic physical problems, basic psychological problems, philosophical, visual art appreciative, visual art productive, visual art decorative, amusement appreciative, amusement productive, amusement managerial, literary appreciative, literary productive, musical appreciative, musical performing, musical composing, sports appreciative, sports participative, domestic service, unskilled labor, disciplinary, power seeking, propaganda, self-aggrandizing, supervisory initiative, bargaining, arbitrative, persuasive, disputatious, masculinity (for males only) or femininity (for females only); Thomas N. Jenkins, John H. Coleman (manual), and Harold T. Fagin (manual); Executive Analysis Corporation. *

For additional information, see 7:1022 (2 references); for a review by John R. Hills and an excerpted review by Gordon V. Anderson, see 6:1059 (1 reference); for reviews by Jerome E. Doppelt and Henry S. Dyer, see 5:859.

REFERENCES THROUGH 1971

1. See 6:1059.
2–3. See 7:1022.

CUMULATIVE NAME INDEX

Anderson, G. V.: exc, 6:1059   Hills, J. R.: rev, 6:1059
Doppelt, J. E.: rev, 5:859   Levine, H.: 2
Dyer, H. S.: rev, 5:859   Mendelson, M. A.: 1
Griggs, S. A.: 3   Schwartz, M. M.: 2

[2190]

*Interest Check List.** Grades 9 and over; 1946–67; ICL; interviewing aid; 1967 revision identical with 1957 edition except for instructions and coding structure; developed by the United States Employment Service; United States Government Printing Office. *

For additional information on the 1957 edition, see 5:860; for reviews by Milton L. Blum and Howard R. Taylor of the original edition, see 4:741.

REFERENCES THROUGH 1971

1. HENDERSON, BRUCE, AND MADAY, DAVID. "Interest Check List Responses of Three Youth Groups." *J Employ Counsel* 4:122–6 D '67. *
2. DAVIS, STEPHEN P. "Analysis of the Interest Check List for Indications of Bias." *J Employ Counsel* 8(2):50–8 Je '71. * (*PA* 47:11865)

CUMULATIVE NAME INDEX

Blum, M. L.: rev, 4:741   Maday, D.: 1
Davis, S. P.: 2   Taylor, H. R.: rev, 4:741
Henderson, B.: 1

[2191]

★Interest Questionnaire for Indian South Africans.** Standards 6–10; 1969–71; IQISA; 7 scores: language, arts, social service, science, mechanics, business, office work; S. Oosthuizen; Human Sciences Research Council [South Africa]. *

[2192]

Inventory of Vocational Interests: Acorn National Aptitude Tests. Grades 7–16 and adults; 1943–60; 5 scores: mechanical, academic, artistic, business and economic, farm-agricultural; 1957 test identical with test copyrighted 1943; 1960 manual identical with manual copyrighted 1943; Andrew Kobal, J. Wayne Wrightstone, and Karl R. Kunze; Psychometric Affiliates. *

For additional information and a review by John W. French, see 6:1060; for reviews by Marion A. Bills, Edward S. Bordin, Harold D. Carter, and Patrick Slater, see 3:638.

[2193]

Kuder General Interest Survey. Grades 6–12; 1934–70; KGIS; also called *Kuder E*; revision and downward extension of *Kuder Preference Record—Vocational*, Form C; 11 scores: outdoor, mechanical, computational, scientific, persuasive, artistic, literary, musical, social service, clerical, verification; G. Frederic Kuder; Science Research Associates, Inc. *

For additional information, reviews by Barbara A. Kirk, Paul R. Lohnes, and John N. McCall, and excerpted reviews by T. R. Husek and Robert F. Stahmann, see 7:1024 (8 references).

REFERENCES THROUGH 1971

1–8. See 7:1024.

CUMULATIVE NAME INDEX

Carrett, P.: 7   Kirk, B. A.: rev, 7:1024
Cronbach, L. J.: 8   Lohnes, P. R.: rev, 7:1024
Husek, T. R.: exc, 7:1024   McCall, J. N.: rev, 7:1024

Mooney, R. F.: 2, 5
Plotkin, A. L.: 1
Replogle, J. R.: 3
Schneider, D. L.: 4

Shann, M. H.: 6
Shapiro, R. M.: 7
Stahmann, R. F.: *exc*, 7:1024
Tillinghast, B. S.: 7

[2194]

Kuder Occupational Interest Survey. Grades 11–16 and adults; 1956–70; KOIS; also called *Kuder DD;* items same as those in *Kuder Preference Record—Occupational* but differently scored; 106 scales for men: 77 occupational, 29 college major; 84 scales for women: 57 occupational, 27 college major; G. Frederic Kuder; Science Research Associates, Inc. *

For additional information, reviews by Robert H. Dolliver and W. Bruce Walsh, and excerpted reviews by Frederick G. Brown and Robert F. Stahmann, see 7:1025 (19 references).

REFERENCES THROUGH 1971

1–19. See 7:1025.
20. JOHNSON, CLARICE WELLS. *Nonintellective Factors Related to College Achievement and Attrition.* Doctor's thesis, University of South Carolina (Columbia, S.C.), 1970. (*DAI* 31:5129A)
21. COLE, NANCY S., AND HANSON, GARY R. "An Analysis of the Structure of Vocational Interests." *ACT Res Rep* 40:1–17 Ja '71. * (*PA* 47:1843)
22. COLE, NANCY S., AND HANSON, GARY R. "An Analysis of the Structure of Vocational Interests." *J Counsel Psychol* 18(5): 478–86 S '71. * (*PA* 47:3679)
23. DIAMOND, ESTHER E. "Occupational Interests: Male-Female or High Level-Low Level Dichotomy." *J Voc Behav* 1(4):305–15 O '71. * (*PA* 48:5928)
24. FLOWERS, HENRY MOSES. *The Relationship of Parental Identification to Parental Vocational Interest Similarity.* Doctor's thesis, University of Kansas (Lawrence, Kan.), 1971. (*DAI* 32:1851A)
25. GOLDMAN, BERT A., AND VICINANZA, PAUL. "A Scoring System for Measuring College Interest With the Kuder Occupational Interest Survey Form DD." *J Ed Res* 65(3):101–2 N '71. * (*PA* 48:1734)
26. HARRINGTON, THOMAS F.; LYNCH, MERVIN D.; AND O'SHEA, ARTHUR J. "Factor Analysis of Twenty-Seven Similarly Named Scales of the Strong Vocational Interest Blank and the Kuder Occupational Interest Survey, Form DD." *J Counsel Psychol* 18(3):229–33 My '71. * (*PA* 46:5555)
27. HAVENS, JANET M. *Relationship Between Some Intellective and Nonintellective Factors of Disadvantaged High Risk Students and Their Success in College.* Doctor's thesis, Rutgers —The State University (New Brunswick, N.J.), 1971. (*DAI* 32:6201A)
28. HORNADAY, JOHN A., AND ABOUD, JOHN. "Characteristics of Successful Entrepreneurs." *Personnel Psychol* 24(2):141–53 su '71. * (*PA* 49:3400)
29. JOHNSON, RICHARD W. "Congruence of Strong and Kuder Interest Profiles." *J Counsel Psychol* 18(5):450–5 S '71. * (*PA* 47:3697)
30. LOADMAN, WILLIAM EARL, II. *A Comparison of Several Methods of Scoring the Kuder Occupational Interest Survey.* Doctor's thesis, Michigan State University (East Lansing, Mich.), 1971. (*DAI* 32:6810A)
31. NELSON, A. GORDON. "Discrepancy Between Expressed and Inventoried Vocational Interests." *Voc Guid Q* 20(1):21–4 S '71. * (*PA* 48:1755)
32. PLATA, MAXIMINO. *A Comparative Study of the Occupational Aspirations and Interests of High School Age Emotionally Disturbed, Vocational-Technical and Regular Academic Students.* Doctor's thesis, University of Kansas (Lawrence, Kan.), 1971. (*DAI* 32:5684A)

CUMULATIVE NAME INDEX

Aboud, J.: 28
Anderson, T. E.: 5
Brown, F. G.: *exc*, 7:1025
Bunker, C. S.: 17
Cain, E. T.: 12
Clemans, W. V.: 6
Cole, N. S.: 21–2
Dauw, D. C.: 3
Diamond, E. E.: 7, 16, 23
Dolliver, R. H.: *rev*, 7:1025
Drum, D. J.: 13
Flowers, H. M.: 24
Goldman, B. A.: 25
Hanson, G. R.: 21–2
Harrington, T. F.: 19, 26
Havens, J. M.: 27
Hornaday, J. A.: 17, 28
Johnson, C. W.: 20

Johnson, R. W.: 29
Kaiser, H. E.: 10
Kuder, F.: 14
Kuder, G. F.: 2
Lefkowitz, D. M.: 18
Loadman, W. E.: 30
Lynch, M. D.: 26
Nelson, A. G.: 31
O'Shea, A. J.: 19, 26
Plata, M.: 32
Richard, J. T.: 8
Ritchie, C. M.: 9
Stahmann, R. F.: *exc*, 7:1025
Vicinanza, P.: 25
Viswanathan, K.: 1
Walsh, R. J.: *rev*, 7:1025
Wilson, R. N.: 4, 10
Zytowski, D. G.: 11, 15

[2195]

Kuder Preference Record—Vocational. Grades 9–16 and adults; 1934–70; KPR-V; G. Frederic Kuder; Science Research Associates, Inc. *
a) FORM B. 1934–60; also called *Kuder B;* 9 scores: mechanical, computational, scientific, persuasive, artistic, literary, musical, social service, clerical; masculinity-femininity score also obtainable. *Out of print.*
b) FORM C. 1934–70; also called *Kuder C;* for revision and downward extension, see 2193; 11 scores: same as for Form B plus outdoor, verification.

For a review by Martin Katz, see 6:1063 (148 references); for reviews by Clifford P. Froehlich and John Pierce-Jones, see 5:863 (211 references); for reviews by Edward S. Bordin, Harold D. Carter, and H. M. Fowler, see 4:742 (144 references); for reviews by Ralph F. Berdie, E. G. Chambers, and Donald E. Super and an excerpted review by Arthur H. Brayfield of *a*, see 3:640 (60 references); for reviews by A. B. Crawford and Arthur E. Traxler of an earlier edition, see 2:1671 (2 references).

REFERENCES THROUGH 1971

1–2. See 2:1671.
3–62. See 3:640.
63–208. See 4:742.
209–419. See 5:863.
420–567. See 6:1063.
568. SHULTZ, IRVIN T., AND RUSH, HARVEY. "Comparison of the Occupational Ranking and Interests, Education and Intelligence of Patients at Sunnyside Sanatorium." *J Appl Psychol* 26:218–26 Ap '42. * (*PA* 16:4184)
569. FRANDSEN, ARDEN. "Appraisal of Interests in Guidance." *J Ed Res* 39:1–12 S '45. * (*PA* 20:555)
570. WOODY, CLIFFORD. *Aptitudes, Achievements and Interests of High School Pupils.* University of Michigan, Bureau of Educational Reference and Research Bulletin No. 157. Ann Arbor, Mich.: School of Education, the University, 1945. Pp. vi, 159. *
571. LARSEN, ARTHUR H.; LOVELASS, HARRY D.; AND WALTER, LOWELL. "Some Characteristics of Veterans Applying for Vocational Rehabilitation." *Sch & Soc* 66:299–303 O 18 '47. * (*PA* 22:2645)
572. HAYES, SAMUEL P. "An Interest Inventory for the Educational and Vocational Guidance of the Blind." *Outl Blind* 42:95–104 Ap '48. * (*PA* 22:5553)
573. SPAULDING, V. V. "A Study of Nurse and Police Applicants." *Delaware State Med J* 20:177–8 Ag '48. * (*PA* 23: 2945)
574. HAYES, SAMUEL P. "What Mental Tests Should We Use?" *Outl Blind* 43:271–9 D '49. * (*PA* 24:3355)
575. BARNETTE, W. LESLIE, JR. "Occupational Aptitude Pattern Research." *Occupations* 29:5–12 O '50. * (*PA* 25:3239)
576. COTTLE, WM. C. "A Factorial Study of the Multiphasic, Strong, Kuder, and Bell Inventories Using a Population of Adult Males." *Psychometrika* 15:25–47 Mr '50. * (*PA* 24:4492)
577. OSBORNE, R. T.; GREENE, J. E.; AND SANDERS, WILMA B. "Are Disabled Veterans Significantly Different From Nondisabled Veterans in Occupational Preferences, Employment Histories, Aptitudes, and College Achievements?" *Sch & Soc* 72: 8–11 Jl 1 '50. * (*PA* 26:2992)
578. CAMPBELL, JESSE FRANK. *Determination of the Predictive Relationship of Selected Factors to the Scholastic Achievement of 456 Veterans With Service-Connected Disabilities.* Doctor's thesis, University of Michigan (Ann Arbor, Mich.), 1952. (*DA* 12:148)
579. HEALY, IRENE, AND BORG, WALTER R. "Personality and Vocational Interests of Successful and Unsuccessful Nursing School Freshmen." *Ed & Psychol Meas* 12:767–75 w '52. * (*PA* 27:6221)
580. PEARLMAN, SAMUEL. *An Investigation of the Problem of Academic Underachievement Among Intellectually Superior College Students.* Doctor's thesis, New York University (New York, N.Y.), 1952. (*DA* 12:599)
581. PRINCENTHAL, HERMAN H. *Response to Vocational Guidance: Veterans With Functional Psychiatric Disorders Compared With Other Disabled Veterans.* Doctor's thesis, New York University (New York, N.Y.), 1952. (*DA* 13:127)
582. WHITTOCK, JOHN MELVILLE, JR. *Study of the Interests of the Female Students Enrolled in the School of Library Science, Drexel Institute of Technology, as Measured by the Strong Vocational Interest Blank and the Kuder Preference Record.* Master's thesis, Drexel Institute of Technology (Philadelphia, Pa.), 1952.
583. DELISLE, FRANCES HELEN. *A Study of the Relationship of the Self-Concept to Adjustment in a Selected Group of College*

Women. Doctor's thesis, Michigan State College (East Lansing, Mich.), 1953. (*DA* 13:719)

584. KULICK, WILLIAM. *Personality Traits and Academic Standing of Probationary Engineering Students Before and After Counseling: An Evaluation of the Effectiveness of Non-Directive Counseling by Means of the Rorschach Test.* Doctor's thesis, New York University (New York, N.Y.), 1953. (*DA* 13:584)

585. McCARTHY, MARY VITERBO. "An Empirical Study of the Personality Profiles Characterizing Differential Quantitative and Linguistic Ability." *Studies Psychol & Psychiatry* 8(4):1–45 Ja '53. * (*PA* 28:4043)

586. MARTINSON, FLOYD M. *Some Personality Adjustment Differences of Rural Nonmigrants and Migrants.* Doctor's thesis, University of Minnesota (Minneapolis, Minn.), 1953. (*DA* 13:1291)

587. BITNER, HAROLD MILLER. *Ethnic Inter-Group Differences in Personality, General Culture, Academic Ability, and Interests in a Geographically Restricted Area.* Doctor's thesis, Ohio State University (Columbus, Ohio), 1954. (*DA* 20:772)

588. CAREY, JOAN. *An Analysis of Certain Traits as Exhibited by a Group of Women Selected for Elementary Education at Syracuse University.* Doctor's thesis, Syracuse University (Syracuse, N.Y.), 1954. (*DA* 15:1356)

589. HILL, JULIUS MATHEW. *The Effects of Artificially Measured Low Aptitude Test Scores on Change in Vocational Interest.* Doctor's thesis, University of Michigan (Ann Arbor, Mich.), 1954. (*DA* 14:781)

590. LaBUE, ANTHONY CHARLES. *An Analysis of Some Factors Associated With Persistence of Interest in Teaching as a Vocational Choice.* Doctor's thesis, Syracuse University (Syracuse, N.Y.), 1954. (*DA* 14:2001)

591. TANNER, WILLIAM C., JR. "Personality Bases in Teacher Selection." *Phi Delta Kappan* 35:271–4+ Ap '54. *

592. ARMSTRONG, MARION ELIZABETH. *A Comparison of the Interests and Social Adjustment of Underachievers and Normal Achievers at the Secondary School Level.* Doctor's thesis, University of Connecticut (Storrs, Conn.), 1955. (*DA* 15:1349)

593. CARMAN, PHILIP McCELLAN. *The Relationship of Individual and Husband-Wife Patterns of Personality Characteristics to Marital Stability.* Doctor's thesis, University of Washington (Seattle, Wash.), 1955. (*DA* 15:113)

594. GENGERELLI, J. A., AND BUTLER, BRUCE V. "A Method for Comparing the Profiles of Several Population Samples." *J Psychol* 40:247–68 O '55. * (*PA* 30:6534)

595. HYMAN, BERNARD. *The Relationship of Social Status and Vocational Interest.* Doctor's thesis, Columbia University (New York, N.Y.), 1955. (*DA* 15:1354)

596. JOHNSON, RALPH HAAKON. *Factors Related to the Success of Disabled Veterans of World War II in the Rehabilitation Training Program Approved for Mechanics and Repairmen, Motor Vehicle.* Doctor's thesis, University of Minnesota (Minneapolis, Minn.), 1955. (*DA* 15:2460)

597. LODATO, FRANCIS JOSEPH. *The Relationship Between Interest and Personality as Measured by the Kuder and the Heston and Gordon Inventories.* Doctor's thesis, St. John's University (Jamaica, N.Y.), 1955.

598. MARTINSON, FLOYD M. "Ego Deficiency as a Factor in Marriage." *Am Sociol R* 20:161–4 Ap '55. * (*PA* 31:912)

599. STOREY, JOHN STUART. *The Validity of Counseling Variables Considered in the Advisement of Disabled Veterans Entering Terminal Business Training.* Doctor's thesis, Michigan State University (East Lansing, Mich.), 1955. (*DA* 15:1019)

600. GORMAN, WILLIAM EDWARD. *The Effect of Occupational Information in English Classes on High School Juniors.* Doctor's thesis, Northwestern University (Evanston, Ill.), 1956. (*DA* 17:301)

601. KNAAK, NANCY KATHERINE. *A Study of the Characteristics of Academically Successful and Unsuccessful Freshmen Women Who Entered Northwestern University in the Fall of 1954.* Doctor's thesis, Northwestern University (Evanston, Ill.), 1956. (*DA* 17:304)

602. LEE, MARILYN CAIRNS. *Configural vs. Linear Prediction of Collegiate Academic Performance.* Doctor's thesis, University of Illinois (Urbana, Ill.), 1956. (*DA* 17:397)

603. PATTERSON, C. H. "A Kuder Pattern for Bakers and Baking Students." *Personnel & Guid J* 35:110–1 O '56. * (*PA* 31:8188)

604. POLLAN, WILLIAM D. *Stability of Interest of College Students.* Doctor's thesis, North Texas State College (Denton, Tex.), 1956. (*DA* 17:673)

605. VAN DALSEM, ELIZABETH LOU. *Factors Related to Low Achievement in High School English.* Doctor's thesis, Stanford University (Stanford, Calif.), 1956. (*DA* 16:1233)

606. CURRIE, CAROLINE. *The Relationship of Certain Selected Factors to Achievement in Freshman Composition.* Doctor's thesis, Northwestern University (Evanston, Ill.), 1957. (*DA* 18:884)

607. DIENER, CHARLES L. *A Comparison of Over-Achieving and Under-Achieving Students at the University of Arkansas.* Doctor's thesis, University of Arkansas (Fayetteville, Ark.), 1957. (*DA* 17:1692)

608. JENSEN, VERN HARMON. *An Analysis and Comparison of the Adjustment Problems of Nonachieving College Students of Low Scholastic Ability and Other Groups of Achieving and Nonachieving Students.* Doctor's thesis, University of Colorado (Boulder, Colo.), 1957. (*DA* 19:70)

609. KEMP, CLARENCE GRATTON. *Changes in Patterns of Personal Values in Relation to Open-Closed Belief Systems.* Doctor's thesis, Michigan State University (East Lansing, Mich.), 1957. (*DA* 19:271)

610. LAY, ARCHIE WILSON. *A Study of the Influence of an Interest Inventory on Choice of Major and Subsequent Academic Behavior.* Doctor's thesis, University of Houston (Houston, Tex.), 1957. (*DA* 17:1707)

611. PATTERSON, C. H. "Interest Tests and the Emotionally Disturbed Client." *Ed & Psychol Meas* 17:264–80 su '57. * (*PA* 32:5620)

612. ROOKS, ILA. *Teaching Satisfaction in Relation to Intelligence, Interests, and Grade-Point Average of Selected University of Georgia Graduates.* Doctor's thesis, University of Georgia (Athens, Ga.), 1957. (*DA* 17:1953)

613. ROWE, FREDERICK B. *The Selection of Psychiatric Aides: Criterion Development and Prediction.* Doctor's thesis, University of Maryland (College Park, Md.), 1957. (*DA* 17:2674)

614. SIDNEY, GEORGE PAUL. *A Study of Psychological Test and Biographical Variables as Possible Predictors of Successful Psychiatric Aide Performance.* Doctor's thesis, Pennsylvania State University (University Park, Pa.), 1957. (*DA* 18:289)

615. SMITH, ROBIN NELSON. *The Evaluation of a Less Structured Form of Interest Test Item.* Doctor's thesis, Columbia University (New York, N.Y.), 1957. (*DA* 17:1709)

616. BRADLEY, ARTHUR DICKINSON. *Estimating Success in Technical and Skilled Trade Courses Using a Multivariate Statistical Analysis.* Doctor's thesis, University of Minnesota (Minneapolis, Minn.), 1958. (*DA* 21:313)

617. CANNON, DEORE J. *The Concepts of Interest and Need Held by Two Occupational Groups.* Doctor's thesis, University of Texas (Austin, Tex.), 1958 (*DA* 19:2283)

618. FRANKEL, EDWARD. *A Comparative Study of Achieving and Underachieving High School Boys of High Intellectual Ability.* Doctor's thesis, Yeshiva University (New York, N.Y.), 1958. (*DA* 20:956)

619. HENNESSY, THOMAS, AND BLUHM, HAROLD. "Using Interest Inventories in Religious and Sacerdotal Counseling." *Cath Counselor* 2:46–9 w '58. *

620. MAHONEY, STANLEY C., AND AUSTON, CHARLES A. "The Empathy Test and Self-Awareness of Kuder Interest Pattern." *Psychol Rep* 4:422 S '58. * (*PA* 33:6265)

621. REINHARD, NORMAN F. *The Validation of Several Procedures for Selecting Student Leaders in a Secondary School Level Naval Military Academy.* Doctor's thesis, Temple University (Philadelphia, Pa.), 1958. (*DA* 19:357)

622. BARSHAY, HELEN BERNADETTE. *An Evaluation of the Contribution of Selected Factors to the Job Satisfaction of Transcribing Typists Who Are Blind.* Doctor's thesis, New York University (New York, N.Y.), 1959. (*DA* 20:1221)

623. BERRYESSA, MAX JOSEPH. *Factors Contributing to the Competency of Elementary Teachers in Teaching Science.* Doctor's thesis, Stanford University (Stanford, Calif.), 1959. (*DA* 20:558)

624. GORDON, BARBARA JANE ARTHUR. *The Determination and Study of Academic Underachievement in the New York State College of Home Economics at Cornell University With Implications for Counseling and Admissions.* Doctor's thesis, Cornell University (Ithaca, N.Y.), 1959. (*DA* 20:1675)

625. MORTOLA, DORIS S. *A Study Employing the Kuder Preference Record for the Purpose of Comparing the Interest Patterns of Two Groups of College Freshmen: Accounting Majors and Marketing Majors.* Master's thesis, Fordham University (New York, N.Y.), 1959.

626. O'HARA, ROBERT P., AND TIEDEMAN, DAVID V. "The Vocational Self-Concept in Adolescence." *J Counsel Psychol* 6:292–301 w '59. * (*PA* 35:3279)

627. VILLEME, MELVIN G. *A Study of the Problems Associated With Various Types of Interest Patterns on the Kuder Preference Record as Indicated by the Mooney Problem Checklist.* Master's thesis, University of Kansas (Lawrence, Kan.), 1959.

628. WALCH, SHELBY LEWIS. *Self-Estimates of Aptitudes and Preferences and Test-Score Defensiveness.* Doctor's thesis, University of Texas (Austin, Tex.), 1959. (*DA* 20:210)

629. BELL, MYRTLE LEE. *The Relationship of Selected Variables to Success of Part-Time Recreation Personnel Employed as Summer Playground Leaders.* Doctor's thesis, University of Texas (Austin, Tex.), 1960. (*DA* 21:2528)

630. FRANKEL, EDWARD. "A Comparative Study of Achieving and Underachieving High School Boys of High Intellectual Ability." *J Ed Res* 53:172–80 Ja '60. * (*PA* 35:7115)

631. GRAY, BENJAMIN GALBREATH. *Characteristics of High and Low Achieving High School Seniors of High Average Academic Aptitude.* Doctor's thesis, University of Southern California (Los Angeles, Calif.), 1960. (*DA* 21:1459)

632. NAUSS, ALLEN HENRY. *Scholastic Ability, Self-Concept and Occupational Plans.* Doctor's thesis, University of Missouri (Columbia, Mo.), 1960. (*DA* 21:2596)

633. ROSEN, MORTON HAROLD. *The Relationship Between Unevenness of Cognitive Functioning as Derived From Verbal-Spatial Discrepancy Scores and Measures of Personality Func-*

Kuder Preference Record—Vocational

tioning. Doctor's thesis, New York University (New York, N.Y.), 1960. (*DA* 20:4724)

634. WAGNER, EDWIN E. "Predicting Success for Young Executives From Objective Test Scores and Personal Data." *Personnel Psychol* 13:181-6 su '60. * (*PA* 36:2LD81W)

635. CAMPBELL, MARY GREGORY. *A Comparative Study of Mental Ability, Personality, and Interests of First-Year Nursing Students in the Diploma and the Baccalaureate Programs.* Doctor's thesis, Fordham University (New York, N.Y.), 1961. (*DA* 26:7152)

636. CARMICAL, LaVERNE LATHROP. *The Identification of Certain Characteristics of Selected Achievers and Underachievers of Bellaire Senior High School.* Doctor's thesis, University of Houston (Houston, Tex.), 1961. (*DA* 22:2244)

637. DARTER, CLARENCE LESLIE, JR. *A Comparative Study of Over-Achieving and Under-Achieving Ninth-Grade Students.* Doctor's thesis, Texas Technological College (Lubbock, Tex.), 1961. (*DA* 22:1462)

638. FIRKINS, CURTIS JAMES. *Factors Related to Change of Major by College Students.* Doctor's thesis, North Texas State College (Denton, Tex.), 1961. (*DA* 22:2287)

639. GOLBURGH, STEPHEN JON. "Vocational Interests of Psychiatric Patients." *Rehabil Counsel B* 4:130-2 S '61. *

640. RISHEL, DARRELL FRED. *The Development and Validation of Instruments and Techniques for the Selective Admission of Applicants for Graduate Studies in Counselor Education.* Doctor's thesis, Pennsylvania State University (University Park, Pa.), 1961. (*DA* 22:2271)

641. SHNEIDMAN, EDWIN S. "The Case of El: Psychological Test Data." *J Proj Tech* 25:131-54 Je '61. * (*PA* 36:21K31S)

642. ABRAHAMS, INA. "Vocational Interests of Selected Indian College Students as Measured by the Kuder Preference Record." *J Am Indian Ed* 2:20-4 O '62. *

643. FRINSKO, WILLIAM. *Experimental Post-Degree Program at Wayne State University—An Analysis of the Selective and Predictive Factors in Student Teaching.* Doctor's thesis, Wayne State University (Detroit, Mich.), 1962. (*DA* 24:1901)

644. JONES, J. B. "Some Personal-Social Factors Contributing to Academic Failure at Texas Southern University," pp. 135-6. (*PA* 37:5606) In *Personality Factors on the College Campus: Review of a Symposium.* Edited by Robert L. Sutherland and Others. Austin, Tex.: Hogg Foundation for Mental Health, 1962. Pp. xxii, 242. * (*PA* 37:5621)

645. MARSH, STEWART H. "Validating the Selection of Deputy Sheriffs." *Pub Personnel R* 23:41-4 Jl '62. * (*PA* 37:2051)

646. PERRY, JAMES OLDEN. *A Study of a Selective Set of Criteria for Determining Success in Secondary Student Teaching at Texas Southern University.* Doctor's thesis, University of Texas (Austin, Tex.), 1962. (*DA* 23:1617)

647. POOR, FREDERICK ALBERT. *The Similarities and Differences in the Successful and Unsuccessful Second-Semester Accounting Students at Northern Illinois University.* Doctor's thesis, University of Minnesota (Minneapolis, Minn.), 1962. (*DA* 23:2381)

648. TERWILLIGER, JAMES SHAW. *Dimensions of Occupational Preference.* Doctor's thesis, University of Illinois (Urbana, Ill.), 1962. (*DA* 23:4424)

649. BECKER, JAMES A. "Interest Pattern Faking by Female Job Applicants." *J Indus Psychol* 1:51-4 Je '63. * (*PA* 38:10455)

650. D'AOUST, THÉRÈSE. *Predictive Validity of Four Psychometric Tests in a Selected School of Nursing.* Master's thesis, Catholic University of America (Washington, D.C.), 1963.

651. DUSTAN, LAURA CORBIN. *Characteristics of Students in Three Types of Nursing Education Programs.* Doctor's thesis, University of California (Berkeley, Calif.), 1963. (*DA* 24:3697)

652. MACLEAN, MURDOCH JOSEPH. *An Investigation of the Factors Influencing the Occupational Choices of Selected College Students.* Doctor's thesis, Fordham University (New York, N.Y.), 1963. (*DA* 25:2351)

653. MAGEE, PAULINE CECILIA. *Cooperation, Background Factors, Personality, and Interests of Senior and Junior College Students in Three Achievement Categories.* Doctor's thesis, Fordham University (New York, N.Y.), 1963. (*DA* 24:630)

654. RICHARDSON, JOHN FRANCIS, III. *A Comparison of Certain Characteristics of a Group of Negro Education and Non-Education College Students: An Investigation to Determine the Nature and Significance of the Differences in Various Characteristics Between Negro College Students Who Select Teaching and Those Who Choose Other Vocational Goals.* Doctor's thesis, New York University (New York, N.Y.), 1963. (*DA* 24:2789)

655. WOOD, PAUL LESLIE. *The Relationship of the College Characteristics Index to Achievement and Certain Other Variables for Freshmen Women in the College of Education at the University of Georgia.* Doctor's thesis, University of Georgia (Athens, Ga.), 1963. (*DA* 24:4558)

656. WYNN, DAN CAMP. *Factors Related to Gain and Loss of Scientific Interest During High School.* Doctor's thesis, University of Georgia (Athens, Ga.), 1963. (*DA* 24:4491)

657. ATTY, JAMES CHARLES. *A Study of the Scatter of Kuder Preference Scores and Their Relationship to Academic Achievement and Mental Ability.* Doctor's thesis, University of Pittsburgh (Pittsburgh, Pa.), 1964. (*DA* 26:485)

658. BALL, MARY K. *The Relation of Identification to Voca-*

tional Interest Development. Master's thesis, Ohio University (Athens, Ohio), 1964.

659. BUCK, JAMES R., JR. *Some Identifiable Characteristics of Students Entering Negro Senior Colleges in Mississippi.* Doctor's thesis, George Peabody College for Teachers (Nashville, Tenn.), 1964. (*DA* 25:5039)

660. CALLIS, ROBERT; WEST, DORAL N.; AND RICKSECKER, E. L. *The Counselor's Handbook: Profile Interpretation of the Strong Vocational Interest Blanks.* Urbana, Ill.: R. W. Parkinson & Associates, 1964. Pp. 100. *

661. CARMICAL, LAVERNE. "Characteristics of Achievers and Under-achievers of a Large Senior High School." *Personnel & Guid J* 43:390-5 D '64. * (*PA* 39:10711)

662. CHATTERJI, S., AND MUKERJEE, MANJULA. "Stability of Measured Interests." *J Voc & Ed Guid* (India) 10:10-4 F '64. * (*PA* 39:1722)

663. DENTON, MARY JANE. *Identification of Characteristics Associated With Discrepancy Between Self-Estimated and Measured Interests.* Doctor's thesis, Oklahoma State University (Stillwater, Okla.), 1964. (*DA* 26:1474)

664. DRASGOW, JAMES, AND CARKHUFF, ROBERT R. "Kuder Neuropsychiatric Keys Before and After Psychotherapy." Comments by Robert S. Waldrop. *J Counsel Psychol* 11:67-71 sp '64. * (*PA* 38:8485)

665. DREW, ALFRED S. "The Relationship of General Reading Ability and Other Factors to School and Job Performance of Machine Apprentices." *J Indus Teach Ed* 2:47-60 f '64. *

666. DUSTAN, LAURA C. "Characteristics of Students in Three Types of Nursing Programs." *Nursing Res* 13:159-66 sp '64. *

667. EDENS, LESTER WILLIAM. *An Analysis of Certain Socio-Psychological Characteristics of Unwed Mothers Referred to Private Agencies in Washington and Idaho.* Doctor's thesis, University of Idaho (Moscow, Idaho), 1964. (*DA* 25:5730)

668. FANGMAN, ELMER G. *A Comparison of Kuder Preference Record-Vocational Scores for Groups of Ninth Grade Boys and Girls Who Differ in Aptitude on Two Scales of the Differential Aptitude Tests.* Master's thesis, University of Kansas (Lawrence, Kan.), 1964.

669. FEINBERG, M. R., AND PENZER, W. N. "Factor Analysis of a Sales Selection Battery." *Personnel Psychol* 17:319-24 au '64. * (*PA* 39:8794)

670. FINLEY, PETER J. "Performance of Male Juvenile Delinquents on Four Psychological Tests." *Training Sch B* 60:175-83 F '64. * (*PA* 39:5704)

671. FORNESS, STEPHEN R., AND MIMS, THOMAS S. "A Comparison of Interest Areas on the Kuder Preference Record With Responses on an Educational Planning Questionnaire for Ninth Grade Students." *J Res Services* 4:21-2 D '64. *

672. GOBETZ, WALLACE. "Suggested Personality Implications of Kuder Preference Record (Vocational) Scores." *Personnel & Guid J* 43:159-66 O '64. *

673. HOLTAN, BOYD. "Motivation and General Mathematics Students." *Math Teach* 57:20-5 Ja '64. *

674. HUGHES, HEIDI B., AND DOLEYS, ERNEST J. "Interest, Set, and Incidental Learning." *Psychol Rep* 15:47-51 Ag '64. * (*PA* 39:587)

675. JONES, KENNETH J. "Interest, Motivation, and Achievement in Science." *J Exp Ed* 33:41-53 f '64. * (*PA* 39:6097)

676. KLUGMAN, SAMUEL F. "Intra-Individual Variability Findings for a Psychotic Population on Vocational Interest Inventories." *J Counsel Psychol* 11:191-3 su '64. *

677. KOBLER, FRANK J. "Screening Applicants for Religious Life." *J Relig & Health* 3:161-70 Ja '64. * (*PA* 40:1793)

678. KRAUSKOPF, C. J.; ELDER, DOROTHY; AND MAPELI, DELIA. "Some Characteristics of Students Who Transfer From Engineering to Arts and Sciences." *Voc Guid Q* 12:187-91 sp '64. * (*PA* 39:5981)

679. KUNZLER, H. GRANT. *Self Rated Vocational Interests vs. Measured Vocational Interests and Implications for High School Guidance.* Master's thesis, University of Utah (Salt Lake City, Utah), 1964.

680. LISKE, RALPH E.; ORT, ROBERT S.; AND FORD, AMASA B. "Clinical Performance and Related Traits of Medical Students and Faculty Physicians." *J Med Ed* 39:69-80 Ja '64. *

681. LONG, JOHN M. "Sex Differences in Academic Prediction Based on Scholastic, Personality and Interest Factors." *J Exp Ed* 32:239-48 sp '64. * (*PA* 39:6058)

682. McMAHON, WILLIAM JOSEPH. *Differential Analysis of Nonintellective Factors Associated With Identified Scholastic Talent in a High School.* Doctor's thesis, Fordham University (New York, N.Y.), 1964. (*DA* 26:873)

683. MAYESKE, GEORGE W. "The Validity of Kuder Preference Record Scores in Predicting Forester Turnover and Advancement." *Personnel Psychol* 17:207-10 su '64. *

684. MEYER, PRISCILLA R. "The Kuder 'V' Scale as a Predictor of Discharge and Rehospitalization." *Newsl Res Psychol* 6:48 Ag '64. *

685. MILLSAP, CARL SHELBY. *Selected Characteristics and Post-Secondary School Educational Plans of Polk County Secondary Public School Graduates.* Doctor's thesis, University of Missouri (Columbia, Mo.), 1964. (*DA* 25:5639)

686. NEAL, CAROLYN MAE. *A Study of the Relationship of Personality Variables to Reading Ability Utilizing Tests Adminis-*

tered College Freshmen. Doctor's thesis, University of Illinois (Urbana, Ill.), 1964. (*DA* 25:4480)

687. POOL, DONALD A., AND BROWN, ROBERT A. "Kuder-Strong Discrepancies and Personality Adjustment." *J Counsel Psychol* 11:63–6 sp '64. * Supplementary letter to the editor. 11:298 f '64. * (*PA* 38:8596)

688. RONAN, W. W. "Evaluation of Skilled Trades Performance Predictors." *Ed & Psychol Meas* 24:601–8 f '64. * (*PA* 39:6074)

689. SPITZER, MORTON EDWARD, AND MCNAMARA, WALTER J. "A Managerial Selection Study." *Personnel Psychol* 17:19–40 sp '64. * (*PA* 39:2945)

690. STEPHAN, EARL E. *A Study of the Relationship of the Social Status of Ninth Grade Students and Their Interests as Measured by the Kuder Preference Record.* Master's thesis, Winona State College (Winona, Minn.), 1964.

691. SWEENEY, ROBERT HOWARD. *Testing Seminarians With the MMPI and Kuder: A Report of Ten Years of Testing.* Master's thesis, Loyola University (Chicago, Ill.), 1964.

692. TILLMAN, KENNETH GENE. *The Relationship Between Physical Fitness and Selected Personality Traits.* Doctor's thesis, University of New Mexico (Albuquerque, N.M.), 1964. (*DA* 25:276)

693. TURO, JOANN K. *The Relationship of Differential Value and Interest Patterns to Authoritarian Attitudes.* Master's thesis, Ohio University (Athens, Ohio), 1964.

694. TYLER, LEONA E. "The Antecedents of Two Varieties of Vocational Interests." *Genetic Psychol Monogr* 70:177–227 N '64. * (*PA* 39:10878)

695. WAGMAN, MORTON. "Persistence in Ability-Achievement Discrepancies and Kuder Scores." *Personnel & Guid J* 43:383–9 D '64. * (*PA* 39:10730)

696. WINICK, CHARLES. "Personality Characteristics of Embalmers." *Personnel & Guid J* 43:262–6 N '64. * (*PA* 39:10222)

697. ZECH, JAMES C. *The Kuder Preference Record as a Predictor of Occupational Choice.* Master's thesis, State College of Iowa (Cedar Falls, Iowa), 1964.

698. BALL, MARY K., AND RUSSELL, DAVID L. "Relationships Between Measures of Identification and Vocational Interests." Abstract. *Proc Ann Conv Am Psychol Assn* 73:339–40 '65. * (*PA* 39:16497)

699. DENT, ORAN B., AND ELDER, R. F. "A Vocational Preference Rank Technique." *Personnel & Guid J* 43:801–3 Ap '65. *

700. DRASGOW, JAMES, AND DREHER, ROBERT G. "Predicting Client Readiness for Training and Placement in Vocational Rehabilitation." *Rehabil Counsel B* 8:94–8 Mr '65. *

701. HANNA, GERALD STANLEY. *An Investigation of Selected Ability, Aptitude, Interest, and Personality Characteristics Relevant to Success in High School Geometry.* Doctor's thesis, University of Southern California (Los Angeles, Calif.), 1965. (*DA* 26:3152)

702. HARRANGUE, M. DAMIAN. *Developmental Changes in Vocational Interests and Work Values as Related to the Vocational Choices of College Women.* Doctor's thesis, Catholic University of America (Washington, D.C.), 1965. (*DA* 26:2050)

703. HARTMAN, BERNARD J. "A Comparison of Implied Interest and Measured Interest." *J Ed Res* 58:380 Ap '65. *

704. IVEY, ALLEN E., AND PETERSON, MARK B. "Vocational Preference Patterns of Communications Graduates." *Ed & Psychol Meas* 25:849–56 au '65. * (*PA* 40:3422)

705. JOHANSEN, ANSGAR NICHOLAS. *An Investigation of the Relationship of Childhood Identification to Language Interest and Ability.* Doctor's thesis, University of North Dakota (Grand Forks, N.D.), 1965. (*DA* 26:5869)

706. KNUDSEN, ROBERT G. *A Study of the Relationship Between Personality as Measured by the Minnesota Multiphasic Personality Inventory and Interest as Measured by the Kuder Preference Record-Form C.* Master's thesis, Utah State University (Logan, Utah), 1965.

707. LAWSON, EDWIN D. "Faking on the Kuder Preference Record." *B Maritime Psychol Assn* 14:3–8 sp '65. * (*PA* 39:15245)

708. MCCALL, JOHN N., AND MOORE, GILBERT D. "Do Interest Inventories Measure Estimated Abilities?" *Personnel & Guid J* 43:1034–7 Je '65. * (*PA* 39:15365)

709. MOUL, EDWARD CLINTON. *Analysis of Scores Made on the Kuder Preference Record, Vocational, by a Group of Negro High School Students.* Master's thesis, University of Texas (Austin, Tex.), 1965.

710. MURTAUGH, JAMES J. *A Longitudinal Study Investigating the Predictability of the MMPI and Kuder for Diocesan Seminaries.* Master's thesis, Loyola University (Chicago, Ill.), 1965.

711. NASH, ALLAN N. "Vocational Interests of Effective Managers: A Review of the Literature." *Personnel Psychol* 18:21–37 sp '65. * (*PA* 39:16589)

712. PALMER, DENSLEY HARLEY. *A Comparison of the Consistency of the Self-Judgments of Physically Disabled and Non-Disabled Male College Students.* Doctor's thesis, University of Oregon (Eugene, Ore.), 1965. (*DA* 26:4456)

713. PEDERSEN, DARHL M. "The Measurement of Individual Differences in Perceived Personality-Trait Relationships and Their Relation to Certain Determinants." *J Social Psychol* 65:233–58 Ap '65. * (*PA* 39:14976)

714. PHILLIPS, LEONARD WARREN. *A Study of the Relations Between Tentative Occupational Choice-Vocational Interests Congruency and Selected Variables.* Doctor's thesis, Michigan State University (East Lansing, Mich.), 1965. (*DA* 26:4507)

715. POOL, DONALD A. "The Kuder Social Service Scale and Hospitalization." *Rehabil Counsel B* 9:47–52 D '65. *

716. RAYGOR, ALTON L., AND WATLEY, DONIVAN J. "Height and Weight in Relation to the Development of Vocational Interests." *J Ed Res* 59:73–5 O '65. * (*PA* 40:2667)

717. SAVASTANO, HELENA. "Interests of a Group of Dental Medicine Students Studied Through the Kuder Preference Record—Some Reasons for Choosing Their Profession." *Congr Inter-Am Soc Psychol* 9(1964):628–32 ['65]. *

718. SLAYTON, WILFRED GEORGE. *A Comparison of Successful and Unsuccessful Bible College Students With Respect to Selected Personality Factors.* Doctor's thesis, University of Arizona (Tucson, Ariz.), 1965. (*DA* 26:1487)

719. SPIERS, DUANE EDWIN. *A Study of the Predictive Validity of a Test Battery Administered to Theological Students.* Doctor's thesis, Purdue University (Lafayette, Ind.), 1965. (*DA* 26:1488)

720. STAPLES, JOHN DIXON. *An Experimental Study to Identify the Basic Abilities Needed to Detect Typescript Errors With Implications for the Improvement of Instruction in Typewriting.* Doctor's thesis, University of North Dakota (Grand Forks, N.D.), 1965. (*DA* 27:1693A)

721. TARPEY, M. SIMEON. "Personality Factors in Teacher Trainee Selection." *Brit J Ed Psychol* 35:140–9 Je '65. * (*PA* 39:16480)

722. TILLMAN, KENNETH. "Relationship Between Physical Fitness and Selected Personality Traits." *Res Q* 36:483–9 D '65. * (*PA* 40:4613)

723. TRAVERS, KENNETH JOSEPH DEAN. *Forced-Choice Preferences for Problem-Solving Situations in Mathematics.* Doctor's thesis, University of Illinois (Urbana, Ill.), 1965. (*DA* 26:7161)

724. VERGER, DON MARSHALL. *A Study of the Relationships of Birth Order to the Development of Interests.* Doctor's thesis, University of Oregon (Eugene, Ore.), 1965. (*DA* 26:5544)

725. WIESNER, EUGENE FRANCIS. *Multilevel Personality Descriptions of Domiciled Men With Selected Kuder Preference Record-Vocational Profiles: A Predictive Study in Interpersonal Theory.* Doctor's thesis, University of Kansas (Lawrence, Kan.), 1965. (*DA* 26:3159)

726. ZYTOWSKI, DONALD G. "Characteristics of Male University Students With Weak Occupational Similarity on the Strong Vocational Interest Blank." *J Counsel Psychol* 12:182–5 su '65. * (*PA* 39:12374)

727. BANKS, ROBERT RICHARD. *Selected Social and Psychological Variables Related to Role Satisfaction Among Graduate Ministerial Students in a Seventh-Day Adventist Seminary.* Doctor's thesis, University of Notre Dame (Notre Dame, Ind.), 1966. (*DA* 27:2384A)

728. BARE, CAROLE E. "Counselor Sensitivity to the Counselor-Client Communication Process." Abstract. *Proc 74th Ann Conv Am Psychol Assn* 1:301–2 '66. * (*PA* 41:6145)

729. BEATON, MARY ANNE. *A Study of Underachievers in Mathematics at the Tenth Grade Level in Three Calgary High Schools.* Doctor's thesis, Northwestern University (Evanston, Ill.), 1966. (*DA* 27:3215A)

730. BELL, EVERETTE LYLE. *Factors Relating to Employment of Graduates of Des Moines Technical High School.* Doctor's thesis, Iowa State University (Ames, Iowa), 1966. (*DA* 27:892A)

731. BROADBENT, LEE ARTHUR. *The Relationship Between Self-Ratings of Interests and Measured Interests.* Master's thesis, University of California (Los Angeles, Calif.), 1966.

732. DRISCOLL, JOHN. *The Dimensions of Satisfaction With the Religious Life Among Scholastics in a Community of Teaching Brothers: A Descriptive Study.* Doctor's thesis, University of Notre Dame (Notre Dame, Ind.), 1966. (*DA* 27:1653A)

733. FINCO, ARTHUR ANTHONY. *Mathematics Majors and Transfers From the Mathematics Major at Purdue University: Temperament, Interest, Value, and Student Questionnaire Differences at the Exploratory Stage.* Doctor's thesis, Purdue University (Lafayette, Ind.), 1966. (*DA* 27:327A)

734. GASH, IRA ARNOLD. *The Stability of Measured Interests as Related to the Clinical Improvement of Hospitalized Psychiatric Patients.* Doctor's thesis, Temple University (Philadelphia, Pa.), 1966. (*DA* 27:1290B)

735. GOLDEN, JAMES FRANKLIN. *Aspirations and Capabilities of Rural Youth in Selected Areas of Arkansas in Relation to Present and Projected Labor Market Requirements.* Doctor's thesis, University of Arkansas (Fayetteville, Ark.), 1966. (*DA* 27:1199A)

736. GOSS, ALLEN MILES. *Predicting Work Success for Patients on an Industrial Rehabilitation Ward in a Neuropsychiatric Setting.* Doctor's thesis, University of Texas (Austin, Tex.), 1966. (*DA* 27:2511B)

737. HANNA, GERALD A. "An Attempt to Validate an Empirically-Derived Interest Scale and Standard Kuder Scales for Predicting Success in High School Geometry." *Ed & Psychol Meas* 26:445–8 su '66. * (*PA* 40:12781)

738. HARDING, WILLIAM THOMAS. *Differential Verbal and Quantitative Scores and Interests.* Master's thesis, Illinois State University (Normal, Ill.), 1966.

Kuder Preference Record—Vocational

739. HOLMES, JACK A., AND SINGER, HARRY. *Speed and Power of Reading in High School.* Cooperative Research Monograph No. 14. Washington, D.C.: United States Government Printing Office, 1966. Pp. xii, 183. *

740. IVANOFF, JOHN M.; MONROE, GERALD D.; AND MARITA, M. "Use of Intellective and Non-Intellective Factors in Classifying Female Elementary and Secondary Teacher Trainees." *J Exp Ed* 34:55–61 su '66. * (*PA* 40:11511)

741. KEIM, LAWRENCE. *A Study of Psychometric Profile Patterns of Selected Associate Degree Technology Majors.* Doctor's thesis, Purdue University (Lafayette, Ind.), 1966. (*DA* 27: 2049A)

742. KERR, WILLIAM D., AND WILLIS, WARREN K. "Interest and Ability: Are They Related?" *Voc Guid Q* 14:197–200 sp '66. * (*PA* 40:10493)

743. KLUGMAN, SAMUEL F. "Differential Preference Patterns Between Sexes for Schizophrenic Patients." *J Clin Psychol* 22: 170–2 Ap '66. * (*PA* 40:5715)

744. LEWIS, LESLIE. *A Multivariate Analysis of Variables Associated With Academic Success Within a College Environment.* Doctor's thesis, Oklahoma State University (Stillwater, Okla.), 1966. (*DA* 27:4134A)

745. MICHAL, ROBERT D. *A Study of the Prediction of Interest Stability Using Multivariate Procedures.* Doctor's thesis, University of Kansas (Lawrence, Kan.), 1966. (*DA* 28:969A)

746. MILLER, ADAM W., JR. "Proposals for Interest Test Development and Experimentation." *Personnel & Guid J* 45: 231–7 N '66. *

747. PARKER, ADAH DONOHUE. *Projections for the Selection, Training and Retention of Sub-Professional Recreation Leaders Based on an Analysis of Personality, Interest, Aptitude, and Preference Data.* Doctor's thesis, University of Illinois (Urbana, Ill.), 1966. (*DA* 27:2059A)

748. RENFER, MARY EMMA FEWELL. *Predicting Success in the Study of Descriptive Linguistics.* Doctor's thesis, University of Southern California (Los Angeles, Calif.), 1966. (*DA* 27:1268A)

749. RYDER, ANN D. *An Inquiry Into the Kuder Preference Record-Vocational Verification Scale and the Guilford-Zimmerman Temperament Survey Falsification Scale.* Master's thesis, University of Richmond (Richmond, Va.), 1966.

750. SAVASTANO, HELENA. "Interests of a Group of Dental Medicine Students Studied Through the Kuder Preference Record: Some Reasons for Choosing Their Profession." *Revista de Psicologia Normal e Patológica* 11:67–89 Ja–S '66. * (*PA* 41: 849, title only)

751. STALANS, VIRGIL, JR. *A Comparative Study of Characteristics of Students Who Made a Low Invalid V-Score and a Valid V-Score on the Kuder Preference Record.* Master's thesis, University of Tennessee (Knoxville, Tenn.), 1966.

752. VAUGHAN, RICHARD P. "Personality Characteristics of Exceptional College Students." Abstract. *Proc 74th Ann Conv Am Psychol Assn* 1:281–2 '66. * (*PA* 41:6255)

753. WEIS, SUSAN F. *An Exploratory Study of the Nature of the Occurrence of Creativity and Self Actualization Among College Students Making Vocational Selections in Home Economics Fields.* Master's thesis, Pennsylvania State University (University Park, Pa.), 1966.

754. WHITTEMORE, ROBERT G.; ECHEVERRIA, BEN P.; AND GRIFFIN, JOHN V. "Can We Use Existing Tests for Adult Basic Education?" *Adult Ed* 17:19–29 au '66. *

755. BENTZ, V. JON. Chap. 7, "The Sears Experience in the Investigation, Description, and Prediction of Executive Behavior," pp. 147–205; critique by Ross Stagner, pp. 206–27. In *Measuring Executive Effectiveness.* Edited by Frederic R. Wickert and Dalton E. McFarland. New York: Appleton-Century-Crofts, 1967. Pp. viii, 242. *

756. BINGMAN, RICHARD MARVIN. "Aptitude and Interest Profiles of Biology Participants in Montgomery County (Pennsylvania) Science Fairs." *J Res Sci Teach* 5(2):245–52 '67–68 ['68]. *

757. BINGMAN, RICHARD MARVIN. *Aptitude and Interest Profiles of Tenth Grade Biology Students Participating in the Montgomery County, Pennsylvania Science Fairs (1962–1966).* Doctor's thesis, Temple University (Philadelphia, Pa.), 1967. (*DA* 28:4039A)

758. CASTRICONE, NICHOLAS RAYMOND. *A Study of Intrateacher Group Variations: The Measured Interests of Teachers of the Educable Mentally Handicapped.* Doctor's thesis, University of Virginia (Charlottesville, Va.), 1967. (*DA* 28:3879A)

759. GOSS, ALLEN M., AND PATE, KENTON D. "Predicting Vocational Rehabilitation Success for Psychiatric Patients With Psychological Tests." *Psychol Rep* 21:725–30 D '67. * (*PA* 42:7550)

760. HUSTON, BEATRICE MOORE. *A Normative Survey of the Personal and Academic Characteristics of the Freshmen Women Students Enrolled in Mary Hardin-Baylor College, 1966–1967.* Doctor's thesis, Baylor University (Waco, Tex.), 1967. (*DA* 28:1209A)

761. KARPOFF, JOHN T. *Aptitudes for Achievement in the Vocational Programs of One Composite High School in Alberta.* Master's thesis, University of Alberta (Edmonton, Alta., Canada), 1967.

762. KISH, GEORGE B., AND BUSSE, WILLIAM. "Interest and Stimulus-Seeking." *Newsl Res Psychol* 9:13–5 N '67. *

763. LUCAS, DONALD HERBERT. *Personality Correlates of Agreement and Nonagreement Between Measures of Ability and Interest for Two Groups of Institutionalized Males.* Doctor's thesis, University of Kansas (Lawrence, Kan.), 1967. (*DA* 28:2986A)

764. McGUNNIGAL, JAMES V. *An Investigation to Determine the Relationship Between Science Achievement and Scientific Interest as Expressed by the Kuder Preference Record-Vocational.* Master's thesis, Northern Illinois University (DeKalb, Ill.), 1967.

765. MADAUS, GEORGE F., AND O'HARA, ROBERT P. "Contrasts Between High School Boys Choosing the Priesthood as Their Occupational Choice and Boys Choosing Eight Other Occupational Categories." *Cath Psychol Rec* 5:41–51 sp '67. *

766. MADAUS, GEORGE F., AND O'HARA, ROBERT P. "Vocational Interest Patterns of High School Boys: A Multivariate Approach." *J Counsel Psychol* 14:106–12 Mr '67. * (*PA* 41: 7885)

767. MARGOLIS, VICTOR HERBERT. *Kuder-Strong Discrepancy in Relation to Conflict and Congruence of Vocational Preference.* Doctor's thesis, Columbia University (New York, N.Y.), 1967. (*DA* 28:1685B)

768. MARSDEN, RALPH DAVENPORT. *Topological Representation and Vector Analysis of Interest Patterns.* Doctor's thesis, Utah State University (Logan, Utah), 1967. (*DA* 28:4004A)

769. MOWBRAY, JEAN K., AND TAYLOR, RAYMOND G. "Validity of Interest Inventories for the Prediction of Success in a School of Nursing." *Nursing Res* 16:78–81 w '67. * (*PA* 42:4634)

770. NEAL, CAROLYN M. "The Relationship of Personality Variables to Reading Ability." *Calif J Ed Res* 18:133–44 My '67. * (*PA* 41:12578)

771. NEAL, CAROLYN M. "Student Ability: Its Effect on Reading-Personality Relationships." *Ed & Psychol Meas* 27: 1145–53 w '67. * (*PA* 42:8985)

772. O'HARA, ROBERT P. "Vocational Self Concepts of Boys Choosing Science and Non-Science Careers." *Ed & Psychol Meas* 27:139–49 sp '67. * (*PA* 41:9476)

773. PEDERSEN, DARHL M. "Acquiescence and Social Desirability Response Sets and Some Personality Correlates." *Ed & Psychol Meas* 27:691–7 au '67. * (*PA* 42:739)

774. REZLER, AGNES G. "Characteristics of High School Girls Choosing Traditional or Pioneer Vocations." *Personnel & Guid J* 45:659–65 Mr '67. * (*PA* 41:9472)

775. REZLER, AGNES G. "The Joint Use of the Kuder Preference Record and the Holland Vocational Preference Inventory in the Vocational Assessment of High School Girls." *Psychol Sch* 4:82–4 Ja '67. * (*PA* 41:5031)

776. SINGH, N. P. "A Hindi Adaptation of Kuder Preference Record-Vocational Form CH." *Manas* (India) 14:81–9 D '67. * (*PA* 43:11959)

777. SLAUGHTER, KENNETH BROOKS. *A Study of Male Dropouts From Selected Public Secondary Schools of Mississippi.* Doctor's thesis, University of Southern Mississippi (Hattiesburg, Miss.), 1967. (*DA* 28:3443A)

778. STEIN, KENNETH B. "Correlates of the Ideational Preference Dimension Among Prison Inmates." *Psychol Rep* 21:553–62 O '67. * (*PA* 42:5757)

779. SWANSON, FERN TALENT. *Typewriting Achievement of Post-Secondary Students at the American Institute of Business Compared With Reading Scores, IQ's, and Academic Interests.* Master's thesis, State College of Iowa (Cedar Falls, Iowa), 1967.

780. THOMPSON, JAMES NEWTON. *Stability and Change in Measured Attitudes and Vocational Interests of Women in a Teacher Education Program.* Doctor's thesis, University of Missouri (Columbia, Mo.), 1967. (*DA* 28:4035A)

781. WINDHOLZ, GEORGE. *Divergent and Convergent Abilities of Semantic Content as Related to Some Personality Traits of College Students.* Doctor's thesis, Columbia University (New York, N.Y.), 1967. (*DA* 28:2130B)

782. WINDHOLZ, GEORGE. "Divergent and Convergent Abilities of Semantic Content as Related to Some Personality Traits of College Students." *Ed & Psychol Meas* 27:1015–23 w '67. * (*PA* 42:8976)

783. WINTER, GERALD DAVID. *Intelligence, Interest, and Personality Characteristics of a Selected Group of Students: A Description and Comparison of White and Negro Students in a Vocational Rehabilitation Administration Program in Bassick and Harding High Schools, Bridgeport, Connecticut.* Doctor's thesis, Columbia University (New York, N.Y.), 1967. (*DA* 28: 4920A)

784. ANDERSON, THOMAS EDWIN, JR. *The Effect of Reading Skill on the Comparability of the Kuder Preference Record and the Occupational Interest Survey.* Master's thesis, University of Texas (Austin, Tex.), 1968.

785. ATKINSON, GILBERT, AND LUNNEBORG, CLIFFORD E. "Comparison of Oblique and Orthogonal Simple Structure Solutions for Personality and Interest Factors." *Multiv Behav Res* 3:21–35 Ja '68. * (*PA* 42:11349)

786. BAGGALEY, ANDREW R. "Congruent Validity of the Milwaukee Academic Interest Inventory." *Ed & Psychol Meas* 28:1207–11 w '68. * (*PA* 44:6786)

787. BENTZ, V. JON. Chap. 3, "The Sears Experience in the Investigation, Description and Prediction of Executive Be-

havior," pp. 59–152. In *Predicting Managerial Success.* Edited by John A. Myers, Jr. Ann Arbor, Mich.: Foundation for Research on Human Behavior, April 1968. Pp. v, 173. *

788. BLANK, STANLEY S. "An Examination of the Usefulness of Various Psychological Instruments for Predicting Department Managers' Ratings of Clerical Sales Personnel." *Can Counsellor* 2:46–50 Ja '68. *

789. BRADSHAW, OTTIE LEON. *The Relationship of Selected Measures of Aptitude, Interest, and Personality to Academic Achievement in Engineering and Engineering Technology.* Doctor's thesis, Oklahoma State University (Stillwater, Okla.), 1968. (*DAI* 30:979A)

790. CAHOON, D. D.; PETERSON, LARS P.; AND WATSON, CHARLES G. "Relative Effectiveness of Programmed Text and Teaching Machine as a Function of Measured Interests." *J Appl Psychol* 52:454–6 D '68. * (*PA* 43:3145)

791. CLEMANS, WILLIAM V. "Interest Measurement and the Concept of Ipsativity." *Meas & Eval Guid* 1:50–5 sp '68. * (*PA* 44:7280)

792. COTTLE, WILLIAM C. *Interest and Personality Inventories,* pp. 30–49, 56–60. Guidance Monograph Series, Series 3, Testing, [No. 6]. Boston, Mass.: Houghton Mifflin Co., 1968. Pp. xi, 116. *

793. FINEGAN, ANNE L. *A Comparison Between the Cleeton Vocational Interest Inventory and the Kuder Preference Record in Assessing the Interests of College Freshmen.* Master's thesis, Colgate University (Hamilton, N.Y.), 1968.

794. FRANDSEN, ARDEN, AND SORENSON, MAURICE. "Interests as Motives in Academic Achievement." *J Sch Psychol* 7(1):52–6 '68–69. * (*PA* 43:10415)

795. GOSS, ALLEN M. "Importance of Diagnostic Categories in Evaluating Psychological Data." *J Counsel Psychol* 15:476–8 S '68. * (*PA* 42:19121)

796. GOSS, ALLEN M. "Predicting Work Success for Psychiatric Patients With the Kuder Preference Record." *Ed & Psychol Meas* 28:571–6 su '68. * (*PA* 42:19110)

797. HALL, SIDNEY G. *The Kuder Preference Record-Vocational and Its Relationship to Academic Success.* Master's thesis, East Tennessee State University (Johnson City, Tenn.), 1968.

798. HEDLEY, CAROLYN NEAL. "Learning Relationship Differences and Curriculum Choice." *Improving Col & Univ Teach* 16:268–72 au '68. *

799. HEDLEY, CAROLYN NEAL. "The Relationship of Personality Factors to Scientific and Mathematical Ability Factors." *Sch Sci & Math* 68:265–71 Ap '68. *

800. HEIBERG, DAVID ALLISON. *Psychometric Correlates Within a Youthful Offender Population.* Doctor's thesis, University of Minnesota (Minneapolis, Minn.), 1968. (*DAI* 30:382B)

801. HEILMAN, HENRIETTA. *A Study of the Relationships Between Certain Factors Associated With Employability and the Rehabilitation Status of Selected Psychiatric Clients in a Vocational Rehabilitation Program.* Doctor's thesis, New York University (New York, N.Y.), 1968. (*DA* 29:2564A)

802. LoMONACO, LEON JOHN. *Response Levels of Disadvantaged Ninth-Grade Negro Boys to Both Standard and Oral-Visual Administrations of Two Vocationally Relevant Instruments.* Doctor's thesis, New York University (New York, N.Y.), 1968. (*DA* 29:3004A)

803. MEHROTRA, CHANDRA MOHAN NATH. *Behavioral Cognition as Related to Interpersonal Perception and Some Personality Traits of College Students.* Doctor's thesis, Ohio State University (Columbus, Ohio), 1968. (*DAI* 30:372B)

804. NEAL, CAROLYN M. "Sex Differences in Personality and Reading Ability." *J Read* 11:609–14 My '68. * (*PA* 42:17204)

805. NUGENT, FRANK A. "Relationship of Kuder Preference Record Verification Scores to Adjustment: Implications for Vocational Development Theory." *J Appl Psychol* 52:429–31 D '68. * (*PA* 42:3082)

806. PALLONE, NATHANIEL J., AND BANKS, R. RICHARD. "Vocational Satisfaction Among Ministerial Students." *Personnel & Guid J* 46:870–5 My '68. * (*PA* 42:16191)

807. STAUFFER, E. "The Validity of Measured Vocational Interests in the Selection of Nonprofessional Trainees." *Proc Inter Congr Appl Psychol* 16:316–21 '68. *

808. STEIN, FRANKLIN. *Consistency of Cognitive, Interest, and Personality Variables With Academic Mastery: A Study of Field-Dependence-Independence, Verbal Comprehension, Self-Perception, and Vocational Interest in Relation to Academic Performance Among Male Juniors Attending an Urban University.* Doctor's thesis, New York University (New York, N.Y.), 1968. (*DA* 29:1429A)

809. TALLMADGE, G. K. "Relationships Between Training Methods and Learner Characteristics." *J Ed Psychol* 59:32–6 F '68. * (*PA* 42:7932)

810. TARRIER, RANDOLPH BRENAN. *Vocational Counseling: A Comparative Study of Different Methods.* Doctor's thesis, Case Western Reserve University (Cleveland, Ohio), 1968. (*DAI* 30:938A)

811. WILSON, ROBERT N., AND KAISER, HERBERT E. "A Comparison of Similar Scales on the SVIB and the Kuder, Form DD." *J Counsel Psychol* 15:468–70 S '68. * (*PA* 42:19287)

812. WINDHOLZ, GEORGE. "The Relation of Creativity and Intelligence Constellations to Traits of Temperament, Interest, and Value in College Students." *J General Psychol* 79:291–9 O '68. * (*PA* 43:3998)

813. BAILEY, HOWARD CLARK. *The Kuder Preference Record as an Instrument for Diagnosing Maladjustment in Prospective Members of the Helping Professions.* Doctor's thesis, Florida State University (Tallahassee, Fla.), 1969. (*DAI* 32:550B)

814. BATEMAN, HILMA B. *Stability of Interests and Direction of Change in Brigham Young University Seniors.* Master's thesis, Brigham Young University (Provo, Utah), 1969.

815. BENJAMIN, JEANETTE ANN. *A Study of the Social Psychological Factors Related to the Academic Success of Negro High School Students.* Doctor's thesis, Northwestern University (Evanston, Ill.), 1969. (*DAI* 30:3543A)

816. BIDWELL, GLORIA P. "Ego Strength, Self-Knowledge, and Vocational Planning of Schizophrenics." *J Counsel Psychol* 16(1):45–9 Ja '69. * (*PA* 43:5726)

817. BUTCHER, H. J. "The Structure of Abilities, Interests and Personality in 1,000 Scottish School Children." *Brit J Ed Psychol* 39(2):154–65 Je '69. * (*PA* 44:7217)

818. BUTCHER, H. J., AND PONT, H. B. "Predicting Arts and Science Specialisation in a Group of Scottish Secondary School Children: Some Preliminary Results." *Scottish Ed Studies* 1(3):3–10 Je '69. *

819. CARRON, THEODORE J. "Validity of Tests for Chemical Plant Personnel." *Personnel Psychol* 22(3):307–12 au '69. * (*PA* 44:9414)

820. FOREMAN, MILTON E., AND JAMES, LEONARD E. "Vocational Relevance and Estimated and Measured Test Scores." *J Counsel Psychol* 16(6):547–50 N '69. * (*PA* 44:4197)

821. HARRINGTON, JOSEPH ANDREW. *Multivariate Test Score Patterns on the KPR-V, the KPR-P, and Both Combined for College Women in Four Curriculum Groups and College Men in Five Curriculum Groups.* Doctor's thesis, Boston College (Chestnut Hill, Mass.), 1969. (*DAI* 30:3784A)

822. HUCKABEE, MALCOM W. "Personality and Academic Aptitude Correlates of Cognitive Control Principles." *South J Ed Res* 3(1):1–9 Ja '69. *

823. KISH, GEORGE B. "Obscure Figures Test (OFT): 4, Relationships With Kuder-Measured Interests." *Newsl Res Psychol* 11(2):18 My '69. *

824. KISH, GEORGE B., AND DONNENWERTH, GREGORY V. "Interests and Stimulus Seeking." *J Counsel Psychol* 16(6):551–6 N '69. * (*PA* 44:4260)

825. KISH, GEORGE B., AND LEAHY, LOUIS. "Stimulus-Seeking, Interests, and Aptitudes: A Replication." *Newsl Res Psychol* 11(4):22–4 N '69. *

826. LaGRONE, C. W. "Sex and Personality Differences in Relation to Feeling for Direction." *J General Psychol* 81(1):23–33 Jl '69. * (*PA* 44:5150)

827. LATHROP, ROBERT CHARLES. *A Study of Various Characteristics of Vocational-Technical Students and Community College Students.* Doctor's thesis, Washington State University (Pullman, Wash.), 1969. (*DAI* 30:4225A)

828. MORTON, JOYCE. *Stability of High School Kuder Vocational Interests as Related to Edwards Personality Needs.* Master's thesis, East Tennessee State University (Johnson City, Tenn.), 1969.

829. POSTON, WILLIAM KENNETH, JR. *Educational Administrator Job Performance and Training Program Admission Criteria.* Doctor's thesis, Arizona State University (Tempe, Ariz.), 1969. (*DAI* 30:532A)

830. RAVENSBORG, MILTON R. "Psychiatric Technicians' Ranking of Five Potential Employment Screening Tests." *Personnel J* 48(1):39–41 Ja '69. * (*PA* 44:2910)

831. SINGH, R. P. "Stability of Interest Patterns." *Indian Psychol R* 6(1):14–5 Jl '69. * (*PA* 46:11594)

832. STALLINGS, WILLIAM M., AND ANDERSON, FRANCES E. "Some Characteristics and Correlates of the Meier Art Test of Aesthetic Perception Under Two Systems of Scoring." *J Ed Meas* 6(3):179–85 f '69. * (*PA* 44:14571)

833. WALKER, RONALD E.; NICOLAY, ROBERT C.; KLUCZNY, RITA; AND RIEDEL, ROBERT G. "Psychological Correlates of Smoking." *J Clin Psychol* 25(1):42–4 Ja '69. * (*PA* 43:9698)

834. WILLMARTH, JOHN GARY. *Factors Affecting the Vocational Choice of Women of Different Ages Selecting Clerical and Secretarial Occupations.* Doctor's thesis, Washington State University (Pullman, Wash.), 1969. (*DAI* 30:991A)

835. CARLSON, STANLEY LLOYD. *Differences in Aptitude, Previous Achievement, and Nonintellectual Traits (Personality, Values, Interest, and Attitude Toward Mathematics) of Freshmen Mathematics Majors and Transfers From the Mathematics Major at the University of Northern Colorado.* Doctor's thesis, University of Northern Colorado (Greeley, Colo.), 1970. (*DAI* 31:3768A)

836. CRONBACH, LEE J. *Essentials of Psychological Testing, Third Edition,* pp. 457–86. New York: Harper & Row, Publishers, Inc., 1970. Pp. xxxix, 752. *

837. CROWELL, ORVILLE. *An Analysis of the Relationship of Measured Interests of Entering College Freshmen to Choice of Occupation Approximately Forty-Four Months Later.* Doctor's thesis, University of Arkansas (Fayetteville, Ark.), 1970. (*DAI* 31:2680A)

838. DUNHAM, PHIL RANDOLPH. *A Comparison of Interests for Selected College Majors at Southeastern State College.* Doc-

tor's thesis, Oklahoma State University (Stillwater, Okla.), 1970. (*DAI* 31:5122A)

839. ELBERFELD, STEPHAN, AND LOVE, BETHOLENE. "Identification of Aptitude Criteria for Medical Technology." *Am J Med Technol* 36(8):388–99 Ag '70. *

840. FLYE, LINDA M. *Knowledge of Aptitude as a Source of Change in Inventoried Interests.* Master's thesis, East Tennessee State University (Johnson City, Tenn.), 1970.

841. HAKANSON, IRVING STEARNS. *Influences of Parent Education and Occupation Upon Eventual Occupational Choice and Interest Patterns of Students.* Doctor's thesis, University of Oregon (Eugene, Ore.), 1970. (*DAI* 32:176A)

842. JONES, KENNETH J., AND JONES, PRISCILLA P. "Contribution of the Rorschach to Description of Personality Structure Defined by Several Objective Tests." *Psychol Rep* 26(1):35–45 F '70. * (*PA* 45:4281)

843. KEOUGH, M. ADRIENNE. *Dimensionalities and Discrepancies in Maternal Perception of the Vocational Interests of Caucasian and Negro Mothers.* Doctor's thesis, Catholic University of America (Washington, D.C.), 1970. (*DAI* 31:2109A)

844. KISH, GEORGE B. "Cognitive Innovation and Stimulus-Seeking: A Study of the Correlates of the Obscure Figures Test." *Percept & Motor Skills* 30(1):95–101 F '70. * (*PA* 46:9304)

845. KISH, GEORGE B. "Oral Passivity, Interests, and Aptitudes." *Newsl Res Psychol* 12(1):22–3 F '70. *

846. KISH, GEORGE B., AND LEAHY, LOUIS. "Stimulus-Seeking, Age, Interests, and Aptitudes: An Amplification." *Percept & Motor Skills* 30(2):670 Ap '70. * (*PA* 46:7567)

847. LAHEY, HENRY CHARLES. *Personality Differentiation of Elevated Outdoor and Literary Kuder Preference Record Scales in an Urban Population.* Doctor's thesis, University of Connecticut (Storrs, Conn.), 1970. (*DAI* 31:1014A)

848. LINDEMAN, ROBERT PAUL. *A Study of Selected Non-Intellectual Variables Among Classes of Students in a College of Engineering.* Doctor's thesis, Oklahoma State University (Stillwater, Okla.), 1970. (*DAI* 31:5852A)

849. NICOL, DONALD D., AND WARD, GEORGE, II. "A Canonical Correlation Analysis of the Minnesota Multiphasic Personality Inventory and the Kuder Preference Record." *Proc W Va Acad Sci* 41(1969):214–8 '70. *

850. REFICE, RONALD J. *A Study of the Relationship of Interest and Personality Variables Using a Multimethod Factor Analysis.* Doctor's thesis, University of Kansas (Lawrence, Kan.), 1970. (*DAI* 31:5777A)

851. RESNICK, HARVEY; FAUBLE, MARIANNE LEESON; AND OSIPOW, SAMUEL H. "Vocational Crystallization and Self-Esteem in College Students." *J Counsel Psychol* 17(5):465–7 S '70. * (*PA* 45:3008)

852. SMITH, I. MACFARLANE. "The Use of Diagnostic Tests for Assessing the Abilities of Overseas Students Attending Institutions of Further Education, Part I." *Voc Aspect Ed* (England) 22(51):1–8 Mr '70. *

853. WRIGHT, FRED H., AND L'ABATE, LUCIANO. "On the Meaning of the MMPI Mf and SVIB MF Scales." *Brit J Social & Clin Psychol* 9(2):171–4 Je '70. * (*PA* 44:16718)

854. ZENGER, WELDON F. *A Study of the Influence of Vocational and Occupational Exploration and Self-Appraisal Activities Upon the Vocational Choices and Vocational Interests of High School Seniors.* Doctor's thesis, University of Kansas (Lawrence, Kan.), 1970. (*DAI* 31:2627A)

855. BESWICK, DAVID G., AND TALLMADGE, G. KASTEN. "Re-examination of Two Learning Style Studies in the Light of the Cognitive Process Theory of Curiosity." *J Ed Psychol* 62(6):456–62 D '71. * (*PA* 47:8153)

856. BREIDENBAUGH, BARRY E., AND BROZOVICH, RICHARD W. "Self-Rated and Test Interest Patterns Among Students Referred for Vocational Rehabilitation Services." *Sch Counselor* 18(3):185–8 Ja '71. *

857. DORRIS, COLEEN WALL. *An Investigation of Vocational Interests Patterns Associated With Perceived Parent-Child Relationships of High School Adolescents of Clarksville-Montgomery County, Tennessee.* Master's thesis, University of Tennessee (Knoxville, Tenn.), 1971.

858. GABLE, ROBERT KEITH. *A Multivariate Study of Work Value Orientations.* Doctor's thesis, State University of New York (Albany, N.Y.), 1971. (*DAI* 32:1997A)

859. GARBER, JOHN RODNEY. *Characteristics of Students Enrolled in the Guided Studies Program at Rockingham Community College and Their Implications for Curriculum Development.* Doctor's thesis, North Carolina State University (Raleigh, N.C.), 1971. (*DAI* 32:3555A)

860. HARDY, RICHARD E., AND CULL, JOHN G. "Vocational Satisfaction Among Alcoholics." *Q J Studies Alcohol* 32(1A):180–2 Mr '71. * (*PA* 46:7098)

861. LEVITT, EUGENE E.; LUBIN, BERNARD; AND DEWITT, KATHRYN N. "An Attempt to Develop an Objective Test Battery for the Selection of Nursing Students." *Nursing Res* 20(3):255–8 My–Je '71. * (*PA* 51:3969)

862. LINN, MOTT ROBERTSON. *Achievement, Aptitude, Interest, and Personality Variables as Predictors of Curriculum, Graduation, and Placement.* Doctor's thesis, University of Pennsylvania (Philadelphia, Pa.), 1971. (*DAI* 32:1857A)

863. MORRIS, J. L., AND PARKINSON, M. "Vocational Interests

of Data Processing Personnel." *Austral Psychologist* 6(1):19–25 Mr '71. * (*PA* 47:3839)

864. MORRISON, JOHN WESLEY, JR. *An Investigation of Relationships Between the Experiences of High School Students and Changes in Their Vocational Interest Profiles.* Doctor's thesis, University of Connecticut (Storrs, Conn.), 1971. (*DAI* 33:2770A)

865. MULDER, FRANS. "Characteristics of Violators of Formal Company Rules." *J Appl Psychol* 55(5):500–2 O '71. * (*PA* 47:7906)

866. SAMPLE, DUANE, AND HOTCHKISS, SALLY M. "An Investigation of Relationships Between Personality Characteristics and Success in Instrumental Study." *J Res Music Ed* 19(3):307–13 f '71. * (*PA* 48:5871)

867. SMITH, I. MACFARLANE. "The Use of Diagnostic Tests for Assessing the Abilities of Overseas Students Attending Institutions of Further Education, Part II." *Voc Aspect Ed* (England) 23(54):39–48 Ap '71. *

868. VANDER WOUDE, JACK DALE. *The Relationship Between an Electro-Oculographic Measure of Interest and a Measure of Expressed and Inventoried Interests.* Doctor's thesis, University of Kansas (Lawrence, Kan.), 1971. (*DAI* 32:5685A)

869. WILKINSON, A. EARL; PRADO, WILLIAM M.; WILLIAMS, WOODROW O.; AND SCHNADT, FREDERICK W. "Psychological Test Characteristics and Length of Stay in Alcoholism Treatment." *Q J Studies Alcohol* 32(1A):60–5 Mr '71. * (*PA* 46:7116)

CUMULATIVE NAME INDEX

[2196]

★**Milwaukee Academic Interest Inventory.** Grades 12–14; 1973; MAII; 8 scores: 6 "field variable" scores (physical science, healing occupations, behavorial science, economics, humanities-social studies, elementary education) plus 2 "discriminant variable" scores (commercial vs. nurturant interests, natural science vs. social studies interests) ; Andrew R. Baggaley ; Western Psychological Services. *

REFERENCES THROUGH 1971

1. BAGGALEY, ANDREW R. "Development of a Predictive Academic Interest Inventory." *J Counsel Psychol* 10:41–6 sp '63. * (*PA* 38:10151)
2. BAGGALEY, ANDREW R., AND CAMPBELL, JAMES P. "Multiple-Discriminant Analysis of Academic Curricula by Interest and Aptitude Variables." *J Ed Meas* 4:143–9 f '67. * (*PA* 42:4434)
3. BAGGALEY, ANDREW R. "Congruent Validity of the Milwaukee Academic Interest Inventory." *Ed & Psychol Meas* 28:1207–11 w '68. * (*PA* 44:6786)
4. CAMPBELL, JAMES P. "Test-Space Prediction of Major Field of Study." *Ed & Psychol Meas* 28:887–9 au '68. * (*PA* 43:4460)

CUMULATIVE NAME INDEX

Baggaley, A. R.: 1–3   Campbell, J. P.: 2, 4

[2197]

Minnesota Vocational Interest Inventory. Males ages 15 and over not planning to attend college ; 1965–66 ; MVII ; abbreviated version of *Navy Vocational Interest Inventory;* 30 scores : 21 occupational scales (baker, food service manager, milk wagon driver, retail sales clerk, stock clerk, printer, tabulating machine operator, warehouseman, hospital attendant, pressman, carpenter, painter, plasterer, truck driver, truck mechanic, industrial education teacher, sheet metal worker, plumber, machinist, electrician, radio-TV repairman) and 9 area scales (mechanical, health service, office work, electronics, food service, carpentry, sales-office, clean hands, outdoors) ; Kenneth E. Clark and David P. Campbell (manual) ; Psychological Corporation. *
For additional information, reviews by John O. Crites and Bert W. Westbrook, and excerpted reviews by Donald W. Hall and John W. M. Rothney (reply by David P. Campbell), see 7:1026 (45 references). For excerpts from related book reviews, see 6:B126 (2 excerpts).

REFERENCES THROUGH 1971

1–45. See 7:1026.
46. CLARK, KENNETH E., AND GEE, HELEN H. "Selecting Items for Interest Inventory Keys." *J Appl Psychol* 38:12–7 F '54. * (*PA* 29:1044)
47. MAYO, GEORGE DOUGLAS, AND THOMAS, DAVID S. "Agreement Between Counselor-Counselee Vocational Decisions and Interest Inventory Scores." *Personnel & Guid J* 35:37–8 S '56. * (*PA* 31:8183)
48. MAYO, GEORGE DOUGLAS, AND GUTTMAN, ISAIAH. "Faking in a Vocational Classification Situation." *J Appl Psychol* 43:117–21 Ap '59. * (*PA* 34:2776)
49. CHRISTIANSEN, HARLEY D. "Inventoried and Claimed Interests." *Voc Guid Q* 9:128–30 w '60–61. *
50. SPIES, CARL JOSEPH. *Some Non-Intellectual Predictors of Classroom Success.* Doctor's thesis, Washington University (St. Louis, Mo.), 1965. (*DA* 26:7442)
51. LAROSE, MICHAEL JOSEPH. *The Effect of Occupational Information and Counseling Upon the Vocational Interest Patterns of Adolescent Boys in a High School Special Education Program for Educable Mentally Retarded.* Master's thesis, Catholic University of America (Washington, D.C.), 1968.
52. COLE, NANCY S., AND HANSON, GARY R. "An Analysis of the Structure of Vocational Interests." *ACT Res Rep* 40:1–17 Ja '71. * (*PA* 47:1843)
53. COLE, NANCY S., AND HANSON, GARY R. "An Analysis of the Structure of Vocational Interests." *J Counsel Psychol* 18(5): 478–86 S '71. * (*PA* 47:3679)
54. KAUPPI, DWIGHT RANDOLPH. *The Development of Instrument-Specific Reading and Comprehension Pre-Tests for Standardized Questionnaires and Inventories.* Doctor's thesis, University of Minnesota (Minneapolis, Minn.), 1971. (*DAI* 32:4844B)
55. LAU, ALAN W., AND ABRAHAMS, NORMAN M. "Stability of Vocational Interests Within Nonprofessional Occupations." *J Appl Psychol* 55(2):143–50 Ap '71. * (*PA* 46:3902)
56. RYAN, JOSEPH ADRIAN. *Vocational Preferences of Public School Special Class Students.* Doctor's thesis, Boston College (Chestnut Hill, Mass.), 1971. (*DAI* 32:1367A)

CUMULATIVE NAME INDEX

Abrahams, N. M.: 55   Blank, P. M.: 43
Barclay, J. R.: 26   Bonfield, J.: 31
Barnette, W. L.: 22, 45   Bradley, A. D.: 7
Beal, L. E.: 39   Campbell, D.: 16, 18

Campbell, D. P.: 10, 19–20, 23, 25; *exc*, 7:1026
Cardon, B. W.: 32
Christiansen, H. D.: 8, 49
Clark, K. E.: 1, 13, 46
Cole, N. S.: 52–3
Crites, J. O.: *rev*, 7:1026
Dawis, R. V.: 37
Doerr, J. J.: 27
French, J. L.: 32
Gee, H. H.: 3, 46
Ghei, S.: 9, 11
Guttman, I.: 48
Hale, P. P.: 39
Hall, D. W.: *exc*, 7:1026
Hanson, G. R.: 52–3
Johnson, R. W.: 35, 44
Kauppi, D. R.: 40–1, 54
Larose, M. J.: 51
Lau, A. W.: 55
Lowman, C. L.: 28
McCall, J. N.: 22, 24
Mahlman, R. W.: 14
Martin, G. R.: 33
Mayo, G. D.: 47–8
Messman, W. B.: 21
Michie, J.: 34
Nelson, H. F.: 17
Norman, W. T.: 6, 12
Olson, D. W.: 35
Passmore, J. L.: 36
Perry, D. K.: 4–5
Ravensborg, M. R.: 42
Rothney, J. W. M.: *exc*, 7:1026
Ryan, J. A.: 56
St. John, D. E.: 44
Schenkel, K. F.: 2
Scott, T. B.: 15
Silver, H. A.: 29, 45
Sorenson, W. W.: 19
Spies, C. J.: 50
Stafford, R. E.: 30
Thomas, D. S.: 47
Thorndike, R. M.: 37
Trockman, R. W.: 20
Vandenberg, S. G.: 30
Weiss, D. J.: 37, 40–1
Westbrook, B. W.: *rev*, 7:1026
Zytowski, D. G.: 38

[2198]

19 Field Interest Inventory. Standards 8–10 and college and adults ; 1970–71 ; 19FII ; 21 scores : fine arts, performing arts, language, historical, service, social work, sociability, public speaking, law, creative thought, science, practical-male, practical-female, numerical, business, clerical, travel, nature, sport, work-hobby, active-passive ; F. A. Fouché and N. F. Alberts ; Human Sciences Research Council [South Africa]. *
For additional information, see 7:1027.

[2199]

Occupational Interest Inventory, 1956 Revision. Grades 7–16 and adults, 9–16 and adults ; 1943–58 ; 10 scores grouped in 3 categories : fields of interests (personal-social, natural, mechanical, business, the arts, the sciences), types of interests (verbal, manipulative, computational), level of interest ; Edwin A. Lee and Louis P. Thorpe ; CTB/McGraw-Hill. *
For additional information, see 6:1064 (6 references) ; for reviews by Martin Katz and Wilbur L. Layton, see 5:864 (20 references) ; for a review by Arthur H. Brayfield of the original edition, see 4:743 (19 references) ; for reviews by Edward S. Bordin and Stanley G. Dulsky, see 3:643.

REFERENCES THROUGH 1971

1–20. See 4:743.
21–40. See 5:864.
41–46. See 6:1064.
47. HUTSON, BILLY T., AND VINCENT, NICHOLAS M. "Motivation and Prognosis in Shorthand." *J Bus Ed* 33:29–31 O '57. *
48. BONNEY, WARREN CHESTER. *An Investigation of Factors Associated With Changes in Inventoried Interests During the First Semester of College.* Doctor's thesis, University of Texas (Austin, Tex.), 1958. (*DA* 18:1718)
49. SWANSON, ROBERT ALLEN. *A Study of Factors Related to the Distortion of Interest Inventory Information Interpreted to Individuals and to Groups.* Doctor's research study No. 1, Colorado State College (Greeley, Colo.), 1963. (*DA* 25:304)
50. HELTON, WILLIAM BERNARD. *A Comparative Analysis of Selected Characteristics of Intellectually Superior Male Students Who Persist and Those Who Do Not Persist in an Advanced Placement Program.* Doctor's thesis, North Texas State University (Denton, Tex.), 1964. (*DA* 25:3394)
51. KLUGMAN, SAMUEL F. "Intra-Individual Variability Findings for a Psychotic Population on Vocational Interest Inventories." *J Counsel Psychol* 11:191–3 su '64. *
52. MORRIS, RUBY PEARL. *A Comparative Analysis of Selected Characteristics of Intellectually Superior Female Students Who Persisted and Those Who Did Not Persist in an Advanced Placement Program.* Doctor's thesis, North Texas State University (Denton, Tex.), 1964. (*DA* 25:3402)
53. STOKER, H. W.; KROPP, R. P.; AND BASHAW, W. L. "A Comparison of Scores Obtained Through Normal and Visual Administrations of the Occupational Interest Inventory." *Fla J Ed Res* 6:63–72 Ja '64. *
54. STRATTON, HERBERT B. *A Study of Vocational Interest Stability of Secondary School Students.* Master's thesis, Brigham Young University (Provo, Utah), 1964.

55. BELL, EVERETTE LYLE. *Factors Relating to Employment of Graduates of Des Moines Technical High School.* Doctor's thesis, Iowa State University (Ames, Iowa), 1966. (*DA* 27: 892A)

56. BISSETT, SHIRLEY JEFFREYS. *The Relationship of Occupational Value Orientation to Vocational Choice.* Master's thesis, Southern Methodist University (Dallas, Tex.), 1967.

57. MARSDEN, RALPH DAVENPORT. *Topological Representation and Vector Analysis of Interest Patterns.* Doctor's thesis, Utah State University (Logan, Utah), 1967. (*DA* 28:4004A)

58. PRICE, THOMAS HUGH. *Psychological Case Studies of Successful Workers in the Field of Retailing.* Doctor's thesis, University of North Carolina (Chapel Hill, N.C.), 1967. (*DA* 28: 4790B)

59. STAHMANN, ROBERT F. *Choice of Major Field: A Study of Four Systems of University Entrance Data as Predictors of Major Field at Graduation.* Doctor's thesis, University of Utah (Salt Lake City, Utah), 1967. (*DA* 28:2571A)

60. CLARK, JAMES VAL. *Characteristics Related to Preferences for Different Procedural Approaches to Counseling.* Doctor's thesis, University of Texas (Austin, Tex.), 1968. (*DA* 29:476A)

61. FREEDMAN, SAUL. *The Relationship Between Selected Variables and Success in Transcribing Typing for Trainees Who Are Blind.* Doctor's thesis, New York University (New York, N.Y.), 1968. (*DA* 29:3000A)

62. MAZUREK, FREDERICK H. *The Occupational Interests of Superior Ninth-Grade Boys as Related to Their Aspects of Adjustment.* Master's thesis, Catholic University of America (Washington, D.C.), 1968.

63. NADEL, ROBERT S. *Social Responsibility as a Criterion for the Prediction of Success of Volunteers: A Study of the Characteristics of People Who Volunteer to Serve.* Doctor's thesis, New York University (New York, N.Y.), 1969. (*DAI* 30:3549A)

64. SHERMAN, LILLIAN LASKAW. *Movers and Perseverers in Education: An Investigation of Interests, Values, Personality Factors, Self-Actualization, Need Satisfaction and Job Satisfaction Among Movers Into Counseling and Into Administration and Among Perseverers in Teaching.* Doctor's thesis, New York University (New York, N.Y.), 1969. (*DAI* 31:1023A)

65. STAHMANN, ROBERT F. "Occupational Interest Inventory 'Fields of Interests' Scores and Major Field of Study." *Ed & Psychol Meas* 29(4):987–91 w '69. * (*PA* 44:21005)

66. STAHMANN, ROBERT F. "Predicting Graduation Major Field From Freshman Entrance Data." *J Counsel Psychol* 16(2): 109–13 Mr '69. * (*PA* 43:10376)

67. LEUNES, ARNOLD, AND CHRISTENSEN, LARRY. "Reliability and Inmate Test Results." *Correct Psychologist* 4(3):85–93 N–D '70. * (*PA* 49:2670)

68. NICHOLSON, EVERARD. *Final Report of the Study of Success and Admission Criteria for Potentially Successful Risks.* Providence, R.I.: Brown University, 1970. Pp. iv, 264. *

69. JACKSON, ARTHUR MELLS. *The Effects of Three Group Approaches in Effecting Change Among Black Students.* Doctor's thesis, Indiana University (Bloomington, Ind.), 1971. (*DAI* 32: 4351A)

CUMULATIVE NAME INDEX

[2200]

Occupational Interest Survey (With Pictures): Individual Placement Series. Industrial applicants and employees; 1959–66; OIS; 9 scores: scientific, social service, literary, agricultural, business, mechanical, musical, clerical, artistic; J. H. Norman; Personnel Research Associates, Inc. *

For additional information and reviews by Robert H. Dolliver and David O. Herman, see 7:1028.

[2201]

***Ohio Vocational Interest Survey.** Grades 8–12; 1969–72; OVIS; 24 scores: manual work, machine work, personal services, caring for people or animals, clerical work, inspecting and testing, crafts and precise operations, customer services, nursing and related technical services, skilled personal services, training, literary, numerical, appraisal, agriculture, applied technology, promotion and communication, management and supervision, artistic, sales representative, music, entertainment and performing arts, teaching-counseling-social work, medical; Ayres G. D'Costa, David W. Winefordner, John G. Odgers, and Paul B. Koons, Jr.; Harcourt Brace Jovanovich, Inc. *

For additional information and reviews by Thomas T. Frantz and John W. M. Rothney, see 7:1029 (4 references).

REFERENCES THROUGH 1971

1–4. See 7:1029.

5. FERENCE, CAMILLE. *Prediction of Creativity by Means of Interest Measures.* Doctor's thesis, Ohio State University (Columbus, Ohio), 1971. (*DAI* 32:3685A)

6. HOUSLEY, WARREN FRANK. *The Narrowing Process of Vocational Decision-Making as a Function of Rejecting Attitudes.* Doctor's thesis, University of Arkansas (Fayetteville, Ark.), 1971. (*DAI* 32:2418A)

7. KARLSON, LARRY AXEL. *A Comparison of Vocational Interests of High School Juniors With Projected Manpower Needs.* Doctor's thesis, Washington State University (Pullman, Wash.), 1971. (*DAI* 32:2420A)

CUMULATIVE NAME INDEX

[2202]

Phillips Occupational Preference Scale. Ages 14 and over; 1959–65; POPS; 10 scores: clerical, computational, practical, scientific, mechanical (males), medical (females), persuasive, social service, literary, artistic, outdoor; G. R. Phillips; Australian Council for Educational Research [Australia]. *

For additional information, see 7:1030.

[2203]

Pictorial Interest Inventory. Adult males, particularly poor readers and nonreaders; 1959; for research use only; 11 scores: clerical and sales, personal service, protective and custodial, farming, mechanical, building and maintenance, skilled-sedentary, vehicle operators, electrical workers, natural processors, assembly line workers; Barron B. Scarborough; the Author. *

REFERENCES THROUGH 1971

1. YOUNG, G. W. *Preliminary Standardization of an Interest Inventory for Use in a Correctional Institution.* Master's thesis, Florida State University (Tallahassee, Fla.), 1961.

2. SCARBOROUGH, B. B. "Measurement of Interest With Pictures." *Percept & Motor Skills* 15:122 Ag '62. * (*PA* 37:4994)

3. CHANSKY, NORMAN M. "Race, Aptitude and Vocational

Interests." *Personnel & Guid J* 43:780–4 Ap '65. * (*PA* 39: 16499)

4. ZURICK, GEORGE T. *The Relationship of the Pictorial Test of Intelligence With Reading Achievement.* Master's thesis, Pennsylvania State University (University Park, Pa.), 1968.

CUMULATIVE NAME INDEX

Chansky, N. M.: 3   Young, G. W.: 1
Scarborough, B. B.: 2   Zurick, G. T.: 4

[2204]

★**Pictorial Inventory of Careers.** Grades 3–14 and disadvantaged adults; 1972; PIC; developmental edition called *Pictorial Inventory of Occupational Training Interest;* 21 scores: agriculture, business and office (data processing, secretarial), communications (fine arts, media), criminal justice, electrical/electronics, engineering technology (applied, civil/drafting), environmental and natural resources, health services, home economics and food service, mid-management and supervision, science and laboratory, service (air transportation, fire science, personal, public), trade and industry construction, mechanics, metal trades; slide projector necessary for administration; Tom Kosuth and Earl Clancy; Educators Assistance Institute. *

[2205]

Picture Interest Inventory. Grades 7 and over; 1958; PII; 9 scores: interpersonal service, natural, mechanical, business, esthetic, scientific, verbal, computational, time perspective; Kurt P. Weingarten; CTB/McGraw-Hill. *

For additional information, reviews by Ralph F. Berdie and Donald E. Super, and an excerpted review by Laurence Siegel, see 6:1066 (4 references).

REFERENCES THROUGH 1971

1–4. See 6:1066.
5–6. HOUSTON, LAWRENCE N. "Vocational Interest Patterns of Institutionalized Youthful Offenders as Measured by a Nonverbal Inventory." *J Clin Psychol* 21:213–4 Ap '65. * (*PA* 39: 12778)
7. BLAKE, RICHARD HALEY. *A Comparison of the Test-Retest Reliability of Picture and Verbal Forms of Occupational Interest Inventories.* Doctor's thesis, University of Missouri (Columbia, Mo.), 1966. (*DA* 27:2868A)
8. CHANSKY, NORMAN M. "Sex Differences and the Picture Interest Inventory." *Voc Guid Q* 15:71–4 S '66. *
9. CHANSKY, NORMAN M. "Work-Oriented Interest Scales." *Percept & Motor Skills* 23:1189–90 D '66. * (*PA* 41:5256)
10. MIHALKA, JOSEPH ALEXANDER. *Interests and the Disadvantaged.* Master's thesis, Ohio State University (Columbus, Ohio), 1966.
11. BLAKE, RICHARD. "Comparative Reliability of Picture Form and Verbal Form Interest Inventories." *J Appl Psychol* 53(1):42–4 F '69. * (*PA* 43:7416)
12. RAVENSBORG, MILTON R. "Psychiatric Technicians' Ranking of Five Potential Employment Screening Tests." *Personnel J* 48(1):39–41 Ja '69. * (*PA* 44:2910)

CUMULATIVE NAME INDEX

Berdie, R. F.: *rev,* 6:1066   Houston, L. N.: 4–5
Blake, R.: 11   Mihalka, J. A.: 10
Blake, R. H.: 7   Ravensborg, M. R.: 12
Cassel, R. N.: 3   Siegel, L.: *exc,* 6:1066
Chansky, N. M.: 8–9   Super, D. E.: *rev,* 6:1066
Hendsch, G.: 3   Weingarten, K. P.: 1–2

[2206-7]

Preference Analysis. Standards 8 and over; 1968–69; PA; 11 or 13 scores: adventurous, outdoors, clerical, domestic-decorative (females only), domestic routine (females only), fine arts and music, natural sciences, persuasion, social sciences, technical, altruistic, verbal, mathematical interest; P. Lourens; National Institute for Personnel Research [South Africa]. *

For additional information, see 7:1031.

[2208]

Rothwell-Miller Interest Blank. Ages 13 and over; 1958; RMIB; formerly called *Rothwell Interest Blank, Miller Revision;* 12 scores: outdoor, mechanical, computational, scientific, personal contact, aesthetic, literary, musical, social service, clerical, practical, medical; Kenneth M. Miller and J. W. Rothwell; Australian Council for Educational Research [Australia]. *

For additional information, see 5:867.

[2209]

Rothwell-Miller Interest Blank, [British Edition]. Ages 11 and over; 1958–68; British adaptation of original Australian edition; 12 scores: outdoor, mechanical, computational, scientific, persuasive, aesthetic, literary, musical, social service, clerical, practical, medical; original test by J. W. Rothwell; 1958 and 1968 revisions by Kenneth M. Miller; NFER Publishing Co. Ltd. [England]. *

For additional information and reviews by A. W. Heim and Clive Jones, see 7:1034 (2 references).

REFERENCES THROUGH 1971

1–2. See 7:1034.

CUMULATIVE NAME INDEX

Heim, A. W.: *rev,* 7:1034   Miller, K. M.: 1
Jones, C.: *rev,* 7:1034   Nelson, D. M.: 2

[2210]

Safran Student's Interest Inventory. Grades 8–12; 1960–69; SSII; revision of *Safran Vocational Interest Test;* 11 scores: 7 interest scores (economic, technical, outdoor, service, humane, artistic, scientific) and 4 ability self-ratings (academic, mechanical, social, clerical); Carl Safran and Edgar N. Wright; Thomas Nelson & Sons (Canada) Ltd. [Canada]. *

For additional information and a review by Thomas T. Frantz, see 7:1035; see also 6:1069 (1 reference).

REFERENCES THROUGH 1971

1. See 6:1069.

CUMULATIVE NAME INDEX

Frantz, T. T.: *rev,* 7:1035   Stewart, J. A.: 1
Safran, C.: 1

[2211]

★**The Self Directed Search: A Guide to Educational and Vocational Planning.** High school and college and adults; 1970–73; SDS; "a self-administered, self-scored, and self-interpreted vocational counseling tool"; 18 scores: 6 scores (realistic, investigative, artistic, social, enterprising, conventional) for each of 3 scales (activities, competencies, occupations); John L. Holland; Consulting Psychologists Press, Inc. *

REFERENCES THROUGH 1971

1. HOLLAND, JOHN L. "A Theory-Ridden, Computerless, Impersonal Vocational Guidance System." *J Voc Behav* 1(2):167–76 Ap '71. * (*PA* 47:11854)

CUMULATIVE NAME INDEX

Holland, J. L.: 1

[2212]

Strong Vocational Interest Blank for Men. Ages 16 and over; 1927–71; SVIB; 84 scoring scales (22 basic interests, 54 occupational, 8 nonoccupational) and 6 administrative indices; BASIC INTERESTS: adventure ('69), agriculture ('69), art ('69), business management ('69), law/politics ('69), mathematics ('69), mechanical ('69), medical service ('69), merchandising ('69), military activities ('69), music ('69), nature ('69), office practices ('69), public speaking ('69), recreational leadership ('69), religious activities ('69), sales ('69), science ('69), social service ('69), teaching ('69), technical supervision ('69), writing ('69); OCCUPATIONAL: *group 1, biological science:* dentist ('32–66), osteopath ('47–66), veterinarian ('49–66, original scale by T. E. Hannum), physician ('28–66), psychiatrist ('52–66), psychologist ('28–66, original scale by

P. H. Kriedt), biologist ('62–66, original scale by Carl A. Lindsay, Louis M. Herman, and Martin L. Ziegler) ; *group 2, physical science:* architect ('28–66), mathematician ('30–66), physicist ('30–66), chemist ('28–66), engineer ('28–66) ; *group 3, technical supervision:* production manager ('38–66), army officer ('52–66), air force officer ('66) ; *group 4, technical and skilled trades:* carpenter ('33–66), forest serviceman ('38–66), farmer ('28–66), math-science teacher ('38–66), printer ('38–66), policeman ('34–66) ; *group 5, social service:* personnel director ('28–66), public administrator ('44–66), rehabilitation counselor ('50–66, original scale entitled vocational counselor by Nathan E. Acree), YMCA secretary ('28–66), social worker ('54–66), social science teacher ('38–66), school superintendent ('30–66), minister ('28–66) ; *group 6, aesthetic-cultural:* librarian ('63–66), artist ('33–66), musician performer ('33–66), music teacher ('54–66) ; *group 7, CPA owner:* CPA owner ('49–66) ; *group 8, business and accounting:* senior CPA ('49–66), accountant ('32–66), office worker ('30–66), purchasing agent ('28–66), banker ('38–66), pharmacist ('49–66, original scale by Milton Schwebel), mortician ('46–66) ; *group 9, sales:* sales manager ('38–66), real estate salesman ('28–66), life insurance salesman ('28–66) ; *group 10, verbal-linguistic:* advertising man ('28–66), lawyer ('28–66), author-journalist ('28–66) ; *group 11, president, manufacturing concern:* president, manufacturing ('38–66) ; *group 12, supplementary occupational:* credit manager ('59–66), chamber of commerce executive ('62–66), physical therapist ('58–66), computer programmer ('66), business education teacher ('59–66, original scale by Robert V. Bacon), community recreation administrator ('66) ; NONOCCUPATIONAL: academic achievement ('66), age related interests ('69), diversity of interests ('69), masculinity-femininity II ('34–69), managerial orientation ('69), occupational introversion-extroversion ('66), occupational level ('39–66), specialization level ('52–66, original scale by Milton G. Holmen) ; ADMINISTRATIVE INDICES: total responses ('69), unpopular responses ('69), form check ('69), like percentage ('69), indifferent percentage ('69), dislike percentage ('69) ; Edward K. Strong, Jr. (except 1969 supplement), David P. Campbell, Ralph F. Berdie (1966 test), and Kenneth E. Clark (1966 test) ; Stanford University Press. *

For additional information, reviews by Martin R. Katz and Charles J. Krauskopf, and excerpted reviews by David P. Campbell and John W. M. Rothney, see 7:1036 (485 references) ; for reviews by Alexander W. Astin and Edward J. Furst of earlier editions, see 6:1070 (189 references) ; see also 5:868 (153 references) ; for reviews by Edward S. Bordin and Elmer D. Hinckley, see 4:747 (98 references) ; see also 3:647 (102 references) ; for reviews by Harold D. Carter, John G. Darley, and N. W. Morton, see 2:1680 (71 references) ; for a review by John G. Darley, see 1:1178. For excerpts from related book reviews, see 7:B127 (1 excerpt), 6:B304 (2 excerpts), 6:B305 (2 excerpts), 5:B115 (5 excerpts), 5:B414 (4 excerpts), 4:748 (2 excerpts), 3:648 (2 excerpts), 3:650 (1 excerpt), and 3:652 (11 excerpts).

REFERENCES THROUGH 1971

1–71. See 2:1680.
72–175. See 3:647.
176–273. See 4:747.
274–426. See 5:868.
427–614. See 6:1070.
615–1099. See 7:1036.
1100. OLIVER, R. A. C. "The Traits of Extroverts and Introverts." *J Social Psychol* 1:345–66 Ag '30. * (*PA* 5:308)
1101. ROSENSTEIN, ISABEL. *The Vocational Interests of Freshmen Engineers and the Development of a Short Method for Scoring Strong's Vocational Interest Test.* Master's thesis, University of Minnesota (Minneapolis, Minn.), 1930.
1102. ALLEN, GRACE E. "Plane Geometry and Character Education." *J Ed Sociol* 7:254–8 D '33. * (*PA* 8:2254)
1103. SEGEL, DAVID. "Differential Prediction of Scholastic Success." *Sch & Soc* 39:91–6 Ja 20 '34. *
1104. DYER, DOROTHY TUNELL. *The Relation Between Vocational Interests of Men in College and Their Subsequent Occupational Histories for Ten Years.* Master's thesis, University of Minnesota (Minneapolis, Minn.), 1937.
1105. FINCH, F. H., AND ODOROFF, M. E. "Sex Differences in Vocational Interests." *J Ed Psychol* 30:151–6 F '39. * (*PA* 13:4353)
1106. THOMSON, WILLIAM A. "An Inventory for Measuring Socialization—Self-Seeking and Its Relationship to the Study of Values Test, the ACE Psychological Examination, and the Strong Vocational Interest Blank." *J Appl Psychol* 25:202–12 Ap '41. * (*PA* 15:4285)
1107. ARSENIAN, SETH. "Own Estimate and Objective Measurement." *J Ed Psychol* 33:291–302 Ap '42. * (*PA* 17:934)
1108. SPOERL, DOROTHY TILDEN. "The Academic and Verbal Adjustment of College Age Bilingual Students." *J Genetic Psychol* 64:139–57 Mr '44. * (*PA* 18:2275)
1109. TODD, J. E. "Measurement in the Continuous Selection and Counseling of Students in a College of Physical Education and Social Work." *Ed & Psychol Meas* 4:233–43 au '44. * (*PA* 19:1810)
1110. FRANDSEN, ARDEN. "Appraisal of Interests in Guidance." *J Ed Res* 39:1–12 S '45. * (*PA* 20:555)
1111. GORY, ADRIAN E., AND McCLELLAND, DAVID C. "Characteristics of Conscientious Objectors in World War II." *J Consult Psychol* 11:245–57 S–O '47. * (*PA* 22:604)
1112. GUEST, LESTER. "A Study of Interviewer Competence." *Int J Opin & Attitude Res* (Mexico) 1:17–30 S '47. * (*PA* 22:4361)
1113. TERMAN, LEWIS M., AND OGDEN, MELITA H. Chap. 15, "Vocational Interests Tests," pp. 196–203. In their *Genetic Studies of Genius: Vol. 4, The Gifted Child Grows Up.* Stanford, Calif.: Stanford University Press, 1947. Pp. xiv, 448. *
1114. COTTLE, WM. C. "A Factorial Study of the Multiphasic, Strong, Kuder, and Bell Inventories Using a Population of Adult Males." *Psychometrika* 15:25–47 Mr '50. * (*PA* 24:4492)
1115. ADAMSON, DERYCK. "Selection and Appraisal of Engineering Graduates: A Case Study." *Personnel* 29:175–93 S '52. * (*PA* 27:3797)
1116. SHAW, JACK. "The Function of the Interview in Determining Fitness for Teacher-Training." *J Ed Res* 45:667–81 My '52. * (*PA* 27:3007)
1117. McCORNACK, ROBERT, AND KIDNEIGH, JOHN C. "The Vocational Interest Patterns of Social Workers." *Social Work J* 35:160–3 O '54. * (*PA* 29:6448)
1118. CROSS, THEODORE RYLAND. *An Exploratory Investigation of the Personality and Background Factors Characterizing Entering College Men Who Possess a Low Intensity of Vocational Interests.* Doctor's thesis, University of Minnesota (Minneapolis, Minn.), 1955. (*DA* 15:2467)
1119. PERSON, GERALD ALTON. *A Comparative Study of University of Minnesota Physical Education Graduates Employed in Related Occupations and Those in Other Vocations.* Doctor's thesis, University of Minnesota (Minneapolis, Minn.), 1955. (*DA* 16:705)
1120. GOSWITZ, CHARLES R. *An Evaluation of the Simplified Method for Scoring the Strong Vocational Interest Blank.* Master's thesis, University of Arizona (Tucson, Ariz.), 1956.
1121. JONES, ROBERT L. "A Psychometric Study of Minnesota Industrial Editors." *Journalism Q* 34:253–5 sp '57. * (*PA* 32:5616)
1122. YESLIN, ARTHUR R.; VERNON, LEROY N.; AND KERR, WILLARD A. "The Significance of Time Spent in Answering Personality Inventories." *J Appl Psychol* 42:264–6 Ag '58. * (*PA* 33:9369)
1123. WHERRY, ROBERT J. "An Evaluative and Diagnostic Forced-Choice Rating Scale for Servicemen." *Personnel Psychol* 12:227–36 su '59. * (*PA* 34:3632)
1124. HANNUM, THOMAS E. "Correlates of Achievement in a Veterinary Medicine Curriculum." *Proc Iowa Acad Sci* 67:459–62 '60. *
1125. HERMAN, LOUIS M., AND ZEIGLER, MARTIN L. "Comparison of Academic Achievement, Aptitudes, and Interest Patterns of Two-Year Technical Students and Four-Year Degree Candidates in Engineering." *J Exp Ed* 29:81–7 S '60. * (*PA* 36:2KL81H)
1126. SHEEHAN, JOSEPH G.; HADLEY, ROBERT G.; AND WHITE, GERALD R. "The Speech Pathologist: His Interests, Activities and Attitudes." *J Speech & Hearing Disorders* 25:317–22 N '60. * (*PA* 35:3762)
1127. SHNEIDMAN, EDWIN S. "The Case of El: Psychological Test Data." *J Proj Tech* 25:131–54 Je '61. * (*PA* 36:21K31S)
1128. MARKS, EDMOND; VAIRO, JOHN D.; AND ZEIGLER, MARTIN L. "Scholastic Aptitudes, Vocational Interests, and Personality Characteristics of Journalism Students." *J Ed Res* 56:37–40 S '62. *
1129. GOSNEY, CHARLES ALAN. *Vocational Interest Patterns of Indiana County Agricultural Extension Agents.* Master's thesis, Purdue University (Lafayette, Ind.), 1963.

Strong Vocational Interest Blank for Men

1130. GOTTERER, MALCOLM, AND STALNAKER, ASHFORD W. "Predicting Programmer Performance Among Non-Preselected Trainee Groups." *Proc Ann Conf Computer Personnel Group* 2:29-44 '64. *

1131. CANNON, W. M. "Toward A New Vocational Interest Scale for Computer Programmers—A Procedural Report." *Proc Ann Computer Personnel Res Conf* 3:60-7 '65. *

1132. HEATH, DOUGLAS H.; WITH THE ASSISTANCE OF HARRIET E. HEATH. *Explorations of Maturity: Studies of Mature and Immature College Men.* New York: Appleton-Century-Crofts, 1965. Pp. xv, 423. * (*PA* 39:12057)

1133. PERRY, DALLIS K., AND CANNON, WILLIAM M. *Heterogeneous Key Development: Vocational Interests of Computer Programmers.* Technical Memorandum TM-2655/003/33. Santa Monica, Calif.: System Development Corporation, 1965. Pp. 11. *

1134. RYDEN, E. R. "Predicting Successful Performance." *J Coop Exten* 3:103-9 su '65. *

1135. BERDIE, RALPH F., AND STEIN, JUNE. "A Comparison of New University Students Who Do and Do Not Seek Counseling." *J Counsel Psychol* 13:310-7 f '66. * (*PA* 40:12631)

1136. CANNON, WILLIAM M., AND PERRY, DALLIS K. "A Vocational Interest Scale for Computer Programmers." *Proc Ann Computer Personnel Res Conf* 2:61-82 '66. *

1137. MILLER, ADAM W., JR. "Proposals for Interest Test Development and Experimentation." *Personnel & Guid J* 45:231-7 N '66. *

1138. PERRY, DALLIS K., AND CANNON, WILLIAM M. *Relationships Among Programmers' Background and Interest Characteristics: Vocational Interests of Computer Programmers.* Technical Memorandum TM-2655/004/00. Santa Monica, Calif.: System Development Corporation, 1966. Pp. 33. *

1139. PERRY, DALLIS K., AND CANNON, WILLIAM M. *Vocational Interests of Female Computer Programmers.* Technical Memorandum TM-2655/005/00. Santa Monica, Calif.: System Development Corporation, 1966. Pp. 22. *

1140. DEB, MAYA. "Interest Patterns of High Achievers in Natural Science Course." *Indian J Psychol* 42(1-4):97-100 '67. *

1141. MAYER, DAVID B., AND STALNAKER, ASHFORD W. "Computer Personnel Research—Issues and Progress in the 60's." *Proc Ann Computer Personnel Res Conf* 5:6-41 '67. *

1142. TILLMAN, CARROLL ALTON. *Interest Patterns of Industrial Engineers as Measured by the Strong Vocational Interest Blank.* Master's thesis, Sacramento State College (Sacramento, Calif.), 1967.

1143. AMICUCCI, EDWARD. *Masculinity Interest in High School Athletes.* Master's thesis, Allegheny College (Meadville, Pa.), 1968.

1144. ATHELSTAN, GARY T. *The Vocational Interests, Values, and Career Development of Specialists in Physical Medicine and Rehabilitation.* CEPM&R Bulletin 9. Minneapolis, Minn.: Commission on Education in Physical Medicine and Rehabilitation, 1968. Pp. vii, 63. *

1145. BERGER, RAYMOND M. "Selection of Systems Analysts and Programmer Trainees." *Proc Ann Computer Personnel Res Conf* 6:44-63 '68. *

1146. MALONE, JAMES H. *Interests and Effectiveness of Residence Hall Counselors.* Master's thesis, Kent State University (Kent, Ohio), 1968.

1147. CAMPBELL, DAVID. "A Psychological Profile of the Money Manager." *Institutional Investor* 3(9):29-36 S '69. *

1148. McCUNE, CORNELIA D., AND RAUSCH, VERNA L. "Vocational Interests of Pre-Medical Technology Students." *Am J Med Technol* 35(10):634-51 O '69. *

1149. SLIVINSKI, L. W., AND DESBIENS, B. "Interests of Managers in the Canadian Public Service." *Studies Personnel Psychol* 1(2):93-120 O '69. *

1150. WILEY, NANCY NEWELL. *A Comparison of Certain Personality Traits and Academic Performance in Freshman Students Who Do and Do Not Seek Counseling.* Master's thesis, Southern Methodist University (Dallas, Tex.), 1969.

1151. ANDERSON, RICHARD J. "Stability of Student Interests in General Psychology." *Am Psychologist* 25(7):630-2 Jl '70. * (*PA* 45:1365)

1152. BALLOU, SUSAN I.; ALSIP, JONATHAN E.; AND HANNUM, THOMAS E. "A Longitudinal Study of the Interests of Veterinarians." *Proc Iowa Acad Sci* 77:322-30 '70. *

1153. BIEDENKAPP, MILDRED SPIER. *Measured Masculinity and Related Variables of a Group of Male Elementary School Educators.* Doctor's thesis, University of Maryland (College Park, Md.), 1970. (*DAI* 31:4375A)

1154. BRASINGTON, CHOLTON REGINALD. *Comparison of the Predictive Validity of the SVIB With Achievement and Aptitude Variables for University of South Carolina Freshman Males.* Doctor's thesis, University of South Carolina (Columbia, S.C.), 1970. (*DAI* 31:5117A)

1155. CARROLL, DELBERT L. *An Investigation of the Relationship Between Undergraduate GPA and High and Low Scorers on the Specialization Level Scale of the Strong Vocational Interest Blank Among Male Psychology Majors at East Tennessee State University.* Master's thesis, East Tennessee State University (Johnson City, Tenn.), 1970.

1156. CASSON, ABRAHAM MORTIMER. *The Negro Law Student: His Childhood Experience, Vocational Interests and Professional Concerns.* Doctor's thesis, University of Michigan (Ann Arbor, Mich.), 1970. (*DAI* 31:7590B)

1157. FLOM, PENELOPE KEGEL. *Performance in the Medical Internship.* Doctor's thesis, University of California (Berkeley, Calif.), 1970. (*DAI* 32:1188B)

1158. FOSTER, JAMES ANDREW. *An Exploratory Study of Holland's Theory of Vocational Choice and Rotter's Social Learning Theory.* Doctor's thesis, University of North Dakota (Grand Forks, N.D.), 1970. (*DAI* 31:4458A)

1159. GERSTEIN, OFFRA BILHA. *The Relationship Between Perception of Parental Behavior, Level of Dependency, and Vocational Interest Pattern in Hemophilic Young Adults.* Doctor's thesis, New York University (New York, N.Y.), 1970. (*DAI* 31:6401A)

1160. HANSON, GARY RANDALL. *Empirical Exploration of the Correlates of Academic Predictability.* Doctor's thesis, University of Minnesota (Minneapolis, Minn.), 1970. (*DAI* 32:177A)

1161. HARRINGTON, CHARLES CHRISTOPHER. *Errors in Sex-Role Behavior in Teen-Age Boys.* New York: Teachers College Press, 1970. Pp. viii, 109. * (*PA* 44:21190, title only)

1162. HOLLAND, PAUL LaVERNE. *A Study of Factors Predictive of Persistence in the Parish Ministry of United Presbyterian Clergymen.* Doctor's thesis, University of Illinois (Urbana, Ill.), 1970. (*DAI* 31:6426A)

1163. IM, IN JAE. *A Multivariate Analysis of the Relationship of Academic, Personality, and Family Background Variables to the Different Patterns of Collegiate Attendance.* Doctor's thesis, University of Minnesota (Minneapolis, Minn.), 1970. (*DAI* 32:240A)

1164. IRWIN, TOM JAY. *An Investigation of the Expression of Empathy of A and B Therapists in a Quasi-Therapeutic Encounter.* Doctor's thesis, University of Missouri (Columbia, Mo.), 1970. (*DAI* 31:5128A)

1165. JOHNSON, JAMES CLIFTON. *Differences in the Vocational Interests of Engineers Engaged in Research, Development, Production, and Sales Functions.* Doctor's thesis, University of Minnesota (Minneapolis, Minn.), 1970. (*DAI* 31:5687B)

1166. LEE, DAVID LAWRENCE. *Selected Interest Factors Related to Academic Achievement at the University of North Dakota.* Doctor's thesis, University of North Dakota (Grand Forks, N.D.), 1970. (*DAI* 32:6762A)

1167. LEON, HERMAN. *Factors Predictive of Successful Educational Performance in Social Work School.* Doctor's thesis, Columbia University (New York, N.Y.), 1970. (*DAI* 31:6724A)

1168. LIBBY, BRUCE C. *The AB Dimension in a Counseling Analogue.* Doctor's thesis, University of Minnesota (Minneapolis, Minn.), 1970. (*DAI* 31:6262B)

1169. McARTHUR, CHARLES. "Vocational Guidance in the Ivy League," pp. 111-23. *Int Psychiatric Clinic* 7(3):83-131 '70. *

1170. MORRIS, J. L., AND PARKINSON, M. "Vocational Interests of Computer Programmers." *Austral Computer J* 2(3):139-42 Ag '70. *

1171. NAOR, NEHAMA KLIBAN. *Configurational Analysis of the Strong Vocational Interest Blank (SVIB) and Concomitant Personality Correlates.* Doctor's thesis, University of North Carolina (Chapel Hill, N.C.), 1970. (*DAI* 31:6908B)

1172. QUIRING, RICHARD G. *The A.A.C.H. Scale on the Strong Vocational Interest Blank.* Master's thesis, Fresno State College (Fresno, Calif.), 1970.

1173. SCHILLINGER, MORTON. *Cotherapist Value Similarity as a Determinant of Combined Therapy Outcome.* Doctor's thesis, New York University (New York, N.Y.), 1970. (*DAI* 31:7612B)

1174. SCHULZETENBERGE, ANTHONY C. *Interests and Background Variables Characterizing Secondary School Librarians Who Work With Teachers in Curriculum Development and Improvement of Instruction.* Doctor's thesis, University of North Dakota (Grand Forks, N.D.), 1970. (*DAI* 32:7019A)

1175. STEPHENSON, PATRICIA M. *The Relationship of Personality Congruence and Achievement Profile to Upper-Division Change of Major.* Doctor's thesis, Florida State University (Tallahassee, Fla.), 1970. (*DAI* 31:4497A)

1176. THOMAS, CAROLINE BEDELL; FARGO, ROGER; AND ENSLEIN, KURT. "Personality Characteristics of Medical Students as Reflected by the Strong Vocational Interest Test With Special Reference to Smoking Habits." *Johns Hopkins Med J* 127(6):323-35 D '70. *

1177. WARD, WILLIAM P. *A Study of the Interests of the Priests of the Diocese of Scranton Using the Strong Vocational Interest Blank and Catholic Priest Scale.* Master's thesis, University of Scranton (Scranton, Pa.), 1970.

1178. WILLOUGHBY, THEODORE C. "Needs, Interests, and Reinforcer Preferences of Data Processing Personnel." *Proc Ann Computer Personnel Res Conf* 8:119-43 '70. *

1179. ABRAHAMS, N. M.; NEUMANN, IDELL; AND GITHENS, W. H. "Faking Vocational Interests: Simulated Versus Real Life Motivation." *Personnel Psychol* 24(1):5-12 sp '71. * (*PA* 47:3671)

1180. ANDERSON, SUSAN C., AND APOSTAL, ROBERT A. "Occupational Introversion-Extroversion and Size of Hometown." *Voc Guid Q* 20(2):138-40 D '71. *

1181. ATHELSTAN, GARY T., AND PAUL, GERALD J. "New Approach to the Prediction of Medical Specialization: Student-Based Strong Vocational Interest Blank Scales." *J Appl Psychol* 55(1):80-6 F '71. * (*PA* 46:1249)

Strong Vocational Interest Blank for Men

1182. BAILEY, ROGER L. "Testing Holland's Theory." *Meas & Eval Guid* 4(2):107–14 Jl '71. *

1183. BENJAMIN, DARRELL R. "On Engineers' Interest Patterns." Letter. *Meas & Eval Guid* 4(2):69 Jl '71. *

1184. BENTON, ARTHUR LOUIS. *The Inventoried Interests of Cartographers.* Doctor's thesis, American University (Washington, D.C.), 1971. (*DAI* 32:6093B)

1185. BORGEN, FRED H. "Predicting Career Choices of Able College Men From Occupational and Basic Interest Scales of the SVIB." *NMSC Res Rep* 7(9):1–14 '71. * (*PA* 47:5870)

1186. CAMPBELL, DAVID P. "Admissions Policies: Side Effects and Their Implications." *Am Psychologist* 26(7):636–47 Jl '71. * (*PA* 47:11560)

1187. CHARTIER, GEORGE M. "A-B Therapist Variable: Real or Imagined?" *Psychol B* 75(1):22–33 Ja '71. * (*PA* 45:8313)

1188. CLAR, PHILIP NORMAN. *The Relationship of Psychological Differentiation to Client Behavior in Vocational Choice Counseling.* Doctor's thesis, University of Michigan (Ann Arbor, Mich.), 1971. (*DAI* 32:1837B)

1189. COLE, NANCY S., AND HANSON, GARY R. "An Analysis of the Structure of Vocational Interests." *ACT Res Rep* 40:1–17 Ja '71. * (*PA* 47:1843)

1190. COLE, NANCY S., AND HANSON, GARY R. "An Analysis of the Structure of Vocational Interests." *J Counsel Psychol* 18(5):478–86 S '71. * (*PA* 47:3679)

1191. COLLINS, JAMES AMBROSE. *A Configural Approach to the Strong Vocational Interest Blank.* Doctor's thesis, University of Minnesota (Minneapolis, Minn.), 1971. (*DAI* 32:2996B)

1192. FERENCE, CAMILLE. *Prediction of Creativity by Means of Interest Measures.* Doctor's thesis, Ohio State University (Columbus, Ohio), 1971. (*DAI* 32:3685A)

1193. FRANK, AUSTIN C. "Men's Strong Vocational Interest Blank Academic Achievement Scale: An Attempted Validation." *J Counsel Psychol* 18(4):324–31 Jl '71. * (*PA* 46:11572)

1194. GANTZ, BENJAMIN S., JR.; ERICKSON, CLARA; AND STEPHENSON, ROBERT W. "Measuring the Motivation to Manage in a Research and Development Population." Abstract. *Proc 79th Ann Conv Am Psychol Assn* 6(1):129–30 '71. * (*PA* 46:3949)

1195. GROSZ, RICHARD D. "Vocational Interests of Freshman Engineering, Business, and Arts and Sciences Students." *Eng Ed* 62(3):297–8 D '71. *

1196. HAAKENSTAD, KENNETH W., AND APOSTAL, ROBERT A. "Acquiescence and Nonoccupational Interests." Abstract. *J Counsel Psychol* 18(5):501–2 S '71. * (*PA* 47:3602)

1197. HAASE, RICHARD F. "Canonical Analysis of the Vocational Preference Inventory and the Strong Vocational Interest Blank." *J Counsel Psychol* 18(2):182–3 Mr '71. * (*PA* 46:1819)

1198. HAGER, PAUL C., AND ELTON, CHARLES F. "The Vocational Interests of Black Males." *J Voc Behav* 1(2):153–8 Ap '71. * (*PA* 47:11701)

1199. HALL, DAVID HENRY. *The Effect of Occupational Information on the Inventoried Interests of Eleventh Grade Boys.* Doctor's thesis, Columbia University (New York, N.Y.), 1971. (*DAI* 32:3682B)

1200. HARRINGTON, THOMAS F.; LYNCH, MERVIN D.; AND O'SHEA, ARTHUR J. "Factor Analysis of Twenty-Seven Similarly Named Scales of the Strong Vocational Interest Blank and the Kuder Occupational Interest Survey, Form DD." *J Counsel Psychol* 18(3):229–33 My '71. * (*PA* 46:5555)

1201. HUGHES, HENRY MICHAEL, JR. *Vocational Choice Level, and Consistency: A Test of Holland's Theory on an Employed Sample.* Doctor's thesis, State University of New York (Albany, N.Y.), 1971. (*DAI* 32:1999A)

1202. HULTGREN, DAYTON DELANO. *Interests and Job Activities of Ministers in a Variety of Preferred Roles.* Doctor's thesis, University of Minnesota (Minneapolis, Minn.), 1971. (*DAI* 32:5038A)

1203. IVERS, KENNETH JOHN. *An Investigation of Holland's (S) Social and (A) Artistic Personality Types With Music and Art Education Majors, and Applied Music and Art Majors.* Doctor's thesis, University of Kansas (Lawrence, Kan.), 1971. (*DAI* 32:1854A)

1204. JACKSON, DOUGLAS N. "The Dynamics of Structured Personality Tests: 1971." *Psychol R* 78(3):229–48 My '71. * (*PA* 46:4995)

1205. JOHANSSON, CHARLES B. "Cognitive Interest Styles of Students." *Meas & Eval Guid* 4(3):176–83 O '71. * (*PA* 49:11957)

1206. JOHANSSON, CHARLES B., AND CAMPBELL, DAVID P. "Stability of the Strong Vocational Interest Blank for Men." *J Appl Psychol* 55(1):34–6 F '71. * (*PA* 46:1925)

1207. JOHANSSON, CHARLES B., AND ROSSMANN, JACK E. "Interest Patterns Among Economists." *J Counsel Psychol* 18(3):255–61 My '71. * (*PA* 46:5827)

1208. JOHANSSON, CHARLES B.; CHAPMAN, CAROL R.; AND CAMPBELL, DAVID P. "College Professors—Their Likes and Dislikes." *Am Psychologist* 26(5):486–8 My '71. * (*PA* 47:3734)

1209. JOHNSON, RICHARD W. "Measurement of Sex and Age Differences on the Strong Vocational Interest Blank for Men." Abstract. *J Counsel Psychol* 18(5):498–500 S '71. * (*PA* 47:3698)

1210. KEMP, DAVID E., AND STEPHENS, JOSEPH H. "Which AB Scale? A Comparative Analysis of Several Versions." *J Nerv & Mental Dis* 152(1):23–30 Ja '71. * (*PA* 46:9381)

1211. KIRK, KENNETH W.; OHVALL, RICHARD A.; AND JOHNSON, RICHARD W. "Vocational Interests of Pharmacy Students." *Am J Pharm Ed* 35(4):564–70 N '71. *

1212. LANTAY, GEORGE CHARLES VON WAGNER. *Academic Underachievement: When It Appears in Male Junior High School Students of Superior Intelligence, Correlates Significantly With Poor Father Identification as Measured by the Strong Vocational Interest Blank.* Master's thesis, University of Illinois (Urbana, Ill.), 1971.

1213. LIPS, ORVILLE JAMES. *An Empirical Test of Hershenson and Roth's Vocational Decision Process Model.* Doctor's thesis, Iowa State University (Ames, Iowa), 1971. (*DAI* 32:4845B)

1214. MIRELS, HERBERT L., AND GARRETT, JAMES B. "The Protestant Ethic as a Personality Variable." *J Consult & Clin Psychol* 36(1):40–4 F '71. * (*PA* 45:9987)

1215. MUSSIO, JERRY J., AND WAHLSTROM, MERLIN W. "Predicting Performance of Programmer Trainees in a Post-High School Setting." Discussion by Charles D. Lothridge. *Proc Ann Computer Personnel Res Conf* 9:26–53 '71. *

1216. NAVRAN, LESLIE, AND KENDALL, LORNE M. "A Canonical Correlational Analysis of the Strong Vocational Interest Blank, the Holland Vocational Preference Inventory, and the Edwards Personal Preference Schedule." *J Counsel Psychol* 18(6):514–9 N '71. * (*PA* 47:7653)

1217. OSTRAND, JANET LOUISE. *Change in Counselor Trainee Personality Variables After Practicum as Measured by the California Psychological Inventory and Subjects Most Amenable to Change According to Interests Measured by the Strong Vocational Interest Blank.* Master's thesis, University of Illinois (Urbana, Ill.), 1971.

1218. PAGE, MARY JEAN. *A Descriptive Analysis of Selected Attitudes, Interests, and Personality Characteristics of Mature College Women.* Doctor's thesis, North Texas State University (Denton, Tex.), 1971. (*DAI* 32:3699A)

1219. RAZIN, ANDREW M. "A-B Variable in Psychotherapy: A Critical Review." *Psychol B* 75(1):1–21 Ja '71. * (*PA* 45:8344)

1220. ROHLF, RICHARD J. "A Higher-Order Alpha Factor Analysis of Interest, Personality, and Ability Variables, Including an Evaluation of the Effect of Scale Interdependency." *Ed & Psychol Meas* 31(2):381–96 su '71. * (*PA* 46:11516)

1221. ROSSMANN, JACK E.; LIPS, ORVILLE J.; AND CAMPBELL, DAVID P. "Vocational Interests of Political Scientists." *J Appl Psychol* 55(2):135–7 Ap '71. * (*PA* 46:3904)

1222. ROTH, NEIL CHARLES. *An Investigation of the Effects of Cognitive Dissonance Upon the Variables: Basic Values, Vocational Interest, and Vocational Choice.* Doctor's thesis, University of Idaho (Moscow, Idaho), 1971. (*DAI* 32:3039A)

1223. SHEPPARD, NATHANIEL ALAN. *Educational-Vocational Decision and Indecision in College Freshmen.* Doctor's thesis, Ohio State University (Columbus, Ohio), 1971. (*DAI* 32:3040A)

1224. SIESS, THOMAS F., AND JACKSON, DOUGLAS N. Chap. 6, "The Personality Research Form and Vocational Interest Research," pp. 109–32. In *Advances in Psychological Assessment, Vol. 2.* Edited by Paul McReynolds. Palo Alto, Calif.: Science and Behavior Books, Inc., 1971. Pp. xii, 395. *

1225. WAGMAN, MORTON. "Clinical and Research Use of the Strong Vocational Interest Blank Academic Achievement Scale." *J Counsel Psychol* 18(4):337–430 Jl '71. * (*PA* 46:11599)

1226. WEINERT, JANE ROSE. *A Factor Analytic Comparison of the Structure of Form M and Form T of the Strong Vocational Interest Blank.* Master's thesis, Boston College (Chestnut Hill, Mass.), 1971.

1227. WELSH, GEORGE S. "Vocational Interests and Intelligence in Gifted Adolescents." *Ed & Psychol Meas* 31(1):155–64 sp '71. * (*PA* 46:10645)

1228. WHITTAKER, DAVID. "The Psychological Adjustment of Intellectual, Nonconformist, Collegiate Dropouts." *Adolescence* 6(24):415–24 w '71. * (*PA* 48:7723)

1229. WIGGINS, JERRY S.; GOLDBERG, LEWIS R.; AND APPELBAUM, MARK. "MMPI Content Scales: Interpretative Norms and Correlations With Other Scales." *J Consult & Clin Psychol* 37(3):403–10 D '71. * (*PA* 47:8950)

1230. WILLOUGHBY, THEODORE CRAWFORD. *Needs, Interests, Reinforcer Patterns and Satisfaction of Data Processing Personnel.* Doctor's thesis, University of Minnesota (Minneapolis, Minn.), 1971. (*DAI* 32:5421A)

1231. WRIGHT, WILBERT. "Vocational and Learning Attitudes of Black Students." *J Col Stud Personnel* 12(4):253–8 Jl '71. * (*PA* 47:7674)

1232. YURA, MICHAEL THOMAS. *The Personality Traits and Vocational Interests of Guidance Students.* Doctor's thesis, Ohio State University (Columbus, Ohio), 1971. (*DAI* 32:3711A)

CUMULATIVE NAME INDEX

Strong Vocational Interest Blank for Men

Whitlock, G. E.: 475, 579, 613
Whitney, D. R.: 1039
Whittaker, D.: 1128
Whittaker, D. N. E.: 889
Whittock, J. M.: 617
Wiens, A. N.: 704
Wientge, K. M.: 608
Wiggins, J. S.: 1229
Wiley, N. N.: 1150
Wilkinson, M. A.: 362
Williams, C. L.: 673
Williams, F. J.: 651, 722
Williams, P.: 522
Williams, P. A.: 523, 723, 825, 961
Williams, R. E.: 426
Williamson, E. G.: 48, 58, 63
Willis, C. H.: 850–1, 1096
Willoughby, T. C.: 1178, 1230
Wilson, R. N.: 890, 962
Winn, A.: 273
Winter, F.: 674
Winters, J. S.: 580
Wisdom, J. R.: 280
Witkin, A. A.: 402–3
Wittenborn, J. R.: 149
Woehr, H. J.: 385

Wolins, L.: 496, 746
Wollowick, H. B.: 1058
Wood, B. D.: 23
Woods, J. E.: 581
Woodward, C. L.: 317
Woolf, J. A.: 386
Woolf, M. D.: 386
Woo-Sam, J. M.: 652
Worley, B.: 858
Worley, B. H.: 805
Wrenn, C. G.: 202
Wright, F. H.: 1097
Wright, R. M.: 453
Wright, W.: 1231
Wynne, J. T.: 1098
Yanis, M.: 826
Yeslin, A. R.: 1122
Young, C. W.: 49
Young, K. M.: 747
Yura, M. T.: 1232
Zahn, J. C.: 891
Zeigler, M. L.: 553, 1125, 1128
Zektick, I. N.: 849
Zubin, J.: 480
Zuckerman, M.: 476
Zytowski, D. G.: 599, 772, 892–3, 963, 1040–1

[2213]

Strong Vocational Interest Blank for Women.
Ages 16 and over; 1933–71; SVIB-W; 81 scoring
scales (19 basic interests, 58 occupational, 4 nonoccupational) and 6 administrative indices; BASIC INTER-
ESTS: art ('69), biological science ('69), homemaking
('69), law/politics ('69), mechanical ('69), medical
service ('69), merchandising ('69), music ('69), numbers ('69), office practices ('69), outdoors ('69), performing arts ('69), physical science ('69), public speaking ('69), religious activities ('69), social service
('69), sports ('69), teaching ('69), writing ('69);
OCCUPATIONAL: *group 1, music-performing:* music
teacher ('54–69), entertainer ('69), musician performer
('54–69), model ('69); *group 2, art:* art teacher ('69),
artist ('35–69), interior decorator ('69); *group 3,
verbal-linguistic:* newswoman ('35–69), original scale
entitled author), English teacher ('35–69), language
teacher ('69); *group 4, social service:* YWCA staff
member ('35–69, original scale entitled YWCA secretary), recreation leader ('69), director-Christian education ('69), nun-teacher ('62–69, original scale entitled sister teacher by Sister Mary David Olheiser),
guidance counselor ('69), social science teacher ('35–
69), social worker ('35–69); *group 5, verbal-scientific:*
speech pathologist ('66–69), psychologist ('46–69),
librarian ('35–69), translator ('69); *group 6, scientific:* physician ('35–69), dentist ('35–69), medical
technologist ('69), chemist ('69), mathematician ('69),
computer programmer ('67–69), math-science teacher
('35–69), engineer ('54–69); *group 7, military-mana-
gerial:* army-enlisted ('69), navy-enlisted ('69), army-
officer ('69), navy-officer ('69); *group 8, business:*
lawyer ('35–69), accountant ('69), bankwoman ('69),
life insurance underwriter ('35–69, original scale entitled life insurance saleswoman), buyer ('46–69), business education teacher ('38–69, original scale by H. F.
Koepke); *group 9, home economics:* home economics
teacher ('46–69), dietician ('46–69); *group 10, health-
related services:* physical education teacher ('41–69,
original scale by Patricia Collins), occupational therapist ('46–69), physical therapist ('58–69), public health
nurse ('35–69), registered nurse ('35–69), licensed
practical nurse ('35–69), radiologic technologist ('69),
dental assistant ('69); *group 11, nonprofessional:*
executive housekeeper ('69), elementary teacher ('41–
69, original scale by Ralph Bedell), secretary ('35–69,
original scale entitled stenographer-secretary), saleswoman ('69), telephone operator ('69), instrument
assembler ('69), sewing machine operator ('69), beau-

tician ('69), airline stewardess ('69); NONOCCUPA-
TIONAL: academic achievement ('66–69), diversity of
interests ('69), femininity-masculinity II ('35–69),
occupational introversion-extroversion; ADMINISTRA-
TIVE INDICES: total responses ('69), unpopular responses ('69), form check ('69), like percentage ('69),
indifferent percentage ('69), dislike percentage ('69);
Edward K. Strong, Jr. (except supplement) and David
P. Campbell; Stanford University Press. *

For additional information and reviews by Dorothy
M. Clendenen and Barbara A. Kirk, see 7:1037 (92
references); see also 6:1071 (12 references) and 5:869
(19 references); for a review by Gwendolen Schneidler Dickson of an earlier edition, see 3:649 (38 references); for a review by Ruth Strang, see 2:1681 (10
references); for a review by John G. Darley, see
1:1179. For excerpts from related book reviews, see
7:B127 (1 excerpt), 6:B304 (2 excerpts), 6:B305 (2
excerpts), 3:650 (1 excerpt), and 3:652 (11 excerpts).

REFERENCES THROUGH 1971

1–9. See 2:1681.
10–45. See 3:649.
46–64. See 5:869.
65–76. See 6:1071.
77–168. See 7:1037.
169. NOTTINGHAM, RUTH D. "A Psychological Study of Forty
Unmarried Mothers." *Genetic Psychol Monogr* 19:157–228 My
'37. * (*PA* 11:4670)
170. BEDELL, RALPH. "The Science Interests of Successful
Elementary Teachers." *Sci Ed* 24:193–9 Ap '40. *
171. CARTER, H. D.; TAYLOR, K. VON F.; AND CANNING, L. B.
"Vocational Choices and Interest Test Scores of High School
Students." *J Psychol* 11:297–306 Ap '41. * (*PA* 15:3573)
172. MCCARTHY, MARY VITERBO. "An Empirical Study of the
Personality Profiles Characterizing Differential Quantitative and
Linguistic Ability." *Studies Psychol & Psychiatry* 8(4):1–45
Je '53. * (*PA* 28:4043)
173. MCCORNACK, ROBERT, AND KIDNEIGH, JOHN C. "The Vocational Interest Patterns of Social Workers." *Social Work J*
35:160–3 O '54. * (*PA* 29:6448)
174. LEAHY, DOROTHY M. "The Need for Selective Recruitment in Home Economics." *J Ed Res* 52:293–8 Ap '59. *
175. KENTZ, MARY JOAN. *The Relationship of Masculine and
Feminine Interests to Adjustment in Career-Oriented Women.*
Master's thesis, Catholic University of America (Washington,
D.C.), 1965.
176. LUNDGREN, ELIZABETH J. "Predicting Student Success
in Medical Technology and Clinical Laboratory Assistant Programs." *Am J Med Technol* 34:349–61 Je '68. *
177. GREENWOOD, KATHRYN B. *A Study of Personality Traits
and Interest of Prospective Teachers.* Master's thesis, University
of Tennessee (Knoxville, Tenn.), 1969.
178. WILLIAMS, HELEN B. *Interests and Prediction of Academic Performance of Associate Degree Nursing Students.* Master's thesis, Alfred University (Alfred, N.Y.), 1969.
179. BOAZ, JACQUELYN ANNE. *A Comparison of the Interests
of Female Professional Personnel in Community Recreation to
Other Occupations Described by the Strong Vocational Interest
Blank for Women.* Doctor's thesis, University of Minnesota
(Minneapolis, Minn.), 1970. (*DAI* 31:5220A)
180. HUGHES, LOIS JUNE. *Selected Factors as Related to Success in Student Teaching of Home Economics.* Doctor's thesis,
University of Missouri (Columbia, Mo.), 1970. (*DAI* 31:5249A)
181. KOELLING, JOHN ALBERT. *A Differential Study of Prospective Elementary School Teachers at the University of Oregon:
A Comparison of Those Preferring Lower and Upper Teaching
Levels.* Doctor's thesis, University of Oregon (Eugene, Ore.),
1970. (*DAI* 31:5251A)
182. KOLPACK, KAREN CARLA. *The Relationship Between Vocational Interest Patterns and Performance Appraisals of Women
Resident Assistants on the Wisconsin State University-Oshkosh
Campus.* Master's thesis, Wisconsin State University (Oshkosh,
Wis.), 1970.
183. LEON, HERMAN. *Factors Predictive of Successful Educational Performance in Social Work School.* Doctor's thesis, Columbia University (New York, N.Y.), 1970. (*DAI* 31:6724A)
184. OKUN, BARBARA FRANK. *A Study of the Variables Affecting the Occupational Choice of Women 12–20 Years After College Graduation.* Doctor's thesis, Northwestern University
(Evanston, Ill.), 1970. (*DAI* 31:5960A)
185. PRATT, ANN BOGUE. *Meanings of Popular and Unpopular Occupations on the Strong Vocational Interest Blank for
Women.* Doctor's thesis, University of Minnesota (Minneapolis,
Minn.), 1970. (*DAI* 31:6317B)
186. SCHILLINGER, MORTON. *Cotherapist Value Similarity as
a Determinant of Combined Therapy Outcome.* Doctor's thesis,
New York University (New York, N.Y.), 1970. (*DAI* 31:
7612B)

187. SCHULZETENBERGE, ANTHONY C. *Interests and Background Variables Characterizing Secondary School Librarians Who Work With Teachers in Curriculum Development and Improvement of Instruction.* Doctor's thesis, University of North Dakota (Grand Forks, N.D.), 1970. (*DAI* 32:7019A)

188. ANDERSON, SUSAN C., AND APOSTAL, ROBERT A. "Occupational Introversion-Extroversion and Size of Hometown." *Voc Guid Q* 20(2):138–40 D '71. *

189. BECKER, STEVEN JOEL. *A Comparison of Body Attitudes in Women With Masculine Vocational Interests and Those With Feminine Vocational Interests.* Doctor's thesis, University of Maryland (College Park, Md.), 1971. (*DAI* 32:5421B)

190. CAMPBELL, DAVID P. "Admissions Policies: Side Effects and Their Implications." *Am Psychologist* 26(7):636–47 Jl '71. * (*PA* 47:11560)

191. COCKRIEL, IRVIN W. "A Question About the Usefulness of the SVIB's Academic Achievement Scale for Women in Education." *J Stud Pers Assn Teach Ed* 10(1):14–5 f '71. *

192. FAUNCE, PATRICIA SPENCER. "Vocational Interests of High Ability College Women." *J Col Stud Personnel* 12(6):430–7 N '71. * (*PA* 47:9758)

193. HARMON, LENORE W. "The Childhood and Adolescent Career Plans of College Women." *J Voc Behav* 1(1):45–56 Ja '71. * (*PA* 47:3693)

194. JOHNSON, RICHARD W. "Congruence of Strong and Kuder Interest Profiles." *J Counsel Psychol* 18(5):450–5 S '71. * (*PA* 47:3697)

195. SHARF, RICHARD S. "Computer-Based Report for the Strong Vocational Interest Blank for Women." *Meas & Eval Guid* 4(1):9–17 Ap '71. *

196. STEELE, CAROLYN I. "Sexual Identity Problems Among Adolescent Girls in Institutional Placement." *Adolescence* 6(24):509–22 w '71. * (*PA* 48:7393)

197. STROOPS, SYLVIA LYNN. *Personality Types and Vocational Interests of Women Students Majoring in Two Different Areas of Teacher Education.* Doctor's thesis, University of Alabama (University, Ala.), 1971. (*DAI* 32:5027A)

198. WONG, JOHN C. *The Effect of Instruction in Health Occupations and of Vocational Interest Appraisal on the Preference of Health Occupations Among Female College Freshmen and Sophomores.* Doctor's thesis, University of Missouri (Columbia, Mo.), 1971. (*DAI* 33:233A)

CUMULATIVE NAME INDEX

[2214]

Thurstone Interest Schedule. Grades 9–16 and adults; 1947; 10 scores: physical science, biological science, computational, business, executive, persuasive, linguistic, humanitarian, artistic, musical; L. L. Thurstone; Psychological Corporation. *

For additional information and reviews by Norman Frederiksen and Donald E. Super, see 4:745 (1 reference).

REFERENCES THROUGH 1971

1. See 4:745.

2. THURSTONE, L. L. "A Vocational Interest Schedule." Abstract. *Psychol B* 32:719 N '35. * (*PA* 10:1152, title only)

3. LAYCOCK, S. R., AND HUTCHEON, N. B. "A Preliminary Investigation Into the Problem of Measuring Engineering Aptitude." *J Ed Psychol* 30:280–8 Ap '39. * (*PA* 13:5899)

4. ROEBER, EDWARD C. "A Comparison of Seven Interest Inventories With Respect to Word Usage." *J Ed Res* 42:8–17 S '48. * (*PA* 23:2915)

5. JOSÉ, ALICIA B. *A Study of the Vocational and Avocational Interests of Eleventh-Grade Pupils in a Diocesan High School.* Doctor's thesis, Fordham University (New York, N.Y.), 1950.

6. DALY, JOAN M. *A Comparison of the Relation of the Thurstone Interest Schedule to the Kuder Preference Record and to Self-Estimated Interests.* Master's thesis, Fordham University (New York, N.Y.), 1951.

7. NEWMAN, SIDNEY H.; FRENCH, JOHN W.; AND BOBBITT, JOSEPH M. "Analysis of Criteria for the Validation of Selection Measures at the United States Coast Guard Academy." *Ed & Psychol Meas* 12:394–407 au '52. * (*PA* 27:6159)

8. SKARD, ØYVIND. "Measurement of Students' Interests." *Acta Psychologica* (Netherlands) 8(4):264–78 '52. * (*PA* 27:5400)

9. TORR, DONALD V. "A Factor Analysis of Selected Interest Inventories." Abstract. *Am Psychologist* 7:296 Jl '52. *

10. SKARD, ØYVIND; AURSAND, INGER MARIE; AND BRAATEN, LEIF J. "Development and Application of Tests for University Students in Norway: A Report on Parts of a Research Project." *Psychol Monogr* 68(12):1–54 '54. * (*PA* 29:7971)

11. KEELER, HAROLD JAY. *Predicting Teacher Effectiveness of Graduates of the State University of New York Teachers Colleges.* Doctor's thesis, Cornell University (Ithaca, N.Y.), 1956. (*DA* 17:545)

12. EASTON, JUDITH C. "Some Personality Traits of Underachieving and Achieving High School Students of Superior Ability." *B Maritime Psychol Assn* 8:34–9 Ap '59. * (*PA* 34:4786)

13. SPRINGFIELD, FRANKLYN BRUCE. *Concept of Father and Ideal Self in a Group of Criminals and Non-Criminals.* Doctor's thesis, New York University (New York, N.Y.), 1960. (*DA* 21:1258)

14. FISHER, SEYMOUR. "Front-Back Differentiations in Body Image and Body Reactivity." *J General Psychol* 64:373–9 Ap '61. * (*PA* 36:1HE73F)

15. PHILIPPUS, MARION JOHN. *A Study of Personality, Value and Interest Patterns of Student Teachers in the Areas of Elementary, Secondary and Special Education.* Doctor's thesis, University of Denver (Denver, Colo.), 1961. (*DA* 22:3926)

16. PHILIPPUS, MARION JOHN, AND FLEIGLER, LOUIS. "A Study of Personality, Value and Interest Patterns of Student Teachers in the Areas of Elementary, Secondary, and Special Education." *Sci Ed* 46:247–52 Ap '62. *

17. BARBERA, RICHARD CARLTON. *The Influence of the Use of Gestalt Teaching Methods Upon the Achievement of Certain Outcomes of Instruction in Junior High School Physical Science.* Doctor's thesis, Boston University (Boston, Mass.), 1968. (*DAI* 30:611A)

18. BARRY, JOHN R.; DUNTEMAN, GEORGE H.; AND WEBB, MARVIN W. "Personality and Motivation in Rehabilitation." *J Counsel Psychol* 15:237–44 My '68. * (*PA* 42:12535)

19. ROSEN, JULIUS. "School Counselor Dogmatism and Vocational Identity." *Psychol Rep* 23:24–6 Ag '68. * (*PA* 43:7350)

20. ISABELLE, LAURENT A., AND DICK, WILLIAM. "Clarity of Self-Concepts in the Vocational Development of Male Liberal Arts Students (An Abstract)." *Can Psychologist* 10(1):20–31 Ja–F '69. * (*PA* 43:16396)

21. KUMAR, K. "Influence of Intelligence on the Vocational Interests of School Children." *J Ed Res & Exten* (India) 8(1):1–8 Jl '71. *

CUMULATIVE NAME INDEX

Aursand, I. M.: 10
Barbera, R. C.: 17
Barry, J. R.: 18
Bobbitt, J. M.: 7
Braaten, L. J.: 10
Daly, J. M.: 6
Dick, W.: 20
Dunteman, G. H.: 18
Easton, J. C.: 12
Fisher, S.: 14
Fleigler, L.: 16
Frederiksen, N.: *rev*, 4:745
French, J. W.: 7
Hutcheon, N. B.: 3
Isabelle, L. A.: 20
José, A. B.: 5
Keeler, H. J.: 11
Kumar, K.: 21
Laycock, S. R.: 3
Newman, S. H.: 7
Philippus, M. J.: 15–6
Roeber, E. C.: 4
Rosen, J.: 19
Skard, O.: 8, 10
Springfield, F. B.: 13
Super, D. E.: *rev*, 4:745
Thurstone, L. L.: 2
Torr, D. V.: 9
Webb, M. W.: 18
Zwilling, V. T.: 1

[2215]

VALCAN Vocational Interest Profile (VIP). Ages 15 and over; 1960–61; title on manual and profile is *PSYCAN Vocational Interest Profile;* formerly called *WIPCO Vocational Interest Profile;* 9 scores: numerical, mechanical, scientific, clerical, persuasive, musical, literary, artistic, service; 1961 test essentially the same as 1960 research edition; R. N. Smith and J. R. McIntosh; distributed by University of British Columbia Bookstore [Canada]. *

For additional information, see 6:1072.

[2216]

The Vocational Apperception Test: Advanced Form. College; 1949; VAT; 2 forms; Robert B. Ammons, Margaret N. Butler, and Sam A. Herzig; Psychological Test Specialists. *

a) [FORM FOR MEN.] Preferences in 8 areas: teacher, executive or office worker, doctor, lawyer, engineer, personnel or social worker, salesman, laboratory technician.

b) [FORM FOR WOMEN.] Preferences in 10 areas: laboratory technician, dietician, buyer, nurse, teacher, artist, secretary, social worker, mother, housewife.

For additional information, see P:492 (3 references); for reviews by Benjamin Balinsky and William E. Henry and an excerpted review by George S. Rhodes, see 4:146 (1 reference).

REFERENCES THROUGH 1971
1. See 4:146.
2–4. See P:492.

CUMULATIVE NAME INDEX

Ammons, R. B.: 1
Balinsky, B.: *rev*, 4:146
Butler, M. N.: 1
Clark, E. T.: 4
Goldstein, A. P.: 3
Henry, W. E.: *rev*, 4:146
Herzig, S. A.: 1
Rhodes, G. S.: *exc*, 4:146
Stowe, E. W.: 2

[2217]

Vocational Interest and Sophistication Assessment. Retarded adolescents and young adults; 1967–68; VISA; 2 forms; Joseph J. Parnicky, Harris Kahn, and Arthur D. Burdett; Joseph J. Parnicky. *

a) FORM FOR MALES. Interest and knowledge scores in each of 7 areas: garage, laundry, food service, maintenance, farm and grounds, materials handling, industry.

b) FORM FOR FEMALES. Interest and knowledge scores in each of 4 areas: business and clerical, housekeeping, food service, laundry and sewing.

For additional information, see 7:1039 (2 references).

REFERENCES THROUGH 1971
1–2. See 7:1039.
3. PARNICKY, JOSEPH J.; KAHN, HARRIS; AND BURDETT, ARTHUR D. "Standardization of the VISA (Vocational Interest and Sophistication Assessment) Technique." *Am J Mental Def* 75(4):442–8 Ja '71. * (*PA* 46:3618)

CUMULATIVE NAME INDEX

Burdett, A.: 1, 3
Burdett, A. D.: 2
Kahn, H.: 1–3
Parnicky, J. J.: 1–3

[2218]

Vocational Interest Profile. Ages 15 and over; 1960–66; VIP; 9 scores: numerical, mechanical, scientific, clerical, persuasive, musical, artistic, literary, service; Robin N. Smith and J. R. McIntosh (test and user's guide); distributed by University of British Columbia Bookstore [Canada]. *

For additional information, see 7:1040 (1 reference).

REFERENCES THROUGH 1971
1. See 7:1040.

CUMULATIVE NAME INDEX

Henry, S.: 1

[2219]

★**Wide Range Interest-Opinion Test.** Grades 8–12 and adults; 1970–72; WRIOT; 25 scores: 18 occupational interests (art, literature, music, drama, sales, management, office work, personal service, protective service, social service, social science, biological science, physical science, number, mechanics, machine operation, outdoor, athletics), 7 vocational attitudes (sedentariness, risk, ambition, chosen skill level, activity by sex, agreement, interest spread); Joseph F. Jastak and Sarah R. Jastak; Guidance Associates of Delaware, Inc. *

[2220]

***William, Lynde & Williams Analysis of Interest.** Male adults; 1956–71; 8 scores: management, accounting, engineering, mechanical, sales, service, teaching, writing; R. W. Henderson; William, Lynde & Williams. *

For additional information and a review by Ralph F. Berdie, see 7:1041.

[2221]

Work Values Inventory. Grades 7–16 and adults; 1968–70; WVI; 15 scales: altruism, esthetics, creativity, intellectual stimulation, independence, achievement, prestige, management, economic returns, security, surroundings, supervisory relations, associates, variety, way of life; Donald E. Super; Houghton Mifflin Co. *

For additional information, reviews by Ralph F. Berdie and David V. Tiedeman, and an excerpted review by John W. French, see 7:1042 (33 references).

REFERENCES THROUGH 1971

1–33. See 7:1042.

34. WOODBURY, ROGER WILLIAM. *Sex Differences, Parental Occupational Level, and Intelligence as Measured by Super's Work Values Inventory on 379 Southern Rural, Caucasian, Protestant 9th Graders of North Carolina.* Master's thesis, North Carolina State University (Raleigh, N.C.), 1966.

35. JORDAN, MARCELLA JULIE. *The Relationship of Life Values and Work Values of College Women to Their Vocational Preferences.* Master's thesis, Catholic University of America (Washington, D.C.), 1967.

36. BROWN, FREDERICK G. "Work Values Inventory: A Review." *Meas & Eval Guid* 4(3):189–90 O '71. *

37. DENDALUCE, IGNATIUS. *Industrialization Level, Socioeconomic Class and Work Values.* Doctor's thesis, Columbia University (New York, N.Y.), 1971. (DAI 32:5470B)

38. DONAHUE, MICHAEL A. *College Placement: An Exploratory Investigation of the Employment Selection Process and Certain Correlates of Vocational Development.* Doctor's thesis, Purdue University (Lafayette, Ind.), 1971. (DAI 32:735A)

39. GABLE, ROBERT K., AND PRUZEK, ROBERT M. "Super's Work Values Inventory: Two Multivariate Studies of Interitem Relationships." *J Exp Ed* 40(1):41–50 f '71. *

40. GABLE, ROBERT KEITH. *A Multivariate Study of Work Value Orientations.* Doctor's thesis, State University of New York (Albany, N.Y.), 1971. (DAI 32:1997A)

41. HALL, JOHN ARLIS. *The Influence of School Desegregation on the Work Values and Occupational Aspiration Levels of Twelfth-Grade Negro Males in Texas Public High Schools.* Doctor's thesis, East Texas State University (Commerce, Tex.), 1971. (DAI 32:5545A)

42. LUCIANO, WILSON. *A Comparative Analysis of the Occupational Values of Male High School Seniors in Urban and Rural Areas of Puerto Rico.* Doctor's thesis, University of New Mexico (Albuquerque, N.M.), 1971. (DAI 32:741A)

43. SHEPPARD, NATHANIEL ALAN. *Educational-Vocational Decision and Indecision in College Freshmen.* Doctor's thesis, Ohio State University (Columbus, Ohio), 1971. (DAI 32:3040A)

44. TEBO, JACK. *An Assessment of Work Values Held by Future, Junior, Field, and Senior Grade Air Force Officers in Flying and Non-Flying Categories.* Doctor's thesis, Florida State University (Tallahassee, Fla.), 1971. (DAI 32:5556A)

45. UNDERWOOD, K. L. "Work Values of University Entrants." *J Col Stud Personnel* 12(6):455–9 N '71. * (PA 47:9626)

CUMULATIVE NAME INDEX

[Out of Print Since TIP I]

MANUAL DEXTERITY

[2222]

*****APT Manual Dexterity Test.** Automobile and truck mechanics and mechanics' helpers; 1960–63; Bentley Barnabas (supplement); Associated Personnel Technicians, Inc. *

For additional information, see 6:1076.

[2223]

Crawford Small Parts Dexterity Test. High school and adults; 1946–56; 2 scores: pins and collars, screws; John E. Crawford and Dorothea M. Crawford; Psychological Corporation. *

For additional information and a review by Neil D. Warren, see 5:871 (8 references); for a review by Raymond A. Katzell, see 4:752; for a review by Joseph E. Moore, see 3:667.

REFERENCES THROUGH 1971

1–8. See 5:871.

9. CRAWFORD, JOHN E., AND CRAWFORD, DOROTHEA M. "Small Parts Dexterity Test." Comment by Walter R. Miles. *Meth Med Res* 3:195–7 '50. * (PA 26:3238)

10. OLLRICH, ARTHUR H. *A Validation of the Stromberg Manual Dexterity Test and the Crawford Small Parts Test (Pins and Collars) for Use in Selecting Female Packaging and Packing Employees.* Master's thesis, Drake University (Des Moines, Iowa), 1962.

11. RIM, Y. "The Predictive Validity of Seven Manual Dexterity Tests." *Psychologia* (Japan) 5:52–5 Mr '62. * (PA 38:1417)

12. PETERSON, FLOYD E. "Identification of Sub-Groups for Test Validation Research." *J Indus Psychol* 2:98–101 D '64. * (PA 40:10636)

13. KEBBON, LARS. *The Structure of Abilities at Lower Levels of Intelligence: A Factor-Analytical Study.* Stockholm, Sweden: Skandinaviska Testförlaget AB, 1965. Pp. 112. *

14. JONES, D.; BENTON, A. L.; AND MACQUEEN, J. C. "Hand Preference and Manipulative Dexterity in Normal and Retarded Children." *J Mental Def Res* 11:49–53 Mr '67. * (PA 41:14118)

15. ELKIN, LORNE. "Predicting Performance of the Men-

tally Retarded on Sheltered Workshop and Non-Institutional Jobs." *Am J Mental Def* 72:533–9 Ja '68. * (*PA* 42:76₂8)

16. ZIMMERMAN, JOHN JAMES. *Relationships Among Scholastic Aptitude, Attitudes Toward Various Facets of College Life, and Academic Performance of Students at Lycoming College.* Doctor's thesis, Pennsylvania State University (University Park, Pa.), 1969. (*DAI* 30:4792A)

17. GRANT, DONALD L., AND BRAY, DOUGLAS W. "Validation of Employment Tests for Telephone Company Installation and Repair Occupations." *J Appl Psychol* 54(1):7–14 F '70. * (*PA* 44:5738)

18. NORDÉN, K. "The Structure of Abilities in a Group of Deaf Adolescents." *Ed & Psychol Interactions* (Sweden) 32:1–22 '70. * (*PA* 44:15094)

19. MECKLER, ROY STEWART. *The Effects of Perceptual-Motor Training on the Development of Fine Motor Proficiency of Trainable Mentally Retarded Adolescents.* Doctor's thesis, George Peabody College for Teachers (Nashville, Tenn.), 1971. (*DAI* 32:1946A)

20. ZULLO, THOMAS G. "A Factor Analysis of Perceptual and Motor Abilities of Dental Students." *J Dental Ed* 35(6):356–61 Je '71. *

CUMULATIVE NAME INDEX

Bauman, M. K.: 8
Benton, A. L.: 14
Bray, D. W.: 17
Bruce, M. M.: 1, 3–4
Crawford, D. M.: 9
Crawford, J. E.: 9
Elkin, L.: 15
Fitzpatrick, E. D.: 2
Grant, D. L.: 17
Jones, D.: 14
Katzell, R. A.: *rev,* 4:752
Kebbon, L.: 13
McCarty, J. J.: 2
MacQueen, J. C.: 14

Meckler, R. S.: 19
Miles, W. R.: 9
Moore, J. E.: *rev,* 3:667
Nordén. K.· 18
Ollrich, A. H.: 10
Osborne, R. T.: 5
Peterson, F. E.: 12
Rim, Y.: 11
Sanders, W. B.: 5
Speer, G. S.: 7
Walker, F. C.: 6
Warren, N. D.: *rev,* 5:871
Zimmerman, J. J.: 16
Zullo, T. G.: 20

[2224]

Crissey Dexterity Test. Job applicants; 1964; CDT; Orlo L. Crissey; Psychological Services, Inc. *

For additional information and a review by Lyle F. Schoenfeldt, see 7:1043 (1 reference).

REFERENCES THROUGH 1971

1. See 7:1043.

CUMULATIVE NAME INDEX

Crissey, O. L.: 1   Schoenfeldt, L. F.: *rev,* 7:1043

[2225]

Hand-Tool Dexterity Test. Adolescents and adults; 1946–65; HTDT; George K. Bennett; Psychological Corporation. *

For additional information, see 7:1044 (4 references); for reviews by C. H. Lawshe, Jr. and Neil D. Warren, see 3:659 (2 references).

REFERENCES THROUGH 1971

1–2. See 3:659.
3–6. See 7:1044.

CUMULATIVE NAME INDEX

Bennett, G. K.: 1–2
Elkin, L.: 5
Fear, R. A.: 1
Laney, A. R.: 3
Lawshe, C. H.: *rev,* 3:659

Payton, O. D.: 6
Rim, Y.: 4
Warren, N. D.: *rev,* 3:659
Wesman, A. G.: 2

[2226]

Manipulative Aptitude Test. Grades 9–16 and adults; 1967; MAT; 3 scores: left hand, right hand, total; Wesley S. Roeder; distributed by Western Psychological Services. *

For additional information, see 7:1045.

[2227]

Minnesota Rate of Manipulation Test, 1969 Edition. Grade 7 to adults; 1931–69; MRMT; revision of *Minnesota Manual Dexterity Test;* 5 scores: placing, turning, displacing, 1-hand turning and placing, 2-hand turning and placing; test by Minnesota Employment Stabilization Research Institute; American Guidance Service, Inc. *

For additional information and a review by Lyle F. Schoenfeldt, see 7:1046 (10 references); see also 6:1077 (24 references); for reviews by Edwin E. Ghiselli and John R. Kinzer and an excerpted review, see 3:663 (23 references); for reviews by Lorene Teegarden and Morris S. Viteles, see 2:1662 (4 references).

REFERENCES THROUGH 1971

1–4. See 2:1662.
5–26. See 3:663.
27–50. See 6:1077.
51–60. See 7:1046.

61. SHEPARD, EUGENE L. "Measurements of Certain Non-verbal Abilities of Urban and Rural Children." *J Ed Psychol* 33:458–62 S '42. * (*PA* 17:809)

62. STEEL, MARION; BALINSKY, BENJAMIN; AND LANG, HAZEL. "A Study on the Use of a Work Sample." *J Appl Psychol* 29:14–21 F '45. * (*PA* 19:1779)

63. ELLIS, DOUGLAS S. "Speed of Manipulative Performance as a Function of Work-Surface Height." *J Appl Psychol* 35:289–96 Ag '51. * (*PA* 26:3078)

64. HOFFMAN, SIMON. "Some Predictors of the Manual Work Success of Blind Persons." *Personnel & Guid J* 36:542–4 Ap '58. * (*PA* 33:8922)

65. CANTOR, GORDON N. "Motor Performance of Defectives as a Function of Competition With Same- and Opposite-Sex Opponents." *Am J Mental Def* 65:358–62 N '60. * (*PA* 35:3775)

66. DREWES, DONALD W. "Development and Validation of Synthetic Dexterity Tests Based on Elemental Motion Analysis." *J Appl Psychol* 45:179–85 Je '61. *

67. WASSENAAR, G. M. C. "The Effect of General Anxiety as an Index of Lability on the Performance of Various Psychomotor Tasks." *J General Psychol* 71:351–7 O '64. * (*PA* 39:3667)

68. ZIMMERMAN, JOHN JAMES. *Relationships Among Scholastic Aptitude, Attitudes Toward Various Facets of College Life, and Academic Performance of Students at Lycoming College.* Doctor's thesis, Pennsylvania State University (University Park, Pa.), 1969. (*DAI* 30:4792A)

69. DAVIDS, ANTHONY, AND BRENNER, DAVID. "Competition and the Premedical Student." *J Consult & Clin Psychol* 37(1):67–72 Ag '71. * (*PA* 47:1722)

70. ZULLO, THOMAS G. "A Factor Analysis of Perceptual and Motor Abilities of Dental Students." *J Dental Ed* 35(6):356–61 Je '71. *

CUMULATIVE NAME INDEX

Balinsky, B.: 62
Barre, M. F.: 9
Bauman, M. K.: 15, 21, 34, 40
Bellows, R. M.: 6
Bennett, G. K.: 8
Bergen, G. L.: 1
Berman, I. R.: 2
Bialer, I.: 60
Bingham, W. V. D.: 3
Blum, M.: 7
Bodley, E. A.: 36
Bourassa, G. L.: 43
Brenner, D.: 69
Candee, B.: 7
Cantor, G. N.: 65
Clark, G. R.: 59
Clawson, L. E.: 56–7
Cook, D. W.: 9
Cooper, J. H.: 6
Crites, J. O.: 49
Cruikshank, R. M.: 8
Davids, A.: 69
Deutsch, M. R.: 60
Distefano, M. K.: 41
Drewes, D. W.: 66
Drussell, R. D.: 44
Dvorak, B. J.: 6
Ellis, D. S.: 63
Ellis, N. R.: 41
Ellison, G. D.: 48
Endler, O. L.: 6
Finley, P. J.: 54
Fleishman, E. A.: 37–8, 47–8
Floor, L.: 59
Geist, H.: 32
Ghiselli, E. E.: 10, 12; *rev,* 3:663
Green, H. J.: 2
Guion, R. M.: 43
Hackman, R. C.: 28
Harrell, W.: 5

Hempel, W. E.: 38
Hoffman, S.: 64
Jayalakshmi, G.: 45–6
Johnson, D. L.: 18
Jurgensen, C. E.: 13
Kinzer, J. R.: *rev,* 3:663
Kivitz, M. S.: 59
Kolbe, L. E.: 6
Lang, H.: 62
McCoy, W. L.: 58
MacKinney, A. C.: 50
McMurray, R. M.: 18
Moore, J. E.: 27
Osborne, H. F.: 6
Otis, J. L.: 6
Oxlade, M. N.: 23, 30
Parker, J. F.: 47
Paterson, D. G.: 4
Peterson, F. E.: 55
Rim, Y.: 52
Roberts, J. R.: 15
Rogers, H. B.: 29
Rosen, M.: 59
Sartain, A. Q.: 31
Schneidler, G. G.: 4
Schoenfeldt, L. F.: *rev,* 7:1046
Seashore, H. G.: 25–6
Shartle, C. L.: 6
Shepard, E. L.: 61
Shore, R. P.: 42
Sloan, W.: 41
Sprague, A. L.: 51
Stead, W. H.: 6
Steel, M.: 62
Sternlicht, M.: 60
Strange, J. R.: 31
Super, D. E.: 33, 49
Surgent, L. V.: 24
Teegarden, L.: 11, 11a, 14; *rev,* 2:1662
Tiffin, J.: 29
Topetzes, N. J.: 39

Tuckman, J.: 16–7, 22
Viteles, M. S.: rev, 2:1662
Walker, K. F.: 23, 30
War Manpower Commission,
  Division of Occupational
  Analysis, Staff: 19
Ward, R. S.: 6
Wassenaar, G. M. C.: 67

Williamson, E. G.: 4
Wilson, G. M.: 20
Winschel, J. F.: 53
Wolins, L.: 50
Wyndham, A. J.: 35
Zimmerman, J. J.: 68
Zullo, T. G.: 70

Kolbe, L. E.: 20
Laney, A. R.: 36
Lang, H.: 50
McCullough, C. M.: 16
Morrow, R. S.: 23
Muenter, M. D.: 57
Neeman, R. L.: 60
Nordén, K.: 55
O'Connor, J.: 1–2, 12, 19, 24, 30
Osborne, H. F.: 20
Otis, J. L.: 20, 48
Parker, J. F.: 44
Paterson, D. G.: 7, 13
Prakash, J. C.: 40
Rim, Y.: 46
Rinsland, H. D.: 34

Ross, L. W.: 31
Salvendy, G.: 56
Schneidler, G. G.: 13
Seymour, W. D.: 56
Shartle, C. L.: 20
Stead, W. H.: 20
Steel, M.: 50
Super, D. E.: 35, 47
Surgent, L. V.: 32
Thompson, C. E.: 17, 27
Tiffin, J.: 14, 33
Viteles, M. S.: rev, 2:1659
Ward, R. S.: 20
Wells, F. L.: 49
Williamson, E. G.: 13
Zimmerman, J. J.: 54
Zullo, T. G.: 61

[2228]

O'Connor Finger Dexterity Test. Ages 14 and over; 1920–26(?); Johnson O'Connor; Stoelting Co. (Also published by Lafayette Instrument Co.) *

For additional information, see 6:1078 (32 references); for a review by Morris S. Viteles, see 2:1659 (15 references).

REFERENCES THROUGH 1971

1–15. See 2:1659.
16–47. See 6:1078.
48. OTIS, JAY L. "The Prediction of Success in Power Sewing Machine Operating." J Appl Psychol 22:350–66 Ag '38. * (PA 13:1688)
49. WELLS, F. L. "Clinical Aspects of Functional Transfer. (Psychometric Practice in Adults of Superior Intelligence, IV.)" Am J Orthopsychiatry 9:1–22 Ja '39. * (PA 13:3317)
50. STEEL, MARION; BALINSKY, BENJAMIN; AND LANG, HAZEL. "A Study on the Use of a Work Sample." J Appl Psychol 29: 14–21 F '45. * (PA 19:1779)
51. JOHNSON, RALPH HAAKON. Factors Related to the Success of Disabled Veterans of World War II in the Rehabilitation Training Program Approved for Mechanics and Repairmen, Motor Vehicle. Doctor's thesis, University of Minnesota (Minneapolis, Minn.), 1955. (DA 15:2460)
52. KEBBON, LARS. The Structure of Abilities at Lower Levels of Intelligence: A Factor-Analytical Study. Stockholm, Sweden: Skandinaviska Testförlaget AB, 1965. Pp. 112. *
53. ELKIN, LORNE. "Predicting Performance of the Mentally Retarded on Sheltered Workshop and Non-Institutional Jobs." Am J Mental Def 72:533–9 Ja '68. * (PA 42:7638)
54. ZIMMERMAN, JOHN JAMES. Relationships Among Scholastic Aptitude, Attitudes Toward Various Facets of College Life, and Academic Performance of Students at Lycoming College. Doctor's thesis, Pennsylvania State University (University Park, Pa.), 1969. (DAI 30:4792A)
55. NORDÉN, K. "The Structure of Abilities in a Group of Deaf Adolescents." Ed & Psychol Interactions (Sweden) 32:1–22 '70. * (PA 44:15094)
56. CORLETT, E. N.; SALVENDY, G.; AND SEYMOUR, W. D. "Selecting Operators for Fine Manual Tasks: A Study of the O'Connor Finger Dexterity Test and the Purdue Pegboard." Occup Psychol (England) 45(1):57–65 '71. * (PA 48:3929)
57. DAVIS, LEO J., JR., AND MUENTER, MANFRED D. "Psychomotor Performances of Patients Undergoing L-Dopa Therapy." Percept & Motor Skills 33(3):1303–8 D '71. * (PA 48:3518)
58. GLUSKINOS, URY, AND BRENNAN, THOMAS F. "Selection and Evaluation Procedure for Operating Room Personnel." J Appl Psychol 55(2):165–9 Ap '71. * (PA 46:3909)
59. INSKEEP, GORDON C. "The Use of Psychomotor Tests to Select Sewing Machine Operators—Some Negative Findings." Personnel Psychol 24(4):707–14 w '71. *
60. NEEMAN, RENATE L. "Manipulative Dexterity and Perceptual-Motor Abilities of Mentally Retarded Adolescents and Young Adults: Perceptual-Motor Attributes of Mental Retardates, Part II." Am J Occup Ther 25(6):309–12 S '71. * (PA 49:10347)
61. ZULLO, THOMAS G. "A Factor Analysis of Perceptual and Motor Abilities of Dental Students." J Dental Ed 35(6): 356–61 Je '71. *

CUMULATIVE NAME INDEX

Balinsky, B.: 50
Bellows, R. M.: 20
Bennett, G. K.: 25
Bergen, G. L.: 4
Berman, I. R.: 6
Bingham, W. V. D.: 8
Blum, M.: 10, 21
Blum, M. L.: 15, 22
Bodley, E. A.: 37
Bourassa, G. L.: 41
Brennan, T. F.: 58
Brown, F.: 9
Candee, B.: 10, 21–2
Cooper, J. H.: 20
Corlett, E. N.: 56
Crites, J. O.: 47
Cruikshank, R. M.: 25
Darley, J. G.: 7
Davis, L. J.: 57
Douglass, H. R.: 11

Dvorak, B. J.: 5, 20
Elkin, L.: 53
Elliott, R. M.: 7
Ellison, G. D.: 45
Endler, O. L.: 20
Fleishman, E. A.: 38–9, 44–5
Ghiselli, E. E.: 26, 28
Gluskinos, U.: 58
Green, H. J.: 6
Greenly, R. J.: 14
Guion, R. M.: 41
Hackman, R. C.: 18
Hayes, E. G.: 3
Hempel, W. E.: 39
Hines, M.: 1
Inskeep, G. C.: 59
Jacobsen, E. E.: 29
Jayalakshmi, G.: 42–3
Johnson, R. H.: 51
Kebbon, L.: 52

[2229]

O'Connor Tweezer Dexterity Test. Ages 14 and over; 1920–28(?); Johnson O'Connor; Stoelting Co. (Also published by Lafayette Instrument Co.) *

For additional information, see 6:1079 (23 references); for a review by Morris S. Viteles, see 2:1678 (13 references).

REFERENCES THROUGH 1971

1–13. See 2:1678.
14–36. See 6:1079.
37. OTIS, JAY L. "The Prediction of Success in Power Sewing Machine Operating." J Appl Psychol 22:350–66 Ag '38. * (PA 13:1688)
38. WELLS, F. L. "Clinical Aspects of Functional Transfer. (Psychometric Practice in Adults of Superior Intelligence, IV.)" Am J Orthopsychiatry 9:1–22 Ja '39. * (PA 13:3317)
39. STEEL, MARION; BALINSKY, BENJAMIN; AND LANG, HAZEL. "A Study on the Use of a Work Sample." J Appl Psychol 29: 14–21 F '45. * (PA 19:1779)
40. JOHNSON, RALPH HAAKON. Factors Related to the Success of Disabled Veterans of World War II in the Rehabilitation Training Program Approved for Mechanics and Repairmen, Motor Vehicle. Doctor's thesis, University of Minnesota (Minneapolis, Minn.), 1955. (DA 15:2460)
41. KAPOOR, K. "A Study on Relation Between Tests of Manual Dexterity and General Mental Ability." Indian J Psychol 39:59–64 Je '64. *
42. PETERSON, FLOYD E. "Identification of Sub-Groups for Test Validation Research." J Indus Psychol 2:98–101 D '64. * (PA 40:10636)
43. GEORGE, E. I., AND DEVADASAN, K. "A Comparative Study of Tweezer Dexterity in Two Selected Groups." J Ed & Psychol (India) 26:149–52 Jl '68. *
44. ZIMMERMAN, JOHN JAMES. Relationships Among Scholastic Aptitude, Attitudes Toward Various Facets of College Life, and Academic Performance of Students at Lycoming College. Doctor's thesis, Pennsylvania State University (University Park, Pa.), 1969. (DAI 30:4792A)
45. ZULLO, THOMAS G. "A Factor Analysis of Perceptual and Motor Abilities of Dental Students." J Dental Ed 35(6):356–61 Je '71. *

CUMULATIVE NAME INDEX

Albright, L. E.: 30–1
Balinsky, B.: 39
Beamer, G. C.: 27
Bellows, R. M.: 18
Bennett, G. K.: 21
Bergen, G. L.: 3
Berman, I. R.: 5
Bingham, W. V. D.: 7
Blum, M.: 9
Blum, M. L.: 13
Bourassa, G. L.: 33
Brown, F.: 8
Candee, B.: 9
Cooper, J. H.: 18
Crissey, O. L.: 22
Crites, J. O.: 36
Cruikshank, R. M.: 21
Darley, J. G.: 6
Devadasan, K.: 43
Dvorak, B. J.: 4, 18
Edmonson, L. D.: 27
Elliott, R. M.: 6
Endler, O. L.: 18
George, E. I.: 43
Green, H. J.: 5
Guion, R. M.: 33
Hackman, R. C.: 16
Harris, A. J.: 10
Jacobsen, E. E.: 24
Johnson, R. H.: 40

Kapoor, K.: 41
Kolbe, L. E.: 18
Lang, H.: 39
Lee, T.: 34
McCullough, C. M.: 14
Morrow, R. S.: 19
O'Connor, J.: 1, 11, 17, 20, 25
Osborne, H. F.: 18
Otis, J. L.: 18, 37
Paterson, D. G.: 6, 12
Peterson, F. E.: 42
Petrie, A.: 29
Powell, M. B.: 29
Prakash, J. C.: 32
Rim, Y.: 35
Schneidler, G. G.: 12
Shartle, C. L.: 18
Stead, W. H.: 18
Steel, M.: 39
Strother, G. B.: 27
Super, D. E.: 28, 36
Surgent, L. V.: 26
Thompson, C. E.: 15, 23
Viteles, M. S.: rev, 2:1678
Ward, R. S.: 18
Wells, F. L.: 2, 38
Williamson, E. G.: 12
Zimmerman, J. J.: 44
Zullo, T. G.: 45

[2230]

★**One Hole Test.** Job applicants; 1972; OHT; 2 machines; Gavriel Salvendy and W. Douglas Seymour; Lafayette Instrument Co., Inc. *

a) LEVEL ONE. 3 scores: number of pins inserted in first and last of 7 or 15 one-minute trials, total.
b) LEVEL TWO. 9 scores: same as above plus first and last trial time for each of 3 categories (grasp, position, reach and move).

REFERENCES THROUGH 1971

1. SALVENDY, GAVRIEL; SEYMOUR, W. DOUGLAS; AND CORLETT, E. NIGEL. "Comparative Study of Static Versus Dynamic Scoring of Performance Tests for Industrial Operators." *J Appl Psychol* 54(2):135–9 Ap '70. * (*PA* 44:11490)

CUMULATIVE NAME INDEX

Corlett, E. N.: 1   Seymour, W. D.: 1
Salvendy, G.: 1

[2231]

Pennsylvania Bi-Manual Worksample. Ages 16 and over; 1943–45; 2 scores: assembly, disassembly; John R. Roberts; American Guidance Service, Inc.*

For additional information and reviews by Edwin E. Ghiselli, Thomas W. Harrell, Albert Gibson Packard, and Neil D. Warren, see 3:665 (3 references).

REFERENCES THROUGH 1971

1–3. See 3:665.
4. GEIST, HAROLD. "The Performance of Amputees on Motor Dexterity Tests." *Ed & Psychol Meas* 9:765–72 w '49. * (*PA* 26:2950)
5. BAUMAN, MARY K. Chap. 8, "Mechanical and Manual Ability Tests for Use With the Blind," pp. 97–113. (*PA* 26:487) In *Psychological Diagnosis and Counseling of the Adult Blind: Selected Papers From the Proceedings of the University of Michigan Conference for the Blind, 1947.* Edited by Wilma Donahue and Donald Dabelstein. New York: American Foundation for the Blind, Inc., 1950. Pp. vii, 173. * (*PA* 26:493)
6. BAUMAN, MARY K. *A Manual of Norms for Tests Used in Counseling Blind Persons.* AFB Publications, Research Series, No. 6. New York: American Foundation for the Blind, Inc., 1958. Pp. 40. * (*PA* 32:1949)
7. HOFFMAN, SIMON. "Some Predictors of the Manual Work Success of Blind Persons." *Personnel & Guid J* 36:542–4 Ap '58. * (*PA* 33:8922)
8. RIM, Y. "The Predictive Validity of Seven Manual Dexterity Tests." *Psychologia* (Japan) 5:52–5 Mr '62. * (*PA* 38:1417)
9. RONAN, W. W. "Evaluation of Skilled Trades Performance Predictors." *Ed & Psychol Meas* 24:601–8 f '64. * (*PA* 39:6074)
10. GHOSH, S. N., AND TRIPATHI, R. C. "Perceptual—Motor Speed Ratio and Accident Proneness." *Indian J Appl Psychol* 2:10–6 Ja '65. * (*PA* 39:10937)
11. FREEBERG, NORMAN E. "Construct Validity of a Paper-and-Pencil Test of Manual Dexterity." *Percept & Motor Skills* 22:200 F '66. * (*PA* 40:4761)

CUMULATIVE NAME INDEX

Bauman, M. K.: 1–2, 5–6   Maher, H.: 3
Fife, I. E.: 3   Packard, A. G.: *rev*, 3:665
Freeberg, N. E.: 11   Rim, Y.: 8
Geist, H.: 4   Roberts, J. R.: 1
Ghiselli, E. E.: *rev*, 3:665   Ronan, W. W.: 9
Ghosh, S. N.: 10   Tripathi, R. C.: 10
Harrell, T. W.: *rev*, 3:665   Warren, N. D.: *rev*, 3:665
Hoffman, S.: 7

[2232]

Practical Dexterity Board. Ages 8 and over; 1962; John G. Miller; SPECO Educational Systems. *
For additional information, see 7:1047.

[2233]

★**Purdue Hand Precision Test.** Ages 17 and over; 1941; 3 scores: attempts, correct responses, error time; Joseph Tiffin; Lafayette Instrument Co. *
For additional information, see 6:1080 (2 references).

REFERENCES THROUGH 1971

1–2. See 6:1080.

CUMULATIVE NAME INDEX

Rogers, H. B.: 1   Tiffin, J.: 1–2

[2234]

★**Purdue Pegboard.** Grades 9–16 and adults; 1941–68; PP; 5 scores: right hand, left hand, both hands, right plus left plus both hands, assembly; Purdue Research Foundation under the direction of Joseph Tiffin; Science Research Associates, Inc. *

For additional information, see 6:1081 (15 references); for a review by Neil D. Warren, see 5:873 (11 references); see also 4:751 (12 references); for reviews by Edwin E. Ghiselli, Thomas W. Harrell, and Albert Gibson Packard, see 3:666 (3 references).

REFERENCES THROUGH 1971

1–3. See 3:666.
4–15. See 4:751.
16–26. See 5:873.
27–41. See 6:1081.
42. BARNETTE, W. LESLIE, JR. "Occupational Aptitude Pattern Research." *Occupations* 29:5–12 O '50. * (*PA* 25:3239)
43. KING, H. E., AND CLAUSEN, J. "Finger Dexterity." *Meth Med Res* 3:193–4 '50. * (*PA* 26:3242)
44. CHRISWELL, M. IRVING. "Validity of a Structural Dexterity Test." *J Appl Psychol* 37:13–5 F '53. * (*PA* 28:1618)
45. DUNHAM, RALPH E. "Factors Related to Recidivism in Adults." *J Social Psychol* 39:77–91 F '54. * (*PA* 28:8866)
46. KAPLAN, HARRY A.; MACHOVER, SOLOMON; AND RABINER, ABRAHAM. "A Study of the Effectiveness of Drug Therapy in Parkinsonism." *J Nerv & Mental Dis* 119:398–411 My '54. * (*PA* 29:4555)
47. VAN BILJON, I. J. "The Influence of Emotional Tension and Lability Upon the Performance of Certain Aptitude Tests." *J Social Res* (South Africa) 5:51–9 Je '54. * (*PA* 30:2331)
48. SEYMOUR, JOHN H. *Some Changes in Psychometric, Perceptual and Motor Performance as a Function of Sleep Deprivation.* Doctor's thesis, New York University (New York, N.Y.), 1956. (*DA* 16:2169)
49. HOFFMAN, SIMON. "Some Predictors of the Manual Work Success of Blind Persons." *Personnel & Guid J* 36:542–4 Ap '58. * (*PA* 33:8922)
50. HABER, WILFRED. *The Contribution of Selected Variables to Success or Failure in a Vocational Rehabilitation Evaluation.* Doctor's thesis, New York University (New York, N.Y.), 1959. (*DA* 20:4171)
51. KIESSLING, RALPH J., AND MAAG, CLINTON H. "Performance Impairment as a Function of Nitrogen Narcosis." *J Appl Psychol* 46:91–5 Ap '62. *
52. CLARK, MERVIN L.; RAY, THOMAS S.; AND RAGLAND, ROBERT E. "Chlorpromazine in Chronic Schizophrenic Women: Rate of Onset and Rate of Dissipation of Drug Effects." *Psychosom Med* 25:212–7 My–Je '63. * (*PA* 38:4397)
53. COSTA, LOUIS D.; SCAROLA, LOUISE M.; AND RAPIN, ISABELLE. "Purdue Pegboard Scores for Normal Grammar School Children." *Percept & Motor Skills* 18:748 Je '64. * (*PA* 39:5045)
54. TAYLOR, JAMES BENTLEY. "The Structure of Ability in the Lower Intellectual Range." *Am J Mental Def* 68:766–74 My '64. * (*PA* 39:1793)
55. SCHWARTZ, ALFRED H. "Pegboard Changes." Letter and reply by Ronald M. Schwartz. *Am Psychologist* 20:366 My '65. *
56. EIDLE, WILLIAM REYNOLDS. *The Effects of a Mild Alcohol Dose on Tactual Vernier Acuity, Simple Addition, and Purdue Pegboard Performance.* Doctor's thesis, Fordham University (New York, N.Y.), 1966. (*DA* 27:622B)
57. FERNALD, L. DODGE, JR.; FERNALD, PETER S.; AND RINES, W. BRIAN. "Purdue Pegboard and Differential Diagnosis." Abstract. *J Consult Psychol* 30:279 Je '66. * (*PA* 40:8253, title only)
58. FREEBERG, NORMAN E. "Construct Validity of a Paper-and-Pencil Test of Manual Dexterity." *Percept & Motor Skills* 22:200 F '66. * (*PA* 40:4761)
59. PAREDES, ALFONSO; BAUMGOLD, JOHN; PUGH, LAWRENCE A.; AND RAGLAND, ROBERT. "Clinical Judgment in the Assessment of Psychopharmacological Effects." *J Nerv & Mental Dis* 142:153–60 F '66. * (*PA* 41:11294)
60. RAPIN, ISABELLE; TOURK, LESTER M.; AND COSTA, LOUIS D. "Evaluation of the Purdue Pegboard as a Screening Test for Brain Damage." *Develop Med & Child Neurol* (England) 8:45–54 F '66. * (*PA* 40:6962)
61. CLAWSON, LaVERE EDWIN. *A Study of the Clawson Worksample Tests for Measuring Manual Dexterity of the Blind.* Doctor's thesis, University of Utah (Salt Lake City, Utah), 1967. (*DA* 28:2548A)
62. KAHN, HARRIS, AND BURDETT, ARTHUR D. "Interaction of Practice and Rewards on Motor Performance of Adolescent Mental Retardates." *Am J Mental Def* 72:422–7 N '67. * (*PA* 42:7649)
63. MAYHUGH, JAMES CARROL. *The Relationship Between Normals and Subnormals Involving Tapping, the Purdue Pegboard, and Simple and Complex Reaction Times.* Doctor's thesis, University of Oklahoma (Norman, Okla.), 1967. (*DA* 28:1231B)

64. PHILLIPS, BEATRICE K., AND HOLDEN, RAYMOND H. "Relationship Between Fine Manipulative Ability and Intelligence in Adults in a Vocational Rehabilitation Setting." *Voc Guid Q* 15:213–6 Mr '67. * (*PA* 42:9542)

65. RAPIN, I.; SCAROLA, L. M.; AND COSTA, L. D. "The Purdue Pegboard as a Screening Test for Brain Damage and Mental Retardation in Nonverbal Children." *Volta R* 69:635–8 D '67. *

66. WAGNER, HILMAR ERNEST. *A Study of Physical, Mental and Musical Characteristics of Selected Band Members.* Doctor's thesis, North Texas State University (Denton, Tex.), 1967. (*DA* 28:2285A) [Reviewed by James M. Shugert, *Council Res Music Ed B* 24:27–35 sp '71. *]

67. CLAWSON, LAVERE E. "A Study of the Clawson Worksample Tests for Measuring the Manual Dexterity of the Blind." *New Outl Blind* 62:182–7+ Je '68. *

68. ELKIN, LORNE. "Predicting Performance of the Mentally Retarded on Sheltered Workshop and Non-Institutional Jobs." *Am J Mental Def* 72:533–9 Ja '68. * (*PA* 42:7638)

69. FREEDMAN, SAUL. *The Relationship Between Selected Variables and Success in Transcribing Typing for Trainees Who Are Blind.* Doctor's thesis, New York University (New York, N.Y.), 1968. (*DA* 29:3000A)

70. GILBERSTADT, HAROLD. "Relationships Among Scores of Tests Suitable for the Assessment of Adjustment and Intellectual Functioning." *J Gerontol* 23:483–7 O '68. *

71. PELOSI, JOHN WILLIAM. *A Study of the Effects of Examiner Race, Sex, and Style on Test Responses of Negro Examinees.* Doctor's thesis, Syracuse University (Syracuse, N.Y.), 1968. (*DA* 29:4105A)

72. REPOVICH, LIEBER DON. *Effect of Practice Upon Motor Skills and Spatial Relationship of Hard-Core Poverty Adult Basic Education Trainees.* Doctor's thesis, University of Mississippi (University, Miss.), 1968. (*DA* 29:3008A)

73. AFTANAS, M. S., AND ROYCE, J. R. "A Factor Analysis of Brain Damage Tests Administered to Normal Subjects With Factor Score Comparisons Across Ages." *Multiv Behav Res* 4(4):459–81 O '69. * (*PA* 44:11030)

74. COSTA, LOUIS D.; VAUGHAN, HERBERT G., JR.; HORWITZ, MORTON; AND RITTER, WALTER. "Patterns of Behavioral Deficit Associated With Visual Spatial Neglect." *Cortex* (Italy) 5(3): 242–63 S '69. * (*PA* 44:13142)

75. MACK, JAMES L. "Validity of the Purdue Pegboard as a Screening Test for Brain Damage in a Psychiatric Population." *Percept & Motor Skills* 28(3):832–4 Je '69. * (*PA* 43:17622)

76. SHIH, WEI-TUN. *The Correlation Among Factors Related to Measuring Ability.* Doctor's thesis, Texas A & M University (College Station, Tex.), 1969. (*DAI* 30:4804A)

77. STERNE, DAVID M. "The Purdue Pegboard and MacQuarrie Tapping and Dotting Tasks as Measures of Motor Functioning." *Percept & Motor Skills* 28(2):556 Ap '69. * (*PA* 43:15143)

78. VEGA, ARTHUR. "Use of Purdue Pegboard and Finger Tapping Performance as a Rapid Screening Test for Brain Damage." *J Clin Psychol* 25(3):255–8 Jl '69. * (*PA* 44:4019)

79. ZIMMERMAN, JOHN JAMES. *Relationships Among Scholastic Aptitude, Attitudes Toward Various Facets of College Life, and Academic Performance of Students at Lycoming College.* Doctor's thesis, Pennsylvania State University (University Park, Pa.), 1969. (*DAI* 30:4792A)

80. BURGESS, MICHAEL M.; KODANAZ, ALTAN; AND ZIEGLER, DEWEY K. "Prediction of Brain Damage in a Neurological Population With Cerebrovascular Accidents." *Percept & Motor Skills* 31(2):595–601 O '70. * (*PA* 45:6841)

81. BURGESS, MICHAEL M.; KODANAZ, ALTAN; ZIEGLER, DEWEY; AND GREENBURG, HOWARD. "Prediction of Brain Damage in Two Clinical Populations." *Percept & Motor Skills* 30(2): 523–32 Ap '70. * (*PA* 46:7299)

82. MCCOY, WESLEY LAWRENCE. *A Comparison of Select Psychomotor Abilities of a Sample of Undergraduate Instrumental Music Majors and a Sample of Undergraduate Non-Music Majors.* Doctor's thesis, Louisiana State University (Baton Rouge, La.), 1970. (*DAI* 31:1833A)

83. PHILBRICK, BARBARA BRINKMAN. *Self-Concept and Its Relation to Selected Movement Performances of 4th Grade Girls.* Doctor's thesis, Purdue University (Lafayette, Ind.), 1970. (*DAI* 31:1605A)

84. PITTMAN, FRANK MALLORY, JR. *An Investigation of the Predictive Value of Selected Factors on Achievement in Beginning Woodworking, Metalworking, and Electricity-Electronics Courses at the College Level.* Doctor's thesis, Texas A & M University (College Station, Tex.), 1970. (*DAI* 31:2149A)

85. ROSEN, MARVIN; KIVITZ, MARVIN S.; CLARK, GERALD R.; AND FLOOR, LUCRETIA. "Prediction of Postinstitutional Adjustment of Mentally Retarded Adults." *Am J Mental Def* 74(6): 726–34 My '70. * (*PA* 44:17195)

86. SALVENDY, GAVRIEL; SEYMOUR, W. DOUGLAS; AND CORLETT, E. NIGEL. "Comparative Study of Static Versus Dynamic Scoring of Performance Tests for Industrial Operators." *J Appl Psychol* 54(2):135–9 Ap '70. * (*PA* 44:11490)

87. BOLTON, BRIAN. "A Factor Analytic Study of Communication Skills and Nonverbal Abilities of Deaf Rehabilitation Clients." *Multiv Behav Res* 6(4):485–501 O '71. * (*PA* 47:11373)

88. CORLETT, E. N.; SALVENDY, G.; AND SEYMOUR, W. D.

"Selecting Operators for Fine Manual Tasks: A Study of the O'Connor Finger Dexterity Test and the Purdue Pegboard." *Occup Psychol* (England) 45(1):57–65 '71. * (*PA* 48:3929)

89. DAVIS, LEO J., JR., AND MUENTER, MANFRED D. "Psychomotor Performances of Patients Undergoing L-Dopa Therapy." *Percept & Motor Skills* 33(3):1303–8 D '71. * (*PA* 48:3518)

90. NEEMAN, RENATE L. "Manipulative Dexterity and Perceptual-Motor Abilities of Mentally Retarded Adolescents and Young Adults: Perceptual-Motor Attributes of Mental Retardates, Part II." *Am J Occup Ther* 25(6):309–12 S '71. * (*PA* 49:10347)

91. TARTER, RALPH E., AND JONES, BEN M. "Motor Impairment in Chronic Alcoholics." *Dis Nerv System* 32(9):632–6 S '71. * (*PA* 48:1249)

92. ZULLO, THOMAS G. "A Factor Analysis of Perceptual and Motor Abilities of Dental Students." *J Dental Ed* 35(6):356–61 Je '71. *

CUMULATIVE NAME INDEX

[2235]

Stromberg Dexterity Test. Trade school and adults; 1945–51; SDT; Eleroy L. Stromberg; Psychological Corporation. *

For additional information and a review by Julian C. Stanley, see 4:755 (1 reference).

REFERENCES THROUGH 1971

1. See 4:755.
2. ELDEEN, MUSTAFA HUSAM, AND TARVIN, JOHN C. "Validity Information Exchange, No. 9-14: D.O.T. Code 5-24, Mason." *Personnel Psychol* 9:123 sp '56. *
3. ELDEEN, MUSTAFA HUSAM, AND TARVIN, JOHN C. "Validity Information Exchange, No. 9-19: D.O.T. Code 7-88.410, Lift Truck Operator." *Personnel Psychol* 9:129 sp '56. *
4. BOLIN, S. F. "Validity Information Exchange, No. 13-04: D.O.T. Code 6-001A, Trainees in Basic Metal Work." *Personnel Psychol* 13:451-3 w '60. *
5. OLLRICH, ARTHUR H. *A Validation of the Stromberg Manual Dexterity Test and the Crawford Small Parts Test (Pins and Collars) for Use in Selecting Female Packaging and Packing Employees.* Master's thesis, Drake University (Des Moines, Iowa), 1962.
6. RIM, Y. "The Predictive Validity of Seven Manual Dexterity Tests." *Psychologia* (Japan) 5:52-5 Mr '62. * (*PA* 38:1417)
7. PETERSON, FLOYD E. "Identification of Sub-Groups for Test Validation Research." *J Indus Psychol* 2:98-101 D '64. * (*PA* 40:10636)
8. TAYLOR, JAMES BENTLEY. "The Structure of Ability in the Lower Intellectual Range." *Am J Mental Def* 68:766-74 My '64. * (*PA* 39:1793)
9. KAHN, HARRIS, AND BURDETT, ARTHUR D. "Interaction of Practice and Rewards on Motor Performance of Adolescent Mental Retardates." *Am J Mental Def* 72:422-7 N '67. * (*PA* 42:7649)

CUMULATIVE NAME INDEX

Bolin, S. F.: 4
Burdett, A. D.: 9
Eldeen, M. H.: 2-3
Kahn, H.: 9
Ollrich, A. H.: 5
Peterson, F. E.: 7
Rim, Y.: 6
Stanley, J. C.: *rev,* 4:755
Stromberg, E. L.: 1
Tarvin, J. C.: 2-3
Taylor, J. B.: 8

[2236]

Yarn Dexterity Test. Textile workers and applicants; 1964-65; YDT; Robert L. Brown; Brown & Associates, Inc. *

For additional information, see 7:1048.

[Out of Print Since TIP I]

Benge Han-Dexterity Test (status unknown), 3:656 (2 reviews)
Martin Peg Board (Finger Dexterity Test) (status unknown), 4:749
Mellenbruch Curve-Block Series, 3:662 (2 reviews, 1 reference)
Minnesota Manual Dexterity Test, T:1902; for a revision, see *Minnesota Rate of Manipulation Test,* 2227
Motor Skills Tests Adapted to the Blind, T:1905

MECHANICAL ABILITY

[2237]

A.C.E.R. Mechanical Comprehension Test. Ages 13.5 and over; 1942-53; Australian Council for Educational Research [Australia]. *

For additional information and reviews by John R. Jennings and Hayden S. Williams, see 5:874 (2 references); for a review by D. W. McElwain, see 4:756.

REFERENCES THROUGH 1971

1-2. See 5:874.

CUMULATIVE NAME INDEX

Hohne, H. H.: 2
Jennings, J. R.: *rev,* 5:874
McElwain, D. W.: *rev,* 4:756
Oxlade, M.: 1
Williams, H. S.: *rev,* 5:874

[2238]

A.C.E.R. Mechanical Reasoning Test. Ages 13-9 and over; 1951-62; abbreviated adaptation of *A.C.E.R. Mechanical Comprehension Test;* T. M. Whitford (revised manual) and Research and Guidance Branch, Queensland Department of Public Instruction (test);

Australian Council for Educational Research [Australia]. *

For additional information, see 6:1082; for reviews by John R. Jennings and Hayden S. Williams, see 5:875.

REFERENCES THROUGH 1971

1. CHAPPEL, SUSAN. "Pre-Selection of Apprentice Motor Mechanics—A Preliminary Validation Study." *Personnel Prac B* (Australia) 23:204-13 S '67. *
2. STAVELEY, BRYAN. *The Abilities and Interests of Craft and Technician Students of Mechanical Engineering.* Master's thesis, University of Manchester (Manchester, England), 1967. (Abstract: *Brit J Ed Psychol* 38:324)
3. BILES, DAVID. "Test Performance and Imprisonment." *Austral & N Zeal J Criminol* (Australia) 1:46-58 Mr '68. *

CUMULATIVE NAME INDEX

Biles, D.: 3
Chappel, S.: 1
Jennings, J. R.: *rev,* 5:875
Staveley, B.: 2
Williams, H. S.: *rev,* 5:875

[2239]

Bennett Mechanical Comprehension Test. Grades 9-12 and adults; 1940-70; BMCT; revision of *Tests of Mechanical Comprehension,* Forms AA, BB, W1; Form CC (entitled *Mechanical Comprehension Test*) for men in engineering schools, is still available; George K. Bennett and William A. Owens (Form CC); Psychological Corporation. (British manuals: 1973; Peter Saville; NFER Publishing Co. Ltd. [England].) *

For additional information, reviews by Harold P. Bechtoldt and A. Oscar H. Roberts, and an excerpted review by Ronald K. Hambleton, see 7:1049 (22 references); see also 6:1094 (15 references) and 5:889 (46 references); for a review by N. W. Morton of earlier forms, see 4:766 (28 references); for reviews by Charles M. Harsh, Lloyd G. Humphreys, and George A. Satter, see 3:683 (19 references).

REFERENCES THROUGH 1971

1-19. See 3:683.
20-47. See 4:766.
48-93. See 5:889.
94-108. See 6:1094.
109-130. See 7:1049.
131. LANE, G. GORHAM. "Studies in Pilot Selection: 1, The Prediction of Success in Learning to Fly Light Aircraft." *Psychol Monogr* 61(5):1-17 '47. * (*PA* 22:5166)
132. BARNETTE, W. LESLIE, JR. "Occupational Aptitude Pattern Research." *Occupations* 29:5-12 O '50. * (*PA* 25:3239)
133. WEIDER, ARTHUR. "Some Aspects of an Industrial Mental Hygiene Program." *J Appl Psychol* 35:383-5 D '51. * (*PA* 26:6560)
134. DUNHAM, RALPH E. "Factors Related to Recidivism in Adults." *J Social Psychol* 39:77-91 F '54. * (*PA* 28:8866)
135. JOHNSON, RALPH HAAKON. *Factors Related to the Success of Disabled Veterans of World War II in the Rehabilitation Training Program Approved for Mechanics and Repairmen, Motor Vehicle.* Doctor's thesis, University of Minnesota (Minneapolis, Minn.), 1955. (*DA* 15:2460)
136. KIRKPATRICK, JAMES J. "Validation of a Test Battery for the Selection and Placement of Engineers." *Personnel Psychol* 9:211-27 su '56. * (*PA* 31:8964)
137. YESLIN, ARTHUR R.; VERNON, LEROY N.; AND KERR, WILLARD A. "The Significance of Time Spent in Answering Personality Inventories." *J Appl Psychol* 42:264-6 Ag '58. * (*PA* 33:9369)
138. FOREHAND, G. A., JR., AND McQUITTY, LOUIS L. "Configurations of Factor Standings as Predictors of Educational Achievement." *Ed & Psychol Meas* 19:31-43 sp '59. * (*PA* 34:119)
139. SPARKS, CHARLES P. "Validity of Psychological Tests." *Personnel Psychol* 23(1):39-46 sp '70. * (*PA* 44:17556)

CUMULATIVE NAME INDEX

Albright, L. E.: 94
Anderson, R. G.: 17, 20
Ash, P.: 98
Barnabas, B.: 12
Barnette, W. L.: 27, 43, 132
Barrett, R. S.: 91
Bechtoldt, H. P.: *rev,* 7:1049
Bennett, G. K.: 2-3, 5, 18
Berg, I. A.: 59
Black, J. D.: 119
Bond, G. L.: 48
Borg, W. R.: 35-6
Bradley, A. D.: 112
Bradshaw, O. L.: 126
Bray, D. W.: 130
Bruce, M. M.: 60, 64-5, 81-2, 109
Campbell, J. T.: 107
Carter, G. C.: 52
Carter, L.: 29

Case, H. W.: 53
Cass, J. C.: 99
Chandler, R. E.: 111
Clegg, H. D.: 102
Cohen, R. M.: 45
Coleman, W.: 61
Cottingham, H. F.: 22, 25
Crane, W. J.: 103
Crannell, C. W.: 34
Crites, J. O.: 105
Cronbach, L. J.: 55, 129
Cruikshank, R. M.: 2–3
Cuomo, S.: 72–4
Decker, R. L.: 92, 102
Dicken, C. F.: 119
Drew, A. S.: 104, 115
DuBois, P. H.: 37, 66
Dunham, R. E.: 134
Durrett, H. L.: 101
Ewing, T. N.: 55
Fear, R. A.: 5
Ferson, R. F.: 50
Finch, C. R.: 127
Fiske, D. W.: 23
Fitzpatrick, E. D.: 70, 75, 83
Fletcher, F. M.: 38, 45
Forehand, G. A.: 138
Forster, C. R.: 76
Gilbert, H. B.: 44, 54
Gilbert, W. M.: 55
Glennon, J. R.: 94
Goodner, S.: 124
Gordon, T.: 30
Grant, D. L.: 130
Greene, R. R.: 21
Grohsmeyer, F. A.: 67
Halliday, R. W.: 38, 45
Halstead, H.: 39
Hambleton, R. K.: exc, 7:1049
Hanes, B.: 110
Harrison, R.: 77
Harsh, C. M.: rev, 3:683
Hinman, S. L.: 122
Hodgson, R. W.: 116
Holmes, J. L.: 71
Hueber, J.: 68
Humphreys, L. G.: rev, 3:683
Hunt, W.: 77
Jackson, T. A.: 77
Jacobsen, E. E.: 6
Jensen, M. B.: 19
Johnson, D. L.: 10
Johnson, R. H.: 48, 84, 135
Juergenson, E. M.: 95
Jurgensen, C. E.: 26
Kazmier, L. J.: 96
Kerr, W. A.: 137
Kirkpatrick, J. J.: 136
Krathwohl, D. R.: 55
Lane, G. G.: 15, 131
Laney, A. R.: 46
Lee, M. C.: 49, 56
Lingwood, J.: 57
Lipsman, C. K.: 123
Littleton, I. T.: 58

McCarty, J. J.: 69–70, 75, 83, 87
McDaniel, J. W.: 8
McElheny, W. T.: 28
McGehee, W.: 4
MacKinney, A. C.: 100
McMurry, R. N.: 10
MacNaughton, J. F.: 128
McQuitty, L. L.: 138
Meadow, L.: 117
Meyer, H. H.: 73–4
Miller, G. E.: 51
Moffie, D. J.: 4, 124
Mollenkopf, W. G.: 88
Moore, B. V.: 1
Moore, C. L.: 128
Morton, N. W.: rev, 4:766
Nair, R. K.: 40
Nixon, M.: 29
North, A. J.: 47
Onarheim, J.: 24
Osburn, H. G.: 128
Otterness, W. B.: 84
Owens, W. A.: 41, 97
Patterson, C. H.: 78, 84–5
Penfield, R. V.: 120
Peterson, L. R.: 84
Poe, W. A.: 59
Reynolds, W. A.: 8
Riland, L. H.: 93
Rinsland, H. D.: 31
Roberts, A. O. H.: rev, 7:1049
Ronan, W. W.: 118
Rotter, J. B.: 19
Sartain, A. Q.: 11, 16
Satter, G. A.: rev, 3:683
Saunders, W. J.: 89
Schmitz, R. M.: 71
Shukla, N. N.: 113
Shultz, I. T.: 12
Shuman, J. T.: 9, 13–4
Smith, O. B.: 79
Smith, W. J.: 94
Sorenson, W. W.: 121
Sparks, C. P.: 139
Super, D. E.: 32, 105
Taylor, D. W.: 108
Tiedeman, D. V.: 99
Topetzes, N. J.: 90
Torres, L.: 114
Travers, R. M. W.: 42
Traxler, A. E.: 7
Upshall, C. C.: 93
Vernon, L. N.: 137
Vernon, P. E.: 33
Walker, F. C.: 86
Wallace, W. L.: 42
Watson, R. I.: 37, 66
Weider, A.: 133
Welsch, L. A.: 125
Wesman, A. G.: 18
Westberg, W. C.: 70
Whitlock, J. B.: 34
Wolff, W. M.: 47
Wolins, L.: 100
Yeslin, A. R.: 137

test available to colleges for local administration; program administered for the College Entrance Examination Board by Educational Testing Service. * For the testing program entry, see 1051.

For additional information, see 7:1050; see also 6:1084 (4 references). For a review of the testing program, see 7:665. For a review of the *College Board Special Aptitude Test in Spatial Relations,* see 4:808.

REFERENCES THROUGH 1971

1–4. See 6:1084.

CUMULATIVE NAME INDEX

Blade, M. F.: 3–4
Bobbitt, J. M.: 1
French, J. W.: 1
Myers, C. T.: 2
Newman, S. H.: 1
Thorndike, R. L.: rev, 4:808
Watson, W. S.: 3–4

[2242]

[Cox Mechanical and Manual Tests.] Boys ages 10 and over, 11–14, 14 and over; 1928–34; 6 tests; J. W. Cox; Charles J. Cox [England]. *
a) COX MECHANICAL TEST M. Ages 11–14, 14 and over.
b) MECHANICAL DIAGRAMS TEST. Ages 14 and over.
c) MECHANICAL EXPLANATION TEST I. Ages 14 and over.
d) COX EYEBOARD TEST NO. 2. Ages 10 and over.
e) COX NAILBOARD TEST. Ages 10 and over.
f) COX NAILSTICK TEST. Ages 10 and over.

For additional information and reviews by C. A. Oakley and Alec Rodger, see 2:1652 (4 references). For excerpts from related book reviews, see 2:B872.1 (2 excerpts) and 1:B336 (12 excerpts).

REFERENCES THROUGH 1971

1–4. See 2:1652.
5. HOLLIDAY, FRANK. "An Investigation Into the Selection of Apprentices for the Engineering Industry." *Occup Psychol* (England) 14:69–81 Ap '40. * (*PA* 14:3710)
6. SLATER, PATRICK. "Some Group Tests of Spatial Judgment or Practical Ability." *Occup Psychol* (England) 14:40–55 Ja '40. * (*PA* 14:2644)
7. BRUSH, EDWARD N. "Mechanical Ability as a Factor in Engineering Aptitude." *J Appl Psychol* 25:300–12 Je '41. * (*PA* 15:4377)
8. KERR, GEORGE. "Aptitude Testing for Secondary Courses: An Essay in Control Under War-Time Difficulties." *Occup Psychol* (England) 16:73–8 Ap '42. * (*PA* 16:3290)
9. SHUTTLEWORTH, CLIFFORD W. "Tests of Technical Aptitude." *Occup Psychol* (England) 16:175–82 O '42. *
10. OXLADE, M. "An Experiment in the Use of Psychological Tests in the Selection of Women Trainee Telephone Mechanics." *B Indus Psychol & Personnel Prac* 2:26–32 Mr '46. * (*PA* 20:4838)
11. VERNON, P. E. "The Structure of Practical Abilities." *Occup Psychol* (England) 23:81–96 Ap '49. * (*PA* 23:5313)
12. YELA, MARIANO. "Application of the Concept of Simple Structure to Alexander's Data." *Psychometrika* 14:121–35 Je '49. * (*PA* 24:1066)

CUMULATIVE NAME INDEX

Blackburn, J. M.: exc, 1:B336
Brush, E. N.: 7
Cox, J. W.: 1, 3
Earle, F. M.: exc, 1:B336
Garrett, H. E.: exc, 1:B336
Greene, E. B.: exc, 1:B336
Harvey, O. L.: 2
Holliday, F.: 5
Hutcheon, N. B.: 4
Kerr, G.: 8
Laycock, S. R.: 4
Martin, A. H.: exc, 1:B336
Oakley, C. A.: rev, 2:1652
Oberlin, K. W.: exc, 1:B336
Oxlade, M.: 10
Pear, T. H.: exc, 1:B336
Rodger, A.: rev, 2:1652
Shuttleworth, C. W.: 9
Slater, P.: 6
Slocombe, C. S.: exc, 1:B336
Vernon, P. E.: 11; exc, 1: B336
Yela, M.: 12

[2240]

Chriswell Structural Dexterity Test. Grades 7–9; 1953–63; manual title is *Structural Dexterity Test of Mechanical Ability;* 1963 revision identical with 1953 edition except for additional norms and technical data in manual; M. Irving Chriswell; Vocational Guidance Service. *

For additional information, see 6:1083 (1 reference); for a review by A. Pemberton Johnson, see 5:876.

REFERENCES THROUGH 1971

1. See 6:1083.

CUMULATIVE NAME INDEX

Chriswell, M. I.: 1
Johnson, A. P.: rev, 5:876

[2241]

*College Placement Test in Spatial Relations. Entering college freshmen; 1962–72, c1954–72; reprintings of inactive 1954 and 1955 forms of *College Board Special Aptitude Test in Spatial Relations;*

[2243]

[Curtis Object Completion and Space Form Tests.] Applicants for mechanical and technical jobs; 1960–61; 2 tests; James W. Curtis; Psychometric Affiliates. *
a) OBJECT-COMPLETION TEST.
b) SPACE FORM TEST.

For additional information and reviews by Richard S. Melton and I. Macfarlane Smith, see 6:1085.

Bennett Mechanical Comprehension Test

[2244]

Detroit Mechanical Aptitudes Examination, Revised. Grades 7–16; 1928–39; 12 scores: motor (circles, classification, total), visual imagery (disarranged pictures, sizes, pulleys, total), mechanical information (tool recognition, tool information, total), arithmetic, total; Harry J. Baker, Paul H. Voelker, and Alex C. Crockett; Bobbs-Merrill Co., Inc. *

For additional information and reviews by Lloyd G. Humphreys and Dewey B. Stuit, see 3:668 (4 references); for a review by Irving Lorge and an excerpted review by J. Wayne Wrightstone, see 2:1656.

REFERENCES THROUGH 1971

1–4. See 3:668.
5. MILLER, ANDREW J., AND MANWILLER, C. E. "A Study of Trade School Pupils." *Pittsburgh Sch* 6:219–69 My–Je '32. *
6. WILLIAMS, RAY A. *The Prognostic Value of the Detroit Mechanical Aptitude Test Battery in the Vocational Education of the American Indian.* Master's thesis, University of South Dakota (Vermillion, S.D.), 1934.
7. MURPHY, LAURA WHITE. "The Relation Between Mechanical Ability Tests and Verbal and Non-Verbal Intelligence Tests." *J Psychol* 2:353–66 Mr '36. * (*PA* 11:3928)
8. GARRISON, K. C. "The Use of Psychological Tests in the Selection of Student-Nurses." *J Appl Psychol* 23:461–72 Ag '39. * (*PA* 13:6426)
9. NEMZEK, CLAUDE L., AND DE HEUS, JOHN H. "The Prediction of Academic and Non-Academic Marks in Junior High Schools." *Sch & Soc* 50:670–2 N 18 '39. * (*PA* 14:1598)
10. BOWN, MAX DUANE. "Variability as a Function of Ability and Its Relation to Personality and Interests." *Arch Psychol* 262:1–45 Jl '41. * (*PA* 16:493)
11. COTTINGHAM, HAROLD F. *The Predictive Value of Certain Paper and Pencil Mechanical Aptitude Tests in Relation to Woodworking Achievement of Junior High School Boys.* Doctor's thesis, Indiana University (Bloomington, Ind.), 1947.
12. BROADHURST, JOHN C. *A Differential Prediction of Success in Vocational-Technical and Vocational-Industrial Courses in a Vocational High School.* Doctor's thesis, New York University (New York, N.Y.), 1948.
13. COTTINGHAM, H. F. "Paper-and-Pencil Tests Given to Students in Woodworking." *Occupations* 27:95–9 N '48. * (*PA* 23:4408)
14. NAIR, RALPH KENNETH. *Predictive Value of Standardized Tests and Inventories in Industrial Arts Teacher Education.* Doctor's thesis, University of Missouri (Columbia, Mo.), 1950. (*DA* 10:77)
15. CANTONI, LOUIS J. "High School Tests and Measurements as Predictors of Occupational Status." *J Appl Psychol* 39:253–5 Ag '55. * (*PA* 30:4722)

CUMULATIVE NAME INDEX

Baker, H. J.: 1	Manwiller, C. E.: 5
Bennett, G. K.: 2	Miller, A. J.: 5
Bown, M. D.: 10	Murphy, L. W.: 7
Broadhurst, J. C.: 12	Nair, R. K.: 14
Cantoni, L. J.: 15	Nemzek, C. L.: 9
Cottingham, H. F.: 11, 13	Portenier, L. G.: 4
Cruikshank, R. M.: 2	Preische, W. A.: 3
de Heus, J. H.: 9	Stuit, D. B.: *rev,* 3:668
Garrison, K. C.: 8	Williams, R. A.: 6
Humphreys, L. G.: *rev,* 3:668	Wrightstone, J. W.: *exc,* 2:1656
Lorge, I.: *rev,* 2:1656	

[2245]

Flags: A Test of Space Thinking. Industrial employees; 1959, c1956–59; L. L. Thurstone (test), T. E. Jeffrey (test), and Measurement Research Division, Industrial Relations Center, University of Chicago (manual); the Center. * [The publisher has not replied to our four requests to check the accuracy of this entry.]

For additional information and a review by I. Macfarlane Smith, see 6:1086.

REFERENCES THROUGH 1971

1. EL-ABD, HAMED A. "The Intellect of East African Students." *Multiv Behav Res* 5(4):423–33 O '70. * (*PA* 45:8037)

CUMULATIVE NAME INDEX

El-Abd, H. A.: 1	Smith, I. M.: *rev,* 6:1086

[2246]

Form Perception Test. Illiterate and semiliterate adults; 1966–68; J. M. Schepers; National Institute for Personnel Research [South Africa]. *

For additional information, see 7:1051.

[2247]

Form Relations Group Test. Ages 14 and over; 1926–46; National Institute of Industrial Psychology; NFER Publishing Co. Ltd. [England]. *

For additional information and a review by A. T. Welford, see 4:757 (10 references).

REFERENCES THROUGH 1971

1–10. See 4:757.
11. MEHROTRA, S. N. "Predicting Intermediate Examination Success by Means of Psychological Tests: A Follow-Up Study." *J Voc & Ed Guid* (India) 4:157–65 My '58. * (*PA* 34:3442)
12. FRISBY, C. B.; VINCENT, D. F.; AND LANCASHIRE, RUTH. *Tests for Engineering Apprentices: A Validation Study.* National Institute of Industrial Psychology, Report 14. London: the Institute, 1959. Pp. iii, 24. *
13. MEHROTRA, S. N. "An Educational-Vocational Guidance Project for Intermediate Students: A Follow-Up Study." *Indian J Psychol* 34:148–62 pt 3 '59. * (*PA* 36:4KJ48M)
14. VENABLES, ETHEL C. "Placement Problems Among Engineering Apprentices in Part-Time Technical College Courses: Part II, Level of Ability Needed for Success in National Certificate Courses." *Brit J Ed Psychol* 31:56–8 F '61. * (*PA* 36:1KJ56V)
15. MONTGOMERY, G. W. G. "Predicting Success in Engineering." *Occup Psychol* (England) 36:59–68 Ja–Ap '62. *
16. ROSS, JEAN. "Predicting Practical Skill in Engineering Apprentices." *Occup Psychol* (England) 36:69–74 Ja–Ap '62. *
17. JOG, R. N. "An Attempt to Predict Success at the 'First Year Engineering Examination.'" *J Voc & Ed Guid* (India) 9:142–8 Ag '63. * (*PA* 38:6643)
18. JOG, R. N., AND AGA, H. "A Comparative Study of the Prediction of Academic Achievement of Engineering." *J Voc & Ed Guid* (India) 12:45–50 My '66. *
19. MILLER, EDGAR. "Handedness and the Pattern of Human Ability." *Brit J Psychol* 62(1):111–2 F '71. * (*PA* 46:795)

CUMULATIVE NAME INDEX

Aga, H.: 18	Miller, E.: 19
Frisby, C. B.: 12	Montgomery, G. W. G.: 15
Harding, D. W.: 8	Moore, B. G. R.: 10
Holliday, F.: 2, 4–5, 9	Peel, E. A.: 10
Hutcheon, N. B.: 1	Ross, J.: 16
Jog, R. N.: 17–8	Shuttleworth, C. W.: 7
Kerr, G.: 6	Slater, P.: 3
Lancashire, R.: 12	Venables, E. C.: 14
Laycock, S. R.: 1	Vincent, D. F.: 12
Mehrotra, S. N.: 11, 13	Welford, A. T.: *rev,* 4:757

[2248]

Group Test 80A. Ages 15 and over; 1943–51; spatial perception; National Institute of Industrial Psychology; NFER Publishing Co. Ltd. [England]. *

For additional information and reviews by E. G. Chambers and John Liggett, see 5:877.

REFERENCES THROUGH 1971

1. FOULDS, G. A., AND CAINE, T. A. "Personality Factors and Performance on Timed Tests of Ability." *Occup Psychol* (England) 32:102–5 Ap '58. *
2. FRISBY, C. B.; VINCENT, D. F.; AND LANCASHIRE, RUTH. *Tests for Engineering Apprentices: A Validation Study.* National Institute of Industrial Psychology, Report 14. London: the Institute, 1959. Pp. iii, 24. *

CUMULATIVE NAME INDEX

Caine, T. A.: 1	Lancashire, R.: 2
Chambers, E. G.: *rev,* 5:877	Liggett, J.: *rev,* 5:877
Foulds, G. A.: 1	Vincent, D. F.: 2
Frisby, C. B.: 2	

[2249]

Group Test 81. Ages 14 and over; 1949; spatial perception; National Institute of Industrial Psychology; NFER Publishing Co. Ltd. [England]. *

For additional information and a review by E. G. Chambers, see 4:758 (5 references).

REFERENCES THROUGH 1971

1–5. See 4:758.
6. SHUTTLEWORTH, CLIFFORD W. "Tests of Technical Aptitude." *Occup Psychol* (England) 16:175–82 O '42. *

7. WRIGLEY, JACK. "The Factorial Nature of Ability in Elementary Mathematics." *Brit J Ed Psychol* 28:61–78 F '58. * (*PA* 33:6845)

8. LEWIS, D. G. "The Factorial Nature of Attainment in Elementary Science." *Brit J Ed Psychol* 34:1–9 F '64. * (*PA* 38:9173)

9. JAMIESON, G. H. "Psychological Aspects of Craftsmanship in Pottery-Making at a Secondary School." *Brit J Ed Psychol* 35:179–82 Je '65. * (*PA* 39:16457)

10. SMITH, I. MACFARLANE. "The Use of Diagnostic Tests for Assessing the Abilities of Overseas Students Attending Institutions of Further Education, Part I." *Voc Aspect Ed* (England) 22(51):1–8 Mr '70. *

11. SMITH, I. MACFARLANE. "The Use of Diagnostic Tests for Assessing the Abilities of Overseas Students Attending Institutions of Further Education, Part II." *Voc Aspect Ed* (England) 23(54):39–48 Ap '71. *

CUMULATIVE NAME INDEX

Chambers, E. G.: *rev*, 4:758
Holliday, F.: 1, 3–5
Jamieson, G. H.: 9
Lewis, D. G.: 8
Shuttleworth, C. W.: 6
Slater, P.: 2
Smith, I. M.: 10–1
Wrigley, J.: 7

[2250]

Group Test 82. Ages 14.5 and over; 1959–70; subtest of *N.I.I.P. Engineering Apprentice Selection Test Battery;* spatial perception; National Institute of Industrial Psychology; NFER Publishing Co. Ltd. [England]. * For the complete battery entry, see 2345. For additional information, see 7:1052.

[2251]

MacQuarrie Test for Mechanical Ability. Grades 7 and over; 1925–43; 8 scores: tracing, tapping, dotting, copying, location, blocks, pursuit, total; T. W. MacQuarrie; CTB/McGraw-Hill. *

For additional information, see 4:759 (15 references); for reviews by John R. Kinzer, C. H. Lawshe, Jr., and Alec Rodger, see 3:661 (43 references). For an excerpt from a related book review, see 4:760.

REFERENCES THROUGH 1971

1–43. See 3:661.

44–58. See 4:759.

59. FULLER, FLORENCE D. "A Study of the Minnesota Paper Formboard Test." *Ed Res B* (Los Angeles City Schools) 7:4–5 Je '28. *

60. WALTON, MAUD SMITH. "The Correlation of Teacher Ratings in Vocational Exploratory Courses With Test Scores of Mechanical Ability." *Ed Res B* (Los Angeles City Schools) 8:2–4 O '28. *

61. LINDSEY, T. T. "Do the White and Colored Races Differ in Mechanical Ability?" *Peabody J Ed* 7:160–3 N '29. *

62. STEDMAN, MELISSA BRANSON. "A Study of the Possibility of Prognosis of School Success in Typewriting." *J Appl Psychol* 13:505–15 O '29. * (*PA* 4:891)

63. GARRETSON, OLIVER KELLEAM. "Relationships Between the Expressed Preferences and the Curricular Abilities of Ninth Grade Boys." *J Ed Res* 23:124–32 F '31. * (*PA* 5:2537)

64. EELLS, WALTER CROSBY. "Mechanical, Physical, and Musical Ability of the Native Races of Alaska." *J Appl Psychol* 17:493–506 O '33. * (*PA* 8:2669)

65. ANDERSON, H. DEWEY, AND EELLS, WALTER CROSBY. *Alaska Natives: A Survey of Their Sociological and Educational Status,* pp. 298–370. Stanford, Calif.: Stanford University Press, 1935. Pp. xvi, 472. * (*PA* 9:2346)

66. HOWARD, JOSEPHINE THEO. *The Mechanical Aptitudes of Indian Boys of the Southwest.* Master's thesis, George Washington University (Washington, D.C.), 1940.

67. GUINN, MARY PAULINE. *Aids for the Prognosis of Success in Typewriting.* Master's thesis, Kansas State Teachers College (Pittsburg, Kan.), 1948.

68. HELLEBRANDT, F. A.; HOUTZ, SARA JANE; AND PEDERSEN, THELMA. "Sex and Age Differences in the Mechanical Ability of Physical Therapy Matriculants." *Arch Phys Med* 32:567–71 S '51. *

69. MARTIN, GLENN C. "Test Batteries for Trainees in Auto Mechanics and Apparel Design." *J Appl Psychol* 35:20–2 F '51. * (*PA* 25:7123)

70. AMERICAN GAS ASSOCIATION, PERSONNEL COMMITTEE. *Personnel Testing in the Gas Industry.* New York: the Association, January 1952. Pp. 10. *

71. BALINSKY, BENJAMIN, AND HUJSA, CHARLES. "Performance of College Students on a Mechanical Knowledge Test." *J Appl Psychol* 38:111–2 Ap '54. * (*PA* 29:3028)

72. HELLEBRANDT, F. A., AND HOUTZ, SARA JANE. "Applications of the MacQuarrie Test for Mechanical Ability." *Am J Occup Ther* 9:259–63+ N–D '55. * (*PA* 30:7198)

73. LIPTON, ROBERT LAWRENCE. "A Study of the Effect of Exercise in a Simple Mechanical Activity on Mechanical Aptitude as Is Measured by the Subtests of the MacQuarrie Test for Mechanical Ability." *Psychol Newsl* 7:39–42 Ja–F '56. * (*PA* 31:1758)

74. SINICK, DANIEL. "Encouragement, Anxiety, and Test Performance." *J Appl Psychol* 40:315–8 O '56. * (*PA* 31:7972)

75. JAEGER, MARTHA. *Some Aspects of Relationship Between Motor Coordination and Personality in a Group of College Women.* Doctor's thesis, Columbia University (New York, N.Y.), 1957. (*DA* 17:2065)

76. ARNOLDI, J. "The Vocational Choices, Interests, and Aptitudes of Secondary School Boys, With Special Reference to the Consistency of These Factors." *J Social Res* (South Africa) 9:1–22 My '58. * (*PA* 34:6552)

77. SHORE, RICHARD P. "Validity Information Exchange, No. 11-22: D.O.T. Code 1-02.01, Bookkeeping-Machine Operator (Banking)." *Personnel Psychol* 11:435–6 au '58. *

78. SHORE, RICHARD P. "Validity Information Exchange, No. 11-23: D.O.T. Code 1-06.02, Teller." *Personnel Psychol* 11:437 au '58. *

79. SHORE, RICHARD P. "Validity Information Exchange, No. 11-24: D.O.T. Code 1-25.68, Proof-Machine Operator." *Personnel Psychol* 11:438–9 au '58. *

80. BUSCH, ALLEN C., AND WOODWARD, RICHARD H. "Validity Information Exchange, No. 12-18: D.O.T. Code 0-18.01, Industrial Engineer." *Personnel Psychol* 12:481 au '59. *

81. HANEY, RUSSELL; MICHAEL, WILLIAM B.; AND JONES, ROBERT A. "Identification of Aptitude and Achievement Factors in the Prediction of the Success of Nursing Trainees." *Ed & Psychol Meas* 19:645–7 w '59. * (*PA* 34:6164)

82. MICHAEL, WILLIAM B.; JONES, ROBERT A.; AND HANEY, RUSSELL. "The Development and Validation of a Test Battery for Selection of Student Nurses." *Ed & Psychol Meas* 19:641–3 w '59. * (*PA* 34:6171)

83. RACKY, DONALD J. "Predictions of Ninth Grade Woodshop Performance From Aptitude and Interest Measures." *Ed & Psychol Meas* 19:629–36 w '59. * (*PA* 34:6572)

84. GARRETT, WILEY S. "Prediction of Academic Success in a School of Nursing." *Personnel & Guid J* 38:500–3 F '60. * (*PA* 35:3954)

85. MARTIN, JACK R. "The Correlation Between Preadmission Tests and Graduation From Nursing School." *J Nursing Ed* 1:3–4+ D '62. *

86. SUPER, DONALD E., AND CRITES, JOHN O. *Appraising Vocational Fitness by Means of Psychological Tests, Revised Edition,* pp. 256–72. New York: Harper & Brothers, 1962. Pp. xv, 688. * (*PA* 37:2038)

87. MATTSON, DALE E.; REILLY, ROBERT R.; AND STACHNIAK, JOSEPH J. "The MacQuarrie Test of Mechanical Ability as a Predictor of Technic Course Grades in Dental School." *J Dental Ed* 27:327–31 D '63. *

88. TAYLOR, JAMES BENTLEY. "The Structure of Ability in the Lower Intellectual Range." *Am J Mental Def* 68:766–74 My '64. * (*PA* 39:1793)

89. DARBES, ALEX. "Some Test Characteristics of Female Student Beauticians." *Proc W Va Acad Sci* 37:286–8 F '66. * (*PA* 40:8250)

90. McRAE, JAMES A. *The Relationship of Mathematical Ability and Physical Coordination.* Master's thesis, North Carolina State University (Raleigh, N.C.), 1966.

91. PETERSON, MARVIN ANHILM. *Correlates of Size of Course Offerings in California's Public Junior Colleges.* Doctor's thesis, Stanford University (Stanford, Calif.), 1967. (*DA* 29:518A)

92. O'CONNOR, GAIL. "Problems of Optimum Selection." *Percept & Motor Skills* 27:715–20 D '68. * (*PA* 43:7528)

93. STOCK, WILLIAM H., JR. *Some Psychological and Physiological Factors Affecting Excellence in Acting.* Doctor's thesis, Michigan State University (East Lansing, Mich.), 1968. (*DA* 29:3716A)

94. STERNE, DAVID M. "The Purdue Pegboard and MacQuarrie Tapping and Dotting Tasks as Measures of Motor Functioning." *Percept & Motor Skills* 28(2):556 Ap '69. * (*PA* 43:15143)

95. McCOY, WESLEY LAWRENCE. *A Comparison of Select Psychomotor Abilities of a Sample of Undergraduate Instrumental Music Majors and a Sample of Undergraduate Non-Music Majors.* Doctor's thesis, Louisiana State University (Baton Rouge, La.), 1970. (*DAI* 31:1833A)

96. STRAUSS, RALPH JOSEPH. *Biographical Factors and Performance: How Are They Related? A Study of the Relationship Between Various Subcultural Factors, Aptitude Test Performance and Job-Success Ratings of Repair and Assembly Workers.* Doctor's thesis, New York University (New York, N.Y.), 1971. (*DAI* 32:5899A)

CUMULATIVE NAME INDEX

American Gas Association,
 Personnel Committee: 70
Anderson, H. D.: 65
Anderson, R. G.: 40, 48
Arnoldi, J.: 76
Babcock, H.: 17, 54
Balinsky, B.: 71
Barrett, D. M.: 36
Beamer, G. C.: 50
Bellows, R. M.: 22, 25
Bennett, G. K.: 26
Bingham, W. V.: 13
Bingham, W. V. D.: 15
Blum, M. L.: 30
Burr, M.: 11
Busch, A. C.: 80

Chapman, R. L.: 51
Cooper, J. H.: 22
Crawford, J. E.: 23
Crites, J. O.: 86
Cruikshank, R. M.: 26
Curtis, H. S.: 27
Darbes, A.: 89
Duran, J. C.: 55
Dvorak, B. J.: 22
Edmonson, L. D.: 50
Eells, W. C.: 64–5
Emerson, M. R.: 17
Endler, O. L.: 22
Faubion, R.: 21
Fife, I. E.: 43
Fuller, F. D.: 59
Garretson, O. K.: 63
Garrett, W. S.: 84
Ghiselli, E. E.: 24, 28
Goodman, C. H.: 37, 41–2, 56
Griffitts, C. H.: 9
Guinn, M. P.: 67
Haney, R.: 81–2
Harrell, W.: 16, 19–21
Hellebrandt, F. A.: 68, 72
Holcomb, G. W.: 10
Horning, S. D.: 1
Houtz, S. J.: 68, 72
Howard, J. T.: 66
Hujsa, C.: 71
Jaeger, M.: 75
Jones, R. A.: 81–2
Jorgensen, C.: 12
Kefauver, G. N.: 5
Kinzer, J. R.: rev, 3:661
Klugman, S. F.: 31
Kolbe, L. E.: 22
Lackey, F. W.: 18
Laney, A. R.: 58
Laslett, H. R.: 10
Lawshe, C. H.: rev, 3:661
Lindsey, T. T.: 61
Lipton, R. L.: 73
McCoy, W. L.: 95
McDaniel, J. W.: 32
MacQuarrie, T. W.: 2
McRae, J. A.: 90
Maher, H.: 43
Martin, G. C.: 69

Martin, J. R.: 85
Mattson, D. E.: 87
Mercer, M.: 46
Michael, W. B.: 81–2
Mitrano, A. J.: 29
Moodie, M.: 47
Morgan, W. J.: 33
Murphy, L. W.: 45
O'Connor, G.: 92
Osborne, H. F.: 22
Otis, J. L.: 22
Pedersen, T.: 68
Peterson, M. A.: 91
Racky, D. J.: 83
Raubenheimer, A. S.: 6
Reilly, R. R.: 87
Reynolds, W. A.: 32
Robinson, J. B.: 25
Rodger, A.: rev, 3:661
Sartain, A. Q.: 35, 38
Scudder, C. R.: 6
Shaffer, L. F.: exc, 4:760
Shartle, C. L.: 22
Shore, R. P.: 77–9
Shultz, I. T.: 49
Sinick, D.: 74
Skolnik, R. F.: 14
Stachniak, J. J.: 87
Stannard, C.: 44
Stead, W. H.: 22
Stedman, M. B.: 7, 62
Stein, M. L.: 3
Sterne, D. M.: 94
Stock, W. H.: 93
Stoy, E. G.: 4
Strauss, R. J.: 96
Strother, G. B.: 50
Super, D. E.: 52, 86
Taylor, D. H.: 8
Taylor, J. B.: 88
Thompson, C. E.: 34
Travers, R. M. W.: 57
Tuckman, J.: 39
Wallace, W. L.: 57
Walton, M. S.: 60
Ward, R. S.: 22
Woodward, R. H.: 80
Zakolski, F. C.: 53

[2252]

Mechanical Aptitude Test: Acorn National Aptitude Tests. Grades 7–16 and adults; 1943–52; 5 scores: comprehension of mechanical tasks, use of tools and materials (verbal), matching tools and operations, use of tools and materials (nonverbal), total; 1952 test identical with test copyrighted 1943; Andrew Kobal, J. Wayne Wrightstone, and Karl R. Kunze; Psychometric Affiliates. *

For additional information, see 5:878; for reviews by Reign H. Bittner, James M. Porter, Jr., and Alec Rodger, see 3:669.

[2253]

Mechanical Comprehension Test, Second Edition. Male technical apprentices and trainee engineer applicants; 1966–68; manual by P. D. Griffiths; National Institute for Personnel Research [South Africa]. *

For additional information, see 7:1053.

[2254]

Mechanical Information Test. Ages 15 and over; 1948–70; MIT; subtest of *N.I.I.P. Engineering Apprentice Selection Test Battery;* National Institute of Industrial Psychology; NFER Publishing Co. Ltd. [England]. * For the complete battery entry, see 2345.

For additional information, see 7:1054 (1 reference).

REFERENCES THROUGH 1971

1. See 7:1054.

CUMULATIVE NAME INDEX

Frisby, C. B.: 1
Lancashire, R.: 1
Vincent, D. F.: 1

[2255]

Mechanical Movements: A Test of Mechanical Comprehension. Industrial employees; 1959–63, c1956–63; abbreviated version of a Thurstone test developed about 1918; L. L. Thurstone (test), T. E. Jeffrey (test), and Measurement Research Division, Industrial Relations Center, University of Chicago (manual); the Center. * [The publisher has not replied to our four requests to check the accuracy of this entry.]

For additional information and a review by William A. Owens, see 6:1089.

[2256]

*Mechanical Reasoning: Differential Aptitude Tests. Grades 8–12 and adults; 1947–73; 2 editions; George K. Bennett, Harold G. Seashore, and Alexander G. Wesman; Psychological Corporation. * For the complete battery entry, see 1069.

a) FORM A. 1947–59. *Out of print.*

b) FORM T. 1947–73; revision of Forms L and M ('62).

For reviews of the complete battery, see 7:673 (1 review, 1 excerpt), 6:767 (2 reviews), 5:605 (2 reviews), 4:711 (3 reviews), and 3:620 (1 excerpt).

REFERENCES THROUGH 1971

1. "Results of the Space Relations, Mechanical Reasoning, and Clerical Speed and Accuracy Tests of the Differential Aptitude Test Battery in Six Public Schools." *Ed Rec B* 58:79–84 F '52. * (*PA* 26:7240)
2. "Validity Information Exchange, No. 7-094: D.O.T. Code 7-80.120, Beginner Mechanics." *Personnel Psychol* 7:572 w '54. *
3. "Validity Information Exchange, No. 7-095: D.O.T. Code 7-94.112 and 7-94.100, Tool and Die and Machinist Apprentice." *Personnel Psychol* 7:573 w '54. *
4. "Validity Information Exchange, No. 7-096: D.O.T. Code 9-03.01, Riveter Assistants (Rivet-Buckers)." *Personnel Psychol* 7:574 w '54. *
5. MENDICINO, LORENZO. "Mechanical Reasoning and Space Perception: Native Capacity or Experience." *Personnel & Guid J* 36:335–8 Ja '58. * (*PA* 33:6837)
6. JAYALAKSHMI, G. "Correlation of Tests of Psychomotor Ability With Intelligence and Non-motor Tests." *J Psychol Res* (India) 3:78–84 S '59. *
7. FOOTE, RICHARD PAUL. *The Prediction of Success in Automotive Mechanics in a Vocational-Industrial Curriculum on the Secondary School Level.* Doctor's thesis, New York University (New York, N.Y.), 1960. (*DA* 21:3014)
8. McGUIRE, CARSON. "The Prediction of Talented Behavior in the Junior High School." *Proc Inv Conf Testing Probl* 1960: 46–67 '61. *
9. JONES, CHARLES W., AND McMILLEN, DAN. "Engineering Freshman Norms for the D.A.T. Mechanical Reasoning and Space Relations Tests Utilizing Fifteen-Minute Time Limits." *Ed & Psychol Meas* 25:459–64 su '65. * (*PA* 39:16507)
10. PARMENTER, WILLIAM H. *An Investigation of the Predictive Validity of the Spatial and Mechanical Tests of the Differential Aptitude Tests in Regard to Success in Industrial Arts.* Master's thesis, California State College (Long Beach, Calif.), 1966.
11. IRVINE, FLEET RAYMOND. *A Study of Creative Thinking Ability, and Its Relationship to Psychomotor Ability, Mechanical Reasoning Ability, and Vocational Aptitude of Selected High School Industrial Arts Students.* Doctor's thesis, Utah State University (Logan, Utah), 1968. (*DA* 29:1768A)

CUMULATIVE NAME INDEX

Foote, R. P.: 7
Irvine, F. R.: 11
Jayalakshmi, G.: 6
Jones, C. W.: 9
McGuire, C.: 8
McMillen, D.: 9
Mendicino, L.: 5
Parmenter, W. H.: 10

[2257]

Mellenbruch Mechanical Motivation Test. Grades 6–16 and adults; 1944–57; formerly called *Mellenbruch Mechanical Aptitude Test for Men and Women;* P. L. Mellenbruch; Psychometric Affiliates. *

For additional information and reviews by Arthur H. Brayfield and John B. Morris, see 5:879; for reviews by Lloyd G. Humphreys and C. A. Oakley of the original edition, see 3:670.

REFERENCES THROUGH 1971

1. COTTINGHAM, HAROLD F. *The Predictive Value of Certain Paper and Pencil Mechanical Aptitude Tests in Relation to Wood-*

working Achievement of Junior High School Boys. Doctor's thesis, Indiana University (Bloomington, Ind.), 1947.

2. COTTINGHAM, H. F. "Paper-and-Pencil Tests Given to Students in Woodworking." *Occupations* 27:95–9 N '48. * (*PA* 23:4408)

CUMULATIVE NAME INDEX

Brayfield, A. H.: *rev,* 5:879
Cottingham, H. F.: 1–2
Humphreys, L. G.: *rev,* 3:670

Morris, J. B.: *rev,* 5:879
Oakley, C. A.: *rev,* 3:670

[2258]

Minnesota Spatial Relations Test. Ages 11 and over; 1930; revision of H. C. Link's *Spatial Relations Test* ('19); 2 scores: time, error; M. R. Trabue, Donald G. Paterson, Richard M. Elliott, L. Dewey Anderson, Herbert A. Toops, and Edna Heidbreder; American Guidance Service. *

For additional information and a review by Milton L. Blum, see 3:664 (18 references); for a review by Lorene Teegarden, see 2:1663 (10 references).

REFERENCES THROUGH 1971

1–10. See 2:1663.
11–28. See 3:664.
29. VANDEN BOOGERT, ALYCE W. *The Significance of the Minnesota Spatial Relations Test With a Group of First and Second-Grade Children.* Master's thesis, University of Michigan (Ann Arbor, Mich.), 1934.
30. BRODY, DAVID. "Twin Resemblances in Mechanical Ability, With Reference to the Effects of Practice on Performance." *Child Develop* 8:207–16 S '37. * (*PA* 12:565)
31. GREENE, EDWARD B. "Practice Effects on Various Types of Standard Tests." *Am J Psychol* 49:67–75 Ja '37. * (*PA* 11:2482)
32. PRITCHARD, MIRIAM C. "The Mechanical Ability of Subnormal Boys." *Teach Col Contrib Ed* 699:1–73 '37. * (*PA* 11:4608)
33. OTIS, JAY L. "The Prediction of Success in Power Sewing Machine Operating." *J Appl Psychol* 22:350–66 Ag '38. * (*PA* 13:1688)
34. HACKMAN, RAY CARTER. *The Differential Prediction of Success in Two Contrasting Vocational Areas.* Doctor's thesis, University of Minnesota (Minneapolis, Minn.), 1940.
35. SHEPARD, EUGENE L. *Measurements of Certain Nonverbal Abilities of Urban and Rural Children.* Doctor's thesis, New York University (New York, N.Y.), 1940.
36. CRISSEY, ORLO L. "Test Predictive of Success in Occupation of Job-Setter." Abstract. *Psychol B* 39:436 Jl '42. * (*PA* 16:4971, title only)
37. ROSS, LAWRENCE W. "Results of Testing Machine-Tool Trainees." *Personnel J* 21:363–7 Ap '43. * (*PA* 17:2459)
38. STEEL, MARION; BALINSKY, BENJAMIN; AND LANG, HAZEL. "A Study on the Use of a Work Sample." *J Appl Psychol* 29:14–21 F '45. * (*PA* 19:1779)
39. WITTENBORN, J. R. "Mechanical Ability, Its Nature and Measurement: 1, An Analysis of the Variables Employed in the Preliminary Minnesota Experiment." *Ed & Psychol Meas* 5:241–60 au '45. * (*PA* 20:2925)
40. WITTENBORN, J. R. "Mechanical Ability, Its Nature and Measurement: 2, Manual Dexterity. *Ed & Psychol Meas* 5:395–409 w '45. * (*PA* 20:2926)
41. HALSTEAD, H., AND SLATER, PATRICK. "An Experiment in the Vocational Adjustment of Neurotic Patients." *J Mental Sci* (England) 92:509–15 Jl '46. * (*PA* 21:281)
42. BARNETT, ALBERT. "A Note on Mechanical Aptitude of West Texans." *J Appl Psychol* 33:316–8 Ag '49. * (*PA* 24:2363)
43. GEIST, HAROLD. "The Performance of Amputees on Motor Dexterity Tests." *Ed & Psychol Meas* 9:765–72 w '49. * (*PA* 26:2950)
44. RINSLAND, HENRY D. "The Prediction of Veterans' Success From Test Scores at the University of Oklahoma." Part 1, pp. 59–72. In *The Sixth Yearbook of the National Council on Measurements Used in Education, 1948–1949.* Fairmont, W.Va.: the Council, Fairmont State College, 1949. Pp. v, 140. *
45. SUPER, DONALD E. *Appraising Vocational Fitness by Means of Psychological Tests,* pp. 285–97. New York: Harper & Brothers, 1949. Pp. xxiii, 727. * (*PA* 24:2130)
46. LANEY, ARTHUR R., JR. "Validity of Employment Tests for Gas-Appliance Service Personnel." *Personnel Psychol* 4:199–208 su '51. * (*PA* 26:1735)
47. TIZARD, J., AND LOOS, F. M. "The Learning of a Spatial Relations Test by Adult Imbeciles." *Am J Mental Def* 59:85–90 Jl '54. * (*PA* 29:4278)
48. JOHNSON, RALPH HAAKON. *Factors Related to the Success of Disabled Veterans of World War II in the Rehabilitation Training Program Approved for Mechanics and Repairmen, Motor Vehicle.* Doctor's thesis, University of Minnesota (Minneapolis, Minn.), 1955. (*DA* 15:2460)
49. SUPER, DONALD E., AND CRITES, JOHN O. *Appraising Vocational Fitness by Means of Psychological Tests, Revised Edition,*

pp. 281–90. New York: Harper & Brothers, 1962. Pp. xv, 688. * (*PA* 37:2038)
50. FINLEY, PETER J. "Performance of Male Juvenile Delinquents on Four Psychological Tests." *Training Sch B* 60:175–83 F '64. * (*PA* 39:5704)
51. ZIMMERMAN, JOHN JAMES. *Relationships Among Scholastic Aptitude, Attitudes Toward Various Facets of College Life, and Academic Performance of Students at Lycoming College.* Doctor's thesis, Pennsylvania State University (University Park, Pa.), 1969. (*DAI* 30:4792A)

CUMULATIVE NAME INDEX

Anderson, L. D.: 1–2
Balinsky, B.: 38
Barnett, A.: 42
Bates, J.: 24
Bellows, R. M.: 14
Bennett, G. K.: 19
Bergen, G. L.: 5
Berman, I. R.: 7
Bingham, W. V. D.: 8
Blum, M. L.: *rev,* 3:664
Brody, D.: 30
Brown, F.: 9
Brush, E. N.: 15
Cooper, J. H.: 14
Crissey, O. L.: 36
Crites, J. O.: 49
Cruikshank, R. M.: 19
Dvorak, B. J.: 6, 14
Elliott, R. M.: 2
Endler, O. L.: 14
Finley, P. J.: 50
Geist, H.: 43
Ghiselli, E. E.: 16
Green, H. J.: 7
Greene, E. B.: 31
Hackman, R. C.: 34
Halstead, H.: 26, 41
Harmon, J. B.: 17
Harmon, L. R.: 17
Harrell, W.: 13
Harvey, O. L.: 4
Heidbreder, E.: 2
Henderson, M. T.: 24
Johnson, A. P.: 20–1
Johnson, R. H.: 48
Kolbe, L. E.: 14

Laney, A. R.: 46
Lang, H.: 38
Loos, F. M.: 47
Morrow, R. S.: 18
Myklebust, H. R.: 28
Osborne, H. F.: 14
Otis, J. L.: 14, 33
Page, M. L.: 11
Paterson, D. G.: 2, 7, 10
Pritchard, M. C.: 32
Rinsland, H. D.: 44
Ross, L. W.: 37
Schieffelin, B.: 3
Schneidler, G. G.: 10
Schwesinger, G. C.: 3
Shartle, C. L.: 14
Shepard, E. L.: 35
Slater, P.: 26, 41
Stanton, M. B.: 12
Stead, W. H.: 14
Steel, M.: 38
Super, D. E.: 45, 49
Teegarden, L.: 22–3, 25; *rev,* 2:1663
Tizard, J.: 47
Toops, H. A.: 2
Trabue, M. R.: 7
Vanden Boogert, A. W.: 29
Wallace, M.: 24
War Manpower Commission, Division of Occupational Analysis, Staff: 27
Ward, R. S.: 14
Williamson, E. G.: 10
Wittenborn, J. R.: 39–40
Zimmerman, J. J.: 51

[2259]

O'Connor Wiggly Block. Ages 16 and over; 1928–51; Johnson O'Connor; Stoelting Co. (Also published by Lafayette Instrument Co.) *

For additional information, see 6:1091 (27 references).

REFERENCES THROUGH 1971

1–27. See 6:1091.
28. LINDSEY, T. T. "Do the White and Colored Races Differ in Mechanical Ability?" *Peabody J Ed* 7:160–3 N '29. *
29. GOODRICH, JOHN RICHARD. *The Prediction of Mechanical Ability in Ninth Grade Boys by Means of a Block Assembly Test.* Master's thesis, University of Cincinnati (Cincinnati, Ohio), 1935.
30. WELLS, F. L. "Clinical Aspects of Functional Transfer. (Psychometric Practice in Adults of Superior Intelligence, IV.)" *Am J Orthopsychiatry* 9:1–22 Ja '39. * (*PA* 13:3317)

CUMULATIVE NAME INDEX

Bates, J.: 16
Bennett, G. K.: 14
Bittel, J.: 22
Brush, E. N.: 12
Bunch, R. H.: 25
Cruikshank, R. M.: 14
Estes, S. G.: 15
Foley, J.: 23
Frye, E. K.: 8
Giese, W. J.: 13
Goodrich, J. R.: 29
Green, M. C.: 27
Harrell, W.: 9, 11
Harris, A. J.: 10
Henderson, M. T.: 16
Keane, F. L.: 1
Khan, H. I. A.: 20

Kjerland, R. N.: 25–7
Lauer, A. R.: 21, 25
Licht, M.: 18–9
Lindsey, T. T.: 28
McIntosh, W. J.: 24
Miller, C.: 21
O'Connor, J.: 1, 5, 17
Philip, B. R.: 6
Phillips, J. J.: 27
Remmers, H. H.: 3, 7
Schell, J. W.: 3
Smith, J. M.: 7
Stoy, E. G.: 2
Viteles, M. S.: 4
Wallace, M.: 16
Wells, F. L.: 30

[2260]

O'Rourke Mechanical Aptitude Test. Grades 7–12 and adults; 1926–57; some forms entitled *O'Rourke*

Mellenbruch Mechanical Motivation Test

Mechanical Aptitude Test—Junior Grade; L. J. O'Rourke; O'Rourke Publications. *

For additional information, see 5:882; for reviews by Jay L. Otis and George A. Satter, see 3:672 (8 references); for a review by Herbert A. Landry, see 2:1668.

REFERENCES THROUGH 1971
1–8. See 3:672.
9. SUPER, DONALD E., AND CRITES, JOHN O. *Appraising Vocational Fitness by Means of Psychological Tests, Revised Edition,* pp. 232–42. New York: Harper & Brothers, 1962. Pp. xv, 688. * (PA 37:2038)

CUMULATIVE NAME INDEX

Bennett, G. K.: 3	Raubenheimer, A. S.: 1
Bingham, W. V. D.: 2	Reynolds, W. A.: 6
Crites, J. O.: 9	Sartain, A. Q.: 8
Cruikshank, R. M.: 3	Satter, G. A.: *rev,* 3:672
Hanman, B.: 4	Scudder, C. R.: 1
Landry, H. A.: *rev,* 2:1668	Super, D. E.: 9
Lawshe, C. H.: 5	Thornton, G. R.: 5
McDaniel, J. W.: 6	Tuckman, J.: 7
Otis, J. L.: *rev,* 3:672	

[2261]
Perceptual Battery. Job applicants with at least 10 years of education; 1961–63; spatial relations; National Institute for Personnel Research [South Africa]. *

For additional information, see 7:1055.

[2262]
Primary Mechanical Ability Tests. Applicants for positions requiring mechanical ability; 1940–50; 4 tests, 5 scores: 4 scores listed below, total; J. H. Hazelhurst; Stevens, Thurow & Associates, Inc. *
a) TEST 1, CROSSES.
b) TEST 2, BOLTS.
c) TEST 3, TOOLS.
d) TEST 4, MISSING LINES.
For additional information, see 6:1087.

[2263]
Purdue Mechanical Adaptability Test. Males ages 15 and over; 1945–50; C. H. Lawshe, Jr. and Joseph Tiffin; University Book Store. *

For additional information, see 4:762 (6 references); for reviews by Jay L. Otis and Dewey B. Stuit, see 3:676.

REFERENCES THROUGH 1971
1–6. See 4:762.
7. BRUCE, MARTIN M. "Validity Information Exchange, No. 7-079: D.O.T. Code 7-83.058, Electrical Appliance Serviceman." *Personnel Psychol* 7:425–6 au '54. *
8. HUEBER, JOANNE. "Validity Information Exchange, No. 7-089: D.O.T. Code 5-83.641, Maintenance Mechanic II." *Personnel Psychol* 7:565–6 w '54. *
9. DREW, ALFRED STANISLAUS. *The Relationship of General Reading Ability and Other Factors to School and Job Performance of Machinist Apprentices.* Doctor's thesis, University of Wisconsin (Madison, Wis.), 1962. (DA 23:1261)
10. CAMPBELL, JOEL T. "Validity Information Exchange, No. 16-04: D.O.T. Code 7-36.250, Gas Deliveryman." *Personnel Psychol* 16:181–3 su '63. *
11. DREW, ALFRED S. "The Relationship of General Reading Ability and Other Factors to School and Job Performance of Machine Apprentices." *J Indus Teach Ed* 2:47–60 f '64. *

CUMULATIVE NAME INDEX

Belman, H. S.: 4	Otis, J. L.: *rev,* 3:676
Bruce, M. M.: 7	Rothe, H. F.: 5
Campbell, J. T.: 10	Semanek, I. A.: 1
Drew, A. S.: 9, 11	Stuit, D. B.: *rev,* 3:676
Evans, R. N.: 4	Super, D. E.: 3
Hueber, J.: 8	Tiffin, J.: 1–2
Lawshe, C. H.: 1–2	Wells, R. G.: 6

[2264]
RBH Three-Dimensional Space Test. Industrial workers in mechanical fields; 1950–63; Richardson, Bellows, Henry & Co., Inc. *

For additional information, see 6:1095.

[2265]
RBH Two-Dimensional Space Test. Business and industry; 1948–63; Richardson, Bellows, Henry & Co., Inc. *

For additional information, see 6:1097.

[2266]
Revised Minnesota Paper Form Board Test. Grades 9–16 and adults; 1930–70; original test by Donald G. Paterson, Richard M. Elliott, L. Dewey Anderson, Herbert A. Toops, and Edna Heidbreder; revision by Rensis Likert and William H. Quasha; Psychological Corporation. *

For additional information, see 7:1056 (19 references); see also 6:1092 (16 references); for a review by D. W. McElwain, see 5:884 (29 references); for reviews by Clifford E. Jurgensen and Raymond A. Katzell, see 4:763 (38 references); for a review by Dewey B. Stuit, see 3:677 (48 references); for a review by Alec Rodger, see 2:1673 (9 references).

REFERENCES THROUGH 1971
1–9. See 2:1673.
10–57. See 3:677.
58–95. See 4:763.
96–124. See 5:884.
125–140. See 6:1092.
141–159. See 7:1056.
160. STOY, E. G. "Tests for Mechanical Drawing Aptitude." *Personnel J* 6:93–101 Ag '27. * (PA 2:816)
161. CARTER, HAROLD DEAN. "The Organization of Mechanical Intelligence." *J Genetic Psychol* 35:270–85 Je '28. * (PA 2:3743)
162. FULLER, FLORENCE D. "A Study of the Minnesota Paper Formboard Test." *Ed Res B* (Los Angeles City Schools) 7:4–5 Je '28. *
163. PETERSON, JOSEPH, AND LANIER, LYLE H. Part 2, "Comparisons of Certain Mental Abilities in White and Negro Adults," pp. 103–56. In their *Studies in the Comparative Abilities of Whites and Negroes.* Mental Measurements Monographs. Serial No. 5. Baltimore, Md.: Williams & Wilkins Co., 1929. Pp. vi, 156. * (PA 3:2316)
164. HALL, O. MILTON. "An Aid to the Selection of Pressman Apprentices." *Personnel J* 9:77–85 Je '30. * (PA 4:3994)
165. GARRETSON, OLIVER KELLEAM. "Relationships Between the Expressed Preferences and the Curricular Abilities of Ninth Grade Boys." *J Ed Res* 23:124–32 F '31. * (PA 5:2537)
166. DuBois, PHILIP HUNTER. "A Speed Factor in Mental Tests." *Arch Psychol* 141:1–38 Je '32. * (PA 7:3591)
167. RUGGLES, EDWARD W. "An Analytical Study of Various Factors Relating to Juvenile Crime." *J Juvenile Res* 16:125–32 Ap '32. * (PA 6:4501)
168. SORENSON, HERBERT. "Some Factors for Pupil Control Measured and Related." *J Ed Psychol* 23:1–10 Ja '32. * (PA 6:2027)
169. PRITCHARD, MIRIAM C. "The Mechanical Ability of Subnormal Boys." *Teach Col Contrib Ed* 699:1–73 '37. * (PA 11:4608)
170. OTIS, JAY L. "The Prediction of Success in Power Sewing Machine Operating." *J Appl Psychol* 22:350–66 Ag '38. * (PA 13:1688)
171. MORRIS, CHARLES M. "A Critical Analysis of Certain Performance Tests." *J Genetic Psychol* 54:85–105 Mr '39. * (PA 13:5387)
172. BOWN, MAX DUANE. "Variability as a Function of Ability and Its Relation to Personality and Interests." *Arch Psychol* 262:1–45 Jl '41. * (PA 16:493)
173. BEAN, KENNETH L. "Negro Responses to Verbal and Non-Verbal Test Materials." *J Psychol* 13:343–53 Ap '42. * (PA 16:3487)
174. SHEPARD, EUGENE L. "Measurements of Certain Non-verbal Abilities of Urban and Rural Children." *J Ed Psychol* 33:458–62 S '42. * (PA 17:809)
175. EBERT, ELIZABETH, AND SIMMONS, KATHERINE. *The Brush Foundation Study of Child Growth and Development: 1, Psychometric Tests.* Monographs of the Society for Research in Child Development, Vol. 8, No. 2, Serial No. 35. Washington, D.C.: the Society, National Research Council, 1943. Pp. xiv, 113. * (PA 18:3322)
176. OSBORNE, AGNES ELIZABETH. "The Relationship Between Certain Psychological Tests and Shorthand Achievement." *Teach Col Contrib Ed* 873:1–58 '43. *
177. BARNETTE, W. LESLIE, JR. "Occupational Aptitude Pattern Research." *Occupations* 29:5–12 O '50. * (PA 25:3239)
178. LEE, EVERETT S. "Negro Intelligence and Selective Migration: A Philadelphia Test of the Klineberg Hypothesis." *Am Sociol R* 16:227–33 Ap '51. * (PA 27:1093)

179. DUNHAM, RALPH E. "Factors Related to Recidivism in Adults." *J Social Psychol* 39:77–91 F '54. * (*PA* 28:8866)

180. ABRAMSON, H. A.; JARVIK, M. E.; HIRSCH, M. W.; AND EWALD, A. T. "Lysergic Acid Diethylamide (LSD-25): 5, Effect on Spatial Relations Abilities." *J Psychol* 39:435–42 Ap '55. * (*PA* 29:8316)

181. BARRATT, ERNEST S. "The Space-Visualization Factors Related to Temperament Traits." *J Psychol* 39:279–87 Ap '55. * (*PA* 29:8424)

182. JOHNSON, RALPH HAAKON. *Factors Related to the Success of Disabled Veterans of World War II in the Rehabilitation Training Program Approved for Mechanics and Repairmen, Motor Vehicle.* Doctor's thesis, University of Minnesota (Minneapolis, Minn.), 1955. (*DA* 15:2460)

183. RABE, AUSMA. "Individual Differences in Orientation in Perceptual and Cognitive Tasks." *Can J Psychol* 9:149–54 S '55. * (*PA* 30:3923)

184. BAIR, JOHN T.; LOCKMAN, ROBERT F.; AND MARTOCCIA, CHARLES T. "Validity and Factor Analyses of Naval Air Training Predictor and Criterion Measures." *J Appl Psychol* 40:213–9 Ag '56. * (*PA* 31:6701)

185. WITHERSPOON, Y. T. "The Measurement of Indian Children's Achievement in the Academic Tool Subjects." *J Am Indian Ed* 1:5–9 My '62. *

186. LEVITA, ERIC; RIKLAN, MANUEL; AND COOPER, IRVING S. "Cognitive and Perceptual Performance in Parkinsonism as a Function of Age and Neurological Impairment." *J Nerv & Mental Dis* 139:516–20 D '64. * (*PA* 39:10554)

187. MOLOMO, RAYMOND R-S. *Two Spatial Factors in Two-Dimensional and Three-Dimensional Spatial Aptitude.* Master's thesis, University of Ottawa (Ottawa, Ont., Canada), 1964.

188. DAWSON, JOHN L. M. "Cultural and Physiological Influences Upon Spatial-Perceptual Processes in West Africa, Part II." *Int J Psychol* (France) 2(3):171–85 '67. * (*PA* 43:5194)

189. GEORGE, E. I.; PILLAY, P. GOPALA; AND DHARMANGADAN, B. "Effect of Physical Disability on Personality Adjustment and Achievement of Secondary School Pupils." *J Ed & Psychol* (India) 24:180–7 Ja '67. *

190. MARTIN, BERNARD L. "Spatial Visualization Abilities of Prospective Mathematics Teachers." *J Res Sci Teach* 5(1):11–9 '67. *

191. BILES, DAVID. "Test Performance and Imprisonment." *Austral & N Zeal J Criminol* (Australia) 1:46–58 Mr '68. *

192. WIGGINS, NANCY; HOFFMAN, PAUL J.; AND TABER, THOMAS. "Types of Judges and Cue Utilization in Judgments of Intelligence." *J Pers & Social Psychol* 12(1):52–9 My '69. * (*PA* 43:11266)

193. DEE, H. L. "Visuoconstructive and Visuoperceptive Deficit in Patients With Unilateral Cerebral Lesions." *Neuropsychologia* (England) 8(3):305–14 Jl '70. * (*PA* 44:21403)

194. BOLTON, BRIAN. "A Factor Analytic Study of Communication Skills and Nonverbal Abilities of Deaf Rehabilitation Clients." *Multiv Behav Res* 6(4):485–501 O '71. * (*PA* 47:11373)

195. WERNER, LAWRENCE KURT. *The Relationships Among the Psycho-Motor, Motor Coordination, Personality, and Intellectual Domains of Development in Preadolescent Children.* Doctor's thesis, Purdue University (Lafayette, Ind.), 1971. (*DAI* 32:4435A)

196. ZULLO, THOMAS G. "A Factor Analysis of Perceptual and Motor Abilities of Dental Students." *J Dental Ed* 35(6):356–61 Je '71. *

CUMULATIVE NAME INDEX

[2267]

SRA Mechanical Aptitudes. Grades 9–12 and adults; 1947–50; 4 scores: mechanical knowledge, space relations, shop arithmetic, total; Richardson, Bellows, Henry & Co., Inc.; Science Research Associates, Inc. *

For additional information and reviews by Alec Rodger and Douglas G. Schultz, see 4:764.

REFERENCES THROUGH 1971

1. FERSON, REGIS F. *The Probabilities of Success in Trade Training as Estimated by Standardized Tests.* Doctor's thesis, University of Pittsburgh (Pittsburgh, Pa.), 1951.
2. LITTLETON, ISAAC T. "Prediction in Auto Trade Courses." *J Appl Psychol* 36:15–9 F '52. * (*PA* 26:7256)
3. BALINSKY, BENJAMIN, AND HUJSA, CHARLES. "Performance of College Students on a Mechanical Knowledge Test." *J Appl Psychol* 38:111–2 Ap '54. * (*PA* 29:3028)
4. VOPATEK, S. H. "Normative Data Information Exchange, No. 36." *Personnel Psychol* 9:551 w '56. *
5. FOOTE, RICHARD PAUL. *The Prediction of Success in Automotive Mechanics in a Vocational-Industrial Curriculum on the Secondary School Level.* Doctor's thesis, New York University (New York, N.Y.), 1960. (*DA* 21:3014)
6. MACKINNEY, ARTHUR C., AND WOLINS, LEROY. "Validity Information Exchange, No. 13–01, Foreman II, Home Appliance Manufacturing." *Personnel Psychol* 13:443–7 w '60. *
7. FRITZ, KENTNER V., AND FRITZ, MARTIN F. "Untimed Norms for the SRA Mechanical Knowledge and Shop Arithmetic Tests." *J Psychol* 72(1):115–8 My '69. * (*PA* 43:16495)
8. PITTMAN, FRANK MALLORY, JR. *An Investigation of the Predictive Value of Selected Factors on Achievement in Beginning Woodworking, Metalworking, and Electricity-Electronics Courses at the College Level.* Doctor's thesis, Texas A & M University (College Station, Tex.), 1970. (*DAI* 31:2149A)

[2268]

*Space Relations: Differential Aptitude Tests. Grades 8–12 and adults; 1947–73; 2 editions; George K. Bennett, Harold G. Seashore, and Alexander G. Wesman; Psychological Corporation. * For the complete battery entry, see 1069.

a) FORM A. 1947–59. *Out of print.*

b) FORM T. 1947–73; 1972 test identical with Form M copyrighted 1962 except for item sequence.

For reviews of the complete battery, see 7:673 (1 review, 1 excerpt), 6:767 (2 reviews), 5:605 (2 reviews), 4:711 (3 reviews), and 3:620 (1 excerpt).

REFERENCES THROUGH 1971

1. GLASER, ROBERT. "The Application of the Concepts of Multiple-Operation Measurement to the Response Patterns on Psychological Tests." *Ed & Psychol Meas* 11:372–82 au '51. * (*PA* 27:5522)
2. GLASER, ROBERT. "Predicting Achievement in Medical School." *J Appl Psychol* 35:272–4 Ag '51. * (*PA* 26:3046)
3. GLASER, ROBERT. "The Validity of Some Tests for Predicting Achievement in Medical School." Abstract. *Am Psychologist* 6:298 Jl '51. *
4. "Results of the Space Relations, Mechanical Reasoning, and Clerical Speed and Accuracy Tests of the Differential Aptitude Test Battery in Six Public Schools." *Ed Rec B* 58:79–84 F '52. * (*PA* 26:7240)
5. GLASER, ROBERT. "The Reliability of Inconsistency." *Ed & Psychol Meas* 12:60–4 sp '52. * (*PA* 27:5523)
6. GLASER, ROBERT, AND JACOBS, OWEN. "Predicting Achievement in Medical School: A Comparison of Preclinical and Clinical Criteria." *J Appl Psychol* 38:245–7 Ag '54. * (*PA* 29:6271)
7. HARRISON, ROSS; HUNT, WINSLOW; AND JACKSON, THEODORE A. "Profile of the Mechanical Engineer: 1, Ability." *Personnel Psychol* 8:219–34 su '55. * (*PA* 30:5414)
8. MENDICINO, LORENZO. "Mechanical Reasoning and Space Perception: Native Capacity or Experience." *Personnel & Guid J* 36:335–8 Ja '58. * (*PA* 33:6837)
9. HORN, FERN MAY. *A Study of the Relationships Between Certain Aspects of Clothing and the Ability to Handle Selected Clothing Construction Tools With the Developmental Levels of Early Adolescent Girls.* Doctor's thesis, Michigan State University (East Lansing, Mich.), 1959. (*DA* 20:3278)
10. JAYALAKSHMI, G. "Correlation of Tests of Psychomotor Ability With Intelligence and Non-motor Tests." *J Psychol Res* (India) 3:78–84 S '59. *
11. JONES, CHARLES W., AND MCMILLEN, DAN. "Engineering Freshman Norms for the D.A.T. Mechanical Reasoning and Space Relations Tests Utilizing Fifteen-Minute Time Limits." *Ed & Psychol Meas* 25:459–64 su '65. * (*PA* 39:16507)
12. MARTIN, BERNARD LOYAL. *Spatial Visualization Abilities of Central Washington State College Prospective Elementary and Secondary Teachers of Mathematics.* Doctor's thesis, Oregon State University (Corvallis, Ore.), 1966. (*DA* 27:2427A)
13. PARMENTER, WILLIAM H. *An Investigation of the Predictive Validity of the Spatial and Mechanical Tests of the Differential Aptitude Tests in Regard to Success in Industrial Arts.* Master's thesis, California State College (Long Beach, Calif.), 1966.
14. MARTIN, BERNARD L. "Spatial Visualization Abilities of Prospective Mathematics Teachers." *J Res Sci Teach* 5(1):11–9 '67. *
15. ROSS, DONALD RUFUS. *Test Performance of Deaf Adults Under Two Modes of Test Administration.* Doctor's thesis, University of Arizona (Tucson, Ariz.), 1967. (*DA* 28:2992A)
16. SCHROTH, MARVIN L. "Spatial Aptitude and Its Relationship to Art Judgment." *Percept & Motor Skills* 24:746 Je '67. * (*PA* 41:13608, title only)
17. NELSON, LEONARD THEODORE, JR. *The Relationship Between Verbal, Visual-Spatial, and Numerical Abilities and the Learning of the Mathematical Concept of Function.* Doctor's thesis, University of Michigan (Ann Arbor, Mich.), 1968. (*DAI* 30:218A)
18. HARTLAGE, LAWRENCE C. "Nonvisual Test of Spatial Ability." Abstract. *Proc 77th Ann Conv Am Psychol Assn* 4(1):163–4 '69. * (*PA* 43:16635)

[2269]

Spatial Tests EG, 2, and 3. Ages 10-0 to 13-11 and 15-0 to 18-0; 1950–63; 3 tests; published for the National Foundation for Educational Research in England and Wales; Ginn & Co. Ltd. [England]. *

a) SPATIAL TEST EG. Ages 11-0 to 13-11; 1950–59; formerly called *Spatial Test 1;* I. Macfarlane Smith.

b) SPATIAL TEST 2 (THREE-DIMENSIONAL). Ages 10-7 to 13-11; 1950–56; distribution restricted to directors of education and colleges of further education; A. F. Watts with the assistance of D. A. Pidgeon and M. K. B. Richards.

c) SPATIAL TEST 3 (NEWCASTLE SPATIAL TEST). Ages 10-0 to 11-11 and 15-0 to 18-0; 1958–63; distribution restricted to directors of education and colleges of further education; I. Macfarlane Smith and J. S. Lawes.

For additional information, see 7:1057 (1 reference); see also 6:1093 (4 references); for reviews by E. G. Chambers and Charles T. Myers of tests 1 and 2, see 5:885; for a review by E. A. Peel of test 1, see 4:753.

REFERENCES THROUGH 1971

1–4. See 6:1093.
5. See 7:1057.
6. SMITH, I. MACFARLANE. "The Development of a Spatial Test." *Durham Ed R* (England) 1(5):19–33 S '54. * (*PA* 29:7298)
7. BULL, K. R. "An Investigation Into the Relationship Between Physique, Motor Capacity and Certain Temperamental Traits." *Brit J Ed Psychol* 28:149–54 Je '58. * (*PA* 33:7655)

[2270]

Spatial Visualization Test: The Dailey Vocational Tests. Grades 8–12 and adults; 1964–65; SVT; John T. Dailey and Kenneth B. Hoyt (manual); Houghton Mifflin Co. * For the complete battery entry, see 2105.

For reviews of the complete battery, see 7:976 (2 reviews, 2 excerpts).

[2271]

Vincent Mechanical Diagrams Test. Ages 15 and over; 1936–70; VMD; based upon *The Vincent Mechanical Models Test A;* subtest of *N.I.I.P. Engineering Apprentice Selection Test Battery;* National Institute of Industrial Psychology; NFER Publishing Co. Ltd. [England]. * For the complete battery entry, see 2345.

For additional information, see 7:1058.

[2272]

Weights and Pulleys: A Test of Intuitive Mechanics. Engineering students and industrial employees; 1959, c1956–59; L. L. Thurstone (test), T. E. Jeffrey (test), and Measurement Research Division, Industrial Relations Center, University of Chicago (manual); the Center. * [The publisher has not replied to our four requests to check the accuracy of this entry.]

For additional information and a review by William A. Owens, see 6:1098.

[Out of Print Since TIP I]

Mechanical Information Questionnaire (status unknown), 6:1088
Mechanical Knowledge Test, T:1925
Minnesota Assembly Test, 3:671 (1 review, 11 references)
Moray House Space Test 2, 6:1090 (1 review, 4 references)
N.I.I.P. Squares Test, 5:880 (1 review, 9 references)
Paper Puzzles: A Test of Space Relations, T:1935
Prognostic Test of Mechanical Abilities, 4:761 (2 reviews, 1 excerpt, 1 reference)
Purdue Mechanical Performance Test, 5:883 (1 reference)
RBH Tool Knowledge Test, 6:1096
Stenquist Mechanical Assembling Test, 3:679 (1 review, 10 references)
Survey of Mechanical Insight, 5:886 (4 reviews, 3 references)
Survey of Object Visualization, 5:887 (5 reviews, 5 references)
Survey of Space Relations Ability, 5:888 (4 reviews, 4 references)
Tool Knowledge Test, 5:890 (2 reviews)
V.G.C. Object Visualization Indicator, 4:767
V.G.C. Space Relations Ability Indicator, 4:768
Vincent Mechanical Models Test A (Industrial), 4:769 (1 review, 7 references)

MISCELLANEOUS

[2273]

Alpha Biographical Inventory. Grades 9–12; 1968, c1966–68; ABI; earlier experimental editions called *Biographical Inventory,* Forms A, B, C, C–1, J, K, L, M, N, O; 2 scores: creativity, academic performance in college; Institute for Behavorial Research in Creativity. *

For additional information and reviews by John K. Hemphill and William C. Ward, see 7:975 (16 references).

REFERENCES THROUGH 1971

1–16. See 7:975.
17. COUNTS, PERRY DALMOND. *A Study of the Relationship Between Academic Achievement and Creativity.* Doctor's thesis, University of Tennessee (Knoxville, Tenn.), 1971. (*DAI* 32: 4342A)
18. DAVIS, GARY A., AND BELCHER, TERENCE L. "How Shall Creativity Be Measured? Torrance Tests, RAT, Alpha Biographical, and IQ." *J Creative Behav* 5(3):153–61 '71. *

19. LUNNEBORG, C. E. "Alpha Biographical Inventory: A Review." *J Ed Meas* 8(3):233–4 f '71. *

CUMULATIVE NAME INDEX

Abe, C.: 2, 13	Hinman, S. L.: 6
Belcher, T. L.: 18	James, L. R.: 10, 15–6
Carron, T. J.: 15	Lunneborg, C. E.: 19
Cline, V. B.: 2, 4, 9	McDonald, B. W.: 10
Counts, P. D.: 17	Moffie, D. J.: 7
Damm, V. J.: 14	Mulaik, S. A.: 4
Davis, G. A.: 18	Price, J. S.: 12
Ellison, R. L.: 1, 3, 5, 8, 10, 15–6	Richards, J. M.: 2
	Schmitt, J. R.: 9
Fox, D. G.: 16	Taylor, C. W.: 5, 8, 10, 16
Goodner, S.: 7	Tucker, M. F.: 4–5, 9
Harrington, C.: 11	Ward, W. C.: *rev,* 7:975
Hemphill, J. K.: *rev,* 7:975	

[2274]

The Biographical Index. College and industry; 1961–62; 5 scores: drive to excel, financial status, human relations orientation, personal adjustment, stability; Willard A. Kerr; Psychometric Affiliates. *

For additional information and reviews by John K. Hemphill and Richard S. Melton, see 6:1099.

[2275]

Business Judgment Test, Revised. Adults; 1953–69; BJT; Martin M. Bruce; Martin M. Bruce, Ph.D., Publishers. *

For additional information, a review by Jerome E. Doppelt, and an excerpted review by Kenneth D. Orton, see 7:1059 (1 reference); see also 6:1101 (4 references); for a review by Edward B. Greene, see 5:893.

REFERENCES THROUGH 1971

1–4. See 6:1101.
5. See 7:1059.
6. BASS, BERNARD M. "Validity Information Exchange, No. 10–25; D.O.T. Code 1–85.22, Salesman, Foodstuffs." *Personnel Psychol* 10:343–4 au '57. *

CUMULATIVE NAME INDEX

Bass, B. M.: 6	Greene, E. B.: *rev,* 5:893
Bruce, M. M.: 1–2	Martin, H. T.: 4
Doppelt, J. E.: *rev,* 7:1059	Orton, K. D.: *exc,* 7:1059
Friesen, E. P.: 2	Watley, D. J.: 3–5

[2276]

*The Conference Evaluation.** Conference participants; 1969–71; ratings by participants; Psychologists and Educators, Inc. *

For additional information, see 7:1060.

[2277]

Conference Meeting Rating Scale. Conference leaders and participants; 1959; B. J. Speroff; Psychometric Affiliates. *

For additional information, see 6:1103.

[2278-9]

★**Continuous Letter Checking and Continuous Symbol Checking.** Ages 12 and over; 1967–72; "capacity to stick to a tedious task"; 2 tests; 7 scores: speed, accuracy, neatness, curve of work (4 scores); H. Reuning; National Institute for Personnel Research [South Africa]. *

a) CONTINUOUS LETTER CHECKING. High school educational level; 1967–72; CLC.
b) CONTINUOUS SYMBOL CHECKING. Any educational level; 1972; CSC.

[2280]

Gullo Workshop and Seminar Evaluation. Workshop and seminar participants; 1969; ratings by participants; John M. Gullo; Psychologists and Educators, Inc. *

For additional information, see 7:1061.

[2281]

Job Attitude Analysis. Production and clerical workers; 1961–70; an inventory for employment interviewing and vocational counseling; 1970 test materials identical with materials published 1965 except for cover design; P. L. Mellenbruch; Psychometric Affiliates. *

For additional information, see 7:980 (1 reference).

REFERENCES THROUGH 1971
1. See 7:980.

CUMULATIVE NAME INDEX
Mellenbruch, P. L.: 1

[2282]

Mathematical and Technical Test. Ages 11 and over; 1948; also called *M-T Test;* 11 scores: completing pictures, copying models, calculations, completing the series, continuing patterns, filling up gaps, technical insight, figure series, geometrical figures, remembering drawings, total; manual out of print; J. Luning Prak; George G. Harrap & Co. Ltd. [England]. *

For additional information and reviews by Charles R. Langmuir and F. W. Warburton, see 4:779.

[2283]

***Minnesota Importance Questionnaire, 1967 Revision.** Vocational counselees; 1967–71; MIQ; intrapersonal vocational needs of an individual for specified job-related reinforcers; 21 scores (20 of which parallel scores of *Minnesota Job Description Questionnaire* and *Minnesota Satisfaction Questionnaire*): ability utilization, achievement, activity, advancement, authority, company policies and practices, compensation, coworkers, creativity, independence, moral values, recognition, responsibility, security, social service, social status, supervision—human relations, supervision—technical, variety, working conditions, validity; David J. Weiss, Rene V. Dawis, Lloyd H. Lofquist, Evan G. Gay, and Darwin D. Hendel (manual); Vocational Psychology Research. *

For additional information, see 7:1063 (29 references).

REFERENCES THROUGH 1971
1–29. See 7:1063.
30. ELO, MARGARET REED. *The Relationship of Counselor and Client Needs to Occupational Outcomes.* Doctor's thesis, University of Minnesota (Minneapolis, Minn.), 1970. (*DAI* 32:1838B)
31. WARREN, LYNDA WALKER. *The Prediction of Job Satisfaction as a Function of the Correspondence Between Vocational Needs and Occupational Reinforcers.* Doctor's thesis, University of Minnesota (Minneapolis, Minn.), 1970. (*DAI* 32:608B)
32. WILLOUGHBY, THEODORE C. "Needs, Interests, and Reinforcer Preferences of Data Processing Personnel." *Proc Ann Computer Personnel Res Conf* 8:119–43 '70. *
33. GAY, EVAN G.; WEISS, DAVID J.; HENDEL, DARWIN D.; DAWIS, RENÉ V.; AND LOFQUIST, LLOYD H. *Manual for the Minnesota Importance Questionnaire.* University of Minnesota Industrial Relations Center Bulletin 54; Minnesota Studies in Vocational Rehabilitation 28. Minneapolis, Minn.: the Center, June 1971. Pp. x, 83. *
34. KAUPPI, DWIGHT RANDOLPH. *The Development of Instrument-Specific Reading and Comprehension Pre-Tests for Standardized Questionnaires and Inventories.* Doctor's thesis, University of Minnesota (Minneapolis, Minn.), 1971. (*DAI* 32:4844B)
35. LYBARGER, ALVIN EUGENE. *A Comparison of Job Satisfaction Needs of Selected Rural and Urban Industrial Education Students in the State of Utah.* Doctor's thesis, Utah State University (Logan, Utah), 1971. (*DAI* 32:3746A)
36. SIMPSON, ALAN ROGER. *A Comparison of Selected Characteristics of Counselors Leaving the State Rehabilitation Agency With Counselors Who Stay.* Doctor's thesis, University of Iowa (Iowa City, Iowa), 1971. (*DAI* 32:4362A)
37. WILLOUGHBY, THEODORE CRAWFORD. *Needs, Interests, Reinforcer Patterns and Satisfaction of Data Processing Personnel.* Doctor's thesis, University of Minnesota (Minneapolis, Minn.), 1971. (*DAI* 32:5421A)

CUMULATIVE NAME INDEX
Anderson, L. L.: 2
Betz, E. L.: 10, 20
Borgen, F. H.: 11
Carlson, R. E.: 2

Dauw, D. C.: 4, 6
Dawis, R. V.: 2–3, 5–6, 8–9, 11, 13–4, 18–9, 33
Dressler, R. M.: 12
Elo, M. R.: 30
Elster, R. S.: 2–3, 5
England, G. W.: 2–3, 5, 8
Fisher, S. T.: 13
Gay, E. G.: 25, 33
Graen, G. B.: 14
Hendel, D. D.: 15, 26–7, 33
Katz, M.: 21
Kauppi, D. R.: 22, 34
Kohlan, R. G.: 7, 16
Lofquist, L. H.: 2–3, 5, 8, 11, 33

Lybarger, A. E.: 35
Muthard, J. E.: 23
Richardson, B. K.: 24
Salomone, P. R.: 17, 23
Shapiro, S.: 1
Simpson, A. R.: 36
Stone, G. V.: 28
Thorndike, R. M.: 9, 18–9
Tinsley, H. E. A.: 11
Warren, L. W.: 31
Weiss, D. J.: 2–3, 5, 8–9, 11, 13–5, 18–9, 22, 25–7, 33
Willoughby, T. C.: 32, 37
Zytowski, D. G.: 29

[2284]

★Minnesota Job Description Questionnaire. Employees and supervisors; 1967–68; MJDQ; for research use only; primarily for group measurement of occupational reinforcer patterns (ORP's) to match with intrapersonal vocational needs as measured by *Minnesota Importance Questionnaire;* 22 scores (20 of which parallel scores of *Minnesota Importance Questionnaire* and *Minnesota Satisfaction Questionnaire*): ability utilization, achievement, activity, advancement, authority, company policies and practices, compensation, coworkers, creativity, independence, moral values, recognition, responsibility, security, social service, social status, supervision—human relations, supervision—technical, variety, working conditions, autonomy, neutral point; separate forms for employees, supervisors; Fred H. Borgen, David J. Weiss, Howard E. A. Tinsley, Rene V. Dawis, and Lloyd H. Lofquist; Vocational Psychology Research. *

REFERENCES THROUGH 1971
1. BORGEN, FRED H., AND WEISS, DAVID J. "Application of the Method of Multiple-Rank Orders to the Scaling of Environmental Characteristics." Abstract. *Proc 76th Ann Conv Am Psychol Assn* 3:197–8 '68. * (*PA* 43:52, title only)
2. BORGEN, FRED H.; WEISS, DAVID J.; TINSLEY, HOWARD E. A.; DAWIS, RENE V.; AND LOFQUIST, LLOYD H. *The Measurement of Occupational Reinforcer Patterns.* University of Minnesota, Industrial Relations Center, Bulletin 49; Minnesota Studies in Vocational Rehabilitation 25. Minneapolis, Minn.: the Center, October 1968. Pp. x, 89. * (*PA* 43:4560)
3. BORGEN, FRED H.; WEISS, DAVID J.; TINSLEY, HOWARD E. A.; DAWIS, RENE V.; AND LOFQUIST, LLOYD H. *Occupational Reinforcer Patterns (First Volume).* University of Minnesota, Industrial Relations Center, Bulletin 48; Minnesota Studies in Vocational Rehabilitation 24. Minneapolis, Minn.: the Center, October 1968. Pp. x, 263. *
4. BETZ, ELLEN L. "Need-Reinforcer Correspondence as a Predictor of Job Satisfaction." *Personnel & Guid J* 47(9):878–83 My '69. *
5. STONE, GAYLE VAUGHN. *The Relationship Between Personality and Work Need-Reinforcer Correspondence.* Doctor's thesis, University of Minnesota (Minneapolis, Minn.), 1970. (*DAI* 31:4346B)
6. WILLOUGHBY, THEODORE C. "Needs, Interests, and Reinforcer Preferences of Data Processing Personnel." *Proc Ann Computer Personnel Res Conf* 8:119–43 '70. *
7. TINSLEY, HOWARD E. A., AND WEISS, DAVID J. "A Multitrait-Multimethod Comparison of Job Reinforcer Ratings of Supervisors and Supervisees." *J Voc Behav* 1(3):287–99 Jl '71. * (*PA* 48:3967)
8. WILLOUGHBY, THEODORE CRAWFORD. *Needs, Interests, Reinforcer Patterns and Satisfaction of Data Processing Personnel.* Doctor's thesis, University of Minnesota (Minneapolis, Minn.), 1971. (*DAI* 32:5421A)

CUMULATIVE NAME INDEX
Betz, E. L.: 4
Borgen, F. H.: 1–3
Dawis, R. V.: 2–3
Lofquist, L. H.: 2–3

Stone, G. V.: 5
Tinsley, H. E. A.: 2–3, 7
Weiss, D. J.: 1–3, 7
Willoughby, T. C.: 6, 8

[2285]

Minnesota Satisfaction Questionnaire. Business and industry; 1963–67; MSQ; satisfaction with specific aspects of work and work environments; 2 editions; David J. Weiss, Rene V. Dawis, George W. England, and Lloyd H. Lofquist; Vocational Psychology Research. *

a) LONG FORM. 21 scores (20 of which parallel scores of *Minnesota Importance Questionnaire* and *Minnesota Job Description Questionnaire*): ability utilization, achievement, activity, advancement, authority, company policies and practices, compensation, coworkers, creativity, independence, moral values, recognition, responsibility, security, social service, social status, supervision—human relations, supervision—technical, variety, working conditions, general satisfaction.

b) SHORT FORM. 3 scores: intrinsic, extrinsic, general.

For additional information and reviews by Lewis E. Albright and John P. Foley, Jr., see 7:1064 (18 references).

REFERENCES THROUGH 1971

1–18. See 7:1064.
19. ELO, MARGARET REED. *The Relationship of Counselor and Client Needs to Occupational Outcomes.* Doctor's thesis, University of Minnesota (Minneapolis, Minn.), 1970. (*DAI* 32: 1838B)
20. LEE, LA JUANA WILLIAMS. *Personality Characteristics and Job Satisfactions of Certified Professional Secretaries and Non-Certified Secretaries.* Doctor's thesis, University of Northern Colorado (Greeley, Colo.), 1970. (*DAI* 31:6220A)
21. MACE, RICHARD EDWARD. *Factors Influencing the Decisions of Teachers to Become Administrators: A Study of the Differences in Self-Actualization and Job Satisfaction Occurring Between Future Administrators and Career Teachers.* Doctor's thesis, Syracuse University (Syracuse, N.Y.), 1970. (*DAI* 32: 132A)
22. WARREN, LYNDA WALKER. *The Prediction of Job Satisfaction as a Function of the Correspondence Between Vocational Needs and Occupational Reinforcers.* Doctor's thesis, University of Minnesota (Minneapolis, Minn.), 1970. (*DAI* 32:608B)
23. WILLOUGHBY, THEODORE C. "Needs, Interests, and Reinforcer Preferences of Data Processing Personnel." *Proc Ann Computer Personnel Res Conf* 8:119–43 '70. *
24. BETZ, ELLEN L. "An Investigation of Job Satisfaction as a Moderator Variable in Predicting Job Success." *J Voc Behav* 1(2):123–8 Ap '71. * (*PA* 47:11882)
25. GRAY, BONNIE L., AND WEISS, DAVID J. "Pilot Study of the Measurement of Job Satisfaction of Mentally Retarded Adults." Abstract. *Proc 79th Ann Conv Am Psychol Assn* 6(2):611–2 '71. * (*PA* 46:5373, title only)
26. HERSHEY, GERALD LEE. *Experiential Attributes and Attitudinal Postures of Indiana University Academic Secretaries.* Doctor's thesis, Indiana University (Bloomington, Ind.), 1971. (*DAI* 32:4180A)
27. KARASICK, BERNARD WOLFE. *Organizational Climate and Its Relationship to Managerial Behavior.* Doctor's thesis, Purdue University (Lafayette, Ind.), 1971. (*DAI* 32:1266B)
28. MACTAGGERT, DONALD STUART. *Job Satisfaction and Organizational Openness as Perceived by Elementary Teachers in a Florida School System.* Doctor's thesis, University of Miami (Coral Gables, Fla.), 1971. (*DAI* 32:3622A)
29. WILLOUGHBY, THEODORE CRAWFORD. *Needs, Interests, Reinforcer Patterns and Satisfaction of Data Processing Personnel.* Doctor's thesis, University of Minnesota (Minneapolis, Minn.), 1971. (*DAI* 32:5421A)

CUMULATIVE NAME INDEX

Albright, L. E.: *rev,* 7:1064
Anderson, L. M. L.: 11
Bates, G. L.: 12, 18
Becvar, R. J.: 13
Betz, E.: 4
Betz, E. L.: 7, 14, 24
Carlson, R. E.: 15
Dawis, R. V.: 1, 3–4, 6, 9, 15
Elo, M. R.: 19
Elster, R. S.: 1
England, G. W.: 1, 3, 6
Foley, J. P.: *rev,* 7:1064
Golie, B. N.: 8
Graen, G. B.: 9
Gray, B. L.: 25
Hamlin, M. M.: 2

Hershey, G. L.: 26
Karasick, B. W.: 27
Lee, L. J. W.: 20
Lofquist, L. H.: 1, 3–4, 6
McCoy, J. F.: 18
Mace, R. E.: 21
MacTaggert, D. S.: 28
Olson, H.: 5, 16
Parker, H. J.: 18
Poley, J. P.: *rev,* 7:1064
Taylor, K. E.: 17
Warren, L. W.: 22
Weiss, D. J.: 1, 3–4, 6, 9–10, 15, 17, 25
Willoughby, T. C.: 23, 29

[2286]

Per-Flu-Dex Tests. College and industry; 1955; 7 tests; Frank J. Holmes; Psychometric Affiliates. *
a) PER-SYMB TEST. Symbol number substitution.
b) PER-VERB TEST. Letter perception and counting.
c) PER-NUMB TEST. Number counting and perception.
d) FLU-VERB TEST. Word completion and verbal fluency.
e) FLU-NUMB TEST. Arithmetic computation.
f) THE DEX-MAN SCALE. Manual speed of movement.

Minnesota Satisfaction Questionnaire

g) DEX-AIM TEST. Aiming accuracy and speed.

For additional information and reviews by Andrew L. Comrey and John W. French, see 5:901.

REFERENCES THROUGH 1971

1. KERR, WILLARD A., AND McGEHEE, EDWARD M. "Creative Temperament as Related to Aspects of Strategy and Intelligence." *J Social Psychol* 62:211–6 Ap '64. * (*PA* 39:5126)
2. KELLEHER, EDWARD J.; KERR, WILLARD A.; AND MELVILLE, NORBERT T. "The Prediction of Subprofessional Nursing Success." *Personnel Psychol* 21:379–88 au '68. * (*PA* 47:4063)

CUMULATIVE NAME INDEX

Comrey, A. L.: *rev,* 5:901
French, J. W.: *rev,* 5:901
Kelleher, E. J.: 2

Kerr, W. A.: 1–2
McGehee, E. M.: 1
Melville, N. T.: 2

[2287]

RBH Breadth of Information. Business and industry; 1957–63; "practical intelligence and attention to the ordinary happenings of the world"; Richardson, Bellows, Henry & Co., Inc. *

For additional information, see 6:1100.

[2288]

A Self-Rating Scale for Leadership Qualifications. Adults; 1942–48; E. J. Benge; National Foremen's Institute, Inc. *

For additional information, see 5:906.

[2289]

The Tear Ballot for Industry. Employees in industry; 1944–62; TBI; job satisfaction questionnaire; Willard A. Kerr; Psychometric Affiliates. *

For additional information and an excerpted review by John O. Crites, see 7:1065; for a review by Raymond A. Katzell, see 6:1108 (5 references); for a review by Brent Baxter, see 4:783 (4 references).

REFERENCES THROUGH 1971

1–4. See 4:783.
5–9. See 6:1108.
10. GROVE, BYRON A., AND KERR, WILLARD A. "Specific Evidence of Origin of Halo Effect in Measurement of Employee Morale." *J Social Psychol* 34:165–70 N '51. * (*PA* 26:5871)

CUMULATIVE NAME INDEX

Baxter, B.: *rev,* 4:783
Crites, J. O.: *exc,* 7:1065
Griffith, J. W.: 1
Grove, B. A.: 10
Katzell, R. A.: *rev,* 6:1108
Kerr, W. A.: 1–2, 4–5, 8, 10
Koppelmeier, G. J.: 2

Mayo, T. B.: 1
Pressel, G. L.: 7
Speroff, B. J.: 9
Sullivan, J. J.: 2
Topal, J. R.: 1, 6
Van Zelst, R.: 3
Zintz, F. R.: 4

[2290]

Test Orientation Procedure. Job applicants and trainees; 1967; TOP; job applicants needing practice taking tests; no scores; George K. Bennett and Jerome E. Doppelt with the assistance of A. B. Madans and R. G. Buchanan; Psychological Corporation. *

For additional information and a review by Lewis E. Albright, see 7:1066.

[2291]

[Tests A/9 and A/10.] Applicants for technical and apprentice jobs; 1955–57; interest in scientific fields; 2 parts; tests in English and Afrikaans; no manual; National Institute for Personnel Research [South Africa]. *
a) TEST A/9: [TECHNICAL AND SCIENTIFIC KNOWLEDGE].
b) TEST A/10: [TECHNICAL READING COMPREHENSION].
For additional information, see 6:1109.

[2292]

Whisler Strategy Test. Business and industry; 1959–61, c1955–61; "intelligent action"; 6 scores: 4 direct scores (number circled-boldness, number attempted-speed, number right-accuracy, net strategy) and 2 derived scores (caution, hypercaution) ; Laurence D. Whisler ; Psychometric Affiliates. *

For additional information and reviews by Jean Maier Palormo and Paul F. Ross, see 6:1110 (1 reference).

REFERENCES THROUGH 1971

1. See 6:1110.
2. KERR, WILLARD A., AND McGEHEE, EDWARD M. "Creative Temperament as Related to Aspects of Strategy and Intelligence." *J Social Psychol* 62:211–6 Ap '64. * (*PA* 39:5126)

CUMULATIVE NAME INDEX

Abrams, P.: 1　　　　　　　Palormo, J. M.: *rev*, 6:1110
Kerr, W. A.: 1–2　　　　　Ross, P. F.: *rev*, 6:1110
McGehee, E. M.: 2

[2293]

Work Information Inventory. Employee groups in industry ; 1958 ; morale ; Raymond E. Bernberg ; Psychometric Affiliates. *

For additional information, see 6:1111.

[Out of Print Since TIP I]

Cancellation Test, 5:894 (2 reviews)
Cardall Test of Practical Judgment (status unknown), 6:1102 (2 reviews, 10 references)
Dartnell Self-Administered Employee Opinion Unit, 6:1104 (1 review)
Diagnostic Counseling Form for Educational, Preventive, and Remedial Counseling, T:1957
Employee Opinion Survey, 6:1105
Five Factor Inventory, T:1959
General Information Survey, T:1960
Guidance Summary Form for Use in Vocational and Educational Counseling, 3:446 (1 review, 1 excerpt)
Jenkins Job Attitudes Survey, 7:1062 (1 review, 4 references)
Labor Turnover Tests, T:1962
Observation Test, T:1964
Organization Survey (status unknown), 6:1107
Q-Sort Cards for Executive Position, T:1967
SRA Employee Inventory, 5:905 (2 reviews, 10 references)

SELECTION AND RATING FORMS

[2294]

APT Controlled Interview. Applicants for employment ; 1945–56 ; revision of *APT Quick Screening Interview;* 19 ratings : job experience (2 ratings), work history, financial status (2 ratings), marital status, voice (3 ratings), appearance (4 ratings), health (2 ratings), family background, relations with the law, social history, total ; distribution restricted to clients ; Associated Personnel Technicians, Inc. *

For additional information, see 6:1112.

[2295]

Application Interview Screening Form. Job applicants ; 1965 ; 10 ratings by interviewer : work experience, previous education and training, job knowledge, intelligence, sociability, ambition, emotional stability, fluency, maturity, leadership capacity ; Psychological Publications Press. *

For additional information, see 7:1067.

[2296]

Career Counseling Personal Data Form. Vocational counselees ; 1962 ; no manual ; John B. Ahrens ; Martin M. Bruce, Ph.D., Publishers. *

For additional information, see 6:1113.

[2297]

Employee Competency Scale. Employees ; 1969 ; ECS ; ratings by supervisors ; 6 scores : communication, dependability, attitude, job competence, leadership, total ; William T. Martin ; Psychologists and Educators, Inc. *

For additional information, see 7:1068.

[2298]

Employee Evaluation Form for Interviewers. Adults ; 1943 ; Richard A. Fear and Byron Jordan ; Psychological Corporation. *

For additional information, reviews by Douglas H. Fryer and C. H. Ruedisili, and excerpted reviews by Kenneth Byers and Martin L. Reymert, see 3:686.

[2299]

Employee Performance Appraisal. Business and industry ; 1962 ; 7 merit ratings by supervisors : quantity of work, quality of work, job knowledge, initiative, inter-personal relationships, dependability, potential ; no manual ; Martin M. Bruce, Ph.D., Publishers. *

For additional information and a review by Jean Maier Palormo, see 6:1116.

[2300]

★**Employee Progress Appraisal Form.** Rating of office employees ; 1944 ; Albert N. Gillett ; National Foremen's Institute, Inc. *

[2301]

*****[Employee Rating and Development Forms.]** Executive, industrial, office, and sales personnel ; 1950–65 ; all current forms, except *c,* identical with forms copyrighted 1950–59 ; Robert N. McMurry ; Dartnell Corporation. *

a) [PATTERNED MERIT REVIEW FORMS.] 1950–64 ; 5 forms ; no manual.
　1) *Patterned Merit Review—Executive.* 1955–59.
　2) *Patterned Merit Review Form—Plant and Office.* 1950–64.
　3) *Patterned Merit Review—Sales.* 1955–59.
　4) *Patterned Merit Review—Technical, Office, Special Skills.* 1956–64.
　5) *Statement of Supervisory Expectancies.* 1958–64.
b) PATTERNED EXIT INTERVIEW. 1953–65.
c) PERSONAL HISTORY REVIEW FORM. 1957 ; no manual.

For additional information and a review by Richard S. Barrett, see 6:1117 ; for reviews by Harry W. Karn and Floyd L. Ruch, see 4:781.

[2302]

*****[Executive, Industrial, and Sales Personnel Forms.]** Applicants for executive, industrial, office, or sales positions ; 1949–68 ; most current forms are essentially the same as or identical with earlier forms ; Robert N. McMurry ; Dartnell Corporation. *

a) [EXECUTIVE PERSONNEL FORMS.] 1949–68 ; 7 forms.
　1) *Application for Executive Position.* 1949–64.
　2) *Patterned Interview Form—Executive Position.* Applicants for management positions ; 1949–65.
　3) *Patterned Interview Form.* Applicants for positions of supervisor, foreman, engineer ; 1955–68.
　4) *Telephone Check on Executive Applicant.* 1950–64.
　5) *Selection and Evaluation Summary.* 1950–64.
　6) *Position Analysis.* 1956–58.
　7) *Physical Record.* 1958.
b) [INDUSTRIAL PERSONNEL FORMS.] 1949–64 ; 10 forms.
　1) *Application for Position.* 1950–64.
　2) *Application for Employment.* 1950–59.
　3) *Application for Office Position.* 1953–64.

4) *Patterned Interview (Short Form)*. 1949–64.
5) *Patterned Interview Form*. Same as *a*(3) above.
6) *Telephone Check [With Previous Employers]*. 1949–59.
7) *Telephone Check With Schools*. 1949–57.
8) *Selection and Evaluation Summary*. Same as *a*(5) above.
9) *Position Analysis*. Same as *a*(6) above.
10) *Physical Record*. Same as *a*(7) above.
c) [SALES PERSONNEL FORMS.] 1949–68; 10 forms.
  1) *Application for Sales Position*. 1950–67.
  2) *Patterned Interview Form—Sales Position*. 1950–64.
  3) *Telephone Check on Sales Applicant*. 1949–64.
  4) *Sales Application Verification*. 1953–59.
  5) *Home Interview Report Form*. 1954–59.
  6) *Selection and Evaluation Summary*. Same as *a*(5) above.
  7) *Sales Position Analysis*. 1962–65.
  8) *Physical Record*. Same as *a*(7) above.
  9) *Salesman Performance Inventory*. 1965; 20 scores: general appraisal, physical and personal factors, external influences, job knowledge, motivational factors, identification with the company, company policies, planning and organization, administrative duties, personal relationships, prospecting, sales approaches, analyzing prospect needs, product presentation, handling objections, closing skills, follow-ups and call-backs, customer relations, special situations, related duties.
  10) *Man Specification Sheet—Sales*. 1968.
For additional information and a review by John P. Foley, Jr., see 6:1119 (1 reference); for a review by Floyd L. Ruch, see 4:773.

REFERENCES THROUGH 1971
1. See 6:1119.

CUMULATIVE NAME INDEX
Foley, J. P.: *rev*, 6:1119   Ruch, F. L.: *rev*, 4:773
McMurry, R. N.: 1

[2303]
*[Job Application Forms.] Job applicants and employees; 1957–71; 8 application forms; no manual for *b–h;* Hilton Shepherd Co., Inc. *
a) JOB APPLICATION FORM. Job applicants; [1960].
b) PERSONNEL INVENTORY FORM. Employees being considered for transfer or promotion; [1960].
c) EMPLOYMENT APPLICATION FORM. Job applicants; 1960–66.
d) PERSONNEL RECORD FOLDER. 1960–68.
e) CONTENT CONTROL SHEET. 1960–68.
f) MEDICAL EMPLOYMENT FORM. Administrators, nurses, and technologists; 1960–67.
g) EMPLOYMENT APPLICATION. Nonmedical personnel; 1960–67.
h) BANK EMPLOYMENT FORM. Applicants for positions in banks and financial institutions; 1971.
For additional information, see 7:1069.

[2304]
Lawshe-Kephart Personnel Comparison System. For rating any aspect of employee performance by the paired comparison technique; 1946–48; C. H. Lawshe, Jr. and N. C. Kephart; Village Book Cellar. *
For additional information and a review by Reign H. Bittner, see 4:778 (1 reference).

REFERENCES THROUGH 1971
1. See 4:778.

CUMULATIVE NAME INDEX
Bittner, R. H.: *rev*, 4:778   Lawshe, C. H.: 1
Kephart, N. C.: 1   McCormick, E. J.: 1

[2305]
★**The McCormick Job Performance Measurement "Rate-$-Scales."** Employees; 1971; 5 ratings by supervisors: responsibility, attitude, time in grade, efficiency, total; Ronald R. McCormick; Trademark Design Products, Inc. *

[2306]
The McQuaig Manpower Selection Series. Applicants for office and sales positions; 1957; 4 parts in 2 booklets; no manual; Jack H. McQuaig; McQuaig Institute of Executive Development. *
a) [PARTS 1–3.]
  1) *Part 1, The McQuaig Telephone Reference Check List.*
  2) *Part 2, The McQuaig Screening Interview Guide.*
  3) *Part 3, Personal History and Experience Record.*
b) PART 4, THE MC QUAIG OCCUPATIONAL TEST.
For additional information, see 6:1122.

[2307]
***The Martin Performance Appraisal.** Employees; 1966–69; MPA; ratings by supervisors; William T. Martin; Western Psychological Services. *
For additional information, see 7:1070.

[2308]
Merit Rating Series. Industry; 1948–59; formerly called *Employee Evaluation Series;* 5 scales; Joseph E. King; Industrial Psychology, Inc. *
a) PERFORMANCE: CLERICAL. 1956; 5 scores: quantity, accuracy, job knowledge, personal-work habits, overall.
b) PERFORMANCE: MECHANICAL. 1953–57; 5 scores: production, quality, job knowledge, personal-work habits, overall.
c) PERFORMANCE: SALES. 1953–57; 5 scores: volume, accuracy, job knowledge, personal-work habits, overall.
d) PERFORMANCE: TECHNICAL. 1953–57; 5 scores: same as for *b*.
e) PERFORMANCE: SUPERVISOR. 1953–57; 4 scores: department operation, employee relations, job knowledge, personal-work habits.
For additional information and a review by Seymour Levy, see 6:1123; for a review by Brent Baxter of the original series, see 4:770 (1 reference).

REFERENCES THROUGH 1971
1. See 4:770.

CUMULATIVE NAME INDEX
Baxter, B.: *rev*, 4:770   Levy, S.: *rev*, 6:1123
King, J. E.: 1

[2309]
The Nagel Personnel Interviewing and Screening Forms. Job applicants; 1963; 4 forms; Jerome H. Nagel Associates; Western Psychological Services. *
a) THE NAGEL INITIAL INTERVIEW DATA FORM. 10 ratings: first impression, physical appearance, voice and speech, educational background, poise and self-confidence, ambition-motivation, intelligence, knowledge of company, maturity, total impression.
b) THE NAGEL PERSONAL HISTORY INVENTORY.
c) THE NAGEL DEPTH INTERVIEW FORM. Ratings in 8 areas: work factors, social and educational factors, economic factors and goals, personal factors, ability to do job, motivation to do job, likelihood to remain on job, suitability of personality.
d) THE NAGEL EMPLOYMENT REFERENCE CHECK.
For additional information, see 6:1124.

[2310]
[Performance Review Forms.] Employees, managers; 1960–61; 2 forms; Seymour Levy; Martin M. Bruce, Ph.D., Publishers. *

a) COUNSELING INTERVIEW SUMMARY. Employees, managers; 1960; for summarizing a performance review interview; 2 editions: forms for employees, managers.
b) MANAGERIAL PERFORMANCE REVIEW. Managers; 1961; ratings by supervisors preparatory to performance review interview.
For additional information, see 6:1125.

[2311]
Personal Data Blank. Counselees ages 15 and over; 1934–52; J. Gustav White; Consulting Psychologists Press, Inc. *
For additional information and a review by Arthur E. Traxler, see 5:903; for reviews by Edward S. Jones and Donald G. Paterson of an earlier edition, see 2:1669.

[2312]
[Personnel Interviewing Forms.] Business and industry; 1956; 4 forms; no manual; Judd-Safian Associates; Martin M. Bruce, Ph.D., Publishers. *
a) INITIAL INTERVIEW TABULATION. For recording ratings in 10 areas: appearance, voice and speech, poise, health, education, manner, responsiveness, experience, job stability, motivation.
b) PERSONAL HISTORY AUDIT. Job applicants.
c) DEPTH INTERVIEW PATTERN. For interviewing in 5 areas: work evaluation, educational and social evaluation, economic evaluation, personality evaluation, ambitions evaluation.
d) EMPLOYMENT REFERENCE INQUIRY. For securing employee evaluation from previous employers.
For additional information, see 6:1127.

[2313]
Personnel Rating Scale. Employees; 1965–66; 11 ratings by supervisors: cooperativeness, quality of work, adaptability, dependability, emotional stability, quantity of work, sociability, persistence, initiative, work knowledge, overall; Psychological Publications Press. *
For additional information, see 7:1071.

[2314]
RBH Individual Background Survey. Business and industry; 1949–69; 3 editions; Richardson, Bellows, Henry & Co., Inc. *
a) FORM T. Business and industry; 1952–63; 4 scoring keys: female clerical, male clerical, male industrial, male sales-supervisory-professional.
b) FORM M-E. Managers and executives; 1962. *Out of print.*
c) FORM W-E. Wage earner level applicants; 1965–69.
For additional information, see 7:1072 (2 references).

REFERENCES THROUGH 1971
1–2. See 7:1072.
CUMULATIVE NAME INDEX
Harrell, T. W.: 1–2

[2315]
San Francisco Vocational Competency Scale. Mentally retarded adults; 1968; SFVCS; for rating workers in "sheltered workshops"; Samuel Levine and Freeman F. Elzey; Psychological Corporation. *
For additional information and an excerpted review by N. M. Downie, see 7:1073.

REFERENCES THROUGH 1971
1. LEVINE, SAMUEL, AND ELZEY, FREEMAN F. "Factor Analysis of the San Francisco Vocational Competency Scale." *Am J Mental Def* 73:509–13 N '68. * (*PA* 43:8592)

CUMULATIVE NAME INDEX
Downie, N. M.: *exc,* 7:1073   Levine, S.: 1
Elzey, F. F.: 1

[2316]
[Selection Interview Forms.] Business and industry; 1962; 2 forms; Benjamin Balinsky; Martin M. Bruce, Ph.D., Publishers. *
a) SELECTION INTERVIEW FORM.
b) INTERVIEW RATING FORM.
For additional information, see 6:1128.

[2317]
Speech-Appearance Record. Job applicants; 1967; SAR; evaluation of young adults for employability; George K. Bennett and Jerome E. Doppelt with the assistance of A. B. Madans; Psychological Corporation. *
For additional information, see 7:1074.

[2318]
*[Stevens-Thurow Personnel Forms.] Business and industry; 1951–72; 12 record and rating forms; Stevens, Thurow & Associates, Inc. *
a) PERSONAL HISTORY RECORD. Applicants, employees; 1951–72; 1972 form essentially the same as form copyrighted 1967 except for 4 new items and adaptation of 2 items concerning age.
b) APPLICATION FOR POSITION. Applicants for clerical positions; 1951.
c) APPLICATION FOR EMPLOYMENT. Applicants for shop or plant positions; 1951.
d) PRELIMINARY INTERVIEW. Prospective employees; 1954.
e) INTERVIEWER'S GUIDE AND RATING FORM FOR PROSPECTIVE EMPLOYEES. Prospective employees; 1956–67; 1963 form essentially the same as form published 1956.
f) EMPLOYMENT INTERVIEW SCHEDULE. Prospective employees; 1956.
g) WORK REFERENCE INVESTIGATION. 1951–63.
h) JOB DESCRIPTION [SHORT FORM]. 1956.
i) JOB DESCRIPTION QUESTIONNAIRE [LONG FORM]. 1952.
j) APPRAISAL REPORT FOR MANAGEMENT PERSONNEL. Manager's rating of employees; 1959.
k) APPRAISAL REPORT FOR MANAGEMENT PERSONNEL (SUPPLEMENTARY FORM FOR SALES MANAGERS). 1959.
l) WORK BEHAVIOR INVENTORY. Supervisor's rating of employees; 1951–63.
For additional information, see 6:1129.

[2319]
★Tickmaster. Job applicants; 1954–65; environmental conditions under which applicant will be most productive; Roland Ballen; the Author. *

[2320]
Wonderlic Personnel Selection Procedure. Applicants for employment; 1967–69; WPSP; 8 parts; E. F. Wonderlic & Associates. *
a) P-1: INTRODUCTORY APPLICATION.
b) P-2: PERSONNEL APPLICATION.
c) P-3: WONDERLIC PERSONNEL TEST, FORM I. See 482.
d) P-4: PERSONNEL INTERVIEWER'S GUIDE. 1967 guide identical with *Diagnostic Interviewer's Guide* copyrighted 1937 and 1942.
e) P-5: HEALTH QUESTIONNAIRE.
f) P-6: [WRITTEN REFERENCE REPORTS].
g) P-7: TELEPHONE REFERENCE CHECK.
h) P-8: PRE-EMPLOYMENT SUMMARY.
For additional information, see 7:1075.

[2321]
Work Reference Check. Job applicants; 1965; information and ratings by former employer; Psychological Publications Press. *
For additional information, see 7:1076.

[Out of Print Since TIP I]
Application-Interview Series, 5:892
Cardall Interviewing Aids (status unknown), 6:1114
Diagnostic Interviewer's Guide, 6:1115 (3 reviews, 2 references)
Employee Merit Report, 4:771
Employee Rating Forms, 6:1118
Hiring Summary Worksheet, 5:898
Job Description Forms, T:1983
Job Description Questionnaire, 6:1121
Occupational Adjustment Forms, T:1988
Performance Record, 5:902 (2 reviews, 1 reference)
Personal History Record [Richardson, Bellows, Henry & Co., Inc.], 6:1126

SPECIFIC VOCATIONS

[Out of Print Since TIP I]
Probst Rating System, 4:785 (2 reviews, 2 references)

ACCOUNTING

[2322]
Account Clerk Test. Job applicants; 1957–66; 1966 edition identical with test copyrighted 1959; distribution restricted to member public personnel agencies and nonmember agencies approved by the publisher; International Personnel Management Association. *
For additional information, see 7:1077.

[2323]
American Institute of Certified Public Accountants Testing Programs. Grades 13–16 and accountants; 1946–72; 2 programs: College Accounting Testing Program (tests available at any time) and Professional Accounting Testing Program (tests available to accountant employers at any time and also administered at regional testing centers); 3 tests; Committee on Personnel Testing, American Institute of Certified Public Accountants; distributed by Psychological Corporation. *
a) ORIENTATION TEST. 3 scores: verbal, quantitative, total.
b) ACHIEVEMENT TEST: LEVELS I AND 2.
c) STRONG VOCATIONAL INTEREST BLANK FOR MEN. See 2212; scored for 34 scales and plotted on an accountant's profile.
For additional information concerning earlier forms, see 5:911 (6 references); see also 4:787 (15 references).

REFERENCES THROUGH 1971
1–15. See 4:787.
16–21. See 5:911.
22. BEAMER, GEORGE C., AND ROSE, TOM. "The Use of the GATB and the AIA Tests in Predicting Success in Accounting." *Acctg R* 30:533–5 Jl '55. *
23. NORTH, ROBERT D. "Relation Between Scores on the AIA Elementary and Advanced Accounting Achievement Tests." *Acctg R* 31:50–5 Ja '56. *
24. RILEY, ROBERT C. "Comparison of Results of AIA Achievement Test and ACE Psychological Examination." *Acctg R* 33:128–30 Ja '58. *
25. TRAXLER, ARTHUR E. "Testing for the Professions: Accounting." *J Exp Ed* 27:341–6 Je '59. * (*PA* 35:1280)
26. COOPER, CHARLES LEWIS. *A Study of the Relationship of*

the American Institute of Certified Public Accountants College Tests and Other Selected Factors to Success in Accounting. Doctor's thesis, University of Pittsburgh (Pittsburgh, Pa.), 1961. (*DA* 22:3545)
27. AHOLA, VIRGINIA I. *Achievement and Aptitude in Accounting of Junior College Accounting of Junior College Transfer Students and SDSC Students.* Master's thesis, San Diego State College (San Diego, Calif.), 1967.
28. DAILY, VICTORIA LEE DEFORE. *The Effect of Programmed Instruction in the Teaching of Principles of Accounting.* Doctor's thesis, Colorado State College (Greeley, Colo.), 1969. (*DAI* 30:4061A)

CUMULATIVE NAME INDEX
Ahola, V. I.: 27
American Institute of Accountants, Committee on Selection of Personnel: 2
Ankers, R. G.: 13
Beamer, G. C.: 22
Budd, T. A.: 3
Caffyn, H. R.: 6, 10
Cooper, C. L.: 26
Daily, V. L. D.: 28
Frederick, M. L.: 19
Hassler, R. H.: 12
Hendrix, O. R.: 16–7
Jacobs, R.: 7, 11, 15, 18
Morici, A. R.: 20
Nissley, W. W.: 5
North, R. D.: 21, 23
Riley, R. C.: 24
Rose, T.: 22
Schmidt, L. A.: 8
Strong, E. K.: 9
Traxler, A. E.: 1, 4-5, 10, 14–15, 25
Ward, L. B.: 12
Wood, B. D.: 5

[2324]
CLEP Subject Examination in Introductory Accounting. 1 year or equivalent; 1970–73; for college accreditation of nontraditional study, advanced placement, or assessment of educational achievement; tests administered monthly at centers throughout the United States; program administered for the College Entrance Examination Board by Educational Testing Service. * For the testing program entry, see 1050.
For additional information, see 7:1079. For reviews of the testing program, see 7:664 (3 reviews).

[Out of Print Since TIP I]
Accounting Orientation Test, 7:1078 (5 references)

BUSINESS

[2325]
Admission Test for Graduate Study in Business. Business graduate students; 1954–73; ATGSB; test administered 4 times annually (January, March, July, November) at centers established by the publisher; 3 scores: quantitative, verbal, total; Educational Testing Service. *
For additional information and reviews by Jerome E. Doppelt and Gary R. Hanson, see 7:1080 (10 references).

REFERENCES THROUGH 1971
1–10. See 7:1080.
11. FOSTER, PHILLIP B. "Management Perspective: Predicting Academic Performance of Foreign and Non-Foreign Students in Graduate Business School." *Acad Mgmt J* 8:319–23 D '65. *
12. BASS, BERNARD M. "Ability, Values, and Concepts of Equitable Salary Increases in *Exercise Compensation.*" *J Appl Psychol* 52:299–303 Ag '68. * (*PA* 42:16239)
13. BASS, BERNARD M. "How to Succeed in Business According to Business Students and Managers." *J Appl Psychol* 52:254–62 Je '68. * (*PA* 42:12889)
14. PAGE, ALFRED N., AND WEST, RICHARD R. "Evaluating Student Performance in Graduate Schools of Business." *J Bus* 42(1):36–41 Ja '69. *
15. CRAVENS, DAVID W. "Predicting Performance of Information Specialists." *J Am Soc Inf Sci* 22(1):5–11 Ja–F '71. *

CUMULATIVE NAME INDEX
Bass, B. M.: 12–3
Cravens, D. W.: 15
Curtis, K. C.: 9
Doppelt, J. E.: *rev,* 7:1080
Foster, P. B.: 11
Gruber, E. C.: 2
Hanson, G. R.: *rev,* 7:1080
Harrell, T. W.: 1
Hinton, B. L.: 7
Lewis, J. W.: 4–6
Mittman, A.: 6
Page, A. N.: 14
Pounders, C. J.: 10
Rudman, J.: 3
West, R. R.: 14

[2326]

*CLEP Subject Examination in Introduction to Business Management. 1 semester or equivalent; 1969–73; for college accreditation of nontraditional study, advanced placement, or assessment of educational achievement; tests administered monthly at centers throughout the United States; program administered for the College Entrance Examination Board by Educational Testing Service. * For the testing program entry, see 1050.

For additional information, see 7:1081. For reviews of the testing program, see 7:664 (3 reviews).

[2327]

*CLEP Subject Examination in Introductory Business Law. 1 semester or equivalent; 1970–73; for college accreditation of nontraditional study, advanced placement, or assessment of educational achievement; tests administered monthly at centers throughout the United States; program administered for the College Entrance Examination Board by Educational Testing Service. * For the testing program entry, see 1050.

For additional information, see 7:1082. For reviews of the testing program, see 7:664 (3 reviews).

[2328]

*CLEP Subject Examination in Introductory Marketing. 1 semester or equivalent; 1968–73; for college accreditation of nontraditional study, advanced placement, or assessment of educational achievement; tests administered monthly at centers throughout the United States; program administered for the College Entrance Examination Board by Educational Testing Service. * For the testing program entry, see 1050.

For additional information, see 7:1083. For reviews of the testing program, see 7:664 (3 reviews).

[2329]

*CLEP Subject Examination in Money and Banking. 1 semester or equivalent; 1967–73; for college accreditation of nontraditional study, advanced placement, or assessment of educational achievement; tests administered monthly at centers throughout the United States; program administered for the College Entrance Examination Board by Educational Testing Service. * For the testing program entry, see 1050.

For additional information, see 7:1084. For reviews of the testing program, see 7:664 (3 reviews).

[2330]

Organizational Value Dimensions Questionnaire: Business Form. Adults; 1965–66; OVDQ; for research use only; attitudes toward business and industrial firms in general; manual title is *Value Scale—The Business Firm;* 9 scores: organizational magnitude and structure, internal consideration, competition and strategy, social responsibility, quality, change, member identification and control, external political participation, member equality and participation; Carroll L. Shartle and Ralph M. Stogdill; University Publications Sales, Ohio State University. * For additional information, see 7:1085.

COMPUTER PROGRAMMING

[2331]

Aptitude Assessment Battery: Programming. Programmers and trainees; 1967–69; AABP; no manual; distribution restricted to employers of programmers, not available to school personnel; Jack M. Wolfe; Programming Specialists, Inc. *

For additional information, see 7:1087 (1 reference).

REFERENCES THROUGH 1971
1. See 7:1087.

CUMULATIVE NAME INDEX
Wolfe, J. M.: 1

[2332]

*CLEP Subject Examination in Computers and Data Processing. 1–2 semesters or equivalent; 1968–73; for college accreditation of nontraditional study, advanced placement, or assessment of educational achievement; tests administered monthly at centers throughout the United States; program administered for the College Entrance Examination Board by Educational Testing Service. * For the testing program entry, see 1050.

For additional information, see 7:1088. For reviews of the testing program, see 7:664 (3 reviews).

[2333]

★CLEP Subject Examination in Elementary Computer Programming—Fortran IV. 1 semester or equivalent; 1971–73; for college accreditation of nontraditional study, advanced placement, or assessment of educational achievement; tests administered monthly at centers throughout the United States; program administered for the College Entrance Examination Board by Educational Testing Service. * For the testing program entry, see 1050.

[2334]

*Computer Programmer Aptitude Battery. Applicants for computer training or employment; 1964–67; CPAB; 6 scores: verbal meaning, reasoning, letter series, number ability, diagramming, total; Jean Maier Palormo; Science Research Associates, Inc. (British edition: 1964–71; standardization supplement by Peter Saville; NFER Publishing Co. Ltd. [England].) *

For additional information and reviews by Richard T. Johnson and Donald J. Veldman of *a,* see 7:1089 (2 references).

REFERENCES THROUGH 1971
1–2. See 7:1089.
3. MARTIN, MAURICE A. "A Study of the Concurrent Validity of the Computer Programmer Aptitude Battery." *Studies Pers Psychol* (Canada) 3(1):69–76 Ap '71. * (*PA* 46:11831)
4. MUSSIO, JERRY J., AND WAHLSTROM, MERLIN W. "Predicting Performance of Programmer Trainees in a Post-High School Setting." Discussion by Charles D. Lothridge. *Proc Ann Computer Personnel Res Conf* 9:26–53 '71. *

CUMULATIVE NAME INDEX
Cronbach, L. J.: 2
Johnson, R. T.: *rev,* 7:1089
Lothridge, C. D.: 4
Martin, M. A.: 3
Mussio, J. J.: 4
Palormo, J. M.: 1
Veldman, D. J.: *rev,* 7:1089
Wahlstrom, M. W.: 4

[2335]

The Diebold Personnel Tests. Programmers and systems analysts for automatic data processing and computing installations; 1959; 5 tests; John Diebold & Associates. *
a) SYMBOLS BLOCK DIAGRAM TEST.
b) CODE INDEX TEST.
c) RELATIONS IN NUMBERS TEST.
d) CODE MATCHING TEST.
e) WORD SEQUENCE TEST.
For additional information, see 6:1142.

[2336]

★Programmer Aptitude/Competence Test System. Computer programmers and applicants for programmer training; 1970; PACTS; 2 tests; Haverly Systems Inc. *

a) PACTS APTITUDE TEST. Applicants for programmer training; "ability to learn programming"; 3 scores (correctness, quality, overall grade) for each of 15 problems plus a single overall aptitude rating.

b) PACTS COMPETENCE TEST. Experienced programmers; tests tailored to meet individual needs, local objectives, and time available by selecting 5 to 9 problems in programming (a maximum of 20 may be selected) out of 30 available; a work performance test which requires the use of computer facilities; 5 scores (percent correct, percent of objective, straight score, numeric grade, letter grade) for each problem and 3 final scores (straight score, numeric grade, letter grade).

REFERENCES THROUGH 1971

1. SEINER, J. P. "Programmer Aptitude and Competence Test System (PACTS)." Discussion by Charles D. Lothridge. *Proc Ann Computer Personnel Res Conf* 9:3-25, 47-53 '71. *

CUMULATIVE NAME INDEX

Lothridge, C. D.: 1   Seiner, J. P.: 1

[Out of Print Since TIP I]

Aptitude Test E51 for Electronic Data-Processing Programmers (status unknown), T:2015
Card Punch Operator Aptitude Test, 7:1103 (2 reviews, 4 references)
IBM Aptitude Test for Programmer Personnel, 7: 1090 (1 review, 14 references)
Punched Card Machine Operator Aptitude Test, 5:941
Revised Programmer Aptitude Test, 6:1153 (2 references)

DENTISTRY

[2337]

*Dental Admission Testing Program. Dental school applicants; 1946-72; DATP; formerly called *Dental Aptitude Testing Program;* tests administered 3 times annually (January, April, September or October) at centers established by the publisher; 4 tests, 12 scores: 11 scores listed below and academic average (average of *a-c*); Division of Educational Measurements, Council on Dental Education, American Dental Association. *

a) SURVEY OF THE NATURAL SCIENCES. 1951-72; 4 scores: biology, inorganic chemistry, organic chemistry, total.

b) READING COMPREHENSION. 1953-69; 2 forms.
  1) *Reading Comprehension in the Natural Sciences.* 1953-65.
  2) *Reading Comprehension in the Basic Sciences.* 1968-69.

c) COOPERATIVE SCHOOL AND COLLEGE ABILITY TESTS. 1961; 3 scores: quantitative reasoning, verbal reasoning, total.

d) PERCEPTUAL-MOTOR ABILITY TEST. 1968-72; 3 scores: 2-dimensional problem solving, 3-dimensional problem solving, average.

For additional information, see 7:1091 (28 references); see also 5:916 (6 references) and 4:788 (2 references).

REFERENCES THROUGH 1971

1-2. See 4:788.
3-8. See 5:916.
9-36. See 7:1091.
37. PETERSON, SHAILER. "Dental Aptitude Testing Program: A Report of Progress." *J Am Dental Assn* 35:175-84 Ag 1 '47. *
38. PETERSON, SHAILER. "The Aptitude Testing Program of the American Dental Association." *Col & Univ* 23:212-6 Ja '48. * (*PA* 22:4671)

39. PETERSON, SHAILER. "Forecasting the Success of Freshman Dental Students Through the Aptitude Testing Program." *J Am Dental Assn* 37:259-65 S '48. *
40. DWORKIN, SAMUEL F. "Further Correlational and Factor Analyses of the DAT as a Predictor of Performance: Conclusions and Summary." *J Dental Ed* 34(4):358-64 D '70. *
41. FULL, CLEMANS A., AND FOLEY, WALTER J. "Selection and Performance: A Factorial Study of Dental Students." *J Dental Ed* 35(9):563-6 S '71. *
42. PYSKACEK, ROBERT A. "The Dental Admission Testing Program and Proposed Changes." *J Dental Ed* 35(4):237-41 Ap '71. *
43. ZULLO, THOMAS G. "A Factor Analysis of Perceptual and Motor Abilities of Dental Students." *J Dental Ed* 35(6):356-61 Je '71. *
44. ZULLO, THOMAS G. "Principal Components Analysis of the Dental Aptitude Test Battery." *J Dental Ed* 35(3):144-8 Mr '71. *

CUMULATIVE NAME INDEX

Anderson, A. V.: 5	Layton, W. L.: 7
Carson, R. L.: 20	Lorencki, S. F.: 30
Chen, M. K.: 24, 32	McDonald, R. E.: 27
DeRevere, R. E.: 13	Manhold, B. S.: 19, 21
Douglas, B. L.: 20	Manhold, J. H.: 19, 21
Dworkin, S. F.: 34, 40	Marles, L.: 3
Endey, M. W.: 14	Mundy, P.: 26
Ference, L. W.: 35	Parkins, G. L.: 10
Fernandez-Pabon, J. J.: 25	Peterson, S.: 1, 2, 4, 37-9
Fishman, R.: 28	Phillip, P. J.: 31
Foley, W. J.: 41	Phipps, G. T.: 28
Fredericks, M. A.: 26	Podshadley, D. W.: 24, 32
Friedman, S.: 5	Pyskacek, R. A.: 42
Full, C. A.: 41	Reinke, B. C.: 14
Ginley, T. J.: 22	Rudman, J.: 15
Gough, H. G.: 36	Scott, R. H.: 28
Gruber, E. C.: 16	Shrock, J. G.: 24, 32
Hall, D. S.: 23	Thomassen, P. R.: 14
Heller, D. B.: 20	Timmons, G. D.: 11
Hood, A. B.: 17	Tocchini, J. J.: 14
Huck, F. T.: 9	Vinton, P. W.: 19
Hutton, J. G.: 29	Webb, S. C.: 8, 12
Kirk, B. A.: 36	Weiss, I.: 6
Kreit, L. H.: 27	Zimmerman, J. J.: 33
Land, M.: 18	Zullo, T. G.: 43-4

[2338]

Dental Hygiene Aptitude Testing Program. Dental hygiene school applicants; 1947-72; DHATP; tests administered 3 times anually (February, May, November) at centers established by the American Dental Hygienists' Association; 4 scores: numerical ability, study-reading, science, general information; prepared for the American Dental Hygienists' Association by Psychological Corporation. *

For additional information, see 7:1092.

[2339]

★Ohio Dental Assisting Achievement Test. Grades 11-12; 1970-73; ODAAT; available only as a part of the *Ohio Trade and Industrial Education Achievement Test Program* (see 2431 for more complete information); 16 scores: orientation, ethics, dental anatomy, dental and laboratory materials, microbiology and sterilization, preventive dentistry, operative-chairside assisting, specialties-chairside assisting, radiology, pharmacology, oral pathology, diet and nutrition, first aid and dental emergencies, human relations, office practice, total; Instructional Materials Laboratory, Ohio State University. *

ENGINEERING

[2340]

AC Test of Creative Ability. Engineers and supervisors; 1953-60; 9 scores: quantity (3 scores), uniqueness (4 scores), quality, total; subtests yielding quantity scores may be administered alone for quantity scores only; Richard H. Harris (test), A. L. Simberg (test), and Measurement Research Division, Industrial

Relations Center, University of Chicago (manual) ; the Center. * [The publisher has not replied to our four requests to check the accuracy of this entry.]

For additional information and reviews by Samuel T. Mayo, Philip R. Merrifield, and Albert S. Thompson, see 6:1130 (1 reference).

REFERENCES THROUGH 1971

1. See 6:1130.
2. MAIZELL, ROBERT EDWARD. *Information Gathering Patterns and Creativity: A Study of Research Chemists in an Industrial Research Laboratory.* Doctor's thesis, Columbia University (New York, N.Y.), 1957. (*DA* 18:1802)
3. MEADOW, ARNOLD, AND PARNES, SIDNEY J. "Evaluation of Training in Creative Problem-Solving." *J Appl Psychol* 43:189–94 Je '59. * (*PA* 34:5568)
4. MEADOW, ARNOLD; PARNES, SIDNEY J.; AND REESE, HAYNE. "Influence of Brainstorming Instructions and Problem Sequence on a Creative Problem Solving Test." *J Appl Psychol* 43:413–6 D '59. * (*PA* 34:7338)
5. ANTLEY, ELIZABETH MARTIN. *Creativity in Educational Administration.* Doctor's thesis, University of Southern Mississippi (Hattiesburg, Miss.), 1962. (*DA* 23:3707)
6. LOCKE, EDWIN A. "Some Correlates of Classroom and Out-of-Class Achievement in Gifted Science Students." *J Ed Psychol* 54:238–48 O '63. * (*PA* 38:4649)
7. DUNNETTE, MARVIN D.; WERNIMONT, PAUL; AND ABRAHAMS, NORMAN. "Further Research on Vocational Interest Differences Among Several Types of Engineers." *Personnel & Guid J* 42:484–93 Ja '64. * (*PA* 39:6040)
8. GERLACH, VERNON S.; SCHUTZ, RICHARD E.; BAKER, ROBERT L.; AND MAZER, GILBERT E. "Effects of Variations in Test Direction on Original Test Response." *J Ed Psychol* 55:79–83 Ap '64. * (*PA* 39:734)
9. RAPP, MARJORIE LEE. *Factors Related to the Impressions Made on One Another by Members of a Discussion Group.* Doctor's thesis, University of California (Los Angeles, Calif.), 1965. (*DA* 25:7087)
10. TUCKER, CASEY ALLEN. *Creativity and Its Relationship to Success in College as Measured by the Grade Point Average.* Doctor's research study No. 1, Colorado State College (Greeley, Colo.), 1965. (*DA* 26:5275)
11. WHITTEMORE, ROBERT G., JR., AND HEIMANN, ROBERT A. "Modification of Originality Responses." *J Counsel Psychol* 13:213–8 su '66. * (*PA* 40:8833)
12. CRAFT, CLYDE O'BRIEN. *Creativity in Engineering Graphics: An Experimental Comparison of Two Types of Graphics Problems.* Doctor's thesis, Texas A & M University (College Station, Tex.), 1967. (*DA* 28:2435A)
13. MAGOWAN, ROBERT EVAN. *A Comparison of Pragmatical and Hypothetical Problems for Developing Creativity in Design.* Doctor's thesis, Texas A & M University (College Station, Tex.), 1967. (*DA* 28:1992A)
14. MILES, DAVID T. *An Experimental Investigation of Programed Creativity.* Doctor's thesis, Southern Illinois University (Carbondale, Ill.), 1967. (*DA* 28:2099A)
15. BUCKEYE, DONALD ANDREW. *The Effects of a Creative Classroom Environment on the Creative Ability of Prospective Elementary Mathematics Teachers.* Doctor's thesis, Indiana University (Bloomington, Ind.), 1968. (*DA* 29:1801A)
16. TURNER, THOMAS B. "The Creative Process." *J Creative Behav* 2:63–70 w '68. * (*PA* 42:13766)
17. BAEHR, MELANY E.; FURCON, JOHN E.; AND FROEMEL, ERNEST C. *Psychological Assessment of Patrolman Qualifications in Relation to Field Performance.* Washington, D.C.: United States Government Printing Office, 1969. Pp. vii, 246. *
18. GOODMAN, P.; FURCON, J.; AND ROSE, J. "Examination of Some Measures of Creative Ability by the Multitrait-Multimethod Matrix." *J Appl Psychol* 53(3):240–3 Je '69. * (*PA* 43:11327)
19. CARLETON, FREDERICK O. "Relationships Between Follow-Up Evaluations and Information Developed in a Management Assessment Center." Abstract. *Proc 78th Ann Conv Am Psychol Assn* 5(2):565–6 '70. * (*PA* 44:19655)
20. ERICKSON, CLARA; GANTZ, BENJAMIN S.; AND STEPHENSON, ROBERT W. "Logical and Construct Validation of a Short-Form Biographical Inventory Predictor of Scientific Creativity." Abstract. *Proc 78th Ann Conv Am Psychol Assn* 5(1):151–2 '70. * (*PA* 44:18715)
21. McNEILL, JOSEPH GERARD. *The Development of Creative Abilities of Personnel in Professional Occupations.* Doctor's thesis, Rutgers—The State University (New Brunswick, N.J.), 1970. (*DAI* 32:674A)
22. REESE, HAYNE W., AND PARNES, SIDNEY J. "Programming Creative Behavior." *Child Develop* 41(2):413–23 Je '70. * (*PA* 44:15509)
23. ROSSITER, CHARLES M., JR. "Creativity and Achievement in Speech." *Today's Speech* 18(3):15–7 su '70. *
24. GLUSKINOS, URY M. "Criteria for Student Engineering Creativity and Their Relationship to College Grades." *J Ed Meas* 8(3):189–95 f '71. *

CUMULATIVE NAME INDEX

Abrahams, N.: 7	Maizell, R. E.: 2
Antley, E. M.: 5	Mayo, S. T.: *rev,* 6:1130
Baehr, M. E.: 17	Mazer, G. E.: 8
Baker, R. L.: 8	Meadow, A.: 1, 3–4
Buckeye, D. A.: 15	Merrifield, P. R.: *rev,* 6:1130
Carleton, F. O.: 19	Miles, D. T.: 14
Craft, C. O.: 12	Parnes, S. J.: 1, 3–4, 22
Dunnette, M. D.: 7	Rapp, M. L.: 9
Erickson, C.: 20	Reese, H.: 4
Froemel, E. C.: 17	Reese, H. W.: 22
Furcon, J.: 18	Rose, J.: 18
Furcon, J. E.: 17	Rossiter, C. M.: 23
Gantz, B. S.: 20	Schutz, R. E.: 8
Gerlach, V. S.: 8	Stephenson, R. W.: 20
Gluskinos, U. M.: 24	Thompson, A. S.: *rev,* 6:1130
Goodman, P.: 18	Tucker, C. A.: 10
Heimann, R. A.: 11	Turner, T. B.: 16
Locke, E. A.: 6	Wernimont, P.: 7
McNeill, J. G.: 21	Whittemore, R. G.: 11
Magowan, R. E.: 13	

[2341]

Engineering Aide Test. Engineering aides; 1957–60; distribution restricted to member public personnel agencies and nonmember agencies approved by the publisher; International Personnel Management Association. *

For additional information, see 6:1131.

[2342]

***Garnett College Test in Engineering Science.** 1–2 years technical college; 1966–71; GCTES; 3 scores: mechanics, heat-electricity-magnetism, total; I. Macfarlane Smith; NFER Publishing Co. Ltd. [England]. *

For additional information concerning the earlier edition, see 7:1093.

[2343]

***The Graduate Record Examinations Advanced Engineering Test.** Graduate school candidates; 1939–73; 3 scores: engineering, mathematics usage, total; Educational Testing Service. * For the testing program entry, see 1053.

For additional information concerning earlier forms, see 7:1094. For reviews of the testing program, see 7:667 (1 review) and 5:601 (1 review).

[2344]

Minnesota Engineering Analogies Test. Candidates for graduate school and industry; 1954–70; MEAT; distribution restricted and test administered at specified licensed university centers; Marvin D. Dunnette; Psychological Corporation. *

For additional information, see 7:1095 (2 references) ; see also 6:1133 (2 references) ; for reviews by A. Pemberton Johnson and William B. Schrader, see 5:933 (6 references).

REFERENCES THROUGH 1971

1–6. See 5:933.
7–8. See 6:1133.
9–10. See 7:1095.

CUMULATIVE NAME INDEX

Abrahams, N.: 9	Pesci, M. L.: 10
Aylward, M. S.: 5	Reynolds, H. J.: 8
Dunnette, M. D.: 1–5, 9	Schrader, W. B.: *rev,* 5:933
Johnson, A. P.: *rev,* 5:933	Spencer, G. M.: 8
MacKinnon, D. W.: 7	Wernimont, P.: 9
Owen, M. L.: 6	

[2345]

***N.I.I.P. Engineering Apprentice Selection Test Battery.** Engineering apprentices; 1936–72; 6 tests, 7 scores: 6 scores listed below and combined score for *a–e;* subtests available only as separates; National Institute of Industrial Psychology; NFER Publishing Co. Ltd. [England]. *

a) GROUP TEST 82. Spatial perception; see 2250.

b) GROUP TESTS 90A AND 90B. Verbal intelligence; see 390.

c) GROUP TESTS 70 AND 70B. Nonverbal intelligence; see 388.

d) ARITHMETIC TESTS EA2A AND EA4. Arithmetic attainment; see 702.

e) VINCENT MECHANICAL DIAGRAMS TEST. Mechanical ability; see 2271.

f) MECHANICAL INFORMATION TEST. See 2254.

For additional information, see 7:1096 (1 reference).

REFERENCES THROUGH 1971
1. See 7:1096.

CUMULATIVE NAME INDEX
Frisby, C. B.: 1   Vincent, D. F.: 1
Lancashire, R.: 1

[2346]
*National Engineering Aptitude Search Test: The Junior Engineering Technical Society. Grades 9–12; 1963–71, c1947–68; tests administered each spring at chapter centers of the Junior Engineering Technical Society; 5 scores: verbal, numerical, science, total, mechanical comprehension; Psychological Corporation. *

For additional information concerning an earlier form, see 6:1134.

[2347]
Purdue Creativity Test. Applicants for engineering positions; 1960, c1957–60; test booklet title is *Creativity Test;* 3 scores: fluency, flexibility, total; C. H. Lawshe and D. H. Harris; distributed by University Book Store. *

For additional information and reviews by Samuel T. Mayo and Philip R. Merrifield, see 6:1136 (2 references).

REFERENCES THROUGH 1971
1–2. See 6:1136.
3. GLUSKINOS, URY M. "Criteria for Student Engineering Creativity and Their Relationship to College Grades." *J Ed Meas* 8(3):189–95 f '71. *

CUMULATIVE NAME INDEX
Gluskinos, U. M.: 3   Mayo, S. T.: *rev,* 6:1136
Harris, D.: 2   Merrifield, P. R.: *rev,* 6:1136
Harris, D. H.: 1

[2348]
*The Undergraduate Program Field Tests: Engineering Test. College; 1969–73; formerly called *The Undergraduate Record Examinations: Engineering Test;* test available to colleges for local administration; Educational Testing Service. * For the testing program entry, see 1062.

For additional information concerning an earlier form, see 7:1097. For reviews of the testing program, see 7:671 (2 reviews).

[Out of Print Since TIP I]
Engineering Aide Test, 6:1131
Engineering and Physical Science Aptitude Test, 4:810 (3 reviews, 6 references)
Engineering Interest Comparisons, T:2002
Owens' Creativity Test for Machine Design, 6:1135 (2 reviews, 1 reference)
Pre-Engineering Ability Test, 4:812 (2 reviews, 11 references)
Professional Employee Inventory, T:2007
Stanford Scientific Aptitude Test, 4:813 (3 reviews, 7 references)

LAW

[2349]
*Law School Admission Test. Law school applicants; 1948–73; LSAT; 2 scores: aptitude (commonly referred to as the LSAT score), writing ability; test administered 5 times annually (February, April, July, October, December) at centers established by the publisher; Educational Testing Service. *

For additional information and a review by Leo A. Munday of earlier forms, see 7:1098 (23 references); see also 5:928 (7 references); for a review by Alexander G. Wesman, see 4:815 (6 references).

REFERENCES THROUGH 1971
1–6. See 4:815.
7–13. See 5:928.
14–36. See 7:1098.
37. BURNHAM, PAUL S., AND CRAWFORD, ALBERT B. "Law School Prediction at Mid-Century (With Particular Reference to Experience at Yale)." *J Legal Ed* 10(2):189–200 '58. *
38. FREEDMAN, MONROE H. "Testing for Analytic Ability in the Law School Admission Test." *J Legal Ed* 11(1):24–42 '58. *
39. HILLS, JOHN R., AND RAINE, WALTER J. "Pair-Comparisons Consistency and Grades in Law School." *J Appl Psychol* 44:94–6 Ap '60. * (*PA* 35:3956)
40. LUNNEBORG, CLIFFORD E., AND LUNNEBORG, PATRICIA W. "Relations of Background Characteristics to Success in the First Year of Law School." *J Legal Ed* 18(4):425–36 '66. *
41. LUNNEBORG, PATRICIA W., AND RADFORD, DONNA. "The LSAT: A Survey of Actual Practice." *J Legal Ed* 18(3):313–24 '66. *
42. GOOLSBY, THOMAS M., JR.; FRARY, ROBERT B.; AND LASCO, RICHARD A. "Factorial Structure and Principal Correlates of the Florida Bar Examination." *Ed & Psychol Meas* 28:427–32 su '68. * (*PA* 42:19400)
43. KLEIN, STEPHEN P.; ROCK, DONALD A.; AND EVANS, FRANKLIN R. "Predicting Success in Law School With Moderators." *J Legal Ed* 21(3):304–13 '69. *

CUMULATIVE NAME INDEX
Andrulis, R. S.: 31   Lasco, R. A.: 42
Bass, B. M.: 14   Lewis, J. W.: 21
Braden, G. D.: 2   Ludlow, H. G.: 29
Braskamp, L.: 21   Lunneborg, C. E.: 26–8, 40
Breslow, E.: 13   Lunneborg, P. W.: 26–8, 40–1
Buckton, L.: 9   Miller, P. V. R.: 22
Burnham, P. S.: 37   Munday, L. A.: *rev,* 7:1098
Chase, C. I.: 29   Olsen, M. A.: 1, 4, 7–8, 11–2
Crawford, A. B.: 37   Pugh, R. C.: 29, 36
Demaree, R. G.: 20   Radford, D.: 41
Distefano, M. K.: 14   Raine, W. J.: 39
Doppelt, J. E.: 9   Ramsey, R. R.: 16–7
Evans, F. R.: 33, 35, 43   Rees, V. M.: 23
Feeney, B. J.: 5   Rock, D. A.: 35, 43
Frary, R. B.: 42   Rudman, J.: 19
Freedman, M. H.: 38   Schrader, W. B.: 4, 8
Fricke, B. G.: 15   Schweiker, R. F.: 20
Goolsby, T. M.: 32, 42   Shah, M.: 20
Gruber, E. C.: 18   Statler, C.: 21
Halfter, I. T.: 25   Thomson, J. E.: 30
Hart, F. M.: 34   Warkov, S.: 24
Hills, J. R.: 39   Wesman, A. G.: *rev,* 4:815
Johnson, A. P.: 3, 6–7, 10–1   Winterbottom, J. A.: 11
Klein, S. P.: 33–5, 43

[Out of Print Since TIP I]
Iowa Legal Aptitude Test, 4:814 (1 review, 5 references)

MEDICINE

[2350]
★CLEP Subject Examination in Clinical Chemistry. Medical technologists; 1972–73; for college accreditation of nontraditional study, advanced placement, or assessment of educational achievement; tests administered monthly at .centers throughout the United States; program administered for the College Entrance Examination Board by Educational Testing Service. * For the testing program entry, see 1050.

[2351]

★CLEP Subject Examination in Hematology.
Medical technologists; 1972-73; for college accreditation of nontraditional study, advanced placement, or assessment of educational achievement; tests administered monthly at centers throughout the United States; program administered for the College Entrance Examination Board by Educational Testing Service. * For the testing program entry, see 1050.

[2352]

★CLEP Subject Examination in Immunohematology and Blood Banking. Medical technologists; 1972-73; for college accreditation of nontraditional study, advanced placement, or assesment of educational achievement; tests administered monthly at centers throughout the United States; program administered for the College Entrance Examination Board by Educational Testing Service. * For the testing program entry, see 1050.

[2353]

★CLEP Subject Examination in Microbiology.
Medical technologists; 1972-73; for college accreditation of nontraditional study, advanced placement, or assessment of educational achievement; tests administered monthly at centers throughout the United States; program administered for the College Entrance Examination Board by Educational Testing Service. * For the testing program entry, see 1050.

[2354]

＊Colleges of Podiatry Admission Test. Grades 14 and over; 1968-72; CPAT; tests administered 3 times annually (February, June, October) at centers established by the publisher; 4 scores: verbal aptitude, quantitative aptitude, natural science, spatial relations; program administered for The American Association of Colleges of Podiatric Medicine by Educational Testing Service (Midwestern Office). *

For additional information, see 7:1099.

[2355]

＊Medical College Admission Test. Applicants for admission to member colleges of the Association of American Medical Colleges; 1946-74; MCAT; 4 scores: verbal, quantitative, general information, science; administered 2 times annually (spring, fall) at centers established by the publisher; program administered for the Association of American Medical Colleges by American College Testing Program.

For additional information and reviews by Nancy S. Cole and James M. Richards, Jr. of earlier forms, see 7:1100 (57 references); for reviews by Robert L. Ebel and Philip H. DuBois, see 6:1137 (43 references); for a review by Alexander G. Wesman, see 5:932 (4 references); for a review by Morey J. Wantman, see 4:817 (11 references).

REFERENCES THROUGH 1971

1-11. See 4:817.
12-15. See 5:932.
16-58. See 6:1137.
59-115. See 7:1100.
116. STALNAKER, JOHN M. "The Study of Applicants for Admission to United States Medical Colleges, Class Entering in 1952-1953." *J Med Ed* 28:21-8 F '53. *
117. STALNAKER, JOHN M. "The Study of Applicants for Admission to United States Medical Colleges, Class Entering in 1953-54." *J Med Ed* 29:13-20 Ap '54. *
118. DYKMAN, ROSCOE A., AND STALNAKER, JOHN M. "The History of the 1949-50 Freshman Class." *J Med Ed* 30:611-21 N '55. * (*PA* 30:5234)
119. GEE, HELEN HOFER, AND COWLES, JOHN T., EDITORS. *The Appraisal of Applicants to Medical Schools: Report of the Fourth Teaching Institute, Association of American Medical Colleges, Colorado Springs, Colorado, November 7-10, 1956.*

Evanston, Ill.: Association of American Medical Colleges, 1957. Pp. xix, 228. * (*PA* 32:3345)
120. ANDERSON, DONALD O., AND RICHES, ELEANOR. "A Decade of Experience With Medical School Applicants at the University of British Columbia." *Can Med Assn J* 88:693-700 Ap 6 '63. *
121. JAMES, FLEMING, III. "A Study of the Relationship Between Grades in Medical School and Certain Predictor Variables." Abstract. *Univ Va Ed R* 1:94-5 '63. *
122. WEITMAN, MORRIS. "A Study of Long-Term Retention in Medical Students." *J Exp Ed* 33:87-91 f '64. * (*PA* 39:3959)
123. JOHNSON, DAVIS G. "The Study of Applicants, 1964-65." *J Med Ed* 40:1017-30 N '65. *
124. SCHOTTSTAEDT, WILLIAM W. "Some Factors Affecting Performance in Medical School." *Trans Am Clin & Climatol Assn* 77:137-49 '65. *
125. ANDERSON, DONALD O.; RICHES, ELEANOR; AND EVANS, ROBERT K. "Applications and Enrollments at the Western Medical Schools: A Study of Medical Matriculants for 1964." *Can Med Assn J* 95:1368-74 D 24 & 31 '66. *
126. "Relationship Between Number of Applications, MCAT Performance and Admission to Medical Schools." *J Med Ed* 43:1268-9 D '68. *
127. JARECKY, ROY K.; JOHNSON, DAVIS G.; AND MATTSON, DALE E. "The Study of Applicants, 1967-68." *J Med Ed* 43:1215-28 D '68. *
128. "Application Activity and MCAT Data of Applicants to the Class of 1969-70." *J Med Ed* 45(12):1071-3 D '70. *
129. CARTWRIGHT, LILLIAN KAUFMAN. *Women in Medical School.* Doctor's thesis, University of California (Berkeley, Calif.), 1970. (*DAI* 31:6237B)
130. FLOM, PENELOPE KEGEL. *Performance in the Medical Internship.* Doctor's thesis, University of California (Berkeley, Calif.), 1970. (*DAI* 32:1188B)
131. GALLAGHER, RICHARD EUGENE. *An Exploration of the Prediction of Academic Performance in Medical School Through the Use of Adjusted Pre-Medical Grades.* Doctor's thesis, Ohio State University (Columbus, Ohio), 1970. (*DAI* 31:4488A)
132. MENSH, IVAN N. "Orientation of Social Values in Medical Student Assessment." *Social Sci & Med* (England) 3(3):339-48 Ja '70. *
133. NELSON-JONES, RICHARD, AND FISH, DAVID G. "Social Characteristics of Applicants to Canadian Medical Schools." *J Med Ed* 45(11):918-28 N '70. *
134. NELSON-JONES, RICHARD, AND FISH, DAVID G. "Women Students in Canadian Medical Schools." *Brit J Med Ed* 4(2):97-108 Je '70. *
135. "Medical College Admission Test." *J Med Ed* 46(5):472-4 My '71. *
136. BEST, WILLIAM R.; DIEKEMA, ANTHONY J.; FISHER, LAWRENCE A.; AND SMITH, NAT E. "Multivariate Predictors in Selecting Medical Students." *J Med Ed* 46(1):42-50 Ja '71. *
137. BRADING, PAUL LEE. *The Relationship Between Success in Medical School and Both Selected Academic and Non-Academic Prediction Factors.* Doctor's thesis, University of Southern California (Los Angeles, Calif.), 1971. (*DAI* 32:747A)
138. DUBE, W. F.; STRITTER, FRANK T.; AND NELSON, BONNIE C. "Study of U.S. Medical School Applicants, 1970-71." *J Med Ed* 46(10):837-57 O '71. *
139. ERDMANN, JAMES B.; MATTSON, DALE E.; HUTTON, JACK G., JR.; AND WALLACE, WIMBURN L. "The Medical College Admission Test: Past, Present, Future." *J Med Ed* 46(11):937-46 N '71. *
140. HALEY, HAROLD B.; JUAN, ISABEL R.; AND PAIVA, ROSALIA E. A. "MCAT Scores in Relation to Personality Measures and Biographical Variables." *J Med Ed* 46(11):947-58 N '71. *
141. HAMBERG, RONALD L.; SWANSON, AUGUST G.; AND DOHNER, CHARLES W. "Perceptions and Usage of Predictive Data for Medical School Admissions." *J Med Ed* 46(11):959-63 N '71. *
142. MOFFATT, D. J.; JACOBS, A. W.; AND METCALF, W. K. "Predictors of Academic Performance in Gross Anatomy." *J Med Ed* 46(6):545-8 Je '71. *
143. PAIVA, ROSALIA E. A., AND HALEY, HAROLD B. "Intellectual, Personality, and Environmental Factors in Career Specialty Preferences." *J Med Ed* 46(4):281-9 Ap '71. * (*PA* 46:6947)
144. STEFANU, CONSTANTINE, AND FARMER, T. ALBERT, JR. "The Differential Predictive Validity of Science MCAT in the Admissions Process." *J Med Ed* 46(5):461-3 My '71. *
145. STRITTER, FRANK T., HUTTON, JACK G., JR.; AND DUBE, W. F. "Study of U.S. Medical School Applicants, 1969-70." *J Med Ed* 46(1):25-41 Ja '71. *

CUMULATIVE NAME INDEX

Ceithaml, J.: 38
Chapman, J. E.: 84
Coisman, F. G.: 80
Cole, N. S.: rev, 7:1100
Colten, T.: 63
Conger, J. J.: 51
Cowles, J. T.: 119
Crowder, D. G.: 23
Davis, J. R.: 15
Diekema, A. J.: 136
Dohner, C. W.: 141
Doppelt, J. E.: 14
Dube, W. F.: 138, 145
DuBois, P. H.: rev, 6:1137
Dykman, R. A.: 60, 118
Ebel, R. L.: rev, 6:1137
Erdmann, J. B.: 139
Evans, L. R.: 82, 97
Evans, R. K.: 125
Farmer, T. A.: 144
Faterson, H. F.: 109
Fish, D. G.: 113, 133–4
Fisher, L. A.: 136
Fitz, R. H.: 51
Flom, P. K.: 130
Flowers, J. F.: 114
Fredericks, M. A.: 75, 95–6, 111
Funkenstein, D. H.: 76, 83
Gallagher, R. E.: 131
Garfield, S. L.: 31
Gee, H. H.: 20, 25, 28–9, 32, 34, 39, 42, 59, 119
Geertsma, R. H.: 84
Geiger, J.: 63
Gilbert, J. A. L.: 85
Glaser, R.: 8
Glaser, R. J.: 21
Gough, H. G.: 52, 66
Graves, G. O.: 67, 77, 97
Groff, M.: 40
Gruber, E. C.: 40
Hain, J. D.: 71
Haley, H. B.: 112, 140, 143
Hall, W. B.: 52, 66
Hamberg, R. L.: 141
Harris, R. E.: 52
Hetherington, R. W.: 61
Hill, J. K.: 24
Hoffman, E. L.: 53
Howell, M. A.: 98
Hunka, S.: 85
Hunter, R. C. A.: 35, 47–8
Hurd, A. W.: 4
Hutchins, E. B.: 32, 41–2, 54–6, 58, 68, 86, 89
Hutton, J. G.: 139, 145
Ingersoll, R. W.: 67, 77, 82, 97
Jackson, G. G.: 22
Jacobs, A. W.: 142
Jacobson, M. D.: 104
James, F.: 121
Jarecky, R. K.: 127
Johnson, D. G.: 27, 43, 86, 107, 123, 127
Juan, I. R.: 112, 140
Kellow, W. F.: 22
Kelly, E. L.: 69
Klinger, E.: 25, 28, 59
Korman, M.: 106
Kosa, J.: 111
Levitt, E. E.: 44
Lief, H. I.: 53, 78
Lief, V. F.: 78
Little, J. M.: 29

Lohrenz, J. G.: 47–8
Lyden, F. J.: 63
McGuire, F. L.: 70
Macleod, J. W.: 61
Martin, L. W.: 106
Mattson, D. E.: 107, 127, 139
Mensh, I. N.: 132
Merwin, J. C.: 88
Metcalf, W. K.: 142
Michael, W. B.: 100
Moffatt, D. J.: 142
Moldowski, E. W.: 109
Moldowski, L. H. K.: 109
Moore, R. A.: 45
Morris, W. W.: 9, 56, 87, 99
Mundy, P.: 95–6, 111
Nelson, B. C.: 138
Nelson-Jones, R.: 113, 133–4
Netsky, M. G.: 71, 104
Novick, M. R.: 29
Opdyke, D.: 103
Paiva, R. E. A.: 140, 143
Peterson, O. L.: 63, 74
Pierson, G. A.: 3
Pollack, S.: 100
Price, P. B.: 46
Prince, R. H.: 35
Ralph, R. B.: 5, 12
Richards, J. M.: 33, 46; rev, 7:1100
Riches, E.: 62, 91, 120, 125
Robertson, L. S.: 111
Roemer, R. E.: 79
Rohrer, J. H.: 2
Rothman, A. I.: 114
Rudman, J.: 57
Sanazaro, P. J.: 58
Schofield, W.: 88, 115
Schottstaedt, W. W.: 124
Schultz, D. G.: 10
Schumacher, C. F.: 34, 39, 72
Schwartzman, A. E.: 35, 47–8
Scott, J. A.: 16
Scott, W.: 70
Sedlacek, W. E.: 89, 101–2, 107
Shatin, L.: 103
Shoemaker, H. A.: 2
Smith, E. J.: 82
Smith, N. E.: 136
Solkoff, N.: 108
Stalnaker, J. M.: 6, 11, 13, 17–8, 116–8
Stefanu, C.: 144
Stritter, F. T.: 138, 145
Stubblefield, R. L.: 106
Swanson, A. G.: 141
Taylor, C. W.: 5, 7, 12, 33, 46
Trainer, J. B.: 37
Tyler, E. A.: 44
Vaughn, K. W.: 1
Vincent, J. W.: 98
Wallace, W. L.: 139
Wantman, M. J.: rev, 4:817
Watson, R. I.: 19
Weitman, M.: 80, 122
Wesman, A. G.: rev, 5:932
Wilson, J. W. D.: 60
Wing, C. W.: 13
Wolpin, M.: 31
Woods, B. T.: 104
Work, H. H.: 49
Young, K. M.: 78
Young, R. H.: 3
Zickmantel, R.: 62

[2356]

Medical School Instructor Attitude Inventory. Medical school faculty members; 1961; 6 scores: democratic-autocratic attitude toward teaching, critical-complimentary attitude toward medical schools, liberal-traditional attitude toward medical education, appreciative-depreciative attitude toward medical students, favorable-unfavorable attitude toward full-time teachers, favorable-unfavorable attitude toward part-time teachers; Edwin F. Rosinski; the Author. *

For additional information, see 6:1138 (1 reference).

REFERENCES THROUGH 1971

1. See 6:1138.

Medical College Admission Test

CUMULATIVE NAME INDEX

Rosinski, E. F.: 1

[2357]

★**Optometry College Admission Test.** Optometry college applicants; 1971–73; OCAT; tests administered 3 times annually (January, March, November) at centers established by the publisher; 6 scores: verbal ability, quantitative ability, biology, chemistry, physics, study-reading; sponsored by the Association of Schools and Colleges of Optometry; prepared and administered by Psychological Corporation. *

[2358]

***Veterinary Aptitude Test.** Veterinary school applicants; 1951–73; VAT; tests administered at centers established by the publisher; 5 scores: reading comprehension, quantitative ability, science information, verbal memory, total; original test by William A. Owens and Loyal C. Payne; Psychological Corporation. *

For additional information, see 7:1101; see also 6:1139 (3 references) and 5:957 (3 references).

REFERENCES THROUGH 1971

1–3. See 5:957.
4–6. See 6:1139.
7. OWENS, WILLIAM A. "Development of a Test of Aptitude for Veterinary Medicine." Abstract. *Am Psychologist* 4:240 Jl '49. * (*PA* 23:6530, title only)

CUMULATIVE NAME INDEX

Brown, F. G.: 5   Payne, L. C.: 3
Layton, W. L.: 2   Ray, D. K.: 6
Owens, W. A.: 1, 4, 7

[Out of Print Since TIP I]

Medical Preference Inventory, T:2012

MISCELLANEOUS

[2359]

***Architectural School Aptitude Test.** Architectural school applicants; 1963–73; ASAT; tests administered 2 times annually (February, December) at centers established by the publisher; program administered for the Association of Collegiate Schools of Architecture by Educational Testing Service. *

For additional information, see 7:1102 (2 references).

REFERENCES THROUGH 1971

1–2. See 7:1102.

CUMULATIVE NAME INDEX

Lunneborg, C. E.: 1–2   Lunneborg, P. W.: 1–2

[2360]

Chemical Operators Selection Test, Revised Edition. Chemical operators and applicants; 1958–71; test by M. A. Storr, J. H. McPherson, P. A. Maschino, and R. G. Garner; manual by J. I. Wegener; Dow Chemical Co. *

For additional information, see 7:1104; see also 6:1141 (1 reference).

REFERENCES THROUGH 1971

1. See 6:1141.

CUMULATIVE NAME INDEX

Coats, J. E.: 1   Garner, R. G.: 1

[2361]

Fire Promotion Tests. Prospective firemen promotees; 1960–69; 5 tests; McCann Associates. *
a) LIEUTENANT. 1962–69; 4 scores: pre-fire practices, extinguishment practices, fire supervision, total.
b) CAPTAIN. 1962–69; 5 scores: pre-fire practices, extinguishment practices, overhaul-salvage-rescue, fire supervision, total.

c) ASSISTANT FIRE CHIEF. 1961–69; 5 scores: fire administration, firefighting knowledge, fire prevention, fire supervision, total.
d) DEPUTY FIRE CHIEF. 1967–69; test also used for battalion chief; 5 scores: same as for *c*.
e) FIRE CHIEF. 1969; 5 scores: same as for *c*.
For additional information, see 7:1106.

[2362]

*Firefighter Test. Prospective firemen; 1954–72; distribution restricted to member public personnel agencies and nonmember agencies approved by the publisher; International Personnel Management Association. *
For additional information, see 6:1143.

[2363]

Fireman Examination. Prospective firemen; 1961–62; 8 or 9 scores: learning ability (verbal, quantitative, total), fireman aptitude (interest, common sense, mechanical, total), easy verbal learning (form 70 only), total; distribution restricted to civil service commissions and municipal officials; McCann Associates. *
For additional information, see 6:1145.

[2364]

General Municipal Employees Performance (Efficiency) Rating System. Municipal employees; 1967–69; ratings by immediate supervisors; 8 summary ratings: quality of work, quantity of work, work habits, personal traits, relationships with people, supervisory ability, administrative ability, total; McCann Associates. *
For additional information, see 7:1107.

[2365]

Journalism Test. High school; 1957; 16 scores: news values, arrangement of facts, paragraphing, sentence variety, news source, sports, feature values, speech-interview, editorials, news style, columns, advertising, makeup, headlines, terminology, copyreading; no manual; Frances Miller and Kenneth Stratton; Stratton-Christian Press. *
For additional information, see 7:1108.

[2366]

★Law Enforcement Perception Questionnaire. Law enforcement personnel; 1970; LEPQ; attitudes toward law enforcement and law enforcement personnel; Frank Lee; Psychometric Affiliates. *

[2367]

Memory and Observation Tests for Policeman. Prospective policemen; 1962; for use with *Policeman Examination;* 2 tests; distribution restricted to civil service commissions and municipal officials; McCann Associates. *
a) MEMORY TEST FOR POLICEMAN.
b) OBSERVATION TEST FOR POLICEMAN.
For additional information, see 6:1146.

[2368]

Police Performance Rating System. Policemen; 1964–69; PPRS; ratings by immediate supervisors; 7 summary ratings: quality of work, interpersonal relationship traits, quantity of work, character traits, quality of supervision given, quality of administrative work, total; McCann Associates. *
For additional information, see 7:1109.

[2369]

Police Promotion Tests. Prospective policemen promotees; 1960–69; 6 tests; McCann Associates. *

a) SERGEANT. 1962–69; 6 or 7 scores: patrol, other police knowledges, crime investigation, law, supervision, reading comprehension (Form B only), total.
b) LIEUTENANT. 1962–69; 6 or 8 scores: same as for *a* plus administration (Form B only).
c) DETECTIVE. 1962–69; 4 scores: crime investigation, investigative judgment, law, total.
d) CAPTAIN. 1962–68; 6 scores: police supervision, police administration, crime investigation, other police knowledges, law (Form A only), reading comprehension (Form B only), total.
e) ASSISTANT CHIEF. 1968–69; 6 scores: same as for *d*.
f) CHIEF OF POLICE. 1960–69; 6 scores: same as for *d*.
For additional information, see 7:1110.

[2370]

Policeman Examination. Prospective policemen; 1960–62; 8 or 9 scores: learning ability (verbal, quantitative, total), police aptitude (interest, common sense, public relations, total), easy verbal learning (forms 70 only), total; distribution restricted to civil service commissions and municipal officials; McCann Associates. *
For additional information, see 6:1150.

[2371]

Policeman Test. Policemen and prospective policemen; 1953–65; distribution restricted to member public personnel agencies and nonmember agencies approved by the publisher; International Personnel Management Association. *
For additional information, see 7:1111.

[2372]

The Potter-Nash Aptitude Test for Lumber Inspectors and Other General Personnel Who Handle Lumber. Employees in woodworking industries; 1958; test booklet title is *The P-N Test;* arithmetic; F. T. Potter and N. Nash; N. Nash. *
For additional information, see 6:1152.

[2373]

★Test for Firefighter B-1. Firemen and prospective firemen; 1973; test booklet title is *Firefighter;* no manual; test rented to member public personnel agencies and nonmember agencies approved by the publisher; International Personnel Management Association. *

[2374]

★Test for Police Officer A-1. Policemen and prospective policemen; 1973; test booklet title is *Police Officer A-1;* no manual; test rented to member public personnel agencies and nonmember agencies approved by the publisher; International Personnel Management Association. *

[2375]

Visual Comprehension Test for Detective. Prospective police detectives; 1963; no manual; McCann Associates. *
For additional information, see 6:1154.

[Out of Print Since TIP I]

Air Force Preference Inventory, T :2014
Fire Performance Rating System, 7:1105
NCR Test Battery for Prospective Check-Out Cashiers (status unknown), 6:1147 (1 review)
P-L-S Journalism Test, 3:149
Personnel Service Rating Report, 5:939
Store Personnel Test, 5:954 (2 reviews, 1 reference)

NURSING

[2376]

Achievement Tests in Nursing. Students in schools of registered nursing; 1952–71; tests administered at any time by individual schools; 14 tests; Psychological Corporation. *
a) ANATOMY AND PHYSIOLOGY. 1953–68.
b) CANCER NURSING. 1967.
c) GENERAL CHEMISTRY. 1954–64.
d) ORGANIC AND INORGANIC CHEMISTRY. 1964.
e) COMMUNICABLE DISEASES. 1953–61.
f) MEDICAL NURSING. 1952–68.
g) MICROBIOLOGY. 1952–68.
h) NUTRITION AND DIET THERAPY. 1952–68.
i) OBSTETRICAL NURSING. 1952–68.
j) PEDIATRIC NURSING. 1952–68.
k) PHARMACOLOGY. 1952–68.
l) PSYCHIATRIC NURSING. 1952–71.
m) PSYCHOLOGY AND SOCIOLOGY. 1957–68.
n) SURGICAL NURSING. 1952–68.
For additional information, see 7:1112.

[2377]

Achievement Tests in Practical Nursing. Practical nursing students; 1957–67; tests administered at any time by individual schools; Psychological Corporation. *
For additional information, see 7:1113 (1 reference).

REFERENCES THROUGH 1971
1. See 7:1113.

CUMULATIVE NAME INDEX
Cavallo, M.: 1   Sternlicht, M.: 1

[2378]

Empathy Inventory. Nursing instructors; 1966–70; EI; empathy for nursing school students; John R. Thurston, Helen L. Brunclik, and John F. Feldhusen (manual); Nursing Research Associates. *
For additional information, see 7:1114 (2 references).

REFERENCES THROUGH 1971
1–2. See 7:1114.

CUMULATIVE NAME INDEX
Brunclik, H.: 1   Feldhusen, J. F.: 2
Brunclik, H. L.: 2   Thurston, J. R.: 1–2
Feldhusen, J.: 1

[2379]

Entrance Examination for Schools of Nursing. Nursing school applicants; 1938–70; EESN; tests administered at centers established by the publisher; 13 scores: 7 ability scores (verbal, numerical, science, reading comprehension, arithmetic processes, general information, scholastic aptitude total) and 6 personality scores (achievement, orderliness, persistence, congeniality, altruism, respectfulness); Psychological Corporation. *
For additional information, see 7:1115 (3 references); see also 6:1156 (2 references).

REFERENCES THROUGH 1971
1–2. See 6:1156.
3–5. See 7:1115.
6. NLN MEASUREMENT AND EVALUATION SERVICE. "The Predictive Validity of Two Entrance Examinations in a School of Practical Nursing." *Nursing Outl* 19(9):611 S '71. *

CUMULATIVE NAME INDEX
Carruth, M. S.: 1   NLN Measurement and Eval-
Lyman, H. B.: 5   uation Service: 6
Meadow, L.: 3   Sartain, A. Q.: 2
Mueller, E. J.: 4–5

[2380]

Entrance Examination for Schools of Practical Nursing. Practical nursing school applicants; 1942–69; tests administered at regional centers established by the publisher; 12 scores: 6 ability scores (verbal, numerical, science, reading, arithmetic fundamentals, total) and 6 personality scores (achievement, orderliness, persistence, congeniality, altruism, respectfulness); Psychological Corporation. *
For additional information, see 7:1116 (2 references).

REFERENCES THROUGH 1971
1–2. See 7:1116.

CUMULATIVE NAME INDEX
Cavallo, M.: 1   Sternlicht, M.: 1
Sitzmann, M. R.: 2

[2381]

George Washington University Series Nursing Tests. Prospective nurses; 1931–50; 5 tests; Thelma Hunt; Center for Psychological Service. *
a) APTITUDE TEST FOR NURSING. 1931–50; F. A. Moss (Form 1).
b) ARITHMETIC TEST FOR PROSPECTIVE NURSES. 1940–50.
c) READING COMPREHENSION TEST FOR PROSPECTIVE NURSES. 1940–50.
d) GENERAL SCIENCE TEST FOR PROSPECTIVE NURSES. 1944–50.
e) INTEREST-PREFERENCE TEST FOR PROSPECTIVE NURSES. 1944–50.
For additional information, see 4:818 (2 references); see also 3:699 (6 references).

REFERENCES THROUGH 1971
1–6. See 3:699.
7–8. See 4:818.
9. FAHRIG, MARJORIE W. *A Preliminary Study of the Aptitude Test (Form 2) of the George Washington University Series of Nursing Tests, in Five Canadian Hospitals.* Master's thesis, Dalhousie University (Halifax, N.S., Canada), 1951.
10. LEPLEY, WILLIAM M. "Predicting Success in Nurses Training." *J Psychol* 48:121–4 Jl '59. * (*PA* 34:6169)
11. GARRETT, WILEY S. "Prediction of Academic Success in a School of Nursing." *Personnel & Guid J* 38:500–3 F '60. * (*PA* 35:3954)

CUMULATIVE NAME INDEX
Berg, I. A.: 6–7   Lepley, W. M.: 10
Douglass, H. R.: 5   McCullough, C. M.: 5
Fahrig, M. W.: 9   Merrill, R. A.: 2, 5
Fiss, C. B.: 3   Rhinehart, J. B.: 1
Ford, A. H.: 8   Stover, R. D.: 3
Garrett, W. S.: 11   Williamson, E. G.: 3
Kraft, L.: 4

[2382]

Luther Hospital Sentence Completions. Prospective nursing students; 1959–70; LHSC; nonquantitative interpretations of responses in 7 attitudinal areas: nursing, self, home-family, responsibility, others, classwork and studies, love and marriage; an abbreviated edition, consisting of 40 of the 90 items, is also available under the title *Nursing Sentence Completions* (NSC); these 40 items may be scored quantitatively in either edition to obtain a score for predicting success in training; the authors refer to the scoring key as the *Nursing Education Scale* (NES); John R. Thurston, Helen L. Brunclik, P. A. Finn (test), and John Feldhusen (manual); Nursing Research Associates. *
For additional information, see 7:1117 (5 references).

REFERENCES THROUGH 1971
1–5. See 7:1117.
6. THURSTON, JOHN R.; FINN, PATRICIA A.; AND BRUNCLIK, HELEN L. "A Method for Evaluating the Attitudes of Prospective Nursing Students." *J Nursing Ed* 2:3–7+ My–Je '63. *
7. LOWE, BARBARA W. *A Comparison of Responses on Selected Items From the Luther Hospital Sentence Completions Form for a Group of Successful Nursing Students and Drop-Outs.* Master's thesis, University of Tennessee (Knoxville, Tenn.), 1971.

[2383]

*NLN Achievement Tests for Schools Preparing Registered Nurses. Students in state-approved schools preparing registered nurses; 1943–73; tests loaned to schools for their own use; 3 levels; National League for Nursing, Inc. *

a) [BASIC ACHIEVEMENT TESTS.] Course-end tests; 1943–73; 9 tests.
   1) *Anatomy and Physiology.* 1943–64.
   2) *Chemistry.* 1943–63; 4 scores: inorganic, organic, biochemistry, total.
   3) *Microbiology.* 1943–71.
   4) *Normal Nutrition.* 1946–72; formerly called *Nutrition and Diet Therapy.*
   5) *Basic Pharmacology.* 1944–67; formerly called *Pharmacology and Therapeutics.*
   6) *Medical-Surgical Nursing.* 1956–62; 4 scores: medical nursing, surgical nursing, medical-surgical nursing, total.
   7) *Obstetric Nursing.* 1945–68; 4 scores: antepartal care, partal and postpartal care of mothers, care of newborn, total.
   8) *Nursing of Children.* 1945–68; 3 scores: growth and development, care of the sick child, total.
   9) *Psychiatric Nursing.* 1945–73; 3 scores: psychiatric nursing practices, facts and principles, total.
b) COMPREHENSIVE ACHIEVEMENT TESTS. Students about to graduate; 1957–68; 8 tests.
   1) *Diet Therapy and Applied Nutrition.* 1962.
   2) *Pharmacology in Clinical Nursing (Application of Facts and Principles).* 1960–67.
   3) *Natural Sciences in Nursing.* 1957–68; 3 scores: facts and principles (knowledge, application, total).
   4) *Maternity and Child Nursing.* 1958–67; 3 scores: care of the normal pregnant woman and normal child, care of sick children, total.
   5) *Disaster Nursing.* 1961; 3 scores: general nursing applied to disasters, facts and principles of disasters and disaster nursing, total.
   6) *Medical-Surgical Nursing, Part 1.* 1961; 4 scores: orthopedic nursing, neurological-neurosurgical nursing, eye-ear-nose-and-throat nursing, total.
   7) *Medical-Surgical Nursing, Part 2.* 1962; 3 scores: medical nursing, surgical nursing, total.
   8) *Communicable Disease Nursing.* 1946–63; 3 scores: prevention and transmission, disease manifestations and other aspects, total.
c) [BACCALAUREATE LEVEL TESTS.] For baccalaureate programs only; 1956–73; 5 tests.
   1) *Maternal-Child Nursing.* 1964; 4 scores: growth and development (including pregnancy), conditions and care of the sick child, other relevant aspects, total.
   2) *Medical-Surgical Nursing.* 1967; 4 scores: part A, part B, knowledge, application.
   3) *Applied Natural Sciences.* 1967; 4 scores: part A, part B, knowledge, application.
   4) *Community Health Nursing.* 1956–73; earlier forms called *Public Health Nursing;* 4 scores: family health, community health, science and general information, total.
   5) *Psychiatric Nursing.* 1972; 3 scores: facts and principles, psychiatric nursing practice, total.
   For additional information, see 7:1118 (10 references); see also 6:1157 (1 reference).

REFERENCES THROUGH 1971

1. See 6:1157.
2–11. See 7:1118.

12. "Science and Nursing Knowledge of Graduate Students." *Nursing Outl* 15:53 D '67. *
13. "A Study Which Used the NLN Microbiology Achievement Test." *Nursing Outl* 15:73 Je '67. *
14. "The Relationship of State Boards and Achievement Test Performance." *Nursing Outl* 18(8):61 Ag '70. *
15. MUHLENKAMP, ANN F. "Prediction of State Board Scores in a Baccalaureate Program." *Nursing Outl* 19(1):57 Ja '71. *

[2384]

NLN Aide Selection Test. Applicants for aide positions in hospitals and home health agencies; 1970; AST; National League for Nursing, Inc. *

For additional information, see 7:1119.

[2385]

NLN Practical Nursing Achievement Tests. Students in state-approved schools of practical nursing; 1950–64; tests loaned to schools for their own use; 3 tests; National League for Nursing, Inc. *

a) THREE UNITS OF CONTENT. 1957–64; TUC; 4 scores: body structure and function, basic nursing procedures, nutrition and diet therapy, total.
b) NURSING INCLUDING ASPECTS OF PHARMACOLOGY. 1950–64; NIP; 4 scores: medical-surgical, maternal-child, pharmacology, total.
c) ELEMENTARY PSYCHIATRIC NURSING. 1958; for aide-training programs.
   For additional information, see 7:1120 (1 reference).

REFERENCES THROUGH 1971

1. See 7:1120.
2. "Factors in the Success of Students in Schools of Practical Nursing." *Nursing Outl* 2:423–7 Ag '54. *
3. THOMAS, MARTHA J., AND WEINSTEIN, ABBOTT S. "Comparison of Test Scores in Psychiatric Nursing." *Nursing Outl* 13:38–41 My '65. *

[2386]

NLN Pre-Admission and Classification Examination. Practical nursing school entrants; 1950–63; PACE; tests administered throughout the year at centers established by the publisher; 2 tests, 8 scores: 7 scores listed below, composite; National League for Nursing, Inc. *

a) GENERAL INFORMATION AND JUDGMENT TEST. 4 scores: science and health, general information, arithmetic, total.
b) VOCABULARY AND READING TEST. 3 scores: vocabulary, reading, total.
   For additional information, see 6:1161 (1 reference).

REFERENCES THROUGH 1971

1. See 6:1161.
2. "Factors in the Success of Students in Schools of Practical Nursing." *Nursing Outl* 2:423–7 Ag '54. *
3. MEADOW, LLOYD. "Assessment of Students for Schools of Practical Nursing." *Nursing Res* 13:222–9 su '64. *
4. BAILEY, LARRY J. "Factors Related to Success in Practical Nursing Programs." *Nursing Outl* 16:59 N '68. *
5. "The Interpretation of Scores on the NLN Pre-Admission and Classification Examination." *Nursing Outl* 18(12):47 D '70. *
6. NLN MEASUREMENT AND EVALUATION SERVICE. "The Predictive Validity of Two Entrance Examinations in a School of Practical Nursing." *Nursing Outl* 19(9):611 S '71. *

[2387]

*NLN Pre-Nursing and Guidance Examination.
Applicants for admission to state-approved schools preparing registered nurses; 1941–72; PNG; tests administered throughout the year at centers established
by the publisher; 4 tests, 7 scores: 6 scores listed
below, composite; National League for Nursing, Inc. *
a) NLN TEST OF ACADEMIC APTITUDE. Special printing
of level 1 (for grades 12–14) of *Cooperative School and
College Ability Tests: Series 2;* 3 scores: quantitative,
verbal, total.
b) NLN READING TEST. Special printing of level 1 (for
grades 12–14) of *Sequential Tests of Educational Progress, Series 2: Reading.*
c) NLN SCIENCE TEST. Special printing of level 1 (for
grades 12–14) of *Sequential Tests of Educational Progress, Series 2: Science.*
d) NLN SOCIAL STUDIES TEST. Special printing of level
1 (for grades 12–14) of *Sequential Tests of Educational
Progress, Series 2: Social Studies.*
For additional information, see 6:1162 (8 references).

REFERENCES THROUGH 1971
1–8. See 6:1162.
9. JOEL, M. LAMPEN. *The Validity of the NLN PNG Examination and Some Other Factors in a School of Nursing.* Doctor's
thesis, Loyola University (Chicago, Ill.), 1964.
10. NATIONAL LEAGUE FOR NURSING. *The NLN Pre-Nursing
and Guidance Examination, Fourth Edition. The Use of Tests in
Schools of Nursing,* Pamphlet No. 1. New York: the League,
1965. Pp. vii, 37. *
11. MADAUS, GEORGE F. "The Predictive Validity of the National League for Nursing, Pre-Nursing and Guidance Examination for Different Criteria of Success in a Three Year Diploma
Program." *Ed & Psychol Meas* 26:431–7 su '66. * (*PA* 40:
12764)
12. "The Interpretation of Scores on the NLN Pre-Nursing
and Guidance Examination." *Nursing Outl* 15:51 Mr '67. *
13. "Multiple Regression and Multiple Cutoffs." *Nursing
Outl* 15:61 O '67. *
14. "PNG, HSR, and Licensure Examination Results." *Nursing Outl* 15:66 N '67. *
15. BAZIAK, ANNA T. "Developing Reliable Indices to Predict
Success on Psychiatric Nursing State Board Examinations." *J
Psychiatric Nursing* 6:79–85 Mr–Ap '68. * (*PA* 42:18848)
16. CRUTCHLOW, MARY ANN. "Validation of Entrance Examination by School Faculties." *Nursing Outl* 16:58–9 O '68. *
17. KIRKPATRICK, JAMES J.; EWEN, ROBERT B.; BARRETT,
RICHARD S.; AND KATZELL, RAYMOND A. *Testing and Fair Employment: Fairness and Validity of Personnel Tests for Different
Ethnic Groups,* pp. 22–3, 25–7, 95–122. New York: New York
University Press, 1968. Pp x, 145. *
18. THURSTON, JOHN R.; BRUNCLIK, HELEN L.; AND FELD-
HUSEN, JOHN F. "The Relationship of Personality to Achievement
in Nursing Education, Phase 2." *Nursing Res* 17:265–8 My–Je
'68. * (*PA* 42:17997)
19. MIKAN, CAROLYN JANE. *High School Biology and Chemistry Grades and the NLN Pre-Nursing and Guidance Examination as Predictors of Achievement in a Diploma School of Nursing.* Master's thesis, St. Joseph College (West Hartford, Conn.),
1969.
20. NLN MEASUREMENT AND EVALUATION SERVICES. "The
Relationship of PNG and Achievement Test Scores." *Nursing
Outl* 17(3):52 Mr '69. *
21. NLN MEASUREMENT AND EVALUATION SERVICES. "PNG
Performance and Academic Ratings." *Nursing Outl* 18(5):66
My '70. *
22. NLN MEASUREMENT AND EVALUATION SERVICES. "PNG
Performance and Performance in a School of Nursing." *Nursing
Outl* 18(4):55 Ap '70. *
23. NLN MEASUREMENT AND EVALUATION SERVICES. "PNG
Performance and Race." *Nursing Outl* 18(7):41 Jl '70. *
24. NLN MEASUREMENT AND EVALUATION SERVICES. "Per-
formance on the PNG and the State Board of Examination."
Nursing Outl 18(6)62–3 Je '70. *
25. NLN MEASUREMENT AND EVALUATION SERVICES. "The
Validity of NLN Pre-Nursing and Guidance Examination."
Nursing Outl 18(3):56 Mr '70. *
26. NATIONAL LEAGUE FOR NURSING. *A Validation Study of
the NLN Pre-Nursing and Guidance Examination and Related
Studies Emerging From Data Gathered From the Validation
Study.* New York: the League, 1970. Pp. v, 58. *

[2388]

**Netherne Study Difficulties Battery for Student
Nurses.** Student nurses; 1964–69; SDB; also called
Study Difficulties Battery; 15 scores: understanding of
words, use of words, scientific information, learning
from a text, checking correctness of spelling, checking
accuracy of numbers, checking accuracy of names,
learning from a diagram, summarizing a paragraph,
following directions, summarizing drawings and diagrams, speed of associations, speed and legibility of
handwriting, speed and accuracy of freehand drawing,
total; James Patrick S. Robertson; Psychological Research Department, Netherne Hospital; distributed by
NFER Publishing Co. Ltd. [England]. *
For additional information, see 7:1121.

[2389]

Nurse Attitudes Inventory. Prospective nursing students; 1965–70; NAI; a multiple choice test based
upon *Luther Hospital Sentence Completions;* 9 scores:
attitudes (nursing, self, home-family, responsibility,
others-love-marriage, academic), verification (V-1,
V-2), total; the authors refer to the scoring key used
to obtain the total score as the *Nursing Education
Scale,* abbreviated NES-NAI to distinguish it from the
Nursing Education Scale based upon either the *Luther
Hospital Sentence Completions* or the *Nursing Sentence Completions;* John R. Thurston, Helen L. Brunclik, and John F. Feldhusen (manual); Nursing Research Associates. *
For additional information, see 7:1122 (5 references).

REFERENCES THROUGH 1971
1–5. See 7:1122.

[2390]

***PSB-Aptitude for Practical Nursing Examina-
tion.** Applicants for admission to practical nursing
schools; 1961–72; revision of *PSB-Entrance Examination for Schools of Practical Nursing;* 5 scores: general mental ability, spelling, natural sciences, judgment
in practical nursing situations, personal adjustment
index; Anna S. Evans, Joan R. Yanuzzi, and George
A. W. Stouffer, Jr., with the technical assistance of
the Psychological Services Bureau; the Bureau. *
For additional information concerning the earlier
edition, see 6:1163.

[Out of Print Since TIP I]

*Basic Nursing Procedures and Elementary Nutrition:
NLN Achievement Tests for Psychiatric Aides,*
6:1158b
NLN Graduate Nurse Examination, 6:1159 (4 references)

RESEARCH

[2391]

Research Personnel Review Form. Research and
engineering and scientific firms; 1959–60; for super-

visor's evaluation of research personnel in preparation for a performance review interview; Morris I. Stein; the Author. *

For additional information, see 6:1164.

[2392]

Supervisor's Evaluation of Research Personnel. Research personnel; 1960; SERP; ratings by supervisors; William D. Buel; Byron Harless, Schaffer, Reid & Associates, Inc. *

For additional information, a review by John W. French, and an excerpted review by Laurence Siegel, see 6:1165 (3 references).

REFERENCES THROUGH 1971

1-3. See 6:1165.
4. BUEL, WILLIAM D. "Biographical Data and the Identification of Creative Research Personnel." *J Appl Psychol* 49:318-21 O '65. * (*PA* 40:787)
5. BUEL, WILLIAM D.; ALBRIGHT, LEWIS E.; AND GLENNON, J. R. "A Note on the Generality and Cross-Validity of Personal History for Identifying Creative Research Scientists." *J Appl Psychol* 50:217-9 Je '66. * (*PA* 40:8829)

CUMULATIVE NAME INDEX

Albright, L. E.: 5　　　French, J. W.: *rev*, 6:1165
Bachner, V. M.: 3　　　Glennon, J. R.: 5
Buel, W. D.: 1-5　　　Siegel, L.: *exc*, 6:1165

[2393]

Surveys of Research Administration and Environment. Research and engineering and scientific firms; 1959-60; 2 forms for gathering information and opinions on the company and its research activities; Morris I. Stein; the Author. *
a) STEIN SURVEY FOR ADMINISTRATORS. Supervisors and administrators; also part of *Technical Personnel Recruiting Inventory.*
b) STEIN RESEARCH ENVIRONMENT SURVEY. Research and technical personnel.

For additional information, see 6:1166.

[2394]

Technical Personnel Recruiting Inventory. Research and engineering and scientific firms; 1959-60; 3 parts; Morris I. Stein; the Author. *
a) INDIVIDUAL QUALIFICATION FORM. Supervisors; description of an available research position.
b) PERSONAL DATA FORM FOR SCIENTIFIC, ENGINEERING, AND TECHNICAL PERSONNEL. Job applicants.
c) STEIN SURVEY FOR ADMINISTRATORS. Administrators; description of company's research environment; also part of *Surveys of Research Administration and Environment.*

For additional information, see 6:1167.

SELLING

[2395]

Aptitudes Associates Test of Sales Aptitude: A Test for Measuring Knowledge of Basic Principles of Selling. Applicants for sales positions; 1947-60; for a revised edition, see 2406; 1960 manual identical with manual copyrighted 1958 excerpt for format, modification in some normative tables, and extension of bibliography; Martin M. Bruce; Martin M. Bruce, Ph.D., Publishers. *

For additional information, see 6:1169 (6 references); for reviews by Milton E. Hahn and Donald G. Paterson, see 4:824. For reference to a review of the revised edition, see 2406.

REFERENCES THROUGH 1971

1-6. See 6:1169.

CUMULATIVE NAME INDEX

Bruce, M. M.: 1, 4　　　Rosen, J. C.: 3
Gray, E. J.: 3　　　　　Speer, G. S.: 5
Hahn, M. E.: *rev*, 4:824　United States Employment
Harless, B. B.: 4　　　　　Service: 2
Paterson, D. G.: *rev*, 4:824

[2396]

Combination Inventory, Form 2. Prospective debit life insurance salesmen; 1954-66; CI; 6 scores: arithmetic, general knowledge, sales aptitude (interest, reaction, personal history, total); interest items selected from *Strong Vocational Interest Blank for Men, Revised;* distribution restricted to home offices of member life insurance companies; Life Insurance Agency Management Association. *

For additional information, see 7:1123; see also 6:1170 (1 reference).

REFERENCES THROUGH 1971

1. See 6:1170.

CUMULATIVE NAME INDEX

Ferguson, L. W.: 1

[2397]

Detroit Retail Selling Inventory. Candidates for training in retail selling; 1940, c1939; 5 scores: personality, intelligence, checking, arithmetic, total; Harry J. Baker and Paul H. Voelker; Bobbs-Merrill Co., Inc. *

For additional information, reviews by Milton E. Hahn and Floyd L. Ruch, and excerpted reviews by William J. Jones and one other, see 3:697.

REFERENCES THROUGH 1971

1. BOUCK, WALTER C. *The Predictive Value of the Detroit Retail Selling Inventory for Success in the College of Business Administration at the University of Toledo.* Master's thesis, University of Toledo (Toledo, Ohio), 1953.
2. STOTSKY, BERNARD A. "Vocational Tests as Measures of Performance of Schizophrenics in Two Rehabilitation Activities." *J Clin Psychol* 12:236-42 Jl '56. * (*PA* 31:6447)

CUMULATIVE NAME INDEX

Bouck, W. C.: 1　　　　Ruch, F. L.: *rev*, 3:697
Hahn, M. E.: *rev*, 3:697　Stotsky, B. A.: 2
Jones, W. J.: *exc*, 3:697

[2398]

The Evaluation Record. Prospective life insurance agency managers; 1947-63; combination of evaluation procedures yielding a composite score; 3 parts; distribution restricted to home offices of member life insurance companies; Life Insurance Agency Management Association. *
a) EXPERIENCE FORM. Completed by candidates.
b) STRONG VOCATIONAL INTEREST BLANK FOR MEN. See 2212; scored for production manager only.
c) HOME OFFICE RATING CHART. Ratings of personal qualities by 1-3 supervisors.

For additional information, see 6:1172.

[2399]

Hall Salespower Inventory. Salesmen; 1946-57; test booklet title is *Salespower Inventory;* 10 scores: background, intelligence, aggressiveness, dominance, sales temperament, sales interest, introversion-extroversion, motivation, emotional, total; Clifton W. Hall and Richard M. Page; Hall & Liles. *

For additional information, see 5:924.

[2400]

Hanes Sales Selection Inventory, Revised Edition. Insurance and printing salesmen; 1954-55; 3 scores: verbal, personality, drive; Bernard Hanes; Psychometric Affiliates. *

For additional information and reviews by William E. Kendall and Albert K. Kurtz, see 6:1173.

[2401]

*Information Index. Life and health insurance agents; 1951–72; 2 editions; distribution restricted to home offices of member life and health insurance companies; Life Insurance Agency Management Association. *

a) LIFE EDITION. 1951–72; life insurance information.

b) HEALTH EDITION. 1966; health insurance information.

For additional information regarding an earlier edition of a, see 6:1174 (1 reference); see also 5:927 (3 references).

REFERENCES THROUGH 1971

1–3. See 5:927.
4. See 6:1174.
5. THAYER, PAUL W.; ANTOINETTI, JOHN A.; AND GUEST, THEODORE A. "Product Knowledge and Performance—A Study of Life Insurance Agents." Personnel Psychol 11:411–8 au '58. * (PA 33:11230)

CUMULATIVE NAME INDEX

Antoinetti, J. A.: 5   Guest, T. A.: 1, 5
Baier, D. E.: 2–4   Thayer, P. W.: 5
Dugan, R. D.: 2–4

[2402]

LIAMA Inventory of Job Attitudes. Life insurance field personnel; 1956–70; IJA; group measurement of company performance; job attitude scores in 10 areas; distribution restricted to home offices of member life insurance companies and research personnel; Life Insurance Agency Management Association. *

For additional information, see 7:1124.

[2403]

Personnel Institute Hiring Kit. Applicants for sales positions; 1954–62; 1957 manual identical with manual copyrighted 1956 except for one minor change; Personnel Institute, Inc. *

a) PRELIMINARY SCREENING INTERVIEW. 1957.

b) PERSONAL HISTORY INVENTORY. 1957–62; 1962 form identical with form copyrighted 1957.

c) DIAGNOSTIC INTERVIEWER'S GUIDE. 1956–57.

d) PERSONAL OR TELEPHONE WORK REFERENCE INVESTIGATION. 1957–59; formerly called Work Reference Investigation.

e) SELECTOR TEST BATTERY. Applicants for routine selling jobs; 1955–57; 3 tests.

1) EM-AY Inventory. Reprint of Otis Employment Tests, Test 2, Form A ('22); mental alertness.

2) ESS-AY Inventory. Sales aptitude.

3) The Personality Inventory. See 1320; 4 scores: extroversion, dominance, self-confidence, social dependence.

f) COMPREHENSIVE TEST BATTERY. Applicants for complex selling jobs; 1954–62; 6 tests.

1) Same as e(1) above.

2) Same as e(2) above.

3) Same as e(3) above.

4) Vocabulary Inventory. 1956 test identical with test copyrighted 1954.

5) ESS-EYE Inventory. Reprint of the SP (Special) Edition of the Social Intelligence Test: George Washington University Series, Revised Form ('47); 3 scores: social judgment, social observation, total.

6) B-B-ESS Inventory. Business skills; 8 scores: comparing, computation, reading, spelling, vocabulary, arithmetical reasoning, English, total; 1956 test identical with test copyrighted 1954.

For additional information, see 6:1176 (3 references).

REFERENCES THROUGH 1971

1–3. See 6:1176.
4. BRUCE, MARTIN MARC. The Importance of Certain Personality Characteristics, Skills and Abilities in Effectiveness as a

Factory Foreman. Doctor's thesis, New York University (New York, N.Y.), 1952. (DA 13:116)

CUMULATIVE NAME INDEX

Bruce, M. M.: 1–4

[2404]

SRA Sales Attitudes Check List. Applicants for sales positions; 1960; modification of Sales Personnel Description Form; Erwin K. Taylor and the Personnel Research & Development Corporation; Science Research Associates, Inc. *

For additional information and a review by John P. Foley, Jr., see 6:1177.

[2405]

*Sales Aptitude Test: ETSA Test 7A. Job applicants; 1960–72, c1957–59; 8 scores: sales judgment, interest in selling, personality factors, occupational identification, level of aspiration, insight into human nature, awareness of sales approach, total; manual and technical handbook by S. Trevor Hadley and George A. W. Stouffer, Jr.; test by Psychological Services Bureau; Educators'-Employers' Tests & Services Associates. * For the complete battery entry, see 2106.

For reviews of the complete battery, see 6:1025 (2 reviews).

[2406]

*Sales Comprehension Test. Applicants for sales positions; 1947–71; revision of the still-in-print Aptitudes Associates Test of Sales Aptitude; 1971 test identical with test copyrighted 1953 except for format and 1 new item; Martin M. Bruce; Martin M. Bruce, Ph.D., Publishers. *

For additional information, see 6:1178 (7 references); for a review by Raymond A. Katzell, see 5:947 (10 references). For reference to reviews of the original edition, see 2395.

REFERENCES THROUGH 1971

1–10. See 5:947.
11–17. See 6:1178.
18. BASS, BERNARD M. "Validity Information Exchange, No. 10-25: D.O.T. Code 1-85.22, Salesman, Foodstuffs." Personnel Psychol 10:343–4 au '57. *
19. BLANK, STANLEY S. "An Examination of the Usefulness of Various Psychological Instruments for Predicting Department Managers' Ratings of Clerical Sales Personnel." Can Counsellor 2:46–50 Ja '68. *
20. DEWITT, CHARLES JAY. A Study of Selected Variables in Discriminating Between Contrasting Levels of Student Teaching Performance. Doctor's thesis, University of Virginia (Charlottesville, Va.), 1969. (DAI 31:260A)

CUMULATIVE NAME INDEX

Albright, L. E.: 8, 10   Dugan, R. D.: 16
Aron, J.: 11   Friesen, E. P.: 4
Ash, P.: 14–5   Glennon, J. R.: 8, 10
Bass, B. M.: 17–8   Hecht, R.: 6, 11
Blank, S. S.: 19   Katzell, R. A.: rev, 5:947
Bruce, M. M.: 1–7, 9, 12–3   Murray, L. E.: 7, 12–3
DeWitt, C. J.: 20   Smith, W. J.: 8, 10

[2407]

*Sales Method Index. Life insurance agents; 1948–71; continuous work-diary record of specific sales procedures and effectiveness for supervisory and self-analysis; distribution restricted to home offices of member life insurance companies; Life Insurance Agency Management Association. *

[2408]

*Sales Motivation Inventory, Revised. Applicants for sales positions; 1953–69; SMI; Martin M. Bruce; Martin M. Bruce, Ph.D., Publishers. *

For additional information and a review by S. Rains Wallace, see 5:948 (2 references).

REFERENCES THROUGH 1971

1–2. See 5:948.
3. BRUCE, MARTIN M. "Normative Data Information Exchange, No. 12-24." *Personnel Psychol* 12:506 au '59. *
4. MURRAY, L. E., AND BRUCE, MARTIN M. "Normative Data Information Exchange, No. 12-18." *Personnel Psychol* 12:334 su '59. *
5. MURRAY, LESTER E., AND BRUCE, MARTIN M. "A Study of the Validity of the Sales Comprehension Test and Sales Motivation Inventory in Differentiating High and Low Production in Life Insurance Selling." *J Appl Psychol* 43:246–8 Ag '59. * (*PA* 34:6609)
6. BRAUN, JOHN R., AND ASTA, PATRICIA. "Effects of Faking Instructions on Sales Motivation Inventory Scores." *J Ed Meas* 5:339–40 w '68. * (*PA* 44:11210)
7. DEWITT, CHARLES JAY. *A Study of Selected Variables in Discriminating Between Contrasting Levels of Student Teaching Performance.* Doctor's thesis, University of Virginia (Charlottesville, Va.), 1969. (*DAI* 31:260A)

CUMULATIVE NAME INDEX

Asta, P.: 6
Braun, J. R.: 6
Bruce, M. M.: 1–5
DeWitt, C. J.: 7
Murray, L. E.: 2, 4–5
Wallace, S. R.: rev, 5:948

[2409]

The Sales Sentence Completion Blank. Applicants for sales positions; 1961; Norman Gekoski; Martin M. Bruce, Ph.D., Publishers. *

For additional information, a review by William E. Kendall, and an excerpted review by John O. Crites, see 6:1181.

[2410]

Steward Life Insurance Knowledge Test. Applicants for life insurance agent or supervisory positions; 1952–56; 5 scores: arithmetic, vocabulary, principles, functions, total; Verne Steward; Steward-Mortensen & Associates. *

For additional information, see 5:950.

[2411]

Steward Occupational Objectives Inventory, 1957 Edition. Applicants for supervisory positions in life insurance companies or agencies; 1956–57; formerly called *Steward Supervisory Personnel Inventory;* ratings in 8 areas: caliber level, life insurance knowledge, selling skills, leadership ability, supervisory skills, personal adjustment, survival on job, supplementary items; Verne Steward; Steward-Mortensen & Associates. *

For additional information, see 5:951.

[2412]

Steward Personal Background Inventory (1960 Revised Edition). Applicants for sales positions; 1949–60; revision of *Personal Inventory of Background Factors;* ratings of 5 factors (caliber, aptitude, adjustment, survival, supplementary) in 7 areas (health, education, experience, financial status, activities, family status, miscellaneous); 1960 manual identical with manual copyrighted 1957 except for minor changes; Verne Steward; Steward-Mortensen & Associates. *

For additional information and reviews by Leonard V. Gordon and Lyman W. Porter, see 6:1183.

[2413]

Test for Ability to Sell: George Washington University Series. Grades 7–16 and adults; 1929–50; F. A. Moss, Herbert Wyle, William Loman, William Middleton, Thelma Hunt, Robert George, and William Schnell; Center for Psychological Service. *

For additional information, see 4:829; for a review by Floyd L. Ruch, see 3:705.

[2414]

★Test of Retail Sales Insight. Retail clerks and students; 1960–71; TRSI; earlier form called *Test of Sales Insight;* 6 scores: sales knowledge, customer

motivation, merchandise procurement, sales promotion, sales closure, total; Russell Cassel; Psychologists and Educators, Inc. *

[Out of Print Since TIP I]

Aptitude Index Selection Procedure, 6:1168 (2 reviews, 21 references)
Bigelow Hiring Kit (status unknown), 4:826
Dealer Inventory (status unknown), 6:1171
How to Develop Sales Ability, T:2053
Interviewer's Impressions—Sales Applicants (status unknown), 6:1175
Measure of Consociative Tendency, 5:931
Personnel Research Institute Area Interview, T:2059
Sales Employee Inventory (status unknown), 6:1179
Sales Personnel Description Form, 6:1180 (1 review, 2 references)
Sales Situation Test, 4:827 (1 reference)
Test of Sales Ability, T:2074
Test of Sales Judgment (status unknown), 4:830
Word Check Forms (status unknown), 6:1184

SKILLED TRADES

[2415]

Electrical Sophistication Test. Job applicants; 1963–65; Stanley G. Ciesla; Psychometric Affiliates. *

For additional information and a review by Charles F. Ward, see 7:1125.

[2416]

The Fiesenheiser Test of Ability to Read Drawings. Trade school and adults; 1955; Elmer I. Fiesenheiser; Psychometric Affiliates. *

For additional information and a review by Joseph E. Moore, see 6:1186.

[2417]

*Mechanical Familiarity Test: ETSA Test 5A. Job applicants; 1960–72, c1957–59; manual and technical handbook by S. Trevor Hadley and George A. W. Stouffer, Jr.; test by Psychological Services Bureau; Educators'-Employers' Tests & Services Associates. * For the complete battery entry, see 2106.

For reviews of the complete battery, see 6:1025 (2 reviews).

[2418]

Mechanical Handyman Test. Maintenance workers; 1957–65; distribution restricted to member public personnel agencies and nonmember agencies approved by the publisher; International Personnel Management Association. *

For additional information, see 7:1126.

[2419]

*Mechanical Knowledge Test: ETSA Test 6A. Job applicants; 1960–72, c1957–59; manual and technical handbook by S. Trevor Hadley and George A. W. Stouffer, Jr.; test by Psychological Services Bureau; Educators'-Employers' Tests & Services Associates. * For the complete battery entry, see 2106.

For reviews of the complete battery, see 6:1025 (2 reviews).

[2420]

*Ohio Auto Body Achievement Test. Grades 11–12; 1969–73; OABAT; available only as a part of the *Ohio Trade and Industrial Education Achievement Test Program* (see 2431 for more complete information); 16 scores: welding, metal forming, body filler, refinishing, trim and hardware, parts replacement, alignment, glass replacement, fiber glass repair, frame and unit body, electrical system, cooling and conditioning, shop management, applied science, applied math, total; Instructional Materials Laboratory, Ohio State University. *

For additional information, see 7:1127.

[2421]

*Ohio Automotive Mechanics Achievement Test. Grades 11-12; 1959-73; OAMAT; available only as a part of the *Ohio Trade and Industrial Education Achievement Test Program* (see 2431 for more complete information); 15 scores: applied math, basic operations, general service, engine, cooling system, electrical system, applied science, fuel system, emission system, power train, suspension system, steering system, brakes, ventilation, total; Instructional Materials Laboratory, Ohio State University. *

[2422]

★Ohio Carpentry Achievement Test. Grades 11-12; 1970-73; OCAT; available only as a part of the *Ohio Trade and Industrial Education Achievement Test Program* (see 2431 for more complete information); 14 scores: orientation, blueprint reading, applied math, applied science, foundations, floor framing, roofing, insulation, exterior finish, interior finish, wall framing, roof framing, special operations, total; Instructional Materials Laboratory, Ohio State University. *

[2423]

★Ohio Communication Products Electronics Achievement Test. Grades 11-12; 1973; OCPEAT; available only as a part of the *Ohio Trade and Industrial Education Achievement Test Program* (see 2431 for more complete information); 12 scores: orientation, D/C electricity, A/C electricity, electron tubes, semi-conductors, vacuum tube and solid state circuitry, audio devices, receivers, transmitters, television, business practices, total; Instructional Materials Laboratory, Ohio State University.

[2424]

★Ohio Construction Electricity Achievement Test. Grades 11-12; 1973; OCEAT; available only as a part of the *Ohio Trade and Industrial Education Achievement Test Program* (see 2431 for more complete information); 19 scores: orientation, D/C electricity, magnetism, D/C power sources, D/C motors and controllers, instrumentation, A/C electricity, A/C circuits, three-phase A/C electricity, transformers, A/C motors and starters, electronics, planning and layout, branch circuits, wiring methods, lighting, heating and air conditioning, low-voltage systems, total; Instructional Materials Laboratory, Ohio State University.

[2425]

*Ohio Cosmetology Achievement Test. Grades 11-12; 1967-73; OCAT; available only as a part of the *Ohio Trade and Industrial Education Achievement Test Program* (see 2431 for more complete information); 14 scores: scalp, hands and feet, hair, hair tints and bleach, face information, facial, make-up, sanitation and bacteriology, applied science, anatomy and physiology, shop management, trade math, legal guidance, total; Instructional Materials Laboratory, Ohio State University. *

For additional information, see 7:1129.

[2426]

★Ohio Industrial Electronics Achievement Test. Grades 11-12; 1973; OIEAT; available only as a part of the *Ohio Trade and Industrial Education Achievement Test Program* (see 2431 for more complete information); 19 scores: orientation, D/C electricity, A/C electricity, electron tubes, semi-conductors, schematic drawings, power supplies, D/C timers, A/C timers, heavy current conductors, sequence timers, welding, sensors, heaters, magnetics, rotating machinery, servos, logic systems, total; Instructional Materials Laboratory, Ohio State University.

[2427]

*Ohio Machine Trades Achievement Test. Grades 11-12; 1958-73; OMTAT; available only as a part of the *Ohio Trade and Industrial Education Achievement Test Program* (see 2431 for more complete information); 18 scores: applied math, layout, hand tools, measuring, power sawing, drilling, shaping, heat treating, trade science, machining-lathe, milling, blueprint reading, grinding (bench, surface, tool and cutter, cylindrical, internal), total; Instructional Materials Laboratory, Ohio State University. *

For additional information, see 7:1130.

REFERENCES THROUGH 1971

1. KAPES, JEROME T., AND LONG, THOMAS E. "An Assessment of the Criterion-Related Validity of the Ohio Trade and Industrial Education Achievement Test Battery." *J Indus Teach Ed* 9(1):6-14 f '71. *
2. RAU, GERALD NORMAN. *The Relationship of Occupational Experience and Professional Preparation of Machine-Trades Teachers to the Achievement of Machine-Trades Students.* Doctor's thesis, University of Missouri (Columbia, Mo.), 1971. (*DAI* 32:3175A)

CUMULATIVE NAME INDEX

Kapes, J. T.: 1   Rau, G. N.: 2
Long, T. E.: 1

[2428]

*Ohio Mechanical Drafting Achievement Test. Grades 11-12; 1962-73; OMDAT; available only as a part of the *Ohio Trade and Industrial Education Achievement Test Program* (see 2431 for more complete information); 19 scores: materials and equipment, dimensioning, auxiliary views, threads and fasteners, production or working drawings, machine elements, auxiliary information, industrial processes, materials of industry, applied science, orthographic projection, sectional views, pictorial drawings, intersections and developments, goemetric drawing, lettering, reproduction of drawings, functions of mathematics, total; Instructional Materials Laboratory, Ohio State University. *

For additional information, see 7:1131.

REFERENCES THROUGH 1971

1. KAPES, JEROME T., AND LONG, THOMAS E. "An Assessment of the Criterion-Related Validity of the Ohio Trade and Industrial Education Achievement Test Battery." *J Indus Teach Ed* 9(1):6-14 f '71. *

CUMULATIVE NAME INDEX

Kapes, J. T.: 1   Long, T. E.: 1

[2429]

*Ohio Printing Achievement Test. Grades 11-12; 1963-73; OPAT; available only as a part of the *Ohio Trade and Industrial Education Achievement Test Program* (see 2431 for more complete information); 17 scores: orientation, printing planning, composition (hand, machine, photo), camera operation, film processing, letterpress (platemaking, presswork), applied science, lithograph (stripping and platemaking, presswork), bindery work, paper technology, ink technology, applied math, total; Instructional Materials Laboratory, Ohio State University. *

For additional information, see 7:1132.

REFERENCES THROUGH 1971

1. KAPES, JEROME T., AND LONG, THOMAS E. "An Assessment of the Criterion-Related Validity of the Ohio Trade and Industrial Education Achievement Test Battery." *J Indus Teach Ed* 9(1):6–14 f '71. *

CUMULATIVE NAME INDEX

Kapes, J. T.: 1   Long, T. E.: 1

[2430]

*Ohio Sheet Metal Achievement Test.** Grades 11–12; 1964–73; OSMAT; available only as a part of the *Ohio Trade and Industrial Education Achievement Test Program* (see 2431 for more complete information); 15 scores: blueprint reading, applied science, applied math, hand tool operations, machine operations, soldering, special operations, mechanical drawing, freehand sketching, metals, non-metallic, layout, fabricating, welding, total; Instructional Materials Laboratory, Ohio State University. *

For additional information, see 7:1133.

REFERENCES THROUGH 1971

1. KAPES, JEROME T., AND LONG, THOMAS E. "An Assessment of the Criterion-Related Validity of the Ohio Trade and Industrial Education Achievement Test Battery." *J Indus Teach Ed* 9(1):6–14 f '71. *

CUMULATIVE NAME INDEX

Kapes, J. T.: 1   Long, T. E.: 1

[2431]

*Ohio Trade and Industrial Education Achievement Test Program.** Grades 11–12; 1958–73; tests administered annually in March at participating schools; each student must take 2 tests: the intelligence test and a trade test; Instructional Materials Laboratory, Ohio State University.

a) INTELLIGENCE TEST. *Short Form Test of Academic Aptitude,* Level 5 (grades 9–12); see 458.

b) TRADE TESTS. 1958–73; 13 tests based on course outlines prepared for use in Ohio.

1) *Ohio Auto Body Achievement Test.* See 2420. *
2) *Ohio Automotive Mechanics Achievement Test.* See 2421. *
3) *Ohio Carpentry Achievement Test.* See 2422. *
4) *Ohio Cosmetology Achievement Test.* See 2425. *
5) *Ohio Dental Assisting Achievement Test.* See 2339. *
6) *Ohio Mechanical Drafting Achievement Test.* See 2428. *
7) *Ohio Construction Electricity Achievement Test.* See 2424.
8) *Ohio Communication Products Electronics Achievement Test.* See 2423.
9) *Ohio Industrial Electronics Achievement Test.* See 2426.
10) *Ohio Machine Trades Achievement Test.* See 2427. *
11) *Ohio Printing Achievement Test.* See 2429. *
12) *Ohio Sheet Metal Achievement Test.* See 2430. *
13) *Ohio Welding Achievement Test.* See 2432. *
For additional information, see 7:1134.

REFERENCES THROUGH 1971

1. KAPES, JEROME T., AND LONG, THOMAS E. "An Assessment of the Criterion-Related Validity of the Ohio Trade and Industrial Education Achievement Test Battery." *J Indus Teach Ed* 9(1):6–14 f '71. *

CUMULATIVE NAME INDEX

Kapes, J. T.: 1   Long, T. E.: 1

[2432]

*Ohio Welding Achievement Test.** Grades 11–12; 1969–73; OWAT; available only as a part of the *Ohio Trade and Industrial Education Achievement Test Program* (see 2431 for more complete information); 12 scores: blueprint reading, flame cutting, oxy-acetylene, arc welding, resistance welding, gas tungsten—arc welding process, gas metal arc welding, equipment, labor and management, applied math, applied science, total; Instructional Materials Laboratory, Ohio State University. *

For additional information, see 7:1135.

[2433]

Purdue Industrial Training Classification Test. Grades 9–12 and adults; 1942; shop mathematics; C. H. Lawshe and A. C. Moutoux; University Book Store. *

For additional information and reviews by D. Welty Lefever and Charles I. Mosier, see 3:675 (2 references).

REFERENCES THROUGH 1971

1–2. See 3:675.
3. LITTLETON, ISAAC T. "Prediction in Auto Trade Courses." *J Appl Psychol* 36:15–9 F '52. * (*PA* 26:7256)
4. LAWSHE, C. H., AND PATINKA, PAUL J. "An Empirical Comparison of Two Methods of Test Selection and Weighting." *J Appl Psychol* 42:210–2 Je '58. * (*PA* 33:9093)

CUMULATIVE NAME INDEX

Lawshe, C. H.: 1–2, 4   Mosier, C. I.: *rev,* 3:675
Lefever, D. W.: *rev,* 3:675   Patinka, P. J.: 4
Littleton, I. T.: 3   Thornton, G. R.: 2

[2434]

Purdue Interview Aids. Applicants for industrial employment; 1943; 3 tests; C. H. Lawshe; distributed by University Book Store. *

a) CAN YOU READ A WORKING DRAWING?
b) CAN YOU READ A MICROMETER?
c) CAN YOU READ A SCALE?

For additional information and a review by William W. Waite, see 4:775.

[2435]

Purdue Trade Information Test for Sheetmetal Workers. Sheetmetal workers; 1958; Joseph Tiffin, B. R. Modisette, and Warren B. Griffin; University Book Store. *

For additional information, see 5:942.

[2436]

Purdue Trade Information Test in Carpentry. Vocational school and adults; 1952; Joseph Tiffin and Robert F. Mengelkoch; University Book Store. *

For additional information and a review by P. L. Mellenbruch, see 5:943 (1 reference).

REFERENCES THROUGH 1971

1. See 5:943.

CUMULATIVE NAME INDEX

Mellenbruch, P. L.: *rev,*   Mengelkoch, R. F.: 1
5:943

[2437]

Purdue Trade Information Test in Engine Lathe Operation. Vocational school and adults; 1955; Robert Cochran and Joseph Tiffin; University Book Store. *

For additional information and a review by William J. Micheels, see 5:944.

[2438]

Purdue Trade Information Test in Welding, Revised Edition. Vocational school and adults; 1952;

Joseph Tiffin and Warren B. Griffin; distributed by University Book Store. *

For additional information, see 5:945.

REFERENCES THROUGH 1971

1. GRIFFIN, WARREN B. *A Trade Information Test for Welders.* Master's thesis, Purdue University (Lafayette, Ind.), 1952.

CUMULATIVE NAME INDEX

Griffin, W. B.: 1

[2439]

Short Occupational Knowledge Test for Auto Mechanics. Job applicants; 1969–70; score is pass, fail, or unclassifiable; Bruce A. Campbell and Suellen O. Johnson; Science Reasearch Associates, Inc.

For additional information and a review by Emory E. Wiseman, see 7:1137.

[2440]

Short Occupational Knowledge Test for Carpenters. Job applicants; 1969–70; score is pass, fail, or unclassifiable; Bruce A. Campbell and Suellen O. Johnson; Science Research Associates, Inc. *

For additional information, see 7:1138.

[2441]

Short Occupational Knowledge Test for Draftsmen. Job applicants; 1969–70; score is pass, fail, or unclassifiable; Bruce A. Campbell and Suellen O. Johnson; Science Research Associates, Inc. *

For additional information, see 7:1139.

[2442]

Short Occupational Knowledge Test for Electricians. Job applicants; 1969–70; score is pass, fail, or unclassifiable; Bruce A. Campbell and Suellen O. Johnson; Science Research Associates, Inc. *

For additional information and a review by Charles F. Ward, see 7:1140.

[2443]

Short Occupational Knowledge Test for Machinists. Job applicants; 1969–70; score is pass, fail, or unclassifiable; Bruce A. Campbell and Suellen O. Johnson; Science Research Associates, Inc. *

For additional information, see 7:1141.

[2444]

Short Occupational Knowledge Test for Plumbers. Job applicants; 1970; score is pass, fail, or unclassifiable; Bruce A. Campbell and Suellen O. Johnson; Science Research Associates, Inc. *

For additional information, see 7:1142.

[2445]

Short Occupational Knowledge Test for Tool and Die Makers. Job applicants; 1970; score is pass, fail, or unclassifiable; Bruce A. Campbell and Suellen O. Johnson; Science Research Associates, Inc. *

For additional information, see 7:1143.

[2446]

Short Occupational Knowledge Test for Welders. Job applicants; 1969–70; score is pass, fail, or unclassifiable; Bruce A. Campbell and Suellen O. Johnson; Science Research Associates, Inc. *

For additional information, see 7:1144.

[2447]

Technical Tests. Standards 6–8 (ages 13–15); 1962; 5 scores: arithmetic, mechanical insight, spatial relations (2 scores), tool test; Human Sciences Research Council [South Africa]. *

For additional information, see 6:1187.

Purdue Trade Information Test in Welding

[Out of Print Since TIP I]

Automotive Mechanic Test, 6:1185
Garage Mechanic Test, 5:573
Ohio Basic Electricity and Electronics Achievement Tests, 7:1128
Purdue Blueprint Reading Test, 4:782
Purdue Test for Electricians, 7:1136 (2 reviews)
Purdue Test for Machinists and Machine Operators, 4:816 (1 review)
Written Trade Tests, 6:1188

SUPERVISION

[2448]

*How Supervise? Supervisors; 1943–71; Quentin W. File and H. H. Remmers (manual); Psychological Corporation. (Australian edition: Australian Council for Educational Research [Australia]). *

For additional information and a review by Joel T. Campbell, see 6:1189 (9 references); see also 5:926 (18 references); for a review by Milton M. Mandell, see 4:774 (8 references); for reviews by D. Welty Lefever, Charles I. Mosier, and C. H. Ruedisili, see 3:687 (5 references).

REFERENCES THROUGH 1971

1–5. See 3:687.
6–13. See 4:774.
14–31. See 5:926.
32–40. See 6:1189.
41. WYLAND, ROBERT R. "A Way to Measure the Results of Supervisory Training." *Factory Mgmt & Maint* 110:110–1 Ja '52. * (*PA* 26:6588)
42. DI VESTA, FRANCIS J. "Instructor-Centered and Student-Centered Approaches in Teaching a Human Relations Course." *J Appl Psychol* 38:329–35 O '54. * (*PA* 29:6161)
43. JOHNSON, ROSSALL J. "Relationship of Employee Morale to Ability to Predict Responses." *J Appl Psychol* 38:320–3 O '54. * (*PA* 29:6372)
44. BASS, BERNARD M. "Validity Information Exchange, No. 10–25: D.O.T. Code 1-85.22, Salesman, Foodstuffs." *Personnel Psychol* 10:343–4 au '57. *
45. MOSEL, JAMES N., AND TSACNARIS, HARRY J. "Evaluating the Supervisors Training Program." *Eng & Ind Psychol* 1:18–23 sp '59. * (*PA* 34:4852)
46. DICKEN, CHARLES F., AND BLACK, JOHN D. "Predictive Validity of Psychometric Evaluations of Supervisors." *J Appl Psychol* 49:34–47 F '65. * (*PA* 39:8793)
47. HESTER, EDWARD J. *A New Method of Scoring the How Supervise Test.* Master's thesis, Loyola University (Chicago, Ill.), 1965.
48. PEARSON, WILLIAM W. *Creating Change in Performance of Supervisors in the Electrical Trades Through Human Relations Training.* Doctor's thesis, New York University (New York, N.Y.), 1967. (*DA* 28:4749B)
49. PARRY, MARY ELLEN. "Ability of Psychologists to Estimate Validities of Personnel Tests." *Personnel Psychol* 21:139–47 su '68. * (*PA* 42:14727)
50. RONAN, W. W. "Evaluation of Three Criteria of Management Performance." *J Indus Psychol* 5(1):18–28 Mr '70. * (*PA* 45:7148)
51. HAYES, WILLIAM G., AND WILLIAMS, EUGENE I. "Supervisory Training—An Index of Change." *Training & Develop J* 25(4):34–8 Ap '71. *

CUMULATIVE NAME INDEX

Albright, L. E.: 34–5	Hayes, W. G.: 51
Barthol, R. P.: 25	Hester, E. J.: 47
Bass, B. M.: 44	Hilton, A. C.: 32
Belman, H. S.: 10–1	Holmes, F. J.: 14
Black, J. D.: 46	Johnson, R. J.: 23, 43
Bolin, S. F.: 32	Jurgensen, C. E.: 7
Campbell, J. T.: *rev*, 6:1189	Karn, H. W.: 8
Canter, R. R.: 12	Katzell, R. A.: 6
Carter, G. C.: 16	Kirchner, W. K.: 31
Cook, J. M.: 28	Lefever, D. W.: *rev*, 3:687
Decker, R. L.: 26, 36	McCormick, E. J.: 27
Dicken, C. F.: 46	Maloney, P. W.: 17
Di Vesta, F. J.: 42	Mandell, M. M.: *rev*, 4:774
Dunn, R. E.: 37	Meyer, H. H.: 33
Dunnette, M. D.: 31	Middaugh, R. W.: 27
Evans, R. N.: 10–1	Millard, K. A.: 18
Farbro, P. C.: 28	Miller, F. G.: 15
File, Q. W.: 1–3	Mosel, J. N.: 45
Glennon, J. R.: 34–5	Mosier, C. I.: *rev*, 3:687

Mowry, H. W.: 29
Neel, R. G.: 37
Nuckols, R. C.: 21
Parker, J. W.: 32
Parry, M. E.: 49
Patton, W. M.: 24
Pearson, W. W.: 48
Pond, B. B.: 13
Remmers, H. H.: 3, 9, 15
Remmers, L. J.: 9
Ronan, W. W.: 50
Rosen, N. A.: 38–9
Ruedisili, C. H.: *rev*, 3:687

Sartain, A. Q.: 4
Saunders, W. J.: 30
Slocombe, C. S.: 2, 5
Smith, W. J.: 34–5
Taylor, E. K.: 32
Tsacnaris, H. J.: 45
Walker, W. B.: 32
Weitz, J.: 21
Wickert, F. R.: 19–20
Wiener, D. N.: 40
Williams, E. I.: 51
Wyland, R. R.: 41
Zeigler, M.: 25

[2449]

Ideal Leader Behavior Description Questionnaire. Supervisors; 1957; ILBDQ; employee ratings of a supervisor; test booklet title is *Ideal Leader Behavior (What You Expect of Your Leader)*; same as *Leader Behavior Description Questionnaire* except that the responses indicate what a supervisor ought to be rather than what he is; original edition by John K. Hemphill and Alvin E. Coons; current edition by Personnel Research Board, Ohio State University; University Publications Sales, Ohio State University. *

For additional information, see 7:1145 (10 references).

REFERENCES THROUGH 1971

1–10. See 7:1145.
11. MORROW, HOWARD GLENN. *Consensus of Observed Leader Behavior and Role Expectations of the Elementary School Principal.* Doctor's thesis, University of Oklahoma (Norman, Okla.), 1970. (*DAI* 31:5856A)
12. DALTON, SAMUEL L. *Perception of the Leadership Behavior of the School Business Manager: A Team Approach.* Doctor's thesis, Miami University (Coral Gables, Fla.), 1971. (*DAI* 32:2338A)
13. JOHNSON, MARY MAGDALENE. *Role Expectations That Supervisors, Teachers and Elementary School Principals Have for the Supervisor of Special Classes for Mentally Retarded Children.* Doctor's thesis, University of Maryland (College Park, Md.), 1971. (*DAI* 32:3613A)
14. MCLENNAN, THOMAS DAVID. *An Analysis of the Leader Behavior Preferences of Selected Suburban Residents From Three Socio-Economic Levels.* Doctor's thesis, Wayne State University (Detroit, Mich.), 1971. (*DAI* 32:2358A)
15. REED, ROY LAWRENCE. *A Study of Relationships Among Certain Aspects of Teacher Perceived Role Discrepancies of Western New York Secondary Principals, Teachers' Stated Satisfaction With Work, and Certain Self-Reported Factual Data About Teachers.* Doctor's thesis, State University of New York (Buffalo, N.Y.), 1971. (*DAI* 32:1808A)
16. SWENSON, JAMES KENNETH. *An Analysis of Leader Behavior and Organizational Climate of the Central Office Administration in a North Dakota School District.* Doctor's thesis, University of North Dakota (Grand Forks, N.D.), 1971. (*DAI* 33:128A)

CUMULATIVE NAME INDEX

Beer, M.: 6
Black, D. O.: 9
Bryant, G. W.: 8
Coady, N. P.: 10
Dalton, S. L.: 12
Gott, C. M.: 7
Halpin, A. W.: 1, 3
Hemphill, J. K.: 2, 4

Johnson, M. M.: 13
Luckie, W. R.: 5
McLennan, T. D.: 14
Morrow, H. G.: 11
Reed, R. L.: 15
Stogdill, R. M.: 10
Swenson, J. K.: 16

[2450]

★**In-Basket Test.** Applicants for high level executive positions; 1961–66; managerial ability; no manual; National Institute for Personnel Research [South Africa]. *

[2451]

Leader Behavior Description Questionnaire. Supervisors; 1957; LBDQ; for a later edition, see 2452; employee ratings of a supervisor; 2 scores: consideration, initiating structure; scores are based upon responses by 4 to 10 raters; original edition by John K. Hemphill and Alvin E. Coons; manual by Andrew W. Halpin; current edition by Personnel Research Board, Ohio State University; University Publications Sales, Ohio State University. *

For additional information, see 7:1146 (108 references).

REFERENCES THROUGH 1971

1–108. See 7:1146.
109. FLEISHMAN, EDWIN A. *The Relationship Between Leadership Climate and Supervisory Behavior.* Doctor's thesis, Ohio State University (Columbus, Ohio), 1951.
110. HALPIN, ANDREW W. "The Superintendent's Effectiveness as a Leader." *Administrator's Notebook* 7(2):1–4 O '58. *
111. BAILEY, BENJAMIN H. "Personality Rigidity, Patterns of Operation and Leadership Effectiveness of Secondary School Principals." *Fla J Ed Res* 2:1–7 Ja '60. *
112. BARNHART, ALVIN E., AND WISCH, PAUL J. "Perceptual Behavior Patterns and the Influence of Value Systems." *J Res Services* 4:9–14 D '64. *
113. STOGDILL, RALPH M.; GOODE, OMAR S.; AND DAY, DAVID R. "The Leader Behavior of Presidents of Labor Unions." *Personnel Psychol* 17:49–57 sp '64. * (*PA* 39:2971)
114. CROFT, JOHN C. "Dogmatism and Perceptions of Leader Behavior." *Ed Adm Q* 1:60–71 au '65. *
115. THORNTON, MERVIN F. *Values and the Perception of Leader Behavior.* Master's thesis, University of Alberta (Edmonton, Alta., Canada), 1967.
116. LOWIN, AARON; HRAPCHAK, WILLIAM J.; AND KAVANAGH, MICHAEL J. "Consideration and Initiating Structure: An Experimental Investigation of Leadership Traits." *Adm Sci Q* 14(2):238–53 Je '69. * (*PA* 44:11503)
117. COOK, RICHARD PAUL. *The Relationship of Principal Leader Behavior and Teacher Morale to Certain Other Variables in Selected Urban Elementary Schools.* Doctor's thesis, Purdue University (Lafayette, Ind.), 1970. (*DAI* 31:5063A)
118. COTTRELL, DAVID ALTON. *The Relationship Between Superintendents' Role Conflict Resolution Orientation and Their Perceived Leader Behavior.* Doctor's thesis, University of Akron (Akron, Ohio), 1970. (*DAI* 32:119A)
119. DOWNEY, RICHARD DELAINE. *A Study of the Leader Behavior of Special Education Administrators in Illinois Public Schools.* Doctor's thesis, Southern Illinois University (Carbondale, Ill.), 1970. (*DAI* 31:5065A)
120. GREEN, PAUL C., JR. *The Effectiveness of Supervisory Style When Leader, Group and Situational Variables Are Considered.* Doctor's thesis, Memphis State University (Memphis, Tenn.), 1970. (*DAI* 31:7659B)
121. JOHNSON, PAUL O'NEAL. *Relationships Between the Morale of Georgia Extension Agents and the Leader Behavior of Georgia County Agent Chairman.* Doctor's thesis, University of Georgia (Athens, Ga.), 1970. (*DAI* 31:5748A)
122. LUCIETTO, LENA L. "Speech Patterns of Administrators." *Administrator's Notebook* 18(5):1–4 Ja '70. *
123. MAGLARAS, TOM. *Leadership Traits and Characteristics of Principals in Secondary Schools of Varying Degrees of Effectiveness.* Doctor's thesis, University of Colorado (Boulder, Colo.), 1970. (*DAI* 31:4423A)
124. MORROW, HOWARD GLENN. *Consensus of Observed Leader Behavior and Role Expectations of the Elementary School Principal.* Doctor's thesis, University of Oklahoma (Norman, Okla.), 1970. (*DAI* 31:5856A)
125. OBORNY, WILLIAM JOSEPH. *The Relationship of Teachers' Perceptions of Their Professionalism, the Organizational Structure of Schools, and the Leadership Behavior of Their Principals.* Doctor's thesis, Oklahoma State University (Stillwater, Okla.), 1970. (*DAI* 31:5090A)
126. SULLIVAN, BLOOMER DON. *The Correlates of Leadership Behavior of Chief Administrative Officers in Selected Junior Colleges.* Doctor's thesis, University of Missouri (Columbia, Mo.), 1970. (*DAI* 31:5736A)
127. VROOMAN, THEODORE HERBERT. *The Perceptions and Expectations of Superintendents and Their High School Principals With Regard to Leadership Style and Delegated Formal Task-Performance.* Doctor's thesis, Syracuse University (Syracuse, N.Y.), 1970. (*DAI* 31:6326A)
128. BEATTY, RICHARD W. "First- and Second-Level Supervision and the Job Performance of the Hard-Core Unemployed." Abstract. *Proc 79th Ann Conv Am Psychol Assn* 6(1):479–80 '71. * (*PA* 46:5873)
129. BRICKNER, CHARLES ELIAS. *An Analysis of Organizational Climate and Leader Behavior in a North Dakota School System.* Doctor's thesis, University of North Dakota (Grand Forks, N.D.), 1971. (*DAI* 33:96A)
130. CORPUS, MARY CYRIL. *Leader Behavior, Teachers' Behavior, and Organizational Climate in St. Paul Secondary Schools.* Doctor's thesis, Catholic University of America (Washington, D.C.), 1971. (*DAI* 32:1214A)
131. DALTON, SAMUEL L. *Perception of the Leadership Behavior of the School Business Manager: A Team Approach.* Doctor's thesis, Miami University (Coral Gables, Fla.), 1971. (*DAI* 32:2338A)
132. GILLESPIE, JOHN OWEN. *Administrative Theory and Policy Patterns of Secondary School Administrators as Factors in Administrative Performance.* Doctor's thesis, West Virginia University (Morgantown, W.Va.), 1971. (*DAI* 32:4283A)
133. HOUSE, ROBERT J.; FILLEY, ALAN C.; AND GUJARATI, DAMODAR N. "Leadership Style, Hierarchical Influence, and the

Satisfaction of Subordinate Role Expectations: A Test of Likert's Influence Proposition." *J Appl Psychol* 55(5):422–32 O '71. * (*PA* 47:7914)

134. HOUSE, ROBERT J.; FILLEY, ALAN C.; AND KERR, STEVEN. "Relation of Leader Consideration and Initiating Structure to R and D Subordinates' Satisfaction." *Adm Sci Q* 16(1):19–30 Mr '71. *

135. LANDSWERK, DAVID RICHARD. *A Study of the Self Perceptions of School Executives and Their Perceptions of Corporate Executives, and the Self Perceptions of Corporate Executives and Their Perceptions of School Executives in Owatonna, Minnesota.* Doctor's thesis, University of Iowa (Iowa City, Iowa), 1971. (*DAI* 32:1229A)

136. LONG, CLIFFORD DAYTON. *Leader Behavior as Perceived by Junior College Professionals.* Doctor's thesis, University of Tulsa (Tulsa, Okla.), 1971. (*DAI* 32:1231A)

137. MCGHEE, PAUL RALPH. *An Investigation of the Relationship Between Principals' Decision-Making Attitudes, Leader Behavior and Teacher Grievances in Public Schools.* Doctor's thesis, Syracuse University (Syracuse, N.Y.), 1971. (*DAI* 32: 4294A)

138. OUSLEY, JACK M. *Behavior Patterns and Operational Effectiveness of Foremen: An Inter-Organizational Analysis.* Doctor's thesis, Boston University (Boston, Mass.), 1971. (*DAI* 32:1833A)

139. REED, ROY LAWRENCE. *A Study of Relationships Among Certain Aspects of Teacher Perceived Role Discrepancies of Western New York Secondary Principals, Teachers' Stated Satisfaction With Work, and Certain Self-Reported Factual Data About Teachers.* Doctor's thesis, State University of New York (Buffalo, N.Y.), 1971. (*DAI* 32:1808A)

140. SIMPSON, DOUGLAS BARRY. *Leadership Behavior, Need Satisfactions, and Role Perceptions of Labor Leaders: A Behavorial Analysis.* Doctor's thesis, University of Washington (Seattle, Wash.), 1971. (*DAI* 32:2248A)

141. SWENSON, JAMES KENNETH. *An Analysis of Leader Behavior and Organizational Climate of the Central Office Administration in a North Dakota School District.* Doctor's thesis, University of North Dakota (Grand Forks, N.D.), 1971. (*DAI* 33: 128A)

142. WALTER, JOHN EDWARD. *The Relationships Between the Personality Characteristics, Personal Factors, and Effectiveness of Community School Directors.* Doctor's thesis, Utah State University (Logan, Utah), 1971. (*DAI* 32:3644A)

143. WASDYKE, RAYMOND G. *Self Role Perception and Leadership Behavior of Area Vocational School Principals in New Jersey.* Doctor's thesis, Rutgers—The State University (New Brunswick, N.J.), 1971. (*DAI* 33:129A)

[2452]

Leader Behavior Description Questionnaire, Form 12. Supervisors; 1957–63; LBDQ–12; revision of still-in-print *Leader Behavior Description Questionnaire* with 10 additional scores; for research use only; employee ratings of a supervisor; 12 scores: representation, demand reconciliation, tolerance of uncertainty, persuasiveness, initiation of structure, tolerance of freedom, role assumption, consideration, production emphasis, predictive accuracy, integration, superior orientation; scores are based upon responses of 4 to 10 raters; original edition by John K. Hemphill and Alvin E. Coons; manual by Ralph M. Stogdill; current edition by Bureau of Business Research, Ohio State University; University Publications Sales, Ohio State University. *

For additional information, see 7:1147 (48 references).

REFERENCES THROUGH 1971

1–48. See 7:1147.

49. STOGDILL, RALPH M.; GOODE, OMAR S.; AND DAY, DAVID R. "The Leader Behavior of Presidents of Labor Unions." *Personnel Psychol* 17:49–57 sp '64. * (*PA* 39:2971)

50. STOGDILL, RALPH M.; IN COLLABORATION WITH DAVID R. DAY, DONALD A. GAAL, NORMAN GEORGE, AND OMAR S. GOODE. *Managers, Employees, Organizations: A Study of 27 Organizations.* Bureau of Business Research Monograph No. 125. Columbus, Ohio: Bureau of Business Research, Ohio State University, 1965. Pp. xiii, 315. *

51. SERGIOVANNI, THOMAS J.; METZCUS, RICHARD; AND BURDEN, LARRY. "Toward a Particularistic Approach to Leadership Style: Some Findings." *Am Ed Res J* 6(1):62–79 Ja '69. * (*PA* 44:13356)

52. FEITLER, FRED CROOHE. *A Study of Relationships Between Principal Leadership Styles and Organizational Characteristics of Elementary Schools.* Doctor's thesis, Syracuse University (Syracuse, N.Y.), 1970. (*DAI* 32:123A)

53. SCHOTT, JAMES LAWRENCE. *The Leader Behavior of Non-White Principals in Inner-City Elementary Schools With Integrated Teaching Staffs Under Conditions of High and Low Morale.* Doctor's thesis, Purdue University (Lafayette, Ind.), 1970. (*DAI* 31:5097A)

54. BRAINARD, STEPHEN RICHARD. *Correlates of Leadership Effectiveness in Personnel Assistants.* Doctor's thesis, University of Missouri (Columbia, Mo.), 1971. (*DAI* 32:2542A)

55. CELASCHI, DONALD ALBERT. *The Relationships Between the Receptivity-to-Change of Public Elementary School Principals in Montgomery County and Their Ages, Sex, and Lengths of Tenure in Their Present Positions.* Doctor's thesis, American University (Washington, D.C.), 1971. (*DAI* 32:6703A)

56. DOW, JOHN, JR. *A Comparative Study of Inner-City Elementary Teachers' and Principals' Perceptions of and Role Expectations for the Leadership Behavior of Selected Inner-City Elementary Principals.* Doctor's thesis, Michigan State University (East Lansing, Mich.), 1971. (*DAI* 32:4869A)

57. FOLEY, GERALD FRANCIS. *A Study of the Relationships Between Team Leaders' Leadership Behavior and the Morale and Effectiveness of Their Team Members.* Doctor's thesis, State University of New York (Buffalo, N.Y.), 1971. (*DAI* 32: 2944A)

58. FULTINEER, JAMES DEAN. *School Principals Look at Leader Behavior: The Problem of Interpersonal Needs.* Doctor's thesis, West Virginia University (Morgantown, W.Va.), 1971. (*DAI* 32:6036A)

59. GUBASTA, JOSEPH LEE. *The Leader and Planning Behaviors of College and University Chief Executives.* Doctor's thesis, University of Wisconsin (Madison, Wis.), 1971. (*DAI* 32:5497A)

60. HEFTY, JOHN CHARLES. *The Relationships Between the Value Orientations, Leader Behavior, and Effectiveness of Secondary School Principals in Selected Middle Sized School Systems.* Doctor's thesis, University of Wisconsin (Madison, Wis.), 1971. (*DAI* 32:4286A)

61. LEDGERWOOD, LESLIE BRYANT. *An Analysis of the Leader Behavior of Middle Managers in Selected Public Four-Year Colleges.* Doctor's thesis, University of Oklahoma (Norman, Okla.), 1971. (*DAI* 32:1881A)

62. NULL, ELDON J., AND SMEAD, WILLIAM H. "Relationships Between the Political Orientation of Superintendents and Their Leader Behavior as Perceived by Subordinates." *J Ed Res* 65(3): 103–6 N '71. * (*PA* 48:1776)

63. PRYER, MARGARET W., AND DISTEFANO, M. K., JR. "Perceptions of Leadership Behavior, Job Satisfaction, and Internal-External Control Across Three Nursing Levels." *Nursing Res* 20(6):534–7 N–D '71. * (*PA* 48:3086)

64. SOLBACH, M. THERESA. *Elementary School Principals' Perception of Their Administrative Performance as Related to Their Staff's Perception of Their Leader Behavior.* Doctor's thesis, Purdue University (Lafayette, Ind.), 1971. (*DAI* 32:2983A)

65. SPENCE, BETTY A. *Sex of Teachers as a Factor in Their Perception of Selected Leadership Characteristics of Male and Female Elementary School Principals.* Doctor's thesis, Purdue University (Lafayette, Ind.), 1971. (*DAI* 32:2985A)

66. VAN MEIER, EDWARD JAMES, JR. *Leadership Behavior of Male and Female Elementary Principals.* Doctor's thesis, Northern Illinois University (DeKalb, Ill.), 1971. (*DAI* 32:3643A)

67. WHITE, RICHARD KENNETH. *The Relationship Among Secondary School Teachers' and Departmental Chairmen's Educational Attitudes, Teacher Perceptions of Leadership Style, and Teacher Ratings of the Chairman.* Doctor's thesis, New York University (New York, N.Y.), 1971. (*DAI* 33:131A)

CUMULATIVE NAME INDEX

[2453]

Leadership Evaluation and Development Scale. Prospective supervisors; 1964–65; LEADS; Harley W. Mowry (question booklet and casebook, from materials prepared by the Armstrong Cork Company); Psychological Services, Inc. *

For additional information and a review by Cecil A. Gibb, see 7:1148 (1 reference).

REFERENCES THROUGH 1971

1. See 7:1148.

Gibb, C. A.: *rev,* 7:1148   Tenopyr, M. L.: 1

[2454]

Leadership Opinion Questionnaire. Supervisors and prospective supervisors; 1960–69; LOQ; 2 scores: consideration, structure; Edwin A. Fleishman; Science Research Associates, Inc. *

For additional information and a review by Cecil A. Gibb, see 7:1149 (41 references); for reviews by Jerome E. Doppelt and Wayne K. Kirchner, see 6:1190 (6 references).

REFERENCES THROUGH 1971

1–6. See 1190.

7–47. See 7:1149.

48. FLEISHMAN, EDWIN A. *The Relationship Between Leadership Climate and Supervisory Behavior.* Doctor's thesis, Ohio State University (Columbus, Ohio), 1951.

49. ARKOFF, ABE, AND SHEARS, LOYDA M. "Conceptions of 'Ideal' Leadership in Accepted and Rejected Principal Training Candidates." *J Ed Res* 55:71–4 O '61. *

50. PERRY, SIMON D., AND WARD, GEORGE, II. "An Evaluation of the Leadership Opinion Questionnaire as Related to Dogmatism and Authoritarianism." *Proc W Va Acad Sci* 35(1963): 216–8 '64. *

51. ASQUITH, RONALD H., AND HEDLUND, DALVA E. "Laboratory Training and Supervisory Attitudes." *Psychol Rep* 20:618 Ap '67. * (*PA* 41:9496)

52. BONS, PAUL M.; BASS, ALAN R.; AND KOMORITA, S. S. "Changes in Leadership Style as a Function of Military Experience and Type of Command." *Personnel Psychol* 23(4):551–68 w '70. * (*PA* 46:7893)

53. CUMMINS, ROBERT CRAIG. *An Investigation of a Model of Leadership Effectiveness.* Doctor's thesis, Purdue University (Lafayette, Ind.), 1970. (*DAI* 31:6313B)

54. FLORESTANO, THOMAS E. *The Relationship of College Leadership and Post-College Leadership as Measured by the Leadership Opinion Questionnaire and a Leadership Inventory.* Doctor's thesis, University of Maryland (College Park, Md.), 1970. (*DAI* 32:173A)

55. STELTER, MERVYN WALTER. *Changes in Self-Perception, Interpersonal Orientation, and View of the Nature of Man of Residence Hall Personnel.* Doctor's thesis, East Texas State University (Commerce, Tex.), 1970. (*DAI* 31:4476A)

56. BEATTY, RICHARD W. "First- and Second-Level Supervision and the Job Performance of the Hard-Core Unemployed." Abstract. *Proc 79th Ann Conv Am Psychol Assn* 6(1):479–80 '71. * (*PA* 46:5873)

57. CUMMINS, ROBERT C. "Relationship of Initiating Structure and Job Performance as Moderated by Consideration." *J Appl Psychol* 55(5):489–90 O '71. * (*PA* 47:7898)

58. DENNIS, JAMES MERCER. *Administrative Behavior of Successful and Unsuccessful Athletic Directors in Small Colleges and Universities.* Doctor's thesis, University of Southern California (Los Angeles, Calif.), 1971. (*DAI* 32:5015A)

59. NIEBUHR, HAROLD EMIL. *Effects of Short Term Rational Counseling in an Industrial Setting.* Doctor's thesis, East Texas State University (Commerce, Tex.), 1971. (*DAI* 32:5551A)

60. OUSLEY, JACK M. *Behavior Patterns and Operational Effectiveness of Foremen: An Inter-Organizational Analysis.* Doctor's thesis, Boston University (Boston, Mass.), 1971. (*DAI* 32:1833A)

61. TRANG, MYRON LEE. *The Effects of a Small Group Leadership Experience Upon Selected Upper Division Education Students at Washington State University.* Doctor's thesis, Washington State University (Pullman, Wash.), 1971. (*DAI* 32:4386A)

62. TURNER, JOHN NICHOLAS. *Relationship Between Supervisors' Orientation and Correlations Between Ratings Given and Objective Production Data.* Doctor's thesis, Wayne State University (Detroit, Mich.), 1971. (*DAI* 32:3052B)

CUMULATIVE NAME INDEX

Litzinger, W. D.: 11, 18
McClung, J. A.: 24
McNamara, W. J.: 17, 34, 41
Mann, W. G.: 44
Niebuhr, H. E.: 59
Oaklander, H.: 16
Ousley, J. M.: 60
Parker, T. C.: 9, 12
Peirce, J. R.: 47
Penfield, R. V.: 25
Perry, S. D.: 50
Peters, D. R.: 6
Rim, Y.: 19
Rowland, K. M.: 30
Schenk, K. N.: 38
Scott, W. E.: 30

Seiler, D. A.: 31
Shears, L. M.: 49
Siegel, J. P.: 32
Skinner, E. W.: 39
Spitzer, M. E.: 17
Stanton, E. S.: 5
Stelter, M. W.: 55
Stephenson, H. B.: 26
Tenopyr, M. L.: 40
Trang, M. L.: 61
Turner, J. N.: 62
Ward, G.: 50
Weissenberg, P.: 22, 27
Wollowick, H. B.: 41
Yeager, J. C.: 42

[2455]

★**Leadership Practices Inventory.** Supervisors; 1955–67; LPI; for use with the author's management development program in leadership and communication; 2 scores (desirable practices marked as ideal, desirable practices marked as in actual practice) for each of: 4 leadership styles (using style answer form), 5 management areas (using area answer form), and 2 derived totals; Charles W. Nelson; Management Research Associates. *

[2456]

Managerial Scale for Enterprise Improvement. Supervisors; 1955; job satisfaction; Herbert A. Kaufman, Jr.; Psychometric Affiliates. *
For additional information and reviews by Brent Baxter and Edward B. Greene, see 5:930.

[2457]

The RAD Scales. Supervisors; 1957; RAD; self-ratings of perceived degrees of responsibility, authority, and delegation of authority; 3 scores: responsibility, authority, delegation; Ralph M. Stogdill; University Publications Sales, Ohio State University. *
For additional information, see 7:1150 (20 references).

REFERENCES THROUGH 1971
1-20. See 7:1150.
21. BROWNE, C. G. "Study of Executive Leadership in Business: 4, Sociometric Pattern." *J Appl Psychol* 35:34-7 F '51. * (PA 25:7151)
22. OTIS, JAY L.; CAMPBELL, JOEL; AND PRIEN, ERIC. Sect. 7, "Leadership Characteristics of Chief Executives," pp. 149-77. In *Small Business Success: Operating and Executive Characteristics: A Study of 110 Successful Metalworking Plants in Ohio.* Edited by Kenneth Lawyer. Cleveland, Ohio: Bureau of Business Research, School of Business, Western Reserve University, 1963. Pp. xii, 183. *
23. STOGDILL, RALPH M.; IN COLLABORATION WITH DAVID R. DAY, DONALD A. GAAL, NORMAN GEORGE AND OMAR S. GOODE. *Managers, Employees, Organizations: A Study of 27 Organizations.* Bureau of Business Research Monograph No. 125. Columbus, Ohio: Bureau of Business Research, Ohio State University, 1965. Pp. xiii, 315. *
24. DENNIS, JAMES MERCER. *Administrative Behavior of Successful and Unsuccessful Athletic Directors in Small Colleges and Universities.* Doctor's thesis, University of Southern California (Los Angeles, Calif.), 1971. (DAI 32:5015A)
25. PFANSTIEL, EVERETT EARL, JR. *A Discriminant Analysis of the Orientation of Principals and Teachers in Changing and Stable Schools.* Doctor's thesis, University of Kentucky (Lexington, Ky.), 1971. (DAI 32:4898A)

CUMULATIVE NAME INDEX
Bowman, H. J.: 14
Browne, C. G.: 1, 3-4, 21
Campbell, D. T.: 6
Campbell, J.: 22
Coons, A. E.: 11
Day, D. R.: 23
Dennis, J. M.: 24
Fleishmann, E. A.: 7
Gaal, D. A.: 23
George, N.: 23
Glogau, L. F.: 18
Goode, O. S.: 23
Jaynes, W. E.: 10-2

Morsink, H. M.: 15
Neitzel, B. J.: 4
Otis, J. L.: 22
Pfanstiel, E. E.: 25
Prien, E.: 22
Schroeder, G. B.: 19
Scott, E. L.: 8, 10-1, 13
Shartle, C. L.: 2, 5, 9, 11
Stogdill, R. M.: 2, 5, 9-13, 17, 23
Tribble, J. S.: 20
Wherry, R. J.: 12
Zinn, L. A.: 16

Leadership Opinion Questionnaire

[2458]

RBH Test of Supervisory Judgment. Business and industry; 1949–63; Richardson, Bellows, Henry & Co., Inc. *
For additional information, see 6:1195.

REFERENCES THROUGH 1971
1. SPITZER, MORTON EDWARD, AND MCNAMARA, WALTER J. "A Managerial Selection Study." *Personnel Psychol* 17:19-40 sp '64. * (PA 39:2945)

CUMULATIVE NAME INDEX
McNamara, W. J.: 1   Spitzer, M. E.: 1

[2459]

Supervisory Index. Supervisors; 1960–69; SI; 5 attitude scores: management, supervision, employees, human relations practices, total; Norman Gekoski and Solomon L. Schwartz; Science Research Associates, Inc. *
For additional information, see 7:1151 (1 reference); for reviews by Arthur H. Brayfield and Albert K. Kurtz, see 6:1192 (1 reference).

REFERENCES THROUGH 1971
1. See 6:1192.
2. See 7:1151.
3. ASQUITH, RONALD H., AND HEDLUND, DALVA E. "Laboratory Training and Supervisory Attitudes." *Psychol Rep* 20:618 Ap '67. * (PA 41:9496)

CUMULATIVE NAME INDEX
Asquith, R. H.: 3
Brayfield, A. H.: *rev,* 6:1192
Gekoski, N.: 1
Hedlund, D. E.: 3
Kurtz, A. K.: *rev,* 6:1192
Schwartz, S. L.: 1-2

[2460]

*Supervisory Inventory on Communication.** Supervisors and prospective supervisors; 1965–72; SIC; Donald L. Kirkpatrick; the Author. *
For additional information, see 7:1152 (1 reference).

REFERENCES THROUGH 1971
1. See 7:1152.

CUMULATIVE NAME INDEX
Kirkpatrick, D. L.: 1

[2461]

★**Supervisory Inventory on Discipline.** Supervisors; 1973; manual subtitle is (*For Union and Non-Union Firms*); SID; Earl J. Wyman; the Author. *

[2462]

★**Supervisory Inventory on Grievances.** Supervisors; 1970; SIG; Earl J. Wyman and Donald L. Kirkpatrick; Earl J. Wyman. *

[2463]

*Supervisory Inventory on Human Relations.** Supervisors and prospective supervisors; 1960–72; SIHR; Donald L. Kirkpatrick and Earl Planty (test); Donald L. Kirkpatrick. *
For additional information and a review by Seymour Levy of the original edition, see 6:1193 (1 reference).

REFERENCES THROUGH 1971
1. See 6:1193.
2. THUMIN, F. J., AND PAGE, D. S. "A Comparative Study of Two Tests of Supervisory Knowledge." *Psychol Rep* 18:535-8 Ap '66. * (PA 40:8273)

CUMULATIVE NAME INDEX
Benson, D.: 1
Hanson, R.: 1
Kirchner, W.: 1
Levy, S.: *rev,* 6:1193
Page, D. S.: 2
Thumin, F. J.: 2

[2464]

★**Supervisory Inventory on Labor Relations.**
Supervisors in unionized firms; 1972; SILR; Earl J.
Wyman; the Author. *

[2465]

Supervisory Inventory on Safety. Supervisors and
prospective supervisors; 1967–69; SIS; Donald L.
Kirkpatrick; the Author. *

For additional information, see 7:1153.

[2466]

Supervisory Practices Test. Supervisors; 1957–64;
SPT; Martin M. Bruce; Martin M. Bruce, Ph.D.,
Publishers. *

For additional information, see 6:1194 (4 references); for reviews by Clifford E. Jurgensen and
Mary Ellen Oliverio, see 5:955.

REFERENCES THROUGH 1971

1–4. See 6:1194.
5. BRUCE, ROBERT LEE. *Predicting Administrative-Supervisory
Effectiveness in Senior County Agricultural Extension Agents.*
Doctor's thesis, Cornell University (Ithaca, N.Y.), 1962. (*DA*
23:3221)
6. THUMIN, F. J., AND PAGE, D. S. "A Comparative Study of
Two Tests of Supervisory Knowledge." *Psychol Rep* 18:535–8
Ap '66. * (*PA* 40:8273)

CUMULATIVE NAME INDEX

Bruce, M. M.: 1–2   Oliverio, M. E.: *rev,* 5:955
Bruce, R. L.: 5   Page, D. S.: 6
Jurgensen, C. E.: *rev,* 5:955   Thumin, F. J.: 6
Learner, D. B.: 2   Watley, D. J.: 3–4
Martin, H. T.: 4

[2467]

★**Survey of Management Perception.** Supervisors;
1956–58; SMP; a projective test requiring the subject to write stories (setting, characters, plot, outcome) about 9 pictures and a story "that could happen
in your own company"; no manual; Charles W.
Nelson; Management Research Associates. *

[2468]

**The WPS Supervisor-Executive Tri-Dimen-
sional Evaluation Scales.** Supervisors; 1966; TES;
the same questions about the individual being rated
are answered by 3 persons—his supervisor, a colleague, and himself; 12 scores for each of the 3 forms:
knowledge, planning, results, delegating, leadership,
morale, training, adaptability, communication, emotionality, growth, total; Western Psychological Services. *

For additional information, see 7:1154.

[Out of Print Since TIP I]

Chart for the Rating of a Foreman (status unknown),
5:915
Personal Development Record, 6:1191
Supervisory Aptitude Test, T:2093
Test of Supervisory Ability, T:2098
WLW Supervisor Survey, 6:1196

TRANSPORTATION

[2469]

[American Transit Association Tests.] Transit
operating personnel; 1941–51; 4 tests; Glen U.
Cleeton, Merwyn A. Kraft, and Robert F. Royster;
American Transit Association. *
a) STANDARD EXAMINATION FOR TRANSIT EMPLOYEES.
1941–46; intelligence.
b) PERSONAL REACTION TEST FOR TRANSIT EMPLOYEES.
1943–46; personality.

c) THE PLACEMENT INTERVIEW FOR TRANSIT EMPLOYEES.
1946; 9 ratings (moral character, mental ability,
motor ability, health, motivation, stability, maturity,
sociability, manner and appearance) in 3 areas (work
experience, schooling and childhood, personal history).
d) A STANDARDIZED ROAD TEST FOR BUS OPERATORS. 1951.

For additional information, see 5:912; for reviews
by Harold G. Seashore, Morris S. Viteles, and J. V.
Waits of *a-c,* see 3:696 (1 reference).

REFERENCES THROUGH 1971

1. See 3:696.
2. SEELEY, W. H. C., AND KRAFT, MERWYN A. "Selecting
Transit Operators." *Mgmt Rec* 10:191–3 Mr '48. *

CUMULATIVE NAME INDEX

Kraft, M. A.: 2   Viteles, M. S.: *rev,* 3:696
Seashore, H. G.: *rev,* 3:696   Waits, J. V.: 1; *rev,* 3:696
Seeley, W. H. C.: 2

[2470]

*****[Driver Selection Forms and Tests.]** Truck
drivers; 1943–73; all revised forms essentially the
same as or identical with earlier forms; no manual;
Dartnell Corporation. *
a) EMPLOYMENT APPLICATION. 1946–64.
b) TELEPHONE CHECK. 1946–73; Robert N. McMurry.
c) DRIVER INTERVIEW. 1946–64.
d) PHYSICAL EXAMINATION RECORD. 1946–54.
e) SELECTION AND EVALUATION SUMMARY. 1950–72;
Robert N. McMurry.
f) STANDARDIZED TEST: TRAFFIC AND DRIVING KNOW-
LEDGE FOR DRIVERS OF MOTOR TRUCKS. 1946–64; Amos
E. Neyhart and Helen L. Neyhart.
g) ROAD TEST IN TRAFFIC FOR TESTING, SELECTING,
RATING, AND TRAINING TRUCK DRIVERS. 1943–64; 3
scores: specific driving skills, general driving habits
and attitudes, total; Amos E. Neyhart.

For additional information and a review by Joseph
E. Moore, see 6:1197; for a review by S. Rains Wallace, Jr., see 4:789.

[2471]

**[McGuire Safe Driver Scale and Interview
Guide.]** Prospective motor vehicle operators; 1961–
62; 2 parts; Frederick L. McGuire; Western Psychological Services. *
a) THE MCGUIRE SAFE DRIVER SCALE. Test booklet title
is *The McGuire S D Scale;* items selected in part
from *Kuder Preference Record—Personal* and *Minnesota Multiphasic Personality Inventory.*
b) THE MCGUIRE SAFE DRIVER INTERVIEW GUIDE.

For additional information and reviews by Willard
A. Kerr and D. H. Schuster, see 6:1198 (1 reference).

REFERENCES THROUGH 1971

1. See 6:1198.
2. McGUIRE, FREDERICK. "Psychological Comparison of Automobile Drivers: Accident- and Violation-Free Versus Accident-
Violation-Incurring Drivers." *U S Armed Forces Med J* 7:1741–
8 D '56. * (*PA* 31:3949)

CUMULATIVE NAME INDEX

Kerr, W. A.: *rev,* 6:1198   McGuire, F. L.: 1
McGuire, F.: 2   Schuster, D. H.: *rev,* 6:1198

[2472]

**Road Test Check List for Testing, Selecting,
Rating, and Training Coach Operators.** Bus drivers; 1958; 3 or 4 scores: general attitude and driving
practices, specific driving errors, total, errors on an
actual bus run (optional); Amos E. Neyhart; published jointly by American Automobile Association
and Institute of Public Safety. *

For additional information, see 5:946.

[2473]

Road Test in Traffic for Testing, Selecting, Rating and Training Truck Drivers [1955 Revision]. Truck drivers; 1943-55; 3 scores: specific skills, general habits and attitudes, total; Amos E. Neyhart; published jointly by American Automobile Association and Institute of Public Safety. *

For additional information, see 4:790.

[2474]

Short Occupational Knowledge Test for Truck Drivers. Job applicants; 1970; score is pass, fail, or unclassifiable; Bruce A. Campbell and Suellen O. Johnson; Science Research Associates, Inc. *

For additional information, see 7:1155.

[2475]

★**Truck Driver Test.** Drivers of light and medium trucks; 1957-72; distribution restricted to member public personnel agencies and nonmember agencies approved by the publisher; International Personnel Management Association. *

For additional information and reviews by Willard A. Kerr and D. H. Schuster of an earlier form, see 6:1199.

[2476 ¹]

*****Wilson Driver Selection Test.** Prospective motor vehicle operators; 1961-72; 6 scores (visual attention, depth visualization, recognition of simple detail, recognition of complex detail, eye-hand coordination, steadiness) and safety aptitude rating (based on number of subtests passed); Clark L. Wilson; Martin M. Bruce, Ph.D., Publishers. *

For additional information and reviews by Willard A. Kerr and D. H. Schuster, see 6:1200.

1 After all tests were numbered, 11 additional test entries were inserted and 20 were deleted, leaving a total of 2467 test entries in this volume. The inserted entries are 63A, 341A, 386A, 419A, 560A, 781A, 997A, 1025A, 1040A, 1354A, and 2027A. The deleted test entries are indicated by the compound numbers assigned to the immediately preceding entries: 93-4, 108-9, 365-6, 376-7, 666-7, 732-3, 748-9, 956-66, 2063-4, 2206-7, and 2278-9.

APA-AERA-NCME STANDARDS

FORTY-NINE years ago, Giles M. Ruch, a well-known testing specialist and author of numerous tests, severely criticized test authors and publishers for not providing adequate data on the construction, validity, and use of their tests. In 1925, he wrote:

Two things [should] be done at once: first, that a set of working *criteria* for test construction be established....and second, that test authors, test publishers, test users, and test investigators adopt some fairly uniform practices in reporting on tests, at least to the extent of a few *minimum essentials.* * Where should the....data be published? The best place, theoretically and practically, is in the manual. * The next best procedure is probably that of publishing abstracts of the complete description of the test in the manual of directions, reserving the details for articles in standard journals or for publication in a separate monograph. The important thing is that full accounts be made accessible to the critical user or student of tests. To the user of tests should be extended the privilege of choice with open eyes, namely, with the "cards all on the table." * Non-publication of such data....is really a violation of the ethical codes of scientific procedures and not to be condoned by virtue of the fact that users of tests generally will not understand the technicalities. * The test buyer is surely entitled to the same protection as the buyer of food products, namely, *the true ingredients printed on the outside of each package.*[1]

Despite the criticisms and suggestions Ruch presented in 1925, nothing of consequence was done in the next thirteen years. In a paper read in February 1935 at the annual conference of the Progressive Education Association, this Editor said:

Today, it is practically impossible for a competent test technician or test consumer to make a thorough appraisal of the construction, validation, and use of most standard tests being published because of the limited amount of trustworthy information supplied by test publishers and authors. * If testing is to be of maximum value to schools, test authors and publishers must give more adequate information concerning the construction, validation, and use of their tests. It would be advantageous....if test authors would construct only one-fourth to one-half as many tests as at present and use the time saved for presenting the detailed information needed by test consumers.[2]

The publication of *The 1938 Mental Measurements Yearbook* was the first breakthrough in the sporadic campaign to impel test authors and publishers to prepare better tests documented by more informative manuals. In *The 1938 Mental Measurements Yearbook,* the Editor reiterated his views on the need for more adequate manuals:

Test users have every right to demand that test authors and publishers present full particulars concerning the methods used in constructing and validating the tests which they place on the market. Tests not accompanied by detailed data on their construction, validation, uses, and limitations should be suspect.[3]

Typescripts of all test reviews written for *The 1938 Yearbook* were submitted to publishers "with the request that they carefully search the reviews for errors of fact." An inappreciable number of errors were found, but the Editor reported that at least some test publishers would begin supplying more adequate information in future test manuals:

The most frequent objection raised by publishers and authors against the reviews submitted to them was that the reviewers were ignorant of unpublished research data in the possession of the test authors and publishers. The Editor has little sympathy for this type of objection. *It is the responsibility of test authors and publishers to furnish in the test manual whatever data they wish to have considered by reviewers and test purchasers.* *

[1] Ruch, G. M. "Minimum Essentials in Reporting Data on Standard Tests." *J Ed Res* 12:349–58 D '25.

[2] Buros, Oscar Krisen. *The 1938 Mental Measurements Yearbook,* p. 3. Highland Park, N.J.: Gryphon Press, 1938. Pp. xv, 415.

[3] Ibid., pp. xiii–xiv.

Because of the test reviews, three publishers have already informed the Editor that they plan to be more careful in the future about publishing data concerning the construction and validation of their tests. Another publisher admitted that they probably had erred in publishing a test a year or so in advance of the publication of the monograph reporting in detail the supporting research.[4]

Beginning with *The 1940 Mental Measurements Yearbook,* every yearbook has included among the MMY objectives the following two relevant to test manuals:

a) To impel authors and publishers to place fewer but better tests on the market and to provide test users with detailed and accurate information on the construction, validation, uses, and limitations of their tests at the time they are first placed on the market.
b) To impress test users with the desirability of suspecting all standard tests—even though prepared by well-known authorities—unaccompanied by detailed data on their construction, validation, use, and limitations.[5]

Each person invited to review for an MMY is given a list of suggestions for preparing his review. The 1940 suggestions included the following statement regarding test manuals:

Attention should be called to a lack, if any, of accompanying data concerning the test. Frequently, it will be found that a test manual fails to give certain information needed to evaluate the test adequately. Reviews should call attention to these omissions if it is thought test authors and publishers should provide such information. It is the opinion of the Editor that the yearbooks can and will render test users a great service by persuading test publishers to present full particulars concerning the construction, validation, and use of their tests. The reviewer can help both test publishers and test users by specifically pointing out the lack of such data in the test manual.[6]

Similar suggestions have been sent to reviewers for all later yearbooks.

The campaign for more adequate reporting of data in test manuals was accelerated greatly in 1954 and 1955 with the publication of two small monographs prepared jointly by three professional organizations in education and psychology: the American Psychological Association, American Educational Research Association, and National Council on Measurements Used in Education. Their first report, *Technical Recommendations for Psychological Tests and Diagnostic Techniques* [7] published twenty years ago, was prepared by the APA Committee on

Test Standards—Edward S. Bordin, R. C. Challman, Herbert S. Conrad, Lee J. Cronbach (Chairman), Lloyd G. Humphreys, Paul E. Meehl, and Donald E. Super. Although many others helped with criticisms and suggestions, these seven men deserve the greatest praise and recognition for their pioneering work. A shorter adaptation covering achievement tests only was published the following year under the title *Technical Recommendations for Achievement Tests.*[8] This second monograph was prepared by Robert L. Ebel, Jacob S. Orleans (Chairman), and Saul B. Sells for the American Educational Research Association and the National Council on Measurements Used in Education.

Although the scope of these two monographs is much narrower than implied by their titles, they were rightly acclaimed as landmarks in the history of testing. Finally, almost thirty years after Ruch's plea for immediate action, the three leading professional organizations most involved with testing took action and provided test authors, publishers, and users with authoritative recommendations for the preparation and evaluation of test manuals.

Although there have been 1966 and 1972 revisions of these first two monographs, the original 1954 monograph makes the clearest statement of the objectives of the series:

The essential principle that sets the tone for this document is that a test manual should carry information sufficient to enable any qualified user to make sound judgments regarding the usefulness and interpretation of the test. This means that certain research is required prior to release of a test for general use by psychologists or school personnel. The results must be reported or summarized in the manual, and the manual must help the reader to interpret these results. A manual is to be judged not merely by its literal truthfulness, but by the impression it leaves with the reader. * It is not appropriate to call for a particular level of validity and reliability, or to otherwise specify the nature of the test. It *is* appropriate to ask that the manual give the information necessary for the user to decide whether the accuracy, relevance, or standardization of the test makes it suitable for his purposes. These recommendations, then, suggest standards of *test description and reporting* without stating minimum statistical specifications.[9]

Within six or seven years after the publication of the Technical Recommendations, the three cooperating associations set up a joint committee to prepare a single monograph revision of the 1954 and 1955 reports. This new committee

4 Ibid., pp. 5–6.
5 Buros, Oscar Krisen. *The 1940 Mental Measurements Yearbook,* p. xviii. Highland Park, N.J.: Gryphon Press, 1941. Pp. xxv, 674.
6 Ibid., p. 15.
7 *Technical Recommendations for Psychological Tests and Diagnostic Techniques.* Prepared by a Joint Committee of the American Psychological Association, American Educational Research Association, and National Council on Measurements Used in Education. Lee J. Cronbach, Chairman. Supplement to the *Psychological Bulletin,* Vol. 51, No. 2, March 1954. Washington, D.C.: American Psychological Association, Inc., March 1954. Pp. ii, 38. (Reprinted in the 1961 *Tests in Print.*)

8 *Technical Recommendations for Achievement Tests.* Prepared by the Committees on Test Standards of the American Educational Research Association and the National Council on Measurements Used in Education. Jacob S. Orleans, Chairman. Washington, D.C.: American Educational Research Association, 1955. Pp. 36. (Reprinted in the 1961 *Tests in Print.*)
9 *Technical Recommendations for Psychological Tests and Diagnostic Techniques,* p. 2.

consisted of Oscar K. Buros, Herbert S. Conrad, Lee J. Cronbach, Max D. Engelhart, John W. French (Cochairman), J. Raymond Gerberich, William B. Michael (Cochairman), and Willard G. Warrington. Their report, *Standards for Educational and Psychological Tests and Manuals*,[10] was published in 1966. In the words of the revising committee:

This second report brings the first ones up to date and takes account of 12 years of progress and of the helpful criticisms of many test publishers and users. * In view of the similarity in the nature of many (but not all) problems in both educational and psychological measurement, the joint committee....decided....to issue one set of standards to cover both educational and psychological tests. The basic structure and format of the first report have been retained. However, many of the recommendations and standards have been substantially modified; others have been dropped; a few new ones have been added. Despite changes in psychological points of view in the theoretical and technical phases of educational and psychological measurement, the principal subdivisions for classifying types of standards still appeared to be sufficiently intact in current testing practices to be retained.[11]

A revision of the 1966 *Standards* was published in May 1974 under the title *Standards for Educational and Psychological Tests*.[12] A joint committee of eleven persons prepared the new revision: Philip Ash, Joan K. Bollenbacher, Frederick B. Davis (Chairman), Robert L. Ebel, Edmund W. Gordon, Robert M. Guion, George F. Madaus, William A. Mehrens, Doris P. Mosby, James H. Ricks, and E. Belvin Williams. In his Foreword to the 1974 revision, Frederick B. Davis states:

By 1971, it had become apparent that problems and issues in testing, especially problems in selection for employment or for admission to educational institutions, had outdated the 1966 publication.[13]

Some of the major differences in this latest edition are described in the Introduction:

The present document is both a revision and an extension of the 1966 *Standards*. It presents standards for test use as well as for test manuals; it is intended to guide both test developers and test users. * The authors of the 1966 *Standards* declared that a test producer has an obligation to provide enough information about a test so that a qualified user will know what reliance can safely be placed on it; they also provided statements of

consensus concerning the information that should be in a manual. It now appears desirable to provide similar statements of consensus concerning competency in testing practices. Part of the stimulus for revision is an awakened concern about problems like invasion of privacy or discrimination against members of groups such as minorities or women.[14]

There can be no question but that the *Technical Recommendations* and *Standards* have been effective in complementing the *Mental Measurements Yearbooks* in the drive for more honest and informative test manuals. Test manuals—*as inadequate as most of them still are*—would certainly have been even poorer had it not been for the *Technical Recommendations, Standards,* and the *Mental Measurements Yearbooks*. Nevertheless, it is discouraging that greater progress has not been made. The test entries in the MMY's are replete with statements such as: "no manual," "no data on reliability," "no data on validity," "no description of normative population," "no norms," "no norms for part scores," and "reliability data based upon earlier experimental forms."

It is a very simple task to give at least some, even though quite inadequate, information on reliability. Yet despite the APA-AERA-NCME efforts over the past twenty years and the MMY efforts over the past thirty-six years, 22 percent of the manuals for 115 recent nonprojective personality tests, listed for the first time in either *Personality Tests and Reviews* or *The Seventh Mental Measurements Yearbook,* reported no reliability information whatsoever. The non-observance of the APA-AERA-NCME and MMY standards by test authors, publishers, and users is shocking. When will test users make it unprofitable for publishers to market tests without reporting even the barest essentials of the data which were considered minimal forty-nine years ago?

Unfortunately, the publisher of a poor test is likely to publish as little factual data as possible. The poorer the test, the more damaging will be the research evidence if honestly gathered and reported. Lack of data on reliability can be criticized but it does not necessarily follow that the test is unreliable. Hence, if a test has low reliability, it is more profitable for the test publisher to report no data than to report data which clearly reflects the unreliability of the test. Every test failing to present data of the type considered essential in the *Standards* should be shunned until data supporting claims for validity become available.

10 *Standards for Educational and Psychological Tests and Manuals.* Prepared by a Joint Committee of the American Psychological Association, American Educational Research Association, and National Council on Measurement in Education. John W. French and William B. Michael, Cochairmen. Washington, D.C.: American Psychological Association, Inc., 1966. Pp. iii, 40. (Reprinted in *Personality Tests and Reviews.*)
11 Ibid., p. 1 (sequence changed).
12 *Standards for Educational and Psychological Tests.* Prepared by a Joint Committee of the American Psychological Association, American Educational Research Association, and National Council on Measurement in Education. Frederick B. Davis, Chair. Washington, D.C.: American Psychological Association, Inc., 1974. Pp. iv, 76.
13 Ibid., p. iii.
14 Ibid., p. 1.

It must be remembered, however, that a test may be poor even though its manual has done a fairly good job in reporting the kinds of information called for by the *Standards*. The information presented in the manual must still be evaluated.

Most testing specialists will find themselves in disagreement with some of the standards set forth in the 1974 monograph as well as in earlier editions. The revised *Standards* must represent many compromises and majority opinions of the eleven committee members, especially since the scope of the *Standards* was enlarged to include test users and the uses of tests. The earlier monographs attempted only to list the kinds of data that a test user would need to determine the suitability of a test for whatever purpose he wished to use it. The 1974 monograph, however, is also concerned with the more controversial questions of how tests should be used and by whom.

Although the Editor strongly endorses the 1974 *Standards,* he does wish to point out one omission of special concern. For many years the Editor has been campaigning to persuade publishers to include copyright dates on all test materials and to report these dates in their catalogs. Twenty years ago, it was not uncommon for publishers to update copyright dates on reprintings of tests. Many test entries in the *Mental Measurements Yearbooks* contain statements such as: "Form B ('54, identical with test copyrighted in 1939)," "Form 3 ('55, same as 1940 test)," "Form Y-2 ('51, same as 1949 edition)," "Form R ('51, same as test copyrighted in 1942)," and "Form S ('42, some printings bear 1949 or 1950 copyright)." This publicity in the MMY's has certainly made publishers more careful about reporting correct dates, but the practice has not been completely eliminated. Today, the abuse consists largely of updating copyright dates on reprintings involving inappreciable corrections or changes and dropping earlier copyright dates on revised materials.

The 1954 *Technical Recommendations* listed as essential: "The copyright date of the manual or the date of the latest revision should be clearly indicated." [15] A similar statement appeared in the 1966 *Standards*.[16] Nothing, however, is said in the 1974 *Standards* about dating test materials. This probably was an oversight—surely honest copyright and publication dates should appear on all test materials.

The Editor also wishes an essential requirement had been included that publishers date all test materials listed in their catalogs. Over the past fifteen years or so, the Editor has been trying to persuade test publishers, in letters and orally, to report dates in their catalogs. Some large publishers have joined the very few who follow this practice. Harcourt Brace Jovanovich deserves to be singled out as a model for other publishers to follow—they report the earliest and latest copyright for each test. A further improvement would be to give the range of dates for each item—specific test forms, manuals, and other accessories.

The Editor is most pleased to have received the permission of the publisher, the American Psychological Association, to reprint the 1974 *Standards.* Their inclusion in *Tests in Print II* will help give them the widest possible distribution. Certainly, every responsible user of tests should consider the *APA-AERA-NCME Standards* must reading.

15 *Technical Recommendations for Psychological Tests and Diagnostic Techniques,* p. 9.
16 *Standards for Educational and Psychological Tests and Manuals,* p. 8.

STANDARDS FOR EDUCATIONAL AND PSYCHOLOGICAL TESTS

Prepared by a Joint Committee (Frederick B. Davis, Chair) of the American Psychological Association, American Educational Research Association, and National Council on Measurement in Education.

CONTENTS

FOREWORD

This document is the lineal descendant of *Technical Recommendations for Psychological Tests and Diagnostic Techniques,* prepared by a committee of the American Psychological Association and published by that organization in 1954, and of *Technical Recommendations for Achievement Tests,* prepared by committees of the American Educational Research Association and the National Council on Measurements Used in Education and published by the National Education Association in 1955. In 1966, the American Psychological Association, the American Educational Research Association, and the National Council on Measurement in Education published *Standards for Educational and Psychological Tests and Manuals* (through the American Psychological Association) to replace the two earlier documents.

By 1971, it had become apparent that problems and issues in testing, especially problems in selection for employment or for admission to educational institutions, had outdated the 1966 publication. Consequently, the Committee on Psychological Tests of the American Psychological Association (later merged with the Committee on Assessment) made contact with the American Educational Research Association and the National Council on Measurement in Education to form a joint committee for the revision of *Standards for Educational and Psychological Tests and Manuals.* The members of the joint committee were: Philip Ash (APA),

Joan K. Bollenbacher (NCME), Frederick B. Davis, Chairman (APA), Robert L. Ebel (APA), Edmund W. Gordon (APA), Robert M. Guion (APA), George F. Madaus (NCME), William A. Mehrens (AERA), Doris P. Mosby (APA), James H. Ricks (AERA), and E. Belvin Williams (liaison with the APA Board of Scientific Affairs).

The principal author of *Standards for Educational and Psychological Tests* is Professor Robert M. Guion, Bowling Green State University, Bowling Green, Ohio. The committee expresses to him and to dozens of other psychologists and educators who provided comments and suggestions with respect to early drafts of the document its deep appreciation for their contributions. Special gratitude is owing to the following who generously read and commented on the final draft: Anne Anastasi, Nancy Cole, Lee J. Cronbach, Robert L. Linn, Julian C. Stanley, and Robert L. Thorndike. The joint committee is deeply indebted to Miriam F. Kelty and Willo P. White of the Central Office of the American Psychological Association for their assistance throughout the project.

Because some members of the joint committee judged that certain aspects of program evaluation and of the interpretation of scores derived from content-referenced tests have not been treated adequately within the scope of the present document, the committee has suggested that publication of a companion volume be considered by a succeeding joint committee.

The major financial support for development of the *Standards* was provided by a grant from the Russell Sage Foundation.

Finally, the chairman of the committee wishes to express to members of the present committee his deep appreciation of their long hours of critical reading and committee discussion.

FREDERICK B. DAVIS
University of Pennsylvania

INTRODUCTION

In March, 1954, the American Psychological Association issued the *Technical Recommendations for Psychological Tests and Diagnostic Techniques,* endorsed by the American Educational Research Association and the National Council on Measurement in Education. In January, 1955, the latter two organizations published a further document, *Technical Recommendations for Achievement Tests.* Subsequently, a joint committee of the three organizations consolidated, modified, and revised the two documents and in 1966, through the American Psychological Association, published the *Standards for Educational and Psychological Tests and Manuals.* The present document is both a revision and an extension of the 1966 *Standards.* It presents standards for test use as well as for test manuals; it is intended to guide both test developers and test users.

A test user is one who chooses tests, interprets scores, or makes decisions based on test scores. (People who do only routine administration or scoring of tests are not included in this definition, although test users often do both.) Test users include clinical or industrial psychologists, research directors, school psychologists, counselors, employment supervisors, teachers, and various administrators who select or interpret tests for their organizations. The audience for the *Standards* is, therefore, broad and cuts across publics with varying backgrounds and different training in measurement and statistics. Sections of the *Standards,* particularly those related to validity and reliability, are necessarily technical. These two sections should be meaningful to readers who have training approximately equivalent to a level between the master's degree and the doctorate in education or psychology. However, the remaining sections—the greater part of the document—are generally nontechnical and may be read with profit by all users.

The authors of the 1966 *Standards* declared that a test producer has an obligation to provide enough information about a test so that a qualified user will know what reliance can safely be placed on it; they also provided statements of consensus concerning the information that should be in a manual. It now appears desirable to provide similar statements of consensus concerning competency in testing practices.

Part of the stimulus for revision is an awakened concern about problems like invasion of privacy or discrimination against members of groups such as minorities or women. Serious misuses of tests include, for example, labeling Spanish-speaking children as mentally retarded on the basis of scores on tests standardized on "a representative sample of American children," or using a test with a major loading on verbal comprehension without appropriate validation in an attempt to screen out large numbers of blacks from manipulative jobs requiring minimal verbal communication.

These are specific examples of a general problem of test appropriateness. A test score describes but it does not explain a level of performance. Test performance may be influenced by many factors such as amount and quality of certain kinds of training, distractions during testing, sensory defects, inability to hear instructions because of poor administration, inappropriate language in instructions or in the test, inability to read, brain damage, motivation level, illumination level, cultural background of the examinee, or test-taking strategies.

Some unfairness may be built into a test, for example, requiring an inordinately high level of verbal ability to comprehend the instructions for a nonverbal test. Many of the social ills attributed to tests, however, seem more a result of the ways in which tests have been used than of characteristics of the tests themselves; for example, errors in administration, failure to consider the appropriateness of normative data, failure to choose an appropriate test, use of incorrect assumptions about the causes of a low or deviant test score, or administrative rigidity in using test scores for making decisions.

TESTS AND TEST USES TO WHICH THESE STANDARDS APPLY

It is intended that these standards apply to any assessment procedure, assessment device, or assessment aid; that is, to any systematic basis for making inferences about characteristics of people.

A test is a special case of an assessment procedure. It may be thought of as a set of tasks or questions intended to elicit particular types of behavior when presented under standardized conditions and to yield scores that will have desirable psychometric properties such as high reliability and high validity.

Tests include standardized aptitude and achievement instruments, diagnostic and evaluative devices, interest inventories, personality inventories, projective instruments and related clinical techniques, and many kinds of personal history forms. It was pointed out in the 1966 *Standards* that the same general types of information are needed for all these varieties of published diagnostic, prognostic, and evaluative devices. It is equally appropriate to point out that unpublished assessment devices can be better used if the same kind of information is available to users.[1]

There are wide variations in the sophistication of assessment techniques. At one extreme is the test that has gone through several revisions based on many research studies. Such a test may provide normative data based on thousands of cases classified into dozens of subpopulations. At the other extreme is the casual interview that provides assessments based on varying and unsystematically observed cues.

These standards are written specifically to apply to standardized tests. They apply in varying degrees, however, to the entire range of assessment techniques. If it is required that a relationship be demonstrated between scores (assessments) on an employment test and subsequent performance on a job, the requirement should in principle also apply to the judgments (assessments) of the employment interviewer. It may not be possible to apply the standards with the same rigor, but the kind of judgments the interviewer is to make can be identified;

the time and procedures for developing and recording them can be standardized; and they can be validated in the same ways that scores are validated. When someone who makes personnel decisions develops his own assessment techniques (a practice not discouraged intentionally in these standards), he will find the standards useful guides for developing information similar to that in good test manuals; the principles are as relevant to him as to the professional test developer. If he chooses to use a test that has been developed by someone else, he may find the standards helpful in evaluating alternatives from which he may choose; moreover, the standards may help in developing a program of application.

There are many dimensions along which measuring instruments can be classified. Some are designed to measure abilities, some to measure accomplishments, others to measure attitudes or interests. Some are inventories, interview aids, biographical data forms, and experimental diagnostic devices, and are not called tests. Generally, however, the word "test" is used in these standards to apply to all kinds of measurement. What these different kinds have in common is that scores with desirable psychometric properties may be derived from each.

These standards also apply to *criterion measures*. Studies evaluating uses of well-developed tests too often employ inadequate criterion data. A criterion measure should have the psychometric properties expected of any other measurement, such as validity, including in special instances some form of criterion-related validity, for example, the relationship of an immediate criterion measure to an intermediate or more nearly ultimate measure. Criterion development should be guided by the standards guiding test development.

Some assessment techniques are used as interview aids. The intent of such use is an idiographic analysis of an individual—an approach to assessment which places special reliance on the skill of the clinician. It is often argued that this use is so unlike the use of other testing procedures that it cannot be judged by essentially psychometric standards. The qualitative nature of the assessment is less the point at issue than the distinction that can be made between clinical and actuarial prediction. When tests, projective or otherwise, are used as aids to an interviewer's assessment, the interviewer is himself the final assessment de-

1 It is sometimes suggested in response to perceptions of test abuse and unfair uses of tests that a moratorium on testing be observed until better and more appropriate instruments are developed and more equitable procedures can be instituted. The suggestion of such an extreme measure may be indicative of the growing sense of frustration and indignation felt particularly by some minority group members who sense that testing has had a disproportionately negative impact on their opportunities for equal access to success in education and employment. This suggestion, although well intended, seems futile for several reasons: First, it fails to consider unfairness resulting from the misuses of tests. If new and better tests were subject to the same sorts of misuse, they might well produce the same sorts of errors (or errors of the same magnitudes) in the decisions based on them.

Second, it requires a corresponding but unlikely moratorium on decisions. Employers will continue to make employment decisions with or without standardized tests. Colleges and universities will still select students, some elementary pupils will still be recommended for special education, and boards of education will continue to evaluate the success of specific programs. If those responsible for making decisions do not use standardized assessment techniques, they will use less dependable methods of assessment.

Third, tests are often useful for *finding* talent but are too often used only as devices for rejecting those with low scores; they can also be used to discover potential for performance that might not otherwise be observed. In this way, the use of tests may sometimes improve the prospects of minority group members and women.

vice, and his assessments become the "scores." These assessments can and should be validated like other psychometric measures.

Component bits of information may be analyzed somewhat as items are analyzed. Proposals for arriving at idiographic interpretations are almost always based partially upon a nomothetic premise; for example, that a Rorschach determinant correlates with a specified internal factor. The usual standards can be applied to premises of this kind. Therefore, although interview aids can present unusual problems, their user requires the same information about them that he requires for any test score, and his use of them is subject to some of the same psychometric considerations (e.g., reliability) applicable to other test scores.

The developer of such an interview aid need not indicate his test's validity by correlating it with any simple criterion. But if he goes so far as to make any generalization about what "most people see" or what "schizophrenics rarely do," he is making a statistical claim and should be held to the usual rules for supporting it. Moreover, when on the basis of projective test data, biographical information, or various behavioral cues elicited during an interview the interviewer makes a statement such as "this man will fail or be subject to severe depression if placed in this situation," he is making a prediction based on his assessment and should be held to the standards for demonstrating the validity of his prediction.

A comment also seems appropriate about hidden tests (such as an interviewer's systematic attempt to assess a trait within the context of the interview) or other unobtrusive or observational measures. Some of these may raise ethical problems, but they do not differ, in principle, from other tests, and the standards apply as much to these unseen or unrecognized tests as to those more clearly perceived by the examinee. Therefore, the psychologist who counts examples of a specific type of response in a behavior-modification setting is as much responsible for the validity of his interpretations of change or the basic reliability of his observations as is any other test user.

In short, the standards are intended to be widely applicable both to standardized tests and a wide variety of other assessment techniques. The degree of applicability of individual standards to nontest assessments will vary; developers and users of such assessment procedures should at least observe the spirit of the standards.

Tests are used for basic research purposes as well as for practical purposes. Although these standards were not written with research purposes in mind, the qualified investigator should be able to determine the manner in which they apply to his research.

These standards cannot replace instructional material on test development; therefore, there are no specific statements directly related to such procedures as item writing or item analysis.

INFORMATION STANDARDS AS A GUIDE TO TEST DEVELOPERS

For each test there should be a test manual, perhaps with supplements, to provide enough information for a qualified user to make sound judgments regarding the usefulness and interpretation of test scores. Research is required prior to the release of the test or test scores for operational use.

A manual is to be judged not merely by its literal truthfulness, but by the impression it leaves with the reader. If the typical professional user for whom the manual is prepared is likely to obtain an inaccurate impression of the test from the manual, the manual is poorly written. The standards apply to the spirit and tone of the manual (or supplemental publication) as well as to its literal statements.

A manual must often communicate information to many different groups. Many tests are used by people with limited training in testing. These users may not follow technical discussion or understand detailed statistical information. Other users are measurement specialists; they seek information on which to judge the technical adequacy of the test. Sometimes technical information can be presented in a supplementary handbook. Whatever the form, the prospective test user must have available to him the information needed for making whatever judgments his use of the test requires. Even when the test (or test battery) is developed for use within a single organization, a manual can often be helpful; preparation of a manual helps the test developer organize his thinking, codify his procedures, and communicate his ideas and intentions to his assistants.

It is not appropriate for this publication to call for a particular level of validity or reliability, or otherwise to establish technical test specifications for specific tests, but it is appropriate to ask that any test manual provide the information necessary for a test user to decide whether the consistency, relevance, or standardization of a test makes it suitable for his purpose. These standards need not prescribe minimum statistical specifications. Rather, their intent is to describe in an explicit and conveniently available form the information required by test users. In arriving at those requirements, it has been necessary to judge what is a reasonable compromise between pressures of cost and time, on the one hand, and the ideal, on the other. The test producer ordinarily spends large sums of money in developing and standardizing a test. Insofar as these recommendations indicate the kind of information that is most valuable to test users, authors and publishers can more efficiently allocate funds for gathering and reporting data of greatest value. Some provisions are more applicable than others in any specific case. The completion of predictive validity studies related to job criteria, for example, is essential before a vocational interest inventory can be used properly, but it may be only desirable for a values inventory and irrelevant for an inventory designed to diagnose mental disorders. These standards, therefore, represent an attempt to state what type of studies should be completed before a test is ready for release to the profession. They can serve as a similar guide for those who are developing tests for their own use.

PROCEDURAL STANDARDS AS A GUIDE TO TEST USERS

The test user, in selecting, administering, scoring, or interpreting a test, should know his purposes, what he is doing to achieve those purposes, and their probable consequences. It is not enough to have benign purposes; the user must know the procedures necessary to maximize effectiveness and to minimize unfairness in test use. He must evaluate the many factors that may have influenced test performance in light of his purposes. Where he finds that certain factors would unfairly influence performance, his procedures for using the test and interpreting the scores should be designed to minimize such influences.

Competence in test use is a combination of knowledge of psychometric principles, knowledge of the problem situation in which the testing is to be done, technical skill, and some

wisdom. Although it is not appropriate to tell a test user that he needs particular levels of validity and reliability, it is appropriate to ask him to ascertain that his procedures result in reasonably valid predictions or reliable classifications, or otherwise conform to the purposes of his testing. These standards of practice are written more as guidelines than as commandments. It is as necessary to make cost-benefit compromises in test use as in test development. These standards provide useful guidelines for test users as well as for test developers.

THREE LEVELS OF STANDARDS

Manuals can never give all the information, and test users can never follow all the procedures that might be desirable. At the same time, restricting this statement of recommendations solely to essential or indispensable information and practices might tend to discourage development and reporting of additional information. The standards are, therefore, grouped in three levels: ESSENTIAL, VERY DESIRABLE, and DESIRABLE. Each proposed requirement is judged based on its importance and the feasibility of attaining it.

The statements listed as ESSENTIAL are intended to represent the consensus of present-day thinking concerning what is normally required for competent use of a test. Any test or testing situation may present some unique problems; it is undesirable for the standards to be treated as unduly rigid; for example, they should not bind the producer of a novel test to an inappropriate procedure or form of reporting. The ESSENTIAL standards indicate what information or practices will be needed for most tests in most applications. When a test developer or test user fails to satisfy these requirements, he should do so only as a considered judgment. In any single test or testing situation, there may be some ESSENTIAL standards that do not apply. It should be noted that many of these standards require thought rather than specific action as an outcome of thought; for example, "A test user should consider . . ." In most cases, such statements are listed as ESSENTIAL.

If some type of ESSENTIAL information is not available on a given test, it is important to help the reader recognize that the research on the test is incomplete in this respect. A test manual should include clear statements of what research has been done and avoid misleading statements.

The category VERY DESIRABLE is used to draw attention to types of information or practices that contribute greatly to the user's understanding of the test and to competence in its use. Standards in this category have not been listed as ESSENTIAL if their usefulness is debatable.

The category DESIRABLE includes information and practices that are helpful but not ESSENTIAL or VERY DESIRABLE.

When a test is widely used, the developer has a greater responsibility for investigating it thoroughly and providing more extensive reports about it than when the test is limited in use. Large sales make research financially possible. Therefore, the developer of a popular test can add information in subsequent editions of the manual. For tests having limited sales, it is unreasonable to expect that as much information will be furnished.

CAUTIONS TO BE EXERCISED IN THE USE OF THESE STANDARDS

Almost any test can be useful for some function and in some situations, but even the best test can have damaging consequences if used inappropriately. Therefore, the primary responsibility for the improvement of testing continues to rest on the shoulders of test users. It is hoped that these standards will be used to extend the professional training of many test users who are not now being trained appropriately. Professional training of personnel managers, school administrators, and classroom teachers should prepare them to better understand information about tests, test interpretations, and these standards. Such training will do much to improve the quality of test use and to minimize the extent of test misuse. The standards draw attention to recent developments in thinking about tests, test analysis, and test use. A comparison of these standards with those in earlier editions should remind test developers and test users that testing is a stable but not a static enterprise and that, in fact, there is room for improvement in the quality of assessments that are being made.

Tests are often developed and used in circumstances that lead to maintaining less than the highest standards of technical excellence. We do not intend to discourage those who must make assessments of people from doing the best they can with whatever training and collaborative resources are available to them. These standards, however, are written to promote excellence. They provide a kind of checklist of factors to be considered in designing, standardizing, validating, scoring, and interpreting tests. They may help test developers and test users decide what studies are needed and how those studies might best be recorded in manuals or in validation reports. Test users who are not going to do independent research on a test should refer to these standards for guidance in the choice, administration, scoring, and interpretation of tests.

It is conceivable that a test developer could fulfill most of the standards presented and still produce a test that would fall short of his intended or stated objectives. Care should be exercised to adhere, both in test development and test use, to the spirit as well as to the letter of these standards. Because of the possibility of misunderstanding or misinterpretation, it would not be appropriate for test developers or test users to state that a manual or procedure "satisfies" or "follows" these standards. There would be no objection to a statement that one has "taken into account or considered" these standards.

A final caveat is necessary in view of the prominence of testing issues in litigation. This document is prepared as a technical guide for those within the sponsoring professions; it is *not* written as law. What is intended is a set of standards to be used in part for self-evaluation by test developers and test users. An evaluation of their competence does not rest on the literal satisfaction of every relevant provision of this document. The individual standards are statements of ideals or goals, some having priority over others. Instead, an evaluation of competence depends on the degree to which the intent of this document has been satisfied by the test developer or user.

STANDARDS FOR TESTS, MANUALS, AND REPORTS

Tests vary in the amount of knowledge and research required to develop them. Much background work is needed for a test that is published or otherwise distributed for widespread use. Less work need be done for a test developed for local use. At any level, however, better tests and testing can be expected where test developers have been guided by fundamental considerations and have demonstrated this in writing.

A test user needs information describing a test's rationale, development, technical characteristics, administration, and interpretation. Such information is ordinarily expected in a test manual or in its supplements. This information is also needed by those using a test or test battery that has not been published but which is used within an organization to aid in making decisions. For these uses, a properly prepared manual reports to local users and to other interested persons (colleagues in other organizations, representatives of governmental agencies, representatives of citizen's groups, etc.) the procedures followed in construction of the test, in its use, and in the interpretation of scores derived from it. In certification or selection programs, a manual can present information about the program as a whole as well as about component tests. Data supporting claims for the program, procedures followed, kinds of tests used, and related information should be recorded not only to provide an adequate basis for the proper use of tests but also to make the information available for public scrutiny.

The development of a test or testing program is based on research; the report of that research is often contained in a manual. These standards, therefore, concentrate on the manual (and any supplementary publication) as the full and proper report of what was done in test development; they specify standards of reporting from which one may infer standards for research.

A. DISSEMINATION OF INFORMATION

A test user needs information to help him use the test in standard ways and to evaluate a test relative to others he might select for a given purpose. The information that he needs to select a test or to use it must come, at least in part, from the test developer. Practices of authors and publishers in furnishing information have varied. Sometimes the test manual offers only vague directions for administering and scoring, norms of uncertain origin, and perhaps nothing more. In contrast, some manuals furnish extensive information on test development, validity, reliability, bases for normative information, appropriate kinds of inter-

pretations and uses, and they present all such information in detail.

★A1. When a test is published or otherwise made available for operational use, it should be accompanied by a manual (or other published or readily available information) that makes every reasonable effort to follow the recommendations of these standards and, in particular, to provide the information required to substantiate any claims that have been made for its use. ESSENTIAL

[Comment: The term "operational use" refers to making practical decisions about the evaluation or handling of individuals, groups, curricula, therapeutic treatments, and so on.

The term "manual" refers to documents describing procedures of test development, use, interpretation, relevant research, normative data, and related information. Depending on such things as the amount of information to report and the diversity of uses and users, the term may designate a document entirely within one cover or a series of separately bound pamphlets. This term might also be extended to include procedural manuals governing the use of tests or of test batteries in, for example, selection situations; the wording and importance of many of these standards would be different for a procedural manual, but the principles applicable to test manuals would at least, therefore, be analogous.

Not all of the standards in this report will apply to any one particular test. A standard may be ignored if it is irrelevant in light of the purpose of the test and the claims made for it, but it may not be ignored merely because it is difficult to meet or has not usually been met by a similar test.]

★A1.1. If information needed to support interpretations suggested in the manual cannot be presented at the time the manual is published, the manual should satisfy the intent of standard A1 by pointing out the absence and importance of this information. ESSENTIAL

*A1.2. Where the information is too extensive to be fully reported in the manual, the essential information should be summarized and accompanied by references to other sources of information, such as technical supplements, articles, or books. VERY DESIRABLE

[Comment: Developers of some well known tests provide extensive technical manuals, make further research data available through other sources (such as the Education Resources Information Center), prepare annotated bibliographies, or include relevant information in technical books which users are encouraged to consult. In other instances, the essential information is given in the manual sold with the instrument, along with references to other useful sources.

Publications by persons other than the author of the test frequently fulfill many functions of a manual. If a book about a test is designed to serve as a manual, its author and publisher have the same responsibility in preparing it as do the author and publisher of a test.]

★A1.2.1. When information about a test is provided in a separate publication, that publication should meet the same standards of accuracy and freedom from misleading impressions that apply to the manual. ESSENTIAL

★A1.2.2. Promotional material for a test should be accurate and should not give the reader false impressions. ESSENTIAL

[Comment: One publisher presents an extensive and complete bibliography, without comment or annotation, of research involving a test; he does *not* mention that many of the entries are studies with negative findings. The impression is one of extensive use, not of limitations to the usefulness of the test.]

★A1.2.3. Informational material distributed within a using organization should be accurate, complete for the purposes of the reader's need, and written in language that will not give the reader a false impression. ESSENTIAL

[Comment: Such information is often given in brief memoranda. In preparing these brief reports, the technical capability of the readers may be kept in mind, but this does not suggest that essential information be either omitted or distorted in the interest of simplicity. Where a reader may be expected to receive such reports regularly, efforts can be made to increase his ability to understand technical detail.]

★A2. A test manual should describe fully the development of the test: the rationale, specifications followed in writing items or selecting observations, and procedures and results of item analysis or other research. ESSENTIAL

★A2.1. Data gathered during the process of developing a test before it is in final form should be clearly distinguished from data pertaining to the test in final form. ESSENTIAL

*A2.2. A test manual should specify the need for maintaining necessary test security. VERY DESIRABLE

[Comment: For example, a manual might describe some acceptable coaching practices. If so, it would be appropriate to add warnings against unacceptable practices that might jeopardize test security.]

*A2.3. A test manual or supplementary document should provide representative sample items and a statement of the intended purpose of the test in a form that can be made available to those concerned about the nature and quality of a testing program. VERY DESIRABLE

[Comment: The evaluation of a test may not fall exclusively to those who are technically trained. Examinees, members of citizen panels, civil rights advocates, and parents are among those who may have reason to make judgments about the appropriateness of a test. Their right to do so need not conflict with the necessity to maintain test security if descriptive and explanatory materials are made available.
One publisher of educational tests has published descriptive material in nontechnical language for a wide variety of tests; pamphlets include information on test development and rationale as well as examples of items and suggestions on test-taking strategies.]

A2.4. The identity and professional qualifications of item writers and editors should be described in instances where they are relevant; for example, when adequacy of coverage of a subject-matter achievement test cannot appropriately or practically be measured against any external criterion. DESIRABLE

*A3. The test and its manual should be revised at appropriate intervals. The time for revision has arrived whenever changing conditions of use or new research data make any statements in the manual incorrect or misleading. VERY DESIRABLE

[Comment: The technical characteristics and the appropriateness of a test may change as social conditions and attitudes, job definitions, educational pressures, or the composition of relevant school populations change.]

*A3.1. Competent studies of the test following its publication, whether the results are favorable or unfavorable to the test, should be taken into account in revised editions of the manual or its supplementary reports. Pertinent studies by investigators other than the test authors and publishers should be included. VERY DESIRABLE

[Comment: The developer of one test has published a comprehensive review of validity studies of the test covering a 15-year period.]

★A3.2. When the test is revised or a new form is issued, the manual should be suitably revised to take those changes into account. In addition, the nature and extent of the revision and the comparability of data from the old test and the revised test should be explicitly stated. ESSENTIAL

[Comment: It is useful for publishers to identify revisions of test manuals in their catalogs and to take other steps to increase the probability that test users have current information.]

★A3.2.1. If a short form of a test is prepared by reducing the number of items or organizing a portion of the test into a separate form, new evidence should be obtained and reported for that shorter test. ESSENTIAL

[Comment: It is especially important to report the reliability and other technical data for the test in its shorter form, since placing items in a new context may alter responses to them.
In the manual for one test that has two alternate forms, the validity data presented were obtained using the sum of the scores of the two forms. It would have been more appropriate to have presented the data for each form independently.]

*A3.2.2. When a short form is prepared from an established test, the manual should

present evidence that the items in the short form represent the items in the long form or measure the same characteristics as the long form. VERY DESIRABLE

[Comment: When no short form of a test has been prepared but there is reason to believe that it is commonly used in a shortened form, the manual should remind the reader that data in the manual may not be applicable to results of administration of a shortened form.

One revision of a long-established achievement test battery illustrates a desirable practice by listing all previous editions and then describing in detail the relation of the new revision to the previous editions.]

B. AIDS TO INTERPRETATION

The responsibility for making inferences about the meaning and legitimate uses of test results rests primarily with the user. In making such judgments, however, he must depend in part on information about the test made available by its developer.

The manual or report form from a scoring service cannot fully prepare the user for interpreting the test. He will sometimes have to make judgments that have not been substantiated by published evidence. Thus, the vocational counselor cannot expect to have validity data available for each job about which he makes tentative predictions from test scores. The counselor or employment interviewer will have examinees who do not fit into any group for which normative or validity data are available. The teacher will have to evaluate the content of an achievement test in terms of his instructional goals and emphasis. The clinician must bring general data and theory into his interpretation of data from a personality inventory. The degree to which the manual can be expected to prepare the user for accurate interpretation and effective use of the test varies with the type of test and the purpose for which it is used. It is the test developer's responsibility to provide the information necessary for good judgment; in fact, developers should make tests as difficult to misuse and to misinterpret as they can.

★B1. The test, the manual, the record forms, and other accompanying material should help users make correct interpretations of the test results and should warn against common misuses. ESSENTIAL

★B1.1. Names given to published tests, and to parts within tests, should be chosen to minimize the risk of misinterpretation by test purchasers and subjects. ESSENTIAL

[Comment: It is desirable that names carry no unwarranted suggestion as to the characteristics measured. Such descriptions as "culture-free," "intelligence," "introversion," "creativity," "primary mental abilities," or "productivity quotients" are questionable for published tests, unless there is appropriate evidence of construct validity, since they may suggest interpretations going beyond the demonstrable meaning of the scores.]

*B1.1.1. Devices for identifying interests and personality traits through self-report should be entitled "inventories," "questionnaires," or "checklists" rather than "tests." VERY DESIRABLE

[Comment: In referring to such instruments in textual material, however, as in these standards, the word "test" may be used to simplify the language even where it is properly avoided in the title.]

*B1.2. The manual should draw the user's attention to data that especially need to be taken into account in the interpretation of test scores. VERY DESIRABLE

[Comment: Many test manuals point out variables that should be considered in the interpretation of a test score, such as information about school record, recommendations, or clinically relevant history.

A personality assessment manual may provide data to show that the psychologist should consider such facts as the sex and age of the subject, whether his parents are dead or separated, the ages and sexes of his siblings, or his vocational or marital status.]

★B1.3. The manual should call attention to marked influences on test scores known to be associated with region, socioeconomic status, race, creed, color, national origin, or sex. ESSENTIAL

[Comment: Social or cultural factors known to affect performance on the test differentially, administrator errors that are frequently repeated, examiner-examinee differences, and other factors that may result in spurious or unfair test scores should, for example, be clearly and prominently identified in the manual.]

★B1.4. The manual should draw attention to, and warn against, any serious error of interpretation that is known to be frequent. ESSENTIAL

[Comment: Some users of general intelligence tests think of the score as a direct measure of inherent native ability, given and unchanging; manuals of such tests may be expected to caution against this interpretation and to do so with reference to appropriate data. They should clearly warn users against unwarranted assumptions about the generality of normative data, particularly avoiding the impression that national norms are genuinely representative when in fact they are not.

Manuals for interest inventories can apply this standard by stressing the fact that interest does not necessarily imply ability and is only one of many factors to be considered in choosing among occupations.]

★B2. The test manual should state explicitly the purposes and applications for which the test is recommended. ESSENTIAL

[Comment: A clear statement of a test's purposes will help prevent the misapplication of test scores. It will alert the user to the kind and extent of evidence he should expect to find in the manual in support of the claims made for the test by the author and publisher. For example, if an achievement test is recommended as a survey test of what students know, an accurate description of its content is important. If, on the other hand, it is recommended as a diagnostic test or one that predicts performance, data on its relationship with one or more criteria are required. See Section E on validity.]

★B2.1. If a test is intended for research use only and is not distributed for operational use, that fact should be prominently stated in the accompanying materials. ESSENTIAL

[Comment: If the developer of a new device (e.g., for studying personality) releases his instrument for studies by other investigators before he considers it ready for operational use, it is appropriate to print "distributed for research use only" on the test package, on the cover of the booklet of directions, and in any catalog where it is listed. This cautions against premature use of the instrument in guidance or selection.]

★B3. The test manual should describe clearly the psychological, educational, or other reasoning underlying the test and nature of the characteristic it is intended to measure. ESSENTIAL

[Comment: There ordinarily are explicit reasons for setting up the test as it has been done; it may be assumed that certain psychological processes are required in taking the test and that certain traits are being measured as a result. The identification of these processes may be based on a theory, empirical research, or empirical processes internal to the test itself. In any case, a clear description of the construct or content and of the manner of measurement enables a user to judge the test by its conformity to his own psychological or educational insight as well as by statistical evidence of its efficacy.]

★B3.1. In the case of tests developed for content-referenced interpretation, special attention should be given to defining the content domain in operational terms. In the case of a mastery test, the test developer's rationale for any cutting score that he suggests should be specified, or the procedures that the user might employ to establish mastery levels should be described. ESSENTIAL

[Comment: The test user needs such information so that he can compare his concept of mastery or competence with that of the test author.]

★B4. The test manual should identify any special qualifications required to administer the test and to interpret it properly. ESSENTIAL

[Comment: One manual differentiates psychologists who work with children from those who work only with adults in identifying qualifications needed to use an individually administered test for children. Another offers specifications for administering the test to non-English-speaking students.
User qualifications might be described in terms of special training generally thought necessary to achieve competence. It may be possible for some test manuals

to identify the most frequent sources of error in test use and to specify the kind of user training necessary to eliminate these common errors.]

★B4.1. The test manual should not imply that a test is "self-interpreting." It should specify information to be given about test results to persons who lack the training usually required to interpret them. ESSENTIAL

[Comment: It is not ordinarily desirable to entrust interpretation of scores to an untrained person. There are, of course, tests that can be scored by the examinee, and it is often useful to give scores to students or parents. Where these practices are followed, the sense of this standard is that interpretative aids should also be given.
The manual should indicate what may be done by untrained persons and what should not be done. The manual for one well-known interests test, for example, indicates that examinees may perform the mechanics of scoring their own tests but properly stresses that they need the help of a trained teacher or counselor in making interpretations and future plans.]

★B4.2. Where a test is recommended for a variety of purposes or types of inference, the manual should indicate the amount of training required for each use. ESSENTIAL

*B4.3. The manual should draw the user's attention to references with which he should become familiar before attempting to interpret the test results. VERY DESIRABLE

[Comment: The references might be to books or articles dealing with related psychological theory or with the particular test in question.]

★B5. Evidence of validity and reliability, along with other relevant research data, should be presented in support of any claims being made. ESSENTIAL

[Comment: Standards for validity and reliability are extensive. Moreover, they are as applicable to research reports prepared by test users as to test manuals. For these reasons, and because of their overreaching importance, a major section of this document presents standards for reports of research on validity and reliability. Adherence to the intent of this standard requires adherence to the appropriate standards in that section.]

★B5.1. Statements in the manual reporting relationships are by implication quantitative and should be stated as precisely as the data permit. If data to support such statements have not been collected, that fact should be made clear. ESSENTIAL

[Comment: Writers sometimes say, for example, "Spatial ability is required for architectural engineering," or, "Bizarre responses may indicate schizophrenic tendencies." Such statements by themselves are quantitatively inadequate. In what proportion of cases giving bizarre responses has schizophrenia been shown to develop? How much has architectural success been found to depend upon spatial ability? Numerical data relating the test scores to definite criteria would help to provide the answers.]

★B5.2. Statistical procedures that are well known and readily interpreted should be preferred for reporting any quantitative information. Any uncommon statistical techniques should be explained, and references to descriptions of them should be given. ESSENTIAL

[Comment: Publishers need not uniformly adhere to the procedures commonly used for reporting data, but terminology and procedures should be sufficiently common in practice to permit adequate judgment by reasonably competent users.

This standard is an elaboration of the principle that data presented in a manual should not be misleading. For example, it is misleading to show the value of combining tests in a battery in a regression equation by using data where intercorrelations are lower than those reported elsewhere in the manual.]

★B5.3. When the statistical significance of a relationship is reported, the statistical report should be in a form that makes clear the sensitivity or power of the significance test. ESSENTIAL

[Comment: Statistical significance that has no practical usefulness can often be obtained by using a very large number of cases. For example, a well-known inventory yields statistically significant differences between large samples of males and of females, but the differences are too small to be of practical importance. Conversely, one who uses an insensitive statistical test can falsely conclude that there is no difference of practical importance. In general, it is more appropriate in reporting test data to state a confidence interval or the likelihood function for the parameter of interest than to report only that the null hypothesis can or cannot be rejected.]

*B5.4. The manual should differentiate between an interpretation that is applicable only to average tendencies of a group and one that is applicable to an individual within the group. VERY DESIRABLE

★B5.5. The manual should state clearly what interpretations are intended for each subscore as well as for the total test. ESSENTIAL

[Comment: Where subscores are obtained only for convenience in scoring the test, and no interpretation is intended, this should be made clear. For some tests, keys are provided for subscores that have possible research use but are not intended to be interpreted; this should be made clear.]

★B6. Test developers or others offering computer services for test interpretation should provide a manual reporting the rationale and evidence in support of computer-based interpretations of scores. ESSENTIAL

[Comment: A computer makes possible the storage and recall of large amounts of data; test interpretation can be greatly assisted by the use of computer data banks. Computer scoring services may provide lengthy printouts of descriptive and prognostic information from individual profiles on a test battery or personality inventory. The user of such printouts needs to know the reasoning and the evidence supporting the suggested interpretations because they are as fallible as other subjective interpretations.]

C. DIRECTIONS FOR ADMINISTRATION AND SCORING

Interpretations of test and measurement techniques, like those of experimental results, are most reliable when the measurements are obtained under standardized or controlled conditions. To be sure, there are circumstances in testing where it may be important to change conditions systematically for maximum understanding of the performance of an individual. For example, an examiner may systematically modify procedures in successive readministrations of a test to explore the limits of a child's mastery of a specific content area such as a set of concepts. Nevertheless, the test developer should provide a standard procedure from which modifications can be made. Without standardization, the quality of interpretations will be reduced to whatever extent differences in procedure influence performance.

For most purposes, great emphasis is properly placed on strict standardization of procedures for administering a test and reciting its instructions. If a test is to be used for a wide range of subpopulations, these procedures should be wholly comprehensible to all examinees in each subpopulation.

★C1. The directions for administration should be presented in the test manual with sufficient clarity and emphasis so that the test user can duplicate, and will be encouraged to duplicate, the administrative conditions under which the norms and the data on reliability and validity were obtained. ESSENTIAL

[Comment: Because persons administering tests in schools and industry sometimes may not follow instructions rigidly and may not understand the need for doing so, it is necessary that the manual be insistent and persuasive on this point. Some tests are fully administered by tape recordings to insure standardization of procedure.]

★C1.1. The directions published in the test manual should be complete enough that persons tested will understand the task as the author intended. ESSENTIAL

[Comment: For example, in a personality inventory, it may be intended that the subject give the first response that occurs to him. If so, this expectation should be made clear in the directions read by or to the subject. Directions for interest inventories should specify whether the person is to mark what things he would ideally like to do or whether he is also to consider the possibility that he would have the opportunity and ability to do them. Likewise, the directions should specify whether the person is to mark those things he would like to do and does occasionally, or only those things he would like to do and does regularly.]

★C1.1.1. The directions should clearly point out such critical matters as instructions on guessing, time limits, and procedures for marking answer sheets. ESSENTIAL

*C1.1.2. The directions to the test administrator should include guidance for dealing with questions from examinees. VERY DESIRABLE

★C1.2. If expansion or elaboration of instructions described in the test manual is permitted, the conditions under which this may be done should be clearly stated either in the form of general rules or in terms of giving numerous examples, or both. ESSENTIAL

C2. Instructions should prepare the examinee for the examination: Sample material, practice use of answer sheets or punch cards, sample questions, etc., should be provided. DESIRABLE

[Comment: The extent and nature of such material depends on expected levels of knowledge among examinees. For example, extensive practice material might be wasteful if developed for frequently tested school children and for a commonly encountered type of test; it may be very important for a novel test format to be administered to older job applicants.]

★C3. The procedures for scoring the test should be presented in the test manual with a maximum of detail and clarity to reduce the likelihood of scoring error. ESSENTIAL

*C3.1. The test manual should furnish scoring instructions that maximize the accuracy of scoring an objective test by outlining a procedure for checking the obtained scores for computational or clerical errors. VERY DESIRABLE

*C3.2. Where subjective processes enter into the scoring of a test, evidence on the degree of agreement between independent scorings under operational conditions should be presented in the test manual. If such evidence is not provided, the manual should draw attention to scoring variations as a possible significant source of errors of measurement. VERY DESIRABLE

*C3.2.1. The bases for scoring and the procedures for training scorers should be presented in the test manual in sufficient detail to permit other scorers to reach the level of agreement reported in studies of scorer agreement given in the manual. VERY DESIRABLE

C3.2.2. If persons having various degrees of supervised training are expected to score the test, studies of the interscorer agreement at each skill level should be presented in the test manual. DESIRABLE

★C3.3. If the test is designed to use more than one method for the examinee's recording of his responses, such as hand-scored answer sheets, or entering of responses in the test booklet, the test manual should report data on the degree to which results from these methods are interchangeable. ESSENTIAL

[Comment: The different amounts of time required for responding to items in forms adapted to different scoring methods may affect the reliability or validity of the test or the applicability of the test norms.]

C3.4. If an unusual or complicated scoring system is used, the test manual should indicate the approximate amount of time required to score the test. DESIRABLE

C3.5. "Correction-for-guessing" formulas should be used with multiple-choice and true-false items when the test is speeded. DESIRABLE

D. NORMS AND SCALES

Interpretations of test scores traditionally have been *norm referenced;* that is, an individual's score is interpreted in terms of comparisons with scores made by other individuals. Alternative interpretations are possible. *Content-referenced* interpretations are those where the score is directly interpreted in terms of performance at each point on the achievement continuum being measured. *Criterion-referenced* interpretations are those where the score is directly interpreted in terms of performance at any given point on the continuum of an *external* variable. An external criterion variable might be grade averages or levels of job performance.[2]

The standards in this section refer principally to tests intended for norm-referenced test interpretations rather than for content-referenced interpretations.

★D1. Norms should be published in the test manual at the time of release of the test for operational use. ESSENTIAL

D1.1. Norms should be established even for a test developed only for local use or only for predictive purposes. DESIRABLE

2 Current usage in educational measurement commonly refers to "criterion-referenced" interpretations for *both* alternatives to interpretations requiring norms. The different meanings of the word "criterion," however, produce some confusion; some measurement specialists have therefore turned to the term "content referenced" and this usage is adopted here. The word "criterion," as it is used in the phrase "criterion-related" validity (that is, an external variable) has suggested a similar but distinguishable alternative to normative interpretation; therefore, "content-referenced and criterion-referenced" are not interchangeable terms as used in this document.

[Comment: It is sometimes forgotten that norms tables provide information useful for purposes other than comparing one individual with group data. For example, a test user can derive information from a normative table about the score levels at which the discrimination power of the measurement is good or poor.]

*D1.2. Even though a test is expected to be used primarily with local norms, the test manual should nevertheless provide normative data to aid the interpreter who lacks local norms. VERY DESIRABLE

[Comment: The manual for one instrument designed to measure employee aptitude stresses the value of local norms but also includes norms based on a wide variety of occupational and educational classifications.]

★D2. Norms presented in the test manual should refer to defined and clearly described populations. These populations should be the groups with whom users of the test will ordinarily wish to compare the persons tested. ESSENTIAL

[Comment: It should be noted that "populations" are plural; in nearly all instances of tests developed for other than purely local use, the user needs to know the applicability of the test to different groups. For tests developed with a view to widespread use in schools or industry, information is needed about differences or similarities of normative data for appropriate subgroups such as sex, ethnic, grade, or age groups. Users need to be alert to situations when norms are less extensive for one group than another.

For example, the manual for an occupational interest inventory, or for an aptitude test particularly useful in certain occupations, should point out that a person who has a high degree of interest or aptitude in a curriculum or occupation when compared to people in general will usually have a lower degree of interest or aptitude compared to persons actually engaged in that field. Thus, a high percentile score on a scale reflecting musical interest, in which the examinee is compared with people in general, may be equivalent to a low percentile where the examinee is compared with professional musicians.]

★D2.1. Care should be taken to avoid misleading impressions about the generality of normative data. ESSENTIAL

[Comment: Truly representative national norms, for example, are rarely if ever obtained; normative data collected from people or schools with specific characteristics, however, are frequently used as if they were taken from a representative national group. Thus, we have test users who may say that an examinee's performance is at a "tenth-grade reading level," without qualification when the norms are in fact obtained only from superior schools voluntarily participating in the test research. It is an error of interpretation to assume that the norms of the volunteer group of schools apply to schools in general; the incidence of such errors may be reduced by manuals that clearly define the characteristics of the normative populations.]

★D2.1.1. The test manual should report the method of sampling from the population of examinees and should discuss any probable bias in this sampling procedure. ESSENTIAL

★D2.1.2. Norms reported in any test manual should be based on well-planned samplings rather than on data collected primarily because it is readily available. Any deviations from the plan should be reported along with descriptions of actions taken or not taken with respect to them. ESSENTIAL

[Comment: Occupational and educational test norms have often been based on scattered groups of test papers, for authors sometimes have requested that all users mail in results for use in subsequent reports of norms. Distributions so obtained are subject to unknown degrees and types of biases. Hence, the methods of obtaining such samples should be clearly described.]

★D2.1.3. In addition to reporting the number of individuals in a set of normative data, the manual should also report the number of sampling units from which those individuals were drawn along with the numbers of individuals in each unit. ESSENTIAL

★D2.2. The description of the norms group in the test manual should be complete enough so that the user can judge its appropriateness for his use. The description should include number of cases, classified by one or more of such relevant variables as ethnic mix, socioeconomic level, age, sex, locale, and educational status. If cluster sampling is employed, the description of the norms group should state the number of separate groups tested. ESSENTIAL

[Comment: Manuals often use too gross a classification system in describing their normative data. For example, the manual for one employee aptitude test provides a variety of normative data for many occupational and educational groupings. However, the lack of information as to sex, ethnic origins, age, education, and experience levels within these groupings considerably reduces the usefulness of the norms.]

★D2.2.1. The populations upon which the psychometric properties of a test were determined and for which normative data are available should be *clearly and prominently described* in the manual. Any accompanying report forms should provide space for identifying the normative groups used in interpreting the scores. ESSENTIAL

[Comment: The intent of this standard is to provide a warning to consumers (users and examinees) against unwarranted interpretations. If a standard report form results in percentile-rank or standard-score interpretations by consistently using the same normative population, the definition of that population, with an indication of the time period of data collection, would be sufficient.]

*D2.3. If the sample on which norms are based is small or otherwise undependable, the user should be cautioned explicitly in the test manual regarding the possible magnitude of errors arising in the interpretation of scores. VERY DESIRABLE

★**D2.4.** Norms on subtests or groups of test items should be reported in the test manual only if the validity and reliability of such subtests or groups of items are also indicated. ESSENTIAL

[Comment: The test user is justified in assuming that, when norms are given for part of a test, the author implies their usefulness for interpreting performance. The reliability and validities of such scores should be reported.]

★**D2.5.** The significant aspects of conditions under which normative data were obtained should be reported in the test manual. ESSENTIAL

[Comment: Some tests are standardized on job-applicant groups, others on groups that have requested vocational guidance, and, still others, on groups that realized that they were experimental subjects. While precise description of levels is probably not always possible, motivation for taking tests, test-taking attitudes, abilities, and personality characteristics often differ within these groups and from group to group.]

★**D3. In reporting norms, test manuals should use percentiles for one or more appropriate reference groups or standard scores for which the basis is clearly set forth; any exceptional type of score or unit should be explained and justified. Measures of central tendency and variability always should be reported.** ESSENTIAL

D3.1. In the case of tests used for prediction, expectancy tables or experience tables translating obtained scores into probabilities of success or into proficiency levels should be included whenever possible. DESIRABLE

*__D4. Local norms are more important for many uses of tests than are published norms. A test manual should suggest using local norms in such situations.__ VERY DESIRABLE

★**D5. Derived scales used for reporting scores should be carefully described in the test manual to increase the likelihood of accurate interpretation of scores by both the test interpreter and the examinee.** ESSENTIAL

[Comment: It would be helpful if the number of kinds of derived scales could be reduced to a few with which testers can become familiar. The present variety makes description necessary in each manual. In part the problem is that many different systems are now used that have no logical advantage over others; some may have outlived their usefulness. New scaling methods may be used in attempts to overcome presumed difficulties with older ones. The variety of scales for reporting test scores can create confusion and misinterpretation unless the scales recommended for a given test are clearly and fully explained.]

★**D5.1.** Derivation of any scale from normative data should be clearly and unambiguously described in terms likely to prevent user misinterpretations or overgeneralization. ESSENTIAL

[Comment: Derived scores can be very useful for drawing inferences. Too often, however, they are treated as if they had absolute meaning independent of a particular test or normative population. An example is the IQ; it is often simply a standard score, but it is frequently reified and interpreted as representing an unchanging and unchangeable characteristic of the person tested. Grade-equivalent scores or even percentile ranks may also be misinterpreted as absolute entities unless the manual makes clear the reference group on which they were based.]

*__D5.2.__ When standard scores are used, the system should be consistent with the purposes for which the test is intended and should be described in detail in the test manual. The reasons for choosing one scale in preference to another should also be made clear in the manual. VERY DESIRABLE

★**D5.2.1.** The manual should specify whether standard scores are linear transformations of raw scores or are normalized. ESSENTIAL

D5.2.2. The choice of a standard scale should be based upon either the standard error of measurement of raw scores or on some other basis that is clearly defined. DESIRABLE

[Comment: There are many standard-score scales in use. The scale for reporting scores on one widely used test is so designed that each unit of the scale is equal to about one thirtieth of the overall standard error of measurement; a different test used for similar purposes is scaled so that one unit is equal to about one third the overall standard error of measurement. The former scale suggests a greater degree of precision than the latter, but this implication is unwarranted.]

*__D5.2.3.__ Interpretive scores that lend themselves to gross misinterpretations, such as mental-age or grade-equivalent scores, should be abandoned or their use discouraged. VERY DESIRABLE

[Comment: When, despite this recommendation, such scores are included in a manual, their relationship to standard scores or percentile ranks, within each category and within an appropriate norm group, should also be provided in tabular form. For example, the table might show, in addition to a grade-equivalent score, the corresponding percentile rank within the examinee's own age or grade level for each raw score. At the high school level, norms within courses (for example, second-year Spanish) may be more appropriate than norms within grades.]

*__D5.3.__ When it is suggested in the test manual that percentile ranks are to be plotted on a profile sheet, the profile sheet should be based on the normal probability scale or some other appropriate nonlinear transformation. VERY DESIRABLE

*D5.4. Normative data should be provided in a form that emphasizes the fallibility of an obtained score. VERY DESIRABLE

[Comment: Some publishers provide norms showing ranges of standard scores or percentile ranks that have designated probability levels of including the true score. A norms table might show for each raw score, not only the associated standard score or percentile rank but also the values for raw scores at plus and at minus one standard error of measurement for each raw score.]

D6. If scales are revised, new forms added, or other changes made, the revised test manual should provide tables of equivalence between the new and the old forms. This provision is particularly important in cases where data are recorded on cumulative records. DESIRABLE

[Comment: New forms of a test should be equated to *recently determined* standard-score scales of other forms, in order that the user may be confident that the scores furnished by the new forms are comparable with those of earlier forms.]

★D6.1. When a new form is equated with an older form of a test, the revised manual should describe the content of both old and new forms and the nature of the norms group for each form. ESSENTIAL

[Comment: Changes in knowledge, technology, or curricula may require that new editions of a test differ in important respects from earlier editions, and the demand for continuity may require that the scales for reporting scores be equated. There is some doubt as to whether meaningful comparability of scores is possible with changed content, however, and a user should be able to evaluate claims of equivalency in terms of the kinds of content changes that have occurred.]

*D6.2. The manual should describe the method used to establish equivalent or comparable scores and should include an assessment of the accuracy of the equating procedure. VERY DESIRABLE

★D7. Where it is expected that a test will be used to assess groups rather than individuals (i.e., for schools or programs), normative data based on group summary statistics should be provided. ESSENTIAL

[Comment: For example, it is inappropriate to evaluate schools by using norms developed for the evaluation of individuals. It is also inappropriate to compute group means for nonlinear scales such as percentile ranks derived for individual norms.]

STANDARDS FOR REPORTS OF RESEARCH ON RELIABILITY AND VALIDITY

A test developer must provide evidence of the reliability and validity of his test; it is usually reported in the test manual. Many test users should do similar research on their own application of the test. Their reports often differ from those in test manuals by being more detailed or more specific to a particular problem, or by validating test batteries rather than individual tests. Despite such differences, the standards of research, and of research reporting, should be generally similar in the two situations.

E. VALIDITY

Questions of validity are questions of what may properly be inferred from a test score; validity refers to the appropriateness of inferences from test scores or other forms of assessment. The many types of validity questions can, for convenience, be reduced to two: (*a*) What can be inferred about what is being measured by the test? (*b*) What can be inferred about other behavior?

The first question inquires into the intrinsic nature of the measurement itself. The measuring instrument is an operational definition of a specified domain of skill or knowledge, or of a trait, of interest to the test developer or user. The essential problem in this context is to reach some conclusion as to how faithfully the scores represent that domain, and it is appropriate to speak of the validity of the measurement.

The second question inquires into the usefulness of the measurement as an indicator of some other variable, for example, as a predictor of behavior. In this context, the essential problem is to reach some conclusion about how well scores on the test are related to some other performance, and it is appropriate to speak of the closeness of the relationship.

The two questions are not necessarily independent. For example, where the test is a sample of the "other behavior," the answer is the same for either question. Moreover, answers to both questions may require a knowledge of the interrelationships between the test scores and other variables. A thorough understanding of validity may require many investigations. The investigative processes of gathering or evaluating the necessary data are called validation. There are various methods of validation, and all, in a fundamental sense, require a definition of what is to be inferred from the scores and data to show that there is an acceptable basis for such inferences.

It is important to note that validity is itself inferred, not measured. Validity coefficients may be presented in a manual, but validity for a particular aspect of test use is inferred from this collection of coefficients. It is, therefore, something that is *judged* as adequate, or marginal, or unsatisfactory.

The kinds of validity depend upon the kinds of inferences one might wish to draw from test scores. Four interdependent kinds of inferential interpretation are traditionally described to summarize most test use: the *criterion-related* validities (*predictive* and *concurrent*); *content* validity; and *construct* validity.[3] (So-called "face" validity, the mere appearance of validity, is not an acceptable basis for interpretive inferences from test scores.)

These aspects of validity can be discussed independently, but only for convenience. They are interrelated operationally and logically; only rarely is one of them alone important in a particular situation. A thorough study of a test may often involve information about all types of validity. In developing or choosing a test for prediction, one should first postulate the constructs likely to provide a basis for useful prediction of the variable of interest; the measures chosen should have adequate construct validity. The content universe from which items are sampled may also be an important early step in producing a predictive test, in evaluating a test considered for use as a predictor, or in developing the criterion measure to be predicted. Even if the accuracy of prediction is good, information about construct validity may make a test more useful. To evaluate construct validity, all knowledge regarding validity is relevant. A reading comprehension test, for example, may be used and validated for all three types of inference: how well it predicts future academic performance, how well it samples a defined content area of material to read, and how well it measures the construct of comprehension.

Criterion-Related Validities

Criterion-related validities apply when one wishes to infer from a test score an individual's most probable standing on some other variable called a criterion. Statements of predictive va-

lidity indicate the extent to which an individual's future level on the criterion can be predicted from a knowledge of prior test performance; statements of concurrent validity indicate the extent to which the test may be used to estimate an individual's present standing on the criterion. The distinction is important. Predictive validity involves a time interval during which something may happen (e.g., people are trained, or gain experience, or are subjected to some treatment). Concurrent validity reflects only the status quo at a particular time. Under appropriate circumstances, data obtained in a concurrent study may be used to estimate the predictive validity of a test. However, concurrent validity should not be used as a substitute for predictive validity without an appropriate supporting rationale.

For many test uses, such as for selection decisions or assignment to treatment, predictive validity provides the appropriate model for evaluating the use of a test or test battery. In employment testing, for example, use of any procedure implies prediction to some degree. Whether one uses a carefully developed test or casual judgments of interviewers, their use for selection purposes assumes that applicants who obtain high scores will become better employees than applicants who obtain low scores.

Other forms of validity are not substitutes for criterion-related validity. In choosing a test to select people for a job, for example, an abundance of evidence of the construct validity of a test of flexibility in divergent thinking, or of the content validity of a test of elementary calculus, is of no predictive value without reason to believe that flexibility of thinking or knowledge of calculus aids performance on that job. The *model* of predictive validity should guide thinking about validity in such applications even where circumstances preclude an actual criterion-related validation study. Whatever other validity information a manual may include, one or more studies of criterion-related validity must be included for any test developed for prediction and for many tests intended for diagnosis; otherwise, such tests can only be regarded as experimental.

Many factors may make a single, obtained validity coefficient questionable. First, the conditions of a validation study are never exactly repeated. Rapidly changing conditions may limit the usefulness of a predictive study. The

3 Many other terms have been used. Examples include synthetic validity, convergent validity, job-analytic validity, rational validity, and factorial validity. In general, such terms refer to specific procedures for evaluating validity rather than to new kinds of interpretive inferences. Any specially-named procedures, including these examples, should meet the standards of investigation contained in this section. These standards apply generally to the various statistics or procedures that might be used in support of one or more classes of inferences from test scores.

logic of predictive validation assumes that conditions existing at the start of the time sequence will exist again after the study is completed.

Second, the logic of criterion-related validity assumes that the criterion possesses validity. All too often, tests are validated against any available criterion with no corresponding investigation of the criterion itself. The merit of a criterion-related validity study depends on the appropriateness and quality of the criterion measure chosen. In applied research, the criterion should be chosen with reference to the problem at hand, and the test or other assessment technique should be chosen with reference to the criterion. If the study is done primarily to enhance understanding of what a test measures, criteria should be selected in terms of beliefs about the nature of the construct reflected by the test scores. In either case, the adequacy of the study depends on the adequacy of the criterion. Criterion-related validity studies based on the "criterion at hand," chosen more for availability than for a place in a carefully reasoned hypothesis, are to be deplored.

Third, the logic of criterion-related validity assumes that the sample is truly representative of the population for which the later inferences are to be drawn. In practice, samples are often nonrepresentative because of, for example, restricted range, preselection, or attrition before a predictive study can be completed.

Fourth, in many practical situations validity studies cannot be done with adequate numbers of cases, and the investigators must do the best they can with the data at hand. It may be better to try to investigate criterion-related validity, even if imperfectly, than to accept totally untested hypotheses. However, "doing something" is not necessarily better than doing nothing; the results of an inadequate study may be quite misleading. Results of validation studies with severely restricted ranges or small Ns are especially open to question.

Content Validity

Evidence of content validity is required when the test user wishes to estimate how an individual performs in the universe of situations the test is intended to represent. Content validity is most commonly evaluated for tests of skill or knowledge; it may also be appropriate to inquire into the content validities of personality inventories, behavior checklists, or measures of various aptitudes. The present discussion will be directed toward the more typical case of achievement testing.

To demonstrate the content validity of a set of test scores, one must show that the behaviors demonstrated in testing constitute a representative sample of behaviors to be exhibited in a desired performance domain. Definitions of the performance domain, the users' objectives, and the method of sampling are critical to claims of content validity. An investigation of content validity requires that the test developer or test user specify his objectives and carefully define the performance domain in light of those objectives. The definition should ordinarily specify the results of learning rather than the processes by which learning is either acquired or demonstrated. It should be sufficiently detailed and organized to show the degree to which component tasks make up the total domain.

Definition of the performance domain is relatively simple where it is finite and unambiguous, as in a simple test of addition for elementary-school use. Depending upon instructional objectives, the performance domain might be defined as *all* addition problems of three to five single-integer addends. The total number of problems and the relative frequency of occurrence of specific integers or pairs of integers within that total are known, and the representativeness of any sample of such problems can be easily judged.

If a test is used to estimate achievement in American history in grade 12, the performance domain is less objectively defined. Given agreement on instructional objectives, it could be defined in terms of the types and quantities of the skills, facts, and concepts of American history, as determined by the pooled judgments of authorities, experienced teachers, and competent curriculum makers in that field. A definition of the total universe might well be tempered by the specific instructional objectives accepted by the panel. A definition appropriate for evaluation of performance at the end of the year of study would differ from the definition appropriate for developing an examination over knowledge of the colonial period. Within such limits, the performance domain requires definition so carefully detailed that rules for item writing will assure appropriate representation of all facets of the definition. It should be noted that an achievement test so constructed would not necessarily constitute a representative sample of the skills, facts, and concepts taught by any particular teacher during any particular year. Consequently, a definition of the performance domain of interest must always be provided by a test user so that the content of a test may be checked against an appropriate task universe.

It is appropriate to inquire into the content validity of many employment tests. Examples would include tests of typing skill, driving ability, or knowledge of certain regulatory laws. The performance domain for published tests might be defined by the pooled judgments of job designers, incumbents, and supervisors. Test users might define the performance domain of interest to them in terms of judgments of similar people in their own organizations or, preferably, in terms of appropriately detailed and comprehensive job analyses. The question of objectives would again enter into the definition; unless only fully trained and experienced people are to be hired, applicants cannot be expected to demonstrate proficiency in all facets of a job. The performance domain would need definition in terms of the objectives of measurement, restricted perhaps only to critical, most frequent, or prerequisite work behaviors.

It should be clear that content validity is quite different from face validity. Content validity is determined by a set of operations, and one evaluates content validity by the thoroughness and care with which these operations have been conducted. In contrast, face validity is a judgment that the requirements of a test merely *appear* to be relevant. The writing of items in terms used in a particular job or by a particular subgroup of the population may give an appearance of relevance while contributing nothing to content validity or indeed to any other useful validity information (although such items may serve a useful public-relations function).

In defining the content universe, a test developer or user is accountable for the adequacy of his definition. An employer cannot justify an employment test on grounds of content validity if he cannot demonstrate that the content universe includes all, or nearly all, important parts of the job.

Construct Validity

A psychological construct is an idea developed or "constructed" as a work of informed, scientific imagination; that is, it is a theoretical idea developed to explain and to organize some aspects of existing knowledge. Terms such as "anxiety," "clerical aptitude," or "reading readiness" refer to such constructs, but the construct is much more than the label; it is a dimension understood or inferred from its network of interrelationships.[4] It may be necessary to postulate several different constructs to account for the variance in any given set of test scores. Moreover, different constructs may be required to account for the variance in different tests of the same general type, or a given test may provide evidence relating to several constructs. For example, given proper evidence, scores on vocabulary tests might be used to infer (*a*) the level of present vocabulary; (*b*) the existence of pathology, interests, or values; or (*c*) intellectual capacity.

Construct validity is implied when one evaluates a test or other set of operations in light of the specified construct. Judgments of construct validity are useful in efforts to improve measures for the scientific study of a construct. They are also useful when a test developer or test user wishes to learn more about the psychological qualities being measured by a test than can be learned from a single criterion-related validity coefficient.

Evidence of construct validity is not found in a single study; rather, judgments of construct validity are based upon an accumulation of research results. In obtaining the information needed to establish construct validity, the investigator begins by formulating hypotheses about the characteristics of those who have high scores on the test in contrast to those who have low scores. Taken together, such hypotheses form at least a tentative theory about the nature of the construct the test is believed to be measuring. In a full investigation, the test may be the dependent variable in some studies and the independent variable in others. Some hypotheses may be "counterhypotheses" suggested by competing interpretations or theories.

Such hypotheses or theoretical formulations lead to certain predictions about how people at

4 This is an admittedly restricted statement of the nature of scientific constructs, which may include entities as well as dimensions. Constructs of interest in the present context are, however, primarily quantitative.

different score levels on the test will behave on certain other tests or in certain defined situations. If the investigator's theory about what the test measures is essentially correct, most of his predictions should be confirmed. If they are not, he may revise his definition of the construct, or he may revise the test to make it a better measure of the construct he had in mind. Through the process of successive verification, modification, or elimination of hypotheses, the investigator increases his understanding of the qualities measured by the test. Through the process of confirmation or disconfirmation, test revision, and new research on the revised instrument, he improves the usefulness of the test as a measure of a construct.

It is important to note in this that the investigation of construct validity refers to a specific test and not necessarily to any other test given the same label.

Evidence of construct validity may also be inferred from the procedures followed in developing a test. For example, in a measure of mechanical interest, a double item analysis may be used to reduce the effect of verbal ability. A preliminary item analysis might be done using a standard verbal-comprehension test as an external criterion. Those items with a very low discrimination index in this analysis could then be subjected to a second item analysis, a conventional internal-consistency analysis. Only those items with a low discrimination index in the first analysis and a high discrimination index in the second analysis would be included in the final item pool.

Although evidence of construct validity may be developed on the basis of a series of criterion-related studies, it is important to note that evidence of the construct validity of a test is *not* adequate evidence of the usefulness of the construct in specific further hypotheses. In the selection of salespersons, for example, it is often hypothesized that success is a function of sociability. If one has a measure of sociability with generally acceptable evidence of its validity as a measure of that construct, he may expect to find it useful as a predictor of sales success; perhaps some of the evidence of the construct validity of that measure came, in fact, from confirmation of such an expectation. However, the test may have no predictive validity against the criterion of success in an engineering sales job. In such a case it is not the construct validity of the sociability measure that is to be questioned.

General Principles

A test developer, or anyone who conducts validation research, should provide as much validity information as possible so the user can evaluate the test or the research for his own purposes. A test manual can provide evidence that will enable the user to evaluate the appropriateness of the item content, to determine whether the test is an acceptable measure of a specified construct, and to decide whether the test has provided useful predictive validities in situations similar to his own. An adequate research report can help the user decide whether to go ahead with the use of the test or to seek another predictor.

★**E1. A manual or research report should present the evidence of validity for each type of inference for which use of the test is recommended. If validity for some suggested interpretation has not been investigated, that fact should be made clear.** ESSENTIAL

[Comment: Validation studies are a part of the process of test development; test users expect them to be reported in detail by the developer, preferably in the manual itself. At the very least, the manual should summarize competent research reported elsewhere, either by the test developer or by others. Preferably, the manual will report on individual studies and provide summaries of validity data for various kinds of interpretations or inferences.]

★**E1.1.** Statements about validity should refer to the validity of particular interpretations or of particular types of decisions. ESSENTIAL

[Comment: It is incorrect to use the unqualified phrase "the validity of the test." *No test is valid for all purposes or in all situations or for all groups of individuals.* Any study of test validity is pertinent to only a few of the possible uses of or inferences from the test scores.

If the test is likely to be used incorrectly for certain areas of decision, the manual should include specific warnings. For example, the manual for a writing-skills test stated that the test apparently was not sufficiently difficult to discriminate among students "at colleges that have selective admissions."]

★**E1.2.** Wherever interpretation of subscores, score differences, or profiles is suggested, the evidence justifying such interpretation should be made explicit. (See also B5.5.) ESSENTIAL

★**E1.2.1.** If the manual suggests that the user consider an individual's responses to specific items as a basis for assessment, it should either present evidence supporting this use or call attention to the absence of such data. The manual should warn the reader that inferences based on responses to single items are subject to extreme error. Hence, they should be used only to direct further inquiry, perhaps in a counseling interview. ESSENTIAL

*E1.3. To insure the continued correct interpretation of scores, the validity of suggested interpretations should be rechecked periodically; test developers should report results in subsequent editions of the manual. VERY DESIRABLE

[Comment: Job duties, conditions of work, and the types of individuals entering an occupation often change materially with the passage of time. Similarly, the meanings of clinical categories, the nature of therapeutic treatment, and the objectives of academic programs change. The difficulty and psychological meaning of test items will also change. Hence, the reader should be in a position to judge the extent to which tests are obsolete.]

*E1.3.1. If factors that may affect test performance or the validity of a suggested test interpretation have changed, and validity studies have not been repeated for the changed conditions, the test should be withdrawn from general sale and distributed, if at all, only to persons who will conduct their own validity studies. VERY DESIRABLE

[Comment: It should be noted that no specific time interval is mentioned. Test developers and publishers should know the relevant conditions and should be able and willing to obtain new validity information when such conditions have changed. It is not necessary to repeat every part of the validation; what is needed is a repetition of those studies most likely to have been rendered obsolete. In the case of some inventories and biographical-data forms, scoring keys should be reevaluated after relatively brief periods of time.]

★E1.4. Correlations of item scores with total scores on the test in which the item is included (or a parallel form of that test) may be presented as item-discrimination coefficients, but they should not be presented or used as item-validity coefficients. ESSENTIAL

[Comment: Item-discrimination coefficients are useful in reasoning about construct validity, and such information is appropriately included in a manual. However, they are indicators of internal consistency, not of validity.]

★E2. A test user is responsible for marshalling the evidence in support of his claims of validity and reliability. The use of test scores in decision rules should be supported by evidence. ESSENTIAL

[Comment: It is a basic responsibility of a test user to read, understand, and evaluate the manual, the research, and the literature to show the appropriateness of the test for the intended use. A large-scale user may have the added responsibility for empirical research bearing on his claims of test validity. Evidence of valid-

ity is needed for *all* bases for decision, not merely those that are easy to study. It is a peculiar paradox that many employers and schools are abandoning the use of standardized tests and are turning instead to casual assessment techniques likely to be less valid. Many employers use procedures with no validity, or biased selection procedures of unknown validity rather than objective procedures for which evidence of validity could have been assembled.]

*E2.1. Test users are responsible for gathering data on the validity and reliability of their assessment techniques. VERY DESIRABLE

[Comment: For many individual test users, this may be a nearly impossible requirement. It would seem, however, that a test user has an obligation to gather data, at least on an informal basis, in an effort to evaluate his work. In even the most difficult circumstances, a test user can be alert to data suggesting possible lack of validity.]

*E2.2. If a user wants to use a test in a situation for which the use of the test has not been previously validated, or for which there is no supported claim for validity, he is responsible for validation. VERY DESIRABLE

[Comment: He who makes the claim for validity is responsible for providing the evidence. Evidence of validity sufficient for test use may often be obtained in a well-documented manual. If the test user wishes to claim that the validity generalizes beyond the evidence for the kinds of situations reported in the manual, it is his responsibility to demonstrate it.]

★E2.3. When a test user plans to make a substantial change in test format, instructions, language, or content, he should revalidate the use of the tests for the changed conditions. ESSENTIAL

Criterion-Related Validity

★E3. All measures of criteria should be described completely and accurately. The manual or research report should comment on the adequacy of a criterion. Whenever feasible, it should draw attention to significant aspects of performance that the criterion measure does not reflect and to irrelevant factors likely to affect it. ESSENTIAL

[Comment: Desirable practices are illustrated in a manual for a test designed to measure abstract intelligence. Several validity studies relating this instrument to criteria are reported, some involving concurrent measures and others involving predictions over periods of time. Limitations of the studies are recognized, and it is stated that "no one criterion is uniquely appropriate." The value of local norms is stressed, and an example of a local expectancy table is provided.

In the case of interest measures, it is sometimes not made clear whether the criterion indicates satisfaction, success, or merely continuance in the activity under examination. When criterion groups include people in a given occupation and when a comparison of such groups is made to people in general, the manual should point out the distinction between working in an occupation and success in it or satisfaction with it.]

*E3.1. When the validity of a test for predicting occupational performance is reported, the manual should describe the duties of the workers as well as give their job titles. VERY DESIRABLE

[Comment: The principle is that information should be given from which the reader can make judgments of the relevance of the criterion. The description of a criterion is often incomplete without such information.]

★E3.1.1. Where a wide range of duties is subsumed under a given occupational label, the test user should be warned against assuming that only one pattern of interests or abilities is compatible with the occupation. ESSENTIAL

*E4. A criterion measure should itself be studied for evidence of validity and that evidence should be presented in the manual or report. VERY DESIRABLE

[Comment: Criterion measures are forms of assessment and are subject to the same standards governing the development and use of any assessment technique. For many employment and educational purposes, the ideal criterion may be an achievement test or work sample judged acceptable in terms of content validity. Supervisory or instructor ratings are more common but may be questioned in terms of construct validity. For example, a rating of proficiency may be defined to include elements of both speed and accuracy, but to exclude elements of dependability. A judgment of acceptable construct validity might be based on evidence of high correlations of the ratings with production data or work samples and of independence from seniority or attendance data.]

★E4.1. Particular attention should be given to potential sources of criterion contamination; results of investigations of contamination should be reported. ESSENTIAL

[Comment: Results of such investigations are often ambiguous, and readers should be warned of this fact. For example, an investigation of possible sex differences in criterion ratings might show significant differences between men and women. That fact in itself, however, is not sufficient evidence of criterion contamination; it might reflect actual sex differences in performance.]

★E4.1.1. The criterion score should be determined independently of test scores. The manual should describe precautions taken to avoid contamination of the criterion or should warn the reader of possible contamination. ESSENTIAL

[Comment: When the criterion is based on judgment, the manual should state whether the test data were available to the judge or were capable of influencing the judgments in any other way. If the test data could have influenced the criterion rating, the user should be warned that the reported validities are likely to be spuriously high.]

★E4.2. The basis for judgments of criterion relevance should be clearly set forth. ESSENTIAL

*E4.3. Criterion-related validation should ordinarily consider more than a single global criterion. VERY DESIRABLE

[Comment: In most situations where decision rules based on testing are worthwhile, performance falls along many dimensions that may be independent. Combining unrelated aspects of behavior into a single composite criterion may obscure important relationships and reduce a test user's opportunity to identify and understand valid test interpretations.

A problem exists in that single decisions must frequently be made on multivariate bases. Nevertheless, it is preferable to find a decision rule for combining predictions than to use a decision rule for combining predictors of ambiguous validity.]

*E4.4. In criterion-related validation, it is important that the criterion measure have substantial reliability. VERY DESIRABLE

[Comment: Since corrections for unreliability of a criterion can be made with generally reasonable statistical assumptions, the degree of reliability of a criterion is perhaps less important than the degree of reliability of the predictor. Nevertheless, reliability is not a trivial consideration; reasonable effort should be made to assure a level of reliability such that statistical corrections are unlikely to change interpretations markedly.]

*E4.4.1. Since the criterion measure is a sample of all possible measures of the same criterion construct, reliability should be reported in terms of the agreement of that sample with other similar samples where feasible. If such evidence cannot be given, the author should make this clear and should discuss the probable extent of agreement of the sample with other samples as judged from indirect evidence. VERY DESIRABLE

[Comment: When validity is measured by agreement of the test with psychiatric judgment, for example, the degree of agreement among judges should be described. Where a published achievement test is used as a criterion measure, the form-to-form agreement or the reliability reported by the test's author may be used as a basis for evaluating the criterion, due regard being given to the effect of differences between the present sample of persons and the original sample.]

*E4.4.2. When validity is appraised by agreement of test results with psychiatric diagnoses, the diagnostic terms or categories should be defined specifically and described clearly. VERY DESIRABLE

[Comment: For example, "paranoid schizophrenia, chronic" is preferable as a category to "schizophrenia." Since the types of patients included in specific diagnostic classifications depend to some extent on the point of view of the classifying psychiatrist, an amplified description of each diagnostic category used in the validity study should be presented.]

*E4.4.3. When validity is appraised by the agreement of test results with psychiatric judgments, the training, experience, and professional status of the judge(s) should be stated, and the nature and extent of his contacts with the patients and other factors influencing the interaction should be reported. VERY DESIRABLE

*E5. The manual or research report should provide information on the appropriateness of or limits to the generalizability of validity information. VERY DESIRABLE

★E5.1. A test manual should report evidence of validity for each type of criterion about which a recommendation is made. If validity for some recommended interpretation has not been tested, that fact should be made clear. ESSENTIAL

[Comment: This principle should not be interpreted as license to present as validity information various correlations with irrelevant variables. Data should be presented with reference to recommended interpretations, either supporting those interpretations or suggesting limitations to them.]

★E5.2. For any type of prediction, a test manual should report criterion-related validities for a variety of institutions or situations. Where validity studies have been confined to a limited range of situations, the manual should remind the reader of the risks involved in generalizing to other types of situations. ESSENTIAL

*E5.2.1. Validity coefficients are specific to the situations in which they are obtained. If the manual is to suggest generalization of validity for prediction of a given kind of criterion construct, it must present data suggesting the limits of generalizability regarding population or sample characteristics, situational context variables, or variations in criterion measurement. VERY DESIRABLE

E5.2.2. Local collection of evidence on criterion-related validity is frequently more useful than published data. In such cases the manual should suggest appropriate emphasis on local validity studies; and test users should, where feasible, conduct such studies. DESIRABLE

[Comment: In cases where criteria differ from one locality to another or from one institution to another, no published validity data can serve all localities. For example, the validity of a certain test for predicting grades at a college with a unique kind of curriculum may be quite different from the published validities of the same test based on a more conventional curriculum. Some publishers have made available advice on local validation studies, including information on the preparation of expectancy tables.]

★E6. The sample employed in a validity study and the conditions under which testing is done should be consistent with recommended test use and should be described sufficiently for the reader to judge its pertinence to his situation. ESSENTIAL

★E6.1. Any selective factor determining the composition of the validation sample should be indicated in a manual or research report. The sample should be described in terms of those variables known as thought to affect validity, such as age, sex, socioeconomic status, ethnic origin, residential region, level of education, or other demographic or psychological characteristics. ESSENTIAL

[Comment: If a validity study uses patients as subjects, the diagnoses of the patients would usually be important to report. The severity of the diagnosed condition should be stated when feasible. For tests used in industry the employment status, occupational experience, and the sex and ethnic composition of the sample should be described. For tests used in educational settings, relevant information may include community characteristics or any selection policies.]

★E6.1.1. Evidence of validity should be obtained for subjects who are of the same age or in the same educational or vocational situation as the persons for whom the test is recommended. Any deviation from this requirement should be described in the manual or research report. ESSENTIAL

[Comment: Validity information for tests intended for guidance should generally be determined on subjects tested prior to or near the time when they are making educational or vocational choices.

One interest inventory was first standardized on men currently employed in the occupation in question. The ability of these scales to differentiate between occupational groups did not, in and of itself, warrant using the inventory in the counseling of high school or college students. Better evidence was obtained later by administering the inventory to students, determining the nature of their later employment, and then establishing the relation between preoccupational score and later occupation.

If an interest inventory uses a criterion of enrollment or nonenrollment in a certain occupation, the sample used in its validation should include only the range of mental ability appropriate to the occupational group. For example, college students are not suitable subjects with whom to estimate the validity of an inventory of interest in manual skills, even though some of them later enter manual occupations.]

*E6.1.2. If an ability test is to be used for educational or occupational selection, its validity should be established using subjects who are actual candidates and who are therefore ordinarily motivated to perform well. If the subjects used in a validity study are volunteers or were told that their test scores would not be used in making decisions about them, this fact should be made clear. VERY DESIRABLE

[Comment: Widespread use is made in industrial selection of the "present-employee method" of validation. Typically, this involves administering the tests to present employees who are told that their performance on the test will not influence their employment situation. The motivational difference may distort sample characteristics in that it introduces a completely new variable to the testing situation.]

*E6.2. Basic statistics should be reported in describing the sample, including numbers of cases (and the reasons for any eliminated cases) and measures of central tendency and variability. A description of the distribution, perhaps with measures of skewness and kurtosis, should also be included. VERY DESIRABLE

[Comment: The smaller the number of cases in a validation sample, the less reliable the statistics. Consider, for example, the effect of the number of cases on the 95% confidence interval when the obtained correlation coefficient is .30. With 250 pairs of observations, the interval runs from .18 to .41. Where $N = 50$, the interval runs from .02 to .53; where $N = 25$, the interval runs from −.10 to +.62.

When N is very small, an obtained correlation coefficient of zero may result in the erroneous rejection of a valid test.]

★E6.2.1. If the distribution of test scores in a validation sample is markedly different from the distribution of scores in the group with whom the test is ordinarily used, data based on these scores, including estimates of population parameters, should be interpreted with great caution. Reports of parameter estimates should cite the original statistics, the distribution characteristics used in making the new estimate, and the statistical procedures employed. ESSENTIAL

[Comment: The reader of the manual or research report needs to evaluate any adjustments made because of atypical sample characteristics. The assumptions underlying such adjustments are frequently ignored; the resulting errors are of undetermined size and direction. Despite such difficulties, an estimate of the appropriate statistic is often needed. The reported validity coefficient, for example, should reflect the predictive power of a test in the group to which it will be applied.]

*E6.2.2. Statistical corrections, such as those for restriction of range, should not be made in situations where mean performance in the sample in the validation study is so different from the mean performance of the population in which it is to be used as to suggest differences in parent populations. VERY DESIRABLE

[Comment: A validation study was conducted on a sample of applicants hired in a period when the rejection ratio was very high, resulting in a serious restriction of range. However, the passage of time brought with it changes in performance standards and in recruiting activities; the variance was greater and the mean was lower in a new sample than in the sample used in the validation study. The situational and psychometric facts together identify a change in groups more important than differences in variance alone, and a "correction" based on sample variances is therefore inappropriate.

In this situation it would be more appropriate to replicate the study with the new applicant population than to "correct" data obtained from the old population for restriction of range.]

★E7. The collection of data for a validity study should follow procedures consistent with the purposes of the study. ESSENTIAL

E7.1. Where feasible, a test should not be used as a basis for decision while its proposed use is being validated. DESIRABLE

[Comment: In many practical situations, decisions must be made whether or not there is a validated basis for them. In some circumstances, high costs may necessitate the use of a test even though it has not been validated, but great caution should then be exercised. In a selection situation, for example, decisions should not be so highly selective that restriction of range makes discovery of validity impossible. Wherever possible, at least some validation research should be done before a test is put to use as a decision instrument, and further data should be gathered subsequently.]

★E7.2. If the validity sample is made up of records accumulated haphazardly or voluntarily submitted by test users, this fact should be stated in the manual or research report, and the test user should be warned that the group is not a systematic or random sample of any specifiable population. Probable selective factors and their presumed influence on the test variable should be stated. ESSENTIAL

[Comment: While it is entirely appropriate to include in the manual such phrases as "the author and publisher of this test would welcome additional data derived from its use," it is difficult to judge the quality and representativeness of most of the resulting reports.]

*E7.3. In collecting data for a validity study, the person who interprets the test results should have only that information about the examinees that is ordinarily expected to be available in practical use of the test, or he should be sufficiently trained and disciplined to disregard information ordinarily not available to him. If there is any possible contamination associated with prior favorable or unfavorable knowledge about the examinees, the manual should discuss its effect on the outcome of the study. VERY DESIRABLE

★E7.4. The time elapsing between the test administration and the collection of criterion data should be reported in the manual. If the criterion data are collected over a period of time, beginning and ending dates should be included. ESSENTIAL

★E7.4.1. Validation reports should be clearly dated, with the time interval given during which the data were collected. ESSENTIAL

[Comment: Validity may deteriorate over time; in employment testing, for example, changes in jobs, work aids, and in the ability levels of applicant populations tend to change the circumstances in which validity information is developed.]

★E7.4.2. In general, a test user should be cautious in making long-term predictions. ESSENTIAL

[Comment: Short-term predictions are much more likely to be valid than are long-term predictions because they are less subject to influences other than the characteristics measured.]

★E7.4.3. If a test is recommended for long-term predictions, but comparisons with concurrent criteria only are presented, the manual should emphasize that the validity of long-term predictions is undetermined. ESSENTIAL

*E7.4.4. The amount and kind of any experience or training received by the subjects between the time of testing and the time of criterion measurement should be stated. VERY DESIRABLE

*E7.4.5. When validity for predicting grades in a course is reported, reasonably clear information should be provided regarding the types of performance required in the course, the nature of the instructional method, and the way in which performance is measured. If the test was administered after the course was started, this fact should be made clear. VERY DESIRABLE

★E8. Any statistical analysis of criterion-related validity should be reported in the manual in a form that enables the reader to determine how much confidence is to be placed in judgments or predictions regarding the individual. ESSENTIAL

★E8.1. A report of criterion-related validity should give full information about the statistical analysis and should ordinarily include, in addition to such basic descriptive statistics as means and standard deviations, one or more of the following: (a) one or more correlation coefficients of a familiar type, (b) descriptions of the efficiency with which the test separates criterion groups, (c) expectancy tables, or (d) charts that graphically illustrate the relationship between test and criterion. ESSENTIAL

[Comment: Full information includes data on the reliability, the strength, and the nature of the relationship. In correlational terms, this would imply information about the statistical significance and magnitude of the correlation coefficient and about the regression equation.

Reports solely of differences between group means give inadequate information regarding validity; if variance is large, classification may be inaccurate even if means differ considerably. The strength of the relationship may be indicated by describing the amount of misclassification or of overlapping. Expectancy tables may provide information about the nature of the predictions.

In general, since manuals and research reports are often directed to test users who have limited statistical knowledge, every effort should be made to communicate validity information clearly.]

*E8.1.1. Errors of prediction should be estimated and reported; a validity coefficient should be supplemented with reports of the regression slope and intercept and of the standard error of estimate. VERY DESIRABLE

[Comment: The required information could be presented in an expectancy table showing the range of possible criterion values for each of several points on the score range. The standard error of estimate at different points along the score range is often helpful.

For a dichotomous criterion, this objective might be achieved by indicating the proportion of hits, misses, and false inclusions at various cutting scores.]

*E8.1.2. For some users, analysis of test variance according to the following sources is appropriate: variance relevant to the criterion, variance explained as form-to-form or trial-to-trial inconsistency, and a reliable but irrelevant remainder. VERY DESIRABLE

[Comment: Such an analysis is more complete and less subject to misinterpretation than a correlation coefficient, including even a "corrected" validity coefficient, or a comparison of group means.]

★E8.1.3. The method of statistical analysis should be chosen with due consideration of the characteristics of the data and of the assumptions of the method. ESSENTIAL

[Comment: Data may often depart from the assumed characteristics with little ill effect. Some violation of assumptions may, however, be seriously misleading. For example, the use of predictions based on the assumption of a normal bivariate correlation surface may seriously overestimate the mean performance of high-scoring candidates if the data are markedly heteroscedastic (as in triangular scatter distributions). In such cases, a method of analysis not based on assumptions about the bivariate distribution would present a more accurate statement of validity.]

★E8.2. If validity coefficients are corrected for errors of measurement *in the criterion,* the computation of the reliability coefficient of the criterion should be explained, and both corrected and uncorrected coefficients should be reported. ESSENTIAL

[Comment: Coefficients corrected for errors of measurement in the *test* are not estimates of the criterion-related validity for the existing test and should not be reported. Corrections for attenuation are very much open to misinterpretation, especially if based on obtained correlation coefficients that are very low or from a small or otherwise inappropriate sample; if misinterpreted, they give an unjustifiably favorable impression of the validity of the test scores. The hazard is illustrated in the manual for an adjustment inventory. The author reported correlation coefficients between inventory scores and criterion ratings; also reported were estimated coefficients between "true" inventory and criterion scores. He then commented that the augmented correlation coefficients "are as high as those often secured between college aptitude tests and college grades." The comparison is improper, in part, because the test author compared augmented coefficients with uncorrected coefficients for ability tests.]

★E8.2.1. Where correlation coefficients are corrected for attenuation or restricted range, full information relevant to the correction should be presented. If such corrections are made, significance tests should be made with the uncorrected correlation coefficients. ESSENTIAL

[Comment: Corrections should be applied only to obtained coefficients. It is ordinarily unwise to make sequential corrections, as in applying a correction for attenuation to a coefficient already corrected for restriction of range. Chains of corrections may be useful in considering possible further research, but their results should not be seriously reported as estimates of population correlation coefficients.]

*E8.3. If validity is demonstrated by comparing groups that differ on the criterion, the manual should report whether and by how much the groups differ on other available variables that are relevant. VERY DESIRABLE

[Comment: Since groups that differ on a criterion may also differ in other respects, the test may be discriminating on a quality other than that intended. Types of mental disorders, for instance, are associated with age, education, and length of time in the hospital. Confounding of this sort should be taken into account when the usefulness of a test for diagnosis is appraised.]

★E8.3.1. If a test is suggested for the differential diagnosis of patients, the manual should include evidence of the test's ability to place individuals in diagnostic groups rather than merely to separate diagnosed abnormal cases from the normal population. ESSENTIAL

[Comment: When a test is recommended for the purpose of assigning patients to discrete categories, such statistics as contingency coefficients, phi coefficients, or discriminant functions should be supplemented by a table of misclassification rates giving, for example, the proportion of patients falsely included in a category or falsely excluded from it. Such proportions should be compared with base rates, that is, the proportions of correct classifications made possible by a mere knowledge of the sizes of the categories.]

*E8.3.2. If validity is demonstrated by comparing groups that differ on the criterion (e.g., where one group is identified as a high-performance group and another as a low-performance group), all cases should be assigned to one or the other of the groups. VERY DESIRABLE

[Comment: The most reliable statistics are obtained if all cases are used; validity coefficients derived from extreme groups may be misleading. In some situations, analyses using extreme groups may be useful for identifying predictors, but generally the validity reported for any given predictor should be based on all cases. If the use of extreme groups is deemed necessary or appropriate to a particular study, appropriate estimates of correlation should be used. The typical product-moment and biserial estimates are *not* appropriate in this situation.]

★E8.4. When information other than the test scores is known to have an appreciable degree of criterion-related validity and is ordinarily available to the prospective test user, the user should consider both the validity of the other information and the resulting multiple correlation when the new test information is combined with it. ESSENTIAL

[Comment: Whether a test should be used for prediction and classification when other information is readily available sometimes depends not on the validity of the test but on its "incremental validity," that is, what it adds to the soundness of the judgment that would otherwise be made.

For a questionnaire intended to predict marital success, delinquency, and similar behavioral variables, the investigator should find out how much the questionnaire enhances prediction over that provided by base rates developed from demographic variables such as socioeconomic status.]

★E8.5. Where more than one test is to be used, validity information should report the validity of the combination actually used. Where composite scores are developed, the basis for weighting (e.g., multiple regression equations) should be given. ESSENTIAL

[Comment: In one organization, a composite was developed and validated by multiple regression in which the optimal weighting of one test was negative. Nevertheless, the organization added unweighted scores to form a different composite for use in making decisions. The multiple correlation coefficient did not, therefore, describe the validity of the test battery as it was actually used. Where a given method of combination is to be used, that method should be validated.

When multiple regression is used and one predictor in a battery is evaluated, the beta weight is a better index of its contribution to the validity of the test in that combination than is its original validity coefficient.]

★E9. A test user should investigate the possibility of bias in tests or in test items. Wherever possible, there should be an investigation of possible differences in criterion-related validity for ethnic, sex, or other subsamples that can be identified when the test is given. The manual or research report should give the results for each subsample separately or report that no differences were found. ESSENTIAL

[Comment: For many uses, regulations published pursuant to civil rights legislation require that validity studies be performed separately on samples differing in national origin, race, sex, or religious affiliation, when technically feasible.

The concept of fairness may involve other sources of inappropriate discrimination. For example, placing a hand-dexterity test on a low table may unfairly bias the test against tall people. The test user should try to identify potentially unfair influences on test scores in his situation. Variables which may contribute inappropriate variance may be used for subgrouping in investigation of fairness.

However, caution must be exercised in evaluating the possibility of bias. A simple difference in group means does *not* by itself identify an unfair test, although it should stimulate research to explore the question of fairness. Evidence of differential validity is developed by comparing, for example, correlation coefficients, regression equations, and means and variances for each variable.

The proper statistical test for such a difference is, for any parameter, the test of the hypothesis of no true difference between the groups, for example, a test of no difference between correlation coefficients, slopes, or intercepts. Some investigators have attempted to examine such differences by comparing in each subgroup independently the validity statistic (e.g., the correlation coefficient) to a postulated true value of zero. This is not a proper procedure; it does not answer the question at issue of *differences* in the characteristics of validity. It is impossible to demonstrate such differences by showing that one correlation coefficient, for example, is significantly different from zero while the other is not.

Users should routinely investigate differences in validity when it is technically feasible to do so, that is, when Ns are sufficient for reliable comparisons and when criteria are reasonably valid in each group. Users should be aware, however, that a too-hasty acceptance of bias or of differential validity, if used in decision making, may be as likely to produce unfair test use as is failure to consider the possibility.

For example, to avoid unfairness in test use for blacks, an employer may investigate the possibility of differential validity and find not only differences in means between black and white applicants but also differences in intercepts of the regression. Some definitions of fairness require that predictions for applicants in either group should be based on the regression line developed for his own group. If the differences in intercepts are statistical artifacts (due, for example, to unreliability), the result might be considered unfair to blacks (if they have the lower regression line) since their performance might be systematically under predicted. The effect can, of course, work both ways depending on the direction of differences in regression.

It is important to recognize that there are different definitions of fairness, and whether a given procedure is or is not fair may depend upon the definition accepted. Moreover, there are statistical and psychometric uncertainties about some of the sources of apparent differences in validity or regression. Unless a difference is observed on samples of substantial size, and unless there is a reasonably sound psychological or sociological theory upon which to explain an observed difference, the difference should be viewed with caution.

Bias is not necessarily detected by criterion-related validity alone; cf. E12.1.2.]

★E10. When a scoring key, the selection of items, or the weighting of tests is based on one sample, the manual should report validity coefficients based on data obtained from one or more independent cross-validation samples. Validity statements should not be based on the original sample. ESSENTIAL

★E10.1. If the user recommends certain regression weights for combining scores on a test or for combining the test with other variables, the statement of the validity of the composite should be based on a cross-validation sample. ESSENTIAL

[Comment: Cross validation is particularly necessary when the number of predictors entering the study (not the final equation) is greater than 4 or 5 and when the sample size is less than 200.]

★E10.1.1. When the scoring of tests in a battery is based on regression coefficients, negative scoring weights should be used only if they have been verified by cross validation in

large samples and if their use will not be invalid (and thus unfair) to one or more subgroups in the population to be tested. ESSENTIAL

★E10.2. If it is proposed that decisions be based on a complex nonlinear combination of scores, it should be shown that this combination has greater validity than a simpler linear combination, that the equation can be logically explained, and that the procedures for combining scores have been cross validated. ESSENTIAL

[Comment: The use of "moderator variables," for example, is to be recommended only where a moderator is shown to produce a clear improvement in validity in a cross-validation sample. Similarly, when it is proposed that some pattern of scores (e.g., high standing in scores on both variables 2 and 5) is an indicator of success, it is necessary to show that the proportion of successful persons in the group so identified is higher than would be expected from the regression of frequency of success on a linear combination of variables 2 and 5.]

E11. To the extent feasible, a test user who intends to continue employing a test over a long period of time should develop procedures for gathering data for continued research. DESIRABLE

[Comment: Validity data may become obsolete. The relationship between test performance and criterion performance may be influenced by many factors, such as changes in populations, recruiting sources, the economy, organizational characteristics, processes, or tasks. Moreover, validity studies are often based on relatively few cases. A plan for the systematic collection of further data after the test has been placed into operational use may be useful both for the development of a more reliable data base and for information on changes in the trends of relationships over time.

Operational use may, however, result in severe restriction of range. Continuing research may be less necessary if the original data are based on a relatively large sample, if the bases for generalizing validity are well established, and if evidence shows a relatively slight rate of change in variables likely to limit the generalizability of validity information. When these favorable conditions do not exist, it may be possible to plan for small replications from time to time rather than for a continuous program of research.]

Content Validity

★E12. If test performance is to be interpreted as a representative sample of performance in a universe of situations, the test manual should give a clear definition of the universe represented and describe the procedures followed in the sampling from it. ESSENTIAL

[Comment: The definition of the universe of tasks represented by the test scores should include the identification of that part of the content universe represented by each item. The definition should be operational rather than theoretical, containing specifications regarding classes of stimuli, tasks to be performed and observations to be scored. The definition should not involve assumptions regarding the psychological processes employed since these would be matters of construct rather than of content validity.]

*E12.1. When experts have been asked to judge whether items are an appropriate sample of a universe or are correctly scored, the manual should describe the relevant professional experience and qualification of the experts and the directions under which they made their judgments. VERY DESIRABLE

E12.1.1. When items are selected by experts, the extent of agreement among judges should be reported. DESIRABLE

★E12.1.2. Test content should be examined for possible bias. ESSENTIAL

[Comment: Bias may exist where items do not represent comparable tasks and therefore do not sample a common performance domain for the various subgroups (cf. B1.3). One may investigate such bias in terms of carefully developed expert judgments; studies of the attitudes or interpretations of items in different subgroups might also present useful information (although care must be taken to assure that the investigation is clearly directed to an analysis of content in relation to an adequately defined performance domain). The judgment of bias may itself be biased; the principle here is that, when it is possible, such judgments should be supported by data.]

E12.2. In achievement tests of educational outcomes, the manual should report the classification system used for selecting items. DESIRABLE

*E12.2.1. When an achievement test has been prepared according to a two-way content-by-process outline, that outline should be presented in the manual, with a list of the items identified with each cell of the outline. VERY DESIRABLE

★E12.3. Any statement in the manual of the relation of items to a course of study (or other source of content) should mention the date when the course of study was prepared. ESSENTIAL

[Comment: In achievement testing, it is frequently the practice to identify significant topics for items by a careful sampling from textbooks. Textbooks and courses of study change, however, and the test that was once an excellent sample becomes out of date. The manual might therefore report such information as the range and median of copyright dates of the textbooks examined, or the date at which the experts judged the items to be representative.

One checklist concerns problems common to students. The manual for this checklist properly reports the date when the list was assembled. From time to time, it will be necessary to determine whether student problems have changed and, if so, to change the test accordingly.

It should be recognized that this standard implies that definitions of a content universe are subject to change as jobs, society, or curricula change.]

★E12.4. When a test is represented as having content validity for a job or class of jobs, the evidence of validity should include a complete description of job duties, including relative frequency, importance, and skill level of such duties. ESSENTIAL

Construct Validity

★E13. If the author proposes to interpret scores on a test as measuring a theoretical variable (ability, trait, or attitude), his proposed interpretation should be fully stated. His theoretical construct should be distinguished from interpretations arising on the basis of other theories. ESSENTIAL

[Comment: For example, if a test is intended to measure the construct of anxiety, the test author should distinguish his formulation of the construct from other possible meanings of the term and should relate his concept to measures of anxiety discussed in the literature.

The description of a construct may be as simple as the identification of "creativity" with "making many original contributions." Even this definition provides some basis for judging whether various pieces of empirical evidence support the proposed interpretation. Ordinarily, however, the test author will have a more elaborate conception. He may wish to rule out such originality as derives only from a large and varied store of information. He may propose explicitly to identify the creative person as one who produces numerous ideas, whether of high or low quality. He may propose to distinguish the ability to criticize ideas from the ability to be "creative." He may go on to hypothesize that the person who shows originality in identifying or describing pictures will also have unconventional preferences in food and clothing. All such characterizations or hypotheses are part of the author's concept of "what the test measures" and are needed in designing and in drawing conclusions from empirical investigations of the psychological interpretation of the construct.]

★E13.1. The manual should indicate the extent to which the proposed interpretation has been substantiated and should summarize investigations of the hypotheses derived from the theory. ESSENTIAL

*E13.1.1. Each study investigating a theoretical inference regarding the test should be summarized in a way that covers both the operational procedures of the study and the implications of the results for the theory. VERY DESIRABLE

*E13.1.2. The manual should report correlations between the test and other relevant tests for which interpretations are relatively clear. VERY DESIRABLE

*E13.2. The manual should report evidence about the extent to which constructs other than those proposed by the author account for variance in scores on the test. VERY DESIRABLE

[Comment: Although it is unreasonable to require a test author to anticipate or to include every counter-interpretation in a test manual, he ought to present data relevant to those counterhypotheses most likely to account for variance in the test scores.]

*E13.2.1. The manual for any specialized test or inventory used in educational selection and guidance should report the correlation of scores derived from it with well-established measures of verbal and quantitative ability in an appropriately representative population. VERY DESIRABLE

[Comment: Verbal and quantitative abilities are specified here because their importance in educational performance is recognized, because they often account for much of total test variance, and because numerous tests of these abilities are already available. To be of practical value, a new test designed to measure other constructs (e.g., spatial abilities) must not closely duplicate the measurement of verbal and quantitative ability.]

E13.2.2. If a test has been included in factorial studies that indicate the proportion of the test variance attributable to widely known reference factors, such information should be presented in the manual. DESIRABLE

*E13.2.3. For inventories such as personality, interest, or attitude measures, evidence should be presented of the extent to which scores are susceptible to an attempt by the examinee to present a socially desirable, conforming, or false picture of himself, or to which the scores may reflect other response sets or styles. Such response patterns should be studied for identifiable subgroups rather than for a more general sample. VERY DESIRABLE

[Comment: Correlational or experimental studies might be reported. Appropriate evidence of acquiescence might, for example, be the proportion of the total test variance in the number of "yes" responses to the test, or by the correlation of the test scores with one or more independent measures of the acquiescence tendency, or by experimental procedures designed to induce acquiescence.]

★E13.2.4. If a test given with a time limit is to be interpreted as measuring a hypothetical psychological attribute not specifically related to speed, evidence should be presented in the manual concerning the effect of speed on the test scores and on their correlation with other variables. ESSENTIAL

[Comment: The most complete evidence of the effect of speed would be the comparison of scores on one form, using the usual time limit, with scores on another form having unlimited time. The correlation of scores at the end of the usual time with scores obtained with extra time on the same trial is of limited meaning because the two scores are not independent. Less complete evidence would consist of data on the percentage of examinees who attempt the last item or some item very near the end of the test. If the percentage is below 90, a more penetrating study is needed to show that individual differences on the test do not reflect speed to any great extent.]

*E13.2.5. Where differences in test-taking strategies that might influence the interpretation of scores are associated with identifiable subgroup characteristics, this information should be clearly presented or its absence clearly noted. VERY DESIRABLE

E13.2.6. Where a low correlation or small difference between groups is advanced as evidence *against* some counterinterpretation, the manual should report the confidence interval for the parameter. The manual should also correct for or discuss any errors of measurement that may have lowered the apparent relationship. DESIRABLE

F. RELIABILITY AND MEASUREMENT ERROR

Reliability refers to the degree to which the results of testing are attributable to systematic sources of variance. Classical methods of estimating reliability coefficients call for correlating at least two sets of similar measurements.

One method of obtaining the two sets of measurements is by retesting with the identical test. Aside from practical limitations, theoretically, retesting is not ordinarily a desirable method of estimating reliability because the examinee may remember his or her responses to items from one testing to the next. Hence, memory becomes a systematic source of variance and the correlation of the two sets of scores may be higher than the correlation of two sets of scores based on two different but parallel sets of items drawn from the population of items in the same way.

If we want to eliminate memory as a systematic source of variance and to include the effects of item sampling and response variation over time as sources of variance, we may use two sets of items developed or selected according to the same specifications. These are called parallel forms of the test.

If the effect of content sampling *alone* is sought without the effects of memory or response variability over time, or if it is not practical to administer two parallel forms with separate time limits, reliability can be estimated from a single administration of an unspeeded test. The test may be divided into two sets of items of equal, or approximately equal, length that are judged by competent authorities to sample as nearly as possible the same functions. Any items based on the same source of data (such as a reading passage) must be assigned to the same set. Then the correlation between scores on the two parallel halves is a matched-half coefficient from which an estimate of the parallel-forms reliability coefficient for the total test may be obtained by a procedure that does not assume that the numbers of items or the variances of the two sets are exactly equal.

Estimates of reliability from a single administration may also be obtained by analysis-of-variance procedures. Such estimates will be spuriously high if the test is speeded or if the items are not independent of each other. On the other hand, for unspeeded tests, such estimates will tend to be lower than matched-half coefficients because they constitute, given certain assumptions, the mean of coefficients obtained by correlating scores on all possible pairs of halves of the test.

From the preceding discussion, it is clear that *different methods of estimating reliability take account of different sources of error.* Thus, from one testing to the other, the result is affected not only by random response variability and changes in subjects over time but also by differences in administration (especially if different persons administer the test on the two occasions). Reliability coefficients based on a single administration of a test exclude response variability over time; these effects on scores do not appear as errors of measurement. Hence, "reliability coefficient" is a generic term. It can be based on various types of evidence; each type of evidence suggests a different meaning. It is essential that any method used to estimate reliability be clearly described.

The estimation of clearly labeled components of score variance is the most informative outcome of a reliability study, both for the test developer wishing to improve the reliability of his instrument and for the user desiring to interpret test scores with maximum understanding. The analysis of score variance calls for the use of an appropriate experimental design. There are many different multivariate designs that can be used in reliability studies; the choice of design for studying a particular test is determined by its intended interpretation and by practical limitations.

It is recommended that test authors describe the meanings of any coefficients they report as accurately and precisely as possible. It is informative to say, for example, "This coefficient indicates the stability of measurement of equivalent scores based on parallel forms of the test administered 7 days apart, without intervening practice or instruction." Although lengthy,

such a description is reasonably free from ambiguity.

Reliability coefficients have limited practical value for test users. The standard error of measurement ordinarily is more useful; it has great stability across populations since it is relatively independent of range of talent, and it may be used to identify limits that have a defined probability of including the true score. Test users may use reliability coefficients in comparing tests, but they use standard errors of measurement in interpreting test scores. Information in a test manual about a standard error of measurement may often be more important than information about a reliability coefficient.

General Principles

★**F1. The test manual or research report should present evidence of reliability, including estimates of the standard error of measurement, that permits the reader to judge whether scores are sufficiently dependable for the intended uses of the test. If any of the necessary evidence has not been collected, the absence of such information should be noted.** ESSENTIAL

[Comment: It is most helpful to the user when several types of reliability estimates are reported. Reports of standard errors of measurement in different groups are also helpful.]

F1.1. The test manual should furnish, insofar as feasible, a quantitative analysis of the total inconsistency of measurement into its major identifiable components; namely, inconsistency in responses of the subject; inconsistency or heterogeneity within the sample of test content (such as the stimulus items, questions, and situations); inconsistencies in administration of the test; inconsistency among scorers, raters, or units of apparatus; and mechanical errors of scoring. DESIRABLE

[Comment: In general, the desired analysis will not be feasible unless scores are expressed in quantitative, as distinguished from categorical or nonparametric, terms and the design of data collection includes the necessary controls.

With group tests of school achievement, the principal sources of error to be evaluated usually include: (*a*) inconsistency of test content; (*b*) inconsistencies in test administration; and (*c*) inconsistency in responses of the examinee over time, that is, instability. The collection of data should be designed to permit evaluation of these three factors. Fluctuation or inconsistency in the responses of the subject may be an important variable by itself; it is often a major source of random error to be evaluated. Inconsistency among scorers or raters should also be evaluated.]

★F1.2. Standard errors of measurement and reliability coefficients should be provided for every score, subscore, or combination of scores (such as a sum, difference, or quotient) that is recommended by the test manual (either explicitly or implicitly) for other than merely tentative or pilot use. ESSENTIAL

★F1.3. For instruments that yield a profile having a low reliability of differences between scores, the manual should explicitly caution the user against interpretation of such differences, except as a source of tentative information requiring external verification. ESSENTIAL

*F1.4. The manual should state the minimum difference between two scores ordinarily required for statistical significance at a designated level. VERY DESIRABLE

[Comment: A nomograph or table for determining the significance of any given score difference would be a very useful addition to a test manual. "Change" or "growth" scores require careful attention to Standards F1.3 and F1.4.]

★F2. The procedures and samples used to determine reliability coefficients or standard errors of measurement should be described sufficiently to permit a user to judge the applicability of the data reported to the individuals or groups with which he is concerned. ESSENTIAL

[Comment: The mean and variance of the sample and information about its composition should be provided. Reliability data should be obtained from "natural" groups such as examinees of a single age or grade level. Estimates of the reliability of a test to be used in selecting employees should be based on scores of applicants for positions rather than scores obtained by testing college students or workers already employed.

If a test claims to be appropriate for groups from the fourth grade through graduate school, the manual should provide reliability data for each grade or age level.]

★F2.1. Any identifying characteristics of the sample that may be related to consistency of performance on the test should be described in the test manual. ESSENTIAL

[Comment: Demographic information, such as distributions of the subjects with respect to age, sex, socioeconomic level, intellectual level, locale, employment status or history, and minority group membership should be given in the test manual. For standardized tests, the samples used to compute reliability coefficients and standard errors of measurement should be drawn at random from the norms groups.]

★F2.2. If reliability coefficients are corrected for restriction of range, both the uncorrected and the corrected coefficients should be reported in the test manual together with the standard deviations of the group actually tested and of the group to which the corrected coefficients are applicable. ESSENTIAL

[Comment: When variances differ and there seem to be other justifications for such a correction, the superiority of the standard error of measurement should be noted; it is largely unaffected by differences in variance.]

★F2.3. When a test is recommended or ordinarily employed in homogeneous subsamples, the reliability and standard error of measurement should be independently investigated within each subsample and reported in the test manual. ESSENTIAL

[Comment: The mechanical reasoning section of a well-known aptitude test yields scores that have significantly different reliability coefficients for boys and for girls. The manual reports the reliability coefficients for each sex in each grade.]

★F2.3.1. At least one estimate of the standard error of measurement should be provided in the manual for every group for which reliability data are given. ESSENTIAL

[Comment: When it is specifically recommended that scores be transformed to a particular metric, the standard errors should be presented in that metric.]

F2.3.2. The test manual should report the standard errors of measurement at different score levels. DESIRABLE

[Comment: The manual for one test of college aptitude reports standard errors of measurement for three score levels: the mean, one standard deviation above the mean, and one standard deviation below the mean. Since more important changes in the standard error of measurement are associated with extreme scores, it might be better to use more widely separated score levels if the number of cases available justifies this action.]

F2.4. Item statistics (such as difficulty or discrimination indices, etc.) should be presented in at least summary form in a test manual. DESIRABLE

★F3. Reports of reliability studies should ordinarily be expressed in the test manual in terms of variances of error components, standard errors of measurement, or product-moment reliability coefficients. Unfamiliar expressions of data should be clearly described, with references to their development. ESSENTIAL

[Comment: Test authors and publishers should avoid unconventional statistics unless conventional statistics are inappropriate. If unusual statistical analyses are presented, explanations should minimize the likelihood of misinterpretation.]

Comparability of Forms

★F4. If two or more forms of a test are published for use with the same examinees, information on means, variances, and characteristics of items in the forms should be reported in the test manual along with the coefficients of correlation among their scores. **If necessary evidence is not provided, the test manual should warn the reader against assuming equivalence of scores.** ESSENTIAL

[Comment: Information to be examined would include a summary of item statistics for each form, such as a frequency distribution of item difficulties and of indices of item discrimination. Content analyses of each of the forms should be presented. Thus, both frequency distributions of item statistics and a tabulation of items by categories of subject-matter content and of behavioral or instructional objectives should be furnished.

The forms should represent different samples of items within each category of content. Insofar as one's concern is for error arising from sampling a content universe, the forms to be compared should have been developed from a common universe according to an appropriate plan. An artificially close similarity between forms will result from item-by-item matching or by creating a second form merely by rephrasing items on a first form. A reliability coefficient based on forms created in this way will be spuriously high because it does not properly take into account sampling error in drawing items from the universe of items.]

Internal Consistency

*F5. Evidence of internal consistency should be reported for any unspeeded test. VERY DESIRABLE

[Comment: Internal consistency is important if items are viewed as a sample from a relatively homogeneous universe, as in a test of addition with integers, a test of general high school vocabulary, or a test presumed to measure introversion. Nevertheless, estimates of internal consistency should not be regarded as a substitute for other measures.]

*F5.1. Estimates of internal consistency should be determined by matched-half or random-half methods or by analysis of variance procedures, if these can properly be used with the data. Any additional measure of internal consistency that the author wishes to report should be carefully explained in the test manual. VERY DESIRABLE

[Comment: Matched-half coefficients reflect expert judgment and tend to be higher in value than random-half coefficients. Analysis of variance procedures tend to yield lower values than matched-half procedures. In unusual circumstances, special coefficients may provide useful information; if used, such coefficients should be described so the reader will be able to understand them in relation to more conventional estimates.]

★F5.2. Internal reliability estimates should not be obtained for highly speeded tests. ESSENTIAL

*F5.3. When a test consists of separately scored parts or sections, the correlation between the parts or sections should be reported in the test manual along with relevant reliability estimates, relevant means, and relevant standard deviations. VERY DESIRABLE

★F5.3.1. If a test manual reports the correlation between a subtest and a total score, it should call attention to the fact that the coefficient is spuriously high because it is based partly on the perfect correspondence of identical errors of measurement in the subtest and in the total score. ESSENTIAL

*F5.4. If several questions within a test are experimentally linked so that the reaction to one question influences the reaction to another, the entire group of questions should be assigned to one of the two halves of the test when random-half or matched-half procedures are used. VERY DESIRABLE

[Comment: In a reading test, several questions about the same paragraph are ordinarily experimentally dependent. All of these questions should be placed in the same half test in using the split-half method. The fact that the test halves do not have exactly equal numbers of items need not be troublesome if an appropriate step-up procedure is used.]

Comparisons Over Time

★F6. The test manual should indicate to what extent test scores are stable, that is, how nearly constant the scores are likely to be if a parallel form of a test is administered after time has elapsed. The manual should also describe the effect of any such variation on the usefulness of the test. The time interval to be considered depends on the nature of the test and on what interpretation of the test scores is recommended. ESSENTIAL

[Comment: For many purposes, reliability coefficients and standard errors of measurement should be based on parallel-forms procedures, with a period of perhaps 2 to 4 weeks elapsing between the administration of two parallel forms. In some situations, when test scores are obtained for changing characteristics of individuals, reliability coefficients or standard errors of measurement based on the administration of parallel forms on successive days or weeks may be desirable. A reading-readiness test used only for initial tentative assignment of first-grade pupils to instructional groups is an example. In experiments on the effects of drugs, it may be desirable to measure changes in two sets of test scores obtained before and after a time lapse of only a few minutes.

It seems reasonable to require an assessment of stability for projective techniques and other devices for assessing personality dynamics, even though it is recognized in some instances that low stability of scores over a substantial period may reflect true trait fluctuation. Clinical practice rarely presumes that the inferences from projective tests are to be applied on the very day the test is given. Realistically, one must recognize that pragmatic decisions are being made from test data which are meaningful only in terms of at least days, and usually weeks or months of therapy. If scores on a certain test are found to be highly unstable from day to day, this evidence casts doubt upon the utility of the test for most purposes, even if some fluctuation might be explained by the hypothesis of trait inconstancy. An investigator may be concerned with a psychological characteristic or educational effect which changes rapidly over a short period of time. In this instance it is important not to confuse the inconstancy of the trait with the instability of the measuring instrument.]

*F6.1. Determination of the stability of scores by repeated testing should make use of parallel forms of the test to minimize recall of specific answers, especially if the time interval is short. VERY DESIRABLE

★F6.2. The report in a test manual of a study of consistency of scores over time should state what period of time elapsed between tests and should give the mean and standard deviation of scores at each testing as well as the correlation coefficient. ESSENTIAL

*F6.3. If it is reasonable to expect scores on a test to change significantly over some time interval in response to developmental or educational influences, the manual should call the test user's attention to this possibility and advise care in the use of old scores. VERY DESIRABLE

[Comment: Since some schools administer aptitude, achievement, or interest tests only at intervals of 2 or 3 years, the manual for such tests should report correlations and changes in means and standard deviations between tests administered 1 year apart, 2 years apart, and 3 years apart. From these data the user can learn how rapidly test records become obsolete with the passage of time.]

F6.3.1. In reporting on stability, the test manual should describe relevant experience, education, or treatment intervening between administrations of the test, if known. DESIRABLE

★F6.4. Where a test is to be used to compare groups rather than individuals, standard errors and standards errors of measurement of group means and related statistics should be presented. ESSENTIAL

STANDARDS FOR THE USE OF TESTS

There are many kinds of test use. As one example, test scores are used for decisions to select or to reject applicants for jobs, schools, or other opportunities. In such use, the test score is a basis for a prediction, one that is either explicit or strongly implied. The test score is used to estimate or predict a likely level of performance on some criterion variable external to the test itself.

Another use is as a prescriptive aid where different scores imply different treatments. For example, elementary school pupils may be classified according to reading ability on the basis of test scores; they may be assigned to different books or to different kinds of instruction. Job applicants may be classified as marginally employable and assigned to programs of remedial vocational training on the basis of test scores. Disturbed persons with one profile of scores may be assigned to treatments different from those for people with different profiles. Each of these examples implies a hypothesis that people with a specific set of attributes will perform a task or achieve a goal more effectively with one form of treatment than with another. The test user in an applied setting may not have the power, the resources, or the training to carry out the necessary experimental work for testing these hypotheses; he may simply accept them as part of the prevailing scientific or professional body of knowledge and use tests accordingly.

A test score may be used to certify that an individual has met some designated standard, that a person is qualified to perform certain skilled tasks, that a child is qualified for a remedial program, or that a defendant can stand trial.

The basic use of tests is descriptive or evaluative. A test score provides a description of the individual who obtained it and can help the test user to understand, analyze, or help that individual. Test scores may be used by a counselor to help a student make a vocational choice or to help a couple in marriage counseling communicate more clearly with each other. They may help a teacher work more effectively with a pupil. These are clinical, diagnostic, and individualistic uses of tests in a continuing relationship between a test user and an individual. Because the relationship is a continuing one, tentative decisions or judgments can be modified as new information is accumulated.

Test scores may constitute the dependent variable or criterion measure in an institutional research study. A program may be continued or terminated on the basis of test results; an institution may receive more or less funding because of test results; test results may be considered in organizational analysis or in making program changes. These *Standards* do not deal fully with these problems; their emphasis is more on the interpretation of scores of individuals. A companion volume is planned dealing with standards for test use in program evaluation, policy-related research, and curriculum evaluation; it will also address issues of research design and of data analysis.

The standards in the present volume are to varying degrees directed to all forms of use.

As the use of tests moves along a continuum from the description of a single individual, in a situation allowing for corrections of erroneous interpretations, to making decisions about large numbers of people, the test user must apply more of the standards and, perhaps, apply them more rigorously. Such decisions may profoundly influence the lives of those tested, such as decisions for employment or for attendance at college, or decisions to assign a person to one treatment or opportunity rather than to another (e.g., tracking in a school system), or decisions to continue or terminate a program or to regulate its funds. The cost of error, in money and in human suffering, may be great. A test user cannot abdicate the responsibilities described in these standards by subscribing to external testing services or test suppliers.

The standards of test use may not have to be so rigidly followed when the purpose of testing is the understanding of an individual. Sometimes such testing is less standardized than is usually recommended. For example, a school counselor may be interested in assessing the maximum performance capability of a single student. To get a full understanding of that student, he must be able to elicit new information, perhaps even through an embellishment of a standardized test, to seek the broadest possible understanding of the level of mastery and of the generalizability of the situations in which mastery can be demonstrated. Interpretation of test scores in such cases is not made in terms of norms but in terms of a counselor's analysis of what mastery of a particular skill entails (even a social skill, not likely to be measured by tests ordinarily used for content-referenced interpretations). In short, exploration of an individual case is different from standardized testing. The *user who develops test embellishments must know the difference;* that is, he must have a clear rationale for what he is doing when he departs from standard procedure, and he must be able to apply that rationale consistently and sensibly. Such individualized testing does not require less skill than does testing broadly for institutional decisions; it requires a different kind of skill (cf. I1).

The standards necessary for using tests for making decisions are not different from the standards necessary when tests are used simply for understanding, but the emphasis within a standard may be different. A test user should be familiar with the standards governing test use in general, and he should pay particular attention to those standards most nearly fitting his own specific type of application.

In doing so, he should realize that the standards are intended to apply, in principle, to *all forms* of assessment. In choosing from alternative methods of assessment, the test user should consider the differences in the ease of applying these standards.

G. QUALIFICATIONS AND CONCERNS OF USERS

Assessing others is an occupational activity for teachers, parents, clergymen, shopkeepers, correction officers, etc. Some people assess with remarkable skill; others are inept and have little or no training to help them. Users of educational and psychological tests in schools, places of employment, clinics, laboratories, prisons, and other places where educators and psychologists work should have had at least some formal training.

A test user, for the purposes of these standards, is one who chooses tests, interprets scores, or makes decisions based on test scores. He is not necessarily the person who administers the test following standard instructions or who does routine scoring. Within this definition, the basic user qualifications (an elementary knowledge of the literature relating to a particular test or test use) apply particularly when tests are used for decisions, and such uses require additional technical qualifications as well. A recurring phrase in discussions about testing is "the legitimate uses of a test." One cannot competently judge whether his intended use is among those that are "legitimate" (however defined) without the technical skill and knowledge necessary to evaluate the validity of various types of inferences.

★**G1. A test user should have a general knowledge of measurement principles and of the limitations of test interpretations.** ESSENTIAL

[Comment: The required level of knowledge will vary with the complexity of the evaluations to be made and the responsibility of the user. At a minimum, the user must be knowledgeable about testing principles, understand the concept of measurement error, and be able to interpret an obtained test score. He should realize that there are alternative explanations for a given score and should have a pool of knowledge from which to evaluate some of the alternatives.]

★**G1.1. A test user should know his own qualifications and how well they match the** qualifications required for the uses of specific tests. ESSENTIAL

*G2. A test user should know and understand the literature relevant to the tests he uses and the testing problems with which he deals. VERY DESIRABLE

[Comment: A broad connotation is intended for this standard. The test user should have some acquaintance with the relevant findings of behavioral sciences, such as those related to the roles of heredity and environment, when using aptitude tests; some understanding of physiology is useful when one is using tests of motor skills. A very narrow interpretation of "the literature relevant to the test" is inadequate.

Unfortunately, it seems that ignorance of the literature requires that old information be rediscovered. For over 40 years, for example, it has been known that children with limited or restricted cultural exposure, such as children on canal boats or in isolated mountain communities, make low scores on intelligence tests standardized on more advantaged populations. The point has been made repeatedly in research reports and textbooks. Nevertheless, many black and Spanish-speaking children with limited cultural exposure who receive low scores on intelligence tests standardized on more advantaged groups are improperly classified as mentally retarded.]

★G3. One who has the responsibility for decisions about individuals or policies that are based on test results should have an understanding of psychological or educational measurement and of validation and other test research. ESSENTIAL

[Comment: A test user should have acquired the technical understanding appropriate to his responsibilities. Test users within organizations or regulatory agencies should have enough technical knowledge to be able to evaluate competently the tests and testing procedures relevant to the decisions they must make. If their technical training is limited, they should seek refresher training or work under the guidance of another test user whose training is adequate.]

★G3.1. The principal test users within an organization should make every effort to be sure that all those in the organization who are charged with responsibilities related to test use and interpretation (e.g., test administrators) have received training appropriate to those responsibilities. ESSENTIAL

[Comment: Serious misuse and distortion in interpretation may occur when people are not properly trained to carry out their responsibilities. The level of training needed varies with the complexity of a testing program, the level of the individual's responsibility for it, and the nature and intensity of possible adverse consequences. Test users should provide at least a basic orientation for administrators or executives who decide whether to test or not to test, to approve or to disapprove specific assessment procedures, to appropriate funds for necessary research, or to decide how test or research results will be used in the organization. Similar knowledge is needed by compliance officers who may have a detrimental influence on testing programs because of unreasoned and unreasoning demands for interpretation of data, who might disapprove of a testing program without adequate consideration of the alternatives, or

who might approve faulty and unfair uses of tests out of ignorance.]

*G3.1.1. A test user should have sufficient technical knowledge to be prepared to evaluate claims made in a test manual. VERY DESIRABLE

[Comment: A test user must accept some responsibility for the choice when a test is chosen. The user must also be able to exercise some judgment concerning descriptions of intended populations that appear in a manual. If he is using the test to evaluate a remedial program for low-performing pupils in the fourth grade, it is not necessarily appropriate to select a test standardized on "children in grades 4 through 6."]

★G3.2. Anyone administering a test for decision-making purposes should be competent to administer that test or class of tests. If not qualified, he should seek the necessary training regardless of his educational attainments. ESSENTIAL

[Comment: Some tests are easily administered, and a brief explanation of the instructions and of the necessity for standardization may be sufficient training for administering them. The use of other tests or assessment procedures may require more specific or unique kinds of training, for example, individually administered intellectual or personality measures or some work samples. It should be recognized that the administration and scoring of a test may not require any specific academic degree; conversely, possession of a degree is not necessarily evidence of qualifications to administer a particular test.]

★G4. Test users should seek to avoid bias in test selection, administration, and interpretation; they should try to avoid even the appearance of discriminatory practice. ESSENTIAL

[Comment: This is a difficult standard to apply. Sources of item or test bias are neither well understood nor easily avoided. The very definition of bias is open to question. The competent test user will accept the obligation to keep abreast of developments in the literature and, at the very least, to demonstrate a sensitivity to the problem and to the feelings of examinees.]

★G5. Institutional test users should establish procedures for periodic internal review of test use. ESSENTIAL

[Comment: The competent use of tests and test scores requires regular review of procedures and of concepts that may change with the advent of new knowledge. A practice that might have been considered acceptable or appropriate at an early period may be found to be either harmful or ineffective in light of subsequent findings in psychometric theory or criticisms of test use. The review should examine the soundness of procedures used in test administration, the modes of assessment, the bases for inferences drawn from test scores, and the relative quality of various validation strategies.]

H. CHOICE OR DEVELOPMENT OF TEST OR METHOD

Standardized tests constitute one class of assessment procedures available to the user. He may also choose various kinds of ratings, personal history information, reference information, or "unobtrusive measures." He may also elect to develop his own tests. His choice depends upon what is available for assessing the characteristics of concern, ethical considerations, and his own knowledge and competency. Among standardized tests there are usually many alternatives: different dimensions to be measured, different methods of measurement, and different forms of tests. Choices should be made as deliberately and carefully as circumstances permit; test users should not use habitually the same test or method of assessment for all purposes; neither should they assess only those characteristics that are easily or conveniently assessed and fail to consider other, possibly more important, characteristics. Standards refer to the process of choice, not to the choices themselves.

★**H1. The choice or development of tests, test batteries, or other assessment procedures should be based on clearly formulated goals and hypotheses.** ESSENTIAL

[Comment: There is usually an assumption that one's goals are good, and that the method of assessment chosen will help one achieve those goals. In choosing or building a test one should be able to articulate such assumptions and values. As a general rule, the assumptions take the form of at least an implicit hypothesis: "If I come to a clearer understanding of this individual, in terms of the characteristic or set of characteristics assessed, I will be able to infer something about his vocational success, or his academic problems, or his prognosis in marriage, or whatever."

The use of a test in a decision context implies a hypothesis of the form that a designated outcome is a function of the test variable. A test user should be able to state clearly the desired outcome, the nature of the variables believed to be related to it, and the probable effectiveness of alternative methods of assessing those variables.

The purpose of administering a test should be explicit. In some school systems, it has been alleged, tests are routinely administered with no purpose other than an apparent hope that they will someday be useful. Such routine testing is unwise.]

*H1.1. The test user should formulate goals clearly enough so that he can later evaluate his success in achieving them and can communicate that evaluation to other qualified persons. VERY DESIRABLE

[Comment: In a clinical or counseling situation, there is a continuing relationship with a person who has been tested. If a test user has clear purposes, later events can provide evidence of some success in achieving goals or information for changing inferences or procedures. Without a clear idea of what is to be learned about a person, and why, there will be no clear direction in the counseling relationship.

One's purposes in developing a testing program define his criteria, and the nature of the criteria should suggest to the informed user hypotheses, that is, test variables, that might be associated with them. Such

hypotheses should be reasonable. There is no clear reason, for example, to use a mechanical-aptitude test to try to predict performance in English classes. Similarly, it is not easy to see what purpose is intended when a vocabulary test is adopted for use in the selection of rolling-mill employees.

Some hypotheses are much more easily justified than others. Few people will quarrel with the suggestion that applicants who type rapidly with few errors will become preferred employees in a stenographic pool. The hypotheses that those who are likely to work with greater persistence at a routine, manipulative task can be identified by scores on a very long but easy perceptual speed and accuracy test may require a more detailed explanation of the logic and background data.]

★H1.2. The test user should consider the possibility that different hypotheses may be appropriate for people from different populations. ESSENTIAL

★**H2. A test user should consider more than one variable for assessment and the assessment of any given variable by more than one method.** ESSENTIAL

[Comment: For most purposes, the evaluation of a person requires description that is both broad and precise; a single assessment or assessment procedure rarely provides all relevant facets of a description.

Decisions about individuals should ordinarily be based on assessment of more than one dimension; when feasible, all major dimensions related to the outcome of the decision should be assessed and validated. This is the principle of multivariate prediction; where individual predictors have some validity and relatively low intercorrelations, the composite is usually more valid than prediction based on a single variable. It is not always possible to conduct the empirical validation study (certainly not in working with problems of individuals one at a time), but the principle can be observed.

In any case, care should be taken that assessment procedures focus on important characteristics; decisions are too often based on assessment of only those dimensions that can be conveniently measured with known validity. For example, mental retardation is often defined as both deficiency in tested intelligence and poor adaptive behavior. If both parts of this definition are accepted, then both variables should be considered in deciding whether an individual is to be classified as a mental retardate, even though it is much more difficult to measure adaptive behavior than to find an acceptable scale for testing intelligence.

Test users should also consider more than one method of assessment. Even a test yielding generally valid scores may in an individual case be susceptible to idiosyncratic errors of interpretation, and a pattern of confirming or modifying assessments may be useful. Confidence in inferences drawn from assessments may be increased by varying the sources and increasing the amount of information on which the inferences are made. In addition to tests, one might consider ratings, references, observations of actual performance, etc. Of these, a test is probably most valid. If the others add to the validity of an assessment, they should be systematically considered in statistical prediction; otherwise, they should be ignored. Frequently, however, one will not have enough confidence in test interpretations to justify overlooking other data. In particular, when using a given test with minorities, one may question the validity of test inferences for those populations and want to get as much additional information as possible before making decisions.]

★H2.1. In choosing a method of assessment, a test user should consider his own degree of experience with it and also the prior experience of the test taker. ESSENTIAL

[Comment: Inexperience of the test user can be alleviated by reading, practice, and training. Warm-up tests or other methods of acclimatization are advocated to alleviate the inexperience of test takers. In addition, attention should be given to the degree of interaction between test user and test taker; there may be special sources of anxiety in situations where they are of different cultural or ethnic background.]

*H2.2. The choice or development of a test or test procedure, or the addition of a test or test procedure to existing assessments, should involve consideration of the relationship between the cost of the choice and the benefit expected. VERY DESIRABLE

[Comment: Both costs and benefits may involve broader considerations than the specific problem at hand. Although quantification may be difficult and even unreliable, costs and benefits to the individuals tested and to the broader society should enter into consideration.]

★H3. In choosing an existing test, a test user should relate its history of research and development to his intended use of the instrument. ESSENTIAL

[Comment: A school system was faced with the necessity of reducing its faculty. Reductions in force, according to policy, were to be based on teacher competence. However, decisions were in fact based on scores on a test that had been developed to evaluate the educational backgrounds of new teachers-college graduates. Nothing about the test established its validity as a measure of classroom effectiveness, nor was any local research conducted on this point. Its choice was, therefore, inappropriate.

In a different situation, a decision had been made to use a standard achievement test to evaluate pupil progress. Upon investigation of the test's development, it was found inconsistent with the curriculum objectives of that school. Other tests were examined and an alternative test was chosen that more closely matched the curriculum content. (In some cases, closely matching curriculum content may not be advantageous since it prevents one from knowing the extent to which pupils may be deficient in skills or knowledge not deliberately specified in the local curriculum objectives.)

This standard calls for a general evaluation of the validity of the proposed use of a test. Such an evaluation includes evaluation of the procedures followed in the development of the test and of the quality and relevance of the research that has been done with it.]

★H4. In general a test user should try to choose or to develop an assessment technique in which "tester-effect" is minimized, or in which reliability of assessment across testers can be assured. ESSENTIAL

[Comment: In general, the less the influence of the tester on scores, the fairer the test. The influence of the tester is obviously greater in an unstructured interview than in a structured one, and there may be more tester effect in a structured interview than in a structured personal history form. Tester effect is most likely to be minimized by standardized testing. In using tests, some organizations have turned to tape-recorded instructions in an effort to minimize further possible tester effect.]

H5. Test scores used for selection or other administrative decisions about an individual may not be useful for individual or program evaluation and vice versa. DESIRABLE

[Comment: The purposes of institutional testing and of evaluative testing are not always compatible. Whereas the typical evaluative use is intended to help the individual (or program), institutional decisions frequently have the apparent effect of hurting, even if the decision may have unseen long-term benefits to the individual (such as avoidance of an unnecessary failure experience). These seemingly contradictory functions may prevent effective interpretation in either instance.]

I. ADMINISTRATION AND SCORING

A test user may delegate to someone else the actual task of administering or scoring tests, but he retains the responsibility for these activities. In particular, he has the responsibility for ascertaining the qualifications of such agents. Standards for administration apply not only to the act of testing but also to more general matters of test administration. The basic principle is standardization; when decisions are based on test scores, the decision for each individual should be based on data obtained under circumstances that are essentially alike for all.

★I1. A test user is expected to follow carefully the standardized procedures described in the manual for administering a test. ESSENTIAL

[Comment: It may in rare cases be necessary to modify procedures. When there is any deviation from standard practice, it should be duly noted, and interpretations of scores should not be made in terms of normative data provided in the manual. Modifications may be standardized for specific purposes. For example, modifications were necessary for testing a group of deaf mutes, but the modified procedures were applied in the same way to all children in the group.

Standardization of procedure is particularly important when decisions are based on test scores. Nevertheless, known examples of failure to follow standardized procedures are numerous. In one organization, when test supplies were depleted, mimeographed versions of uneven quality were prepared. (In addition to being a violation of copyright laws, the result was a markedly changed set of stimulus materials.) One test administrator tried to relieve the monotony of the repeated verbatim instructions by giving a shorter and varied version.]

★I1.1. A test user must fully understand the administrative procedures to be followed. ESSENTIAL

[Comment: The test user should be fully trained to do whatever is required for competent administration of the test. The administration of many tests requires nothing more than the ability to read and understand routine instructions, that of others requires extensive supervised practice. Whatever the requirement, the test user lacking such training should seek it.]

*I1.2. A test user should maintain consistent conditions for testing. VERY DESIRABLE

[Comment: Situational variables should be reasonably controlled. For example, there should be no great variation in temperature or humidity; noises and other distractions should be as nearly eliminated as possible. Interadministrator reliability should be high. In general, testing conditions should minimize variations in the testing procedure.]

★I1.3. A test user should make periodic checks on material, equipment, and procedures to maintain standardization. ESSENTIAL

[Comment: This standard refers, for example, to the constancy of graphics and of printing, or the accuracy of stop watches. It also seeks the elimination of bad habits that may creep into administrative procedures. It applies particularly to any testing procedures that make use of physical equipment which is subject to wear. Such equipment should be regularly examined to assure that its characteristics remain within acceptable tolerances; for example, a pegboard should be replaced if holes become enlarged or beveled through use.]

★I2. The test administrator is responsible for establishing conditions, consistent with the principle of standardization, that enable each examinee to do his best. ESSENTIAL

[Comment: In a negative sense, the goal of this standard is that conditions inhibiting maximum performance should be avoided. The principle can be followed in part simply by being sure that all materials—such as answer sheets, pencils, and erasers—are on hand and that precautions have been taken to avoid distractions. In a more positive sense, the administrator should be sure that the examinee understands the tasks involved in taking the test: what kinds of responses are to be made and on what answer sheets, the implications for test-taking strategy of erasures or multiple marking or guessing, and how to know whether the test has been completed.

The tester should try to create a nonhostile environment; standardized procedures are impersonal, but the test administrator must avoid being either patronizing or unresponsive to the examinees, especially when the tester and the examinee differ in race, sex, or status. A testing situation contains elements that are nonrecurring and unique to the persons tested. Although these may have negligible effects on test reliability, they may include events perceived as denigrating or questioning of the worth of the individual. A complete catalog of such events is not possible or easily described. In general, however, the social amenities of respect, politeness, and due regard for extenuating circumstances are relevant guides for insuring the dignity of persons. While it may not be demonstrated that abuse of these principles leads to poor test performance, such abuse is not likely to enhance performance.

It is often difficult to maximize the motivation of the examinees. The attempt is important; a major source of error may arise when examinees do not like or trust the test, tester, or test situation, and therefore make no special effort to do well in it.]

*I2.1. Procedures manuals should be prepared for use in organizations when there is repeated testing. VERY DESIRABLE

[Comment: Just as a manual is needed for a test, a manual is needed for a testing program. Changes in personnel or lapses in memory make a record of procedures developed and followed necessary for standardization. Such a manual might indicate appropriate circumstances for testing or for referral for testing, standard sequences of tests, or guides to interpretations of test batteries in addition to instructions for administering and scoring tests taken or adapted from individual test manuals.]

★I3. A test user is responsible for accuracy in scoring, checking, coding, or recording test results. ESSENTIAL

[Comment: Any agent of the user shares this responsibility. The clerk who scores a test must understand and accept the necessity for accuracy. The test user, who may or may not do the actual scoring, nevertheless has the responsibility to be sure that procedures are established and followed for verifying accuracy. It is unfair to individuals or organizations when decisions are based on avoidable error.]

★I3.1. When test scoring equipment is used, the test user should insist on evidence of its accuracy; when feasible, he should make spot checks against hand scoring or develop some other system of quality control. ESSENTIAL

[Comment: The frequency of such checks will depend on what is known of the procedures on checking within the scoring service. Commercial scoring services may be queried about their procedures if they have not already announced them; if the procedures seem well designed, such spot checks may be needed only infrequently. Some computer services, on the other hand, may be less meticulous, and some hand scoring may be required in each batch of tests scored by machine. One test user in a certification program, where machine analysis of answers not only yields individual scores but also supplies data for analysis prior to revisions, has adopted the policy of hand scoring as well as machine scoring each test. This assures the accuracy of every score used in individual decisions, and it also assures the accuracy of the computer data used in the continuing research program.]

*I3.2. When test scoring requires judgment, the test user should determine interscorer or intrascorer reliability. VERY DESIRABLE

[Comment: When the test user does his own scoring, he should make periodic comparisons of scores he has determined against scores on the same sets of responses determined by other scorers or by himself at other times.]

★I4. If specific cutting scores are to be used as a basis for decisions, a test user should have a rationale, justification, or explanation of the cutting scores adopted. ESSENTIAL

[Comment: When a cutting score is adopted, the effect is to reduce scoring to a scale of only two points: pass and fail. The validity of the test scored in this way is different at different cutting scores and, in general, is different from the validity found with continuous scores.

The test user should have some justifiable reason for the adoption of a given cutting score. Many kinds of arguments might be used. In a content-referenced interpretation of a mastery test, such a score might be determined as the obtained score at which one can reject, at a preselected level of probability, the hypothesis that a predesignated confidence interval for that score includes the perfect score on the test. If interpretations are referenced against an external criterion, the cutting score might be one where there is a designated probability of achieving a specified level of success (e.g., "We do not admit students who have less than a 30-per-cent chance of graduating"). Decision theory principles can be used to find a cutting score that will maximize the discrimination between high- and low-criterion groups. One might base the cutting score simply on a distribution of scores in a "predicted-yield" situation; for example, the proportion of job applicants who accept offered employment, the number of new employees who will be needed, predictions of growth or reduction in force, and related information can be used to determine the "predicted yields" of new employees at different cutting scores. The determination of a cutting score on this basis may result in using the test in a range where it is less than maximally effective; its validity should be determined in light of its actual use.

This standard does not attempt to recommend a specific procedure for developing cutting scores where they are to be used. The intent is to recommend that test users avoid the practice of designating purely arbitrary cutting scores they can neither explain nor defend. Cutting scores adopted with reference to those used in another organization or for another purpose, or by a casual glance at normative tables, are usually unsatisfactory.]

*I4.1. A validity coefficient for each criterion for which a predictor test is recommended should be provided at each one of several points on the score continuum that may be used as cutting scores. VERY DESIRABLE

★I4.1.1. If examinees are to be selected on the basis of a set of scores that displays different regression lines for use in predicting the same criterion in different subgroups of an applicant population, cutting scores should be established with great caution to avoid unfairness to members of one or more of the subgroups. ESSENTIAL

[Comment: There are many defensible definitions of "unfairness" in the literature, and techniques have been developed for setting cutting scores to minimize "unfairness" as defined in these ways. Test users should keep abreast of the rapidly developing literature on this topic.]

★I5. The test user shares with the test developer or distributor a responsibility for maintaining test security. ESSENTIAL

[Comment: Test security is a problem whenever a lapse in security can result in changing an individual's score without making a change in his true score. For some kinds of tests a lapse of security would not be serious. If one is to be tested for achieved skill, for example, knowing and practicing the test samples might be highly recommended. In many cases, however, prior knowledge of test items or scoring procedures could destroy validity. The problem is not simply one of cheating. Security may be compromised where examinees have had much prior experience with a popular test, have been taught specific test items, or have heard a lot about the test.]

*I5.1. Where a probable breach of security may invalidate test inferences, the test user should employ other methods of assessment; that is, he should seek a basis for more valid inferences. VERY DESIRABLE

★I5.2. All reasonable precautions should be taken to safeguard test material. ESSENTIAL

[Comment: The use of locked files is a minimal requirement in maintaining test security. It is important to know the recipient whenever tests are out of the filing cabinets. In a test-taking situation, examinees should be proctored. When a test is mailed out to other locations, the recipient should be known and trusted. The ubiquitous copying machine has intensified the problem of safeguarding test materials.]

*I5.3. The test user should avoid basing decisions on scores obtained from insecure tests. VERY DESIRABLE

[Comment: A test may be designated insecure because it is known that unauthorized copies have gone astray. Another test might be considered insecure because it is so widely used that a test taker may have had ample opportunity to practice it in other test-taking situations previously and be able to recognize items. Some employment tests, for example, are so widely used that a job applicant may have taken them several times while applying to various employers.]

J. INTERPRETATION OF SCORES

Standards in this section refer to the interpretation of a test score by the test user and to reports of interpretations. Reports may be made to the person tested, to his agent, or to other affected people: teachers, parents, supervisors, and various administrators and executives.

★J1. A test score should be interpreted as an estimate of performance under a given set of circumstances. It should not be interpreted as some absolute characteristic of the examinee or as something permanent and generalizable to all other circumstances. ESSENTIAL

★J1.1. A test user should consider the total context of testing in interpreting an obtained score before making any decisions (including the decision to accept the score). ESSENTIAL

[Comment: The standard is that one must avoid the abdication of responsibility by relying exclusively on an obtained score. Users should, in particular, look for contaminating or irrelevant variables that may have influenced obtained scores; for example, in testing to classify school children, scores may be influenced by behavior problems, visual or hearing defects, language problems, and racial or cultural factors, as well as by ability.]

★J2. Test scores should ordinarily be reported only to people who are qualified

to interpret them. **If scores are reported, they should be accompanied by explanations sufficient for the recipient to interpret them correctly.** ESSENTIAL

[Comment: There are difficult problems associated with the question of who should have access to test scores within an organization. Certainly, curious peers should not have access to them. An individual who must make the ultimate decision to admit or to reject or to hire or to reject, or to certify or not to certify, must have the interpretation. One useful (and unanswered) question is whether such a person who lacks the training necessary for the interpretation of scores should be given that training or should be given only the interpretations of scores.]

J2.1. An individual tested (or his agent or guardian) has the right to know his score and the interpretations made. In some instances, even scores on individual items should be made known. DESIRABLE

[Comment: Strictly speaking, this is an ethical standard rather than a standard of competent test use; it is stated here because it conflicts with technical considerations of test security. If the standard is followed, test interpretations and their foundations will be made available to those with a "need to know"; certainly, the individual whose future is affected by the decision is among those with a "need to know." The test user should take any precautions he can, when the demand for information is severe, to protect test security, but he should not do so at the expense of an individual's right to understand the bases for decisions that affect him adversely. Such understanding may be better promoted, with less threat to test security, by using qualified persons sympathetic to the individual's interests. For example, when there is a civil-rights issue, it would be most useful to have items examined by a qualified testing specialist who is known to be both concerned and knowledgeable.]

★J2.2. A system of reporting test results should provide interpretations. ESSENTIAL

[Comment: Although the form of a report will differ for different audiences (examinees, teachers, parents, supervisors), it should communicate the interpretation in a form that will be clear and easily understood.]

*J2.2.1. Scores should ordinarily be interpreted in light of their confidence intervals rather than as specific values alone. VERY DESIRABLE

J2.3. In general, test users should avoid the use of descriptive labels (e.g., retarded) applied to individuals when interpreting test scores. DESIRABLE

[Comment: The standard applies to the use of summary diagnoses in general. For nearly all purposes, it is better to describe behavior and to differentiate such description from inference. Summary labels tend to be inferences treated as if they were descriptions.

The use of a summary label generally connotes value judgments; unfortunately, most are words used in everyday language and therefore subject to inaccurate interpretation. A test maker may know precisely what he means when he uses the term "retarded," but he has no influence over the interpretation of the same word by a judge, teacher, parent, or child.]

★J3. The test user should recognize that estimates of reliability do not indicate criterion-related validity. ESSENTIAL

[Comment: Reliability is a necessary but not a sufficient condition of validity. Reliability coefficients are pertinent to validity in the negative sense that unreliable scores cannot be valid; but reliable scores are by no means *ipso facto* valid.]

★J4. A test user should examine carefully the rationale and validity of computer-based interpretations of test scores. ESSENTIAL

[Comment: The user of a special service has the obligation to be thoroughly familiar with the principles on which such interpretations are derived, and he should have the ability to evaluate a computer-based interpretation of test performance in light of other evidence he may have.]

★J5. In norm-referenced interpretations, a test user should interpret an obtained score with reference to sets of norms appropriate for the individual tested and for the intended use. ESSENTIAL

[Comment: The reverse is also a standard of competent test use: The test user ordinarily should not interpret an obtained score with reference to a set of norms that is inappropriate for the individual tested or for the purposes of the testing. This is a relatively simple standard to state, but it often is difficult to apply. Contemporary social problems suggest that men and women or members of different ethnic groups should for some purposes be evaluated in terms of several norms groups. For other purposes, such as vocational counseling, students should know how they stand relative to those in or entering a relevant occupation, regardless of their ethnic background. Of course, women or members of minority groups should not be counseled to avoid nontraditional occupations (e.g., women in engineering) merely for lack of appropriate norms.

It is by no means certain that sex or race is the crucial variable in interpreting a given score. It may well be that more important variables for differential norms would be breadth of cultural exposure (or degree of cultural isolation), skill and experience in the use of standard English, interests, or similar variables which may seem to be related to sex or racial differences in test performance.]

★J5.1. It is usually better to interpret scores with reference to a specified norms group in terms of percentile ranks or standard scores than to use terms like IQ or grade equivalents that may falsely imply a fully representative or national norms group. ESSENTIAL

★J5.2. Test users should avoid the use of terms such as IQ, IQ equivalent, or grade equivalent where other terms provide more meaningful interpretations of a score. ESSENTIAL

[Comment: Such scores are objectionable for several reasons. Most important, they generally involve spurious projections of growth. They involve an interpretation which is at best awkward. (To illustrate: It is much simpler to ask, in interpreting a score, "Where does this person stand in relation to specific norm groups?" than to ask, "What group is this person's performance like the average of?" The semantic awkwardness of the latter question illustrates its psychometric awkwardness as well.) They are labels to which the general public attaches many different inappropriate meanings.

Some of these scores, such as mental age or grade equivalent scores, involve severe technical problems. For example, serious misinterpretations occur when grade levels are extrapolated beyond the range for which the test is designed. Moreover, it should be recognized that the standard error of measurement for some widely used standardized achievement tests may be equal to one grade level.

If a test user, either because of his own limitations or because of rigid institutional policies, feels that he must use such terms, he should be sure that interpretations are also given in standard scores or percentile ranks with reference to the specific norms group used in deriving them. The specific test, test form, time of testing, and nature of the test situation should be included in the statement.]

★J5.3. A test user should examine differences between characteristics of a person tested and those of the population on whom the test was developed or norms developed. His responsibility includes deciding whether the differences are so great that the test should not be used for that person. ESSENTIAL

*J5.3.1. If no standardized approach to the desired measurement or assessment is available that is appropriate for a given individual (e.g., a child of Spanish-speaking migrant workers), the test user should employ a broad-based approach to assessment using as many methods as are available to him. VERY DESIRABLE

[Comment: The standard is to do the best one can. This may perhaps include the use of a test, even though no appropriate normative data are available, simply as a means of finding out how the individual approaches the task of the test. It might include references, extensive interviews, or perhaps some ad hoc situational tasks. Efforts to help solve educational or psychological problems should not be abandoned simply because of the absence of an appropriate standardized instrument.]

*J5.4. Local normative data or expectancy tables should ordinarily be developed, if possible, when administrative decisions are based on test scores. VERY DESIRABLE

[Comment: Expectancy tables may be more useful than norms. When decisions are based on test scores (with the possible exception of content-referenced interpretations), the test user has ordinarily hypothesized that some outcome on an external criterion is related to performance on the test. Decision makers will have a more useful interpretation of a test score if it is expressed in terms of an expected level of performance on the criterion than if it is expressed in terms of relative standing.]

★J5.5. Ordinarily, normative interpretations of ability-test scores should not be made for scores in the chance range. ESSENTIAL

[Comment: On one reading test for elementary school students, a child who cannot read, and therefore gives truly random responses, would be most likely to obtain a grade-equivalent score, according to the norms, of 2.2; that is, second month of second grade. Quite apart from the usual difficulties with grade-equivalent scores, the example demonstrates the impropriety of trying to make a normative interpretation of a test score obtained in a chance range. One test manual for a widely used test of general mental ability has provided a useful guide to the interpretation of "range-of-chance" scores.]

★J6. Any content-referenced interpretation should clearly indicate the domain to which one can generalize. ESSENTIAL

★J7. The test user should consider alternative interpretations of a given score. ESSENTIAL

[Comment: In a sense, a test-score interpretation implies the hypothesis that the score obtained is a function of the trait level "really" possessed. Alternative hypotheses can be suggested. The obtained score might be a function of anxiety, prior knowledge of the test, inadequate understanding of the instructions, a general sort of test wiseness, deliberate faking, or any of several other possibilities. The test user needs to consider more than the obvious interpretation and to have the skill and sensitivity necessary to develop alternative explanations and to evaluate them.]

J7.1. Where cutting scores are established as guides for decision, the test user should retain some degree of discretion over their use. DESIRABLE

[Comment: The point bears repeating that a test user cannot abdicate the responsibility for the decision to use the test. In most circumstances, there are alternatives. Despite the fact that a given test may have a high predictive validity for a specific function, it may represent a trait which is not the only path to success in the predicted venture; and its validity for a given individual, tested at a particular time and under particular circumstances, may be in doubt.

This standard may not be taken as a license to discriminate; it is to be used sparingly in recognition that excessive subjectivity can reduce rather than enhance validity. The intent is to avoid a mechanical rigidity in using test scores of imperfect validity. See also H2.]

J7.2. A person tested should have more than one kind of opportunity to qualify for a favorable decision. DESIRABLE

[Comment: In some situations, a candidate might be given the option to qualify on the basis of characteristics other than those measured by the test. If a person with a score so low that his best prognosis is academic failure, nevertheless succeeds in college, he may have demonstrated qualities necessary for success other than those measured by the test, and the fact might well be considered.

Again, the standard must be judiciously applied. In general, the most valid methods available should guide decisions; the subjective use of information not validated can reduce validity. When compelling information exists, however, it should not be ignored in individual cases. It should be noted that it would be unethical as well as invalid to invoke this principle in the application of particular biases of the test user.]

J7.3. A procedure for reporting test results should include checks on accuracy and make provision for retesting. DESIRABLE

[Comment: Errors in procedures and in test scoring occur; procedures should be available for checking. Retesting is one form of checking results. There should be some limits to a retesting provision. The number of allowable retests may be limited by the number of parallel forms available. Certain types of assessments (e.g., personal-history data) are inappropriate for "retesting." Moreover, a true score is likely to be closer to the mean than is its corresponding obtained score. This fact has important implications for extremely low scores; they will tend to be increased in a retest.

In general, however, opportunities for retesting should be permitted without major obstacles. The principle is that no one should be a victim, without recourse, of an adverse decision on the basis of faulty and correctable psychological assessment. Nor should such decisions be permanent; over a period of time, individuals should have a chance for reevaluation on the basis of new learning or new experience.]

*J8. The test user should be able to interpret test performance relative to other measures. VERY DESIRABLE

[Comment: For many uses, one should be able to interpret test scores in terms of external criteria. The necessary data may be in a test manual; manuals for some academic aptitude tests provide expectancy charts useful for such interpretations. When an assessment of performance on an external criterion is also available, and when there is a wide discrepancy between actual and predicted criterion performance, the test user should investigate possible reasons for the discrepancy. Furthermore, there should be no *a priori* assumption that either the test or the criterion is the instrument in error.]

*J8.1. A test user should be able to use and interpret data regarding the statistical significance of differences between scores. VERY DESIRABLE

[Comment: A test user may observe differences in scores made by two individuals on the same test. There may be differences in the scores made by an individual on a pretest and a posttest after some intervening treatment or training. He may be interested in comparing the individual's performance on one test with the same person's performance on still another test. In such cases, the test user should know how much confidence to place in an observed score difference.]

★J9. A test user should develop procedures for systematically eliminating from data files test-score information that has, because of the lapse of time, become obsolete. ESSENTIAL

[Comment: Data should not even be available for consideration in decision making after an invalidating period of time. Scores on early achievement tests in areas where later learning or forgetting is to be expected (e.g., an old typing-test score) are no longer likely to be valid.

Not all data are equally susceptible to obsolescence. Information of a highly subjective nature might be judged to become obsolete in a shorter time than more objective items of information. Information about young children might be judged to become obsolete in a shorter period of time than comparable kinds of information about adults.

In the case of data that have potential value for research or for survey purposes, the purging may consist of destroying the link between a person's name and the information relevant to the test rather than destroying the information itself.]

INDEX

PUBLISHERS DIRECTORY AND INDEX

This directory and index gives the addresses and tests of all publishers represented in this volume. References are to entry numbers, not to page numbers. Stars indicate test publishers with test catalogs listing 10 or more tests. Tests not originating in the country of publication are identified by listing in brackets the country in which the test was originally prepared and published. All foreign tests distributed by United States publishers are listed; however, United States tests distributed by foreign publishers are listed only if the tests have been revised or supplemented for foreign use.

Road Test Check List for Testing, Selecting, Rating, and Training Coach Operators, 2472
Road Test in Traffic for Testing, Selecting, Rating and Training Truck Drivers, 2473
Simplified Road Test, 851

American Chemical Society. *See* Examinations Committee.

American College Testing Program (The), P.O. Box 168, Iowa City, Iowa 52240:
ACT Assessment, 1044
ACT Assessment of Career Development, 2100
ACT Career Planning Program, 2101
ACT Guidance Profile, 2167
ACT Mathematics Placement Examination, 596
Institutional Self-Study Service Survey, College Student Form, 1236
Medical College Admission Test, 2355

American Council on Education, 1 Dupont Circle, Washington, D.C. 20036 (*See also* General Educacational Development Testing Service.):
American Council on Education Cumulative Record Folders, 1008

American Dental Association. *See* Division of Educational Measurements.

American Foundation for the Blind, Inc., 15 West 16th St., New York, N.Y. 10011:
Anxiety Scale for the Blind, 1100
Braverman-Chevigny Auditory Projective Test, 1449
Maxfield-Buchholz Scale of Social Maturity for Use With Preschool Blind Children, 1276
Stanford Multi-Modality Imagery Test, 773

★American Guidance Service, Inc., Publishers' Bldg., Circle Pines, Minn. 55014:
A/9 Cumulative Record Folder, 1007
California Algebra Aptitude Test, 671
Chronological Age Computer, 804
Doren Diagnostic Reading Test of Word Recognition Skills, 1627
Essentials of English Tests, 81
First Grade Screening Test, 979
Goldman-Fristoe Test of Articulation, 2075
Goldman-Fristoe-Woodcock Test of Auditory Discrimination, 2037
I.Q. Calculator, 807
KeyMath Diagnostic Arithmetic Test, 721
Kuhlmann-Finch Tests, 399
Maturity Level for School Entrance and Reading Readiness, 1715
Mental Age Calculator, 808
Minnesota High School Achievement Examinations
    Advanced Mathematics, 597
    Biology, 1803
    Bookkeeping, 776
    Chemistry, 1836
    Elementary Algebra, 678
    Geometry, 748
    Language Arts, 90
    Mathematics, 631
    Physics, 1871
    Science, 1791
    Social Studies, 1949
    Social Studies Grade 10 (American History), 1999
    Social Studies Grade 11 (World History), 2000
    Social Studies Grade 12 (American Problems), 2015
    Trigonometry, 765
Minnesota Preschool Scale, 509
Minnesota Rate of Manipulation Test, 2227
Minnesota Spatial Relations Test, 2258
Oseretsky Tests of Motor Proficiency, 1898
Peabody Individual Achievement Test, 26
Peabody Picture Vocabulary Test, 516
Pennsylvania Bi-Manual Worksample, 2231
Preschool Attainment Record, 519
Ratio I.Q. Computer, 812
Verbal Language Development Scale, 2098
Woodcock Reading Mastery Tests, 1656

American Institutes for Research, 8555 Sixteenth St., Silver Spring, Md. 20910 (*See also* Project Talent Office.):
Orr-Graham Listening Test, 995

American Language Institute (The), Georgetown University, 3605 O St. N.W., Washington, D.C. 20007:
English Usage Test for Non-Native Speakers of English, 230
Oral Rating Form for Rating Language Proficiency in Speaking and Understanding English, 234
Vocabulary and Reading Test for Students of English as a Second Language, 239

American Optical Corporation, Instrumental Division, Box A, Buffalo, N.Y. 14215:
AO Sight Screener, 1906
Pseudo-Isochromatic Plates for Testing Color Perception, 1924

American Orthopsychiatric Association, Inc., 1775 Broadway, New York, N.Y. 10019:
Visual Motor Gestalt Test, 1447a

American Printing House for the Blind, Inc., 1839 Frankfort Ave., Louisville, Ky. 40206:
Colorado Braille Battery: Literary Code Tests, 769
Colorado Braille Battery: Nemeth Code Tests, 770
Cooperative School and College Ability Tests, 361
Diagnostic Reading Tests, 1626
Iowa Tests of Basic Skills, 19
Roughness Discrimination Test, 772
Sequential Tests of Educational Progress, 35
    Listening, 997
    Mathematics, 652
    Reading, 1599
    Science, 1794
    Social Studies, 1948
    Writing, 113
Stanford Achievement Test, 36
    Mathematics Tests, 655
    Reading Tests, 1603
    Science, 1796
    Social Studies Tests, 1953
    Spelling and Language Tests, 115

American Testing Co., 6301 S.W. Fifth St., Fort Lauderdale, Fla. 33317:
Language Arts Diagnostic Probes, 89
Mathematics Inventory Tests, 630
National Test of Basic Words, 1667
National Test of Library Skills, 1762
Reading Diagnostic Probes, 1642
Reading Inventory Probe 1, 1725

American Transit Association, 465 L'Enfant Plaza West S.W., Washington, D.C. 20024:
Personal Reaction Test for Transit Employees, 2469b
Placement Interview for Transit Employees, 2469c
Standard Examination for Transit Employees, 2469a
Standardized Road Test for Bus Operators, 2469d

Anand Agencies, 1433 A Shukrawar, Poona 2, India:
Draw-A-Man Test for Indian Children, 372

Aptitude Test Service, Inc., P.O. Box 16, Golf, Ill. 60029:
Business Test, 345
Hay Clerical Test Battery, 2132
Stenographic Skill-Dictation Test, 2159
Typing Skill, 2163

Arden Press, 8331 Alvarado Drive, Huntington Beach, Calif. 92646:
Academic Readiness and End of First Grade Progress Scales, 1693
Burks' Behavior Rating Scale for Organic Brain Dysfunction, 1114
Burks' Behavior Rating Scales, 1115
School Attitude Survey, 1364
Teacher Self-Rating Inventory, 903

Armed Forces Vocational Testing Group, Randolph Air Force Base, Tex. 78148:
Armed Services Vocational Aptitude Battery, 1067

Associated Personnel Technicians, Inc., Box 1036, Wichita, Kan. 67201:
APT Controlled Interview, 2294
APT Dictation Test, 2119
APT Manual Dexterity Test, 2222
APT Performance Test, 332

Associated Publishers, 355 State St., Los Altos, Calif. 94022:
Client-Centered Counseling Progress Record, 1130

Association Press, 291 Broadway, New York, N.Y. 10007:
Personal Adjustment Inventory, 1313

Attwood (Madge Louise), School of Education, University of Michigan, Ann Arbor, Mich. 48104:
Drug Abuse Knowledge Test, 922

Audio-Visual Services, Pennsylvania State University, 6 Willard Bldg., University Park, Pa. 16802:
Rock-A-Bye, Baby: A Group Projective Test for Children, 1497

★Australian Council for Educational Research, P.O. Box 210, Hawthorn, Vic. 3122, Australia:
A.C.E.R. Advanced Test B40, 323
A.C.E.R. Advanced Tests AL and AQ, 324
ACER Higher Tests, 325
A.C.E.R. Intermediate Test A, 326
A.C.E.R. Intermediate Tests C and D, 327
A.C.E.R. Junior Non-Verbal Test, 328
A.C.E.R. Junior Test A, 329
A.C.E.R. Lower Grades General Ability Scale, 330
A.C.E.R. Lower Grades Reading Test, 1529
ACER Mathematics Tests: AM Series Topic Tests, 595

A.C.E.R. Mechanical Comprehension Test, 2237
A.C.E.R. Mechanical Reasoning Test, 2238
A.C.E.R. Number Test, 691
ACER Primary Reading Survey Tests, 1530
ACER Short Clerical Test—Form C, 2117
A.C.E.R. Speed and Accuracy Tests, 2118
A.C.E.R. Word Knowledge Test—Adult Form B, 163
Advanced Test N, 338
Classification Tasks, 488
Cooperative Reading Comprehension Test, Forms L and M [United States], 1545
Cooperative Reading Comprehension Test, Form Y [United States], 1544
Diagnostic Decimal Tests 1–3, 714
Diagnostic Fractions Test 3, 715
Diagnostic Number Tests 1–2, 716
Diagnostic Test in Basic Algebra, 674
Diagnostic Test in Basic Geometry, 747
Franck Drawing Completion Test, 1463
How Supervise [United States], 2448
Individual Reading Test, 1557
Jenkins Non-Verbal Test [England], 415a1
Kindergarten Behavioural Index, 1708
Mill Hill Vocabulary Scale [England], 403
Object Sorting Scales, 1299
Otis Self-Administering Tests of Mental Ability [United States], 426
Pacific Design Construction Test, 514
Pacific Reasoning Series Tests: Pacific Test Series, 427
Pacific Tests of English Attainment and Skills: Pacific Test Series, 102
Phillips Occupational Preference Scale, 2202
Progressive Achievement Tests of Reading [New Zealand], 1579
Queensland Test, 520
Rothwell-Miller Interest Blank, 2208
Shorthand Aptitude Test, 793
Stamp Behaviour Study Technique, 1388
Student Attitude Inventory, 1399
Vineland Social Maturity Scale [United States], 1428
W.A.L. English Comprehension Test, 1613
Wechsler Intelligence Scale for Children [United States], 533

Automata Corporation, 2952 George Washington Way, Richland, Wash. 99352:
Automata EDT 1200 Educational Data Terminal, 1030

Ballen (Roland), P.O. Box 11209, Palo Alto, Calif. 94306:
Tickmaster, 2319

Baptist Book Store, 1010 Broadway, Nashville, Tenn. 37203:
Bible and You, 1023

Bausch & Lomb, Inc., Rochester, N.Y. 14602:
Ortho-Rater, 1923
School Vision Tester, 1925

Baylor University Press, 5th and Speight, Waco, Tex. 76703:
Biblical Survey Test, 1024

Bealls (J. & P.) Ltd., Gallowgate, Newcastle Upon Tyne, Northumberland, England:
Self Valuation Test, 1505

Behavior Arts Center, 77 Lyons Place, Westwood, N.J. 07675:
Nurses' Observation Scale for Inpatient Evaluation, 1298

Behavioral Publications, Inc., 2852 Broadway, New York, N.Y. 10025:
Baker-Schulberg Community Mental Health Ideology Scale, 1106
Community Adaptation Schedule, 1137
Educational Values Assessment Questionnaire, 860
Gerontological Apperception Test, 1464

Behaviordyne, Inc., P.O. Box 3689, Stanford, Calif. 94305:
Behaviordyne Psychodiagnostic Lab Service (CPI), 1122
Behaviordyne Psychodiagnostic Lab Service (MMPI), 1282

Bell Therapeutic Supplies, Inc., 396 Rockaway Ave., Valley Stream, N.Y. 11581:
Hoffer-Osmond Diagnostic Test [Canada], 1215

Beltone Electronics Corporation, 4201 West Victoria St., Chicago, Ill. 60646:
Beltone Audiometers, 2032

Belwin-Mills Publishing Corporation, 25 Deshon Drive, Melville, N.Y. 11746:
Belwin-Mills Singing Achievement Test, 195
Kwalwasser Music Talent Test, 203

Bennett (Chas. A.) Co., Inc., 809 West Detweiller Drive, Peoria, Ill. 61614:
Visualization Test of Three Dimensional Orthographic Shape, 1935

Berry Language Tests, 4332 Pine Crest Road, Rockford, Ill. 61107:
Berry-Talbott Language Test, 55

Better Reading Program, Inc., 8 South Michigan Ave., Chicago, Ill. 60603:
Reader Rater With Self-Scoring Profile, 1670

Bienvenu (Millard J.), Sr., 710 Watson Drive, Natchitoches, La. 71457:
Interpersonal Communication Inventory, 1241

Bingham Button Test, 46211 North 125th St. East, Lancaster, Calif. 93534:
Bingham Button Test, 485

Biometrics Research, New York State Psychiatric Institute, 722 West 168th St., New York, N.Y. 10032:
Current and Past Psychopathology Scales, 1150
Mental Status Schedule, 1278
Psychiatric Evaluation Form, 1339
Psychiatric Status Schedules, 1340

Blackwell (Basil), Publisher, 5 Alfred St., Oxford, England:
Swansea Test of Phonic Skills, 1652

★Bobbs-Merrill Co., Inc. (The), 4300 West 62nd St., Indianapolis, Ind. 46268:
Achievement Examinations for Secondary Schools
    Advanced Algebra, 664
    Bookkeeping, 775
    Business Relations and Occupations, 779
    Chemistry, 1834
    Economic Geography, 1974
    Elementary Algebra, 677
    English IX–XII, 74
    French I and II, 251
    General Mathematics III, 617
    General Science III, 1786
    German I and II, 268
    Latin I and II, 294
    Modern World History, 1997
    Physics, 1870
    Plane Geometry, 756
    Solid Geometry, 758
    Spanish I and II, 320
Algebra Readiness Test, 665
American School Achievement Tests, 4
    Arithmetic, 695
    Arithmetic Readiness, 694
    Language and Spelling, 52
    Reading, 1532
    Social Studies and Science, 1937
American School Intelligence Test, 339
American School Reading Readiness Test, 1694
American School Reading Tests, 1533
Analytical Survey Test in Computational Arithmetic, 696
Analytical Survey Test in English Fundamentals, 53
Baltimore County French Test, 241
Baltimore County Spanish Test, 303
Bobbs-Merrill Arithmetic Achievement Tests, 705
Breslich Algebra Survey Test, 669
Brief Survey of Arithmetic Skills, 706
Buckingham Extension of the Ayres Spelling Scale, 146
Cattell Culture Fair Intelligence Test, 364b
Detroit Adjustment Inventory, 1155
Detroit Clerical Aptitudes Examination, 782
Detroit General Aptitudes Examination, 1068
Detroit General Intelligence Examination, 370
Detroit Mechanical Aptitudes Examination, 2244
Detroit Retail Selling Inventory, 2397
Detroit Tests of Learning Aptitude, 493
Diagnostic Chart for Fundamental Processes in Arithmetic, 713
Gray Oral Reading Test, 1681
Illinois Algebra Test, 680
Jr.-Sr. High School Personality Questionnaire, 1253
Lee Test of Algebraic Ability, 684
Monroe's Standardized Silent Reading Test, 1569
Patterson Test or Study Exercises on the Constitution of the United States, 2011
Pressey Classification and Verifying Tests, 438
Pressey Diagnostic Reading Tests, 1576
Pressey Diagnostic Tests in English Composition, 104
Public School Achievement Tests, 28
    Arithmetic Computation, 697
    Arithmetic Reasoning, 698
    Reading, 1590
Public School Primary Intelligence Test, 441
Schrammel-Gray High School and College Reading Test, 1598
Self-Analysis Inventory, 1371
Standardized Oral Reading Check Tests, 1689
Standardized Oral Reading Paragraphs, 1690
Traxler High School Reading Test, 1610
Traxler High School Spelling Test, 162
Traxler Silent Reading Test, 1611
Tressler English Minimum Essentials Test, 121

Vocabulary Test for High School Students and College Freshmen, 176
Williams Primary Reading Test, 1615
Williams Reading Test for Grades 4–9, 1616

Book Society of Canada Ltd. (The), 4386 Sheppard Ave. East, P.O. Box 200, Agincourt, Ont. M1S 3B6, Canada:
Watson Diagnostic Mathematics Test: Computation, 663
Watson English Usage and Appreciation Test, 123
Watson Number-Readiness Test, 741
Watson Reading-Readiness Test, 1734

Boyle (Mrs. John H.), 944 Bryant Ave., Chico, Calif. 95926:
Shipley-Institute of Living Scale for Measuring Intellectual Impairment, 1380

Brador Publications, Inc., Livonia, N.Y. 14487:
Reading Skills Diagnostic Test, 1644

Brandywine Achievement Test, Box 526, Coatesville, Pa. 19320:
Brandywine Achievement Test in Geography for Secondary Schools, 1973

Brigham Young University Press, 205 UPB, Provo, Utah 84601:
Sucher-Allred Reading Placement Inventory, 1604

Brook Educational Publishing Ltd., P.O. Box 1171, Guelph, Ont., Canada:
Test of Motor Impairment, 1904

Brown & Associates, Inc., P.O. Box 5092, Station B, Greenville, S.C. 29606:
Yarn Dexterity Test, 2236

Brown (Wm. C.) Co. Publishers, 2460 Kerper Blvd., Dubuque, Iowa 52001:
Classroom Reading Inventory, 1618

★Bruce (Martin M.), Ph.D., Publishers, 340 Oxford Road, New Rochelle, N.Y. 10804:
Aptitudes Associates Test of Sales Aptitude, 2395
Association Adjustment Inventory, 1445
Bruce Vocabulary Inventory, 165
Business Judgment Test, 2275
Career Counseling Personal Data Form, 2296
Clerical Skills Series, 2121
Employee Performance Appraisal, 2299
Industrial Sentence Completion Form, 1477
Modern Photography Comprehension Test, 766
Performance Review Forms, 2310
Personnel Interviewing Forms, 2312
Polyfactorial Study of Personality, 1328
Sales Comprehension Test, 2406
Sales Motivation Inventory, 2408
Sales Sentence Completion Blank, 2409
Selection Interview Forms, 2316
Subsumed Abilities Test, 582
Supervisory Practices Test, 2466
Test of Social Insight, 1419
Trait Evaluation Index, 1424
Wilson Driver Selection Test, 2476

Brunner/Mazel, Inc., 64 University Place, New York, N.Y. 10003:
Family Relations Indicator [England], 1459

Buktenica (Norman A.), Department of Psychology, George Peabody College, Nashville, Tenn. 37203:
Test of Non-Verbal Auditory Discrimination, 2057

★Bureau of Educational Measurements, Kansas State Teachers College, 1200 Commercial, Emporia, Kan. 66802:
Barrett-Ryan English Test, 54
Borman-Sanders Elementary Science Test, 1778
Cass-Sanders Psychology Test, 1004
Emporia American History Test, 1993
Emporia Arithmetic Tests, 719
Emporia Biology Test, 1809
Emporia Chemistry Test, 1841
Emporia Clothing Test, 949
Emporia Elementary Health Test, 924
Emporia First Year Latin Test, 292
Emporia Foods Test, 950
Emporia General Science Test, 1783
Emporia High School Health Test, 925
Emporia Industrial Arts Test, 969
Emporia Physics Test, 1864
Emporia Reading Tests, 1549
Emporia Second Year Latin Test, 293
First Year French Test, 249
First Year Spanish Test, 309
Hiett Simplified Shorthand Test (Gregg), 784
Hollingsworth-Sanders Geography Test, 1978
Hollingsworth-Sanders Intermediate History Test, 1995
Hollingsworth-Sanders Junior High School Literature Test, 136
Hoskins-Sanders Literature Test, 137

Hoyum-Sanders English Tests, 85
Kansas Spelling Tests, 150
Meares-Sanders Junior High School History Test, 1996
Reicherter-Sanders Typewriting I and II, 789
Russell-Sanders Bookkeeping Test, 790
Sanders-Buller World History Test, 1998
Sanders-Fletcher Spelling Test, 156
Sanders-Fletcher Vocabulary Test, 172
Sare-Sanders American Government Test, 2013
Sare-Sanders Constitution Test, 2014
Sare-Sanders Sociology Test, 2019
Second Year French Test, 259
Second Year Spanish Test, 319
Walton-Sanders English Test, 122
Zimmerman-Sanders Social Studies Test, 1957

★Bureau of Educational Research and Service, University of Iowa, Iowa City, Iowa 52240:
Ayres Measuring Scale for Handwriting, 908
Iowa Algebra Aptitude Test, 681
Iowa Geometry Aptitude Test, 751
Iowa High School Content Examination, 18
Iowa Placement Examinations
  Chemistry Aptitude, 1844
  Chemistry Training, 1845
  English Aptitude, 86
  English Training, 87
  Foreign Language Aptitude, 220
  French Training, 254
  Mathematics Aptitude, 621
  Mathematics Training, 622
  Physics Aptitude, 1867
  Physics Training, 1868
  Spanish Training, 313
Iowa Spelling Scales, 149
Iowa Tests of Music Literacy, 199
Kepner Mid-Year Algebra Achievement Tests, 682
Kwalwasser-Ruch Test of Musical Accomplishment, 204
Kwalwasser Test of Music Information and Appreciation, 205
Meier Art Tests, 189
New Iowa Spelling Scale, 155
Templin-Darley Tests of Articulation, 2095

Butler (Edward), 1355 Hunter Ave., Columbus, Ohio 43201:
Level of Aspiration Board, 1261

CAL Press, Inc., 76 Madison Ave., New York, N.Y. 10016:
Reading/Everyday Activities in Life, 1744

C.P.S., Inc., P.O. Box 83, Larchmont, N.Y. 10538:
Bellak TAT and CAT Blank, Short Form, 1519b
Children's Apperception Test, 1451
Psychodiagnostic Test Report Blank, 1018

★CTB/McGraw-Hill, Del Monte Research Park, Monterey, Calif. 93940:
Animal Crackers, 1099
Aptitude Tests for Occupations, 1066
California Achievement Tests, 7
  Language, 61
  Mathematics, 603
  Reading, 1536
California Phonics Survey, 1617
California Short-Form Test of Mental Maturity, 348
California Test of Mental Maturity, 349
California Test of Personality, 1123
Career Maturity Inventory, 2103
Comprehensive Tests of Basic Skills, 11
  Arithmetic, 707
  Language, 68
  Reading, 1542
  Study Skills, 1752
Diagnostic Reading Scales, 1624
Diagnostic Tests and Self-Helps in Arithmetic, 717
Educational Skills Tests, 13
Health Behavior Inventory, 927
Lee-Clark Reading Readiness Test, 1711
Lee-Clark Reading Test, 1563
MacQuarrie Test for Mechanical Ability, 2251
Multiple Aptitude Tests, 1082
Occupational Interest Inventory, 2199
Picture Interest Inventory, 2205
Prescriptive Mathematics Inventory, 647
Prescriptive Mathematics Inventory Interim Evaluation Tests, 648
Prescriptive Reading Inventory, 1639
Prescriptive Reading Inventory Interim Tests, 1640
Short Form Test of Academic Aptitude, 458
Survey of Reading Achievement, 1606
Survey Test of Algebraic Aptitude, 689
Tests of Adult Basic Education, 45
Tests of Basic Experiences, 47
  Language, 120
  Mathematics, 661
  Science, 1857
  Social Studies, 1956

CTB/McGraw-Hill Ryerson Ltd., 330 Progress Ave., Scarborough, Ont., Canada:
Pre-Reading Assessment Kit, 1719

Cal-State Bookstore, 25776 Hillary St., Hayward, Calif. 94542:
McHugh-McParland Reading Readiness Test, 1713

Campus Publishers, 711 North University Ave., Ann Arbor, Mich. 48104:
Pupil Behavior Inventory, 1347

Canadian Association for Health, Physical Education and Recreation, 333 River Road, Vanier City, Ont. K1L 8B9, Canada:
CAHPER Fitness-Performance Test, 919
Modified Sjöstrand Physical Work Capacity Test, 936

Canter (Arthur), 500 Newton Road, Iowa City, Iowa 52240:
Canter Background Interference Procedure for the Bender Gestalt Test, 1447f

Careers Research and Advisory Centre, Bateman St., Cambridge, England:
Connolly Occupational Interests Questionnaire, 2175
Crowley Occupational Interests Blank, 2176

Carlile (A. B.), Box 314, Jetmore, Kan. 67854:
Weighted-Score Likability Rating Scale, 1436

Carlisle Graphics, 645 Harrison St., San Francisco, Calif. 94107:
California Cumulative Record and Health Insert, 1009

Case Western Reserve University. *See* Personnel Research Institute.

Catholic University of America Press (The), 620 Michigan Ave. N.E., Washington, D.C. 20017:
Test for Developmental Age in Girls, 1416

Center for Psychological Service, 1835 Eye St. N.W., Washington, D.C. 20006:
George Washington University Series Nursing Tests, 2381
Interest Inventory for Elementary Grades, 1238
Social Intelligence Test, 1386
Teaching Aptitude Test, 904
Test for Ability to Sell, 2413

Center for Safety (The), New York University, New York, N.Y. 10003:
Hannaford Industrial Safety Attitude Scales, 847
McGlade Road Test for Use in Driver Licensing, Education and Employment, 848
Siebrecht Attitude Scale, 850

Central Iowa Associates, Inc., 1408 Meadowlane Ave., Ames, Iowa 50010:
College Student Satisfaction Questionnaire, 1136

Centre de Psychologie Appliquee, Department Editions, Square Jouvenet, Paris 16e, France:
Toy World Test [United States], 1523

Chambers (Jay L.), Center for Psychological Services, College of William and Mary, Williamsburg, Va. 23185:
Picture Identification Test, 1490

Character Research Association, 6251 San Bonita, St. Louis, Mo. 63105:
C-R Opinionaire, 1116
Teacher Opinionaire on Democracy, 901

Chatterji (S.), Indian Statistical Institute, 203 Barrackpore Trunk Road, Calcutta-35, India:
English Knowledge and Comprehension Test, 228
Scientific Knowledge and Aptitude Test, 1793

Chronicle Guidance Publications, Inc., 105 North Virginia Ave., Falls Church, Va. 22046:
Guidance Cumulative Folder and Record Forms, 1013

Churchill Livingstone, 23 Ravelston Terrace, Edinburgh EH4 3TL, Scotland:
Edinburgh Articulation Test, 2070

Clinical Psychology Publishing Co., Inc., 4 Conant Square, Brandon, Vt. 05733:
Howard Ink Blot Test, 1473
Integration Level Test Series, 1237
M-B History Record, 1265
Minnesota Percepto-Diagnostic Test, 1485
Vane Kindergarten Test, 528

Cognitive Test Center, East Neck Road, Huntington Bay, N.Y. 11743:
Willner Instance Similarities Test, 593

Colgate University Testing Service, Hamilton, N.Y. 13346:
Personal Values Inventory, 1318

College Entrance Examination Board, 888 Seventh Ave., New York, N.Y. 10019:
Advanced Placement Examinations, 1045
  American History, 1980
  Art, 183
  Biology, 1800
  Chemistry, 1832
  Classics, 288
  English, 51
  European History, 1981
  French, 240
  German, 262
  Mathematics, 742
  Music, 193
  Physics, 1858
  Spanish, 302
CLEP General Examinations
  English Composition, 58
  Humanities, 6
  Mathematics, 601
  Natural Sciences, 1779
  Social Sciences and History, 1938
CLEP Subject Examinations
  Afro-American History, 1985
  American Government, 2004
  American History, 1986
  American Literature, 127
  Analysis and Interpretation of Literature, 128
  Biology, 1804
  Clinical Chemistry, 2350
  College Algebra, 670
  College Algebra and Trigonometry, 602
  Computers and Data Processing, 2332
  Educational Psychology, 1002
  Elementary Computer Programming—Fortran IV, 2333
  English Composition, 59
  English Literature, 129
  Freshman English, 60
  General Chemistry, 1833
  General Psychology, 1003
  Geology, 1849
  Hematology, 2351
  History of American Education, 853
  Human Growth and Development, 920
  Immunohematology and Blood Banking, 2352
  Introduction to Business Management, 2326
  Introductory Accounting, 2324
  Introductory Business Law, 2327
  Introductory Calculus, 743
  Introductory Economics, 1963
  Introductory Marketing, 2328
  Introductory Sociology, 2017
  Microbiology, 2353
  Money and Banking, 2329
  Statistics, 1042
  Tests and Measurements, 854
  Trigonometry, 762
  Western Civilization, 1987
College Board Achievement Tests
  American History and Social Studies, 1939
  Biology, 1805
  Chemistry, 1837
  English Composition, 64
  European History and World Cultures, 1940
  French Listening-Reading, 243
  French Reading, 244
  German Listening-Reading, 263
  German Reading, 264
  Hebrew, 279
  Latin, 289
  Literature, 130
  Mathematics, Level 1, 607
  Mathematics, Level 2, 608
  Physics, 1859
  Russian Listening-Reading, 295
  Spanish Listening-Reading, 304
  Spanish Reading, 305
College Board Admissions Testing Program, 1048
College Board Scholastic Aptitude Test, 357
College-Level Examination Program, 1050
College-Level Examination Program General Examinations, 10
College Placement Tests, 1051
  Advanced Mathematics, 609
  American History and Social Studies, 1941
  Biology, 1806
  Chemistry, 1838
  English Composition, 67
  European History and World Cultures, 1942
  French Listening Comprehension, 245
  French Listening-Reading, 246
  French Reading, 247
  German Listening Comprehension, 265
  German Listening-Reading, 266
  German Reading, 267
  Greek Reading, 277
  Hebrew Reading, 280
  Intermediate Mathematics, 610

Cox (Charles J.), Beaufort House, Marlborough Rd., Bowdon, Altrincham, Cheshire WA14 2RW, England:
Cox Mechanical and Manual Tests, 2242

Crawford (Paul L.), Department of Psychology, West Virginia State College, Institute, W.Va. 25112:
Crawford Psychological Adjustment Scale, 1148

Creative Arts Research Associates, Inc., P.O. Box 117, Monmouth, Ore. 97361:
Knuth Achievement Tests in Music, 201
Snyder Knuth Music Achievement Test, 212

Crippled Children and Adults of Rhode Island, Inc., Meeting Street School, 333 Grotto Ave., Providence, R.I. 02906:
Meeting Street School Screening Test, 984

Critical Thinking Project, 371 Education Bldg., University of Illinois, Urbana, Ill. 61801:
Cornell Class-Reasoning Test, 1753
Cornell Conditional-Reasoning Test, 1754
Cornell Critical Thinking Test, 1755

Croft Educational Services, Inc., 100 Garfield Ave., New London, Conn. 06320:
Cooper-McGuire Diagnostic Word-Analysis Test, 1619
McGuire-Bumpus Diagnostic Comprehension Test, 1635

Crosby Lockwood Staples, Frogmore, St. Albans, Herts, AL2 2NF, England:
Figure Reasoning Test, 375

Cutronics Educational Institute, 128 West 56th St., Bayonne, N.J. 07002:
Cutrona Child Study Profile of Psycho-Educational Abilities, 978

Dartnell Corporation (The), 4660 Ravenswood Ave., Chicago, Ill. 60640:
Driver Selection Forms and Tests, 2470
Employee Rating and Development Forms, 2301
Executive, Industrial, and Sales Personnel Forms, 2302

Delaware County Reading Council, Delaware County Public Schools, Sixth and Olive Sts., Media, Pa. 19063:
Delaware County Silent Reading Test, 1547

Delco Readiness Test, 111 Linda Lane, Media, Pa. 19063:
Delco Readiness Test, 1701

Dennis (William H.), Trumbull County Reading Clinic, 255 Bonnie Brae Ave. N.E., Warren, Ohio 44483:
Dennis Test of Scholastic Aptitude, 369

Dent (J. M.) & Sons (Canada) Ltd., 100 Scarsdale Road, Don Mills, Ont. M3B 2R8, Canada:
Ford-Hicks French Grammar Completion Tests, 250
Ohio Tests of Articulation and Perception of Sounds [United States], 2023

Denver Public Schools, 414 Fourteenth St., Denver, Colo. 80202:
Denver Public Schools Reading Inventory, 1621

De Palma (Nicholas), Metro Bordeaux Hospital, Nashville, Tenn. 37208:
Rorschach Combined Location and Record Form, 1499h

Department of Psychological Testing, De Paul University, 25 East Jackson Blvd., Chicago, Ill. 60604:
Commerce Reading Comprehension Test, 1538

Department of Research, Stockton State Hospital, 510 East Magnolia St., Stockton, Calif. 95202:
Stockton Geriatric Rating Scale, 1396

De Paul University. *See* Department of Psychological Testing.

Developmental Reading Distributors (DRD Press), 1944 Sheridan Ave., Laramie, Wyo. 82070:
Maintaining Reading Efficiency Tests, 1566

Devereux Foundation Press (The), Devon, Pa. 19333:
Devereux Adolescent Behavior Rating Scale, 1157
Devereux Child Behavior Rating Scale, 1158
Devereux Elementary School Behavior Rating Scale, 1159
Devereux Test of Extremity Coordination, 1894

Diebold (John) & Associates, 430 Park Ave., New York, N.Y. 10022:
Diebold Personnel Tests, 2335

Division of Educational Measurements, Council on Dental Education, American Dental Association, 211 East Chicago Ave., Chicago, Ill. 60611:
Dental Admission Testing Program, 2337

Dow Chemical Co. (The), Midland, Mich. 48640:
Chemical Operators Selection Test, 2360

Dreier Educational Systems, Inc., 320 Raritan Ave., Highland Park, N.J. 08904:
Group Phonics Analysis, 1632
Instant Word Recognition Test, 1664
Oral Reading Criterion Test, 1684
Phonics Criterion Test, 1636

Drew (Edward) Co., P.O. Box 553, Jacksonville, Fla. 32201:
Florida Cumulative Guidance Record, 1011

Eckstein Bros., Inc., 4807 West 118th Place, Hawthorne, Calif. 90250:
Eckstein Audiometers, 2034

Ecodyne Corporation, 1 City Blvd. West, Suite 935, Orange, Calif. 92668:
APELL Test, 1692

Editest, rue General Capiaumont 94, 1040-Brussels, Belgium:
Test of Family Attitudes [England], 1518

Educational and Industrial Test Services, 83 High St., Hemel Hempstead, Herts, England:
Differential Test Battery, 1070

★Educational and Industrial Testing Service, P.O. Box 7234, San Diego, Calif. 92107:
Biographical Inventory—Creativity, 544
Bristol Social Adjustment Guides [England], 1112
California Occupational Preference Survey, 2170
Caring Relationship Inventory, 815
Comrey Personality Scales, 1139
Concept Assessment Kit—Conservation, 549
Depression Adjective Check Lists, 1154
Eysenck Personality Inventory [England], 1174a
Fear Survey Schedule, 1185
Junior Eysenck Personality Inventory [England], 1252a
Maudsley Personality Inventory [England], 1275b
Multiple Affect Adjective Check List, 1293
Pair Attraction Inventory, 837
Personal Orientation Inventory, 1315
Profile of Mood States, 1337
Queensland Test [Australia], 520
Rhodes WAIS Scatter Profile, 530
Rhodes WISC Scatter Profile, 535
Study Attitudes and Methods Survey, 1766
Tests of Achievement in Basic Skills: Mathematics, 660

Educational Developmental Laboratories, 1221 Avenue of the Americas, New York, N.Y. 10020:
Flash-X Sight Vocabulary Test, 1678
Reader's Inventory, 1671
Reading Eye II, 1672
Reading Versatility Test, 1673
Word Clue Tests, 180

Educational Evaluation Enterprises, 5 Marsh St., Bristol 1, Glos., England:
English Picture Vocabulary Test, 495

Educational Guidance, Inc., P.O. Box 511, Main Station, Dearborn, Mich. 48120:
Career Guidance Inventory, 2172
Educational Interest Inventory, 2178

Educational Opportunities Division. *See* Follett Publishing Co.

Educational Performance Associates, Inc., 563 Westview Ave., Ridgefield, N.J. 07657:
Permanent Record Folder, 1017
Preschool and Kindergarten Performance Profile, 1722
T.M.R. Performance Profile for the Severely and Moderately Retarded, 1412
Y.E.M.R. Performance Profile for the Young Moderately and Mildly Retarded, 1443

Educational Programs Improvement Corporation, P.O. Box 3406, Boulder, Colo. 80303:
Biological Science: Interaction of Experiments and Ideas, 1802

Educational Publications, Dublin, N.H. 03444:
Test of Active Vocabulary, 174

Educational Records Bureau, Box 619, Princeton, N.J. 08540:
Chemistry Achievement Test for CHEM Study or Equivalent, 1835
Cooperative Biology Test, 1807
Cooperative Chemistry Test, 1839
Cooperative Physics Test, 1861
ERB Modern Arithmetic Test, 718
ERB Modern Elementary Algebra Test, 675
ERB Modern Mathematics Test, 616
ERB Modern Second Year Algebra Test, 676
Junior Scholastic Aptitude Test, 394
Lincoln Diagnostic Spelling Tests, 152

Sipay Word Analysis Tests, 1648
Specific Language Disability Test, 990
Edwards (Carl N.), P.O. Box 86, Village Station, Medway, Mass. 02053:
Situational Preference Inventory, 1382
Eidsmoe (Russell M.), Morningside College, Sioux City, Iowa 51106:
Student's Rating Scale of an Instructor, 896
English Universities Press Ltd. (The), St. Paul's House, Warwick Lane, London EC4P 4AH, England:
Objective Tests in Physics, 1869
Essay Press, Inc., P.O. Box 5, Planetarium Station, New York, N.Y. 10024:
Roswell-Chall Auditory Blending Test, 1674
Roswell-Chall Diagnostic Reading Test of Word Analysis Skills, 1643
★Examinations Committee, American Chemical Society, University of South Florida, Tampa, Fla. 33620:
ACS Cooperative Examinations
Analytical Chemistry, Graduate Level, 1815
Biochemistry, 1816
Brief Course in Organic Chemistry, 1814
Brief Physical Chemistry, 1817
Brief Qualitative Analysis, 1818
General Chemistry, 1819
Inorganic Chemistry, 1820
Inorganic Chemistry, Graduate Level, 1821
Inorganic-Organic-Biological Chemistry (for Paramedical Programs), 1822
Instrumental Analysis, 1823
Organic Chemistry, 1824
Organic Chemistry, Graduate Level, 1825
Physical Chemistry, 1826
Physical Chemistry, Graduate Level, 1827
Qualitative Analysis, 1828
Quantitative Analysis, 1829
ACS-NSTA Cooperative Examinations
High School Chemistry, 1830
High School Chemistry: Advanced Level, 1831
Toledo Chemistry Placement Examination, 1847
Executive Analysis Corporation, 50 East 42nd St., New York, N.Y. 10017:
How Well Do You Know Your Interests? 2189
How Well Do You Know Yourself?, 1220
Expression Co., 155 Columbus Ave., Boston, Mass.:
Robbins Speech Sound Discrimination and Verbal Imagery Type Tests, 2052
Speech Defect Questionnaire, 2093
Speech Diagnostic Chart, 2094
Fairview State Hospital, Research Department, 2501 Harbor Blvd., Costa Mesa, Calif. 92626:
Fairview Development Scale, 1177
Fairview Language Evaluation Scale, 2072
Fairview Problem Behavior Record, 1178
Fairview Self-Help Scale, 1179
Fairview Social Skills Scale, 1180
Family Life Publications, Inc., P.O. Box 427, Saluda, N.C. 28773:
Courtship Analysis, 816
Dating Problems Checklist, 817
Drug Knowledge Inventory, 923
Love Attitudes Inventory, 821
Marital Communication Inventory, 823
Marriage Adjustment Form, 826
Marriage Analysis, 829
Marriage Expectation Inventories, 830
Marriage Prediction Schedule, 832
Marriage Role Expectation Inventory, 833
Parent-Adolescent Communication Inventory, 1310
Religious Attitudes Inventory, 1026
Sex Knowledge Inventory, 838
Social Competence Inventories, 1385
Tests for Venereal Disease Education, 943
VD Knowledge Test, 946
Federation of Societies for Paint Technology, 121 South Broad St., Philadelphia, Pa. 19107:
Inter-Society Color Council Color Aptitude Test, 1915
Fels Research Institute (The), Yellow Springs, Ohio 45387:
Fels Parent Behavior Rating Scales, 1186
Fetler (Daniel), Deer Ridge Drive, Staatsburg, N.Y. 12580:
Style of Mind Inventory, 1405
Fischer (Carl), Inc., 56–62 Cooper Square, New York, N.Y. 10003:
Jones Music Recognition Test, 200
Kwalwasser-Dykema Music Tests, 202

Florida Educational Research and Development Council, College of Education, University of Florida, Gainesville, Fla. 32601:
How I See Myself Scale, 1219
Follett Publishing Co., 1010 West Washington Blvd., Chicago, Ill. 60607:
Adult Basic Education Student Survey, 2
Reading, 1742
Basic Concept Inventory, 1697
Botel Reading Inventory, 1658
Developmental Test of Visual-Motor Integration, 1875
Individual Reading Placement Inventory, 1663
Kindergarten Auditory Screening Test, 2041
Music Achievement Tests, 207
Follett's Michigan Book Store, Inc., 322 South State St., Ann Arbor, Mich. 48108:
English Placement Test, 229
Examination in Structure (English as a Foreign Language), 231
Michigan Test of Aural Comprehension, 232
Michigan Test of English Language Proficiency, 233
Test of Aural Perception In English for Japanese Students, 236
Test of Aural Perception In English for Latin-American Students, 237
Fordham University, Department of Psychology, Bronx, N.Y. 10458:
Psychiatric Attitudes Battery, 1496
Foundation for Research in Mental Development (The), Box 1483, Wilmington, Del. 19809:
D-K Scale of Lateral Dominance, 1874
Freund Brothers, 1514 Pacific Ave., Atlantic City, N.J. 08401:
Atlantic City Eye Test, 1907
Fritz (Martin F.), Iowa State University, Ames, Iowa 50010:
Practical Policy Test, 1330
Gallagher (Ralph), 613 North Mountain Ave., Bound Brook, N.J. 08805:
Guidance Inventory, 1203
Galloway (June P.), University of North Carolina at Greensboro, Greensboro, N.C. 27412:
Attitude Inventory, 916
Garrard Publishing Co., 1607 North Market St., Champaign, Ill. 61820:
Basic Sight Word Test, 1657
General Educational Development Testing Service, American Council on Education, 1 Dupont Circle, Washington, D.C. 20036:
Tests of General Educational Development, 48
Gibson (Robert) & Sons, Glasgow, Ltd., 17 Fitzroy Place, Glasgow G37SF, Scotland:
Cotswold Junior Ability Tests, 362
Cotswold Junior Arithmetic Ability Tests, 710
Cotswold Junior English Ability Test, 71
Cotswold Measurement of Ability, 363
Arithmetic, 711
English, 72
Cotswold Personality Assessment P.A.1, 1147
Kelvin Measurement of Ability in Arithmetic, 720
Kelvin Measurement of Ability in Infant Classes, 395
Kelvin Measurement of Mental Ability, 396
Kelvin Measurement of Reading Ability, 1561
Kelvin Measurement of Spelling Ability, 151
"Orton" Intelligence Test, No. 4, 422
Ryburn Group Intelligence Tests, 448
★Ginn & Co. Ltd., Elsinore House, Buckingham St., Aylesbury, Bucks, England:
Basic Mathematics Tests, 599
Clerical Tests FG and 2, 781A
Decimal Currency Test, 760
English Progress Tests, 75
English Test FG, 76
English Tests (Adv.), 79
English Tests 14–20 and 22, 80
General Verbal Practice Tests G1–G3, 379
Mathematics Attainment Test EF, 626
Mathematics Attainment Tests C1 and C3, 627
Mathematics Attainment Tests DE1 and DE2, 628
Mathematics Attainment Tests (Oral), 629
Mathematics Test (Adv.) 6, 632
Mathematics Tests 20–22, 636
Non-Verbal Tests, 415
Number Test DE, 725
Picture Test A, 434
Reading Comprehension Test DE, 1585
Reading Test AD, 1591
Reading Tests A and BD, 1594
Reading Tests EH 1–3, 1595

Senior English Test, 111
Senior Mathematics Test, 651
Spatial Tests EG, 2, and 3, 2269
Verbal Tests (Adv.), 474
Verbal Tests BC, CD, C, and D, 475
Verbal Tests EF and GH, 476
Verbal Tests 15–23 and 69, 477

Girona (Ricardo), 204 Bank of Wood County Bldg., Bowling Green, Ohio 43402:
Affect Scale, 1097

Gleser (Goldine C.), Department of Psychiatry, Cincinnati General Hospital, Cincinnati, Ohio 45229:
Defense Mechanism Inventory, 1152

Gordon (Ira J.), Institute for Development of Human Resources, University of Florida, Gainesville, Fla. 32611:
How I See Myself Scale, 1219

Gough (Harrison G.), 2240 Piedmont Ave., University of California, Berkeley, Calif. 94720:
Home Index, 1040A

Graham-Field Surgical Co., Inc., 415 Second Ave., New Hyde Park, N.Y. 11040:
Test for Colour-Blindness [Japan], 1932

Grason-Stadler Co., Inc., Concord, Mass. 01742:
Grason-Stadler Audiometers, 2038

Gretsch (Fred) Co., Inc., 1801 Gilbert Ave., Cincinnati, Ohio 45202:
Gretsch-Tilson Musical Aptitude Test, 198

Grune & Stratton, Inc., 111 Fifth Ave., New York, N.Y. 10003:
Behn-Rorschach Test [Switzerland], 1499a
Bender Gestalt Test, 1447b
Bender Gestalt Test for Young Children, 1447e
Color Pyramid Test [Switzerland], 1452
Developmental Potential of Preschool Children, 1156
Diagnostic Test of Speechreading, 2021
Freeman Anxiety Neurosis and Psychosomatic Test, 1188
HFD Test, 1468
Hutt Adaptation of the Bender-Gestalt Test, 1447c
Picture Story Language Test, 103
Primary Visual Motor Test, 1882
Psychodiagnostic Plates [Switzerland], 1499f
Pupil Rating Scale, 987
Rorschach Location Charts (Beck's Scoring Areas), 1499j
Szondi Test [Switzerland], 1516
Tree Test [Switzerland], 1524

Guidance Associates of Delaware, Inc., 1526 Gilpin Ave., Wilmington, Del. 19806:
Jastak Test of Potential Ability and Behavior Stability, 1077
Wide Range Achievement Test, 50
Wide Range Employment Sample Test, 2116
Wide Range Interest-Opinion Test, 2219

★Guidance Centre, University of Toronto, 1000 Yonge St., Toronto, Ont. M4W 2K8, Canada:
CGA Mental Ability Tests, 346
Canadian Academic Aptitude Test, 350
Canadian Achievement Test in English, 62
Canadian Achievement Test in French, 242
Canadian Achievement Test in Mathematics, 604
Canadian Achievement Test in Technical and Commercial Mathematics, 605
Canadian English Achievement Test, 63
Canadian Mathematics Achievement Test, 606
Canadian Test Battery, Grades 8–9, 1047
Canadian Test Battery, Grade 10, 1046
Diagnostic Test in Mathematics, 615
Dominion Table for Converting Mental Age to I.Q., 805
G.C. Anecdotal Record Form, 1012
Group Test of Learning Capacity, 387
Group Test of Reading Readiness, 1704
Institute of Child Study Security Test, 1233
OISE Achievement Tests in Silent Reading, 1575
OISE Picture Reasoning Test, 417
Ontario School Record System, 1016
Reading Comprehension: Canadian English Achievement Test, 1582
Survey Tests of Arithmetic Fundamentals, 739

Guidance Testing Associates, 6516 Shirley Ave., Austin, Tex. 78752:
Comprehension of Oral Language: Inter-American Series, 2033
Test of Reading and Number: Inter-American Series, 43
Tests of General Ability: Inter-American Series, 468
Tests of Reading: Inter-American Series, 1609

Hahnemann Medical College and Hospital, Community Mental Health Center, 314 North Broad St., Philadelphia, Pa. 19102:
Hahnemann High School Behavior Rating Scale, 1209

Halgren Tests, 873 Persimmon Ave., Sunnyvale, Calif. 94087:
Rokeach Value Survey, 1355

Hall & Liles, 411 Sandra Drive, Oxford, Ohio 45056:
Hall Salespower Inventory, 2399

★Harcourt Brace Jovanovich, Inc., 757 Third Ave., New York, N.Y. 10017:
Adult Basic Learning Examination, 3
Analysis of Learning Potential, 340
BSCS Achievement Tests: Yellow Version, 1801b
Blyth Second-Year Algebra Test, 668
Brown-Carlsen Listening Comprehension Test, 993
Classification and Placement Examination, 9
Columbia Mental Maturity Scale, 489
Crary American History Test, 1992
Dubins Earth Science Test, 1853
Dunning-Abeles Physics Test, 1863
Durrell Analysis of Reading Difficulty, 1628
Durrell Listening-Reading Series, 1660
Durrell-Sullivan Reading Capacity and Achievement Tests, 1661
Dvorine Pseudo-Isochromatic Plates, 1911
Gilmore Oral Reading Test, 1679
Goodenough-Harris Drawing Test, 381
Gordon Occupational Check List, 2182
Gordon Personal Inventory, 1193
Gordon Personal Profile, 1194
Howell Geometry Test, 750
Iowa Silent Reading Tests, 1560
Lankton First-Year Algebra Test, 683
Metropolitan Achievement Tests, 22
    Mathematics Tests, 637
    Reading Tests, 1567
Metropolitan Readiness Tests, 1716
Mid-Year Algebra Test, 685
Mid-Year Geometry Test, 752
Murphy-Durrell Reading Readiness Analysis, 1717
Nelson Biology Test, 1812
Ohio Vocational Interest Survey, 2201
Orleans-Hanna Algebra Prognosis Test, 688
Orleans-Hanna Geometry Prognosis Test, 755
Otis Employment Tests, 423
Otis-Lennon Mental Ability Test, 424
Otis Quick-Scoring Mental Ability Tests, 425
Otis Self-Administering Tests of Mental Ability, 426
Pimsleur French Proficiency Tests, 258
Pimsleur German Proficiency Tests, 275
Pimsleur Language Aptitude Battery, 223
Pimsleur Spanish Proficiency Tests, 318
Pintner-Cunningham Primary Test, 435
Rorschach Method of Personality Diagnosis: Individual Record Blank, 1499k
Stanford Achievement Test, 36
    Mathematics Tests, 655
    Reading Tests, 1603
    Science, 1796
    Social Studies Tests, 1953
    Spelling and Language Tests, 115
Stanford Achievement Test: High School Basic Battery, 37
    English and Spelling, 114
    Mathematics Tests, 653
    Numerical Competence Test, 654
    Reading Test, 1602
    Science Test, 1795
    Social Studies Test, 1952
Stanford Diagnostic Arithmetic Test, 738
Stanford Diagnostic Reading Test, 1651
Stanford Early School Achievement Test, 38
Stanford Modern Mathematics Concepts Test, 656
Stanford Test of Academic Skills, 39
Thurstone Employment Tests, 2162
Turse Shorthand Aptitude Test, 798
Watson-Glaser Critical Thinking Appraisal, 1775

Harless (Byron), Schaffer, Reid & Associates, Inc., 3106 Morrison Ave., Tampa, Fla. 33609:
Supervisor's Evaluation of Research Personnel, 2392

Harper & Row, Publishers, Inc., 10 East 53rd St., New York, N.Y. 10022:
LRS Seriation Test, 1710
Test of Phonic Skills, 1654

★Harrap (George G.) & Co. Ltd., P.O. Box 70, 182/4 High Holborn, London WC1V 7AX, England:
Cattell Intelligence Tests, 354
Deeside Non-Verbal Reasoning Test, 367
Deeside Picture Puzzles, 368
Holborn Reading Scale, 1682
Kingston Test of Intelligence, 397
Kingston Test of Silent Reading, 1562
Mathematical and Technical Test, 2282
Measures of Musical Abilities, 206
Northumberland Mental Tests, 416
Porteus Maze Test [United States]: British Edition, 518e
Revised Southend Attainment Test in Mechanical Arithmetic, 730
Simplex GNV Intelligence Tests, 459

Simplex Group Intelligence Scale, 460
Simplex Junior Intelligence Tests, 461
Sleight Non-Verbal Intelligence Test, 462
Southend Attainment Test in Mechanical Arithmetic, 736
Southend Test of Intelligence, 463
Staffordshire Arithmetic Test, 737
Stanford-Binet Intelligence Scale [United States], 525

Hart-Davis Educational Ltd., Frogmore, St. Albans, Herts AL2 2NF, England:
Standard Reading Tests, 1650

Harvard University Press, 79 Garden St., Cambridge, Mass. 02138:
Thematic Apperception Test, 1519

Harvey (O. J.), Department of Psychology, University of Colorado, Boulder, Colo. 80302:
This I Believe Test, 1521

Haskins (Mary Jane), Department of Health, Dance and Women's Physical Education, Lamar University, Beaumont, Tex. 77710:
Action-Choice Tests for Competitive Sports Situations, 915

Haverly Systems, Inc., 4 Second Ave., Denville, N.J. 07834:
Programmer Aptitude/Competence Test System, 2336

Hayes Educational Test Laboratory, 7040 North Portsmouth Ave., Portland, Ore. 97203:
Minimum Essentials for Modern Mathematics, 638
Portland Prognostic Test for Mathematics, 646

Heath (D. C.) & Co., 125 Spring St., Lexington, Mass. 02173:
Tasks of Emotional Development Test, 1517

Heath (S. Roy), Jr., 1193 South East St., Amherst, Mass. 01002:
Rail-Walking Test, 1900

Heinemann Educational Australia Pty Ltd., Box 173, South Yarra, Vic. 3141, Australia:
GAP Reading Comprehension Test, 1550a
GAPADOL, 1551

Heinemann Educational Books Ltd., 48 Charles St., London W1X 8AH, England:
GAP Reading Comprehension Test [Australia], 1550b

Henry (William E.), Committee on Human Development, University of Chicago, 5730 Woodlawn Ave., Chicago, Ill. 60637:
Group Projection Sketches for the Study of Small Groups, 1467

Higgins-Wertman Associates, P.O. Box 9012, Delaware Station, Albany, N.Y. 12209:
Higgins-Wertman Test: Threshold of Visual Closure, 560

Hiskey (Marshall S.), 5640 Baldwin, Lincoln, Neb. 68508:
Hiskey-Nebraska Test of Learning Aptitude, 499

★**Houghton Mifflin Co., 110 Tremont St., Boston, Mass. 02107:**
A-S Reaction Study, 1090
Agribusiness Achievement Test: Content Evaluation Series, 768
Analysis of Readiness Skills: Reading and Mathematics, 1695
Appraisal of Occupational Aptitudes, 2120
BSCS Achievement Tests: Blue Version, 1801a
Cognitive Abilities Test, 356
College English Placement Test, 65
Dailey Vocational Tests, 2105
  Business English Test, 57
  Spatial Visualization Test, 2270
  Technical and Scholastic Test, 974
Fisher-Logemann Test of Articulation Competence, 2073
Harrison-Stroud Reading Readiness Profiles, 1705
Henmon-Nelson Tests of Mental Ability, 391
Iowa Tests of Basic Skills, 19
Language Arts Tests: Content Evaluation Series, 91
Lorge-Thorndike Intelligence Tests, 400
Lorge-Thorndike Intelligence Tests, College Edition, 401
Mathematics Test: Content Evaluation Series, 633
Modern Algebra Test: Content Evaluation Series, 686
Modern Economics Test: Content Evaluation Series, 1966
Modern Geometry Test: Content Evaluation Series, 753
Modern Mathematics Supplement to the Iowa Tests of Basic Skills, 639
Musical Aptitude Profile, 209
Nelson-Denny Reading Test, 1572
Nelson Reading Test, 1573
New Purdue Placement Test in English, 99
Office Information and Skills Test: Content Evaluation Series, 788
Pictorial Test of Intelligence, 517
Primary Reading Profiles, 1641
Primary Social Studies Test, 1946
Purdue High School English Test, 105
Reading Aptitude Tests, 1724

Remote Associates Test, 574
School Interest Inventory, 1365
Science Tests: Content Evaluation Series, 1792
Stanford-Binet Intelligence Scale, 525
Study of Values, 1403
Tests of Academic Progress, 44
  Composition, 119
  Literature, 143
  Mathematics, 659
  Reading, 1608
  Science, 1799
  Social Studies, 1955
Work Values Inventory, 2221

Houston Test Co., P.O. Box 35152, Houston, Tex. 77035:
Houston Test for Language Development, 2077

Huber (Hans), Langgassstrasse 76, 3000 Bern 9, Switzerland:
Behn-Rorschach Test, 1499a
Color Pyramid Test, 1452
Psychodiagnostic Plates, 1499f
Rorschach Location Charts, 1499j
Szondi Test, 1516
Tree Test, 1524
Zulliger Individual and Group Test, 1528

Human Engineering Laboratory Inc., 347 Beacon St., Boston, Mass. 02116:
Johnson O'Connor English Vocabulary Worksamples, 167
Johnson O'Connor Vocabulary Tests, 168

Human Resources Center, Albertson, N.Y. 11507:
Scale to Measure Attitudes Toward Disabled Persons, 1363

★**Human Sciences Research Council, Private Bag 41, Pretoria, Republic of South Africa:**
Academic Proficiency Battery, 1
Academic-Technical Aptitude Tests, 1064
Aptitude Test for Junior Secondary Pupils, 1065
Children's Personality Questionnaire [United States], 1129
Diagnostic Arithmetic Tests, 712
General Tests of Language and Arithmetic, 14
General Tests of Language and Arithmetic for Students, 862
Group Test for Indian South Africans, 383
Guidance Test for Junior Secondary Bantu Pupils in Form III, 16
IPAT Anxiety Scale Questionnaire [United States], 1225
Individual Scale for Indian South Africans, 501
Interest Questionnaire for Indian South Africans, 2191
Junior Aptitude Tests for Indian South Africans, 1079
Jr.-Sr. High School Personality Questionnaire [United States], 1253
N.B. Aptitude Tests (Junior), 1083
N.B. Arithmetic Tests, 724
N.B. Group Tests, 410
N.B. Mathematics Tests, 642
N.B. Silent Reading Tests (Beginners), 1570
N.B. Spelling Tests, 153
New South African Group Test, 411
New South African Individual Scale, 511
19 Field Interest Inventory, 2198
Non-Verbal Intelligence Tests for Deaf and Hearing Subjects [The Netherlands], 512
PHSF Relations Questionnaire, 1308
Scholastic Proficiency Battery, 34
Senior Aptitude Tests, 1088
Silent Reading Tests, 1600
Technical Tests, 2447
Tests of Arithmetic and Language for Indian South Africans, 46

Humm Personnel Consultants, P.O. Box 75938, Sanford Station, Los Angeles, Calif. 90075:
Humm-Wadsworth Temperament Scale, 1222

Indiana Public Health Foundation, Inc., 1330 West Michigan St., Indianapolis, Ind. 46207:
Indiana Physical Fitness Test, 932

Industrial Psychological Services, Box 9571, Johannesburg, Republic of South Africa:
African T.A.T., 1444
Social Relations Test, 1509

Industrial Psychology, Inc., 515 Madison Ave., New York, N.Y. 10022:
Employee Attitude Series: C.P.F., 1226
Employee Attitude Series: 16 P.F., 1383
Job-Tests Program, 1078
Merit Rating Series, 2308

★**Industrial Relations Center, University of Chicago, 1225 East 60th St., Chicago, Ill. 60637 (This publisher has not replied to our four requests to check the accuracy of the entries for the tests listed below. Entries 1149, 1747, 2076, 2079, and 2110 were checked by test authors.):**
AC Test of Creative Ability, 2340
Closure Flexibility (Concealed Figures), 547

Closure Speed (Gestalt Completion), 548
Cree Questionnaire, 1149
Emo Questionnaire, 1170
Flags: A Test of Space Thinking, 2245
Halstead Aphasia Test, 2076
Language Modalities Test for Aphasia, 2079
Mechanical Movements: A Test of Mechanical Comprehension, 2255
Non-Verbal Reasoning Test, 414
Perceptual Speed (Identical Forms), 570
Personal History Index, 2110
Press Test, 1333
Temperament Comparator, 1413
Understanding Communication (Verbal Comprehension), 1747
Verbal Reasoning, 472
Weights and Pulleys: A Test of Intuitive Mechanics, 2272
Word Fluency, 594

Institute for Behavioral Research in Creativity, 1417 South 11th East, Salt Lake City, Utah 84105:
Alpha Biographical Inventory, 2273

★Institute for Personality and Ability Testing, 1602 Coronado Drive, Champaign, Ill. 61820:
Children's Personality Questionnaire, 1129
Clinical Analysis Questionnaire, 1131
Early School Personality Questionnaire, 1163
IPAT Anxiety Scale Questionnaire, 1225
IPAT Contact Personality Factor Test, 1226
IPAT Culture Free Intelligence Test, 364a
IPAT 8-Parallel-Form Anxiety Battery, 1227
IPAT Humor Test of Personality, 1228
IPAT Neurotic Personality Factor Test, 1229
Jr.-Sr. High School Personality Questionnaire, 1253
Motivation Analysis Test, 1291
Neuroticism Scale Questionnaire, 1295
Objective-Analytic (O-A) Anxiety Battery, 1300
School Motivation Analysis Test, 1367
Sixteen Personality Factor Questionnaire, 1383

Institute of Clinical Analysis, 1000 East Broadway, Glendale, Calif. 91205:
MMPI-ICA Computer Report, 1283

★Institute of Psychological Research, Inc., 34 Fleury St. West, Montreal, Que. H3L 1S9, Canada:
Ligondé Equivalence Test, 21
Q-Tags Test of Personality, 1351
Test of Work Competency and Stability, 1420

Institute of Public Safety, Pennsylvania State University, University Park, Pa. 16802:
Driving Skill Exercises, 845
Road Test Check List for Passenger Car Drivers, 849
Road Test Check List for Testing, Selecting, Rating, and Training Coach Operators, 2472
Road Test in Traffic for Testing, Selecting, Rating and Training Truck Drivers, 2473

Instructional Materials Laboratory, Ohio State University, 1885 Neil Ave., Columbus, Ohio 43210:
Ohio Trade and Industrial Education Achievement Test Program, 2431
  Auto Body, 2420
  Automotive Mechanics, 2421
  Carpentry, 2422
  Communication Products Electronics, 2423
  Construction Electricity, 2424
  Cosmetology, 2425
  Dental Assisting, 2339
  Industrial Electronics, 2426
  Machine Trades, 2427
  Mechanical Drafting, 2428
  Printing, 2429
  Sheet Metal, 2430
  Welding, 2432

International Business Machines Corporation, Armonk, N.Y. 10504:
IBM 1230 Optical Mark Scoring Reader, 1032
IBM 3881 Optical Mark Reader, 1033

International Personnel Management Association, 1313 East 60th St., Chicago, Ill. 60637:
Account Clerk Test, 2322
Engineering Aide Test, 2341
Firefighter Test, 2362
Mechanical Handyman Test, 2418
Office Worker Test, 2137
Policeman Test, 2371
Test for Firefighter B-1, 2373
Test for Police Officer A-1, 2374
Truck Driver Test, 2475

International Society for General Semantics, P.O. Box 2469, San Francisco, Calif. 94126:
"Is of Identity" Test, 1246
Uncritical Inference Test, 1774

International Tests, Inc., Box 634, Stevens Point, Wis. 54481:
International Primary Factors Test Battery, 1076

International Universities Press, Inc., 239 Park Ave. South, New York, N.Y. 10003:
Zulliger Individual and Group Test [Switzerland], 1528

Interstate Printers & Publishers, Inc. (The), 19–27 North Jackson St., Danville, Ill. 61832:
Applied Biological and Agribusiness Interest Inventory, 2169
Forms From Diagnostic Methods in Speech Pathology, 2074
Multiple-Choice Intelligibility Test, 2022
Photo Articulation Test, 2086
Remmlein's School Law Test, 885
Washington Speech Sound Discrimination Test, 2060

Joint Council on Economic Education, 1212 Avenue of the Americas, New York, N.Y. 10036:
Primary Test of Economic Understanding, 1967
Test of Elementary Economics, 1969
Test of Understanding in College Economics, 1970
Test of Understanding in Personal Economics, 1971

Jones Teaching Aids, 3442 Avenue C, Council Bluffs, Iowa 51501:
Jones Personality Rating Scale, 1251

Jossey-Bass Inc., Publishers, 615 Montgomery St., San Francisco, Calif. 94111:
Washington University Sentence Completion Test, 1527

Jung (C. G.) Educational Center, 4803 Montrose Blvd., Houston, Tex. 77006:
Ruth Fry Symbolic Profile, 1502

K & W Products Co., Inc., 403 Salisbury Road, Wyncote, Pa. 19095:
General Aptitude Test Battery
  Finger Dexterity Board, 1073c5
  Pegboard, 1073c4
Nonreading Aptitude Test Battery
  Finger Dexterity Board, 10861
  Pegboard, 1086k

KDS Systems, Inc., 7 Parkview Court, Farmingdale, N.Y. 11735:
Kupfer-Detre System, 1258

Kanehara Shuppan Co., Ltd., 31–14, 2-chome Yushima, Bunkyo-ku, Tokyo 113–91, Japan:
Test for Colour-Blindness, 1932

Kaneko Shobo Publisher, 3–7, 3-chome Otsuka, Bunkyo-ku, Tokyo 112, Japan:
Ka-Ro Inkblot Test, 1479

Kansas State Teachers College. See Bureau of Educational Measurements.

Karger (S.), AG, Arnold-Bocklin-Strasse 25, 4000 Basel 11, Switzerland:
Columbus: Picture Analysis of Growth Towards Maturity, 1453

Katz (Martin M.), Clinical Research Branch, National Institute of Mental Health, Chevy Chase, Md. 20203:
Katz Adjustment Scales, 1255

Keeler Instruments Ltd., Clewer Hill Road, Windsor, Berks SL4 4AA, England:
Guy's Colour Vision Test for Young Children, 1914
Sheridan Gardiner Test of Visual Acuity, 1926

Keeler Optical Products Inc., 456 Parkway, Lawrence Park Industrial District, Broomall, Pa. 19008:
Guy's Colour Vision Test for Young Children [England], 1914
Sheridan Gardiner Test of Visual Acuity [England], 1926

Kemper Psychological Services, Long Grove, Ill. 60049:
Selection Tests for Office Personnel, 2150

Kennedy-Galton Centre, Harperbury Hospital, Harper Lane, Shenley, Radlett, Herts WD7 9HQ, England:
Pattern Perception Test, 428

Kew (Clifton E.), 245 East 19th St., New York, N.Y. 10003:
Group Psychotherapy Suitability Evaluation Scale, 1202

Keystone View, 2212 East 12th St., Davenport, Iowa 52803:
Keystone Ready-to-Read Tests, 1916
Keystone Tests of Binocular Skill, 1917
Keystone Visual Screening Tests, 1918
Leavell Hand-Eye Coordinator Tests, 1878
Spache Binocular Reading Test, 1929

Kirkpatrick (Donald L.), 4380 Continental Drive, Brookfield, Wis. 53005:
Supervisory Inventory on Communication, 2460
Supervisory Inventory on Human Relations, 2463
Supervisory Inventory on Safety, 2465

Klamath Printing Co., 320 Lowell St., Klamath Falls, Ore. 97601:
Standard Reading Inventory, 1649

Knauber (Alma Jordan), 9871 Lorelei Drive, Cincinnati, Ohio 45231:
Knauber Art Ability Test, 187
Knauber Art Vocabulary Test, 188

Knobloch (Hilda), Albany Medical College, Albany, N.Y. 12208:
Developmental Screening Inventory, 494

Kreul (E. James), Sensory Sciences Research Center, Stanford Research Institute, Menlo Park, Calif. 94025:
Modified Rhyme Hearing Test, 2046

Kundu (Ramanath), Department of Psychology, University of Calcutta, 92 Acharya Prafulla Chandra Road, Calcutta-9, India:
Kundu's Neurotic Personality Inventory, 1257

L & L Associates, P.O. Box 20473, Charlotte, N.C. 28202:
Executive Employment Review, 374
L & L Clerical Tests, 2133

Ladoca Project and Publishing Foundation, Inc., East 51st Ave. and Lincoln St., Denver, Colo. 80216:
Denver Developmental Screening Test, 492

Lafayette Instrument Co., P.O. Box 1279, North 9th St. Road and Sagamore Parkway, Lafayette, Ind. 47902:
Jensen Alternation Board, 560A
Manual Accuracy and Speed Test, 1896
O'Connor Finger Dexterity Test, 2228
O'Connor Tweezer Dexterity Test, 2229
O'Connor Wiggly Block, 2259
One Hole Test, 2230
Purdue Hand Precision Test, 2233

LaForge (Rolfe), 83 Homestead Blvd., Mill Valley, Calif. 94941:
Interpersonal Check List, 1240

Language Research Associates, Inc., 175 East Delaware Place, Chicago, Ill. 60611:
Auditory Discrimination Test, 2028
Auditory Memory Span Test, 2029
Auditory Sequential Memory Test, 2030
Hollien-Thompson Group Hearing Test, 2040
Spatial Orientation Memory Test, 1888

Lawrence (Trudys), 5532 Poplar Blvd., Los Angeles, Calif. 90032:
Getting Along, 1190

Layton (Wilbur L.), 3604 Ross Road, Ames, Iowa 50010:
Minnesota Scholastic Aptitude Test, 405
Ohio College Association Rating Scale, 1301
Ohio State University Psychological Test, 419
Study Performance Test, 1769

Lea & Febiger, Washington Square, Philadelphia, Pa. 19106:
Boston Diagnostic Aphasia Examination, 2066

Leach (Glenn C.), Publisher, 116 North Pleasant Ave., Ridgewood, N.J. 07450:
Information Test on Drugs and Drug Abuse, 933
Information Test on Human Reproduction, 934
Kilander-Leach Health Knowledge Test, 935
Nutrition Information Test, 953

Lear Seigler, Inc./Fearon Publishers, 6 Davis Drive, Belmont, Calif. 94002:
Basic Screening and Referral Form for Children With Suspected Learning and Behavioral Disabilities, 977
Inventory of Primary Skills, 1707
Psychoeducational Inventory of Basic Learning Abilities, 985

Learning Concepts, 2501 North Lamar, Austin, Tex. 78705:
Oral School Attitude Test, 878
Primary Self-Concept Inventory, 1334
School Attitude Test, 888
Tests for Auditory Comprehension of Language, 997A
Tri-Cultural Attitude Scale, 1426

Learning Pathways, Inc., Evergreen, Colo. 80439:
Individual Learning Disabilities Classroom Screening Instrument, 983

Learning Research and Development Center, University of Pittsburgh, Pittsburgh, Pa. 15213:
Rosner Perceptual Survey, 1884

Learning Research Associates, Inc., 1501 Broadway, New York, N.Y. 10036:
LRA Standard Mastery Tasks in Language, 1633

Learning to Learn School, Inc., 1936 San Marco Blvd., Jacksonville, Fla. 32207:
Sprigle School Readiness Screening Test, 1731

Leonard (Hal) Music Co., Inc., 64 East Second St., Winona, Minn. 55987:
Watkins-Farnum Performance Scale, 216

Lewis (H. K.) & Co. Ltd., P.O. Box 66, 136 Gower St., London WC1E 6BS, England:
Crichton Vocabulary Scale, 491
Mill Hill Vocabulary Scale, 403
Progressive Matrices, 439
Test for Colour-Blindness [Japan], 1932

Life Insurance Agency Management Association, 170 Sigourney St., Hartford, Conn. 06105:
Combination Inventory, 2396
Evaluation Record, 2398
Information Index, 2401
LIAMA Inventory of Job Attitudes, 2402
Sales Method Index, 2407

Lincoln Test Service, 304 West Iowa St., Urbana, Ill. 61801:
Quantitative Evaluative Device, 443

Lippincott (J. B.) Co., East Washington Square, Philadelphia, Pa. 19105:
Lippincott Reading Readiness Test, 1712

Longman Inc., 72 Fifth Ave., New York, N.Y. 10011:
Edinburgh Articulation Test [Scotland], 2070

Lucas Brothers Publishers, 909 Lowry, Columbia, Mo. 65201:
Inventory of Teacher Knowledge of Reading, 1665

Lyons & Carnahan, 407 East 25th St., Chicago, Ill. 60616:
New Developmental Reading Tests, 1574
Silent Reading Diagnostic Tests, 1647

M.A.A. Committee on High School Contests, University of Nebraska, Lincoln, Neb. 68508:
Annual High School Mathematics Examination, 598

MKM, Inc., 809 Kansas City St., Rapid City, S.D. 57701:
MKM Binocular Preschool Test, 1919
MKM Monocular and Binocular Reading Test, 1920
MKM Picture Arrangement Test, 1879

★McCann Associates, 2755 Philmont Ave., Huntington Valley, Pa. 19006:
Clerical Worker Examination, 2125
Fire Promotion Tests, 2361
Fireman Examination, 2363
General Municipal Employees Performance (Efficiency) Rating System, 2364
McCann Typing Tests, 2134
Memory and Observation Tests for Policeman, 2367
Police Performance Rating System, 2368
Police Promotion Tests, 2369
Policeman Examination, 2370
Stenographic Dictation Test, 2158
Visual Comprehension Test for Detective, 2375

McCartney (William A.), P.O. Box 507, Kaneohe, Hawaii 96744:
Grammar, Usage, and Structure Test and Vocabulary Test, 84
Reading Comprehension Test, 1584

McFarland (Ross A.), Harvard School of Public Health, 665 Huntington Ave., Boston, Mass. 02115:
Psycho-Somatic Inventory, 1344

McGrath Publishing Co., P.O. Box 535, Whitmore Lake, Mich. 48189:
McGrath Test of Reading Skills, 1564

McGraw-Hill Book Co., Inc., 1221 Avenue of the Americas, New York, N.Y. 10020:
Attitude-Interest Analysis Test, 1101
Comprehensive English Language Test for Speakers of English as a Second Language, 226
Diagnostic Test for Students of English as a Second Language, 227
McGraw-Hill Basic Skills System
  Mathematics Test, 635
  Reading Test, 1593
  Spelling Test, 160
  Study Skills Test, 1771
  Vocabulary Test, 177
  Writing Test, 125

McGraw-Hill Ryerson Ltd., 330 Progress Ave., Scarborough, Ont., Canada:
Canadian Intelligence Test, 486

McMenemy (Richard A.), 3028 Northeast Brazee St., Portland, Ore. 97212:
McMenemy Measure of Reading Ability, 1565

Macmillan Education Ltd., Houndmills, Basingstoke, Hants RG21 2XS, England:
Neale Analysis of Reading Ability, 1683

O'Rourke Mechanical Aptitude Test, 2260
Survey Test of Vocabulary, 173
Survey Tests of English Usage, 116
Survey Tests of Reading, 1607
Parnicky, (Joseph J.), Nisonger Center, Ohio State University, 1580 Cannon Drive, Columbus, Ohio 43210:
Vocational Interest and Sophistication Assessment, 2217
Pennsylvania State University. *See* Audio-Visual Services, Institute of Public Safety, and Speech and Hearing Clinic.
Perceptual Learning Systems, P.O. Box 4209, Dearborn, Mich. 48126:
Flowers-Costello Tests of Central Auditory Abilities, 2035
Perfection Form Co. (The), 214 West Eighth St., Logan, Iowa 51546:
American History: Junior High—Objective, 1982
American History: Senior High—Objective, 1983
American Literature Anthology Tests, 126
Economics/Objective Tests, 1964
English Literature Anthology Tests, 133
Government/Objective Tests, 2008
Grammar and Usage Test Series, 83
Library Tests, 1760
Literature Tests/Objective, 140
Objective Tests in Constructive English, 100
Objective Tests in Punctuation, 101
Poetry Test/Objective, 142
World History/Objective Tests, 2002
World Literature Anthology Tests, 145
Personal Growth Press, Inc., Box M, Berea, Ohio 44017:
Albert Mate Selection Check List, 813
College Adjustment and Study Skills Inventory, 1751
College Interest Inventory, 2174
Henderson Analysis of Interest, 2188
I-Am Sentence Completion Test, 819
Marriage Skills Analysis, 835
Personnel Institute, Inc., 908 Fox Plaza, San Francisco, Calif. 94102:
Personnel Institute Clerical Tests, 2139
Personnel Institute Hiring Kit, 2403
Personnel Press, Education Center, P.O. Box 2649, Columbus, Ohio 43216:
Bowman Chronological Age Calculator, 802
Bowman M.A. and I.Q. Kalculator, 803
Clymer-Barrett Prereading Battery, 1699
Kuhlmann-Anderson Test, 398
McCullough Word-Analysis Tests, 1634
Thinking Creatively With Sounds and Words, 587
Torrance Tests of Creative Thinking, 589
Personnel Research Associates, Inc., 701 Metropolitan Bldg., 1407 Main St., Dallas, Tex. 75202:
Individual Placement Series, 2108
  Academic Alertness "AA," 334
  Occupational Interest Survey, 2200
  Performance Alertness "PA," 429
  Reading Adequacy "READ" Test, 1741
  Shorthand Test, 2156
  Survey of Clerical Skills, 2161
  Survey of Personal Attitude "SPA," 1408
  Typing Test, 2165
Personnel Research Institute, Case Western Reserve University, 1695 Magnolia Drive, Cleveland, Ohio 44106:
Personnel Research Institute Classification Test, 431
Personnel Research Institute Clerical Battery, 2140
  Arithmetic Reasoning Test, 699
  Spelling Test for Clerical Workers, 159
Personnel Research Institute Factory Series Test, 432
Personnel Research Institute Test of Shorthand Skills, 2141
Person-O-Metrics, Inc., 20504 Williamsburg Road, Dearborn Heights, Mich. 48127:
Self-Concept and Motivation Inventory, 1373
Peters and Associates, 328 Huckleberry Hill Road, Avon, Conn. 06001:
Scale of Socio-Egocentrism, 1362
Peterson (Shailer), University of Texas Dental School at San Antonio, 7703 Floyd Curl Drive, San Antonio, Tex. 78284:
Word Dexterity Test, 181
Phonovisual Products, Inc., 12216 Parklawn Drive, Rockville, Md. 20852:
Phonovisual Diagnostic Test, 1638
Physical Education and Industrial Fitness Unit, Loughborough University of Technology, Loughborough, Leics, England:
Swimming Ability Scales for Boys in Secondary Schools, 941

Pikunas (Justin), Psychology Department, University of Detroit, Detroit, Mich. 48221:
Graphoscopic Scale, 1465
Pimm Consultants Ltd., Suite 211, 85 Sparks St., Ottawa 4, Ont., Canada:
Ottawa School Behavior Check List, 1307
Prentice-Hall, Inc., Englewood Cliffs, N.J. 07632:
Basic Fitness Tests, 917
Priority Innovations, Inc., P.O. Box 792, Skokie, Ill. 60076:
Multidimensional Maturity Scale, 1292
Parent Readiness Evaluation of Preschoolers, 1718
Primary Academic Sentiment Scale, 1723
Screening Test for the Assignment of Remedial Treatments, 988
Screening Test of Academic Readiness, 1730
Programming Specialists, Inc., P.O. Box 160, Brooklyn, N.Y. 11234:
Aptitude Assessment Battery: Programming, 2331
Programs for Education, Lumberville, Pa. 18933:
Gesell Developmental Tests, 1703
Project Talent Office, American Institutes for Research, P.O. Box 1113, Palo Alto, Calif. 94302:
Project Talent Test Battery, 1058
Psychodiagnostic Test Co., Box 859, East Lansing, Mich. 48823:
Organic Integrity Test, 1305
Psychodynamic Instruments, Box 1221, Ann Arbor, Mich. 48106:
Blacky Pictures, 1448
Psychological Business Research, 11000 Cedar Ave., Cleveland, Ohio 44106:
Employment Aptitude Inventory, 2102b
Management Aptitude Inventory, 2102a
Sales Aptitude Inventory, 2102c
★Psychological Corporation (The), 304 East 45th St., New York, N.Y. 10017:
A-B-C Vision Test for Ocular Dominance, 1905
Academic Promise Tests, 1063
Achievement Tests in Nursing, 2376
Achievement Tests in Practical Nursing, 2377
American Institute of Certified Public Accountants Testing Programs, 2323
Arthur Point Scale of Performance Tests, 483
Bayley Scales of Infant Development, 484
Bellak TAT Blank, 1519c
Bennett Mechanical Comprehension Test, 2239
Benton Visual Retention Test, 543
Boehm Test of Basic Concepts, 344
Cattell Infant Intelligence Scale, 487
Chicago Non-Verbal Examination, 355
College Qualification Tests, 358
Concept Mastery Test, 359
Cornell Index, 1144
Crawford Small Parts Dexterity Test, 2223
Davis Reading Test, 1546
Dental Hygiene Aptitude Testing Program, 2338
Differential Aptitude Tests, 1069
  Abstract Reasoning, 333
  Clerical Speed and Accuracy, 781
  Language Usage, 93
  Mechanical Reasoning, 2256
  Numerical Ability, 644
  Space Relations, 2268
  Spelling, 157
  Verbal Reasoning, 473
Doppelt Mathematical Reasoning Test, 371
Driscoll Play Kit, 1457
Edwards Personal Preference Schedule, 1164
Employee Evaluation Form for Interviewers, 2298
Entrance Examination for Schools of Nursing, 2379
Entrance Examination for Schools of Practical Nursing, 2380
Examining for Aphasia, 2071
Farnsworth Dichotomous Test for Color Blindness, 1912
Fundamental Achievement Series, 376
General Clerical Test, 2129
Gesell Developmental Schedules, 497
Goldstein-Scheerer Tests of Abstract and Concrete Thinking, 1192
Graves Design Judgment Test, 185
Hand-Tool Dexterity Test, 2225
Harris Tests of Lateral Dominance, 1877
Harrower's Group Rorschach, 1499c
Harrower's Multiple Choice Test, 1499d
Holtzman Inkblot Technique, 1471
How Supervise?, 2448
Kent Series of Emergency Scales, 503
McCarthy Scales of Children's Abilities, 506
Make A Picture Story, 1482
Miller Analogies Test, 404
Minnesota Clerical Test, 2135
Minnesota Counseling Inventory, 1280

English Test: Municipal Tests, 77
First Year Algebra Test, 679
General Biology Test, 1810
General Chemistry Test, 1842
General Physics Test, 1865
General Science Test, 1785
Geography Test, 1976
Geography Test: Municipal Tests, 1975
Health and Safety Education Test, 926
Health Education Test, 928
Health Knowledge Test for College Freshmen, 929
Health Test, 930
High School Reading Test, 1556
History and Civics Test, 1943
Literature Test, 139
Plane Geometry, 757
Plane Trigonometry, 764
Reading Comprehension Test [Crow, Kuhlmann, and Crow], 1586
Reading Comprehension Test [Speer and Smith], 1587
Reading Test (Comprehension and Speed), 1592
Social Studies Test, 1951
Solid Geometry, 759
Spelling Test, 161
Vocabulary Test, 178
Office Skills Achievement Test, 2136
Ohio Penal Classification Test, 418
Per-Flu-Dex Tests, 2286
Pictographic Self Rating Scale, 879
Pictorial Study of Values, 1325
Power of Influence Test, 1329
Purpose in Life Test, 1350
Quick Screening Scale of Mental Development, 521
Ring and Peg Tests of Behavior Development, 523
Rutgers Social Attribute Inventory, 1357
SAQS Chicago Q Sort, 1358
Science Research Temperament Scale, 1368
Self-Interview Inventory, 1375
Tapping Test, 796
Tear Ballot for Industry, 2289
Test for High School Entrants, 42
Triadal Equated Personality Inventory, 1425
Tulane Factors of Liberalism-Conservatism, 1427
Weidner-Fensch Speech Screening Test, 2099
Whisler Strategy Test, 2292
Work Information Inventory, 2293
Psychometric Techniques Associates, 710 Chatham Center Office Bldg., Pittsburgh, Pa. 15219:
Tapping Test, 796
Public Personnel Association. *See* International Personnel Management Association.
Pumroy (Donald K.), University of Maryland, College Park, Md. 20742:
Maryland Parent Attitude Survey, 1273
Rand McNally & Co., P.O. Box 7600, Chicago, Ill. 60680:
BSCS Achievement Tests: Green Version, 1801c
Random House, Inc., 201 East 50th St., New York, N.Y. 10022:
Lüscher Color Test, 1263
Reading Laboratory and Clinic, University of Florida, Gainesville, Fla. 32601:
Group Diagnostic Spelling Test, 148
Incomplete Sentence Test, 1476
Spelling Errors Test, 158
Test on Use of the Dictionary, 1773
Reid (John E.) and Associates, Suite 700, 600 South Michigan Ave., Chicago, Ill. 60605:
Reid Report, 1353
Remediation Associates, Inc., P.O. Box 318, Linden, N.J. 07036:
School Survey of Interpersonal Relationships, 890
Research and Development Center for Teacher Education, University of Texas, Austin, Tex. 78712:
Self-Report Inventory, 1378
Research Concepts, 1368 East Airport Road, Muskegon, Mich. 49444:
ABC Inventory to Determine Kindergarten and School Readiness, 1691
Hartman Value Profile, 1211
Measurement of Self Concept in Kindergarten Children, 1483
School Readiness Checklist, 1728
Research Department, Fairview State Hospital. *See* Fairview State Hospital.
Research Media, Inc., 4 Midland Ave., Hicksville, N.Y. 11801:
Rapid-Rater, 811
Research Psychologists Press, Inc., 36 St. John St., Goshen, N.Y. 10924:
Personality Research Form, 1322

Psychological Screening Inventory, 1342
Similes Test, 580
Revrac Publications, 1535 Red Oak Drive, Silver Spring, Md. 20910:
Basic Reading Rate Scale, 1748
Carver-Darby Chunked Reading Test, 1537
Reading Progress Scale, 1589
★Richardson, Bellows, Henry & Co., Inc., 1140 Connecticut Ave. N.W., Washington, D.C. 20036:
Language Perception Test, 92
RBH Arithmetic Fundamentals Test, 727
RBH Arithmetic Reasoning Test, 728
RBH Basic Reading and Word Test, 1580
RBH Breadth of Information, 2287
RBH Checking Test, 2143
RBH Classifying Test, 2144
RBH Individual Background Survey, 2314
RBH Number Checking Test, 2145
RBH Scientific Reading Test, 1740
RBH Shop Arithmetic Test, 729
RBH Spelling Test and Word Meaning Test, 106
RBH Test of Chemical Comprehension, 1846
RBH Test of Dictation Speed, 2146
RBH Test of Language Skills, 107
RBH Test of Learning Ability, 444
RBH Test of Non-Verbal Reasoning, 445
RBH Test of Reading Comprehension, 1581
RBH Test of Supervisory Judgment, 2458
RBH Test of Typing Speed, 2147
RBH Three-Dimensional Space Test, 2264
RBH Two-Dimensional Space Test, 2265
RBH Vocabulary Test, 171
Roche Psychiatric Service Institute, Roche Laboratories, Nutley, N.J. 07110:
Roche MMPI Computerized Interpretation Service, 1285
Rocky Mountain Behavioral Science Institute, Inc., P.O. Box 1066, Fort Collins, Colo. 80521:
Concept-Specific Anxiety Scale, 1141
Counseling Services Assessment Blank, 857
Mathematics Anxiety Rating Scale, 1274
Suinn Test Anxiety Behavior Scale, 1406
Rosenzweig (Saul), 8029 Washington St., St. Louis, Mo. 63114:
Rosenzweig Picture-Frustration Study, 1500
Rosinski (Edwin F.), School of Medicine, University of California, 50 Kirkham St., San Francisco, Calif. 94143:
Medical School Instructor Attitude Inventory, 2356
Runner Associates, 2628 Deerpark Drive, San Diego, Calif. 92110:
Runner Studies of Attitude Patterns, 1356
SEFA (Publications) Ltd., 240 Holliday St., Birmingham 1, England:
Progress Assessment Chart of Social Development, 1338
S-O Publishers, 1822 Old Canyon Drive, Hacienda Heights, Calif. 91745:
Structured-Objective Rorschach Test, 1513
SPECO Educational Systems, 1230 North Industrial, Dallas, Tex. 75207:
Practical Dexterity Board, 2232
Safran (C.), Calgary School Board, Calgary, Alta., Canada:
Safran Culture Reduced Intelligence Test, 453
Sage Publications, 275 South Beverly Drive, Beverly Hills, Calif. 90212:
Hill Interaction Matrix, 1214
Scarborough (Barron B.), Florida State University, Tallahassee, Fla. 32306:
Pictorial Interest Inventory, 2203
Scherer (Isidor W.), 231 Wells Road, Palm Beach, Fla. 33480:
Northampton Activity Rating Scale, 1297
★Scholastic Testing Service, Inc., 480 Meyer Road, Bensenville, Ill. 60106:
Adult Basic Reading Inventory, 1736
Burnett Reading Series, 1535
Diagnostic Reading Test, 1625
Hall Occupational Orientation Inventory, 2187
STS Closed High School Placement Test, 32
STS Educational Development Series, 33
STS Junior Inventory, 1360
STS Youth Inventory, 1361
Scholastic Mental Ability Tests, 454
Steinbach Test of Reading Readiness, 1732
Schubert (Herman J. P.), 500 Klein Road, Buffalo, N.Y. 14221:
Draw-A-Person Quality Scale, 1456
Schubert General Ability Battery, 455

★Science Research Associates, Inc., 259 East Erie St., Chicago, Ill. 60611 :
Adaptability Test, 337
Army General Classification Test, 342
Basic Skills in Arithmetic Test, 704
College Guidance Program, 1049
Computer Programmer Aptitude Battery, 2334a
Edwards Personality Inventory, 1165
Flanagan Aptitude Classification Tests, 1072
Flanagan Industrial Tests, 2107
Iowa Tests of Educational Development, 20
  Ability to Do Quantitative Thinking, 623
  Ability to Interpret Literary Materials, 138
  Ability to Interpret Reading Materials in the Natural Sciences, 1738
  Ability to Interpret Reading Materials in the Social Studies, 1737
  Correctness and Appropriateness of Expression, 88
  General Background in the Natural Sciences, 1787
  General Vocabulary, 166
  Understanding of Basic Social Concepts, 1944
  Use of Sources of Information, 1758
Junior College Placement Program, 1054
Kuder General Interest Survey, 2193
Kuder Occupational Interest Survey, 2194
Kuder Preference Record—Personal, 1256
Kuder Preference Record—Vocational, 2195
Leadership Opinion Questionnaire, 2454
National Educational Development Tests, 24
Personal Audit, 1314
Principles of Democracy Test, 2012
Purdue Pegboard, 2234
Reading for Understanding Placement Test, 1588
SRA Achievement Series, 29
  Arithmetic, 731
  Language Arts, 108
  Reading, 1596
  Science, 1790
  Social Studies, 1947
  Work-Study Skills, 1765
SRA Arithmetic Index, 732
SRA Assessment Survey, 30
SRA Clerical Aptitudes, 791
SRA High School Placement Test, 31
SRA Mechanical Aptitudes, 2267
SRA Nonverbal Form, 449
SRA Pictorial Reasoning Test, 450
SRA Primary Mental Abilities, 1087
SRA Reading Index, 1746
SRA Reading Record, 1597
SRA Sales Attitudes Check List, 2404
SRA Short Test of Educational Ability, 451
SRA Typing Skills, 792
SRA Verbal Form, 452
Short Occupational Knowledge Tests
  Auto Mechanics, 2439
  Bookkeepers, 2152
  Carpenters, 2440
  Draftsmen, 2441
  Electricians, 2442
  Machinists, 2443
  Office Machine Operators, 2153
  Plumbers, 2444
  Secretaries, 2154
  Tool and Die Makers, 2445
  Truckdrivers, 2474
  Welders, 2446
Short Tests of Clerical Ability, 2155
Study Habits Checklist, 1767
Supervisory Index, 2459
Survey of Interpersonal Values, 1407
Survey of Personal Values, 1409
Test of Economic Understanding, 1968
Test of Family Life Knowledge and Attitudes, 956
Tests of General Ability, 467
Thurstone Temperament Schedule, 1423
Thurstone Test of Mental Alertness, 469
Vocational Planning Inventory, 2114
What I Like to Do, 1439
Writing Skills Test, 124

Scoptec Labs, Inc., 18 Southwest 13th St., Fort Lauderdale, Fla. 33315 :
Grassi Basic Cognitive Evaluation, 980
Grassi Block Substitution Test, 1196

Scott, Foresman & Co., 1900 East Lake Ave., Glenview, Ill. 60025 :
Initial Survey Test, 1706
Inventory-Survey Tests, 1559
Primary Mathematics Survey Tests, 649
Primary Reading Survey Tests, 1577
Primary Survey Tests, 27
Seeing Through Arithmetic Tests, 735
Vocabulary Survey Test, 175

Service for Admission to College and University, 151 Slater St., Ottawa 4, Ont., Canada :
Canadian English Language Achievement Test, 63A
Canadian Scholastic Aptitude Test, 353
Service for Admission to College and University Testing Program, 1060

Shepherd (Hilton) Co., Inc., P.O. Box 846, Fort Worth, Tex. 76101 :
Job Application Forms, 2303

★Sheridan Psychological Services, Inc., P.O. Box 6101, Orange, Calif. 92667 :
Alternate Uses, 542
Army Alpha Examination: First Nebraska Revision, 341A
Christensen-Guilford Fluency Tests, 546
Consequences, 551
Correct Spelling, 147
Creativity Tests for Children, 554
DF Opinion Survey, 1151
Decorations, 555
Driver Attitude Survey, 844
Gregory Academic Interest Inventory, 2183
Guilford-Holley L Inventory, 1204
Guilford-Martin Inventory of Factors GAMIN, 1205
Guilford-Martin Personnel Inventory, 1206
Guilford-Shneidman-Zimmerman Interest Survey, 2184
Guilford-Zimmerman Aptitude Survey, 1074
Guilford-Zimmerman Interest Inventory, 2185
Guilford-Zimmerman Temperament Survey, 1207
Immediate Test, 500
Inventory of Factors STDCR, 1245
Logical Reasoning, 1761
Making Objects, 562
Match Problems, 564
Match Problems 5, 565
Memory for Events, 566
Memory for Meanings, 567
New Uses, 568
Pertinent Questions, 571
Plot Titles, 572
Possible Jobs, 573
Seeing Problems, 577
Ship Destination Test, 457
Simile Interpretations, 579
Sketches, 581
Symbol Identities, 583
Tests of Social Intelligence, 1421
Utility Test, 591

Shurrager (Harriett C.), Department of Psychology and Education, Illinois Institute of Technology, Chicago, Ill. 60616 :
Haptic Intelligence Scale for Adult Blind, 498

Silliman (Henrietta), 404 North Washington, Toulon, Ill. 61483 :
English Tests for Outside Reading, 134

Sines (Jacob O.), P.O. Box 1031, Iowa City, Iowa 52240 :
Missouri Children's Picture Series, 1287

Skandinaviska Testförlaget, Box 461, S-126 04 Hägersten 4, Sweden :
Reversal Test, 1726
Seven Squares Technique, 1508
Trankell's Laterality Tests, 1890

Slosson Educational Publications, Inc., 140 Pine St., East Aurora, N.Y. 14052 :
Slosson Drawing Coordination Test for Children and Adults, 1384
Slosson Intelligence Test, 524
Slosson Oral Reading Test, 1688

Society for New Guinea Psychological Research and Publications, P.O. Box 5008, Boroto, Papua New Guinea :
New Guinea Performance Scales, 510

Sound Apperception Test Distributor, 3505 Oakdale, Temple, Tex. 76501 :
Sound-Apperception Test, 1510

Specialty Case Manufacturing Co., P.O. Box 3067, Philadelphia, Pa. 19150 :
General Aptitude Test Battery
  Finger Dexterity Board, 1073c5
  Pegboard, 1073c4
Nonreading Aptitude Test Battery
  Finger Dexterity Board, 1086l
  Pegboard, 1086k

Speech and Hearing Clinic, Pennsylvania State University, 110 Psychology Bldg., University Park, Pa. 16802 :
Discrimination by Identification of Pictures, 2039b
Threshold by Identification of Pictures, 2039a

Springer Publishing Co., Inc., 200 Park Ave. South, New York, N.Y. 10003:
Interpersonal Perception Method [England], 1243
Miner Sentence Completion Scale, 1484
Polarity Scale, 1327
School Apperception Method, 1503
Structured and Scaled Interview to Assess Maladjustment, 1397
Structured Clinical Interview, 1398
Tomkins-Horn Picture Arrangement Test, 1522
Ward Behavior Inventory, 1435

Stanford University Press, Stanford, Calif. 94305:
College Health Knowledge Test, 921
Patient's Self-History Form, 939
Strong Vocational Interest Blank for Men, 2212
Strong Vocational Interest Blank for Women, 2213

Stanwix House, Inc., 3020 Chartiers Ave., Pittsburgh, Pa. 15204:
Deep Test of Articulation, 2069
Ohio Tests of Articulation and Perception of Sounds, 2023
Screening Deep Test of Articulation, 2090
Word Intelligibility by Picture Identification, 2061

Starr (Anna Spiesman), 126 Montgomery St., Highland Park, N.J. 08904:
Rutgers Drawing Test, 575

Statistical Publishing Society, 204/1 Barrackpore Trunk Road, Calcutta-35, India:
Non-Language Test of Verbal Intelligence, 412

Steck-Vaughn Co., P.O. Box 2028, Austin, Tex. 78767:
Gray-Votaw-Rogers General Achievement Tests, 15
High School Fundamentals Evaluation Test, 17

Stein (Morris I.), Department of Psychology, New York University, 4 Washington Place, New York, N.Y. 10003:
Research Personnel Review Form, 2391
Surveys of Research Administration and Environment, 2393
Technical Personnel Recruiting Inventory, 2394

Stephenson (Richard R.), 2560 First Ave., San Diego, Calif. 92103:
Psychological Audit for Interpersonal Relations, 1341

Stevens, Thurow & Associates, Inc., 105 West Adams St., Chicago, Ill. 60603:
Clerical Tests, 2122
Clerical Tests, Series N, 2123
Clerical Tests, Series V, 2124
Inventory No. 2, 393
Primary Mechanical Ability Tests, 2262
Stevens-Thurow Personnel Forms, 2318

Steward-Mortensen & Associates, 232 North Lake Ave., Pasadena, Calif. 91101:
Steward Basic Factors Inventory, 2111
Steward Life Insurance Knowledge Test, 2410
Steward Occupational Objectives Inventory, 2411
Steward Personal Background Inventory, 2412
Steward Personnel Tests (Short Form), 2112

Stockton State Hospital. *See* Department of Research.

★Stoelting Co., 1350 South Kostner Ave., Chicago, Ill. 60623:
Arthur Point Scale of Performance Tests, 483
Behavior Cards, 1110
Block-Design Test, 545
Concept Formation Test, 1140
Diagnostic Reading Examination for Diagnosis of Special Difficulty in Reading, 1623
Feature Profile Test, 556
Healy Pictorial Completion Tests, 558
Horn Art Aptitude Inventory, 186
Kent-Rosanoff Free Association Test, 1480
Leiter Adult Intelligence Scale, 504
Leiter International Performance Scale, 505
Lincoln-Oseretsky Motor Development Scale, 1895
Manikin Test, 563
Merrill-Palmer Scale of Mental Tests, 507
O'Connor Finger Dexterity Test, 2228
O'Connor Tweezer Dexterity Test, 2229
O'Connor Wiggly Block, 2259
Passalong Test, 515
Perrin Motor Coordination Test, 1899
Porteus Maze Test: Vineland Revision, 518a
Scott Company Mental Alertness Test, 456
Seguin-Goddard Formboard, 578
Smedley Hand Dynamometer, 1901
Two-Figure Formboard, 590

Stogdill (Ralph M.), 3658 Olentangy Blvd., Columbus, Ohio 43214:
Attitudes Toward Parental Control of Children, 1103

Stone (LeRoy A.), 1720 Cottonwood St., Grand Forks, N.D. 58201:
Hellenic Affiliation Scale, 1213

Stratton-Christian Press, Box 1055, University Place Station, Des Moines, Iowa 50311:
Journalism Test, 2365

Swets & Zeitlinger B. V., Keizersgracht 487, Amsterdam-C, The Netherlands:
Non-Verbal Intelligence Tests for Deaf and Hearing Subjects, 512
South African Picture Analysis Test, 1511

Syracuse University. *See* Psychological Research Center.

TACA Development Fund, University of Missouri, 8001 Natural Bridge, St. Louis, Mo. 63121:
Test of Adult College Aptitude, 465

TAV Selection System, 12807 Arminta St., North Hollywood, Calif. 91605:
TAV Selection System, 2113

Tabin (Johanna Krout), 162 Park Ave., Glencoe, Ill. 60022:
Personal Preference Scale, 1316
Symbol Elaboration Test, 1514

Teachers College Press, 1234 Amsterdam Ave., New York, N.Y. 10027:
Foreign Language Prognosis Test, 218
Gates-MacGinitie Reading Tests, 1552
    Readiness Skills, 1702
    Survey F, 1553
Gates-McKillop Reading Diagnostic Tests, 1629
Library Orientation Test for College Freshmen, 1759
Phonics Knowledge Survey, 1637
Phonics Test for Teachers, 1669
Symonds Picture-Story Test, 1515

Teaching Aids Co., 2511 Marquette St., Davenport, Iowa 52804:
Grade Averaging Charts, 806

Teaching and Testing Resources, P.O. Box 77, Fortitude Valley, Qld. 4006, Australia:
Concise Word Reading Tests, 1677
Moreton Arithmetic Tests, 723
Moreton Mathematics Tests, 641
St. Lucia Graded Word Reading Test, 1687

Teaching Resources Corporation, 100 Boylston St., Boston, Mass. 02116:
Lindamood Auditory Conceptualization Test, 2042

Technisonic Studios, Inc., 1201 Brentwood Blvd., St. Louis, Mo. 63117:
Auditory Tests, 2031
Rush Hughes (PB 50), 2053

Test Analysis and Development Corporation, 855 Inca Parkway, Boulder, Colo. 80303:
Classroom Atmosphere Questionnaire, 855
Conceptual Systems Test, 1142
Course Evaluation Questionnaire, 858
School Atmosphere Questionnaire, 887
Self-Esteem Questionnaire, 1374

Test Developments, P.O. Box 167, Burlingame, Calif. 94012:
Structured Doll Play Test, 1512

Test of Musicality, 2515 Arkansas, Lawrence, Kan. 66044:
Test of Musicality, 214

Testscor, Inc., 2312 Snelling Ave., Minneapolis, Minn. 55404:
Hankes Scoring Service, 1031

Theological Schools Scoring Service, P.O. Box 1201, Southern Methodist University, Dallas, Tex. 75275:
Theological School Inventory, 1028

Thomas (Charles C), Publisher, 301-327 East Lawrence Ave., Springfield, Ill. 62703:
Machover Draw-A-Person Test, 1481
Teaching Research Motor-Development Scale, 1903

Thompson (Clem W.), Mankato State College, Mankato, Minn. 56001:
Thompson Smoking and Tobacco Knowledge Test, 944

Time, Inc., Time and Life Bldg., Rockefeller Center, New York, N.Y. 10020:
Time Current Affairs Test, 1961
Time Monthly News Quiz, 1962

Titmus Optical Co., Inc., Petersburg, Va. 23803:
Titmus Vision Tester, 1934

Tracor, Inc., 6500 Tracor Lane, Austin, Tex. 78721:
Tracor Audiometers, 2058

Trademark Design Products, Inc., P.O. Box 2010, Boca Raton, Fla. 33432:
McCormick Job Performance Measurement "Rate-$-Scales," 2305

Tree of Life Press (The), 1309 Northeast Second St., P.O. Box 447, Gainesville, Fla. 32601:
Bzoch-League Receptive-Expressive Emergent Language Scale, 2067

Twitchell-Allen (Doris), RFD #1, Box 147A, Ellsworth, Me. 04605:
Twitchell-Allen Three-Dimensional Personality Test, 1525

United States Government Printing Office, Washington, D.C. 20402:
General Aptitude Test Battery, 1073
Interest Check List, 2190
Nonreading Aptitude Test Battery, 1086
USES Clerical Skills Tests, 2166

★University Book Store, 360 State St., West Lafayette, Ind. 47906:
Handicap Problems Inventory, 1210
Purdue Clerical Adaptability Test, 2142
Purdue Creativity Test, 2347
Purdue Industrial Mathematics Test, 650
Purdue Industrial Supervisors Word-Meaning Test, 170
Purdue Industrial Training Classification Test, 2433
Purdue Instructor Performance Indicator, 880
Purdue Interview Aids, 2434
Purdue Master Attitude Scales, 1348
Purdue Mechanical Adaptability Test, 2263
Purdue Non-Language Personnel Test, 442
Purdue Rating Scale for Administrators and Executives, 1349
Purdue Rating Scale for Instruction, 881
Purdue Reading Test for Industrial Supervisors, 1739
Purdue Student-Teacher Opinionaire, 882
Purdue Teacher Evaluation Scale, 883
Purdue Teacher Opinionaire, 884
Purdue Trade Information Test for Sheetmetal Workers, 2435
Purdue Trade Information Test in Carpentry, 2436
Purdue Trade Information Test in Engine Lathe Operation, 2437
Purdue Trade Information Test in Welding, 2438

University Counseling Center, University of Maryland, College Park, Md. 20742:
Psychometric Behavior Checklist, 1343

University of British Columbia Bookstore, Vancouver 8, B.C., Canada:
VALCAN Vocational Interest Profile, 2215
Vocational Interest Profile, 2218

University of California Press, 2223 Fulton St., Berkeley, Calif. 94720:
Gottschalk-Gleser Content Analysis Scales, 1195

University of Chicago. *See* Industrial Relations Center.

University of Florida. *See* Florida Educational Research and Development Council and Reading Laboratory and Clinic.

University of Illinois. *See* Measurement and Research Division.

University of Illinois Press (The), Urbana, Ill. 61801:
Filmed Demonstration of the ITPA, 982
Illinois Test of Psycholinguistic Abilities, 981

University of Iowa. *See* Bureau of Educational Research and Service.

★University of London Press Ltd., St. Paul's House, Warwick Lane, London EC4P 4AH, England:
A.P.U. Occupational Interests Guide, 2168
Bristol Social Adjustment Guides, 1112
Edinburgh Reading Tests, 1548
Eysenck Personality Inventory, 1174b
Eysenck-Withers Personality Inventory, 1175
Gibson Spiral Maze, 1191
Graded Arithmetic-Mathematics Test, 618
Graded Word Reading Test, 1680
Group Mathematics Test, 620
Group Reading Assessment, 1554
Group Reading Test, 1555
Hostility and Direction of Hostility Questionnaire, 1218
Hysteroid-Obsessoid Questionnaire, 1224
Junior Eysenck Personality Inventory, 1252b
Leicester Number Test, 625
Maudsley Personality Inventory, 1275a
Moray House Arithmetic Test, 722
Moray House English Tests, 95
Moray House Mathematics Tests, 640
Moray House Picture Tests, 408
Moray House Verbal Reasoning Tests, 409
New Junior Maudsley Inventory, 1296a
Non-Readers Intelligence Test, 413
Objective Tests in Mathematics
   Algebra, 687
   Arithmetic and Trigonometry, 645
   Geometry, 754
   Statistics, 1043
Oral Verbal Intelligence Test, 419A

Reading Comprehension Test for Personnel Selection, 1743
Southgate Group Reading Tests, 1601
Symptom Sign Inventory, 1601
Systematic Interview Guides, 1411
Word Recognition Test, 1676

University of Maryland. *See* University Counseling Center.

University of Minnesota Press, 2037 University Ave. S.E., Minneapolis, Minn. 55455:
Aliferis Music Achievement Test, 194a
Aliferis-Stecklein Music Achievement Test, 194b
Minnesota Check List for Food Preparation and Serving, 951
Minnesota Rating Scale for Personal Qualities and Abilities, 1286
Minnesota Reading Examination for College Students, 1568
Minnesota Speed of Reading Test for College Students, 1749
Minnesota Test for Differential Diagnosis of Aphasia, 2080
Scales for Appraising High School Homemaking Programs, 954

University of Natal Press, P.O. Box 375, Pietermaritzburg, Republic of South Africa:
Thematic Apperception Test for African Subjects, 1520

University of Texas. *See* Research and Development Center for Teacher Education.

University of Toronto. *See* Guidance Centre.

University of Utah. *See* Middle East Center.

University Publications Sales, Ohio State University, 20 Lord Hall, 124 West 17th Ave., Columbus, Ohio 43210:
Ideal Leader Behavior Description Questionnaire, 2449
Junior Index of Motivation, 867
Leader Behavior Description Questionnaire, 2451
Leader Behavior Description Questionnaire, Form 12, 2452
Ohio Teaching Record, 877
Organizational Value Dimensions Questionnaire, 2330
Problem Check List: Form for Rural Young People, 1335
RAD Scales, 2457
Robinson-Hall Reading Tests, 1745

Van Wagenen Psycho-Educational Research Laboratories, 1729 Irving Ave. South, Minneapolis, Minn. 55403:
Comprehensive Primary Reading Scales, 1540
Comprehensive Reading Scales, 1541
Diagnostic Examination of Silent Reading Abilities, 1622
Van Wagenen Analytical Reading Scales, 1612
Van Wagenen Reading Readiness Scales, 1733

Village Book Cellar, 308 West State St., West Lafayette, Ind. 47906:
Lawshe-Kephart Personnel Comparison System, 2304

Vocational Guidance Service, 8845 Sheridan Drive, Williamsville, N.Y. 14221:
Chriswell Structural Dexterity Test, 2240

Vocational Psychology Research, Elliott Hall, University of Minnesota, Minneapolis, Minn. 55455:
Minnesota Importance Questionnaire, 2283
Minnesota Job Description Questionnaire, 2284
Minnesota Satisfaction Questionnaire, 2285

Wagner (Mazie Earle), 500 Klein Road, Buffalo, N.Y. 14221:
Buffalo Reading Test for Speed and Comprehension, 1534

Walther (Regis H.), Manpower Research Projects, George Washington University, Washington, D.C. 20006:
Job Analysis and Interest Measurement, 1250

Wardell Associates Inc., P.O. Box 1171, Guelph, Ont., Canada:
Test of Motor Impairment, 1904

Warwick Products Co., 7909 Rockside Road, Cleveland, Ohio 44131:
General Aptitude Test Battery
   Finger Dexterity Board, 1073c5
   Pegboard, 1073c4
Nonreading Aptitude Test Battery
   Finger Dexterity Board, 1086l
   Pegboard, 1086k

Webster Division, McGraw-Hill Book Co., Inc., 1221 Avenue of the Americas, New York, N.Y. 10020:
Kindergarten Evaluation of Learning Potential, 1709

Western Michigan University. *See* Continuing Education Office.

★Western Psychological Services, 12031 Wilshire Blvd., Los Angeles, Calif. 90025:
Alcadd Test, 1098
Anton Brenner Developmental Gestalt Test of School Readiness, 1696
Arizona Articulation Proficiency Scale, 2065

Auditory Apperception Test, 1446
Ayres Space Test, 1104
Babcock Test of Mental Efficiency, 1105
Bender Visual Motor Gestalt Test for Children, 1447d
Buttons, 1450
California Abbreviated WISC, 534
California Life Goals Evaluation Schedules, 1118
California Marriage Readiness Evaluation, 814
California Medical Survey, 1119
California Pre-Counseling Self-Analysis Protocol Booklet, 2171
Cassel Group Level of Aspiration Test, 1124
Child Behavior Rating Scale, 1126
Curtis Completion Form, 1454
Davis Rorschach Miniature Location Charts in Color, 1499b
Demos D Scale, 1153
Dennis Visual Perception Scale, 1910
Draw-A-Person, 1455
Education Apperception Test, 1458
El Senoussi Multiphasic Marital Inventory, 818
Elizur Test of Psycho-Organicity, 1168
Five Task Test, 1460
Forer Structured Sentence Completion Test, 1461
Forer Vocational Survey, 1462
Forty-Eight Item Counseling Evaluation Test, 1187
Geist Picture Interest Inventory, 2180
Geist Picture Interest Inventory: Deaf Form, 2181
Grayson Perceptualization Test, 1197
H-T-P: House-Tree-Person Projective Technique, 1469
Hahn Self Psychoevaluation Materials, 1208
Hand Test, 1470
Harrower's Psychodiagnostic Inkblot Test, 1499e
Hooper Visual Organization Test, 1216
Hunt-Minnesota Test for Organic Brain Damage, 1223
Illinois Index of Scholastic Aptitude, 392
Illinois Ratings of Character in Physical Education, 931
Illinois Ratings of Teacher Effectiveness, 865
Individual and Family Developmental Review, 820
Inferred Self-Concept Scale, 1231
KD Proneness Scale and Check List, 1254
Leadership Ability Evaluation, 1259
MACC Behavioral Adjustment Scale, 1264
McGuire Safe Driver Scale and Interview Guide, 2471
Male Impotence Test, 822
Manipulative Aptitude Test, 2226
Manson Evaluation, 1271
Marital Diagnostic Inventory, 824
Marital Roles Inventory, 825
Marriage Adjustment Inventory, 827
Marriage Adjustment Sentence Completion Survey, 828
Martin Performance Appraisal, 2307
Milwaukee Academic Interest Inventory, 2196
Mother-Child Relationship Evaluation, 1290
Motor Problems Inventory, 1897
Nagel Personnel Interviewing and Screening Forms, 2309
Object Relations Technique [England], 1486
Ohwaki-Kohs Tactile Block Design Intelligence Test for the Blind [Japan], 513
Oregon Academic Ranking Test, 420
Orzeck Aphasia Evaluation, 2085
Pain Apperception Test, 1488
Personality Evaluation Form, 1319
Philo-Phobe, 1324
Picture World Test, 1494
Psychotic Inpatient Profile, 1345
Psychotic Reaction Profile, 1346
Revised Rorschach Evalograph, 1499g
Richardson Emergency Psychodiagnostic Summary, 1354
Riley Articulation and Language Test, 2089
Riley Preschool Developmental Screening Inventory, 1727
Rohde Sentence Completions Test, 1498
Rorschach Concept Evaluation Technique, 1499i
Rorschach Miniature Inkblots in Color, 1499l
Sexual Development Scale for Females, 839
Sherman Mental Impairment Test, 1379
Sklar Aphasia Scale, 2092
Southern California Figure-Ground Visual Perception Test, 1928
Southern California Kinesthesia and Tactile Perception Tests, 1885

Southern California Motor Accuracy Test, 1902
Southern California Perceptual-Motor Tests, 1886
Southern California Sensory Integration Tests, 1887
Stanford-Ohwaki-Kohs Block Design Intelligence Test for the Blind [Japan], 527
Study Skills Counseling Evaluation, 1770
Symbol Digit Modalities Test, 1889
Test of Concept Utilization, 585
Thorman Family Relations Conference Situation Questionnaire, 841
Time Appreciation Test, 588
Verbal Power Test of Concept Equivalence, 471
Visual Motor Gestalt Test Two-Copy Drawing Form, 1447g
Visual-Verbal Test, 1429
WPS Supervisor-Executive Tri-Dimensional Evaluation Scales, 2468
Wahler Physical Symptoms Inventory, 1432
Wahler Self-Description Inventory, 1433
Walker Problem Behavior Identification Checklist, 1434
Western Personality Inventory, 1438
Western Personnel Tests, 481
Whitaker Index of Schizophrenic Thinking, 1440

Williams and Associates, 7201 Creveling Drive, St. Louis, Mo. 63130:
BITCH Test, 343

Williams & Wilkins Co., 428 East Preston St., Baltimore, Md. 21202:
Szondi Test [Switzerland], 1516

William, Lynde & Williams, 153 East Erie St., Painesville, Ohio 44077:
Personal Classification Test, 430
WLW Employment Inventory, 2115
WLW Employment Inventory III, 478
WLW Mental Alertness Inventory, 479
WLW Personal Attitude Inventory, 1431
William, Lynde & Williams Analysis of Interest, 2220
William, Lynde & Williams Analysis of Personal Values, 1441

Winter Haven Lions Research Foundation, Inc., P.O. Box 111, Winter Haven, Fla. 33880:
Perceptual Forms Test, 1881

Wonderlic (E. F.) & Associates, Inc., Box 7, Northfield, Ill. 60093:
Wonderlic Personnel Selection Procedure, 2320
Wonderlic Personnel Test, 482

Woodruff (Asahel D.), 485 North Hills Drive, Salt Lake City, Utah 84103:
Study of Choices, 1402

Woolner (Rosestelle B.), 3551 Aurora Circle, Memphis, Tenn. 38111:
Preschool Self-Concept Picture Test, 1332

Wyman (Earl J.), Box 200, Delafield, Wis. 53018:
Supervisory Inventory on Discipline, 2461
Supervisory Inventory on Grievances, 2462
Supervisory Inventory on Labor Relations, 2464

Youth Research Center, 122 West Franklin Ave., Minneapolis, Minn. 55404:
Youth Research Survey, 1029

Zaner-Bloser Co., 612 North Park St., Columbus, Ohio 43215:
Expressional Growth Through Handwriting Evaluation Scale, 909

Zenith Hearing Instrument Corporation, 6501 West Grand Ave., Chicago, Ill. 60635:
Four Tone Screening for Older Children and Adults, 2036
Verbal Auditory Screening for Children, 2059
ZECO Pure Tone Screening for Children, 2062
Zenith Audiometers, 2063

Zung (William W. K.), Veterans Administration Hospital, Fulton St. and Erwin Road, Durham, N.C. 27705:
Self-Rating Depression Scale, 1377

INDEX OF TITLES

American Council Solid Geometry Test, T:1101
American Council Trigonometry Test, 2:1473
American Government and Citizenship: Every Pupil Test, 6:1014
American Government: Cooperative Social Studies Tests, 2005
American Government: Every Pupil Scholarship Test, 6:1015
American Handwriting Scale, 6:712
American History: Achievement Examinations for Secondary Schools, *see* Social Studies Grade 10 (American History), 1999
American History: Cooperative Social Studies Tests, 1988
American History: Every Pupil Scholarship Test, 6:996
American History: Every Pupil Test, 6:997
American History–Government–Problems of Democracy: Acorn Achievement Tests, 1936
American History: Junior High—Objective, 1982; Senior High—Objective, 1983
American History: Midwest High School Achievement Examinations, *see* Social Studies Grade 10, 1999
American History Test: Affiliation Testing Program for Catholic Secondary Schools, 6:998
American History Test for Catholic Elementary Schools, 35:285
American History Test: National Achievement Tests, 1984
American History Test: State High School Tests for Indiana, 4:682
American History: 20th Century Test, *see* Semester Test for American History, T:1780, 4:683
American Home Scale, 1039
American Institute of Certified Public Accountants Testing Programs, 2323
American Literacy Test, 164
American Literature Anthology Tests, 126
American Literature: Every Pupil Scholarship Test, 5:208
American Literature: Every Pupil Test, 6:294
American Numerical Test, 693
American School Achievement Tests, 4
American School Achievement Tests: Arithmetic, 695
American School Achievement Tests: Arithmetic Readiness, 694
American School Achievement Tests: Language and Spelling, 52
American School Achievement Tests: Reading, 1532
American School Achievement Tests: Social Studies and Science, 1937
American School Intelligence Test, 339
American School Reading Readiness Test, 1694
American School Reading Tests, 1533
American Transit Association Tests, 2469
Analysis of Choices (status unknown), T:1855
Analysis of Controversial Writing: Test 5.31, R:255, 2:1527
Analysis of Learning Potential, 340
Analysis of Readiness Skills: Reading and Mathematics, 1695
Analysis of Relationships, 341
Analysis Sheet for the Thematic Apperception Test, 1519a
Analytic Geometry: Cooperative Mathematics Tests, 745
Analytical Geometry Test: ERB Mathematics Tests, 7:467a
Analytical Scales of Attainment in American History, 2:1631
Analytical Scales of Attainment in Arithmetic, 2:1447
Analytical Scales of Attainment in Elementary Science, 2:1598

Analytical Scales of Attainment in Geography, 2:1625
Analytical Scales of Attainment in Literature, 2:1295
Analytical Survey Test in Computational Arithmetic, 696
Analytical Survey Test in English Fundamentals, 53
Anatomy and Physiology: Achievement Tests in Nursing, 2376a
Anatomy and Physiology: NLN Achievement Tests, 2383a1
Ancient History: Every Pupil Scholarship Test, 6:999
Anderson Chemistry Test, *see* Anderson-Fisk Chemistry Test, 7:840
Anderson-Fisk Chemistry Test, 7:840
Andover School-Entrance Test, *see* Kent Series of Emergency Scales, 503a
Anecdotal Observation Form: Ohio Teaching Record, 877
Anglo American Cultural Attitude Scale, 1426a
Animal Crackers, 1099
Animal Husbandry Test: State High School Tests for Indiana, 3:365
Animal Puzzles, P:493, 1:1057
Annual High School Mathematics Examination, 598
Annual Scholastic News Examination, 36:622
Anton Brenner Developmental Gestalt Test of School Readiness, 1696
Anxiety Scale for the Blind, 1100
Apparatus Test, Sep-1, 561s1
Application for Position: Clerical Tests, Series N, 2123f; Series V, 2124f
Application Interview Screening Form, 2295
Application-Interview Series, 5:892
Application-Interview Series: Job-Tests Program, 1078c
Application of Certain Principles of Logical Reasoning: Test, 5.12, R:256, 2:1528
Application of Principles in Biological Science: Test 1.33A, 2:1584; in Physical Science, Test 1.34, 2:1606; in Science, Test 1.3b, 2:1599
Applied Biological and Agribusiness Interest Inventory, 2169
Applied Natural Sciences: NLN Achievement Tests, 2383c3
Applied Reading for Junior-Senior High School: Every Pupil Test, R:257, 3:534
Appraisal of Occupational Aptitudes, 2120
Appraisal of Reading Versatility, *see* Reading Versatility Test, 1673
Aptitests, *see* ETSA Tests, 2106
Aptitude Assessment Battery: Programming, 2331
Aptitude Index, 6:1168b
Aptitude Index for Life Insurance Salesmen, *see* Aptitude Index Selection Procedure, 6:1168
Aptitude Index Selection Procedure, 6:1168
Aptitude-Intelligence Tests, *see* Factored Aptitude Series, 1078a
Aptitude Inventory, 2102
Aptitude Test C.P.66, *see* C.P.66 Test, 347
Aptitude Test E51 for Electronic Data-Processing Programmers (status unknown), T:2015
Aptitude Test for Elementary School Teachers-in-Training, 4:792
Aptitude Test for Junior Secondary Bantu Pupils in Form I, *see* Aptitude Test for Junior Secondary Pupils, 1065
Aptitude Test for Junior Secondary Pupils, 1065
Aptitude Test for Nursing, 2381a
Aptitude Test: Undergraduate Record Examinations, *see* Undergraduate Program Aptitude Test, 470
Aptitude Tests for Occupations, 1066
Aptitudes and Abilities: A Rating Procedure, 1208d
Aptitudes Associates Test of Sales Aptitude, 2395
Archery Skills Test, 913a
Architectural School Aptitude Test, 2359

Automata EDT 1200 Educational Data Terminal, 1030
Automata 450 Test Scorer, *see* Automata EDT 1200 Educational Data Terminal, 1030
Automated Graphogestalt Technique, 976
Automotive Mechanic Test, 6:1185
Awareness Test in 20th Century Literature, 4:182
Axiometric Test, *see* Hartman Value Profile, 1211
Ayer Standardized Spelling Test, 6:317
Ayer's Cumulative Records, T:1302
Ayres Handwriting Scale, *see* Ayres Measuring Scale for Handwriting: Gettysburg Edition, 908
Ayres Measuring Scale for Handwriting: Gettysburg Edition, 908
Ayres Space Test, 1104

B-B-ESS Inventory, 2403f6
BEC Personality Rating Schedule, P:297, 1:915
BITCH Test, 343
BSCS Achievement Tests, 1801
BSCS Quarterly Achievement Tests, *see* BSCS Achievement Tests, 1801
Babcock Test of Mental Deterioration, *see* Babcock Test of Mental Efficiency, 1105
Babcock Test of Mental Efficiency, 1105
Babcock's Mental Deterioration Scale, *see* Babcock Test of Mental Efficiency, 1105
Baby Grid, 947a
Baker-Schulberg Community Mental Health Ideology Scale, 1106
Ballard's Mental Tests, T:1356
Ballard's New Examiner Tests, T:1361
Ballard's Reading Tests, R:88
Balthazar Scales of Adaptive Behavior, 1107
Baltimore Age Calculator, T:1147
Baltimore County French Test, 241
Baltimore County Spanish Test, 303
Barclay Classroom Climate Inventory, 1108
Barr-Harris Teacher's Performance Record, 4:793
Barrett-Ryan English Test, 54
Barrett-Ryan Literature Test, 3:139
Barrett-Ryan-Schrammel English Test, 5:176
Barron-Welsh Art Scale, 1109
Basic Arithmetic Skills: Iowa Every-Pupil Tests of Basic Skills, 4:408
Basic Concept Inventory, 1697
Basic Employment Test, 3:221b
Basic Fitness Tests, 917
Basic Interest Questionnaire, 3:633
Basic Language Skills: Iowa Every-Pupil Tests of Basic Skills, 4:150
Basic Mathematics Tests, 599
Basic Number Skills Test for Employee Selection (status unknown), 5:466
Basic Nursing Procedures and Elementary Nutrition, 6:1158b
Basic Pharmacology: NLN Achievement Tests, 2383a5
Basic Reading Inventory, *see* Adult Basic Reading Inventory, 1736
Basic Reading Rate Scale, 1748
Basic Reading Tests, R:89, 1:1096
Basic Screen Test—Vision: Measurement of Skill Test 12, 1908
Basic Screening and Referral Form for Children With Suspected Learning and Behavioral Disabilities, 977
Basic Sight Word Test, 1657
Basic Skills in Arthmetic Test, 704
Basketball Scale for Women, 918a
Basketball Skills Test, 913b
Baxter Parent-Teacher Test of Child Feelings, P:298c, 4:32c
Baxter Test of Child Feelings, P:298b, 4:32b
Bayley Scales of Infant Development, 484
Beach Music Test, 3:174
Bear Test on United States Constitution, T:1798

Beard-Erbe Social Science Tests, 2:1614
Becker-Schrammel Plane Geometry, 2:1465
Beginner's Clerical Test, 6:1032
Behavior Cards, 1110
Behavior Description, P:299, 1:898
Behavior Interpretation Inventory (status unknown), T:114
Behavior Maturity Blank, P:300, 2:1209
Behavior Maturity Rating Scale for Nursery School Children, P:301, 2:1210
Behavior Preference Record, P:302, 5:32
Behavior Ratings of Pupils, 1336a
Behavior Status Inventory, 1111
Behavioral Complexity Test, P:494, 6:202
Behavioral Values Inventory, *see* Risk-Taking-Attitude-Values Inventory, 1354a
Behaviordyne Psychodiagnostic Lab Service (CPI), 1122; (MMPI), 1282
Behn-Rorschach Test, 1499a
Beliefs About School Life: Test 4.6, P:303, 2:1211
Bellak TAT and CAT Blank, Short Form, 1519b
Bellak TAT Blank, 1519c
Belmont Measures of Athletic Performance, 918
Beltone Audiometers, 2032
Belwin-Mills Singing Achievement Test, 195
Bender Gestalt Test, 1447b
Bender Gestalt Test for Young Children, 1447e
Bender Visual Motor Gestalt Test for Children, 1447d
Benge Employment Tests (status unknown), 3:221
Benge Han-Dexterity Test (status unknown), 3:656
Benge Two Hand Coordination Test, 3:657
Bennett Mechanical Comprehension Test, 2239
Bennett Use of Library Test, R:258, 4:578
Benton Visual Retention Test, 543
Bernreuter Personality Inventory, *see* Personality Inventory, 1320
Bero-Test, *see* Behn-Rorschach Test, 1499a
Berry-Talbott Language Test, 55
Best Thing to Do: A Test of Knowledge of Social Standards, 4:471
Best Thing to Do: Northwestern University Citizenship Tests, 35:87
Betts Ready to Read Tests, 1:1097
Bible and You, 1023
Bible History Tests, 5:589
Biblical Survey Test, 1024
Bicycle Safety—Performance and Skill Tests, 843
Billett-Starr Youth Problems Inventory, P:304, 6:66
Bingham Button Test, 485
Binion-Beck Reading Readiness Test, 1698
Binocular Reading Test, *see* Spache Binocular Reading Test, 1929
Biographical Index, 2274
Biographical Inventory [CEEB], 1052a1
Biographical Inventory—Creativity, 544
Biographical Inventory for Students, 7:43, P:17
Biographical Inventory, Forms A–C, C–I, and J–O, *see* Alpha Biographical Inventory, 2273
Biographical Profile, 6:1168a
Biological Science: Interaction of Experiments and Ideas, 1802
Biological Science: Patterns and Processes, 7:810
Biology and General Science: National Teacher Examinations, 1788; Teacher Education Examination Program, 1797
Biology: Cooperative Science Tests, 1808
Biology: Every Pupil Scholarship Test, 6:888
Biology: Every Pupil Test, 6:889
Biology: Minnesota High School Achievement Examinations, 1803
Biology Test: Affiliation Testing Program for Catholic Secondary Schools, 6:891
Biology Test: State High School Tests for Indiana, 4:598

Case Study Tests in Human Growth and Development, T :1180
Cass-Sanders Psychology Test, 1004
Cassel Developmental Record, 1010
Cassel Group Level of Aspiration Test, 1124
Cassel Psychotherapy Progress Record, P :33, 6 :74
Catholic Book Tests, 6 :296
Cattell Culture Fair Intelligence Test, 364b
Cattell Infant Intelligence Scale, 487
Cattell Intelligence Tests, 354
Cause and Effect Relationship Test in Science, 2 :1600
Center-Durost Literature Acquaintance Test, 5 :210
Central Wisconsin Colony Scales of Adaptive Behavior, *see* Balthazar Scales of Adaptive Behavior, 1107
Chapin Social Insight Test, 1125
Chapman-Cook Speed of Reading Test, R :232, 3 :522
Chapman Reading Comprehension Test, R :91, 5 :623
Chapman Unspeeded Reading Comprehension Test, *see* Chapman Reading Comprehension Test, R :91, 5 :623
Character and Inventory Chart, P :308, 1 :917
Character and Personality Rating Scale, P :307, 2 :1215
Character-Conduct Self-Rating Scale for Students, T :127
Chart for Diagnosing Defects in Buttonholes, T :1256
Chart for the Rating of a Foreman, 5 :915
Chart of Significant Variations in Severity of the Stuttering Problem Since Onset, 2074a
Charts for Analysis Group Test Results, 35 :428
Chatterji's Non-Language Preference Record, 2173
Check List for Self-Guidance in Choosing an Occupation, 2 :1649
Check List of Novels, 4 :183
Check List of Occupations, 2 :1650
Check List of Stuttering Reactions, 2074m
Check List Review : L & L Clerical Tests, 2133b
Checking : Short Tests of Clerical Ability, 2155b
Checking Test, *see* RBH Checking Test, 2143
Checklist of One Hundred Magazines, 2 :1297
Chemical Operators Selection Test, 2360
Chemistry : Achievement Examinations for Secondary Schools, 1834
Chemistry Achievement Test for CHEM Study or Equivalent, 1835
Chemistry Aptitude : Iowa Placement Examinations, 1844
Chemistry : Cooperative Science Tests, 1840
Chemistry : Every Pupil Scholarship Test, 6 :910
Chemistry : Every Pupil Test, 6 :911
Chemistry : Minnesota High School Achievement Examinations, 1836
Chemistry : NLN Achievement Tests, 2383a2
Chemistry, Physics and General Science : National Teacher Examinations, 1789 ; Teacher Education Examination Program, 1798
Chemistry Test : Affiliation Testing Program for Catholic Secondary Schools, 6 :913
Chemistry Test : State High School Tests for Indiana, 4 :616
Chemistry Test : Undergraduate Program Field Tests, 1848
Chemistry Training : Iowa Placement Examinations, 1845
Chicago Algebra Test, *see* Illinois Algebra Test, 680
Chicago Arithmetic Readiness Test, 3 :337
Chicago Arithmetic Survey Tests, 3 :338
Chicago Non-Verbal Examination, 355
Chicago Plane Geometry Test, 5 :491
Chicago Reading Tests, R :92, 3 :478
Chicago Tests of Primary Mental Abilities, *see* SRA Primary Mental Abilities, 1087
Child Behavior Rating Scale, 1126
Child Development, 7 :615

Child Development : State High School Tests for Indiana, *see* Child Development, 7 :615
Child in Residential Care : Bristol Social Adjustment Guides, 1112b
Child in School : Bristol Social Adjustment Guides, 1112a
Child in the Family : Bristol Social Adjustment Guides, 1112c
Child Personality Scale, *see* Personality Rating Scale, 1321
Children 10 O-A Battery, P :344d, 5 :90e
Children 14 O-A Battery, P :344c, 5 :90d
Children's Apperception Test, 1451
Children's Auditory Test, 6 :944
Children's Behavior Rating Scale, T :116e
Children's Embedded Figures Test, 1127
Children's Hypnotic Susceptibility Scale, 1128
Children's Perceptual Achievement Forms, *see* Perceptual Forms Test, 1881
Children's Personality Questionnaire, 1129
Children's Picture Information Test, 6 :516
Choosing a Path, Ss-2, 561t2
Christensen-Guilford Fluency Tests, 546
Christian Democracy Test (Civics, Sociology, Economics) : Affiliation Testing Program for Catholic Secondary Schools, 6 :964
Chriswell Structural Dexterity Test, 2240
Chronological Age Computer, 804
Cicero Test, 2 :1363
Circles Test : Classification Test Battery, 2104c
Citizenship : Every Pupil Scholarship Test, 6 :965
Civic Vocabulary Test, 5 :830
Civics : Cooperative Social Studies Tests, 2006
Civics : Every Pupil Test, 1 :1145
Civics : 20th Century Test, *see* 20th Century Test for Civics, T :1814
Clapp-Young Arithmetic Test, 3 :339
Clapp-Young English Test, 3 :117
Class Activity-Analysis Chart, T :1181
Class Pictures, 1336b1
Classification and Placement Examination, 9
Class Play, 1336b2
Classification Tasks, 488
Classification Test Battery, 2104
Classification Test for Beginners in Reading, R :202, 3 :515
Classification Test for Industrial and Office Personnel, *see* Personnel Research Institute Classification Test, 431
Classification Test 40-A, 6 :448
Classifying Test, *see* RBH Classifying Test, 2144
Classroom Atmosphere Questionnaire, 855
Classroom Environment Index, 1395a
Classroom Reading Inventory, 1618
Cleeton Vocational Interest Inventory, 3 :635
Clerical Aptitude Test, 780
Clerical Perception Test, 3 :624
Clerical Problems : O'Rourke Clerical Aptitude Test, 2138a
Clerical Routine Aptitude : Aptitude Tests for Occupations, 1066d
Clerical Skills Series, 2121
Clerical Speed and Accuracy : Clerical Skills Series, 2121c
Clerical Speed and Accuracy : Differential Aptitude Tests, 781
Clerical Test D (status unknown), 3 :625
Clerical Tests, 2122
Clerical Tests FG and 2, 781A
Clerical Tests 1 and 2, *see* Clerical Tests FG and 2, 781A
Clerical Tests, Series N, 2123 ; Series V, 2124
Clerical Worker, *see* Clerical Worker Examination, 2125

5:477; Oral Diagnostic Test in Addition, 3:348; Survey Test of Arithmetic Fundamentals, 739

Dominion Tests [Miscellaneous]: Group Achievement Test, 1934 Edition, 5:12; Group Achievement Tests: Niagara Edition, 5:13

Dominion Tests [Reading]: Achievement Test in Silent Reading, R:5, 5:619; Group Test of Reading Readiness, 1704; Oral Diagnostic Test of Word-Analysis Skills, Primary, R:170, 5:673

Dominion Tests [Social Studies]: World Geography Test, 3:603

Dominion Tests of Learning Capacity, *see* Group Test of Learning Capacity: Dominion Tests, 387

Doppelt Mathematical Reasoning Test, 371

Doren Diagnostic Reading Test of Word Recognition Skills, 1627

Drake Musical Aptitude Tests, 5:245

Drake Musical Memory Test, 3:175

Drama and Theatre Test: Undergraduate Program Field Tests, 2096

Draw-A-Man Test for Indian Children, 372

Draw-A-Person, 1455

Draw-A-Person Quality Scale, 1456

Drawing Aptitute Test, 2:1512.1

Drawing-Completion Test, P:496, 5:130

Drawing: Cooperative Industrial Arts Tests, 967

Driscoll Play Kit, 1457

Driver Attitude Survey, 844

Driver Education Teacher Performance Inventory, 7:575

Driver Scalogram, T:1163

Driver Selection Forms and Tests, 2470

Driving Attitude Inventory, *see* Lauer Driver Reaction Inventory, 5:593

Driving Skill Exercises, 845

Drug Abuse Knowledge Test, 922

Drug Abuse Test, *see* Drug Abuse Knowledge Test, 922

Drug Knowledge Inventory, 923

Dubins Earth Science Test, 1853

Duke University Political Science Information Test (American Government), 6:1017

Dunlap Academic Preference Blank, P:315, 3:35

Dunlap-Abeles Physics Test, 1863

Dunning Physics Test, *see* Dunning-Abeles Physics Test, 1863

Duplex Series of Ability Tests, 4:289

Durost-Center Word Mastery Test, 6:330

Durrell Analysis of Reading Difficulty, 1628

Durrell Listening-Reading Series, 1660

Durrell-Sullivan Reading Capacity and Achievement Tests, 1661

Dvorak-Van Wagenen Diagnostic Examination of Silent Reading Abilities, *see* Diagnostic Examination of Silent Reading Abilities, 1622

Dvorine Animated Fusion Training Charts (status unknown), T:1683

Dvorine Color Discrimination Screening Test, 3:461a

Dvorine Color Perception Testing Charts, *see* Dvorine Pseudo-Isochromatic Plates, 1911

Dvorine Color Vision Test, *see* Dvorine Pseudo-Isochromatic Plates, 1911

Dvorine Pseudo-Isochromatic Plates, 1911

Dynamic Personality Inventory, 1162

Dynamicube Test of Power to Visualize, 1:1167

Dyslexia Schedule, 1662

EB Punch-Key Scoring and Answer Sheet System, 6:663

EM-AY Inventory, 2403e1

ERB Mathematics Tests, 7:467

ERB Modern Arithmetic Test, 718

ERB Modern Elementary Algebra Test, 675

ERB Modern Mathematics Test, 616

ERB Modern Second Year Algebra Test, 676

E.R.C. Stenographic Aptitude Test, 3:372

ESS-AY Inventory, 2403e2

ESS-EYE Inventory, 2403f5

ETSA Tests, 2106

Eames Eye Test, 6:956

Ear Tests in Harmony, 1:1084

Early Childhood Education: National Teacher Examinations, 870; Teacher Education Examination Program, 899

Early Detection Inventory, 7:746, R:183

Early Primary Mathematics Survey Test, 649a

Early Primary Reading Survey Test, 1577a

Early Primary Survey Test, 27a

Early School Personality Questionnaire, 1163

Earth Science Test: Content Evaluation Series, 1792b

Easel Age Scale, 5:332

Easy Steps in Arithmetic, T:1058

Eaton Book-Report, 35:212

Eaton Book-Report System, 1:972

Eaton Diagnostic-Accomplishment Tests in English, T:421

Eaton Literature Tests, T:496

Eaton Self-Correcting Literature Tests, 35:214

Eckstein Audiometers, 2034

Economic Distance, P:381d, 4:88d

Economic Geography: Achievement Examinations for Secondary Schools, 1974

Economics: Every Pupil Scholarship Test, 35:154

Economics/Objective Tests, 1964

Economics Test: State High School Tests for Indiana, 4:670

Economics Test: Undergraduate Program Field Tests, 1972

Economics: 20th Century Test, 4:671

Edinburgh Articulation Test, 2070

Edinburgh Reading Tests, 1548

Edmiston How to Study Test, R:262, 4:580

Edmiston Inventory of Interest, 4:738

Edmiston Motor Capacity Test, 4:649

Edmiston RO Inventory, T:1863

Education Apperception Test, 1458

Education in an Urban Setting: National Teacher Examinations, 871

Education in the Elementary School: National Teacher Examinations, 872

Education of Mentally Retarded: National Teacher Examinations, 873

Education Test: Undergraduate Program Field Tests, 906

Educational Administration and Supervision: National Teacher Examinations, 874

Educational Aptitude Test, 3:400

Educational Background Questionnaire, 1:869b

Educational Evaluation of Preschool Children, *see* Developmental Potential of Preschool Children, 1156

Educational Guidance Test: Kefauver-Hand Guidance Tests and Inventories, 2:1661a

Educational Interest Inventory [Oliver], 2178

Educational Interest Inventory [Symonds and others], 5:535

Educational Planning Questionnaire, 24b

Educational Progress Sheet: Michigan Adult Profile, 1:1171a

Educational Skills Tests, 13

Educational Tests for New York Stock Exchange Member Organization Employees (status unknown), T:2019

Educational Values, *see* VAL-Ed, 1176g

Educational Values Assessment Questionnaire, 860

Edwards Personal Preference Schedule, 1164

Edwards Personality Inventory, 1165

Effectiveness of Expression: Cooperative English Test, 5:179c

English Placement Test for Iowa Universities and Colleges, 1:958

English Progress Tests, 75

English Reading Test for Students of English as a Foreign Language (status unknown), 5:258

English Recognition Vocabulary Test, 3:161

English Survey Test: Ohio Senior Survey Tests, 5:188

English Test FG, 76

English Test (Four-Year Course): Affiliation Testing Program for Catholic Secondary Schools, 6:263

English Test: Municipal Tests, 77

English Test: National Achievement Tests, 78

English Test 2, *see* English Test FG, 76

English Tests (Adv.), 79

English Tests for Outside Reading, 134

English Tests 14–20 and 22, 80

English: Thanet Mental Tests, 2:1279

English Training: Iowa Placement Examinations, 87

English: Understanding and Appreciation of Poetry: State High School Tests for Indiana, 3:143

English Usage: Every Pupil Test, 6:265

English Usage Test for Non-Native Speakers of English, 230

English Vocabulary Tests for High School and College Students, T:565

Entrance and Classification Examination for Teachers Colleges: Elementary Test, 2:1185

Entrance and Classification Examination for Teachers Colleges: English Test, 2:1280

Entrance Examination for Schools of Nursing, 2379

Entrance Examination for Schools of Practical Nursing, 2380

Entrance Questionnaire and Experience Record, 2:1658

Environment Inventory for College and University Students, P:316, 2:1218

Environmental Participation Index, 1040

Essential High School Content Battery, 4:9

Essential Intelligence Test, 373

Essential Junior Intelligence Test, *see* Essential Intelligence Test, 373

Essential Mechanical Arithmetic Test, 3:342a

Essential Problem Arithmetic Test, 3:342b

Essentials of English Tests, 81

Estimation of Length Test, Le-1, 561hl

Ethical Judgment Test, 35:93

Ethnic Distance Scale, P:381a, 4:88a

Euphrorimeter, P:317, 3:36

European and American Literature Test, 144b

European and American Literature Test: A Modular Test, 144b

Evaluating the Effectiveness of Oral English, T:522

Evaluation and Adjustment Series [English]: Center-Durost Literature Acquaintance Test, 5:210; Durost-Center Word Mastery Test, 6:330; Greene-Stapp Language Abilities Test, 5:195

Evaluation and Adjustment Series [Mathematics]: Blyth Second-Year Algebra Test, 668; Davis Test of Functional Competence in Mathematics, 5:422; Howell Geometry Test, 750; Lankton First-Year Algebra Test, 683; Madden-Peak Arithmetic Computation Test, 6:624; Seattle Algebra Test, 6:601; Seattle Plane Geometry Test, 5:497; Shaycoft Plane Geometry Test, 5:498; Snader General Mathematics Test, 5:439

Evaluation and Adjustment Series [Miscellaneous]: Brown-Carlsen Listening Comprehension Test, 993; Engle Psychology Test, 5:582; Kilander Health Knowledge Test, 5:562

Evaluation and Adjustment Series [Personality]: Billett-Starr Youth Problems Inventory, P:304, 6:66

Evaluation and Adjustment Series [Reading]: Kelley-Greene Reading Comprehension Test, R:35, 5:636; Spitzer Study Skills Test, R:244, 6:864

Evaluation and Adjustment Series [Science]: Anderson-Fisk Chemistry Test, 7:840; Dubins Earth Science Test, 1853; Dunning-Abeles Physics Test, 1863; Nelson Biology Test, 1812; Read General Science Test, 7:796

Evaluation and Adjustment Series [Social Studies]: Crary American History Test, 1992; Cummings World History Test, 7:917; Dimond-Pflieger Problems of Democracy Test, 5:833; Peltier-Durost Civics and Citizenship Test, 6:1019

Evaluation Aptitude Test, 1757

Evaluation in the Eight Year Study Tests [English]: Alphabetical List of 1000 Fiction Authors Classified by Subject and Maturity Level, 2:1294; Checklist of One Hundred Magazines, 2:1297; Interpretation of Literature: Test 3.1, 4:187; Judging the Effectiveness of Written Composition: Test 3.8, 2:1283; Literary Information Test: American Literature: Test 3.5, 2:1288; Literary Information Test: English Literature: Test 3.4, 2:1289; Literature Questionnaire: The Drama: Test 3.21, 2:1302; Literature Questionnaire: The Novel: Test 3.2a, 2:1303; Questionnaire on Voluntary Reading: Test 3.31, 2:1305

Evaluation in the Eight Year Study Tests [Fine Arts]: Seven Modern Paintings: Test 3.9, 2:1328

Evaluation in the Eight Year Study Tests [Personality]: Beliefs About School Life: Test 4.6, P:303, 2:1211; Interest Index: Test 8.2a, P:329, 2:1226; Interest Questionnaire: Games and Sports: Test 8.3, P:330, 2:1227; Interests and Activities: Tests 8.2b and 8.2c, P:332, 2:1225; Radio Checklist, P:368, 2:1245; Scale of Beliefs: Tests 4.21 and 4.31, P:375, 2:1250; Scale of Beliefs for Junior High School: Tests 4.4 and 4.5, P:374, 2:1251; Social Problems: Test 1.42, P:385, 2:1254

Evaluation in the Eight Year Study Tests [Reading]: Analysis of Controversial Writing: Test 5.31, R:255, 2:1527; Application of Certain Principles of Logical Reasoning: Test 5.12, R:256, 2:1528; Critical-Mindedness in the Reading of Fiction: Test 3.7, R:261, 2:1530; Interpretation of Data: Tests 2.51 and 2.52, 3:535; Interpretation of Data: Test 2.71, R:265, 2:1545; Nature of Proof: Test 5:22, R:270, 2:1556; Test on the Use of Books and Libraries: Test 7.3, R:281, 2:1577

Evaluation in the Eight Year Study Tests [Science]: Application of Principles in Biological Science: Test 1.33A, 2:1584; Application of Principles in Physical Science: Test 1.34, 2:1606; Application of Principles in Science: Test 1.3b, 2:1599; Test of Application of Principles in Physical Science, 4:594

Evaluation Modality Test, 1172

Evaluation of Attitudes Toward Home and Family Life, T:150

Evaluation Record, 2398

Evaluation Scales for Guiding Growth in Handwriting, *see* Expressional Growth Through Handwriting Evaluation Scale, 909

Evanston Early Identification Scale, 7:747

Evening College Characteristics Index, 1395e

Every-Day Life, P:75, 4:41

Every Pupil Achievement Test: Elementary Reading, R:23, 6:788; Primary Reading, R:52, 6:803

Every Pupil Primary Achievement Test, 3:7

Every Pupil Scholarship Tests [Business Education]: Bookkeeping, 6:34; Business Arithmetic, 36:582; Commercial Law, 6:38; General Business, 6:31; Stenography, Gregg, 35:135; Typewriting, 6:54

Every Pupil Scholarship Tests [English]: American Literature, 5:208; Elementary English Test, 35:182; English and American Literature, 35:215; English, 6:257; Literature, 6:301; Spelling, 6:325; Vocabulary, 6:339

Record for High School and College Students, R :144, 5 :666

Examining for Aphasia, 2071

Exceptional Teacher Service Record, 4 :796

Executive Employment Review, 374

Executive, Industrial, and Sales Personnel Forms, 2302

Exercises in the Use of Historical Evidence, 35 :301

Existential Analysis, *see* Existential Study : Integration Level Test Series, 1237f

Existential Study : Integration Level Test Series, 1237f

Experience Variables Record, P :318, 2 :1219

Experiential World Inventory, 1173

Experimental Comparative Prediction Batteries, 7 :674

Expression : Flanagan Aptitude Classification Tests, 1072a14

Expression : Flanagan Industrial Tests, 2107a6

Expression Grouping : Tests of Social Intelligence, 1421b

Expressional Fluency : Christiansen-Guilford Fluency Tests, 546d ; [Fe-1], 561d1

Expressional Fluency, [Fe-1], 561d1

Expressional Growth Through Handwriting Evaluation Scale, 909

Expressive Movement Chart, P :497, 4 :104

Eye-Hand Accuracy : Clerical Skills Series, 2121e

Eye Movement Camera, T :1686

Eysenck Personal Inventory, *see* Eysenck Personality Inventory, 1174

Eysenck Personality Inventory, 1174

Eysenck-Withers Personality Inventory, 1175

"F" [Fluency of Association] Test, P :498, 2 :1220

FIRO Scales, 1176

FIRO-B : Fundamental Interpersonal Relations Orientation—Behavior, 1176a

FIRO-BC, 1176b

FIRO-F : Fundamental Interpersonal Relations Orientation—Feelings, 1176c

FR-CR Test, 4 :339; now available only as a subtest of Leiter Adult Intelligence Scale, 504

Factored Aptitude Series, 1078a

Factorial Interest Blank, 2179

Factory Terms : Factored Aptitude Series, 1078a3

Facts About Science Test, 6 :921

Faculty Morale Scale for Institutional Improvement, 861

Fairfield Block Substitution Test, *see* Grassi Block Substitution Test, 1196

Fairview Development Scale, 1177

Fairview Language Evaluation Scale, 2072

Fairview Problem Behavior Record, 1178

Fairview Self-Help Scale, 1179

Fairview Social Skills Scale, 1180

Family Adjustment Test, 1181

Family Life, 7 :622

Family Relations Indicator, 1459

Family Relations Test, 1182

Famous Sayings, 1183

Fantasy Scale (status unknown), T :156

Farm Shop Tools : State High School Tests for Indiana, 4 :441

Farnsworth Dichotomous Test for Color Blindness : Panel D-15, 1912

Farnsworth-Munsell 100-Hue Test for the Examination of Color Discrimination, 1913

Farnum Music Notation Test, 5 :246

Fatigue Scales Kit, 1184

Fear Survey Schedule, 1185

Feature Profile Test : Pintner-Paterson Modification, 556

Federal Constitution Scale, P :371

Fels Parent Behavior Rating Scales, 1186

Femininity Study : Integration Level Test Series, 1237h

Ferguson Formboards, 2 :1394

Fernald Weights Discrimination Test, T :923

Fetler Self-Rating Test, *see* Style of Mind Inventory, 1405

Field Hockey Scale, 918b

Fields of Occupational Interest, T :1864

Fiesenheiser Test of Ability to Read Drawings, 2416

Fife Tests of Ability, 4 :713

Figure Classification, I-3, 561g3

Figure Reasoning Test, 375

Fiji Test of General Ability, 2 :1395

Filing 7A : Selection Tests for Office Personnel, 2150g

Filing : Short Tests of Clerical Ability, 2155c

Filing Test : National Clerical Ability Tests, *see* Filing Test : United-NOMA Business Entrance Tests, 3 : 379

Filing Test : Personnel Research Institute Clerical Battery, 2140d

Filing Test : United-NOMA Business Entrance Tests, 3 :379

Filmed Demonstration of the ITPA, 982

Finding A's Test, P-1, 561n1

Finger Dexterity Board : General Aptitude Test Battery, 1073c

Finger Dexterity Test, *see* O'Connor Finger Dexterity Test, 2228

Fire Performance Rating System, 7 :1105

Fire Promotion Tests, 2361

Firefighter Test, 2362

Firefighting Promotion Tests, *see* Fire Promotion Tests, 2361

Fireman Examination, 2363

First and Last Names Test, Ma-3, 561i3

First and Second Year French : Every Pupil Test, 35 :233

First and Second Year Latin : Every Pupil Test, 6 :407

First and Second Year Latin Tests : State High School Tests for Indiana, *see* Latin Test : State High School Tests for Indiana, T :679

First and Second Year Spanish : Every Pupil Test, 35 :477

First Grade Screening Test, 979

First Year Algebra : Every Pupil Scholarship Test, 6 :599

First Year Algebra Test : National Achievement Tests, 679

First Year Algebra Test : State High School Tests for Indiana, *see* Algebra Tests, 7 :496a–b

First Year Algebra : 20th Century Test, *see* 20th Century Test for First Year Algebra, T :1012

First Year Arabic Final Examination, 224

First-Year Arabic Qualifying Examination, *see* First Year Arabic Final Examination, 224

First-Year Bookkeeping : Every Pupil Test, 6 :37

First Year French : State High School Tests for Indiana, T :639, 1 :987

First Year French Test, 249

First Year German Test, 5 :274

First Year Latin : Every Pupil Scholarship Test, 6 :408

First Year Latin : State High School Tests for Indiana, 4 :252

First Year Reading Test, *see* Garrison First Year Reading Test, R :96, 3 :483

First Year Shorthand : Every Pupil Test, 6 :42

First Year Spanish Test, 309

First Year Spanish Test : State High School Tests for Indiana, 4 :261

First Year Typewriting : Every Pupil Test, 6 :49

Fisher-Logemann Test of Articulation Competence, 2073

Five Factor Inventory (status unknown), T :1959

Five Task Test, 1460

Flags : A Test of Space Thinking, 2245

Flanagan Aptitude Classification Tests, 1072

General Business: Every Pupil Scholarship Test, 6:31

General Chemistry: Achievement Tests in Nursing, 2376c

General Chemistry Test: National Achievement Tests, 1842

General Classification Battery, 6:1026a

General Clerical Ability Test: ETSA Test, 2128

General Clerical: Every Pupil Test, 1:937

General Clerical Test, 2129

General Clerical Test, PCI Selection Form 20, *see* General Clerical Test, 2129

General Concepts Test, *see* Tests of Basic Experiences, 47

General Education Series [English]: Check List of Novels, 4:183; Interpretation of Literature Test, 4:187; Inventory of Satisfactions Found in Reading Fiction, 4:188

General Education Series [Miscellaneous]: Health Inventories, 4:484

General Education Series [Personality]: General Goals of Life Inventory, P:320, 4:45; Interest Index, P:329, 4:58; Inventory of Personal-Social Relationships, P:333, 4:60

General Education Series [Reading]: Interpretation of Data Test, R:264, 4:581; Logical Reasoning Test, R:269, 4:582; Test on the Use of Books and Libraries, R:281, 4:585

General Education Series [Science]: Test of Application of Principles in Biology, 4:606; Test of Application of Principles in General Science, 4:629; Test of Application of Principles in Physical Science, 4:594

General Employment Review, *see* Executive Employment Review, 374

General First-Aid Test for Senior-High-School Students, 2:1522

General Goals of Life Inventory, P:320, 4:45

General Home Economics: State High School Tests for Indiana, 1:1030

General Industrial Arts: Cooperative Industrial Arts Tests, 970

General Information and Judgment Test: NLN Pre-Admission and Classification Examination, 2386a

General Information Survey, T:1960

General Information Test, *see* Business Fundamentals and General Information Test, 778

General Information Test: National Clerical Ability Tests, 2:1485

General Intelligence: Northumberland Standardised Tests, T:760

General Intelligence Test for Africans, 2:1396

General Interest Review, *see* Executive Employment Review, 374

General Knowledge Test of Local, State, and National Government, 5:834

General Mathematical Ability, 5:426; now available only as a subtest of Tests of General Educational Development, 48

General Mathematics: Every Pupil Scholarship Test, 6:575

General Mathematics: Every Pupil Test, 6:576

General Mathematics III: Achievement Examinations for Secondary Schools, 617

General Mental Ability Test: ETSA Test, 378

General Municipal Employees Performance (Efficiency) Rating System, 2364

General Office Clerical Test: National Business Entrance Tests, 783

General Physics: Every Pupil Test, *see* Physics: Every Pupil Test, 6:933

General Physics Test: National Achievement Tests, 1865

General Professional Examinations: Teacher Education Examination Program, 41

General Reading Test: Ohio Senior Survey Tests, R:99, 4:534

General Reasoning, *see* Guilford-Zimmerman Aptitude Survey, 1074b

General Safety Education Test for Junior-High-School Pupils, 2:1523

General Sales Aptitude: Aptitude Tests for Occupations, 1066c

General Scholarship Test for High School Seniors, 6:8a

General Science: Cooperative Science Tests, 1781

General Science: Every Pupil Scholarship Test, 6:873

General Science: Every Pupil Test, 6:874

General Science Scales, T:1559

General Science Test for Prospective Nurses, 2381d

General Science Test: Gibson's Attainment Tests, 1:1129

General Science Test: National Achievement Tests, 1785

General Science Test [National Institute for Personnel Research], 1784

General Science Test: State High School Tests for Indiana, 4:592

General Science III: Achievement Examinations for Secondary Schools, 1786

General Speech Behavior Rating, 2074b

General Test of Business Information, 3:380

General Test on Traffic and Driving Knowledge, 846

General Test T, *see* A.C.E.R. Junior Test A, 329

General Tests of Language and Arithmetic, 14

General Tests of Language and Arithmetic for Students, 862

General Verbal Practice Tests G1-G3, 379

General Vocabulary: Iowa Tests of Educational Development, 166

General Voice Quality Examination, 2074e

Generalized Attitude Scales, *see* Purdue Master Attitude Scales, 1348

Geography Ability Test: Gibson's Attainment Tests, 1:990

Geography Achievement Test for Beginning High School Students, 7:904

Geography: Every Pupil Scholarship Test, 6:991

Geography of the Americas: Every Pupil Test, 6:992a1

Geography of the Eastern Hemisphere: Every Pupil Test, 6:992a2

Geography of the World: Every Pupil Test, 6:992b

Geography Test: Ballard's New Examiner Tests, T:1361g

Geography Test: Municipal Tests: National Achievement Tests, 1975

Geography Test: National Achievement Tests, 1976

Geography Test: New Examiner Tests, T:1361g

Geography Test: Undergraduate Program Field Tests, 1979

Geology Test: Undergraduate Program Field Tests, 1851

Geometry and Graphs: N.B. Mathematics Tests, 642g

Geometry Attainment Test, 4:424

Geometry: Cooperative Mathematics Tests, 746

Geometry: Every Pupil Test, 6:646

Geometry (Including Plane and Solid Geometry): Minnesota High School Achievement Examinations, 748

Geometry: Objective Tests in Mathematics, 754

Geometry Survey Test, T:1107

Geometry Test, 7:535

George Washington University Series [Education]: Educational Aptitude Test, 3:400; Teaching Aptitude Test, 904

George Washington University Series [Foreign Languages]: Language Aptitude Test, 3:179

George Washington University Series [Intelligence]: Mental Alertness Test, 3:238

Gray Oral Reading Test, 1681
Gray-Votaw General Achievement Tests, *see* Gray-Votaw-Rogers General Achievement Tests, 15
Gray-Votaw-Rogers General Achievement Tests, 15
Grayson Perceptualization Test, 1197
Greene-Stapp Language Abilities Test, 5:195
Gregory Academic Interest Inventory, 2183
Gregory Diagnostic Tests in Language, 2:1282
Greig Social Studies Test, 5:788
Gretsch-Tilson Musical Aptitude Test, 198
Grid for Evaluating Physical Fitness in Terms of Physique (Body Build), Development Level and Basal Metabolism, 947b
Grid Test of Schizophrenic Thought Disorder, 1198
Griffiths Mental Development Scale for Testing Babies From Birth to Two Years, 6:523
Grossnickle Test of Concepts Found in Social Uses of Arithmetic, 36:535
Group Achievement Tests: Dominion Tests, 1934 Edition, 5:12; Niagara Edition, 5:13
Group Cohesiveness: A Study of Group Morale, 1199
Group Diagnostic Reading Aptitude and Achievement Tests, 1631
Group Diagnostic Spelling Test, 148
Group Dimensions Descriptions Questionnaire, 1200
Group Embedded Figures Test, 1201
Group Mathematics Test, 620
Group Personality Projective Test, 1466
Group Phonics Analysis, 1632
Group Picture Impressions, T:346
Group Projection Sketches for the Study of Small Groups, 1467
Group Psychotherapy Suitability Evaluation Scale, 1202
Group Reading Assessment, 1554
Group Reading Test, 1555
Group Selective Test No. 1, 5:337
Group Test for Indian South Africans, 383
Group Test in Siddur Reading, 3:195
Group Test of General Intelligence: AH4, 331a
Group Test of High-Grade Intelligence: AH5, 331b
Group Test of Intelligence, *see* Group Test of Learning Capacity, 387
Group Test of Learning Capacity: Dominion Tests, 387
Group Test of Reading Readiness: Dominion Tests, 1704
Group Test of Speed and Accuracy in Arithmetic Computation, 5:477
Group Tests [Intelligence]: Group Tests 33 and 33B, 5:339; Group Test 36, 384; Group Tests 70 and 70B, 388; Group Tests 72 and 73, 389; Group Test 75, 385; Group Tests 90A and 90B, 390; Group Test 91, 386; Group Test 95, 386A
Group Tests of High-Level Intelligence: AH6, 331c
Group Tests [Vocations]: Group Test 20, 2130; Group Test 25 (Clerical), 4:724; Group Tests 61A, 64, and 66A, 2131; Group Test 80A, 2248; Group Test 81, 2249; Group Test 82, 2250
Guidance Counselor: National Teacher Examinations, 875
Guidance Cumulative Folder and Record Forms, 1013
Guidance Inventory, 1203
Guidance Questionnaire, 2:1659.1
Guidance Questionnaire for Students of Speech, 3:150
Guidance Summary Form for Use in Vocational and Educational Counseling, 3:446
Guidance Test for Junior Secondary Bantu Pupils in Form III, 16
Guide to Employment Decision, 4:828c
Guilford-Holley L Inventory, 1204
Guilford-Martin Inventory of Factors GAMIN,
Guilford-Martin Personnel Inventory, 1206
Guilford-Martin Temperament Profile Chart, 3
Guilford-Shneidman-Zimmerman Interest Surve

Guilford-Zimmerman Aptitude Survey, 1074; Part 5, Spatial Orientation, [S-3], 561r3
Guilford-Zimmerman Interest Inventory, 2185
Guilford-Zimmerman Temperament Survey, 1207
Gulick Vocabulary Survey, 6:331
Gullo Workshop and Seminar Evaluation, 2280
Guy's Colour Vision Test for Young Children, 1914

HFD Test, 1468
H-T-P: House-Tree-Person Projective Technique, 1469
Hackman-Gaither Vocational Interest Inventory, 2186
Haggerty-Olson-Wickman Behavior Rating Schedules, P:321, 2:1222
Haggerty Reading Examination, R:100, 4:535
Hahn Self Psychoevaluation Materials, 1208
Hahnemann High School Behavior Rating Scale, 1209
Hall Occupational Orientation Inventory, 2187
Hall Salespower Inventory, 2399
Halstead Aphasia Test, 2076
Halstead-Wepman Aphasia Screening Test, *see* Halstead Aphasia Test, 2076
Hamilton Cumulative Record Folder, 3:447
Hamilton Student Information Form, *see* Hamilton Cumulative Record Folder, 3:447
Hammond Matrix Sorter, T:1151
Hand Test, 1470
Hand-Tool Dexterity Test, 2225
Handicap Problems Inventory, 1210
Hanes-Benz Biology Test, 2:1586
Hanes Sales Selection Inventory, 2400
Hankes Answer Sheets, *see* Hankes Scoring Service, 1031
Hankes Scoring Service, 1031
Hannaford Industrial Safety Attitude Scales, 847
Haptic Intelligence Scale for Adult Blind, 498
Harlow Achievement Tests for First and Second Grades, 36:506
Harlow Achievement Tests for Texas, 4:13
Harlow Battery Achievement Test, 4:14
Harris Tests of Lateral Dominance, 1877
Harrison-Stroud Reading Readiness Profiles, 1705
Harrower-Erickson's Group Rorschach, *see* Harrower's Group Rorschach, 1499c
Harrower-Erickson's Multiple Choice Test, *see* Harrower's Multiple Choice Test, 1499d
Harrower's Group Rorschach, 1499c
Harrower's Multiple Choice Test, 1499d
Harrower's Psychodiagnostic Inkblot Test, 1499e
Hartman Value Inventory, *see* Hartman Value Profile, 1211
Hartman Value Profile, 1211
Harvard Group Scale of Hypnotic Susceptibility, 1212
Harvard-MLA Tests of Chinese Language Proficiency, 225
Hay Clerical Test Battery, 2132
Hay Tests for Clerical Aptitude, *see* Hay Clerical Test Battery, 2132
Hazlehurst Primary Mechanical Ability Tests, *see* Primary Mechanical Ability Tests, 2262
Health and Safety Education Test: National Achievement Tests, 926
Health and Safety Education Test: State High School Tests for Indiana, 3:420
Health Awareness Test, 2:1501
Health Behavior Inventory, 927
Health Education and Hygiene: Every Pupil Test, 6:725
Health Education Test: Knowledge and Application: Acorn National Achievement Tests, 928
Health Guidance Test: Kefauver-Hand Guidance Tests and Inventories, 2:1661b
Health Inventories, 4:484
Health Inventory for High School Students, 3:422

Iowa Performance Test of Selected Manual Activities, 2074t

Iowa Placement Examinations [English]: English Aptitude, 86; English Training, 87

Iowa Placement Examinations [Foreign Languages]: Foreign Language Aptitude, 220; French Training, 254; Spanish Training, 313

Iowa Placement Examinations [Mathematics]: Mathematics Aptitude, 621; Mathematics Training, 622

Iowa Placement Examinations [Science]: Chemistry Aptitude, 1844; Chemistry Training, 1845; Physics Aptitude, 1867; Physics Training, 1868

Iowa Plane Geometry Aptitude Test, *see* Iowa Geometry Aptitude Test, 751

Iowa Primary Language Test, T:446, 36:642

Iowa Scale of Attitude Toward Stuttering, 2074O

Iowa Silent Reading Tests, 1560

Iowa Spelling Scales, 149

Iowa Tests of Basic Skills, 19

Iowa Tests of Basic Skills: Modern Mathematics Supplement, 639

Iowa Tests of Educational Development, 20

Iowa Tests of Educational Development [English]: Ability to Interpret Literary Materials, 138; Correctness and Appropriateness of Expression, 88; General Vocabulary, 166

Iowa Tests of Educational Development [Mathematics]: Ability to Do Quantitative Thinking, 623

Iowa Tests of Educational Development [Reading]: Ability to Interpret Reading Materials in the Natural Sciences, 1738; Ability to Interpret Reading Materials in the Social Studies, 1737; Use of Sources of Information, 1758

Iowa Tests of Educational Development [Science]: General Background in the Natural Sciences, 1787

Iowa Tests of Educational Development [Social Studies]: Understanding of Basic Social Concepts, 1944

Iowa Tests of Music Literacy, 199

Iowa Unimanual Hand Usage Questionnaire, 2074s

Ishihara Test for Colour-Blindness, *see* Test for Colour-Blindness, 1932

"Is of Identity" Test, 1246

It Scale for Children, 1247

Italian: MLA Cooperative Foreign Language Proficiency Tests, 286

Italian: MLA-Cooperative Foreign Language Tests, 287

JIM Scale Student Questionnaire, *see* Junior Index of Motivation, 867

JNB Psychograph, P:334, 3:56

JNB Time Test, *see* Time Appreciation Test, 588

Jastak-King Work Samples, *see* Wide Range Employment Sample Test, 2116

Jastak Test of Potential Ability and Behavior Stability, 1077

Jenkins Job Attitudes Survey, 7:1062

Jenkins Non-Verbal Test, *see* Non-Verbal Test 1, 415a1

Jenkins Oral Reading Test, R:177, 2:1548

Jensen Alternation Board, 560A

Jensen I.Q. Dial, T:1156

Jesness Behavior Checklist, 1248

Jesness Inventory, 1249

Jewish Home Environment Test, 3:453

Jewish Information Test, 4:518

Jewish Life and Observances: Uniform Achievement Tests, 5:278b

Jewish People: Uniform Achievement Tests, 5:278c

Job Alertness Tests, T:776

Job Analysis and Interest Measurement, 1250

Job Analysis Form for the Study of Engineering and Scientific Positions, T:1983a

Job Application Forms, 2303

Job Attitude Analysis, 2281

Job Choice Inventory, *see* RBH Job Choice Inventory, 7:1032

Job Description Forms, T:1983

Job Description Questionnaire, 6:1121

Job Qualification Inventory, 3:639

Job Satisfaction Inquiry Blank, *see* Survey of Company Morale, 3:693

Job-Tests Program, 1078

John Bidwell and the Trail to California, *see* Test of Individual Needs in Reading, 1653

Johnson Home Economics Interest Inventory, 5:570

Johnson O'Connor English Vocabulary Worksamples, 167

Johnson O'Connor Vocabulary Tests, 168; Architecture, 168b; Mathematics, 168a; Music, 168c; Physics, 168d; Radio and Physics, 168e; Sports, 168f

Johnson Temperament Analysis, *see* Taylor-Johnson Temperament Analysis, 840

Jones Book-A-Day Tests, 4:189

Jones Music Recognition Test, 200

Jones Personality Rating Scale, 1251

Journalism Test, 2365

Judging the Effectiveness of Written Composition: Test 3.8, 2:1283

Judgment and Comprehension: Flanagan Aptitude Classification Tests, 1072a8

Judgment and Comprehension: Flanagan Industrial Tests, 2107a9

Judgment: Factored Aptitude Series, 1078a7

Judgment Test on Safe Driving Practices, 2:1525

Junior Aptitude Tests for Indian South Africans, 1079

Junior Arithmetic A-F, 710

Junior Chemistry Test, 5:747

Junior College Placement Program, 1054

Junior Eysenck Personality Inventory, 12⁵2

Junior High School Civics Test: State High School Tests for Indiana, 4:704

Junior High School Mathematics Test, 624

Junior High School Record, 1015

Junior Index of Motivation, 867

Junior Math Reasoning Test (status unknown), 6:580

Junior Mathematics Tests A1 and B1 (Oral), *see* Mathematics Attainment Tests (Oral), 629

Junior Mathematics Tests C1 and C3, *see* Mathematics Attainment Tests C1 and C3, 627

Junior Maudsley Inventory, *see* New Junior Maudsley Inventory, 1296

Junior Mental Ability A and B, *see* Cotswold Junior Ability Tests, 362

Junior Mental Ability D and F, *see* Cotswold Junior Ability Tests, 362

Junior Personality Quiz, *see* Jr.-Sr. High School Personality Questionnaire, 1253

Junior Physics Test, 5:755

Junior Scholastic Aptitude Test, 394

Junior School Grading Test, 2:1400

Jr.-Sr. High School Personality Questionnaire, 1253

Jurgensen Classification Inventory, P:335, 4:63

KAS Behavior Inventories, *see* Katz Adjustment Scales, 1255

KD Proneness Scale and Check List, 1254

KDS System, *see* Kupfer-Detre System, 1258

K.N.P.I., *see* Kundu's Neurotic Personality Inventory, 1257

Kahn Career Orientation Questionnaire, 4:777

Kahn Intelligence Tests, 502

Kahn Stick Figure Personality Test, *see* Group Personality Projective Test, 1466

Kahn Test of Symbol Arrangement, 1478

Kansas American History Test, 3:610

Kansas Arithmetic Test, 2:1457

Arithmetic, T:1046, 36:532; First Year Algebra, T:997, 36:521; General High School Mathematics, 35:381; Plane Geometry, T:1116, 36:686; Second Year Algebra, T:1010; Solid Geometry, T:1126, 36:689; Trigonometry, T:1135

Manchester Semester-End Achievement Tests [Miscellaneous]: General Shop Woodworking, T:1276; Health, T:1236, 36:708; Ninth Grade Industrial Arts, 36:752; Safety Education, T:1173; Twelfth Year Health, 36:708

Manchester Semester-End Achievement Tests [Science]: Biology, T:1582, 36:549; First Year Chemistry, T:1617, 36:575; Physics, T:1645, 36:795

Manchester Semester-End Achievement Tests [Social Studies]: High School Economics, T:1738; Ninth Grade Civics, 36:843; Twelfth Year High School Economics, 36:627; United States Government, T:1815, 36:848; United States History, T:1787, 36:724; World History, T:1791, 36:717

Mandel Social Adjustment Scale, 1270

Maniken Test, 563

Manipulative Aptitude Test, 2226

Manson Evaluation, 1271

Manual Ability Test Series (Psycho-Motor Profile), see V.D.L. Psychomotor Scale for the Measurement of Manual Ability, 4:653

Manual Accuracy and Speed Test, 1896

Manual Speed and Accuracy: Employee Aptitude Survey, 1071i

Manwiller Word Recognition Test, 35:412

Map Planning Test, Ss-3, 561t3

Mare and Foal Formboard, T:929

Marianne Frostig Developmental Test of Visual Perception, 1921

Marital Attitudes Evaluation, see MATE, 1176f

Marital Communication Inventory, 823

Marital Diagnostic Inventory, 824

Marital Roles Inventory, 825

Marriage Adjustment Form, 826

Marriage Adjustment Inventory, 827

Marriage Adjustment Sentence Completion Survey, 828

Marriage Analysis, 829

Mariage Expectation Inventories, 830

Marriage-Personality Inventory, 831

Marriage Prediction Schedule, 832

Marriage Role Expectation Inventory, 833

Marriage Scale, 834

Marriage Skills Analysis, 835

Marseille Rorschach Mail Interview, 3:73g

Martin Alphabetizing Test (status unknown), 4:726g

Martin Arithmetic Reasoning Test (status unknown), 4:726f

Martin Name Checking Test (status unknown), 4:726b

Martin Number Checking Test (status unknown), 4:726a

Martin Number Facility Test (status unknown), 4:726c

Martin Numerical Operations Test (status unknown), 4:726d

Martin Numerical Order Test (status unknown), 4:726h

Martin Office Aptitude Tests (status unknown), 4:726

Martin Peg Board (status unknown), 4:749

Martin Performance Appraisal, 2307

Martin S-D Inventory, 1272

Martin Stenographic Test (status unknown), 4:726i

Martin Typing Test (status unknown), 4:726j

Martin Vocabulary Test (status unknown), 4:726e

Maryland Parent Attitude Survey, 1273

Maryland Test Behavior Checklist, see Psychometric Behavior Checklist, 1343

Massachusetts Hearing Test, 2045

Massachusetts Vision Test, 1934a–c

Master Achievement Tests, 1:873

Master Ophthalmograph, R:162, 4:660

Master Ortho-Rater, 1923a

Match Problems, 564; 2, Xa-1, 561w1; 5, 565; 5, Xa-2, 561w2

Match Problems 2, see Match Problems, 564

Maternal-Child Nursing: NLN Achievement Tests, 2383c1

Maternity and Child Nursing: NLN Achievement Tests, 2383b4

Mathematical Ability Test, 1:1075

Mathematical and Technical Test, 2282

Mathematical Literacy for High School Seniors: Ohio Senior Survey Tests, 5:431

Mathematics and Reasoning: Flanagan Industrial Tests, 2107a10

Mathematics Anxiety Rating Scale, 1274

Mathematics Aptitude: Iowa Placement Exminations, 621

Mathematics Aptitude Test, R-1, 561o1; R-2, 561o2

Mathematics Attainment Test EF, 626

Mathematics Attainment Tests C1 and C3, 627

Mathematics Attainment Tests DE1 and DE2, 628

Mathematics Attainment Tests (Oral), 629

Mathematics, Biology, Physical Science, R:225, 2:1550

Mathematics: Bristol Achievement Tests, 600

Mathematics: CLEP General Examinations, 601

Mathematics: California Achievement Tests, 603

Mathematics: Cooperative General Achievement Tests [Proficiency Series], 6:573

Mathematics: Cooperative Primary Tests, 614

Mathematics: Every Pupil Test, 6:581

Mathematics for High School Seniors, see Mathematical Literacy for High School Seniors, 5:431

Mathematics Inventory Tests, 630

Mathematics Literacy for High School Seniors: [Ohio Senior Survey Tests], 5:431

Mathematics: Minnesota High School Achievement Examinations, 631

Mathematics: National Teacher Examinations, 643

Mathematics: Sequential Tests of Educational Progress, 652

Mathematics: Teacher Education Examination Program, 657

Mathematics Test (Adv.) 6, 632

Mathematics Test: Content Evaluation Series, 633

Mathematics Test for Grades Four, Five and Six, 634

Mathematics Test: McGraw-Hill Basic Skills System, 635

Mathematics Test: Ohio Senior Survey Tests, 3:313

Mathematics Test 1, 5:436

Mathematics Tests: Metropolitan Achievement Tests, 637

Mathematics: Tests of Academic Progress, 659

Mathematics: Tests of Achievement in Basic Skills, 660

Mathematics: Tests of Basic Experiences, 661

Mathematics Tests: Stanford Achievement Test, 655

Mathematics Tests 20–22, 636

Mathematics Tests: Undergraduate Program Field Tests, 662

Mathematics Training: Iowa Placement Examinations, 622

Maturity Level for School Entrance and Reading Readiness, 1715

Maudsley Personality Inventory, 1275

Maxfield-Buchholz Scale of Social Maturity for Use With Preschool Blind Children, 1276

Maxfield-Fjeld Adaptation of the Vineland Social Maturity Scale, see Maxfield-Buchholz Scale of Social Maturity for Use With Preschool Blind Children, 1276

Maze Tracing Speed Test, Ss-1, 561t1

Meaning Reading Vocabulary Scale, 1540c

Michigan Occupational Preferences Check List, 1: 1171b

Michigan Picture Test, P:455, 5:150

Michigan Pre-School Vision Test, 1934b-c

Michigan Speed of Reading Test, R:233, 3:523

Michigan Test of Aural Comprehension, 232

Michigan Test of English Language Proficiency, 233

Michigan Vocabulary Profile Test, 4:216

Microbiology: Achievement Tests in Nursing, 2376g

Microbiology: NLN Achievement Tests, 2383a3

Middlesex Hospital Questionnaire, 1279

Middleton Industrial Arts Test, 4:504

Midland Attainment Tests [English]: Grammar and Style, 1:962; Knowledge of Literature, 1:973; Vocabulary, 1:980

Midland Attainment Tests [Mathematics]: Arithmetic, 2:1448

Midland Attainment Tests [Reading]: Reading Comprehension, R:95, 1:1101

Midwest High School Achievement Examinations, *see* Minnesota High School Achievement Examinations

Mid-Year Algebra Test, 685

Mid-Year Geometry Test, 752

Miles Career Evaluation Inventory, 4:780

Mill Hill Vocabulary Scale, 403

Miller Analogies Test, 404

Miller-Davis French Test, 2:1355

Milne Arithmetic Test, 5:479

Milwaukee Academic Interest Inventory, 2196

Miner Sentence Completion Scale, 1484

Minimum Essentials for Modern Mathematics, 638

Minnesota Assembly Test, 3:671

Minnesota Check List for Food Preparation and Serving, 951

Minnesota Child Development Inventory, 508

Minnesota Clerical Test, 2135

Minnesota Counseling Inventory, 1280

Minnesota Engineering Analogies Test, 2344

Minnesota Food Score Cards, 3:439

Minnesota High School Achievement Examinations [Business Education]: Bookkeeping, 776

Minnesota High School Achievement Examinations [English]: Language Arts, 90

Minnesota High School Achievement Examinations [Mathematics]: Advanced Mathematics (Including Trigonometry), 597; Elementary Algebra, 678; Geometry (Including Plane and Solid Geometry), 748; Mathematics [Grades 7–9], 631; Trigonometry, 765

Minnesota High School Achievement Examinations [Science]: Biology, 1803; Chemistry, 1836; Physics, 1871; Science Grade 7 (Life Science), 1791a; Science Grade 8 (Earth Science), 1791b; Science Grade 9 (Physical Science), 1791c

Minnesota High School Achievement Examinations [Social Studies]: Social Studies [Grades 7–9], 1949; Social Studies Grade 10 (American History), 1999; Social Studies Grade 11 (World History), 2000; Social Studies Grade 12 (American Problems), 2015

Minnesota Home Status Index, 1:983

Minnesota House Design and House Furnishing Test, 1:1031

Minnesota Importance Questionnaire, 2283

Minnesota Inventory of Social Attitudes; of Social Behavior; of Social Preferences, P:340, 4:70

Minnesota Job Description Questionnaire, 2284

Minnesota MAST, *see* Manual Accuracy and Speed Test, 1896

Minnesota Manual Dexterity Test, *see* Minnesota Rate of Manipulation Test, 2227

Minnesota Mechanical Assembly Test, *see* Minnesota Assembly Test, 3:671

Minnesota Multiphasic Personality Inventory, 1281; scoring services, 1282–5

Minnesota Occupational Rating Scales and Counseling Profile, 3:689

Minnesota Paper Form Board Test, *see* Revised Minnesota Paper Form Board Test, 2266

Minnesota Percepto-Diagnostic Test, 1485

Minnesota Personality Scale, P:341, 5:87

Minnesota Preschool Scale, 509

Minnesota Rate of Manipulation Test, 2227

Minnesota Rating Scale for Personal Qualities and Abilities, 1286

Minnesota Reading Examination for College Students, 1568

Minnesota Satisfaction Questionnaire, 2285

Minnesota Scale for the Survey of Opinions, P:342, 1:901

Minnesota Scholastic Aptitude Test, 405

Minnesota Spatial Relations Test, 2258

Minnesota Speed of Reading Test for College Students, 1749

Minnesota T-S-E Inventory, P:171, 6:144

Minnesota Teacher Attitude Inventory, 868

Minnesota Test for Differential Diagnosis of Aphasia, 2080

Minnesota Tests of Creative Thinking, *see* Torrance Tests of Creative Thinking, 589

Minnesota Vocational Interest Inventory, 2197

Minnesota Vocational Test for Clerical Workers, *see* Minnesota Clerical Test, 2135

Missing Cartoons: Tests of Social Intelligence, 1421c

Missing Pictures: Tests of Social Intelligence, 1421d

Missouri Children's Picture Series, 1287

Missouri College English Test, 7:201

Mitchell Vocabulary Test, 406

Modern Algebra Test: Content Evaluation Series, 686

Modern Economics Test: Content Evaluation Series, 1966

Modern English Usage Test, 5:198

Modern European History: Cooperative Social Studies Tests, 1989

Modern European History: Every Pupil Scholarship Test, 35:309

Modern Geography and Allied Social Studies, 4:678

Modern Geometry Test: Content Evaluation Series, 753

Modern History: Every Pupil Test, 1:1023

Modern Language Aptitude Test, 221

Modern Language Aptitude Test—Elementary, 222

Modern Mathematics Supplement to the Iowa Tests of Basic Skills, 639

Modern Photography Comprehension Test, 766

Modern School Achievement Tests, 4:19

Modern World History: Achievement Examinations for Secondary Schools, 1997

Modification of the Kent-Shakow Formboard, 2:1408

Modified Alpha Examination Form 9, 407

Modified Ortho-Rater, 1923b

Modified Rhyme Hearing Test, 2046

Modified Rhyme Test, *see* Modified Rhyme Hearing Test, 2046

Modified Sjöstrand Physical Work Capacity Test, 936

Money and Banking: Every Pupil Scholarship Test, 35:157

Monroe Reading Aptitude Tests, *see* Reading Aptitude Tests, 1724

Monroe's Standardized Silent Reading Test, 1569

Mood Altering Substances, 1288

Mooney Problem Check List, 1289

Moore Eye-Hand Coordination and Color-Matching Test, 1880

Mooseheart Graphic Rating Scale for Housemothers and Housefathers, 1:1172

Moray House Adult Intelligence Test, *see* Moray House Verbal Reasoning Test (Adult) 1, 409e

Moray House Arithmetic Test, 722

National Achievement Tests [English] : College English Test, 66; English Test, 78; English Test: Municipal Tests, 77; Literature Test, 139; Literature Test: Municipal Tests, 4:191; Spelling Test, 161; Vocabulary Test, 178

National Achievement Tests [Mathematics] : Algebra Test for Engineering and Science, 666; Arithmetic Test, 701; Arithmetic Test (Fundamentals and Reasoning): Municipal Tests, 700; First Year Algebra Test, 679; Plane Geometry, 757; Plane Trigonometry, 764; Solid Geometry, 759

National Achievement Tests [Miscellaneous] : Health and Safety Education Test, 926; Health Knowledge Test for College Freshmen, 929; Health Test, 930; Municipal Battery, 5:18; Municipal Tests, 1592; Test for High School Entrants, 42

National Achievement Tests [Reading] : High School Reading Test, 1556; Reading Comprehension Test [Crow, Kuhlmann, and Crow], 1586; Reading Comprehension Test [Speer and Smith], 1587; Reading Speed Test, 3:525; Reading Test (Comprehension and Speed): Municipal Tests, 1592

National Achievement Tests [Science] : Elementary Science Test, 1782; General Biology Test, 1810; General Chemistry Test, 1842; General Physics Test, 1865; General Science Test, 1785

National Achievement Tests [Social Studies] : American History Test, 1984; Geography Test, 1976; Geography Test: Municipal Tests, 1975; History and Civics Test: Municipal Tests, 1943; Social Studies Test, 1951

National Bicycle Tests, 2:1526

National Business Entrance Tests, 786; Bookkeeping Test, 777; Business Fundamentals and General Information Test, 778; General Office Clerical Test, 783; Machine Calculation Test, 785; Stenographic Test, 795; Typewriting Test, 799

National Clerical Ability Tests, *see* National Business Entrance Tests, 786

National Council of Geography Teachers Geography Test, *see* Fourth Grade Geography Test, 3:599

National Educational Development Tests, 24

National Engineering Aptitude Search Test, 2346

National German Contest for High School Students, *see* National German Examination for High School Students, 273

National German Examination for High School Students, 273

National Guidance Testing Program, 1055

National Institute for Personnel Research High Level Battery, *see* High Level Battery: Test A/75, 1075

National Institute for Personnel Research Intermediate Battery, 1084; Normal Battery, 1085

National Institute of Industrial Psychology Clerical Test, 6:1041

National Inventory of Aptitudes and Abilities : Project Talent Test Battery, 1058

National Merit Scholarship Qualifying Test, *see* Preliminary Scholastic Aptitude Test/National Merit Scholarship Qualifying Test, 436

National Science Foundation Graduate Fellowship Testing Program, 1056

National Science Foundation Testing Program, T:1360

National Spanish Examination, 316

National Teacher Examinations, 869

National Teacher Examinations : Business Education, 787

National Teacher Examinations [Education] : Early Childhood Education, 870; Educational Administration and Supervision, 874; Education in an Urban Setting, 871; Education in the Elementary School, 872; Education of Mentally Retarded, 873; Guidance Counselor, 875; Media Specialist—Library and Audio-Visual Services, 876

National Teacher Examinations : English Language and Literature, 96

National Teacher Examinations [Fine Arts] : Art Education, 190; Music Education, 210

National Teacher Examinations [Foreign Languages] : French, 257; German, 274; Spanish, 317

National Teacher Examinations [Home Economics] : Home Economics Education, 952

National Teacher Examinations [Mathematics] : Mathematics, 643

National Teacher Examinations [Miscellaneous] : Common Examinations, 25; Industrial Arts Education, 972; Men's Physical Education, 937; Women's Physical Education, 938

National Teacher Examinations [Reading] : Reading Specialist, 1571

National Teacher Examinations [Science] : Biology and General Science, 1788; Chemistry, Physics and General Science, 1789

National Teacher Examinations [Social Studies] : Social Studies, 1945; Texas Government, 2010

National Teacher Examinations [Speech] : Audiology, 2047; Speech-Communication and Theatre, 2081; Speech Pathology, 2082

National Test in Driver Education, 6:692

National Test of Basic Words, 1667

National Test of Library Skills, 1762

Nationwide Current Events Examination, 6:982

Nationwide English Composition Examination, 97

Nationwide English Grammar Examination, 98

Nationwide English Vocabulary Examination, 169

Nationwide Library Skills Examination, 1763

Nationwide Speech Examination, 2083

Nationwide Spelling Examination, 154

Natural Science: Cooperative General Achievement Tests [Proficiency Series], 6:870

Natural Sciences: CLEP General Examinations, 1779

Natural Sciences in Nursing: NLN Achievement Tests, 2383b3

Nature of Proof: Test 5.22, R:270, 2:1556

Navy Vocational Interest Inventory, *see* Minnesota Vocational Interest Inventory, 2197

Neale Analysis of Reading Ability, 1683

Near-Point Visual Acuity Test, 1918a9

Nearer Point Test, Le-3, 561h3

Nebraska Personality Inventory, P:343, 1:922

Nebraska Test of Learning Aptitude, *see* Hiskey-Nebraska Test of Learning Aptitude, 499

Necessary Arithmetic Operations Test, R-4, 56104

Needs: A Rating Procedure, 1208f

Nelson Biology Test, 1812

Nelson-Denny Reading Test, 1572

Nelson-Lohmann Reading Test, R:104, 6:801

Nelson Reading Test, 1573

Nelson-Richardson Plane Geometry Readiness Test, 1:995

Nelson Silent Reading Test, *see* Nelson Reading Test, 1573

Nelson's High School English Test, 2:1290

Nemeth Code Tests: Colorado Braille Battery, 770

Netherne Study Difficulties Battery for Student Nurses, 2388

Neuroticism Scale Questionnaire, 1295

New Air World, 4:632

New Century Social Conduct Test, 5:547

New Developmental Reading Tests, 1574

New Eaton Literature Tests, 1:978

New Group Pure Tone Hearing Test, 2048

New Guinea Performance Scales, 510

New Iowa Spelling Scale, 155

New Junior Maudsley Inventory, 1296

New Mexico Career Education Test Series, 2109

New Patterson Test or Study Exercises on the United States Constitution, 4:705

New Purdue Placement Test in English, 99

New Rhode Island Intelligence Test, 5:354

New Road Test for Use in Driver Licensing, Education & Employment, *see* McGlade Road Test for Use in Driver Licensing, Education and Employment, 848

New South Achievement Tests, *see* Gray-Votaw-Rogers General Achievement Tests, 15

New South African Group Test, 411

New South African Individual Scale, 511

New Standard High School Spelling Scale, 4:206

New Standard Vocabulary Test, 6:336

New Stanford Achievement Test, *see* Stanford Achievement Test, 36

New Test for the Detection of Colorblindness, 3:469

New Uses, 568

New York Rating Scale for School Habits, T:232

New York Test of Arithmetical Meanings, 5:480

New York Times Current Affairs Test, *see* School Weekly News Quiz, 1960

New York Times Current Affairs Test for Colleges, 6:984

Newcastle Spatial Test, *see* Spatial Test 3, 2269c

Newkirk-Stoddard Home Mechanics Test, 2:1516

Newspaper Reading Survey, 5:837

Newsweek Current News Test, *see* Current News Test, 1958

Newsweek Monthly Objective Test, *see* Newsweek NewsQuiz, 1959

Newsweek NewsQuiz, 1959

Nines, *see* Spiral Nines, 464

19 Field Interest Inventory, 2198

Non-Language Multi-Mental Test, 3:243

Non-Language Test of Verbal Intelligence, 412

Non-Readers Intelligence Test, 413

Nonreading Aptitude Test Battery, 1086

Nonsense Syllogisms Test, Rs-1, 561q1

Non-Verbal Intelligence Tests for Deaf and Hearing Subjects, 512

Non-Verbal Perception Scale, 35:361

Non-Verbal Reasoning Test, 414

Non-Verbal Test 3, *see* Non-Verbal Test DH, 415b

Non-Verbal Tests, 415

Normal Handwriting Scale, 6:714

Normal Nutrition: NLN Achievement Tests, 2383a4

Normal Percentile Chart, T:1159

North Carolina High School Senior Examination, 35:14

North Central Individual Test of Mental Ability, *see* Pictorial Test of Intelligence, 517

Northampton Activity Rating Scale, 1297

Northamptonshire Composition Scale, 35:169

"Northern" Test of Educability, T:805

Northox Group Intelligence Test, 2:1410

Northport Record, *see* Inpatient Multidimensional Psychiatric Scale, 1232

Northumberland Mental Tests, 416

Northwestern Intelligence Tests, 5:411

Northwestern Syntax Screening Test, 2084

Northwestern University Citizenship Tests: Best Thing To Do, 35:87; How I Feel About It, 35:94; My Code, 35:96

Northwestern University Religious Education Tests, T:1326

Novelty Grammar Tests (status unknown), 6:273

Nufferno Tests of Speed and Level, 6:555

Number Checking Test, *see* RBH Number Checking Test, 2145

Number Comparison Test, 35:496

Number Comparison Test for Clerical and Industrial Inspection Operations, 2140a

Number Comparison Test, P-2, 561n2

Number Fact Check Sheet, 4:417

Number Perception Test: Hay Clerical Test Battery, 2132b

Number Series Completion Test: Hay Clerical Test Battery, 2132d

Numbers: Factored Aptitude Series, 1078a5

Number Test DE, 725

Number Test 1, *see* Number Test DE, 725

Numerical Ability: Differential Aptitude Tests, 644

Numerical Ability: Employee Aptitude Survey, 1071b

Numerical Operations, *see* Guilford-Zimmerman Aptitude Survey, 1074c

Numerical Reasoning: Employee Aptitude Survey, 1071f

Numerical Reasoning: Multiple Aptitude Tests, 1082c

Nurse Attitudes Inventory, 2389

Nurses' Observation Scale for Inpatient Evaluation, 1298

Nursing Education Scale, *see* Luther Hospital Sentence Completions, 2382

Nursing Education Scale: NAI, *see* Nurse Attitudes Inventory, 2389

Nursing Including Aspects of Pharmacology: NLN Practical Nursing Achievement Tests, 2385b

Nursing of Children: NLN Achievement Tests, 2383a8

Nursing Sentence Completions, *see* Luther Hospital Sentence Completions, 2382

Nutrition and Diet Therapy: Achievement Tests in Nursing, 2376h

Nutrition Information, 4:502

Nutrition Information Test, 953

OC Diagnostic Dictionary Test, 1764

OC Diagnostic Syllabizing Test, 1668

OC Diagnostic Syllable Test, *see* OC Diagnostic Syllabizing Test, 1668

OISE Achievement Tests in Silent Reading, 1575

OISE Picture Reasoning Test: Primary, 417

OPTIMUM Psychodiagnostic Consultation Service, *see* Behaviordyne Psychodiagnostic Lab Service, 1282

Oberlin Test of Music and Art, 6:344

Object-Completion Test, 2243a

Object Naming, Xs-3, 561x3

Object-Number Test, Ma-2, 561i2

Object Relations Technique, 1486

Object Sorting Scales, 1299

Object Synthesis, Re-2, 561p2

Objective-Analytic (O-A) Anxiety Battery, 1300

Objective-Analytic Personality Test Batteries, P:344, 5:90

Objective Test in Grammar, *see* Grammar and Usage Test Series, 83b

Objective Tests for English Classics, 36:666

Objective Tests in American Anthology, *see* American Literature Anthology Tests, 126

Objective Tests in American History—Jr. H.S., *see* American History: Junior High—Objective, 1982

Objective Tests in American History, *see* American History: Senior High—Objective, 1983

Objective Tests in American Literature, T:512

Objective Tests in Constructive English, 100

Objective Tests in English Anthology, *see* English Literature Anthology Tests, 133

Objective Tests in English Literature, T:513

Objective Tests in English (status unknown), 4:172

Objective Tests in Mathematics: Algebra, 687; Arithmetic and Trigonometry, 645; Geometry, 754

Objective Tests in Mathematics: Statistics, 1043

Objective Tests in Physics, 1869

Objective Tests in Punctuation, 101

Objective Tests in World Anthology, *see* World Literature Anthology Tests, 145

Objective Tests in World History, *see* World History/Objective Tests, 2002

Observation Test, T:1964

Obstetric Nursing: NLN Achievement Tests, 2383a7

Obstetrical Nursing: Achievement Tests in Nursing, 2376i

Occupation Distance, P :381b, 4 :88b

Occupational Adjustment Forms, T :1988

Occupational Analysis Form, 2 :1665.1

Occupational Interest Blank, 2 :1666

Occupational Interest Blank for Women, 3 :642

Occupational Interest Comparisons, T :1877

Occupational Interest Inventory, 2199

Occupational Interest Survey (With Pictures), 2200

Occupational Interests: Self Analysis Scale (status unknown), 3 :644

Occupational Orientation Inquiry, 2 :1667

Occupational Personality Inventory, P :345, 2 :1232

Occupational Satisfactions Inventory, T :1881

O'Connor Finger Dexterity Test, 2228

O'Connor Tweezer Dexterity Test, 2229

O'Connor Wiggly Block, 2259

Office Ability Review: L & L Clerical Tests, 2133c

Office Arithmetic Test: ETSA Test, 726

Office Information and Skills Test, 788

Office Occupational Interests of Women, T :1882

Office Skills Achievement Test, 2136

Office Terms: Factored Aptitude Series, 1078a1

Office Worker Test, 2137

Ohio Auto Body Achievement Test, 2420

Ohio Automotive Mechanics Achievement Test, 2421

Ohio Basic Electricity Achievement Test, 7 :1128a

Ohio Basic Electronics Achievement Test, 7 :1128b

Ohio Carpentry Achievement Test, 2422

Ohio Classification Test, *see* Ohio Penal Classification Test, 418

Ohio College Association Rating Scale, 1301

Ohio Communication Products Electronics Achievement Test, 2423

Ohio Construction Electricity Achievement Test, 2424

Ohio Cosmetology Achievement Test, 2425

Ohio Dental Assisting Achievement Test, 2339

Ohio Diagnostic Reading Test (status unknown), R :129

Ohio District-State Scholarship Tests, T :1362

Ohio District-State Scholarship Tests [Business Education]: Bookkeeping, T :58-9

Ohio District-State Scholarship Tests [English]: English, T :425, T :427

Ohio District-State Scholarship Tests [Foreign Languages]: French, T :640, T :643; Latin, T :675, T :678; Spanish, T :700, T :703

Ohio District-State Scholarship Tests [Mathematics]: Advanced Algebra, T :981-2; First Year Algebra, T :998-9; Plane Geometry, T :1114, T :1119

Ohio District-State Scholarship Tests [Science]: Biology, T :1580, T :1584; Chemistry, T :1607, T :1610; General Science, T :1557-8; Physics, T :1643, T :1647

Ohio District-State Scholarship Tests [Social Studies]: American History, T :1755, T :1757; Senior Social Studies, T :1717-8; World History, T :1790, T :1792

Ohio Eighth Grade Test, *see* Eighth Grade Test, 6 :8

Ohio General Scholarship Test for High School Seniors, *see* General Scholarship Test for High School Seniors, 6 :8a

Ohio Guidance Tests for Elementary Grades, P :346, 3 :63

Ohio History: Every Pupil Test, T :1779

Ohio Individual Summary Sheet for Committee Selections, P :346b, 3 :63f

Ohio Industrial Electronics Achievement Test, 2426

Ohio Interest Inventory for the Intermediate Grades, P :346a, 3 :63a

Ohio Machine Trades Achievement Test, 2427

Ohio Mechanical Drafting Achievement Test, 2428

Ohio Penal Classification Test, 418

Ohio Printing Achievement Test, 2429

Ohio Recognition Scale for Intermediate Grades, P : 346d, 3 :63d

Ohio Senior Survey Tests: English Survey, 5 :188

Ohio Senior Survey Tests [Mathematics]: Mathematical Literacy for High School Seniors, 5 :431; Mathematics, 3 :313

Ohio Senior Survey Tests [Reading]: General Reading, R :99, 4 :534; Reading Speed and Comprehension, R :234, 3 :524; Special Reading, R :275, 3 :539

Ohio Sheet Metal Achievement Test, 2430

Ohio Social Acceptance Scale for the Intermediate Grades, P :346c, 3 :63c

Ohio State University Psychological Test, 419

Ohio Survey Tests, 1057

Ohio Teaching Record, 877

Ohio Tests of Articulation and Perception of Sounds, 2023

Ohio Thinking Checkup for Intermediate Grades, P : 346e, 3 :63e

Ohio Trade and Industrial Education Achievement Test Program, 2431

Ohio Vocational Interest Survey, 2201

Ohio Welding Achievement Test, 2432

Ohwaki-Kohs Tactile Block Design Intelligence Test for the Blind, 513

Oliphant Auditory Discrimination Memory Test, 2049

Oliphant Auditory Synthesizing Test, 2050

Omnibus Personality Inventory, 1302

One Hole Test, 2230

One Minute Oral Addition and Subtraction Tests: Ballard's New Examiner Tests, T :1361i

One-Minute Reading Scale, R :88a, T :1361j

Onomatopeia and Images, 587b

Ontario School Ability Examination, 2 :1411

Ontario School Record System, 1016

Ophthalmograph, *see* Master Ophthalmograph, R :162, 4 :660

Opinion, Attitude, and Interest Survey, 1303

Opinion Survey, 4 :519

Opinions Toward Adolescents, 1304

OpScan Test Scoring and Document Scanning System, 1037

Optometry College Admission Test, 2357

Oral Diagnostic Test in Addition, 3 :348

Oral Diagnostic Test of Word-Analysis Skills, R :170, 5 :673

Oral Directions Test, *see* PTI-Oral Directions Test, 433c

Oral English Observation Schedule, 1 :1094

Oral Rating Form for Rating Language Proficiency in Speaking and Understanding English, 234

Oral Reading Criterion Test, 1684

Oral School Attitude Test, 878

Oral Verbal Intelligence Test, 419A

Oral Word Reading Test, 1685

Oral Word-Recognition Test: Standard Reading Tests, 1650h

Orally Presented Group Test of Intelligence for Juniors, 5 :360

Oregon Academic Ranking Test, 420

Organic and Inorganic Chemistry: Achievement Tests in Nursing, 2376d

Organic Integrity Test, 1305

Organization Attitude Survey, *see* Organization Survey (status unknown), 6 :1107

Organization Survey (status unknown), 6 :1107

Organizational Climate Index, 1395f

Organizational Value Dimensions Questionnaire, 2330

Orientation Inventory, 1306

Orleans Algebra Prognosis Test, *see* Orleans-Hanna Algebra Prognosis Test, 688

Orleans Geometry Prognosis Test, *see* Orleans-Hanna Geometry Prognosis Test, 755

Orleans-Hanna Algebra Prognosis Test, 688

Primary Arithmetic: Every Pupil Scholarship Test, 6:630

Primary Business Interests Test (status unknown), 6:1067

Primary Classification Test, 438a

Primary Empathic Abilities, *see* Diplomacy Test of Empathy, 1160

Primary Mathematics Survey Tests, 649

Primary Mechanical Ability Tests, 2262

Primary Mental Abilities, *see* SRA Primary Mental Abilities, 1087

Primary Progress Assessment Chart, 1338a

Primary Progress Evaluation Index, *see* Primary Progress Assessment Chart, 1338a

Primary Reading: Every Pupil Achievement Test, R:52

Primary Reading: Every Pupil Scholarship Test, 6:803

Primary Reading: Every Pupil Test, R:105, 6:804

Primary Reading Profiles, 1641

Primary Reading Survey Tests, 1577

Primary Reading Test, R:106, 3:494

Primary Reading Test: Acorn Achievement Tests, 1578

Primary Reading Tests 1 and 2, *see* Reading Tests A and BD, 1594

Primary School Verbal Intelligence Test 1, *see* Verbal Test BC, 475a

Primary Self-Concept Inventory, 1334

Primary Social Studies Test, 1946

Primary Survey Tests, 27

Primary Survey Tests, *see* Primary Mathematics Survey Tests, 649

Primary Test of Economic Understanding, 1967

Primary Verbal Tests 1, 2, 2G, and 3, *see* Verbal Tests BC, CD, C, and D, 475

Primary Visual Motor Test, 1882

Principles of American Citizenship Test, 5:841

Principles of Democracy Test, 2012

Principles of Organization and Management in Secondary Education, 35:162

Pritchard-Fox Phoneme Auditory Discrimination Tests, 2051

Probability and Statistics: ERB Mathematics Tests, 7:467c

Probes Into Auditory Discrimination, 1642a

Probes Into Capitalization, 89a

Probes Into Punctuation, 89b

Probes Into Structural Analysis, 1642b

Problem Arithmetic Graded Test: Burt Scholastic Tests, T:3f

Problem Check List: Form for Rural Young People, 1335; Form for Schools of Nursing, P:365, 4:82

Problem Check List for Student Teachers and Intern Teachers (status unknown), T:1194

Problems in Quantitative Thinking, 1:1077

Problems of Democracy: Cooperative Social Studies Tests, 2007

Probst Rating System, 4:785

Process for In-School Screening of Children With Emotional Handicaps, 1336

Processes of Science Test, 7:795

Professional Employee Inventory (status unknown), T:2007

Profile Chart for Individual Diagnosis, 1:1121

Profile for the Stanford Binet (L-M), *see* Clinical Profile for the Stanford Binet Intelligence Scale (L-M), 526

Profile of Mood States, 1337

Profion Deallwriaeth Cyfaddasiad Cymbraeg, 3:257

Prognostic Test of Mechanical Abilities, 4:761

Programmer Aptitude/Competence Test System, 2336

Programmers Aptitude Test, *see* Revised Programmer Aptitude Test, 6:1153, and IBM Aptitude Test for Programmer Personnel, 7:1090

Programming: Aptitude Assessment Battery, 2331

Progress Assessment Chart of Social Development, 1338

Progress Evaluation Index 1 and 2, *see* Progress Assessment Charts, 1338b, 1338d

Progressive Achievement Tests, *see* California Achievement Tests, 7

Progressive Achievement Tests of Listening Comprehension, 996

Progressive Achievement Tests of Reading, 1579

Progressive Arithmetic Tests, *see* California Achievement Tests: Mathematics, 603

Progressive Education Association Tests, *see* Evaluation in the Eight Year Study Tests

Progressive Language Tests, *see* California Achievement Tests: Language, 61

Progressive Mathematics Test, *see* California Achievement Tests: Mathematics, 603

Progressive Matrices, 439

Progressive Reading Tests, *see* California Achievement Tests: Reading, 1536

Progressive Tests in the Social and Related Sciences, *see* California Tests in Social and Related Sciences, 5:4

Project Talent Test Battery, 1058

Proverbs Test, 440

Providence Inventory Test in Music, 2:1337

Pseudo-Isochromatic Plates for Testing Color Perception, 1924

Psi-Lambda Foreign Language Aptitude Battery, *see* Modern Language Aptitude Test, 221

Psychiatric Attitudes Battery, 1496

Psychiatric Evaluation Form, 1339

Psychiatric Evaluation Form—Diagnostic Version, *see* Current and Past Psychopathology Scales, 1150

Psychiatric History Schedule, *see* Current and Past Psychopathology Scales, 1150

Psychiatric Nursing: Achievement Tests in Nursing, 2376l; NLN Achievement Tests, 2383a9, 2383c5

Psychiatric Outpatient Mood Scale, *see* Profile of Mood States, 1337

Psychiatric Status Schedules: Subject Form, 1340

Psychodiagnostic Inkblots, *see* Harrower's Psychodiagnostic Inkblot Test, 1499e

Psychodiagnostic Plates, 1499f

Psychodiagnostic Test Report Blank, 1018

Psychoeducational Inventory of Basic Learning Abilities, 985

Psychoeducational Profile of Basic Learning Abilities, 986

Psychological Audit for Interpersonal Relations, 1341

Psychological Corporation General Clerical Test, *see* General Clerical Test, 2129

Psychological Corporation MMPI Reporting Service, 1284

Psychological Examination, 2:1418

Psychological Publications Press Achievement Test in General Psychology, 7:645

Psychological Resources, 1038

Psychological Resources Support Systems, *see* Psychological Resources, 1038

Psychological Screening Inventory, 1342

Psychological Vocabulary and Information Test, T:1298

Psychology and Sociology: Achievement Tests in Nursing, 2376m

Psychology Test: Every Pupil Scholarship Test, 6:744

Psychology Test: Undergraduate Program Field Tests, 1006

Psychometric Behavior Checklist, 1343

Psychometric Research and Service Chart Showing the Davis Difficulty and Discrimination Indices for Item Analysis, 810

Psycho-Somatic Inventory, 1344

Psychotherapy Inventory, 7:569

Rating Instrument for the Evaluation of the Reactions of College Students, 2:1498

Rating Language Proficiency in Speaking and Understanding English, *see* Oral Rating Form for Rating Language Proficiency in Speaking and Understanding English, 234

Rating Scale for Automobile-Driver Skills, The Abercrombie Driver Tests, 4:524

Rating Scale for Pupil Adjustment, P:226, 5:102

Rating Scale for Teachers of Home Economics, *see* Minnesota Rating Scale for Personal Qualities and Abilities, 1286

Rating Scales of Vocational Values, Vocational Interests and Vocational Aptitudes, 7:1033, P:227

Ratio I.Q. Computer, 812

Reactions to Everyday Situations, 1352

Read General Science Test, 7:796

Reader Rater With Self-Scoring Profile, 1670

Reader's Inventory, 1671

Readiness and Achievement Tests in Arithmetic, T:1080

Reading Achievement Test: Durrell-Sullivan Reading Capacity and Achievement Tests, 1661b

Reading Adequacy "READ" Test, 1741

Reading: Adult Basic Education Student Survey, 1742

Reading: American School Achievement Tests, 1532

Reading and Construction of Tables and Graphs, R:273, 1:1165

Reading and Mathematics: Analysis of Readiness Skills, 1695

Reading Aptitude Tests, 1724

Reading: California Achievement Tests, 1536

Reading Capacity Test: Durrell-Sullivan Reading Capacity and Achievement Tests, 1661a

Reading Comprehension: Canadian English Achievement Test, Part 1, 1582

Reading Comprehension: Cooperative English Tests, 1583

Reading Comprehension: Midland Attainment Tests, R:95, 1:1101

Reading Comprehension Scale, 1540a

Reading Comprehension Test, 1584

Reading Comprehension Test: Burt Scholastic Tests, R:9b, T:3c

Reading Comprehension Test DE, 1585

Reading Comprehension Test for Personnel Selection, 1743

Reading Comprehension Test for Prospective Nurses, 2381c

Reading Comprehension Test: N.B. Silent Reading Tests (Beginners), 1570

Reading Comprehension Test: National Achievement Tests [Crow, Kuhlmann, and Crow], 1586

Reading Comprehension Test: National Achievement Tests [Speer and Smith], 1587

Reading Comprehension Test 1, *see* Reading Comprehension Test DE, 1585

Reading Comprehensive Tests of Basic Skills, 1542

Reading: Cooperative Primary Tests, 1543

Reading Diagnostic Probes, 1642

Reading Diagnostic Record for High School and College Students, R:144, 5:666

Reading Evaluation and Diagnostic Inventory, *see* Reading Inventory Probe 1, 1725

Reading: Every Pupil Scholarship Test, 35:421

Reading/Everyday Activities in Life, 1744

Reading Eye II, 1672

Reading for Understanding Placement Test, 1588

Reading Inventory Probe 1, 1725

Reading Miscue Inventory, 1686

Reading Progress Scale, 1589

Reading: Public School Achievement Tests, 1590

Reading Readiness Test, R:203, 6:849

Reading Readiness Test, *see* Van Wagenen Reading Readiness Scales, 1733b

Reading: SRA Achievement Series, 1596

Reading Scales in History, R:226, 3:530; Literature, R:227, 3:531; Science, R:228, 3:532

Reading: Sequential Tests of Educational Progress, 1599

Reading: Seven Plus Assessment, R:63, 4:548

Reading Skills Diagnostic Test, 1644

Reading Specialist: National Teacher Examinations, 1571

Reading Speed and Accuracy: Burt Scholastic Tests, R:9a, T:3b

Reading Speed and Comprehension: Ohio Senior Survey Tests, R:234, 3:524

Reading Speed Test: National Achievement Test, R:235, 3:525

Reading Test AD, 1591

Reading Test (Comprehension and Speed): Municipal Tests, 1592

Reading Test: McGraw-Hill Basic Skills System, 1593

Reading Tests A and BD, 1594; EH 1-3, 1595

Reading Tests: Metropolitan Achievement Tests, 1567

Reading: Tests of Academic Progress, 1608

Reading Tests: Stanford Achievement Test, 1603

Reading Versatility Test, 1673

Reading Vocabulary Test: Burt Scholastic Tests, T:3a

Ready or Not, *see* School Readiness Checklist, 1728

Ready Record Forms, T:1316

Real Analysis 1 and 2: Modular Tests, 662b3-4

Reaman Personality Rating Chart, 36:566

Reasoning Arithmetic Test: Ballard's New Examiner Tests, T:1361d

Reasoning: Flanagan Aptitude Classification Tests, 1072a15

Reasoning Test: O'Rourke Clerical Aptitude Test, 2138b

Reasoning Tests for Higher Levels of Intelligence, 446

Reconstruction Puzzle, *see* Dearborn-Anderson Formboards 2 and 2b, 2:1390

Record Booklet for Reading Diagnosis, 35:423

Record for Reading Diagnosis, R:145, 3:512

Recreation Inquiry, P:369, 3:70

Recreational Guidance Test: Kefauver-Hand Guidance Tests and Inventories, 2:1661e

Reicherter-Sanders Typewriting I and II, 789

Reid Report, 1353

Religion Essentials Test, 3:455

Religion Test for Grades Two and Three, 5:591

Religion Test for High Schools, 5:592

Religion Test (Four-Year Course): Affiliation Testing Program for Catholic Secondary Schools, 6:751

Religious Attitudes Inventory, 1026

Religious Distance, P:381c, 4:88c

Remmlein's School Law Test, 885

Remote Associates Test, 574

Renfrow Survey Tests of Mathematical Skills and Concepts, 3:349

Report Form on Temperament and Social Behavior, P:370, 2:1247

Research Personnel Review Form, 2391

Retail Arithmetic Worksample, 4:418

Retrospective Work Curve Feelings for National Research Program on Employee Feelings at Work, 1184b

Revere Safety Test, 4:525

Reversal Test, 1726

Revised Alpha Examination, Form 5, 4:315; Form 6, Short Form, 4:316

Revised Bender Gestalt, *see* Hutt Adaptation of the Bender-Gestalt, 1447c

Revised Beta Examination, 447

Revised Minnesota Paper Form Board Test, 2266

Revised Passalong Test, 6:519e

SRA Tests of Primary Mental Abilities for Ages 5 and 6, *see* SRA Primary Mental Abilities, 1087
SRA Typing Adaptability Test, 5:518
SRA Typing Skills, 792
SRA Verbal Classification Form, *see* SRA Verbal Form, 452
SRA Verbal Form, 452
SRA Youth Inventory, *see* STS Youth Inventory, 1361
S.R.T., *see* Social Relations Test, 1509
SRT Scale, *see* Science Research Temperament Scale, 1368
SSRC S-A Schedule, *see* Stereopathy-Acquiescence Schedule, 1399
STAR Score Teach Answer Record, 6:674
STS Closed High School Placement Test, 32
STS Educational Development Series: Scholastic Tests, 33
STS Junior Inventory, 1360
STS Youth Inventory, 1361
Safran Culture Reduced Intelligence Test, 453
Safran Student's Interest Inventory, 2210
Safran Vocational Interest Test, *see* Safran Student's Interest Inventory, 2210
St. Lucia Graded Word Reading Test, 1687
Sales Aptitude Inventory, 2102c
Sales Aptitude Test: ETSA Test, 2405
Sales Comprehension Test, 2406
Sales Employee Inventory (status unknown), 6:1179
Sales Method Index, 2407
Sales Motivation Inventory, 2408
Sales Personnel Description Form, 6:1180
Sales Questionnaire, 3:703
Sales Sentence Completion Blank, 2409
Sales Situation Test, 4:827
Sales Terms: Factored Aptitude Series, 1078a2
Salespower Inventory, *see* Hall Salespower Inventory, 2399
San Francisco Vocational Competency Scale, 2315
Sanders-Buller World History Test, 1998
Sanders-Fletcher Spelling Test, 156
Sanders-Fletcher Vocabulary Test, 172
Sanders-Schrader General Mathematics Test, 7:486
Sangren-Reidy Survey Tests in Arithmetic, 2:1460
Sangren-Woody Reading Test, R:107, 4:551
Sare-Sanders American Government Test, 2013
Sare-Sanders Constitution Test, 2014
Sare-Sanders Sociology Test, 2019
Scale for Evaluating Student-Efficiency in the Home Economics Laboratory, 36:748
Scale for Evaluating the School Behavior of Children Ten to Fifteen, P:373, 1:926
Scale for Measuring Attitude Toward Any Advertisement, 4:46a; Defined Group, 1348d; Disciplinary Procedure, 4:46b; Home-Making Activity, 1348g; Institution, 1348c; Play, 4:46e; Practice, 1348f; Proposed Social Action, 1348e; Selection of Poetry, 2:1202k; Social Situation, 4:46k; Teacher, 4:46l; Vocation, 1348b
Scale for Measuring Attitude Toward Any School Subject, 1348a
Scale for Measuring Attitude Toward Races and Nationalities, *see* Scale for Measuring Attitude Toward Any Defined Group, 1348d
Scale for Measuring Attitude Toward Teaching, 35:70
Scale for Measuring Developmental Age in Girls, *see* Test for Developmental Age in Girls, 1416
Scale for Measuring Individual and Group "Morale," 1348h
Scale for Rating Effective Teacher Behavior, 4:804
Scale for Rating Severity of Stuttering, 2074n
Scale of Beliefs for Junior High School: Tests 4.4 and 4.5, P:374, 2:1251
Scale of Beliefs: Tests 4.21 and 4.31, P:375, 2:1250
Scale of Non-Verbal Mental Ability, *see* Non-Verbal Tests 1-2, 415a

Scale of Problems in Commercial Arithmetic, 2:1489
Scale of Socio-Egocentrism, 1362
Scale to Measure Attitude Toward Any School Subject, *see* Scale for Measuring Attitude Toward Any School Subject, 1348a
Scale to Measure Attitudes Toward Disabled Persons, 1363
Scales: Flanagan Aptitude Classification Tests, 1072a6
Scales: Flanagan Industrial Tests, 2107a16, 2107b7
Scales for Appraising High School Homemaking Programs, 954
Scales of Functional Independence: Balthazar Scales of Adaptive Behavior, 1107a
Scales of Social Adaptation: Balthazar Scales of Adaptive Behavior, 1107b
Scholarship Qualifying Test, 5:379
Scholastic Achievement Series, 6:23
Scholastic Achievement Series: Arithmetic, 6:633
Scholastic Achievement Series: English-Spelling, 6:278
Scholastic Achievement Series: Religion, 6:752
Scholastic Diagnostic Reading Test, R:146, 5:650
Scholastic Mental Ability Tests, 454
Scholastic Philosophy Test: Undergraduate Program Field Tests, 1000
Scholastic Proficiency Battery, 34
Scholastic Reading Readiness Test, R:204, 6:850
Scholastic Tests: STS Educational Development Series, 33
Schonell Diagnostic Arithmetic Tests, 734
Schonell Diagnostic English Tests, 110
Schonell Reading Tests, 1646
School Adjustment Questionnaire, 36:568
School Administration and Supervision, 886
School Apperception Method, 1503
School Aptitude Test: Thanet Mental Tests, 2:1422
School Atmosphere Questionnaire, 887
School Attitude Survey, 1364
School Attitude Test, 888
School Attitude Test: Oral Version, *see* Oral School Attitude Test, 878
School Entrance Check List, *see* Dyslexia Schedule, 1662
School Equivalence Test, *see* Ligondé Equivalence Test, 21
School Interest Inventory, 1365
School Inventory, 1366
School Motivation Analysis Test, 1367
School Personnel Research and Evaluation Services, 889
School Practices Questionnaire, 1:869d
School Readiness Checklist, 1728
School Readiness Inventory, *see* Maturity Level for School Entrance and Reading Readiness, 1715
School Readiness Survey, 1729
School Records (status unknown), T:1317
School Survey of Interpersonal Relationships, 890
School Vision Tester, 1925
School Weekly News Quiz, 1960
Schorling-Clark-Potter Arithmetic Test, *see* Hundred-Problem Arithmetic Test, 3:344
Schrammel General Ability Test, 6:498
Schrammel-Gorbutt Personality Adjustment Scale, P:376, 3:92
Schrammel-Gray High School and College Reading Test, 1598
Schrammel-Otterstrom Arithmetic Test, 6:634
Schrammel-Reed Solid Geometry Test, 5:496
Schrammel-Wharton Vocabulary Test, 2:1321
Schubert General Ability Battery, 455
Science Applications Test: Gibson's Attainment Tests, 1:1132
Science Aptitude Examination, 6:765
Science Attitude Questionnaire, 1855
Science Background, 6:880
Science Grade 7 (Life Science), 1791a

Standardized Oral Reading Paragraphs, 1690
Standardized Road-Map Test of Direction Sense, 7:880
Standardized Road Test for Bus Operators, 2469d
Standardized Test: Traffic and Driving Knowledge for Drivers of Motor Trucks, 2470f
Stanford Achievement Test, 36
Stanford Achievement Test: Arithmetic Tests, 7:527
Stanford Achievement Test: High School Arts and Humanities Test, 7:26
Stanford Achievement Test: High School Basic Battery, 37
Stanford Achievement Test: High School Business and Economics Test, 7:559
Stanford Achievement Test: High School English and Spelling Tests, 114
Stanford Achievement Test: High School Mathematics Test, 653
Stanford Achievement Test: High School Numerical Competence Test, 654
Stanford Achievement Test: High School Reading Test, 1602
Stanford Achievement Test: High School Science Test, 1795
Stanford Achievement Test: High School Social Studies Test, 1952
Stanford Achievement Test: High School Technical Comprehension Test, 7:633
Stanford Achievement Test: Language Arts, 4:174
Stanford Achievement Test: Literature, 4:195
Stanford Achievement Test: Mathematics Tests, 655
Stanford Achievement Test: Modern Mathematics Concepts Test, *see* Stanford Modern Mathematics Concepts Test, 656
Stanford Achievement Test: Reading Tests, 1603
Stanford Achievement Test: Science, 1796
Stanford Achievement Test: Social Studies Tests, 1953
Stanford Achievement Test: Spelling and Language Tests, 115
Stanford Achievement Test: Study Skills, R:276, 5:698
Stanford Arithmetic Tests, *see* Stanford Achievement Test: Arithmetic Tests, 7:527
Stanford-Binet Intelligence Scale, 525
Stanford-Binet Scale, *see* Stanford-Binet Intelligence Scale, 525
Stanford Diagnostic Arithmetic Test, 738
Stanford Diagnostic Phonics Survey, 5:670
Stanford Diagnostic Reading Test, 1651
Stanford Early School Achievement Test, 38
Stanford Educational Aptitudes Test, 3:404
Stanford High School Arts and Humanities Test, *see* Stanford Achievement Test: High School Arts and Humanities Test, 7:26
Stanford High School Basic Battery, *see* Stanford Achievement Test: High School Basic Battery, 37
Stanford High School Business and Economics Test, *see* Stanford Achievement Test: High School Business and Economics Test, 7:559
Stanford High School English and Spelling Tests, *see* Stanford Achievement Test: High School English and Spelling Tests, 114
Stanford High School Mathematics Test, *see* Stanford Achievement Test: High School Mathematics Test, 653
Stanford High School Numerical Competence Test, *see* Stanford Achievement Test: High School Numerical Competence Test, 654
Stanford High School Reading Test, *see* Stanford Achievement Test: High School Reading Test, 1602
Stanford High School Science Test, *see* Stanford Achievement Test: High School Science Test, 1795
Stanford High School Social Studies Test, *see* Stanford Achievement Test: High School Social Studies Test, 1952

Stanford High School Technical Comprehension Test, *see* Stanford Achievement Test: High School Technical Comprehension Test, 7:633
Stanford Hypnotic Susceptibility Scale, 1389
Stanford Language Tests, *see* Stanford Achievement Test: Spelling and Language Tests, 115
Stanford Modern Mathematics Concepts Test, 656
Stanford Multi-Modality Imagery Test, 773
Stanford-Ohwaki-Kohs Block Design Intelligence Test for the Blind, 527
Stanford Profile Scales of Hypnotic Susceptibility, 1390
Stanford Reading Tests, *see* Stanford Achievement Test: Reading Tests, 1603
Stanford Revision of the Binet-Simon Intelligence Test, *see* Stanford-Binet Intelligence Scale, 525
Stanford Science Tests, *see* Stanford Achievement Test: Science, 1796
Stanford Scientific Aptitude Test, 4:813
Stanford Social Studies Test, *see* Stanford Achievement Test: Social Studies Tests, 1953
Stanford Spanish Tests, 4:266
Stanford TASK, *see* Stanford Test of Academic Skills, 39
Stanford Test of Academic Skills, 39
Stanford Test of Comprehension of Literature, 2:1306
Stanford Tests for Junior Colleges: Test in English, 35:175
State High School Tests for Indiana [Business Education]: Bookkeeping, 3:367; Commercial Arithmetic, 4:448; Shorthand, 3:388; Simplified Shorthand, 4:457; Typewriting, 4:463
State High School Tests for Indiana [English]: English: Understanding and Appreciation of Poetry, 3:143; Mechanics of Written English, 7:199; Tools of Written English, 4:177
State High School Tests for Indiana [Foreign Languages]: First Year French, T:639, 1:987; First Year German, 36:698; First Year Latin, 4:252; First Year Spanish, 4:261; French Recognition Vocabulary, 4:240; Second Year French, 1:988; Second Year German, T:2389, 36:699; Second Year Latin, 4:257
State High School Tests for Indiana [Home Economics]: Assisting With Care and Play of Children, 3:427; Assisting With Clothing Problems, 3:428; Child Development, 7:615; Clothing I and II, 7:616-7; Clothing Problems, 7:618; Family Life, 7:622; Food in the Home, 7:623; Foods I and II, 7:624-5; General Home Economics, 1:1030; Helping With Food in the Home, 4:498; Helping With the Housekeeping, 4:499; Home Care of the Sick, 4:500; Housing the Family, 4:501
State High School Tests for Indiana [Mathematics]: Advanced Algebra, 4:382; Algebra, 7:496; Arithmetic Fundamentals, 7:512; First Year Algebra, 4:391; Geometry, 7:535; Plane Geometry, 4:429; Solid Geometry, 4:435; Trigonometry, 4:440
State High School Tests for Indiana [Miscellaneous]: Animal Husbandry, 3:365; Farm Shop Tools, 4:441; Health and Safety Education, 3:420; Mechanical Drawing, 4:503
State High School Tests for Indiana [Science]: Biology, 4:598; Chemistry, 4:616; General Science, 4:592; Physics, 4:642
State High School Tests for Indiana [Social Studies]: American History, 4:682; Economics, 4:670; Junior High School Civics, 4:704; Senior High School Civics, 4:706-7; World History, 4:696
State-Trait Anxiety Inventory, 1391; for Children, 1932
Statement of Further Educational Intentions, 36:812
Staticube Test of Power to Visualize, 1:1177

Tests A/9 and A/10, 2291

Tests AH4 and AH5, *see* AH4, AH5, and AH6 Tests, 331

Tests for Auditory Comprehension of Language, 997A

Tests for Color-Blindness, Visual Acuity, and Astigmatism, 36:783

Tests for Primary Mental Abilities, *see* SRA Primary Mental Abilities, 1087

Tests for the Appreciation of Literature, 2:1307

Tests for the Hearing of Speech by Deaf People, 2:1526.1

Tests for Venereal Disease Education, 943

Tests in Comprehension of Patterns, 2:1510

Tests in Fundamental Abilities of Visual Arts, 2:1329

Tests of Academic Progress, 44

Tests of Academic Progress: Composition, 119

Tests of Academic Progress: Literature, 143

Tests of Academic Progress: Mathematics, 659

Tests of Academic Progress: Reading, 1608

Tests of Academic Progress: Science, 1799

Tests of Academic Progress: Social Studies, 1955

Tests of Achievement in Basic Skills: Mathematics, 660

Tests of Adult Basic Education, 45

Tests of Arithmetic and Language for Indian South Africans, 46

Tests of Basic Experiences, 47

Tests of Basic Experiences: Language, 120

Tests of Basic Experiences: Mathematics, 661

Tests of Basic Experiences: Science, 1857

Tests of Basic Experiences: Social Studies, 1956

Tests of General Ability [SRA], 467

Tests of General Ability: Cooperative Inter-American Tests, *see* Tests of General Ability: Inter-American Series, 468

Tests of General Ability: Inter-American Series, 468

Tests of General Educational Development, 48

Tests of General Educational Development: Correctness and Effectiveness of Expression, 5:181; now available only as a subtest of Tests of General Educational Development, 48

Tests of General Educational Development: General Mathematical Ability, 5:426; now available only as a subtest of Tests of General Educational Development, 48

Tests of General Educational Development: Interpretation of Literary Materials, 5:216; now available only as a subtest of Tests of General Educational Development, 48

Tests of General Educational Development: Interpretation of Reading Materials in the Natural Sciences, 7:770, R:210; now available only as a subtest of Tests of General Educational Development, 48

Tests of General Educational Development: Interpretation of Reading Materials in the Social Studies, 7:771, R:211; now available only as a subtest of Tests of General Educational Development, 48

Tests of Human Growth and Development, 3:406; *see* Case Study Tests in Human Growth and Development, T:1180

Tests of Language Usage: Cooperative Inter-American Tests, 4:176

Tests of Mechanical Arithmetic, *see* Mechanical Arithmetic Tests, 6:626

Tests of Mechanical Comprehension, *see* Bennett Mechanical Comprehension Test, 2239

Tests of Mental Development, 2:1426

Tests of Natural Sciences: Vocabulary and Interpretation of Reading Materials, R:221, 4:576

Tests of Primary Mental Abilities, *see* SRA Primary Mental Abilities, 1087

Tests of Reading Ability for Art, Fiction, Geology, and History, *see* Robinson-Hall Reading Tests, 1745

Tests of Reading: Cooperative Inter-American Tests, *see* Tests of Reading: Inter-American Series, 1609

Tests of Reading: Inter-American Series, 1609

Tests of Social Intelligence, 1421

Tests of Social Studies: Vocabulary and Interpretation of Reading Materials, R:222, 4:577

Tests of the Physical Science Study Committee, 1872

Tests of the Socially Competent Person, P:395, 2:1259

Test on Biblical Information, *see* Concordia Bible Information Inventory, 1025

Tests on English Classics, 35:223

Texas Government: National Teacher Examinations, 2010

Thanet Mental Tests: Arithmetic, 2:1450

Thanet Mental Tests: English, 2:1279

Thanet Mental Tests: School Aptitude Test, 2:1422

Thematic Apperception Test, 1519

Thematic Apperception Test for African Subjects, 1520

Thematic Apperception Test: Thompson Modification, P:486, 5:166

Theme Test, Fi-2, 561e2

Theological School Inventory, 1028

Thing Categories Test, Fi-3, 561e3

Thinking About Yourself, 1336c2

Thinking Creatively With Pictures, *see* Torrance Tests of Creative Thinking, 589b

Thinking Creatively With Sounds and Words, 587

Thinking Creatively With Words, *see* Torrance Tests of Creative Thinking, 589a

This I Believe Test, 1521

Thomas Self-Concept Values Test (status unknown), 7:153

Thompson Business Practice Test, 1:942

Thompson Smoking and Tobacco Knowledge Test, 944

Thorman Family Relations Conference Situation Questionnaire, 841

Thorman Family Relations Evaluation, *see* Thorman Family Relations Conference Situation Questionnaire, 841

Thorndike Dimensions of Temperament, 1422

Thorndike Intelligence Examination for College Entrance, 35:354

Thorndike-Lorge Reading Test, R:111, 4:558

Thorndike Scale for Handwriting of Children, 4:477

3-D Test of Visualization Skill, 1933

Three-Dimensional Space Test, *see* RBH Three-Dimensional Space Test, 2264

Three-Minute Arithmetic Test: Ballard's Mental Tests, T:1356c

Three Units of Content: NLN Practical Nursing Achievement Tests, 2385a

Threshold by Identification of Pictures, 2039a

Thurstone Employment Tests, 2162

Thurstone Examination in Clerical Work, *see* Thurstone Employment Tests: Examination in Clerical Work, 2162a

Thurstone Examination in Typing, *see* Thurstone Employment Tests: Examination in Typing, 2162b

Thurstone Interest Schedule, 2214

Thurstone Personality Schedule, *see* Personality Schedule, P:360, 6:159

Thurstone Personality Schedule: Clark Revision, 35:107

Thurstone Scoring Board, 3:398

Thurstone Temperament Schedule, 1423

Thurstone Test of Mental Alertness, 469

Tickmaster, 2319

Tiedeman Arithmetical Knowledge and Information Test, 5:490

Tien's OIT, *see* Organic Integrity Test, 1305

Time Appreciation Test, 588

Time Current Affairs Test, 1961

Time Monthly News Quiz, 1962

Time-Saver Grade Averaging Chart, 806c

Tinker Speed of Reading Test, R:231, 5:687

Titmus Vision Tester, 1934

Toledo Chemistry Placement Examination, 1847

ACRONYMS

GREAT, Graduate Record Examinations Aptitude Test, 382
GWRT, Graded Word Reading Test, 1680
GZAS, Guilford-Zimmerman Aptitude Survey, 1074
GZTS, Guilford-Zimmerman Temperament Survey, 1207
HABGT, Hutt Adaptation of the Bender-Gestalt Test, 1447c
HAS, Hospital Adjustment Scale, 1217
HAT, Halstead Aphasia Test, 2076
HDHQ, Hostility and Direction of Hostility Questionnaire, 1218
HFDT, HFD Test, 1468
HFT, Hidden Figures Test, 559
HGR, Harrower's Group Rorschach, 1499c
HGSHS, Harvard Group Scale of Hypnotic Susceptibility, 1212
HGVII, Hackman-Gaither Vocational Interest Inventory, 2186
HIM, Hill Interaction Matrix, 1214
HIS, Haptic Intelligence Scale for Adult Blind, 498
HIT, Holtzman Inkblot Technique, 1471
HMCT, Harrower's Multiple Choice Test, 1499d
HNTLA, Hiskey-Nebraska Test of Learning Aptitude, 499
HOD, Hoffer-Osmond Diagnostic Test, 1215
HOQ, Hysteroid-Obessoid Questionnaire, 1224
HPIT, Harrower's Psychodiagnostic Inkblot Test, 1499c
HRI, Human Relations Inventory, 1221
HSPQ, Jr.-Sr. High School Personality Questionnaire, 1253
HT, Hand Test, 1470
HVOT, Hooper Visual Organization Test, 1216
HWTS, Humm-Wadsworth Temperament Scale, 1222
IAAT, Iowa Algebra Aptitude Test, 681
ICA, Inventory of College Activities, 1244
ICL, Interpersonal Check List, 1240
ILBDQ, Ideal Leader Behavior Description Questionnaire, 2449
ILTS, Integration Level Test Series, 1237
IMPS, Inpatient Multidimensional Psychiatric Scale, 1232
IPAT ASQ, IPAT Anxiety Scale Questionnaire, 1225
ISRT, Iowa Silent Reading Tests, 1560
ITBS, Iowa Tests of Basic Skills, 19
ITED, Iowa Tests of Educational Development, 20
ITPA, Illinois Test of Psycholinguistic Abilities, 981
ITSC, It Scale for Children, 1247
JAIM, Job Analysis and Interest Measurement, 1250
JEPI, Junior Eysenck Personality Inventory, 1252
JI, Jesness Inventory, 1249
KAS, Katz Adjustment Scales, 1255
KAT, Kuhlmann-Anderson Test, 398
KDPCL, KD Proneness Check List, 1254b
KDPS, KD Proneness Scale, 1254a
KLHKT, Kilander-Leach Health Knowledge Test, 935
KOIS, Kuder Occupational Interest Survey, 2194
KPR-P, Kuder Preference Record—Personal, 1256
KPR-V, Kuder Preference Record—Vocational, 2195
K-R, Kent-Rosanoff Free Association Test, 1480
KTSA, Kahn Test of Symbol Arrangement, 1478
LAB, Level of Aspiration Board, 1261
LAIS, Leiter Adult Intelligence Scale, 504
LBDQ, Leader Behavior Description Questionnaire, 2451
LBDQ-12, Leader Behavior Description Questionnaire, Form 12, 2452
LCRRT, Lee-Clark Reading Readiness Test, 1711
LMTA, Language Modalities Test for Aphasia, 2079
LOQ, Leadership Opinion Questionnaire, 2454
LSAT, Law School Admission Test, 2349

LTIT, Lorge-Thorndike Intelligence Tests, 400
MAACL, Multiple Affect Adjective Check List, 1293
MACC, MACC Behavioral Adjustment Scale, 1264
MAP, Musical Aptitude Profile, 209
MAPS, Make A Picture Story, 1482
MAT, Metropolitan Achievement Tests, 22
MAT, Miller Analogies Test, 404
MAT, Motivation Analysis Test, 1291
MAT, Music Achievement Tests, 207
MBHR, M-B History Record, 1265
MBTI, Myers-Briggs Type Indicator, 1294
MCAT, Medical College Admission Test, 2355
MCI, Minnesota Counseling Inventory, 1280
MDAP, Machover Draw-A-Person Test, 1481
ME, Manson Evaluation, 1271
MEAT, Minnesota Engineering Analogies Test, 2344
MFD, Memory-For-Designs Test, 1277
MHQ, Middlesex Hospital Questionnaire, 1279
MIQ, Minnesota Importance Questionnaire, 2283
MLAT, Modern Language Aptitude Test, 221
MMA, Measures of Musical Abilities, 206
MMPI, Minnesota Multiphasic Personality Inventory, 1281
MPAS, Maryland Parent Attitude Survey, 1273
MPCL, Mooney Problem Check List, 1289
MPDT, Minnesota Percepto-Diagnostic Test, 1485
MPI, Maudsley Personality Inventory, 1275
MPS, Minnesota Preschool Scale, 509
MRHT, Modified Rhyme Hearing Test, 2046
MRMT, Minnesota Rate of Manipulation Test, 2227
MRT, Metropolitan Readiness Tests, 1716
MSAT, Minnesota Scholastic Aptitude Test, 405
MSCS, Miner Sentence Completion Scale, 1484
MSQ, Minnesota Satisfaction Questionnaire, 2285
MSS, Mental Status Schedule, 1278
MTAI, Minnesota Teacher Attitude Inventory, 868
MTDDA, Minnesota Test for Differential Diagnosis of Aphasia, 2080
MVII, Minnesota Vocational Interest Inventory, 2197
NDRT, Nelson-Denny Reading Test, 1572
NJMI, New Junior Maudsley Inventory, 1296
NOSIE, Nurses' Observation Scale for Inpatient Evaluation, 1298
NSQ, Neuroticism Scale Questionnaire, 1295
NTE, National Teacher Examinations, 869
OAAB, Objective-Analytic (O-A) Anxiety Battery, 1300
OAIS, Opinion, Attitude, and Interest Survey, 1303
OI, Orientation Inventory, 1306
OIT, Organic Integrity Test, 1305
OPI, Omnibus Personality Inventory, 1302
ORT, Object Relations Technique, 1486
OSS, Object Sorting Scales, 1299
OSUPT, Ohio State University Psychological Test, 419
PA, Personal Audit, 1314
PAB, Psychiatric Attitudes Battery, 1496
PAI, Personal Adjustment Inventory, 1313
PAT, Pain Apperception Test, 1488
PAT, Tompkins-Horn Picture Arrangement Test, 1522
PFT, Perceptual Forms Test, 1881
PI, Personality Inventory, 1320
PII, Picture Interest Inventory, 2205
PIL, Purpose in Life Test, 1350
PIT, Picture Identification Test, 1490
PM, Progressive Matrices, 439
PMA, SRA Primary Mental Abilities, 1087
PMAS, Purdue Master Attitude Scales, 1348
PMT, Perceptual Maze Test, 1311
PMT, Porteus Maze Test, 518
PNG, NLN Pre-Nursing and Guidance Examination, 2387
POI, Personal Orientation Inventory, 1315
POMS, Profile of Mood States, 1337

INDEX OF NAMES

This analytical index indicates whether a citation refers to authorship of a test, a test review, an excerpted review, or a reference dealing with a specific test. In addition to listing authors of tests, reviews, and references for all tests in this volume, the index covers out of print (or status unknown) tests listed in earlier volumes in this series. Numbers without colons refer to in print tests; these numbers refer to test entries, not to pages. The abbreviations and numbers following the names may be interpreted thus: "test, 168" indicates authorship of test 168; "rev, 472," authorship of a review of test 472; "exc, 368," authorship of an excerpted review of test 368; and "ref, 1275," authorship of one or more references for test 1275 (the Cumulative Name Index for the test must be consulted to identify the references). Numbers with colons refer to out of print tests not listed in this volume; readers interested in these tests are referred to the last volume listing the test. For example, "test, 36:782" refers to test 782 in Educational, Psychological, and Personality Tests of 1936; "rev, 1:925" to a review of test 925 in the first yearbook (1938 Yearbook); "ref, 2:1243(10)" to reference 10, test 1243 in the second yearbook (1940 Yearbook); "rev, 5:7" to a review of test 7 in the Fifth Yearbook; "test, R:170" to test 170 in Reading Tests and Reviews; "ref, P:230(2)" to reference 2, test 230 in Personality Tests and Reviews; and "test, T:577" to test 577 in the 1961 edition of Tests in Print.

AAHPER Youth Fitness Project: *test,* 914
ALA Board on Personnel Administration: *test,* 5:939
Aalto, E. E.: *ref,* 1281
Aamodt, G. P.: *ref,* 426, 684, 688
Aaron, I. E.: *rev,* 1637, 1643, 1658, 1669, 1674
Aaron, N. S.: *ref,* 1501, 1519
Aaron, P. G.: *ref,* 1519
Aarons, W. B.: *ref,* 1095
Aaronson, B. S.: *ref,* 518, 1094, 1281, 1380, 1387, 1447
Abate, M.: *ref,* 1164
Abbate, M. S.: *test,* 2023
Abbatiello, A. A.: *test,* 2120
Abbey, D. S.: *ref,* 1499
Abbott, A.: *test,* 2:1270
Abbott, C. F.: *ref,* 1133
Abbott, E.: *ref,* 1471
Abbott, G. V. C.: *ref,* 1499
Abbott, G. W.: *ref,* 20
Abbott, K. A.: *ref,* 1121
Abbott, P. S.: *ref,* 1217, 1232, 1255, 1264, 1346, 1435, P:41(10), P:408(30)
Abbott, R. D.: *ref,* 1121, 1165, 1281, 1403
Abbott, R. F.: *ref,* 525, 1447, 1716
Abbott, W. D.: *ref,* 1380, 1499

Abboud, R. D.: *ref,* 1281
Abdel-Ghaffar, A. S. A. K.: *ref,* 400, 1253, 2185
Abdel-Meguid, S. G. M.: *ref,* 1281, 2180
Abdel-Razik, T. M.: *ref,* 542, 546, 551
Abe, C.: *ref,* 551, 564, 1044, 1430, 1466, 2273
Abe, J. D.: *ref,* 1499
Abe, K.: *ref,* 1275, 1474
Abe, S. K.: *ref,* 1164, 1281
Abegg, G. L.: *ref,* 1856
Abegglen, J. C.: *ref,* 1519
Abel, H.: *ref,* 1289, 6:186(4)
Abel, T. M.: *ref,* 381, 483, 525, 558, 578, 1474, 1499, 1516, 1519, 6:228(64), P:450(85)
Abeles, N.: *ref,* 1164, 1205-6, 1245, 1281, 1403, 1415, 1471, 1491, 1519
Abeles, S.: *test,* 1863
Abell, A. P.: *ref,* 357-8, 1044, 1583
Abell, E. L.: *exc,* 7, 1610, 1:876, 1:917, 1:936, 1:1083, 1:1170, 2:1196, 3:35
Abell, J. M.: *ref,* 1133, 1135
Abell, W. R.: *ref,* 1044
Abelson, H. H.: *rev,* 3:30, 3:105; *ref,* 525
Abenson, M. H.: *ref,* 1346

Aber, W. E.: *ref,* 1499
Abercrombie, M. L.: *ref,* 381
Abercrombie, M. L. J.: *ref,* 533, 1921
Abercrombie, S. A.: *test,* 4:524
Aberman, H. M.: *ref,* 1356, 1383
Abernethy, E. M.: *ref,* 525, 1095, 1205, 1320
Abernethy, J.: *ref,* 1053
Abidin, R. R.: *ref,* 522, 529, 1281, 1478
Ables, B. S.: *ref,* 381, 525, 533
Abney, C. W.: *ref,* 574
Aborn, M.: *rev,* 532; *ref,* 525, 532
Abou-Allam, R. M.: *ref,* 1281, 1383
Aboud, J.: *ref,* 1164, 1407, 2194
Abou-Ghorra, I. M.: *ref,* 542, 1151, 1164, 1207
Abraham, C.: *ref,* 542, 546, 551, 1407
Abraham, H. H. L.: *ref,* 1164
Abraham, H. J.: *ref,* 3:617(1)
Abrahams, D.: *ref,* 1280-1
Abrahams, I.: *ref,* 2195
Abrahams, N.: *ref,* 404, 480, 1121, 1403, 2212, 2340, 2344
Abrahams, N. M.: *ref,* 2197, 2212
Abrahamsen, D.: *ref,* 1499
Abram, H. S.: *ref,* 529, 1447, 1470, 1474, 1519

884

Aiken, W. J.: *ref,* 1281
Aikman, A. L.: *ref,* 1123
Ainley, R. G.: *ref,* 1913
Ainsworth, L. H.: *ref,* 1474, 1500, 1519
Ainsworth, L. L.: *ref,* 404, 425, 1626, 1772
Ainsworth, M.: *ref,* 1253
Ainsworth, M. D.: *rev,* 1520, 5:166; *ref,* 1451, 1474, 1499–500, 1519
Ainsworth, M. E.: *ref,* 364, 1253, 1291
Ainsworth, P.: *ref,* 1205
Air, D. H.: *ref,* 439, 529
Air Force Personnel Research Laboratory: *test,* 6:1023
Aita, J. A.: *ref,* 532, 1223, 1380, 1499
Aitken, R. C. B.: *ref,* 1174, 1218, 1225
Ajax, E. T.: *ref,* 1277
Akamine, T.: *ref,* 69, 6:438(457)
Akel, M.: *ref,* 489
Akerman, R. H.: *ref,* 1073
Akers, D. R.: *ref,* P:321(21)
Akers, J. C.: *ref,* 1716
Akers, S. J.: *ref,* 1289
Akhtar, S. N.: *ref,* 1174, 1275, 1451
Al-Amir, H.: *ref,* 382
Alarcon, J.: *ref,* 1377
Albee, G. W.: *exc,* 1499; *ref,* 532, 1095, 1281, 1474, 1499–500
Albert, A.: *ref,* 7:659(1)
Albert, G.: *test,* 813, 819; *ref,* 1501
Albert, K.: *ref,* 525
Alberts, N. F.: *test,* 1, 34, 1088, 2198
Albertson, R. G.: *ref,* 1302
Albizu-Miranda, C.: *ref,* 1320
Albott, W. L.: *ref,* 1447
Albrecht, K. J.: *ref,* 1519
Albrecht, R.: *ref,* 592, 1499
Albright, G. A.: *ref,* 1164, 1281
Albright, L. E.: *rev,* 481, 1091, 2285, 2290; *ref,* 337, 482, 1171, 1348, 1923, 2229, 2234, 2239, 2266, 2392, 2406, 2448, 6:1140(2)
Albright, M. J.: *ref,* 1387, 1485
Albright, N. A.: *rev,* 2:1508, 2:1511
Albright, R. J.: *ref,* 592, 1281, 1293
Alcock, A. T.: *ref,* 1486, 1499
Alcock, T.: *exc,* 1499; *ref,* 1499
Alcorn, D.: *ref,* 1363
Alcorn, J. D.: *test,* 1242; *ref,* 3, 364, 516, 1242, 1536
Aldag, J.: *ref,* 1281
Aldag, J. C.: *ref,* 2212–3
Aldag, J. C. K.: *ref,* 1164, 2212–3
Alden, C. L.: *ref,* 1661
Alden, E.: *ref,* 1123
Alden, P.: *ref,* 1499
Alden, P. J.: *ref,* 1171
Alder, L. O.: *ref,* 1289, 1415
Alderdice, E. T.: *ref,* 525, 532
Alderfer, R. D.: *ref,* 2103
Alderman, E.: *ref,* 2234
Aldrich, A.: *ref,* 1123
Aldrich, C. G.: *ref,* 497, 507
Aldrich, C. K.: *ref,* 1140, 1499
Aldridge, B. G.: *ref,* 6:18(2, 5–6)
Aleamoni, L. M.: *test,* 864; *ref,* 245, 247, 256, 265, 267, 272, 296, 299, 301, 306, 308, 315, 361, 864, 1044, 1281

Alegre, C. E.: *ref,* 551, 574
Alessi, S.: *ref,* 1281
Alessi, S. L.: *ref,* 447, 532, 1499
Alexakos, C. E.: *ref,* 22, 359, 382, 1073, 1546, 1768, 1775
Alexander, A. A.: *ref,* 1281, 1415
Alexander, B. B.: *ref,* 1176, 1294
Alexander, D.: *test,* 7:880; *ref,* 381, 533, 543, 1087, 1447, 1474, 7:880(1–3)
Alexander, D. A.: *ref,* 1191, 1277
Alexander, E. B.: *ref,* 5:326(19)
Alexander, F.: *ref,* 1499
Alexander, F. D.: *ref,* 1383
Alexander, F. S.: *ref,* 532, 1499
Alexander, I. E.: *ref,* 1294, 1519
Alexander, J. F.: *ref,* 439, 914, 1281
Alexander, L.: *ref,* 1499
Alexander, L. A.: *ref,* 1968
Alexander, L. B.: *ref,* 1281
Alexander, M.: *ref,* 1519
Alexander, R. L.: *ref,* 1415
Alexander, S.: *ref,* 525, 529, 1193, 1499
Alexander, S. M.: *ref,* 529, 561, 1169
Alexander, T.: *test,* 6:202; *ref,* 381, 1519, 6:202(1–2)
Alexander, V. K.: *ref,* 1522
Alexander, W. A.: *ref,* 1475
Alexander, W. P.: *test,* 515, 2:1279, 2:1400, 2:1422, 2:1450, 6:514; *exc,* 1320; *ref,* 515, 2:1376(1–3)
Alexandra, M.: *ref,* 1123
Alexiou, N. G.: *test,* 940; *ref,* 940
Aley, T. H.: *ref,* 6:18(7–8), 7:670(13)
Alford, B. A.: *ref,* 1415
Alford, M. L.: *ref,* 185, 1072
Alft, E. C.: *test,* 6:988
Ali, F.: *ref,* 516
Ali, M. B.: *ref,* 672, 709, 746
Aliferis, J.: *test,* 194; *ref,* 194
Alimena, B.: *ref,* 529, 532–3, 1320, 1499
Aliotti, N. C.: *ref,* 589
Al-Issa, I.: *ref,* 1174, 1198, 1275, 1281
Alker, H. A.: *rev,* 1291, 1318; *ref,* 357, 542, 1519
Alker, L. N.: *ref,* 1447
Alkoff, T. D.: *ref,* 1499
Allan, J. H.: *ref,* 529, 1447, 1470, 1474, 1519
Allan, M. E.: *ref,* 507, 525
Allan, T. K.: *ref,* 1094, 1121, 1240, 1273
Allardice, B. S.: *ref,* 1471
Allebach, N. L.: *ref,* 439, 1087
Allebrand, G. N.: *ref,* 1123
Allee, L. D.: *ref,* 1176
Allee, R.: *ref,* 1499
Allee, W. L.: *ref,* 1499
Allen, A.: *ref,* 331, 589
Allen, B. M.: *test,* 1:1064
Allen, B. V.: *ref,* 529, 1145, 1164, 1281, 1499, 2212
Allen, C. E.: *ref,* 1428
Allen, C. H.: *ref,* 1689
Allen, C. L.: *ref,* 1123, 2195, 2212–3
Allen, D. A.: *exc,* 113
Allen, D. H.: *ref,* 1121
Allen, D. J.: *ref,* 1289
Allen, D. T.: *ref,* 1525
Allen, F. H.: *exc,* 1336; *ref,* 1105

Allen, F. J.: *test,* 1:931; *ref,* 1819, 2:1492(14)
Allen, G. E.: *ref,* 1320, 2212
Allen, G. J.: *ref,* 1275, 1391
Allen, G. W.: *ref,* 1911
Allen, H. E.: *ref,* 1281
Allen, J.: *test,* 1776; *ref,* 533
Allen, J. C.: *ref,* 525, 1921
Allen, J. C. Y.: *ref,* 20, 348
Allen, J. E.: *ref,* 1383, 1552, 3:613(4)
Allen, J. G.: *ref,* 1293
Allen, K.: *ref,* 529
Allen, L.: *ref,* 525, 532
Allen, L. R.: *ref,* 1094, 1121
Allen, L. W.: *test,* 1557
Allen, M.: *ref,* 525, 538
Allen, M. H.: *ref,* 1240, 1281
Allen, M. K.: *ref,* 525, 1094, 1109, 1281
Allen, M. M.: *ref,* 398
Allen, R.: *ref,* 1415
Allen, R. D.: *ref,* 525; *test,* 2:1337
Allen, R. J.: *ref,* 357, 1134, 2195
Allen, R. L.: *exc,* 1:1002
Allen, R. M.: *ref,* 355, 375, 391, 407, 425, 439, 487, 489, 496–7, 505, 516, 529, 532–3, 1164, 1237, 1281, 1320, 1387, 1403, 1428, 1447, 1499, 1921
Allen, R. P.: *ref,* 1281
Allen, R. R.: *ref,* 1176
Allen, S.: *ref,* 529, 592
Allen, T. W.: *ref,* 1499
Allender, J. S.: *ref,* 2355
Aller, F. D.: *ref,* 1121
Allerdice, M. E.: *ref,* 914
Allerhand, M. E.: *ref,* 490, 516, 1281, 1499
Alley, G. R.: *ref,* 543, 1447
Allgaier, E.: *ref,* 842
Allgood, E. V.: *ref,* 361
Alling, R. L.: *ref,* 489, 525
Allison, D. E.: *ref,* 400
Allison, E. E.: *exc,* 538
Allison, G.: *ref,* 4:277(158)
Allison, H. W.: *ref,* 1499
Allison, J.: *ref,* 529, 533, 1499, 1519
Allison, J. R.: *ref,* 914
Allison, L.: *ref,* 1320
Allison, R. B.: *ref,* 357, 1499, 1519
Allison, R. N.: *ref,* 1140
Allison, S. G.: *ref,* 1499
Allman, R. W.: *ref,* 1626
Allman, T. S.: *ref,* 1383
Allmandinger, M. F.: *ref,* 1074
Allor, B. A.: *ref,* 533
Allport, F. H.: *test,* 1090, 2:1199; *ref,* 1090
Allport, G. W.: *test,* 1090, 1403–4, 2:1199; *ref,* 1090, 1403, 2:1243(1)
Allred, D. L.: *ref,* 1499
Allred, G. H.: *ref,* 1121
Allred, R. A.: *test,* 1604
Allred, R. C.: *ref,* 1149, 1225
Alltop, L. B.: *ref,* 1281
Alluisi, E. A.: *ref,* 419
Allumbaugh, J.: *ref,* 1164
Allyn, N. C.: *ref,* 1050
Alm, O. W.: *ref,* 1123
Almack, J. C.: *rev,* 1:1159, 2:1310, 2:1315, 2:1499
Almgren, P. E.: *ref,* 439
Almond, C. H.: *ref,* 1281

Ashcroft, L. M.: *ref*, 1281
Ashcroft, S. C.: *ref*, 655
Ashe, M. R.: *ref*, 1073
Ashe, M. R. B.: *ref*, 1253
Asher, E. J.: *test*, 3:132, 3:234, 3:311; *ref*, 525, 1519, 2234, 2:1284 (1), 2:1402(2), 4:660(25)
Asher, J. J.: *ref*, 551
Asher, J. W.: *ref*, 357, 589, 688
Asher, P.: *ref*, 525
Asher, W.: *ref*, 357, 361, 425
Ashford, T. A.: *rev*, 1832, 1844–5, 3:568, 5:737; *test*, 3:557, 3:559; *ref*, 1818–9, 3:565(1), 4:607(2), 4:608(2), 4:611(1), 4:612(1)
Ashford, Z. W.: *ref*, 36, 1123, 1603
Ashlock, P.: *ref*, 493, 533
Ashlock, P. R.: *ref*, 493, 533
Ashmore, B. J.: *ref*, 1164, 1193–4, 1281
Ashmore, D. L.: *ref*, 1121
Ashworth, M. G.: *ref*, 1705
Askar, A. M.: *ref*, 532, 1192, 1281
Askov, E.: *test*, 1655, 1776
Aslin, N. C.: *ref*, 48
Asprey, G. M.: *ref*, 1281
Aspridy, C.: *ref*, 1716
Asquith, R. H.: *ref*, 2454, 2459
Assael, M.: *ref*, 1499
Assawamatiyanont, S.: *ref*, 1127
Asso, D.: *ref*, 529, 1275
Associated Personnel Technicians, Inc.: *test*, 2119, 2294
Association of American Medical Colleges: *test*, 2355
Association of Collegiate Schools of Architecture: *test*, 2359
Association of Schools and Colleges of Optometry: *test*, 2357
Asta, P.: *ref*, 1193, 1280, 1315, 1322, 2408
Asthana, H. S.: *ref*, 1499
Astill, D. E.: *ref*, 981
Astin, A. W.: *rev*, 1050, 1091, 2212; *test*, 1244; *ref*, 49, 357, 1044, 1121, 1133, 1244, 1281, 1302, 1383, 1430, 2212, 7:670(19, 21–2)
Astin, H. S.: *ref*, 1094
Aston, P. J.: *ref*, 1486
Astrachan, M.: *exc*, 1499
Astrachan, M. A.: *ref*, 497
Åström, J.: *ref*, 1275
Atar, H.: *ref*, 1169, 1499
Ataullah, K.: *ref*, 5:326(2)
Atchison, C. O.: *ref*, 533, 1415, 1501
Atha, D. R.: *ref*, 944
Atha, J.: *test*, 941
Athanasiou, R.: *ref*, 1302
Athanassiades, J. C.: *ref*, 1194, 1370
Athelstan, G. T.: *ref*, 1403, 2212–3
Athey, E. B.: *ref*, 1281
Athey, I. J.: *ref*, 1603
Atkey, R. R.: *ref*, 532
Atkins, R.: *ref*, 440, 1380
Atkins, S. D.: *rev*, 291, 2:1363, 2:1367
Atkinson, B. H.: *ref*, 361, 546, 561, 577
Atkinson, E.: *ref*, 2195
Atkinson, G.: *ref*, 1164, 1256, 1403, 2195, 2212
Atkinson, G. C.: *ref*, 1281
Atkinson, J. A.: *ref*, 2195, 6:438 (501)

Atkinson, J. W.: *ref*, 1164, 1519
Atkinson, K. W.: *ref*, 1337
Atkinson, R. M.: *ref*, 1281
Atkinson, S. L.: *ref*, 981
Atkinson, S. M.: *ref*, 439
Attea, M.: *ref*, 1624, 1628–9
Attea, W. J.: *ref*, 1403
Attkisson, C. C.: *ref*, 1474
Attwell, A. A.: *ref*, 7, 50, 364, 439, 496, 1087, 1225, 1724
Attwood, M. L.: *test*, 922
Atty, J. C.: *ref*, 2195
Atwell, C. R.: *test*, 179, 4:316; *exc*, 532; *ref*, 179, 525, 3:220(44), 4:315(3), 4:316(1)
Atwood, G. E.: *ref*, 1154, 1281
Atwood, R. W.: *ref*, 1281, 1470
Auble, D.: *ref*, 5:66(11)
Aubry, W. E.: *ref*, 1176, 1315
Aucker, J. R.: *ref*, 20, 1073
Aucutt, J. P.: *ref*, 1478
Audiometer Sales Corporation: *test*, 5:762
Audivox, Inc.: *test*, 6:942
Audubon, J. J.: *ref*, 1499
Auerbach, A. H.: *ref*, 1232
Auerbach, S. M.: *ref*, 1391
Auger, R.: *ref*, 1216
Augoustaki, O.: *ref*, 518, 529, 533
Augspurger, E. F.: *test*, 1950
August, I.: *ref*, 1716, 1883, 1921
August, J.: *ref*, 1499, P:450(81, 90)
Aukerman, R. C.: *ref*, 1536, 1610
Auld, F.: *exc*, 1195; *ref*, 1499, 1519
Aull, G.: *test*, 1516
Aumack, F. L.: *test*, T:2017
Aumack, L.: *ref*, 1281, 1516
Auman, R.: *ref*, 1295
Aungst, L. F.: *ref*, 2069
Auria, C.: *ref*, 533, 1087
Auricchio, E. W.: *ref*, 381
Aursand, I. M.: *ref*, 482, 2214, 5:308(366), 5:615(10)
Ausdenmoore, R. J.: *ref*, 1469
Austin, A. S.: *ref*, 1918
Austin, B. A.: *ref*, 1315
Austin, C. J.: *ref*, 1289
Austin, C. N.: *ref*, 1403
Austin, G. R.: *ref*, 361
Austin, J. J.: *test*, 1728
Austin, L. J.: *ref*, 1207
Austin, M. C.: *rev*, 1881, 1921
Austin, R. L.: *ref*, 1302
Auston, C. A.: *ref*, 1171, 2195
Australian Council for Educational Research: *test*, 323, 326, 328–9, 338, 1613, 2117–8, 2237–8, 2:1309, 4:272–3, 4:398, 5:173, 5:222, 5:298, 5:330, 5:616, 6:282, 6:435–6, 6:592, 6:782, 6:886, 6:978
Ausubel, D. P.: *ref*, 1281, 1499, 2195, 2199
Auten, R. T.: *ref*, 1164
Automata Corporation: *test*, 1030
Auvenshine, C. D.: *test*, 1122, 1282; *ref*, 1044, 1164, 1281–2
Avakian, S. A.: *ref*, 435, 1087, 1223, 1716
Averill, J. R.: *ref*, 1121, 1281
Averill, L. A.: *ref*, 69
Avery, C.: *ref*, 529, 1428
Avery, C. B.: *ref*, 1428
Avery, C. D.: *ref*, 498, 529

Avery, G. T.: *ref*, 525, 2:1399(3), 2:1424(3)
Avila, D.: *ref*, 50, 1690
Avila, D. L.: *ref*, 1302, 1519
Avirett, P.: *test*, 676
Avrill, D. V.: *ref*, 1711
Awduche, E. O.: *ref*, 1913
Ax, A.: *exc*, 1499
Ax, A. F.: *ref*, 364, 529, 1261, 1295, 1383, 1499
Axel, G. R.: *ref*, 1519
Axelbaum, E. M.: *ref*, 525, 545
Axelrod, D. W.: *test*, T:2026
Axelrod, H. C.: *test*, 2:1244; *ref*, 2:1244(1)
Axelrod, J.: *ref*, 1499
Axmaker, L. W.: *ref*, 1291, 1415
Axtell, B.: *ref*, 1499
Axtell, B. A.: *ref*, 1499
Axtell, S. B.: *ref*, 1281
Ayad, J. M.: *ref*, 1499
Ayer, F. C.: *test*, 6:317; *ref*, 4:198 (1)
Ayer, F. L.: *rev*, 3:10, 4:66, 4:702
Ayer, M. J.: *ref*, 1281
Ayers, A. W.: *ref*, 1918, 2454
Ayers, F. W.: *ref*, 1281
Ayers, H. B.: *ref*, 890
Ayers, J. B.: *ref*, 404, 516, 869, 1383, 1716
Ayers, J. D.: *rev*, 63, 549, 6:5; *ref*, 559, 561, 1383
Ayers, L. D.: *ref*, 20, 1073
Ayers, M. A.: *ref*, 533
Aylaian, A.: *ref*, 529, 1447
Aylesworth, H. C.: *ref*, 342
Aylward, M. S.: *ref*, 1121, 2212, 2344
Aymat, F.: *ref*, 381, 1447, 1921
Ayres, A. J.: *test*, 1104, 1885–7, 1902, 1928; *ref*, 50, 497, 981, 1073, 1104, 1885–7, 1902, 1921, 1928, 2028
Ayres, L. P.: *test*, 908
Ayres, R. W.: *ref*, 1109, 1315
Ayudhaya, N.: *ref*, 1305
Azancot, C. A.: *ref*, 1474
Azar, G. J.: *ref*, 1145
Azcarate, E.: *ref*, 1470, 1499
Azima, F. C.: *ref*, 532, 1447, 1499
Azimi, C.: *ref*, 1281
Azzi, E.: *ref*, 1449, P:502(11)

BAAS, M. L.: *ref*, 2195
Baasel, P. B.: *ref*, 1281
Babbott, E. F.: *ref*, 69, 152, 425
Babcock, F. C.: *ref*, 914
Babcock, H.: *test*, 1105; *ref*, 525, 1105, 1320, 2251
Babcock, J. C.: *rev*, 2:1372, 2:1375
Babcock, M. E.: *ref*, 518, 1313
Babcock, V. F.: *test*, 3:550
Babigian, H.: *ref*, 440, 1380
Babikow, P. W.: *ref*, 1281, 7:55 (25)
Babladelis, G.: *ref*, 1164
Babson, S. G.: *ref*, 525
Bach, G. L.: *test*, 1968; *ref*, 1968
Bach, G. W.: *ref*, 1281
Bach, L. C.: *ref*, 381, 499, 516, 525, 538, 981
Bachelis, F. G.: *ref*, 1499–500
Bachelis, L.: *ref*, 529
Bachelis, L. A.: *ref*, 542, 546, 551, 1499

Balinsky, B.: *rev,* 1462, 1476, 2216, 4:359; *test,* 2316; *ref,* 426, 525, 529, 532, 1499, 2227–9, 2251, 2258, 2266–7
Balint, M.: *ref,* 1516
Balken, E. R.: *exc,* 1515; *ref,* 483, 1519
Ball, B.: *ref,* 1281
Ball, F. J.: *ref,* 1087
Ball, H.: *ref,* 1281
Ball, J. C.: *ref,* 1281
Ball, J. M.: *ref,* 1074
Ball, L.: *ref,* 1320
Ball, M. E.: *ref,* 1281, 1380
Ball, M. K.: *ref,* 1121, 1415, 2195
Ball, M. T.: *ref,* 1516
Ball, R. L.: *ref,* 868, 1294
Ball, R. S.: *rev,* 509; *test,* 2:1242; *exc,* 487; *ref,* 487, 497, 507, 525, 2:1242(1)
Ball, T. S.: *ref,* 525, 1192, 1446, 1883
Ballachey, E.: *ref,* 1217
Ballachey, E. L.: *test,* 1217
Ballantyne, R. H.: *ref,* 69, 357, 1074, 1164
Ballard, H. T.: *ref,* 529, 1145, 1289
Ballard, K. B.: *ref,* 1121
Ballard, P. B.: *test,* R:88, T:1356, T:1361; *ref,* 416
Ballard, R. E.: *ref,* 1350
Ballard, R. G.: *ref,* 1281
Ballard, S. N.: *ref,* 1164, 1415
Ballas, A. C.: *ref,* 1281
Ballen, R.: *test,* 2319
Ballenger, H. L.: *test,* 4:165; *ref,* 1569
Baller, W. R.: *rev,* 1008–9, 1360, 1371, 4:583; *test,* 5:533; *ref,* 5:533(2)
Ballif, B. L.: *test,* 1099
Ballinger, T.: *ref,* 381
Ballo, G. R.: *ref,* 1478
Balloch, J. C.: *ref,* 1499
Ballou, S. I.: *ref,* 2212
Balodimos, M. C.: *ref,* 1281
Balogh, B.: *ref,* 1101, 1516
Balogh, J. K.: *ref,* 1254
Balow, B.: *test,* 1574, 1647; *ref,* 1567, 1574, 1877
Balow, I. H.: *test,* 22, 637, 1567; *ref,* 400, 1702, 1877
Balshan, I. D.: *ref,* 1207
Balsley, I. W.: *rev,* 2141
Baltes, P. B.: *ref,* 1087, 1418
Balthazar, E. E.: *test,* 1107; *ref,* 532–3, 1107
Baltimore County French Language Committee: *test,* 241, 303
Balyeat, R. M.: *ref,* 426
Bamford, J. L.: *ref,* 364, 529, 1261, 1295, 1383
Ban, T. A.: *ref,* 1298
Banaghan, W. F.: *ref,* 533
Banaka, W. H.: *ref,* 529, 1380
Banas, N.: *ref,* 493, 533, 981
Banas, P.: *ref,* 796, 2151, 7:1103 (3)
Banas, P. A.: *ref,* 1073, 1281, 2212
Banathy, B. H.: *test,* 7:253, 7:272, 7:286, 7:317
Band, R. I.: *ref,* 439, 1281
Bandler, L.: *ref,* 1519
Banducci, R.: *ref,* 1430

Bandura, A.: *ref,* 1499
Banerjee, C.: *ref,* 2173
Banerjee, D.: *ref,* 1164, 1275, 1289, 1500
Banford, S. A.: *ref,* 1390
Bangas, M. V.: *ref,* 1500
Banghart, F. W.: *ref,* 1121, 2355
Bangs, A. J.: *ref,* 1095, 1772
Banham, K. M.: *test,* 521, 523, 1385, 1715; *ref,* 1715, 6:849(1)
Banik, S. N.: *ref,* 1499
Banikiotes, P. G.: *ref,* 1174, 1501
Banker, H. J.: *ref,* 3:247(1)
Banker, M. H.: *ref,* 1313
Banks, C.: *rev,* 439, 491; *ref,* 331, 439, 446, 1320
Banks, C. E. K.: *rev,* 368, 434
Banks, E. M.: *test,* 1708
Banks, H. C.: *ref,* 1499
Banks, M. H.: *ref,* 1218, 1275, 1279, 1383
Banks, R. R.: *ref,* 1383, 1403, 2195
Bannatyne, A. D.: *ref,* 981, 1277
Banner, R. H.: *ref,* 1281
Bannister, D.: *test,* 1198; *ref,* 439, 1198, 1281
Bannochie, M. N.: *ref,* 22, 50, 103, 381, 493, 503, 505, 533, 558, 1087, 1552, 1629
Bannon, C. J.: *ref,* 1863, 7:840(1)
Bannon, M. M.: *ref,* 2221
Bannon, W. J.: *ref,* 439, 495, 525, 1680
Bansavage, J. C.: *ref,* 1123
Banta, T. J.: *ref,* 1164
Bar, A.: *ref,* 1474
Barabasz, A. F.: *ref,* 525, 589
Baratz, S. S.: *ref,* 1516
Barba, M. A.: *ref,* 1293
Barbe, W.: *ref,* 391, 1560
Barbe, W. B.: *ref,* 426
Barbee, E. W.: *ref,* 349, 533
Barbee, R. E.: *ref,* 1176
Barber, D.: *ref,* 15, 36
Barber, H. O.: *ref,* 36
Barber, L. W.: *ref,* 497
Barber, T. X.: *ref,* 1164, 1207, 1240
Barbera, R. C.: *ref,* 2214
Barberousse, E. H.: *ref,* 1294
Barbour, M. A.: *ref,* P:390(23)
Barbour, R. F.: *exc,* 1451, 1459, 1489
Barclay, A.: *exc,* 1471, 1882; *ref,* 381, 522, 525, 529, 533, 538, 543, 981, 1277, 1428, 1499, 1519
Barclay, A. G.: *rev,* 1158; *ref,* 381
Barclay, A. M.: *ref,* 1519
Barclay, G. L.: *ref,* 1215
Barclay, J. E.: *ref,* 518
Barclay, J. R.: *test,* 1108; *ref,* 1121, 1430, 2197
Barclay, L. K.: *test,* 1108
Barcus, C. G.: *ref,* 1281
Bard, M.: *ref,* 1094, 1145, 1499, 1519
Bar-David, D.: *ref,* 2079
Bardecki, A.: *ref,* 1175
Barden, D. M. F.: *ref,* 1265
Barden, H. E.: *ref,* 3:678(9)
Barden, J. W.: *ref,* 2451
Bardis, P. D.: *ref,* P:381(27, 32, 34)
Bardon, E. J.: *ref,* 1281
Bardwick, J. M.: *ref,* 1195

Bare, C. E.: *ref,* 1123, 1164, 1193–4, 1403, 1407, 1499, 2195
Barendregt, J. T.: *ref,* 1499
Barger, B.: *ref,* 361, 1281, 1490
Barger, P. M.: *ref,* 1281, 1471
Barham, R.: *ref,* 559
Barik, H.: *ref,* 592
Barile, P. A.: *ref,* 1383
Barillas, M. G.: *ref,* 1098
Barker, A. J.: *ref,* 1481
Barker, C.: *ref,* 4:472(1)
Barker, D.: *test,* 569
Barker, D. G.: *ref,* 914
Barker, G. B.: *ref,* 532, 1499
Barker, H. R.: *ref,* 1281
Barker, J.: *ref,* 2065
Barker, J. O.: *ref,* 2065
Barker, L. L.: *ref,* 542, 561, 1775
Barker, R. F.: *ref,* 1194
Barker, R. G.: *ref,* 426, 1320, 1416
Barkley, B. J.: *ref,* 1447
Barkley, M. J.: *ref,* 355, 439, 1711
Barkman, P. F.: *ref,* 1403
Barksdale, A.: *ref,* 2199
Barksdale, M. W.: *ref,* 1428
Barlow, D. H.: *ref,* 357, 425
Barlow, D. L.: *ref,* 1383
Barlow, F. P.: *ref,* 525
Barna, J. D.: *ref,* 1164, 1281
Barnabas, B.: *test,* 332, 2222, 4:38; *ref,* 426, 482, 1281, 1320, 2212, 2239
Barnard, B.: *test,* 75; *ref,* 202
Barnard, E. L.: *test,* 725, 1585
Barnard, H. B.: *test,* 35:192–3
Barnard, L. W.: *ref,* 2098
Barnard, W. H.: *ref,* 1576
Barnes, A. C.: *ref,* 840
Barnes, C. A.: *ref,* 1207
Barnes, C. M.: *ref,* 543, 1471
Barnes, D. F.: *ref,* 1322
Barnes, D. J.: *ref,* 1519
Barnes, E. H.: *ref,* 1281
Barnes, E. J.: *ref,* 1447
Barnes, J. M.: *ref,* 29
Barnes, J. R.: *ref,* 1144, 1289
Barnes, K. D.: *ref,* 1123
Barnes, L. B.: *ref,* 1383, 1403, 1519
Barnes, M. R.: *ref,* 1105
Barnes, M. W.: *ref,* 3:217(114–5)
Barnes, P. J.: *ref,* 425
Barnes, T. C.: *ref,* 1095, 1223, 1447, 1499
Barnes, T. J.: *ref,* 1121
Barnes, W.: *rev,* 1:949
Barnes, W. E.: *ref,* 688
Barnett, A.: *ref,* 2258, 2266, 4:277 (158)
Barnett, C. D.: *ref,* 1289
Barnett, G. J.: *ref,* 2212
Barnett, I.: *ref,* 532, 1499
Barnett, L. C. F.: *ref,* 1315
Barnett, M.: *test,* 1549, R:52
Barnett, R.: *ref,* 1094, 1121, 1403
Barnett, T. M.: *ref,* 69, 348, 1044
Barnette, W. L.: *ref,* 87, 342, 425, 621, 1090, 1101, 1121, 1281, 1844, 2129, 2135, 2195, 2197, 2212, 2234, 2239, 2266, 2:1377(43), 4:277 (200, 261), 4:810(3, 5)
Barnette, Z. B.: *ref,* 1918
Barney, O. P.: *ref,* 1254
Barnhart, A. E.: *ref,* 2451
Barnhart, E. L.: *ref,* 1583, 6:255 (15), 6:438(491)

Batt, H. V.: *ref,* 1499
Battersby, W. S.: *ref,* 1924
Battin, R.: *ref,* 381, 533, 981
Battle, E. S.: *ref,* 497, 525, 532, 1087
Batts, V.: *ref,* 331
Baty, M. A.: *ref,* 1466, 1519
Bat-Zion, N.: *ref,* 1447
Bauer, D. H.: *ref,* 361
Bauer, G. R.: *ref,* 1394–5
Bauer, J.: *ref,* 1469
Bauer, M. L.: *ref,* 1121
Bauer, N. J.: *ref,* 1123
Bauer, R.: *ref,* 358, 2212, 7:1090 (10)
Bauer, R. W.: *ref,* 439, 529
Bauer, W. W.: *exc,* 2:1501, 2:B835, 3:419
Bauermeister, P. J.: *ref,* 1281
Bauernfeind, R. H.: *rev,* 4, 420, 1321, 5:100; *test,* 1369; *exc,* 2170; *ref,* 31, 1360, 1403, 2195
Baugh, A. P.: *ref,* 1481, 1499
Baugh, V. S.: *ref,* 447, 1481, 1499
Baughman, E. E.: *exc,* 1499; *ref,* 36, 525, 1087, 1121, 1281, 1499, 1519
Baukol, J. H.: *ref,* 1281
Baum, M. P.: *ref,* 5:766(9)
Baum, R. C.: *ref,* 1176
Bauman, E.: *ref,* 1447, 1485, 1921
Bauman, G.: *ref,* 1169, 1499
Bauman, M. H.: *ref,* 1281
Bauman, M. J.: *ref,* 1225
Bauman, M. K.: *test,* T:1905, *ref,* 2223, 2227, 2231
Baumann, K. S.: *ref,* 516, 533, 1447
Baumann, M. L.: *ref,* 1123
Baumberger, T. S.: *ref,* 1499
Baumeister, A.: *ref,* 533, 1387
Baumeister, A. A.: *ref,* 35, 361, 533
Baumgartel, H.: *ref,* 1176
Baumgarten, D. L.: *ref,* 525, 533
Baumgold, J.: *ref,* 529, 2234
Baumrind, D.: *ref,* 6:223(14)
Baur, L. M.: *ref,* 1475
Baurer, H. T.: *ref,* 3:678(12)
Bausch & Lomb, Inc.: *test,* 1923, 1925
Bavelas, A.: *ref,* 381
Bawden, H. T.: *test,* 1:953
Baxter, B.: *rev,* 1091, 2289, 2308, 2456, 3:221, 3:252; *ref,* 426, 1207
Baxter, E. D.: *test,* 4:32; *ref,* 4:32(1–2)
Baxter, E. W.: *test,* 2:1514; *ref,* 2:1514(1)
Baxter, J. C.: *ref,* 1240, 1281, 1471, 1482, 1499, 1519
Baxter, J. L.: *ref,* 2195
Bay, J. H.: *ref,* 1121, 1164
Bay, M. S.: *ref,* 532
Baye, A. Y. O.: *ref,* 1794, 1844
Bayer, A. E.: *ref,* 1058, 1244
Bayes, A. H.: *ref,* 1164
Bayles, E. E.: *rev,* 1:1088, 1:1091
Bayley, N.: *rev,* 497, 507, 509, 529, 3:285, 5:404, 5:411; *test,* 484, 2:1382; *exc,* 497, 509; *ref,* 359, 484, 487, 497, 525, 529, 532, 1121, 1320, 2195, 2:1382(1), 4:324(60)
Bayley, S. J.: *ref,* 1281
Baylor, C. C.: *ref,* 349
Bayroff, A. G.: *ref,* 1067

Bayti, J. L.: *ref,* 2173
Bayton, J. A.: *ref,* 1207
Bayuk, R. J.: *ref,* 36, 400, 424, 1716
Baziak, A. T.: *ref,* 2383, 2387
Bazik, A. M.: *ref,* 1095, 1403, 2212
Baznik, C. A.: *ref,* 1164
Beach, F. A.: *test,* 3:174
Beach, H. D.: *ref,* 439, 532
Beach, J. E.: *ref,* 439, 529
Beach, L.: *ref,* 1162, 1499
Beach, L. R.: *ref,* 1245, 1302, 1320
Beach, S.: *ref,* 398, 5:326(33)
Beal, A. E.: *ref,* 1095
Beal, L. E.: *ref,* 2197
Beal, M. A.: *ref,* 1280
Bealer, J. E.: *ref,* 1302
Beales, B. B.: *ref,* 1222
Beall, H. S.: *ref,* 1281
Beall, L.: *ref,* 1281
Beals, E. W.: *ref,* 357
Beals, L.: *ref,* 1123
Beaman, G. C.: *ref,* 3:217(81)
Beamer, B. A.: *ref,* 1572, 1583
Beamer, G. C.: *ref,* 425–6, 868, 1069, 1073, 2135, 2195, 2212, 2229, 2251, 2266, 2323
Beamish, J. J.: *ref,* 850, 1207, 1280–1
Beamish, P.: *ref,* 1275
Beamon, W. S.: *ref,* 1403
Bean, A. G.: *ref,* 357, 1356
Bean, K. L.: *rev,* 211, 1446, 5:246, 6:125; *test,* 1510; *ref,* 211, 426, 525, 1510, 2266
Bean, W. J.: *ref,* 533
Beans, D. T.: *ref,* 505
Bear, M. V.: *test,* T:1798
Bear, R. B.: *ref,* 426
Bear, R. M.: *rev,* 1583, 1745, 3:509, 4:586; *exc,* 1:1108; *ref,* 426, 1560, 1626, 1867, 2:1559(1)
Beard, B. B.: *ref,* 529
Beard, B. H.: *ref,* 1240
Beard, E.: *test,* 1558
Beard, J. G.: *ref,* 361
Beard, M. R.: *test,* 2:1614
Beard, M. T.: *ref,* 1298
Beard, R. B.: *ref,* 1073
Beard, R. M.: *ref,* 217, 331, 525, 1070, 1311
Beardslee, D. C.: *ref,* 1519
Beardsley, J. V.: *ref,* 529, 1281
Beardsley, K.: *ref,* 529, 1499, 1516
Beardsley, K. P.: *ref,* 1090
Beardsley, S. W.: *ref,* 4:10(2)
Beasley, S. R.: *ref,* 1044
Beatley, B.: *ref,* 2:1342(3)
Beatley, R.: *test,* 1:1073, 2:1440
Beaton, A. E.: *ref,* 1403
Beaton, M. A.: *ref,* 2195
Beattie, A. D.: *test,* 779
Beattie, H. R.: *test,* 5:440
Beatty, B. C.: *ref,* 1281
Beatty, L. S.: *test,* 738
Beatty, R. W.: *ref,* 2451, 2454
Beatty, W. W.: *ref,* 908
Beauchamp, J. M.: *ref,* 435, 1717
Beaujour, M.: *ref,* 255
Beaumont, H.: *ref,* 1932
Beaumont, J. G.: *ref,* 1293, 1337
Beaupre, R. G.: *ref,* 1716
Beaupre, W. J.: *ref,* 1207
Beaver, A. P.: *ref,* 1090, 1207, 1281, 2195, 5:308(401)

Beaver, M. L.: *ref,* 2069
Beavers, I.: *ref,* 5:570(3)
Bebeau, D. E.: *ref,* 233
Becher, B. A.: *ref,* 1480
Bechtel, J.: *test,* 3:127
Bechtel, L. P.: *ref,* 1164, 1403
Bechtel, R.: *ref,* 1087
Bechtel, R. B.: *ref,* 1519
Bechtel, R. D.: *ref,* 2212
Bechtold, D. W.: *ref,* 357, 1044, 1291
Bechtold, L. A.: *ref,* 1176
Bechtold, M. L.: *ref,* 1254
Bechtoldt, H.: *rev,* 1069, 1074; *test,* 36:582, 1:1018, 3:598
Bechtoldt, H. P.: *rev,* 1072–3, 1078, 2239; *ref,* 1121, 1281
Becica, B.: *ref,* 364, 574
Beck, A. G.: *ref,* 1499
Beck, A. T.: *ref,* 529
Beck, B. S.: *test,* 6:283
Beck, E. C.: *ref,* 525, 529, 533, 1277, 1418
Beck, E. J.: *ref,* 439, 525, 589
Beck, F.: *ref,* 533
Beck, H. S.: *ref,* 533, 1447, 1469
Beck, I. H. H.: *ref,* 1087, 1151, 1207, 1403
Beck, J. D.: *ref,* 1145
Beck, K. W.: *ref,* 1121
Beck, M.: *ref,* 1474
Beck, M. P.: *ref,* 1101
Beck, N.: *ref,* 1499
Beck, R.: *ref,* 516, 1921
Beck, R. C.: *ref,* 1174, 1383
Beck, R. L.: *rev,* 15, 2:1272, 2:1278, 3:6; *test,* 1578, 1698, 2:1293, 3:17, 6:283; *ref,* 419, 2:1271(4–5), 2:1293(1–3)
Beck, S. J.: *rev,* 1095, 1499, 2:1240; *exc,* 507, 1448, 1499, 6:72; *ref,* 1499
Beck, Y. M.: *test,* 1435
Becker, A. J.: *ref,* 1281, 1423
Becker, B.: *ref,* 1281, 1469, 1499, 1519
Becker, B. C.: *ref,* 529
Becker, C. J.: *ref,* 1121, 1293
Becker, G.: *ref,* 1121, 1164, 1207, 1281
Becker, G. J.: *ref,* 532, 1087, 1386, 1499, 1519
Becker, I. S.: *test,* 2:1465; *ref,* 2:1465(1)
Becker, J.: *ref,* 1169, 1281, 1499, 1519
Becker, J. A.: *ref,* 426, 1164, 1207, 1314, 2195, 2213
Becker, J. T.: *ref,* 516, 533, 981, 1447
Becker, M.: *ref,* 1090, 1320
Becker, M. A.: *ref,* 2045
Becker, P. H.: *ref,* 1429
Becker, P. W.: *ref,* 1193
Becker, S. J.: *ref,* 2213
Becker, S. L.: *ref,* 1281, 1395
Becker, W.: *ref,* 1499
Becker, W. C.: *rev,* 1183, 1320; *ref,* 1186, 1207, 1281, 1383, 1471, 1499
Becker-Carus, C.: *ref,* 1169
Beckerle, G. P.: *ref,* 559
Beckert, C. B.: *ref,* 1280, 1415
Beckett, P. G. S.: *ref,* 1281

Bennett, E. M.: *ref,* 381, 1451, 1499–500

Bennett, G.: *ref,* 1519

Bennett, G. K.: *rev,* 574, 1091, 2184, 3:645, 3:690, 4:355, 6:18; *test,* 93, 157, 333, 358, 376, 473, 644, 781, 794, 1063, 1069, 2148, 2151, 2225, 2239, 2256, 2268, 2290, 2317, 2:1233, 3:446; *exc,* 1516; *ref,* 358, 407, 447, 529, 794, 1069, 1320, 2129, 2135, 2148, 2151, 2225, 2227–9, 2239, 2244, 2251, 2258–60, 2266, 2:1233(5), 3:61(7), 3:159 (2), 3:658(3), 3:660(12), 3:671 (10), 3:678(17), 3:679(10), 5:954(1)

Bennett, H. J.: *ref,* 518, 1380

Bennett, J. L.: *ref,* 1232, 1346

Bennett, J. W.: *ref,* 1044, 1394–5

Bennett, L. A.: *ref,* 1121, 1275, 1281, 1500

Bennett, M. C.: *ref,* 1247

Bennett, M. G.: *test,* 358, 1063

Bennett, M. J.: *ref,* 427

Bennett, M. W.: *ref,* 3:263(44, 49)

Bennett, R.: *ref,* 529

Bennett, R. C.: *ref,* 1447

Bennett, R. E.: *test,* 5:497

Bennett, R. M.: *ref,* 1881

Bennett, T.: *ref,* 5:87(27)

Bennett, V. D. C.: *ref,* 1474

Bennett, W.: *ref,* 1320, 1499

Benning, J. J.: *ref,* 1254

Benninger, C. A.: *ref,* 516

Bennis, W.: *ref,* 1164, 1176, 1383

Benoit, E. P.: *ref,* 349, 489, 505, 525

Bensberg, G. J.: *ref,* 4, 364, 483, 496, 505, 525, 532–3, 1447

Benson, A. L.: *ref,* 869

Benson, C. E.: *ref,* 3:220(19)

Benson, D.: *ref,* 170, 445, 482, 914, 1739, 2212, 2463

Benson, G. B.: *ref,* 868, 1281

Benson, J. P.: *ref,* 1634

Benson, L.: *ref,* 1044, 1048

Benson, P. H.: *ref,* 357

Benson, R. R.: *ref,* 525, 529

Benson, R. W.: *ref,* 2031

Benson, S.: *ref,* 532

Benson, W. W.: *ref,* 1403

Bent, R. J.: *ref,* 1499

Bentall, G.: *ref,* 20, 1603

Bentler, P. M.: *rev,* 1240, 1326, 1415; *test,* 549; *ref,* 516, 549, 1212, 1240, 1275, 1281, 1322, 1389, 1471

Bentley, A.: *test,* 206; *ref,* 206

Bentley, C. S.: *ref,* 1923

Bentley, J. C.: *ref,* 404, 2212

Bentley, M.: *exc,* 518, 1515; *ref,* 1207, 1480

Bentley, R. R.: *test,* 882–4; *exc,* 206; *ref,* 203, 214, 217, 884, 5:246 (1), 6:352(2)

Benton, A. L.: *rev,* 1281, 1384, 1447, 1519, 2092, 3:29; *test,* 543; *exc,* 1105; *ref,* 426, 503, 525, 529, 532–3, 543, 545, 1192, 1277, 1281, 1311, 1380, 1447, 1471, 1499, 2212, 2223, 4:813(4)

Benton, C. D.: *ref,* 1921

Benton, J. A.: *ref,* 1519

Benton, J. E.: *ref,* 589

Benton, J. G.: *ref,* 381, 489, 525, 529, 1447, 1474, 1499, 1501

Benton, J. L.: *ref,* 1151

Benton, R. G.: *ref,* P:381(50)

Benton Review Publishing Co.: *test,* 4:430, 4:599, 4:643, 4:671

Bentovim, L.: *ref,* 1499

Bentsen, I. B.: *ref,* 1519

Bentz, D. D.: *ref,* 1716

Bentz, V. J.: *ref,* 469, 1205–6, 1245, 1403, 1423, 2195, 5:308(313)

Benveniste, S. J.: *ref,* 1499

Ben-Yishay, Y.: *ref,* 529, 1447

Benz, D. A.: *ref,* 1647

Benz, H. E.: *rev,* 713, 2:1457; *test,* 2:1586

Benz, S. C.: *test,* 4:798; *ref,* 4:798 (1–2)

Beran, M.: *ref,* 447, 592, 1281, 1499

Berbiglia, J. C.: *ref,* 840

Bercegeay, W. J.: *ref,* 1289

Bercel, N. A.: *ref,* 1499

Berdie, R. F.: *rev,* 358, 1069, 1072, 1082, 1087, 2195, 2205, 2220–1, 3:639; *test,* 1280, 2212; *ref,* 48, 69, 357, 381, 404–5, 1044, 1069, 1087, 1133, 1280–1, 1403, 2195, 2212, 2266, 3:217(109), 4:277 (233, 263), 4:618(3), 5:87(29), 5:308(291), 6:438(502)

Bereiter, C. E.: *ref,* 545

Berenbaum, H. L.: *ref,* 1109

Berenberg, A. N.: *ref,* 1101, 1474, 1519

Berends, E. H.: *ref,* 1383

Berens, A. E.: *ref,* 361, 1164

Berens, C.: *ref,* 3:470(3–4)

Berenson, B. G.: *test,* 1343; *ref,* 1343

Beretta, S.: *ref,* 589

Berg, B. C.: *ref,* 435

Berg, D. A.: *ref,* 1499

Berg, H. D.: *rev,* 1943, 1945, 1953, 1955, 1980, 3:593, 3:596, 4:23, 5:832, 7:888; *test,* 1:1020, 4:663, 4:684

Berg, I. A.: *exc,* 1281; *ref,* 69, 337, 348, 1205–6, 1320, 1403, 2195, 2212, 2239, 2381, 3:217(139), 4:277(172), 5:886(2), 5:888(4)

Berg, J.: *ref,* 1499

Berg, K. A.: *test,* 1870

Berg, N. L.: *ref,* 516, 1094, 1174, 1358

Berg, O. D.: *ref,* 1069

Berg, P. C.: *rev,* 1702, 1711

Berg, P. S. D.: *ref,* 1275, 1281, 1519

Berg, S. D.: *ref,* 516

Berg, T.: *ref,* 449, 452

Berg, V.: *ref,* 533

Berg, W.: *ref,* 1447

Berg, W. A.: *ref,* 1501

Bergan, A.: *ref,* 533

Bergan, J. R.: *ref,* 1499

Bergee, H. O.: *test,* 5:741

Bergem, J.: *ref,* 1123, 1423, 1536

Bergemann, K.: *ref,* 1193–4, 1320

Bergen, G. L.: *ref,* 189, 211, 1320, 2135, 2212, 2227–9, 2258

Bergeon, J. B.: *ref,* 1045

Berger, A.: *rev,* 1547, 1605; *ref,* 381, 525, 1281, 1481

Berger, A. S.: *ref,* 1281

Berger, B.: *ref,* 1499

Berger, D.: *ref,* 349, 1387, 1499

Berger, D. F.: *ref,* 1164

Berger, D. G.: *ref,* 532, 1499

Berger, E. H.: *ref,* 884, 1164

Berger, E. J.: *test,* 756, 758

Berger, E. M.: *ref,* 1281

Berger, I. L.: *ref,* 1501

Berger, J.: *ref,* 1499

Berger, J. V.: *ref,* 1133

Berger, L.: *ref,* 529, 532, 1448, 1499

Berger, M.: *ref,* 525, 538

Berger, R. A.: *ref,* 914, 1121

Berger, R. M.: *test,* 564, 571–2; *ref,* 457, 551, 564, 1074, 1761, 2212

Berger, S.: *ref,* 1499

Berger, S. E.: *ref,* 525, 529, 1380

Berger, S. I.: *ref,* 1499

Berger, S. R.: *ref,* 1129, 1313

Berger, V. F.: *ref,* 391

Berger, W. G.: *ref,* 1355

Bergerson, W. L.: *ref,* 69

Berges, J.: *ref,* 483

Bergin, A. E.: *ref,* 1164, 1281

Bergman, L. M. E.: *ref,* 1775

Bergman, M.: *ref,* 1281, 1519

Bergman, P.: *ref,* 1281

Bergman, P. S.: *ref,* 1924

Bergman, R. L.: *ref,* 525

Bergmann, A. M. W.: *ref,* 1383

Bergmann, I.: *exc,* 1243

Bergmann, K.: *ref,* 529, 1281

Bergmann, M. S.: *ref,* 1499, 1519

Bergquist, W. H.: *ref,* 1499

Bergren, V. I.: *ref,* 1716

Bergstein, V.: *ref,* 533, 2039

Bergstresser, J.: *ref,* 1320

Bergstresser, J. L.: *ref,* 4:60(2)

Berk, N.: *ref,* 1474, 1499–500, 1519

Berk, R. L.: *ref,* 525, 532, 1898

Berk, T. J. C.: *ref,* 1129

Berke, N. D.: *ref,* 504, 529

Berkeley, M. H.: *ref,* 1228

Berkey, R.: *ref,* 357

Berkman, P. L.: *ref,* 503

Berko, M. J.: *ref,* 489, 497, 525, 578, 1428

Berkowitz, B.: *ref,* 529, 532

Berkowitz, H.: *ref,* 902, 1519

Berkowitz, L.: *ref,* 1207, 1471

Berkowitz, M.: *ref,* 1499

Berkowitz, M. C.: *ref,* 381

Berkowitz, P. H.: *test,* 1450; *ref,* 592, 1447

Berkowitz, W. R.: *ref,* 1164

Berks, M. D.: *ref,* 532

Berks, M. D. D.: *ref,* 4:354(5)

Berkshire, R.: *ref,* 2135, 4:277 (234)

Berkun, M. M.: *ref,* 1500, 1519

Berle, B. B.: *ref,* 1182

Berlew, D. E.: *ref,* 1519

Berlfein, H. P.: *ref,* 2454

Berlin, A. J.: *ref,* 1281

Berlin, C. I.: *ref,* 2028

Berlin, M. A.: *ref,* 533

Berliner, A.: *ref,* 1499

Berlow, N.: *ref,* 1499

Berman, A.: *ref,* 489, 1232

Berman, A. B.: *ref,* 525, 1095, 1474

Berman, D.: *ref,* 1447

Berman, G.: *ref,* 391, 1121

Berman, I.: *ref,* 529, 533

Berman, I. R.: *ref,* 438, 518, 525, 532, 1123, 1223, 1447, 2135, 2212–3, 2227–9, 2258, 3:642(4)

Biller, H. B.: *ref*, 1121, 1247, 1463, 1474
Billeter, P. E.: *ref*, 342
Billett, R. O.: *test*, 6:66
Billhartz, W. H.: *ref*, 36
Billig, A. L.: *ref*, 1095, 1320
Billig, O.: *ref*, 1499
Billing, P. S.: *ref*, 2195
Billinger, L. W.: *ref*, 1360
Billings, E. L.: *ref*, 2:1675(3)
Billingslea, F. Y.: *exc*, 1447; *ref*, 1320, 1447
Billingsly, L. C.: *ref*, 868, 1403
Billington, D. R.: *ref*, 1275
Bills, M. A.: *rev*, 336-7, 421, 780, 2192, 3:221; *ref*, 1222, 1320, 2212, 3:220(20, 48), 4:320(1), 5:913 (20)
Bills, N.: *ref*, 1519
Bills, R. E.: *ref*, 1499, 1519
Billy, H. T.: *ref*, 516
Bilmes, M.: *ref*, 1499
Bilodeau, I. M.: *ref*, 503, 532
Bilon, L. R.: *ref*, 589
Bilorusky, J.: *ref*, 1302
Bilovsky, D.: *ref*, 981
Bilsky, H. B.: *ref*, 1101
Bilyeu, E. E.: *exc*, 318
Binder, A.: *ref*, 1087, 1281, 1499
Binder, H.: *ref*, 1499
Bindman, S. S.: *ref*, 1281
Bindon, D. M.: *ref*, 1482, 1499
Binford, M. L.: *ref*, 404
Bingham, C. W.: *ref*, 211
Bingham, W. C.: *rev*, 2012; *ref*, 342, 439, 529
Bingham, W. J.: *test*, 485
Bingham, W. V.: *rev*, 1:1174; *test*, 3:691; *ref*, 189, 342, 2135, 2212-3, 2227-9, 2251, 2258, 2260, 2266, 2:1325(9), 2:1676(3), 2:1683 (2), 3:220(32), 3:637(5), 3:642 (5), 3:671(6), 3:678(10), 3:689 (4), 3:691(1-2)
Bingman, R. M.: *ref*, 1069, 2195
Bininger, M. L.: *ref*, 425, 3:581(1), 4:618(2), 4:634(1), 4:718(3)
Binion, H. S.: *test*, 1698; *ref*, 1698
Binkley, M. E.: *ref*, 1123
Binks, N.: *ref*, 1200, 1259, 1291
Binks, V.: *ref*, 533, 1626
Binks, V. M.: *ref*, 532
Binnewies, E. R.: *test*, 3:556
Binnewies, W. G.: *ref*, 426
Binz, E.: *ref*, 1499
Biological Sciences Curriculum Study: *test*, 1801-2, 7:795, 7:810, 7:815
Birch, C. M.: *ref*, 1320
Birch, H. C.: *ref*, 1428
Birch, H. G.: *ref*, 516, 525, 529, 532-3, 1499
Birch, J. R.: *ref*, 36, 505
Birch, J. W.: *ref*, 36, 381, 505, 525
Birch, L. B.: *rev*, 8, 495, 1650; *exc*, 525
Birch, R.: *ref*, 1447
Birch, R. W.: *ref*, 1164
Birchenough, C.: *exc*, 3:776
Birchler, G. R.: *ref*, 1433
Bird, A. M.: *ref*, 1121
Bird, D. J.: *ref*, 1289, 2213
Bird, E. I.: *ref*, 1164, 1322, 1383
Bird, G. E.: *test*, 5:354; *ref*, 908, 5:354(2-3)

Bird, H. B.: *ref*, 1121, 2355
Bird, K. L.: *ref*, 1844
Bird, M. H.: *ref*, 187, 189, 2:1325 (2), 2:1329(5)
Bird, R. B.: *ref*, 1320
Bird, R. G.: *ref*, 1073
Birds, V. G.: *ref*, 1281, 1283
Bireley, M. B.: *ref*, 1192
Birge, W. R.: *ref*, 1256
Birjandi, P. F.: *ref*, 1499
Birkemeyer, F.: *ref*, 439, 525, 533
Birkemeyer, F. W.: *ref*, 1439
Birkmaier, E. M.: *test*, 268, 320
Birkner, E. C.: *ref*, 1281
Birnbaum, J.: *ref*, 529, 533, 1169
Birnberg, V. K.: *ref*, 1281
Birnbrauer, J. S.: *ref*, 516
Birney, R. C.: *ref*, 542, 561, 572
Birney, S. D.: *ref*, 489, 538, 1141
Birns, B.: *ref*, 487, 525
Birren, J. E.: *ref*, 439, 529, 532, 1105, 1144, 1480, 1901
Birsh, E.: *test*, 1370
Birtchnell, J.: *ref*, 1377
Bisbee, E. V.: *test*, 1:936; *ref*, 1:936(1)
Bischof, L. J.: *ref*, 1073, 4:277 (235)
Bish, G. G.: *ref*, 349, 589
Bishop, F. V.: *ref*, 1162
Bishop, H.: *ref*, 2:1402(3), 2:1424 (24)
Bishop, H. C.: *ref*, 1315
Bishop, H. M.: *ref*, 483
Bishop, J. B.: *ref*, 1207
Bishop, J. L.: *ref*, 1370
Bishop, J. S.: *ref*, 381
Bishop, L. K.: *ref*, 1383
Bishop, M. P.: *ref*, 1281, 1298, 1346, 1469
Bishop, R.: *ref*, 404
Bishop, R. L.: *test*, T:1330
Bishop, T. J. S.: *ref*, 1275
Bishop, W. E.: *ref*, 1164
Bissett, S. J.: *ref*, 2199
Bissiri, G. R.: *ref*, 1294
Bitcon, L. E.: *ref*, 914
Bither, S. W.: *ref*, 1322
Bitner, G. H.: *ref*, 1403
Bitner, H. M.: *ref*, 1205-6, 1245, 2195
Bittel, J.: *ref*, 2259
Bitterman, M. E.: *ref*, 447, 1281, 4:281(84)
Bittner, J. R.: *ref*, P:63(1)
Bittner, R. H.: *rev*, 2132, 2159, 2252, 2304, 3:680; *ref*, 342, 2:1225(4), 4:317(2)
Bixby, A. P.: *ref*, 868
Bixenstine, V. E.: *ref*, 1281
Bixler, H. H.: *rev*, 159, 2140, 3:158, 3:162, 3:164, 3:268, 4:198, 4:204; *test*, 22, 637, 1567, 2:1312, 2:1313.1, 4:206, 6:877; *ref*, 2:1312 (2)
Bixler, J.: *ref*, 209
Bjerring, J.: *ref*, 533
Bjerstedt, A.: *rev*, 1164, 1329, 1500, 5:33, 6:186; *ref*, 1452
Bjorkman, M. A.: *test*, 7:616
Bjorksten, C.: *ref*, 1499
Blacharsky, E.: *ref*, 1501
Blacher, R. S.: *ref*, 1469
Blachley, P. H.: *ref*, 1093
Black, A. D.: *ref*, 496

Black, A. H.: *ref*, 532
Black, B. G.: *ref*, 533, 1716
Black, D. A.: *ref*, 1281
Black, D. B.: *rev*, 350, 387, 1550, 1593; *ref*, 64, 69, 244, 349, 357, 361, 525, 603, 1048, 1536, 1837, 1859, 6:291(1), 6:438(458, 477), 6:568(8, 10), 6:569(6)
Black, D. O.: *ref*, 2449, 2451
Black, E. L.: *test*, 1539
Black, F. W.: *ref*, 533
Black, H.: *rev*, 113
Black, H. O.: *ref*, 1281
Black, H. P.: *ref*, 105, 361
Black, I. S.: *ref*, 525
Black, J.: *ref*, 1500
Black, J. D.: *rev*, 1259, 1368, 1419, 5:570; *test*, 365; *ref*, 425, 1281, 2129, 2135, 2212, 2239, 2448
Black, J. M.: *ref*, 1281, 1500
Black, J. W.: *test*, 2022; *ref*, 2022
Black, M. D.: *ref*, 1500
Black, M. H.: *ref*, 2135
Black, R. B.: *ref*, 492
Black, R. D.: *test*, 36:575
Black, R. W.: *ref*, 1135, 1415
Black, S.: *ref*, 1275
Black, T. R.: *ref*, 1123
Black, W.: *ref*, 6:159(64)
Black, W. A.: *test*, 4:708
Black, W. G.: *ref*, 1281
Black, W. W.: *ref*, 908
Blackburn, A. R.: *ref*, 532
Blackburn, H.: *ref*, 1281
Blackburn, H. L.: *ref*, 529, 1073
Blackburn, I.: *ref*, 381, 525
Blackburn, J. B.: *ref*, 1073
Blackburn, J. M.: *rev*, 2:1220, 2:1376; *exc*, 2242
Blackburn, J. R.: *ref*, 1073
Blackburn, L. F.: *ref*, 1164
Blackburn, M.: *ref*, 382, 1005, 1303
Blackburn, R.: *ref*, 1218, 1275, 1281
Blacker, E.: *ref*, 1499
Blackham, G. J.: *ref*, 1499, 1519, P:339(9)
Blackhurst, A. E.: *ref*, 542, 546, 551, 561, 577, 594
Blackhurst, J. H.: *rev*, 1:994
Blacklock, C.: *exc*, 486
Blackman, C. T.: *ref*, 1709
Blackman, L. S.: *ref*, 7, 50
Blackman, S.: *ref*, 1281
Blackshire, R. E.: *ref*, 1181
Blackstone, E. G.: *rev*, 799, 3:378, 3:382-3
Blackwell, A. C.: *test*, 3:558
Blackwell, E. B.: *ref*, 1499
Blackwell, R. B.: *ref*, 868, 1164
Blackwell, S.: *test*, 954
Blackwell, T. B.: *ref*, 1499
Blade, M. F.: *ref*, 2241
Blahd, W.: *ref*, 1499
Blai, B.: *ref*, 35, 361
Blaine, G. R.: *ref*, 1499
Blaine, H. M.: *ref*, 484
Blair, C. E.: *ref*, 1315
Blair, F. X.: *ref*, 1277
Blair, G. E.: *ref*, 1383
Blair, G. M.: *exc*, 2:1263; *ref*, 426, 1123, 1499, 2:1263(3)
Blair, J. R.: *ref*, 519
Blair, M.: *ref*, 1225
Blair, M. S. M.: *ref*, 868
Blair, N. J.: *test*, 4:6

Breen, L. J.: *ref,* 358, 1383
Breese, F. H.: *test,* 1186; *ref,* 1087, 1186
Breeskin, J.: *ref,* 533, 1471
Breger, I.: *ref,* 1449
Breger, L.: *ref,* 1121, 1519
Bregman, E. O.: *test,* 35:334, 36:809, 1:1116, 4:317; *ref,* 655, 4:281(76)
Bregman, M.: *ref,* 1281, 1772, 5:308(418)
Bregoli, E. J.: *ref,* 348
Brehm, M. L.: *ref,* 1281
Breidenbaugh, B. E.: *ref,* 2195
Breidenbaugh, V. E.: *test,* 2:1477
Breiger, B.: *ref,* 532, 1499
Breimeier, K. H.: *ref,* 382, 419, 1028, 1164, 1207, 1281, 1294, 2212
Breithaupt, J. F.: *ref,* 1500
Brembeck, W. L.: *ref,* 1775
Bremer, N.: *ref,* 1716
Bremner, E. A.: *ref,* 1499
Brendemuehl, F. L.: *ref,* 349, 400, 1087
Brenden, H. A.: *ref,* 1315
Brender, W. J.: *ref,* 1519
Brener, E. M.: *ref,* 1471, 1519
Brener, R.: *ref,* 1499
Brengelmann, J. C.: *ref,* 439, 489, 505, 516, 525, 529, 543, 1121, 1226, 1275, 1281, 1447
Brenke, W. C.: *rev,* 3:321
Brenkus, P. M.: *ref,* 2355
Brenman, M.: *ref,* 1499, 1519
Brenna, D. W.: *ref,* 48, 1073
Brennan, E. P.: *ref,* 1389
Brennan, J. G.: *ref,* 529
Brennan, J. T.: *ref,* 425, 637, 1087
Brennan, M. J.: *ref,* 1281
Brennan, T.: *ref,* 1174, 1403, 1772
Brennan, T. F.: *ref,* 482, 1121, 2228
Brennan, W. K.: *ref,* 1112, 1269
Brenner, A.: *test,* 1696; *ref,* 381, 435, 947, 1696, 1716, 1724
Brenner, A. R.: *ref,* 1480
Brenner, B.: *ref,* 1499
Brenner, D.: *ref,* 2227
Brenner, L. O.: *ref,* 1499
Brenner, M. S.: *ref,* 1519
Brenner, M. W.: *ref,* 381, 543, 1447
Brenner, R.: *ref,* 1519
Brentlinger, W. H.: *ref,* 438, 2135
Bresee, C. W.: *ref,* 1194, 1370, 1500, 1583, 5:597(8)
Breskin, S.: *ref,* 398, 1169, 1418
Breslich, E. R.: *test,* 669, T:1107
Breslow, A.: *ref,* 1169
Breslow, A. K.: *ref,* 1499
Breslow, E.: *ref,* 2349
Bresnahan, T. J.: *ref,* 1499
Bressler, M. B.: *ref,* 532, 1140
Bretnall, D.: *ref,* 69
Bretnall, E. P.: *ref,* 2212
Bretnall, P.: *ref,* 1169
Breton, G. R.: *ref,* 1302, 1395
Bretsch, H. S.: *ref,* 1289
Breuer, C. E.: *ref,* 424
Brewer, B.: *ref,* 2212
Brewer, C.: *ref,* 529, 543
Brewer, E. J.: *ref,* 533, 1499
Brewer, J.: *ref,* 1499
Brewer, J. H.: *ref,* 1394-5
Brewer, J. J.: *ref,* 1281, 1500
Brewer, J. J. A.: *ref,* 1500

Brewer, J. M.: *ref,* 2195, 2212, 3:635(11)
Brewer, J. W.: *test,* 2:1499
Brewer, T. E.: *ref,* 1207
Brewington, A.: *rev,* 795, 2148
Brewington, W. I.: *ref,* 1164
Brewster, E. S. G.: *ref,* 1383
Brewster, E. T.: *ref,* 1281, 1383
Brewster, H. W.: *ref,* 1289
Brewton, B. C.: *ref,* 589
Briar, S.: *ref,* 1240
Brice, B. C.: *ref,* 1519
Brice, M. M.: *ref,* 425-6, 5:308 (417)
Brick, H.: *ref,* 1281, 1447, 1499
Bricker, A. L.: *ref,* 50
Bricklin, B.: *ref,* 1470, 1499
Brickman, L.: *ref,* 981
Brickman, P.: *ref,* 357
Brickman, R. L.: *ref,* 1207
Brickner, A.: *rev,* 2054, 2056
Brickner, C. A.: *ref,* 1129, 1672
Brickner, C. E.: *ref,* 2451
Brickner, S. A. M.: *ref,* 868, 1164
Bridge, L.: *ref,* 2199
Bridger, W.: *ref,* 487, 525
Bridges, A. F.: *test,* 929
Bridges, C.: *ref,* 22, 532-3
Bridges, C. C.: *ref,* 533
Bridges, C. I.: *ref,* 553
Bridges, F.: *ref,* 929
Bridges, J. S.: *ref,* 516, 1447, 1711
Bridges, J. W.: *ref,* 1480, 3:220(9)
Bridges, P. K.: *ref,* 1174
Bridgewater, E.: *test,* 2002
Bridgham, R. G.: *rev,* 7:792
Bridgman, C. S.: *ref,* 482, 2195
Bridgman, J. N.: *ref,* 868, 1403, 1437
Brierley, H.: *ref,* 331, 532, 1383, 6:555(6)
Brierley, J.: *ref,* 532
Brigden, R. L.: *ref,* 2:1217(2-3)
Brigger, G.: *ref,* 525
Briggs, A. P.: *ref,* 1932
Briggs, D. A.: *ref,* 1394
Briggs, D. L.: *ref,* 1144, 1448, 1519
Briggs, K. C.: *test,* 1294
Briggs, K. R.: *ref,* 1403
Briggs, L.: *ref,* 3:653(10)
Briggs, L. D.: *ref,* 1123, 1499
Briggs, M. S.: *ref,* 1164
Briggs, P. F.: *test,* 1265, 1896; *ref,* 381, 518, 529, 533, 1073, 1265, 1270, 1281, 1896, 1921, P:408 (26, 29)
Brigham, B. W.: *ref,* 529, 559, 1499, 1918
Brigham, C. C.: *ref,* 357, 426
Brigham, L. H.: *ref,* 786
Brigham, R. G.: *rev,* 1795
Bright, C. J.: *ref,* 1281
Bright, H. A.: *ref,* 533
Bright, H. F.: *ref,* 5:530(49)
Bright, I. J.: *ref,* 2:1424(1)
Brighton and Hove Teacher's Association: *test,* 2:1529
Brilhart, B. L.: *ref,* 559, 561
Brilhart, J. K.: *ref,* 559, 561
Brill, I.: *ref,* 1281
Brill, M.: *ref,* 381, 525, 2:1388(2), 2:1401(6)
Brill, N. Q.: *ref,* 1232, 1281, 1519
Brill, R. G.: *ref,* 529, 533

Brilliant, P. J.: *ref,* 543, 1240, 1277, 1281, 1447
Brillinger, E. V.: *ref,* 3:470(8)
Brim, B. J.: *ref,* 868
Brim, C. W.: *ref,* 1069
Brimble, A. R.: *ref,* 439, 464, 1085
Brimer, A.: *test,* 5, 56, 600, 1614, 1750
Brimer, M. A.: *rev,* 52, 71-2, 95, 111, 1683, 1743; *test,* 75, 495; *ref,* 495
Brimm, J. L.: *ref,* 1044
Brinegar, V.: *ref,* 419, 1844-5
Bringmann, W. G.: *ref,* 1281, 1293, 1322
Brinitzer, W.: *ref,* 1447
Brink, D. C.: *ref,* 1403
Brink, R. W.: *ref,* 1447
Brinkley, S. G.: *ref,* 868
Brinkman, M. J.: *ref,* 884
Brintle, S. L.: *ref,* 2212
Brinton, G.: *ref,* 559, 1169
Brinton, G. A.: *ref,* 1932
Briskin, G. J.: *ref,* 1281, 1447
Brislin, R.: *ref,* 561
Brister, D. M.: *ref,* 1281
Bristol, A. S.: *test,* T:908
Bristol, H.: *ref,* 354, 507
Bristol, J. L.: *ref,* 7, 348, 751
Bristol, M.: *ref,* 1499
Bristol, R. W.: *test,* 3:303
Bristow, D.: *ref,* 1145
Bristow, M. R.: *ref,* 1469
Bristow, R. B.: *ref,* 1469
Bristow, R. M.: *ref,* 1044
Bristow, W. H.: *test,* 23
Britain, S. D.: *ref,* 1474
British Psychological Society, English Division of Professional Psychologists (Educational and Clinical): *ref,* 525, 529
Brito, H.: *ref,* 517, 533
Brittain, M.: *ref,* 525, 533, 538
Brittain, W. L.: *ref,* 542, 551, 564
Britton, J. H.: *ref,* 381, 592, 1087, 1145, 1164, 1207, 1418, 1519, P:411(7)
Britton, J. O.: *ref,* 2451
Britton, P. G.: *ref,* 529, 1281
Broad, E. J.: *ref,* 361, 6:438(459)
Broadbent, F. W.: *ref,* 868
Broadbent, L. A.: *ref,* 2195
Broadbent, T. H.: *ref,* 1144-5
Broadhead, G. D.: *ref,* 914
Broadhurst, A.: *ref,* 439, 1174, 1275, 1447
Broadhurst, J. C.: *ref,* 650, 2244, 2266
Broadhurst, N. A.: *ref,* 1775, 1856
Broadway, C. M.: *ref,* 1121, 1383
Brochu, E. W.: *ref,* 981
Brockopp, G. W.: *ref,* 1315
Brockway, A. L.: *ref,* 1499
Brockway, R. L.: *ref,* 533
Brod, D.: *ref,* 357, 1281
Brode, E. L.: *ref,* 868
Brodie, F. H.: *ref,* 487, 1276, 1428
Brodie, R. E.: *ref,* 1499
Brodie, T. A.: *ref,* 1280
Brodman, K.: *test,* 1144-5; *ref,* 1144-6
Brodsack, J.: *ref,* 1471
Brodsky, A. M.: *ref,* 1281, 1470
Brodsky, M.: *ref,* 349, 381, 1499

Brodsky, S. L.: *ref,* 361, 1281, 1470, 1519
Brodsky, S. M.: *ref,* 361
Brodsly, W. J.: *ref,* 1478
Brodt, A.: *ref,* 533
Brodt, A. M.: *ref,* 533
Brody, A. B.: *ref,* 532, 1087, 1499
Brody, C. M.: *ref,* 5:147(44)
Brody, C. M. H.: *ref,* 1499
Brody, D.: *ref,* 2258
Brody, D. S.: *ref,* 1281, 2195
Brody, E. B.: *ref,* 357, 574, 868, P:381(36, 40)
Brody, E. E. B.: *ref,* 868
Brody, G. F.: *ref,* 1273
Brody, G. G.: *ref,* 1499
Brody, H.: *ref,* 1499, 1519
Brody, J. R.: *ref,* 1499, 1519
Brody, L.: *test,* 2:1524; *ref,* 525
Brody, M. B.: *exc,* 3:29; *ref,* 525, 1105
Brody, R. P.: *ref,* 1164
Broe, J. R.: *ref,* 361, 1071, 1513
Broedel, J. W.: *ref,* 1499
Broekhoff, J.: *ref,* 1121
Broekmann, N. C.: *ref,* 1499
Broen, W. E.: *ref,* 1281
Brogden, H. E.: *rev,* 220, 482, 1205, 1245, 3:179; *ref,* 1320, 1403, 2195
Broida, D. C.: *ref,* 1281, 1499, 1519
Broida, H.: *ref,* 1247, 1481
Broiles, M. R.: *ref,* 993
Brollier, C.: *ref,* 1164
Brolyer, C. R.: *ref,* 357
Broman, H. J.: *ref,* 50, 342, 529, 1073
Broman, S. H.: *ref,* 484, 525
Bromberg, P. M.: *ref,* 1162
Bromer, J. A.: *ref,* 400, 1069, 1164
Bromet, E. J.: *ref,* 1192, 1499
Bromley, A.: *ref,* 1622, 4:5(8), 4:277(236), 6:573(2)
Bromley, D. B.: *ref,* 439, 518, 532, 1140
Bromley, E.: *ref,* 1198
Bromwich, R. M.: *ref,* 381, 516
Bronner, A. F.: *ref,* 2:1390(3), 2:1391(6), 2:1394(3), 2:1401(2)
Bronson, L.: *ref,* 1145, 1303, 2212
Bronte-Stewart, J.: *ref,* 1913
Bronte-Stewart, J. M.: *ref,* 1913
Bronzaft, A.: *ref,* 1090, 1275
Bronzo, A. F.: *ref,* 1407, 1409, 1442
Brook, D. F.: *ref,* 1113
Brook, J. G.: *ref,* 1145
Brook, R. C.: *ref,* 1415
Brook, R. R.: *ref,* 1164
Brooke, J. D.: *ref,* 1174
Brooke, K. M.: *ref,* 1129
Brooke, M. L.: *ref,* 1133, 1403
Brooker, R. A.: *ref,* 1395
Brookhouse, D. B.: *ref,* 533
Brooks, B. R.: *ref,* 525
Brooks, B. S.: *ref,* 1133
Brooks, C. R.: *ref,* 1887, 1928
Brooks, E.: *ref,* 2213, 3:217(56) 4:96(3), 6:159(44)
Brooks, E. M.: *ref,* 426, 447, 529, 533
Brooks, F. D.: *ref,* 426, 525, 908, 1569, 2:1424(8)
Brooks, F. O.: *ref,* 1227, 1403
Brooks, G. C.: *test,* 1381; *ref,* 1381
Brooks, G. W.: *ref,* 1073, 1121

Brooks, J.: *ref,* 1174, 1224, 1383
Brooks, J. B.: *ref,* 1415
Brooks, J. J.: *ref,* 1428, 2:1201(4), 2:1222(8)
Brooks, J. N. B.: *ref,* 1044
Brooks, K. P.: *test,* 1:1124
Brooks, L. E.: *ref,* 532, 1223
Brooks, L. M.: *ref,* 4:88(8)
Brooks, M.: *ref,* 1240, 1499
Brooks, M. O.: *ref,* 1499
Brooks, M. S.: *ref,* 2195
Brooks, N.: *rev,* 227, 241, 249, 252, 1:984-5, 2:1343, 2:1354, 3:183, 3:185, 4:242-3; *test,* 248; *ref,* 244, 1924
Brooks, R.: *ref,* 1169, 1207, 1315, 1924
Brooks, R. D.: *ref,* 1403
Brooks, R. S.: *ref,* 2031, 2052
Brooks, S.: *ref,* 516
Brooks, S. T.: *ref,* 516
Brooks, W. D.: *ref,* 997
Brooks, W. N.: *ref,* 357, 1044
Broom, E.: *test,* T:704; *ref,* 518, 525, 545
Broom, M. E.: *rev,* 2:1310, 2:1534; *exc,* 2:1559; *ref,* 36, 211, 426, 525, 1090, 1386, 1603, 1615, 2:1508 (1), 2:1565(5), 3:470(10), 4:535(4), 4:542(1)
Broome, B. J.: *ref,* 50, 6:793(7)
Broome, L. W.: *ref,* 589
Broomhead, E.: *ref,* 1499
Broota, A.: *ref,* 1519
Broota, K. D.: *ref,* 1519
Brosin, H.: *ref,* 1499
Brosin, H. W.: *ref,* 1499
Broskowski, A.: *ref,* 1281, 1342
Brosseau, J. F.: *ref,* 516
Brotemarkle, R. A.: *rev,* 1205-6, 1245; *ref,* 1320
Brothers, C. T.: *ref,* 357
Brothers, W. L.: *ref,* 69, 1281, 1583, 4:6(23), 4:277(237), 4:581(16)
Brotman, S.: *ref,* 1281
Broudy, H. S.: *ref,* 3:613(6)
Broughton, A.: *ref,* 1121
Broughton, E.: *ref,* 525, 538
Brouillette, O. J.: *ref,* 1775
Broussard, L. J.: *ref,* 1490
Brousseau, M. A.: *ref,* 357, 1094
Brousseau, P. J.: *ref,* 349, 1660
Brouwer, P. J.: *ref,* 4:60(2)
Broverman, D. M.: *ref,* 381, 518, 532, 1087
Brower, D.: *ref,* 426, 532, 1090, 1095, 1116, 1146, 1281, 1428, 1499, 1519
Brower, E.: *ref,* 1519
Brower, J. F.: *ref,* 1428
Brower, J. L.: *ref,* 1090, 1164
Brown, A. C.: *ref,* 1145
Brown, A. E.: *ref,* 484
Brown, A. F.: *ref,* 868, 1164, 1403, 2452
Brown, A. J.: *ref,* 545, 2:1394(4)
Brown, A. M.: *ref,* 538
Brown, A. S.: *rev,* 1826
Brown, A. W.: *rev,* 483, 2:1399; *test,* 355; *ref,* 36, 211, 355, 426, 483, 525, 1194, 3:256(2)
Brown, B.: *ref,* 400
Brown, B. H.: *ref,* 1499
Brown, B. J.: *ref,* 912
Brown, B. S.: *ref,* 1094

Brown, C.: *ref,* 50, 533, 1275, 1377, 1447, 1887, 1902, 7:55(21)
Brown, C. C.: *ref,* 532, 1275, 1377, 1499
Brown, C. H.: *ref,* 1716
Brown, C. M.: *rev,* 1638, 1658, 1:1030, 2:1505, 2:1508; *test,* 1286, 1:1031, 2:1511, 3:439; *ref,* 1073, 1286
Brown, C. P.: *ref,* 1289, 1361
Brown, C. R.: *ref,* 1247
Brown, C. T.: *ref,* 1164
Brown, C. W.: *ref,* 497
Brown, D.: *test,* 4:435; *ref,* 1095, 1439
Brown, D. A.: *ref,* 529
Brown, D. G.: *test,* 1247; *ref,* 1145, 1162, 1174, 1245, 1247, 1275, 1344, 1481, 1499
Brown, D. J.: *ref,* 419, 1095, 1164, 1207, 1281, 1403, 1415, 2212
Brown, D. L.: *ref,* 525
Brown, D. R.: *ref,* 1094, 1121, 1133, 1135, 1302, 1403
Brown, D. V.: *ref,* 532, 1499
Brown, E.: *ref,* 1499
Brown, E. A.: *ref,* 419, 1164
Brown, E. C.: *ref,* 2028
Brown, E. J.: *test,* T:1181; *ref,* 1240, 1281
Brown, F.: *test,* 5:36; *exc,* 5:130; *ref,* 525, 529, 532-3, 1447, 1469, 1481, 1499, 2228-9, 2258, 2:1240 (1-6), 5:36(9, 12-3), P:321(12)
Brown, F. G.: *rev,* 11; *exc,* 2194; *ref,* 11, 69, 405, 419, 1044, 1280-1, 1772, 2212, 2221, 2358
Brown, F. T.: *ref,* 1499
Brown, G.: *ref,* 1252
Brown, G. A.: *test,* 2:1196
Brown, G. D.: *ref,* 1240
Brown, G. G.: *ref,* 1499
Brown, G. I.: *ref,* 1109, 1437
Brown, G. J.: *ref,* 1164
Brown, G. K.: *ref,* 4:45(5, 7)
Brown, G. L.: *ref,* 525
Brown, G. M.: *test,* 1617, 5:670
Brown, H. S.: *ref,* 1281, 4:277 (238)
Brown, I.: *ref,* 1192
Brown, I. D.: *ref,* 1348, 1439
Brown, J.: *ref,* 525, 1499
Brown, J. B.: *ref,* 1176, 1240, 1306
Brown, J. C.: *ref,* 868
Brown, J. E.: *ref,* 1176, 1320, 1415, 1519, 2212
Brown, J. F.: *exc,* 1447; *ref,* 532, 1140, 1192, 1500
Brown, J. I.: *test,* 65, 993, 1572; *ref,* 99, 993
Brown, J. L.: *ref,* 357, 1679, 1921
Brown, J. M.: *ref,* 1394-5
Brown, J. R.: *ref,* 914, 1281, 1501
Brown, L.: *ref,* 69, 529, 1674, 1755, 1761, 1775
Brown, L. B.: *ref,* 1225, 1275, 1281, 1403, 1481, 1499-500, 1519
Brown, L. F.: *ref,* 516, 981
Brown, L. N.: *test,* 35:287
Brown, L. P.: *ref,* 1123
Brown, L. S.: *ref,* 1875
Brown, M.: *ref,* 209, 1281, 1302, 1499

Burns, L. M.: *ref,* 524
Burns, M. H.: *ref,* 1321
Burns, N. M.: *ref,* 1281
Burns, P. P.: *ref,* 505
Burns, R. C.: *ref,* 533
Burns, R. J.: *ref,* 1256, 1403
Burns, R. K.: *test,* 2110, 5:905,
  6:1107, 6:1171; *ref,* 5:902(1)
Burns, R. L.: *ref,* 357, 1044, 1053
Burns, S. T.: *ref,* 211
Burns, W. H.: *ref,* 50, 532, 1469
Burnside, L. H.: *ref,* 525
Burnstein, E.: *ref,* 1519
Burr, E.: *ref,* 1105
Burr, E. T.: *rev,* 469, 3:222; *test,*
  1:1032; *ref,* 1:1032(1)
Burr, M.: *ref,* 2251
Burrall, L.: *ref,* 7, 1087, 1123
Burrell, L. F.: *ref,* 404
Burrow, W. H.: *ref,* 981
Burrows, B.: *ref,* 1281, 1519
Bursch, C. W.: *ref,* 1281, 2195
Bursill, A.: *exc,* 1275
Burson, G. E.: *ref,* 525
Burson, S. L.: *exc,* 1819
Burstein, A. G.: *rev,* 529, 533, 1104,
  1499, 1887; *ref,* 1499
Burstiner, I.: *ref,* 589
Burt, C.: *rev,* 348, 1087, 5:326;
  test, 36:708, 4:295, R:9, R:176,
  T:3, T:428, T:760, T:1026; *exc,*
  217, 525, 3:283, 4:345, 6:B449;
  ref, 518, 525, 533
Burt, R. B.: *ref,* 1294, 1501
Burt, S. M.: *ref,* 1073
Burton, A.: *ref,* 525, 532, 1281,
  1474, 1499, 1519, 1775
Burton, D. A.: *ref,* 529, 1164, 1383
Burton, E. C.: *ref,* 1391
Burton, J. G.: *ref,* 1164
Burton, J. H.: *ref,* 1716
Burton, J. L.: *ref,* 1240
Burton, L.: *ref,* 1112, 1519
Burton, M.: *ref,* 173
Burton, M. V.: *ref,* 1320
Burton, N. W.: *rev,* 141
Burton, R. L.: *ref,* 2212
Burton, R. V.: *ref,* 1207
Burton, T. M.: *test,* 3:558
Burtt, H. E.: *ref,* 3:220(10)
Burwell, E.: *ref,* 533
Busbice, J. J.: *ref,* 833
Busby, W. A.: *ref,* 473, 1069
Busch, A. C.: *ref,* 482, 2251
Busch, J. C.: *ref,* 400
Busch, J. G.: *ref,* 914
Buscher, R. E.: *ref,* 868
Bush, H.: *ref,* 1123
Bush, J. J.: *ref,* 1227
Bush, M.: *ref,* 1294, 1303
Bush, M. L.: *ref,* 357
Bush, W. J.: *ref,* 533
Bushey, J. T.: *ref,* 348, 1465, 1696,
  1716, 1724
Bushnell, R. J.: *ref,* 1932
Bushong, G. E.: *ref,* 18, 391
Buskirk, E.: *ref,* 533, 2039
Buss, A.: *ref,* 1281
Buss, A. H.: *ref,* 1499
Buss, F. H.: *ref,* 364
Busse, E. W.: *ref,* 529
Busse, T. V.: *ref,* 542, 564, 574,
  1087
Busse, W.: *ref,* 1073, 1281, 2195

Bussis, A. M.: *ref,* 436
Buswell, G. T.: *test,* 713, 1597; *ref,*
  449, 713, 1596, 1622, 2:1559
Buszek, B. R.: *ref,* 7, 36, 357–8, 425
Butcher, H. J.: *rev,* 361; *ref,* 80,
  364, 477, 636, 1087, 1253, 1291,
  1383, 1403, 2195
Butcher, J.: *ref,* 1281
Butcher, J. N.: *ref,* 1281, 1342
Butcher, T.: *ref,* 1499
Butcofsky, D.: *ref,* 1767
Butcofsky, D. L.: *ref,* 1289
Butler, A.: *ref,* 532
Butler, A. C.: *ref,* 1350
Butler, A. J.: *ref,* 525, 529, 532–3,
  1277, 1281, 1387, 1447, 1560, 1900
Butler, B. V.: *ref,* 381, 484, 516,
  533, 1281, 1447, 1474, 2195
Butler, D. C.: *ref,* 1281, 1501
Butler, D. F.: *test,* 1852
Butler, E. A. (W.): *ref,* 1716
Butler, E. S.: *ref,* 1499
Butler, E. W.: *ref,* 1249
Butler, G. A.: *ref,* 1519
Butler, G. D.: *ref,* 533
Butler, J.: *ref,* 997, 1275
Butler, J. H.: *ref,* 194, 211, 357,
  1383
Butler, J. R.: *ref,* 1094, 1281, 1469
Butler, K. G.: *rev,* 2097–8; *ref,* 533
Butler, M. J.: *ref,* 404, 546, 551, 574
Butler, M. N.: *test,* 2216; *ref,* 2216
Butler, O. P.: *ref,* 1415, 1519
Butler, P. C.: *ref,* 482
Butler, P. E.: *ref,* 1281, 1391
Butler, R. B.: *ref,* 391
Butler, R. D.: *ref,* 1133
Butler, R. E.: *ref,* 1932
Butler, R. L.: *ref,* 1451, 1481
Butler, R. R.: *ref,* 1133
Butler, S.: *ref,* 538
Butler, W. R.: *ref,* 5:77(5)
Butsch, R. L. C.: *ref,* 18, 2:1377
  (37)
Butt, D. S.: *ref,* 1121, 1275, 1320,
  1322, 1383, 1423
Buttenweiser, P.: *ref,* 1320, 2212
Butterfield, C. C.: *ref,* 525
Butterfield, E. C.: *exc,* 1077; *ref,*
  525, 533, 1281, 1447
Butterfield, M.: *ref,* 69
Butterfield, M. L.: *ref,* 1415
Butterfield, W. H.: *test,* 2:1337
Butters, F. K.: *test,* 1:908
Butterworth, A. T.: *ref,* 1377
Buttiglieri, M. W.: *ref,* 1281
Buttimore, D. J.: *ref,* 1123, P:353
  (7)
Buttle, D.: *ref,* 439, 529
Button, A. D.: *ref,* 1281, 1499
Button, H. W.: *ref,* 868
Butts, E. M.: *ref,* 917
Butts, F. E.: *ref,* 7:1078(4)
Butts, H. F.: *ref,* 1123
Butts, T. M.: *ref,* 981
Butzow, J. W.: *ref,* 357
Buxbaum, J.: *ref,* 1164
Buxbaum, R. C.: *ref,* 2355
Buynitzky, K. C.: *test,* 3:179
Buzahora, R. G.: *ref,* 914
Buzby, D. E.: *ref,* 1169, 1474
Buzzard, G. A.: *test,* 3:601
Byars, H.: *ref,* 1415
Byas, W. H.: *ref,* 1121

Byerly, C.: *test,* 35:320
Byerly, R. L.: *ref,* 405
Byers, A. P.: *ref,* 1164
Byers, E. E.: *test,* 6:41; *ref,* 6:41
  (1)
Byers, J. L.: *ref,* 359
Byers, K.: *exc,* 2298
Byler, J. T.: *ref,* 35, 361
Byram, N. K.: *ref,* 1383
Byrd, C.: *ref,* 381, 533
Byrd, E.: *ref,* 525, 1383, 1447, 1451
Byrd, O. E.: *test,* 939, 3:418, 4:487;
  ref, 3:418(1)
Byrne, A. E.: *ref,* 1478
Byrne, A. V.: *ref,* 522, 529
Byrne, D.: *ref,* 1121, 1240, 1281,
  1519
Byrne, J. A.: *test,* 1673
Byrne, K. M.: *ref,* 1087
Byrne, M. A.: *ref,* 542, 546, 561
Byrne, M. C.: *rev,* 2075, 2077; *ref,*
  211, 981, 1623, 2028
Byrne, P. S.: *ref,* 331
Byrns, R.: *ref,* 391
Byrns, R. K.: *ref,* 419
Byrum, M.: *ref,* 518, 1281
Bystryn, D.: *ref,* 1094, 1121
Bytheway, B.: *ref,* 95, 373, 408–9,
  722
Bzoch, K. R.: *test,* 2067; *ref,* 2067

CTB/McGRAW-HILL: *test,* 11,
  13, 45, 68, 707, 1542, 1639–40,
  1752, 4:464, 7:462–4, 7:499; *ref,*
  349, 1123
Cabanski, C. L.: *ref,* 398
Cabanski, S. J.: *ref,* 1281
Cabat, L.: *ref,* 244, 305
Cabe, P. A.: *ref,* 559, 1169
Cabeen, C. W.: *ref,* 1281
Cabot, P. S. de Q.: *ref,* 1090, 1320
Cabot, R.: *test,* 1633
Cabrer, S. M.: *ref,* 1164
Cacavas, P. D.: *ref,* 1481
Caccamo, J. M.: *ref,* 981
Caccavo, E.: *ref,* 533, 1649
Cacha, F. B.: *ref,* 589, 1129
Caditz, S. B.: *ref,* 1164, 1281
Cadman, W. H.: *ref,* 532, 1499
Cady, L. D.: *ref,* 1383
Caffey, E. M.: *ref,* 1232, 1255, 1281,
  1346
Caffrey, B.: *ref,* 1383
Caffrey, C. B.: *ref,* 1383
Caffrey, J.: *ref,* 349, 5:326(11, 18)
Caffyn, H. R.: *ref,* 2323
Cagle, B. G.: *ref,* 1306, 1403
Cahen, E. R.: *ref,* 1281, 1499–500,
  1519
Cahen, L. S.: *rev,* 9; *ref,* 709
Cahill, C. A.: *ref,* 1281, 1285
Cahill, G. B.: *ref,* 3:35(5)
Cahill, R.: *ref,* 1281
Cahill, R. F.: *ref,* 1516
Cahoon, D. D.: *ref,* 447, 529, 981,
  2195
Cahoon, G. P.: *rev,* 1863, 1868, 3:
  581, 3:585; *test,* 1:1137; *ref,* 1320
Cahoon, R. L.: *ref,* 1169
Cahow, A. C.: *ref,* 419, 2:1182(3),
  2:1225(5), 2:1250(5), 2:1544(9)
Cain, A. C.: *ref,* 1451
Cain, E. R.: *ref,* 533
Cain, E. T.: *ref,* 1094, 2194

Carson, R. C.: *ref,* 1281, 2212
Carson, R. L.: *ref,* 1164, 2337
Carssow, K. P.: *ref,* 1281
Carstairs, G. M.: *ref,* 1499
Cartee, J. K.: *ref,* 525, 533, 1626
Carter, A. R.: *ref,* 1519
Carter, C. D.: *ref,* 1123
Carter, C. E.: *ref,* 1200, 2451
Carter, C. O.: *ref,* 525, 1428
Carter, D.: *ref,* 1923
Carter, F. H.: *ref,* 1094
Carter, G. C.: *ref,* 881, 1281, 1622, 2195, 2239, 2448, 4:5(8), 4:277 (236), 6:573(2)
Carter, H. D.: *rev,* 1238, 1610, 2192, 2195, 2212, 1:1170, 1:1180, 2:1679, 3:655; *test,* 6:857; *exc,* 2212–3; *ref,* 1320, 1499, 2195, 2212–3, 2266, 5:689(1–7), 6:857(8–9)
Carter, H. E.: *test,* 3:556
Carter, H. L.: *ref,* 1123, 1127, 1415
Carter, J. D.: *ref,* 545, 1499
Carter, J. F.: *ref,* 2079
Carter, J. L.: *ref,* 981
Carter, J. P.: *ref,* 525
Carter, J. W.: *test,* 2:1518; *ref,* 2:1518(2)
Carter, K.: *ref,* 211
Carter, K. W.: *ref,* 1302
Carter, L.: *ref,* 1087, 1090, 1101, 1403, 2135, 2195, 2239
Carter, L. F.: *rev,* 4:56
Carter, R. E.: *ref,* 1346, 1383, 1499
Carter, R. S.: *ref,* 425, 1123
Carter, T. E.: *ref,* 1281
Carter, W. R.: *ref,* 419
Carton, A. S.: *ref,* 1480
Cartwright, C. W.: *ref,* 2:1372(2)
Cartwright, D. S.: *ref,* 529, 1281, 1499, 1519
Cartwright, G. P.: *ref,* 516
Cartwright, J. L.: *ref,* 529
Cartwright, L. K.: *ref,* 1094, 1121, 2355
Cartwright, R. D.: *ref,* 1499, 1519
Cartwright, R. W.: *ref,* 1499
Cartwright, W. H.: *rev,* 3:591, 3:610, 3:618
Caruth, E.: *ref,* 1499
Carver, C.: *test,* 1676
Carver, R. P.: *test,* 995, 1537, 1589, 1748; *ref,* 361, 917, 995, 997, 1537, 1572
Cary, L. A.: *ref,* 36, 355
Cary, T. C.: *ref,* 1383
Casanova, T.: *test,* 36:616
Casciani, J. A.: *ref,* 914
Case, H. W.: *test,* 5:888; *ref,* 426, 2195, 2239, 5:888(1, 3)
Case, J. L.: *ref,* 2097–8
Case, L. D.: *ref,* 947
Casella, C.: *ref,* 1164
Casella, C. F.: *ref,* 1499
Casey, D. D.: *ref,* 1772
Casey, D. L.: *ref,* 325, 439, 2266
Casey, E. W.: *ref,* 2195
Casey, J.: *ref,* 1252
Casey, J. E.: *ref,* 5:308(344)
Casey, J. F.: *ref,* 1232, 1346
Casey, M. L.: *ref,* 525
Casey, T. M.: *ref,* 1281
Cash, W. L.: *ref,* 69, 404, 419, 1320, 1626, 6:438(504)
Cashdan, A.: *ref,* 439, 489, 516, 2025

Cashdan, S.: *ref,* 1094, 1109, 1403, 1437
Cashen, V. M.: *ref,* 348–9
Cashman, J. P.: *ref,* 425, 1281, 1447, 1583, 1877, 1918
Casjens, C. C.: *ref,* 499
Casner, D.: *ref,* 1095, 1281, 2195
Casola, A. S.: *ref,* 1915
Cason, E. B.: *ref,* 1480
Cason, H.: *ref,* 1480
Caspari, I. E.: *ref,* 1499
Cass, D. H.: *test,* 1004
Cass, J. C.: *ref,* 425, 2135, 2195, 2239, 2266
Cass, W. A.: *ref,* 1281, 1499
Cassaretto, F. P.: *rev,* 1819, 5:744
Casse, R. M.: *ref,* 1428
Cassel, J. C.: *ref,* 1281
Cassel, M. E.: *ref,* 1428
Cassel, R.: *test,* 1756, 2414; *ref,* 1259–60, 1466, 1756
Cassel, R. H.: *ref,* 50, 439, 532, 1087, 1428, 1469, 1898
Cassel, R. N.: *test,* 1010, 1124, 1126, 1130, 1166–7, 1259–60, 1419, 1466, 5:81, 6:74; *ref,* 7, 20, 22, 349, 357–8, 361, 391, 1044, 1069, 1073, 1123–4, 1126, 1166–7, 1259–60, 1419, 1466, 1499–500, 1583, 1756, 2195, 2199, 2205, 5:81(1), P:381 (24)
Cassel, W.: *ref,* 1394–5
Cassell, W. A.: *ref,* 1499
Casselman, G. G.: *ref,* 357
Casserly, P. L.: *ref,* 1045
Cassidy, V. M.: *ref,* 4:468(3)
Cassingham, C. C.: *ref,* 525
Cassius, J.: *ref,* 1281
Casson, A. M.: *ref,* 2212
Cassotta, L.: *ref,* 1225
Castanos, J.: *ref,* 1174
Castell, J. H. F.: *ref,* 525, 529
Castelli, C. D.: *ref,* 542, 551
Castellow, W. A.: *ref,* 1094, 1174, 1387
Castelnuovo-Tedesco, P.: *ref,* 1281, 1499, 1519
Castetter, J. S.: *ref,* 439
Castiglione, L. V.: *ref,* 425, 546, 574
Castiglione, P. B.: *ref,* 286
Castka, J. F.: *test,* 5:744
Castle, E. H.: *test,* 2:1495
Castle, M.: *ref,* 185, 1109
Castle, P. F. C.: *ref,* 386, 389
Castles, C.: *ref,* 1185
Castleton, B.: *ref,* 543
Castner, B. M.: *rev,* 507, 2:1383; *ref,* 497
Casto, G. W.: *ref,* 1281
Caston, J.: *ref,* 1281, 1469, 1471
Caston, W. F.: *ref,* 1516
Castor, M.: *ref,* 2212
Castore, C. H.: *ref,* 2452
Castricone, N. R.: *ref,* 2195
Castro, P. N.: *ref,* 1499
Castrogiovanni, P.: *ref,* 1499
Catalano, F. L.: *exc,* 1451, 1519, 5:B370
Catalano, J. F.: *ref,* 1164
Cate, C. A.: *test,* T:1320
Cate, C. C.: *ref,* 364, 439, 467, 529, 533
Catellier, E.: *ref,* 1403

Catford, J. C.: *ref,* 1519
Cathcart, R.: *ref,* 113, 997, 1044, 1599
Cathcart, R. S.: *rev,* 2099
Cato, J. L.: *ref,* 1471
Catron, D. W.: *ref,* 1094
Cattell, A. K. S.: *test,* 364
Cattell, M. D.: *ref,* 1253
Cattell, M. D. L.: *test,* 1253
Cattell, P.: *rev,* 398, 425, 1:1044, 3:256, 3:274; *test,* 487; *ref,* 36, 398, 426, 487, 525
Cattell, R. B.: *rev,* 349, 1095, 1123, 2:1389; *test,* 354, 364, 1078, 1129, 1131, 1163, 1225–9, 1253, 1291, 1295, 1300, 1367, 1383, 1:962, 1:973, 1:980, 1:1101, 2:1220, 2:1448, 4:287, 5:90, 6:125; *exc,* 525; *ref,* 354, 364, 388, 439, 473, 525, 709, 1069, 1087, 1129, 1131, 1151, 1163, 1205, 1207, 1225–9, 1245, 1253, 1281, 1291, 1295, 1300, 1367, 1383, 1499–500, 1519, 1583, 1781, 1988, 2:1220(9–10), 3:228 (1, 4), 5:73(1–3), 5:90(1–2, 4–6), 6:125(7), P:41(3), P:344(7, 11, 13, 16–7, 19–21)
Catterall, C. D.: *test,* 1108; *ref,* 532, 1281
Cauble, B. L.: *ref,* 19, 348, 1123
Caudill, A. C.: *ref,* 1395
Caudill, W.: *ref,* 1499, 1519
Cauffiel, P. W.: *ref,* 1281, 1344
Cauffman, P. F.: *ref,* 48
Cauffman, W. J.: *ref,* 1144
Causey, G. D.: *ref,* 2045
Cautela, J. R.: *ref,* 357, 425
Cauthen, N. R.: *ref,* 1281, 1481, 1499
Cava, E. L.: *ref,* 1094, 1261
Cavallo, M.: *ref,* 2377, 2380, 2383
Cavan, R. S.: *test,* 4:100; *exc,* 1416; *ref,* 4:100(1)
Cavanagh, P.: *ref,* 1469, 1932
Cavanaugh, J. O.: *ref,* 1320, 3:70 (1)
Cavanaugh, M. C.: *ref,* 487
Cave, R.: *ref,* 1232
Cave, R. L.: *ref,* 400, 589, 1232, 1346
Cavell, A. C.: *ref,* 398
Cavins, L. V.: *ref,* 104
Cavior, N.: *ref,* 1281, 1481
Cawley, A.: *ref,* 2213
Cawley, A. M.: *ref,* 1320, 2213
Cawley, J. F.: *ref,* 29, 589, 981, 1087, 1716, 1921
Cawte, J. E.: *ref,* 520, 1145
Cay, L.: *ref,* 1218, 1383
Cayley, W. E.: *ref,* 1327
Cazden, C. B.: *rev,* 47
Cazier, V. O.: *test,* 983
Cazzelle, J. G.: *ref,* 1302, 1772
Cech, E. J.: *ref,* 1395
Cecil, C. E.: *ref,* 1281
Ceithaml, J.: *ref,* 2355
Celaschi, D. A.: *ref,* 2452
Celebre, G.: *ref,* 981
Celliers, C. P.: *test,* 1064
Cellura, A. R.: *ref,* 1447
Center, C. C.: *ref,* 7, 349
Center, S. S.: *rev,* 1:1108; *test,* 5:210, 6:330
Center, W. R.: *ref,* 981, 1087

6:964, 6:998, 6:1013; *ref,* 357, 1048, 1939
Chauncey, M. R.: *ref,* 36
Chausow, H. M.: *ref,* 48
Chave, E. J.: *test,* 35:66; *ref,* 35: 66(1)
Chaves, J. F.: *ref,* 1389–90
Chawla, T. R.: *ref,* 502, 533, 1478, 1501
Chazan, B. I.: *ref,* 1281
Chazan, M.: *rev,* 1252; *exc,* 1269; *ref,* 1112
Checov, L.: *test,* 5:90
Chedekel, D. S.: *ref,* 1153, 1225, 1315
Cheek, F.: *ref,* 404, 1403, 2212
Cheek, F. E.: *ref,* 361, P:327(24, 30)
Cheers, A. L.: *ref,* 361
Cheifetz, D. I.: *ref,* 1094, 1281, 1293, 1447
Chelnek, I.: *ref,* 1499
Chen, A.: *exc,* 4:101
Chen, M. K.: *ref,* 1121, 2337
Chen, S. A.: *ref,* 1121, 1403
Chen, W.: *ref,* 1281, 1499
Chenault, J.: *ref,* 6:223(17)
Chenault, V. M.: *ref,* 468, 1609
Cheney, T. M.: *ref,* 1069, 1073, 1289
Chenoweth, E. C.: *ref,* 1320
Cheong, G. S. C.: *ref,* 324, 1069
Cheraskin, E.: *ref,* 1145–6
Cherdack, A. N.: *ref,* 357
Cherry, A. L.: *ref,* 105, 357, 1144, 1383
Cherry, M.: *ref,* 1275
Cherry, N.: *ref,* 529, 545, 1499
Cherymisin, D. G.: *ref,* 1474
Chesire, L. E.: *test,* 2:1184, 4:387–8; *ref,* 507, 525, 2:1241(1)
Chesler, D. J.: *test,* 159, 431, 699, 2140; *ref,* 431, 482
Cheslock, L.: *exc,* 216
Chesrow, E. J.: *ref,* 532, 1499
Chess, S. B.: *ref,* 1293
Chestek, A.: *test,* 4:410
Chester, R. D.: *test,* 1776
Chestnut, W. J.: *ref,* 1164
Chevigny, H.: *test,* 1449
Chevrette, J. M.: *ref,* 914
Cheydleur, F. D.: *test,* 2:1345–6; *ref,* 2:1345(1–3, 5), 2:1348(3)
Cheyne, W. M.: *ref,* 439, 495
Chia, F.: *ref,* 1281
Chiappa, J.: *test,* 946
Chiappone, A. D.: *ref,* 493, 533
Chiasson, J. W.: *ref,* 1361
Chickering, A. W.: *ref,* 1133, 1302
Chiga, D. E.: *ref,* 1121
Child, D.: *ref,* 331, 516, 1174, 1296
Child, I. L.: *test,* 3:291; *ref,* 357, 1090, 1101, 1294, 1320, 1448, 1519, 6:159(52), P:363(13)
Child, S. E. A.: *ref,* 1174
Childers, B.: *ref,* 1264
Childers, H. E.: *ref,* 1121, 1281, 1471, 7:55(13)
Childers, P. R.: *ref,* 516, 997, 1095, 1403
Childers, R.: *ref,* 1259, 1419, 1466
Childers, R. D.: *ref,* 1365, 1383
Childs, C. A.: *ref,* 216
Childs, F. V.: *ref,* 1649

Childs, H. G.: *ref,* 525
Childs, R. de S.: *test,* 1630
Childs, S. B.: *test,* 1630
Chiles, D. R.: *ref,* 1254, 1361
Chiles, G.: *ref,* 1121
Chille, R. A.: *ref,* 2212
Chilman, C. S.: *ref,* 1361, 1394
Chilton, B. S.: *ref,* 1123
Chimbidis, M. E.: *ref,* 589
Chimonides, S. G.: *ref,* 105, 382
Chinnian, R. R.: *ref,* 1224
Chin-Shong, E. T.: *ref,* 1340
Chinsky, J. M.: *ref,* 1094, 1264
Chipman, A.: *ref,* 1094, 1281, 1293, 1363
Chipman, C. E.: *ref,* 525, 1499, 1519
Chipman, L. P.: *ref,* 1193–4
Chiriboga, D.: *ref,* 1519
Chisholm, A.: *ref,* 1913
Chisholm, I. A.: *ref,* 1913
Chisholm, M. (M.): *ref,* 1094
Chissom, B. S.: *rev,* 1875, 1921; *ref,* 365, 424–5, 1921
Chittenden, E. W.: *test,* 621–2, 1: 1073, 2:1440, 3:547
Chiu, A.: *ref,* 1166
Cho, W. K.: *ref,* 1932
Choate, H. H.: *ref,* 349, 981
Choate, M. S.: *ref,* 1469
Chodorkoff, B.: *ref,* 1380
Chodorkoff, J.: *ref,* 381, 525, 533
Choppy, M.: *ref,* 1275
Chopra, S. L.: *ref,* 439
Chorny, H. H.: *ref,* 1519
Chorost, S. B.: *ref,* 1447, 1500
Chothia, F. S.: *ref,* 1069, 2266
Chotlos, J. W.: *ref,* 1281
Chou, K. P.: *test,* 225
Chou, S. K.: *ref,* 6:159(45)
Choungourian, A.: *ref,* 1275
Chovan, W. L.: *ref,* 502, 981, 1192
Chowdhury, U.: *ref,* 1519
Chown, S.: *ref,* 403, 439, 1277, 1311, 1387
Choynowski, M.: *ref,* 1275, 1447
Chrisien, G.: *ref,* 533
Chrisman, J. W.: *ref,* 1164
Christ, A. E.: *ref,* 533, 1499, 1519
Christ, A. F.: *ref,* 391
Christakos, A. C.: *ref,* 503, 1225, 1240, 1281
Christel, R. I.: *ref,* 1068
Christenfeld, R. M.: *ref,* 1225
Christensen, A. H.: *ref,* 1499, 1519, 4:142(3)
Christensen, A. M.: *ref,* 1320
Christensen, C.: *ref,* 1281
Christensen, C. M.: *ref,* 1134, 1164, 1281, 2195
Christensen, D.: *ref,* 2212
Christensen, F. A.: *test,* 1751
Christensen, G. M.: *ref,* 1281
Christensen, H. T.: *ref,* 826
Christensen, L.: *ref,* 425, 1174, 1281, 1383, 1403, 1422, 2199
Christensen, P. R.: *test,* 457, 542, 546, 551, 561c2, 561d1, 561m3, 561o3, 561x2, 579, 1151; *ref,* 457, 546, 551, 561, 564, 571, 1074, 1403, 1761, 2185, 2195
Christensen, R. M.: *ref,* 1281
Christensen, T. E.: *ref,* 342, 2195
Christenson, J. A.: *ref,* 1499, 1519

Christenson, J. M.: *ref,* 1044, 1281, 2212
Christeson, B.: *test,* 325
Christian, Q. A.: *ref,* 1415
Christiansen, A. O.: *ref,* 2:1390 (1), 2:1391(1)
Christiansen, B.: *ref,* 1448
Christiansen, C.: *ref,* 1281, 1499
Christiansen, H. D.: *ref,* 2197
Christiansen, J. R.: *ref,* 1123
Christiansen, K.: *ref,* 1281, 1519
Christiansen, K. M.: *ref,* 1281
Christiansen, M. A.: *ref,* 1383
Christiansen, T.: *ref,* 533
Christie, R.: *test,* 1393
Christine, C.: *ref,* 2028
Christine, D.: *ref,* 2028
Christner, C. A.: *ref,* 2452
Christofanelli, D. J.: *ref,* 20
Christoff, P. L.: *ref,* 357, 1133, 1236
Christofferson, H. C.: *test,* 696, 35: 44–8
Christopher, S. A.: *ref,* 1240
Christy, E. G.: *ref,* 1519
Christy, L. J.: *ref,* 211
Christy, W. J.: *ref,* 1123, 1313
Chriswell, M. I.: *test,* 2240; *ref,* 2234, 2240
Chronicle Guidance Publications: *test,* 1013
Chronister, G. M.: *ref,* 1123, P: 302(3)
Chrysler, J. D.: *ref,* 1133
Chu, C.: *ref,* 1519
Chu, C. L.: *ref,* 1281
Chu, C. P.: *ref,* 1519
Chu, H. M.: *ref,* 1145
Chu-chang, C.: *ref,* 1499
Chun, K.: *ref,* 1121, 1281
Chun, R. W. M.: *ref,* 50, 439, 518, 525, 533
Chung, B. M.: *ref,* 1499
Chung, K. H.: *ref,* 1383
Chung, W. S.: *ref,* 1169
Chung, Y. E.: *ref,* 1121
Chuprayoon, L.: *ref,* 1305
Church, A. M.: *ref,* 7, 349, 4:2(7)
Church, H. V.: *ref,* 3:220(2)
Church, J. C.: *ref,* 525, 1281
Church, J. J.: *ref,* 1063
Church, N. L.: *ref,* 211
Churchill, E. P.: *rev,* 621–2, 3:323
Churchill, F. J.: *ref,* 255–6, 271–2, 314–5
Churchill, J. A.: *ref,* 533
Churchill, R.: *ref,* 1501
Churchill, R. D.: *rev,* 3:136, 5:615
Churchill, W. D.: *ref,* 525, 1403
Churukian, G. A.: *ref,* 1176
Chused, T. M.: *ref,* 543, 1478
Chute, E.: *ref,* 1499
Chyatte, C.: *ref,* 342, 1281
Chylinski, J.: *ref,* 1164, 1281
Cibelli, L. A.: *ref,* 1337
Cicchetti, D. V.: *ref,* 400
Cicero, J.: *ref,* 381
Cicirelli, J. S.: *ref,* 574, 589, 868
Cicirelli, V. G.: *ref,* 7, 348, 574, 589, 868, 981
Cieboter, F. J.: *ref,* 382
Ciesla, S. G.: *test,* 2415
Cieutat, V. J.: *ref,* 69, 221, 525
Ciocco, A.: *ref,* 3:475(2–3, 5, 8)
Circle, D. E.: *ref,* 207

Ciruti, J. E.: *ref,* 314
Cisler, L. E.: *ref,* 525
Cisney, H. N.: *test,* 3:689; *ref,* 1923, 2212–3, 3:689(2)
Claasen, B. S.: *test,* 862
Clack, G. S.: *ref,* 1127, 1478, 1480
Claeys, W.: *ref,* 1275, 1499
Clagett, A. F.: *ref,* 1281
Claghorn, J.: *ref,* 1281
Clair, T. N.: *ref,* 1887, 1928
Claire, C.: *ref,* 1275
Clancy, D. D.: *ref,* 1281, 1481, 1499
Clancy, E.: *test,* 2204
Clancy, J.: *ref,* 1281
Clancy, M.: *ref,* 1281
Clapp, B. E.: *ref,* 1716
Clapp, F. L.: *test,* 3:117, 3:339
Clapp, H. L.: *ref,* 4:260(2)
Clapp, H. S.: *ref,* 1499
Clapp, R. C.: *ref,* 1121
Clapp, R. K.: *ref,* 1885, 1887
Clapp, R. R.: *ref,* 1133
Clapper, I. W.: *ref,* 1123
Clapperton, G.: *ref,* 1519
Clapson, L.: *ref,* 551
Clar, P. N.: *ref,* 1164, 1169, 1303, 2212
Clardy, E. R.: *ref,* 1499
Claridge, G.: *ref,* 1226, 1275, 1281
Claridge, G. S.: *ref,* 1275, 1387
Clark, A.: *ref,* 50, 981
Clark, A. B.: *ref,* 2212
Clark, A. D.: *ref,* 2028
Clark, A. L. H.: *ref,* 1164, 1294
Clark, A. T.: *ref,* 1403
Clark, B.: *ref,* 525, 538
Clark, B. P.: *ref,* 7, 349
Clark, C. A.: *rev,* 1478, 5:131
Clark, C. G.: *ref,* 1281
Clark, C. M.: *ref,* 1164, 1207, 1253, 1281, 1471, 1881
Clark, D. F.: *rev,* 1191; *ref,* 1164, 1275, 1279, 1281
Clark, D. L.: *ref,* 1281
Clark, D. W.: *ref,* 2028
Clark, E. A.: *ref,* 525
Clark, E. J.: *ref,* 1205–6, 1245
Clark, E. L.: *ref,* 1377
Clark, E. T.: *ref,* 525, 532, 1123, 1164, 1247, 1474, 1519, 1526, 1716, 2216
Clark, E. W.: *ref,* 64, 357
Clark, F. E.: *ref,* 371, 404
Clark, G. C.: *ref,* 1281
Clark, G. D.: *ref,* 1305
Clark, G. E.: *ref,* 425, 5:326(29)
Clark, G. R.: *ref,* 22, 518, 529, 2227, 2234
Clark, G. W.: *rev,* 784, 5:518; *test,* 4:197
Clark, G. Y.: *ref,* 419, 426, 438
Clark, H.: *ref,* 1053
Clark, H. C.: *ref,* 1679
Clark, H. G.: *ref,* 1121
Clark, H. V.: *test,* 448, 3:257
Clark, I. S.: *ref,* 1218
Clark, J. B.: *ref,* 6:1135(1)
Clark, J. F.: *rev,* 5:880, 5:890
Clark, J. H.: *ref,* 349, 525, 532, 1095, 1123, 1281, 1499, 1932
Clark, J. L. D.: *rev,* 258–9; *exc,* 256, 272, 287, 301, 315; *ref,* 219, 253, 270, 299, 312
Clark, J. M.: *ref,* 504, 529

Clark, J. P.: *ref,* 1069
Clark, J. R.: *rev,* 669, 2:1442; *test,* 1909, 3:344; *ref,* 409, 1909
Clark, J. V.: *ref,* 1315, 1403, 2199
Clark, J. W.: *ref,* 1087, 1098, 1271, 1281, P:344(8)
Clark, K.: *ref,* 357
Clark, K. B.: *ref,* 1320, 1499
Clark, K. C.: *ref,* 558
Clark, K. E.: *rev,* 1348, 1361, 4:52; *test,* 2197, 2212; *ref,* 2195, 2197, 2212, P:342(15)
Clark, L. F.: *ref,* 838, 1421
Clark, M.: *test,* 4:706–7; *ref,* 364, 1499
Clark, M. G.: *test,* 35:301; *ref,* 221
Clark, M. H.: *ref,* 69, 1281
Clark, M. L.: *test,* 325, 327, 330, 595, 1529–30, 1579; *exc,* 1579; *ref,* 529, 1298, 2234
Clark, M. N.: *ref,* 1383
Clark, M. P.: *ref,* 1087
Clark, N. C.: *ref,* 361, 1391
Clark, P. E.: *test,* 3:563
Clark, P. J.: *ref,* 439, 1087
Clark, P. M.: *ref,* 574, 589
Clark, P. N.: *ref,* 2212
Clark, R. A.: *ref,* 1519
Clark, R. B.: *ref,* 1351
Clark, R. M.: *ref,* 1519
Clark, R. T.: *ref,* 914
Clark, R. W.: *ref,* 1123, 1499
Clark, S.: *rev,* 605–6, 674, 680, 683, 4:386–7; *ref,* 525
Clark, S. G.: *ref,* 1281, 1499
Clark, S. L.: *ref,* 1169, 1225
Clark, T. J. H.: *ref,* 1174
Clark, V.: *exc,* 1499
Clark, W. A.: *ref,* 1095
Clark, W. B.: *ref,* 868, 1407
Clark, W. C.: *ref,* 1293
Clark, W. D.: *ref,* 1499
Clark, W. H.: *ref,* 426, 1121, 1403
Clark, W. M.: *ref,* 525, 533
Clark, W. W.: *rev,* 24; *test,* 7, 61, 348–9, 458, 603, 1123, 1536, 1563, 1606, 1711, 3:222, 3:345, 3:690, 4:538, 4:645, 6:4, 6:141, 6:280, 6:503, 6:591, 6:622, 6:638; *ref,* 7, 349, 525, 1123, 1711, 3:15(3), 4:2(5)
Clarke, A. D. B.: *ref,* 525, 529, 532
Clarke, A. M.: *ref,* 532
Clarke, A. T.: *ref,* 868
Clarke, B.: *exc,* 6:B449
Clarke, B. R.: *ref,* 533, 1277, 1447
Clarke, C. T.: *ref,* 2180
Clarke, D. F.: *ref,* 589
Clarke, D. H.: *ref,* 6:141(2)
Clarke, D. P.: *ref,* 525
Clarke, F. H.: *ref,* 167, 426, 1320, 2135, 2212, 2266, 4:668(2)
Clarke, F. M.: *test,* 2:1343; *ref,* 1320, 2:1343(2–3)
Clarke, F. R.: *ref,* 525, 532–3
Clarke, G. E.: *ref,* 868
Clarke, H. H.: *rev,* 921, 4:480; *ref,* 1360–1, 6:82(3), 6:141(2), P:312(3)
Clarke, H. J.: *ref,* 532, 1313, 1499–500
Clarke, J. I. C.: *ref,* 1499
Clarke, J. R.: *ref,* 1447
Clarke, L.: *ref,* 1281, 1322

Clarke, N. B.: *ref,* 1499
Clarke, R. B.: *ref,* 361, 1069
Clarke, R. R.: *ref,* 382, 404, 869
Clarke, R. V.: *ref,* 1415
Clarke, R. V. G.: *ref,* 1191, 1249, 1253, 1296
Clarke, S. C. T.: *ref,* 1281, 1501
Clarke, T. A.: *ref,* 1904
Clarke, W. J.: *ref,* 1469
Clarke, W. M.: *ref,* 533
Clarke, W. V.: *exc,* 532; *ref,* 1069, 1080, 1091, 1094, 1383
Clarke (Walter V.) Associates, Inc.: *test,* 1080, 1091, 1908, 2157
Clarkson, Q. D.: *ref,* 1474
Clary, E. G.: *ref,* 1164
Clasen, R. E.: *ref,* 981, 1383
Class, L.: *ref,* 1499
Claus, K. E.: *ref,* 589, 1164
Clausen, J.: *ref,* 1087, 2234
Clawar, H. J.: *ref,* 36, 357, 360, 394, 436, 1546, 1626
Clawson, A.: *test,* 1447d; *ref,* 50, 381, 533, 1447
Clawson, L. E.: *ref,* 2227, 2234
Claycamp, H. J.: *ref,* 1164
Claycomb, C. M.: *ref,* 868
Claye, C. M.: *ref,* 1415, 2451
Clayman, D. P. G.: *ref,* 1447, 1643, 1681
Claypool, A. M.: *ref,* 1439
Clayton, D. E.: *ref,* 1383
Clayton, H.: *ref,* 529, 1121
Clayton, H. D.: *ref,* 1383
Clayton, J.: *ref,* 1419
Clayton, T. E.: *ref,* 1499
Clayton, W. H.: *ref,* 1232, 1264
Claytor, M. P.: *test,* 4:507, 5:834
Cleak, R. E.: *ref,* 206
Cleare, J. A.: *ref,* 1281
Cleary, M. E. L.: *ref,* 1135
Cleary, T. A.: *ref,* 357, 436
Cleeland, C. S.: *ref,* 529, 1281, 2076
Cleere, W. R.: *ref,* 1383
Cleeton, G. U.: *rev,* 1386, 3:645, 3:694; *test,* 2469, 3:224, 3:635, 3:695; *ref,* 18, 2:1679(2–3), 3:695(4)
Clegg, H. D.: *ref,* 348, 1281, 2239
Clegg, S. J.: *ref,* 505
Cleghorn, J. M.: *ref,* 1195, 1278, 1383
Cleland, C. C.: *ref,* 1471, 1519
Cleland, D. L.: *exc,* 1618; *ref,* 525, 695, 997, 1087, 1661, 6:793(5)
Cleland, V.: *ref,* 6:1159(3)
Clem, J. E.: *test,* 2:1480
Clemans, W. V.: *rev,* 371, 1583; *ref,* 2194–5, 2212
Clemens, B.: *ref,* 2212
Clemens, B. T.: *ref,* 2212
Clemens, T.: *ref,* 1499
Clement, E.: *ref,* 1145
Clements, B. E.: *ref,* 1403
Clements, D.: *ref,* 3:217(55)
Clements, G. R.: *ref,* 533
Clements, H. M.: *ref,* 1289
Clements, L. J.: *exc,* 1452
Clements, S. D.: *ref,* 533, 1253–4, 1313, 1447
Clements, W. H.: *ref,* 1195, 1383, 1519
Clemes, S.: *ref,* 1499

Cowen, L.: *ref,* 1293
Cowgill, S.: *ref,* 1281
Cowie, V.: *ref,* 1275
Cowin, M.: *exc,* 1499; *ref,* 1499
Cowles, J. T.: *ref,* 2355, 4:812(10)
Cowles, K.: *ref,* 518
Cowley, J. J.: *ref,* 439, 532, 1403
Cowne, L.: *ref,* 348, 1992
Cox, A.: *ref,* 357
Cox, B.: *ref,* 1519
Cox, B. F.: *ref,* 1519
Cox, B. J.: *ref,* 1932
Cox, C.: *ref,* 1403
Cox, F. N.: *exc,* 1519; *ref,* 1499–
    500, 1519
Cox, G. M.: *ref,* 497
Cox, J.: *ref,* 1912–3
Cox, J. A.: *rev,* 5:256–8; *ref,* 144,
    868
Cox, J. F.: *ref,* 525
Cox, J. W.: *test,* 2242; *ref,* 2242
Cox, K. J.: *ref,* 1499, 2135, 2195,
    4:315(8)
Cox, L.: *ref,* 1094, 1164, 1394
Cox, M.: *ref,* 1281
Cox, M. M.: *rev,* 1702, 1711, 1918,
    3:515, 3:521
Cox, O.: *ref,* 349, 424, 589
Cox, R. C.: *exc,* 356, 1730; *ref,* 1730
Cox, R. D.: *ref,* 1499, 1519
Cox, R. H.: *ref,* 1121, 1289
Cox, S. G.: *ref,* 1430, 2103, 2105
Cox, S. H.: *ref,* 1326, 1519
Cox, S. M.: *ref,* 1499
Cox, T.: *ref,* 525
Cox, W. H.: *ref,* 1176
Cox, W. K.: *ref,* 482, 1383
Coxe, R. C.: *ref,* 1377
Coxe, W. W.: *test,* 2:1388, 2:1507,
    3:399, T:232; *ref,* 2:1388(1), 3:
    399(1), 6:480(8–9)
Coxford, L. M.: *ref,* 1069
Coy, M.: *ref,* 69, 357
Coy, R. V.: *ref,* 211
Coyle, F. A.: *ref,* 516, 522, 533–4,
    1031, 1035, 1216, 1281, 1285, 1474,
    1499, 1775
Coyle, F. P.: *ref,* 2135
Coyle, P. J.: *ref,* 35
Coyne, L.: *ref,* 532
Coyne, W. J.: *ref,* 532
Cozad, M. S.: *ref,* 5:570(4)
Cozan, L. W.: *ref,* 504
Cozens, F. W.: *test,* 36:707, 1:1003–
    4, 1:B338; *ref,* 36:707(1)
Crabbé-Declève, G.: *ref,* 1499
Crabtree, A. P.: *ref,* 48
Crabtree, B. D. D.: *ref,* 1207, 1280
Crabtree, M.: *test,* 2077
Crabtree, M. C.: *ref,* 2077
Crabtree, P. D.: *ref,* 1430
Craddick, R.: *ref,* 1281
Craddick, R. A.: *ref,* 357, 529, 532–
    3, 1277, 1281, 1474, 1478, 1480–1,
    1499
Craft, C. O.: *ref,* 2340
Craft, M.: *ref,* 518, 529, 1112, 1281,
    1499
Crager, R. L.: *test,* 585, 6:516; *ref,*
    585, 6:516(2)
Crago, P. H.: *ref,* 50
Craig, A. L.: *ref,* 505
Craig, C. R.: *test,* 5:354
Craig, G.: *ref,* 1519

Craig, G. S.: *test,* 2:1190
Craig, H.: *ref,* 1932
Craig, J.: *ref,* 532, 1499, 1519
Craig, J. O.: *ref,* 1913
Craig, K. D.: *ref,* 1306
Craig, M. J.: *ref,* 1044
Craig, R. J.: *ref,* 529, 1192, 1346
Craig, W. J.: *ref,* P:408(31)
Craik, K. H.: *ref,* 1121
Cram, F. D.: *test,* 4:164
Crambert, A. C.: *ref,* 1073, 2166
Cramblett, H.: *ref,* 50, 533, 1447
Cramblett, H. G.: *ref,* 1447
Cramer, J. F.: *ref,* 36
Cramer, W. F.: *ref,* 211, 1313
Cramer-Azima, F.: *ref,* 529, 532,
    592, 1447, 1499
Cramer-Azima, F. J.: *ref,* 1481
Cramond, W. A.: *ref,* 1281
Crandall, E.: *test,* 4:492
Crandall, E. B.: *ref,* 1320
Crandall, F. E.: *ref,* 529
Crandall, J. E.: *ref,* 1240
Crandall, J. H.: *ref,* 7, 19, 22, 29,
    36
Crandall, V.: *ref,* 1519
Crandall, V. C.: *ref,* 497, 525, 532,
    1087, 1121
Crandall, V. J.: *ref,* 1164, 1169,
    1186, 1501, 1519
Crandell, J. M.: *ref,* 524
Crane, J. M.: *ref,* 621
Crane, L.: *ref,* 1164
Crane, M. M.: *ref,* 1906, 1918, 1923,
    5:781(9, 12)
Crane, M. P.: *ref,* 755
Crane, W. E.: *test,* 1026
Crane, W. J.: *ref,* 87, 426, 868,
    1164, 1386, 1403, 1560, 1775, 2135,
    2195, 2239, 6:113(24)
Cranford, V.: *ref,* 1499
Crannell, C. W.: *ref,* 185, 189, 1320,
    1380, 1474, 2239
Cranny, C. J.: *ref,* 1044, 1225, 1768,
    2212
Crary, H. L.: *ref,* 543, 592, 1087,
    1277, 1447
Crary, J. O.: *ref,* 1253
Crary, R. W.: *test,* 1992
Crary, W. G.: *ref,* 1447
Crasilneck, H. B.: *ref,* 1447, 1499,
    1519
Craske, S.: *ref,* 1174
Crathorne, A. R.: *test,* 1:1073, 2:
    1440
Craven, D. D.: *ref,* 1281
Craven, E. C.: *ref,* 2195
Craven, G. F.: *ref,* 1755, 1856
Cravens, D. W.: *ref,* 2325
Cravens, R. B.: *ref,* 525
Craver, A. A.: *ref,* 542, 574
Crawford, A.: *ref,* 439, 1911, 1932
Crawford, A. B.: *rev,* 2195, 2:1676;
    test, 5:615; *exc,* 1087; *ref,* 48,
    357, 1048, 1053, 1087, 1320, 2212,
    2349, 3:217(131), 4:718(4), 5:
    615(8)
Crawford, A. E.: *ref,* 1519
Crawford, C. D.: *ref,* 1403, 1775
Crawford, C. S.: *ref,* 1281, 1499
Crawford, D.: *test,* 3:658
Crawford, D. M.: *test,* 2223; *ref,*
    2223
Crawford, E. E.: *ref,* 1447

Crawford, F. W.: *ref,* 382, 1005
Crawford, G. L.: *ref,* 919
Crawford, J.: *ref,* 1906, 1918, 1923
Crawford, J. E.: *test,* 2223, 3:658;
    ref, 2223, 2251, 2266, 3:224(2),
    3:658(1–2, 4)
Crawford, J. M.: *ref,* 354, 439, 518,
    525, 545, 1073, 1900
Crawford, J. P. W.: *test,* 2:1371
Crawford, L. E.: *ref,* 2195
Crawford, P. L.: *test,* 1148; *ref,*
    504, 518, 529, 850, 1148
Crawford, R. E.: *ref,* 1155, 1281,
    1313
Crawford, V. B.: *ref,* 516, 525, 533,
    538
Crawford, W. R.: *rev,* 1830, 1847,
    6:591, 7:840; *ref,* 20, 361
Crawshaw, J. E.: *ref,* 331
Crawshaw, T. C.: *ref,* 19, 221
Creager, J. A.: *ref,* 49, 382, 881,
    1053, 1244, 1499
Creamer, D. G.: *ref,* 1395
Creamer, W.: *ref,* 2186
Creaser, J.: *ref,* 1044, 1164, 1572
Creasy, M. A.: *ref,* 1281
Creed, C. D.: *ref,* 495, 533
Creek, R. J.: *ref,* 1123, 1326
Creekmore, A. M.: *ref,* 1383, 1403
Creekmore, F.: *ref,* 589
Creelman, A. G.: *ref,* 426
Crego, C. A.: *ref,* 559
Creighton, S. L.: *ref,* 357
Cremer, A. G.: *ref,* 927, 1471
Crenshaw, W.: *ref,* 1383
Creutzer, W. A.: *ref,* 3:217(61)
Crew, J. L.: *ref,* 1253, 1383
Crewe, N. L. M.: *ref,* 1280
Crewe, N. M.: *ref,* 1280
Cribb, G. R.: *ref,* 1044
Crickmore, L.: *ref,* 217, 439, 1275
Crider, A.: *ref,* 1281
Crider, B.: *ref,* 426, 1095, 1572,
    2213, 3:344(2)
Crider, M. M.: *ref,* 1123
Crighton, J.: *ref,* 1185, 1293
Cripe, A. G.: *ref,* 981
Crisp, A. H.: *test,* 1279; *ref,* 1174,
    1279, 1295
Crissey, O. L.: *test,* 2224; *ref,* 398,
    525, 2135, 2212–3, 2224, 2229, 2258
Crissy, W. J.: *ref,* 786
Crissy, W. J. E.: *rev,* 4:63, 4:418;
    ref, 69, 869, 1403, 2213, 3:2(9–
    10), 3:4(6–7)
Crist, R. L.: *ref,* 868, 1207, 1394
Cristantiello, P. D.: *ref,* 6:438(505)
Criswell, C. E.: *ref,* 1121
Criswell, R. L.: *rev,* 2:1501
Critchfield, J. B.: *ref,* P:200(3)
Crites, J. O.: *rev,* 1187, 1303, 2182,
    2197; *test,* 2103; *exc,* 391, 1071,
    1121, 1295, 1322, 1415, 1475, 1572,
    1775, 2113, 2289, 2409; *ref,* 20,
    189, 211, 342, 419, 426, 1069, 1073,
    1087, 1121, 1123, 1164, 1256, 1281,
    1403, 1499, 2103, 2135, 2195, 2212,
    2227–9, 2234, 2239, 2251, 2258,
    2260, 2266, 6:438(513), P:346
    (17)
Crites, K. R.: *ref,* 1240
Crittenden, J. B.: *ref,* 533, 981, 1883,
    1921, 2028
Crocker, L.: *ref,* 6:309(1)

Curr, W.: *rev,* 710, 5:461; *ref,* 439, 461, 525, 1646
Curran, A. M.: *ref,* 1134, 1205, 1772
Curran, E. E.: *ref,* 1052
Curran, G. T.: *ref,* 1123
Curran, J. P.: *ref,* 2195
Curran, P. M.: *ref,* 1164
Currens, W. C.: *ref,* 1281
Current, W. F.: *ref,* 1603, 1724, 4: 535(2)
Currie, C.: *ref,* 425, 1073, 1207, 1572, 1772, 2195
Currie, J. S.: *ref,* 342
Currier, A. J.: *test,* 1:933
Currier, W. D.: *ref,* 1281
Curry, D. R.: *ref,* 516, 538, 2028
Curry, E. M.: *ref,* 1123
Curry, E. T.: *ref,* 2031, 2052
Curry, G. I.: *test,* 1881
Curry, R. L.: *ref,* 7, 349
Curry, R. St. C.: *ref,* 1129
Curti, M.: *exc,* 497
Curti, M. W.: *ref,* 381, 497, 509
Curtin, J. T.: *ref,* 349
Curtin, M. E.: *ref,* 381, 439, 525, 533, 1164
Curtis, E. L.: *ref,* 1121, 1403
Curtis, F. D.: *rev,* 1785, 1:907, 1: 1139, 2:1598
Curtis, G.: *ref,* 1225, 1240
Curtis, G. C.: *ref,* 1154, 1225, 1281, 1293, 1471, 1519
Curtis, H. A.: *ref,* 359, 361
Curtis, H. S.: *ref,* 1499, 2251
Curtis, J. M.: *ref,* 1499
Curtis, J. T.: *ref,* 2212
Curtis, J. W.: *test,* 1454, 2126-7, 2177, 2243, 4:338; *ref,* 2234
Curtis, K. C.: *ref,* 2325
Curtis, Q. F.: *ref,* 1281
Curtis, W. S.: *ref,* 498
Curtiss, D. W.: *test,* 1759
Cushman, C. L.: *ref,* 426, 525
Cushna, B.: *ref,* 1447
Cuthbert, B. L.: *ref,* 838
Cutler, C.: *ref,* 1519
Cutler, G. H.: *ref,* 1923
Cutler, R.: *ref,* 1499
Cutler, T. H.: *ref,* 3:635(4)
Cutright, P.: *test,* 2:1197
Cutrona, M. P.: *test,* 978
Cutsumbis, M. N.: *ref,* 1289
Cutter, F.: *ref,* 1281, 1474, 1499
Cutter, H.: *ref,* 1164, 1176, 1383
Cutter, H. S. G.: *ref,* 1281, 1500
Cutts, R. A.: *ref,* 525, 532, 1499
Cvetkovich, G. T.: *ref,* 1281
Cynamon, M.: *ref,* 4:812(10)
Cytanovich, K.: *ref,* 36
Czaczkes, J. W.: *ref,* 381, 439, 545, 1499
Czajkowski, T. J.: *ref,* 868, 1164

DAANE, C. J.: *ref,* 1281, 1403
Dabas, Z. S.: *ref,* 5:905(4, 10)
Dabelstein, D. H.: *ref,* 2195, 2: 1214(1)
Dable, R. R.: *ref,* 5:766(16)
Dacey, J.: *ref,* 331, 589
Dacey, J. S.: *ref,* 331, 400, 574, 589
Dachowski, M. M.: *ref,* 1281, 1519
da Costa, M. I. L.: *test,* 1898; *ref,* 1898
Dacus, W. P.: *ref,* 1123

Daffron, M. R.: *ref,* 589
Dager, E. Z.: *ref,* 1123
Daggett, C. J.: *test,* 2:1638
Dague, D. M.: *ref,* 2046
Dahl, R. L.: *ref,* 914
Dahl, T.: *ref,* 1775, 1970
Dahle, A. J.: *ref,* 2039
Dahlgren, H.: *ref,* 518, 529, 543, 592, 1192, 1277, 1281, 1447
Dahlin, D. D.: *ref,* 1289
Dahlin, G.: *ref,* 1471, 1519
Dahlke, A. B.: *ref,* 533, 1624
Dahlke, A. E.: *ref,* 361, 1121, 1281
Dahlstrom, W. G.: *rev,* 1124, 1170, 1228, 1445; *exc,* 1281; *ref,* 36, 525, 1087, 1281, 1447
Dai, B.: *ref,* 1499
Dailey, C. A.: *ref,* 1205
Dailey, J. T.: *rev,* 342, 357, 382, 404, 4:281; *test,* 57, 974, 2078, 2105, 2270; *ref,* 1058
Daily, V. L. D.: *ref,* 2323, 7:1078 (5)
Daingerfield, M.: *ref,* 1499
Dalack, J. D.: *ref,* 1519
Dale, A. B.: *test,* 2:1381; *ref,* 460, 2:1381(1)
Dale, E.: *rev,* 3:160-1; *test,* 35: 174
Dale, F. W.: *test,* 1894
Dale, R. R.: *rev,* 446, 1591
Dale, V. M.: *ref,* 1315
Dales, R. J.: *ref,* 497
Daley, M. F.: *ref,* 532, 1123
Daley, R. F.: *ref,* 2212
Dallek, J. I.: *ref,* 1164
Dallenbach, K. M.: *ref,* 342, 4:277 (170)
Dallmann, M.: *rev,* 6:274
Dalton, G. W.: *ref,* 1383, 1403, 1519
Dalton, M. M.: *ref,* 1918
Dalton, S. L.: *ref,* 2449, 2451
Daly, E. J.: *ref,* 1415
Daly, J. L.: *ref,* 69
Daly, J. M.: *ref,* 1281, 2195, 2214
Daly, R. J.: *ref,* 1218, 1383
Daly, S. S.: *rev,* 598
Daly, W.: *ref,* 1481
Daly, W. C.: *ref,* 50, 1474
Damankos, F. J.: *ref,* 1207, 1281
Damarin, F.: *ref,* 1281, 1499-500, 1519
Damgaard, T. L. J.: *ref,* 211
D'Amico, D. J.: *ref,* 1394-5
D'Amico, L.: *ref,* 1164
D'Amico, L. A.: *ref,* 48, 1082
Damm, V. J.: *ref,* 349, 574, 1164, 1315, 2273
Damodar, V. N.: *ref,* 1387
Dampel, D. D.: *ref,* 361
Damrin, D. E.: *test,* P:230; *ref,* 1095, 1320, P:230(1-3)
Dana, J. M.: *ref,* 529, 1499
Dana, L.: *ref,* 1298
Dana, R. H.: *rev,* 1499-500, 1514, 1519; *ref,* 361, 529, 532, 574, 1095, 1109, 1121, 1164, 1169, 1275, 1281, 1294, 1389, 1437, 1447, 1499, 1508, 1519, 6:228(72)
Dancey, T. E.: *ref,* 1499
Dandes, H. M.: *ref,* 1315
D'Andrade, R. G.: *exc,* 1499
Dane, M. W. A.: *test,* 1:1169
Daneel, D.: *test,* 569

Danek, T. A.: *ref,* 1430
Danenhower, H. S.: *ref,* 1087, 1428
Danesino, A.: *ref,* 1519
Danet, B. N.: *ref,* 1281
Danford, B. H.: *ref,* 381, 516
Danforth, L.: *ref,* 2:1492(11)
Dangel, H. L.: *ref,* 533
D'Angelo, R.: *ref,* 528, 1921
D'Angelo, R. D.: *ref,* 357
D'Angelo, R. Y.: *ref,* 381, 1253
Dani, S. K.: *ref,* 1164
Daniel, J.: *ref,* 1174
Daniel, J. L.: *ref,* 1121
Daniel, K. B.: *ref,* 361, 1193-4
Daniel, K. laV. B.: *ref,* 361, 1193-4
Daniel, W. J.: *ref,* 2213
Daniels, A.: *ref,* 529
Daniels, C. W.: *ref,* 1281
Daniels, E. E.: *ref,* 1281
Daniels, J. C.: *rev,* 71, 462, 5:392; *test,* 375, 1650; *ref,* 375, 1650
Daniels, J. L.: *ref,* 1133
Daniels, L. K.: *ref,* 1481
Daniels, R. S.: *ref,* 1195, 1281
Danielson, E. L.: *ref,* 868
Danielson, H. A.: *ref,* 1164
Danielson, J. R.: *ref,* 1281
Danielson, R. H.: *ref,* 1281
Daniere, A.: *ref,* 357
Danish, S. J.: *ref,* 1315
Danks, J. H.: *ref,* 574
Danowski, T. S.: *ref,* 1281, 1383, 1519
Dans, C.: *ref,* 516
Dansereau, R. A.: *ref,* 1281
Dansinger, S.: *ref,* 2059
Danskin, D. G.: *ref,* 1044, 6:438 (478)
Danwitz, M. W.: *ref,* 1474
Danzer, H.: *test,* 4:6, 5:179
D'Aoust, B. R.: *ref,* 1296
D'Aoust, T.: *ref,* 1069, 1775, 2195
Dar, R. J.: *ref,* 1772
Darbes, A.: *ref,* 36, 425, 525, 529, 532, 1121, 1123, 1183, 2251, 6: 438(479)
Darbonne, A. R.: *ref,* 1499
Darby, C. A.: *test,* 1537; *ref,* 1537, 1572
Darby, H. E.: *ref,* 505
Darby, J.: *ref,* 1499
Darby, J. A.: *ref,* 1471
Darcy, N. T.: *ref,* 525, 5:368(19)
D'Arcy, P. F.: *ref,* 2195, 2212
Dargel, R.: *ref,* 559, 561
Darke, R. A.: *ref,* 381, 1144
Darley, F. L.: *test,* 2074, 2095; *ref,* 533, 2074, 2095
Darley, J. G.: *rev,* 1095, 2212-3, 1:1171, 2:1492; *test,* 4:70, 5:87; *exc,* 2212-3; *ref,* 342, 357-8, 361, 419, 426, 1095, 1320, 2212-3, 2228-9, 3:61(1-5), 3:642(4), 4: 70(1-8), 5:87(21), 6:438(506), P:342(2-6, 8)
Darley, S. A.: *ref,* 1281
Darling, C. D.: *ref,* 1095, 1281, 1289, 1344
Darling, H. W.: *ref,* 1207
Darlington, M. D.: *ref,* 1169
Darnell, A.: *test,* 4:370
Darnell, D. K.: *ref,* 238
Daroff, R. B.: *ref,* 529, 592, 1281, 1447, 1499

Darr, R. F.: *ref,* 1275
Darrow, H. D.: *ref,* 20, 868
Darsie, M. L.: *ref,* 36, 525
Darter, C. L.: *ref,* 1361, 1560, 1772, 2195
Das, A. K.: *ref,* 1365, 2103
Das, G.: *ref,* 1275
Das, J. P.: *ref,* 439, 1275
Das, R. S.: *test,* 118; *ref,* 388, 439, 1095, 1383, 1932
Das Gupta, B.: *test,* 810
Dasgupta, J.: *ref,* 439
Dash, H. H.: *test,* 3:556
Dash, S. C.: *ref,* 439
Dashiell, J. F.: *ref,* 525
Dass, S. L.: *ref,* 1207, 1519
Daston, P.: *ref,* 1337
Daston, P. G.: *ref,* 496, 518, 592, 1499
Datel, W. E.: *ref,* 1121, 1293, 1499
Datta, A.: *ref,* 381
Datta, L.: *ref,* 381, 490, 1121
Datta, L. E.: *ref,* 348, 516, 574, 1121, 1403, 1481
Datwyler, D.: *ref,* P:381(45)
Dau, A. W.: *ref,* 947
Daugherty, B. N.: *ref,* 1403
Daugherty, J. H.: *rev,* 3:561, 3:565
Daugherty, R. A.: *ref,* 547, 1164
Daughtrey, A. S.: *ref,* 1968
Daughtrey, J. P.: *ref,* 4:277(177)
Dauterman, W.: *ref,* 513, 529
Dauterman, W. L.: *test,* 527, 773; *ref,* 498, 773
Dauw, D. C.: *ref,* 589, 1356, 1383, 2194, 2283
Davage, P. P. E.: *ref,* 439
Dave, I.: *ref,* 1289
Dave, P. N.: *ref,* 525
Davenport, B. F.: *ref,* 1519
Davenport, C. A.: *ref,* 1121
Davenport, C. B.: *ref,* 525
Davenport, C. M.: *ref,* 1365
Davenport, E. L.: *ref,* 381
Davenport, G.: *ref,* 1169
Davenport, K. S.: *ref,* 881, 4:277 (203), 4:799(2), 6:879(2)
Davert, E. C.: *ref,* 1389
Daves, E.: *test,* 35:289, 35:311
Davey, H.: *ref,* 529
Davey, J. B.: *ref,* 1923
David, C.: *ref,* 1519, 6:223(18)
David, H. P.: *exc,* 1499, 1516; *ref,* 1516
David, K.: *ref,* 518
David, K. H.: *ref,* 518, 542, 574, 1281, 2212
Davidoff, M. D.: *ref,* 1348, 4:88 (17)
Davidoff, P.: *ref,* 3:110(7)
Davidov, W. H.: *ref,* 1169
Davids, A.: *ref,* 1094, 1121, 1164, 1281, 1344, 1387, 1448, 1481, 1499-500, 1519, 2227
Davids, I.: *ref,* 211
Davidson, A. J.: *ref,* 1474
Davidson, C. M.: *ref,* 421, 1320, 2135, 2162, 2212, 3:220(56-7, 60)
Davidson, C. W.: *ref,* 868
Davidson, G. M.: *ref,* 1499
Davidson, H.: *ref,* 1499
Davidson, H. H.: *test,* 1499k; *ref,* 1474, 1499

Davidson, H. P.: *ref,* 525
Davidson, J.: *ref,* 529
Davidson, J. F.: *ref,* 525, 533
Davidson, J. L.: *ref,* 532, 1140
Davidson, K.: *ref,* 1474, 1499, 5: 36(18)
Davidson, K. S.: *ref,* 518, 532, 1087, 1281, 1499
Davidson, M.: *ref,* 439, 525
Davidson, M. A.: *ref,* 331, 1281
Davidson, N.: *ref,* 1499
Davidson, N. L.: *ref,* 529
Davidson, P. O.: *ref,* 1275, 1293, 1391
Davidson, R. A.: *ref,* 1123, 1325
Davidson, W.: *ref,* 1499
Davidson, W. N.: *ref,* 1516
Davies, A. D. M.: *ref,* 403, 439, 1225, 1275, 1277, 1311, 1383, 1387
Davies, B.: *ref,* 1145, 1174
Davies, B. M.: *ref,* 1145, 1174
Davies, B. N.: *ref,* 1302
Davies, E.: *ref,* 1200, 1259, 1291
Davies, F. R. J.: *ref,* 426, 4:272(2)
Davies, J.: *ref,* 381, 533, 1447
Davies, J. E.: *ref,* 2:1377(25)
Davies, J. F.: *ref,* 1121
Davies, J. G. V.: *ref,* 1281
Davies, L. S.: *ref,* 868, 1174, 1225, 1383
Davies, M.: *ref,* 1174, 1249
Davies, M. G.: *ref,* 1311
Davies, M. H.: *ref,* 1275, 1387
Davies, M. M.: *ref,* 1315
Davies, R.: *ref,* 1499
Davies-Eysenck, M.: *ref,* 403, 439
Davis, A.: *test,* 5:326; *ref,* 348, 391, 398, 425, 1087
Davis, A. D.: *ref,* 1499
Davis, A. F.: *ref,* 2028
Davis, A. J.: *ref,* 525, 1094
Davis, A. L.: *test,* 227
Davis, B.: *ref,* 1536, 1542, 1603
Davis, B. H.: *ref,* 398
Davis, B. J.: *ref,* 1428
Davis, B. S.: *ref,* 1542, 1567, 1603
Davis, C. C.: *rev,* 64, 105, 113, 4: 153-4, 4:175; *test,* 1546, 4:213, 5:179, 5:645
Davis, C. E.: *ref,* 1094, 1281, 1469, 2212
Davis, C. H.: *ref,* 1281
Davis, C. J.: *ref,* 36, 1923, 1925, 5:781(19)
Davis, C. R.: *ref,* 1294
Davis, C. W. C.: *rev,* 3:125
Davis, D.: *test,* 4:493; *ref,* 1281
Davis, D. J.: *test,* 5:422; *ref,* 589
Davis, D. R.: *rev,* 1105, 1197, 1379, 2071; *ref,* 525, 533
Davis, D. S.: *ref,* 211, 1123, 1500
Davis, E. A.: *ref,* 525
Davis, E. W.: *rev,* 3:113, 3:634
Davis, F. B.: *rev,* 49, 64, 357, 361, 1536, 1560, 1574, 1611, 1622, 1626, 1749, 2:1529, 3:507; *test,* 1544, 1546, 4:184, 4:213, 5:179, 5:645; *exc,* 398; *ref,* 69, 525, 869, 1058, 1320, 1546, 1572, 1583, 4:7(2), 4:213(3), 4:277(239), 5:87(19)
Davis, F. G.: *ref,* 1164
Davis, G. A.: *ref,* 391, 542, 574, 589, 2273
Davis, G. C.: *ref,* 1281

Davis, G. N.: *exc,* 275
Davis, H.: *ref,* 1281, 1486, 2031, 3:220(21)
Davis, H. B.: *ref,* 1499
Davis, H. C.: *ref,* 1281, 1363, 1447
Davis, H. G.: *ref,* 1281, 1383
Davis, H. L.: *ref,* 4:301(4)
Davis, H. S.: *ref,* 1499
Davis, H. T.: *ref,* 1164, 1240
Davis, J.: *ref,* 1240
Davis, J. A.: *ref,* 357, 433, 1133, 1135, 1169
Davis, J. B.: *test,* 1242; *ref,* 1315, 1383
Davis, J. C.: *test,* 1499b, 1499j; *ref,* 532, 2057
Davis, J. D.: *ref,* 1281
Davis, J. E.: *ref,* 1474
Davis, J. K.: *ref,* 559, 561, 1129
Davis, J. M.: *ref,* 69
Davis, J. R.: *ref,* 1176, 1383, 2355
Davis, K. A.: *ref,* 499
Davis, K. E.: *ref,* 1176
Davis, K. G.: *ref,* 1281, 1383
Davis, K. L.: *ref,* 868, 1207, 1281, 1403
Davis, K. M.: *ref,* 1044
Davis, K. R.: *ref,* 1281
Davis, L.: *ref,* 439, 1435
Davis, L. E.: *ref,* 69, 361, 1207, 1583
Davis, L. F.: *test,* 4:696
Davis, L. J.: *ref,* 50, 532-3, 592, 1281, 2076, 2228, 2234
Davis, L. W.: *ref,* 6:159(31)
Davis, M.: *ref,* 1522
Davis, M. A.: *ref,* 1289
Davis, M. C. E.: *ref,* 1603, 1658
Davis, M. G.: *ref,* 211
Davis, M. L. F.: *ref,* 1123, 1313
Davis, M. R.: *ref,* 1087
Davis, N. E.: *ref,* 1516
Davis, N. W.: *ref,* 1281, 1572
Davis, O. L.: *ref,* 19, 589, 868, 1032, 1716
Davis, O. U.: *test,* 4:301
Davis, P.: *rev,* 1324
Davis, P. C.: *rev,* 365, 504; *ref,* 532
Davis, R.: *ref,* 525, 545
Davis, R. A.: *rev,* 3:536, 3:592; *ref,* 798, 1320
Davis, R. E.: *ref,* 1281
Davis, R. K.: *ref,* 1121
Davis, R. M.: *ref,* 525, 912, 1428, 1471
Davis, R. W.: *ref,* 1499
Davis, S. C.: *ref,* 1044
Davis, S. E.: *rev,* 879, 1770; *ref,* 64, 211, 361, 2212
Davis, S. F.: *ref,* 1225
Davis, S. P.: *ref,* 2190
Davis, S. S.: *ref,* 2195
Davis, S. W.: *ref,* 1383
Davis, T. N.: *ref,* 1383
Davis, T. R.: *ref,* 36, 426
Davis, V.: *test,* 2:1273, 2:1355, 3: 133, 4:199
Davis, V. A.: *ref,* 349, 391, 398, 425, 1087, 4:324(59)
Davis, W. A.: *ref,* 439, 522, 529, 1281, 3:678(14)
Davis, W. L.: *ref,* 1273
Davis, W. M.: *ref,* 528

Davis, W. N.: *ref,* 1207, 1403, 1775
Davis, W. Q.: *ref,* 1536, 1552, 1567, 1596, 1603
Davis, W. R.: *ref,* 755, 1394-5
Davis, W. T.: *ref,* 3:220(32)
Davison, A. H.: *ref,* 1519
Davison, D. G.: *test,* 1967; *ref,* 467, 1967
Davison, K.: *ref,* 1383
Davison, L.: *ref,* 439, 1281
Davison, M.: *ref,* 1480
Davol, S. H.: *ref,* 6:186(5)
Daw, R. P.: *ref,* 1471, 1499
Dawald, V. F.: *test,* 36:725
Dawe, H. C.: *rev,* 3:427, 3:429
Dawes, J. W.: *ref,* 1145
Dawes, R. M.: *ref,* 529, 1281, 1499
Dawis, R. V.: *test,* 2283-5; *ref,* 561, 1071, 1073, 2197, 2212, 2283-5
Dawson, A.: *ref,* 533, 1447
Dawson, C. D.: *ref,* 525
Dawson, D. D.: *ref,* 1501
Dawson, F.: *ref,* 1315
Dawson, J. G.: *ref,* 1281, 1448, 1470, 1499
Dawson, J. L. M.: *ref,* 545, 1169, 2266
Dawson, R. I.: *ref,* 1193
Dawson, S.: *test,* 2:1389; *ref,* 525
Day, B. R.: *ref,* 1164
Day, C. W.: *ref,* 1281, 1519
Day, D.: *ref,* 914
Day, D. R.: *ref,* 2451-2, 2457
Day, F.: *ref,* 1499
Day, F. E.: *test,* 35:241, 35:291, 35:457
Day, H.: *ref,* 1109, 1174
Day, H. G.: *test,* 3:556
Day, H. I.: *ref,* 574, 1380
Day, H. P.: *ref,* 868
Day, J. E.: *test,* 1:933
Day, J. F.: *ref,* 2195, 4:277(204)
Day, M.: *ref,* 1383
Day, M. E.: *ref,* 1281, 2195
Day, R.: *ref,* 525
Day, R. H.: *ref,* 1387
Day, R. T.: *ref,* 1052
Dayal, P.: *ref,* 473, 644, 1069
Dayan, M.: *ref,* P:319(3)
Dayley, A. J.: *ref,* 2212
Dayries, J. L.: *ref,* 1281
Dayton, C. M.: *ref,* 1430
Dayton, L. L.: *ref,* 1164
D'Costa, A.: *ref,* 2201
D'Costa, A. G.: *test,* 2201
D'Costa, A. G. J. E.: *ref,* 2201
De, B.: *ref,* 1095, 1174, 1275
Deabler, H. L.: *ref,* 1073, 1277, 1281, 1383, 1387, 1403, 1447, 1469, 1481, 1499, 1519, 2212
de Aboitiz, F. S.: *ref,* 1519
Deacon, K. F.: *ref,* 1428
Deahl, K.: *ref,* 483, 525
Deak, M. R.: *ref,* 1164
Deal, M.: *ref,* 533
Dean, C. C.: *ref,* 505
Dean, C. D.: *ref,* 211, 1716, 1724, 1918
Dean, C. H.: *ref,* 104
Dean, C. W.: *ref,* 1320
Dean, D. A.: *ref,* 525, 1087
Dean, D. G.: *ref,* 1095
Dean, G. S.: *ref,* 1133

Dean, J. T.: *ref,* 1407
Dean, J. W.: *ref,* 2212
Dean, K. I.: *ref,* 1281
Dean, R. B.: *ref,* 1281
Dean, R. F. A.: *ref,* 497
Dean, S.: *ref,* 525, 533
Dean, S. I.: *ref,* 1281, 1448, 1501, 5:143(6)
Dean, W. H.: *ref,* 1499
de Andrade, E. M.: *ref,* 1383
de Andrade, L. D.: *ref,* 1499
Deane, M. A.: *ref,* 532, 1281
DeAngelis, L.: *ref,* 1320
Deanovich, B. F.: *ref,* 1482
Dear, R. E.: *ref,* 357
Dearborn, L. W.: *rev,* 826, 832
Dearborn, T. H.: *test,* 921; *ref,* 921
Dearborn, W. F.: *test,* 2:1390-1; *ref,* 36, 525, 1560, 1572, 2:1390 (1-2), 2:1391(1-2), 3:507(3)
Deatherage, D.: *ref,* 1207, 1403
Deb, M.: *ref,* 1174, 1320, 2212
Deb, S.: *ref,* 515
DeBerardinis, A.: *ref,* 349
De Beruff, E.: *ref,* 361, 404
DeBlassie, R.: *ref,* 533
DeBlassie, R. R.: *ref,* 36, 451, 1383
De Boer, D. L.: *ref,* 19, 349
de Bottari, L.: *ref,* 22, 425
DeBroder, G. W.: *ref,* 211, 1275
DeBruler, R. M.: *ref,* 533
DeBurger, R. A.: *ref,* 381, 439, 525, 533
DeBusk, B. W.: *ref,* 525
DeCamp, J. E.: *ref,* 525, 3:220(22)
de Castro, F. J.: *ref,* 503
DeCencio, D. V.: *ref,* 1207, 1281, 1403, 2186, 2212
DeCharms, R.: *ref,* 439
de Cillis, O. E.: *ref,* 1101, 1281, P:294(6)
Deckard, N. S.: *ref,* 1200, 1403
Decker, A. I.: *ref,* 36
Decker, C. E.: *ref,* 1090, 1403, 2212
Decker, R. L.: *ref,* 348, 482, 1281, 2239, 2448
Deckner, C. W.: *ref,* 1480
DeCosse, J.: *ref,* 1281
DeCosta, F. A.: *ref,* 382, 863, 869
DeCoster, D. T.: *ref,* 1121, 1176
Dedmon, D.: *ref,* 993
Dee, H. L.: *ref,* 543, 2266
Deeble, C. T.: *ref,* 1383
Deed, M. L.: *ref,* 1164
Deemer, W. L.: *test,* 3:372, 7:987
Deer, G. H.: *ref,* 3:538(2)
Dees, M. H.: *ref,* 935
Deese, J.: *rev,* 1772, 5:697
Deese, J. C.: *ref,* 981
DeFazio, V. J.: *ref,* 1169
DeForrest, R.: *ref,* 507, 509
Defrain, D. M.: *ref,* 1044, 1123, 1572
de Francis, J.: *test,* 225
Degenhardt, F. J.: *ref,* 1474
Degering, E. F.: *test,* 3:556, 3:558, T:1616
Degerman, R.: *ref,* 1127
DeGideo, J.: *ref,* 1121, 1164, 2212
DeGooyer, M. H.: *ref,* 497, 5:6 (11), 6:573(1)
De Graaf, C.: *ref,* 1775
De Haan, H.: *ref,* 532
DeHart, A. L.: *ref,* 69, 361

DeHaven, G. E.: *test,* 1894; *ref,* 1894
de Heus, J. H.: *ref,* 22, 2244, 5: 329(5)
de Hirsch, K.: *ref,* 1447, 1702, 2028
Deich, R. F.: *ref,* 50, 349, 516, 1174
Deignan, F. J.: *ref,* 1403, 6:438 (462)
Deignan, M. C.: *ref,* 981, 1921
Deihl, N. C.: *ref,* 214
Deisher, R. W.: *ref,* 947
Deissler, K. L.: *ref,* 20
Deitche, J. H.: *ref,* 1415
Deiulio, R. S.: *ref,* 1135, 1164, 1315
deJesús, C.: *ref,* 381
Dejmek, F. W.: *ref,* 349, 2266
deJung, J. E.: *ref,* 6:186(2, 8, 13-6), P:390(17, 21)
Dekker, J. H.: *ref,* 1121, 1403, 2212
Dekker, L. C.: *ref,* 355, 439
DeKoninck, J. M.: *ref,* 1499
de Lacey, P. R.: *ref,* 516
Delancy, E. O.: *ref,* 425, 1087, 1694
Delaney, E. C.: *ref,* 869
Delaney, J. F.: *ref,* 1133
Delaney, J. J.: *ref,* 1176, 2454
Delaney, R. J.: *ref,* 538
DeLange, W. H.: *ref,* 532, 1240
Delany, F. I.: *ref,* 1192
Delany, L. T.: *ref,* 1499
DeLapa, G.: *ref,* 524-5
Delattre, L.: *ref,* 532-3
Delauretis, R. J.: *ref,* 357, 1303
De Lay, F. P.: *rev,* 2:1269, 2:1290
Delay, J.: *ref,* 1499
del Carlo-Giannini, G.: *ref,* 1499
DeLeon, G.: *ref,* 1293
DeLeon, P.: *ref,* 1281
DeLeon, P. H.: *ref,* 1275, 1415
de Leonard, C. C.: *ref,* 1471
De-Levie, A.: *ref,* 1447
Del Gaudio, A. C.: *ref,* 574, 1169, 1474
Delhees, K. H.: *test,* 1131; *ref,* 1281, 1300, 1383
de L. Horne, D. J.: *ref,* 592
DeLiberty, W. F.: *ref,* 603
de Lint, J.: *ref,* 529
DeLisle, F. H.: *ref,* 2195
DeLisser, O.: *ref,* 1183, 1281
Dell, D.: *ref,* 517, 533
Dell, H. L. D.: *ref,* 1144, 1383, 1403
della Cioppa, M.: *ref,* 1240, 1281, 1519, 6:223(12)
Della-Piana, G.: *ref,* 1623, 1628
Della Piana, G. M.: *rev,* 1629; *ref,* 532, 868
Dellas, M.: *ref,* 542, 551
Delli Colli, P.: *ref,* 532
Dellis, N. P.: *ref,* 1499
Delman, L.: *ref,* 1087
DeLong, J. J.: *ref,* 358
DeLong, R. D.: *ref,* 1391
de Lopategui, M. N.: *ref,* 1361
Deloria, D. J.: *rev,* 1696, 1728
Delp, H. A.: *rev,* 504, 533; *test,* 4:465; *ref,* 503, 533
Delph, D. J.: *ref,* 1123, 1439
Del Popolo, J. A.: *ref,* 868
DeLuca, J.: *ref,* 529, 1448
De Luca, J. N.: *ref,* 349, 529, 1448, 1499
Demand, J. W.: *ref,* 391, 407
De Marco, W.: *ref,* 533

Dittes, J. E.: *test,* 1028; *ref,* 419, 1028, 1164, 1207, 1281, 1294
Dittmar, N. S.: *ref,* 1716
Dittrick, A. R.: *ref,* 48
DiTullio, W. M.: *ref,* 7:55(15)
DiVesta, F. J.: *ref,* 419, 1094, 1164, 1386, 1394, 1402, 2448, 4:370(4), 5:308(346), 6:870(1)
Divney, H. P.: *ref,* 1499
Dixit, R. C.: *ref,* 1247, 1403
Dixon, A. S.: *ref,* 1069
Dixon, D. H.: *ref,* 2187
Dixon, J. C.: *ref,* 439, 522, 529, 542, 592, 1105, 1380, 1519
Dixon, P.: *ref,* 403, 439
Dixon, P. T.: *ref,* 48
Dixon, P. W.: *ref,* 361, 1164
Dixon, S. D.: *ref,* 1674, 1724
Dixon, S. L.: *ref,* 1152
Dixon, T. R.: *ref,* 221
Dixon, W. R.: *ref,* 48, 4:660(23)
Dizney, H.: *ref,* 7, 233, 238, 349, 1672
Dizney, H. F.: *ref,* 7, 19, 238, 255, 271, 314, 348, 398, 1032, 1044, 1059, 1240, 1403
Dizzone, M. F.: *ref,* 439, 522, 529
Dlabal, J. J.: *ref,* 1121
Dlodlo, M. S.: *ref,* 1508
Dobbins, H. J.: *ref,* 1044
Dobbins, R. D.: *ref,* 1281
Dobbs, D. D.: *ref,* 1499
Dobbs, N. J.: *ref,* 1281
Dobell, H. R.: *ref,* 1205
Dobruszek, Z.: *ref,* 1207, 1306
Dobson, J. C.: *ref,* 50, 525, 981, 1711
Dobson, W. R.: *ref,* 1281
Dobyns, Z. P.: *ref,* 1294
Dockar-Drysdale, B. E.: *test,* 6:244
Dockrell, W. B.: *ref,* 95, 409, 516, 533, 722
Docter, R.: *ref,* 1499
Docter, R. F.: *rev,* 518; *ref,* 518, 1281, 1471, 1519, P:41(6)
Doctor, R. M.: *ref,* 1169, 1499
Dodd, B. E.: *ref,* 1881
Dodd, C.: *test,* 5:179
Dodd, J.: *ref,* 1281
Dodd, J. M.: *ref,* 381, 1281
Dodd, M. R.: *ref,* 3:399(2)
Dodd, S. C.: *exc,* 1:983
Dodd, W. E.: *ref,* 426, 1193-4, 1407, 2212
Dodds, J. B.: *test,* 492; *ref,* 492
Dodge, A. B.: *ref,* 3:242(2)
Dodge, A. F.: *test,* 2:1232; *ref,* 167, 438, 1320, 2135, 2:1232(1-3)
Dodge, D. W.: *ref,* 1275
Dodge, G. R.: *ref,* 1281
Dodgens, C. E.: *ref,* 1121
Dodson, M. H.: *ref,* 391, 5:308 (277)
Dodson, R. G.: *ref,* 32
Doehne, E. F.: *ref,* 1281
Doehring, D. G.: *ref,* 496, 532, 1140, 1281
Doerman, L. H.: *ref,* 504, 4:350(4)
Doermann, H.: *ref,* 357
Doerr, J. J.: *test,* 7:904; *ref,* 2105, 2197
Doerries, L. E.: *ref,* 1350
Doerring, P. L.: *ref,* 504, 1196, 1216
Doherty, A.: *ref,* 1121, 1164, 1240
Doherty, D.: *ref,* 1415

Doherty, M. A.: *ref,* 529, 574, 1267, 1281, 1383
Doherty, V. W.: *ref,* 400
Dohner, C. W.: *ref,* 69, 1044, 1303, 1775, 2355
Dohrenwend, B. P.: *ref,* 1340
Doidge, W. T.: *ref,* 1281
Doig, M.: *ref,* 1032
Dokecki, P. R.: *ref,* 381, 525, 538, 1480
Dolan, F. A.: *ref,* 1121, 1164, 1403
Dolan, R. E.: *ref,* 1236
Dolby, J. R.: *ref,* 1164
Dolby, L. L. L.: *ref,* 574
Dolch, E. W.: *test,* 1657, 1:1096, 2: 1575; *exc,* 2:1539, 2:1559; *ref,* 1657, 1690, 2:1559(2), 2:1575(1)
Dolcini, M. E.: *ref,* 997
Dole, A. A.: *test,* 6:1073; *ref,* 357, 361, 364, 525, 868, 1069, 1194, 1471, 1500, 6:1073(1, 3-4), P: 381(33)
Doleys, E. J.: *ref,* 361, 1164, 1281, 1289, 1499, 2195
Dolgan, J.: *ref,* 1121, 1471
Dolinsky, R.: *ref,* 1480
Dolio, A. J.: *test,* 4:52
Dolke, A. M.: *ref,* 1174
Doll, E. A.: *test,* 519, 1428, T:921; *exc,* 497; *ref,* 497, 507, 519, 525, 545, 1428, 1898
Doll, P. A.: *ref,* 516, 1247, 1403, 1519
Doll, R. C.: *test,* 1262
Doll, R. E.: *ref,* 1176
Dollar, R. J.: *ref,* 1133, 1135, 1207, 1394, 1407, 1772
Dollard, J.: *ref,* 1094, 1437
Dollarhide, R. S.: *ref,* 50, 1679
Dollin, A.: *ref,* 1519
Dollin, A. P.: *ref,* 1519
Dollins, J. G.: *ref,* 1123
Dolliver, R. H.: *rev,* 2194, 2200; *ref,* 2212
Dolly, A.: *ref,* 497
Dombrose, L. A.: *test,* 1475; *ref,* 1475
Domenichetti, M.: *ref,* 2103
Domincovich, H. A.: *test,* 4:184
Domino, G.: *rev,* 238; *ref,* 357, 364- 5, 439, 447, 525, 529, 1094, 1117, 1121, 1281, 1350, 1463, 2212
Domrath, R. P.: *ref,* 381, 399, 533, 543
Donabedian, A.: *ref,* 5:781(17)
Donaghy, R. T.: *ref,* 382, 404, 1499, 1519
Donahue, D.: *ref,* 529
Donahue, M. A.: *ref,* 2103, 2221
Donahue, M. C.: *ref,* 1254
Donahue, M. M.: *ref,* 1291, 1403
Donahue, W. T.: *ref,* 48
Donald, G.: *ref,* 3:688(3-4)
Donald, M. W.: *ref,* 1087
Donat, G. M.: *ref,* 868, 1281
Donato, D. J.: *ref,* 1395
Donceel, J. F.: *ref,* 1320
Donelan, J. R.: *ref,* 1137
Donelson, K. L.: *ref,* 20, 426
Donini, G.: *ref,* 1481
Donlon, T. F.: *ref,* 357
Donnan, H.: *ref,* 357, 1303
Donnan, H. H.: *ref,* 1303, 1383
Donnan, S. P. B.: *ref,* 1174

Donnell, G.: *ref,* 497
Donnelly, E. F.: *ref,* 532, 1281
Donnelly, E. M.: *ref,* 1186
Donnelly, F.: *ref,* 381, 1696, 1921
Donnelly, M. C.: *ref,* 18, 87, 621, 1560
Donnelly, M. M.: *ref,* 1193-4
Donnenwerth, G.: *ref,* 1044, 2213
Donnenwerth, G. V.: *ref,* 2195, 2212-3
Donnerstein, E.: *ref,* 1281
Donofrio, A. F.: *ref,* 497
Donofrio, I. A.: *ref,* 1519
Donoghue, J. R.: *ref,* 1281
Donohue, H. H.: *ref,* 425, 1281
Donoian, G.: *ref,* 1394
Donovan, G. L.: *ref,* 1121
Doob, L. W.: *exc,* 1444; *ref,* 1499
Dooley, B. J.: *ref,* 1291
Dooley, L. B.: *ref,* 1351
Dooley, M. D.: *ref,* 529
Dooley, R. J.: *exc,* 451
Doongaji, D. R.: *ref,* 1499
Doorack, R.: *ref,* 1281
Doorbar, R. R.: *ref,* 529, 1469, 1519
Doost, R. M.: *ref,* 1355
Dootjes, I.: *ref,* 1094
Doppelt, J. E.: *ref,* 532-3
Doppelt, J. E.: *rev,* 170, 394, 500, 1739, 2189, 2275, 2325, 2454, 4: 812; *test,* 371, 376, 433, 1063, 2164, 2290, 2317; *ref,* 69, 404, 433, 447, 529, 1069, 2151, 2212, 2349, 2355, 5:7(30), 5:954(1)
Doran, S.: *test,* 3:179, 3:238
Doran, W. J.: *ref,* 1133
Dorcus, M. D.: *ref,* 558
Dorcus, R. M.: *ref,* 532, 1206, 1222, 1320, 1499
Dore, J. J.: *ref,* 532
Dore, P. D.: *ref,* 1519
Dore, R. L.: *ref,* 2212
Doren, M.: *test,* 1627
Doress, I.: *ref,* 1121, 1315
Dorfman, E.: *ref,* 1313
Dorfman, M. B.: *ref,* 1281
Doris, J.: *ref,* 1471
Doris, R. E.: *ref,* 381, 533
Dörken, H.: *exc,* 1499; *ref,* 381, 532, 1499, 5:147(19, 49)
Dorman, D.: *ref,* 1225, 1293, 1499
Dorn, D. S.: *ref,* P:381(45)
Dorpat, T. L.: *ref,* 1281
Dorr, D. A.: *ref,* 1307
Dorris, C. W.: *ref,* 2195
Dorsey, H. A.: *ref,* 2069
Dorsey, J. M.: *test,* 4:492
Dorsey, R. N.: *ref,* 1499
Dorsey, T. E.: *ref,* 489
Dorworth, T. R.: *ref,* 1133
Dosajh, N. L.: *ref,* 1069, P:441(7)
Dosey, M. A.: *ref,* 1499, 1519
Dosier, C. H.: *ref,* 1447
Doss, L.: *test,* 36:506
Dotson, E.: *ref,* 1174
Dotson, E. J.: *ref,* 1245, 1383, 6: 113(14)
Dotterer, J. E.: *test,* 35:381, 36:516, 36:521, 36:686, T:1126
Doty, B. A.: *ref,* 529, 1164, 1207, 1281
Doty, C. N.: *ref,* 1164
Doub, B. A.: *ref,* 482, 2132
Doub, W. H.: *ref,* 1281

1683; *exc*, 1911; *ref*, 1911, 1932,
3 :461a(1)
Dwarshuis, L.: *ref*, 439, 1447
Dwinell, A. J.: *ref*, 1481
Dwivedi, C. B.: *ref*, 1772
Dworkin, S. F.: *ref*, 1069, 1394, 2337
Dworsky, A.: *ref*, 1140
Dwyer, P. S.: *ref*, 2212
Dwyer, R. C.: *ref*, 533
Dye, G. M.: *ref*, 1127
Dye, H. A.: *ref*, 1164
Dye, J. M.: *ref*, 357
Dyer, A. M.: *ref*, 1480
Dyer, D. T.: *ref*, 1095, 1281, 1403,
2212
Dyer, E. D.: *ref*, 1121
Dyer, F. N.: *ref*, 1127, 1169
Dyer, G. B.: *ref*, 400, 533, 1895
Dyer, H. S.: *rev*, 22, 1533, 2189;
test, 2 :1485, 6 :708; *ref*, 19, 48,
64, 244, 264, 305, 357, 1048
Dyer, P. T.: *ref*, 1135
Dyett, E. G.: *ref*, 381
Dyk, R. B.: *ref*, 1169, 1519
Dyke, R. G.: *ref*, 525, 533, 1474,
1499, 1519
Dykema, P. W.: *test*, 202; *ref*, 205
Dyken, M. L.: *ref*, 532
Dykman, R. A.: *ref*, 533, 1281, 1447,
2355
Dykstra, R.: *rev*, 1702; *ref*, 400,
435, 570, 1603, 1629, 1679, 1702,
1705, 1716-7, 1724
Dymond, R.: *ref*, 1281
Dymond, R. F.: *ref*, 1519
Dynes, J. B.: *ref*, 1144
Dyrhaug, D. R.: *ref*, 1044
Dysinger, D. W.: *ref*, 525, 532,
1192, 1222
Dzendolet, E.: *ref*, 1281
Dziuban, C. D.: *ref*, 1439
D'Zmura, T.: *ref*, 1195
D'Zmura, T. L.: *ref*, 1195

EACHUS, H. T.: *ref*, 1164
Eaddy, M. L.: *ref*, 1281, 2212
Eads, L. K.: *test*, 2 :1259
Eager, M. F.: *ref*, 1123
Eagle, C. J.: *ref*, 1127, 1169
Eagle, M.: *ref*, 1169
Eagle, N.: *rev*, 418, 1054; *ref*, 19,
22, 400
Eagleson, O. W.: *ref*, 1320, 1403
Eakins, L. M.: *test*, 677
Eames, T. H.: *test*, 6 :956; *ref*, 1447,
1918, 3 :463(2, 4-5), 3 :468(3), 6 :
956(8)
Earhart, E. L. M.: *ref*, 1921
Earhart, R. H.: *ref*, 525
Earl, C. J.: *ref*, 1499
Earl, C. J. C.: *exc*, 525, 1499; *ref*,
381, 515, 518, 525, 545, 2 :1401(7)
Earl, R. B.: *ref*, 1415
Earl, R. D.: *ref*, 1121
Earle, E. S.: *ref*, 505
Earle, F. M.: *test*, 3 :114, 3 :356, 3 :
546, 4 :289, 4 :380, 4 :713; *exc*,
2242; *ref*, 3 :114(1), 3 :356(1-2),
3 :546(1-2), 4 :289(1-2), 4 :380
(1-2), 4 :713(1-2)
Earle, J. B.: *ref*, 1281, 1499
Earley, S. R.: *ref*, 1281
Early, F. G.: *ref*, 989

Early, G. H.: *ref*, 533, 981, 989,
1628
Early, R. G.: *ref*, 935
Earth Science Curriculum Project:
test, 7 :803
Easley, G. T.: *ref*, 381
Easley, H.: *rev*, 391, 2 :1418, 2 :1424
East, R.: *ref*, 1093, 1144
Easter, L. V.: *ref*, 1519
Easterbrook, C. M.: *ref*, 574, 868,
1281
Eastern Commercial Teachers' As-
sociation: *ref*, 786
Eastes, S. H.: *ref*, 2212
Eastman, D. F.: *ref*, 1448
Eastman, F.: *ref*, 2199
Eastman, F. C.: *ref*, 1480
Eastman, W. F.: *ref*, 1281
Eastman Kodak Co.: *test*, 4 :660
Easton, J. C.: *ref*, 1123, 1519, 2214
Easton, K.: *ref*, 1499
Easton, R.: *ref*, 1383
Easton, Z. F.: *ref*, 1281
Eastwood, G. R.: *ref*, 589
Eastwood, M. R.: *ref*, 1145
Eaton, A. E.: *ref*, 522, 533
Eaton, E. L.: *test*, 1549
Eaton, H. T.: *test*, 35 :214, 1 :972,
1 :978, T :421, T :496; *ref*, 525
Eaton, M. J.: *ref*, 1481
Eaton, M. T.: *ref*, 36, 69, 1560, 4 :
174(1)
Eattell, E. A.: *ref*, 525
Eaves, L.: *ref*, 533
Eaves, L. C.: *ref*, 381, 525, 533,
1428, 1447
Ebaugh, F. G.: *ref*, 1499
Ebel, R. L.: *rev*, 1765, 1795, 2355,
4 :491, 4 :582, 5 :698, 7 :792; *test*,
4 :4, 4 :7, 4 :15; *exc*, 1968, 7 :659
Eber, H.: *ref*, 1383
Eber, H. W.: *test*, 1038, 1383, 6 :
125, P :246; *ref*, 449, 498, 529,
1281, 1383
Eber, M.: *ref*, 1447
Eberdt, M. G.: *ref*, 1294, 1403
Eberhart, W.: *ref*, 2 :1294(1), 4 :
58(5)
Eberlein, E. L.: *ref*, 1164
Eberlein, L.: *ref*, 1240
Eberly, C. G.: *ref*, 1395
Eberly, J. W.: *ref*, 211
Ebert, E.: *ref*, 7, 426, 507, 518, 525,
545, 2266, 3 :660(15)
Ebert, E. H.: *ref*, 525, 1499
Ebert, F. J.: *ref*, 404, 868, 1164,
1403
Ebert, J. N.: *ref*, 1232
Ebinger, R. D.: *ref*, 1469
Eble, S. J.: *ref*, 1499, 1528
Eby, J. M.: *ref*, 214, 1358
Eby, K.: *test*, 36 :724
Eccker, W. F.: *ref*, 1519
Eccles, A. M.: *ref*, 558
Echeverria, B. P.: *ref*, 348, 425, 447,
1069, 1073, 1121, 1560, 2195
Eck, R. A.: *ref*, 1471
Eckelberry, R. H.: *ref*, 48, 869,
1053
Eckermann, A. C.: *ref*, 3 :217(64)
Eckerson, L. D.: *test*, 3 :161; *ref*,
2 :1319(1-2), 3 :161(8)
Eckert, D. Z.: *ref*, 36
Eckert, R. E.: *test*, 2 :1265

Eckert, R. G.: *ref*, 1095, 1320
Eckert, W. J.: *test*, 1 :1126
Eckhardt, W.: *ref*, 1499
Eckhoff, C. M.: *ref*, 404
Eckman, K. M.: *ref*, 1225, 1281,
1293, 1471, 1519
Eckman, R.: *ref*, 525, 533, 538
Eckstein, C.: *ref*, 1657
Eckstein, C. G.: *ref*, 1657
Eckstein Bros., Inc.: *test*, 2034
Economidou, J.: *ref*, 518, 529, 533
Edberg, G.: *ref*, 20, 48, 419
Eddins, E. L.: *ref*, 2186
Edds, J. H.: *ref*, 2 :1272(3), 6 :
480(30)
Eddy, B.: *ref*, 2212
Eddy, B. B.: *ref*, 361
Eddy, H. M.: *test*, 1 :1069
Eddy, R.: *ref*, 1095
Eddy, R. T.: *ref*, 2212
Edelman, F.: *ref*, 1123
Edelman, R. I.: *ref*, 1391
Edelman, S. K.: *ref*, 1499
Edelstein, G.: *ref*, 348, 439
Edelstein, R. R.: *ref*, 1519
Edens, F. N.: *ref*, 1394
Edens, L. W.: *ref*, 1281, 1447, 1481,
2195
Eder, S. C.: *ref*, 1391
Edfeldt, A. W.: *test*, 1726
Edgar, C. L.: *ref*, 1482, 1883
Edgar, J. W.: *test*, 5 :699
Edgar, M.: *ref*, 348, 399, 425
Edgar, M. S.: *ref*, 1447
Edgecombe, W. D.: *ref*, 884, 1383
Edgerly, J.: *ref*, 1499
Edgerton, H. A.: *test*, 6 :765; *ref*,
419, 1087, 1101, 1745
Edgerton, R. B.: *ref*, 1499
Edgington, M.: *test*, 36 :639, 36 :
644, 36 :646
Edholm, O. G.: *ref*, 439
Edington, E. D.: *ref*, 1069, 1073,
2135
Edlow, D. W.: *ref*, 1519
Edman, M.: *ref*, 1281
Edminster, I. F.: *ref*, 1281
Edmiston, R. W.: *test*, 4 :580, 4 :
649, 4 :738, T :1863; *ref*, 1123, 4 :
179(7), 4 :738(1), 6 :265(1)
Edmonds, P.: *ref*, 516
Edmonds, W. S.: *ref*, 361
Edmondson, H. S.: *ref*, 211
Edmondson, M. B.: *ref*, 525
Edmonson, B. W.: *ref*, 1499
Edmonson, L. D.: *test*, 478-9, 1431;
ref, 86, 426, 621, 1572, 2135, 2195,
2229, 2251, 2266, 4 :216(12)
Edmonston, W.: *test*, 7 :957
Edmonston, W. E.: *ref*, 532-3,
1164, 1212, 1225, 1383, 1389, 1499
Edmunds, P. K.: *ref*, 1240
Edmunds, R.: *ref*, 1447
Edrington, T. C.: *ref*, 532, 1140
Edson, K. C.: *ref*, 1133
Edson, L. N.: *ref*, 1910
Edson, R. C.: *ref*, 211
Educational Institute of Scotland:
test, 1548, 35 :411, 3 :124
Educational Performance Associ-
ates, Inc.: *test*, 1017
Educational Records Bureau: *test*,
616, 675, 718, 1807, 1839, 1861,

Everett, R. B.: *ref,* 1281, 1391
Everhart, R. W.: *ref,* 1702
Eversmeyer, G. J.: *ref,* 1281
Everson, R.: *ref,* 1387
Everson, R. R.: *ref,* 532
Everstein, L.: *ref,* 1448
Everstine, L.: *ref,* 518, 1275
Eveson, M. B.: *ref,* 1245, 1275, 1300, 1383
Evvard, E.: *ref,* 1447
Ewald, A. T.: *ref,* 2266
Ewald, H. H.: *ref,* 1069, 1519
Ewalt, J. R.: *ref,* 1217
Ewell, J. W.: *ref,* 1145
Ewen, R. B.: *ref,* 333, 382, 404, 449, 1005, 1069, 2151, 2387
Ewens, W. P.: *ref,* 2195
Ewert, J. C.: *ref,* 439, 529, 592, 1281, 1380, 1447, 1499
Ewert, L. D.: *ref,* 1499
Ewing, D. B.: *ref,* 1249
Ewing, D. R.: *ref,* 1281
Ewing, J. A.: *ref,* 518, 1281, 1295
Ewing, J. H.: *ref,* 1232
Ewing, R. M.: *ref,* 355, 1499
Ewing, T. N.: *ref,* 1281, 1383, 2239, 5:6(16), 5:308(300)
Exline, R. V.: *ref,* 1176, 1281
Exner, J. E.: *exc,* 6:72; *ref,* 533, 1281, 1481, 1499
Exton, A. H.: *test,* 432
Eyde, L. D.: *ref,* 2212
Eygenstein, W. F.: *ref,* 1499
Eyley, H. E.: *ref,* 1499
Eyman, R. K.: *ref,* 2234
Eynon, T. G.: *ref,* 1207
Eysenck, H. J.: *rev,* 1144, 1205, 1218, 1222, 1224, 1245, 1281, 1410, 1423, 1471, 1499, 4:50, 5:90, 5:123; *test,* 1174, 1275; *exc,* 509, 1087, 1499; *ref,* 185, 381, 403, 425, 439, 1109, 1174–5, 1205–6, 1226, 1232, 1245, 1252, 1275, 1281, 1296, 1383, 1387, 1499, 4:115(4), P:343(2)
Eysenck, M. D.: *ref,* 439
Eysenck, S. B. G.: *test,* 1174–5, 1252; *ref,* 381, 1174–5, 1205–6, 1245, 1252, 1275, 1383, 1387

FABIAN, A. A.: *ref,* 1447
Fabian, H.: *ref,* 1508
Fabian, J. J.: *ref,* 1139, 1174 ,1295, 1300
Fabian, W. A.: *ref,* 1090, 1499
Fabisch, W.: *ref,* 518, 1112, 1281, 1499
Fabrega, H.: *ref,* 1298, 1471
Fabrikant, B.: *ref,* 1499
Fabrikant, M. B.: *ref,* 1447
Fadale, V. E.: *ref,* 1415
Fadiman, J.: *ref,* 1240, 1281
Faeth, H. W.: *ref,* 1519
Fagan, E. C.: *ref,* 1225, 1383
Fagan, J.: *ref,* 525, 538, P:381(41)
Fagan, L. B.: *test,* 35:285
Fager, R. E.: *ref,* 1499
Fagerburg, J. E.: *ref,* 1207
Fagert, C. M.: *ref,* 524, 533
Fagin, H. T.: *test,* 1220, 2189, 7: 1062
Fagin, M. C.: *ref,* 10, 1050
Fagin, W. B.: *ref,* 2212
Faglioni, P.: *ref,* 439, 1192, 1311
Fagot, H. J.: *ref,* 516, 1247

Fahey, G. L.: *ref,* 404
Fahmy, M.: *ref,* 381, 515, 518, 578
Fahrig, M. W.: *ref,* 2381
Fahrion, S. L.: *ref,* 1171
Fahrner, B. G.: *ref,* 1415
Fahrner, C. J.: *ref,* 914
Fahs, H.: *ref,* 1281
Fahy, T. J.: *ref,* 1278
Faibish, G.: *ref,* 1281
Failor, L. M.: *ref,* 349, 391, 426, 4:315(6)
Fair, D. C.: *ref,* 2212
Fair, D. T.: *ref,* 36
Fair, M. H.: *ref,* 1095, 1320
Fairbairn, V. J.: *test,* 1352
Fairbanks, G.: *ref,* 1560, 3:163(3)
Fairbrother, C. J.: *ref,* 217
Fairchild, C. M.: *ref,* 1499
Fairchild, M. R.: *ref,* 981
Fairchild, P. C.: *ref,* 425, 1044
Fairfield, P. D.: *ref,* 1164
Fairweather, G. W.: *ref,* 1281, 1430, 1519
Faison, C.: *ref,* 1905
Falberg, R. M.: *ref,* 529
Falck, F. E.: *ref,* 1403, 1772, 2212
Falck, V. T.: *ref,* 2038
Falconer, A. D.: *ref,* 518, 543, 592
Falconer, G. A.: *ref,* 2031
Falek, A.: *ref,* 525, 529, 532, 1281
Falik, L. H.: *ref,* 1696
Falk, G.: *ref,* 1499
Falk, H. B.: *ref,* 1281, 1448
Falk, L. J.: *ref,* 493, 516, 533, 1428, 1875, 2028
Falk, R.: *ref,* 525, 3:242(2)
Fallers, J.: *ref,* 1895
Fallon, J. M.: *ref,* 1280
Falls, H. B.: *ref,* 914
Falls, R. P.: *ref,* 1500
Falstein, E. K.: *ref,* 483
Faltz, C. A.: *ref,* 1281
Familant, R. P.: *ref,* 516, 2095
Family Life Publications: *test,* 817
Fancher, E. C.: *ref,* 1516
Fand, A. B.: *test,* 1267; *ref,* 1267
Fandal, A. W.: *test,* 492
Fanelli, G. C.: *ref,* 592, 1223
Fangman, E. G.: *ref,* 1069, 2195
Fangman, M. W.: *ref,* 543
Fantel, E.: *ref,* 1482
Fantl, E.: *exc,* 1447
Faragher, J. P.: *ref,* 361
Farahmand, S. S.: *ref,* 1281
Farber, I. E.: *ref,* 532
Farber, N.: *ref,* 2234
Farber, R. H.: *ref,* 69, 2195, 4:277 (267), 5:6(14), 5:66(3)
Farberow, N. L.: *ref,* 1281, 1482, 1499–500, 1519
Farbro, P. C.: *ref,* 423, 1194, 1205–6, 1403, 2448
Fare, D. E.: *ref,* 1383
Fargo, G.: *ref,* 516
Fargo, G. A.: *ref,* 516
Fargo, G. E.: *ref,* 1315
Fargo, R.: *ref,* 2212
Farina, A.: *ref,* 1519
Farkas, E.: *ref,* 1281
Farkas, R.: *ref,* 1268
Farkas, T.: *ref,* 1340
Farley, E. J.: *ref,* 48
Farley, E. S.: *test,* 2:1642; *ref,* 2: 1642(1)

Farley, F. H.: *ref,* 403, 1044, 1164, 1174, 1185, 1275, 1281
Farley, G. A.: *ref,* 1225
Farley, J.: *ref,* 361, 1519, 6:468(6)
Farley, N. B.: *ref,* 1519
Farley, R. E.: *ref,* 1499
Farley, S. V.: *ref,* 1174
Farls, R. J.: *ref,* 1326
Farmelant, M. C. S.: *ref,* 1500
Farmer, C. R.: *ref,* 1447
Farmer, E.: *ref,* 4:295(1)
Farmer, H. S.: *ref,* 2213
Farmer, L.: *ref,* 1044
Farmer, P.: *ref,* 64
Farmer, R. G.: *ref,* 1275, 1499
Farmer, T. A.: *ref,* 2355
Farnen, R. F.: *ref,* 2007
Farnham, L. J.: *exc,* 1281; *ref,* 518
Farnsworth, D.: *test,* 1912–3; *ref,* 1912–3, 1923
Farnsworth, K. E.: *ref,* **2213**
Farnsworth, P. R.: *rev,* 189, 194, 203, 211, 214, 1:1087, 2:1330, 3: 54, 6:125; *exc,* 206, 217; *ref,* 189, 202, 211, 419, 1320, 2212–3, 4: 96(4)
Farnum, H. B.: *ref,* 426, 1499, 1583
Farnum, S. E.: *test,* 216, 5:246; *ref,* 211, 216
Faroqi, M. A.: *exc,* 372; *ref,* 439
Farquhar, W. G.: *ref,* 1772
Farquhar, W. W.: *ref,* 1303, 1772
Farr, J. L.: *ref,* 425, 469, 1423
Farr, R.: *rev,* 1535, 1699; *test,* 1560; *ref,* 1536, 1552, 1560, 1567, 1572–3, 1583, 1603, 1634, 1702, 1705, 1711, 1716–7
Farr, R. S.: *ref,* 559, 1101
Farr, S. D.: *exc,* 361; *ref,* 1302
Farrah, G. A.: *test,* 1373
Farram, F.: *ref,* 1090, 2:1243(13)
Farrant, R. H.: *ref,* 355, 364, 381, 1087
Farrar, R. D.: *ref,* 361
Farrell, B. A.: *exc,* 1499
Farrell, G. E.: *ref,* 1475
Farrell, J. R.: *ref,* 1515
Farrell, M.: *ref,* 381, 1447
Farrell, M. L.: *ref,* 1087
Farrell, R. M.: *ref,* 1165
Farren, P. J.: *ref,* 1133
Farrington, A. D.: *ref,* 1091
Farris, J. D.: *ref,* 921
Farrow, B. J.: *ref,* 1121, 1123, 1169
Farrow, E. G.: *ref,* 2195
Farson, M. R.: *ref,* 525
Farthing, M.: *ref,* 525
Farwell, E. D.: *ref,* 1302
Farwell, H. W.: *test,* 1:870b, 1: 1126, 2:1607, 3:582, 5:751
Fassett, K. K.: *ref,* 532, 1281, 2212, 5:143(1, 3)
Fast, I.: *ref,* 1499, 1519, 2212
Fast, R. E.: *ref,* 533
Fate, W. H.: *ref,* 1920
Faterson, H.: *ref,* 1481
Faterson, H. F.: *exc,* 1481; *ref,* 525, 529, 533, 1169, 1474, 1499, 1519, 2355
Fattu, N. A.: *ref,* 69, 2195, 6:438 (532)
Fatzinger, F. A.: *ref,* 1073
Faubion, R.: *ref,* 1087, 2251
Fauble, M. L.: *ref,* 1415, 2195

Ferrell, J. G.: *ref,* 1127, 1169
Ferrell, R. H.: *rev,* 1994
Ferrier, E. E.: *ref,* 981
Ferriman, M. R.: *ref,* 1478
Ferris, A. H.: *test,* 6:708
Ferris, D. R.: *ref,* 589
Ferris, F. L.: *test,* 6:936
Ferris, M. J.: *ref,* 361, 652, 1383
Ferritto, M. C.: *ref,* 1447
Ferry, R. D.: *ref,* 1403
Ferson, R. F.: *ref,* 342, 2199, 2239, 2266-7
Fertman, M. H.: *ref,* P:363(15-6)
Feshbach, S.: *ref,* 529, 1519
Fessenden, S. A.: *test,* 5:33; *exc,* 2:1535
Fessler, M. H.: *ref,* 4:95(18)
Fest, B.: *ref,* 1499-500, 1519
Fetler, D.: *test,* 1405
Fetter, M. C.: *ref,* 1932
Fetterman, J. L.: *ref,* 1105
Feuers, S.: *ref,* 1546, 1572
Feurfile, D.: *ref,* 1499
Fewell, M.: *ref,* 1320
Fey, W. F.: *ref,* 532, 1164, 1281, 1380
Fialkin, H. N.: *ref,* 438
Fialkow, P. J.: *ref,* 1932
Ficca, S. C.: *ref,* 532, 1499
Fick, D. J.: *ref,* 1133, 1194, 5:66(6)
Fick, R. L.: *ref,* 1289, 1361
Ficken, C. E.: *rev,* 2:1342, 2:1349; *ref,* 2:1349(2)
Fiddleman, P. B.: *ref,* 1281, 1499
Fidel, Y.: *ref,* 529, 533
Fidler, M.: *test,* 5c, 1750
Fiebert, M.: *ref,* 1127
Fiebert, M. S.: *ref,* 1127
Fiedler, E. R.: *ref,* 439, 496, 1087, 1092
Fiedler, F. E.: *ref,* 381, 1474, 1519
Fiedler, G. O.: *ref,* 1073
Fiedler, M.: *ref,* 484, 525
Fiedler, M. F.: *ref,* 1447, 1499
Field, A.: *ref,* 914
Field, A. E. J.: *ref,* 914
Field, H. E.: *ref,* 2:1519(1)
Field, J.: *ref,* 1447
Field, J. A.: *rev,* 1980
Field, J. G.: *ref,* 529, 532-3, 1226, 1275, 1281
Field, L. W.: *ref,* 1448, 2212
Field, P. B.: *ref,* 1212, 1389, 1519, P:327(25)
Field, T. W.: *ref,* 1856
Field, W. F.: *ref,* 1519
Fielder, D. W.: *ref,* 1207, 1281, 2212
Fielder, W. R.: *ref,* 467, 868
Fieldhouse, A. E.: *test,* 690, 1531, 1685
Fielding, B.: *ref,* 1499
Fielding, B. B.: *ref,* 1515
Fielding, J. R.: *ref,* 1145
Fields, D. L.: *ref,* 525
Fields, F. R. J.: *ref,* 529, 592
Fields, S. J.: *ref,* 1281
Fieldsteel, N. D.: *test,* 5:585; *ref,* 1499
Fiesenheiser, E. I.: *test,* 2416
Fieve, R. R.: *ref,* 1281, 1293 1339, 1398
Fife, I. E.: *ref,* 469, 2135, 2231, 2251
Fife, J.: *ref,* 1711

Fife, P. B.: *ref,* 5:570(5)
Fife, R. H.: *ref,* 468, 1609, 4:176 (3), 4:576(4), 4:577(4)
Fifer, G.: *rev,* 652, 5:421; *test,* 5: 535
Figetakis, N.: *ref,* 1281, 1448, 1474
Figura, C. J.: *ref,* 1281
Fike, D.: *ref,* 1194
Filbeck, R. W.: *ref,* 2212
File, Q. W.: *test,* 2448; *ref,* 2448
Filella, J.: *ref,* 1499
Filella, J. F.: *ref,* 1069
Filer, R. J.: *ref,* 452
Filicetti, P. J.: *ref,* 1280
Fillenbaum, S.: *ref,* 1281
Filler, M. G.: *ref,* 3:220(3)
Filley, A. C.: *ref,* 2451
Filley, M. E.: *ref,* 167
Fillmore, A. R.: *ref,* 496, 533
Filmer-Bennett, G.: *ref,* 1499, 1519
Filmer-Bennett, G. T.: *ref,* 1499
Fils, D. H.: *ref,* 50, 1478
Finch, C. R.: *ref,* 650, 868, 1073, 1403, 1407, 2239, 2266
Finch, F. H.: *test,* 399; *ref,* 426, 438, 1039, 1105, 1320, 2212, 2:1424(19, 22), 3:220(52, 58)
Finch, K.: *ref,* 1164, 1281
Finco, A. A.: *ref,* 1207, 1403, 2195
Findikyan, N.: *ref,* 1200
Findley, D. G.: *ref,* 1164
Findley, W. G.: *rev,* 7, 15, 22, 29, 48, 358, 1044-5, 1050, 2:1259, 2: 1619, 4:2; *test,* 3:127; *ref,* 7, 36, 48, 1053, 3:397(34), 6:291(3)
Fine, B. J.: *ref,* 559, 561, 1275, 1281, 1383, 1500, 1519, P:344(22)
Fine, E. W.: *ref,* 1447
Fine, H. J.: *ref,* 1499, 1515, 5:77 (12)
Fine, J. L.: *test,* 7:573; *ref,* 7:573 (1-2)
Fine, M. J.: *ref,* 381, 496, 1233
Fine, R.: *ref,* 1482, 1499, 1519
Fine, S. A.: *ref,* 1073
Finegan, A.: *ref,* 1318
Finegan, A. L.: *ref,* 2195
Fineman, C. A.: *ref,* 1261
Finesinger, J. E.: *ref,* 1499, 3:688 (2), 5:76(11)
Finger, J. A.: *test,* 1318; *ref,* 357, 1032, 1037, 1318
Fingerle, C. O.: *ref,* 2079-80
Fingert, H. H.: *ref,* 381
Fink, D. D.: *ref,* 1069
Fink, D. M.: *ref,* 1169, 1281
Fink, H. H.: *ref,* 1478, 1519
Fink, J. H.: *ref,* 1281, 1380, 1481, 1499, 1519
Fink, M.: *ref,* 532, 1121, 1232, 1499
Fink, M. A.: *ref,* 1499
Fink, M. B.: *ref,* 1121
Fink, R. W.: *ref,* 1383
Fink, S. L.: *ref,* 529, 1447
Finkbeiner, D. T.: *ref,* 742
Finkelstein, M.: *ref,* 532
Finkelstein, P.: *ref,* 1898
Finkenbinder, R. L.: *ref,* 981
Finkle, R. B.: *ref,* 1207
Finlay, G. C.: *test,* 4:52
Finlayson, D. S.: *ref,* 1252
Finlayson, L.: *test,* 1253
Finley, C.: *ref,* 533

Finley, C. J.: *test,* 534; *ref,* 7, 19, 22, 348, 381, 525, 533
Finley, J. R.: *ref,* 357, 1207
Finley, K. H.: *ref,* 525, 533
Finley, M. H.: *ref,* 1430
Finley, P. J.: *ref,* 1087, 2195, 2227, 2258
Finn, F.: *ref,* 1383
Finn, J. A.: *ref,* 1281, 1499
Finn, P.: *ref,* 1254
Finn, P. A.: *test,* 2382; *ref,* 1281, 2382
Finnegan, S. B.: *ref,* 1658
Finnegan, S. D.: *ref,* 1481
Finnerty, R.: *ref,* 1161
Finnerty, R. J.: *ref,* 50, 533
Finney, B. C.: *ref,* 1121, 1499
Finney, B. J.: *ref,* 439
Finney, H. C.: *ref,* 1302
Finney, J. C.: *test,* 1122, 1282; *ref,* 1121, 1281-2
Finney, R. M.: *exc,* 1499
Finnie, F. R.: *ref,* 439, 529, 1169, 1499
Finnigan, D. W.: *ref,* 1123
Finzi, H.: *ref,* 1499
Fionda, A. J.: *ref,* 1174
Fiondo, J. P.: *ref,* 1447, 1469, 1499
Fiorentino, D.: *ref,* 439, 1227, 1281
Fireman, J.: *ref,* 1232
Firestone, M. H.: *exc,* 497
Firestone, R. W.: *ref,* 342
Firetto, A.: *ref,* 1281
Firetto, A. C.: *ref,* 529
Firkins, C. J.: *ref,* 2195
Firnberg, J. W.: *ref,* 1044
Firnhaber, E. P.: *ref,* 525
Fisch, R. I.: *ref,* 1499
Fischer, A.: *ref,* 503, 592, 1281, 1447, 1481, 1499
Fischer, D. G.: *ref,* 1293
Fischer, E. C.: *ref,* 1280
Fischer, F. A. P.: *test,* 2:1515
Fischer, H.: *ref,* 1499
Fischer, H. L.: *ref,* 1275, 1293, 1499
Fischer, L. K.: *ref,* 1523
Fischer, R.: *ref,* 1281, 1294
Fischer, R. F.: *ref,* 19, 400, 404
Fischer, R. P.: *ref,* 1289, 1403
Fischer, W. E.: *ref,* 868
Fischle, M. J.: *ref,* 868, 1315
Fish, B.: *ref,* 497, 947
Fish, C. C.: *ref,* 518, 1499
Fish, D. G.: *ref,* 2355
Fish, F.: *ref,* 1447
Fish, H. L.: *ref,* 407, 1320, 1386
Fish, J. P.: *ref,* 69
Fish, K. D.: *ref,* 1094, 1121
Fishbein, G. M.: *ref,* 1169
Fishbein, M.: *ref,* 574
Fishbein, S.: *ref,* 532
Fishburn, W. R.: *ref,* 1289, 1403
Fisher, A. C.: *ref,* 1101
Fisher, B.: *ref,* 1112, 1398
Fisher, C.: *ref,* 529, 592
Fisher, D.: *ref,* 1519
Fisher, E. J.: *ref,* 2212
Fisher, F.: *ref,* 167
Fisher, G.: *ref,* 529, 1164, 1281, 1315, 1481
Fisher, G. C.: *ref,* 532
Fisher, G. M.: *ref,* 496, 525, 529, 532-3, 1225, 1281, 1481, 1519
Fisher, H.: *ref,* 1474

Flory, C. D.: *rev*, 433, 482, 1 :1116–7, 1 :1120, 3 :251; *ref*, 1123, 2: 1377(44)
Flottman, E. A.: *ref*, 36, 426
Flournoy, R. L.: *ref*, 1428
Flower, R. M.: *ref*, 522, 533, 1628
Flowers, A.: *test*, 2035
Flowers, H. M.: *ref*, 2194
Flowers, J. F.: *ref*, 1256, 1322, 1383, 2355
Floyd, A.: *ref*, 1398
Floyd, H.: *test*, 35 :486
Floyd, J. A.: *test*, 5 :389
Floyd, W.: *ref*, 1923
Floyd, W. A.: *ref*, 357, 516, 1073
Flügel, J. C.: *exc*, 1101
Flye, L. M.: *ref*, 1069, 2195
Flynn, A. P.: *ref*, P :455(11)
Flynn, C.: *ref*, 1281
Flynn, E.: *ref*, 525
Flynn, J. D.: *ref*, 1281
Flynn, J. J.: *ref*, 532, 1499
Flynn, J. T.: *ref*, 1094, 1164
Flynn, P. S.: *ref*, 1277
Flynn, P. T.: *ref*, 211, 981, 1623, 2028
Flynn, W. F.: *ref*, 529
Flynn, W. R.: *ref*, 1281
Foa, U. G.: *ref*, 1240
Fode, K.: *ref*, 1519
Fode, K. L.: *ref*, 1281
Fogarty, B. M.: *ref*, 1383, 2451
Fogel, J.: *ref*, 532
Fogel, M.: *ref*, 1225, 1240
Fogel, M. E.: *ref*, 1291
Fogel, M. L.: *exc*, 1499; *ref*, 440, 529, 543, 1154, 1210, 1293, 1311, 1519
Fogelson, R.: *ref*, 1519
Fogelson, S.: *ref*, 1377
Fogey, E. W.: *ref*, 1281, 1499, 1519
Fogg, C. P.: *ref*, 1164
Folds, J. H.: *ref*, 361, 1164
Foley, A. W.: *ref*, 2195
Foley, G. F.: *ref*, 884, 2452
Foley, J.: *ref*, 2259
Foley, J. M.: *ref*, 425, 529, 1421
Foley, J. P.: *rev*, 482, 1349, 2285, 2302, 2404, 5 :395; *exc*, 5 :130; *ref*, 1474
Foley, L.: *ref*, 2 :1272(2)
Foley, L. J.: *ref*, 1480
Foley, M. V.: *ref*, 533
Foley, P. M.: *ref*, 1365
Foley, W. J.: *ref*, 1207, 1281, 2337
Folk, E. D.: *ref*, 50, 532
Folkins, C. H.: *ref*, 1094, 1293
Follett, G. C.: *ref*, 1499
Follman, J.: *ref*, 22, 69, 361, 400, 1572, 1755, 1761, 1775
Follman, J. C.: *ref*, 69, 1572, 1755, 1761, 1775
Folsom, A. T.: *ref*, 1499
Folsom, C. H.: *ref*, 1121, 1135, 1430
Folsom, M. O.: *rev*, 731
Folstrom, R. J.: *ref*, 194
Fonda, C. P.: *ref*, 1205–6, 1499
Fong, L. J.: *ref*, 516
Fong, S. L. M.: *ref*, 1121
Font, M.: *exc*, 5 :137; *ref*, 1499
Font, M. M.: *ref*, 525, 1380
Fontana, A. F.: *ref*, 1281
Fontes, P. J.: *ref*, 361
Fooks, G.: *ref*, 518

Foose, R. L.: *ref*, 1044, 1048
Foote, F. M.: *ref*, 1906, 1918, 1923, 5 :781(9, 12)
Foote, R. P.: *ref*, 449, 1069, 2195, 2256, 2267
Footlik, S. W.: *ref*, 1475
Forader, A. T.: *ref*, 1363
Foran, T. G.: *rev*, 1 :1159; *ref*, 36, 435, 438, 1569, 1576, 1603, 1616, 2 :1190(2), 2 :1197(1), 2 :1539(1, 3), 2 :1565(4)
Forbes, A. R.: *ref*, 439, 1281, 1383
Forbes, M. M.: *test*, 294
Forbes, T. W.: *ref*, 1934
Force, R. C.: *ref*, 2195
Ford, A. B.: *ref*, 1164, 1403, 2195
Ford, A. H.: *ref*, 1087, 2195, 2381
Ford, C. A.: *ref*, 525, 1403
Ford, C. F.: *ref*, 1101
Ford, C. V.: *ref*, 1281
Ford, D. H.: *ref*, 529
Ford, E. D.: *ref*, 562, 564, 1109
Ford, G. C.: *ref*, 786
Ford, H. E.: *test*, 250; *ref*, 2 :1342 (7)
Ford, J. B.: *ref*, 533, 981
Ford, J. J.: *ref*, 1383
Ford, J. S.: *test*, 1071
Ford, L. H.: *ref*, 1164, 1281, 1293
Ford, M.: *ref*, 1499
Ford, M. E. N.: *ref*, 1499
Ford, R. M.: *ref*, 1227
Ford, R. N.: *ref*, 361, 4 :88(11)
Ford, R. R.: *ref*, 868
Ford, R. W.: *ref*, 1315
Ford, T. G.: *ref*, 20
Ford, Z. B.: *ref*, 361
Forden, H. G.: *ref*, 1253
Fordham, M.: *ref*, 1121
Fordham, S. L.: *ref*, 361
Fordyce, W. E.: *ref*, 1164, 1281
Fordyce, W. G.: *test*, 3 :63; *ref*, 3: 63(1)
Foree, S. S.: *ref*, 357
Forehand, G. A.: *ref*, 361, 2239
Forehand, R.: *ref*, 525
Foreman, M. E.: *ref*, 1094, 1164, 1500, 2195, 2212
Foreman, P. B.: *exc*, 4 :57
Forer, B.: *ref*, 1499
Forer, B. R.: *rev*, 1445, 1471; *test*, 1461–2; *exc*, 1524; *ref*, 1461, 1482, 1499, 1519, 2195, 2212
Foresman, C. S.: *ref*, 1318
Forget, F.: *ref*, 1499
Forgy, E.: *ref*, 1281, 1519
Forlano, G.: *test*, 2 :1201, 2 :1244; *ref*, 426, 525, 850, 1095, 1101, 1123, 1313, 1320, 1403, 2 :1201 (1–3), 2 :1243(28), 2 :1244(1), 3 :97(10), 3 :110(10), 5 :421(6), 6 :159(51, 60), P :294(8–9), P: 346(14), P :367(3)
Forman, H.: *ref*, 211
Formanek, R.: *ref*, 490
Formica, L. A.: *ref*, 1289, 2212
Formicola, A. J.: *ref*, 1164
Forness, S. R.: *ref*, 1877, 2195
Forney, R. B.: *ref*, 1093, 1144
Forney, R. S.: *ref*, 36
Fornoff, F. J.: *rev*, 1820, 1830–1; *ref*, 1872
Forrer, G. R.: *ref*, 1499
Forrest, A.: *ref*, 1447

Forrest, A. R.: *ref*, 1249, 1252, 1296
Forrest, D. R.: *ref*, 652
Forrest, D. V.: *ref*, 361, 2212
Forrest, D. W.: *ref*, 1164, 1275, 1499
Forrest, G. G.: *ref*, 1164, 1281
Forrest, G. L.: *ref*, 1227, 1383
Forrest, G. M.: *ref*, 1383, 1403, 2195
Forrest, L. C.: *ref*, 884
Forrest, M.: *ref*, 1391
Forrest, T.: *ref*, 50, 381, 533, 1447
Forsius, H.: *ref*, 1913
Forsleff, L. P.: *ref*, 1240
Forster, C. R.: *ref*, 532, 2135, 2195, 2239
Forster, M. C.: *ref*, 2212
Forster, M. H.: *ref*, 1499
Forsyth, D. R.: *ref*, 1281
Forsyth, E.: *rev*, 1976, 3 :599; *test*, 4 :663
Forsyth, R.: *ref*, 19
Forsyth, R. A.: *rev*, 633, 1610; *test*, 20
Forsyth, R. P.: *ref*, 1281, 1430, 1499, 1519
Fort, D. J.: *ref*, 1281
Fort, G. M.: *ref*, 1281
Fort, T.: *rev*, 2 :1431
Fortenberry, W. D.: *ref*, 50, 6 :793 (7)
Fortier, R.: *ref*, 1499
Fortier, R. H.: *ref*, 1499, 5 :147(31)
Fortin, C. C.: *ref*, 1403
Fortna, R. O.: *ref*, 35, 361, 1599
Fortney, H. M.: *ref*, 1280
Fortson, C. B.: *ref*, 532
Fortson, L. R.: *ref*, 589
Fortune, D. M.: *ref*, 1222
Fosa, E. J.: *test*, 1898
Fosberg, I. A.: *ref*, 1140, 1499, 1516
Fosha, R. L.: *ref*, 209
Foshee, D. P.: *ref*, 1164
Foshee, J. G.: *ref*, 1499
Foss, A.: *ref*, 1281
Fosse, J. B.: *ref*, 1281
Fosselius, E. E.: *ref*, 2195
Fosshage, J. L.: *ref*, 2212
Foster, A.: *ref*, 447, 529, 532, 1499
Foster, A. L.: *ref*, 532, 1447, 1499–500
Foster, C.: *test*, 2 :1458; *ref*, 532
Foster, C. G.: *ref*, 532
Foster, D.: *ref*, 533, 1626
Foster, D. V.: *ref*, 532–3
Foster, G. M.: *ref*, 1499, 1519
Foster, G. R.: *ref*, 22, 361
Foster, H.: *ref*, 1924, 1932, 3 :473 (7)
Foster, H. C.: *ref*, 1451
Foster, J.: *test*, 2 :1294; *ref*, 50, 981
Foster, J. A.: *ref*, 2212
Foster, J. D.: *ref*, 1716
Foster, J. M.: *ref*, 1044, 1499
Foster, K. E.: *ref*, 2184
Foster, L.: *ref*, 1264
Foster, L. E. C.: *ref*, 868
Foster, L. F.: *ref*, 1837
Foster, L. S.: *test*, 1 :933; *ref*, 1819, 1845, 3 :217(86)
Foster, M. E.: *ref*, 348–9, 425, 603, 1531, 1536
Foster, P.: *ref*, 1281

Freed, E. S.: *ref,* 1499
Freed, E. X.: *ref,* 1197, 1216, 1363, 1380, 1407, 1447
Freed, G. O.: *ref,* 1499, 1519
Freed, H.: *ref,* 1469, 1481, 1499, 1519
Freed, L. B.: *test,* 36:549
Freedheim, D. K.: *ref,* 487, 525, 533, 1428, 2080
Freedman, J. L.: *ref,* 574
Freedman, L. Z.: *ref,* 1500
Freedman, M.: *test,* 1240; *ref,* 1121, 1281
Freedman, M. B.: *ref,* 1121, 1281, 1302, 1519, 5:144(1–2), P:384 (13)
Freedman, M. H.: *ref,* 2349
Freedman, M. J.: *ref,* 1174, 1315
Freedman, N.: *ref,* 1519
Freedman, S.: *ref,* 529, 2199, 2234
Freedman, S. A.: *ref,* 1121, 1207
Freehill, M. F.: *ref,* 69, 1572–3, 2195, 5:308(295, 348)
Freeman, A. V.: *ref,* 532
Freeman, E.: *test,* 5:776–8; *ref,* 1387, 1906, 4:659(1–2)
Freeman, E. H.: *ref,* 1281
Freeman, F. N.: *test,* 909, 2:1256; *exc,* 525; *ref,* 525, 909
Freeman, F. S.: *rev,* 349, 400, 1361, 4:794; *exc,* 344; *ref,* 419, 525, 529, 532–3, 1499, 1519, 2195, 2212, 2:1377(11)
Freeman, H.: *ref,* 1298, 1499
Freeman, H. R.: *ref,* 1315
Freeman, J.: *ref,* 331, 439, 529
Freeman, J. A.: *ref,* 1087
Freeman, K. H.: *ref,* 87, 426
Freeman, L. C.: *ref,* 1145
Freeman, M. J.: *test,* 1188; *ref,* 1188
Freeman, P.: *ref,* 331, 1162, 1164
Freeman, R. A.: *ref,* 1281
Freeman, T. S.: *ref,* 1289
Freer, F. J.: *ref,* 533, 538, 543, 2028
Freides, D.: *rev,* 525, 533
Freinek, W. R.: *ref,* 439, 529, 1281
Fremer, J.: *ref,* 357, 1048
Fremont, T.: *ref,* 1275, 1293
Fremont, T. S.: *ref,* 1275
French, D. T.: *test,* 7:512
French, E.: *test,* 4:480; *ref,* 4:480 (1–2)
French, E. G.: *ref,* 532, 1164
French, E. I.: *ref,* 211, 214
French, F. E.: *ref,* 487, 1428
French, J.: *ref,* 489
French, J. G.: *ref,* 439
French, J. L.: *rev,* 26, 490; *test,* 391, 517; *exc,* 7:880; *ref,* 7, 349, 517, 981, 1253, 1787, 1895, 1898, 2195, 2197
French, J. W.: *rev,* 1151, 1867, 2170, 2174, 2192, 2286, 2392, 3: 61–2, 3:701, 4:810, 6:1053; *test,* 559, 561, 7:674; *exc,* 2221; *ref,* 64, 357, 1095, 1939, 2214, 2241, 2266, 5:308(296, 302), 7:674(1–3)
French, L. A.: *ref,* 518, 525, 529, 532, 592, 1277, 1281, 1428
French, N. H.: *ref,* 1435
French, R. L.: *rev,* 382, 1430; *ref,* 1500
French, S. J.: *rev,* 1819

French, T. M.: *exc,* 1087, 1140
French, V. V.: *ref,* 1320, 1324, 1344, 1403, 1480, 1499, 1519
Frengel, B. A.: *ref,* 589
Frenkel-Brunswik, E.: *ref,* 1499, 1519
Fresco, R.: *ref,* 2212
Freshour, F. W.: *ref,* 1716
Freston, C. W.: *ref,* 518
Fretwell, L. N.: *ref,* 502, 525, 529, 589
Fretz, B. R.: *ref,* 533, 1121, 1164, 1281, 1294, 1447, 1885, 1887, 1921
Freud, S. L.: *ref,* 529, 1281, 1387, 1447
Freudenberg, R.: *ref,* 1499
Freudenberg, R. K.: *ref,* 545, 1281, 1447
Freudenberger, H. J.: *ref,* 1499, 1519
Frevert, R. K.: *ref,* 19
Frey, A. H.: *ref,* 1207
Frey, J. H.: *ref,* 489
Frey, R. M.: *ref,* 1911
Freyberg, P. S.: *ref,* 439, 1087
Freyd, M.: *ref,* 1480
Freyermuth, R. A.: *ref,* 589
Freyman, L.: *test,* 91
Freymark, B. A.: *ref,* 529
Friberg, R. R.: *ref,* 1281
Frick, J. W.: *ref,* 457, 546, 551, 561, 571, 1074, 1281, 1761, 5: 308(406)
Frick, N. K.: *test,* 2:1322
Frick, R. C.: *ref,* 589
Fricke, B. G.: *rev,* 930, 1048, 1193–4, 5:20; *test,* 1303; *ref,* 69, 357, 868, 1281, 1303, 1583, 2195, 2349
Fridiana, M.: *ref,* 3:486(3)
Fried, C.: *exc,* 1499; *ref,* 1519
Fried, E. G.: *ref,* 1499
Fried, R.: *ref,* 947
Friedberg, J.: *ref,* 2:1225(2, 6–7), 2:1226(2–4)
Friedemann, A.: *test,* 1516; *ref,* 1499
Friedemann, T. E.: *ref,* 1281
Friedersdorf, N. W.: *ref,* 2213
Friedhoff, W. H.: *ref,* 5:597(7)
Friedl, F. P.: *ref,* 2212
Friedlander, D.: *ref,* 1192
Friedlander, G. H.: *ref,* 2045
Friedline, C. L.: *ref,* 525
Friedman, A. L.: *ref,* 1240, 1281, 1519
Friedman, A. R.: *ref,* 1499
Friedman, A. S.: *ref,* 529, P:41(2, 4)
Friedman, B.: *ref,* 1500, 1516
Friedman, C. J.: *ref,* 1519
Friedman, E.: *ref,* 1516
Friedman, E. C.: *ref,* 529, 533, 543, 1277
Friedman, G.: *ref,* 1447–8, 1499
Friedman, G. H. P.: *ref,* 50, 533, 981
Friedman, H.: *ref,* 1499
Friedman, I.: *ref,* 532, 1499, 1519
Friedman, J.: *ref,* 529, 1194, 1207, 1225, 1447–8, 1519
Friedman, M.: *ref,* 545, 1121
Friedman, M. B.: *ref,* 1320
Friedman, M. I.: *ref,* 1176
Friedman, M. L.: *ref,* 1380

Friedman, P.: *ref,* 5:598(6)
Friedman, R.: *ref,* 533
Friedman, S.: *ref,* 2337
Friedman, S. B.: *ref,* 1281
Friedman, S. H.: *ref,* 1281
Friedman, S. M.: *ref,* 361, 1176, 1583
Friedman, S. R.: *ref,* 1261
Friedman, T. I.: *test,* 976
Friedman, V. S.: *ref,* 1383
Friedman, W. H.: *ref,* 543, 1478
Friedrich, D.: *ref,* 533, 1485
Friedrich, G.: *ref,* 1045
Friedrichs, T. D.: *ref,* 348, 1711, 1716
Friel, C. M.: *ref,* 1519
Frields, S. I.: *ref,* 357, 436
Frieman, B. B.: *ref,* 1403
Friend, C. M.: *ref,* 1775
Friend, R. S.: *ref,* 211
Fries, M. E.: *ref,* 1499
Friesen, D.: *ref,* 1069
Friesen, E. C.: *ref,* 1921
Friesen, E. P.: *ref,* 2275, 2406
Friesen, E. W.: *ref,* 1363, 1407
Friesen, W. S.: *ref,* 993, 1044
Friesen, W. V.: *ref,* 1094, 1281
Friis, R. H.: *ref,* 1244
Frinsko, W.: *ref,* 868, 2195, 2212
Frisbie, K. G.: *ref,* 884
Frisby, C. B.: *ref,* 384, 388, 439, 2247–8, 2254, 2345
Frisch, G. R.: *ref,* 1481
Frisell, W. R.: *exc,* 1816
Frisk, G. C.: *ref,* 1387
Fristoe, M.: *test,* 2037, 2075; *ref,* 2037, 2075
Fristoe, M. W.: *ref,* 2037, 2075
Fritchey, K. H.: *ref,* 1281
Frith, C. D.: *ref,* 1174
Fritz, K. V.: *ref,* 2267
Fritz, M. F.: *test,* 1330; *ref,* 1330, 2267, 5:308(349)
Fritz, R. A.: *ref,* 36, 3:217(52)
Fritzky, F. J.: *ref,* 1201
Fritzler, D. E.: *ref,* 1499
Frobarj, G.: *ref,* 1499
Froebe, D. J.: *ref,* 1199
Froehle, T. C.: *ref,* 1176
Froehlich, A.: *ref,* 1221, 1519
Froehlich, C. P.: *rev,* 1066, 1073, 2195, 4:798; *ref,* 1069, 2195, 3: 397(35), 3:655(3)
Froehlich, G. J.: *rev,* 20, 48, 341, 358, 3:10, 4:577, 5:319; *test,* 3: 22, 3:138, 3:330, 3:362, 3:555, 3:577, 3:589; *exc,* 509; *ref,* 391, 525, 3:22(1–2), 3:217(82), 4: 238(2)
Froemel, E. C.: *ref,* 414, 547–8, 570, 1149, 1164, 1275, 1333, 1413, 1419, 1470, 1475, 1747, 2110, 2340
Froese, V.: *ref,* 1649
Frogner, E.: *test,* 4:8
Frohman, C. E.: *ref,* 1281
Froiland, D. J.: *ref,* 1095
Fromhart, M. V.: *ref,* 1281
Fromm, D. M.: *ref,* 1447
Fromm, E.: *exc,* 1499; *ref,* 487, 525, 1499
Fromm, E. O.: *ref,* 1499, 1516, 1519
Fromme, D. K.: *ref,* 1519
Frommelt, L. A.: *ref,* 533
Frook, W. F.: *ref,* 391

Gerson, M. J.: *ref,* 1499
Gerstein, A. I.: *ref,* 364, 532, 1499, 1626, 2213
Gerstein, O. B.: *ref,* 1295, 1383, 2212
Gerstein, R. A.: *ref,* 487, 497, 532
Gerstein, S.: *ref,* 525
Gersten, J.: *ref,* 1499
Gerstman, L.: *ref,* 529, 1447
Gerstman, L. J.: *ref,* 529
Gertler, M. M.: *ref,* 1101, 1383
Gertz, B.: *ref,* 1164, 1217, 1232, 1387
Gerum, E.: *ref,* 2212
Gerver, D.: *ref,* 533, 1646
Gerver, J. M.: *ref,* 525, 1499, 1519
Gery, F. W.: *ref,* 1044, 1968, 1970
Gesell, A.: *test,* 497; *ref,* 497
Gesell, A. L.: *ref,* 497
Gesler, H. L.: *ref,* 211
Gessel, J.: *test,* 647–8
Gessner, T.: *ref,* 1281
Gessner, T. L.: *ref,* 1281
Getman, G. N.: *ref,* 1921
Getoff, L.: *ref,* 1499
Getter, H.: *ref,* 1501
Gettinger, T.: *ref,* 603, 1536
Gettys, R. H.: *ref,* 357
Gettys, V. C.: *ref,* 1501
Getz, S. B.: *ref,* 532, 1481
Getzels, J. W.: *ref,* 482, 533, 542, 546, 868, 1074, 1109, 1123, 1205, 1245, 1281, 1383, 1403, 1499–500, 2195
Geuting, M. P.: *ref,* 533
Gewinner, M. N.: *ref,* 868, 1383
Gewirtz, H.: *ref,* 1281, 1294, 1403, 1859, 2212
Gewirtz, J. L.: *ref,* 525
Geyer, D. L.: *exc,* 2:1619; *ref,* 6: 480(14)
Geyer, J. J.: *rev,* 1671–3
Geyer, M. L.: *ref,* 2043, 2045
Ghannad, R. H.: *ref,* 1164, 1281, 1415
Ghei, S.: *ref,* 2197
Ghei, S. N.: *ref,* 1164
Ghiselli, E. E.: *rev,* 2227, 2231, 2234; *test,* 341; *ref,* 341, 438, 2135, 2212, 2227–8, 2251, 2258, 2266
Ghosh, S.: *ref,* 416, 1320
Ghosh, S. N.: *ref,* 2231
Ghosh, S. P.: *ref,* 525
Ghozeil, S.: *ref,* 525, 533, 1716
Giampa, F. L.: *ref,* 1117, 1428
Giampiccolo, J. S.: *test,* 1180; *ref,* 1179
Giangreco, C. J.: *ref,* 499
Giannell, A. S.: *ref,* 529, 532, 1164, 6:438(522)
Giannitrapani, D.: *ref,* 529
Gianturco, J.: *ref,* 529
Gianturco, J. A.: *ref,* 1281, 1377
Gibb, C. A.: *rev,* 1199, 1259–60, 1467, 2453–4, 5:76–7; *ref,* 1253, 1499
Gibb, E. G.: *test,* 27, 649, 735, 1577, 1706
Gibb, L. L.: *ref,* 1315
Gibbens, T. C. N.: *ref,* 439, 518, 1281
Gibbins, K.: *ref,* 1174
Gibbins, R. J.: *ref,* 1271

Gibbons, B. D.: *ref,* 49, 382, 1151, 1205, 1207, 1245, 1383
Gibbons, C. C.: *ref,* 398, 2:1233(2), 2:1250(6)
Gibbons, C. W.: *ref,* 1123
Gibbons, D.: *ref,* 1185
Gibbons, K. C.: *ref,* 331, 1772
Gibbs, D. N.: *ref,* 1123, 1164
Gibbs, J. M.: *ref,* 1174
Gibby, M. K.: *ref,* 868
Gibby, R.: *ref,* 1499
Gibby, R. G.: *ref,* 425, 532, 1240, 1281, 1447, 1499
Gibeau, P. J.: *ref,* 529, 1169, 1281, 1499
Gibel, I. L.: *ref,* 1050
Gibilisco, J. A.: *ref,* 1281
Giblette, J. F.: *ref,* 1171, 1423, 2195
Gibney, E. F.: *ref,* 1087, 6:647(3)
Gibson, A. M.: *ref,* 1073
Gibson, D.: *ref,* 525
Gibson, D. L.: *ref,* 1214
Gibson, F. J.: *ref,* 525, 532
Gibson, F. W.: *ref,* 1164
Gibson, G. C.: *ref,* 1669
Gibson, H. B.: *test,* 1191, 1296; *exc,* 518, 1249; *ref,* 403, 439, 1145, 1174, 1191, 1275, 1296, P:294(14)
Gibson, J.: *ref,* 529
Gibson, J. J.: *ref,* 1499
Gibson, J. W.: *ref,* 542, 561, 1775
Gibson, N. L. B.: *ref,* 1123
Gibson, Q. H.: *ref,* 364, 439
Gibson, R. E.: *ref,* 1921
Gibson, R. L.: *ref,* 1313, 1499
Gibson, R. M.: *ref,* 503
Gibson, R. W.: *ref,* 1499
Gibson, W. D.: *ref,* 1572
Gibson, W. M.: *ref,* 50, 533, 1447, 1887, 1902
Gibson (Robert) & Sons, Glasgow, Ltd.: *test,* 422, 1:990, 1:1036, 1:1045, 1:1086, 1:1129, 1:1132
Giddan, J. J.: *test,* 992
Giddings, J. W.: *ref,* 1322
Giddings, W. V.: *ref,* 1225
Giddon, D. B.: *ref,* 1293
Giduz, H.: *ref,* 2:1344(2), 2:1349(4)
Giebink, J. W.: *ref,* 516, 868, 981, 1281, 1447
Giedt, F. H.: *ref,* 1264, 1281, 1474, 1499
Giedt, H. M.: *ref,* 532
Giel, R.: *ref,* 1410
Gier, D. L.: *ref,* 1094
Gier, J. D.: *ref,* 1469, 1501, 1519
Giese, R. N.: *ref,* 868, 1207
Giese, W. J.: *ref,* 337, 1314, 1923, 2129, 2259, 5:513(2)
Giesecke, G. E.: *ref,* 18, 87, 220, 1560
Gieseke, M.: *ref,* 1084, 1784
Gieseking, C. F.: *ref,* 1293
Giessow, F. J.: *ref,* 357
Giesz, W. G.: *ref,* 1448, 2212
Giffen, M. B.: *ref,* 1478
Giffin, K.: *ref,* 1519
Gifford, B. M.: *ref,* 1133
Gifford, C. A.: *ref,* 1603, 1615
Gifford, D. W.: *ref,* 3:217(83)
Gifford, E.: *ref,* 525
Gifford, E. V.: *ref,* 525
Gikas, A. M.: *ref,* 6:1075(1)

Gil, S. H.: *ref,* 1281
Gilbart, T. E.: *ref,* 1094, 1109, 1281
Gilberg, R. L.: *ref,* 2199, 2212
Gilberstadt, H.: *ref,* 518, 529, 592, 1281, 1380, 1387, 1447, 1481, 2234
Gilberston, V. A.: *ref,* 1281
Gilbert, A. C. F.: *ref,* 357, 742, 1522, 1583, 1832, 1837, 1858–9, 2212, 6:568(9)
Gilbert, A. E.: *ref,* 1133
Gilbert, A. R.: *ref,* 1028, 1281, 1423
Gilbert, A. S.: *ref,* 1164
Gilbert, C.: *ref,* 1186, 1206–7, 1320
Gilbert, C. D.: *ref,* 868, 1121
Gilbert, C. F.: *ref,* 1207, 1320
Gilbert, G. M.: *ref,* 202
Gilbert, H. B.: *ref,* 480, 2239, 5:87 (22, 24)
Gilbert, J.: *ref,* 7, 426, 1289, 1403, 2195, 6:438(497)
Gilbert, J. A. L.: *ref,* 2355
Gilbert, J. G.: *ref,* 381, 533, 1105, 1281, 1387, 1447, 1474–5, 1915
Gilbert, M. D.: *test,* 4:450
Gilbert, M. M.: *ref,* 1499
Gilbert, O. E.: *ref,* P:496(14)
Gilbert, V. R.: *ref,* 1716
Gilbert, W. M.: *ref,* 1240, 1281, 1383, 2239, 5:6(16), 5:308(300)
Gilberts, R. A.: *ref,* 1164, 1281, 1403
Gilberts, R. D.: *ref,* 1176
Gilbreath, S. H.: *ref,* 1281, 1394
Gilchrist, A.: *ref,* 1519
Gilchrist, A. A.: *ref,* 1519
Gilden, J. B.: *ref,* 1281
Gildersleeve, G.: *test,* 2:1336
Gildston, H. M.: *ref,* 1207
Giles, A. S.: *ref,* 2025
Giles, G. C.: *ref,* 31, 333, 439, 1069
Giles, H. H.: *rev,* 139, 1:949, 2: 1296
Giles, M. T.: *test,* 983; *ref,* 1875, 1895
Giles, P. G.: *ref,* 1281
Gilgash, C. A.: *ref,* 532
Gilger, G. A.: *ref,* 3:635(5)
Gilham, S. M.: *ref,* 1519
Gilhooly, F. M.: *ref,* 532, 1499, 1519
Gilkinson, H.: *test,* 3:150; *ref,* 211, 1095, 1101, 1320, 2212–3, 3:150 (2–3), 3:151(2), 3:152(2), 4: 70(9), P:342(10)
Gill, A.: *test,* 35:222
Gill, E. M.: *test,* 5:554
Gill, G.: *ref,* 404
Gill, H. S.: *ref,* 1499
Gill, L. J.: *ref,* 1121
Gill, L. N.: *ref,* 398
Gill, M.: *ref,* 532, 1105, 1140, 1192, 1499, 1516, 1519
Gill, M. J.: *ref,* 589
Gill, M. M.: *ref,* 532, 1105, 1192, 1499, 1519
Gill, M. P.: *test,* 387; *ref,* 398
Gill, M. R.: *ref,* 439, 525
Gill, N.: *ref,* 29
Gill, N. T.: *ref,* 868, 1370, 1921
Gill, W. S.: *ref,* 1499, 1519
Gillam, E. S.: *ref,* 1069
Gillenson, G.: *ref,* 1499
Giller, D. W.: *ref,* 1144, 1281
Gillespie, F. H.: *test,* 1348; *ref,* 1348

Gillespie, H. F.: *ref,* 69, 6:438 (507)
Gillespie, J. O.: *ref,* 2451
Gillespie, P. H.: *ref,* 524
Gillespie, W. H.: *exc,* 1140
Gillett, A. N.: *test,* 2300
Gillett, R.: *ref,* 214
Gillette, A. L.: *ref,* 525
Gillette, A. P.: *ref,* 1281
Gillham, C.: *test,* 625
Gilliard, S. B.: *ref,* 1314
Gillies, J.: *ref,* 1474, P:450(91)
Gilliland, A. R.: *test,* 5:411; *ref,* 211, 532, 904, 1222, 1281, 1320, 4:354(1-4, 6-9)
Gilliland, H.: *test,* 380, 1653
Gilliland, J.: *ref,* 1277
Gilliland, S. F.: *ref,* 1403
Gillin, J.: *ref,* 1499
Gillingham, A.: *test,* 1630
Gillingham, W. H.: *ref,* 533
Gillion, H. E. J.: *ref,* 1883
Gillis, J.: *ref,* 1394
Gillis, J. S.: *ref,* 1383
Gillis, R.: *ref,* 1298
Gillis, R. D.: *test,* 1298; *ref,* 1298
Gillman, R. D.: *ref,* 1447, 1499, 1501
Gillman, S.: *ref,* 381, 543, 1447
Gilman, R. H.: *ref,* 349, 529
Gilman, S. F.: *ref,* 1121
Gilmer, R.: *ref,* 1918
Gilmore, D.: *ref,* 1281
Gilmore, E. C.: *test,* 1679
Gilmore, J. V.: *test,* 1679; *ref,* 1679
Gilmore, M.: *ref,* 1471
Gilmore, S. I.: *ref,* 516, 2095
Gilmore, S. K.: *ref,* 1121
Gilner, F. H.: *ref,* 1240, 1281
Ginett, L. E.: *ref,* 532
Ging, R.: *ref,* 1232
Gingerich, C. N.: *ref,* 4:179(7), 6:265(1)
Gingles, R.: *ref,* 1289
Gingles, R. H.: *ref,* 5:66(13)
Gingrich, D. D.: *ref,* 1289
Giniger, S.: *ref,* 436, 529, 1772, 1775
Ginley, T. J.: *ref,* 1303, 2337
Ginsberg, A.: *test,* 35:170; *ref,* 1499
Ginsberg, A. M.: *ref,* 1499, P:502 (11)
Ginsburg, G. P.: *ref,* 574
Ginsburg, N.: *ref,* 1275
Ginsparg, H. T.: *ref,* 1451
Ginther, M. L.: *ref,* 361
Gioioso, J. V.: *ref,* 489, 496, 525, 533
Giolas, T. G.: *ref,* 2031, 2053
Giovino, R.: *ref,* 1651
Gipson, T. H.: *ref,* 904
Girard, F. G.: *ref,* 1294, 1383
Girard, J. A. F.: *ref,* 340, 1552
Girdany, B. R.: *ref,* 497, 525
Girdner, J.: *ref,* 592
Girdner, J. B.: *ref,* 4:115(9)
Gire, E.: *ref,* 5:766(7)
Girona, R.: *test,* 1097
Gislason, S.: *ref,* 1232
Gisvold, D.: *ref,* 1164
Githens, W. H.: *ref,* 382, 2212
Gitlin, S.: *ref,* 1447, 2185, 2195
Gitlitz, H. B.: *ref,* 381
Gittelman, M.: *ref,* 525, 533

Gittinger, J. W.: *rev,* 1522; *ref,* 529, 1095
Giuliani, G. A.: *ref,* 1716
Givens, P. R.: *ref,* 542, 546, 551, 1383, 2195
Givone, R.: *ref,* 1383
Gjernes, O.: *ref,* 1073
Glad, D. D.: *ref,* 1281, 1403, 1423, 1499, 1516, 1519
Glad, J. R. B.: *ref,* 359, 400, 1164
Gladfelter, J. H.: *ref,* 1144
Gladfelter, M. E.: *ref,* 69, 1560, 2: 1271(6)
Glading, J. C.: *ref,* 404
Gladney, M. B.: *ref,* 357
Gladstein, G. A.: *ref,* 5:326(4)
Gladston, E. R.: *ref,* 1486, 1499, 1528, 6:228(65)
Gladstone, R.: *ref,* 1499, 6:1102 (7)
Gladwin, T.: *ref,* 1499, 1519
Glaister, B. R.: *ref,* 543, 1277
Glanville, A. D.: *ref,* 525
Glasberg, H. M.: *ref,* 1162
Glaser, E. M.: *test,* 1775, 3:53; *ref,* 1775, 3:53(1-2, 4)
Glaser, N. A.: *ref,* 1624
Glaser, N. M.: *ref,* 1499
Glaser, R.: *ref,* 48, 342, 404, 482, 1069, 1123, 1281, 2199, 2268, 2355
Glaser, R. J.: *ref,* 2355
Glasgow, A. D.: *ref,* 2451
Glasnapp, D. R.: *ref,* 1716
Glasner, S.: *ref,* 1348
Glass, A.: *ref,* 1275
Glass, B.: *ref,* 1192
Glass, C. F.: *ref,* 2212
Glass, D. C.: *ref,* 1164, 1383
Glass, G. V.: *rev,* 1365, 1409; *ref,* 589
Glass, H.: *ref,* 1499
Glass, H. L.: *ref,* 1499, 1519
Glass, K. D.: *ref,* 1225
Glasscock, E. M.: *ref,* 1281
Glasser, A. J.: *ref,* 533
Glassman, B. M.: *ref,* 1121
Glassman, S.: *ref,* 1387
Glassman, S. M.: *ref,* 1281
Glatt, C. T.: *ref,* 1499
Glatt, K. M.: *ref,* 1281
Glatt, M. M.: *ref,* 1499–500
Glatter, A. M.: *ref,* 1474
Glaudin, V.: *ref,* 1240, 1281
Glavin, J. P.: *ref,* 7, 1123
Glazer, M. W.: *ref,* 1275
Glazer, S. H.: *ref,* 2195
Gleason, J. B.: *ref,* 516
Gleason, W. J.: *ref,* 1499
Glenn, E. R.: *test,* 2:1596
Glenn, I.: *ref,* 525
Glenn, J.: *test,* 4:658
Glenn, R.: *ref,* 1281
Glenn, R. T.: *ref,* 505, 525
Glenn, W. D.: *ref,* 525
Glennon, J. R.: *rev,* 431, 1222; *ref,* 482, 1171, 2239, 2266, 2392, 2406, 2448, 6:1140(2)
Gleser, G.: *ref,* 1499–500
Gleser, G. C.: *rev,* 551, 1339, 1345, 1470; *test,* 1152, 1195; *exc,* 1524, 5:130; *ref,* 1152, 1169, 1195, 1225, 1278, 1281, 1383, 1474, 1499, 1519
Glick, H. L.: *ref,* 1501
Glick, H. N.: *test,* 2:1186; *ref,* 525

Glick, I. D.: *ref,* 529
Glick, R.: *ref,* 2213
Glick, W. P.: *ref,* 2212
Glickstein, M.: *ref,* 1499
Glidden, G. W.: *ref,* 391, 1546, 1772, 1775
Glik, E. E.: *ref,* 532, 1499
Glixman, A. F.: *ref,* 1407
Glober, G. A.: *ref,* 1281
Glock, M. D.: *rev,* 90, 693, 1565, 1608, 5:666, 5:699; *ref,* 1772
Gloeckler, T.: *ref,* 516, 533
Glofka, P. T.: *ref,* 1415
Glogau, L. F.: *ref,* 2451, 2457
Glorfeld, P.: *ref,* 1647
Glorig, A.: *test,* 2027
Glosser, E. A.: *ref,* 2213
Glotzbach, C. J.: *ref,* 868, 1281, 2213
Glover, J. A.: *test,* 35:112, 35:393
Glovsky, L.: *ref,* 981
Glowatsky, E.: *ref,* 381, 483, 533
Gloye, E. E.: *ref,* 1281, 1474
Gluck, M. R.: *ref,* 1499, 1519
Gluck, Z.: *ref,* 1447, 1499, 1519
Glucksberg, S.: *ref,* 574, 1164
Glucksman, M. L.: *ref,* 381, 1499
Glueck, B. C.: *ref,* 1150, 1281
Glueck, E.: *ref,* 36, 532, 1499
Glueck, E. T.: *ref,* 1499
Glueck, S.: *ref,* 36, 532, 1499
Gluskinos, U.: *ref,* 482, 1121, 2228
Gluskinos, U. M.: *ref,* 1121, 2340, 2347
Glymour, C.: *ref,* 1499, 1519
Gnagey, W. J.: *ref,* 868, 1281
Gnauck, J.: *ref,* 19, 400, 435
Go, E.: *ref,* 1169, 1380
Gobetz, W.: *ref,* 1447, 2195
Goble, R. L.: *ref,* 1073
Goche, L. N.: *ref,* 1205, 1245, 2195
Gochman, D. S.: *ref,* 1499
Gochros, H. L.: *ref,* 1281
Gocka, E.: *ref,* 1281
Gocka, E. F.: *ref,* 1121, 1164, 1240, 1281, 1383
Godbold, D. H.: *ref,* 1394-5
Goddard, E. R.: *ref,* 2:1342(8)
Goddard, H. H.: *test,* 578, 1103, 2: 1204
Goddeyne, L. M.: *ref,* 6:647(2)
Godec, F.: *ref,* 7:1062(4)
Godfrey, A. E.: *ref,* 1281, 1519
Godfrey, L. L.: *ref,* 525
Godfrey Thomson Unit. See University of Edinburgh.
Godin, J. D.: *ref,* 244, 305
Godin, M. A.: *ref,* 1087
Godsey, E. R.: *test,* 4:253
Godshall, T. A.: *ref,* 1129, 1383
Goebel, A. K.: *ref,* 981, 1447
Goebel, R. A.: *ref,* 1212
Goeckerman, R. W.: *ref,* 419
Goedicke, R.: *ref,* 361, 1174
Goen, J. N.: *ref,* 1094
Goens, B. D.: *ref,* 533, 538
Goering, O. J.: *ref,* 1164
Goertzel, V.: *ref,* 1499
Goertzen, S. M.: *ref,* 503
Goetzinger, C. P.: *ref,* 355, 439, 532, 543, 1513, 1900, 2028, 2031, 2053
Goetzinger, M. R.: *ref,* 439
Goewey, G. I.: *ref,* 211

Grace, A. G.: *ref*, 426
Grace, D. P.: *ref*, 1281
Grace, E. R.: *ref*, 1207, 2212
Grace, G. L.: *ref*, 1313
Grace, J. L.: *ref*, 1775
Graczykowska-Koczorowska, A.: *ref*, 532, 1519
Grad, B.: *ref*, 529, 532, 592, 1447, 1499
Gradel, D. V.: *ref*, 1394–5
Grady, M. J.: *ref*, 1394
Grady, W. E.: *ref*, 1044, 1176
Graebner, O. E.: *test*, 7:649
Graef, J. R.: *ref*, 1448
Graen, G. B.: *ref*, 2283, 2285
Graf, R. G.: *ref*, 1121
Graff, F.: *test*, 6:1051
Graff, F. A.: *ref*, 1289, 2212
Graff, H.: *ref*, 1225
Graff, H. F.: *ref*, 1980
Graff, J. R.: *ref*, 2065
Graff, R. L.: *ref*, 1240
Graff, R. W.: *ref*, 357, 1134, 1303, 1315
Grafton, T. D.: *ref*, 1225
Gragg, D. B.: *ref*, 525, 3:217(75)
Graham, A. W.: *ref*, 1123
Graham, C.: *ref*, 403, 533
Graham, D.: *ref*, 354, 373, 408, 425, 462
Graham, D. D.: *ref*, 525
Graham, E.: *ref*, 1499
Graham, E. E.: *ref*, 529, 532–3, 1499
Graham, F. K.: *test*, 1277; *ref*, 1277
Graham, G.: *rev*, 2:1632; *test*, 36: 716
Graham, G. A.: *ref*, 538
Graham, H.: *ref*, 1499
Graham, H. B.: *test*, 1066
Graham, J.: *exc*, 2:1477, 2:1480–1, 2:1489; *ref*, 559, 1471
Graham, J. A.: *ref*, 1240
Graham, J. L.: *ref*, 426, 1480
Graham, J. R.: *ref*, 1281
Graham, L. E.: *ref*, 1295, 1394
Graham, L. F.: *ref*, 2266, 5:308 (385)
Graham, L. R.: *ref*, 1281
Graham, M. J.: *ref*, 1174
Graham, S. R.: *ref*, 1447, 1474, 1499
Graham, V. T.: *ref*, 525, 545, 1480, 1499
Graham, W. K.: *ref*, 1094
Graham, W. R.: *test*, 995; *ref*, 48, 361, 995, 997, 1599, 2135, 5:308 (350)
Graine, G. N.: *ref*, 1164, 1500
Grainer, H. M.: *ref*, 1499
Grais, M. L.: *ref*, 1281
Grajales, M. C.: *ref*, 518, 532
Graley, J.: *ref*, 1499
Graliker, B.: *ref*, 497
Graliker, B. V.: *ref*, 497
Gralnick, A.: *ref*, 1232
Grams, A.: *ref*, 1481
Grande, P. P.: *ref*, 1133, 1164, 1318, 1383
Grandovic, M. C.: *ref*, 381, 533, 1447
Grangaard, G. H.: *ref*, 1151, 1281
Granger, G. W.: *ref*, 185
Granger, R.: *ref*, 981

Granick, S.: *ref*, 381, 439, 496, 525, 529, 1281, 1448, 1481, 1499, 6:342 (6), P:41(2)
Granitz, D. W.: *ref*, 2038
Granlund, E.: *ref*, 1095
Grant, A.: *test*, 6:714; *exc*, 1573; *ref*, 435, 1573, 1716, 3:255(9–10)
Grant, A. D.: *ref*, 1164
Grant, A. K.: *ref*, 1295
Grant, B.: *test*, 2170–1, 7:1033
Grant, C. H.: *ref*, 1415
Grant, C. O.: *ref*, 1164, 1448
Grant, C. R. H.: *ref*, 1383, 1415
Grant, C. W.: *ref*, 1044, 1133
Grant, D. A.: *ref*, 1281
Grant, D. L.: *ref*, 333, 361, 1069, 1164, 1205–6, 1403, 1501, 1519, 2195, 2223, 2239
Grant, G. V.: *test*, 584, 7:438–9; *ref*, 541, 1073
Grant, H.: *ref*, 1144, 1281
Grant, J. D.: *ref*, 1499
Grant, J. G.: *ref*, 1281
Grant, J. N.: *ref*, 2212
Grant, M. Q.: *ref*, 1499
Grant, R. A.: *ref*, 1516
Grant, T. F.: *ref*, 1281
Grant, T. N.: *ref*, 543
Grant, W. H.: *ref*, 1294
Grant, W. V.: *ref*, 1073, 4:277 (242)
Grant, W. W.: *ref*, 497
Grantham-McGregor, S. M.: *ref*, 497
Granville, A. C.: *ref*, 1176
Grapko, M. F.: *test*, 1233; *ref*, 1123, 1233
Grasberger, J. C.: *ref*, 1232, 1346
Graser, E.: *test*, 91
Grason-Stadler Co., Inc.: *test*, 2038
Grass, P. L.: *ref*, 1294, 1302
Grassi, J. R.: *test*, 980, 1196; *ref*, 532, 1196, 1499
Grasty, W. K.: *ref*, 997
Grat, E. C.: *ref*, 1164
Grater, H.: *ref*, 1164, 1281, 2212, 5:308(379)
Grater, M. R.: *ref*, 1315
Gratton, L.: *ref*, 1182
Graubard, P. S.: *ref*, 516, 533, 981
Grauer, D.: *ref*, 1499
Graumann, H. M.: *ref*, 1499
Gravatt, A. E.: *ref*, 1240
Gravem, H.: *ref*, 484, 525
Graves, B. C.: *ref*, 1281, 1478
Graves, G. O.: *ref*, 1302–3, 2355
Graves, G. R.: *ref*, 516, 533
Graves, K. B.: *ref*, 525
Graves, M.: *test*, 185; *ref*, 185
Graves, W. H.: *ref*, 1094
Graves, W. S.: *ref*, 211, 214, 1499
Gravitz, H. L.: *ref*, 1447
Gravitz, M. A.: *ref*, 1281, 1474, 1481
Gray, B.: *ref*, 1069
Gray, B. G.: *ref*, 1207, 1281, 2195
Gray, B. L.: *ref*, 2285
Gray, C. F.: *ref*, 1164
Gray, C. T.: *ref*, 211, 908, 1690
Gray, C. V.: *ref*, 532, 1380
Gray, C. W.: *ref*, 2212
Gray, D. M.: *ref*, 1474
Gray, E. A.: *ref*, 533, 1447

Gray, E. J.: *ref*, 2395
Gray, H.: *test*, 15
Gray, J.: *ref*, 525, 532, 3:217(98)
Gray, J. A.: *ref*, 7, 348, 1174
Gray, J. E.: *ref*, 381, 439
Gray, J. J.: *ref*, 546, 561, 572–3, 591, 1471
Gray, J. T.: *ref*, 1164
Gray, M. G.: *ref*, 503
Gray, P. L.: *ref*, 525
Gray, S. C.: *ref*, 1044
Gray, S. L.: *ref*, 1176
Gray, S. W.: *ref*, 1403
Gray, W. H.: *test*, 1598, 2:1534
Gray, W. M.: *ref*, 868
Gray, W. S.: *rev*, 1552, 1661, 1705, 3:493, 4:535; *test*, 1681, 1689–90, 1:1006; *ref*, 1690
Graybiel, A.: *ref*, 1499
Grayden, C.: *ref*, 1281, 1448
Grayson, H.: *ref*, 1281
Grayson, H. M.: *test*, 1197; *ref*, 1144, 1281, 1298, 1380, 1499
Grayson, H. T.: *ref*, 1481, 1499, 1519
Graziano, A.: *ref*, 1499
Graziano, A. M.: *ref*, 1499, 1528
Greaves, G.: *ref*, 1281, 1521
Greaves, S. T.: *ref*, 1499
Grebstein, L. C.: *ref*, 1499
Greco, G. F.: *ref*, 35, 361
Gredler, G. R.: *exc*, 1466, 1468; *ref*, 533, 1485
Greemore, R.: *ref*, 516
Green, C.: *test*, 81
Green, C. T.: *ref*, 1499
Green, C. W.: *ref*, 425
Green, D. A.: *ref*, 20
Green, D. D.: *ref*, 1121
Green, E.: *ref*, 525
Green, E. B.: *ref*, 1498
Green, E. J.: *ref*, 382, 1315
Green, E. L.: *ref*, 1906, 1918, 1923, 5:781(9)
Green, H. B.: *ref*, 529, 533, 1281, 1403, 2212
Green, H. J.: *ref*, 438, 525, 2135, 2212, 2227–9, 2258
Green, J. B.: *ref*, 50, 1428, 2008
Green, J. H.: *ref*, 425, 1044, 1363, 1407, 1572
Green, J. L.: *ref*, 361, 1772, 7:904 (1)
Green, L. A.: *ref*, 1095
Green, L. H.: *ref*, 1430
Green, L. R.: *ref*, 1174
Green, M.: *ref*, 1281
Green, M. A.: *ref*, 1144
Green, M. C.: *ref*, 2259
Green, M. E.: *ref*, 1281, 4:95(25)
Green, M. F. F.: *ref*, 1378
Green, M. G.: *ref*, 1253
Green, M. L.: *ref*, 1123
Green, M. W.: *ref*, 439
Green, P. A.: *ref*, 868
Green, P. C.: *ref*, 1383, 2451
Green, R.: *ref*, 532
Green, R. B.: *ref*, 400, 439, 1603
Green, R. F.: *rev*, 361, 451, 468, 6:468; *ref*, 529, 532, 1205, 1245, 2195
Green, R. M.: *ref*, 538
Green, R. V.: *ref*, 1315
Green, S.: *ref*, 1281, 1403, 2212

Hager, C. W.: *ref,* 1069
Hager, P. C.: *ref,* 2212
Haggard, E. A.: *ref,* 1318, 1451, 1499
Haggerty, A. D.: *ref,* 532, 1481, 1519
Haggerty, L. C.: *test,* 4:535
Haggerty, M. E.: *test,* 1568, 2:1222, 4:535; *ref,* 2:1222(1), 4:535(1)
Haggerty, M. J.: *test,* 1997, 5:807
Hagin, R. A.: *ref,* 381, 538, 1447
Hagiwara, M. P.: *rev,* 256, 258
Haglund, C. A.: *ref,* 1499
Hagman, H.: *ref,* 1281
Hagness, D. E.: *ref,* 2046
Hagstrom, D. A.: *ref,* 1133
Hague, H. R.: *ref,* 1196
Haguenauer, G.: *ref,* 1499, 1528
Hahn, B. M.: *test,* 35:223
Hahn, C. W.: *ref,* 20
Hahn, F.: *ref,* 1499–500
Hahn, H.: *ref,* 1275, 1486
Hahn, H. R.: *ref,* 981
Hahn, J. M.: *ref,* 2031, 2046
Hahn, K.: *ref,* 1164
Hahn, K. V.: *ref,* 1471
Hahn, M.: *ref,* 529
Hahn, M. E.: *rev,* 2180, 2395, 2397, 3:704, 4:798; *test,* 1118, 1208, 3:689; *ref,* 404, 1095, 1118, 1139, 2135, 2195, 2212, 3:62(4), 5:87 (10), P:340(13)
Hahn, M. S.: *ref,* 589, 1069
Hahn, P.: *ref,* 1275, 1281
Haigh, G. V.: *ref,* 1403
Haimes, P. E.: *test,* 1157
Haimowitz, M. L.: *ref,* 1499
Haimowitz, N. R.: *ref,* 1499
Hain, J. D.: *ref,* 1121, 1281, 1447, 2355
Haine, S. E.: *ref,* 1093, 1144
Haines, E. M.: *ref,* 3:217(143)
Haines, J.: *test,* 1703
Haines, L. E.: *ref,* 1164, 1176
Haines, M. S.: *ref,* 507
Haines, R. B.: *ref,* 529, 1069
Hainsworth, M.: *ref,* 984
Hainsworth, P.: *ref,* 984
Hainsworth, P. K.: *test,* 984; *ref,* 984
Hairston, P.: *ref,* 1281
Hakanson, I. S.: *ref,* 1256, 2195
Hake, D.: *ref,* 439
Hake, D. T.: *ref,* 1519, 2195
Hakel, M. D.: *ref,* 405, 1164
Hakenwerth, Q. W.: *ref,* 1281
Hakerem, G.: *test,* 1435; *ref,* 1435
Hakes, J. E.: *ref,* 1027
Hakkinen, S.: *ref,* 2266, 6:232(10)
Hakstian, A. R.: *rev,* 222–3; *exc,* 258, 275, 318
Halberstam, J. L.: *ref,* 1194, 1281
Halbower, C. C.: *ref,* 1281
Halcomb, C. G.: *ref,* 1121
Halcrow, J. H.: *ref,* 361, 1281
Hale, J. R.: *ref,* 516
Hale, P. P.: *ref,* 1501, 2195, 2197, 5:308(319)
Hales, N. M.: *ref,* 3:220(41)
Hales, W. M.: *ref,* 398, 1281, 1499, 2135, 2162
Haley, E. M.: *ref,* 1499
Haley, G.: *test,* 35:454, 35:456

Haley, G. A.: *ref,* 1218, 1322
Haley, H. B.: *ref,* 1403, 1407, 2355
Haley, M. J.: *ref,* 2031
Halfter, I. T.: *test,* 1538; *ref,* 1538, 2349
Hall, A. E.: *ref,* 574
Hall, B. W.: *ref,* 361
Hall, C. C.: *ref,* 1094, 1415
Hall, C. E.: *ref,* 1069, 1080, 1091
Hall, C. L.: *ref,* 1094, 1281
Hall, C. W.: *test,* 2399
Hall, D. H.: *ref,* 2212
Hall, D. J.: *ref,* 1291
Hall, D. M.: *ref,* 1499
Hall, D. S.: *ref,* 1164, 1403, 2337
Hall, D. W.: *exc,* 2197; *ref,* 2103
Hall, E.: *ref,* 361, 382, 404, 1252, 1281, 1490
Hall, E. E.: *ref,* 1281
Hall, F. D.: *ref,* 1121
Hall, F. P.: *ref,* 1699
Hall, G. C.: *ref,* 1499
Hall, H. E.: *ref,* 425, 1171, 1277, 1387
Hall, H. S.: *ref,* 1171
Hall, J.: *ref,* 1121, 1183
Hall, J. A.: *ref,* 2221
Hall, J. C.: *ref,* 381, 439, 516, 529, 532, 543, 1573
Hall, J. D.: *ref,* 1275, 1415
Hall, J. G.: *ref,* 863
Hall, J. W.: *exc,* 3
Hall, K. R. L.: *ref,* 532
Hall, L. G.: *test,* 2187; *ref,* 867, 2187
Hall, L. H.: *ref,* 1515, 1519
Hall, L. P.: *ref,* 533, 1468
Hall, L. T.: *ref,* 35, 113, 348, 361, 1069, 1560
Hall, M.: *ref,* 1247, 1447
Hall, M. D.: *ref,* 1281
Hall, M. E.: *ref,* 1105, 2:1243(22)
Hall, M. M.: *ref,* 1499
Hall, M. R.: *ref,* 381, 1474
Hall, O. A.: *ref,* 1207, 2213
Hall, O. M.: *ref,* 2266
Hall, P.: *test,* 1745; *ref,* 1745
Hall, R. A.: *ref,* 1406
Hall, R. C.: *ref,* 1069
Hall, R. L.: *ref,* 1513
Hall, R. T.: *ref,* 18
Hall, R. W.: *ref,* 1215
Hall, S. G.: *ref,* 2195
Hall, S. M.: *ref,* 947
Hall, T.: *ref,* 1174
Hall, T. W.: *ref,* 1471
Hall, V. C.: *exc,* 549
Hall, W. A.: *ref,* 1044
Hall, W. B.: *rev,* 1171; *ref,* 1094, 1121, 1176, 1281, 1294, 1345–6, 1403, 2212, 2355
Hall, W. E.: *rev,* 48, 1622; *ref,* 529, 1087, 1447, 1470, 1474, 1519, 1745, 4:216(10)
Hall, W. J.: *ref,* 2212–3
Halladay, R. E.: *ref,* 64, 357
Hallberg, M. C.: *ref,* 532
Hallenbeck, C. E.: *ref,* 529
Haller, A. O.: *ref,* 1123, 1383
Haller, R. M.: *rev,* 2089, 2095
Halley, E. E.: *test,* 35:445–6
Halliday, M. F.: *ref,* 884
Halliday, R. W.: *ref,* 426, 2239
Hallock, G. A.: *ref,* 1123

Halloran, A. V.: *ref,* 1281
Hallow, W. C.: *ref,* 1499
Hallowell, A.: *ref,* 1499
Hallowell, A. I.: *ref,* 1499
Hallowell, D. K.: *ref,* 525
Hall-Smith, P.: *ref,* 1218, 1410
Hallworth, H. J.: *ref,* 95, 409, 439, 446, 722, P:294(15)
Halmiova, O.: *ref,* 1174
Halperin, S.: *ref,* 1123
Halperin, S. L.: *ref,* 532, 1447, 1499
Halpern, A. S.: *ref,* 529, 1428
Halpern, C.: *ref,* 1164
Halpern, F.: *ref,* 525, 532, 1140, 1447, 1499, 1519
Halpern, F. C.: *ref,* 1499
Halpern, G.: *ref,* 1194, P:329(9)
Halpern, H. M.: *ref,* 1205, 1403, 1499
Halpern, S. H.: *test,* 1667
Halpern, S. K.: *ref,* 574
Halpin, A.: *ref,* 1629, 1702, 1733, 1918, 3:515(2)
Halpin, A. W.: *test,* 2451; *ref,* 2449, 2451–2
Halpin, J. W.: *ref,* 1519
Halpin, V. G.: *ref,* 1192, 1447
Halsall, E.: *ref,* 221
Halsey, H.: *ref,* 1069
Halstead, H.: *ref,* 354, 403, 439, 532, 1174, 1205, 1380, 1499, 2239, 2258, 3:273(5)
Halstead, M. B.: *ref,* 1932
Halstead, W. C.: *test,* 2076; *ref,* 2076
Halverson, D. E.: *ref,* 914
Halverson, H. M.: *ref,* 497
Ham, D. G.: *ref,* 574
Hama, H.: *ref,* 1281
Hamachek, D. E.: *ref,* 1123, 1164
Hamaluk, O. J.: *ref,* 981
Hamaty, G. G.: *ref,* 1394–5
Hamberg, R. L.: *test,* 1265; *ref,* 2355
Hambidge, G.: *ref,* 1195, 1519
Hambleton, R. K.: *exc,* 2239
Hamblin, R. L.: *ref,* P:327(18)
Hamby, R.: *ref,* 1499
Hamby, T. M.: *ref,* 589
Hamely, E. J.: *ref,* 1174
Hamer, C.: *test,* 35:320
Hamer, O. S.: *test,* 36:848
Hamerlynck, L. A.: *ref,* 1281
Hames, C. G.: *ref,* 1121, 1281
Hamilton, B. A.: *test,* 3:611
Hamilton, D. D. H.: *ref,* 20, 391, 1253
Hamilton, D. L.: *ref,* 1121, 1240
Hamilton, E. L.: *ref,* 1499
Hamilton, E. W.: *rev,* 637, 731
Hamilton, H. A.: *ref,* 783
Hamilton, J.: *ref,* 532, 1275, 1281, 1499
Hamilton, J. T.: *ref,* 1315, 1516
Hamilton, L. K.: *ref,* 1275, 1295
Hamilton, M.: *ref,* 1145, 1377
Hamilton, M. E.: *ref,* 483, 525
Hamilton, R.: *ref,* 1471, 1519
Hamilton, R. G.: *ref,* 1471
Hamilton, R. J.: *ref,* 1320
Hamilton, V.: *ref,* 331, 403, 439, 1162, 1164
Hamilton, W. F.: *ref,* 1932

Hardy, C. A.: *ref,* 1252
Hardy, J.: *ref,* 868
Hardy, J. B.: *ref,* 50, 381, 484, 525, 533, 981, 1447
Hardy, L. H.: *test,* 1924, 5:768; *ref,* 1912, 1924, 1932, 3:473(5, 8–9), 4:661(14, 17), 5:768(27)
Hardy, M. C.: *ref,* 36, 525
Hardy, M. J.: *ref,* 1500
Hardy, M. P.: *ref,* 50, 516, 533, 981, 1681
Hardy, M. W.: *ref,* 1277, 1387, 1474
Hardy, R. E.: *test,* 1100; *ref,* 500, 529, 1100, 1207, 1481, 2195
Hardy, V. T.: *ref,* 1090, 1101, 1500, P:129(6)
Hardyck, C.: *ref,* 529
Hardyck, C. D.: *ref,* 551, 1121, 1281, 1499
Hare, A. P.: *ref,* 1474, P:326(30), P:327(15, 27)
Hare, E. H.: *ref,* 1174, 1275
Hare, J.: *test,* 331
Hare, R. D.: *ref,* 361, 1281
Hare, R. T.: *ref,* 1474
Harford, T.: *ref,* 439, 529, 1346, 1380, 1428, 1471, 2212
Harford, T. C.: *ref,* 1073, 1383, 1403, 2212
Hargadon, K.: *ref,* 1499
Hargan, J.: *ref,* 1320
Hargrave, H.: *test,* 4:696
Hargreaves, D. H.: *ref,* 1113
Hargreaves, H. L.: *ref,* 2:1220(2)
Haring, N. G.: *ref,* 1394
Haritos-Fatouros, M.: *ref,* 518, 529, 533
Hariu, T.: *ref,* 513
Harker, J. B.: *ref,* 1091, 2132, 2151, 2212
Harkey, S. M.: *ref,* 440
Harkless, R.: *ref,* 1281, 1775
Harlan, C. L.: *ref,* 1569
Harlan, G.: *ref,* 1383
Harlan, G. E.: *ref,* 1383, 2103, 2221
Harlen, W.: *test,* 5c, 1750
Harless, B. B.: *test,* 5:394; *ref,* 2395
Harley, R. K.: *ref,* 489, 496, 516, 6:537(5)
Harlow, G.: *ref,* 1222, 1281
Harlow, J. E.: *ref,* 525, 533
Harlow, J. G.: *test,* 36:534
Harlow, R. G.: *ref,* 1519
Harlow, S. D.: *ref,* 19, 382, 404, 551, 561, 591, 863
Harlow Publishing Corporation: *test,* 4:13–4
Harman, C. E.: *ref,* 381, 1447
Harman, H. H.: *ref,* 525
Harman, R. L.: *ref,* 20, 857, 1044
Harman, W.: *ref,* 1281
Harmatz, J. S.: *ref,* 1121, 1225, 1281
Harmatz, M. G.: *ref,* 1346
Harmeling, J. D.: *ref,* 1415
Harmes, H. M.: *ref,* 2451
Harmeson, V. F.: *ref,* 1123
Harmon, J. B.: *ref,* 2258
Harmon, J. E.: *ref,* 1471
Harmon, J. S.: *ref,* 1073, 1164
Harmon, L. A. W.: *ref,* 2213

Harmon, L. R.: *test,* 3:251; *ref,* 1281, 2195, 2258
Harmon, L. W.: *ref,* 2212–3
Harms, C. R.: *ref,* 36, 400
Harms, I. E.: *ref,* 487
Harney, J.: *ref,* 1207
Harney, J. B.: *ref,* 1207
Haronian, F.: *ref,* 529, 1474
Harootunian, B.: *ref,* 349, 425, 1069
Harootunian, B. A.: *ref,* 349, 425
Harper, A. E.: *test,* 118, 810; *ref,* 532
Harper, B. P.: *exc,* 2212; *ref,* 2212–3
Harper, F. B. W.: *ref,* 1121
Harper, J. A.: *ref,* 1164
Harper, J. C.: *ref,* 36
Harper, J. H.: *ref,* 1164
Harper, M.: *ref,* 525, 1275
Harper, P.: *ref,* 494, 497
Harper, P. A.: *ref,* 50, 533, 1447
Harper, R. A.: *rev,* 814, 817, 825, 829
Harper, R. J. C.: *ref,* 36
Harper, R. T.: *ref,* 1499
Harrangue, M. D.: *ref,* 2195, 2221
Harrell, M. S.: *ref,* 342
Harrell, T. W.: *rev,* 2231, 2234; *ref,* 342, 423, 1207, 1222, 1281, 1320, 2212, 2314, 2325, 2454, P:399(31)
Harrell, W.: *ref,* 426, 1087, 1386, 2212, 2227, 2251, 2258–9, 3:671(8), 3:678(11, 15)
Harries, W. T.: *ref,* 981
Harrigan, J. E.: *ref,* 1500, P:381(33)
Harrigan, M.: *ref,* 1519
Harrill, J. E.: *ref,* 1121
Harriman, B. L.: *ref,* 1167, 1260, 1466
Harriman, M.: *ref,* 1447
Harriman, P. L.: *rev,* 1247, 1456, 1469, 1481, 4:108, 5:131, 5:137, 6:232; *exc,* 1499; *ref,* 525, 1447, 1499, 1932
Harrington, C.: *ref,* 1044, 2212, 2273
Harrington, C. C.: *ref,* 1121, 1463, 2212
Harrington, C. J.: *ref,* 209
Harrington, D.: *ref,* 914
Harrington, H.: *ref,* 1164, 1176, 1383
Harrington, J. A.: *ref,* 1256, 2195
Harrington, J. J.: *ref,* 1415
Harrington, M. A. C.: *ref,* 1281
Harrington, M. J.: *ref,* 425
Harrington, R. L.: *ref,* 1499
Harrington, R. W.: *ref,* 1474, 1499
Harrington, S. A.: *exc,* 1772
Harrington, T. F.: *ref,* 1164, 1207, 2194, 2212
Harris, A. E.: *test,* 4:793
Harris, A. J.: *rev,* 380, 1634, 1679, 1681, 1929, 3:496, 3:511, 3:530; *test,* 1714, 1877; *ref,* 364, 425–6, 525, 533, 1877, 2229, 2259, 2:1243.1(2)
Harris, A. S.: *ref,* 19, 22
Harris, B. R.: *ref,* 381, 400, 533, 575, 1895, 1898
Harris, C. D.: *ref,* 1164
Harris, C. S.: *ref,* 1383

Harris, C. W.: *rev,* 73, 3:139–40, 3:143; *ref,* 457, 561, 1576, 1761, 4:58(5), 5:631(8)
Harris, D.: *ref,* 238, 1403, 2347
Harris, D. B.: *rev,* 1182, 1186, 1254, 1290, 1321, 1455, 1468, 1882; *test,* 381, 1326; *exc,* 525, 1447; *ref,* 381, 439, 507, 1087, 1095, 1474, 2:1214(1), P:306(3), P:363(12, 23)
Harris, D. H.: *test,* 2347; *ref,* 1144, 2347
Harris, D. J.: *ref,* 947
Harris, D. P.: *rev,* 59, 7:200; *test,* 69, 73, 226, 230, 234, 239, 1545, 1583, 7:263
Harris, D. V.: *ref,* 1164
Harris, E. F.: *ref,* 2454
Harris, E. H.: *ref,* 2452
Harris, E. M.: *ref,* 1281
Harris, E. M. K.: *ref,* 1281
Harris, F. E.: *ref,* 1513
Harris, F. J.: *ref,* 1499–500
Harris, F. W.: *ref,* P:446(27)
Harris, G.: *ref,* 1044, 1291, 1295, 1415
Harris, G. A.: *ref,* 1291, 1295
Harris, H.: *ref,* 533
Harris, H. I.: *ref,* 503
Harris, H. J.: *ref,* 1144
Harris, H. R.: *ref,* 1254
Harris, J.: *test,* 233; *ref,* 357
Harris, J. A.: *ref,* 382, 1560
Harris, J. D.: *ref,* 503
Harris, J. E.: *ref,* 1481, 1499
Harris, J. G.: *rev,* 1473, 1513; *ref,* 1281, 1499
Harris, J. H.: *ref,* 202, 211
Harris, J. J.: *ref,* 1275
Harris, J. M.: *ref,* 1403
Harris, J. S.: *ref,* 1499
Harris, J. W.: *ref,* 2103
Harris, L. A.: *rev,* 1634, 1653
Harris, L. C.: *ref,* 1121
Harris, L. L.: *ref,* 1499, 1519, 4:142(1)
Harris, M. L.: *test,* 1655
Harris, M. M.: *ref,* 1383
Harris, M. W.: *ref,* 1261, 1500
Harris, N.: *ref,* 1519
Harris, P.: *ref,* 1196
Harris, P. T.: *ref,* 1403
Harris, R.: *test,* 6:621; *ref,* 532–3, 574, 1499
Harris, R. C.: *rev,* 967
Harris, R. E.: *exc,* 1499; *ref,* 381, 532, 1281, 1499, 1519, 2355
Harris, R. H.: *test,* 2340; *ref,* 1924, 1932, 3:473(4)
Harris, R. J.: *ref,* 1281
Harris, R. M.: *ref,* 1447
Harris, S.: *ref,* 1326, 1499, 1519
Harris, T. L.: *rev,* 909, 6:712, 6:714; *ref,* 1437
Harris, T. M.: *ref,* 1499
Harris, V.: *test,* 4:4
Harris, V. W.: *ref,* 1192, 1447, 1481, 1499
Harris, W. E.: *ref,* 1499
Harris, Y. Y.: *ref,* 361, 1069
Harrison, A. W.: *ref,* 403, 1198
Harrison, B.: *ref,* 19, 426
Harrison, C. E.: *ref,* 2031
Harrison, C. F.: *ref,* 993

Hatfield, J. S.: *ref,* 1121, 1281
Hatfield, R. C.: *ref,* 349, 589, 1294
Hatfield, W. G.: *ref,* 209
Hathaway, M. L.: *ref,* 502
Hathaway, S. R.: *rev,* 1101, 3:93; *test,* 1281; *ref,* 1095, 1222, 1281, 1320, 1499
Hatlestad, S. L.: *ref,* 5:766(8)
Hatt, E.: *ref,* 507, 525, 2:1241(1)
Hattem, J. V.: *ref,* 1207, 1240, 1519
Hatton, R. O.: *ref,* 1281
Hattwick, L. A.: *ref,* P:321(11)
Hattwick, L. W.: *ref,* P:406(2–3)
Hauck, H.: *ref,* 1519
Hauck, J. M.: *ref,* 1356
Hauck, P.: *ref,* 1474
Hauck, P. A.: *ref,* 1447, 1481, 1499
Hauck, W. E.: *ref,* 1210
Hauenstein, F. B.: *ref,* 1303
Hauff, A. C.: *ref,* 869
Haugen, E. S.: *ref,* 35, 361, 529
Haugen, R. F.: *ref,* 914
Haugh, O. M.: *test,* 44, 65, 119, 143
Haughey, C.: *ref,* 19, 391, 533
Haun, K. W.: *ref,* 357, 1275, 1281
Haupt, I.: *ref,* 1932
Haupt, T. D.: *ref,* 516, 533, 1237, 1383, 1921
Haury, G.: *ref,* 525
Hause, E.: *ref,* 3:242(5)
Hauselman, A. J.: *ref,* 1044, 1302
Hausenfluck, E.: *test,* 36:765, 36:771
Hauser, L. J. M.: *ref,* 4:277(207)
Hauser, R. J.: *ref,* 532, 1499
Havel, J.: *ref,* 1499
Haven, G. A.: *ref,* 589, 1403
Havener, P. H.: *ref,* 1415
Havens, J. M.: *ref,* 1407, 2194
Havens, N. H.: *ref,* 1365
Havens, R. I.: *ref,* 419, 1281
Havens, V.: *ref,* 69, 1583, 4:277(187)
Haverly Systems Inc.: *test,* 2336
Havighurst, R. J.: *test,* 4:100; *exc,* 2212–3; *ref,* 348–9, 381, 391, 398, 425, 483, 518, 525, 532, 1087, 1121, 1123, 1560, 2266, 3:161(13), 4:100(1–2, 4), 4:324(59)
Haviland, F. H.: *ref,* 4:825(7)
Havlena, R. A.: *ref,* 1169
Havlicek, L. L.: *ref,* 2212
Havlin, N. J.: *ref,* 1123
Haw, A. B.: *ref,* 525
Haward, L. R. C.: *test,* 1743; *ref,* 381, 532, 1174, 1305, 1316, 1481, 1499, 1519, 1743
Hawk, J.: *ref,* 1073, 1086
Hawk, J. A.: *ref,* 1073
Hawke, W. A.: *ref,* 497
Hawkes, G. R.: *ref,* 1123, 1281, 1313
Hawkes, H. E.: *test,* 4:422
Hawkes, N. J.: *ref,* 426, 1069
Hawkins, C. C.: *test,* 4:523
Hawkins, D. B.: *ref,* 1471
Hawkins, D. R.: *ref,* 1121, 1215, 1281, 1499, 1519
Hawkins, G. E.: *rev,* 2:1473–4
Hawkins, H. M.: *ref,* 518, 532, 1232, 1277, 1499
Hawkins, L. G.: *ref,* 1224
Hawkins, N. E.: *ref,* 1403
Hawkins, R.: *ref,* 1470

Hawkins, R. E.: *ref,* 2454
Hawkins, R. R.: *ref,* 2028
Hawkins, W. A.: *ref,* 482, 1499
Hawkins, W. C.: *ref,* 1207, 1499
Hawkins, W. F.: *ref,* 533, 1468, 1485
Hawkridge, D. G.: *rev,* 2168, 2175
Hawks, D. V.: *ref,* 1105, 1192
Haworth, M. R.: *rev,* 525, 1469, 6:537; *test,* 1451, 1497, 1882; *ref,* 381, 525, 533, 1451, 1481, 1497, 1499, 1519, 1882
Hawthorne, R. E.: *ref,* 1109, 1403, 1437
Hay, E. N.: *rev,* 786, 791, 2129, 2142, 3:624, 3:631; *test,* 345, 2132, 2159, 2163; *exc,* 525, 1087; *ref,* 341A, 426, 482, 791, 1519, 2132, 2135
Hay, J. E.: *ref,* 1073, 1294, 1383, 1407, 2454
Hay, L.: *ref,* 868, 1474
Hayasaka, K.: *ref,* 513
Hayashi, K.: *ref,* 1500
Hayashi, S.: *ref,* 1499
Hayden, B. S.: *ref,* 533, 1447
Hayden, C. E.: *ref,* 1164
Hayden, D. L.: *ref,* 50, 425, 533, 981, 1115, 1447, 1679, 7:880(4–6)
Hayden, J. R.: *rev,* 32, 896, 907, 5:23
Hayden, L. A.: *ref,* 1626
Hayden, M. P.: *ref,* 543, 1277, 1447
Hayden, S. J.: *ref,* 532
Hayes, A. B.: *ref,* 1403, 2212
Hayes, B.: *ref,* 1383
Hayes, C. V.: *ref,* 1293
Hayes, D. D.: *ref,* 1403
Hayes, E.: *test,* 638, 646
Hayes, E. G.: *ref,* 2228
Hayes, E. M.: *ref,* 29, 361, 400, 1560
Hayes, M. E.: *ref,* 981
Hayes, M. L.: *test,* 1:926; *ref,* 1500, P:373(1)
Hayes, M. P.: *ref,* 2180
Hayes, M. T.: *test,* 1660; *ref,* 1660
Hayes, P. L.: *ref,* 1315
Hayes, R.: *ref,* 1090, 1275
Hayes, S. P.: *ref,* 22, 36, 525, 532, 1320, 2195
Hayes, V.: *ref,* 1044, 1383
Hayes, W. G.: *ref,* 1513, 2448
Haymaker, W.: *exc,* 1499
Hayman, M.: *ref,* 1105, 1380
Haynes, C. R.: *ref,* 542, 546, 573, 1772
Haynes, E. F.: *ref,* 349, 1560
Haynes, J. O.: *ref,* 69, 1583, 5:308(380)
Haynes, J. R.: *ref,* 1074, 1383, 1447
Haynes, L. M.: *rev,* 691, 798
Haynes, R. C.: *ref,* 868
Hays, B. B.: *ref,* 1193–4, 2451
Hays, J. R.: *ref,* 1499
Hays, W.: *ref,* 532, 1499, 1519
Hayter, W. H.: *ref,* 1622
Haythorn, W. W.: *ref,* 1471
Hayward, A. E.: *ref,* 1383
Hayward, M. L.: *ref,* 1164
Hayward, P.: *ref,* 1599
Hayweiser, L.: *ref,* 525
Haywood, H. C.: *ref,* 516
Haywood, N. R.: *ref,* 538

Hazard, L.: *ref,* 36, 3:10(8)
Hazari, A.: *ref,* 439, 1095, 1174, 1499
Hazelhurst, J. H.: *test,* 2262
Hazelton, J. E.: *ref,* 1275, 1499, 1519
Heacock, D. D.: *ref,* 1281, 1363
Headlee, M. K.: *ref,* 2195
Headley, E. B.: *ref,* 1278
Headrick, E. B.: *ref,* 1121, 1383
Heal, L. W.: *ref,* 516
Heald, J. E.: *ref,* 1164, 1192
Healey, G. W.: *ref,* 1415
Healey, R. E.: *ref,* 5:147(23)
Healey, R. M.: *ref,* 1970
Health, D.: *ref,* 1499
Healy, B. C.: *ref,* 1501, 1519
Healy, C. C.: *test,* 2109; *ref,* 2212
Healy, I.: *ref,* 1205–6, 1245, 2195
Healy, M. M. I.: *ref,* 1383, 1394
Healy, W.: *test,* 558, T:929; *exc,* 1499; *ref,* 558, 2:1390(3), 2:1391(6), 2:1394(3), 2:1401(2)
Heap, R. F.: *ref,* 1281
Heard, W. G.: *ref,* 357, 1207
Hearn, J. L.: *ref,* 1164
Heater, W. H.: *ref,* 1407
Heath, D.: *ref,* 1519
Heath, D. D.: *ref,* 1123
Heath, D. H.: *ref,* 1094, 1281, 1320, 1403, 1499, 1519, 2212
Heath, E. D.: *test,* 6:694; *ref,* 1423
Heath, E. J.: *ref,* 868, 989
Heath, F. A.: *test,* 3:562
Heath, H.: *ref,* 1256
Heath, H. A.: *ref,* 1164, 1207, 1281, 1423, 1471, 1474, 1499
Heath, H. E.: *ref,* 1094, 1281, 1320, 1403, 1499, 1519, 2212
Heath, R. W.: *ref,* 1599
Heath, S. R.: *test,* 1900; *ref,* 1900
Heathers, G. L.: *ref,* 1144
Heathers, L. B.: *ref,* 532, 1164, 1281, 5:308(328)
Heaton, J. M.: *ref,* 361, 1315
Heaton, K. L.: *rev,* 881, 1349
Heaton-Ward, W. A.: *ref,* 525
Heaxt, S.: *ref,* 357, 1358
Heber, R. F.: *ref,* 398
Heberlein, M.: *ref,* 1481
Hebert, D. J.: *ref,* 869, 1164, 1415
Hebert, J. A.: *ref,* 1164, 1772
Hebron, M. E.: *test,* 397, 463, 730, 736–7, 1560; *ref,* 1275
Hechlik, J. E.: *ref,* 1306
Hecht, C. A.: *ref,* 1320
Hecht, I.: *ref,* 532, 1499
Hecht, P. J.: *ref,* 533
Hecht, R.: *ref,* 426, 1386, 2406
Hecht, R. M.: *ref,* 423
Hecht, S.: *ref,* 1281
Heck, E. M.: *ref,* 1181
Heck, E. T.: *ref,* 1281
Heckel, R. V.: *ref,* 1281, P:327(23)
Hecker, A. O.: *ref,* 532, 1499
Hecker, M. H. L.: *ref,* 2046
Heckler, V. J.: *ref,* 1499
Heckman, S. B.: *ref,* 381, 435, 438, 525
Hector, H.: *test,* 1508, 6:459; *ref,* 1508, 6:459(1)
Hedberg, R.: *ref,* 1207, 1407, 1500
Heddendorf, R.: *ref,* 1383

Henmon, V. A. C.: *rev,* 1:956, 1:1038; *test,* 2:1271, 2:1342, 2:1346, 2:1357–8, 2:1371; *ref,* 69, 391, 438, 525, 2:1271(7), 2:1342(4), 2:1343(1), 2:1345 (4), 2:1357(2), 2:1371(2), 2:1377(28)
Henneberry, J. K.: *ref,* 1391
Hennessy, J.: *ref,* 1052
Hennessy, R. M.: *ref,* 1281
Hennessy, T.: *ref,* 2195, 2212
Henning, J. A.: *ref,* 36, 426
Henning, J. J.: *ref,* 529, 533, 1253
Henning, R. L.: *ref,* 532
Henning, W. D.: *ref,* 1383
Hennis, G. M.: *test,* 5:565; *ref,* 5:565(1)
Henrichs, T.: *ref,* 1281
Henrichs, T. F.: *ref,* 1281, 1481
Henrickson, P. R.: *ref,* 589
Henricksson, N. G.: *ref,* 1275, 1387
Henrikson, L. V.: *ref,* 1144
Henry, A. F.: *ref,* 1519
Henry, D. R.: *ref,* 1164
Henry, E. M.: *ref,* 1499
Henry, E. R.: *rev,* 4:316–7
Henry, G. H.: *ref,* 1094, 1403
Henry, J.: *ref,* 1499
Henry, J. A.: *ref,* 525
Henry, J. L.: *ref,* 1133, 1303
Henry, L. J.: *ref,* 69, 1583
Henry, L. K.: *ref,* 1164
Henry, M.: *ref,* 1320, 1336, 1383
Henry, M. B.: *ref,* 398
Henry, P. M.: *ref,* 868, 1281
Henry, S.: *ref,* 2043, 2218
Henry, W. E.: *rev,* 1010, 2216, 5:102, 5:150; *test,* 1467; *ref,* 1467, 1499, 1519
Henry, W. O.: *ref,* 2195
Henry, Z.: *ref,* 1499
Henrysson, S.: *ref,* 1275
Henshaw, J. H.: *test,* 674, 747
Hensley, M.: *ref,* 1135
Hensley, R.: *ref,* 1320
Hensman, C.: *ref,* 1275
Henson, J. P.: *ref,* 589
Hensrud, N. B.: *ref,* 868, 1121
Henze, A. L.: *ref,* 1289
Henze, M. V.: *ref,* 1439
Hepburn, A. W.: *ref,* 381, 981, 1696, 1921
Hepner, H. W.: *test,* 36:564, 36:845, 36:866; *ref,* 36:564(1)
Heppell, H. K.: *ref,* 1519
Herber, H. L.: *ref,* 1775
Herbert, M.: *ref,* 1500, 1519
Herbert, N.: *ref,* 409, 868, 1320, 1386, 1500
Herbert, R. A.: *test,* 1642
Herbstritt, R. L.: *ref,* 357
Herd, J.: *ref,* 1500
Herdt, B. F.: *ref,* 1207, 1499
Herdtner, T. J.: *ref,* 1921
Hered, W.: *rev,* 1819, 1830–1, 1837; *ref,* 3:564(1)
Heredero, J. M.: *ref,* 1403, 1519
Herer, G.: *ref,* 2038
Herfindahl, O. C.: *ref,* 3:397(31)
Herger, J.: *ref,* 1481
Hering, F. J.: *exc,* 1281
Heriot, J. T.: *ref,* 1428, 1883
Heriot, M. R.: *ref,* 1069
Heritage, L. J. G.: *ref,* 1383

Herke, M. L.: *ref,* 1053, 5:308 (322)
Herkelmann, L. E.: *ref,* 3:397(15)
Herkenhoff, L. H.: *ref,* 2213
Herkness, W. W.: *ref,* 2195, 2212, 3:635(6, 8), 3:637(6), 3:653 (8, 11), 3:655(2, 4)
Herlin, W. R.: *ref,* 1623, 1628
Herman, D. O.: *rev,* 847, 2200, 6:1147, 7:1032; *ref,* 538, 1383
Herman, G. N.: *ref,* 1519
Herman, H.: *exc,* 1451
Herman, J.: *ref,* 1499
Herman, J. L.: *ref,* 1499
Herman, K.: *ref,* 532, 592
Herman, L.: *ref,* 1232, 1346, 1365
Herman, L. M.: *test,* 2212; *ref,* 2212
Herman, P. S.: *ref,* 1499, 1519
Herman, R. S.: *ref,* 2028
Herman, S.: *ref,* 1394
Herman, S. J.: *ref,* 484
Herman, W. L.: *ref,* 868
Hermann, A. L.: *ref,* 981
Hermann, M. G.: *ref,* 357, 542
Hermann, R. S.: *ref,* 496
Hermans, H. J. M.: *ref,* 1519
Hermsen, L. P.: *ref,* 69, 1123
Hernández, C.: *ref,* 1360
Hernandez, D.: *ref,* 22, 361, 1755, 1775
Hernandez, D. E.: *ref,* 1775
Hernández, O. F.: *test,* 309, 319
Hernandez, P. E.: *ref,* 1711
Herndon, C. N.: *ref,* 532
Herndon, J. D.: *ref,* 516, 533
Herod, J.: *ref,* 2451
Heron, A.: *ref,* 403, 439, 1073, 1277, 1311, 1387
Herr, E. L.: *ref,* 1394–5
Herr, S. E.: *ref,* 435, 1716
Herr, V. V.: *ref,* 1090, 1281, 1480
Herrans, L. L.: *ref,* 529
Herreid, C. F.: *ref,* 1281
Herreid, J. R.: *ref,* 1281
Herrell, J. M.: *ref,* 529, 533, 1281
Herrera, J. A.: *ref,* 1519
Herrick, C. J.: *ref,* 505, 518, 525, 1428, 1499
Herrick, V. E.: *rev,* 4, 19, 36; *ref,* 348, 391, 398, 425, 908, 1087
Herrin, B.: *test,* 35:476, 35:480
Herring, F. H.: *ref,* 532, 1205, 1245, 1281, 1285, 1499, 1519
Herring, J. P.: *test,* 1:869, 2:1399; *ref,* 518, 525, 1:869(1–2), 2:1399 (1, 4–7)
Herrington, R. N.: *ref,* 1275, 1387
Herriott, R. E.: *ref,* 1302
Herrman, W. L.: *ref,* 1365
Herrmann, M.: *ref,* 349, 532
Herrmann, R. S.: *ref,* 1499
Herrmann, W. C.: *ref,* 621, 4:718 (1)
Herrmann, W. M.: *ref,* 884
Herron, E. W.: *test,* 1471; *ref,* 1275, 1281, 1293, 1471
Herron, M. K.: *test,* 1255
Herron, W. G.: *ref,* 381, 440, 529, 533, 1127, 1169, 1281, 1383, 1447, 1475, 1478, 1499, 1519
Herrscher, B. R.: *ref,* 1133
Hersch, C.: *ref,* 1499

Hersch, P. D.: *ref,* 1094, 1121, 1501, 2212–3
Hersemann, D. D.: *ref,* 1133
Hersen, M.: *ref,* 1185, 1281, 1499, 1519
Hersh, J. B.: *ref,* 525
Hershberger, T. J.: *ref,* 1281
Hershenson, D. B.: *ref,* 533, 1481, 2212
Hershenson, J. R.: *ref,* 1499
Hershey, C. F.: *test,* 796
Hershey, G. L.: *ref,* 2285
Hershey, H.: *ref,* 1383
Herskovitz, F. S.: *ref,* 1415
Hertel, C. G.: *ref,* 981
Hertel, J. P.: *ref,* 419, 4:370(4), 6:870(1)
Hertel, R. K.: *ref,* 533
Hertz, H.: *ref,* 1499
Hertz, M. R.: *ref,* 1499
Hertzberg, O. E.: *ref,* 507, 525, 2:1243(6)
Hertzig, M. E.: *ref,* 525, 533
Hertzka, A. F.: *test,* 561q2, 1761
Hertzman, M.: *exc,* 1499; *ref,* 1169, 1481, 1499, 1519
Herz, A. J.: *ref,* 1121
Herz, M. I.: *ref,* 1339–40, 5:123 (8)
Herzberg, B.: *ref,* 1275
Herzberg, B. N.: *ref,* 1174
Herzberg, F.: *ref,* 1087, 1207, 2195
Herzberg, F. I.: *ref,* 1281, 1499
Herzberg, I.: *ref,* 1499
Herzig, S. A.: *test,* 2216; *ref,* 2216
Hesbacher, P.: *ref,* 1377
Hesch, G. P.: *ref,* 1207, 2212
Heseltine, G. F.: *ref,* 1218, 1275
Heseltine, G. F. D.: *ref,* 1185, 1225, 1281
Heskett, S. L.: *ref,* 1133
Heskin, K. J.: *ref,* 1275
Hesler, A. P.: *ref,* 6:159(39)
Heslet, F. E.: *ref,* 1174
Heslin, P.: *ref,* 2386
Heslin, R. E.: *ref,* 1121, 1521
Heslop, J. R.: *ref,* 1140
Hespelt, E. H.: *test,* 35:473, 2:1373, 4:245
Hespelt, M. V.: *test,* 4:245; *ref,* 4:245(6)
Hess, A. H.: *test,* 2:1508
Hess, A. L.: *ref,* 1094
Hess, A. W.: *ref,* 2186
Hess, D. W.: *ref,* 1482
Hess, M.: *ref,* 1915
Hess, R. D.: *ref,* 5:326(3)
Hess, T.: *ref,* 1123
Hesse, K. A.: *test,* 625
Hessel, M. G.: *ref,* 1499
Hessemer, M.: *ref,* 1087
Hester, E. J.: *ref,* 2448
Hester, R.: *ref,* 2195
Heston, J. C.: *test,* 6:113; *ref,* 48, 69, 419, 518, 525, 1053, 1281, 2195, 2212, 4:5(2), 4:11(1), 4:50(1), 4:277(179, 188), P:363 (17)
Heston, L. L.: *ref,* 1281
Hetherington, E. L.: *ref,* 1151, 1383
Hetherington, E. M.: *ref,* 1121, 1164, 1281
Hetherington, M.: *ref,* 1164

Hinds, E.: *ref,* 1101, 1499–500, 1519, 2212
Hindsman, E.: *ref,* 349, 542, 551, 997, 1069, 1253, 1772
Hine, W. D.: *ref,* 533, 1112
Hine, W. W.: *ref,* 589
Hinely, R. T.: *ref,* 868, 1164
Hiner, D. L.: *ref,* 1281
Hiner, E. S.: *ref,* 1394–5, 1403
Hinerman, C. O.: *ref,* 1794
Hines, A. C.: *ref,* 688
Hines, D. A.: *ref,* 1923
Hines, H. C.: *ref,* 2:1424(4)
Hines, M.: *ref,* 2228
Hines, M. P.: *ref,* 1194, 1500
Hines, T. F.: *ref,* 1164, 1500
Hines, V. A.: *ref,* 1205
Hinkel, H.: *ref,* 1281, 1342
Hinkelman, E. A.: *ref,* 398, 840, 1123
Hinkle, J. E.: *ref,* 1500
Hinkson, J.: *ref,* 1240
Hinman, E. F.: *ref,* 1383
Hinman, M. E. H.: *ref,* 525
Hinman, S. L.: *ref,* 426, 1320, 2212, 2239, 2273
Hinrichs, J. R.: *ref,* 359, 361, 1194, 1403, 2454
Hinrichs, W. E.: *ref,* 381
Hinshaw, A. L.: *test,* T:1088
Hinson, R. G.: *ref,* 1499
Hinton, B. L.: *ref,* 542, 551, 564, 1207, 1281, 2212, 2325
Hinton, E. A.: *ref,* 1626
Hinton, G. G.: *ref,* 50, 516, 533
Hinton, J.: *ref,* 1275
Hinton, M. A.: *ref,* 1280
Hinton, M. E.: *ref,* 1123
Hinton, N. H.: *test,* 2:1264
Hinton, R. T.: *ref,* 483, 525
Hinton, T. E.: *ref,* 207
Hinz, S. M.: *test,* 2:1357
Hinzman, J. L.: *ref,* 1281
Hippe, D. L.: *ref,* 364, 574
Hipple, J. L.: *ref,* 1145, 1176
Hipskind, M. J. F.: *ref,* 859
Hipwood, S. J.: *ref,* 1121
Hire, A. W.: *ref,* 1499, 1519
Hirning, L. C.: *ref,* 1499
Hirsch, E. A.: *ref,* 532–3, 1447, 1451, 1481, 1499, 1519
Hirsch, I.: *ref,* 1281
Hirsch, I. J.: *ref,* 2031
Hirsch, J.: *ref,* 381, 1499
Hirsch, M. J.: *ref,* 349, 525, 1207, 1918
Hirsch, M. W.: *ref,* 2266
Hirsch, N. D. M.: *ref,* 435, 3:255 (2)
Hirsch, S.: *ref,* 1481, 1499
Hirsch, S. R.: *ref,* 1499
Hirschenfang, S.: *ref,* 381, 489, 525, 529, 1447, 1474, 1499, 1501
Hirschhorn, B.: *ref,* 2234
Hirschman, W.: *ref,* 1174
Hirschstein, R.: *ref,* 1499
Hirsh, E.: *ref,* 1370
Hirshoren, A.: *ref,* 525, 981
Hirst, L. S.: *ref,* 533
Hirst, W. E.: *ref,* 1703, 1716
Hirt, M.: *ref,* 1073, 1196, 1281, 1383, 1448, 1471, 1499, 2195
Hirt, M. L.: *ref,* 529, 532, 1073, 1121, 1196

Hirt, Z. I.: *ref,* 525
Hiscox, E. A. W.: *ref,* 1394
Hiskey, M. S.: *rev,* 489, 498, 1117; *test,* 499; *ref,* 499, 525
Hispanicus, P.: *ref,* 1281
Hitch, K. S.: *ref,* 1499
Hitchcock, C. S.: *test,* 3:561
Hitchman, I.: *ref,* 1481
Hite, L.: *ref,* 533
Hitti, F. J.: *ref,* 19
Hittinger, J.: *ref,* 525, 532, 3:217 (98)
Hittleman, D. R.: *ref,* 1686
Hittler, G. M.: *ref,* 786
Hittson, R. J.: *ref,* 1253
Hitz, J. B.: *ref,* 1918
Hjelle, L. A.: *ref,* 1121, 1164, 1302
Hjelmhaug, N. N.: *ref,* 1775
Hlavaty, J. H.: *test,* 679, 757, 759, 764
Ho, D.: *ref,* 496, 525
Ho, M. K.: *ref,* 1772
Ho, W. C.: *test,* 225
Hoag, A.: *test,* 4:539
Hoag, R. L.: *ref,* 1900, 2234
Hoagland, R. M.: *ref,* 884
Hoakley, Z. P.: *ref,* 483, 525
Hoard, J.: *rev,* 104, 2:1285
Hobbs, D. J.: *ref,* 1073
Hobbs, G. E.: *ref,* 532
Hobbs, G. W.: *ref,* 838, 1415
Hobbs, P. J.: *ref,* 2451
Hobby, A. K.: *ref,* 1121
Hobson, J. R.: *rev,* 1087, 1536, 1567, 1587, 1599, 1603, 1641, 1711, 2:1539, 2:1567, 3:501; *ref,* 1087
Hobson, R. L.: *test,* 1349, 4:800; *ref,* 1349
Hobson, S.: *ref,* 1254, 1500
Hoch, P.: *ref,* 525
Hoch, P. H.: *ref,* 1474, 1499
Hoch, P. M.: *ref,* 532
Hochberg, A. C.: *ref,* 1192, 1302
Hochman, L.: *ref,* 1383
Hochman, S. H.: *ref,* 559, 561, 1418
Hocker, M. E. M.: *ref,* 1447
Hockett, H. D.: *ref,* 1519
Hockey, S. W.: *ref,* 409, 1113
Hocking, E.: *rev,* 251, 3:199, 4:238
Hoddick, N. A.: *ref,* 1164
Hodge, J. R.: *ref,* 1470, 1499
Hodge, S. E.: *ref,* 2212
Hodges, J. D.: *ref,* 603, 1536
Hodges, J. M.: *ref,* 1069, 1087
Hodges, L. R.: *ref,* 1133
Hodges, W. F.: *ref,* 529, 1293, 1391
Hodgins, A. S.: *ref,* 516, 525, 981
Hodgson, E. W.: *ref,* 1094, 1273
Hodgson, G. L.: *ref,* 532
Hodgson, J.: *ref,* 655
Hodgson, R. W.: *ref,* 482, 1205, 1245, 2239
Hoedt, K. C.: *ref,* 1176
Hoefer, C. F.: *ref,* 36, 507, 525
Hoeflin, R.: *test,* 6:225; *ref,* 6:225(1)
Hoeflin, R. M.: *ref,* 1164
Hoehn, A. J.: *ref,* 1039, 1499
Hoehn, J. G.: *ref,* 1303, 1415
Hoekstra, C. S.: *ref,* 1499
Hoeltzel, P. R.: *ref,* 4:45(5, 7)

Hoene, E.: *ref,* 1281
Hoening, J.: *ref,* 1232
Hoepfner, R.: *test,* 147, 182, 184, 567–8, 579, 583, 586, 1239; *exc,* 589; *ref,* 19, 349, 457, 542, 546, 551, 561, 572, 577, 579, 581, 591, 1069, 1421
Hoepner, B. J.: *ref,* 1164, 1383
Hoerl, J. B.: *ref,* 1281
Hoerres, M. A.: *ref,* 5:308(354)
Hoey, H. P.: *ref,* 1281
Hoff, A. L.: *ref,* 1034, 1073
Hoffberg, C.: *ref,* 1519
Hoffeditz, E. L.: *ref,* 398, 503, 1320
Hoffer, A.: *test,* 1215; *ref,* 1215
Hoffer, B. D.: *ref,* 1499
Hoffman, B.: *ref,* 1275
Hoffman, C. B.: *ref,* 349, 525
Hoffman, E. G.: *ref,* 2212
Hoffman, E. L.: *ref,* 1281, 1499, 2212, 2355
Hoffman, H.: *ref,* 1380
Hoffman, H. E.: *ref,* 1094, 1227
Hoffman, H. J.: *ref,* 1281
Hoffman, J.: *ref,* 1164, 1176, 1383
Hoffman, J. L.: *ref,* 1275
Hoffman, L. R.: *ref,* 1207
Hoffman, M.: *ref,* 532
Hoffman, M. F. J.: *ref,* 1095
Hoffman, M. L.: *ref,* 1320, 1519
Hoffman, M. N. H.: *test,* 35:227; *ref,* 35:227(1)
Hoffman, N.: *ref,* 1447
Hoffman, P. J.: *ref,* 364, 1071, 1183, 1281, 1437, 2266
Hoffman, S.: *ref,* 1164, 2227, 2231, 2234
Hoffman, S. D.: *ref,* 1447
Hoffmann, H.: *ref,* 1164, 1281, 1322
Hoffmeister, J. K.: *test,* 855, 858, 887, 1142, 1374; *ref,* 589, 1142, 1521
Hofforth, R. A.: *ref,* 339
Hofland, D. M.: *ref,* 1044, 1303
Hofman, K.: *ref,* 1499
Hofmann, H.: *ref,* 1696
Hofmann, L. J.: *ref,* 533, 1164
Hofmann, R. J.: *ref,* 1407
Hofmeister, A.: *ref,* 50, 525, 981, 1697, 1895
Hofstaetter, P. R.: *ref,* 391, 1087, 1123, 1423
Hogadone, E.: *ref,* 4:784(2)
Hogan, E. E.: *ref,* 1164
Hogan, H. P.: *ref,* 503, 525
Hogan, I.: *test,* 5:584
Hogan, J.: *ref,* 1281, 2212
Hogan, M. J.: *ref,* 1275
Hogan, R.: *rev,* 1403, 7:69; *ref,* 1121, 1253, 1275, 1281, 1294, 1403
Hogan, R. A.: *ref,* 868, 1164, 1281, 1403
Hogan, T. P.: *ref,* 496, 529, 1240
Hogan, V.: *ref,* 1448
Hogarty, G. E.: *test,* 1161; *ref,* 1161, 1255, 1278
Hogben, D.: *ref,* 323, 1583
Hogg, M. I.: *ref,* 2212
Hoggart, K.: *ref,* 518, 529, 1499
Hoggatt, W. E.: *test,* 36:515
Hoghughi, M. S.: *ref,* 1252, 1296
Hogue, J. P.: *ref,* 1164, 1207, 1519
Hogue, R. J.: *test,* 1:1124

Hoops, H. R.: *ref*, 490, 981
Hoover, B.: *ref*, 1207, 1395, 1772
Hoover, C. R.: *test*, 1:933
Hoover, E. B.: *ref*, 1281
Hoover, H. D.: *test*, 639; *ref*, 19
Hoover, H. M. P.: *ref*, 1044, 1315
Hoover, K. H.: *ref*, 2195
Hoover, M.: *ref*, 357
Hoover, N. K.: *test*, 7:1038
Hoover, T. O.: *ref*, 1499
Hope, A. G.: *ref*, 1294
Hope, K.: *test*, 1218, 1224, 1410;
　ref, 1105, 1198, 1218, 1224, 1275,
　1281, 1302, 1410
Hope, L. H.: *ref*, 357
Hopen, H. M.: *ref*, 731
Hopewell, E.: *ref*, 1281, 1499, 1519
Hopka, E.: *ref*, 349
Hopkins, B.: *ref*, 403, 439, 532, 1192
Hopkins, B. R.: *exc*, 656
Hopkins, C. R.: *ref*, 1968
Hopkins, G. W.: *ref*, 1281
Hopkins, J.: *ref*, 1486
Hopkins, J. H.: *ref*, 1383, 1499
Hopkins, J. J.: *ref*, 4:825(19)
Hopkins, K. D.: *rev*, 15, 465, 1552;
　exc, 360; *ref*, 7, 19-20, 29, 35,
　50, 348-9, 361, 391, 400, 533, 603,
　731, 1567, 1679, 1711
Hopkins, N. R.: *ref*, 1281
Hopkins, R. F.: *ref*, 1246
Hopkins, R. W.: *ref*, 1281
Hopkins, T. R.: *ref*, 1169, 1225,
　1275, 1281, 1293, 1403, 1471, 1519
Hopkinson, D. D.: *ref*, 1212
Hopkinson, N. T.: *ref*, 2038
Hopper, C. L.: *ref*, 529, 1281, 2076
Hopper, G. C.: *ref*, 1133
Hopper, H. E.: *ref*, 1281
Hoppock, M. E.: *test*, 2:1650
Hoppock, R.: *test*, 2:1649, 3:693;
　ref, 36:868(1), 3:693(1)
Horan, K.: *ref*, 1629, 1702, 1733,
　1918, 3:515(2)
Horchow, R.: *ref*, 2:1492(7)
Hord, C. L.: *ref*, 2057
Hore, B. D.: *ref*, 1275
Horgan, C. M.: *ref*, 1123
Horgan, J. F.: *ref*, 1281, 1403
Horine, I.: *ref*, 1383
Horiuchi, H.: *ref*, 1499
Horlick, R. S.: *ref*, 532, 1123, 1281,
　1380, 1499
Horn, B. J.: *ref*, 1302
Horn, C. C.: *test*, 186; *ref*, 186
Horn, D.: *test*, 1522; *ref*, 2212
Horn, D. M.: *ref*, 1422
Horn, E.: *test*, 4:15, 4:150, 4:408,
　4:554, 4:588; *ref*, 1572, 2:1271
　(2-3)
Horn, F. M.: *ref*, 1069, 2268
Horn, G.: *test*, 100-1
Horn, J.: *ref*, 1291, 1383
Horn, J. B.: *ref*, 1164
Horn, J. F. H.: *ref*, 1194
Horn, J. L.: *rev*, 518; *test*, 1291;
　exc, 450, 2107; *ref*, 364, 868, 1281,
　1300, 1480, 1499
Horn, R. M.: *ref*, 1164
Horn, T. D.: *rev*, 156, 160
Horn, W. A.: *ref*, 981, 1629
Horn, W. O.: *test*, 1076
Hornaday, J. A.: *ref*, 69, 357, 361,
　1164, 1407, 2194-5

Horne, A. M.: *ref*, 1225
Horne, B. M.: *ref*, 525, 529
Horne, B. N.: *ref*, 3:61(6)
Horne, D.: *ref*, 1921
Horne, D. J. D.: *ref*, 1174
Horne, D. L.: *ref*, 1289
Horne, E. P.: *ref*, 1923, 5:147(45),
　6:228(66-7)
Horne, I. E.: *ref*, 495, 1447
Horne, R. R. C.: *test*, 1065
Horner, A. J.: *ref*, 1281, 1499
Horner, G. C.: *ref*, 1281
Horner, J. T.: *test*, 768
Horner, R. D.: *ref*, 981
Horney, A. G.: *test*, 1:933
Horning, S. D.: *ref*, 2251
Hornung, P. E.: *ref*, 1121, 2213
Hornyak, D. J.: *ref*, 1844
Horobin, G.: *ref*, 95, 373, 408-9,
　722
Horowitz, F. D.: *ref*, 529, 532-3
Horowitz, H.: *ref*, 1058, 1471
Horowitz, I. A.: *ref*, 1419
Horowitz, J. Z.: *ref*, 1228, 1383
Horowitz, M. J.: *ref*, 1499
Horrall, B. M.: *ref*, 1090, 1289,
　1499, 1519, 4:277(208)
Horrocks, C.: *ref*, 589, 1109, 1123
Horrocks, J. E.: *rev*, 467, 5:83, 6:
　495; *test*, T:1180; *ref*, 868, 1519,
　3:406(1-3), P:390(22)
Horrocks, W. B.: *test*, T:1180
Horsch, A. C.: *ref*, 1320
Horsley, J. A.: *ref*, 1428
Horsman, V. G.: *ref*, 2212
Horst, P.: *ref*, 592, 1087, 1164, 1418
Horton, C. P.: *ref*, 357, 382, 507
Horton, C. W.: *rev*, 1800, 1805,
　1810-2, 2:1586, 2:1589, 3:550, 3:
　552-4, 4:606; *test*, 1:908
Horton, D. L.: *ref*, 221, 1480
Horton, K. B.: *ref*, 525
Horton, M.: *ref*, 1281
Horton, S. P.: *ref*, 447, 2:1325(13)
Horvat, G. L.: *ref*, 1383, 1430
Horvath, W. J.: *ref*, 1480
Horwitz, M.: *ref*, 439, 529, 532,
　2234
Hosford, P. M.: *ref*, 1513, 2195, 6:
　113(21)
Hosford, R. E.: *ref*, 1073
Hoshaw, L. D.: *test*, 4:461; *ref*,
　881, 1348
Hosic, J. F.: *ref*, 4:179(1)
Hosinski, M.: *ref*, 1383
Hoskins, J. E.: *ref*, 482, 1281
Hoskins, T.: *test*, 137
Hosler, R. J.: *ref*, 798, 3:372(1),
　3:392(4)
Hostetler, D. K.: *ref*, 1407
Hotchkiss, S. M.: *ref*, 1253, 2195
Hottel, J. V.: *ref*, 516
Houchins, R. R.: *ref*, 439
Houck, R. L.: *ref*, 1174
Houk, C. C.: *ref*, 69, 419
Houk, T. W.: *ref*, 1281
Houlahan, F. J.: *exc*, 1515
Houlihan, M. B.: *ref*, 1123
Houlihan, R. A. M.: *ref*, 525
Hountras, P. T.: *ref*, 404, 1044,
　1073, 1121, 1281
House, B.: *ref*, 529
House, B. J.: *ref*, 525
House, F. R.: *ref*, 525

House, H. P.: *test*, 2027
House, R. J.: *ref*, 2451
Houser, J. D.: *ref*, 525
Houser, R. L.: *ref*, 868, 1207
Housley, W. F.: *ref*, 2201
Houston, B. K.: *ref*, 1169, 1281,
　1293
Houston, C.: *ref*, 522, 524, 533
Houston, D. E.: *ref*, 884
Houston, H. S.: *ref*, 1182, 1247
Houston, J. P.: *ref*, 574
Houston, L. N.: *ref*, 2205
Houston, S. R.: *ref*, 49, 382, 863
Houston, T. J.: *ref*, 1320, 5:76(14)
Houston, V. M.: *ref*, 1289
Houtchens, H. M.: *ref*, 1095, 1222,
　1480
Houts, D. C.: *ref*, 1028, 1281
Houts, P. S.: *ref*, 1121, 1176, 1214
Houtz, S. J.: *ref*, 2251
Houwink, R.: *test*, 6:213
Hover, G. L.: *ref*, 532, 1281
Hovey, H. B.: *test*, 1375; *ref*, 532,
　1277, 1281, 1375
Hovey, N. W.: *test*, 1847; *ref*,
　1818, 1847
Hovland, C. I.: *rev*, 382, 404, 1775,
　3:218, 3:263; *ref*, 426, 482, 6:
　1115(2)
Hovosel, M.: *ref*, 1145
Howald, B. L.: *ref*, 1519
Howard, A. R.: *ref*, 592, 1277
Howard, D. P.: *ref*, 1360
Howard, D. S.: *ref*, 1423
Howard, E.: *ref*, 1383
Howard, E. A.: *ref*, 914
Howard, F. M.: *ref*, 1281
Howard, G.: *test*, 1319; *ref*, 1475
Howard, G. H.: *ref*, 1499
Howard, J.: *ref*, 1447
Howard, J. L.: *ref*, 516-7, 525
Howard, J. M.: *ref*, 2451
Howard, J. O.: *ref*, 499, 525
Howard, J. S.: *ref*, 382
Howard, J. T.: *ref*, 2251
Howard, J. W.: *test*, 1473; *ref*,
　1473
Howard, K.: *ref*, 1164
Howard, K. G.: *ref*, 1519
Howard, K. I.: *ref*, 1228, 1281,
　1383, 1499, 1519
Howard, L.: *ref*, 525
Howard, L. A.: *ref*, 1106
Howard, L. H.: *ref*, 1164, 1403, 2212
Howard, L. L.: *ref*, 1133
Howard, M. J.: *ref*, 490, 981
Howard, M. L.: *ref*, 1164, 1207,
　1403
Howard, M. T.: *ref*, 518, 529, 578,
　592, 1277, 1281
Howard, R. W.: *rev*, 66, 2:1278
Howard, S. J.: *ref*, 1281, 1481,
　1499, 1519
Howard, T. W.: *ref*, 1499
Howard, V. M.: *ref*, 211
Howard, W.: *ref*, 529, 532
Howard, W. H. R.: *ref*, 497
Howard, W. T.: *ref*, 869
Howarth, E.: *ref*, 1129, 1174, 1275,
　1294, 1383
Howden, J. R.: *ref*, 1302
Howe, M. E.: *test*, T:1189
Howell, A. A.: *ref*, 525
Howell, E. N.: *test*, 750

Howell, I. L.: *ref,* 532, 545, 1192, 1380, 1499
Howell, J. J.: *ref,* 36, 357
Howell, J. O.: *ref,* 1044
Howell, L. M.: *ref,* 1164
Howell, M. A.: *ref,* 1073, 1094, 1109, 1121, 1194, 1281, 1403, 1407, 1437, 2355, 7:1090(7)
Howell, M. C.: *ref,* 1519
Howell, M. L.: *ref,* 936
Howell, R. J.: *ref,* 440, 529, 532, 1281, 1389, 1499
Howell, R. W.: *ref,* 533, 1279
Howell, W. J.: *ref,* 357
Howell, W. S.: *ref,* 1775
Howells, J. G.: *test,* 1459; *ref,* 1459
Howie, D.: *rev,* 324, 1761; *ref,* 328
Howie, M. M.: *ref,* 1499
Howitt, C.: *test,* 5:13
Howland, R. H.: *ref,* 2212
Howlett, J. L.: *ref,* 357, 1044, 1583, 7:670(24)
Hoy, P.: *ref,* 1121, 1281
Hoy, R. M.: *ref,* 1383
Hoy, W. K.: *ref,* 1121
Hoye, M. M.: *rev,* 3:343, 3:345
Hoyt, C. J.: *rev,* 31, 419, 646, 681, 684, 688-9, 4:422-3, 4:433; *test,* 1574, 1647; *ref,* 868
Hoyt, D.: *ref,* 1281
Hoyt, D. B.: *ref,* 1475
Hoyt, D. P.: *test,* 1236; *ref,* 357, 419, 1044, 1164, 1281, 2212-3, 5:308(356), 6:438(478)
Hoyt, K. B.: *rev,* 2182, 2185; *test,* 57, 974, 2105, 2270; *ref,* 1034, 1073
Hoyt, M. F.: *ref,* 1164
Hoyt, R. L.: *ref,* 1121, 1256
Hoyt, T. E.: *ref,* 1469, 1481
Hoyt, W. G.: *ref,* 6:669(53)
Hoyum, V. D.: *test,* 85, 5:196
Hozier, A.: *ref,* 381, 1474, 1482
Hrapchak, W. J.: *ref,* 2451
Hrdlicka, A.: *exc,* 497
Hritzuk, J.: *ref,* 1174
Hrychuk, W.: *ref,* 1232, 1346
Hsiao, H. H.: *ref,* 525, 1932, 3:220(45)
Hsiao, S.: *ref,* 1499
Hsiao, S. L.: *ref,* 447
Hsien, R.: *ref,* 1499
Hsu, C.: *ref,* 1499
Hsu, E. H.: *ref,* 1499, 2:1243(20), 6:159(66)
Hsu, F.: *ref,* 1499
Hsu, F. L. K.: *ref,* 1499
Huang, D. D.: *ref,* 840, 1403, 2170
Huang, S. C.: *ref,* 1164, 1403
Hubbard, B. L.: *ref,* 1162
Hubbard, L. M.: *ref,* 1480
Hubbard, O. S.: *ref,* 525
Hubbell, M. B.: *ref,* 1403
Hubele, G. E.: *ref,* 1383
Huber, J. T.: *ref,* 382, 1005
Huber, N. A.: *ref,* 2110
Huber, T. G.: *ref,* 543
Huber, W.: *ref,* 1481
Huber, W. G.: *ref,* 1123
Huber, W. K.: *ref,* 1298
Huberman, J.: *ref,* 1470, 1499
Hubert, W. J.: *ref,* 1207
Huberty, C. J.: *rev,* 635, 659
Hubertz, L.: *test,* 1:1029

Hubschman, E.: *ref,* 516, 981
Huck, C. S.: *ref,* 7, 400, 1123
Huck, F. T.: *ref,* 2337
Huckabee, M. W.: *ref,* 69, 559, 561, 1044, 1164, 1169, 1314, 1383, 1403, 1772, 2195
Huddleston, E.: *ref,* 1386
Huddleston, E. M.: *rev,* 4:507, 4:678; *ref,* 64
Huddy, J. A.: *ref,* 1073
Hudelson, E.: *test,* 4:179; *ref,* 4:179(1-2)
Hudesman, J.: *ref,* 2212
Hudgins, B. B.: *ref,* 1361
Hudson, A.: *ref,* 1569, 1690
Hudson, D. K.: *ref,* 1069
Hudson, E.: *test,* 36:626
Hudson, F. G.: *ref,* 425, 493, 516, 533
Hudson, H. H.: *ref,* 1087
Hudson, J.: *ref,* 529
Hudson, L.: *ref,* 331
Hudson, M. M. C.: *ref,* 1207, 1403, 1407
Hudson, W.: *ref,* 1508
Hudspeth, M. A. B.: *ref,* 1471
Hueber, J.: *ref,* 1205, 2239, 2263, 2266
Huebert, A.: *test,* 3:164
Huebner, M. H.: *rev,* 1730, 7:746
Huebner, R.: *ref,* 1716
Hueftle, M. K.: *ref,* 533, 981, 1921
Huelsman, C. B.: *test,* 1675; *ref,* 533, 1675, 1918, 1923, 1929, 5:774(7), 5:781(11)
Huesing, R.: *ref,* 381
Huff, B.: *ref,* 349, 361, 652, 1069, 1560
Huff, F. W.: *ref,* 529, 1240, 1281, 1481
Huff, J.: *ref,* 211
Huffer, V.: *ref,* 1281
Huffman, A. V.: *ref,* 1095, 1245
Huffman, E.: *test,* 4:46k
Huffman, E. S.: *ref,* 1348
Huffman, W. J.: *ref,* 1281, 1403, 2195, 5:308(284)
Hug, G. S.: *test,* 1:1145
Huggan, R. E.: *ref,* 1225, 1295
Huggan, R. R.: *ref,* 1275
Huggett, A. J.: *ref,* 1716, 1733, 5:354(6)
Hughes, B. E.: *ref,* 69, 419, 868, 1207
Hughes, D.: *ref,* 529, 1447, 1470, 1474, 1519
Hughes, D. H.: *ref,* 533, 1192
Hughes, D. L.: *ref,* 69, 361
Hughes, H.: *ref,* 1499
Hughes, H. B.: *ref,* 2195
Hughes, H. H.: *ref,* 1069, 1164
Hughes, H. M.: *ref,* 1383, 1430, 2212
Hughes, H. O.: *ref,* 408
Hughes, J. B.: *ref,* 2195
Hughes, J. L.: *test,* 6:1153; *ref,* 1194, 2129, 2151, 2212, 6:1140(1), 6:1153(1)
Hughes, J. M.: *ref,* 426, 1207
Hughes, L. J.: *ref,* 419, 868, 1164, 2213
Hughes, L. S.: *ref,* 381
Hughes, M. L.: *ref,* 1225
Hughes, R. B.: *ref,* 516, 533

Hughes, R. M.: *ref,* 1499
Hughes, T.: *ref,* 1164
Hughes, T. H.: *ref,* 868
Hughes, T. M.: *ref,* 1415
Hughes, V.: *rev,* 2:1300
Hughes, V. A.: *ref,* 533
Hughes, W. G.: *ref,* 1275
Hughes, W. H.: *ref,* 398, 684
Hughley, R. C.: *ref,* 1428
Hugo, J. A.: *ref,* 1281
Hugo, M. J.: *ref,* 1326
Huguelet, P. W.: *ref,* 589
Huisinga, V. N.: *ref,* 1481
Huizinga, R. J.: *ref,* 525, 533, 981, 1499
Hujsa, C.: *ref,* 2251, 2266-7
Hukins, A. A.: *ref,* 1794, 1856
Hulac, G. M.: *ref,* 1094
Hulac, V.: *ref,* 1474
Hulbert, M. B.: *ref,* 211
Hulbert, S.: *ref,* 1923
Hulek, J. E.: *ref,* 1474
Hulicka, I. M.: *ref,* 529, 592
Hulin, C. L.: *ref,* 1091
Hull, A.: *ref,* 255
Hull, J.: *ref,* 1164, 1281, 1423
Hull, J. S.: *ref,* 1240, 2212
Hullett, J.: *ref,* 381
Hulling, R. H.: *ref,* 681
Hulme-Moir, I.: *ref,* 1174
Hulse, J.: *ref,* 1281
Hulse, S. H.: *ref,* 1281
Hulse, W. C.: *ref,* 1474
Hult, E.: *ref,* 69, 391, 1583, 4:6(17)
Hulten, C. E.: *ref,* 1569, 4:179(3-4)
Hultgren, D. D.: *ref,* 1025A, 2212
Hultsch, C. L.: *ref,* 483, 525
Human Engineering Laboratory: *ref,* 211, 1386
Human Sciences Research Council: *test,* 14, 46, 153, 383, 410-1, 511, 642, 712, 724, 1083, 1570, 1600, 2447
Humber, W. J.: *ref,* 69, 1560, 1583, 1768, 4:184(4), 4:216(9)
Humbert, J. T.: *ref,* 2221
Humble, E.: *test,* 2:1458, 4:539
Hume, C. D.: *test,* 4:816
Humes, C. W.: *ref,* 1515, 1519
Humm, D. G.: *rev,* 1090, 1095, 1344, 2:1199; *test,* 1222, 5:931; *ref,* 1222
Humm, K. A.: *test,* 1222, 5:931; *ref,* 483, 1222
Hummel, R.: *ref,* 1207, 1403, 1519, 2212
Hummel, T. J.: *ref,* 36, 1603
Hummers, J. A.: *ref,* 1135
Humphrey, B. M.: *ref,* 1320
Humphrey, E. M.: *ref,* 1320
Humphrey, M.: *ref,* 1289, 1377
Humphreys, J. A.: *ref,* 48
Humphreys, L. G.: *rev,* 404, 1066, 1069, 1073, 1080, 2239, 2244, 2257; *ref,* 364, 525, 1044, 1087, 1253, 1403, 2212
Humphries, C. C.: *ref,* 592
Humphries, G. R.: *test,* 1:1065
Humphries, O.: *ref,* 1281
Hundal, P. S.: *ref,* 364, 439, 1090, 1225, 1275, 1383, 1403

Hundleby, J. D.: *rev*, 442, 1403,
  6:491; *ref*, 1087, 1129, 1253, 1275,
  1281, 1300, 1367, 1383, P:344(17)
Hundleby, J. H.: *ref*, 1383
Hundley, J. W.: *ref*, 1499
Hundrichs, W. A.: *ref*, 1281, 1499
Hundziak, M.: *ref*, 981, 1232
Huneryager, S. G.: *ref*, 1176, 2454
Hung, T. P.: *ref*, 1447
Hungerman, A. D.: *ref*, 603, 7:463
  (1)
Hungerman, J. M.: *ref*, 1302
Hunka, S.: *rev*, 6:337, 6:1032; *ref*,
  561, 2355
Hunkin, V.: *ref*, 381
Hunley, P. J.: *ref*, 1094, 1281
Hunsicker, A. L.: *rev*, 1098, 1271
Hunsicker, L.: *ref*, 2:1377(14)
Hunsicker, P.: *ref*, 914
Hunsicker, P. A.: *ref*, 914
Hunsucker, F.: *test*, 4:704
Hunt, B.: *ref*, 381
Hunt, B. M.: *ref*, 505, 525
Hunt, D.: *ref*, 525, 533
Hunt, D. H.: *ref*, 1194
Hunt, E. H.: *ref*, 1968
Hunt, E. J.: *ref*, 1775
Hunt, E. L.: *ref*, 1281
Hunt, E. P.: *rev*, 2:1400, 2:1410;
  exc, 483
Hunt, F. D.: *ref*, 1281, 1320
Hunt, H. F.: *test*, 1223; *ref*, 1105,
  1223, 1277, 1281, 1380, 1448
Hunt, J. E.: *ref*, 2451
Hunt, J. G.: *ref*, 1121
Hunt, J. M.: *ref*, 1281, 1383, 1499
Hunt, J. T.: *ref*, 1583
Hunt, J. V.: *rev*, 523–4; *ref*, 484
Hunt, J. W.: *ref*, 1474
Hunt, K.: *test*, 4:15
Hunt, M. B.: *ref*, 1281
Hunt, N. J.: *ref*, 1133
Hunt, R. A.: *ref*, 1403
Hunt, R. G.: *ref*, 1187, 1281, 1481,
  1519
Hunt, T.: *rev*, 2129, 2135; *test*, 904,
  1386, 2381, 2413, 3:179, 3:400;
  ref, 211, 904, 1386, 1499
Hunt, W.: *ref*, 482, 1069, 1380,
  2212, 2239, 2268
Hunt, W. A.: *rev*, 1380; *ref*, 503,
  525, 529, 532, 1275, 1281, 1499
Hunt, W. L.: *ref*, 532
Hunt, W. O.: *ref*, 1394–5
Hunter, A. D.: *ref*, 1320
Hunter, C.: *exc*, 381
Hunter, D.: *ref*, 529
Hunter, E. C.: *test*, 2:1260; *ref*,
  869, 1123, 3:217(102), P:394(1–
  2)
Hunter, E. J.: *ref*, 533
Hunter, G. W.: *rev*, 1785, 1:907,
  1:910, 2:1601, 2:1603
Hunter, H.: *ref*, 518, 529, 1499
Hunter, H. T.: *ref*, 3:220(4)
Hunter, J. W.: *ref*, 3:10(2)
Hunter, K. J.: *ref*, 1121
Hunter, M.: *ref*, 505, 518, 525, 533,
  1428, 1499
Hunter, M. C.: *ref*, 1447
Hunter, N. W.: *ref*, 1069, 1073,
  1775
Hunter, R. C. A.: *ref*, 529, 2355
Hunter, T. A.: *ref*, 426

Hunter, W. A.: *ref*, 1281
Hunting, R. S.: *test*, 7:199
Huntington, D. A.: *ref*, 2031
Huntley, C. W.: *ref*, 1403
Huntley, J. R.: *ref*, 1174
Huntley, R. M. C.: *ref*, 525, 1428,
  2025
Huntress, D. W.: *ref*, 533
Hurd, A. W.: *rev*, 1:1088, 1:1091;
  test, 2:1611; *ref*, 425–6, 1095,
  2355
Hurd, D. E.: *ref*, 1135, 1315
Hurley, J. D.: *ref*, 589, 1109
Hurley, J. R.: *ref*, 349, 1123, 1164,
  1516, 1519
Hurley, M. E.: *ref*, 1447
Hurley, O. L.: *ref*, 981
Hurley, R. B.: *ref*, 2221
Hurst, J. C.: *test*, 857; *ref*, 857
Hurst, J. F.: *ref*, 1519
Hurst, J. G.: *ref*, 419, 507, 525, 868,
  1428, 1895
Hurst, M. E.: *test*, 35:389
Hurster, M.: *ref*, 947
Hurt, M.: *ref*, 22, 1716
Hurt, R. W.: *ref*, 349
Hurvich, M. S.: *test*, 1451; *ref*,
  1451
Hurvitz, N.: *test*, 825; *ref*, 825
Hurwitz, H. L.: *ref*, 357
Hurwitz, I.: *ref*, 1499
Hurwitz, J. I.: *ref*, P:446(28)
Husain, M. Q.: *ref*, 1095
Husband, R. W.: *ref*, 6:159(31)
Husek, E.: *test*, 5:90
Husek, T. R.: *exc*, 2193; *ref*, 1183,
  1207, 1383, 1423
Husemoller, K. E.: *ref*, 20, 69, 361,
  1207
Huset, M. K.: *ref*, 1674
Huskey, J. F.: *ref*, 426
Husman, B. F.: *ref*, 1500, 1519
Husted, D.: *ref*, 4:95(19)
Husted, G. P.: *ref*, 1519
Husted, J.: *ref*, 487
Hustmyer, F. E.: *ref*, 529, 1169
Huston, B. M.: *ref*, 425, 1044, 1289,
  2195
Huston, P. E.: *ref*, 1499
Hutchcraft, G.: *ref*, 357, 607
Hutchens, W. H.: *ref*, 503
Hutcheon, J. F.: *ref*, 1087
Hutcheon, N. B.: *ref*, 1320, 2214,
  2242, 2247, 2:1683(4), 4:277
  (154)
Hutcherson, D.: *ref*, 20, 1176
Hutcherson, D. E.: *ref*, 1176
Hutchings, E. M. J.: *test*, 1548
Hutchings, M.: *ref*, 3:242(2)
Hutchings, M. J.: *test*, 1548
Hutchins, B. E.: *ref*, 361, 439
Hutchins, E. B.: *ref*, 1164, 1395,
  1403, 2212, 2355
Hutchins, H. C.: *ref*, 357–8, 1044,
  1583
Hutchinson, B. B.: *ref*, 2028
Hutchinson, D.: *exc*, 1:983
Hutchinson, J.: *ref*, 1377
Hutchinson, J. C.: *ref*, 2213
Hutchinson, M. E.: *test*, 2:1367;
  ref, 2:1367(1)
Hutchison, M. H.: *test*, 5:188
Hutchison, R. S.: *ref*, 1164, 1403
Huth, R. W.: *ref*, 496

Hutslar, J. L.: *ref*, 1164, 1207, 1383
Hutson, B. T.: *ref*, 425, 2199
Hutson, K.: *ref*, 2057
Hutson, P. W.: *ref*, P:200(3)
Hutt, M. L.: *test*, 1447c, 5:102, 5:
  150; *exc*, 1451, 1519; *ref*, 525,
  545, 1447, 1499, 1519, 5:150(1–2,
  4), P:455(8)
Hutt, S. J.: *ref*, 1174, 1275
Hutter, A.: *ref*, 1474
Hutter, J. I.: *ref*, 1164
Huttner, L.: *test*, T:2093; *ref*, 482,
  1087, 2212
Hutton, C.: *ref*, 2031
Hutton, D. C.: *ref*, 1469, 1499
Hutton, D. E.: *ref*, 2451
Hutton, E. L.: *ref*, 1499, 1519
Hutton, G. H.: *ref*, 529
Hutton, J. B.: *ref*, 524–5, 533, 1225,
  1447, 1730–1
Hutton, J. G.: *ref*, 2337, 2355
Hutton, R. D.: *ref*, 543, 1437, 1478
Hutton, W. O.: *ref*, 981
Huysamen, G. K.: *ref*, 381
Huyser, B. H.: *ref*, 199
Huzioka, Y.: *ref*, 1499
Hvistendahl, J. K.: *ref*, 6:438(448)
Hwang, C.: *ref*, 1164
Hwang, C. H.: *ref*, 439, 1500
Hwang, K. Y.: *ref*, 238
Hyatt, I.: *ref*, 1515
Hyble, A. R.: *ref*, 1500
Hyde, G. G.: *ref*, 1121
Hyde, J. C.: *ref*, 1281
Hyde, M. R.: *ref*, 516
Hying, J. A.: *ref*, 1159
Hylan, N. W.: *ref*, 426
Hylbert, K. W.: *ref*, 342, 1281
Hyman, B.: *ref*, 2195, P:341(32)
Hyman, I.: *ref*, 538, 578, 1447, 1921,
  2028
Hyman, J. R.: *ref*, 489
Hyman, M.: *ref*, 1225, 1281
Hyman, S. R.: *ref*, 404, 1583

IACONO, C.: *ref*, 1281
Iacono, J. M.: *ref*, 1195
Iannaccone, L.: *ref*, 868, 1383, 2212
Iannotti, M. M.: *ref*, 1383, 1395
Iazetta, V.: *ref*, 1519
Ibeling, F. W.: *test*, 6:756
Ibrahim, H.: *ref*, 1121, 1205, 1207
Ibrahim, M. A.: *ref*, 1281
Ichikawa, H.: *ref*, 1932
Ichimura, J.: *ref*, 1499
Ichimura, K.: *ref*, 1508
Ichitani, T.: *ref*, 1500
Iglinsky, C. L.: *ref*, 1242, 1415
Ignatieff, E.: *ref*, 300
Ignatovich, F. R.: *ref*, 2452
Ihilevich, D.: *test*, 1152; *ref*, 1152,
  1169, 1281
Ihinger, R. F.: *ref*, 7
Ihlanfeldt, W. I.: *ref*, 357, 1121,
  1135
Ikeda, M.: *ref*, 981
Ikenberry, S. O.: *ref*, 358
Iker, H.: *ref*, 1281
Iker, H. P.: *ref*, 1281
Ilanit, N.: *ref*, 529, 1281, 1380
Ilardi, R. L.: *ref*, 1315, 1403
Ilg, F. L.: *test*, 1703; *ref*, 497, 1499,
  1703, 1724, 6:228(71), P:450
  (79–81, 87–8, 94)

Ilika, J.: *ref,* 1617
Illesley, R.: *ref,* 373, 408–9
Illingworth, R. S.: *ref,* 497
Illinois Council on Economic Education: *test,* 6:988
Ilyus, R. B.: *ref,* 1169
Im, I. J.: *ref,* 405, 1044, 1280–1, 2212
Imber, S. D.: *ref,* 1447
Imboden, J. B.: *ref,* 1145, 1281
Imig, C.: *ref,* 1281
Imig, D. R.: *ref,* 1121
Immergluck, L.: *rev,* 1192; *ref,* 1499
Impellitteri, J. T.: *ref,* 31, 1073
Imre, P.: *ref,* 1496
Imre, P. D.: *ref,* 529, 1496
Imus, H. A.: *rev,* 1906, 1923; *exc,* 1:1108; *ref,* 1560, 1906, 1918, 1923, 2:1559(1)
Inaba, K.: *test,* 6:491
Incardona, J. S.: *ref,* 2451
Indermill, R. R.: *ref,* 1281
Indow, T.: *ref,* 533
Industrial Relations Center: *test,* 414, 472, 547, 594, 1149, 1170, 1333, 1747, 2245, 2255, 2272, 2340, T:2007
Ingebo, G. S.: *ref,* 400
Ingebregtsen, E.: *ref,* 1499
Ingenito, J.: *test,* 1258
Ingenohl, I.: *ref,* 1320
Ingersoll, R. W.: *ref,* 69, 1073, 1302–3, 1775, 2355
Ingham, J. G.: *ref,* 533, 1275, 1499
Ingham, J. M.: *ref,* 1519
Ingham, R. J.: *ref,* 1225
Ingle, D. J.: *ref,* 1320
Ingle, J.: *ref,* 1281
Ingling, J. H.: *ref,* 1447
Inglis, A.: *test,* 5:234, T:1155; *ref,* 3:163(1)
Inglis, J.: *ref,* 496, 529, 532, 1073, 1275, 1447
Inglis, J. D.: *ref,* 868
Inglis, R. B.: *test,* 35:170
Ingmire, B. D.: *ref,* 589
Ingraham, J. E.: *test,* 4:538, 4:541–2
Ingram, G. L.: *ref,* 1164
Ingram, J. A.: *ref,* 69, 361
Ingram, L. M.: *ref,* 419
Ingram, M.: *ref,* 1499
Ingram, O. K.: *ref,* 1281
Ingram, R. T.: *ref,* 1430
Ingram, T. T. S.: *test,* 2070; *ref,* 381, 525
Ingram, W.: *ref,* 1447, 1499
Inman, G. D.: *ref,* 868, 1164
Inoue, A.: *ref,* 1403
Insel, P.: *ref,* 1143
Insel, S. A.: *ref,* 1176, 1294
Inskeep, G. C.: *ref,* 2228
Insko, W. R.: *ref,* 1315
Institut Pedagogique Saint-Georges: *test,* 5:115
Institute for Behavioral Research in Creativity: *test,* 2273
Institutional Research Program for Higher Education: *test,* 867, 894, 1235
Instructional Materials Laboratory, Ohio State University: *test,* 2339, 2420–32, 7:1128

International Business Machines Corporation: *test,* 1032–3, 6:669; *ref,* 2:1492(4)
International Personnel Management Association: *test,* 2137, 2322, 2341, 2362, 2371, 2373–4, 2418, 2475
International Psychological Service Center: *ref,* 504, 1499, 4:339(1)
Iorns, M. E.: *ref,* 1222
Ipson, W. M.: *ref,* 532
Ireland, E. C.: *ref,* 1921
Ireton, H.: *ref,* 381, 484, 525
Ireton, H. R.: *test,* 508
Irish, T. E.: *ref,* 482
Irizarry, R.: *ref,* 1471, 1499, 1519
Irons, J. L.: *ref,* 589
Ironside, W.: *ref,* 1281
Irvin, F. S.: *test,* 1507; *ref,* 1044, 1507, 1519, 2212
Irvine, D. J.: *ref,* 542, 546, 551, 1109
Irvine, D. W.: *ref,* 35, 357
Irvine, F. R.: *ref,* 589, 1069, 2256
Irvine, J.: *ref,* 516, 533, 989, 1921, 2028
Irvine, S. H.: *ref,* 361, 439, 464, 1085
Irving, D. D.: *ref,* 1127, 1474
Irving, G.: *ref,* 403, 439
Irving, R. W.: *ref,* 1516
Irving, S. G.: *ref,* 1281, 1293
Irwin, D. O.: *ref,* 533
Irwin, E. C.: *ref,* 1123
Irwin, I. A.: *ref,* 48, 2199, 2212
Irwin, J. L.: *ref,* 1716
Irwin, J. M.: *ref,* 1095, 1123
Irwin, J. T.: *ref,* 1069
Irwin, O. C.: *test,* 6:311; *exc,* 497; *ref,* 516, 525, 533, 6:311(1–9)
Irwin, R. B.: *test,* 2023; *ref,* 2023
Irwin, T. C.: *ref,* 1448
Irwin, T. J.: *ref,* 2212
Isaac, B. K.: *ref,* 1447
Isaac, D. M.: *ref,* 532
Isaac, S. W.: *ref,* 1294
Isaacs, A.: *ref,* 426
Isaacs, S.: *ref,* 2:1519(1)
Isaacson, L. E.: *ref,* 1073, 1207, 2195, 5:308(298)
Isaacson, R. L.: *ref,* 1383, 1519
Isabelle, L. A.: *ref,* 1094, 1403, 2212, 2214
Isard, E. S.: *ref,* 381, 419, 1356
Isbell, S. R.: *ref,* 211
Isbitz, S. F.: *ref,* 1603
Iscoe, I.: *exc,* 1428; *ref,* 349, 355, 381, 439, 532–3, 542, 1123, 1169, 1256, 1403, 1428, 1499
Isele, F. W.: *ref,* 1281
Isenberger, W.: *ref,* 868, 2213
Isenberger, W. E.: *ref,* 868, 2213
Isham, A. C.: *ref,* 1481, 1499, 1519
Ishihara, S.: *test,* 1932
Ishikawa, A.: *ref,* 1383
Ishikawa, W.: *ref,* 1281
Islam, A F M S: *ref,* 1121
Ismail, A. H.: *ref,* 36, 364, 425, 914, 1129, 6:82(1–2), 6:83(2)
Ismir, A. A.: *ref,* 1121, 1281, 1519
Ison, M. G.: *ref,* 529, 533
Israel, H.: *ref,* 525, 532
Israel, H. M.: *ref,* 1499

Israël, M.: *ref,* 1499
Israelite, J.: *ref,* 381
Issel, R. P.: *ref,* 1094
Ivanoff, J.: *ref,* 524, 529
Ivanoff, J. M.: *ref,* 64, 357, 361, 516, 1094, 1281, 2195, 6:438(494), P:339(20)
Ivers, K. J.: *ref,* 1164, 1430, 2212
Iversen, I.: *ref,* 525, 1702
Iverson, E. W.: *ref,* 7, 36
Iverson, I. A.: *ref,* 533
Iverson, M. A.: *ref,* 1225, P:381(31)
Iverson, N. E.: *ref,* 1519
Ives, K. H.: *ref,* 1320
Ives, L. A.: *ref,* 1921
Ives, M.: *rev,* 1223, 1380; *exc,* 1498
Ives, R. K.: *ref,* 1471
Ives, V.: *ref,* 1499
Ives, V. M.: *ref,* 1281, 1499
Ivey, A. E.: *ref,* 357, 1395, 2195, 2221, P:200(5)
Ivey, M. E.: *ref,* 1195
Ivinskis, A.: *ref,* 217, 529, 592
Ivy, A. C.: *ref,* 1281
Iwahara, S.: *ref,* 1164
Iwawaki, S.: *ref,* 1275, 1499
Izard, C. E.: *ref,* 1164, 1205–6, 1245, 1320, 1415, 2195
Izard, J.: *test,* 595
Izner, S. M.: *ref,* 1499

JABS, M. L.: *ref,* 868, 1775, 2454
Jachevasky, L.: *ref,* 1499
Jachuck, K.: *ref,* 439
Jackli, E.: *ref,* 1499
Jackman, A. J.: *ref,* 1499
Jackman, K.: *test,* 1835
Jackman, S.: *ref,* 1281
Jacks, I.: *ref,* 1469, 1499
Jackson, A. M.: *ref,* 1315, 1407, 2199
Jackson, A. S.: *ref,* 917
Jackson, B. J.: *ref,* 349
Jackson, B. R.: *ref,* 2065, 2086, 2095
Jackson, B. T.: *ref,* 1225
Jackson, C. L.: *test,* 2:1513; *ref,* 496, 516, 533
Jackson, C. V.: *ref,* 532
Jackson, C. W.: *ref,* 1069, 1499, 2195
Jackson, D.: *ref,* 1281
Jackson, D. N.: *rev,* 1253, 1421; *test,* 1322; *ref,* 561, 1121, 1164, 1169, 1281, 1322, 1437, 1471, 1499, 2212
Jackson, E.: *ref,* 1182
Jackson, E. M.: *ref,* 533
Jackson, G. D.: *ref,* 1281
Jackson, G. G.: *ref,* 2355
Jackson, H. D.: *ref,* 1968
Jackson, H. O.: *test,* 664
Jackson, J.: *ref,* 1123, 1207, 2135, 2195, 3:397(26)
Jackson, J. F.: *rev,* 2:1348–9, 3:180, 3:184
Jackson, J. K.: *ref,* 1240, 1281
Jackson, J. M.: *exc,* 1200; *ref,* 1207
Jackson, J. T.: *ref,* 1499
Jackson, K. R.: *ref,* 1281
Jackson, L.: *test,* 1518; *exc,* 5:B274; *ref,* 1518
Jackson, L. F.: *test,* 36:752

Kahler, R. A.: *ref,* 1281
Kahn, D. F.: *ref,* 337, 1206, 2195, 4:825(11, 13–4)
Kahn, D. M.: *ref,* 1281, 1499, 1519
Kahn, E.: *ref,* 529, 592
Kahn, E. M.: *ref,* 2212
Kahn, H.: *test,* 2217; *ref,* 516, 532, 1281, 1447, 1499–500, 2217, 2234–5, 4:277(210)
Kahn, I.: *ref,* 1281
Kahn, J. H.: *ref,* 533
Kahn, M.: *ref,* 529, 1225, 1519
Kahn, M. W.: *ref,* 529, 532, 1281, 1481, 1499, 1519
Kahn, P.: *ref,* 1499
Kahn, R. L.: *ref,* 1121, 1145, 1225, 1281, 1383, 1499
Kahn, S.: *ref,* 1164, 1499
Kahn, T. C.: *test,* 502, 1466, 1478, 4:777; *ref,* 502, 1466, 1478
Kahne, M. J.: *ref,* 1302
Kahnk, D. L.: *ref,* 1044
Kahrs, K. A.: *ref,* 1320
Kaim, S. C.: *ref,* 1499
Kaiman, B. D.: *ref,* 1145, 1289
Kainer, R. K.: *ref,* 518
Kaiser, C.: *ref,* 1293
Kaiser, H. E.: *ref,* 2194–5, 2212
Kaiser, H. F.: *ref,* 457, 542, 551, 561, 564, 571–2, 1207, 1383, 1423, 1775
Kaiser, M. D.: *ref,* 533
Kaiser, R. L.: *test,* 479, 1431
Kakkar, A.: *ref,* 439
Kakkar, S. B.: *ref,* 364, 400, 868, 1095, 1281, 1289, 1403–4, 1407
Kalakian, L. H.: *ref,* 1883
Kaldegg, A.: *exc,* 1499, 1519; *ref,* 439, 529, 532, 1447, 1499, 1516, 5:127(1, 6), P:450(92)
Kaldenberg, D. E.: *test,* 1102
Kalehoff, D. W.: *ref,* 364, 1383
Kales, A.: *ref,* 1281, 1298
Kalhorn, J.: *test,* 1186; *ref,* 1186, 1281
Kalhorn, J. C.: *ref,* 1186
Kaliappan, K. V.: *ref,* 592, 1281, 1447
Kalil, A. J.: *ref,* 1447
Kalil, J.: *ref,* 1447
Kalimo, E.: *ref,* 1145
Kalin, R.: *ref,* 1519
Kalinkowitz, B. N.: *ref,* 532, 1499
Kalis, B. L.: *ref,* 1121, 1281
Kalisch, B. J.: *ref,* 1171
Kalish, R. A.: *ref,* 6:113(22)
Kaliski, M. S.: *ref,* 516, 981
Kallingal, A.: *ref,* 358
Kallingal, A. K.: *ref,* 358
Kallmann, F. J.: *ref,* 525, 532, 1499
Kallos, G. L.: *ref,* 533
Kallstedt, F. E.: *ref,* 1499
Kalman, B. A.: *ref,* 1123, 1415
Kalman, K. S.: *test,* 676
Kalnius, D.: *ref,* 1519
Kaloger, J. H.: *ref,* 357, 361, 1069
Kalt, N. C.: *ref,* 1302
Kalter, N.: *ref,* 533, 1499, 1519
Kalton, G.: *ref,* 1145
Kaltsounis, B.: *ref,* 589
Kamano, D.: *ref,* 529
Kamano, D. K.: *ref,* 1164, 1281, 1474, 1499
Kamat, V. V.: *ref,* 525

Kambly, P. E.: *rev,* 1796, 4:481; *test,* 1:910, 4:601, 4:623–4
Kamen, G. B.: *ref,* 1391, 1471
Kamenetzky, J.: *ref,* 1500
Kamerschen, K. S.: *ref,* 1240
Kamii, C. K.: *ref,* 19, 349, 525
Kamil, L. J.: *ref,* 1185, 1499, 1519
Kamin, H. S.: *ref,* 498
Kamin, L. J.: *ref,* 1087
Kaminsky, B. P.: *test,* 1412, 1443, 1722
Kamiya, M.: *ref,* 1499–500
Kamm, K.: *test,* 1655, 1776
Kamman, G. R.: *ref,* 532, 1281, 1447, 1499, 1519
Kamman, J. F.: *ref,* 220, 426
Kammann, R. A.: *ref,* 1044, 6:438 (524)
Kammeier, M. L.: *ref,* 1280, 1315
Kampsen, A.: *ref,* 1716, 1881
Kandel, A.: *ref,* 349, 400, 425, 525, 532, 1275
Kandel, I. L.: *ref,* 869
Kanderian, S. S.: *ref,* 364, 561–2, 591, 1087
Kandil, B. A.: *ref,* 1519
Kandler, H.: *ref,* 1403
Kane, A. S.: *ref,* 211
Kane, B. H.: *ref,* 688, 755
Kane, F. J.: *ref,* 518, 1281, 1295
Kane, J.: *ref,* 1383
Kane, J. E.: *ref,* 917, 1383
Kane, J. G.: *ref,* 1135
Kane, R. B.: *ref,* 542, 546, 561
Kanekar, S.: *ref,* 1174
Kaneko, Z.: *ref,* 1499, 1519
Kanfer, F. H.: *ref,* 489, 1144, 1281, 1306, 1480
Kangas, B. B.: *ref,* 1169, 1403
Kangas, J.: *ref,* 525, 529
Kangas, J. A.: *ref,* 525, 529
Kangas, R. D.: *ref,* 19, 400
Kania, W.: *ref,* 1225, 1281
Kanitz, H. E.: *ref,* 589, 1164, 1294
Kannapell, B.: *ref,* 1603, 1948
Kannenberg, K. M.: *ref,* 1519
Kanner, L.: *ref,* 1515
Kanter, H. M.: *ref,* 529
Kanter, V. B.: *ref,* 1275, 1499, 1519
Kanthamani, B. K.: *ref,* 1253
Kantner, L. A.: *ref,* 1471
Kantor, H. I.: *ref,* 1217
Kantor, N. J.: *test,* 548, 570
Kantor, R.: *ref,* 1281
Kantor, R. E.: *ref,* 532, 1281, 1383, 1447, 1499, 1519
Kantrowitz, J. L.: *ref,* 357, 1499, 1519
Kanun, C.: *ref,* 1281
Kanungo, R.: *ref,* 439
Kanungo, R. N.: *ref,* 1275
Kao, K. S.: *ref,* 3:242(2)
Kao, Y. K.: *test,* 225
Kapat, G.: *ref,* 515
Kapel, D. E.: *ref,* 22, 281, 524
Kapel, M. B.: *ref,* 22, 281, 524
Kapes, J. T.: *ref,* 655, 1073, 2103, 2427–31
Kapfer, E. L.: *ref,* 1499
Kaplan, A.: *ref,* 1447, 1481, 1499
Kaplan, A. H.: *ref,* 1499
Kaplan, A. M.: *ref,* 1474, 1481, 1499, 1519
Kaplan, B.: *ref,* 1499, 1519

Kaplan, B. E.: *ref,* 516, 1237
Kaplan, D. M.: *ref,* 868, 1499
Kaplan, E.: *test,* 2066; *ref,* 525, 1281
Kaplan, H.: *ref,* 1519
Kaplan, H. A.: *ref,* 1129, 1169, 1911, 2234
Kaplan, H. H.: *ref,* 2221
Kaplan, H. K.: *ref,* 543, 1087, 1387, 1447
Kaplan, J. E.: *ref,* 1281, 1370
Kaplan, M.: *ref,* 357, 482, 561, 574, 1281, 1499
Kaplan, M. F.: *ref,* 574, 1094, 1164, 1519
Kaplan, M. J.: *ref,* 1519
Kaplan, M. L.: *ref,* 529, 1447, 1474, 1499, 1519
Kaplan, M. S.: *exc,* 381; *ref,* 1361, 1471
Kaplan, O.: *ref,* 525
Kaplan, R.: *ref,* 993, 1536
Kaplan, R. B.: *ref,* 993
Kaplan, S. M.: *ref,* 1195, 1499–500
Kaplon, M. D.: *ref,* 2212
Kapoor, K.: *ref,* 1295, 1383, 2229
Kapoor, S. D.: *ref,* 1295, 1383
Kappea, M.: *ref,* 205, 211
Kappeler, T.: *ref,* 1281, 1294
Kappelman, M. M.: *ref,* 533
Kapur, M.: *ref,* 1481, 1499, 1519
Kapur, R. L.: *ref,* 1481, 1499, 1519
Karabelas, M. J.: *ref,* 1281
Karadenes, M.: *ref,* 50, 525
Karas, S. F.: *ref,* 357, 1039, 1253, 1772
Karasick, B. W.: *ref,* 1164, 2285
Karat, A. B. A.: *ref,* 1174, 1383
Karbe, W. W.: *ref,* 1225
Kardak, V.: *ref,* 1383
Kardak, V. S.: *ref,* 331, 446
Kardiner, A.: *ref,* 1499
Kardos, M. S.: *ref,* 525, 533
Karelitz, R.: *ref,* 487, 525
Karelitz, S.: *ref,* 487, 525
Karen, R. L.: *ref,* 1461
Karioth, E. J.: *ref,* 589
Karioth, J.: *ref,* 589
Kark, E.: *ref,* 1145
Kark, S. L.: *ref,* 1145
Karlan, S. C.: *ref,* 1222, 1499
Karle, H.: *ref,* 532
Karlin, I. W.: *ref,* 529
Karlin, J. E.: *ref,* 211, 3:175(1)
Karlin, L.: *ref,* 1500
Karlin, R.: *ref,* 1536, 1596, 1716
Karlins, M.: *ref,* 357, 482, 561, 574
Karlsen, B.: *test,* 3, 36, 655, 1603, 1651; *ref,* 381, 533, 1447, 1499, 1629, 1647, 1794
Karlson, L. A.: *ref,* 2201
Karmel, L. J.: *ref,* 1281
Karn, H. W.: *rev,* 2301; *ref,* 1403, 2448
Karnes, E.: *ref,* 1169
Karnes, L. R.: *ref,* 365, 400, 1437
Karnes, M. B.: *ref,* 516, 525, 981
Karnes, M. R.: *rev,* 4:441
Karni, E. S.: *ref,* 1121
Ka-Ro Research Group: *test,* 1479
Karon, B. P.: *ref,* 1448, 1499, 1519, 1522
Karp, R. E.: *ref,* 1069, 1560
Karp, S. A.: *test,* 1127, 1169, 1201;

ref, 525, 529, 533, 547, 1127, 1169, 1474, 1481, 1499, 1519
Karpeles, L. M.: *ref,* 518
Karpoff, J. T.: *ref,* 1069, 2195
Karr, B.: *ref,* 1164, 2212
Karr, C.: *ref,* 1164
Karr, S. K. S.: *ref,* 981
Karras, A.: *ref,* 529, 1499
Karras, E. J.: *ref,* 1383
Karslake, R. H.: *ref,* 1348
Karson, S.: *ref,* 529, 532, 1129, 1253, 1281, 1383, 1499
Karsten, M. O.: *ref,* 561–2, 577, 591
Karstendiek, B.: *ref,* 482, 548, 1171, 1194, 1386, 1501
Kartye, J.: *ref,* 1117
Karve, B. D.: *ref,* 2:1220(4)
Karzen, J. M.: *ref,* 400, 1716
Kasambi, K.: *ref,* 497
Kasanin, J.: *test,* 1140; *ref,* 1140
Kasanin, J. S.: *ref,* 1140
Kasdon, L. M.: *rev,* 1625, 1651; *ref,* 1649, 1681
Kaser, H.: *test,* 3:127
Kashefi-Zihagh, M.: *ref,* 1355
Kashiwagi, S.: *ref,* 1087
Kashuba, M.: *ref,* 1624, 1649, 1658
Kasin, E. D.: *ref,* 1519
Kaskoff, Y. D.: *ref,* 1387
Kasl, S.: *ref,* P:41(5)
Kasl, S. V.: *ref,* 1073, 1121
Kaspar, E. A.: *ref,* 1395
Kaspar, J. C.: *ref,* 381, 516, 525, 533, 1447
Kasper, E. C.: *ref,* 1395
Kasper, S.: *ref,* 439, 529
Kass, C. E.: *ref,* 533, 981
Kass, E. H.: *ref,* 1281
Kass, E. L.: *ref,* 1391
Kass, W.: *rev,* 1494, 1519; *exc,* 1499, 1516, 4:109, 5:130; *ref,* 532, 1499, 1515
Kassarjian, H. H.: *ref,* 1145, 1207, 1281, 1403, 2212
Kassarjian, W. M.: *ref,* 1281, 1403, 2212
Kassebaum, G. G.: *ref,* 1281
Kassen, T. L.: *ref,* 1207
Kassera, W. J.: *ref,* 1121
Kassinove, H.: *ref,* 529, 1040
Kaste, C. M. M.: *ref,* 1281
Kastein, S.: *ref,* 211
Kastl, A. J.: *ref,* 529, 592, 1281, 1447, 1499
Kastner, H. H.: *ref,* 1968
Kastner, S. B.: *ref,* 981
Kastrinos, W.: *ref,* 1805, 1812
Kasturi, H. Y.: *ref,* 1380
Kaswan, J.: *ref,* 529, 1169, 1500
Kataguchi, Y.: *test,* 1479; *ref,* 1479, 1499
Katahn, M.: *ref,* 1391, 1499
Kataja, R.: *ref,* 5:579(2)
Katakis, H.: *ref,* 529, 1519
Kates, S. L.: *ref,* 1123, 1192, 1447, 1474, 1480, 1499–500, 2212
Kates, W. W.: *ref,* 1192
Kathleen, M.: *ref,* 1569
Katkin, E. S.: *ref,* 1281, 1293
Katkin, S.: *ref,* 1281
Katkovsky, W.: *rev,* 1459, 1475; *ref,* 1281, 1501, 1519
Kato, J. G.: *ref,* 525

Katō, K.: *ref,* 1499
Kato, N.: *ref,* 1451, 1499, 1519
Katsuki, S.: *ref,* 2080
Katter, R. V.: *ref,* 1121, 1207, 1383
Katz, A.: *ref,* 1499
Katz, D.: *ref,* 404, 1281
Katz, E.: *test,* 431; *ref,* 525, 1117
Katz, E. M.: *ref,* 688
Katz, E. W.: *ref,* 1519
Katz, F. M.: *ref,* 516, 981, 1395
Katz, G.: *ref,* 1232, 1281
Katz, H.: *ref,* 1469
Katz, I.: *ref,* 1164
Katz, I. S.: *ref,* 496
Katz, J.: *test,* 2041; *exc,* 1244, 4:109; *ref,* 532, 1281, 1447, 1474, 1481, 1499, 1516, 1519
Katz, K.: *ref,* 357
Katz, L.: *ref,* 503
Katz, L. F.: *ref,* P:390(20)
Katz, M.: *rev,* 2195, 2199; *ref,* 2195, 2212, 2283
Katz, M. M.: *test,* 1255; *ref,* 1195, 1232, 1255, 1278, 1435, 1474, 1499, 1519, P:41(9)
Katz, M. R.: *rev,* 2212
Katz, N.: *ref,* 1395
Katz, S. E.: *ref,* 1192, 1320, 2:1243 (11)
Katz, S. S.: *ref,* 61, 361, 603, 1536
Katz, W. D.: *ref,* 1474, 1499
Katzell, M.: *ref,* 2386
Katzell, M. E.: *ref,* 1164, 1281
Katzell, R. A.: *rev,* 450, 2106, 2129, 2138, 2223, 2266, 2289, 2406, 3:624, 5:954, 6:1104; *ref,* 333, 449, 1069, 1164, 1281, 2151, 2387, 2448
Katzenmeyer, W. G.: *ref,* 400, 2195
Katzman, R.: *ref,* 1281
Katzoff, E. T.: *ref,* 1320
Kauffman, G. B.: *exc,* 1820
Kauffman, J. M.: *ref,* 400, 1182
Kaufman, A.: *ref,* 1519
Kaufman, A. S.: *ref,* 400, 1703
Kaufman, H.: *ref,* 524, 529
Kaufman, H. A.: *test,* 2456
Kaufman, H. I.: *ref,* 50, 516, 529
Kaufman, J.: *ref,* 1447
Kaufman, J. B.: *ref,* 1448
Kaufman, L. W.: *ref,* 1499
Kaufman, M.: *ref,* 1281, 1499, 1567
Kaufman, M. J.: *ref,* 533
Kaufman, M. R.: *ref,* 532, 1447, 1469, 1499
Kaufmann, C.: *ref,* 1240, 1281, 1519, 6:223(12)
Kaufmann, H. J.: *test,* 3:274
Kaufmann, J. D.: *ref,* 357, 436
Kaufmann, P.: *ref,* 1281
Kaul, M. M.: *ref,* P:321(20)
Kaulfers, W. V.: *rev,* 218, 244, 248, 252, 310, 314, 316, 1:986, 1:1156–7, 2:1341, 2:1355, 3:211, 4:176, 7:253; *test,* T:704; *ref,* 2:1341(1), 3:263(30)
Kaunitz, R. M.: *ref,* 525, 4:281 (79)
Kauppi, D. R.: *ref,* 1073, 1281, 2197, 2283
Kaur, R.: *ref,* 1370
Kausch, D. F.: *ref,* 1281
Kausler, D. H.: *ref,* 6:67(4–5)
Kauzer, A.: *test,* 3:382

Kavajecz, L. G.: *ref,* 538
Kavanagh, M. J.: *ref,* 2451
Kavazanjian, T.: *ref,* 1499
Kavkewitz, H.: *ref,* 1499
Kavruck, S.: *ref,* 525
Kawa, T.: *test,* 1855
Kawai, H.: *ref,* 1499
Kawakami, D.: *ref,* 1281
Kawamura, W.: *ref,* 1281
Kawash, G. F.: *ref,* 1393
Kawin, E.: *test,* 2:1256; *exc,* 525; *ref,* 507, 1716
Kay, B.: *ref,* 1121
Kay, B. A.: *ref,* 1121
Kay, D. W. K.: *ref,* 529, 1275, 1281
Kay, E.: *ref,* 1481, 1499, 1501, 1519
Kay, G. M.: *test,* 1:1126, 3:579
Kay, L. W.: *exc,* 1481; *ref,* 1499
Kay, P. M.: *ref,* 655, 1602
Kaya, E.: *exc,* 12, 361
Kayani, M. R.: *ref,* 69, 473, 1069
Kaye, J. D.: *ref,* 1499
Kays, D.: *ref,* 574
Kayser, K.: *test,* 3:7
Kayton, R.: *ref,* 1094, 1121
Kazan, A. T.: *ref,* 1281
Kazelskis, R.: *ref,* 559, 561, 1169
Kazmier, L. J.: *ref,* 337, 423, 482, 1164, 2239
Keach, C. C.: *ref,* 349, 400, 425, 525
Keane, F. L.: *ref,* 2259
Keany, M.: *ref,* 524, 1688
Kear-Colwell, J. J.: *ref,* 403, 439, 1229, 1295, 1383, 1410
Kearney, C. P.: *ref,* 646, 681
Kearney, D. L.: *ref,* 1121, 1772, 2212
Kearney, G. E.: *test,* 520; *ref,* 364, 514, 520
Kearney, H. M.: *ref,* 1207
Kearney, J. E.: *ref,* 512, 520, 533
Kearney, N. C.: *ref,* 868
Kearns, H. H.: *ref,* 868
Kearsley, R. B.: *ref,* 522, 533
Keating, F. R.: *ref,* 1281
Keating, G. W.: *ref,* 1281
Keating, T. J.: *rev,* 439, 515, 2:1385
Keats, J. A.: *rev,* 331, 359, 546, 1069; *ref,* 1646, 1680, 1685
Kebbon, L.: *ref,* 439, 525, 1069, 1073, 1087, 2223, 2228
Kedar, H.: *ref,* 439
Keddy, M.: *ref,* 1320
Kedzuf, M. A.: *ref,* 1407, 1409
Kee, B. E.: *ref,* 1054, 2167
Keefe, J. F.: *ref,* 1240, 1519
Keefe, K.: *ref,* 529, 1281
Keefe, M. K.: *ref,* 529
Keefer, K. E.: *ref,* 1044
Keegan, M.: *ref,* 1320
Keehn, J. D.: *ref,* 364–5, 439, 532, 1174, 1275, 1447, 1499
Keeler, B. T.: *ref,* 2451
Keeler, C. E.: *ref,* 364, 505, 529
Keeler, H. J.: *ref,* 1123, 2214, 5:308(408)
Keeler, M. H.: *ref,* 1281
Keeley, T. D.: *ref,* 1499
Keeley, W. E.: *test,* 5:4, 6:885, 6:897

Kennedy, V.: *ref,* 525
Kennedy, W.: *ref,* 7, 525
Kennedy, W. A.: *ref,* 7, 359, 381, 525, 529, 533, 1123, 1164, 1281, 1403, 1501, 6:225(2)
Kennedy, W. D.: *ref,* 681
Kennedy, W. R.: *ref,* 1302
Kennedy-Frazer, D.: *ref,* 525
Kennett, K. F.: *ref,* 425
Kenney, C. E.: *ref,* 2195, 2212
Kenney, E. T.: *ref,* 981
Kenney, J. B.: *ref,* 1383
Kenney, R. A.: *ref,* 7, 22, 36, 3:15 (4), 4:205(1)
Kenney, R. C.: *ref,* 1164, 1207
Kennon, L. H. V.: *test,* 3:165; *ref,* 3:165(1)
Kenny, D. T.: *rev,* 1451, 5:81; *ref,* 1499, 1519
Kenny, F.: *ref,* 1185, 1225, 1281
Kenny, J. A.: *ref,* 1478
Kenny, J. T.: *ref,* 505, 525, 529
Kenny, T. J.: *ref,* 1447
Kenoyer, M. F.: *ref,* 1207, 1775
Kent, D. R.: *ref,* 1225
Kent, E. G.: *ref,* 342
Kent, G. H.: *rev,* 515, 2:1390-1, 2:1394, 2:1426, 3:273; *test,* 503, 1480, 3:660; *exc,* 525, 532; *ref,* 503, 525, 545, 1480, 2:1401(1, 3)
Kent, N.: *ref,* 525, 533
Kent, R.: *ref,* 1499
Kent, R. A.: *ref,* 2:1377(5)
Kenton, R. W.: *ref,* 1164, 1407
Kentz, M. J.: *ref,* 2213
Kenworthy, J. A.: *ref,* 1164, 1403, 2212
Kenyon, E. L.: *ref,* 1428
Kenyon, F. E.: *ref,* 1145, 1275
Keochakian, S. V.: *ref,* 69, 357
Keogh, B. K.: *ref,* 381, 1127, 1447
Keogh, J.: *ref,* 914, 1121, 1281
Keogh, J. F.: *ref,* 381, 914, 1121, 1447
Keogh, R. P.: *ref,* 1232
Keohane, R. E.: *rev,* 2:1642
Keough, B. J.: *ref,* 1123
Keough, M. A.: *ref,* 2195
Keough, M. J.: *ref,* 419
Kepecs, J.: *ref,* 1281, 1499
Kepecs, J. G.: *ref,* 1281, 1519
Kephart, N. C.: *rev,* 1885, 1887, 1902, 1921; *test,* 1883, 2304; *ref,* 1095, 1480, 1883, 1923-4, 1932, 2304, 5:768(26)
Kepka, E. J.: *ref,* 357
Kepner, H. S.: *test,* 682
Kepner, R. D.: *ref,* 518, 525
Kerchner, L.: *ref,* 1302
Kerckhoff, A. C.: *ref,* 1176, 1519
Kerckhoff, R. K.: *test,* 7:615, 7:622
Kerenyi, A. B.: *ref,* 1245
Kerfoot, J. F.: *ref,* 400, 1702, 1705, 1717, 1724
Kerl, J. M.: *ref,* 1716
Kerley, S. A.: *ref,* 357
Kermeen, B. G.: *ref,* 1069, 2195
Kermoian, S. B.: *ref,* 1716
Kern, D. W.: *ref,* 69, 1597, 2195, 5:308(324)
Kern, F. E.: *ref,* 50, 439, 529
Kern, K.: *ref,* 1918
Kern, K. C.: *ref,* 533

Kern, K. R.: *ref,* 1403
Kern, W. H.: *ref,* 1123
Kernaleguen, A. P.: *ref,* 589, 1169, 1370, 1471
Kernan, J. B.: *ref,* 1193-4
Kernan, J. P.: *ref,* 2129, 2454
Kernan, J. S.: *ref,* 381
Kernen, P. J.: *ref,* 1430
Kerner, O. J. B.: *ref,* 1519
Kernoff, P.: *ref,* 357, 1281
Kernohan, W.: *ref,* 1278
Kerns, R. D.: *ref,* 2195
Kerpelman, L. C.: *ref,* 1135, 1194, 1407
Kerr, G.: *ref,* 425, 2130, 2242, 2247
Kerr, M.: *ref,* 1281, 1311, 1403, 1499, 4:115(1)
Kerr, S.: *ref,* 2451
Kerr, T. A.: *ref,* 1275
Kerr, W.: *ref,* 1171
Kerr, W. A.: *rev,* 1581, 2471, 2475-6, 3:662, 4:525, 4:761; *test,* 1039, 1160, 1171, 1184, 1427, 2274, 2289; *ref,* 418, 1039, 1149, 1160, 1171, 1184, 1325, 1333, 1368, 1427, 1923, 2177, 2212, 2239, 2286, 2289, 2292
Kerr, W. D.: *ref,* 1087, 2195
Kerrick, J. S.: *ref,* 1519
Kerridge, D.: *ref,* 518, 1112, 1281, 1499
Kerridge, P. M. T.: *test,* 2:1526.1; *ref,* 2:1526.1(1)
Kerry, R. J.: *ref,* 1281
Kersh, B. Y.: *ref,* 1749
Kershner, K. M.: *test,* 1874; *ref,* 1874
Kessel, N.: *ref,* 1275
Kessel, P.: *ref,* 1403, 1499
Kessell, R.: *ref,* 518, 529, 1105
Kessler, C. R.: *ref,* 1499
Kessler, J. W.: *ref,* 1499
Kessler, M. R.: *ref,* 545
Kessler, R. T.: *ref,* 381
Kessler, S.: *ref,* 1091, 1164
Kestner, R. A.: *ref,* 914
Keston, M. J.: *ref,* 525
Ketcham, H. E. (Mrs.): *ref,* 357, 419, 1546
Ketcham, W. A.: *ref,* 1087
Ketcherside, W. J.: *ref,* 589, 1280
Kettelkamp, G. C.: *rev,* 264, 273
Kettell, M. E.: *ref,* 529, 1499, 1911
Kettering, W. R.: *ref,* 1463, 1474
Ketterling, M. E.: *ref,* 1164
Kettner, N. W.: *ref,* 457, 551
Keuthe, J. L.: *ref,* 1281
Keutzer, C. S.: *ref,* 1174, 1225
Kew, C. E.: *test,* 1202; *ref,* 1202
Keyes, E. J.: *ref,* 1499, 5:137(6)
Keynes, R.: *ref,* 919
Keys, A.: *ref,* 1281, 1499
Keys, N.: *test,* 671, 2:1237; *ref,* 211, 1095, 1320, 2:1237(2-3), 2:1424(25), 3:263(42), P:321(9)
Keys, S. R.: *ref,* 2451
Keystone View: *test,* 1916-8, 6:957
Keyt, N. L.: *ref,* 1428
Keyton, F. R.: *ref,* 868, 1302
Khalique, N.: *ref,* 1370
Khan, A. A.: *ref,* 1174
Khan, A. R.: *ref,* 1403
Khan, E. U.: *ref,* 1415
Khan, H. I. A.: *ref,* 2259

Khan, J. A. G.: *ref,* 1383, 1421
Khan, L.: *ref,* 1082, 1207, 1513
Khan, R. Z.: *test,* 1526; *ref,* 1526
Khan, S. B.: *ref,* 350, 361, 561, 1772
Khanna, A.: *ref,* 1257, 1320
Khanna, J. L.: *ref,* 1121, 1217, 1281, 1499
Khanna, P.: *ref,* 1499
Khare, P. G.: *ref,* 1403
Khatena, J.: *test,* 587; *ref,* 381, 439, 587, 589, 1356
Khatun, S.: *ref,* 1281
Khorana, S.: *ref,* 1499
Khullar, B. M. P.: *ref,* 545
Kian, M.: *ref,* 1519
Kiang, C. G.: *ref,* 439
Kibbey, S.: *ref,* 2088
Kibler, R. J.: *ref,* 542, 561, 1775
Kicklighter, R.: *ref,* 529, 533
Kicklighter, R. H.: *ref,* 1415
Kicklighter, R. M.: *ref,* 516, 525
Kidd, A. H.: *ref,* 364, 525, 1169, 1174, 1281, 1471, 1474
Kidd, C. B.: *ref,* 1229
Kidd, J. E.: *ref,* 1164
Kidd, J. S. H.: *ref,* 1275
Kidd, K. A. J.: *ref,* 1133, 1135
Kidd, L. R. R.: *ref,* 50, 1542, 1603
Kidd, R. M.: *ref,* 1471
Kidder, J. W.: *ref,* 516, 525
Kidneigh, J. C.: *ref,* 2212-3
Kidson, M. A.: *ref,* 1145, 1174, 1383
Kiefer, C. W.: *ref,* 1519
Kiefer, R.: *ref,* 1519
Kiely, M. H.: *test,* 35:160
Kienlen, J. S.: *ref,* 391, 755
Kiesler, C. A.: *ref,* 1281, 1519
Kiesler, D. J.: *ref,* 1281
Kiessling, R. J.: *ref,* 2234, 6:113 (22)
Kiesz, T. D.: *ref,* 211
Kiev, A.: *ref,* 2212
Kievit, M. B.: *ref,* 1395
Kight, H. R.: *ref,* 1394-5
Kiker, V.: *ref,* 1281
Kikuchi, A.: *ref,* 1176, 1407, 1442
Kikuchi, M.: *ref,* 1275
Kikuchi, T.: *ref,* 1499
Kilander, H. F.: *test,* 933-5, 953; *ref,* 929, 934-5, 953
Kilanski, D. M.: *ref,* 868
Kilborne, L.: *ref,* 1185
Kilbride, J. E.: *ref,* 484
Kilbride, P. L.: *ref,* 484
Kilburn, K. L.: *ref,* 439, 516, 525, 1121, 1254, 2212
Kilby, C. S.: *ref,* 69, 3:4(12)
Kilby, R. W.: *ref,* 1560
Kilcawley, M. P.: *ref,* 1121, 1430
Kildahl, J. P.: *ref,* 1281
Kilduff, C. T.: *ref,* 524, 1688
Kilgore, J. H.: *test,* 1967; *ref,* 467, 1967
Kilgore, L. L.: *ref,* 400
Killcross, M. C.: *test,* 2168; *ref,* 2168
Kille, F. R.: *ref,* 1048
Killen, J. R.: *ref,* 22, 50, 103, 381, 493, 503, 505, 533, 558, 1087, 1552, 1629
Killian, C. D.: *ref,* 525
Killian, D. L.: *ref,* 7:69(3)

Killian, L. R.: *ref,* 533, 981, 1447, P:344(21)
Killian, W. D.: *ref,* 1123
Killinger, G. G.: *ref,* 1320
Killough, C. B.: *ref,* 1219
Kilman, B. A.: *ref,* 525, 529, 533
Kilman, M. D.: *ref,* 1087
Kiloh, L. G.: *ref,* 1145
Kilpatrick, A. R.: *ref,* 361
Kilpatrick, D. G.: *ref,* 1281, 1481
Kilpatrick, J.: *rev,* 7:462
Kiltz, K. W.: *test,* 3:365
Kim, I. C.: *ref,* 1447
Kim, K. S.: *ref,* 1183, 1772, 5:308(423)
Kim, S. S.: *ref,* 1232, 1298, 1398
Kimball, A. J.: *ref,* 1499
Kimball, C. P.: *ref,* 529, 545, 1145, 1174, 1275, 1293
Kimball, C. S.: *exc,* 1366
Kimball, I.: *ref,* 1232
Kimball, J. E.: *ref,* 1032, 1044
Kimball, J. N.: *test,* 35:132
Kimball, W. H.: *ref,* 69, 361
Kimbell, F. T.: *ref,* 69, 361, 652, 1207, 2195
Kimbell, I.: *ref,* 1232
Kimbell, I. H.: *ref,* 1232
Kimbell, V. W.: *ref,* 1703, 1724
Kimber, G. C.: *test,* 2:1580
Kimber, J. A. M.: *ref,* 1123, 1281, 2195
Kimber, J. M.: *ref,* 3:61(9)
Kimber, M.: *ref,* 1123
Kimberlin, C. C.: *ref,* 487, 525
Kimble, G.: *ref,* 1281, 5:308(438)
Kimble, G. A.: *ref,* 1499
Kimble, J. P.: *ref,* 561
Kimbles, S. L.: *ref,* 361
Kimbreall, G. M.: *ref,* 529
Kimbrell, D. L.: *ref,* 496, 516, 525, 533, 1499
Kimbrough, B. M.: *ref,* 868
Kimeldorf, C.: *ref,* 1448
Kimmel, G. M.: *test,* 2054; *ref,* 2054
Kimmel, J.: *ref,* 1474, 1499
Kimmel, P. B.: *ref,* 1383
Kimura, T.: *ref,* 1403
Kinard, F. W.: *ref,* 1924
Kincaid, W. D.: *ref,* 1480
Kincannon, J. C.: *ref,* 1281
Kincannon, S. G.: *ref,* 357
Kinder, E. F.: *rev,* 1428; *ref,* 518, 525, 532
Kinder, L. M.: *ref,* 2056
Kindred, M. I.: *ref,* 1923
King, A. J.: *ref,* 381
King, A. R.: *ref,* 364
King, C. D.: *ref,* 1123
King, C. E.: *ref,* 832, 1069
King, C. W.: *ref,* 1395
King, D. B.: *ref,* 69
King, D. C.: *ref,* 382, 482, 1071, 1320, 1448, 2195
King, D. E.: *test,* 2116
King, D. J.: *ref,* 1212
King, D. M.: *ref,* 532
King, D. T.: *ref,* 69, 6:438(525)
King, D. W.: *ref,* 1053
King, E.: *test,* 2:1637
King, E. M.: *test,* 8
King, E. S.: *ref,* 69
King, E. V.: *ref,* 1240

King, F. J.: *ref,* 349, 382, 542, 551, 869, 997, 1069, 1087, 1121, 1123, 1253, 1772
King, F. W.: *ref,* 522, 1281, 1448, 1469, 1474
King, G. F.: *ref,* 496, 532, 1281, 1437, 1499
King, H. B.: *test,* T:908
King, H. E.: *ref,* 2234
King, H. H.: *ref,* 1123, 1281, 1481, 1499, 1501
King, H. V.: *test,* 3:120, 3:203, 4:251, 4:547, 5:258; *ref,* 869
King, I.: *ref,* 908
King, J.: *ref,* 1069
King, J. D.: *ref,* 525, 533, 538, 981, 1336
King, J. E.: *rev,* 3:166, 3:684; *test,* 449, 1078, 1226, 1229, 2308, 5:892, 5:898, 6:781; *ref,* 1078, 2308
King, J. H.: *ref,* 1395
King, J. W.: *test,* 1879, 1919–20
King, L. A.: *ref,* 2212
King, M.: *ref,* 1069, 1396
King, M. L.: *ref,* 7, 400, 1123
King, N.: *ref,* 1139, 1207
King, N. W.: *ref,* 409
King, P.: *ref,* 349, 404, 1164, 1281, 1423, 2195, 2212, 6:438(467)
King, P. T.: *ref,* 1123, 1289, 1403, 2212
King, R.: *ref,* 868, 1370
King, R. G.: *ref,* 64, 264, 357, 1048
King, S.: *ref,* 1499
King, S. H.: *ref,* 505, 516, 981, 1176, 1294, 1394, 2065
King, S. P.: *ref,* 1302, 1403
King, W. H.: *ref,* 439, 461
Kinget, G. M.: *test,* 5:130; *ref,* 5:130(1, 3)
Kingsbury, F. A.: *rev,* 1222, 2:1682
Kingsbury, W. T.: *ref,* 1121
Kingsley, L.: *ref,* 342, 439–40, 532, 1196, 1281, 1499, P:327(31)
Kingsley, R. F.: *ref,* 1087
Kingsmore, J. M.: *ref,* 1519
Kingston, A. J.: *rev,* 1626, 1647, 1663, 1736; *ref,* 221, 419, 868, 997, 1383, 1546, 1716, 2195, 2199, 6:113(23)
Kinnane, J. F.: *ref,* 1207, 1403, 1501, 2212, 2221
Kinne, S.: *ref,* 1121, 1281
Kinnear, P. R.: *ref,* 1913
Kinneman, J. A.: *test,* 3:593
Kinney, J. C. M.: *ref,* 1389–90
Kinney, L. B.: *rev,* 2:1432, 2:1436, 4:388; *test,* 2:1489; *ref,* 2:1489(1–3)
Kinnick, B. C.: *ref,* 1164, 1403
Kinnie, E. J.: *ref,* 538
Kinnison, A. L.: *ref,* 2028
Kinsbourne, M.: *ref,* 439
Kinsella, N. A.: *ref,* 1383
Kinsey, D. R.: *ref,* 1069
Kinsinger, J. R.: *ref,* 1240, 1281
Kinslinger, H. J.: *ref,* 1499, 2212
Kintner, M.: *ref,* 189, 2:1325(5), 2:1329(6)
Kinzer, J. R.: *rev,* 2227, 2251; *ref,* 419
Kinzer, L. G.: *ref,* 419
Kinzer, S. M.: *ref,* 1302

Kinzie, W. B.: *ref,* 529, 1281
Kiplinger, G. F.: *ref,* 1093, 1144
Kipnis, D.: *ref,* 357, 1121
Kipper, D. A.: *ref,* 1478
Kirby, B. J.: *ref,* 361, 1572
Kirby, C. L.: *ref,* 1679, 1681
Kirby, C. L. L.: *ref,* 1679, 1681
Kirby, M. E.: *ref,* 400
Kirby, T. J.: *test,* T:448, T:684
Kirchman, M. M.: *ref,* 1383
Kirchner, E. P.: *ref,* 574, 1109, 1164, 1275, 1407, 1409
Kirchner, J. H.: *ref,* 425, 439, 1164, 1383, 1403, 1469
Kirchner, R.: *ref,* 1225
Kirchner, W.: *ref,* 170, 445, 482, 1739, 2212, 2463
Kirchner, W. K.: *rev,* 2454, 6:1180; *ref,* 404, 480, 529, 796, 1069, 1078, 1091, 1121, 1164, 1513, 2151, 2212, 2448, 7:1103(3–4)
Kiresuk, T. J.: *ref,* 518, 1281, 1380, 1499
Kirk, B.: *ref,* 1281, 1349
Kirk, B. A.: *ref,* 2193, 2213; *exc,* 2212; *ref,* 358–9, 361, 382, 391, 1121, 1164, 1281, 1294, 1302, 2212–3, 2266, 2337
Kirk, C. R.: *ref,* 357
Kirk, D.: *ref,* 2212
Kirk, G. E.: *ref,* 516
Kirk, H. A.: *ref,* 419, 6:480(41)
Kirk, J.: *ref,* 403, 439
Kirk, J. G.: *ref,* 908
Kirk, J. P.: *ref,* 2212
Kirk, K. W.: *ref,* 2212
Kirk, L.: *ref,* 1281
Kirk, R. E.: *ref,* 559, 561, 1121
Kirk, R. F.: *ref,* 1383
Kirk, S. A.: *test,* 981; *ref,* 499, 981, 1320, 1428, 1724, 2:1222(6.1)
Kirk, W. D.: *test,* 981; *ref,* 981
Kirk, W. E.: *ref,* 1164
Kirkendall, D. R.: *ref,* 36, 357, 364, 425, 1129, 1253
Kirkham, S. L.: *ref,* 1469
Kirkland, M. C.: *ref,* 1394–5
Kirkner, F. J.: *ref,* 1499
Kirkpatrick, D. L.: *test,* 2460, 2462–3, 2465; *ref,* 2135, 2460
Kirkpatrick, E. L.: *test,* 3:568; *ref,* 3:568(1)
Kirkpatrick, F. H.: *exc,* 525; *ref,* 419, 426, 1095, 1320, 2:1243(18), 3:110(10), 3:217(73), 3:255(12), 5:368(14)
Kirkpatrick, J. J.: *ref,* 333, 342, 449, 1069, 1207, 1499, 2151, 2239, 2387, 4:63(5, 10), 6:155(1)
Kirkpatrick, M. S.: *test,* 4:586
Kirkpatrick, P. R.: *ref,* 1394
Kirkwood, J. W.: *ref,* 1281
Kirman, W. J.: *ref,* 1164
Kirsch, A. D.: *ref,* 1348
Kirsch, J. M.: *ref,* 1250
Kirschner, D.: *ref,* 529, 532, 1192
Kirschner, E. E.: *test,* 6:601
Kirschner, F. E.: *ref,* 381
Kirschner, R.: *ref,* 1500
Kirsh, J. L.: *ref,* 589, 1423
Kirtland, J. C.: *test,* 3:204
Kirtley, D.: *ref,* 1281, 1775
Kirtner, W. L.: *ref,* 529, 1281, 1499, 1519

Knight, M. W.: *ref,* 483, 525
Knight, R.: *ref,* 391, 398
Knight, R. P.: *ref,* 532, 1105, 1140, 1499, 1516, 1519
Knights, R. M.: *ref,* 50, 516, 533
Knill, F. P.: *ref,* 1281
Knipe, C. S.: *ref,* 1603
Kniss, F. R.: *test,* 3:612; *ref,* 3: 612(1)
Knittel, M. G.: *ref,* 1363
Knittle, J. L.: *ref,* 381, 1499
Knobloch, H.: *test,* 494; *ref,* 494, 497
Knoblock, P.: *ref,* 1499
Knoll, D. B.: *ref,* 538, 1691
Knollin, H. E.: *ref,* 525
Knopf, I. J.: *exc,* 1499, 1516; *ref,* 532–3, 1474, 1499
Knott, D. P.: *test,* 4:696
Knott, J. R.: *ref,* 503, 532–3
Knott, T. G.: *ref,* 1028, 1164
Knott, V. B.: *test,* 1014
Knotts, J. D.: *ref,* 1293
Knower, F. H.: *test,* 3:150–2; *ref,* 1095, 1101, 1320, 2212–3, 3:150 (1–3), 3:151(1–2), 3:152(1–2), 4:70(9), P:342(10)
Knowles, J.: *ref,* 1275
Knowles, J. B.: *ref,* 532, 1174, 1225, 1275, 1281, 1387
Knowles, L.: *test,* 735; *ref,* 1095
Knowles, R. H.: *ref,* 1281, 1320, 2212
Knox, A.: *exc,* 2095; *ref,* 1377
Knox, A. B.: *ref,* 529, 7:378(4)
Knox, A. E.: *ref,* 1281
Knox, A. W.: *ref,* 1877
Knox, D.: *test,* 821
Knox, D. H.: *ref,* 821
Knox, J. B.: *ref,* 1164, 1403
Knox, P.: *ref,* 20, 22, 391
Knox, S.: *ref,* 525
Knox, S. J.: *ref,* 529, 1145
Knox, W. H.: *ref,* 1164, 1289, 1415
Knox, W. J.: *ref,* 529, 1277, 1391
Knudsen, A. K.: *ref,* 1471, 1499
Knudsen, C. W.: *ref,* 4:179(5)
Knudsen, R. G.: *ref,* 1281, 2195
Knupfer, G.: *ref,* 5:598(6)
Knuth, A. S.: *test,* 212
Knuth, W. E.: *test,* 201; *ref,* 201
Knutson, C. S.: *ref,* 1275
Knutson, J. F.: *rev,* 1499
Knuttgen, H. G.: *ref,* 914
Ko, Y.: *ref,* 1164, 1281, 1447, 1499
Ko, Y. H.: *ref,* 529, 1447
Kobal, A.: *test,* 335–6, 780, 2192, 2252
Kobasigawa, A.: *ref,* 1247
Kobayashi, M. J.: *ref,* 589
Kobler, A. L.: *ref,* 1516
Kobler, F. J.: *ref,* 398, 439, 496, 525, 1144, 1281, 1289, 1380, 1499, 2195
Kobos, J. C.: *ref,* 1240
Kobrick, J. L.: *ref,* 1281, 1383
Koch, C.: *test,* 1524; *ref,* 1524
Koch, C. C.: *exc,* 1911
Koch, D. G.: *test,* 4:592
Koch, H. L.: *exc,* 497; *ref,* 435, 507, 1087, 1186, 1451
Koch, R.: *ref,* 497, 1499
Kochar, D. C.: *ref,* 1275, 1370
Kochnower, W.: *ref,* 1253

Kodama, H.: *ref,* 2212
Kodama, M.: *ref,* 1281
Kodanaz, A.: *ref,* 529, 543, 1277, 1447, 1485, 2234
Kodman, F.: *ref,* 489, 525, 1281, 1499
Koechel, J. W.: *ref,* 1210
Koegler, R. R.: *ref,* 1169, 1380
Koehler, L. E.: *ref,* 48
Koehn, E. B.: *ref,* 19
Koelega, H. S.: *ref,* 1275, 1281
Koelling, J. A.: *ref,* 1164, 2213
Koenig, F. B.: *ref,* 1253
Koenig, F. G.: *ref,* 1499
Koenig, F. J.: *ref,* 503
Koenig, K.: *ref,* 1121, 1519
Koenig, R.: *ref,* 1281
Koenigsberg, L. A.: *ref,* 1164
Koeninger, R. C.: *ref,* 2:1544(8)
Koepke, H. F.: *test,* 2213; *ref,* 2213
Koerth, W.: *ref,* 3:220(31)
Koestline, W. C.: *ref,* 529
Koeth, F. J.: *ref,* 1923
Koff, S. A.: *ref,* 1499
Koffman, G.: *ref,* 1169
Kogan, K. L.: *rev,* 592, 1140, 1192, 4:339; *test,* 6:516; *ref,* 211, 381, 426, 483, 525, 532, 1068, 1240, 1281, 1320, 1403, 1499–500, 1519, 1523, 2212, 6:516(1–2)
Kogan, L.: *ref,* 2212
Kogan, N.: *ref,* 35, 361, 533, 1281
Kogan, W.: *ref,* 1499
Kogan, W. S.: *rev,* 1140, 4:339; *ref,* 532, 1240, 1281, 1499, 5:123 (11)
Kogen, J. B.: *ref,* 1281
Koh, T. H.: *ref,* 516, 525
Kohen-Raz, R.: *ref,* 484, 1499
Kohfeld, D. L.: *ref,* 1121
Kohl, R. N.: *ref,* 1281
Kohlan, R. G.: *ref,* 1164, 2212, 2283
Kohlberg, L.: *exc,* 549
Kohle, K.: *ref,* 1516, 1519
Kohler, A. T.: *ref,* 1118, 1214, 2212
Kohler, E. T.: *ref,* 559, 561
Kohli, P. E.: *ref,* 1069
Kohn, H.: *ref,* 1519
Kohn, H. A.: *test,* 1:1172; *ref,* 419, 2:1377(34), 3:218(3)
Kohn, M.: *ref,* 1499
Kohn, N.: *ref,* 2195, 2212
Kohr, M. C.: *ref,* 1289
Kohrt, C. F.: *ref,* 1289
Kohs, S. C.: *test,* 545; *ref,* 525
Kohut, S.: *ref,* 489, 1313
Koile, E. A.: *ref,* 1289
Koken, J. E.: *ref,* 419, 5:308(402)
Kokosh, J.: *ref,* 1281
Kokovich, S.: *ref,* 884, 2451
Kolasa, B. J.: *ref,* 4:277(245)
Kolb, A.: *ref,* 2212
Kolb, L.: *ref,* 525
Kolbe, L. E.: *ref,* 2135, 2227–9, 2251, 2258, 2266
Koldjeski, T.: *ref,* 1164, 1380
Kole, D.: *ref,* 1145
Kole, D. M.: *ref,* 529, 1145, 1164, 2212
Kolesnik, P. E.: *ref,* 603, 1536
Kolho, P.: *ref,* 1499
Kolin, E. A.: *ref,* 1169, 1293
Kollar, E. J.: *ref,* 1281, 1298, 1471, 1519, P:41(6)

Kollar, F. J.: *ref,* 1281
Koller, J. R.: *ref,* 525
Koller, K. M.: *ref,* 1174
Kollmeyer, L. A.: *ref,* 1123
Kolpack, K. C.: *ref,* 2213
Kolstoe, O. P.: *exc,* 1428; *ref,* 525, 533, 543, 1087, 1116
Kolstoe, R. H.: *ref,* 1281
Koltuv, M.: *ref,* 1090, 1275
Koltveit, T. H.: *ref,* 404
Kolvin, I.: *ref,* 1275
Komatsu, R.: *ref,* 1275
Komich, M. P.: *ref,* 984
Komlos, E.: *ref,* 1383
Komorita, S. S.: *ref,* 2454
Konecny, P. W.: *ref,* 1073
Konick, A.: *ref,* 1183
Konietzko, K.: *ref,* 1418
Konstadt, N.: *test,* 1127
Konstans, D. J.: *ref,* 525
Konttinen, R.: *ref,* 1275, 1469, 1481, P:496(19)
Koo, G. Y.: *ref,* 348, P:406(4)
Kooi, K. A.: *ref,* 1281
Kooiker, J. E.: *ref,* 1154
Kooker, E. W.: *ref,* 361, 404, 1073, 1207, 1772, 1775
Kool, K. A.: *ref,* 532
Kools, J. A.: *ref,* 516, 1451, 2095
Koonce, M.: *ref,* 1320
Koons, N.: *ref,* 589
Koons, P. B.: *test,* 2201; *ref,* 1164
Koontz, E. R.: *ref,* 1716
Koopman, M.: *test,* 1:1147
Koopman, P. R.: *exc,* 361
Koos, E. M.: *ref,* 533
Koos, F. H.: *ref,* 908
Koos, L. V.: *ref,* 908
Kooser, E. D.: *ref,* 1463
Kooyumjian, M. L. V. H.: *ref,* 1294
Kopas, J. S.: *ref,* 2212
Kopel, D.: *rev,* 1690, 1918, 1:1097, 1:1108, 2:1548; *test,* 1:1117; *exc,* 349; *ref,* 1918, 1:1117(1–2)
Koper, C.: *ref,* 1519
Kopff, R. G.: *ref,* 348, 482, 1207
Koplin, J. H.: *ref,* 1480
Koplyay, J. B.: *ref,* 425
Koponen, A.: *ref,* 1164
Kopp, H.: *ref,* 1898
Kopp, T.: *ref,* 2195, 3:635(17)
Koppel, M. A.: *ref,* 1275
Koppell, B.: *ref,* 1281
Koppelmeier, G. J.: *ref,* 2289
Koppitz, E. M.: *test,* 1447e, 1468; *ref,* 381, 525, 533, 1313, 1447, 1468, 1474, 1481, 1519, 1711, 1716, 2028
Kopra, L. L.: *ref,* 2031
Koprowski, E. J.: *ref,* 2212
Koran, M. L.: *ref,* 561
Koran, S.: *ref,* 5:36(11)
Koran, S. W.: *ref,* 2:1492(8), 3: 397(21)
Korchin, S.: *ref,* 1482, 1519
Korchin, S. J.: *ref,* 1447, 1480, 1499–500, 1519, 4:138(3)
Kordasz, F.: *ref,* 1154, 1293
Kordinak, S. T.: *ref,* 489, 538
Korella, K.: *ref,* 1383, 1466, 1501
Koret, S.: *ref,* 1499
Koriat, A.: *ref,* 574

Kroll, W.: *ref*, 1281, 1383, 1403
Krom, A. B.: *test*, 36:549
Kronenberg, M.: *ref*, 1144, 1146
Kronenberg, M. H.: *ref*, 1144, 1146
Kronenberger, E. J.: *ref*, 545, 1181, 1240, 1447, 2180
Krop, H.: *ref*, 349, 551, 1109, 1164
Krop, H. D.: *ref*, 381, 551, 574, 1447
Kropp, H.: *ref*, 1415
Kropp, R. P.: *rev*, 5:623, 5:636; *ref*, 20, 349, 359, 361, 561, 1087, 1499, 2199
Kroske, W. H.: *ref*, 502, 525, 529
Kroth, J. A.: *ref*, 1225, 1391
Krouner, P. J.: *ref*, 1315
Krout, B. M.: *ref*, 1281, 1499, 1519
Krout, J.: *test*, 1316, 1514; *ref*, 1499, 1514
Krout, M. H.: *test*, 1316; *ref*, 482, 1316, 1499, 2195, 4:784(5)
Krueger, A.: *ref*, 1281
Krueger, A. F.: *ref*, 419
Krueger, B.: *ref*, 1281
Krueger, E. S.: *ref*, 935
Krueger, G. R.: *ref*, 1281
Krueger, R. L.: *ref*, 426
Krueger, W. C. F.: *ref*, 426
Krug, E. A.: *test*, 2:1182-3
Krug, J. E.: *ref*, 1499
Krug, O.: *ref*, 1499
Krug, R. E.: *ref*, 1164, 1207
Krug, R. S.: *ref*, 1281
Krug, S.: *ref*, 1383
Krug, S. E.: *test*, 1367
Kruger, A. K.: *ref*, 1499
Kruger, B. L.: *ref*, 1222
Kruglak, H.: *exc*, 1872
Kruglov, L.: *ref*, 1499
Krugman, A. D.: *ref*, 1261, 1380, 1447, 1481, 1498-9
Krugman, J. I.: *ref*, 525, 533, 1499
Krugman, M.: *rev*, 1289, 1469, 1499, 4:29, 5:102, 5:150; *exc*, 525, 1428, 1499, 5:B274; *ref*, 525, 533, 1499, 1519
Krumbein, E.: *ref*, 1519
Krumboltz, H. B.: *ref*, 868
Krumboltz, J. D.: *rev*, 879, 6:857; *ref*, 1303, 1772
Krumm, R. L.: *ref*, 1207, 2195
Krupp, N. E.: *ref*, 1281
Krupski, A.: *ref*, 1174
Krusen, M. M. M.: *ref*, 538
Kryter, K. D.: *test*, 2046; *ref*, 2046
Kubala, A. L.: *ref*, 532
Kubany, A. J.: *ref*, 1281
Kubiniec, C. M.: *ref*, 1032
Kubis, J.: *ref*, 1499
Kubis, J. F.: *ref*, 1073, 1499
Kucera, G. A.: *ref*, 1253
Kuder, F.: *rev*, 425-6; *ref*, 2194
Kuder, G. F.: *rev*, 1068, 2:1267, 3:248; *test*, 1256, 2193-5, 6: 1062; *exc*, 2212-3; *ref*, 357, 1087, 1256, 2194-5, 2212, 2:1492(5), 3:217(92), 6:1062(12)
Kuder, J. M.: *ref*, 1135
Kuderna, J. G.: *ref*, 3:220(25)
Kueffer, E. A.: *ref*, 1474
Kuehn, A. A.: *ref*, 1164
Kuehn, J. A.: *ref*, 1604
Kuehn, J. P.: *ref*, 1123
Kuethe, J. L.: *ref*, 1281, 1499-500

Kuethe, J. W.: *ref*, 1281
Kugel, R. B.: *ref*, 497
Kugler, J. E.: *ref*, 1302
Kuhlen, R. G.: *ref*, 1164, 1289, 1313, 1499, P:363(14, 20-1)
Kuhlmann, F.: *rev*, 349, 425; *test*, 398, 2:1426; *ref*, 398, 426, 435, 441, 525, 2:1424(12), 3:255(4), 4:288(1), 6:480(26)
Kuhlmann, F. M.: *ref*, 1499
Kuhlmann, M. J.: *test*, 1586
Kuhn, E.: *ref*, 1145, 1174, 1240
Kuhn, H. S.: *ref*, 1918, 1923
Kuhn, J. P.: *ref*, 1281
Kuhn, M. V.: *ref*, 1716
Kuhn, R.: *ref*, 1499
Kuhns, F.: *ref*, 1499
Kukkonen, S.: *ref*, 592, 1499
Kukuk, W. D.: *ref*, 1519
Kulberg, G. E.: *ref*, 2212
Kuldau, V. D.: *ref*, 1383
Kulick, W.: *ref*, 1499, 2195
Kulik, J. A.: *ref*, 1094, 1121, 1133, 1135, 1302, 2212-3
Kulis, J. C.: *ref*, 1383
Kulkarni, S. S.: *ref*, 1361
Kullberg, G.: *ref*, 439
Kumar, B.: *ref*, 1451
Kumar, K.: *ref*, 1095, 1174, 1185, 2214
Kumar, K. V.: *ref*, 1174
Kumar, M.: *ref*, 1499
Kumar, P.: *ref*, 439, 1403, 1499-500, P:450(93)
Kumar, S.: *ref*, 1139
Kumar, V. K.: *ref*, 1500
Kumariah, V.: *ref*, 1224, 1410
Kumin, E.: *ref*, 2:1394(10)
Kunce, J.: *ref*, 1145, 1281, 2212
Kunce, J. T.: *ref*, 529, 1281, 1469, 2212
Kundu, C. L.: *ref*, 1499
Kundu, R.: *test*, 1257; *ref*, 439, 515, 525, 532, 1095, 1257, 1320
Kunert, K. M.: *ref*, 1121
Kunhart, W. E.: *ref*, 69
Kunke, T.: *ref*, 1499, 1524, P:431 (8)
Kunkel, R.: *ref*, 1195
Kunkle, E. C.: *ref*, 1281
Kuntz, A. H.: *ref*, 6:186(6, 9, 14-5)
Kuntz, J. E.: *ref*, 1772, 3:397(17)
Kuntz, K. J.: *ref*, 1499
Kuntz, P.: *ref*, 1465
Kuntz, R. H.: *ref*, 1073
Kuntzelman, W. P.: *ref*, 1395
Kunze, K. R.: *test*, 335-6, 780, 2192, 2252
Kunze, L. H.: *ref*, 981
Kunzler, H. G.: *ref*, 2195
Kuo, Y. Y.: *ref*, 589
Kupfer, D. J.: *test*, 1258; *ref*, 1258
Kuppuswamy, B.: *test*, 1041
Kurcz, I.: *ref*, 1480
Kurek, A.: *ref*, 349, 1069, 1121
Kureth, G.: *ref*, 525, 533
Kurfman, D. G.: *rev*, 1978, 7:904
Kurger, B.: *ref*, 2031
Kurie, G. D.: *ref*, 1169
Kurk, M.: *ref*, 1918
Kurko, V. K.: *ref*, 525
Kurland, A.: *ref*, 1281, 7:55(25)

Kurland, A. A.: *ref*, 439, 529, 1232, 1255, 1264, 1281, 1346, 1499
Kurland, H. D.: *ref*, 1121, 1281, 1447
Kurlander, E. D.: *ref*, 221
Kurle, H. B.: *ref*, 914, 947
Kuroda, J.: *ref*, 439
Kuroda, M.: *ref*, 1499
Kuroiwa, Y.: *ref*, 2080
Kurpius, D. J.: *ref*, 1395
Kurth, C. J.: *ref*, 1281
Kurth, G. M.: *exc*, 1499
Kurtz, A. K.: *rev*, 1087, 2140, 2400, 2459, 5:902, 6:1115; *ref*, 1101, 1499, 2212, 2:1646(5), 2:1670 (5), 4:825(6, 8-9, 12)
Kurtz, E. S.: *test*, 4:501
Kurtz, J. C.: *ref*, 1499
Kurtz, K. H.: *ref*, 5:123(8)
Kurtz, R.: *ref*, 1281, 1383, 1471
Kurtz, R. R.: *ref*, 1281, 1415
Kurtzberg, R. L.: *ref*, 1281, 1481
Kurtzke, J. F.: *ref*, 1387
Kurtzman, K. A.: *ref*, 1253
Kurz, R. B.: *ref*, 1499
Kushinka, M.: *ref*, 24, 1560
Kushmar, H. S.: *ref*, 482, 1423
Kushner, E. N.: *ref*, 1164, 1281, 1471
Kushner, R.: *ref*, 525
Kushner, R. E.: *ref*, 426
Kuske, I. I.: *ref*, 981
Kusyszyn, I.: *ref*, 1322
Kutash, S. B.: *test*, 5:137; *exc*, 1486, 1519; *ref*, 525, 532, 1499, 1519, 5:137(1-3, 5, 7)
Kutner, B.: *ref*, 1519
Kutner, M.: *ref*, 2195, 2212-3
Kutner, S. J.: *ref*, 1185
Kutsche, R. P.: *ref*, 1499
Kutscher, A. H.: *ref*, 1281
Kuttner, R. E.: *ref*, 1499
Kuusinen, S.: *ref*, 1302
Kuznets, G.: *ref*, 1320
Kuznets, G. M.: *ref*, 2:1243(23), 6:159(40)
Kvaraceus, W. C.: *rev*, 86-7, 1110, 3:35, 4:254; *test*, 1254; *ref*, 525, 1254, 4:15(11)
Kwall, D. S.: *ref*, 1123
Kwalwasser, J.: *test*, 202-5; *ref*, 204
Kweller, I. I.: *ref*, 1164
Kyle, D. G.: *ref*, 1474
Kyle, N. L.: *ref*, 1281
Kyriazis, C.: *ref*, 1500
Kyriazis, P. W.: *ref*, 1281
Kyte, G. C.: *test*, T:1189; *ref*, 525, 4:205(2)

L & L ASSOCIATES: *test*, 374, 2133
Laane, C. L.: *ref*, 1474
LaBach, P. A.: *ref*, 1135, 1315
Labak, A. S.: *ref*, 529
LaBarba, R. C.: *ref*, 518, 1499
LaBarre, E. D.: *ref*, 1320
LaBarre, W.: *ref*, 1499
L'Abate, L.: *ref*, 381, 440, 489, 516, 529, 532-3, 543, 1281, 1313, 1437, 1478, 1485, 2195, 2212
LaBelle, J. E.: *ref*, 1395
Laberteaux, T. E.: *ref*, 529
Labib, M. A.: *ref*, 1281

Lee, J. M.: *rev*, 20, 1:872, 5:18; *test*, 684, 1563, 1711, 3:17, 3:345, 6:647; *ref*, 398, 684, 1711, 2:1195 (1), 6:647(1)

Lee, K. T.: *ref*, 1253, 1280

Lee, L.: *test*, 2084

Lee, L. J. W.: *ref*, 2285

Lee, L. L.: *ref*, 2084

Lee, M. C.: *ref*, 914, 935, 1101, 1256, 2135, 2195, 2239

Lee, M. V.: *ref*, 525

Lee, N.: *ref*, 1447, 1631

Lee, P. J.: *ref*, 2135, 2195, 5:308 (358)

Lee, R.: *ref*, 517, 533

Lee, R. E.: *ref*, 209, 1240, 1346, 1691, 1716

Lee, R. G.: *ref*, 914

Lee, R. J.: *ref*, 2212

Lee, R. R.: *ref*, 1281, 1499

Lee, S. E.: *ref*, 1544

Lee, S. G.: *rev*, 1263, 1452, 1511, 6:213; *test*, 1520; *exc*, 1444; *ref*, 1164, 1519–20

Lee, T.: *ref*, 428, 2130, 2229

Lee, W. H.: *ref*, 1281

Lee, W. M.: *ref*, 1281

Lee, W. S.: *ref*, 868

Lee, Y. B.: *ref*, 603, 1281, 1383, 1536, 1766

Leeds, C. H.: *test*, 868; *ref*, 868, 1207

Leeds, D. P.: *ref*, 1169, 1383, 1499

Leeds, D. S.: *ref*, 981, 1480, 1921

Leek, W. R.: *ref*, 1447

Leep, A. G.: *ref*, 35, 105, 361, 868, 1151, 1281

Leeson, H. J.: *ref*, 947

Lee-Teng, E.: *ref*, 1281, 1389

Lefcoe, N. M.: *ref*, 1383

Lefcourt, H. M.: *ref*, 574, 1121, 1261, 1499, 1519

Lefeber, J. A.: *ref*, 1415

Lefebvre, A.: *ref*, 1415

Lefever, D. W.: *rev*, 7, 391, 425, 863, 1078, 2433, 2448, 1:876, 2:1197, 3:695, 4:726, 6:480; *test*, 29, 108, 731, 1596, 1765, 1790, 1921, 1947, 5:668, 6:237b; *ref*, 1499, 1921

Lefever, W.: *ref*, 1921

Leff, B.: *ref*, 6:514(10)

Leff, J. P.: *ref*, 1383, 1499

Lefford, A.: *ref*, 1516

Lefkovits, A. M.: *ref*, 1144, 1499–500, 1519

Lefkowitz, D. M.: *ref*, 2194, 2212

Lefkowitz, M. M.: *ref*, 518, 1255, 1281, 1474, 1528

Lefley, H. P.: *ref*, 1101

Leftwich, W. H.: *ref*, 880–1, 1471

Legg, D.: *ref*, 529

Leherissey, B. L.: *ref*, 1293, 1391

Lehman, C. F.: *ref*, 202, 1281

Lehman, E. B.: *ref*, 381, 533, 1471

Lehman, P. R.: *rev*, 207, 210; *exc*, 217

Lehman, R. T.: *ref*, 2195

Lehmann, H.: *ref*, 1215

Lehmann, H. E.: *ref*, 1298

Lehmann, I. J.: *rev*, 1799, 1830–1, 1871, 6:885, 7:796; *exc*, 1780–1, 1808, 1840, 1862; *ref*, 36, 358, 400, 525, 529, 1073, 1451

Lehmann, M. M.: *ref*, 525, 533

Lehmann, P. W.: *test*, 174

Lehmkuhl, C. B.: *ref*, 69, 404

Lehndorff, A.: *ref*, 1500

Lehner, G. F. J.: *ref*, 1123, 1281, 1474

Lehrer, A. C.: *ref*, 542, 546, 564, 1471

Lehrer, B. E.: *ref*, 400

Lehrer, M. C. B.: *ref*, 1121

Leib, J. W.: *ref*, 1315

Leiberman, H.: *ref*, 1164

Leibert, R. E.: *ref*, 1921

Leibman, O. B.: *ref*, 1123, 1313, 1499

Leibowitz, M.: *ref*, 518

Leichman, N. S.: *ref*, 529, 1447

Leichtman, S. R.: *ref*, 533

Leichty, M. M.: *ref*, 1448, 1519

Leiding, W. C.: *ref*, 532, 1499

Leigh, D.: *ref*, 1145, 1275

Leigh, K. B.: *ref*, 2212

Leighton, A. M.: *ref*, 1164

Leighty, D. L.: *ref*, 1123

Leihy, R.: *ref*, 1281

Leiman, A. H.: *ref*, 1519

Leiman, C. J.: *ref*, 1499, 1519

Leiner, M.: *ref*, 1281

Leipold, V.: *ref*, 1474

Leipold, W. D.: *ref*, 532, 1275, 1474, 1481

Leischuck, G. S.: *ref*, 1044

Leiser, R.: *ref*, 1499

Leisner, R.: *ref*, 1275, 1281

Leitch, M.: *ref*, 525, 1499, 1519

Leiter, N. Z.: *ref*, 1415

Leiter, R. G.: *test*, 504–5, 4:339, 4:347–8, 4:355; *exc*, 497; *ref*, 504–5, 4:359(3)

Leiterman, P. H.: *ref*, 1176

Leith, G. O. M.: *ref*, 1174

Leithwood, K. A.: *ref*, 525, 1383

LeJeune, S. J.: *test*, 634

Leland, B.: *test*, 493

Leland, E. M.: *ref*, 1499

Leland, H.: *test*, 1092; *ref*, 1092

Leland, L. A.: *ref*, 5:147(29, 46, 54)

Lelos, D.: *ref*, P:446(28)

LeMaistre, E. H.: *test*, 927

LeMaistre, G.: *ref*, 1121, 1281–2

Leman, J. E.: *ref*, 1519

LeMaster, J. L.: *test*, 2:1479

LeMay, M.: *ref*, 357, 1281

LeMay, M. L.: *ref*, 1164, 1281, 1315

Lembeck, M.: *ref*, 1847

Lembke, R. T.: *ref*, 1133

Lemeshnik, S.: *ref*, 1474

Lemke, E. A.: *ref*, 7, 29, 36, 425, 439, 457, 561, 1164, 1383, 1761

Lemley, D. W.: *ref*, 1481

Lemmon, D. B.: *ref*, 1380

Lemon, H. B.: *test*, 3:582

Lemons, C. D.: *ref*, 357

Lempérière, J.: *ref*, 1499

Lenfestey, F. T.: *ref*, 1281

Lenke, J. M.: *ref*, 424, 688, 755

Lenneberg, E. H.: *ref*, 1913

Lenning, O. T.: *test*, 1236; *ref*, 1044

Lennon, L. J.: *ref*, 1320, 1932

Lennon, R. T.: *rev*, 4:7, 4:66, 5:20, 5:379; *test*, 424; *ref*, 22, 425, 4:324(62), 5:368(17–8, 23)

Lennox, W. G.: *ref*, 525, 532

LeNoue, D.: *ref*, 1499

Lent, A.: *ref*, 1501

Lentz, E. M.: *ref*, 1164

Lentz, R. J.: *ref*, 1298

Lentz, T. F.: *rev*, 1289, 3:70; *test*, 901, 1116; *ref*, 36, 1116, 1320, 3:653(5)

Leon, D. A.: *ref*, P:406(4)

Leon, H.: *ref*, 2212–3

Leon, H. V.: *ref*, 1383, 1423

Leon, J. F.: *ref*, 398

Leon, R. L.: *ref*, 1144

Leonard, E. W.: *ref*, 1116

Leonard, J. P.: *rev*, 61, 69, 2:1282, 3:125; *test*, 2:1285; *ref*, 2:1285 (1–2)

Leonard, L. B.: *ref*, 2095

Leonard, L. C.: *ref*, 358, 1383, 2213

Leonard, M.: *test*, 1009

Leonard, M. R.: *exc*, 2:B835

Leonard, R. J.: *ref*, 2195

Leonard, R. L.: *ref*, 1044

Leonard, S.: *ref*, 1424

Leonard, S. A.: *test*, 2:1271

Leonetti, R.: *test*, 1334

Leonhardt, T. M.: *ref*, 516

Leonhardy, A.: *ref*, 655

Lepak, R. C.: *ref*, 2212

Lependorf, S.: *ref*, 1280

Lepine, L. T.: *ref*, 1281, 1499

Lepkin, M.: *ref*, 1087

Lepkowski, J. R.: *ref*, P:411(9)

Lepley, A. R.: *ref*, 1824, 1826

Lepley, W. M.: *test*, 1314; *ref*, 1314, 2381, 6:438(469), 6:870 (2)

Leppel, L.: *ref*, 1481

Lepper, C.: *ref*, 1163

Lepper, R. E.: *ref*, 1303

Leppke, R. D.: *ref*, 381, 516, 1921

Lerand, L. W.: *ref*, 533

Lerche, M.: *ref*, 3:242(2)

Lerea, L.: *ref*, 489, 1281, 1313

Lerman, J.: *test*, 2061; *ref*, 2061

Lerman, J. W.: *ref*, 2061

Lerner, A.: *test*, 827–8

Lerner, B.: *ref*, 1471, 1499

Lerner, B. A.: *ref*, 1499

Lerner, D.: *exc*, 4:57

Lerner, E.: *ref*, 400

Lerner, M. S.: *ref*, 1474

Lerner, P. M.: *ref*, 1499

Lescarbeau, W. J.: *ref*, 361

Lesh, T. V.: *ref*, 1420

LeShan, L.: *ref*, 342, 1499

Leshner, B.: *ref*, 1281

Leshner, M.: *ref*, 1281

Leshner, S. S.: *ref*, 2195

Leskosky, R.: *ref*, 381, 538

Leskosky, R. J.: *ref*, 381

Lesley, E. L.: *ref*, 1499

Leslie, L. A.: *ref*, 3:136(2)

Leslie, P. T.: *ref*, 533, 1277, 1447

Lessa, W. A.: *ref*, 1519

Lesser, E.: *ref*, 1499

Lesser, G. S.: *ref*, 1500, 1519, P:408(17–8)

Lesser, R. A.: *ref*, 1121

Lewis, M. D.: *ref,* 1383
Lewis, M. M.: *test,* 5:337
Lewis, M. P.: *ref,* 1281
Lewis, N. D. C.: *exc,* 2071; *ref,* 1281, 1469, 1499-500, 1516
Lewis, N. P.: *ref,* 1109, 1127
Lewis, O. F.: *ref,* 561, 591, 1281, 1293, 1377, 1499
Lewis, P.: *ref,* 1499
Lewis, R.: *ref,* 525, 1031, 1035, 2212
Lewis, R. B.: *ref,* 589, 1394-5, 1499
Lewis, R. D.: *rev,* 1772, 5:92; *ref,* 1281
Lewis, R. E.: *ref,* 1207
Lewis, R. L.: *ref,* 1415
Lewis, R. W.: *ref,* 1430, 1772
Lewis, S. C.: *ref,* 357
Lewis, S. O.: *ref,* 1315
Lewis, T.: *test,* 1:872
Lewis, V.: *ref,* 381, 525, 533
Lewis, V. G.: *ref,* 529, 533
Lewis, W. A.: *ref,* 1164, 1281
Lewis, W. B.: *ref,* 1447, 1499
Lewis, W. C.: *ref,* 1281
Lewis, W. D.: *ref,* 398
Lewis, W. M.: *ref,* 529, 1383
Lewis, W. W.: *ref,* 1207, 1281
Ley, P.: *ref,* 403, 439, 1225, 1275, 1383
Lezak, M. D.: *exc,* 1168; *ref,* 1281, 1499
Lezak, R. J.: *ref,* 2039
Lézine, I.: *ref,* 483
Lezotte, L.: *ref,* 2212
Lhota, B.: *ref,* 2212
Li, A. K.: *ref,* 439
Li, A. K. F.: *ref,* 331, 868
Liakos, A.: *ref,* 1174, 1279, 1295
Libb, J. W.: *exc,* 1281; *ref,* 447, 522, 529, 592, 1281, 1481
Libby, B. C.: *ref,* 2212
Libby, D. F.: *ref,* 1044
Libby, W. L.: *ref,* 35, 69, 361, 574, 1383
Libenson, M. A.: *ref,* 1315
Liberman, R.: *ref,* 1240
Liberman, R. P.: *ref,* 1240
Liberthson, L.: *ref,* 1499
Liberty, P.: *ref,* 1519
Liberty, P. G.: *ref,* 1164, 1205, 1245, 1281, 1403
Libo, L.: *test,* T:346
Libo, L. M.: *rev,* 1106, 1137; *test,* 1491; *ref,* 1491
Libowitz, M.: *ref,* 529
Librach, S. J.: *ref,* 1499
Liccione, J. V.: *ref,* 1519
Licht, L.: *ref,* 542, 1480
Licht, M.: *ref,* 2259
Lichtenberger, E. W.: *ref,* 1176
Lichtenstein, D.: *ref,* 1499
Lichtenstein, E.: *ref,* 1121, 1281
Lichtenstein, K. R.: *ref,* 1499
Lichtman, M.: *test,* 1744
Lichtman, M. V.: *ref,* 538, 589, 2078
Lickorish, J. R.: *test,* 1459; *ref,* 1459
Liddell, W. W.: *ref,* 1176
Liddicoat, R.: *ref,* 497, 532
Liddle, G.: *ref,* 1121
Liddle, G. P.: *ref,* 1121, 1123
Liddle, L. R.: *ref,* 2113
Lidz, T.: *ref,* 525, 545, 1192, 1299, 1481, 1499, 1501, 1519

Lieberman, J. N.: *ref,* 516
Lieberman, L. R.: *ref,* 361, 1164, 1281, 1293, 1447, 1490, 1519
Lieberman, M.: *ref,* 655, 1500
Lieberman, M. A.: *ref,* 1447, 1474, 1519
Liebert, R.: *ref,* 1481
Liebert, R. M.: *ref,* 529, 1185
Liebert, R. S.: *ref,* 1474
Liebowitz, B.: *ref,* 1519
Liebroder, M. N.: *ref,* 1214
Liechti, R.: *ref,* 1281
Liedtke, W.: *ref,* 348, 1123, 1603
Lief, H. I.: *ref,* 404, 1281, 1469, 1499, 2212, 2355
Lief, V. F.: *ref,* 404, 1499, 2212, 2355
Liefeld, T. S.: *ref,* 211
Lien, A. J.: *ref,* 69, 391, 1320, 2199
Lien, L. J.: *ref,* 5:308(301)
Lietz, E. S.: *ref,* 1883
Lievens, S.: *ref,* 1500
Life Insurance Agency Management Association: *test,* 2396, 2398, 2401-2, 2407, 2:1670, 6: 1168; *ref,* 2:1646(1-4), 2:1670 (1-4)
Liff, Z. A.: *exc,* 1499
Lifrak, S. T.: *ref,* 1293
Lifton, W. M.: *ref,* 1314
Liggett, J.: *rev,* 331, 390, 2248, 5: 340, 5:357, 6:207; *test,* 1505; *ref,* 1499, 1505
Liggitt, W. A.: *ref,* 361, 652, 1794, 1948
Light, B. H.: *ref,* 1451, 1499, 1519, 5:166(8), 6:228(59)
Light, C. S.: *ref,* 1499
Light, L. L.: *ref,* 1768
Light, M. L.: *ref,* 529, 532
Light, P.: *ref,* 529
Lightfoot, F. L.: *ref,* 1281
Lighthall, F.: *ref,* 425, 1474, 1499, 5:36(18)
Lighthall, F. K.: *ref,* 518, 1087, 1281
Lightsey, R.: *ref,* 357, 365, 425
Ligondé, P.: *test,* 21
Ligthelm, G. J.: *test,* 16, 1065
Lijtmaer, N.: *ref,* 1499
Likert, R.: *test,* 2266; *ref,* 1348, 2266
Liles, P.: *ref,* 786
Liljebald, M. T.: *ref,* 1403
Lillian, K. K.: *ref,* 1499
Lillie, D. L.: *ref,* 1895
Lilliston, L.: *ref,* 1447
Lilliston, L. G.: *ref,* 1277, 1447
Lilly, R. S.: *ref,* 561, 1109, 1129, 1281
Lim, D.: *ref,* 1121
Limbert, P. M.: *rev,* 1:948
Limuaco, J. A.: *ref,* 1481, 1499
Lin, J. Y.: *ref,* 1305
Lin, L.: *ref,* 1164
Lin, P.: *ref,* 1281
Lin, T. T.: *ref,* 529, 1380
Lin, Y. G.: *ref,* 357, 529, 1121, 1164, 1383, 1519, 1772
Lincoln, A. L.: *test,* 152
Lincoln, E. A.: *ref,* 525, 1048, 2: 1390(2), 2:1391(2), 3:273(3)
Lincoln, H.: *ref,* 2:1388(3)
Lind, A.: *ref,* 1164, 1403, 2212
Lind, A. I.: *ref,* 1164, 1403, 2213

Lind, C.: *ref,* 36, 2:1190(3)
Lindahl, C.: *ref,* 1133
Lindahl, L. E. H.: *ref,* 439, 1275
Lindamood, C. H.: *test,* 2042
Lindamood, P. C.: *test,* 2042
Lindauer, M. S.: *ref,* 1174
Linde, L. M.: *ref,* 487, 497, 525, 936
Linde, T.: *ref,* 1281
Linde, T. F.: *ref,* 1281
Lindeman, R. H.: *ref,* 357
Lindeman, R. P.: *ref,* 1302, 1403, 2195
Lindemann, E.: *ref,* 3:688(2), 5: 76(10-1)
Lindemann, S. J.: *ref,* 1123
Lindemuth, M. H.: *ref,* 1133, 2451
Lindén, Å.: *ref,* 1275
Linden, A. V.: *test,* 1:873, 2:1257
Linden, J.: *exc,* 1174; *ref,* 2212
Linden, J. D.: *ref,* 868, 1164, 1174, 1207, 1281, 1470-1, 1501
Linden, K. W.: *ref,* 868, 1207
Linder, M. G.: *ref,* 507
Linder, R.: *ref,* 1447
Linder, T. D.: *ref,* 1499
Linderfelt, F. M.: *ref,* 1499
Lindesmith, A. R.: *exc,* 1499
Lindgren, H. C.: *ref,* 1094-5, 1123, 1281, 2195, 2199, 2212
Lindholm, B. W.: *ref,* 525
Lindley, M. R.: *ref,* 1415, 1572
Lindley, S. B.: *ref,* 1232
Lindlof, J.: *ref,* 7, 19, 22
Lindner, H.: *ref,* 1448
Lindner, L. A.: *ref,* 1281
Lindner, R.: *ref,* 525, 529, 1281, 1499
Lindner, R. M.: *test,* 447; *exc,* 1499; *ref,* 447, 1499
Lindner, R. S.: *ref,* 381
Lindquist, E. F.: *rev,* 993, 997; *test,* 8, 19-20, 88, 138, 166, 623, 639, 1737-8, 1758, 1787, 1944, 35: 294-5, 1:951, 2:1184, 2:1299, 2: 1618, 2:1633, 2:1635-6, 4:4, 4:7, 4:15, 4:150, 4:408, 4:554, 4:588, 4:685, 6:255; *ref,* 357, 1044, 1560, 1610, 1749, 3:604(1), 4:15(10)
Lindsay, C.: *ref,* 1320
Lindsay, C. A.: *test,* 2212; *ref,* 1135, 2212-3
Lindsay, J.: *ref,* 1447
Lindsay, R. B.: *ref,* 69, 5:6(10)
Lindsey, J. F.: *ref,* 589
Lindsey, J. M.: *ref,* 496, 516, 533
Lindsey, T. T.: *ref,* 2251, 2259
Lindvall, C. M.: *rev,* 44
Lindy, J.: *ref,* 1711, 1716
Lindzey, G.: *test,* 1403-4; *ref,* 482, 1121, 1403, 1448, 1482, 1499-500, 1516, 1519
Lindzey, G. E.: *ref,* 482, 532, 1918, 1923
Line, W.: *rev,* 2:1411; *exc,* 349, 483, 497, 507, 1447; *ref,* 525, 1320, 1499
Lines, J.: *ref,* 2:1394(8-9)
Linfert, H. E.: *test,* 3:285; *ref,* 3: 285(2)
Linfoot, K. W.: *ref,* 1646
Lingoes, J. C.: *rev,* 1174, 1275, 1281; *ref,* 1281, 1516
Lingren, R. H.: *ref,* 1447, 1468, 1499, 2028

Lupfer, M. B.: *ref*, 1306
Lupp, J.: *ref*, 1447
Lupton, D. E.: *ref*, 1240, 1281, 1519
Luria, M. A.: *test*, 2:1341
Lurie, L. A.: *exc*, 1499; *ref*, 1428
Lurie, W. A.: *ref*, 1403
Lüscher, M.: *test*, 1263
Lushene, R.: *test*, 1391
Lushene, R. E.: *test*, 1392; *ref*, 1281, 1391
Lusienski, D. R.: *ref*, 533
Lussiev, G.: *ref*, 1315
Lustbader, L.: *ref*, 1451, 1519
Lustgarten, B. J.: *ref*, 1499, 1519
Lustig, F. M.: *ref*, 1281
Lustig, P.: *ref*, 1164
Luszki, M. B.: *ref*, 529
Luszki, W. A.: *ref*, 487, 525, 529, 533
Luther, B. R.: *ref*, 1281
Lutjemeier, J. A.: *ref*, 1176
Luton, J. N.: *ref*, 69, 404, 868, 1403, 1499, 1775, 2195
Luttgen, G.: *ref*, 1696
Lutz, R. E.: *test*, 4:370
Lutz, S. W.: *ref*, 1044, 1430, 2167
Lutz, W. W.: *ref*, 1281
Lutzker, D. R.: *ref*, 1281
Lutzky, H. L.: *ref*, 1448
Luyster, R. J.: *ref*, 1095
Luzzi, M. H.: *ref*, 1315, 1403
Lybarger, A. E.: *ref*, 2283
Lyden, B. A.: *ref*, 357
Lyden, F. J.: *ref*, 2355
Lyder, W.: *ref*, 1716, 1881
Lyerly, O.: *ref*, 342
Lyerly, S. B.: *test*, 1255; *ref*, 1217, 1232, 1255, 1264, 1346, 1435, 2212, P:41(10), P:408(30)
Lykken, D. T.: *rev*, 1145, 1375, 6: 72, 7:55; *ref*, 1281
Lyle, C.: *ref*, 1264, 1281, 1383
Lyle, F. A.: *ref*, 1306
Lyle, J.: *exc*, 1499; *ref*, 1519
Lyle, J. G.: *exc*, 1447, 1451, 1499, 1519; *ref*, 509, 533, 1277, 1499, 1519
Lyle, W. H.: *ref*, 1144, 1281, 1500
Lyles, W. K.: *ref*, 1451
Lyman, G.: *ref*, 525
Lyman, H. B.: *rev*, 342, 380, 516, 529; *test*, 4:301; *exc*, 26; *ref*, 1383, 2379, 2383
Lyman, H. W.: *ref*, 1481
Lyman, R. C.: *ref*, 1478
Lynch, B. L.: *ref*, 5:887(3)
Lynch, D. J.: *ref*, 1121, 1193, 1475
Lynch, G. B.: *ref*, 1164
Lynch, H.: *ref*, 1370
Lynch, K.: *test*, 1:873
Lynch, M. D.: *ref*, 574, 2194, 2212
Lynch, P. L.: *ref*, 419
Lynch, R.: *ref*, 1281
Lynch, R. C.: *ref*, 1133
Lynch, T.: *test*, 1318
Lynch, W. J.: *ref*, 529, 1281
Lynch, W. W.: *ref*, 5:533(1)
Lynd, C.: *ref*, 529
Lynde, R. E.: *ref*, 1439
Lynn, B.: *ref*, 1469
Lynn, D. B.: *test*, 1512; *ref*, 1451, 1499, 1512, 1519
Lynn, G.: *ref*, 2053

Lynn, R.: *ref*, 403, 439, 1174, 1275, 1383, 1387, 1512
Lynn, T. N.: *ref*, 1145
Lyon, B.: *ref*, 1144, 1448
Lyon, J. B.: *ref*, 1281, 2212
Lyon, J. T.: *ref*, 361, 1164
Lyon, V. E.: *ref*, 391, 419
Lyon, V. W.: *ref*, 426, 6:159(37)
Lyon, W.: *ref*, 1500
Lyons, E. A.: *ref*, 104
Lyons, E. R.: *ref*, 981
Lyons, J.: *ref*, 1281, 1469, 1499
Lyons, R. A.: *ref*, 361, 1348
Lyons, T. J.: *ref*, 529, 7:378(5)
Lyons, W. A.: *ref*, 357, 6:18(12)
Lysaught, J. P.: *ref*, 425, 1306, 1320, 1403, 1775
Lytle, M. B.: *ref*, 1281
Lytton, H.: *ref*, 409, 462, 525, 533, 589, 1296, 1499

M.A.A. COMMITTEE on High School Contests: *test*, 598
Maag, C. H.: *ref*, 2234
Maas, H. S.: *rev*, 1039
Maas, M. G.: *ref*, 1133
Mabee, D.: *ref*, 914
Mabee, D. D.: *ref*, 914
Maberly, N. C.: *ref*, 49, 382, 1812
Mabli, J.: *ref*, 1293
Mabry, M.: *ref*, 1469
Mabry-Hall, M.: *ref*, 1499
McAdam, W.: *ref*, 403, 439, 1499
McAdams, C. D.: *ref*, 1176
McAdams, H. E.: *ref*, 20, 6:438 (495)
McAdoo, W. G.: *ref*, 1391
McAdory, M.: *test*, 2:1325; *ref*, 2: 1325(1)
Macaitis, L.: *test*, 452
MacAllister, A. T.: *ref*, 286
McAllister, C. E.: *ref*, 1281
McAllister, J.: *ref*, 1174, 1225, 1296, 1383
McAllister, J. G.: *ref*, 1171, 1207, 1225, 1370
McAllister, R. J.: *ref*, 1095
McAloon, F. W.: *ref*, 518
McAlpin, A. S.: *ref*, 398
McAmmond, D. M.: *ref*, 1391
McAndless, T.: *test*, 2:1583.1
MacAndrew, C.: *ref*, 1281
McAndrew, H.: *ref*, 1499
McAndrew, W.: *exc*, 1366, 36: B79, 36:B211
McAninch, M.: *ref*, 381
McAnulty, E. A.: *ref*, 525, 1101
McAree, C. P.: *ref*, 1281
Macari, L. M.: *ref*, 1499
McArthur, C.: *exc*, 1281, 1519; *ref*, 1164, 1499, 1519, 2212-3
McArthur, C. C.: *rev*, 1499; *ref*, 1499, 1519
McArthur, C. R.: *ref*, 516, 525, 533
MacArthur, R.: *ref*, 364, 400, 425, 439, 453, 1169
MacArthur, R. S.: *ref*, 7, 348-9, 364, 400, 425, 439, 453, 464, 1085
McAuliffe, M. E.: *ref*, 1090, 1403
McBeath, M.: *ref*, 533, 1921
McBeath, P. M. L.: *ref*, 1921
McBee, G.: *ref*, 349, 603, 1536, 1794, 1948
McBeth, M. R.: *exc*, 2:1291

MacBrayer, C. T.: *ref*, 1519
McBrearty, J. F.: *ref*, 483, 533, 1403
McBride, D. W.: *ref*, 505, 1281
McBride, G. M.: *ref*, 2057
McBride, J. F.: *test*, 1548
McBride, J. R.: *ref*, 1499
McBride, J. W.: *ref*, 533
MacBride, K.: *ref*, 426
McBride, K.: *ref*, 525
McBride, K. E.: *ref*, 36, 381, 518, 525, 655, 1690
McBride, R.: *test*, 1777
McBride, R. S.: *ref*, 1194
McBroom, M.: *test*, 4:15, 4:150, 4: 408, 4:554, 4:588; *ref*, 1657
McBroom, P.: *ref*, 1499
McCabe, F. J.: *ref*, 1207
McCabe, M. S.: *ref*, 681
McCabe, O. L.: *ref*, 1174, 1255, 1281, 1315
McCall, C. I.: *ref*, 516, 981
McCall, C. M.: *ref*, 1281
McCall, J. N.: *rev*, 2182, 2193; *ref*, 64, 69, 357, 1281, 2195, 2197, 5: 308(340)
McCall, J. R.: *ref*, 349, 5:368(22)
McCall, R. A.: *ref*, 349, 1627, 1634, 1643, 1647, 1716
McCall, R. B.: *ref*, 349, 1627, 1634, 1643, 1647, 1716
McCall, R. J.: *rev*, 1499; *test*, 1538; *exc*, 1471; *ref*, 1281, 1499, 2213
McCall, W. A.: *rev*, 1768, 2:1580; *test*, 1:869, 2:1501, 3:242-3, 4: 205, 4:421; *ref*, 1:869(1-2), 3: 242(1-2)
McCall, W. C.: *rev*, 1568, 2:1632; *ref*, 2195, 36:716(2), 3:61(6)
McCall, W. M.: *ref*, 2:1272(3), 6: 480(30)
McCallister, J. M.: *rev*, 1568, 1598, 3:505
McCallon, E.: *test*, 888
McCallum, J. W.: *ref*, 1289
MacCalman, D. R.: *ref*, 1499
McCambell, R. H.: *ref*, 1499
McCamey, J. E.: *ref*, 869
McCampbell, M. K.: *ref*, 2212
McCandless, B.: *exc*, 1499
McCandless, B. R.: *rev*, 344, 521-2, 525, 533, 1247, 1697; *ref*, 483, 525, 1094, 1247, 1499
McCandless, J. B.: *ref*, 1403
McCandlish, L. A.: *ref*, 1519
McCann, B.: *ref*, 542
McCann, D. C.: *ref*, 1856
McCann, W. H.: *ref*, 1320, 2:1243 (26)
McCann Associates: *test*, 2125, 2134, 2158, 2361, 2363-4, 2367-70, 2375, 6:1185, 6:1188, 7:1105
McCants, A. J.: *ref*, 1281
McCarbery, R. J.: *ref*, 881
McCardle, H. J.: *ref*, 868
McCarley, W. W.: *ref*, 1207, 2169
McCart, P. A.: *ref*, 1395
McCarter, R. E.: *ref*, 1522
McCarthy, B. W.: *ref*, 1501
McCarthy, C. E.: *ref*, 1281
McCarthy, D.: *test*, 506; *ref*, 211, 381, 529, 533, 1101, 1121, 1205, 1281, 1463

McDonald, D.: *ref,* 7, 349, 1044, 3: 15(2)
McDonald, D. C.: *ref,* 574
MacDonald, E.: *test,* 2:1504; *ref,* 2:1504(1)
McDonald, E. T.: *test,* 2069, 2090; *ref,* 2069, 2090
McDonald, F. J.: *ref,* 561, 589
McDonald, F. R.: *ref,* 1474, 1482, 1499, 1519
MacDonald, G. L.: *ref,* 419, 1095, 1281, 1572
Macdonald, H. A.: *ref,* 22, 439
Macdonald, J.: *ref,* 1281
McDonald, J. R.: *ref,* 518, 545
McDonald, K.: *ref,* 1253
McDonald, K. G.: *ref,* 529, 1191, 1275
McDonald, K. L.: *ref,* 1073
McDonald, M. A.: *ref,* 543, 1447
McDonald, N. L. H.: *ref,* 50, 589
MacDonald, P.: *ref,* 1383, 1500
McDonald, P. J.: *test,* 830
MacDonald, R.: *test,* 5:325
McDonald, R. D.: *ref,* 1519
McDonald, R. E.: *ref,* 2337
McDonald, R. L.: *ref,* 503, 1164, 1169, 1225, 1240, 1281, 6:223(13, 16), P:446(25)
McDonald, R. P.: *ref,* 439
MacDonald, W. R.: *ref,* 1403
McDonnell, I.: *ref,* 1254
McDonnell, M. W.: *ref,* 348, 439
McDonough, D. B.: *ref,* 1447
McDonough, J. M.: *ref,* 1387
McDonough, J. P.: *ref,* 1176
McDonough, J. R.: *ref,* 1281
McDonough, L. B.: *ref,* 1500
MacDorman, C. F.: *ref,* 1253, 1281
McDougal, C. R.: *test,* 3:576
McDougal, L.: *ref,* 2212
McDougal, R.: *test,* 4:592
McDougall, C. E. A.: *ref,* 1275
MacDougall, M. J.: *ref,* 589
McDougall, W. P.: *ref,* 1302
McDowall, W. H.: *ref,* 1430
McDowell, E.: *ref,* 1281
McDowell, E. D.: *ref,* 36, 1480
McDowell, F.: *ref,* 529
McDowell, G. M.: *ref,* 1500
McDowell, J.: *ref,* 1133, 1302
McDowell, J. V.: *ref,* 1519
McDowell, R. L.: *ref,* 1137, 1264
McDuffie, F. C.: *ref,* 1281
Mace, N. C.: *ref,* 1499
Mace, R. E.: *ref,* 1315, 2285
Maceachern, D. G.: *ref,* 1474
McElhaney, M.: *ref,* 1474
McElhaney, M. L.: *ref,* 533, 1447, 1499
McElheny, W. T.: *ref,* 2239
McElroy, A. A.: *ref,* 22
McElvain, J. L.: *ref,* 589
McElvaney, M. B.: *ref,* 1457
McElwain, D. W.: *rev,* 2118, 2237, 2266, 5:888; *test,* 520; *ref,* 520, 1145
McElwee, A. R.: *ref,* 1087
McElwee, E. W.: *ref,* 381, 525, 1480, 3:679(6)
McEntire, E. M.: *ref,* 357
McEvedy, C. P.: *ref,* 1174
MacEvitt, M.: *ref,* 529
McEvoy, D.: *ref,* 1225, 1240

McEvoy, T. L.: *ref,* 1499, 1519
McEwen, W. E.: *ref,* 1383
McEwin, T.: *ref,* 868
McFadden, J. D.: *ref,* 868, 1121, 1407
McFadden, J. H.: *exc,* 518; *ref,* 525, 1123, 1480
McFall, R. M.: *ref,* 1164
McFall, R. W.: *ref,* 1302
McFarland, C. J.: *ref,* 1280
McFarland, J. A.: *ref,* 419
McFarland, M. G.: *test,* 36:748, 1: 1029–30, 3:427, 3:429, 4:498–501, 7:616
McFarland, R. A.: *test,* 1344; *ref,* 1344, 3:470(3–4)
McFarland, R. L.: *ref,* 532, 1087, 1499, 1519
Macfarlane, J. W.: *ref,* 525, 532
McFarlane, M.: *ref,* 2:1394(2)
McFate, M. Q.: *ref,* 1499
McFee, A.: *ref,* 1394–5
McFie, J.: *ref,* 525, 532–3, 545, 1105, 1192, 1499
Macfie, J. L.: *ref,* 1403
McGahan, C.: *test,* 7:746
McGahan, F. E.: *test,* 7:746
McGann, J. R.: *ref,* 2213
McGann, M.: *ref,* 69
McGannon, J. B.: *ref,* 6:742(1–2)
McGarrett, V.: *test,* 1936, 2003
McGarry, M. E.: *ref,* 484
McGarry, N. M.: *ref,* 1289
McGarry, R. J.: *ref,* 216
McGary, P. W.: *ref,* 1415
McGaughey, M. V.: *ref,* 574
McGaughran, L. S.: *ref,* 1192
McGauvran, M. E.: *test,* 1716
McGavin, R. J.: *ref,* 1133
McGavren, M.: *ref,* 543
McGee, E.: *ref,* 439, 518, 525, 532, 1192, 1428, 1447, 1469
McGee, J. E.: *ref,* 69, 361
McGee, S.: *ref,* 1281
McGee, T. E.: *ref,* 869
McGee, T. F.: *ref,* 1217, 1232
McGehearty, L. I. D.: *ref,* 1164, 1207, 1281, 1306
McGehee, C. R.: *ref,* 1207, 1499
McGehee, E. M.: *ref,* 418, 1333, 1368, 2286, 2292
McGehee, W.: *ref,* 69, 426, 621, 1845, 2135, 2239, 2266, 2:1377 (35), 3:217(117)
McGeoch, J. A.: *ref,* 426, 1090, 3: 220(30), 6:480(22)
Mcghee, P. E.: *ref,* 1519
McGhee, P. R.: *ref,* 2451
McGhie, A.: *ref,* 1499
McGibbeny, H. G.: *ref,* 1395
McGillicuddy, K.: *test,* 4:499
McGilligan, R.: *ref,* 381
McGilligan, R. P.: *ref,* 381, 1087, 1121
MacGillivray, M. C.: *ref,* 1599
MacGinitie, W. H.: *test,* 1552–3, 1702
Mc Ginn, N. F.: *ref,* 1383
McGinnies, E.: *ref,* 1403
McGinnis, C. A.: *ref,* 1281
McGinnis, E.: *ref,* 211
McGinnis, N. A.: *ref,* 1225
McGinnis, N. H.: *ref,* 1415
McGlade, C. A.: *ref,* 1716

McGlade, F. S.: *test,* 848; *ref,* 848
McGlothlin, D. E.: *ref,* 209
McGlothlin, L. E.: *ref,* 1711
McGlothlin, M. S.: *ref,* 542, 546, 551, 574, 1300, 1500
McGlothlin, W. H.: *ref,* 542, 546, 551, 574, 1095, 1294, 1300, 1500
McGoldrick, D. T.: *ref,* 1583
McGough, W. E.: *ref,* 1281
McGovern, J. D.: *ref,* 1499
McGovney, W. C.: *ref,* 1121
McGowan, B.: *ref,* 1383
McGowan, J. F.: *ref,* 1481, 2195
McGowan, J. R.: *ref,* 36, 400, 424, 1716
McGowan, K.: *ref,* 1225
McGowan, R. P.: *ref,* 1207, 1403
Mc Gown, W. P.: *ref,* 559, 561
McGrail, R. F.: *ref,* 1383, 1395
McGrath, F.: *test,* 1370
McGrath, J. E.: *test,* 1564
McGrath, J. H.: *ref,* 1281
McGrath, R. F.: *ref,* 525
McGrath, R. L.: *ref,* 1254
McGraw, J. J.: *ref,* 533
McGraw, J. P.: *ref,* 1281
McGraw, M. L.: *ref,* 435, 438
McGraw-Hill Book Co., Inc.: *test,* 635
McGreevey, J. C.: *ref,* 1519, 6:141 (5)
McGreevy, C. P.: *ref,* 404, 1164, 1281
MacGregor, B.: *ref,* 211, P:406(5)
McGregor, J. R.: *ref,* 1281, 1501
MacGregor, R.: *ref,* 1499
McGuire, C.: *rev,* 1980, 2009, 5: 835, 6:980, 6:1019; *ref,* 61, 349, 542, 551, 603, 997, 1069, 1253, 1394, 1519, 1772, 1794, 1948, 2256
McGuire, C. H.: *rev,* 1968, 1970
McGuire, D.: *ref,* 361
McGuire, E. C.: *ref,* 1121
McGuire, F.: *ref,* 1281, 1500, 2471
McGuire, F. L.: *test,* 2471; *ref,* 1256, 1281, 1447, 1500, 1546, 2355, 2471
McGuire, L.: *ref,* 533
McGuire, M. L.: *test,* 1619, 1635
McGuire, R. J.: *ref,* 1275
McGuire, S. H.: *ref,* 4:188(2)
McGuirl, D.: *ref,* 1481
McGunnigal, J. V.: *ref,* 2195
McGurk, E.: *ref,* 1094, 1121
McGurk, E. L.: *ref,* 1094, 1121
McGurk, W. S.: *ref,* 1499
Mach, B. K.: *ref,* 1094
McHale, A.: *ref,* 1428
McHale, K.: *test,* 3:654; *ref,* 3: 654(1–2)
Machen, L. H.: *ref,* 4:277(247)
McHenry, E. W.: *ref,* 947
McHenry, T. B.: *ref,* 1121
Machi, V. S.: *ref,* 533, 1499
Machir, D.: *ref,* 1471
Machl, M.: *ref,* 1499
Machover, K.: *test,* 1481; *exc,* 1466, 1468; *ref,* 1169, 1281, 1474, 1481, 1499, 1519
Machover, S.: *ref,* 532, 1101, 1169, 1281, 1448, 1474, 1481, 1499, 1519, 2234
McHugh, A. F.: *ref,* 348–9, 381, 533, 1469, 1474, 1481

Mai, F. M. M.: *ref,* 1383
Maico Hearing Instruments: *test,* 2043-4
Maier, G. E.: *ref,* 2195, 2212
Maier, J.: *test,* 2155, 7:987
Maier, L. J.: *ref,* 516, 1447
Maier, L. R.: *ref,* 1281, 1499
Maier, N. R. F.: *ref,* 357, 1303
Maijgren, R.: *ref,* 1480
Mailer, A. B.: *ref,* 532
Mailloux, N.: *exc,* 1481
Main, C. L.: *ref,* 1383
Main, H. V.: *ref,* 426
Main, N. J.: *ref,* 1044
Maine, R. F.: *ref,* 1281
Mainord, F. R.: *ref,* 1164, 1451, 1481
Mainord, W. A.: *ref,* 532
Mains, M. A.: *test,* 7:616-8, 7:623-5
Mainwaring, J.: *rev,* 460, 463, 5:245
Mair, J. M. M.: *ref,* 1198
Maire, F.: *ref,* 1906
Mais, R. D.: *ref,* 4:63(9, 11)
Maisel, R. N.: *ref,* 505, 1164, 1499-500
Maitra, A. K.: *ref,* 439, 1109, 1437, 1463, 1499, 1516
Maity, H.: *ref,* 525
Maizell, R. E.: *ref,* 2340
Maizlish, I. L.: *ref,* 525, 532
Maj, G.: *ref,* 1474
Majer, K.: *ref,* 1135, 1302
Majesky, S. W.: *ref,* 1123, 1383
Majima, A.: *ref,* 1932
Major, C. L.: *ref,* 419
Majumdar, A. K.: *ref,* 1095, 1499
Majumdar, P. K.: *ref,* 439, 529, 1499
Majumdar, S. K.: *ref,* 372, 381
Majzoub, H. S.: *ref,* 529
Makey, H. O.: *test,* 36:639, 36:644, 36:646-7, 36:655, 36:658
Maki, B.: *ref,* 1281, 1403
Makita, H.: *ref,* 1519
Makley, M.: *ref,* 1536
Makovic, M. V.: *ref,* 868, 1164
Maksimczyk, W. J.: *ref,* 532
Malamud, D.: *ref,* 1499
Malamud, D. I.: *ref,* 1499
Malamud, R. F.: *ref,* 1223, 1499
Malamud, W.: *ref,* 525
Malan, D. H.: *ref,* 1499
Malasky, C.: *ref,* 1281, 1519
Malatesha, R. N.: *ref,* 1519
Malcolm, D. D.: *ref,* 2195, 2199, 2212
Malcolm, R. W.: *ref,* 357, 1772
Malcolm, T.: *ref,* 185
Malcom, E. V.: *ref,* 1447, 1499, 1519
Malcomesius, N.: *test,* 990
Malcove, L.: *exc,* 497
Maldonado-Sierra, E. D.: *ref,* 1519
Malecki, G. S.: *ref,* 357, 5:308 (359)
Malecki, H. R.: *ref,* 1073
Malek, Z.: *ref,* 1217
Malerstein, A. J.: *ref,* 516, 529, 1380
Malev, J. S.: *ref,* 1499
Maley, M.: *ref,* 1281
Maley, R. F.: *ref,* 529, 1164, 1281

Malfetti, J. L.: *test,* 7:573, 7:575; *ref,* 850, 1207, 1280-1, 7:573(2)
Malin, A. J.: *ref,* 533
Maliphant, R.: *ref,* 1281
Maliver, B. L.: *ref,* 1519
Malkenson, L.: *exc,* 1499
Maller, J. B.: *rev,* 1366, 2:1237; *test,* 35:86, 35:91, 35:93, 1:903, 1:925, 2:1214-5, 2:1244, 3:53; *ref,* 426, 35:91(1), 2:1244(1), 3:53(2)
Mallett, D. R.: *ref,* 1095, 2:1243 (17), 6:159(41)
Malley, P. B.: *ref,* 1121, 1164
Mallick, A. K.: *ref,* 1275
Mallinger, B. R.: *ref,* 1499
Mallinson, G. G.: *rev,* 1794, 1872, 6:877, 7:795-6; *ref,* 419, 2195
Mallinson, J. V.: *rev,* 1787, 1791-2, 1796
Mallory, B.: *rev,* 2:1510
Mallory, E. B.: *test,* 5:232; *ref,* 1320
Malloy, H.: *ref,* 1499
Malloy, H. T.: *ref,* 1499
Malloy, J. P.: *ref,* 64, 357, 2266, 5:308(326, 384-5)
Malloy, M.: *ref,* 1516
Malmivaara, K.: *ref,* 1499
Malmo, R. B.: *ref,* 1519
Malmquist, C.: *ref,* 2031
Malmquist, C. P.: *ref,* 518, 1281, 1380, 1499
Malmquist, E. J. T.: *ref,* 1918
Malmstrom, E. J.: *ref,* 1281
Malnig, L. R.: *ref,* 361
Malo, A. H.: *test,* 2150
Malone, F. E.: *ref,* 2103, 2105, 2221
Malone, J. H.: *ref,* 2212
Malone, R. L.: *ref,* 2212
Maloney, M. P.: *ref,* 381, 516, 522, 1164, 1447, 1883
Malony, P. W.: *ref,* 2448
Malos, H. B.: *ref,* 532, 1281
Malpass, L. F.: *ref,* 439, 1895
Malphurs, O.: *ref,* 2071
Maltzman, I.: *ref,* 542, 574, 1480
Malueg, E.: *ref,* 6:438(466)
Malumphy, T. M.: *ref,* 1383
Man, E. B.: *ref,* 484
Manahan, N.: *ref,* 496
Manas, L.: *ref,* 1881
Mancott, A.: *ref,* 400
Mandel, H. P.: *ref,* 1499, 1519
Mandel, K.: *ref,* 1281
Mandel, N.: *ref,* 1270, 1281, 1469
Mandel, N. G.: *test,* 1270; *ref,* 1281
Mandel, R.: *ref,* 349, 439, 516
Mandelbaum, D.: *ref,* 517
Mandell, A. J.: *ref,* 1281, 1471, 1519, P:41(6)
Mandell, E. R.: *ref,* 1519
Mandell, M. M.: *rev,* 2448, 4:785; *ref,* 3:217(134), 3:535(13)
Mandell, W.: *ref,* 5:123(8)
Mandeville, K.: *test,* 1460
Mandeville, P. F.: *ref,* 1499
Mandleberg, I.: *ref,* 529
Mandler, G.: *ref,* 532, 545, 1499, 1519, P:408(19)
Mandler, J. M.: *ref,* 1499
Mane, K. L.: *ref,* 1281, 1407
Mangan, G. L.: *ref,* 542, 546-7, 551,

561, 572, 591, 1087, 1174, 1275, 1403, P:344(8)
Mangan, J. C.: *ref,* 1303
Mangan, M. R.: *ref,* 202
Mangold, K. M.: *ref,* 1475
Mangold, M. C.: *ref,* 435, 438
Mangus, A. R.: *ref,* 1240
Manheim, H. L.: *ref,* 1207
Manhold, B. S.: *ref,* 1164, 1225, 1403, 2337
Manhold, J. H.: *ref,* 1164, 1225, 1403, 2337
Mankin, D.: *ref,* 1121
Manley, D. R.: *ref,* 95, 409, 722
Mann, A.: *ref,* 525
Mann, A. W.: *ref,* 947
Mann, C. V.: *test,* 1:1167, 1:1173, 1:1175, 1:1177; *ref,* 2212, 1:1173(1), 1:1175(1)
Mann, C. W.: *test,* 2:1395; *ref,* 525, 2:1395(1-2)
Mann, E.: *exc,* 1499
Mann, E. B.: *exc,* 1499
Mann, E. T.: *ref,* 529, 1478
Mann, G. T.: *ref,* 1624, 1672
Mann, H. P.: *ref,* 525, 1560, 1583
Mann, I.: *ref,* 1932
Mann, J. H.: *ref,* 1164, 5:77(13)
Mann, K. W.: *ref,* 1205
Mann, L.: *rev,* 991, 1881, 1921; *ref,* 19, 36, 391, 400, 424, 533, 981, 1063, 1387, 1499, 1716, 1921
Mann, M. J.: *rev,* 1794; *ref,* 357, 361
Mann, N. A.: *ref,* 1281, 1499
Mann, P. A.: *ref,* 1121, 1302
Mann, R. D.: *ref,* 1090, 1207, 1383
Mann, W. A.: *ref,* 1144
Mann, W. G.: *ref,* 2454
Mann, W. R.: *ref,* 1303
Manne, S. H.: *ref,* 532, 1275, 1499
Mannen, G. T.: *ref,* 1473
Mannheim, B. F.: *ref,* 2451
Manning, E. J.: *ref,* 1164
Manning, F. L.: *ref,* 69, 426
Manning, G. C.: *ref,* 516, 532
Manning, H. M.: *ref,* 1281-2, 1284-5
Manning, I.: *test,* 3:556
Manning, J.: *rev,* 1989, 1998, 2003, 5:820, 7:917; *ref,* 426
Manning, J. C.: *test,* 27, 175, 649, 1577, 1706
Manning, W. H.: *rev,* 1091; *ref,* 357, 436
Mannix, M.: *test,* 1:917
Manno, J. E.: *ref,* 1093, 1144
Manocha, S. N.: *ref,* 1275
Manolakes, G.: *ref,* 7, 349, 483, 525
Manor, H. C.: *ref,* 211
Manos, N. E.: *ref,* 1164
Manosevitz, M.: *ref,* 1185, 1281
Mansfield, J.: *ref,* 914
Mansfield, N. S.: *ref,* 1368
Manske, M. E.: *ref,* 542
Mansmann, J. A.: *ref,* 1499
Manson, G. E.: *test,* 3:642; *ref,* 3:220(34), 3:642(2)
Manson, G. G.: *ref,* 361
Manson, M. P.: *test,* 481, 814, 827-8, 1098, 1119, 1271, 1438, 1494, 1499g, 1499l, 4:467; *ref,* 349, 1098, 1144, 1271, 1281, 1380, 1494
Manson, P. D.: *ref,* 1691

Manson, W. Y.: *ref,* 1560
Mansour, J. M.: *ref,* 2452
Mantell, D.: *ref,* 1275
Manuel, H. T.: *rev,* 227, 504, 2:
1190, 2:1428, 2:1492, 3:634, 5:
261; *test,* 43, 468, 1609, 2033, 2:
1521, 3:50, 4:176, 4:576-7, 4:632,
5:389, 5:699; *exc,* 221; *ref,* 69,
189, 361, 381-2, 468, 525, 655, 863,
908, 1603, 1609, 3:217(75), 4:176
(3), 4:576(4), 4:577(4), 5:308
(327, 427), 5:389(1)
Manus, G. I.: *ref,* 1499
Manwiller, C. E.: *test,* 35:412; *ref,*
426, 655, 2244
Many, W.: *ref,* 981
Many, W. A.: *ref,* 589, 981
Manzano, I. B.: *ref,* 1205-6, 1245,
1281, 2195
Manzer, C. W.: *ref,* 202, 1090
Mao, W. S.: *ref,* 1932
Mapeli, D.: *ref,* 2195, 2212
Maples, V. S.: *ref,* 349
Mapou, A.: *ref,* 1073
Maradie, L. J.: *ref,* 1499
Marais, H. C.: *ref,* 1456
Marasciullo, D. L.: *ref,* 1123
Marascuilo, L. A.: *ref,* 404
Marburg, G. S.: *ref,* 589
Marcantonio, C.: *ref,* 1164, 1521
March, C.: *ref,* 2059
March, J. V.: *ref,* 1519
Marchand, J. W.: *ref,* 271
Marches, J. R.: *ref,* 6:438(484)
Marcheschi, M.: *ref,* 1499
Marchi, J. U.: *ref,* 533
Marchionne, A. M.: *ref,* 1281
Marcia, J. E.: *ref,* 1380, 1471
Marco, G. L.: *ref,* 135, 998, 1005,
1053, 1843, 1994
Marcotte, Y.: *ref,* 1499
Marcus, A. S.: *ref,* 1164
Marcus, B.: *ref,* 439
Marcus, J.: *ref,* 1474
Marcus, J. J.: *test,* 3:563
Marcus, M.: *ref,* 1481, 1921
Marcus, M. M.: *ref,* 1448
Marcus, N. S.: *ref,* 1164
Marcus, S. I.: *ref,* 1499, 1519
Marcuse, F. L.: *ref,* 447, 1320, 1451,
1454, 1481, 1519, 4:281(84)
Marden, M. L.: *ref,* 516, 981, 1447
Mardenes, J.: *ref,* 1913
Marder, E.: *ref,* 2452
Mardis, V.: *ref,* 1447, 1711, 1716
Maresca, V. K.: *ref,* 2076
Margach, C.: *ref,* 533
Marggraff, W. M.: *ref,* 1281
Margolese, A.: *ref,* 2028
Margolet, B. L.: *exc,* 1516
Margolin, J. B.: *ref,* 1499
Margolis, M. F.: *ref,* 1481
Margolis, M. O.: *ref,* 1448
Margolis, P.: *ref,* 1281
Margolis, P. M.: *ref,* 1281
Margolis, R. H.: *ref,* 2031
Margolis, V. H.: *ref,* 2195, 2212
Margoshes, A.: *ref,* 1281, 1481,
1499
Margulies, H.: *ref,* 1499
Margulies, N.: *ref,* 1315, 2221
Margulis, M.: *ref,* 1315
Mar'i, S. K.: *ref,* 589
Mariani, E. L.: *ref,* 1499

Mariani, R. R.: *ref,* 532, 1499
Maricle, L. R.: *ref,* 1320, 2212
Marie, J.: *ref,* 1830
Mariglio, A. J.: *ref,* 19
Marihal, V. G.: *ref,* 1519
Marin, G.: *ref,* 1430
Marinaccio, L. V.: *ref,* 425
Marine, E. L.: *ref,* 525
Marini, J. L.: *ref,* 31
Marinkov, M.: *ref,* 1499
Marino, C.: *ref,* 542
Marino, D. R.: *ref,* 1169
Marinosson, G.: *ref,* 981
Marinow, A.: *ref,* 1481
Maris, I.: *test,* 35:23, 35:403
Marita, M.: *ref,* 1281, 2195, P:339
(20)
Marjerrison, G.: *ref,* 1232, 1346,
1447
Marjoribanks, K.: *ref,* 1087
Marjoribanks, K. M.: *ref,* 1087
Mark, J. C.: *ref,* 532, 1447
Marke, S.: *ref,* 1222
Markel, N. N.: *ref,* 1281
Markenson, D.: *ref,* 1500, 1519
Markey, O. B.: *ref,* 1144, 1499
Markham, S.: *ref,* 532, 1469, 1499,
1519
Markham, S. J.: *ref,* 7:1090(14)
Markham, W. T.: *test,* 2:1196, T:
565
Markides, M.: *ref,* 496
Markin, K. E.: *ref,* 532
Marking, K. C.: *ref,* 1403
Markkanen, T.: *ref,* 1281, 1499-500,
1519, P:327(14)
Markowitz, A.: *ref,* 1293
Markowitz, J.: *ref,* 1281
Markowski, E.: *ref,* 1281
Marks, A.: *ref,* 457, 542, 551, 561,
564, 571-2, 1207
Marks, C. H.: *ref,* 542, 546, 551,
561, 577, 594
Marks, C. S.: *ref,* 592, 1281, 1293
Marks, E.: *ref,* 357, 529, 1133, 1320,
1322, 2212
Marks, E. S.: *ref,* 525
Marks, I.: *ref,* 1145, 1174, 1275
Marks, I. M.: *ref,* 1145, 1174
Marks, J.: *ref,* 1217, 1232, 1264,
1281, 1383
Marks, J. B.: *ref,* 533, 1217, 1281,
1383, 1499
Marks, L. G.: *ref,* 2110
Marks, M. R.: *rev,* 431, 786; *ref,*
532
Marks, P. A.: *ref,* 1281, 1447, 1449,
1516, 1519, 2212
Marks, S. B.: *ref,* 1225, 1423, 1500
Marks, V.: *ref,* 1218, 1383
Markt, A. R.: *ref,* 904
Markus, E.: *ref,* 1127
Markus, E. J.: *ref,* 1127
Markwardt, F. C.: *test,* 26; *ref,*
868, 1281, 1583, 2212, 6:438(485)
Markwell, E. D.: *ref,* 532, 1094,
1281
Marlens, H. S.: *ref,* 1474, 1481,
1499, 1519
Marler, R. M.: *ref,* 1164
Marles, L.: *ref,* 2337
Marley, A. D.: *ref,* 489, 516, 533
Marley, E.: *ref,* 1145, 1275
Marlowe, D.: *ref,* 419, 1094, 1121,

1164, 1261, 1281, 1448, 1480, 1499,
1501, 1519
Marlowe, G. H.: *ref,* 1281, 1285
Marmis, C.: *ref,* 914
Marmorale, A. M.: *ref,* 1207
Marmorston, J.: *ref,* 439, 529, 1447,
1481, 1499
Maroc, J.: *ref,* 1293
Marone, J.: *ref,* 1154, 1377
Maroney, K. A.: *ref,* 1164
Maronpot, R. P.: *ref,* 218
Marowitz, S.: *ref,* 202
Marquardt, C. R.: *test,* 6:756
Marquardt, W. F.: *ref,* 221
Marquart, D. I.: *ref,* 364, 525, 1320
Marquette, A. J.: *ref,* 357
Marquette, C. H.: *ref,* 1281
Marquette, G. R.: *ref,* 1356
Marquis, D. G.: *ref,* 1121, 1164,
1281, 1383
Marquis, D. P.: *ref,* 381, 1205, 1448,
1499, 1519
Marquis, F. N.: *ref,* 1087
Marquis, J. N.: *ref,* 1519, P:450
(78)
Marr, E.: *ref,* 388, 439
Marriage, A.: *ref,* 439, 518, 1281
Marrington, D. J.: *ref,* 1356
Marron, J. P.: *ref,* 1176
Mars, P. A.: *ref,* 348, 603, 1536
Marsan, C. A.: *ref,* 529, 592, 1192
Marsch, G. G.: *ref,* 1194
Marschak, M.: *ref,* 487, 525
Marsden, G.: *ref,* 533, 1499
Marsden, R. D.: *ref,* 2195, 2199,
2212
Marsden, R. E.: *ref,* 525
Marseille, W. W.: *test,* 3:73g
Marset, P.: *ref,* 1174
Marsh, C. J.: *ref,* 518, 558, 1095,
1289, 3:110(8)
Marsh, F. E.: *ref,* 357, 1164
Marsh, J. S.: *ref,* 2212
Marsh, J. T.: *ref,* 1281, 1482, 1499,
1519
Marsh, L. F.: *ref,* 1499
Marsh, M. E.: *ref,* 1094
Marsh, M. M.: *ref,* 1069, 1281, 2195
Marsh, R. W.: *ref,* 1112, 1579
Marsh, S. H.: *ref,* 1207, 1281, 2195
Marshak, M. D.: *ref,* 532
Marshall, A.: *test,* 35:242-4; *ref,*
381, 495, 525, 578, 1112, 1338
Marshall, F. B.: *ref,* 497
Marshall, H.: *ref,* 359, 525, 1186,
1222, 1320
Marshall, H. E.: *test,* 1:1122
Marshall, I. N.: *ref,* 1383
Marshall, J. C.: *ref,* 1164, 1289,
2212
Marshall, J. F.: *ref,* 1133, 1394
Marshall, J. J.: *ref,* 64, 349, 1044,
1383, 1572, 1772
Marshall, J. L.: *test,* 1776
Marshall, J. W.: *ref,* 1383
Marshall, M. L.: *ref,* 1095, 1144,
1519
Marshall, M. S.: *ref,* 516
Marshall, M. V.: *ref,* 3:136(1),
3:217(123)
Marshall, N. J. C.: *ref,* 1294
Marshall, R. J.: *ref,* 529, 1281, 1500
Marshall, S.: *ref,* 1164
Marshall, S. V.: *ref,* 1164

Matell, M. S.: *ref,* 1403
Mates, C. G.: *ref,* 1253, 1415
Mathae, D. E.: *ref,* 407, 1380
Mathai, K. V.: *ref,* 1499
Mathematical Association of America: *test,* 2:1440, 4:369; *ref,* 2: 1440(1)
Matheny, A. P.: *ref,* 487, 516, 525, 533, 538
Matheny, K. B.: *ref,* P:496(9, 15)
Matheny, P. A.: *test,* 2068
Mather, L. J.: *ref,* 439, 505, 533
Mather, M.: *ref,* 1281
Mather, M. D.: *ref,* 592, 1275, 1277
Mather, M. E.: *ref,* 2212
Matheson, W.: *ref,* 1240
Mathew, P. M.: *ref,* 1174, 1383
Mathews, A.: *ref,* 533, 1281
Mathews, B. H.: *ref,* 1281
Mathews, C. O.: *ref,* 1320
Mathews, D. L.: *ref,* 543, 1437, 1478
Mathews, J.: *ref,* 525
Mathews, J. B.: *ref,* 1210
Mathews, J. E.: *ref,* 2451
Mathews, M.: *ref,* 997
Mathews, P. R.: *ref,* 981
Mathews, T. W.: *ref,* 1205, 1245
Mathias, R. E. S.: *ref,* 1281, 1499
Mathieu, P.: *ref,* 1281
Mathieu-Fortin, C.: *ref,* 1499
Mathis, A. G.: *ref,* 1474, 1481
Mathis, C.: *ref,* 357, 1121, 1123, 1289, 1772
Mathis, H.: *test,* 1040
Mathis, H. I.: *ref,* 1040, 1073
Mathis, J. K.: *ref,* 1481
Mathis, J. L.: *ref,* 1281
Mathis, J. O.: *ref,* 1207, 1370
Mathur, K.: *ref,* 1095, 1370
Mathur, R. K.: *ref,* 1320
Mathur, S.: *ref,* 1451, 1499, 1519
Matis, E. E.: *ref,* 1281, 1394, 2213
Matkom, A. J.: *ref,* 1499
Matlin, A. H.: *ref,* 1123
Matsch, P. L.: *ref,* 1121
Matsunaga, A.: *ref,* 245, 247, 265, 267, 296, 299, 306, 308
Matsunaga, A. S.: *ref,* 1121
Matsuuro, L. N.: *ref,* 1521
Mattar, J. C.: *ref,* 532
Matteson, R. W.: *rev,* 1366, 4:726; *ref,* 2195
Matthew, J.: *ref,* 525
Matthews, C. G.: *ref,* 50, 439, 516, 518, 525, 529, 532–3, 578, 1281, 2076
Matthews, C. V.: *ref,* 1121, 1123
Matthews, D. R.: *ref,* 1383
Matthews, E. J.: *test,* 1869
Matthews, J.: *ref,* 505
Matthews, L. B.: *ref,* 948, 1090, 1169, 1225, 1370
Matthews, R. E.: *ref,* 1281, 2135
Mattick, W. E.: *ref,* 348, 400, 1563, 1716
Mattie, E. C.: *ref,* 1383
Mattoon, P. F.: *ref,* 1275
Mattson, B. D.: *ref,* 1407
Mattson, D. E.: *ref,* 1164, 2251, 2355
Mattsson, A.: *ref,* 1471
Mattsson, K. D.: *ref,* 1280, 1383
Mattsson, N.: *ref,* 1232, 1435

Mattsson, N. B.: *ref,* 1232, 1435
Mattussek, P.: *ref,* 504, 1105, 1192, 1429, 6:555(4)
Matulef, N. J.: *ref,* 1499
Matunas, M. I.: *ref,* 543, 1447
Matyas, R. P.: *ref,* 525, 533
Matzler, F.: *ref,* 1302, 1403, 2212
Maucker, W.: *test,* 1:872
Maul, T. L.: *ref,* 589, 1315
Maulsby, A.: *ref,* 1194
Mauney, J. E.: *ref,* 1320
Maupin, E. W.: *ref,* 529
Maurath, J. D.: *ref,* 1164
Maurer, H.: *ref,* 1281, 1500
Maurer, K. M.: *test,* 509; *ref,* 381, 509, 525
Maurer, R.: *ref,* 981
Maurer, S.: *ref,* 483
Mauser, A. J.: *ref,* 516, 1716
Mausner, B.: *ref,* 189, 559, 1471, 1500
Maw, E. W.: *ref,* 1123–4, 1129, 1233
Maw, W. H.: *ref,* 1123–4, 1129, 1233
Mawardi, B. H.: *ref,* 1403
Maxey, E. J.: *ref,* 20, 1044, 1430, 1628, 2167
Maxey, J.: *test,* 751
Maxfield, F. N.: *rev,* 525, 1:1061, 2:1388, 2:1426; *exc,* 391, 483, 525, 1:B335; *ref,* 349, 525
Maxfield, K. E.: *test,* 1276; *ref,* 529, 1276, 1428, 2234
Maxon, L. M.: *ref,* 1291, 1626
Maxson, L. S.: *ref,* 1281
Maxwell, A.: *ref,* 238
Maxwell, A. E.: *ref,* 439, 518, 525, 529, 532–3, 1105, 1245, 1281
Maxwell, E.: *ref,* 529
Maxwell, E. S.: *ref,* 1469
Maxwell, J.: *rev,* 375, 1628, 1661, 3:8, 3:59, 4:85; *exc,* 525; *ref,* 525
Maxwell, J. W.: *ref,* 1181
Maxwell, M. J.: *test,* 1343; *ref,* 1121, 1343, 1745, 6:438(486)
Maxwell, M. T.: *ref,* 524–5, 533
Maxwell, R. E.: *ref,* 868
Maxwell, W. C.: *test,* T:87
May, A. E.: *ref,* 440, 1164, 1192, 1275, 1277
May, D. R.: *ref,* 1131
May, G.: *test,* 233
May, J. G.: *ref,* 1474
May, L. L.: *ref,* 546, 1044
May, M. B.: *ref,* 1121
May, M. J.: *ref,* 1291, 1383
May, P. R. A.: *ref,* 529, 1264, 1281, 1380, P:41(7)
May, R.: *ref,* 1519
May, R. B.: *ref,* 1232
May, S. B.: *ref,* 1144
May, W. T.: *ref,* 489, 525, 981, 1315, 1403
Mayans, A. E.: *ref,* 516, 1716
Maycock, G. A.: *ref,* 36, 533, 1253
Mayer, A. D.: *ref,* 503, 1169
Mayer, B. A.: *ref,* 525
Mayer, C. L.: *ref,* 1326
Mayer, D.: *ref,* 1194, 1403
Mayer, D. B.: *ref,* 2212, 7:1090(8)
Mayer, E.: *ref,* 1387
Mayer, J.: *ref,* 357, 1499

Mayer, J. J.: *ref,* 1913, 1924, 5:768 (28), 5:778(4)
Mayer, M. F.: *ref,* 947
Mayer, R. W.: *ref,* 361, 533, 1599
Mayer, W. K.: *ref,* 2213
Mayer, W. V.: *exc,* 1805
Mayeske, G. W.: *ref,* 2195, 6:125 (9)
Mayfield, D. G.: *ref,* 1471, 7:55 (16–7)
Mayfield, E. C.: *ref,* 2212
Mayfield, R. A.: *ref,* 1289
Mayhon, W. G.: *ref,* 20, 348, 589
Mayhugh, J. C.: *ref,* 2234
Mayman, M.: *exc,* 1499; *ref,* 525, 529, 532, 1105, 1140, 1192, 1499, 1519
Maynard, P. E.: *ref,* 2103
Mayo, C. C.: *ref,* 1281
Mayo, C. D.: *ref,* 1281
Mayo, G. D.: *ref,* 1281, 2197
Mayo, P. R.: *ref,* 1105, 1174, 1191, 1198, 1218, 1224, 1410
Mayo, S. T.: *rev,* 1740–1, 2340, 2347, 6:1135, 7:775
Mayo, T. B.: *ref,* 1184, 2289
Mays, A. B.: *rev,* 2:1516; *exc,* 1: 1034
Mayzner, M. S.: *ref,* 1403, 1480
Mazak, R. M. J.: *ref,* 1403, 2212
Mazer, G. E.: *exc,* 1291; *ref,* 1315, 1383, 2340
Mazer, M.: *ref,* 516, 1121
Mazur, J. L.: *ref,* 398
Mazur, J. M.: *ref,* 69, 709, 1073
Mazur, S.: *ref,* 1164
Mazurek, F. H.: *ref,* 1095, 2199
Mazzitelli, D.: *ref,* 868
Mazzoni, H. A.: *ref,* 1923
Mead, A. R.: *ref,* 419
Mead, D. E.: *ref,* P:505(5)
Mead, D. F.: *ref,* 496
Mead, L. C.: *ref,* 1918
Mead, M.: *ref,* 497, 1499
Mead, P. G.: *ref,* 1281, 1293
Meade, R. A.: *rev,* 5:195, 5:236
Meade, R. G.: *ref,* 314
Meaders, W.: *ref,* 1164
Meadors, P. R.: *ref,* 898
Meadow, A.: *ref,* 529, 542, 561, 572, 1121, 1145, 1164, 1281, 1499, 1519, 2340, 3:97(8)
Meadow, L.: *ref,* 1073, 1164, 1519, 2213, 2239, 2379, 2386
Meadows, A. W.: *rev,* 1151, 1463; *ref,* 1499
Meadows, G. D.: *ref,* 1447
Meadows, M. E.: *ref,* 357, 1207, 2212
Meagher, D. W.: *test,* 35:258
Mealiea, W. L.: *ref,* 1174, 1185
Meals, D. W.: *ref,* 532
Means, C. E.: *ref,* 1679
Means, G. H.: *ref,* 1275, 1293
Means, H. R.: *ref,* 35, 361, 1095, 1133, 1772
Means, J. E.: *ref,* 1225
Means, R. S.: *ref,* 1275, 1293
Meara, N. M.: *ref,* 1294
Meares, R.: *ref,* 1174, 1499
Meares, S.: *test,* 1993, 1996, 6:1005
Mearig, J. S.: *ref,* 589, 1069, 1087
Mears, F. G.: *ref,* 439

525, 529, 532, 1499–500, 1516, 1519, 2213, 2251, 2266
Meredith, C. G. W.: *ref,* 1383
Meredith, G.: *ref,* 1164
Meredith, G. M.: *rev,* 865; *ref,* 864, 896, 1101, 1164, 1225, 1383
Meredith, H. E.: *ref,* 1164
Meredith, H. V.: *test,* 1014; *ref,* 947, 1014
Meredith, L. M.: *ref,* 36
Meredith, P.: *ref,* 1087
Meredith, W. V.: *ref,* 1709
Merenda, P. F.: *exc,* 36, 522, 2212–3; *ref,* 19, 382, 522, 1005, 1069, 1080, 1091, 1094
Merigold, F. A.: *ref,* 1121
Meriwether, S.: *test,* 35:319
Merkin, M.: *ref,* 1856
Merkle, R. W.: *ref,* 2213
Merle, S.: *ref,* 404
Merlin, S. B.: *ref,* 981, 1624
Merlis, M.: *ref,* 439, 1281
Merlis, S.: *ref,* 439, 1227, 1281, 1447, 1480
Mermelstein, M. D.: *ref,* 1499
Mermis, B.: *ref,* 1185
Mermis, W. L.: *ref,* 1214
Merrens, M. R.: *ref,* 1320, 1322, 1499
Merriam, S. L.: *test,* 5:497
Merrick, H. A.: *ref,* 1281
Merrick, R. A.: *ref,* 1164
Merrifield, P. R.: *rev,* 2340, 2347, 6:1135; *test,* 542, 551, 554–5, 561m3, 561x2, 562, 565, 571, 577, 581, 591; *ref,* 457, 546, 551, 561, 571, 1032, 1044, 1074, 1109, 1129, 1761, 1772
Merrill, C. C.: *ref,* 1133, 1395
Merrill, E. H.: *test,* 2003
Merrill, E. J.: *test,* 1:1124
Merrill, J. D.: *ref,* 1711
Merrill, K. E.: *ref,* 1302, 2212
Merrill, M. A.: *test,* 525; *ref,* 36, 525, 1101
Merrill, P. F.: *ref,* 1391
Merrill, R. A.: *ref,* 87, 2381, 4:623 (1)
Merrill, R. M.: *ref,* 419, 532, 1164, 1281, 5:308(328)
Merriman, C.: *ref,* 525
Merriman, J. B.: *ref,* 1121
Merritt, C. B.: *ref,* 2212
Merritt, M. A.: *ref,* 1121
Merritt, N.: *test,* T:1791
Merritt, R. K.: *ref,* 1448
Merritt, W. R.: *ref,* 1394
Merry, R. V.: *ref,* 211
Merryman, E. P.: *ref,* 589
Merryman, P.: *ref,* 529, 592
Merton, E. L.: *test,* T:1080
Merton, R. K.: *ref,* 5:598(6)
Merwin, J.: *test,* 114
Merwin, J. C.: *rev,* 7, 50, 1054, 6:20; *test,* 36–7, 39, 653–5, 1602–3, 1795, 1952, 7:26, 7:559, 7:633; *exc,* 480, 613, 672–3, 709, 744–6, 763, 1069, 2105, 7:378; *ref,* 69, 357, 404–5, 1031, 1069, 1207, 1281, 2212, 2355
Mery, M.: *exc,* 549
Merz, W. R.: *ref,* 381
Merz, W. S.: *ref,* 1403
Meshke, E.: *test,* 4:494

Meshover, L.: *test,* 1637
Mesinger, J. F.: *ref,* 524
Meskin, J.: *ref,* 525
Meskin, J. D.: *ref,* 589
Meskin, L. H.: *ref,* 1281
Mesner, D. M.: *ref,* 1583, 5:308 (413)
Mesnikoff, A.: *test,* 1339; *ref,* 1339–40
Messenheimer, M. G.: *ref,* 1281
Messer, A. L.: *ref,* 1320
Messer, M. E.: *ref,* 375, 516
Messerley, S.: *ref,* 1169, 1499
Messick, D.: *ref,* 1176
Messick, D. M.: *ref,* 1281
Messick, S.: *ref,* 1121, 1164, 1169, 1201, 1281
Messick, S. J.: *ref,* 561, 1164, 1169, 1281
Messier, M.: *ref,* 1161
Messina, V. J.: *ref,* 914
Messineo, J. F.: *ref,* 981
Messineo, L. V.: *ref,* 981
Messman, W. B.: *ref,* 1164, 2197
Metcalf, L.: *ref,* 4:98(1)
Metcalf, W. K.: *ref,* 2355
Metcalfe, M.: *exc,* 1499; *ref,* 1174, 1275
Metcalfe, Z. F.: *test,* 1:1032; *ref,* 655, 1:1032(1), 3:679(8)
Metfessel, N. S.: *ref,* 364, 400, 561–2, 591
Methvin, M.: *ref,* 522
Metivier, L. G.: *ref,* 1207, 1383
Metraux, R.: *ref,* 1499, 1516
Metraux, R. W.: *ref,* 1499
Metsky, M.: *ref,* 1516
Mettee, D. R.: *ref,* 1121
Mettler, F. A.: *ref,* 1499, 5:123(4)
Metwally, A.: *ref,* 1073, 1387, 1447
Metz, J. F.: *ref,* 1133
Metz, J. R.: *ref,* 6:228(69)
Metz, K. F.: *ref,* 914
Metzcus, R.: *ref,* 2452
Metzger, P. L.: *ref,* 2212
Metzger, R.: *ref,* 522
Metzger, S. M.: *ref,* 69, 6:438 (449)
Metzner, R.: *ref,* 1121, 1281
Metzner, S.: *ref,* 868
Meuser, M. F.: *ref,* 1225
Meux, M. O.: *ref,* 1169
Mewes, G. E.: *ref,* 216, 1877
Meyer, A. E.: *ref,* 1275
Meyer, B.: *rev,* 170, 2163; *ref,* 1281, 2387, 6:438(470)
Meyer, B. C.: *ref,* 1469
Meyer, B. T.: *ref,* 1499
Meyer, C. A.: *exc,* 4:786
Meyer, C. T.: *ref,* 1186
Meyer, D. L.: *rev,* 679, 689; *test,* 1395
Meyer, F.: *ref,* 1232
Meyer, G.: *ref,* 1499
Meyer, G. L.: *ref,* 1044
Meyer, H.: *ref,* 1182
Meyer, H. H.: *ref,* 445, 447, 482, 729, 1087, 2239, 2266, 2448
Meyer, H. J.: *ref,* 1164, 1200, 1207, 1383, 1423
Meyer, J. G.: *test,* 35:241, 35:291, 35:457, 36:848
Meyer, J. H.: *rev,* 3:182, 3:186
Meyer, J. K.: *ref,* 1361

Meyer, K. C.: *ref,* 1123
Meyer, M.: *ref,* 1207
Meyer, M. E.: *ref,* 1164, 1403
Meyer, M. L.: *ref,* 1383, 1499
Meyer, M. M.: *exc,* 1486, 1499, 1519; *ref,* 532, 1182, 1461, 1474, 1499, 1519
Meyer, P. E.: *ref,* 36
Meyer, P. G.: *ref,* 1294
Meyer, P. R.: *ref,* 2195
Meyer, R. E.: *ref,* 1227, 1281, 1337, 7:55(24)
Meyer, R. G.: *ref,* 1383, 1519
Meyer, S. R.: *test,* 1968
Meyer, V.: *ref,* 403, 439, 532, 592, 1275
Meyer, W. J.: *ref,* 525, 1087, 1207, 1447, 2195, 6:186(3, 10, 16), P:390(23)
Meyering, C.: *ref,* 1403
Meyers, C. E.: *test,* 1439; *ref,* 7, 20, 349, 400, 525, 533, 672, 683, 755, 981, 1069, 1087, 1608
Meyers, E.: *ref,* 364, 439, 496, 1087, 1724
Meyers, E. S.: *ref,* 2195
Meyers, H. W.: *ref,* 1052
Meyers, R.: *ref,* 1480
Meyers, W. J.: *ref,* 1188
Meyersburg, H. A.: *ref,* 1164, 1281
Meyerson, L.: *ref,* 2045
Mezei, A.: *ref,* 1499
Mezei-Erdeley, E.: *ref,* 1499
Mezey, A. G.: *ref,* 1275
Mezzano, J.: *ref,* 1403
Mi, C. Y.: *ref,* 6:159(45)
Miale, F. R.: *ref,* 1499
Miceli, F.: *ref,* 1567
Michael, C. M.: *ref,* 1217, 1447
Michael, J.: *ref,* 1192
Michael, J. C.: *ref,* 1281, 1499, 1519, 1523
Michael, J. F.: *ref,* 1499
Michael, J. J.: *rev,* 91, 7:153; *test,* 1766; *ref,* 516, 603, 1281, 1383, 1536, 1716, 1731, 1766, 1948
Michael, L. D.: *test,* 1879, 1919–20
Michael, N.: *ref,* 1499
Michael, R. E.: *test,* 36:561
Michael, V.: *ref,* 1281
Michael, W. B.: *rev,* 185, 218, 360, 398, 401, 1072, 5:308–9, 5:377; *test,* 1766; *ref,* 7, 20, 49, 113, 349, 357, 361, 364, 382, 400, 439, 457, 525, 533, 542, 551, 561–2, 564, 571–2, 591, 603, 660, 672, 683, 755, 993, 997, 1032, 1044, 1071, 1074, 1087, 1123, 1133, 1164, 1207, 1281, 1293–4, 1315, 1383, 1423, 1447, 1536, 1599, 1608, 1766, 2251, 2355, 4:761(1)
Michaelis, J. U.: *ref,* 840, 1281, 4:50(2)
Michaels, J. J.: *ref,* 525
Michaels, R. G.: *ref,* 1164
Michaelson, S.: *ref,* 1277
Michal, R. D.: *ref,* 2195
Michalski, S. F.: *ref,* 214, 357
Michal-Smith, H.: *ref,* 1448, 1469
Michaux, M. H.: *ref,* 1232, 1255, 1346
Michaux, W.: *ref,* 2195
Michaux, W. W.: *test,* 1255; *ref,* 1255

Moore, T. I.: *ref,* 533, 1069, 1169
Moore, W. B.: *ref,* 529, 1474
Moore, W. E.: *ref,* 426, 447, 449, 529, 533, 1320
Moore, W. J.: *rev,* 141
Moorman, J. D.: *ref,* 2195
Moos, J. C.: *ref,* 211
Moos, R.: *ref,* 1281, 1380
Moos, R. H.: *ref,* 1281, 1499
Moosbruker, J. B.: *ref,* 1164
Morales, N.: *ref,* 1428
Moran, F. A.: *ref,* 532
Moran, G.: *ref,* 1200
Moran, J. K.: *ref,* 1519, P:446(26)
Moran, L. J.: *ref,* 440, 532, 561, 1192, 1471, 1519
Moran, M. J.: *ref,* 4:115(10, 42)
Morán, R. E.: *ref,* 439, 525, 533
Moran, S. M.: *ref,* 1289
Moran, T. F.: *ref,* 2:1243(14)
Morano, N. T.: *ref,* 1109, 1121, 1437, 1519
Morant, R. B.: *ref,* 1387
Moravek, M.: *ref,* 1415
Moray House College of Education: *test,* 1548
Mordkoff, A.: *ref,* 1281
Mordkoff, A. M.: *ref,* 1121, 1169, 1281, 1471, 1500, 7:55(18)
Mordock, J. B.: *ref,* 533, 1121, 1447, 1894
Mordy, F. E.: *test,* 3:618-9, T: 1807
More, A.: *ref,* 349, 361, 425
More, D. M.: *ref,* 1519
More, G. V. D.: *ref,* 202, 211
Morea, P. C.: *ref,* 2175
Moreau, M.: *ref,* 435, 1711
Morello, M.: *ref,* 1206, 1500
Morency, A.: *test,* 2029-30; *ref,* 2028
Moreno, J. L.: *exc,* 3:37
Moreton, C. A.: *ref,* 80, 477, 636
Moretz, W. J.: *ref,* 1193-4
Morey, E. A.: *ref,* 1320, 2195, 2213
Morf, M. E.: *ref,* 1281, 1383
Morgan, A. B.: *test,* 4:204, 4:776, 5:198, 5:395, 5:466; *ref,* 1471
Morgan, A. H.: *test,* 1390; *ref,* 1389
Morgan, A. L.: *ref,* 1906, 1918, 1923
Morgan, A. T.: *ref,* 981, 2028, 2035
Morgan, B. Q.: *test,* 2:1357
Morgan, C. D.: *ref,* 1519
Morgan, C. E.: *ref,* 533, 1281
Morgan, C. L.: *ref,* 1560, 1923, 6: 480(43)
Morgan, D. H.: *ref,* 69, 1572, 1844, P:353(6)
Morgan, D. W.: *ref,* 529
Morgan, E.: *ref,* P:305(20)
Morgan, E. F.: *ref,* 435, 496, P: 305(21)
Morgan, F.: *ref,* 3:263(43)
Morgan, G. A. V.: *rev,* 5, 19, 1112, 1147, 1269, 5:405, 6:620; *test,* 76, 79, 781A, 6:610, 6:626; *ref,* 415
Morgan, G. D.: *ref,* 7
Morgan, G. G.: *ref,* 1403
Morgan, H. H.: *exc,* 5:B370; *ref,* 1281, 1519, 2212
Morgan, H. K.: *test,* 3:65
Morgan, J. B.: *ref,* 1164

Morgan, J. C.: *ref,* 1207, 1289
Morgan, J. J. B.: *ref,* 1313, 4:354 (1)
Morgan, J. M.: *ref,* 64, 357, 1805, 1837, 1939
Morgan, J. P.: *ref,* 1073
Morgan, L. B.: *ref,* 357
Morgan, M.: *ref,* 1073
Morgan, M. E.: *test,* T:1123
Morgan, M. K.: *ref,* 1044, 1302
Morgan, P.: *ref,* 1508
Morgan, P. K.: *ref,* 1281
Morgan, R.: *ref,* 1123
Morgan, R. E.: *ref,* 357, 1430
Morgan, R. R.: *ref,* 1164
Morgan, S. A.: *test,* 2:1493
Morgan, W. G.: *ref,* 1923
Morgan, W. J.: *test,* 4:170, 4:204, 4:776, 5:395, 5:437, 5:466; *ref,* 220, 2251, 2266, 3:220(71)
Morgan, W. P.: *ref,* 672, 1174, 1227, 1281, 1377
Morgart, H. S.: *ref,* 425, 1072, 1074, 1383
Morgenson, D. F.: *ref,* 1174
Morgenstern, F. B.: *ref,* 1474
Morgenstern, G.: *ref,* 1127
Morgenstern, M.: *ref,* 1469
Morgenthaler, W.: *ref,* 1499
Morgenthau, D. R.: *ref,* 518, 525, 558
Mori, T.: *ref,* 1123, 1164
Moriarty, A.: *ref,* 487, 497, 507, 525, 533, 1471, 1499, 1519
Moriarty, A. E.: *rev,* 492, 1731; *ref,* 1451
Morice, H. O.: *ref,* 69, 6:438(527)
Morici, A. R.: *ref,* 2323, 5:907(2)
Morison, L. J.: *test,* 4:82; *ref,* 4: 82(1)
Morison, N. E.: *test,* 1529
Moritz, C.: *test,* 150
Moritz, F. C.: *ref,* 868, 1315
Moriwaki, S. Y.: *ref,* P:381(49)
Morledge, J.: *ref,* 529, 533
Morley, C. A.: *ref,* 36, 426
Morley, D. I.: *ref,* 1932
Morman, R.: *ref,* 2113
Morman, R. R.: *test,* 2113; *ref,* 2113
Morningstar, M.: *ref,* 69, 357
Morningstar, M. E.: *ref,* 1430
Moroney, F. M.: *ref,* 1164
Moroney, W. F.: *ref,* 1169
Morony, J. H.: *ref,* 1383
Morosko, T.: *ref,* 1164, 1389
Morosko, T. E.: *ref,* 1281
Morper, J.: *ref,* 361, 400, 533
Morrice, J. K. W.: *ref,* 1281
Morril, R. A.: *ref,* 1164, 1415, 2212
Morrill, R.: *ref,* 1240
Morrill, W. H.: *ref,* 857, 2178, 2213
Morris, A. B.: *ref,* 439
Morris, B. B.: *ref,* 1407
Morris, B. E. J. VanC.: *ref,* 499
Morris, C.: *ref,* 1423
Morris, C. E.: *ref,* 1129
Morris, C. M.: *ref,* 391, 518, 2266, 5:36(10)
Morris, C. S.: *test,* 36:795
Morris, D.: *ref,* 1069
Morris, F.: *ref,* 532
Morris, G. L.: *ref,* 499

Morris, H. L.: *exc,* 2069, 2090; *ref,* 525, 533, 1428, 2095
Morris, J.: *ref,* 1377, 1471, 1500
Morris, J. B.: *rev,* 2257, 5:954
Morris, J. E.: *test,* 772; *ref,* 772
Morris, J. L.: *ref,* 2180, 2195, 2212
Morris, J. R.: *ref,* 884, 1516
Morris, J. W.: *test,* 35:247
Morris, K. L.: *ref,* 1281
Morris, K. T.: *ref,* 1164, 1407
Morris, L. A.: *ref,* 1281
Morris, L. W.: *ref,* 529, 1391
Morris, M.: *test,* 437
Morris, M. J.: *ref,* 881, 914
Morris, M. L.: *ref,* 1383
Morris, P. R.: *ref,* 1904
Morris, R. O.: *ref,* 35, 361
Morris, R. P.: *ref,* 1121, 1294, 1370, 2199
Morris, W. W.: *ref,* 1281, 1474, 1499, 2355
Morrisby, J. R.: *test,* 1070; *ref,* 1070
Morrisey, R. J.: *ref,* 1135
Morrish, R. B.: *ref,* 1174
Morrison, C.: *rev,* 1552, 1563
Morrison, D.: *ref,* 1499
Morrison, D. E.: *ref,* 1519
Morrison, D. F.: *ref,* 529
Morrison, D. H.: *ref,* 532-3
Morrison, E.: *ref,* 1519
Morrison, E. B.: *ref,* 533
Morrison, E. J.: *ref,* 1500
Morrison, F. C.: *rev,* 604, 606; *test,* 615
Morrison, F. G.: *ref,* 1164
Morrison, H. B.: *rev,* 2:1534, 2: 1575
Morrison, H. E.: *ref,* 36, 425, 1164
Morrison, I. E.: *ref,* 7, 348, 1536
Morrison, J.: *ref,* 6:438(528)
Morrison, J. C.: *test,* 4:205; *ref,* 6:480(23)
Morrison, J. H.: *test,* 1266, 1417; *ref,* 1266
Morrison, J. S.: *ref,* 1207, 1281, 2201, 2212
Morrison, J. W.: *ref,* 357, 2195
Morrison, L. M.: *ref,* 1499-500, 1519
Morrison, L. P.: *test,* 840
Morrison, M.: *ref,* 439, 533
Morrison, M. J.: *ref,* 1447
Morrison, M. M.: *ref,* 69, 529, 1069
Morrison, N.: *rev,* 3:304, 3:329
Morrison, N. C.: *ref,* 3:242(2)
Morrison, R. H.: *test,* 1:955, 2: 1218
Morrison, R. L.: *ref,* 1499
Morrison, R. T.: *ref,* 1831
Morrison, T. F.: *rev,* 2:1587-8; *test,* 3:550
Morrison, W. E.: *ref,* 482, 2135
Morrison, W. J.: *ref,* 2:1411(2)
Morrison, W. L.: *test,* 840; *ref,* 868, 1044, 1383
Morrissette, M. P.: *ref,* 1465
Morrow, G. M.: *ref,* 1150, 1281
Morrow, H. G.: *ref,* 2449, 2451
Morrow, J. M.: *ref,* 1430
Morrow, M.: *exc,* 1499
Morrow, R.: *test,* 1753-4
Morrow, R. S.: *ref,* 189, 211, 532,

Myers, B. J.: *ref,* 497
Myers, C.: *exc,* 1499
Myers, C. E.: *test,* 2:1192; *ref,* 533, 981
Myers, C. R.: *ref,* 525
Myers, C. S.: *exc,* 2212–3
Myers, C. T.: *rev,* 2269; *ref,* 357, 1169, 2241
Myers, H. F.: *ref,* 1164
Myers, I. B.: *test,* 1294
Myers, J. H.: *ref,* 1121
Myers, J. L.: *ref,* 1164
Myers, J. S.: *ref,* 1499, 1519
Myers, J. W.: *ref,* 1164, 1394
Myers, K. R.: *ref,* 1129
Myers, M.: *ref,* 1069
Myers, M. C.: *ref,* 1499
Myers, M. J.: *ref,* 2028
Myers, N. K.: *ref,* 1123
Myers, P.: *ref,* 981
Myers, P. I.: *ref,* 516, 981
Myers, R. A.: *ref,* 447, 529, 1240, 1281, 1395, 1403
Myers, R. C.: *ref,* 357
Myers, R. E.: *ref,* 206, 391, 589
Myers, R. L.: *ref,* 1499, 1519
Myers, R. W.: *ref,* 1073
Myers, S. S.: *rev,* 654, 759, 6:601, 7:499; *ref,* 529
Myers, T. I.: *ref,* 1499
Myers, W.: *test,* 1725
Myers, W. P.: *ref,* 2103
Myers, W. R.: *test,* 1642
Myerson, P. G.: *ref,* 1499
Myklebust, H. R.: *test,* 103, 987, 2021; *ref,* 22, 50, 103, 381, 483, 493, 503, 505, 533, 558, 1087, 1281, 1428, 1552, 1629, 1900, 2258, 2266, 3:671(11), 3:678(18), P:321(13, 16)

NCS INTERPRETIVE Scoring Systems: *test,* 1035–6
NLN Measurement and Evaluation Service: *ref,* 2379, 2383, 2386–7
Naar, R.: *ref,* 533, 1469
Naboisek, H.: *ref,* 1281, 1519, 5:144(2)
Nabors, M. G.: *ref,* 211, 2080
Nace, E. P.: *ref,* 1389
Nacewski, R. M.: *ref,* 1478
Naches, A. M.: *ref,* 1447
Nachmann, B.: *ref,* 529
Nachtman, W.: *test,* 721
Nackenson, B. L.: *ref,* 1169, 1423
Nackes, M.: *ref,* 2031
Nacman, M.: *ref,* 1164, 1281
Naddeo, C. L.: *ref,* 498
Nadeau, C.: *ref,* 349, 364, 400
Nadeau, G. G.: *ref,* 1281
Nadel, A. B.: *ref,* 545, 1192, 1499
Nadel, R. S.: *ref,* 529, 2199
Nadel, S. F.: *ref,* 1499
Nadler, E. B.: *ref,* 529, 1447
Naffziger, J. V.: *ref,* 1281
Nagae, K.: *ref,* 2080
Nagalakshmi, S. V.: *ref,* 1383
Nagel, E. H.: *ref,* 1289
Nagel, T. S.: *ref,* 36, 1129
Nagel (Jerome H.) Associates: *test,* 2309
Nagelberg, L.: *ref,* 1499
Nagge, W. W.: *ref,* 1519
Nagler, E.: *ref,* 525

Nahinsky, I. D.: *ref,* 1499
Nahum, L. H.: *ref,* 1281, 1284
Naiman, D. W.: *ref,* 1169, 1499
Nair, R. K.: *ref,* 349, 1320, 2199, 2239, 2244, 2266
Naitoh, P.: *ref,* 1281, 1298
Najarian, P.: *ref,* 381, 487, 518
Najjar, B. E.: *ref,* 1519
Nakagawa, O.: *ref,* 1932
Nakajima, A.: *ref,* 1932
Nakamoto, K.: *ref,* 1145
Nakamura, C. Y.: *ref,* 1121, 1281
Nakamura, H.: *ref,* 525
Nakanishi, N.: *ref,* 1478
Nakshian, J.: *ref,* 1164
Nalder, W. K.: *ref,* 2451
Nale, S.: *ref,* 525, 533
Nale, S. L.: *ref,* 525
Nalven, F. B.: *ref,* 533, 1158, 1281
Namani, A. K.: *ref,* 2195, 2212
Namkin, S.: *ref,* 655, 1603
Namy, E.: *ref,* 533
Nanassy, L. C.: *rev,* 345, 1739
Nance, E. E.: *ref,* 1174, 1275
Nance, R. D.: *ref,* 1205, 1281, 2212
Nance, W. D.: *test,* 35:284, 35:311
Nandy, A.: *ref,* 1481
Naor, N. K.: *ref,* 1094, 1281, 1437, 2212
Napp, F. P.: *ref,* 5:308(389)
Narciso, J. C.: *ref,* 1281
Nardi, A. H.: *ref,* 1087, 1322, 1418
Nardi, N.: *test,* 3:195–8, 3:452a, 3:453, 4:518–9; *ref,* 3:196(1)
Narosny, E. H.: *ref,* 483, 525
Narramore, S. B.: *ref,* 1921
Nase, R. R.: *ref,* 381, 538
Nash, A. N.: *ref,* 482, 1073, 1121, 1171, 1403, 2195, 2212
Nash, C. B.: *ref,* 1169, 1207, 1281, 1474
Nash, C. S.: *ref,* 1169, 1207, 1474
Nash, D.: *ref,* 1499
Nash, D. C.: *ref,* 1164
Nash, D. J.: *ref,* 1499
Nash, E. A.: *ref,* 1:915
Nash, H.: *ref,* 381
Nash, H. T.: *ref,* 1499
Nash, J.: *ref,* 543
Nash, J. M.: *ref,* 361, 1044, 1181, 1273
Nash, M. J.: *ref,* 1069
Nash, M. S.: *ref,* 524, 1127, 1923
Nash, N.: *test,* 2372
Nash, P. G.: *ref,* 398, 2199
Nash, P. N.: *ref,* 525, 1716
Nasiadka, M. J.: *ref,* 1395
Naslund, R. A.: *test,* 29, 108, 731, 1596, 1765, 1790, 1947, 5:668
Nason, H. M.: *test,* 1673
Nassiakos, M.: *ref,* 1519
Nastri, L. S.: *ref,* 1724
Natale, G. M.: *ref,* 795, 799
Natalicio, L. F. S.: *ref,* 1391
Nataraj, P.: *ref,* 1095, P:381(43)
Nathan, P.: *ref,* 529, 1500
Nathan, P. E.: *ref,* 1337, 1500
Nathan, S.: *ref,* 381, 1499
Nathanson, I. A.: *ref,* 529, 1380
Nathanson, S. N.: *ref,* 1423
Nathanson, Y. S.: *ref,* 211
Nathawat, S. S.: *ref,* 1499
Nation, J. E.: *ref,* 516
National Association of Secondary-

School Principals: *test,* 1015, 1019, 1400, 4:78, 4:513, 4:515, T: 1311, T:1918
National Bureau of Educational and Social Research: *test,* 5:31, 5:479, 5:604, 6:1028
National Business Education Association: *test,* 777–8, 783, 785–6, 795, 799
National Cash Register Co.: *test,* T:2015
National Council for Geographic Education: *test,* 7:904
National Council of Business Education. See Joint Committee on Tests.
National Council of Geography Teachers: *ref,* 3:599(1)
National Council of Teachers of English: *test,* 141
National Foundation for Educational Research in England and Wales: *test,* 75, 79–80, 111, 379, 474–7, 599, 626–9, 632, 636, 651, 760, 1594, 5:393, 6:610, 6:626
National Institute for Personnel Research: *test,* 235, 402, 464, 529, 557, 658, 703, 708, 740, 1784, 2104, 2261, 2291, 2450, 6:1026
National Institute of Industrial Psychology: *test,* 384–6, 386A, 388–90, 702, 2130–1, 2247–50, 2254, 2271, 2345, 4:724, 4:769, 5:339–40, 5:880
National Institute of Mental Health Psychopharmacology Service Center Collaborative Study Group: *ref,* 1232, 1435
National League for Nursing, Inc.: *test,* 2383–7, 6:1158b, 6:1159; *ref,* 2383, 2385, 2387, 6:1159(2, 4)
National Merit Scholarship Corporation: *test,* 436
National Office Management Association. See Joint Committee on Tests.
National Research Council: *test,* 4:281
Nau, L. Y.: *ref,* 1513
Naughton, J.: *ref,* 1069
Naugle, F.: *ref,* 1394
Naugle, F. W.: *ref,* 1394
Nauman, C.: *ref,* 1519
Naumann, T. F.: *rev,* 272–3, 1149; *ref,* 516, 533
Naumberg, M.: *ref,* 1499, 1519
Nauss, A. H.: *ref,* 2195, 2212
Navran, L.: *test,* 824; *ref,* 1164, 1281, 1430, 2212–3
Nawas, M. M.: *ref,* 1447, 1519
Nayar, P. P.: *ref,* 1775
Naylor, G. F. K.: *ref,* 529
Naylor, H. K.: *ref,* 1519
Naylor, J. C.: *ref,* 1403
Naylor, W. M.: *ref,* 1281
Nazario-Ortiz, I.: *ref,* 1469
Nazzari, R. H.: *ref,* 1164
Neal, C. D.: *ref,* 439, 1174, 1380
Neal, C. M.: *ref,* 1281, 2195
Neal, J. A.: *ref,* 589
Neal, L. R.: *ref,* 65
Neal, P. E.: *ref,* 1164
Neal, R. G.: *ref,* 1430, 2212
Neal, W. R.: *ref,* 2095

Neale, C. R.: *ref,* 1281
Neale, D. C.: *ref,* 29, 914
Neale, M. D.: *test,* 1683; *exc,* 525; *ref,* 1646, 5:632(9)
Nealy, S. M.: *ref,* 2451
Neary, J. R.: *ref,* 2452
Neary, R. S.: *ref,* 1437
Neaves, A. I.: *ref,* 533, 1129, 1253, 1898
Nebelkopf, E.: *ref,* 1127
Nebelkopf, E. B.: *ref,* 533, 1127
Nebergall, R. E.: *ref,* 419
Neckere, E. D.: *test,* 20
Nedd, A. N. B.: *ref,* 1169, 1207
Nedelcu, A.: *ref,* 1305
Nedelsky, L.: *rev,* 1858, 1866, 1872
Nedler, S.: *ref,* 505, 516
Neeb, M. M.: *ref,* 1716
Needelman, S. D.: *ref,* 1519
Needham, N. R.: *ref,* 381, 525, 1192
Needham, R. F. H.: *ref,* 1298
Needham, W. E.: *ref,* 349, 525, 529, 533, 551, 559, 561, 564, 577, 1074, 1277, 1407
Neel, A. F.: *ref,* 1499
Neel, M. O.: *ref,* 419
Neel, R. G.: *ref,* 482, 2448
Neely, J. H.: *ref,* 489, 525
Neeman, R. L.: *ref,* 1883, 2228, 2234
Neff, B. E.: *ref,* 2031, 2046
Neff, J. D.: *ref,* 742
Neff, J. W.: *ref,* 1501
Neff, M. C.: *test,* 2, 1742
Neff, W. S.: *ref,* 1499
Negrete, A.: *ref,* 1281
Neher, G.: *test,* 3:422; *ref,* 3:422 (1)
Neher, L. A.: *ref,* 529, 533
Neher, O. W.: *test,* 36:549, 36:752
Nehowig, D.: *ref,* 914
Neiberg, N. A.: *ref,* 1500
Neice, T. E.: *ref,* 194
Neidich, J. F.: *ref,* 1176
Neidig, P. H.: *ref,* 1474
Neidt, C. O.: *rev,* 7, 31, 399, 1059; *test,* 1330; *ref,* 357, 359, 455, 1164, 1281, 1330
Neiger, S.: *ref,* 1499
Neild, M.: *ref,* 1626
Neilen, G. C.: *ref,* 1205-6, 1245, 1383
Neill, J. A.: *ref,* 1322
Neilsen, M. K.: *ref,* 529
Neilson, J. B.: *ref,* 51
Neilson, J. R.: *ref,* 512
Neilson, N. P.: *test,* 36:707, 1: 1003, 1:B338; *ref,* 36:707(1)
Neisworth, J. T.: *ref,* 542, 546, 551, 561-2, 577, 589
Neithercutt, M. G.: *ref,* 1094, 1121
Neitzel, B. J.: *ref,* 2457
Nel, B. F.: *test,* 1511
Nelsen, E. A.: *ref,* 357, 1281
Nelsen, H. M.: *ref,* 1289
Nelson, A. E.: *ref,* 1330
Nelson, A. G.: *exc,* 3:635; *ref,* 349, 1430, 2194
Nelson, A. H.: *ref,* 1164
Nelson, A. K.: *exc,* 497; *ref,* 419
Nelson, A. R.: *test,* 1424
Nelson, B.: *ref,* 1145, 1275, 1303
Nelson, B. C.: *ref,* 2355
Nelson, B. E.: *ref,* 357, 607

Nelson, C. C.: *ref,* 533, 1207, 6:514 (11)
Nelson, C. D.: *ref,* 981
Nelson, C. H.: *rev,* 926, 1777, 1781, 1790, 1800, 3:551, 3:554, 4:576, 4:606, 5:554, 6:897; *test,* 1812; *exc,* 1780-1, 1808, 1840, 1862
Nelson, C. L.: *ref,* 532, 1087
Nelson, C. M.: *ref,* 425, 493, 516, 533, 1158, 1240
Nelson, C. W.: *test,* 809, 897, 2455, 2467; *ref,* 3:217(106)
Nelson, D.: *ref,* 533, 1275, 1281
Nelson, D. A.: *ref,* 503, 1044, 1391
Nelson, D. D.: *ref,* 1280
Nelson, D. M.: *ref,* 2209
Nelson, D. O.: *ref,* 1225, 1383
Nelson, D. T.: *ref,* 1164, 1403
Nelson, E.: *ref,* 1116, 2:1492(10)
Nelson, E. A.: *ref,* 1403
Nelson, E. H.: *ref,* 1105, 5:357(3)
Nelson, E. N. P.: *ref,* 1116
Nelson, E. V.: *test,* 6:801
Nelson, F. S.: *test,* 1:995
Nelson, G. K.: *ref,* 532, 6:459(3)
Nelson, G. W.: *ref,* 1253
Nelson, H. A.: *ref,* 1403
Nelson, H. F.: *ref,* 2197
Nelson, J.: *test,* 1710
Nelson, J. A.: *ref,* 1121, 1176
Nelson, J. A. R.: *ref,* 1921
Nelson, J. C.: *ref,* 50, 1087, 1383
Nelson, J. H.: *ref,* 786, 795, 799
Nelson, J. I.: *ref,* 1322
Nelson, J. V.: *ref,* 1499
Nelson, J. W.: *ref,* 1121
Nelson, K. B.: *ref,* 525
Nelson, K. G.: *ref,* 1281, 2212
Nelson, L. A.: *ref,* 529, 592, 2071
Nelson, L. G.: *ref,* 1145
Nelson, L. T.: *ref,* 473, 644, 1069, 2268
Nelson, L. W.: *test,* 5:116
Nelson, M. J.: *test,* 391, 1572-3, 2: 1290, 2:1543; *ref,* 18, 87, 391, 1499, 1572, 2:1377(2), 2:1424 (10)
Nelson, M. O.: *ref,* 348, 439, 1245, 1281, 1499
Nelson, N. J.: *ref,* 884
Nelson, O. D.: *ref,* 1289
Nelson, P.: *ref,* 1194, 1499
Nelson, P. C.: *ref,* 516, 1164, 1281, 1380
Nelson, P. D.: *ref,* 1176, 1403, 1407
Nelson, R.: *ref,* 1403
Nelson, R. A.: *ref,* 1164
Nelson, R. E.: *ref,* 868, P:390(18)
Nelson, R. J.: *ref,* 240, 404
Nelson, S.: *ref,* 381, 5:83(1)
Nelson, S. E.: *test,* T:526; *ref,* 1281, 1380, 1447
Nelson, T.: *ref,* 914
Nelson, T. D.: *ref,* 1281, 1383
Nelson, T. M.: *ref,* 525, 1164
Nelson, V.: *ref,* 497, 525
Nelson, V. L.: *ref,* 497, 525, 1499, 1519
Nelson, W.: *ref,* 525, 529, 1281, 1499
Nelson, W. D.: *ref,* 1499
Nelson, W. H.: *ref,* 1069
Nelson-Jones, R.: *ref,* 2355
Nemes, L.: *ref,* 1499

Nemeth, G.: *ref,* 1499
Nemzek, C. L.: *ref,* 22, 36, 398, 426, 438, 525, 1101, 1320, 2244, 2:1399 (11, 13), 3:163(2), 3:220(47), 5:329(5), 6:647(2), P:347(11)
Nencini, R.: *ref,* 1281
Neprash, J. A.: *ref,* 2:1243(15)
Nerlove, M. E.: *ref,* 1724
Nesbitt, J. D.: *ref,* 1073
Nesbitt, J. E.: *ref,* 1253
Nesbitt, M. C.: *ref,* 516, 1716
Ness, J. H.: *ref,* 1775
Nesselroade, J. R.: *ref,* 1207, 1383
Nester, E. W.: *ref,* 1519
Nesvig, D.: *ref,* 532, 1447, 1474
Netherton, A. H.: *ref,* 22, 439
Netley, C.: *ref,* 1683
Netley, C. T.: *ref,* 403, 1275
Netsky, M. G.: *ref,* 1121, 2355
Nett, E. W.: *ref,* 1499
Netterberg, E. E.: *ref,* 1143
Neu, R. A.: *exc,* 1499
Neubeck, G.: *ref,* 1281
Neubeck, R. C.: *ref,* 1281, 1481, 1501
Neuber, J. L.: *ref,* 1470
Neubert, F. R.: *ref,* 1924, 1932, 4: 661(12)
Neubert, J.: *ref,* 496, 529
Neufeld, G. G.: *ref,* 221, 1383
Neufeld, J. A.: *ref,* 1121, 1403
Neufeld, K. A.: *test,* 7:495
Neugarten, B. L.: *ref,* 1519
Neuhaus, E. C.: *ref,* 1499, 5:36 (17), P:305(19)
Neuhaus, J. O.: *ref,* 1087
Neuhaus, M.: *ref,* 512, 533, 1363
Neuhof, M.: *ref,* 3:535(12)
Neulinger, J.: *ref,* 1281, 1499, 1519
Neuman, G. G.: *ref,* 1448, 1499
Neumann, H.: *exc,* 3:37
Neumann, I.: *ref,* 2212
Neumann, T. M.: *ref,* 1245, 2195
Neuringer, C.: *ref,* 529, 532, 1164, 1169, 1205, 1240, 1281, 1293, 1387, 1403, 1451, 1482, 1499-501
Nevill, D. D.: *ref,* 1169
Nevill, E. M.: *exc,* 525
Neville, C. W.: *ref,* 1383
Neville, D.: *ref,* 533, 2028
Neville, H. A.: *ref,* 1281, 1465
Neville, H. R.: *test,* 5:179, 5:645
Neville, M. H.: *ref,* 453, 603, 1536
Neville, W. G.: *ref,* 1294
Nevin, D. A.: *ref,* 1478
Nevins, F. A.: *ref,* 525
Nevis, E. C.: *exc,* 1486; *ref,* 1164
New York Public Schools, Division of Tests and Measurements: *ref,* 525
New York Times: *test,* 1960, 3: 613, 6:984
New Zealand Council for Educational Research: *test,* 426, 690
Newall, K.: *ref,* 2266
Newberry, L. A.: *ref,* 1094, 1281, 1501
Newbert, N.: *ref,* 1129, 1163
Newbigging, P. L.: *ref,* 1403, 1519
Newbrough, J. R.: *ref,* 439
Newburg, A. S.: *ref,* 1519
Newburg, J. E.: *test,* 1547
Newburger, M.: *ref,* 1428
Newburn, H. K.: *ref,* 1222

Newbury, D. N.: *ref*, 1365
Newcomb, R. W.: *test*, 35:30
Newcomb, T.: *rev*, 1320
Newcomb, T. M.: *rev*, 1348; *ref*, 1133, 1135, 1164, 1302, 1383, 1395, 1403
Newcomb, W. B.: *ref*, 439, 1216
Newcombe, F.: *ref*, 1277
Newcomer, C. A.: *ref*, 1356, 1407
Newell, A.: *ref*, 1281
Newell, G.: *ref*, 1214
Newell, J. M.: *ref*, 1516
Newham, V.: *ref*, 538
Newhauser, D.: *ref*, 1281
Newkirk, L. V.: *test*, 2:1516; *ref*, 2:1515(1)
Newland, T. E.: *rev*, 489, 499, 517, 540, 6:516; *ref*, 355, 525, 529, 533, 538
Newlyn, D.: *ref*, 525
Newman, A.: *ref*, 1164
Newman, A. P.: *ref*, 533, 1603, 1717
Newman, B. H.: *rev*, 790, 7:552
Newman, C.: *ref*, 1164, 1519
Newman, D. A.: *ref*, 1320
Newman, D. K.: *ref*, 1519
Newman, E. N.: *ref*, 1423
Newman, J.: *rev*, 543, 592; *ref*, 1164, 2195, 3:660(19)
Newman, J. R.: *ref*, 532-3
Newman, M.: *ref*, 1164
Newman, P. M.: *ref*, 1094, 1281
Newman, R. E.: *ref*, 1227, 1499
Newman, R. I.: *ref*, 382, 1005
Newman, S. E.: *ref*, 419, 1222
Newman, S. H.: *ref*, 64, 357, 1095, 1939, 2214, 2241, 2266, 5:308(296, 302)
Newman, W. H.: *ref*, 868, 1164, 1403, 2451
Newmark, C. S.: *ref*, 1281, 1391
Newmark, M.: *ref*, 262
Newnam, B. L.: *ref*, 1383
Newport, D. L.: *ref*, 1394-5
Newport, G.: *ref*, 2451
Newsom, N. W.: *test*, 35:162, 1:953
Newsome, G. L.: *ref*, 868, 1403
Newsweek Educational Division: *test*, 1958-9
Newton, B. M.: *ref*, 152, 400
Newton, B. W.: *ref*, 532, 1499, 1516
Newton, D.: *ref*, 1302
Newton, D. R.: *ref*, 1501
Newton, G. E.: *ref*, 914
Newton, G. M.: *ref*, 500, 529
Newton, J. A.: *ref*, 1466
Newton, J. R.: *ref*, 1281
Newton, K. R.: *rev*, 1448, 1515; *ref*, 1481
Newton, M.: *ref*, 1281
Newton, P. M.: *ref*, 1471
Newton, R. H.: *test*, 3:559
Newton, R. L.: *ref*, 532, 1105, 1499
Neyhart, A. E.: *test*, 845, 849, 2470, 2472-3
Neyhart, H. L.: *test*, 2470
Neyhus, A. I.: *test*, 2021; *ref*, 1482, 1499, 1501
Neyman, C. A.: *ref*, 1058
Neymann, C. A.: *ref*, 1499
Nhan, N.: *ref*, 1225, 1320
Ni, L.: *ref*, 447, 1519

Nias, D. K. B.: *ref*, 1252
Niblock, M. W.: *ref*, 1207
Nicely, R. E.: *ref*, 1174
Nichol, J. S.: *ref*, 2103
Nicholas, A. L.: *ref*, 1474, 1481, 1499
Nicholas, D. J.: *ref*, 1281
Nicholi, A. M.: *ref*, 357
Nicholls, J. G.: *ref*, 1087, 1499, 1599
Nichols, A. C.: *ref*, 211, 2095
Nichols, A. S.: *ref*, 869
Nichols, C. D.: *ref*, 1403
Nichols, C. H.: *ref*, 1281
Nichols, D. C.: *ref*, 1275, 1471
Nichols, D. S.: *ref*, 1281
Nichols, E. G.: *ref*, 1499
Nichols, E. J.: *ref*, 1281, 1293
Nichols, J. E.: *ref*, 532
Nichols, R. C.: *rev*, 1188, 1522; *ref*, 357, 382, 440, 1094, 1121, 1164, 1205, 1217, 1225, 1232, 1281, 1294, 1380, 1383, 1430, 1481, 1499, 1501, 6:113(25), 7:670(15, 25)
Nichols, W. A.: *ref*, 1847
Nichols, W. R.: *ref*, 1430, 1447
Nicholson, A.: *ref*, 349, 425, 1717
Nicholson, C. L.: *ref*, 439, 489, 516, 524-5
Nicholson, E.: *ref*, 357, 1048, 2199, 2212
Nicholson, E. R.: *ref*, 1921
Nicholson, J.: *ref*, 357, 361, 7:201(1)
Nicholson, L. O.: *ref*, 1499
Nicholson, R. C.: *ref*, 1501
Nickel, H. J.: *ref*, 1232
Nickel, T.: *ref*, 1169
Nickels, J. B.: *ref*, 1281, 1403, 2212
Nickerson, E. T.: *ref*, 1207, 1499, P:331(8)
Nickerson, R. S.: *ref*, 1247
Nickeson, R. C.: *ref*, 1164
Nickols, J.: *ref*, 439, 529, 533, 543, 1095, 1481, 1499, P:339(21)
Nickols, J. E.: *ref*, 439, 529, 1475, 6:141(8)
Nickols, M.: *ref*, 533
Nickore, A.: *ref*, 1123
Nicksick, T.: *ref*, 1073
Nicol, D. D.: *ref*, 1281, 2195
Nicol, G. C.: *ref*, 1174
Nicolay, G. C.: *ref*, 542, 551, 1261
Nicolay, R. C.: *ref*, 529, 1281, 1289, 1403, 1519, 2195
Nidorf, L.: *ref*, 1316
Nidorf, L. J.: *ref*, 1094, 1316
Niebuhr, H.: *ref*, 1447
Niebuhr, H. E.: *ref*, 2454
Niederkorn, R. H.: *ref*, 19
Nield, M. A.: *ref*, 1225, 1293
Nielsen, G. S.: *ref*, 1519
Nielsen, H. H.: *ref*, 381, 1192, 1447, 1481, 1921
Nielsen, J. K.: *ref*, 1207, 1256, 1361, 1423
Nielsen, W.: *ref*, 382, 1320
Nielson, C. L.: *ref*, 1044, 2212
Nielson, J. R.: *test*, 220
Nielson, L. J.: *ref*, 1281
Niemela, W. A.: *ref*, 3:217(67)
Niemeyer, K. P.: *ref*, 2451
Niemi, G. M.: *ref*, 426

Niemiec, C. J.: *ref*, 1403
Niess, R. J.: *ref*, 240
Nihira, K.: *test*, 1092; *ref*, 1092
Nijhawan, H. K.: *ref*, 416
Nikas, G. B.: *ref*, 400, 1716
Nikelly, A. G.: *ref*, 1499
Nikkari, J. G.: *ref*, 1302
Nikolaisen, K.: *ref*, 1499
Nila, M.: *test*, 5:682
Nilson, K.: *ref*, 398
Nilsson, A.: *ref*, 1275, 1387
Nimkoff, M. F.: *ref*, 1095, 1403
Nimnicht, G. P.: *ref*, 1164, 1403
Nims, J.: *ref*, 1447
Ninemeier, J. D.: *ref*, 1073
Nisbet, J.: *rev*, 331, 415, 474-5, 5:224, 5:398, 7:695; *ref*, 95, 409, 722, 1174, 1772
Nisbet, J. D.: *ref*, 95, 373, 408-9, 415, 459, 722
Nisbet, S.: *rev*, 75, 79-80, 476, 618, 1682, 6:621, 7:342
Nisbet, S. D.: *rev*, 4:24, 4:289
Nisenson, R.: *ref*, 1500
Nissley, W. W.: *ref*, 2323
Niswander, G. D.: *ref*, 1281
Nitardy, J. R.: *ref*, 1073
Nitsche, C. J.: *ref*, 1499
Nittoli, M. J.: *ref*, 1552
Nix, A. P.: *ref*, 533
Nixon, G. F.: *ref*, 1391
Nixon, J. C.: *test*, 2046; *ref*, 2046
Nixon, M.: *test*, 488; *ref*, 488; 1087, 1090, 1101, 1403, 2135, 2195, 2239
Nixon, M. E.: *ref*, 2195
Nixon, W. L. B.: *ref*, 529, 1311
Nixon, W. W.: *ref*, 1360-1
Niyekawa, A. M.: *ref*, 1121, 1124, 1499
Noak, J. R.: *ref*, 1485
Nobechi, M.: *ref*, 1403
Nober, E. H.: *ref*, 2031, 2095
Nober, L. W.: *ref*, 2031
Noble, E. L.: *ref*, 3:220(14)
Noble, E. P.: *ref*, 1195
Noble, F. C.: *ref*, 1415
Noble, H.: *ref*, 525
Noblin, C. D.: *ref*, 1448
Noe, A. P.: *test*, 35:381, 36:516, 36:521, 36:686, 36:689
Noe, P.: *test*, 4:435
Noffsinger, G. M.: *test*, T:472
Nolan, C. Y.: *test*, 772; *ref*, 36, 655, 772
Nolan, E. G.: *ref*, 189, 349, 1403, 1516, 1519, 2212
Nolan, J. D.: *ref*, 1192
Nolan, P.: *ref*, 1924, 1932, 4:658(1), 5:768(22)
Nolan, R. D.: *ref*, 1451
Nolan, R. E.: *ref*, 1207
Noland, S. J.: *ref*, 1094
Nolasco, J. B.: *ref*, 1932
Nolder, E. L.: *ref*, 1123
Nolen, D. R.: *ref*, 1073
Noll, A.: *ref*, 1451, 1519
Noll, G. A.: *ref*, 1403
Noll, R. P.: *ref*, 868, 1403, P:411(11)
Noll, V. H.: *rev*, 15, 17, 164, 1556, 1852, 1856, 1:1137, 2:1589, 2:1596, 2:1598, 3:564, 3:569, 3:573, 4:493, 4:581; *test*, 1:807b,

1:1126, 2:1263, 3:561; *exc*, 344;
ref, 868, 1144, 1403, 2:1263(1–
2), 5:87(23)
Nollen, M.: *ref*, 1320, 1348
Noller, P. A.: *ref*, 525, 533, 1474
Nolting, E.: *ref*, 2213
Noonan, J. D.: *ref*, 1717
Noonan, J. R.: *ref*, 1363
Noonan, M. E.: *test*, 4:535
Noone, A.: *ref*, 381
Norcross, C. E.: *rev*, 36
Nordan, R. W.: *ref*, 1499
Nordén, K.: *ref*, 381, 439, 1447,
2223, 2228
Nordmark, T.: *ref*, 1403
Nordvik, H.: *ref*, 529
Norenberg, C. D.: *ref*, 2212
Norfleet, M. A.: *ref*, 1447, 1712,
1716
Norfleet, M. A. W.: *ref*, 1094, 1121
Norgarb, B. A.: *ref*, 1499
Norgarb, B. N.: *ref*, 1499, 1519
Norland, C. R.: *ref*, 637
Norman, J.: *ref*, 1447
Norman, J. H.: *test*, 334, 429, 1408,
1741, 2108, 2156, 2161, 2165, 2200
Norman, M.: *ref*, 1519
Norman, R. D.: *ref*, 7, 349, 381,
439, 496–7, 525, 529, 532, 1123,
1140, 1205, 1281, 1407, 1499–500,
3:639(2)
Norman, R. M.: *ref*, 525, 6:480(33,
37–8)
Norman, R. P.: *ref*, 529, 1281,
1499, 1519
Norman, W. T.: *rev*, 1090, 1165,
1204, 1281, 2177; *ref*, 419, 1281,
1437, 2197, 5:308(356)
Normile, R. H.: *ref*, 2221
Normington, C. J.: *ref*, 1448, 1481
Norred, R. G.: *ref*, 1044, 1394
Norrell, G.: *ref*, 349, 1164, 1281,
1423, 2195, 2212, 6:438(467)
Norris, B. N.: *ref*, 357
Norris, H. T.: *ref*, 211
Norris, M.: *ref*, 487, 1276, 1428
Norris, N. P.: *ref*, 1313
Norris, R. C.: *rev*, 1221, 5:354, 5:
793; *ref*, 516, 1702
Norris, V. L.: *ref*, 1281
Norsted, L. V.: *ref*, 1383
Norsworthy, N.: *test*, 578
North, A. J.: *ref*, 1516, 2195, 2239
North, G. E.: *ref*, 532, 981, 1499,
1519
North, R. D.: *rev*, 7, 33, 469, 603,
731, 6:4; *test*, 4:301; *ref*, 22, 36,
69, 348, 361, 398, 400, 425, 652,
746, 997, 1245, 2195, 2323, 5:308
(409, 428), 5:610(3), 6:438
(529), 6:495(1), 6:574(1–2), 6:
790(4), 6:792(10), P:352(2)
North Carolina College Confer-
ence: *test*, 35:14
Northrop, P. A.: *rev*, 1:1089, 2:
1611–2
Northway, M. L.: *ref*, 1499
Northwestern University, Division
of Research: *test*, T:1326
Norton, A. K.: *ref*, 1471
Norton, B. M.: *test*, 3:559; *ref*,
1819
Norton, D. P.: *ref*, 425, 681, 1069,
1560

Norton, E. D.: *ref*, 2212
Norton, F. E.: *ref*, 1281
Norton, H. W.: *ref*, 1253
Norton, J.: *ref*, 1164, 1225, 1293,
1499, 1519
Norton, J. A.: *ref*, 533, 1154
Norton, J. B.: *ref*, 1232, 1336, 1921
Norton, J. K.: *ref*, 525, 6:480(10)
Norton, J. L.: *ref*, 1513
Norton, R.: *ref*, 1513
Norton, W. K.: *ref*, 1294
Norwalk-Polsky, Z.: *ref*, 868, 1403
Nosik, W. A.: *ref*, 1380, 1499
Notcutt, B.: *ref*, 381, 439
Notestine, E. B.: *ref*, 357
Nott, P. N.: *ref*, 592
Nottingham, R. D.: *ref*, 22, 525,
558, 578, 1320, 1480, 2213
Noty, C.: *ref*, 1383
Novack, H. S.: *ref*, 1087
Novak, B. J.: *ref*, 2195, 2266
Novak, D. F.: *ref*, 2195
Novak, J. D.: *exc*, 1812
Novak, M. L. B.: *ref*, 65
Novello, R. R.: *ref*, 6:598(2)
Novick, J. I.: *ref*, 1499
Novick, M. R.: *ref*, 1044, 2355
Novik, E.: *ref*, 1447
Nowakiwska, M.: *ref*, 529, 533
Nowell, A.: *ref*, 1123, 1313, 1499,
1519, 5:36(15)
Nowicki, S.: *ref*, 1164, 1275, 1281
Nowka, H. E.: *ref*, 357
Nowlis, D. P.: *ref*, 1212, 1389
Noyes, A. P.: *ref*, 1105
Noyes, E. S.: *rev*, 69, 2:1272, 2:
1298; *ref*, 64
Noyes, M.: *ref*, 516
Noyes, M. H.: *ref*, 516
Noyes, R. C.: *ref*, 1391
Nucho, A. O.: *ref*, 1090, 1256
Nuckols, R.: *ref*, 482, 1206, 2135
Nuckols, R. C.: *ref*, 2448
Nudd, E.: *ref*, 1313
Nugent, F. A.: *ref*, 1069, 1074,
1121, 2195
Nugent, G. R.: *ref*, 529
Nuhn, D.: *ref*, 113, 349, 1599
Null, E. J.: *ref*, 868, 1383, 2452
Nunnally, J.: *ref*, 1207, 1383, 1423
Nunnally, J. C.: *rev*, 995, 7:378;
ref, 525, 529, 533, 1164, 1281,
1395, 1480, 1499
Nunnery, M. Y.: *ref*, 69, 404, 868,
1164, 1403, 1423, 1499, 1775, 2195
Nurcombe, B.: *ref*, 516, 538, 981,
1275
Nurnberger, J. I.: *ref*, 1281, 1293
Nurss, J. R.: *ref*, 36, 516, 525, 533,
981, 1447, 1629, 1921, 2028
Nussbaum, H.: *ref*, 1121
Nussbaum, K.: *ref*, 1232, 1264,
1346
Nuthmann, C.: *ref*, 1281
Nuttall, D.: *test*, 1855
Nuttall, E. V.: *ref*, 589
Nuttall, J. C.: *ref*, 381, 525, 533,
1428, 1447
Nuttall, R. L.: *ref*, 1073, 1383
Nutting, M. L.: *ref*, 621
Nutting, R. E.: *ref*, 426, 1123, 2213
Nuzum, R. E.: *ref*, 2213
Nyaard, M.: *ref*, 529
Nyblade, O. W.: *ref*, 1403

Nye, M. R.: *ref*, 400
Nyman, A.: *ref*, 1281
Nyman, A. J.: *ref*, 857
Nyman, E. L.: *ref*, 868
Nyman, G. E.: *ref*, 439

OAK, L.: *ref*, 1918, 3:468(2)
Oakes, F.: *ref*, 19, 1069, 1194, 2195
Oakes, M. R.: *ref*, 1094, 1195
Oakes, R. H.: *ref*, 1358
Oakes, W. F.: *ref*, 1281, P:327
(22)
Oakey, R. C.: *ref*, 1144, 1289
Oakland, J. A.: *ref*, 533, 1164–5
Oakland, T. D.: *ref*, 525, 533, 538,
2028
Oaklander, H.: *ref*, 2451, 2454
Oakley, C. A.: *rev*, 2242, 2257, 3:
635; *ref*, 381
Oakley, C. O.: *rev*, 3:357–8
Oana, R. G.: *ref*, 868
Oas, R. T.: *ref*, 348, 400
Oates, W. E.: *ref*, 357
Obelkevich, H.: *ref*, 525
Ober, S. S.: *test*, 676
Oberheim, G. M.: *ref*, 1095, 3:217
(107), 3:628(3–4, 6)
Oberholzer, E.: *ref*, 1499
Oberlander, M.: *ref*, 1123, 1129
Oberlander, M. I.: *ref*, 1256, 1499
Oberle, J. B.: *ref*, 1363
Oberleder, M.: *ref*, 529, 1447, 1464,
1471, 1474, 1499, 1519
Oberlin, D. S.: *ref*, 507
Oberlin, K. W.: *exc*, 2242
Oberlin College: *test*, 6:344
Oberstein, R. M.: *ref*, 349, 1447
Oberteuffer, D.: *exc*, 36:B79
Oblinger, B.: *ref*, 525
O'Block, F. R.: *ref*, 1077
Oborny, W. J.: *ref*, 2451
O'Brien, B. J.: *ref*, 1281
O'Brien, C. C.: *ref*, 69, 86, 202,
532, 1121
O'Brien, C. K.: *ref*, 1253
O'Brien, F. P.: *ref*, 3:263(29)
O'Brien, F. W.: *exc*, 1499
O'Brien, J.: *test*, 6:23, 6:278, 6:
633, 6:752
O'Brien, J. A.: *test*, 5:589
O'Brien, J. F.: *ref*, 1281
O'Brien, M. C.: *ref*, 1087
O'Brien, T. C.: *rev*, 639, 7:463
O'Brien, T. G.: *ref*, 381
Obrist, W. D.: *ref*, 529
O'Bryan, K.: *ref*, 400, 589
Obrzut, J. E.: *ref*, 1379, 1387
Obst, F.: *ref*, 358, 1121, 1403, 1583,
1775, 2213, 6:438(471)
Obuchowski, K.: *ref*, 532, 1519
Ochs, E.: *ref*, 381
O'Connell, A. W.: *ref*, 533, 1447
O'Connell, D. N.: *ref*, 1212, 1281,
1389, 1500, 1519
O'Connell, E.: *test*, 1792
O'Connell, M. M.: *ref*, 798
O'Connell, T. J.: *ref*, 1044
O'Connell, W. E.: *ref*, 1121, 1164,
1281, 1500
O'Connor, C. A.: *ref*, 1164
O'Connor, D. J.: *ref*, 425, 1591
O'Connor, G.: *ref*, 516, 525, 2251
O'Connor, H. A.: *ref*, 7, 603, 1536

Osipow, S. H.: *ref,* 555, 589, 1415, 1430, 1480, 2103, 2195, 2212
Oskamp, S.: *rev,* 1466; *ref,* 1281, 1393, 1447, 1474, 1499, 1516, 1519
Oskamp, S. W.: *ref,* 1281
Osman, H. H.: *ref,* 533, 589
Osmon, R. V.: *ref,* 868
Osmon, W. R.: *ref,* 1383
Osmond, H.: *test,* 1173, 1215; *ref,* 1215, 1480
Osmond, W. M. G.: *ref,* 1281
Osofsky, H.: *ref,* 1183, 1281, 1403, 1423, 1471, 1519
Osofsky, H. J.: *ref,* 1499
Ossorio, A. G.: *ref,* 5:144(1)
O'Steen, A.: *rev,* 2:1331, 2:1335
Oster, Z. H.: *ref,* 439
Osterberg, E.: *ref,* 1275
Osterberg, M. N.: *ref,* 1519
Osterberg, W.: *exc,* 4:57
Osterhouse, R.: *ref,* 1121, 1134
Ostfeld, A. M.: *ref,* 1281, 1383, 1499, P:41(1)
Ostlund, J. A.: *ref,* 2195
Ostrand, J. L.: *ref,* 1121, 2212
Ostrander, J. M.: *ref,* 532, 1499
Ostreicher, L. M.: *ref,* 868, 1474
Ostrom, S. R.: *ref,* 2212
Ostrow, A. C.: *ref,* 1164, 1519
Ostrow, J.: *ref,* 20, 532
Ostwalt, J. H.: *ref,* 36
O'Sullivan, M.: *test,* 1421; *ref,* 1421
Oswald, M. O.: *ref,* 1470
Oswald, N. C.: *ref,* 1174, 1225
Oswald, R. M.: *ref,* 1302
Ota, K. Y.: *ref,* 1232, 1281, 1346
Ota, Y. K.: *ref,* 1069, 1844
Otis, A. S.: *test,* 423-6, 3:247-8, 4:386, 6:480, T:41, T:1078, T:1159; *ref,* 146, 525, 6:480(1)
Otis, J. L.: *rev,* 1880, 2260, 2263, 3:680, 4:776; *test,* 159, 431-2, 699, 2140-1; *ref,* 426, 431, 1164, 1207, 1519, 1583, 2135, 2227-9, 2251, 2258, 2266, 2457, 6:438(503), 6:1062(8)
Otis, L. S.: *ref,* 1499
Otis, M.: *ref,* 1480
Otness, H. R.: *ref,* 1428
O'Toole, C. E.: *test,* 4:761
O'Toole, D. M.: *ref,* 1775, 1968, 1970
O'Toole, J. J.: *ref,* 2212
O'Toole, T. J.: *ref,* 103
Otsuka, F.: *ref,* 1499
Otsuka, Y.: *ref,* 1499
Ott, V. E.: *test,* 5:4
Otte, A. W.: *ref,* 1259
Otte, H. W.: *ref,* 361, 1028, 1207
Otten, M. W.: *ref,* 1471, 1499
Ottenstein, D.: *ref,* 1137
Otterness, W. B.: *ref,* 342, 2239, 2266
Otterstrom, R.: *test,* 719, 2:1457, 6:634
Ottinger, D. R.: *ref,* 1225
Ottman, D. K.: *ref,* 480, 5:308 (422)
Ottman, R. W.: *ref,* 211, 1572
Otto, F.: *ref,* 255
Otto, H. A.: *test,* 836; *ref,* 836
Otto, J. E.: *ref,* 1164

Otto, W.: *test,* 1655, 1776; *ref,* 36, 522, 524, 533
Ottoson, J. W.: *ref,* 1289
O'Tuel, F. S.: *ref,* 868, 1383
Ouellette, E. G.: *ref,* 1121
Ouellette, F. E.: *ref,* 381
Ouellette, L. A.: *ref,* 1915
Oury, T. H.: *ref,* 1164
Ousley, J. L.: *ref,* 1245
Ousley, J. M.: *ref,* 2451, 2454
Outcalt, L. C.: *ref,* 1428
Outhit, M. C.: *ref,* 525
Outland, R. W.: *ref,* 1289
Outridge, M.: *ref,* 981, 1227
Ouzts, D. H.: *ref,* 1394
Overall, J. E.: *ref,* 447, 529, 1232, 1281, 1471-2, 2195
Overdeer, A. R.: *ref,* 1447
Overlade, D. C.: *ref,* 1446
Overley, H. M.: *test,* 6:44
Overley, T. M.: *ref,* 1389
Overn, A. V.: *ref,* 1361
Overs, R. P.: *ref,* 5:597(9)
Overstreet, G. C.: *ref,* 589
Overstreet, P. L.: *ref,* 1289, 1501
Overton, E. C.: *ref,* 1087, 1923
Overton, R. K.: *ref,* 1924
Owen, A.: *ref,* 403, 518, 1218, 1224, 1410
Owen, C.: *ref,* 361, 561, 564, 1294, 1437
Owen, D. R.: *ref,* 533, 1281, 1287
Owen, F. W.: *ref,* 50, 381, 533, 1447
Owen, H. F.: *test,* 4:782, 4:816
Owen, J. C.: *ref,* 349, 400, 1661
Owen, K.: *test,* 1064
Owen, M. L.: *ref,* 2344
Owen, R.: *ref,* 3:242(2)
Owen, S. V.: *ref,* 542, 551, 2389
Owenby, D. J.: *ref,* 1383, 1403
Owens, C. D.: *ref,* 1087
Owens, C. E.: *ref,* 1370
Owens, E.: *ref,* 1200, 2031, 2053
Owens, E. P.: *ref,* 519, 532, 1488
Owens, K. D.: *ref,* 533
Owens, N. F.: *ref,* 1383
Owens, R. E.: *ref,* 589
Owens, R. T.: *ref,* 50, 439, 543, 1277, 1481, 1889
Owens, T. R.: *ref,* 419, 1775
Owens, W. A.: *rev,* 2255, 2272; *test,* 2239, 2358, 6:1135; *ref,* 1281, 2212, 2239, 2358, 2:1377(3), 3:220(35), 4:277(212), 4:281(87), 5:87(16), 6:1135(1)
Owens, W. S.: *ref,* 1164, 1383
Oxford, L. C.: *ref,* 1123, 1313
Oxhorn, J. L.: *ref,* 1481
Oxlade, M.: *ref,* 426, 439, 1932, 2237, 2242
Oxlade, M. N.: *ref,* 426, 2227, 2266
Ōyama, M.: *ref,* 1499
Oyama, T.: *ref,* 1275
Oyamada, T.: *ref,* 1275
Ozaki, R. H.: *ref,* 1135, 1403
O'Zee, W. F.: *ref,* 357
Ozehosky, J. R.: *ref,* 1164
Ozehosky, R. J.: *ref,* 1716
Ozer, M. N.: *ref,* 516
Oziel, L. J.: *ref,* 439, 533, 1447

PABLE, M. W.: *ref,* 2221
Pabst, J.: *ref,* 1281

Pabst, R. L.: *ref,* 20, 1572
Pace, C. R.: *rev,* 48, 880-1, 901, 1052, 1427, 1883, 3:619, 4:45, 5:33, 5:116; *test,* 1133, 1395; *ref,* 1133, 1395, 1568, 1749, 4:6(24)
Pace, J. L.: *ref,* 361, 1403
Pace, L. T.: *ref,* 1133, 1164
Pace, T.: *ref,* 1133
Pace, W. T.: *ref,* 1394-5
Pacella, B. L.: *ref,* 1281, 1499
Pacella, M. J.: *ref,* 1447
Pacht, A. R.: *ref,* 50, 364, 426, 529, 1237, 1249, 1280, 1383
Pacine, L.: *ref,* 1121
Pacinelli, R. N.: *ref,* 2451
Pack, M. E.: *ref,* 1170
Packard, A. G.: *rev,* 2231, 2234
Packer, M.: *ref,* 1391, 1430
Paddack, J. D.: *ref,* 1395
Paden, D. W.: *ref,* 1044, 1968
Padgett, H. G.: *ref,* 1415
Padover, A. F.: *ref,* 868, 1240, 1403
Paepe, C.: *ref,* 1169, 2212
Paeratakul, C.: *ref,* 69, 419
Page, A. N.: *ref,* 2325
Page, B. H.: *ref,* 348, 655, 1603
Page, C. W.: *ref,* 1188, 1281, 1499
Page, D. S.: *ref,* 2463, 2466
Page, E. B.: *rev,* 15, 20, 119
Page, E. R.: *ref,* 981, 1092
Page, H.: *ref,* 1281
Page, H. A.: *ref,* 525, 1044, 1387, 1499, 1516, 1519
Page, H. E.: *ref,* 337, 650, 1320, 1344
Page, H. F.: *ref,* 439, 1294
Page, J.: *ref,* 1101, 1380
Page, J. D.: *ref,* 525, 1095
Page, K.: *ref,* 532
Page, M.: *ref,* 1191, 1320
Page, M. H.: *ref,* 1499
Page, M. J.: *ref,* 1164, 1403, 2212
Page, M. L.: *ref,* 2258
Page, R. B.: *ref,* 1281
Page, R. M.: *test,* 2399
Page, S.: *ref,* 529, 533, 1380
Pagedar, R. M.: *ref,* 529
Pagola, M.: *ref,* 1499
Pai, T.: *ref,* 2:1243(20)
Paige, P. E.: *ref,* 1281
Pain, R. F.: *ref,* 1934
Paine, H. E.: *ref,* 1516
Paine, R. W.: *ref,* 529, 533, 1123, 1281, 1403
Painter, G.: *ref,* 381, 981
Painter, I.: *test,* 4:252
Painter, J. J.: *ref,* 1194
Painter, P.: *ref,* 533, 1679
Painter, R.: *test,* 36:705
Painton, M. B.: *ref,* 1516
Pais, C. M.: *ref,* 1499
Paisios, J. P.: *ref,* 1361
Paisley, J. D.: *ref,* 1214
Paitich, D.: *ref,* 439, 1281, 1383
Paiva, R. E. A.: *ref,* 1403, 1407, 2355
Paivio, A.: *ref,* 1383, 1403
Pal, S.: *ref,* 525
Pal, S. K.: *ref,* 1403, 1499, 1519
Palacios, J. R.: *ref,* 105, 868, 1207, 1572, 6:589(8)
Palasek, J. R.: *ref,* 2069
Palate, E. L.: *ref,* 61

Palermo, D. S.: *ref,* 1480
Palermo, R. R.: *ref,* 589
Paley, H. M.: *ref,* 1293
Paley, H. W.: *ref,* 1281
Palkes, H.: *ref,* 518
Pallister, H.: *ref,* 1095
Pallone, N. J.: *ref,* 357, 1318, 1383, 1403, 2195, 2221
Palm, H. J.: *ref,* 1383
Palm, R.: *exc,* 1499; *ref,* 1499
Palmer, A.: *test,* 233
Palmer, A. B.: *ref,* 525, 1094, 1164
Palmer, B.: *ref,* 1499
Palmer, C. E.: *ref,* 3:475(8)
Palmer, D. A.: *ref,* 1164
Palmer, D. H.: *ref,* 1403, 2195
Palmer, E. M.: *ref,* 525
Palmer, F.: *test,* 3:582
Palmer, F. H.: *ref,* 516, 525, 533, 1519
Palmer, G. J.: *ref,* 1183
Palmer, G. T.: *test,* 1:1002
Palmer, I.: *ref,* 1320
Palmer, J.: *ref,* 1240
Palmer, J. D.: *ref,* 1383
Palmer, J. M.: *ref,* 2053
Palmer, J. O.: *ref,* 532, 1144, 1281, 1380, 1471, 1499–500, 1519, P:41 (6)
Palmer, L. A.: *test,* 226, 230, 233, 239, 7:263; *ref,* 238
Palmer, M.: *test,* 3:559
Palmer, O.: *rev,* 186; *ref,* 64
Palmer, O. E.: *rev,* 65–6, 119, 121, 124, 5:195, 5:236
Palmer, R. D.: *ref,* 1094, 1281, 1389, 1519
Palmer, R. H.: *ref,* 382
Palmer, R. J.: *ref,* 19, 424, 518
Palmer, W. F.: *ref,* 868, 1281
Palmer, W. H.: *ref,* 1281
Palmerton, K. E.: *ref,* 1363
Palmore, C. B.: *ref,* 1921
Palmore, E. B.: *ref,* 529
Palola, E. G.: *ref,* 1281
Palormo, J. M.: *rev,* 2292, 2299; *test,* 2334; *ref,* 2334
Palubinskas, A. L.: *ref,* 2212, 5:87 (25–6, 28)
Pam, E.: *ref,* 1361, 1383
Pan, J. S.: *ref,* P:411(6, 8)
Pancella, J. R.: *ref,* 7:795(1)
Panda, T. P.: *ref,* 439
Pande, C. G.: *ref,* 439, 1169
Pandey, J.: *ref,* 1095, 1289, 1383, 1772, P:340(16–8)
Pandey, R. E.: *ref,* 361
Pandey, R. N: *ref,* 1041
Pandya, D. N.: *ref,* 1121
Pane, J. B.: *rev,* 286–7
Panek, R. E.: *ref,* 1245
Panepinto, J. V.: *ref,* 1129, 1176
Paney, H.: *ref,* 589, 1109, 1123
Pang, H.: *ref,* 589, 815, 1109, 1407
Pangle, R.: *ref,* 921
Pankaskie, M.: *exc,* 1560; *ref,* 87, 621, 1087, 1560
Pankove, E. W.: *ref,* 542
Panos, R.: *ref,* 1244
Panos, R. J.: *ref,* 49, 1244, 7:670 (22)
Panther, E. E.: *ref,* 381, 400, 516, 575, 1711
Pantleo, P. M.: *ref,* 1106

Panton, J. H.: *ref,* 50, 447, 529, 1093, 1281
Paolino, A. F.: *ref,* 532, 1499
Papadopoulou, E.: *ref,* 381, 1875
Papageorgis, D.: *ref,* 1471
Papajohn, J. C.: *ref,* 1499
Papalia, A. S.: *ref,* 1164
Papaloizos, A.: *ref,* 1275
Papania, N.: *ref,* 525, 1499, 5:326 (15–6)
Papastergiou, C.: *ref,* 1499
Papavassiliou, I. T.: *ref,* 381
Papert, A.: *ref,* 1032
Pappanikou, A. J.: *ref,* 1281
Pappas, A. J.: *ref,* 2212
Pappas, J. G.: *ref,* 1044, 1121
Pappas, N.: *ref,* 1164, 1281
Papurt, M. J.: *ref,* 525
Paquette, F. A.: *ref,* 255–6, 271–2, 286, 300, 314–5
Paquin, L. G.: *ref,* 1289
Paradis, R. L.: *ref,* 914
Paramesh, C. R.: *ref,* 1109
Parameswaran, E. G.: *exc,* 1041; *ref,* 1090, 1403, P:381(44)
Paraskevopoulos, I.: *ref,* 1294
Paraskevopoulos, J.: *ref,* 1044
Paraskevopoulos, J. N.: *ref,* 981
Paravonian, S. D.: *ref,* 1176
Pardes, H.: *ref,* 1169
Pardes, M.: *ref,* 1275
Pardon, C. D.: *ref,* 1883
Pardthaisong, T.: *ref,* 1419
Paredes, A.: *ref,* 529, 1281, 2234
Pareek, U.: *test,* 1041; *ref,* 1041, 1500
Pareek, U. N.: *ref,* 1500
Pareis, E. N.: *ref,* 1471, 1499
Pargellis, S.: *ref,* 1939
Parham, K. J.: *ref,* 1281
Parikh, B. S.: *ref,* 1499
Paris, J. A.: *ref,* 1129
Parish, R. L.: *ref,* 349
Parisi, G.: *rev,* 311, 318
Park, C. V.: *test,* 1:1164
Park, G. R.: *ref,* 349, 652
Park, J.: *ref,* 1240
Park, J. C.: *test,* 6:79
Park, P. D.: *ref,* 1519
Park, S.: *ref,* 1932
Park, Y. H.: *ref,* 357
Parke, L. A.: *test,* 35:126, 3:385
Parke, R. D.: *ref,* 1275, 1281
Parker, A. D.: *ref,* 349, 1164, 1191, 1275, 2195
Parker, A. L.: *ref,* 518, 1247
Parker, A. W.: *ref,* 1040A, 1164, 1447, 2213
Parker, B. T.: *ref,* 1923
Parker, C.: *test,* 6:1104
Parker, C. A.: *ref,* 1121, 1281, 1395
Parker, C. M.: *test,* T:1399
Parker, D. H.: *ref,* 1500
Parker, D. H. H.: *ref,* 206, 415, 1682
Parker, D. L.: *ref,* 1536, 1918
Parker, E. B.: *ref,* 2212
Parker, F. B.: *ref,* 1098, 1101
Parker, G.: *exc,* 1281
Parker, G. V. C.: *ref,* 1094, 1121, 1164, 1378, 1519
Parker, H. J.: *ref,* 381, 489, 1087, 1094, 1123, 1182, 1383, 1394, 1428, 1430, 2285

Parker, H. T.: *ref,* 525
Parker, J.: *ref,* 533, 1294, 1403
Parker, J. A.: *ref,* 868
Parker, J. B.: *ref,* 1499
Parker, J. F.: *ref,* 2227–8, 2234
Parker, J. W.: *ref,* 431, 532, 592, 1164, 1192, 1207, 1380, 1403, 1447, 2140, 2195, 2212, 2448
Parker, L. L.: *ref,* 425
Parker, M. M.: *exc,* 532
Parker, R. S.: *ref,* 529, 1499
Parker, S.: *ref,* 1164, 1355
Parker, T. C.: *ref,* 2454
Parkes, E. H.: *ref,* 1281
Parkhurst, N. M.: *test,* 4:441; *ref,* 4:441(1)
Parkins, G. L.: *ref,* 2337
Parkinson, L.: *ref,* 1121
Parkinson, M.: *ref,* 2180, 2195, 2212
Parkman, J. E.: *ref,* 914
Parkman, M. C.: *test,* 949–50
Parks, A. B.: *ref,* 1289
Parks, D. J.: *ref,* 1176, 2452
Parks, E.: *ref,* 435
Parks, E. L.: *ref,* 36
Parks, J. A.: *ref,* 36
Parks, J. C.: *ref,* 1214
Parks, K. J.: *ref,* 1044
Parks, P.: *ref,* 561
Parkyn, G. W.: *ref,* 525
Parlagreco, M. L.: *ref,* 1145
Parlanti, I. A.: *ref,* 1499
Parlett, T. A. A.: *ref,* 559, 561, 1383
Parloff, M. B.: *ref,* 1121
Parmelee, A. H.: *ref,* 497
Parmenter, M. D.: *test,* 3:451–2, 4: 327, 4:517, 6:1053, P:397
Parmenter, W. H.: *ref,* 1069, 2256, 2268
Parmer, C. H.: *ref,* 838
Parmon, R. E.: *ref,* 1069
Parnell, R. W.: *ref,* 331, 1281
Parnes, P. S.: *ref,* 1280, 1295
Parnes, S. J.: *ref,* 542, 546, 551, 561, 572, 1121, 1519, 2340
Parnicky, J. J.: *test,* 2217; *ref,* 2217
Parr, F. W.: *test,* 2:1321.1, 2: 1559.1
Parres, J. G.: *ref,* 357
Parrillo, V. N.: *ref,* 1164
Parrino, J. J.: *ref,* 1391
Parrish, C. E.: *ref,* 1499
Parrish, J.: *ref,* 1281, 1519
Parrish, M. C.: *ref,* 1164
Parrish, R. E.: *ref,* 1447
Parrott, L.: *ref,* 1289
Parry, D. F.: *ref,* 2212
Parry, J. B.: *ref,* 388, 439, 4:295 (2), 4:724(1)
Parry, M. E.: *ref,* 357, 480, 482, 1407, 2129, 2448
Parsek, A.: *rev,* 2:1626
Parsley, J. F.: *ref,* 361, 1775, 1948
Parsley, K. M.: *ref,* 7, 525, 603, 1536, 1711
Parsons, A. R.: *ref,* 28
Parsons, D. R.: *ref,* 1383
Parsons, E. T.: *ref,* 1499–500
Parsons, G. E.: *ref,* 2451
Parsons, J. L.: *ref,* 1915
Parsons, L. B.: *ref,* 1094, 1447

Pearce, K. I.: *ref, 1281*
Pearl, D.: *ref,* 529, 532, 543, 592, 1140, 1232, 1499, 1516
Pearl, H.: *ref,* 1403
Pearlman, S.: *ref,* 1499, 2195
Pearman, R.: *ref,* 1895
Pearson, A. N.: *ref,* 868
Pearson, C. A.: *test,* 3:550-1, 3:561, 3:571, 3:581, 4:5, 4:623, 6:870; *ref,* 869
Pearson, D. N.: *ref,* 1281
Pearson, D. R.: *ref,* 1454
Pearson, D. T.: *ref,* 2195
Pearson, E.: *ref,* 1383
Pearson, H.: *test,* 5:283
Pearson, I. B.: *ref,* 1174
Pearson, J.: *ref,* 2039
Pearson, J. M.: *ref,* 755
Pearson, J. S.: *test,* 1284; *ref,* 525, 1281, 1284
Pearson, L. W.: *ref,* 1302
Pearson, M. A.: *ref,* 361
Pearson, O.: *ref,* 1315
Pearson, P. H.: *ref,* 1165, 1322, 1394
Pearson, P. R.: *ref,* 529, 1174, 1383
Pearson, R.: *ref,* 64, 357, 1044-5, 1048
Pearson, R. E.: *ref,* 391
Pearson, W.: *ref,* 529
Pearson, W. O.: *ref,* 1207, 1281, 1500
Pearson, W. W.: *ref,* 2448
Pease, D.: *ref,* 487, 497
Pease, D. A.: *ref,* 1176
Pease, K.: *ref,* 4:10(1)
Pease, P. M.: *test,* 719
Peatman, J. G.: *rev,* 1068, 2:1667; *exc,* 497; *ref,* 525
Peatman, L. B.: *test,* T:908; *ref,* 525
Peavy, R. V.: *ref,* 1294, 1383
Peccolo, C. M.: *ref,* 868
Pechstein, L. A.: *ref,* 202
Peck, A.: *ref,* 1227
Peck, C. P.: *ref,* 1499
Peck, D. F.: *ref,* 403, 529
Peck, D. J.: *ref,* 1253
Peck, I. D.: *ref,* 1430
Peck, J. H.: *ref,* 1164
Peck, L.: *ref,* 1711, 6:159(42)
Peck, R.: *ref,* 381, 533
Peck, R. F.: *ref,* 1069, 1121, 1378, 1383, 1394-5, 1519, 1572
Peckens, R. G.: *ref,* 1164
Pecsok, J. D.: *ref,* 1923
Pedder, D.: *ref,* 1447, 1921
Pedersen, D. M.: *ref,* 361, 533, 1094, 1109, 1123, 1206-7, 1227, 1245, 1281, 1315, 1389, 1407, 2195
Pedersen, E. C.: *ref,* 1069
Pedersen, F.: *ref,* 419, 1448
Pedersen, F. A.: *ref,* 1281
Pedersen, R. A.: *test,* 792, 3:388c, 4:454; *exc,* 1095; *ref,* 69, 1095, 3:2(10), 3:4(6), 4:454(1)
Pedersen, T.: *ref,* 2251
Pederson, M. G.: *ref,* 1094
Pederson, W.: *test,* 320
Pederson-Krag, G.: *exc,* 5:127
Pedigo, L.: *ref,* 1499
Pedley, J. C.: *ref,* 1275
Pedrini, D. T.: *ref,* 50, 381, 516, 525, 529, 532, 1428, 1481

Pedrini, L. N.: *ref,* 525, 1428, 1481
Peebles, R. R.: *ref,* 1499, 1519
Peek, R. M.: *ref,* 1281, 1447
Peel, E. A.: *rev,* 415, 1070, 2269, 5:357, 5:377; *test,* 4:313; *ref,* 95, 189, 354, 373, 408-9, 415, 425, 439, 462-3, 2247, 4:313(2)
Peel, R. A.: *ref,* 1069
Peerson, R. H.: *ref,* 1044
Pegg, J. L.: *ref,* 1415
Pegnato, C. V.: *ref,* 425
Pegram, E. L.: *ref,* 525
Pehle, J. W.: *ref,* 1281
Pehrson, P. J.: *ref,* 798, 1044
Peirce, J. R.: *ref,* 2451, 2454
Peiser, W. G.: *ref,* 3:217(57)
Peisner, E. F.: *ref,* 505
Peixotto, H. E.: *ref,* 64, 69, 357, 532, 1447, 1457, 1519, 1583
Pekarek, R. C.: *ref,* 1415
Pelc, R. E.: *ref,* 381, 1447
Pellegreno, D. D.: *ref,* 1315
Pellegrin, V. B. H.: *ref,* 1164, 1281, 1294, 1315
Pelletier, H. W.: *ref,* 208
Pelosi, J. W.: *ref,* 364, 529, 2234
Pelser, A. J. K.: *test,* 1511
Peltier, C. L.: *test,* 6:1019
Pelton, R. B.: *ref,* 364
Pelz, D. C.: *ref,* 574
Pelz, K.: *ref,* 497, 533, 1499, 1724
Pelz, K. S.: *ref,* 497, 533, 1499, 6:228(70, 74)
Pemberton, C. L.: *ref,* 1205-6, 1245, 1403, 2195
Pemberton, D. A.: *ref,* 1275, 1383
Pemberton, W.: *ref,* 1499
Pemberton, W. A.: *ref,* 49, 361, 1164, 1772
Pemberton, W. H.: *ref,* 1281, 1499
Peña, C. D.: *ref,* 1164, 1499
Penberthy, D. K.: *ref,* 1281
Pence, R. W.: *test,* 6:283
Pender, F. R.: *ref,* 1069, 2195
Pendergast, K.: *test,* 2086
Pendergast, M. C.: *ref,* 419, 1145, 1281
Pendergraph, A.: *ref,* 1069
Pendergrass, P. W.: *ref,* 1415
Penfield, R. V.: *ref,* 482, 2107, 2212, 2239, 2454
Penfold, D. J.: *ref,* 391, 439, 533
Penfold, D. M.: *ref,* 1294
Penfold, V.: *ref,* 1174
Penk, W.: *ref,* 1471
Penk, W. E.: *ref,* 1471
Penman, A. S.: *ref,* 1281
Penn, L.: *ref,* 1383
Penn, M. P.: *ref,* 1281
Penn, N. E.: *ref,* 404, 1281, 1499
Pennebaker, W. K.: *ref,* 884
Pennell, L. A.: *ref,* 1121
Penner, C. L.: *ref,* 1315
Penner, L.: *ref,* 1355
Pennington, A. L.: *ref,* 2212
Pennington, D. F.: *test,* 1285
Pennington, H.: *ref,* 1499
Pennington, L. W.: *ref,* 1469
Pennington, M. H.: *ref,* 1281
Pennington, V.: *ref,* 1232, 1281
Pennscott, W. W.: *ref,* 1303
Penny, R.: *ref,* 1140
Penny, R. K.: *ref,* 542
Penny, S.: *ref,* 543, 1447

Penrose, L. S.: *rev,* 1281, 3:228; *test,* 428; *ref,* 428, 439, 518, 525
Penry, I. F.: *ref,* 1521
Penzer, W. N.: *ref,* 529, 1144, 1183, 1363, 1403, 2195
Peoples, C.: *ref,* 1447
Peoples, L. C.: *ref,* 1447
Pepin, L. A.: *ref,* 1447
Pepin, R. R.: *ref,* 1289
Pepinsky, A.: *exc,* 216
Pepinsky, H. B.: *ref,* 1164, 1499
Pepinsky, H. N.: *ref,* 404
Pepitone, A.: *ref,* 1474
Peploe, E.: *ref,* 1567, 1574
Peppard, P. L.: *ref,* 69
Pepper, L. J.: *ref,* 1281, 1437
Pepper, R. S.: *ref,* 1164, 1626, 1772
Perce, F. C.: *ref,* 525
Percival, T. S.: *test,* 6:380-1; *ref,* 6:380(1), 6:381(1)
Percy, L. M.: *ref,* 533
Percy, R. L.: *ref,* 1383
Perczel, L.: *ref,* 1500
Perczel, T.: *ref,* 1500
Perdue, W. C.: *ref,* 840, 1281, 1499
Peres, S. H.: *ref,* 2212, 7:1090(3)
Peretz, D.: *ref,* 518, 2234
Perez, E.: *ref,* 2046
Perez, F.: *ref,* 1281
Pérez, R. L. C.: *ref,* 1169
Perfection Form Co.: *test,* 83, 140, 142, 1760, 1964, 1982-3, 2002, 2008
Periaswamy, T. M.: *ref,* 439
Perin, C. T.: *ref,* 1212
Perkins, C. W.: *ref,* 1164, 1481
Perkins, D. W.: *ref,* 1123
Perkins, E. R.: *ref,* 1176
Perkins, J. A.: *ref,* 255, 271, 300, 314
Perkins, J. C.: *ref,* 447, 592, 1281, 1499
Perkins, J. E.: *ref,* 1281
Perkins, K. A.: *ref,* 1519
Perkins, K. J.: *test,* 4:799; *ref,* 4:799(1)
Perkins, R. E.: *ref,* 525
Perkins, S. A.: *ref,* 574
Perkins, W. H.: *rev,* 103, 2097-8
Perkinson, P. R.: *ref,* 1469
Perl, M. L.: *ref,* 1403
Perl, R. E.: *ref,* 1320, 3:217(60)
Perler, H.: *ref,* 2031
Perley, J.: *ref,* 1195
Perlitsh, H. D.: *ref,* 1240, 1281
Perlman, J. A.: *ref,* 1499
Perlman, L. G.: *ref,* 342, 1281
Perlman, R. M.: *ref,* 1087
Perlman, S. E.: *ref,* 1499
Perloe, S. I.: *ref,* 1448
Perloff, R.: *ref,* 342
Pernell, E.: *ref,* 1303, 1415
Perozzi, J. A.: *ref,* 981
Perr, H. M.: *ref,* 1240, 1281, 1519
Perret, K. N.: *rev,* 248, 5:291
Perrett, L.: *ref,* 529, 543
Perrin, F. A. C.: *test,* 1899
Perrine, G.: *test,* 35:230
Perrine, M. W.: *ref,* 444, 480, 844, 1069, 1174, 2195, 2266
Perris, C.: *ref,* 1275, 1281
Perrodin, A. F.: *ref,* P:302(1)
Perrone, J. V.: *ref,* 574
Perrone, P. A.: *ref,* 1073, 1289
Perrow, M. V.: *ref,* 1383

Phifer, M. P.: *ref*, 1129, 1289
Philbrick, B. B.: *ref*, 2234
Philbrick, E. B.: *ref*, 1387
Philbrick, R. E.: *ref*, 826
Philip, A. E.: *ref*, 1218, 1224, 1227, 1281, 1295, 1383, 1410
Philip, B. R.: *ref*, 1519, 1932, 2259
Philip, F. J.: *ref*, 1281
Philip, R.: *ref*, 1281
Philipp, J. A.: *ref*, 589
Philippopoulos, G. S.: *ref*, 1481, 1499
Philippus, M. J.: *ref*, 1164, 1225, 1228, 1281, 1403, 2214
Philips, B. U.: *ref*, 1094, 1181, 1275, 1281
Philleo, C.: *ref*, 36
Phillip, P. J.: *ref*, 2337
Phillips, A.: *ref*, 525
Phillips, A. J.: *test*, 35:417; *ref*, 387, 3:242(8)
Phillips, A. R.: *ref*, 1281
Phillips, B.: *ref*, 981
Phillips, B. K.: *ref*, 2234
Phillips, B. N.: *ref*, 36, 1123, 1129, 1513
Phillips, B. S.: *ref*, 1145
Phillips, C.: *ref*, 1583
Phillips, C. E.: *ref*, 1281
Phillips, C. J.: *ref*, 439, 495, 525, 981, 1447, 1680
Phillips, D. C.: *ref*, 519, 525, 981, 1314
Phillips, D. L.: *ref*, 1281
Phillips, E. L.: *ref*, 518, 525, 532, 1123, 1223, 1281, 1447
Phillips, G. H.: *test*, 3:149
Phillips, G. O.: *ref*, 1772
Phillips, G. R.: *test*, 2202; *ref*, 325, 439, 2266
Phillips, H. E.: *ref*, 1883
Phillips, J. A.: *ref*, 1968
Phillips, J. C.: *ref*, 482, 5:308(436)
Phillips, J. D.: *ref*, 1383
Phillips, J. E.: *ref*, 1380
Phillips, J. J.: *ref*, 2259
Phillips, J. L.: *ref*, 1164
Phillips, J. S.: *ref*, 1044, 1499, 5:76(23-5), P:326(26, 31)
Phillips, L.: *exc*, 1499; *ref*, 1428, 1499
Phillips, L. N.: *ref*, 357
Phillips, L. W.: *ref*, 2195
Phillips, M.: *ref*, 1031, 1035, 1207, 1275, 1281, 1294, 1383, 2212
Phillips, R.: *ref*, 449, 452
Phillips, R. L.: *ref*, 1281
Phillips, R. M.: *ref*, 361, 447, 449, 452, 529
Phillips, R. V.: *ref*, 868, 1194
Phillips, R. W.: *ref*, 1145
Phillips, T. G.: *rev*, 1859, 1863-6, 5:751
Phillips, V. A.: *ref*, 1281
Phillips, V. K.: *ref*, 574, 589
Phillips, W. S.: *ref*, 2195
Phillipson, H.: *test*, 1243, 1486; *exc*, 1522, 4:138, 5:137; *ref*, 1243, 1486, 1499, 1519
Philo, T. F.: *ref*, 1469
Philpott, S. J. F.: *exc*, 4:345
Phipps, G. T.: *ref*, 425, 1072, 1074, 1363, 1383, 2337
Pian, R. C.: *test*, 225

Piccard, L. A.: *ref*, 1135
Picerno, V. J.: *ref*, 868
Piche, M.: *ref*, 1355, 1403
Pichot, P.: *ref*, 439, 1499
Pick, T.: *ref*, 1499
Pickard, H. A.: *ref*, 1383
Pickard, L.: *test*, 35:234
Pickard, P. M.: *ref*, 1499
Pickering, C. T.: *ref*, 12
Pickering, W. D.: *ref*, 1499, 1519
Pickett, B. J.: *ref*, 1500
Pickett, E.: *test*, 4:682
Pickett, H. C.: *rev*, 3:359
Pickett, L. M.: *ref*, 1073
Pickett, W. W.: *ref*, 1320
Pickford, A. S.: *exc*, 1140
Pickford, J. H.: *ref*, 1207
Pickford, R. W.: *test*, 1489; *exc*, 1140, 5:127; *ref*, 1489, 1932
Pickle, J. H.: *ref*, 69
Pickles, D. G.: *ref*, 525, 533
Pickup, A. J.: *ref*, 1252
Pickup, K. T.: *ref*, 381, 525, 533
Piddington, M.: *ref*, 518
Piddington, R.: *ref*, 518
Pidgeon, D. A.: *rev*, 328, 398, 400, 652, 1743; *test*, 415, 474-5, 2269; *ref*, 415
Piel, G.: *ref*, 3:688(5)
Pienaar, W. D.: *ref*, 1499
Pierce, C. M.: *ref*, 1281
Pierce, D. R.: *ref*, 1572
Pierce, H. O.: *exc*, 1519; *ref*, 525
Pierce, J.: *ref*, 1253
Pierce, J. V.: *ref*, 1121, 1123
Pierce, K. K.: *ref*, 1207, 1281
Pierce, R. A.: *ref*, 518, 1207, 1302, 1322, 1394-5
Pierce, R. C.: *ref*, 503, 529
Pierce, R. M.: *ref*, 529, 1281, 1499
Pierce, W. E.: *ref*, 1281
Pierce, W. O.: *ref*, 1095
Pierce-Jones, J.: *rev*, 1357, 1419, 2195, 5:100; *ref*, 364, 533, 542, 1095, 1121, 1281, 2195, 4:277(251)
Piercy, M.: *ref*, 529
Piercy, M. F.: *ref*, 525, 532, 545, 1105, 1192, 1499
Piercy, M. M.: *ref*, 439, 529, 532, 1192
Pierleoni, R. G.: *ref*, 425, 1306, 1320, 1403, 1775
Pierloot, R. A.: *ref*, 1500
Piers, E. V.: *rev*, 516, 522, 6:537; *test*, 1326; *ref*, 574, 1109, 1275
Pierson, E.: *test*, 1028
Pierson, G.: *ref*, 1383
Pierson, G. A.: *ref*, 69, 2355, 4:812(11)
Pierson, G. R.: *ref*, 1253, 1367
Pierson, H.: *ref*, 113
Pierson, J. S.: *ref*, 1164, 1281, 2212
Pierson, L. R.: *ref*, 419
Pierson, R. R.: *ref*, 2212
Pietrofesa, J. J.: *ref*, 1164
Piety, K. R.: *ref*, 1469
Pigg, E. E.: *ref*, 1281
Pignatelli, M. L.: *rev*, 355, 2:1426; *ref*, 525
Pihkanen, T. A.: *ref*, 1281, 1499-500, 1519, P:327(14)
Pihl, R. O.: *ref*, 529, 533
Pihlblad, C. T.: *ref*, 419

Pikaart, L.: *rev*, 654, 7:479
Pike, A.: *ref*, 1383
Pike, F.: *ref*, 497, 533, 1499, 1724, 6:228(70, 74)
Pike, H.: *ref*, 202
Pike, R. E.: *test*, 2:1277
Pikunas, J.: *test*, 1465; *ref*, 1465
Pilapil, B.: *ref*, 1044, 1280-1, 2212
Pilberg, R.: *ref*, 2069, 2095
Pilch, A.: *ref*, 1291
Pilch, J.: *test*, 281
Pildner, H.: *ref*, 1344, 1519
Pile, E.: *ref*, 1519
Pile, E. N.: *ref*, 1281
Pilgram, M. A. G.: *ref*, 1207
Piliavin, I.: *ref*, 1121
Pilkey, L.: *ref*, 1519
Pilkington, G. W.: *ref*, 331, 446
Pillai, N. P.: *ref*, 1775
Pillard, R. C.: *ref*, 1337
Pillay, P. G.: *ref*, 1095, 1275, 2266
Pilley, J. G.: *ref*, 869
Pilliner, A. E. G.: *rev*, 5, 79, 338, 358, 5:351, 6:469; *ref*, 95, 409, 525, 722
Pilling, L. F.: *ref*, 1281
Pilowsky, I.: *ref*, 1145, 1383, 1519
Pimm, J. B.: *test*, 1307; *ref*, 1307
Pimsleur, P.: *rev*, 255; *test*, 223, 258, 275, 318; *ref*, 211, 221, 223, 258, 457, 1074
Pinchard, A. G.: *ref*, 1281
Pinckers, A.: *ref*, 1912-3
Pinckney, G. A.: *ref*, 1387, 1475
Pincus, M.: *test*, 5:480
Pindner, G. D.: *ref*, 381
Pine, F.: *ref*, 1437, 1499, 1519
Pine, I.: *ref*, 532, 1499, 1519
Piness, G.: *ref*, 525
Pinkard, C. A.: *ref*, 542, 546, 551, 1383
Pinkerton, P.: *ref*, 403, 439
Pinkham, T. C.: *ref*, 20
Pinkston, J. R.: *ref*, 1207
Pinneau, S. R.: *test*, 525; *ref*, 525, 533, 1281, 1499, 2212
Pinney, E. L.: *ref*, 50
Pino, C. J.: *ref*, 1281
Pinsker, E. J.: *ref*, 981
Pinson, R. B.: *test*, 35:50
Pintel, G.: *ref*, 357
Pintner, R.: *rev*, 349, 419, 425; *test*, 435, 556, 563, 590, 1:1061, 2:1201, 2:1244, 3:254, 3:256, 5:368, T:928; *exc*, 518, 36:B77; *ref*, 435, 525, 558, 908, 1101, 1320, 1386, 1403, 1:1061(1), 2:1201(1-3), 2:1243(28), 2:1244(1-2), 3:97(10), 3:255(1, 3), 3:256(1, 3-4), 3:263(38), 4:477(3), 6:159(32, 51, 60), P:294(7-9), P:367(3)
Pinto, A.: *ref*, 1232, 1281, 7:55(25)
Pinto, P.: *ref*, 1318
Piotrowski, Z.: *ref*, 1281, 1499
Piotrowski, Z. A.: *exc*, 1499, 1519; *ref*, 525, 1281, 1469-70, 1499, 1519, 2195
Piper, A. H.: *ref*, 681
Piper, W. E.: *ref*, 1293
Pipher, J. A.: *ref*, 357, 361, 387, 1572
Pipho, C. C.: *ref*, 48
Pippert, R. R.: *ref*, 391, 644, 1069

Port, Y. I.: *ref,* 1499
Portenier, L.: *ref,* 1095, 1281, 1320, 1403
Portenier, L. G.: *ref,* 18, 419, 1095, 1281, 1320, 1403, 1572, 1768, 2244, 4:277(191–2)
Porter, A.: *ref,* 419, 2212
Porter, A. C.: *ref,* 357
Porter, C. M.: *ref,* 589
Porter, E. H.: *ref,* 2:1426(1)
Porter, F. S.: *ref,* 1519
Porter, H. M.: *ref,* 1499
Porter, J. B.: *ref,* 1164
Porter, J. H.: *ref,* 868
Porter, J. M.: *rev,* 2252, 3:678, 3:682
Porter, J. P.: *ref,* 419
Porter, K. D.: *ref,* 1281
Porter, L. G.: *ref,* 1207
Porter, L. W.: *rev,* 2111–2, 2412
Porter, M. P.: *ref,* 435, 3:255(6)
Porter, M. R.: *ref,* 7:840(3)
Porter, R. B.: *test,* 339, 1129; *ref,* 1129, 1253, 1383
Porter, T. A.: *ref,* 2031
Porter, T. L.: *ref,* 498, 529, 1253
Porter, W.: *test,* 4:4
Porterfield, A. L.: *ref,* 1377
Porterfield, C. L.: *ref,* 439, 538, 1447, 1451, 1468
Porteus, S. D.: *rev,* 355, 447; *test,* 518; *ref,* 381, 505, 518, 525, 545, 578, 1428, 1499
Portnoy, B.: *ref,* 532–3, 1500
Portwood, P. F.: *ref,* 525, 533
Poruben, A.: *ref,* 426, 480
Posavac, E. J.: *ref,* 1164, 1240
Poser, E. G.: *ref,* 1499, 1519
Poshek, N. A.: *ref,* 1281
Posner, R.: *ref,* 1090, 1500, 1519
Post, A. W.: *ref,* 1174, 1315
Post, F.: *ref,* 403, 439, 532, 1192, 1447
Post, H. H.: *ref,* 1315
Post, J. M.: *ref,* 533
Post, M.: *ref,* 525
Post, W. L.: *rev,* 61, 78, 108, 4:195
Postel, H.: *exc,* 3:110
Postema, L. J.: *ref,* 1281, 1519
Poster, D. C.: *ref,* 1169, 1481
Posthuma, A. B.: *ref,* 1164, 1430, 2212
Postlethwaite, T. N.: *test,* 475
Postman, L.: *ref,* 1403
Poston, A. M.: *ref,* 914
Poston, F. L.: *ref,* 3:486(4, 6), 3:494(1)
Poston, W. K.: *ref,* 69, 404, 1383, 2195
Potash, H. M.: *ref,* 1474
Poteet, J. A.: *ref,* 1087, 1447
Pothast, M. D.: *ref,* 1281, 1499
Potkay, C. R.: *ref,* 1499
Pottas, A. P. J.: *test,* 16
Pottash, M. E.: *ref,* 439
Potter, A. A.: *ref,* 881
Potter, C. S.: *ref,* 1281
Potter, D. R.: *ref,* 868
Potter, E. H.: *ref,* 545, 1499
Potter, F. H.: *test,* 1:1069
Potter, F. T.: *test,* 2372
Potter, H. W.: *ref,* 1481
Potter, M. A.: *test,* 3:344

Potter, M. C.: *ref,* 425, 1711
Potter, N. R.: *ref,* 1164
Potter, R. E.: *ref,* 1428, 2089
Pottharst, K.: *ref,* 1499
Pottharst, K. E.: *ref,* 1499
Potts, E.: *ref,* 408, 1646, 1680
Potts, L.: *ref,* 592, 1277
Potts, M.: *ref,* 1603
Poulakakis, G. M.: *ref,* 1232
Poull, L. E.: *test,* T:908; *ref,* 518, 525, 5:354(4)
Poulton, I. A.: *ref,* 1499
Pouncey, A. T.: *ref,* 1087, 1121
Pounders, C. J.: *ref,* 440, 1071, 2325
Pounds, R. L.: *ref,* 69, 5:308(391)
Povey, R. M.: *ref,* 311
Powell, A.: *ref,* 1447
Powell, B. J.: *ref,* 529, 1169, 1281, 1921
Powell, D. B.: *ref,* 4:277(213)
Powell, D. H.: *ref,* 529, 1164, 1194, 1447, 1481, 1499, 1519
Powell, E.: *test,* 35:281
Powell, E. K.: *ref,* 1314, 1344, 1448
Powell, E. M.: *ref,* 1133
Powell, F. V.: *ref,* 2212
Powell, G.: *ref,* 1164
Powell, H. L.: *ref,* 1044
Powell, J.: *ref,* 1133, 1135, 1289
Powell, J. A.: *ref,* 525, 532
Powell, J. A. J.: *ref,* 868, 1281
Powell, J. C.: *ref,* 440
Powell, J. D.: *ref,* 316
Powell, J. O.: *ref,* 1095, 1281, 2195, 2212
Powell, K.: *ref,* 533, 1447, 1596, 2028
Powell, K. S.: *ref,* 1451, 1519
Powell, L.: *ref,* 1428, P:373(2)
Powell, M.: *exc,* 1515; *ref,* 7, 348, 525, 603, 1095, 1123, 1423, 1499, 1536, 1711
Powell, M. B.: *ref,* 403, 428, 2135, 2229
Powell, M. G.: *ref,* 1320
Powell, R. K.: *ref,* 1281
Powell, R. R.: *ref,* 364
Powell, V. M.: *ref,* 1095, 3:423(2)
Powell, W. D.: *ref,* 1430
Powell, W. R.: *exc,* 1552; *ref,* 1618, 1624, 1628–9, 1649, 1679, 1681
Power, D. J.: *ref,* 868, 1383
Power, F. F.: *test,* 2:1370
Power, L.: *ref,* 36
Power, M. E. F.: *ref,* 1253
Power, R. P.: *ref,* 1174, 1198, 1275
Powers, C. A.: *ref,* 1481
Powers, G. F.: *ref,* 6:438(531)
Powers, G. P.: *ref,* 2195, 2212
Powers, G. R.: *ref,* 2095
Powers, J. H.: *ref,* 1281
Powers, J. R.: *ref,* 1176
Powers, M. E.: *ref,* 1403
Powers, M. K.: *ref,* 2212
Powers, R. J.: *ref,* 357, 1135
Powers, S. M.: *ref,* 528
Powers, S. R.: *test,* 1:870b, 2:1591, 2:1601, 3:550, 3:561
Powers, W. T.: *ref,* 1499
Poyntz, L.: *ref,* 5:766(9)
Prabhu, G. G.: *ref,* 1174, 1447, 1485, 1499
Prado, W. M.: *ref,* 529, 532, 1164, 1256, 1281, 1380, 1403, 1447, 2195

Prados, M.: *ref,* 1499
Prager, D.: *ref,* 525, 532
Prager, R. A.: *ref,* 1281
Prahl, M. R.: *ref,* 1082
Prak, J. L.: *test,* 2282
Prakash, J.: *ref,* 1090, 1519, P:381(48)
Prakash, J. C.: *ref,* 2228–9
Prandoni, J. R.: *ref,* 381, 1481
Prange, A. J.: *ref,* 518, 1281, 1377, 7:55(23)
Pranis, R. W.: *test,* 1413
Prasad, C.: *ref,* 1123
Prasad, K.: *ref,* 1499
Prasad, R.: *ref,* 525
Prasad, S. C.: *ref,* 1370
Pratap, S.: *ref,* 1499
Prater, G. F.: *ref,* 1474
Prather, E.: *test,* 2060
Prather, M.: *ref,* 1142, 1521
Prather, M. S.: *ref,* 1142, 1521
Pratt, A. B.: *ref,* 2213
Pratt, B. M.: *ref,* 2:1217(1)
Pratt, C.: *ref,* 1499
Pratt, C. C.: *ref,* 525
Pratt, E. W.: *ref,* 1318
Pratt, H. G.: *ref,* 36
Pratt, I. E.: *ref,* 381
Pratt, K. C.: *test,* 1:1163; *ref,* 3:217(62)
Pratt, M.: *ref,* 361, 1044
Pratt, M. A.: *ref,* 1095
Pratt, N. T.: *rev,* 291, 2:1366, 2:1370
Pratt, R. T. C.: *ref,* 529
Pratt, S.: *ref,* 1217, 1281
Pratt, W. E.: *test,* 4, 52, 339, 694–5, 1532–3, 1694, 1937; *ref,* 1694
Praul, J. A.: *ref,* 1294
Preas, N. B.: *ref,* 69, 357
Preble, E.: *ref,* 20
Pred, A. L. S.: *ref,* 1320
Pred, G. D.: *ref,* 99, 337, 4:63(3), 4:277(252)
Prediger, D.: *test,* 2100
Prediger, D. J.: *ref,* 361, 404, 419, 1583
Preededilok, K. P.: *ref,* 1383
Preische, W. A.: *ref,* 425, 1560, 2244
Prelinger, E.: *ref,* 1516
Prell, A. E.: *ref,* 1281
Prema, P.: *ref,* 1499
Prensky, S. J.: *ref,* 1499–500
Prentice, N. M.: *ref,* 22, 381, 525, 529, 532–3, 1344, 1501
Prentiss, R. J.: *ref,* 1121, 1281
Prescott, D. A.: *rev,* 1222, 1:928
Prescott, G. A.: *test,* 22, 340, 637, 1567; *ref,* 22, 1716, 5:855(1)
Prescott, H.: *test,* 36:666
Prescott, P. L.: *ref,* 203, 211
Presel, R.: *ref,* 262
Presher, C. H.: *ref,* 6:223(13)
Presly, A. S.: *ref,* 403, 439, 1198, 1218, 1383, 1410
Presnell, M.: *ref,* 1121, 1281
Press, I.: *ref,* 1519
Pressel, G. L.: *ref,* 2289
Pressey, A. W.: *ref,* 1169
Pressey, L. C.: *test,* 104, 438, 1576, 2:1196, 2:1243.1; *ref,* 435, 438, 2:1243.1(1), P:363(6–7)
Pressey, L. W.: *ref,* 438, 1569

Puletti, F.: *ref,* 529, 1281
Pulleine, R. H.: *ref,* 518
Pullen, J. R.: *ref,* 1383
Pullen, M.: *ref,* 1277, 1447
Pullias, C.: *ref,* 1032
Pullias, C. M.: *ref,* 382, 1032
Pullias, E. V.: *rev,* 22, 28; *ref,* 22, 28, 36
Pulos, L.: *ref,* 1164, 1232, 1380
Pulver, H. E.: *test,* 1834
Pulvermacher, G. D.: *ref,* 1281
Pulvino, C. J.: *ref,* 1394-5
Pum, R. J.: *ref,* 868, 1383, 1403
Pumfrey, P. D.: *ref,* 408
Pummell, M. F.: *test,* 5:13
Pumroy, D. K.: *test,* 1273, 1343; *ref,* 1121, 1273, 1281, 1343
Pumroy, S. S.: *ref,* 5:123(11)
Punwar, A.: *ref,* 1104, 1887
Puranajoti, V. P.: *ref,* 1121
Purcell, C. K.: *ref,* 532, 1281, 1499
Purcell, E. W.: *ref,* 1123, 1536
Purcell, J. F.: *ref,* 1094, 1225, 1423
Purcell, K.: *ref,* 518, 532, 1129, 1164, 1253, 1281, 1499, 1519
Purcell, T. D.: *ref,* 1164
Purdom, G. A.: *ref,* 529, 1281, 1500
Purdue Research Foundation: *test,* 2234, 6:703
Purdue University, Personnel Evaluation Research Service: *test,* 5:532
Purdy, B. F.: *ref,* 425, 2135
Purdy, P. A.: *ref,* 1044, 1294, 1383
Purdy, R. D.: *test,* 1:944
Purdy, R. S.: *ref,* 532
Puri, P.: *ref,* 1500
Purin, C. M.: *test,* 2:1357, 2:1359
Purinton, D. E.: *ref,* 1415
Purkey, W. W.: *ref,* 1121
Purkhiser, C. A.: *ref,* 981
Purohit, A. P.: *ref,* 1275
Purseglove, E. M.: *ref,* 516, 525
Purves, A. C.: *rev,* 137, 143; *ref,* 130
Purvis, L. C.: *ref,* 1123
Puryear, H. B.: *ref,* 1225, 1281, 1437
Pusey, C. R.: *exc,* 258
Pusey, H. C.: *ref,* 1123, P:321(15)
Puskin, R.: *ref,* 1110
Pustel, G.: *ref,* 1277, 1447, 1469, 1474
Pustell, T. E.: *ref,* 1281
Putnam, P. H.: *ref,* 48
Putnam, T. J.: *ref,* 483, 525, 532, 1499
Putney, S.: *ref,* 1320
Putthoff, R.: *ref,* 36
Puttick, W. H.: *ref,* 1295
Puzzo, F.: *ref,* 532
Puzzo, F. S.: *ref,* 532, 1281, 1448, 1481, 1499, 1519
Pyecha, J.: *ref,* 1383
Pyecha, J. N.: *ref,* 1383
Pyle, R. F.: *ref,* 533
Pyle, S. I.: *test,* T:1312; *ref,* 947
Pyle, W. H.: *ref,* 525
Pyles, M. K.: *ref,* 2212
Pyron, B.: *ref,* 1370, 1403
Pyskacek, R. A.: *ref,* 2337
Pytkowicz, A. R.: *ref,* 1519

QASHU, M. F.: *ref,* 1403
Quadfasel, A. F.: *ref,* 532, 592
Quagliotti, C. A.: *ref,* 1164, 1281
Quaid, T. D. D.: *ref,* 99, 419, 3: 217(58, 63)
Qualls, L. J.: *ref,* 656
Qualtere, T.: *ref,* 1519
Qualtere, T. J.: *ref,* 439, 525
Quan, J.: *ref,* 1121
Quandt, R. E.: *ref,* 357
Quarrington, B.: *ref,* 1164, 1281, 1499-500
Quarrington, B. J.: *ref,* 1196
Quarrington, M.: *ref,* 1499
Quasha, W. H.: *test,* 2266; *ref,* 2266
Quasha, W. R.: *ref,* 2266
Quass, R. M.: *ref,* 1145, 1278
Quast, W.: *ref,* 381, 1281, 1447
Quatman, G. L.: *ref,* 2180
Quattlebaum, L. F.: *ref,* 522, 529, 1277, 1447
Quay, A. T.: *ref,* 1133
Quay, H.: *ref,* 1281, 1307, 1500
Quay, H. C.: *ref,* 529, 532, 1121, 1186, 1254, 1275, P:353(8)
Quay, L. C.: *ref,* 525
Quayle, M. S.: *ref,* 426, 1090, 2135
Queen, R.: *ref,* 1415
Queeney, D. S. S.: *ref,* 189, 1315
Queensland Department of Public Instruction: *test,* 793, 2238, 5:890
Quello, D. Y.: *ref,* 1164, 1281
Quenk, N. L.: *ref,* 1094, 1281, 1294
Quereshi, M. Y.: *rev,* 1069, 1087, 1139; *ref,* 525, 529, 532-3, 981
Query, J. H.: *ref,* 211
Query, W. T.: *ref,* 518, 533, 1121
Quesnell, J. G.: *ref,* 1281
Quevillon, S. M.: *ref,* 1281
Quidwai, A. A.: *ref,* 1069
Quill, L. L.: *test,* 1:933
Quiller, G. F.: *ref,* 20, 357
Quimby, N. F.: *ref,* 2195
Quinlan, C. A.: *ref,* 35, 357, 1044, 1164
Quinlan, D.: *ref,* 1481, 1499
Quinlan, P.: *ref,* 529
Quinn, A. W.: *ref,* 1121
Quinn, B.: *ref,* 1499
Quinn, L. W.: *ref,* 1281
Quinn, O. W.: *exc,* 1481
Quinn, P. J.: *ref,* 868
Quinn, P. V.: *ref,* 1775
Quinn, R. P.: *ref,* 1121, 1145, 1225, 1281, 1383
Quinn, S. B.: *ref,* 1281
Quinn, T. L.: *ref,* 1519
Quintar, B.: *ref,* 1225
Quiring, R. G.: *ref,* 2212
Quirk, D.: *ref,* 1499
Quirk, D. A.: *ref,* 1499
Quirk, E. L.: *ref,* 1469

RAAB, W. E.: *ref,* 1394-5
Raaheim, K.: *ref,* 439
Raban, R.: *ref,* 1519
Rabbitt, P. H.: *ref,* 2028
Rabe, A.: *ref,* 2266
Rabie, L.: *ref,* 1499, 1519
Rabin, A.: *ref,* 50, 1144, 1499
Rabin, A. I.: *rev,* 1451-2, 1482, 1499, 1516; *exc,* 1489, 1499; *ref,*

341A, 496, 525, 529, 532-3, 1105, 1428, 1448, 1451, 1481, 1499, 1516, 1519
Rabin, H. M.: *ref,* 1895
Rabindradas, L. D.: *ref,* 1261
Rabiner, A.: *ref,* 2234
Rabiner, E. L.: *ref,* 1232
Rabinovich, D.: *ref,* 1499
Rabinovitch, M. S.: *ref,* 1499
Rabinovitch, V.: *ref,* 1360
Rabinovitz, A.: *ref,* 532, 1223, 1380
Rabinovitz, G.: *ref,* 1499
Rabinowitz, G.: *ref,* 1499
Rabinowitz, J.: *ref,* 533
Rabinowitz, W.: *ref,* 868, 1474, 1516, 2212, 5:597(10)
Rabon, A. M.: *ref,* 1232, 1281
Race, R.: *ref,* 1281
Rachiele, L. D.: *ref,* 496, 533, 1281
Rachman, S.: *rev,* 6:447; *ref,* 533, 1683
Racky, D. J.: *ref,* 398, 1087, 2195, 2251
Racusen, F. R.: *ref,* 1499, 1519
Radatz, G.: *test,* 36:586
Radcliffe, J. A.: *rev,* 1164, 1193-4, 1221, 1403; *test,* 533, 1291; *ref,* 529, 1164, 1275, 1291, 1367, 1383, 1403, 2195
Radcliffe, R. D.: *ref,* 1546
Radebaugh, B. F.: *ref,* 1775
Raden, B.: *ref,* 1237, 1519
Rader, B. B.: *ref,* 1123, 1164, 1294, 1403
Rader, G. E.: *ref,* 1499
Radford, D.: *ref,* 2349
Radford, E.: *ref,* 1499
Radford, G.: *ref,* 1415
Radford, J.: *ref,* 439
Radhakrishnan, B. K.: *ref,* 1232
Radin, N.: *ref,* 516, 525
Radin, N. L.: *ref,* 525
Radley, S.: *ref,* 2234
Radus, L.: *ref,* 211, 981, 2079
Radzan, M.: *ref,* 439
Rae, J. B.: *ref,* 1164, 1281
Raffel, S. C.: *ref,* 433, 447, 529, 592, 2135
Rafferty, J.: *exc,* 1527
Rafferty, J. E.: *test,* 1501; *ref,* 1501
Rafi, A. A.: *ref,* 365, 439, 529, 1275
Raftery, F. M.: *ref,* 1281
Ragland, G.: *ref,* 981
Ragland, G. G.: *ref,* 981
Ragland, R.: *ref,* 529, 2234
Ragland, R. E.: *ref,* 529, 2234
Ragouzis, P. N.: *ref,* 589
Ragsdale, N. L.: *ref,* 1716, 1921
Rahe, R. H.: *ref,* 1145
Raia, J. R.: *ref,* 555, 589
Raiche, A.: *ref,* 868, 1383
Raifman, I.: *ref,* 1261, 1499, 1519
Raim, R. L.: *ref,* 209
Raimy, V. C.: *exc,* 1516; *ref,* 1516, 1519
Rain, M. E.: *ref,* 1428
Raina, M. K.: *ref,* 589
Raina, T. N.: *ref,* 868, 1164
Rainaldi, F. D.: *ref,* 1395
Rainbow, I.: *ref,* 211
Raine, L. M.: *ref,* 532
Raine, W. J.: *ref,* 2349
Raines, B.: *ref,* 1395

Ravenette, A. T.: *ref,* 491, 533
Ravensborg, M. R.: *ref,* 1161, 1281, 1298, 1407, 1430, 2195, 2197, 2205
Ravsten, L. A.: *ref,* 1214, 1281
Rawl, M. F.: *ref,* 381, 516
Rawlings, G.: *exc,* 1:1043
Rawlings, J. S.: *ref,* 2452
Rawlings, T. D.: *ref,* 349, 1073, 1087
Rawlins, G. M.: *ref,* 868
Rawlinson, M. E.: *ref,* 1240
Rawls, D. J.: *ref,* 382, 404, 1121, 1164, 1519
Rawls, J. R.: *ref,* 382, 404, 1121, 1164, 1499, 1519
Rawn, M. L.: *ref,* 532, 1225, 1447, 1474
Rawnsley, K.: *ref,* 1145, 1340
Ray, A. B.: *ref,* 1499
Ray, C. D.: *ref,* 1499
Ray, D. K.: *ref,* 2358
Ray, E.: *nef,* 1281
Ray, J. B.: *ref,* 525, 1121, 1164, 1499, 1516
Ray, J. J.: *ref,* 1143
Ray, J. R.: *ref,* 22, 400
Ray, M.: *ref,* 1186
Ray, M. R.: *ref,* 349
Ray, O.: *ref,* 1275
Ray, O. S.: *ref,* 1275
Ray, P. B.: *ref,* 405, 589, 1044
Ray, P. C.: *ref,* 1499
Ray, T.: *ref,* 515
Ray, T. S.: *ref,* 529, 1516, 2234
Ray, W. J.: *ref,* 357, 1391
Ray, W. S.: *ref,* 542
Raybold, E.: *ref,* 435, 525, 545
Raychaudhuri, M.: *ref,* 1109, 1289, 1437, 1463, 1499, 1516, 1519
Raychaudhuri, S.: *ref,* 1499
Ray-Chowdhury, K.: *ref,* 515, 545, 1090, 1095, 1320, 1403
Raygor, A. L.: *rev,* 1546, 6:864; *test,* 125, 160, 177, 1593, 1771; *ref,* 1281, 1383, 2195
Raygor, B. R.: *ref,* 1281
Raymaker, H.: *ref,* 1281
Raymond, C. S.: *ref,* 381, 1447
Rayner, E. H.: *ref,* 1486
Rayner, S. A.: *rev,* 1685, 1948, 5:673; *test,* 5:830; *ref,* 5:830(1)
Raynor, G. H.: *ref,* 1281
Raynor, J. E.: *ref,* 981
Razin, A. M.: *ref,* 2212
Razor, B. A. L.: *ref,* 1074
Read, C. B.: *ref,* 18, 99, 419, 1560
Read, H. S.: *test,* 4:533
Read, J. G.: *test,* 6:877, 7:15, 7:200, 7:479, 7:792, 7:796, 7:888; *ref,* 5:715(1)
Read, J. M.: *ref,* 3:613(13)
Read, J. W.: *ref,* 211, 1044
Reader, N.: *ref,* 1090, 1499, P:384 (12)
Reagan, B. V.: *ref,* 1469
Reahard, R. R.: *ref,* 884
Ream, M. J.: *ref,* 3:220(23)
Reaman, G. E.: *test,* 36:566
Reams, J. W.: *ref,* 361
Reardon, B.: *ref,* 589
Reaser, V.: *ref,* 1475
Reatig, N.: *ref,* 1232, 1435
Reaume, R.: *ref,* 1145
Reavis, L. D.: *ref,* 1207

Reber, D. C.: *test,* 36:765, 36:771
Reber, P.: *test,* 36:575
Rebhun, A. M.: *ref,* 525, 533
Rebish, D.: *ref,* 533
Rebstock, C. W.: *ref,* 868, 1164, 1403
Rechenberg, W.: *ref,* 1164
Rechner, J.: *ref,* 981, 2095
Rechnitzer, P. A.: *ref,* 1383
Rechter, B.: *test,* 595, 1530
Rechtschaffen, A.: *ref,* 1281, 1519
Reck, J. J.: *ref,* 1500
Reck, M.: *ref,* 357
Reckless, W. C.: *ref,* 1121
Recktenwald, L. N.: *ref,* 3:635 (14–5, 18)
Record, J. N.: *ref,* 914
Rector, A. P.: *ref,* 1069
Rector, W.: *ref,* 1358
Red, S. B.: *ref,* 1124
Redbird, H. M.: *ref,* 381, 525
Reddell, R. C.: *ref,* 2031
Redden, J. W.: *ref,* 1164
Reddig, G. L.: *ref,* 1087
Reddin, E.: *ref,* 997
Redding, A. J.: *ref,* 1383
Redding, J. F.: *ref,* 1129
Reddy, B. G.: *ref,* P:381(48)
Reddy, I. K. S.: *ref,* 439
Reddy, K. M.: *ref,* 1403
Reddy, M. J.: *ref,* 532, 1281, 1294
Reddy, P. V.: *ref,* 1451
Redel, M. C.: *ref,* 1121
Redfearn, L.: *ref,* 3:678(13)
Redford, J.: *ref,* 1044
Reding, G. R.: *ref,* 1145, 1281
Redlener, J.: *ref,* 2195, 2212
Redlich, F. C.: *test,* 3:291; *exc,* 1499
Redlo, M.: *ref,* 1281, 1499
Redman, B. D. K.: *ref,* 1403
Redman, B. K.: *ref,* 1403
Redman, D. R.: *ref,* 1174, 1225
Redman, R. S.: *ref,* 1281
Redmond, F. A.: *test,* 2:1269
Redmond, J.: *ref,* 1448
Redmond, J. F.: *ref,* 2212
Redmond, M.: *ref,* 426, 4:272(2)
Redmond, N. J.: *ref,* 533, 1499
Redmore, C.: *test,* 1527; *ref,* 1527
Redmount, R. S.: *ref,* 1499
Reeb, M.: *ref,* 1516
Reece, M.: *ref,* 1164
Reece, M. M.: *ref,* 1164, 1499
Reed, A. A.: *test,* 2:1277
Reed, C. F.: *ref,* 1121
Reed, C. L.: *ref,* 1569
Reed, C. R.: *ref,* 869
Reed, G. F.: *ref,* 1140, 1275, 1296
Reed, H. B.: *ref,* 1053, 1320, 3:166(6), 3:653(6, 9), 3:678(16)
Reed, H. B. C.: *ref,* 211, 529, 532, 578
Reed, H. C.: *ref,* 532
Reed, H. R.: *ref,* 525, 532
Reed, J. C.: *rev,* 1384, 7:880; *ref,* 50, 529, 532–3, 1407, 1626, 2076
Reed, J. D.: *ref,* 1924, 5:768(20)
Reed, J. L.: *ref,* 440
Reed, K.: *ref,* 1499
Reed, K. E.: *ref,* 1164, 1171
Reed, M. R.: *ref,* 1247, 1281, 1463, 1481, 1499
Reed, P. C.: *ref,* 1281, 1285

Reed, P. H.: *ref,* 1222
Reed, P. R.: *ref,* 914
Reed, R. B.: *ref,* 1931
Reed, R. D.: *test,* 1:933, 3:562; *ref,* 1818–9, 4:608(1)
Reed, R. L.: *ref,* 1164, 1281, 2449, 2451
Reed, V. M.: *test,* 5:496, 6:634
Reed, W. W.: *ref,* 1448, 2195
Reeder, C. W.: *ref,* 1768
Reeder, D. E.: *ref,* 1766
Reeder, E. H.: *rev,* 1975, 3:598, 3:603, 4:678
Reekie, E.: *ref,* 1294, 1315
Reeling, G. E.: *ref,* 1164
Reeling, P. A.: *ref,* 357, 1164, 1403
Reem, L. E.: *ref,* 1519
Rees, A. H.: *ref,* 525, 533, 1519
Rees, L.: *ref,* 1499
Rees, M. B.: *ref,* 1281
Rees, M. E.: *ref,* 1207, 1281
Rees, R. E.: *ref,* 1536
Rees, V. M.: *ref,* 2349
Rees, W. L.: *ref,* 403, 439, 1205, 1499
Reese, C. S.: *ref,* 1176, 1294
Reese, D. G.: *ref,* 1499
Reese, E.: *ref,* 1918
Reese, H.: *ref,* 2340
Reese, H. W.: *ref,* 542, 546, 551, 561, 1121, 2340
Reese, J. L.: *ref,* 1044
Reese, P. M.: *ref,* 1281
Reeve, E. B.: *test,* 2:1511
Reeve, R. R.: *ref,* 2092
Reeves, E. A.: *ref,* 1250
Reeves, M. P.: *ref,* 1519
Reeves, R.: *test,* 91
Reeves, R. J.: *ref,* 997
Reeves, T. G.: *ref,* 1133
Reeves, W. P.: *ref,* 1481
Reevy, W. R.: *rev,* 816, 836
Refice, R. J.: *ref,* 1164, 2195
Regal, J.: *ref,* 1281
Regal, L. H.: *ref,* 1281
Regan, G.: *ref,* 1253, 1296
Regelin, C.: *ref,* 1222, 1281
Reger, R.: *ref,* 22, 50, 179, 516, 533, 1447
Rehder, H.: *ref,* 271
Rehfeld, F. W.: *ref,* 1560, 3:217 (108)
Rehfisch, J. M.: *ref,* 1121, 1281
Rehm, L. P.: *ref,* 1094, 1185
Rehmstedt, H.: *ref,* 1705, 1711
Reich, H.: *ref,* 532
Reich, R. D.: *ref,* 1164
Reichard, J. D.: *ref,* 518, 525
Reichard, J. R.: *ref,* 262
Reichard, S.: *exc,* 1519; *ref,* 532, 1140, 1192, 1499, 1516, 1519, 2266, 3:159(3)
Reichart, R. R.: *ref,* 5:308(293)
Reichenberg-Hackett, W.: *ref,* 381
Reicherter, R. F.: *test,* 789
Reichman, W.: *ref,* 436, 529, 1772, 1775
Reid, A. R.: *ref,* 1281
Reid, B.: *ref,* 1281
Reid, B. A.: *ref,* 1044
Reid, C. P.: *test,* 927
Reid, E. B.: *test,* 3:558
Reid, H. T.: *ref,* 868
Reid, I. E.: *ref,* 902

Rhoderick, W. A.: *ref*, 532
Rhodes, F.: *test*, 530, 535; *ref*, 1281
Rhodes, G. S.: *exc*, 2216; *ref*, 2212
Rhodes, H. E.: *ref*, 1196
Rhodes, H. K.: *ref*, 1133
Rhodes, J. M.: *ref*, 1281
Rhodes, L. E.: *ref*, 533
Rhodes, R. G.: *ref*, 1383
Rhodes, R. J.: *ref*, 1145, 1169, 1232, 1281, 1298, 1447
Rholl, K. N.: *ref*, 1240
Rhone, D. E.: *ref*, 529, 533
Rhudick, P. J.: *ref*, 529, 1145, 1281, 1519
Rhum, G.: *ref*, 20
Ribal, J. E.: *ref*, 1164
Ribbeck, J. C.: *ref*, 868
Ribble, M. A.: *exc*, 497
Ribler, R. I.: *ref*, 1196, 1223, 1447, 1474
Ricard, E. L.: *ref*, 2212, 7:1090(3)
Ricci, J.: *ref*, 1192, 1299
Riccio, A. C.: *ref*, 868, 1403
Riccio, P.: *test*, 3:199
Ricciuti, E. A.: *ref*, 1123, 1500
Ricciuti, H.: *ref*, 1499, 1519
Ricciuti, H. N.: *ref*, 1499, 1519
Rice, C. E.: *ref*, 1232, 1435
Rice, C. L.: *ref*, 1819, 4:618(1)
Rice, D.: *ref*, 1281
Rice, D. B.: *ref*, 533
Rice, D. G.: *ref*, 1281, 1499
Rice, D. L.: *ref*, 1361
Rice, D. M.: *ref*, 516, 1921
Rice, D. P.: *ref*, 1306
Rice, G. A.: *ref*, 254, 313
Rice, J.: *ref*, 543, 1447
Rice, J. A.: *ref*, 50, 209, 424, 516, 543, 981, 1447
Rice, M.: *ref*, 1471
Rice, M. E.: *ref*, 1320
Rice, M. L.: *ref*, 361
Rice, P. J.: *ref*, 1281
Rice, P. L. K.: *ref*, 1240
Rice, R. R.: *test*, 2:1481
Rice, V.: *ref*, 19, 400, 1069
Rice, W.: *ref*, 503, 529
Rice, W. H.: *exc*, 3:211
Rich, A. E.: *ref*, 36
Rich, C.: *ref*, 1320
Rich, C. C.: *ref*, 439, 533, 1281
Rich, C. L.: *test*, 2:1612, 4:383
Rich, D. C.: *ref*, 1145, 1278
Rich, G. J.: *rev*, 3:113; *exc*, 497
Rich, J. M.: *ref*, 1171
Rich, K. D.: *ref*, 398
Rich, M. P.: *ref*, 1105, 1380
Rich, R.: *ref*, 1289
Rich, T. A.: *ref*, 381, 542, 546, 551, 1145, 1383
Rich, V.: *test*, 4:207
Richard, J. T.: *ref*, 2194
Richard, W.: *ref*, 529
Richard, W. A.: *ref*, 2183
Richard, W. C.: *ref*, 1253, 1415
Richards, A. B.: *ref*, 1093, 1144
Richards, B. F.: *ref*, 7, 525, 1123
Richards, B. W.: *ref*, 525
Richards, C. B.: *ref*, 1281, 1377
Richards, C. J.: *ref*, 2028
Richards, E. A.: *ref*, 1403
Richards, H. E.: *ref*, 533
Richards, J. M.: *rev*, 2355, 7:43;

ref, 69, 179, 349, 419, 551, 559, 561, 564, 1044, 1133, 1430, 2273, 2355
Richards, J. N.: *ref*, 69
Richards, J. T.: *ref*, 538
Richards, M. K. B.: *test*, 781A, 2269
Richards, O. W.: *ref*, 1912-3, 1915
Richards, P. N.: *ref*, 409, 589
Richards, R. A.: *rev*, 53, 90, 121, 995
Richards, R. C.: *test*, 4:693
Richards, T. D.: *ref*, 559, 561, 1201
Richards, T. W.: *rev*, 4:108; *exc*, 1481, 1519; *ref*, 497, 525, 532-3, 1144, 1281, 1474, 1499, 1519, 2: 1209(2), P:358(4)
Richards, W. S.: *ref*, 1320, 1322, 1499
Richardson, B. K.: *ref*, 482, 1094, 2283
Richardson, Bellows, Henry & Co., Inc.: *test*, 92, 106-7, 171, 444-5, 727-9, 791, 1580-1, 1740, 1846, 2143-7, 2264-5, 2267, 2287, 2314, 2458, 6:155, 6:1096, 6:1126, 6: 1191, 7:982, 7:996, 7:1032
Richardson, C. A.: *test*, 459-61; *ref*, 461, 525
Richardson, C. E.: *ref*, 1281, 1499
Richardson, D.: *ref*, 993
Richardson, D. H.: *ref*, 1247
Richardson, E. J.: *ref*, 439, 496, 525
Richardson, F. C.: *ref*, 1164
Richardson, H.: *ref*, 532, 1121, 1254, 1281, 1499
Richardson, H. D.: *test*, 1:995, 1: 1120, 2:1645, 2:1658, 2:1660; *ref*, 218, 2:1645(1), 2:1658(1), 2: 1660(1), 4:324(54)
Richardson, H. M.: *ref*, 533, 1320, 1403, 1516
Richardson, H. W.: *ref*, 1206
Richardson, I. F.: *ref*, 1121, 1207, 1383
Richardson, J.: *test*, 5:474; *ref*, 1121, 5:308(371)
Richardson, J. A.: *rev*, 5:173, 5: 222; *test*, 6:620; *ref*, 1924
Richardson, J. F.: *ref*, 868, 1174, 1423, 2195
Richardson, J. S.: *rev*, 4:623, 4: 628
Richardson, J. W.: *ref*, 1145
Richardson, L.: *ref*, 1302, 1501
Richardson, L. H.: *ref*, 1164, 1245, 1302, 1499, 1519
Richardson, M. W.: *rev*, 681, 782, 1:870, 1:882, 1:1071, 1:1073; *test*, 792, 3:388c, 4:454; *ref*, 525
Richardson, O. R.: *test*, 1354
Richardson, P. C.: *ref*, 1387
Richardson, R. A.: *ref*, 1481
Richardson, R. L.: *ref*, 1281, 1294
Richardson, S.: *test*, 1404
Richardson, S. A.: *ref*, 1519
Richardson, S. C.: *rev*, 72, 76
Richardson, S. K.: *exc*, 1:B335
Richardson, T. E.: *ref*, 1133, 1135
Richardson, W.: *test*, 36:843; *ref*, 1447, 1883
Richek, H. G.: *ref*, 1121, 1281, 1294, 1378

Richer, H. M.: *ref*, 1281, 1320, 1499
Riches, E.: *ref*, 2355
Riches, R. C.: *ref*, 1129
Richey, M. H.: *test*, 1343; *ref*, 381, 1343, 1474
Richie, A.: *ref*, 398, 5:326(9)
Richie, J.: *ref*, 1277
Richman, A.: *ref*, 1145
Richman, B. J.: *ref*, 1164
Richman, E.: *ref*, 357
Richman, J.: *ref*, 529, 1394-5, 1499
Richman, J. T.: *ref*, 157, 1069
Richman, V.: *test*, 1884
Richmond, A. M.: *ref*, 2212
Richmond, B. O.: *ref*, 400, 542, 551, 589, 1350, 1403
Richmond, D. M.: *ref*, 328, 723, 1550, 1646
Richmond, E.: *ref*, 1181
Richmond, W.: *exc*, 532
Richmond, W. V.: *ref*, 525, 1105
Richter, P. D.: *ref*, 1164
Richter, R. H.: *ref*, 1294, 1471
Richter, W. R.: *ref*, 382
Richtmeyer, C. C.: *test*, 1:894
Richtsmeier, H. L.: *ref*, 20
Rickard, F. S.: *ref*, 2221
Rickard, G.: *ref*, 1517
Rickard, H. C.: *ref*, 1164, 1281
Rickels, K.: *ref*, 1225, 1227, 1295, 1300, 1377, 1499, P:41(3, 11), P:344(19)
Rickers-Ovsiankina, M.: *ref*, 1499
Rickers-Ovsiankina, M. A.: *exc*, 1447, 1499; *ref*, 1499
Ricks, D. F.: *ref*, 1281, 1383, 1499-500, 1519
Ricks, D. R.: *ref*, 1519
Ricks, J. H.: *rev*, 255, 345, 4:472-3, 5:490; *test*, 1063; *ref*, 529
Ricksecker, E. L.: *ref*, 2195, 2212
Riddell, S. A.: *ref*, 543
Ridding, L. W.: *ref*, 1253, 1275
Riddle, C. W.: *ref*, 1069
Riddle, L.: *ref*, 1394
Riddle, W. T.: *ref*, 1679
Rider, P. R.: *rev*, 2:1434, 2:1440
Rider, R.: *ref*, 494, 497
Rider, R. V.: *ref*, 525, 533, 1447
Rider, W. V.: *ref*, 50
Ridge, R. A.: *ref*, 1315
Ridgway, R. W.: *ref*, 543, 592, 1087, 1277, 1447
Ridley, D. R.: *ref*, 542, 561, 572
Ridley, D. W.: *ref*, 1121, 1181
Ridley, W. N.: *ref*, 18, 425, 1560
Rieber, M.: *ref*, 516
Riechard, D. E.: *ref*, 361
Rieck, E. C.: *ref*, 1281
Ried, B. R.: *ref*, 1193-4
Riedel, R. G.: *ref*, 1281, 1289, 1403, 2195
Riedel, W. W.: *ref*, 1261, 1281
Riedesel, C. A.: *rev*, 655, 705, 707, 6:638
Riegel, E. J.: *ref*, 4:367(2), 4:368 (1)
Riegel, K. F.: *ref*, 529, 532, 1303, 1480
Riegel, R. H.: *ref*, 1905
Riegel, R. M.: *ref*, 529, 532, 1303
Rieger, A. F.: *ref*, 1499
Rieker, G. A.: *ref*, 533

Roberts, K. E.: *test,* 2:1242; *ref,* 2:1242(1)
Roberts, L. F.: *ref,* 868
Roberts, L. H.: *ref,* 981
Roberts, L. K.: *ref,* 1281, 1499
Roberts, M. J. R.: *ref,* 1389
Roberts, M. K.: *ref,* 1094
Roberts, M. R.: *ref,* 1212, 1389
Roberts, P. C.: *ref,* 1383
Roberts, P. T.: *ref,* 382
Roberts, R.: *ref,* 1499
Roberts, R. C.: *ref,* 3:217(90)
Roberts, R. K.: *ref,* 2212
Roberts, R. W.: *ref,* 529, 1121, 1281
Roberts, S. O.: *ref,* 357, 382, 1087, 2195, 4:277(194)
Roberts, T. G.: *ref,* 981
Roberts, W. H.: *ref,* 482, 2195
Robertson, C. V.: *ref,* 1164
Robertson, G. J.: *ref,* 1069
Robertson, J. M.: *ref,* 1281
Robertson, J. P. S.: *test,* 2388; *ref,* 529, 545, 1198, 1281, 1380, 1447
Robertson, J. R.: *ref,* 20, 1164
Robertson, J. W.: *ref,* 400
Robertson, L. S.: *ref,* 2355
Robertson, M.: *ref,* 382, 404, 1471, 1500, 1519
Robertson, M. H.: *ref,* 358, 529, 1069, 1240, 1281, 1471, 1626, 5: 147(53)
Robertson, P. C.: *ref,* 1281
Robertson, T. G.: *ref,* 1389
Robertson, T. S.: *ref,* 1121
Robertson, Y.: *ref,* 1281
Robey, A.: *ref,* 1281
Robey, D. L.: *ref,* 1069, 1123, P: 302(2)
Robin, A. A.: *ref,* 1275, 1380, 1499, 1519
Robinault, I. P.: *ref,* 381
Robinovich, D.: *ref,* 1499
Robinowitz, R.: *ref,* 503, 532-3, 1281
Robins, S.: *ref,* 1293
Robinson, A.: *test,* 150
Robinson, A. B.: *test,* 35:327, 2: 1508
Robinson, B.: *test,* 4:539
Robinson, B. V.: *ref,* 357
Robinson, B. W.: *ref,* 1281
Robinson, C.: *ref,* 3:242(2)
Robinson, C. A.: *ref,* 1123
Robinson, C. D.: *ref,* 884, 1252
Robinson, D. J.: *ref,* 1121
Robinson, D. W.: *ref,* 382, 404, 1133, 1164
Robinson, E. B.: *ref,* 1281
Robinson, E. E.: *ref,* 655
Robinson, E. L.: *ref,* 525
Robinson, F. K.: *ref,* 357, 1044, 1069
Robinson, F. P.: *test,* 1745; *ref,* 1087, 1560, 1745, 1918, 4:216(10)
Robinson, G. E.: *rev,* 668, 744
Robinson, H.: *ref,* 1383
Robinson, H. A.: *rev,* 1567, 1573, 1649; *exc,* 2212; *ref,* 381, 489, 1474, 1567, 1675, 1716, 1923, 2028, 2043
Robinson, H. B.: *ref,* 484, 490, 505, 516, 538, 1921
Robinson, H. M.: *rev,* 1603, 1628,

1661, 1694, 1881, 1925, 1929, 6: 956; *test,* 1681; *ref,* 1689, 1881, 1906, 1917-8, 1923, 1929, 5:774 (6-7), 5:781(10-1)
Robinson, H. P.: *ref,* 1499
Robinson, H. W.: *ref,* 2451
Robinson, J. B.: *ref,* 1087, 2212, 2251
Robinson, J. F.: *ref,* 1499
Robinson, J. M.: *ref,* 1087
Robinson, J. O.: *ref,* 1275
Robinson, J. S.: *ref,* 484
Robinson, J. T.: *ref,* 1174, 1225, 1519
Robinson, L.: *ref,* 1133, 1174, 1253
Robinson, L. F.: *ref,* 1044
Robinson, L. G. M.: *ref,* 1073
Robinson, M.: *ref,* 1094, 1207
Robinson, M. E.: *ref,* 6:228(63)
Robinson, M. F.: *ref,* 4:44(2)
Robinson, M. L.: *ref,* 398
Robinson, M. S.: *ref,* 525
Robinson, N.: *ref,* 525, 1322
Robinson, N. M.: *ref,* 484, 490, 505, 516, 525, 529, 538, 1447, 1921
Robinson, R.: *ref,* 349
Robinson, R. A.: *ref,* 403, 439
Robinson, R. V.: *ref,* 1649, 1688
Robinson, S. A.: *ref,* 1448
Robinson, S. J.: *ref,* 525, 533
Robinson, T. C.: *ref,* 1394-5
Robinson, T. R.: *ref,* 1207
Robinson, W.: *ref,* 868, 1207, 1572
Robinson, W. A.: *ref,* 2169
Robinson, W. P.: *ref,* 495, 533
Robischon, P.: *ref,* 492
Robison, J. O.: *ref,* 1073
Robison, R. K.: *exc,* 532
Robitaille, H. J.: *ref,* 525
Robles, A.: *ref,* 1499, P:450(82)
Robles, A. G.: *ref,* 1380
Roby, A. R.: *ref,* 194, 211
Roby, T. B.: *ref,* 1151, 1519, 1775
Rocchio, P. D.: *ref,* 868
Roche, D.: *ref,* 381, 1447
Roche, D. D. J.: *ref,* 1182
Roche, P. J. D.: *ref,* 381
Rochefort, G.: *test,* 35:303, 35:404
Rochefort, R.: *test,* 35:404
Rochester, D. E.: *ref,* 447, 529, 1403
Rochester Datronics, Inc.: *test,* 7: 652A
Rochlin, G. N.: *ref,* 1499
Rochlin, I.: *ref,* 1087, 1499
Rochlin, M.: *ref,* 1249
Rochman, J. E.: *ref,* 1280
Rochwarg, H.: *ref,* 1499
Rock, D.: *ref,* 49
Rock, D. A.: *ref,* 357, 2212, 2349
Rock, M. L.: *test,* 4:827; *ref,* 1519, 4:827(1)
Rock, M. R.: *ref,* 1499
Rock, R. J.: *ref,* 1576, 1616
Rock, R. T.: *ref,* 2212, 2:1539(3), 2:1565(4)
Rock, R. W.: *ref,* 1395
Rockberger, H.: *ref,* 1499
Rockett, F. C.: *ref,* 1471
Rockey, M. A.: *ref,* 1281
Rockliff, B. W.: *ref,* 1377
Rockwell, F. V.: *exc,* 1499; *ref,* 1499
Rockwell, G. J.: *ref,* 533

Rockwell, J. G.: *test,* 35:361
Rodahl, K.: *ref,* 439, 1294
Rodd, W. G.: *ref,* 364, 1403, 1775
Rodda, B. E.: *ref,* 1093, 1144
Rode, A.: *ref,* 1383
Rodell, C.: *ref,* 1499
Roden, A. H.: *ref,* 359, 1090, 1121
Roderick, J. A.: *ref,* 589
Roderick, J. L.: *ref,* 589
Rodger, A.: *rev,* 2142, 2242, 2251-2, 2266-7
Rodger, A. G.: *ref,* 409
Rodgers, C. W.: *ref,* 1164, 1212
Rodgers, D. A.: *rev,* 1281; *ref,* 1121, 1281, 1499
Rodgers, D. C.: *ref,* 400, 1552, 2028
Rodgers, F. P.: *ref,* 1164, 2212
Rodgers, R. F.: *ref,* 1094, 1176
Rodgers, W. L.: *ref,* 1073
Rodies, H.: *exc,* 1499
Rodil, D.: *ref,* 1932
Rodnick, E. H.: *ref,* 1499-500, 1519
Rodrigues, M. C.: *test,* 1695
Roe, A.: *ref,* 36, 381, 518, 525, 655, 1499, 1519, 1690
Roe, K. V.: *ref,* 497
Roeber, E. C.: *test,* 5:870; *ref,* 48, 2195, 2199, 2212, 2214, 4:737(7)
Roebuck, J.: *ref,* 1121, 1281
Roeder, W.: *test,* 1329
Roeder, W. S.: *test,* 1066, 2226
Roehlke, A.: *ref,* 1031, 1035, 2212
Roehrig, W. C.: *ref,* 1387, 1499
Roelfs, P.: *test,* 895
Roelke, P.: *ref,* 1536, 1552, 1634
Roelke, P. L.: *ref,* 542, 1552, 1567
Roemer, G. A.: *ref,* 1499
Roemer, R. E.: *ref,* 2355
Roemmich, H.: *ref,* 371, 1164
Roen, S. R.: *test,* 1137; *ref,* 1137
Roesel, H. A.: *ref,* 5:308(305)
Roessel, F. P.: *ref,* 1281
Roessler, R.: *ref,* 1121, 1281, 1293, 1471, 7:55(13)
Roff, M.: *ref,* 400, 525, 1186
Roffee, D. T.: *ref,* 1123
Roffers, T.: *ref,* 1214
Roffman, P. O.: *ref,* 502
Rogal, R.: *ref,* 532
Rogal, R. A.: *ref,* 1281, 1499
Rogers, A. H.: *ref,* 1281, 1500
Rogers, A. L.: *test,* 2:1343; *ref,* 525, 2:1343(3)
Rogers, B. E.: *ref,* 545
Rogers, B. G.: *ref,* 1121
Rogers, C. A.: *rev,* 415; *ref,* 354, 1087
Rogers, C. R.: *rev,* 2:1237, 2:1240; *test,* 1313; *ref,* 1313, 1519
Rogers, D. C.: *ref,* 357, 426
Rogers, D. W.: *ref,* 189, 589
Rogers, F. R.: *rev,* 2:1499-500; *exc,* 1:B455
Rogers, H. B.: *ref,* 2227, 2233
Rogers, J. L.: *test,* 15; *ref,* 3:10 (1)
Rogers, K. E.: *ref,* 1164
Rogers, L. L.: *ref,* 364
Rogers, L. S.: *ref,* 532, 1499
Rogers, M. E.: *ref,* 1320
Rogers, M. E. P.: *ref,* 1133, 1135
Rogers, M. I.: *ref,* 551, 1121, 1315
Rogers, M. S.: *ref,* 1121, 1281
Rogers, V. M.: *rev,* 1946, 1953

Rogers, V. R.: *ref,* 868
Rogers, W. A.: *ref,* 1302, 1403
Rogers, W. T.: *rev,* 738
Rogge, H.: *ref,* 2195
Rogge, H. J.: *ref,* 533, 1281, 2195
Roggenkamp, R. R.: *ref,* 357, 425, 1044
Rogo, R. A.: *ref,* 1626, 5:308(362)
Rogolsky, M. M.: *ref,* 1499
Rohaly, K. A.: *ref,* 1315, 1391
Rohan, J. C.: *ref,* 354, 525
Rohan, W. P.: *ref,* 1281
Rohde, A. R.: *test,* 1498; *ref,* 1498
Rohde, R. H.: *ref,* 1407
Rohila, P.: *ref,* 1164, 2173
Rohila, P. K.: *ref,* 1121, 1281, 2212
Rohlf, R. J.: *ref,* 359, 1281, 2212
Rohovit, D. D.: *ref,* 1195
Rohr, M. E.: *ref,* 1383, 1415, 1499
Rohrer, G.: *test,* 36:752
Rohrer, J. H.: *ref,* 48, 381, 426, 1499, 2212, 2355
Rohrer, P. L.: *test,* 355
Rohrs, D. K.: *ref,* 211, 2195, 6:438 (512), P:399(33)
Rohrs, F. W.: *ref,* 381, 525, 533, 1275
Rohwer, W. D.: *ref,* 400, 439, 516, 1603
Roitman, R. T.: *ref,* 1474
Roitzsch, J. C.: *ref,* 1281
Rokeach, M.: *test,* 1355; *ref,* 1121, 1355
Rokicki, R. R.: *ref,* 503
Rokosz, S.: *ref,* 529
Roland, N. L.: *ref,* 1289
Roland, W. A.: *ref,* 381, 1481
Rolfe, J. F.: *ref,* 1320, 3:110(12), 3:217(125), 3:404(4), 4:66(1)
Rolland, J. C.: *ref,* 516
Roller, R. D.: *ref,* 525
Rollins, R. W.: *ref,* 2195
Rollinson, E. A.: *test,* 35:133
Rolston, R. H.: *ref,* 1519
Roman, M.: *ref,* 1499
Roman, P. M.: *ref,* 1281, 1383, 7:55 (22)
Romanella, A. E.: *ref,* 1207, 1499
Romaniuk, A.: *ref,* 1716
Romano, E.: *ref,* 1240
Romano, R. J.: *ref,* 1315
Romano, R. L.: *ref,* 6:223(15)
Romanowski, W. V.: *ref,* 879
Romberg, T. A.: *rev,* 763; *exc,* 7:464; *ref,* 709
Rome, H. P.: *ref,* 1281, 1284
Romero, T. D.: *ref,* 2212
Romine, B. H.: *ref,* 1133, 1135
Romine, P. G.: *ref,* 1044, 1164, 1275
Rommel, R. C. S.: *ref,* 1281
Romney, A. K.: *ref,* 2195, 4:88 (19)
Romney, D.: *ref,* 403, 439, 1198, 1299
Romo, B. E.: *ref,* 1137
Romoser, R. C.: *ref,* 868, 1044, 1383
Ronan, R. J.: *ref,* 361
Ronan, W. W.: *ref,* 482, 1074, 1078, 1087, 1206-7, 2195, 2231, 2239, 2266, 2448
Rondberg, S. R.: *ref,* 532-3
Rondeau, J. H.: *ref,* 868

Rondinella, O. R.: *ref,* 908
Ronning, R. R.: *ref,* 419, 868
Rood, T. M.: *ref,* 516
Roody, S. I.: *test,* 4:116; *ref,* 4: 116(1-2)
Rook, L. H.: *ref,* 1499
Rooker, J. L.: *ref,* 1519, 2452
Rooks, I.: *ref,* 348, 2195
Rooks, J. E.: *ref,* 869
Rooney, J. J.: *ref,* 1225, 1281
Roorda, T.: *ref,* 1430
Roos, P.: *exc,* 1499; *ref,* 426, 1232, 1447
Root, A. R.: *ref,* 87, 6:159(43)
Root, E. L.: *ref,* 1044
Root, W. T.: *ref,* 525, 6:480(18)
Roper, G. E.: *ref,* 355
Rorabaugh, M. E.: *ref,* 1281
Rorer, L. G.: *rev,* 1094, 1383; *ref,* 1121, 1164, 1281
Rorison, J. R.: *ref,* 1281
Rorschach, H.: *test,* 1499f; *ref,* 1499
Ros, P. de M. M.: *ref,* 1123
Rosander, A. C.: *test,* 1:902
Rosanes, M. B.: *ref,* 1499-500
Rosanoff, A. J.: *test,* 1480; *ref,* 525, 1480
Rosanoff, I. R.: *ref,* 1480
Rosauer, J. K.: *ref,* 487, 497
Roscoe, D. L.: *ref,* 1293
Roscoe, J. T.: *ref,* 49, 382, 755, 863
Rose, A.: *ref,* 1293
Rose, A. A.: *ref,* 1095, 1281, 1499
Rose, A. L.: *test,* 35:160
Rose, A. M.: *ref,* P:381(21)
Rose, A. W.: *ref,* 1499, 1519
Rose, C. L.: *ref,* 1073, 1383
Rose, D.: *ref,* 1499, P:450(82)
Rose, D. E.: *ref,* 2038
Rose, D. M.: *ref,* 532
Rose, E.: *ref,* 993
Rose, F. H.: *ref,* 1320
Rose, G.: *ref,* 1171
Rose, H. A.: *ref,* 1044, 1302, 1430, 1501, 1626, 2212
Rose, J.: *ref,* 561, 574, 577, 2340
Rose, J. R.: *ref,* 64, 357
Rose, J. T.: *ref,* 1277
Rose, N. H.: *ref,* 1245
Rose, R.: *ref,* 1281
Rose, R. M.: *ref,* 1281
Rose, T.: *ref,* 1073, 2323
Rose, W.: *ref,* 2195
Roseborough, M. E.: *ref,* 4:56(3)
Rosecrans, C. J.: *ref,* 1281, 1447, 1499
Rosemier, R. A.: *ref,* 1647
Rosen, A.: *ref,* 1281, 1387, 1474
Rosen, A. C.: *ref,* 1281, 1499
Rosén, A. S.: *ref,* 518
Rosen, C. L.: *rev,* 1910, 1925, 1934; *ref,* 400, 1574, 1716, 1921
Rosen, C. M.: *ref,* 1544
Rosen, E.: *rev,* 1469, 4:105; *exc,* 1448; *ref,* 1281, 1463, 1480, 1499, 2212
Rosen, E. K.: *ref,* 381
Rosen, G.: *ref,* 1145, 1500
Rosen, G. P.: *ref,* 1140, 1192
Rosen, H.: *ref,* 1164, 1277, 1281, 1293, 1471, 1480
Rosen, I. C.: *ref,* 1281, 1448, 1499

Rosen, J.: *ref,* 868, 1164, 1403, 1499, 2212, 2214
Rosen, J. C.: *ref,* 1109, 1437, 2395
Rosen, J. L.: *ref,* 1519
Rosen, M.: *ref,* 22, 518, 529, 533, 1281, 2227, 2234
Rosen, M. H.: *ref,* 1073, 1481, 2195
Rosen, M. S.: *ref,* 1499
Rosen, N. A.: *test,* 6:879; *ref,* 357, 574, 2448
Rosen, R. A. H.: *ref,* 1281
Rosenau, C. B.: *ref,* 400, 1073
Rosenbach, J. H.: *rev,* 349, 401
Rosenbaum, B. B.: *ref,* 6:159(47)
Rosenbaum, G.: *ref,* 1281
Rosenbaum, I.: *ref,* 868, 1474, 2212, 5:597(10)
Rosenbaum, I. S.: *ref,* 1499
Rosenbaum, M. E.: *ref,* 1519
Rosenberg, A. M.: *ref,* 1121, 1447
Rosenberg, B.: *ref,* 1139
Rosenberg, B. G.: *ref,* 532, 1121, 1164, 1281, 1437, 1447, P:305(20-1)
Rosenberg, C. M.: *ref,* 439, 981, 1164, 1174, 1225, 1275, 1383
Rosenberg, C. Y.: *ref,* 1474, 1499
Rosenberg, E.: *ref,* 529, 1040
Rosenberg, J. B.: *ref,* 516
Rosenberg, J. J.: *ref,* 1164
Rosenberg, J. L.: *ref,* 1121
Rosenberg, J. M.: *ref,* 1176
Rosenberg, L.: *test,* 1192
Rosenberg, L. A.: *ref,* 489, 516, 525, 1121, 1281, 1447
Rosenberg, L. M.: *ref,* 1192
Rosenberg, L. R.: *ref,* 1474
Rosenberg, M.: *ref,* 525, 533, 1094, 1121
Rosenberg, N.: *ref,* 1205-6, 1245, 1281, 1320, 2195
Rosenberg, P.: *ref,* 2195
Rosenberg, S.: *ref,* 1232, 1499
Rosenberg, S. J.: *ref,* 1499
Rosenberger, P. B.: *ref,* 533
Rosenblatt, B.: *ref,* 1499
Rosenblatt, B. P.: *ref,* 1474
Rosenblatt, D.: *ref,* 1519
Rosenblatt, H. S.: *ref,* 1129
Rosenblatt, J. B.: *ref,* 1163
Rosenblatt, M. S.: *ref,* 1451
Rosenblatt, S. M.: *ref,* 532, 1169, 1474, 1499
Rosenblith, J. F.: *ref,* 484
Rosenbloom, A. A.: *ref,* 1881, 1929
Rosenbloom, P. C.: *rev,* 619
Rosenblum, J.: *ref,* 489
Rosenblum, M. P.: *ref,* 1232, 1298, 1346
Rosenblum, S.: *ref,* 1140, 5:326(15-6)
Rosenbrock, P. A.: *ref,* 1383
Rosenfeld, G. B.: *ref,* 487, 489, 525
Rosenfeld, H. M.: *ref,* 1121, 1207, 1370, 1463, 1519
Rosenfeld, I. J.: *ref,* 1169, 1481, 1519
Rosenfeld, L. B.: *ref,* 1176
Rosenfeld, L. S.: *ref,* 5:781(17)
Rosenfeld, M.: *ref,* 35, 361
Rosenfield, A. G.: *ref,* 981
Rosenfield, L.: *ref,* 487, 525
Rosengren, W. R.: *ref,* 1519
Rosenhan, D.: *ref,* 1121, 1212, 1519

Rowe, F. B.: *ref,* 482, 1133, 1281, 1395, 2195
Rowe, H. R.: *ref,* 2387
Rowe, J.: *ref,* 1281
Rowe, L. A.: *ref,* 1447, 1499, 1519
Rowe, L. M.: *ref,* 357
Rowe, R.: *ref,* 1225, 1227
Rowe, W.: *ref,* 1315
Rowe (H. M.) Co.: *test,* 36:588
Rowell, D.: *ref,* 1134
Rowell, J. T.: *ref,* 1281
Rowell, W. J.: *ref,* 1094
Rowland, A. L.: *ref,* 869
Rowland, C.: *test,* 4:473
Rowland, G. W.: *ref,* 1039, 1794
Rowland, K. M.: *ref,* 2454
Rowland, M. M.: *ref,* 1164
Rowland, M. S.: *ref,* 525
Rowland, W. M.: *ref,* 1906, 1923
Rowles, E.: *ref,* 419
Rowley, I. F.: *ref,* 1262
Rowley, J. V.: *ref,* 1207
Rowley, V. N.: *ref,* 50, 533, 543, 1281
Rowntree, J. P.: *ref,* 206
Roy, A. B.: *ref,* 1499
Roy, E. A.: *ref,* 1572
Roy, H.: *ref,* 1232
Roy, H. L.: *ref,* 1281
Roy, J. P.: *ref,* 1109
Roy, J. R.: *ref,* 1275
Roy, S.: *ref,* 1383
Royal, E. A.: *ref,* 1469
Royal, R. E.: *ref,* 1474, 1499
Royce, J. R.: *ref,* 439–40, 518, 1196–7, 1216, 1277, 1305, 1478, 1485, 2234
Royer, E. B.: *ref,* 1320
Royer, F. L.: *ref,* 529
Royer, H. L.: *rev,* 776
Royer, J. E.: *ref,* 69, 5:308(393)
Royer, O. O.: *ref,* 2:1182(4)
Royo, D.: *ref,* 439, 532, 1447
Roys, K. B.: *ref,* 2212
Royse, A. B.: *rev,* 461, 477, 5:857, 6:470
Royse, N. D.: *ref,* 1395
Royster, R. F.: *test,* 2469
Royster, S.: *test,* 3:147, 4:190
Rozan, G. H.: *ref,* 1144
Rozehnal, B. J.: *ref,* 840
Rozynko, V.: *ref,* 349, 1073, 1121, 1164, 1281
Rozynko, V. V.: *ref,* 1073, 1121, 1281
Rubenstein, B. B.: *ref,* 1499
Rubin, B.: *ref,* 1105
Rubin, D.: *ref,* 1772
Rubin, E. J.: *ref,* 407, 440, 529, 533, 1478
Rubin, E. Z.: *ref,* 1499
Rubin, G.: *ref,* 1094
Rubin, H.: *ref,* 532, 1281, 1469, 1499
Rubin, H. K.: *ref,* 1519
Rubin, H. S.: *ref,* 7, 1315
Rubin, J.: *ref,* 439, 529
Rubin, R. A.: *ref,* 1069
Rubin, R. T.: *ref,* 1281, 1298
Rubin, S. B.: *ref,* 1281
Rubin, S. E.: *ref,* 1383
Rubin, S. I.: *rev,* 1078
Rubin, S. S.: *ref,* 349, 1169, 1519
Rubino, C.: *ref,* 1447, 1883
Rubino, C. A.: *ref,* 505, 529, 532–3

Rubin-Rabson, G.: *ref,* 532, 1320
Rubinroit, C. I.: *ref,* 1121
Rubinstein, E. A.: *ref,* 532, 1232
Rubisoff, R.: *ref,* 3:53(5)
Ruble, R. A.: *ref,* 20, 400, 1082, 1121
Ruby, T. M.: *ref,* 529, 1300
Ruby, W. M.: *ref,* 1383, 1519
Ruch, C. P.: *ref,* 1133
Ruch, F.: *ref,* 1123
Ruch, F. L.: *rev,* 1222, 2301–2, 2397, 2413, 3:704; *test,* 1071, 3: 631, 5:888; *ref,* 525, 1071, 1101, 1281, 1320
Ruch, G. M.: *rev,* 2:1433, 2:1458, 2:1619; *test,* 18, 204, 2:1192, 2: 1454–5, 2:1588, 3:353, 4:174, 4: 195, 5:698; *ref,* 18, 36, 211, 525, 1603, 1611, 1724, 2:1588(1–2), 3:220(15, 31), 4:535(2)
Ruch, J. C.: *ref,* 1389
Ruch, W. W.: *ref,* 1071, 1281
Ruchti, G. E.: *ref,* 1121
Rucker, M. H.: *ref,* 1207
Ruckhaber, C. J.: *ref,* 1447
Ruda, E.: *ref,* 482
Rudd, J. P.: *ref,* 69, 361, 655, 1069, 1599
Rudd, M.: *ref,* 2:1565(5), 4:535(4)
Rudder, J.: *ref,* 1336
Rude, H. N.: *ref,* 1071
Rudel, R. G.: *ref,* 533
Ruderman, V.: *ref,* 1281
Rudhe, L.: *ref,* 1516
Rudloff, J. S.: *ref,* 2212–3
Rudman, H. C.: *test,* 36, 115, 655–6, 1603, 1796, 1953
Rudman, J.: *ref,* 382, 2325, 2337, 2349, 2355
Rudnick, M.: *ref,* 19, 400
Rudoff, A.: *ref,* 1121, 1500
Rudolf, G. de M.: *ref,* 439, 503, 525, 532, 1428
Rudolph, L.: *ref,* 524, 529, 1044
Rudolph, R.: *ref,* 6:244(2–3)
Rudorfer, L.: *ref,* 1293
Ruebush, B.: *ref,* 425
Ruebush, B. K.: *ref,* 518, 1087, 1281, 1471
Ruedisili, C. H.: *rev,* 2298, 2448; *ref,* 2195, 3:217(78), 4:277(162–3)
Ruesch, H. A.: *ref,* 1499
Ruesch, J.: *ref,* 1281, 1499, 1519
Ruess, A. L.: *ref,* 497, 533, 1499, 1519, 5:326(35)
Rufe, C. P.: *ref,* 1121
Ruff, W. H.: *ref,* 5:530(45)
Rugen, M. E.: *rev,* 928, 3:422
Rugg, H.: *ref,* 525
Rugg, L. S.: *ref,* 525
Rugg, R. H.: *ref,* 496, 516
Ruggles, E. W.: *ref,* 2266
Ruggles, R.: *ref,* 1090
Ruhlen, H.: *test,* 104
Ruhling, R. O.: *ref,* 1281
Ruisanchez-Lopez, L.: *ref,* 314
Ruiz, R. A.: *ref,* 1281, 1380
Rule, E. T.: *ref,* 1499
Rulon, P. J.: *test,* 1:915, 2:1485; *ref,* 1320, 2212, P:297(1)
Rumage, C. J.: *ref,* 1254
Rumbaugh, D. M.: *test,* P:30; *ref,* 1207, P:30(1)

Rumley, E.: *ref,* 589
Rump, E. E.: *ref,* 1174
Rumrill, C.: *ref,* 1281
Runde, R. E.: *ref,* 1474
Runde, R. M.: *ref,* 1044
Rundquist, E. A.: *rev,* 794, 3:372; *test,* 1:901; *ref,* 1281, P:342(1)
Runner, K.: *test,* 1356
Runner, K. R.: *ref,* 1356
Runte, R. M.: *ref,* 1407
Rupe, J. C.: *ref,* 1349
Rupert, H. A.: *ref,* 981
Rupiper, O. J.: *ref,* 7, 382, 1207, 1403, 2195, 2212
Rupp, L. G.: *ref,* 1216
Rupp, R. A.: *ref,* 3:255(12)
Ruppel, R. W.: *ref,* 1281, 1378
Rupprecht, P.: *ref,* 1281
Rusalem, H.: *ref,* 529
Rusch, C. E.: *ref,* 603
Rusch, R. R.: *ref,* 560
Ruschival, M. L.: *ref,* 533, 538
Rush, A. C.: *ref,* 349, 1164, 1281, 1403
Rush, B. H.: *ref,* 1519
Rush, C. H.: *ref,* 1200, 1572, 2451
Rush, H.: *ref,* 438, 2195
Rushall, B. S.: *ref,* 1383
Rushing, J. R.: *test,* 6:601
Rushton, C. S.: *ref,* 525
Rushton, J.: *ref,* 1129, 1383
Rushton, J. G.: *ref,* 1281
Rushton, S. Y.: *ref,* 543
Rusk, M. T.: *ref,* 1123, 1469
Ruskin, H. D.: *ref,* 1281
Rusmore, J.: *ref,* 482, 2135, 2151
Rusmore, J. T.: *ref,* 482, 1194, 3: 658(7), 6:1102(8, 10)
Rusnak, A. W.: *ref,* 1499
Russel, J. H.: *ref,* 1289
Russell, C. A.: *ref,* 525, 533
Russell, D.: *ref,* 2195
Russell, D. H.: *rev,* 1689, 1694, 1711, 1715, 1733, 2:1309, 3:515, 4:551; *test,* 6:318; *ref,* 1087, 1629, 1661, 1702, 1733, 1918, 3:515(2), 4:200(1)
Russell, D. L.: *ref,* 2195
Russell, E. C.: *ref,* 497
Russell, E. W.: *ref,* 529, 1499
Russell, G. E.: *ref,* 532
Russell, G. H.: *ref,* 1499
Russell, G. W.: *ref,* 1275, 1383
Russell, H. H.: *ref,* 387, 425
Russell, H. J.: *rev,* 313, 2:1372–3, 3:209
Russell, I. L.: *ref,* 1447, 5:326(24)
Russell, J.: *ref,* 518, 1383, 1772
Russell, J. A.: *ref,* 529, 1275
Russell, J. B.: *ref,* 416
Russell, J. D.: *ref,* 908
Russell, J. L. A.: *test,* 1529
Russell, J. M.: *ref,* 1174, 1501
Russell, J. W.: *ref,* 357, 652, 1794, 1948
Russell, K. R.: *ref,* 1474
Russell, L.: *ref,* 532, 592, 1447, 1499
Russell, M. A.: *ref,* 1500
Russell, R. B.: *test,* 790
Russell, R. W.: *ref,* 381, 1261
Russell, T.: *ref,* 381, 1252
Russell, T. S.: *ref,* 5:766(3)
Russell, W. A.: *ref,* 1480
Russell, W. J. C.: *ref,* 1164, 1315

Russell, W. P.: *ref,* 69, 361, 1095, 1572
Russo, J. F.: *ref,* 48, 1044
Russo, J. R.: *ref,* 1073, 6:1023(1)
Russo, W. J.: *ref,* 1253
Russon, A. R.: *ref, 69,* 5:6(18)
Rust, M. M.: *ref,* 1320
Rust, R.: *ref,* 1499
Rust, R. M.: *ref,* 1121, 1281, 1499, 2212
Rust, V. I.: *ref,* 1775
Rustin, S. L.: *ref,* 439, 529, 1464
Rutan, J. S.: *ref,* 1240
Ruter, M. D.: *ref,* 1123
Ruth, J. M.: *ref,* 1499
Ruth, R. A.: *rev,* 991
Rutherford, B. M.: *ref,* 425
Rutherford, E.: *ref,* 1247
Rutherford, R. C.: *ref,* 1281
Rutherford, W. L.: *ref,* 1716
Rutland, E.: *ref,* 436
Rutledge, A. L.: *test,* 7:569
Rutledge, C. W.: *ref,* 1289
Rutledge, J. A.: *ref,* 1281
Rutledge, L.: *ref,* 1387
Rutschmann, D. F.: *ref,* 1315
Rutschmann, J.: *ref,* 1387
Rutstein, E. H.: *ref,* 1094, 1293, 1499
Rutt, R. J.: *ref,* 1069
Rutter, D.: *ref,* 409
Rutter, E.: *ref,* 1094
Rutter, M.: *exc,* 1411; *ref,* 516, 533, 1145, 1428, 1646
Rutter, W. A.: *ref,* 1474
Ruttiger, K. F.: *ref,* 1275
Ruuth, E.: *ref,* 1387
Ruzicka, W. J.: *ref,* 868
Ruzicka, W. R.: *ref,* 522, 533, 1628
Ryan, B.: *ref,* 361
Ryan, B. A.: *ref,* 1176, 1499
Ryan, C. W.: *ref,* 1281
Ryan, F.: *ref,* 146
Ryan, F. J.: *ref,* 1499, 2212
Ryan, H. J. L.: *ref,* 1672
Ryan, J. A.: *ref,* 2197
Ryan, J. R.: *ref,* 1281
Ryan, L. C.: *test,* 926
Ryan, M. A.: *ref,* 1123
Ryan, M. S.: *exc,* 497
Ryan, P. L.: *ref,* 1176, 1306
Ryan, P. M.: *ref,* 1403
Ryan, R. D.: *ref,* 1044
Ryan, R. P.: *ref,* 1383, 1519
Ryan, S. E.: *ref,* 69, 419
Ryan, S. R.: *ref,* 1127
Ryan, T. A.: *exc,* 2212
Ryan, T. G.: *ref,* 2212
Ryan, T. M.: *test,* 54, 3:139, 5:176; *ref,* 1176
Ryan, V.: *ref,* 1906, 1918, 1923, 5: 769(4), 5:781(16)
Ryan, V. I.: *ref,* 1906
Ryan, W.: *ref,* 1499
Ryans, D. G.: *rev,* 414, 472, 1423, 3:399, 3:403–4, 6:448; *exc,* 497; *ref,* 69, 398, 869, 1095, 1320, 1366, 1583, 3:2(8–9), 3:4(5, 7)
Ryback, D.: *ref,* 1121
Ryback, R. S.: *ref,* 561, 591, 1281, 1293, 1377, 1499
Ryberg, D. C.: *exc,* 223
Rybolt, G. A.: *ref,* 1164

Rychlak, J. F.: *ref,* 533, 1129, 1164, 1205, 1253, 1281, 1499, 1519
Ryckman, D. B.: *ref,* 981, 1875
Ryden, E. R.: *test,* 879, 4:240; *ref,* 2212, 4:240(1)
Ryder, A. D.: *ref,* 1207, 2195
Ryder, F. G.: *ref,* 271
Ryder, R. G.: *ref,* 1281
Ryle, A.: *ref,* 1145, 1174, 1218, 1410
Ryman, D. H.: *ref,* 1176
Rymsza, J. S. D.: *ref,* 533, 1451
Rystrom, R.: *rev,* 1537
Rytel, M. W.: *ref,* 1281

SAAM, T.: *ref,* 525
Sabatino, D. A.: *ref,* 50, 516, 533, 981, 1115, 1447, 1679, 1887, 1902, 7:880(4–6)
Sabeh, R.: *ref,* 419, 532
Saber-Motamedi, H.: *ref,* 529
Sabers, D.: *test,* 681–2, 751
Sabers, D. L.: *ref,* 19–20, 681
Sablosky, L.: *ref,* 1377
Sabourin, G. J.: *ref,* 1320
Sachs, D. A.: *ref,* 533
Sachs, K. S.: *ref,* 1499
Sachs, L. B.: *ref,* 1389
Sachtlebon, C. C.: *ref,* 357
Sackett, E. B.: *rev,* 49, 1:1176
Sackman, H.: *ref,* 1499
Sacks, E. L.: *ref,* 525
Sacks, H.: *ref,* 1499
Sacks, J.: *ref,* 1447
Sacks, J. G.: *ref,* 1499
Sacks, J. M.: *ref,* 518, 1499
Sacks, L.: *ref,* 533, 1447, 1469, 1499, 1519
Saddler, J.: *test,* 4:494
Saddler, L. E.: *test,* 479, 1431; *ref,* 2212
Sadler, P. M.: *ref,* 1121, 1403
Sadler, T. G.: *ref,* 1174
Sadnavitch, J. M.: *test,* 7:253, 7: 272, 7:286, 7:317; *ref,* 525, 1073
Sadowsky, D.: *ref,* 532, 1281
Saelens, E. A.: *ref,* 1481
Saenger, E. L.: *ref,* 1195
Saetveit, T. G.: *test,* 211; *ref,* 211
Safer, D. J.: *ref,* 1281
Saffer, J. B.: *ref,* 1121
Saffir, M. A.: *ref,* 525
Safford, H. W.: *ref,* 529
Safian, M. Z.: *ref,* 1447, 1499, 1519
Safran, C.: *test,* 453, 2210; *ref,* 453, 2210
Safrin, R. K.: *ref,* 533, 1447
Sage, E. H.: *ref,* 1280
Sage, J. N.: *ref,* 1121
Sagen, H. B.: *rev,* 40, 1052, 1306, 1430; *ref,* 1394–5
Sager, C. J.: *ref,* 1499, 1519
Sager, G.: *ref,* 1247
Saguiguit, G. F.: *ref,* 1320, 2212
Saha, G. B.: *ref,* 1320, 1428
Saha, R. P.: *ref,* 1320
Sahu, S.: *ref,* 1174
Sai-Halász, A.: *ref,* 1499
Sailor, P. J.: *ref,* 1471
Sainsbury, P.: *ref,* 1275
St. Clair, J. K.: *ref,* 2451
St. Clair, N. E.: *ref,* 5:597(9)
St. Clair, W.: *ref,* 1320
St. Clair, W. F.: *ref,* 1320, 1499
St. Denis, G. C.: *ref,* 1094

St. George, R.: *ref,* 981
St. John, D. E.: *ref,* 2197
St. John, J.: *ref,* 1447, 1485, 1921
Sainte-Laure, *Sister: ref,* 1320
Sainty, G. E.: *ref,* 1351
Sainty, J. E.: *ref,* 1351
Sainz, A.: *ref,* 1281
Sait, E. M.: *ref,* 1164
Saito, C. H.: *ref,* 1474
Saito, K.: *ref,* 1499
Sak, H. G.: *ref,* 381, 533, 1447
Sakalosky, J. C.: *ref,* 1069, 1073
Sakheim, G.: *ref,* 1447, 1481, 1499
Sakheim, G. A.: *ref,* 1499
Sako, Y.: *ref,* 529, 1281
Sakoda, J. M.: *ref,* 1499
Salas, R. G.: *ref,* 1174, 1240, 1295, 1383
Salasin, S.: *ref,* 1281
Salber, E. J.: *ref,* 1280
Salcines, R. A.: *ref,* 1281, 1499
Sälde, H.: *ref,* 1499
Saleh, S. D.: *ref,* 1164, 1194
Sales, R. C.: *ref,* 879
Salfield, D.: *ref,* 1499
Salfield, D. J.: *ref,* 1499
Salier, M. W.: *ref,* 1430
Salinda, J. F.: *ref,* 69
Salisbury, D. L.: *ref,* 533
Salisbury, F. S.: *ref,* 211
Salisbury, L. H.: *ref,* 529
Salisbury, R.: *rev,* 2:1273, 2:1580
Salk, L.: *ref,* 1499, 1519
Salkind, C. T.: *ref,* 598
Sallade, J. B. R.: *ref,* 1123
Sallak, V. J.: *test,* 6:729
Sallery, R. D. H.: *ref,* 1469
Salley, R. E.: *exc,* 1366; *ref,* 3:217 (130), 4:277(217)
Salman, A. R.: *ref,* 1519
Salmi, I.: *test,* 159
Salmon, C.: *test,* T:1266
Salmon, P.: *ref,* 1281
Salomon, F.: *test,* 1528; *ref,* 1528
Salomone, P. R.: *ref,* 1121, 1145, 1210, 1225, 1383, 1430, 2283
Salop, P.: *ref,* 1281
Salopek, T. F.: *ref,* 50, 525, 533
Sals, D. K.: *test,* 1776
Salter, M. D.: *ref,* 1499
Saltiel, S.: *ref,* 1069
Saltz, E.: *ref,* 1164
Saltz, G.: *ref,* 1519
Saltzgaver, L. D.: *ref,* 6:438(443)
Saltzman, E. S.: *ref,* 1500, 1519
Saltzman, S.: *ref,* 525, 1145, 1500
Saltzmann, S. S.: *ref,* 1499, 1519
Salva, D. M.: *ref,* 1315, 2212
Salvati, S. R.: *ref,* 533
Salvatore, J. C.: *ref,* 1448
Salvendy, G.: *test,* 2230; *ref,* 2228, 2230, 2234
Salvia, J.: *ref,* 1911–2, 1932
Salvia, J. A.: *ref,* 1924
Salyers, M. H.: *ref,* 1123
Salzinger, K.: *exc,* 1195; *ref,* 36, 518, 2234
Salzinger, S.: *ref,* 518, 2234
Salzman, L. F.: *ref,* 440, 1281, 1380, 1447, 1474
Salzman, M.: *ref,* 1133, 1164
Samborski, G.: *ref,* 1403
Samenfeld, H. W.: *ref,* 419, 5:308 (331)

Saum, J. A.: *ref,* 382, 863, 4:10 (4)
Sauna, V. D.: *ref,* 1363, 1519
Saunders, A.: *ref,* 1185
Saunders, A. W.: *rev,* 189, 2:1329
Saunders, B. T.: *ref,* 1281
Saunders, C. B.: *ref,* 1383
Saunders, D. R.: *rev,* 1207, 1368; *test,* 5:90, 5:112; *ref,* 529, 532, 1087, 1383, 1394-5, 2212, 5:73(2)
Saunders, F. F.: *ref,* 1363
Saunders, H. R.: *ref,* 357
Saunders, J. C.: *ref,* P:326(29, 33)
Saunders, M. H.: *ref,* 381, 1469, 1481
Saunders, P.: *ref,* 1968
Saunders, R.: *ref,* 1516
Saunders, R. E.: *ref,* 1516
Saunders, R. J.: *ref,* 914
Saunders, W. J.: *ref,* 423, 426, 2239, 2448
Saunders, W. L.: *ref,* 1121
Saunders, W. W.: *ref,* 1516
Sauté, G. D.: *ref,* 1281
Sauté, L.: *ref,* 1164
Savage, B. M.: *ref,* 407
Savage, C.: *ref,* 1240, 1281, 7:55 (25)
Savage, E.: *ref,* 1281
Savage, H. W.: *ref,* 69, 1704, 1772
Savage, R. D.: *ref,* 331, 425, 529, 533, 1129, 1174, 1252, 1275, 1281, 1447, 1485, 1591, 1772, 1895
Savage, W.: *ref,* 532-3
Savard, J. G.: *rev,* 255
Savastano, H.: *ref,* 2195
Savering, F. R.: *ref,* 1447
Saville, P.: *test,* 331, 529, 533, 538, 1253, 1383, 1552, 2239, 2334
Savitsky, J. C.: *ref,* 357, 1044
Savitz, R. A.: *ref,* 1931
Savoiardo, M.: *ref,* 1192
Sawa, H.: *ref,* 533
Sawin, E. I.: *ref,* 1626
Sawin, M. M.: *ref,* 868, 1164
Sawrey, J. M.: *ref,* 435, 532, 5:326 (17)
Sawrey, W. L.: *ref,* 1281, 1403, 1423, 1512
Sawyer, C. R.: *ref,* 398, 1225, 5:329 (3)
Sawyer, G. W.: *ref,* 1500
Sawyer, J.: *ref,* 170, 1314, 2135
Sawyer, M. O.: *ref,* 4:468(4)
Sawyer, R.: *ref,* 533
Sawyer, R. I.: *ref,* 533
Sawyer, R. N.: *ref,* 517, 533, 2212
Sawyier, W. G.: *ref,* 1519
Sax, A. B.: *ref,* 1123, 1289
Sax, G.: *exc,* 7:378; *ref,* 391
Saxe, C. H.: *ref,* 1519
Saxe, E. L. G.: *ref,* 529
Saxena, B. M.: *ref,* 1298
Saxena, K. N.: *ref,* 2266
Saxena, P. C.: *ref,* 1226
Saxon, J. P.: *ref,* 498, 529
Saxon, S. V.: *ref,* 1280
Saxton, D. F.: *ref,* 1164
Saxton, G. H.: *ref,* 7, 50
Sayer, K. E.: *ref,* 1300
Sayers, M. P.: *ref,* 497
Sayons, K.: *ref,* 1499
Sayons, Z.: *ref,* 1499
Sayre, M. L.: *ref,* 993

Scagnelli, D. P.: *ref,* 5:123(9)
Scagnelli, J. M.: *ref,* 1281
Scalea, C. J.: *ref,* 6:186(7)
Scales, E. E.: *ref,* 1164
Scales, J. L.: *ref,* 1225
Scales, M. B.: *ref,* 1499
Scallon, R. J.: *ref,* 533, 1127, 1169
Scammon, M. W.: *ref,* 1164
Scandary, E. J.: *ref,* 1696
Scandrette, O.: *ref,* 1164
Scandrette, O. C.: *ref,* 1123
Scanlan, J. W.: *ref,* 1281
Scanlon, J. C.: *ref,* 1394
Scanlon, S. L.: *ref,* 1900
Scannell, D. P.: *test,* 44, 119, 143, 659, 1608, 1799, 1955; *ref,* 19-20
Scarborough, B. B.: *test,* 2203; *ref,* 49, 532, 2195, 2203, 5:66(12)
Scarborough, R. L.: *ref,* 1560
Scarbrough, J. P.: *ref,* 881
Scarf, R. C.: *ref,* 6:438(444)
Scarola, L. M.: *ref,* 2234
Scarpitti, F. R.: *ref,* 1121
Scarr, E. H.: *ref,* 525
Scarr, H. A.: *ref,* 1281
Scarr, S.: *ref,* 1094, 1186
Scates, D. E.: *rev,* 15, 1768, 1:1154, 3:538, 3:542, 5:833
Schaaf, W. L.: *rev,* 4:407, 4:450
Schaar, W. G.: *ref,* 1121
Schachtel, A.: *ref,* 1499
Schachtel, A. H.: *ref,* 1499
Schachtel, E.: *ref,* 1499
Schachtel, E. G.: *exc,* 1499; *ref,* 1499
Schachter, F. F.: *ref,* 525, 533, 1447
Schachter, J.: *ref,* 1150, 1227
Schachter, J. S.: *ref,* 1227
Schachtitz, E.: *ref,* 1501
Schackow, C. F.: *ref,* 1383
Schacter, M.: *ref,* 1499
Schadler, M. M.: *ref,* 1883
Schaefer, B. R.: *ref,* 1403
Schaefer, C. E.: *test,* 544, 553, 580; *ref,* 381, 542, 544, 551, 553, 580, 587, 1090, 1109, 1121, 1437, 1463, 1519
Schaefer, E.: *ref,* 348, 1232
Schaefer, E. S.: *ref,* 484, 1186, 1232, 1499
Schaefer, H. H.: *ref,* 1281
Schaefer, J. B.: *ref,* 1519
Schaefer, J. H.: *ref,* 1383
Schaefer, S.: *ref,* 868
Schaefer, T.: *ref,* 2059
Schaefer, W. C.: *rev,* 452, 4:281; *ref,* 1087, 5:530(46)
Schaeffer, D. L.: *ref,* 1448
Schaeffer, R. F.: *ref,* 4:245(7)
Schaeffer, R. W.: *ref,* 1481
Schafer, E. W. P.: *ref,* 425, 533, 1087
Schafer, R.: *rev,* 1499; *exc,* 1516, 1519; *ref,* 529, 532, 1105, 1140, 1192, 1499, 1519
Schafer, S.: *ref,* 525, 1299, 1499, 1519
Schafer, T.: *ref,* 1383
Schafer, W. E.: *test,* 1347
Schaffer, H. B.: *ref,* 1447
Schaffer, M. C.: *ref,* 1087, 1169
Schaffer, R. E.: *ref,* 1387
Schaie, K. W.: *test,* 1418, 1452;

ref, 22, 36, 50, 592, 1087, 1121, 1129, 1145, 1163-4, 1253, 1383, 1418, 1452
Schalk, M. C.: *ref,* 2023
Schall, R. P.: *ref,* 868, 1415
Schalling, D.: *ref,* 365, 518, 529, 532, 543, 1087, 1196, 1277
Schalock, R.: *ref,* 1217
Schalock, R. L.: *ref,* 1380, 1383, 1500
Schalon, C. L.: *ref,* 529, 1094, 1281, 1415
Schanberger, W. J.: *ref,* 5:147(27)
Schapero, M.: *ref,* 1207
Schapira, K.: *ref,* 1275
Scharf, G. C.: *ref,* 1403
Scharf, M. C.: *ref,* 1121
Scharf, M. P.: *ref,* 516
Scharles, H. G.: *ref,* 1164
Schatia, V.: *ref,* 1499
Schatz, L.: *ref,* 1164
Schauble, P. G.: *ref,* 1281
Schauder, D. E.: *ref,* 1923
Schaw, L. C.: *ref,* 1519
Schechter, M. D.: *ref,* 1281, 1391
Scheck, R. R.: *ref,* 1536, 1599
Scheckel, R.: *ref,* 1500
Scheel, W. P.: *ref,* 1133
Scheerer, M.: *test,* 1192; *ref,* 1192
Scheflen, N. A.: *ref,* 1448
Scheibe, K. E.: *ref,* 1094, 1121, 1281, 1501, 2212-3
Scheibner, R. M.: *ref,* 547, 1356
Scheide, E. J.: *ref,* 1499
Scheidel, T. M.: *ref,* 1164, 1403
Scheidemann, N. V.: *test,* 35:166-7
Scheider, R. M.: *ref,* 244, 262, 306, 6:384(1)
Scheier, I.: *ref,* 1383
Scheier, I. H.: *test,* 1225, 1227, 1295, 1300; *exc,* 1295; *ref,* 388, 439, 473, 1069, 1225, 1227, 1229, 1295, 1300, 1383, P:344(7, 11, 15)
Schein, E. H.: *ref,* 532, 1281, 1499, 1519
Schein, J.: *ref,* 1387
Schein, J. D.: *ref,* 1387
Scheinberg, P.: *ref,* 1499
Scheiner, S. B.: *ref,* 1240, 1499
Scheinker, J. L.: *ref,* 1281
Schell, J. W.: *ref,* 2259
Schell, M.: *ref,* 525
Schell, R. E.: *ref,* 349, 518, 1247, 1281, 2212
Schellenberg, E. D.: *ref,* 7, 349, 1447, 1921, 4:2(8)
Schellenberg, P. E.: *ref,* 1480
Scheller, T. G.: *ref,* 2212
Schellhammer, J. R.: *ref,* 357
Schemmel, D.: *ref,* 981
Schena, R. A.: *ref,* 398, 525
Schenck, H. U.: *ref,* 516, 522
Schendel, J.: *ref,* 1121
Schendel, J. S.: *ref,* 1094, 1121
Schenk, K. N.: *ref,* 1315, 2454
Schenk, Q. F.: *ref,* 4:88(19)
Schenke, L. W.: *ref,* 1447
Schenkein, D.: *ref,* 1164
Schenkel, K. F.: *ref,* 1073, 2197
Schepers, J. M.: *rev,* 1511, 6:213; *test,* 550, 1414, 2246; *ref,* 439, 1075

Scherer, G. A. C.: *ref,* 221, 357, 993
Scherer, I. W.: *test,* 1297; *ref,* 50, 504, 525, 532, 1105, 1192, 1223, 1281, 1380, 1428, 1499, 1516
Scherer, P.: *ref,* 262
Scheuerman, E. L.: *ref,* 1320
Scheuhing, M. A.: *ref,* 2195, 2266
Schiebel, D. R.: *ref,* 1471
Schieffelin, B.: *ref,* 558, 2258, 2: 1390(4), 2:1391(8), 2:1394(5), 2:1401(4)
Schiele, B. C.: *ref,* 1281, 1345–6
Schiele, W.: *ref,* 1320
Schifani, J. W.: *ref,* 981
Schiff, D.: *ref,* 533, 1447
Schiff, H.: *test,* 5:90
Schiff, H. M.: *ref,* 1281, 1499, 2195, 2199
Schiff, S.: *ref,* 529, 1499
Schiffman, D. C.: *ref,* 868, 1164, 1383, 1415, 1519
Schiffman, G. B.: *ref,* 1921
Schiffman, H.: *ref,* 1294, 1480
Schiffman, H. M.: *ref,* 1522
Schild, A. H.: *test,* 44, 1955
Schilder, P.: *ref,* 381, 1447
Schildhaus, A. F.: *ref,* 1281
Schill, T.: *ref,* 529, 1225, 1281, 1448, 1500
Schill, T. R.: *ref,* 1500
Schiller, A.: *test,* 27, 649, 1577
Schiller, B.: *ref,* 381, 713
Schiller, J. J.: *ref,* 981, 1921
Schiller, J. R.: *ref,* 1478
Schiller, M.: *ref,* 1281
Schilling, M.: *ref,* 1169, 1275, 1281, 1293, 1403, 2212
Schilling, M. E.: *ref,* 525
Schillinger, M.: *ref,* 2213
Schillo, R. J.: *ref,* 532
Schiltz, J. H.: *ref,* 917
Schimek, J. G.: *ref,* 1169, 1499, 1519
Schindler, A. W.: *rev,* 7, 1:1125, 2:1608, 2:1610, 4:2, 4:8; *test,* 1: 1091, 1:1126, 1:1131
Schindler, M. D.: *ref,* 1207
Schindler, R.: *ref,* 439
Schiphorst, B.: *ref,* 1338
Schipman, W. G.: *ref,* 1499
Schipper, L. M.: *ref,* 1322
Schiro, F. M.: *ref,* 529, 1101, 1205, 1281
Schissel, R. F.: *ref,* 2212
Schlachet, P. J.: *ref,* 1164
Schlachter, L. C.: *ref,* 1225
Schlaff, A.: *test,* 1207; *ref,* 1207
Schlag, M.: *ref,* 1164, 1403
Schlanger, B. B.: *ref,* 2028, 2095
Schleifer, M. J.: *ref,* 1499
Schlesinger, B.: *ref,* 1499
Schlesinger, H. J.: *ref,* 1499
Schlesinger, K.: *ref,* 1281
Schlesinger, R. J.: *ref,* 1499
Schlesser, G. E.: *test,* 1318, T: 1204; *ref,* 357, 1318, 3:217(90), 4:277(254)
Schletzer, V. M.: *ref,* 1281, 2212
Schleuter, S. L.: *ref,* 199, 209, 1253
Schlicht, W. J.: *ref,* 364, 574, 1501, 1513
Schlick, E. F.: *ref,* 48, 1044
Schloener, C. J.: *ref,* 1289

Schlosser, J. R.: *ref,* 532, 1499
Schluck, C. G.: *ref,* 1281
Schludermann, E.: *ref,* 1121, 1370
Schludermann, S.: *ref,* 1121, 1370
Schlueter, M. P.: *ref,* 400, 1123
Schmale, A. H.: *ref,* 1281
Schmale, H. T.: *ref,* 4:115(3)
Schmalzried, N. T.: *ref,* 881
Schmauk, F. J.: *ref,* 1281
Schmeidler, D.: *ref,* 1212, 1389, 1481
Schmeidler, G. R.: *ref,* 1403, 1448, 1499–500
Schmickel, C. A.: *ref,* 1428
Schmid, A. C.: *ref,* 1142
Schmid, F. W.: *ref,* 1499, 1528
Schmid, J.: *ref,* 48, 50, 496, 518, 1281, 1289, 1880, 4:95(22, 26)
Schmidl, F.: *ref,* 1499
Schmidl-Waehner, T.: *ref,* 1474, 1499
Schmidt, A. G.: *test,* 3:455, 5:592; *exc,* 497, 507, 518, 532, 1192, 1348, 1366, 1702, 36:B79, 2:1228, 2: 1264, 2:1426, 2:1535; *ref,* 3:455 (1)
Schmidt, D. G.: *ref,* 532
Schmidt, D. J.: *ref,* 1856
Schmidt, E. P.: *ref,* 1447
Schmidt, G. L.: *ref,* 1423
Schmidt, H. E.: *test,* 552, 576; *ref,* 1183
Schmidt, H. O.: *ref,* 1225, 1281, 1320, 1499
Schmidt, L. A.: *ref,* 2323
Schmidt, L. D.: *ref,* 1164, 1294, 1481
Schmidt, L. G.: *ref,* 48, 868, 1087, 1121, 1281, 1403
Schmidt, M. A.: *ref,* 36
Schmidt, M. M.: *ref,* 1315
Schmidt, M. R.: *ref,* 1430
Schmidt, R. H.: *ref,* 589, 1856
Schmidt, R. H. H.: *ref,* 1281
Schmidt, W. G.: *ref,* 2452
Schmidt, W. H. O.: *ref,* 1646, 1680
Schmieding, A.: *test,* 4:80; *ref,* 4:80(1), P:211(2)
Schmitt, J. A.: *ref,* 404, 1294, 1501
Schmitt, J. R.: *ref,* 2273
Schmitt, P. A.: *ref,* 868
Schmitt, R. L.: *ref,* 1403
Schmitt, W. C.: *ref,* 1499
Schmitz, R. M.: *ref,* 419, 2239, 2266, 5:308(363)
Schmitz, S. B.: *ref,* 426, 1560, 2: 1377(30), 3:220(59)
Schmitz, S. M.: *ref,* 204, 211
Schmitz, T. J.: *ref,* 1519
Schmolke, M. F.: *ref,* 1447
Schmotz, R. R.: *ref,* 1123
Schmuck, R. A.: *ref,* 399
Schmuck, R. W.: *ref,* 399
Schmuckler, J.: *exc,* 1830
Schnack, G. F.: *ref,* 525, 1480, 1499, 1519
Schnadt, F.: *ref,* 529, 532, 1481
Schnadt, F. W.: *ref,* 1164, 1256, 1281, 1380, 1403, 2195
Schnall, M.: *ref,* 1474
Schnebly, L. M.: *ref,* 2195
Schneck, J.: *ref,* 1519
Schneck, J. M.: *ref,* 1281, 1469, 1499, 1519

Schneck, M. R.: *ref,* 2266, 2:1394 (6), 2:1399(12)
Schnee, R. G.: *ref,* 1395
Schneideman, N. V.: *exc,* 487
Schneider, A. E.: *rev,* 3:379, 3:387
Schneider, B.: *ref,* 532–3
Schneider, B. H.: *ref,* 1403, 1499
Schneider, D. E.: *ref,* 2195, 6:1180 (1)
Schneider, D. L.: *ref,* 2193
Schneider, F. A.: *ref,* 2451
Schneider, J. H.: *ref,* 533
Schneider, J. M.: *ref,* 1471
Schneider, L. I.: *ref,* 1499
Schneider, L. R.: *ref,* 1295
Schneider, M.: *ref,* 1192
Schneider, R. A.: *ref,* 532, 1281
Schneider, S. F.: *ref,* 1499
Schneider, W. F.: *ref,* 1164
Schneiderhan, R. M.: *ref,* 1536, 1658
Schneiderman, A.: *ref,* 1913
Schneiderman, N.: *ref,* 211, 6:537 (3)
Schneidler, G. G.: *rev,* 1:1170; *test,* 3:689; *ref,* 7, 22, 69, 189, 211, 438, 1095, 1222, 1348, 1568, 1749, 1932, 2135, 2212–3, 2227–9, 2258, 2266, 2:1182(1), 2:1184 (2), 2:1193(1), 2:1197(2), 2: 1271(9), 2:1325(11), 2:1360(2), 2:1401(8), 2:1424(23), 3:217 (109)
Schnell, D.: *test,* 4:491
Schnell, L. H.: *rev,* 701, 2:1467, 3:334, 3:339
Schnell, R. R.: *ref,* 439, 1121, 1164, 1207
Schnell, W.: *test,* 2413
Schnepp, A.: *test,* 2:1520
Schneps, A.: *ref,* 1469
Schneyer, J. W.: *ref,* 357, 1772
Schneyer, S.: *ref,* 532
Schnitzen, J. P.: *ref,* 144, 1164
Schnitzer, L. P.: *ref,* 551, 561, 572, 1121
Schnobrich, J.: *ref,* 1475
Schnobrich, J. N.: *ref,* 381, 516, 529, 981, 1281, 1475
Schnore, M. M.: *ref,* 529, 543
Schobel, J. A.: *ref,* 1044, 1303
Schoch, E. W.: *ref,* 1193–4, 1225
Schock, N. H.: *ref,* 867, 1812
Schoeberle, E. A.: *ref,* 1474
Schoel, D. R.: *ref,* 542, 574
Schoemer, J. R.: *ref,* 357
Schoen, M.: *ref,* 202, 211
Schoen, W. T.: *ref,* 1133
Schoenberg, B.: *ref,* 1281, 1499, 1519
Schoendube, R.: *ref,* 5:766(16)
Schoenfeld, H.: *ref,* 1289
Schoenfeldt, L. F.: *rev,* 2224, 2227; *ref,* 1058
Schoeninger, D.: *ref,* 1281
Schoeninger, D. W.: *ref,* 516, 1447, 1711
Schoer, L. A.: *ref,* 533
Schofield, J.: *test,* 7:416
Schofield, L. F.: *ref,* 529
Schofield, M.: *test,* 450, 452
Schofield, W.: *rev,* 543, 1197, 1130, 1215, 1379, 1501, 6:74; *ref,* 69, 404, 532, 1281, 2212, 2355

Scholastic Testing Service, Inc.: *test*, 32–3

Scholl, C. E.: *ref*, 1207, 1256, 2212

Scholl, G.: *ref*, 533, 1905, 1320

Scholl, G. T.: *ref*, 36

Scholl, P. C.: *ref*, 5:570(6)

Scholter, A. J.: *test*, 2:1659.1, 2:1679.1

Schommer, C. O.: *ref*, 1281

Schon, M.: *ref*, 532, 1447, 1481, 1499

Schonbar, R. A.: *ref*, 1164, 1169, 1225, 1281

Schonell, F. E.: *test*, 110; *ref*, 110, 525, 734, 1646

Schonell, F. J.: *rev*, 1702, 2:1448, 2:1450, 4:272, 5:616–7; *test*, 373, 734, 1646, 3:342, 5:224, 5:474, 6:620, 6:642; *ref*, 734, 1646

Schonhorn, R.: *ref*, 533

Schooff, K.: *ref*, 1281

School Administrator's Service: *test*, T:1317

School Library Association of California: *test*, 3:536

Schooler, C.: *ref*, 529, 1232

Schooler, N. R.: *ref*, 1232, 1255, 1435

Schooley, M.: *ref*, 1403

Schoolfield, L. D.: *test*, 1638, 2094

Schoolman, D. A.: *ref*, 1237, 1499

Schoon, C. G.: *ref*, 1342

Schoonover, C.: *test*, 2:1513

Schoonover, S. M.: *ref*, 36, 525, 533

Schopler, E.: *ref*, 1299

Schopler, J. H.: *ref*, 1240

Schor, T.: *ref*, 868, 1423

Schorer, C. E.: *ref*, 1447, 1481

Schorling, R.: *test*, 3:306, 3:344

Schorr, C. A.: *ref*, 1499

Schorr, M.: *ref*, 348

Schott, E. L.: *exc*, 1519; *ref*, 525, 2:1243(21)

Schott, J. L.: *ref*, 884, 2452

Schottstaedt, W. W.: *ref*, 1281, 2355

Schpoont, S.: *ref*, 1499

Schrader, C. H.: *ref*, 2103, 2212

Schrader, D. R.: *ref*, 20, 349, 400, 672, 683, 755, 1164, 1608

Schrader, E. N.: *ref*, 3:217(91)

Schrader, H. E.: *test*, 7:486

Schrader, P. J.: *ref*, 4:44(2)

Schrader, W. A. B.: *ref*, 2:1250 (6–7)

Schrader, W. B.: *rev*, 335–6, 404, 455, 457, 2344, 4:329; *ref*, 135, 357, 998, 1005, 1048, 1053, 1843, 1994, 2349, 4:10(3), 5:308(294)

Schrader, W. J.: *ref*, 1121

Schrag, C.: *exc*, 1281

Schrager, J.: *ref*, 1711, 1716

Schram, H. J.: *ref*, 1499

Schramm, T. A.: *ref*, 525, 533

Schrammel, H. E.: *rev*, 1:877; *test*, 54, 784, 1598, 35:463, 1:1018, 1:1040, 2:1273, 2:1321, 2:1363, 2:1366, 2:1437, 2:1457–8, 2:1465, 2:1499, 2:1513, 2:1534, 2:1589, 2:1610, 2:1641, 3:7, 3:92, 3:133, 3:139, 3:149, 3:153, 3:164, 3:174, 3:206, 3:315, 3:326, 3:381–2, 3:387, 3:426, 3:456, 3:568, 3:576,

3:598, 3:610–1, 3:618–9, 4:199, 4:207, 4:254, 4:281, 4:472, 4:504, 4:539, 4:578, 4:673, 4:708, 5:176, 5:196, 5:430, 5:496, 5:554, 5:584, 6:297, 6:498, 6:634, T:1807

Schreck, J. F.: *ref*, 361

Schreck, T. C.: *ref*, 69, 333, 1069

Schreffler, R. H.: *ref*, 525

Schreiber, E. H.: *ref*, 1121, 1123, 1225

Schreiber, E. W.: *ref*, 426

Schreiber, H.: *ref*, 1499, 1519

Schreiber, M.: *ref*, 1499

Schreiber, P. R.: *ref*, 36

Schreiner, F.: *ref*, 1470

Schreiner, J. O.: *ref*, 2452

Schreiner, R. L.: *ref*, 19

Schreurs, E.: *ref*, 2:1377(5)

Schriefer, L.: *ref*, 525, 558

Schrier, M.: *ref*, 1934

Schroedel, E. C.: *ref*, 2:1492(2, 6.1)

Schroeder, B. L. F.: *ref*, 1315

Schroeder, C. E.: *ref*, 1403, 1499

Schroeder, C. R.: *ref*, 1121, 1383

Schroeder, D. F.: *exc*, 838

Schroeder, G. B.: *ref*, 2451, 2457

Schroeder, H.: *ref*, 1471

Schroeder, H. E.: *ref*, 1281

Schroeder, H. G.: *ref*, 1499

Schroeder, P.: *ref*, 69, 1256, 1281

Schroeder, R.: *ref*, 1883

Schroeder, W. L.: *ref*, 391

Schroth, M. L.: *ref*, 189, 1069, 2268

Schubert, C. C.: *test*, 36:575, 36:795

Schubert, D. G.: *ref*, 1536, 1918

Schubert, D. S. P.: *test*, 455, 1534; *ref*, 1281

Schubert, E. D.: *test*, 2046; *ref*, 2046

Schubert, H. J. P.: *test*, 455, 1456, 35:337, 35:496; *ref*, 1456

Schubert, J.: *exc*, 1499; *ref*, 533, 1499, 1516

Schubert, J. D.: *ref*, 1403

Schubert, P. W.: *ref*, 1176, 1214, 1407

Schubot, E.: *ref*, 1390

Schuchman, B. J. E.: *ref*, 1133

Schucker, R. E.: *ref*, 1739

Schucman, H.: *ref*, 529, 532

Schueler, H.: *rev*, 262, 264, 271, 3:191–3, 4:245, 5:274, 6:384

Schuell, H.: *test*, 2080; *ref*, 50, 496, 2079–80, 2213

Schuerger, J. M.: *ref*, 1059

Schuerhoff, C.: *ref*, 357, 482, 561, 574

Schuessler, K. F.: *exc*, 1281

Schuettler, A. K.: *test*, 1078, 1226, 1229

Schuh, A. J.: *ref*, 482

Schuh, B.: *ref*, 3:242(2)

Schulberg, H. C.: *test*, 1106; *ref*, 529, 1106, 1447

Schuldt, D. L.: *ref*, 1430

Schuldt, W. J.: *ref*, 1164, 1280–1

Schulman, D.: *ref*, 1451, 1499, 1519

Schulman, I.: *ref*, 1192, 1499

Schulman, J.: *ref*, 1069

Schulman, J. L.: *ref*, 381, 516, 525, 533, 1447

Schulman, M. J.: *ref*, 3:161(13)

Schulman, P.: *ref*, 1499

Schulman, R. E.: *ref*, 1281, 1389, 1499

Schulman, W. J.: *ref*, 1121, 1281

Schulte, F. J.: *ref*, 497

Schulterbrandt, J.: *ref*, 1435

Schulterbrandt, J. G.: *ref*, 1232

Schultz, C.: *ref*, 6:125(10–1)

Schultz, C. B.: *ref*, 357, 436, 542, 561, 1109, 1230, 1281

Schultz, D.: *ref*, 1394

Schultz, D. G.: *rev*, 2136–7, 2143–5, 2267, 4:761; *ref*, 357, 2355, 4:367 (4), 4:368(2)

Schultz, D. P.: *ref*, 1281, 1383

Schultz, E. W.: *ref*, 1176

Schultz, F. G.: *ref*, 48

Schultz, H. A.: *rev*, 189–90

Schultz, K. V.: *test*, 831; *ref*, 1437

Schultz, M. C.: *ref*, 2031

Schultz, M. K.: *ref*, 269, 382, 619, 863, 1053

Schultz, R. E.: *ref*, 2212, 2451, 6:202(3)

Schultz, R. S.: *ref*, 1090, 1403, 2212, 2266, 2:1199(2, 4), 3:220 (49), 4:277(147)

Schultz, S. D.: *ref*, 1281

Schultz, W.: *ref*, 529

Schulz, E. D.: *ref*, 1164

Schulz, E. F. D.: *ref*, 1164

Schulz, H.: *ref*, 1091, 1275

Schulz, R. E.: *ref*, 1519, 5:308 (394)

Schulzetenberge, A. C.: *ref*, 2212–3

Schumacher, A.: *ref*, 1499

Schumacher, C. F.: *ref*, 1164, 1403, 2212, 2355, 6:1135(1)

Schumacher, H. C.: *exc*, 1499

Schumacher, J.: *ref*, 1519

Schuman, E. P.: *ref*, P:500(12)

Schumann, D.: *ref*, 2383

Schumann, W. D.: *ref*, 1496

Schumer, F.: *ref*, 1448, 1451, 1482, 1499–500, 1519

Schumer, F. C.: *ref*, 1499

Schumer, H.: *ref*, 1164

Schunert, J. R.: *test*, 5:425, 5:493

Schurdak, J. J.: *ref*, 391

Schurr, E.: *ref*, 1123

Schurr, W. E.: *ref*, 1121

Schusler, M. M.: *ref*, 361, 425, 1069

Schusler, R. A.: *ref*, 1164

Schuster, C. R.: *ref*, 1093

Schuster, D. H.: *rev*, 2471, 2475–6, 7:573, 7:575; *test*, 844; *ref*, 844, 1151, 1204, 1207, 1383, 1403

Schuster, L.: *ref*, 1383

Schut, D.: *ref*, 439, 532, 1528

Schutte, E. P.: *ref*, 1164, 1281, 1403

Schutte, T. H.: *ref*, 426

Schutter, C. H.: *test*, 680, 5:491

Schutz, J. R.: *test*, 36:627

Schutz, R. A.: *ref*, 2212

Schutz, R. E.: *rev*, 61, 467–8, 1069, 1087; *ref*, 425, 1033, 1207, 2212, 2340, 5:368(23), 6:1062(9–10), P:304(2–3)

Schutz, W. C.: *test*, 1176; *exc*, 1240, 5:B261; *ref*, 1176

Schwaab, E. L.: *ref*, 1305

Schwab, D. P.: *ref*, 1193–4

Sedberry, M. E.: *ref,* 381
Seder, M.: *ref,* 2212-3, 2:1377(40, 45), 2:1433(1-2)
Seder, R. W.: *ref,* 2170
Sedlacek, C. G.: *ref,* 1164, 2213
Sedlacek, G.: *ref,* 1281
Sedlacek, G. M.: *ref,* 1281
Sedlacek, W. E.: *test,* 1381; *ref,* 357, 1133, 1381, 2355
Sedman, G.: *ref,* 1224, 1275
Seech, P.: *ref,* 1232, 1435
Seefelt, E. R.: *ref,* 1911, 1924
Seegars, J. E.: *ref,* 1240, 1281, 1626, 6:223(17)
Seeger, R. E.: *exc,* 3:538
Seegers, J. C.: *ref,* 1320
Seeley, J. R.: *ref,* 1271
Seeley, M. S.: *ref,* 1383
Seeley, W. H. C.: *ref,* 2469
Seeling, K. D.: *test,* 5:789
Seelye, B. J.: *ref,* 525, 981
Seeman, J.: *ref,* 1499, 1519
Seeman, M.: *ref,* 1123, 2451
Seeman, W.: *rev,* 1314, 4:95; *ref,* 532, 1101, 1281, 1403, 1447-8, 1499, 1516, 1519, 2212
Seevers, C. J.: *ref,* 1094, 1289
Sefer, J. W.: *test,* 2080
Segal, A. S. B.: *ref,* 1448, 1519
Segal, B. E.: *ref,* 1281
Segal, D.: *ref,* 2212
Segal, P.: *ref,* 1499
Segal, S. J.: *rev,* 1489, 1526; *ref,* 529, 532, 1447, 1499, 1519, 2212
Segel, D.: *rev,* 398, 671, 681, 1: 1037, 4:216; *test,* 1082, 35:175; *ref,* 18, 20, 48, 400, 1082, 1121, 2212, 2:1377(16)
Segel, R. H.: *ref,* 529, 1039, 1044, 1513
Segner, E. F.: *rev,* 2:1507, *test,* 4: 491
Segner, V. C.: *ref,* 1121, 1164, 1383
Segraves, R. T.: *ref,* 1174
Segrist, A. E.: *ref,* 1044
Seguin, E.: *test,* 578
Seguin, E. L.: *ref,* 265, 267
Seibel, D. W.: *ref,* 404, 436, 868, 1281
Seibert, E. W.: *ref,* 840, 2195, 3: 470(16), 3:639(1, 3)
Seibert, L. C.: *test,* 2:1347; *ref,* 2:1342(8)
Seidel, C.: *ref,* 1499
Seidel, H. E.: *ref,* 355, 439, 1711
Seiden, R.: *ref,* 1464
Seidenberg, B.: *ref,* 1403
Seidenfeld, M. A.: *ref,* 426, 1105, 1123
Seidenross, H.: *ref,* 1252
Seidl, J. C.: *ref,* 483, 525
Seidman, E.: *ref,* 1500, 2212
Seidman, S. K.: *ref,* 1415
Seidner, R.: *ref,* 1519
Seifert, G. G.: *ref,* 185
Seifert, J. G.: *ref,* 1447, 1672
Seifert, K. R.: *ref,* 1403
Seigle, W. F.: *ref,* 69, 5:308(365)
Seiler, D. A.: *ref,* 2454
Seiler, J.: *ref,* 1073, 1086, 7:1090 (9)
Seim, S.: *ref,* 439, 1499
Seiner, J. P.: *ref,* 2336
Seither, F. G.: *ref,* 349, 1123, 1536

Seitz, C.: *ref,* 1344
Seitz, C. P.: *test,* 1344; *ref,* 1344, 1499
Seitz, E. K.: *ref,* 538, 1331
Seitz, F. C.: *ref,* 522, 529, 1281, 1377, 1499
Seitz, M. J.: *ref,* 1073
Seitz, P. F. D.: *ref,* 1500
Seitz, R.: *ref,* 1169
Seitz, T. L.: *ref,* 542, 546, 551, 1123
Sekyra, F.: *ref,* 489, 525, 533
Selden, E. H.: *ref,* 1124
Selders, G. R. W.: *ref,* 1289, 1597
Seldman, M.: *ref,* 1109, 1176
Selecki, B. R.: *ref,* 529
Selesnick, S. T.: *ref,* 1281
Self, L. V.: *ref,* 1133
Selig, K.: *ref,* 1499
Seliger, R. V.: *ref,* 1499
Seligman, M.: *ref,* 1214
Seligman, R.: *ref,* 1133
Seligsohn, H. C.: *ref,* 1095, 1133
Selinsky, H.: *ref,* 1499
Selkin, J.: *ref,* 1377, 1471, 1500, 1519
Selkirk, S. A.: *ref,* 1255
Sell, D. E.: *test,* 418, 1757
Sella, A. P.: *ref,* 490, 525
Selland, C. T.: *ref,* 19, 398
Seller, M. A.: *test,* 2:1363, 3:206
Sellers, D. J.: *ref,* 1240, 1281
Sellers, H.: *ref,* 1474
Sellers, J. R.: *ref,* 391, 1775, 7:378 (7)
Sellers, L. B.: *ref,* 1435
Sellin, D. F.: *ref,* 1412
Sellinger, S.: *ref,* 1225
Sells, J. A.: *ref,* 929
Sells, M. A.: *ref,* 1123
Sells, S. B.: *rev,* 1146, 1162, 1195, 1226, 1229, 1398; *exc,* 1394-5, 1486; *ref,* 50, 381, 400, 533, 1146, 1200, 1205-7, 1245, 1281, 1320, 1383, 1519
Selman, R. L.: *ref,* 516
Selmar, J. W.: *test,* 2086
Selover, M. S.: *ref,* 36
Selover, R. B.: *rev,* 2135, 3:628; *ref,* 419, 3:4(8), 3:141(1)
Seltzer, C. C.: *ref,* 357, 407
Seltzer, S. S.: *test,* 36:786; *ref,* 36: 786(1)
Selvey, C. L.: *ref,* 1519
Selvini-Palazzoli, M.: *ref,* 1499
Semanek, I. A.: *ref,* 2263
Semeonoff, B.: *test,* 6:519; *exc,* 522, 1182, 1252, 1281, 1451, 1486, 1499, 1519, 1528; *ref,* 205, 406, 1140, 1192, 1499, 1513, 1519, 1528, 6:519(1)
Semler, I. J.: *ref,* 20, 439, 533, 1123, 2103, P:226(1-2), P:346(15-7)
Semmel, M. I.: *rev,* 575, 1092; *ref,* 981
Semon, R. G.: *ref,* 1217
Semper, L. T.: *ref,* 1383
Sempert, E. L.: *ref,* 1164
Semrow, J. J.: *ref,* 1383
Sen, A.: *ref,* 439, 1499, 1519
Sen, M.: *ref,* 1140
Sen, R.: *ref,* 525
Sender, S.: *ref,* 1499
Senf, R.: *ref,* 1281, 1499
Sengstake, C. B.: *ref,* 1140, 1499

Sengstock, W. L.: *ref,* 914
Senior, N.: *ref,* 1073
Senk, H. M.: *ref,* 1716
Senn, D. J.: *ref,* 1176
Senoff, G.: *ref,* 868
Senour, A. C.: *ref,* 1716, 3:256(5)
Senoussi, A. E.: *test,* 818, 822, 839
Senseman, L. A.: *ref,* 1174, 1383
Sensibar, M. R.: *ref,* 1519
Senter, D. R.: *ref,* 1794, 1856
Senti, M. M.: *ref,* 503, 532
Senturia, A. G.: *ref,* 1281
Seppala, J.: *ref,* 603, 1536
Serafetinides, E. A.: *ref,* 532, 1298
Sereda, L.: *ref,* 1302
Seret, C. J.: *ref,* 1500
Sergeant, R. L.: *ref,* 1095, 1320
Sergiovanni, T. J.: *ref,* 2452
Serijan, K. T.: *ref,* 22, 36
Serl, J. W.: *ref,* 914, 947
Sermat, V.: *ref,* 1281
Serot, N. M.: *ref,* 1123
Serota, K. E.: *ref,* 525
Serpento, S. T.: *ref,* 1123
Service for Admission to College and University: *test,* 63A, 353, 1060
Servis, M.: *ref,* 425, 1403
Servis, M. A.: *ref,* 1403, 1423
Sessions, A.: *ref,* 1499
Sessions, A. D.: *ref,* 2195
Sethi, B. B.: *ref,* 1499, 1519
Setyaadmadja, A. T. S. H.: *ref,* 1146
Setze, K. D.: *ref,* 1499
Setze, L. A.: *ref,* 1499
Severance, K. M.: *ref,* 99, 5:308 (334)
Severinsen, K. N.: *ref,* 529, 1044
Severson, R.: *ref,* 1281
Severson, R. A.: *ref,* 543, 981, 1169, 1447
Severson, W. E.: *ref,* 1499
Sevier, F. A. C.: *ref,* 357
Sevilla, S. A.: *ref,* 1883
Seville, E. W.: *test,* 714-6
Sevransky, P.: *ref,* 400, 1069, 1164, 1275
Sevren, M.: *ref,* 1121
Sevringhaus, E. L.: *ref,* 1499
Seward, G. H.: *ref,* 1481, 1499, 1519
Seward, H.: *ref,* 1500
Seward, J. P.: *ref,* 1448
Seward, T. C.: *ref,* 868
Sewell, W. H.: *exc,* 5:B140; *ref,* 391, 1123, P:342(14)
Sexology Corporation: *test,* 6:688
Sexson, J. A.: *test,* 5:4, 6:884-5, 6:897, 6:994, 6:1010
Seybold, A.: *test,* 1549
Seybold, F. R.: *ref,* 50, 532
Seymore, S.: *ref,* 542, 1480
Seymour, J. H.: *ref,* 532, 592, 1245, 1499, 1519, 2234
Seymour, M.: *ref,* 1164
Seymour, O. J.: *ref,* 4:277(144)
Seymour, P. J.: *ref,* 1280, 1775
Seymour, R. B.: *ref,* 1145
Seymour, W. D.: *test,* 2230; *ref,* 2228, 2230, 2234
Seymour, W. R.: *ref,* 361, 1395
Sferra, A.: *ref,* 1164
Sgan, M. R.: *ref,* 357
Shaalan, M.: *ref,* 532, 1192

Shearn, C. R.: *ref*, 496, 1474, 1478
Shears, L. M.: *ref*, 2454
Shebesta, D. F.: *ref*, 1121
Shechori, H.: *ref*, 1474
Shechtman, A. M.: *ref*, 483, 525, 1123
Shedd, C. L.: *ref*, 1500, 5:326(10)
Sheddan, B. R.: *ref*, 419, 1386
Sheehan, J.: *ref*, 1499, 2212
Sheehan, J. G.: *ref*, 1261, 1499–500, 1519, 2212
Sheehan, P. W.: *ref*, 542, 1212, 1240, 1389, 1499, 1519
Sheeley, E. C.: *rev*, 2037, 2039
Sheer, D.: *ref*, 1499, 1519
Sheer, D. E.: *ref*, 1499
Sheets, C. S.: *ref*, 1232
Sheffield, B. F.: *ref*, 1275
Sheffield, E. F.: *ref*, 1095, 1768, 4: 277(165)
Sheffield, J.: *ref*, 1121
Sheinberg, I. M.: *ref*, 1281
Shekelle, R. B.: *ref*, 1281, 1383
Shelden, M. A.: *ref*, 1164
Sheldon, A.: *ref*, 1145, 1176
Sheldon, E.: *ref*, 589
Sheldon, F. A.: *ref*, 1069
Sheldon, H. J.: *ref*, 533, 1716
Sheldon, J. M.: *ref*, 211
Sheldon, M. J. R.: *ref*, 589
Sheldon, M. S.: *ref*, 533, 868, 1164, 1281, 1403, 1519
Sheldon, P. M.: *ref*, 1499
Sheldon, R.: *ref*, 1164
Sheldon, W. D.: *rev*, 1573, 4:553; *ref*, 7, 349, 483, 525, 1628
Sheldon, W. H.: *ref*, 357, 525, 1090, 1101
Shell, S. A.: *ref*, 1370, 1501
Shelley, E. L. V.: *ref*, 1469, 1499, 1519
Shellhaas, M.: *test*, 1092; *ref*, 1092
Shellhaas, M. D.: *ref*, 1092
Shellow, R. S.: *ref*, 1448
Shellow, S. M.: *ref*, 2212
Shelly, C. H.: *ref*, 211, 529, 1164, 1205, 1240, 1281, 2076
Shelly, M. B.: *ref*, 1044
Shelsky, I.: *ref*, 1094
Shelsky, I. M.: *ref*, 1281
Shelton, H. W.: *ref*, 1133
Shelton, J.: *ref*, 1232, 1281, 1447, 1468
Shelton, J. E.: *ref*, 1383
Shelton, P. B.: *ref*, 1519
Shelton, R. L.: *rev*, 2037, 2075
Shemberg, K. M.: *ref*, 1207
Shemky, R. W.: *ref*, 1133
Shemwell, E. C.: *test*, 3:387
Shen, F.: *ref*, 1094
Shepard, E. L.: *ref*, 202, 425, 2227, 2258, 2266
Shephard, R. J.: *ref*, 914, 1275, 1383
Shepherd, C. W.: *ref*, 50, 524, 1921
Shepherd, D. C.: *ref*, 1227, 1281, 2038
Shepherd, E. M.: *ref*, 1689
Shepherd, I. L.: *ref*, 1207, 1281
Shepherd, J. E. D.: *ref*, 1252
Shepherd, J. R.: *ref*, 1164, 1403, 1499
Shepherd, J. W.: *test*, 3:136
Shepherd, L. A.: *test*, T:446
Shepherd, L. M.: *ref*, 1044

Shepherd, M.: *ref*, 1145
Shepherd (Hilton) Co., Inc.: *test*, 2303
Shepler, B.: *ref*, 1370
Shepler, B. F.: *ref*, 1101, 1281, 1463, 2212–3
Shepler, M. P.: *ref*, 1302
Shepley, G. B.: *test*, 1:970
Sheppard, C.: *ref*, 7, 349, 439, 1227, 1281, 1447, 1536
Sheppard, D. C.: *ref*, 255, 271, 286, 300, 314
Sheppard, N. A.: *ref*, 1121, 2212, 2221
Shepps, F. P.: *ref*, 1772
Shepps, R. R.: *ref*, 1772
Sher, M. A.: *ref*, 1247
Sherard, E. S.: *test*, 494; *ref*, 494, 497
Sherburne, J. W.: *test*, 3:524, 3: 539
Shere, E. S.: *ref*, 1499
Shereshevski-Shere, E.: *ref*, 1499
Sherfey, M. J.: *ref*, 1499
Sherick, I. G.: *ref*, 1281, 1499
Sheridan, K.: *ref*, 1315
Sheridan, M. D.: *test*, 1926, 1931, 2055; *ref*, 1926, 1931
Sherin, C. R.: *ref*, 1164, 1207, 1240, 1415
Sherk, J. K.: *ref*, 1921
Sherman, A. R.: *ref*, 529
Sherman, A. W.: *ref*, 1281, 1320
Sherman, C. E.: *ref*, 1407, 1409
Sherman, D.: *exc*, 2075; *ref*, 1911, 1932
Sherman, D. M.: *ref*, 361
Sherman, E. A.: *ref*, 349, 1123, 1519
Sherman, E. C.: *ref*, 2195
Sherman, E. E.: *test*, 1631
Sherman, G. L.: *ref*, 1281
Sherman, I.: *test*, 1:1095, 1:1104
Sherman, J. E.: *ref*, 1499
Sherman, L. J.: *ref*, 1121, 1232, 1281, 1305, 1471, 1474, 1481
Sherman, L. L.: *ref*, 1315, 1383, 1403, 2199
Sherman, M.: *ref*, 1499, 4:79(1–2)
Sherman, M. H.: *test*, 1379; *ref*, 1379, 1499
Sherman, O.: *ref*, 1560, 4:277(155)
Sherman, R. A.: *ref*, 1923, 1934
Sherman, R. C.: *ref*, 405, 1094, 1164
Sherman, R. L.: *ref*, 1499, 1515
Sherman, R. W.: *ref*, 1471
Sherman, S. E.: *ref*, 1058
Sherman, V. M. S. R.: *ref*, 361, 1519
Shero, L. R.: *ref*, 289
Sherr, R. D.: *ref*, 1073, 2186
Sherr, R. L.: *ref*, 1363
Sherrick, M. F.: *ref*, 1121
Sherriffs, A. C.: *ref*, 1519
Sherrill, D.: *ref*, 357, 1394
Sherron, R. H.: *ref*, 357, 1303
Sherry, N. M.: *ref*, 1302, 2212
Sherry, P. J.: *ref*, 1519
Shertzer, B.: *ref*, 1069, 1225, 2212
Sherwood, D. W.: *ref*, 589, 1470
Sherwood, E. J.: *ref*, 419, 1356
Sherwood, E. T.: *ref*, 1519
Sherwood, J. C.: *rev*, 67, 73, 143, 6:283

Sherwood, J. J.: *ref*, 1519
Shetterly, H. T.: *ref*, 1253, 1289
Shevel, L. R.: *test*, 596; *ref*, 596, 1044
Sheverbuch, R. L.: *ref*, 525
Sheviakov, G. V.: *ref*, 2:1225(2, 6–7), 2:1226(2–4)
Shevrin, H.: *ref*, 1499
Sheya, J. A.: *ref*, 1164
Shibuya, R. R.: *ref*, 1383
Shick, J.: *ref*, 1923
Shiek, D. A.: *ref*, 1129
Shields, D. L.: *ref*, 1519
Shields, J.: *ref*, 1281
Shields, J. B.: *ref*, 533
Shields, R. V.: *ref*, 349
Shientag, I.: *ref*, 1499
Shier, D. A.: *ref*, 532
Shierson, H. E.: *ref*, 2195, 2199
Shigaki, I. S.: *ref*, 400, 589
Shih, W.: *ref*, 2234, 2266
Shillinger, D.: *ref*, 1109
Shils, E. A.: *ref*, 5:77(8)
Shimabukuro, S.: *ref*, 1164
Shimberg, B.: *rev*, 1206, 1361, 2105, 2180, 3:65, 3:695, 4:484, 7:633; *ref*, 1361
Shimberg, M. E.: *ref*, 2:1390(3), 2:1391(6), 2:1394(3), 2:1401(2)
Shimkunas, A. M.: *ref*, 440, 529, 1232, 1281
Shimota, H. E.: *ref*, 518, 532, 2234
Shinagawa, F.: *ref*, 533
Shine, A.: *ref*, 525
Shine, A. E.: *ref*, 525
Shine, R. E.: *rev*, 2056
Shinedling, M.: *ref*, 1164
Shinedling, M. M.: *ref*, 524, 533, 1481
Shinn, B. M.: *ref*, 1716
Shinn, E. O.: *ref*, 1087, 2195
Shinn, S. M.: *ref*, 357, 529
Shinohara, M.: *ref*, 1281
Shipe, D.: *ref*, 516, 518, 525, 538, 981, 1281, 1921
Shipe, D. M.: *ref*, 516, 533
Shipley, T. E.: *ref*, 1519
Shipley, W. C.: *rev*, 439, 447, 3: 228; *test*, 1380; *ref*, 525, 1380
Shipman, E. A.: *ref*, 1164
Shipman, V. C.: *ref*, 1073
Shipman, W. G.: *ref*, 1094, 1164, 1207, 1281, 1383, 1423, 1471, 1474, 1499, 1516, 1519
Shipp, D. E.: *ref*, 381
Shipper, J. C.: *ref*, 1281, 1501
Shirahata, E.: *ref*, 1499
Shire, A.: *ref*, 1205, 1448, 1499
Shirley, J. H.: *ref*, 1207, 1281, 1403, 2212
Shirley, M.: *ref*, 497
Shirley, M. G.: *ref*, 1133
Shirts, R. G.: *ref*, 2103
Shivadasani, H. K.: *ref*, 1499
Shively, J. E.: *ref*, 589
Shlaudeman, K. W.: *ref*, 1320, 1480, 2212
Shlien, J. M.: *ref*, 1519
Shmavonian, B. M.: *ref*, 1481
Shmelzer, J. L.: *ref*, 1232
Shmukler, B. C.: *ref*, 1918
Shmukler, D.: *ref*, 1508
Shneidman, E.: *test*, 2184

Silberberg, N.: *ref,* 525, 533, 1447, 1702
Silberberg, N. E.: *ref,* 483, 516, 533, 1447
Silbergeld, S.: *ref,* 1195
Silberman, L.: *ref,* 533, 1169
Silcock, A.: *ref,* 1544
Sill, J. B.: *ref,* 1499
Siller, J.: *ref,* 1094, 1281, 1293, 1363
Silliman, H.: *test,* 134
Sills, F. D.: *test,* 913
Siloac, K. T.: *ref,* 516, 1921, 2097
Silva, J. J.: *ref,* 592, 1499
Silvaroli, N. J.: *test,* 1618; *ref,* 425, 1519
Silveira, A.: *ref,* 1499
Silver, A. A.: *ref,* 381, 497, 538, 1447
Silver, A. W.: *ref,* 1240, 1281, 1499, 1515, 1519
Silver, C. E.: *ref,* 348, 532, 5:308 (280)
Silver, H.: *ref,* 1474
Silver, H. A.: *ref,* 2195
Silver, I. H.: *ref,* 1499
Silver, I. O.: *ref,* 20
Silver, M.: *ref,* 981
Silver, M. J.: *ref,* 1389, 1499
Silver, M. R.: *ref,* 342
Silver, R. J.: *ref,* 1270, 1281, 1469, 2195
Silverberg, J.: *ref,* 1499
Silverberg, R. A.: *ref,* 589
Silverberg, W. V.: *exc,* 1101
Silverblank, F.: *ref,* 1194, 1225
Silverman, A. J.: *ref,* 1192, 1281, 1447-8, 1481, 1499
Silverman, B.: *ref,* 1519
Silverman, D. K.: *ref,* 1192, 1499
Silverman, E. H.: *ref,* 2186
Silverman, E. M.: *ref,* 1451
Silverman, H.: *ref,* 532, 1499
Silverman, H. L.: *rev,* 820; *ref,* 1205, 1403
Silverman, I.: *ref,* 1094
Silverman, I. W.: *ref,* 1261
Silverman, J.: *ref,* 529, 1232, 1281
Silverman, L.: *ref,* 1481
Silverman, L. H.: *ref,* 1192, 1281, 1469, 1499, 1519
Silverman, M.: *ref,* 940, 1318, 1519
Silverman, P.: *ref,* 1256, 1403
Silverman, P. L.: *ref,* 1121, 1281
Silverman, R.: *ref,* 1281, 1342
Silverman, R. E.: *ref,* 1164, 1281
Silverman, R. H.: *test,* 182, 184; *ref,* 185, 1082
Silverman, S. A.: *ref,* 1281
Silverman, S. M.: *ref,* 1924
Silverman, S. R.: *ref,* 2031, 3:475 (6)
Silvers, D.: *ref,* 1478
Silvers, D. L.: *ref,* 1478
Silverstein, A. B.: *rev,* 534, 538; *exc,* 525, 1447; *ref,* 381, 496, 516, 525, 529, 532-3, 538, 543, 981, 1087, 1192, 1315, 1428, 1447, 1474, 1480, 1488, 1500, 1516, 1519, 1921
Silverstone, J. T.: *ref,* 1145
Silverstone, S.: *ref,* 1169
Silvert, D. M.: *ref,* 1164
Silvey, H. M.: *ref,* 1572, 2195, 4: 277(218, 270)

Sim, M.: *ref,* 529
Simberg, A. L.: *test,* 2340
Simes, F. J.: *ref,* 1320, 2212
Simkevich, J. C.: *ref,* 2212
Simkin, J. S.: *ref,* 532
Simkins, L.: *ref,* 496, 1471
Simkins, L. D.: *ref,* 1471
Simmer, L.: *ref,* 31
Simmers, C. P.: *ref,* 525, 533
Simmins, C. A.: *test,* 2:1220
Simmonds, V.: *test,* 331, 1113; *ref,* 1113
Simmons, A. A.: *ref,* 211, 532, 1140, 1560
Simmons, A. D.: *ref,* 1281, 1474
Simmons, A. J.: *ref,* 1499
Simmons, C.: *ref,* 1105
Simmons, D. D.: *ref,* 1164, 1240, 1281, 1302, 1451
Simmons, E. P.: *test,* 4:206; *ref,* 2:1312(2)
Simmons, H.: *ref,* 529, 981, 1380
Simmons, H. E.: *ref,* 1133
Simmons, J. E.: *ref,* 1225
Simmons, J. R.: *ref,* 1294
Simmons, K.: *ref,* 7, 426, 507, 518, 525, 545, 2266, 3:660(15)
Simmons, M.: *ref,* 1123
Simmons, M. D.: *ref,* 1383, 1394
Simmons, P. W.: *ref,* 525
Simmons, R.: *ref,* 435
Simmons, W. L.: *ref,* 1519
Simms, J. T.: *ref,* 542, 546, 1151, 2185
Simms, L. G.: *ref,* 543
Simon, A.: *ref,* 439, 532, 1281, 1646
Simon, A. J.: *ref,* 487, 497
Simon, B.: *ref,* 5:123(9)
Simon, G. B.: *test,* 2:1485; *ref,* 3: 397(24)
Simon, L. M.: *ref,* 532
Simon, L. R.: *ref,* 574
Simon, N. M.: *ref,* 1281
Simon, R. J.: *ref,* 1398
Simon, S.: *ref,* 1519
Simon, W.: *ref,* 1281
Simon, W. B.: *ref,* 1240
Simon, W. E.: *ref,* 533, 1403
Simon-Hermann, *Sister: ref,* 248
Simonian, C.: *ref,* 1044
Simonian, K.: *ref,* 487, 1087, 1428, 1447
Simono, R. B.: *ref,* 1281
Simons, B.: *test,* 1718
Simons, C.: *ref,* 1516, 1519
Simons, J. B.: *ref,* 1318, 1383, 1403
Simons, W. S.: *ref,* 1207, 1281, 1403
Simonton, K. M.: *ref,* 2059
Simopoulos, A. M.: *ref,* 1232, 1281, 1346, 7:55(25)
Simos, A. T.: *ref,* 1447
Simos, I.: *ref,* 1500
Simpkins, R. E.: *ref,* 1121
Simpson, A. R.: *ref,* 1094, 2283
Simpson, C. D.: *ref,* 529
Simpson, D.: *ref,* 1069
Simpson, D. B.: *ref,* 2451
Simpson, D. J.: *ref,* 542, 546, 562, 573
Simpson, D. M.: *ref,* 1716
Simpson, E. J.: *ref,* 1289
Simpson, E. L.: *ref,* 1303
Simpson, G. M.: *ref,* 1232, 1298

Simpson, H. D.: *ref,* 869
Simpson, J.: *ref,* 1145
Simpson, J. E.: *ref,* 1121, 1207
Simpson, M.: *ref,* 1380
Simpson, M. M.: *ref,* 532, 1380
Simpson, R. G.: *ref,* 69, 1583, 4: 213(2), 4:660(20)
Simpson, R. L.: *ref,* 50, 529, 533, 1679
Simpson, R. M.: *ref,* 3:678(8)
Simpson, S. A.: *ref,* 543, 1447
Simpson, S. E.: *ref,* 202
Simpson, W. H.: *ref,* 533, 1447, 1516
Sims, A. G.: *ref,* 1048
Sims, B. W.: *ref,* 1164
Sims, D. M.: *ref,* 1133
Sims, J. H.: *ref,* 1519
Sims, N.: *test,* 1652
Sims, N. B.: *ref,* 529, 1383, 1499
Sims, V. M.: *rev,* 17, 50, 173, 1039, 1123, 1:869, 1:983, 3:159, 4:29, 4:70, 4:78; *test,* 5:597; *ref,* 426, 1095, 1569, 5:597(1-6)
Sinaiko, H. W.: *ref,* 561, 1500, 4: 798(3)
Sinatra, L. J.: *ref,* 1176
Sinay, R. D.: *ref,* 1074, 1207, 2212
Sinclair, G. R.: *ref,* 2142
Sinclair, J.: *ref,* 1499
Sinclair, J. K.: *ref,* 489
Sinclair, W. A.: *ref,* 1921
Sinco, E. D.: *ref,* 1394-5
Sindberg, R. M.: *ref,* 1387
Sindt, D. M.: *ref,* 1164, 1207, 1294
Sindwani, K. L.: *ref,* 2452
Sineps, J.: *ref,* 1281
Sines, J. O.: *test,* 1287; *exc,* 1281; *ref,* 533, 1281, 1287, 1499
Sines, L. K.: *test,* 1287; *ref,* 529, 532, 1281, 1380, 1499
Singer, A.: *ref,* 1123, 1281
Singer, B. A.: *ref,* 1174
Singer, C. R.: *ref,* 1583, 1672
Singer, E.: *ref,* 532, 1151, 1281, 1499, 1775, 4:277(210)
Singer, H.: *rev,* 1716-7; *ref,* 202, 1087, 1361, 1474, 1499, 1622, 1661, 2195
Singer, J. L.: *ref,* 1181, 1207, 1225, 1275, 1281, 1499, 1519
Singer, M.: *ref,* 1299, 1499
Singer, M. I.: *ref,* 1281
Singer, M. M.: *ref,* 1470
Singer, M. T.: *ref,* 381, 532, 1192, 1281, 1499, 1519
Singer, P. R.: *ref,* 529, 1225, 1499, 1519
Singer, R. D.: *ref,* 1164, 1519
Singer, R. H.: *ref,* 1469, 1474, 1499
Singer, R. N.: *ref,* 1164
Singer, S.: *ref,* 1121, 1302
Singer, S. K.: *ref,* 1094, 1121, 1281
Singer, S. L.: *ref,* 1207, 1289, 2199
Singh, A.: *ref,* 331, 364, 1225, 1275, 1383, 1403
Singh, A. J.: *ref,* 1225, 1275, 1403
Singh, B.: *ref,* 381, 914, 1281, 1447
Singh, J.: *ref,* 1519
Singh, M.: *ref,* 439, 1225, 1275, 1383, 1403
Singh, N. P.: *ref,* 2195
Singh, P. N.: *ref,* 1164, 1403
Singh, R.: *ref,* 1095

Smalheiser, L.: *ref,* 1275

Small, I. F.: *ref,* 543, 592, 1277, 1447

Small, J. F.: *ref,* 348, 981

Small, J. G.: *ref,* 529, 543, 592, 1277, 1281, 1447

Small, J. J.: *ref,* 323, 1281

Small, K.: *ref,* 518

Small, L.: *ref,* 1499

Small, R. M.: *ref,* 7:69(4)

Small, S. M.: *ref,* 592, 1305, 1447

Small, V.: *test,* 2035

Smallegan, M.: *ref,* 1176

Smallenburg, H. W.: *ref,* 1123, 3: 635(13), 4:58(6)

Smalley, N. S.: *ref,* 1240

Smarr, R. G.: *ref,* 1387

Smart, D. W.: *ref,* 1182

Smart, J. C.: *ref,* 1044, 1302

Smart, R. C.: *ref,* 525

Smart, R. G.: *ref,* 529, 1098, 1271, 1275, 1281, 1519

Smathers, S.: *ref,* 1281

Smead, W. H.: *ref,* 2452

Smedley, F.: *test,* 1901

Smee, P. G.: *ref,* 1164

Smelser, W.: *ref,* 1281

Smelser, W. T.: *ref,* 1121, 1240

Smeltzer, C. H.: *test,* 35:162, 1: 953

Smillie, D.: *ref,* 947

Smith, A.: *test,* 1889; *ref,* 518, 529, 532, 1192, 1501, 1519, 1889

Smith, A. A.: *ref,* 381, 533, 1447, 1519

Smith, A. B.: *ref,* 69, 419, 1221, 1519, 1583

Smith, A. C.: *ref,* 1164

Smith, A. E.: *exc,* 424; *ref,* 532, 1087, 1256

Smith, A. F.: *ref,* 1094

Smith, A. H.: *ref,* 359, 1164, 1281, 1403

Smith, A. J.: *ref,* 1403, 1519, 1968

Smith, A. M. B.: *ref,* 1430

Smith, A. M. W.: *ref,* 1383

Smith, A. P.: *ref,* 1280

Smith, B. B.: *ref,* 1093, 6:244(4)

Smith, B. F.: *ref,* P:399(28)

Smith, B. J.: *ref,* 1905

Smith, B. M.: *ref,* 529, 1447, 1470, 1474, 1519

Smith, B. S.: *ref,* 50, 489, 496, 533

Smith, C.: *ref,* 357, 1121, 1383

Smith, C. A.: *ref,* 354

Smith, C. B.: *ref,* 1572

Smith, C. E.: *rev,* 409, 734, 2:1279, 2:1422, 2:1450; *exc,* 1087; *ref,* 1264, 1447

Smith, C. F.: *ref,* 868

Smith, C. J.: *ref,* 1923

Smith, C. L.: *ref,* 1318, 1552, 1660

Smith, C. M.: *ref,* 981, 1275, 1281, 1499, 1567, P:408(24, 27)

Smith, C. O.: *ref,* 1240

Smith, C. P.: *ref,* 1302

Smith, C. R.: *ref,* 1225, 1415, 1447

Smith, C. S.: *ref,* 525

Smith, C. T.: *test,* 5:497

Smith, D.: *ref,* 357

Smith, D. C.: *ref,* 1094, 1240, 1447, 1519

Smith, D. D.: *ref,* 1069, 1087, 1194,

1256, 1294, 1572, 1772, 2195, 4: 277(256)

Smith, D. E.: *ref,* 64, 244, 357, 361, 1145, 1805, 1837, 1859, 2195, 5: 308(433), 5:417(7), 5:418(5)

Smith, D. E. P.: *rev,* 1533, 1747, 5:666, 6:857; *test,* 1633; *ref,* 1610

Smith, D. F.: *test,* 1122, 1282; *ref,* 1044, 1121, 1129, 1164, 1281-2

Smith, D. J.: *ref,* 1165

Smith, D. L.: *ref,* 589, 868, 1403

Smith, D. M.: *ref,* 358, 1499, P: 324(4)

Smith, D. P.: *ref,* 1281

Smith, D. V.: *test,* 81, 4:8, 5:180

Smith, D. W.: *ref,* 1281

Smith, E.: *ref,* 517, 533, 1474

Smith, E. E.: *ref,* 1281

Smith, E. H.: *test,* 1663; *ref,* 51

Smith, E. J.: *ref,* 1281, 1289, 1302-3, 2355

Smith, E. L.: *ref,* P:294(13)

Smith, E. P.: *ref,* 1294

Smith, E. R.: *test,* 1:898, 2:1287, 3:537, 4:182, 4:190, 4:196, 4:217; *ref,* 1215, 4:581(14), 4:582(5), 4:585(1), 4:594(3), 4:606(4), 4:629(3)

Smith, F. F.: *ref,* 1560, 4:277(171)

Smith, F. J.: *ref,* 1171

Smith, F. M.: *rev,* 29; *exc,* 7:464

Smith, F. O.: *ref,* 381

Smith, F. P.: *ref,* 3:181(5-6)

Smith, F. R.: *ref,* 35, 868, 1207

Smith, F. W.: *ref,* 525

Smith, G.: *test,* 3:2, 3:5, 4:683, 4: 697, 4:701; *ref,* 1069, 1222, 1516, 1519

Smith, G. B.: *ref,* 69, 5:308(411)

Smith, G. G.: *ref,* 1499

Smith, G. H.: *ref,* 1095, 1377

Smith, G. J. W.: *ref,* 439

Smith, G. M.: *ref,* 1164, 1383, 1499

Smith, G. P.: *ref,* 589

Smith, G. R.: *ref,* 398, 1087, 1603

Smith, G. V.: *ref,* 1437

Smith, H.: *ref,* 525, 529, 533, 1123, 1281, 1403

Smith, H. A.: *ref,* 349

Smith, H. B.: *ref,* 211

Smith, H. C.: *ref,* 1087, 1370, 1386, 1403, 1480, 1499

Smith, H. E.: *test,* 3:268; *ref,* 447, 529

Smith, H. J.: *ref,* 1921

Smith, H. L.: *ref,* 69, 1219, 1240, 1560

Smith, H. N.: *ref,* 2:1243(8)

Smith, H. P.: *rev,* 4:529, 4:541; *test,* 44, 1608; *ref,* 419, 1095

Smith, H. T.: *ref,* 1044

Smith, H. W.: *ref,* 525, 981

Smith, I. F.: *test,* 1138

Smith, I. L.: *ref,* 400, 404, 551, 573-4, 1164, 1952

Smith, I. M.: *rev,* 354, 364, 2243, 2245, 4:424, 4:713; *test,* 415, 2269, 2342, 5:436; *ref,* 409, 415, 425, 439, 618, 1070, 1174, 1536, 2195, 2245, 2249, 2269, 6:1090(4)

Smith, I. R.: *ref,* 1337

Smith, J.: *test,* 1311; *ref,* 503, 1281

Smith, J. A.: *ref,* 868, 1519, 2186, 2199

Smith, J. B.: *ref,* 532

Smith, J. E.: *rev,* 7:803; *ref,* 1164, 1403

Smith, J. F.: *ref,* 1474

Smith, J. G.: *ref,* 7, 1499

Smith, J. H.: *ref,* 492, 1101, 1121

Smith, J. J.: *ref,* 1480

Smith, J. L.: *ref,* 1499

Smith, J. M.: *test,* 1633; *ref,* 981, 1095, 1121, 1519, 1560, 2259, 3: 217(93)

Smith, J. M. M.: *ref,* 1169

Smith, J. O.: *ref,* 981

Smith, J. P.: *ref,* 1387, 1447

Smith, J. R.: *ref,* 1281, 1482, 1499, 1775, 1895

Smith, J. S.: *ref,* 357, 1135

Smith, J. T.: *ref,* 1123

Smith, J. W.: *ref,* 1913, 1932

Smith, K.: *ref,* 440, 529, 1232

Smith, K. D.: *ref,* 1225, 1281, 1293

Smith, K. H.: *ref,* 1109, 1205, 1207, 1227, 1315, 1407

Smith, K. J.: *rev,* 1679, 1699; *test,* 1654

Smith, L.: *ref,* 358

Smith, L. B.: *test,* 7:495

Smith, L. C.: *ref,* 440, 529, 543, 1428, 1447, 1478, 1499

Smith, L. D.: *ref,* 1121, 1281, 1499, 1519

Smith, L. E.: *ref,* 1275

Smith, L. F.: *ref,* 186, 1095, 2266, 4:784(2)

Smith, L. J.: *rev,* 1062; *ref,* 1281, 1481

Smith, L. M.: *ref,* 404, 496, 533, 1123, 1313, 1361, 1500, 2212, 2451

Smith, M.: *ref,* 525, 529, 533, 1123, 1281, 1403

Smith, M. A.: *ref,* 1164, 1560, P: 425(7)

Smith, M. D.: *ref,* 1500

Smith, M. E.: *ref,* 1403, 1519, 4: 277(167)

Smith, M. H.: *ref,* 1716

Smith, M. K.: *ref,* 2:1319(3), 3: 161(9-10, 12)

Smith, M. L.: *ref,* 1500

Smith, M. L. H.: *ref,* 1315

Smith, M. M.: *ref,* 533

Smith, M. P.: *ref,* 516, 525

Smith, M. S.: *ref,* 1519

Smith, N. B.: *rev,* 4:539, 4:542, 4: 565; *ref,* 1387

Smith, N. C.: *ref,* 533

Smith, N. E.: *ref,* 2355

Smith, N. P.: *ref,* 1164, 1403

Smith, N. R.: *ref,* 1484

Smith, N. V. O.: *ref,* 1228

Smith, O. B.: *ref,* 22, 2239, 2266

Smith, O. D.: *ref,* 3:256(6)

Smith, O. M.: *test,* 1:933, 2:1593; *exc,* 2:1596; *ref,* 1844-5

Smith, O. P.: *ref,* 1315, 1415

Smith, O. W.: *ref,* 211

Smith, P.: *rev,* 2:1381, 2:1389

Smith, P. A.: *ref,* 529, 533, 981, 1164, 1387

Smith, P. B.: *ref,* 516, 981, 1176, 1672, 2095

Smith, P. C.: *ref,* 1044, 1225, 1768

Smith, P. D.: *ref,* 221, 255-6, 271-2, 348-9

Sonstroem, R. J.: *ref,* 914
Sontag, L. W.: *ref,* 525, 1186, 1499, 1519
Sontag, M.: *ref,* 490, 525
Sopchak, A. L.: *ref,* 61, 1123, 1281, 1451, 1474, 1481, 1499–500, 1519, 1536, 5:308(437)
Soper, M. E.: *ref,* 2234, 5:308(336)
Soper, W.: *test,* 2:1336
Sorauf, T.: *ref,* 1281
Sorber, E. R.: *ref,* 1164
SoRelle, E.: *test,* 1024
Sorensen, M. A.: *ref,* 529
Sorensen, M. B.: *ref,* 211
Sorenson, A. G.: *ref,* 868, 1073
Sorenson, D. P.: *ref,* 1164
Sorenson, G.: *ref,* 868, 1073
Sorenson, H.: *ref,* 404, 1568, 2266
Sorenson, M.: *ref,* 20, 2195
Sorenson, M. A.: *ref,* 1303
Sorenson, W. W.: *ref,* 2197, 2239
Sorey, K. E.: *ref,* 1207
Sorge, D. H.: *ref,* 868
Sorhaindo, A. L.: *ref,* 1403
Sorribas, E.: *ref,* 1499
Sorsby, F. B.: *ref,* 532
Soskin, R. A.: *ref,* 1281, 1383
Soskin, W. F.: *ref,* 1499, 1519
Soskis, D. A.: *ref,* 1255
Sostek, A. B.: *ref,* 1403
Sosulski, M. C.: *ref,* 533
Soucar, E.: *ref,* 1302, 1501
Soueiff, M. I.: *ref,* 1073, 1174, 1205–6, 1245, 1281, 1320, 1383, 1387, 1447
Souelem, O.: *test,* 1496
Soufi, A.: *ref,* 1281
Soule, D. H.: *ref,* 5:593(2)
Sours, C. F. R.: *ref,* 361
Sours, J. A.: *ref,* 1281
South, D. R.: *ref,* 1306
South, E. B.: *ref,* 419, 426, 438
Southall, B. J.: *ref,* 1069
Southard, J. K.: *ref,* 1176, 1403
Souther, S. P.: *ref,* 4:490(1)
Southern, J. A.: *ref,* 2195
Southern, M. L.: *ref,* 516–7, 525, 533, 538, 981, 1121, 1403
Southgate, V.: *test,* 1601
Southwick, R. N.: *ref,* 1073
Southwick, W. O.: *ref,* 1258
Southworth, H. C.: *ref,* 1164, 1403
Southworth, J. A.: *ref,* 69, 357, 838, 1430
Souza, S. P.: *ref,* 6:1073(2)
Sowada, L.: *ref,* 981
Spaan, M.: *test,* 229, 232–3
Space, M. N.: *ref,* 20, 69, 405, 1281
Spache, G.: *rev,* 152; *test,* 158, 1476; *ref,* 22, 398, 525, 532, 1500, 1567, 1626, 1689, 1724, 1929
Spache, G. D.: *rev,* 1552, 1628–9, 1638, 1653, 1660, 1672, 3:485; 4:200, 6:274; *test,* 1624, 1671, 1678, 1773, 1929; *ref,* 533, 1500, 1628, 1672, 1923, 3:463(1, 3)
Spadafore, G. J.: *ref,* 381
Spaeth, C. F.: *ref,* 1313
Spaeth, J. W.: *ref,* 289
Spaethe, M.: *ref,* 482
Spafford, R. R.: *test,* 35:75, 35:249–50
Spahr, B. J. W.: *ref,* 99
Spaights, E.: *ref,* 7, 868, 1123

Spaner, F. E.: *ref,* 529, 532, 1232, 1499
Spaner, S. D.: *ref,* 522, 1303
Spaney, E.: *rev,* 597, 681, 683, 688, 696; *test,* 2:1434, 3:3, 3:304, 3:316, 4:423; *ref,* 869, 1314, 6:438(440), P:331(7)
Spangenberg, H. H.: *ref,* 1444, 1509
Spangler, D.: *ref,* 1499
Spangler, D. P.: *ref,* 1164
Spanier, S. W.: *ref,* 532
Spanner, M.: *ref,* 1094, 1240
Spano, R. M.: *ref,* 518, 1281, 1380, 1499
Spanos, N. P.: *ref,* 1389–90
Spare, G. H.: *ref,* 1281, 1294, 1499
Sparer, P. J.: *ref,* 1144, 1500
Sparks, C. P.: *ref,* 444, 729, 1320, 2239
Sparks, D. L.: *ref,* 1193–4
Sparks, J. N.: *ref,* 1164
Sparks, L.: *ref,* 1281
Sparks, R. E.: *exc,* 1:B338; *ref,* 914
Sparks, T. P.: *ref,* 1044
Sparling, E. J.: *ref,* 456, 518, 4:281(78)
Sparling, M. E.: *ref,* 525
Sparrow, J.: *ref,* 1657
Sparrow, J. L.: *ref,* 1657
Sparrow, N. H.: *ref,* 1121, 1275
Spaulding, G.: *rev,* 254, 259, 3:187, 5:201; *test,* 394, 1544, 2:1276, 2:1286, 2:1373–4, 3:4, 3:180–1, 3:203, 4:238, 4:245, 4:251, 4:260, 5:179, 5:645, 6:255; *ref,* 7, 36, 69, 248, 357, 394, 398, 869, 1059, 1087, 1705, 4:2(11)
Spaulding, H.: *ref,* 357–8, 419
Spaulding, P. J.: *ref,* 487, 525, 1276, 1428
Spaulding, R. L.: *ref,* 22, 981
Spaulding, V. V.: *ref,* 2195
Speaks, C.: *ref,* 2031
Speal, S. A.: *ref,* 1171
Spear, J. E.: *ref,* 981
Spearman, C.: *rev,* 425, 1087; *exc,* 525; *ref,* 439
Spearman, C. E.: *ref,* 439
Spearman, L. H. O.: *ref,* 525, 533
Spearritt, D.: *rev,* 2142, 5:855; *test,* 324–5, 327–8, 426, 691, 5:890; *ref,* 327–8, 415, 997, 5:298(1), 6:435(1)
Spears, B. G.: *ref,* 1044
Spears, J. B.: *ref,* 1169
Spector, N. J.: *ref,* 1240, 1281
Speedie, S.: *ref,* 1254, 1500
Speedie, S. M.: *ref,* 589
Speegle, J. R.: *ref,* 1133, 1395
Speer, D. C.: *ref,* 1281
Speer, G. S.: *ref,* 425, 525, 1053, 1320, 1923, 2195, 2223, 2266, 2395
Speer, R. K.: *rev,* 2:1196, 2:1295; *test,* 77–8, 139, 161, 178, 700–1, 930, 1556, 1587, 1592, 1785, 1943, 1951, 1975–6, 1984, 3:525, 4:191, 5:18
Speer, S. C.: *ref,* 1366, 1519
Speer, V. J.: *ref,* 1121
Speerstra, B. T.: *ref,* 1133
Spees, E. R.: *ref,* 1315
Speevack, M.: *ref,* 525

Speigler, M. D.: *ref,* 1185
Speilberg, M. J.: *ref,* 1249
Speisman, J. C.: *ref,* 1281, 1499
Spellacy, F. J.: *ref,* 211
Spelman, M. S.: *ref,* 403, 439, 1198, 1225, 1275, 1383
Spence, A. G.: *ref,* 525, 533, 1716
Spence, B. A.: *ref,* 2452
Spence, C. C.: *ref,* 1133
Spence, D. P.: *ref,* 1169, 1499
Spence, J. T.: *ref,* 529, 1275
Spence, K. W.: *ref,* 1275
Spence, R. B.: *test,* 2:1259, 4:19; *ref,* 426, 2:1259(1)
Spencer, D.: *rev,* 1123, 2:1233, 2:1243.1, 3:59
Spencer, G. M.: *ref,* 1134, 2344
Spencer, L.: *ref,* 1092
Spencer, P. A.: *ref,* 1281
Spencer, P. L.: *rev,* 637, 2:1463
Spencer, R. E.: *test,* 864, 866; *ref,* 221, 255–6, 265, 267, 271–2, 301, 314–5, 864, 1037, 1044
Spencer, R. F.: *ref,* 1121
Spencer, R. L.: *ref,* 1240, 2451
Spencer, S. J.: *ref,* 1073
Spencer, S. J. G.: *ref,* 331, 1281
Spencer, T. D.: *ref,* 1247
Spencer, V.: *ref,* 1469
Spennato, N. A.: *test,* 1547
Sperber, Z.: *ref,* 529, 1240
Spergel, P.: *ref,* 1073, 1447, 2186
Sperlich, W. C.: *ref,* 914
Sperling, A.: *ref,* 1095, 6:159(58)
Sperling, A. P.: *ref,* 1090, 1403
Spero, J. A.: *ref,* 1921
Spero, J. R.: *ref,* 1240, 1281, 1519
Speroff, B. J.: *test,* 1171, 2277; *ref,* 1171, 2289
Sperrazzo, G.: *ref,* 439, 1121, 1281
Spevacek, J. D.: *ref,* 1094
Speyer, H.: *exc,* 487
Spiaggia, M.: *ref,* 1281
Spicher, R. S.: *ref,* 1471
Spicker, H. H.: *ref,* 981
Spiegel, A. R.: *ref,* 1447
Spiegel, D.: *ref,* 1118, 1121, 1281, 1283, 1298, 1370, 1380, 1403, 1499
Spiegel, D. E.: *ref,* 1281, 1298
Spiegel, D. K.: *ref,* 1471, 2079
Spiegel, E. A.: *ref,* 1499
Spiegel, H.: *ref,* 525
Spiegel, J. A.: *ref,* 357, 1281, 2212
Spiegel, J. P.: *ref,* 1499
Spiegelman, J. M.: *ref,* 1499
Spiegelman, M.: *ref,* 1482, 1499, 1519, 6:213(6)
Spielberg, M. J.: *ref,* 1447, 1499
Spielberger, C. D.: *test,* 1391–2; *ref,* 324, 357, 404, 529, 1281, 1293, 1391, 1447, 1499, 1519, 6:438(452)
Spiers, D. E.: *ref,* 349, 1028, 1116, 1207, 2195
Spies, C. J.: *ref,* 1164, 1207, 2197
Spies, K. E.: *ref,* 1499
Spies, T. D.: *ref,* 947
Spieth, P. E.: *ref,* 525, 529
Spieth, W.: *ref,* 529
Spiker, C. C.: *ref,* 487
Spilka, B.: *ref,* 1121, 1123, 1164, 1240, 1245, 1281, 1355, 1370, 1499–500, 5:308(438), 6:438(453)
Spilker, O. H.: *ref,* 914

Star, K. H.: *ref,* 1275
Starbuck, E. O.: *ref,* 2212
Starch, D.: *ref,* 908
Starch, T. W.: *ref,* 1225, 1293, 1499
Starcher, G.: *ref,* 869
Starer, E.: *ref,* 532, 1090, 1499–500, 1516, 1525
Stark, H.: *ref,* 1164
Stark, I.: *exc,* 532
Stark, J.: *rev,* 2024; *test,* 992; *ref,* 516, 981, 993
Stark, L.: *test,* 251
Stark, M.: *ref,* 1289
Stark, M. J.: *ref,* 1281, 1501
Stark, R.: *test,* 1328; *ref,* 533, 1355
Stark, S.: *ref,* 1499
Stark, T. F.: *ref,* 1123
Starke, E. P.: *rev,* 4:369, 4:388
Starker, S.: *ref,* 1519
Starkman, S. S.: *ref,* 357
Starks, D. D.: *ref,* 881
Starks, W. L.: *ref,* 1044, 1207, 1407, 1772
Starnes, T. A.: *ref,* 868
Starr, A. M.: *test,* 1136; *ref,* 1136
Starr, A. S.: *rev,* 1428; *test,* 575; *ref,* 575
Starr, B. D.: *test,* 1503; *ref,* 1503
Starr, D. F.: *ref,* 1174
Starr, F. H.: *ref,* 997, 1772
Starr, H.: *ref,* 1164, 1207
Starr, H. M.: *ref,* 914
Starr, I. S.: *test,* 6:66
Starr, J. W.: *ref,* 1383
Starr, S.: *ref,* 1481, 1519
Starr, W. H.: *ref,* 255, 271, 286, 300, 314
Starry, A. R.: *test,* 883
Start, K. B.: *ref,* 323, 1383
Starzynski, S.: *ref,* 1499
Stasser, D. A.: *ref,* 1121, 1164
Staskey, P. J.: *ref,* 914
Statler, C.: *ref,* 2349
Statler, C. R.: *ref,* 48
Statman, J. M.: *ref,* 1403
Staton, J. T.: *ref,* 1044
Staton, T. F.: *ref,* 419, 904, 1095, 1320, 1768, 3:399(3), 4:96(5)
Staton, W. M.: *ref,* 1281
Staubach, F. W.: *ref,* 1906
Staudt, V. M.: *ref,* 426, 1095, 1281
Stauffacher, J. C.: *ref,* 1164, 1264, 1281, 1383, 1499, 2195
Stauffer, E.: *ref,* 2195
Stauffer, R. G.: *rev,* 1532, 1605, 5:650
Stauffer, R. W.: *ref,* 1291
Staunton, G. J.: *ref,* 1486, 1499, 1519
Staveley, B.: *ref,* 1087, 1253, 1275, 2238
Stavrakey, K. M.: *ref,* 1281
Stavrianos, B.: *ref,* 1499
Stavrianos, B. K.: *ref,* 1447, 1469, 1499
Stayton, W. E.: *test,* 1578
Stead, L. S. G.: *ref,* 532, 1499
Stead, W. H.: *ref,* 173, 2135, 2227–9, 2251, 2258, 2266
Steadman, R. F.: *test,* 3:591; *ref,* 3:591(1)
Stearns, K. E.: *ref,* 981
Stecher, L. I.: *ref,* 525

Stechler, G.: *ref,* 497
Steck Co.: *test,* T:1302
Steckel, M. L.: *ref,* 398, 426, 497, 6:480(28)
Steckle, L. C.: *test,* 430, 478–9, 1431, 7:399
Stecklein, J. E.: *rev,* 35; *test,* 194; *ref,* 194
Stedman, D. J.: *ref,* 22, 381, 516, 519, 981
Stedman, L. A.: *ref,* P:296(3)
Stedman, M. B.: *ref,* 2162, 2251, 3:263(35)
Stedtfeld, R. W.: *ref,* 868, 1176
Steel, M.: *ref,* 2227–9, 2258
Steele, C. I.: *ref,* 1121, 1519, 2213
Steele, F. I.: *ref,* 1294
Steele, I.: *ref,* 1090, 2:1243(12)
Steele, J.: *ref,* 1169, 1281
Steele, J. R.: *ref,* 1169, 1281
Steele, M.: *test,* 3:534
Steele, M. W.: *ref,* 1291
Steele, N. M.: *ref,* 1499
Steele, R. E.: *ref,* 1281
Steen, F. H.: *ref,* 2212
Steenbarger, C. J.: *ref,* 1499
Steer, M. D.: *ref,* 381, 426, 1428
Steere, J. L.: *ref,* 1028, 1281
Steeves, H. R.: *test,* 2:1270
Steeves, R.: *ref,* 1403
Stefanich, G. P.: *ref,* 1044
Stefanu, C.: *ref,* 2355
Steffe, L. P.: *rev,* 613, 7:485
Steffen, H. H. J.: *ref,* 1073
Steffen, J. D.: *ref,* 1214
Steffenhagen, R. A.: *ref,* 1281
Stefflre, B.: *ref,* 404, 1164, 1207, 1289, 1403, 2195, 2199, 2212, 3:634(6), 3:635(19)
Steffy, R. A.: *ref,* 1261, 1346, 1471
Stefic, E. C.: *ref,* 532, 1121, 1164, 1281
Steggerda, M.: *ref,* 497, 509, 2:1325(7, 12)
Stegman, E. J.: *ref,* 54, 1598, 5:6(19), 5:308(341)
Stegman, W. N.: *ref,* 1394–5
Stehbens, J. A.: *ref,* 1281
Steiber, J. K.: *ref,* 1281
Steige, R.: *ref,* 357
Steigelman, G. W.: *ref,* 2135
Steimel, R. J.: *ref,* 1164, 1281, 2212
Stein, B.: *ref,* 1169, 1320, 1499
Stein, C. I.: *ref,* 1073
Stein, D. D.: *ref,* 1094
Stein, E. J.: *ref,* 1281
Stein, F.: *ref,* 1201, 1315, 2195
Stein, H.: *ref,* 529, 1499
Stein, H. L.: *rev,* 5:462, 5:619, 6:1032, 6:1041; *ref,* 349, 868
Stein, J.: *ref,* 405, 1044, 1280, 2212
Stein, J. B.: *ref,* 1280
Stein, J. M.: *rev,* 270, 275; *ref,* 1192
Stein, J. U.: *ref,* 914
Stein, K.: *ref,* 1499
Stein, K. B.: *exc,* 1422; *ref,* 1094, 1121, 1281, 2195
Stein, L. L.: *ref,* 1281
Stein, M.: *test,* 1370; *ref,* 1162, 1370, 1519, 5:76(22)
Stein, M. D.: *ref,* 1499
Stein, M. I.: *test,* 2391, 2393–4;

ref, 404, 532, 1394, 1403, 1498–9, 1519
Stein, M. J.: *ref,* 1281, 1499, 1519
Stein, M. L.: *ref,* 545, 2251, 3:220(36), 3:678(3)
Stein, R. F.: *ref,* 382, 1164
Stein, R. S.: *test,* 1038
Stein, S.: *ref,* 426, 1386
Stein, S. H.: *ref,* 1275, 1281
Stein, S. L.: *ref,* 1407, 1409
Stein, S. P.: *test,* 355
Stein, Z.: *ref,* 525, 529
Steinau, B.: *ref,* 1499
Steinbach, A. A.: *ref,* 525
Steinbach, M. N.: *test,* 1732; *ref,* 1732
Steinbach, R. R.: *ref,* 20
Steinbaum, M.: *ref,* 1918
Steinberg, A.: *ref,* 1499, 1516, 2195
Steinberg, B.: *ref,* 1277
Steinberg, D.: *ref,* 113, 361, 652, 1599
Steinberg, D. L.: *ref,* 1095, 1245
Steinberg, J.: *ref,* 578
Steinberg, M.: *ref,* 529, 1039, 1044, 1513
Steinberg, M. D.: *ref,* 2142
Steinbook, R. M.: *ref,* 1281
Steinbrecher, A. W.: *ref,* 1044
Steindler, F. M.: *ref,* 357, 529
Steiner, A. F.: *ref,* 2212
Steiner, B. J.: *ref,* 2195
Steiner, F.: *ref,* 529, 1281
Steiner, G. A.: *ref,* 1164
Steiner, I. D.: *ref,* 1281
Steiner, J.: *ref,* 1281
Steiner, M.: *ref,* 1499
Steiner, M. A.: *ref,* 525
Steiner, M. E.: *test,* 4:117d–e, 5:154c, 5:154e; *ref,* 1499
Steiner, S. R.: *ref,* 981, 1631
Steiner, V. G.: *test,* 2024
Steingart, J. N.: *ref,* 1169
Steinhard, M.: *ref,* 1277
Steinhardt, R. W.: *ref,* 1145
Steinhelber, J. C.: *ref,* 529, 543, 592, 1192, 1277, 1447
Steinhilber, R. M.: *ref,* 1281
Steinhoff, C. R.: *test,* 1395f; *ref,* 1394–5
Steininger, E. H.: *ref,* 1281
Steininger, M.: *ref,* 357
Steinkamp, S. W.: *ref,* 1164
Stein-Lewinson, T.: *ref,* 1499
Steinman, C. C.: *ref,* 1560, 6:480(43)
Steinman, K.: *ref,* 1474
Steinman, W. M.: *ref,* 381, 529, 1447, 1499
Steinmann, A.: *test,* 1267–8; *ref,* 1267–8
Steinmetz, A.: *ref,* 547
Steinmetz, C. S.: *ref,* 589
Steinmetz, H. C.: *test,* 4:66; *ref,* 1499, 2212
Steinmetz, J. R.: *ref,* 439, 1294
Steinzor, B.: *ref,* 1499
Steisel, I.: *ref,* 1499
Steisel, I. M.: *ref,* 532, 1499
Stekert, E. J.: *ref,* 1519
Stelle, W. W.: *ref,* 1169
Stellern, J. T.: *ref,* 1499
Stellwagen, W.: *ref,* 1394
Stelmachers, Z. T.: *ref,* 1281

Stillion, G. W.: *ref,* 1133, 1403
Stillman, B. W.: *test,* 1630
Stillman, N.: *ref,* 1361
Stillwell, D. J.: *ref,* 1069
Stillwell, L.: *ref,* 5:326(36)
Stillwell, L. M.: *ref,* 1447
Stillwell, W. E.: *test,* 1108
Stilson, D. W.: *ref,* 1217, 1232, 1387
Stimeling, W. F.: *ref,* 589
Stimson, J.: *ref,* P:327(17)
Stimson, R. C.: *ref,* 357, 542, 546, 1094, 1519
Stinchfield, S. M.: *ref,* 211
Stine, J.: *ref,* 1474
Stinnett, N.: *ref,* 1306
Stinson, M. C.: *ref,* 2195
Stinson, P. J.: *ref,* 69, 529, 1069, 1074, 2195, 6:438(454)
Stirrup, W.: *ref,* 1275
Stirton, M. E.: *ref,* 1646, 1680
Stith, D.: *ref,* 355, 439, 1711
Stitt, C. L.: *ref,* 211
Stitt, J. D.: *ref,* 1471
Stivers, E. R.: *ref,* 361
Stix, D. L.: *ref,* 357, 1281, 1356
Stochl, J. E.: *test,* 735
Stock, J. C.: *ref,* 2076
Stock, M. J. S.: *ref,* 1291, 1383
Stock, W. H.: *ref,* 211, 425, 574, 1121, 2251
Stockdill, J. L.: *ref,* 914
Stockey, M. R.: *ref,* 1164
Stockford, L. B. O.: *ref,* 426, 1749
Stockman, I. M. J.: *ref,* 2088, 2090
Stockridge, H. C. W.: *ref,* 2168
Stockstill, K.: *ref,* 1069
Stockton, G. E.: *ref,* 913
Stockton, R. A.: *ref,* 868, 1315
Stockwell, K. W.: *ref,* 19, 1794
Stockwell, R. P.: *ref,* 221, 223
Stockwin, A. E.: *ref,* 525
Stoddard, A. J.: *ref,* 869
Stoddard, G. D.: *test,* 86–7, 220, 254, 313, 621–2, 1844–5, 1867–8, 2:1516; *exc,* 497; *ref,* 18, 86–7, 211, 220, 254, 313, 621–2, 1611, 1844–5, 1867–8, 2:1588(2)
Stoegbauer, M. K.: *ref,* 1207
Stoer, L.: *ref,* 1447
Stoess, A. W.: *ref,* 1522
Stoffel, C. M.: *ref,* 533
Stoffer, S. S.: *ref,* 1281
Stogdill, E. L.: *exc,* 532, 1:983; *ref,* 1320
Stogdill, R. M.: *test,* 1103, 1110, 2330, 2452, 2457, 2:1204; *ref,* 1103, 1110, 2449, 2451–2, 2457, 2:1204(1–2)
Stogsdill, J. W. E.: *test,* 35:112, 35:393
Stohs, R. V.: *ref,* 1303
Stojanovic, L.: *ref,* 1499
Stoke, S. M.: *ref,* 64, 525, 1048
Stoker, H. W.: *ref,* 20, 361, 561, 2199
Stokes, C. W.: *ref,* 461
Stokes, J.: *ref,* 1340
Stokvis, B.: *ref,* 1499
Stolberg, H.: *ref,* 1232, 1298
Stoler, N.: *ref,* 1281, 2212
Stollak, G. E.: *ref,* 1094, 1164
Stoller, F. H.: *ref,* 1214
Stolorow, R. D.: *ref,* 1519

Stolper, B. J. R.: *test,* 2:1294
Stolper, R.: *ref,* 1171
Stoltz, R. E.: *ref,* 1164, 1481, 1500
Stolurow, K. A.: *ref,* 1471
Stolz, A.: *ref,* 189
Stolz, L. M.: *ref,* 50, 381, 533, 1447
Stone, A. R.: *test,* 1397
Stone, B.: *ref,* 533
Stone, C. H.: *ref,* 1031, 2212
Stone, C. L.: *exc,* 518; *ref,* 357, 426, 1095, 1403, 3:220(27)
Stone, C. P.: *test,* 592; *ref,* 426, 532, 592, 1320, 1416, 4:281(85)
Stone, C. R.: *rev,* 1689–90, 2:1548; *test,* 3:504, 3:512, 3:515, 5:682; *ref,* 4, 1567, 1689–90, 3:483(2), 3:486(5), 3:504(1)
Stone, D. B.: *ref,* 69, 361, 1318
Stone, D. R.: *ref,* 533, 1281, 1446
Stone, F. B.: *ref,* 50, 533, 1281
Stone, G.: *ref,* 1499
Stone, G. B.: *ref,* 1499, 1519
Stone, G. C.: *ref,* 868
Stone, G. P.: *ref,* 1094
Stone, G. V.: *ref,* 1281, 2283–4
Stone, H.: *ref,* 1499, 1519
Stone, H. K.: *ref,* 1499
Stone, I. R.: *exc,* 1470; *ref,* 426
Stone, J. B.: *test,* 1513; *ref,* 1164, 1207, 1513, 5:7(29), 5:308(368)
Stone, J. T.: *ref,* 1499
Stone, L. A.: *test,* 1213; *ref,* 529, 533, 1044, 1213, 1281, 1380, 1394–5, 1447
Stone, L. G.: *ref,* 1289, 4:660(21)
Stone, L. J.: *rev,* 1451, 1523; *exc,* 1499; *ref,* 1499
Stone, M. H.: *ref,* 357, 1303
Stone, P.: *ref,* 1174
Stone, P. A.: *ref,* 381
Stone, P. M.: *ref,* 1474
Stone, R.: *test,* 676
Stone, S.: *ref,* 1423, 2195, 5:87 (31), 5:308(429)
Stone, T. C.: *ref,* 20, 1044, 1073, 2105
Stone, T. E.: *ref,* 1499
Stone, T. H.: *ref,* 2213
Stone, T. K.: *ref,* 1133, 1135
Stone, V. W.: *ref,* 2212
Stone, W.: *test,* 36:705
Stone, W. H.: *exc,* 2212–3
Stone, W. M.: *ref,* 1195
Stone, W. N.: *ref,* 1195, 1278, 1383
Stonehill, E.: *ref,* 1174, 1279
Stoner, M.: *ref,* 1164
Stoner, W. G.: *ref,* 18, 1121, 1626
Stones, E.: *ref,* 1140
Stonesifer, F. A.: *ref,* 381, 592, 1087, 1196
Stonesifer, J. N.: *exc,* 1087
Stonum, M. M.: *ref,* 1320
Stoops, J. A.: *ref,* 2195
Stopher, E. C.: *ref,* 419, 3:217(95)
Stopol, M. S.: *ref,* 1499
Storch, H. R.: *ref,* 1877
Storck, J.: *test,* 1:871
Stordahl, K. E.: *ref,* 404, 2212
Storey, A. G.: *test,* 1351; *ref,* 1351, 1599
Storey, J. S.: *ref,* 2135, 2195
Storey, S. E.: *ref,* 1289
Storlie, T. R.: *ref,* 868, 1356, 1383
Storm, T.: *ref,* 1185, 1275, 1519

Storment, C. T.: *ref,* 1205–6, 1245, 1499
Storment, R. C.: *ref,* 1222
Stormer, G. E.: *ref,* 525
Storms, L. H.: *ref,* 1275, 1281, 1447
Storr, M. A.: *test,* 2360
Storrs, S.: *ref,* 1073
Storrs, S. V.: *ref,* 532, 1073
Storseth, M. C.: *ref,* 914
Stortroen, M.: *ref,* 1281
Story, J. L.: *ref,* 518
Story, R. I.: *ref,* 1447
Story, W. E.: *ref,* 1796
Stothers, C. E.: *ref,* 486
Stotland, E.: *ref,* 1281, 1380
Stotsky, B. A.: *ref,* 447, 518, 529, 532, 1271, 1499, 2397
Stott, D.: *ref,* 1112
Stott, D. H.: *test,* 1411, 1904; *ref,* 525, 1112, 1898, 1904
Stott, L. H.: *test,* 4:41; *ref,* 487, 497, 507, 525, 1123, 1205, 3:38 (1–4, 6), P:306(2)
Stott, M. B.: *ref,* 525
Stott, S. S.: *ref,* 1403
Stott, W. W.: *ref,* 1499
Stoudenmire, J. A.: *ref,* 1391
Stouffer, G. A. W.: *test,* 339, 378, 437, 726, 1312, 2106, 2128, 2160, 2390, 2405, 2417, 2419
Stouffer, G. W.: *test,* 1694
Stouffer, S. A.: *test,* 24, 6:1075
Stough, K. F.: *ref,* 467, 1572
Stoughton, R. W.: *ref,* 1069
Stoup, D. D.: *ref,* 1281
Stout, C.: *ref,* 1145
Stout, D. H.: *ref,* 533
Stout, M.: *ref,* 1281
Stout, R.: *test,* 36:717
Stout, R. J.: *ref,* 1315, 1471
Stoutenborough, A.: *ref,* 423
Stovall, E. L.: *test,* 4:190
Stovall, E. M.: *ref,* 357
Stovall, F. L.: *ref,* 468
Stover, D. O.: *ref,* 1281
Stover, D. W.: *ref,* 607–8
Stover, L.: *ref,* 1240
Stover, R. D.: *ref,* 2381
Stover, R. M.: *ref,* 1133
Stowe, E. W.: *ref,* 2195, 2216
Stoy, E. G.: *ref,* 2251, 2259, 2266
Strabel, E.: *ref,* 18, 69, 419, 3:4 (3), 3:217(54, 59)
Strachan, E. D.: *ref,* 216
Strachan, L.: *ref,* 525, 3:220(15)
Strag, G. A.: *ref,* 2028
Strahan, R.: *ref,* 357
Strahl, G. T.: *ref,* 1240
Straight, B.: *ref,* 1194
Straight, G. H.: *ref,* 1281, 1320, 6:144(11)
Strain, J. E.: *ref,* 236
Strain, J. J.: *ref,* 543, 592
Strainge, R. E.: *ref,* 1724
Straits, B. C.: *ref,* 1281
Strandberg, T. E.: *ref,* 516, 522
Strang, H.: *ref,* 1281
Strang, R.: *rev,* 1568, 1749, 2213, 2:1672, 5:698; *test,* 4:474, 4:481, 5:666; *ref,* 349, 1386, 1560, 1568, 1572, 2:1553(2), 4:474(1), 4:481(1)
Strang, R. M.: *rev,* 1765

Tausig, T. N.: *ref,* 1164, 1281
Tauss, W.: *ref,* 1275
Tava, E. G.: *ref,* 533
Tavernier, A.: *ref,* 532
Tavris, E.: *ref,* 525, 532
Tavris, E. C.: *ref,* 2195
Taylor, A.: *ref,* 1499
Taylor, A. B.: *ref,* 1240
Taylor, A. J. W.: *ref,* 439, 545, 1129, 1228, 1253, 1281, 1383
Taylor, A. L.: *ref,* 29, 35, 349, 361, 400, 1069, 1121, 1560
Taylor, C.: *ref,* 529, 1123
Taylor, C. C.: *ref,* 2269
Taylor, C. D.: *ref,* 1716
Taylor, C. W.: *rev,* 359; *ref,* 349, 357, 1073, 1245, 2273, 2355
Taylor, D.: *test,* 4:156
Taylor, D. A.: *ref,* 1164, 1281, 1391, 1471
Taylor, D. B.: *ref,* 1913
Taylor, D. H.: *ref,* 426, 1307, 2251, 2266
Taylor, D. S.: *ref,* 1133
Taylor, D. W.: *ref,* 359, 2212, 2239
Taylor, E. A.: *test,* 6:835; *ref,* 7, 19, 22, 29, 36, 348, 489, 4:660(18), P:346(11-2)
Taylor, E. E.: *ref,* 1164, 1519
Taylor, E. G.: *ref,* 409
Taylor, E. K.: *rev,* 433, 444-5, 471, 480-1, 1071, 2135, 3:624, 3:631, 4:276, 5:905; *test,* 2404; *ref,* 431, 1207, 1403, 2140, 2195, 2212, 2448, 3:397(33), 6:1180(1-2)
Taylor, E. M.: *exc,* 1703; *ref,* 202, 211
Taylor, E. S.: *ref,* 1073
Taylor, E. W.: *ref,* 1176
Taylor, F. R.: *ref,* 1073, 1277
Taylor, G. A.: *ref,* 36, 525
Taylor, G. B.: *ref,* 1044
Taylor, G. J.: *ref,* 532, 1407, 2212, 4:648(1)
Taylor, G. M.: *ref,* 1447, 2212
Taylor, G. P.: *ref,* 1281
Taylor, G. R.: *ref,* 1117
Taylor, H.: *rev,* 486; *test,* 4:658
Taylor, H. C.: *ref,* 497, 525
Taylor, H. L.: *ref,* 1281, 1383
Taylor, H. R.: *rev,* 1073, 1386, 2190, 3:694; *ref,* 3:217(53)
Taylor, J.: *test,* 5c, 1750; *ref,* 69, 1069
Taylor, J. A.: *ref,* 1281
Taylor, J. B.: *ref,* 50, 381, 529, 1281, 1447, 1499, 2234-5, 2251
Taylor, J. F.: *ref,* 525, 529, 533, 1470, 3:242(4)
Taylor, J. G.: *ref,* 2212, 5:913(20)
Taylor, J. H.: *ref,* 868
Taylor, J. K.: *ref,* 1745
Taylor, J. N.: *ref,* 1169
Taylor, J. P.: *ref,* 1281
Taylor, J. R.: *ref,* 516, 1447
Taylor, J. W.: *ref,* 532, 1499
Taylor, K. E.: *ref,* 1281, 1448, 1499, 2285
Taylor, K. L.: *ref,* 1133
Taylor, K. V. F.: *ref,* 2212
Taylor, K. von F.: *ref,* 2213
Taylor, L. C.: *ref,* 948, 1306, 1403
Taylor, L. L.: *ref,* 1519
Taylor, M.: *ref,* 868, 1394, 2451

Taylor, M. F.: *ref,* 1519
Taylor, M. P.: *test,* P:460, P:483
Taylor, M. V.: *ref,* 1095, 1500
Taylor, M. W.: *ref,* 507
Taylor, O. M.: *ref,* 1500
Taylor, P. A.: *exc,* 11; *ref,* 1383, 1403, 1775
Taylor, P. H.: *ref,* 357
Taylor, P. J.: *ref,* 1174
Taylor, P. L.: *ref,* 1087, 2195
Taylor, P. S.: *ref,* 936
Taylor, R. E.: *ref,* 1094, 1281, 1294, 1452, 1474, 1499
Taylor, R. G.: *ref,* 405, 1044, 1063, 1280, 2195, 2212-3, 2383
Taylor, R. L.: *ref,* 1123
Taylor, R. M.: *test,* 840
Taylor, R. S.: *ref,* 1499
Taylor, S. E.: *test,* 180, 1671-2, 1678; *ref,* 1672
Taylor, S. St. C.: *ref,* 890
Taylor, T. D.: *ref,* 1415
Taylor, V.: *ref,* 1499
Taylor, V. C.: *ref,* 538
Taylor, V. H.: *ref,* 1447, 1499
Taylor, W.: *rev,* 1984; *test,* 36: 619, 1:1021, 2:1635, 2:1641, 4: 685, 5:814
Taylor, W. C.: *ref,* 533
Taylor, W. F.: *ref,* 1159
Taylor, W. W.: *rev,* 3:609, 3:612
Teachers College, Columbia University, Citizenship Education Project: *test,* 5:829, 5:832, 5: 837, 5:841; *ref,* 5:841(1)
Teachers College Personnel Association: *test,* 2:1185, 2:1280, 2:1418
Teagarden, F. M.: *rev,* 487, 497, 507, 509, 1428, 5:34, 5:332; *ref,* 503, 525
Teahan, J. E.: *ref,* 533
Teal, C. E.: *ref,* 1164
Teasdale, G. R.: *ref,* 516, 981
Teasdale, J. D.: *ref,* 1240, 1293, 1337
Tebo, J.: *ref,* 2221
Tebor, I. B.: *ref,* 1121
Tecce, J. J.: *ref,* 1281
Tedeschi, J. T.: *ref,* 1291, 1519
Tedford, W. H.: *ref,* 542, 1471, 1499
Teegarden, L.: *rev,* 2258, 2:1401; *ref,* 2227, 2258, 3:660(13-4, 16)
Teel, J. R.: *ref,* 2059
Teel, S. K.: *ref,* 1281
Teepe, E. A.: *ref,* 426
Teeter, B.: *ref,* 1281
Teeter, B. S.: *ref,* 1447
Teeter, V. A.: *test,* 35:153, 35: 466
Teevan, R.: *ref,* 1519
Teevan, R. C.: *ref,* 1123, 1448, 1519
Tegnell, J. E.: *ref,* 1447
Teicher, M. I.: *ref,* 532
Teichman, M.: *ref,* 1500
Teichman, Y.: *ref,* 1499
Teichner, W.: *ref,* 1519
Teigen, K. H.: *ref,* 1471
Teigland, J. J.: *ref,* 533, 868, 1123
Tejessy, C.: *ref,* 1500, 1519
Tekane, I.: *ref,* 6:459(2)
Telder, T. V. D.: *ref,* 1474
Teledgi, M. S.: *ref,* 574

Telegdy, G. A.: *ref,* 533
Telfer, M. A.: *ref,* 1281
Telford, A.: *ref,* 1311
Telford, C. W.: *ref,* 381, 518, 1121, 1403
Telford, N. J.: *ref,* 1123
Tellegen, A.: *test,* 1896; *ref,* 529, 533, 1073, 1281, 1896, 1921
Teller, J. D.: *ref,* 3:535(10)
Teltscher, H. O.: *ref,* 1499
Temmer, H. W.: *ref,* 529, 1447
Temp, G.: *ref,* 357
Tempero, H. E.: *ref,* 361, 516
Templer, A. J.: *test,* 1492; *ref,* 1225, 1275, 1414
Templer, D. I.: *ref,* 503, 529, 543, 1145, 1174, 1281
Templeton, G.: *ref,* 1499
Templin, M. C.: *rev,* 499, 4:354; *test,* 2095; *ref,* 496, 2095
Ten Brink, T. D.: *ref,* 981
Tendler, A. D.: *ref,* 1480
Tenhoff, M. L.: *ref,* 516, 1715
Tenney, E. A.: *ref,* 2:1299, 2:1561
Tennison, J. C.: *ref,* 1164
Tennyson, R. D.: *ref,* 1391
Tennyson, W. W.: *rev,* 31, 419
Tenopyr, M. L.: *ref,* 35, 113, 361, 652, 1071, 1207, 1421, 1599, 2453-4
Tepper, B. S.: *ref,* 1121
Terespolsky, L.: *ref,* 1145
ter Hoevan, B.: *ref,* 1275
Terleski, D. R.: *ref,* 1176, 1214
Terman, E. L.: *test,* 3:243; *ref,* 3: 243(1)
Terman, L. M.: *test,* 359, 525, 1101, 4:174, 4:195, 4:324, 5:698; *ref,* 36, 359, 525, 1101, 1320, 2212, 3: 220(1)
Terman, S. W.: *ref,* 1932
Terrell, G.: *ref,* 1123
Terrell, R. E.: *ref,* 914
Terrill, J. L.: *ref,* 1294
Terrill, J. M.: *ref,* 1240, 1519, P: 446(22)
Terrill, L. L.: *ref,* 914
Terrill, P. A.: *ref,* 1447
Terris, J. E.: *ref,* 1499
Terry, D.: *ref,* 1519
Terry, D. J.: *ref,* 1519
Terry, J. H.: *ref,* 1447
Terry, P. W.: *ref,* 1560, 6:480(32)
Terry, R. L.: *ref,* 1383
Terry, T. R.: *ref,* 1302
Terwilliger, J. S.: *ref,* 361, 1403, 2195, 6:1062(13)
Terwilliger, R. F.: *ref,* 357, 1281
Tesch, M. J.: *ref,* 1315
Tesi, G.: *ref,* 439
Teska, J. A.: *ref,* 7, 50, 516, 525, 981
Teska, P. T.: *ref,* 381, 1469
Tesseneer, R.: *ref,* 1281
Testin, R.: *ref,* 1499
Testin, R. F.: *ref,* 1499, 1519
Testing Bureau of the National Curriculum Research Institute: *test,* 278, 1021-2
Teter, J. T.: *ref,* 1281
Teuber, H. L.: *ref,* 342, 533, 578
Tew, B. O.: *ref,* 1281, 1289
Tewari, J. G.: *ref,* 1475, 1500, 1519
Tewari, J. N.: *ref,* 1475, 1500, 1519
Thacker, J. A.: *ref,* 869

Thomson, M.: *ref,* 1281
Thomson, R. W.: *ref,* 2212
Thomson, W. A.: *ref,* 1403, 2212, 2:1233(4), 2:1377(47), 4:277 (157)
Thomson, W. D.: *ref,* 1069, 1121
Thomure, E.: *ref,* 499
Thorderson, P. E.: *ref,* 20
Thoren, A.: *ref,* 1516
Thoresen, C. E.: *ref,* 1121, 2212
Thoresen, P. W.: *ref,* 1094
Thoreson, R. W.: *ref,* 1281
Thorman, G.: *test,* 841
Thorn, K. F.: *ref,* 1281
Thorndike, E. L.: *test,* 35:354, 4: 477, 4:558; *ref,* 655, 1480, 1572, 2:1271(1), 4:477(1, 4)
Thorndike, R. L.: *rev,* 50, 589, 1121, 1160, 1171, 1183, 1386, 1413, 1939, 2241, 2:1377, 3:244, 3:263; *test,* 351–2, 356, 400–1, 525, 1422, 2241, 6:342; *ref,* 22, 357, 359, 426, 490, 525, 1194, 1383, 1386, 1416, 1422, 2:1243.1(4–5), 4:277(182, 197), 6:342(1–3)
Thorndike, R. M.: *ref,* 2197, 2212, 2283
Thorne, D. E.: *ref,* 1389
Thorne, F. C.: *test,* 1237; *ref,* 1237, 1281, 1469, 1499, 1519
Thorne, F. M.: *ref,* 1447
Thorne, G. D.: *ref,* 532–3
Thorne, G. L.: *ref,* 1121, 1281
Thorne, W. E.: *ref,* 1469
Thornton, C. C.: *ref,* 1395
Thornton, C. L.: *ref,* 533, 559, 1169, 1470
Thornton, D.: *ref,* 1293
Thornton, D. R.: *ref,* 1164, 1281
Thornton, G. R.: *ref,* 337, 421, 1499, 2260, 2433
Thornton, M. F.: *ref,* 2451
Thornton, S. M.: *ref,* 1447
Thornton, T. E.: *ref,* 496, 532
Thoroughman, J. C.: *ref,* 1447
Thorp, T. R.: *ref,* 532
Thorpe, J. A.: *ref,* 1164
Thorpe, J. A. L.: *ref,* 1164
Thorpe, J. G.: *ref,* 1175, 1281
Thorpe, J. S.: *test,* 1471; *ref,* 381, 533, 1094, 1169, 1253, 1437, 1471
Thorpe, L. P.: *rev,* 50; *test,* 29, 108, 731, 1123, 1439, 1596, 1765, 1790, 1947, 2199, 3:690, 5:668, 5: 870, 6:141, 6:352; *exc,* 1240, 5: B261; *ref,* 1123, 6:352(1)
Thorsen, E. E.: *ref,* 439, 589
Thorton, C. C.: *ref,* 1395
Thorup, R. F. H.: *ref,* 868
Thouless, R. H.: *rev,* 110, 1775, 3: 124
Thrall, J. B.: *ref,* 2212
Thrall, J. R.: *ref,* 2212
Thralls, Z. A.: *test,* 3:599
Thrash, P. A.: *ref,* 1207, 1403, 2195
Thrasher, R.: *test,* 232–3
Threadcraft, M. H.: *ref,* 1289
Threatt, R.: *ref,* 357
Throne, F. M.: *ref,* 381, 516, 525, 533, 1447
Throne, J. M.: *ref,* 533
Throneberry, C. A.: *ref,* 1207
Throp, J. L.: *ref,* 529
Thrower, F. L.: *ref,* 1519

Thrush, R. S.: *ref,* 2212
Thuline, H. C.: *ref,* 1932
Thumin, F.: *ref,* 482, 1206, 2151
Thumin, F. J.: *ref,* 404, 426, 482, 792, 1071, 1206, 1281, 1583, 2151, 2463, 2466
Thune, J.: *ref,* 529, 545, 1499
Thurlow, B. H.: *ref,* 1129
Thurlow, H. J.: *ref,* 1281
Thurman, C. G.: *ref,* 1073
Thurston, D.: *ref,* 533, 1679
Thurston, D. R.: *ref,* 840, 1205, 1245, 1281
Thurston, H. I.: *ref,* 1281
Thurston, J.: *ref,* 1254, 1281, 1500
Thurston, J. R.: *test,* 2378, 2382, 2389; *ref,* 532, 542, 551, 1254, 1281, 1501, 1519, 2378, 2382, 2387, 2389
Thurstone, L. L.: *test,* 452, 469, 547–8, 570, 1087, 1423, 2162, 2214, 2245, 2255, 2272, 3:398, 3:653, 5: 309, 5:899, 5:905, 6:159, 6:438, 6:495, T:1935; *ref,* 69, 525, 1087, 1205–6, 1245, 1423, 1499, 1583, 2162, 2195, 2212, 2214, 35:66(1), 2:1243(2), 2:1377(1, 4, 7, 10, 12–3, 17, 21, 24, 27, 31, 36, 41, 48), 2:1378(1–2), 2:1683(1), 3:217 (96, 112, 118, 124, 127, 136), 3: 218(8), 6:159(29)
Thurstone, T. G.: *test,* 24, 452, 469, 1087, 1149, 1588, 1747, 3:478, 5: 309, 5:899, 6:438, 6:495; *ref,* 1087, 2:1243(2), 2:1377(10, 12–3, 17, 21, 24, 27, 31, 36, 41, 48), 2:1378(1–2), 3:217(96, 112, 118, 124, 127, 136), 3:218(8), 3:478 (1), 6:159(29)
Thweatt, R. C.: *ref,* 525, 1379, 1387, 1447
Thwing, E.: *ref,* 484, 525
Thwing, E. J.: *test,* 508
Tiahrt, H. G.: *ref,* 533
Tibbetts, J. W.: *ref,* 589
Tiber, N.: *ref,* 525
Tidey, W. J.: *ref,* 1063
Tidyman, W. F.: *ref,* 149
Tiebout, C.: *ref,* 381, 398, 426
Tiedeman, D. V.: *rev,* 18, 358, 1059, 2221, 4:301, 5:319, 6:11, 7: 1033; *exc,* 1044, 1058, 2180; *ref,* 357, 425–6, 1040A, 1069, 1302, 1403, 2135, 2195, 2221, 2239, 2266, 5:308(364)
Tiedeman, H. R.: *test,* 5:490
Tiege, E.: *ref,* 1281
Tieger, M. E.: *ref,* 1499–500
Tiegs, E. W.: *rev,* 1:869, 2:1192, 3:5, 3:22; *test,* 7, 61, 348–9, 458, 603, 1123, 1536, 1606, 3:59, 3: 222, 3:690, 4:645, 6:4, 6:280, 6: 503, 6:591, 6:638; *ref,* 349, 1123
Tiel, E. M.: *ref,* 981
Tieman, N.: *ref,* 1123
Tiemeyer, E. B.: *ref,* 1519
Tien, H. C.: *test,* 1305; *ref,* 1305
Tierney, R. W.: *ref,* 1281
Tieszen, M. J.: *ref,* 1923–4, 1932, 5:768(26)
Tietze, C.: *ref,* 525, 545, 1192
Tiffany, L. H.: *test,* 1:908
Tiffany, T. L.: *ref,* 1254, P:353(8)
Tiffin, J.: *rev,* 1:1108; *test,* 170,

337, 442, 1739, 2142, 2233–4, 2263, 2435–8, 1:871, 4:782, 4:816, 6: 491, 7:1136; *ref,* 337, 426, 1573, 1918, 1923, 2142, 2195, 2227–8, 2233–4, 2263, 6:480(40)
Tigay, B.: *ref,* 533
Tikofsky, R.: *ref,* 547
Tikofsky, R. S.: *ref,* 496, 547, 2071, 2076
Tilis, H. S.: *ref,* 489, 516, 525
Tilker, H. A.: *ref,* 349, 518, 1383
Tilleard, D. L.: *ref,* 1915
Tiller, T. C.: *ref,* 1394–5
Tillinghast, B. S.: *ref,* 357, 516, 2193
Tillman, C. A.: *ref,* 2212
Tillman, C. E.: *ref,* 1923
Tillman, C. G.: *ref,* 532
Tillman, H. M.: *ref,* 533
Tillman, K.: *ref,* 914, 1090, 1383, 1403, 2195
Tillman, K. G.: *ref,* 914, 1090, 1383, 2195
Tillman, M. H.: *ref,* 533
Tillman, T. W.: *ref,* 2031
Tillmans, S. J.: *ref,* 516, 981
Tillquist, P. F.: *ref,* 1395
Tilson, L. M.: *test,* 198; *ref,* 198, 202, 211
Tilton, J. W.: *exc,* 518; *ref,* 22, 398, 441, 4:324(57), 5:368(15)
Timberlake, J. B.: *test,* 1638
Time, Inc.: *test,* 1961–2
Timmermans, G. B.: *ref,* 1033
Timmermans, H. M.: *ref,* 1207
Timmermans, P. R.: *ref,* 1033
Timmons, E. O.: *ref,* 1448
Timmons, F.: *ref,* 1121
Timmons, G. D.: *ref,* 2337
Timmons, W. M.: *ref,* 1320
Timson, I. M.: *ref,* 868
Tindall, R. H.: *ref,* 1123, 1499, 1501, 5:66(9), P:321(18)
Tine, S.: *ref,* 529, 545, 1499
Tinio, F.: *ref,* 1519
Tinio, F. S.: *ref,* 1519
Tinker, K. J.: *ref,* 1877
Tinker, M. A.: *rev,* 1611, 1628, 1877, 1905, 1:1108, 3:524, 3:539, 4:660; *test,* 1748, 5:687; *exc,* 1447, 1629, 1911; *ref,* 419, 881, 1560, 1918, 1924, 1932, 2266, 3: 470(7), 4:660(22), 5:768(23)
Tinley, J.: *ref,* 1422
Tinley, J. J.: *ref,* 1303, 1376
Tinsley, D. G.: *ref,* 2057
Tinsley, D. J.: *ref,* 1044
Tinsley, H. E. A.: *test,* 2284; *ref,* 2283–4
Tinsley, W. V.: *test,* 4:491, 4:502
Tippett, J. S.: *ref,* 525, 6:480(13)
Tipton, R. M.: *ref,* 1073
Tireman, L. S.: *ref,* 1661
Tirman, R. J.: *ref,* 2221
Tirpak, R. D.: *ref,* 1383
Tisdale, J. C.: *ref,* 35, 361, 1052
Tisdale, J. R.: *ref,* 1164, 1403
Tisdall, W. J.: *ref,* 542, 546, 551, 561, 577, 594
Tisdel, L. D.: *ref,* 1350, 1403
Tismer, W.: *ref,* 29
Titler, N. A.: *ref,* 1337
Titmus Optical Co., Inc.: *test,* 1934
Tittle, C. J.: *ref,* 655, 1602

Trapp, E. P.: *ref,* 533, 1281, 1469, 1500, 2095, 6:67(5)
Traster, S.: *ref,* 4:324(51)
Trattner, M. H.: *ref,* 1073
Traub, R. E.: *test,* 387
Traut, G. M.: *ref,* 36
Travernier, A.: *ref,* 1499
Travers, K. J.: *rev,* 672, 683
Travers, K. J. D.: *ref,* 2195
Travers, R. M. W.: *rev,* 1785, 1794, 1863, 1867, 3:698, 4:792; *ref,* 48, 69, 404, 902, 1095, 1474, 1499, 2239, 2251, 2266, 4:277(257)
Travis, L. E.: *test,* 5:169; *ref,* 211, 426, 1499, 5:169(4)
Travis, V. A.: *ref,* 1164
Traweek, M. W.: *ref,* 1123
Traxler, A.: *ref,* 69, 1320, 1583, 1611
Traxler, A. E.: *rev,* 24, 1574, 1603, 2195, 2311, 1:1171, 2:1321, 3:397, 3:635, 3:641, 4:468, 4:738, 4:777, 5:650, 6:791; *test,* 162, 176, 706, 1610-1, 2:1196, 3:17, 4:583; *exc,* 525; *ref,* 35-6, 69, 152, 176, 248, 291, 349, 357, 360-1, 394, 398, 400, 426, 652, 706, 746, 908, 1087, 1095, 1281, 1320, 1366, 1403, 1560, 1572, 1583, 1610-1, 1622, 1626, 1716, 1768, 1807, 1839, 1861, 2195, 2212, 2239, 2266, 2323, 2:1299(2), 2:1377(42), 2:1567(3), 3:181 (7), 3:217(79, 97, 113, 119, 128), 3:397(25, 36), 3:604(2-3), 3: 613(16), 4:238(1), 4:251(1-2), 4:260(3), 4:583(1), 5:308(307, 397-8, 412), 5:530(47, 51), 5:817 (1), 5:907(1)
Traxler, H. W.: *ref,* 1073
Traxler, R. J.: *ref,* 20
Treacy, J. P.: *ref,* 698, 863, 1622
Treadway, C. R.: *ref,* 518, 1281, 7:55(23)
Treadwell, Y.: *ref,* 574, 1121
Treanor, C. C.: *ref,* 1302
Treat, K.: *ref,* 518
Trebbe, E. S.: *ref,* 357, P:200(5)
Tredgold, R. F.: *ref,* 1275
Tredick, V. D.: *ref,* 1087
Treece, J. M.: *ref,* 1133
Treece, R. R.: *ref,* 1281
Treesh, E. O.: *ref,* 1164, 1403
Treffinger, D. J.: *ref,* 35, 361, 542, 551, 589, 881
Trefsgar, T. F.: *ref,* 19, 391, 533
Trehub, A.: *ref,* 532, 1164
Trejdosiewicz, L.: *ref,* 1448, 1475
Trela, T. M.: *ref,* 138, 1599, 1603, 1624, 1628-9, 1647, 1658, 1679, 1775, 6:793(6)
Trella, S. C.: *test,* 7:615, 7:622
Tremain, D. L.: *ref,* 1281
Trembath, M. F.: *ref,* 2195
Trembath, W. E.: *ref,* 1499
Trembly, W. A.: *ref,* 1766
Tremel, J. G.: *ref,* 1069
Trent, J.: *ref,* 1856
Trent, J. H.: *ref,* 1856
Trent, J. W.: *ref,* 1302, 2212
Trent, R.: *test,* 1057
Trent, R. D.: *ref,* 1448
Trent, S. J.: *ref,* 1383
Trentini, G.: *ref,* 1500
Treppa, J. A.: *ref,* 1519

Tresselt, M. E.: *ref,* 1090, 1205-6, 1245, 1320, 1403, 1480
Tressler, J. C.: *test,* 121, 3:17
Tretakoff, M. I.: *ref,* 7, 50
Treumann, M. J.: *ref,* 1560, 4:277 (211), 4:810(4)
Trever, R. W.: *ref,* 1281
Trevorrow, R. L.: *ref,* 36, 400, 424, 1716
Trezise, R. L.: *ref,* 1302
Triandis, H. C.: *ref,* 1240
Triandis, L. M.: *ref,* 1500
Tribble, J. S.: *ref,* 2457
Trice, E. W.: *ref,* 935
Trice, H. M.: *ref,* 1281, 1383, 1519, 7:55(22)
Trider, M. S.: *ref,* 424, 1603
Trieb, M. H.: *test,* 36:707, 1:B338; *ref,* 36:707(1)
Trieglaff, A. L.: *ref,* 36, 533, 1603
Trier, T. R.: *ref,* 1499
Trieschmann, R. B.: *ref,* 529, 1281
Trifari, T. E.: *ref,* 6:66(1)
Trigg, C. W.: *ref,* 4:324(53)
Triggs, F.: *ref,* 532-3, 1626
Triggs, F. O.: *rev,* 1597, 3:642, 3: 654; *ref,* 152, 525, 533, 1626, 1918, 2195, 2212-3, 3:639(4), 4:277 (256, 272)
Trigos, M. G.: *test,* 1211
Trilling, M.: *test,* 2:1508, 2:1510
Trimble, C.: *ref,* 2451
Trimble, H. C.: *rev,* 655, 6:638, 6: 641; *ref,* 3:535(11), 4:606(3)
Trimble, H. M.: *ref,* 1844-5
Trimble, J. E.: *ref,* 1121
Trimble, J. T.: *ref,* 2212
Trimble, M. G.: *ref,* 1133, 1394
Trimble, O. C.: *test,* 36:748
Trimble, R. R.: *ref,* 868
Trimble, R. W.: *ref,* 1293, 1377, 1499
Trimble, W. E.: *ref,* 1599
Trinkhaus, W. K.: *ref,* 2212
Trione, V.: *ref,* 48, 1073
Tripathi, R. C.: *ref,* 2231
Triplett, B.: *ref,* 1073
Triplett, R. J.: *ref,* 426, 1403
Tripp, C. A.: *ref,* 1447
Trippe, M. J.: *ref,* 1448, 1499
Trismen, D. A.: *ref,* 35
Trist, E.: *test,* 6:519; *ref,* 406, 6: 519(1)
Trist, E. L.: *ref,* 532
Trites, D. K.: *ref,* 349, 1069, 1121, 1146, 4:277(222)
Trivedi, G.: *test,* 1041; *ref,* 1041
Trobman, P. B.: *ref,* 1716
Trockman, R. W.: *ref,* 2197
Troffer, S. H.: *ref,* 1121, 1176
Troisi, N. F.: *ref,* 868
Trojanowicz, R. C.: *ref,* 1250
Tronca, W. F.: *ref,* 404
Tronsue, M. E.: *ref,* 20
Tronzo, R. G.: *ref,* 1500
Troop, J.: *ref,* 1145, 1275
Trosman, H.: *ref,* 1281, 1499, 1519
Trost, H.: *ref,* 525
Trost, M. E.: *rev,* 2:1626
Trott, D. M.: *ref,* 1322
Trotter, A. B.: *ref,* 1315
Troup, E.: *ref,* 1428, 1499
Trousdale, W.: *ref,* 1298
Trousdale, W. W.: *ref,* 1383

Trout, R. W.: *ref,* 1052
Trouton, D. S.: *ref,* 1387
Trowbridge, L.: *ref,* 503
Trowbridge, N.: *ref,* 349, 381
Trown, E. A.: *ref,* 1174
Troxel, L. L.: *ref,* 1134, 2195
Troxel, V. A.: *ref,* 1775, 1819, 1856
Troxel, W. D.: *ref,* 1207, 1281
Troy, E. M.: *ref,* 69, 358, 1572
Troyer, M. E.: *rev,* 18, 3:22; *test,* 928, 3:125, 4:468, 4:534, T:1180; *ref,* 928, 3:406(3), 4:6(24), 4: 468(1)
Truax, C. B.: *ref,* 1280-1
Truax, W. E.: *ref,* 1281
Trubin, B.: *ref,* 1428
Truby, H. M.: *test,* 1654
Truchses, R. E.: *ref,* 1383
Truckenmiller, J. L.: *ref,* 1240, 1519
Trudeau, P.: *ref,* 529, 1040
True, G. L.: *ref,* 914
True, S.: *ref,* 589
True, S. R.: *ref,* 589
Trueblood, G. E.: *ref,* 2212
Truelove, J. W.: *ref,* 1281
Trujillo, C. M.: *ref,* 1207
Trumbull, R.: *ref,* 1087, 1205, 1281
Trumm, O.: *ref,* 1281
Trump, P. L.: *ref,* 1044, 1048
Trunnell, J. B.: *ref,* 1499-500, 1519
Truog, A. L.: *ref,* 1044, 1174
Trusler, V. T.: *test,* 3:426
Truss, C. V.: *ref,* 1387
Trussell, E. M.: *ref,* 1895, 1898, 1921
Trussell, W. D.: *exc,* 533
Truumaa, A.: *ref,* 1121
Tryk, H. E.: *ref,* 533, 589
Tryon, R. C.: *rev,* 1087; *ref,* 1281, 6:159(40)
Tryon, R. M.: *rev,* 1:1017, 2:1183, 2:1616
Tsacnaris, H. J.: *ref,* 2448
Tsai, L. S.: *ref,* 529, 1069
Tsao, D. F.: *ref,* 381
Tschechtelin, M. A.: *ref,* 859, 1321
Tschritter, R. E.: *ref,* 1294
Tseng, M.: *ref,* 361
Tseng, M. S.: *ref,* 1164, 1383, 1519
Tsubouchi, K.: *ref,* 1281
Tsuda, K.: *ref,* 1499
Tsuji, K.: *ref,* 1474
Tsuji, S.: *ref,* 1451, 1499, 1519
Tsujioka, B.: *ref,* 1205-6, 1245, 1383
Tsushima, W.: *ref,* 529, 1447, 1481, 1499
Tsushima, W. T.: *ref,* 1519
Tuason, V. B.: *ref,* P:326(32)
Tubbs, V. K.: *ref,* 981
Tubbs, W. R.: *ref,* 1314, 1320
Tuchman, S. B.: *ref,* 525
Tuck, J. A.: *ref,* 532, 1281
Tucker, A. C.: *ref,* 2212
Tucker, B. Z.: *ref,* 1094
Tucker, C. A.: *ref,* 589, 2340
Tucker, C. B.: *test,* 7:511, 7:541
Tucker, D. A.: *ref,* 496
Tucker, D. W.: *ref,* 202, 217
Tucker, F. C.: *ref,* 1315
Tucker, G.: *ref,* 1275, 1481, 1499
Tucker, G. J.: *ref,* 1499
Tucker, H.: *ref,* 69, 382

Tucker, J.: *ref,* 1499
Tucker, J. E.: *ref,* 1289, 1447, 1499
Tucker, L. R.: *ref,* 244, 264, 289, 305, 529, 5:308(296)
Tucker, M. F.: *ref,* 2273
Tucker, N. M.: *ref,* 914
Tucker, S. B.: *ref,* 1133, 1302
Tucker, W. F.: *ref,* 35, 425, 1069
Tucker, W. H.: *ref,* 1327
Tucker, W. L.: *ref,* 1164, 1207
Tucker, W. T.: *ref,* 1193–4
Tucker, W. V.: *ref,* 1383
Tuckman, B. W.: *ref,* 967–8, 970–1, 975, 1164
Tuckman, J.: *ref,* 798, 1095, 1144–5, 1474, 2195, 2227, 2251, 2260, 2266, 3:392(2)
Tuddenham, R. D.: *exc,* 529, 532, 1112, 1447; *ref,* 342, 439, 1105, 1121, 1164, 1281, 1437, 4:315(10)
Tuel, J. K.: *ref,* 525, 1087
Tueller, R. L.: *ref,* 542, 1315
Tuft, E. N.: *ref,* 1560, 1610, 1749, 1768, 4:660(24)
Tuft, L. H.: *ref,* 1281
Tuinman, J. J.: *ref,* 1599
Tukey, R. S.: *ref,* 1164, 1253
Tulchin, S. H.: *rev,* 1110, 2:1233, 2:1244, 3:98; *ref,* 525, 1499
Tulkin, S. R.: *ref,* 439
Tullos, S. J.: *ref,* 869
Tully, A. G.: *ref,* 869
Tully, G. E.: *ref,* 49, 349, 361, 382, 404, 439, 869, 1032
Tully, M.: *test,* 2:1337
Tuma, A. H.: *ref,* 529, 1121, 1264, 1281, 1380, P:41(7)
Tuma, J. W.: *ref,* 1383
Tumampos, R. S.: *ref,* 1383
Tumangday, M. G.: *ref,* 19
Tumen, E.: *ref,* 1519
Tunis, M. M.: *ref,* 1499
Tunney, T. E.: *ref,* 1499
Tunstall, O. A.: *ref,* 425, 439, 1174
Tupes, E. C.: *ref,* 1205, 1244
Tupin, J.: *ref,* 1192, 1519
Turaids, D.: *test,* 1888
Turberg, J.: *ref,* 1313, 1519
Turbeville, W. C.: *ref,* 211
Turbovsky, J. M.: *ref,* 1281
Tureen, L. L.: *ref,* 1144
Tures, R. S.: *ref,* 7, 20, 1383
Turgut, M. F.: *ref,* 1164
Turille, S. J.: *test,* 3:380
Turk, E.: *ref,* 1232
Turk, H.: *ref,* 1281
Turknett, R. L.: *ref,* 589
Turland, D. N.: *ref,* 1277
Turley, D. L.: *ref,* 1121, 1164
Turnbull, G. H.: *ref,* 409, 868, 1320, 1386, 1500
Turnbull, J. W.: *ref,* 518, 1129, 1253, 1499
Turnbull, M. E.: *rev,* 241–2, 249, 251, 4:236; *ref,* 1048
Turnbull, W.: *ref,* 1109, 2212
Turnbull, W. W.: *rev,* 31, 433, 1063, 1534, 1560, 1597, 1626; *ref,* 1048, 1859
Turner, A. J.: *ref,* 525, 1383
Turner, A. R.: *ref,* 302
Turner, C.: *ref,* 1932
Turner, C. B.: *ref,* 1423
Turner, C. E.: *rev,* 253, 259, 2:

1347, 2:1351, 3:180, 3:184, 4:234, 4:240, 5:261
Turner, C. J.: *ref,* 489, 1087
Turner, C. P.: *ref,* 48
Turner, D.: *ref,* 61, 1123, 1536, 1560
Turner, D. M.: *test,* 2:1457
Turner, D. R.: *ref,* 1499
Turner, E.: *ref,* 529
Turner, G. C.: *ref,* 1519
Turner, G. H.: *ref,* 391, 439, 533
Turner, J.: *ref,* 525, 529, 1281, 1447
Turner, J. F.: *ref,* 1073
Turner, J. N.: *ref,* 2454
Turner, L. N.: *ref,* 1240, 1281
Turner, M. L.: *rev,* 5:747, 5:755
Turner, M. M.: *ref,* 1095, 1383
Turner, N. D.: *ref,* 598
Turner, R. D.: *ref,* 882, 884
Turner, R. K.: *ref,* 533, 1683
Turner, T. B.: *ref,* 2340
Turner, T. N.: *ref,* 589
Turner, V. D.: *ref,* 1044
Turner, W. D.: *ref,* 1320
Turner, W. J.: *ref,* 440, 1227, 1380, 1383
Turner, W. S.: *ref,* 1121, 1164
Turney, A. H.: *rev,* 398, 1095, 1:1006, 2:1378, 2:1500; *ref,* 426, 1320, 2:1424(16), 3:242(7)
Turney, J. R.: *ref,* 574
Turnipseed, J. P.: *ref,* 1044
Turo, J. K.: *ref,* 1403, 2195
Turrell, E. S.: *ref,* 1281, 1403, 1423, 1519
Turrentine, E. M.: *ref,* 357, 419, 425
Turse, P. L.: *test,* 798, 3:392, 5:855; *ref,* 798, 3:392(1)
Tursky, B.: *ref,* 1275, 1471
Turteltaub, A.: *ref,* 1293
Turton, L. J.: *rev,* 2077, 7:957
Turula, E.: *ref,* 1121
Tuska, S. A.: *test,* 796; *ref,* 381, 796
Tussey, S. C.: *ref,* 914
Tussing, L.: *ref,* 1095, 1320, 1348, 1403, 2195, 2212, 3:635(17)
Tustin, F.: *ref,* 1499
Tuthill, C. E.: *ref,* 2212
Tuthill, E. W.: *ref,* 1281
Tutko, T.: *ref,* 1164
Tutko, T. A.: *ref,* 1164, 1192, 1499, 1501, 1519
Tuton, K.: *ref,* 1237
Tutoo, D. N.: *ref,* 1191
Tutt, M. L.: *ref,* 533, 1087
Tuttle, C. E.: *ref,* 404
Tuttle, H. S.: *test,* 1:903
Tuttle, L. E.: *ref,* 489, 516, 533
Tuttle, L. L.: *ref,* 1123
Tutton, M. E.: *ref,* 2195
Twain, D. C.: *ref,* 426, 447, 529, 533
Twarog, L. I.: *ref,* 300
Tweeten, P. W.: *ref,* 1787
Twichell, C. M.: *ref,* 4:825(18)
Twining, G. A.: *ref,* 1123
Twitchell-Allen, D.: *test,* 1525; *ref,* 1525
Twogood, A. P.: *test,* 2:1665.1
Twomey, A. E.: *ref,* 1403
Twomey, J. F.: *ref,* 1225, 1281

Twyman, J. P.: *ref,* 1044, 1164, 1403
Tyagi, A. K.: *ref,* 1519
Tycko, M.: *ref,* 1499
Tydlaska, M.: *test,* 5:518; *ref,* 1281
Tyl, M. M.: *ref,* 1500
Tyler, D. J.: *ref,* 2266
Tyler, D. W.: *ref,* 1281
Tyler, E. A.: *ref,* 2355
Tyler, F.: *ref,* 1403
Tyler, F. T.: *rev,* 387, 3:237, 3:268; *ref,* 20, 364, 840, 1281, 2195, 3:263(48), 4:50(2), 4:277(251), 5:66(5), 5:87(18), 6:144(9)
Tyler, H. E.: *ref,* 48
Tyler, H. T.: *test,* 2:1580; *ref,* 1095, 1366
Tyler, I. K.: *test,* 1:873
Tyler, J. D.: *ref,* 1519
Tyler, L. E.: *rev,* 391, 547–8, 1053, 1169, 1320, 2177, 4:45, 5:570; *ref,* 20, 361, 589, 1087, 1101, 1121, 1123, 1164, 1238, 2195, 2212–3
Tyler, R. W.: *rev,* 1939, 1948, 2:1182, 2:1585, 3:5; *test,* 1:870b, 1:908–9, 1:933, 2:1593, 3:313; *ref,* 48, 348, 391, 398, 425, 1087, 4:581(14), 4:582(5), 4:585(1), 4:594(3), 4:606(4), 4:629(3)
Tyler, V.: *ref,* 1918
Tyler, V. O.: *ref,* 1253
Tynes, D. E.: *ref,* 1232
Tyre, B. B.: *ref,* 1617, 1669
Tyson, M.: *ref,* 331, 1162
Tyson, M. C.: *ref,* 381
Tyson, M. H.: *ref,* 533
Tzuo, H. Y.: *ref,* 1499

UBER, T. B.: *ref,* 1365
Uchiyama, A.: *ref,* 1094
Udry, J. R.: *ref,* 1383, 1403
Uecker, A. E.: *ref,* 525, 532, 592, 1281, 1428, 1485, 2195
Uehling, H. F.: *ref,* 1499
Ueno, H.: *ref,* 1499
Uffelmann, R.: *ref,* 1447
Ufford, M. S.: *ref,* 533, 2095
Uherik, A.: *ref,* 1174
Uhes, M. J.: *ref,* 1306, 1315
Uhl, H. J.: *ref,* 1403
Uhl, N. P.: *ref,* 36, 516, 981, 1430, 1921, 2028
Uhl, W. L.: *ref,* 1690
Uhlaner, J. E.: *ref,* 1923
Uhlenhuth, E. H.: *ref,* 2212
Uhlig, G. E.: *ref,* 1315
Uhlin, D. M.: *ref,* 1469
Uhlinger, C. A.: *ref,* 1164
Uhlir, G. A.: *ref,* 1164
Uhlmann, F. W.: *ref,* 547
Uhr, L.: *ref,* 1121, 1164, 1281, 1383, 2212
Uhrbrock, R. S.: *exc,* 1101; *ref,* 18, 86–7, 167, 354, 419, 621–2, 755, 1090, 1320, 1403, 1844–5, 1867–8, 2212, 4:422(1), 4:718(7), 4:813(7), 5:234(10)
Uleman, A. L.: *ref,* 439, 532, 1528
Uleman, J. S.: *ref,* 1519
Ulett, G.: *ref,* 1499
Ulett, G. A.: *test,* 1499g; *exc,* 1499; *ref,* 1499
Ulfeldt, V.: *ref,* 1921

Ulin, R. O.: *ref,* 357
Ullman, B. L.: *test,* 4:197, T:684
Ullman, R. R.: *ref,* 1386
Ullman, R. W.: *ref,* 1044, 6:8a(2)
Ullmann, L.: *ref,* 1499
Ullmann, L. P.: *exc,* 1522; *ref,*
  1121, 1176, 1281, 1471, 1499, 1519
Ullsvik, B. R.: *test,* 3:22; *ref,* 3:
  22(4)
Ulmer, G.: *test,* 44, 633, 659
Ulmer, R. A.: *ref,* 1519
Ulrich, R. F.: *test,* 1161
Ulseth, S.: *ref,* 1121
Umberger, J. P.: *ref,* 503, 532
Umphress, A.: *ref,* 1095
Underhill, O. E.: *test,* 1:870b, 2:
  1601
Underwood, A. G.: *ref,* 1133
Underwood, H. L.: *ref,* 1403
Underwood, J. R.: *ref,* 1415
Underwood, K.: *ref,* 1113
Underwood, K. L.: *ref,* 2221
Underwood, S. S.: *ref,* 1781, 1794
Underwood, W. J.: *ref,* 1176
Unger, B. L.: *ref,* 1281, 1293
Unger, S.: *ref,* 1281
United Business Education Asso-
  ciation. See Joint Committee on
  Tests. United Consultants: *test,*
  1425
United States Armed Forces Insti-
  tute, Examinations Staff: *test,*
  3:119–30, 3:183–5, 3:191–3, 3:
  200–2, 3:208–10, 3:323–5 3:343,
  3:354–5, 3:358–9, 3:364, 3:373–8,
  3:401, 3:407–16, 3:440, 3:528, 3:
  552–4, 3:564–5, 3:573–4, 3:578,
  3:580, 3:583–6, 3:607–9, 3:616–7,
  5:181, 5:216, 5:426
United States Employment Service: *test,* 1073, 1086, 2166, 2190,
  4:717, 4:735, 4:767–8; *ref,* 1073,
  2395
U.S. Naval Personnel Research
  Field Activity: *ref,* 1194, 1206
U.S. Province Brothers of Holy
  Cross: *test,* 6:296
University of Chicago. See Industrial Relations Center.
University of Edinburgh, Godfrey
  Thomson Unit: *test,* 95, 409, 640,
  722, 1548, 6:628, 6:1090
University of Michigan. See English Language Institute.
University of Illinois Press: *test,*
  982
University of Pennsylvania, Subur-
  ban School Study Council: *test,*
  5:100
University of Toronto, Ontario
  College of Education, Depart-
  ment of Educational Research:
  test, 739, 805, 35:251, 35:290, 3:
  186–8, 3:348, 3:603, 5:12–3, 5:
  462, 5:473, 5:477, 5:619, 5:673,
  6:5, 6:337; *ref,* 387, 798
University of Wisconsin, School of
  Education, Bureau of Guidance
  and Records: *test,* 3:138, 3:330,
  3:362, 3:555, 3:569, 3:577, 3:589
University Publications Sales, Ohio
  State University: *test,* 877
Unoh, S. O.: *ref,* 981
Unruh, L. D.: *ref,* 1069

Unser, M. C.: *ref,* 189
Unwick, D.: *test,* 1550
Unwin, S. M.: *test,* 75
Upadhyaya, O. P.: *ref,* P:381(35)
Upadhyaya, S.: *ref,* 1387
Upchurch, W. B.: *ref,* 1087, 1895,
  2028
Updegraff, R.: *ref,* 507, 525, 1428,
  1905
Upham, E. V.: *ref,* P:304(4)
Upper, D.: *ref,* 1281
Upshall, C. C.: *rev,* 650, 778, 3:
  379; *ref,* 1386, 1572, 2239, 2:1377
  (32), 2:1580(1)
Upshaw, H. S.: *ref,* 1281
Upshur, J.: *test,* 232–3
Upton, V.: *ref,* 1240
Uras, A.: *ref,* 1474
Uray, R. M.: *ref,* 425, 2212
Urbach, N.: *ref,* 185, 532, 1281
Urbaitis, J. C.: *ref,* 1499
Urban, H. B.: *ref,* 1500
Urban, T. S.: *ref,* 1164, 1264
Urban, W. H.: *test,* 1455; *ref,* 1145
Urbas, R.: *ref,* 1626
Urbina, S.: *ref,* 1463
Urdan, J. A.: *ref,* 1121, 1403
Urlocker, W. T.: *ref,* 425
Urmer, A. H.: *ref,* 439, 529, 1217,
  1281
Urquhart, A.: *ref,* 1277
Urquhart, D.: *ref,* 1387
Urschalitz, M. O.: *ref,* 2195
Ursua, A. R.: *ref,* 233
Usui, K.: *ref,* 1403
Utgard, R. O.: *ref,* 357
Utley, J. L.: *test,* 5:579; *ref,* 5:
  579(1)
Utsugi, E.: *ref,* 381
Uttley, M.: *rev,* 3:601–2; *test,* 3:
  599
Utz, V. R.: *ref,* 1164, 1403
Uyeno, E.: *ref,* 1281, 1485

V. NORREN, C.: *ref,* 1144, 1499
Vaage, M.: *ref,* 487, 1428
Vacc, N. A.: *ref,* 50
Vacca, E.: *ref,* 1499
Vaccaro, J. J.: *ref,* 426, 433, 1101,
  1500, 2199
Vacchiano, R. B.: *ref,* 868, 1164,
  1281, 1383, 1395, 1415, 1490, 1519
Vacek, W. L.: *ref,* 1164
Vacher, C. J. D.: *ref,* 1094
Vadum, A. C.: *ref,* 1121, 1281
Vahar, M.: *ref,* 381
Vail, C. C. D.: *rev,* 1:999–1001
Vail, J. P.: *ref,* 1095
Vaillant, P.: *test,* 35:230, 3:181
Vairo, J. D.: *ref,* 1320, 2212
Valadian, I.: *ref,* 1931
Valdes, A. L.: *ref,* 2028
Vale, C. A.: *ref,* 1044, 1225, 1768
Válek, J.: *ref,* 1145, 1174, 1240
Valenti, J. J.: *test,* 897
Valentine, C. W.: *test,* 446, 2:1247,
  5:405; *exc,* 497, 509; *ref,* 446, 2:
  1247(1), 4:343(2–3), 5:405(4–5)
Valentine, J. A.: *ref,* 6:289(2)
Valentine, J. H.: *ref,* 1232
Valentine, L. D.: *test,* 1067; *exc,*
  1322
Valentine, M.: *ref,* 439, 1275, 1499,
  1519

Valerius, E.: *ref,* 1293
Valesio, P.: *rev,* 283, 285
Valett, R.: *ref,* 991
Valett, R. E.: *rev,* 990, 1718; *test,*
  526, 977, 985–6, 991, 1707; *ref,*
  525
Valette, R. M.: *ref,* 255
Vallance, R. C.: *ref,* 1249, 1275
Valles, J.: *ref,* 1281
Valley, J. R.: *ref,* 240, 262, 302,
  742, 1800, 1832, 1858
Van Allyn, K.: *test,* 3:633, 3:639,
  4:771, 6:1049, 6:1068; *ref,* 3:
  639(5)
Van Alphen der Veer, M. R.: *ref,*
  1144, 1499
Van Alstyne, D.: *test,* 1:929, 6:
  537; *ref,* 36, 525, 6:537(1), P:
  321(11), P:406(1–2)
Van Andel, G. A.: *ref,* 1144, 1499
Van Atta, E. L.: *ref,* 1499
Van Atta, R. E.: *ref,* 1164, 1281
Van Bark, B.: *ref,* 1499
van Bavinckhove-Ossola: *ref,* 1500
van Biljon, I. J.: *ref,* 2234
Van Blaricom, V. L.: *test,* 1655,
  1776
Vanbramer, P. J.: *ref,* 533
Van Buren, J. D.: *ref,* 1207
VanBuskirk, C.: *ref,* 1160, 1394,
  1499
Van Buskirk, W. L.: *ref,* 1194,
  1403
Van Camp, S. S.: *ref,* 1087, 2028
VanCampen, J.: *ref,* 492
Vance, E. M. B.: *ref,* 1315, P:339
  (22)
Vance, F. L.: *rev,* 1094–5, 1361;
  ref, 1281
Vance, S. B.: *ref,* 489, 533
Vance, T. F.: *ref,* 507, 578
Vancini, J. P.: *ref,* 533
Van Dalsem, E.: *ref,* 1121
Van Dalsem, E. L.: *ref,* 1281, 2195
Van de Castle, R.: *ref,* 1499
Van de Castle, R. L.: *ref,* 518,
  1164, 1281, 1295, 1437, 1471, 1499,
  1519
Van De Mark, S. N.: *ref,* 1499
Van den Akker, J. A.: *ref,* 1924,
  1932, 4:658(1), 5:768(22)
Vanden Belt, B. H.: *test,* 2:1583.1
Vandenberg, S.: *ref,* 525
Vandenberg, S. G.: *exc,* 1452, 1491;
  ref, 439, 457, 529, 533, 561, 1069,
  1087, 1253, 1281, 1294, 1394, 1423,
  1499, 1761, 1895, 2197, 2212, 2269
Vanden Boogert, A. W.: *ref,* 2258
Vandenbos, G. R.: *ref,* 1519
van den Broek, P.: *ref,* 1499
Vander Beke, G. E.: *test,* 220, 254,
  313
Vanderberg, S. G.: *ref,* 484
Vandergriff, J. C.: *ref,* 1383
Vanderhoof, E.: *ref,* 1281
Vanderhoof, T. J.: *ref,* 1133
Vanderhost, L.: *ref,* 532–3
Vanderhost, L. L.: *ref,* 1240
Van De Riet, H.: *ref,* 529, 533,
  1123, 1281, 1403
Van De Riet, V.: *ref,* 7, 525, 529,
  533, 1123, 1281, 1403
Van Der Jagt, E. R.: *ref,* 1583,
  5:308(413)

Vernon, P. E.: *rev*, 574, 1070, 1074, 1087, 1123, 1222, 1253, 1275, 1296, 2:1201, 2:1220, 5:610; *test*, 618, 1403–4, 1680; *exc*, 217, 525, 1112, 1601, 2242, 4:289; *ref*, 381, 388, 439, 515, 518, 525, 558, 578, 734, 1403, 1447, 1499, 1680, 2239, 2242, 4:295(2), 4:724(1)
Vernson, E. E.: *ref*, 2213
Veroff, J.: *ref*, 1403, 1519
Veroff, J. B.: *ref*, 1519
Verrier, R.: *ref*, 1415
Verriest, G.: *ref*, 1912–3
Verrill, B. V.: *ref*, 518, 1164, 1475, 1499, P:500(11)
Vertein, L. D.: *ref*, 349, 868, 1281
Very, P. S.: *ref*, 457, 561, 1074, 1281, 1761
Vesprani, G. J.: *ref*, 1164, 1281
Vest, M. L. R.: *ref*, 981
Vest, T. J.: *ref*, 1383
Vestling, C. S.: *test*, 3:556
Vestre, N. D.: *test*, 1345; *ref*, 1164, 1207, 1255, 1265, 1281, 1345–6
Vetter, G. B.: *ref*, 1090, 1480
Vetter, H. J.: *ref*, 1499
Vetter, L.: *ref*, 1207, 2213
Via, M. E.: *ref*, 1225, 1302, 1415
Vialle, H. D.: *ref*, 1281
Vicent, P.: *ref*, 1921
Vicinanza, P.: *ref*, 2194
Vicino, F. L.: *ref*, 1380
Vick, G.: *ref*, 525, 532, 3:217(98)
Vick, M. C.: *ref*, 69, 357, 361
Vickers, M. J.: *ref*, 516, 2095
Vickers, V. S.: *ref*, 5:766(9)
Vickery, A.: *ref*, 1519
Vickery, V. L.: *rev*, 1627, 1641
Vicon Instrument Co.: *test*, T: 1662
Vics, I. I.: *ref*, 1932
Victor, G. C.: *ref*, 3:10(3), 3:116 (2)
Victor, M.: *ref*, 532, 592
Victoreen, J. A.: *test*, T:1663
Vidor, M.: *ref*, 1281
Vidulich, R.: *ref*, 1306
Vidulich, R. N.: *ref*, 1183
Viehweg, R.: *ref*, 522, 533, 1628
Viel, B.: *ref*, 439
Viele, A. B.: *ref*, 435
Vielhaber, D. P.: *ref*, 1395
Vienna, P.: *ref*, 1469
Viers, R. F.: *ref*, 1470
Vietze, P. M.: *ref*, 1415
Viewag, W. E.: *ref*, 1696
Vignolo, L. A.: *ref*, 1192
Vignos, P. J.: *ref*, 525
Vigotsky, L. S.: *ref*, 1140
Viitamäki, R. O.: *ref*, 533, 592, 1447, 1486, 1499, 1519, P:496(6, 13)
Vilhotti, A. J.: *ref*, 1481
Villa-Landa, I.: *ref*, 1447
Villalobos, M.: *ref*, 914
Villard, H. H.: *ref*, 1968, 1970
Villarreal, J. A.: *ref*, 255, 271, 314
Villaveces, H. J.: *ref*, 2212
Villeme, M. G.: *ref*, 1289, 2195
Vimal, K.: *ref*, 1275
Vinacke, W. E.: *ref*, 1228, 1500, P: 381(33)
Vincent, C. E.: *ref*, 1121
Vincent, D. F.: *test*, 4:769; *ref*,

384, 388, 390, 2247–8, 2254, 2345
Vincent, J.: *ref*, 1121, 1370, 1383, 1415
Vincent, J. W.: *ref*, 1073, 2355, 7: 1090(7)
Vincent, L.: *ref*, 361, 5:308(439)
Vincent, L. E.: *test*, 3:226
Vincent, M. J. P.: *ref*, 1121, 1370, 1383, 1415
Vincent, M. O.: *ref*, 1218, 1275, 1281, 1380
Vincent, M. S.: *ref*, 1499
Vincent, N. L.: *ref*, 480
Vincent, N. M.: *ref*, 425, 2199
Vincent, N. M. P.: *ref*, 1281
Vincent, V.: *ref*, 1303
Vincent, W. J.: *ref*, 1074
Vineberg, S. E.: *ref*, 1281, 1363
Vines, R. H.: *ref*, 1391
Vinette, R.: *rev*, 3:182, 3:188
Viney, L. L.: *ref*, 1121, 1195, 1291, 1383
Vineyard, E. E.: *ref*, 69, 157, 997, 1069, 1164, 1207, 1519, 1572, 6: 438(488)
Vingoe, F. J.: *ref*, 489, 538, 1121, 1174, 1389
Vinitsky, M. H.: *ref*, 2212
Vinoda, K. S.: *ref*, 403, 1218, 1224, 1410, 1447
Vinson, D. B.: *ref*, 504, 1275, 1499, 1513
Vinson, L.: *test*, 5:389
Vinsonhaler, J. F.: *ref*, 358, 2212, 7:1090(10)
Vint, V. H.: *ref*, 561, 572, 1437, 1463
Vinter, R. D.: *test*, 1347
Vinton, K. W.: *ref*, 1819, 4:618(1)
Vinton, P. W.: *ref*, 2337
Virene, E. P.: *ref*, 357
Virgil, *Sister*: *ref*, 218
Virmani, V.: *ref*, 529
Virtue, C. F. S.: *ref*, 4:45(5, 9)
Visotsky, H. M.: *ref*, 1281, 1499, P:41(1)
Vistica, N. J.: *ref*, 532
Viswanathan, K.: *ref*, 2194
Vitale, J.: *ref*, 1499
Vitale, J. H.: *ref*, 529, 543, 592, 1192, 1277, 1281, 1447
Vitanza, A. A.: *ref*, 1447
Viteles, M. S.: *rev*, 2227–9, 2469; *ref*, 211, 1222, 2259, 2266, 3:220 (28), 3:679(7), 6:480(19)
Vitola, B. M.: *ref*, 1281
Vittenson, L. K.: *ref*, 1289
Vitz, P. C.: *ref*, 1121, 1281
Vivers, B. B.: *ref*, 469, 1403
Voas, R. B.: *ref*, 1207, 1281, 2195
Voas, W. H.: *test*, 36:618; 36:817
Vocational Guidance Centre: *test*, 3:447, 4:470, 4:735, 4:767–8
Vocolo, J. M.: *ref*, 256
Vodacek, J.: *ref*, 1176
Vodde, T.: *ref*, 1519
Vodde, T. W.: *ref*, 1281
Voelker, C. H.: *ref*, 3:475(9)
Voelker, P. H.: *test*, 370, 782, 1068, 2244, 2397
Vogel, B.: *ref*, 1164
Vogel, B. S.: *ref*, 2212
Vogel, F. X.: *ref*, 381, 1481
Vogel, J. L.: *ref*, 1281, 1519

Vogel, L.: *ref*, 1293
Vogel, M. D.: *ref*, 1275
Vogel, M. J.: *ref*, 1215
Vogel, R. B.: *ref*, 1164, 1281
Vogel, W.: *ref*, 1281
Vogelsang, M. P.: *ref*, 533
Voggenthaler, A. L.: *ref*, 439
Vogler, J. D.: *ref*, 517
Vogler, R. E.: *ref*, 543, 1281, 1478
Vogler, W. H.: *test*, 1695
Vohs, A. P.: *ref*, 358
Voight, W. H.: *ref*, 1164, 1499, 1508
Vojtisek, J. E.: *ref*, 1169
Vokas, C. S.: *ref*, 209
Volberding, E.: *ref*, 1123, P:294 (11)
Voldseth, E. V.: *ref*, 1281
Volk, D.: *ref*, 1932
Volkin, L. A.: *ref*, 1072
Volkman, A. P.: *ref*, 1281
Volksdorf, N. R.: *ref*, 1291, 1383
Volle, F. O.: *exc*, 533
Vollmar, J.: *ref*, 1281
Volsky, T. C.: *ref*, 1480
Vonachen, H. A.: *ref*, 1144, 1146
Von Arnold, B.: *ref*, 1499
Von Bulow, H.: *ref*, 1428
von der Lippe, R. P.: *ref*, 1094
Vondracek, F. W.: *ref*, 1281
Von Drach, R. B.: *ref*, 7
von Felsinger, J. M.: *ref*, 1499
von Holt, H. W.: *ref*, 1140, 1499, 1519
Von Lackum, W. J.: *ref*, 1499
von Singer, R.: *ref*, 1094
Von Wittich, B.: *ref*, 223, 425, 1044
Voor, J. J.: *ref*, 1427
Voorhees, S. F.: *ref*, 492
Voors, A. W.: *ref*, 1281
Voots, R. J.: *ref*, 2038
Vopatek, S. H.: *ref*, 2195, 2267
Vordenberg, W.: *ref*, 69, 4:738(1)
Vorhaus, P. G.: *ref*, 532, 1499, 1519
Vormeland, O.: *ref*, 381, 1447
Vorreyer, W. J.: *ref*, 419, 1095
Vorwaller, D. J.: *test*, 1347
Voss, B.: *ref*, 1805
Voss, C. E.: *ref*, 349, 5:326(27)
Voss, D. H.: *ref*, 1394–5
Voss, J. R. H.: *ref*, 1121
Voss, M. D.: *ref*, 2:1325(8)
Votaw, D. F.: *test*, 15, 17, 35:165, 3:457, 4:632, 6:603, 6:710, 6: 849; *ref*, 15, 17, 69, 404, 1583, 2: 1492(11), 3:217(137–8), 4:586 (1)
Voth, H. M.: *ref*, 1169, 1499
Vraa, C. W.: *ref*, 1044, 1176
Vrana, M.: *ref*, 1499
Vreeland, F. M.: *ref*, 1386
Vroegh, K.: *ref*, 381, 1129, 1163, 1253, 1474
Vroman, C.: *ref*, 238, 357, 364
Vroom, A. L.: *ref*, 1448
Vroom, A. L. W.: *ref*, 1448
Vrooman, T. H.: *ref*, 2451
Vuorinen, V.: *ref*, P:496(11)

WAAG, W. L.: *ref*, 1121, 1275, 1291, 1322, 1383
Waage, L.: *ref*, 840
Wachs, H.: *ref*, 1481
Wachs, S. R.: *ref*, 1856

48, 69, 404, 529, 1583, 2212, 2239, 2251, 2266, 2355, 4:277(223, 257, 273-4)
Wallach, E. S.: *ref,* 516, 1921
Wallach, M. A.: *ref,* 35, 357, 361, 533, 589, 1164, 1245, 1275, 1281
Wallach, M. S.: *ref,* 1281
Wallar, G. A.: *ref,* 2212
Wallbrown, F. H.: *ref,* 533
Wallen, N. E.: *rev,* 391, 1302; *ref,* 359, 404, 589, 902, 1281, 1500
Wallen, R.: *ref,* 1499, 1516, 2195
Wallen, R. W.: *ref,* 1499, 1519
Wallen, V.: *ref,* 1499
Waller, G. A.: *test,* 2:1667; *ref,* 2:1667(1)
Waller, L. T.: *ref,* 1289
Waller, P. F.: *ref,* 1499
Waller, R. C.: *ref,* 1169, 1192
Waller, R. E.: *ref,* 1174, 1225
Wallihan, R. S.: *ref,* 398, 435
Wallin, J. E. W.: *ref,* 483, 525, 1690
Wallin, K.: *ref,* 487
Wallin, P.: *ref,* 826, 6:519(62)
Wallmark, M.: *ref,* 255-6, 271-2, 286, 314-5
Wallmark, M. M.: *ref,* 1053
Wallner, C. A.: *ref,* 1073
Wallner, J. M.: *ref,* 1499
Wallon, E. J.: *ref,* 1481, 1500
Walnut, F.: *ref,* 1281
Walraven, M. P.: *ref,* 1447
Walsh, A. K.: *test,* 35:185
Walsh, D. D.: *ref,* 305
Walsh, E. P.: *ref,* 1430
Walsh, J.: *ref,* 528-9, 1281, 1403, 1501
Walsh, J. A.: *rev,* 1152; *ref,* 1121, 1275, 1281, 2212
Walsh, J. E.: *ref,* 1225
Walsh, J. F.: *ref,* 528, 1921
Walsh, J. J.: *ref,* 382
Walsh, J. M.: *test,* 35:185, 35:216
Walsh, M. A.: *ref,* 532
Walsh, N. E.: *ref,* 349
Walsh, R.: *ref,* 499, 507
Walsh, R. P.: *ref,* 1164, 1264, 1430
Walsh, T. M.: *ref,* 1183, 1192, 1281
Walsh, W. B.: *rev,* 2194; *exc,* 1394-5; *ref,* 1094, 1121, 1133, 1164, 1289, 1430
Walshaw, J. B.: *ref,* 403
Walsmith, C. R.: *ref,* 1207, 1403, P:339(19)
Walster, E.: *ref,* 1280-1
Walston, A.: *test,* 35:35, 35:262
Walston, R. L.: *test,* 2:1184, 3:141
Walsworth, B. M.: *ref,* 1313, 1320, 1499
Walter, C. J. S.: *ref,* 1275
Walter, D.: *ref,* 1501
Walter, H.: *ref,* 1921
Walter, H. J.: *test,* 932
Walter, J. E.: *ref,* 881, 1403
Walter, J. I.: *ref,* 1294, 1383
Walter, L.: *ref,* 2195
Walter, L. J.: *test,* 1903
Walter, P. B.: *ref,* 1281
Walter, R. J.: *ref,* 913
Walter, R. W.: *test,* 5:234
Walter, S.: *ref,* 1121, 1280
Walter, V. A.: *ref,* 1501
Walters, A.: *ref,* 4:45(2, 5, 10)
Walters, A. W.: *ref,* 1044

Walters, C. A.: *ref,* 1499
Walters, C. E.: *ref,* 497, 1277
Walters, F. C.: *ref,* 36, 525
Walters, J.: *ref,* 5:87(27)
Walters, J. E.: *exc,* 1366
Walters, N. R.: *ref,* 69, 357
Walters, R. H.: *exc,* 1281; *ref,* 532, 1087, 1275, 1281, 1499
Walters, S. M.: *ref,* 1281
Walters, W. M.: *ref,* 1281
Walthall, N.: *ref,* 1289
Walther, E. C.: *test,* 2:1261, 3:602
Walther, R.: *test,* 1250
Walther, R. H.: *ref,* 1250
Walthew, J. K.: *ref,* 868
Waltmann, R. H.: *ref,* 1281, 1283
Waltner, S. K.: *ref,* 1403
Walton, A. J.: *ref,* 1254
Walton, C. E.: *test,* 122
Walton, D.: *ref,* 439, 525, 592, 1275, 1281, 1451, 1499
Walton, D. F.: *ref,* P:339(17)
Walton, F. X.: *ref,* 1121, 1775
Walton, H. F.: *ref,* 1275, 1302
Walton, H. J.: *ref,* 1218, 1275, 1302, 1383, 1410
Walton, H. N.: *ref,* 1918
Walton, J. M.: *ref,* 589, 1164, 1294
Walton, M. S.: *ref,* 2251
Walton, R. D.: *test,* 4:424
Walton, R. E.: *test,* 5:102, 5:150; *ref,* 5:150(1-2, 4), P:455(8)
Walton, W. E.: *ref,* 1320
Waltz, M. F.: *ref,* 1856
Wamba, D. E.: *ref,* 439
Wambach, H.: *ref,* 1306
Wambach, H. S.: *ref,* 1499
Wampler, J. F.: *ref,* 50, 561
Wanderer, Z. W.: *ref,* 1474, 1481
Wandt, E.: *rev,* 869, 4:796, 4:804
Wandzek, F. P.: *ref,* 2178
Wang, C.: *ref,* 381, 1481
Wang, C. K. A.: *test,* 1:927; *ref,* 1090, 1386, P:378(1)
Wang, F. Y.: *ref,* 439
Wang, H. A.: *ref,* 529
Wang, H. S.: *ref,* 529
Wang, M.: *ref,* 1519
Wang, R. P.: *ref,* 1499
Wanger, R. S.: *ref,* 1044, 1073
Wann, H. V.: *test,* 1:987-8
Wannemacher, J. T.: *ref,* 2059
Wanner, P. W.: *ref,* 1481
Wanser, B. R.: *ref,* 1207
Wantman, M. J.: *rev,* 99, 1552, 1759, 1944, 2355, 5:837, 5:841; *ref,* 786
Waples, D.: *test,* 2:1294
Wapner, I.: *ref,* 533
Wapner, S.: *ref,* 529, 1169, 1474, 1481, 1499, 1519
War Manpower Commission, Division of Occupational Analysis, Staff: *ref,* 173, 1073, 2227, 2258, 2266
Warburton, F. W.: *rev,* 373, 475, 2282, 5:325; *ref,* 439, 525, 1383, 1403, 2195
Warburton, J. W.: *ref,* 1105
Warburton, M. A.: *ref,* 1094, 1121
Ward, A. J.: *ref,* 1499
Ward, A. W.: *ref,* 399, 5:326(12)
Ward, B.: *ref,* 1145
Ward, B. J.: *ref,* 533, 1716

Ward, C. A.: *ref,* 1253
Ward, C. F.: *rev,* 2415, 2442, 7:1136
Ward, D. B.: *ref,* 1275, 1281
Ward, D. J.: *ref,* 1275
Ward, D. V.: *ref,* 404
Ward, G.: *ref,* 69, 361, 365, 400, 1044, 1164, 1183, 1281, 1293, 2195, 2454
Ward, G. R.: *ref,* 6:1062(6)
Ward, J.: *ref,* 35, 361, 533, 981, 1281, 1383, 1921
Ward, J. E.: *ref,* 914
Ward, J. H.: *ref,* 404, 532
Ward, J. L.: *ref,* 1215
Ward, L. B.: *ref,* 1320, 2323
Ward, L. C.: *ref,* 1519
Ward, L. R.: *ref,* 1626
Ward, L. W.: *ref,* 1320, 2212
Ward, M. P.: *ref,* 516, 522, 1447
Ward, P.: *ref,* 868
Ward, P. L.: *ref,* 1164, 1256, 1403
Ward, R. S.: *ref,* 2135, 2227-9, 2251, 2258, 2266
Ward, W. C.: *rev,* 2273; *ref,* 516
Ward, W. D.: *ref,* 529, 840, 881, 1164, 5:308(339)
Ward, W. J.: *ref,* 1447
Ward, W. P.: *ref,* 2212
Warde, S.: *ref,* 1191
Warden, P. G.: *ref,* 981
Warder, J.: *ref,* 403, 439, 1218, 1410
Wardeska, B. C.: *ref,* 574, 1164
Wardlaw, H. P.: *ref,* 48
Wardlow, M. E.: *ref,* 1256, 1289, 1361, 1366, P:346(13)
Ware, F. E.: *ref,* 5:630(3), 5:632(8)
Ware, G. C.: *test,* 2:1590
Ware, J. G.: *ref,* 1281
Ware, K. E.: *ref,* 1499
Ware, R.: *ref,* 1521
Ware, W. B.: *ref,* 516
Warfel, C. I.: *ref,* 1475
Wargo, D. G.: *ref,* 1280-1
Warhapdande, N. R.: *ref,* 545
Warheit, G. J.: *ref,* 1225
Warhime, R. G.: *ref,* 1315
Warinner, E. M.: *ref,* 525, 533
Wark, D. M.: *rev,* 1671; *ref,* 1281
Warkentin, J.: *ref,* 1101
Warkov, S.: *ref,* 2349
Warman, R. E.: *ref,* 1073, 1101, 1281, 1474, 2212
Warnath, C. F.: *rev,* 6:1049, 6:1068
Warne, E.: *ref,* 1407
Warne, E. K.: *ref,* 1194, 1407
Warner, B. E.: *ref,* 6:141(6)
Warner, F. L.: *ref,* 1516
Warner, J. K.: *ref,* 2084
Warner, N.: *ref,* 1144
Warner, R. W.: *ref,* 1134, 1394-5, 1415
Warner, S.: *test,* 1725
Warner, S. B.: *test,* 89, 1642
Warner, S. J.: *ref,* 532, 1499
Warner, W. L.: *ref,* 1519
Warr, C. F.: *ref,* 1930
Warr, P. B.: *ref,* 1094, 1174, 1363
Warren, A. B.: *ref,* 1281
Warren, E. C.: *ref,* 4:277(150)
Warren, J.: *test,* 895

5:7(32), 5:308(340, 414), 5:887
(4)
Webb, W. B.: *ref,* 425, 532, 1500,
1519, 1901
Webb, W. D.: *ref,* 1289
Webb, W. W.: *test,* 979; *ref,* 979
Webber, V. L.: *ref,* 6:438(455)
Webberley, M.: *ref,* 323, 364, 559,
561, 564, 1069, 1383, 1403
Weber, C. O.: *ref,* 244, 357, 1048,
1090, 1480, 1837, 1859, 1939, 4:
277(169)
Weber, D. S.: *ref,* 425
Weber, E. G.: *ref,* 425, 3:217(129)
Weber, G. H.: *ref,* 532, 1499, 1519,
5:166(6)
Weber, J. C.: *ref,* 1383
Weber, J. R.: *ref,* 1281
Weber, L. A.: *ref,* 361, 1044
Weber, L. C.: *ref,* 1499
Weber, L. E.: *ref,* 425
Weber, M. A.: *ref,* 981, 1895
Weber, R. G.: *ref,* 1164, 1403, 2451
Weber, R. J.: *ref,* 1281
Weber, T. R.: *ref,* 1073
Weber, W. A.: *ref,* 589
Webersinn, A. L.: *ref,* 1164, 1474
Webster, A. C.: *ref,* 1143, 1164,
1315, 1383
Webster, A. S.: *ref,* 1281
Webster, B. S.: *ref,* 202
Webster, E. C.: *ref,* 404, 2195, 2212
Webster, H.: *rev,* 1303, 1370, 5:91;
test, 1302, 1393; *ref,* 1121, 1281,
1302, 1519, P:384(13)
Webster, H. D.: *ref,* 1519
Webster, J. C.: *ref,* 2046
Webster, J. D.: *ref,* 1363
Webster, R. B.: *ref,* 1469, P:341
(35)
Webster, R. L.: *ref,* 1499
Webster, S. W.: *ref,* 1176
Webster, W. J.: *rev,* 1988, 7:917
Wechsberg, F. O.: *ref,* 1144, 1500
Wechsler, D.: *rev,* 403, 439, 447,
3:228; *test,* 529, 532-3, 538, 592,
1144, 1146; *exc,* 1499, 6:B343;
ref, 525, 529, 532-3, 545, 556, 563,
592, 1144, 1146, 3:220(42)
Wechsler, I. R.: *ref,* 482
Wechsler, R. R.: *ref,* 1499, 1519
Weckowicz, T. E.: *ref,* 547, 1192,
1275, 1281, 1379
Weddell, J. M.: *ref,* 1883
Weddington, R. T.: *exc,* 5:B140
Wedell, K.: *ref,* 495, 1447
Wedemeyer, B.: *ref,* 1499
Weede, G. D.: *ref,* 1395
Weedon, V.: *test,* 35:174
Weeks, A.: *test,* 676
Weeks, A. L.: *ref,* 525
Weeks, E. E.: *ref,* 1717
Weeks, J. S.: *ref,* 361, 6:438(476)
Weeks, L. E.: *ref,* 1264
Weeks, L. V.: *test,* 3:558
Weeks, R. W.: *ref,* 516
Weeks, W. R.: *ref,* 1069
Weems, L. B.: *ref,* 1519
Weener, P.: *ref,* 981
Wegelius, C.: *ref,* 936
Wegener, J. I.: *test,* 2360
Wegman, M.: *ref,* 447, 525
Wegner, K. W.: *ref,* 1164, 2212-3
Wehmer, G. M.: *ref,* 1281

Weiant, E. A.: *ref,* 1383
Weible, E.: *test,* 1776
Weick, D. V.: *ref,* 1281
Weick, K.: *ref,* 1176, 1306
Weick, L. K.: *ref,* 1164
Weick, R. K.: *ref,* 1403
Weide, M.: *ref,* 1217, 1499
Weidemann, C. C.: *rev,* 751, 755,
1:993, 2:1470; *ref,* 2:1499(1)
Weider, A.: *test,* 1144, 1446; *ref,*
482, 525, 532-3, 592, 1144, 1146,
1474, 2239
Weider, N.: *ref,* 1144, 1146
Weidman, A. H.: *ref,* 36
Weidner, B. V.: *test,* 3:563
Weidner, W. E.: *test,* 2099; *ref,*
2069
Weigel, R.: *ref,* 1031, 1035, 2212
Weigel, R. G.: *test,* 857; *ref,* 857,
1031, 1035, 1164, 1281, 1772, 2212
Weigel, V. M.: *ref,* 1164, 1772
Weigl, E.: *ref,* 1192
Weijola, M. J.: *ref,* 1044, 1121
Weikart, D. P.: *rev,* 1691, 1718;
ref, 19, 349
Weiking, M. L.: *ref,* 1289
Weil, A. A.: *ref,* 1499
Weil, F. S.: *exc,* 1499
Weil, G.: *ref,* 1121, 1281
Weil, G. R.: *test,* 1517; *ref,* 1517
Weil, M. C.: *ref,* 1877
Weil, P. G.: *ref,* 1420
Weil, W. B.: *ref,* 525
Weiland, E. J.: *ref,* 1123
Weimer, L. B.: *ref,* 1361
Weinbaum, L.: *ref,* 1281
Weinberg, G. H.: *ref,* 1499
Weinberg, H.: *ref,* 529
Weinberg, J.: *ref,* 1447
Weinberg, J. R.: *ref,* 1370
Weinberg, N.: *ref,* 1121, 1240
Weinberg, N. H.: *ref,* 1192, 1499
Weinberg, R. M.: *ref,* 1499
Weinberg, R. S.: *ref,* 533
Weinberg, S.: *ref,* 533
Weinberg, S. L.: *ref,* 1281
Weinberg, W. L.: *ref,* 1500
Weiner, A. S.: *ref,* 1253
Weiner, G.: *test,* 940
Weiner, H.: *ref,* 532, 1145, 1447-8,
1481, 1499, 1519
Weiner, I. B.: *ref,* 529, 1474, 1499-
500
Weiner, I. W.: *ref,* 1281
Weiner, L.: *ref,* 1499
Weiner, L. H.: *ref,* 36
Weiner, M.: *ref,* 22, 36, 391, 425,
655, 1048, 1073, 1602
Weiner, P. S.: *ref,* 439, 505, 516,
533, 981, 1428, 1447, 2028, 2098
Weiner, S.: *ref,* 1225, 1293, 1499
Weinert, J. R.: *ref,* 2212
Weingarten, G.: *ref,* 439
Weingarten, K. P.: *test,* 2205; *ref,*
2205
Weingarten, L. L.: *ref,* 1448
Weingold, H. P.: *ref,* 1377, 1380,
1499
Weinhold, C. E.: *ref,* 48
Weinhouse, I.: *ref,* 2031, 2053
Weinick, G. D.: *ref,* 1164
Weinik, H. M.: *ref,* 341A
Weinland, J. D.: *ref,* 1901
Weinlander, A. A.: *ref,* 1513

Weinlander, M. M.: *ref,* 525, 1513
Weinreb, A. C.: *ref,* 1225, 1295
Weinstein, A. D.: *ref,* 1500
Weinstein, A. S.: *ref,* 2383, 2385
Weinstein, B.: *ref,* 525, 1281, 1293,
1339-40, 1398
Weinstein, E. A.: *ref,* 1499
Weinstein, F. T.: *ref,* 1174
Weinstein, G. J.: *ref,* 1337
Weinstein, J.: *ref,* 1121, 1281
Weinstein, M.: *ref,* 1516
Weinstein, M. R: *ref,* 503, 592,
1281, 1447, 1481, 1499
Weinstein, M. S.: *ref,* 1121, 1164
Weinstein, P.: *ref,* 1391, 1430
Weinstein, S.: *ref,* 342, 578, 1447,
1474
Weinstock, C.: *ref,* 529
Weinstock, C. S.: *ref,* 529, 1278
Weinstock, H. I.: *ref,* 1144
Weinstock, H. R.: *ref,* 868
Weinthaler, J.: *ref,* 981
Weintraub, R. G.: *ref,* 3:217(130),
4:277(217)
Weintraub, S.: *ref,* 489, 589, 1923,
2028
Weintraub, S. A.: *rev,* 1127, 1249
Weintraub, W.: *ref,* 1281
Weir, A. J.: *ref,* 1499, 5:127(7)
Weir, C. E.: *ref,* 1095
Weir, J. R.: *ref,* 2212
Weir, M. W.: *ref,* 381
Weir, W.: *ref,* 1315
Weir, W. R.: *ref,* 1315
Weis, S. F.: *ref,* 1315, 2195
Weisberg, M.: *ref,* 1394-5
Weisberger, S. E.: *ref,* 1519, 1898
Weisbrod, K. C.: *ref,* 1336
Weisbrodt, J. A.: *test,* 881; *ref,*
1361
Weise, C. C.: *ref,* 1377
Weise, I. B.: *ref,* 2212
Weise, P.: *ref,* 525, 533, 1087, 2212
Weisenburg, T.: *ref,* 36, 381, 518,
525, 655, 1690
Weiser, J. C.: *ref,* 589, 868, 1094,
2178
Weiser, M. G.: *ref,* 1716
Weisgerber, C.: *ref,* 1028
Weisgerber, C. A.: *ref,* 138, 361,
525, 532-3, 1281, 1403
Weisman, F.: *ref,* 525
Weisman, L. L.: *ref,* 3:535(11),
4:581(15), 4:606(3)
Weisman, S.: *ref,* 1281
Weisman, S. E.: *ref,* 525
Weismar, R.: *ref,* 492
Weiss, A.: *ref,* 1499
Weiss, A. A.: *ref,* 1169, 1192, 1447,
1499
Weiss, A. D.: *ref,* 529
Weiss, A. J.: *ref,* 1095, 1320
Weiss, B. A.: *ref,* 1499
Weiss, D. J.: *test,* 2283-5; *ref,* 561,
1071, 1073, 1281, 2197, 2212,
2283-5
Weiss, G.: *ref,* 1500
Weiss, I.: *ref,* 48, 2337, 5:308(308),
5:887(1)
Weiss, J.: *ref,* 529, 533, 1499
Weiss, J. H.: *ref,* 1499
Weiss, J. L.: *ref,* 1448
Weiss, K. P.: *ref,* 357
Weiss, L.: *ref,* 1090, 1499

West, K. L.: *ref,* 1281
West, L. J.: *rev,* 2164, 7:559A; *ref,* 1281
West, L. L.: *ref,* 1281
West, L. W.: *ref,* 348, 400, 439, 453
West, P. C.: *ref,* 381
West, P. M.: *ref,* 1281
West, P. V.: *test,* 6:712; *ref,* 908, 1569
West, R. L.: *ref,* 6:480(12)
West, R. R.: *ref,* 2325
Westberg, W. C.: *ref,* 482, 1206, 2151, 2195, 2239
Westbrook, B.: *test,* 2100
Westbrook, B. W.: *rev,* 2182, 2197; *ref,* 391, 1033, 1775, 7:378(7)
Westbrook, C. H.: *exc,* 532
Westbrook, J. W.: *ref,* 1348
Westby, G.: *rev,* 388, 439, 1486, 4:313, 6:227-8
Westcott, M. R.: *ref,* 357
Westerhold, R.: *ref,* 532
Western, J. S.: *test,* 1399; *ref,* 1399
Western Electric Co.: *test,* 3:475
Western Psychological Services: *test,* 1446, 1447g, 2468
Western Reserve University, Psychological Research Services: *test,* T:1983
Westfall, H. R.: *ref,* 884
Westfall, R.: *ref,* 1423
Westie, C. M.: *test,* 1200; *ref,* 1200
Westlake, E. J.: *ref,* 1395
Westler, L.: *ref,* 1356
Westmoreland, L.: *ref,* 2195
Weston, D. L.: *ref,* 1499
Weston, L. D.: *ref,* 400, 1087
Westover, F. L.: *rev,* 1609
Westover, H. T.: *ref,* 48
Westphal, G.: *ref,* 1901
Westphal, J. H.: *ref,* 32
Westphal, M. E.: *ref,* 19, 211, 391, 400
Westrope, M. R.: *ref,* 1499
Westwood, D.: *ref,* 1073, 1471, 1499
Wetherell, J.: *ref,* 981
Wetherell, R. H.: *ref,* 349, 1536, 1918
Wetherhorn, M.: *ref,* 1499
Wetherick, N. E.: *ref,* 439
Wetsel, H.: *ref,* 1470
Wetterberg, L.: *ref,* 1275
Wetzel, K. H.: *ref,* 1447
Wetzel, N. C.: *test,* 947; *ref,* 947
Wetzel, R. J.: *ref,* 1499
Wevrick, L.: *ref,* 482, 1386, 1775
Wexberg, E.: *ref,* 525, 1192
Wexler, A. H.: *ref,* 357
Wexler, M.: *ref,* 532, 1474, 1499
Wexler, N.: *ref,* 404, 1480
Wexler, R. M.: *ref,* 1481, 1499
Wexner, L. B.: *ref,* 1281
Weybrew, B. B.: *ref,* 1164, 1403
Weychert, M. C.: *ref,* 981
Weymouth, F. W.: *ref,* 1918
Weynand, R. S.: *ref,* 2195
Whalen, E. M.: *ref,* 1377
Whaley, D.: *ref,* 1277
Whaley, E. R.: *ref,* 69, 6:438(517)
Wharry, R. E.: *ref,* 989, 1883
Wharton, L.: *test,* 1:1018, 3:598
Wharton, L. H.: *ref,* 543, 1481
Wharton, L. P.: *test,* 2:1321

Wharton, M. C.: *ref,* 1240
Wharton, M. H.: *ref,* 914
Wharton, W. L.: *ref,* 1281
Wharton, W. P.: *ref,* 1303
Whatley, A. A.: *ref,* 1415
Whatley, C. E.: *ref,* 1877
Whatley, R. G.: *ref,* 533
Wheat, H. G.: *rev,* 603, 637
Wheat, L. B.: *test,* 1:1120
Wheatley, L. A.: *ref,* 1320, 1403
Wheatley, M. M.: *ref,* 532, 1087
Wheaton, C. H.: *ref,* 1519
Wheeler, D. K.: *rev,* 1685, 5:222, 5:617; *ref,* 1164, 1583, 6:782(1)
Wheeler, E. T.: *ref,* 532, 1281, 1380, 1499, 1519
Wheeler, F.: *ref,* 113
Wheeler, G. R.: *test,* 1:1124; *ref,* 529
Wheeler, H. E.: *ref,* 1519
Wheeler, J. A.: *ref,* 503
Wheeler, J. E.: *ref,* 1044
Wheeler, J. I.: *ref,* 381, 532, 1499, 1519
Wheeler, L.: *ref,* 529, 1164, 1281, 1391, 1471, 2076
Wheeler, L. R.: *ref,* 201, 211, 1560, 4:277(224-5, 275)
Wheeler, M. D.: *ref,* 1499
Wheeler, M. F.: *ref,* 1193-4
Wheeler, N. C.: *ref,* 1281
Wheeler, R. G.: *ref,* 357
Wheeler, R. W.: *ref,* 469, 1194
Wheeler, V. D.: *ref,* 201, 211, 1560, 4:277(225, 275)
Wheeler, W. M.: *ref,* 532, 1281, 1451, 1499
Whelan, R. F.: *ref,* 929
Whellams, F. S.: *ref,* 217
Wherry, R. J.: *ref,* 1281, 1906, 1918, 1923, 2212, 2452, 2457, 5:905(3, 7)
Whetstone, B. D.: *ref,* 1407, 1500
Whetstone, R. D.: *ref,* 357
Whigham, B. R.: *ref,* 1407
Whigham, N.: *ref,* 1772
Whinery, S. M.: *ref,* 419
Whipkey, K. L.: *ref,* 622, 1044
Whipple, B.: *ref,* 1519
Whipple, C. I.: *ref,* 489, 516, 1447
Whipple, C. M.: *ref,* 1499
Whipple, G. M.: *test,* 3:507; *ref,* 1480, 1901
Whisenton, J. T.: *ref,* 1394
Whiskin, F. E.: *ref,* 1145, 1281
Whisler, L.: *test,* 1348; *ref,* 1348, 2:1243(25)
Whisler, L. D.: *test,* 2292; *ref,* 1091, 1348
Whisler, R. H.: *ref,* 1281
Whistler, H. S.: *test,* 6:352; *ref,* 6:352(1)
Whitacre, R. L.: *ref,* 524-5
Whitaker, L.: *ref,* 1471, 1481, 1499
Whitaker, L. C.: *test,* 1440
Whitcomb, C. E.: *ref,* 1207
Whitcomb, M. A.: *ref,* 525, 532, 1428, 6:669(52)
Whitcraft, C. J.: *ref,* 981, 1716
Whitcraft, J. E.: *test,* 3:387
Whitcraft, L. H.: *ref,* 1048
White, A.: *ref,* 194
White, A. A.: *ref,* 1281
White, A. J.: *ref,* 361, 533, 1072

White, A. W.: *ref,* 1395
White, B. A.: *ref,* 1370
White, B. J.: *ref,* 589, 1142, 1521, 2213
White, B. O.: *ref,* 1370
White, C.: *test,* 5:518; *ref,* 1145, 1281
White, C. A.: *ref,* 1281
White, C. W.: *ref,* 1690
White, D. K.: *ref,* 1123
White, D. S.: *test,* 4:258
White, D. T.: *ref,* 496, 525
White, E. B.: *ref,* 1281
White, E. E.: *ref,* 532, 592
White, E. L.: *ref,* 1053
White, G.: *ref,* 381, 525
White, G. R.: *ref,* 2212
White, G. W.: *ref,* 382, 681
White, H. G.: *ref,* 1087, 2195
White, H. I.: *ref,* 1911
White, H. M.: *ref,* 1293, 1315
White, H. R.: *rev,* 1447
White, H. W.: *ref,* 1121, 1164, 1407
White, I. W.: *ref,* 1087
White, J.: *ref,* 1403, 1521
White, J. A.: *ref,* 981, 1121
White, J. C.: *ref,* 7, 525, 1205
White, J. G.: *test,* 834, 2311; *exc,* 1473; *ref,* 529, 1224, 1275, 1277
White, J. H.: *ref,* 1044, 1174
White, J. L.: *ref,* 1448
White, J. M.: *ref,* 868, 1499
White, K.: *ref,* 542, 551, 1383, 1415
White, K. D.: *ref,* 1174, 1383
White, L.: *ref,* 1298
White, L. A.: *ref,* 525, 533, 538
White, L. E.: *ref,* 542, 574
White, M.: *ref,* 1205-6, 1245
White, M. A.: *ref,* 1499, 1519
White, M. F.: *ref,* 1249
White, M. F. R.: *ref,* 381
White, M. L.: *ref,* 525
White, M. R.: *ref,* 1094, 1281
White, M. S.: *ref,* 1924, 4:661(10)
White, N.: *test,* 1:1031
White, P.: *test,* 3:50
White, P. D.: *ref,* 1101
White, P. O.: *ref,* 1174, 1205-6, 1245, 1383, 1478
White, P. T.: *ref,* 532
White, R.: *ref,* 1225, 7:55(19)
White, R. A. M.: *ref,* 1135, 1403
White, R. C.: *exc,* 1:983
White, R. E.: *ref,* 1395
White, R. K.: *ref,* 1480, 1482, 1499, 1519, 2452
White, R. M.: *ref,* 1280, 2195
White, R. R.: *ref,* 525
White, T. R.: *ref,* 868, 1403
White, V.: *exc,* 11; *ref,* 3:130(1-4)
White, W. C.: *ref,* 1281, 1500
White, W. F.: *ref,* 221, 349, 505, 522, 529, 561, 572, 591, 1192, 1253, 1277, 1291, 1383, 1403, 1415, 1447, 1499, 1546
White, W. J.: *ref,* 1474, 1481
Whitehill, R. P.: *ref,* 1174
Whitehorn, J. C.: *ref,* 2212
Whitehouse, D.: *ref,* 533
Whitehouse, E.: *ref,* 1519
Whiteley, D. P.: *ref,* 1091, 1256
Whiteley, G. C.: *test,* 1835

Whiteley, J. M.: *ref,* 382, 404, 1499, 1519
Whitelock, P. R.: *ref,* 1281
Whitely, P. L.: *ref,* 1090, 1403
Whiteman, D. B.: *ref,* 532, 1499
Whiteman, G. L.: *ref,* 1474
Whiteman, M.: *ref,* 532
Whiteman, P. H.: *ref,* 1516
Whiteman, S. L.: *ref,* 1500
Whiteside, O. R.: *ref,* 6:438(514)
Whitford, T. M.: *test,* 163, 2118, 2238
Whiting, H. T. A.: *ref,* 1191, 1296, 1904
Whiting, J. F.: *ref,* 1469, 1499, 1519
Whitinger, B. R.: *test,* 5:719
Whitla, D. K.: *rev,* 1048; *ref,* 357
Whitley, M. T.: *ref,* 202, 211
Whitlock, G. E.: *ref,* 1121, 2212
Whitlock, J. B.: *ref,* 1320, 2239
Whitman, A. D.: *ref,* 1048
Whitman, C. P.: *ref,* 1403
Whitman, D.: *ref,* 1499
Whitman, E. B.: *ref,* 1519
Whitman, E. C.: *ref,* 2046
Whitman, G. L.: *ref,* 1281, 1481
Whitman, J. R.: *ref,* 529, 1500
Whitman, M. A.: *ref,* 516
Whitman, R. M.: *ref,* 1195, 1499
Whitmer, C. A.: *rev,* 483, 2:1388, 3:243, 3:254, 3:256; *test,* 1694
Whitmore, E. L.: *ref,* 1281
Whitmore, H. L.: *ref,* 1176
Whitmore, L. C.: *ref,* 1403
Whitmyre, J. W.: *ref,* 529, 1387, 1474, 1516
Whitney, D. R.: *test,* 596; *ref,* 20, 596, 1044, 1430, 2212
Whitney, E.: *ref,* 1481
Whitney, G.: *ref,* 981, 1716, 1921
Whitney, V.: *ref,* 522
Whitsett, D. A.: *ref,* 1315
Whittaker, D.: *ref,* 1094, 1302, 1403, 2212
Whittaker, D. N. E.: *ref,* 1094, 1302, 1403, 2212–3
Whittaker, E. W.: *ref,* 1302
Whittaker, R. D.: *ref,* 1275
Whittaker, S.: *ref,* 1499
Whittemore, R. G.: *ref,* 348, 425, 447, 551, 574, 587, 1044, 1069, 1073, 1109, 1121, 1281, 1294, 1403, 1437, 1560, 2195, 2340
Whitten, C. F.: *ref,* 381, 525, 533
Whitten, L.: *ref,* 1253, 1415
Whittenbaugh, J.: *ref,* 1144
Whittenbaugh, J. A.: *ref,* 1281
Whittington, H. G.: *ref,* 1281
Whittington, R. W. T.: *ref,* 217
Whittlesey, J.: *ref,* 1921
Whittlesey, J. R. B.: *ref,* 1921
Whittlesey, R. B.: *test,* 1921
Whittlesey, R. R.: *ref,* 1430
Whittock, J. M.: *ref,* 2195, 2212
Whooley, J. P.: *ref,* 1281
Whorton, J. E.: *ref,* 1044
Whybrow, P. C.: *ref,* 518, 1281, 7:55(23)
Wiant, H. V.: *ref,* 1242, 1415
Wicas, E. A.: *ref,* 1513
Wich, R.: *ref,* 1519
Wichiarajote, N. K.: *ref,* 1253
Wichiarajote, P.: *ref,* 981, 1277
Wickersham, B.: *ref,* 935

Wickersham, F. M.: *ref,* 1144
Wickert, F.: *ref,* 1403, 3:653(7)
Wickert, F. R.: *ref,* 2448
Wickes, T. A.: *ref,* 1499
Wickham, M.: *ref,* 439
Wickham, W.: *ref,* 50, 533, 1447, 1887, 1902
Wickiser, R.: *ref,* 31
Wickman, E. K.: *test,* 2:1222; *ref,* 2:1222(2)
Wickramasekera, I.: *ref,* 1389
Wicks, J. H.: *ref,* 1207
Wicks, N.: *test,* 1:1022–3
Wickstrom, M. L.: *ref,* 529, 1519
Wickwire, P.: *ref,* 1253, 1772
Wickwire, P. J. N.: *ref,* 349, 381, 981, 1129
Widdop, J. H.: *ref,* 914
Wideen, M. F.: *ref,* 435
Wideman, H.: *ref,* 1499
Wideman, H. R.: *exc,* 1473; *ref,* 5:147(34–5, 47)
Widener, S. E.: *ref,* 404
Widlak, F. W.: *ref,* 529, 532–3
Widman, J. B.: *ref,* 533
Widmar, G. E.: *ref,* 1135
Wiechers, J. E.: *ref,* 439, 533
Wiedefeld, M. T.: *test,* 3:602
Wiedeman, J. S.: *ref,* 1499
Wieder, G. S.: *ref,* 1281
Wiederholt, J. L.: *ref,* 22, 1716, 1921
Wiegel, D. F.: *ref,* 48
Wiegerink, R.: *ref,* 981
Wiemann, C. B.: *ref,* 1164
Wiemer, M. J.: *ref,* 1281
Wiemers, I. H.: *ref,* 487, 497
Wiener, D. J.: *ref,* 1240
Wiener, D. N.: *ref,* 1281, 1380, 2195, 2448
Wiener, G.: *ref,* 50, 525, 529, 533, 940, 1447, 1499
Wiener, M.: *ref,* 202, 1164
Wiener, M. L.: *ref,* 1144
Wiener, W. K.: *ref,* 1176
Wiens, A. N.: *ref,* 529, 1145, 1164, 1281, 1380, 1499, 1519, 2212, P: 326(36)
Wientge, K. M.: *test,* 465; *ref,* 2212
Wiersma, W.: *ref,* 221, 357, 1123
Wierson, P. W.: *ref,* 1164
Wiersteiner, S. R.: *ref,* 1407
Wierzbinski, E. J.: *ref,* 1194
Wiese, H.: *ref,* 1133
Wiesen, L. E.: *ref,* 1281
Wiesenthal, D. L.: *ref,* 1094
Wiesner, C. W.: *ref,* 1176
Wiesner, E. F.: *ref,* 2195
Wig, N. N.: *ref,* 1275
Wigdor, B. T.: *ref,* 592, 1447, 1499
Wiggenhorn, A. H.: *ref,* 1481
Wiggett, R.: *ref,* 914
Wiggin, M. K.: *ref,* 487
Wiggins, C. A.: *ref,* 1225
Wiggins, G. E.: *ref,* 1121, 1281
Wiggins, J. G.: *test,* 835; *ref,* 532
Wiggins, J. S.: *rev,* 1322, 1480, 6:223; *ref,* 1094, 1121, 1164, 1281, 2212
Wiggins, N.: *ref,* 364, 382, 1005, 1071, 1164, 1281, 1303, 1437, 2266
Wiggins, N. A.: *ref,* 1240

Wiggins, N. W.: *ref,* 69, 532, 6:438(456)
Wiggins, P. Y.: *ref,* 529, 592, 1499, 1519
Wiggins, R. E.: *ref,* 2195
Wiggins, T. W.: *ref,* 1176, 1407
Wight, B.: *ref,* 1499
Wight, B. W.: *ref,* 496, 516, 533
Wightman, N.: *test,* 5:13
Wightwick, B.: *ref,* 426, 794, 2135, 2266
Wightwick, M. I.: *ref,* 2213
Wijesinghe, B.: *ref,* 1275, 1281
Wikler, A.: *ref,* 1499
Wikoff, R. L.: *ref,* 525, 1475
Wilborn, B. L.: *ref,* 868
Wilburn, R. G.: *ref,* 868, 1370
Wilcock, J. C.: *ref,* 439, 525
Wilcock, K. D.: *ref,* 1121, 1281
Wilcock, W. W.: *ref,* 1281
Wilcocks, A. M.: *test,* 1084, 7:1005
Wilcott, R. C.: *ref,* 518
Wilcox, A. H.: *ref,* 1121
Wilcox, E. T.: *ref,* 1045
Wilcox, G. M.: *ref,* 48
Wilcox, G. T.: *ref,* 1281
Wilcox, H. E.: *test,* 3:559; *exc,* 1829
Wilcox, K. W.: *rev,* 1469, 3:112; *ref,* 1447
Wilcox, L.: *ref,* 238, 357, 364
Wilcox, P. H.: *test,* 4:44; *ref,* 4:44(1)
Wilcox, R.: *ref,* 211, 1281
Wilcox, R. M.: *ref,* 1499
Wilcox, W. W.: *ref,* 1281
Wild, C.: *ref,* 1192, 1299
Wilde, G. J. S.: *ref,* 1499
Wilder, A. M.: *ref,* 1121
Wilder, D. H.: *ref,* 426
Wilder, J. F.: *ref,* 1339–40
Wilderson, F. B.: *exc,* 1336
Wildman, L. R.: *ref,* 1133, 1403
Wildman, R. W.: *ref,* 1164, 1469, 1474
Wile, D. B.: *ref,* 1447
Wile, I. S.: *exc,* 497, 525, 545, 1499; *ref,* 1428
Wile, M. Z.: *ref,* 1583
Wilensky, H.: *ref,* 529, 1499, 1519
Wiley, E. S.: *ref,* 796
Wiley, J. M.: *ref,* 1499
Wiley, L. N.: *ref,* 349, 532, 4:277(258)
Wiley, N. N.: *ref,* 1207, 2212
Wiley, R.: *ref,* 400, 1572
Wiley, R. E.: *ref,* 221
Wilfong, H. D.: *ref,* 1281
Wilgus, G.: *ref,* 2:1492(12)
Wilhelm, H. M.: *ref,* 357
Wilhelm, R.: *ref,* 533, 1918
Wilhelm, R. M.: *ref,* 1918
Wilhide, E. R.: *ref,* 1073
Wilk, E. K.: *ref,* 1281, 1499–500, 1519, 5:123(9)
Wilk, W. S.: *ref,* 525, 533
Wilk, X. G.: *ref,* 1499
Wilke, M. M.: *ref,* 1281
Wilke, W. H.: *test,* 2:1308
Wilkenson, J. C. M.: *ref,* 1185
Wilkerson, C. D.: *ref,* 1069
Wilkerson, C. J.: *ref,* 7
Wilkes, E.: *ref,* 1281
Wilkie, F.: *ref,* 529

Wilkin, W. R.: *ref*, 342, 439
Wilking, S. V.: *ref*, 1560
Wilkins, G. W.: *ref*, 314
Wilkins, L. G.: *ref*, 1169, 1383, 1519, 1911
Wilkins, M. F.: *ref*, 1087
Wilkins, P. E.: *ref*, 2213
Wilkins, T. B.: *ref*, 69, 3:217(87)
Wilkins, W. L.: *ref*, 439, 503, 532, 1499
Wilkinson, A. E.: *ref*, 1164, 1256, 1281, 1380, 1403, 1481, 1499, 2195
Wilkinson, B.: *ref*, 2151
Wilkinson, D.: *ref*, 1174
Wilkinson, J. C. M.: *ref*, 1174
Wilkinson, M. A.: *ref*, 1499, 2212
Wilkinson, N. W.: *ref*, 1499
Wilkinson, R.: *test*, 3:70
Wilkinson, V. J.: *ref*, 439
Wilks, S. S.: *rev*, 684, 688, 1:870, 1:880-1, 1:993, 1:1073-4, 2:1436
Will, D. P.: *ref*, 1205-7, 1245, 1383
Will, L. M.: *test*, 2:1361
Willard, D. W.: *ref*, 3:263(27)
Willard, L. A.: *ref*, 364, 532-3, 1063
Willard, N.: *ref*, 1923
Willcutt, H.: *ref*, 529, 6:225(2)
Willcutt, H. C.: *ref*, 1281
Wille, G. R.: *ref*, 482, 2129
Wille, W. S.: *ref*, 1481
Willems, P. J.: *ref*, 1144, 1499
Willenson, D.: *ref*, 532, 1261, 1298
Willerman, B.: *ref*, 1281, 1501
Willerman, L.: *ref*, 484, 525, 533, 1281
Willerscheidt, M. M.: *ref*, 1403
Willett, E. A.: *ref*, 358, 1383
Willett, G. W.: *ref*, 4:277(226)
Willett, R. A.: *ref*, 1226, 1275, 1281
Willhauk, R. C.: *ref*, 468
Willi, J.: *ref*, 1499
William, R. L.: *ref*, 1499
Williams, A. F.: *ref*, 516, 1094, 1293, 2095
Williams, A. J.: *test*, 1615-6, 2:1196, 2:1310
Williams, A. P.: *ref*, 390, 1275
Williams, B.: *ref*, 1225
Williams, B. K.: *ref*, 381
Williams, B. L.: *ref*, 400
Williams, B. M.: *ref*, 1044
Williams, B. R.: *ref*, 1281, 1775
Williams, C.: *ref*, 1174, 1499, 1519
Williams, C. A.: *test*, 3:194
Williams, C. B.: *ref*, 1281
Williams, C. D.: *ref*, 551, 574, 1164, 1291, 1519
Williams, C. E.: *ref*, 1094, 2046
Williams, C. L.: *ref*, 361, 1281, 2212, 6:438(445)
Williams, C. M.: *ref*, 357
Williams, C. M. D.: *ref*, 1383, 1403, 1430
Williams, C. O.: *ref*, 202, 211
Williams, C. R.: *ref*, 1474
Williams, C. T.: *ref*, 2195
Williams, D. E.: *ref*, 868, 1123, 1207, 1451
Williams, E.: *ref*, 1198
Williams, E. B.: *ref*, 1499
Williams, E. I.: *ref*, 2448
Williams, F. C.: *ref*, 1661
Williams, F. E.: *ref*, 589, 1383

Williams, F. J.: *ref*, 2212
Williams, G.: *ref*, 1499
Williams, G. B.: *ref*, 2110
Williams, G. J.: *ref*, 1499
Williams, G. P.: *test*, 35:169, 2:1410
Williams, G. W.: *ref*, 1090, 1403, 2:1394(8-9)
Williams, H. B.: *ref*, 357, 2213
Williams, H. H.: *ref*, 1499-500
Williams, H. L.: *ref*, 1044, 1121, 1281, 1499
Williams, H. M.: *ref*, 447, 507, 525, 1095, 1428, 3:475(1)
Williams, H. N.: *ref*, 2043
Williams, H. S.: *rev*, 2237-8
Williams, H. V.: *ref*, 391
Williams, H. Y.: *ref*, 1383
Williams, J.: *ref*, 425, 868, 1044, 1423, 3:617(1)
Williams, J. C.: *test*, 486, 923; *ref*, 357
Williams, J. D.: *ref*, 19, 382, 400, 404, 447, 551, 561, 591, 863, 1073, 1383
Williams, J. E.: *ref*, 49, 69, 480, 516, 1281, 1447, 5:308(309), 6:7(25), 6:438(534)
Williams, J. G.: *ref*, 1225, 1252
Williams, J. H.: *ref*, 381, 525
Williams, J. L.: *ref*, 1095, 1275, 1536, 1567
Williams, J. M.: *ref*, 533, 1164, 1182, 1383, 1451, 1499
Williams, J. R.: *rev*, 1336, 6:141; *test*, 2:1589; *ref*, 349, 439, 525, 529, 1383, 1499, 2:1589(1)
Williams, J. T.: *ref*, 1281
Williams, K. C.: *ref*, 425, 688, 6:793(2)
Williams, L.: *ref*, 914
Williams, L. A.: *ref*, 1469
Williams, L. E.: *ref*, 1134
Williams, M.: *test*, 540; *exc*, 1452, 1516; *ref*, 439, 503, 525, 532, 540, 592, 1174, 1217, 1232, 1322, 1380, 1499
Williams, M. E.: *ref*, 1144, 1344
Williams, M. F.: *ref*, 1123
Williams, M. G.: *ref*, 1499
Williams, M. H.: *ref*, 1499
Williams, M. J.: *ref*, 1123
Williams, M. L.: *ref*, 381
Williams, M. S.: *ref*, 1121, 1183
Williams, M. T.: *test*, 150
Williams, M. W.: *ref*, 1305
Williams, N.: *ref*, 333, 473, 1069
Williams, O. C.: *ref*, 1044
Williams, O. H.: *ref*, 382
Williams, P.: *test*, 1652; *ref*, 1302, 1403, 2212
Williams, P. A.: *ref*, 1302, 1403, 2212
Williams, P. J.: *ref*, 1469
Williams, P. L.: *ref*, 1164
Williams, P. R.: *ref*, 349, 364
Williams, R.: *test*, 343; *ref*, 522, 529, 1073, 1716
Williams, R. A.: *ref*, 69, 361, 1470, 2244
Williams, R. B.: *ref*, 1519
Williams, R. C.: *ref*, 1383
Williams, R. D. B.: *ref*, 525

Williams, R. E.: *ref*, 194, 868, 1164, 2212, 6:125(5)
Williams, R. H.: *test*, 35:473, 2:1373-4; *ref*, 357, 2103
Williams, R. J.: *ref*, 533, 1499
Williams, R. K.: *ref*, 1320
Williams, R. L.: *ref*, 533, 589, 1174, 1281, 1415
Williams, R. M.: *ref*, 505
Williams, S. B.: *exc*, 1519; *ref*, 342, 503, 1380
Williams, S. G.: *ref*, 1500
Williams, S. I.: *ref*, 742
Williams, T. A.: *ref*, 1227
Williams, T. M.: *ref*, 516
Williams, V.: *ref*, 69, 1572
Williams, W. A.: *ref*, 1880
Williams, W. C.: *ref*, 398
Williams, W. G.: *ref*, 2098
Williams, W. O.: *ref*, 1164, 1256, 1281, 1380, 1403, 2195
Williams, W. S.: *ref*, 1123
Williams, W. W.: *ref*, 1499
Williamson, D. A.: *ref*, 357
Williamson, D. B.: *ref*, 1090, 1116, 1123, 1519
Williamson, E. G.: *rev*, 1:904, 1:921, 1:1181, 2:1214, 2:1218, 2:1661; *test*, 4:70; *ref*, 7, 22, 189, 211, 438, 1095, 1222, 1281, 1348, 1568, 1749, 1932, 2135, 2212-3, 2227-9, 2258, 2266, 2381, 1:904(2), 2:1182(1), 2:1184(2), 2:1193(1), 2:1197(2), 2:1271(9), 2:1325(11), 2:1360(3), 2:1401(8), 2:1424(23), 4:70(4-5), P:342(7)
Williamson, H. M.: *ref*, 1164
Williamson, H. T.: *ref*, 400, 542
Williamson, J. A.: *ref*, 1164
Williamson, J. F.: *ref*, 1207
Williamson, M. L.: *ref*, 19, 361, 603, 731
Williamson, R. W.: *ref*, 1281
Williamson, T. L.: *ref*, 1856
Willig, S. N.: *ref*, 50, 516, 533, 981, 1681
Willing, M. H.: *rev*, 115; *test*, 2:1271; *ref*, 104, 4:179(1)
Willingham, D. C.: *ref*, 881
Willingham, G. W.: *ref*, P:339(18)
Willingham, M. E.: *ref*, 1415
Willingham, W. W.: *rev*, 382, 404; *ref*, 357, 425, 1193-4, 1837
Willis, C. B.: *ref*, 3:268
Willis, C. G.: *rev*, 602; *ref*, 357, 361, 7:201(1)
Willis, C. H.: *ref*, 1073, 1383, 1403, 2212
Willis, D. J.: *ref*, 528, 1447
Willis, J.: *ref*, 400, 533, 1275
Willis, J. D.: *ref*, 1275, 1519
Willis, M.: *rev*, 2:1631, 2:1633; *test*, 2:1184, 2:1618, 2:1635, 3:3, 3:548, 3:592, 3:596-7, 3:604, 4:184, 4:213, 5:179, 5:645
Willis, R. N.: *ref*, 7, 1281
Willis, W. K.: *test*, 2178; *ref*, 1087, 2195, 6:1153(2)
Willits, J. M.: *rev*, 337, 2162, 3:625, 5:389
Willman, C. E.: *ref*, 868, 1164
Willman, M. D.: *ref*, P:365(2)

Winston, C. M.: *ref*, 1499
Winston, W. E.: *ref*, 61, 211, 425
Winter, C.: *ref*, 997
Winter, F.: *ref*, 2212
Winter, G. D.: *ref*, 529, 1499, 2195
Winter, I.: *ref*, 1275, 1481
Winter, K. S.: *ref*, 529
Winter, L. M.: *ref*, 1448
Winter, P. M.: *ref*, 592, 1305, 1447
Winter, S. K.: *ref*, 1519
Winter, W. D.: *ref*, 381, 1205, 1281, 1293-4, 1447-8, 1471, 1499, 1519, P:327(32)
Winter, W. N.: *ref*, 525
Winterbottom, J. A.: *ref*, 2349
Winterbottom, M. T.: *ref*, 1302
Winterbourn, R.: *rev*, 329, 373, 5:300
Winterrose, H. G.: *ref*, 1123
Winters, A. W.: *ref*, 1123
Winters, C. L.: *test*, 1395e
Winters, J. S.: *ref*, 2212
Winters, S.: *ref*, 533, 1169, 1281
Winthrop, H.: *ref*, 496, 1095
Wipf, A.: *test*, 4:539
Wirls, C. J.: *ref*, 522, 529, 1474, 1478, 1499
Wirt, A. L.: *ref*, 1281
Wirt, R.: *ref*, 439, 1716
Wirt, R. D.: *rev*, 1129, 1175, 1252, 1296, 1313, 1451; *ref*, 1265, 1281, 1499
Wirt, S. E.: *ref*, 1923
Wirth, G.: *ref*, 529
Wirth, J. W.: *ref*, 589
Wirthlin, L. D.: *ref*, 1716, 1921
Wirths, C. G.: *ref*, 1474
Wirwick-Van Dusen, M.: *ref*, 574
Wisch, P. J.: *ref*, 2451
Wischner, G. J.: *ref*, 1164, 1447, 1499, 1501
Wisconsin Education Association, State Science Committee: *test*, 1:1135-6, 2:1600
Wisdom, B.: *ref*, 1174
Wisdom, J. R.: *ref*, 2195, 2212
Wise, F.: *ref*, 1499
Wise, J. B.: *ref*, 1912
Wise, J. H.: *ref*, 525, 1447, 1481, 1716
Wise, L. M.: *ref*, 1144
Wise, R. M.: *ref*, 1073
Wisecup, P.: *ref*, 1281, 1294
Wiseman, D. E.: *ref*, 981
Wiseman, E. E.: *rev*, 2439
Wiseman, R. J.: *ref*, 1499
Wiseman, S.: *rev*, 20, 736, 1591, 1599, 3:342; *test*, 5:857, 6:470, 6:796, 7:520, 7:695; *ref*, 409, 5:857(2-3)
Wiser, W. C.: *ref*, 525, 529, 533
Wisham, W.: *ref*, 1499
Wisham, W. W.: *ref*, 1499
Wishner, J.: *ref*, 532, 1499
Wiskoff, M.: *ref*, 382
Wisland, M.: *ref*, 981
Wisland, M. V.: *ref*, 981
Wisler, M. L.: *ref*, 483, 525
Wisner, R. W.: *ref*, 1050
Wisocki, P. A.: *ref*, 1406
Wisotsky, M.: *ref*, 1481
Wissel, J. W.: *ref*, 1923
Wisser, R. E.: *ref*, 533, 1123
Wissner, F.: *ref*, 1447

Withall, J.: *exc*, 4:53
Witham, E. C.: *rev*, 2:1625; *ref*, 1569
Withers, G. P.: *test*, 1530
Witherspoon, P.: *ref*, 1207, 1289, 6:438(531)
Witherspoon, R. L.: *ref*, 1451
Witherspoon, R. P.: *ref*, 1207, 2195, 6:438(499)
Witherspoon, Y. T.: *ref*, 50, 533, 1631, 2266
Withrow, C. Q.: *ref*, 1164
Withycombe-Brocato, C. J.: *ref*, 1403
Witkin, A. A.: *ref*, 1320, 2212
Witkin, H. A.: *test*, 1127, 1169, 1201; *ref*, 525, 529, 533, 1169, 1474, 1481, 1499, 1519
Witmer, H. L.: *exc*, 1281
Witmer, J. M.: *ref*, 533
Witmer, L.: *ref*, 525
Witmer, L. R.: *ref*, 419, 1386
Witryol, S. L.: *ref*, 425, 1207, 1386, 1403
Witsaman, L. R.: *ref*, 489
Witt, E. L.: *ref*, 532, 1499
Witt, G.: *ref*, 1356
Witt, H. F.: *ref*, 1176
Witt, N. E.: *ref*, 426, 1222
Witt, R. E.: *ref*, 1121
Witte, E. T.: *ref*, 1164
Witten, G. L.: *test*, 1864
Wittenberg, A.: *ref*, 482, 1206, 1281
Wittenborn, J. R.: *rev*, 1228, 1383, 1499, 1519; *test*, 5:123; *exc*, 1499; *ref*, 18, 86-7, 220, 425, 497, 529, 532, 1215, 1281, 1499-500, 1519, 1560, 2195, 2212, 2258, 2266, 5:123(1-9, 15), P:408(16-23, 25)
Wittich, J. J.: *ref*, 1095
Wittick, M. L.: *ref*, 1881
Wittig, B.: *ref*, 1232, 1264, 1346
Wittkower, E. D.: *ref*, 1481, 1499
Wittman, M. P.: *ref*, 1095, 1245
Wittman, P.: *ref*, 532, 1105, 1222, 1499
Wittmer, J.: *test*, 890; *ref*, 382, 1164, 1281, 1383
Wittmer, R. E.: *ref*, 31
Wittmeyer, A. L.: *ref*, 1044, 1294, 1383
Wittner, W.: *ref*, 1281
Wittner, W. K.: *ref*, 1214
Witton, K.: *ref*, 1281
Wittson, C. L.: *ref*, 503, 1499
Witty, P. A.: *rev*, 7, 1694, 1698, 1702, 3:15; *test*, 1:1117; *ref*, 36, 525, 1918, 1:1117(1-2), 3:242(4)
Witzeman, B. E.: *ref*, 3:470(15)
Witzke, D. B.: *ref*, 1471
Wladkowsky, E.: *ref*, 525, 532
Wober, M.: *ref*, 439
Wodin, M. H.: *ref*, 1192
Wodtke, K. H.: *ref*, 589, 902
Wodtli, T.: *ref*, 1164
Woehlke, A. B.: *ref*, 426
Woehr, H. J.: *ref*, 1207, 2212
Woelfel, F.: *ref*, 1932
Woellner, R. C.: *exc*, 3:639
Woerdehoff, F. J.: *ref*, 1207
Woerner, E. M.: *ref*, 3:217(121)
Woerner, M. G.: *ref*, 529
Woestehoff, E. S.: *ref*, 1647
Wofford, J. C.: *ref*, 1207

Wogan, M.: *ref*, 1281, 1293
Wohl, J.: *ref*, 1094, 1164, 1225, 1281, 1419, 1447, 1499, 1519
Wohl, T. H.: *ref*, 1195
Wohlford, P.: *ref*, 1277, 1281, 1447, 1519
Wohlford, P. F.: *ref*, 1519
Wolaver, K. E.: *ref*, 868, 1207
Wolbach, A. B.: *ref*, 1093
Wolcott, C. M.: *ref*, 1123
Wold, A. A.: *ref*, 20
Wold, J. A.: *ref*, 1223
Wold, O.: *test*, 36:568
Wold, R. M.: *test*, 1891-3
Wold, S. G.: *ref*, 185
Woldt, A. L.: *ref*, 1253
Wolf, C. W.: *ref*, 533
Wolf, E. B.: *ref*, 1499
Wolf, G. P.: *ref*, 516
Wolf, I.: *ref*, 1499
Wolf, I. W.: *ref*, 1448
Wolf, L.: *test*, 3:556
Wolf, M. G.: *ref*, 1499, 1519
Wolf, R.: *ref*, 489, 525
Wolf, R. C.: *ref*, 884
Wolf, R. R.: *ref*, 357
Wolf, S.: *ref*, 439, 529, 1145, 1281, 1496
Wolf, S. J.: *ref*, 525, 1155, 1313
Wolf, S. R.: *ref*, 1447, 1481, 1499, 1501, 1519
Wolf, W.: *ref*, 7, 400, 439, 505, 1123
Wolf, W. C.: *ref*, 525
Wolf, W. S.: *ref*, 439, 505
Wolfe, D. M.: *ref*, 1121, 1145, 1225, 1281, 1383
Wolfe, J. M.: *test*, 2331; *ref*, 2331
Wolfe, L. M.: *ref*, P:411(12)
Wolfe, L. S.: *ref*, 1905
Wolfe, R. N.: *ref*, 433
Wolfe, S.: *ref*, 1395
Wolfensberger, W.: *ref*, 516, 1428, 1911-2
Wolfensberger, W. P.: *ref*, 532, 1499
Wolfenstein, C. M.: *ref*, 1499
Wolff, B. B.: *ref*, 529
Wolff, C.: *ref*, 1480
Wolff, C. E.: *ref*, 1123, 1383
Wolff, F.: *ref*, 1448, 5:147(48)
Wolff, H.: *test*, 1146
Wolff, H. G.: *test*, 1144-5; *ref*, 1144-6
Wolff, R.: *ref*, 529
Wolff, S. J.: *ref*, 532
Wolff, W.: *test*, 4:104; *ref*, 4:104(1-2)
Wolff, W. M.: *ref*, 1281, 2195, 2239
Wolfgang, A.: *ref*, 1519
Wolfle, D.: *rev*, 407, 1:909, 2:1587-9, 4:315-6; *ref*, 5:530(42)
Wolfson, B. N.: *ref*, 901, 1171
Wolfson, R.: *ref*, 1499
Wolfson, W.: *ref*, 529, 1448, 1469, 1481, 1499
Wolins, L.: *rev*, 570, 1082; *ref*, 7, 69, 342, 348, 423, 482, 487, 497, 1044, 1078, 1164, 1206-7, 1280, 1320, 1812, 2132, 2195, 2199, 2212, 2227, 2234, 2239, 2266-7, 6:870(3), 7:840(4)
Wolins, M.: *ref*, 439
Wolitzer, M.: *ref*, 1121

Wright, F.: *ref,* 533, 1898
Wright, F. A.: *ref,* 211
Wright, F. H.: *ref,* 1281, 2195, 2212
Wright, G. N.: *test,* 1210; *ref,* 1210
Wright, H. C.: *ref,* 533, 1447
Wright, H. F.: *ref,* 503, 532
Wright, H. M.: *test,* 2:1512; *ref,* 2:1512(1)
Wright, H. T.: *ref,* 7, 6:8(1)
Wright, J. A.: *ref,* 1294
Wright, J. C.: *ref,* 49, 1626, 2195, 5:66(12), 6:113(17)
Wright, J. H.: *ref,* 361, 482, 1427
Wright, J. J.: *ref,* 1281
Wright, J. M.: *ref,* 1500
Wright, J. M. C.: *ref,* 1499
Wright, L.: *test,* 918; *ref,* 533, 918, 1447, 1921
Wright, M. A.: *ref,* 1145
Wright, M. E.: *ref,* 1380, 1499
Wright, M. L.: *ref,* 1254
Wright, M. M.: *test,* 2:1307
Wright, M. R.: *ref,* 1500
Wright, M. S.: *ref,* 1281
Wright, M. T.: *ref,* 382, 404
Wright, M. W.: *ref,* 1164, 1281, 1386, 1519
Wright, N. A.: *ref,* 1164, 1281, 1423, 1499
Wright, P. H.: *ref,* 1164
Wright, P. K.: *test,* 918; *ref,* 918
Wright, P. M.: *test,* 3:559
Wright, R. E.: *ref,* 525, 1087
Wright, R. L.: *rev,* 7:26; *ref,* 2195
Wright, R. M.: *ref,* 2212
Wright, S.: *ref,* 1281, 1383, 1499–500
Wright, S. C.: *ref,* 532, 1499, 1516, 1519
Wright, W.: *ref,* 1302, 2212
Wright, W. D.: *ref,* 1911, 1932
Wright, W. R.: *ref,* 1395
Wright, W. W.: *ref,* 36, 1716
Wrighter, J.: *ref,* 1123
Wrightsman, L. S.: *ref,* 337, 1415
Wrightstone, J. W.: *rev,* 1759, 1: 950, 2:1306, 2:1581, 3:535, 3:537, 3:545, 5:458; *test,* 22, 335–6, 637, 780, 1262, 1567, 2192, 2252, 2: 1266, 2:1615, 2:1619, 4:761, 5: 480, 6:877; *exc,* 435, 532, 1610–1, 2244, 2:1196, 2:1291, 2:1293, 2: 1416, 2:1453; *ref,* 391, 425, 525, 533, 850, 1123, 1567, 2:1266 (1–3), 5:368(21), P:346(10, 14)
Wrigley, C.: *ref,* 1087
Wrigley, J.: *rev,* 5:436, 5:489; *test,* 7:520, 7:695; *ref,* 409, 2249, 6: 470(1), 6:796(1), 6:1090(3)
Wrinkle, W. L.: *test,* 704
Wrinn, M. J. J.: *test,* 4:190
Wrong, E.: *ref,* 5:147(16)
Wu, C. Y.: *ref,* 1499
Wu, J. J.: *ref,* 589
Wu, T. M.: *ref,* 525
Wubbolding, R. E.: *ref,* 1164, 1193–4
Wuebben, P. L.: *ref,* 1033
Wunderlich, E.: *ref,* 1663
Wunderlin, R. J.: *ref,* 533
Wurmser, J. H.: *ref,* 1383
Wursten, H.: *ref,* 1499
Wussler, M.: *ref,* 533, 981

Wyatt, F.: *exc,* 1519; *ref,* 532, 1499, 1519
Wyatt, H. G.: *ref,* 1101
Wyatt, L. D.: *ref,* 1207
Wyatt, R.: *ref,* 211
Wyatt, R. F.: *ref,* 211
Wyatt, T. C.: *ref,* 1407
Wycis, H. T.: *ref,* 1499
Wyeth, E. R.: *ref,* 69, 382, 1176, 1294
Wyke, M.: *ref,* 529
Wykoff, G. S.: *test,* 99, 105, 3:143; *ref,* 881
Wyland, R. R.: *ref,* 2448
Wyle, H.: *test,* 2413
Wylie, A. A.: *ref,* 1499
Wylie, A. E.: *ref,* 1724
Wylie, H. W.: *ref,* 1195
Wylie, R. C.: *ref,* 1519, 3:660(18, 20)
Wyman, B. A. W.: *ref,* 1478
Wyman, B. W.: *ref,* 1478
Wyman, E. J.: *test,* 2461–2, 2464
Wyman, J. B.: *ref,* 1569
Wyndham, A. J.: *ref,* 2227
Wyndham, J.: *ref,* 1200, 1259, 1291
Wyne, M. D.: *ref,* 533
Wynn, D. C.: *ref,* 2195
Wynn Jones, L.: *rev,* 2:1220, 2: 1430; *exc,* 3:776; *ref,* 2:1220(3, 6)
Wynne, J. T.: *ref,* 1044, 2212
Wynne, L. C.: *ref,* 1499, 1519
Wynne, R. D.: *ref,* 1480
Wyrick, W.: *ref,* 1881, 1898
Wysocki, A. C.: *ref,* 532
Wysocki, B.: *ref,* 2266
Wysocki, B. A.: *ref,* 439, 532, 1481, 1499, 5:308(385)
Wysong, H. E.: *ref,* 1073

XYDIAS, N.: *ref,* 364
Xydis, G. A.: *ref,* 533, 1123, 1499

YACORZYNSKI, G. K.: *exc,* 1105; *ref,* 532, 545, 1105
Yadoff, B.: *ref,* 1164
Yager, R. E.: *ref,* 20, 1044, 1775, 1856
Yagoda, G.: *ref,* 1469, 1481
Yahav, A. L.: *ref,* 574
Yakub, S.: *ref,* 2135
Yalom, I. D.: *ref,* 1121, 1176, 1214
Yalowitz, J. M.: *ref,* 533
Yamaguchi, H.: *ref,* 1500
Yamahiro, R.: *ref,* 1281
Yamahiro, R. A.: *ref,* 1281
Yamahiro, R. S.: *ref,* 529, 532, 1281, 1499
Yamamoto, J.: *ref,* 1101, 1281
Yamamoto, K.: *ref,* 7, 19–20, 348, 398, 400, 589, 868, 1121, 1240, 1403, 1463
Yamamoto, S.: *ref,* 1499
Yamarat, V.: *ref,* 533
Yamashita, I.: *ref,* 1403
Yamashita, T.: *ref,* 1281
Yanagi, G. H.: *ref,* 1261, 1447, 1481
Yang, K.: *ref,* 1164, 1499
Yang, K. C.: *ref,* 1232
Yang, K. S.: *ref,* 1499
Yanis, M.: *ref,* 2212
Yankauer, A.: *ref,* 2043, 2045
Yanuzzi, J. R.: *test,* 2390

Yap, P. M.: *ref,* 403, 439, 1205, 1499
Yarborough, O. J.: *ref,* 3:146(1)
Yardley, A.: *test,* 35:302, 35:304
Yarington, D. J.: *ref,* 1044
Yarnell, H.: *ref,* 1499
Yarnell, T.: *ref,* 1094
Yarnell, T. D.: *ref,* 1094, 1350, 1499
Yarnold, J. K.: *ref,* 1228
Yarrow, W. H.: *ref,* 1289
Yaryura-Tobias, J. A.: *ref,* 1480
Yaskin, J. C.: *ref,* 1105, 1499
Yatabe, T.: *ref,* 1205–6, 1245
Yater, A. C.: *ref,* 381, 525, 538, 1073, 1129, 1281, P:408(29)
Yates, A.: *rev,* 425, 5:857
Yates, A. J.: *rev,* 1105, 1168, 1311, 1380; *ref,* 403, 439, 532, 545, 592, 1192, 1223, 1296, 1380, 1499
Yates, L. G.: *ref,* 36, 525, 1087
Yauch, W. A.: *test,* 3:63; *ref,* 3: 63(4)
Yaukey, D. W.: *ref,* 1164
Yawger, N. S.: *ref,* 1499
Yeager, C. T.: *ref,* 1121, 1447
Yeager, J. C.: *ref,* 1315, 2454
Yearsley, M.: *exc,* 2:1526.1
Yeats, L. C.: *ref,* 532
Yeatts, P. P.: *ref,* 914, 1219
Yee, A. H.: *rev,* 160; *ref,* 868
Yee, G. F.: *ref,* 589, 1123
Yela, M.: *ref,* 426, 515, 545, 2242, 4:324(61), 4:334(8)
Yellen, S.: *test,* 927; *ref,* 927
Yelsky, M.: *ref,* 1448, 1519
Yen, F.: *ref,* 1281
Yen, S. M. Y.: *ref,* 381, 516, 525
Yen, Y.: *ref,* 1499
Yen, Y. S.: *ref,* 1499
Yengo, C.: *ref,* 868
Yeomans, W. N.: *ref,* 1281
Yepsen, L. N.: *test,* 35:139; *ref,* 381
Yerbury, E. C.: *ref,* 447, 1499
Yeremian, T. S.: *ref,* 357
Yerkes, R. M.: *ref,* 447, 525, 2:1391 (3–4), 3:220(18a, 25a)
Yeslin, A. R.: *ref,* 2212, 2239
Yingst, C. E.: *ref,* 1254
Ylitalo, S. H.: *ref,* 1129, 1336
Yntema, O.: *test,* 2:1497–8; *ref,* 2: 1497(2), 2:1498(2)
Yoakum, C. S.: *ref,* 447, 2:1391 (3), 3:220(18a)
Yoder, D.: *rev,* 4:785
Yoder, L. J.: *test,* 36:516, 36:521, 36:686, 36:689
Yoesting, C.: *ref,* 1775
Yoloye, E. A.: *ref,* 400
Yonce, C. W.: *ref,* 1383
Yonge, G.: *test,* 1302
Yonge, G. D.: *ref,* 1133, 1281, 1302
Yonge, K. A.: *ref,* 1275
Yorioka, G. N.: *ref,* 1169
York, D. H.: *ref,* 496, 529
York, L. J. N.: *ref,* 1164
York, M. W.: *ref,* 496, 518
York, P. W.: *ref,* 1573
York, R. H.: *ref,* 1499
Yorkston, N. J.: *test,* 1397
Yormak, B. B.: *ref,* 1261
Yoshimura, S.: *ref,* 1281
Yoshpe, S. R.: *ref,* 1501
Yost, M. A.: *ref,* 1275

SCANNING INDEX

This scanning index is an expanded table of contents listing all tests in this volume. Foreign tests are identified by listing the country of origin in brackets immediately after the title. The population for which a test is intended is presented to facilitate the search for tests for use with a particular group. Stars indicate tests not previously listed in a Mental Measurements Yearbook; *asterisks indicate tests revised or supplemented since last listed. Numbers refer to test entries, not to pages.*

ACHIEVEMENT BATTERIES

Tests of Adult Basic Education, adults at reading levels of children in grades 2–9, see 45
★*Tests of Arithmetic and Language for Indian South Africans* [South Africa], standards 6–8, see 46
Tests of Basic Experiences, prekgn–grade 1, see 47

Tests of General Educational Development, candidates for high school equivalency certificates, see 48
Undergraduate Program Area Tests, college, see 49
Wide Range Achievement Test, ages 5 and over, see 50

ENGLISH

Advanced Placement Examination in English, high school students desiring credit for college level courses or admission to advanced courses, see 51
American School Achievement Tests: Language and Spelling, grades 4–9, see 52
Analytical Survey Test in English Fundamentals, grades 9–13, see 53
Barrett-Ryan English Test, grades 7–13, see 54
★*Berry-Talbott Language Test: Comprehension of Grammar,* ages 5–8, see 55
Bristol Achievement Tests: English Language [England], ages 8–13, see 56
Business English Test: Dailey Vocational Tests, grades 8–12 and adults, see 57
CLEP General Examinations: English Composition, 1–2 years of college or equivalent, see 58
CLEP Subject Examination in English Composition, 1 year or equivalent, see 59
★*CLEP Subject Examination in Freshman English,* 1 year or equivalent, see 60
California Achievement Tests: Language, grades 1–14, see 61
Canadian Achievement Test in English [Canada], grade 10, see 62
Canadian English Achievement Test [Canada], grades 8.5–9, see 63
★*Canadian English Language Achievement Test* [Canada], candidates for college entrance, see 63A
College Board Achievement Test in English Composition, candidates for college entrance, see 64
College English Placement Test, college entrants, see 65
College English Test: National Achievement Tests, grades 12–13, see 66
College Placement Tests in English Composition, entering college freshmen, see 67
Comprehensive Tests of Basic Skills: Language, grades 2.5–12, see 68
Cooperative English Tests, grades 9–14, see 69
Cooperative Primary Tests: Writing Skills, grades 2.5–3, see 70
Cotswold Junior English Ability Test [Scotland], ages 8.5–10.5, see 71
Cotswold Measurement of Ability: English [Scotland], ages 10–12, see 72
English Expression: Cooperative English Tests, grades 9–14, see 73
English IX–XII: Achievement Examinations for Secondary Schools, grades 9–12, see 74
English Progress Tests [England], ages 7-3 to 15-6, see 75
English Test FG [England], ages 12–13, see 76
English Test: Municipal Tests, grades 3–8, see 77
English Test: National Achievement Tests, grades 3–12, see 78
English Tests (Adv.) [England], ages 12–13, see 79
English Tests 14–20 and 22 [England], ages 10–11, see 80
Essentials of English Tests, grades 7–13, see 81
★*Functional Grammar Test,* high school and college, see 82
Grammar and Usage Test Series, grades 7–12, see 83

Grammar, Usage, and Structure Test and Vocabulary Test, college entrants, see 84
Hoyum-Sanders English Tests, 1–2 semesters in grades 2–8, see 85
Iowa Placement Examinations: English Aptitude, grades 12–13, see 86
Iowa Placement Examinations: English Training, grades 12–13, see 87
Iowa Tests of Educational Development: Correctness and Appropriateness of Expression, grades 9–12, see 88
★*Language Arts Diagnostic Probes,* grades 3–9, see 89
Language Arts: Minnesota High School Achievement Examinations, grades 7–12, see 90
Language Arts Tests: Content Evaluation Series, grades 7–9, see 91
Language Perception Test, business and industry, see 92
Language Usage: Differential Aptitude Tests, grades 8–12 and adults, see 93–4
Moray House English Tests [England], ages 8.5–14, see 95
National Teacher Examinations: English Language and Literature, college seniors and teachers, see 96
Nationwide English Composition Examination, grades 4–12, see 97
Nationwide English Grammar Examination, grades 4–12, see 98
New Purdue Placement Test in English, grades 11–16, see 99
Objective Tests in Constructive English, grades 7–12, see 100
Objective Tests in Punctuation, grades 7–12, see 101
Pacific Tests of English Attainment and Skills: Pacific Test Series [Australia], job applicants in Papua New Guinea, see 102
Picture Story Language Test, ages 7–17, see 103
Pressey Diagnostic Tests in English Composition, grades 7–12, see 104
Purdue High School English Test, grades 9–12, see 105
RBH Spelling Test and Word Meaning Test, business and industry, see 106
RBH Test of Language Skills, business and industry, see 107
SRA Achievement Series: Language Arts, grades 2–9, see 108–9
Schonell Diagnostic English Tests [Scotland], ages 9.5–16, see 110
Senior English Test [England], technical college entrants, see 111
★*Sequential Tests of Educational Progress, Series 2: English Expression,* grades 4–14, see 112
Sequential Tests of Educational Progress: Writing, grades 4–14, see 113
Stanford Achievement Test: High School English and Spelling Tests, grades 9–12, see 114
Stanford Achievement Test: Spelling and Language Tests, grades 4–9, see 115
Survey Tests of English Usage, grades 9–13, see 116
Teacher Education Examination Program: English Language and Literature, college seniors preparing to teach secondary school, see 117

LITERATURE

SPELLING

VOCABULARY

FINE ARTS

ART

FOREIGN LANGUAGES

SPANISH

INTELLIGENCE

GROUP

Preliminary Scholastic Aptitude Test/National Merit Scholarship Qualifying Test, grades 10–12, see 436

★*Preschool and Early Primary Skill Survey*, ages 3-3 to 7-2, see 437

Pressey Classification and Verifying Tests, grades 1–12 and adults, see 438

Progressive Matrices [England], ages 5 and over, see 439

Proverbs Test, grades 5–16 and adults, see 440

Public School Primary Intelligence Test, grades 2–4, see 441

Purdue Non-Language Personnel Test, business and industry, see 442

Quantitative Evaluative Device, entering graduate students, see 443

RBH Test of Learning Ability, business and industry, see 444

RBH Test of Non-Verbal Reasoning, business and industry, see 445

Reasoning Tests for Higher Levels of Intelligence [Scotland], college entrants, see 446

Revised Beta Examination, ages 16–59, see 447

Ryburn Group Intelligence Tests [Scotland], ages 6.5–15.5, see 448

SRA Nonverbal Form, ages 12 and over, see 449

SRA Pictorial Reasoning Test, ages 14 and over, see 450

SRA Short Test of Educational Ability, grades kgn–12, see 451

SRA Verbal Form, grades 7–16 and adults, see 452

Safran Culture Reduced Intelligence Test [Canada], grades 1 and over, see 453

Scholastic Mental Ability Tests, grades kgn–8, see 454

Schubert General Ability Battery, grades 12–16 and adults, see 455

Scott Company Mental Alertness Test, applicants for office positions, see 456

Ship Destination Test, grades 9 and over, see 457

Short Form Test of Academic Aptitude, grades 1.5–12, see 458

Simplex GNV Intelligence Tests [England], ages 11–12, see 459

Simplex Group Intelligence Scale [England], ages 10 and over, see 460

Simplex Junior Intelligence Tests [England], ages 7–14, see 461

Sleight Non-Verbal Intelligence Test [England], ages 6–10, see 462

Southend Test of Intelligence [England], ages 10–12, see 463

Spiral Nines [South Africa], job applicants with 7–8 years of education, see 464

Test of Adult College Aptitude, evening college entrants, see 465

Test of Perceptual Organization, ages 12 and over, see 466

Tests of General Ability, grades kgn–12, see 467

Tests of General Ability: Inter-American Series, preschool and grades kgn–13.5, see 468

Thurstone Test of Mental Alertness, grades 9–12 and adults, see 469

Undergraduate Program Aptitude Test, grades 15–16, see 470

Verbal Power Test of Concept Equivalence, ages 14 and over, see 471

Verbal Reasoning, job applicants and industrial employees, see 472

Verbal Reasoning: Differential Aptitude Tests, grades 8–12 and adults, see 473

Verbal Tests (Adv.) [England], ages 12–13, see 474

Verbal Tests BC, CD, C, and D [England], ages 8–11, see 475

Verbal Tests EF and GH [England], ages 11–14, see 476

Verbal Tests 15–23 and 69 [England], ages 10–12, see 477

★*WLW Employment Inventory III*, job applicants, see 478

★*WLW Mental Alertness Inventory*, job applicants, see 479

Wesman Personnel Classification Test, grades 8–16 and adults, see 480

Western Personnel Tests, college and adults, see 481

Wonderlic Personnel Test, adults, see 482

INDIVIDUAL

Arthur Point Scale of Performance Tests, ages 4.5 to superior adults, see 483

Bayley Scales of Infant Development, ages 2–30 months, see 484

★*Bingham Button Test*, disadvantaged children ages 3–6, see 485

Canadian Intelligence Test [Canada], ages 3–16, see 486

Cattell Infant Intelligence Scale, ages 3–30 months, see 487

★*Classification Tasks* [Australia], ages 5–9, see 488

Columbia Mental Maturity Scale, ages 3.5–9, see 489

Cooperative Preschool Inventory, ages 3–6, see 490

Crichton Vocabulary Scale [England], ages 4–11, see 491

Denver Developmental Screening Test, ages 2 weeks to 6 years, see 492

Detroit Tests of Learning Aptitude, ages 3 and over, see 493

Developmental Screening Inventory, ages 1–18 months, see 494

English Picture Vocabulary Test [England], ages 5 and over, see 495

Full-Range Picture Vocabulary Test, ages 2 and over, see 496

Gesell Developmental Schedules, ages 4 weeks to 6 years, see 497

Haptic Intelligence Scale for Adult Blind, blind and partially sighted adults, see 498

Hiskey-Nebraska Test of Learning Aptitude, ages 3–17, see 499

Immediate Test: A Quick Verbal Intelligence Test, adults, see 500

★*Individual Scale for Indian South Africans* [South Africa], ages 8–17, see 501

Kahn Intelligence Tests, ages 1 month and over (particularly the verbally or culturally handicapped), see 502

Kent Series of Emergency Scales, ages 5–14, see 503

Leiter Adult Intelligence Scale, adults, see 504

Leiter International Performance Scale, ages 2–18, see 505

★*McCarthy Scales of Children's Abilities*, ages 2.5–8.5, see 506

Merrill-Palmer Scale of Mental Tests, ages 24–63 months, see 507

★*Minnesota Child Development Inventory*, ages 1–6, see 508

Minnesota Preschool Scale, ages 1.5–6.0, see 509

New Guinea Performance Scales [Papua New Guinea], pre-literates ages 17 and over, see 510

New South African Individual Scale [South Africa], ages 6–17, see 511

Non-Verbal Intelligence Tests for Deaf and Hearing Subjects [The Netherlands], ages 3–16, see 512

Ohwaki-Kohs Tactile Block Design Intelligence Test for the Blind, blind ages 6 and over, see 513

Pacific Design Construction Test [Australia], illiterates and semiliterates in Papua New Guinea, see 514

SPECIFIC

MATHEMATICS

ALGEBRA

ARITHMETIC

CALCULUS

GEOMETRY

SPECIAL FIELDS

TRIGONOMETRY

MISCELLANEOUS

AGRICULTURE

BLIND

BUSINESS EDUCATION

COMPUTATIONAL & TESTING DEVICES

★*Bowman Chronological Age Calculator,* see 802
Bowman M.A. and I.Q. Kalculator, see 803
*Chronological Age Computer, ages 3-7 to 19-5, see 804
Dominion Table for Converting Mental Age to I.Q. [Canada], see 805
Grade Averaging Charts, see 806
I.Q. Calculator, see 807
★*Mental Age Calculator,* see 808
*Multiple Purpose Self Trainer, high school and adults, see 809
Psychometric Research and Service Chart Showing the Davis Difficulty and Discrimination Indices for Item Analysis [India], see 810
Rapid-Rater, see 811
★*Ratio I.Q. Computer,* see 812

COURTSHIP & MARRIAGE

★*Albert Mate Selection Check List,* premarital counselees, see 813
California Marriage Readiness Evaluation, premarital counselees, see 814
Caring Relationship Inventory, marital counselees, see 815
Courtship Analysis, adults, see 816
Dating Problems Checklist, high school and college, see 817
El Senoussi Multiphasic Marital Inventory, premarital and marital counselees, see 818
★*I-Am Sentence Completion Test,* marital counselees, see 819
Individual and Family Developmental Review, counselees and therapy patients, see 820
★*Love Attitudes Inventory,* grades 12-16, see 821
Male Impotence Test, adult males, see 822
Marital Communication Inventory, adults, see 823
★*Marital Diagnostic Inventory,* marital counselees, see 824
Marital Roles Inventory, marital counselees, see 825
Marriage Adjustment Form, adults, see 826
Marriage Adjustment Inventory, marital counselees, see 827
Marriage Adjustment Sentence Completion Survey, marital counselees, see 828
Marriage Analysis, married couples in counseling, see 829
★*Marriage Expectation Inventories,* engaged and married couples, see 830
Marriage-Personality Inventory, individuals and couples, see 831
Marriage Prediction Schedule, adults, see 832
Marriage Role Expectation Inventory, adolescents and adults, see 833
*Marriage Scale (For Measuring Compatibility of Interests), premarital or married counselees, see 834
★*Marriage Skills Analysis,* marital counselees, see 835
Otto Pre-Marital Counseling Schedules, adult couples, see 836
★*Pair Attraction Inventory,* college and adults, see 837
Sex Knowledge Inventory, sex education classes in high school and college and adults, see 838
Sexual Development Scale for Females, adult females, see 839
*Taylor-Johnson Temperament Analysis, grades 7-16 and adults, see 840
Thorman Family Relations Conference Situation Questionnaire, families receiving therapy, see 841

DRIVING & SAFETY EDUCATION

*American Automobile Association Driver Testing Apparatus, drivers, see 842
*Bicycle Safety—Performance and Skill Tests, ages 10-16, see 843
Driver Attitude Survey, drivers, see 844
★*Driving Skill Exercises,* automobile drivers, see 845
General Test on Traffic and Driving Knowledge, drivers, see 846
Hannaford Industrial Safety Attitude Scales, industry, see 847
McGlade Road Test for Use in Driver Licensing, Education and Employment, prospective drivers, see 848
Road Test Check List for Passenger Car Drivers, passenger car drivers, see 849
Siebrecht Attitude Scale, grades 9-16 and adults, see 850
★*Simplified Road Test,* drivers, see 851

EDUCATION

Academic Freedom Survey, college students and faculty, see 852
*CLEP Subject Examination in History of American Education, 1 semester or equivalent, see 853
*CLEP Subject Examination in Tests and Measurements, 1 semester or equivalent, see 854
★*Classroom Atmosphere Questionnaire,* grades 4-9, see 855
★*Comprehensive Teaching and Training Evaluation,* college and training programs, see 856
★*Counseling Services Assessment Blank,* college and adult counseling clients, see 857
★*Course Evaluation Questionnaire,* high school and college, see 858
Diagnostic Teacher-Rating Scale, grades 4-12, see 859
★*Educational Values Assessment Questionnaire,* adults, see 860
Faculty Morale Scale for Institutional Improvement, college faculty, see 861
★*General Tests of Language and Arithmetic for Students* [South Africa], first and second year Bantu candidates for primary teacher's certificate, see 862
*Graduate Record Examinations Advanced Education Test, graduate school candidates, see 863
*Illinois Course Evaluation Questionnaire, college, see 864
Illinois Ratings of Teacher Effectiveness, grades 9-12, see 865
Illinois Teacher Evaluation Questionnaire, grades 7-12, see 866
*Junior Index of Motivation, grades 7-12, see 867
Minnesota Teacher Attitude Inventory, elementary and secondary school teachers and students in grades 12-17, see 868
*National Teacher Examinations, college seniors and teachers, see 869
*National Teacher Examinations: Early Childhood Education, college seniors and teachers, see 870
*National Teacher Examinations: Education in an Urban Setting, college seniors and teachers, see 871
*National Teacher Examinations: Education in the Elementary School, college seniors and teachers, see 872
*National Teacher Examinations: Education of Mentally Retarded, college seniors and teachers, see 873
★*National Teacher Examinations: Educational Administration and Supervision,* prospective principals, see 874
★*National Teacher Examinations: Guidance Counselor,* prospective guidance counselors, see 875

HANDWRITING

HEALTH & PHYSICAL EDUCATION

HOME ECONOMICS

INDUSTRIAL ARTS

LEARNING DISABILITIES

LISTENING COMPREHENSION

PHILOSOPHY

PSYCHOLOGY

RECORD & REPORT FORMS

RELIGIOUS EDUCATION

Achievement Test in Jewish History, junior high school, see 1020
★*Achievement Test—Jewish Life and Observances,* grades 5–7, see 1021
★*Achievement Test—The State of Israel,* "pupils who have completed an organized course of study on the State of Israel," see 1022
★*Bible and You,* ages 13 and over, see 1023
★*Biblical Survey Test,* college, see 1024
Concordia Bible Information Inventory, grades 4–8, see 1025
Inventory of Religious Activities and Interests, high school and college students considering church-related occupations and theological school students, see 1025A
Religious Attitudes Inventory, religious counselees, see 1026
Standardized Bible Content Tests, Bible college, see 1027
Theological School Inventory, incoming seminary students, see 1028
Youth Research Survey, ages 13–19, see 1029

SCORING MACHINES & SERVICES

Automata EDT 1200 Educational Data Terminal, see 1030
Hankes Scoring Service, see 1031
IBM 1230 Optical Mark Scoring Reader, see 1032
★*IBM 3881 Optical Mark Reader,* see 1033
MRC Scoring and Reporting Services, see 1034
NCS Scoring and Reporting Services, see 1035
NCS Sentry 70, see 1036
OpScan Test Scoring and Document Scanning System, see 1037
Psychological Resources, see 1038

SOCIOECONOMIC STATUS

American Home Scale, grades 8–16, see 1039
Environmental Participation Index, culturally disadvantaged ages 12 and over, see 1040A
Home Index, grades 4–12, see 1040A
Socio-Economic Status Scales [India], urban students, adults, and rural families, see 1041

STATISTICS

CLEP Subject Examination in Statistics, 1 semester or equivalent, see 1042
★*Objective Tests in Mathematics: Statistics* [England], ages 15 and over, see 1043

TEST PROGRAMS

ACT Assessment, candidates for college entrance, see 1044
Advanced Placement Examinations, high school students desiring credit for college level courses or admission to advanced courses, see 1045
Canadian Test Battery, Grade 10 [Canada], see 1046
Canadian Test Battery, Grades 8–9 [Canada], grades 8.5–9.0, see 1047
College Board Admissions Testing Program, candidates for college entrance, see 1048
★*College Guidance Program,* grade 11, see 1049
College-Level Examination Program, 1–2 years of college or equivalent, see 1050
College Placement Tests, entering college freshmen, see 1051
Comparative Guidance and Placement Program, entrants to two-year colleges and vocational-technical institutes, see 1052
Graduate Record Examinations: National Program for Graduate School Selection, graduate school candidates, see 1053
Junior College Placement Program, junior college entrants, see 1054
National Guidance Testing Program, grades 1.5–14, see 1055
National Science Foundation Graduate Fellowship Testing Program, applicants for N.S.F. fellowships for graduate study in the sciences, see 1056
★*Ohio Survey Tests,* grades 4, 6, 8, and 10, see 1057
Project Talent Test Battery, grades 9–12, see 1058
Secondary School Admission Test, grades 5–10, see 1059
★*Service for Admission to College and University Testing Program* [Canada], candidates for college entrance, see 1060
★*Testing Academic Achievement,* high school students desiring credit for college level courses or advanced placement, entering college freshmen, and 1–2 years of college or equivalent, see 1061
Undergraduate Program for Counseling and Evaluation, college, see 1062

MULTI-APTITUDE BATTERIES

Academic Promise Tests, grades 6–9, see 1063
★*Academic-Technical Aptitude Tests* [South Africa], "coloured pupils" in standards 6–8, see 1064
★*Aptitude Test for Junior Secondary Pupils* [South Africa], Bantus in Form I, see 1065
Aptitude Tests for Occupations, grades 9–13 and adults, see 1066
★*Armed Services Vocational Aptitude Battery,* high school, see 1067
Detroit General Aptitudes Examination, grades 6–12, see 1068
Differential Aptitude Tests, grades 8–12 and adults, see 1069
Differential Test Battery [England], ages 7 to "top university level," see 1070
Employee Aptitude Survey, ages 16 and over, see 1071

Flanagan Aptitude Classification Tests, grades 9–12 and adults, see 1072
General Aptitude Test Battery, grades 9–12 and adults, see 1073
Guilford-Zimmerman Aptitude Survey, grades 9–16 and adults, see 1074
High Level Battery: Test A/75 [South Africa], adults with at least 12 years of education, see 1075
★*International Primary Factors Test Battery,* grades 5 and over, see 1076
Jastak Test of Potential Ability and Behavior Stability, ages 11.5–14.5, see 1077
Job-Tests Program, adults, see 1078
★*Junior Aptitude Tests for Indian South Africans* [South Africa], standards 6–8, see 1079
Measurement of Skill, adults, see 1080

PERSONALITY

NONPROJECTIVE

Developmental Potential of Preschool Children, handicapped children ages 2–6, see 1156

Devereux Adolescent Behavior Rating Scale, normal and emotionally disturbed children ages 13–18, see 1157

Devereux Child Behavior Rating Scale, emotionally disturbed and mentally retarded children ages 8–12, see 1158

Devereux Elementary School Behavior Rating Scale, grades kgn–6, see 1159

Diplomacy Test of Empathy, business and industry, see 1160

★*Discharge Readiness Inventory,* psychiatric patients, see 1161

Dynamic Personality Inventory [England], ages 15 or 17 and over with IQ's of 80 and over, see 1162

Early School Personality Questionnaire, ages 6–8, see 1163

Edwards Personal Preference Schedule, college and adults, see 1164

Edwards Personality Inventory, grades 11–16 and adults, see 1165

Ego-Ideal and Conscience Development Test, ages 12–18, see 1166

Ego Strength Q-Sort Test, grades 9–16 and adults, see 1167

Elizur Test of Psycho-Organicity, ages 6 and over, see 1168

Embedded Figures Test, ages 10 and over, see 1169

Emo Questionnaire, adults, see 1170

Empathy Test, ages 13 and over, see 1171

Evaluation Modality Test, adults, see 1172

★*Experiential World Inventory,* disturbed adolescents and adults, see 1173

Eysenck Personality Inventory [England], grades 9–16 and adults, see 1174

Eysenck-Withers Personality Inventory [England], institutionalized subnormal adults, see 1175

FIRO Scales, grades 4–16 and adults, see 1176

★*Fairview Development Scale,* infirm mentally retarded, see 1177

★*Fairview Problem Behavior Record,* mentally retarded, see 1178

★*Fairview Self-Help Scale,* mentally retarded, see 1179

★*Fairview Social Skills Scale,* mentally retarded, see 1180

Family Adjustment Test, ages 12 and over, see 1181

Family Relations Test [England], ages 3 and over, see 1182

Famous Sayings, grades 9–16 and business and industry, see 1183

Fatigue Scales Kit, adults, see 1184

Fear Survey Schedule, college and adults, see 1185

Fels Parent Behavior Rating Scales, parents, see 1186

Forty-Eight Item Counseling Evaluation Test, adolescents and adults, see 1187

Freeman Anxiety Neurosis and Psychosomatic Test, mental patients, see 1188

★*Frost Self Description Questionnaire* [Canada], ages 8–14, see 1189

Getting Along, grades 7–9, see 1190

Gibson Spiral Maze [England], ages 8.5 and over, see 1191

Goldstein-Scheerer Tests of Abstract and Concrete Thinking, brain damaged adults, see 1192

Gordon Personal Inventory, grades 9–16 and adults, see 1193

Gordon Personal Profile, grades 9–16 and adults, see 1194

Gottschalk-Gleser Content Analysis Scales, ages 14 and over, see 1195

Grassi Block Substitution Test, mental patients, see 1196

Grayson Perceptualization Test, detection of cortical impairment, see 1197

Grid Test of Schizophrenic Thought Disorder [England], adults, see 1198

Group Cohesiveness: A Study of Group Morale, adults, see 1199

Group Dimensions Descriptions Questionnaire, college and adult groups, see 1200

★*Group Embedded Figures Test,* ages 10 and over, see 1201

Group Psychotherapy Suitability Evaluation Scale, patients in group therapy, see 1202

Guidance Inventory, high school, see 1203

Guilford-Holley L Inventory, college and adults, see 1204

Guilford-Martin Inventory of Factors GAMIN, grades 12–16 and adults, see 1205

Guilford-Martin Personnel Inventory, adults, see 1206

Guilford-Zimmerman Temperament Survey, grades 12–16 and adults, see 1207

★*Hahn Self Psychoevaluation Materials,* ages 40 and over, see 1208

★*Hahnemann High School Behavior Rating Scale,* grades 7–12, see 1209

Handicap Problems Inventory, ages 16 and over with physical disabilities, see 1210

Hartman Value Profile, ages 12 and over, see 1211

Harvard Group Scale of Hypnotic Susceptibility, college and adults, see 1212

Hellenic Affiliation Scale, college, see 1213

Hill Interaction Matrix, psychotherapy groups, see 1214

Hoffer-Osmond Diagnostic Test, mental patients, see 1215

Hooper Visual Organization Test, ages 14 and over, see 1216

Hospital Adjustment Scale, mental patients, see 1217

Hostility and Direction of Hostility Questionnaire [England], mental patients and normals, see 1218

★*How I See Myself Scale,* grades 3–12, see 1219

How Well Do You Know Yourself?, high school, college, office and factory workers, see 1220

Human Relations Inventory, grades 9–16 and adults, see 1221

Humm-Wadsworth Temperament Scale, adults, see 1222

Hunt-Minnesota Test for Organic Brain Damage, chronological ages 16–70 and mental ages 8 and over, see 1223

Hysteroid-Obsessoid Questionnaire [England], mental patients and normals, see 1224

IPAT Anxiety Scale Questionnaire, ages 14 and over, see 1225

IPAT Contact Personality Factor Test, high school and adults, see 1226

IPAT 8-Parallel-Form Anxiety Battery, ages 14 or 15 and over, see 1227

IPAT Humor Test of Personality, high school and adults, see 1228

IPAT Neurotic Personality Factor Test, grades 9–16 and adults, see 1229

Independent Activities Questionnaire, high school and college, see 1230

★*Inferred Self-Concept Scale,* grades 1–6, see 1231

Inpatient Multidimensional Psychiatric Scale, hospitalized mental patients, see 1232

Institute of Child Study Security Test [Canada], grades 1–8, see 1233

Institutional Functioning Inventory, college faculty and administrators, see 1234

★*Institutional Goals Inventory,* college faculty and students, see 1235

Institutional Self-Study Service Survey, college students, see 1236

Integration Level Test Series, adults, see 1237

Interest Inventory for Elementary Grades, grades 4–6, see 1238

PROJECTIVE

Social Relations Test [South Africa], adult males, see 1509

Sound-Apperception Test, ages 16 and over, see 1510

South African Picture Analysis Test [The Netherlands], ages 5–13, see 1511

Structured Doll Play Test, ages 2–6, see 1512

Structured-Objective Rorschach Test, adults, see 1513

Symbol Elaboration Test, ages 6 and over, see 1514

Symonds Picture-Story Test, grades 7–12, see 1515

Szondi Test [Switzerland], ages 5 and over, see 1516

Tasks of Emotional Development Test, ages 6–11 and adolescents, see 1517

Test of Family Attitudes [Belgium], ages 6–12, see 1518

Thematic Apperception Test, ages 4 and over, see 1519

Thematic Apperception Test for African Subjects [South Africa], ages 10 and over, see 1520

★*This I Believe Test*, grades 9 and over, see 1521

Tomkins-Horn Picture Arrangement Test, ages 10 and over, see 1522

Toy World Test [France], ages 2 and over, see 1523

Tree Test [Switzerland], ages 9 and over, see 1524

Twitchell-Allen Three-Dimensional Personality Test, ages 3 and over (sighted and sightless), see 1525

Visual Apperception Test '60, ages 6 and over, see 1526

Washington University Sentence Completion Test, ages 12 and over, see 1527

Zulliger Individual and Group Test [Switzerland], ages 3 and over, see 1528

READING

A.C.E.R. Lower Grades Reading Test: Level 1 [Australia], grade 1, see 1529

★*ACER Primary Reading Survey Tests* [Australia], grades 3–6, see 1530

A.C.E.R. Silent Reading Tests: Standardized for Use in New Zealand [New Zealand], ages 9–12, see 1531

American School Achievement Tests: Reading, grades 2–9, see 1532

American School Reading Tests, grades 10–13, see 1533

Buffalo Reading Test for Speed and Comprehension, grades 9–16, see 1534

Burnett Reading Series: Survey Test, grades 1.5–12, see 1535

California Achievement Tests: Reading, grades 1–14, see 1536

Carver-Darby Chunked Reading Test, grades 9–16 and adults, see 1537

Commerce Reading Comprehension Test, grades 12–16 and adults, see 1538

Comprehension Test for Training College Students [England], training college students and applicants for admission, see 1539

Comprehensive Primary Reading Scales, grade 1, see 1540

Comprehensive Reading Scales, grades 4–12, see 1541

Comprehensive Tests of Basic Skills: Reading, grades kgn–12, see 1542

Cooperative Primary Tests: Reading, grades 1.5–3, see 1543

Cooperative Reading Comprehension Test, Form Y [Australia], secondary forms 5–6 and university, see 1544

Cooperative Reading Comprehension Test, Forms L and M [Australia], secondary forms 2–4, see 1545

Davis Reading Test, grades 8–13, see 1546

Delaware County Silent Reading Test, grades 1.5–8, see 1547

★*Edinburgh Reading Tests* [England], ages 8.5–12.5, see 1548

Emporia Reading Tests, grades 1–8, see 1549

GAP Reading Comprehension Test [Australia], grades 2–7, see 1550

★*GAPADOL* [Australia], ages 10 and over, see 1551

Gates-MacGinitie Reading Tests, grades 1–9, see 1552

Gates-MacGinitie Reading Tests: Survey F, grades 10–12, see 1553

Group Reading Assessment [England], end of first year junior school, see 1554

Group Reading Test [England], ages 6–10, see 1555

High School Reading Test: National Achievement Tests, grades 7–12, see 1556

Individual Reading Test [Australia], ages 6-0 to 9-9, see 1557

★*Informal Reading Assessment Tests* [Canada], grades 1–3, see 1558

★*Inventory-Survey Tests*, grades 4–8, see 1559

Iowa Silent Reading Tests, grades 4–16, see 1560

Kelvin Measurement of Reading Ability [Scotland], ages 8–12, see 1561

Kingston Test of Silent Reading [England], ages 7–11, see 1562

Lee-Clark Reading Test, grades 1–2, see 1563

McGrath Test of Reading Skills, grades 1–13, see 1564

McMenemy Measure of Reading Ability, grades 3 and 5–8, see 1565

Maintaining Reading Efficiency Tests, grades 7–16 and adults, see 1566

Metropolitan Achievement Tests: Reading Tests, grades 2–9, see 1567

Minnesota Reading Examination for College Students, grades 9–16, see 1568

Monroe's Standardized Silent Reading Test, grades 3–12, see 1569

N.B. Silent Reading Tests (Beginners): Reading Comprehension Test [South Africa], substandard B, see 1570

National Teacher Examinations: Reading Specialist, college seniors and teachers, see 1571

Nelson-Denny Reading Test, grades 9–16 and adults, see 1572

Nelson Reading Test, grades 3–9, see 1573

New Developmental Reading Tests, grades 1–6, see 1574

OISE Achievement Tests in Silent Reading: Advanced Primary Battery [Canada], grade 2, see 1575

Pressey Diagnostic Reading Tests, grades 3–9, see 1576

★*Primary Reading Survey Tests*, grades 2–3, see 1577

Primary Reading Test: Acorn Achievement Tests, grades 2–3, see 1578

Progressive Achievement Tests of Reading [New Zealand], standards 2–4 and Forms I–IV (ages 8–14), see 1579

RBH Basic Reading and Word Test, disadvantaged adults, see 1580

RBH Test of Reading Comprehension, business and industry, see 1581

Reading Comprehension: Canadian English Achievement Test [Canada], grades 8.5–9.0, see 1582

Reading Comprehension: Cooperative English Tests, grades 9–14, see 1583

Reading Comprehension Test, college entrants, see 1584

Reading Comprehension Test DE [England], ages 10–12.5, see 1585

Reading Comprehension Test: National Achievement

DIAGNOSTIC

MISCELLANEOUS

SCIENCE

BIOLOGY

Cooperative Biology Test: Educational Records Bureau Edition, high school, see 1807

Cooperative Science Tests: Biology, grades 10–12, see 1808

Emporia Biology Test, 1–2 semesters high school, see 1809

General Biology Test: National Achievement Tests, high school, see 1810

Graduate Record Examinations Advanced Biology Test, graduate school candidates, see 1811

Nelson Biology Test, grades 9–13, see 1812

Undergraduate Program Field Tests: Biology Test, college, see 1813

CHEMISTRY

ACS Cooperative Examination Brief Course in Organic Chemistry, 1 semester college, see 1814

ACS Cooperative Examination in Analytical Chemistry, Graduate Level, entering graduate students, see 1815

ACS Cooperative Examination in Biochemistry, college, see 1816

ACS Cooperative Examination in Brief Physical Chemistry, 1 semester college, see 1817

ACS Cooperative Examination in Brief Qualitative Analysis, college, see 1818

ACS Cooperative Examination in General Chemistry, 1 year college, see 1819

ACS Cooperative Examination in Inorganic Chemistry, grades 15–16, see 1820

ACS Cooperative Examination in Inorganic Chemistry, Graduate Level, entering graduate students, see 1821

ACS Cooperative Examination in Inorganic-Organic-Biological Chemistry (for Paramedical Programs), 1–2 semesters of chemistry for nursing, home economics, and other paramedical students, see 1822

ACS Cooperative Examination in Instrumental Analysis, grades 15–16, see 1823

ACS Cooperative Examination in Organic Chemistry, 1 year college, see 1824

ACS Cooperative Examination in Organic Chemistry, Graduate Level, entering graduate students, see 1825

ACS Cooperative Examination in Physical Chemistry, 1 year college, see 1826

ACS Cooperative Examination in Physical Chemistry, Graduate Level, entering graduate students, see 1827

ACS Cooperative Examination in Qualitative Analysis, college, see 1828

ACS Cooperative Examination in Quantitative Analysis, college, see 1829

ACS-NSTA Cooperative Examination in High School Chemistry, 1 year high school, see 1830

ACS-NSTA Cooperative Examination in High School Chemistry: Advanced Level, advanced high school classes, see 1831

Advanced Placement Examination in Chemistry, high school students desiring credit for college level courses or admission to advanced courses, see 1832

CLEP Subject Examination in General Chemistry, 1 year or equivalent, see 1833

Chemistry: Achievement Examinations for Secondary Schools, high school, see 1834

Chemistry Achievement Test for CHEM Study or Equivalent, high school, see 1835

Chemistry: Minnesota High School Achievement Examinations, high school, see 1836

College Board Achievement Test in Chemistry, candidates for college entrance, see 1837

College Placement Test in Chemistry, entering college freshmen, see 1838

Cooperative Chemistry Test: Educational Records Bureau Edition, high school, see 1839

Cooperative Science Tests: Chemistry, grades 10–12, see 1840

Emporia Chemistry Test, 1–2 semesters high school, see 1841

General Chemistry Test: National Achievement Tests, grades 10–16, see 1842

Graduate Record Examinations Advanced Chemistry Test, graduate school candidates, see 1843

Iowa Placement Examinations: Chemistry Aptitude, grades 12–13, see 1844

Iowa Placement Examinations: Chemistry Training, grades 12–13, see 1845

RBH Test of Chemical Comprehension, employee applicants and applicants for nurses' training, see 1846

Toledo Chemistry Placement Examination, college entrants, see 1847

Undergraduate Program Field Tests: Chemistry Test, college, see 1848

GEOLOGY

CLEP Subject Examination in Geology, 1 year or equivalent, see 1849

Graduate Record Examinations Advanced Geology Test, graduate school candidates, see 1850

Undergraduate Program Field Tests: Geology Test, college, see 1851

MISCELLANEOUS

Butler Life Science Concept Test, grades 1–6, see 1852

Dubins Earth Science Test, grades 8–12, see 1853

★*NM Concepts of Ecology Test*, grades 6–8, see 1854

★*Science Attitude Questionnaire* [England], secondary school, see 1855

Test on Understanding Science, grades 9–12, see 1856

Tests of Basic Experiences: Science, prekgn–grade 1, see 1857

PHYSICS

Advanced Placement Examination in Physics, high school students desiring credit for college level courses or admission to advanced courses, see 1858

College Board Achievement Test in Physics, candidates for college entrance, see 1859

College Placement Test in Physics, entering college freshmen, see 1860

Cooperative Physics Test: Educational Records Bureau Edition, high school, see 1861

Cooperative Science Tests: Physics, grades 10–12, see 1862

Dunning-Abeles Physics Test, grades 10–13, see 1863

Emporia Physics Test, 1–2 semesters high school, see 1864

General Physics Test: National Achievement Tests, grades 10–16, see 1865

Graduate Record Examinations Advanced Physics Test, graduate school candidates, see 1866

Iowa Placement Examinations: Physics Aptitude, grades 12–13, see 1867

Iowa Placement Examinations: Physics Training, grades 12–13, see 1868

★*Objective Tests in Physics*, high school, see 1869

Physics: Achievement Examinations for Secondary Schools, high school, see 1870

Physics: Minnesota High School Achievement Examinations, high school, see 1871

Tests of the Physical Science Study Committee, high school, see 1872

Undergraduate Program Field Tests: Physics Test, college, see 1873

SENSORY-MOTOR

MOTOR

VISION

SOCIAL STUDIES

and World Cultures, candidates for college entrance, see 1940

College Placement Test in American History and Social Studies, entering college freshmen, see 1941

College Placement Test in European History and World Cultures, entering college freshmen, see 1942

History and Civics Test: Municipal Tests, grades 3–8, see 1943

Iowa Tests of Educational Development: Understanding of Basic Social Concepts, grades 9–12, see 1944

National Teacher Examinations: Social Studies, college seniors and teachers, see 1945

Primary Social Studies Test, grades 1–3, see 1946

SRA Achievement Series: Social Studies, grades 4–9, see 1947

Sequential Tests of Educational Progress: Social Studies, grades 4–14, see 1948

Social Studies: Minnesota High School Achievement Examinations, grades 7–9, see 1949

Social Studies Test: Acorn National Achievement Tests, grades 7–9, see 1950

Social Studies Test: National Achievement Tests, grades 4–9, see 1951

Stanford Achievement Test: High School Social Studies Test, grades 9–12, see 1952

Stanford Achievement Test: Social Studies Tests, grades 5.5–9, see 1953

Teacher Education Examination Program: Social Studies, college seniors preparing to teach secondary school, see 1954

Tests of Academic Progress: Social Studies, grades 9–12, see 1955

Tests of Basic Experiences: Social Studies, prekgn–grade 1, see 1956

Zimmerman-Sanders Social Studies Test, grades 7–8, see 1957

CONTEMPORARY AFFAIRS

Current News Test, grades 9–12, see 1958

Newsweek NewsQuiz, grades 9–12, see 1959

School Weekly News Quiz, high school, see 1960

Time Current Affairs Test, grades 9–12 and adults, see 1961

★*Time Monthly News Quiz,* grades 9–12 and adults, see 1962

ECONOMICS

CLEP Subject Examination in Introductory Economics, 1 year or equivalent, see 1963

★*Economics/Objective Tests,* 1 semester high school, see 1964

Graduate Record Examinations Advanced Economics Test, graduate school candidates, see 1965

★*Modern Economics Test: Content Evaluation Series,* grades 10–12, see 1966

★*Primary Test of Economic Understanding,* grades 2–3, see 1967

Test of Economic Understanding, high school and college, see 1968

★*Test of Elementary Economics,* grades 4–6, see 1969

Test of Understanding in College Economics, 1–2 semesters college, see 1970

★*Test of Understanding in Personal Economics,* high school, see 1971

Undergraduate Program Field Tests: Economics Test, college, see 1972

GEOGRAPHY

Brandywine Achievement Test in Geography for Secondary Schools, grades 7–12, see 1973

Economic Geography: Achievement Examinations for Secondary Schools, high school, see 1974

Geography Test: Municipal Tests, grades 3–8, see 1975

Geography Test: National Achievement Tests, grades 6–8, see 1976

Graduate Record Examinations Advanced Geography Test, graduate school candidates, see 1977

Hollingsworth-Sanders Geography Test, grades 5–7, see 1978

Undergraduate Program Field Tests: Geography Test, college, see 1979

HISTORY

Advanced Placement Examination in American History, high school students desiring credit for college level courses or admission to advanced courses, see 1980

Advanced Placement Examination in European History, high school students desiring credit for college level courses or admission to advanced courses, see 1981

★*American History: Junior High—Objective,* grades 7–9, see 1982

American History: Senior High—Objective, 1–2 semesters high school, see 1983

American History Test: National Achievement Tests, grades 7–8, see 1984

★*CLEP Subject Examination in Afro-American History,* 1 semester or equivalent, see 1985

CLEP Subject Examination in American History, 1 year or equivalent, see 1986

CLEP Subject Examination in Western Civilization, 1 year or equivalent, see 1987

Cooperative Social Studies Tests: American History, grades 7–8, 10–12, see 1988

Cooperative Social Studies Tests: Modern European History, grades 10–12, see 1989

Cooperative Social Studies Tests: World History, grades 10–12, see 1990

Cooperative Topical Tests in American History, high school, see 1991

Crary American History Test, grades 10–13, see 1992

Emporia American History Test, 1–2 semesters high school, see 1993

Graduate Record Examinations Advanced History Test, graduate school candidates, see 1994

Hollingsworth-Sanders Intermediate History Test, grades 5–6, see 1995

Meares-Sanders Junior High School History Test, grades 7–8, see 1996

Modern World History: Achievement Examinations for Secondary Schools, high school, see 1997

Sanders-Buller World History Test, 1–2 semesters high school, see 1998

Social Studies Grade 10 (American History): Minnesota High School Achievement Examinations, grade 10, see 1999

Social Studies Grade 11 (World History): Minnesota High School Achievement Examinations, grade 11, see 2000

Undergraduate Program Field Tests: History Test, college, see 2001

World History/Objective Tests, 1–2 semesters high school, see 2002

World History Test: Acorn National Achievement Tests, high school and college, see 2003

POLITICAL SCIENCE

CLEP Subject Examination in American Government, 1 semester or equivalent, see 2004
Cooperative Social Studies Tests: American Government, grades 10–12, see 2005
Cooperative Social Studies Tests: Civics, grades 8–9, see 2006
Cooperative Social Studies Tests: Problems of Democracy, grades 10–12, see 2007
★*Government/Objective Tests,* 1 semester grades 11–12, see 2008
Graduate Record Examinations Advanced Political Science Test, graduate school candidates, see 2009
★*National Teacher Examinations: Texas Government,* college seniors and teachers, see 2010
Patterson Test or Study Exercises on the Constitution of the United States, grades 9–16 and adults, see 2011
Principles of Democracy Test, grades 9–12, see 2012

Sare-Sanders American Government Test, high school and college, see 2013
Sare-Sanders Constitution Test, high school and college, see 2014
Social Studies Grade 12 (American Problems): Minnesota High School Achievement Examinations, grade 12, see 2015
Undergraduate Program Field Tests: Political Science Test, college, see 2016

SOCIOLOGY

CLEP Subject Examination in Introductory Sociology, 1 year or equivalent, see 2017
Graduate Record Examinations Advanced Sociology Test, graduate school candidates, see 2018
Sare-Sanders Sociology Test, high school and college, see 2019
Undergraduate Program Field Tests: Sociology Test, college, see 2020

SPEECH AND HEARING

★*Diagnostic Test of Speechreading,* deaf children ages 4–9, see 2021
★*Multiple-Choice Intelligibility Test,* college, see 2022
★*Ohio Tests of Articulation and Perception of Sounds,* ages 5–8, see 2023
Preschool Language Scale, ages 2–6, see 2024
Reynell Developmental Language Scales [England], children ages 1–5 with delayed or deviant language development, see 2025
Undergraduate Program Field Tests: Speech Pathology and Audiology Test, college, see 2026

HEARING

Ambco Audiometers, ages 10 and over, see 2027
Ambco Speech Test Record, ages 3 and over, see 2027A
Auditory Discrimination Test, ages 5–8, see 2028
★*Auditory Memory Span Test,* ages 5–8, see 2029
★*Auditory Sequential Memory Test,* grades 5–8, see 2030
Auditory Tests, grades 2 and over, see 2031
Beltone Audiometers, grades kgn and over, see 2032
Comprehension of Oral Language: Inter-American Series, grade 1, see 2033
Eckstein Audiometers, grades kgn and over, see 2034
★*Flowers-Costello Tests of Central Auditory Abilities,* grades kgn–6, see 2035
★*Four Tone Screening for Older Children and Adults,* ages 8 and over, see 2036
Goldman-Fristoe-Woodcock Test of Auditory Discrimination, ages 4 and over, see 2037
Grason-Stadler Audiometers, ages 6 and over, see 2038
Hearing of Speech Tests, ages 3–12, see 2039
Hollien-Thompson Group Hearing Test, grades 1 and over, see 2040
★*Kindergarten Auditory Screening Test,* grades kgn–1, see 2041
★*Lindamood Auditory Conceptualization Test,* grades kgn–12, see 2042
Maico Audiometers, grades kgn and over, see 2043
Maico Hearing Impairment Calculator, see 2044
Massachusetts Hearing Test, grades 1–16 and adults, see 2045
Modified Rhyme Hearing Test, grades 4 and over, see 2046

National Teacher Examinations: Audiology, college seniors and teachers, see 2047
New Group Pure Tone Hearing Test, grades 1 and over, see 2048
★*Oliphant Auditory Discrimination Memory Test,* grades 2–6, see 2049
★*Oliphant Auditory Synthesizing Test,* grade 1, see 2050
Pritchard-Fox Phoneme Auditory Discrimination Tests: Test Four, kgn and over, see 2051
Robbins Speech Sound Discrimination and Verbal Imagery Type Tests, ages 4 and over, see 2052
Rush Hughes (PB 50): Phonetically Balanced Lists 5–12, grades 2 and over, see 2053
Screening Test for Auditory Perception, grades 2–6, see 2054
Stycar Hearing Tests [England], ages 6 months to 7 years, see 2055
Test of Listening Accuracy in Children, ages 5–9, see 2056
★*Test of Non-Verbal Auditory Discrimination,* ages 6–8, see 2057
★*Tracor Audiometers,* infants and older, see 2058
Verbal Auditory Screening for Children, ages 3–8, see 2059
★*Washington Speech Sound Discrimination Test,* ages 3–5, see 2060
★*Word Intelligibility by Picture Identification,* hearing impaired children ages 5–13, see 2061
★*ZECO Pure Tone Screening for Children,* ages 3–8, see 2062
Zenith Audiometers, preschool and over, see 2063–4

SPEECH

Arizona Articulation Proficiency Scale, mental ages 2–14 and over, see 2065
★*Boston Diagnostic Aphasia Examination,* aphasic patients, see 2066
★*Bzoch-League Receptive-Expressive Emergent Language Scale: For the Measurement of Language Skills in Infancy,* birth to age 3, see 2067
Communicative Evaluation Chart From Infancy to Five Years, see 2068
Deep Test of Articulation, all reading levels, see 2069

★*Edinburgh Articulation Test* [Scotland], ages 3–5, see 2070
Examining for Aphasia, adolescents and adults, see 2071
★*Fairview Language Evaluation Scale,* mentally retarded, see 2072
★*Fisher-Logemann Test of Articulation Competence,* preschool and over, see 2073
Forms From Diagnostic Methods in Speech Pathology, children and adults with speech problems, see 2074
Goldman-Fristoe Test of Articulation, ages 2 and over, see 2075
Halstead Aphasia Test, adults, see 2076
Houston Test for Language Development, ages 6 months to 6 years, see 2077
Language Facility Test, ages 3 and over, see 2078
Language Modalities Test for Aphasia, adults, see 2079
Minnesota Test for Differential Diagnosis of Aphasia, adults, see 2080
National Teacher Examinations: Speech-Communication and Theatre, college seniors and teachers, see 2081
National Teacher Examinations: Speech Pathology, college seniors and teachers, see 2082
Nationwide Speech Examination, grades 4–12, see 2083
★*Northwestern Syntax Screening Test,* ages 3–7, see 2084

Orzeck Aphasia Evaluation, mental and brain damaged patients, see 2085
Photo Articulation Test, ages 3–12, see 2086
Porch Index of Communicative Ability, adults, see 2087
Predictive Screening Test of Articulation, grade 1, see 2088
Riley Articulation and Language Test, grades kgn–2, see 2089
Screening Deep Test of Articulation, grades kgn and over, see 2090
Screening Speech Articulation Test, ages 3.5–8.5, see 2091
Sklar Aphasia Scale, brain damaged adults, see 2092
Speech Defect Questionnaire, ages 6 and over, see 2093
Speech Diagnostic Chart, grades 1–8, see 2094
Templin-Darley Tests of Articulation, ages 3 and over, see 2095
★*Undergraduate Program Field Tests: Drama and Theatre Test,* college, see 2096
Utah Test of Language Development, ages 1.5 to 14.5, see 2097
Verbal Language Development Scale, birth to age 15, see 2098
Weidner-Fensch Speech Screening Test, grades 1–3, see 2099

VOCATIONS

★*ACT Assessment of Career Development,* grades 8–11, see 2100
★*ACT Career Planning Program,* entrants to postsecondary educational institutions, see 2101
Aptitude Inventory, employee applicants, see 2102
★*Career Maturity Inventory,* grades 6–12, see 2103
★*Classification Test Battery* [South Africa], illiterate and semiliterate applicants for unskilled and semiskilled mining jobs, see 2104
Dailey Vocational Tests, grades 8–12 and adults, see 2105
ETSA Tests, job applicants, see 2106
Flanagan Industrial Tests, business and industry, see 2107
Individual Placement Series, high school and adults, see 2108
★*New Mexico Career Education Test Series,* grades 9–12, see 2109
Personal History Index, job applicants, see 2110
Steward Basic Factors Inventory, applicants for sales and office positions, see 2111
Steward Personnel Tests, applicants for sales and office positions, see 2112
TAV Selection System, adults, see 2113
Vocational Planning Inventory, vocational students in grades 8–12 and grade 13 entrants, see 2114
WLW Employment Inventory, adults, see 2115
★*Wide Range Employment Sample Test,* ages 16–35 (normal and handicapped), see 2116

CLERICAL

ACER Short Clerical Test—Form C [Australia], ages 13 and over, see 2117
A.C.E.R. Speed and Accuracy Tests [Australia], ages 13.5 and over, see 2118
APT Dictation Test, stenographers, see 2119
★*Appraisal of Occupational Aptitudes,* high school and adults, see 2120
Clerical Skills Series, clerical workers and applicants, see 2121

Clerical Tests, applicants for clerical positions, see 2122
Clerical Tests, Series N, applicants for clerical positions not involving frequent use of typewriter or verbal skill, see 2123
Clerical Tests, Series V, applicants for typing and stenographic positions, see 2124
Clerical Worker Examination, clerical workers, see 2125
Cross Reference Test, clerical job applicants, see 2126
Curtis Verbal-Clerical Skills Tests, applicants for clerical positions, see 2127
General Clerical Ability Test, job applicants, see 2128
General Clerical Test, grades 9–16 and clerical job applicants, see 2129
Group Test 20 [England], ages 15 and over, see 2130
Group Tests 61A, 64, and 66A [England], clerical applicants, see 2131
Hay Clerical Test Battery, applicants for clerical positions, see 2132
L & L Clerical Tests, applicants for office positions, see 2133
McCann Typing Tests, applicants for typing positions, see 2134
Minnesota Clerical Test, grades 8–12 and adults, see 2135
Office Skills Achievement Test, employees, see 2136
Office Worker Test, office workers, see 2137
O'Rourke Clerical Aptitude Test, Junior Grade, applicants for clerical positions, see 2138
Personnel Institute Clerical Tests, clerical personnel and typists-stenographers-secretaries, see 2139
Personnel Research Institute Clerical Battery, applicants for clerical positions, see 2140
Personnel Research Institute Test of Shorthand Skills, stenographers, see 2141
Purdue Clerical Adaptability Test, applicants for clerical positions, see 2142
RBH Checking Test, applicants for clerical and stenographic positions, see 2143
RBH Classifying Test, business and industry, see 2144
RBH Number Checking Test, business and industry, see 2145

INTERESTS

MANUAL DEXTERITY

MECHANICAL ABILITY

MISCELLANEOUS

SELECTION & RATING FORMS

APT Controlled Interview, applicants for employment, see 2294

Application Interview Screening Form, job applicants, see 2295

Career Counseling Personal Data Form, vocational counselees, see 2296

Employee Competency Scale, employees, see 2297

Employee Evaluation Form for Interviewers, adults, see 2298

Employee Performance Appraisal, business and industry, see 2299

★*Employee Progress Appraisal Form,* rating of office employees, see 2300

Employee Rating and Development Forms, executive, industrial, office, and sales personnel, see 2301

Executive, Industrial, and Sales Personnel Forms, applicants for executive, industrial, office, or sales positions, see 2302

Job Application Forms, job applicants and employees, see 2303

Lawshe-Kephart Personnel Comparison System, for rating any aspect of employee performance by the paired comparison technique, see 2304

★*McCormick Job Performance Measurement "Rate-$-Scales,"* employees, see 2305

McQuaig Manpower Selection Series, applicants for office and sales positions, see 2306

Martin Performance Appraisal, employees, see 2307

Merit Rating Series, industry, see 2308

Nagel Personnel Interviewing and Screening Forms, job applicants, see 2309

Performance Review Forms, employees and managers, see 2310

Personal Data Blank, counselees ages 15 and over, see 2311

Personnel Interviewing Forms, business and industry, see 2312

Personnel Rating Scale, employees, see 2313

RBH Individual Background Survey, business and industry, see 2314

San Francisco Vocational Competency Scale, mentally retarded adults, see 2315

Selection Interview Forms, business and industry, see 2316

Speech-Appearance Record, job applicants, see 2317

Stevens-Thurow Personnel Forms, business and industry, see 2318

★*Tickmaster,* job applicants, see 2319

Wonderlic Personnel Selection Procedure, applicants for employment, see 2320

Work Reference Check, job applicants, see 2321

SPECIFIC VOCATIONS

ACCOUNTING

Account Clerk Test, job applicants, see 2322

American Institute of Certified Public Accountants Testing Programs, grades 13–16 and accountants, see 2323

CLEP Subject Examination in Introductory Accounting, 1 year or equivalent, see 2324

BUSINESS

Admission Test for Graduate Study in Business, business graduate students, see 2325

CLEP Subject Examination in Introduction to Busi-ness Management, 1 semester or equivalent, see 2326

CLEP Subject Examination in Introductory Business Law, 1 semester or equivalent, see 2327

CLEP Subject Examination in Introductory Market-ing, 1 semester or equivalent, see 2328

CLEP Subject Examination in Money and Banking, 1 semester or equivalent, see 2329

Organizational Value Dimensions Questionnaire, adults, see 2330

COMPUTER PROGRAMMING

Aptitude Assessment Battery: Programming, programmers and trainees, see 2331

CLEP Subject Examination in Computers and Data Processing, 1–2 semesters or equivalent, see 2332

★*CLEP Subject Examination in Elementary Computer Programming—Fortran IV,* 1 semester or equivalent, see 2333

Computer Programmer Aptitude Battery, applicants for computer training or employment, see 2334

Diebold Personnel Tests, programmers and systems analysts for automatic data processing and computing installations, see 2335

★*Programmer Aptitude/Competence Test System,* computer programmers and applicants for programmer training, see 2336

DENTISTRY

Dental Admission Testing Program, dental school applicants, see 2337

Dental Hygiene Aptitude Testing Program, dental hygiene school applicants, see 2338

★*Ohio Dental Assisting Achievement Test,* grades 11–12, see 2339

ENGINEERING

AC Test of Creative Ability, engineers and supervisors, see 2340

Engineering Aide Test, engineering aides, see 2341

Garnett College Test in Engineering Science [England], 1–2 years technical college, see 2342

Graduate Record Examinations Advanced Engineering Test, graduate school candidates, see 2343

Minnesota Engineering Analogies Test, candidates for graduate school and industry, see 2344

N.I.I.P. Engineering Apprentice Selection Test Battery [England], engineering apprentices, see 2345

National Engineering Aptitude Search Test: The Junior Engineering Technical Society, grades 9–12, see 2346

Purdue Creativity Test, applicants for engineering positions, see 2347

Undergraduate Program Field Tests: Engineering Test, college, see 2348

LAW

Law School Admission Test, law school applicants, see 2349

MEDICINE

★*CLEP Subject Examination in Clinical Chemistry,* medical technologists, see 2350

★*CLEP Subject Examination in Hematology,* medical technologists, see 2351

★*CLEP Subject Examination in Immunohematology and Blood Banking,* medical technologists, see 2352

★*CLEP Subject Examination in Microbiology,* medical technologists, see 2353

MISCELLANEOUS

Colleges of Podiatry Admission Test, grades 14 and over, see 2354
Medical College Admission Test, applicants for admission to member colleges of the Association of American Medical Colleges, see 2355
Medical School Instructor Attitude Inventory, medical school faculty members, see 2356
★*Optometry College Admission Test,* optometry college applicants, see 2357
Veterinary Aptitude Test, veterinary school applicants, see 2358

MISCELLANEOUS

Architectural School Aptitude Test, architectural school applicants, see 2359
Chemical Operators Selection Test, chemical operators and applicants, see 2360
Fire Promotion Tests, prospective firemen promotees, see 2361
Firefighter Test, prospective firemen, see 2362
Fireman Examination, prospective firemen, see 2363
General Municipal Employees Performance (Efficiency) Rating System, municipal employees, see 2364
Journalism Test, high school, see 2365
★*Law Enforcement Perception Questionnaire,* law enforcement personnel, see 2366
Memory and Observation Tests for Policeman, prospective policemen, see 2367
Police Performance Rating System, policemen, see 2368
Police Promotion Tests, prospective policemen promotees, see 2369
Policeman Examination, prospective policemen, see 2370
Policeman Test, policemen and prospective policemen, see 2371
Potter-Nash Aptitude Test for Lumber Inspectors and Other General Personnel Who Handle Lumber, employees in woodworking industries, see 2372
★*Test for Firefighter B-1,* firemen and prospective firemen, see 2373
★*Test for Police Officer A-1,* policemen and prospective policemen, see 2374
Visual Comprehension Test for Detective, prospective police detectives, see 2375

NURSING

Achievement Tests in Nursing, students in schools of registered nursing, see 2376
Achievement Tests in Practical Nursing, practical nursing students, see 2377
Empathy Inventory, nursing instructors, see 2378
Entrance Examination for Schools of Nursing, nursing school applicants, see 2379
Entrance Examination for Schools of Practical Nursing, practical nursing school applicants, see 2380
George Washington University Series Nursing Tests, prospective nurses, see 2381
Luther Hospital Sentence Completions, prospective nursing students, see 2382
NLN Achievement Tests for Schools Preparing Registered Nurses, students in state-approved schools preparing registered nurses, see 2383
NLN Aide Selection Test, applicants for aide positions in hospitals and home health agencies, see 2384
NLN Practical Nursing Achievement Tests, students in state-approved schools of practical nursing, see 2385
NLN Pre-Admission and Classification Examination, practical nursing school entrants, see 2386
NLN Pre-Nursing and Guidance Examination, applicants for admission to state-approved schools preparing registered nurses, see 2387
Netherne Study Difficulties Battery for Student Nurses [England], student nurses, see 2388
Nurse Attitudes Inventory, prospective nursing students, see 2389
PSB-Aptitude for Practical Nursing Examination, applicants for admission to practical nursing schools, see 2390

RESEARCH

Research Personnel Review Form, research and engineering and scientific firms, see 2391
Supervisor's Evaluation of Research Personnel, research personnel, see 2392
Surveys of Research Administration and Environment, research and engineering and scientific firms, see 2393
Technical Personnel Recruiting Inventory, research and engineering and scientific firms, see 2394

SELLING

Aptitudes Associates Test of Sales Aptitude, applicants for sales positions, see 2395
Combination Inventory, Form 2, prospective debit life insurance salesmen, see 2396
Detroit Retail Selling Inventory, candidates for training in retail selling, see 2397
Evaluation Record, prospective life insurance agency managers, see 2398
Hall Salespower Inventory, salesmen, see 2399
Hanes Sales Selection Inventory, insurance and printing salesmen, see 2400
Information Index, life and health insurance agents, see 2401
LIAMA Inventory of Job Attitudes, life insurance field personnel, see 2402
Personnel Institute Hiring Kit, applicants for sales positions, see 2403
SRA Sales Attitudes Check List, applicants for sales positions, see 2404
Sales Aptitude Test, job applicants, see 2405
Sales Comprehension Test, applicants for sales positions, see 2406
Sales Method Index, life insurance agents, see 2407
Sales Motivation Inventory, applicants for sales positions, see 2408
Sales Sentence Completion Blank, applicants for sales positions, see 2409
Steward Life Insurance Knowledge Test, applicants for life insurance agent or supervisory positions, see 2410
Steward Occupational Objectives Inventory, applicants for supervisory positions in life insurance companies or agencies, see 2411
Steward Personal Background Inventory, applicants for sales positions, see 2412
Test for Ability to Sell: George Washington University Series, grades 7-16 and adults, see 2413
★*Test of Retail Sales Insight,* retail clerks and students, see 2414

SKILLED TRADES

Electrical Sophistication Test, job applicants, see 2415
Fiesenheiser Test of Ability to Read Drawings, trade school and adults, see 2416
Mechanical Familiarity Test, job applicants, see 2417
Mechanical Handyman Test, maintenance workers, see 2418
Mechanical Knowledge Test, job applicants, see 2419

SUPERVISION

TRANSPORTATION

1. This volume presents a comprehensive bibliography of all in print tests published as separates for use with English-speaking subjects.

2. *Tests in Print II* (TIP II) serves as a master index to the test reviews, excerpts, and references in the seven *Mental Measurements Yearbooks* (MMY), *Personality Tests and Reviews* (PTR), and *Reading Tests and Reviews* (RTR).

3. Verified bibliographies through 1971 on the construction, use, and validity of specific tests are given for all tests for which references were located. These bibliographies supplement earlier bibliographies in the MMY's and PTR. A Cumulative Name Index is presented for each specific test bibliography.

4. TIP II serves as an index to out of print tests once listed as in print in an MMY, PTR, RTR, or TIP I. The volume also includes classified listings of tests which have gone out of print since the 1961 *Tests in Print*.

5. The 1974 APA-AERA-NCME *Standards for Educational and Psychological Tests* has been reprinted with the permission of the American Psychological Association.

6. The Expanded Table of Contents opposite presents a complete list of all categories under which tests have been classified. The numbers cited, as in all the indexes and cross references, are test numbers (the numbers in the running heads next to the outside margins), not page numbers. Tests are listed alphabetically by title within a classification.

7. The Scanning Index, the last index in the book, presents a classified listing of all tests along with a description of the population for which each test is intended. Stars indicate tests not previously listed in one of our publications and asterisks indicate tests new or supplemented since last listed. Foreign tests are identified by reporting the country of origin in brackets immediately after the test title.

8. The test write-ups, called entries, report the following information when applicable: (*a*) test title; (*b*) population for which suitable; (*c*) range of copyright dates; (*d*) acronym; (*e*) part scores; (*f*) absence of a manual; (*g*) questionable updating of test materials; (*h*) authors; (*i*) publisher; (*j*) country if not the United States; (*k*) cross references to MMY's and PTR for more informative entries, test reviews, excerpted test reviews, and references. The names of authors of reviews and excerpts are reported. As in the Scanning Index, titles of new tests are preceded by stars; revised or supplemented tests by asterisks. An asterisk following the publisher's name indicates that all test materials have been examined in the MMY office.

9. Necessary directions for the use of the four indexes (Publishers Directory and Index, Index of Titles, Index of Names, and Scanning Index) are summarized at the beginning of each index. More detailed information on the indexes is given in the Introduction.

10. All indexes and cross references refer to test numbers, not to page numbers. In the running heads, test numbers are next to the outside margins; page numbers are next to the inside margins.

11. In the indexes, all cited numbers which contain colons refer to out of print tests; for further information about these tests, earlier volumes must be consulted. For 4:385, for example, see test 385 (now out of print) in *The Fourth Yearbook*.

12. The name and title indexes cover out of print tests as well as the in print tests listed in this volume. The comprehensive name index is analytical in that each cited number is labeled to indicate whether it refers to authorship of a test, review, excerpt, or reference. Further information about where to find authors' reviews and excerpts are given in the test entries; information about an author's references for a specific test is given in the Cumulative Name Index for that test.

13. The Publishers Directory and Index lists each publisher's tests alphabetically.

14. The Preface presents a statement on the history and objectives of this series and plans for the preparation and publication of *Tests in Print III, The Eighth Mental Measurements Yearbook,* and a series of monographs in specific areas.

15. The Introduction first presents a capsule history of our publications. This is followed by detailed information about *Tests in Print II*. Many readers will find the seven tables of statistics on tests, countries, references, and publishers of interest. Next is a section called Editorial Reiterations, containing the Editor's objectives and some of his concerns about testing. Last is a bibliography of books listing information on unpublished tests—an area not covered by our publications.